Peake's
Commentary on the Bible

Peake's Commentary on the Bible

General Editor and New Testament Editor

Matthew Black

D.D. D.Litt. D.Theol. F.B.A.

Old Testament Editor

H. H. Rowley

D.D. B.Litt. Theol.D. F.B.A.

London

First published in 1962
Van Nostrand Reinhold (UK) Co. Ltd.
Molly Millars Lane, Wokingham, Berkshire, England

Reprinted by Routledge in 1990
11 New Fetter Lane, London EC4P 4EE

Reprinted 1962, 1963, 1964, 1967, 1972, 1975, 1976, 1977,
1980, 1981, 1982, 1984, 1985, 1986, 1987

Printed in Hong Kong

British Cataloguing in Publication Data
Available on Request

ISBN: 0 415 05147 9

Advisory Board

List of Contributors

Contributor	Contribution
ACKROYD, Rev. Peter R., M.A., PH.D., Samuel Davidson Professor of Old Testament, London University	Hosea ; Haggai ; Zechariah
ALBRIGHT, William F., PH.D., LITT.D., D.H.L., TH.D., LL.D., Professor Emeritus of Semitic Languages, Johns Hopkins University, Baltimore	The Archaeology of the Ancient Near East
ANDERSON, Rev. George W., M.A., D.D., Professor of Old Testament Literature and Theology, Edinburgh University	The Religion of Israel; The Historical Books of the Old Testament; The Psalms
BALSDON, John P. V. D., M.A., Fellow of Exeter College, Oxford	The Roman Empire in the First Century
BARR, Rev. James, M.A., B.D., W. H. Green Professor of Old Testament Literature, Princeton Theological Seminary, New Jersey	Daniel
BARRETT, Rev. C. Kingsley, M.A., D.D., F.B.A., Professor of Theology, Durham University	John
BEASLEY-MURRAY, Rev. George R., M.A., M.TH., PH.D., Principal of Spurgeon's College, London	Philippians
BLACK, Rev. Matthew, D.D., D.LITT., D.THEOL., F.B.A., Professor of Biblical Criticism and Principal of St Mary's College, St Andrews University	The Development of Judaism in the Greek and Roman Periods (*c.* 196 B.C.–A.D. 135)
BOOBYER, George H., B.A., B.D., D.TH., Lecturer and Head of the Department of Divinity, King's College, Newcastle-upon-Tyne	II Peter ; Jude
BOWMAN, Rev. John W., D.D., Professor of New Testament Interpretation, San Francisco Theological Seminary, San Anselmo, California	The Life and Teaching of Jesus
BRIGHT, Rev. John, TH.D., PH.D., D.D., Cyrus H. McCormick Professor of Hebrew and the Interpretation of the Old Testament, Union Theological Seminary, Richmond, Virginia	Isaiah—I
BROCKINGTON, Rev. Leonard H., M.A., B.D., Senior Lecturer in Aramaic and Syriac, Oxford University	I and II Samuel; Joel; Obadiah; Jonah; Malachi
BROWNE, Rev. Laurence E., M.A., D.D., Emeritus Professor of Theology, Leeds University; Vicar of Highbrook, Sussex	History of Israel—II Post-Exilic ; Ezra and Nehemiah ; Esther
BRUCE, Frederick F., M.A., D.D., Rylands Professor of Biblical Criticism and Exegesis, Manchester University	The Epistles of Paul ; Hebrews
BURROWS, Rev. Millar, M.A., B.D., PH.D., Winkley Professor Emeritus of Biblical Theology, Yale University; Vice-Chairman of the Standard Bible Committee of the National Council of the Churches of Christ in America	The Social Institutions of Israel
CANTERBURY, Archbishop of (Most Reverend Arthur M. Ramsey, P.C., M.A., D.D.)	The Authority of the Bible
CHADWICK, Rev. Canon Henry, MUS.B., D.D., F.B.A., Regius Professor of Divinity and Canon of Christ Church, Oxford	Ephesians
CLARK, Kenneth W., A.B., B.D., PH.D., Professor of Biblical Literature, Duke University, Durham, North Carolina	The Textual Criticism of the New Testament
CRANFIELD, Rev. Charles E. B., M.A., Lecturer in Theology, Durham University	The Catholic Epistles ; I Peter

LIST OF CONTRIBUTORS

DAVIES, Rev. G. Henton, M.A., B.LITT., D.D., Principal of Regent's Park College, Oxford	Deuteronomy
DAVIES, Rev. William D., M.A., D.D., Professor of Biblical Theology, Union Theological Seminary, New York	The Jewish State in the Hellenistic World ; Contemporary Jewish Religion ; The Apostolic Age and the Life of Paul
DINKLER, Erich, Professor of New Testament, Ancient Church History and Archaeology (Faculty of Evangelical Theology), Rheinische Friedrich-Wilhelms-Universität, Bonn	Form Criticism of the New Testament
ELLIOTT-BINNS, Rev. Leonard E., Canon Emeritus of Truro Cathedral	James
GADD, Cyril J., C.B.E., M.A., D.LITT., F.B.A., F.S.A., Professor of Ancient Semitic Languages and Civilisations, School of Oriental and African Studies, London University, and Hon. Fellow of Brasenose College, Oxford	Israel's Neighbours—I Mesopotamia
GRAY, Rev. John, M.A., B.D., PH.D., Professor of Hebrew and Semitic Languages, Aberdeen University	The Archaeology of Palestine—II The Biblical Period ; Chronology of the Old Testament ; Israel's Neighbours—III The Levant
HENN, Thomas R., C.B.E., M.A., Lecturer in Poetry and Drama, St Catharine's College, Cambridge	The Bible as Literature
HERBERT, Rev. Arthur S., M.A., B.D., Professor of Old Testament Literature and Religion, Selly Oak Colleges, Birmingham	Ruth ; I and II Chronicles ; The Song of Solomon ; Lamentations
HIGGINS, Rev. Angus J. B., M.A., B.D., PH.D., Lecturer in New Testament, Theological Department, Leeds University	The Pastoral Epistles—I, II Timothy and Titus
HOOKE, Samuel H., M.A., D.D., TH.D., F.S.A., Professor Emeritus of Old Testament Studies, London University	The Religious Institutions of Israel ; Introduction to the Pentateuch ; Genesis
HYATT, Rev. J. Philip, M.A., B.D., PH.D., Professor of Old Testament Studies and Chairman of the Graduate Department of Religion, Vanderbilt University, Nashville, Tennessee	Amos ; Nahum ; Habakkuk ; Zephaniah
IRWIN, Rev. William A., M.A., B.D., PH.D., Professor Emeritus of Chicago University, and of the Southern Methodist University, Dallas, Texas	Job
JOHNSTON, Rev. George, M.A., B.D., PH.D., Principal of United Theological College, and Professor of New Testament Studies, McGill University, Montreal	The Doctrine of the Church in the New Testament ; The Constitution of the Church in the New Testament ; I, II, III John
JONES, Rev. Douglas R., M.A., Lecturer in Theology, Durham University	Isaiah—II and III
KENYON, Kathleen M., C.B.E., M.A., D.LIT., F.B.A., F.S.A., Lecturer in Palestinian Archaeology, Institute of Archaeology, London University, Director of the British School of Archaeology, Jerusalem	The Archaeology of Palestine—I Prehistoric and Early Phases
LAMPE, Rev. Geoffrey W. H., M.C., D.D., Ely Professor of Divinity, Cambridge University	Luke ; Acts
† MANSON, Rev. Thomas W., M.A., D.LITT., D.D., TH.D., F.B.A., Rylands Professor of Biblical Criticism and Exegesis, Manchester University	Romans
MARSH, Rev. John, M.A., D.PHIL., D.D., Professor and Principal, Mansfield College, Oxford	The Theology of the New Testament
MAUCHLINE, Rev. John, M.A., D.D., Professor of Old Testament Language and Literature and Principal of Trinity College, Glasgow University	I and II Kings
MAY, Rev. Herbert G., A.B., A.M., PH.D., D.D., Finney Professor of Old Testament Language and Literature, School of Theology, Oberlin College, Ohio	History of Israel—I To the Exile ; Joshua
METZGER, Bruce M., M.A., PH.D., D.D., Professor of New Testament Language and Literature, Princeton Theological Seminary, New Jersey	The Early Versions of the New Testament

LIST OF CONTRIBUTORS

MOULE, Rev. Professor Charles F. D., B.A., M.A., D.D., Lady Margaret's Professor of Divinity and Fellow of Clare College, Cambridge	Colossians and Philemon
MUILENBURG, James, M.A., PH.D., L.H.D., D.D., Davenport Professor of Hebrew and Cognate Languages, Union Theological Seminary, New York	Old Testament Prophecy; Ezekiel
NEIL, William, M.A., B.D., PH.D., D.D., Warden of Hugh Stewart Hall, Nottingham University	I and II Thessalonians
OGG, Rev. George, B.SC., D.D., D.LITT., formerly Minister of Anstruther Easter, Fife	The Chronology of the New Testament
PATERSON, Rev. John, M.A., PH.D., D.D., Professor Emeritus of Hebrew and Old Testament Exegesis, Drew University, Madison, New Jersey	Jeremiah
PORTEOUS, Rev. Norman W., M.A., D.D., Professor of Hebrew and Semitic Languages, Edinburgh University	The Theology of the Old Testament
ROBERTS, Rev. Bleddyn J., M.A., D.D., Professor of Hebrew, University College of North Wales, Bangor	Canon and Text of the Old Testament; The Ancient Versions of the Old Testament
ROWLEY, Rev. Harold H., M.A., B.LITT., D.D., THEOL.D., LL.D., F.B.A., Professor Emeritus of Hebrew Language and Literature, Manchester University	The Literature of the Old Testament; Apocalyptic Literature
RYDER, Rev. Edwin T., M.A., B.D., Lecturer in Semitic Languages, University College, Cardiff	The Languages of the Old Testament; Form Criticism of the Old Testament; Ecclesiastes
RYLAARSDAM, Rev. J. Coert, B.D., PH.D., Professor of Old Testament Theology, Chicago University	Hebrew Wisdom; The Proverbs
SANDERS, Rev. Joseph N., M.A., Dean, Domestic Bursar and Fellow of Peterhouse College, University Lecturer in Divinity, Cambridge	The Literature and Canon of the New Testament; Galatians
SCHOFIELD, Rev. John Noel, M.A., B.D., Lecturer in Hebrew and Old Testament, Cambridge University	The Geography of Palestine; Judges
SCOTT, Robert B. Y., B.A., M.A., PH.D., D.D., F.R.S.C., Danforth Professor of Religion, Princeton University, New Jersey	Weights, Measures, Money and Time
SNAITH, Rev. Norman H., M.A., D.D., Principal of Wesley College, Headingley, Leeds	Leviticus; Numbers
STALKER, Rev. David M. G., M.A., B.D., Senior Lecturer and Head of the Department of Biblical Studies, Edinburgh University	Exodus
STENDAHL, Krister, PH.D., THEOL.D., Associate Professor of New Testament Studies, Harvard University	Matthew
THACKER, Thomas W., M.A., Director of the School of Oriental Studies and Professor of Semitic Philology, Durham University	Israel's Neighbours—II Egypt
THOMAS, D. Winton, M.A., Regius Professor of Hebrew and Fellow of St Catharine's College, Cambridge	Micah
TURNER, Rev. Nigel, B.D., M.TH., PH.D., formerly Vicar of Diseworth, nr Derby	The Language of the New Testament; Revelation
WIKGREN, Allen P., M.A., PH.D., Associate Professor of New Testament Language and Literature, Chicago University	The English Versions of the Bible
WILLIAMS, Rev. C. S. C., M.A., Chaplain of Merton College, Tutor in Theology and Divinity Lecturer, Oxford University	The Synoptic Problem; I and II Corinthians
WILSON, Robert McL., M.A., B.D., PH.D., Lecturer in New Testament Language and Literature, St Andrews University	Pagan Religion at the Coming of Christianity; Mark

Preface

IT is now nearly sixty years since the first appearance of Peake's *Commentary on the Bible.* Although one-volume commentaries were not unknown at the time, Peake's Commentary achieved an immediate success: its standards of scholarship were high (some of the most famous names among contemporary scholars, G. A. Cooke, Wheeler Robinson, James Moffatt, J. H. Moulton, Gilbert Murray, to name only a few, were enlisted among its contributors); and it succeeded, as no other one-volume commentary had done, in presenting the results of modern scholarship in simple, intelligible terms to the general reader. It has been described as the stand-by of countless students who could not afford a large library, and it has been said that it was Peake's work which did most to preserve religion in this country from an outbreak of the Fundamentalist controversy. It was not surprising that a revised edition was called for, and in 1937 it was reprinted with a Supplement edited by the assistant editor of the original Commentary, A. J. Grieve, at that time Principal of Lancashire Independent College, Manchester. Since that date the Commentary with its Supplement has been regularly reprinted.

In 1952 discussion began between the publishers and interested scholars about the future of this famous work. There was complete agreement that the time had come to replace the old Peake by an entirely new work. Since the first appearance of the Commentary, scholarship had made notable advances in almost every field of Biblical study. The publication, under the auspices of the Old Testament Society, of *The Old Testament and Modern Study* in 1951 (edited by Professor H. H. Rowley), showed how great was the need for the replacement of many of the articles and commentaries on the Old Testament. This was particularly true of the developments in Biblical Archaeology, while the new emphasis on Biblical Theology made a reassessment and rewriting of much in the old Peake an urgent task. Everything pointed to the desirability of an entirely new work on both the Old Testament and the New Testament: there were the new manuscript and textual discoveries, the Chester Beatty papyri and the Dead Sea Scrolls; the publication of new exegetical commentaries and translations; the availability since 1919 of such indispensable *instrumenta studiorum* as Strack-Billerbeck's *Kommentar zum Neuen Testament aus Talmud und Midrasch* and of Kittel's *Theologisches Wörterbuch*, the accumulating knowledge of the historical and religious background of the Scriptures, etc.

About one thing there was no question: there could be no departure from the Peake tradition of accurate and reliable popular scholarship, or from the aim and purpose of the original Commentary. What was written by A. S. Peake himself in his Preface still holds for the new Peake and deserves to be quoted in full:

> The present work is designed to put before the reader in a simple form, without technicalities, the generally accepted results of Biblical Criticism, Interpretation, History and Theology. It is not intended to be homiletic or devotional, but to convey with precision, and yet in a popular and interesting way, the meaning of the original writers, and reconstruct the conditions in which they worked and of which they wrote. It will thus, while not explicitly devotional or practical, provide that accurate interpretation of the text through which alone the sound basis for devotional use and practical application can be laid. It has been the desire of the promoters that it should be abreast of the present position of scholarship, and yet succeed in making the Scriptures live for its readers with something of the same significance and power that they possessed for those to whom they were originally addressed. While it is intended in the first instance for the layman, and should prove specially helpful to day and Sunday school teachers, to lay preachers, to leaders of men's societies, brotherhoods, and adult Bible classes, and to Christian workers generally, it should also be of considerable use to clergymen and ministers, and in particular to theological students.

The original Peake's Commentary was based on the text (including the marginal readings) of the Revised Version. The new Commentary is based on the text of the Revised Standard Version, but contributors were free to cite or make use of any of the English versions then available, and, where anyone considered it to be necessary or desirable, to give preference to any of these in his exposition.

The original Peake was the work of a group of British scholars. Modern Biblical scholarship is now more international in character, and since the new Commentary was designed for the whole English-speaking world, and is based on the Revised Standard Version, it seemed desirable to include scholars from the U.S.A. and the Commonwealth on the Advisory Board and among the contributors. The Commentary is also appearing in a German translation, edited by Professor Kurt Aland of the University of Münster and published by Töpelmann and Co., Berlin.

In the old Peake the work of editing was in the hands of A. S. Peake with the assistance of A. J. Grieve. In the new Peake the General Editor has also been responsible for the New Testament: the Old Testament Editor has generously shared the task of editing the whole Commentary, as well as making himself responsible for completing the index.

The original design of the old Commentary has been adopted, with some slight modifications only. In the old Commentary, in order to simplify the exposition, general questions of background, social and political questions, historical and religious development, etc. were dealt with in a series of introductory articles. This method has also been followed in the new Commentary: articles are now, however, arranged into General Articles, Old Testament Articles and New Testament Articles, and more attention has been given to questions of Biblical and Near Eastern Archaeology, and the two chief authorities in these fields, Professor W. F. Albright and Dr Kathleen Kenyon, have contributed two of the relevant articles. In view of the present-day interest in the English Bible, more attention has been paid in the new Peake to the English Bible as literature and to the English versions: the article on 'The Bible: its Meaning and Aim' in the old Commentary has been replaced by one on 'The Authority of the Bible', contributed by Dr Ramsey, Archbishop of Canterbury. A completely new feature, reflecting present-day interests and emphases, is the space allotted to discussions of questions of Biblical Theology. Professor Norman Porteous of Edinburgh writes on 'The Theology of the Old Testament' and Dr John Marsh, Principal of Mansfield College, Oxford, on 'The Theology of the New Testament'.

The work has taken approximately seven years to complete and during that period three deaths have occurred among our advisers and contributors: the Very Reverend Dr E. G. Selwyn of Winchester, Professor William Manson of New College, Edinburgh and Professor T. W. Manson of Manchester University were all members of the Advisory Board. Professor T. W. Manson contributed the commentary on Romans; it was the last thing he wrote, and it was only completed shortly before his death.

The preparation of the index, a very formidable task, was begun by the Rev. George Farr of Manchester; Mr Farr was compelled by ill health to give up the work, and it has been completed by Professor Rowley, the Old Testament Editor, who, in spite of his many other commitments, volunteered to undertake this heavy additional burden. For any disuniformities in the index, inevitable in the circumstances of its preparation, we crave the reader's indulgence.

The maps which accompany the Commentary have been prepared by the cartographic staff of Nelson's; they are based on the maps of the Nelson *Atlas of the Bible*, but have been checked, revised and adapted.

At the early stages of planning and consultation help was given by the Rev. Dr G. D. Kilpatrick, Dean Ireland's Professor of Biblical Exegesis in the University of Oxford, and by the Rev. Dr W. D. McHardy, now Regius Professor of Hebrew in Oxford.

Acknowledgment is also due to those who have provided secretarial assistance to the editors in the typing of manuscripts and with the voluminous correspondence: Miss Dorothy Taylor and Miss Gillian Unwin, former secretaries in St Mary's College, Miss Ann Ruscoe (now Mrs Kelly) of Manchester and Miss Mary Blackwood, also secretary in St Mary's College.

Finally mention must be made of the skill and labour of the editorial and printing staff of Thomas Nelson and Sons, who have worked in the closest harmony and co-operation with the editors. One name deserves to be singled out for special mention, that of Mr G. S. Dickson, a senior member of the editorial staff of Thomas Nelson, whose painstaking and devoted reading of all the manuscripts and proofs of the new Peake has greatly lightened the burden of the General and Old Testament Editors.

In taking leave of his task the General Editor wishes to thank all the contributors to this volume for their co-operation, patience and forbearance, in what has proved to be a work of immense labour and industry.

MATTHEW BLACK

St Mary's College
University of St Andrews

Contents

CONTENTS

INTRODUCTORY ARTICLES TO THE NEW TESTAMENT

COMMENTARIES—NEW TESTAMENT

Abbreviations

BOOKS OF THE BIBLE

Old Testament

OT	Old Testament	2 Sam.	2 Samuel	Prov.	Proverbs	Am.	Amos
Gen.	Genesis	1 Kg.	1 Kings	Ec.	Ecclesiastes	Ob.	Obadiah
Exod.	Exodus	2 Kg.	2 Kings	Ca.	(Canticles) Song of Solomon	Jon.	Jonah
Lev.	Leviticus	1 Chr.	1 Chronicles	Isa.	Isaiah	Mic.	Micah
Num.	Numbers	2 Chr.	2 Chronicles	Jer.	Jeremiah	Nah.	Nahum
Dt.	Deuteronomy	Ezr.	Ezra	Lam.	Lamentations	Hab.	Habakkuk
Jos.	Joshua	Neh.	Nehemiah	Ezek.	Ezekiel	Zeph.	Zephaniah
Jg.	Judges	Est.	Esther	Dan.	Daniel	Hag.	Haggai
Ru.	Ruth	Job	Job	Hos.	Hosea	Zech.	Zechariah
1 Sam.	1 Samuel	Ps.	Psalms	Jl	Joel	Mal.	Malachi

Apocrypha

Apoc.	Apocrypha	Ad. Est.	Additions to Esther	Bar.	Baruch	Man.	The Prayer of Manasseh
1 Esd.	1 Esdras	Wis.	The Wisdom of Solomon	S 3 Ch.	Song of the Three Holy Children	1 Mac.	1 Maccabees
2 Esd.	2 Esdras	Sir.	Ecclesiasticus	Sus.	Susanna	2 Mac.	2 Maccabees
Tob.	Tobit			Bel	Bel and the Dragon		
Jdt.	Judith						

New Testament

NT	New Testament	Rom.	Romans	1 Th.	1 Thessalonians	1 Pet.	1 Peter
Mt.	Matthew	1 C.	1 Corinthians	2 Th.	2 Thessalonians	2 Pet.	2 Peter
Mk	Mark	2 C.	2 Corinthians	1 Tim.	1 Timothy	1 Jn	1 John
Lk.	Luke	Gal.	Galatians	2 Tim.	2 Timothy	2 Jn	2 John
Jn	John	Eph.	Ephesians	Tit.	Titus	3 Jn	3 John
Ac.	Acts of the Apostles	Phil.	Philippians	Phm.	Philemon	Jude	Jude
		Col.	Colossians	Heb.	Hebrews	Rev.	Revelation
				Jas	James		

STANDARD WORKS OF REFERENCE

AAA	*Annals of Archaeology and Anthropology*
AASOR	*Annual of the American Schools of Oriental Research*
AC	*The Abingdon Bible Commentary*
Adv. Haer.	Irenaeus, *Adversus Haereses*
AJSL	*American Journal of Semitic Languages and Literature*
ANEP	Pritchard, *Ancient Near East in Pictures*
ANET	Pritchard, *Ancient Near Eastern Texts*
ANF	*Ante-Nicene Fathers*
AOT	Gressmann, *Altorientalische Texte* (1926)
APB	Albright, *Archaeology of Palestine and the Bible*
Aq.	Aquila's version
ARA	Luckenbill, *Ancient Records of Assyria*
Aram.	Aramaic
ARE	Breasted, *Ancient Records of Egypt*
ARI	Albright, *Archaeology and the Religion of Israel*
Assy.	Assyrian
ASV	American Standard Version
ATD	*Das Alte Testament Deutsch*
AV	Authorised Version
BA	*Biblical Archaeologist*
Bab.	Babylonian
Barn.	*The Epistle of Barnabas*

BASOR	*Bulletin of the American Schools of Oriental Research*
BBSAJ	*Bulletin of the British School of Archaeology, Jerusalem*
BCP	Book of Common Prayer
BDB	Brown, Driver, Briggs, *Hebrew Lexicon*
BGDW	Bauer, *Griechisch-deutsches Wörterbuch* (1937)
BH	Biblia Hebraica
Bi.	*Biblica*
BJRL	*Bulletin of the John Rylands Library*
BK	*Biblischer Kommentar, Altes Testament*
BWANT	*Beiträge zur Wissenschaft vom Alten und Neuen Testament*
BWAT	*Beiträge zur Wissenschaft vom Alten Testament*
BZAW	*Beihefte zur Zeitschrift für die alttestamentliche Wissenschaft*
BZNW	*Beihefte zur Zeitschrift für die neutestamentliche Wissenschaft*
CAH	*Cambridge Ancient History*
CAP	Charles, *Apocrypha and Pseudepigrapha*, 2 vols. (1913)
CB	*The Cambridge Bible*
CBer.	*Corpus Berolinense* (*Die griechischen christlichen Schriftsteller der ersten drei Jahrhunderte* (1897–))
CBQ	*Catholic Biblical Quarterly*
CBSC	*Cambridge Bible for Schools and Colleges*
Cent.B	*The Century Bible*
CGT(C)	*Cambridge Greek Testament* (*Commentary*)
CH	Code of Ḫammurabi
CIL	*Corpus Inscriptionum Latinarum*
CIS	*Corpus Inscriptionum Semiticarum*
CNT	*Commentaire du Nouveau Testament*
CQR	*Church Quarterly Review*
CSEL	*Corpus Scriptorum Ecclesiasticorum Latinorum*
DAC	*Dictionary of the Apostolic Church*
DAr. Ch.	Cabrol, *Dictionnaire d'archéologie chrétienne et de Liturgie* (1907–)
DB	*Dictionary of the Bible*
DCG	*Dictionary of Christ and the Gospels*
Did.	*The Didache*
*DSS	Dead Sea Scrolls
EB	Cheyne and Black, *Encyclopaedia Biblica*
EBib.	*Études Bibliques*
EBrit.	*Encyclopaedia Britannica*
Ech.B	*Echter Bibel*
Ed.	Edersheim, *Jesus the Messiah*, 2 vols.
EGT	*Expositor's Greek Testament*
EHAT	*Exegetisches Handbuch zum Alten Testament*
ERE	*Encyclopaedia of Religion and Ethics*
ET	*The Expository Times*
EV(V)	English Version(s)
Ex.B	*Expositor's Bible*
Exp.	*The Expositor*
FSAC	Albright, *From the Stone Age to Christianity* (1940)
GAB	Grollenberg, *Atlas of the Bible*
Ges.	Gesenius' *Thesaurus linguae hebr. et chald.* (1835–53)
GK	Gesenius' *Hebrew Grammar*, ed. Kautzsch (tr. Cowley)
Gr.	Greek
HAT	*Handbuch zum alten Testament*
HC	*Hand-Commentar*
HDB	Hastings' *Dictionary of the Bible*
HE	Eusebius, *Historia Ecclesiastica*
Hex.	Hexateuch
HJ	*Hibbert Journal*
HKAT	*Handkommentar zum Alten Testament*
HKNT	*Handkommentar zum Neuen Testament*
HNT	Lietzmann, *Handbuch zum NT*
HRCS	Hatch and Redpath, *Concordance to the Septuagint* (1897–1906)
HSAT	Kautzsch, *Die heilige Schrift des alten Testaments*
HSATes	*Die Heilige Schrift des Alten Testamentes* (Bonner Bibel)
HSDB	Hastings' *One Volume Dictionary of the Bible*
HTR	*Harvard Theological Review*
HUCA	*Hebrew Union College Annual*
IB	*Interpreter's Bible*
ICC	*International Critical Commentary*
IH	*International Handbooks to the NT*
ILS	*Inscriptiones Latinae Selectae*
INT	*Introduction to the New Testament*
Inter.	*The Interpreter*
IOT	*Introduction to the Old Testament*
ISNT	Metzinger, *Introductio Specialis in Novum Testamentum*
JAOS	*Journal of the American Oriental Society*
JBL	*Journal of Biblical Literature*
JE	*Jewish Encyclopedia*
Jer.	St Jerome
Jer.B	*Jerusalem Bible*
JJS	*Journal of Jewish Studies*
JNES	*Journal of Near Eastern Studies*
Jos. Ant.	Josephus, *Antiquities*
Jos.BJ	Josephus, *De Bello Judaico*
Jos.c.Ap.	Josephus, *Contra Apionem*
JPOS	*Journal of the Palestine Oriental Society*
JQR	*Jewish Quarterly Review*
JR	*Journal of Religion*
JSS	*Journal of Semitic Studies*
JTS	*Journal of Theological Studies*
JV	Jewish Version
KAT	*Kommentar zum Alten Testament*
K-B	Koehler-Baumgartner, *Lexicon in Veteris Testamenti Libros*
KEH	*Kurzgefasstes exegetisches Handbuch*
KHC	*Kurzer Hand-Commentar zum Alten Testament*
KHS	*Kurzgefasster Kommentar zu den heiligen Schriften des Alten und Neuen Testamentes*

* See special abbreviations at the end of this list

ABBREVIATIONS

LOT	Driver, *Introduction to the Literature of the Old Testament* (1929)
LTK	Buchberger, *Lexicon für Theologie und Kirche*
LXX	The Septuagint
LXX[A]	Septuagint, Codex Alexandrinus
LXX[B]	Septuagint, Codex Vaticanus
LXX[L]	Lucianic Recension of the Septuagint
Mey.	Meyer, *Kommentar über das NT*
MGC	Moulton and Geden's *Concordance to Greek NT*
MMV	Moulton and Milligan's *Vocabulary of the Greek Testament* (1930)
MNTC	Moffatt's *New Testament Commentary*
MT	Massoretic Text
NT	New Testament
NTD	*Das Neue Testament Deutsch*
NTS	*New Testament Studies*
NTT	New Testament Theology
OL	Old Latin Version
Orig.	Origen
OT	Old Testament
OTJC	Robertson Smith, *The OT in the Jewish Church*
OTMS	Rowley, *Old Testament and Modern Study*
OTT	Old Testament Theology
PAAJ	*Proceedings of the American Academy for Jewish Research*
PBV	Prayer Book Version
PC	*Pulpit Commentary*
PEF	*Palestine Exploration Fund Quarterly Statement* (1855–1937)
PEQ	*Palestine Exploration Quarterly* (1937–)
PG	Migne, *Patrologia Graeca*
PJB	*Palästina-Jahrbuch*
PL	Migne, *Patrologia Latina*
PSBA	*Proceedings of the Society of Biblical Archaeology*
PW	Pauly-Wissowa, *Real-encyclopädie der classischen Altertumswissenschaft* (1894–)
QL	Qumrân literature
R.	Redactor or editor
RB	*Revue Biblique*
RBn	*Revue Bénédictine*
RGG	*Die Religion in Geschichte und Gegenwart*
RHPR	*Revue d'Histoire et de Philosophie religieuses*
RHR	*Revue de l'Histoire des Religions*
RS	Robertson Smith, *The Religion of the Semites*
RSR	*Recherches de Science Religieuse*
RSV*n*	Revised Standard Version, footnote
RTP	*Review of Theology and Philosophy*
RV	Revised Version
RVm	Revised Version, margin
Sam.	Samaritan
SAT	*Die Schriften des Alten Testaments in Auswahl*
SB	Strack und Billerbeck, *Kommentar zum NT aus Talmud und Midrasch* (1922–8)
SDB	Smith's *Dictionary of the Bible*
SHG	G. A. Smith, *Historical Geography of the Holy Land*
SJTh.	*Scottish Journal of Theology*
SNTS	*Studiorum Novi Testamenti Societas*
Sp.	*Speaker's Commentary*
Syr.	Syriac Version
Tert.	Tertullian
ThRs (NF)	*Theologische Rundschau* (*Neue Folge*)
TLZ	*Theologische Literaturzeitung*
TR	Textus Receptus
TS	*Texts and Studies*
TU	*Texte und Untersuchungen zur Geschichte der altchristlichen Literatur* (3 series), ed. Harnack and others (1883–)
TWNT	Kittel, *Theologisches Wörterbuch zum Neuen Testament*
VSS	Versions
VT	*Vetus Testamentum*
Vulg.	Vulgate
WBA	Wright, *Biblical Archaeology*
WC	*Westminster Commentaries*
WH	Westcott and Hort, *The New Testament in Greek*
WNT	*Westminster New Testament*
WW	Wordsworth and White's Vulgate NT
ZATW	*Zeitschrift für die alttestamentliche Wissenschaft*
ZDMG	*Zeitschrift der deutschen morgenländischen Gesellschaft*
ZDPV	*Zeitschrift des deutschen Palästina-Vereins*
ZK	Zahn, *Kommentar zum Neuen Testament*
ZNTW	*Zeitschrift für die neutestamentliche Wissenschaft*

ABBREVIATIONS REFERRING TO THE DEAD SEA SCROLLS

1QIs[a]	First Isaiah Scroll
1QIs[b]	Second Isaiah Scroll
1QLevi	Testament of Levi
1QpHab	Habakkuk Commentary
1QS	Rule of the Community (Manual of Discipline)
1QSa (= 1Q28a)	Rule of the Community (Appendix)
1QSb (= 1Q28b)	Collection of Benedictions
1QM	War of the Sons of Light against the Sons of Darkness
1QH	Hymns of Thanksgiving
CD	Fragments of a Zadokite work (Damascus Document)

THE AUTHORITY OF THE BIBLE

By The ARCHBISHOP OF CANTERBURY

I

1a The Bible is the sacred book of the Christian Church. The familiar English word comes from the Greek through the Latin. The Greek original, *Biblia*, meant simply 'the books', and when the word was transliterated into Latin it came to be a singular feminine noun. Two collections of books are embraced within the Bible—those of the Old Testament, which were formed into the Canon of Scripture within the Jewish Church and subsequently came to be received within the Christian Church also, and those of the New Testament, which were written within the Christian Church and therein were accepted as sacred scripture along with the earlier collection.

The early Church used language ascribing high authority to both parts of the Bible (for the special problem of the difference between the Hebrew and the Greek forms of the Canon of the Old Testament, see §§57–63). The books were described by the early Fathers as 'holy scriptures', 'sacred books', 'sacred writings', 'divine scriptures', and as written by divine inspiration—the Holy Spirit both prompting the authors to write and directing their minds to write as they did. Subsequently, the Bible has been cherished in every part and in every phase of Christendom as possessing an authority which is divine. Within the history of the Church, the most debated questions concerning the Bible have been the various modes in which it conveys truth (such as literal, or symbolic, or allegorical) and the relation between the authority of the Bible and the authority of the Church. In modern times there have been also the questions created by the relation between the authority of the Bible and the impact of historical and literary criticism, which in its investigations has treated the Bible in the same way as other ancient documents.

b It would, however, be wrong to infer from the exalted place of the Bible in every form of Christianity that Christianity is the religion of a Book. The central fact of Christianity is not a Book but a Person—Jesus Christ, himself described as the Word of God. The books of the Old Testament came to have authority within the Church because Jesus Christ set the seal of his own authority upon them and interpreted them as preparing the way for himself. The books of the New Testament came to have authority because the Church recognised in them the testimony of the apostles to Jesus Christ. It is the relation of the books to the person which makes them very different from a collection of oracles such as itself provides the basis for a religion. Indeed, both in the Jewish Church and in the Christian Church, the religion preceded the making and the canonisation of the books.

The method of inquiry into the nature of the authority of the Bible in this article will be an historical one. How did the books, first of the Old Testament, and then of the New, come to be treated as possessing authority? What was the relation of the two covenants to one another, to the Church and to Jesus Christ? If it is here that we look in order to understand how the Bible came to be itself, it is here also that we may look if we are to understand the nature of its authority today.

II

Long before the Old Testament came into existence as a collection of sacred books, it was the belief of Israel that God had spoken to her with authority in law and in prophecy. The collection of sacred books was not the basis of the belief in a divine revelation, but its consequence. 2a

It was the belief of Israel that God had chosen her from among the nations, set her free by a wonderful act of deliverance in the Exodus from Egypt, and given her through Moses the law and the covenant at Mount Sinai. Throughout her history Israel looked back to these events as conveying to her the proof of Yahweh's graciousness and of his imperious, moral claim. But the revelation was not given all at once, and by subsequent events and by men who interpreted their significance Yahweh made known to the people his character and purpose. He used human agents who conveyed his truth, and through those human agents he was himself believed to 'speak'.

The media of Yahweh's speech to Israel were Law and Prophecy. The word *Tôrāh*, rendered 'law' in the English versions of the Old Testament, properly means 'direction' or 'teaching'. Moses had given decisions on particular matters of dispute, and also general precepts forming a code of conduct for the community, known comprehensively as 'the law of Yahweh' and 'the law of Moses'. After the entrance of Israel into Canaan, the priests gave torah on matters of ritual and morals. The idea of a closed corpus of torah was not in view. Yet there was probably never a time from Moses onwards when the nation was without some written documents of torah, and indeed it is recorded that Moses himself wrote the laws of God upon tables of stone. The idea that Israel possesses torah and yet looks forward to the delivery of more is seen in Dt. 18:18. b

Prophecy, though it had been linked with law in Moses who was both prophet and lawgiver, came to stand in contrast with law as the other medium of Yahweh's speech to Israel. The prophets claimed to speak with Yahweh's authority. Their utterances were frequently introduced by the formula 'Thus saith Yahweh'; and their adherents who edited their prophecies in writing described how 'the word of Yahweh came' to them. In contrast with torah the prophets were concerned less with the giving of moral directions than with the affirmation of Yahweh's fundamental relation with Israel. They spoke of Yahweh's graciousness in his call of Israel and care for her, of the grievousness of her disobedience, of Yahweh's demand for her practical repentance, of his holiness, righteousness and love, of his government of the nations and the processes of nature, of his judgments in the form of calamities both national and cosmic, and of his future vindication of his justice in a 'day of Yahweh' which will come. The prophets spoke too of the sovereignty of God to be realised on earth in a cleansed and restored Israel, and finally of the bringing of all the nations to know Yahweh and of the role of Israel to be Yahweh's messenger to them. c

The term 'word of Yahweh' has special significance for the understanding of the prophetic message.

2c It is used both of the message of Yahweh which comes to a prophet and is delivered by him, and also the divine activity whereby the world is created and sustained, the events of history are controlled and nations are delivered or judged. Indeed the word *dābhār* itself means etymologically both 'saying' or 'message' and 'event' or 'thing'. This connection between event and message is fundamental in the Hebrew conception of Yahweh's revelation of himself. On the one hand his actions in history, interpreted by the prophets, are the means of his disclosure of himself in the world. On the other hand his word spoken by a prophet can have a mighty potency in effect upon the course of events. The word of Yahweh shall not return to him void (Isa. 55:11) : it is a destroying fire, before which the people are as fuel (Jer. 5:14). Event and message are often inseparable.

d The prophets claimed to be the mouthpieces of Yahweh. 'Inspiration' had not for the Hebrew mind the refinement of conception which it has since come to have. The spirit of Yahweh was held to be the source of many kinds of extraordinary strength and skill. To it was ascribed the weird and ecstatic behaviour of the early bands of prophets whose role it was to stir up enthusiasm for Yahweh rather than to give any particular ethical or theological message. Thus the significant element in the authority of the great prophets is to be seen not in the claim, in itself, to have the spirit of Yahweh (cf. Mic. 3:8) so much as in their manner of speaking of their relation to Yahweh and his message. The prophet was conscious of a divine summons to speak in his name, and a divine guiding as to what to say (cf. Am. 7:15), an overwhelming divine constraint (cf. Jer. 23:9–29) and a personal converse with Yahweh, wherein his mind and speech were brought into relation with Yahweh's word (cf. Am. 7:2–9, Isa. 6:5–12, Jer. 1:6–14, 15:10–21). The criteria of authenticity were found not in the particular media of communication, whether dream or ecstasy or audition or impulse, but in the fulfilment of things which the prophet declared would happen (cf. Zech. 1:6, Dt. 18:22, 1 Kg. 22:1–28). It was not so much in the foreseeing of the details of events that this predictive element lay as in the proclaiming of the divine rule over future history. To discern that rule was to have confirmation that the prophet spoke true, and that the word of Yahweh had come to him.

3a Law and prophecy were thus the primary agents of Yahweh's revelation of himself to Israel. Both were at first given orally. Both came to be collected in writing. As to *Law*, there were probably written laws in existence from the time of Moses, and written collections were added at various dates. Elsewhere in this Commentary is to be found the evidence for the making of these collections and for the influence of prophetic teaching upon their content. It was after the return of Israel from the Babylonian exile that the collection of the Books of the Law into the present corpus was made, and it is known that this was done at some date before the Samaritan schism, *c.* 250 B.C. As to *Prophecy*, it seems that prophets sometimes wrote collections of their own prophecies (Jer., Ezek., Hag., Zech.), though more often their disciples wrote collections of them. Such collections were in course of time combined and enlarged. By the time of the Son of Sirach, who wrote the book commonly called Ecclesiasticus, *c.* 180 B.C., the Book of the Prophets existed as a corpus. This corpus included what we now call the 'historical books', 1 and 2 Samuel and 1 and 2 Kings. This fact is very significant. It shows that the history was not separated from its interpretation as the record of Yahweh's word in the events ; so close was the unity believed to exist between history and message.

b Thus were Law and Prophecy assembled in authoritative collections, and became the first two elements in the Bible of the Jewish Church. The third collection —the books known as the *writings*—was made, at least, at some date earlier than the time of Jesus Christ (cf. Lk. 24:44). This collection included (in the Hebrew 3b
Canon) the Psalms ; the three Wisdom books, Job, Proverbs and Ecclesiastes ; three books of history, Chronicles, Ezra and Nehemiah ; and Daniel, Canticles, Ruth, Lamentations and Esther. The inclusion of these indicated the belief that God's revelation came through media of speech and writing other than the law and the prophets. Without being themselves law or prophecy, these other books served the word of Yahweh which law or prophecy proclaimed. These books bear witness to the doctrine of the prophets, or to the prophetic view of history, or to the national cultus which law had ordered and prophecy had deeply affected, or to the aspirations of men towards God which both law and prophecy had evoked in psalm and hymn, or to the tenacious loyalty of Israel to the law in patriotic fervour (Esther), or to the lesson of friendship with other nations (Ruth). All this served and witnessed to the action of the word of Yahweh in Israel, the word which not only created the response of righteousness but also exposed and judged failure : the word which is seen not only in moral achievements but also in the half-lights of Israel's struggles. The inclusion of the writings shows how comprehensive was that action in Israel of the word which prophecy interpreted.

The threefold collection of books formed the Canon c
of Sacred Scripture. The assumption behind the making of the Canon was that prophecy had ceased to happen ; and henceforth it is in Holy Scripture that the people must find the word of Yahweh. The source of the authority of scripture was held to be divine inspiration, for the written Books had an authority no less than and no different from that of the prophets themselves. The Books were sacred. They were the Word of God. To learn what is divine truth, it was necessary to inquire as to 'what is written'. The scriptures 'cannot be broken'.

It does not lie within our scope to trace the beliefs d
held within Judaism about the authority of the Sacred Scriptures. Our concern is with these scriptures as what they were to become for the Christian Church— 'the Old Testament'. The Christian Church received from the Jewish Church both these books and the belief that they were the inspired word of God. But there was this difference. To the Christian Church these books were God's word not in its completeness, but as the word of his promise : their significance lay not in themselves, but in a fulfilment which was beyond them. Hence the Christian reader of these books, which he calls the 'Old Testament', notices within them signs of longing for the future and predictions of things to come : the kingdom of God, the day of Yahweh, a new covenant, a new temple, an outpouring of spirit, a re-creation of the world. He notices also the passage in Isa. 52:12–53:end, which tells of the suffering servant of Yahweh, whose suffering issued in peace for the people and his own exaltation and triumph. In these ways he reads these scriptures as God's word of promise, and looks to Jesus Christ and the apostles for the exposition of their fulfilment. But he notices also that, in their teaching of the fulfilment, Jesus Christ and the apostles appealed not only to the text of the scriptures but to the dynamic history of law and prophecy which lay behind them and had preceded the formation of the Canon.

III

In John the Baptist the Jews were startled by a 4a
revival of the role of the prophet which had long been in abeyance. John proclaimed the divine judgment upon the nation with the long-forgotten directness of the 'Word of the Lord'. John was followed by Jesus of Nazareth, also a prophet (Mk 6:4, Lk. 4:24). He spoke with authority in the name of God, he uttered predictions of judgment, and he claimed to be himself an instrument of judgment by his presence and teaching

4a (Lk. 12:49–53). But his claims went beyond those which belong to the category of a prophet. He claimed that in him and his works the kingdom of God was now present (Mt. 12:28, Lk. 11:20), that the era of unfulfilled longing had now been replaced by the era of fulfilment (Mt. 13:16–17, Lk. 10:23–4). On the night before the crucifixion, Jesus made in the sacrificial blood of his death the new covenant which Jeremiah had foretold (Mk 14:24). After his death, resurrection and exaltation, the apostles witnessed the promised outpouring of spirit (Ac. 2:14–21).

b What was the attitude of Jesus Christ towards the Old Testament? He treated it as possessing divine authority (Mt. 4:3–10, Lk. 4:3–12 ; Mk 12:10, 26, Mt. 12:7, Mk 7:9–13). Particularly, he found in it the declaration of the divine purpose for his own mission to die (Mk 14:21, Lk. 22:22, 37). He accepted all the three divisions of the scriptures—law, prophets, writings—as the divine word (Lk. 24:44).

c As to the law, Jesus Christ came to fulfil it (Mt. 5:17). This he did by teaching and practising a more radical obedience to the divine demand which the law had set forth. This more radical obedience is described in the Sermon on the Mount (Mt. 5:21–48). It involves both (*a*) the right dispositions of the heart in matters where the law had enjoined right actions, (*b*) positive actions of righteousness in matters where the law had condemned actions of unrighteousness. In two instances Jesus Christ goes even farther in his radical treatment of the law. He abrogates the rules of the law concerning meats clean and unclean (Mk 7:14–23). He says that the law, in allowing divorce, had been making a concession to human weakness, whereas the divine institution of marriage as a permanent union had been given at the creation (Mk 10:1–10). Elsewhere, Jesus Christ summarises the moral demand of the law in the twofold command of love towards God and love towards neighbour (Mk 12:28–31).

From the attitude of Jesus Christ towards the law, it is evident that there is a big difference between his use of the scriptures and a literalistic exegesis. For this reason it seems precarious to try to settle questions about the historicity of Old Testament narratives by the citations which Jesus Christ makes of particular passages. Thus, when he says, 'as Jonah was three days and three nights in the belly of the whale' (Mt. 12:40), the force of the analogy which he was teaching does not turn upon a question of history, about which he was not teaching ; and when he cites Psalm 110 as written by David (Mk 12:36) he is not giving teaching about the authorship of the Psalm, but conducting an *ad hominem* argument with the Pharisees.

d Yet the scriptures were for Jesus Christ the word of God. Upon him there rested the obligation to fulfil them. This he did finally by his death, the necessity of which he saw in the application to himself of the words of Isaiah 53. The fulfilment in its completeness and in its effects is seen only when Jesus Christ had died and had risen again and given the Holy Spirit to his Church, the new Israel which he had constituted from the remnant of the old Israel which had rejected him. Living under the new covenant, the Church was able to use the ancient scriptures in the new way which the Gospel of Christ had created.

5a The Church of the apostolic age accepted the books of the Old Testament as sacred scriptures, and every New Testament writer cites them or alludes to them as having divine authority. Their inspiration is explicitly defined in 2 Tim. 3:16, 2 Pet. 1:20–1.

(1) First, there are passages cited as prophecies of the events of the Gospel. Thus, Isaiah 53 was used to tell of Christ's sufferings and death (Ac. 8:32–3). Psalm 2:7 was used of the vindication of his divine sonship at the resurrection (Ac. 13:33, Heb. 5:5). Psalm 118:22 was used of the vindication by the resurrection of him who had been rejected (Ac. 4:11, 1 Pet. 2:7). Psalm 110:1 was used of the exaltation of Jesus to the right hand of God (Ac. 2:34). The passages were used almost as descriptions of the great 5a
events of the Gospel as belonging to the agelong purpose of God. Besides those often-quoted passages, there were many correspondences of detail noticed between texts in the scriptures and incidents in the Gospel history (cf. Mt. 21:4–5, 26:15, 27:34).

(2) We also see in the apostolic Church the drawing b
out of correspondences between events, institutions and conceptions in the scriptures, and events, institutions and conceptions which have come under the new covenant. These correspondences were conspicuous in the minds of the early Christians. Thus the Exodus from Egypt has its counterpart in the deliverance effected by Jesus Christ (cf. 1 C. 10:1–10, 1 Pet. 1:2, 2:9–10). The temple in Jerusalem has its counterpart in the temple of the Church composed of the living stones who are its members (Eph. 2:20–2, 1 Pet. 2:5). The manna from heaven has its counterpart in Jesus as the living bread from heaven (Jn 6:32–40). The creation of mankind has its counterpart in the new creation wrought by Jesus Christ (2 C. 5:17). Adam, as the head of a race sinful and subject to death, has his counterpart in Christ, the second Adam, the New Man, the head of a race restored to life (1 C. 15:45–9). In all these ways the new covenant recapitulated the old.

Noteworthy also are the images from the scriptures which are applied to Jesus Christ. He is priest and also victim (Heb. 8–10). He is sacrificial lamb, and also victorious king (Jn 18–19). He is the Son of Man, destined like the Son of Man in Daniel 7:13–14 to possess the kingdom, and like the Son of Man in Psalm 2 to reign over God's creation, but first humiliated and put to death like the servant in Isaiah 53 (Mk 14:21, Heb. 2:5–9). This imagery seems to show Jesus fulfilling the role of Israel in attaining to triumph, but attaining it only through humiliation.

(3) Besides these broad and conspicuous corres- c
pondences between the two covenants, the apostolic writers used the scriptures for the proving and illustrating of points in theological or moral arguments. Sometimes methods of exegesis were used *akin to those of the Rabbis* and the Alexandrine exegetes ; and in some instances the exegesis seems strangely inconsequent (e.g. 1 C. 9:9, Gal. 4:30). There are also instances of a use of the scriptures which is strictly *theological*, as when Paul in Gal. 3 and Rom. 4 draws from the story of Abraham the principle of justification by faith in antecedence to the works of the law. There are instances also of a use of the scriptures which is not more than *illustrative*, as when Paul uses a passage not to prove a point, but to put into vivid language a point already established (cf. 1 C. 9:8–10, Eph. 4:8–11).

The use of the scriptures within the Church was thus 6a
wide and varied. It might seem that the scriptures were used merely as a collection of texts to be drawn upon where fancy dictated ; but this is far from being so : there were factors at work which deeply influenced the Church's use of the scriptures.

(1) There was in the Church a heightened sense of history which the Gospel had created. The Church's concern was with events which had recently happened : events in which God was the author and agent. He had raised up Jesus. He is the God of mighty acts. He had always been the God of mighty acts. *That* was the significance of the scriptures. They mattered to the apostles not just as a volume for the discovery of proof-texts, but as the record of the mighty acts of God. Thus the prophetic conception of the might of the divine word, at work in the continuous movement of events, revived in the apostolic Church. This is seen in the recapitulation of continuous phases of Israel's history in Stephen's speech (Ac. 7), in a similar recapitulation in Paul's speech at Antioch in Pisidia (Ac. 13), in the drawing out of the successive epochs from the Creation to Moses, from Moses to the Advent in Romans (Rom. 5), and in the tracing of the series of heroes of faith from the patriarchs, through the exodus, the conquest of Canaan, and the monarchy down to

6a the Maccabean martyrs in Hebrews (Heb. 11). There was thus an awareness of the fulfilment in the Gospel not only of a collection of scriptures but of a series of historical events in whose sequence the mighty hand of God had been at work.

b (2) There was also the conviction in the Church that Jesus Christ himself was the Word (Jn 1:14, 1 Jn 1:1, Rev. 19:13). He was himself the utterance of God's grace and truth in the world. The implications of this were realised to be considerable. There was in Jesus a finality of the divine utterance, in relation to which the utterances in the Old Testament had been fragmentary and preparatory (Heb. 1:1). There was in Jesus the divine utterance not only in his teaching and message, but in *himself*: the word and the person were utterly one. Furthermore, the word, who was made flesh, had himself been 'in the beginning with God' (Jn 1:1), at work in the creation of the world, and in the giving of life and light to mankind. Thus, in a sense hard to describe and faintly yet decisively perceived, the scriptures of the Old Testament not only prepared the way for Christ but also revealed *him*, as the word, now incarnate in him, had been at work from the beginning.

IV

7a We pass on now to the scriptures of the New Testament themselves. As in the case of those of the Old Testament, the divine revelation implicit in the covenant began to be received by the Church before ever the scriptures were written or formed into a Canon; and the process which preceded the writing of the books throws light upon the nature of their authority.

From the earliest days the Christian Church possessed the sacraments of Baptism and the Eucharist, an oral tradition of teaching about Jesus Christ, and an apostolic ministry. By all of these the Gospel was mediated to the Church.

b 1. By Baptism, converts were on profession of faith admitted to the Church as the Body of Christ, and to union with Christ crucified and risen (Rom. 6:1–11, 1 C. 12:13). By means of the Eucharist, the members of the Church shared together in partaking in the body of Christ and the blood of Christ, and showed forth his death (1 C. 10:16–17, 11:26).

2. The preaching of the apostles set forth the Gospel of divine salvation through the life, death and exaltation of Jesus Christ in fulfilment of the scriptures, and his gift of the Holy Spirit. In the preaching, the death and the resurrection had a central place (cf. 1 C. 15:3–5). There was also oral teaching within the Church about the things which Jesus did and taught in his life on earth. There is some evidence that Christian teachers made use of written credal or catechetical summaries as an aid in the process of oral teaching.

3. There were also men commissioned by Jesus Christ with authority to teach and to rule in the Church, the apostles (Mk 3:14–19, Lk. 22:29–30, Ac. *passim*, 1 C. *passim*). Exercising their authority in the name of Christ, with personal humility and self-effacement, they served the unity of the Church and its adherence to the historic Jesus Christ.

c Sacraments, oral teaching, apostolic ministry were all means whereby the word of the Gospel ruled in the Church. But while these 'norms' had their indispensable role, their role was exercised within the Church, in all of whose members there was the Holy Spirit whose office it was to glorify Christ and to guide the Church into all the truth. Distributed amongst the members of the Church were many gifts of the Holy Spirit; and among these were the speaking with tongues, whereby members of the Church testified to the divine leading, and prophecy whereby they foretold the future and interpreted the will of God.

d It was therefore within a Church already ruled by the divine word that the writings were made which 7d were to become the new Holy Scriptures. The *Epistles* were written as the letters of an apostle to churches, and to individuals. Their recipients would have held them to possess authority in so far as they contained directions from an apostle which called for obedience, or in so far as they gave reminders of the authority of Jesus Christ and his Gospel or of the Holy Scriptures. But they were no more than letters, and it would seem that they were written with no sort of consciousness that they were or would ever become 'sacred scripture'. The four *Gospels* were a novel kind of literature: they were written to provide not biographies of Jesus Christ so much as presentations of how the Gospel of God came through his life, teaching, passion and resurrection. The motive and method of the writing of a gospel are described in the prologue of the Gospel of Luke: without any claim to inspiration, the writer set out to get the best information that he could and to use the previous attempts which had been made. The narrative was not designed to be sacred scripture: it was a record of the events wherein the sacred scriptures were fulfilled (Lk. 24:44). On the other hand the *Apocalypse*, bearing the name of John, claimed to be the work of a prophet, revealing to the Church the visions which had been granted to him.

As the generation of the apostles died out, the e Church was compelled to think about the nature and the source of its doctrine. There was no doubt as to the answer. The doctrine was that which Christ had brought, by his teaching and person, and the authorities for it were the prophets who preceded him, and the apostles who followed him. Polycarp urged the Church at Philippi to accept Christ as their standard, along with 'the apostles who preached the gospel to us, and the prophets who announced our Lord's coming in advance' (Ep. Phil. 6:3). The Old Testament was a doctrinal norm, through the Church's belief that it was a Christian book and that it testified to Christ and his glory. The apostles were a doctrinal norm, on account of their relation to Christ and the first-hand character of their testimony to the true gospel (cf. 1 Clem. 42, Justin 1 Apol. 42:4, 50:12. Ign. Eph. 11:2, Trall. 7:1). Authority therefore belonged to what was 'handed over' from Christ to the apostles, and from the apostles to the Church. Here in embryo is the conception of 'tradition', though the Greek verb 'to hand over' (*paradidonai*) was used frequently of the handing over of the apostolic testimony before the noun (*paradosis*) came to be used in a technical sense.

Authority belonged to the testimony of the apostles, handed down in the Church. It was handed down in many ways: by oral teaching, by liturgical forms, by baptismal creeds, by customs, by the special role of the monarchical bishops whose succession to one another in their sees from apostolic times was valued as a means of securing the true teaching (cf. Irenaeus, Adv. Haer. 3, 2, 2; 3, 3, 3; 3, 4, 1). As evidence of the testimony of the apostles, the Books which were believed to have been written by them, or by their immediate followers (such as Mark in relation to Peter, or Luke in relation to Paul), were recognised to possess authority. By the middle of the second century references begin to be made to a Canon of such books. But the process of defining the limits of the collection of books deemed to have apostolic authority was a gradual one, and the first official document which prescribes the twenty-seven Books of our New Testament as alone canonical is Athanasius' 'Easter letter' for the year 367.

What was the relation of the scriptures to the Church? 8a There was at first little sense of a contrast, and still less of a conflict, between the Books and the rest of the tradition. The true doctrine was what the apostles had delivered, whether it was since handed down in the Books or in the oral teaching. But a tendency to contrast the Books and the other means of tradition arose. Since heretics were able to misinterpret the Books for their own ends, an emphasis upon the

8a necessity of interpreting the Books according to tradition arose as a safeguard ; and this emphasis is seen in the second century in both Irenaeus and Tertullian, who urged that scripture must be understood in the light of the Church's unwritten Rule of Faith. But after the dangers of Gnosticism passed there was less hesitancy about the direct appeal to scripture as providing the content of the Church's doctrine, and there follow both a heightened definition of the authority of scripture and, at the same time, a broader and more explicit description of the medium of tradition. If it is from within tradition that sureness of interpretation of the scriptures must come, there is no hesitancy in describing the scriptures as divine and sufficient. In the classic statement of patristic teaching, the *Commonitorium* of Vincent of Lerinum (*c.* A.D. 450), it is stated that ' scripture is sufficient and more than sufficient ', though its right interpretation is to be found by reference to the ' agreement of the whole Church in all times and places ', ' what has been believed, everywhere, always and by all '.

b Though the Church made the Canon of the New Testament, it was not thereby conferring authority on the Books. Rather was it acknowledging the Books to possess authority in virtue of what they were, and it was an authority supreme and divine. Typical of the belief of the Fathers is the statement of Origen, ' the sacred books were not the works of men : they were written by inspiration of the Holy Spirit, at the will of the Father of all through Jesus Christ ' (*De Princip.* 4:9). The conception of inspiration was applied to them not by intuitive criteria in connection with the authors, so much as on the principle that where there is divine authority it is from the Holy Spirit that it comes. Inspiration was thought of as a form of special possession. Favourite analogies are ecstasy, as when God's spirit seizes a man so that he speaks words not his own but God's, or musical instruments in which men are the chords and the Holy Spirit is the player. Since this theory of inspiration was the dominant one, it is the more significant that often the Fathers pleaded for leaving room for the rationality, the human volition, the thought and literary methods of the individual writers of scripture. While, however, the problems posed by Divine Inspiration and the writers' human freedom were realised, there was no effort to probe them deeply.

c In their treatment of the doctrine of Inspiration, the patristic theologians show themselves grappling without final success with the problems to which the doctrine gives rise. Difficult questions arose. What is to be said of historical discrepancies in the scriptural narratives ? Is it possible that some portions of scripture express the truth about God more adequately than others ? Is it possible that truth may be recognised in a passage of scripture in more senses than one ? The Fathers gave various answers to those questions. Thus we find some of them decrying the Old Testament sacrifices, scriptural ordinances though they were, as being an imperfect compliance with the will of God. We find Origen teaching that the scriptures ' have two senses, the literal and the hidden, whereof the latter can be known only to those to whom is given the grace of the Holy Spirit in the word of wisdom and knowledge ' (*De Princip.* 1, prol.). In accord with this theory there came about a considerable use of allegorical interpretation, particularly in the school of Alexandria. In reaction, the school of Antioch insisted upon the need for historical exegesis, and for the primacy of the literal meaning. An instance of a foreshadowing of ' critical ' method is seen when Chrysostom deals with the problem of alleged discrepancies in detail in the Gospel narratives by saying that their existence makes more noteworthy the consensus of the Gospels to the ' important facts ' (In Matt. Hom. 1:2). These different modes of interpretation of the truth of the scriptures all lay within the belief in their divine authority and inspiration. The source of the belief had been the apostolic 8c
testimony to Christ.

V

It is beyond the scope of this article to trace the 9a
ways in which the authority of the Bible has been regarded within the various theological systems in the history of Christendom. Something, however, is here said about the movements of thought which have created the chief contemporary problems concerning the authority of the Bible.

In what sense is the Bible true ? Though from early times there had been within the Church the acknowledgment that literal history is not the only kind of truth which the Bible presents, the overwhelmingly prevailing view of the Bible in the Churches of the Reformation, no less than in the Roman Catholic Church, ascribed to its contents the character of literal history throughout. In the nineteenth century there came about the clash between this view of the Bible as an inerrant volume and the discoveries of biology, geology and literary and historical criticism. Thus the theory of the evolution of species taught by Charles Darwin challenged a literal acceptance of the account of the creation of the world. The investigation of the documents of the Old Testament by the same criteria as were applied to other ancient documents showed that books which had been held to be of single authorship were compiled by different writers at different dates ; and in particular the belief that Moses was the author of the Pentateuch was challenged. It came to be held that the laws ascribed to Moses were compilations at different periods under the influence of the teaching of the prophets. In the study of the New Testament literary criticism also had its effects. In particular, light was thrown upon the process by which the Gospels were compiled by the editing of earlier sources, and apart from more radical tendencies there came about a widespread readiness to see within the Gospels the presence of elements belonging to the Church's interpretation of the history as well as those which were strictly historical. Particularly was this so in the case of the Fourth Gospel.

One general effect of the critical revolution has been b
to enhance the awareness and understanding of the *human elements* in the Bible, and to enable it to be read less as a uniform volume of oracles than as a library of books of very different kinds, each in its particular human setting. But when critical methods are thus used and their results accepted, what becomes of belief in the *divine authority* of the Bible ? If a man is compelled as the price of his intellectual integrity to reject the literal belief in the creation of the world in six days, and in the story of Adam and Eve and the inerrancy of the Biblical narratives as a whole, is he thereby involved in rejecting the divine authority of the Bible ? This has been a crucial question. Without the doctrine of inerrancy, how may the belief in the divine authority of the Bible be held ?

One view of Biblical authority which has been very prominent is that which may be called evolutionary liberalism. This view sees the significance of the Bible as the record of the progress of religious and moral ideas amongst the Jews, using the idea of evolution as the key to religion and morals no less than to the origin of species. Thus it has been possible to trace Jewish ideas of God from stages which were crude and primitive through a steady progress up to the high achievements of the more enlightened writers, and to regard the latter alone as inspired. This view of the Bible commonly allowed no room for the supernatural activity of God in history, and treated the kingdom of God in terms of man's moral progress and not in terms of God's own action in salvation and judgment. In the field of the New Testament there is a similar tendency to take the moral teaching and example of Jesus as the core of the Gospel and to regard the

9b christological and soteriological elements in the records as unhistorical accretions made by the Early Church. Here is a way of treating the Bible which sees divine authority in portions of it, but fails to do justice to these things which had caused the Bible to come into existence, and incurs the charge that it is using criticism with arbitrary presuppositions. None the less, it was for many people the only known alternative to the dilemma of fundamentalism versus total scepticism.

c In the last few decades, however, another alternative has appeared, in reaction from extreme liberalism. There has been study of the Bible rigorous in critical methods, but using those methods without negative presuppositions against the intervention of God in the providential direction of history and in mighty acts of redemption such as the election of Israel and the resurrection of Jesus Christ. Hence there have come expositions of the Old Testament which emphasise the mighty act of God in the deliverance of Israel as providing the clue to the subsequent prophetic message and to the existence of the Old Testament books themselves, even though the historical records may be criticised and not accepted at face value. Equally, there have come expositions of the New Testament which, while allowing considerations of historical criticism to affect the assessment of the various books and their contents, hold that the explanation of the New Testament lies in the divine salvation brought by the unique event of the mission of Jesus, the Word-made-Flesh.

It is against the background of all these tendencies that the contemporary student of the Bible finds himself, together with some reassertion in recent times of a conservative position such as had prevailed before these newer tendencies appeared. The reader of the present edition of *Peake's Commentary* will find in its pages scientific criticism using its own methods and calling for the conclusions to which it leads. He will find, no less, the exposition of the Bible as an authoritative word of God. But how are these two attitudes held together, and what conception of the authority of the Bible do they together point to?

d The answer to the question is assisted by the process of historical inquiry which the previous sections of this article have followed, tracing what happened so as to cause the books of the Bible to be written and to come to be accepted as sacred scripture. It was the belief in a revelation through Law and Prophecy in the history of Israel which caused the books of the Old Testament first to be written, and finally to be formed in the Canon. It was the belief that these same books bear witness to Jesus Christ and were fulfilled by him which caused them to remain sacred scripture within the Christian Church. Similarly, the books of the New Testament were received as sacred scripture because they recorded the apostolic witness to Jesus Christ. Thus the process of historical inquiry helps us to understand the nature of the authority of the scriptures. Their authority lies in their relation to Jesus Christ who is the truth. Here is the clue to our understanding of the way in which the scriptures are *inspired*, *true* and the *Word of God*.

10a (1) In what sense are the scriptures *true*? They contain the truth of history, and it is fundamental to their existence as sacred scripture that God was active in real events whereby Israel was chosen, set free, given the law and the covenant, and ruled providentially by God in happenings such as the exile and the restoration which the prophets interpreted as his self-manifestation in mercy and judgment. It is no less fundamental that God uniquely manifested himself in the actual life, death and resurrection of Jesus Christ and in the subsequent endowment of the Church with the Holy Spirit. Without true facts of history, the sacred scriptures would not be what they are. But to accept this is not to deny that the recording of history may in the scriptures be mingled with symbolic interpretation which itself may be a vehicle of truth. Nor is it to deny that the records may 10a
contain details which are not factually correct, for indeed the discrepancies in some of the narratives make the acceptance of them all as factually correct to be virtually impossible. This admission does not, however, invalidate the belief that the scriptures are 'true' when we go on to recall that there are other aspects of truth besides historical fact. The scriptures can convey truth about God and man through poetry, drama, allegory and story. Furthermore, their status lies in the claim to convey 'the truth of God'. It is important to study the meaning of this phrase in the Bible itself. It there means the reality of God himself, made known in the impact of his righteous purpose upon Israel. To this impact of the reality of God the various books of the Bible bear witness; but they do so with various degrees of apprehension and response. No words, even inspired words, are wholly adequate to convey the reality of God: it transcends the media which convey it, and amongst those media the use of imagery and parable has its place.

(2) In what sense are the scriptures *inspired*? b
Modern critical study has led to an emphasis upon the human characteristics of the writers, which is congruous with the belief that inspiration does not involve the overriding of those human characteristics—a belief which indeed existed within the ancient Church. This has sometimes been expressed in modern times by saying that it was the writers, and not the words, which were inspired. It is rather doubtful whether this distinction can be pressed, since it is hard thus to separate thought from its clothing in words, or meaning from language. The essential point at stake, however, is that inspiration need not imply verbal inerrancy. Another conception to which modern critical study has given encouragement is that of 'degrees' of inspiration between the books of the Bible. Now plainly there *are* 'degrees' within the Bible—'degrees' of significance, as for instance between Exodus and Ruth, or between Isaiah and Esther, or between Matthew and 2 Peter. There are also degrees of approximation to the final revelation of the Word in Jesus Christ, as when the zeal for Yahweh in some of the Biblical writers goes with an apprehension of his character far short of the fuller apprehension which was to come. These differences are, it has been said, explained by degrees of inspiration of the writers. But this position has its difficulties. It is hard to distinguish quantities of 'more' and 'less' in the activity of the Holy Spirit. It is arbitrary to distinguish 'more' and 'less' in the responses of persons to the Holy Spirit in circumstances of which our knowledge is small. It is unsafe to be sure that the Holy Spirit is more concerned with products of 'genius' in religion, thought or language than with the work of grace in the moral struggles of writers of less 'genius' or none. For these reasons, the idea of 'degrees' of inspiration seems precarious.

Another approach to the inspiration of the scriptures c
has been through the evidence of the Books themselves as to the mark of inspiration in their writers. Amongst the Old Testament writers the prophets specially claimed inspiration, and the accounts of them describe supernatural experiences suggestive of the Spirit of God. Amongst the New Testament writers, Paul the apostle claims to speak under the direct influence of the Holy Spirit, and so does John, the author of the Apocalypse. Not so, however, the author of Luke and Acts, who claimed no inspiration as he describes his method of historical investigation in the compiling of his book. It seems arbitrary either to limit inspiration to the particular writers whose mode of inspiration is described, or to take their mode of inspiration as being universally applicable to the writers of scripture. Rather does there seem more warrant for understanding the inspiration of the scriptures from their place within the process of divine revelation in the old Israel and the new. God made himself known in the history of Israel, in Jesus Christ, and in the testimony

10c of the apostolic Church to him, and used many writers and books as witnesses to his self-disclosure. It was through the activity of the Holy Spirit in them and their writings that he enabled their witness to be given, a witness greatly varying in significance and in insight, and yet all part and parcel of the process of revelation. This inspiration is to be defined not in terms of the personal qualities of each writer, but in terms of the Canon as a whole. The key is found in the making of the Canon, itself a product of inspiration in the Church.

d (3) In what sense is there *revelation* in the scriptures? Here modern critical studies have led to an emphasis upon revelation being a process, and upon the disparity of its phases. The Song of Deborah and Barak, for instance, teaches that Yahweh is God, and that zeal for him is right: but it reveals this amid imperfect apprehension of his character. The Sermon on the Mount reveals that Yahweh is still God, and that zeal for him is right, but amid the revelation of the full demands of his righteousness. Clearly the revelation in the Bible possesses stages. It is doubtful however whether the phrase often used in modern discussion, 'progressive revelation', is satisfying. It suggests that God disclosed portions of his being or character at various times, while withholding other portions; and it is hard, on reflection, to see meaning in so quantitative a view of divine attributes. Rather is revelation to be thought of as the presence and impact of God himself amongst his people as he gives himself to them, never present with less than his whole self. It seems, therefore, that where there is advance in the Bible it is advance not in God's revelation but in the witness of Israel to it and to the inspired deductions which Israel draws from it. Here indeed is the light and shade of historical movement, in the midst of which God is ever present striving ceaselessly with men.

e In all these ways the methods and the conclusions of modern critical study may be shown to compel no denial of the authority of the Bible, but rather to assist our understanding of the ways in which it is *true*, *inspired* and the word of God in *revelation*. It is an understanding different in many ways from that which existed in the ancient Church, and yet based upon fresh knowledge of the processes whereby the ancient Church came to believe as it did.

In like manner, modern critical study, while it has given the analysis of the many diverse portions of the Bible, can yet serve our understanding of its unity. The unity is that of Promise and Fulfilment. The deliverance of Israel from Egypt in the exodus, and the giving to her of the law and the covenant have their counterpart in the deliverance of mankind in the death and resurrection of Jesus Christ and the giving through him of the new covenant in his blood and the new commandment which fulfils the law. The Old Testament is a book 'about Christ' inasmuch as its record is not self-explanatory but explicable as the preparation for Christ, and inasmuch as the divine word was himself present making ready for the Incarnation.

VI

11a The authority of the Bible is thus the authority of God who speaks through it to mankind. He speaks in the Old Testament the word of promise, and in the New Testament the word of apostolic witness; 11a
and both the promise and the witness enable us to hear the word who is Jesus Christ himself.

The hearing of the word in the Bible, and the pursuit of critical study are in no way incompatible. It is necessary to reject the idea that a firm faith implies the repelling from the mind of the queries raised by criticism—for the faith of a Christian is faith in God, and God is the giver of the scholar's quest for truth as he sets out in search of it, as one not knowing whither he goes. It is required of faith that it does not deny the spirit of inquiry; and conversely it is required of the spirit of inquiry that it does not cling to prejudices as to what God can or cannot do in the sovereign activity of his word. The problem of the synthesis of faith and criticism seems to be one aspect of the larger problem of divine grace in its relation to human freedom.

The reader of the Bible has the Church to guide him. b
The relation of the authority of the Bible to the authority of the Church is a subject treated differently by different theological traditions within the history of Christendom, and it cannot be pursued fully here. Suffice it to notice, from the earlier portions of this article, that the connection between Bible and Church is inherent in the existence of both, and the one cannot be explained without the other. Under both the Old Covenant and the New, the Church preceded the Bible. It was within Israel, with its prophets and priests, its oral traditions and its cultus, that the Old Testament was made. It was within the new Israel, with its apostles and prophets, its sacraments and oral traditions, that the New Testament was made. The mission of the Church to interpret the Bible means this at least: that it is the man who lives truly in the fellowship of the Church and shares in the privileges of the covenant who has his mind attuned to the understanding of the scriptures as the books of the people of the covenant.

Within the Church of God Word and Sacrament c
interpret one another. The word of the Gospel, read and preached, is the story of a past event, yet it has its present impact in grace and power upon the hearers. Christ, whose Word is preached, is himself present in the Eucharist in the Sacrament of his body and blood wherein his death is shown forth until his coming again. Thus the Church's understanding of the Word in the scriptures is reinforced by the contemporary action of Christ in Word and Sacrament. This action sustains the common life of the Church, and it is in that common life that there is continuity with the life of the Israel of God in the Bible.

It is to men and women not *in vacuo* but in the contemporary context of their existence that the Word in the Bible speaks. The light which critical study can bring, the light which comes from the mind and experience of the Church, these illumine the meaning of the Bible for those who would understand it—but it is to *them* that it speaks the divine Word of love and judgment: 'today if you will hear his voice, harden not your hearts.'

Bibliography—C. H. Dodd, *The Authority of the Bible* (rev. ed. 1938); C. W. Dugmore (ed.), *The Interpretation of the Bible* (1943); A. G. Hebert, *The Authority of the OT* (1947); J. K. S. Reid, *The Authority of Scripture* (1957); W. Sanday, *Inspiration* (1893).

THE BIBLE AS LITERATURE

By T. R. HENN

12a This brief essay can do no more than touch upon some few aspects of a vast subject, and indeed each of its headings could be expanded many times. It seemed necessary to inquire first how and in what sense we may consider the Bible as literature today; thereafter, its themes and the language in which they are set out. Here, as in the second section called 'The Forge of Style', the AV has been used as the norm, with some consideration, so far as space allowed, of earlier and later versions. The third section, 'The Holy War', is designed to exemplify the language and imagery deriving from that activity, culminating, perhaps, in the great exhortation of St Paul. In the fourth, 'Image and Archetype', an attempt has been made to suggest something of the mysterious perennial quality of the imagery of the Bible, and the organic aspect of language with which so much literary criticism is concerned today. 'Proverbs and Prophecy' in the fifth section are grouped together to suggest a related but independent mode of statement; leading to the last section, 'Visions', that comprehends (in one sense) the intention of the Bible; the progress of man's tentative and intermittent knowledge, the search through spiritual warfare and faith, for 'the city that hath foundations, whose builder and maker is God'.

Any attempt to exemplify standards of literary excellence by comparison with other works did not appear to be a practical technique; and for this there seemed to be two main reasons. First, there is no other work of comparable size, manner, structure and intention. We may on occasion point to the Koran, or to the Granth, or to the Upanishads, or to the Bhagavadgita, or to *The Book of the Dead*; but such comparisons are not fruitful. In its range, its unity, its divergence, its two major symphonic movements of promise and fulfilment, its avoidance (in general) of those tedious and childish deserts common in other great religious books, the Bible remains unique.

Secondly (and this is the chief obstacle to any attempt at an aesthetic evaluation), the character of the Bible is burned into the timber of English; and this is not wholly because of its character as a sacred book. At the lowest level, its proverbs and its parables, its episodes sacred or profane, have been expounded pictorially, mimetically, or verbally from our beginnings. It has supplied the themes for epic, satire, tragedy, comedy, farce, ballet, oratorio. One might say, at a guess, that one-third of the poems in our language bear traces of its imagery or thought; perhaps two-thirds of the world's greatest graphic and plastic works have drawn upon it. It seems probable that its rhythms are embedded in us (first through the Latin of ritual, and their transpositions into the English Liturgy) so firmly as to condition our recognition, and response to, all other rhythms of a similar nature. This point is elaborated in §13*a*. But all questions of our responses to rhythm are still speculative.

The word 'burned' has been used of the mark set upon English literature and life, with some thought of Isaiah's coal; but we must recognise two currents of opposing thought. One is that which proclaims, and laments, the present lack of knowledge of the Bible, as of the Greek and Latin Classics; and indicates regretfully the mass of English literature that is made 12a
sterile, in whole or in part, by that ignorance. It is indeed possible that students of English literature may one day come to the stage at which references to the Tree of Knowledge, the Fiery Furnace, the Journey of the Magi or the Last Supper, require explanatory footnotes. Even today a biblical allusion, used directly, or ironically, or to give 'depth', is not always recognised. We cannot count on a reasonable response, say, to A. E. Housman's

> Ho, every one that thirsteth
>   And hath the price to give,
> Come to the stolen waters,
>   Drink and your soul shall live—

in terms of the relevant passages from Isaiah (Isa. 55:1), or to Dryden's *Absalom and Achitophel*, or to Kipling's satire *Gehazi*; though it is probable that most would still recognise an allusion to the Valley of Dry Bones (Ezek. 37:1) or to the Crowing of the Cock.

There is another and more formidable thought: b
the argument that the **literary influence** of the Bible has been overestimated in the past, and will decrease in the future; and here the protagonist is C. S. Lewis (*The Literary Impact of the Authorised Version*). He has argued that 'the Authorised Version as a strictly literary influence has mattered less than we have often supposed'; suggesting that 'the modern approach, or what was till lately the modern approach, to the Bible is deeply influenced by the Romantic movement . . . that taste for the primitive and passionate which can be seen growing through nearly the whole of the 18th cent. It may be asked whether now, when only a minority of Englishmen regard the Bible as a sacred book, we may anticipate an increase of its literary influence. I think we might if it continued to be widely read. But this is not very likely. Our age has, indeed, coined the expression "the Bible as literature". It is very generally implied that those who have rejected its theological pretensions nevertheless continue to enjoy it as a treasure house of English prose. It may be so. There may be people who, not having been forced upon familiarity with it by believing parents, have yet been drawn to it by its literary charms and remained as constant readers. But I never happen to meet them.'

It is a case that is cogently argued, but I cannot find support for it in my own experience; nor can I agree that the Bible is 'so remorselessly and continuously sacred that it does not invite, it excludes or repels, the merely aesthetic approach'; for I believe that the term 'aesthetic' is, in the context, misleading. We shall attempt, in the rest of this essay, to suggest its peculiar blend of 'aesthetic' and moral values. Yet there are certain difficulties which we must face at the outset.

We must be prepared to read and value a literature that is set very far apart from our own, because it is a **literature of simplification and simplicity**. It communicates thought and feeling arising out of limited situations, and out of a world view that is characterised by profundity without complexity. This very

12b profundity would appear to involve the reader in the assumption of a corresponding simplicity (but not *naïveté*) of mind: for, if not, that which the Bible has to communicate will lose its power to move to action, or to meditation upon action, in ' the strange mutations of the world '. Some of us believe that, when civilisations in their great wave-motions exhibit complexities so great as to be unbearable to the individual mind, we are given by poets and artists, or make for ourselves, some framework of thought and action that may enable us to achieve again a real or imagined simplicity. Once we are so prepared, the literature that is presented within the Bible does, I think, fall into place. But it does not so fall without difficulties. We must, I believe, accept the sinfulness of man, for the Bible is in one sense the record of this. We must accept, as a consequence, the trajectory of nations and individuals, through the classic sequence of wrong-doing, punishment, repentance, purification, redemption.

We must accustom ourselves to the short double blows of the verse-form, so like a trip-hammer in a forge; to a prose-structure limited in its capacity to the cadences, some of which I have tried to discuss; to the Eastern repetition, parallel or incremental, which sounds, at times, as if it carried some ancient spell; to words that sing with a strange music, though their sense may at times hardly be recovered by the labour of scholars. We must accustom ourselves to think metaphysically or parabolically, allowing text and counter-text, cliché or poetic diction, to certify one another, as they do in Homer.

This, then, is the first background, the conditions of our reading. The second involves some consideration of the manner in which this mass of literature takes its relatively final shape. It is written out of fallible human memories; cross-hatched with interpolations; edited and re-edited with intention. It is the fragmentary history of a small tribe of the Eastern Mediterranean, who had amalgamated some of their epic traditions with the compressed and skeletal myths, common to many of their neighbours, of the Creation and the Flood. It concerns a people who are at first (whether by choice or chance) nomadic; and, to the end, largely pastoral. Their strategical position had made them a buffer state, lying on the line of march between Egypt and Syria, between Persia and the coast; living always uneasily with their neighbours; and liable always to invasion, subjection or captivity as the great empires about them rose and fell. To survive unbroken, slavery, occupation, dispersion, they must be conscious always of a spiritual unity in the nation, fostered by the tradition and by the moral and physical superiority of their God; out of which grew the sense of unity as a nation and as an army, so that they might speak with their enemies in the gate.

When they occupy, tentatively and with divided forces, their promised land, they are cut off from the sea by the Philistines of the coastal plain: so that their literature speaks of the sea, its storms and its monsters, of ships and of merchandise, with something like awe (e.g. Ps. 104:26). The horses and chariots of the plain become an emblem of fear, joining the perpetual mystery of the horse-image in dream and nightmare. In time of peace their traffic with the neighbouring peoples (as well as the pressure to conform to their conquerors in the long captivities) invites continually those restless experiments with alien religions, that might conquer or transform (whenever their faith in His omnipotence wavered) their own God, as in the proverb still current in the East: ' Your gods or my gods—how do I know which are the stronger? ' So the worship of the Golden Calf, and of every kind of image, totem or fetish that man's fear or lust could imagine or approve. We may remember the long struggles of Mohammedanism with idolatry, and the achieved corruption of Hindu doctrine. As always the temptation is strengthened by marriage or concubinage, so that the common image 12b
is of whoring after strange gods.

Their civilisation becomes stabilised, and community life tends to what we may call a settled pastoral; the cities at first few and of no great account, but increasing in size and importance as the narrative progresses. Wealth is mainly of flocks and herds, and save under Solomon's extended kingdom, not greatly multiplied by trade. Their defence is that of small mobile bands, levied when need arises; though their warfare is always complicated, after the immemorial fashion of the East, by tribal and intertribal dissensions, jealousies, treacheries.

Their history is written, in general, long after the events that are commemorated. Therefore it is perceived in terms of action; the acid of time eating away all save irrelevancies and fortuitous traces of personality, that survive mysteriously and irregularly in a narrative concerned with action. That narrative moves simply and strongly through time; its gaps compressed to throw into relief the more vivid and memorable peaks of warfare, prophecy, codifications of their Law, or those genealogies that are so important to the East as certifying continuity of spirit and blood.

The narrative moves, a little spasmodically, towards its objective, the Messianic promise that will one day be fulfilled. Its track through history is maintained (as it were) by constant retrospective correction of the course; through back-references to history, recalled as a national epic, and the finding of past promise or prophecy fulfilled in the present. So there is no cyclic philosophy, no birth or recreation or reinterpretation of the fixed Law; only the intermittent backslidings, by people or king, from a known ideal, and their return to grace. Events in time fall like beads down taut wires, from Past-in-Memory into Past-in-History, to be seen eventually as patterns or *exempla* that certify, by their powerful accumulation, the promise of the future.

We have, therefore, **a narrative that is highly** e
selective, concerned with the skeletons of action yet with a peculiar retrospective unity; simple, direct, and vivid, with the language and imagery of a people living in close and toilsome contact with agriculture and war. They are intensely aware of the rhythm of the seasons; of the fear that seed-time or harvest may fail, the fear of famine and pestilence, the destruction of the locust or of the unreturning cloud (Ec. 12:2). Their flocks are guarded against eagle, lion, wolf; serpent and scorpion are emblems of pain and death; net, snare, hook, are familiar as emblems of the hunter, fisher, fowler, who garnered those wild fruits. Thus their imagery is drawn from flocks and herds, the immemorial routine of shepherds and herdsmen seeking pasture for their flocks in Mediterranean lands, and giving rise, then as now, to a peculiar rough kindly relationship between man and beast; of the valleys that stand thick with corn; of the grape and olive that comfort the toiler of the terraced slopes. Metals seem to denote value; gold and precious stones, purity and incorruptibility; iron may stand for the sword, or strength, or captivity, or death. The OT questions continually the mystery of man's alternating experiences of pleasure and pain. It is aware, like Synge's peasants, of ' the coming of grey hairs, and the loosening of the teeth '. It speculates little, save in the Psalms, Job, and Ecclesiastes, on cosmic matters; but the stars carry a sense of steadfastness and wonder (as they must to those who navigate by them through sea or desert, or sow and reap by them), and God Himself may answer out of the whirlwind or the fire or the storm. Beyond these physical phenomena are the creatures of the penumbral world, many of them, significantly, of the sea: Leviathan, the Great Fishes, Dragons, Serpents, that shew and praise His mystery.

Against the background the individual matters little; saving his place as king, judge, leader, and the *exempla* which his actions give. He is gathered to his

12c fathers, goes to his long home, or goes down into the pit ; and ceases to give thanks to God. He knows only the immortality in which his actions live, to be recited, generation after generation, to stiffen the national will, to proclaim the care of Yahweh, and the relationship of that care to the continuing righteousness of his people.

When we turn to the NT we are, in some measure, in another world : in some measure only, since the continuity of the Jewish tradition is emphasised by genealogy, quotation of the Law, the triumphant fulfilment of prophecy. Perhaps the works of Josephus form a link between Old and New : for in the New the battle-clouds, the thunder of Yahweh, the pessimism and exaltation of the Prophets, seem to have yielded to a quieter air. The soldiery and their arms seem to stand a little in the background, as in a country occupied by a conquering but civilised nation ; we are conscious of their pressure on the perimeter, but they do not often come forward. A little behind the middle ground of our canvas we are aware of the jarring Jewish sects, the Law with its tendency to the aridity of ritual ; nationalist pressure ebbing and flowing beneath the Roman sway. But the foreground has a sweeter light upon it. The pastoral world is painted in softer, more peaceful shades ; parables are built on the incidents and problems of normal quiet living. There is—even inland—a smell of ships and fishermen; the boundaries have extended to the Mediterranean, and let in something of the Greek in thought as well as in tongue. It is true that the impending fall of Jerusalem casts a shadow in prophecy, and the tragedy of the Crucifixion is the crisis of each Gospel ; but as we travel over Greece and Asia Minor we move to the new, struggling, dissentious Churches, beset with every sort of practical and heretical problem ; the vicissitudes of missionary work lightening the narrative prose and strengthening the doctrine that grows in the minds and mouths of its preachers. At the end, we pass from narrative and doctrine and exhortation to phantasy in Revelation ; to recapture momentarily the atmosphere of Ezekiel or Daniel in the island of Patmos. We are aware of a new lyric pressure forced (as it were) through the relatively unhelpful medium of NT Greek ; yet at its best with a moving simplicity of its own.

Against some such backgrounds we may see the Language of the Themes : their statements of men in action, and the desires, adorations, persuasions, ecstasies proper to them.

13a **I The Themes and their Language**—The main theme of the Bible could, perhaps, be described very crudely as the relationship of Man to God : Man's perception (growing slowly in the direction of understanding and love) of the nature of God. This nature is exemplified, illuminated, urged forward in human comprehension, by a multitude of actions : each one illuminating (as it might be the facets of a slowly turning crystal) some attribute or intention or characteristic of Him ; so far as the capacity of Man allowed him to deduce such qualities or perceive them in moments of insight. It would be proper to see the whole pattern as, ultimately, subordinated to such an end ; a vast fragmentary epic, moving with spasmodic jerks through time ; its intellectual unity arising from a dominating monotheistic concept ; its literary unity, though in the last resort a loose one, built on its peculiar method of retrospective composition selected out of oral tradition.

Within such a major framework we can distinguish a number of contributory themes. The cosmic 'mythologem' (to use a term established by Jung) of Creation and the version of the Flood is on a scale and of a scope of which the ἔκστασις (in the sense used by Longinus) may be thought to lend to the book of Genesis its distinctive style. The escape from Egypt, the Red Sea Crossing, the Wandering in the Wilderness, constitute another action fused, as it were, by the Sinaitic Commandments. We have then a series of minor 'trajectories', those curves of development 13a
common to all living ; that may be roughly denoted by the sequence of achievement, disobedience, disaster, regeneration, at the hands of the God who, like the Zeus of Aeschylus, had 'bound fast learning to suffering'.

Across these run the minor related actions, **adventures in spiritual and moral evil** ; the art and b
practice of ritual living in contaminated surroundings ; *exempla* of offensive and defensive campaigns, with the sins and virtues of their leaders ; the individual tragedy of Job (the sole drama among countless dramatic incidents) ; ballads, sacred songs, rhapsodies, oracular utterances ; all interspersed with the codified wisdom, the proverbial distillation of experience, from which the Hebrew tradition renewed continually its characteristic life.

But there is another aspect of the Bible that we must include among its themes. There is, indeed, hardly an aspect of human evil that cannot be found in the Bible ; and without this component the book would suffer infinitely in stature. The simplicity, directness and matter-of-fact character of its statement rob this vision of evil of any pejorative influence. More serious (and a perpetual stumbling-block to many readers) has been the objective bloodthirstiness of many narrated incidents ; the defenestration of Jezebel ; the Psalmist's vision of the children dashed against the stones (outdoing Lady Macbeth) ; the wholesale massacre of enemies. These things we cannot today condone ; we must try to understand, and it is helpful to remember the savagery that even today lies so close to the surface of civilised man. Of human ingenuity in torture, save of mutilation, fire or stone, there is happily nothing. We have savagery, but not sadism.

Indeed, every provision of the Decalogue is broken many times. Idolatry, blasphemy, drunkenness, concupiscence, harlotry (setting aside the approved plurality of wives and concubines) ; cheating of every kind, from deceit to the instances of 'sharp practice' that are sometimes viewed with approval ; witchcraft and divination (this latter shading into legitimate prophecy). It is also difficult to condone 'heroic' treachery, Jael's murder of Sisera, Judith's of Holofernes, unless we remember, not only the tradition in so much Eastern literature of this sacrificial seduction by the woman-liberator, but this mysterious archetypal pattern of the Severed Head that is apparent everywhere.

Yet it is not enough to see all this in its historical context ; we must see it as among the great qualities of the OT. The evils, exemplified in action, are those of the human situation, born of the eternal conflict between man's erected wit and his infected will (I use the term of Sidney's *Apologie for Poetry*). They are not, as in Greek and Roman literature, the product of the caprice or petulance or lust of those multiform deities ; though indeed, like them, the Hebrew is aware of the retribution which follows ritual neglect, or the greater sin of *hubris*. Evil is an essential component of this microcosm. So long as the conception of Yahweh, jealous always but constant in his guardianship of his perverse people, is unmodified by the conception of love, so long Yahweh's attributes of victory and vengeance must seem of paramount importance to his people.

We must also perceive this component as part of the supreme objectivity of biblical narrative. If we were to imagine it purged, by selection or editing, we should lose not only its moral and aesthetic balance but also an essential component of the simplification which it presents. Evil of this kind is deeply rooted in a universal experience, of which the complex psychological motivations are perceived, quite simply, as the responsibility of the individual Will. Evil is an intrinsic product of the primary appetencies of living : food, desire, power, security. It is seen in terms of action which arises from individual or collective wickedness (for it is shown, rightly, as having always

13b a strong infective aspect) or from the power-lust of an enemy. A king desires his neighbour's vineyard, or his wife ; a prophet convicts a whole people of corruption, ritual and moral ; a captivity (and it is difficult to imagine the detailed horror of those scenes) is the direct outcome of Yahweh's turning aside from his people. The ethic which emerges, whether by the *exempla* in suffering or at the mouths of the long succession of prophets, those Secretaries of the Holy Ghost (the phrase is Donne's), is the ethic of Sinai, sharply focused by ritual and the Law, pressed home by a real or imagined system of rewards and punishments. Slowly the thinkers of the OT confront the ethical problem in its full perspectives ; the perceived lines of the Godhead are seen to expand, as the burnt-offerings smell less sweet. The evil sent upon Job is in part capricious, but his story is of the beginning of the Tragic Hero : and in the λύσις of that drama there is the dawning consciousness of its nature :

> Suffering is permanent, obscure, and dark,
> And shares the nature of infinity.
>
> Wordsworth, *The Borderers*

Evil and suffering are shewn as a mystery, and there is no scale by which they may be measured and weighed.

e But again we must correct the perspective of the themes. There is, I think, no humour, but there are the **gracious songs** of rejoicing, of gratitude, and a keen delight in the observed world : whether as a source of awe, or gratitude at deliverance from famine, or the mere liberty to dwell at peace in their habitations. There is the ecstasy of the **love poetry,** calling in the delighted senses to decorate the Beloved (there are a few comparable things in English : we may think of Spenser's *Prothalamion*, Keats' *Eve of St Agnes*, Meredith's *Love in a Valley*) ; the tenderness of the story of Ruth, the pathos of her desire and loyalty fixed for ever in a single epithet of Keats ; stories of compassion, of friendships, of loyalty and fortitude. There is the **theme of death** ; carrying no great charge of emotion save the simplicity of loss : for the thought of eternity does not often come in the OT to bring the fears and hopes from beyond the grave. Men are gathered to their fathers, or go down into the darkness. Exceptions are the famous Isa. 26:19 and Dan. 12:2.

The epithets used of ' the Bible as Literature ' are usually ' sublime ', ' magnificent ', ' awe-inspiring '. They have little validity as terms of criticism unless we attempt to look at them a little more closely. And since **sublime** is the first of these, and perhaps the commonest (serving for Genesis, Job, Isaiah, the beginning of the Fourth Gospel, or the Vision of St John) we may consider it first and see what light is shed.

The περὶ ὕψους of ' Longinus ', that mysterious Greek or Sicilian critic, was the first to use the term, which achieved its greatest popularity, and perhaps effectiveness, in the work of Blair, Burke, Reynolds, Ruskin. ' Longinus ' had defined sublimity as ' the true ring of a noble mind ', ' the echo of a great soul '. The mind of the great writer must be ' neither small nor ignoble '. Yet the last test is the power of ' sublime ' writing to lead us, not to ' persuasion ' (the province of rhetoric) but to ' ecstasy ' : an exalted and valuable state of mind. ' Sublime sayings naturally fall to men of spirit.' But it is not necessarily built on the ' grand style ', or upon grandiloquence ; indeed the turgid and tumid styles are in his view special vices to which writers who attempt the sublime are always subject. On the contrary, the sublime may use common words, ' which are not vulgar because they are so expressive '. In the prelude to the famous passage on Genesis he first quotes Hesiod on the Horses of Heaven, then—from the Battle of the Gods—one of the passages which, in his view, far surpasses that of Hesiod, Homer's lines on Poseidon, as representing what he calls ' the divine nature in its true attributes, pure, majestic and 13e
unique '.

> Then were the woods and the long-lying ranges a-tremble,
> Aye, and the peaks and the city of Troy and the ships of Achaia,
> 'Neath the immortal feet and the oncoming march of Poseidon.
> He set him to drive o'er the swell of the sea, and the whales at his coming
> Capering leapt from the deep and greeted the voice of their master.
> Then the sea parted her waves for joy, and they flew on the journey.
>
> (trans. Hamilton Fyfe)

There is some shadow of comparison possible with the description of Leviathan in Job 41. But consider in general the function of the poetic statement of the environment and attributes (in all literatures) of a god. ' So, too, the Jewish lawgiver, no ordinary man, having formed a worthy conception of divine power, gave expression to it at the very threshold of his *Laws* where he says : " God said "—what ? " Let there be light ", and there was light. " Let there be earth, and there was earth ".' It is, I think, clear from the context that ' Longinus ' has in mind two thoughts. Here is a fragment of Jewish literature that conveys, by its ' eminence and excellence of language ', the fact of divine omnipotence : as surely as Dante contracted all Christian philosophy into the line

> In la sua volontade è nostra pace.

The words ' Let there be light, and there was light ' is just this gesture of finality, beyond comprehension, the expression of that which is and must remain penumbral to the understanding. We might set beside it that other ' dark abstraction ' :

> And the Spirit of God moved upon the face of the waters.

This sense of mysterious power, finding its expression not in magniloquence but in simplicity and compression, adjusts itself to a particular rhythmic phrasing : nor can we separate words and rhythm from the total statement, or judge how those same rhythms may, by custom and inheritance, become an integral part of our way of thinking. In the last-quoted sentence we may, if we wish, note how the movement is in fact anapaestic :

> And the Spirit of God . . .

and how its continuance is rightly denied by substituting *upon* for the possible *on* : how the vowels lengthen and fall in the scale from

> Spirit of God moved upon

to the final cadence of

> the face of the waters

and mark how strangely the conjunctive *ands* carry their peculiar weight in this narrative of man's derivation from the dust. But of the final force we have explained nothing.

Sometimes the addition of the image seems to lend additional rhythmic sublety, as in the two phrases :

> And Moses stretched forth his hand over the sea, and the sea *returned to his strength* when the morning appeared. (Exod. 14:27)

Sometimes there is a strict simplicity born of the understatement that in its turn communicates the intensity of the unspoken. So Judas' departure after the Last Supper :

13c He then having received the sop went immediately out : and it was night. (Jn 13:30)

or

And immediately the cock crew. (Mt. 26:74)

or

So I spake unto the people in the morning : and at even my wife died ; and I did in the morning as I was commanded. (Ezek. 24:18)

recalling, perhaps, the line of Wordsworth's *Michael* that Arnold praised for just such a distilled essence,

And never lifted up a single stone.

or the Epitaph at Marathon

O stranger, tell the Spartans we lie here
Obedient to their will.

or that more modern epigram in Greek, on the Miracle in Cana,

The modest water saw its Lord, and blushed.

For one quality of the understatement of this kind is its expansive power : the ripples spread outward from the stone thrown into the pool of the mind, and we do not know the further shores.

d Of this **expansive** quality we may consider for a moment some aspects of the imagery which, as we have said, is born of simplicity of environment and concreteness of thinking. Its characteristic effects are in some sort accountable to certain qualities in the original tongues, as well as to their relationship to Elizabethan English. Hebrew is poorly supplied with adjectives and with adverbs ; the concrete must often be adopted to serve these purposes. Emotional states are constantly expressed in physical terms ; as in Elizabethan thinking, psychology and physiology are intermingled in the motions of body and soul. In consequence, we are left to deduce, or recreate, the emotion communicated from the bare bones of the situation, stated but not directly charged with feeling ; and even where there is direct expression there is still the component of the thing that is unsaid, yet alive with its latent quality of extension. Two passages may help to illustrate this : the first is from Job :

They cause the naked to lodge without clothing, that they have no covering in the cold.
They are wet with the showers of the mountains, and embrace the rock for want of a shelter.
They pluck the fatherless from the breast, and take a pledge of the poor . . .
Men groan from out of the city, and the soul of the wounded crieth out : yet God layeth not folly to them. (Job 24:7–9, 12)

Consider beside this a passage from *King Lear* :

Poor naked wretches, wheresoe'er you are,
That bide the pelting of this pitiless storm,
How shall your houseless heads and unfed sides,
Your loop'd and window'd raggedness, defend you
From seasons such as these ? O ! I have ta'en
Too little care of this. Take physic, pomp ;
Expose thyself to feel what wretches feel,
That thou mayst shake the superflux to them,
And show the heavens more just.

Both themes deal with pity. The rich Shakespearean complexity of image and attitude makes the comparison unfair, but it does bring out one matter of great importance. The parallel structure of the biblical verses, the two balanced clauses, the incremental or contrasting repetition, has its own peculiar formal qualities. By repeating or enlarging the thing said, it conveys a characteristic precision and finality of statement. For slightly different reasons it can carry, 13d
within fairly narrow limits of intention, the lyric qualities of lament, love-poetry, elegy, and gnomic sayings. Again, for different reasons, it can compass admirably simple consecutive narrative ; a campaign, a siege, the building of a wall, a sea voyage, a shipwreck, a rioting trade-guild. For proverbs (as the survival of the form in English shows) its terse illumination and expansive analogical power make it almost supreme, rivalled only by the heroic couplet at its best.

But when we have said all this, we must confess the e
grave limitations of the verse structure, which can never be wholly overcome by writing it as consecutive prose. If we set beside it any passage of English prose, of comparable subject and intention, we are immediately made aware of the resources of the larger paragraphic structure, the subtleties and overtones and richness of the adjectives (consider the adjectives, one by one, in the *Lear* passage). We are confronted with the certainty that the range is narrow ; that we must judge it by the depth of simplicity and of certain effects of imagery ; and that very little English prose, written after 1611, can legitimately be used for a touchstone.

Yet the very simplicity, limited vocabulary, narrative and dramatic clichés, and the comparative poverty of resources in imagery combine to produce certain literary effects of importance. Both words and imagery acquire ' depth ' by repetition, or incremental repetition. We become accustomed to old usages, and graft new shades of meaning upon their stocks, in accordance with the context. Even verses or phrases which are logically separated from the remainder of the passage may become, as it were, *assimilated* to their position so that a kind of metaphysical relationship may grow up. We might, for example, check at the imagery of this passage :

By reason of the voice of my groaning my bones cleave to my skin.
I am like a pelican of the wilderness ; I am like an owl of the desert.
I watch, and am as a sparrow alone upon the house top. (Ps. 102:5–7)

The bones that cleave to the skin is expressive enough of wasted cattle or man in famine : the water-bird in a waterless country, the night predator where there is no life, are expressive : the sparrow on the housetop an emblem of loneliness. But behind them, as we search our memories, there is the pelican (coupled with the swan as unclean) as a mysterious symbol in Elizabethan literature ; the owl as Athene's bird ; God's care for the sparrow (five for two farthings) in the NT : and the pattern draws closer, becomes credible because of such associations. In something of the same way, it seems possible that ' blurred ' or indeterminate, or even corrupt imagery, may acquire a meaning from such usage.

As regards Wordsworth's definition of poetry, the f
' best words in the best order ', we may consider a familiar passage from the Psalms :

Such as sit in darkness and in the shadow of death, being bound in affliction and iron ;
Because they rebelled against the words of God, and contemned the counsel of the most High ;
Therefore he brought down their heart with labour ; they fell down, and there was none to help.
(Ps. 107:10–12)

and set it against this Tate and Brady's paraphrase of this passage :

Some lie, with darkness compass'd round,
In death's uncomfortable shade,
And with unwieldy fetters bound,
By pressing cares more heavy made.

13f Because God's counsel they defied,
And lightly priz'd his holy word,
With their afflictions they were tried :
They fell, and none could help afford.

It would not be easy to find a more striking example of the poetic diction of the 18th cent. playing havoc with the simplicity and directness of the original. The flattening effect of the *appliqué'd* adjectives and adverbs, the circumlocutions demanded by the rhyme, are clear enough. Our mind and ear will reject indignantly 'death's uncomfortable shade' for 'in the shadow of death' ; yet the very rejection may give us pause to think. Why do we accept unhesitatingly the 'comfortable words' of the Liturgy, and reject 'uncomfortable' here, since both carry their earlier and stronger meaning ? Has not the *shade* a suggestion of the classical underworld, the ghosts, that might once have been valuable ? I suppose it is because the *shadow* of death has become familiar through the *valley of the shadow* . . ., because *shadow* suggests a warning of something progressive, menacing, whereas *shade* is static. *Pressing cares* is hopelessly wide of *affliction*, which is bodily torment as well as mental ; the zeugma of *bound in affliction and iron* give as it were a reciprocal intensification to each ; and the *iron* is not, I believe, limited in the original to fetters (however unwieldy) but has the wider meaning of the *mental* bitterness, the iron that enters into the soul (and, perhaps, an overtone of the *rusting* of the spirit.)

As a more complex example, we may consider the following :

> O my God, my soul is cast down within me : therefore will I remember thee from the land of Jordan, and of the Hermonites, from the hill Mizar.
> Deep calleth unto deep at the noise of thy waterspouts : all thy waves and thy billows are gone over me. (Ps. 42:6, 7)

The first-quoted verse employs the traditional and abundantly justified nostalgia of locality—the historic river, the sacred hill. The second appears to be disjointed ; perhaps we pass over it recalling our proverbial 'deep calling unto deep' (though it means something quite different) : but here we are, surely, left with a triple image. The waterspouts dragged up into the sky contain or carry the water of the unplumbed depths : the waves and billows (longer, more powerful, smoother than a wave) overwhelm the poet (as in that astonishing description of Jonah) : waterspouts and waves are of God and of His commanding ; and we recall the description in Genesis of the waters before creation, with the spirit of God moving upon their face. Given the fear of an inland people for the great waters, the suggestion of the powerlessness of the drowned mind could not be stronger.

14a Because of the parallelism, and for other reasons which we shall discuss later, the **rhythmic effects** of biblical prose are peculiar, though again limited. Dr Daiches (*Literary Essays* (1956)) has suggested that the translators attempted at times to reproduce some of the cadences of the Hebrews : as in Isa. 40 : 'Comfort ye, comfort ye, my people', corresponding to the Hebrew '*Naḥ[a]mû naḥ[a]mû* ʿ*ammî*'. They can be best considered by some brief reference to the *cursus* of Medieval Latin, which was a striking feature of rhetorical literature, and which had left traces, through the Mass, in much of the English Liturgy.

The cursus is in essence a rhythmical arrangement of the concluding words of any period or phrase. It is based on the stressed syllables (in Latin the long syllable) counting *backwards* from the end of the sentence : so that it is usually described by counting the accents, and denoting them numerically in relationship to the sentence-ending. There are in Late Latin three traditional forms of this :

the *cursus planus* (lóngum sermónem, víncla perfrégit) 14a
denoted by 5:2 (the penultimate being long or stressed),
the *cursus tardus* (ráro justítia, fórtis operátio) denoted by 6:3,
and the *cursus velox* (témpore ópportúno) denoted by 7:4:2.

Now the cursus is a peculiarly Latin rhythm, because of b
the case-endings which so often bring the stress on the penultimate. It is less common in English because of the frequent 'strong' ending, particularly in a vocabulary which has a high proportion of Anglo-Saxon words. We may, however, perceive it in such phrases as :

Cóuntless misfórtunes (5:2)
Vísion of mémory (6:3)
Vápour upón the móuntains (7:4:2)

Of the effect of these rhythms upon us we know little ; yet it is clear that they include a species of 'free' poetic rhythm, that this rhythm checks and controls the emotional pressure, and at the same time may generate a peculiar exaltation proper to the 'chant'. Any *strict* repetition of the cursus pattern, any tendency to break into metrical units, would result in 'poetic' prose which, by its inflexibility, tends to become an ineffective hybrid form. But when it is used sparingly and with subtlety, the cadence appears to offer musical analogies to a resolution of chords, which conveys both finality and a sense of elevation proper to the semi-liturgical character of many of the contexts in which the cursus seems to appear. We may hold for a moment in our ears the cadences and metrics of

Hóly, hóly, hóly, (6:4:2)
Lord God of hosts,

Heaven and earth
are fúll of Thy glóry : (5:2)
Glory be to thee, O Lord most high.

and then consider two passages from Isaiah :

Crý aloúd, spáre not ; (5:(½):2)
lift up thy vóice like a trúmpet, (5:2)
and shéw my péople their transgréssion, (8:5:2)
and the house of Jacob their sins. . . . (Isa. 58:1)

and the Lórd shall gúide thee contínually, (9:6:3)
and sátisfy thy sóul in drý pláces (9:5:2)
and make strong thy bones.

This last verse (Isa. 58:11) is taken, deliberately, from RV to demonstrate a subtlety which is lacking (for once) in AV, which has *drought* for *dry places*, and *fat* for *strong*.

Of the seven lines, five end in formal cadences : and they are so placed that the non-cadenced lines—which end in strong monosyllables—break up and vary the passages. In lines 5, 6 and 7 there is a diminishing number of strong accents, to slow up and make firm the climax of the last line ; and we may notice, too, the packed alliterative sibilants—

satisfy thy soul in dry places
and make strong thy bones

decreasing in emphasis towards the line-ending ; as well as of the falling tone of the *o* vowel as between *soul*, *strong*, *bones*. That such effects were, consciously or unconsciously, sought by the translators is, I believe, clear from a comparison between the Authorised and earlier versions ; the filing and adjustment to produce these strange and definite rhythms seems to be part of the response to the exaltation of just these kinds of passages. That the word *exaltation* can be used as a critical term is a proposition that one

14b can, I believe, defend : having in mind Wordsworth's experience among the mountains :

> . . . for I would walk alone
> Under the quiet stars, and at that time
> Have felt whate'er there is of power in sound
> To breathe an elevated mood, by form
> Or image unprofaned. (*Prelude* ii, 302)

For it seems to me that Wordsworth, of all modern poets, is best fitted to prepare us for just this state of mind, an awareness of the numinous that is often intermittent (' gleams like the flashings of a shield '), and may well proceed by slow integration of such perceptions at long intervals of time.

15a **II The Forge of Style**—'. . . neither did we disdaine to revise that which we had done, and to bring back to the anvil that which we hammered.'

(*Address to the Reader* by Dr Smith)

The Committee under the chairmanship of Miles Smith and Thomas Wilson, charged with the forging of the King James Bible, were ordered to use the previous English translations, of which the chief is Tyndale's. We can do no more than hint at the many influences that determined this characteristic style, and glance at some more recent versions : bearing always in mind the conservatism of the ear for rhythmic effects, and that of the mind for idiom and image which have become so familiar through use.

The translators of the OT had certain advantages which we can hardly overestimate. The Versions before them had clear-cut characteristics : the homely, even warm quality of Wycliff's Anglo-Saxon, from which the archaisms had to be almost wholly purged ; the sonority of Tyndale, itself permeated with Latin rhythms which (restrained, compressed and weighted by the crisp verse structure) was to achieve its own peculiar heightened style.

b Let us consider a single passage :

> And he said, Go forth, and stand upon the mount before the Lord. And, behold, the Lord passed by, and a great and strong wind rent the mountains, and brake in pieces the rocks before the Lord ; but the Lord was not in the wind : and after the wind an earthquake ; but the Lord was not in the earthquake :
> And after the earthquake a fire, but the Lord was not in the fire : and after the fire, a still small voice. (1 Kg. 19:11, 12)

The whole dramatic lyric achieves its force from its setting : from its balanced statements and negations : from the famous final words. In the Coverdale Bible they are rendered as ' a styll soft hyssinge '. The Matthew Bible has :

> And after the fyre / came a small still voice.

By what magic of perception was the final cadence achieved, so that the vowels *i-a-oi* drop in a descending scale, whereas the Matthew Bible breaks them with *a-i-oi*? It is this subtlety of rhythm and vowel sound that appears to give the AV its finality. So in Isaiah 35:1, in Coverdale's version :

> But the deserte & wilderness shal reioyse, ye waist grounde shal be glad, and florish as the lilly. She shal florish pleasauntly, and be ioyful, and euer be geuinge of thankes more and more.

set against this :

> The wilderness and the solitary place shall be glad for them ; and the desert shall rejoice, and blossom as the rose. It shall blossom abundantly, and rejoice even with joy and singing . . .

RV is identical here in the first sentence except that it omits the words *for them* : losing perhaps the cadence of AV and an indefinable shade of meaning. Now **15b**
both versions seem to have felt the need to ring the changes between *desert, wilderness* and the sense of *solitary place* : but the *blossoming of the desert* is more vivid and compressed than that of the *waist place* of Coverdale. The old sense of *pleasauntly* which includes the idea of ' generous delight ' has yielded to *abundantly*. We may note how the weak *geuing of thankes more and more* has given place to the stronger *rejoice even with joy and singing*, though we may regret the clash of *joy* and *rejoice*.

For another example of this filing and fitting of **e**
language, with a blend of the dramatic and phonetic, we may consider the description of the War Horse in Job 39:23–5, and note the compression, the elimination of archaisms, between the Wycliffite Bible of 1395 and the AV :

> An arowe caas schal sowne on hym ; a spere and scheeld schal florische. He is hoot, and gnastith, and swolewith the erthe ; and he arettith not that the crie of the trompe sowneth. Whanne he herith a clarioun, he seith, Joie ! he smellith batel afer ; the excitying of duykis, and the yellyng of the oost.

contrasted with :

> The quiver rattleth against him, the glittering spear and the shield. He swalloweth the ground with fierceness and rage ; neither believeth he that it is the sound of the trumpet. He saith among the trumpets, Ha, ha : and he smelleth the battle afar off, the thunder of the captains, and the shouting.

I have quoted these two passages because, in one **d**
mood, we may admire the energy and ' quaintness ' of the early version. There is a peculiar vividness in

> Whanne he herith a clarioun, he seith, Joie !

and the *excitying of dukys* has a delightful Chaucerian freshness, as also the *yellyng of the oost*. We are for a moment in Chaucer's world, where the Latin cadences do not yet govern the prose. And while we may approve (through long familiarity)

> The thunder of the captains, and the shouting

we may, in cold blood, question the propriety of this human *thunder*, and the flatness of the *shouting*.

The 23rd, which has been, perhaps, more paraphrased and versified than any other Psalm, shows very clearly both the forging of the language, and the characteristic tone of 17th-cent. religious writing at its best. Yet the Latin text differs at several points from the Hebrew, and both from the King James version, which contains characteristic emphases.

We may consider first a version from the English **e**
Primers, based upon the Latin ' Book of Hours ' (A.D. 1410) :

> Oure Lord gouerneth me
> and nothyng schal lacke me ;
> in place of pasture there he hath sett me.
> He hath browghte me foorth up on the water of rehetynge ; [1]
> he conueertede my soule.
> he ladde me upon the paths of rightwesnesse ;
> for his naame.
> For whi though y go in myddes the schadwe of deeth;
> Y schal nought dreede yveles.
> for thou art with me. Thy yerde and thi staf ;
> they han comforted me.[2]

We may note the literal rendering of the Latin *Dominus regit me* ; and in the feeling towards the finality of the

[1] *Super aquam refectionis* (Vulgate) ; *up on the water of refreshment* (Douay)

[2] For this and other comparisons I am indebted to the tabulations given by G. C. Butterworth, *The Literary Lineage of the King James Bible* (Philadelphia 1941).

15e familiar *green pastures*, ' goodly lusty pasture ', ' pasture full of grasse ', Coverdale and the Geneva Bible furnishing the phrase the Forty-Seven retained. So we can trace successively ' & fullest my cuppe full ' through ' and my cuppe shalle brymme full ', ' and my chalice inebriating how goodlie it is ' to the final ' my cuppe runneth over ' ; how, too, the Prayer Book version returns to that of the Great Bible of 1539, ' & my cuppe shalbe full ' : achieving two different meanings as well as two different rhythms.

f ' The Bible is not only what modern scholarship holds the text to mean : it is also what the text has meant to many generations of devout readers ' (Daiches, *Literary Essays*). This is true ; and we may consider this curious patina of meaning, penumbral or multiplex in character, which much of the Bible has acquired. The Translators respected the originals : they returned to the forge to reshape with sureness, tact, precision and an impeccable auditory sense the work of their predecessors. Many phrases in the AV are obscure ; many have acquired this patina as of a rich antique bronze. ' The Ancient of Days ' is no longer —as it was—a synonym for ' old ' : its meaning is perhaps born of man's imagination striving to picture that God that answered Job out of the whirlwind, perhaps as Blake saw him. Phrases such as the ' waters of Babylon ' or ' the fleshpots of Egypt ' have grown into each other, and are never to be separated again ; and for layered or laminated meaning, each phrase dependent on its remembered context, we may quote Kipling's ' The Vineyard ' :

> At the eleventh hour he came
> But his wages were the same
> As ours who all day long had trod
> The winepress of the wrath of God.

Yet much that is mysterious, much that is irrational is left ; and—for poetry may rightly be prophecy too—the penumbral meaning may extend (to our mind) far beyond an ' accurate ' modern version. A single example, from Ec. 12:5 in the AV must suffice :

> Also when they shall be afraid of that which is high, and fears shall be in the way, and the almond tree shall flourish, and the grasshopper shall be a burden, and desire shall fail ; because man goeth to his long home, and the mourners go about the streets.

The dominant feeling appears to be that of pessimism at the coming of an evil time, rising through acceptance to a kind of ecstasy communicated by the lyric statement. The half-deserted village : its few inhabitants overcome with fear (cf. Isa. 33:8 : ' The highways lie waste, the wayfaring man ceaseth '), the seasons gone awry (' nor the clouds return after the rain ') : poverty-stricken, defenceless, its crops destroyed by locusts. We are puzzled, but do not question, the cryptic almond-tree, for we do not know the East. The *long home* seems deliberately ambivalent : the eternity of the grave, and Shakespeare's

> But now two paces of the vilest earth
> Is room enough . . .
>
> (*1 Henry IV*, v. 4)

and a final Blake-like vision of the streets filled with black-hooded figures that complete this lyric Life-in-Death.

But, we are told, in the interpretation of Robert Gordis (*Ecclesiastes* (1945)), it really means this :

> When one fears to climb a height,
> And terrors lurk in a walk.
>
> The hair grows white, like ripe almond blossom,
> The frame, bent like a grasshopper, becomes a burden,
> And the caper-berry can no longer stimulate desire.
>
> So man goes to his eternal home
> While the hired mourners walk about in the street.

Consider for a moment our gains and losses. The 15f
almond-tree is now clear. We lose the ambiguity of ' that which is high ' (the ' terror of the skies ', storms, divine vengeance ?) : as well as the ' fears in the wayside ' (as of the traveller rather than the casual stroller). Our ear may disapprove the cacophony of *lurk-walk* : we may think that man bent in old age is by no means like a grasshopper : we may be slightly revolted by the idea of an eastern aphrodisiac, measured against the far-reaching and noble image, ' and desire shall fail '. But who shall judge ?

It has long been recognised that the Greek of the g
NT is colloquial, of the ' book of the people ' : and we can estimate the stylistic value of a typical modern version (J. B. Phillips, *Letters to Young Churches*) by a brief comparison, from Rom. 13:11.

' Why all this stress on behaviour ? Because, as I think you have realised, the present time is of the highest importance—it is time to wake up to reality. Every day brings God's salvation nearer.

' The night is nearly over, the Day has almost dawned. Let us therefore fling away the things that men do in the dark, let us arm ourselves for the fight of the Day ! '

Set against this the AV rendering :

' And that, knowing the time, that now it is high time to awake out of sleep : for now is our salvation nearer than when we believed.

' The night is far spent, the day is at hand : let us therefore cast off the works of darkness, and let us put on the armour of light.'

We have, I think, to attempt to balance gain and loss : and the matter is not simple. ' It is high time to awake out of sleep ' is both wider in meaning, more economical in statement than the modern version. The idiom of ' high time ' is still a living one ; the sleep image (= unawareness, sloth) is still valid, and I doubt if anything is added by ' wake up to *reality* ' : which, we might argue, means something quite different.

In the second verse there are differences of great importance. The Phillips rendering has imposed a purely *verse* rhythm in the lines : ' The night is nearly over, the Day has almost dawned '—an iambic beat with a feminine ending, as against the purely prose rhythm of ' The night is far spent, the day is at hand '. And ' spent ' has its special overtones, of the exhaustion, as it were, of force ; we may consider the force of *is at hand* (waiting, eagerness) with the entirely different ' the Day ' (is anything gained by capitalising ?) ' has almost dawned '. *Cast off* still survives (as of garments) and seems more fitted to the image than the apparently more colloquial *fling away*. But it is the *works of darkness* that must give us pause ; for I take these to be not only ' the things that men do in the dark ' (murder, adultery ?) but everything that proceeds, positively or negatively, from the unenlightened soul. By changing it we have lost the whole point of the night-day antinomy, which carries on (through *cast off-put on) the armour of light.*

I have taken these random examples in order to suggest two points. First, the whole fabric of the AV and RV is often a great deal more complex than appears at first sight : in the precision of meaning, in the deliberate imprecision (as in the ' works of darkness ' which involves an accepted series of references) and in the function of the rhythms in leading to an acceptance of the thing said. The more closely the fabric is examined, the more certain we become that we are dealing only with a translation, and that no less knowledge than that of Hebrew will suffice. But the *idiom* of the AV is—except for a few obscure passages—much less antiquated than we might suppose ; and custom and usage have in fact developed and fixed (I use the image from photography) meanings ' in depth ' with which it may be thought unwise to tamper.

III The Holy War—' The Lord your God which 16a
goeth before you, he shall fight for you, according to all that he did for you in Egypt before your eyes '

16a (Dt. 1:30). 'And when the Lord thy God shall deliver them before thee; thou shalt smite them, and utterly destroy them; thou shall make no covenant with them, nor shew mercy unto them' (Dt. 7:2).

An incident in a contemporary novel depicts the Headmaster of an infamous preparatory school at Morning Prayers, who reads aloud, 'with obvious distaste, a chapter of bloodcurdling military history'. It would indeed be easy to compile an anthology of passages of blood: extermination, revenge, treachery; savage exaltation over the humiliated enemy; a blessing on those who take the children of the foemen and dash them against the stones. We are familiar with the texts used, say, for the New Model Army of Cromwell, by the Covenanters' forces, and even by a leader in the Far Eastern Campaign of the Second World War, to inculcate what might be termed a 'ferocity of righteousness'. It is clear that in many of the episodes and phrases that glorify the defeat of an enemy there is a strong and heady wine, the more violent in its effects for being thought an incitement to a divine mission (Ps. 18:34ff.). It is well to stand back a little and consider something of the setting.

An invading army, the spearhead of a migrating host, is lured on, as always, by the need for room, the promise of higher standards of living, the assurance of divine protection in their multiplying seed. That protection will be a stronger hope if it can be shown as something continuous in the history of a people. The inhabitants whom they dispossess, enslave, exterminate, are of an inferior race; idolaters, liable to contaminate pure religion by their more spectacular practices of worship, and racial purity by the perpetual risk of intermarriage. Therefore massacre is the normal culmination of victory; that, and the spoiling of the vanquished, in goods and cattle, disarmament by breaking the spears and burning the chariots. The story is familiar in history. With recent examples in our minds, we need not wonder at its objects, nor blame, beyond reason, its cruelty.

b It is possible to picture much of the OT as a sort of dual epic, of invasion and defence. Once colonised, the land is held uneasily, much as the Elizabethans held parts of 16th-cent. Ireland: raids, burnings, cattle-lifting, counter-raids, always liable to swell into some type of Holy War. We may quote Doughty (*Arabia Deserta*, i, 43), as much for the accent that he has caught as for the compression of biblical narrative:

> Edom and Jeshurun are rivals, and great was the cruelty of the Hebrew arms in these countries. When David was king, his sister's son Joab went and killed of Edomites in the Ghror twelve thousand men, and Joab's brother Abishai killed of them his eighteen thousand, if the Semitic numbers were aught; Edom, be it remembered, and Moab and Ammon, were states to be compared with our smaller counties. Joab's sword went through Edom six months, until he had made an end of killing every male of Esau, and belike he made then sure of Doeg the king's adversary, and the righteous laughed to the ears, at his calamity; but all was contrary to Moses' word, 'Thou shalt not abhor the Edomite for he is thy brother'.

Of the unsuccessful battles we hear little; of the successful, the formula is: 'The Lord hath delivered them into our hand'. The reliance placed upon Him appears to have been complete: and we have in a few verses of 2 Sam. 5:17ff. (AV) what is almost a microcosm of the pattern of a battle-sequence:

> But when the Philistines heard that they had anointed David king over Israel, all the Philistines came up to seek David; and David heard of it, and went down to the hold. The Philistines also came and spread themselves in the valley of Rephaim.
>
> And David enquired of the Lord, saying, Shall I go up to the Philistines? wilt thou deliver them into mine hand? And the Lord said unto David, Go up: for I will doubtless deliver the Philistines 16b into thine hand.
>
> And David came to Baal-perazim, and David smote them there, and said, The Lord hath broken forth upon mine enemies before me, as the breach of waters. Therefore he called the name of that place Baal-perazim.
>
> And there they left their images, and David and his men burned them.
>
> And the Philistines came up yet again, and spread themselves in the valley of Rephaim.
>
> And when David enquired of the Lord, he said, Thou shalt not go up; but fetch a compass behind them, and come upon them over against the mulberry trees.
>
> And let it be, when thou hearest the sound of a going in the tops of the mulberry trees, that then thou shalt bestir thyself: for then shall the Lord go out before thee, to smite the host of the Philistines.
>
> And David did so, as the Lord had commanded him; and smote the Philistines from Geba until thou come to Gazer.

I have chosen this passage because it embodies many c of the typical features of this warfare. The Philistines are the people of the plains, strong in cavalry and armour. David has recovered from the defeat under Saul; he has occupied a fortified area on the high ground. The Philistines decide to forestall his growing strength, and challenge him to battle in the valley. In the first action the Philistines are routed; possibly they took up an unfavourable position. They challenge a second time, probably with reinforcements. This time they have learnt their tactical lesson, and the position is unfavourable for a frontal attack. So the light-armed Israelites attack by the familiar right- or left-hook tactics, under the screen of the mulberry grove, that gives somehow a feeling of precision and actuality to the narrative. But the supernatural is always present; the signal for attack is the mysterious 'sound of a going' in the trees (was it a rustling, as in the Oak at Dodona?), and the defeat of the Philistines follows.

Local strategy in this warfare is often interesting, and not without profit to the student of these arts. There is the tactical withdrawal before Ai, where the defensive troops are lured in pursuit from their city while an assault party takes it from the rear (Jos. 8:4). There is Gideon's classic night attack with shock-troops (such an attack on a rocky hill must have demanded picked and highly disciplined men) and the stratagem of making the enemy attack one another in the confusion. The dramatic incident in the valley of Gilboa, when sun and moon stand still so that the Israelites may complete the defeat of the enemy, is one of the most vivid of all incidents; the solution of the classic problem of all generalship, 'Ask of me anything but time'.

But as a rule the narrative of warfare seems to d follow a fairly constant pattern. It is seasonal; it is defensive or aggressive as the political situation requires; it communicates the historical narratives with a bare minimum of essentials. Yet these are broken from time to time, whether by chance or art, with vivid detail that brings character to life, and has an air of authenticity. The message from the battle, the stride of a well-known runner, the confused intelligence of the dusty fight, the dramatic arrival of the hopeful word that is later annihilated to despair; all these can be seen in this episode (2 Sam. 18:24):

> And David sat between the two gates: and the watchman went up to the roof over the gate unto the wall, and lifted up his eyes, and behold a man running alone.
>
> And the watchman cried, and told the king. And the king said, If he be alone, there is tidings in his mouth. And he came apace, and drew near.
>
> And the watchman saw another man running:

16d and the watchman called unto the porter, and said, Behold another man running alone. And the king said, He also bringeth tidings.

And the watchman said, Me thinketh the running of the foremost is like the running of Ahimaaz the son of Zadok. And the king said, He is a good man, and cometh with good tidings.

And Ahimaaz called, and said unto the king, All is well.

And he fell down to the earth upon his face before the king, and said, Blessed be the Lord thy God, which hath delivered up the men that lifted up their hand against my lord the king.

And the king said, Is the young man Absalom safe? And Ahimaaz answered, When Joab sent the king's servant, and me thy servant, I saw a great tumult, but I knew not what it was.

And the king said unto him, Turn aside, and stand here. And he turned aside, and stood still.

And behold Cushi came; and Cushi said, Tidings, my lord the king, for the Lord hath avenged thee this day of all them that rose up against thee.

And the king said unto Cushi, Is the young man Absalom safe? And Cushi answered, The enemies of my lord the king, and all that rise up against thee to do thee hurt, be as that young man is.

And the king was much moved, and went up to the chamber over the gate, and wept: and as he went, thus he said, O my son Absalom, my son, my son Absalom! would God I had died for thee, O Absalom, my son, my son!

The texture of this passage includes all the artistic devices which lend urgency and verisimilitude to the narratives: the first runner, standing anxiously while the second approaches; the quick interrogation by David; Cushi's attempt both to veil his ill news, and to direct the king's mind to his victory; the supreme economy of the whole narrative; and that last achievement of the lyric lament, wrought to that pitch that is rendered only by the barest simplicity.

In the NT there is no war; only the images of warfare used parabolically to image the Christian life. In the background there are the Roman forces of occupation, ready to suppress an uproar, to scourge, imprison, rescue from the violence of the mob. Their cold justice runs throughout the narrative of Acts with a restrained dignity. In any military occupation, the informer-collaborator is a vicious figure:

And when he was come, the Jews which came down from Jerusalem stood round about, and laid many grievous complaints against Paul, which they could not prove.

While he answered for himself, Neither against the law of the Jews, neither against the temple, nor yet against Caesar, have I offended anything at all.

But Festus, willing to do the Jews a pleasure, answered Paul, and said, Wilt thou go up to Jerusalem, and there be judged of these things before me?

Then said Paul, I stand at Caesar's judgment seat, where I ought to be judged: to the Jews have I done no wrong, as thou very well knowest.

For if I be an offender, or have committed anything worthy of death, I refuse not to die: but if there be none of these things whereof these accuse me, no man may deliver me unto them. I appeal unto Caesar. (Ac. 25:7–11)

The contempt for the puppet governor who seeks popularity, the injustice that may arise from the local trial, the strong confidence in Rome's justice—these are set out with an economy and precision of language that are above criticism.

It is fitting to conclude the images of the holy war with that archetypal image which Sir Thomas Browne calls 'the armature of St Paul' (Eph. 6:11–17). There is some difficulty in recapturing in imagination the attitude of all ages (till, say, the later 17th cent.) towards arms. 16d

Put on the whole armour of God, that ye may be able to stand against the wiles of the devil.

For we wrestle not against flesh and blood, but against principalities, against powers, against the rulers of the darkness of this world, against spiritual wickedness in high places.

Wherefore take unto you the whole armour of God, that ye may be able to withstand in the evil day, and having done all, to stand.

Stand therefore, having your loins girt about with truth, and having on the breastplate of righteousness.

And your feet shod with the preparation of the gospel of peace;

Above all, taking the shield of faith, wherewith ye shall be able to quench all the fiery darts of the wicked,

And take the helmet of salvation, and the sword of the Spirit, which is the word of God.

In a mosaic in the Archbishop's palace at Ravenna e
there is a representation of Christ as a Roman soldier: unhelmeted, for sufficient reason. The image of the armour is primarily a defensive one: attack is sudden, directed at vulnerable points: therefore the armour must be *whole*. *Wrestle* suggests, not a ritual sport, but an involvement in violent activity of the whole being: as when the adversary, having attacked with missiles, closes hand to hand. The injunction is repeated, emphasising the need for the *whole* armour: *withstand* is the act of repulsing the attack, *stand* is the retention of the secure position. Again this is repeated, and the emblems develop. The loins, always prone to deceit, are girt about with truth, for the defender is poised in readiness against all attack. The breastplate of righteousness carries, perhaps, many meanings: it could recall that notable ceremonial breastplate of the high priest; it is that part of the armour which confronts the opponent; it protects the most precious, honourable and vital part of the body. The shod feet again seem to suggest the Roman legionary, together with the preparation for the journey that is to spread the gospel. The shield of faith, perhaps of bull's hide to 'quench' arrow or javelin, is a kind of mobile defence; the helmet of salvation secures against the deadly stroke against the head. The sword of the spirit would again recall many previous usages, from the Psalms onward; the archetypal image of power, purification, justice. But what felicity of the translators produced that astonishing rhyme that draws *sword* and *word* together, as spirit and God bind themselves 'in this strange finality of the Logos that cleanses, transfixes, annihilates'?

IV Image and Archetype—By *image* I mean in this 17a
section both simile and metaphor: by *parable* that method of communicating, by means of simple narrative, transferred applications of the narrative to the activities of body or soul. In either, the values of a *symbol* may attach themselves to, or grow about, certain recurrent images; which may in their turn be linked to basic and apparently universal images which represent conscious or subliminal thoughts and emotions of man. I am using in this section the terms of Jung, to whom I am much indebted: as well as to Miss Bodkin, particularly in her *Archetypal Patterns in Poetry*. But I must emphasise again that the approach is in terms of literature, not of theology.

We have seen that the **images**, both of the OT and b
the NT, are devised, not from literary sources, but from the everyday life of a people in action. Examples are infinite; and many are familiar to us from the Psalms, where, indeed, we should expect the lyrical pressure to bring them forth. Yet it may be that some of them are staled by familiarity, so that we miss the full implications of the images. One or two instances may serve:

Our bones are scattered at the grave's mouth, as when one cutteth and cleaveth wood upon the earth. (Ps. 141:7)

17b To an Eastern people, burying in tombs built above ground on rocky (and therefore least valuable) soil, the spectacle of the desecrated grave was both familiar, and horrible in prospect and reality. We may remember Browne's *Hydriotaphia* :

> To be knaved out of graves, to have our skulls made drinking bowls, and our bones turned into pipes, to delight and sport our enemies, are tragical abominations escaped in burning burials.

Yet the fate was a common one, in all ages : whether by the action of tomb-robbers or outcasts seeking shelter in the cities of tombs, or by wild beasts, or by succeeding grave-hungry generations. It is possible that we commonly miss the depth-imagery in the second of the clauses quoted ; the bones suggest, in their aimless scattered whiteness, slivers and chips of wood, while the image of man as tree, and tree as man, is one of the most ancient and constant in poetry. Similarly when the Psalmist says (Ps. 22:15)

> My strength is dried up like a potsherd

we may not at once recognise the train of images related to that fragment of baked clay. For the potter can be the emblem or parable of the Creator, moulding man out of the dust to which he must return : and the potter's vessel, containing water or wine (both emblems of life) is, when full, tempered or made whole with that which it contains.

c I am aware of the difficulty and complexity of any account of the **archetypes** : but I believe that in our growing knowledge of their nature we can find one important reason for the appeal of the Bible as literature, and an explanation of its permanent value as such. I must first recapitulate, using, in the main, the words of others.

'The "archetype"—indicated by Jung through various metaphors and approaches—is a term hard to define, because of the elusive, interpenetrative, character of the spiritual life to which it applies. In its subjective aspect the archetype can be described as a psychophysical disposition. Objectively it appears in images preserved through words and pictorial forms. Beyond this characterisation, we may recognise the archetypes of Wisdom, and of the Divine birth, as communicated through the encounter of finite beings, and through this, of finite with infinite spirit' (Maud Bodkin, *Studies of Type-Images in Poetry, Religion and Philosophy*, xii).

'In the individual, the archetypes occur as involuntary manifestations of unconscious processes whose existence and meaning can only be inferred' (Jung and Kerényi, *Towards a Science of Mythology*, 100).

'What an archetypal content is always expressing is first and foremost a *figure of speech*. If it speaks of the sun and identifies it with the lion, the king, the hoard of gold guarded by the dragon, or the force that makes for the life and health of man, it is neither the one thing nor the other, but the unknown third thing that finds more or less adequate expression in all these similes, yet—to the perpetual vexation of the intellect —remains unknown and not to be fitted into a formula (ibid., 105).

We have, then, a series of mythologems in the Bible ; which find analogies or parallels in every literature and which are, in many instances, closely linked to similar mythologems among the peoples that had traffic with the Jews. To call them thus, to point to sources or similarities, does not invalidate them in any possible sense in which we are considering them here. The Creation, the Flood, the Fall, the Child-Redeemer, appear in many forms : just as the trajectory of the Hero, his birth, upbringing, warfare, rule and death obeys a well-defined common pattern. In and inextricably fused with them are the images, metaphor or simile, which lead us to 'the unknown third thing'.

d Some of these images are so obvious, whether in secular or divine writing, that we pass them by without 17d
any *conscious* attempt at examining their implications. Of such are the Rose-Woman image (with the complications of rosebud-virginity), the 'eating canker' at the heart, the swift decay of beauty ; and we are led onwards to the whole flower-woman group, with the same general theme. So is that of the clay and the potter and his vessel—the container of life (often, as Sir Thomas Browne noted, in the shape of the womb) ; the clay embodying (as in Plato) some principle recalcitrant to the potter's shaping hand. So the complexities of the ship's voyage as an emblem of life ; the sea as the matrix and the giver of life, but also that which harbours the monstrous enemies, Leviathan, Behemoth, the White Whale. Tunnel and cave may stand for rebirth, death ; sword, spear and arrow are power, death, or the sexual principles ; honey and honeycomb stand for wisdom or longevity ; the hierarchy of animals into whose semblance, as many poets have seen, the evil latent in man may so easily cause him to pass. The serpent, and indeed, many things that go in the dust, may signify the adversary, the principle of evil ; that dominant archetype, the dragon, which Otto describes as a 'numen of terror', has already acquired a considerable literature of its own. He may be of the land or of the waters : an agent of God, like Satan in the Book of Job.

> And though they hide themselves in the top of Carmel, I will search and take them out thence ; and though they be hid from my sight in the bottom of the sea, thence will I command the serpent, and he shall bite them. (Am. 9:3)

But as the adversary—who may be many-headed like that other image of evil, the hydra—he is finally destroyed by God :

> . . . thou brakest the heads of the dragons in the waters.
> Thou brakest the heads of leviathan in pieces,
> and gavest him to be meat to the people inhabiting the wilderness. (Ps. 74:13)

Subtlety, speed, crookedness, are his attributes ; and above all a fascinated sensual attraction and repulsion that has caused man to concentrate on this dragon-figure every possible extension of the creative imagination.

So in Isaiah's image of judgment :

> For, behold, the Lord cometh out of his place to punish the inhabitants of the earth for their iniquity ; the earth also shall disclose her blood, and shall no more cover her slain. (Isa. 26:21)

(We need not labour the blood-stain-guilt-sacrifice-purification as an archetypal image : it is enough to remember the hands of Lady Macbeth, and those of the conspirators in *Julius Caesar* : the blood of Abel, and the blood of Zacharias) :

> In that day the Lord with his sore and great and strong sword shall punish leviathan the piercing serpent, even leviathan that crooked serpent ; and he shall slay the dragon that is in the sea. (Isa. 27:1)

Sometimes the archetypal image is nobly and e
unashamedly sexual, with the hard purity of Blake ; complex in its juxtapositions, alive with an exaltation of its own :

> Who is she that looketh forth as the morning,
> fair as the moon,
> clear as the sun,
> and terrible as an army with banners?
> I went down into the garden of nuts
> To see the fruits of the valley,
> And to see whether the vine flourished.
> And the pomegranates budded.
>
> (Ca. 6:10)

17e It is the astonishing profusion of the images in such a passage as this that makes it seem as if the mind were throwing out a series of flexing tentacles in the attempt to attain to a meaning which, of its very nature as poetic statement, can never be encompassed or enclosed. We are concerned with the unconscious, in some or other of its Protean manifestations. And here it is fitting to quote some sentences from Austin Farrer (*A Rebirth of Images*, 14).

> Nowhere are the images in more vigour than in the Old Testament, when they speak of God, but are not he . . .
> The images are not through all ages absolutely invariable, and there is no historical study more significant than the study of their transformations. Such a transformation finds expression in the birth of Christianity ; it is a visible rebirth of images.

We may refer to the exegesis of *Revelation* as seen by this writer : for the moment we should probably agree in perceiving that the most important of the archetypes are the Virgin and the Child, Mother and Saviour. In its simplest terms, every detail of the annunciation and nativity, in every version, are given with a nobility, dignity, restraint which are without parallel. From the prophecy

> Behold, a virgin shall conceive and bear a son . . .
> (Isa. 7:14)

it is not, I believe, sentimental or rhetorical to say that a new light begins to illuminate the Bible. An angel appears, or a star falls, to signify that heaven and earth meet in the only symbols that could express that union. For the child-saviour-victim is as it were a microcosm of the most profound truths of man's progress, dreams, tested realities. In the Christian story, the conception, and its very familiarity, so often passes over the upper layers of our perceptions. Of the richness of accomplished pattern it is enough to name a few instances. That shepherds should be the first to hear the heavenly announcement ; that desert, hills, fishing villages, the Temple and its precincts, should symbolise portions of the ministry ; that two malefactors should frame God's death upon a hill (I remind the reader, without comment, of Frazer's saying : ' Many seemingly divergent lines converge towards the Cross on Calvary') ; that woman's fate of pain, service, exaltation and sorrow beyond all bearing should be etched with bare noble strokes upon the background of His life ; all these are (if at no other level) the eternal symbols of the human situation. Again and again the essential humanity is emphasised :

> Woman, what have I to do with thee ? Mine hour is not yet come.
> My house is a house of prayer, but ye have made it a den of thieves.
> Let this cup pass from me.
>
> My God, my God, why hast thou forsaken me ?

18a Throughout the visions of the OT and NT there passes a strange procession of images which alone can shadow forth man's groping recognition of all kinds of hidden life. I believe it to be true, as many critics have argued (echoing the less explicit statements of poets and artists) that it is essential for us to recognise, and learn to use, these taproots that the images send deep into our minds to draw from them something that satisfies, we do not know how or whence, the deepest needs of the psyche. Without the links with the past which the archetypes give us, we are apt to remain there, with an accompanying malaise which many moralists have discerned as the prevalent distraction of our time. It is possible, as a recent writer has argued, that the individual of today who cannot completely accept the teaching of the Christian churches may yet in his encounter through literature with thinkers past and present, or in personal relationships with present-day leaders and friends, so realise the nature of the archetypes of saving wisdom and of spiritual rebirth as to share in the religious life and fellowship that to others has been indicated by the Christian churches. In so arguing, I have not written of the realisation of the archetypes as a meeting simply of subjective human need and objective traditional image. I have assumed, with Jung, that the individual mind brings to the encounter a creative activity, whatever thought or word fashioned the image in the past. ' But also I have come to believe that in the encounter there is the co-operation of an influence, termed by the philosopher Whitehead the Divine Persuasion, and, by theologians, the Grace of God ' (Maud Bodkin, *Studies of Type-Images*, 175). 18a

Yet it is perhaps in the simple imagery that is compelled into the service of persuasion that we may find the most notable achievement of the Bible, both in the OT and the NT. We find it in the appeal to the seasons and their relation to the cycle of human life :

> For as the rain cometh down, and the snow from heaven, and returneth not thither, but watereth the earth, and maketh it bring forth and bud, that it may give seed to the sower, and bread to the eater :
> So shall my word be that goeth forth out of my mouth : it shall not return to me void, but it shall accomplish that which I please, and it shall prosper in the thing whereto I sent it. (Isa. 55:10, 11)

Then suddenly comes a transposition into lyric harmony which (while projecting the image of the fructifying rain) leads to the transcendency of the poet's statement :

> For ye shall go out with joy, and be led forth with peace :
> the mountains and the hills shall burst forth before you into singing and all the trees of the field shall clap their hands.

I do not think the antithesis between *go* and *led* is fortuitous : in the one instance suggesting a delight in energy, in the other safety in submission to God's will.

Yet this prose of the NT has one particular quality b
that arises perhaps out of its quiet illumination—again remembering Longinus and his encomium of Genesis—of the holy vision ; of man who is shown, not a promised land, but a promised eternity. And eternity is seen, perhaps, from two angles ; the holy life of which it is the end and the beginning, built upon the simple yet most profound detail of parable and incidents of daily living, rooted in the earth, yet spreading branches of grace abundantly. So the parables have the layered and complex quality, the extreme simplicity that contains, and reveals on meditation, its endless meanings. And again there is this mysterious quality of naked graceful ease in the NT as in the OT, that we accept unconsciously, until we start to analyse its peculiar ' rightness '. So a parable of seed on stony ground, or an image (remembering the Psalm) of man as grass, is clothed again in simplicity like the lilies themselves ; images from the craft of the fisherman, from the hardships of the traveller, the foundations of a building.

We do not always realise the classical economy of understatement, this dramatic compression, this apparently unfailing touch of the right word ; whether in narrative, sermon, exhortation, rebuke, prophecy. I can do no more than suggest at this point some of these qualities, in the first instance by comparison. Here is a paraphrase by an eminent novelist of a familiar incident (Lloyd C. Douglas, *The Big Fisherman*. This passage comes from a novel of the author's creation, and the author is here doing no more than fulfilling his intention) :

18b When they arrived at the house where John and James were standing at the gate they found that Jesus had already entered and was waiting for them at the doorway of the upper room. He had provided himself with towels and a basin of water. It was customary, when guests were expected, to station a servant at the door to wash the visitors' dusty feet. The disciples were appalled to find that the Master intended to perform this menial service. Peter, when his turn came, stoutly refused to consent, but yielded reluctantly when Jesus insisted.

> . . . He riseth from supper, and laid aside his garments ; and took a towel, and girded himself.
> After that he poureth water into a bason, and began to wash the disciples' feet, and to wipe them with the towel wherewith he was girded.
> Then cometh he to Simon Peter : and Peter saith unto him, Lord, dost thou wash my feet ?
> Jesus answered and said unto him, What I do thou knowest not now, but thou shalt know hereafter.
> Peter saith unto him, Thou shalt never wash my feet. Jesus answered, If I wash thee not, thou hast no part with me. (Jn 13:5)

c I have chosen these two versions to suggest several things. The ceremonial and symbolic washing is given an entirely different emphasis. The mixture of the actions in the historic present, the suggestion (but no more) of the sequence of action that makes the scene so vivid. But the actual words in St John's narrative are almost wholly verbs and nouns ; adjectives and adverbs are few. There is no need to point out that the service is ' menial ' ; Peter's ' stoutly ' and ' reluctantly ' fail to throw that strong light upon his character that is given by St John.

Again and again in the NT narrative we can perceive this exquisite *rightness* that comes from supreme economy allied to complete knowledge of the essence of the known action. A single example must again suffice :

> But when the fourteenth night was come, as we were driven up and down in Adria, about midnight the shipmen deemed that they drew near to some country ;
> And sounded, and found it twenty fathoms : and when they had gone a little further, they sounded again, and found it fifteen fathoms.
> Then fearing lest we should have fallen upon rocks, they cast four anchors out of the stern, and wished for the day.
> And as the shipmen were about to flee out of the ship, when they had let down the boat into the sea, under colour as though they would have cast anchors out of the foreship,
> Paul said to the centurion and to the soldiers, Except these abide in the ship, ye cannot be saved. (Ac. 27:27)

In this lean and sinewy prose nouns and adjectives work together to produce an objective harmony. It is the shipmen who sense the distant roar of the surf, or perceive, through a sixth sense, the presence of the land. A ship on a rocky coast *falls* upon rocks, is lifted by the surf and crashed down on them ; therefore she must be held off if possible and the panic rush of the crew frustrated, until the dawn shows them the creek into which the ship could be driven. This vivid bare economy, this ability to communicate the experience felt and known in all its details of action, can be paralleled again and again from the Elizabethan and Jacobean voyagers ; and, in this kind, remains a model of what supremely good prose can be.

But it is perhaps in the Lesson for the Burial of the Dead (1 C. 15) that the variety and scope of the prose is most clearly seen. We have the archetypal image of sower and seed, the quickening spirit recalling the miracle of resurrection ; the Anglo-Saxon vocabulary proper to that theme giving place, as need arises, to 18e the sonority of the Latin polysyllables : *corruption, inherit, immortality*, the writer ranging deliberately through the whole gamut of scorn, metaphor, pleading, and triumphant assertion, to be modulated downwards, as it were, to the quiet intimate certainty of the close :

> Therefore, my beloved brethren, be ye stedfast, unmoveable.

V Proverbs and Prophecy—For any Eastern people 19a their proverbs are a kind of pillar of social intercourse, and their judicious quotation extends beyond a mere grace of social intercourse to become an index to the speaker's wit, poise, and wisdom. As common currency they cover an infinite number of situations and problems of conduct. Thus memorable qualities are achieved by vividness of imagery, by sheer compression ; and, to the Western mind, they often attain a persuasive force that has been dulled in our pallid counterparts. ' The words of the wise are as goads, and as nails fastened by the masters of assemblies . . .' (Ec. 12:11). In range they extend from that prudential wisdom which has been, throughout history, a characteristic of the Jews, up to the highest ethical problems. Even though the scale may run, in Proverbs and Ecclesiastes, from the practical to the numinous, there is nothing incongruous, to such a people, in the juxtapositions of the two extremes.

In general they appear to be regarded as components of the quality described as wisdom ; towards which, if they are assimilated and practised, they conduce. This wisdom is often associated with a material prosperity arising from what we should now describe as a prudential morality : the wise man, the righteous man, may usually be recognised by his honourable position in the community. We may indeed see traces of an ' impure ' wisdom, perceived thus in some aspects of Victorian England, in which prosperity and riches certified, as it were, a supposed observance of divine law. The desuetude of these proverbs in our own century has various interesting causes : it is sufficient for the moment to note their replacement by the expressively named ' wisecrack '.

There are perhaps two main types. One is the b
' worldy wisdom ' proverb, not far removed in intention from ' A stitch in time . . .' or ' A rolling stone . . .' We may glance at some of them :

> A fool's wrath is presently known : but a prudent man covereth shame. (Prov. 12:16)
> Hast thou found honey ? Eat so much as is sufficient for thee, lest thou be filled therewith, and vomit. (Prov. 25:16) (So much more memorable, because more dramatic, than ' Enough is as good as a feast '.)
> Get thyself the love of the congregation, and bow thy head to a great man. (Sir. 4:7)
> For children begotten of unlawful beds are witnesses of wickedness against their parents in their trial. (Wis. 4:6)
> Do nothing without advice, and when thou hast once done, repent not. (Sir. 32:19)
> He that sinneth before his Maker, let him fall into the hands of the physician. (Sir. 38:15)

It is significant that the richest treasure-house of these sayings is the Apocrypha ; the poorest, the NT.

At the opposite extreme there is the proverb which is, as it were, spirit-borne : the protest of God against human stupidity. And to disregard the voice of wisdom, crying in the streets or through the mouths of the prophets, is to invite the nemesis of God :

> Turn you at my reproof : behold, I will pour out my spirit unto you, I will make my words known unto you.
> Because I have called, and ye refused ; I have stretched out my hand, and no man regarded . . .
> But whoso hearkeneth unto me shall dwell safely, and be quiet from fear of evil.' (Prov. 1:23, 33)

19b The *fear of evil* may be thought of, primarily, as a dread of punishment, of the vengeance of God ; that threat which is ever in the mouths of the prophets. But it is, perhaps, capable of extension to the individual conscience, the fear of being led into temptation. And for the most part the injunctions are the familiar ones, an expansion of the Decalogue into the recesses of human evil : enjoining honour to parents, charity to the poor, justice in the household ; and above all the restraint from false witness ; a little strange, this, to the Western mind, but of cardinal importance in the multiplex disputes of the East. Sometimes these are in strange language, as this :

> A man that beareth false witness against his neighbour is a maul, and a sword, and a sharp arrow. (Prov. 25:18)

Does this suggest three types of slander? The ideal portrayed is the just, the reasonable man ; less subject, perhaps, to the positive Aristotelian virtues than to the prohibitions conducing to that end :

> Thus saith the Lord, Stand ye in the ways, and see, and ask for the old paths, where is the good way, and walk therein and ye shall find rest for your souls. But they said, We will not walk therein. (Jer. 6:16)

c Much proverbial wisdom is concerned with women ; warnings against the evil, the tedious, the ill-tempered, the spendthrift, the vain ; anticipating the famous satire of Juvenal, and the long tradition that arises from it. Sometimes the imagery is picturesque to the limits of imagination :

> As a jewel of gold in a swine's snout, so is a fair woman which is without discretion. (Prov. 11:22)

The ideal wife, she whose price is far above rubies, is literally a source of wealth : through spinning, weaving, household husbandry, and trade.

> She openeth her mouth with wisdom ; and in her tongue is the law of kindness. (Prov. 31:26)

But it is against the 'strange woman', the harlot, that so much proverbial wisdom is levelled : and as we read the writing seems to take on a fiercer, more compelling, rhythm, a new intensity of imagery. Is she indeed something more than the mere harlot ; the outlawed woman, the foreigner, perhaps as Jezebel was, who could (being freed from God's vengeance) commit abominable crimes? Or was the exogamous marriage the main danger to the solidarity of Israel, the subtle infiltration into monotheistic purity? A passage from Hosea may suggest this :

> Then said the Lord unto me, Go yet, love a woman beloved of her friend, yet an adulteress, according to the love of the Lord toward the children of Israel, who look to other gods, and love flagons of wine.
>
> So I bought her to me for fifteen pieces of silver, and for an homer of barley, and an half homer of barley. And I said unto her, Thou shalt abide for me many days ; thou shalt not play the harlot, and thou shalt not be for another man : so will I also be for thee. (Hos. 3:1)

Here the parabolic meaning is apparent, though its details are obscure. But the following passage suggests a wider meaning than appears on the surface :

> (Discretion) . . . shall . . . deliver thee from the strange woman, even from the stranger that flattereth with her words . . . For her house inclineth unto death, and her paths unto the dead. None that go unto her return again, neither take they hold of the paths of life . . . (Prov. 2:16)
>
> For the lips of a strange woman drop as an honeycomb (how ancient is the emblem of honey 19c
> as sexual potency, the bee's sting for love or death ?) and her mouth is smoother than oil ; but her end is bitter as wormwood, sharp as a twoedged sword. (Prov. 5:4)
>
> . . . Lust not after her beauty in thine heart, neither let her take thee with her eyelids ; for by means of a whorish woman a man is brought to a piece of bread, and the adulteress will hunt for the precious life. Can a man take fire in his bosom, and his clothes not be burned ? (Prov. 6:25)

As to **Prophecy**, we must, I believe, attempt to see d
this form in a certain perspective. It is not merely, and seldom only, an apocalyptic vision. It is rather a lyrical cry : reproof, malediction, exhortation, promise ; made out of the bitterest contemplation of evil and bondage, or of the most exalted assurance of the Divine Love. The following passage shows this double aspect :

> Woe be unto the pastors that destroy and scatter the sheep of my pasture ! saith the Lord.
>
> Therefore thus saith the Lord God of Israel against the pastors that feed my people, Ye have scattered my flock, and driven them away, and have not visited them : behold, I will visit upon you the evil of your doings, saith the Lord.
>
> And I will gather the remnant of my flock out of all countries whither I have driven them, and will bring them again to their folds ; and they shall be fruitful and increase.
>
> And I will set up shepherds over them which shall feed them : and they shall fear no more, nor be dismayed, neither shall they be lacking, saith the Lord.
>
> Behold, the days come, saith the Lord, that I will raise unto David a righteous Branch, and a King shall reign and prosper, and shall execute judgment and justice in the earth. (Jer. 23:1–5)

We may note in passing the reiterated emphasis on the image of the sheep and the shepherd : the rhythms of

> and will bring them again to their folds

and

> and a King shall reign and prosper

and recall in a more famous passage (Isa. 11:1f.) the recurrent tree-image on which the spirit rests.

There are few touchstones for prophecy in literature. Few writers after the 17th cent. offer a parallel in the *furor poeticus* of the prophet :

> Therefore I am full of the fury of the Lord ; I am weary with holding in. (Jer. 6:11)

But have not all prophecies this in common? to enable men to look through and beyond adversity, beyond the overthrow of evil ; and to that end to exalt the heart of man through those intricate and strange marshallings of words that, through setting the imagination aflame, lift their hearts in ecstasy. Let us gather some of the sentences :

> Then thou shalt see, and flow together, and thine heart shall fear, and be enlarged. . . . (Isa. 60:5)
>
> Thus saith the Lord of hosts ; There shall yet old men and old women dwell in the streets of Jerusalem, and every man with his staff in his hand for very age.
>
> And the streets of the city shall be full of boys and girls playing in the streets thereof. (Zech. 8:4, 5)

It is such things as these that are more vivid to us today than the tedious railings of the prophets against their own people or their enemies : a joy suggesting a Blake engraving from the *Songs of Innocence*, and that grow more elaborate and more mysterious in the Visions.

20a **VI Visions—**

The burden of the valley of vision. (Isa. 22:1)
Your old men shall dream dreams, your young men shall see visions. (Jl 2:28)

It may be objected that *prophecy* and *vision* overlap in both the OT and NT; but I wish to use the term 'vision' in a special sense, and to attempt to see it in some perspective in relation to the 'idealistic' philosophy of the Bible. To the Hebrew mind, the *spirit* is usually the impelling power, distinct from the soul or psyche, and drawing directly upon the supranatural for its source. They had found—in common with the neighbours—many channels that might pierce 'the vast dim veil uncertain' of the future and of the φύσις, the order, harmony, justice, that reveals itself so incompletely and perplexingly in individual saga and in national history. Astrology, numerology, oracles, witchcraft, had all, at one time or another, been laid under contribution. But the most important sources were the vision which came in a dream, or as the result of the voice of God in a waking dream, or in some ecstatic condition not far removed from trance.

If we try to disentangle the things thus seen we can perhaps distinguish the following:

A vision of the world turning to its God-appointed perfectibility: in which perfect justice, truth, material satisfaction of the needs of the body, should reign supreme as a revelation of the justice of God.

As a prelude to this, a series of events which would comprise the defeat of Israel's enemies, the unification of the kingdoms, the restoration of Jerusalem to her supreme place as a symbol of national and spiritual unity.

The rebuilding of the Temple, as a symbol within a symbol: embodying the real presence as well as the masonic exemplar (through its ritual precision of measurement and architectural-ritual detail) of Order.

On the trajectory of the path to perfect unity, we can perceive a broad developing rhythm: battles, with final victory; repentance, and glorification of God; His visitation of His People and abiding sojourn with them; the final resolution in an imprecise (because necessarily symbolic) assertion of a final harmony.

b In the NT, the Vision of St John, conditioned by the destruction of the Temple and the purer vision of the multiplex temple of man's body and of the New Jerusalem, follows a more complicated but broadly similar trajectory; warfare, destruction, judgment, interspersed with periods of suffering described in aeonic language, to culminate in the supreme vision of the new Heaven and the new Earth.

Now the difficulty with all who deal in visions—Virgil, Dante, Milton, Blake, Shelley—is the difficulty of transmitting into words the outline of the thing seen, and the need to communicate the emotion inherent in the thing seen by means of symbols which may be thought of as approximating, in some sense, to the use of colour. For these symbols the writer of visions must use traditional material, attempting to give it the peculiar contextual significance which can —by its nature—be only a shadow of what he has seen, perpetually weakened or distorted by its imprisonment in words. It is possible that his usage was clarified by a knowledge which his original audience had, and which is now lost. He may even, on occasion, be inventing (as Blake sometimes did) a spiritualised idiom. And when the whole statement may be darkened by interpolations, textual corruptions, the tendency of subsequent generations to look for gnomic utterances, and to adjust their behaviour some thousands of years later to a subjective interpretation of those utterances, it is clear that we labour in a great darkness.

Obscurity, complex symbolism, nobility, and a curious penumbral exaltation are, perhaps, blended in Dan. 12:

And at that time shall Michael stand up, the great prince which standeth for the children of thy people; and there shall be a time of trouble, such as never was since there was a nation even to that same time: and at that time thy people shall be delivered, every one that shall be found written in the book. 20b

And many of them that sleep in the dust of the earth shall awake, some to everlasting life, and some to shame and everlasting contempt.

And they that be wise shall shine as the brightness of the firmament; and they that turn many to righteousness, as the stars for ever and ever.

I take these three passages to be a kind of microcosm of the vision. Hosea, Joel, Amos, Zephaniah, are of this patterning: their emphasis mainly on the wickedness of backsliding Israel, and their time of trouble. The common theme is emphasised with every resource of imagery: the spoiled vineyard, the waterless land, the 'day of the trumpet and alarm against the fenced cities, and against the high towers' (Zeph. 1:16). c

The prophet or seer is moved to his dream or vision under conditions similar to those wrought by all mystics or ascetics: Daniel mourns and fasts (Dan. 10:3), the mouth of the prophet is purified by a live coal (Isa. 6:7). We cannot easily conjecture the meaning of the strange cosmic symbols, the winged creatures and their wheels, in the first chapter of Ezekiel; and there are many instances as difficult or even fantastic to the Western mind. Perhaps Blake, also a visionary, can show us something of their nature, as in certain of his illustrations to Dante. And whatever the symbolism, whatever the significance evocative or historical, of the names and places that roll through the interminable complexities, they have little interest for us. By contrast, the calm lyricism of a passage such as this lives and redeems itself by its integrity of image and rhythm:

And there shall come forth a rod out of the stem of Jesse, and a Branch shall grow out of his roots:

And the spirit of the Lord shall rest upon him, the spirit of wisdom and understanding, the spirit of counsel and might, the spirit of knowledge and of the fear of the Lord;

. . . and he shall not judge after the sight of his eyes, neither reprove after the hearing of his ears:

But with righteousness shall he judge the poor, and reprove with equity for the meek of the earth: and he shall smite the earth with the rod of his mouth, and with the breath of his lips shall he slay the wicked.

And righteousness shall be the girdle of his loins, and faithfulness the girdle of his reins.

(After this difficult, perhaps incomprehensible, image of the girdle, we move into the natural world, the new Eden: the sustained clauses falling into lyrical cadences.)

The wolf also shall dwell with the lamb, and the leopard shall lie down with the kid; and the calf and the young lion and the fatling together; and a little child shall lead them.

And the cow and the bear shall feed; their young ones shall lie down together: and the lion shall eat straw like the ox.

And the sucking child shall play on the hole of the asp, and the weaned child shall put his hand on the cockatrice' den.

They shall not hurt nor destroy in all my holy mountain; for the earth shall be full of the knowledge of the Lord, as the waters cover the sea. (Isa. 11:1–9)

In no verses of the Bible have the rhythms of English been used with more consummate art and restraint: swelling and ebbing, yet held back perpetually from any suggestion of pseudo-verse.

20d Of St John's vision on Patmos I have neither speech nor learning to write. The apocalyptic vision is centred on symbols which do not wholly conceal moments of comprehensible beauty : as of the river of life, or the New Jerusalem. The archetypal horses, the dragons, horned beasts, the seven candlesticks, form mysterious patterns in our minds.

Yet within the general trajectory of sin, punishment, the justification of God's wrath, and His redemption, there are—in both OT and NT—these mysterious symbolic visions. Of them we may complain that we have lost the key to their esoteric meaning, and ransack comparable literatures to recover it ; or hold that they are textually corrupt, or represent intermingled versions ; or reckon them as prophecy and therefore legitimate objects for subjective interpretation, so that they may still be 'pyramidally extant', or a prey to the numerologist. There are few who would not question the legitimacy, or at times the sanity, of such interpretings.

e But perhaps there is another aspect. I find in many of the visions a curious sense of pattern which we may, one day, find to be akin to the *mandala* symbolism which, in Jung's psychology, represents deep-rooted formations of fear, hope, security. That the city or temple should be built in a square or rectangular pattern, box within box, the mystery at the centre ; that man should see himself wading through rising waters, and confronted at last by an impassable river ; that the dream of fear should take shape in a clay-footed image or a felled tree ; that the symmetrical four and the asymmetrical seven should appear so constantly : these I find no stranger than scores of dream-symbols in the case-books of the psychologists. We cannot know why the mysterious horses (Zech. 1:8ff., 6:1ff.) came in groups of four, unless it be that they come from the four quarters of the world : we know only that an archer on a red horse may still symbolise war, death on the pale horse stand for pursuing fear. It is not easy to speculate as to whether the prophecies and visions may reflect aspects of the subliminal depths of the human mind : or whether they were implanted in it by just such mythologems, visions, prophecies. But what if these things help us to reach, perhaps to release, certain 20e
depths in ourselves?

> And hardly do we guess aright at things that are upon earth, and with labour do we find the things that are before us : but the things that are in heaven who hath searched it?

I have called this, the concluding section of my f
essay, *Visions* rather than *Vision* : since it seems to me that, at the last, we must regard the Bible as a book which reflects and communicates the image of man's conflict with himself, and with the human situation : his quest for a city that hath foundations : his wonder, awe, pity and terror before the natural universe, the unfolding of history, the mysteries of birth and death ; his intermittent certainties through visions, his faith, or its loss, through darkness. That the Bible should, at the appropriate times, work through the obscure, the gnomic, the penumbral, seems to me the natural outcome of the attempt to express transcendental things ; nor do I find it helpful to use in this context the word 'romantic'. That its approach to the spiritual should be poetic, allowing simplicity to mirror the transcendental through the image, through the appeal of understatement to the imagination, these seem to me conditions which one must accept when we approach it.

For the visions of the Bible are diverse and multiform. They have the power of making men see high things, the visions of terror or exaltation or delight, behind which lay the mystery of God. Jehovah is high and lifted up : to his strength the hills belong, and the laughter of the valleys, the peace of the streams of the south : much of the scene fitting easily in tone and key to the temper of 17th-cent. metaphysical writing, or the grave contemplations of the early 19th cent. And indeed we may remember Izaak Walton, 'That when God intended to reveal any future events or high notions to his prophets, he carried them either to the deserts or the sea-shore, that having so separated them from amidst the press of people and business, and the cares of the world, he might settle their mind in a quiet repose, and thus make them fit for revelation.'

THE ENGLISH VERSIONS OF THE BIBLE

By A. WIKGREN

21a For a long time after the introduction of Christianity into Britain the Bible was made known to the people through the spoken word, aided by minstrel song, church ritual, art and drama, and picture-books for the poor (*biblia pauperum*). Manuscripts were difficult to produce, and few could read. The church also was dubious about lay use of the Scriptures, especially in the 'profane' vernacular dialects. When interlinear glosses, paraphrases, and partial translations appeared in the Anglo-Saxon of the 9th and following centuries, they were designed primarily to serve the priest in his interpretation of the Latin text.

b From this early period little survives. A 10th-cent. manuscript of the metrical paraphrases of **Cædmon,** 7th-cent. swineherd, exemplifies his 'inspired' retelling of the stories of Gen., Exod., Dan., and the Gospels. Tradition about him we owe to the churchman and historian Bede. **Bede** himself is credited with what may have been the first prose translation of a biblical book, a Gospel of John completed traditionally on the day of his death in A.D. 735. He also translated the Lord's Prayer and the Apostles' Creed. Tradition assigns a translation of the Psalter to the abbot and minstrel Aldhem of south England, and biblical paraphrases to the poet Cynewulf, both of *c.* A.D. 700. In this same period Egbert, erstwhile bishop of Lindisfarne, is supposed to have paraphrased the Gospels. To **King Alfred** (*c.* A.D. 900) is ascribed an incomplete Psalter, as well as the extant Decalogue prefixed to his Book of Laws, and a version of the Ten Commandments and of the Lord's Prayer.

c From the 9th and 10th cent. several glosses on the Psalter and the Gospels are extant. The anonymous **Vespasian Psalter** (Mercian) of the 9th cent. and the **Paris Psalter** (south England) of the 9th or 10th are important examples. The oldest extant version of the Gospels is the 10th-cent. Northumbrian gloss in the beautiful **Lindisfarne** or **Durham Gospels,** a Latin manuscript of the late 7th cent. produced under Eadfrith, bishop of Lindisfarne (A.D. 698–721), and glossed by Aldred, bishop of Durham. It is also known as the 'Book of St Cuthbert', in honour of Aldred's predecessor and assistant. An independent Mercian version of Mt. is found in the 'Rushworth Gospels' of the late 10th cent., otherwise a transcript of the Lindisfarne gloss. The first complete translation is the **Wessex Gospels** attributed to the prominent scholar and churchman Ælfric (*c.* A.D. 1000). At least 7 manuscript copies are known from the 11th and 12th cent. From Ælfric also come paraphrases of several OT books and biblical quotations in sermons and commentaries.

d In the important transition period of the 11th and following centuries, the Norman conquest and the partial suppression of the Anglo Saxon were unfavourable to literary production in 'English'. But biblical quotation and allusion continue, significant extant examples appearing in the 11th-cent 'Blickling Homilies' and in the 'Ormulum', a paraphrase of the Gospels and Ac. in the transitional Anglo-Norman dialect by Orm, an Augustinian monk. But the development of the language in this period made new 21d translation possible and necessary. The 14th cent. provides the first independent translation of the Ps., the Latin-English 'Midland Psalter' (*c.* A.D. 1320), questionably attributed to William of Shoreham, and a gloss recopied several times and ascribed to the Yorkshire hermit and preacher, Richard Rolle of Hampole. Other work surviving from this time includes an Apocalypse, a Gospel 'Harmony', several manuscripts of Ac. and the Epistles from the 14th and 15th cent., and the usual devotional texts.

But the signal achievement of this period was the e complete translation of the Bible into English under the sponsorship of the Oxford scholar and reformer **John Wycliffe.** A pupil, Nicholas of Hereford, had a large part in the enterprise, and a friend of the latter, John Purvey, probably participated. The translation was made from the Latin and was originally over-literal. A greatly improved revision, attributed to Purvey, became the prevalent form. It included, as did the Vulgate, the OT Apocrypha. A complete Bible was now available to the layman, and thanks to the Lollards or 'poor priests', followers of Wycliffe who carried on his work, it came to circulate in a surprisingly large number of copies. When Forshall and Madden brought out the first complete printing of the Wycliffe Bible in 1850—distinguishing the original and the revision—they were able to consult 170 manuscripts.

The importance of this Bible was manifold. Religiously it helped to prepare for the reform movement in England and elsewhere. It exerted a significant moulding influence upon the English of the period, of which it is itself a great monument. Much of its phraseology was reproduced in subsequent translations. Wycliffe's writings were banned, and in 1428 his bones were exhumed and burned, but that fire which he and his colleagues kindled was destined with the work of the reformers and the advent of printing to blaze into an inextinguishable flame.

Printing was introduced into England in 1477 by f the merchant-scholar William Caxton, and the first printed portions of the Scriptures (chiefly Genesis and Exodus) appeared in his *Golden Legende* (1483), a collection of medieval legends. While other portions also were printed, an edict of 1408 banning the unauthorised publication of the Bible in the vernacular discouraged the printing of a complete Bible or even NT in English in the 15th cent.

The outlook in the early 16th cent. was still dis- 22a couraging. But the Renaissance and Reformation movements had released forces which were to make inevitable the legal publication of the Scriptures in English and other vernacular tongues. Agitation for lay reading of the Bible increased, the vernaculars themselves developed into media appropriate for literary expression, and the veneration for the Latin text was breaking down as Hebrew and Greek texts became available.

In this situation the man of the hour was **William** b **Tyndale,** well equipped by education and conviction

22b to advance the cause of the English Bible. Educated at Oxford and Cambridge, he concluded from his experience as a tutor and chaplain that the Scriptures must be 'playnely layde before their eyes in their mother tongue' if the people were to apprehend religious truth. According to John Foxe he declared to a contemporary churchman that 'If God spare my lyfe, ere many years I wyl cause a boye that dryveth the plough shall know more of the Scripture than thou doest!' Encountering strong opposition because of his Protestant views, he was compelled to carry out his proposed work on the Continent, although with the aid of certain London merchants.

c In 1525–6 in Germany he completed and published the first printed English NT. A quarto edition of probably 3,000 copies was printed at Cologne and Worms, and an octavo of the same extent in Worms. But so proficient were Tyndale's enemies in destroying them that of the former edition only one 31-leaf fragment of Mt. (1:1–22:12) survives (Brit. Mus. Grenville 12179), and of the latter only two copies are known, one in the Baptist College at Bristol and the other in St Paul's in London. The version itself was a creative and vigorous work. Based on the Greek texts of Erasmus—unfortunately uncritical—it also made use of Wycliffe, the Vulgate, Erasmus' own Latin version, and Luther. The format, the contents of the Prologue, the prefaces to individual books and the controversial notes in the quarto edition (omitted in the octavo) reflect clearly the influence of Luther's 1522 NT. This plus Tyndale's known association with Luther at Wittenberg made him a heretic in the eyes of the authorities. They objected also to his substitutions for ecclesiastically charged terms, e.g. 'repentance' for 'penance', 'elder' for 'priest', 'congregation' for 'church'. But through revised editions of his own (especially 1534, 1535) and others his work lived on as a formative influence upon subsequent revision and translation.

Tyndale also made a valuable contribution to the OT in English, publishing the Pentateuch in 1530 and Jon. in 1531. But his enemies through the treachery of a friend accomplished his imprisonment. During this period he apparently carried his work to the end of Chr. Condemned for heresy he was put to death in 1536. Strangely enough, at the time of his death a complete English Bible was being allowed to circulate in England, whose basis in the NT and Pentateuch was his own work!

Meanwhile, also, George Joye, a collaborator of Tyndale's who had fallen out with him by pirating editions of his NT, contributed some translations of his own in the OT. These included Jer., Lam., Isa., a separately published Psalter (1534) and an edition of Prov. and Ec. (1535). An anonymous Psalter of 1530, the first printed in English, has also been ascribed to him. Joye apparently worked entirely from the Latin.

d But it was **Miles Coverdale**, scholar and churchman, who in the very year of Tyndale's imprisonment, 1535, was instrumental in producing the first complete printed Bible in English. Coverdale was not a controversialist, but he shared enough of the viewpoint of Tyndale to make it politic to leave England for a time. When the situation changed under Thomas Cromwell, and king and archbishop appeared to favour a Bible in English done by 'the proper persons', he returned to carry out the work. He secured unimpeded circulation for his edition, notwithstanding dependence upon Tyndale, by eliminating controversial material and by humbly disclaiming sectarian intentions. He also restored the terms which Tyndale had altered.

Coverdale made an enduring contribution to subsequent editions through his facile handling of English phraseology; and his Psalter became a permanent part of the Anglican Prayer Book. Where not using Tyndale he worked from the Latin and German, a fact indicated on the title page. New printings in the same year omitted the reference to the 'Douche and

Latyn', doubtless to avoid implications of Lutheran 22d
and Catholic influences. Otherwise he seems chiefly to have consulted Pagninus' Latin of 1528 and, especially in the OT, the Zürich Swiss-German Bible of 1527–9. He included the Apocrypha with no particular hesitation, but, except for Bar., he placed them at the end of the OT as Luther had done.

The relatively favourable climate of opinion now e
encouraged other publications. Editions of Coverdale in 1537 by James Nicholson and by Tyndale's friend John Rogers circulated with official approval. The second, issued under the pseudonym of Thomas Matthew, was apparently the first English Bible formally to be licensed by the king. This resulted from Cranmer's desire for an 'official' version to serve until one requested from the clergy could be prepared. Whether he knew it or not, the Matthew Bible incorporated for the first time Tyndale's unpublished OT work, except Jon. Yet, through Cranmer's endorsement, it came to serve as the chief foundation for the next official revision. Another revision was published in 1539 by **Richard Taverner**, a University-trained scholar and member of Cromwell's staff. It was the first English Bible completely to be printed in England, and contained a number of independent renderings of merit and lasting influence.

These productions were now overshadowed in 1539 f
by the long-awaited official version. It became known as the **Great Bible** because of its large folio size, or as 'Cranmer's Bible', from the Archbishop's preface in the second edition (1540). Coverdale, at Cranmer's request, had undertaken the responsibility for the work, and the result was in the Tyndale-Coverdale-Matthew tradition, with influence also apparent from the Vulgate, the Complutensian Polyglot, Erasmus' Latin, and the Latin OT of Sebastian Münster (1534–5). But who the 'dyverse excellent learned men' otherwise were, to whom the title page alludes, is not known. Prologues and explanatory notes were omitted, and in the Preface the people were enjoined to seek the counsel of 'men of higher judgment' in difficult passages. Seven editions of the Great Bible were published between 1539 and 1541, and it was, so far as extant records indicate, the first and only Bible formally authorised by king and parliament, i.e. 'apoynted to the use of the churches', as the 1540 and following title pages indicate.

Unfortunately, however, the Roman Catholic reaction which characterised the later years of Henry VIII, and which saw the execution of Cromwell in 1540, involved a virtual ban on popular use of the English Bible. A brief respite under Edward VI (1547–52) proved to be the prelude to severe persecution of Protestants under Queen Mary (1553–8). Some 300 suffered martyrdom, including Cranmer, Latimer, Ridley and Rogers. Many others fled to the Continent.

Among refugees in Geneva a significant edition of 23a
the English Bible was next prepared. Involved also in the undertaking were Calvin, Beza, Knox, and perhaps Coverdale. The NT (1557), was the work mainly of William Whittingham, a brother-in-law of Calvin; the OT was done by a committee, of which the only other certain names are Anthony Gilbey and Thomas Sampson. The *editio princeps* of the completed Bible (1560) contained a carefully revised NT. The work was of high scholarly quality and made the most important contribution to the English text since Tyndale. Yet it stood well within the tradition, being based chiefly on Tyndale's 1534 NT and on the Great Bible in the OT. Other important sources used were Beza's Latin NT text and commentary (first published in 1556), and the OT Latin of the Zürich and Münster Bibles. The version is often called the **Breeches Bible** from the translation in Gen. 3:7, although 'breeches' had been read here by Wycliffe and Caxton.

Just before publication Queen Elizabeth came to b
the throne (1558) and cautiously re-established the

23b Church of England. To her the **Geneva Bible** was dedicated in a strongly Protestant statement. But the many ' moste profitable annotations upon all the hard places ' were often polemical in nature and offensive to the authorities. The people, however, liked them, as well as the maps and other ' helps ', octavo size, attractive price, and the roman type and verse divisions which here appeared for the first time. Only the chapters had been indicated previously. This Bible, therefore, soon came into common usage among English-speaking Protestants, and so remained for about a century. Some 96 editions were published, and another 75 or so of the NT or other parts. The popularity of such a strongly Protestant production led the authorities to seek a rehabilitation of the authorised Bible through a new revision.

c Thus it came about that a second ' authorised ' English Bible was published in 1568, the work of a committee under the supervision of Archbishop Matthew Parker. Because of the large number of bishops involved it became known as the **Bishops' Bible**. Its basis was the Great Bible, but the influence of Pagninus, Münster, and even of the Geneva Bible is apparent. Most of the ' helps ' found in the Geneva were present, although controversial notes were disallowed. The traditional folio format and type were used. The text itself was uneven in character and without particular distinction. It is not strange, therefore, that it failed to replace the Geneva in popular favour. Nevertheless it became a link in the chain of official revisions, and the 2nd edition (1572) of the 20 or so published between 1568 and 1606 served as the formal basis for that version which eventually found popular acceptance.

d Meanwhile the need for an official English Bible was also felt in Roman Catholic circles, especially in connection with the aim to re-establish the Catholic faith in England. This time Catholic refugees were responsible for the work, chiefly two Oxford men, Gregory Martin and William Allen. In 1582 the NT was published at **Rheims** ; the OT, delayed by lack of funds, appeared in 1609–10 at **Douai**. The basis of the translation was the ' authentical Latin ', although other texts were consulted, as the title page indicates. Unfortunately the close adherence to the Latin often resulted in an over-literal rendering, sometimes simply transliteration of the text, as in phrases like ' supersubstantial bread ' (Mt. 6:11), or ' the similitude of the prevarication of Adam ' (Rom. 5:14). In format the edition was similar to the Geneva, to which it also appears indebted for certain readings. Strongly anti-Protestant prefaces and marginalia were included, and for some years by these media a Catholic-Protestant disputation was carried on in editions of the Geneva and Douai Scriptures. The Douai version was the first printed Catholic Bible, and also became the basis for all subsequent official revisions.

24a **The Authorised Version**—Circumstances in England had now become propitious for a new attempt to displace the Geneva Bible. James of Scotland, who succeeded Queen Elizabeth in 1603, had shown considerable interest in biblical studies, and Puritan dissatisfaction with the previous versions became the occasion in 1604 (Hampton Court Conference) for his support of a new revision. By July he had appointed a committee of about 50 men to do the work. After some delay the revision was carried through in amazingly short time between 1608 and 1611, and the 1st edition was published in the latter year in the traditional format and folio size. Controversial notes were excluded.

The long Preface by the learned committee member, Miles Smith, unfortunately omitted in most modern editions, explains that the edition was a *revision* greatly indebted to its predecessors. He found it necessary also still to defend a Bible in English ! Officially based on the Bishops' Bible (2nd edition 1572), the version actually made more use of other sources, except as it carried forward the basic Tyndale-Coverdale text. Evidently consulted were the Geneva Bible, Luther, 24a
the Rheims-Douai Bible (especially NT), and the usual Latin texts. The Preface also alludes to the use of French, Italian and Spanish translations. The Apocrypha appear without comment.

In qualities of literary style and accuracy the new version was the undoubted acme of the early efforts to render the Bible into English. Of course it was still based on uncritical texts, and the study of Greek and Hebrew was in its infancy. A desire for variety and enrichment of English often led to inconsistencies, especially apparent in proper names and in parallel passages in the Synoptic Gospels. Printing errors were numerous in the early editions. Sharp criticism of these and other matters led to several revisions, much of which consisted of modernised spelling. The chief of these were issued by Thomas Paris (Cambridge 1762) and Benjamin Blaney (Oxford 1769). The latter became the standard and virtually fixed form. After a half-century or so the Authorised Version (AV) began to displace the Geneva Bible, becoming the popular as well as official Bible. Its long ascendancy, involving as it did private and liturgical usage, literary associations, and general cultural penetration, made definitive revision of it next to impossible, when times and circumstances again made this advisable.

In this period, however, many private attempts b
were made to improve it or to make new translations (dated editions refer to NT unless otherwise indicated). The earliest (17th cent.) were adaptations consisting of interpolated paraphrases. Modifications of language followed, as in the NT of William Whiston (1745) and of John Wesley (1755), and in the Bible of Noah Webster (1833) and of A. C. Kendrick (1842). Some were too literal, e.g. Robert Young of concordance fame (Bible 1862) ; others were too free and familiar (Mace 1729 ; Harwood 1768 ; Scarlett 1798). Yet the latter group, and others such as Worsley (1770), Newcome (1796), and the Americans, Dickinson (1833), A. Norton (Gospels 1855), Sawyer (1858), Woodruff (1852), and Worrell (1904) were based on improved texts and began the use of modern idiom. A few, though textually better, preferred the traditional English, e.g. Penn (1836–7), Sharpe (1840–65), Noyes (1869), Ainslie (1869), Alford (1869–70), and Conant and others involved in the ambitious American Bible Union Version (1865, 1912). Other translators deserving mention were, in the 18th cent., Wakefield, Purver, Campbell, and MacKnight ; and in the 19th, Doddridge, Moberly, Ellicott, Humphry, Barrow, and Mrs Spurrell. Still unique in the annals of the English Bible is the translation of the Greek OT (1808) made by Charles Thomson, secretary of the Continental Congress.

Among English-speaking Jews the AV was used at c
first, with some adaptations. Independent translation began with renderings of the Pentateuch by Delgado (1785) and David Levi (1851), and the complete Scriptures by Benisch (1851) and by Friedlaender (1883). In America the edition of Leeser (1853) came into general use. Not until 1917 was an edition published which could be called an ' official ' Bible. This work was ably executed in America by a committee of seven scholars between 1908 and 1915 and published in 1917 by the Jewish Publication Society. Chairman and chief contributor was Professor Max Margolis. The version retained the ' biblical ' style. Jewish scholars in America have also undertaken a translation of the *Jewish Apocryphal Literature*. Six volumes have appeared (1950–8), comprising 1–4 Mac., Aristeas, Wis., and Tob., under the editorship of Professor S. Zeitlin.

Among Roman Catholics no revision was permitted d
until the 18th cent., when the obvious defects of the Douai Bible led to several attempts at improvement. Among these were the NT of Nary (1718) and Witham (1730), and the Bibles of Challoner (1749–50, 1752–64), McMahon (1783–1810) and Geddes (1786–1802). Most important were the first three editions of Richard

24d Challoner, whose work became the basis of most subsequent revision. But throughout the 19th cent. great confusion resulted from the huge number of editions and the inconsistent endorsements of prelates of the church. The widely used 3rd edition of Challoner was gradually displaced by the 1st through the influence of the 'Catholic Board' edition (1815) of the Roman Catholic Bible Society.

e Even while the AV reigned supreme much advance was made in studies closely related to translation. Especially significant were the discovery of early manuscripts and the publication of critical texts of the Hebrew and Greek. Also the English of the 'Authorised Version', notwithstanding orthographical modernisation, had become increasingly obsolete and obscure. Growing concern for this situation is reflected in the private revisions; but efforts for an 'official' revision proved unavailing until 1870.

f In that year a Convocation of Canterbury endorsed such an undertaking and arranged for its execution by a well-qualified committee of scholars and divines. This group, numbering 24 to 28, laboured for 14 years (10½ on the NT) to produce the **Revised Version**. Non-Anglicans participated, and collaboration with an American committee was developed. The latter consisted of some 19 active members under the leadership of the eminent church historian Philip Schaff. The new edition was published and copyrighted by the University presses of Cambridge and Oxford, the NT appearing in 1881 (17 May), the OT in 1885 (19 May), and the Apocrypha in 1895. Readings preferred by the American committee were given in an Appendix, and 14 years later—as agreed upon—an American edition, the **American Standard Version**, was published (26 August 1901), which incorporated these and other changes.

The revision was at first enthusiastically received and saw wide adoption and usage, especially in the United States. But it failed to supplant the AV in public favour; for in spite of improvements in underlying texts and in a clearer and more consistent English, it was justly criticised for being over-literal and for introducing many unnecessary changes, especially in view of the stated purpose of the committee to alter the AV only where necessary. On the other hand the proponents of modern idiom deprecated the continued use of archaic speech.

The need, then, for a generally acceptable revision continued, and was accentuated in the 20th cent. by new evidence for the text and its meaning. Many private translations appeared, representing various interests and idiosyncrasies. A number were revisions of the AV. Some are too literal, e.g. the 'Concordant Version' (1921–7); the renderings of J. B. Phillips were very free but had a wide appeal. The Basic English version edited by S. H. Hooke (NT 1941; OT 1950) is surprisingly clear and vigorous in spite of the limited vocabulary. Modern idiom is represented in F. S. Ballentine (Bible 1899–1901); in American speech, C. B. Williams (1937); the *Letters* by J. W. C. Wand (1943); the 'Letchworth' NT of T. F. and R. E. Ford (1948); Charles F. Kent's *Shorter NT* (1919), and the 'Berkeley' version (NT 1945; OT in progress), by a committee with Gerrit Verkuyl as editor. The 'plain English' NT of C. K. Williams (1952) and the Penguin Gospels of E. V. Rieu (1953) also deserve mention.

Some measure of popularity was achieved by the version of Ferrar Fenton (NT 1885; OT 1903), a London business-man, and by the *20th Cent. NT* (1898–1901, 1904), published anonymously by a capable committee of some 35 persons, mostly non-Anglicans and laymen, whose moving spirits were Ernest Malan and Mrs Mary K. Higgs. Comparable editions in America approaching modern idiom were William G. Ballantine's *The Riverside NT* (1923, revised 1934) and *The Centenary NT* of Mrs Helen Barrett Montgomery (1923–4).

Most widely used of the modern-speech versions have been those of **R. F. Weymouth, James Moffatt,** and **E. J. Goodspeed.** While free and idiomatic renderings, their essential accuracy is guaranteed by the scholarly competence of the translators. Weymouth translated his own *Resultant Greek Testament*, based on other modern editions. His version, supplied with a number of helpful notes, was published posthumously in 1903. A revised edition came out in 1924. Professor Moffatt published an edition of the entire Bible (NT 1913; OT 1924). The NT was based on the text of von Soden and contained a few notes, mainly textual. Professor Goodspeed produced *An American Translation* in 1923, closely following the Westcott-Hort Greek text. A somewhat less free rendering of the OT followed in 1927, the work of Professors J. M. P. Smith (editor), Leroy Waterman, Theophile J. Meek, and Alexander R. Gordon. *The Complete Bible . . .*, containing also the Apocrypha in a new version prepared by Goodspeed, was issued in 1939 by the University of Chicago Press. 24f

Among Roman Catholics the Douai-Challoner tradition continued well into the 20th cent. An exception is F. A. Spencer's modern-speech version (Gospels 1898; NT edited by Callan and McHugh, 1937). *The Westminster NT*, edited by Lattey and Keating (1913–35), though based on the Greek, was conservative in English. Publication in the OT here continues, based on the Hebrew. Ps., Ru., Dan. and most of the Minor Prophets appeared between 1934 and 1953. More advance is marked by the version of the 'Episcopal Committee of the Confraternity of Christian Doctrine'. The NT (1941), while based on the Vulgate, made full use of Greek texts. The OT, of which Ps.-Ca., the Octateuch and the Wisdom Books appeared between 1950 and 1955, is being rendered primarily from the Hebrew and into completely modern idiom. An independent work, officially sponsored in England, came from **Ronald Knox** (NT 1944; OT 1948–50), whose literary *savoir-faire* is reflected in a highly readable translation aimed at 'timeless English'. The American Kleist-Lilly NT (1954) also represents modern idiom, especially good in the Gospels. g

Eventually, 'official' efforts were again made among Protestants in both England and America to meet the need for modern and accurate editions. In America a revision of the ASV known as the **Revised Standard Version** was prepared under the sponsorship of the National Council of the Churches of Christ in the U.S.A., by a committee of scholars under the leadership of Dean Luther Weigle. This representative body had received the copyright of the ASV upon its expiration in 1928 from the publishers, Thomas Nelson and Sons, New York. The work was begun in 1930 and, after an interruption (1932–7) occasioned by the economic recession, the NT was completed and published in 1946 and the OT in 1952, the complete Bible now incorporating some 80 changes in the NT. The Apocrypha, undertaken at the request of the Protestant Episcopal Church, came out in 1957. h

The new version was well received both by scholars and the public. While based naturally upon modern critical texts and scholarship, the version aimed to retain such traditional phraseology as might be consonant with modern idiom and intelligibility, thus hoping to serve for public worship as well as private reading and study. The difficulties of attaining this ideal led easily to charges of unevenness and inconsistency. Yet the total result represented a tremendous achievement, the language was generally clear and idiomatic, and provision was made for improvement through a continuing supervisory committee.

The **British revision** was initiated in 1947 after a discussion in the General Assembly of the Church of Scotland and authorisation by a Convocation of Canterbury. A joint supervisory committee includes representatives of the 'free' churches and the Scottish and British Bible Societies. Two committees of i

24i scholars organised in four panels (OT, NT, Apoc., Literary) are at work under the general chairmanship of Professor C. H. Dodd. This version aims to provide a new translation into modern English without necessary dependence upon previous efforts and is designed primarily for private use. In 1961 the first volume of this translation appeared, *The New English Bible—New Testament.*

Bibliography—F. F. Bruce, *The English Bible* (1961) ; C. C. Butterworth, *The Literary Lineage of the King James Version of the Bible*, 1340–1611 (1941) ; John Eadie, *The English Bible* (2 vols. 1876) ; F. G. Kenyon, *Our Bible and the Ancient Manuscripts* (5th ed. by A. W. Adams, 1958) ; N. R. Ker, *Catalogue of Manuscripts Containing Anglo-Saxon* (1957) ; H. G. May, *Our English Bible in the Making* (1952) ; A. W. Pollard, *Records of the English Bible . . . 1525–1611* (1911) ; H. Pope, *English Versions of the Bible* (rev. and amplified by S. Bullough, 1952) ; I. M. Price, *The Ancestry of our English Bible* (3rd rev. ed. by W. A. Irwin and A. Wikgren, 1955) ; H. W. Robinson (ed.), *Our Bible in its Ancient and English Versions* (1940) ; P. Schaff, *A Companion to the Greek Testament and the English Versions* (1883) ; L. A. Weigle, *The English NT from Tyndale to the RSV* (1949), *An Introduction to the RSV NT* (1946), *An Introduction to the RSV OT* (1952) ; B. F. Westcott, *A General View of the History of the English Bible* (3rd rev. ed. by W. A. Wright, 1905, 1916).

THE GEOGRAPHY OF PALESTINE

By J. N. SCHOFIELD

25a **The Biblical World**—' Biblical geography is not a study by itself but the natural introduction to all other Biblical studies ' (C. F. Kent, *Biblical Geography and History* (1911), vi). In a commentary on the Bible the geography of Palestine must be confined to Biblical geography, seeking to describe the earthly stage whereon were made the initial acts of man's salvation recorded in the Bible. The Bible world extended from Tarshish in southern Spain eastward to the Persian Gulf, and from Cush (Ethiopia) in the south to the Black Sea and Caspian Sea in the north. Palestine, at the eastern end of the Mediterranean, lay at the centre of this area, and through it passed many of the roads, the military and trade routes, linking the three continents of Africa, Asia, and Europe ; from all three continents came military conquerors who left their mark on the history of the little country, and archaeology is continually yielding fresh evidence of the presence of traders, both in the wares they brought and in the influence of those wares on local products. On the west and the east lay two ancient river civilisations, linked by the ' Fertile Crescent ' formed by the upper reaches of the Euphrates, the Orontes and the Jordan
b Valley. The land on the west was known as **Egypt** throughout biblical history. It is a narrow strip of alluvial soil on both sides of the Nile, broadening into the everchanging Delta at the northern end where it enters the Mediterranean. Biblical writers were conscious of the contrast between Egypt and Palestine : ' For the land which you are entering to take possession of it is not like the land of Egypt, from which you have come, where you sowed your seed and watered it with your feet, like a garden of vegetables ; but the land which you are going over to possess is a land of hills and valleys, which drink water by the rain from heaven, a land which the Lord your God cares for ; the eyes of the Lord your God are always upon it, from the beginning of the year to the end of the year ' (Dt. 11:10 ff.) ; Egypt was a man-made country, dependent on the Nile floods and the man-made irrigation channels ; Palestine was God-made, dependent for its life and prosperity on the God-given rain from heaven (Dt. 11:14 ; Am. 4:7 ; Zech. 14:17 ; Mt. 5:45), and needing his constant care. From the fourth millennium B.C. there are records of Egyptian troops and traders entering Palestine by land and sea to exploit mines in the south and forests in the north ; political refugees fled from one country to the other ; from Egypt came Sinuhe in about 2200 B.C., and to Egypt Uriah fled from Palestine (Jer. 26:21) ; Palestinians were driven to Egypt for food (Gen. 42) and sold there as slaves (Gen. 39 ; Dt. 17:16). The fact that Egypt was the nearest great power to Palestine tempted the Hebrews to rely on her military aid. Though ' like a dove, silly and without sense ', she called to Egypt and went to Assyria (Hos. 7:11), it was intrigues with Egypt that caused disaster to Palestine from Assyrian, Babylonian and Greek invaders, and proved Egypt to be ' that broken reed of a staff, which will pierce the hand of any man who leans on it ' (Isa. 36:6).

c In **Mesopotamia** on the east the climate and the physical features are in many ways comparable to those in Egypt : a warm climate, and fertile alluvial soil brought down each year by the flood waters of 25c two great rivers. The Tigris and the Euphrates both rise in the mountains south of the Caspian Sea ; the former flows south-east for about 1,100 miles, the latter flows westward toward the Mediterranean before turning east-south-east to flow, in most of the lower part of its course, through desert to join the Tigris in the Persian Gulf. Life was not so stable in the valley between the two rivers as round the Nile. There were no natural marshes to control the flood waters of these two rivers like those near the head-waters of the Nile ; the desert on the west was not so impenetrable a barrier, and from the hills on the north and east successive invaders entered and conquered the land. Sumerians in the south were later rivalled by Akkadians from Assyria in the north ; semitic nomads, called Westerners (Amurru) or Amorites, pressed in from the west and founded dynasties ; the first Babylonian dynasty was overthrown by Hittites from Asia Minor, who in their turn gave way to more Indo-Aryan invaders from the hills south of the Caspian Sea ; later Assyrian, Babylonian and Persian conquerors followed each other, until Alexander the Greek swept across the whole Near East. At the end of the Bible period Parthians were successfully challenging Roman supremacy and checking Roman movement toward the east. The influences of all these peoples are discernible in Palestine, in degrees that vary with the length of their domination and with the extent of their conquests : the influence was less strong and less permanent if Palestine was the limit of their empire and a buffer state between them and Egypt than if they extended beyond the country, including Egypt under their dominion, and Palestine as an integral part of their empire.

To the north lay **Syria**, the gateway through which d came not only the conquerors from Mesopotamia but those from Asia Minor and Europe. The word has no fixed geographical content, and may be used for the whole strip of land between the eastern Mediterranean coast and the Arabian desert from Amanus in the north to Sinai in the south, or at the other extreme be limited in meaning to the small modern republic of Syria. In the Bible the word usually denotes the larger area, but excluding Palestine and Transjordan. The Hebrew name was *Aram* because of the Aramaeans, who had established themselves in the area from about the 13th cent. B.C. and whose kingdom, centering at Damascus, was founded at about the same time as David established the Hebrew monarchy. The name Syria comes from the LXX translation of Aram, perhaps influenced by a Babylonian name, Suri, for part of the north-west Euphrates valley. In the RSV the word is variously translated as Aram, Mesopotamia, Syria and Syrians. The land is dominated by the Lebanon and Anti-Lebanon ranges and the broad valley between them which is continued southward in the deepening valley of the Jordan and the Dead Sea. In this valley rise, not only the Jordan, but the two rivers Orontes and Lītânī, the one flowing north and the other south from a watershed near Ba'albek ; the former (Nahr el-'Aṣi) after running northward for about 160 miles through Lake Homs

25d and the plain of Antioch, turns suddenly south-west to enter the Mediterranean four miles south of Seleucia, the ancient port of Antioch ; the Lītānī flows south and makes a similar abrupt turn westward at the southern end of the Lebanon, entering the sea between Tyre and Sidon. The coastline varies from rugged headlands to sandy beaches with natural harbours at Acre, Tyre, Sidon, Beirût, Tripoli, and Alexandretta. The Lebanon rises steeply to a plateau about 8,000 ft. high with its highest peaks over 10,000 ft., and the main pass from Damascus to Beirût about 5,000 ft. The upper slopes are desolate, but below 5,000 ft. they are cultivated, wooded with the trees so often mentioned in the Old Testament, and well populated. Parallel with the Lebanon on the eastern side of the valley runs the Anti-Lebanon, rising steeply about 17 miles south of Homs and sinking after 65 miles to the pass, south of which stands Hermon, 9,232 ft. high. North-west of Damascus the range fans out eastward, one ridge stretching 130 miles to Palmyra. Damascus is watered by streams from Hermon, of which Abana (Baradā) and Pharpar (A'waj) are mentioned in the Bible (2 Kg. 5:12 ; Ca. 4:8). North of Syria lay the Taurus mountains and Asia Minor whence came the conquering Hittites ; to the north-west, the Aegean islands, from which the Sea Peoples—known in the OT as Philistines—swarmed in, and Macedonia, the home of Alexander the Great, who made it part of his Greek empire in the 4th cent. ; westward was Rome, which made Syria a province in the 1st cent. B.C.

e South and east of Palestine lay **desert** ; it ran down into the Arabian peninsula and across to Mesopotamia. Across it no routes ran, nor did tracks penetrate far into it until the 11th cent., when the camel was domesticated and bedouin life was revolutionised. Both the Syrian desert on the east and Arabia in the south support a considerable population at oases where springs or lakes allow irrigation ; some of these have over 15,000 inhabitants. In large areas, especially in the west and south, there are long periods of drought, and the land is empty except for a few visiting bedouin ; in other areas the rainfall is sufficient to provide pasture in the winter. To Palestine the desert was a protecting barrier, but it was feared because of its mystery, its demons, and its inhospitability ; and because from it came the hungry nomads to raid or to settle (Jg. 6:1–6).

f On the west was another barrier equally feared and mysterious—**the sea**. Lack of harbours prevented the Hebrews from becoming a maritime people like their Phoenician neighbours ; for them paradise was a place where there was no more sea, and the mythological language ascribing to God the conquest of the sea, its control, and the fixing of limits it could not pass, was readily and frequently adapted in Jewish devotion and used as a description of Israel's God.

26 **The Name of the Country**—The *Land of Israel*, the term by which that part of it in Jewish hands is today designated, is used for the country both in the OT and the NT, but the commonest name for it in the OT is *Land of Canaan*. The word may be connected with the name for the purple dye used by the inhabitants, but it is clearly an ancient name, being used by Egyptians from the early 20th cent. and in the Tell el-Amarna letters. In the OT the word is used both for the lowlands, the coastal plain and the Jordan valley, and sometimes for the whole territory west of the Jordan. Another name, *Amorite*, appears to have originated from the eastern side of Palestine and describes the people as ' westerners '. As originally it referred to the inhabitants of the hill country of Syria and northern Palestine it may have had a nuance of ' highlander ' in contrast to the Canaanite ' lowlander '. In the OT it is used of the people in Transjordan ruled by Sihon and Og, as a general term for the pre-Israelite inhabitants of all Palestine, and as the name of one of the nations dispossessed by Israel. The common name Palestine by which the land was known until recently is quoted by the Jewish historian Josephus as used by Herodotus for the whole land, 26
including both the coast land and Judaea. It originated from the name of the Philistines, the Sea Peoples who swarmed into the coastal plain at the end of the 13th cent. B.C. ; used by Greeks as an adjective to distinguish southern from northern Syria, it was later used by Romans as the name of a province.

Boundaries—There is only one definite and certain 27
boundary to Palestine : the Mediterranean on the west ; elsewhere boundaries may be drawn wherever political propaganda requires. In the south the land shades off into the desert of Sinai with no barrier until the Suez Canal is reached. In the OT the two **southern** limits mentioned are Beersheba, the outpost town where desert and cultivation meet ; and the Brook of Egypt, not the Nile but the Wâdī el-'Arîsh about half-way between Gaza and the Suez Canal. The **north,** too, has no simple natural limits. There is a break at the plain of Esdraelon at the foot of the Carmel range and the Nazareth hills ; and another where the Orontes turns abruptly to the west ; but neither break has been historically the limit. Here also the OT mentions two limits, Dan, north of Lake Huleh, near the modern Bâniyâs, known in the NT as Caesarea Philippi ; and ' The entering of Hamath '—not, probably, the city of Hamath in Syria but the beginning of the valley between the Lebanons and Anti-Lebanons leading up to Hamath. (An alternative view is that ' the entering of Hamath ' should be rendered Lebo-hamath, and understood as a place name.) From Dan to Beersheba (Jg. 20:1) or from the entrance of Hamath to the Brook of Egypt (1 Kg. 8:65) may have been at various times the actual or ideal limits of the Israelite kingdom, but they correspond to no pronounced geographical boundaries. On the **east** the ideal limit was even more ambitious, ' the great river, the river Euphrates ' (Dt. 1:7). Nearer home was the Jordan, but that was never a boundary or barrier. Israelite tribes settled on both sides of it ; Roman and Turkish administration governed some of Transjordan from the western side, and now the kingdom of Jordan controls much of the western side from 'Ammân on the east. If we take the usual limits, from Dan to Beersheba and from the Mediterranean to the Jordan, the length is 130 miles, the breadth at its widest in the south 90 miles, narrowing to less than 40 in the north. Roughly there are 6,000 sq. miles, of which, according to the Hope Simpson report, about 3,000 are cultivable—thus Palestine is about the same size as Wales and just about as fertile.

Natural Divisions—A relief map or a flight over the 28a
country makes clear the four natural sections of the land running north and south : the coastal plain, the central hill country, the deep Jordan valley, and the hill country of Transjordan. These dominating divisions, caused by a geological fault—a deep fracture of the earth's surface resulting in the shifting of the strata of underlying rocks—and secondary fracture lines, some running north and south parallel to the fault and others east and west, have produced ' a land of brooks of water, of fountains and springs, flowing forth in valleys and hills ' (Dt. 8:7) ; they have also produced a great variety of soils and of climate. Bethlehem, 14 miles from the Dead Sea, is 3,842 ft. above the level of its waters and 5,150 ft. above the deepest point of its bed ; snow can be falling in Jerusalem, while 15 miles away Jericho can be sweltering in almost tropical heat.

The Coastal Plain, of varying width, stretches b
between the central hills and the sea. On the Syrian border at Râs en-Nāqûrah—the Ladder of Tyre—the Galilean hills run out in precipitous cliffs to the sea and there is no coastal plain, but southward it widens to the plain of Acre where it is nearly 5 miles in breadth. At Haifa it is still wider, opening out to the broad plain of Esdraelon which stretches through the vale of Jezreel to the Jordan Valley. Immediately south of Haifa, the long arm of Carmel reaches to within 200 yards of the sea, but at 'Athlît, 9 miles

28b south of Carmel, the plain is 2 miles wide and gradually widens to a maximum width of 30 miles at the southern end. Numerous wadis or river beds have been cut through the limestone and run across the plain, but most of them are only winter torrents, and the only permanent water supply is at Râs el-'Ain north-east of Jaffa.

The actual coast is sandy, and south of Jaffa a widening belt of sand dunes, like those on the south coast of England near Rye and Winchelsea, intervenes between the plain and the sea and merges into the Sinai desert. The absence of navigable river estuaries or rock-protected bays means that there are no harbours south of Carmel. Even the harbour at Haifa, north of Carmel, despite the expenditure of millions of pounds and continual dredging, cannot accommodate a large vessel except in the calmest weather. The currents flow northward parallel to the coast, bringing tons of Nile mud which, mingling with sand blown from the south by the prevailing wind, deposit large quantities of silt, discouraging efforts to build harbours. From the east, too, fertile soil is washed down from the hills by heavy winter rains, making the plain one of the most fertile parts of Palestine. Much of it, including the lovely plain of Sharon north of Jaffa, was allotted to Israel by the United Nations commission in 1947, and more was taken over by Israel at the armistice two years later.

c The maritime plain itself can be divided into **three parts** : the Philistine plain, the plain of Sharon, and the land north of Carmel which has already been described. The largest is the **Philistine plain** in the south, stretching 40 miles from the Wâdī el-'Arîsh to the low hills, which form the watershed between the Valley of Sorek and the Wâdī Nuṣrah just south of Ramleh. The extreme south is called *wilderness* in the RSV, but the Hebrew word denotes '*a place where cattle are led out to pasture*'—land that after the winter rain can be covered with pasture. Abraham and his son found food for their herds there, dug wells, and reaped a hundredfold (Gen. 26). With careful water conservation and irrigation, as in Roman times, this area supported a large population ; for 30 miles south even of Beersheba there are remains of villages and towns clustering round wells, and in one of them, Esbaita, remains of three large Christian churches witness to the size of the community that once inhabited it. North of Gaza the whole area can be cultivated ; citrus fruits, oranges, lemons, and grapefruit grow on the light sandy soils near the coast, and wheat on the plain. Almost everywhere wells can be bored and water obtained. The climate is always temperate with an average temperature of about 65°F. In the winter, west and south-west winds bring the rains from October to April ; in summer cool winds from the north-west are dry ; the central hills protect the plain from the hot, sandy, violent, east winds from the desert.

d Here lay the **five cities of the Philistines** : Gaza, Ashkelon, Ashdod, Ekron and Gath. Gaza, the most southerly, probably occupied the same site as the modern town, a mound 3 miles from the coast and on the edge of the desert. Roads from Egypt and Syria, as well as through Beersheba to Elath on the Gulf of 'Aqaba, met there. Vitally important to an army invading Palestine from the south, Egypt, then as now, held Gaza whenever possible. Ashkelon, 17 miles north of Gaza, was the only port of the five cities, and excavations have shown that during the Philistine period trade from the western islands flowed into the country through it. The main road northward, avoiding the deep western end of the Wâdī el-Ḥesī, missed Ashkelon and went straight to Ashdod, which like Gaza lay inland, although few traces of it remain, for sand has almost covered the old site. Later it was called Azotus, the town where Philip was found after his encounter with the eunuch on the Gaza road (Ac. 8:40) At Ashdod the roads branch ; the coast road runs north through Jamnia to Jaffa and another road north-east to Lydda through 'Âqir, probably the ancient **28d**
Ekron, about 5 miles north of the Valley of Sorek. Like Ekron, Gath has not been certainly identified ; it disappeared from history at the end of the 8th cent. B.C., but the biblical contexts of the name suggest that its most probable identification is with 'Arâq el-Menshîyeh, 8 miles due west of Beit Jibrîn at the edge of the foothills.

These low foothills, between the western edge of the **e**
plain and the central hills, are an important feature of this section of Palestine ; they are called the **Shephelah** (the lowland, Dt. 1:7). Through them run wadis, cut into the soft limestone and forming the passes into the hills ; on them stand many of the cities famous in Jewish history, guarding these entrances to Judaea. The Wâdī el-Afranj leads down from Hebron through Beit Jibrîn into the valley of Zephathah. Tell ed-Duweir, the ancient Lachish, 5 miles south-south-west of Beit Jibrîn, guards the entrance to another smaller valley leading through to the same Wâdī el-Afranj. Northward from this wadi is the valley of Elah, up which roads run south-east to Hebron, north-east to Jerusalem, and eastwards to Gibeah and Bethlehem. Guarding its entrance at the foot of the Shephelah stands the large crescent-shaped limestone mound of Tell eṣ-Ṣâfī, possibly the ancient Libnah, and farther east along the valley at the foot of the next ridge, 940 ft. above sea level, is the fortress of Azekah (Tell Zakarîyah). Five miles north is the vale of Sorek, the scene of Samson's exploits, carrying the main road to Jerusalem through Beth-shemesh and Kiriath-jearim. Farthest north is the vale of Aijalon, defended at the edge of the Shephelah by Gezer, which was handed over to Solomon by the Egyptian Pharaoh as a wedding dowry, and at the foot of the central hill range by Upper and Lower Beth-horon. Northward of Aijalon the distinctive characteristic of the Shephelah ceases ; that is, the fact that the valleys, instead of running eastward straight up into the hill country, turn south and south-east running parallel to the central range, thus forming easily defended barriers protecting the hills from attack from the plain and even cutting them off from easy infiltration by culture or traders. This geographical peculiarity had considerable influence on the history of the southern Jewish kingdom called Judah, perched on these hills east of the Shephelah, and on the development of its religion and literature. These wadis from the hills through the Shephelah carried swift torrents of water across the plain during the heavy winter rains, cutting deep channels there, making traffic along it difficult except on clearly defined routes, which could thus be guarded by lines of fortresses across the country from west to east. Hence were developed such lines as Gerar, Bethpelet, Beersheba in the south ; Gath, Lachish, Hebron ; Libnah, Azekah, Socoh ; Beth-shemesh, Kiriath-jearim, Jerusalem ; Ekron, Aijalon, Beth-horon and Michmash ; and at the northern end of the plain, the line of Carmel across Esdraelon to Beth-shan. The mild western slopes of the Shephelah, with vineyards and cornfields, were Judah's most important economic possession.

North of the valley of Aijalon, which runs to the sea **f**
in the Wâdī Nuṣrah lies the beautiful fertile **plain of Sharon,** in biblical times covered with an oak forest. Southward are the towns of Jaffa, Lydda, and Ramleh, and to the north lies the Wâdī ez-Zerkâ (Crocodile River) breaking to the sea through wild marshes about 3 miles north of the ruins of Herod's famous port of Caesarea. It is well watered and, especially in the south, cultivated in palm and orange groves, with fields of corn and melons. Wadis run straight across the central hills : the Wâdī Deir Ballûṭ almost due west from a watershed east of Shiloh, from which other streams flow east into the Jordan valley. Well-worn passes cross the Carmel range into the plain of Esdraelon. The widest pass follows the Wâdī Selhab through the Plain of Dothan, where Joseph's brothers

28f fed their flocks and met the Ishmaelite caravan or the Midianite traders (Gen. 37); it enters the plain of Esdraelon at Jenîn. North-west the Wâdī 'Ârah leads through to Megiddo. The most westerly pass crosses from Subbarin to Tell Keimun, enters the narrow northern end of the plain near Harosheth, and is the shortest route from the coastal plain to Acre.

29a **The Central Hills** are the next main division of the country, in which also there are **three** clearly marked sections—Judah, Samaria, and Galilee. Like a gigantic backbone the rugged limestone hills continue the line of the Lebanon range, broken by the deep gorge of the Lītânī river and the wide plain of Esdraelon, varying considerably in height but rising to a maximum of 3,600 ft. The climate is mild apart from the hot sandy Sirocco wind from the east, and there is ample rainfall except in the extreme south, but the soft limestone soon absorbs any water not carried in torrents down the hillsides, which have been washed bare since the old terraces were broken and the trees cut down. Rain water is stored in rock-hewn cisterns, and the early Israelite invaders in the 13th cent. B.C. were able to populate the hills because of the discovery at that time of the art of making slaked-lime waterproof plaster with which to line the cisterns. **Judah** at the southern end of the hills covered about 1,350 sq. miles but half of it is desert; its length from south to north, from Beersheba to Bethel, is 55 miles, and no part is more than 25 miles across. The eastern side is wilderness, leading down to the Dead Sea, formed by deep valleys whose sides are too steep for cultivation; there is five to eight hours of desolate waterless waste between the gates of Hebron, Bethlehem and Jerusalem, and the Dead Sea providing 'the appearance of devastated war-scarred country unhealed by the gentleness of time'. The whole area is known as Jeshimon, translated 'wilderness' in RSV —the howling waste of the wilderness (Dt. 32:10)— and consists of the wilderness of Maon, the wilderness of Ziph east of Hebron, the wilderness of Jeruel, and the wilderness of Tekoa. In the shallow soil vegetation dies during the summer months, reviving again after the autumn rains, and giving pasture to bedouin goats and hardy mountain sheep such as Amos tended.

b Beersheba, at the southern end of Judah, stands at the edge of the desert with which it has its closest affinities. Allotted to the Arabs by the United Nations, it was taken over by Israel in 1949 together with about half the twenty miles between it and Hebron. Beersheba is the centre of the district known as the Negeb (Gen. 12:9), and through it run roads westward to Suez and El-'Arîsh, the pilgrim route to Sinai, and the old Roman road to 'Aqaba, the port at the northern end of the Red Sea. Wells at Beersheba are traditionally linked with Abraham, known by his Arab name of El-Khalîl—the Friend of God—but the water supply is poor and, even with careful conservation, life is precarious. From it the hills rise gradually to Hebron, 3,000 ft. above sea level, and continue to rise another 350 ft. before sinking to 2,550 ft. at Bethlehem and Jerusalem. At Hebron is the patriarchal burial-place, the Cave of Machpelah (Gen. 25:9) and the town is famous for its primitive wheel-made pottery. From it roads lead down westward to the coastal plain, and eastward a steep track, dropping 4,000 ft. in 15 miles, runs down to Engedi on the shore of the Dead Sea. West of the road from Beersheba to Hebron lies the important site of Tell Beit-Mirsim, the ancient Debir or Kiriath-sepher, attacked by Judah and Caleb in their initial drive into the south (Jg. 1:11). About 3 miles to the east of the road and 6 miles south of Bethlehem lies Tekoa, on the edge of the desert, about 2,780 ft. above sea level, famous for its wisdom and as the home of Amos. Bethlehem is lovely, clustered on a terraced hill with wide views across the fields where 'shepherds watched their flocks by night'; from the tower of the Church of the Nativity which crowns the hill it is possible to see down to the shores of the Dead Sea near Qumrân, the site of the monastery of the sect whose literary 29b treasures have been discovered in caves in the desolate hillside. Six miles farther north is Jerusalem where the Prince of Peace died, and the scene of so many bitter conflicts. West of the road is the Valley of Rephaim up which the railway from the coast climbs and in which Philistine forces encamped against David. The old city of Jerusalem and the Temple area stand on a hill surrounded on three sides by valleys; the Tyropoeon valley on the west continues the valley of Rephaim, the valley of Hinnom on the south where the city's rubbish was burned and which gave its name, Gehenna, to the picture of the abode of the wicked in the after-life, and the valley of the Kidron or the vale of Jehoshaphat on the east, across which runs the path to the Mount of Olives and the village of Bethany. On the western slopes, in the valleys built round springs on the wooded hillsides, are many pleasant villages; one of them, 'Ain Kârim—the reputed birthplace of John the Baptist—was for many years the home of old Russian nuns of the Eastern church who are now, at last, helped by young sisters from the Soviet Union.

North of Jerusalem is the real centre of Judah, the c rocky, broken tableland from 2,000 to 3,000 ft. high with small cultivated patches, a few remains of ruined terraces, flocks of sheep and goats, and houses concentrated in many villages scattered over the hills. In biblical days the district was well populated and many of the villages were walled and fortified, forming the northern boundary between the kingdoms of Judah and Israel. Anathoth, Gibeah of Saul (Tell el-Fûl), Ramah, Michmash, and Bethel lay on the east of the main road, Mizpah (Tell en-Naṣbeh) was on the western side close to the road, and farther west lay the dominating height of Nebī Samwîl, perhaps the high place of Gibeon where Solomon offered his coronation sacrifices (2 Chr. 1:3). On this more open plateau there was no natural border between north and south; Baasha of Israel was fortifying Ramah when attacked in the rear by Benhadad of Syria at the instigation of Asa of Judah, and when he withdrew, Asa used the same stones and timber to fortify Geba and Mizpah as frontier towns (1 Kg. 15:22).

North of Mizpah is the highland known as the Mount 30a of Ephraim, where we enter the northern kingdom of **Samaria**. On this highland are three ancient holy places, Bethel, Shiloh (Seilûn), and Shechem (Nâblus), approached by wadis from both east and west. From Jericho the road to Bethel, probably used by Joshua's invading army, runs through Michmash and the ruin of et-Tell, probably the ancient Ai which had been destroyed before the Israelites entered Palestine, and which was used as a strong point to protect Bethel, less than a mile away. From Bethel the road north drops slowly. Shiloh is 10 miles north of Bethel on the east of the main road, at the head of the Wâdī Deir Ballûṭ and the Wâdī el-Kub running straight up from the coastal plain. Destroyed in the 11th cent. by the Philistines (1 Sam. 4), Shiloh was still an important religious centre in the time of Jeremiah (Jer. 41:5). Northward the hills become more open and fertile; the cultivated areas become larger, wadis to east and west are less precipitous leading down to fertile plains even on the eastern side. It is more accessible on all sides than Judah.

Northward for another 10 miles the road falls rapidly b to Balâṭāh, the site of ancient Shechem in the south-eastern end of the narrow pass between the twin mountains of Ebal and Gerizim, 3,077 and 2,850 ft. respectively. Here roads from all directions meet, and the central importance of the town in Palestine's history is readily understood. It was an Egyptian fortress after the XVIII Dynasty had expelled the Hyksos; the Tell el-Amarna tablets mention it; stories link Abraham and Jacob with it; and there Joshua and the Israelites made their covenant (Jos. 24). Thither Rehoboam had to go to confirm his kingship, and there the break between the two kingdoms took

30b place. The small Samaritan community still hold their annual Passover on Mount Gerizim overlooking the ancient site. It could not easily be defended and when Omri revolted and seized the northern throne, he built a new centre at Samaria, 7 miles north-west on the hills 1,450 ft. above sea level (1 Kg. 16:24). Like Jerusalem, this site was protected by valleys on three sides with a narrow neck joining it to the hills on the fourth, so strong a position that even the Assyrians took three years to subdue it. From it the sandy shore of the Mediterranean at Caesarea is visible ; roads run through to the coast, zigzag down the steep slopes to the plain of Dothan, and follow the Roman track eastward along the broad valley of the Wâdî Fār'ah to the Jordan ford at ed-Dâmîyeh, opposite the valley of the Jabbok. In the kingdom of Samaria the plains are wider than in Judah, the ground more fertile, so that the whole land was more accessible to troops and traders, and to the infiltration of culture and religious ideas from both Egypt and Mesopotamia. The country's links were closer with foreigners north, east, and west, than with brothers on the south, and the rebellion against Rehoboam was the natural revolt of a people with different racial origin, geographical environment, racial symbols and linguistic dialects against eighty years of military domination under David and Solomon.

c At the north-eastern end of the plain of Dothan, where its low foothills drop to the great plain of Esdraelon, stands the important town of Jenîn, with its few tall palm trees standing near the road as evidence of a milder climate than the hills allow. In the OT, under the name En-gannim, it formed a southern limit of the land of the northern tribe of Issachar (Jg. 19:21), being one of Issachar's four Levitical cities (Jg. 21:29). Perhaps it should be regarded as on the boundary between Samaria and **Galilee,** the third main section of the central hill country. In fact the plain belongs to neither north nor south, but is the break between them. On its western side the central hills continue beyond the pass of Dothan to Carmel, rising to over 1,800 ft. ; on the east the hills are broken by three deep, wide valleys from the Jordan. North-east of Jenîn, the hills rise to Mount Gilboa, where Israel's first king Saul met his death trying to break through the Philistine lines and unite Galilee and Samaria. Beyond Gilboa is the valley of Jezreel, about 12 miles long, guarded at the western end by Ahab's royal town of Jezreel, and at the east by the great fortress of Beth-shan or Scythopolis, where excavations since 1921 have yielded evidence of a long religious and political history. Lying at the eastern end of the line of fortresses from Dor on the Mediterranean through Megiddo and Taanach, it was often the centre of government for both sides of the Jordan, controlling one of the main routes from the coast which at Pella in Transjordan branches north to Damascus and south to 'Aqaba. North of the valley the hills rise again to 1,700 ft. between Shunem and Nain before dropping again at Endor to the narrower valley of the Sherrar and Bireh. At the north-western end of this valley Mount Tabor rises suddenly from the plain to a height of 1,850 ft., like some great domed fortress. From its wooded slopes Deborah's Israelites swooped on Sisera's chariots, held fast in the Kishon swamps. The third break in the hills, 5 miles to the north, runs down from Adamah to the southern end of the Sea of Galilee, carrying the road from Acre to Transjordan through the valley north of Sepphoris and Cana of Galilee, beyond the plain of Esdraelon. The plain itself, about 200 ft. above sea level, forms a triangle : its base 20 miles long runs north-east at the foot of the Carmel hills, the other two sides, each 15 miles long, lie one at the foot of the steep hills rising 1,000 ft. to Nazareth, and the other along the broken eastern side. It drains north-west in the Kishon to the swamps between Haifa and Acre, and contains some of the most fertile land in Palestine ; but it was also Palestine's greatest battlefield for 'those armies of all nations whose ceaseless contests have rendered this plain the classic battleground of Scripture' (cf. SHG, chap. xix). 30c

31a The main road northwards twists and turns as it climbs to Nazareth through the young forest of fir trees, as we pass from the OT background to that of the NT. The hills here in southern Galilee are broken, rising to isolated rounded knolls, sometimes 1,800 ft. high, separated by level plains and rolling country capable of intense cultivation, altogether more mild than northern Galilee. Nazareth, like Bethlehem, is a pleasant place. It nestles in a cup-shaped hollow surrounded by hills, some of which are steep and precipitous (Lk. 4:29), one rising to 1,600 ft. The main road north to Syria passes through its winding streets to Cana of Galilee, 4 miles away, and thence eastward to Magdala and Capernaum on the lovely shore of the Sea of Galilee, another 18 or 20 miles away. Most of this area was taken over by Israel in 1949, but before that the district had changed but little. From the hills round Nazareth, it was possible to watch the long camel trains carrying loads of grain along the broad valleys from the Hauran in Transjordan ; shepherd boys watched their flocks on the steep slopes decked with the gayest of wild flowers whose beauty even Solomon in all his glory could not rival (Mt. 6:29). A characteristic of the district is the way in which the hills isolate the many small towns from each other. Driven out from Nazareth, it would be possible for Jesus to settle in Cana, or westward along the same valley at Sepphoris (Ṣeffûriyeh), or in one of the lakeside towns, almost in a different community. In the 1st cent. A.D. this part was only superficially Jewish. Its name Galilee (the circle) of the Gentiles (Isa. 9:1 ; Mt. 4:15) reminds us that Israelites had been deported and foreigners settled there by the Assyrians in the 8th cent. B.C., and a large Roman population later stretched across it to winter resorts at the hot springs of Tiberias, and on the mild shore of the Sea of Galilee. Josephus states that Galilee was thick with cities and that even the least of the villages had over 15,000 inhabitants ; the NT speaks of Nazareth and Capernaum as cities, not villages ; Sepphoris, now a small village in olive groves on a mound surmounted with the stump of a crusader castle, was the capital of the tetrarchy of Herod Antipas until he had built Tiberias.

Northern Galilee is more rugged and wild. It forms the foothills of the Lebanons and rises to 4,000 ft. at Jebel Jermuk west of Safed, 'the city set upon a hill, that cannot be hid'. As the road from Nazareth to Capernaum is dominated by the remains of the great Bronze Age fortress of Hattin rising 1,040 ft. above sea level, so off the road, about 9 miles north of the lake and 5 miles west of Lake Huleh, are the ruins of the ancient city of Hazor mentioned in Egyptian literature from the 19th cent. B.C. execration texts until it was destroyed in the 13th cent. B.C., perhaps by the Israelites. In the ruins are two distinct areas : a tell or city ruin covering 25 acres, and a much larger rectangular plateau, capable of holding 30,000 men with horses and chariots, enclosed on the west by a beaten earth wall and on the other three sides by steep ravines that had been fortified. The whole 170-acre enclosure provides an excellent example of the fortifications provided by the Hyksos conquerors of the near east ; it was worthy to be head of all those kingdoms of the north (Jos. 11:10). Northern Galilee is a high tableland broken by stony valleys, but with a mild climate, well watered and wooded, and with numerous villages. The contours link it clearly with the eastern side ; its less accessible cliffs running out to the Mediterranean, discouraged the Phoenicians from colonising it, though often they spread southwards and held the Carmel hill to control the bay of Haifa. It has a natural northern barrier, at the Lîtânî river, but that is not today, nor was it in biblical times, a political boundary. b

The third main division is **the Jordan Valley** extend- 32a

32a ing the valley between the Lebanons for 350 miles to the Gulf of 'Aqaba through the three lakes and the 'Arabah. The river itself has its source in the many springs at the foot of Hermon, which rises to 9,100 ft. at the southern end of the Anti-Lebanon range. The valley between the Lebanon and Anti-Lebanon turns eastward at the foot of Hermon, and most of the water from the mountain is drained into this valley. One source of the Jordan is Nahr Ḥâṣbânī, rising in the Anti-Lebanon, fed by streams from Hermon, and dropping from 1,700 ft. to 6 ft. above sea level where it enters the swampy plain of Huleh. Two other sources spring from the plain itself, both of them on the east of the line of the Ḥasbânī river : one near the mound of Tell el-Qâḍī, probably the site of ancient Dan or Laish, and the other from Bâniyâs, ancient Caesarea Philippi, on the edge of a rocky gorge, where the foothills of Hermon enter the plain. These two sites mark the twin gateway from the north into the Jordan valley, and are almost as important for Palestine's history as the passes leading into the plain of Esdraelon. The malarial swamp at the north of Lake Huleh was allotted to Israel in 1947, and much of it has been drained by colonists. At the southern end of Lake Huleh the river enters the gorge, falling over the rocky river bed into the beginning of the cultivated Jordan valley, and later enters, through a marshy delta, the Sea of Galilee 682 ft. below the level of the Mediterranean.

b This lake, 13 miles long and 8 across at its widest, was called the sea of Chinnereth (Num. 34:11 ; Jos. 12:3 ; 13:27), perhaps from the name of a city on its shore (Dt. 3:17). In the NT it is called the lake of Gennesaret (Lk. 5:1), and the sea of Galilee (Mt. 4:18). After the building of Tiberias in A.D. 30 the lake became known by the name of this most important town upon its shore as the Sea of Tiberias (Jn 21:1) ; it is referred to as ' the sea of Galilee which is the sea of Tiberias ' in Jn 6:1. Firm banks or sandy shores have prevented the growth of reeds, and the clear pure waters take their colour from the changing lights on the surrounding hills. Its warm, pleasant climate made it a populous winter resort in Roman times, when a prosperous fishing industry supported a considerable Jewish population, and its shores and cities were the scene of many stories and parables of Jesus. The cities, made famous by his ministry, have disappeared into unidentified mounds, but the calm beauty of the lake is still suddenly lashed into fury by tempestuous winds drawn down the neighbouring hillsides ; numerous coves along the lakeside, forming perfect natural amphitheatres, show where a boat could have been ' thrust out a little from the shore ', enabling thousands to listen to his parables before he fed them with loaves and fishes, or resisted their attempt to take him by force and make him king. The fertile land around the shore, fed by many springs, can support rich subtropical vegetation, and warm healing springs still flow from near the ruins of ancient Tiberias, once a famous Roman spa.

c **The Jordan** river earns its name as '*the Descender*' by the speed with which it rushes out at the southern end of the lake, cutting its way into the valley like a mill stream, first westward, and then turning south along the foot of the hills. The valley is about 65 miles long from Galilee to the Dead Sea, and varies in width from 3 to 14 miles, but the river itself winds and twists along its length for a distance of nearly 200 miles like a huge serpent. The valley drops about 590 ft. or approximately 9 ft. per mile ; the swiftly flowing stream eats into the whitish grey marl banks and, depositing the mud on the other side, makes the zigzag course ever more tortuous. The clear rapid stream as it leaves the lake is about 95 ft. wide, varying in depth from 3 to 10 ft., but about 5 miles southward the waters of the Yarmuk, flowing in from the east, make it muddy and more swift. Stretching both sides of the river is an older river bed, usually about 200 ft. wide but in some places extending to a mile, filled with coarse rank vegetation and dense tangled thorn bushes growing 6 ft. high in the tropical heat. 32c
This area, called the ' Pride ' or ' Jungle ' of the Jordan (Jer. 12:5) is flooded each year when the river ' overfloweth all its banks all the time of harvest ' (Jos. 3:15). This tropical useless flood plain is itself set in the broader Jordan valley, bounded on each side by steep hills towering 2,000 ft. above the valley. At Beisân (Beth-shan) in the eastern end of the valley of Jezreel, and at Jericho in the south, the valley widens to a plain where there is evidence of extensive irrigation and where good crops are grown. Excavations in the valley (N. Glueck, *The River Jordan*) have revealed that it was one of the earliest parts of the country to be inhabited ; it contains some of the richest land in the whole of Palestine or Transjordan, justifying the description of it as ' well watered everywhere like the garden of the Lord ' (Gen. 13:10). Everywhere there are ancient mounds, testifying to the density of the population and the prosperity of the valley from as early as the fourth millennium B.C. On the eastern side alone seventy such sites have been noted. One site, Tell ed-Dâmîyeh, on the east of the Jordan near the Jabbok, probably to be identified with Adam (Jos. 3:16), dominates the surrounding area and a ford across the Jordan. Great slag heaps give evidence of metal refineries in the age of Solomon and during the monarchy, until these cities ceased to exist in the 6th cent. B.C.

Below Jericho, where the valley opens out to its greatest width of 14 miles, the river runs into the **Dead Sea,** whose surface is nearly 1,300 ft. below the level of the Mediterranean and its bed as deep again, forming the deepest cleft in the earth's surface yet discovered. This sea, 53 miles long and 10 across at its widest, has no outlet except by evaporation, which has left the water four times as salt as the Atlantic. ' The streams that feed the Dead Sea are unusually saline ; they flow through nitrous soil, and they are fed by sulphurous springs. Chemicals, too, have been found in the water of the sea, which are not traceable in its tributaries, and probably are introduced by hot springs in the sea bottom. Along the shore are deposits of sulphur and petroleum springs. The surrounding strata are rich in bituminous matter, and after earthquakes lumps of bitumen are often found floating on the water ' (SHG, 500f.). The sea is divided into two sections by a long peninsula of gravel, marl and bitumen, jutting out from the eastern side and rising to 60 ft. South of this tongue—El-Lisân—the water is shallower, not more than 14 ft. deep and running off into marshes, which in flood time extend 2 or 3 miles. The banks are formed of greasy, barren marl backed by steep limestone and basalt cliffs towering to 3,000 ft. On the west the rugged cliffs are unbroken, except where wadis have cut into the limestone ; on the east is the deep narrow gorge of the Arnon. Qumrân, the home of the Jewish community whose scrolls were discovered in 1947, lies at the foot of a fresh-water wadi about 4 miles from the northern end of the sea. d

South of the Dead Sea the valley is called **El-'Arabah,** as distinct from El-Ghôr, the name of the remainder of the Jordan Valley. This name, Arabah, has persisted from Biblical times (Dt. 1:7) although there is evidence that it was then also applied to the Jericho plain north of the Dead Sea (Dt. 11:30). The Arabah is desert land, uninhabited except after the rains, when Bedouin move in to pasture their flocks on the meagre covering of grass and shrubs. There are some springs where remains of walls show that during Nabataean and Roman occupation there was intensive cultivation. At Feinân about 27 miles south of the Dead Sea (possibly Punon, Num. 33:42) there was sufficient water to irrigate a large area, which was occupied from as early as 2200 B.C. ; a track runs through it to rich agricultural land on the east. Other ancient caravan centres can be traced on the route leading south to the gulf of 'Aqaba, where springs and reservoirs made cultivation possible. Such places are Bir Madkhûr e

32e 15 miles south of Feinân, Ṭaiyibeh another 6 miles south-west with a track leading east to Petra, 'Ain Gharandel, and Ghadyân a few miles nearer the Gulf of 'Aqaba. The Arabah was an important route carrying traders from the Red Sea to Damascus, with side tracks to the Mediterranean at Gaza and Ashkelon on the west, and through Teimâ to Babylonia and the Persian Gulf. But archaeological evidence (cf. N. Glueck, *The Other Side of the Jordan* (1940)) has revealed that the main importance of the Arabah was for mining and smelting copper and iron. A continuous line of mining centres with furnaces still standing have been traced from the Dead Sea to Ezion-geber (Tell Kheleifeh) in the valley between the two horns of the Red Sea. The presence of copper and iron ores in the hills of the Arabah suggests that it was to this region that the Deuteronomist referred when describing Palestine as ' a land whose stones are iron and out of whose hills you can dig copper ' (Dt. 8:9). The two largest centres were Khirbet en-Naḥās (the Copper Ruin) about 22 miles south of the Dead Sea, and Meneiyeh about 30 miles from the north-western end of the Gulf of 'Aqaba. Glueck suggests that the ores were partially smelted or roasted at these many smelting settlements and taken to Ezion-geber for further purification at the elaborate refinery built in the reign of King Solomon. Pottery remains indicate that his reign witnessed the period of greatest industrial activity in the Arabah.

33a The fourth main division of Palestine is **Transjordan,** the highland between the Jordan valley and the Syrian Desert, stretching 150 miles from Hermon to the southern end of the Dead Sea, varying in breadth from 30 to 80 miles, and rising to an average height of 2,000 ft. above sea level. The climate is temperate, with cooling breezes from the west and more rain than west of the Jordan. Numerous perennial streams and springs make its pastures more green and give to its soil greater fertility, while its shady oaks bring memories of parts of southern England.

b The deep wide gorges of its four main rivers, Wâdī Ḥesā, Arnon, Jabbok, and Yarmuk, form natural boundaries dividing the land into clear sections. At the extreme south lay **Edom.** The desert from the Red Sea and Arabia ends abruptly at the steep, often sheer, hills leading up to the high Edomite plateau, which ends at the Wâdī Ḥesā running NW. into the southern end of the Dead Sea. These hills provided a formidable barrier on the south of Edom, reinforced by numerous fortresses built on the higher peaks, and make it easy to understand why the invading Israelites compassed Edom and turned north only when her eastern border had been reached. Glueck identifies Wâdī Ḥesā with the brook Zered (Dt. 2:13) (*The Other Side of the Jordan* (1940), 8), and it is possible to regard its upper south-eastern end as the place where Israel crossed into Moabite territory. The eastern boundary of Edom was also well fortified ; caravan tracks led down on the west into the Arabah, controlled by fortresses of which the strongest was Bozrah (Am. 1:12) the modern Buṣeira. Edom itself contains fertile, agricultural land, with trees and springs.

c North of the Wâdī Hesā, between it and the Arnon (Wâdī Môjib), lay the land of **Moab,** into which that nation had been driven by the conquests of Sihon, king of the Amorites, who at the time of the Israelite invasion held what had been the northern part of Moab between the Arnon and the Jabbok (Wâdī ez-Zerkâ) ; later Moab regained some of this land from Israel (2 Kg. 3). The land south of the Arnon is fruitful, the soil is good, and there are numerous springs. Remains of terraces on the hillsides, now broken or washed away by the sudden rush of the winter rains, are evidence that once the land was more intensively cultivated. The Arnon, from its mouth, about half-way along the eastern side of the Dead Sea, lies in a gorge 1,700 ft. deep, 2 miles across at the top and about 40 ft. across at the bottom. About 13 miles from the mouth the gorge divides, one branch going NE. and the other SSE. and later both branches divide again, making the whole area well watered, and easily protected from the east, where lay probably the wilderness of Kedemoth (Dt. 2:26). 33c

North of the Arnon lay the country known in the OT as the Mishor, or Tableland (Dt. 3:10, 4:43), or half-Gilead (Jos. 12:2) and, in the NT as Peraea. Probably at the time of the Israelite invasion under Joshua, Sihon held the western half down to the Jordan valley, while Ammon was on the east with its capital at Rabbath Ammon, the modern 'Ammân ; perhaps the dividing line was the upper part of the Jabbok, where the flow is from south to north. The land consists of high treeless moors and limestone ridges, excellent for pasturing large flocks. There Reuben tarried among the sheepfolds at the hour of Israel's need (Jg. 5:16) and Mesha, king of Moab, reared his thousands of lambs (2 Kg. 3:4). Only low rolling hills separate it from the desert, whose hordes of hungry nomads have always made the prosperity of Transjordan precarious, and life there insecure. On the west, limestone ridges run out overlooking the Jordan valley and the towers of western Palestine, providing such vantage points as Râs es-Siâghah and Râs Nebâ, opposite the northern end of the Dead Sea ; either of them may be the Pisgah from which Moses viewed the promised land he could not enter (Dt. 34:1). d

The northern half of Gilead between the Jabbok and the Yarmuk was also part of Peraea. Here the high limestone hills are more thickly wooded, as in the days when the trees rather than David's soldiers defeated Absalom's dangerous revolt (2 Sam. 18:8). There are fields of wheat and maize, vineyards and olive yards, and orchards of apricots and pomegranates, and the hills are still fragrant with herbs—perhaps the balm of Gilead (Jer. 8:22). The Jabbok, like most of the rivers of Transjordan, flows at first parallel to the Jordan in a northerly direction ; rising only 18 miles from the Jordan valley it flows NW. around the ancient city of Rabbath Ammon, now the capital of the kingdom of Jordan, rich in Roman remains, as is all the central and northern part of Transjordan. The river flows through 60 miles, fed by numerous small streams ; one of these, coming south from Jebel Ajlûn, flows through the lovely ruins of the Roman city of Jerash (Gerasa) and joins the main river at the point where it turns west toward the Jordan. In Gilead lay most of the Greek cities forming the confederacy known as the Decapolis. Philadelphia ('Ammân) and Gerasa (Jerash) were the most southerly; Scythopolis (Beth-shan or Beisân) was the only member in western Palestine, and Damascus, at one time a member of the league, was the most northern. Most of the sites of towns in Gilead mentioned in the Bible have not been identified with any certainty, but many of the roads crossing the country from east to west must have followed, as today, the main river valleys ; and the line of the King's Highway (Num. 21:22), used successively by all the conquerors of Transjordan, still runs north and south through the whole length of the land. e

The Yarmuk is the largest river in Transjordan. It rises far to the south in Gilead, flows north till it is joined by tributaries from the east and north draining the water-bearing volcanic region of the Hauran ; then, turning west and south-west, carries into the Jordan south of the Sea of Galilee as great a quantity of water as flows from the Sea. It is the swift flow of the Yarmuk waters down the steep falls from the Hauran plain that changes the character of the Jordan to a muddy zigzag river.

North of the Yarmuk is the land known in the OT as **Hauran** (Ezek. 47:16) or more commonly as **Bashan** (Dt. 3) ; it included the territory spoken of as the region of Ituraea and Trachonitis and Abilene in the NT (Lk. 3:1). Israel claimed to have captured this land from Og, king of Bashan, whose two most important towns were Ashtaroth (Tell 'Ashtarah) and f

33f Edrei (Der'ā), both in the Yarmuk valley: Edrei was at the southern edge of the Hauran, covering a great complex of caves which form a large underground city easily defended as a refuge from invading nomads, and in modern times a railway junction where the line from Haifa branches north to Damascus and south to 'Ammân. All this land from the Yarmuk to Hermon, to which it owes much of its fertility, shows evidence of ancient volcanic activity. Along the eastern edge of the Jordan valley, as well as on the desert border, are craters of extinct volcanoes; hard black basalt rock covers the softer limestone hills, and on the east of the Hauran the district called the Leja is a long sea of lava, comprising about 350 sq. miles, terminating southward in the higher Jebel Drûz. The Hauran itself has rich, fertile, volcanic soil, cultivated for wheat or providing excellent pasture for the sleek cows of Bashan, likened by Amos to the ladies of Samaria (4:1ff.), and the powerful bulls used by the Psalmists as a symbol of Israel's enemies. Except in the Leja there are few springs, but the harder volcanic rock holds the moisture more than the limestone of western Palestine, making this plain a granary of the Near East, and its threshing-floors proverbial. Rising 2,700 ft. above the Jordan 33f
and in wide terraces from the Pharpar river (Nahr el-A'waj) in the north, the high open plain stretches about 50 miles north and south; it is 20 miles wide and, unlike the area south of the Yarmuk, is practically treeless. It has retained its fertility through the ages and is still dotted with many villages, but for prosperity it needs, as all Transjordan does, the security it enjoyed under Roman rule, to which numerous tomb inscriptions and most of the roads still in use pay tribute.

Bibliography—F.-M. Abel, *Géographie de la Palestine*, 2 vols. (1933, 1938); D. Baly, *Geography of the Bible* (1957); M. du Buit, *Géographie de la Terre Sainte* (2 vols. 1958); N. Glueck, *The Other Side of the Jordan* (1940); N. Glueck, *The River Jordan* (1946); L. H. Grollenberg, *Atlas of the Bible* (1956); E. G. Kraeling, *Rand McNally Bible Atlas* (1956); M. Noth, *Die Welt des ATs* (1957); G. A. Smith, *Historical Geography of the Holy Land* (1896), and *Atlas to the Historical Geography of the Holy Land* (1915); G. E. Wright and F. V. Filson, *The Westminster Historical Atlas to the Bible* (2nd ed. 1957).

WEIGHTS, MEASURES, MONEY AND TIME

By R. B. Y. SCOTT

34a Biblical metrology cannot pretend to an exactness which is denied it at many points by the ambiguity and incompleteness of the evidence. Mensuration tables are misleading if ratios are given with greater definiteness than is warranted, and if the figures for several terms are deduced from one which is itself uncertain. Only occasionally in the Bible is one term of measurement defined in relation to another, as in Ezek. 45:11–12. There is no assurance that such ratios were constant throughout the biblical period, or were more than the defining of what had previously been approximate, or even different. Except for some inscribed weights which do not correspond exactly and can be evaluated only by striking a mean, no Hebrew standards of measurement have been recovered intact. Their relationship to better-known metrological systems of the ancient world can only be inferred, or reckoned from approximate equivalents given by Josephus and other authors of the Graeco-Roman period. 'Natural' terms of measurement like *homer* ('donkey-load') and *cubit* ('forearm'), under the necessities of commerce, taxation and architecture, came to have more specific meanings, and were brought into relationships to one another which in some cases at least were artificial. Finally, as with terms of measurement in use today (e.g. mile, gallon), the same term was used in contemporary systems for different measures, and might have more than one meaning in the same country at the same time (cf. Ezek. 40:5).

b **I Linear Measures**—Length and distance are often indicated informally: 'some distance' (Gen. 35:16); 'a pace' (2 Sam. 6:13); 'a step' (1 Sam. 20:3); 'an (ascending) step' (Exod. 20:26); 'a stone's throw' (Lk. 22:41); 'a bowshot' (Gen. 21:16); 'a furrow's length' (1 Sam. 14:14); 'a day's journey' (Lk. 2:44).

c The most important formal measurement of length was the **cubit** (Heb. *'ammāh*, Lat. *cubitus*), a unit common to the Near Eastern and Graeco-Roman civilisations. Like the smaller related units—**span, palm** or **handbreadth, finger**—the cubit was at first an informal or 'natural' measure, the length of a man's forearm, usually measured to the tip of the middle finger. This 'natural' cubit, 17–18 in., is called 'a man's cubit' in Dt. 3:11, and its use is to be inferred in references to the height of a man (e.g. 1 Sam. 17:4), depth of water (Gen. 7:20), and approximate distances (Jn 21:8). A more exact unit was required for detailed dimensions such as those of the ark of Noah (Gen. 6:15–16), the tabernacle (Exod. 26), the Temple and its furnishings (1 Kg. 6:2ff.; Ezek. 40:5ff.), and the walls of Jerusalem (Neh. 3:13). As in Babylonia and Egypt, there were longer and shorter cubits. Ezek. 40:5 specifies the use of a cubit which was 'a (common) cubit and a handbreadth', i.e. a cubit of 7 palms rather than of 6, and the Chronicler in 2 Chr. 3:3 refers to this as 'the old standard' which (in his view) was used in the construction of Solomon's Temple. A 7-palm cubit of 20·6 in. (524 mm.) was early used in Egyptian achitecture, as appears from surviving cubit-rods and measurements of pyramids of the III and IV Dynasties; this is the 'royal cubit' 34c
of which Herodotus (Hist. i, 178) speaks in describing Babylon, and which he reckons as longer by 3 fingers than the Greek cubit of 18.2 in. The unit of 6 palms is witnessed to in Egypt by the 17·7-in. cubit of the Nilometer, and is the neo-Babylonian common cubit.

d The Siloam inscription states that the length of Hezekiah's tunnel was 1,200 cubits. This is a round number, and the limits of the distance measured are not precise; nevertheless the modern measurement of 1,749 ft. (533·1 m.) cannot be far out. This gives 1,185 of the 17·7-in. cubit, or 1,200 cubits of 17·49 in. (444 mm.). Again, the volume of the *bath*, 22–3 litres, as calculated by Albright and Barrois from the capacity of the Lachish and Beit Mirsim jars, makes possible a further calculation of the cubit used for the dimensions of the 'molten sea' and the 10 lavers, in 1 Kg. 7:23–6, 38. If the 'sea' was a hemisphere containing 2,000 baths, its cubit was 22·1–22·3 in., a figure impossible to relate to the cubit of the Siloam tunnel or to the 7-palm cubit of 20·6 in. If, however, a scribe has given by mistake the capacity of a sphere instead of a hemisphere of the same dimensions (his $\pi=3$, as the dimensions show), the resulting cubit is 17·5–17·7 in. The same figure accords with the capacity of the 10 lavers, if these were spherical segments with a height of 1½ cubits, It is close also to the figure 17·6 deduced by Kennedy from measurements of Herodian architecture in Jerusalem.

e The remaining units of linear measurement are not defined in the Bible as fractions of the cubit, but their ratios can be inferred. The **span** (*zereth*) or hand-stretch was half the common cubit (cf. 1 Sam. 17:4), and hence the term was not used for this fraction of the 7-palm 'sacred' cubit (cf. Exod. 25:10; Ezek. 40:42). The **handbreadth** or **palm** (*ṭephaḥ, ṭōphaḥ*) was $\frac{1}{6}$ the common cubit and $\frac{1}{7}$ the 'sacred' cubit; it was equivalent to 'four fingers' (1 Kg. 7:15, 26; (cf. Vulg., Exod. 25:25). The *gōmedh* of Jg. 3:16 (RSV 'cubit') is probably another word for 'span', since LXX translates both it and *zereth* by *spithamē*, and since the context makes clear that a short dagger is in question. The **reed** of Ezek. 40:3 and the **rod** of Rev. 21:15, like the 'measuring line' of Zech. 2:1 (Heb. 2:5), are measuring instruments rather than units of measurement.

f Graeco-Roman units mentioned in NT are the **fathom** or arm-stretch (*'orguia*) (Ac. 27:28), 6 Greek ft. or 72·9 in.; the **furlong** (RV) or **stadion** (RSV), 600 Greek ft. or 202·5 yd.; and the Roman **mile** (Mt. 5:41), 8 stadia or 1,620 yd. In the eastern provinces of the Empire a slightly longer mile, approximately ¼ of the Persian *parasang*, was used.

g **II Measures of Area**—The 'cubits' of the Levitical pasture lands (Num. 35:4–5) must be understood as cubit frontages of land, if the passage is not to be reduced to absurdity; i.e. on each side of the city there was to be a block of land with a frontage of 2,000 cubits and a depth of 1,000 cubits.

The only other measures of area are informal. The 'acre', literally 'yoke', of Isa. 5:10 was apparently

34g the area which a yoke of oxen could plough in one day ; in Mesopotamia this was estimated as 6,480 sq. cubits or *c.* $\frac{1}{3}$ an English acre. In 1 Kg. 18:32 and Lev. 27:16 areas are described as equal to what would be sown respectively with 2 seah measures and one homer measure of barley ; on the Mesopotamian analogy this would mean *c.* 10,000 sq. ft. and *c.* $3\frac{1}{2}$ acres.

h **III Measures of Capacity**—Like the informal statements of quantity, 'cupful' (Jg. 6:38), 'bowlful' (Am. 6:6), 'handful' (1 Kg. 20:10), most biblical units of capacity were originally non-specific, and their names were taken from utensils used in commerce or in the household. The *homer* was an ass-load, the *hin* a pot, and the *ephah* perhaps a basket. The ephah and hin were adapted from Egyptian measures, and the *homer-cor* and *seah* from Mesopotamian ; the *lethech* and *log* may be Phoenician.

i **(a) Liquid Measures**—The **bath** (*c.* 5 imper. gal., *c.* 6 U.S. gal.) was the standard unit (cf. Ezek. 45:14). Ezek. 45:10–11 seeks to standardise the bath and the ephah by equating them as $\frac{1}{10}$ homer, the standard of dry measurement, but this does not mean that the homer was used as a liquid measure, for it does not appear to be so used elsewhere in the Bible. The bath appears in multiples up to 20,000 (2 Chr. 2:10 (Heb. 2:9)). The capacity of *c.* 5 gal. is derived from the estimated capacity of broken jars from Lachish and Beit Mirsim marked 'bath' or 'royal bath', *c.* 22–3 litres. This is to be compared with the figure 21·5 litres derived from pottery of the Graeco-Roman period, and with the 21·83 litres of the Egyptian measure corresponding to the ephah ; it is supported also by calculations of the capacity of the 'molten sea' (see above, under *cubit*). The larger figure of 8·6 imper. gal. found in older works was derived from Josephus's approximate equation of the log with the Graeco-Roman *xestes-sextarius*. A still larger figure, *c.* 10 imper. gal., is demanded by the capacity of a jar found at Qumrân marked '2 seah, 7 log' ; this suggests that the Qumrân community operated with standards of capacity double the ancient ones, and used the former dry and liquid measures in combination.

j The two other liquid measures of OT were related to the bath in sexagesimal ratios, the **hin** being $\frac{1}{6}$ bath, and the **log** $\frac{1}{12}$ hin (the bath is divided decimally only in Ezek. 45:14). The hin was $\frac{5}{6}$ imper. gal., 1 U.S. gal. It appears only in P and Ezek., as the unit for small quantities, mainly in connection with offerings (e.g. Num. 15:4–10). The log, $\frac{5}{9}$ imper. pint, $\frac{2}{3}$ U.S. pint, is mentioned only in Lev. 14:10–24.

The bath is mentioned in NT only in Lk. 16:6 (RSV 'measures'). The Hellenistic **metrētēs** of Jn 2:6 (RV 'firkin') is interpreted by RSV as 10 (U.S.) gal. (strictly, 10·3 U.S. gal., 8·6 imper. gal.).

k **(b) Dry Measures**—A decimal system of Assyrian antecedents, 1 homer = 10 ephah = 100 *omer* or *tenths*, was combined with a Babylonian sexagesimal series, 1 *cor* = 30 seah = 180 *kab*. The **homer** and **cor** were equivalent in capacity, 6·3 imper. bushels, reckoned from the value adopted above for the bath-ephah. Both are only dry measures in the Bible, since Ezek. 45:11 simply defines the ephah which is being equated with the bath ; in Ezek. 45:14 and 1 Kg. 5:11 (Heb. 5:12) the text is corrupt. The homer was used of quantities which could be visualised (e.g. Isa. 5:10), the cor as a unit of account (1 Kg. 5:11 ; Heb. 5:25). The lethech, named only in Hos. 3:2 (where LXX differs), is interpreted in Vulg. as $\frac{1}{2}$ homer.

l The **ephah**, $\frac{1}{10}$ homer = approx. $\frac{5}{8}$ imper. bushel ($\frac{2}{3}$ U.S. bushel), is the larger unit for ordinary purposes, and is not used in multiples. In Dt. 25:14 a receptacle of this size is mentioned ; in Zech. 5:6–10 the ephah is a large receptacle with a covering lid, unrelated to the unit of measure. The **seah** (RSV 'measure'), $\frac{1}{30}$ homer, was also called a 'third', i.e. of an ephah (Isa. 40:12 ; RSV 'measure'). The **omer** or 'sheaf', a day's ration (Exod. 16:16ff.), is defined in Exod. 16:36 as $\frac{1}{10}$ ephah, and was thus equivalent to the '*iśśārōn* or
'tenth' of Exod. 29:40 (cf. Num. 28:5). The **kab** 34l
mentioned only in 2 Kg. 6:25 was $\frac{1}{6}$ seah or $\frac{1}{18}$ ephah.

Of the above dry measures only the seah (*saton*, Mt. 13:33) and the cor (*koros*, Lk. 16:7) appear in NT. The Hellenistic *choinix* (RSV 'quart') of Rev. 6:6 was *c.* 2 dry pints. The *xestēs* of Mk 7:4 (RSV 'pot') was a household vessel holding about 1 pint. The *modius* of Mt. 5:15 (RSV 'bushel') held *c.* 1 peck or 2 gal.

IV Weights—The Hebrew system of weights was 35a
taken over from the Canaanites, who in turn had received it from Babylonian traders. The Babylonian system was sexagesimal : 1 *talent* = 60 *minas* = 3,600 *shekels* = 86,400 *girû*, but in Israel and Phoenicia the ratios between the units were different. There is evidence from Ugarit for a mina of 50 shekels. The plain statement in Exod. 38:25–6 that (for P) there were 3,000 shekels to the talent is usually interpreted as meaning 60 minas of 50 shekels, but it could equally well mean 50 minas of 60 shekels. Ezek. 45:12 defines the sacred **shekel** as weighing 20 *gerahs* and the **mina** as 60 shekels (cf. RSV*n*) ; since the Babylonian shekel weighed 24 girû, it is a reasonable inference that the shekel is being reduced in weight by $\frac{1}{6}$ and the number of shekels in the mina increased proportionally from 50 to 60. The evidence of actual stone weights—talent and mina weights from Mesopotamia, and shekel and smaller weights from Palestinian sites—lends colour to the view that the commercial standard in pre-exilic Israel was 1 **talent** = 50 minas = 2,500 shekels. A 2-talent weight from Lagash in the British Museum yields a talent of $66\frac{2}{3}$ lb. or 30·27 kg., and mina weights from periods down to the neo-Babylonian show that a standard talent in the range 28·38–30·27 kg. was maintained for millennia. That this talent was standard in Syria and Palestine also is inherently probable, and gains some support from the fact that the same figure, 'thirty talents of gold', appears as Hezekiah's tribute in 1 Kg. 18:14 and in Sennacherib's account. At the other end of the scale, shekel weights from Palestine, with some examples of the shekel fractions *pim* ($\frac{2}{3}$, cf. 1 Sam. 13:21) and *beka* ($\frac{1}{2}$, cf. Exod. 38:26), point to a shekel of *c.* 12·25 g. which depreciated to *c.* 11·3 g. Thus 2,500 such shekels, like 3,000 Ugarit shekels and 3,600 Babylonian shekels, yield a talent of the same standard noted above. Other weights marked *nṣp* (a weight not mentioned in the Bible) are about $\frac{1}{6}$ smaller than the shekel weights, and thus fit the 1:3,000 ratio of the 'sacred' shekel of Ezek. and P. The commercial shekel is specified once in P as that 'current among the merchants' (Gen. 23:16) in order to distinguish it from the lighter shekel of the sanctuary. The Temple tax in Neh. 10:32 (Heb. 10:33) was $\frac{1}{3}$ shekel, evidently the common shekel, since the corresponding beka or $\frac{1}{2}$-shekel tax in P (Exod. 38:26) by the standard of the sanctuary would be $\frac{5}{12}$ the common shekel. A 5th-cent. beka silver coin weighs $\frac{1}{3}$ the common shekel (see below).

To summarise : in the common system, 1 talent b
= 50 minas = 2,500 shekels = 60,000 gerahs ; in the sanctuary system of Ezek. and P, 1 talent = 50 minas = 3,000 shekels = 60,000 gerahs. Taking the approximate mean weight of the talent as 64 lb. avdp. or 29 kg., the corresponding mina weighed 1 lb. $4\frac{1}{2}$ oz., or 0·58 kg., the common shekel $\frac{2}{5}$ oz. or 11·6 g., and the 'sacred' shekel $\frac{1}{3}$ oz. or 9·7 g. The gerah in both systems would be *c.* 7·3 grains. It must be recognised that these values are approximate only, since a unified, exact and unvarying system cannot be assumed.

The talent as a weight is mentioned in NT only in c
Rev. 16:21 (RSV 'hundred weight'), where obviously a precise figure is not intended. The only other weight named is the *litra* (RSV 'pound'), the Roman pound of $11\frac{1}{2}$ oz. or 327 g.

V Money—The terms *talent*, *mina* and *shekel* denote 36a
in the first instance specific weights, and, in the second, corresponding but not identical weights of precious metal used as standards of value and media of exchange. Of these, only the shekel was eventually coined by the

36a Jews. The word 'money' where it occurs in EVV almost always represents the Hebrew or Greek word for 'silver'. The invention of coinage in Asia Minor in the 7th cent. B.C. resulted from the practice of marking pieces of silver as a guarantee of weight and value. The use of coins spread rapidly, but outside the region of issue coins still were weighed to determine their value, and not infrequently were melted down.

b Since **coinage** was not introduced into Palestine until the Persian period, all earlier references to money in the Bible are to lump silver, or to silver ornaments or utensils valued by weight. Such money silver was carried wrapped in a cloth bundle (Gen. 42:35; Prov. 7:20), and weighed against stone weights taken from a bag (Gen. 23:16; Mic. 6:11). When it is said in 2 Kg. 12:10 that the king's officials 'counted the money', the meaning is that they reckoned the value of the silver by its weight. Gold was valued at about thirteen times the value of the same weight in silver, but was rarely used as a medium of exchange (cf. Isa. 46:6) before the invention of coinage. An ingot or bar (Heb. 'tongue') of gold is mentioned in Jos. 7:21 as a form of treasure. The Heb. word *ḳᵉśîṭāh* (RSV 'piece of money', LXX 'lamb') seems to be a monetary unit (cf. Gen. 33:19; Jos. 24:32); it may represent the value of a sheep in silver. Silver and gold are not found in Palestine, but were introduced from abroad by immigrants and through tribute and commercial payments. In Gen. 13:2 (J) Abram is pictured as arriving in the land, rich in cattle, gold and silver. We are told that Solomon's trade ventures brought gold from distant Ophir, and that he flooded the country with silver (1 Kg. 10:11–29). In the times of the Judges a private citizen might own 1,100 shekels of silver (Jg. 17:2), and even a servant carried on his person $\frac{1}{4}$ shekel as a reserve for emergencies (1 Sam. 9:8). The prophets speak of wealth as accumulated gold and silver (Isa. 2:7), and of silver used as money (Am. 8:6). Though Solomon's assessments were in kind (1 Kg. 4:7ff.), later kings raised taxes in silver (2 Kg. 15:20). Hos. 3:2 illustrates the use of silver in barter rather than as a standard medium of exchange.

c The earliest references to coined money are to the gold **stater** or **daric** introduced by Darius I toward the end of the 6th cent. B.C. (Ezr. 2:69, 8:27; Neh. 7:70–2 (Heb. 7:69–71)). The gold daric weighed 130 g., and was equal in value to 20 silver *sigloi* or 'Median shekels' of 87 g. (roughly $\frac{1}{2}$ the Hebrew shekel weight). The mina of silver mentioned with the daric was not a coin but the weight in silver of 100 sigloi. The shekels of Neh. 5:15 may have been these half-weight 'Median shekels', but the Temple tax of Neh. 10:32 was certainly reckoned by the Jewish shekel weight in silver. What is apparently the oldest Jewish coin known is a silver *beka* or $\frac{1}{2}$ shekel published by Reifenberg and dated in the 5th cent.; its weight of 3·88 g. is $\frac{1}{3}$ the weight of the old Hebrew shekel (see Weights). A few other silver coins of the Persian period bear the inscription *yhd* ('Judah').

d These early Jewish coins imitated Greek silver currency, which circulated widely and introduced the standard of the silver drachma of *c.* 66 g. (later reduced in weight). Since coinage was invented in Asia Minor where the weights were derived from the Babylonian system, the larger units of account were the silver **mina** and **talent**, the ratios being 100 drachmas to the mina and 60 minas to the talent. With the depreciation of the drachma, a silver talent came to be worth 10,000 drachmas. The **stater** or 'double drachma' ($\frac{1}{50}$ mina) was considered by the Jews as equivalent to a shekel, and the term *didrachma* is used as an alternative to *siklos* by some LXX translators. But it is the **tetradrachma** or '4-drachma piece' of 224 g. which in NT is called a *stater* and equated with the 'sacred' shekel (Mt. 17:24, 27). As in OT, 'thirty of silver' meant 30 shekels (Zech. 11:12; Mt. 26:15).

e Beginning with John Hyrcanus (135–104 B.C.), the Hasmonaean princes and the Herods issued coins, in 36e
bronze only and of uncertain denomination. Roman money began to circulate after Pompey's conquest of Palestine in 63 B.C., together with various Hellenistic coinages, especially the Tyrian. The Roman silver **denarius,** rated at $\frac{1}{25}$ the value of the gold denarius or **aureus,** weighed *c.* 60 g. (later depreciated to *c.* 53 g.); it was thus nearly equal to the Tyrian drachma, and was so regarded. In Mt. 10:9 money is of gold, silver and copper. Roman taxes were reckoned by the denarius (RSV 'coin', Mt. 22:19), the temple tax by the shekel-tetradrachma-stater (Mt. 17:24, 27). The remaining coins mentioned in NT were of bronze: the **assarion** (RSV 'penny', Mt. 10:29), a Hellenistic approximation to the Roman *as* = $\frac{1}{16}$ denarius; the **kodrantēs** (RSV 'penny' also, Mt. 5:26), i.e. the Roman *quadrans* = $\frac{1}{4}$ as, probably the denomination of the coins issued by the Roman procurators; and the **lepton** (RSV 'copper coin'), defined in Mk 12:42 as $\frac{1}{2}$ quadrans. The last was 'the widow's mite', called a *pᵉrûṭāh* in the Mishnah.

During the First Jewish Revolt of A.D. 66–70 the f
national-religious spirit showed itself in the issue by the Jews for the first time in their history of a coinage specifically denominated in shekels. There were silver shekels of *c.* 220 g., nearly the weight of the Hellenistic tetradrachma-shekels, together with $\frac{1}{2}$-shekels and $\frac{1}{4}$-shekels in silver, and bronze coins which were either token shekels or fractions of the shekel. During the Second Revolt of A.D. 132–5 Graeco-Roman silver and bronze coins were restruck with Jewish devices and inscriptions.

VI Time and the Calendar—The calendaric data of 37a
the Bible reflect a long development, and behind the finished system of the late post-exilic and NT periods are traces of earlier methods of marking the passage of time. The basic phenomena are universal—the alternation of day and night, the waxing and waning of the moon, and the annual return of the seasons. Day, month and year are natural time divisions, but the week and the hour are not. The seasons fluctuate and differ in the climate of different regions, but the solstices and equinoxes to which they are related are fixed and universal. Societies may disagree about when the new year begins, but that it begins and ends they are unanimous.

The basic difficulty in evolving a calendar is, of course, that of relating to each other in some regular way the three 'natural' time divisions which for astronomical reasons are independent of each other. The number of days in a lunar month is something over $29\frac{1}{2}$, and in a solar year $365\frac{1}{4}$, so that the number of full days reckoned to each must vary. 12 lunar months are too few for a year, but 13 are too many. Moreover, the length of daylight changes with the seasons.

The problem is complicated also by geographical b
factors and climatic differences between neighbouring regions. The annual rhythm of life is not the same in Palestine, Egypt, Anatolia, Mesopotamia and the Arabian peninsula. Yet these regions were in touch with each other, and their calendars, whether primitive or precise, made some impact beyond their frontiers. Another complication arises from the need to provide in one system for the recurring periods and days important to producers, to the priesthood and to the monarchy, and to celebrate anniversaries of events potent in the social memory (e.g. Passover). Finally there was the unresolved question inherited from a dim past—which was the primary determinant of time, the sun or the moon?

The Calendar—Morgenstern, the Lewys and others c
have shown that the developed calendaric legislation of OT preserves traces of earlier stages and differing elements which have contributed to it. Two of the principal festivals of rabbinic Judaism—*Pûrîm* and *Ḥᵃnukkāh*—were added after the latest legislation on the subject in the Pentateuch. From the Book of Enoch and the Qumrân scrolls we learn that Jewish

37e sectarians at the beginning of the Christian era held to a sacred calendar which differed from that of the dominant party which has come down to our day. The following elements may be distinguished in the biblical calendar, which is an amalgam of mementoes of the nation's history :

d (i) **The patriarchal traditions** trace the first Hebrew connection with Canaan to immigration from Upper Mesopotamia. Immigrants of the Amorite period probably brought the **7-day week** (which appears in the Sumerian Deluge story), with its culminating 'sabbath' day of ill omen or religious awe. This 7-day week apparently had nothing to do with the phases of the moon. Like the 'week of years' culminating in the Fallow Year (Exod. 23:10–12 ; cf. Dan.9:24), it belongs rather to a system of reckoning time by the sacred or ominous number seven and its multiples, so that a year was 7 × 7 × 7 days, with a fiftieth day added to each of the 7-week periods, and a *šapattum* or intercalary period after the seventh 50 to fill out the year. This old Mesopotamian pentecontad calendar proved unsuitable to the Palestinian seasons, but traces of it remain in the OT calendar—in the pentecontad culminating in the festival of 'Weeks' (Lev. 23:15–16) ; in the Deuteronomic *sh^{e}miṭṭāh* or 'Release' after 7 years of 7 pentecontads of days (Dt. 15:1) ; and in the 'Year of Jubilee' in P, concluding a pentecontad of years (Lev. 25:8–11).

e (ii) A second prominent element is the lunar festivals of **New Moon** and **Passover** (*pesaḥ*), which came down from the nomadic past and probably from the period of the Exodus and the Conquest. The New Moon festival remained as only a minor feature of the later calendar (cf. Num. 28:11–15), but it was more prominent in earlier times (1 Sam. 20:5 ; Isa. 1:13–14). It left its mark in the lunar reckoning of the dates of major festivals (Exod. 12:2ff. ; Lev. 23:5ff.). *Pésaḥ* was unquestionably a festival of pastoral origin, revived by Josiah, and continued as a cult symbol linking Israel's religion specially with the Exodus and the Wanderings. It may have originated in sacrifice to a protective deity at the lambing season, and for long it continued to be celebrated on 'the new moon of Abib', following the spring equinox (cf. Exod. 13:4 ; Dt. 16:1).

f (iii) The three annual festivals related to agriculture, **Unleavened Bread** (*maṣṣôth*), **Harvest** (*ḳāṣîr*) and **Ingathering** (*'āsîph*), comprise, with *Sabbath*, the complete festal calendar in the Code of the Covenant (Exod. 23:12–17) and the 'Ritual Decalogue' (Exod. 34:18–23). That the three annual pilgrimages were Canaanite festivals taken over by Israel is generally agreed. To begin with, their dates were determined by the state of the crops : Unleavened Bread was held in the month *Abib* when barley came into the ear and the harvest could begin (cf. Dt. 16:9) ; Harvest, called also in Exod. 34:22 'the feast of (the seven) Weeks' was held when the wheat harvest ended ; Ingathering came at the year's end in the autumn when the fruits of garden and vineyard had all been gathered in (Dt. 16:13–15). We may compare the 'Gezer Calendar' of the 10th cent. B.C., with its listing of 12 months according to the appropriate agricultural operations : the 8th was 'barley harvest', the 9th 'harvest and feasting', and the 12th 'summer fruit'. This points to a 12-month solar year ending in the autumn, and to some method of intercalation. Though the name 'Tabernacles' or 'Booths' (*sukkôth*) came to be used for Ingathering, the old Canaanite month names continued in use until after the publication of Dt. The four which happen to be mentioned are : *Abib*, 'green ears' ; *Ziv*, 'brightness' (i.e. prolonged daylight of harvest-time in June) ; *Ethanim*, 'steadily flowing' (i.e. of perennial streams) ; and *Bul*, 'fruit'. These are identified approximately with the 1st, 2nd, 7th and 8th months of the later calendar whose months were numbered from the spring (cf. Dt. 16:1 ; 1 Kg. 6:1, 38 ; 8:2).

g (iv) The erection of Solomon's Temple as a royal shrine with solar associations led, it seems, to the **37g**
introduction at the autumn equinox of a **New Year festival** on the Babylonian model. 1 Kg. 8:2, 62–6 describes the dedication of the Temple in the month Ethanim, apparently for 7 days preceding the festival of Tabernacles (cf. v. 65, RSV*n*). We can take it that the first day marked the New Year. The turn of the year was of capital importance for the institution of monarchy, though its associations were alien to the tradition championed by the prophets. According to Dt. the New Year festival is not a religious obligation of the Covenant People, and in Lev. 23:24–5 it survives only as a special sabbath marking the New Year according to the ancient reckoning.

(v) In the neo-Babylonian period a **new calendar** **h**
was introduced, patterned on the Babylonian. That the months were now designated by ordinal numerals rather than by their Babylonian names was doubtless a compromise to avoid the heathen associations of the latter. The P document specifically authorises the ordering of the festal calendar by this civil year beginning in the spring (Exod. 12:2), but its secular character is evident from the fact that no religious significance was attached to its first day. Only in the Persian period did the Babylonian month names (e.g. Nisan) which have survived until today come into use.

(vi) By NT times additional feasts and fasts had **i**
been inserted in the sacred calendar established by P. *Ḥ^{a}nukkāh*, 'the feast of the **Dedication**' (Jn 10:22), celebrated the anniversary of the rededication of the Temple in December 164 B.C. after its defilement by Antiochus Epiphanes ; this feast at the same time brought into Judaism the age-old recognition in Syria of the winter solstice. The nationalistic feast of Pûrîm, which was initiated in Persian times according to Est. 9:17–19, is not mentioned elsewhere in the Bible.

The Day—It is clear that in the later strata of OT as **j**
well as in NT the day was reckoned from sunset to sunset (Gen. 1:5 ; Lev. 23:5 ; 2 C. 11:25). That it was always so reckoned is doubtful, in the light of 1 Kg. 17:6 ; Ps. 65:8 (Heb. 65:9) ; Jg. 19:9 ; 1 Sam. 28:8, 19. The divisions of the day were at first only the broad 'natural' ones : dawn (Jos. 6:15 ; Mt. 28:1) ; sunrise (Gen. 32:31) ; 'the heat of the day' (Gen. 18:1) or noon (Jer. 20:16) ; 'the cool (wind) of the day', when the sea breeze begins in early afternoon (Gen. 3:8) ; late afternoon, when 'the day declines' (Jg. 19:8) ; evening ; 'between the evenings', or dusk (Lev. 23:5) ; night ; midnight (Exod. 11:4). In OT the night was divided for military purposes into 3 watches (cf. 'middle watch', Jg. 7:19 ; 'morning watch', Exod. 14:24). In NT the 4 night watches of the Romans, 'evening', 'night', 'cock-crow', (early) 'morning', each of 3 hours, are referred to (Mt. 14:25 ; Mk 13:35 ; Lk. 13:35 ; Ac. 23:23). The division of daylight into 12 hours (cf. Jn 11:9 ; Ac. 2:15), though it originated in early times in Babylonia, is not mentioned in OT (unless indirectly with the 'dial of Ahaz', Isa. 38:8). In NT the 3rd, 6th and 9th hours are used broadly for morning, midday and afternoon, but there is reference also to the 7th, 10th and 11th hours.

The Week—The Jewish week, originating in a time **k**
division by the ominous number seven (see §37*d*), consisted of numbered days, as the year at one time of numbered months, to avoid use of the heathen names. The 7th day was designated rather than named 'the sabbath'. By NT times the 6th day was called 'the eve of the sabbath' (Mk 15:42).

The Month—The months at first bore Canaanite **l**
names, and about the time of the Exile began to be designated by ordinal numbers (e.g. 1 Kg. 6:1 ; see under §37*h*). There is no proof that the months with Canaanite names exactly corresponded to the later numbered months, or that the same system of intercalation was maintained. The Passover at first was kept on the new moon of Abib (Exod. 13:4, 34:18),

371 but later on the full moon of the 1st month (Lev. 23:5). The Babylonian month names were introduced in the Persian period, perhaps by Nehemiah as civil governor.

m **The Year**—The festivals of the agricultural year ending with completion of the harvests in the autumn came to form the framework of the sacred calendar (Exod. 23:14–17). From this viewpoint it was the end of the old year rather than the beginning of a new one which was celebrated. For the pastoral nomads among whom it originated, Passover at the new moon nearest the spring equinox may have marked the commencement of the year. The autumn New Year festival associated with the monarchy disappeared with that institution, though it left traces in the festival of Trumpets (Lev. 23:24–5) and possibly in the Day of Atonement (Lev. 25:9 ; cf. Ezek. 40:1). Some of the kings seem to have followed the Assyro-Babylonian practice of reckoning the year from the spring, as in the civil calendar of numbered months referred to above. The intercalation necessary to adjust the lunar to the solar year seems at one time to have been decided by the state of the crops (cf. Dt. 16:9). Later, an extra month was inserted in every 3rd year ; still later, 7 months were inserted in each cycle of 19 years.

Bibliography—Weights and Measures: A.-G. Barrois, *Manuel d'Archéologie Biblique* ii (1953), 243–58, ' La Métrologie dans la Bible ', RB 40 (1931), 185–213, RB 41 (1932) 50–76 ; IB I (1952), 153–7 ; A. E. Berriman, *Historical Metrology* (1953) ; D. Diringer, ' Early Hebrew Weights found at Lachish ', PEQ (1942), 82–103 ; K. Galling, *Biblisches Reallexikon* (1937), 186ff., 366ff. ; F. Nötscher, *Biblische Altertumskunde* (1940), 206ff. ; W. M. F. Petrie, *Ancient Weights and Measures* (1934) ; R. B. Y. Scott, ' The Hebrew Cubit ', JBL 77 (1958), 205–14 ; A. Segrè, ' A Documentary Analysis of Ancient Palestinian Units of Measure ', JBL 64 (1945), 357–75 ; J. Trinquet, ' Métrologie Biblique ', *Dict. de la Bible*, Supp. (ed. L. Pirot), fasc. xxviii (1955), 1212–50 ; O. Viedebantt, *Antike Gewichtswesen und Munzfüsse* (1924) ; articles in EB (Hill), EBrit., 13th ed. (Petrie), and HDB (Kennedy).

Money: J. Babelon, ' Monnaie ', *Dict. de la Bible*, Supp. (ed. L. Pirot), fasc. xxix (1957), 1346–75 ; A.-G. Barrois, *Manuel d'Archéologie Biblique* ii (1953), 258–73 ; IB I (1952), 157–64 ; G. F. Hill, *Brit. Mus. Cat. Coins of Palestine* (1914) ; R. Loewe, ' Earliest Biblical Allusion to Coined Money ? ', PEQ (1955), 141–50 ; A Reifenberg, ' A Hebrew Shekel of the 5th Cent. B.C.', PEQ (1943), 100–4, *Ancient Jewish Coins* (1947) ; article in HDB (Kennedy).

Time and Calendar: H. and J. Lewy, ' Origin of the Week and the Oldest West Semitic Calendar, HUCA 17 (1942–3), 1–152 ; J. Morgenstern, ' Three Calendars of Ancient Israel ', HUCA I (1924), 13–78, 3 (1926), 77–107, 10 (1935), 1–148, ' Chanukkah Festival and the Calendar of Ancient Israel ', HUCA 20 (1947), 1–136, 21 (1948), 365–496 ; J. B. Segal, ' Intercalation and the Hebrew Calendar ', VT 7 (1957), 250–307 ; E. R. Thiele, *Mysterious Numbers of the Hebrew Kings* (1951) ; articles in EB (Marti), ERE (Hommel, Woods, Poznanski) and HDB (Abrahams, Ramsay).

THE ARCHAEOLOGY OF PALESTINE—I

PREHISTORIC AND EARLY PHASES

By KATHLEEN M. KENYON

38a **Introductory**—The scholarly study of Palestinian archaeology dates from the 19th cent. The general interest in the Bible in the Victorian era made it inevitable that the great discoveries bearing on ancient history which were being made in Egypt and Mesopotamia should stimulate the investigation of the land which was the home of the Bible. No-one could expect Palestine to rival its great neighbours in richness of finds, but the discovery of comparatively commonplace objects could illustrate a well-known biblical story.

b But Palestinian archaeology had been actively practised for nearly three-quarters of a century before it in fact became a reliable auxiliary to historical, literary and epigraphical studies. The reason for this is largely the poverty of the country in finds of any kind of written material, a fact which may seem surprising in connection with a country whose written records have come down to us in such detail and whose alphabet is the ancestor of most modern European and Near Eastern scripts. The ancient documents of Mesopotamia were on clay and those of Egypt on papyrus. Semitic documents, more closely connected with those of Egypt, the nearer neighbour, were mainly on papyrus or parchment. Such materials can survive in the dry climate of Egypt, but do so only in very exceptional circumstances in Palestine. The famous Dead Sea Scrolls are an example of such exceptional circumstances, and the fact that, though the oldest date at most from the 2nd or 3rd cent. B.C., these include the earliest biblical manuscripts known, is a good illustration of this lack of really ancient documents.

c Archaeology is relatively useless unless its finds can be tied in with some time scale. In Egypt and Mesopotamia the link was provided by literary documents, in Greece and Rome, and the Roman West, by coins and inscription. But until Greek coins began to circulate there, Palestinian sites provided almost no finds, with the exception of a few ostraca and the very rare inscription or two, which would tell the excavator the period of the settlement he was excavating.

Palestine therefore is an example *par excellence* of a country in which the extraction of history and other information from the material remains is dependent on purely archaeological techniques. One of the most essential of these is a study of pottery types. It can thus be said that Sir Flinders Petrie is the father of Palestinian archaeology, for he, in his excavation of Tell el-Ḥesī in 1890, showed that different layers in the artificial mound created by the ruins of successive stages of the settlement could be associated with distinctive types of pottery. These types he used to establish a time scale by relating some of the finds to those with which he was familiar in Egypt; thus he brought Palestinian archaeology into relationship with a fixed calendar. Some of Petrie's correlations and inferences were wrong, and his early Egyptian chronology very much inflated, but the principle was the key to progress in Palestinian archaeology.

d It was only gradually that Petrie's lesson of the basic importance of common pottery was learnt. 38d Moreover, the accurate use of pottery is dependent on a second archaeological technique, exact stratigraphy. In the detailed identification and interpretation of the different layers on a settlement site, by which pottery changes could safely be associated with building-levels, Palestine and the whole Near East lagged behind the West, and particularly Britain, partly perhaps because plentiful and cheap labour encouraged excavations on such a scale that the niceties which greater stringency demanded in Britain were ignored. Thus, though Professor R. A. S. Macalister excavated Gezer with great thoroughness between 1902 and 1909, and published the finds, including the pottery, with exemplary fullness, very little of value as to the history of the site can in fact be deduced from his finds, since the complications of the stratification of the site were such that his classification of pottery is not based on the evidence of association, except in the case of tomb groups, and it is impossible to date the buildings from the finds. Similarly the value of the Harvard excavations at Samaria between 1908 and 1911 under the great Egyptian archaeologist Dr G. A. Reisner was reduced by the fact that he was unable to interpret the stratification of the summit of the hill, so much more complicated than that of the mud-brick-built sites to which he was accustomed.

That by the time of the 1914–18 war the main outline of a pottery chronology had been built up was largely due to Père Hugues Vincent. His flair for archaeological matters and his close study of the finds of every expedition which visited Palestine gave him, more than anyone else, the co-ordinating influence necessary to evolve a reliable system.

The fruit of these years of pioneer developments was e
born in the years between the two wars, when the British Mandate opened the country to expeditions in a way which had been impossible with the vexatious complications and delays under the Turkish régime. It is the work carried out during these years which makes it now possible to write the history of Palestine in the light of archaeology. The methods of some of the expeditions can be criticised from the point of view of excavation, and particularly stratigraphical technique, but in most cases the material is published in sufficient detail for it to be possible to correct interpretations which are at variance with more recent information.

Of the innumerable excavations which took place f
between the wars, only a few can be mentioned. The first place must be given to the excavations of Tell Beit-Mirsim by Professor W. F. Albright in 1926–32. This is not due to the importance of the site, perhaps the biblical Debir or Kiriath-sepher, but to the fact that careful excavation and thorough publication provided a sequence of pottery forms and other finds from the mid 3rd millennium B.C. to the Second Exile. The pottery chronology built up by Père Vincent and others, and Professor Albright's encyclopaedic knowledge of material which could provide

38f links with dating evidence in adjacent lands, were combined in a manner which made the site for many years the criterion to which all other finds were referred.

g On a very different scale was the expedition of the Oriental Institute of Chicago to Megiddo between 1929 and 1938. The original plan was to excavate the whole of this large and most important site from top to bottom. This scheme was abandoned when clearance had reached a level of about the 10th cent. B.C. and the lower levels were only examined in more restricted areas, of which but one was carried to bedrock. The results, lavishly published, were a magnificent series of finds, covering a period from the late 4th millennium to the 5th cent. B.C. Unfortunately, the clearance was of such a wholesale nature that the exact interpretation of the stratification was often very faulty, and in the succeeding sections of this article interpretations will be offered which will differ from those of the excavators.

h Between 1930 and 1936, Professor John Garstang carried out very important excavations at Jericho. Subsequent investigation has shown that his dating of some of the town walls to the Late Bronze Age, and thus probably to the period of Joshua, was mistaken. A most far-reaching discovery was that at the base of the mound there was a long series of levels of the Neolithic period.

i Another site of the greatest importance to be excavated was Beth-shan, under the auspices of the University of Philadelphia. Again, the lowest levels were only sounded, but produced a valuable sequence of pottery. Unfortunately, the publication of this material is far from complete, with an absolute gap between a publication by Mr G. M. Fitzgerald of pottery from the Strata XVIII to XII, and the publication of the temples of Stratum VIII onwards, a gap covering the whole of the Middle Bronze Age and the beginning of the Late Bronze Age. Moreover, Stratum VIII onwards were misdated, by the ascription to them of the dates of stelae and scarabs found in them, which a greater knowledge of pottery shows to have been derived from earlier levels.

j The excavations of Samaria, carried out by a joint expedition under the direction of Mr J. W. Crowfoot between 1931 and 1935, were concerned with a site of much shorter life. Their importance lies in the close association which can be established with the written record. Since a foundation in 880 B.C. and a destruction in 722 B.C. can be firmly established, building-style, art, pottery and other objects can be dated with a closeness not possible elsewhere.

k In the south of Palestine, the most important site excavated was Tell Duweir, probably to be identified with Lachish. Again, a scheme of complete clearance was frustrated by the tragic death of the director, Mr J. L. Starkey, and only the later Iron Age levels were cleared. The most important find was a series of ostraca dating from the last days of the town before its destruction by the Babylonians. Of the earlier periods, only tombs, part of the Middle Bronze Age defences, and an important Late Bronze Age temple, were cleared.

l Of major importance in the field of Palaeolithic and Mesolithic studies were the excavations between 1929 and 1934 in Wâdī el-Mughârah, on the slopes of Mt Carmel, by the British School of Archaeology in Jerusalem and the American School of Prehistoric Research under the direction of Professor Dorothy Garrod. These excavations for the first time provided a stratified sequence into which hitherto isolated Palaeolithic and Mesolithic finds could be fitted.

m From 1936 to about 1951, archaeological work in Palestine was at a standstill, and it has not yet been resumed on the pre-war scale. The first major excavation to be undertaken was that of the École Biblique, under Père R. de Vaux, at Tell el-Fâr'ah, a site with a history beginning in the 4th millennium, which can probably be identified with Tirzah, the predecessor of Samaria as capital of the Northern Kingdom. In 1952, a new series of excavations was begun at Jericho, under the auspices of the British School of Archaeology in Jerusalem and a number of other bodies, including the American School of Oriental Research. The major importance of the finds concerns the earliest Neolithic levels. At the other end of the history of Palestine are the excavations of Qumrân, the site of a monastery of the first centuries B.C.–A.D., from which the Dead Sea Scrolls were derived. An important excavation begun in 1955 was that of the Hebrew University at Hazor. 38m

Palaeolithic and Mesolithic—During the tens of thousands of years which are covered by the Palaeolithic Age, man in Palestine, as in Europe, lived as a hunter and food gatherer. Conditions were of course different in the Mediterranean area, for instead of successive glaciations, pluvial periods marked the advance of the Ice-cap. The climatic changes were nevertheless sufficiently great to affect human life and habits, particularly in the changes caused in the fauna. 39a

The study of the Palaeolithic goes back at least three-quarters of a century in Palestine. But it was only with Professor Garrod's excavations in the caves of Mount Carmel between 1929 and 1934 that a coherent outline was established. Though much useful work had been done previously, notably by M. René Neuville and Mr F. Turville Petre, much of it dealt with surface finds, or sites covering a limited range of time. In the Wâdī el-Mughârah, Professor Garrod was fortunate enough to find caves which gave an almost complete sequence, thus providing a framework into which other finds could be fitted.

Two of the caves gave a long sequence of deposits. b
In the Tabūn, these extended from the later stages of the Lower Palaeolithic to the Upper Middle Palaeolithic, in Mughâret el-Wad they started at that point and extended to the Neolithic, with a possible gap between the last Upper Palaeolithic level and the Mesolithic. A combination of the deposits in the two caves gave an accumulation of about 21 metres in depth, which represented almost the complete sequence of cultures in Palestine during the food-gathering stage of man's existence. The only stages missing are that represented by the gap already mentioned, and the very earliest stages. Evidence of stages corresponding to the earliest Palaeolithic cultures in Europe, the Abbevillian and Lower Acheulian, has been found in Palestine, but not in a stratified sequence. The most important result to emerge is that throughout the Palaeolithic, the associations of Palestine are with Europe rather than Africa. For the most part, the types of stone implements found can be paralleled by groups in Western Europe, and the evidence of a number of burials shows that Palestine was inhabited during the Middle Palaeolithic by men closely related to the Neanderthal race of Europe, a race which is not directly ancestral to modern man.

The two lowest levels found belong to the Lower c
Palaeolithic, and can be equated with the Tayacian and Upper Acheulian, and belong to a time in which, on the evidence of the fauna, there were tropical conditions. At this stage, there was apparently close contact with Egypt. But from that stage onwards, the contact seems to be broken. A very long period, in which there was a warm climate with heavy rain, supporting forest in which deer were abundant, is represented by a final Lower Palaeolithic level with a culture resembling the Micoquian of France and a long Middle Palaeolithic, to which the name Levalloiso-Mousterian has been given, since it combines the characteristics of the two main European Middle Palaeolithic cultures. At the end of the Levalloiso-Mousterian, the temperature seems to fall, though the rainfall is still high, and the stage is perhaps to be related to a final glaciation in Europe. Thereafter conditions gradually become more arid, and the desert-dwelling gazelle gradually supersedes the forest-dwelling deer. The flint industry of the Upper Palaeo-

39c lithic is of classic Aurignacian type, indicating that the connection with Europe is still close. There is not, however, skeletal evidence to show whether in Palestine, as in Europe, Homo Sapiens had taken the place of men of the divergent Neanderthal type.

d Thus for the very long space of time in which man was a food-gatherer and hunter, the sequence of cultures in Palestine followed closely on the lines of those in Europe. With the beginning of the Mesolithic, there is an almost complete break. The Mesolithic of Europe is the period in which man, still a food-gatherer, was adapting himself to the changed conditions of the end of the Ice Age, and for a time living conditions were worse and cultures poorer. Recent archaeological work in the Near East is tending to suggest that in this phase there was the beginning of the process which gave Western Asia an advantage over Western Europe of several thousand years in the advance towards civilisation.

The first step towards civilisation is the beginning of permanent settlement ; this is dependent on agriculture, for this is essential for the provision of an adequate food supply within a restricted range. The domestication of animals is an ancillary, but primitive non-agricultural pastoralists are seldom permanently settled.

e The Wâdī el-Mughârah excavations provided evidence that in Palestine the beginnings of agriculture may have taken place during the Mesolithic. The flint industry, to which the name Natufian has been given, and the evidence of hunting and fishing show that the culture has the same general characteristics as the Mesolithic of Europe, and both in the Mughâret el-Wad and in another cave not far off, the Mughâret el-Kebârah, sickles were found, consisting of flint blades set in grooved bones with carved heads, and also mortars and pestles which might have been used for grinding grain. It is not certain that ground was yet cultivated to increase the yield of grain, but at least the systematic collection of grain is probable. The first steps towards agriculture had been taken. The evidence from Jericho, described in the following section, shows that progress was comparatively rapid.

f **Neolithic**—The definition of the Neolithic period which is now accepted is that it is a stage marked by an economy based on permanent settlement, supported by agriculture and domesticated animals, and characterised by villages largely self-sufficient and not dependent on trade. The generally accepted date for the end of the Ice Age of Europe and the corresponding Pluvials of the Mediterranean is *c.* 10,000 B.C., followed by a Mesolithic which in Europe lasted down to the 3rd millennium. Until comparatively recently, it was doubted whether Palestine had a true Neolithic. A flint industry had been found, to which the name Tahunian was given, but in caves and on surface sites which did not suggest a village economy. The first indication of a true Neolithic was provided by Professor Garstang's excavations at Jericho in 1935–6. In the lower levels beneath the Bronze Age town he found good buildings, associated with a Tahunian flint industry, but lacking pottery, which is usually found in the other Neolithic sites, both in Europe and the Near East. The subsequent excavations at Jericho, begun in 1952, have considerably extended our knowledge of this culture, and have shown that there were earlier stages.

g A structure has been identified which is probably a sanctuary established beside the spring by Mesolithic hunters. This was succeeded by a long period of increasingly permanent settlement, but only when a mound 4 metres in height had been built up from the debris of slight huts do any houses appear. These houses are solidly built of mud-bricks of plano-convex type, some of them hog-backed in section. The houses are round or curved in plan, and are sunk below the surrounding level, with projecting porches covering steps leading down into them. Some houses are probably single-roomed, but others certainly have more than one compartment. The dead were buried in graves beneath the floors of the houses. The associated flint industry has not yet been fully studied, but seems to resemble the Natufian. There is also a rich bone industry. It is not yet known whether, and to what extent, agriculture or the domestication of animals was practised. The settlement of this period expanded to cover the whole 8 acres of the Tell. 39g

The most remarkable feature of the settlement was a massive defensive wall with external, rock-cut ditch. This has been located at the north, west and south extremities of the Tell, and it would therefore appear to be a town wall, representing a major community undertaking. On the west side, where it is best preserved, it is built against a great stone tower, 9 metres in diameter, with a carefully built staircase penetrating into its heart. The tower is older than the existing wall, and there are probably at least two earlier walls going with it.

From a stage when deposits had risen against the tower to a height of some 5·50 metres above bedrock, charcoal has been obtained which has given a radiocarbon dating of *c.* 6800 B.C. This settlement of Jericho thus appears to be going far to providing a link between the Mesolithic as found in the Mt Carmel caves, presumably dating from the millennia after 10,000 B.C., and the beginnings of permanent settlement which constitute the hall-mark of the Neolithic. h

This phase at Jericho comes to an abrupt end with a period of erosion and destruction, which may indicate an appreciable interval. It is succeeded by a second culture, that discovered by Professor Garstang, which is still Neolithic and still pre-pottery, which appears to arrive at the site fully developed. It is characterised by houses of elaborate architecture, with rectilinear walls and mainly rectangular rooms. Two distinguishing features are plastered walls and floors with highly burnished surfaces, and the use of bricks in shape resembling flattened cigars, with the tops decorated with herring-bone-pattern thumb impressions. The houses of this phase again cover the full 8 acres of the Tell, and the settlement is therefore in the nature of a town rather than a village. In the earlier stages it was undefended, but subsequently a great stone wall was constructed, immediately above the line of the earlier one ; at least one further stage of defences has been traced.

The flint industry associated with this culture is the Tahunian, which is found widespread in Palestine, but not hitherto associated with evidence of permanent settlement. Finely worked stone bowls served as dishes, probably supplemented by other containers in perishable materials. Large numbers of querns of a characteristic form, together with great numbers of sickle blades, are evidence of the use of grain ; the extent to which this was cultivated has yet to be established by the study of samples, but agriculture can be presumed as necessary to support a community of the size indicated by the extent of the settlement. The most outstanding achievement of the inhabitants was a series of plaster portraits, modelled on a basis of human skulls, which show a high degree of artistic powers, and are probably evidence of a form of ancestor worship. i

Two stages in this settlement have provided material for radio-carbon dating, and have given dates of *c.* 6250 B.C. and 5800 B.C. Jericho is thus by far the earliest site to have given proof of fully developed permanent settlement, on a scale which was not reached in the rest of Western Asia till two thousand years or more later. One reason for this was clearly its favourable situation. A copious perennial stream assured the fertility of the adjacent land, and provides a favourable environment for the development of agriculture. It can probably be deduced that irrigation was practised, which would give a stimulus to the community organisation of which the defensive walls are evidence.

The length of time covered by this phase is shown j

39j in that by its end the ruins of successive layers of building had raised a mound 15 metres in height. As in the case of its predecessor, the end is an abrupt one, and is succeeded by a period of denudation. In the following stage pottery for the first time appears. In other respects, however, this stage is one of retrogression, for there are few traces of permanent structures, and the inhabitants appear to have camped on the site.

In due course, a second type of pottery provides evidence of the arrival of a new group, somewhat more advanced, for they built houses, using plano-convex bun-shaped bricks. The importance of this stage is that for the first time it can be linked with other sites. Similar pottery has been found at a site on the Yarmuk, just south of the Sea of Galilee. It also can be linked with the first settlement at Byblos, and through Byblos with the whole phase of Neolithic village settlements which were beginning to grow up round the Fertile Crescent in the mid 5th millennium B.C. This link serves to emphasise the remarkable isolation, as far as present knowledge goes, of the earlier stages at Jericho, both in their antiquity and in their high degree of development.

k **Chalcolithic**—The boundary between the Neolithic and the Chalcolithic is not a clear-cut one. The second of the two early pottery stages at Jericho is sometimes included in the Chalcolithic, and though it seems better to call this Neolithic, it is probable that descendants of this people continued to live side by side with newcomers for much of the 4th millennium. The general character of the period in Western Asia is transitional between the Neolithic and the first Metal Age, with all that this implies in the way of trade, specialist crafts and an economy capable of supplying craftsmen, and urban development. It is this stage in which the great river valleys at either end of the Fertile Crescent begin to outstrip the intervening lands. In the latter, village economy is still predominant, but the breakdown of self-sufficiency results in much more widespread uniformity or at least similarity of culture. It is only comparatively recently that the picture of Palestine at this stage has begun to be clarified.

l The first excavation of a settlement of this period to attract attention was that of Teleilât Ghassûl, a group of low mounds east of the Jordan, a few miles north of the Dead Sea, which were excavated by the Pontifical Biblical Institute between 1929 and 1934. The mounds revealed the remains of a village settlement in which four levels were identified, though only the uppermost was extensively excavated. The architecture was solid but unpretentious, and perhaps the most striking find was fragments of wall plaster with remarkable paintings, apparently of an allegorical nature. The economy was based on agriculture, but a find of two copper celts showed that metal was just appearing. The highly distinctive pottery and flint industry and other characteristics make it clear that the Ghassulians were newcomers to Palestine, though whence is not yet clear.

m When Ghassûl was discovered, it appeared to stand in isolation, and many archaeologists were not prepared to agree that it was earlier than the Early Bronze Age. Since then, however, traces of the same or allied cultures have been found widespread in Palestine, in fact stretching from one end of the country to the other. In the south, Sir Flinders Petrie found a group of settlements in the Wâdī Ghazzeh, in which the same pottery and flint industry is found. It is interesting, however, that these are not village sites but camping-sites, probably occupied seasonally by hunters or pastoralists. The finds from some of the sites were closer to Ghassûl than the others, and it is possible that the latter may be earlier, indicating that the full village development came at a later stage. In the north, Ghassulian pottery and flints have been found at ʿAffûleh and on the edge of the Plain of Esdraelon, on the west at Hederah in the Plain of Sharon, where an interesting find was a number of pottery ossuaries, in
form obviously models of the houses of the period. A 39m
site which has introduced a new variety, though the material equipment is clearly related to Ghassûl, is Tell Abū Maṭar, near Beersheba. The dwelling-places here were elaborately excavated underground dwellings, with entrance shafts, connecting galleries, sunk silos, forming an exceedingly complex layout with a series of occupation stages. At this settlement copper smelting and casting was carried out, presumably with ore brought from the Sinai peninsula.

The Ghassulian groups thus have the general char- n
acteristics of the Chalcolithic phase. In most instances, they were firmly settled, and though still largely agricultural, copper was becoming known and worked, and the trade that this implies shows that self-sufficiency was breaking down. But none of these settlements was anything approaching a town, and the variety of way of life of the different groups of which evidence has been discovered shows that there was as yet no uniform culture. There is little direct evidence as to chronology concerning them. Their occupation of Palestine covers the middle centuries of the 4th millennium, for there are enough contacts to show that there was some overlap with the succeeding groups, who can be dated to the last centuries of the millennium, but so far there is nothing to establish their date of arrival in Palestine.

Though evidence of the Ghassulian people is found o
widespread over Palestine, it cannot yet be said that they contributed anything towards the build-up of civilisation. The first groups which formed the basis of the population which in due course evolved the civilisation of the Early Bronze Age, are those which appear in Palestine in the last two or three centuries of the 4th millennium, and there are no real signs that anything of the Ghassulian culture was absorbed by these new groups. The occasional appearance of a Ghassulian pottery form, the cornet, may show there was some slight contact, but nearly all the typical Ghassulian products disappear. It is, moreover, especially significant that none of the towns of the Early Bronze Age seem to owe their foundation to the Ghassulians ; so far, at any rate, Ghassulian remains have never been found at the base of any of the settlements with a long history which have been excavated. On the other hand, the remains of their successors have been found on the sites of many of the greater towns, for instance Jerusalem, Megiddo, Beth-shan and Jericho.

The process by which the Early Bronze Age civilisation was evolved was a gradual and complex one. The first stage is, as happens so frequently in Palestinian history, the appearance of a number of nomadic groups. Two of them appear at Jericho, and it may be presumed that they have come in from the East. The evidence for this comes from tombs, for they were as yet too near nomadic ways to do much in the way of town-building. But it is a matter of interest that they introduced the practice of burying their dead in rock-cut tombs, which was, with variations in details, to be the standard method almost till the Christian era.

At Jericho, the two groups, who may be called p
A and B, seem to have remained separate, as far as can be judged from their tombs. The A group are distinguished by a rather monotonous range of round-based bowls and little juglets, only crudely decorated, if at all. The B group are distinguished by pottery attractively decorated with patterns, in red or brown, in groups of lines at angles to each other. But it seems probable that as members of the groups pushed farther into Palestine they mingled, and at Ai and Tell en-Naṣbeh, in the central highlands, both are found, while the B group are found at Ophel, the original site of Jerusalem. Other members of the A group went north, and are found at Tell el-Fârʿah, near Nâblus. There, however, they mixed with a third group, who may be called C, and who are characterised by a grey burnished pottery known as Esdraelon ware,

39p from its main distribution in the Plain of Esdraelon. It is therefore to be presumed that they entered the country from the north. They are found at Megiddo and Beth-shan, where they may have mixed with some elements descended from the users of the second type of Neolithic pottery, who it is suggested above may have continued to live in the country side by side with the Ghassulian people.

q The period is therefore one of major immigration into Palestine. Lack of knowledge of the earlier inhabitants of most of the countries to the north and east makes it impossible as yet to trace their origins. The chronology of the period is suggested by imports which show that there were contacts with both Mesopotamia and Egypt. At Megiddo have been found some clay jar sealings bearing impression of stamps dated to the Jemdet-Nasr period, between 3200 and 2800 B.C. At Jericho has been found a stone palette which can be dated to the Late Predynastic period in Egypt, at the end of the 4th millennium. Additional evidence comes from Jericho, where charcoal in a tomb of the A people gave a radio-carbon date of 3260 B.C. ± 110.

r The period is thus the most formative one in Near Eastern history. In both Egypt and Mesopotamia the stage was being reached out of which the great empires of the river valleys emerged in the 3rd millennium. On a smaller scale, the same thing was happening in Palestine. Palestine never developed into an empire, for it had not the resources, nor the economic needs which demanded trade and elaborate communal organisation. For two thousand years it was to be a country of city states, and in this formative period these city states were born. Some confusion has grown up as to the nomenclature of the period. Before it became evident that the groups were contemporary, the A and C groups were ascribed to the Late Chalcolithic, and the B group to Early Bronze Age Ia. To avoid confusion, it seems desirable to give them a different title, and it is suggested that Proto-urban is the most suitable. It emphasises the significance of the period, and it aligns it with the comparable and contemporary periods in Egypt and Mesopotamia, the Proto-dynastic and the Proto-literate.

40a **The Early Bronze Age**—In the course of the Early Bronze Age, covering the period from *c.* 2900 B.C. to *c.* 2300 B.C., nearly all the towns of Palestine which we meet in the biblical record take their origin. As has already been mentioned, settlement on the sites in many cases took place during the Proto-urban stage. But none, as far as we know, were large in size, none were walled, and architecture and the other appurtenances of settled life were simple. The Early Bronze Age is essentially a period of urban development. It is still a pre-literate era as far as Palestine is concerned, and therefore, apart from sparse references in the Egyptian records, we are still dependent on archaeology for the story of the period. The story told by archaeology is by no means complete. In the first place, it is dependent on surviving material remains ; it can show that there appeared to be a more or less uniform culture covering the whole country, but it does not show what alliances existed between the different towns, nor whether any established a hegemony over their neighbours, though we can infer that there was no widespread state, or such would have appeared from contacts with Egypt. Secondly, only a few of the greater city mounds have been excavated to the levels of the 3rd millennium, and then only in soundings. The picture is therefore an incomplete one.

b On many of the sites occupied by these Proto-urban groups, full town life gradually developed. It is possible that the impetus was given by the arrival of yet another group, characterised by the fine red-burnished pottery which is such a feature of the period, but this is not yet clear. The first evidence of the developing towns is the appearance of well-built rectangular houses, either in mud-brick or stone, depending on which was the locally available building-material. At Tell el-Fâr'ah and elsewhere, evidence 40b
is found of central lines of pillars to support the roof. A special feature both at Tell el-Fâr'ah and at Jericho is a number of well-built silos for the storage of corn. At Fâr'ah a kiln for the firing of pottery was found, already in the technically excellent form which continued in use down to the Roman period. Another important advance was the use of the pottery wheel. The use was, however, rather tentative, and did not improve throughout the whole length of the Early Bronze Age ; the wheel was only used on small vessels, and then only for forming the rim, after the lower part of the vessel had been made by hand.

The development towards town life seems to have c
been indigenous, and does not show obvious signs of external influence. It was certainly gradual. At Fâr'ah, it was only in the fourth of the six Early Bronze Age levels that a town wall appears, a massive affair, partly in stone and partly in brick, about 30 feet thick. At Jericho, the position was probably similar, though the house levels have not yet been closely related to the town wall. Jericho provides striking evidence of the importance of town walls as the period develops. Within the Early Bronze Age, the walls were built, rebuilt or strengthened no less than seventeen times. This is no doubt a reflection of the strategic situation of Jericho as a guard to one of the principal routes into coastal Palestine from the east. As an urban and agricultural Palestine developed, it would offer rich booty to the nomadic desert dwellers to the east. In a country of city states, defence would no doubt be necessary in inter-city quarrels, but for Jericho there was the additional need of defence against desert raiders.

The full development of the period comes in Early d
Bronze III. Much of the evidence from many sites belongs to this period, though Tell el-Fâr'ah seems for some reason to have been abandoned. At Megiddo, it is marked by a grandiose town-planning development ; in this interpretation, it should be noted, the views of the excavators have not been followed, but a reassessment has been made of the evidence from the site. The earlier centuries of the Early Bronze Age on the site are marked by a succession of buildings which are ill-preserved. These are buried beneath a series of great terraces with massive retaining walls, which levelled up the hitherto sloping sides of the mound ; in the view here put forward, no town wall has yet been discovered, but there is little doubt that one must have accompanied such an elaborate layout, if not already in existence in the earlier levels.

At Ai, again, a town wall existed now, if not earlier, e
and a great stone-built citadel. An interesting feature at this site is the existence of a sanctuary, which with its outer court, inner room and holy of holies, seems already to be in the form of the typical Semitic sanctuary of later centuries.

Many of the smaller towns seem actually to have been founded in Early Bronze III. The earliest level at Tell Beit Mirsim belongs to this period, and so does that of Tell el-Ḥesī, both in southern Palestine. The latter site is interesting as producing a group of copper weapons. Though the period is conventionally called the Early Bronze Age, there is actually little evidence that bronze was used, and any metal was in fact rare until the later stages. But both Tell el-Ḥesī and Jericho have produced examples of a type of crescentic axe which is ultimately derived from Mesopotamia, and also flat celts, daggers and, in the case of Ḥesī, a spearhead ; metal arrowheads are not however known.

It has already been said that the culture of the f
period was essentially an indigenous one. The weapons just mentioned are, however, evidence of trade connections with the rest of the Fertile Crescent. Connections with Egypt also existed. The chronology of the beginning of the full Early Bronze Age is in fact based on the finding in Palestine, at Megiddo, Jericho and Beth-shan of jugs of a hard metallic ware which are found in I Dynasty tombs at Abydos. The urban

40f development of the Early Bronze Age in Palestine thus runs parallel to the rise of the Old Empire in Egypt. To some extent, Egypt may have exercised control over coastal Palestine, but the archaeological evidence of this is not very clear.

g In Early Bronze III, Palestine seems to have received some new immigrants. On sites in the north, there appears a very finely burnished red and black ware known as Khirbet Kerak ware. This can be traced north through Syria into Anatolia, and perhaps even to the Caucasus. In Syria, the users of this ware seem to have caused major disturbances, but Palestine lay on the fringe of the movement, and the newcomers seem to have been assimilated.

It is usually held that the major element in the population of Early Bronze Age Palestine was the Canaanites, though there is little certain linguistic evidence to support this. It is however probably the case. What is clear is that for the first time the country was fully occupied by a population based on towns and villages. From Jericho there is interesting evidence that between *c.* 3200 B.C. and 2300 B.C. there was very considerable erosion of the surface of the land. Moreover, from the towns, such as Tell el-Fâr'ah and Jericho, we have evidence of a considerable use of timber ; the use of the timber, and the clearance of the land for the agriculture which would be essential to support the sedentary population, would have removed much of the forest and scrub cover, and denudation is the inevitable result of such a process. It was therefore in the Early Bronze Age that the country assumed its present aspect.

41a **Intermediate Early Bronze–Middle Bronze Period**—It is only comparatively recently that it has been recognised that between the Early Bronze Age and the Middle Bronze Age there was a phase which corresponds in significance and approximately in chronology with the First Intermediate of Egypt. Tombs of the period from Tell 'Ajjûl were first published by Petrie ; to the culture he gave the name ' Copper Age ', since in many of the tombs there were copper daggers. The phase was first put in its true setting by Albright in the excavation of Tell Beit Mirsim, where it occurred as Stratum H. Albright designated it Middle Bronze I, in recognition of the complete break with the preceding Early Bronze Age. But the break is even more complete with the Middle Bronze Age, and the term Intermediate Early Bronze–Middle Bronze, first used by J. H. Iliffe in the arrangement of the Palestine Archaeological Museum, is here preferred.

b The excavations at Jericho have thrown much light on the period. The Early Bronze Age town comes to a violent end with the destruction of the latest town wall by fire. The Early Bronze Age levels are succeeded by ones of an entirely different culture. The newcomers were nomads, and a long period elapsed before they started to build houses, during which they camped on the mound and also on the surrounding hillside. Even when they did start to build, the structures are flimsy, and the settlement was apparently never walled. The only structure of any interest is one, incompletely excavated, which may have been a shrine ; in two adjoining rooms were solid blocks of mud-bricks which might be altars. The pottery of the period is quite distinct from that of the Early Bronze Age, especially in its thinness and gritty texture ; in general form it is nearer the pottery of that period than to that of the Middle Bronze Age, but at most the connection may be that of a common ancestry.

c In contrast with the lack of interest in building houses is the astonishing care directed to the excavation of tombs. At Jericho, by far the greatest number of tombs excavated belong to the period, and at almost all other sites most of the evidence comes from tombs. The reason for the multiplicity of tombs is that, in striking contrast to the communal tombs of the Early Bronze Age, each tomb contained a single body only, or at the most two. Though the burial customs of the

period at Jericho have thus the feature of single burial 41c in common, in other respects there is considerable diversity. Five groups of tombs, showing different burial customs, can be recognised, ranging between the two extremes of neat little tombs containing an intact skeleton with a dagger as the sole offering, to very large and roughly cut tombs containing a body buried as a disarticulated bundle of bones, with a group of little pots as the offering. At Tell 'Ajjûl, also, two separate groups of tombs can be recognised, and the same is true of Megiddo.

This feature of diversity of burial customs at the same site is in keeping with the other evidence that the newcomers were nomads. It is probably to be interpreted as evidence that there were several different tribal groups at each place, allied for the purpose of conquest, but retaining separate tribal habits, and that which is preserved by the archaeological record is the tribal burial custom.

The only site in which anything in the way of d substantial buildings are probably to be attributed to the period is Megiddo. Here, three massive temples with a columned porch in front of a spacious sanctuary succeed the level attributed above to Early Bronze III. The archaeological evidence is unfortunately not very clear, but it is probable that two of the temples belong to a first phase, and are succeeded by the third, all within this period ; a rebuild of the third is certainly to be attributed to it, for built into its wall was a fenestrated axehead which is typical of the period. The reason that there are these structural remains at Megiddo and not elsewhere is probably to be accounted for by the fact that one of the groups at Megiddo would appear to have a much more civilised background than those found elsewhere. Their tombs, with shafts with elaborate multiple chambers opening off them, have an architectural quality, and the pottery, much more sophisticated in form and technique than that of the other groups, has links with the settled area of inland Syria.

The tribesmen who thus disrupted the Early Bronze e Age civilisation of Palestine may be identified with great probability as the Amorites. At Râs Shamra in the north and at the great port of Byblos there is archaeological evidence of the same break, and at the end of the millennium the Amorites secured supremacy in Mesopotamia. The Egyptian Execration Texts of the XI Dynasty may provide evidence (though this is not universally agreed) of the presence of Amorite chieftains among the towns on the Syrian coast listed as incurring Egyptian wrath.

The chronological limits of the period are not very closely defined. One of the groups of tombs at Megiddo contains toggle pins which can be linked with Mesopotamia with a date of *c.* 2200 B.C. The other contains a type of pin which occurs at Râs Shamra in graves beneath a temple of the 20th cent. B.C. The beginning of the succeeding Middle Bronze Age can be linked with the period of the Egyptian XII Dynasty ; in Egypt this is to be dated *c.* 1990 B.C. though there may be some time lag before the resultant restoration of stability affected Palestine. It is probable that the beginning of the period is also to be linked with Egyptian history. The VI Dynasty succumbed in 2290 B.C. before attacks of Asiatic barbarians. These barbarian raids must be part of the same movement as that which destroyed the Palestinian Early Bronze Age civilisation, and the raiders must have come through Palestine. The Intermediate Early Bronze–Middle Bronze period is therefore likely to have lasted from *c.* 2300 to *c.* 1900 B.C.

Middle Bronze Age—In about 1900 B.C., or perhaps f a little earlier, a new civilisation was established, which was to last as long as that of the Early Bronze Age. From that date till *c.* 1200 B.C. there is no real break.

The newcomers are characterised by an entirely new type of pottery. For the first time in Palestine, the vessels are entirely wheel-made, on a fast wheel. The

41f vessels are excellently made, the bowls of sharply angular forms, and many are covered with a highly burnished red slip. Metal prototypes lie behind a number of them. The place of origin of the newcomers is clear. At Byblos in tombs contemporary with the XII Dynasty, both the metal prototypes and the pottery copies, as well as other pottery parallels, have been found. The period marks the beginning of a close connection between Palestine and coastal Syria, where the Phoenician seaports were to flourish during the succeeding centuries. The whole forms one continuum of Canaanite culture.

The infiltration of the newcomers was apparently a gradual affair. The early types of the pottery, Middle Bronze I, have so far only been found at comparatively few places, notably Megiddo, Râs el-ʿAin, Tell ʿAjjûl and Tell Beit Mirsim. Nearly all the pottery comes from tombs, and it was probably only gradually that villages grew to towns on the sites of the preceding Early Bronze Age towns.

g By Middle Bronze II, the culture had developed into an urban civilisation at least as impressive as that of the Early Bronze Age. The pottery, directly developed from that of Middle Bronze I, is found widespread. In many cases, the settlements of the period mark the maximum expansion of the sites. The houses are well built, and the practice of building round a courtyard, which was to be a characteristic for many centuries in Palestine, was introduced. At Jericho houses were built in terraces up the side of the mound created by the debris of earlier towns, and opened on to paved streets ascending the mound in a series of shallow steps. The houses were of two storeys, and the ground-floor rooms seem to have been storerooms and shops, with the living-quarters above. At Jericho, finds in the tombs have shown that the houses were furnished with wooden tables, stools and beds, and the inhabitants used wooden bowls, rush baskets and mats, as well as the pottery and alabaster vessels which are ordinarily all that survives.

h The chronology for the end of Middle Bronze I and the beginning of Middle Bronze II is not yet clearly established. Probably the first stage was a short one perhaps from the end of the 20th cent. B.C. to the mid 19th cent. Middle Bronze II was a long period, judging from the pottery stages which can be identified, and pretty certainly overlapped the Egyptian XII Dynasty. Egypt at this time exercised some control over Palestine, but probably this was confined mainly to the coastal area, in which Egypt was interested as controlling the route to Syria. The extent of control may be assumed to be similar to that in the Late Bronze Age, when chiefs acknowledged a suzerainty which may have been little more than nominal. Essentially, it was, as in the Early Bronze Age, a country of city states.

i In *c.* 1730 B.C., the Middle Empire of Egypt fell, and the rule of the alien Hyksos was established. The Hyksos were in Egypt an alien aristocracy of Asiatic origin. They were clearly largely Semitic, but seem to have been of mixed origin. The most probable explanation is that they were warrior bands recruited from various sources, from the nomadic Semites of the Arabian desert, from the Hurrians who in the early centuries of the 2nd millennium were pushing across north Syria, and from groups of outlaws and dispossessed persons. Such groups do not bring a culture or civilisation with them. In Egypt, they adopted Egyptian civilisation. In Palestine, where many of the bands were racially akin to the inhabitants, they adopted the culture of that country, though there is little doubt that it was at this stage that a considerable admixture was introduced into the hitherto predominantly Semitic population. By the time of the Amarna letters in the 14th cent. many of the names of the rulers were Hurrian, and it is probably at this stage that this alien aristocracy is established.

j The most striking element in the culture of Palestine which was introduced at this stage was a new system of defence. Hitherto, the town walls had consisted 41j of a simple wall of stone or mud-brick, crowning the slopes of the natural hill or the mound of earlier debris. The new system is marked by a great artificial bank, usually faced with plaster, at a much steeper angle than the natural slope. These great banks, usually called glacis (though this is an incorrect use of the military term) have been found, for instance, at Tell ʿAjjûl, Tell Fârah, Tell Duweir, Tell Jerîsheh and Jericho. At Jericho, three separate phases can be identified, in each of which there was a massive retaining wall at the foot, a long plastered slope at an angle of *c.* 35°, and a town wall crowning the slope at a height of 15·75 metres above the foot of the defences. The proof that this new system of fortification is to be associated with the Hyksos is provided by the fact that defences based on the same system are found at places as far apart as Qatna in inland Syria and Tell el-Yehûdîyeh in the Egyptian delta ; at these sites, the associated pottery is that of the country ; in Palestine it is that of the Palestinian Middle Bronze Age. The defences were something extraneous, imposed by a warrior aristocracy. It is tempting to ascribe them to a method of defence against chariot warfare, the introduction of which has often been ascribed to the Hyksos, but the evidence of horses at the period is unsatisfactory. Another possibility would be that archery was in use, and the great banks provided the necessary field of fire, but again there is inadequate evidence. A third possibility is that the banks were designed to prevent access to the town walls with battering-rams. Archaeological evidence of this would not survive, but there is evidence for their use in the Egyptian records.

The Hyksos period in Palestine, therefore, is one in k which the native, Semitic, cultures of the country continued uninterrupted, with the superimposition of a warrior aristocracy, partly alien and probably partly drawn from other Semitic groups, of which the best material evidence is the new system of fortification. It is one in which town life flourishes ; all the excavation evidence so far available points to the existence of prosperous towns down to the end of the period. It may not have been one of undisturbed peace, for most of the sites give evidence of destructions and rebuildings ; some of these may have been due to inter-town rivalries, others to conquests by incoming warrior bands. The material evidence does not suggest a very high degree of culture ; there is little evidence of art, or even of imposing buildings. But the general impression is one of reasonable prosperity. The finds suggest that there was considerable contact with Egypt. Egyptian scarabs and local copies are found in great quantities. The finds at Jericho of perishable materials which have not survived elsewhere show that many of the house furnishings may have been of Egyptian types ; the stools, wooden bowls and wooden toilet boxes, for instance, are closely similar. How much of this is due to contacts when there were Hyksos rulers in both countries, and how much to the period of the XII Dynasty, when strong rule would have stimulated trade, is not yet clear, for at most sites it is not yet possible to say at what stage Hyksos rule begins.

In *c.* 1550 B.C. the alien Hyksos were driven out of l Egypt with the re-establishment of the native XVIII Dynasty. Palestine would be affected both by the recoil into it of those Hyksos bands which had settled in Egypt, and by the Egyptian campaigns connected with the expulsion. Two sites, Tell Beit Mirsim and Jericho, show evidence of destructions which can probably be attributed to the Egyptians, which in both instances were followed by periods of abandonment. The evidence of the destruction at Jericho is very dramatic. The whole of the town levels which have survived subsequent denudation give proof of a tremendous conflagration, which brought the upper storeys of the houses toppling down into the burnt remains of the ground floor.

Bibliography

Tell Abū Maṭar: J. Perrot, in *Israel Exploration Journal* 5 (1955), 17–40, 73–84, 167–89

'Ai: Judith Marquet-Krause, *Les Fouilles de 'Ay* (1949)

Tell 'Ajjûl: Sir Flinders Petrie, *Ancient Gaza* I–IV (1931–1934). Kathleen M. Kenyon, in *Annual of the Department of Antiquities of Jordan* 3 (1956), 41–55

Tell Beit Mirsim: W. F. Albright, *Annual of the American School of Oriental Research* 12 (1932), 13 (1933), 17 (1938), 21–2 (1943)

Beth-shan: G. M. Fitzgerald, in *Museum Journal of the University of Pennsylvania* 24 (1935), 5–32

Tell ed-Duweir: Olga Tufnell, *Lachish* IV (1958)

Tell el-Fâr'ah: R. de Vaux, in *Revue Biblique* 54 (1947), 394–433, 573–89, 55 (1948), 544–80, 56 (1949), 102–38, 58 (1951), 393–430, 566–90, 59 (1952), 551–83, 62 (1955), 541–89, 64 (1957), 552–80

Ghassûl: A. Mallon, R. Koeppel and R. Neuville, *Teleilat Ghassul* I and II (1934, 1940)

Tell Ḥesī: F. J. Bliss, *A Mound of Many Cities* (1894). Kathleen M. Kenyon, *Annual Report of the Institute of Archaeology* 11 (1955)

Jericho: J. Garstang, in *Annals of Archaeology and Anthropology* 19 (1932), 3–22, 35–54, 20 (1933), 3–42, 21 (1934), 99–136, 22 (1935), 143–84. Kathleen M. Kenyon, *Digging up Jericho* (1957); *Palestine Exploration Quarterly* (1951), 88–9, 101–38, (1952), 4–6, 62–82, (1953), 81–96, (1954), 45–63, (1955), 108–17, (1956), 67–82, (1957), 101–7

Megiddo: G. Loud, *Megiddo* II (1948). P. L. O. Guy and R. M. Engberg, *Megiddo Tombs* (1938). Kathleen M. Kenyon, in *Eretz Israel* v (1958)

Wâdī Mughârah: Dorothy A. E. Garrod and D. M. A. Bate, *The Stone Age of Mount Carmel* I (1937).

THE ARCHAEOLOGY OF PALESTINE—II

THE BIBLICAL PERIOD

BY J. GRAY

42a Our period begins at the **end of the Early Bronze Age** in the last two centuries of the 3rd millennium and the first century of the 2nd. This is probably earlier than the age of the Hebrew patriarchs, but it was now that the stage was set for their appearance in the history of the Near East. At this time, on the evidence of various sites excavated, the sedentary civilisation of Palestine was rudely disturbed and the regular settlements of the preceding age were apparently occupied by squatters. This suggests one of the periodic irruptions of tribesmen from the desert hinterland, which are a feature of the history of Palestine throughout the ages. More specifically, if we may judge from Egyptian Execration Texts from Luxor and Saqqârah relating to chiefs of Palestine and southern Syria in the 19th cent., these interlopers were Amorites and their movement into Palestine part of the general upheaval in the ancient Near East which brought Semitic Amorites to power in Mesopotamia and inaugurated a dark age in the history of Egypt.

There is no evidence except the problematic passage in Gen. 14 that Abraham or Isaac was associated with folk-movements, but it is suggestive that the patriarchal associations with Mesopotamia, particularly the North, Palestine, and Egypt are just those of the Amorites, whose political consolidation in North Mesopotamia, Syria, and Palestine is attested in the Mari texts in the 18th and 17th cent. and in the Egyptian Execration Texts a century earlier. Here it may be observed that the situation at Gerar, where Abraham (Gen. 20, 21:22–32) and Isaac (Gen. 26) are forces to be seriously reckoned with by the ruler of the town, suggests the situation in the earlier Execration Texts, those from Luxor, which attest a plurality of chiefs in any one locality. This archaeological evidence, together with legal matter in the patriarchal narratives illustrated by documents from Babylon in the time of Ḫammurabi (*fl.* 1700 B.C.) and from the Hurrian community of Nuzu (*c.* 1400 B.C.), indicates that, though there is no direct trace of the Hebrew patriarchs, the scriptural narrative concerning them is in the main a faithful reflection of conditions in the Amorite penetration of Palestine on the eve of the **Middle Bronze Age**.

b The succeeding period was one of political consolidation, and cultural development and urban settlement are attested at all the sites already occupied in the Early Bronze Age. The power of Egypt recovered too from the Amorite irruptions in what is known as the First Intermediate Period, and in the following two centuries Palestine and Syria were spheres of Egyptian influence, at least in the coastal areas and in the inland plains along the great trunk highway between the Nile and the Euphrates. Sphinxes of Egyptian princesses of the XII Dynasty at Râs Shamra (Ugarit) and at Qatna on the Orontes may indicate that the Pharaohs extended their influence over Syria and Palestine by means of intermarriage with the daughters of local rulers, a situation which the misadventures of Sarah (Gen. 20) and Rebekah (Gen. 26) may in some measure reflect. In the domination of Lower Egypt by the foreign Hyksos (*c.* 1730–1580), the recovery of Egypt and the advance **42b**
of her arms to the Euphrates (after 1580) and her clash with the Hittites in Syria (*c.* 1360–1260) until the decisive phase of the Hebrew settlement, associated in scripture with Joshua (*c.* 1225), Palestine was under the domination of Egypt, and phases of Hebrew history are illustrated by Egyptian records rather than by material remains from archaeological sites in Palestine. The most conspicuous monuments of the late XVIII and XIX Dynasties in Palestine are four temples to Canaanite deities at Bethshan and a temple thrice repaired outside Lachish.

Field archaeology, however, has revealed certain **c**
features in this period which illustrate the biblical narrative. The **Hyksos conquerors of Egypt** were apparently to a large extent Semites of Syria and Palestine, the Amorites of the Execration Texts who had now consolidated their power and, probably joined by non-Semitic elements from the north, Armenoid Hurrians (Horites of Scripture) and Aryans, whose distinctive names appear in the nomenclature of Palestinian chiefs in the Amarna Tablets from the post-Hyksos period (1411–1358), had effected the conquest of Lower Egypt. In the Hyksos period conspicuous fortresses appear in Palestine. Certain towns are fortified with a steep, smooth glacis, with or without a counterscarp, in dressed stone as at Jericho, limestone chips and plaster as at Lachish, or simply beaten earth as at Hazor in Upper Galilee. This feature is found at various sites, for instance, at Tell el-ʿAjjûl (old Gaza), Tell el-Fârʿah in the Wâdī Ghazzeh (possibly Sharuhen), Tell Beit Mirsim (possibly Kiriath-sepher, otherwise known as Debir), Tell Jerîsheh at the ford of the ʿAujā River north of Jaffa, Tell el-Qedaḥ (Hazor) south-west of Lake Huleh, Shechem, and Tell el-Fârʿah by Shechem (Tirzah). Such fortifications surmounted by strong walls made a great impression on the Hebrews in their first reconnaissance of the land (Num. 13:28), and many of them were not incorporated in the Hebrew polity until the time of Solomon, and those in the coastal plain never at any time. This situation is reflected in Jg. 1. In this passage the horse and chariot are also a bar to the progress of the Hebrews. This armament was introduced to West Asia by the Aryans from the Iranian plateau *c.* 1800 B.C., and is first mentioned in Egyptian records in an inscription recording the expulsion of the Hyksos. The only evidence of horses in Palestine in the Hyksos period is from Tell el-ʿAjjûl, where a bronze bit and skeletons of horses in multiple graves were found. With the new tactics of chariot warfare a feudal system was introduced to West Asia, into which the administrative and legal texts from Râs Shamra (14th–13th cent.) give us new insight. We should probably regard the above-mentioned fortresses during the Hyksos period and for the whole period of Egyptian domination of Palestine as the centres of feudal baronies. Professor Albright would see evidence of this order of society in the heavily fortified ' castle ' of the chief, the mansions of his entourage in the immediate neighbourhood, and

42c the hovels of the commonalty, which are features of the town plan of sites in this period. The introduction of this feudal order is of significance for the understanding of the situation in Palestine in the days of the Hebrew settlement and early monarchy. The Philistines certainly used it (1 Sam. 27:6), having adopted it together with their settlement of certain of the old Hyksos fiefs in the coastal plain of south Palestine. Saul also was a feudal war-lord (1 Sam. 8:11–18, 17:25), and the feudal system was also the strength of David's monarchy.

d In the 14th and 13th cent. the evidence of the Egyptian archives, the Amarna Tablets, and other historical inscriptions, and of field archaeology in Palestine points to a long period of disturbances. The fall of the **Late Bronze** settlement of Jericho *c.* 1350 and of Bethel a little later may be associated with the inroads of the Ḫabiru of whom there is notice in the Amarna Tablets, and, in view of the association of the Ḫabiru with Shechem in these documents (Knudtzon, *Die El-Amarna Tafeln*, 289:22ff., and possibly 252:9ff.), we might conceivably have a reference to the Hebrew penetration associated with Jacob and at least the elder, or Leah, tribes (Gen. 33:13–35:15). A further reference to elements of this older group of Hebrews, now apparently established in Palestine in the vicinity of Bethshan, may be the notice of 'the ʿApiru of the mountain of Yarmuth' in stelae of Seti I from Bethshan dated 1313 B.C. With the penetration of Palestine by the younger, or Rachel, tribes we may associate the fall of the Late Bronze settlement of Hazor (to Naphtali). The destruction of the Late Bronze settlements of Lachish and Tell Beit Mirsim may relate to a phase of the same Hebrew movements in the south, though the Hebrew traditions of the capture of Hebron (by Caleb) and Kiriath-sepher (by Othniel) suggest that the destruction at Lachish and Tell Beit Mirsim was due not to the Hebrews themselves, but to the Kenizzites, who were affiliated with them. From a conservative point of view the only certain archaeological evidence for **the date of the Exodus** and subsequent Hebrew settlement seems to us that discovered by Professor Glueck in Transjordan that there was a complete recession of sedentary occupation there from the end of the Early Bronze Age to *c.* 1300, after which clearly defined territorial states, Edom and Moab, emerged. Since the presence of these kingdoms largely determined the course and duration of the desert sojourn of the Israelites, this would indicate that the Exodus should be dated early, and the settlement in Palestine late, in the 13th cent.

e Scarcely half a century after the decisive phase of Israelite penetration of the hill-country from the east, the Egyptian records of the reign of Rameses III (1168–1137) attest the settlement of the coastal plain by the Philistines and kindred peoples, whose ultimate origin was apparently the north of the Balkan region. These peoples are first noticed by Egyptian records since the 15th cent. as mercenaries of Egypt and of the Hittites. As mercenaries of the latter they were armed with **weapons of iron,** which was first wrought in Anatolia and guarded by the Hittites as a state secret. By the end of the 13th cent. the Philistines and their kindred had apparently learned the secret of working iron, and they turned their weapons on their masters and destroyed the Hittite Empire. A reminiscence of the Philistine monopoly of iron-working in Palestine is the note in 1 Sam. 13:19 in the account of the reign of Saul (late 11th cent.). The Philistines seem to have been particularly aggressive in the foothills of the interior and by the end of the 2nd millennium apparently occupied Bethshan at the east end of the great central plain, where anthropoid coffins of pottery were found from this period, the corpse being buried with a gold mouthplate, perhaps a vestige of the gold mask found in the royal tombs of the 15th cent. at Mycenae. It will be recollected that the Philistines exposed the bodies of Saul and his sons here after the Battle of Gilboa (1 Sam. 31:9–12). Characteristic of the area of the Philistine occupation in the coastal plain is a very distinctive type of painted pottery decorated in geometric and bird motives. The occurrence of this ware so far inland as Jerusalem and Tell en-Naṣbeh, some nine miles north of Jerusalem, may be evidence of the phase of Philistine expansion when they established garrisons in Geba and Michmash in Saul's own district (1 Sam. 12).

f The divulgence of the secret of iron is a significant event in the history of the Near East. Much more common than copper, iron-ore supplied small ethnic groups with weapons with which they might dispute imperial expansion. With iron tools village communities and individual families might clear and occupy new grounds (Jos. 17:15–18). A good deal of virgin land, in fact, seems to have been occupied in the hills of central Palestine in the first phase of the Iron Age (*c.* 1200–1000), a phase of settlement ascribed by Professor Albright to the discovery of a new technique of watertight lime-plastering of cisterns, which made settlement less dependent on perennial springs. With the settlement of Syria and Palestine by Aramaean tribal confederacies there emerged eventually the kingdoms of Edom, Moab, Israel, and Damascus, and other states in Syria with which we are not immediately concerned. When these groups were armed with the new efficient metal the day of the small nation had dawned.

Another important factor in the cultural life of the small nation and in the eventual emancipation of the individual, with more far-reaching results than the discovery of iron, was the **invention of the alphabet,** apart from the religion of the prophets the one signal contribution of Palestine or Syria to the cultural progress of man. Two experiments were made to reduce the complicated syllabic scripts, the cuneiform of Mesopotamia and the hieroglyphic of Egypt, to a consonantal alphabet. The former resulted in the cuneiform alphabet in which the literature of Canaan has survived in the Râs Shamra Texts, and which has been found in Palestine in very short inscriptions on a potsherd from Beth-shemesh and on a bronze knife-blade from the open country north of Bethshan. The latter was the more successful experiment, resulting in the linear alphabet which is the direct predecessor of the Hebrew alphabet and the Greek and Latin alphabets of the West. The alphabet is the achievement of the Late Bronze Age, but the appropriation of the new script by the Aramaean peoples including the Hebrews has made it possible for us to follow their history and thought in inscriptions from the Iron Age and in the scriptures of the OT.

g The coming of the Philistines is marked by a level of destruction which terminates the Bronze Age settlement of most of the sites in the coastal plain of Palestine. The ensuing phase of occupation is on a definitely lower cultural plane. Recovery here, however, was more rapid, and conditions apparently more stable, than in the mountains, though settlements in both districts reflect the unsettled times of the period of the Hebrew Judges, with raid and counter-raid, as in the narratives of Samson, Samuel, and David in his early days.

The settlement of the Hebrews to the life of the peasant in Palestine is illustrated by the building and modest **fortification of hill-towns** in an area of central Palestine hitherto thinly populated. A feature of these fortifications was casemate walling, that is to say a double wall with chambers between. Of strength more apparent than real, though still quite efficient, this may have been conceived as a quick temporary fortification, to be strengthened as occasion demanded. The space between the walls seems to have served also for storage. Such fortifications may be a development of the temporary *laager* defence of the Hebrew nomads. A good illustration of such a settlement is Tell el-Fûl, some three miles north of Jerusalem, identified by Albright with Gibeah of Saul and excavated by him between 1923 and 1933. The first settlement, of the

42g 12th cent. and apparently unfortified, was destroyed by fire, which may reflect the civil war between the local Benjamites and the rest of the Israelites after the incident of the Levite's concubine (Jg. 19:20). A feature of the next settlement was a considerable fortress with casemate walling. This building, with an inside measurement of 32 × 17 metres and an overall outside measurement including four corner towers of 50 × 34 metres, is generally taken as Saul's palace. The dimensions, however, suggest that it was less palace than fortress, and it may have been the redoubt of the Philistine garrison which occupied Gibeah before Saul and Jonathan dislodged it (1 Sam. 13:3, after the Septuagint). The fortress may have contained Saul's dwelling, and it may be safely assumed that his striking-force of professional soldiers, such as David, was quartered here. Another site of this period to be excavated was Khirbet Seilûn, probably Shiloh, the centre of the Israelite amphictyony, and the seat of the Ark, some twelve miles south of Shechem. This was a case of 'biblical archaeology' in the narrow sense, since the site promised no prospect of the evidence of the interplay of races and cultures. No trace of the sanctuary of the Ark was certainly identified, but it was found that the site was occupied in the first phase of the Early Iron Age (*c.* 1200–1000), but destroyed in the same period, an event to which Jeremiah (7:12) possibly alludes.

h In view of the great significance of David in the political development of Israel we naturally expect archaeology to provide some point of tangible contact with the king. In effect, results are rather negative. At Jerusalem on the Ophel, or South-eastern, Hill certain portions of the old Jebusite wall have been discovered, which, with strong revetments, measure nearly 30 feet in thickness. 'Warren's shaft', leading down from the cover of the city wall to the Spring of Gihon (the Virgin's Fountain) in the Kidron Valley, has been known since 1867, but, like similar, but much more impressive, works at Gezer, Megiddo, and Ibleam, it was from before the time of David, being cut probably by the Canaanites in face of the general insecurity in the land in the Late Bronze and Early Iron Ages. It is generally stated that it was up the watershaft at Jerusalem that Joab led his men when he captured the fortress of the Jebusites (2 Sam. 5:6–8), but the Hebrew text at this point is not absolutely reliable. Other monuments of the reign of David are probably the fortifications of Beth-shemesh and Tell Beit Mirsim, which were repaired at this time with casemate walls, probably to serve as frontier fortresses against the Philistines.

i Monuments of Solomon's reign also are to be found elsewhere than at Jerusalem. The **second phase of the Early Iron Age** (1000–800) is characterised by fresh building activity at Megiddo, Gezer, and Lachish. At Megiddo defences and administrative quarters were built on a much grander scale than in the previous level of occupation, solid bonded masonry being used instead of casemate walling, probably under Phoenician influence (1 Kg. 5:18). Those towns and also Tell el-Kheleifeh (Elath or Ezion-geber) on the Gulf of 'Aqaba were equipped with heavily fortified double gateways with side chambers. Such works are referred to in 1 Kg. 9:15, which states that Solomon fortified Gezer, Hazor, and Jerusalem. At Megiddo a great stable-complex with limestone troughs and pillars perforated at their angles indicates one of the cities in which Solomon quartered his chariotry (1 Kg. 9:19, 10:26). This statement visualises several such chariotry depots, and it is possible that alignments of pillars noted at Tell el-Ḥesī (possibly Eglon) and Taanach are also the relics of such stables.

j Perhaps the most striking monument of Solomon's reign are the opencast **copper and iron mines,** chiefly in the eastern escarpment of the Wâdī 'Arabah, properly in the land of Edom, where copper had been worked by Egypt in the Pyramid Age (3rd millennium). This work in the Israelite period may go back to David, whose subjection of Edom (2 Sam. 7:14; 1 Kg. 11:15–16) would be thus explained. Professor Glueck discovered many of those ancient workings and the remains of furnaces where the ore was first smelted. The surface pottery indicates the 10th cent. B.C. Walled enclosures in the vicinity of the mines suggest that mining was done by slave labour, chiefly, no doubt, by Edomites. At the head of the Gulf of 'Aqaba, in a waterless site and directly in the path of the prevailing wind from the north, Glueck excavated a settlement of the same period which proved to be a great refinery, as was indicated by a series of flues open to the north. The whole settlement was heavily defended and access was through a double, chambered gateway typical of the period. Remains of thick cables, lumps of pitch, and long iron nails suggest shipbuilding, and the site is probably that of Ezion-geber. Here copper and iron ingots and possibly also finished articles were produced for shipment in the trading enterprises of Solomon and his Phoenician allies down the Red Sea to South Arabia and East Africa (1 Kg. 9:26), and the copper for the bronze pillars Jachin and Boaz and other items of the Temple equipment was almost certainly refined here.

On the death of Solomon the tribes of the North with the exception of Benjamin revolted from the House of David, and a leader was found in Jeroboam, who had already headed an abortive rising and had had to seek refuge in Egypt, then under the Libyan usurper Sheshonq I (935–914). An inscription of Sheshonq on the pylon of the Temple of Amon at Karnak agrees with the statement in 1 Kg. 14:25–6, where an Egyptian expedition against Judah is dated in the fifth year of Rehoboam (926). In the Karnak inscription, however, the Pharaoh claims to have reduced certain localities in North Israel too, including the towns along the trunk highway in the plains. The fragment of a stele of Sheshonq at Megiddo bears out this statement and the Egyptian evidence suggests that Sheshonq saw in this crisis in Israel an opportunity to secure Egyptian influence in Palestine through a vassal king, while taking the towns of the plain directly under Egyptian control. Evidence pointing to the same conclusion is found in scarabs and other material remains of the influence of Egypt at this period at Gezer, Beth-shemesh, Tell el-'Ajjûl, Tell Jemmeh, and Tell el-Fâr'ah in the Wâdī Ghazzeh. 43a

The subsequent tension between Israel and Judah is reflected in the fortification of certain towns immediately north of Jerusalem, which was now a frontier area. Bethel was fortified at this time as the southernmost town of the Northern Kingdom and Tell en-Naṣbeh (probably Mizpah of 1 Kg. 15:16–22) as the most northerly town of Judah, an imposing fortress with walls 20 feet thick.

The first capital of the Northern Kingdom was **Shechem,** a tribal centre and probably a shrine of the tribes of the North since the first settlement, traditionally associated with Jacob (Gen. 33:18–20, 34). The refortification of Shechem at this time may probably be associated with this phase of the history of Israel (1 Kg. 12:25). Subsequently the capital of the kingdom until the foundation of **Samaria** in 880 was Tirzah, some 7 miles north-east of Shechem. The Dominican excavations at Tell el-Fâr'ah, almost certainly the site of Tirzah, show that the first stratum of the Iron Age occupation terminates in a burnt level, which may reflect the civil war between Omri and his ephemeral rival Zimri (1 Kg. 16:18). There follows a phase of reconstruction which was, however, abruptly interrupted, the site remaining virtually an open town. The affinities between the pottery of this phase of the settlement of Tell el-Fâr'ah and that of the first two levels at Samaria suggest that this was the point at which Omri transferred his capital to Samaria, where there is evidence of the greatness of this king. The most impressive evidence of the real political significance of Omri and his house, however, comes from beyond Israel, in Assyrian records, which b

43b refer thereafter to Israel as 'the house of Omri', and in the inscription from Dhībân in Moab where Mesha records his war of liberation, probably from Joram, the grandson of Omri, which lie beyond the scope of this assignment.

c Under **Omri** an alliance was effected with the Phoenicians of Tyre (1 Kg. 16:31 ; cf. Jos. Ant.), and the new capital shows many traces of the material culture of Tyre. In spite of the destruction which Samaria suffered, first by the Assyrians in 722 and later by the Jewish prince John Hyrcanus in 134 B.C., fragments of the palace begun by Omri and completed by Ahab remain to suggest the strength and splendour of the city. The summit of the isolated hill was dominated by the palace-complex built of fine bonded masonry. The **palace of Ahab** was indeed a 'palace of ivory' (1 Kg. 22:39), ivory plaques carved in low relief with Phoenician renderings of Egyptian motives having been found here. Letters of the Phoenician, or proto-Hebraic, alphabet on the back of these plaques indicate that they were pieces for inlay of panelling and furniture (Am. 6:4), instances of which are found from roughly the same period in North Syria and Nineveh. The palace-complex was enclosed by a strong wall of fine Phoenician masonry founded on the rock and indeed laid in places in rock-cut foundation trenches. Two other walls and a fortified gateway lower down the hill enclosed the city, which from its situation as well as its fortifications must have been most impressive. The site, of course, had been deliberately acquired—actually bought—by Omri so that in his crown property he might be free to organise his administration as David had done in Jerusalem, which was literally the city of David. A number of inscribed potsherds, which are actually receipts from the royal treasury for corn, wine, and olive-oil from certain districts in the vicinity of Samaria, may indicate a fiscal organisation such as that of Solomon (1 Kg. 4:7ff.), which is illustrated by the fiscal organisation attested in legal and administrative texts from Râs Shamra in the Late Bronze Age. The proximity of the localities in the Samaritan ostraca to the city, however, suggests rather that these are crown estates, and that the system of Solomon may not have been so thoroughly applied after the Disruption. The Samaritan dockets are from a level later than the time of Omri and Ahab and are nearer the time of Jeroboam II, the contemporary of Amos in the first half of the 8th cent. (Am. 7:11).

d On the fall of the House of Omri Israel rapidly sank back into the obscurity of dynastic rivalries and border warfare with Judah and her Aramaean neighbours. The splendour of Omri's Samaria was defaced by poor native building such as had always characterised the provincial towns of Israel and Judah, which were little more than large market villages, the most impressive feature of which was their fortification. Both Israel and Judah soon sank to the status of vassal states to Assyria before Assyria in 732, after the suppression of the revolt of Pekah (2 Kg. 16:5ff.), stripped Israel of Galilee and Transjordan. From Assyrian records we know that the latter became the Assyrian province of Gilzau (Gilead) and the former the province of Megiddo, so called after the provincial capital. This phase is attested by the destruction of the great frontier fortress of **Hazor** in Upper Galilee, where a layer of carbon has sealed off the furniture of the houses of the Israelite city (cf. 2 Kg. 15:29 and probably Isa. 9:1). The third level at Megiddo was destroyed by Tiglath-pileser III and the second level was rebuilt, the most conspicuous feature being a large fort. Samaria, the capital of all that remained of Israel, fell in 722, a layer of carbon indicating the disaster. The city was rebuilt by the Assyrians as the capital of their province Samerina, and here and at the site of Tirzah (Tell el-Fâr'ah) and at Tell Jemmeh on the Wâdī Ghazzeh on the highway to Egypt the presence of the suzerain power is indicated by a type of pottery strange to Palestine, but common from the 43d
excavation of the palace at Nineveh. Two cuneiform deeds of conveyance from Gezer dated in 649 B.C. are further evidence of the Assyrian domination, especially of the districts along the highway to Egypt in the time of Manasseh of Judah, who is known from Assyrian records as a vassal of Assyria.

The insecurity of the period in face of the increasing e
domination of the West by Assyria is probably reflected in the **Siloam tunnel** in Jerusalem, the last development of a series of hydraulic works from the Spring of Gihon. This conduit, totally underground, brought water from east to west of the Ophel Hill to the Pool of Siloam. The script and idiom in which this work is recorded on the wall of the tunnel at its egress indicates the period of Hezekiah, to whom such works are attributed (2 Kg. 20:20 and more precisely 2 Chr. 32:30). The course of Hezekiah's reign is better known from Assyrian records than from the archaeology of Palestine. The most significant events were his unsuccessful revolts against Assyria which brought Sennacherib twice to Palestine. The OT is unclear in the matter of these events at the beginning and towards the end of Sennacherib's long reign. The reference to Tirhakah in 2 Kg. 19:9 indicates an expedition *c.* 689–686, since a recently found inscription of Tirhaqa from the Sudan indicates that he would not have been old enough to take the field against Sennacherib in 701, in the fourteenth year of Hezekiah, when Assyrian annals attest Sennacherib's subjection of Hezekiah and the reduction of Judah from his base at Lachish. In 2 Kg., then, there is a conflation of accounts of two different expeditions in which Hezekiah was involved.

The last phase of the history of the kingdom of f
Judah is graphically illustrated from the excavation of **Lachish**. Two layers of ash, impossible to distinguish but for the fact that the debris of the first destruction had choked the drain at the gate of the city, indicate that the place fell twice to the Babylonians between 597 and 586. The life of the town, then, reflects the divided counsels which Jeremiah witnesses, and this is more particularly revealed by the famous **Lachish Letters**. These documents, brief and to all but contemporaries cryptic, are inscribed potsherds, of which eighteen were found in the ashes of a guard-room flanking the city-gate, and are mostly military dispatches from one Hoshea, the commander of a post between Lachish and Azekah, to Yaush, the governor of Lachish. By a remarkable coincidence both of these places are mentioned together in the account of the final Babylonian campaign against Judah, which we may now, in the light of Nebuchadrezzar's Chronicle, date from 587 to 586, a year and a half. Since Jerusalem fell in the summer of 586 in the eleventh year of the last king Zedekiah, the invasion took place in his ninth year. Since one of the Lachish Letters is dated 'in the ninth year', the documents date probably from 587 and later. In content they refer probably to a delegation to Egypt (cf. Jer. 37:5, 7–9), to the Jewish defence based on Lachish, Azekah, and, of course, Jerusalem, which is not actually mentioned (cf. Jer. 34:7), and to divided counsels on the question of resistance or non-resistance (cf. Jer. 38:4), all of which affords an excellent commentary on the Book of Jeremiah. The idiom is that of his period, and the script—almost a cursive—enables us to visualise the appearance of Jeremiah's oracles written by Baruch on the roll which Jehoiakim slit up as he sat by his winter brazier (Jer. 36). Attempts have been made to particularise and find references to actual personalities of Scripture in these documents, but in the fragmentary state of the evidence this is not possible. Yet in a certain seal-impression of the period from Lachish with the legend 'Belonging to Gedaliah who is over the house' there may be a reference to the notable Gedaliah the son of Ahikam, a high official known for his moderation (Jer. 26:24). The title 'who is over the house' is that of no less a person than the royal chamberlain, and Gedaliah may well have been the

43f same as the native Jewish governor subsequently appointed by the Babylonians who was so brutally murdered at Mizpah (1 Kg. 25:25; Jer. 41). The provincial palace occupied by the royal chamberlain at Lachish is the most conspicuous feature of the site, being the 'palace-fort' on the summit of the mound. This building may have been erected under Solomon in his organisation of the land to incorporate Canaanites in his kingdom, and served probably for fiscal as well as strategic purposes.

g The fate of Lachish in the final collapse of Judah was that of Jerusalem and other settlements in the south. Those which have been excavated and others whose surface potsherds have been examined prove to have been destroyed or abandoned at that time and unoccupied except by squatters for a long period (Am. 9:14; Isa. 61:4). This confirms the biblical statement concerning the general deportation of notables and artisans by the Babylonians (2 Kg. 25:11–12). By contrast the former Assyrian provinces of Megiddo and Samaria remained aloof from the conflict, doubtless under the influence of the Mesopotamian and Aramaean military colonists settled by Assyria (2 Kg. 17:24ff.). Here, consequently, Megiddo, Samaria, and Bethel remained untouched. **Tell en-Naṣbeh** too, which was probably one of the sites named Mizpah (Watchtower), though in Judah, remained intact, probably to serve the purpose its name signifies, and here moderate elements gathered under the native statesman Gedaliah, who may have served as a provincial governor, or possibly a fiscal officer, in the interests of Babylon. Nothing is actually known of Babylonian administration in Judah, but it is likely that the land was administered from one of the former Assyrian administrative centres in the north, probably Samaria, which was the seat of the district officer Sanballat (Sin-uballiṭ) in the Persian period. One of the few relics of the Babylonian period is an Akkadian tablet from the surface of the mound at Gezer.

h **Cyrus the Great,** succeeding to the Empire of Babylon, reversed the policy of Babylon in deporting subject peoples, and a limited number availed themselves of his edict and returned to Palestine. There is little evidence, however, of a general resettlement, and the returned exiles were apparently content to settle in and about Jerusalem. The organisation of Palestine, in fact, now in the fifth Persian satrapy 'beyond the river', did not encourage Jewish settlement elsewhere. Judah was but one district of the province along with Samaria, Ammon, Ashdod, and Arabia, where other racial elements were in the great majority. The Persians apparently made the bold experiment of appointing at first princes of the Davidic House as district governors of Jerusalem and the vicinity, which we know from legends on coins and from official stamps on jar handles to have been called Yehud. From a certain papyrus letter from the elders of an Israelite military colony at **Elephantine** by Assuan it seems that this experiment was given up, and by the end of the 5th cent. the province was under a Persian governor Bigvai (Bagoses of Jos. Ant.), though the Jewish High Priest was probably a not insignificant assessor. The stamps on the jar handles seem to indicate a guarantee of measure, perhaps of tribute in kind paid to the Persian administration. The coins too are significant. They appear now for the first time in the archaeology of Palestine, making it soon possible to date archaeological strata with a precision hitherto seldom possible (*v. infra* on Qumrân). Coined money was a Greek, or rather Lydian, invention, the stamps of individual merchants or of communities and city-states guaranteeing the purity of the specie. So the coins now current in Palestine, in so far as they are not Phoenician, bear the stamps of the Greek city-states most active in the Levant, such as the owl of Athens, but stamped with the name of the province YHD.

i Lachish was reoccupied at this time and its fortifications repaired. It has been suggested that this may have been the seat of the governor of the district 43 'Arabia', who in the time of Nehemiah (*c.* 444 B.C.) was 'Gashmu the Arabian', who joined Sanballat in opposing the refortification of Jerusalem. There was an influx of Edomites into south Palestine at this time and they apparently occupied the hills as far as the country just north of Hebron, where Bethsur, where YHD coins have been found, was apparently a frontier town. Lachish, then, may well have been the capital of the district 'Arabia'. On the other hand it may have been too important a base for operations against the distant Persian province of Egypt to have been entrusted to a native, and perhaps it is thus that we should explain the refortification of the city. The old palace-fort on the summit of the mound was now occupied by a smaller, though still ample, residence, which has all the appearance of the residence and offices of a district governor, and in the vicinity a notable feature is a small shrine. An open courtyard backed by several apartments was the largest part of this complex. Six steps led up to an antechamber, and three more steps to the inner shrine, the holy of holies. A drain in the doorsill of the inner shrine probably indicates that libations were made there. A small limestone altar was found with the relief of a man with arms raised in supplication, and an upraised hand, presumably symbolising the deity blessing his devotee. It is interesting that the entrances to the antechamber and inner shrine were in line from the east, so that the rays of the rising sun could shine into the inner shrine. The passage in Ezek. 8:16 is suggested where the prophet animadverts on a company in the Temple standing with their backs to the Temple and their faces to the east, worshipping the sun.

Further traces of the Persian administration in j Palestine are probably some fine silver bowls with repoussé work and silver ladles with the handles in the form of nude swimming maidens, whose hair-style suggests Persian workmanship, from Tell Jemmeh and Tell el-Fâr'ah in the Wâdī Ghazzeh. The last two places were important fortresses on the limit of the settled land before the ten grim desert marches to the Delta, and it is natural that the Persians, with designs on Egypt, should garrison these. A number of grain silos at Tell Jemmeh, the filling debris of which includes Greek potsherds, probably indicates the significance of these places as Persian bases for provisioning expeditions to Egypt.

The **Greek period** proper begins with Alexander's 44 conquest of the Persians, which was complete in 331 B.C., after which, as agencies of the Hellenisation of his eastern empire, veteran colonies were settled with Hellenistic institutions in various parts of Asia. Such settlements presumably were Dion and Pella in Transjordan, both named after towns in Macedonia. Greek influence, however, may be detected in Palestine even before the time of Alexander, when black-figured glazed Greek pottery characteristic of the 6th cent. is found, and later red-figured black-glazed ware, Greek lamps, and coins are current in the country. Already by the 6th cent. the Greeks had established a trading colony which had grown to a city at Naucratis in the Delta, and to the activities of the merchants and slave-traders of this place Joel (3:6) may refer. Alexander's policy of the Hellenisation of Asia was carried on by his successors, who claimed Palestine as a sphere of influence, the Lagids of Egypt till 198 B.C. and then the Seleucids of Syria. In this period many towns flourished as centres of Hellenism, such as Raphia, Gaza, Ascalon, Ashdod, Joppa (Jaffa), Dor (Ṭanṭûrah), and Ptolemais ('Akkā). Samaria flourished anew under Greek guise, the most conspicuous traces of which are the remains of strong round towers along a new wall which followed the line of the old Israelite fortification of the summit of the mound. Bethshan was rebuilt after over half a millennium of dereliction, and renamed Nysa and Scythopolis. East of the Lake of Galilee was Hippos, while in Transjordan Gadara (Umm Qeis), Gerasa (Jerash), and Philadelphia

44a ('Ammân) took their origin, though what remains there is from the Roman imperial period. Certain of these towns, such as Ptolemais, Joppa, Ascalon, and Gaza, were autonomous and minted their own coins with the image of the suzerain Lagid or Seleucid king. These coins are a conspicuous feature at archaeological stations in this period. They indicate Hellenistic architecture as well as institutions at the various sites, which is confirmed by archaeology. They also reflect religious syncretism of native and Greek deities, e.g. Resheph with Apollo, Baal Melqart with Heracles, Eshmun with Asclepius, Astarte with Aphrodite, etc.

b In this period stratification may be more precisely dated, since coins of the Lagids and Seleucids, and of the Jewish native rulers of the House of Hashmon, become quite common, the last from the time of John Hyrcanus (135–104 B.C.). The records of the times too, for instance the Books of the Maccabees, are very circumstantial and detailed so that in the light of the combined evidence of documents and coinage it is often possible to interpret the archaeological remains of sites most accurately. Bethsur, for instance, a Jewish fortress between the Persian administrative districts of Yehud and Arabia, had its fortifications rebuilt and extended in the 2nd cent. B.C. This is almost certainly the work of **Judas Maccabaeus** in the initial success of the Jewish revolt in 165–163 B.C. (1 Mac. 6:7). The destruction of these fortifications and their subsequent reconstruction may be the work of the Seleucid general Bacchides in 161 B.C. (1 Mac. 9:52). Handles of wine-jars with dates of high priests of Rhodes probably indicate occupation by Seleucid garrisons until, with the establishment of native Jewish rule, the place ceased to serve as a fortress commanding access to Judah by way of the wadis running westward, and, on the evidence of coins, was abandoned *c.* 100 B.C. Other settlements which had a similar history until the extension of Jewish rule made them strategically insignificant were Samaria, Gezer commanding access to Judah by the valleys of Aijalon and Sorek, and Marissa (Tell es-Sandaḥannah) near old Lachish commanding the approach to Hebron by Wâdī el-Afranj (Crusaders' Wadi).

c The last site is an interesting instance of a provincial Hellenistic town in Palestine. Its town plan is much more systematic than in the Oriental period; its houses are arranged in blocks and its streets mostly at right angles and much more spacious than in towns of the preceding ages in Palestine. Here, as indeed in other sites of the period in Western Palestine, scores of Rhodian jar handles were found, testifying to trade with the Aegean and probably to occupation by garrisons of the Ptolemies of Egypt and the Seleucids of Syria until the district was incorporated in the native Jewish state under the Hasmonaeans. The power of the Greek successors of Alexander the Great had opened the coast and western slopes of Palestine to foreign penetration. Already in the Persian period possibly the Phoenicians were established at 'Athlît and Dor, south of the Carmel head, Straton's Tower, the site of later Caesarea, and in the vicinity of Jaffa. Now at Tell es-Sandaḥannah a number of rock-cut family tombs cut in the soft limestone reveals a colony of Phoenicians from Sidon. Their business at Marissa is not revealed by the Greek and Aramaic inscriptions in the tombs, but theophoric names containing the name of Cos, the national deity of Edom, indicate association with the Edomites and may possibly point to an interest in the caravan trade from Arabia via 'Aqaba to the markets of Gaza and the Phoenician settlements already mentioned on the Palestinian coast.

d The archaeological evidence of the Jewish wars of liberation under Judas Maccabaeus and his family and the final triumph and restoration of Jewish independence is largely negative, consisting of settlements deliberately ruined by the Jews or allowed to fall into ruin since after the Jewish triumph they had lost their strategic value. One settlement which apparently assumed a new significance in this age was the settlement of **Khirbet Qumran** overlooking the Dead Sea 44d from the north-west some 8 miles south of Jericho. Some traces have been found of a settlement there in the 8th and 7th cent. B.C., perhaps associated with desert settlements attributed to Jotham, the son and co-regent of Uzziah (2 Chr. 27:4), and possibly 'the City of Salt' of Jos. 15:62, as suggested by Professor Noth. Now in the Hellenistic Age coins of John Hyrcanus (135–104 B.C.) and from all his successors until Herod the Great and his son Archelaus and the Roman procurators of Judah until A.D. 68 indicate a new settlement associated exclusively with the sect which left the celebrated **Dead Sea Scrolls** in caves and crevices of the adjacent cliffs.

As is well known, opinion was violently divided over the date of the manuscripts, biblical and non-biblical, from the first cave to be discovered in the spring of 1947. Sufficient regard was not always paid to the archaeological evidence, meagre as it was. That evidence consisted of the jars in which the scrolls were contained, their lids, a juglet, some lamps, and a cooking-pot. This in itself might have dated the deposit to *c.* 200 B.C.–A.D. 70, the jars finding no exact parallel in Palestine, but being similar in form and purpose to jars used in Egypt in the 2nd cent. B.C., and the rest of the pottery being similar to that found in Jewish tombs about Jerusalem in the 1st cent. A.D. until the destruction of the city in A.D. 70. This finding is confirmed by subsequent excavations at the adjacent settlement of Khirbet Qumrân.

The excavation of this settlement by the Jordan e
Department of Antiquities, L'École Archéologique Française, and the Palestine Archaeological Museum under G. L. Harding and Père R. de Vaux in five campaigns between 1951 and 1956 revealed three main phases of occupation, the first two by the Sect, or Community, of the New Covenant, as they called themselves. It is not possible to determine, either from the excavations or from the documents so far deciphered, when and in what circumstances the Sect took its origin. The whole period of occupation by the Sect is well delimited by coins, and the fact that these, as far as they have been cleaned and deciphered, begin in the time of John Hyrcanus suggests that the settlement dates from this time, the Sect having taken its origin a little earlier, perhaps in protest at the assumption of the high-priesthood by Jonathan as a political bribe at the hands of the Seleucid king in 152 B.C. Non-biblical texts, at any rate, such as the Manual of Discipline and particularly the Commentary on the first two chapters of the Book of Habakkuk, show that for the Sect the legitimacy of the priesthood was a controversial issue. The exploration of caves in the escarpment behind the settlement excavated indicates that the community probably lived in tents with caves as storehouses and dwellings in the winter rains, which are rare enough in that region of rain-shadow. The buildings excavated were a watch-tower, the public meeting-houses, refectory with kitchens and pantries, scriptorium, common bakery, pottery and other workshops, together with the vital cisterns, most of which were used for storage rather than for ceremonial ablution, which we know from the Manual of Discipline of the Sect to have been one of their important rites. There is good evidence that this somewhat modest settlement was disrupted by earthquake. From coins of Herod the Great (37–4 B.C.), which are the last precisely datable evidence from this level, Père de Vaux connects the destruction of Qumrân with the earthquake which Josephus relates in the reign of Herod in 31 B.C. The second phase of occupation begins, after a period of dereliction, in the time of Herod's son Archelaus (4 B.C.–A.D. 6) and, on the evidence of coins, continues to the second year of the Jewish Revolt (A.D. 68). Again Josephus may enable us to particularise, since he records that in that year in his systematic isolation of Jerusalem Vespasian brought the X Legion down the Jordan Valley to Jericho. This phase of the

44e settlement of Qumrân ended in conflagration, and iron arrowheads indicate violence. This is the time when the scriptures of the sect were secreted in the caves, as the archaeological evidence suggests. The Romans apparently did not discriminate between pietists and fanatics. After this a limited area of the site was occupied as a garrison post by troops, apparently of the X Legion, who were occupied in mopping up in this natural refuge for rebels after the fall of Jerusalem in A.D. 70. This was the legion which was quartered in the ruins of Jerusalem, where tiles have been found with the stamp of the legion, LEG X F (i.e. Fretensis). A coin found at Qumrân counter-stamped with X is probably a relic of their occupation. The site was again abandoned towards the end of the 1st cent. but reoccupied by the Jewish insurgents in the Revolt of Bar Cochba (A.D. 132–5). On the suppression of this revolt Qumrân was finally abandoned except by periodic squatters, who left a few coins from the Byzantine (till the 7th cent. A.D.) and Arabic (after A.D. 636) periods.

f In the period of occupation by the Sect the identification of buildings, in so far as that was not suggested by material evidence, was facilitated by the documents found in the caves. Obviously much copying of manuscripts was done, and the scriptorium was indicated by a room with long stone benches and stone tables with inkwells of brass and pottery. The Manual of Discipline of the Sect mentions communal meals, and a certain large room with kitchen and pantry with a great store of various dishes obviously served such a purpose. The careful burial of bones of domestic animals almost certainly indicates the disposal of the remains of such meals. The adjoining cemetery was also interesting. Burials were orientated southwards and there was no grave furniture. Coins were found only in the area of the public buildings and not in the caves, certain of which show signs of habitation. This agrees with the Manual of Discipline, which makes it clear that there was no private property, but all money brought by novices or subsequently earned was paid into a common fund. The fact that this was no ordinary settlement greatly narrowed the field of conjecture as to the purpose of the buildings.

g The date of the deposit of the manuscripts of the Sect has a peculiar significance for textual criticism of the OT. So far it has not proved possible to date the origin of the manuscripts except by the *terminus post quem*, that is the settlement of Qumrân in the Maccabaean period. However, even if we assume that the biblical manuscripts date nearer A.D. 68 than in the 2nd cent. B.C., the gain is enormous. In view of the late manuscript authority for the OT in Hebrew the Greek version of Alexandria (Septuagint) has been greatly valued, particularly where it is at variance with the accepted Hebrew text, the more so as manuscripts of the whole OT antedate the oldest Hebrew manuscripts by over half a millennium. Now the biblical manuscripts of Qumrân, even on their latest dating, carry the tradition of the Hebrew text back two and a half centuries before the Greek codices Sinaiticus (א) and Vaticanus (B). The Hebrew texts of Qumrân substantiate, though they do not absolutely agree with, the Hebrew accepted text. There is, however, a certain fluidity of tradition evidenced particularly in certain Greek versions of the Minor Prophets from the Wâdî Murabba'at in the vicinity of Qumrân, which differ from the Septuagint or any of the Greek versions hitherto known. In particular one Hebrew text of Qumrân supports the Septuagint rather than the accepted Hebrew text, so that it may hardly be said that the discovery of those early Hebrew manuscripts has impaired the worth of the Septuagint. Until more of this material is forthcoming and has been carefully studied judgment on the precise significance of the Qumrân texts for the textual criticism of the OT must be suspended.

h In subject-matter, in view of the late date, the Qumrân texts are likely to prove more useful in elucidating the background of the NT than in elucidating the OT, particularly the Gospel of St John. Here and in the Pauline Epistles the cosmic opposition of the forces of light and darkness finds a parallel in the beliefs of the Qumrân community as expressed chiefly in the non-biblical texts, the War of the Children of Light with the Children of Darkness and the Manual of Discipline. This was a particular development of the ethical dualism which became prevalent in Judaism in the Persian period. The texts also emphasise the keenness of eschatological anticipation in certain quarters in Palestine on the eve of the Gospel. If, as seems likely, the Sect was Essene, then the texts with their pure, simple, if pragmatic, ethic help us to visualise a good proportion of those to whom Jesus addressed his teaching, since Josephus states that the Essenes were to be found throughout the land, presumably in various employments.

i In the **Roman period,** after Pompey's capture of Jerusalem in 63 B.C., we have the advantage of accurate and detailed history, particularly Josephus' history of the events leading up to and culminating in the revolt of A.D. 66–70. In the light of those intimate records it is possible to give often a very accurate interpretation of the remains of this period, many of which are still conspicuous monuments visible without actual excavation. On these monuments inscriptions often admit of particularisation, and in stratified excavation coins of Herod the Great, his family, and the Roman procurators of Judah make precise dating possible within narrow limits.

j The first phase of this period is the reign of **Herod the Great** (37–4 B.C.). Herod has left many monuments, all in the Graeco-Roman style. Samaria was given to Herod as a personal estate by the Roman Emperor Augustus in 30 B.C., and was rebuilt with more extensive walls, a stadium, and a forum. On the top of the mound on the site of the Israelite palace, a temple was erected to Augustus, the steps and part of the platform of which still remain. Caesarea was also built between 25 and 13 B.C. on the site of the Phoenician settlement of Straton's Tower. This city, which was the Roman administrative centre, was also equipped with the typical institutions of Graeco-Roman culture, forum, stadium, amphitheatre, and theatre, all on a grand scale, and a temple to Augustus, with a statue of the Emperor. Marble statuary in the Graeco-Roman style is a specific feature of Palestinian archaeology from now onwards. The place, like modern Haifa, was made into a considerable seaport by the construction of two great moles, remains of which may still be seen. Apparently a great deal of Straton's Tower was devoted without scruple to the construction of Herod's moles. Caesarea is a most inviting site for Jewish archaeology, and all the features mentioned are plainly visible from the air and even from the ground. A splendid palace with ornamental gardens at Jericho, where Herod died, has also been excavated.

From these well-known monuments Herodian work may be detected where it is incorporated into later building, as at Jerusalem, Hebron, in the building which encloses the traditional cave of Machpelah, and at the reputed site of the Oak of Mamre at Râmat el-Khalîl, 2 miles north of Hebron.

k As is well known Herod rebuilt **the Temple** at Jerusalem. Nothing indeed survives of the building itself, but Herod's southern extension of the sacred area remains, underpinned by the vaults known as 'Solomon's Stables', and the lower courses of masonry in the West, or Wailing, Wall are thought to be his work. The pavement of the fortress which commanded the sacred area from the north-west, called Antonia after Herod's patron Mark Antony, may still be seen under the modern convent of the Sisters of Zion. The foundations of one of the three great towers at the western angle of Herod's north wall have been discovered under the Turkish citadel of the city by the Jaffa Gate.

44k Other monuments of Herod are the striking desert fortresses Herodium, where Herod was buried, on that isolated peak south of Bethlehem which resembles an extinct volcano, Qarn Sarṭaba, built on a former Hasmonaean fortress Alexandreion 15 miles south-east of Nablus, Masada overlooking the south of the Dead Sea, where the last remnants of the Jewish resistance forces perished in A.D. 73, and Machaerus overlooking the north of the Dead Sea from the east, where, possibly, John the Baptist was beheaded. None of these sites, however, with the exception of Masada, has been excavated, though surface remains are typical of Herod's building.

l Since the Hellenistic Age the material remains in the various sites excavated in Palestine are more and more typical of the Graeco-Roman world rather than of the East. From Herod's time Western types predominate in art, architecture, and building technique with marginal-drafted masonry, and all but the simplest pottery. The extent of Westernisation is indicated by inscriptions on public buildings, which are in Greek, and it is significant that an inscription from the Temple court warning Gentiles to proceed no farther on pain of death and the inscription from a synagogue built by one Theodotus, son of Vettenus, and possibly the Synagogue of the Freedmen of Acts 6:9, both rather later than Herod the Great, are in Greek. A further indication of the same cultural trend are various Greek versions of the OT, besides the four already known, recently discovered in the Wâdī Murabbaʿat, some 10 miles south of Khirbet Qumrân. Palestine from this time hence is culturally and politically a province of the Roman Empire, and even the synagogues, the earliest remains of which are at Capernaum, Chorazin, and Kefr Birʿim in Upper Galilee from *c.* A.D. 200, are Roman in architecture and decoration.

m East of the Dead Sea, however, in the region occupied by the Nabataeans, who had come from the oases of the Hejaz and ousted the Edomites in the 4th cent. B.C., a distinctively native tradition in architecture and ceramics flourished, though here too from the 1st cent. B.C. till the incorporation of the Nabataean kingdom in the Roman Empire in A.D. 106 Graeco-Roman influences may be detected. Apart, however, from the interesting coins of the Nabataean king Aretas IV, the contemporary of Herod the Great, Jesus, and St Paul, and the father-in-law and later conqueror of Herod Antipas, and the general interest of the works of irrigation and settlement of what is now open desert, this field of archaeology is rather peripheral to our study.

n The studies of Herodian Jerusalem by Père H. Vincent, R. Weil, and J. Simons, the recovery of the Herodian palace at Jericho, and the remains of an aqueduct from ʿAin ʿArrûb, 9 miles SSE. of Bethlehem, to Jerusalem, which was constructed by Pontius Pilate, give us points of contact with our Lord. Both Jesus and John the Baptist would certainly know of the Qumrân community, the latter perhaps being at one time a member, and would no doubt be familiar with the ethical principles by which the Sect was governed. In Galilee the town and palace built by Herod Antipas at Tiberias was contemporary with Jesus, and the site of Cana of Galilee (Khirbet Qânā, some 8 miles north of Nazareth, and not Kefr Kennā) may still be seen, a conspicuous feature of which is plaster-lined cisterns. The site of the Holy Sepulchre is still a matter of controversy; as there is yet no unanimity among archaeologists as to the position of the second and third walls on the north of the city mentioned by Josephus in his account of the Jewish Revolt. The traditional site, however, was certainly an ancient graveyard, and, if the second wall ran from Herod's palace fort at the Turkish citadel to the Antonia, as is certain, then the site of the Church of the Holy Sepulchre might well have been outside the city wall. Recent excavations and surface exploration at the traditional site of the Shepherd's Fields by Bethlehem and in caves in the vicinity have shown evidence in pottery and coins of occupation in the Herodian period and subsequently to A.D. 66–70. The sites of Capernaum (Tell Ḥûm), Chorazin (Khirbet Kerâzeh), and Bethsaida (Eṭ-Ṭâbghah), and other localities around the Lake of Galilee are also fairly certainly located, but the remaining monuments, except at Tiberias, are of a later date.

o In the vicinity of Jerusalem many family tombs have been cleared, especially from the 1st cent. B.C. to the 2nd cent. A.D., and a great number of ossuaries, or bone-caskets, of limestone found. Among these the most interesting was one which was inscribed to the effect that it contained the **bones of King Uzziah.** This king, who died a leper, had been buried outside the city, and at some later time, when his tomb was used for burial, his bones were collected and deposited in the ossuary. Other ossuaries recently found on the slopes of the Mount of Olives bore names familiar in the NT, such as Jairus, Miriam (Mary), Martha, Simon bar Jonah, etc. Not only so, but certain of them are marked with the sign of the cross. The fact that ossuaries are not found after the 2nd cent. A.D. makes it feasible that here is a cemetery in which Christian families of the district had been buried, possibly since the first generation of believers.

Bibliography—W. F. Albright, *The Archaeology of Palestine* (1949); A. G. Barrois, *Manuel d'Archéologie Biblique* i (1939), ii (1953); D. Barthélemy and J. T. Milik, *Discoveries in the Judaean Desert* i: *Qumran Cave I* (1955); M. Burrows, *What mean these Stones?* (1941), *The Dead Sea Scrolls* (1955); J. Finegan, *Light from the Ancient Past* (1946); N. Glueck, *The Other Side of the Jordan* (1940); J. Simons, *Jerusalem in the OT* (1952); L. H. Vincent and A. M. Stève, *Jérusalem de l'AT* I (1954), II (1956); C. Watzinger, *Denkmäler Palästinas* (1935); G. E. Wright, *Biblical Archaeology* (1962).

THE ARCHAEOLOGY OF THE ANCIENT NEAR EAST

By W. F. ALBRIGHT

45a **1 Archaeological Method: Surface Exploration and Excavation**—In this article I shall endeavour to survey the general field of ancient Middle and Near Eastern archaeology, with particular attention to biblical connections. While there will inevitably be some overlapping with articles on 'Mesopotamia', 'Egypt', 'Archaeology of Palestine', etc., I shall try to limit myself as far as practicable to areas in which there is likely to be least repetition. Some repetition of what may be found elsewhere is, of course, desirable, since it is difficult to see things in perspective unless they are treated by different scholars from varying points of view. Our subject is comprehensive in so far as it 'includes both material remains and inscriptions'. Nothing can eliminate the stubborn fact that the Bible is a written document and will thus be illuminated most directly by written sources, especially when they belong to the same period and are in a closely related dialect. This is the reason why the Ugaritic texts have thrown more light on the text of the Bible than all the non-epigraphic finds yet made in Palestine. On the other hand the latter are indispensable for the reconstruction of Hebrew and Israelite history.

b Archaeological method has improved enormously since the surface explorations of the early 19th cent. by such men as Richard Lepsius, J. L. Burckhardt and Edward Robinson, C. J. Rich and Robert Kerr Porter. What these men did for historical geography and topography, for the recording of surface monuments and inscriptions, can never be forgotten; all their successors stood on their shoulders and those who forgot their practice of complete and accurate recording after assimilating the accumulated knowledge of past ages were mostly doomed to oblivion, and their supposed discoveries were generally discarded. The earliest excavators were not in the same class as the giants we have mentioned among surface explorers. The first serious diggers, such as Botta and Layard, Mariette and de Saulcy, had no idea of systematic recording and were looking mostly for treasure and museum objects, though the first two did try to plan important buildings and draw the most interesting monuments. Only the geologist, W. K. Loftus, showed a real grasp of archaeological methodology, though he worked for too short a time and in too many different places to contribute much of tangible nature. Just when there should have been most rapid progress in turning archaeology into a science, came the Crimean War (1854–6), after which Near Eastern archaeology remained virtually stagnant for decades.

c **Modern scientific archaeology** owes most to Flinders Petrie, the greatest single excavating genius of modern times. In 1890 he put his idea that ordinary **pottery** could become a most valuable means of dating, to a test in the Palestine mound of Tell el-Ḥesī. Twenty years before (1870), Heinrich Schliemann had excavated the mound of Troy, but he was to die in the same year that Petrie began stratigraphical work in Palestine, without having convinced more than a small minority of scholars. For that matter, Petrie's
discovery of the pottery clue failed to convince a single 45
expert in Palestinology, and it was a third of a century before he was fully vindicated. Even when Petrie discovered the equally important principle of sequence dating (published in 1901), it was a full quarter of a century before the German Egyptologists (who had made such brilliant contributions to Egyptian philology) began to accept it. These are only a few examples of the principle that revolutionary discoveries require decades for general acceptance, unless they are in a field where they can easily be tested by *both* experiment and mathematical reasoning.

d After Petrie came the period in which the great German historical architects, Dörpfeld and Koldewey, developed a brilliant new method of architectural excavation, best illustrated by the excavations of the Deutsche Orient-Gesellschaft. They were rapidly followed by two American archaeologists, G. A. Reisner and C. S. Fisher, who combined all previous techniques and rationalised excavation by employing the latest methods of accurate recording and card indexing. With the aid of adequate funds they and their imitators were able to turn archaeology into a true science and to publish their excavations in a way which made them really serviceable to coming generations. This new method was most fully developed in the work of the Oriental Institute of Chicago, founded by J. H. Breasted, who employed archaeologists of many backgrounds and many nations in his vast undertakings. To be sure, it sometimes happened, as at Megiddo, that the human equation was disregarded, and men without sufficient knowledge and experience were expected to turn out first-class results merely because of the superior material organisation of the project. We are now discovering that nothing can replace adequate training or exceptional native talent, especially when both are combined.

e This golden age of archaeology in the Near East came to an end at the outbreak of the Second World War. Since then it has proved impossible to bring it back. The nations of the Near East are now independent, and exacerbated nationalism is not favourable to any foreign undertakings. Moreover the absorption of national income by the exigencies of the 'Cold War' makes it virtually impossible to obtain either government or private grants in sufficient quantities to continue excavation along the old lines. Again we turn to new methods—this time to the methods introduced by Sir Mortimer Wheeler and best represented in the Near East by Kathleen Kenyon. These scholars have rehabilitated the old **trenching method**, which fell into disfavour as a result of the work of Reisner and Fisher, and have made it a powerful new tool of the excavator. By sinking deep trenches or leaving banks of earth standing, followed by careful analysis of all significant data visible on their vertical faces, they are able to determine stratification more minutely than was feasible with previous methods. In a way this is a case of getting along as well as possible with inferior means, but since it has resulted in notable refinement of technique, the loss

45e has been turned into gain. To be sure, when the trenching method is exalted into a major goal, as is sometimes done by imitators, there is serious loss of perspective, but the Wheeler-Kenyon refinements are here to stay and will contribute more and more to making archaeology an exact science.

f Another important development of the past quarter-century is the expansion and improvement of **surface exploration**. Here Nelson Glueck leads the way, with his long-continued archaeological explorations in Transjordan and the Negeb of Israel, where he has located and studied some 2,000 sites, mostly unknown before his work. These regions are peculiarly adapted to this form of research, since few sites show any depth of occupation, most of them having a tendency to spread out over the surface and to shift from one point in the vicinity to another. Test soundings have shown that one can almost always tell from surface finds what the occupational history of any given site may have been. When we move northward into central and northern Transjordan or into the Jordan Valley surface exploration proves less satisfactory, though it has everywhere yielded notable results. For demographic studies, the work of Glueck has proved invaluable ; we now know vastly more about the fluctuation of population, the nature of soil and water utilisation in different periods, and the exact boundaries between the different states of the Iron Age and later.

46a **2 Archaeological Method : Comparative Study of Excavated Material**—In the previous section we discussed the progress of excavation toward a sound method of recording successive strata, phases, and stages of occupied sites. In this section we turn to the excavated material itself. The commonest of all classes of material is, of course, pottery, which has become inseparable from stratigraphic method in general. Other classes of material include everything from buildings and fortifications to tools and weapons ; artistic objects are particularly interesting because their nature lends itself so well to historical and aesthetic analysis. But whatever the material is, the archaeologist must analyse it primarily from the standpoint of typology, classifying it in respect to form and function. Since all objects made by the hand of man show similar evolutionary tendencies, whether they are ancient flint tools or modern automotive vehicles, it is possible to construct systems of sequence dating for all material artifacts. To be sure, their evolution is not necessarily steady and regular ; it is more often illustrated by a curve showing brief periods of violent change between longer periods of slow development along recognisable lines. As in all sequence dating, we must have absolute or relative chronological pegs in order to show the direction of change. Such absolute pegs consist of datable radio-carbon counts, inscriptions, or stratigraphic context. Our best relative chronology is derived from stratigraphic context, preferably where a given type of object occurs with sufficient frequency to assure its position in a given series of occupied levels.

b The archaeologist needs careful training in identifying objects by their form, as well as wide acquaintance with pertinent material in order to avoid the innumerable mistakes which lurk around every corner. Knowledge of form is not enough ; he must also have broad general familiarity with the history of arts and crafts in antiquity as well as with less developed branches of modern technology, including if possible a good background in cultural anthropology. He must learn what similarities or differences are chronologically significant, and what classes of material are too uniform to be useful in comparative study.

c We shall have to limit ourselves to one general illustration of method in the field of comparative archaeology and art : the current task of reconstructing the history of **South-Arabian civilisation.** The story of the penetration of South Arabia by modern travellers and expeditions, from Carsten Niebuhr (1761–4) to the present, is so romantic and so 46c spattered with the blood of explorers that it has inevitably captured the imagination of the West. The few inscriptions that were copied or brought back to Europe in the early 19th cent. were deciphered on the basis of Ethiopic and Arabic by the two leading Semitists of Germany, W. Gesenius and E. Rödiger, in independent studies which appeared in 1841–2. In the following decades thousands of new inscriptions were found above ground, and many scholars worked on their interpretation—though without much success until N. Rhodokanakis, an Austrian of Greek origin, began working on them systematically just before the beginning of the First World War. There were no excavations at all before the American expedition organised in 1950 by Wendell Phillips, except for two brief but very productive digs in 1928 and 1937–8. The American expedition (until 1953 and since 1957) has yielded a great mass of material of all kinds, which is in process of publication.

d Until well after 1950 scholarly opinion with regard to South-Arabian chronology ranged widely, for lack of adequate published evidence for any clear absolute or even relative chronology. Exponents of the high chronology often went back before the middle of the 2nd millennium B.C. in dating what they believed to be the earliest inscriptions. Advocates of the low chronology began the story about the 8th cent. B.C., and a few were inclined to go even lower. The high chronologists dated the Kingdom of Maʿin (the Minaeans) before Saba (Sheba) ; their opponents made the Minaeans and Sabaeans contemporaries. After the American excavations had demonstrated the impossibility of the high chronology and had shown that the kings of Maʿin were generally later than the kings of Saba, a new tendency arose, to push down dates still more drastically. The Louvain school of South Arabists began in 1954 to reduce the dates approximately established by the American excavations some 250–300 years, crowding all early material into the period between about 525 B.C. and A.D. 250. Since nearly all synchronisms between South-Arabian kings and cuneiform, Egyptian and Graeco-Roman sources can be twisted to fit widely differing dates (owing particularly to the recurrence of royal names again and again in different periods), the most solid basis for dating is provided by comparative archaeology : architecture, masonry, pottery, comparative art, etc. In this way we can show that there was a wave of influence from the Fertile Crescent, transmitted by innumerable trading caravans, in the 10th and 9th cent. B.C., illustrated by pottery and art. Influence from Syria and Mesopotamia during the 8th and 7th cent. is shown by pottery, masonry, and art. Neo-Babylonian and Persian influence during the 7th–4th cent. is illustrated by architecture, masonry, and art. After tentative acceptance of minor elements of Greek origin, such as Attic coinage (in the 4th cent. B.C.), Greek influence increased rapidly in the Hellenistic period, reaching a climax in the last cent. B.C. and the 1st cent. A.D. With the aid of all other evidence, such as stratigraphy (with radiocarbon dating), palaeography, and reassessment of all known synchronisms, it is now possible to fix dates within 50 years or less from about 800 B.C. onwards, and the chronology of occupation can be pushed back with a probable error of not over two or three centuries to the middle of the 2nd millennium B.C., hundreds of years before the earliest yet known inscription.

47a **3 Chronology : Radiocarbon and Other Scientific Aids to Chronology**—In 1948 the American nuclear physicists, Libby and Arnold, first announced their success in dating ancient material of organic origin by determining the proportion of radioactive carbon (carbon isotope with the atomic weight 14) to ordinary carbon (with the atomic weight 12). During life all plants absorb carbon 14 from outer space in a ratio to carbon 12 which is fixed by computing the proportion with the aid of a Geiger counter. Radio-

47a carbon has a 'half-life' of some 5,600 years, which means that half its mass is dissipated by radiation in that time. Thousands of separate counts of organic material (especially carbonised wood) have now been made, either by the solid carbon or the acetylene method of preparing samples for counting. Both the apparatus and the basic data have been refined, until it has become possible to date within a statistical margin of some 5 per cent of error on either side of the computed date. However, the accuracy of different laboratories and of individual counts varies widely, and where the uncertainty attached to any given chronology is too high, it is generally unsafe to reckon with less than a 10 per cent margin of error on both sides. All dates thus have a 'plus-or-minus' sign attached to them.

b There is no object in using the radiocarbon method where it is possible to date more exactly by other means within a range of one or two centuries. As a rule, therefore, radiocarbon datings are computed only where there is wide disagreement among scholars. For instance radiocarbon counts of the age of linen from **Qumrân I** (the first cave where Dead Sea Scrolls were found in 1947), made in laboratories at Chicago and Pittsburgh, fix a range between about 150 B.C. and A.D. 50 for the cloth in which scrolls had once been wrapped. Since other indications suggest a date somewhere between 50 B.C. and A.D. 50 for the harvesting of the flax from which the linen in question was woven, this is very satisfactory, and is well confirmed by a radiocarbon count of a sample of carbonised wood from Qumrân itself made in London.

c The greatest value of radiocarbon has been in fixing late geological time for the past 70,000 years or so. As a result we now know that the last Ice Age began in both hemispheres at least 45,000 years ago, though probably not over 60,000 years before the present. The age of Neanderthal man was at its height in Palestine some 35,000 years ago in the Levalloisian period. The age of Aurignacian cave paintings seems to have been at its height in southern France some 15,000 before the present, and the end of the last Ice Age fell roughly about 9000 B.C. (11,000 years ago). It is also possible to fix the beginning of town-life in pre-pottery Neolithic before 6000 B.C. and to refine our chronology of the pottery Neolithic, Chalcolithic, and Early Bronze until it becomes possible to date cultures within two or three centuries.

d While there are other terrestrial aids to prehistoric and historic chronology, and new ones turn up every few years, none has yet proved effective within our field. Some day it should prove possible to date wood by dendrochronology, following the method of plotting the curves of growth as represented in the annual rings of wood in trees, which has been so successful in Arizona and New Mexico. Since conditions of rainfall in the central plateau of Anatolia (Turkey) resemble what we find in the former region, there is reason to hope for successful application of the method there.

e Ever since classical antiquity, **astronomical computations** have been of the greatest chronological value. From the 16th cent. on, historians have relied more and more on astronomical data, such as solar and lunar eclipses and planetary phenomena, in order to fix dates. Fortunately many references to celestial events have been found in cuneiform and Egyptian records. For instance, a reference to a solar eclipse in an Assyrian list of annual events has enabled scholars to fix the exact dates of the annual eponyms (officials after whom years were dated) from the late 10th to the late 7th cent. B.C. The famous Venus observations from the reign of Ammiṣaduqa (the fourth successor of Ḫammurapi) are held by several leading authorities on astronomical chronology to provide evidence which some day will enable us to date every year in the I Dynasty of Babylon (low chronology, about 1830–1530) exactly. In Egypt we can now fix many reigns astronomically: e.g. Take-
lothis II became king in 837/6 B.C., Rameses II in **47**
1290, Thuthmosis III in 1490. Cross-dating by the Sothic Cycle (which lasted 1,460 years, the time required for a fixed astronomical event to recur in the Egyptian civil calendar, which was a quarter of a day short each year of the Julian calendar) fixes the accession of Amenophis I, second king of the XVIII Dynasty, in 1545 B.C. and of the founder of the XII Dynasty in 1991 B.C. Dead reckoning on the basis of lists, co-regencies, etc. enables many other dates to be established.

4 Decipherment and Interpretation of New **f**
Scripts and Tongues—One of the most engrossing subjects in our field is the recovery of forgotten scripts and languages. This task, which really began (after many unsuccessful attempts to solve the riddle of different scripts) in 1802 with the partial decipherment of the **Rosetta Stone**, has continued ever since, as unknown scripts have come to light in rapid succession. We now have an impressive list of successes, which almost seems to justify the optimist who declared a century ago, 'If an inscription in unknown characters were to fall from the moon, we should be able to read it.' Among them are Egyptian hieroglyphic, hieratic and demotic; Old Persian cuneiform; Babylonian cuneiform in many different phases from pictographs to cursive characters; Phoenician, South Arabian and many other Semitic alphabets; Lycian and other Anatolian alphabets; Hittite hieroglyphs, Mycenaean Linear B. Many other scripts remain only partially read or wholly enigmatic. For several decades it seemed that two new scripts were discovered for every one which was successfully read.

While many of these scripts were used only to **g**
write their own national languages, others served for different tongues. This was notably true of Babylonian cuneiform, which was employed for over a dozen distinct languages and for more than twice as many dialects. It was also true of the Phoenician and Greek alphabets, as well as of the Aegean linear script underlying Mycenaean B. Often in such cases it proves harder to interpret a new language in a known script than it does to read a new script.

The task of decipherment requires many different **h**
skills: the successful pioneer may be a specialist in decoding ciphers or merely an ingenious soul who delights in attacking riddles; he may be a specialist in linguistics or philology—rarely both. **Ugaritic** was fortunate in being first deciphered by two scholars —E. Dhorme and H. Bauer—who were both cipher experts and eminent Semitists. Old Persian and Cypriote were deciphered by two scholars who did not even know the languages involved (Avestan and Greek respectively). Curiously enough, only the earliest and the most recent decipherments were carried out by men who had devoted many years to patient preparation by learning everything which seemed to show promise of being useful: Champollion's solution of the Egyptian riddle in 1822 and Ventris's decoding of Mycenaean Linear B in 1953. A triumph of patient work on the part of many scholars was the partial interpretation of **hieroglyphic Hittite** by P. Meriggi, I. Gelb, B. Hrozný, and H. Th. Bossert after 1928; it proved to be substantially correct when Bossert discovered the Hittite-Phoenician bilinguals of Karatepe in the late 40s.

Nor should we forget that most efforts at decipher- **i**
ment turn out to be fallacious. The most famous is the grandiose structure of Athanasius Kircher in the 17th cent., not a single stone of which was left standing by Champollion. A successful decipherer may become over-confident, as in the case of Hrozný, who failed completely with Cretan Linear B and the Indus Valley script after his initial successes with cuneiform and (partially) with hieroglyphic Hittite. A. H. Sayce contributed some valuable insights to the solution of the problems of Urartian (Vannic) and hieroglyphic Hittite, but seems to have failed com-

47i pletely in trying to read Carian. Dhorme has certainly failed to decipher the Byblian syllabic script, though he was successful in his initial efforts to read Ugaritic.

j The story of the decipherment of **Proto-Sinaitic** is instructive. First discovered by Flinders Petrie in 1905, it was brilliantly deciphered in part by Alan Gardiner in 1915. Then it stopped because of the lack of material—which did not prevent ingenious scholars like H. Grimme from trying their hands at the problem, with fantastic results. There followed a period of enlarging the available material, in which R. Butin took the leading part. In 1935 the present writer ventured into the task of decipherment, which failed because he then attempted to make the language of the texts conform to the known phenomena of North-west Semitic in the Middle Bronze Age, to which Gardiner had attributed them. Thirteen years later the writer visited Sinai and soon recognised that Petrie's date about 1500 B.C. was the only possible one. Then results came fast—partly utilising the writer's previous finds, published and unpublished. The phonetic values of 19 letters were established, and it became clear that this alphabet had 26 or 27 letters, not merely 22, as in the Iron Age. And yet some of the interpretations failed to convince, and there was not enough material to make it possible to check words and phrases adequately against each other. Toward the end of 1957 the writer tried again, heartened by Virolleaud's discovery that there had been 27 different letters, including the Hebrew 22 in the same order, in the linear alphabet which served as a prototype for the invention of Ugaritic before 1400 B.C. Meanwhile new inscriptions had been found in Palestine and Syria, filling in gaps between the Proto-Sinaitic phase of our ancestral alphabet and the well-known script of the 10th cent. B.C. It now became possible to identify at least three more letters and to correct and extend the earlier interpretation. The phonetic structure, grammar, and vocabulary of the dialect in question turn out to be good South Canaanite of the late Bronze Age, as should have been expected *a priori*.

k The task of interpreting successfully deciphered scripts requires the collaboration of a great many scholars over a long period. It demands not only clever guessing of meanings, but infinite patience, following rigorously precise and logical methods of work. Successful reconstruction of the complex grammar and lexicography of a previously unknown tongue must follow the principles of scientific method which have been found to operate in other areas: exact recording of phenomena, systematic induction, careful deduction, prudent application of analogy, concomitant variation, statistical analysis, etc. Every conjecture and each intuition must be tested in new contexts and under new conditions, in order to subject them to the same processes of verification that are employed in the experimental sciences. The history of philological research in the field of Assyriology is particularly instructive, since Akkadian grammar and lexicography are now far advanced in their development, outstripping progress in any other of the new languages of antiquity which have been recovered. All other ancient Eastern languages, including biblical Hebrew, lag behind Akkadian, and some of the newly deciphered texts, such as the Ugaritic mythological epics, are far from being completely understood.

48a **5 Pre-Patriarchal Times**—Perhaps the most remarkable single product of archaeological research is the steadily increasing respect which we must feel for the cultural achievements of early man in the Fertile Crescent and neighbouring areas. Thanks to the work of Kathleen Kenyon at Jericho we know that urban culture goes back at least to the early centuries of the 7th millennium B.C. and perhaps even farther. We also begin to appreciate the tremendous expansion of civilisation in the Near and Middle East between the 5th and the 2nd millennium. Men were just as inventive as they are today, even if they were not able to stand on the shoulders of scientists and technicians carrying on the Hellenic tradition, as we 48a
are. The inventors of the Bronze Age developed scores of thousands of technical processes in the arts and crafts, involving new uses of old materials and the discovery of new materials; they devised innumerable tools, gadgets, and contrivances. Many of their ideas gave rise to what are now lost arts, especially in metallurgy. While these lost arts would perhaps be rarely of more than casual interest today, their existence at one time should caution us against a totally misleading pride of achievement.

During the Neolithic and Chalcolithic periods, men b
moved around much more freely than later, so these early cultures actually show greater adaptability and mobility than we find in many later ages. At the beginning of the 3rd millennium there was constant intercourse between the Euphrates and Nile Valleys, thanks to which Egypt was flooded with Mesopotamian cultural elements just before the beginning of the I Dynasty. At that time we find great cities, such as Byblos and Beth-yerah, in Syria and Palestine; from them have come objects vividly illustrating the diffusion of culture from the great alluvial centres. Except in times of nomadic irruption, Palestine and Syria were no more 'primitive' during the 4th and 3rd millennia than were Egypt and Babylonia, though we may freely admit that there was much less concentration of wealth and power in the former countries.

Writing had already reached the cursive stage in c
both Egypt and Mesopotamia by about 3000 B.C.; we find clay tablets covered with rapidly impressed wedges in Babylonia well before the end of the 4th millennium, and in Egypt we find cursive hieroglyphs written with ink as early as the 29th cent. B.C. About the same time a still mysterious pictographic script was used at Byblos. Literature also arose about the same time, and Egyptian tradition attributes the composition of some books to the Thinite period (*c.* 29th–27th cent.). The Pyramid Texts, written in a very archaic language, were copied on the walls of pyramids in the 23rd cent. B.C., but part of their contents certainly goes back into predynastic times, not later than about 3000 B.C. The Sumerian heroic age, to events and personalities of which much Sumerian epic literature is devoted, must be dated by archaeological evidence to the general period between 3200 and 2800 B.C., though the language in which these texts were copied between *c.* 1900 and 1650 B.C. (low chronology) reflects a later stage of Sumerian. The oldest Semitic inscriptions hitherto known come from **Mari** on the Middle Euphrates and date from the middle of the 3rd millennium. During the 24th–22nd cent. arose the Empire of Akkad, founded by Sargon I and raised to its acme by his grandson, Naram-Sin. Nearly all south-western Asia was subject to these mighty rulers, whose extraordinarily developed art and architecture are gradually coming to light. Thousands of administrative documents, many of them in Semitic Akkadian, show a remarkable level of culture. To this period Assyriologists now attribute the rise of the beautiful poetic literature which survived in later adaptations (the so-called hymnal-epic style) into the 16th cent. B.C., after which it seems to have perished for ever.

6 The Age of the Patriarchs in the Light of d
Archaeology—For convenience we designate the first half of the 2nd millennium as the Patriarchal Age. While we do not know exactly how to date a single episode in Gen. 12–50, there are a few external pegs. The personal names of this phase of Hebrew history nearly all belong specifically to the Middle Bronze Age, after which they do not appear until revived as archaistic appellations by the Jews of the Hellenistic period. The argument from generations is quite fallacious, since the first few generations reflect the names of tribal and clan founders and the following generations belong to the immediate background of the person whose genealogy is being traced, seldom going back of the latter's grandfather. The intervening

48d generations tended to be telescoped by tradition and generally disappeared, just as we find to have happened often among the Arabs and more primitive peoples as far as Rhodesia.

e Without entering into a discussion of the history of settlement in Palestine or stating the archaeological evidence with regard to the Palestinian towns which figure in Genesis, which does not properly belong in this chapter, we may point out some external connections. It is now reasonably certain that Ur 'in the land of the Chaldees' (as the original text seems to have read) sank into obscurity for several centuries after its total destruction by the Elamites about 1950 B.C. (low chronology). The tradition that the Terachids came to Harran in the north from Ur must, accordingly, be based on an event not later than this date (since the older total rejection of the historicity of these early traditions has now been discredited). Harran itself was a flourishing city in the 19th and 18th cent. B.C. (low chronology), as we know from the tablets of Kanish in Cappadocia and Mari on the Euphrates. For a long time the writer cherished the expectation that it might be possible to date the life of Abraham approximately by fixing the time of the four invading kings mentioned in Gen. 14. This hope has hitherto proved illusory, but the antiquity of the factual and linguistic data preserved in the chapter becomes clearer every year. All the *names* of foreign kings have been identified with probability or certainty. Certain is the name of Tidal (Heb. *Tidh'al*), which appears in Ugarit as *TDGHL* = Hittite *Tudkhaliya* and *Tudkhul'a* in the Spartoli texts; *GH* fell together with *'ayin* in Hebrew and Canaanite about the end of the Bronze Age. This name is common in the Cappadocian texts of the 19th cent. B.C. and appears frequently among the names of Hittite kings and nobles in later centuries. Certain is also the first element of the name of Chedor-laomer, which has long been recognised as *kudur* ('servant' in Elamite), appearing frequently as the first element in Elamite royal names from at least the 17th cent. B.C. down to the 7th. Unfortunately the second element remains uncertain, though a number of scholars consider it as a phonetic and graphic deformation of the second element in the name of the great Elamite conqueror Kudur-Nakhkhundi I (dated in much later times back to the early 23rd cent., but probably several centuries later). 'Arioch' is doubtless *Arriyuk*, which appears as the name of a vassal of Mari about 1700 B.C.; his land, Ellasar, is perhaps Ilanzura in northern Mesopotamia, which is phonetically quite satisfactory, since Hebrew *sāmekh* always reflects cuneiform *z* in Bronze Age tablets. 'Amraphel' almost certainly should be read with *D* instead of *R* (like Greek *Thargal* for Hebrew *Tidh'al*); it is clearly 'Amorite' *Amud-pi-El*, 'Enduring Is the Word of El' (formerly read *Amut-pi-el*, identified with *Amraphel* by F. Böhl), which occurs as a royal name in the Mari tablets about 1700 B.C. Unfortunately we do not know what is meant by 'Shinar' in this chapter; it appears as the name of an important Mesopotamian country in cuneiform and Egyptian documents of the 15th–13th cent. B.C., and was later employed in Hebrew to designate the land of Babylonia. In the writer's opinion the kings of Gen. 14 flourished in the 17th cent. B.C., but whether they are figures in early Hebrew heroic saga which were arbitrarily associated or were really allies in an expedition against the contemporary rulers of Egypt we cannot yet say. Now that we have cuneiform inscriptions from Anatolia and Syria covering every century from *c.* 1900 to *c.* 1200 B.C., a solution is by no means impossible; the latest discoveries throw particular light on the hitherto obscure 17th and 16th cent. B.C.

f As discoveries continue to accumulate, it becomes more and more certain that there is much unmotivated material in the Patriarchal stories which can readily be explained on the basis of parallels from northern Mesopotamia (**Nuzu**), Cappadocia (both Old Assyrian texts from the 19th–18th cent. and later Hittite documents), Syria (Mari, Alalakh, and Ugarit, 18th– **48f**
13th cent. B.C.), and elsewhere. E. A. Speiser and C. H. Gordon have pointed out numerous parallels in customary law between the Horite (Hurrian) culture of northern Mesopotamia and Genesis; Manfred Lehmann has produced a close Hittite parallel to the Machpelah transaction. (Incidentally, we now know that the name 'Hittite' was used in Syria long before the foundation of the Old Hittite Empire by Labarnas, so the difficulty with regard to Hittites at Hebron in the time of Abraham has vanished.) The writer is collecting very striking new material for the earliest stage of oral tradition in the Patriarchal narratives; this line of investigation was inaugurated by the late Albrecht Alt, but can now be carried much farther, showing that there is a solid core of original tradition preserved in the specifically religious episodes and allusions in Gen. 12–50.

7 Light from Ugarit on the Bible—The long- **49a**
continued excavation of Ugarit, modern Râs Shamra, on the North-Syrian coast opposite Cyprus, by C. F. A. Schaeffer since 1929 has yielded several thousand tablets and fragments in Babylonian and Canaanite alphabetic cuneiform (Ugaritic), besides a few in Hittite, Horite (Hurrian), Cypriote, etc. As we have seen above, the script and language were successfully deciphered in 1931, since when much of the material has been published by C. Virolleaud, J. Nougayrol, and others. This entire material dates from between *c.* 1400 and 1200 B.C., and since the Ugaritic dialect of Canaanite differed less from contemporary South Canaanite and the most archaic biblical Hebrew than Low German from High German or Provençal from French, it is not surprising that biblical studies are being revolutionised by it. We find, for example, that the earliest biblical poems, such as the Song of Deborah, and other poems which are traditionally early (though often relegated to a very late period by modern scholarship) are closest stylistically and grammatically to Ugaritic. In view of our ignorance of Hebrew poetic vocabulary, which has led in recent decades to innumerable erroneous emendations, the sudden afflux of over 1,500 new words, practically all well attested in form even when the meaning is not known, is bound to have great significance. It must be remembered that the known biblical Hebrew vocabulary cannot represent over a fifth of the total stock of North-west Semitic words used between 1400 and 400 B.C.

The outstanding characteristic of Hebrew poetic **b**
style is **parallelism**. So far nearly a hundred examples of pairs of words in parallelism have been found to be common to biblical Hebrew and Ugaritic. Moreover, there are long lists of stylistic patterns of repetitive parallelism which are characteristic of both Ugaritic and archaic Hebrew verse (sometimes preserved only in otherwise late compositions of archaising tendency). The best known follows the pattern *abc:abd*, in which each letter stands for a word or pair of short words, the first two of which are repeated in the second colon (poetic unit, sometimes called hemistich or stich). This type may be expanded to a tricolon like the following (Ps. 92:9):

> For see, thine enemies, O Yahweh,
> For see, thine enemies shall perish,
> All doers of evil shall be scattered!

In the Baal Epic of Ugarit we find almost identically the same tricolon:

> See, thine enemies, O Baal,
> See, thine enemies shalt thou crush,
> See, thou shalt smite thy foes!

It will be noted that the later Hebrew form of this ancient tricolon has eliminated any direct allusion to the battles between the lord of the world and the primordial monsters of chaos.

There are many other examples of this particular **c**

49e pattern, as well as of similar patterns. A careful survey of any long Hebrew poem of relatively early date yields scores of patterns of style and syntax, word arrangement, and vocabulary which are also found in Ugaritic. Through systematic analysis of this rich material it is becoming possible to write a chronological history of Hebrew literature, never hitherto possible. In the process nearly all 'accepted' conclusions of critical scholarship are being revised or even completely transformed. For one thing, it is no longer possible to accept a Hellenistic date of any of the biblical Psalms. In scores of passages whose Hellenistic date was formerly taken for granted, difficulties have been cleared up by the identification of obscure words with Ugaritic homonyms. In virtually every case the LXX translators were just as ignorant of the true meaning as were the Massoretes who vocalised the Bible in the 8th–9th cent. A.D. Yet they translated the Hebrew Psalter in the 2nd cent. B.C., at or just after the time in which these Psalms are supposed to have been composed! Needless to say, the religious poems of the Essenes, as now known from the Dead Sea Scrolls, though composed between *c.* 150 and 50 B.C., are not in the least like the Psalter in structure or metre, but show only incidental parallelism and consist mainly of mosaics put together from innumerable biblical reminiscences from all parts of the Hebrew Bible. In the Psalter, wherever we have hymns of undoubted post-exilic date, as in the case of the 'Psalms of Degrees', we find material with prevailingly later extra-biblical analogies and without any trace of the ancient patterns. Even where these Psalms indulge in extensive repetition of words and phrases, the patterns are totally different from the archaic examples with close parallels in Ugaritic.

d **8 Moses and the Exodus**—Both from the standpoint of archaeology and of 'traditio-history' there can be no doubt about the historicity of the sojourn of the Hebrew precursors of Israel in Egypt. We shall not dwell on the Hyksos period and the Egyptian background of the story of Joseph, which belong elsewhere in the present volume. The names found in Exodus and Numbers are often attested in Egyptian sources, from the list of Semitic slave names included in an Egyptian document dating about 1740 B.C. (published in 1954) down into the 13th cent. B.C. Among the most interesting cases is the name of Shiphrah, one of the midwives mentioned in Exod. 1:15, which occurs in the slave list just mentioned as a female name; her companion Puah bears a name familiar as that of the sister of Aqhat (cf. the name of Levi's son Qahat, 'Kohath') in Ugaritic mythology. While the midwives were unimportant persons, the mere fact that they were remembered by Israelite tradition should have prevented a distinguished scholar from writing a few years ago that their names were 'probably artificial'. Historically more significant is the fact that many Semites from Egypt and Canaan were reduced to slavery by the Egyptians after the expulsion of the Hyksos about 1550 B.C. Many names of such slaves from the 16th and 15th cent. B.C. are preserved in Egyptian inscriptions, and a great many more remain unpublished. The Proto-Sinaitic inscriptions (see §47*j*, above) prove that some of these slaves, who were put to forced labour in the turquoise mines, worshipped Egyptian deities (Hathor, Ptah, Osiris, etc.) and set up monuments to them. Their language, however, was Canaanite, and most of the appellations of deity (including probably El-olam and Elyon, both well known from Genesis) are closely related to the Patriarchal Hebrew type. Shaddai, the 'Mountain God', said in Exod. 6:3 to have been the name of the chief Hebrew deity in the Patriarchal Age, is attested for the period of the Exodus by an Egyptian text mentioning a *Sade-ammi* (13th cent. B.C.), which was the South-Canaanite pronunciation at that time of the name appearing in Numbers in the transposed form Ammi-shaddai, belonging to one of the princes of Israel at the time of the Exodus.

While points like these, which may easily be multiplied, are very interesting, they do not begin to be as 49e significant as the indirect evidence from archaeological sources bearing on the Mosaic period. Whatever we may think about the validity of prose tradition, it is generally agreed that poetic tradition tends to carry us much farther back than prose, since it was fixed in its form from the beginning, and only minor changes in wording may be expected. As emphasised above, the discovery of the lost Canaanite (Ugaritic) mythological epics carries our knowledge of North-west-Semitic poetic style and imagery back to before the 14th cent. B.C. It now becomes certain that the **Song of Miriam** (Exod. 15), like the Song of Deborah (Jg. 5), reflects contemporary Canaanite verse forms (especially repetitive patterns), grammar, and vocabulary, and cannot be dated later than the time of the Judges. For instance, the supposed evidence for a date after the building of the Temple contained in v. 17 vanishes when we compare 'the mountain of Thine inheritance' with Baal's 'mountain of mine inheritance' (in which the word for 'inheritance' is the same). Since the burden of proof is logically on those who would date the Song of Miriam late, it is they who must disprove our contentions, not we who must disprove theirs.

If the Song of Miriam is an early and authentic f witness to the crossing of the Sea of Reeds by Israel, we may turn to the traditional itinerary in Exod. 12:37 and 14:2ff., 15:22, with renewed confidence. It is now certain that Rameses was either at Tanis or in its immediate vicinity, that Succoth was at Heroopolis, modern Tell el-Maskhûṭah, and that Baal-zephon was at Daphne (Tahpanhes) or near it. In those days there was no Pelusiac branch of the Nile, as in the Iron Age, and the only body of water that had to be crossed was the Papyrus Marsh, called 'Reed Sea' in Hebrew (the words for 'reed' and 'papyrus' are identical, the Hebrew being a loan from the Egyptian, and Heb. *yam* means 'marsh' and 'lake' as well as 'sea'). The former view that the Red Sea itself was crossed south of the Bitter Lakes and far to the north of its present north end at Suez, was disproved once for all by the results of the American expedition in Sinai (1947–8), where we were able to show that the level of the Gulf of Suez has not fallen over 15 ft. with reference to the shore since the 15th cent. B.C.; even such a fall (and no fall at all can be demonstrated) would not begin to be enough to extend the northern end of the Gulf appreciably at the time of the Exodus. Nelson Glueck has proved the same to be true of the northern end of the Gulf of 'Aqaba, also held by such scholars as H. Guthe to have extended far to the north of its present shore-line in biblical times. It is, therefore, certain that the traditional **route of the Exodus** began in the vicinity of Tanis, continued in a south-east direction into the Wâdi Ṭumilât, was deflected northward by the Egyptian frontier fortifications until it reached the sea near later Daphne, crossed the marshes south-east of the latter and proceeded south on the eastern side of the Wall of the Prince (Heb. *Shûr*) until it reached the region of Mt Sinai proper. It must again be emphasised that Hebrew 'Mount Sinai' is the name of the entire granite massif, just as Seir, Lebanon, Judah, Ephraim, etc. are names of ranges or massifs, not of single peaks. On the other hand, Horeb may be the name of a single peak.

For lack of space we cannot discuss the role of g Moses in the religious and institutional history of Israel. In the writer's present opinion, the role of Moses was more important than is indicated in any of his past publications, and Israelite tradition is substantially correct in its total picture, though details may have been refracted and rearranged. Our present knowledge of North-west-Semitic vocalisation in the Late Bronze Age makes it certain, in the writer's opinion, that *Yahweh* is a causative formation from the verb *HWY*, 'to be, become, come into being'; it

49g may be paraphrased by ' Creator '. B. Balscheit and G. von Rad have stressed the ubiquity of the concept of ' Allkausalität ' in Yahwism from the earliest times (cf. v. Rad, *Theologie des AT*, i (1957), 61). It has been alleged that the concept of ' causing to come into existence, bringing into being ' was too abstract for the time of Moses, but in Egypt we find the corresponding Egyptian causative with the same meaning in use over and over again in the Pyramid Texts, written down not later than the 23rd cent. B.C., and going back to a much older oral tradition. In Babylonia we can trace the theological use of the corresponding Akkadian causative verb back at least to the 18th cent. B.C.

50a **9 Light from Abroad on Early Israel: Joshua to Solomon**—In the nature of the case we learn little directly about the Conquest of Canaan and the Judges of Israel from extra-Palestinian archaeological sources. It is now, however, certain from the excavations at such sites as Lachish, Tell Beit Mirsim (probably Kiriath-sepher), Bethel, and especially Hazor (since 1955), which are dated primarily by Egyptian inscriptions and pottery imported from abroad, that **the main phase of the Conquest is to be fixed about the fourth quarter of the 13th cent. B.C.** The reconquest of the coastal region and of Syria by Rameses III was probably without much effect on the Israelites, who were only beginning to settle down and who therefore offered little attraction to Egyptian tribute collectors. In any case, the Egyptian invasion was completely overshadowed by the irruption of the Sea Peoples (cf. Num. 24:24), including especially the **Philistines**. Thanks to recent discoveries in Cyprus (Sinda and Enkomi) it is possible to show that the Philistines settled there between *c.* 1225 and 1175 B.C., shortly before their occupation of the coast of Southern Palestine. It is also possible to show, with the aid of Greek scholia and personal names preserved in the Wen-amon Report (*c.* 1060 B.C.) and elsewhere, that they came from the Aegean region, where they were already called *Pelast-* (from the better attested *Pelasg-*). There can be little doubt that they will eventually emerge from obscurity, thanks to the decipherment of Mycenaean Linear B and the partial interpretation of Minoan Linear A. We also know, as a result of the comparative studies of Mrs Dothan, that the Philistines were employed as Egyptian garrison troops in Canaan, where their tribes were distinguished by the same special insignia illustrated in the reliefs of Medinet Habu.

b In evaluating the traditions from the period of the Judges, it must be remembered that alphabetic writing was already in regular use during this period (cf. Jg. 8:14, where the Hebrew text has ' he wrote for them '), as we know from many finds of inscribed objects in different parts of Palestine (e.g. the inscribed arrow-heads from near Bethlehem, which were used in belomancy (as shown by S. Iwry), and the Beth-shemesh ostracon. We cannot, therefore, be surprised to find oral and written tradition both playing a role at this time.

c An account of archaeological light on the reigns of Saul and David lies outside our horizon in this chapter, since it comes almost entirely from excavations in Palestine such as the clearance of what was left of Saul's citadel at Gibeah and the recovery of fortifications which cannot well be attributed to anyone but David. On the other hand, there has been a great deal of archaeological light from outside Palestine on the age of Solomon. It is true that both David and Solomon flourished at a time when Egyptian and Assyrian inscriptions are virtually mute. It is also true that no less an authority than the late Henri Frankfort declared repeatedly that there was no architecture or art (presumably of sufficient quality to merit the name) in Syria (including Phoenicia and Palestine), Anatolia, or western Mesopotamia between *c.* 1200 and *c.* 850. If he were right, the Temple of Solomon would be a myth and the description of Solomon's building enterprises, as found in 1 Kg. and 2 Chr., would be strictly legendary. Other scholars 50e
have denied the authenticity of the story of the visit of the **Queen of Sheba** to Solomon. Against all of these unwarranted rejections of Israelite written records and oral traditions the writer has, in a series of studies since 1955, opposed the direct evidence of archaeological monuments and remains. It can be shown that the 10th cent. was a period of rapid advance among Phoenicians, Aramaeans and Hittites of North Syria, when impressive buildings and monumental art were both being created. It can also be shown that the Tyrians were already exploring the recesses of the Mediterranean and establishing trading-posts as far as Sardinia (called ' Tarshish ' in a Phoenician inscription from the 9th cent. which was found long ago at Nora). It can be proved that Sheba (Saba) was already an established state by 800 B.C. and had probably been in existence for some time. Settlement in cities can be traced back archaeologically into the late 2nd millennium and the use of South-Arabic writing goes back at least to the 10th cent. (for South-Arabian culture, see §46*c*). So far from being a fiction of the 6th cent. B.C., concocted by scribes who were already under Greek influence, as maintained by some recent writers, the Temple of Solomon followed a well-known plan, already illustrated by a sanctuary of the 13th cent. found at Hazor in 1957 and with a perfect pre-Hellenic parallel in a chapel of the 9th cent. B.C. which was discovered in 1938 in the lower valley of the Orontes in Syria.

10 Light on the Age of the Prophets—Since d
archaeological data for the Divided Monarchy are derived mostly from excavations in Palestine and from cuneiform sources, themselves being enlarged all the time as new texts from the 9th–6th cent. are published, we refer elsewhere in this volume for details. Here we shall limit ourselves in the main to general observations. For one thing, the time has passed when we can try to solve any chronological or historical question in the period between *c.* 922 and 587 B.C. without drawing on extra-biblical material. Our chronology is established by confronting biblical data with evidence from Assyria, Babylonia, Tyre, and Egypt, with more and more interconnections to consolidate the picture. The names of most of the Israelite kings of this period are found either in cuneiform or in Palestinian inscriptions (especially seals), or in both.

Recent archaeological discoveries are illuminating e
the unique Israelite institution of the ***nᵉbhî'îm* (prophets**). We now know a great deal more about the ancient Oriental background of this system, thanks especially to the Mari tablets from the 18th cent. B.C. Here the diviners or seers (Akkad. *barû*, Heb. *rō'eh*, *ḥōzeh*) and the ecstatic prophets both appear over and over again. While their background is Sumero-Babylonian, they seem to have been much less elaborately trained than in Babylonia and to have been more like the seers of the earliest Hebrew tradition. Since the verbal stem from which the Hebrew word *nābhî'* is derived appears at Mari in North-west-Semitic personal names with the meaning ' to call ' just as in Akkadian, we may now consider the interpretation of the basic meaning of the word as ' one who is called, receives a vocation ', first proposed by H. Torczyner, as virtually certain.

Archaeology is beginning to yield data which will f
eventually clear up many obscurities in the Prophetic literature of Israel. Thanks to the Dead Sea Scroll discoveries, we are beginning to understand difficult passages in the Book of Isaiah, for instance. The reference to Tabeel in Isa. 7:1–9 has been cleared up by a letter found by Mallowan at Nimrud (Calah). The treaties between Arpad and Katka in northern Syria, found at Sudjin and Sefireh near Aleppo in numerous large fragments, explain some otherwise enigmatic expressions in the contemporary prophets Amos, Hosea, and Isaiah. The difficult problem of Hezekiah's Assyrian relations is being settled by archaeo-

50f logical data in favour of the so-called 'two-campaign' view. We now have many indications that the Israelite captives from the provinces of Samaria continued to maintain their identity in Mesopotamia and Media long after the exiles of 733 and 721, etc. New evidence comes from the Nimrud finds and the Dead Sea Scrolls, which prove that the Book of Tobit was composed in the Persian period.

51a **11 Exile and Restoration**—By the 30s of this century extremely drastic reconstructions of Israelite history between 600 and 300 B.C. were in vogue, and eminent scholars supported such positions as the following: there is scarcely a single reliable source in the Bible for this period, except possibly a few chapters of the Memoirs of Nehemiah; Jeremiah and Ezekiel are to be rejected as historical sources and may both be spurious; the original material contained in Chronicles (not found in earlier biblical books) is worthless for historical purposes; Ezra may never have existed and his so-called memoirs are, in any case, worthless; there was no general destruction and depopulation of Judah by the Chaldaeans, but life proceeded very much as before; the accounts of the Restoration are misleading from start to finish and must be completely reconstructed; individual points supported by many eminent names include a destruction of Jerusalem between 515 and the middle of the 5th cent. (in 485, according to the latest writer on the subject), and a lowering of the date of Nehemiah to the late 4th cent. B.C.

b The tide has now completely turned, thanks to archaeology. The publication of the ration lists of Nebuchadnezzar's time from Babylon, and of the Lachish Letters and other inscribed material from Palestine have clinched arguments previously drawn from pottery chronology for the general destruction of the towns of Judah in the early 6th cent. B.C., followed by a period of abandonment. Chronological details have been settled by Donald Wiseman's publication of part of the Nebuchadnezzar Chronicle in 1956. A whole series of minor finds has confirmed the general picture of the Exile and Restoration already known from the Bible.

c Most important of all, of course, is the discovery and publication of a great many **papyri from 5th-cent. Egypt**, mostly from the Jewish colony at **Elephantine** on the Nubian border. These documents have established the antiquity of the language of Ezra, which proves to have been the standard official tongue of the Persian Empire (with some revisions in spelling, just as in our modern English editions of the Authorised Version and of Shakespeare), and have conclusively established the date of Nehemiah in the third quarter of the 5th cent. The Elephantine Papyri have also brought to light a multitude of hitherto unknown facts about the life and religion of the Jews at this period. Their content is, in fact, so rich and many-sided that it is quite impossible to give any idea of it here.

d Owing to restrictions of space we shall, accordingly, limit ourselves here to a few scattered finds which throw light on the Restoration. The Elephantine Papyri have demonstrated the correctness of references to a Sanballat, governor of Samaria, in Nehemiah, and have fixed his period. Next to turn up was Tobiah, the Jewish magnate of Ammon, in an inscription from 'Arâq el-Emir in southern Gilead, now dated confidently in the 5th cent. The third enemy of Nehemiah, Geshem or Gashmu the Arab, was found mentioned in a North-Arabic inscription by Winnett and Grimme (both writing in 1937), but some more recent scholars have denied the antiquity of this text. However, in 1956 Isaac Rabinowitz published silver bowls from the frontier between Egypt and Arabia, dated by script and context to the late 5th cent. B.C., which mention Geshem and call his son 'king of Kedar', thus fixing the historical place of the former. And these are only a few of the recent finds which completely revolutionise our knowledge of the Restoration.

Bibliography—W. F. Albright, *From the Stone Age to Christianity* (1940; latest ed. 1957), *Archaeology and the Religion of Israel* (1942; latest ed. 1953), 'The OT and the Archaeology of the Ancient East', in *The OT and Modern Study*, ed. by H. H. Rowley (1951), *Recent Discoveries in Bible Lands* (3rd ed. 1955–6); L. H. Grollenberg, *Atlas of the Bible*, trans. and ed. by J. M. H. Reid and H. H. Rowley (1956); E. G. Kraeling, *Rand McNally Bible Atlas* (1956); A. Parrot, *Cahiers d'Archéologie Biblique* (since 1952; a series of excellent popular monographs, beginning to appear also in English translation); J. B. Pritchard (ed.), *Ancient Near Eastern Texts Relating to the OT* (2nd ed. 1955), *The Ancient Near East in Pictures* (1954); G. E. Wright (with F. V. Filson), *The Westminster Historical Atlas to the Bible* (rev. ed. 1956), *Biblical Archaeology* (1957).

THE LANGUAGES OF THE OLD TESTAMENT

By E. T. RYDER

52a **The languages of the OT** are Hebrew and, to a limited extent, Aramaic, which apart from sporadic instances of an occasional word, two words at Gen. 31:47 and a verse at Jer. 10:11, is confined to Ezr. 4:8–6:18, 7:12–26 and Dan. 2:4*b*–7:28. Owing to their very close affinity and many common features they are rightly understood only in relation to each other and to the other languages of the Semitic family to which they belong. This has become increasingly apparent through continuing textual, epigraphical and comparative philological study, greatly enhanced by excavation in Syria and Palestine since the First World War, so that much hitherto obscure concerning the origin, history and characteristics of the OT languages is being clarified, thereby deepening our insight into the revelation of which they are the vehicle.

b **The Semitic languages** are thus styled from the name Shem, cf. Gen. 10:21–31, a convenient though hardly accurate designation accepted into regular use from the end of the 18th cent. The groups into which they fall are at present perhaps best regarded as three, namely North-west Semitic, comprising Aramaic, Ugaritic, Canaanite, Phoenician (including Punic), Hebrew and Moabite; East Semitic, comprising Assyrian and Babylonian—often classed together as Akkadian; and South Semitic, comprising Arabic, Old South Arabic and Ethiopic. By joining the first two of these, a twofold grouping into North and South Semitic, or by dividing only the first of them, a fourfold grouping into North, West, East and South Semitic has at different times been advocated. As a working hypothesis it has been assumed that these languages stem from a parent language, once current in Arabia and called Proto-Semitic.

c **Characteristics**—Quite distinctive is the way in which the vocabulary is made up preponderantly of roots consisting of three consonants. In Heb., e.g. the root *ŠBR* when pronounced *ŠāḆaR* means 'he broke', *ŠeḆeR*, 'a fracture', or *miŠBāR*, 'a breaker (of the sea)'. Instances of words having two such radicals and continuing study of triliteral verbal stems point, however, to the probability of biconsonantal forms having been original. Even so the triconsonantal root is the basis of the verbal system, and recent study, taking this into account together with the way in which the different verb-forms are derived from the root, suggests a common ancestry for Semitic and Egyptian. The vowels, not of necessity represented in writing, are important in pronunciation where they serve according to definite grammatical patterns to indicate the different parts of speech formed from the root. Especially is this so with the verb, where along with the required vowel change there take place also doubling of the middle consonant, repetition of one or two of the stem consonants and the addition of preformatives to provide various themes. Thus, e.g. the intensive of *ŠāḆar* is *ŠiBBaR*, 'he shattered', the passive and also reflexive, *niŠBaR*, 'it was broken, broke itself', and the causative, *hiŠBîR*, 'he caused to break'. This ability of the Semitic verb to develop themes offsets its deficiency in the matter of tenses, 52
which are not so developed as in other linguistic groups. Akkadian has three tenses—Present, Preterite and Permansive (expressive of *lasting state* or *condition*). In Heb. their number, until recently thought to be limited to Perfect and Imperfect, now appears to have included Universal and Preterite tenses. Aramaic, through employment of the substantive verb (roughly corresponding to the verb 'to be'), has a more extended range, and it is only in modern usage that, e.g. Arabic has a comparatively full series of tenses. The noun has only the masculine and feminine genders, the masculine taking precedence and the feminine serving as well for the neuter. Peculiar to the noun is the expression of the genitive by what is known as the 'construct state' (§53*d*). With the exception of Aramaic and Arabic, connecting particles are few and in keeping with the simplicity of the syntactical structure, which is characterised by the prevalence of the co-ordinate clause.

HEBREW

The word 'Hebrew' appears as the gentilic term 53
'iḇrî in the OT where it is used by Hebrews of themselves as distinct from non-Hebrews, e.g. Gen. 40:15, etc., by non-Hebrews of Hebrews, e.g. Gen. 39:14, 17, etc., or to differentiate between Hebrews and non-Hebrews, e.g. Gen. 14:13, etc. It would seem to be connected with *'ēḇer*, i.e. Eber, cf. Gen. 10:21, 24f., 11:14ff., 1 Chr. 1:18f. as the eponymous ancestor of the Hebrews. From the root *'br*, 'to cross', *'iḇrî* has also been explained, in line with the LXX rendering of it as ὁ περάτης, cf. Gen. 14:13, as referring to the *crossing* of Abraham and his family from the east of the Euphrates or Jordan, cf. Jos. 24:2f., 14f., or more generally as 'one who *crosses* (from place to place)', i.e. 'a wanderer, nomad'. Many would here discern a connection with the Akkadian *ḫabiru* which by inference means 'a plunderer, brigand, nomad', occurring in cuneiform texts of the 2nd millennium B.C. from many parts of the Near East, as also with the term *'apiru*, having like meaning, and found in Egyptian sources from the latter half of the same period. Originally it would appear to have been an appellative derogatorily employed for aliens and freebooters, not in all cases Semites, which in course of time was ethnically applied to the Hebrews of the OT. The expression *lāšôn 'iḇrîṯ*, 'Hebrew language', does not appear before the Mishnah, and the omission from the OT of *'iḇrîṯ* may be accidental in view of the presence at 2 Kg. 18:26 = Isa. 36:11 of *'ᵃrāmîṯ*, 'Aramaic' and *yᵉhûḏîṯ*, 'Jewish (language)'. Early use of the term appears as ἑβραϊστί in the Prologue to Sir., cf. also Rev. 9:11. In Jn 5:2, 19:13, 17, however, it refers to the Aramaic current in Palestine. There is uncertainty as to whether Heb. or Aramaic is intended in Jn 19:20; Rev. 16:16; as also with regard to Ἑβραῒς φωνή at 4 Mac. 12:7, 16:15 and ἡ Ἑβραῒς διάλεκτος in Ac. 21:40, 22:2, 26:14.

53b **Composite nature**—Especially appropriate is the description of Heb. in Isa. 19:18 as *śᵉpaṯ kᵉna'an*, 'the lip (speech, language) of Canaan', i.e. Canaanite. On their entry into Canaan following the Exodus, the Hebrews brought with them an Aramaeo-Arabic dialect and found already there the language which became in large measure that of the OT. The language current in Palestine at the time was mixed, having features of both East and West Semitic. This is evident from the Tell el-Amarna letters, inscribed in cuneiform on clay tablets from *c.*1375 B.C., containing in a debased form of Akkadian the correspondence of vassal princes in Syria and Palestine. In them also occur explanatory glosses, consisting in part of Canaanite words written in cuneiform, which may provide a linguistic deposit of the prototype of Heb. Similarly the Ugaritic texts from Râs Shamra, *c.*14th–13th cent. B.C., indicate the use in Palestine at the period of a language having at some points close affinity with Heb. The Canaanite native to Palestine was probably successively influenced by Amorite and Phoenician. Of the latter, several inscriptions relating to this time have been recovered, being those of a number of kings of Gebal who reigned from the 17th cent. B.C. A Phoenician coastal town of which the Greek name was Byblos, Gebal is noteworthy for the attempts there made to produce an alphabetic script. Heb., therefore, is composite, reflecting as a language the fusion of the cultures discernible in the history and religion of the people who used it. It must accordingly be studied in relation to the linguistic and cultural *milieu* of the ancient Near East. In view, moreover, of the necessarily restricted nature and scope of the Heb. of the OT such comparative study is all the more imperative for its understanding and interpretation.

c **Characteristics**—The alphabet is limited to 22 *consonants*, and as this is less than the 28 of Arabic, some of them as *ḥêṯ* and *'ayin* serve the dual function of representing both the harsher and the softer sounds. In the matter of the sibilants dialectal variation is illustrated at Jg. 12:6. The 6 consonants *bgdkpt* were aspirated or not according to position (represented in this article by *b ḇ*, *g ḡ*, *k ḵ*, etc., but elsewhere in this volume by *b bh*, *g gh*, *k kh*, etc.), thereby adding to the number of sounds denoted in the alphabet. In the absence of letters for the vowels, the consonants *hē*, *wāw*, *yōḏ* were early adopted to indicate respectively the pure long vowels *â*, *û* and *ô*, *î* and *ê*, cf. e.g. their restricted use in the Siloam inscription (*c.*700 B.C.). These vocalic consonants or vowel letters are also known as *matres lectionis*. From the middle of the 2nd cent. B.C. Heb. was no longer generally spoken and its cessation as a living language led in time to difficulty over pronunciation of the biblical text, since the vocalic consonants failed to represent all the variations of sound. In order to safeguard the pronunciation of the consonantal text, authoritatively fixed about the end of the 1st cent. A.D., a vowel system was devised and elaborated by the Mas(s)oretes, Heb. *mas(s)ōrāh*, *mas(s)ōreṯ*, 'tradition'. As the heirs of the Scribes they were thus engaged from *c.* 5th cent. A.D., the Tiberian system superseding those of Babylon and Palestine in the Mas(s)oretic text which became definitive. This vowel system known as pointing, Heb. *niḵḵēḏ*, consists of a series of strokes and dots below or above the appropriate consonants. For greater precision accents were added, which are of importance especially as marks of punctuation and of the tone. The tone by regulating the stress of the vowels determines inflexional change. Owing to the rigid uniformity thus achieved by the Mas(s)oretes, variation of dialect and changes in pronunciation, which assuredly took place in the Heb. language throughout the thousand or so years of its use in biblical times, have been almost entirely effaced. The meagre traces somewhat fortuitously preserved in the OT are in a measure supplemented by early transliterations of parts of it in Gr. and Lat., by Samaritan renderings—though dialectal idiosyncrasy here needs to be taken into account—and by texts having an 53c earlier Palestinian pointing. These have been augmented by the recovery from the Dead Sea caves of MSS belonging to a period anterior to the fixation of the consonantal text.

d The **noun** includes and is the basis of pronouns, adjectives, adverbs and prepositions. As in Ugaritic, Akkadian and Arabic it has 3 cases, each distinguished by a particular ending. Of these the nominative represented by the termination *-û* has barely survived. The idea of *direction* or *place where* appears to be expressed by the accusative ending *-â*, e.g. *ṣāpôn-āh*, 'northward', *maḥᵃnayim-āh*, 'in Maḥanaim'. This afformative is known as *hē locale* because of the locative use of the *hē* which represents the vowel *â* in Heb. Comparison with Ugaritic, however, suggests that *hē locale* is not an accusative ending, but in fact a distinct consonantal afformative. Nevertheless, the accusative being the adverbial case of Semitic, it seems probable that such a form as *yômām*, 'in the daytime', consists of the noun having the adverbial accusative ending *-â* plus the enclitic *-m* characteristic of Ugaritic. The 3rd case-ending *-î*, denoting the genitive, is distinctive of the masculine plural termination *-îm*. As an extension of the genitive relation the construct state is of special interest. Here the preceding or governing noun is reduced in construction, cf. e.g. *śāp̄āh*, 'lip', which is contracted in the phrase *śᵉpaṯ kᵉna'an*, 'the lip of Canaan'. In such an instance the noun in the genitive, 'Canaan', imparts to the noun in construction preceding it a quality or attribute, the phrase having the force of 'the *Canaanite* language'. The use of the construct in Heb. offsets its deficiency in adjectives and indeed is often preferred, especially in verse. In Ps. 23, e.g. no adjective occurs, there being used such expressions as *mê mᵉnûḥôṯ*, 'waters of stillness', i.e. 'still waters'. The adjective has no comparative or superlative, the preposition *min*, 'from', being given the force of 'than' which is otherwise lacking, and the article being prefixed to the adjective to extend to the superlative degree. Other expedients include recourse to the construct, e.g. *šîr haššîrîm*, 'the song of songs', i.e. 'the most excellent song' and the occasional idiomatic employment of words consonant with the superlative idea. Such are *'ᵉlōhîm*, 'God', *māweṯ*, 'death', and *lāneṣaḥ*, 'for ever', which, suggesting severally excellence, extremity, pre-eminence or the ultimate, are susceptible of being so interpreted, e.g. in Gen. 23:6; Ca. 8:6; Job 14:20.

e The **verb** forms its tenses by the joining of the pronouns to the verbal stem in the Perfect as post-formatives only and in the Imperfect as both pre- and post-formatives. In them as also with the Participle the time reference may be past, present or future, the Perfect applying to event or action as *completed*, the Imperfect to process or action as *uncompleted* and the Participle to *state* or *condition*. Recent study, however, whilst adding to our knowledge of the tenses, renders classification of them less rigid. Instances of verbs seemingly Imperfect in form occur in verse, occasionally preceded by a particle such as *'āz*, 'then', which can only be construed as Preterite. Thus, e.g. in Exod. 15:5, such a past definite sense for *yᵉḵasᵉyūmû*, 'covered them', is required by both context and parallelism since the verb in the corresponding member, *yārᵉḏû*, 'went down', is Perfect. What has hitherto been regarded as Imperfect has the form *yiŠBōR* (*yiḴṬōL* of the paradigm verb) which from consideration of the verb in Ugaritic may more fittingly be called the Universal tense because of its past, present and future reference. On this assumption the Preterite and Imperfect having the same form are to be regarded as special applications of it. It should be noted, however, that the *Present-future* tense (see below) has also been regarded as a Universal tense, instances of which have been cited in connection with the so-called Prophetic Perfect. Examples occur of such a Perfect with a future reference, cf. Am. 5:2, where the force of 'has fallen' is '*shall* fall'. This *Prophetic* Perfect

53e indicates idiomatically the certainty of the speaker who regards oracularly the event he mentions as having already taken place. The mixed character of the Heb. verbal system is seen in the use of *wāw*, 'and', with Perfect and Imperfect forms. Here the construction with simple or weak *wāw* is traceable to Aramaic as is that with consecutive or strong *wāw* to Akkadian influences. What was long regarded as strong *wāw* with the Perfect used in a future sense is now recognised to be *wāw* with a *Present-future* tense on the analogy of the Akkadian *ū* with the Permansive state of the verb. Similarly *wāw* with the Imperfect is actually *wāw* with the *Preterite*, the construction here being the equivalent of the Akkadian *-ma* used *enclitically* with the Preterite. Of the two Infinitives the Infinitive Construct is applied both verbally and nominally, being capable of use in construction. The Infinitive Absolute which is not inflected is one of the most ancient of the Semitic verb-forms. In full use only in Heb. it is employed immediately before or after the verb to signify intensity or prolongation of action. It also functions as an adverb—helping to compensate for their lack in Heb.—and does duty independently for a tense or mood of the verb. The Imperative is limited to the 2nd person, of which Akkadian parallels show the Cohortative and Jussive to be extensions respectively for the 1st and 3rd persons.

f The **vocabulary** of biblical Heb. is relatively small, only about a tenth of its five thousand-odd words being found with any frequency. There are, however, indications of a more extensive vocabulary than what has survived in the OT, cf. e.g. the Gezer calendar and Siloam inscriptions. Similarly in the Lachish Letters there occur words unknown to biblical Heb., e.g. the name *Ṭōḇšillēm* and the expression *lᵉhašḵîṯ yᵉdê*, 'to make rest, depress the hands of'. Words found but once in the OT were not necessarily rare in contemporary usage, corresponding terms appearing and with the meaning more extensively represented in the Râs Shamra texts. Apart from such epigraphical evidence the findings of comparative philology point in the same direction, in many instances indeed obviating the need for emendation in resolving obscurities of the Heb. text. Certain words have thus been discovered to have more than one meaning since they represent roots with identical spelling. A case in point is *yāḏa'*, having the same consonants as *yāḏa'*, 'to know', with an Arabic equivalent, 'to be still, humiliated', a sense required, e.g. in Jg. 16:9, rendering 'his strength was not *brought low*'. Of importance also in the recovery of this vocabulary are the ancient versions, especially the LXX. In them differences of rendering from that of the MT often point to a meaning in one or more of the Semitic languages once current in Heb.

g The mixed heredity and environment of the vocabulary appear in the duplicate forms of the 1st person singular of the pronoun and the differing negative particles, and likewise with a number of synonyms as e.g. the two words for 'sun'; *šemeš* is common to Aramaic, Akkadian, and Arabic whilst *ḥeres* is peculiar to Heb. So well known a word as 'Eden' is illuminated by its discovery in Akkadian with the meaning of 'a sandy desert' in which (cf. Gen. 2:8) 'God planted a garden'. Ethiopic similarly has much to contribute to Heb. lexicography, one instance from a number that have been cited showing that in 1 Sam. 19:20 *lahᵃqaṯ* is not by metathesis *qᵉhillaṯ*, 'company of', as earlier supposed, but a *hapax legomenon* in the OT which has clearly to do with '*the senior ones* among (the prophets)'. Examples of loan words from outside the Semitic family are *barzel*, 'iron', of Hittite derivation; *tēḇāh*, 'ark', of palatial dimensions in Gen. 6:14–9:18 and of humbler proportions at Exod. 2:3, 5, from two quite distinct Egyptian words, having the sense respectively of 'palace' and 'box'; and *hêḵāl*, 'palace, temple', going back through Akkadian to the Sumerian compound *E.GAL*, 'house.great' = 'palace', which in Heb. alone has acquired the significance of 'temple'.

The concrete quality of its vocabulary with its use 53h of physical terms for the emotional and psychical as well as the simplicity of its syntactical structure combined to make Heb. a superb instrument for vivid and picturesque narration, ill suited though it was for sustained argument and the articulation of abstract thought, owing to its paucity of connecting particles and preponderance of co-ordinate over subordinate clauses. Much of the dramatic force of Heb. prose was further heightened by such simple expedients as the circumstantial clause, the preparatory mention of a subject in isolation from its predicatory sentence as in *casus pendens*, the emphatic repetition of significant words and appropriate changes in word order along with its marked preference for direct speech as against indirect statement. So with the poetry for which Heb. was singularly fitted with its correspondences of sound issuing in rhythm controlled by the tonal factor, and of thought expressed in parallelism, taking the form in balanced series of repetition, contrast or completion. The understanding of Heb. metrics has been enhanced by the discovery of strikingly similar features in the poetical texts from Râs Shamra, and a number of psalms, like so early a poem as the Song of Deborah (Jg. 5), have thus been found to belong to a period not later than the 10th cent. B.C.

ARAMAIC

Unlike the term 'Hebrew' the word 'Aramaic' 54a occurs in a linguistic sense as *'ᵃrāmîṯ* in the OT in 2 Kg. 18:26 = Isa. 36:11; Ezr. 4:7, 7; Dan. 2:4, and is to be distinguished from the gentilic adjective *'ᵃrammî* in Gen. 25:20, etc. In the Talmud likewise it is so employed, although sometimes it is there called 'Targum' and occasionally as also in the LXX 'Syriac'. 'Chaldee' standing for 'Old Syriac' is now and then met with in Syriac literature.

History and extent—The Aramaeans who used this b language were a prominent branch of the Semitic family whose earliest tribal movements in the Fertile Crescent belong to the 1st quarter of the 3rd millennium B.C. Much later, during the 12th cent. B.C., when the great powers in Asia Minor, Mesopotamia and Egypt were in decline, they swarmed into eastern Syria. It is in connection with this movement that certain of their settlements which throve *c.*1000 B.C., notably at Damascus, Beth-Rehob and Zobah, are familiar from the allusions to them (in the English versions as 'Syrians') in 2 Sam. 8:5, 10:6, 8.

In use over a wide area from an early period, c Aramaic was becoming from the end of the 8th cent. B.C. the international language of diplomacy and commerce as is evident from the incident recorded in 2 Kg. 18:26 and from inscriptions on weights and seals besides endorsements on documents, all of Babylonian and Assyrian origin. Indeed one of the oldest known Aramaic papyri in the form of a letter found in 1942 at Saqqara in Egypt points to the fact that a century later it was in this respect supplanting Akkadian. Subsequently under the Persian empire it was the language of administration for the western part of the realm, a stereotyped form of it becoming in effect a specialised dialect employed for all types of documents. This is apparent, e.g. in two series of connected papyri of the 5th cent. B.C. recovered from Elephantine and especially in the recently edited leather documents of the same cent., relating to Persian administration in Egypt. Inscribed on seals, stone, clay tablets, ostraca, papyri and leather from the 9th cent. B.C. to the 3rd cent. A.D., the Aramaic so far recovered includes such material as official communications, legal transactions, public documents, literary pieces, propagandist writing and personal notes. The widespread employment of Aramaic is still further demonstrated by the number and geographical extent of its dialects. Of these Syriac, Babylonian Talmudic, and Mandaean form an eastern

54c group, whilst to a western group belong Palmyrene, Nabataean, Samaritan, Targumic, Palestinian Christian and Egyptian Aramaic. Beyond Mesopotamia, Egypt, Palestine and Syria, inscriptions have been located in countries so widely separated as India, Persia, Arabia, Sinai, Armenia, Asia Minor, Greece and Italy.

d **Characteristics**—Within the Semitic family Nabataean inscriptions, representing a North Arabian dialect, and to a lesser extent Palmyrene inscriptions from the Syrian desert, together covering the period from the 1st cent. B.C. to the 3rd cent. A.D., exhibit the linguistic affinity of Aramaic with Arabic, and similarity of vocabulary indicates its close relationship with Heb. For so long the *lingua franca* of the ancient Near East, it probably took in more foreign elements than any other Semitic language of antiquity, a feature sufficiently apparent, e.g. in the Aramaic portions of Ezr. and Dan. where there are clear instances of Akkadian, Persian and Greek borrowing. Its employment of the substantive verb in combination with the Active Participle, the Perfect, and Imperfect to form compound tenses gave it flexibility and precision. The number and diversity of conjunctions and an extensive vocabulary bound up with its elasticity and capacity for absorption gained for Aramaic a cosmopolitan quality. These traits contributed to its supplanting of Heb. in which they were lacking. Correspondingly its use of a simple alphabetic script led to the popular ascendancy of Aramaic over Akkadian with its complicated and much less practical cuneiform system of writing.

e **Relation to Hebrew**—Aramaic was from the beginning a constituent of Heb. and this together with the fact of its early and wide distribution is reflected in the Aramaisms of such pre-exilic writings as Jg. and Hos., so that they are not to be looked upon as indicating a late date. The settlement of Aramaic-speaking foreigners to replace the Israelites deported from the Northern Kingdom after the fall of Samaria in 721 B.C., cf. 2 Kg. 17:24, resulted in the spread of Aramaic there and its use concurrently with Heb. This was not without effect in due course on the inhabitants of the Southern Kingdom. Certain it is that the Exiles, returning from Babylon with Heb. still their mother-tongue as Deutero-Isaiah makes clear, found Aramaic firmly established in their homeland. From then on both languages were jointly current, with Heb. gradually yielding to the popular pressure of Aramaic. So in Neh. 13:24 there is mention of some who could not speak the Jews' language. Est., Ec., and a few psalms are unmistakably tinged with Aramaic. On the other hand the Heb. of Ecclesiasticus indicates that the purer form of the language was written and understood early in the 2nd cent. B.C. Yet, as noted above, during this cent. Aramaic almost entirely ousted Heb. as the spoken language of Palestine. By the time of the NT it was the language of ordinary speech throughout the country, Heb. being retained as the language of scholarship and worship.

f **Old Testament Aramaic**—Comparison of the linguistic features of biblical Aramaic with the related dialects has shown it to have a closer affinity with what is found in the later sources of the western group than with that of the earlier period belonging to Mesopotamia. Thus examination of consonantal mutations as also of grammatical and syntactical traits points definitely to its having come somewhere chronologically between the Aramaic of the Egyptian papyri of the 5th cent. B.C. and that of the Nabataean, Palmyrene, and Targumic dialects from *c.* 1st cent. B.C. On this linguistic evidence it appears that the Aramaic of Ezr. may well be a 4th cent. product and that there is nothing to preclude that of Dan. from being 2nd cent., so that whilst it cannot be of Babylonian origin it is certainly Palestinian and could be Maccabaean. 54f

Writing—Heb. and Aramaic in common with the majority of Semitic languages are written from right to left. Almost all Heb. MSS and fragments of the OT and all printed editions of the Heb. Bible are in *k^{e}ṯāḇ m^{e}rubbā'*, 'square writing, script'. Of Aramaean origin this was known also as *k^{e}ṯāḇ 'aššûrî*, 'Assyrian script', because of its employment in Mesopotamia from the 8th cent. B.C. It appears to have come into use in Palestine with the spread there of Aramaic, superseding gradually after the Exile the Phoenician-Old Hebrew script in which a considerable part of the OT was originally written. Mt. 5:18 indicates that the square script was common in NT times although there is evidence, e.g. in the Dead Sea Scrolls, of the earlier script having been used archaically both then and later. Specimens of this older script are preserved, e.g. in the Gezer calendar-inscription (*c.*950 B.C.), ostraca from Samaria (*c.*770 B.C.), the Siloam inscription (*c.*700 B.C.), the Lachish Letters (*c.*590 B.C.), and certain biblical fragments from the Dead Sea caves. It also occurs in a number of Phoenician and Aramaic inscriptions, dating respectively from the middle of the 2nd millennium B.C. and the beginning of the 1st millennium B.C. as well as on the Moabite Stone (*c.*850 B.C.). The alphabet thus used, which was of West Semitic invention, was the outcome of a long process of experimentation between the middle of the 3rd and the middle of the 2nd millennium B.C., arising through contact with and simplification of the more elaborate systems of Babylonia and Egypt. Subsequently inherited by modern civilisation via Greece and Rome it is in itself one of the great bequests of the Semitic peoples to the human race besides being the instrument whereby the Scriptures were transmitted. g

Bibliography—GRAMMAR : H. Bauer and P. Leander, *Grammatik des Biblisch-Aramäischen* (1927), *Kurzgefasste biblisch-aramäische Grammatik* (1929) ; G. Beer, *Hebräische Grammatik* I (2nd ed. 1952), II (2nd ed. 1955) ; G. Bergsträsser, *Hebräische Grammatik usw.* I (1918–26), II (1929) ; C. Brockelmann, *Hebräische Syntax* (1956) ; A. B. Davidson, *An Introductory Heb. Grammar*, 21st and foll. edd., revised by McFadyen (1921ff.), *Heb. Syntax*, (3rd ed. 1901) ; G. R. Driver, *Problems of the Heb. Verbal System* (1936) ; S. R. Driver, *A Treatise on the Use of the Tenses in Heb.* (3rd ed. 1892) ; E. Kautzsch, *Gesenius' Heb. Grammar*, 2nd Eng. ed., revised by A. E. Cowley (1910) ; J. Weingreen, *A Practical Grammar for Classical Heb.* (1929).

LEXICONS : F. Brown, S. R. Driver, and C. A. Briggs, *A Heb. and English Lexicon of the OT* (reprint 1951) ; L. Koehler and W. Baumgartner, *Lexicon in VT Libros* (1953), *Supplementum* (1958) ; F. Zorell and L. Semkowski, *Lexicon Hebraicum et Aramaicum VT* (1946–).

OTHER WORKS : M. Black, *An Aramaic Approach to the Gospels and Acts* (2nd ed. 1954) ; G. R. Driver, 'The Modern Study of the Heb. Language', in *The People and the Book*, ed. A. S. Peake (1925) ; A. Dupont-Sommer, *Les Araméens* (1949) ; H. H. Rowley, *The Aramaic of the OT* (1929) ; D. W. Thomas, 'The Languages of the OT', in *Record and Revelation*, ed. H. W. Robinson (1938).

G. A. Cooke, *A Textbook of North Semitic Inscriptions* (1903) ; D. Diringer, *The Alphabet : A Key to the History of Mankind* (1948) ; G. R. Driver, *Semitic Writing* (2nd ed. 1954) ; A. M. Honeyman, 'Semitic Epigraphy and Heb. Philology', in *The OT and Modern Study*, ed. H. H. Rowley (1951) ; M. Lidzbarski, *Handbuch der nordsemitischen Epigraphik* (1898).

CHRONOLOGY OF THE OLD TESTAMENT

By J. GRAY

55a With Jacob and the tribes traditionally associated with him we see the first emergence of Israel in the politics of the ancient Near East, and it is noteworthy that, whatever the actual significance of the earlier patriarchs may have been, for the pre-Exilic prophets at least the practical beginning of the political development of Israel was the Aramaean agglomeration associated with Jacob. Here are folk-movements which fit into the political map as known in general outline from historical records of the imperial powers of the Late Bronze Age (1600–1200 B.C.). The question of the date of these movements is relative to that of the Exodus.

The numerical **date of the Exodus,** 480 (12 × 40) years before the foundation of the Temple in the fourth year of Solomon (1 Kg. 6:1) in 967, is obviously the artificial reconstruction of some pious antiquary, like such specific numbers in the P source of the Pentateuch. Actually in the earlier sources of the Pentateuch, which are more faithful to tribal tradition, there are statements at variance with such specific dating. It is stated (Gen. 15:16) that the Exodus would take place in the fourth generation, though, to be sure, the sojourn in Egypt is given as 400 years (v. 13). Gen. 50:23–C implies that Joseph's descendants of the third generation took part in the Exodus, and this is supported by the statement that Moses lived in the third generation after Levi (Exod. 6:16–20), though again the period is said to amount to 407 years. Thus a maximum of a century and a half may reasonably be allowed between the Exodus and the descent of Jacob to Egypt. As against the artificial computation of 1 Kg. 6:1, which would yield a 15th-cent. date, the weight of evidence from the OT regarding conditions in Egypt, Palestine, and Transjordan implies a date in the XIX Dynasty in the 13th cent. for the Exodus, with the main phase of the Hebrew settlement in Palestine after the campaigns of Rameses II (1289–1224 B.C.). We cannot date those events, however, more accurately than within the limits of certain periods, and to this extent archaeology supports our conclusions. The decisive phase of the Israelite penetration of Palestine, then, and the settlement in the time of the Judges coincides with the general Aramaean movements into the settled lands at the beginning of the Iron Age (*c.*1200 B.C.), while the movements of the Jacob-tribes in Palestine and Egypt are part of the Ḫabiru inroads in the Amarna Age (*c.*1400 B.C.).

b In the Hebrew Monarchy there is more specific chronological detail. The reigns of **David and Solomon** are noted according to their duration, though in the number forty for each reign we may suspect generalisation, and those of subsequent kings of Israel and Judah are noted by their duration and are synchronised. Often there is double corroboration of dates, but on the sole evidence of Kings these precise figures often confuse rather than elucidate Hebrew chronology, which, consequently, is one of the notorious problems of OT scholarship.

Fortunately there are certain synchronisms with Assyrian and Babylonian history. Here there is a firm chronology based on accurate lists of Assyrian eponyms (*limmu*), *limmu* annals recording events in the eponym's year of office, royal annals, with cross-references to the *limmu* annals, and finally lists of kings with the duration of their reigns. Of the last the most significant is the Khorsabad King-list which, though noting only the names and sequence of the first thirty-two kings of Assyria, continues with the duration of the reigns until 738 B.C. Into these records dates are introduced relative to the solar eclipse noted in the month Simanu in the *limmu*-ship of Pur-Sagale (ninth year of Ashur-dan III). This may be dated by astronomical calculation on 15 June, 763 B.C. Calculating back and forward from the accession of Ashur-dan III we may establish a firm Assyrian chronology from a period contemporary with the foundation of the Hebrew monarchy to the year of the last *limmu* recorded (649 B.C.). This chronological scheme is supplemented and continued by that of the Alexandrine Ptolemy (A.D. 70–161), who utilised local annals and astronomical observations to give a chronology from 747 B.C. to the Roman Imperial era. Within this framework of Assyrian, Babylonian, Persian, Ptolemaic, and Seleucid history there are determinable synchronisms with Hebrew history. 55b

Of these the first and most significant is the **Battle of Qarqar** on the Orontes in the sixth year of Shalmaneser III (853 B.C.), who mentions Ahab of Israel among his opponents. The same king lists Jehu among his tributaries in his eighteenth year (841 B.C.). Now between Ahab and Jehu fell the reigns of Ahaziah and Joram, given respectively as two (1 Kg. 22:51) and twelve years (2 Kg. 3:1). Since there is evidence that Judaean scribes, accustomed to reckon a king's reign from the first New Year after his accession (accession-reckoning), added a year to the official Israelite figures for the reigns of Amaziah and Joram, which were given from their natural accession (non-accession reckoning), the interval between Ahab and Jehu is twelve years, exactly the interval between the two events recorded in the Assyrian inscriptions associated with Ahab and Jehu. Ahab, then, must have died in 853 and Jehu's first year is 841.

Reckoning back from Ahab's death in 853 on the basis of statements in Kings as to the duration of the reigns of the kings of Israel and Judah, and allowing for the extra years allowed to each Israelite king by the Judaean scribes, we arrive at the date 931 for the accession of Jeroboam I of Israel and the death of Solomon, whose son Rehoboam officially acceded as King of Judah in 930 at the Autumnal New Year in Tishri, probably on the occasion of the Festival of the Enthronement of Yahweh.

In the account of the Hebrew Monarchy there are many **chronological discrepancies.** These are, however, largely more apparent than real and may be explained as Thiele has done, by recognising that an event may be dated so long after a king's accession or, alternatively, so long after another event, e.g. Baasha of Israel died in the twenty-sixth year of Asa of Judah (1 Kg. 16:6, 8); Baasha raided Judah in the thirty-sixth year of Asa (2 Chron. 16:6). The first date is reckoned from Asa's accession; the second really from the Disruption. So too in the case of Omri. Dating back from the death of Ahab (853) on the basis of statements about the length of the reigns of Omri and Ahab, and c

55c allowing for the Judaean reckoning of two extra accession years we arrive at 885 B.C. for the accession of Omri. This agrees with the statement that Zimri, the ephemeral predecessor of Omri, slew King Elah in the twenty-seventh year of Asa (1 Kg. 16:10, 15). In 1 Kg. 16:23, however, the reign of Omri is dated from the thirty-first year of Asa. The first date is from the time that Omri ruled with a rival king Tibni ; the second relates to the accession of Omri as sole ruler. Similarly order may be introduced into the chaos of OT chronology in the late 8th cent. by recognising that dates relative to the reign of Pekah of Israel (e.g. 2 Kg. 15:33) are reckoned not from 740/39, when Pekah became undisputed ruler, but from 752, when he had been frustrated in his ambitions by Menahem with the support of Assyria. Similarly an event may be reckoned from the date when a prince became co-regent with his father, as was occasionally the practice, or, alternatively, from the time when he became sole ruler. Such co-regencies were those of Jeroboam II, and Azariah (Uzziah) and Jotham of Judah.

d In the last phase of the Jewish Monarchy and into the Babylonian Exile there are more detailed synchronisms with Babylonian history, where chronology is fixed by **Ptolemy's canon.** Accurate cross-references to regnal years of Babylonian and, later, Persian kings in the records of the end of the Jewish Monarchy and of the Exilic and post-Exilic periods doubtless reflect the intense editorial activity which was a feature of the Exile, the Books of Kings, for instance, being finally edited in that period, the last historical reference being the alleviation of Jehoiachin's lot in the first year of Awil-Marduk (2 Kg. 25:27) in 561 B.C.

The restoration of the Jewish community in the **Persian period** is synchronised with the regnal years of the Achaemenid kings. Ezr. (1:1ff., 6:3) refers to a royal directive regarding the building of the Temple in Jerusalem in Cyrus' first year. The reference is to Cyrus' first year as suzerain of Babylon, i.e. 538 B.C., when a foundation cylinder of Cyrus from Ur records his decree of tolerance for minorities with option to return to their ancestral homes. A limited number of Jews apparently availed themselves of this and returned under Sheshbazzar (Ezr. 1:8, 11), but it is questionable, in the light of the evidence of the Books of Haggai and Zechariah, if the restoration of the Temple was contemplated as early as 538 as Ezr. 1:1ff. and Ezr. 6:3 state. The specification regarding the Temple betrays the predominant interest of the Chronicler, a much later and less reliable authority for this period than the contemporaries Haggai and Zechariah. The rebuilding of the Temple, then, was undertaken, not without much prophetic urging, under Zerubbabel and Joshua (Hag. 1:1, 12, 2:2–4 ; Zech. 3:8–9 ; Ezr. 3:2, 8, 4:2–3, cf. Ezr. 3:8–13) in the sixth month of the second year of Darius (I), i.e. 520 (Hag. 1:1, 5). Ezr. (3:8) refers to the activity of Joshua and Zerubbabel in the second year after their return. Possibly the Chronicler (the compiler of Ezr.) is thinking of the foundation of the Temple the year after the return of Sheshbazzar in 538. On the other hand, it may be that there had been a fresh influx of exiles under Joshua and Zerubbabel in 522, fresh hopes having been excited by the convulsions in the Persian Empire before and immediately after Darius suppressed the impostor Gaumata. The Temple thus begun in 520 was finished in the sixth year of Darius I in 516 (Ezr. 6:15) in the month Adar.

e The next phase of Jewish history was the fortification of Jerusalem and the promulgation of the revision of the Law. In spite of the superficial impression conveyed by Ezr.-Neh., there is good internal evidence in these books that Nehemiah's work in Jerusalem preceded Ezra's. The activity of both is synchronised with Persian chronology, but there is a certain amount of ambiguity. Nehemiah's permission for his journey to Jerusalem is dated in the first month of the twentieth year of Artaxerxes (Neh. 2:1). Unfortunately it is 55e not said which Artaxerxes. If the first is indicated the date would be 444 B.C. ; if the second, 384 is the date. Ezra left Babylon on the first day of the first month of the seventh year of Artaxerxes (again unspecified), arriving, no doubt, after a mission through the Jewish communities of Mesopotamia, on the first of the fifth month (Ezr. 7:7–8). If the first Artaxerxes is meant, 457 is the date ; if the second, 397. That Nehemiah's mission fell in 444 and Ezra's in 397 is indicated by a critical appreciation of internal Biblical evidence and by the fact that in the papyri of the Israelite military colony of Elephantine, the High-priest in Jerusalem in 411 is Johanan, probably Jehohanan the contemporary of Ezra (10:6) and the grandson of Eliashib (Neh. 12:22) the contemporary of Nehemiah (Neh. 3:1).

As far as concerns historical references and synchronisms with contemporary history the following period of Jewish history is a dark age. To be sure, the Book of Daniel five times over (chs. 2, 7, 8, 9, 11), albeit somewhat cryptically, gives a synopsis of the period from Nebuchadrezzar to Antiochus Epiphanes (175–163) with a wealth of precise dating in the regnal years of kings from the third year of Jehoiakim, King of Judah (Dan. 1:1), hence 606, to the first year of Darius 'the son of Ahasuerus' (Dan. 9:1). These dates, however, are confined to verses introducing various visions (modern chapter-headings) and may well be editorial and secondary. In any case they are flagrantly unreliable, the first, to take but one of many examples, being a glaring anachronism, since the third year of Jehoiakim fell before the accession of Nebuchadrezzar (605). Nor was Jehoiakim deported, as is stated in Dan. 1:2, but died in Jerusalem in 597 (2 Kg. 24:6).

By contrast, however, the Book of Daniel, especially 11:2–45, abounds in specific allusions to the period of the Diadochi, particularly to the career of the Seleucid Antiochus IV, Epiphanes (175–163 B.C.), 'the little horn with a mouth speaking great things' (Dan. 7:8). The last topical reference in the OT is probably to his death in Ispahan in 163 (Dan. 11:44–5).

CHRONOLOGICAL TABLE[1] 56a

Exodus	13th cent. B.C.
David	c.1010–970
Solomon	c.970–931

Israel

Jeroboam I	931/30–910/09
Nadab	910/9–909/8
Baasha	909/8–886/5
Elah (reigned hardly two years)	886/5–885/4
Zimri (reigned seven days)	885/4
Tibni and Omri reign independently	885/4–880
Omri sole ruler	880–874/3
Ahab	874/3–853
Ahaziah	853–852
Joram	852–841
Jehu	841–814/13
Jehoahaz	814/13–798
Jehoash	798–782/1
Jeroboam II co-regent with Jehoash	793/2–782/1
Jeroboam II	782/1–753
Zechariah (reigned six months)	753/2
Shallum (reigned one month)	752
Menahem	752–742/1
Pekahiah	742/1–740/39
Pekah (having unsuccessfully asserted authority in 752)	740/39–732/1
Hoshea	732/1–723/2

[1] [For the period of the Hebrew monarchy, where it is difficult to reconcile all the Biblical data, Dr Gray here follows the views of Thiele, who presumes a number of co-regencies. These views are not accepted by all scholars, and hence in other parts of this volume different dates will be found assigned to some of the kings.—H.H.R.]

56a **Judah**

Rehoboam	930–913
Abijam	913–911/10
Asa	911/10–870/69
Jehoshaphat co-regent with Asa	873/2–870/69
Jehoshaphat	870/69–848
Jehoram co-regent with Jehoshaphat	853–848
Jehoram	848–841
Ahaziah	841
Athaliah	841–835
Joash	835–796
Amaziah	796–767
Azariah co-regent with Amaziah	791/90–767
Azariah (Uzziah)	767–740/39
Jotham co-regent with Azariah	750–740/39
Jotham	740/39–732
Ahaz co-regent with Jotham	735–732
Ahaz	732/1–716
Hezekiah	716/15–687/6
Manasseh co-regent with Hezekiah	696/5–687/6
Manasseh	687/6–642/1
Amon	642/1–640/39
Josiah	640/39–608
Jehoahaz (reigned three months)	608
Jehoiakim	608–597
Jehoiachin (reigned three months)	597
Zedekiah	597–586

b SOME SYNCHRONISMS IN THE HISTORY OF THE ANCIENT NEAR EAST

Invasion of Sheshonq (935–914) in fifth year of Rehoboam	926/5
Ahab at the Battle of Qarqar in sixth year of Shalmaneser III (858–824)	853
Jehu pays tribute to Shalmaneser in the latter's eighteenth year	841
Fall of Samaria to Sargon II (722–705), brother of Shalmaneser V (725–721), probably during campaigns in the West between 725 and 723, in the ninth year of Hoshea of Israel	723/2
Invasion of Judah by Sennacherib (705–681) in his third campaign, the fourteenth year of Hezekiah	702/1
Fourth year of Jehoiakim coincides with the first year of Nebuchadrezzar (605–561)	605
Deportation of Jehoiachin in Nebuchadrezzar's eighth year	597
Fall of Jerusalem in the nineteenth year of Nebuchadrezzar, the eleventh year of Zedekiah	586
Edict (in favour of deported minorities) of Cyrus in his first year (as ruler of Babylon) ; Jewish return under Sheshbazzar	538
Rebuilding of the Temple between the second and the sixth years of Darius I (522–486)	520–516
Nehemiah's journey to Jerusalem in the twentieth year of Artaxerxes I (464–424)	444
Ezra's journey to Jerusalem in the seventh year of Artaxerxes II (404–359)	397
Death of Antiochus Epiphanes (cf. Dan. 11:44–5)	163

56b

Bibliography—J. Lewy, *Die Chronologie der Könige von Israel und Juda* (1927) ; V. Coucke, 'Chronologie Biblique', *Dictionnaire de la Bible*, ed. F. Vigouroux (*Supplément*, ed. L. Pirot) i (1928) ; S. Mowinckel, 'Die Chronologie der israelitischen und jüdischen Könige', *Acta Orientalia* 9 (1931), 161–277 ; A. Poebel, 'The Assyrian King-list from Khorsabad', JNES 1 (1942), 247–306, 460–92, 2 (1943), 56–90 ; W. F. Albright, 'The Chronology of the Divided Monarchy of Israel', BASOR 100 (1945), 16–22 ; 'New Light from Egypt on the Chronology and History of Israel and Judah', BASOR 130 (1953), 4–8 ; M. B. Rowton, 'Manetho's Date for Ramesses II', JEA 34 (1948), 54–74 ; 'The Date of the Founding of Solomon's Temple', BASOR 119 (1950), 20–2 ; H. H. Rowley, *From Joseph to Joshua* (1950) ; E. R. Thiele, *The Mysterious Numbers of the Hebrew Kings* (1951) ; P. Van der Meer, *The Chronology of Ancient Western Asia and Egypt*, 2nd ed. (*Documenta et Monumenta Orientis Antiqui* v (1955)) ; D. J. Wiseman, *Chronicles of Chaldaean Kings (626–555 B.C.) in the British Museum* (1956).

CANON AND TEXT OF THE OLD TESTAMENT

By B. J. ROBERTS

57a **The Canon**—The word ' canon ' is derived from the Greek κάννα, ' reed ' or ' cane ', with the idea of measuring-rod, and it was first used in this sense when Athanasius applied it to the books of the NT. But it is obvious from the Rabbinic writings of the early Christian era, especially the Mishnah codified in the 2nd cent. A.D., that a closed corpus of writings was known as ' Holy Scriptures ' (Shab. 16:1 ; Yad. 3:5), and defined as books ' which defile the hands '. It has been suggested that the word ' canon ', too, has Semitic ancestry, and it is consistent with this that during the later stages of its development Judaism was greatly exercised about the inclusion of some of its religious books in its official Scriptures, or their exclusion from their number. Down to the period of Biblical Criticism in the 16th–18th cent., Christian teachers accepted Rabbinic assertions that after the time of Ezra, or the Great Synagogue traditionally attributed to his influence, no books were included in Scripture, but, of course, literary and historical analysis has made this dogma untenable. But it will be seen that it was the Rabbinic list which, in the last resort, dictated the number of books which were included in the accepted Canon, at least of the Protestant Churches.

b Non-canonical books form the **Apocrypha,** a word whose function has changed during its complicated history. An early reference (2 Esd. 14:44–7) is best explained as distinguishing between canonical books and apocalyptic writings which were regarded as ' to be hidden from all except the wise ', and it is demonstrable that the NT contains quotations from and echoes of both types. Origen, too, in the 3rd cent. uses the word for apocalyptic books, and he even expands it to include heretical works. The range of apocalyptic works of this kind current in the Early Church cannot be estimated, though some of them have been included in individual LXX MSS, and they are also well represented in the Qumran scrolls. At a later stage, however, the term apocrypha was used to denote a totally different collection of books, namely those which were contained only in the Greek Bible, and the apocalyptic books conventionally came to be called **Pseudepigrapha.** That is, as the apocalyptic writings were originally ' hidden ', and then ' refused ', the books in the Greek Bible which were not also in the Heb. Canon came to be regarded as outside the Canon, though not exactly ' hidden ' or totally ' refused '.

The arrangement of the books in the English Bible, in both Roman Catholic and Protestant forms, points to a scheme of editing which is basically educational and didactic ; its setting is the schoolroom, and the reader is taught by means of it to trace the whole history of the divine revelation down to the time of Christ. So far as is known, the only organised religious institution which has adopted the scheme is the Christian Church, for it is demonstrable that Judaism has transmitted a different scheme, with, apparently, a different function. The actual basis of the present order is in the collection of OT Scriptures in Greek, the Septuagint (LXX), which presumably was the Bible of the Early Church, and is conventionally 57b
known as the Alexandrian Canon because the version itself originally came from Alexandria. Prior to it, however, is the Heb. Canon.

c **The Hebrew Canon**—Jos., in c.Ap., book 1, *c.* A.D. 100, seems to have been the first to refer explicitly to a collection of books in the Heb. OT, saying that it consisted of 22 books, that they were composed in the time between Moses and Artaxerxes (i.e. the period of prophetic activity, and consequently ' inspired '), that they were sacred and their text inviolable. This statement agrees, except for the number of books being 24 and not 22, with others which are roughly contemporary, especially 2 Esd. 14:45 in the Apocrypha and *Baba Bathra* 14*b*–15*a* in the Babylonian Talmud. The idea of the sanctity of the books is further elucidated in Mishnaic writings, where it is stated that the scriptures are those books ' which defile the hands ', i.e. render the reader ritually unclean because they are tabu. The discrepancy about the number of books is capable of different explanations. It may be that Josephus, with his Hellenistic background, adopted the LXX order of combining Ru. with Jg., and Lam. with Jer., and Ezr.-Neh. as one book ; it may also be that current Jewish debates were reflected in his statement, for we know that during the 1st cent. A.D. Ec. and Ca. were in dispute between the two major Pharisaic schools, Hillel and Shammai. Other books, such as Est. and even the prophecy of Ezek., were challenged from time to time, but it is generally assumed that when the Rabbinic academy was reassembled in Jamnia (Jabneh) in Palestine after the fall of Jerusalem in A.D. 70 (i.e. A.D. 90 to 100), steps were taken under the leadership of Rabbi Johanan ben Zakkai to fix the canon of OT Scripture as far as Jewish worship was concerned. It must be stressed that there is no explicit statement to this effect, and many writers have doubted the conclusion, but it is at least convenient to regard this event as the *terminus ad quem* for the history of the growth of the canon among orthodox Jewish leaders.

The passage in Jos.c.Ap. mentioned above divides d
the canon into three parts : the Pentateuch, thirteen books of Prophecy and four books of hymns and precepts. It is the last part that occasioned most controversy among the Rabbis. The usual name is *Kethubim*, i.e. **Writings,** also rendered Hagiographa. In the Massoretic OT it contains The Psalter, Prov., Job, the Five Rolls (*Megillôth*, i.e. Ca., Ru., Lam., Ec., Est.), Dan., and the historical collection Chr., Ezr.–Neh. At least two of these groups suggest that the collection had to do with ritual, viz. the Psalter and the Five Rolls. Of the latter, Est. has always been connected with the celebration of the festival of Purim, and the others have been used by the Rabbis, at least since the Middle Ages, in connection with annual festivals ; e.g. Lam. from an early time has been read at the annual commemoration of the fall of Jerusalem. They could quite well have been regarded as ' Song ', and in this respect the phrase in Lk. 24:44 which

57d refers to the Law of Moses, the Prophets, and the Psalms might have relevance. Furthermore, the reference in Mt. 23:35 includes as Jewish history the stretch from Cain and Abel to Zachariah son of Barachiah, and since the latter is described in Chr. (2 Chr. 24:20f.) it is reasonable to conclude that all the books at present in the Hagiographa were regarded as Scripture in NT times. At the same time, Josephus' reference to four books of 'hymns' might be explained by reference to Ps., Prov., Job, and the Five Rolls.

e The second part of the Canon, the Prophets, is more clearly defined and probably goes back to an earlier period in the story of the OT Scriptures. In one important respect however our view of this section might be modified because of a significant, though badly neglected, fact. It is that the division of the books into **Former** and **Latter Prophets** cannot be traced back farther than the 8th cent. A.D., and it probably rested on the difference in character of the two groups of books. Consequently, the common division into 'Former Prophets', i.e. historical books, and 'Latter Prophets', i.e. prophetical books, reflects a Western, or Hellenistic, standpoint rather than a Hebraic one. It would appear that, whatever function is to be attributed to this section of the Canon in the Hebraic tradition, it does not reflect a division into historical prose and prophetic writing but regards both as having equal value and having one common purpose. Furthermore, it is known that throughout the history of the synagogue the books of the Prophets provided the 'second lesson' for the liturgy, and it lies to hand to suggest that the function of this section, historical and prophetical writings alike, was ritual and liturgical rather than educational; that is, tradition, which was meant to accompany the recitation of the Torah in the official Temple worship.

f There are a few points to notice about the collection of this section of the Canon. The first has to do with date. The prologue of Sir. says that the Pentateuch and the Prophets were in existence in ben Sirach's lifetime, i.e. *c.*200 B.C., if the present Greek rendering belongs to a date after 117 B.C. It is sometimes argued from this that the reason for the exclusion of Dan. is that it was composed after 200, and confirmation is derived from the absence of Dan. from the list of praiseworthy Fathers in Sir. 48:22–49:12. This however is conjecture, because, by the same token at least Deutero-Zech. (9–14) should not have been added to that book, since it, too, was composed after 200 B.C. It does not seem right to counter by suggesting that it was only new books that were excluded, because the Rabbis state clearly that the texts of the accepted books were sacrosanct, and any attempt to add substantially to them must have been impossible. What is more likely to support the usual *ad quem* dating of this Canon is the attitude of the OT itself to prophecy in those sections and passages which can independently be dated *c.*200 B.C. A study of the canonical prophets demonstrates the extent to which glosses and even lengthy passages were sporadically added to the text to form a transition from prophecy to apocalyptic (cf. Isa. 24–7; Zech. 9–14; Hab. 3). But as the latter increased in authority true prophecy tended to lose caste, so that it became possible for one passage (Zech. 13:2–4) even to discredit prophecy with poignant sarcasm. It was then high time that prophecy, a most important part of the divine revelation, should be declared inviolable and sacred, and that the apocalyptic writings, such as Dan. and the Pseudepigrapha, if they were to be included at all, should find a home in another collection. It is in the Greek Bible that Dan. ranks among the Prophets, and there the whole standpoint differs fundamentally from the standpoint adopted in the Heb. Canon.

Whether or not such a conclusion helps us to reconstruct the still earlier history of the second section of the Heb. Canon is a moot point. Sir. 49 refers to Jer., Ezek. and 'the Twelve Prophets', and it is more than likely that the Heb. tradition 57f has always regarded the Twelve as forming a single collection by their filling a single scroll. But at what period such a collection could have been made, or when these and other books stopped being expandable is beyond demonstration. Future research into the cultic background of prophetic writings might open up interesting possibilities. Another possible clue might be discovered in the Dead Sea scrolls, especially in the *pesher* scrolls where we find evidence of at least sectarian tendency to regard the prophetical books as oracles to be interpreted in terms of contemporary circumstances.

Finally, the **Torah.** The *terminus ad quem* of the g canonical Five Books of Moses is dependent on the date of the Samaritan Schism, for it is well known that that community adopted for its own use, and transmitted throughout the generations, a text of the Torah which in contents is practically identical with that of the Rabbis. If the Schism be regarded as having taken place *c.* mid-4th cent. B.C., it is likely that the Torah Canon was fixed at a considerably earlier date.

Indeed, it is difficult to think of Jewish religion without a sacred Torah at any time in its history, and the word *Torah* is frequently used in pre-exilic prophetic writings, e.g. Hos. 4:6; Jer. 2:8, for a corpus of instruction relating to sacred institutions. The question of the date of composition of the Pentateuch lies outside the scope of the present article, but it is relevant to suggest that whenever *Torah* or *Sepher Torah* is used of a collection of laws it constitutes a canonical corpus. Thus we have the Torah of the Stone Tablets (Exod. 24:12), the book of the Torah of God (Jos. 24:26, an E narrative); frequently of the Deuteronomic code (Dt. *passim*, 2 Kg. 22:8); and the Divine or Mosaic Law which refers, according to the contexts, to either D or P or the whole Torah. If, as is likely, Judaism emerged in its final form in the time of Ezr., it is equally likely that the canonical Torah belongs to the same time and to the same occasion.

In §57*a* reference was made to the Rabbinic dogma that Ezr. was the *terminus ad quem* to the canon of Scripture: this has been refuted, but it may be permitted to refer to it again as containing a basic truth, as far as the Rabbinic principles of canon are concerned. Jewish ritual and worship postulate the acceptance of an authoritative Torah, and in so far as Ezr. and/or the Great Synagogue saw the final emergence of Judaism, it seems right to regard them as the definitive authorities in the composition of the Pentateuch, i.e. of the Scriptures *par excellence.* What was added was interpretative—the Prophets gave 'tradition', the second lesson in the worship; and the Writings were used sporadically as addenda, and indeed, some of them never were included in the synagogue lectionary.

The Alexandrian Canon—The LXX was produced 58a for the Jewish-Hellenistic Diaspora, but little or nothing is directly known of its transmission apart from its use by the Christian Church. By implication, however, it is possible to conclude that the main importance was attached to the Pentateuch. The philosopher Philo, the most eminent product of the Diaspora, was concerned to present the Pentateuch as the epitome of all truth. It is significant, too, that the name '*Septuaginta*' in the Letter of Aristeas (cf. §64*c*) is applied only to the Pentateuch. But there were other books in the LXX, and there is mention even of a tripartite division into Torah, Prophecy and 'other books', as the grandson of Jesus ben Sirach explains in the prologue of his book. It may be argued, however, that ben Sirach did not himself deem the 'Prophets' and 'the others' to constitute a defined and officially exclusive group of writings, for his grandson proceeds to explain that ben Sirach 'was drawn on to write somewhat pertaining to instruction and wisdom, in order that others . . . might make progress much more by living according to the Law'.

58a This was the book Ecclesiasticus, and its survival is due to the fact that it was included in the Alexandrian Canon, for though some portions of the Heb. original text have been recovered among the MSS of Qumrân and the Cairo Geniza it does not appear likely that it ever found a place in any orthodox Jewish collection of books ' which defile the hands '.

The Alexandrian Canon has always been amorphous, and the only means of determining its scope has been the older MSS of the LXX. These vary both in the arrangement of books and also in content. Indeed, a survey of the MSS will show how misleading it is to refer to an Alexandrian Canon in the precise sense which attaches to the word in the Heb. OT. A bare outline of the books in one of the best-known LXX MSS, the *Codex Vaticanus* from the 4th cent. A.D., shows the following lay-out for the Greek OT: 1. Pentateuch. 2. Prose history: Jos. to Chr., 2 Esd. (Ezr.-Neh.). 3. Poetry: Ps., Prov., Ec., Ca., Job, Wis., Sir. 4. Narratives: Est., Jdt., Tob. 5. Prophecy: The Minor Prophets, Isa., Jer., Bar., Lam., Epistle of Jeremy, Ezek., Dan. (with addition of S 3 Ch., Sus., and Bel). The fact that most printed editions follow roughly this order, with the addition of Late History in 1–4 Mac. probably reflects the prestige achieved by this particular MS (cf. §64*n*).

b It is impossible to discover when the process of segregating the books of the LXX into canonical and apocryphal began. At the synod of Hippo, 393, and of Carthage, 397, the OT was decreed to contain all the books of the Alexandrian Canon. In the late 4th cent. the question seems to involve side-issues; particularly on the one hand the date and character of the Syriac Version known as the **Peshitta,** and on the other the work of Jerome and the **Vulgate** translation. The relevance of the former lies in the absence from its earlier form of all the books at present found in the Apocrypha, as well as Chr., and if it could be proved that the Peshitta was from the outset a Christian work, it would follow that at an early date at least one branch of the Church distinguished between the canonical and apocryphal books. But this is unlikely, not only because of the probable Jewish provenance of the Version but also because there was a later alignment of the Peshitta with the LXX of Western Christendom, and the Peshitta *Codex Ambrosianus* from the 6th cent. contains the Apocrypha and some Pseudepigrapha as well. The story of how Jerome resorted to the Heb. text in order to produce his Vulgate translation is told elsewhere (§65*c*); here it must be noted that his preference for the Heb. text over the LXX is reflected also in his attitude to those books which were absent from the Heb. Bible. In the general introduction to his translation, *Prologus Galeatus* (the Preface to 1–4 Kg.) he explains that the books not contained in the Heb. Canon should be relegated ' *inter apocrypha* ', and it will be seen that the speed with which he ' translated ' these books is evidence of the little importance he attributed to them (§65*c*).

c But Jerome had comparatively little authority in the ecclesiastical councils of his day, and official Roman policy was dictated by his great contemporary St Augustine and the African Church, where the Greek Bible had been originally produced and which had never doubted its divine inspiration. St Augustine probably had but little patience with any desire to have its prestige shared at all with a Bible in Latin and derived from Heb. Although Jerome's distinction between *libri canonici* and *libri ecclesiastici* had come to stay, and the term ' Apocrypha ' used as a title for the latter, the Roman Church adhered to the wider Greek canon; and the form now found in the Vulgate, the Douay English, and the latest version by Mgr Knox conforms to this custom. The Council of Trent (1546) and the Vatican Council (1870) seem to have saved the Greek Bible as a Christian heritage by insisting at least on the ' deutero-canonicity ' of the Apocrypha.

When Protestants produced translations of the OT based on the Heb. original text, they were naturally limited to the books which constituted the Heb. Canon, but even this development was not allowed to interfere with the general order. Consequently there arose the convenient compromise whereby the order of the Alexandrian Canon was retained, but was confined to the thirty-nine books of the Heb. Canon; the other books were largely retained and deemed to be ' good and useful to read ' and put in the Apocrypha. Thus Luther kept the Apocrypha in his Bible but explained they were for edification: Calvin excluded them. In this country the Anglican Church has declared in the Thirty-nine Articles (Article 6) that it retains them in the lectionary but they are to be read ' for example of life and instruction of manners, but yet doth it not apply them to establish any doctrine '. On the other hand the British and Foreign Bible Society cannot by charter include the Apocrypha in its Bibles. Nevertheless the books of the Apocrypha are contained in the main translations into English, including both AV and RV, and the latest translation now in preparation will also contain them. 58d

The Text—The story of the transmission of the text follows to some extent that of the Canon; it may be actually subservient to it, for in its attitude to the text the Church may be said to reflect its more general attitude to the Canon. Consequently, the present résumé must follow the two main divisions accepted above, and trace the more liberal story of the Greek text as well as the more rigid one of the Heb. text. 59a

It must be assumed that as the OT of the Early Church was composed of the books of the Alexandrian Canon, so also the text was that of the LXX. With minor, though intrinsically significant, divergences, the Fathers quoted the LXX scriptures at least in Western Christendom. When Latin became increasingly popular in North Africa and Western Europe, and the Scriptures were rendered in the vernacular, it was the Greek texts that were at first translated.

From the very outset, and certainly from a very early time in the Christian era, the text transmission of the LXX was far from strict: indeed from the early 3rd cent. A.D. we have a comment by Origen, the first scholar, in our sense of the word, in the history of Christendom, that the MSS showed the greatest divergence, due both to scribal errors and, what is worse, to revision of the text and additions and omissions of ' whatever seems right ' to the revisers. Again, as the article on the OT Versions will demonstrate in greater detail, the Church in various areas adopted different recensions of the LXX, which further added to the chaos. After the Edict of Milan in A.D. 313 and the consequent acceptance of Christianity by Constantine as an empire religion, there was an attempt to secure for the OT, just as for the NT, a semi-standardisation of the text; but one need only look at the **Great Codices** of the Greek Bible which were produced as a result of the Edict, to realise that there was very little consistency used in the production of such a text, and still less success in establishing the textual minutiae. Codices Sinaiticus and Vaticanus from the 4th cent., Alexandrinus, Ephraemi, and others from the 5th show little textual improvement on the earlier text forms which have been discovered in the papyri from the 2nd and 3rd cent. b

Because of this deterioration it is impossible to exaggerate the importance of Jerome's work on the **Vulgate** in the late 4th and early 5th cent. He was commissioned by the then Pope to produce a Latin rendering of the whole of the Bible, and he began by revising for the NT and the Psalter the existing translations into Latin, the so-called **Old Latin texts,** to bring them into line with the LXX. He then again revised the Psalter and possibly other parts of the OT according tot he Hexaplaric text (cf. §65*c*). But between the years 390 and 405, whilst he lived in Palestine, he produced a Latin translation based not c

59c on any LXX MS or edition but on the Heb. text. It is unlikely that he resorted to the Heb. text from any desire to introduce any revolutionary principle of scholarship, for he stressed that, in translating, ' if we follow the syllables we lose the understanding ', and there are innumerable instances of departure from the Heb. text to accommodate Christian dogma and interpretation. He appreciated, rather, that in the Heb. he found a stabilised, well-defined text-form. This, in turn, led him to contrast the Heb. text with the Greek and Latin renderings, and to declare his preference for ' the source of truth ' (the Heb. text) over the ' opinion of mere rivulets ' (the LXX recensions). We have seen how the same preference is shown by him in his attitude to the Canonical books over the books of the Apocrypha.

d But the history of the Vulgate shows that as a Version it was premature and that Jerome himself was not the theologian to carry through its implications. We have seen how his attitude to the Canon was rejected by his contemporaries, especially St Augustine, and in the same way his Vulgate was very quickly modified to accommodate the LXX and even the popular local renderings of the Old Latin Version. The Council of Trent made the Vulgate the ' official ' Bible of the Roman Church, but an examination of this text shows that it is far removed from any Latin text which can reasonably be assumed to have been Jerome's. And it is significant that the latest move to reconstruct the ' original ' text of Jerome, by the Benedictines (1907 on) shows that the attempt has met with considerable criticism even among some Roman Catholic scholars, and it is already commonly accepted that the edition is unlikely to be definitive.

e During the Renaissance, and particularly by the Reformers, another significant step was taken when new translations were produced deliberately based on Heb. In England the renderings into English had previously rested on the Vulgate, with the monks diligently keeping one eye on the popular Old Latin Versions. The 16th cent., however, saw **Tyndale's NT** translated from Greek, and later the OT translated from Heb. It was not a solitary venture, and the earliest extant notice of the work, a note sent to Wolsey by his agent in Antwerp in May 1527, refers to a combined effort by 'some Englishmen, Luther, his disciples . . . to translate the bible into English ', and it is well known that Tyndale's OT was not only slightly later than Luther's German translation, but frequently influenced by it. Indeed, comments were passed, especially by Roman leaders, that both were really but different forms (English and German) of the same translation. It is generally allowed, however, that there is also considerable independence in Tyndale's rendering over against Luther's. And it is fair to quote from a letter sent by Tyndale in May 1535, when he was imprisoned in the Castle of Vilvord, asking that he be permitted to have ' my Hebrew Bible, my Hebrew Grammar and Hebrew Dictionary, that I may pass the time in that study '.

The translation was a typical piece of Renaissance-Reformation work. There was obvious and deep interest in Heb. words, syntax and the verbal system, and also in the orthography of proper names—including the word Jehovah which Tyndale seems to have introduced and explained independently of Luther.

f Subsequent revisers, especially in the **Geneva Bible,** and through various phases to the final emergence of the **AV**, declare in their prefaces that Heb. scholarship claimed due importance in their preparation, but the fact remains that the purpose of the renderings, and especially the AV itself, was liturgical and consequently avoided wherever possible any drastic changes in the current version. The **Bishops' Bible** of 1568 which was the official basis of the AV was itself ' a backward looking version ', and ' the Rules to be observed in the Translation of the Bible ' (the AV) state that not only was the Bishops' Bible to be followed, but also ' when a word hath divers Significations, that to be kept which hath been most commonly used by the most of the Ancient Fathers, being agreeable to the Propriety of the Place and the Analogy of the Faith '. That is, compromise was accepted and fidelity to the Heb. text was subservient to continuity of doctrine. The innumerable marginal notes of the edition, however, indicate the will of the translators themselves to go much farther than their terms of reference, and in them we find much scholarly information which even today has considerable lexicographical interest. 59f

A fair number of translations from the Heb. were prepared during the 17th, 18th, and 19th cent., but they were eclipsed by the appearance at the end of the 19th of the **RV.** Textually, the number of changes introduced is smaller than for the NT but the general change of attitude to the original text is far reaching. Here the Heb. diction and even the idiom has greater control. Any student who uses the RV as a crib for the Heb. text knows how much easier it is to get away with the misdemeanour than if he uses the AV, and, by the same token, the sensitive reader will quickly put aside the RV and return to the AV for the aesthetic pleasure of reading Scripture ; the Hebraic flavour of the former is too strong. Again, as with the AV, the marginal entries of the RV are particularly important, especially for lexicographical purposes. g

The influence of Biblical Criticism, especially the urge to alter the text by conjectural emendation, is evident in most of the OT renderings of the present century, and, despite temporary popularity, most of them are sooner or later forgotten. Ferrar Fenton's translation shows considerable originality, while Paul Haupt's Polychrome Bible (incomplete) makes important scholarly contributions. Moffatt's rendering has retained its popularity because of its felicity, but its departures from the standard parent text makes its use in the classroom precarious. The same is patently true of translations contained in the weightier commentaries, particularly the ICC, and to a lesser though more useful extent, in the notes in the Cambridge and Century Bibles. The latest rendering, the **RSV,** is certainly the best in English, and suffers only because it is a revision of a previously accepted version, and one is left wondering how much better the rendering might have been, had the eminent scholars responsible for it been given their head. h

In some ways the story of the OT text in English might be regarded as a digression, but it does serve the purpose of demonstrating how the history of Bible study in Protestant England increasingly underlines the importance of the Heb. text. And it is for this reason alone that a survey of the transmission of the Heb. text is relevant in an article such as this : normally its interest is confined to the Hebraist, who, at every stage, must rely on a good working-knowledge of the language. The present outline must necessarily ignore or pass lightly over some of the more important technical aspects, but the interest of the general reader will be met by indicating how the Heb. transmission fared at its various stages. 60a

The oldest extant **MSS of the Heb. Bible** are the Qumrân biblical MSS from the **Dead Sea Scrolls.** They include examples of practically every book in the OT, many of them in more than one copy. At present only two MSS of Isa. from Cave 1 have appeared in facsimile : A(1QIs[a]), in *The Dead Sea Scrolls of St Mark's Monastery*, vol. 1, *The Isaiah Manuscript and the Habakkuk Commentary*, ed. M. Burrows (1950), and B(1QIs[b]), in *The Dead Sea Scrolls of the Hebrew University*, ed. E. L. Sukenik (1955), with further fragments from the same scroll in *Discoveries in the Judaean Desert I, Qumrân Cave I*, ed. D. Barthélemy and J. T. Milik (1955), Section 8, Plate XII. They are designated here as texts A and B respectively. Special interest attaches also to scrolls of Sam. from Cave 4, as yet unpublished but described by F. M. Cross in JBL 74 (1955), 147–72, with additional details in BA 19 (1956), 84f. This b

60b MS contains sections of practically the whole of the books of Sam.

These three MSS may be used to illustrate what must be regarded as a provisional picture of the state of the Heb. text in the late pre-Christian era—provisional because until many more manuscripts are available in published form it is impossible to give any kind of overall survey. At the same time it is a most instructive picture that does emerge from these three documents.

c Firstly, the Isa. A document, which contains the whole of Isa. apart from a few minor lacunae due to wear and tear of the MS. It was the first biblical MS of the scrolls to be published, and even now it is by far the best known. The average person who reads about the Dead Sea Scrolls—and his number is legion—is reassured by the authorities that the scroll agrees to a remarkable degree with the text of the standard Heb. Bible, and there is no need to dispute this verdict, at least as far as the average reader is concerned. But textual criticism is a detailed study, and from this standpoint it is quite misleading to emphasise this very great measure of agreement. Apart from scribal errors which are numerous, the following divergences stand out: (*a*) the scroll, especially in the second half, presents a widely divergent orthography and grammar from that of the classical text; (*b*) there are numerous divergent readings, some of which correspond to known alternatives, e.g. in the LXX and in the *Ḳ^{e}rê* and *K^{e}thîbh* variants, whereas others were previously unknown; (*c*) in some instances the proper names agree not with the form they have in the common Isa. text but with that in later books, e.g. Chr. That is, the text in MS A might be regarded as a recension, approximating to the classical form, but by no means identical with it.

Secondly, the Sam. document, which agrees very frequently with the LXX over against the classical text. It has always been suspected that behind the LXX lies a different recension of the Heb. text, but it has been a moot point whether any given variant reflects the recension or represents an interpretation introduced by the Greek translator. The present discovery has tilted the balance very strongly in favour of the former view, and in future, at least for the books of Sam., LXX divergences are likely to be taken as representing a divergent Heb. underlying text. *A fortiori*, the same principle will be followed for other books. In other words, the existence of recensions, already indicated by the Isa. MS A, must be assumed to a still greater degree, with qualitative as well as quantitative variants from the traditional Heb. text.

Thirdly, Isa. MS B, which contains fragments of chs. 7–8, 12–13, 15–16, 19, 22, 24–5, in one collection, and of chs. 10, 13, 16, 19, 22–3, 26, 28, 29–30, 35, 37–9, 40 and long, almost continuous sections of 41–63, 65–6 in another. Contrary to the two examples described above, the significance of this scroll, with its substantial amount of text, is that it has a remarkable degree of agreement with the classical, Massoretic text. There are minor divergences, but they are no different in character, and no more numerous than those in medieval biblical MSS. The conclusion clearly indicated is that there was in existence among sectarian Jews, in pre-Christian times, a text-form which coincided with the form of the text which was later transmitted by the Rabbinic scribes of orthodox Judaism. We shall have to return to this point.

d Apart from the Qumrân Scrolls the only example of a Heb. biblical text generally thought to belong to pre-Christian times is the **Nash papyrus** in the University Library of Cambridge, and its main interest now lies in the palaeographical indication it gives for dating the scrolls. A much more important witness for the text, however, is the Greek translation in the LXX, and this will be discussed in the section given to the ancient Versions.

Otherwise the available information about the Heb. 60d
text is culled from statements in the Mishnah, for there are no extant Heb. MSS until well on in the Christian era.

The text was written on scrolls, probably parchment, e
and the square, so-called Aramaic alphabet was used; an earlier, Phoenician script was expressly proscribed by the Rabbis, though it is interesting to note that among the sectarian scrolls from Qumran this prohibition was either unknown or ignored, as witness some fragments of Lev. in the early script. At the same time, it is unlikely that the Aramaic script was in regular use until NT times, for the script of the scrolls does not quite agree with it in all details.

Rabbinic writings tell us of two important steps in 61a
the **history of the text.** The first is that from three copies of the Torah which were kept in the Temple, a definitive form was adduced, thus stabilising the text (Pal. Talm. Ta'anith, 4:2). The second is that Rabbi Aqiba (2nd cent. A.D.) spent many years in scrutinising the use of the particles in the text, with a view to establishing a definitive text-form. On the basis of this information a theory was evolved, which, especially under the influence of de Lagarde late in the 19th cent., was held until comparatively recently, that since the 2nd cent. A.D. a standardised text was scrupulously transmitted by Judaism. But the theory has been considerably modified, mainly as a result of the work of Paul Kahle during the present century, who has shown that the authoritative text is actually an emergent text-form which presupposes centuries of gradual development from the time of Aqiba onward. The phases in this emergence will be described later in this article, but before it can be discussed, it should be noted that the discovery of Isa. MS B mentioned above may well bring about yet another modification, this time of Kahle's hypothesis. The very close affinity between MS B of Isa. and the classical text shows that the latter text had been in existence in pre-Christian times, and since it circulated outside orthodox circles, it is right to assume that it was accepted by Rabbinic orthodoxy. At least, it would be passing strange if orthodox Judaism, at a subsequent stage, adopted a text-form which had been current only among Sectarians. Furthermore, the canonical sanctity of Scripture postulates, as we have seen, a considerable degree of inviolability of text, and questions of 'sanctity' were practically settled by the time of Aqiba.

The view might now be advocated that when Aqiba b
and the scribes of the 2nd cent. were concerned about a standardised text-form, the text was already in existence and accepted as authoritative, but required to be firmly established, even as the books of the Canon and even as Judaism itself required consolidation, because of the moral and spiritual chaos which had followed the fall of Jerusalem in A.D. 70.

Thus, after the fall of the state Judaism put its c
house in order, and henceforth the transmission of Scriptures was more than ever the concern of professional scribes. They scrutinised the columns of script, counted words and letters, established which was the middle consonant and the middle word, noted various grammatical forms, listed words which denoted divergent traditions. These and similar activities were practised, not from any desire to collect curiosities but to ensure correct and careful copying. The scribes came to be regarded as the authorities *par excellence* in the transmission of Scriptures, and their close connection with the Pharisees shows how deeply rooted was their adoration of Scripture.

But their transmission was not uniform, for they d
worked at different centres and reflected divergent traditions. Rabbinic scholarship was conducted not only at Jamnia in Palestine, but also in Babylon, where there flourished two academies, one at Nehardea and later at Pumbeditha, and another at Sura. Thus it is necessary to think of two main lines of transmission, Western and Eastern. They show divergence not only

61d in minutiae but even in major matters, such as the division of the Torah for lectionary purposes. Another witness of the extent of divergence is the production of the Jerusalem and Babylonian Talmuds, both based on the standard Rabbinic codification of the oral tradition, the Mishnah, which they had in common. The two transmissions must be followed independently for some centuries until there did emerge a standardised form, some time in the 11th cent.

e The tradition was technically known as **Massorah**—a word which goes back to the OT, but in this specific sense to the Mishnah. It served to safeguard the transmission by delimiting, defining and excluding all possible interpretations and corruptions which might endanger the technical sanctity of the text. The people responsible for it were *Ba'ale Ha-Massoreth*—its masters (not creators); and the text that they guarded and transmitted was the Massoretic Text—which is, of course, still the technical name for the classical Heb. text of the OT. The word Massorah is also used for the collection of Massoretic data which was collected and transmitted on the margins and at the end of MSS, and which was, until the researches of Paul Kahle, erroneously regarded as uniform for all transmissions of the text. There were Massoroth for the Babylonian and for the Palestinian transmissions, and the latter, after the Islamic conquest of Palestine in 638, came into considerable prominence in Tiberias.

62a Some time in the 7th cent., probably under the indirect influence of Islam and of developments in the Syriac language, a rough and ready beginning was made to vocalise the consonantal text by the addition of vowel signs. It happened concurrently in Babylon and in Palestine, but the schemes differed though each was supralineal. Some time later, under the influence of a Jewish biblical but non-Rabbinical sect called the Karaites, both schemes were drastically modified to produce a careful, elaborate and subtle vocalisation, but still divergent, with the Babylonian adhering to supralineal marks and the Tiberian devising a scheme of punctuation. Accents were introduced, and gradually the whole complicated Tiberian pointing was evolved which replaced the Babylonian in all official manuscripts, especially after the decline of Babylon in the 10th cent. The result of vocalisation, of course, was to establish further the recitation of the text and to increase enormously the data of Massoretic notes, which now had to be assembled in separate MSS.

b There was still, however, some conflict even in the successful Tiberian academy, and we know of two families of Massoretes from the 9th cent. whose transmissions varied. They were ben Naphtali and ben Asher, and though the former's text-form has disappeared, partial lists of discrepancies between the two are extant. It was ben Asher's text that emerged, and received official blessing, as it were, by Maimonides and other Rabbinic authorities. An actual copy of the ben Asher text, it is claimed, was kept in Aleppo until it was destroyed by fire in 1949, but a copy of the text, preserved in Leningrad, and dated A.D. 1008 was adopted by Kahle as the text for Kittel's *Biblia Hebraica*, 3rd (1937) and subsequent editions. Other manuscripts from the same group include the British Museum MS of the Pentateuch (Or 4445), for which a 9th-cent. date has been claimed, but which is probably later. It should be noted, however, that recent examination, especially by Teicher, has queried this dating of ben Asher MSS.

c Subsequent MSS are not particularly interesting for the present purpose, nor are the earlier printed editions of the Heb. OT, until the second Rabbinic Bible especially prepared for the printing-press of Daniel Bomberg in Venice in 1524–5. It was edited by Jacob ben Chayim, and, despite its having been based on recent and poor MSS it became the basis for most of the textual work in subsequent centuries. It was used by C. D. Ginsburg for his special edition for the centenary celebrations of the British and Foreign Bible Society in 1926, and for the first two editions of 62c
Biblia Hebraica (1905, 1912).

d Another interesting edition was that included in the Complutensian Polyglot (1514–17), but its claim to be an authoritative text-form cannot be highly estimated, and subsequent Polyglots show considerable influence by the ben Chayim text. It is also significant that the early Protestant translators preferred editions produced by Jews to the Catholic Polyglot texts, and it has been so throughout the centuries. The text reprinted by the British and Foreign Bible Society since 1866, edited by Letteris (1852), is a version by van der Hooght (1705) which, in turn, goes back ultimately to an edition by Buxtorf (1611) based on ben Chayim and the Complutensian Polyglot.

e It is amazing that during the past two centuries so much textual criticism has been based on a text whose prototype existed only in such recent editions. But the fact is that there are no really early Massoretic MSS extant. Biblical MSS were sacred, and when they had become ragged and worn by synagogue use they were not destroyed, but placed reverently in a room in the synagogue, called the Geniza, or treasure-place, and when the Geniza was full, advantage was taken of the burial of a Rabbi to fill his grave with discarded MSS. By a remarkable accident, an old synagogue in Cairo was examined during the latter part of the last century, and its Geniza was half full of MSS from before the late 9th cent., when the building had first become a synagogue (it was previously a church). Obviously some of the MSS were about two hundred years old before they had been discarded, so the cache contains fragments from the 7th cent. and later. There are about two hundred thousand of them, containing religious poetry, private papers, even children's exercises, but particularly biblical fragments. These are now deposited in great libraries, in Leningrad, in the U.S.A., and particularly in Britain, where the University Library in Cambridge, the British Museum, and (latterly) the John Rylands Library, in that order, have some thousands of fragments. Of course, their date is too late for them to be of great textual significance, but a scrutiny will show a surprising degree of textual variations, especially in the writing of the Divine Name: Adonay, YHWH and Elohim seem to be easily and frequently interchangeable. (An examination of fragments of the Pentateuch would be interesting in view of the dependence of Pentateuchal criticism on the use of Divine Names!) But important information can be derived from these fragments about the later phases of the story of the transmission. By means of them Kahle was able to reconstruct the history of vocalisation in a way previously impossible, for they contain actual examples of early and later Babylonian, Palestinian and Tiberian vocalisations; and they also became the mainstay of his hypothesis for the various phases in the history of the transmission of the text and the Massoroth. For this reason Kahle's 1941 Schweich Lectures, *The Cairo Geniza* (published 1947) is probably the most important study for the history of the text that has appeared for many centuries.

63a Because so much material is available for the history of the text most of the available space to be devoted to the subject of this article has been taken up with its survey. It is impossible to do more than mention another aspect of OT textual criticism, the classification of **scribal errors** and the attempts made to emend the text. That such errors exist is not doubted, and textual emendation is still legitimate. But it is now realised that their incidence is not nearly as common as was once thought, and leading scholars today are far less inclined than were their predecessors to interfere with the MT.

b A glance at the *apparatus criticus* of Kittel's *Biblia Hebraica*, 3rd edition (1937) or later will show it divided into two sections, the upper consisting of textual variants in the Massoretic transmission and a few from the Versions, and the lower, according

63b to the Preface the more important, of textual changes. There are scholars who would reverse the order, and argue that the upper section is the more important because the merely conjectural emendations of the lower discredit it. Without sharing in the rather extreme iconoclasm of this view, it is nevertheless necessary to mention one of the most common errors. In the use of Versions it is frequently given that a number of Versions support a reading when actually only one Version could legitimately be quoted, because the others simply reproduce it. Thus, in 2 Sam. 13:21, 27, and possibly 31, LXX, OL, and Vulg. show that there are lacunae in the MT, whereas actually it is the LXX which alone provides the variants whence the readings were adopted in the other Versions. There are other instances where LXX daughter translations are involved, where the *apparatus criticus* quotes LXX, Syr., and Vulg., but this really means only one Version, because of the admitted dependence of the other two on the LXX. The fact that the Versions, especially those with Christian transmissions, are so interlocked despite their independent origins, means that each of them must be individually examined to establish whether or not it can provide independent textual evidence on any particular reading.

c **Textual criticism,** or Lower Criticism as it used to be called to distinguish it from Higher, Literary Criticism, is an established science, and can be surveyed as a historical study.

For the MT it can be divided into two sections : (*a*) changes in the text due to deliberate alterations by the scribes, and (*b*) accidental changes.

d (*a*) Long before the text assumed its present form it was modified for reasons known to us and unknown. Glosses were added, explanatory, pious, habit (e.g. the adding of the words ' of the covenant ' to ' ark ' in many places), and others. Unfortunately, some commentaries in the past have shown an undue enthusiasm for this class of textual corruption, and any phrase in the text which might contradict a preconceived theory was apt to be dismissed as a gloss : on the other hand it is generally recognised that, e.g. the book of Ezek. contains numerous instances of the glossator's work. Other early interferences were made by scribes who expunged the names of foreign deities and substituted for them the word *bôsheth* ('shame'), e.g. Mephibosheth for Meribaal.

e From the period which followed the fixing of the consonantal text we have Rabbinic evidence of textual criticism. *Tikkûnê ha-Sôph^{e}rîm* (emendations of the scribes), mentioned in Rabbinic commentaries, refer to attempts to avoid anthropomorphisms in the text by a change of suffix, in as many as eighteen passages. *'Ittûrê ha-Sôph^{e}rîm* (omissions of the Scribes) refer to grammatical points. *S^{e}bhîrîn* are marginal notes inserted in the Massorôth to indicate that the form is ' unexpected ' and should probably be replaced by another word. *N^{e}kuddôth* (*puncta extraordinaria*) are dots placed over words in ten passages in the Pentateuch which were queried by the Massoretes on textual or exegetical grounds, and the fact that they are frequently mentioned in the Mishnah and other Rabbinic writings shows that they were commonly acknowledged. Again, the retention of *K^{e}rê* and *K^{e}thîbh* variants shows Massoretic concern for textual criticism.

f There are other places where the scribes can be held responsible for textual corruption. There are innumerable instances where a vocalisation is queried on the basis of an LXX reading, and it lies to hand to suggest that if any case is to be made for a ' recension ' in the Massoretic text, it is in the interpretation given to it by the Massoretes responsible for the Tiberian vocalisation. On the other hand, it is sometimes thought these late Massoretes confused the meaning of a passage because they had failed to understand it and consequently pointed it wrongly.

g It is in this context, too, that mention should be made of collections of textual variants. In the general survey (§62*a-c*) it was suggested that after the emergence of the final vocalisation and accentuation in the ben Asher text, the MSS and printed editions show uniformity. Nevertheless variants do occur, and they form the basis of two massive works from the 18th cent. Kennicott published in 1776–80 his *VT Hebraicum cum variis lectionibus*, based on 615 MSS and 52 printed editions. De Rossi, *Variae lectiones VT* (1784–8), is more thorough, based on 731 MSS and 300 other editions. Furthermore, as G. R. Driver has pointed out, Kennicott's variants sometimes preserve old lost words, e.g. in Prov. 1:27, or preferable forms, e.g. in Jg. 4:18. Finally C. D. Ginsburg, in his British and Foreign Bible Society edition of the Heb. OT (1926), includes a full treatment of variants in the *apparatus criticus*.

(*b*) The possibility of involuntary scribal errors is well demonstrated by the very carelessly written Qumrân Scroll 1QIs^{a}, and in a recent introduction to the study, *The Text of the OT*, by E. Würthwein (Eng. tr. by P. R. Ackroyd, 1957), very good use is made of the manuscript to demonstrate the types and classes of error in the Heb. MT. The only caveat which might be entered is that 1QIs^{a} is not a Massoretic MS nor does it belong to Judaism but rather to a sect, and perhaps it is not fair to the Massoretes to put them to this undeserved disrepute. A better source would be the fragments from the Cairo Geniza, where the same types of error occur, but the incidence is not nearly so common. h

There have been useful manuals of textual corruption published—one in English by J. Kennedy (ed. by N. Levison), *An Aid to the Textual Amendment of the OT* (1928). It discusses such errors as confusion of similar letters, in both the archaic and Aramaic scripts, e.g. *Beth* and *Kaph*, *Daleth* and *Resh* ; inversion of letters ; haplography (writing a letter once where it should be repeated, or the omission of a word which is similar to the adjacent word) ; dittography (the reverse of the previous error) ; homoeoteleuton (where phrases and even passages have been omitted from between two similar words or even endings of words). How such omissions could have taken place in such official texts as the prototype of the present *Biblia Hebraica* and all the MSS supporting it defies explanation, because the Rabbis were strict in the matter of checking and correcting standard MSS, but it is a fact that they exist. For instance in 1 Sam. 14:41 a lengthy passage has disappeared by homoeoteleuton with the word ' Israel ', which occurs immediately before the beginning of the lost passage and which ends the passage. i

Other assumed errors or sources of error are disputed among scholars. It is sometimes thought that abbreviations, particularly in the divine names, coupled with the wrong division of words constitute a possible error. That such abbreviations occur in the Geniza Fragments is demonstrable, but it is still open to argue that they did not occur in more official MSS. Another debatable point is whether or not MSS were copied by dictation. This could have been a common source of corruption and would account for the numerous variations between similarly sounding gutturals ; but, again, there is scepticism among scholars on the possibility. j

The final note, however, in any discussion of textual errors must be one of caution. The prestige of the Massoretic scribal activity, increasingly recognised of recent years, makes the *a priori* likelihood of errors less than was previously believed. Increased study of Heb. philology and semantics, and better acquaintance with cognate languages show that departure from the accepted text is frequently hazardous, and fresh information, particularly from the Dead Sea Scrolls and the Cairo Geniza, makes the history of the text not only more interesting but enhances its standing as a text-form, the early standardisation of which made it unique among all textual transmissions. k

Bibliography—A. Bentzen, *Introduction to the OT* (2nd ed. 1952) ; O. Eissfeldt, *Einleitung in das AT*

(2nd ed. 1956); E. E. Flack and others, *The Text, Canon and Principal Versions of the Bible* (Reprint from *20th-Cent. Encyc. of Religious Knowledge*) (1956); W. O. Oesterley and T. H. Robinson, *An Introduction to the Books of the OT* (1935); R. H. Pfeiffer, *Introduction to the OT* (2nd ed. 1952); H. R. Willoughby (ed.), *The Study of the Bible Today and Tomorrow* (1947).

CANON: F. Buhl, *Canon and Text of the OT* (Eng. tr. 1892); G. Hölscher, *Kanonisch und Apokryph* (1905); J. L. Koole, *Het Probleem van de Canonisatie van het OT* (1955); G. Östborn, *Cult and Canon: a Study in the Canonisation of the OT* (1950); H. H. Rowley, *The Growth of the OT* (1950); H. E. Ryle, *The Canon of the OT* (2nd ed. 1899); G. Wildeboer, *The Origin of the Canon of the OT* (Eng. tr. 1895); S. M. Zarb, *Historia Canonis Utriusque Testamenti* (1934).

TEXT AND VERSIONS: D. R. Ap-Thomas, *A Primer of OT Criticism* (1947); F. F. Bruce, *The Books and the Parchments* (1950); C. D. Ginsburg, *Introduction to the Massoretico-Critical Edition of the Heb. Bible* (1897); P. Kahle, *Masoreten des Ostens*, BWAT 15 (1913), *Masoreten des Westens*, I, BWAT (N.F. 8) (1927), II, BWANT 14 (1930), *The Cairo Geniza* (1947); F. G. Kenyon, *Our Bible and the Ancient MSS* (1948); I. M. Price (rev. W. A. Irwin, A. P. Wikgren), *The Ancestry of our English Bible* (3rd ed. 1956); B. J. Roberts, *The OT Text and Versions* (1951); E. Robertson, *The Text of the OT and the Methods of Textual Criticism* (1939); H. W. Robinson (ed.), *The Bible in its Ancient and English Versions* (2nd ed. 1954); L. A. Weigle (ed.), *An Introduction to the RSV* (1952); E. Würthwein (Eng. tr. P. R. Ackroyd), *The Text of the OT* (1957).

OTHER WORKS: H. S. Gehman, 'Manuscripts of the OT in Hebrew', BA 8 (1945), 100–3; J. L. Teicher, 'The Ben Asher Bible MSS', JJS 2 (1950), 17–25 (cf. P. Kahle, 'The Hebrew Ben Asher Bible MSS', VT 1 (1951), 161–7); D. W. Thomas, 'The Textual Criticism of the OT', OTMS (1951), 238–64.

C. H. Dodd, *The Bible and the Greeks* (1934); G. Gerleman, *Studies in the LXX: Job, II Chronicles* (1946), *Proverbs* (1956); H. G. Meecham, *The Oldest Version of the Bible* (1932); H. M. Orlinsky, *The LXX: the Oldest Translation of the Bible* (1949); R. R. Ottley, *A Handbook to the LXX* (1920); I. L. Seeligmann, *The LXX Version of Isaiah* (1948); H. B. Swete, *An Introduction to the OT in Greek* (3rd ed. 1914); H. St. J. Thackeray, *Some Aspects of the Greek OT* (1927).

F. V. Filson, 'The LXX and the NT', BA 9 (1946), 34–42; H. S. Gehman, 'The Theological Approach of the Greek Translator of Job 1–15', JBL 68 (1949), 231–40; P. Katz, 'The Recovery of the Original LXX', *Actes du Premier Congrès de la Fédération Internationale d. Assoc. d'Études Classiques* (1951), 165–82; H. M. Orlinsky, 'The Use of the Versions in Translating the Holy Scriptures', *Religious Education*, 47 (1952), 253–9; H. H. Rowley, 'The Proto-LXX Question', JQR, NS 33 (1943), 497–9); J. W. Wevers, 'Septuaginta Forschungen', ThRS (N.F. 22) (1954), 85–138, 171–90.

P. Benoît, 'Editing the Manuscript Fragments from Qumran', BA 19 (1956), 75–96; P. Churgin, *Targum Jonathan to the Prophets* (1927); F. M. Cross, 'The Oldest MSS from Qumran', JBL 74 (1955), 147–72; A. Díez Macho, 'Una copia completa del Targum palestinense al Pentateuco en la Biblioteca Vaticana', *Sefarad* 17 (1957), 119–21; P. Kahle, *Die Hebräischen Hss. aus der Höhle* (1951); A. Sperber, 'The Targum Onkelos in its Relation to the Masoretic Heb. Text', *Proc. Amer. Acad. f. Jewish Research* (1934–5), 309–51; J. F. Stenning, *The Targum of Isaiah* (1949).

THE ANCIENT VERSIONS OF THE OLD TESTAMENT

BY B. J. ROBERTS

64a Two important benefits derive from the study of the Ancient Versions : (*a*) source material for a study of the interpretation of the OT at formative stages in the growth of Christian and Jewish doctrine ; (*b*) readings which provide variants for the Heb. OT text itself. Both, however, are conditioned by the history of the individual versions, and the present survey is intended to outline the history in order to stress that neither benefit should be used indiscriminately, but should be assessed each against its own background. That is, each version is an entity in itself, and it is wrong to patch up one text with a piece from another without first scrutinising both.

b The most important and the most interesting of the Versions is the Greek, mainly in the **LXX.** Its original setting is Egypt, particularly Alexandria, in the Hellenistic period, but the main background is provided by the Early Church throughout the Middle East, and the course of the version's history is largely governed by Christian interests.

c It is difficult to know when Jewish communities first settled in Egypt, but by the middle of the 3rd cent. B.C. there was in Alexandria an important establishment, which enjoyed considerable autonomy, and which had become acclimatised to its Hellenistic surroundings. From the period *c.*150 B.C. comes one of the OT Pseudepigrapha (cf. §57*b*), the *Letter of Aristeas*, which describes how Ptolemy II Philadelphus (285–246 B.C.) arranged to have 72 men sent from Jerusalem to translate the Pentateuch for inclusion in the royal library. At a later period this account was embellished to such an extent that it inevitably became legendary, and subsequent criticism has deprived the Aristeas account of most of its historicity. Almost the only survival is the date, *c.*250 B.C., and the probability that the translators were more familiar with Heb. than Greek. But whether even this is true for the whole of the OT is debatable : in any case the translation varies considerably from one book to another. The translation of the Pentateuch is comparatively literal ; for others, e.g. Sam. and Jer., different recensions of the Heb. text are commonly presupposed ; yet others, e.g. Job and Prov., are so free that some passages are paraphrastic and others draw on classical Greek poets. Furthermore, there is evidence to show that more than one translator was responsible for each book.

d Thus it is obvious that the rendering was not produced at one time, or by one single body, but emerged during the period between 250 B.C. and the end of the 1st cent. B.C. It is likely that in the whole translation a lectionary interest was observed (see H. St John Thackeray, *The Septuagint and Jewish Worship* (1921)), but it is consistent with what we know of synagogue worship in the Diaspora to find in the version also a considerable emphasis on education, and a more liberal attitude to the canon—if, indeed, any principle of selection was observed at all (see §58*a*).

e The specifically Christian adoption of the LXX, and the canonical and textual developments of Judaism
in the 1st and 2nd cent. A.D., brought about an 64e
important change in the history of the Greek OT. The LXX was, like the Church, thrown out of the synagogue, and Greek-speaking Jewish orthodoxy was supplied by the early 2nd cent. with different translations, much more subservient to the authority of the Heb. text, and acceptable to the Pharisaic scribes and Rabbis. The renderings are marked by a rigid adherence to the Heb. text, even in minutiae, though it has been shown that there are sporadic phrases in very good Greek. The first has been attributed to **Aquila,** a proselyte from Pontus, and, according to Jewish belief, a pupil of Rabbi Aqiba. Remains of this rendering can be gleaned from fragments of Origen's *Hexapla* (cf. §64*f*) but the main source of the actual text is the Cairo Geniza (cf. §62*e*) in which some palimpsest copies from the 6th cent. A.D. have been found.

The second version from the same period, though slightly later, is by **Theodotion,** also, presumably, a proselyte. Actually this rendering is more in the nature of an adaptation of an existing Greek text to the Heb., but whether the Greek was the LXX or another version is still an open question. The main source of Theodotion's version is the book of Dan. in the usual LXX editions. It is moreover sufficient in quantity to enable Theodotionic readings to be identified in other sources, with the result that the pre-Theodotion basic text can be found in the NT and some Apostolic Fathers.

The third divergent version is that of **Symmachus,** possibly an Ebionite, or a Jewish proselyte, which belongs to A.D. 179. This rendering, however, is comparatively unknown except for a few Hexaplaric remains. To what extent a new Greek text of the Minor Prophets discovered in Qumrân is going to affect our knowledge of these three renderings cannot be discovered until the text is published, but it has been suggested that all three will be shown to have their basis in this version.

The next step is that taken by **Origen** in A.D. 240–5 f
(cf. §59*b*). In order to establish the LXX text he produced for the whole of the OT a six-columned (hence the technical term **Hexapla**) edition, containing (1) The Heb. text, (2) the same in transcription, (3) Aquila, (4) Symmachus, (5) the LXX, (6) Theodotion. For the Ps. there were three other texts, Quinta, Sexta, and Septima, one of which (Sexta), Origen said, came from a cave near Jericho (Qumrân or Murabba'at?). In order to obtain correspondence between the Heb. text and the LXX he marked the LXX passages omitted from the Heb. with an obelus (÷), passages present in Heb. and not in LXX he translated and marked with an asterisk (*), with a metobelus (⟨) marking the end in each case. The original MS, which must have been immense, was kept at Caesarea in Palestine, and Jerome was able to study it, but nothing is known of it since the Arab conquest of Palestine in 638. But a palimpsest copy discovered in Milan in 1894 contains the text of five of the six columns (the missing column

64f being the Heb. text) for eleven Psalms. Otherwise, extant Greek fragments of the Hexapla were assembled by Field, *Origenis Hexaplorum quae supersunt* (1875).

Origen also produced a shorter edition—whether before or after the Hexapla is not known—in which only the Greek texts were given, and this constitutes the **Tetrapla.**

g The purpose of Origen's work is clear: he wanted to bring the LXX and the Heb. text into line with each other. But what actually happened was that he added to the existing multiplicity of texts by producing yet another. The position was worsened when scribes accepted his readings but dropped the diacritical signs, and consequently made Origen the unwilling author of a Hexaplaric recension of the LXX. To complicate matters still further, two other recensions became current in the 4th cent., the one by **Hesychius** (Bishop of Egypt, *d.*311) and the other by **Lucian** (Presbyter at Antioch, *d.*312). The influence of these recensions is obvious from quotations in the Fathers, but it is also patent that subsequent LXX MSS contain all three recensions, so intertwined that it is now well-nigh impossible to separate them.

h Thus we arrive at the early 4th cent. A.D., a crucial date in the history of the Greek Bible, because it was the time of the Edict of Milan, the so-called conversion of Constantine and the acceptance of Christianity as an official religion in the Roman Empire. The text of the Greek Bible was indeed confusing. If the history of Bible transmission in the Early Church has a lesson to teach, it is that the Early Fathers and biblical authorities were in no way encumbered by strictures limiting the truth to the written words of Scripture. They were modified and changed and interpreted almost at will. Nor were the Fathers as a rule perturbed about this freedom; on the contrary they revelled in it. The idea of literal inspiration is not one that belonged to the Early Church. It is against this background that we look at the next aspect of the study, the **MSS of the Greek Bible.**

i In contrast to the history of the Heb. OT text, some very early MSS of the LXX have been recovered, though the earliest of them are fragments with only a few verses. From the middle of the 2nd cent. B.C. come a papyrus fragment of Dt., now in the Rylands Library in Manchester, and another papyrus fragment, likewise of Dt., in Cairo; and from about a century later (recently estimated between 50 B.C. and A.D. 50) we have a leather scroll of the Minor Prophets which was discovered in 1952 with the Dead Sea Scrolls, but until the MS has been more fully studied its main significance cannot be assessed (see §64*e*).

j The next important group is the early Christian papyri, generally known as the **Chester Beatty Papyri.** They were acquired in 1930 from a dealer in Egypt, and according to Sir Frederic Kenyon, who edited the MSS (*The Chester Beatty Biblical Papyri*, Fascs. i–vii (1933–7)), they presumably come from the library of an early Christian Church in the region of Memphis at the head of the Nile Delta. They are now housed in the magnificent collection of Sir Chester Beatty, in Dublin. They contain portions of seven MSS of the OT, three of the NT, and one of the Greek text of the book of Enoch, and range from the 2nd to the 4th cent. Their importance is many-sided: they teach us much that is new about codex formation; they supply text specimens from the period before Origen and the recensions; one of them provides a genuine LXX text of Dan. The significance of the last point is that whereas normally the LXX MSS and editions give Theodotion's translation, there is in this MS, P967, a genuine and almost complete LXX text of Dan. 3:72–8:27 from the early 3rd cent.; otherwise the extant sources for this text are the Chigi MS (*Codex Chisianus*, 11th cent. in Rome, edited by Cozza (1877)), which is based on the Hexapla, and the Syro-Hexaplar of Paul of Tella, 616/17 (see §65*j*), which, in turn, was used to correct the Chigi MS.

Other fragments from the same collection are in Princeton and Vienna; and yet other small fragments 64j
of papyri, independent of the above, belong to the 3rd cent. A.D.

Then came the new era in biblical MSS. Papyrus k
gave way to vellum, and MSS were produced for the official use of the Church. Constantine commissioned fifty copies for the churches in Constantinople, and though not one of them has survived, the **Great Codices** of the 4th and 5th cent. reflect the importance of this step.

The MSS, transmitted in codices, i.e. in book form, are divided into two groups, according to the nature of the script, uncials or majuscules (capitals) and cursives or minuscules (small letters). The siglum for the uncials is normally a letter, or, less frequently, a number based on the collection by **Holmes and Parsons** in 1798–1827. The cursives are still given by numbers. A much more comprehensive list of MSS appeared in 1914 as part of the great German LXX undertaking, bearing the title *Verzeichnis d. LXX HSS d. AT* with A. Rahlfs, probably the most eminent LXX scholar of this century, as editor. The main uncials have been frequently described. The older MSS are called Great Codices—because of their eminence or because they contain the whole Bible, and from among them the following should be noted as basis for LXX study:

(1) **Codex Sinaiticus** (*Aleph* also *S*), now in the l
British Museum, generally dated late 4th or early 5th cent. The story of its discovery on Mt Sinai, some scandal connected with its subsequent history, and the final acquisition of it by the British Museum in 1933, makes one of the most romantic stories about the Bible, and can challenge even the discovery of the Dead Sea Scrolls. More relevant for us is the fact that three correctors, working at different stages, *c.* 6th cent., modified the text, and it is claimed for one of them that his corrections go back to Origen's *Hexapla.*

(2) **Codex Alexandrinus** (A), again in the British Museum, where it was one of the foundation gifts. It belongs to the early 5th cent.

(3) **Codex Vaticanus** (B), in the Vatican. A 4th cent. MS, it is generally regarded as the oldest and best of the LXX MSS, and it will be seen that current editions of the Version are either based on it or very largely depend on its readings.

(4) **Codex Ephraemi** (C), Paris. A palimpsest, with the biblical text forming the nether script. 5th cent.

(5) **Codex Marchalianus** (Q), Vatican, 6th cent.: the text, containing Prophets only, is Hesychian (cf. §64*g*), and the margins contain a great number of readings from a copy of the *Hexapla.*

Most of the uncials have been published in facsimile m
and in printed editions. The cursives of course are later and much more numerous: their main use is for collation after kinship has been established for them with either recensions or uncial MSS.

The history of the printed editions ranges from the n
Complutensian Polyglot (1514–17) down to two major editions which are in the process of publication. With two exceptions, which will be discussed later (§64*o*), the practice has been to print the text of one important uncial, which, since the appearance of the official Sixtine text of Rome (1587) has been Codex B for the editions of Holmes and Parsons (1798–1827), Swete (*The OT in Greek* (1887–91, with later editions)), Brooke-McLean-Thackeray (the so-called *Cambridge LXX* (1906–)) later under the editorship of T. W. Manson, and of which up to the present Gen. to Tob. (1940) have appeared. The most convenient edition of the LXX now available is the two-volume text edited by A. Rahlfs (published 1935), based on three uncials, B, Aleph, and A, with a limited *apparatus criticus.*

The editions which do not conform to this practice o
are the so-called Göttingen LXX, and the projected edition of M. L. Margolis. The former was planned

64o by Lagarde in the late 19th cent., followed by Rahlfs and Ziegler in the 20th cent, and discussed in a number of important handbooks (*Mitteilungen d. LXX Unternehmen*). The general principle is that the whole mass of readings from MSS, quotations, and daughter translations is systematically broken down to provide ultimately an eclectic version, which can be regarded as having the most legitimate claim to originality, and the *apparatus criticus*, appropriately sub-divided, not only claims to substantiate the theory but also to supply the student with information; for instance, it is recognised as the best available collection of Hexaplaric remains, thus replacing Field. It is, of course, a colossal undertaking, and the following books have already been published, Ru., Gen., Ps., 1 Mac., Isa., The Minor Prophets, Ezek., Dan., Jer. The Margolis edition is still more ambitious, but follows somewhat similar lines, with a more elaborate *apparatus criticus*, but the publication of an experimental part of Jos. is all that has appeared.

p With all this textual work on the LXX it may appear strange to the average student that there is hardly ever mention of a modern translation of the Version. An English rendering by C. Thomson, in 1808, has, albeit rather unsatisfactorily, been revised by C. A. Muses (*The LXX Bible* (1954)).

q Mention has been made of daughter translations. They include Old Latin, Coptic (Sahidic, Bohairic), Gothic, Armenian, Slavonic, Georgian, Ethiopic, and Arabic, and though intrinsically interesting and important for the history of the Church, it is impossible to deal with them in this survey without loss of perspective. The only exception is the Old Latin, which comes up again in connection with the Vulg. Their general significance is in their antiquity (ranging from the 2nd cent. to the 6th) and their local witness to the basic importance of recensions, e.g. the Bohairic and Sahidic translations are among the most important and oldest witnesses to the Hexaplaric recension of the Minor Prophets, whereas the Ethiopic presupposes in places an old LXX text which has no direct affinities with Manuscript A or Origen or Lucianic recension.

65a **The Vulg. and Peshitta**—These versions, like the LXX, are to be assessed as Christian documents, but in their origins they postulate more or less direct dependence on the Heb. Bible.

b The Latin text of Jerome's **Vulgate** produced between A.D. 390 and 405 can claim to be one of the most significant landmarks in the history of the Bible in Western Christendom. As far back as the second half of the 2nd cent. there were sporadic renderings of the LXX in Latin in S. Europe and N. Africa, and the resultant Old Latin version (or versions, for it is often thought that extant MSS point back to a number of originals) is still regarded as one of the important sources for LXX reconstruction. The OL Bible fragments were collected by P. Sabatier, 1743–9, and this has been brought up to date for the greater part of Gen. in four important volumes by the publication of *Vetus Latina* (1951–4).

c But in 382 Pope Damasus commissioned Jerome to produce a Latin Bible which should be textually more self-consistent than that presented in OL. It is not clear how he proceeded, but the general view today is that he first produced (384) the Psalter, based on the LXX and reflecting the OL renderings, in an edition later called *Psalterium Romanum*. In 386, Jerome, now living in Bethlehem, produced a second revision of the Psalter, this time with reference to Origen's *Hexapla*, and this became the Gallican Psalter, which, incidentally, is the version included in the modern Vulg. Possibly he revised other books of the OT at the same time. He then proceeded to translate the whole of the OT based on the Heb. text. He began in 391 with Sam., which he prefaced (*Prologus Galeatus*) with an explanation of the entire project, and the whole translation was finished in 405. The books of the Apocrypha altogether engaged him for only a few months.

The Version was not immediately accepted by the Church, and during the next two centuries the text was always subject to local accommodation to the OL renderings: a recent authority has stated that 'whole sections of some Vulg. MSS are pure OL, and few have escaped a modicum of OL admixture in isolated passages' (H. F. D. Sparks, 'The Latin Bible', in *The Bible in its Ancient and English Versions*, ed. Robinson (2nd ed. 1954), 118). Moreover subsequent revisions in the early 9th cent. made no attempt to reconstruct Jerome's text; thus Alcuin based his text on English MSS and Theodulf on Spanish. In the 13th cent. Stephen Langton produced at the new University of Paris an edition which saw the introduction of chapter divisions, but which textually was no improvement on its predecessors. The Council of Trent in 1546 made the Vulg. the authoritative text of the Roman Church, but though it produced the Sixtine of 1590 and the Clementine editions of 1592 and later, its claims to textual authenticity have never been strong. The edition in general use today is a Clementine text, revised by Hetzenauer, 1906. The work of the Benedictines since 1907 'to determine the text of St Jerome' has already been mentioned (§59*d*). 65d

Thus the textual history of the Vulg. shows how precarious it must be simply to take a reading from the version as evidence for or against the Heb. text, particularly if it points away from that text. In other words, when the Vulg. does not support the Heb., it is possible that the variation is more capable of 'inner Latin' explanation than anything else. e

The English renderings of the Vulg. can be very briefly described. The Old English renderings from Cædmon through the Venerable Bede and King Alfred, and the Anglo-Saxon interlineal renderings reflect OL rather than the Vulg. But when the translations of the Protestant Reformers turned out to be popular, the Vulg., too, was rendered in an official English Version called the Douay (1609–10) after the Catholic College in Flanders where it was produced. This was drastically revised in the 18th cent., and since that time, too, there have been a fair number of translations, particularly *The Westminster Version* (1913–35); but they are eclipsed by the most recent of them all, Mgr Ronald Knox's *Holy Bible translated from the Latin Vulg. in the Light of the Heb. and Greek Originals* (1945–9), and authorised by the Hierarchy. Whatever its value as a text might be, it is probably the most readable of all English Bibles.

The Peshitta—It is more difficult to begin the story of the Syr. Version than the Vulg., and the authorities are about equally divided on the question of whether it was originally a Jewish or a Christian version. There was strong Jewish proselytism in the Syrian royal house at Adiabene in the 1st cent. A.D. and this may well have occasioned a rendering at least of the Torah. Furthermore, the text agrees closely with the MT, with certain marked exceptions where either Christian replacements have been made, or a revision made on the basis of the LXX (e.g. in Isa. 7:14 the text gives 'virgin', not 'young woman'). Another important point is that the Syr. Canon was originally that of the Palestinian Canon and not the Alexandrian, though some Apocrypha were added soon afterwards. Two eminent Syrian Fathers from the 4th cent. refer to and quote copiously from the OT, and it is likely that the Version was widely known in Syria by that time. It is commonly accepted that the Version, whatever its origin, was current in Christian Churches during the 2nd or early 3rd cent. One other fact is that its text-form reveals a variety of translators. f

Again, as with other Christian Bibles, the subsequent history is one of multiplicity of text-forms and serious, though vain, attempts by leading Church Fathers to stabilise the text, especially by Rabbula, Bishop of Edessa, in the 5th cent., Jacob of Edessa in the early 8th, and bar Hebraeus in the 13th. The position is further complicated by the division of the Syrian Church g

65g in the 5th cent. into Nestorian and Jacobite, each with its own tradition. The name Peshitta (' simple '—probably ' common ' like the Latin ' Vulgate ') was given to the Version in the early 10th cent.

h The British Museum is happily placed in being probably the largest repository of Syr. biblical MSS in the world, and among them is the oldest dated copy of the Bible extant. It is a Pentateuch from A.D. 464, and its text varies considerably from the usual Peshitta MSS. The most important MS, however, is **Codex Ambrosianus** from the 6th cent., in Milan, which was reproduced in a photolithographic edition by Ceriani in 1876–81.

i Despite the numerous and good Syr. MSS, despite, too, the frequently repeated protest of scholars, the history of the printed editions of the Version is a sad one. The first edition was by Sionita, 1625 ; and the Paris Polyglot of 1645 contains a slightly revised edition of Sionita's, and this was reproduced in the Walton Polyglot (1657) and also, though still further corrupted, by Lee for the British and Foreign Bible Society in 1823. Other editions of the 19th cent. are either too dependent on Sionita or too free to be seriously regarded as critical texts.

But there have been important treatises and editions which deal with single books : Ps. (1914) and the Pentateuch (1914) by W. E. Barnes, Isa. by Diettrich (1905), Song of Songs by Bloch (AJSL, 1922), Ezr. by Hawley (1922), 2 Sam. by Englert (1949). Lagarde edited the Syr. Apocrypha in 1861.

j The **Syro-Hexaplar** is of course quite a different Version. It is a literal translation into Syr. of Origen's *Hexapla* (see §64*f*), with the diacritical signs carefully retained, and with references to variants in other Greek versions entered in the margins. It was made by Paul, Bishop of Tella in Mesopotamia, in 616–17. Because of the paucity of Hexaplaric remains, and the inadequacy of those that have been recovered, this version is extremely important. There are extant editions of most of the OT : Ceriani published in 1874 a text based on a Milan MS which contained the OT without Gen.-Kg., Chr.-Neh., Ru., but previously (1868) Gen.-Exod. 33:2 had been published, and Lagarde (1892) published most of the other books based on MSS in London and Paris.

66a It will be realised that the enormous part played in the history of the Versions by the Church and its patent lack of interest in a fixed textual transmission renders their usefulness for the textual study of the Heb. OT at best secondary. But there is a totally different side to the story, which recounts the translations of the Heb. text within the native tradition of Judaism itself. It is divided into two Versions, the **Samaritan** and the **Aramaic Targums.**

b It is probably inaccurate to speak of the Sam. text as a Version though it is quite customary. The rendering is in Heb., in a form of the archaic script, and it has been regarded as authoritative by the Sam. community throughout its history. But it frequently deviates from the MT in matters of orthography, pointing (in MSS since the 12th cent.), text divisions, and in one or two points of teaching, such as reading Gerizim instead of Ebal in Dt. 27:4. The question of the early history of the version has been raised by two recent events. The first is the discovery in the Qumrân MSS of 4QEx[a] (cf. Skehan, ' Exodus in the Samaritan Recension from Qumran ', JBL 74 (1955), 182–7), a fairly lengthy text of Exod. with obvious affinities with the Sam. text. The second consists of two quite independent examinations of photographs of the elusive Abisha scroll in Nablus, for which a very early date has been traditionally claimed. Both experts, P. Castro of Madrid, and E. Robertson, Manchester, have declared in favour of an early, pre-Christian date for the text (cf. R. E. Moody, ' Samaritan Material at Boston University : The Boston Collection and the " Abisha Scroll " ', *Boston University Graduate Journal* 10 (1957)). The text was edited by von Gall (1914–18), and is known also in translations : Greek (*Samaritikon*, whose readings are **66b**
given in Hexaplaric notes), Aramaic, whose text-form, however, was always rather free (edited Petermann u. Vollers, *Pentateuchus Samaritanus*, 1872–1911), and Arabic (Saadya Gaon's 10th-cent. rendering of the MT revised by Abu Sa'id in the late 13th).

Much more important are the direct Aram. render- **c**
ings of the OT, produced for the instruction of Jews under the auspices of the Rabbis themselves, as a result of the adoption of Aram. during the period of the Persian empire and later in Palestine and Mesopotamia generally. (The Qumrân Scrolls, however, show how wrong it is to assume that Heb. was a dead language by the time of Our Lord.)

The Targums, as they are called, fall into two **d**
clearly defined groups : (*a*) free interpretations, with sometimes lengthy interpolations of a midrashic, i.e. didactic, nature and containing all the books of the OT, and (*b*) literal, official translations of the Pentateuch. How far back they go is not known, but there is evidence for their existence in pre-Christian times. There is, moreover, a history of opposition to their use in synagogue worship, at least in their written form (Yad. 4:5). The Talmud states that the oral translation follows the reading of the Torah verse by verse and in the reading of the Prophets after every three verses ; and there is evidence that even the Prophets and the Hagiographa were rendered verse by verse. The existence of an official interpreter, *m[e]thūrg[e]mān*, was recognised, and the word Targum means ' translation '.

(*a*) It would appear that the free Targums are **e**
likely to be older than the more literal and they are available, albeit in late manuscript fragments and editions, for the whole of the OT. For the Pentateuch we have Targum Jerusalem I (or Palestinian Targum), which has also been called Pseudo-Jonathan (the abbreviation T.J. having been wrongly tacked on to a well-known Targumic personality). It contains a text to which later reference will be made, and a considerable amount of paraphrase, popular stories and marginal notes, though how much is later accretion is rightly suspected when we find that it includes in Gen. 21:21 the names of a wife and daughter of Mohammed. Copies of another Jerusalem Targum (Jerusalem II) have appeared in the important Cairo Geniza fragments. Its contents are similar in type to Jerusalem I, but especial interest attaches to its language, thought by Kahle (*Cairo Geniza*, pp. 121ff.) to represent the Palestinian Aram. of the 1st cent. A.D. much more correctly than the later official Targum of Onqelos, which is, Kahle continues, essentially artificial. Considerable importance attaches to a recent (1957) announcement of the discovery in the Vatican Library of a complete MS of this Targum (Neofiti I) from the 15th cent. (cf. P. A. Díez-Macho, ' Una copia completa del Targum palestinense al Pentateuco en la Biblioteca Vaticana ', *Sefarad* 17 (1957), 119–21).

The texts of these Midrashic Targums are found in Rabbinic Bibles from the 16th cent. on, and editions have been produced by Ginsburger (*Das Fragmenten Targum* (1899), and *Jerusalem* I (1903)). But Kahle's publication of the Geniza fragments, *Masoreten d. Westens* II (1930), and the general discussion in *The Cairo Geniza* is an important addition to the earlier material. It is promised that the publication of the edited text of Neofiti I will contribute substantially to the issues raised by Kahle.

There is one complete Targum to the Prophets, **f**
Targum Jonathan, probably Jonathan ben Uzziel, a pupil of Hillel in the early 1st cent. A.D. It is a semi-official rendering, fairly literal for whole sections of text, but suddenly interrupted by insertions of a legendary, or semi-historical kind. Interpretation, too, is prominent, and, e.g. classical place-names are changed for more familiar ones. Targums to the Hagiographa vary considerably, and many of them are patently late, the Targum on Chr. not being known

66f until after the Polyglots, and there is no known Targum for Dan. and Ezr.-Neh.

Targum Jonathan to the Prophets is well represented in Rabbinic Bibles and an edition by Lagarde (*Prophetae Chaldaice* (1872)). But they need further examination, and some of the preparatory work may be found in learned journals (cf. D. W. Thomas's résumé in his article 'The Textual Criticism of the OT' in OTMS, 257). Mention may be made of Stenning's edition of *Isaiah* (1949), which, despite shortcomings, marks an important advance.

g (*b*) The official Targum to the Pentateuch is that by Onqelos, and it is generally assumed that it existed in the 2nd cent A.D., and indeed that its author was to be identified with Aquila (the Greek form of the name) who produced a similarly literal and official rendering in Greek. But Kahle has challenged this view, and has interpreted the version as an emanation from Babylon, given its present form not earlier than the 5th cent., and corresponding to the emergence of the final consonantal form of the MT at that time.

h The official character of the Onqelos text is reflected in at least two ways. Firstly, it replaced the original Aram. translation in Jerusalem I; and secondly, Targum Jonathan follows it in the literal renderings of the Heb. text, and, wherever it quotes the Torah, it is given in Onqelos' rendering. Again the evidence of Neofiti I is likely to be important, for it is claimed that it shows further instances of Onqelos' 'infiltrations' in the text of Jerusalem Targum II. It has also been suggested that not only does Onqelos correspond to Aquila but also that Jonathan is to be identified with Theodotion. Whatever be Onqelos' period and background, the text of this Targum is in principle very close to the MT, consequently its numerous deviations from this text become all the more significant. The edition of Onqelos in general use today is A. Berliner's text (1884), based on the edition of Sabbioneta in 1557.

Still greater interest attaches, however, to the way Targumic texts show theological characteristics of Jewish interpretation. It is well known that anthropomorphisms are scrupulously avoided in these texts. The OT phrase 'trust in God' becomes 'trust in God's Word (*Mēmrā'*)', 'I am with thee' is 'My word will help thee'. It is a substitution that rewards closer examination, and it is significant that whereas in Onqelos *Mēmrā'* occurs 179 times, in well-defined ways, Targum Jerusalem I has it 321 times (cf. for an informative examination of this aspect of Targum study, V. Hamp, *Der Begriff 'Wort' in den Aramäischen Bibelübersetzungen* (1938)).

67a **Conclusion**—Despite the possible impression that all has been chaos in the study of the Versions during the past few years, in general the student of the OT should be reassured that what is actually happening is that the beginnings of order are emerging for the first time. Whereas previously, and occasionally even in the latest edition of *Biblia Hebraica*, the Versions were used quite indiscriminately for the purposes of emending the MT, it is now becoming clear that there is not a single Version that immediately lends itself to this use. The LXX has its own peculiar importance as representing a text apparently older by centuries than the MT, but it does not follow, as was once commonly assumed, that a retranslation into Heb. of any incidental word or phrase would give 'a superior reading'. To use a phrase that was possibly overdone in the 1930s it is necessary 'to get the feel' of the Version, to know how and why a particular rendering was produced in the first place before applying it to the usual purpose of Heb. textual emendation.

b Another aspect that emerges is the difficulty of reconstructing any of the Versions to its hypothetical original text-form. Hypothetical it must be, because there is no MS sufficiently early for the purpose, nor is there a tradition of a scrupulous transmission of the text such as obtains for the MT. It has been argued, for instance by Kahle and his school, that such an original never existed, and that it is unscientific to try to produce an 'artificial' text because it contradicts the whole essence and history of the Versions. But it is becoming necessary to remind students that, although the theory is popular—increasingly popular to judge by recent textbooks—it is not the only solution to the vexed question of 'originals'. The problem can be suitably stated against the background of the LXX, and particularly of the two main editions now being produced, the Göttingen and the Cambridge. The former, as has been shown, tries to reconstruct an eclectic text, after a careful reduction and classification of all the available readings according to recensional and other well-established groupings tabulated in the *apparatus criticus*. The latter adopts an already established text, Codex B, and classifies the readings, again according to established criteria, in the *apparatus criticus*, but does not go beyond a given MS in the reconstruction of the text. But the fact remains that behind all MSS, even the papyri, there is a traditional Version called the LXX, whose extant MS fragments go back far beyond Codex B, even to the pre-Christian era, and that there is partial evidence at least, from the Qumrân MSS, of the existence of a Heb. recension which supports the LXX rendering. It is true that the Göttingen LXX may often be wrong in its eclectic text, but such a reconstructed text is not impossible, and what is more important, it is at least as likely to produce a proper historical perspective for the study of the LXX as the more negative principle that the actual version did not exist until it was 'officially' created.

For the purposes of the history of biblical thought e
and interpretation, the Versions are to be appreciated individually. We have seen that not one of the Versions grew in a vacuum, but always absorbed, and in turn reflected, important movements in the history of the Church and of Judaism. Once more it is the LXX that provides the best example. Analyses such as those of the Scandinavian scholar G. Gerleman and the American H. S. Gehman go far to explain the historical and cultural background of various books, the extent to which Hellenistic influences are reflected in them, and how they nevertheless remained Hebraic. Again, in subsequent phases of the Versions' history, with recensions and deliberate 'corrections', Christian interests are no less clearly reflected. G. F. Moore, in his *Judaism in the First Centuries of the Christian Era* (i, 176), said of the Targums, 'their true value lies in the evidence they give to the exegesis of the Tannaite period—to the real understanding of what the Bible said for itself'. This is equally true of all the Christian versions, from the LXX to the remotest daughter version. Not all have been scrutinised for their 'exegesis', but what is more serious is that the better-known versions still need to be more thoroughly studied. This survey would have served a valuable purpose if it were to suggest to a student that he get Hatch and Redpath, *Concordance to the LXX*, which, though sixty years old, is the most important of all source books next to the text itself, and there examine the variety of ways in which any given Heb. word is rendered. How, for example, does the LXX render technical words connected in Heb. with the cult and cultic acts? In other words, what attitude did the Diaspora Jews adopt to the cult which was so remote from them? What did atonement mean to them? Does it mean the same in the NT? **Once a beginning is made, there is no end to the prospect.**

For **Bibliography,** see preceding article.

THE LITERATURE OF THE OLD TESTAMENT

By H. H. ROWLEY

68a The writings contained in the OT were composed over a very long period of time, and while the older writings have come down to us in a form edited by later hands they still bear the marks of their antiquity. We can no longer think of the entire Pentateuch as the literary composition of Moses (see §§136ff.), but it is likely that we have some fragments from his time, or even earlier. These are principally **the poetic passages embodied in the Pentateuch.** The discovery of the Râs Shamra tablets a generation ago gave us a new insight into the literary creations of a north Syrian city with a language and a culture closely related to the Canaanite language and culture, and since that city was destroyed probably somewhere about the time of the Exodus the many links between its literature and the OT are of the highest interest. They show that the early literature of Israel had behind it a Canaanite literature which in form and style, and often in its expressions, provided the incoming tribes with a heritage whose marks are to be found in the Bible. This does not mean that the Bible is to be explained in terms of Râs Shamra literature, any more than the links with Babylonian literature which were noted half a century ago meant that the Bible was to be read merely as a borrowing from Babylon. Every writer's forms and style owe much to his age and environment ; his significance lies in what he does with those forms and style, and the purpose to which he applies them. The literature of the OT is vastly different from the literature of Râs Shamra, and also from the literature of Babylon. For all is permeated with a religious quality which is quite different, a religious quality which gives meaning to the whole, for which it has been treasured through the centuries and for which it is still treasured. For the OT is still a living book, whereas the Râs Shamra and Babylonian literatures have only an antiquarian interest.

b In many countries the oldest surviving literature is in poetry. It is not, therefore, surprising that ancient poems should provide the earliest parts of the OT. The Song of Deborah in Jg. 5 is probably contemporary with the 12th-cent. events it celebrates. The Balaam Oracles in Num. 23f., as distinct from the narrative in which they are now embedded, may be slightly older. Some writers have thought them to be of much later composition, but Albright has argued on the basis of links with Râs Shamra forms that they may be the oracles of a 12th-cent. diviner from North Syria. Tribal songs such as the Song of Lamech (Gen. 4:23f.), the blessings of Rebekah (Gen. 24:60) and of Jacob by Isaac (Gen. 27:27ff.), may well be of great antiquity, and some of the elements of the Blessing of Jacob (Gen. 49) probably antedate the founding of the monarchy. All these and other poetic passages may have been preserved orally for a long time before they were written down, though some were collected in written works before the oldest of our main Pentateuchal documents were composed. For here we find a citation from the Book of the Wars of the Lord (Num. 21:14f.), which was clearly a written collection. Similarly in the book of Joshua, in what is probably a continuation of the earliest of the main Pentateuchal sources, we find a citation from the Book of Jashar (Jos. 10:12f.). Since the Book of Jashar contained David's lament over Saul and Jonathan (2 Sam. 1:19–27) it could not have been compiled before the reign of David, and indeed it may have been somewhat later.

c This means that the earliest of our **main Pentateuchal sources** is to be placed after David's time. For an account of Pentateuchal criticism the reader is referred to §§136ff. where the reason for the analysis of the Pentateuch into different documents will be found in brief. It should be remembered that the dating of these sources in the period of the monarchy does not mean that they are of little historical worth, or that they were the baseless creations of the compilers. Just as the poems embodied in the Pentateuch were probably handed down orally before they were written, so most probably the traditions embodied in the Pentateuch were handed down orally for long before our present sources were composed. Recent archaeology has brought to light from Mesopotamia in the patriarchal age several customs which figure in the stories of the book of Gen., but which do not appear later in the OT. They are therefore authentic customs of the patriarchal age, but not of the age of the compilers of the Pentateuchal sources, and they probably belonged to the stories as they received them. Since tradition had faithfully preserved obsolete customs, it would seem likely that it had also preserved genuine historical memories of earlier times. While no ingenuity can reconcile all the details of the Pentateuchal story as it now stands, it is probable that many of the difficulties are due to the compilers' attempts to integrate into a single continuous story independent traditions which came from separate sources.

d While the Israelite tribes seem to have been of kindred stock, it is improbable that they entered the land as a united group of tribes, and likely that while two or more of them sometimes combined for mutual help in critical situations, they were not involved in any organised unity of the whole before the establishment of the monarchy. Not all the tribes appear to have gone into Egypt, though it is probable that those that did go there had been in some association with others of the kindred tribes before they went down. The tribe of Judah seems to have been largely isolated from the northern tribes before the founding of the monarchy, and it was the capture of Jerusalem by David and the fact that David was of the tribe of Judah and became acknowledged by all the tribes that brought it into the full current of Israelite life. The traditions which have gone into the Pentateuch were the traditions of all the tribes, and it seems likely that it was during the brief period of the united monarchy that these traditions were collected and pooled. The J source of the Pentateuch is usually connected with Judah and the E source with Ephraim. It is to be emphasised, however, that both were corpora of traditions of all the tribes, and both impose

68d upon the separate traditions of the past the unity of the present. It is probably in this way that we should explain the diverse accounts of the origin of Yahwism given in the Pentateuch. In one source its beginning is dated in the time of Moses and in another in the very beginning of man's existence. We should not suppose that one is historical and the other is not, but should realise that if not all the tribes were in Egypt and came out under the leadership of Moses, for the group he led the worship of Yahweh may have begun in his day, whereas for other tribes it may have begun earlier and its beginnings have been lost in the mists of time and therefore ascribed to the childhood of man.

If it was during the time of the united monarchy that there was a pooling of the traditions of all the tribes, it was probably not until after the Disruption that the two corpora known as J and E took their present shape. Each has the stamp of its own geographical place of compilation upon it. The J source probably received its form in the 9th cent. B.C. and the E source somewhat later.

e It is improbable that these sources ended with the period of Moses. For the tribes had each their post-Settlement traditions, and these would be equally collected and pooled in the period of the united monarchy. Hence it is likely that the J and E compilations covered pre-monarchic traditions of the post-Mosaic period, though this does not mean that they ever formed part of a continuous whole which included the present Pentateuch and more. We must distinguish between the sources of the Pentateuch and the Pentateuch. For the compiler of the latter drew on the former only for what he wanted, and very probably left not a little material unutilised. In any case we have to remember that oral traditions of the post-Settlement period would be handed down in the same way as those of the pre-Settlement period, to be later written down and drawn on by the compilers of the books of Jos. and Jg. More than one set of traditions were certainly used, though whether they were continuous with the J and E corpora of traditions cannot be known with certainty.

f The **legal material in the Pentateuch** is no more to be attributed in its entirety to Moses than is the narrative material. The tribes must have had some customary law even before the time of Moses, and the many links that have been found between the laws and customs of Israel and those of Babylonia and Northern Mesopotamia show that Israelite law had behind it a background of Near Eastern law. Of that background we have an ever fuller knowledge. For the Code of Ḫammurabi is now supplemented by other ancient codes, including a Hittite Code and the Laws of Eshnunna. Some of the laws that have been preserved in the OT may be of pre-Mosaic origin. The present writer holds that in its original form the Decalogue of Exod. 34, the so-called Ritual Decalogue, may be pre-Mosaic. The familiar Decalogue of Exod. 20, again in its original unexpanded form, is probably of Mosaic origin, and this higher Decalogue may be a fitting symbol of the superior level to which Moses lifted the tribes he led. Much, however, was carried on from the past, some things to be gradually modified in the course of time, and especially under Canaanite influence after the Settlement. Alt has argued that all the case law is based on Canaanite legal forms, whereas the apodictic laws of Israel are peculiar to herself in both form and substance. The oldest corpus of legal material in the Pentateuch is the Book of the Covenant which is introduced by the Decalogue of Exod. 20. While in its present form this is not earlier than the united monarchy, it embodies not a little of very ancient origin. Indeed some of the material of the very latest legal collection in the Pentateuch is probably very ancient, just as in any codification of British law today very ancient laws would still be included. The Book of the Covenant is commonly thought to have come down to us through the compiler of the E source of the Pentateuch, but 68f
since we find distributed in it most of the provisions of the Ritual Decalogue, which is believed to have been preserved by J, it cannot be regarded as E in contrast to J, and is frequently attributed to JE.

Perhaps even earlier than the compilation of the 69a
J source the **Court History of David,** from which the compiler of the books of Sam. and the compiler of the books of Kg. drew in 2 Sam. 9–20 and 1 Kg. 1–2, was composed by a brilliant writer who stood close to the events he described, and whose historical fidelity is beyond question. We know that court records were kept during the monarchy, and these probably supplied some of the sources which were later drawn on by the compilers of the historical books. Other literary sources were written during the monarchy, including probably a history of the Ark and the Temple, and various prophetic histories. All of these were used when the historical books came to be compiled in their present form. That seems to have been towards the end of the 7th cent. B.C. and the beginning of the 6th cent. B.C., under the influence of the book of Dt.

Earlier, however, than Dt. we must place the life b
and work of some of **the prophets** whose oracles have been preserved for us in the prophetic books of the OT. We have traditions about Micaiah and Elijah and Elisha and other prophets, but no collections of their oracles similar to the books of Am. and Hos. But with the 8th cent. B.C. we find prophets whose oracles were preserved by their disciples and later collected and handed down to us. We know that in the 7th cent. a collection of many of Jeremiah's oracles had been prepared under his direction, and other prophets may have similarly been responsible for the collection of some of their oracles. Nevertheless we cannot suppose that any of the prophetic books was prepared in its present form by the prophet whose name it bears, though much of the contents of these books may with confidence be accepted as the authentic oracles of the men to whom they are attributed. The 8th and 7th cent. prophets brought new religious insights, but are not to be thought of as the mediators of a new religion, or even as the creators of ethical religion. They recalled men to the principles of Mosaic religion, and applied those principles fearlessly to the situation of their own day, insisting that justice and humanity were the basic requirements of God, without which the most costly religiosity was vain.

It was under the influence of the 8th-cent. prophets c
that the book of **Deuteronomy** was composed, probably early in the 7th cent. The religious group from which it came stressed the prophetic principles of justice and humanity and in harmony with the teaching of the prophets sought to purge the religion of their day of practices of Canaanite origin. Behind them was the abortive effort of Hezekiah to control religion by centralising it in Jerusalem, and Dt. planned a new centralisation, and thought through its consequences. It was towards the end of the 7th cent., in the reign of Josiah, that this programme for reform, by then forgotten since those who had prepared it had most probably all died, was discovered in the Temple and adopted as the programme of Josiah's reform. This work consisted of a new code, based on the Book of the Covenant but modifying its provisions sometimes in the light of later developments and sometimes in the light of the special interests of the compilers in the centralisation of the cultus and the purification of religious practice, and it was introduced by a historical retrospect placed in the mouth of Moses. This retrospect, like the code, shows knowledge of J and E, but only of J and E amongst the other Pentateuchal sources.

The book of Dt. was accepted as the work of Moses, d
and this became the basis of the Pentateuch as a Mosaic collection. We have no evidence that J or E was ever regarded as composed by Moses, but since D is cast in the form of an utterance of Moses and its origin was unknown, it was natural that it should be

69d believed to be his composition. That it was an application of the principles of the Mosaic faith to contemporary circumstances and conditions is beyond question, and it is of the highest importance for the understanding of the literary and religious development of the OT. It is probably from the discovery of this book that the idea of a Canon of Scripture took its rise, though it is misleading to think of more than the seed of the idea at this stage.

e It has already been said that it was under the influence of the book of Dt. that **the historical books,** known as the Former Prophets in the Heb. Canon, came to be compiled, So far as Jos. and Jg. are concerned, the compilers used ancient traditions which had probably been handed down orally for a long time before they were embodied in the written sources now drawn on. So far as the books of Sam. and Kg. are concerned, a great variety of written sources seem to have been used. But the compilers were not writing history as a modern historian would. They were writing with a religious and didactic purpose. They were therefore more interested in the lessons of history than in the facts for their own sake. They passed lightly over what was of no use to them—giving, for instance, only a few verses to the important reign of Omri—and preserving more fully what they found edifying. They did not wilfully distort the facts, as the Chronicler later sometimes did, but they selected them and supplied them with a framework which brought out the lessons in which they were interested. The framework of Jg. was designed to make the stories teach that religious loyalty and national prosperity belonged together, while religious declension inevitably brought national disaster. The framework of the books of Kg. from the Disruption was governed by the acceptance of the principle of the centralisation of worship in a single sanctuary. All of these four historical books were compiled after the discovery of the book of Dt. The last event mentioned in 2 Kg. was the release of Jehoiachin in 561 B.C., but it is possible that the termination of this book is a later addition and that in their original form Jos., Jg., Sam., and Kg. formed a great Deuteronomic history compiled within twenty-five years of the discovery of D. When it is remembered that but a few years after this the Babylonian exile and the destruction of the Temple took place, the importance of the discovery of D for the history of the religion of Israel, and indeed for the world, becomes clear.

70a Meanwhile the work of the prophets continued, and their disciples continued to preserve their oracles in some form. Many of the oracles seem to have been preserved as separate fragments, and so we occasionally find that the same oracle is ascribed independently to two different prophets. Some seem to have been preserved in small collections. With the beginning of the Babylonian exile we come to the priest-prophet **Ezekiel,** whose conception of a restored religion centralised in a new Temple and served by the Zadokite priests—i.e. the former Jerusalem priesthood—while all others should be on a lower level was of great importance for the future development of Jewish religion. His prophetic ministry was exercised in Babylonia, and it was probably in Babylonia that the **Priestly Code** was prepared. This consisted of another code, to take the place of D, together with a new narrative accompaniment prepared to accord with its own principles. Many of the actual laws and rites preserved in P are ancient, but this code sought to control the centralised religion more firmly than D had done, and to regulate it through a priesthood which was graded in accordance with Ezekiel's principle, though not precisely as Ezekiel has proposed. For here the higher ranks were the Aaronites, who included more than Ezekiel's Zadokites. J and E had represented the patriarchs as offering sacrifice themselves, without the need of any priest, and in the book of Jg. we find the beginnings of a preference for Levites as priests, though the priesthood was not limited to them. In D only Levites were contemplated as priests, 70a
but without distinction of rank amongst the Levites. Now the Aaronites were exalted, and Aaron himself was represented as the first legitimate Israelite priest. Hence in the narrative sections of the book of Gen. P does not represent the patriarchs as offering sacrifice. In P, therefore, we have a new programme for the reform and regulation of the cultus and indeed of the administration of the law through the priests, ready to be put into operation when a suitable moment offered.

A further powerful influence and notable literary b
creation came from Babylonia in the 6th cent. in the form of the prophecies of **Deutero-Isaiah.** In that century it was in Babylonia that the creative religious centre of Israel was to be found, and it is probable that both for the preservation of older works and the creation of the new we are indebted to the exiles. Deutero-Isaiah held out to the exiles the hope of return to their own land and proclaimed the call to a mission to the world to lead all men to share the faith of Israel, given to her that she might share it with others. In the Servant Songs he gave expression to an insight of the profoundest significance in the history of Israelite religion, and these passages are of first importance for the study of the relation of the OT and NT. For our Lord claimed that in himself this concept of a mission to the world, achieved through the organ of suffering and death, was actualised, and the Church with confidence maintained the claim.

In the period following the return **Trito-Isaiah,** c
whether that term is understood to denote an individual or a succession, continued the teaching of Deutero-Isaiah, though not on the same high level. That there are links between Trito-Isaiah and Deutero-Isaiah, and between both and Proto-Isaiah, has long been recognised, though those links will be found emphasised in a new way in the present Commentary. It is possible that a continuous stream of disciples had preserved the teaching of Isaiah of Jerusalem, and had thrown up from its numbers Deutero-Isaiah and Trito-Isaiah in the course of time.

With the return under Cyrus prophecy continued d
in Palestine, though the post-exilic prophets were not of the stature of their predecessors. The latest of the prophets whose oracles are preserved in the collection of the twelve Minor Prophets may perhaps be dated towards the end of the 5th cent. B.C., though some would date Jl later than this, and it is probable that the closing chapters of the book of Zech. are later. The compilation of the collection of the Minor Prophets, which is to be thought of as a single compilation rather than as twelve separate books, cannot be placed earlier than the end of the 5th cent., and if it was as early as this we must reckon with the likelihood that some passages were subsequently added. Probably the compilations of the other prophetic collections in Isa., Jer., and Ezek. were made at about the same time. It may well be that just as the Former Prophets were compiled within a short space of time before the exile, the **Latter Prophets** were compiled within a short space of time about the end of the 5th cent. B.C. Here no more than there was the compilation the free composition of any writer, but a collection of older materials, much of which is the authentic work of the prophets to whom it is attributed, though the compiler's attribution of other oracles may be no more reliable than the attribution of a single oracle to Isaiah and to Micah (Isa. 2:1–4 ; Mic. 4:1–4). Here in the prophetic corpus we have a collection of oracles and traditions about the prophets of Israel that is of the highest value. There are passages of high literary quality and sidelights on the history of Israel of great importance. Beyond this these books are of enduring worth for their evidence of the religious life and thought of Israel, and for the spiritual principles which they set forth.

It was in all probability about the beginning of the e
4th cent. B.C. that Ezra came to Jerusalem from the Persian court, bringing a Book of the Law which he was

70e charged to put into effect. That **Ezra's lawbook** was the Priestly Code has long been thought probable. This does not mean that it had just been written, or even that it had just become known. Josiah's lawbook, or D, was put into effect for a short time, after which it ceased to be operated, though it must have continued to be known. Ezra's lawbook may have been similarly known, though until Ezra came armed with authority from the king none had enforced its acceptance. Now it was put into operation, and from this time on it continued to be the recognised law down to NT times, save that in the 2nd cent. B.C. High Priests who were not of the rightful line were appointed by the Seleucids, and then the Hasmonaeans assumed the position, while later the Roman authorities set aside the rules of the high-priestly succession. Since Ezra's lawbook was believed to be of Mosaic origin, it is not surprising that it was accepted by the Samaritans, no less than by the Jews, despite the tension which had more than once developed between Samaria and Jerusalem in the post-exilic period. Probably quite soon after Ezra's mission the Pentateuch reached its present form by the combination of P with the earlier J, E, and D. This Pentateuch was accepted by both Jews and Samaritans, save that in the Samaritan Pentateuch there are some variations in the book of Dt. which reflect the claims of the Samaritan community. The date when the Samaritan schism became final cannot be recovered with certainty, but it must have been after the completion of the Pentateuch, since both parties accepted it.

71a At some time after the completion of the Pentateuch we must place the work of **the Chronicler,** who compiled the books of Chr. and continued the story through Ezr. and Neh. Again we do not have history for its own sake, but history recorded for its lessons, and the compiler does not hesitate to omit what he does not regard as edifying, or to alter the details of what he records when they are at variance with what he thought they ought to be. Like all the other biblical compilers, he uses earlier materials. For much of the story he uses the books of Sam. and Kg., and it is instructive to make a careful comparison of these books to see how he introduces changes to accord with his own principles. These were not his only sources, and he probably used the others as he uses these, faithfully preserving what he found where it did not conflict with his ideas of what was edifying. The story of David's adultery and all the family troubles which he subsequently experienced are entirely omitted, probably because the compiler did not think it edifying to record these things about the king who was now viewed only through the rose-coloured spectacles of time. Similarly the Northern Kingdom is entirely ignored, save where the history of Judah required its mention. Apparently the Samaritan schism was complete, at least for this writer.

b In the continuation of the story in Ezr. and Neh. the same anti-Samaritan bias is also apparent. Here the compiler drew on the memoirs of Nehemiah and of Ezra, and also on some Aramaic documents from older sources. He clearly was under the impression that Nehemiah and Ezra were contemporaries, but it seems unlikely that his sources indicated their relationship to one another, and a large number of modern scholars believe that Nehemiah preceded Ezra by nearly half a century. If this view is right, we must come down to not less than a century after Ezra for the work of the Chronicler, but the fact that he appears to be later than the Samaritan schism, which itself must be later than the completion of the Pentateuch, brings us to a date not earlier than about 300 B.C.

c More difficult to place is the book of **Ruth,** which is a historical story dealing with the period of the Judges, but which does not appear ever to have been a part of the Deuteronomic historian's great survey of history. It would seem to come from a time long after Dt., when customs current when that work was written were now obsolete and in need of explanation, and it is often thought to come from the obscure 5th cent. B.C. 71c
It breathes something of the generous air of the book of **Jonah,** which reflects the missionary spirit of Deutero-Isaiah, and may come from somewhere about the same time. The one expresses a prophetic message in the form of a story about a prophet, while the other recounts a simple story with no propagandist aim—a story which gives a pleasanter picture of the age of the Judges than some of the stories found in the book of Jg. The one story found its home in the prophetic canon, because it was the story of a prophet, but the other does not even mention a prophet, and so went into the miscellaneous collection of the Heb. canon, known as the Writings.

In the same collection we find the book of **Daniel,** d
which in the English Bible stands amongst the prophets. It is really of quite a different *genre* from the prophetic books, though there are passages in the prophetic books which are of a not unrelated character. This book is commonly distinguished as an apocalyptic work. That apocalyptic is the child of prophecy is beyond question, and there are some parts of the prophetic books which partake of the character of apocalyptic in varying measure. The first six chapters of the book of Dan. contain stories about Daniel, and there is nothing to indicate that Daniel was the author. They were probably composed, on the basis of older historical memories and traditions, to encourage the faithful to stand firm in the persecution of the Maccabaean time, and were orally circulated as separate stories. The second half of the book consists of visions attributed to Daniel, in which events subsequent to the age in which Daniel was placed are unfolded. Those events culminate in the Maccabaean age, which is clearly indicated as the age of the composition of these chapters. The attribution of the visions to Daniel was probably not to conceal their authorship, but to declare it, and to make plain that they were by the author of the stories about Daniel, and so to claim the attention of the many who had been heartened by the stories. In the 2nd cent. B.C. and later a whole succession of apocalyptic works appeared, but none of them secured admission to the sacred collection save this one. This may have been in part because the others circulated mainly amongst the groups from which they came, whereas this work achieved a wide popularity amongst all the faithful in the critical days of persecution, and in part owing to its quality.

Even later than Dan. is probably the book of e
Esther, which is of the nature of a historical novel, and which breathes a fierce hostility to Gentiles which may have owed something to the bitter suffering of the Maccabaean days, but which contrasts very strongly with the spirit of the book of Jon. In our Bibles it stands with the historical books, but again in the Heb. canon it stands in the collection of Writings.

We are left with the **poetic books** of the OT. It 72a
has been said that there are poetic passages in the Pentateuch and historical books, and that there were lost collections of poetry. It should be remembered also that much of the oracular material in the prophetic books is cast in poetic form. One of the main features of Heb. poetry is **parallelism,** so that its unit is the balanced couplet—though sometimes a triplet can take the place of a couplet. The terms of the first line are normally balanced by the terms of the second, though it may be a balance of contrast as easily as of similarity. Hence we find synonymous parallelism or antithetic parallelism. Sometimes we have what is called synthetic parallelism, where there may be a certain parallelism of form, but where the thought is continuous rather than balanced. Further special kinds of parallelism are emblematic (where the second line has the form of a figure parallel to the idea of the first line), stair-like (where the second line repeats the actual terms of part of the first line and then proceeds to something fresh), and introverted (where the first line is parallel to the fourth and the second to the third). Further, parallelism is not always complete,

72a with every term in the first line matched by a term in the second. It may be incomplete with something in the first line without its parallel in the second. But here there may be some compensation, which may take many different forms, or there may be no compensation, and the second line be shorter than the first. An almost infinite variety is possible, so that parallelism may be entirely without monotony.

b Heb. poetry also has **rhythm,** though not a rhythm of syllable but of significant elements. The significant element is normally a single word, but particles may be lightly passed over and included with the words that follow, while long words may be given the value of two significant elements. Rigid rules cannot be applied here, and it is unwise to try to force Heb. poetry into the Procrustean bed of any scheme we impose upon it. The major rhythms are 3′ 3′ and 3′ 2′, which Buchanan Gray called Balancing Rhythm and Echoing Rhythm. Further Balancing Rhythms are 4′ 4′ and 2′ 2′. But again, there is constant variety in Heb. poetry, and a 3′ 3′ poem may by catalexis have 3′ 2′ and even 2′ 2′ lines, or by hypercatalexis have 4′ 3′ or 4′ 4′ lines. Particularly common is a longer, or weighted, line at the end of a poem or section. Again, by anacrusis an introductory word in a line may stand outside the poetic scheme.

c Larger units than the couplet are found in some poems, where strophes may be detected. But strophe other than the balanced couplet is not a regular feature of Heb. poetry. Further refinements, such as acrostic structure, are found in a number of poems, but again these are not regular features.

All of these characteristics are to be found in the prophetic books of the OT no less than in the poetic books. The poetic books are Ps., Prov., and Job, and also Lam., Ca., and Ec. The first three of these are given a special accentuation by the Massoretes.

d It will be convenient to mention first the book of **Lamentations,** because, though its authors cannot be known, its approximate date is reasonably sure. Its five separate poems are not all to be attributed to a single author, but some seem to be by eye-witnesses of the destruction of Jerusalem, and all may come from the 6th cent. B.C. All save the last chapter are acrostic in form, but there are technical differences of poetic form as well as of imaginative power and skill. They are not merely descriptive poems, but religious poetry marked by spiritual insight as well as pathos. In our Bible they follow Jer., though there is no reason to ascribe them to that prophet, and in the Heb. Bible they stand in the Writings.

e The **Psalter** in its present form is without question a post-exilic compilation. But this does not mean that the individual psalms are of post-exilic origin. Indeed the present trend is to find very considerable pre-exilic elements in the Psalter, including especially the royal psalms. The present trend is also to find a considerable cultic element in the Psalter, and to regard large numbers of the psalms as having been composed for, and used in, the worship of the Temple. Since we know that religious poetry was composed in early Israel and that such poetry continued to be composed down to the beginning of the Christian era, it is antecedently likely that some poems from many different ages have survived, to be collected in the Psalter. There is evidence that earlier collections of psalms antedated the completion of the Psalter, and since we occasionally find a psalm, or part of a psalm, repeated in the Psalter with indications of editorial modifications, it may well be that other psalms have been edited and are not quite in their original form. It is unprofitable to try to date with precision the individual psalm, and wiser to recognise that here we have an unrivalled collection of sacred and cultic poetry covering a long period, yet timeless in that it was created to express the moods of the religious spirit and to minister to those moods.

f The book of **Proverbs** belongs to what is called the Wisdom Literature. In its present form it is certainly post-exilic, though it doubtless rests on more ancient materials. Many of the individual sayings must be ancient, and we have evidence elsewhere in the Bible that the Hebrews, like others, could coin pithy sayings to embody the lessons of experience. The 'Wise' were found in every age, and collections of wise sayings were probably made at various times. 72f

With the book of **Job** we come to a different type of Wisdom book. Here on the basis of a traditional story a brilliant author created a work in which one of the perennial human problems, the problem of innocent suffering, is discussed. That no philosophical solution of the problem was offered by the book in its original form does not detract from its merit, for it offers a religious message of far more value to the sufferer than an intellectual answer to his questions. Here is wisdom indeed—not the wisdom of acute observation, but the wisdom of profound religious teaching. While it is impossible to date this book with precision, it is almost certainly from the post-exilic period, when the Deuteronomic doctrine of the strict equation of national desert and fortune had been individualised in some circles under the influence of the emphasis on individual responsibility by Jeremiah and Ezekiel. Somewhat later the book seems to have gathered some additions, particularly the Elihu speeches, which seek to give the explanation of the meaning of suffering which the author of Job had wisely refrained from offering. g

Ecclesiastes is quite certainly a late book, which offers a mixture of worldly wisdom, touched by cynicism, and pious observations. The relations between the two have been variously estimated, and do not concern us here. h

The only book which remains to be mentioned is the **Song of Songs,** which is commonly classed with the Wisdom Literature, but which is really of a quite different *genre.* Here we find love songs, both prenuptial and post-nuptial. Again in their present form they are probably of post-exilic date, but they may echo older songs. For love songs belong to no one age exclusively. Here we most likely have a cycle of songs related to one another, and coming in their present form from a single hand, though quite different views have been taken of this book.

From this brief survey it will be clear that the OT covers not alone a wide range of time, but includes many different types of literature. In some of the general articles in this commentary, and in the introductions to the individual books, much will be found to supplement what is here said, and in §§73–5 more information on the types of literature found in the OT is given. The purpose of the present article is but to give a summary view of the whole, and of the growth of this literature and the purposes it served. From this summary it will appear that the OT is a richly varied collection of writings, and that its literary and historical merits are all subordinate to its profoundly religious interest and purpose. It is more than the expression of the human spirit. It is the literature of revelation, through which the word of God was mediated to men, and it is for this revelatory character that it is still cherished. i

Bibliography—A. Bentzen, *Introduction to the OT* (2nd ed. 1952); J. A. Bewer, *The Literature of the OT in its Historical Development* (1922); O. Eissfeldt, *Einleitung in das AT* (2nd ed. 1956); J. Hempel, *Die althebräische Literatur und ihr hellenistisch-jüdisches Nachleben* (1930); A. Lods, *Histoire de la littérature hébraïque et juive* (1950); D. B. Macdonald, *The Hebrew Literary Genius* (1933); J. Meinhold, *Einführung in das AT* (3rd ed. 1932); R. H. Pfeiffer, *Introduction to the OT* (1941); H. H. Rowley, *The Growth of the OT* (1950); A. Weiser, *Einleitung in das AT* (4th ed. 1957).

G. B. Gray, *The Forms of Hebrew Poetry* (1915); W. O. E. Oesterley, *Ancient Hebrew Poems* (1938); G. A. Smith, *The Early Poetry of Israel in its Physical and Social Origins* (1912).

FORM CRITICISM OF THE OLD TESTAMENT

By E. T. RYDER

73a **Form criticism** as a branch of literary science, although of comparatively recent introduction, is complementary to textual, literary, and historical criticism. Its primary concern, as its name implies, is with the forms or literary patterns discernible in ancient prose and poetry, which it seeks to trace back to and evaluate in their original community and cultural setting. As these are often to be found at a prewritten stage of composition, much of its interest centres in oral tradition. Hence the fuller designation of this method as form historical (*formgeschichtliche*) is more apposite in conveying the fact of its preoccupation also with literary origin and growth. From the opening years of the present century its application in the field of OT study has been especially fruitful and indeed highly important, for even as it has helped to widen the horizons of scholarship it has at the same time led, as was its foremost intention, to a truer appreciation and so to an enriched understanding of OT literature from the standpoint of its aesthetic quality, its historical development, and in particular its religious value and significance.

b **The development of form-critical study** of the OT came about mainly through the industry and acumen of German scholars, amongst whom H. Gunkel was the pioneer, architect, and for a generation the presiding genius. The method had already been applied in the sphere of German folklore as also in the field of Classical studies, as a result of which it had been demonstrated that ancient authors, in a way not applicable in modern literary composition, were stylistically bound by conventions of literary form appropriate to the subject they handled. (This has proved important because consideration of subject or theme has frequently helped in the classification of the literary types.) Previously in the 18th cent. R. Lowth had investigated the forms and literary structure of Hebrew poetry, whilst in the early part of the 19th cent. J. G. Herder, with fine appreciation of its literary and spiritual quality, had discerned conventionalised literary forms to be the vehicle of its expression. From then until the present century, however, despite the view put forward at the opening of the 19th cent. by A. Geddes concerning the oral origin of separate literary units underlying the structure of the Pentateuch, the interest of OT scholarship was almost entirely centred in literary criticism with its emphasis on documentary analysis. To be sure such study was of first importance as clearing the site and in large measure laying the foundation on which subsequent inquiry was to build, yet it suffered by being over-analytical and therefore insufficiently appreciative of formative influences and aesthetic values. It failed to concern itself with the literary forms and the manner in which they had taken shape. Thus it was that Gunkel, alive to the pressing need for studying the literature as the expression of the religion, embarked upon his pioneer work, which bore fruit in a series of epochal writings published between 1901 and 1933. This involved together with the investigation of the literary patterns the consideration of the situation in life or occasion and environment of their origin as 73b
also, for comparative purposes necessary to this approach, the examination of similar material in the literary remains of the ancient Near East, examples of which were becoming increasingly available through archaeological discovery. For the first quarter of the present century attention was therefore principally focused on the study of the forms and on the attempt to ascertain the situation in life of each literary type. Thereafter, in accordance with Gunkel's original intention to work out a synthesis of the literary history of the OT, the emphasis shifted to the investigation of the way in which the early material had come to be collected and arranged in written form. Accordingly J. Hempel in his full-length survey of ancient Hebrew literature (1930), paying necessary attention to the contribution of literary criticism, brought together and applied the findings of form-critical study, and O. Eissfeldt in his general introduction to the OT (1934, 2nd edition revised and expanded, 1956), whilst making due allowance for the oral origin of each literary type, concerned himself mainly with the written stages of development. Since then the influence of form criticism, which has contributed so much to a renaissance of OT studies, has been seen increasingly in subsequent introductions to the literature, in commentaries on the individual books, and in important studies on a variety of themes made possible by the hinterland thus opened up. Discussion continues with regard to the classification of the literary types, the matter of the situation in life, the relation to other literature of the ancient Near East, and the interplay of oral and written transmission. In what follows a brief survey is attempted of the application of form criticism to the different kinds of prose and poetical literature in the OT.

PROSE FORMS

Gunkel first examined the book of Genesis with c
regard to the form in which its contents had existed in oral tradition. On the assumption that oral tradition develops according to certain patterns or laws he indicated the short hero story, the more extended legend, and the longer complex of episodes as the main stages in the process. Similar conclusions were reached by H. Gressmann concerning the accounts of Moses in Exod. and Num. The OT narratives thus studied were found to be of a distinct literary *genre*, the characteristic features of which were evolved in the oral stage, and, as such, the product of the community rather than of individual authors. (This view was subsequently modified, Hempel later pointing out that even though in the earlier stages of composition the formal types were dominant, yet as time went on the literature was creatively shaped by writers of outstanding artistic ability.) Others directed their attention to the historical books, e.g. Jg. and 1, 2 Sam., in order to isolate and assess the single narrative as a literary type at the prewritten stage.

73c Such analysis of the literary forms and the tracing of the growth of particular units from the simple to the more complex arrangement of their variants made possible a reconstruction of the history of the literature. Under similar examination also the legal portions of the OT were shown to have developed gradually from oral beginnings to their present shape, through the accumulation of experience rather than by literary processes, and not to be, as held by literary criticism, the product of successive creative epochs.

d In Hebrew the unit of all utterance is the *dābhār*, 'word', which has a wide range of application as employed by God or man, in prose or poetry, as oracle, law or event, whether single word, phrase or number of sentences. It may be said to underlie the prose types as they have been ascertained and classified by form criticism. For present convenience these categories may be somewhat broadly grouped as Speech, Record, Law, and Narrative.

e **(a) Speech**—Instances occur of **Political Speeches**, in which the situation in life is apparent from the context, e.g. those of Jotham (Jg. 9:7–20), the Rabshakeh (2 Kg. 18:19–25, 28–35, Propagandist), Joab (2 Sam. 10:11f., Military), and Joshua (Jos. 23:2–16, 24:2–28, Valedictory). In the two Jos. passages parenetic (or exhortatory) material is discernible, characteristic of yet another type within this class, viz. the **Sermon**. As a mixture of literary types (often combining priestly, prophetic, and wisdom traits with parenesis) the Sermon is generally regarded as of later development, although it probably originated as poetry—cf. the Song of Moses (Dt. 32)—and is found not surprisingly in the prose sections of Jer. and Ezek., related as they are respectively to Dt. (D) and Lev. 17–26 (H), both of which fall within the Sermon category. Also of mixed character is the **Prose Prayer**, e.g. as uttered by Joshua (Jos. 7:7–9), Solomon (1 Kg. 8:22–53), and Jeremiah (Jer. 32:16–25), which shares with the Sermon an interest in historical retrospect, e.g. Neh. 9:6–37.

f **(b) Record**—Within this category, but sparsely represented in the OT, come **Documents** and **Letters**, the forms of which are more amply illustrated in other literary remains of the ançient Near East, e.g. the Elephantine papyri. Jer. 32:6–15 preserves the account of a contract of purchase entered into by the prophet; cf. also Gen. 23:16–18. Of especial interest because of its legal and cultic provisions is the official agreement recorded *in extenso* in Neh. 9:38–10:39. Other related types include divorce contracts, genealogies, and lists of officials. With regard to the Letter, David's grim little note to Joab (2 Sam. 11:15) is one of a few that are mentioned, and some of Jeremiah's correspondence is recorded in Jer. 29:1–32. The actual form of the Letter in the Persian official mode occurs in Ezr. 4:7–16, 17–22, 5:6–17, 6:6–12, 7:12–26.

74a **(c) Law**—Here the significant term is *tôrāh*, 'instruction', embracing short pronouncements of an occasional character, more lengthy utterances by priests, prophets, and the wise, and the Law as a whole. Basically connected with the **Priestly Oracle** it was cultic, and associated with it were such other terms as *miṣwāh*, 'commandment', *mishpāṭ*, 'judgment', *dābhār*, 'word', and *'ēṣāh*, 'counsel'. Comparative study has shown OT laws to have been closely related, by indirect influence rather than by direct borrowing, to those of Mesopotamia and Asia Minor, mediated probably to some extent through Canaanite culture. Of especial significance has been the recognition in the Book of the Covenant (Exod. 20:22–23:19) of two distinct forms of law, the one common to the ancient Near East and the other peculiar to Israel, which A. Alt has classified as casuistic and apodictic, the former being hypothetical or arguable as case law, and the latter being categorical or final as commandments. The casuistic provisions, *mishpāṭîm*, had the popular courts for their situation in life, whereas in the case of the apodictic laws, *d^ebhārîm*, it was the religious congregation. Both types are well illustrated in Exod. 22: cf. (i) for the hypothetical 74a
form vv. 1–17, 'If . . .', with the provision in the 3rd person; (ii) for the categorical form vv. 18, 21f., 'Thou shalt not . . .', with the injunction in the 2nd person; and (iii) for a further mixed form vv. 23ff., 'If you . . .', where hypothesis and injunction are syntactically combined. Originally the legal types appear to have been small units orally transmitted and possibly poetical in form. Thus the civil regulations of Exod. 21:2–22:17 exhibit the short independent section such as is apparent in 21:28–32, relating to the goring of an ox. So also with the cultic requirements which Eissfeldt calls 'Agendas', exemplified in Lev. 6:2–6, where a nucleus of older oral material has been incorporated and a superscription at 6:1, together with a direction to the priest subscribed at 6:7, has been later added; cf. similarly Num. 6:13–21, etc. Between these small units and those of medium length, e.g. the Book of the Covenant, comes the **Decalogue** type (Exod. 20:3–17, 34:14–26; Dt. 5:7–21, 27:15–26) with which, according to Eissfeldt, have been associated 'Laymen's Catechisms', comprising lists of feasts, e.g. Exod. 23:14–17, tables of affinity, e.g. Lev. 18:6–18, and the like. Finally there are the larger legal codes having their own kind of unity and a diversity of style, which distinguishes the law literature of the OT from all other similar material of the ancient Near East; cf. the laws of Exod. 25–31 in categorical style with their counterpart in Exod. 35–40 as narrative. The fact that Israelite law was able to advance, through its being grounded in Yahwism, from a congeries of civil and cultic regulations to a complex system for the ordering of a theocratic state owes much to the creative work of Moses.

(d) Narrative—The major proportion of OT prose b
material belongs to this class, in which legendary and historical writing may be noted as two comprehensive divisions. The former corresponds to what in other literatures takes the form of epic poetry, to which the parallelism of Hebrew verse was unsuited. Analysis of its literary types has been complicated by the criteria and terminology that have been applied. Especially characteristic of it is the **Legend** proper, here understood as an episode having an historical nucleus and intended to instruct as well as to beguile. Thus the Aetiological legend, in which the OT is so rich, serves to explain the origin of place names, local phenomena, sanctuaries, customs, and the like, for which in turn cf. Gen. 16:7–14 (Beer-lahai-roi), Jos. 10:16–27 (great stones), Jg. 6:11–24 (at Ophrah), Gen. 32:22–32 (food taboo). Also distinctive is the so-called Devotional legend, which aiming to edify is dominated by moral and religious motives. To this type, most fully exemplified in the grand stories of Dan. 1–6, belong such variations as the Priest legend, e.g. the rebellion of Korah and its sequel in Num. 16f., the Prophet legend as in the Elijah and Elisha stories of 1 Kg. 17–2 Kg. 13, and what is sometimes known as the Martyr legend, where the hero makes as it were a valiant stand for the faith, e.g. David's triumph over Goliath in 1 Sam. 17:31–54 as well as Daniel's fortitude in the chapters already cited. Coming somewhere between these two categories, though hardly perhaps a distinct type in itself, is the Hero legend with its string of episodes, extensively illustrated in the narratives of Jg. Distantly related to the Legend, although solely by the bond of imaginary creation, are the **Fairy Tale** and the **Myth**. In its longer form the Fairy Tale, wholly fictitious and often grotesque, did not thrive in Semitic as in other literatures, whilst of the shorter type only an occasional feature is discernible in the OT, e.g. the rod which became a serpent (Exod. 4:3). The Myth, which may be regarded as Legend on a supernatural level and is so extensively represented in Babylonian and Canaanite sources, appears only in modified form in the OT, whose monotheistic interests it was made to serve; cf. the Creation and Flood accounts (Gen. 1f., 6–9). It was also explanatory of

74b the ritual enacted at the great festivals, and is thus a vital factor in the cultic background of the Psalter and Prophetic literature (see §75*b*, *d*).

c In the historical narratives of the OT is discernible a quality unequalled in the literature of the ancient Near East and indeed rivalled only, and considerably later in antiquity, by that of the Greek historians. Incorporated in them is earlier material orally delivered. The age of David, in many ways so memorable, may well have provided the incentive for the recounting and writing of history, of which the 'Court History' in 2 Sam. 9–20 and 1 Kg. 1f. is so superb an example. Less inspired and somewhat perfunctory are the 'Annals' of the official archivists, comprising part of the sources of Kg. and Chr., similar material to which has come to light in Egyptian, Mesopotamian, and Canaanite sources. Of a quite different type is the autobiographical narrative in which the 'I'-form appears. Its occurrence in 3rd-millennium Egyptian tomb inscriptions shows it to be early, and it is found in dream and vision narratives (Gen. 37, 40f. ; Isa. 6 ; Am. 7ff.) at the oral stage, and later in more stylised literary form in, e.g., Ezek. 1f. ; Zech. 1–8, after the manner of Apocalyptic ; cf. Dan. 7–12. Partaking of the nature of legend, whilst affecting to be historical, are Ru. and Est., approaching more as regards form the historical novel.

d There can be no doubt that at the oral stage the community played an important part in the preservation of legendary material ; cf. Exod. 12:26f., 13:14–16 ; Jos. 4:4–7, passages which also hint at the situation in life of such narratives, along with the strong religious urge to ensure their faithful transmission. Yet the undoubted artistry of so much of the literature suggests the craftsmanship of the professional story-teller of which there were almost certainly guilds, as was the case in other ancient societies. Complexes of legends probably developed at specific local centres ; cf. Jos. 1–12, apparently associated with the sanctuary at Gilgal. The situation in life of much of this material is cultic, even as the stories themselves, preserved and transmitted by the sanctuary personnel (priestly, prophetic, and lay), were a necessary part of the ritual as interpreting the various cultic acts. Yet the OT makes it clear that the creative factor underlying the ritual was the history. Variations in style and in treatment of the material point to different circles of narrators, who were responsible for the collecting of the stories and in course of time for their fixation in writing. Upon the basis of this oral and written history the major works of history were at successive stages compiled. First and foremost of these is that of the Yahwist (J) who as both collector and author displays superlative literary skill, coupled with a vital religious interest. The religious interest is more developed, though with decreasing artistry, in the Elohist (E), whilst in the writings of the Deuteronomist (D) and Priestly (P) circles the events related are viewed in accordance with their differing theological approach, to which the history and artistry are subordinated. Later still the Chronicler worked over the entire material afresh, putting it in a new garb and bringing it up to date by the inclusion of the Ezr.-Neh. sections, in order to match contemporary requirements.

POETIC FORMS

e From his examination of Genesis, where he had already distinguished between verse types and prose types, Gunkel turned to the form-critical investigation of the Psalter, observing that the literary patterns fixed by long usage from early in the oral period had linguistic characteristics peculiar to each category. Comparison with other OT poetry revealed the possibility that a large number of psalms belonged to the pre-exilic period even though the completed Psalter was post-exilic. Moreover the resemblance of certain literary types to Babylonian and Egyptian thanksgiving hymns 74e
showed the influence of environment, and it became evident that the psalms were originally cultic hymns. This was further supported by the discovery of striking parallels in Ugaritic literature, and the cultic aspect of the Psalter was worked out in very great detail by S. Mowinckel (second only to Gunkel for his contribution to studies in this field), who, regarding the psalms as the product of centuries-old liturgical use, linked them more definitely with specific enactments in the ritual. OT Wisdom literature, similarly investigated, is now realised to have had very early antecedents in the culture of the ancient Near East. Many of its simpler forms belong to the period before the Exile, and it is not therefore in its entirety to be regarded as late, a view formerly held on account of the presence of similar literature in the Apocrypha and subsequent writings. In the matter of the Prophetic literature examination of the forms revealed it to be the end-product of cycles of prophetic tradition assembled from originally small oral units uttered under inspiration. Their situation in life was recognised as being in some cases the shrines, with which in the period of the monarchy associations of cultic prophets were linked (a common enough phenomenon in the ancient Near East), priest and prophet now being demonstrated to have exercised complementary rather than opposed functions. A suggestion by Gunkel that liturgical material was also present in this literature (cf. his interpretation of Mic. 7:2–20) was duly taken up, as a result of which it has been held that Nah., Hab., and part of Jl were composed for use in public worship.

Hebrew poetry, as that of other literatures of the 75a
ancient Near East, is characterised by parallelism or rhythmic balance of thought. Its metre is dependent on accentuation, the unit being the couplet, in which the members may be of equal or varying length. There is often a further arrangement of couplets into strophes. Of this poetry the fundamental category is the *shîr*, 'song, lyric'. The **Song** was accompanied by music, e.g. Gen. 31:27 ; Isa. 30:29 ; Am. 6:5, and associated with the dance, e.g. Exod. 15:20f. ; Ps. 87:7, composition of tune and words possibly being a simultaneous process as in oriental music to this day. Its wide variety of types includes the Workers' song, e.g. the Song of the Well (Num. 21:17f.), the Taunt song, e.g. Num. 21:27–30 ; Isa. 47, the Watchman's song, e.g. Isa. 21:11f., in all of which the content suggests the situation in life. Wedding and Love songs, for such situations in life as described in Gen. 29:27f. ; Jg. 14:10–18, are more extensively represented in the OT, especially in Ca. with its wealth of erotic verse, which is variously interpreted and has undoubtedly cultic elements. In the case of the Mourning song, the funeral provided the situation in life, professional singers being usually engaged, e.g. Jer. 9:17ff. ; Am. 5:16f. David's lament over Saul and Jonathan (2 Sam. 1:17–27) is the classic example of this *genre*, which was taken over by the prophets for their utterances of doom, e.g. Jer. 22:18ff. ; Lam. War songs or chants are widely apparent, e.g. the Song of Deborah (of mixed type) in Jg. 5, Joshua's invocation (incantational) at Jos. 10:12, Balaam's spells (with **Curse** and **Blessing** ; cf. Gen. 9:25–7, 12:2f., etc.) in Num. 23:7–10, 18–24, 24:3–9, 15–24, where in all cases cited the situation in life is suggested by the context.

(a) The Psalter—In his final classification of the b
psalms Gunkel distinguished five principal and five subsidiary types. The major categories comprised (i) the **Hymn**, in praise of God, chanted chorally or as solo in the ritual, but later separated from such cultic associations and made the vehicle of spiritual aspiration (subsequently refuted by Mowinckel). To this category, in which he included 25 psalms, e.g. 8, 19, 29, Gunkel added three subordinate groups : (*a*) Songs of Zion, Ps. 46, 48, 76, 87, (*b*) Enthronement Songs, Ps. 47, 93, 97, 99, dealing with Yahweh's en-

75b thronement as the universal King and eschatological in character, and (*c*) Songs of Deliverance, viz. the Song of the Red Sea (Exod. 15:1–18, 21) and Hannah's Prayer (1 Sam. 2:1–10). (ii) The **Community Lament**, of an expiatory character and having as its situation in life such threats to the national weal as famine or invasion, e.g. Ps. 44, 74. (iii) The **Royal Psalm**, only later included as one of the major types and connected with various cult-functional aspects of the Israelite king in the pre-exilic period, e.g. Ps. 132, 2, 45, 20, 18, dealing respectively with the anniversary of the establishment of the Davidic dynasty and the enthronement, marriage, preparation for war, and triumphant return of the reigning monarch. (iv) The **Individual Lament**, in which the suppliant is in distress and frequently victimised by 'enemies'. These psalms, some 40 in number, e.g. Ps. 3, 5, 6, 13, 17, 22, are of the essence of the Psalter. Characteristic of them is such an utterance as 'Yahweh has heard my supplication' (Ps. 6:9*a*), technically known as 'The Certainty of a Hearing', or 'I will give to Yahweh the thanks due to his righteousness' (Ps. 7:17), termed the 'Vow'. Certain psalms, also within this class, are further designated 'Psalms of Confidence', e.g. Ps. 4, 23. (v) The **Individual Song of Thanksgiving**, a relatively small category, e.g. Ps. 18, 30, 32, and, like the Individual Lament to which it corresponds, cultic and in some instances a royal psalm. Belonging to the minor categories are the **Song of Pilgrimage**, Ps. 84, 122; the **Community Song of Thanksgiving**, Ps. 67, 124; the **Wisdom Poem**, containing Wisdom elements in shorter (Ps. 127, 133) or longer (Ps. 1, 37, etc.) form; the **Liturgy**, developed from antiphonal usage and the blending of literary types as **Torah Liturgies** and **Prophetic Liturgies** (§75*d*); the **Mixed Poem**, where different forms are commingled by assimilation of earlier material (Ps. 40, 89, etc.) or by free composition.

c **(b) The Wisdom Literature** of the OT is, as already indicated, closely related to the common stock of international Wisdom material, which with very early oral beginnings was widely current in the ancient Near East. Prov. 22:17–24:34, which is so closely parallel to the *Wisdom of Amen-em-ope*, an Egyptian text of possibly the 8th or 7th cent. B.C., illustrates the way in which such material was freely handled and adapted to Israel's religious needs. The situation in life of the Wisdom teaching, as the product of a specialist class of wise men, e.g. Jer. 18:18, was the school, conducted out of doors (Prov. 1:20f., 8f.) or later more formally in the *bēth hammidhrāsh*, 'house of instruction, academy' (Sir. 51:23). It may even have had antecedents in the court or Temple in the period of the monarchy, and the possibility of cultic associations is not to be ruled out. Of the Wisdom writings the characteristic literary unit with its basic meaning of 'likeness' is the *māshāl*, which is widely employed in the OT for various types of literature, ranging from the popular proverb, e.g. 1 Sam. 10:12; Ezek. 16:44, to the more extended composition, e.g. Prov. 1–9, and the elaborate didactic poem exemplified in Job. Originally the popular proverb might be either prosaic or poetical in form, but the unit employed in the Wisdom literature is the **Poetical Sentence**, of highly artistic quality with its parallelism, rhythm, and such features of prosody as paronomasia, alliteration, and assonance. Instances of it abound in Prov., and on it, in varying degrees of combination, the collections therein are based. Frequently such Sentences are linked in series, connection being made by repetition of the introductory word (Prov. 12:6f.), by an acrostic device (Prov. 31:10–31), according to which each unit begins with a different letter of the alphabet in complete sequence from *'āleph* to *tāw* or by arrangement in numerical patterns (Prov. 30:15–31), all differently suggesting the employment of the mnemonic principle, which was so important for oral instruction. Another type to which the term *māshāl* is applied in its sense of 'comparison' is the **Parable** often used by the prophets; cf. Ezek. 17:2, although what follows in **75c** vv. 3–10 has features of both **Fable** and **Allegory**. Told as a story and nearer to the NT model is the Parable of Nathan (2 Sam. 12:1–6), almost without peer as a prose poem. The Fable as a related type, where the agents are plants or animals, occurs briefly in prose on the lips of Jehoash at 2 Kg. 14:9, and, as poetry of greater length, is put into the mouth of Jotham in Jg. 9:7–15. Allegory which, as a series of metaphors each with its particular significance, is to be distinguished from the Parable with its single point of comparison, is found, e.g., in Prov. 9:13–18; Ec. 11:9–12:7, and is also of frequent occurrence in the Prophetic literature, e.g. Isa. 5:1–7, and in the form of a **Lament** in Ezek. 19. A further type employed by the wise and associated with the *māshāl* is the *ḥîdhāh*, 'riddle' (Prov. 1:6; Ezek. 17:2). The connection of the **Riddle** with community lore relating to marriage is apparent in, e.g., Jg. 14:12ff. Between Prov. on the one hand, with its rich and varied grouping of maxims and short dissertations, and Job on the other in its unique literary magnificence, stands Ec., which is composed of sayings of differing length, gathered and arranged partly according to content and partly by formal association. A creative climax is reached in Job, whether or not it be regarded as a psalm of Lament elaborately dramatised, in virtue of the consummate artistry with which its author has made use of the most diverse elements. The function of Wisdom writing in Apocalyptic provides a link between this and the concluding section of the present outline.

(c) The Prophetic Literature with the sanctuary **d**
as its situation in life, in which priest and prophet had complementary roles, centres in the **Oracle** which issued as *tôrāh* (Priestly) and *dābhār* (Prophetic). In the **Priestly Oracle**, **Blessing**, e.g. Num. 6:24–7, and **Curse**, e.g. the liturgical series in Dt. 27:15ff., are regular formulae. Here belong also **Torah Liturgies**, dealing with conditions for entering the sanctuary, e.g. Ps. 15, 24; with which cf. prophetic adaptations at, e.g., Isa. 1:10–17; Am. 5:21–4; Mic. 6:6–8. The **Ordeal** (Num. 5:11–31) is a more complex and extended variation, combining with its formulae of cursing, and according to a set form, Confession of Sin (Jos. 7:19f.; Ps. 32:5), Protestation of Innocence (Ps. 7:3ff.), and the Oath of Purification (again Ps. 7 and in great detail Job 31). Characteristic of the **Prophetic Oracle** are the inner compulsion underlying its utterance (Jer. 20:9; Am. 3:8), a certain ruggedness, oscillation between the divine and human 'I', and frequent poetical brilliance, e.g. Jer. 4:19–26. In it are apparent the cryptic use of names (Isa. 7:3, 8:1ff.; Mic. 1:10–16) and the striking epigram, often enhanced by assonance (Isa. 7:9*b*), and having a proverb-like quality, which provided as it were a link between the *māshāl* of the prophets and the wise. Stylistic qualities include the prophetic perfect (Isa. 5:13; Am. 5:2, etc.), the imperative address to an audience vividly imagined (Isa. 8:9f.), and to these must be added the authenticating clause, 'Thus has Yahweh said' or 'Yahweh's oracle'. A significant feature of the Prophetic literature is its extensive use of other literary types already noticed, almost as though everything that could be used for compelling utterance was looked upon as grist to the prophetic mill! Hence are discernible such categories as the **Speech**, of a declamatory kind and frequently in series, e.g. Am. 1:3–2:16 (Reproach), in Isa. 5:8–10, 11f., etc. with an introductory 'Woe' or in Isa. 9:8–12, 13–17, etc. with a concluding refrain (Denunciation), and in Am. 5:4–6, 14f., etc. (Admonition); the **Prayer**, e.g. in addition to the **Prose Prayer** (§73*e*) the Prayer *par excellence* in poetical form, which Jeremiah so especially made his own (Jer. 15:10–18, 17:14–18, etc.); the **Legend**, e.g. Isa. 36–9 (Prophetic); the **Song**, e.g. Hab. 2:6–19 (Taunt); Jer. 22:18–23, 28–30 (Mourning); the **Hymn** (Mic. 7:18–20) and **Community**

75d **Lament** (Jl 1:1–2:27), and the **Poetical Sentence** as popular proverb (Isa. 28:20 ; Am. 6:12) or in more extended form like an extract from an agricultural primer in verse (Isa. 28:23–9). Already mentioned and found in considerable quantity are the **Prophetic Liturgies,** e.g. Isa. 63:7–64:12 ; Hos. 6:1–3, 4–6, which are a fusion of the **Lament** with the **Oracle,** such as characterises certain of the psalms, e.g. Ps. 12, 75.

Finally, if one may propound a *māshāl*, the application with care and skill of the form-critical method is like the restoring by a special technique of an old master, as a result of which its faded colours are able to be seen in something of their original splendour, details obliterated come to light, and its true significance is more readily apparent.

Bibliography—W. Baumgartner, 'The Wisdom Literature' in OTMS (1951) ; A. Bentzen, *Introduction to the OT*, (2nd ed. 1952) ; O. Eissfeldt, *Einleitung in das AT* (2nd ed. 1956), 'The Prophetic Literature' in OTMS (1951) ; H. Gunkel, *Die Genesis* in HAT (1901), *Einleitung in die Psalmen* (1933), *The Legends of Genesis* (1901), 'The Poetry of the Psalms' in *OT Essays* (1927), *What Remains of the OT* etc. (1928) ; H. F. Hahn, *OT in Modern Research* (1954) ; J. Hempel, *Die althebräische Literatur* usw. (1930), 'The Forms of Oral Tradition' in *Record and Revelation*, ed. by H. W. Robinson (1938) ; G. Hylmö, *Gamla Testamentets Litteraturhistoria* (1938) ; A. R. Johnson, 'The Psalms' in OTMS (1951) ; S. Mowinckel, 'Psalm Criticism between 1900 and 1935', VT 5 (1955), 13ff., *Prophecy and Tradition* (1946) ; C. R. North, 'Pentateuchal Criticism' in OTMS (1951) ; T. H. Robinson, *The Poetry of the OT* (1947) ; N. H. Snaith, 'The Historical Books' in OTMS (1951) ; A. Weiser, *Einleitung in das AT* (4th ed. 1957).

ISRAEL'S NEIGHBOURS—I
MESOPOTAMIA

By C. J. GADD

76a Palestine, the geography of which has been described in a preceding article, was but a small part of the landmass conveniently called Western Asia, i.e. the steppe and hill country lying between the parallel ridges of the Zagros Mountains (which now roughly divide the territories of modern Iraq and Iran) and the eastern shores of the Mediterranean Sea. The most striking natural features of this whole tract are the twin rivers of **Tigris** and **Euphrates,** and it was upon the lower courses of these, where they are about to fall into the Persian Gulf, that the country lay which was the focus of all the ancient civilisations that flourished in Western Asia from the beginning of history up to and beyond the intrusion of Greek influence in the 5th cent. B.C. A basically similar culture became the property of the Semitic peoples which inhabited, as they still do, the greatest part of this area. But its origin was in a restricted precinct of what is now southern Iraq. This was called Babylonia (after Babylon, its capital) by classical and subsequent writers, but its name in the cuneiform inscriptions was generally 'the land of Sumer and Akkad', or, at one time, 'the land of Kar(an)duniash', or again, at a late period, it was called 'the land of Kaldi', i.e. Chaldaea. The name **'Mesopotamia'** is often used for convenience in designating the whole Babylonian-Assyrian territory, but is strictly applicable only to the northern plains lying between the upper courses of the two rivers.

b The people among whom this civilisation first evolved were the **Sumerians,** a name given to them after the name of their language and country, although they seem hardly to have called themselves so, but mostly 'the black-headed'. Their origin is unknown and variously conjectured, as are their racial and linguistic affinities, and it will suffice to say that they were in possession of the land as early as any definite identification is possible, and that they must be regarded as the first users, perhaps the inventors, of a material equipment, a religion, a literature, institutions, and a mode of thought which remained dominant in the lives of divers peoples in Western Asia over some three millennia, and have left no slight traces even in the world of today. The Sumerian physical type is characteristically displayed by their own sculptures as short and squat, with heads sunk low upon the shoulders, and long arms. Their heads, often shaved, look full of character, having large eyes, strong brows, and prominent noses. Their dress is equally distinctive; the body is generally shown naked to the waist or with one shoulder covered, and the garment is a thick bunchy skirt of peculiar material, probably the woolly skin of sheep or goats with the fleece generally outside but sometimes reversed.

When first emerging into history, about the middle of the third millennium B.C., the Sumerians dwelt in a number of great cities, each the centre of a restricted territory. All of these shared a common manner of life and similar ideas but contended violently among themselves, both in border disputes and in competition for a certain supremacy, the 'kingship' (*nam-lugal*), which passed by conquest from city to city. The rise and fall of these were recorded by lists of 'dynasties', rehearsing the numbers and names of their kings and the total periods for which each dynasty held sway.

76b In theory these cities were theocracies, owned and patronised by the principal god of the place, who merely leased his authority to a mortal governor (*ensi*), acting in all things as the god's agent. The supreme god Enlil exercised in a like sense 'kingship' over the other gods, but his state was not transitory, and his own city Nippur was withdrawn from the profane strife which agitated the other cities in pursuit of a passing ascendancy.

c As no natural barrier protected Southern Babylonia, it was at all times the goal of immigrants from less advanced districts of Western Asia, who travelled by an easy route down the Euphrates. Most of these immigrants, in all ages, were **Semites,** a name which connotes neither a single physical type nor a common appellation of their own, for Shem, the reputed ancestor, was of course unknown in antiquity to any but the Hebrews. What they had in common was, above all, their language (the dialects of which differed much, as they still do), and this was what most distinguished them from the Sumerians, for the two 'races', mingling since days before history begins, evolved a general mode of life and thought which was of such vitality that successive immigrations were themselves absorbed, and wrought no more than a gradual development over the space of some two and a half millennia. Owing to this continual fusion it is not easy to distinguish in the early art a 'Semitic' type from a 'Sumerian', for most of the outward differences are merely those of costume and conduct upon varying occasions, but in general the Semites do seem to have been marked by a somewhat taller stature, with thinner faces and more frequent wearing of the beard. The most notable effect brought about by the Semitic influx was the early change of language: soon after the beginning of the second millennium, finally submerged by the ubiquitous 'Amorite' invasion, the old **Sumerian language** became defunct or relegated to the extreme south, and the Semitic dialect called **Akkadian,** long in possession of the northern parts, prevailed over the whole land. But the prestige of the old tongue remained supreme, and it abode ever afterwards in honour as the vehicle of religion, literature, and scholarship, occupying a position almost exactly comparable with that of Latin in later Europe.

d The struggles between the Sumerian city-states were of merely local interest, concerning no more than boundaries, tributes, and homages, but in their course events of wider scope sometimes emerged. Lugalzaggisi of Erech, after establishing his 'kingship' in Sumer, accomplished a march up to North Syria and the Mediterranean. But he soon disappeared before a greater figure, the first 'world-conqueror', never afterwards to be forgotten, **Sargon of Agade** (about 2300 B.C.). Legend credited this hero with obscure birth at a place on the upper Euphrates, where he was set adrift in a floating cradle by his mother. Borne down to Babylonia, he was rescued by 'Akki the irrigator', grew up, attained royal favour, usurped the throne, built a new capital, Agade, and established his supremacy over all the cities. His career afterwards was of unequalled military glory, and various sources (the most authentic being copies of his own inscrip-

6d tions) represent him as a world-subduer, whose conquests covered not only all the Mesopotamian lands, but Syria up to the coasts, the south-eastern parts of Asia Minor, and even the island of Crete (**Kaptara**). His two sons, succeeding him, maintained most of his dominions, but the reign of a grandson, **Naram-Sin,** himself almost equally famous in story, seems to have ended in disaster, and the dynasty, after a few more powerless reigns, was extinguished by the barbarous **Gutians,** one of the hill-peoples of the Zagros which, together with the more organised threat of the land of **Elam,** were the standing menace to Mesopotamian powers in all ages. The Gutian domination, bitterly as it was resented by the more civilised subjects, lasted over a century (about 2250–2130), but the hated invaders were at length driven out by a Sumerian revival, and Babylonia came soon after to be ruled by the **III Dynasty of Ur** for another hundred years (about 2120–2010). Flourishing internally, this kingdom seems to have been of limited extent, even under **Shul-gi,** its most powerful monarch, and it was in continual struggle with the menace from the eastern hillmen. There is no sufficient evidence that the kings of Ur ever extended their rule into Syria, much less Palestine, and the last years of the dynasty were caught up in a death-struggle not only with the **Elamites,** but with the forerunners of a new Semitic invasion. Although Ur was captured and utterly destroyed by the Elamites its kingdom over the land was taken by the city of **Isin,** and to this there sprang up, in quick succession, two rival kingdoms in the cities of **Larsa** and of **Babylon** itself, which then entered history for the first time. This parcelling-out of the land into three principal, as well as a number of smaller, kingdoms was paralleled by similar developments in states along the middle Euphrates and in Syria.

7a The Old-Babylonian period, as it is generally called, may be taken as covering, in its greatest extent, the centuries between about 2000 and 1600. It had been brought in by another massive, though apparently slow, pervasion of the whole Syrian and Babylonian territories by another Semitic people whose only distinction is, in fact, their personal names, which differ in certain elements and grammatical forms from the Akkadian, and incorporate some names of non-Akkadian gods. These people are commonly called **Amorites,** because they are supposed to have come from the west (Amurru), although it is very unlikely that they used this style for themselves ; there is, indeed, no evidence that they had any bond of union, or thought themselves distinct from the populations among whom they established their kingdoms. These new immigrants remained partly in a nomadic condition, at least upon the upper course of the Euphrates, but more characteristic was the host of petty princes (all calling themselves 'kings') who seized the rule over cities great and small and engaged in mutual hostilities, partly under the lead of regional potentates whose shifting alliances produced a general instability. In Mesopotamia itself this age culminated in the rule of two commanding figures, **Shamshi-Adad I,** who belongs chiefly to the history of Assyria (§77*d* below), and **Ḫammurabi** the lawgiver of Babylon (about 1790–1750) who, by final victories over two powerful rivals, made himself master not only of Sumer and Akkad, but of Assyria for a time, and of a dominion extending to the middle Euphrates. Concerning this district and its more remote connections a great store of information has recently been gained from the letters and documents found at the site of **Mari,** the capital of that region. These amply confirm what was indeed known already, that it was this period which not only brought into full development a culture with very ancient roots in the Babylonian homeland, but disseminated it over most of the whole area of the ancient Orient. It may be presumed that the influence of Babylonian literature and ideas upon the land of Israel, whatever its inhabitants at that time, dates mainly from these centuries, which are in fact the 'patriarchal' age, the westward spread of Mesopotamian ideas being typified by the migration of Abraham. 77a

The Old-Babylonian period was brought to an end (about 1600) not merely by the capture of Babylon in a foray of the Hittite king from Asia Minor but much more by a general movement of peoples in the Near East, which introduced a period of unsettlement and set-back over the whole of the area. In Babylonia itself a kingdom was established by the **Kassites,** another horde of invaders from the eastern hill-country, of whom little is known either as concerns their origin or their history, especially in the early years of their ascendancy. They spoke a barbarous language, without clear affinity, and their material remains are both few and of poor quality. Despite this their rule lasted for more than five centuries, though the later Kassites became completely assimilated and merged in the Babylonian society of which they adopted and even developed the culture, for considerable changes had come over the land by the time that Kassite documents are more numerous. But the Kassite kings had not the importance in their contemporary world that the kings of Agade or even Ḫammurabi had once commanded. The seats of power were now removed farther west, for this (the 15th–13th cent.) was the age of international conflicts centred upon Syria, in which the contenders were the Egyptians, the Hurrians, the Hittites, and at last the Assyrians. Among these great rivals the Babylonian kings could scarcely assert equality, and they appear variously in the diplomatic correspondences of the age as anxious to claim a recognition which was accorded to them rather by prestige than by power. b

It was **Assyria,** which, from the later years of the Kassites and through the mostly unimportant Babylonian dynasties succeeding them, was to be dominant in the affairs of Western Asia as a whole. The name of Mesopotamia is properly confined, as said above, to the northern part of the lands between the two rivers, and designates the wide tract of steppe and desert extending from northern Syria to the neighbourhood of Mosul on the Tigris ; with this may be included the mountain fringes in the north and east, parts of Armenia and Kurdistan, with which the history of these lands has ever been conjoined. In the pre-classical world this great area was occupied by various inhabitants and transformed by successive invasions, but for the most part its rule was exercised from the east and particularly from the country which had acquired, at a very early time, the name of **Ashur** borne alike by the patron god, by the capital, and by the people. The heart of this country lay in the neighbourhood of Mosul, its original capital, the city of Ashur, being some 60 miles down the river, and its later centres (Kalḫu, Dûr-Sharrukîn, and Nineveh) not far apart, in the district of Mosul. Themselves immigrants, probably from the west, into this land, the Assyrians looked back to a time when their first kings 'dwelt in tents' as nomads of the steppe, but they were settled at Ashur when history first emerges. Under the III Dynasty of Ur (§76*d*) Ashur was for a time the dependency of these kings, but before the end of this dynasty the vigour of Assyrian enterprise was curiously displayed in a far distant country, for it has been revealed that companies of Assyrian merchants were active in trading settlements situated in south-east and even central Anatolia, carrying on a lively and lucrative trade with Ashur mainly in metals and wool, apparently under licence granted by native princes, including the forerunners of the great kings of the Hittites. These trading stations flourished in the 19th cent. B.C., and probably their traffic was interrupted and their fraternity dispersed by the spread of those 'Amorite' immigrants who brought a new age into Western Asia. c

One of the most remarkable of these new dynasts, **Shamshi-Adad I** (*c.*1815–1780), took for himself the d

77d kingdom of Assyria. He has been shewn by recent discoveries to be a ruler of outstanding capacity and certainly the foremost man of his age; he was for a time contemporary with Ḫammurabi, who in comparison looks a smaller figure. Shamshi-Adad controlled not only northern Mesopotamia, being influential in the south as well, but most of the territory along the middle course of the Euphrates, which he ruled under the name of his younger son **Iasmah-Adad,** whom he made king of **Mari,** the principal city of that region, but his influence stopped short of the upper Euphrates and north Syria, which were controlled by another great power centred upon Aleppo.

78a After the death of this great figure the fortunes of Assyria sank. For the rest of the Old-Babylonian period she was partly under Babylonian control, but was soon merged in the confusion of that new migration which profoundly affected the peoples of Western Asia and issued in a situation when power was transferred to the west, and an 'international' rivalry centred upon control of northern Syria, during the 15th–13th cent. In the plains of Mesopotamia east of the Euphrates had been founded the kingdom of **Mitanni,** which consisted mostly of the people called **Hurrians.** These were also of obscure origin and affinities and they spoke a very difficult and uncouth language, still little understood though freely written in cuneiform. They were ruled by a dynasty which shows signs of Indo-Aryan connections in the names of certain kings and gods and in a technical vocabulary. The kingdom of Mitanni, once the rival as well as the ally of Egypt under her XVIII and XIX Dynasties, was subverted by the **Hittites** of Asia Minor, but these in turn soon found themselves faced with a resurgent Assyria, now ruled by **Ashur-uballiṭ I** (about 1355–1320), a king who had thrown off the control of his nominal overlords, the Kassites of Babylon, and now proceeded to take a very effective part in the contention for supremacy in Syria. His effort met with considerable success, but this had no permanence, and Assyria went into a period of decline and obscurity. A succession of three great kings reasserted her power in the first half of the 13th cent. but these, although they extended their conquests up to the Euphrates, were principally occupied in making head against the Kassite rulers of the south, over whom the last of the three, **Tukulti-Ninurta I** (1256–1233), won a signal triumph, after which he sacked Babylon itself and actually set his own governors over the southland for several years.

b During all this period the situation in the whole of Western Asia was being transformed by still another Semitic migration, this time of the people called **Aramaeans.** They had been already present in Syria in the reign of Ashur-uballiṭ I, and in the succeeding centuries their slow invasion went on with increasing pressure, the tribes finally pushing their penetration down the Euphrates, so that the territory of Babylonia was ringed and partly occupied by the **Chaldaeans,** a branch of these immigrants. Assyria was protected by a great champion, **Tiglath-pileser I** (1098–1068), who for a while extended his rule over the west and northern fringes and dealt successfully with some of the Aramaeans. Following him, the next kings of Assyria were all engaged in a desperate struggle to keep out the invaders from the nearer boundaries of their own land and it was not until the reign of **Adad-nirari II** (911–889) that Assyria began to gain the upper hand and expand again towards its ancient boundaries in the west. With the progress of the 9th cent. revival of Assyrian power was made fully effective, and one of her greatest monarchs, **Ashur-naṣir-apli II** (884–859) inaugurated the final period of Assyrian triumph and empire which, despite a setback after the reign of his son, lasted with increasing brilliance until the early 7th cent., when even Egypt itself was for a short time included in the Assyrian empire.

c Since the principal effort of Assyrian campaigns in this last and best-known period was directed to the west, and especially against the Aramaean powers and 78c the cities of Phoenicia, its history is intimately bound up with the history of Israel, which, in resisting Assyrian attacks, was obliged to ally herself, however vainly, with the Aramaean kings of Damascus, whom otherwise she opposed, even by force of arms. Under **Shalmaneser III** there occurred the first clash with the Israelites, as allies of the king of Damascus, at the **battle of Qarqar** (853), when the Assyrians were victorious in the field, though not able to capture Damascus. Most dramatically the relation of Israelites and Assyrians is pictured by the famous scene of **Jehu**'s submission to Shalmaneser sculptured on the '**Black Obelisk**' in the British Museum. The further course of these relations with Assyria, and afterwards with the Chaldaean kings, will be related in the section of this General Introduction devoted to the History of Israel (pre-Exilic), and may be omitted here.

In the intervals of extending their power in the west, d the kings of Assyria were busied, during the 9th to the 7th cent., in fighting, rather to defend themselves than for conquest, on the north and east sides of their home country. Against Babylon too, often allied with Elam, there were intermittent wars, despite the great similarity of culture, religion, and outlook of the two peoples. In this quarter the most persistent and able enemy of the Assyrians was Marduk-apal-iddinna II (**Merodach-baladan**), a Chaldaean prince who, after an early submission to Tiglath-pileser III (745–727), lived to be a constant threat to both Sargon (722–705) and Sennacherib (705–681). In these almost fratricidal struggles between the neighbours and close relations of north and south the advantage was generally with the Assyrians, who indeed at different times took over the kingship of Babylon either in their own monarchs or by nominees, but always to the great resentment of the Babylonians. This situation was repeated, for the last time, when Esarhaddon (680–669) arranged for the twin kingdoms in the north and south to be assumed after his death by his two sons, Ashurbanipal in Assyria and his brother Shamash-shum-ukin in Babylon. After a few years the younger brother, moved rather by the nationalism of his subjects than by family jealousy, revolted and involved the two nations in a conflict which ended with the dramatic capture of Babylon and the death of Shamash-shum-ukin in the flames of his palace (648). More dangerous enemies of the Assyrians were active in the north, where they had known since the days of Shalmaneser I the kings of **Urarṭu** (Ararat, later Armenia) as formidable opponents. The history of Assyrian hostilities with Urarṭu is a long chapter which cannot be related here; in the 9th cent. the Urarṭians rose to a height of power, and the struggle against them lasted for more than a century. In the reign of Esarhaddon the threat from the native kings of Urarṭu was succeeded by the disorderly raids of **Cimmerians** and **Scythians** who had overrun the Urarṭian country and variously threatened the Assyrian territories from the north and north-west. The movement of these nations portended the approach of a great migration which was bringing Indo-European invaders (the **Medes** and subsequently the **Persians**) into the hill-country east of Assyria.

It was these newcomers who finally proved the ruin e of Assyria, which is associated with the name of Kyaxares (called by the Assyrians Umakishtar), a Median prince who became an enemy of the hitherto dominant power, and allied himself with the founder of a new dynasty which had set itself up in Babylonia in defiance of the Assyrians, and was at length able to eject them from the southern kingdom. This founder was Nabopolassar (625–605), whose life was dedicated mostly to his struggle against the traditional enemy. In 612 the alliance of the Medes and Babylonians finally captured Nineveh, and brought to destruction the Assyrian empire, greatest and most powerful that the world had hitherto seen. To most

8e of this the Medes succeeded, although the Babylonian kings were left with wide dominions in Mesopotamia and Syria, and under **Nebuchadrezzar II** (605–561) they were supreme in the whole of the West, defeated the Egyptians at the battle of Carchemish (605), encountered them upon their own borders, and in particular captured Jerusalem and carried away many of the Jews into the Exile. Not long afterwards the Babylonian kingdom itself came to an end, when the last king Nabonidus (556–539) was taken captive, with his city, by **Cyrus** the Persian. Under him, but especially under his successors Cambyses (529–522) and above all **Darius I** (522–496) the Persian empire included Egypt and spread across the whole of the Near and Middle East as far as the north-west of India itself. Its peculiar interest for the history of Israel and of Judaism is that under Artaxerxes I took place the return of the exiles to Jerusalem (Cyrus himself, upon his conquest of Babylon, had proclaimed restoration of all deported gods and peoples). With the establishment of the Persian rule over Asia came a great extension eastwards of the influence, the culture, and the language of the **Greeks,** so that, for example, some leading men in the cities of Babylonia, under the rule of the Persian kings, are found to have adopted Greek names in addition to their own. It is known too that Greeks occupied many positions of trust and confidence at the courts and in the government of the Persian kings. All of this culminated in the final supersession of the Persian power by the Greeks, when the great Macedonian conqueror **Alexander** the son of Philip finally defeated king Darius III and succeeded to all of the Persian dominions, which he set himself to extend even farther to the East in the few years which remained before his early death at Babylon in 323. At this event it is possible to close the survey of Mesopotamian history, for the tracts broadly defined by that name can hardly be said thereafter, until the rise of Islam, to have a history of their own, becoming no more than borderlands between powers centred elsewhere.

9a In order to appreciate the influence of Mesopotamia upon the whole life of ancient Western Asia, and thus upon Israel, it is necessary to give a slight sketch of the high civilisation which developed there, entirely native and original, so far as can be seen, and so strong that not only did it succeed in absorbing a constant influx of less advanced immigrants, but its influence, carried especially by its cuneiform writing and the prestige of its literature, spread far and wide even beyond mountains and deserts. Its foundation was the rich farming and stock-raising of the homeland, and these in turn depended upon the control and utilisation of the two rivers by a vast system of canals and ditches. Grain and wool were the staples of production and trade, by which a great variety of commodities (especially all metals) which the country lacked were obtained from abroad. A community of traders and manufacturers required the opportunities of city life, and from the earliest days the country of Sumer (i.e. Lower Iraq) was a land of cities. About ten of these divided the soil of the country, often with strife, but their daily life and occupations were little interrupted. Essentially they were small states, all of a like pattern. Each was regarded as the property of its own god, who dwelt in its midst in a temple marked externally by one or more of the ziggurrats or staged-towers which rose above it. These gods themselves were a kind of fraternity having its own ranks and functions ; they had, indeed, three overlords, the gods of heaven, the intermediate space, and earth with its waters, to whom a mother-goddess was often joined in pre-eminence. This did not prevent a kind of contest proceeding among the gods for sovereignty, and their struggle was reflected in the wars of their cities. As each of these variously established a leadership, so their patron gods gained or lost the advantage, until with the rise of Babylon, hitherto unknown, its equally obscure god, **Marduk,** won the
reputation of a conqueror and creator, was not deposed 79a
again, and his ' son ' Nabu was established as his heir-apparent. He finally enjoyed such prestige that a kind of henotheism began to prevail, other gods being regarded as merely functions or aspects of this supreme deity.

Each in the temple focusing the activities of his city, b
the Sumerian gods lived a life of ease, for the community existed to serve them. In the earlier Sumerian period the temples actually possessed the greatest part of the city's territory, and the mass of the inhabitants was formed of serfs who laboured for the maintenance or profit of the temple. At the head of these citizens were temporal rulers, called generally governors (*ensi*) or, when aspiring, kings (*lugal*), whose formal position was no more than that of the god's agent. In that capacity the ruler not only supervised the exploitation of the god's estate and the due maintenance of his revenues, but was charged to repel the inroads of encroaching neighbours, and to make good by force, if necessary, his own god's claims to property held by the same neighbours. With time this system was modified, though without losing the character of divine relations with its subjects. Private property became more widespread (it had never been absent), and more of the country's income came to be produced by trade. But the temples kept their wealth and importance, and the god, never ceasing to be a landowner, became more of a merchant and investor. Kings, who had never been divine, now became less closely identified with the god, and approached him rather as priests than agents. Even their warfare had now more of a political and even private character, although the late Assyrian kings still fought in the name of their lord the god Ashur, and even sent to his temple elaborate despatches informing him of the victories won in his honour and to his material gain.

The interest of rulers in the welfare of their subjects made itself felt early, and from the old Sumerian period there is a body of evidence for the enforcement of justice and the rule of law. At first it is the check of administrative abuses which moves the reformer, but soon there begin to appear fragments of written laws, which were, as it seems, set up in the markets or in the temples to be consulted both by traders and by persons suffering wrongs. Although such enactments probably existed, with increasing complexity, from early days their great development came at the time, if not in consequence, of the passing of a Sumerian into a predominantly Semitic society, after the beginning of the second millennium B.C. The famous code of Ḫammurabi, though it remains the best and principal example, is now seen as only the latest of several such compilations of laws. Their most striking features are their selective character (much being left to customary law, when this was not thought in need of amendment), and their purely secular interests. Reinforced by a large mass of surviving legal private documents (which do not, in general, seem to be subject to all the rules given in the codes) and by an almost equal wealth of private letters, mostly concerning business and administration, the laws impart much detailed information upon the structure of society in that age, especially the prevailing division of the subjects into three classes, gentry, commons, and slaves, each having their own privileges in descending order, but also their liabilities for wrongdoing which increase in the contrary direction.

Babylonian society, from the above and many other c
sources, is well known. Upon the whole it was happily endowed, for there is no frequent appearance of poverty and scarcity came only from bad harvests or hostile devastation. Slaves themselves, though bought and sold, had their protection in the law, their right to wives and property, and to benefit by the liberality of masters. Women too, although it is impossible here to sketch their position, possessed many rights and but few disabilities ; in particular, they could hold and inherit property, and their position in marriage and

79c divorce was diligently protected by the law. The privilege of children too was carefully regulated, especially as regards inheritance. There was also a remarkable system of education, which aimed to train boys for the scribal profession. In proportion to the reverence in which writing and learning were held, the scribe was in great honour, for he was not only the medium of all written communication, but an expert in every kind of knowledge, religious, scientific, and mercantile. Priests were attached to every temple with the purpose of performing the daily services of the gods ; their offices were of value, and were often transferred by holders to purchasers whose object was to obtain the portions of sacrifices which were taken by officiants. More influential in the life of the people were certain special classes of priests whose function was to combat the various ills into which the individual might fall. If the sufferer was able to use the assistance of these (which was doubtless expensive) they could both advise him what was amiss and what had been the cause of it and could provide the appropriate remedies. The so-called 'seer' was the interpreter of signs, for it was these, properly understood, which warned of coming fate and also indicated what was amiss at present. All this was the domain of divination, which was looked upon as the supreme science ; its aid was usually called in for affairs of state, but certain kinds of omens were more generally applicable to private affairs. Sickness was the most common cause of distress, and it was combated by means both magical and practical, by incantations (which were the province of the enchanter-priest) and by the compounding of drugs and treatments, the province of the physician. A large literature of both kinds of treatment is still extant, and the medical texts display an extensive pharmacopoeia and an intelligent, if primitive, use of the properties of plants and mineral drugs. The individual seems to have been concerned with his gods principally when in distress. The Babylonians had evolved a characteristic notion of personal gods, who normally made it their business to recommend their charge to the favour of the greater gods, because these seemed unapproachable to the ordinary man, but they could also take offence, and themselves afflict the individual. In that case they were to be reconciled only by submission and by prayer or incantation. Like most ancient religions, the Babylonian laid stress rather upon ritual correctitude than upon moral conduct, but moral reflection is nevertheless shown by a large literature of proverbs and by a number of pieces in the class of 'wisdom' literature, a favourite theme being the problem of suffering apparently undeserved, and the question of divine justice which such affliction seemed to violate.

80a Babylonian literature has survived in an impressive quantity, and owing to the nearly indestructible nature of clay tablets this is being increased almost annually by fresh discoveries. Its most flourishing period was the Old-Babylonian (19th to 17th cent.) when was first composed, or rather first written down, the national mythology, stories of the gods, of heroic men who mingled with them, of former ages and the beginning of things, creation itself, man's destiny, the conduct of life and its end. There were also hymns and prayers, incantations, and a copious scientific literature, embracing both factual and fanciful knowledge ; beside such subjects as mathematics, geometry, medicine, and law, in which the attainments of this people were considerable, many tablets were devoted to the vain study of divinatory arts in various forms. Later ages, though of great length and fruitful of changes in many respects, made no great addition to this literature, which was rather systematised than developed. The chief innovation was in the writing of history, which, under the Assyrian kings, and perhaps with outside influence, attained a scope which had been quite lacking in the earlier and otherwise more creative ages, for it may be said that history is the department which is most deficient over the whole period of Babylonian development. By contrast, the annals of Assyrian kings, however they may be criticised either as compositions or as history, are a rich and copious source of information unparalleled in ancient times, being the direct productions of those who enacted the events described, and whose own statements, even distortions, are the best of first-hand evidence. **80**

b It is perhaps true that the Babylonians, though patient and ingenious craftsmen, had not the gift of fine artistic work in the same degree as, for example, their contemporary Egyptians ; yet, in judging this, it must be remembered that, owing to climatic and soil conditions, very much less of the finest Babylonian work has survived than of the Egyptian. Despite these disadvantages Babylonian art has left a remarkable record of achievement from centuries when most of the world had as yet little or nothing to show. This is especially the case in its earlier ages, for no period was so productive and so rich as that which is called by modern archaeologists Early Dynastic III, and may be placed about the middle of the third millennium B.C. Historically very little known, this age, most strikingly exhibited by the 'Royal Cemetery' of Ur and the earlier discoveries at Tello (Lagash), was a time of unequalled wealth and artistic splendour. Stone-carving was clumsy but gathering confidence, and the great accomplishments were in metal-work (the supply of metal being then, for unknown reasons, at a great height), shell inlay, and stone engraving, with articles of jewellery and personal adornment. Sculpture was to have its triumphs in a succeeding period, the age of Sargon and Naram-Sin, when carving in relief was able to produce masterpieces, and these led onwards, though with slow progression, for about 200 years, to the finest products of Babylonian sculpture, the figures of Gudea, which would now be dated at about 2100. Afterwards there is nothing of great note until the age of Assyrian reliefs, beginning about the 9th cent., when a different nation, under quite other influences, began to translate the acts of the king into pictures as well as words, and to fashion in stone divine forms to guard the entrances of temples. Limited as is the range of these themes, the Assyrian sculptures, apart from their artistic merit, are a rich source of information upon the life of that people and upon their material resources and equipment. These bas-reliefs, originally coloured, are a more permanent and costly form of painting, such as was used to cover the upper parts of walls. Painting had a long history in Babylonia, going back to the prehistoric period, and it was extensively used to decorate walls with subjects sometimes illustrating the activity which was connected with particular rooms ; owing, however, to the perishable nature of these pictures rendered upon the plaster of walls, very little survives, and we have consequently no sufficient idea of the subjects, the methods, and the materials of the ancient artists.

c In even greater measure has the doom of forgetfulness overtaken another art in which the Babylonians took great delight, and were much given to representing —the art of music. They had a variety of harps, flutes, pipes, and drums, but (like the rest of antiquity) no known means of recording tunes in script. One other product is especially characteristic of Babylonia, and well known from the very numerous examples which still exist—the small stone cylinder-seals, which were carried by all persons of any consequence, and used to attest legal and business documents. These were one of the most popular symbols of the spread of Babylonian influence in Western Asia ; they have been found over the whole area from Asia Minor and Palestine to the western borders of Persia, even in lands which themselves favoured the stamp seal. Apart from this cultural and symbolic value the cylinder seals themselves are often remarkable pieces of small craftsmanship. These attained their highest achievement in the early age of Agade (about 2300), when the

80c subjects are taken from mythology, often obscure to us, the execution masterly, and even the materials chosen for their beauty.

Bibliography—G. Contenau, *Everyday Life in Babylon and Assyria* (trans. by K. R. and A. R. Maxwell-Hyslop) (1954) ; L. J. Delaporte, *Mesopotamia* (trans. by V. Gordon Childe) (1925) ; B. Meissner, *Babylonien und Assyrien*, 2 vols. (1920, 1925) ; *The Cambridge Ancient History* i–iv (1923–6) ; A. Moortgat, 'Geschichte Vorderasiens bis zum Hellenismus', in A. Scharff and A. Moortgat, *Ägypten und Vorderasien im Altertum* (1950) ; Sidney Smith, *Early History of Assyria* (1928) ; G. R. Driver and Sir John Miles, *The Assyrian Laws* (1935), and *The Babylonian Laws* (2 vols. 1952, 1955) ; 'Babylonian Law', in *Encyclopaedia Britannica* (1954) ; A. Falkenstein, 'La Cité-Temple sumérienne', in *Cahiers d'Histoire mondiale* i (1954), 784ff. ; C. J. Gadd, *Ideas of Divine Rule in the Ancient East* (1948) ; A. Goetze, *The Laws of Eshnunna* (1956) ; P. Koschaker, 'Keilschriftrecht', in the *Zeitschrift der deutschen morgenländischen Gesellschaft* 89 (1935), 1–39 ; E. Dhorme, *Les Religions de Babylonie et d'Assyrie* (1945) ; S. H. Hooke, *Babylonian and Assyrian Religion* (1953) ; C. F. Jean, *Le Littérature des Babyloniens et des Assyriens* (1924) ; S. N. Kramer, *Sumerian Mythology* (1944), and *From the Tablets of Sumer* (1956) ; B. Meissner, *Die babylonisch-assyrische Literatur* (1930) ; J. B. Pritchard (ed.), *Ancient Near-Eastern Texts* (2nd ed. 1955) (relevant sections) ; G. Contenau, *Manuel d'Archéologie Orientale* (1927–47), 4 vols. ; H. Frankfort, *Art and Architecture of the Ancient Orient* (1954).

ISRAEL'S NEIGHBOURS—II

EGYPT

By T. W. THACKER

81a **Land, Race and Language**—The land of Egypt is situated in the NE. corner of Africa. It is bounded on the N. by the Mediterranean Sea and on the S. by Nubia or, to give it its modern name, the Sudan. On the E. lies the Red Sea and on the W. the Libyan Desert. It is joined on the NE. to the continent of Asia by the Sinai Peninsula, through which runs the land route to Palestine and the Region of the Fertile Crescent. It is a long narrow country, divided throughout its entire length of 600 miles by the river Nile, which enters the Mediterranean Sea through a number of mouths known as the Nile Delta. From the most ancient times the Nile has dominated the economic life of Egypt, both because it provides the most convenient means of transport and communication and also because its waters bring fertility to the otherwise arid valley through which it flows. Each year the melting of the snows and the heavy spring rains at its sources cause it to rise and overflow, depositing rich mud along its banks as it falls. Egypt has always been a predominantly agricultural country, whose fertile stretches have encouraged the settled life essential for the development of civilisation and at the same time have attracted invasions of foreigners from the surrounding countries not so well favoured by nature.

b Civilisation began in the Nile Valley at a very early date. Little can be said with certainty about the Palaeolithic Age, but the Neolithic Age seems to have lasted from 10,000 B.C. to about 5,000 B.C. Somewhere about the latter date the use of copper side by side with the employment of flint began. Civilisation in the prehistoric period advanced more rapidly in the N. than in the S. and two independent kingdoms were evolved. Even in historic times the Egyptians very commonly spoke of their country as the 'two lands', i.e. Upper and Lower Egypt. This is perhaps reflected in the Hebrew word for Egypt, *Miṣrayim*, which may be dual in form. Another name by which Egypt was known was *Kēmet*, i.e. 'the black', referring to the black soil and in contrast to 'the red', the sand of the desert. The name 'Egypt' is derived from the Greek *Aiguptos*, itself derived from *Ḥikuptah*, an ancient Egyptian name for Memphis.

c Anthropological evidence as to the racial affinities of the Egyptians is conflicting. The most favoured theory is that the primitive inhabitants were **Hamitic**, belonging to the same stock as the Gallas and the Somalis to the SE. of Egypt and the Berbers of Libya. At a very early date they were subjected to an invasion of **Semites**, either from the N. via the Peninsula of Sinai or from the E. via the Red Sea and the eastern desert. By 3000 B.C. these two elements had fused into a race which persisted throughout Pharaonic times and members of which may still be encountered today.

d Linguistic evidence lends support to this view. The earliest place of the ancient Egyptian language, known as Old Egyptian, has strong affinities with the Semitic languages on the one hand and the Hamitic languages on the other hand. In general it may be said that the grammatical structure and syntax are predominantly Semitic, while the vocabulary contains a preponderance of non-Semitic words, many of which can be connected with Hamitic. The personal pronouns and the inflexion of nouns stand very close to Semitic. Egyptian shares with Semitic what are demonstrably the most ancient forms of the Semitic verbal system but the Egyptian verb appears to have split from the Semitic verb when the latter was still in an incomplete stage of development and to have followed its own paths. Thus Egyptian has all the characteristics of a language of mixed origins. The Semitic elements portray a much more primitive stage of development than is to be found in any of the surviving Semitic languages. 81d

In historic times the Egyptian language had a continuous history of some 3,800 years. It is now dead, having been gradually superseded by Arabic, the present language of Egypt, after the Arab conquest in A.D. 640. It has five main phases—Old Egyptian (3180–2240 B.C.), Middle Egyptian (2240–1990 B.C.), Late Egyptian (1573–715 B.C.), Demotic (715 B.C.–A.D. 470) and Coptic (*c.* A.D. 300–*c.* A.D. 640). (The dates here given refer to their use as vernacular languages and do not always correspond with their use as written languages.) Late Egyptian and Demotic were the phases current in OT times and in them occur a large number of Semitic loan-words, which owe their presence to the close and frequent intercourse between Egypt and Syria-Palestine. It is interesting to note that there are relatively few Egyptian loan-words in biblical Hebrew, in spite of the fact that Egypt was politically the dominant power. Coptic is Egyptian as spoken and written by the Christian descendants of the ancient Egyptians. It is written in the Greek alphabet supplemented by seven characters derived from the demotic script. The influence of Greek is very strong and a large percentage of the Coptic vocabulary, especially theological terms, is Greek. e

The ancient Egyptians employed three types of scripts. The oldest is **hieroglyphic,** a picture script, which continued in use down to Roman times. A cursive script, used in writing on papyri and ostraca, is known as **hieratic**: it bears roughly the same relation to hieroglyphs as our handwriting does to print. Each period has its own distinctive form of hieratic, which enables documents to be dated with a fair degree of accuracy. A still more cursive script is **demotic,** which grew out of the crabbed hieratic of legal documents. It was used to write the language of the phase of Egyptian named after it, i.e. the vernacular language spoken 715 B.C.–A.D. 470. f

Hieroglyphic writing is pictorial in character. Three classes of signs were used. First came ideograms, which denote objects by pictures of them. At a very early date phonetic characters were devised: these may represent one, two, or three consonantal sounds. Signs known as 'determinatives', which indicate the general meaning or class of the word, became increasingly common throughout the history of Egyptian writing. From Middle Egyptian onwards most words were spelt with phonetic characters or with an ideogram, followed by one or more determinatives. The phonetic characters indicate only the consonantal skeleton of a word, like the Hebrew and Arabic alphabets, though some scholars believe that in certain cases the weak consonants *w* and *y* at the g

81g end of the words were intended to mark vowel sounds, as in the Punic inscriptions. It is also reasonably certain that weak consonants were employed in the Late Egyptian period to indicate the internal vowels of foreign words imported into Egyptian and of foreign names, the pronunciation of which would be quite unfamiliar to the Egyptians.

h The set of characters which denote single consonants is to all intents and purposes an alphabet, but it was never recognised as such by the Egyptians. It was left to the genius of others to evaluate the chance discovery of the Egyptians and to devise a purely alphabetic script. Most scholars are agreed that the notion of alphabetic writing was transmitted from Egypt via the inhabitants of the Sinai peninsula to Syria-Palestine, where a true alphabet was evolved sometime in the second millennium B.C. on the rebus principle.

82a Egyptian history properly begins when the Southern kingdom conquered the Northern kingdom somewhere about 3200 B.C. and the two were united under one rule. It was formerly supposed that this took place under Menes, but it now seems probable that Narmer was the first king of the whole of Egypt. Some scholars have argued that Menes and Narmer are the same person. The seven kings who followed the unifier of Egypt comprise the I Dynasty. (The term ' dynasty ' denotes a family or group of kings. Following the native Egyptian historian Manetho, who lived in the Greek period, the rulers of ancient Egypt to Alexander the Great are divided into 31 dynasties.) The kings of the **I and II Dynasties** reigned *c.* 3000–2778 B.C. at This. Their tombs are in Abydos and the vicinity. Little is known of the political history of this remote period, but already there is evidence of wars with the Libyans on the W. and the marauding Beduin on the E. Art and civilisation made steady progress and stone masonry and the arch were introduced.

b The III–VI Dynasties (*c.* 2778–2263 B.C.) are known as **the Old Kingdom** and cover one of the major epochs of Egyptian history. The first king of the III Dynasty was Djeser. His minister, Imhotep, was revered by Egyptians throughout the ages as a sage, physician and man of letters. Djeser was the builder of the first real pyramid, a so-called ' step-pyramid '. In the Old Kingdom the tombs of the wealthy commonly had a low square building with sloping sides over the shaft which led to the subterranean burial chamber, called a ' mastaba '. Djeser's pyramid was in essence several mastabas placed one on top of another, each being smaller than the one on which it stands. The final development is to be seen in the pyramid of Khufu, the second king of the IV Dynasty, who built the Great Pyramid at Gîzeh. Here the ' steps ' were filled in and the whole cased with polished granite. Smaller pyramids were built by his successors Khafrē (Second Pyramid of Gîzeh) and Menkaure (Third Pyramid of Gîzeh), and other kings and queens of the V and VI Dynasties. The walls of the chambers of some V and VI Dynasty pyramids at Saqqârah are covered with religious texts known as the Pyramid Texts. These are the earliest known religious compositions from Egypt. They are largely magical in character and many of them were clearly composed centuries before the pyramids in which they are inscribed were built. The main purpose of the spells was to assure the continued existence of the owner of the pyramid in the next world.

c Few documents of a historical character have come down to us from the Old Kingdom. The most important are biographical inscriptions from the tombs of the nobles, especially those of the officials Weni and Khewefḥar. Through them we are afforded a glimpse of a state organised on feudal lines. Egypt was divided into districts each governed by a noble responsible to the king, who was regarded as divine. He was at the head of the central government, which was called *per-o*, ' the great house '. In later times this title came to be applied to the king himself and passed into Hebrew in the form of ' Pharaoh '. The main trend of Egypt's foreign policy at this period 82c
seems to have been the conquest and colonisation of Nubia and the lands beyond her southern frontiers. The inscriptions of Weni and Khewefḥar tell of military expeditions in the far south. They also speak of primitive raids against the Beduin in the NE., but in general it would appear that Egypt's relations with her Semitic neighbours were good. At any rate an Egyptian temple existed in Byblos already in the IV Dynasty and there was a flourishing trade with Phoenicia. Civilisation reached a very high peak during the Old Kingdom. Great strides were made in architecture and the arts generally. No literary productions of the Old Kingdom have survived, though the Proverbs of Ptaḥḥotep and Kagemni were probably composed in this period.

The last king but one of the VI Dynasty was Pepi II, d
who reigned more than 90 years. His reign, the longest in history, began brilliantly, but towards the end, enfeebled by old age, he lost his grip over the nobles in charge of the administrative districts, who had been growing steadily more powerful throughout the V and VI Dynasties. The confusion resulting from a more than usually determined series of raids on the part of the Beduin gave the nobles of the N. an opportunity to wrest still further independence. The central government broke down and a period of anarchy followed, in which it seems that the common people rose against the nobles and the organised life of the community collapsed. Nothing is known of Manetho's VII Dynasty—indeed its very existence is doubtful—and hardly anything is known of the kings of the VIII Dynasty beyond their names. During the next 200 years (Manetho's IX, X and the first half of the XI Dynasties) Egypt was divided and the barons of Koptos, Herakleopolis and Thebes struggled for supremacy. Eventually Thebes won the day and Egypt was once more united under Menthuḥotep II, a king of the XI Dynasty, who reigned 2065–2060 B.C.). This troubled period of Egyptian history is known as the **First Intermediate Period** : it lasted roughly 2300–2065 B.C. The overthrow of the old order and the constant strife caused men to challenge accepted moral values and standards of behaviour. Some of the most remarkable literary compositions which ancient Egypt ever produced are probably to be attributed to this age, namely the ' Admonitions of an Egyptian Sage ', the ' Instructions for King Merikare ' and the ' Dispute over Suicide '.

The Middle Kingdom—With Menthuḥotep II a new 83a
era of Egyptian history begins. It is commonly called the ' Middle Kingdom ' and it lasted about 500 years. Menthuḥotep II was followed by three kings who bore the same name and who reigned a total of 60 years. A new dynasty, the XII, was established by Amenemḥet I in 2000 B.C. It is one of the most glorious and its members were characterised by their energy and ability. Amenemḥet I (2000–1970 B.C.) set to work to reorganise and strengthen the administration of the country. He moved the centre of government from Thebes some three hundred miles northwards to a site near the modern Lisht, the better to control and defend his kingdom. His successors continued to live in the same region—between Memphis and the Faiyûm, the development of which was one of the major concerns of the dynasty. He was succeeded by Sesostris I (1970–1936 B.C.), who, having inherited a firmly established kingdom, was at liberty to turn his attention to the colonisation of Nubia, begun by the kings of the VI Dynasty. Amenemḥet II (1938–1904 B.C.) and Sesostris II (1906–1888 B.C.) ruled over a prosperous Egypt and their reigns were uneventful. Sesostris III (1887–1850 B.C.) was a b
dynamic personality who himself led a number of campaigns into Nubia, which was brought under Egyptian rule as far as the Second Cataract. He also directed an expedition into Palestine against a town called Sekmem. His successor Amenemḥet III (1850–1800 B.C.) was mainly concerned with the

83b economic and agricultural development of Egypt. Under him the Lake Moeris of the classical geographers,, a vast irrigation project, was completed, and he it was who built the vast administrative centre, with sets of halls containing shrines for each of the gods of the administrative provinces, called by Greek writers the 'Labyrinth' and compared by them with the Cretan Labyrinth. The last two rulers of the XII Dynasty, Amenemḥet IV (1800–1792 B.C.) and Queen Sebekneferurē (1791–1785 B.C.) have left scarcely any traces of their reign. The XII Dynasty was thus a period of unparalleled prosperity, during which Egypt developed her resources at home and strengthened her position abroad. In spite of the military expedition of Sesostris III into Palestine, it would appear that Egypt's relations with the Semitic kingdoms to the NE. were friendly. It seems likely that Phoenicia was administered by an Egyptian
c governor, at any rate for a while. To this period are to be attributed the so-called **Execration Texts,** curses directed against Asiatic and Nubian princes written on pots and figurines, which were then smashed to bring about by sympathetic magic the downfall of the persons and peoples named on them. These rites were doubtless directed against marauding bands of tribesmen. They throw much interesting light on Semitic names of the time and the Egyptian method of writing them. It would seem that many Semites penetrated peacefully into Egypt and settled there : representations of them are to be found in the tomb of Khnomḥotep at Beni Hasan and elsewhere. Under the able rulers of the XII Dynasty art flourished. Literature attained a standard which was never surpassed. The story of Sinuhe, the Eloquent Peasant, and the Shipwrecked Sailor are outstanding examples of the narrative prose of the period.

d After the XII Dynasty there was a rapid decline. A succession of some 30 kings followed, comprising the XIII and XIV Dynasties (1785–1680 B.C.). So little is known of the 105 years during which these weaklings occupied the throne that even the order in which they came is uncertain. During this period, often named the **Second Intermediate Period**, an influx of Asiatics began. Following Manetho, historians refer to them as the 'Hyksos', which he interprets as 'shepherd kings'. It is, however, much more likely that the second element of the name was not *shasu*, 'nomads, shepherds', but *khasut*, 'foreign countries'. The title *heka-khasut*, 'prince of the foreign countries', occurs in inscriptions of the Middle Kingdom, where it is used of Asiatic chieftains who bring tribute to the governors of Beni Hasan. Dispossessed from their own lands and driven south by waves of Aryan invaders, amongst whom were the Hittites, these people steadily filtered into Egypt and settled in the Delta region. They were Semites interspersed with Asiatic elements who were carried along with them. They appear to have made their first appearance in Egypt about 1730 B.C. The Egyptian kings were too feeble to expel them and they quietly ignored them. The newcomers were allowed to establish a capital at Avaris, where they maintained their Asiatic mode of life. Nevertheless they adopted some Egyptian customs and they wrote their names in hieroglyphs. Sometimes they took purely Egyptian names. The period of infiltration perhaps lasted about 50 years. Eventually, when they became sufficiently numerous, they elected a chieftain, Salatis, according to Manetho, and began the conquest of Egypt. This they effected without any difficulty, partly because of the enfeebled state of the country and partly because of their superior arms. They had brought with them the horse and the war chariot, which were up to that time unknown in Egypt and which they themselves had taken over from the Aryans. Five Hyksos kings are known to have reigned and they comprise Manetho's XV and XVI Dynasties (*c.* 1730–1580 B.C.). They have left few remains, doubtless because the Egyptians did everything possible to expunge the memory of the
hated invaders after their expulsion. It appears that 83
the princes of Thebes enjoyed a certain independence and stood in the relationship of vassals to the Hyksos kings. These, Manetho's XVII Dynasty (?1680–1580 B.C.), kept alive the Egyptian national spirit and fostered the desire for independence. According to a later folk-tale, one of the Theban princes, Sekenenrē, took up arms against the Hyksos overlords. Certainly his son, Kames, the last ruler of the XVII Dynasty, was in conflict with them and appears to have extended the boundary of his domain considerably northwards. It was the brother and successor of Kames, Aḥmosis, who captured Avaris and drove the Hyksos from Egyptian soil. Once again Egypt was united under the rule of a native king.

Period of the Empire—Aḥmosis (1580–1558 B.C.) 84
became the first king of the XVIII Dynasty and was the founder of the empire. Under him Egypt rapidly recovered her prosperity, for the expulsion of the Hyksos had called forth an upsurge of patriotic energy throughout the land. One of his first tasks was the reconquest of Nubia to ensure the security of Egypt's southern frontiers. It was subdued after three campaigns. Hitherto Egypt's relations with the countries of Asia had been mainly commercial and her policy had been defensive rather than aggressive. The invasion of the Hyksos had changed all this and the Egyptians now felt that the best way to prevent a recurrence of their recent unhappy plight was to subdue the Asiatic lands on their NE. border. Towards the end of his reign Aḥmosis undertook an expedition to Phoenicia, doubtless for the purpose of establishing sea-bases for future military operations. He appears to have brought the Phoenician ports under Egyptian domination without any difficulty. Aḥmosis was succeeded by his son Amenophis I (1557–1530 B.C.), who continued his father's internal and external policy. Another campaign in Nubia extended Egypt's influence southwards. There are no records of any Asiatic campaigns, but his son, Ṭhuthmosis I, in the second year of his reign was able to boast that his empire extended from Tombos in upper Nubia to the Euphrates. It therefore seems probable that Amenophis I had at any rate laid the foundations of that empire. Ṭhuthmosis I (1530–1520 B.C.) consolidated the work of his father and grandfather. Having quelled an incipient revolt in Asia, he erected a stele on the upper Euphrates recording his victory.

The succession of the three sovereigns who succeeded b
Ṭhuthmosis I is a much debated question. The simplest theory is the following. Ṭhuthmosis I had no legitimate male issue, but two daughters. The elder daughter, princess Hatshepsut, was married to a young prince Ṭhuthmosis, her half-brother, the son of Ṭhuthmosis I by his concubine Mutnefret. This made him the legitimate heir to the throne and he became Ṭhuthmosis II. When he died (*c.* 1505) he left two daughters and an illegitimate son. Thus the situation at the end of Ṭhuthmosis I's reign was repeated exactly. The son was married to a daughter of Ṭhuthmosis II and Hatshepsut, and his succession as Ṭhuthmosis III was legalised. As he was still a child, his aunt Hatshepsut had herself proclaimed regent and usurped the throne for 22 years (1505–1483 B.C.). On her death in 1483 B.C., Ṭhuthmosis III came into his own and he reigned for over a quarter of a century until he died in 1450 B.C. Ṭhuthmosis II (?1520–1505) found it necessary to quell a revolt in Asia which spread to the very frontiers of Egypt. While the family quarrels after his death were raging, Egypt's power in Asia declined. Queen Hatshepsut, although she dressed as a man and caused herself to be represented on her monuments as a male, had little interest in the maintenance of the empire and the policy of conquest inaugurated by Aḥmosis suffered a temporary check. She turned her attention to building and commerce, and she erected numerous temples, one of which, at Deir el-Baḥari, has carved on its walls the record of the trading expedition she sent to the land of Punt,

84b on the Somali coast. As soon as Hatshepsut died, **Tḥuthmosis III** was free to undertake the reconquest of Asia. He marched against the King of Kadesh, who had organised a coalition of Syrian states against Egypt, and won a decisive victory at Megiddo in 1483 B.C. In all, seventeen campaigns were necessary to smash the power of the Mitanni, an Aryan people who had settled in the great westward bend of the Euphrates, and who were the core of the Asiatic resistance and the instigators of the opposition. When Kadesh finally fell in 1463 the power of Tḥuthmosis III was unchallenged, and he was now undisputed master of all the lands west of the Euphrates. Tḥuthmosis III organised his Asiatic empire with the greatest care. He allowed the native princes to rule, but took their sons to Egypt, where they were educated at the Egyptian court, in order to instil in them a pro-Egyptian outlook. They also served as hostages for the good behaviour of their fathers. Egyptian officials were stationed at various points throughout the empire and there were companies of troops ready to suppress revolts. Rich tribute from the newly conquered lands began to flow into Egypt and the wealth of the nation was enormous. Ancient Egypt reached the summit of her power and prosperity under Tḥuthmosis III.

c Tḥuthmosis III took his son Amenophis II as his co-regent a year before he died. Amenophis II (1450–?1425 B.C.) inherited his father's energetic character and followed his father's internal and external policies. He had occasion to make two punitive expeditions into Syria. He was succeeded by Tḥuthmosis IV (?1425–1408 B.C.), the most significant event in whose reign was his marriage with the daughter of the king of the Mitanni. The marriage was doubtless intended to seal a defensive alliance against the growing power of the Hittites, a potential source of danger both to the kingdom of Mitanni and to the northern provinces of the Egyptian empire.

d Amenophis III (1408–1370 B.C.), the son of Tḥuthmosis IV by his Mitanni wife, succeeded his father. He was of quite a different character from his forebears. It is not impossible that he owed his indolent disposition and his love of luxury to the Aryan blood of his mother. Apart from one expedition to Nubia soon after he came to the throne he never left Egypt during the whole of his long reign. The only physical activity in which he indulged was lion hunting, of which he was very fond. He used the vast revenue which was coming into Egypt on innumerable building projects throughout the land. The famous colossi of Memnon, granite statues of himself, were erected by him on the fertile plain of Thebes. While he led the life of an oriental despot, danger was threaten-
e ing the Asiatic empire. The **Amarna letters**, correspondence written on clay tablets in Babylonian cuneiform mainly by the Asiatic princes to their overlord Amenophis III and his successor which were found at Tell el-Amarna, show that the empire was menaced in two directions. The Hittite King Shubbiluliuma induced the Amorites led by Abdashirta to attack the Phoenician states, thereby affording a screen behind which he could attack the Mitanni. In spite of repeated appeals on the part of the loyal princes Amenophis gave no effective assistance and some of them were forced to renounce their allegiance to Egypt. Similarly in Palestine, the Ḥabiru, bands of desert Semites, identified by many scholars with the ancestors of the Hebrews, were beginning to threaten the security of the country by their steady infiltration. Such was the situation inherited by Amenophis IV (1372–1354 B.C.) on the death of his father, and he did nothing to arrest it. Urgent appeals from the Asiatic princes were unanswered and Egyptian authority in Palestine collapsed. The Ḥabiru overran
f Palestine. Shubbiluliuma conquered the Amorites, now led by Aziru the son of Abdashirta, and so gained control of the greater part of Syria and Phoenicia. Finally he subdued Mitanni, Egypt's ally, and the Hittites became the most powerful nation in Asia.

While all this was going on, Amenophis IV was 84f
occupied in propagating a religious movement. Already in the reign of Tḥuthmosis IV there is evidence of the worship of Aton, the sun's disk, and Amenophis III seems to have had a special affection for the Aton, since the pleasure-boat in which he sailed on the lake near his palace in company with Tiy, his queen, was named by him 'Splendour of Aton'. It has been conjectured that the cult of Amon, the state god of Egypt, was too exclusively Egyptian to become popular with the Asiatics who had settled in Egypt and intermarried with the Egyptians, and that a god with more universal appeal was needed. Amenophis IV therefore exalted the Aton to be the sole god of Egypt and set to work not only to spread the cult of Aton, but actively to suppress the cults of other gods, especially Amon. He changed his name from Amenophis (Amon is content) to Akhenaton (Splendour of Aton). He removed the capital from Thebes and built himself an entirely new city at Tell el-Amarna in Middle Egypt, which he called Akhetaton (Horizon of Aton).
The outstanding features of the new religion are its g
insistence on the uniqueness of Aton, the stress on Aton as the divine creator of the universe, and the love of nature which its devotees displayed. The personality and character of Akhenaton are an enigma. He was obviously a man of energy and he possessed a strong will—his handling of the powerful priesthood of Amon is ample witness of this. Yet he did nothing to save the empire—or if he did act, he acted when it was too late. It has been very plausibly suggested that the reason for this was that he was kept in ignorance of the true state of affairs by the officials of his Foreign Office, who were in sympathy with the Ḥabiru and may themselves have been Semites. When he died he was followed by three nonentities, Semenkhkarē, Tutankhamon and Ai, who between them reigned about 12 years. The priests of Amon began to exert pressure for the restoration of Amon to his former position of supremacy. About four years after the death of Akhenaton, Tutankhamon, who had ascended the throne as Tutankhaton (The Living Image of Aton), abandoned Tell el-Amarna for Thebes, the centre of the cult of Amon, and renounced Atonism. The last king of the XVIII Dynasty, according to Manetho's reckoning, was Horemḥeb (?1344–1314 B.C.). He was not of royal blood, but came of an ancient noble family, and he served as a general in the army during the reigns of his predecessors. Some time right at the end of Akhenaton's reign or during the first years of Tutankhamon's reign he was sent on a military expedition to Asia. He managed to preserve Palestine for Egypt and to save something of the Egyptian empire. After the death of Ai he was elected king by an oracle of Amon. Once on the throne, Horemḥeb set to work to remove all traces of the Aton heresy, and Amon and his priesthood were fully reinstated. It would seem that the local administration and government of the country had fallen into considerable confusion during the Aton period. Horemḥeb limited himself to the task of conducting the necessary reforms and wisely made no attempt to regain the lost parts of the empire.

The first king of the XIX Dynasty was Rameses I h
(1314–1312 B.C.), who belonged to a powerful family living in the Delta and who served in the army under Horemḥeb. He was already an old man when he came to the throne and he reigned but 2 years. He was followed by his son Seti I (1312–1298 B.C.), with whom the second period of the empire begins. The Beduin tribes known as the Shashu had seized 23 fortresses along the military road from Qanṭarah to Gaza. Seti I marched against them in 1316 B.C., retook the fortresses and pressed into Palestine. Here he was met with a coalition of the Amorites and Aramaeans, incited and backed by the Hittites, as their ancestors had been by the Mitanni in the time of Tḥuthmosis IV. Fortunately for Egypt the hostile armies were still dispersed and the Hittites had not been able to send

84h reinforcements in time. By a bold stroke Seti defeated the three armies of the allies and thus gained control of the greater part of Palestine. He pushed on as far as Tyre, but before he could follow up his advantage he was forced to return to Egypt to deal with an invasion of Libyans on Egypt's western border. Having successfully repelled this he returned to Palestine. At Kadesh the Egyptian and the Hittite armies clashed for the first time and the Egyptians were victorious. Nevertheless Hittite influence was still predominant in Syria and Seti failed to bring Syria wholly under the Egyptian yoke. For the rest of his reign he made no further campaigns and the power of the Hittites grew steadily.

i **Rameses II** (1301–1235 B.C.) was a young man when he came to the throne, full of energy and ambition. In the fourth year of his reign he felt himself in a position to follow up the work of his father in Asia, and he marched along the coast almost as far as Byblos. In the meantime the Hittite King Muwattali had hastily organised a coalition of some twenty states. The armies met just outside Kadesh and by supreme feats of personal valour Rameses was able to retrieve the dangerous situation into which he had been tricked by the wily Hittite king and to claim a victory. It was, however, far from a decisive victory and the result of the battle was a stalemate. Rameses was unable to take Kadesh and to push on to his ultimate objective, the Euphrates, while Muwattali was barred from pursuing his ambitions in the south. Between the years 1292–1279 B.C. Rameses II was forced to undertake various campaigns in Syria-Palestine to crush revolts instigated by the Hittites. He failed to make any significant additions to his territories, though several independent kings thought it prudent to send him tribute. In 1278 B.C., alarmed by the growing power of Assyria, the Hittite King Hattusil proposed a treaty with Egypt. Rameses II agreed and thus the Hittite-Egyptian rivalry came to an end. Both sides observed the treaty faithfully, and for nearly half a century there was peace in Western Asia.

j Towards the end of the reign of Rameses II a new threat to the stability of Egypt and her neighbours appeared. Wave after wave of Indo-Europeans from the region of the Balkans and the Black Sea, whom the Egyptians called the 'Peoples of the Sea', began to pour into Asia Minor, the Aegean Islands, Greece and North Africa. They travelled with their families and property, by land or sea, hoping to settle in some fertile spot, but the pressure of each succeeding migration forced them ever farther towards the south. The land of the Hittites was one of the first to be affected and for a time the Hittites managed to check the invaders. Many of them landed in Libya and it was inevitable that the rich lands of Egypt should attract them further. A major invasion of Egypt was attempted in the 5th year of the reign of Merneptah (1234–1224 B.C.), the successor of Rameses II, but it failed utterly. It seems likely that Merneptah had occasion to lead the Egyptian armies into Palestine. On a stele which records his victory over the Libyans he says, 'Canaan is devastated, Ashkelon is fallen, Gezer is ruined, Yenoam is reduced to nothing, Israel is desolate and her seed is no more, Ḥaru (i.e. Syria-Palestine) has become a widow for Egypt : all the countries are unified and pacified.' This is the first time that Israel is mentioned in an Egyptian text. Five kings, of whom hardly anything is known, followed Merneptah. During their reigns foreigners from Asia and from Libya succeeded in penetrating into Egypt under various pretexts. Once in Egypt they refused to pay taxes or to discharge any of their obligations and a state of anarchy resulted. So great was the confusion that it was even possible for a Syrian, Yarsu (1205–1200 B.C.), to seize the throne, oppress the people and disregard the gods. The first king of the XX Dynasty, Setnakht, who reigned only two years (1200–1198), re-established order and

k punished the guilty. His son, **Rameses III** (1198–1166 B.C.), continued his brilliant work. Externally Egypt was now menaced on two sides. On the Libyan frontier the Indo-European settlers were reorganised after their defeat by Merneptah and on the NW. frontier other tribes of these same peoples, who had now overthrown the Hittites and had poured southwards, were threatening to overwhelm Palestine and to pour into Egypt. In 1194 B.C. a coalition of tribes from Libya crossed the frontier with the intention of attacking Memphis. Rameses III reacted violently and inflicted a terrible slaughter on them. Three years later, in 1191 B.C., the Peoples of the Sea attempted an invasion of the Delta by land and sea. This also was decisively defeated, and it appears that they gave up any thought of occupying Syria-Palestine. Only the Peleset settled on the coastal strip between Gaza and Mount Carmel : these are the Philistines of the OT. In 1188 B.C. the Peoples of the Sea in Libya, united under a chieftain named Kaper, once more invaded Egypt. They succeeded in reaching the outskirts of Memphis, where they were annihilated by Rameses III. This was the last time that peoples from Libya attempted to enter Egypt by force. Eight kings, all bearing the name of Rameses, comprise the rest of the XX Dynasty. They reigned 1166–1085 B.C. It was an age of decline, and with it the second half of the Period of the Empire came to a close. The enormous wealth which came into Egypt during the empire enabled its kings to undertake grandiose building projects throughout Egypt, but especially at Thebes, where the vast temples still bear witness to the might of the pharaohs of the XVIII and XIX Dynasties. Egyptian painting, sculpture and craftsmanship reached their summit in the XVIII Dynasty. Literature also flourished. By chance, most of the works of the empire period which have survived date from the second half. Among prose narratives may be mentioned the Taking of Joppa, the Tale of the Two Brothers (with which the story of Joseph and Potiphar's wife has been compared), the Story of Truth and Falsehood, and the Travels of Wen-Amon (which gives a fascinating picture of life in Byblos in the time of Rameses XI and describes an encounter with an ecstatic prophet). Poetical works, letters, annals and various other types of literature are also well represented.

Late Period—There is nothing of importance to record of the seven kings of the XXI Dynasty (1085–950 B.C.). The main seat of the government, if such it can be called, was at Tanis, while the high-priest of Amon enjoyed virtual independence at Thebes and sometimes even employed the royal titulary. So low had Egypt sunk that the main preoccupation of the rulers seems to have been the preservation of the mummies of the great kings of the empire from destruction at the hands of the tomb-robbers, who had already begun their depredations in the previous dynasty. The impotence of Egypt enabled the energetic young King David to establish a powerful kingdom in Palestine. It was probably Psousennes II (984–950 B.C.) to whom the Edomite prince Hadad fled to escape the massacres of Joab (1 Kg. 11:14–22) and who, having taken Gezer and burnt it, gave it to his daughter, the wife of Solomon (1 Kg. 9:16). Neither of these events is known to us from Egyptian sources. 85

b The Libyans had failed to take Egypt by force, but while the feeble kings of the latter half of the XX and XXI Dynasties were on the throne they succeeded in penetrating by peaceful means. By nature warriors, they offered themselves as mercenaries and soon the Egyptian army became almost entirely composed of them. Their leaders were given land as payment for their services, and a number of military colonies grew up, whose power and importance increased rapidly. So it was that Sheshonq I (950–929 B.C.), the Shishak of the OT, was able to seize the throne and to establish the XXII Dynasty (950–730 B.C.), a dynasty of Libyan rulers. His policy towards the newly established

5b kingdom in Palestine was to maintain friendly relations with it, but to watch for signs of internal dissension which might be advantageous to Egypt. He thus hoped to restore Egypt's former position in Asia. Accordingly he welcomed Jeroboam when he fled to Egypt (1 Kg. 11:40) to escape from Solomon. Later, five years after the split of the Southern and Northern Kingdoms in Palestine, he attacked Judah and carried off rich booty (1 Kg. 14:25–6). There is no precise account of the campaign from the Egyptian side, but lists of conquered towns, now incomplete, are engraved on the south wall of the great temple of Karnak. The success of the campaign restored Egypt's prestige in Asia and gave the Asiatic princes quite a false impression of her might—an impression which was later to have disastrous consequences when they were faced with the threat of Assyrian invasion. The plunder which Sheshonq I brought home enabled him and his successors to continue the vast building projects of former dynasties. Lack of royal records makes it impossible to trace the later history of the Libyan period in any detail. After about a century the country appears to have split, with the XXII Dynasty reigning in Bubastis and a XXIII Dynasty (?817–730 B.C.) reigning in Thebes. There are indications that the process of fragmentation went even farther, and that other dynasties of kinglets made their appearance in various places. Thus the country was reduced to impotence, and it was in the hands of weaklings.

e It seems probable that a section of the priesthood of Amon at Thebes disapproved of Sheshonq's usurpation of the throne in 950 B.C. and fled to Nubia, where they established a sanctuary of Amon at Napata, in the region of the Fourth Cataract. Here the worship of Amon was continued in seclusion and Egypt was left to her own devices until Piankhi, the king of Napata, came on the scene two centuries later. In 730 B.C. we find him already in control of the district of Thebes, though there is no record whatever of any campaign. That same year Tefnakht, the first of the two kings of the XXIV Dynasty (730–715 B.C.), had gained control of the Delta and was pressing southwards. News of the fall of Memphis and the submission of the king of Hermolopolis reached Piankhi and he decided to check his advance. Battle was joined, and the Nubians won a complete victory. Piankhi became master of the whole of Egypt and his territory extended from the Mediterranean Sea to the Fourth Cataract. He allowed Tefnakht and his successor Bocchoris (720–715 B.C.) to rule as vassals in the Delta as far as Memphis, while he himself retired to Napata. He seems not to have dispossessed any of the turbulent local princes and to have done nothing to remove the causes of Egypt's internal strife. (Tefnakht was most probably the king with whom Hoshea, king of Israel, made an alliance against Assyria, and Bocchoris the king who incited the coalition of princes to revolt and to challenge the Assyrians at Qarqar. After the defeat of the Egyptian army at Raphia, Bocchoris made no further attempt to interfere in Asia.) Piankhi (730–716 B.C.) was the
d founder of the XXV Dynasty (730–656 B.C.). He was succeeded by Shabaka (716–701 B.C.), who left Napata to take up residence in Thebes. He reaffirmed Piankhi's rule over the whole of Egypt and legend has it that he took Bocchoris prisoner and burnt him at the stake. The rest of his reign was peaceful, and he adopted a conciliatory attitude towards Sargon II of Assyria, exchanging presents with him. He was followed by his son Shabataka (701–689 B.C.), who appears to have been of a retiring disposition, devoting himself to works of piety. When Shabataka died Tirhakah became king and he reigned 690–664 B.C. He preferred to reside in Tanis, the better to watch events and to foment revolt amongst the vassals of Assyria in Tyre and Sidon. When Sennacherib laid siege to Jerusalem he sent an army into Asia, an act which occasioned the Rabshakeh's mocking outburst recorded in 2 Kg. 18:21. The Egyptian and the
Assyrian armies never met, for Sennacherib was 85d
suddenly obliged to abandon his plans for the capture of Jerusalem. It would seem that the writer of the Book of Kings has telescoped two Assyrian campaigns into one. Recent evidence shows that Tirhakah would have been a boy of eight in the 14th year of Hezekiah, when, according to the biblical narrative, he appears to have led his army into Egypt. If one postulates a second Assyrian campaign in the period 689–686 B.C., the difficulty is overcome. In 671 B.C. Esarhaddon marched against Egypt, determined to put an end to the incessant intrigues of Egypt. He captured the Delta and besieged Memphis, which soon fell to him. Tirhakah fled to Thebes. As soon as Esarhaddon left Egypt, Tirhakah began to plot with the Egyptian princes whom Esarhaddon had appointed as governors and Memphis was retaken in 669 B.C. For three years Tirhakah reigned in peace, but in 666 B.C. Ashurbanipal sent an army against Egypt and he was forced to flee to Thebes a second time. He died two years later and was succeeded by his nephew Tanutamon (663–656 B.C.), who was crowned in Napata. His attempts to regain Egypt provoked yet another Assyrian invasion and he fled to Napata. The Assyrians followed him as far as Thebes, which was sacked, an event which made a profound impression on Egypt's Asiatic neighbours, and the memory of which was still vivid half a century later (cf. Nah. 3:8–10). So ended the Ethiopian rule of Egypt and the XXV Dynasty.

The Assyrian domination of Egypt was of short e
duration, lasting probably not more than 10 years. Psammetichus, whom Ashurbanipal had appointed governor of Athribis, revolted against the Assyrians and pursued them into Palestine. Exactly when this happened is unknown, but by 653 B.C. Egypt was entirely freed. Psammetichus I (663–609 B.C.) was thus the founder of the XXVI Dynasty (663–525 B.C.). During his reign Greek traders became numerous in Egypt and close relations between the Egyptians and the Greeks were encouraged by him and his successors. A curious archaising movement began. The language, art forms and even the religion of the Old and Middle Kingdoms were consciously copied, doubtless with the intention of rousing the Egyptians to emulate their former glories. Needless to say, without the dynamism of the earlier periods these efforts were in vain. Towards the end of his reign, Psammetichus became alarmed at the rapid rise of Babylon and in 616 B.C. we find him
rallying to the aid of the Assyrians. This new policy f
was followed by his son and successor, **Neco** (609–594 B.C.). In 608 B.C. he marched into Palestine to support Ashuruballiṭ, not to attack him, as 2 Kg. 23:29 has been thought to assert. He also had dreams of restoring the Egyptian empire in Asia. He defeated Josiah of Judah, a supporter of Babylon, at Megiddo and he exacted heavy tribute from Jerusalem (2 Kg. 23:29–35). He overran Syria and reached the Euphrates. At this point the king of Babylon decided to attack the Egyptian army and his son Nebuchadrezzar inflicted a heavy defeat on the Egyptians at Carchemish (Jer. 46) in 605 B.C. According to Herodotus, Neco planned an invasion of Palestine by sea to avenge his former defeat, but he died before his schemes could be put into operation. Both Psammetichus II (594–588 B.C.) and his successor Apries (588–568 B.C.), Pharaoh Hophra of the OT, made no attempt to invade Palestine, though there is evidence of their intervention farther north. It was during the reign of Apries that Jerusalem fell and numbers of Jews sought refuge in Egypt (Jer. 44:12), where they were treated kindly. Probably some of them founded the Jewish colony at Elephantine which produced the famous documents, written in Aramaic, during the Persian period. Apries was dethroned and killed by Amasis (568–526 B.C.), a general in his army. His long reign was peaceful and prosperous, but hardly had his son Psammetichus III (525 B.C.) ascended the throne than Egypt was invaded by Cambyses. The Persians had little difficulty in defeating the Egyptians

851f and their Greek allies, and Egypt was completely overpowered. She remained effectively under Persian rule till the conquest of Alexander in 332 B.C. Persian domination gave way to Greek, and Greek to Roman. The history of ancient Egypt as an independent nation thus ceases with the fall of the XXVI Dynasty. The period from the XXI–XXVI Dynasties is one of decadence and decline. Only for a short while, during the XXVI Dynasty, did Egypt regain something of her former splendour. As might be expected, the period is barren from the standpoint of art and literature. One work dating from this age is, however, of exceptional interest to students of the OT. This is the Proverbs of Amenemope, a didactic composition in the tradition of the Proverbs of Ptaḥ-ḥotep and the old Egyptian wisdom literature, parts of which are reproduced in a modified form in the OT Book of Proverbs.

Bibliography—J. H. Breasted, *The Dawn of Conscience* (1933), *Development of Religion and Thought in Ancient Egypt* (1912), *A History of Egypt from the earliest times to the Persian Conquest* (2nd ed. 1925) ; *Cambridge Ancient History* (2nd ed. 1924–36) ; E. Drioton and J. Vandier, *L'Égypte*, 3rd ed. (' Clio '. Les peuples de l'orient méditerranéen ii) (1952) ; A. Erman and H. Ranke, *Ägypten und ägyptisches Leben im Altertum* (1923) ; H. Frankfort, *Ancient Egyptian Religion* (1948) ; A. H. Gardiner, *Egyptian Grammar* (3rd ed. 1957) ; L. H. Grollenberg, *Atlas of the Bible*, trans. and ed. by J. M. H. Reid and H. H. Rowley (1956) ; T. E. Peet, *Egypt and the OT* (1922) ; J. B. Pritchard (ed.), *Ancient Near Eastern Texts relating to the OT* (2nd ed. 1955) ; A. Shorter, *Everyday Life in ancient Egypt* (1932) ; G. Steindorff and K. C. Seele, *When Egypt ruled the East* (1945).

ISRAEL'S NEIGHBOURS—III

THE LEVANT

By J. Gray

6a The first definite clue to the ethnology of the Levant is the nomenclature of chiefs of Southern Syria and Palestine in **execration texts** of the 19th cent. B.C. from Luxor and Saqqârah. The names, being theophoric, consisting of a divine name and a predicate which is a noun, adjective, or verb, may be certainly identified according to their linguistic affinity, and are without exception Semitic. More precisely, the deities and their attributes are identical with elements in theophoric names in documents of the First Amorite Dynasty of Babylon (1826–1526 B.C.). A feature of the earlier execration texts from Luxor (*c.*1850) is that in any one locality there may be several chiefs. This may indicate the tribal stage of social and political development of the Amorites in Palestine (so Albright), and reflects the situation depicted at Gerar, where the nomad sheikhs Abraham and Isaac are potential rivals of Abimelech, the ruler of the town (Gen. 20, 26). The fact that in the earlier texts the gods are conceived of as kinsmen is a further indication that the Amorites in Palestine and Syria in the 19th cent. had comparatively recently penetrated from the desert hinterland. They may, in fact, be the final wave of invaders from that quarter whose depredations are attested by archaeology in a general recession of culture in the Near East towards the end of the 3rd millennium.

b The **Amarna Tablets** (*c.*1411–1358) and contemporary documents from Râs Shamra, Taanach, and Shechem indicate a much more complex political situation where Egypt maintained her Asiatic empire through local feudatories in urban fiefs particularly along the trunk highways in the coastal and central plains. The nomenclature of these texts attests a wide variety of races, Amorite (e.g. Mutba'lu, Milkilu, Shammu-Addu, etc.), Indo-Iranian (e.g. Shuwardata, Yashdata), and Hurrian (e.g. Biridiya, Widiya, Tadua, §86*c*). Into the non-Semitic category, particularly Hurrians from the north-east, we would place the 'Hittites', Hivites, Perizzites, Girgashites, and possibly the Jebusites, who are listed with the Semitic Amorites and Canaanites as the inhabitants of pre-Israelite Palestine.

Between the time of the Execration Texts and the Amarna Tablets the power of Egypt in Asia and even in Lower Egypt was eclipsed by the **Hyksos** (*c.*1730–1580). It seems natural to suppose that this invasion introduced the above-mentioned non-Semitic peoples to Palestine. There is, however, no conclusive evidence of the racial identity of the Hyksos ('Rulers of the Foreign Lands'). Their introduction of the horse and light war-chariot to Egypt suggests Aryan affinities. Certain of their kings, however, had Semitic names. Thus it may be said that the racial situation in Palestine was complicated after the Hyksos invasion, but it is not easy to particularise upon the racial elements introduced at the time of the conquest. One significant feature of the Hyksos domination was the control of their territories in Asia and Egypt by a feudal system, whereby specialists in chariot warfare were invested with fiefs at strategic points along the great trunk highways. These cities long defied the Hebrew invaders, and it is probable that the Philistines and their kindred peoples later occupied the old Hyksos fiefs (so Alt), either on their own initiative or by 86b
the authority of Rameses III, as the Pharaoh claims.

The **Hurrians,** first known through their peculiar c
names in cuneiform texts from Mesopotamia, where they were associated with the state of Mitanni with its capital on a tributary of the Habur, where an Aryan military aristocracy ruled a Hurrian subject-people, next emerged in documents from the old Hittite capital of Boghaz-köi as a definite ethnic element in the Near East from the vicinity of Lake Van to Syria. Texts from Kirkuk and Nuzu, about a hundred miles north of Baghdad, enable Hurrian names in other texts to be more precisely determined. Hurrians in Palestine are thus attested in the Amarna Tablets and others of the same period from Taanach and Shechem. They are found again at Râs Shamra, where, by the 15th cent., they were apparently an influential class and an effective power behind the throne. Here also Hurrian texts, syllabaries, and vocabularies indicate the extent of Hurrian cultural influence. Certain of the Amarna Tablets from Qatna and Tunip in central Syria are further evidence of the distribution of the Hurrians. These are probably the Biblical Horites, whom the OT locates in Palestine and Edom, and it is interesting that Palestine is termed *Ḫaru* in Egyptian records.

In spite of the mention of 'Hittites' in the list of pre- d
Israelite inhabitants of Palestine and in Abraham's purchase of the cave at Hebron from 'Ephron the Hittite' (Gen. 23), there is no evidence that the historical **Hittites,** who penetrated Anatolia probably from beyond the Bosphorus towards the end of the 3rd millennium and ruled as an imperial power from *c.* 1900–1200, ever extended their influence to Palestine. Even at the zenith of their Empire under Shubbiluliuma (*fl.*1370) their power did not extend beyond Southern Syria, as is indicated in the Amarna Tablets and Egyptian records of the XIX Dynasty. 'Hittite' in the OT is a geographic rather than a strict ethnic term, denoting a northern race recognised to be non-Semitic. Similarly the Assyrians refer to the West generally, including Syria, as 'the Hittite land' (*mat Ḫatti*). A similar usage is in 1 Kg. 10:29, 'the kings of the Hittites', which denotes the peoples living between north Mesopotamia and Syria who were loosely federated with the Hittites at the height of their power and shared with them certain elements of culture. In the 10th cent., to which this text applies, the Hittite Empire had been destroyed, and the Hittite military and cultural tradition seems to have lived on with Hittite notables in Syria, who either effected their independence in their fiefs there or asserted their influence among the Aramaean tribes who settled there in the Early Iron Age (*c.*1200). This fusion of Hittite and Semitic culture is evidenced by Hittite hieroglyphs in Syrian towns of the Aramaean period, cf. the Hittite(hieroglyphs) - Phoenician bilingual inscription of Kara-Tepe, north of the Plain of Adana. We would explain David's mercenary Uriah the Hittite as such a 'displaced person', an actual Hittite or perhaps a Hurrian, the name being possibly a corruption of *ewir*, found in the Râs Shamra texts as a military title and recognised as a Hurrian term (so J. A. Montgomery).

86e The disorders in Syria and Palestine in the Amarna age are greatly complicated by the **Ḫabiru.** They are mentioned by Abdi-Ḫepa of Jerusalem, and are reported to have occupied Shechem. Amarna tablets from Syria refer to a people of similar nature and habits termed in ideogram SA-GAZ. There the SA-GAZ operate chiefly as mercenaries of various local chiefs ; in Palestine the Ḫabiru seek a home.

87a On the evidence of the Hittite archives and administrative texts from Râs Shamra, both from *c.*1400, there is no doubt that the SA-GAZ and the Ḫabiru were but different groups of the same people. The Ḫabiru, then, are a much larger group than the Biblical Hebrews, with whom they have often been identified. In fact Mesopotamian texts attest the activity of Ḫabiru in Southern Mesopotamia from the end of the 3rd millennium and they are last mentioned as 'Apiru in Egyptian records referring to labour gangs in Egypt in the 11th cent. In Nuzu (*c.*1400) they are found as mercenary soldiers, servants, and even as self-sold slaves.

b Thus the Ḫabiru were apparently a landless people of loose social structure who penetrated the settled lands seeking livelihood, land, or plunder. A class rather than a race, they would normally come from weaker tribes in the desert hinterland, and probably include many, if not most, of the ancestors of the Hebrews. After the decline of the power of Egypt in Asia in the Amarna age their infiltrations reached the proportions almost of an invasion, and with this movement we would associate the coming of Jacob and the tribes to Palestine from the north-east. The traditional provenance of Jacob from North Mesopotamia at this particular time suggests further an association with the Aḫlamu of the Assyrian inscriptions of this period, Aramaean invaders who appear in the 14th cent. and are actually mentioned in one of the Amarna Tablets of unknown, but probably Mesopotamian, origin (Knudtzon, 200).

88a The **Phoenicians,** whose culture in the Late Bronze Age is particularly well illustrated by the excavations of Râs Shamra and Byblos, are associated mainly with the coastal strip from the Gulf of Alexandretta to the headland of Carmel in Palestine. The breadth of this coastal strip varies. In the north there are broad, cultivable plains in the vicinity of Râs Shamra, but in the south the mountains are never more than 30 miles distant, and often drop abruptly into the sea. Phoenicia, then, consists of a chain of coastal plains, each dominated by a fortified city, either a port itself, such as Tyre, Sidon, Beirut, Byblos, Tripoli, or Arvad, or adjacent to one, as Râs Shamra (Ugarit). The cities communicated with one another chiefly by sea, and eventually sought scope for their enterprise in maritime trade with the West and even in colonial expansion, notably in North Africa, where Carthage was founded by the Tyrians *c.*814, itself to be the metropolis of colonies in Sardinia, the Balearic islands, Spain, and Sicily. The Phoenician homeland is named Kinaḫna (hence Canaan) in Akkadian texts, this denoting the trade in purple dye (*kinaḫḫu*) from the murex, for which the Syrian coast was famous. 'Phoenicia' is literally the Greek translation of this term (*φοινίκεος* = purple).

The Phoenicians, however, were also interested in the Asiatic hinterland. In the 12th cent. the Israelites, in occupying the headwaters of the Jordan, found a Phoenician settlement (Jg. 18:7, 28). Hiram of Tyre, who engaged with Solomon in trading ventures down the Red Sea to South Arabia and possibly to East Africa, negotiated the acquisition of a district Kabul in the hinterland of Acco, doubtless to relieve the economic pressure on his limited homeland, a perpetual Phoenician problem (cf. Ac. 12:20). The alliance of Ittobaal of Tyre with Israel in the 9th cent., which was cemented by the marriage of Ahab and Jezebel, was conditioned by similar economic and possibly also commercial considerations, Israel occupying a land traversed by vital trade-routes between Mesopotamia and Egypt and controlling in addition Moab, which commanded an important caravan route from the oases of north Arabia to Damascus. Maritime interest in the West, however, was the principal interest of the Phoenician city-states, where a materialistic and essentially urban civilisation developed under local merchant princes either as monarchs or oligarchs. This seafaring, natural to coast-dwellers, must have been further stimulated by the Aramaean invasions and the establishment of states in the interior like Damascus (Aram), Hamath, Arpad, and others in the 12th cent., and the growing interest of Assyria in the politics and commerce of Western Asia, which dates from the same time.

The specific application of the name Canaan to the Phoenician coast, which we have already noted in Akkadian texts, is known also in the OT, e.g. Jos. 13:4 (the vicinity of Sidon), Isa. 23:11 (Tyre), and possibly Jg. 5:19 ('kings of Canaan' in alliance with Sisera in the west of the great central plain by Megiddo). The last reference extends the application of the name to the inhabitants of the great cities of the plains of Palestine, which maintained contact with the cities of Phoenicia proper and shared in their culture and religion, cf. Num. 13:29, which locates the Canaanites by the seashore and the Jordan, i.e. the natural channels of culture and commerce. Such a centre of Canaanite culture was Hazor in the plain of the upper Jordan commanding the fords south of Lake Huleh, whose king, Jabin, is termed 'the king of Canaan' (Jg. 4:2, 23–4). Here there can be no question of a strictly ethnic category in view of the racial admixture of Semites and non-Semites evidenced by the nomenclature of the Amarna period ; the term connotes a culture rather than a race, and the use of the term Canaan to denote the whole of Palestine, or rather the foreland of the north Arabian desert including Syria, in the OT and certain Egyptian inscriptions, e.g. of Amenhotep II and Merneptah, refers to the predominant culture mediated to the whole of that area by the Phoenician cities and those of the plains of Palestine through the Semites who were the largest ethnic element in the population. This unity of culture is demonstrated by the agreement between the OT references to Canaanite culture, material remains from the various archaeological sites, and the documentary evidence from Râs Shamra. b

The tablets from **Râs Shamra** in the local Semitic language and in alphabetic cuneiform, as apart from Hurrian tablets, which have also been found, may safely be taken as evidence of the culture of the Phoenicians in the 2nd millennium, which we recognise on Biblical evidence to be essentially that of the Canaanites, the native population of Palestine at the Hebrew settlement. c

The religion of the Phoenicians, to judge from the myths of Râs Shamra concerning the vicissitudes of Baal, the god of winter storms and secondarily the vegetation thereby promoted, was largely directed to predisposing Providence in nature. As in Babylonian mythology related to the ritual of the Spring New Year, the gods bow before the threat of Chaos, depicted as unruly waters. The young god Baal, whose proper name was Hadad, champions the cause of Order. He engages the waters ('Sea and River'), and, on his victory, is acclaimed king, the waters being 'scattered', i.e. distributed, so that the potential curse proves a blessing. This theme and imagery was appropriated by the Hebrews with due adaptation to the cult of Yahweh, as appears clearly from psalms celebrating the kingship of Yahweh, e.g. Pss. 93, 96, 97, 98, 22, 47, etc., and other psalms which, though not of this type, borrow its imagery. The Prophets too draw frequently on this source in the language and imagery in which they speak of the 'Day of Yahweh', i.e. the day of his vindication and judgment, e.g. Isa. 2 ; Zeph. 3:15, 17 ; Nah. 1 ; Hab. 3:8 ; Ezek. 32:2f., 29:3f., etc. It recurs also in Wisdom poetry, e.g. Job, and in Jewish and Christian apocalyptic, e.g. Dan. 7:7f.;

8c Jub. 23:11 ; 2 Esd. 8:63–9:6 ; Rev. 20:21, etc., and it is in the ideology of the kingship of God that the influence of Canaanite on Hebrew thought was strongest. Jewish tradition associates the Enthronement Psalms with the New Year festival, cp. Zech. 14:16, which associates the cult of Yahweh as king with the Feast of Tabernacles and the autumn rains. We think it highly probable that the Enthronement Psalms and their Canaanite prototype were relevant to this supreme crisis in the agricultural year.

d The rest of the Ugaritic myths of epic form and proportions relating to Baal dramatise the tension in local agriculture as a conflict between Baal and Mot (Sterility, Death). Here Baal is a vegetation-god, a dying and rising god like the Mesopotamian Tammuz and the Syrian Adonis, whose cult in Graeco-Roman times is known in the vicinity of Beirut, and the myth is obviously related to various phases in the agricultural year. A great part of it, for instance, is concerned with the building of a ' house ' for Baal, a conspicuous feature of which is a roof-shutter, the opening of which, as a rite of imitative magic, coincides with the opening of the clouds and the fall of the vital autumn rains. Baal eventually succumbs to Mot and is sought and, when recovered, is buried and lamented by his sister Anat. The search for the god in the power of the underworld and the mourning by a goddess is a common motive in myth and ritual related to the fertility-cult throughout the Mediterranean world, especially in Egypt and Greece. Anat's vengeance on Mot, whom she cuts with a blade, threshes, winnows, parches, grinds, and scatters for the birds to eat, certainly reflects a ritual of desacralisation of the new crop, cf. Lev. 2:14. Baal, however, rises again and renews his conflict with Mot, which culminates in a ' battle royal ' after seven years. This would seem to have some relation to a seven-year cycle in agriculture, such as was, in fact, known to the Hebrews. In a land exposed to such vicissitudes as sirocco winds, drought, and locusts it was felt that after a few good years a disaster was overdue. This the Hebrews sought to forestall by an artificial famine, the Sabbatical Year, when the land lay fallow ; the peasants of Ugarit seem to have staged a ritual combat, Mot, the power of sterility, being given full scope against Baal, the power of fertility, so that he might be exhausted in the conflict, Baal's victory being, at the same time, an act of imitative magic to predispose the issue for the ensuing time-cycle.

Thus creative symbolism in ritual and the creative word in myth were important principles of Canaanite religion. Sporadic references in OT and Mishnah indicate that there were several such survivals in the religion of Israel, though there the prophetic use of symbolism and the creative word in history and social relations far transcended the ritual and myth of the Canaanite fertility-cult.

e In spite of the preoccupation of the Phoenicians with material values there are certain indications in the Râs Shamra Texts of a social conscience. In two texts relating to ancient kings, Keret and Danel, the king is guarantor of the social order, judging the case of the widow, the orphan, and the oppressed. From the description of the ideal son in the latter text we see that the integrity of the religious and social unit was preserved by common sacramental meals, and the god of the community was regarded as a kinsman, thus standing in an essentially moral relationship to the worshipper. Such social conventions as hospitality and the protection of the guest were ideals of early Phoenician society, as among modern Bedouin. The evidence for the more moral and spiritual aspects of religion is certainly not so strong as for the ritualism of the fertility-cult, but this may signify not that the latter prevailed to the exclusion of the former, but that the former was not readily expressed in myth and ritual which might leave tangible remains.

f Administrative texts in the local cuneiform script and in Akkadian give a fair picture of **Canaanite society.** The king, who was hereditary, stood at the 88f head of the social order. In the heroic past he had been personal leader in war, priest, and judge. By the 14th cent. his military duties were delegated to professional soldiers in a feudal system where land was held in virtue of military status and in lieu of service, the *mariannu*, or chariot specialists, being the highest of various feudal orders. Legal texts from the palace of Ugarit, however, from the 14th cent. show that this system was already breaking down and that the old rigid conditions of land tenure in lieu of personal service were relaxed, so that such property, originally inalienable, could now be bought and sold. Far from the king concentrating the priestly office in his person, there are at that time twelve priestly families named in the administrative texts. Two of these, however, *Ṯ'* and *Dtn*, were probably royal clans and were singled out for special privileges or responsibilities, which indicates that the king still maintained his influence in the cult by 'strategic posting' (so C. H. Gordon). Numerous legal deeds of sale, exchange, emancipation, and adoption issued under the royal authority or citing the king as a witness indicate the royal supervision of justice, though we should not necessarily conclude that the king was personally implicated. There is, however, sufficient evidence to suggest that the king, like Solomon, had sovereign rights over the property of the realm and even over the persons of his subjects, whose social status he could change and whom he could use freely in the *corvée*.

Ugarit, the records of which so well amplify the 89a picture of Canaanite civilisation suggested by Scriptural references and the material remains of archaeological sites in Syria and Palestine, was destroyed *c.*1200, doubtless by the Philistines and other ' Sea-Peoples ' on their southward migration. This date marks an epoch in the political and social history of the Levant, which was, we believe, conditioned largely by the divulgence of the secret of working iron.

Iron, both meteoric and terrestrial, had been known in the Near East already in the 2nd millennium, though at that time it was so rare as to be reserved for ornaments. The economic working of iron-ore seems to have been discovered and developed in the mountains of Armenia, and by the 15th cent. the Hittite armies were using iron weapons. The Hittites, however, guarded the secret of the industry ; but ultimately it was divulged. From the middle of the 15th cent. peoples of the Aegean and the European mainland penetrated Anatolia and settled the coastlands. The Hittites from their seat of empire on the central plateau endeavoured to absorb these new folk-elements by using them as mercenaries, as Egyptian records of the next two centuries show. The mercenaries, however, through the use of iron weapons learned the secret of the smiths, and eventually turned their weapons against their masters, probably on the occasion of a fresh influx of their kinsfolk from beyond the Bosphorus (§89*b*). The result was the collapse of the Hittite Empire. Some of these ' Sea-Peoples ' migrated southwards through Syria to Palestine where they were halted early in the 12th cent. in the eighth year of Rameses III. Among them were the Philistines, who are noted as possessing the art of metal-working which they endeavoured to keep as a monopoly in the days of Saul of Israel (1 Sam. 13:19–22). Archaeology and the records, however, demonstrate that the new technique was soon in the hands of other barbarians. The consequences were revolutionary. Soon the individual peasant could equip himself with iron implements to break new land (cf. Jos. 17:18) and with iron weapons to defend his home. The secret of working iron-ore, so much more common and more widely distributed than copper, released small nations and peoples from the monopolies and domination of the great imperial powers. Now small nations assert themselves. Israel, Judah, Moab, Ammon, Edom, Damascus, Hamath,

89a and the Aramaean states of north Syria maintain their independence against one another and against the imperial designs of Egypt and Assyria. The latter certainly advanced through Syria and Palestine to Egypt, but only after three centuries of warfare, exhausting herself in the effort.

b The **Philistines,** or Pulusatu of the Egyptian records, are depicted in Egyptian sculptures as a race apart from the Semites of Palestine, and they give the impression of an active warrior-race. This is borne out by Egyptian inscriptions of the 15th to the 13th cent., which number the Pulusatu among several peoples subsumed under the name 'Sea-Peoples', who were active around the coasts of Asia Minor and raided the Delta itself. It was probably they who destroyed the Minoan Empire in Crete, whose cities Knossos and Phaestos were destroyed *c.*1400. This would accord with the Hebrew tradition which derives the Philistines from Caphtor (Crete) (Am. 9:7), though the connection of the Philistines with Crete was incidental and secondary. From excavations in the coastal plain between Jaffa and Gaza, where the Philistines during the Hebrew settlement and Monarchy occupied Ekron, Ashdod, Ashkelon, Gaza and Gath, certain features emerge which are distinctive of the Philistines and their kindred peoples. In the Early Iron Age (*c.*1200–1000) a striking bi-chrome pottery associates the Philistines with the Anatolian coast, the Aegean, and even the Greek mainland. The long, leaf-shaped sword depicted in Egyptian sculptures suggests a Danubian provenance. At Gezer and Beth-shan the burial custom of closing the mouth of the corpse with a small gold mouth-plate is thought to be a relic of the gold mask of the royal burials at Mycenae in the 16th cent. This custom is found in Early Iron Age graves in Macedonia, where it is associated with pottery and ornaments of north Balkan affinities. The same association is suggested by the practice of cremation attested at Ashkelon in the Early Iron Age, a practice entirely strange to Palestine and Syria since the Mesolithic Age (before *c.*6000 B.C.) except for single tombs at Jericho and Tell Beit-Mirsim (probably Kiriath-sepher, otherwise known as Debir) from the 15th cent., and from Ḥamā and 'Aṭshāna in north Syria in the same period. More numerous instances of cremation at the same period at Troy indicate the provenance of its exponents from the Bosphorus and beyond. The fact that the rite, commonly attested in the area and period of Philistine occupation in Palestine, is found at the sites above-mentioned two centuries at least before the Philistines occupied Palestine in force indicates that small groups of their kinsfolk had already penetrated, probably as mercenaries of the Hittites in Anatolia and north Syria and of the Egyptians in Palestine, as the inscriptions would suggest. It is possible too that these 'Sea-Peoples' had some connection with the peoples who fought about Troy in the celebrated Trojan War, and the names of some of them, Dardanu, Akhwash, and Danuna, familiar from Egyptian records, suggest the Dardanoi, Achaioi, and Danaoi of the Iliad. The last of these were apparently established near the Phoenician coast, since in his report on that area (Kinaḫna) in the Amarna Tablets the King of Byblos states that the King of Danuna is dead. This early political consolidation of the Danuna is interesting, and the inscription of Azitawwad, King of Danuna, at Kara-tepe in the Taurus foothills north of the Plain of Adana helps us to locate this people more precisely.

c Halted by Rameses III on their southward trek they were, according to Rameses III, 'settled in fortresses bound in his name'. It is not clear whether the Philistines enjoyed the status of the Danuna mentioned above or were in the nature of a police-force, but they do seem to have occupied the old Hyksos fiefs in the central and coastal plains of Palestine and to have been organised on a feudal basis. Significantly enough, when David took service with Achish, the Philistine ruler of Gath, he received the frontier town of Ziklag in the Judaean foothills north-west of Beersheba as a 89 heritable fief (1 Sam. 27:6). Both archaeology and the OT attest the occupation by the Philistines of Beth-shan (1 Sam. 31:10). The Egyptian papyrus relating the misadventures of the envoy Wenamon in Palestine and Syria *c.*1100 gives clear evidence of a strong maritime settlement of a kindred people, the Ṯekel, at Dor in the north of the Plain of Sharon. The consolidation of the various Hebrew tribes under David and the incorporation of the Canaanite cities of the plains of north Palestine in the territorial state of Solomon apparently limited Philistine occupation to the coastal plain between Jaffa and Gaza, where they are found in the period of the Hebrew Judges and the Monarchy.

Almost simultaneously with the 'Sea-Peoples' d there appeared in the settled lands of the Levant other barbarian peoples, the **Aramaeans.** Unlike the former, they were not entire strangers, since their settlement marked one of the periodic culminations of the perpetual seasonal ebb and flow of pastoral tribesmen from the Eastern steppes. They were Semites of kindred stock to the majority in the land, to whom, consequently, they found it easy to assimilate themselves. W. F. Albright has associated this Aramaean influx with the domestication of the camel, which does not appear in Assyrian inscriptions until the 11th cent. Such movements are usually economically conditioned, and the domestication of the camel would admirably account for the greater mobility of the tribes from the north Arabian steppe resulting in longer range in raiding with consequent increase in power of the stronger and greater vulnerability of the weaker tribes, obliging the latter to join larger confederacies for aggression or for protection. Albright's suggestion, therefore, is feasible, though, to be sure, the Aramaeans were active for some three centuries before the camel is mentioned in Assyrian inscriptions. There seems, however, to have been some such consolidation as we have hypothetically outlined, since, when the Aramaeans emerge into the clear light of history, they appear as large, clearly defined confederacies who very soon developed into independent kingdoms.

The first mention of these folk-movements from the desert is in a fragmentary tablet from Tell el-Amarna, where the Aḫlamu are mentioned together with the King of Karduniash (i.e. Babylon). With other desert people, such as the Sutu, the Aḫlamu and Aramaeans are mentioned regularly in Assyrian texts from the end of the 14th cent., and Assyrian inscriptions from the 12th and 11th cent. refer to their building cities and even founding the state of Bīt-Adini on both sides of the Euphrates in the region of the great westward bend south of Carchemish. By the end of the 11th cent. a considerable number of Aramaean states had been established in northern Mesopotamia and even east of the Tigris, and an Aramaean usurper, Adad-apal-iddin (1070–1049) reigned in Babylon and had his daughter married to the King of Assyria. About the same time Aramaeans had merged with Hittite remnants in north Syria, and there emerged the states of Arpad, about Aleppo, and Ya'udi, also called Sam'al, whose capital was Zenjirli. Another Aramaean state was Hamath on the Orontes, where a cultural break *c.*1000, which is attested by archaeology, apparently relates to a decisive phase in the Aramaean settlement. From the Books of Samuel it is well known that by the time of David there were Aramaean states at Damascus and between Damascus and the Sea of Galilee. It seems natural that we should associate with this general folk-movement the settlement of Transjordan and the consolidation of the states of Edom, Moab, and Ammon in the beginning of the 13th cent. and the main phase of the Hebrew settlement of Palestine about a century later.

The Aramaean settlement in Mesopotamia, the e Anatolian foothills, and inland Syria, the consolidation of their several states, and their prolonged resistance to, and final liquidation by, Assyria soon after the middle

89e of the 8th cent. is documented by the Assyrian annals and, to a less extent, by about a dozen local alphabetic inscriptions in Phoenician and Aramaic from Syria. Limited as these are, they give some insight into the culture of the Aramaeans, and this may be amplified by excavations, notably at Tell Ḥalâf (ancient Guzana) in the Habur region of upper Mesopotamia, and at Ḥamâ on the Orontes. These indicate that the Aramaean settlers from the north Arabian desert assimilated the culture of the settled lands, the more readily since they brought from the desert nothing except a virile social ethic and a fierce tribal particularism. Both these factors are found in almost exaggerated degree in Israel, though even she, according to her own records, assimilated the culture of Canaan with alarming thoroughness.

Politically the Aramaeans coalesced into a number of different states thereby preserving, no doubt, their original constitution as free groups of kinsfolk, or at least tribal confederacies. Certain of these, such as Aram Zobah, probably in the Beqʿa north of Damascus, Beth-rehob, probably in the Līṭânī region of south Syria, Maachah, about the upper Jordan, and Geshur, apparently in the Hauran, never seem to have developed beyond a loose tribal constitution before they were absorbed in the kingdom of Aram, the capital of which was Damascus. In north Syria the consolidation of the Aramaean kingdoms was achieved by the 10th cent., this development being, we believe, here facilitated by the political development of old Hittite fiefs, where the great barons and provincial governors had perforce declared their independence after the collapse of the Hittite Empire in Anatolia.

f The Aramaeans, as already observed, assimilated local culture in art and religion in the areas where they settled. In religion, however, the pantheon is distinctively Semitic. The most prominent deity was Baal Shemain ('Lord of the Sky'), the Canaanite Hadad, also called Rimmon ('Thunderer'), especially at Damascus (1 Kg. 5:18). El, the doyen of the Canaanite pantheon, was also worshipped, and Elyon ('Exalted'), who is apparently distinct from El, and astral deities, Shamash (the Sun), Sin the moon-god as Sahar ('Bright') and 'Lord of Haran', together with his consort Nikkal. As Aṭtar the Venus-star was venerated, particularly, we believe in Moab, where we have local evidence of the cult of Aṭtar-Kemosh, and in Ammon, where the god was known by his title Melek-ma ('the King'). Aṭtar was worshipped as a female, Ishtar, in Mesopotamia, and in this form she was syncretised with the Canaanite Anat as Attargatis, whose worship is attested by Lucian of Samosata at Hierapolis (modern Membij) in the 2nd cent. A.D. Resheph, the Canaanite god of pestilence, is prominent in the Aramaic inscriptions, and such names as Yaubidi (also called Ilubidi) and Joram of Hamath, and Azriyau of Sam'al or Ya'udi suggest the cult either of the Canaanite god Yw or of Yahweh. The latter is possible when we consider that Yahweh was not worshipped exclusively by Israel, but also by the Kenites, or desert smiths, who were in fact probably the original worshippers of Yahweh (see Rowley, *From Joseph to Joshua*, 152f., with relevant bibliography). Bearing in mind the provenance of the Aramaeans from the north Arabian desert and also the itinerant habits of the Kenites, there is nothing improbable in the cult of Yahweh among the Aramaeans in North Syria, though we have no means of knowing if the cult in Syria ever reached the high plane of Yahwism as it was practised in Israel.

90a Particularly associated with Israel are Damascus, her inveterate enemy throughout the monarchy, Moab and Ammon, recognised as indirectly akin to Israel (Gen. 19:30–8), and Edom, which was freely acknowledged as the 'brother' of Israel (Gen. 25:23; Dt. 23:7).

It is significant that in the account of David's clashes with the Aramaeans beyond Jordan (2 Sam. 8:3–8, 10:6–19) the region of Damascus plays a minor role, though the city was of strategic significance 90a
for David's control of the Aramaean tribes (2 Sam. 8:6). Whatever may be the actual facts of that ill-defined phase of Hebrew history, Damascus emerges as the centre of a powerful kingdom apparently on the death of David. David's suppression of the Aramaean tribes under the hegemony of Zobah proved to be the genesis of the new state (1 Kg. 11:23–5), which effectively limited the northward extension of the influence of Israel, but also proved a bulwark against Assyrian aggression until Damascus finally succumbed in this age-long conflict in 732. In 853 Israel under Ahab is found in alliance with Damascus and other Syrian states, when the Assyrians were halted at the Battle of Qarqar on the Orontes, and again in 735/4, when Pekah of Israel and Rezin of Damascus united in a similar policy in the days of Isaiah of Jerusalem. Such common action, however, is exceptional in the relationships between Israel and Damascus, which were generally bitterly hostile.

Moab lay east of the Dead Sea with her southern b
border along the Wâdī el-Ḥesā, which flows into the Dead Sea at its south-eastern extremity, and her northern border generally confined to the Wâdī Môjib (Arnon) during the Hebrew Monarchy. This northern border, however, fluctuated. In the period of the early Hebrew Judges, Moab actually occupied Jericho, west of the Jordan (Jg. 3:12–29), and in the 9th cent. Mesha, the King of Moab, was able to occupy territory to the north of the Arnon which had been held by Israel in the time of Omri and Ahab and possibly since the time of David. This war of Moabite independence is recorded on the famous stele of Mesha in language reminiscent of Hebrew historical narrative, and this inscription attests the practice of holy war with its attendant severities, familiar from the history of Israel. This was a consequence of the intense tribal particularism in politics and religion introduced to the Levant by the Aramaeans, which was the germ of Israel's faith in the self-revelation of God in history.

Ammon, with her capital at Rabbath Ammon c
(modern 'Ammân) occupied an undefined area north of Moab and in the time of the Judges and Saul menaced the Israelite settlers in Jabesh Gilead overlooking the north part of the valley of the middle Jordan. Their power, however, was broken by David and, though they continued to harry the Israelites beyond Jordan (cf. Am. 1:13–15) they ceased to be a serious menace to Israel. It is significant that Ammon is generally referred to as Bene Ammon, 'the Sons of Ammon', which probably indicates that they had never really developed politically beyond the tribal stage.

Edom, with her capital at Ṣelaʿ ('the Rock'), i.e. d
Petra in its impressive sandstone canyon, lay to the south of the Wâdī el-Ḥesā and extended to the Gulf of ʿAqaba. There being no sedentary occupation south of this region except in isolated oases deep into the territory now known as the Hejaz, the southern frontier of Edom was vague, and certain passages suggest that certain of these, e.g. Teman, Dedan, Dumah, if not actually under Edomite control, were certainly in contact with her. Like Moab, Edom enjoyed a fair precipitation of rain on the plateau and on the Western escarpment. (The writer has been snowed up for a week in Petra early in January.) Like Moab, Edom either carried, or controlled in her desert hinterland, the caravan routes from the oases of Arabia to Damascus (Jer. 49:7–8; Ezek. 25:13), the metropolis of the north Arabian desert, but she had further advantages in that the route which diverged to cross the north Sinai desert to Gaza or directly to Egypt ran through her territory. The copper beds of the Wâdī ʿArabah also lay in Edomite territory. This probably occasioned the Hebrew subjection of Edom in the time of David (2 Sam. 8:14), after which Israel enjoyed this asset. There is unfortunately no monument from Edom like the Moabite

90d stone to elucidate local culture. From theophoric names and from Josephus (*Ant.* XV, vii, 9) it appears that the national god of Edom was Kos. The OT, however, gives no hint of the god of Edom, which, significantly perhaps, is never reproached for idolatry. Hebrew tradition consistently accredits the Edomites with wisdom (e.g. Jer. 49:7), which indicates a certain preoccupation with moral issues, so that Edomite religion may have had much in common with the religion of Israel. In taking advantage of the ruin of Judah in 586 it was considered that Edom was guilty of an unnatural outrage. Actually by that time the Edomites themselves were under pressure from the Nabataeans, a virile stock from the Hejaz, and were soon forced to seek new homes in the south of Palestine. This district was consequently termed Idumaea, a name which applies as far north even as Hebron in the time of the great Jewish revolt (Josephus, *War* IV, ix, 7). The Hasmonaean John Hyrcanus in 109 B.C. dealt with this problem by forcibly converting the Idumaeans, or Edomites, to Judaism, and from one of these converts Herod the Great was descended.

e In the south Palestine is open to the desert, and under these conditions there is a continual movement of nomads between the desert and the sown, partly to seek pasture and water according to climatic fluctuations and partly to find a market for their stock. In the days before the Zionist occupation Beersheba and Gaza were overrun by nomads from the southern deserts every Friday, the Arab holy day and weekly market. So in antiquity there were various nomadic or semi-nomadic elements in the south, some of them actually federated with Judah, and others, notably the Amalekites, inveterate enemies.

In the first category are the **Kenizzites.** Their home must be sought both east and west of the Wâdī 'Arabah, the great rift valley between the Dead Sea and the Gulf of 'Aqaba, since they were an influential element both in Judah and Edom (Gen. 36:11, 42). According to Hebrew tradition the Kenizzites penetrated Palestine with Judah from the south and occupied Hebron and Kiriath-sepher (Jos. 15:17; Jg. 1:13), exploits associated respectively with Caleb and Othniel. They were soon fused into kinship with Judah, as is indicated by the fact that Caleb is reckoned of the tribe of Judah (Num. 13:6) and Othniel one of the Judges of Israel (Jg. 3:8–11), while Hebron itself was the first seat of the House of David.

f Also associated with Judah in the penetration of Palestine from the region of 'Aqaba were the **Kenites,** who were affiliated with Israel through the marriage of Moses with the daughter of their chief (Jg. 1:16). They do not seem to have settled in the land, however, since they are found among the Amalekites in the north Sinai desert in the time of Saul (1 Sam. 15:16; cf. 1 Sam. 27:10). An isolated Kenite family is mentioned in south-eastern Galilee in the time of the Judges, when Jael, the redoubtable Kenite woman, slew Sisera in her tent (Jg. 4:11, 5:24). The etymology 90f of the name suggests that they were smiths or artificers, a theory which is supported by their association with the Wâdī 'Arabah, where there were copper deposits which had been worked by the Egyptians since the middle of the 3rd millennium. The nature of such craftspeople and their itinerant habits is illustrated at the present day by the desert tinkers, the Nawwar and Sulayb, and doubtless the family of Jael was one of these.

Associated with the Kenites in the north Sinai desert were the **Jerahmeelites** (1 Sam. 27:10), to whom the Hebrews were well disposed (1 Sam. 30:29), and who, like Caleb the Kenizzite, were reckoned in late Jewish tradition as of the kinship of Judah (1 Chr. 2:9f.).

The **Amalekites,** who also occupied north Sinai, g
were the inveterate enemies of Israel. The two peoples came into conflict in Israel's desert sojourn in north Sinai, possibly over the control of the oasis of Kadesh (so Mowinckel), the most desirable part of the region and an important desert sanctuary, as well as a vital point on the desert route between Edom and Egypt. We hear of campaigns against them in the time of Saul (1 Sam. 15:2f.), and David (1 Sam. 30:1f.), but after this time they play no part in Hebrew history. The explanation is that the eastern part of the north Sinai desert was occupied by the Kenizzites, Kenites, and Jerahmeelites, who were friendly to Israel, and the Amalekites, largely by the campaigns of Saul and David, had been confined to the west, where they would neighbour the Philistines.

Bibliography—From the foregoing it will be apparent that any study of the ethnology and culture of the ancient Near East depends greatly on the results of archaeology. In the scope of the present article it is impossible to cite all the publications in this field which contribute directly and indirectly to the subject, and the following bibliography is necessarily selective:

W. F. Albright, *Archaeology and the Religion of Israel* (2nd ed. 1946), *The Archaeology of Palestine* (1949); A. Alt, *Völker und Staaten Syriens im frühen Altertum* (1936), *Die Landnahme der Israeliten in Palästina* (1925); V. G. Childe, *The Aryans* (1926), *What Happened in History* (1950); G. Contenau, *La Civilisation Phénicienne* (1949); A. Dupont-Sommer, *Les Araméens* (1949); R. Dussaud, *Les découvertes de Ras Shamra et l'Ancien Testament* (2nd ed. 1941); C. H. Gordon, *Ugaritic Literature* (1949); N. Glueck, *The Other Side of the Jordan* (1940); A. Goetze, *Hethiter, Churriter, und Assyrer* (1936); O. R. Gurney, *The Hittites* (1952); J. A. Knudtzon, *Die El-Amarna Tafeln* (1908–15); R. A. S. Macalister, *The Philistines* (1914); M. Noth, *Die Welt des Alten Testaments* (3rd ed. 1957); R. T. O'Callaghan, *Aram-Naharaim* (1948); J. B. Pritchard, *Ancient Near Eastern Texts relating to the Old Testament* (1950); H. H. Rowley, *From Joseph to Joshua* (1950); G. E. Wright, *Biblical Archaeology* (1957).

HISTORY OF ISRAEL—I
TO THE EXILE

By H. G. MAY

91a **THE EXODUS AND THE CONQUEST OF CANAAN**

Moses and the Exodus—The origins of the Heb. people are obscure. Certain it is that they did not appear all at once and in full flower, even though the theological concept of the ' people of the Lord ' may have had a definite, traceable beginning. In general, we may regard the 14th and 13th cent. as the time when the Hebrews came on the historical scene. This is the period of the New Kingdom in Egypt, the XVIII and XIX Dynasties. Some Heb. tribes may have entered Canaan in the early part of this period and others near its end. The latter were those under the leadership of Joshua and who had been led from Egypt by Moses. The relationship between these two groups, and the specific tribes in each are debated by biblical historians. Without discussing here the pros and cons of the variant views, we may refer the reader to the comprehensive treatment of the problems involved by H. H. Rowley, *From Joseph to Joshua* (1950).

b During the reigns of Amenhotep III (1413–1377) and particularly of Akhenaton (1377–1360) the city-kings of Canaan wrote letters to the Egyptian Pharaohs seeking help and referring to the Ḫapiru (or Ḫabiru) and SA-GAZ people who were a threat to the Canaanite cities and to the Egyptian overlordship of Canaan. These letters have been found at Tell el-Amarna, ancient Akhetaton, Akhenaton's capital. Ḫapiru occurs as 'Apiru in the Egyptian records, largely of the XIX Dynasty. Although the Ḫapiru people cannot be narrowly identified with the biblical Hebrews and are mentioned frequently in early inscriptions of Mesopotamia, there may be a relationship between the words themselves, and the biblical data are better understood if it is presumed that there were Hebrew tribes entering Canaan in the 14th cent., although probably not the kind of organised force represented in the Joshua stories.

c There can now be little doubt but that the **Exodus from Egypt** occurred in the 13th cent., with Rameses II (1301–1234) the Pharaoh of the oppression. As slaves in Egypt the Hebrews built the cities of Pithom and Raamses (Exod. 1:11), the latter in all probability modern Ṣân el-Ḥagar, known in the Hyksos period, at the time of the patriarchs, as Avaris and later as Tanis, the biblical Zoan. The city was started by Seti I but made more splendid by Rameses II, as evidenced by statues and architectural remains bearing the cartouches of Rameses II and his successors. Either Rameses II or his successor Merneptah (1235–1227) was the Pharaoh of the Exodus, probably the former. A stele of Merneptah makes the first non-biblical allusion to Israel (already in Canaan). The explorations of Nelson Glueck in the areas of Edom, Moab, and southern Transjordan point to no sedentary occupation in these areas between the end of the 20th cent. and the beginning of the 13th cent. (see AASOR 18–19 (1939)) ; yet at the time of the Exodus the kingdoms of Edom and Moab and the Amorite kingdom of Sihon south of the Jabbok were in existence. This supports a 13th-cent. Exodus date, as do the destructions of Hazor and Bethel, and 91c
probably also Lachish, revealed by the excavations. Consonant with this date is the fact that eight kings reigned over Edom before there was a king over Israel (Gen. 36:31–9 ; Num. 20:14–21). The building of the Temple 480 years after the Exodus (1 Kg. 6:1) would place the Exodus earlier, but this datum has scanty support.

It is difficult to separate the Moses of history from d
the Moses of tradition. While the story of his rescue from the bulrushes may reflect a legend about Sargon of Agade (*c.* 2400 B.C.) and gives a Heb. etymology (' drawn out ') to an Egyptian name ('Moses' is from an Egyptian word meaning ' to bear ' or ' beget ', found in such names as Aḥmosis, Ṭhuthmosis, etc.), there is no reason to doubt his training in the Egyptian court, his flight from Egypt, his marriage and residence with the Midianites, his leadership of Heb. slaves and his welding them into a ' people ', and his role as the founder of Heb. religion. Scholars may differ on whether he led one or more tribes from Egypt, but it is generally agreed that not all the twelve tribes were involved. The essential characteristics of Heb. religion introduced by Moses were those which set it apart at significant points from the pagan religions ; it involved a monolatrous theology and a deity without consort, image, or mythology who was bound to his people by a covenant. The antiquity of the covenant ideology in Israel has been questioned, but recent studies support possible Mosaic origin. The ultimate origins of the worship of Yahweh and of the name are obscure. The most probable meaning of the name is ' He brings into existence ', i.e. as the creator God.

The time of the **descent into Egypt** is uncertain. e
It may have been some of the Heb. tribes who entered Canaan in the Amarna period who shortly moved on down into Egypt. A common opinion is that the Heb. tribes (i.e. the sons of Jacob) entered Egypt in the Hyksos period (*c.* 1720–1580), and that Joseph should be placed at this time, about 400 years before the Exodus (see Gen. 15:13 ; Exod. 12:40). The Joseph story might seem to support the hypothesis that it was primarily the Joseph (and Benjamin) tribes who were in Egypt and who therefore formed the Exodus party, along with the Levites, whose presence in Egypt cannot be denied in view of the role of Moses and Levitic names of Egyptian origin, such as Moses, Hophni, Pashhur, Phinehas, and Merari. On the other hand, some scholars maintain it was the southern tribes (Judah, Simeon, Reuben) who, along with the Levites, were with Moses and who entered Canaan in the latter part of the 13th cent. The identification of the tribes who entered Canaan in the Amarna period depends in part on the reconstruction of the Exodus narrative : were they all the tribes, some of whom went on to Egypt (Joseph and Benjamin), or were they the northern tribes only ?

It is common for scholars today to speak of an f
amphictyonic organisation of the Heb. tribes, i.e. a league of tribes organised in a covenant around a central sanctuary (see A. Alt, *Die Staatbildung der Israeliten in Palästina* (1930)). T. J. Meek (*Hebrew*

91f *Origins* (rev. ed. 1950)) presumes such a confederacy of northern tribes at Shechem under Joshua (14th cent.) and a later one of the southern tribes under Moses at Kadesh-barnea. Hebron is sometimes regarded as an amphictyonic sanctuary for the southern confederacy of tribes. The importance of Shechem as an Israelite covenant centre is reflected in Jos. 8:30–5, 24:1–28. Its pre-Exodus occupation by Heb. tribes is evidenced in Gen. 24. The city also had Canaanite associations with covenant ideology, for its patron deity was Baal-berith (El-berith), Lord of the Covenant (Jg. 9:4, 46). Perhaps both Sinai and Kadesh-barnea were covenant-making sites of Moses and the tribes under him ; Exod. 15:22–5 may reflect an earlier account of the incident at Meribah (cf. Exod. 17:7 ; Num. 20:1–13). It is futile to try to reconstruct the original legislation associated with the Mosaic covenant.

g **The Conquest of Canaan**—Messengers from Moses from Kadesh-barnea asked the king of Edom in vain for permission to pass along the King's Highway (Num. 20:14ff.), the main trade and travel route that led from the Gulf of 'Aqaba through Edom and Moab up the length of Transjordan to Damascus. It was known in Roman times as Trajan's Road and in modern times as the Sultan's Road and Abdullah's Road. In the path of Israel was not only the kingdom of Edom, but also the kingdom of Moab and the kingdom of Sihon, the last of these extending from the Arnon to the Jabbok. North of these was the kingdom of Bashan where Og ruled. Skirting Edom and Moab, the Israelites defeated Sihon, who also had forbidden access to the King's Highway, and Og was also conquered (Num. 21). When a conflict with Moab seemed imminent, Balak of Moab sent to the Euphrates region for Balaam to give oracles against Israel, but the expected curses proved to be blessings on Israel (Num. 22–4). Nelson Glueck's explorations have disclosed the line of border fortresses of Moab and Edom, built one in sight to the other, protecting the Sown from the Desert.

h The course of the conquest of Cisjordan after the death of Moses on Mt Nebo cannot be reconstructed with assurance. (See §250) What took more than one generation to accomplish has been telescoped into one generation, in the two great campaigns of Joshua. After being tricked into making a treaty with the Gibeonites, Joshua is pictured defeating a coalition of southern kings of the cities Jerusalem, Hebron, Jarmuth, Lachish, and Eglon. The northern coalition he next subdued centred around Hazor, Madon, Shimron, and Achshaph. His two major antagonists were Adonizedek of Jerusalem and Jabin of Hazor.

i The stories of the preceding conquest of Jericho and Ai may be, as Noth believes and as the excavations at present seem to indicate, largely aetiological tales. The fall of Jericho cannot be illustrated archaeologically. The presumed double-wall fortifications of the Joshua period at Jericho belong to the 3rd millennium and to two different periods of the city's occupation. The evidences of a catastrophic destruction within the city previously connected with Joshua belong to the 16th cent. Jericho of Joshua's day may have been little more than a fort! Ai (et-Tell) disclosed no signs of occupation between *c.* 2400 and 1000. A terrific destruction and conflagration evident at Bethel and probably due to the Israelites is datable to the 13th cent., and may be the ultimate source of the Ai story. Lachish (Tell ed-Duweir) perhaps fell in the latter half of the 13th cent., *c.* 1220, and Eglon (Tell el-Ḥesī) and Debir (Tell Beit Mirsim) were destroyed in this same period, as also was Hazor (Tell el-Qedaḥ) in the north. Nothing is said in Joshua about the conquest of central Palestine where the tribes Ephraim and Manasseh settled ; this may already have been in the hands of people friendly to the Israelites, as Gen. 34 suggests, and as noted above. If so, we can better understand Joshua's use of Shechem for the covenant rite despite the fact that its capture is not recounted. It has been suggested 91 that it was here that the tribes who were not in Egypt were brought under the Exodus covenant.

When the Israelites entered Canaan they found there a very mixed population, generally designated by the term Amorite or Canaanite. They included particularly Semites and Horites (Hurrians), the latter playing a much larger role in the Near East than was formerly known.

Hebrew Antecedents—The tribes which thus conquered or occupied Canaan were by the Heb. tradition j reckoned to be descended from eponymous ancestors, the sons of Jacob and Joseph. This is historical fiction, comparable to that which gave eponymous ancestors to nations and even to cities. The stories of the 'births' of the tribes in Gen. 29, 30 may be reminiscent of the origin of some of the Israelite tribes in Mesopotamia. The sons of Jacob's concubines have been thought to represent Canaanite tribes assimilated to the Israelites after the conquest of Canaan. The insistent tradition of the association of the patriarchs with the Haran-Nahor territory is significant. Not only did Abraham come into Canaan from Haran, but the wife of Isaac also came from there, and there Jacob spent more than a score of years. Haran and Nahor, the two brothers of Abraham, are the names of cities. Something of the culture and religion of the Paddan-aram area at the time of the Patriarchs is disclosed by the excavations at Mari (Tell Ḥarîrī) on the Middle Euphrates. Thousands of tablets were recovered from the palace, a building of more than 250 rooms. They illuminate especially the period of Ḫammurabi (*c.* 1728–1686), when the Amorite Zimri-lim was king of Mari. Mari seems to have controlled the territory of Haran. The inscriptions mention the city of Nahor and refer to an Amorite tribe of Benjamin (Banu-yamina) raiding Zimri-lim's territory, and the correspondence with the warlike character of Benjamin in the biblical narratives has been noted. The relationship to the later Heb. tribe is obscure, and Benjamin is pictured as 'born' in Canaan (Gen. 35:18). See G. Mendenhall, 'Mari', BA 11 (1948), 1ff. ; ANET, p. 482. David has been mistakenly found as the designation of a chieftain (*dawidum*) of the Benjaminites of Mari. Abraham may have been among Amorite invasions from this area, and perhaps at this time myths and legends of Sumerian and Babylonian origin were also coming to Canaan. The patriarchal names are 'at home' in this period. The name Jacob appears in contemporary inscriptions from Chagar Bazar in the area between Mari and Haran, while Jacob-el appears as a place name in Palestine in the 15th cent. The name Abram is found on 16th-cent. tablets.

The patriarchal narratives reflect customs and k situations known to have been contemporary with the patriarchs, illustrating that legends and traditions may preserve valid historical reminiscences. The marriage of Jacob conforms closely to the *errebu*-marriage of ancient Mesopotamia, according to which the family in which there were no sons might be continued through a daughter taking a husband into her father's family, as also in the case of the modern Palestinian 'visiting husband'. The teraphim or household gods stolen by Rachel from Laban have their parallel in the Nuzu tablets where possession of personal gods constituted the title to the chief inheritance portion and leadership in the family (C. H. Gordon, BASOR 66 (1937), 25ff.). The explorations of Nelson Glueck have disclosed the cities and agricultural activities which once existed in the now desert-like Jordan valley and which made it Lot's choice (Gen. 13:10–12). Canaanite mythological texts from Ugarit (Râs Shamra) illuminate the role of the god Shalem who gave his name to Jerusalem (Salem) and of El-Elyon (God-Most-High), whose priest-king Melchizedek met Abraham after the defeat of the invaders from the east (Gen. 14). The ruins of Sodom and Gomorrah lie in all probability beneath the waters at the southern k end of the Dead Sea, and a nearby sanctuary with standing stones at Bab-edh-Dhra is mute evidence of this. It was in the days of Jacob that the name of the city of Luz was changed to Bethel, although the reason may have been to honour the Canaanite god Bethel. Archaeological research gives a picture of Middle Bronze Age (*c.* 2000–1550) Palestine in general consonant with the biblical picture of the patriarchs, even if we must discount the references to domesticated camels and the Philistines and remember that the stories are told to illustrate the theology of a later period, that of the writers.

THE SETTLEMENT OF CANAAN

2a **The Times of the Judges**—When the Israelites entered Canaan there was no central government, but rather there were many city-states, each with its king, as we know from the Amarna letters, the Egyptian records, and the biblical account. Jos. 12:7ff. lists the city-kings defeated by Joshua in Cisjordan. The conquest did not result in the annihilation of the Canaanites; the biblical historian acknowledges numerous cities where the Israelites did not drive out the native inhabitants (Jg. 1:16–36). Even as the Jebusites at Jerusalem conquered by David were not killed but were eventually absorbed within the Heb. community, so the Canaanites in other parts of Canaan were similarly assimilated. The destruction of the Canaanites was by no means as thorough as the Deuteronomic historian pictures it. The Hebrews were long a minority group in the country. When they entered Canaan they first occupied the sparsely populated hill-country.

b For a considerable time after their entrance they retained something of their tribal character. Conducive to this was the at least eventual occupation of more or less specific areas by the individual tribes; territorial factors would help keep tribal differentiations alive. Canaan had never had a native, unified overall government, and although the presence of a common enemy such as the Philistines might result in occasional united action, it produced no real organisational unification for almost two centuries. The Song of Deborah (Jg. 5) illustrates co-operation among some of the tribes in conquering a specific area, and the tribes who did not participate are chided. The Ephraimites might even attack the Gileadites for not permitting them to participate in the war against Ammon (Jg. 12). The Israelites assembled together as tribes at Mizpah before the war against one of their number, the Benjaminites. There are elements of both tribal unity and conflict in these narratives. The institution of judgeship might mean the rule of one man over several tribes, but his rule was fairly localised, involving no general governmental organisation or political differentiation, and it did not affect deeply the economic or social life of the people. In this respect it was quite different from the kingship. Allegiance to the judge was a voluntary affair, and the person rather than the office bore the authority.

c The period of the Judges lies within the Iron Age, between *c.* 1200 and 1020. The Philistines, who came from Caphtor (Crete), entered Canaan early in this period. The records of Rameses III (1180–1149) refer to the defeat of the 'Sea Peoples', among whom were the Philistines. They settled on the southern coastland of Canaan where their pentapolis (Gaza, Ashdod, Ashkelon, Gath, and Ekron) was located. North of the Philistines and south of Carmel, at Dor on the Plain of Sharon, were the Tjeker, another group of Sea Peoples. Although the Deuteronomic historian places the judges in succession, one after the other, and presumes a much longer period, it must be recognised that the judges often possessed a local authority and some judges were contemporary with others. The Deuteronomic chronology is schematised, rather than accurate.

The Judges—Othniel, the first judge, had captured 92d
the city of Debir, also called Kiriath-sepher, modern Tell Beit Mirsim, where the poorly and perhaps hastily constructed casemate walls, silos, iron implements, and some Philistine pottery have been uncovered. Israel's adversary Cushan-rishathaim of Aram-naharaim is unknown, although a district of Qusana-ruma in north Syria is known from contemporary Egyptian records. The judgeship of Ehud is next reported; he slew with his two-edged sword Eglon of Moab who had taken possession of the Jericho area. Of Shamgar son of Anath (i.e. inhabitant of the city of Beth-anath in Galilee) it is recorded only that he slew 600 Philistines with an ox-goad (Jg. 3).

One of the most important events of this period is e
preserved in prose and in ballad form (Jg. 4, 5). In the struggle for the possession of the fertile Plain of Megiddo (Plain of Esdraelon), Deborah's commander Barak led the Israelites against the forces of Sisera and his coalition of Canaanite kings (see Jg. 5:19). The ballad suggests that Megiddo was in ruins at the time, and the most probable date for the battle would be *c.* 1125 B.C., between city levels VII and VI. The later prose account introduces Jabin of Hazor into the narrative and represents only the tribes Zebulun and Naphtali as participants. More historical is the ballad, composed soon after the event, breathing the spirit of the occasion and written in exciting, contemporary diction. At Deborah's call Ephraim, Benjamin, Machir (Manasseh), Zebulun, Naphtali, and Issachar rallied to defeat Sisera, whose iron chariots were mired in the torrent Kishon, which drains this fertile plain, while Sisera himself was slain by a Kenite woman. The Israelites rebuilt Megiddo along new lines. The pottery from the rebuilt city is comparable to that of the Israelite hill-country. The importance of Israelite possession of this stronghold, which controlled not only the fertile plain but a significant trade-route leading from Egypt to Syria and Mesopotamia, is obvious.

The exploit which brought Gideon forward as judge f
involved the Valley of Jezreel, just east of the scene of the battle with Sisera, a part of the same break in the central highlands. Here he defeated the Midianites, who along with Amalekites and Kedemites were raiding Israel, making extensive use, perhaps for the first time, of the domesticated camel. Gideon, whose earlier (not later) name Jerubbaal honoured the Canaanite god, rallied the Israelites to Yahweh, routed the Midianites, and pursued their two kings Zebah and Zalmunna into Transjordan. There he slew them and punished the Gileadite cities Succoth and Penuel for not assisting him (Jg. 6–8).

Although Gideon rejected the request that he assume the kingship, his authority seems to have surpassed that of other judges; he took a harem and had seventy sons, and established a religious centre at Ophrah, where he made a cult object, an ephod, a divination instrument comparable to an ark. The fact that he named a son Abimelech, honouring God as Father and King, may hint at increasing royal ideology. Jg. 9:2 (contrast 8:22–3) has been taken as evidence he may have accepted the kingship. Certainly Abimelech did, with the help of the kinsmen of his Shechemite mother and the treasury of the temple of Baal-berith. This temple has been excavated; its walls were about 17 feet thick, a fortress-type temple or *migdāl*, and it belonged to the Late Bronze Age and the earliest phase of the Early Iron Age. There were what were perhaps three bases for sacred pillars on each side of the door and one in the courtyard. Abimelech's royal residence was at Arumah. Shechem was razed to the ground and its site sown with salt by Abimelech when it revolted against him. The times were not ripe for the monarchy, nor was Abimelech one who could have set it on a firm foundation. The spirit of independence and of tribal autonomy was still too strong, and Abimelech lost his life in an attack against the rebellious city of Thebez. His rule

92f was largely limited to the area of the tribe of Manasseh (Jg. 9).

g Jephthah (Jg. 10–13) ruled as judge in Transjordan over the Gileadites, who were involved in a war with the Ammonites, whose territory lay east of the southern extension of the Jabbok river. The Ammonites claimed the territory between the Arnon and the Jabbok, which Israel had conquered from Sihon (Num. 21:21–31). The Ammonites had also crossed the Jordan and raided Judah, Benjamin, and Ephraim. Jephthah argued the divine right of conquest to substantiate Israel's claim. His victory over the Ammonites was followed by the fulfilment of his vow, and his daughter was sacrificed to Yahweh. Her death was commemorated by a four-day annual lamentation festival, perhaps an adaptation of an early pagan rite. The narrative of the subsequent war between the Ephraimites and Gileadites illustrates dialectic differences between the two areas (Shibboleth, Sibboleth) as well as the bitter intertribal conflicts which sometimes characterised this period (see also Jos. 22 ; Jg. 19–21).

h Samson (Jg. 14–16) was a popular folk-tale figure. Despite legendary accretions, the narrative reflects the stresses and strains which existed in the territory bordering on Philistia. Intermarriage with a Philistine woman, association with a Gaza harlot, the willingness of the men of Judah to deliver one of their number to the Philistines, domination of the Israelites in neighbouring areas by the Philistines, slaughter of Philistines by a lone ' infiltrator ', enslavement of a Heb. captive—these all hint the complicated relationships of Philistines and Israelites in the early days of their settlement. Although some earlier critics have regarded Samson as a depotentised solar deity, Samson was an historic figure, even though myth motifs may appear in the legends and Samson may have been named after the sun-god Shemesh, who gave his name to Beth-shemesh, a city just across the valley from Zorah, the home of Samson's parents. Samson is a Canaanite personal name, appearing as *šmšyn* in Ugaritic texts. Samson was a Nazirite for life, as possibly also was Samuel, and the Nazirites may have played a larger role in Israel than our present sources indicate (cf. Am. 2:11, 12). Of the ' minor ' judges little is known.

i **Supplemental Narratives**—Samson was a Danite, and perhaps because of pressures from these same Philistines, the Danites were forced to migrate from their original ' allotment ' adjacent to the Philistines to the far north at the source of the Jordan, where they captured the city of Laish and gave it the name Dan (Jg. 17–18). The story was originally told to explain the origins of the sanctuary at Dan, one of the two royal sanctuaries of the kingdom of Israel, and its Levitic priesthood. The Deuteronomic historian obliquely criticises it and its graven image, which is apparently regarded as a prototype of the later calf image that was there, and suggests the legitimate contemporary sanctuary was at Shiloh (18:31). The narrative may indicate the northward spread of the Levitic priesthood from Judah and the gradual gain of Levitic authority throughout Israel. Neither Micah nor the Danites seemed conscious of the existence of the Shiloh sanctuary, perhaps for the obvious reason that it as yet had not attained its later significance. The incident belongs early in the period of the judges.

j Another Levite sojourning in Ephraim, and who had as concubine a girl from Judah, was the cause of an intertribal war which nearly resulted in the annihilation of Benjamin (Jg. 19–21). When his concubine was violated and killed at Gibeah of Benjamin, he called the tribes to Holy War by distributing the twelve parts of her body throughout Israel, as Saul was later to summon the tribes to Holy War by distributing the pieces of his oxen through Israel. Bethel, before the days of Eli perhaps a more important sanctuary than Shiloh, was the scene of the gathering of the tribes and the invoking of an oracle (Mizpah is a later addition to the narrative). The first assault of the Israelites against Gibeah was unsuccessful, but after a fast-rite and second oracle at Bethel the battle was successful and Gibeah was put to the sword. The account pictures but 600 Benjaminites surviving. The first city at Tell el-Fûl, the site of Gibeah, was only a village, belonging to the 12th cent. It was destroyed at this time by fire, and rebuilt at the end of the following century. (The allusion to the Ark and Phinehas in 20:27, 28 comes from a later source.) The account of the attack on Jabesh-gilead, which secured wives for 400 of the Benjaminites, and the seizure of maidens at the annual festival at Shiloh for wives for the rest of the Benjaminites, is embellished by folklore, but subsequent events substantiate special relationships between the people of Gibeah and those of Jabesh-gilead.

BEGINNINGS OF THE HEBREW MONARCHY

Samuel and Saul—The role of Samuel was in some ways more significant than the present narrative presumes, and in other ways less significant. The late source pictures him as a prophet of almost unlimited authority, whose consent, albeit reluctant, was necessary before a king could be selected, who made the selection by lot, and the king was at once accepted. It was he who gave approval of the kingship of David and thereby legitimated the not completely clear claims of the Davidic dynasty. Some of the details of the story of Samuel's birth were probably originally told of Saul rather than Samuel, for the explanation of the name of Samuel in 1 Sam. 1:20ff. fits Saul (' Asked ') rather than Samuel (' Name of God ' or better ' The Unnamed God is God '). Historically, it seems to have been Samuel, rather than the people, who saw the need of the kingship, and who took the initiative in its institution. 93

Rameses III in the period of the judges had re-established control over parts of Egypt's Asiatic empire. The Egyptian story of Wenamon illustrates how the prestige and power of Egypt had declined by the latter part of the 12th cent. and the beginning of the 11th cent. (ANET, pp. 25–9). Assyria, following a period of expansion under Tiglath-pileser I (*c.* 1116–1078), was likewise in a period of decline. It was not, however, merely lack of outside interference which made possible a centralised government in Canaan. The pressures of enemies on Israel were the primary motivation. A system of more or less localised judges could not cope with the situation. Samuel witnessed the destruction of Shiloh, a religious and political centre of Israel under the leadership of Eli and his sons. To judge from the excavations, Shiloh was destroyed around 1050, doubtless in the war between the Philistines and Israel recorded in 1 Sam. 4–6. b

The Philistines, whose entrance into Canaan coincides with the introduction of the techniques of iron metallurgy, for a long time seem to have succeeded in keeping the production of the new metal under their control. They forced the Israelites to come to them for the sharpening of iron implements, and the Israelites were deficient in military equipment, iron swords, and spears because of the Philistine monopoly (Jg. 5:8 ; 1 Sam. 13:19–22). Although their headquarters were on the coastland, the Philistines roved inland, and in the latter half of the 11th cent. controlled Beth-shan at the eastern end of the Plain of Jezreel. Early in the reign of Saul Philistine garrisons were at Geba and Michmash (1 Sam. 13, 14, 31). In the battle of Ebenezer the Ark was captured by the Philistines, but was returned when it was associated by them with a plague ravaging their cities. The plague seems to have followed the Ark to Beth-shemesh, and it was put by the Israelites into temporary retirement at Kiriath-jearim. This Ark may have originated at Shiloh, although it must have had Canaanite analogies. The earlier allusions to the Ark are historically questionable. c

93d After Eli's death Samuel served as judge and prophet, as well as in some priestly function. He may be credited perhaps with the organisation of the ecstatic prophets into bands or guilds, the sons of the prophets, who appear now for the first time and under some sort of leadership from Samuel. They were associated with Samuel in the instigation of the kingship, for they participated in the sign given to Saul that he had been selected as king, and Saul joined them in prophecy. The later source, which regards the kingship as a rejection of Yahweh as king, may reflect opposition to the kingship by those who preferred the ways of patriarchal and tribal organisation and the more informal administration of the judges (1 Sam. 8). The earlier narrative depicts Samuel taking the initiative (9:1–10:16) ; the anointing was done privately, and the official announcement of Saul's selection was not made until after the Jabesh incident (1 Sam. 9:27ff., 11:15 ; contrast 10:20–7).

e Saul of Gibeah in Benjamin came to the fore when Jabesh-gilead was threatened by the Ammonites. His eagerness to help Jabesh when he heard of the threat of Nahash of Ammon may have been in part because of previous associations of Gibeah and Jabesh noted above. 1 Chr. 7:12, 15 implies earlier marriage relations between Gilead (Machir) and Benjamin. Saul summoned the tribes to Holy War by distributing pieces of his oxen through Israel (see §92*j*). After the defeat of Ammon, Saul's next battle was against the Philistines at Michmash ; the Philistines were defeated and forced to return 'to their own place' (1 Sam. 13, 14). Saul's capital was at Gibeah (Tell el-Fûl), three miles north of Jerusalem, where the castle or citadel of Saul has been uncovered. Saul's fortress-citadel, in the second city on the mound, had a double or casement wall with great towers at each corner. Although only one corner was excavated, its general measurements can be estimated to have been *c.* 170 by 110 ft. The outer casement wall was about 4½ ft. thick, and the inner wall narrower, with transverse partitions between the two.

f Early in Saul's reign conflicts arose between Saul and Samuel. In the first of apparently duplicate tales of the Lord's rejection of Saul as king, Saul made a sacrifice at Gilgal without benefit of Samuel's ministrations (1 Sam. 13:8–15), and in the second Saul disobeyed Samuel's orders to make a complete destruction, a *ḥerem*, of the Amalekites after their defeat (ch. 15). While these narratives are in part the background of the Judaean attempt to authenticate David's kingship, Saul must have in various ways antagonised his Yahwist supporters. The priesthood at Nob gave David more than tacit support, to read between the lines in 1 Sam. 21:1–9, and after Saul's slaughter among them, the priest Abiathar, who escaped, went over to David (1 Sam. 22:11–23), and with him must have gone much of the sympathy of the true Yahwist elements. If the name of Saul's son and successor, Ish-baal (Man of Baal) honours the Canaanite deity, the disaffection of loyal Yahwists from Saul could more easily be understood, although Saul is not accused of pagan worship.

Saul was subject to strong emotional disturbances, anticipated in his participation in the ecstasy of the itinerant bands of prophets (1 Sam. 10:9–13 ; see also 19:23–4). The historian interprets the emotional aberrations of Saul to be the result of the departure of the spirit of Yahweh from him and the coming of an evil spirit from Yahweh upon him. It was to soothe him during these spells that David was chosen as court musician to play the lyre. A lyre is being played before an enthroned Canaanite king on a 12-cent. ivory inlay found at Megiddo. David was selected not only because of his musical ability, but also because of his general qualifications as a courtier ; he was a man of valour, a soldier, prudent in speech, and of goodly presence. David became Saul's armour-bearer. A later tradition ascribed to David the exploit of one of his officers, also a Bethlehemite, Elhanan, the son of Jaareoregim, who slew Goliath 93f
the Gittite, the shaft of whose spear was like a weaver's beam (2 Sam. 21:19). The transfer of this event to David (1 Sam. 17) is understandable, and attempts to explain the discrepancy by positing that David was his throne name, or by eliminating the name Goliath from 1 Sam. 17, or by giving Goliath a brother for Elhanan to slay (1 Chr. 20:5) are unnecessary. The story of David and Goliath serves to picture David as one possessed of the grace of the Lord after the manner of the judges, a shepherd unused to war, rescuing Israel from its enemy not by force of arms, but in the name of the God of Israel (1 Sam. 17:45–7).

While the account of David's anointment by Samuel g
before his introduction to Saul's court is questionable (1 Sam. 16:1–13), David seems early to have had his eye on Saul's throne. Jonathan's friendship was soon regarded with disapproval by Saul, who recognised that David was a menace to himself and his dynastic hopes (1 Sam. 20:30ff.). Saul's attempts to do away with David were justified from his viewpoint. The open praise of David as a greater warrior than Saul made Saul fear for his throne. David's professed reluctance to marry into Saul's family was not such as to prevent his marriage to Saul's daughter. Saul may have been playing on his knowledge of David's hopes for the throne when he offered to David in turn his two daughters, using them as a snare to try to bring about David's death. The importance of his marriage to Michal for David's claim on Saul's throne is evident in subsequent events (2 Sam. 3:12–17). When Saul gave Michal to another after the open break between him and David, it was to weaken David's pretensions to the throne. Saul's drastic treatment of the priests at Nob and his pursuit of David show how seriously he took David's threat to his throne. David's cutting off the skirt of Saul's robe was the equivalent of a claim to wear the royal robe. The author makes the story climax in Saul's acknowledgment of David's claim, as an added justification of David's succession to Saul (1 Sam. 24). The Nabal incident not only illustrates David's means of support of himself and his men, but anyone who paid for the 'protection' offered by David would presumably be reckoned not unsympathetic to David's cause. Nabal regarded David as a slave who had broken away from his master. He obviously was not of David's party, and this may help explain David's role in the story. Abigail's politics obviously differed from those of her husband ! See 1 Sam. 25.

Plausible explanations have been given for David's h
vassalage to Achish, the Philistine king of Gath. Only thus perhaps could David have escaped death at the hands of Saul, i.e. by leaving Israel's borders. There is no evidence that David ever intended to side with Israel's enemies against Israel, and he did use his stay with the Philistines as a cover for activities on behalf of Judah. Still, the story is not as savoury as one might wish, and David was seeking the promotion of his own personal ambitions, which were in conflict with Saul's interests. It is futile to conjecture what David's role would have been had he been permitted to remain with the Philistines in the battle on Mt Gilboa. Certainly all but Achish believed he might turn against the Philistines, but this does not mean that he would have given his support to Saul. It is difficult to see David at this point fighting Saul's battles. These contacts with the Philistines may be a part of the background which explain how David later had a bodyguard of Cherethites and Pelethites, Aegaean peoples related to the Philistines, and the role of Gathites or Gittites in the later David story in 2 Sam. 6:10–11, 15:18–22, 18:2.

Saul's consultation with the medium of En-dor because no answer was received from the normal means of divination reflects a lack of confidence on the part of those who manipulated the oracles ; dubious of the outcome, they preferred to make no prediction. Although weakened and without hope, Saul fought

93h valiantly. When he was wounded he fell on his own sword rather than allow himself to be degraded as a Philistine captive. As his public activity had begun when he came to the aid of Jabesh-gilead, so the curtain drops on the drama of his life when the men of Jabesh-gilead rescued the bodies of Saul and his sons from the wall of Beth-shan and burnt them in Jabesh and buried them under the tamarisk tree there, fasting seven days.

THE UNITED MONARCHY

94a **The Reign of David (c. 1000-961)**—Saul was unable to bring the kingship to full flower. This was done by David. Although David must have secretly rejoiced at the death of his enemy, he must preserve the sacred character of the kingship to which he aspired. So he slew the Amalekite who claimed, probably falsely, that he had dispatched the wounded Saul on Mt Gilboa. David's lament over Saul and Jonathan, preserved in the Book of Jashar, is one of the oldest and finest pieces of Hebrew poetry. A Canaanite poem has assisted the RSV in reconstructing a corrupted line (2 Sam. 1:21*c*). Whatever his opinion of Saul, David's grief at Jonathan's death was genuine.

b David had won the support of Judah, and now Judah made David its king at Hebron. The city was selected by Yahweh's oracle, doubtless by Abiathar's ephod. David gave a gentle hint to the citizens of Jabesh-gilead that they should follow him (2 Sam. 2:4–7), but Ish-baal, Saul's son, became king over Israel, i.e. Cisjordan north of Judah and Transjordan, with his capital at Mahanaim in Transjordan. Abner, Saul's commander of the army, who now served Ish-baal, met with Joab, David's army commander, at the pool in Gibeon (2 Sam. 2:12ff.), which has been recovered in the recent excavations. The subsequent battle marked the beginning of war between the house of Saul and the house of David. Abner, chided by Ish-baal for taking one of Saul's concubines, offered to turn the kingdom over to David and secured for David Saul's daughter Michal. But Joab doubted Abner's motives and feared for his own position, and he slew Abner. Two Israelites brought to David the head of Ish-baal, but David rewarded them by slaying them, for as king he could hardly countenance regicide. Israel now came to David at Hebron, and in accord with Israel's more democratic procedures, a covenant was agreed upon, and David was anointed king of Israel.

c After seven years at Hebron, David moved his capital to Jerusalem, just north of the old tribal boundary of Judah. The city was in the hands of the Jebusites, but was taken by entrance through the water-shaft which led from the spring Gihon into the city, a type of water system known also at Megiddo, Gibeon, Gezer, and Ibleam. Here David built himself a palace. He made the city a religious centre of his kingdom, moving to it the Ark of the covenant and building an altar at the site where later Solomon's Temple was to stand. The site for the altar was selected after a plague which had followed the taking of a census (2 Sam. 24), and the figures for the census may perhaps now be found in Num. 1 and 26. The census was to make possible the conscription of an army, and was also for taxation purposes and the imposition of forced labour (cf. 2 Sam. 20:23–5). Israel was to learn for the first time the real costs of a kingdom. A well-trained personal army with foreign mercenaries in it (Cherethites, Pelethites, and Philistines) formed the hard core of David's military machine with which he and Joab were to produce phenomenal results.

d David subdued the Philistines and conquered the Canaanite cities still holding out in Cisjordan. He defeated the Edomites in the Valley of Salt, putting garrisons in Edomite cities and extending his rule southward to the Gulf of 'Aqaba. In Transjordan the Moabites and Ammonites were defeated and brought 94d within his kingdom, and also the Aramaean states of Zobah and Damascus. David's control was established up to the vicinity of the Euphrates, and even Toi, king of Hamath on the Orontes River, felt the need of placating David by sending him congratulations through his son, who brought to David articles of silver, gold, and bronze (2 Sam. 8–10). David also concluded a treaty with Hiram of Tyre.

An early source (2 Sam. 9–20 and 1 Kg. 1–2) presents graphic and perhaps eye-witness reports of the inner court and family life of David. The sordid incident of David's sin with Bath-sheba and his murder of her husband Uriah forms a fitting prelude to the narratives which involve the sons of David. The crown prince Amnon dishonoured his half-sister Tamar, and was slain by his brother Absalom. Absalom, after returning from exile in Geshur, as crown prince prepared a chariot and horses and fifty runners to run before him. He tried to win from David to himself the sympathies of those bringing a suit to David for judgment, seeking to undermine his father's prestige and power. So he 'stole the hearts of the men of Israel' from David. Dissatisfaction with David's reign must have helped make this possible. After four years of this Absalom deemed the time ripe and had himself proclaimed king at Hebron and had the news announced throughout Israel. He moved north against Jerusalem, from which David fled to Transjordan, to Mahanaim, and Absalom took over his father's harem. e

As David had once been pursued by Saul, he was now pursued by Absalom, who made Amasa commander of his army. But Amasa proved to be no equal to the seasoned warrior Joab, and Absalom's army was defeated in the Battle of the Wilderness. Absalom met his death at the hands of Joab when his head was caught in a great oak and his mule moved on. The weakened and ungrateful David asked the Judaeans, who apparently had been Absalom's chief supporters, rather than the Israelites to return him to Jerusalem, and he made Amasa his army commander. The spurned Israel now revolted under the Benjaminite Sheba, raising a war-cry against David and his house. But Amasa was killed by Joab and it was Joab who put down the revolt and saved David's kingdom for him. f

With the death of Absalom, Adonijah could now legitimately assume the role of crown prince. David's preference was for Solomon, son of Bath-sheba, who had remained his favourite wife since he had secured her by having her husband placed in a position where he would inevitably be killed in battle. Nathan, the prophet who is reported to have castigated David for this incident, gave his support to Solomon, as did the army officer Benaiah, who was hoping for Joab's job (everyone seems to have wanted it!), and Zadok the priest, who hoped to be something more than co-priest with Abiathar. Possibly Zadok was of Canaanite rather than Aaronite ancestry, belonging to Melchizedek's line. Adonijah was supported by Joab and Abiathar. With David on his death-bed Adonijah was crowned king, but before the coronation feast was over Solomon was anointed king by Zadok with David's permission. Adonijah sought the sanctuary of the altar. It was not long before Solomon, now king, found opportunity to do away with Adonijah. The altar did not save Joab even temporarily. Abiathar was banished to Anathoth. Shimei of the house of Saul and a possible threat to the throne was executed for violating house arrest. Not by the power of the spirit, like the judges or even Saul, and not by covenant, but by right of succession and ruthless removal of possible claimants, Solomon became ruler. Politically, Israel had what she is reported to have asked for, 'a king to govern us like all the nations' (1 Sam. 8:4). g

Solomon (*c.* 961–922) received from David a kingdom h
extending from the entrance to Hamath to the Gulf of 'Aqaba, an air distance of about 400 miles, in

4h contrast with the usual ' Dan to Beer-sheba ' limits of about 150 miles. Through astute administration, state monopolies, and an extensive forced-labour policy, Solomon brought to his capital at Jerusalem power and wealth beyond that achieved by a native government in Palestine before or since. In part through diplomatic marriages, as when he married the daughter of Pharaoh, he strengthened his international ties. He divided the country into 12 administrative districts under 12 officers. Only roughly did the districts accord with tribal boundaries, for empire interests were not consonant with tribal loyalties ; the 5th district extended from Jokneam by Mt Carmel in the west across the Jordan to Abel-meholah (Tell el-Maqlûb) in the east. The administrative officers were each responsible for providing food supplies for the palace one month of each year, i.e. some 5,850 bushels of flour, 11,700 bushels of wheat, 300 fat oxen, 600 pasture-fed cattle, and 3,000 sheep, besides harts, gazelles, roebucks, and fatted fowl (see 1 Kg. 4:7, 22–3, and reckoning a cor at 6½ bushels). They also provided barley and straw for Solomon's horses. The drain on the countryside must have been a terrible burden for the people to bear. An overall official was in charge of the forced labour. Descendants of the Canaanites were made state slaves and a levy of forced labour was drawn from the Israelites. This free labour was used in Solomon's building activities in Jerusalem and in other cities, including his store cities and cities for horses and chariots, as well as in his lumber camps, quarries, mines, and maritime commerce. The picture of all Judah and Israel eating, drinking, and being happy (1 Kg. 4:20) is an idealisation, and the oppressive rule of Solomon was to have inevitable repercussions in revolt and revolution. There is no question of the splendour of the court of Solomon, with his great wealth and his large harem.

i The best evidenced of Solomon's activities archaeologically are his building of cities, his horse and chariot trade, and his mining industries. The well-planned Stratum IVB at Megiddo, with its elaborately fortified gateway, its city wall (11½ ft thick), its fine masonry, and its extensive installations for housing horses illustrate the first two of these. The most reliable report gives Solomon 1400 chariots, 4000 stalls for horses, and 12,000 horses (1 Kg. 10:26 after LXX^{B}; cf. 5:26). Solomon's import of horses was from Kue (Cilicia) and of chariots from Egypt, and they were exported to the kings of the Hittites and Syria (1 Kg. 10:28–9). In the Negeb and particularly in the Arabah south of the Dead Sea, in Edomite territory, Solomon exploited the rich copper and iron deposits. Guarding the northern approach to the Arabah mining area was a fortress at modern Khirbet Ḥamr Ifdān. A few miles below is the large ruined site of Khirbet en-Naḥās (literally, Copper Ruin), a great copper-mining and -smelting site. A large enclosure marks the mining camp site, and inside are ruins of miners' huts and smelting furnaces, and heaps of slag. This was but one of the many mining- and smelting-sites discovered by modern exploration (see N. Glueck, *The Other Side of the Jordan* (1940), 50ff.). Control of these resources was a major reason for the long warfare between Edom and the Israelites.

j The Phoenicians and Egyptians carried on the sea commerce in the Mediterranean, but Solomon realised the potentialities in trade via the Gulf of 'Aqaba and the Red Sea. The copper and iron resources of Wâdī 'Arabah, of which the Gulf of 'Aqaba was really a geologic extension, made this both a natural and a highly profitable development. At the head of the Gulf of 'Aqaba Solomon built the city of Ezion-geber (Tell el-Kheleifeh), in reality a great smelting-plant, and this could serve as the base from which his Tarshish (' Foundry ') ships, built and manned by Phoenicians, could carry the rich metal and manufactured objects as media of exchange. His ships brought back gold from Ophir (Punt), silver, ivory, and two kinds of 94j
monkeys (1 Kg. 10:22). The Queen of Sheba's visit to Solomon was not merely to test his reputation for wisdom, but rather to seek relief from the threat posed by Solomon's traders to her commercial life-line.

These resources, along with a profitable treaty with k
Hiram of Tyre and the use of Phoenician craftsmen, made possible Solomon's building activities. The bronze made from the copper of the Arabah region provided for the Temple so many vessels that the weight of them was not known. There were also the two great pillars of bronze, some 27 ft. high exclusive of their capitals and 18 ft. in circumference, cast, doubtless in ringed sections, in the clay in Transjordan. The glory of Solomon's kingdom was symbolised in part by his palace, the House of the Forest of Lebanon, with its magnificent Hall of Pillars and Hall of the Throne. But above all it was evident in the Temple, overlaid with gold and decorated with palm-tree, cherub, and flower motifs, and in the furnishings of the Temple. Its decorative motifs and its general plan have numerous archaeological parallels. The significance of its symbolism, and that of the two free-standing pillars, the bronze sea, and the great altar of burnt offering, especially its cosmic reference, is illuminated by archaeological and literary studies. The import of the Temple for the development of the religion of Israel must not be underestimated, even though later prophets were to condemn reliance on its rites and ritual.

The Temple was both an expression of and an instrument of national unity. Yahweh, the God of the people of Israel, became the God of the nation Israel. Although Jerusalem was not the sole sanctuary, it was the national religious centre as it was the national political centre. The Temple possessed a cosmic, national, and royal symbolism at one and the same time. Solomon, like David, had a certain priestly function, and it is curious that Zadok is not mentioned in the story of the making or dedication of the Temple in 1 Kg.

Also both an expression of and an instrument of l
unity was the prototype of the later J and E ' histories ' which must have come into existence at the time of the united monarchy. The people of Israel were made to play the central role in an epic of world history which began with creation and ended with the conquest of Canaan. This was not a nationalistic history with monarchic implications. It contained no allusion to a central sanctuary and no royal ideology. In some respects, therefore, it represented a different trend in Heb. thought from that inherent in the Temple. Although of a different character and purpose, the wisdom literature in which Solomon interested himself, perhaps both as patron and author, should be mentioned here (1 Kg. 4:29, 34).

Solomon's ' wisdom ' carried for him no implications m
of democratic government. It was his oppressive rule, rather than his worship of pagan gods and building shrines for them (1 Kg. 11:26–40), that caused Ahijah the prophet to encourage Jeroboam to lead Israel in revolt. The Deuteronomist naturally gives the latter explanation of Ahijah's motives. Solomon nipped in the bud the incipient rebellion, and Jeroboam fled to Egypt, which also had granted asylum to Hadad of Edom. It is difficult for us to appreciate the radical changes which the monarchy made in the daily lives of the Israelites, with the startling commercial and industrial developments and the tightening of administrative supervision. The very structure of society underwent change, and a political and commercial aristocracy arose. In a few decades Israel had moved from a relatively simple agricultural and pastoral people to a highly commercial nation. The covenanted-people concept of Moses would tend to be obscured by the demands of loyalty to the king. Obviously Israel was not of one mind, and the more theocratic views in the new epic of the Heb. people may have been at least tacitly anti-monarchic.

95a **THE KINGDOMS OF ISRAEL AND JUDAH**

Israel and Judah to the Reigns of Jehoram and Ahaziah—The United Monarchy had become the Divided Monarchy. Although the division was inspired by Ahijah the prophet and another prophet, Shemaiah, forbade Solomon's son to try to regain Israel, for the Lord had said, ' This thing is from me ' (1 Kg. 12:22–4), the later Hebrews looked on the division as a major catastrophe (cf. Isa. 7:17). The later prophets were to look forward to a time when the schism would be healed, as in the new age Israel and Judah would once more be under a single head, a king of the line of David. The Deuteronomic castigation of Jeroboam (1 Kg. 13:1–14:20) seems much too severe, but the historian writes from the viewpoint of Judah and one who honours the Davidic dynasty, as well as from the theological standpoint that any sanctuary outside of Jerusalem was contrary to the law of Yahweh. So the unnamed man of God is pictured as addressing the altar at Bethel, predicting its destruction and even mentioning by name king Josiah, who was to desecrate and tear down the altar at Bethel and abolish the local sanctuaries. The chronology of the Divided Monarchy poses many difficult problems. In the main the chronology given below follows Albright in BASOR 100 (1945), 16ff.

b At the death of Solomon **Rehoboam** his son (922–915) was accepted as king by Judah, but Israel demanded a conditional kingship. Rehoboam went to Shechem, the historic covenant centre where Abimelech had ruled. The assembled Israelites demanded that the oppressive rule which had been imposed by Solomon be lightened. Spurning the counsel of his older advisers and accepting that of the younger courtiers who were loth to give up luxuries and privileges drained from the country's resources to Jerusalem, Rehoboam took Israel's request as impertinence and an insult to his royal prerogatives, and promised to increase Israel's yoke. Under the leadership of **Jeroboam**, who had returned from Egypt, Israel raised the same battle-cry it had at the time of Sheba's revolt, when its rights had been by-passed by the Jerusalem throne. Egypt was willing to see the power of the monarchy weakened and may have given Jeroboam encouragement. Rehoboam sent Adoram, taskmaster over the forced labour, into Israel, but he was stoned to death. Jeroboam was called to the Shechem assembly and made king (922–907). He made his capital first at Shechem and then at Tirzah (Tell el-Fâr'ah).

As his own royal shrines, and necessarily in opposition to the Jerusalem sanctuary, Jeroboam built sanctuaries at Dan and at Bethel, placing in the temple at both sites the image of a bull. This was not apostasy from Yahweh, for these were images in the Yahweh cult, perhaps representing the throne of the deity. Yahweh was as truly the national God of Israel as of Judah. While there were cherub images in the holy of holies of Solomon's Temple and bovine symbolism in the oxen beneath the sea of bronze, the bull images at Dan and Bethel did represent closer syncretism with the Baal cult.

c Shishak's policy of dividing and conquering succeeded, for in the fifth year of Rehoboam (918) he invaded both Judah and Israel, including Transjordan which was part of Israel, and also invaded Edom. His conquest is recorded on the walls of his temple at Thebes (Breasted, ARE iv, §§709–22). The biblical account reports only his conquest of Judah. He despoiled the Temple and palace of their treasures, and the five hundred shields of gold made by Solomon for his bodyguard were taken by Shishak and had to be replaced by bronze shields (1 Kg. 14:25–8). So much had the glory of Solomon dimmed. In the excavations at Megiddo in Israel there was found a fragment of a stele set up by Shishak there.

d Abijam (Abijah) (915–912), Rehoboam's son, reigned for three years. They were years of warfare with Israel in which, according to the Chronicler (2 Chr. 13), he had some success. He was succeeded by his brother **Asa** (912–872). In Israel Jeroboam was followed by his son Nadab (901–900), the last of his dynasty. In contrast with the situation in Judah where, with a brief six-year intermission, the Davidic family continued on the throne, dynasties tended to be short-lived in Israel. Nadab's brief reign came to an end when he was slain by Baasha (900–877) when the Israelites were laying siege to the Philistine city of Gibbethon on Israel's border. Asa was the first of the reforming kings of Judah, concerned with the purification of the Jerusalem cultus. The motives for these reforms may have been mixed, for they often involved periods of national crisis, when it was important to stress the national God Yahweh and placate his anger through the repair or the purification of his Temple. Asa abolished male cult-prostitutes and removed idols, deposing the queen mother who had made an image for the goddess Asherah. Baasha was waging war against Judah and had fortified Ramah, only five air miles north of Jerusalem. Asa called in the help of Israel's rival, Syria, ruled by Ben-hadad, the son of Tab-rimmon, whose stele dedicated to the god Melqart has been found at Aleppo. Asa depleted the treasures of the Temple and palace to compensate Ben-hadad, who conquered the cities of northern Israel and forced Baasha to desist. Now Asa fortified the cities of Geba and Mizpah, the latter some distance north of Ramah at Tell en-Naṣbeh, with stones taken from Ramah. Asa's fortifications at Mizpah were so strong that they amazed the excavators. See 1 Kg. 15:9ff. An invasion of Judah under Zera the Ethiopian, perhaps acting as an agent of Osorkon I of Egypt, was repulsed by Asa at Mareshah (2 Chr. 14:9ff.).

e Asa's son **Jehoshaphat** also had a long reign (873–849). He controlled Edom and tried unsuccessfully to revive the Red Sea trade. The ' foundry ships ' he made to go to Ophir were wrecked at Ezion-geber. In Israel regicide seemed the order of the day. Elah, son of Baasha (877–876), was slain by Zimri, and Zimri, after seven days on the throne, was killed by Omri (876–869). **Omri** ruled for six years at Tirzah and then decided to build a new capital befitting his dignity and the role he planned for Israel. He bought a hill from Shemer, and on it he built his city, naming it Shomeron (i.e. Samaria) after the owner of the hill (modern Tell Sebaṣṭiyeh). Here Omri began and his son Ahab completed the construction of the famed ' houses of ivory ' (1 Kg. 22:39 ; Am. 3:15 ; Ps. 45:8), conceived on a scale comparable to that of the palaces of the Assyrian kings. The acropolis or inner wall around the summit had masonry similar to that of the Solomonic buildings at Jerusalem, and the monumental forecourt of the gateway was decorated with pilaster columns topped by proto-Ionic capitals similar to those found in the Solomonic city at Megiddo. Later, probably under Jehu, this acropolis wall was replaced by a casemate wall and the palace was probably rebuilt. In the ornamental gateway there took place the dramatic incident in 1 Kg. 22:5ff. Among the ruins were found numerous artistically carved inlays that had been on panels, on furniture, and on boxes, explaining the designation ' ivory house '. They are comparable to ivories known from Arslan Tash and Nimrud from the same period, the Arslan Tash ivories being of Damascene origin. The Samaria ivories may have been imported from Damascus and Phoenicia.

Omri's conquest of Moab is mentioned on the ' Moabite Stone ', a stele set up by King Mesha (cf. 2 Kg. 3:4), discovered at Dibon in 1868. Omri was apparently victorious over Damascus, and he cemented relations with Phoenicia by marrying his son Ahab to Jezebel, the daughter of Itto-baal (Ethbaal), king of Tyre. His importance was more than is suggested in the few verses given to him by the biblical record. The Assyrians were later often to speak of Israel as ' the land of Omri '.

95f His son **Ahab's** reign (869–850) is the most detailed of the reigns of the Israelite kings, largely because of the historian's interest in Elijah. As usual, Damascus and Israel were rivals, with conflicting claims over northern Transjordan. Ben-hadad of Damascus invaded Israel and even laid siege to Samaria, but Israel was victorious. A second battle took place at Aphek east of the Sea of Galilee, but again Ben-hadad met with defeat. Perhaps because of new threats from Assyria which counselled a common front against a common enemy, Ahab treated his vanquished foe leniently, much to the displeasure of the prophetic guilds (1 Kg. 20). In the year 853 Ahab's chariotry and infantry were part of a coalition with the forces of the kings of Damascus, Hamath, Kue, Muṣri, Arvad, Ammon, and other districts, altogether a total of twelve kings. At Qarqar on the Orontes River they fought with Shalmaneser III, king of Assyria. Shalmaneser in his records claims the victory, but his westward march was temporarily stopped. Ahab lost his life in the battle with the Syrians at Ramoth-gilead, when Jehoshaphat of Judah as a subordinate ally joined forces with him.

g The religious situation in Israel was complicated by the machinations of Jezebel, for whom Ahab built a temple of Baal at Samaria, and who was involved in bitter controversy with Elijah. The Elijah stories may have been preserved in the circles of the prophetic guilds, and the Elisha narratives may come from the same source. Behind the legendary accretions we can see in Elijah a prophet whose concern for Yahwism and the rights of the Israelite citizen make him a worthy forerunner of the 8th-cent. prophets. The folk-tale character of the present narratives is in contrast with the historical data taken from the Book of the Chronicles of the Kings of Israel and the Book of the Chronicles of the Kings of Judah.

h Ahab's son and successor Ahaziah (850–849) was rebuffed in his attempt to join Jehoshaphat's ill-fated Red Sea venture (1 Kg. 22:49). His ineffectual rule was followed by that of his brother Jehoram (849–842), under whom Mesha of Moab revolted (see 2 Kg. 3 and the Moabite Stone). Jehoshaphat of Judah was succeeded by his son Jehoram (Joram) (849–842). Jehoram lost control of Edom. An invasion of Judah by Philistines and Arabs resulted in the despoliation of the treasures of the palace, and the king's sons were carried off (2 Chr. 21:6–17). Jehoram married Athaliah, the daughter of Ahab and Jezebel. His son Ahaziah (842) and Jehoram of Israel were reigning over their respective kingdoms when the revolt of Jehu took place.

96a **From Jehu's Revolt to the Fall of Samaria**—Ahaziah of Judah went with Jehoram of Israel to fight against Hazael of Syria at Ramoth-gilead. Hazael's seizure of the throne of Syria had been instigated by Elisha (2 Kg. 8:7–15). Jehoram was wounded, and went to Jezreel to recover, where he was visited by Ahaziah (2 Kg. 8:28–9). To Elisha the time seemed ripe to strike a fatal blow against the dynasty of Ahab and Omri, and at his behest a member of a prophetic band anointed Jehu as king over Israel (842–815). The methods of Jehu's bloody revolt and reign of terror vitiated any good that his Yahwist supporters hoped might come from it. Elisha's choice was not a good one, to judge from both the religious and political outcome of Jehu's rule, and the prophet Hosea was later to condemn the revolt (Hos. 1:4). Though Jonadab, the founder of the Rechabite sect, rode in Jehu's chariot, and though Jehu slew the prophets of Baal in their temple (after himself making offerings to Baal, 2 Kg. 10:18ff.), the nation did not profit religiously from the revolt.

It would seem that Jehu hoped to set himself up as king of Israel and Judah through the murder of both Jehoram and Ahaziah. But he reckoned without Athaliah, the queen mother in Judah, who could be as ruthless as Jehu himself. Jehu slew Jezebel in a crude and gory incident, and he inspired the slaughter of
the seventy sons of Ahab, whose heads he received in baskets and then pretended innocence. The record reports he slew also all Ahab's great men, his close friends and his priests, ' until he left him none remaining ' (2 Kg. 10:11). In the eighteenth year of the reign of Shalmaneser III (841) the Assyrians besieged Hazael in Damascus and devastated the surrounding area, and took tribute from Tyre, Sidon, and ' Jehu, son of Omri '. On the famous Black Obelisk Shalmaneser lists the tribute, and the relief shows Jehu kissing Shalmaneser's feet, while behind Jehu file Israelites bearing tribute (ANEP, 351–5). Jehu also suffered at the hands of Hazael, and after his unsuccessful rule was followed by his son Jehoahaz (815–801). 96a

Athaliah of Judah slew the royal family to establish her throne (842–837). Ahaziah's infant son Joash (Jehoash) escaped the slaughter and was hidden in the Temple. Under the direction of Jehoiada the priest, the boy prince was proclaimed king in the Temple courts, and Athaliah was murdered. Jehoiada was regent in the early years of Joash's reign (837–800), and Mattan, the priest of Baal established by Athaliah, was slain and the pagan altars and images were destroyed. **Joash** repaired the Temple extensively, beginning in the 23rd year of his reign. Hazael of Damascus invaded Judah and captured Gath, but was bought off by the treasures of the palace and Temple. Dissatisfied with Joash's reign, his servants (officials) slew him, and his son Amaziah became king (800–783). b

Amaziah conquered Edom, defeating the Edomites in the Valley of Salt and taking Sela by storm. This gave him control of Edom's mineral resources. His success was nullified by his foolhardy challenge to **Joash (Jehoash)**, the son of Jehoahaz, king of Israel (802–786). Joash defeated Amaziah at Beth-shemesh, destroyed the fortifications at Jerusalem, and took as spoil the treasures of the palace and Temple, and returned with hostages to Samaria. Judah was still vassal to Israel. As was his father, so Amaziah was slain in a conspiracy, and his son Azariah (Uzziah) became king (783–742). In Israel Jeroboam II, son of Joash, ascended the throne (786–746). c

Both **Azariah** and **Jeroboam** prospered. Judah's economic and military position was improved. Azariah rebuilt Elath (Ezion-geber) on the Gulf of 'Aqaba (2 Chr. 26:2), and what is probably the seal ring of his son, bearing the name Jotham and a figure of a horned ram, was found in the excavations there. In the latter part of his reign Azariah contracted leprosy, and Jotham acted as regent. The personal seals of Abijah and Shebaniah, two of Azariah's officials, have been found. An Aramaic plaque from the 1st cent. A.D. bears the inscription : ' Hither were brought the bones of Uzziah, king of Judah. Do not open.'

Judah and Israel together nearly reached the limits of Heb. domination at the time of the United Monarchy. As predicted by the prophet Jonah, the kingdom of Israel extended from the entrance to Hamath to the Sea of the Arabah (Dead Sea). Israel was victorious over Damascus. The prosperity of Israel in this period is reflected in the book of the prophet Amos, and in Hosea ch. 2. The prosperity was superficial, based on injustice, and Amos and Hosea predicted the end of the ruling dynasty. Hosea prophesied into the period of anarchy following the death of Jeroboam.

Jeroboam's son Zechariah after a six-month reign was slain by Shallum, who was king one month and was slain by Menahem of Tirzah (745–737). Menahem began his reign with atrocities against the expectant mothers of the rebellious city of Tappuah. He was forced to acknowledge the sovereignty of Tiglath-pileser III of Assyria (called Pul in 2 Kg. 15:19ff., this being his Babylonian name, i.e. *Pulu*), who invaded Israel. Tiglath-pileser's annals record his conquest of Gaza and tribute received from Rezin of Damascus, Menahem of Israel, Hiram of Tyre, and others. Another record tells how Menahem fled, and Tiglath-pileser returned him to his throne, imposing tribute on him (ANET, pp. 283–4). Menahem was d

96d followed by Pekahiah, his son, who after a brief reign (738–737) was killed by Pekah (737–732).

e After a successful rule, Jotham of Judah (742–735) was succeeded by his son Ahaz (735–715). Judah was attacked by Pekah of Israel and Rezin of Damascus, who sought to put on Judah's throne 'the son of Tabeel', i.e. a prince of Judah from Tabeel, a territory in northern Transjordan (see BASOR 140 (1955), 34, 35). Isaiah did not believe that the allies would conquer Judah, and predicted that Assyria would subdue Syria, Israel, and also Judah (Isa. 7–8). Ahaz, however, bought the help of Tiglath-pileser with the gold and silver of the Temple and palace. The Assyrians attacked Damascus and Israel, and annexed to the Assyrian empire all but the district of Samaria, turning the rest of Israel into the Assyrian provinces of Dor, Megiddo, Karnaim, Hauran, and Gilead. This we learn from Tiglath-pileser's record which supplements the biblical account in 2 Kg. 15:29, 30. Tiglath-pileser tells us that the Israelites overthrew their king Pekah and that he placed Hoshea on the throne (ANET, p. 284). Pekah was slain by Hoshea who initiated a conspiracy against him (2 Kg. 15:30).

f Hoshea (732–724) after eight years of vassalage to Assyria rebelled with the encouragement of So (Sibe) of Egypt. The siege of Samaria, begun by Shalmaneser V, was brought to a successful conclusion in 722–721 by Sargon II, whose report tells of exiling 27,290 Israelites, defeating Sibe, settling others in Samaria, and rebuilding the city (ANET, pp. 284, 285). Before the beginning of the siege Hoshea had been seized and imprisoned. The exiles were settled in Halah, on the Habor, the river of Gozan, and in Media. The kingdom of Israel had come to an end.

97a **The Kingdom of Judah after the Fall of Samaria**—Israel's fall had brought Assyrian territory just to the north of Judah. Sargon had brought into Israel deportees from Babylon, Cuthah, Avva, Hamath, and Sepharvaim. Sargon writes: 'I settled there people from countries which I myself had conquered, and I placed my officer as governor over them and imposed on them the tribute as for Assyrian citizens.' The new population, obviously a minority, for only a small proportion had been exiled by Sargon or earlier by Tiglath-pileser III, intermarried with the remaining Israelites. The Judaeans came to regard this mixed population as no longer true Hebrews, and they are the Samaritans. Actually, neither the Judaeans nor the Samaritans could claim unmixed racial heritage.

b Not only was Samaria an Assyrian province, but Ahaz was a vassal to Assyria. **Ahaz** had been called to Damascus by Tiglath-pileser III, doubtless to swear his allegiance to Assyria, and it has been plausibly suggested that the subsequent altar he built at Jerusalem honoured the god of Assyria. The removal of the old Yahweh altar from the front of the Temple and the twelve bronze oxen from beneath the sea of bronze has also been interpreted in terms of the lessened prestige of the national God of Judah (2 Kg. 16:10ff.). Judaean border towns were lost to the Philistines, and Edom regained its independence. The biblical chronology is uncertain, but Ahaz, contrary to 2 Kg. 18:10, was on the throne at the time Samaria was taken, for it is known the events in the 14th year of Hezekiah took place in 701 (2 Kg. 18:13). Ahaz's son **Hezekiah** (715–687) began his reign with Judah still acknowledging the sovereignty of Assyria. Ashdod, which revolted against Assyria, was made an Assyrian province in 711. Inspired by prophetic ideals, and also moved by the spirit of independence and restlessness among Assyria's vassals, Hezekiah honoured the national God Yahweh with the most thoroughgoing religious reform to that time, removing high places, cutting down the Asherah, and destroying the bronze image of the (Levite ?) serpent deity Nehushtan. He made Jerusalem's defences more secure by improving its water system, constructing a tunnel from the spring Gihon under the hill a distance of 1,750 feet to bring the water to a pool within the city walls, providing water in time of siege. In 1880 Hezekiah's inscription commemorating the completion of the tunnel was found on the wall of the tunnel, only the lower part of the inscription being preserved (ANET, p. 321). 97

With the encouragement of Merodach-baladan of Babylonia and the assistance of Egypt, Hezekiah joined a revolt of the Philistine cities in the year 701. Sargon had been succeeded by Sennacherib, and Sennacherib's annals complement and at points correct the much edited account in II Kg. 18–19; Isa. 36–7. Neither account is completely objective. The people of Ekron had put their king Padi, who had refused to join the revolt, into fetters, and given him to Hezekiah to hold in prison. On his campaign, Sennacherib received the submission of the Phoenician cities, and conquered the coastland cities of Beth-dagon, Joppa, Benai-barka, Azuru and Ekron, as well as Eltekeh and Timnah. He defeated the Egyptian forces on the plain of Eltekeh. Many Judaean cities were taken, including Lachish, which was made Sennacherib's headquarters in his attack against Jerusalem, to which he laid siege. A relief found at Nineveh depicts the siege and surrender of Lachish (ANEP, 371–4). In the Lachish excavations a pit was discovered containing the remains of some 1,500 persons, perhaps representing the clearance of the city after its capture by Sennacherib. Hezekiah was forced to capitulate, and Sennacherib imposed heavy tribute on him (ANET, pp. 287, 288). Isaiah's role in these events is obscure, but he seems to have recognised that Jerusalem would not be destroyed at this time, although he did not abandon his view that Assyria was the instrument of Yahweh's judgment which was heavy on Judah. Micah's oracle against the Philistine cities in Mic. 1:10ff. may have been composed during Sargon's or Sennacherib's invasion of Philistia. c

Hezekiah's son **Manasseh** (687–642), notorious for his pagan worship, was at first loyal to Assyria, but in the reign of Sennacherib's successor Esarhaddon he revolted. Despite his earlier paganism, he did have a religious reform, perhaps to unite his country around Yahweh in his bid for independence. He also strengthened the fortifications of Jerusalem. But all to no avail, for the commanders of Esarhaddon took him in fetters to Babylon, and after proper indoctrination he was returned to Judah as king (2 Chr. 33). A record of Esarhaddon refers to the assembling of twenty-two kings of Hatti, Beyond the River, and Cyprus, i.e. the kings of Tyre, Edom, Moab, Gaza, Ekron, Byblos, etc., including Manasseh king of Judah, to transport with their labourers timber from the mountains and stone colossi from the quarries for Esarhaddon's palace at Nineveh (ANET, p. 291). A similar list of kings, including Manasseh, comes from the records of Ashurbanipal. d

Manasseh's ineffective son Amon (642–640) was killed in a palace conspiracy and was followed by one of Judah's most important rulers, **Josiah** (640–609). The continuance of pagan elements in the early years of Josiah evidenced in Zephaniah's oracles is explained by Josiah's youth, for he began reigning at the age of eight. A frequently presumed Scythian invasion as the background of the oracles of Zephaniah and the early oracles of Jeremiah is very dubious. Ashurbanipal was the last significant ruler of Assyria (668–633), and with his death Josiah could begin to think in terms of religious reform and independence. 2 Chr. 34:3 has been taken to imply that upon Ashurbanipal's death Josiah cast out the gods of the Assyrian overlord. 2 Chr. 34 pictures a thoroughgoing reform before the discovery of the book of the law in the Temple, but the 2 Kg. 22–3 account more plausibly places the reform after the discovery of the book of the law; the reform was based on the book of the law. Both accounts presume Josiah's authority in the north as well as in Judah. It may be Josiah at first had some e

97e administrative control of Israel with Assyrian permission, and then with the increasing weakness of Assyria he took advantage of this to claim rule over Israel and Judah, in other words, to restore the United Monarchy. Josiah abolished the local sanctuaries and made Jerusalem the only legitimate temple in the kingdom. He removed the pagan paraphernalia from the Jerusalem Temple, and he destroyed and defiled the temple at Bethel. Josiah's book of the law was the legislative core of the Book of Deuteronomy, probably chs. 12–26. Its ultimate origins we cannot discuss here. It has been maintained that Josiah divided Judah into 12 administrative districts, with Jos. 15:21–62 dating from this period. See §257*l*.

The death knell of Assyria began tolling with the fall of Ashur in 614 and Nineveh in 612. The prophet Nahum rejoiced over Nineveh's destruction. In 609 Pharaoh Neco was en route through Palestine to Haran to give support to dying Assyria. Josiah met him at Megiddo, and a battle took place in which Josiah was killed (2 Chr. 35:20–4; cf. 2 Kg. 23:29–30). Josiah very likely felt that the Egyptian king was violating the sovereignty of his kingdom, and he would not have been favourable to Egypt's interest in supporting Assyria, Judah's traditional enemy.

f Josiah's son Shallum, with the throne-name Jehoahaz, was made king by the people, but he was exiled by Neco to Egypt after a three-month reign, and another son of Josiah, Eliakim, now called **Jehoiakim** (608–598), was put on the throne by Neco. Jeremiah's oracles on the Foe from the North (Jer. 4:5–6:26, etc.) belong to this period, and the foe is the Babylonians. In the Babylonian Chronicle important information is available for the history of this period. In May-June in 605 in Jehoiakim's third year (not fourth year) the Egyptians were defeated by Nebuchadrezzar at Carchemish (Jer. 46:2), and Hatti, including Syria and Palestine, came under Babylonian control (cf. 2 Kg. 24:7). Nabopolassar died in the same year, and Nebuchadrezzar became king of Babylonia. Jehoiakim rebelled, perhaps after a defeat of Nebuchadrezzar in 601 by the Egyptians. He died and was succeeded by his son **Jehoiachin** (Jeconiah, Coniah) on 6/7 Dec. 598. In the same month Nebuchadrezzar marched to the 'Hatti-land', and he laid siege to the city of Jerusalem, according to the Babylonian Chronicle. The Chronicle goes on to state that on the second day of the month of Adar (15/16 March 597), Nebuchadrezzar seized the city, captured the king, appointed there a king of his own choice, received its heavy tribute, and sent them to Babylon (see D. J. Wiseman, *Chronicles of the Chaldaean Kings* (1956)). Jehoiachin was carried into exile, along with 3,023 of the leading Jews (Jer. 52:28). Mattaniah, now called Zedekiah (597–586), another son of Josiah and uncle of Jehoiachin, was put on the throne by Nebuchadrezzar as 'a king of his own choice'. Cuneiform tablets found at Babylon listing payments of rations of oil and grain to captives and skilled workmen mention Yaukin (Jehoiachin) king of Judah and his five sons. One of the tablets is dated in 592 (ANET, p. 308). Jehoiachin's return was expected by many of the Jews (see Jer. 28:4, 22:24–30), and the Babylonians themselves may have thought of his exile as temporary, as in the case of Manasseh. 97f

Zedekiah, accepting Jeremiah's advice, remained loyal to Babylonia, but the pro-Egyptian sympathies of his court forced a rebellion in 589. Nebuchadrezzar attacked the cities of Judah, and inscribed potsherds from Lachish, most of them letters from Hoshaiah, the Judaean commander in the field, to Jaosh, the commander of the city of Lachish, shed important light on this period. One of them was written shortly after the situation described in Jer. 34:7, when the city of Azekah had just fallen (ANET, p. 322). In January of 588 the siege of the city of Jerusalem began. Presuming a calendar that began in the autumn rather than the spring, the siege lasted two and one-half years, with a brief respite when the Egyptian army marched up to give futile aid. The city fell in July 586. Zedekiah was brought before Nebuchadrezzar at Riblah on the Orontes, where his sons were killed and his eyes put out, and he was taken in fetters to Babylon. Another deportation took place, this time consisting of 832 persons according to Jer. 52:29. For the role of Jeremiah in these last days of Judah and for the oracles of Ezekiel, who had been carried into exile in the first deportation, see the commentaries on the books of Jeremiah and Ezekiel in this volume. Gedaliah, the son of Ahikam, was appointed governor and made his headquarters at Mizpah. A clay sealing found at Lachish inscribed 'To Gedaliah, who is over the house', was originally attached to an official papyrus document. After a brief rule of perhaps less than three months he was treacherously murdered by one Ishmael of royal blood, who was incited by Baalis, king of the Ammonites (2 Kg. 25:22ff.; Jer. 41). g

Bibliography—W. F. Albright, *From the Stone Age to Christianity* (3rd ed. 1946), *The Archaeology of Palestine* (1949), and 'The Chronology of the Divided Monarchy of Israel', BASOR 100 (1945), 16ff.; A. Alt, *Kleine Schriften zur Geschichte des Volkes Israels* (1953); J. Bright, *Early Israel in Recent History Writing* (1956); N. Glueck, *The Other Side of the Jordan* (1940); E. G. Kraeling, *Bible Atlas* (1956); A. Lods, *Israel from its Beginnings to the Middle of the Eighth Century*, Eng. tr. by S. H. Hooke (1932); T. J. Meek, *Hebrew Origins* (rev. ed. 1950); M. Noth, *Geschichte Israels* (1950; Eng. tr. 1958); A. T. Olmstead, *History of Palestine and Syria* (1931); H. M. Orlinsky, *Ancient Israel* (1954); J. B. Pritchard, *Ancient Near Eastern Texts Relating to the OT* (2nd ed. 1956); T. H. Robinson and W. O. E. Oesterley, *History of Israel* (1932); H. H. Rowley, *From Joseph to Joshua* (1950); E. R. Thiele, *The Mysterious Numbers of the Book of Kings* (1951); G. E. Wright, *Biblical Archaeology* (1957).

HISTORY OF ISRAEL—II

POST-EXILIC

By L. E. BROWNE

98a The four centuries of Jewish history from the fall of Jerusalem in 586 B.C. to the Maccabaean rising in 166 are worthy of serious study, and from the religious point of view exceedingly rewarding. For in that history we see a nation becoming great through weakness. It is a fact which cannot be controverted that within this period, when Israel lacked everything that is usually connected with national greatness, it began to give the world a contribution to the development of religion far outstripping the contributions even of Greece or India. If, when Israel's capital was sacked and the best of its people deported, it had followed the example of other nations in similar plight, it would either have ceased to exist, or else after a lapse of years have crawled back to some semblance of its former state. Familiarity perhaps hides from most of us the amazing result of Israel's defeat by Nebuchadrezzar, that it rose from death to **a veritable resurrection**, and found a kind of greatness that was new to the world. It is our task in this chapter to fit together as in a jigsaw the fragments of history that remain, and then to try to understand how and why this astonishing thing happened.

b Fortunately we have as our guide in this task one of the greatest religious geniuses of all time. Like the compilers of the Book of Judges, Second Isaiah set out to interpret history as showing the hand of God. But, unlike the compilers of Judges, Second Isaiah did not wait till the events were old history before explaining them. Second Isaiah did what so few men can do : he explained contemporary history. And, as if that was not enough, he interpreted history that had not yet happened in terms of an ideal of conduct which no-one had previously thought of.

c Second Isaiah himself was an inheritor of the riches of earlier prophets, particularly Isaiah and Jeremiah. Before Jerusalem fell in 586 some of the Jews had become possessors of a spiritual truth not known anywhere else in the world, viz. that one God of perfect moral character ruled supreme over the whole universe. How many of the Jews knew this it is impossible to say. Of course they were a small minority, but they were either numerous enough, or strong enough in their conviction, to influence history. The great majority of the Jews held the traditional belief that Yahweh was the God of Israel alone. It is possible that even those who accepted the new universalistic truth did not realise that the two views were incompatible. Anyhow, it needed the destruction of the nation and the Temple to free the wider truth from its nationalistic shackles.

d The one thing that held the exiled Jews together was the belief of the minority that Yahweh was the only God in the world, and that no other people worshipped a God of righteousness. The bonds of fatherland and sacrificial worship were broken. The exiles could only bemoan their loss, and hope for a possible restoration some day. But the sense that they alone of all mankind knew the truth about God became a bond that united them into a nation in a way in which they had never been one before.

e Three outward signs marked the Jews off from non-Jews. The first was that they did not use **idols**. The significance of this, as a distinguishing mark of those who held the new belief about God, was seen at 98e
once, and is consequently emphasised by Second Isaiah —not of course to persuade Babylonians to abandon idolatry, but to give the Jews a proper sense of their religious superiority. The second distinguishing mark of the Jews was circumcision. Being in itself a purely external rite, it was chiefly of legal interest. The prophets had no interest in it. Jeremiah twice refers metaphorically to the 'uncircumcised in heart'. Second Isaiah once uses the word 'uncircumcised' as synonymous with 'Gentile', a usage frequently followed by Ezekiel, whose interests were mainly legalistic. The frequent references to circumcision and uncircumcision in St Paul's epistles and the Acts reflect the stranglehold of legalism on the Jews of apostolic times. The third mark of the Jews was sabbath observance. As a distinctive duty of Jews it is prominent in Nehemiah, and just before him in Third Isaiah (Isa. 56–8). It also comes in Jer. 17, a passage usually attributed to Nehemiah's time, and frequently in Ezekiel. It is important to notice that in all these places the sabbath was a legal day of rest, connected, of course, with religious observance. Later on, with the rise of the synagogue, its importance, as a regular weekly act of worship, prayer and study, was greatly enhanced. Thus we may say that up to the first year of Cyrus the chief mark of the Jews was their abhorrence of idolatry. This fact greatly strengthens our contention that the binding-force that united the Jews was closely connected with their high spiritual conception of God.

The northerners, of the old Kingdom of Israel, had f
scarcely had time to assimilate Isaiah's doctrine of God's moral holiness when they were deported to Assyria, and that may explain why Jeremiah's longing for their return and restoration was never as a whole fulfilled.

The history of the Jews from the Exile to the time g
of Christ has so many gaps that we can never hope to gain a complete picture. But it is clear that at certain times the universalistic light was dimmed almost to extinction, while at other times it shone in some sections of the people. It may be that if we had a fuller picture of the history we might find that the intensity of the universalistic hope varied inversely with the nationalistic fervour. It is so easy for us to see the bad effects of national pride, that we are perhaps too ready to assume that nationalism is bound to militate against internationalism. And yet, without a Jewish nation, the Jewish religion could scarcely have survived ; and, even when the world was ready for religion to burst all national boundaries, it was necessary for Christ to be born into the Jewish nation.

Beginning our history with the fall of Jerusalem, 99a
we immediately find ourselves in great lack of material. From **Jeremiah** we learn that it was possible for the Jews in Babylonia to build houses : evidently they were not slaves. Recent work on Ezekiel has thrown so much doubt on the unity and date of the book that it can no longer be used to supply information about the state of affairs in Jerusalem in the early part of the Exile. In particular we no longer feel obliged to believe that actual idolatry was practised in the Temple. What Ezekiel described was a vision, and in any case,

99a whenever he wrote, when he spoke of people taking idols to their hearts, he was probably speaking in metaphors as St Paul was when he said ' covetousness which is idolatry '.

b We learn from Jer. 44 that certain Jews resident in Egypt in his day worshipped the Queen of Heaven, and claimed that they were only continuing a practice which had been current in Judaean cities, including Jerusalem. Aramaic papyri dating from 408 B.C. show that at the Jewish colony at Elephantine in Egypt other Gods were worshipped side by side with Yahweh. This colony may well have started as Jewish mercenary soldiers in the service of Psammetichus II (594–589 B.C.). They may, then, have been the very people against whom Jeremiah inveighed. But Jeremiah's horror and surprise suggest that such polytheism was not known in his day in Jerusalem, and we should be inclined to connect its origin with the syncretistic worship which had so long prevailed in the high places of Judah. (See *Early Judaism*, 170–5. For other views of the origin of the Jewish colony, see Kraeling, *The Brooklyn Museum Aramaic Papyri*, 41ff.)

c An incident is recorded in Jer. 41:5 in which eighty men from Shechem, Shiloh, and **Samaria** came to offer sacrifice in the ruined Temple of Jerusalem. This incident has an important bearing on the relationship between the Jews and the Samaritans at that time. When Samaria fell to the Assyrians in 721 B.C., the territory of the northern Kingdom of Israel was incorporated into the Assyrian Empire, and later, when Babylonia swallowed up Assyria, Samaria became automatically part of the Babylonian Empire. Thus Samaria had come under the ' civilising ' influence of great powers a century and a half earlier than Judah. The boundary between Samaria and Judah in the time of Nebuchadrezzar was not the boundary between two petty states, but simply the western boundary of the Empire. When Judah was first annexed, there could be no question of giving it any important status, certainly not a higher status than that of Samaria. When Jerusalem fell the upper classes of the Jews were mostly deported to Babylonia, so that there would have been no reason to make Judah into a province. Right up to the time of Nehemiah (445 B.C.) Judah seems to have been administered as an annexe to the Province of Samaria. The name of ' Judah ' as the official name of a Province first appears on jug handles about 400 B.C., and soon afterwards on coins. (See ' Die Rolle Samarias bei der Entstehung des Judentums ' in Albrecht Alt's *Kleine Schriften* ii (1953).)

d Yet the incident of Jer. 41 shows that to many minds the religion of Judah and of Samaria was one and the same, and that Samaritans could look on Jerusalem as their mother church. This fact is not so surprising when we remember that many prophets had worked in both kingdoms, and that Jeremiah had longed for the return of Israel from Exile. The contrary view, that the Samaritans were deliberate heretics and schismatics, simply results from the fact that nearly all the surviving literature is Judaean, and reflects the later political animosity.

e We read in Jer. 52:31ff. that, after the death of Nebuchadrezzar, his son and successor Evil-Merodach released Jehoiachin from prison. There is no indication that this made any difference to the other exiled Jews. In any case, they were free men, whose only disability was that they could not get passports for Palestine. Soon afterwards Babylonia suffered two revolutions in quick succession, signs of discontent in the Empire. Nabonidus, who came to the throne in 555 B.C. as the last Babylonian king, spent about half of his reign of seventeen years at Têma in NW. Arabia. He may have chosen this desert oasis as a centre for trade, or merely as a place where he would be personally safer from assassination. For a short time he allied himself with Cyrus. But Cyrus rose to power so rapidly that Nabonidus was obliged to join in a defensive alliance with Croesus of Lydia and Amasis 99e
of Egypt in a vain attempt to stay the inevitable advance (see Oesterley and Robinson, *History of Israel*, ii, 14–18).

This was all common knowledge, and it needed no f
second-sight or divine inspiration for the anonymous Jewish prophet to realise that **Cyrus** would conquer Babylonia. It was probably about 540 B.C., some two years before Cyrus took Babylon, that this prophet addressed himself to his fellow Jews with a twofold message (1) that they should seize the coming opportunity to return to Jerusalem, and (2) that they should proclaim the greatness of Yahweh as seen in these events, and thus bring the other nations of the world to a knowledge of the one true holy God. The writings of this prophet are found in Isa. 40–55 (except 49:14–50:3) and perhaps 65–6, and he is therefore referred to as Second Isaiah. His twofold message shows that he was in the general stream of Jewish nationalistic tradition, and also in the true succession of Isaiah and Amos that looked on Yahweh as the God of the whole earth. His nationalism is tempered by the fact that he calls upon the restored nation to be the evangelist of the world to bring the light of Yahweh to the nations in darkness. Furthermore, the situation of the Jews of his day, as exiles in an idolatrous land, enabled him to see for the first time in history the part that might be played by self-sacrificing service and suffering.

Second Isaiah was writing at the time which is g
generally called the end of the Exile. This is not an inappropriate designation, for when Cyrus entered Babylon the status of the Jews there was immediately altered from that of exiles to that of foreign residents. Physically the difference was negligible, for few took immediate advantage of the new liberty, but mentally there was all the difference in the world : the Exile was over.

What, then, can we learn from Second Isaiah about h
the result on the thoughts and character of the Jews of their half-century's exile? Perhaps the most important fact is that, while Isaiah of Jerusalem had staggered his contemporaries by the boldness of his claim that Yahweh was the holy God whose glory filled the whole earth, Second Isaiah could speak of it as an accepted fact. It needed no proof, for every Jew knew it now. Similarly it is clear that the Jews needed no persuasion to abandon idols or to refrain from falling into idolatry. As far as Judaism was concerned, idolatry was only a memory of former generations. Second Isaiah's violent attacks on idolatry show no understanding of the mental attitude of those who worship idols, and would have been of no value as propaganda against their use. His purpose was to give the Jews a proper sense of value of their own spiritual religion compared with the childish absurdities of the heathen.

But when Second Isaiah turned to his new theme i
of the glory of self-sacrifice, as he wished to see it in the people of Israel acting as **Yahweh's Servant**, and especially when the exaltation of his conception forced him to leave prose behind and burst into poetry or song, we may be sure that he was soaring aloft into the heavens with no followers in his train.

This result is not merely what one might naturally j
have expected. It also tallies with all the evidence we have. Among his followers was Third Isaiah (Isa. 49:14–50:3 and 58–63:6) who wrote about 450 B.C. He knew Second Isaiah's work, and often reflected his language, but he was quite unable to accept the universalistic hope for the Gentiles. There were some voices raised, like the authors of Ruth and Jonah, to support the universalism of Second Isaiah, but they were lone voices in a wilderness of nationalism. The mass of the people, right up to the time of Christ, were nationalistic in their religious outlook. The few who thought of light proceeding from Israel to lighten the Gentiles were of great importance for the future, but must not be regarded as typical of the Judaism of any period before Christ.

100a With this proviso in mind, let us see what happened when Cyrus conquered Babylon and issued his edicts of liberty for captives of the former regime. The actual words of the Cylinder of Cyrus are : 'The gods, who dwelt in all parts, deserted their dwellings in anger because Nabunaid had carried them away to Babylon. Marduk went round to all the dwellings (i.e. the people) whose homes were laid low, and he allowed the people of Sumer and Akkad, who were like corpses, to turn . . . He permitted the return of all of the lands.' 'All gods, which I have returned to their towns, shall daily proclaim before Bel and Nebo the length of my days, and shall declare the word of my grace, and shall thus speak to Merodach my lord "Cyrus the king etc."' (quoted in *Early Judaism*, 43, from Schrader's *Keilinschriftliche Bibliothek*). Ezr. 1 has a story about a certain Sheshbazzar who is said to have brought back sacred vessels to Jerusalem, and to have laid the foundations of the **Temple**. So long as this chapter was read as meaning that a real beginning was made in work on the Temple site, and so long as it was linked with an account of the return of a caravan of eager patriotic Jews from exile, it had to be rejected, as it was plainly contradicted by Haggai. Haggai shows that returned exiles in his day were negligible, and that no work had been done on the Temple. But it is still possible, as Alt suggests (op. cit., 'Die Rolle', 334), that Sheshbazzar's mission was solely concerned with the return of the vessels, and that on arrival he had a purely formal ceremony of laying a foundation-stone. Such a ceremony would have sufficiently complied with the decree of Cyrus, and no-one would have expected it to be followed by any actual work on the site.

b It was not till eighteen years later, 520 B.C., that two vigorous leaders, Haggai and Zechariah, instigated 'the people of the land', i.e. Jewish residents and not returned exiles, to build the Temple, and did it in such a way as to stir up ill feeling between Jews and Samaritans by telling the latter that they had no rights in the city and Temple of Jerusalem. The Samaritans, who had made a quite genuine offer of assisting in the restoration of the Temple, in the spirit of those earlier Samaritans of whom we read in Jer. 41:5, were deeply hurt by their curt rejection by Zerubbabel the Governor and Jeshua the High Priest, who spoke in the name of all the heads of Judaean families (Ezr. 4:3). It has been suggested that in Isa. 63:7–64:12 we have the pathetic response of a truly religious Samaritan, who felt that by their rejection they had been excluded from serving their ancestral God Yahweh. Ezr. 4:4–5 and 5:3–6:14 shows the reaction of other Samaritans who stirred up trouble for the Jews by questioning their authority to build the Temple. The objection of course could not be upheld, and the work on the Temple was allowed to be completed.

c The rebuilding of the Temple, completed we may suppose about 515 B.C., served the useful purpose of providing the Jews once more with a religious centre around which they could rally. Gradually, no doubt, the existence of a temple would allow for something like a school of priests. Such a school would at least have preserved the ancient documents, not only the writings of the pre-exilic prophets and such historical works as Samuel and Kings, but also those documents which later came to be incorporated in the Torah or Pentateuch. But from the ignorance of the people about the Feast of Booths in the days of Ezra, more than a hundred years later, it would be unwise to assume any great study of the scriptures at this time, still less any work towards the completion of the Pentateuch. The building of the Temple was an expensive undertaking, and taxed the resources of Judah, as well as cutting them off from friendly relations with Samaria. Economically and socially it was disastrous, and it is not surprising that there was a long blank in the history for some sixty-five years. It does not seem likely to have been a period of any great events, or marked by any special characteristics,
and we know too little about it to feel inclined to **100**
attribute to it any of the undated pieces of OT literature.

Before we leave the story of the building of the **d**
Temple, we must say a word about Zerubbabel. He is of particular interest because he is the first actual person who was believed in his own days to fulfil the prophecies which are commonly called **Messianic**. Haggai and Zechariah both use language concerning him which is associated with the Messianic prophecies. In the broadest sense the Messianic hope was just a hope for a future time of great prosperity. That, no doubt, might quite reasonably have been looked for through the restoration of the Temple. Whenever there has been a central figure in a Messianic picture, he has almost always been a king of David's line. The claim to Davidic ancestry was certainly made for Zerubbabel at a later time, but it is not altogether certain that it was true. The most constant feature of the Messianic hope was that it would be accompanied by righteousness, both in the Messiah and in all the people. It is this element that is entirely lacking in the Zerubbabel story. He is not represented as a bad man, but he is not outstandingly righteous. The result for us is that we do not feel able to put Haggai and Zechariah on the same high moral level as the earlier prophets.

Let us now turn to the personal details told us of **e**
Zerubbabel. Haggai describes him as son of Shealtiel, and Governor of Judah, and this contemporary evidence cannot be altogether set aside. Zechariah does not specify his office. The list of returned exiles in Neh. 7:7 gives Zerubbabel as the leader of the first convoy, and the parallel list in Ezr. 2:2 adds that he was the son of Shealtiel. We have already seen that it is unlikely that Judah was a separate province till Nehemiah's time. If that is correct, Zerubbabel cannot have been Governor of the Province of Judah, but the word translated 'Governor' is somewhat vague, being even used at times for military captains, and he may have had some temporary authority given to him in connection with the convoy, or with the building of the Temple. Some such position of authority seems necessary to account for the way in which both Haggai and Zechariah speak of him as if he were the coming Messiah. The genealogy in 1 Chr. 3:19 would make Zerubbabel one of the royal Davidic line, which of course is not impossible, though Chronicles disagrees with Haggai in making Shealtiel the uncle instead of the father of Zerubbabel.

The next ray of light that is thrown on Jewish **101**
history is from Third Isaiah, whose writings are found in Isa. 49:14–50:3 and 58–63:6. This writer, as we have already seen, knew the work of Second Isaiah and frequently copied his language, but without rising to his universalistic heights. Third Isaiah's writings are easily distinguished from those of Second Isaiah by the different attitude towards the Gentiles, and by the frequent mention of the ruined state of Jerusalem, and the need to **restore its walls**. Not only do we find frequent reference to the ruins, and hopes of their restoration, but God is appealed to in most fervent terms not to forget them, and the prophet assures his hearers that God has the plan of the city engraved on his hands, and that the builders are hastening to the work. With this prophetic encouragement it seems that the people in Jerusalem actually began to repair the walls, and set up wooden gates ; for in Neh. 1:1–3 we read of the grief of Nehemiah when he learnt that the city gates had been burnt and that the walls were in ruins. The tenses of the verbs imply that the burning of the gates was recent, and that the walls were lying in ruins, either as they had been for many years, or as a result of recent interference.

Ezr. 4:7–23 gives an account of just such an event. **b**
The first part of the narrative is in a bad state of preservation, but it is pretty clear that it meant that a complaint was made by Samaritan officials that Jerusalem was being rebuilt, and would be a menace

1b to the peace of the Persian Empire. Incidentally we notice that a number of names of Samaritan officials are given as the authors of this complaint, and that in the later stories of Sanballat two or three other officials are mentioned by name as associated with him. Kraeling, in his edition of the Brooklyn Papyri (p. 33) says, 'An outstanding characteristic of Persian officialdom was that the presiding individual in every department of government had a group of "colleagues" who shared in the responsibility of decisions and actions. At the head of the chancery from which the satrap's orders were issued was an official called the "chancellor" or *b*^{e}*'ēl ṭ*^{e}*'ēm*. Among the letters published by Sachau was one by this official, on the authorisation of Arsham. Ezr. 4:9, where a man named Rehum, bearing the same title, sends a report to the king, is thus fully confirmed.' As a result of the complaint, the Samaritan officials were given authority to stop the work by force. If, as we suppose, Judah was being administered as part of the Province of Samaria, the narrative is perfectly feasible: it would be the normal procedure to allow the Governor of Samaria to put down what he thought was a threatened rising.

c That then was the position when **Nehemiah** came into the picture. Nehemiah heard the bad news that the attempt to repair the defences of Jerusalem had failed miserably. Very skilfully he proceeded with his plan to redress the damage. We must suppose that, when the Samaritan officials reported the threatened rising to headquarters, it was dealt with departmentally, not being regarded as of any serious importance, and that, although permission to stop the work went out in the name of the king, the king personally was not informed. Nehemiah guessed this might be the case, and so, with some trepidation, he put up a request to the king personally to allow him to restore the place of his ancestral tombs. This request did not go through the usual channels—if it had, the recent events would surely have been disclosed—but was made to the king by Nehemiah, in the course of his duties as a butler, on an informal occasion when the king was dining with his queen. The king suspected nothing, and gave the required permission, including grants of timber from the royal forests, and leave of absence for Nehemiah. At this stage of the narrative there is one curious omission: there is no mention of his appointment as Governor of Judah, although Neh. 5:14 says that he held that office from the twentieth year of Artaxerxes. It looks very much as if he said nothing on first arrival about the document conferring the appointment, and only announced it when his plans were laid. Then, when the work began, and Sanballat and his officials proceeded to interfere as on the previous occasion, Nehemiah disclosed the evidence that he was duly appointed as Governor of Judah, and dismissed them with the words, 'Ye have no portion, nor right, nor memorial, in Jerusalem' (Neh. 2:20).

d There is no need here to describe in detail the skill with which Nehemiah overcame all the plots of the Samaritans, and completed the defences of the city. With the ejection of the Samaritan Governor and his associates, and the successful completion of the walls, the Samaritans lost once and for all the leadership in Palestine, and Neh. 6:16 triumphantly records how they fell in the eyes of the surrounding peoples.

e It is probable that Nehemiah was the first Jewish Governor of Judah, Zerubbabel's position being rather doubtful as we have seen. There is no doubt that Nehemiah was an exceedingly capable man, and to him more than to anyone else was due the establishment of Judah as a distinct Province in the Persian Empire. He was interested in the enforcement of the law of the sabbath, because the sabbath was a distinguishing mark of the Jews, and his chief concern was to make Judah a purely Jewish province. It was for the same reason that he began the movement against mixed marriages, as we realise specially in the case of the marriage of the old High Priest's grandson with 101e
one of Sanballat's daughters, which might easily have enabled the Samaritans to gain control again in Jerusalem. These actions were all taken as part of his political programme to make Judah a nation conscious of itself, and as nearly as possible independent of outside control. Although Nehemiah conformed to the religion of his time, for instance in having a solemn dedication of the walls, he was not a priest, and shows no sign of being moved by purely religious motives. It is as the builder of the city and the restorer of homes that he is remembered in Sir. 49:13, 'Also of Nehemiah the memorial is great; who raised up for us the walls that were fallen, and set up the gates and bars, and raised up our homes again.'

The next series of historical events which have been 102a
preserved is connected with **Ezra**, the priest, the scribe of the law of the God of heaven. As will be seen in the Commentary (§§325*d–e*) this was an official title. It is shown there that he probably held a position at the Persian court which might be described as 'Commissary for Jewish Religious Affairs', and that in this capacity he was sent by Artaxerxes II to inquire into the circumstances which had provoked the High Priest Jehohanan to murder his own brother Jeshua in the Temple. It would appear that there was some feeling that this disgraceful affair would not have taken place if Bagohi, the Governor of Judah, had not interfered in the religion of the Jews by trying to make an appointment to the High-Priesthood. Nehemiah's appointment had been an exceptional one, and was not taken as a precedent that future Governors should be Jews. A foreigner could be expected to be more impartial, but, as in the case of Pilate, the value of impartiality could be outweighed by failure to understand the people, and evidently Bagohi was unaware how strongly the Jews would resent any foreign influence in the appointment of the High Priest.

Ezra's task was not to pass judgment on the High b
Priest for his crime, nor on the Governor for his unwarranted action which had been its occasion, but to set the religious affairs of the Jews in proper order, first so that there should not in future be clashes between the secular and the religious authorities, and secondly so that the religion should be properly regulated by law.

The law promulgated by Ezra, which formed the c
basis of the covenant which he made for the people, was that which is preserved for us in Deuteronomy (§§327*a–e*). There had been general neglect of the law, and the narrative indicates the general surprise and grief when it was publicly recited. Such neglect implicated all the priests, including the High Priest himself, for the people could not be blamed if they had not been instructed. Normally, of course, no-one could have overridden the High Priest, but the official position which we now know Ezra to have held gave him the king's authority to act. The tradition that Ezra had something to do with the Torah, for instance in 2 Esd. 14 that he wrote it all out afresh after it had been lost, is not without some underlying truth. After beginning by expounding the law as it then stood, he probably set on foot the work of addition and revision which resulted, within a generation at most, in the completion of the Pentateuch. If Ezra arrived about 400 B.C., and the Pentateuch was completed by 370, it would allow forty years for it to be generally accepted by Jews and Samaritans alike before the final schism about 330 B.C.

The religious interest of Ezra is shown quite clearly d
in the covenant and in his reforms. Even in his dealing with the mixed-marriage question, in which he followed in the steps of Nehemiah, the difference between these two leaders is clear. For Nehemiah it was primarily a political matter, especially the marriage that might have brought Samaritan influence into the High-Priestly family. Ezra was of course aware of the same danger, but to him the very act of mixed marriage was a pollution of the holy seed (Ezr. 9:2).

102d Nehemiah was the politician who dealt with actions which endangered the state of Israel as a nation. To Ezra it was a matter of principle to keep the blood of Israel free from the pollution of foreign blood, which to his mind was something like injecting the poison of heathenism and idolatry into the holy people. This is the type of religion which might be called an attempt to secure holiness by Act of Parliament, which is characteristic of Ezra, and of the later strands of the Pentateuch, and also of the book of Ezekiel.

e For the 4th cent. B.C. we have little direct information about the Jews. To form the framework for what information we have, we must look into the political events of neighbouring countries. Darius II had a stormy reign of twenty years (425–405 B.C.) during which there were rebellions in various parts including Egypt. It was in 410 B.C., during the unrest in the last years of his reign, that the temple of the Jewish garrison at **Elephantine** was destroyed by Egyptian priests. Information about this event comes from papyri found at Elephantine, or Yeb, an island in the Nile in Upper Egypt. It appears that, after the outrage, the Jews sent letters to Palestine asking that the temple might be rebuilt. They were not asking for money; nor could they have asked for permission, because that would rest with the Persian satrap in Egypt. All they wanted was that letters should be written to them from Palestinian authorities which they could show to the satrap to prove that theirs was genuine Jewish worship. The strange and surprising thing is the people to whom the letters were addressed: first they wrote one letter to Jehohanan (or John) the High Priest of Jerusalem and his associates, and another to the Governor of Judah, Bagohi (or Bagoas). Both of these men we have already met in connection with the murder in the Temple. Neither letter received a reply. We may conjecture that the authorities in Jerusalem could not approve of a temple elsewhere in which sacrifices were offered; or that they could not regard people as true Jews who associated other divine names with that of Yahweh; or merely that they could not be bothered, and were afraid of getting mixed up in politics at a time when Persia was having difficulties in Egypt.

f Two years later further letters were sent. One, as before, was sent to Bagohi; but this time they ignored the High Priest, and sent their other letter to Delaiah and Shelemiah, two brothers who were evidently acting as Governor of Samaria for their aged father Sanballat. Evidently to the Jews of Elephantine an authorisation from Samaria was as good as from Jerusalem, and they regarded the religions of the two as the same. The termination *-iah* of the two names shows at least that Sanballat, who gave such names to his sons, was a worshipper of Yahweh. A joint verbal reply was made by the two Governors, approving the rebuilding of the Temple, but only authorising meal offerings and incense. No mention was made of animal sacrifices. Similarly, another papyrus dated 419 B.C., apparently containing a message from the priests at Jerusalem, gave instructions for the feast of unleavened bread, with no mention of the Passover lamb.

g Thus these papyri, while giving us most valuable information bearing on Jewish and Samaritan relations, leave us with unanswered questions as to how the Deuteronomic law of the one sanctuary was regarded outside Palestine. As far as the future of the Jewish colony is concerned we are left in darkness, and have no knowledge how long it survived, and whether its temple was ever rebuilt.

103a When Artaxerxes II came to the throne in 404 B.C. he still held sway over Egypt, but lost all his authority there before 400 B.C. (Kraeling, op. cit., 31f. and 111f.). Artaxerxes II reigned till 358 B.C., and was never able to reconquer Egypt. He was succeeded as king of Persia by Artaxerxes III (Ochus), the most unscrupulous of all his sons, who got rid of more rightful claimants to the throne, and then, for greater security, massacred other members of the royal family.

Ochus's first attempt to reconquer Egypt was such a **10**
complete failure that there was a general revolt of Syria, Asia Minor, Cyprus, and Sidon. In revenge **Sidon** was subjected to such a terrible siege in 345/4 that the 40,000 inhabitants committed a mass suicide by setting the city on fire. From there Ochus went on in great strength and conquered Egypt in 342 B.C., subjecting its people to cruelty, and infuriating them by slaying the sacred bull at Memphis, and serving it up at a banquet to celebrate his victory.

It was probably between the fall of Sidon and the **b**
conquest of Egypt, in 344 or 343, that Ochus led away a portion of the Jews into **captivity to Hyrcania** near the Caspian Sea. The date given in the existing MSS of Jerome, who preserved this information, is ten years earlier than this; but it is almost impossible that Ochus would have concerned himself with Judah before he had settled with Sidon, and it is probable that a figure '10' has dropped out in transmission. It is generally believed that Judah must have joined in the general revolt to merit such a punishment. 'A portion of the Jews' suggests a considerable number, either all the well-to-do people as Nebuchadrezzar had done, or some large proportion, say one-quarter, of the population of Jerusalem. Seventy years ago that brilliant, though erratic, scholar T. K. Cheyne, in his Bampton Lectures, *The Origin of the Psalter* (p. 53), wrote, 'It was the third of Israel's great captivities.' It seemed a wild judgment to base on a few sentences of rather late authorities, and no-one hitherto has paid much attention to it, but it has now come to the fore in connection with a new theory about the period which is considered below. The possibility must be considered that a really serious calamity befell the Jews at this time, and that it was only lost sight of because the greater disturbance of Alexander's invasion followed only ten or eleven years later, affecting the whole of western Asia, and obliterating both memories and written records.

Artaxerxes Ochus only lived four years after his **c**
barbarous triumphs over Sidon and Egypt. He was a good organiser of the Empire, and had an excellent vizier in Bagoas—the general whom Josephus confused with the earlier and much less important Governor of Judah in Ezra's time. But neither Ochus nor Bagoas could control personal intrigues, which kept growing underground. When finally Bagoas was faced with the prospect of being himself denounced and executed, he took the only alternative that he could think of, and assassinated his master the king, and most of the royal family, keeping only one son, Arses, to be a puppet king. When he found that Arses was unwilling to be a puppet, Bagoas liquidated him too, and put on the throne in 336 B.C. a certain Codomannus, who took the name of Darius III.

In the same year, 336 B.C., **Alexander the Great** **d**
ascended the throne of Macedonia on the death, by assassination, of his father Philip. Philip had reigned for twenty-three years, and all that time had been preparing the military machine that was to crush Persia.

Alexander wasted no time. Early in 334 B.C. he **e**
crossed the Dardanelles, and consolidated his position in western Asia Minor before marching eastwards to meet the Persian forces. The two armies met at Issus in October or November 333 B.C. Our eyes, as we try to reconstruct the scene, should be set, not on the battlefield, but on Egypt, Tyre and Sidon, Philistia, Samaria, Judah, and Edom. None of these loved Persia, and up till three years before they had wished for nothing better than to see Persia utterly defeated. Was not this the time for them all to revolt, while Darius III was fully occupied with the new invader? It seemed impossible that Alexander could win the battle: his forces were only one-tenth the number of those of Darius. Maybe there were rumours from Greece about the new kind of army that Philip had created. Whatever the cause may have been, these semi-independent nations waited, and, whatever their

3e doubts about the outcome of Issus may have been, we may be certain that they waited trembling. The best they could have hoped for would have been an indecisive engagement which would have left both sides much weaker.

f The news when it came was terrible and staggering. The defeat of the Persians was so complete that Darius could not escape fast enough in his chariot. He must needs alight from his chariot, throw away his shield, and flee on horseback. What did the nations do? They must have realised at once that Issus spelt the defeat, not of Persia alone, but of all western Asia. Sidon, inhabited now no doubt by a miserable remnant who had survived the mass suicide of eleven or twelve years before, surrendered to Alexander at once. So did some lesser seaports, and also Samaria. But Tyre, proud unbeaten Tyre whom Nebuchadrezzar had been unable to reduce in a thirteen years' siege, refused to surrender, probably relying more on her natural defences than on the bribe of ten thousand talents which Darius was offering as the price of peace at the moment when Alexander stood at the gates of Tyre. Gaza, farther afield, joined with Egypt in refusing submission. The Jews took a vacillating course. At first, proudly boasting that they could not break their oath of allegiance to Darius, they refused to send the supplies that Alexander demanded ; and then, shortly afterwards, the High Priest and all his company went out in procession from Jerusalem in their priestly robes, and made their abject surrender, which the Jewish historians glozed over by writing it up as a victory for Yahweh that Alexander should bow before the High Priest's breastplate. That, at any rate, is the story as Josephus records it. This surrender was evidently made in the nick of time. The fate of Tyre and of Egypt, who resisted to the end, was too terrible for words.

g One literary work, completed apparently just before the invasion, which includes the name of Jaddua, the High Priest of Alexander's time, was the **Book of Chronicles**. It was a rewriting of the history from Adam to Jaddua, in which the first part, up to David, and the last part, after Nehemiah and Ezra, are only represented by lists of names. Among the names of the heads of fathers' houses, presumably in the compiler's days, is a certain **Ezekiel**, spelt in our English versions as Jehezkel, but in Hebrew the same name as that of Ezekiel the son of Buzi, the author of the great prophetic book. As long ago as 1832 Leopold Zunz noticed that Ezek. 26–8, which speak of the imminent fall of Tyre, must refer to the event of 332 B.C., and not to the unsuccessful siege by Nebuchadrezzar. The present author has suggested that the whole book, or at any rate 1–39, is of the same date, and that the dates given as so many years after Jehoiachin's captivity are a simple code, used for security reasons, indicating the corresponding number of years after the captivity to Hyrcania. [For a different view of the book of Ezekiel, cf. §§494*b–d*.—H.H.R.] Thus, beginning his book less than five years after the terrible catastrophe of Hyrcania, with all its horror fresh in his mind, instead of writing 'In the fifth year of the captivity of Ochus', he substituted the name of Jehoiachin. A few years later Hyrcania and Ochus were almost forgotten, and the name to curse by was not 'Ochus' but 'Alexander'.

h It is from Josephus that we learn that the Samaritans offered their help to Alexander, and received in return permission to build a temple of their own on Mt Gerizim. It was this act which was the final act of schism between the Jews and the Samaritans. It was the logical conclusion (1) of the refusal of the Jews to allow the Samaritans to help build the Temple in 520 B.C., and (2) of the policy of mixed marriages pursued by Nehemiah and Ezra.

i It is well known that Ezekiel ardently wished for a union of Judah and northern Israel, and that he envisaged such a union being centred round a temple which was to be in the midst of the land. It is difficult to think that there was any time early in the Babylonian 103i Exile when such a union could have been practical politics. If, however, the theory that Ezekiel was contemporary with Alexander should prove possible, it would throw much light on his proposed union, for it was obvious that the only hope of resisting the invasion lay in the united efforts of all the western Asiatic powers. We should also have an explanation of the High Priest's sudden change of front. His first refusal to help Alexander would be due to pressure from the prophet, who held an oath in God's name to be inviolable, but, when he saw that Samaria had surrendered, and gained advantage thereby, he determined to ignore the prophet and to surrender to Alexander. It is difficult to imagine any other circumstances in which a prophet would have dared to denounce the High Priest and to demand his deposition in such words as we read in Ezek. 21:25, 'And you, O unhallowed wicked one, prince of Israel, whose day has come, the time of your final punishment, thus saith the Lord Yahweh : Remove the turban, and take off the crown.' The word translated 'turban' is used elsewhere in the OT eleven times in the Priestly Code in Exodus and Leviticus, and always of the High Priest's turban.

We must admit that the choice set before Jaddua j was a difficult one. It is true that he had sworn allegiance to Darius, but Darius was a fugitive. It is true that a nobler course would have been to join with Samaria and others in resisting the invader, but Samaria had already defaulted, so that there was now no hope of a united Israel and Judah. The High Priest, like all his contemporaries who had lived in the reign of Artaxerxes III, would have expected Alexander to be equally cruel in revenge on those who opposed him. The future facts he could not know were that Alexander was in fact a comparatively lenient conqueror, and that Darius III would be dead in less than three years. Would it have made his decision any easier to have known these facts? In any case, the blame for the final schism between Judah and Samaria cannot be put on one man or on one generation. It was due to failings on both sides, and it is certainly true in the lives of nations that the sins of fathers are visited on their children to the third and fourth generation. Any advantage that Samaria might have gained by its immediate adhesion to Alexander was soon lost. For, while he was in Egypt, the Samaritans ambushed and burnt alive the administrator Andromachus whom Alexander had left in charge of Palestine. To prevent a recurrence of such incidents, Alexander stationed a colony of Macedonians in Samaria (Abel, *Histoire de la Palestine*, 13).

A problem which has to be faced without much in 104a the way of direct evidence is the sort of literature that we might expect to find in any particular period. It would seem antecedently probable that, if any literature at all was produced in the midst of the upheaval of Alexander's invasion, it would be something exciting. It is as easy to expect a book of the apocalyptic type like Ezekiel at that time as it is to find Daniel in the Maccabaean crisis. What one would not expect would be a sober book of history, or sermons of the Deuteronomic type, or pithy proverbs, all of which are by their nature suited for peaceful days. It is rather hard to envisage the state of men's minds after the main crisis was over. As far as Judah was concerned, the crisis lasted at least till Jerusalem was taken by Ptolemy, and probably till he had taken possession of all Coele-Syria in 301 B.C. Is it likely that anyone between 333 and 301 B.C. would have had the peace of mind to sit down and edit Chronicles–Ezra–Nehemiah? One would think not. If that editing had been done after 300 B.C. it is inexplicable that the story is not carried on—at least in genealogies—beyond Jaddua. By trying thus to put oneself in the position of men who lived through those days, one is forced to believe that **Chronicles–Ezra–Nehemiah** was finished before Alexander's invasion.

104b The same sort of argument would apply to the last stages of completing the **Pentateuch**. The view has been expressed above that this work was done in the generation after Ezra, leaving, say, thirty or forty years for the completed book to be accepted by both Samaritans and Jews. Some critics disbelieve Josephus's story about the building of the Samaritan temple in the time of Alexander and the schism at that time between Jews and Samaritans. But even if the schism was considerably later it would not be possible to put the completion of the Pentateuch in the stormy years of the crisis; and later than 300 B.C. would bring it too near the time when the Greek translation was begun. The suggestion that the schism might have taken place earlier than Alexander's time is answered by Alt in his essay *Zur Geschichte der Grenze zwischen Judäa und Samaria* (*Kleine Schriften*, ii, 359). His main argument is that if the temple on Mt Gerizim had been built earlier, the Jews at Yeb would have appealed to the High Priest of Samaria as well as to the High Priest of Jerusalem and the Governors of Judah and Samaria.

c Seeing that the Samaritans accept the Law and not the Prophets, it seems most likely that early in the 3rd cent., when life had settled down peacefully under the Ptolemies, there was considerable literary activity consisting first of study of the Law (i.e. the Pentateuch) by the priests and scribes, and then the collection and copying of the Prophets. This study of the Scriptures by the learned would be followed later in the 3rd cent. by the rise of the synagogue and the teaching of the Law to the common people.

d There must have been a great difference between the outside influences impinging on the Jews in the Greek period and what had occurred before. During the two centuries of Persian rule the Jews had received nothing in thought or culture from their political masters. The first reason of course is that they did not want to. The whole tendency from the beginning of the Persian period was based on the belief that all religious truth was with the Jews. We know now that there was some truth of real religious value in Zoroastrianism, a religion based on a belief in one holy God. We know too that Darius I was the first king of all Persia to proclaim himself a worshipper of Zoroaster's God. But that tells us little of the type of religion and religious thought current in Iraq at the time. Herodotus visited Persia about Nehemiah's time, and has left us an account of the religion he found there. It was still the sort of polytheism from which Zoroaster had tried to deliver the Persians of his district (probably the extreme east) some four or five centuries earlier. It is just possible that some of the Jewish belief in angels, and even some picturesque details of Messianic imagery, may have been of popular Persian origin, but if so the borrowing was probably after Alexander's time.

e With the Greek invasion a new spirit entered Asia. What it was is hard to define, because the common Greeks were no more deep thinkers than the common Asiatics. But, even if the common Greek was not a philosopher, at any rate he held philosophy in respect. There were certain ideas called 'principles' which had to be reckoned with. The Asiatic dealt in things. Things needed adjectives to describe them, so that even Asiatics would talk of beautiful women or a true story. But they did not talk of truth or beauty in the abstract, with the result that, when the Greeks talked in terms of abstract principles, it was something unheard of in Asia before. Of all the abstract words that now began to be heard in Asiatic market-places and schools, the most frequent was 'wisdom'. They talked of men who were lovers of wisdom, or of the pursuit of wisdom as if it were the pursuit of hidden treasure. The Jew could only reply that wisdom was the revealed religion of God, and the pursuit of wisdom was obeying the commandments of God. It was not quite what the Greeks meant, for Greek philosophers were conscious of thinking out things for themselves, and the Jewish prophets were conscious of hearing the words of God. **10** There was some common ground, though the Greek was more intellectual, and the Jew more moral. The contact was useful, and issued in a new type of writing among the Jews called the **Wisdom Literature**. Another thing that was new to Asia was a new conception of organised civic life, in cities and in the state.

f At the end of our period, when we come out into the light of history, we find organised resistance in some Jewish religious circles to the whole European influence, not only to the idolatry, but to the dress and the games, and no doubt to the language. The inclusiveness of this resistance shows how strongly the Jews felt the pressure of the new ideas and practices. The attitude of Samaria was the opposite, for, with the settlement of Macedonians, Samaria became the centre for the dissemination of hellenism west of Jordan (Abel, op. cit., 14). It must have been within this period that the Jews began first to distinguish between religious and secular affairs. The OT laws, as they stand written in the Pentateuch, include matters relating to religious practice, belief, ritual, human morals, sanitary regulations, and food laws, without distinguishing between them. It was not at first obvious to the Jews that other customs and other civil laws might be as good as their own. It was only when they began to realise what was wrong with heathenism —the idolatry and the unworthy ideas of God—that they began the process of emancipating their religion from its nationalistic and local setting. An early stage of this process, probably about 200 B.C., is seen in the saying attributed to Antigonos of Socho in *Pirqe Aboth* 1:3, 'Be not like to slaves who serve the master with a view to receiving a present; but be like slaves who serve the master not with a view to receiving a present; and let the fear of heaven be upon you.' It was thus during the Greek period that some of the Jews were beginning to learn that what was worth fighting for was their revealed religion. This was just the first stage of the process which eventually led, in Christianity, to religion bursting all national boundaries.

g But before we turn to follow such trends of thought in the Maccabaean and later periods, we must glance at the external history of Judah. At the death of Alexander in 323 B.C., Ptolemy became the ruler of Egypt. At first, following the arrangement which had obtained under Persian rule, Palestine became part of the Aramaic-speaking province of Syria. But Ptolemy felt the need of Palestine, both for strategic reasons, and also on economic grounds, for instance for the supply of timber. He entered Jerusalem about 312 B.C., and became master of the whole of Palestine by 301. This remained in the hands of the Ptolemies of Egypt, except for occasional intervals, till 198 B.C. An author of the 2nd cent. B.C. tells us that Ptolemy's capture of Jerusalem was made possible by the foolish custom of the Jews of resting on the sabbath day. That may well be true, as it was 150 years later when some of the fanatical Maccabaean warriors allowed themselves to be cut down on the sabbath day rather than lift sword in self-defence. Such behaviour was a considerable extension of the emphasis on the sabbath by Third Isaiah in 450 B.C. (Isa. 56:4–6). We are also told that, when Ptolemy conquered Jerusalem and Palestine, enormous numbers of Jews were taken to Egypt as slaves, or went there voluntarily. Until recently it was agreed that the first mention of **synagogues** was in Egypt in the 3rd cent. B.C., where they were so successful that soon afterwards they were adopted in Palestine (see E. L. Sukenik, *Ancient Synagogues in Palestine and Greece* (1934), 1). It also seems likely that the translation of the OT into Greek, which began in Egypt in the 3rd cent., was connected with the rise of the synagogue. But in 1941 C. C. Torrey suggested that one of the ostraca found at Elath, and probably dating from the 6th cent. B.C. should be read as referring to a *bêth knîshāh* or 'synagogue' there. It is too early yet to say whether this meeting-house in Elath was a sporadic experiment, or a precursor of

104g the synagogues which were later found in every place of any size (BASOR 82 (1941), 11ff., 84 (1941), 4f.).

h At the same time that Ptolemy I became master of Egypt, his foremost general Seleucus gained Babylonia, and founded the Seleucid dynasty. It was one of this dynasty, Antiochus III, who made up his mind to conquer Coele-Syria. His first attack in 221 was a failure, but he made repeated efforts, and was finally successful in 198 B.C. He took Jerusalem in that year, and, in recognition of the Jewish assistance in driving out the Egyptians, gave specially generous terms to the Jews, including remission of certain taxes, the promise of grants for sacrifices, and remission of taxes on building-materials. But most important of all was the decree that those who were of the Jewish nation should be allowed to live under their own laws. These were not unlike the terms granted at the same time to other cities (Abel, op. cit., 90). But they 104h meant much more to the Jews than to any other nation, and they must be borne in mind when, in the reign of Antiochus IV, we come to the militant stage of the hellenising movement, which resulted in attempts to abolish the ancient Jewish law by force.

Bibliography—F. M. Abel, *Histoire de la Palestine* i (1952); Albrecht Alt, *Kleine Schriften zur Geschichte des Volkes Israel* ii (1953); L. E. Browne, *Early Judaism* (1920), *From Babylon to Bethlehem* (2nd ed. 1951), *Ezekiel and Alexander* (1952) ; A. Cowley, *Jewish Documents of the time of Ezra* (1919) ; E. G. Kraeling, *The Brooklyn Museum Aramaic Papyri* (1953) ; Oesterley and Robinson, *History of Israel* ii (1932) ; Sir Percy Sykes, *History of Persia* i (1921).

THE SOCIAL INSTITUTIONS OF ISRAEL

By M. BURROWS

105a **The Social Unit: Family, Clan, Tribe, and Nation**—The basic social unit of the Hebrews was the patriarchal family, which included not only a man with his wives and unmarried children but also his married sons and their wives and children, and also the slaves with their wives and children. Membership in the family therefore did not necessarily mean actual blood relationship. In fact, by drinking blood together or by mingling their own blood, as well as by other forms of covenant, men became brothers. An outsider could be taken into the family also as a ' sojourner ' or resident alien. The family was a religious as well as a social unit. The father acted as priest in the celebration of festivals and in offering sacrifice. All sacrifices and festivals, indeed, were originally affairs of the family.

Kinship ordinarily involved living together. Whether migrating from one place to another or remaining in a more or less permanent place of residence, the members of a family or a clan naturally pitched their tents or built their houses together. In settled life the population of a town might consist of a single family or at least be dominated by it. Thus the local unit of society assumed much of the importance of the family, though the fiction of kinship might be maintained for some time.

b With the disintegration of the old clan organisation went the tendency to form separate small families, each son as he married leaving his parents and establishing a home of his own. The religious function of the patriarch now devolved upon the head of the small family, as in the celebration of the Passover ; yet the annual sacrifice of the large family or clan at the home town was not at once abandoned (1 Sam. 20:6, 29).

In nomadic and semi-nomadic life families and clans were grouped together in tribes, each tribe consisting of the families that migrated and fought together. Living and acting together led to intermarriage, more or less complete fusion, and the assumption of a common descent. The problem of the ethnic and geographical origins of the Hebrew tribes is much too complicated to be treated here. The OT genealogies represent the tribes as expanded families, each descended from a definite ancestor, but the inclusion of geographical terms in the genealogies is enough to show that the actual development was by no means so simple. The varying lists of tribes reflect their uneven fortunes, some growing large and powerful while others sank into a minor status or disappeared.

c The unity of a nomadic tribe often finds expression in a **tribal shrine,** to which the members of the tribe make pilgrimage for their festivals, and beside which they bury their dead. Some of Israel's sacred places were probably tribal sanctuaries before they were adopted by the nation as a whole ; indeed, common use of the same shrine was probably a major factor in the formation of tribal federations. The grouping of tribes indicated by the story of the birth of Jacob's sons (Gen. 29f., 35:16–18) apparently represents their geographical relations, but it may also reflect in part a process of federation among groups of tribes (the sons of Leah, Rachel, Zilpah, and Bilhah respectively). The grouping of twelve tribes as one people, the sons of Israel, is evidently artificial, because the lists of the tribes differ even while maintaining the conventional number. 10 How many tribes were actually united in the Mosaic covenant of Sinai or Kadesh-Barnea is uncertain. There may well have been a previous federation of six or nine tribes with its centre at Shechem. The renewal of the covenant by Joshua (Jos. 24) may reflect a union of this federation with the tribes from the desert who had participated in the covenant of Sinai. Among the motives animating the successive stages of federation, the acceptance of the same deity by several tribes must have played a part. Ultimately the people, the God, and the land were so closely associated as to be practically inseparable (Ru. 1:14ff. ; 1 Sam. 26:19f.).

With the formation of the nation and the growing power of the monarchy, the tribal unit lost all but a traditional, conventional, or eschatological significance. The clan and large patriarchal family had meanwhile broken up, but the smaller, immediate family remained the basic unit of Hebrew society.

Marriage and Family Life—In patriarchal society 10 marriage normally meant the acquisition by one family of a wife for one of its sons from another family. The wife thus became a member of her husband's family. She was not, however, the property of her husband or his family ; if he died, she might either remain in his family by marrying another member of it or return to her father's family. A form of marriage by which the husband entered his wife's family was known in Babylonia, but it was rarely if ever practised among the Hebrews. Jacob's relation to Laban's family was a special case in several respects. A man who was known by the name of his wife's family is mentioned (Ezr. 2:61 ; Neh. 7:63), and there is one instance of a man who, having no son, gave his daughter in marriage to his slave (1 Chr. 2:34f.) ; but these were obviously exceptional.

Preference was given to fairly close relatives ; there were limitations, however, on the degrees of relationship within which marriage was permitted. Marriage of cousins was apparently common. Instances of marriage with a half-sister are related without disapproval (Gen. 20:12 ; cf. also 2 Sam. 13:13), though there seems to have been some misgiving on this point later (Jubilees 4:14f.), and sexual relations between a son and daughter of the same father or mother are condemned as incest by the Holiness Code and Ezek. (Lev. 18:9, 11 ; Ezek. 22:11). Moses' mother was his father's paternal aunt (Exod. 6:20), but this relationship too is condemned by the Holiness Code (Lev. 20:19). A priest was required to marry ' a virgin of his own people ' (Lev. 21:7, 13–15), though Ezek. permits marriage with another priest's widow (Ezek. 44:22).

As a relationship between families rather than b individuals, marriage was ordinarily arranged by the parents of the young couple, though marriage for love was by no means unknown. A man might marry a woman taken captive in war (Dt. 21:10–14), but there is no indication that marriage by capture was ever a recognised practice among the Hebrews. The normal marriage was a matter of contract between the two families. A marriage gift, the *mohar* (cf. Arabic *mahr*), was presented by the bridegroom to his bride's father

106b (Gen. 34:12 ; Exod. 22:16f. ; 1 Sam. 18:25). Modern writers often call it the bride-price, but it was not a price paid for property ; it was the gift which sealed a contract (see §106*f* on the use of the verb 'buy' in Ru. 4:5, 10). The idea of compensation was involved to the extent that the giving up of a daughter to another family was a real loss. There is even some suggestion that the *mohar* might be regarded as compensating the father for the loss of his daughter ; there are also indications, however, that it was intended to be passed on to the bride to be her personal property. When Rachel and Leah tell Jacob that their father 'has been using up the money given for us' (literally 'has eaten our money', Gen. 31:15), the meaning, as shown by Babylonian parallels, is that Laban has appropriated the value of Jacob's labour for himself instead of giving it to his daughters.

The husband's authority over his wife was not that of the owner of property. She had rights, in which her father still took a personal interest (Gen. 31:50). Even a woman bought as a slave, who became the wife of her owner or his son, could not be sold again or mistreated but was allowed to go free if her husband failed to give her the full rights of a wife (Exod. 21:7–11). The rights of a captive of war taken in marriage by her captor were similarly guarded (Dt. 21:10–14).

c The wife's obligation to her husband of course included strict chastity. Adultery incurred the death of both the man and the woman (Lev. 20:10 ; Dt. 22:22). A wife suspected of premarital unchastity was stoned if her father could not produce her 'tokens of virginity' (Dt. 22:13–21). Since the decisive point in making the marriage contract was the betrothal, violation of a betrothed virgin was treated as adultery, though if it took place where no rescue was possible, only the man was put to death (Dt. 22:23–7). This penalty was not exacted if the woman was a slave, according to the Holiness Code ; the man was then required only to bring a guilt offering to the priest (Lev. 19:20–2). Seduction or rape of an unbetrothed virgin obligated the guilty man to marry her and give her father the customary *mohar* ; the father might, however, refuse to let him have her and still exact the equivalent of the *mohar* (Exod. 22:16f. ; Dt. 22:28f.).

d The husband's right of **divorce** is recognised but limited. Nothing is said of a wife's divorcing her husband. Dt. assumes that the man divorcing his wife 'has found some indecency in her', and that he gives her a bill of divorce (Dt. 24:1). Divorce is denied to a man who has falsely accused his wife of unchastity and to a man compelled to marry a girl he has violated (Dt. 22:19, 29). If a divorced woman marries another man, and he dies or divorces her, the first husband cannot marry her again (Dt. 24:1–4). Malachi 2:14–16 associates divorce with marital infidelity as a thing that God hates.

e The purpose of marriage is the continuation of the family. To give her husband a son is a wife's greatest pride ; barrenness is a grievous curse. Various devices for obtaining a son when the wife is barren are attested ; strangely enough, adoption is not one of them, although it was common among neighbouring peoples. A second wife or a concubine might of course provide a son if the first wife was barren. A barren wife might give her slave-girl to her husband to bear him a son (Gen. 16:1ff., 30:1–13). The unique instance of a man who gave his daughter to a slave to get an heir has already been mentioned (1 Chr. 2:34f.).

f The last resort, if a man died leaving no son to succeed him, was **levirate marriage** : the widow was taken by her brother-in-law (Latin *levir*), and their son was considered the son of the deceased husband. This was considered a binding obligation in very early times (Gen. 38). Dt. 25:5–10 subjects to public disgrace a man who refuses to perform this duty. When the inheritance of property and the support of the widow came to be associated with levirate 106f marriage, the institution of 'redemption' (§108*b*) might be combined with it, and a more distant relative might be held responsible for the widow and the property, as in the story of Ruth. Here the widow seems to be regarded as part of the estate, to be purchased with it, yet both are 'bought' from the elder widow, Naomi, and the purpose of the transaction is 'to restore the name of the dead to his inheritance' (Ru. 4:5, 10). In late times the levirate obligation apparently weakened ; the fact, however, that the Holiness Code condemns taking a brother's wife (Lev. 18:16, 20:21) does not imply the abrogation of levirate marriage.

Polygamy was commonly practised in ancient g Israel ; it is nowhere condemned in the OT. Many incidents reflect the domestic complications caused by it. For economic reasons, however, monogamy probably became the rule as time went by. Some passages in the OT presuppose it as normal. The story of the creation of Eve does not even suggest the possibility of having more than one wife ; the first man said to have taken two wives is Lamech (Gen. 4:19). Concubinage is recognised as a fact and nowhere condemned. A concubine's children might inherit property along with the wife's children.

In general the **position of woman** in Hebrew society was not as high as modern standards would require, or even as high as it was among some other ancient peoples. The husband was his wife's lord (*ba'al* ; not *'ādôn*, as a slave's owner was called) ; 'he shall rule over you', she was told (Gen. 3:16). An unmarried woman's vows could be annulled by her father, those of a married woman by her husband (Num. 30:3–15). Yet the wife's importance in home and community is eloquently attested by Prov. 31:10–31. Ruth and Naomi reflect the Hebrew ideals of womanhood. Deborah and Huldah illustrate the influence that could be exerted by women (Jg. 4f. ; 2 Kg. 22:14ff.), to say nothing of Jezebel and Athaliah. The property rights of women in Israel were more limited than in Babylonia, but many OT narratives presuppose the possession of property by women. While a widow did not ordinarily inherit her husband's property (§108*c*), the possibility of her holding his estate, at least as a trustee, appears in the case of Naomi and the incident related in 2 Kg. 8:1–6.

The mother's place in the family was very high. Father and mother are usually mentioned together in exhortations to respect and obey parents (Exod. 20:12 ; Dt. 5:16 ; Lev. 19:3). The father's authority, however, was supreme. He might sell his daughter or son into slavery (Exod. 21:7 ; Neh. 5:5). The extraordinary instances of Abraham (Gen. 22) and Jephthah (Jg. 11:29–40), however, do not imply that a father had the power of life and death over his children. The practice of sacrificing the first-born son may be reflected and by implication superseded in Gen. 22 (cf. Exod. 22:29, 34:20). In later times child-sacrifice was abhorred as a pagan rite (Lev. 18:21, 20:2–5 ; 2 Kg. 23:10 ; Jer. 32:35). Striking or cursing father or mother and even stubborn disobedience were capital crimes (Exod. 21:15, 17 ; Lev. 20:9 ; Dt. 21:18–21). The sages stressed not only respect and obedience but conduct reflecting credit upon one's parents (Prov. 10:1 ; 15:5, 20 ; 17:25 ; 19:26 ; 20:20 ; 23:24f. ; 28:24 ; 30:17).

Strict discipline was commended (Prov. 13:24 ; h 19:18 ; 22:6, 15 ; 23:13f. ; 29:15). The same Hebrew word (*mûsār*) means discipline, training, and instruction. Parental teaching is highly praised in the book of Prov. (1:8f., 6:20–2, 13:1, 23:22) ; in fact, the teaching of the sages themselves often takes the form of fatherly admonition (Prov. 2:1, 3:1, etc.). Religious instruction was given in the home : ceremonies were explained (Exod. 12:26f.), stories were told of what God had done for Israel (Dt. 4:9, 6:20–5 ; Ps. 44:1, 78:2–4, and the commandments were taught (Dt. 6:4–9, 32:46).

106h Other **teachers** also are mentioned (Ps. 119:99 ; Prov. 5:13). A prophet might gather disciples about him (Isa. 8:16), and the sages undoubtedly had followers to whom they gave oral teaching. The priests and Levites were held responsible for teaching the law to the people (Hos. 4:4–6). A public reading of the law every seven years at the feast of booths is enjoined by Dt. 31:9–13 ; on such occasions the Levites helped the people to understand the law's meaning (Neh. 8:7f.). Training for the priests and Levites themselves was doubtless acquired through apprenticeship, as it was by Samuel (1 Sam. 3). Instructors and pupils among the Levites are mentioned in 1 Chr. 25:8. Such an apprenticeship may have existed among the prophets also, but the existence of schools for prophets is a precarious inference from references to 'the sons of the prophets' (1 Kg. 20:35 ; 2 Kg. 2:3, 5, 7, 15 ; 4:38 ; 6:1 ; Am. 7:14).

i The degree and growth of **literacy** in ancient Israel cannot be determined. Much of the material in the OT was no doubt transmitted orally for generations. Written records and memoranda probably existed very early, but they were made by professional scribes. This is true also of the few inscriptions found in Palestine. Isa. 8:1 and Hab. 2:2, however, imply a widespread ability to read. The story of the young man who wrote the names of the officials of Succoth for Gideon (Jg. 8:14) has a similar implication for a surprisingly early time. Josephus mentions schools in the Greek period (Ant. XII, iv, 6). As Ben Sira testifies, however, learning was still a prerogative of the wealthy (Sir. 38:24–39:11). In the days of the Maccabees many people had copies of the sacred books (1 Mac. 1:57), and the library of the Qumrân community evinces an amazing amount of literary activity during that period.

107a **Economic Forms of Life**—When the Hebrews first appeared on the scene of history, they were a semi-nomadic people, tent-dwellers and keepers of sheep and goats. References to camels in this period may be anachronistic, though not necessarily. Wealth was counted in livestock and also in slaves, fine clothing, and even gold and silver jewelry (Gen. 13:2 ; 24:22, 35, 53 ; cf. Job 1:3 ; 42:10–12). Like the semi-nomads of our day, the Hebrews did a little farming (Gen. 26:12–14, 30:14, 37:7), but they did not yet buy or own land except for the burial of their dead (Gen. 23). Such was their life when they went down into Egypt and when they went out again (Gen. 46:33f., 47:1–6 ; Exod. 12:37f.). While wandering through the desert they probably stayed at some places long enough to sow and reap meagre crops of grain. Canaan was thought of at first as a land flowing with milk and honey, the products of cattle and bees, though its grapes also were admired (Num. 13:23, 27 ; Dt. 6:3). The tribes that remained on the eastern side of the Jordan chose that region because of its fitness for pastoral life (Num. 32:1–5). The nomad's dislike and distrust of settled farming life is reflected in the ancient tradition that Yahweh preferred Abel's firstlings of the flock to Cain's fruit of the ground (Gen. 4:3–5). This attitude survived centuries later in the austere ideals of the Rechabites (Jer. 35:8–10).

b In Canaan the Israelites came into contact and inevitable conflict with an old sedentary civilisation. Before the strong Canaanite cities they felt like grass-hoppers (Num. 13:28, 33 ; Dt. 9:1). They could not but admire and covet the solid houses, relatively abundant water, and rich produce of Canaan (Dt. 6:10–12, 8:7–9). During the protracted process of conquest and assimilation they gradually learned the arts and ways of the Canaanite farmers. Most of the laws in the Book of the Covenant presuppose an agricultural mode of life with permanent villages.

Harvest and vintage were now added to the birth of the young of flock and herd as occasions of rejoicing (Jg. 21:19–21 ; Isa. 16:10 ; Jer. 48:33). The fruit of the vine brought not only joy but also drunkenness and the sorrows it caused (Gen. 9:20ff. ; Isa. 5:11f.,
22 ; 28:1, 7 ; Hos. 4:11 ; Hab. 2:5 ; Prov. 20:1 ; **107**
31:4–7). Wine thus came to be associated with everything in Canaanite life that was contrary to Hebrew tradition ; Nazirites and Rechabites, the most zealous representatives of the old ideals, renounced all use of wine (Num. 6:1–4 ; Jg. 13:3–5 ; Jer. 35:8 ; Am. 2:12).

For the average Israelite it was all too easy to suppose that it was not Yahweh, the desert God, that gave the fruits of the earth, but the Canaanite deities of soil, weather, and fertility (Hos. 2:5, 8). The prophets, however, recognised that the products of the soil came from Yahweh, and that it was he who taught the farmer his skill (Jer. 31:12 ; Isa. 28:23–9). Israel was thus able to make the transition from a pastoral to an agricultural economy without losing her religion ; Yahwism was in fact broadened and enriched by the process.

With settled life came also the development of **c**
crafts and trades. Such domestic crafts as weaving and dyeing were of course practised in semi-nomadic life ; in the towns of Canaan they became the vocations of separate, skilled groups. Separate streets were devoted to particular crafts (Jer. 37:21 ; Neh. 3:8, 31f.). Even whole towns specialised in particular trades (1 Chr. 4:21, 23). The first Hebrew pottery is crude as compared with the fine Canaanite product, but more skill was developed as time went by. The OT refers often to the potter with his wheel (Isa. 29:16, 45:9, 64:8 ; Jer. 18:1–4). Working metals was known also before the settlement in Canaan. Tubal-cain is said to have made implements of bronze and even of iron (Gen. 4:22), and the Kenites (Cainites) were probably a tribe of wandering coppersmiths. The story of Bezalel, therefore, need not be anachronistic (Exod. 31:1–5). After the conquest, however, such crafts were no doubt more highly developed.

The Israelite conquest took place just as the Bronze Age was giving way to the Iron Age in Canaan. Exploration in the Arabah has shown that iron and copper were mined there (Dt. 8:9). The Philistines dominated Israel for a while by keeping the black-smith's trade in their own hands (1 Sam. 13:19–21). For the bronze implements of the Temple Solomon had to import a Phoenician craftsman (1 Kg. 7:13f.). In later years, however, the metal-working crafts were cultivated to such a degree that a thousand craftsmen and smiths were numbered among the captives taken to Babylon in 597 (2 Kg. 24:14, 16 ; cf. Jer. 24:1, 29:2). The building trades were of course learned by the Hebrews after the conquest, except for their unwilling apprenticeship in brickmaking in Egypt (Exod. 1:8–14, 5:5–19). The earliest Israelite masonry found in excavations is crude. Even David and Solomon had to get skilled Phoenicians to help build the palaces and Temple (2 Sam. 5:11 ; 1 Kg. 5:6–18). The workers who repaired the Temple under Jehoash and Josiah were presumably Hebrews (2 Kg. 12:11f., 22:5f.).

The division of labour involved in the growth of the crafts necessitated an increase of trading. Even at the pastoral stage there was some commerce. References to buying and selling in the patriarchal period, with silver as the medium of exchange (Gen. 23:16 ; 42:1f., 25–8), need involve no anachronism. An early form of attestation, taking off the sandal and giving it to the receiver of the property or right in question, is recalled in Ru. 4:7. A similar way of claiming ownership appears in Ps. 108:9. By the end of the 7th cent. B.C. written and witnessed deeds were used in real estate transactions (Jer. 32:9–15).

International trade was well developed in western **d**
Asia long before the Hebrews came into Canaan. Palestine is both a bridge between Asia and Africa and a crossroads, where the traffic between Asia and Africa crosses that between Arabia and the Mediterranean. The frequent passage of caravans is illustrated by the Midianites who bought Joseph (Gen. 37:28). Deborah recalls the cessation of such traffic in the

107d disorderly conditions following the Israelite invasion (Jg. 5:6).

Palestine's advantages as a centre of commerce do not include facilities for maritime trade. Aside from the fact that the Canaanites and Philistines allowed Israel no access to the Mediterranean for two centuries, Palestine has no natural harbour. The Hebrews were therefore dependent upon their relations with the Phoenicians for commerce by sea. Only at Ezion-geber on the Gulf of 'Aqaba did they have direct access to maritime commerce, and even here they needed Phoenician assistance (1 Kg. 9:26–8; 10:11, 22).

e David's conquests enabled Solomon to control the trade routes through Palestine and collect tolls from the caravans (1 Kg. 10:15). The wealth of southern Arabia and parts beyond came as imports (1 Kg. 10:10f., 14, 22, 25), and Solomon reaped a profit from the trade in horses and chariots between Egypt and Syria (vv. 28f.). The agricultural products of his kingdom provided exports, supplemented by the output of the copper mines in the Arabah and the smelting-plant at Ezion-geber. Traffic with the south by way of Ezion-geber evidently declined after the division of the kingdom. Jehoshaphat made an unsuccessful effort to revive it (1 Kg. 22:48f.). Judah later lost this territory but regained it under Azariah, who built Elath near the site of Ezion-geber (2 Kg. 14:22).

Commerce with Syria also became important, especially for the Northern Kingdom. Here as always commercial relations were strongly affected by political and military conditions. When the Aramaean kingdom of Damascus had the upper hand over Israel and was able to take several cities from Omri, it also demanded a concession to establish bazaars in Samaria; when Ahab defeated Benhadad and regained the captured cities, he secured a similar concession in Damascus (1 Kg. 20:34).

Judah, farther removed than Israel from Phoenicia and Syria, and better protected by her more rugged terrain, developed more slowly, but the commercial aspect of life became more and more prominent. In both kingdoms avarice begat dishonesty; weights and measures were falsified (Lev. 19:35f.; Dt. 25:13–16; Am. 8:5; Prov. 11:1; 16:11; 20:10, 23). The prophets did not condemn commercial activity or economic prosperity as such; their expectations for the future included not only security but abundance (Isa. 2:4, 32:18; Am. 9:13f.; Mic. 4:3f.). Jeremiah promised the resumption of transactions in real estate (Jer. 32:42–4). The prophets attacked only the concomitant evils of commercialism: selfish luxury, dishonesty, oppression of the poor, and indifference to the plight of the unfortunate (Isa. 3:14–17; Jer. 22:13f.; Am. 2:6–8, 4:1).

f During the later history of Israel and Judah wars and revolutions drained the resources of the rulers and brought much hardship upon the people. Commerce must have been affected as in the days of the Judges. When the Babylonians put an end to the Hebrew monarchy and carried the people into exile, only the poorest were left 'to be vinedressers and plowmen' (2 Kg. 24:14, 25:12). Jeremiah advised the exiles to settle down and to seek the welfare of Babylon (Jer. 29:4–7). On the whole they apparently did so. Some evidently prospered, and to do so they must have adapted themselves to Babylonian forms of business and commerce. When the Persians came, and the exiles were allowed to return to Palestine, relatively few took advantage of the opportunity. The restored community in Judah was poor and weak, harassed by drought, pests, and famine (Neh. 1:3; 4:2; 5:1–5; Jl 1:4, 9–12, 17–20; Hag. 1:6, 9–11; 2:16f.). The peasants brought their produce into the city for sale, as always, and Phoenician traders brought fish and other supplies (Neh. 13:15f.).

g Just as a nostalgia for the old pastoral life accompanied the transition to an agricultural economy, so a desire for the simple life of the farmer persisted after the growth of industry and trade. In fact, the life of trade never became more than a thin coating over the 107g agricultural order. The priestly legislators contemplated only the simplest forms of commercial dealing. Even in the Greek period the hope was expressed that in the coming days there would be no trader in the Lord's house (Zech. 14:21). Many Jews during that period, however, undoubtedly 'went down to the sea in ships, doing business on the great waters' (Ps. 107:23). Ben Sira points out the physical and moral hazards of the trader's life (Sir. 7:15, 26:29, 27:2, 43:24f.). Financial activity by Jews during the dominance of the Ptolemies in Palestine is attested by Egyptian papyri. The Maccabees secured freedom from foreign tribute and taxation, achieving a prosperity which continued into the Roman period but was destroyed then by misgovernment, popular revolt, and widespread lawlessness and brigandage.

Economic Institutions—On the pastoral stage of 108a social evolution everything except the most personal possessions of each member of the family belonged in effect to the whole family. To allow any member of the group to suffer want was unthinkable, unless the whole family, clan, or tribe became destitute through famine or some other general calamity. There was no class division, though differences in economic status appeared from the beginning. Aside from the family cemetery (Gen. 23), there was no ownership of land. Flocks and herds, of course, required water and pasturage, and questions of the right to use these inevitably arose. Abraham and Lot could not maintain their flocks in the same area (Gen. 13:1–12); disputes and agreements concerning wells marked the experiences of Abraham and Isaac at Gerar and Beersheba (Gen. 21:25–32; 26:15–23, 26–33). Normally many families shared more or less peaceably the use of the same wells (Gen. 24:10f., 29:1–10; Exod. 2:15–17).

In settled agricultural life also the situation was at first much the same. Even the land was the property of the family, if not of the whole tribe or village. The Book of the Covenant, however, already recognises individual ownership not only of livestock (Exod. 21:28–36; 22:1–4, 9–15; 23:4f.) but of fields and vineyards (22:5f.; 23:10f., 16, 19). Theoretically the land conquered from the Canaanites had been distributed by lot among the tribes and among the families within each tribe; the lists of allotments and boundaries in Jos. 13–19 probably give the actual possessions of the tribes a few centuries later.

Each family's portion was considered its inalienable b heritage. According to the Holiness Code the land belonged to God, and the Israelites were his tenants; any permanent sale of land was therefore forbidden. If a man became poor and sold a field, his next of kin was obliged to redeem it (Lev. 25:23–7; cf. Jer. 32:6f.). For cases where no kinsman-redeemer was available, and the seller did not regain sufficient prosperity to redeem his own property, the year of Jubilee was devised, though perhaps never put into practice: every fiftieth year was to be a year of liberty, when every man returned to his property and family (Lev. 25:8–17, 28; cf. Ezek. 46:16f.). Sales of land were thus in effect only leases for the number of years remaining until the next Jubilee. Apparently this was an artificial elaboration of the ancient custom by which fields, vineyards, and olive orchards were left fallow every seventh year (Exod. 23:10f.). Whatever may have been the original practice, the Holiness Code clearly intends that all the land shall lie fallow the same year (Lev. 25:1–7, 20–2).

All these regulations sought to preserve the economic c balance of the population and prevent the loss of any family's heritage. The **laws of inheritance** were directed to the same end. The eldest son succeeded his father in the control of the family's property. His was the father's chief blessing (Gen. 27:19, 35; 48:17f.) and the birthright (25:29–34), apparently a double share when there was a division of property (Dt. 21:15–17). The son of a barren wife's slave had the

108c same inheritance as the son of a wife (Gen. 21:10). Even an illegitimate son might share in the inheritance (Jg. 11:1f.). If there was no son, a slave might be his master's heir (Gen. 15:3) ; or levirate marriage might provide an heir (§106*f*). A custom attested at Nuzu, by which possession of the family idols proved an adopted son's right of inheritance, may be reflected in Rachel's theft of her father's idols (Gen. 31:30–5). Daughters might inherit if they had no brother, but they were then required to marry within the family to prevent the alienation of its property (Num. 27:1–11; 36). As we have seen (§106*g*), a widow might inherit her husband's property, at least as trustee for her son or for a possible son or grandson by levirate marriage.

d As economic inequalities developed, **borrowing** and indebtedness were inevitable. In the OT lending to a fellow Israelite is regarded as temporary aid to a brother in need, to be given ungrudgingly (Dt. 15:7f., 10 ; Ps. 112:5). An object of personal property might be taken as a pledge, but the creditor was forbidden to hold anything which the debtor needed (Exod. 22:26f. ; Dt. 24:6, 10–13, 17 ; Job 22:6 ; 24:3, 9 ; Ezek. 18:7, 12, 16 ; Am. 2:8). A friend might be asked to provide surety, but the sages warned against doing so (Prov. 6:1–5, 11:15, 20:16, 27:13 ; Sir. 8:13). Charging interest for loans was known but prohibited (Exod. 22:25 ; Lev. 25:35–7 ; Ps. 15:5 ; Prov. 28:8 ; Ezek. 18:8, 13, 17 ; 22:12) ; Dt., however, permits loans on interest to Gentiles (Dt. 23:19f.). Isa. 24:2 presupposes commercial lending. Dt. provides relief for debtors by demanding that 'Yahweh's release' be proclaimed every seventh year and all debts except those of non-Israelites be cancelled (Dt. 15:1–10). Clearly indebtedness was a serious social problem in ancient Israel. In the adverse conditions after the exile heavy taxes and exorbitant interest caused such hardship that Nehemiah found people mortgaging their property and selling their children to meet their debts. With characteristic vigour he corrected these evils (Neh. 5:1–13, 15).

e **Slavery** was a regular feature of Hebrew society. Joshua's treatment of the Gibeonites (Jos. 9) illustrates the fact that making slaves of defeated enemies is at least more humane than slaughtering them. Evidently the inhabitants of many Canaanite cities were enslaved (Jg. 1:28, 30, 33, 35). Dt., however, demands that they be completely annihilated ; only the people of more distant cities may be taken as slaves (Dt. 20:10–18). A captive woman whom her captor wishes to marry must be treated with respect (21:10–14). Foreign slaves might also be acquired by purchase ; they were then inherited like other property (Lev. 25:44–6), and their numbers were increased by those 'born in the house' (Gen. 14:14 *et passim*).

There were also Hebrew slaves, but they were sharply distinguished from foreign slaves. Stealing and selling a man of Israel was punished by death (Exod. 21:16 ; Dt. 24:7). The most common cause of Hebrew slavery seems to have been debt (Exod. 21:7 ; Lev. 25:39 ; 2 Kg. 4:1 ; Am. 2:6, 8:6). The Hebrew slave served for only six years ; he could then, if he wished, become a slave for life by the ceremony of the doorpost (Exod. 21:2–6). This law was modified by Dt. and the Holiness Code (Dt. 15:12–18 ; Lev. 25:39–43, 47–53 ; cf. Jer. 34:8–16). The law concerning a woman sold by her father assumes that she is to be the wife of her purchaser or his son ; her rights in either case are carefully guarded (Exod. 21:7–11).

f A slave was his master's property (Exod. 20:17 ; 21:21, 32 ; Dt. 5:21) ; the master's power over him, however, was limited. Extreme cruelty was punished (Exod. 21:20f., 26f.). Opportunity for slaves to rest was one of the purposes of the Sabbath (Exod. 20:10, 23:12 ; Dt. 5:14f.). Dt. forbids returning a runaway slave to his master (Dt. 23:15f.). Job recognises an obligation to treat his slaves well because he and they have the same Creator (Job 31:13–15). Slaves were probably as well treated among the Hebrews as anywhere. They were incorporated into the holy people **10** by circumcision (Gen. 17:13, 27) and took part in the festivals (Exod. 12:44 ; Dt. 12:12, 18 ; 16:11–14 ; 29:10f.). A slave might even become his master's heir (Gen. 15:2f.). A priest's slave could partake of the holy food (Lev. 22:11). Yet the slave's freedom from his master is one of the compensations of Sheol (Job 3:19).

The existence of slavery prevented the development of an independent, prosperous wage-earning class. Service for wages was always possible (Gen. 29:15, 30:28, 31:7f. ; Jg. 17:10), but it seems to have been incidental and occasional. The **hired servant** did not partake of the Passover as a member of the household (Exod. 12:45). That his status was higher than that of a slave may be inferred from Lev. 25:39f. ; yet the hard service of the hired worker afforded a figure for human misery in general (Job 7:1f.). A slave's labour cost only half as much as that of a hired worker (Dt. 15:18). Employers had to be warned not to withhold or diminish the wages of their labourers (Lev. 19:13 ; Dt. 24:14f. ; Jer. 22:13 ; Mal. 3:5).

For the ancient Hebrew **wealth** was a blessing and **g**
a mark of divine favour (Gen. 24:1, 35 ; Dt. 8:18; 1 Chr. 29:12 ; Job 1:1–3, 42:10 ; Ps. 37:25, 112:1–3, 115:13f. ; Prov. 10:22, 22:4) ; poverty was an evil and a manifestation of divine displeasure (1 Sam. 2:36 ; Prov. 10:15 ; 19:4, 7). At the same time it was always recognised that some members of society were unfortunate and entitled to help. The temptation to deny a poor man justice is seen in Exod. 23:6. Dt., after promising that there will be no poor in Israel if the commandments are obeyed, continues, 'If there is among you a poor man, one of your brethren, . . .' and concludes, 'For the poor will never cease out of the land ; therefore I command you, You shall open wide your hand to your brother, to the needy and to the poor, in the land' (Dt. 15:4, 7, 11). Several ways of providing for the poor were developed. The land was left fallow every seventh year that the poor might eat (Exod. 23:11). When fields and orchards were harvested, something had to be left for the poor to glean (Lev. 19:9f., 23:22 ; Dt. 24:19–21 ; Ru. 2). Anyone was allowed to step into a vineyard and eat his fill, though not to carry grapes away in a vessel ; passing through a field he might gather grain in his hand, but not reap it with a sickle (Dt. 23:24f. ; cf. Mk 2:23).

Only in a simple peasant community could such means be adequate. Hebrew society did not remain so simple. Varying circumstances made some individuals and families more prosperous, while the fortunes of others declined. Unscrupulous men increased the inequality, even moving the ancient landmarks which delimited the possessions of families (Dt. 19:14, 27:17 ; Job 24:2 ; Prov. 22:28, 23:10). Large estates were accumulated, dispossessing the poor (Isa. 5:8 ; Mic. 2:2). Thus a wealthy class emerged and achieved a hereditary status, becoming almost a feudal nobility. The monarchy, with its court and military establishment, created also a nobility of power and privilege. Nobles appeared beside the elders of the cities (1 Kg. 21:8, 11). Economic differences could no longer be explained on the basis of moral and spiritual merits.

Wealth led to ostentation, luxury, and social **h**
indifference, which the prophets excoriated (Am. 4:1 ; 6:1, 4–6 ; Isa. 3:16–24 ; 32:11). Exploitation of the poor is denounced by prophets and sages alike (Am. 2:6, 5:11, 8:4–6 ; Isa. 3:14f., 10:2, 32:7 ; Ezek. 1812, 22:29 ; Job 20:19, 24:3–12 ; Prov. 14:31, 17:5, 22:22, 30:14, 31:9). Generosity to the poor will be rewarded (Prov. 11:24f., 19:17, 22:9, 28:27 ; Ec. 11:1 ; Ps. 41:1–3, 112:9) ; withholding aid brings calamity (Prov. 21:13, 28:27 ; Ezek. 16:49). Justice to the poor becomes a part of the eschatological hope (Isa. 11:4, 14:30, 29:19). God himself will come to their aid (Ps. 37:6, 49:5f., 72:12). So the old idea of wealth as a sign of divine favour and of poverty as a proof of disfavour was practically reversed. The fact

08h that both poverty and riches involve spiritual dangers was recognised (Prov. 30:9), but toward the end of OT times the rich so often collaborated with foreign oppressors, and those who were loyal to their traditions were so often impoverished, that ' poor ' and ' godly ' became almost synonymous (Ps. 72:2 ; Prov. 19:1, 28:11 ; cf. Am. 2:6, 8:6 ; Isa. 3:15). Thus the ground was laid for the attitudes toward wealth found in the Dead Sea Scrolls and the NT.

i Sympathy for all the **afflicted and helpless** is characteristic of the OT. Especially prominent are the fatherless and widows, mentioned sometimes with the poor, sometimes separately (Job 22:9, 29:12f. ; 31:16 ; Ps. 82:3f. ; Isa. 1:17 ; Jer. 5:28, 7:6, 22:3 ; Zech. 7:10 ; Mal. 3:5). The dissolution of the patriarchal family made their lot precarious. A widow might return to her father's family or remarry (§106*a*). Often, however, she was dependent on charity and an easy prey for the unscrupulous (Job 24:3, 21 ; Ps. 94:6 ; Isa. 1:23 ; 10:1f. ; Ezek. 22:7). The fatherless child was even more helpless (Job 6:27 ; 24:9 ; 31:17f., 21 ; Prov. 23:10). The fatherless and widows are given special assurance of God's protection (Dt. 10:18 ; Ps. 68:5, 146:9 ; Prov. 15:25 ; Jer. 49:11 ; Hos. 14:3). The Deuteronomic code in particular contains various provisions for their need (Dt. 14:29 ; 16:11; 14 ; 24:17–21 ; 26:12f.).

Often included with the poor, the fatherless, and widows are the Levites. They had no tribal territory (Num. 18:20 ; Dt. 10:9, 12:12, 14:27 ; Jos. 13:14, 14:3, 18:7). Forty-eight cities, including the six cities of refuge, were assigned to them to dwell in, according to Num. 35:1–8. A Levite might sell his house in one of these cities and redeem it at any time ; if not redeemed, it returned to him at the year of Jubilee. The common fields of the Levitical cities could not be sold at all (Lev. 25:32–4). Many Levites, however, did not live in such cities. With all the prerogatives assigned to them, it was still deemed necessary to commend them to the charity of their fellow citizens.

j Another group often mentioned along with the fatherless and the widows consisted of the resident aliens in the community, called 'sojourners', ' strangers', or ' guests ' (Heb. *gēr*, cf. Arabic *jār*). The Israelites were exhorted not only to respect the stranger's rights but to love him (Exod. 22:21, 23:9 ; Lev. 19:33f. ; Dt. 10:18f. ; Jer. 7:6, 22:3 ; Zech. 7:10 ; Mal. 3:5). Impartial justice in disputes with aliens was commanded (Dt. 1:16). The sojourner shared many privileges with the Hebrews : rest on the Sabbath (Exod. 20:10 ; Dt. 5:14), the right of gleaning (Lev. 19:9f., 23:22 ; Dt. 24:19–21), the tithe of the third year (Dt. 14:28f. ; 26:12), the joy of the festivals (Dt. 16:11, 14 ; 26:11). He was subject to cultic requirements (Lev. 17:8–16) and included in the atonement made for Israel when sin had involved the whole congregation (Num. 15:26). He was excluded, however, from the law of release for slaves (Lev. 25:45f.). Whether sojourners were included among the foreigners to whom loans with interest might be made (Dt. 15:1–3, 23:20) is not clear. Ezekiel declares that after the exile resident aliens shall have an inheritance ' as native-born sons of Israel ' (Ezek. 47:21–3).

09a **Law and Government, Tribal and Local**—Behind law lies custom. One of the most deeply rooted customs among many peoples is **blood revenge.** A savage lust for revenge is expressed in the song of Lamech (Gen. 4:23f.). The Hebrews had primitive superstitions concerning bloodshed (Gen. 4:10–12 ; Num. 35:33 ; Dt. 19:10 ; Job 16:18). They also believed it was a fundamental divine law that if a man shed human blood, his blood should be shed by man (Gen. 9:6). The person responsible for avenging a man's death was his nearest male relative. The noun used for this ' redeemer ' (*gō'ēl*) was the one used for the redeemer of property (§108*b*) and applied later to Yahweh himself as Israel's Redeemer. Blood revenge was a concern of the family, a matter of restoring its honour and relative strength. It led, however, to continuing 109a
feuds between families and tribes. The need for some limitation must have been felt very early. The right of asylum at the sanctuary (§109*e*) undoubtedly rested on ancient custom. The *lex talionis*, ' eye for eye, tooth for tooth ', was applied also to bodily injuries and damages to property (Exod. 21:23–5 ; Dt. 19:21) ; here too it was a curb on unlimited retaliation. How far such elaborations took place on the plane of custom, however, is uncertain.

Another area in which the unwritten law was clear b
and strong was **hospitality.** Examples of the inviolability of the guest and the courtesy he could expect appear in early narratives (Gen. 18:1–8, 24:15–33 ; Exod. 2:15–21). Violations of hospitality were regarded with horror (Gen. 19:1–11 ; Jg. 19), though less so if committed against an enemy of the nation (Jg. 4:17–22, 5:24–7). The concern for the sojourner noted above was a development of the obligation of hospitality (Job 31:32). In other ways also social life was regulated by custom before the emergence of formal government. The making of **covenants** is a significant example because of its application to the bond between Yahweh and Israel. Many covenants between individuals are mentioned in the OT (e.g. Gen. 21:25–32, 26:26–31, 31:43–54 ; 1 Sam. 18:3).

Custom was supported by public opinion, which c
was usually adequate, but disputes requiring **adjudication** arose, and recalcitrant individuals needed a stronger authority. In the patriarchal family the father's authority was sufficient. In the tribe a council of the heads of families, the elders of the tribe, was needed (Jg. 11:5 ; 1 Sam. 30:26 ; 2 Sam. 19:11). The leaders, commanders, marshals, and princes mentioned in the song of Deborah (Jg. 5:2, 9, 14f.) may have included both the elders and younger men of exceptional prowess. In cases where the elders could not agree and in disputes between tribes the parties might consult a seer or the priest of a common sanctuary. This function was performed by Deborah and Samuel (Jg. 4:4f. ; 1 Sam. 7:15–17) ; it had been performed before them by Moses, who found it necessary to appoint as his assistants ' rulers of thousands, of hundreds, of fifties, and of tens ' (Exod. 18:13–26 ; cf. Num. 11:16f., 24–30).

Moses and Joshua held together the tribes that took part in the Exodus and the conquest. Thereafter each tribe went its own way, except when an emergency united them. Some if not all had separate sanctuaries, perhaps with their own tribal deities (Dt. 33:19 ; Jg. 18:29–31). Yahweh's shrine at Shiloh, however, was a rallying-point. Finally, by the process of federation already outlined (§105*b*), all the tribes were combined into one nation.

The transition to an agricultural economy involved d
dwelling together in villages, from which the farmers went out to their fields (Ru. 2:4). Common local interests developed, and local government became necessary. The elders of the city now largely took the place of the elders of the tribe (Dt. 21:1–9 ; Jg. 8:14, 16 ; Ru. 4:2 ; 1 Sam. 11:3). Both local and tribal elders retained some influence under the monarchy (1 Kg. 8:1, 20:7 ; 2 Kg. 23:1) ; during and after the exile they enjoyed high prestige (Ezr. 5:5, 9 ; 6:7, 14 ; Ezek. 8:1, 11 ; 14:1 ; 20:1, 3).

Religion played a part in the government of the e
community from early times. Priests were consulted in matters of ritual and conduct. In cases of theft or breach of trust the parties were required to ' come near to God ' (Exod. 22:7–9) ; whether this refers to the sacred lot or to an ordeal, as ancient analogies suggest, is uncertain. The sacred lot (Urim and Thummim) gave the priest's directions a divine authority (Exod. 28:30 ; Num. 27:21). The only clear case of the ordeal in the OT is the use of the ' water of bitterness ' (Num. 5:11–31).

The only codifications of law in Israel were apparently the religious codes embodied in the OT. Reproducing in large part what was already time-honoured

109e custom, they gave it the sanction of God's will. They also modified customs. Liability to blood revenge, for example, was limited to the murderer himself instead of his whole family (Gen. 9:5f. ; Dt. 24:16 ; 2 Kg. 14:5f.). Cities of refuge supplemented the sanctuary of the altar for those guilty of manslaughter, but not for murderers (Exod. 21:13f. ; Num. 35 ; Dt. 19:1–13 ; Jos. 20 ; 1 Kg. 1:50, 2:28). The *lex talionis* was softened by provisions for commutation or compensation (Exod. 21:22, 28ff. ; 22:1).

110a **Law and Government, National and International Relations**—In Canaan the invading Israelites encountered small city states with no strong central government. To cope with them the loose tribal federation of the Hebrews was fairly adequate. The Philistine threat, much more formidable, necessitated a stronger union. Saul came to power like one of the Judges and hardly differed from them (1 Sam. 11:1–7). Both strands in the dual tradition of the inauguration of the monarchy may embody truth : many in Israel no doubt believed a **king** was needed (1 Sam. 10:1, 20–4) ; others distrusted and feared the innovation (Jg. 8:23 ; 1 Sam. 8:4–22, 10:17–19, 12:12f.). Certainly the old spirit of independence did not die. Even after the glorious reigns of David and Solomon there was rebellion, and the most powerful kings trembled before Yahweh's prophets.

b The king's authority depended on popular acclamation and a covenant (1 Sam. 10:24 ; 11:15 ; 2 Sam. 5:3 ; 2 Kg. 11:12, 17). His position was made official by anointing (Jg. 9:8 ; 1 Sam. 10:1, 16:13 ; 2 Sam. 2:4, 5:3 ; 1 Kg. 1:39 ; 2 Kg. 9:6, 11:12) ; he was 'Yahweh's anointed' (1 Sam. 2:10 ; 24:6 ; 26:11 ; Ps. 2:2 ; 20:6 ; 89:20, 38, 51). At first Hebrew kingship, like the office of judge or prophet, was charismatic : the Spirit of Yahweh came upon Saul (1 Sam. 10:10, 11:6) and David (1 Sam. 16:13). We are not told that the Spirit came upon Solomon ; with him the kingship in Judah became hereditary. As Alt has shown (VT 1 (1951), 2–22), the charismatic principle survived in the Northern Kingdom : except for a few short-lived efforts to establish dynasties, the kingship passed by a series of revolutions from one family and tribe to another. In Judah the dynastic principle was established, and the covenant with David replaced the gift of the Spirit as the religious sanction of the king's authority (2 Sam. 7:8–16 ; Ps. 89:3f., 28, 34, 39 ; Isa. 55:3).

c Much has been written lately concerning divine kingship. The Hebrew king was God's son (2 Sam. 7:14 ; Ps. 2:7, 89:26f.), but only by adoption ; his sonship meant nothing essentially different from the divine choice and anointing. The prophets and lawgivers sternly reminded the kings that they were the servants of God and his people (Dt. 17:14–20 ; 1 Sam. 15:26 ; 2 Sam. 5:12, 12:7ff. ; 1 Kg. 18:17f. ; Jer. 22:15–17, 23:1f.).

The creation of an aristocracy by the appointment of royal officials has been mentioned above (§108*g*). Various army and court officers are referred to (2 Sam. 8:16–18 ; 20:23–6 ; 1 Chr. 27:29–31 ; 1 Kg. 4:1–6 ; 5:14, 16 ; 12:18 ; 2 Kg. 18:18, 37 ; 19:2 ; 22:3f. ; Isa. 3:3 ; 22:15–25). All this, of course, was a heavy burden on the people (1 Sam. 8:11–18). Solomon's organisation of districts to supply his household with food is recorded (1 Kg. 4:7–19, 22f., 27f.). The maintenance of the army and the building of fortifications and palaces, not to mention the Temple, increased the burden. When the treasuries of the palace and Temple were insufficient to pay tribute to foreign invaders, it had to be raised from the people (2 Kg. 15:20, 23:35). Solomon's exactions led to the division of the kingdom after his death (1 Kg. 12:1–16).

The king was expected, however, to maintain justice (1 Kg. 3:9 ; Ps. 72:1f. ; 82 ; Prov. 31:4f., 9 ; Isa. 11:1–5 ; 32:1 ; Ezek. 45:9). This was the common assumption of the ancient world. The city elders still had local jurisdiction ; Dt. speaks also of special magistrates, who with the priests constituted a court of appeal (Dt. 16:18, 17:8–13, 19:16–20, 21:2 ; cf. 1 Chr. 23:4, 26:29). According to the Chronicler, Jehoshaphat appointed judges in the cities of Judah and a court of appeal at Jerusalem (2 Chr. 19:4–11). The king himself, however, was always expected to be accessible to his people (2 Sam. 15:1–6 ; 1 Kg. 3:16–28; 2 Kg. 6:24–31, 8:1–6).

d Little information is given as to **court procedure.** When an accused person came to trial, his 'adversary' or 'accuser' (Heb. *śāṭān*) stood at his right hand (Ps. 109:6 (RSVn) ; Zech. 3:1 ; cf. Job 1:6–12, 2:1–6). Bribery and corruption were evidently common (Exod. 23:8 ; Dt. 16:19 ; Ps. 15:5 ; Prov. 15:27 ; 17:8, 23 ; 18:16 ; 21:14 ; Ec. 5:8 ; Isa. 1:23 ; 33:15 ; Ezek. 22:12 ; Am. 5:12 ; Mic. 3:11). False testimony also necessitated strict precautions, including the requirement of two witnesses (Exod. 20:16 ; Num. 35:30 ; Dt. 5:20, 17:6f., 19:15–21 ; Prov.19:5, 9.)

The early 'apodictic' laws prescribe death for many offences (Exod. 21:12, 15, 17 ; 22:19, etc.). The obscure priestly formula, 'that person shall be cut off from Israel' or 'from his people' (Gen. 17:14 ; Exod. 12:15, 31:14 ; Lev. 7:20 *et passim*) apparently implies death. For lesser offences stripes were inflicted (Dt. 25:1–3). Offenders and suspects were sometimes imprisoned (Lev. 24:12 ; Num. 15:34 ; 1 Kg. 22:27 ; 2 Chr. 16:10 ; Ps. 102:20, 107:16 ; Isa. 42:7, 49:9, 61:1 ; Jer. 37:15–21) ; confinement in the stocks is mentioned also (2 Chr. 16:10 ; Jer. 20:1f.). Dt. forbids humiliating punishments (25:3).

e No machinery for **legislation** is described in the OT. Custom, precedent, and royal decrees no doubt all played their part. Certain legal standards and forms were generally accepted throughout western Asia. Legislation of some kind is implied by Isaiah's reference to iniquitous decrees (Isa. 10:1). How far the religious codes were intended for the actual administration of justice cannot be determined. Dt.'s demand that the king copy the lawbook and study it (Dt. 17:18–20) was unrealistic, yet the conviction that Moses had proclaimed God's laws, and that the welfare of the nation depended on obeying them, was undoubtedly strong. That much at least may be inferred from the story of Josiah's reformation (2 Kg. 22f.). After the exile the priestly formulation of the laws became the constitution of the Jewish community (Neh. 8:1–8), administered by the high priest, subject to the Persian emperor and the governor appointed by him. After the Macedonian conquest the government of Palestine went through vicissitudes too complicated to be followed here.

f Hebrew history is full of **conflicts with other nations.** Every man of Israel was a warrior ; only the Levites were exempt from military service (Num. 2:33). The considerate provisions of Dt. 20:5–8 and 24:5 were probably never observed. Each tribe and town was expected to furnish its share of fighting-men (Jg. 5:23 ; 1 Kg. 22:36 ; Am. 5:3) ; a tribe not invited to take part in a campaign felt slighted (Jg. 8:1). Something like a standing army, however, appears already under Saul (1 Sam. 14:52 ; 17:55) ; David employed foreign mercenaries (2 Sam. 8:18 ; 15:18 ; 20:23 ; 23:8–39 ; 1 Kg. 1:38, 44). The ancient organisation of the host by thousands, hundreds, and fifties still appears in the divided monarchy (1 Sam. 8:12 ; 2 Kg. 1:9–14, 11:4 (RSV 'captains' for Heb. 'commanders of hundreds') ; Isa. 3:3).

War was by no means considered contrary to the will of God. He was 'a man of war' (Exod. 15:3), 'the Lord of hosts, the God of the armies of Israel' (1 Sam. 17:45). David, even as an outlaw, fought 'the battles of the Lord' (1 Sam. 25:28). War was 'sanctified' (Jl 3:9 (RSVn) ; it was directed by the sacred lot (1 Sam. 14:37 ; 23:2, 4 ; 28:6 ; 30:7f.). Its spoils were often 'devoted' to Yahweh and destroyed (Jos. 6:17–19, 21, 24 ; 7:10–26 ; 1 Sam. 15:1–23). Israelite warfare was fierce and cruel, though not always as unsparing as the prophets and historians thought it should have been (Dt. 2:34 ;

110f Jos. 10:40 ; 11:14 ; Jg. 2:1–3, 20–3 ; 3:1, 4 ; 1 Sam. 15:1–23; 1 Kg. 20:30–43; 2 Kg. 13:14–19). Extreme brutality was condemned (Am. 1:3, 11, 13 ; Hos. 1:4f.). Even the instruments of God's judgment would be punished if they exceeded their commission (Isa. 10:5–19). War remained the principal means used by Yahweh to punish both the enemies of Israel and his disobedient people themselves ; it would be the means of final judgment (Ezek. 38f. ; Jl 3:9–12 ; Ob. 18–21). The Hebrews knew well, however, the horrors of war and the blessings of peace, and some 110f
of the prophets promised a time of peace in the latter days (Isa. 2:2–4 ; 9:5, 7 ; 11:6–9 ; 32:17f. ; Mic. 4:1–4 ; cf. Ps. 46:9).

Bibliography—D. Jacobson, *The Social Background of the OT* (1942) ; A. S. Peake, *Brotherhood in the OT* (John Clifford Lectures for 1923) ; T. G. Soares, *The Social Institutions and Ideals of the Bible* (1915) ; R. de Vaux, *Les institutions de l'AT*, i (1958).

THE RELIGIOUS INSTITUTIONS OF ISRAEL

By S. H. HOOKE

111a Introductory—The Deuteronomic writer, after a considerable period of Israel's history had run its course, speaking with full knowledge of what that history had been, did not shrink from describing Israel (Dt. 14:2) as 'a peculiar people' unto Yahweh (*'am s*^{e}*ghullāh*) (AV). By the use of this epithet he implied that Irsael had from the beginning of its history belonged to God in a way which was unique, the result of the divine choice. The same writer could say, 'Did any people ever hear the voice of a god speaking out of the midst of the fire, as you have heard, and still live? Or has any god ever attempted to go and take a nation for himself from the midst of another nation?' (Dt. 4:33–4). History has answered these questions with an emphatic affirmation: 'He hath not dealt thus with any other nation' (Ps. 147:20). Hence, while the comparison of Israel's religious institutions with those of her neighbours may show borrowings and the working of external influences, yet always there will remain those unique elements which spring from the fact that the religious institutions of Israel were being used by God as a vehicle of revelation.

It is clear that the development of Israel's religious institutions must run parallel with the various stages of her growth into a nation. For the purpose of this study our subject will be treated under the following historical periods: (1) The Patriarchal Period, (2) Israel in the Wilderness, (3) The Tribal Period, embracing the conquest and settlement in Canaan, (4) The Monarchy, subdivided into (*a*) The United Monarchy, (*b*) The Divided Kingdoms, in which the institutions of Israel and Judah will be dealt with separately, (5) The Post-Exilic Period.

b (1) The Patriarchal Period—Our sources for this period consist of the saga cycles of Gen., supplemented by occasional references in the prophetic literature and the Pss. It is generally recognised that the saga material in Gen. has been worked over by various hands, and there is an increasing tendency to find in the final form of Gen. evidence of a single mind at work giving a unity of purpose to the book as a whole, but at the same time imposing here and there upon an earlier age the conceptions and outlook of a much later age.

c (a) The God of the Fathers—The Exod. tradition represents Yahweh as instructing Moses to tell his people in Egypt that the God who had revealed himself in the burning bush was the God of the fathers, the God of Abraham, Isaac, and Jacob (Exod. 3:6, 15). Nevertheless it is not easy to distinguish in the sagas of Gen. the precise nature of the object of the patriarchs' worship. In Jos. 24:2 Joshua is represented as telling the tribes assembled at Shechem that their ancestors in Mesopotamia had served 'other gods'. Various divine names occur in Gen. in connection with the movements of the patriarchs: El 'Elyon (14:22), El Ro'i (16:13), El Shaddai (17:1), El 'Olam (21:33), El Bethel (31:13), Paḥad Isaac (31:42), and 'Abir Jacob (49:24). In Gen. 35:2–4 Jacob is represented as collecting the 'strange gods' possessed by his family and burying them under a sacred tree in Shechem. We also hear of Rachel's theft of Laban's 1
'teraphim' (31:19). These various divine names are d
for the most part found in connection with cult actions or objects, such as altars, sacred trees, or standing stones. The concrete situation underlying these traditions is that the earliest Hebrew settlers, coming partly from an urban environment in Mesopotamia, and partly from a semi-nomad environment in Aramaean Paddan-Aram, found themselves confronted with the various Canaanite gods and their cults, established in various cult-centres such as Bethel, Shechem, and, according to Gen. 14, Jerusalem with its priest-king Melchizedek and its god 'Elyon. We cannot tell what was the nature of the 'other gods' which they brought with them. Albright thinks that El Shaddai was the original god of the immigrant Hebrews, a mountain god, to be identified with Hadad (FSAC, 186); he has also argued that the strange name Paḥad Isaac should not be rendered 'the Fear of Isaac', but 'the Kinsman of Isaac'
(FSAC, 189). From this he proceeds to argue, in e
agreement with Alt, that an important element in the patriarchal religion was the belief in a close relationship between a clan or family and its god. He also adopts Alt's view, based on the evidence of early Aramaic and Arabian inscriptions, that in the patriarchal narratives we have examples of individuals entering into relation by covenant with a particular god who continues to direct their lives. The editor who gave the book of Genesis its present form, in the belief that God's choice of Israel as his special people began with the call of Abraham, has recounted the various experiences of Abraham as the establishing of a personal relation between Yahweh and Abraham; for him the names El Shaddai, El 'Elyon, and El 'Olam, are, so to speak, modes of Yahweh. We have no means of knowing what these names represented to the Canaanites who worshipped at Bethel or Shechem, nor what face they presented to the patriarchs when they first came in contact with them in the course of their wanderings. The character of the God with whom they were brought into relationship by his own action is revealed (*a*) by covenant, and (*b*) by promise. A further characteristic may be described by the term 'exodus'. The most striking result of the divine action upon the lives of those affected by it is a calling out, an exodus, from the social and religious environment in which they are embedded. It is possible to obtain further light on the nature of the God of the patriarchs from the various actions and objects which may, for the purposes of our study, come under the general description of the cult.

(b) The Cult—Most of the religious institutions of 11
Israel can be found in germ in the experiences of the patriarchs. The first element of the cult which calls for consideration is the *b*^{e}*rîth*, the covenant. In Gen. 15 we have the account of the first establishing of a covenant between Yahweh and Abraham, and a description of the ritual which accompanied the making of the covenant. It is not necessary to suppose that the editor has projected into the past a form of

a covenant ritual belonging to a much later period Although a similar form is recorded in Jer. 34:18–19, there is evidence to show that this type of covenant ritual is very ancient and prior to Hebrew settlement in Canaan (ICC, *Genesis*, 281). Both parties to the covenant were supposed to pass between the severed portions of the slain victim, and to invoke upon themselves the fate of the victim in case of a breach of the covenant by either party. There is no need to doubt the possibility of such a ritual being current in Canaan in Abraham's time. The editor of the narrative has represented Yahweh as passing between the pieces of the victims in the symbolic form of a smoking oven and a flaming torch, thus binding himself to the fulfil-
b ment of the promise attached to the covenant. A later version of the covenant is found in Gen. 17 connected with the ritual of **circumcision,** an element in the religious institutions of Israel which, according to the tradition preserved in Jos. 5:2–9, was not introduced into Israel until after the entry into Canaan. The account in Gen. 17, commonly assigned to P, is probably to be regarded as a case of validation of an institution by giving it a patriarchal origin. On the other hand, the episode related in Exod. 4:24–6 suggests an earlier origin for the institution. It is difficult to say with any certainty when this very important element in the religious institutions of Israel was first adopted by the Hebrew people. There is no evidence for its existence among the Babylonians, and hence it is not likely to have been brought by Abraham into Canaan. E. Meyer has given evidence for its early existence among the Phoenicians (ZATW 29 (1909), 152), and it may therefore have been practised in Canaan also. According to the Hebrew tradition of their sojourn in Egypt, the tribes in Egypt were not circumcised and were despised by the Egyptians on that account. According to the law of the Passover in Exod. 12:43–8 (P), no uncircumcised male might keep the Passover, but there is no record of the Israelites being circumcised in order to keep the feast in Egypt. Hence, while it would be rash to assume that circumcision was not practised by the patriarchs, it seems more probable that it was first adopted by the Hebrew tribes after their entry into Canaan. It is generally recognised that some of the tribes which ultimately constituted the nation of Israel did not go down into Egypt, and the fragment of independent tradition in Gen. 34 connected with the Israelite conquest of Shechem may relate to the history of these tribes. If so, and if we do not relegate the narrative to the later conquest and settlement of Canaan by Israel, then it may suggest that circumcision was practised by the tribes which remained in Canaan during the period of the Egyptian bondage, and that those tribes which did go down into Egypt abandoned or lost the practice during their sojourn in Egypt. What may originally have been an initiation ritual ultimately developed, probably after the Exile, into a religious institution of the first importance, second only to the sabbath.

c The next element to be considered in the pattern of patriarchal religion is **sacrifice**. Both Abraham and Jacob are said to have offered sacrifices, Abraham at Mt Moriah (Gen. 22:1–13), and Jacob in connection with his covenant with Laban (Gen. 31:54). The narrative of the offering of Isaac, and the substitution of a ram for the human victim, raises the question of the institution of human sacrifice and its obstinate survival in Israel. Archaeology has given evidence for the existence of child sacrifice in Canaan before the Israelite occupation, and although the motive of the story is clearly to establish by a supreme test the nature of Abraham's faith and obedience, yet it is permissible to use it as evidence for the existence of human sacrifice in Canaan in the patriarchal period, and also as indicating one of the species of clean animal used for sacrifice. It has been suggested that since all the victims used in the covenant ritual of ch. 15 belong to the Levitical list of clean animals, the narrative must
be late. This, however, is an unnecessary conclusion, 112c
the Râs Shamra texts having proved that the technical terms found in the Levitical sacrificial regulations were already in use in Canaan prior to Hebrew settlement there, and that with one exception, namely asses, the same kind of victims were used for sacrifice. But more precise indications as to the practice of sacrifice in the patriarchal period are not to be found in Gen.

Closely associated with the institution of sacrifice is d
the use of **altars.** All the patriarchs are said to have built altars : Abraham at Bethel (Gen. 12:8), Hebron (Gen. 13:18), and Mt Moriah (Gen. 22:9) ; Isaac at Beersheba (Gen. 26:25) ; Jacob at Shechem (Gen. 33:20) and Bethel (Gen. 35:7). Only in the instance of the sacrifice at Mt Moriah is the altar said to have been used for sacrifice ; in all the other instances the altar is connected with an unspecified act of worship addressed to Yahweh, and the regular phrase is ' called on the name of Yahweh '. It is also noteworthy that all the altars are connected with the Canaanite sanctuaries already in existence when the immigrants entered the country. The commonly accepted interpretation of these recorded acts is that they represent an attempt on the part of the later editors of the patriarchal sagas to validate for Israel the use of the ancient Canaanite sanctuaries for its own cult. But it may also be urged that we have here a tradition of the way in which the newcomers adjusted themselves to the religious customs of the country. This is borne out by the fact that Abraham is said to have ' planted a tamarisk tree in Beersheba ' (Gen. 21:33), and erected an altar by the grove of sacred terebinths at Mamre (Gen. 13:18) ; while Jacob is said to have erected a *maṣṣēbhāh*, or sacred pillar, both at Bethel (Gen. 28:18) and at the place of his covenant with Laban (Gen. 31:45). To these instances may be added the mention of at least one sacred well, Beer-lahai-roi (Gen. 16:14). These all represent accommodation to Canaanite cult practices and ideas. The mention of Rachel's theft of Laban's teraphim (Gen. 31:19) may not be pressed as proof of the existence of household gods in the patriarchal circles, since it has been suggested that Rachel's action was intended to secure for her husband the right of inheritance from Laban (E. A. Speiser, ' Ethnic Movements in the Near East in the 2nd Millennium B.C.', AASOR 13 (1933), 44).

(2) Israel in the Wilderness—In considering the 113a
stage of development reached by Israel's religious institutions during the period covered by the sojourn in Egypt and the wilderness wanderings there are certain preliminary observations to be made. First, Israel at this point of its history is an ideal in the mind of the editors of the sagas, not a real entity. There is no nation yet, although the editors may speak of ' the whole congregation of the children of Israel ' (Exod. 12:2). The historical kernel embedded in the saga material relates only to those tribes and clans which left Canaan for Egypt in search of food during one of the periodic famines which afflicted Canaan. From the editorial point of view all that happened to these tribes from the time of Jacob's descent into Egypt up to the entry into Canaan was experienced by the twelve tribes. From the interpretative point of view all this is of great value for the pattern of revelation, but, from the historical point of view it has to be discounted if we are to arrive at any estimate of the real
state of ' Israel's ' religion during this period. It is b
very difficult, in the second place, to establish a continuity between the picture of patriarchal religion and the religion of Moses. For the editors of the material the continuity was the continuity of revelation, and of course they were right. The God who chose Israel in Abraham and called him to be the bearer of what Paul calls ' the covenants of promise ', was the same God who appeared to Moses in the burning bush and called him to be the instrument of redemption. But it is hard to find any continuity between the religion of Moses, when we have done

113b our best to disengage it from the form which the editors have given it, and the religion of Abraham or Jacob. It presents the appearance of a wholly new creation. Thirdly, we have to distinguish between the framework of religious institutions under which the new community brought into existence by Yahweh through the instrumentality of Moses was intended to live, and the actual behaviour of the members of this community. To call only one witness ; Ezekiel, who must have been familiar with the traditions of his people, tells them, 'But the house of Israel rebelled against me in the wilderness : they walked not in my statutes, and they rejected my judgments' (Ezek. 20:13). Hence, both here and in the subsequent stages of the religious development of Israel, we shall have to include under the category of the religious institutions of Israel, not only those which belong to what is sometimes misleadingly called the 'official' religion of Israel, but also those religious customs and practices which the prophets condemn ; these were, however, undoubtedly regarded as part of the religion of Yahweh by those who observed them.

c **(a) The Decalogue**—It is generally admitted that the narrative parts of Exod. 19–24 contain the tradition of an epiphany of Yahweh at Sinai, followed by a covenant ritual whereby the various tribes and clans whom Moses had brought out of Egypt or collected from the nomads of the Sinai peninsula were constituted the people of Yahweh, bound to him by the acceptance of the conditions contained in a prescribed standard of conduct which should accord with the revealed character of Yahweh. Such a code of conduct may rightly be regarded as the first and most important of the religious institutions of Israel. The question is whether the Decalogue, in either of its two forms, Exod. 20:3–17 and Dt. 5:7–21, is to be accepted as representing the original covenant conditions, concerning which the people say, 'All that the Lord hath commanded us we will do'. We have not space here to discuss the various answers which have been given to this question. It must suffice here to say that many scholars are today prepared to admit that the Decalogue of Exod. and Dt. in a shortened form may have been the original basis of the covenant at Sinai. But it must also be recognised that collections such as that contained in Exod. 34, sometimes called the 'ritual decalogue' ; that given in Dt. 27, which is a dodecalogue ; or the short list of conditions for entry into the sanctuary in Ps. 24, may represent codes or lists of ritual or ethical requirements belonging to various cult centres in Israel in the early stages of its history.

d **(b) The Cult**—The Pentateuch in its present form represents the whole nation of Israel with its twelve tribes as entering into the covenant with Yahweh at Sinai, receiving from Moses an ethical code of conduct, the Decalogue, a body of civil and ritual prescriptions, commonly called 'the Book of the Covenant', and instructions for the consecration of the priesthood, the making of a portable sanctuary with all its ritual vessels, and for the institution of an elaborate system of sacrifices and seasonal festivals. All this is represented as being actually carried out during the wilderness wanderings.

When, however, we examine the collection of material contained in Exod., Lev. and Num., and compare it with the later commentary on it in Dt., together with allusions and comments on the wilderness period in the prophets, the possibility of a much simpler order of things emerges.

e In the first place, with regard to the central elements of the cult, we find from Exod. 33:7–11 that what is known as 'the Tent of Meeting' (*'ōhel mō'ēdh*), was an ordinary tent which Moses had pitched outside the camp, probably his own tent. To this tent came those who wished to consult the sacred oracle (*bqš*) and to receive the responses delivered by Moses. The tent probably contained the sacred chest (*'ᵃrôn*), concerning whose making we have the older tradition preserved in Dt. 10:1–5. According to this tradition Moses himself made an ark of acacia wood and placed in 11
it the tablets containing the second version of the Ten Words, after the first had been broken.

With regard to sacrifices we have two well-known f
prophetic comments in Am. 5:25 and Jer. 7:22 which have been interpreted to mean that neither Amos nor Jeremiah accepted the sacrificial system practised in their time as having been divinely ordained or actually carried out during the wilderness period. With regard to seasonal festivals it is obvious that the three main festivals prescribed in Exod. 23 and 34 are agricultural feasts and could not have been celebrated in the wilderness, but we shall return to these later. Lastly, with regard to the institution of priesthood, although there must have been some kind of priesthood in the wilderness, the subsequent history shows that the development of the priesthood with its various orders and grades and rival families belongs to a much later period.

Hence we have to think of the picture of an elaborate sanctuary, priesthood, and sacrificial system, as the idealisation by post-exilic editors of the pattern of Israel's life under God in the wilderness. It may be compared to Ezekiel's vision of the ideal city, sanctuary, and priesthood of the future, the sight of which was to shame Israel into repentance. What actual elements of Mosaic religious organisation and practice were carried into Canaan is a question which may be more conveniently discussed in the next section of our enquiry.

(3) The Tribal Period—The period of Israel's history 11
which lies between the entry into Canaan and the founding of the monarchy confronts us with several difficult problems when we try to gather from the materials in Jos. and Jg. a clear picture of the pattern of religious development characteristic of that period. Much of the material is still saga. In spite of the fact that the compiler represents Israel from time to time as acting as a united nation of twelve tribes, it is clear from such ancient material as the song of Deborah that the consciousness of nationhood had not yet come to birth in Israel. Groups of tribes might take united military action when threatened by raids from the east, or by the danger of Canaanite ascendancy, and Noth's theory of an amphictyony of tribes with a central sanctuary at Shechem has much to commend it (M. Noth, *Das System der Zwölf Stämme Israels*, 45f.). But while the tribes were clearly conscious of a common ancestry, and could look back to the epiphany of Yahweh at Sinai, and further shared a common language, even if differences of dialect existed, tribal loyalties were more powerful than a sense of national unity. The sagas of Jg. are tribal traditions, and preserve the memory of the exploits of tribal heroes. Hence any account of the religious institutions of Israel during this period must reflect a state of things described by the Deuteronomic editor as a time when 'every man did that which was right in his own eyes'. It b
has been suggested (E. Voegelin, *Israel and Revelation*, 212) that this is a nostalgic *cri de cœur*, a wistful looking-back to a time when royal tyranny did not yet exist, but this interpretation of the statement is open to objection. It has been pointed out (E. Voegelin, op. cit. 213) that Israel did not do 'every man what was right in his own eyes' ; on the contrary, behind the tribal traditions collected in the book of Jg. lies the actual situation of a continual struggle to repel invaders from without, until in the end the additional pressure of Philistine invasion made the establishment of a monarchy inevitable. But from the religious point of view there was probably more truth in the statement. What to the Deuteronomic editors appeared as a series of apostasies, punishments, and recoveries, must, from the historical point of view, be regarded as a steady process of assimilation to Canaanite religious practices. The identification of Yahweh with Baal, denounced by Hosea, began in this period. It is, however, permissible to suppose that some knowledge of the essential character of Yahweh as mediated through

114b Moses survived through this period, just as we find Yahweh saying to Elijah in the dark period of the Omri dynasty, 'Yet I will leave seven thousand in Israel, all the knees that have not bowed to Baal, and every mouth that has not kissed him' (1 Kg. 19:18).

c The first element in the religion of Israel during the tribal period that calls for consideration is the **sanctuaries**. Professor Albright has said, 'The central religious institution of Israel after the Conquest was the system of twelve tribes grouped round a central shrine' (ARI, 102). Although classical parallels have been adduced for amphictyonic leagues of twelve tribes or cities, it is doubtful whether the organisation of Israel into twelve tribes belongs to a period earlier than the united monarchy. The tribal structure of Israel during the period of settlement was not so sharply defined and included names, such as Gilead, which never formed part of the classical twelve tribes. It is also probable that Judah lay outside the early circle of associated tribes. A similar uncertainty surrounds the question of the early Israelite central sanctuary. An early tradition attributes considerable importance to Gilgal as a religious centre: there the invading Israelites were circumcised, it was the first place where the Ark was installed, and there the first Passover after the entry into Canaan was celebrated. But side by side with Gilgal the Deuteronomic tradition assigns to Shechem a central place during the early stages of settlement. It has been remarked that there is no record in Jos. of any capture of Shechem; yet we find in Jos. 24 Shechem described as the scene of a covenant between Israel and Yahweh, and spoken of as 'the sanctuary of the Lord', with a pillar and a sacred terebinth. It is the place where the Dodecalogue was to be proclaimed (Dt. 11:29, 27:11f.), and in Jg. 9:4, 46 we hear of a temple of Baal-Berith, who is also called El-Berith. Hence Shechem may well have been a cult centre of Yahweh worship belonging to those tribes which had remained in Canaan when the descent into Egypt took place. Next we find another tradition, starting from Jos. 18:1, which places the tent of meeting, the priesthood, and presumably the Ark, in Shiloh. This strand of tradition reappears in Jg. 18:31, and 21:19, where we are told that there was an annual feast of Yahweh in Shiloh; it continues into 1 Sam. where the destruction of Shiloh by the Philistines and the capture of the Ark are described. One more place is mentioned in Jg. as the seat of the priesthood and the Ark, and as a place of assembly for

d Israel, namely Bethel (20:26–8). Closely connected with the problem of a central sanctuary is the question of the **Ark.** In Jos. and Jg. we hear of the Ark at Gilgal, Shiloh, Bethel, and by implication at Shechem; in 1 Sam. it is at Shiloh until the destruction of the sanctuary by the Philistines. Thereafter it is found for a short time at Beth-shemesh (1 Sam. 6:15), from which place it is carried to Kiriath-jearim, where it seems to have been outside what was reckoned as Israelite territory; that this was the case may be inferred from 1 Sam. 14:18 and 1 Sam. 7:2. E. Nielsen's suggestion (*Shechem*, 302) that a purely Canaanite coalition of cities, Gibeon, Chephirah, Beeroth, and Kiriath-jearim, continued an independent existence within the territory of Benjamin until the time of Saul and David, confirms this view. It seems to have remained there until David brought it to his new capital in Jerusalem. One more place must be mentioned, Nob, which is called in 1 Sam. 22:19 'the city of the priests'. According to the account in 1 Sam. (Eissfeldt's sources I and II: O. Eissfeldt, *Die Composition der Samuelisbücher*, 58), the ritual of 'inquiring of Yahweh' was carried on there, the showbread was laid out, and, in the case of Doeg, ritual purification was carried out there. These details would seem to imply the presence of the Ark at this sanctuary. Arnold's argument that 'ephod' has been substituted for 'ark' in the MT of 1 Sam. 22:18 is not entirely unworthy of consideration (W. R. Arnold, 'Ephod and Ark', *Harvard Theological Studies* iii, 124f.).

From these various traditions, possibly emanating 114e originally from the cult legends of the different sanctuaries concerned, it is permissible to infer that during the pre-monarchic period of Israelite occupation of Canaan, there were various religious centres which served as places of assembly on different occasions, and where the cult of Yahweh was carried on. But the question of the Ark raises a difficulty. When the traditions of Israel were worked over and brought into the form in which we have them now, the view that the ark which had been carried by Israel in the wilderness as the symbol of Yahweh's presence with his people was the same ark which appeared in all the accounts of its presence and fortunes at different centres, and was finally discovered by David and brought to its final resting-place in Jerusalem, had become the accepted belief. But this, the orthodox Jewish view, is open to question. It is highly probable that the various sanctuaries, not including the high-places, belonging to the different tribes or tribal groups, possessed their own sacred chests which were essential cult objects for the carrying out of divination by the sacred lot and other ritual purposes. It was probably the ark belonging to the central sanctuary at Shiloh which, after strange vicissitudes, was ultimately brought to Jerusalem by David, that became the depository of the wilderness traditions. Before we pass on to other elements of Israel's religious institutions during this period one point remains to be dealt with in connection with this central feature of sanctuary and ark. This is the question whether the local habitation of shrine and ark was a tent or a building. In 1 Sam. 2:22 we hear of 'the women who served at the entrance to the tent of meeting' in Shiloh. In 2 Sam. 7:6 Nathan is represented as giving David a message from Yahweh, when the project of building a temple was mooted, to the effect that Yahweh had never dwelt in anything but a tent since the Exodus; further, when David brought the Ark to Jerusalem, we are told that he placed it in the tent that he had pitched for it (2 Sam. 6:17). On the other hand there seem to be archaeological grounds for believing that the Israelites made use of the Canaanite temples for their own cultic purposes (S. A. Cook, *The Religion of Ancient Palestine in the Light of Archaeology*, 95).

There are other features of the religion of Israel f during the period of the Judges which call for mention. Von Rad has called attention to the interesting religious institution of the **Holy War** which he regards as specially characteristic of the period of the Israelite amphictyony (G. von Rad, *Studies in Deuteronomy*, 45f.). Such wars were distinguished from secular wars and were conducted under cultic auspices; the warriors were 'consecrated', allowed their hair to grow, and refrained from sexual intercourse. This special feature of Israel's religion continued under the monarchy, and the circle from which the book of Dt. emanated sought to revive it (cf. Dt. 20).

Although we have no specific evidence that the 115a **three agricultural feasts** prescribed in the Book of the Covenant were observed in Israel during the period of the Judges, it is probable that they were carried out. The 'feast of the Lord' mentioned in Jg. 21:19 as being held annually in Shiloh, at which the maidens came out to dance in the vineyards, may well have been the feast of Ingathering, the great autumn festival which later on became the Feast of Booths and the New Year festival of Israel. It is probably this feast which Amos has in mind when he speaks of the people as desiring the Day of the Lord (Am. 5:18). Another festival is mentioned in Jg. 9:27, also connected with the vintage, as being celebrated at Shechem. It is possible that this feast which was held in the temple of El Berith may have been the great Covenant Festival of the Yahweh amphictyony of which Shechem was the centre (G. von Rad, op. cit., 41).

The story of Jephthah's vow and the somewhat obscure reference to the fate of his daughter (Jg. 11:30,

115a 31, 39), may probably be taken as an indication of the existence of human sacrifice during this period as part of the cult of Yahweh.

b Another element of the cult whose existence in Canaan is attested by the prohibitions in the codes (Lev. 19:29; Dt. 23:17), is the *k^edhēshôth*, or **sacred prostitutes.** It is generally recognised that the sacred marriage was a central feature of the ritual pattern in those religions of the ancient Near East whose main concern was fertility, and the institution of sacred prostitution was the regular accompaniment of the sacred marriage. The story of Judah and Tamar in Gen. 38 shows the existence of this class of sacred persons in Canaan during the patriarchal period, and suggests a connection with a sheep-shearing festival. The allusion to ' the women that did service at the door of the tent of meeting (Exod. 38:8; 1 Sam. 2:22), has been interpreted, probably correctly, as referring to the same class of persons. The presence of such an element in the cult of Yahweh is an evidence of the extent to which the religion of Israel had been assimilated to the fertility cult of Canaan during the early stages of settlement. Hosea's denunciation of the practice (Hos. 4:14) shows that it was still common in the Northern Kingdom in the 8th cent.

c One of the most important elements in the religion of Israel, and one which exercised a decisive influence on its later development, was the institution of **prophecy.** It is not easy to determine how early this feature appears in Israel. The existence of such a class of sacred persons, attached to the temples, is well attested for the neighbouring countries at a date prior to the entry of Israel into Canaan. In the wilderness sagas we have the story of what appears to be an outbreak of the phenomenon of ecstatic prophecy (Num. 11:25), and Moses is represented as saying, ' Would God that all the Lord's people were prophets '. During the period with which we are dealing only one case of prophetic activity is recorded, namely that of Deborah, the prophetess, who was connected with the sacred palm-tree in the territory of the tribe of Ephraim; the children of Israel are said to have resorted to her ' for judgment ', and she was instrumental in stirring up the tribes of Zebulun and Naphtali under the leadership of Barak to throw off the yoke of Jabin, king of Hazor. But the person to whom Hebrew tradition assigned the establishment of the prophetic order as a recognised element in the religious life of Israel was Samuel. His career forms the bridge from the period of unregulated tribalism to the period of the monarchy. From the various traditions which have gathered round the figure of Samuel, three features emerge which throw light on the beginnings of prophecy in Israel.

d The first of these is the picture which is given of Samuel the seer (*rō'eh*) in one of the early traditions concerning the founding of the monarchy. In this narrative (1 Sam. 9–10:16) Samuel is represented as a local seer (the editor of the source inserts a gloss to say that the term *nābhî'*, ' prophet ', was not yet used to denote persons of this type), whose activities appear to have been restricted to a circle of villages round Ramah. He offered sacrifices at the local high-places, and for a small fee would give information about lost property. The second point concerns Samuel's relations to a class of persons who are described as *n^ebhî'îm*, and whose activities appear to have an ecstatic character. In the early narrative already referred to, these people are represented as going about the country ' prophesying ' to the accompaniment of musical instruments. In all probability they were doing what Deborah has been described as doing, inciting the people to resistance against the Philistine invaders. In the same connection it would appear that early tradition attributed to Samuel the organisation of these prophetic bands into guilds, residing at special centres, as we find them later in the Elijah and Elisha sagas (1 Sam. 19:18–24; 2 Kg. 2:3, 5; 6:1). The third point is that the relation of the prophets to the monarchy and to the policy of the state is already 11
prefigured in the activities of Samuel. We shall have more to say on this point in the next section, but the anti-monarchic attitude which we find in the 8th-cent. prophets, and the king-making and revolutionary activities which are characteristic of the prophets of the 9th cent., are both found in the traditions gathered round the figure of Samuel. It is noteworthy that, although in the early traditions about Samuel he is connected with the sanctuary at Shiloh, and is seen performing priestly functions at Ramah, yet he is never represented as having any connection with the priesthood during Saul's reign.

e The last point to be mentioned in connection with the state of religion and the cult during the tribal period arises out of the story of Micah, and belongs to the Danite tribal traditions. The two features of this story which are relevant to our subject are, first, the evidence which the story affords that during the early period of Israelite settlement in Canaan **graven and molten images** (Jg. 17:3–5) could be used in the cult of Yahweh, though it would be going beyond the evidence to say that Micah's images were images of Yahweh. The second feature concerns the **history of the priesthood.** First of all Micah ' consecrates ' one of his sons to be the priest of this family shrine of Yahweh; then a wandering Levite who is said to belong to the ' clan ' of Judah, and later on (Jg. 18:30) said to be the grandson of Moses, is engaged by Micah to be his family priest. The images and the Levite are subsequently carried off by a band of Danites seeking a place to settle in, and according to Danite tradition continue to be a Danite cult centre until the captivity.

11 **(4) Monarchy (*a*) The United Monarchy**—The most important and far-reaching change in the religious institutions of Israel during this period was, of course, the introduction of kingship. It is not necessary to offer evidence here for the established fact that everywhere in the ancient Near East kingship had a religious character. In Egypt the king had been a god from the earliest times; in the city states of Mesopotamia, while deification of kings was sporadic, yet from a very early date the ruler of the state was a sacral person and exercised important functions in the religious life of the state. At the time of Israelite settlement in Canaan, the city states of Canaan were ruled by kings whose sacral character is now clearly established by the evidence of the Râs Shamra texts (J. Gray, ' Canaanite Kingship in Theory and Practice ', *VT* 2 (1952), 193–220). But while the form which kingship took in Israel was to some extent influenced by the pattern of Canaanite kingship, yet the fact that the Kingship of Yahweh always remained an essential element in the religion of Israel caused the institution of kingship to develop a distinctive character in Israel which differentiated it from the general pattern of sacral kingship in Canaan and the ancient Near East. It must also be recognised that after the great schism, kingship in northern Israel developed along different lines from its development in Judah. There is not space here to describe the history of kingship in Israel in detail, so that we can only outline briefly its main characteristics.

b The war-leaders and deliverers of whom we have the records in the book of Jg. were all of a ' charismatic ' type, and their warfare partook in general of the character of the ' holy war ' which has already been mentioned. It is clear that Saul's kingship was of this character. He was anointed and received an access of the spirit of Yahweh in preparation for his task of war-leadership. He exercised priestly functions, and a sacred character attached to his person, as appears from David's words after he had cut off the skirt of Saul's royal mantle in the cave (1 Sam. 24:6). This charismatic conception of kingship persisted, even after the dynastic principle had been established in both Northern and Southern Kingdoms. But it was not until the accession of David that the religious

6b changes caused by the introduction of the kingship, and still further developed under Solomon, take definite shape.

c The first and most important change, bringing other changes with it, was the capture of the old Jebusite city of Jerusalem by David, and the establishment there of the central cult of Yahweh with Ark and priesthood. It has been suggested that the Ark may have been placed in the old Jebusite shrine, and that the Zadokite priesthood established in Jerusalem alongside the Aaronite priesthood represents an accommodation with the old Jebusite cult of El 'Elyon referred to in Gen. 14 (H. H. Rowley, ' Zadok and Nehushtan ', JBL 58 (1939), 113–41). It is also possible that the account of the bringing of the Ark to Jerusalem, and the accompanying ritual in which the king played an important part, may represent the inauguration of the Israelite New Year Feast of the Enthronement of Yahweh, and that this may have been taken over and adapted from a previously existing Jebusite rite (J. R. Porter, ' The Interpretation of 2 Samuel 6 and Psalm 132 ', JTS, N.S. 5 (1954), 161–73). The existence of such a festival and the central part played therein by the king as an essential element in the pattern of Israelite religion under the monarchy is now generally accepted. For the grounds on which this view rests reference may be made to the work of Mowinckel, Johnson, and other scholars (S. Mowinckel, *Psalmenstudien* ii ; A. R. Johnson, *Sacral Kingship in Ancient Israel*).

d The next development resulting from the introduction of kingship was the new relationship established between the king and the prophetic order. We find prophets attached to the court in an official character : Gad is described as the king's seer (S. Mowinckel, op. cit., iii, 10). Under the monarchy the court-prophets would seem to have fulfilled similar functions to those exercised by the *barū* in Assyria on behalf of the king. The Assyrian king never went to war or performed any public act of importance without consulting his staff of *barū*-priests. We shall have more to say on this point when we come to deal with religious institutions in the Northern Kingdom. Modern study on the Psalter has led to the view now generally accepted that many psalms exhibit a pattern of prophetic oracular responses given in answer to inquiry by the king or by individuals.

The centralisation of the cult at Jerusalem and its association with the king and his court naturally led to a more elaborate organisation of the priesthood. The Chronicler attributes the organisation of the priesthood and of the Temple music to David, and while some allowance must be made for the tendency of the later editors to validate institutions by assigning their origin to an early period of Israel's history, as we have seen in the case of circumcision, yet it is most likely that the beginnings of the organisation of the priesthood into courses, and of the Temple musicians, go back to the time of David and Solomon.

e The next change which arose from the introduction of the kingship was the separation between the religious practice of the capital and that of the country. From the evidence of the Deuteronomic editors of the book of Kg. and from the Prophets we know that in the country the local shrines, ' the high places ', with their local priests carried on a form of Yahwistic cult which was strongly influenced by Canaanite practice. Hosea shows to what an extent Yahweh and Baal had become confused in the minds of Israelite worshippers. This state of things persisted, in spite of prophetic denunciations and the efforts of reforming kings, until the fall of Jerusalem in 586 B.C.

f One religious institution which is probably much older than the monarchy, but of whose practice we first have an account under the monarchy, is the method of ascertaining the divine will by means of the sacred lot. The LXX text of 1 Sam. 14:41, where the Massoretic text is defective, gives a description of how the sacred lots, known as Urim and Thummim, were used. The
only other mention under the monarchy is in Chr. 116f
where the priestly courses are said to have been assigned by the casting of the lot. That the custom of divination by Urim and Thummim persisted throughout the monarchy, and that the sacred lots disappeared when the Ark was carried away at the capture of Jerusalem, is implied by the reference in Ezr. 2:63 (Neh. 7:65), where the decision concerning doubtful cases of priestly descent is deferred ' until there stood up a priest with Urim and Thummim '.

The centralisation initiated by David when he brought the Ark to Jerusalem was completed by Solomon in the building of the Temple. Here according to Israelite tradition Yahweh came to take up his abode when the completed Temple was dedicated. Intended at the outset to be a royal chapel, it became in the course of time the symbol of Yahweh's presence among his people, a pledge of safety, a guarantee of Jerusalem's inviolability, until Jeremiah had to remind the religious authorities of his day that what had happened to Shiloh might also happen to Jerusalem. But for over four hundred years it remained the centre of Israel's religious institutions. In vision Ezekiel saw the glory of Yahweh leave the Temple and the city to its doom ; then after many years he saw again in vision the glory return to a restored city and a restored Temple, where Yahweh said he would dwell forever with a repentant and restored people.

(b) The Divided Kingdoms—After Jeroboam's 117a
revolution and the ensuing schism which had prophetic instigation behind it (1 Kg. 11:30f.), the religious institutions of the Northern Kingdom developed along different lines from those of Judah, and we must consider them separately.

(i) The Kingdom of Israel—Jeroboam's first anxiety after the breach was complete was to ensure that his people should not go up to Jerusalem for the great seasonal feasts or other religious occasions. Accordingly he established cult centres at Dan, where the ancient centre whose founding is described in Jg. 18 already existed, and at Bethel, a very ancient Canaanite sanctuary. In these two centres he set up bull images and established a priesthood whose personnel was not drawn from the ranks of the recognised priestly class. Hosea uses the word *k^emārîm* to describe the priests of the sanctuary at Bethel (Hos. 10:5), a word which is only used in the OT of idol priests. Jeroboam also instituted an autumn New Year festival similar to that held in Jerusalem, but a month later, and officiated himself in a priestly capacity (1 Kg. 12:26–33). There can be no doubt that Jeroboam's arrangements were regarded as providing the northern tribes with a genuine worship of Yahweh, and he may even have considered himself as a restorer of the customary form of the cult, as against Solomon's innovations. When Omri built his new capital at Samaria he must have made some provision for the cult, since Hosea speaks of ' the calf of Samaria ' (Hos. 8:6), and there must have been some kind of installation, although the excavation of the site has not so far revealed traces of a temple. The evidence of proper names compounded with Yahweh as compared with those compounded with Baal, shows that the former predominated, so that Yahweh still remained the principal object of worship in the Northern Kingdom (ARI, 160). During the reign of Ahab, as the result of his marriage to a Tyrian princess, Yahweh's supremacy was threatened by the cult of Melqart of Tyre ; but the challenge of Elijah and the revolution headed by Jehu removed this danger. Ezekiel's description of the religion of Samaria under the symbolic name of Oholah (Ezek. 23:1–10) shows the extent to which the religious institutions of the Northern Kingdom had become contaminated by Canaanite and Assyrian cult practices.

The state of the prophetic order in northern Israel b
presents some curious contrasts. Ahab would appear to have maintained a staff of court prophets whom he consulted in the same way as the Assyrian kings did

117b before beginning a campaign. These were not prophets of Baal, but regarded themselves as prophets of Yahweh. Their mode of prophesying consisted in the performance of symbolic acts intended to secure favourable results for those who consulted them (1 Kg. 22:11f.). At the same time the prophetic guilds already mentioned seem to have continued an independent existence at centres like Bethel, Gilgal, and Jericho. Among them the traditions of Israel's past and a purer form of religion were preserved, and it is probable that Elijah with his challenge to the syncretism of the court came from such a circle. From these 'sons of the prophets', as they are called in the Elijah and Elisha sagas, there emerged from time to time individuals, often nameless, who stirred up resistance to the established order, or rebuked kings (1 Kg. 20:13, 38; 2 Kg. 9:4).

c **(ii) The Kingdom of Judah**—In the chapter of Ezek. to which we have already referred, the prophet describes the careers of the two sisters Oholah and Oholibah, whose symbolic names represent Samaria and Jerusalem. According to his estimate Jerusalem, undeterred by the shocking example and dreadful fate of her sister, Samaria, behaved even worse than her sister had done. Nevertheless the so-called Deuteronomic judgments which punctuate the annals of the kings of Israel and Judah suggest that there were redeeming features in the history of the Southern Kingdom, while none appear in the history of the Northern Kingdom.

In the first place, in the religious institutions of Judah, the Davidic kingship became the living centre of a ritual pattern which is reflected in the liturgies of the Psalter. The religious life of the capital gathered round the Temple with its ordered priesthood and its staff of prophets, its seasonal festivals and above all the great New Year festival of the enthronement of Yahweh. It is impossible to say whether anything similar was to be found in northern Israel, although the 2nd book of the Psalter, with its use of the name Elohim, has been assigned to the Northern Kingdom. Several of the royal and kingship psalms which have been used in the reconstruction of the Israelite New Year festival of the enthronement of Yahweh are to be found in the 2nd book of Psalms, and this might be thought to offer a prima facie case for the existence of such a festival in the Northern Kingdom, although Professor Johnson's treatment of the festival limits it to Jerusalem (A. R. Johnson, *Sacral Kingship*, 77, 124).

d With regard to the institution of prophecy, the biographical sections of Jer. show that a staff of court and temple prophets similar to those already mentioned as existing at Ahab's court was functioning in Jerusalem in Jeremiah's time, and his bitter denunciation of them in his oracle 'Concerning the prophets' (Jer. 23:9–40) shows what he thought about them. But it is also clear that, as the records of the careers of Isaiah and Jeremiah show, the religion of Israel continued to produce a succession of 'charismatic' persons, independent of and generally opposed to the 'official' prophets, who exercised a profound influence, not only upon the history of their own time, but upon the whole development of the religion of Israel. The autobiographical elements which have been preserved among their oracles show that all these men had passed through a profound experience of God which both gave them a sense of mission, and set them consciously apart from the official class of *nᵉbhî'îm* of their day. They did not regard themselves as innovators, but as recalling Israel to standards of private and public conduct which went back to the time of the covenant mediated by Moses. Hence, while they were the most trenchant critics of the religious institutions of their time, kings, princes, priests, and prophets, all alike coming under the lash of their denunciation, they themselves cannot be omitted from any account of the religious institutions of Israel.

e The most important change which took place in the order of the priesthood during the period of the monarchy in Jerusalem was the result of Josiah's reforms. We are told that this king destroyed all the high-places both in northern Israel, which by that time had been depopulated after the fall of Samaria in 721, and in Judah, and had brought the priests of those local sanctuaries up to Jerusalem, where they were assigned a lower status in the Jerusalem priesthood. This is what the tradition preserved in the book of Kg. appears to mean. But the actual situation is obscure and complicated. We have already seen that in the period of the Judges Levites were regarded as the proper persons to exercise priestly functions. The Deuteronomic writer regards all Levites as priests but divides them into two classes, country priests, and those attached to the Temple in Jerusalem. For the Priestly writer all Levites are priests but he envisages a priesthood entirely centred in the Temple. Ezekiel introduces a distinction which may never have been carried out in practice. There are the Levites who had officiated in the local sanctuaries which Ezekiel regards as idolatrous places of worship. These persons are forever to be debarred from exercising the full functions of priesthood, though they may perform the more menial duties of the sanctuary. Then there are the 'sons of Zadok' who had remained faithful to the pure Yahweh worship; they are to be rewarded by the promise of a perpetual priesthood in the restored Temple at Jerusalem. It has already been pointed out, however, that the Zadokite priesthood at Jerusalem may have been the continuance of a Jebusite priesthood whose tradition went back to Melchizedek, the priest-king of Salem, and their place in the Israelite tradition may have been validated by giving them a genealogy derived from the Eli priesthood in Shiloh. In the narrative of David's reign, Abiathar and Zadok are represented as accompanying David and as guardians of the Ark. In Solomon's reign Abiathar is shown as displaced because of his adherence to the cause of the rival claimant, Adonijah, so that Zadok becomes the founder of a priestly line whose descent is traced down to the captivity (1 Chr. 6:8–15). Joshua, the high-priest of the return from exile, is the son of Jozadak, the last of the Zadok line before the captivity (Ezr. 3:2). We shall see that after the return from exile important changes in the status of the priesthood took place.

f With regard to the cult under the Davidic monarchy, the New Year festival of the enthronement of Yahweh has already been mentioned; it should be said, however, that the evidence for this feast is drawn mainly from the Psalter, and that evidence for it from the historical books is almost entirely wanting. It would seem that the first of the three great seasonal festivals, the Passover, had fallen into abeyance under the monarchy, and at the time of its revival as part of Josiah's reforms we are told that it had not been kept since the days of the Judges (1 Kg. 23:22); but the Chronicler records that Hezekiah revived the Passover, and remarks that it had not been held since Solomon's reign (2 Chr. 30:26). It has been observed that the Chronicler shows a tendency to exalt the virtues of Hezekiah at the expense of Josiah, and the assignment of a Passover to Hezekiah's reign may be due to this tendency. Moreover a contradiction in the Chronicler's narrative appears in his account of Josiah's Passover when he remarks that no such Passover had been held since the time of Samuel (2 Chr. 35:18). Recent studies have brought to notice the existence of a ritual of covenant renewal, possibly originating at the great central sanctuary at Shechem, and later on becoming a kingship ritual and introduced into the pattern of the autumn New Year festival (G. Widengren, 'King and Covenant', JSS 2 (1957), 1f.). Another element in the cult which is often alluded to by the prophets is the festal celebration of 'new moon and sabbath'. David was expected by Saul to be in his usual place at the king's table for this feast (1 Sam. 20:5). It is possible that the sabbath celebration mentioned by Isaiah (Isa. 1:13; cf. Am. 8:5) is not the seventh-day

7f sabbath of later observance, but a full moon celebration. The full development of the course of the priests and the Temple choirs probably belongs to the post-exilic period, but there is no doubt an historical foundation for the tradition which assigned the beginnings of this organisation to David and Solomon.

8a **(5) The Post-Exilic Period**—The end of the monarchy and the destruction of the Temple put an end to all those elements in the cult in which the king played a central part. It also brought to an end the intimate relation between the king and the priesthood which had developed under the Davidic kings. During the Exile, and after the return until the Temple was rebuilt, sacrifices were no longer possible ; connection between the prophetic guilds and the court was also broken. Hence important changes in the religious institutions of Israel were inevitable.

We have seen that kingship, and the Davidic kingship in particular, had become a religious institution in a very definite sense. The effect of the Exile on the kingship took two forms. In the first place the Messianic character of the Davidic kingship, which had already existed in germ before the Exile, became explicit and deeply rooted in post-exilic prophecy. In the second place the priest's influence and importance increased to such an extent that the rise of a dynasty of priest-kings was only the logical result of this change.

b But other important changes in the character and functions of the priesthood after the return from exile call for notice. Jeremiah's enemies are represented as saying, ' the law shall not perish from the priest ' (Jer. 18:18), and the Chronicler represents Jehoshaphat as sending a mission of priests and Levites to teach *tôrāh* in the cities of Judah (2 Chr. 17:7–9). From such references we may infer that one of the priest's functions was to be the depository of the cultic traditions and to instruct the laity in *tôrāh*. When the captivity put an end to all sacrificial and other cultic activities, this aspect of the priest's functions assumed increased importance, and those collections of *tôrôth* concerning sacrifices, festivals, purificatory rituals, and other cultic activities which have been brought together in Lev. and Num., represent the work of priests during and after the Exile. The figure of Ezra, a priest who could trace his descent from Zadok's line, represents this new aspect of the priest's functions. He is described as ' a ready (*māhîr*) scribe in the law of Moses ' (Ezr. 7:6), and has become for Jewish tradition the archetype of the devoted student of *tôrāh*, the founder of ' the Great Synagogue '.

When the Temple was rebuilt such priests as Ezra were able to ensure that the orders of priests, Levites, and singers were re-established as they had been in pre-exilic times (Ezr. 6:12 ; Neh. 12:44–7), and it is probable that staffs were enlarged and priestly courses reorganised. Much of the Temple arrangements which we find in the Mishnah probably goes back to early post-exilic times.

c A further consequence of changed conditions after the Exile was the emergence of a person who is called ' the high priest ' (*hakkōhēn haggādhôl*). While grades in the priestly hierarchy undoubtedly existed under the monarchy, no priest in pre-exilic times occupied the unique position which the high priest came to occupy after the return from exile. The title ' the anointed one ', which had been the special designation of the king, now becomes the epithet applied to the high priest. Under Persian rule the Jews were allowed to have a governor of their own nationality, who bears the titles, ' prince (*nāśî'*) of Judah ', and Tirshatha, the latter being a Persian loan-word meaning possibly ' the revered one ' (Ezr. 1:8 ; Neh. 8:9), but he was never given the title of king and was under the control of a Persian resident. While the prince was for a time during the early years of the restoration the focus of Messianic hopes, he soon fades out of the picture, and in one of Zechariah's oracles we have the symbolic action of the placing of a crown upon the head of Joshua the high priest, and the prophetic utterance, ' he shall be a priest upon his throne ' (Zech. 6:13, AV). 118c
The highest point of high-priestly authority was reached under the Hasmonaeans, when the high priest added the regal to his priestly title, and for a brief period Judah was again governed by a king of her own race.

Changes also took place with regard to the prophetic d
order and its activities. The removal of the king and his court would involve the dispersion of the prophetic guilds attached to the court and the Temple, and we know from Jeremiah's letter to the exiles in Babylon that many of the prophets against whom he had protested so vigorously had been deported to Babylon, and were continuing the same activities there (Jer. 29:1, 8, 9). There was a great nameless prophet who was active at the time of Cyrus's capture of Babylon and who may have been engaged in stirring up a partisan warfare in support of Cyrus. We know from his oracles that he had reached the highest level attained by the religion of Israel before the coming of Christ. It is more than probable that he was a representative of the school of Isaiah, one of the ' disciples ' among whom that prophet's instruction and witness was preserved (Isa. 8:16). He also, in his turn, may have had a circle of disciples by whom his oracles were collected, and from whose midst came the collection known as Trito-Isaiah. Among the returned exiles we find evidence of both kinds of prophetic activity. There are the two representatives of the school of Isaiah and Jeremiah who are called ' prophets of God ' (Ezr. 5:2), Haggai and Zechariah, who stirred up the discouraged Jews to rebuild the Temple, and whose oracles have been preserved. But we also hear of prophets and a prophetess who sought to hinder Nehemiah's efforts to rebuild the walls of Jerusalem (Neh. 6:14) ; they seem to have been agents of the Samaritan opposition to the restoration of Jerusalem to its former importance. If the 74th Psalm is to be assigned to the 4th cent., it may be regarded as evidence of the decline and disappearance of the prophetic witness by that time. If 2nd Zechariah also belongs to a late date in the Persian period, it affords evidence for the total disrepute into which the prophetic order had fallen (Zech. 13:2–6). The emergence of John the Baptist from ' the wilderness ' makes the surmise not wholly improbable that the settlements in the Jordan valley, where the Essenes are known to have lived, and from whence the much-discussed Dead Sea documents have come, may have been the last refuge of the remnants of the prophetic order.

One more important religious institution which has 119a
its origin in the post-exilic period is the **Synagogue**. Most scholars agree that the synagogal form of worship began in Babylon in answer to the need of the exiles for some means of supporting their religious life. It has also been suggested that the public reading of the Law from a pulpit, accompanied by exposition and possibly by an Aramaic paraphrase (targum), which Ezra is described as carrying out (Neh. 8:2–8), was the first introduction of the synagogue form of worship into Palestine ((W. O. E. Oesterley and T. H. Robinson, *A History of Israel* ii, 137f.). The dispersion of the Jews throughout the Greco-Roman world made the extension of synagogue worship necessary. We know that during the Greek period many synagogues were built in Alexandria, and the excavations at Dura Europos have revealed unexpected characteristics in the synagogue there.

Circumcision and the Sabbath assumed a new b
importance after the Exile. They became the distinctive marks which separated Judaism from the rest of the pagan world. The festal calendar also underwent changes. The simple calendar of the Book of the Covenant was expanded to the elaborate calendar of Lev. 23, which is still in force in orthodox Judaism today, save that additional prayers have been provided to replace the sacrifices which are no longer possible.

5a

119b Also it is possible to gather from the Megillath Ta'anith that a number of new festivals were added to the calendar during the post-exilic period, most of which were intended to celebrate historical events and are still observed in contemporary Judaism. We may also notice the tendency which had already appeared in the course of the development of the religious institutions of Israel, to connect ritual occasions which were much older than Israel's settlement in Canaan, and which had been taken into the pattern of Israel's religion, with historical events. Thus Passover, which was an apotropaic ritual far older than the beginnings of Israel (S. H. Hooke, *Origins of Early Semitic Ritual*, 50) is connected with and celebrates the deliverance of Israel from Egyptian bondage, and the feast of Booths which has its roots in the ritual pattern of Mesopotamia has become a remembrance of the time when Israel lived in tents in the wilderness (Lev. 23:42–3).

c **Conclusion**—When we come to consider the religious institutions of Israel in the light of recent archaeological and historical researches, it is clear that Israel had taken over many elements of the religious pattern of Canaan, Egypt, and Mesopotamia. The relation between its origin-myths and those of Sumer and Babylon is too obvious to be denied ; much of the Pentateuchal legislation has its counterpart in early Babylonian and Assyrian codes ; it is generally admitted that, to say the least, the pattern of the Israelite New Year festival owes much to the Babylonian Akitu festival, although some scholars may have exaggerated the extent of Babylonian influence ; the Israelite pattern of kingship is, by the evidence of their own prophets, derived from the neighbouring form of kingship ; even the institution of prophecy, which was by far the most formative influence in the shaping of Israel's religion, is well known to have had its parallels in the religion of Israel's immediate neighbours. But when all this is recognised, the essential fact remains that something happened in the development of the religious institutions of Israel which is unparalleled in the history of the world. The Psalmist was only stating an inescapable fact when he said of God's dealings with Israel, 'He has not dealt thus
d with any other nation' (Ps. 147:20). God's choice of Israel to be the vehicle of his self-revelation and the channel of his redemptive purpose so wrought in the history of Israel that all her borrowings were transformed. From generation to generation Israel's history
recorded by her own prophets was a tragic story of 119
apostasy and rebellion against her Divine lover and begetter ; the stream of revelation flowed on through an ever-narrowing channel ; but the body of Israel's religious institutions, which had been created by divine action out of the materials of which we have spoken, remained and might be compared to the pattern of the city which Ezekiel saw in vision, and which he was instructed to show to the children of Israel that they might 'be ashamed' (Ezek. 43:10).

The religious institutions of Israel did not come into existence and grow by a natural process, like a tree. Every constituent element in them represents some divine act and some human response. So every detail acquires symbolic significance, a meaning which extends beyond its immediate contemporary meaning. In the sacrifices, the priesthood, the kingship, the prophetic oracle, God was revealing himself ; these things were the language of the divine speech, and it is impossible to say this about the religious institutions of any other people. 'In many and various ways God spoke of old to our fathers by the prophets ; but in these last days he has spoken to us by a Son' (Heb. 1:1).

Bibliography—W. F. Albright, *Archaeology and the Religion of Israel* (3rd ed. 1953), *From the Stone Age to Christianity* (2nd ed. 1946) ; A. Alt, *Kleine Schriften zum Geschichte Israels* I and II (1953) ; S. A. Cook, *The Religion of Ancient Palestine in the Light of Archaeology* (1925) ; H. Frankfort, *Kingship and the Gods* (1948) ; S. H. Hooke, *The Origins of Early Semitic Ritual* (1938), *In the Beginning* (1948) ; A. R. Johnson, *The Cultic Prophet in Ancient Israel* (1944), *Sacral Kingship in Ancient Israel* (1955) ; H. J. Kraus, *Gottesdienst in Israel* (1954) ; A. Lods, *Israel* (Eng. tr. by S. H. Hooke, 1932) ; T. J. Meek, *Hebrew Origins* (2nd ed. 1950) ; E. Meyer, *Die Israeliten und ihre Nachbarstämme* (1906) ; S. Mowinckel, *Psalmenstudien* II (1922), III (1923) ; E. Nielsen, *Shechem* (1955) ; M. Noth, *Das System der Zwölf Stämme Israels* (1930) ; J. Pedersen, *Israel* I–II (1926) ; G. von Rad, *Studies in Deuteronomy* (Eng. tr. by D. M. Stalker, 1953) ; H. H. Rowley, *The Servant of the Lord* (1952), (ed.) *The OT and Modern Study* (1951) ; W. Robertson Smith, *The Religion of the Semites* (3rd ed. 1927) ; E. Voegelin, *Israel and Revelation* (1956) ; G. Widengren, *Sacrales Königtum im AT und im Judentum* (1955).

THE THEOLOGY OF THE OLD TESTAMENT

By N. W. PORTEOUS

120a Old Testament theology is the first part of Biblical theology. It is a commonly held opinion that, if it would keep within its proper limits, it should be strictly objective in character, should, in fact, either take the form of a history of Israel's religion, or, perhaps, provide a description of that religion arranged according to some systematic principle. There was a time when OT theology was a department of dogmatic theology and so, to win for itself the autonomy it needed if it was to develop, it had to make a violent breakaway and deny that it had any normative function. A science of Israel's religion came into being which could use without inhibition all the modern techniques of archaeology and comparative religion, of historical and literary analysis, and which, by giving full scope to its new-found freedom, produced results of the greatest interest and value. That work goes on.

It is coming to be recognised, however, that, close as this necessary science of Israel's religion is to OT theology, the latter is not properly to be regarded as another name for the former. It has indeed a descriptive task to perform, in carrying out which its method may be as systematic as the subject-matter permits. Beyond all this, however—and it is round this point that recent discussion has moved—OT theology has a normative function in respect of which it can claim the right to be regarded as theology.

b As a normative science OT theology will relate what it finds in the OT to the NT in such a way that the OT, instead of being, what it is for many, a stumbling-block and an embarrassment, or of being given an independent authority for the Christian to which it is not entitled, will be seen by him as an enrichment of his religious life and will even be a guide to him in dealing with its problems. Moreover, the proper performance of this task by the OT theologian is essential if Biblical theology, whose function it is to deal with the Bible as a whole, is to make the Biblical material, that of the OT no less than that of the NT, available in proper form for the use of the dogmatic theologian. It may be suggested that it is through lack of the proper functioning of Biblical theology that dogmatic theology at times shows a tendency to mishandle the Bible and thus to endanger the gains which have been so hardly won. The problem which the Biblical theologian has to solve is how best to combine an honest, realistic approach to his material with the right kind of critical evaluation of it. But normative he must be, if the Bible is not to become the kind of authority which makes it difficult for men to hear the living word of God, as it had become in Judaism in the time of Christ. This theological work, of course, can never be done once and for all. Error can scarcely be avoided, yet it need not be deadly error, so long as it is not allowed to harden into dogma but is kept in the moving stream of life.

c OT theology is concerned with the OT as a witness to certain things which God is believed to have done and as the record of the human response to these acts of God. The divine activity and the human
response which it initiates belong together in such a 120c
way that the evidence for the former will largely be found in the latter. It is always difficult to study life, since thought by its very nature tends to view things in their static interrelationships. The process of thought is like stopping the machinery so as to examine the structure or killing the living creature so as to anatomise it. Perhaps more than any other science theology is confronted with this difficulty of procedure. It deals not only with life but with life as the evidence for that very source of life which produces in man his most intense and mysterious activity. It is in that activity and in the forms of life in which it took shape that we shall find our best evidence for the nature of that supernatural power which theology identifies by using the name God.

Theology is by etymology the *logos* of God, 'the study or science which treats of God, His nature and attributes, and His relations with man and the universe', to quote the definition given in the Oxford English Dictionary. While concerned with God, however, there is a very real sense in which theology—and this applies in a very particular way to OT theology—has to proceed by concentrating its attention upon man, since the revelation becomes visible in the human response to it. This does not mean that we commit the grave error of substituting anthropology for theology. In the living event of revelation God always takes the initiative. Yet theology can only deal with what comes within the human range of perception. That is why theology is inevitably anthropomorphic in its language and why, in the last resort and in a very real sense from the outset, it takes the form of Christology which corresponds to the fact that the Word became flesh. It is because the Word became flesh and dwelt among men that we have a light in which to judge the OT that illuminates without distorting. d

The problem of method with which the OT confronts the theologian arises from the way in which it came into existence and from the consequent nature of its contents. The various writings of which it is composed were produced to meet the developing needs of the Hebrew people in the course of its historic existence. Much of the material consists of the record of that history and of the experiences and actions of those who played their parts in it. We have to look, however, not only at the history and the men and women who act on its crowded stage but also at the point of view of those who tell the story, that being a very important part of the evidence with which we are concerned. History is like that; the very telling of it itself becomes history. But the OT contains more than history. There is legal material from which we can make inference to the form of the society in which the events took place and find evidence for the will of God in relation to that society. There is the record of the preaching of that extraordinary succession of men, the Canonical prophets, who both spoke for God and represented the people before God. There is reflective material which in part shows us the religion in action e

120e at the level of popular instruction and in part takes us inside the minds of those who were grappling with life's ultimate problems. There is cultic material, partly consisting of rubrics connected with the forms of worship, partly consisting of sacred songs employed in worship. The Psalms, as we call them, provide some clue to the nature of Hebrew piety both at the popular level, since the priests knew what would best express and foster that piety, and at the more individual level which a man might reach in a moment of inspiration where he might have few to keep him company.

This analysis by no means exhausts the types of literature we find in the OT. It will suffice, however, to make clear how highly complicated must be the method of a discipline which has to use and evaluate such varied material. Moreover, the different writings as they have come down to us have in most cases been subjected to a process of editing and re-editing in which modification, correction, addition, omission, rearrangement and reinterpretation have played their parts. For the unravelling of the process of literary creation and transmission of the OT, the theologian will be in the debt of the science of Biblical introduction. In the complicated story which the critic reconstructs for him he will find invaluable evidence for that movement of life and thought which it is his duty to study from his own particular point of view, and he will have failed in his task if he does not give the impression that what he is studying is no static system of ideas but something intensely alive and on the move, which Unamuno calls ' the man of flesh and bone '.

f It is no doubt a part of the theological task to demonstrate the broad unity of life and thought which is to be found in the OT and even in the Bible as a whole. In spite of differences and changes there is a distinctive pattern which is to be recognised almost everywhere, so that something of a family likeness can be detected as between different parts of the OT and the different periods which it records. In a truly remarkable way the OT mirrors a life which seems to have remained true to type throughout hundreds of years. In the same way there is an undoubted family likeness between the Testaments. It is these features of resemblance which give one the confidence that the Bible does indeed contain the human witness to One who was pursuing a single, self-consistent plan and was getting, in some measure at least, the response that he desired. The response, however, is varied, as men and ages are varied, and it is ambiguous, since human nature has its depths as well as its heights. If it were not for the steady, revealing light which streams from one particular quarter the task of the theologian would be wellnigh impossible. In that light the witness can become witness to One who has a living word to speak to our own and to every day.

121a The first point which has to be grasped if we are to get on the right lines for constructing a theology of the OT has to do with what the OT itself calls ' knowledge of God '. By that is meant not so much an intellectual apprehension of the nature of God—though an intellectual element is undoubtedly present—as a response to God which can most adequately be expressed in terms of conduct. Revelation has to be appropriated by the whole man in thought, emotion, and action, especially in action. When Hosea (4:1–2) declares that there is ' no knowledge of God in the land ', he proceeds immediately to explain what that involves by saying that ' there is swearing, lying, killing, stealing, and committing adultery '. Jeremiah (22:15–16) is even more explicit when he declares an oracle to Jehoiakim : ' Do you think you are a king because you compete in cedar ? Did not your father eat and drink and do justice and righteousness ? Then it was well with him. He judged the cause of the poor and needy ; then it was well. Is not this to know me ? says the Lord.'

This usage is made natural by the fact that, when the Hebrew employed the word which we normally translate by the English word ' know ', he meant 12
something which would often justify us in using the phrase ' to be intimate with '. We may compare the familiar words (Am. 3:2) : ' You only have I known of all the families of the earth ' and the circumstance that the word ' know ' is applied to sexual intimacy. It seems to be clear, then, that, when either of the aforementioned prophets spoke of the knowledge of God, he was thinking of an intimacy of relationship between men and God which on the human side would imply a real understanding of the divine will and would manifest itself in a degree of conformity to that will, namely, in the kind of conduct, the absence of which is destructive of community. It will be found that this word ' community ' takes us very nearly to the heart of OT theology, since the main purpose of God's self-disclosure of his will was clearly the creation of a community obedient to himself. The ethics of community is, therefore, a very central part of OT theology.

To make an important point clear, however, it is not b
necessary to exaggerate it. The emphasis so far has been laid upon the kind of society God expects man to produce, since it is when man makes this response to the revelation of God that one can be sure that in applying high titles to God man is really taking him seriously. The same language used about God inside and outside Israel may mean very different things. What makes the OT of such tremendous importance theologically is that it contains the record of men who in varying measure did take God seriously by allowing their beliefs to determine their conduct, or, when they failed to do so, provide significant examples of what failure involves. There is, however, a primary emphasis upon the initiative of God. Indeed when man responds to God in the way of obedience and in the creation of community, we may in a very real sense include his action in the divine revelatory action to which it bears witness and by which it is elicited. Indeed the human response furnishes the most convincing proof it is possible to give that God is really acting in history.

The primary emphasis, then, in the OT is that the c
God in whom Israel believes is a God who acts and reveals himself in history. The NT *kerygma* or proclamation of the acts of God in Christ is both reinforced by what we may call the OT *kerygma* and supplies us with a criterion by which to measure it, as well as with an experience which predisposes us to accept it.

To say that God reveals himself in history is a very different thing, of course, from saying that history is the revelation of God. Much in history is anything but the self-disclosure of God. What is asserted is that God is a God whose activity may be recognised in certain events in history by that form of apprehension which is called faith, such faith expressing itself not only in word but also in deed.

How does the OT speak of these acts of God ? It d
speaks first and foremost, and indeed repeatedly, of a divine act of deliverance which is best described in the words of the preface to the Decalogue (Exod. 20:2 ; Dt. 5:6) : ' I am the Lord your God, who brought you out of the land of Egypt, out of the house of bondage '. It is true that in certain traditions there were previous acts of God which may be summarised as his dealings in guidance and promise with the Patriarchs. With these the Exodus tradition (Exod. 3:13) links up, though some have regarded this as later construction. Yet that the Israel mutation began with a smaller unit than the people (viz. the family or the clan) is not impossible. But it was the great act of deliverance from the Egyptian servitude, which gave shape to tradition and poetry for centuries, that must be regarded as the decisive event in Israel's history. The evidence points unmistakably to this. From that day onwards Israel was not its own. The first signal act of God was followed, so Israel believed, by others. The people was brought to the mountain of the Law where it received its charter. It was led through the

1d wilderness to the so-called land of promise. It was given that land as a possession. In subsequent events during the period of settlement it recognised the hand of God in disaster and deliverance alike. It may be that it was in the experiences of the institution called the Holy War that Israel found confirmation of its faith. With Israel established in Palestine we may pause for the moment, since what followed raised new problems for Israel which fall to be discussed at a later stage.

e In the OT, then, we have witness to a series of classic events commencing with the call of Abraham, leading on to a new and more decisive beginning at the Exodus from Egypt and culminating in the eventual settlement of Israel in the land which was believed to have been promised to the fathers of the race. One of the most important recent emphases in the field of OT study is the insistence that the so-called *Heilsgeschichte* (sacred history or salvation-history) which we have in narrative form in the Hexateuch has grown from briefer summaries of the crucial events, from recitals of the acts of God on behalf of his people, which played an integral part in the old Hebrew cult. Historical writing in Israel, that is to say, took its origin in worship and so the story which has come down to us is stylised in form and is concerned to concentrate on the divine rather than on the human causation. Two of the best examples of the summary statement of the acts of God are to be found in Dt. 26 and Jos. 24, the former associated with the offering of first-fruits and the latter probably giving us the rubric for use at a ceremony of covenant renewal. There are in the Psalter, too, psalms which proclaim the acts of God for varying purposes, e.g. for thanksgiving (Ps. 105), for confession (Ps. 106).

f Both Testaments, then, have a *kerygma*, a proclamation of the acts of God. In the case of both we are faced with the ultimate question of the truth of the *kerygma* proclaimed. Two questions are in fact involved, the question of the accuracy of the events of history recorded and the question of the relation between these events and the alleged complicity of God in them. The NT by the light it casts on the nature of the divine action in history must surely affect our judgment of the OT *kerygma* and make it impossible for us to accept wholesale the OT view when it is alleged that such and such actions are in accordance with the will of God. That God overruled Israel's history, as he overrules all history, is a truth which is surely indispensable for faith, but merely to add the *kerygma* of the NT to that of the OT is no more satisfactory than merely to add the principles of the Christian way of life to what is enjoined upon Israel in the OT. Even within the limits of the OT we can observe different views of the relation of human acts to the will of God (2 Kg. 10:30; Hos. 1:4). For us to ignore this and accept the OT *kerygma* naïvely, giving up the attempt to find a Christian perspective, would be to lay ourselves open to the attack of some modern Marcion. The witness of the OT must not be identified with the revelation itself.

22a That God acted in Israel's history is, as we have seen, an assertion of faith on the part of the worshipping community. We must now look more closely at the form of this community which was held to have been given it by an initial covenant at Sinai-Horeb through which Israel was constituted as the people of God. The concept of the covenant has been regarded, as for example by Eichrodt, as the most central theological concept in the OT. There is much to be said for this view. The covenant, properly understood, does safeguard the divine initiative and makes it clear that God who is the Lord of the covenant imposes certain conditions on his people. For, while covenants between human beings might be in the nature of a bargain between equals, the covenant at Sinai-Horeb should be regarded as the limiting case of covenants between unequals, as a covenant indeed in which the absolute transcendence of one partner makes it possible for him to lay down the conditions absolutely and of indefeasible right and to demand an obedience which will express itself as conformity to a certain pattern of conduct. 122a

b The people of Israel was taught to recognise that what gave its God the right to impose upon it this covenantal relationship with all that it involved was the decisive act of deliverance by which he freed it from its servitude in Egypt and led it out to a new life of national independence. This conviction as to the way in which Israel came into existence as a people eventually took the form of a belief in election or choice. To this we must return later. At the moment it is only necessary to recognise that the covenant relationship must have implied from the beginning for Israel a sense of obligation towards a God who, though transcendent (*ḳādhôsh*), had intervened on the historical plane on behalf of a particular people. The correlative word to describe the human partner to the covenant is slave or servant (*'Ebhedh*), the word which is generally applied to man in relation to God, while the attitude towards God expected of man within the covenant relationship can best be described as fear of God or reverence before God (*yir'ath 'elōhîm*), the typical Hebrew phrase meaning religion.

c It seems right that we should remind ourselves at this point that, when we view the covenant between God and Israel from the Christian perspective, while there are features in it which have no longer relevance to ourselves, there is much which serves to deepen our own sense of obligation and which can guide our thoughts as we seek to learn God's will for the ordering of life today. Moreover it helps to keep us conscious of the gulf which still separates the transcendent God from his creatures. What God in his grace did under the old covenant to bridge that gulf gains a new significance when we remember him 'who, though he was in the form of God, did not count equality with God a thing to be grasped, but emptied himself, taking the form of a servant (or slave), being born in the likeness of men'. (Phil. 2:6–7) The obedience of Christ, of which St Paul goes on to speak, which entitled him to be acknowledged as Lord, brings us back to that pattern of life which it was the purpose of the covenant to promote and control. The demand for obedience in act made upon Israel of old, especially as it is formulated in the Decalogue and summed up later as the dual injunction to love God and love one's neighbour (Dt. 6:5 and Lev. 19:18), may still serve to remind us that Christ came not to destroy but to fulfil and did so by himself crossing over to be the slave and, through perfect obedience to God's will, inaugurating the new covenant.

d It may be claimed that, when we look at the OT covenant from the Christian point of view, we can see in a clearer light just what that covenant involved, what it was able to do and what it failed to do. That even within the OT period its inadequacy was recognised may be seen from what Jeremiah (31:31ff.) says, though even that great prophet did not foresee that the new covenant would be inaugurated, not by a miraculous change in human nature, such as Ezekiel too hoped would be brought about (36:26f.), but by the obedience of one upon whose heart the law did not require to be written because he himself was one with the Lawgiver and with the Spirit. It is one of the privileges of the OT theologian that he may point out how the human spirit in face of the challenge and claim of God is stirred up and set in motion and enabled to reach forward towards the light. The OT undoubtedly needs the NT, but, on the other hand, it can give depth to our understanding of that new covenant wherein we stand, and it can help to make us aware of the extent and tragedy of our failure to accept the privileges which have been won for us.

e To return to the covenant community of Israel, we must now look more narrowly at the way in which its distinctive life was perpetuated. Though perhaps Noth's theory of a pre-monarchic Israelite amphictyony

122e is open to certain criticisms and modifications and the confederacy was probably less fully developed than he maintains, there seems little doubt of the correctness of his view that, even in the early days of the Israelite settlement in Palestine, there was something in the nature of a common law which was recognised as valid by a group of Hebrew tribes and which was at least as important for determining Israel's consciousness of its distinctiveness as a people as any warlike experiences it may have gone through and interpreted as divine deliverances. If the Holy War, as von Rad believes, was a significant early institution in Israel, and, as such, gave concrete form to Israel's faith in its divine Leader, there were also legal institutions which, for all that they were primitive in form, gave shape to the developing Israelite way of life which was to be Israel's legacy to the world. That there was such an amphictyonic law seems to be implied both by what the prophets of the 8th and 7th cent. had to say and by a characteristic element in the so-called royal theology.

f From the theological point of view it is most important that we should give due weight to the evidence for an early emergence of a distinctive Israelite pattern of life corresponding to the faith that Yahweh had acted and was acting on his people's behalf and indeed constituting that faith as something of real consequence to the world. If we place, as we ought, the evidence of the NT alongside that of the OT, we can see that the proclamation of the NT *kerygma* would have been singularly ineffective without the witness of Christian lives. Another way of putting this is to say that the *kerygma* is not complete unless it includes the outpouring of the Spirit at Pentecost which made possible a fuller human response to what God did in Christ, a response which is of the essence of our Christian knowledge of God. It is indeed in the *koinonia* of the Christian Church that the language of Christian theology can alone be meaningful. OT theology must also reckon with an Israel of the Spirit which, however imperfectly, lived its faith. The imperative of law does imply an indicative. Law leads forward on the road upon which some at least are adventuring.

123a We have concentrated our attention so far on the Israelite community with its consciousness of a unique relationship to a God whom it called Yahweh and of a status, which it defined by the word covenant, into which it had been brought, as it believed, through a signal act of divine deliverance. That it applied to its God names used of deity by other peoples need not surprise us. Israel was linked with the wider world and in various ways was indebted to it. That it used the name Yahweh as its distinctive name for God concerns us theologically, since, whatever its etymology may have been, the name Yahweh was explained (Exod. 3) as meaning that God was ever present with and available for his people. This thought was caught up and carried forward by the 'Immanuel' (God with us) of Isaiah (7 and 8). Later God is thought of as present in his word (Dt. 30:4), which it was specially the duty of the prophet to utter. Along the cultic line of thought, there was belief in the tabernacling Presence in the Temple. As we look back from our vantage point in Christianity we can see both lines of thought converging on the Word who became flesh and tabernacled among men. If we are to do justice to the OT theologically we must listen to both priest and prophet, since the witness of both was fulfilled and, where necessary, corrected in Christ. Moreover the OT can mirror for us the ways in which we too can go wrong in conceiving of God's presence with his people. Both Jeremiah and Ezekiel knew that possession of the Temple was no guarantee of the Presence and Jeremiah knew that God was accessible to prayer wherever man turned to him in faith.

b The Israelite community might not live to itself. It had to meet the challenge of being in the world while not of it. The great theological interest of the superb historical source which critics have labelled the Yahwistic is that it seems to come, in its beginnings at least, from the period during which Israel under the United Monarchy of David and Solomon became conscious of its place in the world and in some measure of its responsibility towards that world. The table of the nations (Gen. 10) may well belong to this time and indicate an international awareness on Israel's part. Above all, the words addressed to Abraham by God (Gen. 12:3)—' By you all the families of the earth will bless themselves ' or ' In you all the families of the earth will be blessed '—seem to imply an early recognition that Israel was in the world not merely for its own sake. Here is a thought that was to bear wonderful fruit in the world vision of the prophets, until in the hope of the second Isaiah we are, as it were, within sight of the NT. As we look back we can see where Israel turned aside from its calling and how our own narrowness of spirit falls under judgment.

c In the Primeval History (Gen. 2–11) which now forms the preface to the Yahwistic source we have the work of one of the greatest Hebrew writers, who tells us in story form what it means to be man in the stream of history under God's care and judgment. He takes a sombre view of human civilisation, underlining the inexorable consequences of sin in a way which reminds us of that other supreme narrator who describes the court history of David (2 Sam. 9–20 ; 1 Kg. 1–2). Narratives like these can only arise out of a profound historical consciousness and seem to imply an audience capable of appreciating them. Here surely we have proof that an Israel after the spirit was emerging. The same is true of the work of the Yahwist as a whole. What kind of people was this for whom such literature was composed ? The story of Joseph shows us in the person of Joseph Israel serving the world and displaying the qualities which made Israel capable of that service. It also reveals an advanced conception of God's providence (Gen. 45:5ff.).

d It was possibly in this humanistic age too, if we may call it such, that the beginnings of Hebrew Wisdom literature are to be found. If that is so, we would have further evidence that Israel was looking beyond its frontiers and becoming aware of its kinship with other peoples. This has a bearing on the origin of the Hebrew morality. Contact with the wider world doubtless helped Israel to universalise an ethic which it learned as God's chosen and covenanted people. It may be too that in the thought of judicial wisdom as specially belonging to the endowment of kings we have the beginning of the train of thought which by devious ways leads to the conception of Christ as the Wisdom of God. Jeremiah knew ' that it is not in man that walks to direct his steps ' and the OT in general challenges us with the great perennial problem of the control of human life. If we may anticipate here, the close of the OT shows us the shadow of legalism descending upon Judaism—one attempted solution of the problem. The alternative was presented in the One whose authority differed from that of the scribes, and in the endowment of the ' messianic ' ruler (Isa. 11:1ff.) we can recognise the hope which Christ fulfilled.

e This brings us to what has been called ' the royal theology ' which early came to be associated with the Davidic House and must be given a significant place in any theological assessment of the OT. With the institution of the monarchy Israel entered into more intimate relation to the world of its day and the danger of assimilating with that world in respect of religion became even more acute than it had been when the settlers were challenged by the Nature cults of the indigenous farming population. That David realised the importance of preserving connection with the Israel of the early amphictyony is shown by the fact that he brought the Ark, the ancient palladium of the tribes and the symbol of Yahweh's presence, to occupy a position of honour in his new capital. But that was not all. We do not know what part David himself may have played in the development which followed. What does seem probable is that there were those

123e intimately associated with the royal house who realised that theological justification must be found for such an innovation in Israel's life as the monarchy represented. Of very great significance is the story of how Nathan conveyed to David the divine promise of permanence for his royal house. How profound was the theology which was worked out is shown by certain of the Psalms (e.g. 2, 72, 89, 110) which, for all their probable links with Canaanite thought about monarchy, show that there were those in Israel who realised that the new covenant with the Davidic house must be linked with the covenant which was the basis of Israel's existence as a people, and that the king would not fulfil his part unless he became the guarantor of the true Israelite way of life. The special significance attached to the Davidic house colours the thought of the Deuteronomic editor of the Books of Kings and the outlook of the Chronicler in whose theological thought David played a central part. It is against the background of this royal theology too that, in the 8th cent. prophets and later, we find the emergence of the 'messianic hope', which, developed within and beyond the OT in various forms, was part of the material which Jesus was to use selectively and creatively in interpreting his own person and task. The use made by Jesus of the 'messianic' ideology, rejecting part of it decisively and combining part of it with ideas from elsewhere, provides us with an object lesson to guide us in our theological handling of the OT. Jesus solved the problems of Scripture in creative action, and theological interpretation must so throw Scripture into relief that its letter will be given the true character of witness to the living God and not become a dead letter to hinder the Church in its task of creative obedience under the guidance of the Spirit working in and through it.

124a The bright hopes which were associated with the Hebrew monarchy were doomed to disappointment and, with the break in the political unity of Israel brought about by the Disruption and various changes in the balance of power beyond Israel's borders, the Hebrew kingdoms found themselves in a struggle for survival in a world which seemed to take no account of the human values for which Israel in the thought of its best representatives stood. The Israelite pattern of life was threatened both from within and from without and it was the danger from within that was the more serious. It was to meet the threat of this internal collapse and to interpret the great movements of world powers in which Israel was inevitably involved that the unique succession of the Hebrew prophets made its appearance and played its part during the centuries when mankind was passing through one of its most decisive periods of transition. A spiritual battle, in which a very few men were the protagonists, was fought and won, and so the stage was set for the supreme historical climax associated with the beginnings of Christianity.

b The detailed story of Hebrew prophecy is dealt with elsewhere. Here in the theological interest it is necessary to emphasise certain points.

It is in Hebrew prophecy that the characteristic Israelite conception of revelation comes most clearly to light. It is true that the Hebrews recognised certain natural phenomena as media of revelation, as did other peoples, while certain artificial symbols, the sacred lots, the Ark, the Tabernacle, and the Temple played their several parts. It was through specially chosen men, however, that God spoke to his people most distinctively and the three classes of men who in their various ways spoke for God were the priests, the prophets and the wise men. The priests supplied *tôrāh* or instruction which was not confined to liturgical matters but included ethical teaching. The wise men seem to have made their greatest contribution later. Yet long before the exile their shrewd observation of life and their gift for expressing religious truth in pithy phrases that brought it within the comprehension of the common man were doubtless put at the service of Yahwism. It was in the prophets, however, that the agents were 124b
found who best combined continuity with Israel's most distinctive past and sensitivity to the living word of God. Recent study of the phenomenon of prophecy in Israel has tended to discard the category of religious genius, which seemed appropriate to an earlier generation of interpreters, and has concentrated rather upon the prophetic tradition by which the prophet received and handed on the insights of Israel's great past when, through the work of Moses and his successors in the pre-monarchic period, the community began to take shape, and upon his obedience to the living word of God even when it took the form of an inexorable warning of judgment. There has been a further emphasis upon the links between prophet and priest with the interesting identification of the person of the so-called cultic prophet. This should serve to keep us, while giving a large place to the prophetic criticism of the Israelite community, from failing to do justice to those who made of the Hebrew cult a real means of grace. The fact that the priest came not unjustly under the lash of the prophet's invective should not make us blind to the revelational value of the Israelite system of worship which, as above all the Psalter shows, can serve us as a guide in piety no less than as a warning.

The criticism of Israelite society by the prophets c
can best be appreciated if we recognise that they were in the first instance applying the criterion of the old amphictyonic law of the confederate tribes to the state of affairs in their own day. The prophet stood for much more than the nomadic ideal in conflict with an agricultural and urban society. His convictions arose from the fact that he had inherited the tradition of a way of life which was incumbent on Israel as the covenanted people of God, a way of life imposed by a God who demanded righteousness because he himself was righteous. We must suppose that they knew the value of this way of life, because, however much the people as a whole had declined in their loyalty to Yahweh, they themselves had been reared in circles in which the old morality was not yet dead and so had learned from living examples what were the values for which Israel was called upon to stand. That there were those who shared the outlook on life of the great prophets we know from the fact that their words were remembered and handed down. Here we have proof of the existence of what we may rightly call an Israel of the spirit.

The great prophets of the 8th and 7th cent. were d
prophets of judgment. They saw what was implicit in the covenantal relationship and proclaimed that a disobedient Israel must come under the flail of whatever avenging power God chose to use. The Day of the Lord would not bring the triumph Israel hoped for. In the 8th cent. the avenger proved to be Assyria, at the beginning of the 6th, Babylon. In thus using the nations as instruments of his purpose and making it clear that his relation to Israel was a moral and not a natural one, Yahweh was, the prophets believed, showing himself as the Lord of history. It was an astonishing faith which, because it represented response to a living God, was capable of surviving the wreck of the earthly fortunes of those who held it. When many of the old forms of life and worship in which Israel's religious beliefs had found concrete expression were swept away in the storm of events it showed itself capable of creating new forms which expressed it even more adequately. What is most remarkable is that, before the final disaster came, there were those in Israel who perceived clearly what must come and could even see beyond the disaster and feel sure that God would recreate the people whose natural existence he must destroy.

We have already seen that these prophets of judgment found one expression of their faith for the future of Israel in the 'Messianic' hope. It was a hope in the historic recovery of Israel under a ruler who would be all that a descendant of David ought to be, and,

124d limited in its horizon though it was, it contained elements with a vitality which enabled them to be used in a new synthesis, when the old limited hope had become a snare and a delusion.

125a Before the final crash came and the kingdom of Judah had gone, there came in Judah the reform movement which was associated with the Deuteronomic Code. Certainty as to the origin of this cannot be reached, but the probability is that it represents the religious and legal traditions of the Northern Kingdom which at some period in Judah prior to the reformation sponsored by Josiah came to be appropriated by a group of faithful men in Judah. One suggestion is that they were the Levites in alliance with the substantial farmers in Judah, another that they belonged to the disciples of Isaiah. Whatever the truth of the matter may be, the Book of Deuteronomy with its code and framework of hortatory chapters is now one of the most central portions of the OT and provides us with a portrait of Israel by looking on which we can clearly see delineated much that was finest in Israel's response to God. We can also recognise features which belong to the limitations of Israel's faith, but even these have much to teach us still.

b It is clear that, just as much that was most significant in the Yahwistic source in the Pentateuch is characteristic of a time when Israel was reaching self-consciousness, becoming more fully aware of the world in which it found itself and asking itself how it had arrived where it now was, so the Book of Deuteronomy represents the profound questioning of those who were deeply concerned to make the people of Israel more conscious of its status as God's people and of all that that involved. We have the emphasis on God's gracious initiative in the deliverance of Israel from Egypt, on the reason for that deliverance in the inscrutable will of God and on the response in gratitude that demanded, a response which must find expression in life. Great prominence is given to the covenant form of Israel's community life, and with the word *b^{e}rîth* (covenant) is linked that rich word *ḥesedh* (steadfast love, covenant love, devotion) which is essentially the bond of the covenant and, as such, corresponds to some extent, to the NT word ἀγάπη. There is little doubt that we are not far from the spiritual milieu to which the prophet Hosea belonged, the prophet who described the required Israelite way of life by using words like *ḥesedh*, *ṣ^{e}dhāḳāh* (righteousness), *'^{e}meth* and *'^{e}mûnāh* (truth and faithfulness), and *da'ath '^{e}lōhîm* (the knowledge of God which is expressed in brotherly conduct within the Community).

c In the Code of Deuteronomy itself we are given numerous concrete examples of what the Israelite pattern of life should look like in detail. Once again, whatever idealisation there may be here, it seems certain that the Code reflects a way of life which was more than an unrealised ideal. The spirit of brotherhood which inspires some of the injunctions in this wonderful book must have animated living men as well. This was not all merely thought out ; it was lived before it was taught. Deuteronomy lays down many regulations, it is true, but much that it requires goes beyond the letter of any possible law and such exhortations would have meant little except among men who had reached a high level of understanding of the nature of community.

d It is important to notice that Deuteronomy is the first book in the OT in which the word *bāḥar* (choose) is used as the characteristic expression to describe Yahweh's relation to Israel. This use of a special technical term suggests that a new level of religious reflection had been reached. This election of Israel is clearly thought of as election for a purpose and the purpose, according to the Book of Deuteronomy, is the conforming of Israel's will to the will of God which is set forth in the injunctions of the code. When one is tempted to dismiss this as legalism, one should remember that the controlling thought is that of God's gracious intervention to make Israel a people and that one motive of obedience ought to be gratitude for all that God has done and is still doing in his providential care for Israel. 12

e Moreover, there is a very practical reason why the injunctions of the law should not be neglected. 'Lay to your heart all the words which I enjoin upon you this day, that ye may command them to your children, that they may be careful to do all the words of this law. For it is no trifle for you, but it is your life' (Dt. 32:46–7). It is quite true that the life meant here is not the ζωὴ αἰώνιος (eternal life) of the Fourth Gospel, but at least our eyes are turned in the direction of the living God of Israel's faith whose will it was that his people should, through their conformity to the terms of the covenant, share in that abundant life which was intended for them. Life is one of the key words of the Bible and what it represents is, in the thought of Deuteronomy, made readily available to Israel since the conditions for obtaining it are no secret. 'For what great nation is there that has a god so near to it as the Lord our God is to us, whenever we call upon him ? And what great nation is there, that has statutes and ordinances so righteous as all this law which I set before you this day ? ' (Dt. 4:7f.). Deuteronomy makes it very clear what is the purpose of God's revelation : 'The secret things belong to the Lord our God ; but the things that are revealed belong to us and to our children for ever, that we may do all the words of this law.' In one passage classic expression is given to the thought of the nearness of God in his word : 'For this commandment which I command you this day is not too hard for you, neither is it far off. It is not in heaven, that you should say, " who will go up for us to heaven, and bring it to us, that we may hear it and do it ? " Neither is it beyond the sea, that you should say, " Who will go over the sea for us, and bring it to us, that we may hear it and do it ? " But the word is very near you ; it is in your mouth and in your heart, so that you can do it. See I have set before you this day life and good, death and evil' (Dt. 30:11–15).

f If there is legalism in this book, it should not be forgotten that it also contains the summary of man's duty to God of which Jesus approved (Dt. 6:5). Although the complementary injunction 'You shall love your neighbour as yourself'—or perhaps better 'You shall love your neighbour with all your might'—(Lev. 19:18) is not given here in so many words, it is clear that a right attitude to the neighbour occupies a central place in the thought of Deuteronomy. The great defect of the book as we look at it from the Christian angle is that it looks inwards and not outwards. There is scarcely a trace of the world view of the Yahwist. Israel is to obey God, but there is no suggestion that God might be desiring that other peoples should obey him too and that Israel had been given the privilege of helping to bring this about. It is strange indeed that in a book of such depth of understanding there should be such narrow horizons. There is also present an intolerance which shocks us until we remember what a very precious treasure of faith it is intended to guard. Yet we must not forget that even within the OT period a deeper understanding of God's will was reached which brought with it once more the vision and challenge of wide horizons.

The Book of Deuteronomy gives the impression of a curious state of equilibrium having been reached. The Land of Promise has to be reoccupied in the sense that Israel is summoned to make good its right to be there by proving itself to be Israel in the fullest sense. But Israel has only to make an act of recollection and bestir itself and all will be well. There is presage of disaster, however, in the clouds of judgment which are piling up, and the age which followed Josiah's reform witnessed the breaking of the storm and the dissolution of the Israelite community in the familiar national form. 126

To help us to understand what happened and how Israel began to be recreated from the ruins, we are b

126b fortunate in having records of the prophecies of Jeremiah and Ezekiel for the beginning of the period and of the Second Isaiah somewhat later. Although there are many things we should like to know about those years when the Israel of the monarchy disappeared and the foundations of Judaism began to be laid, it is possible for us to look out on the world of that day with its problems and crises and reorientations through the eyes of men of extraordinary spiritual insight.

c Hosea in his day had understood that the essence of what God wanted of his people was loyalty to himself and to the way of life which was to reflect his righteousness. Jeremiah is Hosea's spiritual successor and he expresses the same yearning over a people strangely oblivious to what its high calling involved. ' Cross to the coasts of Cyprus and see, or send to Kedar and examine with care ; see if there has been such a thing. Has a nation changed its gods, even though they are no gods ? But my people have changed their glory for that which does not profit. Be appalled, O heavens, at this, be shocked, be utterly desolate, says the Lord, for my people have committed two evils : they have forsaken me, the fountain of living waters, and hewed out cisterns for themselves, broken cisterns, that can hold no water '. Jeremiah and Ezekiel both paint unforgettable pictures of how a wayward and undisciplined people went far astray and make us aware of both the anger and pity of God who found his will thus flouted. While it is true that individualism in Israel did not originate in the thought and experience of these prophets, it is certainly true that they helped to make men more aware of the nature of human responsibility towards a God who made inexorable demands upon man, and, at the same time, of the curious disability in man which prevented him from rendering that due obedience.

d The emphasis on individual responsibility in Ezekiel (see esp. ch. 18) may seem extreme, but we have to remember that the prophet is trying to release his hearers from the fatalism which did not clearly distinguish between society and the units which went to form it and led to the forming of the proverb about the children's teeth being set on edge because of the fathers' having eaten sour grapes (Jer. 31:29f. ; Ezek. 18:2). The theologian must handle such a passage sympathetically and remember that the prophet is not speaking in cold blood but is fighting the despair of those who thought that a new beginning was impossible. That is the meaning too of Ezekiel's vision (ch. 37) of the valley of dry bones which became a great army of living men. Both Jeremiah and Ezekiel believed that the depravity of Israel could only be cured if God himself acted on men's hearts (Jer. 31:33 ; Ezek. 36:26f.) but Jeremiah believed that there was something practical which the exiles in Babylon could do at once : ' Seek the welfare of the city where I have sent you into exile, and pray to the Lord on its behalf, for in its welfare you will find your welfare . . . For I know the plans I have for you, says the Lord, plans for welfare and not for evil, to give you a future and a hope. Then you will call upon me and come and pray to me, and I will hear you. You will seek me with all your heart ' (Jer. 29:7, 11–13). Israel's recovery of its hope and trust in God and its consequent survival as a people in a new form through its discovery that God was available everywhere is an interesting example of how a theological idea becomes important as it is embodied in life. Israel in dispersion became witness to the omnipresence of God and to the universality of his power.

e In the so-called confessions of Jeremiah (11:18–23, 12:1–6, 15:10–21, 17:12–18, 18:18–23, 20:7–18) we are permitted a closer look at the mystery of the prophetic experience than anywhere else. What perhaps strikes one most forcibly is the way in which God, in making his revelation through the prophet, has to take possession of the prophet's personality, without, however, obliterating the distinction between the divine and the human, so that the revelation in the last resort is the 126e
prophet himself. We shall see how, in this way, Jeremiah probably contributed to one of the deepest insights which the OT contains. If we knew more, it would probably have been clear to us that Jeremiah did not stand absolutely alone. There was at least Baruch who believed in him. Yet one does get the impression that in the crisis of its fate Israel's future, humanly speaking, rested upon Jeremiah. So long as he was there there was a response to God on Israel's behalf, and Jeremiah had his spiritual successors who came to themselves in exile and laid hold on the essentials of their faith.

It may well have been, however, that another link f
with Israel's past held firm and assisted recovery. The fact that the great prophet of the exile, to whom we give the name the Second Isaiah, so clearly looks back to, and feels himself in continuity with, Isaiah of the 8th cent. is probably best to be explained by a living prophetic tradition connecting the two men. However that may be, we have now to notice how this unknown prophet gathered together and summed up the essential message which his predecessors had delivered and succeeded in making clearer than ever before what was Israel's calling and task in the world. The Second Isaiah is the theologian *par excellence* of the OT, but his importance for theology lies, not so much in any abstract formulations he may have reached about the oneness and creative power of God, as in the way in which he seems to have given living embodiment to his understanding of Israel's call to be God's servant in the world. We can scarcely doubt that behind his prophecies lies a tremendous personal experience and witness.

In the prophecies of the Second Isaiah we get the g
culmination of the conviction of the First Isaiah that Yahweh was the Lord of History. Then the Assyrian without his own knowledge had been the rod in the hand of God to chastise his people (Isa. 10:5ff.). Now Cyrus, once more unwittingly, was to be God's instrument—he is even called ' his anointed ' (Isa. 45:1)—to restore the fortunes of Israel. Isaiah and those who accepted his insight, his disciples in whom his hope of a remnant realised itself, kept the soul of Israel alive by confessing the justice of God's judgment. The Second Isaiah and those who recovered hope through his inspiration, building again on the foundation of faith which Isaiah had spoken of, ensured the continuance of the Remnant into a new age, even though the brilliant colours with which the prophet painted the future were destined to fade. The Second Isaiah was of those who mount up with wings as eagles, but, in the days that followed, the faithful in Israel belonged to the ranks of those who walk without fainting.

The God of history was one who carried his people, h
unlike the idols of the Babylonians who had to be carried on the shoulders of their priests (Isa. 46:1ff.). The prophet's repeated polemic against images was no mere piece of argument. It reflects the experience of a man who knew what God was doing for him and what he could do for his people. Moreover the folly of the idolaters was shown by the reflection that the God whom they sought to depict was the Creator of all that is as well as the controller of the destiny of all men. These two convictions seem to fuse together in the thought of this prophet and it is difficult to say which was prior to the other. Perhaps the Second Isaiah owed his glowing faith in the creative power of God to the cultic tradition by which the literary types to be found among his prophecies suggest that he was influenced. We have to look to the Psalms to find anything comparable to the first chapter of Genesis which doubtless represents the culmination of generations of reflection in some priestly college.

The climax of the Second Isaiah's thought and, it may be conjectured, of his service to his people, lies in the way in which he broke out of the closed circle in which Deuteronomy had confined Israel (if Judaism later grew a hard shell to protect itself, at

126b least it preserved in writing the vision of the Second Isaiah and included the book of Jonah in its prophetic canon; cf. also Isa. 19:23f. and Ps. 87), asserted that election implied mission and that Israel's failure as the servant to fulfil the task set it by God could only be redeemed by the vicarious suffering of a servant of the Lord who should represent Israel as a covenant of humanity and a light to the nations and seal his witness by his death. No doubt many colours from the palette of history went into this picture. Jeremiah surely provided inspiration by his faithful endurance. We do not know to what extent the prophet himself sought to play a part which was beyond any single man. This at least is surely true, that in this marvellous venture of faith the OT and NT come closest together.

127a We must now look briefly at the institution of Judaism which we find in being after the soaring enthusiasm and glowing hopes of the Second Isaiah have paled into the light of common day. We shall not only look at the institution as it was in these post-exilic centuries but shall look back at the cultic tradition which gave another line of continuity to Israel than that provided by the prophetic tradition.

We have just seen that the theological reflection of some priestly college may have contributed one of the dominant strands in the thought of the Second Isaiah. Belief in God's creative power no doubt owed much to the liturgy of the Temple, especially to the Psalms with their flights of inspired imagination. It should not be forgotten that it was in the priestly tradition that the Hebrew understanding of the nature of man as not just a part of nature like the beasts but as created in the image and likeness of God (Gen. 1:27, 5:1) was reached. It is not surprising that we have a Psalm (8:5) which says the same thing in more poetical language and, like the first Genesis passage, immediately connects the thought of man's likeness to God with his authority over the lower creatures. Whatever else the assertion may mean it is certain that it represents the priestly effort to describe that intimacy of relation between God and man which distinguishes man from every other creature. But intimate as the relationship is, it implies no kind of identity between God and man. Ezekiel, who was a priest turned prophet, knew this well when, in his variation on the Eden story (Ezek. 28), he reminded the king of Tyre that, for all his exaltation, he was but a man and no god. It is from passages like these which confront man with God that we learn best what the OT has to tell us about man. Hebrew psychological thought is by no means unified and self-consistent, but the OT gives classical expression to the belief that man was created by God, is maintained in life by him and lives that life under God's searching scrutiny (see esp. Ps. 139).

b A cult which in ritual, psalmody and instruction gave Israel such profound insights into the status of man and guided and inspired so magnificently man's response to God in adoration, praise, confession and supplication must not be taken lightly in any theological handling of the OT. It should not be forgotten that two of the earliest and most attractive glimpses we get into Hebrew piety are associated with the ritual of sacrifice (Jg. 13; 1 Sam. 1). The Hebrew cultic system does no doubt illustrate the subtle dangers to which the worship of God is exposed when attention is concentrated on what men do. The Hebrew prophets said the final word about that. But, when we read Micah's contrast of the ritual of sacrifice with what God really required of man, we should not forget that the third requirement was that man should walk humbly with God, and that it was in the Temple that Micah's great contemporary, Isaiah, whose insight he may have been echoing in these words, reached his conviction of the transcendence of God, before whom humility was fitting and by whom arrogance was condemned.

c The Hebrew Cult served various ends. It helped to maintain a sense of the Presence of God in the midst of his people, the importance of which we must not minimise. 127c The danger of the symbolism we can see from what Jeremiah said one day in the Temple (7:4) and Ezekiel's dreadful vision of the departing Presence (10:18f., 11:22f.) reminds us how the life can go out of a religious institution. But from the abundant evidence of the Psalter it is possible to gain some idea of the reality of Israel's worship, while the inexhaustible vitality of the Psalter right up to the present day is evidence in defence of those who created it. That the NT calls the living fellowship of the Church the temple of God ought to impress upon us the value of the institution which could supply the metaphor and remind us that institutions have still their value so long as they do not quench the spirit.

There was an elaborate system of sacrifices, the d purpose of which cannot be brought under a single explanation. It seems clear that the motives of obedience, gratitude, desire for communion, desire for forgiveness are all present. It does not seem to be the case that the offering of blood in certain sacrifices had anything to do with any idea of the vicariousness of the death of a victim, since heinous sin which merited the punishment of death could not be atoned for by any sacrifice. In fact the sacrificial system did not properly avail to procure God's forgiveness of sin in the sense in which the prophets spoke of sin as moral offences against God. For the forgiveness of these men had simply to rely on his mercy. 'Nevertheless,' as A. R. S. Kennedy points out (HDB, 1 vol., 818a), although the doctrine that the death of the victim was a vicarious punishment for the sin of the offerer is not to be found in the legislation itself, the thought was one that could scarcely fail to suggest itself to the popular mind—a conclusion to which it was doubtless assisted by the representation of the vicarious sufferings of the Servant in Is. 53.'

This popular tendency illustrates how a superficial e attitude to sin could easily be caused by a system which used the word 'sin' ambiguously. We must not forget, however, that the idea behind the cult was that God himself in his grace had provided a means of fellowship with himself, an opportunity of worship and protection from dangers which primitive thought associated with certain actions. That a Christian today cannot recognise these dangers as real need not prevent him from doing justice to the faith in God's gracious provision for his people's safety which inspired the sacrificial system. The value of trying to work out an elaborate typology from the sacrificial regulations is highly doubtful. That deliberate moral offences, sins committed 'with a high hand' could not be dealt with by propitiatory sacrifice, bears a direct relevance to what the NT has to say about sin. The use made by the author of the Epistle to the Hebrews of the ritual of the Day of Atonement to contrast the efficacy of what was done by Christ with the inefficacy of the sacrificial system of the OT dispensation, should not be used to obscure the important fact that it was not supposed under the OT dispensation that sacrifice could heal the breach of fellowship that sin properly so-called had caused. That sin in all its heinousness was understood for what it was by those in charge of Israel's worship is shown by the inclusion in the Psalter of psalms like 50 and 51. These may have been the composition of cultic prophets but, whoever their authors may have been, they knew what sin was when they wrote as they did.

In this concluding section brief reference must first 128a be made to the Wisdom books of the OT. Among these the Book of Proverbs, in particular, has presented a problem to those who have sought to systematise the teaching of the OT. There seems to be little or nothing here of the distinctive faith of Israel as the covenant people, no mention of the saving acts of God in history, nothing about the characteristic forms of Hebrew life. The book seems to be addressed to man in general and, indeed, it is certain that many of its sayings have been culled from foreign sources. Proverbial literature over-

128a leaps national boundaries and has a universal character. Nevertheless, it is fitting that the Book of Proverbs should have a place in the Canon of the OT. We know from the legal material in the OT that Israel's religion was worked out in the detail of human life and here in the Book of Proverbs we see the process of making the faith concrete being carried into situations with which law could not always deal. If the motive of prudence is frequently prominent, we should remind ourselves that a religion is none the worse for a liberal dash of plain common sense. But the distinctive note of the prophetic teaching keeps breaking through. It might have been an Amos or a Micah who said : 'Diverse weights are an abomination to the Lord, and false scales are not good' (Prov. 20:23) or a Jeremiah who declared : 'The sacrifice of the wicked is an abomination to the Lord, but the prayer of the upright is his delight.' Could the quality of Israel's religion be better expressed than by words like these : 'Righteousness exalts a nation, but sin is a reproach to any people'?

b What the Hebrews called *ḥokhmāh* (wisdom) includes a kind of rudimentary science largely of the observational kind and ethical aphorisms related to the conduct of life. In the Book of Proverbs we can detect the emergence in Israel of rationalism. Men were beginning to face a whole new series of problems which challenged thought and the stirring of the human mind in response to these must have seemed dangerous to many orthodox and pious people. If thinkers were too daring they had to be reminded that 'the fear of the Lord is the beginning of wisdom and the knowledge of the Holy One is insight' (Prov. 9:10). At the end of the Wisdom poem in the book of Job where the inscrutable marvels of the universe are rehearsed, man is reminded that, for all his great achievements in mastering Nature, there is a wisdom which is proper to God alone. Man's true wisdom is of another kind. 'Behold, the fear of the Lord, that is wisdom ; and to depart from evil is understanding' (Job 28:28).

c Perhaps the most remarkable philosophical flight is to be found in the hypostatisation of Wisdom in Prov. 8 which may have helped to supply categories of thought both to St Paul when he spoke of Christ as the power and wisdom of God (1 C. 1:24) and to the author of the Fourth Gospel in the working-out of his doctrine of the Logos. We can see that face to face with the mystery of the world the Hebrew mind could respond with a richness of imagination which anticipated the fuller revelation that was yet to be. But in its handling of the problem of Wisdom the Hebrew was essentially practical and, when the eternal Wisdom became flesh, it was as a man who went about doing good.

d Out on the frontiers of Israel's faith we have the authors of the Books of Job and Ecclesiastes. The former was no detached thinker playing with intellectual problems but was a man for whom it was a very personal question why, in a world where suffering was so often undeserved, one should still do the right and keep his faith. His book stands as a warning of how orthodoxy can browbeat honest doubt and practise the most exquisite cruelty upon those who are caught in the grip of circumstance. A more enigmatic and controversial figure is Ecclesiastes, whoever concealed himself behind that name. Yet, in spite of his agnosticism and disillusionment, he showed by the things he could not surrender how a tradition of faith can keep a man from final despair.

e In an age when new hopes were stirring and the climax of history seemed to many to be at hand, Ecclesiastes retained the negative attitude to death and what lay beyond it which is characteristic of most of the OT. One of the most astonishing things about Israel's religious faith is the warmth and intensity of fellowship with God which was experienced against the sombre background of a belief in nothing but the most shadowy and unsatisfying kind of survival after death. In Amos (ch. 9) and Psalm 139 we find the belief that Yahweh's writ extended even to the underworld

of Sheol, but there is little evidence till near the end of the OT period that there was any belief in a blessed existence after death. It may well be that in these days, when so many men and women of fine character and deep sensitivity of spirit find it difficult, if not impossible, to accept the Christian hope, a wise handling of the OT by the Church might bring such people to a point where the word which transforms everything might have a chance to be heard. Feverish attempts to find the belief in a future life in places where it is almost certainly absent are not very helpful. A long, steady look into the dark through the eyes of an OT saint is a bracing experience. 128e

f It seems to have been in the storm and stress of the struggle with hellenistic paganism that the hope of resurrection made its appearance (Dan. 12:2 ; possibly also Isa. 26:19). Whatever foreign influences may have given form to the hope, there is little doubt that what gave substance to it was that sense of fellowship with the living God which was no new thing. It may have been the sudden conviction that the Judge of all the earth must do right by those valiants for the truth who were suffering martyrdom which enabled men to make the daring leap of faith. We cannot know for certain.

g The prophets of earlier centuries had proclaimed that the Day of the Lord men hoped for would be a day of judgment on God's people as well as on the nations. Some of them too had looked beyond the judgment to the horizon of time when a kingdom of righteousness and peace would be established. In the last centuries before Christ came this hope changed into the expectation of an imminent climax when a new age of supernatural splendour would succeed the age of conflict and distress in which men were involved. God would bring history to its fulfilment. This hope produced the literary type called apocalyptic, of which the most complete example in the OT is the Book of Daniel. It is perhaps not without significance that in a book which tells of the passing pomp of empires, stories are also told of individuals who in an alien world of menacing danger remained faithful to the truth as they knew it. On such loyalty God could build his kingdom and those saints of the Most High are symbolised for us in the mysterious figure of the 'one like a son of man' (Dan. 7:13) who was at least one source of the title which Jesus chose for himself. It was no accident that it was this title and that other one of the Servant which he combined with such of the ideas associated with the title of Messiah as would serve his purpose. As Son of Man and Servant he linked himself with those who in service and sacrifice had proclaimed their faith in deeds and not just in words and, being themselves the true Israel of their day, prepared the way for the fuller revelation and the fuller response that was to come. It is in the light of that fuller revelation that we can best do justice to what they actually did, and estimate truly who the God was who claimed their allegiance.

Bibliography—C. H. Dodd, *The Bible to-day* (1946) ; W. Eichrodt, *Theologie des Alten Testaments* (1933–9), *Man in the Old Testament* (1951) ; P. van Imschoot, *Théologie de l'Ancien Testament* (1954–6) ; E. Jacob, *Théologie de L'Ancien Testament* (1955) ; A. R. Johnson, *Sacral Kingship in Ancient Israel* (1955) ; L. Köhler, *Theologie des Alten Testaments*, 3rd ed. (1953) ; S. Mowinckel, *He that cometh* (1956) ; N. W. Porteous, 'Old Testament Theology', Section XI in *The Old Testament and Modern Study* (1951) ; G. von Rad, *Theologie des Alten Testaments*, i (1957) ; H. W. Robinson, 'The Theology of the Old Testament', Section V in *Record and Revelation* (1938), *Inspiration and Revelation in the Old Testament* (1946) ; H. H. Rowley, *The Biblical Doctrine of Election* (1950), *The Faith of Israel* (1956) ; J. C. Rylaarsdam, *Revelation in the Jewish Wisdom Literature* (1946) ; Th. C. Vriezen, *Theologie des Alten Testaments in Grundzügen* (1956) ; G. E. Wright, *The Old Testament against its Environment* (1950), *God who Acts* (1952).

THE RELIGION OF ISRAEL

By G. W. Anderson

129a The history of Israel's religion is a record of the blending of the indigenous and the borrowed, of the manifestation of the constant in the changing, of continuity in development, and of unity in variety. The material for the study of it is derived on the one hand from the OT documents themselves, sometimes fragmentary and difficult to interpret, and on the other from the evidence provided by archaeological research, also incomplete and sometimes of debatable significance, but now available in increasing profusion. The biblical and extra-biblical sources illuminate the religion both of Israel and of Israel's neighbours. Without some knowledge of the latter the former cannot be adequately understood. Yet the faith of Israel has its own distinctive character, which is displayed both in its OT development and in its sequels in post-biblical Judaism and in Christianity. Any attempt to describe it solely in terms of its environment leaves much unexplained.

b Two factors have contributed greatly to the modern study of Hebrew religion. The first of these is the critical study of OT literature, which, in so far as it enables us to date the various books or parts of books, makes possible some sort of reconstruction of the phases through which Hebrew religion passed. The Graf-Wellhausen hypothesis of the composition of the Pentateuch, which was so ably expounded and so widely accepted in the latter part of the 19th cent., was associated with one theory of the development of Israel's religion, according to which it exhibits three main stages : the primitive or pre-prophetic, the prophetic, and the legalistic. Among the vigorous attacks made on the literary hypothesis in recent decades is the claim that the reconstruction of Israel's religion which is associated with it is artificial, being based on a defective analysis of the documents and a mistaken view of the history of religion in general. At all events there is today a much more cautious attitude to the dating of the documents and a greater reluctance to try to deduce from them an orderly development in the history of Hebrew religion.

c The second factor is the rapid progress of archaeological investigation, which has illuminated not only the specifically religious beliefs and practices but also the whole range of life and experience in the ancient Near East. Of outstanding importance are the discoveries made at Râs Shamra in northern Syria, which include religious texts of great value. In spite of the fact that they come not from Palestine but from Syria and are at least as early as the 14th cent. B.C., they shed valuable light on the religious environment of Israel. Elsewhere, the excavation of sanctuary sites has done much to illustrate cultic praxis. But even discoveries which are not directly or obviously religious contribute to the understanding of our subject, since they help to recreate the setting and the atmosphere of life in ancient Israel and the varied influences to which religion was exposed. Further, the results of archaeological discovery may enable us to correct erroneous conclusions derived from literary analysis, particularly in the early period.

130a **The Religion of the Patriarchs**—The patriarchal narratives in Genesis represent the ancestors of the Hebrews as worshippers of the one true God. If, however, we accept the analysis of the Pentateuch into 130 literary sources composed centuries later than the patriarchal period, or hold that it is derived from a mass of traditions which have passed through a long process of growth and revision, the evidential value of these stories clearly calls for careful scrutiny. The claim has been made that they tell us much more about the religion of the time of the monarchy than about the religion of the patriarchs. References to places such as Shechem, Bethel, Hebron and Beersheba may well owe something to the later traditions of the sanctuaries which flourished there. But archaeological discovery has done much to vindicate the general reliability of the picture which these stories give of the period to which they refer. In particular, the Nuzu tablets show that some of the stories in Genesis reflect the law and custom of Mesopotamian society about the middle of the 2nd millennium B.C. Writers or traditionists of the period of the monarchy would not have imposed on the narratives features unknown in Israelite society in their own time. There is, it is true, no extra-biblical corroboration of the occurrence of any specific event or the existence of any particular person mentioned in the patriarchal stories ; but they cannot simply be dismissed as fabrications ; and it is unwise to treat any element in them as late without good reason.

The stories contain allusions to features which b belonged to Canaanite religion before the Hebrew invasion and which were subsequently adopted by the Hebrews, e.g. the sacred pillar (Gen. 28:18, 33:20), the sacred tree (Gen. 12:6, 13:18, 14:13, 21:33, 35:4), the sacred spring (Gen. 16:14), the teraphim (Gen. 31:19, 34f.) or household idols which, as the Nuzu tablets show, guaranteed the right of inheritance. There are also several divine titles which resemble those found in the Râs Shamra texts. These are compounds of El, the name of the chief god in the Ugaritic pantheon. Thus we find El Elyon (Gen. 14:18–20, 22), El Shaddai (Gen. 17:1, 28:3, 35:11, 48:3, 49:25), El Roi (Gen. 16:13), El Olam (Gen. 21:33), El Bethel (Gen. 31:13, 35:7). Of these, El Elyon and El Shaddai are of special interest and importance. El Elyon, which occurs in the passage about Melchizedek, the priest-king of Salem, was in all probability associated with the pre-Israelite cult at the sanctuary of Jerusalem and survived in Hebrew usage as a title of Yahweh. El Shaddai is said in Exod. 6:3 to be the name by which Yahweh revealed himself to the patriarchs.

Though we cannot exclude the likelihood that some c of the material was embodied in the traditions after the Conquest, these elements give some indication of the environment of the pre-Mosaic Hebrews in Canaan, an environment by which they cannot have been unaffected. In addition to the general picture of the patriarchs as worshippers of the one true God, there are references to idolatry among the ancestors of Israel at this period (Gen. 35:2 ; Jos. 24:2).

We must ask, however, whether there is evidence of d a religious faith distinct from that of Canaan and akin to that of Moses and the prophets. The answer to this question depends to some extent on our belief or disbelief in the existence of the patriarchs as historical

0d individuals. In some stories what is related of an individual is in all probability the record of tribal or national events (Gen. 31:46ff., 34:1ff., cf. 25:23, 27:27–9, 39f., 49:2–27). But this does not by any means apply to all. Again, it has often been claimed that some at least of the patriarchs were originally divine figures. The names Terah, Laban, Sarah, and Milcah may be associated with moon worship; and Abraham (or Abi-ram), Isaac, and Jacob have been thought to be divine names. But there is in fact little or no positive evidence for this: and the supposition is remote from the spirit of the narratives.

e Much nearer the mark is the view which sees in the patriarchs cult-founders. A. Alt has used evidence from Palmyrene and Nabataean texts to suggest that the terms 'Shield of Abraham' (Gen. 15:1), 'Fear (or, perhaps, Kinsman) of Isaac' (Gen. 31:42, 53), 'Mighty One of Jacob' (Gen. 49:24) indicate deities who had revealed themselves to the patriarchs, and that each theophany had given rise to the cult of the deity in question, who was henceforth known by this title. Such a cult differed profoundly from those which were associated with specific regions or particular sanctuaries. Beginning with a personal revelation of the deity to the cult-founder and with an act of choice by the latter, it was personal, and related above all to the family or clan. According to Alt, these patriarchal deities were later fused with the Mosaic Yahweh. Without necessarily accepting every detail of the theory, we may recognise in the character of a faith such as Alt describes, with its emphasis on personal revelation, personal choice, and personal relationship, something which is in harmony with much in the patriarchal narratives themselves and also with the distinctive Hebraic faith of later ages. When all allowance has been made for accretions to the tradition, and for those narratives in which clan history is narrated in individual terms, it is not fanciful to suppose that such men as the patriarchs did exist and did exercise such a faith.

1a **The Religion of Moses**—In turning to the narratives about Moses and the Exodus we do not leave behind the world of saga. The documents are not yet in the strict sense historical documents. But we are on firmer ground, if only because so many other parts of the OT look back to the events of the Exodus and the settlement in Canaan as basic to Israel's faith. We may not have the data for a detailed historical reconstruction, but there can be no reasonable doubt about the fact of the Exodus and its far-reaching significance. It was a new beginning in the religion of the Hebrew tribes, and its influence lasted through all the subsequent developments of Israel's faith.

b If we ask whence the Mosaic religion was derived, the answer may appropriately begin with a significant denial: not from Egypt. Attempts have been made to relate Israel's belief in Yahweh to the so-called monotheism of Ikhnaton; but in spite of the similarity between Ps. 104 and the Egyptian hymn to the sun associated with the heretic Pharaoh, and in spite of other, sometimes striking, indications of Egyptian influence in Israel's Wisdom Literature, there is no trace of Egyptian influence in anything which may be reasonably assumed to have formed part of the religion of Moses. Four factors contributed to that religion (cf. J. Lindblom, *Israels religion i gammaltestamentlig tid*, 2nd ed., p. 48).

c First, there was the faith of the Hebrew fathers. According to two strata in the tradition, Moses announced a hitherto unknown divine name, Yahweh; but he was the envoy not of a new God but of the God of the Fathers. What Moses taught about God could not but be influenced by what he had himself learned from the religious traditions of his people, traditions which would be present to the minds of those to whom he had been sent. As we have seen, this traditional religion included a strongly personal element.

d Second, Moses was probably influenced by those amongst whom he lived while in exile; and it may 131d have been from them that he learned the name Yahweh. The family into which Moses then married is variously described as Midianite (Exod. 2:16, 3:1, 18:1) and Kenite (Jg. 1:16). There is evidence in various passages that at later times the Kenites were thought of as friendly to Israel and zealous for the cause of Yahweh (Jg. 4:11, 17ff.; 1 Sam. 15:6). Further, the story of how the priest Jethro, Moses' father-in-law, came to meet Moses and the Israelite tribes just before they reached the sacred mountain (Exod. 18:1ff.) tells not only that he confessed the greatness of Yahweh (Exod. 18:10f.), but that he took the lead in acts of worship in which Aaron, the father of the Israelite priesthood, joined together with the elders (Exod. 18:12), and that he suggested to Moses, the father of Israelite law, methods of administering justice (Exod. 18:13ff.). It is unlikely that such features would have been imposed on the traditions gratuitously; and although the view that the Mosaic faith owed something to the religion of the Kenites (the Kenite hypothesis) has been strongly criticised, it accords with general probability and with Hebrew tradition. Having said this, however, we must add that it is easier to admit the debt than to establish just what was taken over. If Yahweh was the name of the Kenite deity, the revelation to Moses involved the identification of Yahweh with the God of the Hebrew tribes. But our ignorance of Kenite religion makes it impossible to say which elements in the religion of Israel were of Kenite origin.

Third, the content of Mosaic religion owed much e to the events of the Exodus. The deliverance of the Hebrew tribes was seen as an act of God for the good of those whom he now made his people. Historical events were the field of the divine action and in what God did his nature and purpose were revealed. This affected the entire character and subsequent development of Hebrew religion.

Fourth, Mosaic religion bore the stamp of Moses' f own religious experience. Important as the historical events were, they did not take place unheralded. What Yahweh was about to do was revealed to Moses, who, as his spokesman, foretold what was to happen and interpreted the events as Yahweh's intervention for the deliverance of his people. There is here a link both with that personal communion with God which is a notable feature in the patriarchal narratives and also with the later prophetic tradition in which history was interpreted in terms of the divine purpose. The importance of historical events in the religion of Israel does not mean simply that extraordinary or impressive happenings are automatically regarded as divine acts either because they are unusual or because they are to Israel's immediate advantage. The man who has heard God speak is the herald and interpreter of the divine action; and through his faith and insight he can make plain the place in the divine purpose of disasters and deliverances alike.

What has been said above of the sources of Mosaic g religion is a pointer to much that may be inferred about its content. Four main themes call for consideration: 1 the name and nature of God; 2 the fact of election; 3 the covenant bond; 4 the covenant people.

1 The name and nature of God. Hebrew h tradition as preserved in Exod. 3 and 6:2ff. ascribes particular importance to the revelation of the divine name which is represented by the four consonants YHWH. Most moderns accept 'Yahweh' as the probable vocalisation of the name; but the original form, the etymology, and the meaning are uncertain. These latter questions need not now detain us. For the study of Hebrew religion they are of secondary importance. What matters is the meaning or meanings which the name conveyed to the Israelite worshipper. Probably Exod. 3:13f. is our safest guide. In reply to Moses' question about the divine name, 'God said to Moses, "I AM WHO I AM"'. The implication is

181h that the name is to be understood as a form of the verb 'to be' (*hāyāh*). Yahweh is HE WHO IS. The verb does not simply express static existence, but the existence which is manifested in action. Nor does the present tense alone adequately express the meaning. Yahweh was, is, will be who he was, is, will be. He manifests his nature in the successive situations in which he encounters those with whom he has to do. Thus interpreted, the name aptly expresses the continued manifestation of the divine nature in Yahweh's dealings with his people. He is not a remote, sublime being who car be known only or primarily by intellectual speculation or mystical contemplation. He gives himself in active self-manifestation.

i The mode of his self-manifestation is at times awesome and terrifying, violent and dangerous. He is a holy God. His holiness is his divine character, dynamic and even demonic. He is also a jealous God (*'ēl ḳannā'*) a term which sums up his zealous maintenance of his cause and his claim on the undivided allegiance of his people : him alone they must worship, in him alone they must trust.

j This exclusiveness is an important element in Hebrew monotheism and emphasises its character as essentially practical rather than speculative. To claim that Mosaic religion was fully and consciously monotheistic is to go too far ; to put it on a level with the religion of surrounding peoples is to miss its distinctive character. But in this faith in a God who will brook no rivals, who has no partner or consort, before whom the deities worshipped by other peoples are as nothing, we have the germ of the developed monotheism of later times. Yahweh has sovereign freedom to work his will, in Egypt or elsewhere. To resort to any other is to resort to the ineffectual.

k **2 The fact of election.** Though the vocabulary of election may not belong to the earliest period, the fact of election is an essential element in the Mosaic religion. Before the covenant was made at Sinai, the divine promises were given and the divine deliverance wrought. The emphasis is less on Israel's special place in God's purpose than on the fact that the bond between God and Israel was established by God's compassion for the afflicted tribes in Egypt.

l **3 The covenant bond.** The immediate outcome of the deliverance was the establishment of a covenant between Yahweh and Israel. This involved more than a mere compact or contract. To be in covenant was to share a common life. But it also involved responsibilities. Thus the covenant idea, which some have regarded as central in OT religion, contributed to Israel's faith personal and moral elements, emphasising the consistency of the divine character and purpose (since Yahweh bound himself by the covenant) and imposing on Israel the obligation of obedience.

m **4 The covenant people.** The institution of the covenant created a religious community. The corporate aspect of Hebrew religion was always important and found expression in the life of family, clan, and nation. It may seem that at times the faith was subordinate to nationalism or even that religion was swallowed up in racialism. But the true bond of Israel's common life was not race but the covenant. The nature and number of the tribes which assembled at Sinai are matters of dispute ; but it is clear that the unity into which they then entered was based on the covenant. They belonged to each other because Yahweh had taken them to be his own people (Exod. 6:7 ; cf. Jer. 31:33*b*).

n Later tradition associated with the Mosaic religion a substantial corpus of law, which included detailed though incomplete regulations for the observance of a complicated cultic system. Much of this must be of later origin ; and it is difficult to determine which laws and rites may reasonably be attributed to the Exodus period. Of the three law codes found in the older material in the Pentateuch, the Yahwistic or Ritual Decalogue (Exod. 34:10–28) and the Book of the Covenant (Exod. 20:22–23:33) clearly reflect the conditions of agricultural life and are therefore more appropriate to the period after the Conquest. The third, the Elohistic version of the Decalogue (Exod. 20:1–17), has often been regarded as the deposit of prophetic teaching. If, however, allowance is made for later amplification of some of its commandments, its substance may well be very early. The standard of undivided allegiance to Yahweh in whose worship the use of idols was forbidden, and the laws about life, family, and property accord well with what is known of Mosaic religion and desert life. The tangled question of the nature and early history of the Sabbath makes it somewhat harder, though not unreasonable, to make such a claim for the fourth commandment.

There can be little doubt that sacrifice, at least in simple forms, belonged to Mosaic religion, in spite of the prophetic denials, implied in Am. 5:25 and explicit in Jer. 7:22. Of the great seasonal festivals, Unleavened Bread, Weeks, and Ingathering presuppose agricultural life and were doubtless adopted after the Conquest. Passover, which came to be closely associated with Unleavened Bread, has features in common with apotropaic (i.e. to avert evil) rites in pastoral communities. There is no adequate reason to doubt that it was adopted at the time of the Exodus to commemorate the great deliverance. o

The records tell of a sacred Tent which was of great importance in the religion of the period. In the later account (Exod. 25ff.) it is described as an elaborate structure, resembling the Temple, which was erected in the middle of the camp. In the earlier (Exod. 33:7–11) it is represented in simple terms as a sanctuary outside the camp, at which revelations were received. p

The other important religious object which is associated with the wilderness period is the Ark. The ancient formula contained in Num. 10:35f., together with the evidence of 1 Sam. 4–7 and 2 Sam. 11:11, suggests that it accompanied the Israelite armies in war. According to the Deuteronomic tradition (Dt. 10:1–5), it contained the Tables of the Law. At all events it embodied the active divine presence. Later, when it lay in the Holy of Holies in the Temple, it seems to have been regarded as the throne of the invisible Yahweh. q

Religion after the Conquest—The religion of Canaan presented a sharp contrast to the historical and personal character of Mosaic religion. Its deities were closely associated with the processes of nature, and its festival rituals with the annually recurring cycle of the seasons and not with the events of history. Among its chief concerns was the maintenance of fertility in field, flock, and herd, and among men. By entering Canaan the Israelites could be deemed to have come into the domain of the Canaanite deities. By becoming farmers they were exposed to the temptation to adopt Baal worship in order to ensure fertility, regarding the produce of the land as the gifts of Baal. Baal worship represented a challenge to the absolute supremacy of Yahweh. To that challenge four responses were possible. 132

First, it might be held that the settled agricultural life was contrary to Yahweh's will for his people. As late as the 6th cent. we find this view held by the Rechabites, who would not grow cereals, cultivate the vine, or live in houses (Jer. 35). Thus loyalty to Yahweh was expressed in adherence to a particular mode of life ; and since this in fact limited Yahweh's sway by excluding from it agricultural and urban life, it was a religious cul-de-sac. b

Second, at the other extreme, it was possible to abandon the worship of Yahweh altogether and to adopt Baal worship as the appropriate religion for the new environment. It is unlikely that many went to this extreme. In times of national crisis, Yahweh remained the god of national unity, who led his people to war against their enemies. c

The third response would accordingly be a working compromise. The Hebrew might adopt the fertility d

132d cult of Canaan and worship the Canaanite deities in order to prosper as a farmer and yet retain loyalty of a sort to Yahweh as the national war god. This anticipation of the principle *cuius regio eius religio* must have been widely practised; but it clearly involved a serious limitation of Yahweh's sway.

e Fourth, even those who did not bow the knee to Baal might worship Yahweh under the forms of Baal worship. Syncretism of this kind could corrupt; but it could also enrich. Much that was borrowed from Canaanite religion was later swept away in various Yahwistic reform movements; but much remained as part of the religion of Israel; and even prophetic reformers were indebted to Canaan (e.g. the use of the symbolism of the vine and of the marriage bond).

f The impact of Canaan on Israelite religion must now be considered in greater detail.

The invading Israelites appropriated many Canaanite holy places. Hebron and Beersheba in the south; Bethel, Gilgal, Shechem, and Shiloh in the central region; Dan in the far north; and, finally and most important of all, the ancient Jebusite sanctuary at Jerusalem—all these became centres of Israelite worship, as did many other smaller sanctuaries. Some of them were associated with traditions about the Hebrew fathers. Shechem, which is prominent in the stories about Jacob-Israel, was the site of a great Israelite covenant ceremony (Jos. 24) and also of Canaanite worship of Baal-berith, Lord of the covenant (Jg. 9:4). The important sanctuary of Shiloh, which was the home of the Ark before it was captured by the Philistines, would be the natural centre for the religious life of the Israelite confederacy.

g The normal equipment of the sanctuaries included not only the altar but the standing stone (*maṣṣēbhāh*) and the wooden pole (*'ashērāh*). At first, these and other Canaanite cult objects seem to have been accepted by all but the most austerely puritan Yahwists. Only at a later date were some of them officially condemned and abolished.

h The prophetic polemic against religious infidelity shows the attraction which the Canaanite pantheon had for many Israelites. The violent conflict between Yahwism and the Baal cult ought not, however, to obscure the probability that the conception of Yahweh's nature was influenced by Canaan. The worship of Yahweh at Canaanite sanctuaries led to the application to him of Canaanite divine titles. Foremost among these are the term Baal and compounds of El. The former, a noun meaning 'lord', was applied as a title to different deities, but supremely to Hadad, the storm god, son of Dagon. That the title was applied to Yahweh is evident both from its appearance in the names of children of loyal Yahwists like Saul, Jonathan, and David (1 Chr. 8:33f., 14:7), and from the prophetic protest against its use (Hos. 2:16). El, the generic term for 'god', was the name of the supreme god of the Canaanite pantheon, and was also used in the titles of sundry local deities. We have noted the occurrence of such titles in the patriarchal stories. Of these, El Elyon appears to have been the title of a pre-Israelite deity at Jerusalem. The application of these terms to Yahweh emphasised his connection with nature and his functions as god of the land and promoter of its fertility.

i The appeal of the fertility goddesses, Asherah, Anath, and Astarte, appears to have been widespread. This is amply evidenced by the large numbers of figurines of such goddesses which have been unearthed, as well as by the OT evidence (where, however, Anath is scarcely even mentioned by name). Sacred prostitution formed an important part of the cult of these goddesses.

j The transition to farming life led to the adoption of the great seasonal festivals: Unleavened Bread (barley harvest), Weeks (wheat harvest), Ingathering or Tabernacles (the harvest of fruits at the end of the agricultural year). Here, as elsewhere, however, adoption involved adaptation and interpretation, The heritage of Canaan was baptised into the tradition 132j
of Mosaic Yahwism. These festivals, which were related to the cycle of the seasons, came in time to be linked with the great historic events of Israel's religious experience: Unleavened Bread with Passover and the deliverance from Egypt, Weeks with the giving of the Law, and Tabernacles with the sojourn in the wilderness (though the tabernacles or booths originally represented the bridal bower in the sacred marriage and not the tents of the migrating Israelites).

The third of these has been the subject of much k
research and discussion in recent decades. It has been argued that a New Year Festival was held in the autumn, at which Yahweh's triumph over the powers of chaos was celebrated: in a ritual drama he defeated his enemies, was acclaimed and enthroned as king, and renewed his covenant with his people. Supporting evidence has been adduced from other parts of the ancient Near East, notably from Mesopotamia and Ugarit; and much has been made of rituals connected with the dying and rising again of the fertility god. But Yahweh was not a dying and rising god: he was the living God; and thus any such festival in Israel must have differed significantly from similar rituals elsewhere. The liturgical texts for the cultic enthronement of Yahweh are found in the enthronement psalms (e.g. Ps. 47, 93, 95–100). This festival, with its thought of the decisive day of Yahweh's triumph, the renewal of nature, the reaffirmation of the covenant, and the vindication of Yahweh's people in all probability provided the pattern for the later hope of the eschatological Day of Yahweh. It has, indeed, been claimed that there was an eschatological element in the pre-exilic festival itself.

A most important element borrowed by Israel from l
Canaan was the monarchy. It was established partly because of political developments and for political reasons; but in the ancient Near East, and not least in Israel, the integration of politics and religion was such that religion could not remain unaffected by such an innovation. There is considerable divergence of opinion about the religious meaning of the Israelite monarchy. Strong claims have been made for the 'divine' character of kings in Israel by analogy with their status and functions in neighbouring countries. No simple analogy can in fact be drawn, since usage elsewhere varied. Further, any theory of the 'divine' character of kings in Israel must be qualified by the sharp distinction between God and man which is apparent in Hebrew religion and by the fact that the monarchy and individual kings were subjected to searching criticism by Yahweh's spokesman. Again, it is probable that the monarchy in Israel was not simply borrowed from Canaan but was a fusion of Canaanite kingship with the Israelite tradition of charismatic leadership exemplified in the judges. It has often been pointed out that Saul, the first king, retained much of the character of a judge. Nevertheless it is clear that the kings of Israel performed important cultic functions and possessed a sacral character. The king was the anointed of Yahweh (1 Sam. 24:6, 10, 26:9, 11, 16, 23; 2 Sam. 1:14, 16, etc.). He was also the son of Yahweh. This status seems to have been conferred on him at his accession (Ps. 2:7). It was sonship by adoption. The relationship of the king to Yahweh was a covenant relationship (Ps. 89:26–8). The covenant made with the royal house was a counterpart of the covenant made with all Israel. The presence of the king ruling in vigour, well-being, and righteousness was a token and pledge of Yahweh's continuing goodwill to his people and of his purpose to maintain his covenant promises. It is not surprising that, at a later period, hopes of restoration, of a new age, and of a new or renewed covenant included the expectation of an anointed one (Messiah).

The influence of the monarchy on religion is further m
seen in the building of the Temple at Jerusalem, which was at first primarily a royal chapel but became

132m also the central national sanctuary. Phoenician craftsmen were employed in its construction; and both the plan of the building and its decoration and equipment indicate alien influence. The control exercised by kings over the scope of such influence is evident from the references to the innovation of Ahaz (2 Kg. 16:10ff.), the apostasy of Manasseh (2 Kg. 21:1ff.), and the reforms of Hezekiah (2 Kg. 18:4) and Josiah (2 Kg. 22f.). The account of the religious measures adopted by Jeroboam I (1 Kg. 12:26–33), though marked by the standards of a later time, is further evidence of the important bond between the monarchy and the cult, and seems also to indicate the peculiar importance for the royal house of the Autumnal Festival.

n The nature and structure of that festival and the sacral character of the king have been prominent in discussions of the theory of a myth-and-ritual pattern in the ancient Near East. According to this theory, such a pattern existed, with appropriate variations at different periods and in different regions, and was transmitted to Israel through Canaanite influence. The New Year Festival was the climax of the whole; the myth of creation, with its theme of the triumph over the powers of disorder and destruction, was prominent in it; the king played the part of the dying and rising god in the ritual drama. As we have already seen, the OT itself testifies to extensive influence on Israel from its environment; and, if the evidence of the Psalter is admissible, the myth of creation was a significant feature of Israelite worship. But, as we have noted, the historical character of Israel's religion drastically modified elements which were borrowed from elsewhere; and, further, there is no cogent evidence in the OT to indicate that Yahweh was thought of as a dying and rising god.

133a **Prophecy until the Exile**—The period of the conflict with the Philistines and the establishment of the monarchy saw also the emergence of the prophetic movement. It has often been claimed that this was the most distinctive feature of OT religion. In an important sense this is true; but it has to be admitted that some of the features of Hebrew prophecy are found in religious communities and individuals outside Israel. In the OT itself the term 'prophet' is applied to devotees of Baal as well as to the spokesmen of Yahweh. Like so much else in the religion of Israel, prophecy has important links with the wider background of ancient Near Eastern religion; but its supremely important features are those which belong to the indigenous Israelite tradition. No account of OT religion would be complete without some treatment of prophecy, but since another article in this volume is devoted to the subject, some of its aspects may here be omitted or mentioned only briefly. See §§411–17.

b In the earliest mention of the prophetic movement (1 Sam. 10:5–13), three important characteristics appear. First, the prophets were in a group. Attempts have been made to draw a sharp distinction between gregarious and solitary prophets, but with no great success. Prophetic communities appear to have continued to exist in Israel for centuries; and most of the great individual prophetic figures had some connection with such groups or even helped to bring them into being. Elijah and Elisha were associated with 'the sons of the prophets'; and at a later period Isaiah seems to have gathered round him a group of disciples who owned him as master.

c Second, the word 'prophesying' (1 Sam. 10:5f., 10, 13) denotes not the coherent announcement of a message but the violent bodily movements and frenzied, incoherent utterance which resulted from an abnormal psychological state produced by artificial stimuli (cf. 1 Sam. 19:20–4; 2 Kg. 3:15). The term ecstasy has been widely used to describe this abnormal state. It has been held that all prophets were ecstatic and that ecstasy was a recognised outward mark of a prophet's inspiration. But this is to outrun the evidence. Non-biblical sources show that holy men 13 outside Israel experienced ecstasy. Something similar appears in the stories of the abnormal fits of martial frenzy, coupled with skill, courage, and the gift of leadership, which came upon Israel's national heroes when the Spirit (*rûaḥ*) of Yahweh fell on them (Jg. 3:10, 6:34, 11:29, 13:25, 14:6, 19, 15:14; 1 Sam. 11:6). It was the Spirit, too, which bestowed the divine energy which was manifest in the prophetic frenzy (1 Sam. 10:6, 10; cf. 'the hand of Yahweh was on . . .'; 1 Kg. 18:46; 2 Kg. 3:15; Ezek. 1:3, 3:22, 8:1, 33:22, 37:1, 40:1).

d Third, the prophets were coming down from the sanctuary. The close link between prophets and the sanctuaries has been increasingly emphasised in much recent research. Notwithstanding the violently anti-sacrificial and anti-cultic passages in some parts of the prophetic books, it has been claimed that all prophets were cultic functionaries on the staffs of the sanctuaries; and parallels have been drawn between the Israelite prophetic communities and associations of cultic holy men elsewhere. This, again, is to outrun the evidence; but it is no longer possible to regard the prophets as invariably or usually hostile to the cultic system. The contention that some parts of the Psalter are oracles delivered by sanctuary prophets is both plausible and illuminating. Further, in the activity of the prophets there is much that is akin to the world of cultic ideas and practice. As in the ritual drama of the cult the sacred words of the liturgical formula and the acts of the ritual were potent with divine energy, so the words of the prophetic oracle and the actions which have been described as prophetic symbolism or acted prophecy (e.g. 2 Kg. 13:14–19; Isa. 20; Ezek. 4f., etc.) did not merely describe situations and events but helped to bring them about. This may seem to drag prophecy down to the level of magico-cultic practice, to which, indeed, it did sometimes fall. But, whereas magico-cultic practice aimed at the manipulation of divine power for the furtherance of the aims of individuals or societies, there is in Hebrew prophecy an austere tradition which is concerned above all with the will of Yahweh. In 1 Kg. 22 the words and actions of the prophets led by Zedekiah were aimed at ensuring victory; but Micaiah sought simply to express the will of Yahweh, whatever the consequences to himself (1 Kg. 22:14).

e This concern with the will of Yahweh is central in the work of the great prophets. They were not primarily either foretellers or moral teachers, though they did in fact both predict future events and impart moral teaching. They interpreted historical events in terms of God's will, looking back to Yahweh's past dealings with his people (particularly the Exodus, the wilderness wanderings, and the settlement), and tracing his purpose in the events of their own day, even when they seemed disastrous. The righteousness of Yahweh which they proclaimed was not simply an abstract standard but the active personal power of Yahweh at work in the world. In their ethical teaching they were neither revolutionary reformers nor die-hard conservatives. They protested against alien influence and recalled their contemporaries to the pure worship of Yahweh. They reasserted the moral claims of Yahweh in a society whose structure had undergone and was undergoing drastic change; and they did so, not by advocating a return to earlier conditions, but by applying anew the ancient standards to their own age. The moral standards of their religion were derived not from a particular pattern of social life, but from Yahweh's historic revelation of himself to his people.

f The two aspects of prophetic teaching are seen clearly in the work of Elijah: in his polemic against the Phoenician Baal, Melkart, and in his protest against the judicial murder of Naboth and the appropriation of his land. The cult of Melkart, which Jezebel tried to impose on Israel, represented a more serious

133f challenge to Yahwism than ordinary Baalism. In withstanding it Elijah reasserted the ancient claim for undivided allegiance to Yahweh, and so took his stand in the tradition which went back to Moses. The refusal of Naboth to sell his field represents the strong conservative feeling against selling ancestral property, to which the king, representing a newer outlook, was unsympathetic. Elijah's protest was the expression not of conservatism but of the standards of impartial justice which were inherent in Israel's faith. As a representative of that austere tradition Elijah towers in stature above his disciple Elisha ; but from the stories about the latter we get a vivid picture of something nearer to the normal pattern of prophetic activity, in touch with the common life of the countryside, the towns, and the sanctuaries. Moreover, the influence of Elisha was behind the violent revolt against the house of Omri and the Baal cult (2 Kg. 9f.).

g In the great prophets of the 8th cent. three themes recur : worship, social conditions, and foreign policy. These are closely interrelated in prophetic teaching, as they were in actual experience. Relations with foreign powers could lead to heathen influence in religion. Frequent campaigns and invasions impoverished the yeoman farmer, who, having mortgaged his land, might find the mortgage foreclosed and ultimately lose both his property and his personal independence. So the small farms were swallowed up in the large estates of the rich (Isa. 5:8) and those who had owned them were reduced to the status of hired labourers. In this far-reaching social and economic revolution, the prophets pleaded for the ancient Hebrew standards of justice and covenant faithfulness.

h The plea for social righteousness is particularly prominent in Amos, who denounces unsparingly the flagrant injustices in the Northern Kingdom. The series of oracles with which his book opens, telling of Yahweh's impending punishment of neighbouring nations, implies that the claims of Yahweh are not limited to Israel ; but his denunciation of Israel has as its background God's saving acts (Am. 2:9f.), and the special bond between Yahweh and his people (Am. 3:2), and points forward to certain punishment if Israel does not repent. Yahweh's righteousness is not simply a standard by which men are tested but a power by which they may be either strengthened or broken. Of foreign policy Amos says nothing. His attack on contemporary worship is partly a criticism of heathen practices (Am. 5:26) and partly a condemnation of religious fervour without compassion (Am. 2:8). It appears in its most extreme form in Am. 5:21–5.

i The national background of Hosea's ministry is the political instability and the moral and religious corruption of the closing years of the Northern Kingdom. Its personal background is his broken marriage, which is a counterpart of the covenant bond between Yahweh as Israel's husband (symbolism which probably owes something to the Canaanite fertility cult) and father is based on the Exodus story (Hos. 2:14f., 11:1ff.). Not only is his attack on the Baal cult more explicit than anything in Amos (Hos. 2, *passim*) ; but his denunciation of the bull images at Bethel (Hos. 10:5f.) may indicate a new hostility to cult objects which had previously been taken for granted. The military reverses which Amos prophesied in general terms seem to be nearer at hand in Hosea's predictions. But his searching analysis of Israel's sin and his certainty of divine chastisement do not empty his message of all hope. In spite of Israel's infidelity, Yahweh's covenant love (*ḥesedh*) remains strong : the purpose of his chastisement is restoration (Hos. 2:14f.).

j In the work of Isaiah of Jerusalem, pre-exilic prophecy reaches its most representative and majestic expression. He lashes unsparingly the superficiality and immorality of contemporary religious practice (Isa. 1:10ff., 28:7f.). He exposes the rapacity and cynicism by which the national life was distorted (Isa. 5:1–23 ; in this he is matched by his younger contemporary, Micah, who championed the cause of 133j
the dispossessed). He denounces the policy of alliance with foreign powers : the invocation by Ahaz of Assyrian help against Syria and Ephraim (Isa. 7), and the negotiations of Hezekiah with Egypt (Isa. 30:1ff., 31:1ff.) and Babylon (Isa. 39). The two poles of his thought are the holiness of God and the faith of man. In the crises of his time he sees the hand of Yahweh, who uses even the Assyrian to further his purpose. Beyond the crises Isaiah sees a future of divine blessing for a renewed Israel of which the nucleus already exists in the remnant (those who have faith : Isa. 28:16). The prophecies of deliverance and renewal include the promises of a future ideal king (Isa. 9:2–7, 11:1–9).

Isaiah seems to have exercised some influence on k
Hezekiah ; and this may in part account for the religious reforms carried out in that king's reign (2 Kg. 18:4), which anticipated those of Josiah in that they included suppression of the high places and the purification of worship at Jerusalem. But Hezekiah's successor, Manasseh, undid his father's work. This may be partly explained by the fact that the country was a vassal of Assyria ; but Manasseh was active both in fostering heathen practice and in persecuting faithful Yahwists (2 Kg. 21:1–18). Two features are prominent in the syncretistic worship of the period : the worship of the host of heaven and human sacrifice.

It was in the aftermath of this long period of l
syncretism that Jeremiah's ministry was begun ; and his earliest oracles are directed against the consequent corruption of Judah's worship and morals (Jer. 2, *passim*). Like his predecessors, Jeremiah grounds his rebukes and his appeals on Yahweh's historic acts of deliverance (Jer. 2:2, 6f.) ; and like them he sees in impending invasion and exile Yahweh's continuing action in his people's history. The opposition and ridicule which he encountered made him turn to God in bitter complaint. This experience taught him the lessons of personal communion with God : and probably this is his chief contribution to Hebrew religion, though it is a mistake to suppose that before his time individual experience of God was unknown in Israel. It is characteristic that his vision of the future indicates the promise of the New Covenant, which is marked by its inwardness and its individual character, though it is still a covenant with the *house* of Israel (Jer. 31:31ff.). Jeremiah's emphasis on the inwardness of true religion is also expressed in his attack on false trust in the outward media of religion, notably the Temple and the sacrificial system (Jer. 7:1ff., 21ff.). This has led some to suppose that Jeremiah was necessarily hostile to the Deuteronomic reform, or that, having originally supported it, he later turned against it.

The conditions of the late 7th cent. are also reflected m
in the teaching of Zephaniah, who predicts the Day of Yahweh's judgment, of Nahum, who rejoices fiercely over the fall of Nineveh, and of Habakkuk, who wrestles with the problem of the divorce of might and right. But Jeremiah is supremely the representative prophet of the period.

The Deuteronomic Reform—In spite of arguments n
to the contrary, it is highly probable that the book found in the Temple in Josiah's reign (2 Kg. 22:3ff.) was at least chs. 12–26 of Deuteronomy. The two main principles of the reform were the *purification* of Israelite life and worship from pagan practices and the *centralisation* of sacrificial worship at Jerusalem as the one legitimate sanctuary. Centralisation was not only a practical expedient to ensure cultic correctness : it expressed the theological principle of the unity of Yahweh's being (Dt. 6:4). Here Deuteronomic teaching is in line with that of the prophets ; and there are other similarities in the Deuteronomic concern for the needy and defenceless and in the emphasis on the love of God which is evident in the preamble to the Code (Dt. 1–11).

133o Deuteronomy also marks an important phase in the development of the priesthood. The origins of the Levitical tribe or guild are obscure. It appears that in the period of the judges and the early monarchy the priestly office was not confined to Levites, though Levites were preferred, possibly because they understood the manipulation of the sacred oracle. In Deuteronomy every priest is a Levite and every Levite a priest. The suppression of the high places because of the law of centralisation deprived many Levites of their means of livelihood, and must have inflicted considerable hardship (cf. Dt. 18:6–8 with 2 Kg. 23:9). In fact, one result of the Deuteronomic legislation was the dominance of the Zadokite priests, whose sanctuary was now the only legitimate one. The regulations in Ezek. 40–8 presuppose a purely Zadokite priesthood; but evidently this limitation could not be maintained. The prevailing post-exilic practice is found in the Priestly Code of the Pentateuch in which the priesthood is confined to the house of Aaron, other Levites having subordinate functions to perform.

134a **The Exile**—The fact that the religion of Israel survived the Exile at all is one of the most striking proofs of its vitality. Like the challenge of Canaanite religion at an earlier time, the Exile in fact enriched what it might have been expected to destroy. The Temple at Jerusalem, which had so recently gained added prestige because of the Deuteronomic legislation, was robbed of its treasures and left a ruin. The house of David, to whom Yahweh's promise of unending rule had been made, was no longer on the throne. The promised land was no longer the home of a large part of Yahweh's people. That lofty religious standards survived such a crisis is partly the result of the Deuteronomic reform. Those who went into exile were the upper classes, many of whom must have been profoundly influenced by Josiah's measures. But that faith itself survived the Exile is largely the result of prophetic teaching. The prophets had predicted just such a disaster as Yahweh's chastisement of his people. Events had vindicated the word which they claimed that he had spoken through them, and accordingly the experience, shattering as it was, might not undermine but reinforce belief in his power and his purpose. It is a mark of the centrality of the prophetic tradition in Israel that, having thus prepared the way for the Exile, it reveals in its own subsequent developments some of the most important changes through which the religion of Israel was to pass.

b In spite of debate about the integrity of the book of Ezekiel and the date of his ministry, we may take it that he was a child of the pre-exilic age who went into exile, and, having protested against false hopes of a speedy restoration, sought to deliver his people from paralysing despair by assuring them of the certain fulfilment of God's purpose for them. His sense of the transcendent majesty of Yahweh is expressed in the impressive vision with which the book opens, in his presentation of Yahweh's purpose as accomplished 'for the sake of his name' (Ezek. 20 *passim*) and in the phrase by which the prophet himself is repeatedly addressed: 'Son of man' (i.e. 'mere man', 'mortal man'). His emphasis on individual responsibility is memorably recorded in ch. 18; but the notion that no such awareness of individual responsibility existed in Israel before his time is erroneous. His active interest in the cult appears in his denunciation of the corruption of Temple worship in the last years before the Exile and in the detail of his prophecy of the restoration. Two features of post-exilic Judaism are already present in the prophecies attributed to him. The detailed and fantastic imagery closely resembles apocalyptic; and the description of the new order of things after the restoration accords well with the post-exilic interest in law.

c The great prophet whose teaching is found in Isa. 40–55 belongs to the closing years of the Exile. Faced with the impending triumph of Cyrus and the fall of Babylon, he boldly proclaims that the return of the exiles, and the renewal of Israel's national life and mission are the main objects of these events. True to the great prophetic tradition, he interprets the movement of history in terms of Yahweh's purpose; but now it is a purpose not to chastise but to restore. All nature and all history are dominated by Israel's God. The temptation to be overawed by the magnificence of Babylonian temples and their ritual, or impressed by the prevalent heathen divinatory practices is made to seem ridiculous in the presence of the Creator of the ends of the earth, the God who alone can foretell events, since he controls them. Embedded in the prophecy are the four Servant Songs (Isa. 42:1–4, 49:1–6, 50:4–9 (11), 52:13–53:12). On any reasonable theory of the identity of the Servant, these songs express two great themes: the will of Yahweh that all nations should accept his way, and the power of vicarious suffering to free men from the results of their sin and reconcile them to God. Here an explicitly monotheistic faith is matched by an explicit belief in a positive purpose of God for all nations; and the sense of the divine election of Israel has its complement in Israel's world-wide mission. 13

After the Exile—The prophet's glowing pictures of the restored Jerusalem must have seemed strangely out of touch with reality to those who returned. The frustrations and difficulties which they had to face appear clearly in Haggai and Zechariah (1–8) who prophesied at the beginning of the reign of Darius I, recalling the people and their leaders Joshua and Zerubbabel to the task of rebuilding the Temple and to an active faith in Yahweh's purpose for them. Some sixty years later, we have another glimpse of the restored community in the book of Malachi. Those three prophets of the Persian period indicate the main tendencies in the religious life of the time. All are interested in the Temple, which was rebuilt in the reign of Darius, and in the maintenance of its worship. Particularly in Malachi we see the prophetic teaching acquiring a legal emphasis In all three there is the hope of Yahweh's intervention on behalf of his people. But in Zechariah coming events are depicted in a series of night visions which are full of elaborate and artificial symbolism. Here prophecy is passing into apocalyptic. As a living movement prophecy does not appear to survive much longer. The spoken word of the prophets gives place to the written word of the prophetic epigoni. 13

The integration of the life of the community and the right ordering of its religious expression are the main objects of the work of Nehemiah and Ezra. For our present purpose it is unnecessary to decide whether Ezra came to Jerusalem in 457 or (as an impressive body of scholarly opinion maintains) in 397. His work may conveniently be classed with that of Nehemiah, who, when he had given Jerusalem security by rebuilding its walls, forcefully sought to make its common life conform to the written Law, and to safeguard its religious tradition by forbidding marriages with foreign women. Ezra came to Jerusalem as a scribe, bringing a book of the Law. It is widely agreed that the latest portions of legal material in the Pentateuch (P) had been compiled during or soon after the Exile. What Ezra brought with him was perhaps P or, more probably, the entire Pentateuch. His work is a decisive step in the transformation of Judaism into a religion of the Book, and his influence continued both in the scrupulous transmission of the written Law and in the elaboration of oral expansion and comment. Like Nehemiah he opposed mixed marriages and, indeed, went further in advocating that those which had been contracted should be dissolved. These actions should be understood primarily as a means of ensuring the purity of the religious life of the community. b

Whether the Jew lived in Palestine or elsewhere, his life was constantly open to alien influence. The establishment of Seleucid and Ptolemaic rule in Syria and Egypt and the consequent diffusion of Hellenistic c c culture in Palestine brought new and subtle forms of this influence. It is clear that many of the priests and the aristocracy yielded to it readily. The policy of Antiochus Epiphanes added the pressure of ruthless persecution. The Law and, in particular, those practices which had served to make the distinctive character of the Jewish community (e.g. circumcision and the dietary laws) were the particular objects of his repressive measures. It is from the resistance to this persecution that apocalyptic literature takes its rise ; and it is therefore somewhat ironical that so many traces of alien, mainly Persian, influence have been found in apocalyptic teaching : an almost dualistic view of the world, a determinist view of history which is divided into sharply defined ages, a developed angelology and demonology, and a developed eschatology. But apocalyptic is the child of prophecy ; and most of its characteristics are in some way anticipated in the earlier religion of Israel. In particular it enriched the conception of a coming Day of Yahweh, the hope of the Messiah, and the concept of the Son of Man, and formulated the faith in a future life in which the martyrs would receive the reward of their sufferings.

d It has been customary to associate the Wisdom Literature with the religious development of this period; but part of the Wisdom Literature is pre-exilic, and the work of the Wise in Israel is by no means an exclusively post-exilic phenomenon.

e Not only does Wisdom have its counterpart in neighbouring lands, it is in many ways itself cosmopolitan. It does not emphasise the specifically Hebrew tradition and its ideal character is the Wise Man. Its central theme, Wisdom, is a quality not solely intellectual but religious and practical. One mode of its expression is intelligent and disciplined conduct, commended by the precepts in Proverbs, where it is said that such conduct will be rewarded by prosperity. This view is challenged both by the scepticism of **135e**
Ecclesiastes and also by the passionate theological revolt of Job which raises to a higher plane the whole problem of retribution and reward by denying that suffering is necessarily the result of sin.

Above all, Wisdom is an attribute or activity of **f**
God himself, by which he created all things (Job 28 ; Prov. 8). In post-canonical Wisdom Literature (Wis. 7:22–8:1 ; Sir. 24), this creative Wisdom is presented in personal terms. This conception is an important element in the OT doctrine of creation and a pointer to the NT doctrine of the Logos.

Conclusion—The history of Hebrew religion as it is **g**
presented in the OT is incomplete. It is a story with a double sequel : in post-biblical Judaism and in Christianity. In one sense the principle of its unity lies beyond itself. In another it is already evident in the central themes which recur in its varied phases : the majesty, holiness and righteousness of God ; the saving acts of God ; the people whom he has created for himself ; the world as God's creation and the new creation as the goal of his purpose.

Bibliography—W. F. Albright, *From the Stone Age to Christianity* (1946[2]), *Archaeology and the Religion of Israel* (1946[2]) ; E. Dhorme, *La religion des hébreux nomades* (1937) ; S. H. Hooke (ed.), *Myth, Ritual, and Kingship* (1958) ; A. R. Johnson, *The Cultic Prophet in Ancient Israel* (1944), *Sacral Kingship in Ancient Israel* (1955) ; E. A. Leslie, *OT Religion in the Light of its Canaanite Background* (1936) ; A. Lods, *Israel from its Beginnings to the Middle of the 8th Cent.* (Eng. tr. 1932), *The Prophets and the Rise of Judaism* (Eng. tr. 1937) ; S. Mowinckel, *He That Cometh* (Eng. tr. 1956) ; J. Pedersen, *Israel, its Life and Culture* I–II, III–IV (1926, 1940) ; H. H. Rowley, *The Faith of Israel* (1956) ; E. Sellin, *Israelitisch-jüdische Religionsgeschichte* (1933) ; G. E. Wright, *The OT against its Environment* (1950).

INTRODUCTION TO THE PENTATEUCH

By S. H. HOOKE

136a One of the foremost of modern OT scholars, speaking of the problems connected with the critical analysis of the Pentateuch, has said, ' It is here that the greatest fluidity in the whole field of OT study is to be found today, though it cannot be said that any agreed pattern is emerging from the welter of challenges to the older views ' (H. H. Rowley, *The OT and Modern Study*, xxvii). Another writer has said, ' The Pentateuch reminds one of a medieval cathedral which by good fortune has escaped the vandalism of rigorous restorations and therefore now stands with all its different styles mixed up, so that a very trained eye is needed to discover the original plan. And nevertheless, there is a plan ' (A. Bentzen, *Introduction to the OT*, ii, 12).

b The Jewish name for the Pentateuch is the **Torah, the Law**. Talmudic commentators, speaking of its five constituent parts, call them ' the five fifths of the Law ', and have named them by the first words of each book ; the English titles of the five books are translated from the Vulg. Latin titles, which, again, are translations of the Greek titles given to the books by the LXX translators. As is well known, the Torah occupies the first place in the three divisions of the Heb. canon of scripture, the Law, the Prophets, and the Writings ; according to the Jewish view the Torah, revealed to Moses and written down by him, possesses a higher degree of sanctity and authority than the other two divisions of the canon.

c The LXX translation provides the *terminus ad quem* for the present form of the Pentateuch and its place in the canon, while references to the Exile in Dt. show that its present form must be post-exilic. The first reference to ' the book of the law of Moses ' after the Exile occurs in the account given in Neh. 8 of the public reading of the law to the people at the feast of Tabernacles. It is unlikely that Ezra's book contained much more than the legal material of the Pentateuch, although it may be urged against this view that the prayer of the Levites in Neh. 9 contains elements from every book in the Pentateuch, especially from Dt. This, however, does not prove that the constituent parts of the Pentateuch had been united by this time in one collection. The most that can be said is that the returning exiles brought with them from Babylon a book which was known as the book of the law of Moses, and that the book reached its final form by the time the translation of the OT into Greek began, i.e. about the first half of the 3rd cent. B.C.

d But the real problems of the Pentateuch meet us when we examine the very varied nature of its contents and inquire how this shapeless and heterogeneous mass of material came to be welded into a book with a plan and a purpose. Each of the different elements has its own history and must be considered separately. These elements may be classified as follows :

(*a*) The **myths,** or origin stories, which have been collected and form an introduction to the whole work, in Gen. 1–11.

(*b*) A mass of **saga material** consisting of various cycles : the Abraham sagas ; the Jacob-Israel sagas, forming two distinct cycles linked by floating traditions about Isaac ; the Moses sagas, linked to the sagas of the patriarchs by the Joseph romance.

(*c*) Embedded in the saga material are various **cult-legends** : the Passover legend, the *Landnahme* 13
legend, and the Sinai legend. The importance of these cult-legends has been much stressed in recent work on the Pentateuch.

(*d*) The **legal material** consisting of a number of ' codes ' or collections of laws and prescriptions of a civil and religious nature.

(*e*) A number of **poems and poetical fragments**, e.g. the ancient ' Song of the Sword ' (Gen. 4:23–4) ; the Blessing of Jacob (Gen. 49) ; the Song of Moses (Exod. 15:1–18) ; the ' Song of the Well ' (Num. 21:17–18) and the oracles of Balaam (Num. 23 and 24) ; the Song of Moses and the Blessing of Moses (Dt. 32 and 33).

(*f*) Gen. 14, which has been described as an **erratic block** in the midst of the Abraham cycle of sagas.

(*g*) Blocks of parenetic (or hortatory) and prophetic material found in Dt.

Before we go on to speak of the various theories e
which have been put forward to explain the motives and methods by which this heterogeneous material has been woven into the present form of the Pentateuch, some general remarks may be made. In the first place it must be remembered that all this material has its source in the life and history of a people, and because this people was Israel the cultic and religious motive underlies everything. It has been rightly said that we are not in a position to understand the problems of the Pentateuch aright unless we recognise that the origin of the literature lies in the cult (C. R. North, *The OT in Modern Study*, 73). In the second place it must be remembered that Israel did not attain to national unity until several centuries after its earliest settlement in Canaan, and during that period groups of tribes, individual tribes, and even single clans and families, established themselves in various parts of Canaan, took over the cult centres already existing, or created new ones for themselves, as in the story of Micah in Jg. 17, and in the course of generations developed and handed on traditions about tribal heroes and events in the history of the tribe. Since we now know that not all the tribes went down into Egypt and experienced the Exodus, received the law from Moses, and endured the wilderness wanderings, we may not assume that the Passover legend and the Sinai legend, to take only two of the important cult-legends, were from the first a national possession. One more remark may be added. Although we no longer suppose that Moses wrote the Pentateuch, yet the idea of authorship should not be wholly dismissed from our minds. The process of weaving all these scattered traditions into the whole which is the Pentateuch was not a mechanical one. Collectors were at work with an intelligent purpose, but more than that, writers of the highest literary skill, with a firm belief in the purposes of God for Israel and for all mankind, have left the impress of their creative activity upon the narratives of the Pentateuch.

1 The Documentary Hypothesis—This line of f
approach to the problems of the Pentateuch, generally associated with the names of Graf and Wellhausen, has been accepted for wellnigh a century as critical orthodoxy. It owed its success to the fact that it

36f recognised that Israel's literature grew out of its history, but its chief defect was an over-simplification of that history. This was due in part to its academic and purely literary approach to the material, and also to the lack of knowledge concerning the background of Israel's religious development, which has now been made available through the discovery of so many new original sources. The Graf-Wellhausen hypothesis is so well known that a brief outline may suffice. It assumed a long period of purely oral tradition from the first settlement in Canaan up to the beginning of the monarchy ; then the two earliest written sources came into existence, collecting and combining the oral traditions concerning the early history of Israel into two parallel narratives, distinguished from each other by their respective use of the divine names Yahweh and Elohim, and emanating from the south and north respectively. These two documents, denoted by the symbols J and E, were then combined by a redactor into a single source during the latter period of the monarchy, and in the process they were subjected to a certain amount of revision and interpolation ; this stage of the evolution was
7a denoted by the symbol R^{JE}. A third source came into existence in the 7th cent. from the hands of a reforming circle which produced the book of the Law discovered in the Temple in Jerusalem during the reign of Josiah. This document, which was held to be the nucleus of the present Dt., was denoted by the symbol D. After the return from Babylon D underwent revision and expansion, and the hand of the circle which had produced D was thought to have worked over the earlier historical sources and imposed upon them the Deuteronomist view of history. In the Persian period a priestly school of writers and editors produced a document known as the Priestly writing, denoted by the symbol P, containing a collection of cultic laws and material relating to the history of the cult. The name of Ezra and his associates is attached to the activities of this school, and to it is attributed the genealogies and chronological framework giving some appearance of historical sequence to the earlier narratives. Finally, all these constituent documents were revised and united in the form of the Pentateuch as we now have it, a process which must have been complete before the beginning of the LXX translation in the 3rd cent. B.C.

b This scheme gave to the ' shapelessness ' of the Pentateuchal material an apparent order and rationality which carried conviction, and some of its main contentions have survived and will probably continue to survive the ' welter of challenges ' of which Professor Rowley has spoken. As in the case of NT criticism the use of at least one written source by the Gospel writers cannot be denied, so in the OT the chronicler's use of the books of Sam. and Kg. as written sources is undeniable. Also the discovery of the Râs Shamra texts has made it plain that written sources of cultic material were in existence in Canaan even before Israelite settlement there. The Râs Shamra texts further showed that a number of the technical terms connected with the sacrificial system and regarded as the invention of the Priestly writers were already being used in Ugarit long before the period assigned to the Priestly writing. In addition to the damaging effects of archaeological discoveries such as these, the Documentary hypothesis exhibited in the course of time what may be called a tendency to nuclear fission. Critical analysis of the sources tended to multiply revisers and revisions, and symbols threatening to extend J, E, and P to the *n*th degree, together with the rainbow hues of the Polychrome Bible, bred an increasingly sceptical attitude towards the Documentary theory and a hostility towards the application of the techniques of ' higher criticism ' to the Scriptures. One scholar of early days allowed himself to make the quite irrelevant remark that higher criticism had never saved any souls nor healed any bodies.

c But the reverent critical study of the Scriptures is a part of the life of the Spirit and must go on. The 137c feeling that the Documentary mode of approach had outlived its usefulness led to the search for new insights and fresh modes of approach. The most spectacular attack on the Documentary position has come from Scandinavia, and has been styled by its exponents the ' Traditio-historical ' method ; but before discussing this new line of approach, something must be said about a critical method which has yielded valuable results without abandoning completely the Documentary theory.

2 The Form-critical (*Formgeschichtliche*) **Method** d —This line of approach, which has achieved considerable notoriety through the work of Dibelius and Bultmann in the critical study of the Gospels, had already been applied with much success to the OT, notably by Gunkel in his studies on the Psalms, by Albrecht Alt in his studies on Heb. law, and more recently by Gerhard von Rad in his studies on Dt. There is not space here to describe in detail the methods and results of the Form-critical school, but some important aspects of its work as it affects the Pentateuch must be mentioned. First, we may refer to the examination of the legal formulae used in the various collections of legal material in the Pentateuch by Alt in his *Die Ursprünge des israelitischen Rechts* ; an earlier study along the same lines was made by A. Jirku
in his *Das weltliche Recht im AT*. As a result of his e
investigations Alt put forward the view that, using the criterion of the introductory formulae, the material of the Book of the Covenant, to which his inquiry was mainly limited, could be divided into two different types of law : the first, to which he gave the name of *casuistic*, or case-law, was distinguished by the hypothetical form of its introduction, ' If a man ', followed by a definition of the offence and a statement of the penalty attached to it. A comparison with Mesopotamian and Hittite laws shows that this was the invariable form of legal terminology in use among Israel's neighbours at the time of the settlement in Canaan. A discussion of the contents of these casuistic laws leads to the suggestion that they represent the impact of Canaanite customary law upon the immigrants as they sought to adjust themselves to the new environment. But in contrast to this hypothetical form of legal statement an entirely different form is to be found in the Book of the Covenant side by side with, and occasionally interwoven with, the casuistic form.
This second form is characterised by the address in f
the 2nd person, ' Thou shalt ', or ' Thou shalt not ', and by the introduction of the 1st person ' I ' of Yahweh, although participial and other slightly variant forms occur. The Decalogue is included by Alt among the groups of laws which are characterised by this style, called by him the ' Apodeictic ', or declarative, form. In the collections of laws bearing this apodeictic stamp, he finds no trace of Canaanite influence, and emphatically asserts that their origin is to be sought within the boundaries of Israel. A further important distinction is drawn between the two classes of laws : in the case of the casuistic laws it is assumed that they are to be administered by the local tribunals of elders in the city gate, as was probably already the custom in Canaanite cities ; but, on the other hand, the group of apodeictic laws in Dt. 27 suggests the cultic origin of such laws, and their enforcement by divine sanctions is in the hands of the priesthood ; the scene described in Dt. 27 is laid in what may have been the first Israelite sanctuary in Canaan, Shechem.

It is to be observed that the results of the Form-critical method, of which this is an authoritative example, do not involve the abandonment of the Documentary hypothesis, but illustrate the shift of interest from purely literary analysis to the nature of the contents of the various documents, with a view to discovering their relation to Israel's life and culture.

Another aspect of the Form-critical method as it g
relates to the problems of the Pentateuch is to be found

187g in von Rad's *Studies in Deuteronomy* and in more detail in his *Das formgeschichtliche Problem des Hexateuch*. In this work he follows up the line indicated by Mowinckel in his study *Le Décalogue*. The Scandinavian scholar had put forward the view that, underlying the J and E narratives which have been combined to form the account of the epiphany of Yahweh and the establishment of the covenant, was a yearly cult festival coinciding with the autumn New Year festival, at which the making of the covenant was re-enacted, and the cult legend of Sinai recited. One element of the cult ritual consisted in the recitation of the conditions of the covenant, and Mowinckel suggests that the decalogues of J and E represent the statement of such conditions as recited by the officiating priests. In his Form-critical study of the problem of the Hexateuch, von Rad pointed out that in the various forms of the *Landnahme* legend there was no allusion to the Sinai episode and the making of the covenant. He went on to show that the Sinai pericope (Exod. 19–24) was a cult legend forming part of an Israelite festival of the renewal of the covenant, and that its form was used in the construction of Dt. In support of this view he suggested that Ps. 50 and 81 contained elements, such as the epiphany of Yahweh on Sinai and the pronouncement of the Decalogue, which pointed to their recitation as part of the ritual of a covenant
138a festival. With regard to the problem of the origin of Dt., von Rad has laid stress on the warlike character of Dt., and sees in it an attempt to revive the Holy War and the conditions of the old Israelite amphictyony which he thinks had never completely disappeared. Taking this feature of Dt. together with the strongly parenetic character of so much of the book, he would find the provenance of Dt. among the Levites whom the book represents as living here and there in the country towns. He finds the period from Joash to Josiah as presenting historical and social conditions most favourable to such a movement. Here again the use of the Form-critical technique does not involve abandonment of the Documentary hypothesis, but illustrates the tendency to turn from purely literary analysis to the examination of small units of material with the aim of discovering their setting, their *Sitz im Leben*, in the political, social, and cultic life of Israel at some given point in its history.

b The third line of approach has its source in Scandinavia and presents the most thorough-going challenge to the Documentary hypothesis. Its propounders have given it the name of :

3 The Traditio-historical Method—The names of Engnell and Widengren are those mainly associated with the movement, but its foundations rest upon the work of Gunkel, Mowinckel, Nyberg, and Pedersen, especially the last-named, and a number of younger scholars have been active in developing the ideas of the Uppsala school.

As its name implies, the characteristic feature of the school is its emphasis on the part played by oral tradition in the transmission and shaping of the Pentateuchal material.

c In the course of the development of the Documentary hypothesis, scholars had claimed that the sources into which the Pentateuch had been dissected could be traced on into the book of Jos. and even farther. Hence it had become customary to speak of the Hexateuch. But the Uppsala school's radical break with the Documentary hypothesis involves the rejection of such a conception as the Hexateuch. In its place Engnell puts forward the hypothesis that the mass of tradition material in the OT falls into three divisions : (*a*) Genesis-Numbers, a collection of traditions which he calls the 'P-work', or the Tetrateuch, though it should be noted that the symbol P does not bear for Engnell the meaning which it has in the Documentary theory ; (*b*) Deuteronomy-2 Kings, which he calls the Deuteronomistic history-work ; and (*c*) 1 Chronicles-Nehemiah. The third division does not concern us here, but some account must be given of the implications of this new method of approach to the problems 1:
of the Pentateuch.

Engnell's view is, in the first place, that the P-work d
originated in a traditionist circle which he calls the P-circle. This was a group of persons, sometimes called 'tradents', who preserved a body of traditions, corresponding on the whole to what is contained in the Priestly writing of the Wellhausen school, and combined this with materials collected by other traditionist circles to form the Tetrateuch. This implies that, instead of parallel narratives covering the same period existing side by side and subsequently combined by a redactor into a continuous narrative, we have various traditionist circles each preserving its own body of traditions and interweaving it with the traditions of other circles, until the P-circle combined its own material with the traditions of the other circles and created the Tetrateuch with the stamp of its own interpretation of Israel's history. Following Pedersen, Engnell holds that the nucleus and formative element in this process was the Passover legend of Exod. 1–15, and with Pedersen would maintain that dissection into literary sources cuts across and destroys the cultic unity of what was never meant to be a factual report, but a cultic glorification of Yahweh's mighty acts.

In the same way the view is advanced that the second e
great block of tradition, the Deuteronomist history-work, emanated from a D-circle of traditionists, also drawing on the traditions from other circles, and combining them with their own material into a book which bears the stamp of an interpretation of history which we are accustomed to call the Deuteronomic, and which is specially noticeable in the parenetic parts of Dt. and in the so-called Deuteronomic judgments in the books of Kg. The two circles worked side by side, and their activities were completed in the post-exilic period, when the two collections were combined into one narrative by placing the P-story of the death of Moses at the conclusion of the Deuteronomic speeches. In Engnell's words, 'Once the two great works were united, the original unity of the D-work was forgotten, and it was split up into its present books' (quoted by C. R. North, op. cit., 70).

It may be remarked that both the Documentary f
hypothesis and the Traditio-historical method of approach rest upon assumptions which in their turn are based upon a critical assessment of the existing text of the Pentateuch. Hence our estimate of their comparative merits must depend ultimately upon our judgment of the degree in which each method seems to make the Pentateuch more intelligible as a record of Israel's history and its place in the wider purpose of God. It has to be remembered that the Traditio-historical method is in the formative stage and has not yet received its final exposition, and that it has yet to run the gauntlet of contemporary criticism ; hence any attempt to assess its merits and defects must necessarily be provisional. Critical study of the Documentary hypothesis during the last thirty years has revealed many of its weaknesses ; Volz and Rudolph have challenged the existence of E as an independent source ; the very early date of much of the material of P has been demonstrated ; and, as we have already seen, the fissiparous tendency of source criticism threatens to reduce the whole method to an absurdity ; perhaps the most damaging criticism lies in the charge that the exponents of this method of approach to the Pentateuch have failed to recognise that OT history is not 'pragmatic' history, to use Professor Voegelin's term, but *Heilsgeschichte*. Indeed, the last-named scholar has said, 'The source criticism of the old type, we may say, is indeed dead' (*Israel and Revelation*, 162). It is not easy, at the present stage of g
development, to say what advantages, if any, the Traditio-historical method offers as compared with the source-criticism method of approach. The following advantages have been suggested : the new method is based on a better understanding of the contents of the

8g sources as narratives than the source critics seem to possess; it shows a respect for the Massoretic text, and a reluctance to resort to emendation, which has not always characterised the Wellhausen school; it possesses a thorough knowledge of the comparative material furnished by recent discoveries, enabling it to elucidate symbols and cult patterns; and, finally, the theory of traditionist circles provides a more probable explanation of the various types of traditions to be found, not only in the Pentateuch, but in the OT as a whole. Some of these advantages must be credited to the work of the Form-critical school, whose valuable results can be combined, as we have seen, with an acceptance of the main position of source criticism.

h In criticising von Rad's treatment of the Creation story in Gen. 1 Engnell has said, 'the P-circle is not, as a matter of fact, a very typical priestly circle, but rather—to use a very anachronistic metaphor—of the type of the Israelite 'Academy of Literature, History, and Antiquities', though, of course, with its root and keen interest in the cult' ('Knowledge and Life in the Creation Story', VT 3 (1953), 105). An unkind critic might retort that this observation savours somewhat of the 'desk-logicism' of which Engnell so often accuses the source critics, but it is not without justification; Voegelin has remarked in reference to it, 'One wonders whether the analogy is really so very anachronistic; for the concern with the past as the paradigmatic record of God's way with man, extending over a period of more than a thousand years, could hardly translate itself into practice without a considerable apparatus of both personnel and material installations, for preserving this enormous body of traditions not only mechanically but with the necessary intelligence and erudition' (op. cit., 159–60).

9a It is probable that the main reason for the prevailing note of dissatisfaction with the results of source criticism is the feeling that this method of approach to the Pentateuch has reached a dead end and does not seem capable of offering any fresh light on Israel's history and religious development. While most of the recent German work seems to take the general position of source criticism for granted, its trend seems to be away from further minute dissection of the documents, and towards a study of small units and special phenomena in the documents, such as Noth's study of the personal names in the OT and their significance for the history of the cult, or his study of the early tribal organisation of Israel, resulting in his interesting theory of an early amphictyony of tribes with a central sanctuary; in the same context von Rad's study of the institution of the Holy War in the early history of Israel, and the attempt to revive it, of which he finds evidence in Dt., is an example of the present trend in Pentateuchal studies, outside of Scandinavia, which is yielding results and opening out fresh vistas in a way which source criticism has seemed incapable of doing.

b There is one more issue between the Traditio-historical method and the Documentary hypothesis which calls for comment. The dissection of the Pentateuch into documentary sources rested on the assumption, for which evidence was offered, that in the text of the Pentateuch certain recurring features could be observed, and these provided criteria distinguishing the different written sources. The earliest and best known of such criteria is the use of the names Yahweh and Elohim to distinguish the Yahwist writer, or school, from the Elohist. Other criteria were added in the course of time: where the Yahwist spoke of Sinai as the scene of the divine epiphany, the Elohist used the name Horeb; the Yahwist was more anthropomorphic in his descriptions of Yahweh's intercourse with men, while the Elohist spoke of divine communications as coming to men by means of dreams or angelic intermediaries. The inconsistencies and contradictions in the telling of a story were pointed out and used as further criteria of different sources: for example, the difference in the number of animals taken into the ark, or the discrepant accounts of how Joseph's 139b
brethren disposed of him in Gen. 37. The rejection of c
written sources by the propounders of the Traditio-historical method raises the question of how these criteria, or 'constants', as they are now beginning to be called, are to be explained. With regard to this question, Engnell's main contention is that the existence of such variants and contradictions is best explained on the theory of an original, orally transmitted, tradition or group of traditions. He maintains that in the stage of language and culture which Israel had reached in the OT such contradictions and obscurities were only to be expected, and he appeals here to what he calls 'the epic law of iteration'. It is true that the Râs Shamra texts have demonstrated the epic tendency to iteration, and the frequent repetition of passages has been very useful in enabling lacunae in the texts to be restored by their aid; but, as the repetitions are generally verbatim, they may illustrate the accuracy of oral transmission but do not help to explain the presence of contradictions and variants in a narrative. With regard to the use of the divine names as a criterion Engnell maintains that its validity depends upon the consistency with which the names are used, and he denies that they are so used. He also holds that the differences which the LXX shows in its use of the divine names as compared with the Massoretic text prove that the variations are not original. How d
untenable this last argument is was shown long ago by Skinner's refutation (*The Divine Names in Genesis* (1914)) of Dahse's similar argument in his book, *Textkritische Materialen zur Hexateuchfrage* (1912). Engnell further argues that the variations in the use of the divine names are intentional and imply that the same traditionist is using the names in a different context or with a different 'ideological' reference. Thus he uses Yahweh in a context where Israel's God is contrasted with the gods of other nations, but Elohim in more theological and abstract contexts. But when examined, this distinction proves very difficult to maintain. The use of such differences as criteria for the differentiation of documentary sources is dismissed by Engnell in the words, 'Such criteria rest upon nothing other than an *a priori*, evolutionistic way of looking at things, which goes hand in hand with and dictates the sources-analysis' (quoted by C. R. North, in *The OT and Modern Study*, 67).

While, therefore, the Traditio-historical method does e
offer new insights, and its renewed emphasis on the importance of oral tradition coupled with the results of Form-critical studies is to be welcomed, it does not appear that we can wholly dispense with written sources and the activities of compilers and editors in the course of the production of the Pentateuch in its present form.

As each of the books composing the Pentateuch will be dealt with in a separate commentary, it is not necessary in this article to discuss each book in detail, and we shall now turn to the question of whether a clear plan or purpose directed the activities of the final editors of the Pentateuch, and what place each book occupies in relation to such a plan.

First of all it may be said that whether we agree or f
not with the view that the first four books form a separate unit, and that Dt. comes from another circle and begins a fresh unit of tradition, it remains true **that Dt. has a distinctive character and stands apart from the other books of the Pentateuch.** It may, perhaps, be compared to the Fourth Gospel in relation to the Synoptists. The author of the Fourth Gospel knows and uses the material of the Synoptists, but he imposes a new pattern of symbolism upon the historical material: he sees the earthly life of Jesus of Nazareth as the creative activity of the divine Word, proceeding from the Father, passing through the world, and returning to the Father, having accomplished the work which the Father gave him to do. So the author, or compiler, of Dt., under the device of a farewell discourse delivered by Moses

139f to the children of Israel in the plains of Moab as they are on the eve of entering the Promised Land, recapitulates the Exodus and wilderness experience, as it had been related in the traditions now collected in the four books, and interprets it all in terms of the divine purpose. While the book shows obvious signs of having passed through various stages of editing before reaching the form in which we have it now, and von Rad may well be right in his suggestion that the provenance of the book is to be found in the circle of country Levites, and that Shechem is its cultic centre, whoever affixed the song of Moses to it and gave it its final form looked far beyond any immediate political or cultic situation. They, or more probably he, for the book in its present form bears the stamp of a single mind and a unitary conception, looked at the pattern of the history of Israel as it revealed itself to him in the body of collected traditions before him, and saw that what gave meaning to that pattern was the purpose of
140a Yahweh in choosing Israel. Here it may be remarked that while in its first form or draft the book may have been independent of Engnell's P-work, yet its final form presupposes a knowledge of the *Landnahme* tradition, the Sinai pericope, both the casuistic and the apodeictic collections of laws, the history of the monarchy, and the promises made to the patriarchs, that is, material from all the collected traditions which ultimately constituted the four books of Engnell's Tetrateuch. The Song of Moses is a poem of great power and beauty, and is by an author who is clearly familiar with the later poetry of Israel ; echoes of Deutero-Isaiah and of post-exilic Psalms are heard in the song. But the keynote is to be found in v. 8, ' When the Most High gave to the nations their inheritance, when he separated the sons of men, he fixed the bounds of the peoples according to the number of the sons of God ' ; here the RSV follows the reading of the LXX, found also in a Dead Sea Scrolls fragment, but the Massoretic text has, ' according to the number of the children of Israel '. Even if the LXX represents the original reading, the meaning of v. 9 suggests that the Massoretes were right in interpreting ' the sons of God ' (Heb. *'ēl*) as referring to Israel : ' For the Lord's portion is his people, Jacob
b his allotted heritage '. Hence, for the author of the poem the key to world history lay in God's choice of Israel to be the vehicle of his revelation of himself. The map of the known world unrolled itself before his mind ; there lay Egypt, Ashur, Babylon, Persia, and all the smaller nations, each within the boundaries fixed for them by Yahweh, and at the centre of them lay Yahweh's own portion, Israel. It is, perhaps, not impossible that the author of the poem may be the final editor of Dt., and may be responsible for the final arrangement of the Pentateuch ; but, be that as it may, the person who placed the poem at the end of the book did so because it expressed the central truth which he proclaims with reiterated emphasis in the introductory section of the book, the truth of Yahweh's love for so unlikely an object as Israel. This unmotived choice is the reason which the author gives for Israel's obedience : ' It was not because you were more in number than any other people that the Lord set his love upon you and chose you, for you were the fewest of all peoples ; but it is because the Lord loves you, and is keeping the oath that he swore to your fathers, that the Lord has brought you out with a mighty hand, redeemed you from the house of bondage . . . you shall therefore be careful to do the commandments, and the statutes, and the ordinances, which I command you
c this day ' (Dt. 7:7–11). Hence, in Deuteronomy, as it receives its final form from an editor whose point of view has now been impressed upon the book, we find the directive principle which determined the arrangement and order of the traditional material as we have it now in the four books of the Tetrateuch. There is no reason to suppose that when Dt. received its final form the collected body of traditions had already been divided into four books in the order in which they now stand. We have no means of knowing exactly what had 14
happened to the traditions during the Exile, nor what was the precise form or content of the book which Ezra brought back from Babylon and read to the assembled people at the feast of Tabernacles. Unless, with Torrey, we reject the Ezra-Nehemiah-Chronicles material as fiction, Ezr. 3:2 suggests that part of its contents consisted of the law relating to burnt-offerings; Ezr. 9:1–2 suggests that it contained the prohibition of mixed marriages in Exod. 34:16 and Dt. 7:3 ; Neh. 8:14 indicates that it contained the regulations given in Lev. for the observance of the feast of Tabernacles ; and finally, Neh. 9:7–8 refers to the call of Abraham, his change of name, the covenant, and the promise of the land, embracing material in Gen. from J, E, and P. More references from this late post- d
exilic material could be added to support the view that Ezra's book of the law of Moses contained the main body of tradition arranged in something like the order in which it now appears. Hence, unless we are to assume that the priests and scribes in Babylon had already divided the material into four books and arranged them in the order in which they now stand in the Heb. canon, it will follow that this final stage of editorial activity took place between the return of Ezra, now placed by most scholars after the two visits of Nehemiah, about 397 B.C. (cf. H. H. Rowley, ' The Chronological Order of Ezra and Nehemiah ', in *The Servant of the Lord* (1952), 131–59), and the final split between the Samaritans and the Jews, since the Samaritan Pentateuch, although showing an independent history of textual transmission from that of the Massoretic and LXX forms of the Pentateuchal text, nevertheless has the same division and order of the separate books as the Massoretic and the LXX (cf. E. Würthwein, *The Text of the OT*, 31f.)

At this point of time, then, according to the tradition- e
ists, those responsible for bringing all the collected material into the present form of the Pentateuch must have had before them two great collections, namely, the P-work, and the D-history work headed by Dt. in what we may assume was its penultimate form. It is doubtful whether the P-work had been divided into its separate books before the final stage of editing, and for the purposes of this essay we shall assume that it had not been so divided. Hence the first question that arises is, What led the final editors to detach Dt. from its place at the beginning of the D-history work, give it its present form, and attach it to the end of the P-work ? The answer here suggested is that the final editor or editors of Dt., by affixing to it the Song of Moses and possibly reinforcing it by the parenetic material in the opening sections of the book, gave it a character which it had not previously possessed, and which is not entirely consonant with some of the material embodied in it. The book now expressed the conviction of those who had given it its final form that the meaning, not only of Israel's history, but of all history, was to be found in Yahweh's choice of Israel and his subsequent dealings with her. Hence we suggest that Dt. in its final form provides the motive and directive impulse which explains the order and arrangement of the other four books of the Pentateuch.

The first question that had to be answered by those f
who had taken in hand to give the material the form of a *Heilsgeschichte* was, How did it all begin ? Israel was not the only nation in the world ; there were other nations far more numerous and powerful, and they too had histories and a beginning, and if the purpose of Yahweh gave meaning to history they could not be left out of the picture. Man, the ultimate object of Yahweh's purpose, must have had some kind of a beginning, and the universe, the heavens, and the earth with all their various forms of life, must have had a beginning, and so the person or persons responsible for the final shape of the Pentateuch gathered into one collection all the available traditions about the beginnings of the heavens and the earth and man, and their opening word was, ' In the beginning God '. Ques-

140f tions concerning the origin of these traditions will be dealt with in the commentary on Gen., and need not be discussed here, but it may be pointed out that most, if not all, of this material had already been available, either in the form of cult-traditions preserved in the various cult-centres of Palestine, or, on the Documentary hypothesis, already formed part of the JE narrative. Its final form, however, and its present position as an introduction to the story of the divine choice of Israel, is due to the final editors. In this section answers were given to the fundamental questions: God was shown bringing order out of chaos, making man in his own image, and placing him over the created order; in symbolic form man's relationship with God was shown to rest upon trust and obedience; then, still in symbols, the act of disobedience was shown, breaking the relationship, destroying the created order, and bringing sin into the world with all its disastrous consequences; the section ends with the breaking up of the original unity of mankind into discordant fragments, so that the very existence of the nations was the result of sin, and God had to begin again the work of bringing order out of chaos.

141a How this work began was the next question which the final editors had to answer. Here there were two divergent traditions to be dealt with; according to one tradition the *Heilsgeschichte* began with Abraham; the author of Deutero-Isaiah says to his people, 'Look to the rock from which you were hewn, and to the quarry from which you were digged. Look to Abraham your father and to Sarah who bore you; for when he was but one I called him, and I blessed him and made him many' (Isa. 51:1–2); according to the other tradition the salvation-story began with the redemption of Israel from the bondage of Egypt; Hosea says, 'When Israel was a child, I loved him, and out of Egypt I called my son' (Hos. 11:1). It was necessary for these two traditions to be united, and the second stage of the story began with an act of obedience, an exodus from the chaos of nations; Abraham is shown, in the fragment of cult-tradition in Jos. 24:2–13, as led by Yahweh from beyond the River into Canaan. The relationship based on obedience is re-established and God can begin the work of re-creation. Here there was available for the editors the collection of Abraham and Jacob (Israel) sagas in the form of the JE narrative, which had already undergone considerable revision. It has already been pointed out that the existence of E as an independent source has been questioned, but many scholars today are inclined to find the impress of a single mind of great power and originality in the
b so-called JE narrative. But, for the final editors, this section of the salvation-story showed the development of the fundamental theme of the obedience of faith making possible the covenant relationship and the promise of a seed through whom blessing would come to all the nations; it showed the climax reached when obedience was carried to its utmost limit, and Abraham was seen prepared to give back to God the son upon whom the fulfilment of the promise depended. Another fragment of cult-tradition in Dt., possibly recited at one of the annual festivals, represents the second line of tradition concerning the salvation-story; it runs, 'A wandering Aramaean was my father; and he went down into Egypt and sojourned there' (Dt. 26:5). The Aramaean is Jacob, and the Jacob cycle of sagas shows how the theme of obedience is continued, and Jacob wrestles with his divine antagonist to become Israel. In this way, through the intermediate link of Isaac, whose function in the narrative is to provide this link, Abraham, the subject of the first tradition, and Israel, the subject of the second, are brought
c together into one story. But the next question to be answered by the final editors was, How and why did Israel come to be in Egypt? The question was answered in the Joseph story. It is generally recognised that this narrative is not saga, but of a different literary type; it has been called a romance, and its beginning shows signs of editorial activity and of variant versions.

But it probably lay ready to hand for the final editors, 141c
and it was placed by them at the end of the Abraham-Jacob group of sagas, to show how Jacob-Israel came to be in Egypt. The first stage of the salvation-story ended there, and with it the first book of the Pentateuch received its final shape and place. This was Genesis. Its Heb. title was *B^e^rēshîth*, 'In the beginning'.

Pedersen, whom Engnell follows in this context, d
holds that the Passover legend in Exod. 1–15 is a unit which cuts across the lines of source-analysis, and that it was a nucleus round which various traditions gathered. But whether we agree here with the traditionists or not, the material, either in the form of the continuation of the revised JE narrative, or as an important constituent in the P-work, lay before the final editors, and provided what they required for the next stage of the salvation-history. Israel was in Egypt; even if, historically, only a comparatively small part of what was ultimately to become Israel had gone down into Egypt with Jacob-Israel, for those who were giving its final shape to the Pentateuch that part represented Israel; Israel had to be redeemed if Yahweh was to keep his covenant and fulfil his promise. So the Passover cult-legend and the Sinai pericope were brought together and made the centre round which the saga of Moses and the wilderness experiences were grouped. Moses is shown continuing the line of e
Abraham's faith and obedience, the basis on which the covenant relationship rests, and when the redeemed people are brought by Moses to meet with Yahweh at Sinai, the same basis for the covenant is laid down, 'Now therefore, if you will obey my voice and keep my covenant, you shall be my own possession among all the peoples, for all the earth is mine', and the people accept the condition, 'All that the Lord has spoken we will do' (Exod. 19:5, 8). The testing of the newly established relationship, and its breach, are related, and Moses alone sustains the relationship by his intercession and faith in the purpose of Yahweh. An essential element in that purpose was that Yahweh should dwell among his redeemed people, and the Exodus story reaches its climax with the glory of Yahweh filling the house whose pattern had been revealed to Moses in the Mount. This completed the second stage of the salvation-history and constituted the second book. We call it Exodus, but the Heb. name for it was 'These are the names', because the book opened with the words, 'These are the names of the sons of Israel who came to Egypt with Jacob.' They are the names of the redeemed. This was what 'the beginning' in Gen. had led to.

The next question the final editors had to deal with f
was concerned with the realisation that a holy God had taken up his abode with a sinful people. In one of the 'kingship' psalms which describes Yahweh as enthroned upon the cherubim, the significant words occur, 'Thou wast a forgiving God to them, but an avenger of their wrong-doings' (Ps. 99:8). A necessary part of the salvation-history was an account, which was at the same time an explanation, of how Yahweh made the continuance of forgiving possible, and how it was possible for a sinful people to go on living with a holy God without being destroyed. Here the editors had abundant material at their disposal: there was the accumulation of centuries of priestly *tôrôth* relating to all kinds of things that were unfitting for the divine presence. Much of it was g
already in written collections, such as what is known as the 'Holiness Code' in Lev. 17–26, and some of it might still have been in oral form, as Hag. 2:11–13 suggests; but we are not now concerned with the origin of this material but with the purpose of the final editors in placing it where they have. The second book had closed with the entry of Yahweh into his house; this third book opens with the words, 'The Lord called Moses, and spoke to him from the tent of meeting.' Then follow groups of *tôrôth* intended to provide for every possible contingency, everything in short that concerned the right relationship of Israel

141g with the God who dwelt in their midst. The book closes with the words, 'These are the commandments which the Lord commanded Moses for the people of Israel on Mount Sinai.' Ancient rituals which must have been far older than the time of Moses, and prescriptions which could only relate to a period long after the occupation of Canaan, all are gathered together and presented by the editors as delivered by Yahweh to Moses on Sinai, *for the people.* For the architects of the Pentateuch it is all part of the salvation-history, and it constitutes the third book, Leviticus. The Heb. title is 'And he called'. It is the first word to come from Yahweh in his new house.

142a The point reached at the end of the third book of the Pentateuch leaves Israel still at the foot of Sinai. The salvation-history has shown Israel redeemed from bondage, Moses as the prepared instrument of redemption, the epiphany at Sinai and the ratification of the covenant constituting Israel as Yahweh's chosen people on the condition of obedience; it has shown the pattern of the house revealed to Moses on the Mount, then prepared under the direction of the Spirit of Yahweh, and finally entered by Yahweh in glory. Then comes the record of Yahweh's provision of the means by which he can continue to dwell among a sinful people. Now it becomes necessary for the final editors to bring Israel to the point of fulfilment towards which all the divine activity of redemption had been directed; Israel is to be shown in the ideal order of encampment and the order of march; the story of forty years of testing must be told, and Israel shown standing on the brink of Jordan, ready to enter and take possession of the land which Yahweh had promised to Abraham at the beginning of the salvation-history.

b The material gathered together in this fourth book of the Pentateuch is an extraordinary mixture of very early traditions, extracts from the book of the Wars of Yahweh, which may have been a collection of traditions concerning campaigns waged by the old Israelite amphictyony, of which the campaign described in Jg. 20 is an example, the Song of the Well, the Balaam oracles, and some very late material. But its over-all place in the plan of the final editors seems to be the rounding off of the story of redemption, and the mingling of mercy with judgment; Moses, Aaron, and Miriam are involved in the judgment; the sinful generation falls in the wilderness, and a purged Israel stands in the plains of Moab ready to enter the promised land under the leadership of the man commissioned at the hands of Moses by divine direction, Joshua, whose symbolic name means 'Yahweh is salvation', a name of infinite prefigurative significance. The fourth book of the Pentateuch takes shape, and receives the name Numbers (Ἀριθμοί in the LXX) in our Bibles, but its Heb. title, again taken from its opening words, is 'And Yahweh spoke', i.e. to Moses, giving orders for the numbering of the people.

c The fourth book thus meets the already prepared fifth book, in which Moses is presented as standing before the purged Israel on the plains of Moab, and interpreting for them the meaning of the whole pattern of the salvation-history as it has been unfolded in the four previous books. Deuteronomy (so named from the LXX's mistranslation of 17:18 as τὸ δευτερονόμιον τοῦτο, but of which the Heb. title is 'These are the words') is to be taken, on the view of 14 the origin of the Pentateuch which we are here suggesting, as both the key and the directing impulse of the plan to which Bentzen referred in the quotation which stands at the head of this essay. If the Pentateuch is read as a continuous history it appears to be a confused collection of myths, sagas, legal codes, and cultic legends, the history of whose transmission the Documentary hypothesis on the one hand, and the Traditio-historical method on the other, have sought to explain. But if the five books are seen as a planned salvation-history, giving a panoramic view of the divine purpose for mankind, and of Israel's place in it, the Pentateuch is seen as a planned whole, and becomes charged with meaning.

It has been suggested by von Rad that Joshua's d speech at Shechem, recorded in Jos. 24:2–13, may be regarded as a Hexateuch in miniature (ATD ii, 9), and the proponents of the Documentary hypothesis hold that the final editors of the collected traditions intended to give the completed work the form of a Hexateuch, although some would find the component sources continued into the early historical books. On the other hand, as we have already seen, the traditionists regard their P-work as a Tetrateuch. Whichever of these assumptions be accepted, the question still requires an answer, Why did the final editors detach Dt. in its penultimate form, either from the Hexateuch, or from the Tetrateuch, transform it by the addition of the Song of Moses and other material, and make it the final book of a Pentateuch? We have seen that this must have taken place before the Samaritan schism. What has been written above is an attempt to answer this question.

It is perhaps necessary to add that the process of e transforming the various cult-legends, which were perhaps somewhat naïve and materialistic in character, into salvation-history, did not begin with the post-exilic editors. It can already be seen in the work of the Yahwist, and the 8th- and 7th-cent. prophets show an ever-deepening sense of the purpose of God as giving meaning, not only to the history of Israel, but to all history. What is here claimed is that the post-exilic editors, emerging from the purgation of the Captivity, put the corner-stone on the process, and gave the Pentateuch that cathedral-like character which Bentzen has so happily attributed to it.

Bibliography—A. Alt, *Die Ursprünge des israelitischen Rechts* (1934); A. Bentzen, *Introduction to the OT* (1948); H. Cazelles, *Études sur le Code de l'Alliance* (1946); S. R. Driver, *Introduction to the Literature of the OT* (9th ed. 1913); O. Eissfeldt, *Einleitung in das AT* (2nd ed. 1956); A. Jirku, *Das weltliche Recht im AT* (1927); A. Lods, *Histoire de la littérature hébraïque et juive* (1950); S. Mowinckel, *Le Décalogue* (1927); E. Nielsen, *Oral Tradition* (1954); M. Noth, *Überlieferungsgeschichte des Pentateuch* (1948); W. O. E. Oesterley and T. H. Robinson, *Hebrew Religion, its Origin and Development* (1930); J. Pedersen, *Israel: its Life and Culture* III–IV (1940); H. H. Rowley (ed.), *The OT and Modern Study* (1951); E. Voegelin, *Israel and Revelation* (1956); G. von Rad, *Studies in Deuteronomy* (1953), *Das formgeschichtliche Problem des Hexateuch* (1938); A. Welch, *Deuteronomy: the Framework to the Code* (1932).

GENESIS

By S. H. HOOKE

(In the sections which deal with individual books of the Bible our policy is to give at the top of each page the numbers of the chapters discussed. In the case of Genesis these chapters are not always consecutive. The reason for this treatment will be quite clear to the student as he reads the article.)

143a **General Character**—The post-exilic editors who gave the Pentateuch its final form intended the collection of traditions of which Gen. is composed to serve as an explanation of God's choice of Israel and of his purpose in choosing her. It bears the impress of a mind firmly convinced that all history had a meaning which could only be understood in the light of the divine activity, and that it was Israel's mission to interpret that activity to the world. It was necessary to give an account of how and why the world which was the scene of that activity had come into existence; of how Israel as a people had come into being; and of how the various nations whose relations with Israel formed an essential part of the whole story had come into existence. It was to answer these 'obstinate questionings' that the author of Gen., not in a spirit of objective curiosity like Herodotus, but with a definite religious intention, collected and arranged the floating oral or written traditions of Israel in the form of a book which might stand at the beginning of the story of God's ways with man and with Israel. Hence, although it is the book of divine beginnings, it was probably the last book of the Pentateuch to receive the form in which we have it.

b **Literary Structure**—The book falls into three well-defined divisions:

(A) Chs. 1–11 containing the account of God's activity in bringing order out of primeval chaos; of the creation of man and the place assigned to him in the created order; of man's disobedience and the break up of that order; of the consequences of the break up and the dispersal of mankind into nations and tongues, in open rebellion against the rule of God; of a great symbolic act of judgment, and of the dawn of a new hope.

(B) Chs. 12–36 containing the account of how an act of obedience made possible the first stage in God's work of restoration and redemption. These chapters contain what are called the sagas of the patriarchs. They are not history in the modern sense of the word, but early cultic and tribal traditions, collected and arranged in order to show how, through the response of obedience and faith, God was able to create the people of Israel to be the instrument of his purpose of redemption.

(C) Chs. 37–50 containing the story of Joseph. This is not saga, but what may be called romance with an historical basis. It was intended by the author to form the link between the tradition of the call of Israel in Abraham, and the parallel tradition of the call of Israel in Egypt, as we find it in Hos. 11:1, 'When Israel was a child, I loved him, and out of Egypt I called my son.' Hence the story given in this section provides the explanation of how Israel came to be in Egypt.

c **Literary Sources**—While, as has already been said, the book of Gen. bears the stamp of a single mind, yet it contains a mass of material of very varied character. It is generally accepted that those who gave the OT its
final form had before them certain written sources, 143c
and for many years it has also been the accepted view that the book of Gen. by the application of literary criteria, sometimes called 'constants', can be separated into a number of strands. By this method of literary analysis the narratives of Gen. have been divided into three main sources, denoted by the symbols J, E, and P. The reason for the use of these particular symbols is that at the beginning of the critical analysis of the Pentateuch it was observed that the two usual names which the Hebrews used for God, namely, Yahweh (or Jahveh) and Elohim, were used in such a way as to suggest that they indicated different written sources whose compilers regarded the history of their people from different points of view. By the use of this criterion it was found possible to divide Gen. into two parallel narratives, one of which was assigned to an imaginary writer, or school of writers, called the Yahwist, while the other was similarly assigned to the Elohist writer or school. But it was soon found that the use of the divine name as a criterion led to confusion, and caused certain parts of Gen. to be regarded as early which later on were discovered, by the use of finer criteria, to be late. This led to the separation of the third strand to which the symbol P was allotted, indicating that the material so designated came from the hand of the priestly circles who were engaged in editing the traditions of Israel after the return from the exile in Babylon. It is not necessary to discuss here in detail the implications of the Documentary Hypothesis, as it is generally known, as this has been done in the Introduction to the Pentateuch (§§136*f*, 137*a*), and the characteristics of the different writers will be dealt with in the commentary; but the general position reached as the result of the critical analysis of Gen. is that we have two parallel narratives, J and E, belonging to the south and north of Israel respectively. They may have been committed to writing about the 10th cent. B.C., and were probably combined into a single narrative and considerably revised during the following century. The state of the book at this stage is usually indicated by the symbols R^{JE}. Although the Deuteronomist (see §138*e*) probably knew the book of Gen. in this form, it does not seem to have received any revision or additions from his hand. It received its final form at the hand of the priestly writer after the Exile. His contribution does not seem to have taken the form of a continuous narrative, though this is open to question, but his characteristic additions, indicated by the symbol P, will be noted in the course of the commentary.

Documentary Analysis—While the trend of much OT scholarship today is away from source analysis, yet d
it has by no means been abandoned, and we frequently refer to it in the course of the commentary. Hence it may be useful to set out the generally accepted results of the documentary analysis of Gen. in tabular form, and this is given on the next page.

143d

DOCUMENTARY ANALYSIS OF GENESIS

J	E	P
		1:1–2:4*a*
2:4*b*–4:25		
5:29		5:1–28, 30–2
6:1–8		6:9–22
7:1–5, 12, 16*b*, 17*b*, 22 3		7:6, 13–16*a*, 17*a* (except the words 'forty days', which are a gloss from J), 18–21, 24
8:2*b*–3*a*, 6–12, 13*b*, 20–2		8:1–2*a*, 3*b*–5, 13*a*, 14–19
9:18–27		9:1–17, 28–9
10:1*b*, 8–19, 21, 24–30		10:1*a*, 2–7, 20, 22–3, 31–2
11:1–9, 28–30		11:10–27, 31–2
12:1–4*a*, 6–9, 10–20		12:4*b*–5
13:1–5, 6*b*–11*a*, 12*b*–18		13:6*a*, 11*b*–12*a*
14 (source unknown)		
15:3–4, 6–15, 17–18, 19–21 (Deuteronomic redactor)	15:1 2, 5, 16	
16:1*b*–2, 4–8, 11–14	16:9–10	16:1*a*, 3, 15–16
		17:1–27
18:1–33		
19:1–28, 30–8		19:29
20:18	20:1–17	
21:1*a*, 2*a*, 7, 28–30, 33	21:6, 8–27, 31–2, 34	
22:15–18, 20–4	22:1–14, 19	
		23:1–20 (but this has been questioned)
24:1–67		
25:1–5, 11*b*, 18, 21–25*a*, 26*a*, 28	25:6, 25*b*, 27, 29–34	25:7–11*a*, 12–17, 19–20, 26*b*
26:1–3*a*, 6–14, 16–17, 19–33	26:3*b*–5, 15, 18	26:34–5
27:1*a*, 2–3, 4*b*, 5*b*–7*a*, 15, 18*b*–20, 24–7, 29*ac*, 31*b*–34, 41*b*–42, 43*b*, 45*a*	27:1*b*, 4*a*, 5*a*, 7*b*–14, 16–18*a*, 21–3, 28, 29*b*, 30*b*, 31*a*, 35–41*a*, 43*a*, 44, 45*b*	27:46
28:10, 13–16, 19, 21*b*	28:11–2, 17–18, 20–21*a*, 22	28:1–9
29:2–14, 26, 31–5	29:1, 15–23, 25, 27–28*a*, 30	29:24, 28*b*–29
30:3*b*–16, 22*c*–23*a*, 24–5, 27, 29–31*a*, 34–38*a*, 39–40*ac*, 41–3	30:1–3*a*, 17–20, 22*b*, 23*b*, 26, 28, 31*b*–33, 38*b*, 40*b*	30:21–22*a*
31:1, 3, 10, 12*b*, 17–18*a*, 25, 27, 31, 43–4, 46, 48, 50*ab*	31–2, 4–9, 11–12*a*, 13–16, 19–24, 26, 28–30, 32–42, 45, 47, 49, 51–5	31:18*b*
32:3–7*a*, 13*b*–22*a*, 23*b*, 24–9, 31–2	32:1–2, 7*b*–13*a*, 22*b*–23*a*, 23*c*, 30	
33:1–17	33:18*a*, 18*c*–20	33:18*b*
34:2*b*–3*ac*, 5, 7, 11, 19, 26, 29*b*–31		34:1–2*a*, 3*b*, 4, 6, 8–10, 12–18, 20–5, 27–29*a*
35:14, 16–22*a*	35:1–4, 6*b*–9	35:5–6*a*, 9–12*ab*, 13*ab*, 15, 22*b*–29
36:32–9		36:1–31, 40–3
37:2*b*, 2*d*–4, 12–13*a*, 14*b*, 18*b*, 21, 25*b*–27, 28*b*, 32*a*, 33*b*, 35	37:5–11, 13*b*–14*a*, 15–17*a*, 17*b*–18*a*, 19–20, 22–25*a*, 28*a*, 28*c*–31, 32*b*–33*a*, 34, 36	37:1–2*ac*
38:1–30		
39:1–4*a*, 4*c*–5, 6*b*, 7*b*–23	39:4*b*, 6*ac*, 7*a*	
40:(1, 3, 5, 15, redactor)	40:1–23	
41:31, 34, 35*b*, 36*b*, 41–45*a*, 46*b*–49, 56*a*, 57	41:1–30, 32–3, 35*a*, 36*a*, 37–40, 47–8, 50–5, 56*b*	41:45*b*–46*a*
42:2, 4–5, 7*ac*, 27–28*a*, 38	42:1, 3, 6, 7*b*–26, 29–35, 28*b*, 36–7	
43:1–13, 15–34	43:14	
44:1–34		
45:1*a*, 2*b*, 4–5*ac*, 9–11, 13–14, 19*ab*–21*a*, 28	45:1*b*–2*a*, 3, 5*bd*–8, 12, 15–18, 21*b*–27	
46–1*a*, 28–34	46:1*b*, 2–4, 5*ab*	46:6–27
47:1–4, 6*b*, 12–27*a*, 29–31		47:5–6*a*, 7–11, 27*b*–28
48:2*b*, 9*b*–10*a*, 13–19	48:1–2*a*, 8–9*a*, 10*b*–12, 20–2	48:3–7
49:1*b*–24*a*, 27, 33*b*	49:24*b*–26	49:1*a*, 28*ab*–33*ac*
50:1–11, 14, 18, 21, 24	50:15–17, 19–20, 22–3, 25–6	50:12–13

e **Cultic Traditions**—The general tendency of recent study of the early traditions of Israel has been to turn from the over-elaboration of literary analysis to the different traditions which underlie the literary sources. One of the most important results of this study has been the recognition that the various Canaanite sanctuaries which were taken over by the Israelites during their settlement in Canaan became centres of tradition in which the early episodes in the history of the ancestors of Israel and of Israel's own experiences took the form of cult legends which were recited at the various sanctuaries. Many of the Psalms suggest by

3e their form and contents that they were used in this way. Such cult legends, together with the written sources referred to above, formed the material which was finally woven together into the book of Gen. as we have it now.

(A) The Origin-Stories of Genesis (I-XI)

f This first section of the book falls into the following main divisions :

(*a*) The Priestly writer's account of the six days of Creation, 1–2:4*a*.
(*b*) The J-E account of the Creation of man and the animals, 2:4*b*–25.
(*c*) The J-E story of the Fall and the Expulsion from Eden, ch. 3.
(*d*) The J-E story of Cain and Abel, ch. 4.
(*e*) The P genealogy from Adam to Noah, ch. 5 (exc. v. 29).
(*f*) The J-E myth of the Sons of God and the daughters of men, 6:1–7.
(*g*) The J-E-P story of the Flood, 6:9–8:22.
(*h*) The P account of the Covenant with Noah, 9:1–17.
(*i*) The J-E story of the beginnings of agriculture, 9:18–27.
(*j*) The J-E-P story of the peopling of the earth after the Flood, ch. 10.
(*k*) The J-E story of the Tower of Babel, 11:1–9.
(*l*) The P genealogy of Abraham, linking up the origin-stories with the sagas of the patriarchs, 11:10–32 (exc. vv. 28–30, which belong to J-E).

g Before we deal with the material contained in this section of Gen., something must be said about the general character of the stories here collected by the editor of Gen. What we have called origin-stories represent a type of literature which is not peculiar to the Hebrew people. In the early literature of Egypt, Babylon, and Canaan, and indeed among most so-called primitive peoples, similar stories are to be found, purporting to give an account of the beginning of things. Such stories are commonly known as ' myths ', and it is necessary for us to inquire what place ' myth ' has in the literature of the Hebrews.

4a **The Meaning and Function of Myth**—In common usage, to say that something is a myth, or mythical, implies that it is not true, and hence many thoughtful people feel that to say the Bible contains myths is the same as saying the Bible contains what is not true. But such an attitude is based on a mistaken idea of the true nature of myth, and also on a mistaken idea of what the Hebrew writer had in mind when he made use of myths, not only in the first eleven chapters of Gen., but elsewhere in the Bible.

In the first place, it is of course true that myth is not history, that is, it is not, and does not profess to be, a record of events which happened in a particular place and at a particular date. But historical truth, important though it is, is not the only kind of truth, and **a myth can, and often does, represent a kind of truth which cannot be expressed in historical categories.** When we call the story of the Fall a myth we do not deny its truth ; we imply rather that its truth lies deeper than the kind of historical truth which rests on dates and documentary evidence. Hence, in order to get the term ' myth ' in proper perspective we must inquire into the origin and function of myths in the ancient civilisations which form the background of Hebrew religion and culture.

b Long before Israel settled in Canaan the dwellers in the Nile valley and the Tigris-Euphrates valley had built up an elaborate structure of society which rested ultimately upon agriculture. In achieving this they had discovered the incalculable nature of their environment, and had evolved a pattern of activities by which they believed they could control their environment and secure the prosperity of their communities. This pattern of activities we call *ritual*, and we have abundant evidence to show that while almost every situation in life might call for some kind of ritual, the great ritual occasions coincided with the great turning points of the agricultural year. One of such occasions concerning which we are specially well informed was the Babylonian New Year Festival in the spring. What was done and said on that occasion will illustrate for us the meaning and function of myth. 144b

The first thing to be observed is the **central importance of the king** in the New Year rituals. We shall see later that this point has special significance in relation to the Hebrew attitude towards kingship. But for both the Egyptians and the Babylonians the king had come to have a central place as the focus of the activities intended to secure the well-being of the community. Hence some of the most important ritual acts were intended to ensure that the king continued to be an efficient agent for this purpose. In the second place the king took part in certain ritual acts, one of which was a ritual combat which symbolised the original victory of the god over the forces of chaos. Thirdly, twice, at critical points of the ritual, the priests chanted the ritual chant called *Enuma elish*, in which the victory of the god over the chaos-dragon, Tiamat, and the ensuing act of creation were described. This chant contained the ' myth ', what the Greeks called the ' *muthos* ', or spoken part of the ritual, which, together with the ' *dromenon* ', or acted part, constituted the whole efficacious ritual. The myth described, in symbolic terms, the original situation by which the furious river was tamed, the swamps drained, and order created out of chaos. But while ritual and myth together re-enacted and described the triumphant creative activity of the god, those who carried out the ritual believed that upon its regular seasonal performance the whole created order depended for its perpetuation. Myth and ritual together had power, they did something. Here we have the original meaning and function of myth. The truth of the myth lay in the fact that it described, in symbolic terms, a real situation. The function of the myth lay in its power, in conjunction with the ritual, to maintain that situation in being. c

The next point we have to bear in mind is that, either by direct contact with Babylonian civilisation before their entry into Canaan, or indirectly through Canaanite civilisation after their entry into Canaan, the Hebrew people had taken over into their own body of traditions a number of these myths. What the editor of Gen. did with them and with what intention, we shall inquire later ; but for the present it may suffice to point out that none of the myths in this section of Gen. has been shown to be of distinctively Hebrew origin, while most of them, the Flood story in particular, are of Mesopotamian origin. d

Furthermore it must be recognised that **the use of myths in the Bible** is only a particular case of the larger question of the use of symbols or images as a form of divine speech, an essential vehicle of revelation. We shall be specially concerned with this in Gen. because a large part of the significant symbols and images come to birth in Gen., and it will be one of our objects to observe the conditions under which images arise. Much of the biblical narrative, including the sagas of Gen., is concerned with the relations between God and man, and in the last resort rests upon an historical basis. But there are certain central themes which were of vital significance for the editor or author of Gen., whom we may without prejudice call the Yahwist, and these themes lie beyond the sphere of historical categories. While the sojourn in Egypt might be enshrined in a cult legend, nevertheless it rested upon the tradition of something that had actually happened. The Hebrew poet could say, ' We have heard with our ears, O God, our fathers have told us, what deeds thou didst perform in their days, in the days of old ' (Ps. 44:1) ; but another, perhaps later, poet could also say, ' Where were you when I laid the foundation of the earth ? ' (Job 38:4). Here was e

144e something which only the Sons of God and the morning stars had witnessed, and the only language which the Yahwist could use to describe it was the language of myth and symbol. Again, the presence of sin in the world, with all its dreadful consequences, was a fact of inescapable reality, but the manner and moment of its entry into the world was a timeless reality, only capable of description in terms of myth and symbol. Hence, in such circumstances, myth, so far from being untrue, is the divinely chosen means of expressing truths which lie far deeper than historical truth.

f Again, we have to remember that the Yahwist was not interested, as a Greek might have been, in the problem of the origin of the universe as a matter of intellectual curiosity ; looking back upon as much of Israel's history as had so far unrolled, and being convinced that he saw in it the pattern of divine activity which included not only Israel but the whole world, he was concerned to set it in the larger perspective of its divine origins, and in giving an account of how it all began he used material which lay ready to his hand.

Recent studies give strong grounds for believing that already during the early period of the Hebrew monarchy a great New Year festival was celebrated with appropriate ritual in which the kingship of Yahweh and his triumph over the forces of evil opposing his purposes of blessing for Israel and the world were depicted in the form of a dramatic myth. The evidence in support of this view is drawn mainly from the kingship and royal psalms. For example, in Ps. 74:12–17 we have first the announcement of the kingship of Yahweh, ' Yet God my king is from of old ', then we have a description of Yahweh's triumph over the monster Leviathan, followed by an account of creation. Similarly, in Isa. 51:9–10 we have Yahweh's triumph over the dragon recalled in connection with the cult-legend of the Exodus. This then was the symbolic material which lay ready to the hand of the Yahwist when he set out to give an account of matters which could only be described in terms of symbol and myth.

g **The Chronology of Genesis**—Although, as we have seen, the purpose of the book of Gen. is not history, yet it has an historical background. The movements of the patriarchs, translated by the Yahwist into salvation history, represent significant movements of peoples, and it is possible to give a tentative outline of the chronological order of events underlying the narratives of Gen.:

h (i) 1700–1600 B.C. Entry of Abraham and his clan or tribe into Canaan. Possible descent of some part of the Hebrew people into Egypt, implied in the account of Abraham's descent into Egypt in Gen. 12.

(ii) 1500 B.C. A fresh movement of Aramaean stock from Syria into Canaan, represented by the cycle of Jacob stories. Beginning of the Hebrew settlement and conquest of Canaan. Attempt to conquer Shechem successful at first, but afterwards recovered by the Canaanites.

(iii) 1400–1300 B.C. Movement of Judah and associated tribes from Kadesh northward, and settlement in the Negeb. Northern tribes, Zebulun, Asher, Naphtali, and Dan come in from the north and occupy the north of Canaan. Professor Rowley connects the former movement with the Ḫabiru of the Tell el-Amarna Letters, and the latter with the SA.GAZ.

(iv) 1360–1350 B.C. Joseph in Egypt, and descent into Egypt of some of the Hebrew tribes. Professor Rowley places these events during the period of Akhnaten.

(v) 1250 B.C. Conquest of Canaan still proceeding. Capture of Bethel, Kirjath-sepher, and other cities. As the result of criticism, and of Miss Kenyon's excavation of Jericho, most scholars now reject Garstang's date for the fall of Jericho *c.* 1400 B.C. and assign it to *c.* 1230 B.C.

I 1-II 4a The Priestly Account of Creation—It is 14 both useful and necessary to compare the two accounts of creation in Gen. and to note the differences between them. But before we do so it may be well to remember two things. First, the Priestly writer, presumably collecting and editing the traditions of Israel after the exile, was using the same kind of ancient material as the Yahwist before him. Secondly, it is a mistake to think of the Yahwist and the Priestly writer as regarding the history of their people from opposed points of view. It can be clearly seen from the Priestly prayer in Neh. 9 that, even if there had been, there was no longer any difference between the priestly and the prophetic view of Israel's history, that history was for both completely *Heilsgeschichte* (salvation history). The old controversy reflected in both the 8th- and the 7th-cent. prophets was dead ; the prophetic protest had done its work. In the prayer just referred to the story of creation has its place in the rehearsal of God's ways with Israel, and the book of the Law which Ezra brought with him from Babylon must have had an account of Creation. The suggestion has much to commend it that the Priestly account with its recurring refrains may have been a chant sung or recited at the New Year festival where the victory of Yahweh over the forces of evil and disorder was celebrated. If this is a possible suggestion, and such a festival could only have been celebrated in Jerusalem during the period of the monarchy and in the Temple, then the composition of this chant may have been pre-exilic. It may be remarked in passing that the author or editor whom we are calling the Yahwist, and who has impressed the stamp of his personality and outlook so forcibly upon our book of Gen., need not be the J of the hypothetical document or historical writing composed about the 10th cent. and subsequently combined with the E document to make the main historical source underlying the Pentateuch, or even the Hexateuch, if that hypothetical work ever existed. Our Yahwist would be a prophetic individual looking back over a longer period of Israel's history than one which goes back from the 10th cent., and one whose conception of God as the Judge of all the earth (Gen. 18:25) springs rather from the 7th cent. than the 10th. Hence, even if he did not himself prefix to his own account of Creation this Priestly chant as a magnificent exordium, a suggestion which is probably too questionable to be accepted, we can, nevertheless, be sure that there was no fundamental difference of outlook upon the *Heilsgeschichte* between the Yahwist and the Priestly writer who gave his book its final form.

We can turn to the comparison between the two b accounts of Creation given at the top of the next page.

In the first place it is clear that the setting of both these accounts is Mesopotamian. As the J-E narrative continues to the end of ch. 11, we have to take into account other elements beside those contained in the Creation stories. It is generally accepted that the two accounts of the Flood, and the various Mesopotamian versions, go back to a common source, although the Hebrew versions are obviously related to the account in the Gilgamesh epic. Two of the four rivers in Eden are the Mesopotamian rivers Tigris (Hiddekel) and Euphrates. The story of the Tower of Babel is set in the land of Shinar, an early Hebrew name for Babylonia. Although the Mesopotamian background of the P account is less obvious, yet it may be seen (*a*) in the Hebrew word for ' the deep ', *t*ᵉ*hôm* (1:2), which is generally accepted as being the equivalent of the Babylonian Tiamat, denoting both the underworld ocean, and the Chaos-dragon, vanquished and slain by Marduk before the creation of the world takes place ; (*b*) the way in which an ordered place is assigned to each created thing closely resembles Marduk's ' fixing the destinies ' of each element in creation ; (*c*) it is possible to translate 1:2*a*, ' a great wind swept over the deep ' (so Goodspeed and von Rad), in which case we might have another echo of the Babylonian Epic of Creation where Marduk arms

145c

ACCOUNTS OF THE CREATION

P (1-2:4a)	J-E (2:4b-25)
The original state of the earth is a watery chaos (*tōhû wābhōhû*)	The original state of the earth is a waterless waste, without vegetation
The work of creation is divided into six separate operations, each assigned to one day	The account contains no note of time
The order of creation is : (*a*) Light (*b*) The firmament—heaven (*c*) The dry land—earth. Separation of earth from sea (*d*) Vegetation—three orders (*e*) The heavenly bodies—sun, moon, and stars (*f*) Birds and fishes (*g*) Animals and man—male and female together	The order of creation is : (*a*) Man, made out of the dust, with the breath of Yahweh (*b*) The Garden (Paradise)—to the east—in Eden (*c*) Trees of every kind, including the Tree of Life and the Tree of the Knowledge of Good and Evil (*d*) Animals, beasts and birds (no mention of fishes) (*e*) Woman, created out of man

himself with the winds in order to overcome Tiamat. The point of these parallels is not, however, to emphasise the dependence of Hebrew symbolism upon Babylonian myths, but to emphasise the fact that the Hebrew writers, whether Yahwist or Priestly, did not invent a symbolism to express the various aspects of the divine activity, but took what lay ready to their hand, the material which they had inherited as part of their early cultural contacts, and transformed it into the vocabulary of the divine speech.

d It is a mistake to suggest, as some commentators do, that there is no note of conflict in the Hebrew description of the divine activity in creation, or that the Hebrew word *bārā'* ('made') implies creation *ex nihilo*. Chaos, tempest, and darkness are all symbols of what is opposed to the divine purpose and must be overcome. We hear the same note in Ps. 93:3–4, in symbolism perhaps borrowed from the Canaanite myth in the Râs Shamra texts of the struggle between Baal and the waters, 'The floods have lifted up their voice ; the floods lift up their roaring. Mightier than the thunder of many waters, mightier than the waves of the sea, the Lord on high is mighty.' In Isa. 42:14 we have Yahweh depicted as crying out like a travailing woman, gasping and panting, in his redemptive activity. Hence behind the apparently effortless display of creativity in the Priestly account there lies the symbolism of divine victory over chaos and darkness. The conquered deep becomes his servant ; when he pleases he can unleash the waters of *t*^{e}*hôm* in judgment, but, as the Psalmist says, 'The Lord sat enthroned (as king) over the flood' (Ps. 29:10).

Hence, in the Priestly account we have the stage set for the divine drama, the order displayed, the heavenly bodies making the 'times and seasons' which are the turning-points in the divine plan, man set in his appointed place to rule over the established order of creation as God's representative. It is all very good, and God rests. With this in mind the Psalmist asks, 'What is man ?', and the Yahwist takes up the tale and shows what man is.

146a **II 4b-25 The J-E Account of the Creation**—The Priestly writer had shown man as he is in the purpose of God, what God meant him to be. The Yahwist now proceeds to show in significant symbols the other side of the coin, the constituents of man's nature. The Priestly writer had used the word *bārā'* for the divine activity in making man. The Yahwist uses the word *yāṣar* for the creative act, the word which is regularly used for the potter's work. The Priestly writer had depicted God as taking counsel with his heavenly court about the creation of man, 'Let *us* make man', so that man was there conceived of as forming part of the divine plan ; but the Yahwist represents man as shaped by Yahweh as the potter shapes his vessel out of clay. Man is formed out of the dust of the earth and informed with the breath of life, breathed into him

by Yahweh, so that he becomes 'a living soul'. As 146a
St Paul says, 'the first man was from the earth, a man of dust (1 C. 15:47) ; farther on the Yahwist puts it in another way, 'in his going astray he is flesh' (RVm 6:3). Seen as part of the divine purpose man is meant to show what God is like, a visible image (*ṣelem*) of God ; but in himself he is flesh, with all its possibilities of knowledge, desire, and choice, and also its possibilities of failure and error. Again, the Priestly writer presents male and female as created together in one act, 'male and female created he them, and called their name Adam' ; but the Yahwist represents man as at first 'alone', a state which Yahweh says is not good ; he is incomplete without his counterpart ; so, in one of the profoundest images in the OT, Yahweh builds woman out of man's essential stuff. The most intimate human relationship is established, with all its potentialities for good and ill. Corresponding to the assignment of its place to each element in the created order as described by the Priestly writer, is the vivid picture drawn by the Yahwist of man fulfilling his function as head of the created order by giving names to each of the living creatures, formed like himself out of the dust of the earth. The act of naming is a very important symbol. It has in it an element of creative activity. To know the name of a person or thing is to know its essential nature and to have power over it. In the subsequent narratives and throughout the Bible when God changes a man's name it signifies a creative act, an essential change has been brought about by God in the man's nature. In the Yahwist's narrative the man (*hā'ādhām*) gives two significant names to the woman (*'ishshāh*) whom Yahweh had made to be his counterpart : the first indicates her intimate relation to himself ; she is Ishshah because she has been taken out of Ish, where the generic Adam names himself Ish, a name which signifies man in his humanity, his strength and his weakness ; but he gives her a second name, Eve (*ḥawwāh*), after the Fall and the break-up of the original divine order. It is a name of hope ; the woman who had been a contributory cause to man's disobedience contains the seed of life ; she is to be 'the mother of all living' (3:20), another image of the deepest import.

We must now turn from the Yahwist's account of the b
creation of man to his description of **the scene in which the first act of the drama is set,** the garden of Eden, or in its Persian form, Paradise. In this account the Yahwist has blended elements of myths from various sources. In contrast to the watery chaos of the Priestly setting of the creative activity, the Yahwist describes a waterless, treeless waste upon which Yahweh had not yet caused his rain to fall. This element is clearly Palestinian. Babylon and Egypt depended upon irrigation for their fertility, but Canaan was, as the Deuteronomist says, a land that

146b 'drinks water by the rain from heaven' (Dt. 11:11), and that rain was the gift of Yahweh was a peculiarly Hebrew conception. This waterless waste was nevertheless, before Yahweh had brought rain, mysteriously watered by an agency which is not ascribed to Yahweh. The various English versions render the Hebrew word by 'mist', but the meaning of the word is very uncertain. The only other occurrence of the word in the OT is in Job 36:27, which the RSV renders, 'he distils his mist in rain'; the LXX has 'fountain', and the suggestion seems to be of some underground source breaking through to moisten the soil and make it into soft clay for the activities of the divine Potter. But into this Palestinian setting the Yahwist has worked the myth of the garden of Eden, derived from a different source. In Ezek. 28:12–19 we have a description of 'the garden of God', in which dwells a mysterious semi-divine figure who is the sum of wisdom and beauty, and is ultimately expelled from the garden on account of his pride in aspiring to be like God. Other references in the OT show that the Yahwist is using here a myth which formed part of
c ancient Hebrew tradition. Similarly the analysis of the text has shown that in the original form of the myth there was only one tree whose nature was not disclosed; so that we may assume that it is the Yahwist himself who has shaped the myth so as to present the two contrasted trees with their different properties, one of them containing the fruit of forbidden knowledge, and the other containing the fruit of immortal life. While it is of academic interest to dissect the narrative into its component elements, what is really valuable is to recognise that this narrative is no mere patchwork quilt, but a construction of the highest art in which the author has so blended all these diverse elements in such a way as to present a symbolic pattern of the underlying causes of all God's activity in Creation and Redemption. These things could only be said in myth and symbol, and those who would deny the myth and try to take the story literally lose thereby all the significance of the divine language of symbol. It may be added, finally, that the symbols here brought together and made significant run on through the whole of Scripture, and in the Apocalypse of St John, that book in which all the symbols are reborn, we hear the One who is 'the beginning of God's creation' (Rev. 3:14), who had prevailed where the first man had failed, saying, 'To him who conquers I will grant to eat of the tree of life, which is in the paradise of God' (Rev. 2:7).

d **III The J-E Story of the Fall**—Central elements in the Yahwist's presentation of the human tragedy are the related ideas of the forbidden knowledge and the loss of immortality. In the period in which the Yahwist was writing, the essential knowledge for man, and the knowledge which set Israel apart from all the other nations, was the knowledge of God, and obedience was the condition of life. In Dt. 32:47 Moses is represented as saying, 'Lay to heart all the words which I enjoin upon you this day, that you may command them to your children, that they may be careful to do all the words of this law. For it is no trifle for you, but it is your life.' The prophets repeatedly reproach their people with having lost the knowledge of God (cf. Hos. 4:1, 'There is no knowledge of God in the land'). But there was also a forbidden knowledge, as the Deuteronomist represents Moses as saying, 'the secret things belong to the Lord our God' (Dt. 29:29), and for the Yahwist this was the one forbidden thing, the knowledge of those secrets of life and death which belonged of right to God alone.
e In the myths which the Yahwist is using, knowledge of good and evil was not *moral* knowledge, but knowledge of powerful spells and incantations by which the mysterious forces of the universe could be controlled. This kind of knowledge or wisdom belonged to the god Ea and could be imparted by him to the priests who jealously guarded its secrets. In the myth of Adapa, which has interesting echoes of the Paradise
story, the hero Adapa is the son of Ea, and his name 14
has been equated by some scholars with the name Adam. In the story Ea had given Adapa wisdom but not immortality. It was Adapa's duty to serve the gods by providing them with daily food, which included fish. One day, while Adapa was fishing, the South Wind capsized his boat, and in his anger Adapa uttered a curse which broke the wings of the South Wind so that it did not blow for seven days. Observing this, Anu sent a messenger to find out what had happened, and when he heard who had done it he summoned Adapa to appear before him. Ea prepared his son for the interview by instructing him how to gain the favour of the two gods who kept the gate of Anu's abode; he also told him that he would be offered bread and water which he must refuse, because they would be bread and water of death; he might, however, accept the clothing which would be offered him. He obtained entrance through the favour of Tammuz and Ningizzida whom he had propitiated; they also interceded for him and caused Anu to accept his account of why he had broken the wings of the South Wind. Anu then took counsel with the gods and decided that Adapa should be made a god, and offered him the bread and water of immortality. Adapa, as instructed by his father, refused them, and when Anu asked him why he had done so, he explained what his father Ea had told him. Anu laughed and told him that through his father's guile he had lost the gift of immortality; he then sent him back to earth with the sentence that mankind should henceforth be subject to disease.

Another version of man's loss of immortality is found f
in the Epic of Gilgamesh, to which we shall refer later in connection with the myth of the Flood. In this myth, of which several versions exist, the hero Gilgamesh, distressed by the death of his friend Enkidu, sets out on a long and adventurous journey to find his ancestor Utnapishtim, the only survivor of the Flood. He learns from him that the gods have reserved for themselves the gift of immortality, but also learns from him where to find a magic herb which has the power of renewing life. He finds the herb, but loses it by the guile of the serpent who steals it while Gilgamesh is bathing.

This brings in **the theme of the serpent** and its 14
role in mythology, also its significance as a symbol in Scripture. In Christian symbolism, of course, the serpent has become almost wholly a symbol of evil, the only exception being its use by Jesus in the saying, 'So be as wise as serpents, and innocent as doves', where the serpent is a symbol of wisdom that is not evil (Mt. 10:16). But in ancient mythology it was not by any means always a symbol of evil. In Canaan it was the symbol of the god Eshmun, the equivalent of the Greek Aesculapius, the god of healing, and the rod with its entwined serpent was the god's magic implement of healing. The story of the brazen serpent lifted up by Moses in the wilderness is a reminder that this aspect of serpent symbolism was a part of early Hebrew tradition. Moreover, in Greek mythology the serpent is especially connected with the underworld, with reincarnation because of his power of changing his skin, and with the mysterious knowledge which the spirits of ancestors are supposed to possess. An early Greek coin shows a great coiled snake surrounded by emblems of fertility, with the inscription *Neos Agathos Daimon*; he is a good daimon (J. Harrison, *Themis*, 277).

But to the Yahwist this kind of goodness was only b
evil; the serpent with his magic knowledge, his promises of life and fertility, was the fitting symbol of the guile which would lure men into the ways of death, away from the one truly good God, the only source of life, and the only lawful object of knowledge. Thus we see the Yahwist making skilful use of the old myths, the guile of the serpent, the gods' jealousy of man, and representing the serpent as offering to man the enticing prospect of vital knowledge which was being withheld by Yahweh through jealousy.

7c So the fatal act of disobedience is committed, the free and happy relationship between man and God is broken, and the curse falls. All the good and useful activities are darkened and turned to evil. The pleasant care of the fertile soil becomes a weary toil, a struggle against useless and hurtful weeds for a bare subsistence, until man returns to the dust from which he was taken. The natural desire of the man for the woman becomes a thing of shame, and child-bearing becomes a mortal struggle with pangs of the rending flesh. The serpent becomes the agelong enemy of God and man, the incarnate symbol of evil. Although the cryptic oracle of the perpetual enmity between the serpent and the seed of the woman has been interpreted as a Protevangelium, no hopeful or Messianic meaning was intended by the Yahwist in his picture of the unending fight between the serpent and mankind. Finally man is expelled from the Paradise, the garden of God, where he had dwelt in happy companionship with God, the way to the tree of life is barred by Cherubim and a fiery sword, no return is possible.

d It is hard not to believe that the Yahwist was fully aware that in this wonderful pattern of images he was describing what could only be described in the language of symbols, drawn so skilfully from the ancient myths which had passed from many sources into the traditions of his people. He had to tell how man marred what God had made ; to show how and why the *Heilsgeschichte* began. It would have been possible to go into much fuller detail concerning the rich background of ancient Semitic myth from which this first section of Gen. has been drawn, but space will not allow of this. Enough, however, has been said to show the importance of myth as a vehicle of truths that lie deeper than what may be described as historical truth.

8a **IV The J-E Story of Cain and Abel**—In this section of the Origin stories the Yahwist continues his account of the consequences of the breach in the relationship between man and God, and now describes the first breach in human relationships. It is clear that the story of Cain and Abel has been drawn by the Yahwist from a different source of Hebrew tradition from that from which the accounts of Creation and the Fall are drawn. That the connection is an artificial one is shown by the fact that the story assumes the existence of other people on the earth ; Cain says, ' whosoever finds me will slay me ', whereas the context in which the Yahwist has placed the story supposes no other human beings on earth but Adam and Eve and Cain and Abel. The story presupposes the existence of a clan or tribe who will take up the blood-feud for the slaying of Abel (4:15), also of a tribe among whom Cain may find refuge and a wife. The story also assumes the existence of the institution of sacrifice which implies a settled form of community life and some degree of religious organisation. The name Cain is generally taken by Semitic philologists to mean ' smith ', and regarded as the patronymic of the Kenite clan of smiths. The explanation of the name attributed to Eve, ' I have gotten a man with (the help of) the Lord ', rests upon a questionable derivation from the Hebrew *ḳānāh*, which means (*a*) ' to acquire ', and (*b*) ' to create '. The verse presents many difficulties and is probably an isolated fragment of tradition unconnected with the Cain and Abel story which follows. An interesting suggestion is that it may represent a fragment of another form of the myth of the creation of man in which the goddess Aruru together with Marduk creates man. But the main body of the story in its present form is made up of two strands : vv. 1–15 containing the story of the slaying of Abel by Cain, and the circumstances under which it took place ; in this strand Cain is condemned to nomadism and is a different figure from the Cain of the second strand in vv. 16–26 in which Cain is a city-builder, and his descendants develop the various arts and crafts of a civilised community. These two strands must be treated separately.

(*a*) Since it is clear that the story had no original connection with the Paradise story, but depicts a developed stage of society, with established religious institutions, we must consider what is the situation presented by the story. **Cain and Abel represent two different types of community,** the agricultural and the pastoral, each carrying out its regular ritual of sacrifice. In the story one ritual is successful and the other is not ; this is what is implied when it says that Yahweh accepted Abel's offering but rejected Cain's. Now, as we have already seen, the main purpose of ancient ritual was to secure the well-being of the community ; for the agricultural community the fertility of the crops, and for the pastoral the fertility of the herds and flocks. 148a

b In the Yahwist's narrative the slaying of Abel follows an obscure conversation between Yahweh and Cain. The Hebrew text is in some disorder and has evidently suffered some mutilation in the course of transmission. Its form seems to suggest that the agriculturist whose sacrifice has failed to secure its object, has consulted the oracle to inquire what is to be done, and has received a reply saying that he knows what the proper ritual is, and that there is a *rōbhēṣ*, a hostile demonic power waiting to be propitiated. The word translated ' lieth ' or ' croucheth ' is the same as the Akkadian *rabiṣu*, ' the evil croucher ', who lies in wait for his offering, and is frequently mentioned in Babylonian magical texts.

c The next step is introduced by a significant phrase which is omitted in the Hebrew text but is supplied by the LXX, as the RSV*n* indicates ; it says, ' Cain said unto Abel his brother, Let us go out to the field '. It is in the *field*, the tilled soil whose infertility has brought about the situation, that the slaying of the shepherd takes place, and the suggestion is that, in the source which the Yahwist is using, the slaying was a ritual one, not an impulsive murder instigated by jealousy, but a ceremonial killing intended to fertilise the soil by drenching it with the blood of the victim; in the words of the narrative, ' the ground . . . which has opened its mouth to receive your brother's blood from your hand '.

Then follows in the Yahwist's story the curse pronounced upon Cain, his flight from the scene of the slaying, and the protective mark placed upon him by Yahweh. Here there are more difficulties. Yahweh curses the slayer and at the same time places him under his protection ; the nature and meaning of the mark, too, have been the cause of much speculation. These difficulties disappear if we relate the story to certain ancient ritual practices.

d In the Babylonian New Year Festival, whose original purpose was wholly agricultural, a sacrificing priest and an exorcist purified the shrine of Nabu with the carcase of a slain sheep, smearing the walls of the shrine with the blood of the sheep, after which they were obliged to flee into the desert until the festival was over because they were defiled by their ritual act. In the Hebrew ritual of the Day of Atonement, originally part of the New Year ritual, we find a similar combination of a ritual slaying and a flight, but here the human participants in the ritual are replaced by animal victims, the two goats, one of which is slain, while the other, the scape-goat, is driven out into the desert (cf. Lev. 10). Another ancient parallel is to be found in the Athenian ritual of the Bouphonia, where an ox was ritually slain by two men who were then obliged to flee (cf. J. Harrison, *Themis*, 142).

e It is therefore suggested that the flight of Cain may be explained by the motive of the ritual flight. The sacrificer is defiled by his ritual act and is driven out by the community until he is purified ; his guilt is a communal and not an individual guilt. This explains why the slayer enjoys ritual protection. He is no common murderer but a priest or sacred person who has performed an act for the benefit of the community, an act which involves ceremonial defilement and the consequent temporary banishment of the slayer, but

148e his person is sacrosanct. This also suggests that the most likely explanation of the mark is that it represents a tattoo mark or other indication that the fugitive belonged to a sacred class. We know from Hebrew sources that the prophets bore such marks (cf. Zech. 13:4–6), and the existence of such marks to distinguish the members of temple staffs as the property of the god is abundantly attested in ancient literature.

Thus the original form of the story seems to be based on a ritual myth which depicts a ritual slaying to secure fertility for the crops ; the slaying is followed by the flight of the slayer, who is protected by a mark which indicates his sacred character.

f But, like other ancient myths, before the story was used by the Yahwist for his exposition of the theme of the salvation-history, an aspect of the subject to which we shall return later, it had in the course of transmission acquired other meanings. It had become an aetiological myth intended to explain the agelong feud between the desert and the sown, between the settled peasant, tilling his fields, and the pastoral, half-nomad peoples who lived on the borders of the settled fertile lands, though the distortion of the story is shown by the fact that the agriculturist is the slayer and the pastoral nomad the victim, whereas in the feud between the agriculturist and the nomad it has always been the latter who is the aggressor. The story has also assumed the form of an aetiological myth explaining the origin of the institution of the blood feud. The suggestion that the story was intended to explain why Yahweh preferred animal sacrifices cannot be accepted, since both kinds of sacrifice are prescribed in the Levitical code.

149a (*b*) The second strand of the story in vv. 16–26 evidently comes from a different source. It belongs to **the traditions of the Kenite clan** with whom the Hebrews had early and close associations. But difficulties still remain. The Kenites seem to have been always nomads or half-nomads (cf. Jg. 4:11, 17), but the eponymous ancestor of the Kenite clan is depicted in this strand of the story as a city-builder, a settled inhabitant of the land of Nod, a land which cannot be identified geographically. He is the founder of a line from whence spring the various elements of civilised life. If we compare the genealogy of Cain's descendants given by the Yahwist in 4:17–18, with the Priestly genealogy of Seth in ch. 5, it becomes clear that the two genealogies are parallel forms of the same tradition about the descendants of the first man. This may be seen if we set them out side by side :

	J	P
1	Adam	Adam
2	—	Seth
3	—	Enosh
4	Cain	Kenan
5	Enoch	Mahalalel
6	Irad	Jared
7	Mehujael	Enoch
8	Methushael	Methuselah
9	Lamech	Lamech
10	—	Noah

b If these two lists are compared it will be seen how close is the parallel between them. First, the father of Kenan in P's list is Enosh ; but this is merely another Hebrew word for 'man' and a synonym for Adam, the first man. Kenan is another Hebrew form of Cain, so that in the original form of both lists the first man was the father of Cain. Then Irad is the same as Jared ; Enoch occurs in both lists ; for Mehujael the LXX has Maleleel, i.e. Mahalalel ; and for Methushael it has Mathusala, i.e. Methuselah ; and, finally, Lamech occurs in both lists. Hence it is certain that we have two different versions of the same list, and that J's list is really the genealogy of the first inhabitants of the earth, together with the account of the origin of the various elements of early civilisation.

c We have thus three distinct elements which the Yahwist has either woven together into a connected narrative and linked up with the Paradise story, or found brought together already in the traditions of the Kenite clan, and used for his special religious purpose. The long-standing connection of the Kenites with the Hebrews goes back to the saga of Moses, who is represented as having married into the Kenite clan (cf. Jg. 4:11, where 'brother-in-law' (RV) should be 'father-in-law', as RSV), and this may explain how the Yahwist could find and make use of Kenite traditions in his story of the beginnings of the salvation-history. It may be added that the fragment of ancient poetry preserved in Gen. 4:23–4, where the nomad code of blood-revenge is greatly intensified and referred back to the ancestor of the Kenites, supports the view that it was from Kenite traditions that the Yahwist drew the material for this part of his story. The three elements thus preserved, transformed, and woven into a continuous narrative are (*a*) a story explaining the nomad origin of the blood feud, (*b*) a story containing the motive of the ritual slaying and ritual flight, and (*c*) an ancient genealogical list embodying one of the many traditions concerning the origin of civilisation. One more point calls for remark. The correct rendering of Gen. 4:26*b* is, 'he was the first to call upon the name of Yahweh' (so the LXX and Vulg.) ; the 'he' may refer either to Enosh or Seth. The words 'to call upon the name' are the technical expression for an organised cult ; the Yahwist's point of view is that the knowledge of the name of Yahweh and the origin of his worship could be traced to the beginnings of the salvation-history, in contrast to the Elohist and Priestly view that they were first revealed to Moses as recorded in Exod. 3:13–14.

d **The Yahwist's Purpose in the Story of Cain and Abel**—Before we go on to deal with the rest of the Origin stories in this first section of Gen., we have to inquire why the Yahwist has taken this very varied body of traditions which had no connection with the Paradise story, and has woven them into a connected narrative which continues the Paradise story.

We can assume without question that the Yahwist was not moved by any antiquarian interest in the mere collection of the ancient traditions of Israel. He entirely ignores any technical details as to the type of offering or as to the way in which the acceptance or rejection of the offering was indicated ; the erection of altars is not mentioned, nor is any set time suggested, only the vague expression 'at the end of days', i.e. 'after a lapse of time'. What the Yahwist is concentrating on is that the bond of brotherhood is broken, anger and violence break out, and death enters the world. The theme of the broken relationship with God is now developed in its disastrous and divisive consequences. It is to be remarked that the story is bracketed between two births : Cain's birth in 4:1 and Seth's birth in 4:25. Of Cain his mother says 'I have gotten', of Seth she says 'God has appointed'. The lines divide ; Cain flees from the presence of Yahweh, builds a city, and sets in motion the mechanism of a society without God, where under the veneer of civilisation violence and death lie ready to break out. But God has his own purposes ; he appoints Seth, and with Seth begins the recognition of man's dependence upon God, and the line that is to lead through the symbol of judgment and a new beginning with Noah to the call of Abraham, towards which all this preparatory part of Gen. has been leading up. But the symbolic picture of the consequences of man's disobedience is not yet complete, and we have now to examine the way in which the Yahwist develops the theme of the two lines.

The next three divisions mentioned in §143*f* can be taken together. They are :

V, the P genealogy from Adam to Noah; VI 1-7, the J-E myth of the Sons of God and the daughters of men ; and VI 9-VIII 22, the J-E-P story of the Flood. As in the previous sections so in these the Yahwist has drawn on ancient traditional

150a material and shaped it to make a continuation of the themes already begun. The presence of elements attributed to the Priestly writer is usually explained as the result of the final Priestly editing and revision of all the material which now constitutes the Hebrew canon of scripture. In the main this is probably a correct explanation, but the current dissatisfaction with a purely
b literary analysis opens the door to other possibilities. It is generally recognised that much of the material contained in what is classified as P is very ancient, and we have already suggested that the author whose stamp has been impressed upon Gen., and whom we have called the Yahwist, is not to be identified with the editor or compiler of the hypothetical J history which was, on the Documentary theory, combined with the hypothetical Elohist narrative somewhere about the 10th cent. Our Yahwist may well have known and embodied in his work P material which fitted in with his purpose, and if it was part of that purpose to show the divergence of the lines of Cain and Seth as having a profound theological significance, then he might well have embodied the P genealogy of Seth in the prelude to the Flood story which we are now considering. If then it was the Yahwist who placed the two genealogies side by side, he must have intended to call attention
c to their differences. But something must first be said about the sources which evidently underlie the Priestly material in ch. 5. In the first place it is the line of Seth, and Cain only appears in it in an altered form ; in the second place the P list has ten names instead of the eight of Cain's genealogy, and with the exception of Enoch, the individuals in that list have an extraordinary duration of life assigned to them, each of them being said to have lived little short of a thousand years. Now, in the Sumerian king-lists from Larsa we have the names of ten kings who reigned before the Flood, and the length of their reigns ranges from 10,000 to 60,000 years. The Larsa list ends with the words, ' After the Flood kingship was sent down from on high ', indicating that a new beginning was made after the Flood ; a further point of interest is that the last name in the second Larsa list is Ziusudra, which is another name for Utnapishtim, the hero of the Babylonian story of the Flood which is contained in the 11th tablet of the
d Gilgamesh Epic. A further remarkable correspondence is that the seventh king in the Sumerian list was regarded as possessing special wisdom in matters pertaining to the gods and as being the first of mankind to practise divination ; the seventh name in the P list is Enoch, of whom it is said that ' he walked with God ', and who in later Jewish tradition was held to have been taken up to heaven without dying. These striking correspondences can hardly be due to chance, and there can be little doubt that the Priestly writer was using Sumerian material which had passed into early Hebrew tradition. The reason why he, or the Yahwist using his material, following this tradition, attributed to Seth's descendants before the Flood this abnormal length of life may be in order to emphasise the contrast between the conditions of life before and after the divine judgment in the Flood had taken place. There is, however, another possible reason. It has been conjectured that the astronomical numbers in the Sumerian king-lists may be the product of astrological speculations which applied measurements derived from the observation of the stars to the calculation of mythical regnal periods. In the same way the numbers in the Priestly list may have been arranged to correspond with the Priestly chronology which assigned a fixed number of years from the Creation to the foundation of Solomon's Temple, and divided this period into epochs, the first of which from the Creation to the Flood contained 1,656 years.

e **The Nephilim**—There can be no doubt that the Yahwist regarded the serpent as the symbol of intelligent and evil beings opposed to God, with whom man, by his act of disobedience, had established relations, and in this fragment of tradition concerning the union of divine and mortal beings he sought to
emphasise the increasing violence and lawlessness of 150e
man which finally decided Yahweh to destroy the whole race of mankind.

This myth is found in early Babylonian sources in which the kings before the Flood are represented as gods or semi-divine beings, and was widely diffused at an early date, as Greek mythology bears witness. A similar and related myth underlies this passage. It is the myth of a race of semi-divine and gigantic beings who rebelled against the gods and were cast down into the underworld. This myth is found in Jewish apocalyptic literature, and has passed into early Christian literature (cf. 2 Pet. 2:4 ; Jude 6). The remains of this myth are to be found in Ezek. 32, especially in v. 27, where a slight emendation gives us a definite reference to the Nephilim. The only other reference to the Nephilim occurs in Num. 13:33, which preserves the tradition of a race of giants among the aboriginal inhabitants of Canaan. Arab tradition connects these people with the remains of megalithic culture found in Transjordan. The Hebrew tradition of Og, king of Bashan, who belonged to the race of giants, is connected with this Arab belief ; Og's ' iron bedstead ' is a dolmen.

In early Hebrew tradition the myth of the Nephilim was an aetiological myth intended to explain the existence of a vanished race of giants ; but the Yahwist has used it here to emphasise the widening breach between God and man. The degradation of the sexual instincts, hinted at in the story of the Fall, is here revealed in its disastrous consequences, and is indicated in the words put into the mouth of Yahweh in v. 3, RVm, ' in their going astray they are flesh '.

The J-E-P Story of the Flood—Usener's great study f
of the diffusion of the myth of the Flood has shown how wide is that diffusion. It is now generally accepted that the Hebrew form of the myth is closely related to the Sumerian and Babylonian forms of the myth. The main Babylonian version is found in the Gilgamesh Epic. In this famous classic are related the adventures of the semi-divine king of Erech, whose name occurs in the Sumerian king-lists as the fifth king of Erech, the second dynasty after the Flood. The 11th tablet of the Epic tells how Gilgamesh, distressed by the death of his companion Enkidu, the bull-man, sets out to find his ancestor Utnapishtim, the survivor of the Flood, to learn from him the secret of the immortality which he is said to possess. After many adventures he reaches Utnapishtim and learns from him the story of the Flood, of his escape from it through the intervention of his father, the god Ea, and how the god Enlil conferred upon him and his wife the gift of deification and immortality. While the Flood story is possibly of independent origin and is a later insertion in the Gilgamesh Epic, the motive of the story and the purpose of its insertion are clear. The motive is the familiar one which we have already met with in the Paradise stories, deification and immortality. Utnapishtim, who like Adapa (cf. §§146*ef*) has the title Atrakhasis, ' unsurpassed in wisdom ', attains immortality and deification by passing through the waters of the Flood, symbolic of an initiatory rite, a *rite de passage*, and it is with the object of discovering the knowledge of the necessary ritual that Gilgamesh seeks his ancestor and receives the account of the Flood.

Before we deal with the points of resemblance be- 151a
tween the Hebrew and the Babylonian stories of the Flood, something must be said about the question of their historicity. In the first place it should be remarked that in the various myths of the destruction of mankind a flood is not the only means of bringing about that end. There is no Flood myth in Egypt, but there is a myth of the destruction of mankind in which the goddess Hathor or Sekmet is the agent of the wrath of Ra. Underlying the story of the destruction of the cities of the Plain in Gen. 19, there is a Canaanite myth of the destruction of mankind by a rain of fire and brimstone. Hence it would seem that the Flood element in the widely distributed myth of the destruc-

151a tion of mankind is a local variant which may be carried with the myth into countries where floods are out of keeping with local conditions, so betraying its foreign origin, as in the case of the Greek myth of Deucalion, and the Hebrew Flood story.

b Sir Leonard Woolley's excavation of Ur showed evidence of a destructive flood at a very early date, and that fact has been used to support the belief in the occurrence of a universal deluge. But excavation on the sites of other ancient Mesopotamian cities has shown similar evidence of early destructive floods, but not at the same period. Hence the Mesopotamian evidence only proves that the Tigris-Euphrates valley was subject to severe river-floods, and that this local feature had been taken up into the myth of the destruction of mankind which had a different origin altogether. The fact that the Sumerians could date an epoch from the Flood only proves that one particularly destructive flood had made a landmark in Sumerian history.

c We may now compare the various accounts of the Flood found in the Sumerian, Babylonian, Yahwist, and Priestly sources or traditions :

THE VARIOUS ACCOUNTS OF THE FLOOD

Sumerian	**Babylonian**	**Yahwist**	**Priestly**
Gods decree destruction of mankind by flood	Gods decree flood	Yahweh decrees destruction of man for his wickedness	God decrees destruction of all flesh for its corruption
Nintu protests	Ishtar protests		
Ziusudra, hero of Deluge, king and priest	Utnapishtim, hero of Deluge	Noah, hero of Deluge	Noah, hero of Deluge
Ziusudra's piety		Noah finds favour with Yahweh	Noah the only righteous man
Ziusudra warned by Enki in dream	Utnapishtim warned by Ea in dream		Noah warned by God
Ziusudra's vessel a huge ship	Ship : 120 × 120 × 120; 7 stories ; 9 divisions		Ark : 300 × 50 × 30 ; 3 stories
		Instruction to enter the ark	
	All kinds of animals	7 pairs of clean ; 2 of unclean animals. Yahweh shuts Noah in	2 of all animals
Flood and storm	Flood from heavy rain and storm	Flood from rain	Fountains of great deep broken up, and windows of heaven opened. Exact date of beginning and end of Flood given
Flood lasts 7 days	Flood lasts 6 days	Flood lasts 40 days, retires after 2 (?3) periods of 7 days	Flood lasts 150 days, retires in 150 days
	Ship grounds on Mt Nisir		Ark grounds on Ararat
	Utnapishtim sends out dove, swallow, and raven	Noah sends out raven and dove	
Ziusudra sacrifices to Sun-God in ship	Utnapishtim offers sacrifice on Mt Nisir	Noah offers sacrifices on altar	
	Gods gather like flies to the sacrifice	Yahweh smells sweet savour	
Immortality given to Ziusudra	Immortality and deification for Utnapishtim and his wife	Yahweh resolves not to curse the ground again for man's sake	God makes a covenant with Noah not to destroy the earth again by flood
	Ishtar's necklace of lapis lazuli as sign of remembrance		God gives rainbow as sign of covenant

151d The far earlier date of the Mesopotamian versions, together with the striking correspondences which the Hebrew versions show with the Mesopotamian, clearly prove the dependence of the Hebrew story either directly upon the Mesopotamian form, or upon some earlier Semitic source underlying both. The former alternative is the more probable. The differences between the two Hebrew versions suggest that the Priestly writer is using a different recension of the story from that used by the Yahwist, and that his recension is in some respects closer to the Mesopotamian sources. In later Hebrew literature there are frequent references to the Flood (cf. Ps. 29:10 ; Isa. 54:9), and there may have been several versions of the tradition in existence. It is possible that the Priestly writer does not include in his account any mention of sacrifices or the distinction between clean and unclean animals because he relates these institutions to the time of Moses. As we have already seen, the Yahwist regards the worship of Yahweh and the institution of sacrifice as already existing before the Flood.

e **The Significance of the Flood-story for the Yahwist**—We have remarked that the Yahwist, in attempting to describe the activity of God in Creation, could only do so by using the language of symbols. In the same way he could only depict such a purely spiritual event as the breach in the relationship between man and God in symbolic terms ; the garden, the tree, the serpent, the flaming sword, are all symbols which remain part of the divine speech until the final word is uttered in the Word made flesh. The ancient myths from which the Yahwist drew the material for his picture already expressed something of early man's sense of stress and his strife with malevolent powers, and of a lost immortality. But the symbolic pattern created by the prophetic writer, as we may surely believe the Yahwist to have been, resists all attempts at demythologisation, and in the ancient myth of the Flood he shows the order established at the creation of the world breaking down in ruin. The 'bars and doors' (Job 38:10), fixed at the Creation to keep the turbulent waters in their place, are broken through ; 'the foundations of the great deep' are 'broken up'. The whole story is a symbolic picture of the inevitable consequences of the rejection of the rule of God. Man is overwhelmed by the disorder which he himself has created. But God's purpose for blessing is undefeated, and the principle of the remnant, which was to play so important a part in the development of that purpose, emerges from the wreck, and the way is prepared for the new beginning. It is against the background of this whole symbolic presentation of the entry of sin into the world which made the divine activity in restoration necessary, that the call of Abraham is set. But one more detail remains to be added to the picture, the account of how the various nations of the world, from whom the instrument of the divine purpose was to be called out, came into existence. This is told in the last of the Origin stories. But before we come to this, mention must be made of the three sections which introduce the story of the Tower of Babel.

f **IX 1-17 The P Account of the Covenant with Noah**—Here the principle of the covenant relationship appears for the first time, and it is accompanied by another important feature in God's dealings with man which also appears for the first time, namely, the 'sign' (*'ôth*). The word is also used for the 'mark' which Yahweh puts upon Cain ; but this is a different use of the term. In the OT, and to a certain extent in the NT, a 'sign' is some event which is interpreted as an indication of divine intervention, and we frequently have instances of an individual asking for a sign from Yahweh, as in the case of Gideon (Jg. 6:36–40), or, on the other hand, Yahweh is represented as giving a sign to establish the fact of his intervention, as in the case of Moses on the occasion of his first encounter with Yahweh (Exod. 4:2–8). In this case, although an aetiological motive is apparent in the story, namely
an explanation of the phenomenon of the rainbow, an 151f
element which finds its parallel in the myth of Ishtar's necklace in the Babylonian story of the Flood, yet a deeper significance is to be seen in the emergence of the rainbow as a symbol of the divine activity in mercy enthroned (cf. Ezek. 1:28 and Rev. 4:3). There is also a difference between the covenant with Noah and the next covenant we meet with, namely that with Abraham: the former is a comprehensive one which embraces all created forms of life, while the latter establishes a personal relationship between Yahweh and Abraham. Another aetiological element is also to be seen in connection with the Noachic covenant, namely, the validation of the cultic taboo on the eating of blood. But here, too, we have the emergence of one of the most important of symbols, viz. blood as a symbol of life.

18-27 The J-E Story of the Beginnings of Agri- 152a
culture—It has often been pointed out that the Noah who discovers the culture of the vine and gets drunk is a very different figure from the righteous man of the Flood story. The Yahwist has clearly taken another independent tradition and woven it into his picture designed to show that even in a world purged by the Flood, man remains the same. God's good gift of the vine is turned to shameful uses ; the family relationship is broken up, and the lines begin to divide. Canaan is cursed, and Shem is blessed and marked out as the line along which the purpose of God is to develop. In the next section, compounded of elements from J, E, and P, we are carried on to the climax of man's rejection of God's rule in the story of the Tower of Babel.

X The J-E-P Story of the Peopling of the Earth b
after the Flood—This primitive Hebrew ethnology is introduced by the Yahwist into his picture with a definite purpose. His interest is not antiquarian. In the history which lay behind him, Egypt, Babylon, Assyria, Canaan, and other nations and peoples had become involved in the fortunes of Israel. In the main they had been instruments in the hand of Yahweh for the chastisement of Israel and the working out of his own purposes ; but in the mind of the Yahwist was also the conviction that in Abraham God intended to bless, not Israel alone, but all the nations of the earth. Whether we can date such an oracle as Isa. 19:24–5, 'In that day Israel will be the third with Egypt and Assyria, a blessing in the midst of the earth, whom the Lord of Hosts has blessed, saying, "Blessed be Egypt my people, and Assyria the work of my hands, and Israel my heritage"', early enough for the Yahwist to be acquainted with it, is hard to say ; but, together with such an indication of a similar point of view as we find in Ps. 87:4, it at least points to the existence of such a prophetic outlook. But the origin and character of these nations had to be explained, and their part in the general independence of God which became apparent in the history of man after the Flood had to be indicated. This is the motive which led the Yahwist to embody in his picture the material in Gen. 10. It leads up to the finishing touch in the Yahwist's picture, namely:

XI 1-9 The J-E Story of the Tower of Babel— c
Like the story of the Flood, the story, or myth, of the Tower of Babel is, according to most modern critics, a composite account. Its two strands can be separated with as much plausibility as the J-E and P strands in the Flood story. Nevertheless, by the time the Yahwist used the ancient story to complete his picture of human rejection of the rule of God, the two strands had already been fused into a single narrative. No doubt an aetiological motive underlies the story. It was an attempt to explain the existence of the diversity of languages where once, in the opinion of the original author of the legend, there had been only one language (cf. v. 6) ; it was also an attempt to give a reason for the existence of the ziqqurats, those strange temple-towers whose ruins archaeologists have laid bare in the Tigris-Euphrates valley. But this was not the Yahwist's

152c motive in using the story. In it he found the final touch of that symbolic picture which he had been building up in this first section of the book of Gen. It represented in symbolic terms the final disintegration of that order and unity which God had brought into existence in the primal act of creation. Moreover, like the Flood it was an act of divine judgment. In the heavenly council Yahweh had said, ' Let *us* make man ', and man's creation and the pre-eminent place assigned to him in the order of creation were the result of the divine plan. Now, when the whole story of the disintegration of that order had been unrolled, in the same heavenly council Yahweh says, ' Let *us* go down and there confound their language '. It is well known that the Akkadian Bab-ilu means ' the gate of the god ', and the popular Hebrew etymology which the Yahwist adopts is an erroneous derivation of the name from the Hebrew root *bll* which means ' confusion '. But it correctly represents what Babel meant to the Yahwist. In contrast to Zion whither the prophetic vision saw all nations flowing together in restored peace and primal harmony, Babel was the scene of the final dissolution of that primal harmony, the place from which flowed out the diversified and warring elements of mankind : ' from there the Lord scattered them abroad over the face of all the earth '.

d **10-32 The P Genealogy of Abraham**—All that remained now for the Yahwist was to embody in his narrative the Priestly genealogy of the godly line of Shem, in order to bring Abraham into the setting which the first eleven chapters of Gen. had furnished for him. This genealogy follows the pattern of the genealogy of Seth in ch. 5 and leaves Abraham suspended, so to speak, midway between the scene of disorder and the land of Promise, in Haran.

(B) The Sagas of the Patriarchs (XII-XXXVI)

e **The Meaning of Saga**—Before we begin to deal with the sagas of the patriarchs, something must be said about the meaning of the term saga. The essential difference between myth and saga is that saga has no connection with ritual, and need not have any religious significance, although sagas may be used, as they are in Gen., to convey religious lessons. The saga is primarily a story, transmitted orally from generation to generation, preserving traditions of the wanderings and adventures of clans or tribes, or of the exploits of tribal heroes. For example, we have a group of stories in the book of Jg. which preserve the memory of the exploits of the Danite hero Samson. This is genuine saga material which was once part of the traditions of the tribe of Dan. When the separate tribes became united into a nation in the time of Saul and David, such tribal traditions became part of the national tradition, and Samson became a national hero. It is clear that the Samson-saga has no particular religious significance in itself, although the editor of Jg. has used the stories with a moral purpose and has woven them into the religious pattern of the history of Israel. Hence, for our present purpose saga is a body of early racial and tribal tradition relating to the ancestors of the Hebrew people, and to the earliest period of their settlement in Canaan, preserved orally or in writing, and collected and worked over by later writers with a definite religious purpose.

f We have also to consider the question of the historical value of the sagas of Gen. Much ancient literature which is not history in the strict sense is nevertheless of great historical value. Now the sagas of Gen. are certainly not history. Broadly speaking, history is concerned with public events and rests upon what, in the judgment of the historian, is reliable contemporary evidence. Not all history is good history, nor are even the best historians infallible. An historian's judgment about the value of his sources may be wrong ; he may have a biassed political or religious point of view ; contemporary evidence may be scanty or wholly lacking for some period of which he is
writing ; but if he is describing public events and 15
basing his account upon documents which belong to the periods he is writing about, then we call what he writes history. Now it is clear that, with the exception of Gen. 14 with which we shall deal later on, the stories in Gen. 12–50 cannot be so described ; they are concerned wholly with domestic incidents, conversations, and intimate affairs which can hardly have been accurately reported and transmitted for hundreds of years.

Nevertheless **saga is very valuable to the** 15
historian. Sagas such as the Nibelungen Lied, the Mabinogion, or the Arthurian cycle, throw much light on the social and political conditions of the people among whom they arise, and the sagas of Gen., while they throw light on the religious ideas of the writers who were using this material, also reflect in many ways the customs and social conditions of an age so far removed in time from that of the Hebrew historian who recorded them that he did not always understand what he was recording ; so that we may believe him to have faithfully preserved much of the ancient tradition of his people in its early form. Hence, in studying these stories of Gen. it is necessary to distinguish those elements which reflect the religious and social point of view of the writer from those which truly depict the actual conditions and beliefs of the earliest period of the history of the Hebrew people. This is not always easy, but it is very necessary.

In addition to the saga material of Gen. there is b
another type of material which recent studies have brought to light, namely, **cult legends**. These differ from sagas in that they are from the first of religious origin. Like the term ' myth ', the term ' legend ' thus used does not imply that what is related in a cult legend is untrue. The nature of a cult legend may be best explained by reference to what is said in Dt. 6:20–3 and Exod. 13:14–15 about the observance of the Passover. In those passages a form of question and response is prescribed as part of the Passover ritual. The children were to ask their fathers the meaning of the various elements of the ritual, and the fathers were to reply in a set formula which consisted of a statement of what had happened, according to the tradition, at the Exodus. This short statement of what God had done for his people when he redeemed them from the bondage of Egypt, recited year by year, would tend to assume a stereotyped, liturgical form as the result of repetition, and this is what is meant by a cult legend. Moreover, as most of the feasts and ritual occasions were celebrated at the various local sanctuaries, it would be the priests who would naturally come to be the custodians of such cult legends. The difference between this and saga is obvious, and there is no small amount of the material in Gen. whose source is to be found in the cult centres, such as Bethel, Hebron, and Shechem, rather than in tribal tradition. Such materials, myths, sagas, and cult legends underlie the documentary sources already named.

One more point remains to be dealt with before we c
go on to deal with the patriarchal sagas in detail. The book of Gen. is part of a larger whole, whether that whole be regarded as a Pentateuch or, as many scholars believe, a Hexateuch, or, again, as certain Scandinavian scholars would have it, a Tetrateuch; in any case the editor or author of Gen. must have had the whole in his mind when he gave to that book the form in which we have it now. It is assumed in the book of Exod. that the call of Israel took place in Egypt through the agency of Moses ; but the tradition preserved in Gen. is that the choice and call of Israel began with Abraham. Both these traditions are known to the prophetic writers, and are part of the fixed tradition of Israel. Now it would seem to have been the purpose of the Yahwist to unify these two traditions. He brought the sagas of the patriarchs together and so arranged them as to represent the history of the Hebrews as the continuous unfolding of the purpose of Yahweh from the call of Abraham to

3c the descent of Jacob into Egypt. He used or created the story of Joseph, which, as we shall see, is different in character from the earlier sagas, as the link between the two strands of tradition. It forms the transition from Canaan to Egypt and sets the stage for the call of Israel through Moses and the deliverance from
d Egypt. Hence the Yahwist, throughout the sagas of the patriarchs, makes use of the name Yahweh, since in his view of the religious history of Israel Yahweh was known from the beginning by that name, and it is the activities of Yahweh which these early traditions relate. But the other principal narrator, according to the Documentary theory, the Elohist, avoids the use of the name Yahweh until it has been revealed to Moses at the burning bush, and in this he is followed by the Priestly writer. From the Elohist's point of view the ancestors of the Hebrews did not know God by that name (cf. Exod. 6:3), and for him the call of Israel dates from the Exodus. His narrative in Joshua (cf. Jos. 24:2, 15) states that the ancestors of the Hebrews in Mesopotamia and in Canaan had 'served other gods'.

Hence, apart from such details of the settlement as may be derived from the tradition contained in the sagas of Gen., there lies embedded in the early form of the tradition a picture of the general occupation of Canaan by various groups of Semites, the ancestors of the Hebrews. This occupation, partly peaceful, partly the result of conquest (cf. Gen. 48:22), was, in this earlier tradition, represented as continuous, unbroken by the Egyptian sojourn.

e **Classification of the Sagas**—According to the Yahwist and the Priestly writer, Abraham's group was an offshoot of one of the three main groups of nations as classified by P. These divisions were territorial rather than racial or linguistic, and cut across modern ethnological groupings. They consisted, first, of the mingled group of peoples inhabiting Asia Minor and the Aegean; secondly, the African group, containing Egypt, Arabia, and Canaan; this group also contains, strangely enough to our minds, the Assyrians and the Philistines; and, thirdly, the sons of Shem, consisting of two main groups, the descendants of Eber, and the Aramaeans. By some confusion of thought the Elamites, who belong to none of these groups, and the Assyrians, were included in this group. Probably Assyria came to be included in the second group also through confusion of the African Cush, or Ethiopia, with the northern Cush which represents the Kassites of the Zagros.

f Hence Abraham is brought on to the stage of history as a representative of the Semitic group, and we see him, in obedience to the call of Yahweh, leaving his original home in Mesopotamia and entering Canaan, accompanied by his nephew Lot, who became the ancestor of two kindred groups, the Moabites and the Ammonites (cf. 19:30–8).

The patriarchal sagas fall into four groups, each of which may be subdivided into episodes. The Jacob group seems to be composed of three distinct cycles of stories, probably originally independent of one another. On the assumption that the Yahwist is responsible for the collection and arrangement of the material, we shall have to discuss, as in the previous section, the reasons which led the Yahwist to adopt this arrangement.

54a I **The Abraham Saga**—Chs. 12–24. This contains a number of separate elements or episodes taken from various independent traditions and woven together by the Yahwist into a continuous narrative of the life of Abraham, from his call until his death. The following are the elements referred to:

(*a*) The Call of Abraham: 12:1–9.
(*b*) The Descent into Egypt: 12:10–20.
(*c*) Abraham and Lot: ch. 13.
(*d*) Abraham and the Four Kings: ch. 14. The Melchizedek episode which the Yahwist has inserted into this section is probably a fragment of an independent Jerusalem tradition.
(*e*) The Covenant Ritual and Promise: ch. 15. 154a
(*f*) The Ishmael Tradition: ch. 16 (ch. 17 is an insertion from the Priestly writer) and 21:8–21.
(*g*) The Destruction of Sodom: chs. 18–19.
(*h*) Abraham and Abimelech: chs. 20 and 21:22-34.
(*i*) Abraham and Isaac: chs. 21:1–7 and 22.
(*j*) The Purchase of the Cave of Machpelah: ch. 23.
(*k*) Abraham sends for a Wife for Isaac: ch. 24.

II **The Isaac Saga**—ch. 26, together with fragments which have been incorporated into the Jacob saga. The Isaac material really serves as a link between the two separate traditions of Abraham and Jacob, in the same way as the Joseph story serves as a link between the two traditions of the call of Israel.

III **The Jacob Saga**—This is composed of three b
cycles of episodes:

(*a*) Jacob and Esau:
  (i) The Birthright Stories: chs. 25:21–34 and 27:1–45.
  (ii) The Struggle with Esau: chs. 32–3.
(*b*) Jacob and Laban:
  (i) Jacob's Dream and Flight to Aram: ch. 28.
  (ii) The Outwitting of Laban and the Origin of the Twelve Tribes: chs. 29–31.
(*c*) Jacob in Shechem: chs. 33:19–20 and 34–5.

In their original form these sagas of the patriarchs were a series of unconnected episodes preserved, either as part of the traditions and folklore of the various clans and tribes which claimed descent from the ancestors of the Hebrew people, or as fragments of cult legends preserved at various local cult centres. These were collected and arranged by the Yahwist in the same way and with the same purpose as in his handling of the Origin stories. From the point of view adopted here with regard to the Documentary theory, the Yahwist, in the sense in which we are using the term, had before him the J-E narrative, united about the 10th cent., and arranged it with interpolations from the Priestly material to give it its penultimate form, before its final revision at the hands of the post-exilic editors. We shall return to this question later.

Before we deal with the sagas in greater detail some c
general remarks may be made. If the three groups mentioned above be examined carefully, it will be seen that the only part of the Isaac saga which is unconnected with either the Abraham or the Jacob stories is the short group of episodes in ch. 26. But these episodes are unmistakably duplicates of similar episodes contained in the Abraham saga. The other episodes in which Isaac plays a part, such as Abraham's offering of Isaac, the sending of Eleazar by Abraham to fetch a wife for Isaac, or Jacob's deception of his father in order to obtain the blessing, really belong to the Abraham and the Jacob sagas. So it appears that the figure of Isaac never became the centre of a tradition, and is merely used by the Yahwist to form the necessary link between the two groups of sagas, those connected with Abraham and those connected with Jacob-Israel. Outside of Gen. Isaac is only mentioned separately twice in the OT, in Am. 7:9, 16, where the reference is to Isaac's traditional connection with Beersheba.

Again, there is a noticeable difference between the d
stories about Abraham and those of which Jacob is the centre. Abraham is rather a figure designed to be the pattern of the ideal 'righteous man', the man of faith and obedience, whom God can use as the instrument for the fulfilment of his purposes of restoration and blessing. Jacob, on the other hand, is evidently a figure belonging to a genuine popular tradition, living in the imagination of a pastoral people. It is also a much more complex tradition, as will appear when we come to deal with the Jacob cycle of stories.

Finally, the **Joseph story** is quite distinct in char- e
acter from the other groups. It is not episodical like the Abraham saga, nor is it an interweaving of ancient folk-stories in the manner of the Jacob saga. Although

154e the beginning of the story shows signs of the interweaving of two variant versions, the remainder of the story flows smoothly and presents a continuous romantic narrative dealing with a situation often used by Oriental story-tellers, the rise of a virtuous young man from humiliation to greatness. It is later than the other sagas, and may have been composed by the Yahwist in the same spirit, and with the same end in view, as may be seen in the stories of the first part of the book of Dan., and also to serve as the necessary link between the sagas of the patriarchs and the Moses saga.

155a **XII-XXIV The Abraham Saga**

XII 1-9 The Call of Abraham—With the entry of Abraham upon the stage of Israel's history we are confronted for the first time with a personality. The various figures of the first section of Gen., Adam, Eve, Cain, Abel, and Noah, are all types, not persons. They are the embodiments of early Hebrew ideas and traditions concerning the beginnings of life on the earth. But although, as we have already said, Abraham is the type of the ' righteous man ', the question arises whether he is also to be regarded as an historical person. The further question also arises whether the patriarchal stories are to be regarded as representing the history of the movements of racial or tribal groups. Recent studies have also suggested the possibility, strongest in the case of Jacob, that behind the figures of the patriarchs there lie in the earliest traditions the shadowy forms of local gods or heroes.

It is noteworthy that outside the Pentateuch, it is only in the later books of the OT that Abraham comes into notice as the ancestor of the Hebrews (cf. Isa.51:2 ; Ezek. 33:24). But it would not be safe to infer from this that he is merely the creation of a later idealising age. It is also noteworthy that he is not an eponymous ancestor, no tribe or people takes its name from him.

Hence, while certain elements in the saga suggest that Abraham's movements do reflect the movements of early Semitic groups, there is no good ground for denying the existence of Abraham as an historical person. The suggestion is attractive, although possessing slight foundation in the tradition as we have it, that Abraham was the leader of a religious movement, possibly in revolt from the polytheism of the Babylonians, seeking a new home for a new worship. The phrase used by the Priestly writer in 12:5, ' the persons that they had gotten in Haran ', has been interpreted to mean the adherents of such a movement.

b If we accept the view that Abraham was an historical figure, some attempt must be made to set him in the frame of contemporary history. One of the curious features of the book of Gen. is the absence of any reference to what was going on in the ancient Near East during the 2nd millennium B.C. We should not gather from the narrative of Gen. that Canaan was the scene of an advanced civilisation, and the theatre of great ethnic movements, a country of walled cities, numberless unwalled villages, and full of the activities of an extensive international trade. But this is the picture which archaeology has reconstructed for us, and the movements of Abraham and his followers must be set against this background. The only chapter of Gen. which appears to bring Abraham into direct contact with the ethnic movements of the ancient Near East is ch. 14, a chapter which, owing to its marked difference in style and contents from the rest of the book, has been regarded by most commentators as a separate insertion belonging to a later tradition. Hence, before we examine the rest of the episodes which the Yahwist has brought together to compose the story of Abraham, it will be helpful to discuss the problems raised by this section of the Yahwist's narrative. The two main problems to be discussed are (i) the historical character of the chapter, and (ii) the Yahwist's purpose in making use of this tradition.

c (i) **The Historical Character of Gen. XIV**—The story relates that four kings from the north of Canaan raided the five kings of the cities of the Dead Sea 15
plain, subdued them, took much spoil, and among their captives took Abraham's nephew Lot, who had settled in Sodom. When Abraham heard of it, he led out his clan, numbering 318 men, and with the help of Hittite or Amorite allies defeated the invaders and recovered the spoil, freeing his nephew Lot. The story goes on to relate that on his return he was met by the Jebusite king of Jerusalem, Melchizedek, who blessed him in the name of El Elyon and gave him bread and wine. Abraham gave Melchizedek a tithe of all the spoils, but refused to accept anything from the king of Sodom.

The tradition which the Yahwist is using has d
preserved the names of all the kings except that of the king of the unimportant town of Zoar, or Bela. It may be said at once that none of the names of kings mentioned in this chapter can be identified with any certainty as corresponding to the names of any kings known to us from contemporary records. The name **Amraphel** used to be confidently equated with Ḫammurabi of the first Amorite dynasty of Babylon, famous for his Code ; but the identification is no longer accepted, and we also now know that there were at least three other kings of that name ruling city-states during this period. **Ellasar** is no longer identified with the Mesopotamian city of Larsa, and its king **Arioch** is now connected with a Hurrian king, Ariukki, whose name occurs in the Nuzu tablets. Behind the names Horites and Hivites, frequently mentioned in the OT as dwellers in Canaan at the time of the first Hebrew settlement in the land, lies an important racial group known as the Hurrians, who founded a kingdom of which the principal city was Haran, Abraham's halting-place on his way from Ur to Canaan. Hurrian personal names show that their bearers formed an important part of the population from east of the Tigris to Syria and Asia Minor, and study of the Nuzu tablets has shown striking parallels in Hurrian law and custom with the customs depicted in the sagas of the patriarchs. It has even been e
suggested that it was the invasion of this Hurrian ethnic group and the founding of the Hurrian kingdom in the neighbourhood of Haran which caused the southward movement into Canaan of those Hebrew clans which had Abraham for their leader. The presence of the Hurrians, under the name of Horites, in the south of Palestine may be due to the fact that about 1500 B.C. they, in their turn, were driven out by the Aramaean invasion and dispersed throughout Canaan, where they were gradually absorbed. This, however, is a disputed question. These historical facts provide further support for the view that these racial movements form the background for the Abraham saga. For the close connection between the patriarchs and the Aramaeans reflected in Gen. would have been an anachronism in the time of Ḫammurabi, when the Aramaeans had not yet appeared on the stage of history.

The name of the leader of the raid, **Chedorlaomer,** f
is the Hebrew form of a perfectly good Elamite name, Kudur-Lagamar, although there is no contemporary evidence for an Elamite king of that name during the period under discussion ; nevertheless it is quite in keeping with what is known of the history of the time, that Elam should have been the head of such an alliance as the story depicts.

The last name, **Tidal,** has been identified with the Hittite king Tudhaliash, the first of a line of kings who ruled the Old Hittite Empire. A possible date has been assigned to him between 1700 and 1650 B.C. It is not clear why he should be called ' king of *nations* ', for that is what the Hebrew word **Goiim** means. It may possibly be an honorific title, comparable with the title which the Assyrian kings gave themselves in their inscriptions, ' King of the Four Quarters '.

Little is known of the conditions in Syria at this 15
period. The Amorite dynasty in Babylonia had been overthrown by the Kassites about 1745 B.C. About

6a this time the important Hyksos movement began It is commonly believed that the people known by this name, which is a corruption of the name given to them in Egyptian documents meaning ' princes of the lands ', were a mixture of Canaanite or Amorite stock with people of other races, possibly including Hurrians and even Hebrews. They conquered and ruled Egypt from their capital at Avaris, and have left traces of their presence in Palestine and Syria. The revival of Egyptian power under the XVII and XVIII Dynasties led to the expulsion of the Hyksos from Egypt about 1580 B.C. If, as is possible, there are written sources underlying the present form of Gen. 14, and if Tidal may be reasonably identified with Tudhaliash I, then this disturbed period between 1700 and 1600 B.C. may possibly furnish the background for the movements of Abraham and his group.

b One more point calls for discussion in connection with the historical setting of the Abraham saga. In 14:13 the patriarch is styled ' Abram the Hebrew ' ; this is the first occurrence of the term Hebrew in the OT. The LXX rendering of the word by περάτης, ' the man from beyond ', i.e. ' from beyond the River ', shows that the traditional interpretation of the term derived it from the Hebrew root *'br*, ' to cross ', or ' pass over ', implying that Abraham had come from beyond the River, i.e. the Euphrates. But it is doubtful whether this is the true meaning of the term ' Hebrew '. The mention in the Tell el-Amarna Letters of a people called the Ḫabiru or Ḫabiri, who are described as invading and settling in Palestine during the reigns of Amenophis III and IV, caused many scholars to identify these people with the Hebrews, and to place the entry of the Hebrews into Canaan during the 14th cent. But more recent discoveries have shown that the name is of much wider occurrence than was at first supposed. The Ḫabiru are mentioned in Babylonian documents of the pre-Ḫammurabi period ; the new texts from Mari mention their activities during the reign of Zimri-Lim, the last king of Mari, and contemporary with Ḫammurabi ; in the Hittite records from Boghazköi they are found in the service of the Hittites ; the tablets from Arrapḫa, in the Hurrian district, east of the Tigris, speak of people who are described as Ḫabiru having sold themselves into slavery there ; and if we accept the identification of the *'apiru* of Egyptian sources with the Ḫabiru, they are found in Egypt as late as the time of Rameses IV in the 12th cent. B.C. We do not know the original meaning of the name Ḫabiru, but it is now generally agreed that the Hebrews were a part of the people designated as Ḫabiru, whose activities are found so widely dispersed in space and time. This is probably the original meaning of the appellation ' Hebrew ' as applied to Abraham.

c Hence two alternatives are open to us. Either we may, with many modern scholars, place the movements of Abraham and his followers in the time of the Amorite dynasties in Syria and Babylonia between 1800 and 1600 B.C., or we may assign the activities of Abraham to the disturbed time of the break-up of the Hyksos Empire between two and three hundred years later than the first alternative. The picture which contemporary writers give us of the state of political affairs in the Near East suggests that the latter date is more in accord with the account given in Gen.

One more element in the story calls for comment. An episode is recorded in vv. 18–20 which breaks the connection between vv. 17 and 21 rather awkwardly, and seems to be an independent fragment of tradition. It may be an aetiological legend intended to explain the origin of the institution of tithes and the claim of the Jerusalem priesthood. It may also have had the aim of validating the position of the Zadokite priesthood, and David's action in taking over the old Jebusite priesthood when he made Jerusalem his capital and the official centre of the cult of Yahweh. It represents Abraham as paying tithes to Melchizedek, the priest-king of Jerusalem, and receiving a blessing from him. Later Jewish speculation invested the 156c
figure of Melchizedek with mystical and symbolical significance, as we may see from Ps. 110:4, and from the use made of it by the author of the Epistle to the Hebrews (cf. Heb. 7). The point which concerns us d
here is whether the story has any historical verisimilitude in this setting. We know that Jerusalem was a city-state of some importance at an early date. Letters from Abdi-Ḫiba (or Puti-ḫepa), the king of Jerusalem, are found among the Tell el-Amarna Letters, and in Jos. 10:1 we hear of an Amorite king of Jerusalem, Adoni-zedek, a name of the same form as Melchizedek. Ezekiel knew the tradition that Jerusalem had an Amorite and Hittite background of history (cf. Ezek. 16:3), and even in David's time the city was still in Jebusite (i.e. Hittite) hands. Hence if there is some historical foundation for the tradition here preserved, the king of Jerusalem may have had some share in the league which defeated the four invading kings, and may have had a rightful claim to a share in the spoils. Finally, with regard to the question of the historical character of the chapter, it may safely be said that the old view that ch. 14 is a late midrash is no longer tenable. It suggests a dependence upon written sources and presents a situation which is not historically impossible. Hence the story may legitimately be regarded as throwing some light on the background of Abraham's activities. But the more important question of what was the purpose of the Yahwist in using this isolated fragment of political history remains to be discussed.

(ii) **The Yahwist's Use of Gen. XIV**—We have e
seen that the purpose of the Yahwist in his treatment of the material brought together in the first section of Gen. was to give an account in symbolic terms of the human situation which had made it necessary for God to undertake the work of restoration. He drew a picture of the primal created order destroyed by an act of disobedience, and closed his account of the progressive deterioration of the human situation by showing the earth peopled by divided nations, unable to understand each other's speech, and prepared to display the violence which is seen in action in ch. 14.

10-20 The Descent into Egypt—The first episode f
in the new beginning is an act of faith. In its external character it has the appearance of an exodus ; an act of disobedience had broken up the primal order, and the restoration begins with an act of obedience, prefiguring that great central act of obedience of which St Paul spoke when he said, ' so by one man's obedience many will be made righteous ' (Rom. 5:19). The Yahwist does not tell us what form the divine call took. We may conjecture that Abraham's migration was a small part of the racial movements taking place in the 2nd millennium, or that his departure from the civilisation of Ur had a religious cause ; all that the Yahwist is concerned with is to show the initial act of obedience and its consequences. We are shown Abraham coming out from the man-made order where the rule of God had been rejected, passing as a sojourner and tent-dweller through the land of Canaan, his stages marked by the erection of altars and by acts of worship. ' The Canaanite was then in the land ', says the Yahwist, but Abraham acknowledged the rule of God. Then came the first test and the first failure. The famine was sore in the land, and Abraham leaves the land of Promise and goes down into Egypt. Canaan lies midway between those two symbolic regions, Babylon and Egypt, both of them scenes of exile and bondage for the people of God. In Egypt Abraham denies his relationship with Sarah ; he benefits materially by so doing, but brings the judgment of God upon Egypt. It was not the place to which his first act of faith and obedience had brought him, and to it he must return. That it was a spiritual return is emphasised by the Yahwist in the words, ' to the place where his tent had been at the beginning ', and, ' to the place where he had made an altar ' (13:3f.).

157a **XIII Abraham and Lot**—Then, after a failure and a return, comes the third of the episodes which the Yahwist has selected to illustrate the growth of Abraham's faith and experience of God. We are shown the place where the ways divide. The violence that, ever since the first act of disobedience, always underlay human relations, even between brethren, now breaks out between Abraham's herdmen and Lot's. In the interests of peace between brethren Abraham offers Lot his choice of a place to dwell in, and we are shown Lot choosing the material advantages of the well-watered plain of Jordan. Lot pitches his tent 'as far as Sodom', and in ch. 19 we are shown Lot actually sitting in the gate of Sodom; 'Now', comments the Yahwist, 'the men of Sodom were wicked, great sinners against the Lord' (13:13). The consequences of Lot's choice will be seen later; but the Yahwist leaves the situation to develop, and turns to the consequences of Abraham's choice. As soon as Lot had gone his way, Yahweh came to Abraham and gave him the promise in the most absolute terms of all the land that he had surrendered. In 12:2–3 Yahweh had promised to make Abraham 'a great nation', and that he was to be the source of blessing to all nations; but now the further consequence of his faith is that he receives the promise of the land itself as the inheritance of his descendants who are to be numberless as the dust of the earth. He is told to walk through the length and breadth of the land, taking seisin of it, as it were. From now on Hebron becomes the centre of his movements, and once again his acknowledgment of Yahweh is marked by an altar. He was yet to learn the full significance of the altar.

b **XIV Abraham and the Four Kings**—This brings us to the point of our departure, the episode of the victory over the four kings in ch. 14. In view of what we have so far seen (§§156*ef*), it can hardly be doubted that the Yahwist did not choose this fragment of Hebrew tradition because of his interest in the international situation of Abraham's time. On the historical level the episode is one which must have been of frequent occurrence in those disturbed times. But on the interpretative level the Yahwist sees in it the development of the spiritual forces which he has been describing; in the strength of faith Abraham is victorious over the worldly powers from amongst whom he has been called out. Furthermore, Lot is shown involved in the fate of Sodom. He suffers the loss of all those material goods for the sake of which he had chosen to live in Sodom, and himself becomes a captive of the worldly powers. But his connection with Abraham is not yet completely severed, and he has a share in Abraham's victory. He is delivered and his lost possessions are restored to him. What he did with his deliverance we know from the terrible story in ch. 19; but the Yahwist is not concerned with his fate at present.

c We now get the curious fragment of tradition about Melchizedek introduced into the story of Abraham's victory. The possible significance of the tradition on the historical level was discussed in the previous section; what we are now concerned with is the use which the Yahwist makes of the episode. Jerusalem may have been a Jebusite city in Abraham's time, as it was to remain until David's capture of it, but for the Yahwist it was Zion, 'the city of the great King', and it was of no small symbolic significance that Abraham should be shown as blessed by the king of Salem, 'for there the Lord has commanded the blessing' (Ps. 133:3); it was also significant that Abraham should acknowledge the right of Salem's king to receive the spoils of victory, and should receive from

d his hands bread and wine. Finally, we are shown Abraham refusing to accept from the king of Sodom any share in the spoils which he had recovered, 'lest you should say, "I have made Abram rich"'. He takes over from Melchizedek the name of El Elyon, the Most High God, the maker of heaven and earth, and in so doing places himself in the position of the man in Ps. 91:1, 'He who dwells in the shelter of the Most High, who abides in the shadow of the Almighty'; thus uniting in his experience the first two great names of Israel's God, El Elyon and El Shaddai. El Elyon may have been the name of the Jebusite god of Jerusalem on the historical level, but through Abraham's act of faith and renunciation it is here taken up into the pattern of revelation; similarly, El Shaddai, on the historical level, may mean 'the mountain god', if we accept this as the most probable of the many etymologies which have been proposed for it, and may have been the name of another Canaanite deity; but here, again, the name is taken up into Abraham's experience of God, and is given to him, as we shall see, shortly after the episode of ch. 14, as the name by which Abraham is henceforth to know the God who has called him. It is the name which was to mark the restored relationship until the time for the fresh revelation to Moses, and the call of Israel. Thus in this most significant fragment of world history the Yahwist has shown a great advance in Abraham's experience, and a picture of the faith that overcometh the world. In the next episode we have the answer to Abraham's act of renunciation. 157

e **XV The Covenant Ritual**—There can be little doubt that the Yahwist has intentionally placed the episode of ch. 15 as the immediate consequence of Abraham's act of renunciation in ch. 14. But first a word must be said about the material which the Yahwist has brought together to compose the picture of the next stage in the development of Abraham's growth in the knowledge of God. According to the critical analysis ch. 15 contains material from the E narrative, viz. vv. 1–2, 4–5, 16; vv. 19–21 are from P, and the rest is from the J narrative. In the J narrative a very ancient covenant ritual has been preserved and used by the Yahwist with deep symbolical significance. There is a difficult textual problem in v. 2, where Abraham is represented as saying to Yahweh that his only heir is his house-steward Eliezer, whom he apparently describes as 'Dammesek Eliezer' according to the RV, or 'Eliezer of Damascus' according to RSV. The MT is generally recognised to be corrupt here; RV has simply transliterated the Hebrew, and the RSV rendering is not admissible. If Eliezer was born in Abraham's house, as the RV rendering of the Hebrew would suggest, although the rendering is doubtful, then it is difficult to see how Eliezer could be described as 'of Damascus', or as 'the Damascene'. The LXX is quite unintelligible, and the Syriac gives a paraphrase, 'Eliezer of Damascus, a son of my house, is my heir'. The covenant ritual, f
which the Yahwist has made use of here for its symbolical value, is an ancient Semitic form of covenant making which survived as late as the time of Jeremiah (cf. Jer. 34:18). A similar ritual is recorded for the ratification of a treaty between the Assyrian king Ashur-nirari and the Syrian prince Mati-ilu. But, as we have already remarked, the Yahwist's interest in such matters was not an antiquarian one. The first point in his narrative is that Abraham's renunciation is immediately met by Yahweh's declaration to him, 'Fear not, Abram, I am your shield and your reward shall be very great.' Then follows the first conversation between Abraham and Yahweh in which we can trace a growing intimacy. When Yahweh says, 'Your reward shall be very great', Abraham replies, 'What wilt thou give me?' Yahweh's answer is the promise of a son, and in contrast to the previous promise that his seed should be numberless as the dust of the earth (13:16), he is now told that they shall be as the stars in number. Then we are told, 'he believed the Lord; and he reckoned it to him as righteousness'. It may seem a strange juxtaposition to find, side by side with this great cardinal statement of the restored relationship between God and man, a piece of ancient magical ritual, but both elements in the picture have their place in the design the Yahwist is working out.

The word 'righteousness' has a long philological 158

58a history, but by the time the Yahwist had come to use it here its fundamental meaning was nothing less than the character of God himself in his dealings with man. The original intention in man's creation was that he should be in God's image, after his likeness. By his act of disobedience the image was defaced, the likeness destroyed ; now the work of restoration has begun ; God has found the response of faith and obedience, he has found a man in whom his own character begins to be formed. Then Abraham asks for an assurance of the fulfilment of the promise that his seed should inherit the land, and receives in answer the instructions for the covenant ritual. He is to take three ritually clean animals and divide them into two halves, laying the severed parts opposite to each other. He also takes a turtle dove and a young pigeon, but does not divide the birds. At sunset a supernatural sleep (*tardēmāh*), like the sleep that Yahweh caused to fall upon Adam at the creation of Eve, falls upon Abraham, and he sees in a vision Yahweh passing between the severed pieces of the victims in the form of ' a smoking fire pot and a flaming torch ', thus binding himself to the fulfilment of the covenant which he now makes with Abraham. In the symbolism of the ritual the act of passing between the pieces, which may have the significance of a *rite de passage*, bound the person who passed through. Yahweh himself passed through, and by so doing entered into a new relationship with the man of his choice. Death is implicit in the ratification of the covenant.

b **XVI** records the episode of the birth of Ishmael (see §160*a*), where we are told that Abraham ' hearkened to the voice of Sarai ', who was unable to believe that Yahweh's promise of a child would be fulfilled.

XVII The Institution of Circumcision—A section is introduced from the Priestly material recording the institution of the ritual of circumcision as a ratification of the covenant in ch. 15. The symbolic signification of circumcision is the same as that of the divided victims in the previous narrative. Circumcision was not confined to the Hebrews, and was practised in Egypt in the Old Kingdom period, long before the Hebrews appeared on the stage of history. It is still practised as an initiation rite among many savage tribes. There are various Hebrew traditions concerning the origin of the rite ; apparently the Hebrews born in Egypt were not circumcised, and this was regarded as shameful or barbarian by the Egyptians, hence the expression ' the reproach of Egypt ' in Jos. 5:9, where the circumcision of the Israelites by Joshua is recorded. The obscure fragment of tradition in Exod. 4:24–6 has suggested a possible Midianite origin of the rite among the Hebrews. But the statement in Jos. 5:3 that Joshua used flint knives for the performance of the rite, although the period of the Hebrew invasion of Canaan under Joshua was late in the Bronze Age, and the use of metal was already long known, shows the extreme antiquity of the rite. Whether circumcision had come to be regarded as the sign of the covenant prior to the Exile is not certain, but in Jeremiah's oracles circumcision is spoken of as the distinguishing mark of Israel as Yahweh's people (cf. Jer. 9:25–6), and the same is implied in Dt. 10:16, so that it is not impossible that the Yahwist should have made use of the Priestly material in ch. 17 to establish the ratification of the covenant by another symbolic act, not as a substitute for the ritual act of ch. 15, but as a confirmation of it.

c **XVIII-XIX The Destruction of Sodom**—We have already referred to the revelation of the name El Shaddai to Abraham in connection with the ratification of the covenant, but there is also another important feature of this experience, namely that Yahweh changes Abraham's name from Abram, which is the form used in the Hebrew text up to this point, to the familiar
form Abraham. Scholars are generally agreed that 158c
the form Abram is a contraction of the name Abiram which is found in Assyrian documents as well as in Hebrew. But, like many Hebrew etymologies, the explanation of the name given by the Hebrew writer is doubtful. What is important, however, is that a change of name has great significance, implying a change of personality. Both Abraham and Sarah are here given new names by Yahweh, indicating a change in their personal relation with God. With the establishment of the covenant a new order has begun, and under that new order things may happen which could not happen under the old order, the order of nature. In spite of incredulous laughter on the part of both Abraham and his wife, Yahweh is about to do something which lies beyond the order of nature, and events now move towards the birth of Isaac, the child of promise. But between the renewal of the covenant in ch. 17 and the account of the birth of Isaac, the Yahwist brings together a group of episodes in which the development of Abraham's intimacy with God and his growth in understanding of God's ways is contrasted with the fate of Lot. In chs. 18 and 19 we have the account of the theophany at Mamre and the renewed promise of a son for Sarah, the time of fulfilment being now made definite ; the most probable explanation of the difficult phrase in 18:14, rendered ' in the spring ' by RSV, and ' when the season cometh round ' by RV, is ' according to the time of a pregnant woman ', i.e. ' in nine months '.
Then comes the moving account of Abraham's inter- d
cession for Sodom, in which we see Yahweh admitting Abraham to his inner counsels, ' Shall I hide from Abraham that which I do ? ' and Abraham appealing, with the confidence born of a knowledge of Yahweh's character, to his justice, ' Shall not the Judge of all the earth do right ? ' The scene round Abraham's tent has a touch of a restored Eden ; the simplicity of the divine visit and the homely conversation with Abraham and Sarah remind one of the intimate way in which Yahweh walked in the garden in the cool of the day, and talked with Adam ; we are in the atmosphere of Paradise Regained. The companions of the divine Visitant, appearing human in the intimacy of the tent door, when they turn towards Sodom become messengers of judgment. Just as the Yahwist had used an ancient myth of the destruction of mankind to depict symbolically the inevitable consequences of man's rejection of God's rule, so here he uses a similar myth, only this time of a destruction of mankind by fire, to depict the consequences of Lot's choice. He had failed to profit by his deliverance in ch. 14, and had returned to Sodom ; now he is involved in the final fate of the wicked city and loses everything ; his wife, turning back, becomes the dreadful type of those of whom the author of the Epistle to the Hebrews speaks, ' those who shrink back and are destroyed ' (Heb. 10:39), while he himself is saved ' so as by fire '. That the story is a fragment of a myth of the destruction of mankind is shown by the words of Lot's daughters in 19:31, ' There is not a man on earth to come in to us after the manner of all the earth ', that is to say, Lot and his daughters are the only survivors of the catastrophe, just as Noah and his family were of the Flood. As the final touch of tragedy in the picture, the fruit of the unnatural union of Lot's daughters with their father is the birth of two of the traditional enemies of Israel, namely Moab and Ammon.

XX Abraham in Gerar—In this chapter we have an e
incident, attributed by the critical analysis to the Elohist narrative, which is regarded by most commentators as a duplicate version of the J episode in 12:10–19. A third version of the episode occurs in 26:1–14, and a synopsis of the three versions is given on the next page for comparison :

158e

J **Abraham in Egypt** **Gen. 12:10-20**	E **Abraham in Gerar** **Gen. 20:1-18**	J[R] **Isaac in Gerar** **Gen. 26:1-14**
Famine		Famine (said by the redactor to be a second famine, after the one in Abraham's time)
Abraham arranges with Sarah to say that she is his sister	Abraham says that Sarah is his sister	Isaac says that Rebekah is his sister
Abraham says that he is afraid of being killed for his wife's sake	Abraham says that he is afraid of being killed for his wife's sake. He says that 'there is no fear of God at all in this place'	Isaac says that he is afraid of being killed for Rebekah's sake
Sarah is taken into Pharaoh's house	Sarah is taken by Abimelech	
Pharaoh is plagued by Yahweh, and discovers that Sarah is Abraham's wife	Abimelech is told by God in a dream that Sarah is Abraham's wife. Abimelech's house is smitten with barrenness	Abimelech looks out of a window and discovers that Rebekah is Isaac's wife.
Pharaoh reproves Abraham	Abimelech reproves Abraham and Sarah	Abimelech reproves Isaac
Pharaoh gives presents to Abraham	Abimelech gives presents to Abraham and Sarah	
Wealth of Abraham		Wealth of Isaac, and his agricultural success

159a On the documentary theory the existence of such duplicates is explained as due to the use by J and E of two independent versions of an old folk-story ; a later reviser of the J narrative inserted an altered version of E's story into the narrative of Isaac, and introduced the anachronism of making Abimelech a Philistine king ; then the final Priestly editor after the Exile allowed all three versions to remain side by side as three independent episodes. Whether such an explanation can be considered wholly satisfactory is a question which cannot be discussed here. It will not satisfy those who are already finding the documentary hypothesis inadequate. But it must be confessed that it is also not easy to find a satisfactory explanation for all these duplicates in the Yahwist's intention of writing what is now called, and rightly, *Heilsgeschichte*, salvation history. Some of the duplicates, such as the double genealogies of Cain and Seth (see §149*a*), or the two accounts of the covenant with Abraham in chs. 15 and 17, may be explained in terms of their different symbolic meaning ; but in the case of the triple versions of the denial of the relation between husband and wife, an explanation in terms of a symbolic meaning is not obvious. For the prophets the relation between husband and wife had a profound meaning as a symbol of the relation between Yahweh and Israel, and it may indeed be that the Yahwist intended to emphasise by its repetition the gravity of the denial of the relation, and to suggest in symbolic terms that such a breach would take place whenever Israel abandoned the path marked out for her by Yahweh. However, there we must leave the question.

b **XXI The Birth of Isaac, and the Expulsion of Ishmael**—This episode has its place in the history of revelation. Ishmael was not the child of promise, but the fruit of an act of impatience and unbelief. As St Paul was to say long after, the son of the bondwoman might not inherit with the son of the free woman (cf. Gal. 4:30) ; Hagar and Ishmael must go, even though it was bitter for Abraham to have to reject the son of his flesh. There again, images arise in the pattern of revelation, prefiguring the eternal strife between the flesh and the spirit. It is interesting to observe that in the episodes of Hagar and Ishmael an important symbol makes its appearance for the first time, the symbol of the well. Although Hagar and her son lie outside the main stream of promise, they are not beyond the activities of the divine mercy. The well in the wilderness is revealed to Hagar in her distress by divine agency, 'God opened her eyes' (21:19). Probably behind the name which she is represented as giving to the well, with its doubtful Hebrew etymology, there lies an ancient name of Canaanite origin indicating the occupation of the well by a local deity. But here, as elsewhere, we see Yahweh, so to speak, taking possession of his land ; for the Yahwist and his readers the name becomes significant of a living God who not only had vast purposes of blessing, but who was concerned with the needs of individuals. The Yahwist had already represented Yahweh as interested in the destiny of Ishmael's descendants, and by his insertion in 25:12–17 of a fragment of P material containing Ishmael's genealogy in the regular form of the Priestly genealogies, he brings the Arab tent-dwellers within the ambit of the divine purpose. In Isa. 60:7 the prophet's vision sees the flocks of Kedar and the rams of Nebaioth being brought as acceptable offerings to Yahweh's dwelling-place in Zion.

But we now come to the climax of the Yahwist's picture of the development of Abraham's faith.

XXII The Offering of Isaac—From a literary point **c** of view this is one of the finest pieces of Hebrew prose narrative in the OT. From the anthropological point of view it may be regarded as evidence for the existence of child sacrifice among the Hebrews at an early period of their settlement in Canaan ; it may also be considered as a prophetic protest against that practice which persisted so long in Israel, as the famous passage in Mic. 6:7 shows, 'Shall I give my firstborn for my transgression, the fruit of my body for the sin of my soul?' that is, as late as the time of Hezekiah. But there can be little doubt that, for the Yahwist, the episode was the supreme moment in the spiritual pilgrimage of Abraham. The opening words of the story show this clearly, 'After these things God tested Abraham'. Only twice in Abraham's story does the significant expression 'after these things' occur.

9c They suggest a crisis, something towards which the previous events have been working up. The point has been reached when God sees that Abraham is ripe for testing. A point was reached in the relationship of Jesus with his disciples when he saw that the time had come to test the Father's work in them, and he asked, ' Whom say ye that I am ? ' The answer given by Peter showed that what had been wrought in him enabled Jesus to see that the building of his Church
d was now possible. So God tested Abraham to see whether he could go on to build upon what he had wrought in Abraham's soul. Abraham's response of complete surrender showed the solidity of God's building ; it was now possible for God to reaffirm the promise in the most absolute way, swearing by himself and thus going beyond the guarantee of the promise in ch. 15. Indeed it is perhaps not too much to say that the scene in ch. 22 is the pendant of that in ch. 15. In that first binding of the covenant Yahweh himself passed through the symbols of death ; in this scene the reaffirmation of the covenant is a consequence of Abraham's passing through symbolic death, so to speak ; he and God are bound together by that shared experience. Not only so, but in the development of the pattern a whole constellation of images emerges : the father giving the son, the son yielding himself up to do the father's will, all the symbols of sacrifice, the knife, the wood, the altar, the ram of the burnt-offering ; already, at the very outset of the salvation history, through the faith and obedience of one man, the whole pattern of redemption is prefigured. All that God intended to do through Abraham is done ; nothing remains now for Abraham to do but to provide a wife for the heir of the promises, and to declare how utterly he was a stranger and a pilgrim in the land of Promise by purchasing a burial-place for himself and Sarah. It should be remarked in passing that critical analysis has assigned ch. 22, with the exception of vv. 15–18 and 20–4 to the Elohist, but from the point of view taken in this commentary it is the Yahwist who has made use of the E material and has placed the episode of the testing of Abraham as the climax of the preparation of Abraham as the instrument for the creation of Israel as the vehicle of the divine purpose of restoration and redemption.

e Before bringing our account of the Abraham sagas to a close, a note is called for on the question of **the site of the offering of Isaac** and the name given to it in the Elohist narrative. The original purpose of the story may have been explanatory, like many of the stories composing the patriarchal sagas. In the first instance it may have been intended to explain the origin of a place-name, and it has been suggested that the original name of the site with which the incident is connected was Jeruel, or Jeriel, meaning ' God will see ' or ' provide '. The name Yahweh-yireh is an impossible Hebrew place-name, and it may be presumed that the Elohist would naturally use a name which was compounded with the name El. The name Jeriel occurs in 1 Chr. 7:2 as that of a clan belonging to Issachar, and in 2 Chr. 20:16 we have the name Jeruel given to a place near Tekoa, ' the wilderness of Jeruel '. The situation of the latter would suit the conditions of the saga, where Abraham takes a journey of three days to reach the place. Like Bethel, Lahai-roi, and probably also Penuel, Jeruel may have been an ancient sacred place whose sanctity for the Hebrews was explained by an episode in the life of Abraham. In v. 2 the scene of the episode is said to be a mountain in ' the land of Moriah ', and it is possible that these words and the obscure phrase in v. 14, ' in the Mount (i.e. the Temple Mount) where Yahweh is seen ' (where the Hebrew text has evidently suffered some corruption), may have been inserted by the Priestly editor to carry back the sanctity of the Temple site to the age of Abraham. But it is impossible that the Temple Mount at Jerusalem could have been the scene of the incident for various reasons, one of which is that, as ch. 14 suggests, Jerusalem was already a
Jebusite city. The story may also have been intended 159e
to explain the early Hebrew custom of ransoming the firstborn of male children (cf. Exod. 34:20).

Something may also be said about the place of 160a
Ishmael in early Hebrew tradition. The Yahwist's purpose in interweaving the Ishmael stories with the Abraham sagas has already been pointed out, but the factual material calls for notice. The Ishmael stories clearly reflect early Hebrew and nomad traditions about the group of nomad tribes inhabiting the fringe of steppes bordering Canaan on the east and south-east. In the P genealogy in 25:12–16 the descendants of Ishmael are arranged in a group of twelve, in order to furnish a parallel to the twelve tribes descended from Jacob. Each of the three strands in Gen., J, E, and P, has contributed something to the composition of the Ishmael stories. In 16:1–14 we have the J story of Abraham's taking of Hagar at Sarah's suggestion, and Hagar's flight into the desert to the sacred spring of Beer-lahai-roi, a tradition which is intended to explain the meaning of the name of the spring. Then from the E narrative we have in 21:8–21 a doublet of the story of the expulsion of Hagar. The words ' Return to your mistress ' in 16:9 are a gloss intended to bring the two stories into harmony. That the two stories were originally independent of one another is shown by the discrepancy in the age of Ishmael as
given in P and E respectively. According to P's con- b
tribution to the Ishmael saga, in ch. 17 Ishmael was thirteen at the time of his circumcision before Isaac was born. In ch. 21 the birth of Isaac is related by P as taking place a year after the circumcision of Ishmael. Then, in the E narrative, comes the weaning of Isaac and the expulsion of Hagar and her son, when Ishmael would have been a lad of about sixteen. Yet the E story represents Hagar as carrying the water-skin and the child when she is driven out. In the original tradition, no doubt, Hagar did not return, but settled in the Wilderness of Paran, the home of the various nomad groups whose eponymous ancestor was Ishmael. It may be remarked that Hagar also is the ancestor of a nomad group, for we find in the genealogies in 1 Chr. 5:10, 19 a tribe called the Hagrites, who were dispossessed by the tribe of Reuben. They are also mentioned in Ps. 83:6–8 by the name Hagrites as allied with ' the children of Lot ', i.e. Moab and Ammon. The P genealogy in ch. 25, already mentioned, recognises the kinship of the various nomad stocks with Israel, and traces the origin of Midian, Sheba, Dedan, as well as the descendants of Ishmael, back to Abraham, and introduces Keturah and other concubines of Abraham for this purpose.

An important point to note in the Ishmael stories c
is the insistence on the admixture of Egyptian blood with nomad stocks. Hagar is an Egyptian (16:1, J ; 21:9, E), and Ishmael marries an Egyptian wife (21:21). This is in agreement with the agelong relations between the Bedouins and the Egyptians. It is also borne out by the notice in 25:18, which assigns the traditional limits of the wanderings of the nomad stocks as from Havilah to the wall of Egypt (the *Shûr*), i.e. the fortified boundary which guarded the eastern frontier of the Egyptian territory in Sinai, including the copper and turquoise mines, from Bedouin raids. It may finally be noted that the name Jetur, which occurs in 25:15, is philologically the same as Jethro, the Midianite father-in-law of Moses.

XXIII Abraham's Purchase of the Cave of d
Machpelah—Although documentary analysis has assigned this section of Gen. to the Priestly writer, it presents features which are not usually regarded as characteristic of his style, and it has often been pointed out that God is not mentioned in the episode. Yet the accuracy with which the account of a business transaction corresponds with contemporary records of such transactions suggests that the story is a piece of genuine early tradition. From the historical point of view the presence of Hittites is a difficulty, and is usually explained as an anachronism similar to that which

160d represents Philistines as ruling in Canaan in Abraham's time. But in Num. 13:29, a passage which is usually assigned to E, and therefore to be regarded as early Hebrew tradition, we have Hittites described as occupying the hill-country of Judah, and therefore as settled in that part of Canaan where the present episode is represented as taking place. Recent research, however, has given good grounds for the belief that as the result of certain special circumstances within the Hittite kingdom, isolated Hittite settlements may have taken place in the south of Canaan at a much earlier date than had hitherto been supposed possible. But the allusion to Philistines in Canaan at this period must undoubtedly remain an anachronism. The purpose of the Yahwist in including this episode in his picture of Abraham is not wholly clear, but it does not seem out of keeping with that purpose that the note of detachment and renunciation which he has made so marked a feature of Abraham's spiritual pilgrimage should be maintained to the end. It is a feature which Stephen emphasises in his speech before the Sanhedrin in Ac. 7:5, 'Yet he, God, gave him no inheritance in it, not even a foot's length'. So, at the last, the only inheritance of the man of faith in the land of Promise is a grave.

e **XXIV Abraham sends for a Wife for Isaac**—At the end of ch. 22, after the supreme test of Abraham's faith was over, the Yahwist inserted a genealogy which was intended to provide a link with the further development of the salvation history, the genealogy of Isaac's future wife. Rebekah is represented as being the granddaughter of Abraham's brother Nahor. In the brief cult-legend in Dt. 26:5–10, the Israelite worshipper is represented as declaring before Yahweh that his ancestor had been 'a wandering (i.e. a nomad) Aramaean'. It is a fixed element in early Hebrew tradition that there had been an admixture of Aramaean stock at the very beginning of Israel's history. It has been pointed out that there are discrepancies between P's genealogy in 10:22 and J's genealogy in 22:20–4. The discrepancy may be due to a confusion between the Aramaeans settled in Haran, and the semi-nomad Aramaeans whose habitat was the Syro-Arabian deserts. According to other references in the OT the Syro-Arabian deserts are the home of 'the people of the East' (*b*^{e}*nê ḳedhem*), and in 29:1 Jacob is represented as going to the people of the East to find himself a wife. It is possible that, in spite of the mention of Haran in 29:4 and the connection of Nahor with the Haran tradition, the original form of the tradition traced the Aramaean element in the Hebrew stock to the semi-nomads of the Syro-Arabian deserts, rather than to the settled Aramaeans of Aram-Naharaim and Haran. Nevertheless the tradition that connects Abraham with Ur and Haran is too strong to be set aside, and it seems certain that behind the Jacob sagas there lies the historical fact of two main streams of early Hebrew settlement in Canaan, the first represented by the movements of Abraham and his dependants, and a second, Aramaean, wave of settlement, represented by Jacob and his dependants.

f The story in ch. 24 is assigned to J by the critical analysis, but its style is very different from that of the Abraham sagas hitherto discussed. It has no small resemblance to the Joseph romance, and may well come from a different source from the sagas. Like the Joseph story it is intended to serve as a link. The Joseph story links the patriarchal sagas with the Exodus and the Moses saga; the story in ch. 24 links the Abraham sagas with the Jacob sagas through the figure of Isaac and his wife Rebekah.

For the Yahwist **the purpose of the story** would seem to be a continuation of the theme of detachment. The iniquity of the Amorites is not yet full (15:16), and the time has not yet arrived for the heirs of the promise to take up their inheritance. So Abraham cannot leave the scene of his wanderings without securing that the child of promise shall not intermarry with 'the daughters of the Canaanites'. It is Abraham's last act, and, in keeping with the rest of the Yahwist's picture, it is an act of faith and obedience. The story is a beautiful one, and, like the story of the offering of Isaac, is of a very high literary order.

XXVI The Isaac Saga—For the sake of consistency we have given the name of saga to the material which concerns Isaac, but, as we have already pointed out, most of the episodes into which Isaac enters belong either to the Abraham or the Jacob sagas. The finding of a wife for Isaac is the concluding episode of the Abraham saga, while the stories of the birth of Jacob and Esau, and of Jacob's theft of the birthright, introduce the cycle of Jacob sagas. The material relating to Isaac alone is confined to ch. 26, where Isaac's relations with Abimelech, king of Gerar, are largely a duplication of earlier material in the Abraham story, for which see the synopsis in §158*e*. Amos is the only OT writer who mentions Isaac, and it is clear that the figure of Isaac never became a centre of folk-tradition like Abraham and Jacob. His importance for the Yahwist's salvation history lies in the fact that he is a type figure, the bearer of the promise. We hear comparatively little about the relations of Yahweh with Isaac. In 25:11 we are told that God (E) blessed Isaac, and that he dwelt by the well Beer-lahai-roi; in 26:2–5 (J-E) Yahweh appears to Isaac, tells him not to go down into Egypt, and blesses him for Abraham's sake, 'because Abraham obeyed my voice'; and in the same chapter, v. 24, Yahweh appears to him in Beersheba and again blesses him for Abraham's sake; there Isaac builds an altar and 'calls upon the name' of Yahweh, the only occasion upon which he is recorded as doing this.

The Jacob Saga—(*a*) The first cycle consists of episodes involving the relations between **Jacob and Esau**. In this cycle we have two groups of stories: b

(i) **XXV 21-34, XXVII 1-45 The Birthright Stories**—When we compare the sagas of Abraham and Jacob several significant differences appear. In the first place the material is treated differently. In the Abraham cycle the stories have been much less closely knit together, and often show signs of their original independence of one another. On the other hand, while the material of the Jacob saga is much more complex and varied, it has been much more skilfully woven into a unity. Then there is a great contrast between the two central figures of the sagas. While the figure of Abraham is not entirely without individual traits, yet for the Yahwist he is clearly more a type than an individual. He is the prophetic ideal of the truly righteous man, a fit vehicle of the promises and of God's purposes of restoration, by reason of his obedience, faith, and absolute surrender to the will of God. But, with the possible exception of ch. 14, there is little to suggest that he was ever the hero of popular imagination, or that such a figure lies behind the picture of him in Gen. It might almost be said that he is the ideal Israel. Ancient traditions and popular folk-tales, such as the story of the destruction of the cities of the Plain, or the story of Sarah at the court of Pharaoh, have been attached to his figure by the Yahwist in order to illustrate or develop the design which he is working out, but they do not seem to grow naturally out of Abraham's character.

But the figure of Jacob, on the other hand, is far more personal and individual. Crafty, patient, fearful, faint yet pursuing, he might be said to be the embodiment of the real Israel, the Israel of history and the prophets, continually sinning and suffering, yet ever seeking the birthright and the blessing. One might almost say that the Yahwist has set out to show why the scripture had said, 'Jacob have I loved, and Esau have I hated' (Mal. 1:2, 3). From the point of view of the natural man, Esau is a far more attractive character, generous and impulsive, quick to forget an injury, but for the Yahwist he is in the line of descent represented by Cain and Ishmael, the line of nature c

1c as opposed to the line of grace. Cain and Abel, Ishmael and Isaac, Esau and Jacob, represent the two streams that the Yahwist keeps always before him as he develops his theme.

d Moreover, Abraham is not an eponymous ancestor, and gives his name to no racial group. He is truly 'the father of the faithful'. But Jacob has a double character ; as Jacob he is a very ancient cult-hero, possibly Canaanite in origin, representing the spirit of a people ; as Israel, in opposition to Edom, who is Esau, he is an eponymous ancestor, the traditional source of the very mixed people of Israel.

In the story of the birth of Esau and Jacob we have on the factual level a legend which reflects the undying hatred between Israel and Edom, based on historical events, such as the continual struggle during the monarchy between the two kingdoms, culminating in the behaviour of Edom at the time of the capture of Jerusalem by Nebuchadrezzar. This is summed up in the words of Obadiah, 'For the violence done to your brother Jacob, shame shall cover you, and you shalt be cut off for ever.' But, as in the case of other aetiological stories, the Yahwist uses this story to develop his theme of the two lines, the line of grace and promise, and the line of nature rejecting the rule of God and opposed to his purposes. Like Cain, Esau comes first in point of time, but Jacob, his twin, comes out holding on to his brother's heel ; the struggle begun in the womb is continued from the moment of birth. The etymology of the names raises a problem with regard to both names. It is the name Edom, and not Esau, which is a play on the 'redness', either of hair or complexion, which is said to have been a feature of Esau when he was born ; the names Edom and Adam come from the same Hebrew root *'dm* meaning 'red'. The name Esau has no Hebrew etymology. The name Jacob, of which the meaning is connected in the story with the heel-holding there mentioned, is probably a contraction of a theophorous form Jacobel, a form which finds parallels in both Egyptian and Babylonian sources. It may mean either 'El overreaches', or 'Jacob is El', and the latter interpretation has been used as a ground for the view that in early Hebrew or Canaanite tradition Jacob was a local deity.

e There are several other points of interest in connection with the birth narrative which call for comment. First, the feature of Rebekah's barrenness is a recurrent element in OT birth stories ; we have already had the case of Sarah's barrenness by reason of age, where the birth of a son is regarded as a very special proof of divine purpose ; similarly with the mother of Samson, with Hannah, the mother of Samuel, and, in the NT, with Elizabeth, the mother of John the Baptist. In each case the barrenness is connected with the birth of a child who is destined to fulfil a special role in the history of Israel. Moreover, this barrenness is an image of great importance ; we find it used by the prophets as a symbol of Israel under the judgment of God, and the removal of it is a symbol of the restoration of divine favour, e.g. Isa. 54:1. Then we have a new feature, the consulting of the oracle and an oracular response in the poetic form in which such responses were usually delivered. It is obvious that, on the factual level, Rebekah would have to consult a local Canaanite shrine and receive the response from a member of the staff at such a shrine. But for the Yahwist it is Yahweh who was consulted, and it is Yahweh who replies in terms which refer to his purpose concerning the destiny of the two peoples who were to be the fruit of this birth.

f At the beginning of our discussion of the Abraham sagas the question was raised as to their historical character. The same question arises with regard to the Jacob saga, and again we have to remember that saga is not history. Nevertheless, behind the situations which the saga represents as the adventures and incidents of an individual life there lie historical situations and developments.

It may be remarked that Hosea, in the 8th cent., 161f
was familiar with the Jacob saga, and deals with it in such a way as to show that by that time the prophets were using such material as depicting the character and behaviour of Israel reflected in the story of their ancestor ; so that what we are suggesting as the treatment of the sagas by such a prophetic person as we assume our Yahwist to have been, is only the extension on a larger scale of what the prophets had already begun to do with the same material ; he was building on the foundations of the prophets.

There can be little doubt that **the cycle of Jacob-** 162a
Esau stories reflects early historical traditions about the relations between the Hebrews and a neighbouring people which was closely related to them, namely, the Edomites. In ch. 36 we have an extract from the P material relating to the early history of the Edomites, and from this we learn that Edom was politically an older people than the Hebrews, and that eight kings had reigned in Edom before the monarchy had been established among the Hebrews. In the saga this is represented by making Esau the elder of the two brothers. But in the course of history Israel became more important politically than Edom, and during the earlier period of the Hebrew monarchy Edom was a tributary state, a situation which is represented in the saga by Jacob's acquisition of the birthright and the blessing.

The course of the relations between Jacob and Esau as depicted in the cycle of stories with which we are dealing shows a series of changes : first, we have the transactions by which Jacob succeeds in obtaining for himself both the birthright and the blessing ; then a period during which Jacob is obliged to flee from the wrath of his brother until he has gathered enough strength in Aram to enable him to return and face his brother ; and the cycle closes with a reconciliation between the brothers, a reconciliation which is represented by the Priestly writer, in 36:6–8, as an agreement to separate because there was not room in Canaan for both of them.

Now, in the course of Hebrew history we find a b
series of changes in the relations between Edom and Israel. First, there is a tradition that Edom refused a passage to Israel on their way from Egypt to Canaan (Num. 20:14–21 ; Jg. 11:17) ; then comes the record of David's subjugation of Edom (2 Sam. 8:14) ; next we hear of the revolt of Edom and the recovery of independence (2 Kg. 8:22) ; then about a century later, in the middle of the 8th cent., we learn from an oracle of Amos (Am. 1:11–12) of the undying hostility of Edom towards Israel, 'He pursued his brother with the sword, and cast off all pity.' Finally, as we have already pointed out, at the time of the capture of Jerusalem in 586 B.C., we are told that Edom rejoiced at the disaster which had befallen Israel, a fact which Israel never forgot or forgave (Ps. 137:7 ; Ob. 10–11). In Dt. 23:7 the command is found, 'You shall not abhor an Edomite, for he is your brother.' This would hardly have been written after the Exile when the feeling against Edom had become so bitter. But it might well correspond with the final stage of the saga where the reconciliation between the brothers is depicted. We do not know enough about the early history of Edom to be able to say whether the changes in the relations between Jacob and Esau described in the saga reflect the political vicissitudes in the relations between Israel and Edom, but it is clear that there is a general correspondence which gives support to the view that there is an historical element behind the stories of the individual adventures of the brothers.

(ii) **XXXII-XXXIII Jacob's Meeting with Esau** c
—The cycle of stories dealing with the relations between Jacob and Esau is broken by the account of Jacob's flight from Esau and his adventures in Paddan-aram, to which we shall return. In these two chapters we have the account of Jacob's return to Canaan with sufficient wealth and force to enable him to meet Esau without fear. Nevertheless he is

162c represented as much afraid, and as preparing for the worst. He sends rich gifts ahead of his own advance, in order to propitiate his brother, and the final outcome is the reconciliation already mentioned. But the Yahwist's interest is not so much in the external circumstances of the encounter as in Jacob's encounter with God. As in the Abraham saga there was a climax in his relations with God at the testing moment of the offering of Isaac, so the climax of Jacob's relations with God is reached in the vivid story of his wrestle with a divine antagonist who, under a veil of mystery, is clearly none other than Yahweh himself. A modern commentator has said of this episode, ' Unless we shut our eyes to some of its salient features, we must resign the attempt to translate it wholly into terms of religious experience.' We have already referred to Hosea's acquaintance with the incidents of the Jacob saga, and this particular incident is referred to in Hos. 12:3–4. The rendering of the RSV is, ' In his manhood he strove with God. He strove with the angel and prevailed ', and the context shows that already in the 8th cent. the prophet was interpreting the tradition in a spiritual sense. The Yahwist is only continuing the interpretation of Hosea and expanding it to cover all the experience of Jacob as the development of his salvation history, and regarding it as the continuation of what God had begun to do in his relations with
d Abraham. Undoubtedly behind the Yahwist's treatment of the various episodes of the Jacob saga there lie ancient traditions which depicted Jacob as a deity, as a hero of supernatural strength, or as a typical tribal ancestor, famous for his skill in outwitting his enemies. He also figured in the cult legends of such local sanctuaries as Penuel, Bethel, and Shechem. Finally there was a tradition in which he figured as a warrior, taking possession of a part of Canaan ' with his sword and with his bow ' (Gen. 48:22), probably referring to an early tradition of the conquest of Shechem by the Hebrews. But the Yahwist makes use of all this ancient material with the same purpose in mind as in the case of all the material of the Abraham sagas. What we found absent from the Isaac saga, save in a minor degree, is present in the whole of the Jacob saga in the most marked degree. Jacob's dealings with Yahweh are of the most personal and intimate kind. They begin at the moment of his flight from Esau, at the great experience at Bethel, and continue all through his various adventures, reaching their climax in the struggle at the brook Jabbok, where he declares that he has seen God face to face and still lives, and they end in the night vision at Beersheba, where Yahweh appears to him and tells him
e not to be afraid to go down into Egypt (46:2–4). But there is a noticeable difference between Abraham's relations with God and those which are recorded of Jacob. Abraham receives the title ' the friend of God ' (Isa. 41:8) ; he is made the recipient of God's purposes ; he intercedes with God for the cities of the Plain ; even in the supreme test nothing is revealed of any inward struggle, there is nothing but calm acceptance of the divine command. But all Jacob's encounters with God have something of the character of the struggle which reaches its climax at Penuel. Jacob's will is at work all through ; he is determined to get the birthright and the blessing, and does so by means of questionable morality ; he is determined to get Rachel, the wife of his choice, but is compelled to take Leah whom he did not choose. All through we have the sense of God's shaping hard and refractory material, and of Jacob's acknowledgment of the fact that all through his wanderings and trials God's hand had been over him, guiding him towards an end which only becomes clear in the Joseph story. We must now return to the cycle of stories which relate Jacob's adventures in Paddan-aram.

163a (*b*) **Jacob and Laban**

(i) **XXVIII Jacob's Dream and Flight to Aram** —We have already referred to the fact that there are two traditions relating to the Aramaean strain in the
Hebrew stock. In the J account of Eliezer's mission 16
to find a wife for Isaac, he goes to Aram-naharaim, a name which means Aram of the Two Rivers, and is rendered Mesopotamia by the RSV, and there he finds the family of Bethuel, the son of Abraham's brother Nahor, whose children are Laban and Rebekah. According to 11:31 and 28:4 their home is Haran, which is in NW. Mesopotamia. On the other hand, according to E's account of Jacob's flight from Esau, he finds Laban and his family living in ' the land of the people of the east '. Now, in OT usage this always refers to the NW. part of the Arabian desert, and in the genealogical fragment given in 22:20–4 the names of Nahor's children are place-names or tribal names belonging either to the Syro-Arabian desert, or to the settled regions in northern Syria. Hence we have two apparently divergent regions designated as the home of the Aramaeans, one in NW. Mesopotamia, in Haran, and the other in the NW. Arabian desert, the home of ' the people of the east '.

Recent research has shown that both these traditions b
are based on historical fact. It is now known that the people called in ancient sources Aḫlamu, and by the Assyrians identified with the Aramaeans, played a very important part in the early history of the ancient Near East, and that at different periods we find them settled in Naharin, that is, the district between the Euphrates and the Orontes, corresponding to the biblical Aram-naharaim, which is incorrectly rendered Mesopotamia ; for a time they occupy the region between the Euphrates and the Tigris, and even gain a brief control over Babylon ; then, owing to racial movements southwards from Asia Minor, we find them for a time restricted to the Syrian desert ; finally, from the 11th cent. onwards we find the growth of small city-states, the result of the splitting up of the greater Aramaean tribes and confederations. It was the Aramaean kingdom of Damascus which, in the period of the Omri dynasty of Israel, waged those wars with northern Israel which are described in the books of Kg.

Early sources also show the close relation between c
the Ḫabiru (see §156*b*) and the Aḫlamu or Aramaeans. The Ḫabiru, coming, like the Aramaeans, from the NW. Arabian desert, were the first to move northwards and westwards, and there are grounds for connecting Abraham with this movement of the Ḫabiru. Later on, under the pressure of the movements of population caused by the expulsion of the Hyksos from Egypt, the Aramaeans also began their northward and westward migration about the 16th cent. B.C. Hence it is in accordance with external evidence that the saga of Jacob brings him into contact with Aramaeans to the north and east of Gilead, and that he and Laban, the Aramaean, are represented as fixing by treaty the mountain range of Gilead as the boundary of their respective territories (31:44–53).

Hence, behind the stories of Jacob's adventures d
among ' the people of the east ' there lies some core of historical tradition concerning the movements of the Aramaean ancestors of the Hebrew people, and the relations between a branch of the stock already settled in Canaan and an older branch inhabiting the desert to the east of Gilead and Bashan. In order to bring the two traditions into harmony, i.e. the tradition of Aramaean ancestors settled in Haran in Mesopotamia, and the tradition of Aramaeans of the same stock living in the NW. Arabian desert, the J narrator has inserted in 29:4 an episode making Haran the scene of Jacob's meeting with Laban and his kinsfolk. But the well in that scene is no city well, and the setting is wholly that of an encampment of nomadic Aramaeans about an oasis in the desert, an impression which is borne out by the subsequent course of the narrative. It is also noteworthy that all the sons of Jacob, with the exception of Benjamin, are represented as having been born in this region. It is generally recognised that behind the stories of the birth of Jacob's sons there lie traditions about the origin and early history

3d of the Hebrew tribal divisions and their settlement in Canaan. Hence the account of Jacob's return from his sojourn with Laban, enriched with cattle and a numerous following, may represent the tradition of the entry into Canaan of a second branch of the Hebrew stock, more strongly Aramaic in character, reinforcing the Hebrew elements already settled there and making them strong enough to withstand the pressure of the Edomite element of the population and to force them to surrender Canaan to Hebrew occupation.

It should be remembered that the body of ancient traditions which compose the J-E narrative, and which the Yahwist has used for his own special purpose, with the exception of 15:13–16, which many scholars regard as a later interpolation, knows nothing of a period during which there were no Hebrews in Canaan, all of them having gone down into Egypt. That tradition belonged to another cycle, the Moses saga, and it was the work of the Yahwist to bring these two strands of tradition together by means of the story of Joseph, unless perhaps he found them already united in the J-E narrative.

e Hence this body of tradition which relates to the movements of Jacob and his sons may cover the whole of the early period of Hebrew settlement and conquest in Canaan. The Tell el-Amarna Letters with their accounts of the movements of Ḫabiru and other foreign elements into Canaan in the middle of the 14th cent. B.C. may well reflect in some measure the movements of Aramaean immigrants which underlie the Jacob saga.

The Yahwist could hardly fail to be interested in these traditions relating to the early history and origins of the tribes of Israel ; but for him they are still part of salvation history, and from the very beginning of Jacob's wanderings and trials he keeps ever in view God's purpose of blessing and restoration, in which Jacob, in spite of his wilfulness, must be brought to play the part destined for him ; Jacob has to be created into Israel. What was begun at Bethel is completed at Penuel. There his name is changed to Israel, and we have already seen the important implication of a change of names.

4a It is probable that the original object of the tradition of Jacob's experience at Bethel was a validation of an ancient Canaanite sanctuary as a place for Hebrew worship, a *bêth-'ēl*, a house of God. Behind what the Yahwist has made of the story of Jacob's dream lies what was originally a story of Jacob's consultation of the oracle at the Canaanite sanctuary in Bethel by the method of incubation, that is, by sleeping within the temple enclosure in order to obtain a dream, which would then be interpreted by one of the temple staff. But out of some such tradition the Yahwist has drawn a picture of Jacob's first encounter with the God of whom he was to say at the end of his long and stormy life, ' the God before whom my fathers Abraham and Isaac walked, the God who has led me all my life long to this day, the angel who has redeemed me from all evil, bless the lads ' (Gen. 48:15–16). As the Yahwist tells the story, Bethel and its sanctuary disappear, and Jacob discovers that a God whom he does not know is interested in him, and has actually descended the ladder which leads from heaven to earth in order to stand beside him, for so the Hebrew should be rendered. He finds himself caught up into the vast purposes of God and is afraid, ' How awesome is this place ! ' ; but, in characteristic fashion, he makes a bargain with this unknown God, and promises that if God will keep his word and look after him and bring him safely home again, ' then the Lord shall be my God '. This is the Yahwist's account of Jacob's first encounter with God.

b The ladder is an unusual image, and does not occur again in the OT, but there is an echo of it in Jn 1:51, ' You will see the heaven opened, and the angels of God ascending and descending upon the Son of Man.' It is, however, a symbol which belongs to the religious pattern of Egypt and Babylon. It occurs in the Egyptian coronation ritual of the Ramesseum Payprus as a symbol of the deification of the king, and in the 164b
ziqqurat, the great Babylonian temple tower, the bond between earth and heaven, the stairs or ramps leading to the top of the tower are a characteristic feature. It may have been some such association which led to the prohibition of steps up to the altar in the regulations contained in the Book of the Covenant, Exod. 20:26. No doubt such stairs formed part of the sanctuary at Bethel, and the remains of the steps up to the great altar in the high place at Petra are still to be seen. Moreover, the ' messengers ', which is the meaning of the Hebrew word translated ' angels ', are another element in the ancient pattern ; all the gods had their messengers, who were themselves lesser gods. Hence, behind the simple story into which the art of the narrator has transformed the ancient tradition there appear the traces of the old religion of Canaan with its roots in the ancient religious pattern of Babylon and Egypt.

(ii) **XXIX-XXXI The Outwitting of Laban, and the Origin of the Twelve Tribes**—The documentary analysis of these three chapters is very complicated, and commentators differ considerably in the parts which they assign to J and E respectively. The stories are genuine saga material, such as would be of interest to a pastoral community. It is generally agreed that behind the stories of the births of the sons of Jacob, and the rivalry of the two wives, there lie traditions about the origin of the various Hebrew tribes, and something must now be said about this subject. c

The material here collected by the J-E narrative relates to an early stage of the migration and settlement of the Hebrews in Canaan. It should be compared with the poem in ch. 49 called the Blessing of Jacob. It is clear that the narrator has imposed upon his material a genealogical form which is secondary, and which merely reflects the genuine tradition that the separate political units which in the course of time came to make up the Hebrew people recognised their common ancestry as an historical fact. In the story as we now have it Jacob brings with him from the Aramaean country the eleven sons mentioned in the Blessing of ch. 49, while the twelfth, Benjamin, is said to have been born in Canaan. Behind this story lies a mass of confused traditions, very difficult to disentangle, concerning the early stages of the settlement of the various clans and families composing this wave of migration in different localities in Canaan. For many years it has been held by scholars that the system of twelve tribes was the ideal creation of later writers, and never had an actual existence in the political history of the Hebrews ; but recent research has shown that this view is not well grounded. There d
is good evidence to prove that, not only among the neighbours of the Israelites, such as the Edomites and the Ishmaelites, but also among the Greeks and the Romans, political groups of six and twelve tribal units had arisen at a very early stage of the history of these peoples. Hence there is no reason for rejecting the evidence of the passage in ch. 49 for the early existence of a political system of twelve tribes. From the analogy of similar systems among the Greeks and Romans, together with the evidence from such passages as Jg. 19–21 and Jos. 24, it has been deduced that such leagues of tribes had come into existence for the purpose of common action in time of crisis, were bound together by a solemn covenant ratified at a central sanctuary with the proper ritual, possessed a code of laws regulating their behaviour in matters which concerned the tribes as a whole, and were pledged to the maintenance of the sanctuary which was their centre and meeting-place. Part of the duty of the e
members of such a league was to send representatives to the central meeting-place at regular times, and to unite in common action against any infraction of the league's code or custom by any of its members. With regard to the mention of the Edomites and Ishmaelites in this connection (cf. 25:13–16 and 36:10–14) it should be observed that these lists belong to the traditions of

164e the peoples concerned, and have been incorporated in the story of Jacob because of the traditional relation between Israel, Ishmael, and Edom ; hence the existence of tribal groups of twelve among these peoples may be considered as resting on independent evidence, since there is no reason to suppose that the Yahwist or the Priestly writer would have imposed their own ideal system upon the traditions of other peoples.

165a The period during which such a system could flourish would be the period between the settlement in Canaan and the rise of the monarchy, i.e. roughly between 1400 and 1000 B.C. Before the entry into Canaan it would not have been called into existence, and after the creation of a central despotic authority its usefulness would cease. It has recently been suggested that evidence is to be found in Dt. for an attempt to revive this amphictyonic league during the closing years of the Southern Kingdom. The pre-monarchic period is the time during which the conditions presupposed by the Blessing of Jacob existed. If we compare the list of tribes given in this passage with two other early traditional lists, namely those in Num. 26 and Num. 1, certain facts emerge. There is a group which stands first in all three lists and contains the same names, with one important exception ; it is the list of those sons of Jacob who, according to the account in ch. 29 (JE), were the sons of Leah. This group of six tribes occupies the same place in the three lists, in the same order, save that Issachar changes places with Zebulun in the two later lists, and with the same names, save that Levi disappears in the two later lists and his place is taken by Gad. This is the first result of the examination of the three lists. Next we find that, following the Leah group, there comes in the first list a group of four tribes who according to the account in ch. 29 are the handmaid tribes, i.e. the sons of the two handmaids of Leah and Rachel respectively. In the two later lists Gad has been taken out of this group to replace Levi in the first six, and the remaining three come at the end of the list instead of after the Leah group. Lastly, in the first list the two sons of Rachel, Joseph and Benjamin, complete the tale of twelve. In the second list, Num. 26, the Rachel group comes after the Leah group, and in order to keep the number of twelve tribes, Joseph, who is a tribe in the first list, is divided into two tribes, Manasseh and Ephraim, so that the Rachel group in the second list is composed of Manasseh, Ephraim, and Benjamin, in that order. In the third list, Num. 1, the only change from the arrangement of the second list is that Ephraim has now the precedence over Manasseh.

b Hence these three lists, in the order Gen. 49, Num. 26, and Num. 1, represent three stages of settlement and political development, up to the time of the establishment of the monarchy, in particular the Davidic kingdom, which is reflected in the oracle concerning Judah in Gen., ch. 49. They suggest the view that the first tribes to enter Canaan were those composing the Leah group, namely Reuben, Simeon, Levi, Judah, Zebulun, and Issachar. These tribes, it is suggested, formed a league of six, for mutual protection and support, with a central sanctuary in the neighbourhood of Mt Gerizim ; they remained throughout in Canaan, and an Egyptian sojourn formed no part of their tradition. But, in the course of time, certain changes took place. Owing to causes which are obscure, the tribe of Reuben became small and unimportant (cf. Dt. 33:6, ' let his men be few ') ; Simeon and Levi suffered reverses in the attempt to conquer Shechem, and Levi disappears entirely from the list, while Simeon was apparently absorbed into the territory of Judah, although retaining a nominal place in the list of the six. Levi reappears in Dt. 33
c as the priestly tribe with no territory of its own. In the early stages of settlement the tribe of Issachar was obliged to accept a position of vassalage to the Canaanite inhabitants, as its name implies (*'Ish-śākhār* = ' man of hire '), but later on, probably as the result of Barak's successful revolt, the tribe threw off the Canaanite 16
yoke and became more important than its immediate neighbour, Zebulun, a change which is reflected in the changed order of the two names in the two later lists. In the oracles composing the Blessing of Jacob the oracle concerning Judah is one of the latest. Judah probably suffered severely during the period of Philistine domination, a stage in its history which is possibly reflected in the Blessing of Moses ; but, as the result of the skilful military leadership of David, Judah passed successfully through this difficult period and emerged as the leading tribe, a state of things which is reflected in the Blessing of Jacob.

The status of the four tribes, Dan, Gad, Asher, and d
Naphtali, as ' handmaid ' tribes probably reflects the tradition that they were not of the original stock of Israel, but were related groups which joined themselves to the league of six during the early stages of settlement. Dan was originally a strong clan (*mishpāḥāh*), and not a tribe, as Jg. 18:2 shows, and had found a temporary settlement in the neighbourhood of Asher and Naphtali in the south, in what was afterwards Philistine country. Probably as the result of the Philistine invasion the clan was forced to find a new home, and the tradition preserved in Jg. 18 tells of the Danite settlement in the north, on the Phoenician coast, where, as Gen. 49:16 suggests, it attained the status of a tribe. Gad was taken into the Leah group of six tribes to replace the loss of Levi, and Asher and Naphtali were also probably obliged to find a settlement in the north, as we find them in Isa. 9:1 and Jos. 19:24–39 in the region which was afterwards called Galilee. But the early stages of the settlement of this group are uncertain and obscure. It may be remarked here that the Leah group together with the four handmaid tribes were the first to be exposed to attacks from the Aramaeans and the Assyrians, and the four handmaid tribes disappeared at an early stage from the history of Israel.

Then we come to the ' house of Joseph ', as they are e
regularly called in the early stages of their settlement. It is probable that Benjamin, afterwards associated with the Rachel group, was one of the earliest tribes to settle in Canaan. The story related in Jg. 19–21 preserves a tradition of the united action of the amphictyonic league against Benjamin on account of the violation by that tribe of the covenant of the league ; they are said to have ' committed wanton crime [Heb. *n^{e}bhālāh*, " a shameful thing "] in Israel ' (Jg. 20:10). This would explain why Benjamin, originally a powerful and warlike tribe, is reduced to the position of the smallest of the tribes and is obliged to accept the protection of the powerful ' house of Joseph '.

It may be gathered from the Blessing of Jacob that 16
Joseph was originally, on first entering the land, a single tribe. The two later lists show that this large and powerful group (Jos. 17:14) was later on divided into two groups, Manasseh being at first the more important of the two ; ultimately the position was reversed and Ephraim became the leading tribe of the Rachel group, a change which is reflected in the story of Jacob's blessing the two sons of Joseph (Gen. 48:12–20). It is to this group that the tradition of the sojourn in Egypt belongs, and it was this group which came up from Egypt, and, under the leadership of Joshua, himself an Ephraimite, entered Canaan on the east and settled in the central part of Canaan, the ' hill-country of Ephraim '. The house of Joseph was the last of the component parts of the nation to enter Canaan, and two very important results ensued from their arrival and settlement. These results appear from what is recorded in Jos. 24. In the first place, that chapter preserves a tradition (mainly E) of the circumstances under which the tribes already settled, i.e. the Leah group of six tribes met in solemn assembly at the central sanctuary in Shechem, with the more recently settled ' house of Joseph ', and established for the first time the league of the twelve tribes, on the

6a basis of covenant conditions said to have been recorded by Joshua in writing. The four handmaid tribes, hitherto loosely connected with the six tribes, would have received their places on this occasion as members
b of the full league of twelve. Secondly, we have here the definite acceptance of Yahweh as the God of the united tribes. Joshua is represented as offering the gathered tribes the choice between the cults which they have hitherto followed, that is, the cults of Mesopotamia (v. 15), or the local cults of Canaan, and the cult of Yahweh which the house of Joseph has brought with them into Canaan. He declares that it is the intention of the house of Joseph (' as for me and my house ') to adhere to the cult of Yahweh which they had brought with them from the wilderness. The league then makes choice of Yahweh as the God of the united tribes, and the choice is ratified with due ceremonial at the sanctuary of Shechem. It is noteworthy that the book of Joshua contains no reference to any conquest of Shechem, and this may be taken as an indication that Shechem had already become a centre and a sanctuary for the tribes which had preceded the house of Joseph in finding a settled habitation in Canaan.

c This, briefly, is an account of the early political organisation and stages of settlement whose history underlies the form of the narrative of Gen. as we now have it. While to the later writers the period of settlement seemed a time of lawlessness and chaos, ' when there was no king in Israel ', it may be seen from what has been said that this obscure period, important as the formative period of Hebrew history, was far from being as unregulated as it seemed to later ages, but that it had a principle of unity, a central sanctuary, and a common code of behaviour whose violation entailed disastrous consequences for the violator.

d While this is a possible reconstruction of what underlies the narrative of the outwitting of Laban and the birth of the sons of Jacob, told in saga form and collected or used by the Yahwist, we have still to inquire **how the Yahwist relates this material to the redemptive purpose of God** which he is engaged in tracing out. We have seen that the story begins with a revelation of God to Jacob, and an assurance that heaven is interested in what happens to him. He is told that God will not leave him until he has done what he purposes to do with him. But God is not yet Jacob's God ; when he makes a treaty with Laban he swears by the strange name of ' the Fear (*paḥadh*) of Isaac ', a mysterious designation which has been thought to be the name of a deity worshipped by Isaac. But all through there are no communications between Jacob and God, although at the end of his period of trial he tells his wives that God has spoken to him in a dream, telling him that he is the God who had spoken to him at Bethel, and that it is now time for him to go home. Yet, although through the twenty years of Jacob's service with Laban there is no record of any intercourse between God and Jacob, the Yahwist makes it clear that God had hold of all the tangled threads of Jacob's manoeuvres and was working out his purpose to make Jacob into Israel. God sees that Leah is hated and gives her children ; he has mercy on Rachel's barrenness and gives her Joseph ; his interest in the births of the various children is indicated by their names, even though the interpretation of the names generally rests on doubtful etymologies, and underlying the names there may be references to Canaanite deities (29:31–
e 30:24). On Jacob's way back the angels whom he had seen moving in interested activity on the heavenly ladder at Bethel meet him again, indicating that he is back in the place where God intends him to be, and when he sees them he recognises them and says ' This is God's army ' (32:1–2). But, as we have already seen, the climax is reached at Penuel ; he meets God face to face, seeks to know the secret name of his divine antagonist, and has his own name changed; Jacob becomes Israel, a name of uncertain derivation, but which the Yahwist clearly interprets as a sign 166e
that Jacob has come through the struggle, the contest of wills, and, in the divine judgment, has prevailed ; the operative word is, ' and there he blessed him '. The blessing that he had cheated his father to possess, and had laboured for twenty hard years to acquire, is now his. After the dreaded encounter with Esau is over, and the reconciliation has been effected, Jacob receives a direct order from God to go back to Bethel, where he had first met with God, and there he is to make the formal recognition that he has taken Yahweh to be his God. He is even told to make an altar, a thing which Abraham had never been told to do. So we are shown Jacob returning to Bethel, no longer f
a lonely wanderer, but with all the wealth and the dependants whom he had acquired in Aram. At Bethel he builds the altar, and calls the place El-bethel, ' the God of Bethel ', because, says the Yahwist, there God was revealed to him. Now God reveals his name to him, and it is the name revealed to Abraham when the covenant was reaffirmed in ch. 17, the name El Shaddai, for the Yahwist a name of power ; the immediate consequence of the revelation is that ' a great terror (Heb. ' a terror of God ') fell upon the cities that were round about them. One more important thing took place at Bethel, Jacob cleared his camp of all ' the strange gods ' that they had brought with them from Aram. So the salvation history progresses a stage farther ; from this point Jacob is Israel, and in him Israel's history, its trials and testings are prefigured. Rachel dies in giving birth to Benjamin, the last of Jacob's children, and Reuben, the firstborn, commits an act of shame which deprives him of the birthright ; we are told that Israel, not Jacob, heard of it. The story now runs on, and we do not see a triumphant Israel living up to his new name, but a figure round whom the consequences of other people's sins and failures gather, until he cries out in bitterness, ' All this has come upon me ' (42:36). But the pattern of redemption had to be wrought out in Egypt, and the things that seemed to be against him were all part of the divine purpose to bring him, against his will, to the place where that purpose should find fulfilment.

(*c*) **XXXIII 19-20, 34f. Jacob in Shechem**—This 167a
third section of the Jacob sagas is more fragmentary than the two previous sections, and clearly seems to belong to a different set of traditions from those which concern Israel's relations with Edom or Aram. In the material with which we have been dealing Jacob's activities seem to be connected with three main localities. The hero-tradition and probably the dim figure of Jacob as a local deity have their source in the habitat of the Aramaeans east of Jordan, and were brought into Canaan along with the entry into Canaan of that branch of Hebrew immigration to which the Jacob tribes belonged. Then we have, on the west side of Jordan, a group of traditions connecting Jacob with various cult-centres, but especially with Bethel ; lastly we have this third section of Gen., whose connection with the two previous sections is uncertain chronologically, which represents a settlement of Jacob and his descendants in Shechem. The place of b
Shechem in the early history raises many difficult problems. In the J narrative, incl. 12:6–7, the sanctity of Shechem and its sacred tree are traced back to Abraham ; in 33:18–20 the Elohist assigns it to Jacob, who is there said to have bought a place of settlement from the Hamorites who occupied Shechem. In Jos., as we have already pointed out, no account of its conquest is found among all the other conquered cities of Canaan, yet in the end of Jos. 24:1, Shechem is named as the central gathering-place for all the tribes, and the scene of a covenant between Yahweh and Israel. In 1 Kg. 12:25 Jeroboam is said to have built Shechem, apparently making it the royal city of northern Israel, until it was superseded by Omri's new city of Samaria. Hence, in spite of the obscurity which veils its early history, Shechem was evidently

167b one of the earliest cities in Canaan to be occupied by Israel, and the deliberate omission of any mention of its conquest by Joshua suggests that it had been in Hebrew hands, or at least occupied by a mixed population of Hebrews and Canaanites, from patriarchal times (cf. Jg. 9:26–8).

c It is generally recognised as the result of documentary analysis that 34 does not belong to the J-E narrative, and that its point of view is that of a later period than the patriarchal age. It is concerned, not with the doings of Jacob, but with those of the two tribes, Simeon and Levi, whose early disappearance from the history of Israel is one of the unsolved problems of OT history. The expression, ' he had wrought folly in Israel ', used in 34:7 presupposes Israelite settlement in Canaan, and the existence of a national standard of behaviour, a point of view quite incompatible with that of the J-E narratives (for the same expression cf. Jg. 20:6). In Jg. 9 we have the story of the total destruction of Shechem by Abimelech, and it is possible that, since Hamorites are there represented as still living in Shechem in peaceful relations with Israelites, this perplexing element in the saga of Jacob is another tradition of the catastrophe which befell Shechem in the period of the Judges.

d Hence the question of Jacob's connection with Shechem remains very obscure, and is most probably the reflection of later events in the period of the Judges, one version of which has been inserted by a redactor in the E narrative of Jacob's doings. The reference to Simeon and Levi in the Blessing of Jacob, although Shechem is not mentioned, no doubt refers to the episode and implies that the two tribes involved incurred reprisals from the Canaanites which led to their disappearance as tribes.

We come now to the third main division of Gen., the story of Joseph. This contains two insertions—ch. 38 (see §172*b*), which is part of an early tradition about the tribe of Judah, probably preserved because of its connection with the genealogy of David (cf. Ru. 4:18), and ch. 49 (see §172*d–g*), which contains the ancient poem called the Blessing of Jacob, a series of oracles about the twelve tribes containing valuable historical matter.

(C) The Joseph Story (XXXVII; XXXIX–XLVIII; L)

For Chs. 38 and 49 see §172*a–g*

168a Although there are traces in the beginning of the Joseph story of the use of sources, yet the story as a whole is quite unlike the sagas of Abraham and Jacob. It is not episodic, but is a well-constructed, consecutive narrative, with a plot and a dramatic denouement. It is impossible to say whether the author whose hand is manifest throughout the whole book of Gen., and whom we have called the Yahwist, has written this story; but, whether he wrote it or not, it is clear that he has used it with a deliberate purpose, and that it is an essential part of his salvation history.

b On the factual level it may be compared to the stories in the first part of the book of Daniel. It is generally recognised that the historical setting of the stories of Daniel and his three companions at the court of Nebuchadrezzar and Darius is entirely imaginary. Similarly, the setting of the adventures of Joseph in Egypt at the court of an Egyptian monarch is not based on any knowledge of the contemporary Egyptian scene. No name is given to the Pharaoh, whereas in the accounts which Hebrew historical writers give of the relations between Israel and Egypt, the name of the particular Pharaoh is always given. Most of the Egyptian words and names in the story have baffled all the commentators, and any contemporary colouring has generally been assigned to the XXII Dynasty, i.e. the period of Solomon and Rehoboam. Parallels with the Egyptian *Tale of Two Brothers* are so close as to make it probable that there is some literary dependence of the Hebrew story upon the Egyptian. The story of Joseph raises two important historical problems: first, the question as to 16
what period in the history of Egypt provides the most probable background to the story, and secondly, the question of the historicity of the account of the descent of the entire Hebrew people into Egypt at this period.

(*a*) **The Historical Background of the Story c**
of Joseph—In discussing the historical character of ch. 14 we found that the main difficulty was the absence of any definite contemporary evidence which might help us to arrive at an approximate date for the events described. The same difficulty confronts us in the case of the story of Joseph; there is even less contemporary material available to help us. We have already pointed out that the king of Egypt is simply called Pharaoh, which is merely a title descriptive of all the kings of Egypt. With regard to the personal names occurring in the story, there are only three: Potiphar, the captain of the guard (39:1), a name which seems to be the same as that of the priest of On (41:45); Asenath, the daughter of the priest of On, who is given in marriage to Joseph by Pharaoh; and the name Zaphenath-paneah, which is given to Joseph on his elevation to the viziership. It has already been pointed out that these personal names are characteristic of the XXI or XXII Egyptian Dynasty, contemporary with the 10th cent. of Israelite history.

The place-names mentioned in the story are not d
much more helpful. The two names in question are ' the land of Rameses ' (47:11) where Joseph is said to have settled his father and brothers, and the land of Goshen, which seems to be equated by the narrator with the land of Rameses. There is no Egyptian authority for the name Goshen, but it has been identified by modern archaeologists with a region in the eastern Delta which includes the Wâdī Ṭumilât, and the evidence of a XIX-Dynasty papyrus shows that the Bedouins from the Sinai peninsula were occasionally allowed to enter this district and pasture their flocks. For the other name the difficulty arises that the Ramessids belong to the XIX Dynasty and after, and that a town or region in Egypt would not have received such a name earlier than this period, which is much too late for the story of Joseph. Hence the geographical data lead to the same conclusion as the personal names, namely that both are due to the narrator, who uses in his picture of Egypt such names as would be in use in his own time. Of course, if we assume that the Joseph story received the form in which we have it now at the hands of the J-E narrators, that would give us a date about the 10th cent., according to the usually accepted date for the uniting of the separate J and E histories, and in that case our Yahwist, whom we have distinguished from the J of the J-E history as a later prophetic editor or author, would have left the personal and place names unchanged, since he was not interested in factual details, but in the unfolding of the purpose of God in the whole plan of Gen. In the unfolding of that plan the career of Joseph occupied a decisive place.

The same result is arrived at if we examine the 16
various details of local colour with which the story abounds; everything is entirely in accordance with the Egyptian scene, but, with one exception, there is nothing which gives any indication of date or period; the one exception is the mention of the chariot (41:43) which points to a date later than the Hyksos invasion, when the horse was introduced into Egypt.

The mention of the Hyksos brings us to a period in Egyptian history which many scholars regard as the most probable period for the events described in the story of Joseph. The name Hyksos is formed from the Egyptian words *ḥeq-chasut*, meaning, ' bedouin princes ' or ' princes of the lands ', and is used by the Egyptians to designate a body of invaders, of mixed race, who conquered the Delta and part of Upper Egypt about 1730 B.C. Now it is generally accepted that Semitic elements were to be found among the invaders, and that this would be a period during which Semitic immigrants would be favourably received. Further,

9a it is urged that the change in dynasty which followed
the expulsion of the Hyksos might correspond to the
rise of 'a new king who did not know Joseph' (Exod.
1:8), and that any of the foreign elements left in
Egypt would be liable to such treatment as is described
b in the early chapters of Exod. This view is not without
plausibility, but is nevertheless open to serious objections, both on internal and on chronological grounds. In the Joseph story we are told that Pharaoh gave Asenath, the daughter of the priest of On, to Joseph in marriage. Now we know from Egyptian sources that the Hyksos worshipped Set and despised Ra, the Sun-god, the chief deity of Egypt, whose great temple was at On, more generally known as Heliopolis. Hence we have the difficult supposition of a Hyksos king not only tolerating the continuance of the worship of Ra and the existence of the priesthood, but even sanctioning the marriage of his vizier to the daughter of the priest of Ra. The form which the chronological difficulty takes is as follows: if we assume that the descent of the Hebrew people into Egypt took place during the Hyksos period, this will give us a date for the Joseph story about the middle of the 17th cent B.C. Until recently most scholars, though not all, were inclined to accept the late Professor Garstang's dating
of the fall of Jericho at the beginning of the 14th
c cent. B.C. Hence between the descent of the Hebrews
into Egypt and the capture of Jericho there would be a period of only about 250 years for the sojourn in Egypt, the Exodus, and the wilderness wanderings. But since the results of Miss Kenyon's recent excavations at Jericho have been published, the objections of Rowley, Vincent, and other scholars to Garstang's date have been confirmed, and the old date in the 13th cent. is now generally accepted. But even on that dating the interval is too short, and conflicts with the J tradition of a 400-year-period of bondage in Egypt, as well as with the Priestly chronological framework. But it should be remarked that the 400-year-tradition is inconsistent with other Hebrew traditions, e.g. the genealogy of Moses and Aaron in Exod. 6:14–27, which allows only four generations between Levi and Moses.

d Hence there is nothing in the Joseph story itself to give us any reliable guidance as to the period of Egyptian history in which the events there recorded took place. It seems most probable that J has used a popular folk-story with a motive very common in the East to serve as the basis of a story which provides an explanation for the Hebrew tradition of a sojourn in Egypt, and which serves as a link between the cycle of sagas belonging to the early period of Hebrew settlement in Canaan and the cycle of sagas which have Moses for their central figure, thus unifying two divergent traditions concerning the call of Israel. It should, however, be noted that, although divergent, the two traditions are not incompatible, but represent historical facts concerning the origins of the Hebrew people.

a (*b*) **The Historicity of the Traditions** concerning the Descent of Israel into Egypt.

It has often been remarked that a people will not invent traditions of its own humiliation, and the tradition of the bondage in Egypt and the subsequent deliverance is too deeply rooted in Hebrew memories not to have some historical foundation. What we have to deal with is the special difficulties which the story of Joseph raises in this connection. In the first place the Hebrew tradition presupposes that *all* the Hebrew people went down into Egypt with Jacob. Now the statement is repeated more than once (Gen. 46:27; Exod. 1:5) that the total number of those who went down into Egypt was seventy persons. This involves a double difficulty. We have already seen that the sagas of Abraham and Jacob presuppose the movements, not of individuals, but of clans or tribal groups, hence it can hardly be regarded as historically accurate that during a period of about 200 years' settlement in Canaan the increase of
Hebrew population should have been so small. 170a
Moreover, at the end of the period of bondage this small Hebrew group is represented as having increased to a population estimated, on the basis of the number of men capable of bearing arms (Exod. 12:37), at about two million. This latter difficulty is enhanced if we accept the tradition embodied in Gen. 15:16 (E) and Exod. 6:14–27 (P) that there were only five generations inclusive between Jacob and Moses.

We have already referred to the evidence from b
Egyptian sources that Bedouin tribes were allowed from time to time to enter the region of the Wâdī Ṭumilât for pasture, and the story of Abraham's descent into Egypt (Gen. 12:10–20) has parallels with the story of the general Hebrew sojourn in Egypt which have often been remarked. Moreover, as we have seen, the sagas of the patriarchs at various points imply a continuous occupation of Canaan by the Hebrews, e.g. the relations of the Simeon and Levi tribes with the inhabitants of Shechem, and the story of Judah in ch. 38.

Hence all the evidence seems to point to the conclusion that only a limited portion of the Hebrews who had settled in Canaan went down into Egypt and experienced the events related in the saga of Moses, and further that the tradition of Jacob's descent into Egypt, impelled by famine, may be a telescoping into one story of various entries of Semitic elements into Egypt.

The Pattern of the Joseph Story—The Joseph c
story bears all the marks of a skilful construction. The join with the last cycle of the Jacob saga is cleverly contrived. After the P introductory formula (37:1), 'This is the history of the family' (*tôlᵉdhôth*) of Jacob', Joseph is shown as a lad of seventeen, living with his father and elder brethren in the vale of Hebron. It is implied in 37:10 that his mother is still alive, whereas in 35:18 we are told that Rachel had died in giving birth to Benjamin, an indication that the Joseph story is quite independent of the Jacob saga. Joseph is presented as his father's favourite, and therefore the object of his brothers' envy. The element of significant dreams, which plays very little part in the sagas, makes its appearance at once and is an important element in the pattern of the story. In the sagas the few occasions in which dreams occur are always direct revelations from God to Abraham or Jacob, not cryptic communications which require interpretation. But in the Joseph story we have first Joseph's two prophetic dreams which his father interprets and deprecates, then the dreams of the court baker and cup-bearer in prison, which Joseph interprets with striking success. Then Pharaoh has a double dream which his magicians are unable to interpret, but again Joseph successfully interprets it, and so brings about the peripeteia in his fortunes. The use of dreams in the story has obvious resemblances to the dreams of Nebuchadrezzar which the mages could not interpret, but which Daniel succeeded in interpreting, and was in consequence promoted to a high place in the court. No doubt the author of the book of Dan. used the Joseph story as his model.

Enraged by his dreams Joseph's brethren plot to d
kill him, and an opportunity arises when his father sends him to visit them and bring back a report on their welfare, much as David's father is recorded as doing in 1 Sam. 17:17–18. At this point the sources become extremely tangled. The critics acknowledge that the usual criterion of the divine names fails here, but find that the use of the names Israel and Jacob serves the same purpose. Be that as it may, there seem to be at least two divergent traditions concerning the fate of Joseph. According to one tradition the brethren see him coming and agree to kill him and throw his body into a cistern, and tell his father that he has been killed by a wild beast. Reuben intervenes to save him, and advises that he should be thrown alive into the cistern, intending to come and rescue him subsequently. According to this version of the

170d story, a caravan of Midianites passing by find Joseph in the pit, pull him out, and sell him, either to another caravan of Ishmaelites or into Egypt, but here in v. 28 the confusion is inextricable. Then Reuben returns and finds the pit empty to his great dismay. According to the other version, Judah prevents the others from killing Joseph and suggests that they would do better to make a profit out of his disappearance, and, taking advantage of the opportune arrival of a caravan of Ishmaelites on their way to Egypt with a load of spices, they sell Joseph to the Ishmaelites, dip Joseph's coat in the blood of a goat, and bring it to Jacob as a proof of his son's death. The mention of Jacob's daughters as endeavouring to comfort him is another proof of the independence of the Joseph story. This ends the first act in the drama.

e In the second act we are shown Joseph in Egypt, having been sold by the Ishmaelites to a certain Potiphar, who is said to be a eunuch (Heb. *sārîs*) at Pharaoh's court, and the chief of the butchers (Heb. *ṭabbāḥîm*). If the term ' eunuch ' is to be taken in its usual sense it would conflict with the story of Potiphar's wife, but it may be used here in a wider sense to designate an official of the court. It is usually supposed that the cooks or butchers had become the royal guard. The term *sārîs* is also applied to the chief cup-bearer and the chief baker who come into the story later. Yahweh is said to be with Joseph and to make him prosperous in his new situation, so that his master gives everything into his charge. Potiphar's wife then falls in love with Joseph and endeavours to seduce him. Being unsuccessful, she accuses him to her husband of attempted rape. He is thrown into prison and again Yahweh causes him to find favour with the head gaoler, so that he is put in charge of all the prisoners. The next development in the story is that the two officials referred to above, the chief cup-bearer and the chief baker, incur Pharaoh's displeasure, are cast into prison, and come under Joseph's supervision. Then we have two more dreams. Each of the imprisoned officials has a dream which calls for an interpretation, but none is obtainable. They tell Joseph their dreams, and he says, ' Do not interpretations belong to God ? ' ; he proceeds to interpret the cup-bearer's dream in a favourable sense ; the chief baker, encouraged by the propitious interpretation of his companion's dream, tells his and receives a bodeful interpretation. Both of Joseph's predictions are fulfilled ; the cup-bearer is restored to favour, while the unfortunate chief baker is hanged. Joseph had begged the cup-bearer to speak to Pharaoh on his behalf when he was restored to favour, but the narrator remarks, ' Yet the chief butler did not remember Joseph, but forgot him ', a most artistic touch. This brings the second act of the drama to a close.

f The third chapter in the story opens with two more dreams. After two years, during which Joseph remained in prison, Pharaoh has two dreams, and none of his court magicians can interpret them. Then the chief butler remembers what had happened to him in prison, and tells Pharaoh about it. Joseph is sent for, and when Pharaoh tells him that he has heard that Joseph can interpret dreams he replies, ' It is not in me, God will give Pharaoh a favourable answer '. He then proceeds to interpret Pharaoh's dreams as premonitory of seven years of severe famine to follow after seven years of plenty. He goes on to advise Pharaoh as to the best course to pursue in view of what is to come. Pharaoh is so impressed by Joseph's wisdom that he thereupon appoints him grand vizier of all Egypt, with every mark of honour. Joseph then puts into effect the advice which he had given Pharaoh, and secures Egypt against the coming famine. The narrator also tells us of the birth of Joseph's two sons, and of their significant names, Manasseh, which the author interprets as meaning ' causing to forget ', and Ephraim, from the Hebrew root meaning ' to be fruitful '. It is to be noted that, contrary to
the usage in the sagas, the father here names the **17**
children. The term *'Abhrēkh* in 41:43, which seems to be a cry of homage, has long puzzled the commentators. The rendering ' bow the knee ', unfortunately preserved in both RV and RSV, is erroneous, as the margin of both versions points out. The most probable explanation is Spiegelberg's, who thinks that it is a call to ' Attention ', based on the Egyptian *'b r-k*, meaning, ' thy heart to thee '. The name which Pharaoh gives to Joseph in v. 45, Zaphenath-paneah, is also of doubtful meaning : the best interpretation seems to be, ' the god speaks and lives ', but it has also been explained as meaning, ' he who gives the food of life '. Thus ends triumphantly the third act of the drama, and the narrator now returns to the Canaanite scene.

Joseph's two dreams must now have their fulfilment : **17**
his family must be brought to bow before him. The previous section of the story had closed with the statement that all the surrounding countries were coming to Egypt to buy food. Now we are shown the effects of the famine in Canaan, and the deliberations in Jacob's family about what they shall do. Jacob sends ten of his sons to Egypt to buy corn, but will not allow Benjamin to go. On their arrival the ten brothers are harshly treated and accused of being spies. One commentator remarks that it was natural that ten strange men coming across the border should be suspected of being spies. But this conflicts with the statement in the previous chapter that everyone was coming to Egypt to buy food ; there was no special reason why ten Hebrews coming, among all the other claimants, to buy food should be regarded as spies. This element in the narrative is artificial, and results from Joseph's design to get his brothers in the right condition of penitence. It is implied later on that at their first interview with Joseph they had told Joseph that their youngest brother had been left behind with their father, otherwise Joseph could not have been supposed to know that they had another brother. So, after imprisoning them for three days, Joseph sends them back to their father with injunctions to bring their youngest brother on their next visit as a proof that they are speaking the truth ; meanwhile he retains Simeon as a hostage. The brothers are much disturbed at finding their money in the sacks along with the corn, and they begin to recall their treatment of Joseph, and to think that God is pursuing them with retribution. Their arrival home without Simeon, and their account of what had happened to them in Egypt, occasions much alarm in Jacob's mind, and when the food is exhausted, and the question of going back for more arises, there is a distressing scene. At last Jacob consents to Benjamin's going, as Judah offers to be surety for his safe return ; so they take double money and Benjamin, and once more reach Egypt. Now Joseph is resolved to make himself known to his brethren and to forgive them. After various manoeuvres intended to reduce them to a state of abject terror, the reconciliation is staged and the fourth act of the drama ends with Joseph's brothers being introduced to Pharaoh, who invites them to bring their father and all their goods and settle in Egypt. They then go home and bring their father the good news that Joseph is still alive and has sent for him to come to Egypt.

The last stage of the story brings Jacob and all his **b**
dependants, to the number of seventy souls, into Egypt, where they are settled in ' the land of Rameses ' (cf. §168*d*). Jacob is introduced to Pharaoh and blesses him, and according to the narrator lives seventeen years in Egypt. We have the account of Jacob's blessing the two sons of Joseph, a scene in which there is a recurrence of one of the themes of the salvation history, namely the reversal of the natural order, the preference of the younger over the elder as the recipient of the blessing. Then Jacob dies and his embalmed body is carried by his sons and a great cortège of Egyptians back to Canaan to be buried in the cave of Machpelah with his ancestors. After

b a renewal of the reconciliation between Joseph and his brethren, the Joseph story closes with the account of his death and the promise which he made his brethren give him that when the Israelites left Egypt they should carry his body back to Canaan. So, we are told, 'they embalmed him, and he was put in a coffin in Egypt'. The purpose of the Joseph story has been fulfilled; Israel has been brought to the scene where the redemption of Israel, not as an individual, but as the people of Yahweh, is to be accomplished.

c **The Yahwist's Use of the Joseph Story**—In Ps. 105:16–23 we have an indication, both of the fact that at the time the psalm was composed the Joseph story occupied its present place in the pattern of Gen., and of the way in which the story was being interpreted. The first fifteen verses of the psalm have been incorporated into the liturgy of thanksgiving in 1 Chr. 16:8–22, assigned to the occasion of David's bringing the Ark into Jerusalem. Hence the psalm must be earlier than the Priestly work of Chr.-Ezr.-Neh. It may even be pre-exilic, though most commentators date it after the Exile. But, whether pre- or post-exilic, the story is interpreted as part of the divine plan concerning Israel. The famine is sent by Yahweh to prepare for the next act in the divine drama. Then Joseph is sent, 'He had sent a man ahead of them' (Ps. 105:17); his sufferings and imprisonment are meant to test him: 'until what he had said came to pass, the word of the Lord tested (*ṣāraph*) him' (Ps. 105:19). We have already seen that there are indications in the story as we have it in Gen. that it was originally independent of the patriarchal sagas into which it was inserted. We are assuming, as has already been said, that the book of Gen. bears the impress of a single mind, even though various sources have been used in the making of it. We are also suggesting the view that between the period when, on the documentary hypothesis, the J and E narratives were united, and the final editing which, on the same hypothesis, the book underwent at the hands of the Priestly school of writers after the Exile, a writer of great literary skill and a profoundly spiritual outlook, belonging to a prophetic circle, gave the book its penultimate form, and stamped upon it the character of *Heilsgeschichte*, or salvation history. We have further suggested that, since it is now generally acknowledged that a great deal of the material classed as P by the documentary critics is early and pre-exilic, there is no reason why such material should not have been available to the writer of whom we have spoken, and have been used by him wherever he found it useful for the composition of his design. We have called this writer the Yahwist, with the proviso that he is not to be identified with the J of the J-E narrative.

d We have endeavoured to show that in his choice and arrangement of the myths in the first section of Gen., in his linking of this section to the sagas of the patriarchs, and in his arrangement of those sagas, the writer whom we have called the Yahwist is working out a well-defined plan, which is nothing less than to present to Israel God's purpose in history from Creation up to that point in Israel's history at which he is standing, and from which he surveys and interprets its course. Von Rad may be right in thinking that the author has a Hexateuch in mind, though that view is not without difficulties; but, so far as Gen. is concerned, the Yahwist, having shown how God had so dealt with Jacob as to change him into Israel, had now to find material which would enable him to show the divine purpose so ordering the course of events as to bring Israel from Canaan into Egypt, where the great act of redemption was to be staged. For Abraham and Isaac to go down into Egypt was contrary to the divine plan, but Yahweh himself is shown as ordering Jacob to go down into Egypt because the time had come for it.

e The question now arises as to the way in which the Yahwist met this need. Did he himself write the Joseph story to fill the gap, or did he find this piece of tradition already in literary form and adapt it to his 171e
purpose, skilfully joining it to the Jacob saga? The suggestion has much to commend it that the story might well have been composed in Egypt during the long sojourn of Israel there. Its Egyptian colouring is so truthful, it shows such remarkable resemblances to the Egyptian romance already mentioned (see §168*b*), that this alternative seems preferable to the view that the Yahwist wrote the story himself. It would seem that there was no saga material similar to that which had grown up round the figures of Abraham and Jacob available for the Yahwist to enable him to complete his design for Gen. The Joseph story shows signs, as we have seen, of more than one version having existed, which is a further argument against the view that the Yahwist is the author. How long the story may have circulated, orally or in writing, in Israelite circles before the Yahwist found it and made such skilful use of it is impossible to say. A comparison of the liturgy in 1 Chr. 16 with Ps. 105 shows that the Chr. liturgy breaks off just where the Joseph story begins in the psalm, and suggests the possibility of the Joseph story circulating independently. Be that as it may, the Yahwist must have found the story admirably suited to his purpose, and it is probable that it contains editorial additions and changes from his hand intended to bring it more completely into accordance with his design.

One striking contrast with the patriarchal sagas lies 172a
in the different way in which the relations between Yahweh and those with whom he is dealing are depicted. In the case of Abraham and Jacob, and to a less degree in the case of Isaac, the relations with Yahweh are of a personal and most intimate character. But throughout the Joseph story, although the hand and purpose of God are everywhere evident and explicitly acknowledged, the only way in which God is represented as communicating with anyone is by means of dreams. Direct personal communication is only resumed when we come to the saga of Moses. There is one exception to this characteristic of the Joseph story, namely, in 46:1–4, where God speaks to Jacob 'in visions of the night', and tells him to go down into Egypt; but the style here is not that of the Joseph story, and suggests rather the hand of the Yahwist adapting the story to his purpose.

XXXVIII and XLIX are two insertions in the Joseph story which clearly do not form part of the original story: they are ch. 38 (see 167*d*, 172*b*), a fragment of tradition about the tribe of Judah, and ch. 49 (see 172*d*–*g*), the so-called Blessing of Jacob, about which we have already said something (see §§165*c*, 166*a*, 167*d*). These must now be dealt with, and the question whether they were inserted by the Yahwist as part of his design, or by a later editor, must also be examined.

XXXVIII The Story of Judah and Tamar—It is b
clear that this chapter interrupts the story of Joseph, and comes from an independent source. It contains two elements, originally separate; one is a fragment of the genealogy of the tribe of Judah, and the other is the story of Judah and Tamar. It is clear that the story has no relation to the Joseph story from the fact that the picture of Judah's settlement in the south of Canaan and his activities are not compatible with the part which Judah plays in the story of Joseph. The main part of the chapter, which describes the artifice by which Tamar forces Judah to fulfil his legal obligations to her, makes use of several interesting folk-story motives which are found elsewhere in the OT and the Apocrypha. There is the motive which forms the thread of the story of Ruth, a story which may be a later version of the story of Judah and Tamar. Both stories describe the arts employed by a widow to secure an heir to her dead husband's inheritance. Both also are concerned with the genealogy of Judah, and in particular with David's descent from Judah. Another feature of the story is that Tamar obtains a child by her father-in-law, to which we have a parallel in the story of Lot and his daughters-in-law in Gen.

172b 19:30–8. A third motive finds a parallel in the Apocryphal story of Susanna, and is a common one in folk-tales, namely that of a virtuous woman who risked her reputation and her life in fulfilling her wifely duty, and is vindicated at the last moment. The story also furnishes evidence for the existence at a very early date of two Canaanite customs which were adopted by the Hebrew immigrants. One is the custom of the Levirate form of marriage which continued to prevail in Israel down to the time of Christ. The other is the institution of the *ḳ[e]dhēshôth*, or sacred prostitutes, to which we find frequent references in the legislation and later history of Israel. They were attached to the local sanctuaries, and are frequently denounced by the 8th-cent. prophets. We find the institution forbidden in the Deuteronomic legislation ; cf. Hos. 4:13–14 ; Am. 2:7 ; Dt. 23:18–19.

c We have already seen that in Gen. 34 we have a fragment of tradition about the early attempts of the tribes of Simeon and Levi to conquer the important Canaanite city of Shechem, and of some disaster that befell them in their attempt, which brought about their practical extinction as tribes. Now in ch. 38 we have a similar fragment of tradition concerning the tribe of Judah, which raises problems regarding the settlement of Judah in the south of Canaan. In this chapter we find Judah in a part of Canaan where later on we find that tribe under Philistine domination, in Jg. 14–16. It is also well known that there is no mention of Judah among the tribes that either took part in the campaign of Barak and Deborah against Sisera, or were cursed for not doing so. There is a tradition in Num. 21:1–3 that when the Israelites left Kadesh-barnea they were attacked by the Canaanite king of Arad, and that in retaliation they destroyed Arad and called the name of the place Hormah. In Jg. 1:16 there is another tradition that the tribes of Judah and Simeon went from the city of palm-trees and smote the Canaanites who inhabited Zephath, and called the name of the place Hormah. What lies behind these inconsistent traditions is probably the separate movement of the tribe of Judah with associated tribes and clans, such as the Calebites and the Kenizzites, northward from the Sinai peninsula into the south of Canaan where they settled about the district of Hebron, Adullam, and Timnah. For a long time they were cut off from the northern tribes by a belt of hostile and unconquered 17 territory, and hence would not have been able to take part in the league of tribes against Sisera, and are not therefore mentioned in the Song of Deborah. The tradition in ch. 38 implies friendly relations and intermarriage with the Canaanites inhabiting that region, and it has always been recognised that Judah was an extremely mixed tribe, possibly even not originally of Hebrew stock.

The other insertion into the Joseph story is the collection of oracles, not all of the same date, which have been brought together under the title the Blessing of Jacob, and placed, either by the Yahwist, or by the final editor, in the account of Jacob's last days in Egypt.

XLIX 1-27 The Blessing of Jacob—The editor's d introduction to the oracles is intended to suggest that Jacob was indued with a spirit of prophecy before he died, and that the oracles are intended to forecast the future history of each of the tribes. But it is clear that they represent the early history of each tribe, and the period to which each oracle refers can best be inferred, though not with any certainty, by comparison with the similar collection of oracles attributed to Moses, and called the Blessing of Moses, in Dt. 33, and also with the very early poem known as the Song of Deborah, which gives information about the northern group of tribes at an early period of Hebrew settlement in Canaan. This will best be done in the form of a comparative table (see foot of this page).

The Song of Deborah is probably the earliest of e these documents, and the Blessing of Moses the latest, but they all belong to an early period of Israel's history, and in the two Blessings the individual oracles do not all come from the same period. The most important oracles, and the most difficult, are those relating to Judah and Joseph. As we have already pointed out, Judah is not mentioned in the Song of Deborah, probably because Judah was still cut off from the rest of the tribes by an unsubdued belt of country, and also because of Philistine domination. It is also possible that the oracle in the Blessing of Moses represents an earlier stage of Judah's history than that implied in the Blessing of Jacob. In the latter Judah is established as the leading tribe in virtue of the Davidic kingship, whereas in the Blessing of Moses Judah's place among

Deborah	Jacob	Moses
Ephraim : settled in Amalekite country	Reuben : loss of pre-eminence	Reuben : population shrinking
Benjamin : included in the forces of Ephraim	Simeon : scattered in Israel because of the Shechem episode	Judah : is to be brought to his people by the help of Yahweh
Machir : = Manasseh ; provides lawgivers	Levi : associated with the fate of Simeon	Levi : has become the Priestly tribe
Zebulun : bears the tribal staff, and fights wholeheartedly	Judah : is pre-eminent among the tribes, with the Davidic kingship, and Messianic expectation	Benjamin : under the protection of Yahweh, 'makes his dwelling between his shoulders' (Dt. 33:12)
Issachar : in the lead with Deborah and Barak	Zebulun : settled on the coast, bordering on Sidon	Joseph : echoes the blessing of Jacob. The two horns of Joseph, i.e. the two Joseph tribes, are :
Naphtali : associated with Issachar	Issachar : has become tributary to the Canaanites	Ephraim and Manasseh, together described as victorious in war
Reuben : undecided, but stays with the sheep-folds	Dan : has to struggle for independent existence as a tribe	Zebulun : associated with
Gilead : stays beyond Jordan	Gad : harassed by marauding bands, but resists successfully	Issachar : as prosperous, and profiting by coastal traffic
Dan : remains 'with the ships', i.e. as a resident alien in Phoenicia	Asher : prosperous, and supplies the royal table	Gad : territory enlarged, and tribal independence gained
Asher : remains 'at the coast of the sea', bordering on Tyre (cf. Jos. 19:29)	Naphtali : fertile and free from restraint	Dan : leaps from Bashan
	Joseph : next to Judah in importance ; prosperity attained after a struggle. (But text is very corrupt, and translation doubtful)	Naphtali : prosperous, settled in the southern seaboard (but rendering doubtful)
	Benjamin : lives by the proceeds of marauding raids	Asher : prosperous, 'dips his foot in oil', well fortified

e the tribes does not seem to be fully established. There are some difficulties in the oracle about Judah in the Blessing of Jacob which call for comment.

f The chief crux is in v. 10. The previous verses of the poem have described the warlike prowess of Judah, which would seem to reflect the victories of David; the oracle then goes on to say that the 'sceptre' (*shēbheṭ*) and the 'staff' (*mᵉḥōḳēḳ*) will belong to Judah until . . . The reading and the meaning of the next phrase are still an unsolved riddle. The RV renders the phrase 'until Shiloh come'; the RSV has 'until he comes to whom it belongs'; the LXX reads 'until the things that are his shall come', with variants; the Hebrew has also been rendered 'until he come to Shiloh'. The history of the interpretation is as long and varied as the textual history. The main question is whether the phrase has a Messianic meaning, and this again depends upon the sense attached to the symbols 'sceptre' and 'staff'. If they are royal symbols there might be some justification for the interpretation much favoured by the Fathers of a Messianic king such as the king of Zech. 9:9. But the symbols may equally well be tribal emblems, and the reference may not be to the monarchy at all. Recent studies in the history of the Messianic concept in Israel seem to have established the position that Messianic kingship in Israel is a post-exilic idea, which would exclude a Messianic interpretation for such an early stage in the development of Hebrew religious ideas.

The other difficult passage is the blessing of Joseph. Here the text is extremely corrupt, and it is difficult to avoid emendation. The period to which the oracle refers is apparently a period in the history of the Ephraim-Manasseh tribes—for Joseph never was a tribe—when they were finding it difficult to maintain their position in the new country. The Joseph tribes stood out as leaders in the struggle of the central group of tribes to resist the attacks of the Canaanites, 'the archers'; the epithet 'separate' (*nāzîr*) in v. 26 has been interpreted by Gunkel as meaning 'champion', i.e. as leading the other tribes in war. The same scholar would restore the very corrupt half of v. 24 as 'by the hands of the Bull of Jacob, by the name of the Stone of Israel'.

g Other differences that call for note are the position of Levi; in the Blessing of Jacob the tribe is still associated with Simeon in connection with the Shechem episode; in the Blessing of Moses Levi is a fully Priestly tribe. This change is already evident in the end of Jg. in the story of the Levite who becomes the priest of the tribe of Dan, and whose lineage, according to some MSS, is traced back to Moses. In the Song of Deborah there is a tribal unit mentioned with the name of Gilead, a name which is not found in any later lists of the tribes of Israel.

3a Before bringing this commentary to a close there are two important topics arising out of the narratives in Gen. which call for an additional note. The first is the question of the religion of the patriarchs, and the second is the question of the relation of the patriarchs to the cult-legends of the Canaanite sanctuaries.

I. **The Religion of the Patriarchs**—We have here three separate problems: (*a*) there is the difficult question of the nature of the religion which the immigrant Hebrews and Aramaeans brought with them when they entered Canaan; (*b*) the question of the authenticity of the religious experience of the individual ancestors, Abraham, Isaac, and Jacob; (*c*) the problem of distinguishing the religion of the Yahwist from the two previously mentioned levels.

b (*a*) It should be clear from what has been said that the entry into Canaan of the patriarchs, and their movements in that country, involved the entry and movements of clans and tribes, and not merely of individuals. The tradition preserved in Jos. 24 in the form of an address of Joshua to the assembled tribes at Shechem represents Joshua as saying that the ancestors of the Hebrews, first in Mesopotamia, and then in Egypt, had worshipped the gods of those countries; he further implies that after their settlement in Canaan **173b**
they were worshipping 'the gods of the Amorites, in whose land you dwell' (Jos. 24:15). Ezekiel has the same tradition, both with regard to the sojourn in Egypt, in the wilderness, and in Canaan (Ezek. 20:7, 18, 28). The passage in Joshua referred to above would also seem to imply that he was offering to the tribes the choice between the gods of Canaan, and the worship of Yahweh as practised by himself and his tribe: 'As for me and my house, we will serve the Lord'. Hence, in the light of this tradition it seems certain that the immigrant Hebrews brought with them the gods of the countries from which they had come, and also adopted the gods of Canaan after their entry into the land. We have seen from various allusions in the sagas, such as Jacob's dream at Bethel (see §164*a*), Rachel's theft of her father's teraphim, or Rebekah's consulting of the oracle at some Canaanite sanctuary, that, whatever conclusion we may arrive at with regard to the individual religious experiences of Abraham or Jacob, the general religious practice of their families and adherents would have been in conformity with the religious customs of the country in which they were settling.

(*b*) The second question is more difficult. It will not c
do to dismiss all the accounts of the religious experiences of Abraham or Jacob as merely the reflection of the Yahwist's beliefs at a much later period. It is generally admitted today that although Abraham, and to a greater degree Jacob, were figures round whom folk-stories and tribal traditions had gathered, yet they were both real people. God is not bound by the theory of evolution, and there is no valid reason, except a somewhat slavish adherence to the belief in a progressive revelation, why we should believe that Abraham's faith and obedience, and his intimate relations with God as they are described by the Yahwist, have no foundation in fact. The friend of God was not a lay figure, and though, to outward seeming, he may have presented the appearance of a well-to-do Arab sheikh, yet, in the inscrutable purposes of God, something happened to him which brought him into the pattern of revelation. The same thing, only in a different key, must be said about Jacob. To discuss the question whether they were monotheists or Yahwists is really to miss the essential point of what God was doing in these beginnings of the development of his purposes of redemption. We may believe, surely, that as Abraham visited the various sacred places of Canaan, and built his altars, he became aware of the reality behind these outward trappings of divinity; El Elyon and El Shaddai were for him names that expressed a profound experience of a personal reality to be known, believed in, and obeyed.

(*c*) With regard to the third question, we can hardly d
doubt, unless our approach to the book of Gen. has been wholly mistaken, that the mind which has given its shape to that book was one which was wholly dominated by the prophetic interpretation of history and by a conception of the purposes of God for the ultimate restoration of mankind through the instrumentality of Israel. Hence it was inevitable that such a mind should at times colour the presentation of the experiences of the patriarchs with its own developed conception of the character of God, but that need not prevent us from recognising the reality of those experiences. One further question arises in connection with this subject of the religious outlook of the Yahwist, namely, at what period did the interpretation of history of which we have been speaking find the clear expression which it has received in the book of Gen.? May we attribute it to a prophetic writer living in the later period of the kingdom of Judah, or to a Priestly writer after the return from Exile?

The former of these alternative views has been e
adopted in this commentary, mainly for the reason that it is clear that the 8th- and 7th-cent. prophets knew the material of Gen. much in the form in which we have it now, and had also begun to interpret it in the sense

173e of salvation history. An additional reason is that, as has already been pointed out, it is now recognised that much of the material assigned to P on the documentary hypothesis is pre-exilic, and some of it quite early; hence such material could have been available for such a pre-exilic writer as we have assumed our Yahwist to have been; and what, on stylistic grounds, has been regarded as inserted by a final Priestly editor, need not necessarily have been woven into the book as late as its final stage. On the other hand it is recognised that after the Exile the sharp cleavage between priest and prophet that manifests itself in the writings of the pre-exilic prophets ceased to exist, and such a presentation of Israel's past history as we find in Neh. 9, where all the Gen. material is given in the form of a salvation history, has what we should have to call a Priestly setting. Hence the view that a Priestly writer or school might have given to the book of Gen. the form of a salvation history cannot be ruled out of court.

f II. **The Relation of the Patriarchs to the Cult Legends of the Canaanite Sanctuaries**—The other point upon which an additional note may be given is the nature of the evidence in Gen. concerning the connection of the patriarchs with the various sacred places and sanctuaries in Canaan. At the time when the Hebrews began to settle in Canaan there were many places in various parts of the country which had acquired a sacred character. There were trees, springs, standing stones (*maṣṣēbhôth*), stone circles (*gilgāl*, hence the occurrence of various places in Canaan with this name), caves, mountain tops, and, of course, places which possessed temples of local divinities, which had come to be regarded as possessing special sanctity.

Archaeological evidence shows that there is no clear break in the cultural history of Canaan separating the period of Hebrew occupation from that of Canaanite occupation. The sites, objects, and natural phenomena which had been sacred to the Canaanites became in time sacred for the Hebrews also. Stories whose purpose was to explain how such places or objects became holy arose among the people and were handed on from generation to generation. The more important sanctuaries, when they had been taken over by the Hebrews, became the places where the main seasonal festivals were held, and on the occasion of these festivals, a recitation, probably antiphonal in form, took place, recounting the tradition of the Exodus, or of the covenant at Sinai, or of the taking possession of the land; these recitations assumed a stereotyped form, such as we find in Dt. 26:5–10. These were preserved by the Priestly staffs of the sanctuaries in the form of 'cult-legends', as modern scholars now designate them, and they form an important part of the material which was used by the editors and compilers of the Pentateuch.

g It may be useful to give here a list of **the Canaanite sacred places** which are mentioned in Gen. as connected in some way with each of the patriarchs:

(1) *Abraham*

(*a*) The sacred tree of Moreh, i.e. 'the Instructor's Tree', Gen. 12:6–7. Here there is an appearance of Yahweh, a promise, and the building of an altar (J).

(*b*) A sacred site, a mountain between Bethel and Ai, Gen. 12:8, 13:3–4. The building of an altar and the invocation of Yahweh (J).

(*c*) Hebron and the sacred trees of Mamre, Gen. 13:18. The building of an altar and the invocation of Yahweh (J).

(*d*) The sacred spring of Beersheba, Gen. 21:31–3 (J-E). Planting of a sacred tree, and invocation of Yahweh under the name of El Olam, the name of the Canaanite deity or numen of the spot.

(*e*) The sacred place whose name in the text as we have it was Yahweh-Yireh, but originally was probably Yeruel (or Jeruel). Gen. 22:14 (E), the scene of the offering of Isaac.

(2) *Ishmael* **1**

The sacred spring of Beer-lahai-roi, a name whose original meaning is uncertain, Gen. 16:11–14 (J). This spring seems to have been in the Sinai desert, in the neighbourhood of 'Ain-Qedeis. It is specially connected with Hagar's flight and the promise concerning Ishmael. The two places where the name occurs again, 24:62 and 25:11, are, in the text as we have it now, connected with Isaac, but were probably originally connected with Ishmael.

(3) *Sarah*

The sacred cave of Machpelah, Gen. 23 (P).

(4) *Isaac*

The sacred spring of Beersheba, Gen. 26:23–5 (J). Appearance of Yahweh, building of an altar, and invocation of Yahweh. It seems clear that in the original tradition the special locality with which Isaac was connected was Beersheba.

(5) *Jacob*

(*a*) The sacred standing stone of Bethel, Gen. 28:19–21 (J-E). Appearance of Yahweh in a dream, erection and dedication of a sacred stone. Jacob promises to give tithes to Yahweh. This holy place is the one most definitely connected with Jacob in the tradition; the ancient bull-cult of Bethel, condemned by the 8th-cent. prophets, may have been the original form of the Canaanite cult of the numen of the place.

(*b*) The sacred standing stone of Galeed or Mizpah, in the mountain of Gilead, east of Jordan, Gen. 31:45–54 (J-E). This sacred stone was the traditional ancient boundary between the Aramaeans and the Hebrews. Jacob offers sacrifice there.

(*c*) The sacred place Mahanaim (meaning 'two hosts'), Gen. 32:1–2 (E). Jacob is met by angels.

(*d*) The sacred place Peniel, or Penuel (meaning 'The face of God'), Gen. 32:30 (E). The scene of a conflict between Jacob and an angel or supernatural opponent (evidently Yahweh in the opinion of the narrator).

(*e*) Shechem, Gen. 33:18–20 (E). Jacob sets up a standing stone, not an altar, and calls it El Elohe-Israel, i.e. 'El is the God of Israel'.

It is clear from these instances that all these ancient **1**
sacred places, most of which, if not all, were already sacred when the Hebrews entered Canaan, had become connected in tradition with some religious experience in the lives of the patriarchs, a dream, an appearance, the performance of some ritual act, or what the tradition describes as 'calling on the name of Yahweh'. In this way the narrator, J or E, records the process by which Canaanite holy places became Israelite holy places, and validates the sanctity of such places for Israel's tradition. But the Yahwist's purpose went beyond this. He was not concerned with the sanctity of particular holy places so much as with the reality and significance of the various experiences which tradition had attached to these places. He saw in them part of the purpose of God to choose and fashion for himself an instrument for the accomplishment of his design for the blessing and restoration of mankind.

Bibliography—COMMENTARIES: W. H. Bennett, Cent.B; S. R. Driver, WC (1904); H. Gunkel, HKAT (5th ed. 1922); O. Procksch, KAT (2nd ed. 1924); G. von Rad, ATD (1949–53); H. E. Ryle, CB (1914); C. A. Simpson, IB (1952); J. Skinner, ICC (1912).

OTHER LITERATURE: W. F. Albright, *Archaeology and the Religion of Israel* (2nd ed. 1946); A. Alt, *Der Gott der Väter* (1929); A. Bentzen, *Introduction to the OT* (1948); F. M. Th. Böhl, *Das Zeitalter Abrahams*

(1930); K. Budde, *Die Biblische Paradiesesgeschichte* (1932); C. F. Burney, *Israel's Settlement in Canaan* (1918); E. Dhorme, *La Religion des Hébreux nomades* (1937); O. Eissfeldt, *Hexateuch-Synopse* (1922); R. M. Engberg, *The Hyksos Reconsidered* (1939); H. Gunkel, *Die Urgeschichte und die Patriarchen* (1911); S. H. Hooke, *In the Beginning* (1947); P. Humbert, *Études sur le Récit de Paradis et de la Chute* (1940); A. Jirku, *Geschichte des Volkes Israel* (1931); A. Lods, *Israel* (Eng. tr. 1932); T. J. Meek, *Hebrew Origins* (1936); E. Meyer, *Die Israeliten und ihre Nachbarstämme* (1906); M. Noth, *Das System der zwölf Stämme Israels* (1930); T. H. Robinson, *History of Israel* I (1932); H. H. Rowley, *From Joseph to Joshua* (1950); C. A. Simpson, *The Early Traditions of Israel* (1948); S. Smith, *Alalakh and Chronology* (1940); E. A. Speiser, *Ethnic Movements in the Near East in the 2nd Millennium B.C.* (1933).

EXODUS

By D. M. G. STALKER

175a The Book of Exodus is one of the most important in the OT, and indeed in the whole Bible. For the event from which, in the English Bible, it takes its name, the latinised form of the Greek word 'exodos' which stands in LXX 19:1 for 'had gone forth out', thrills through the whole of the OT tradition as the great constitutive action of God by which he not only brought the nation of Israel into being, but also gave his plan for the salvation of mankind its final shape. In the OT prophet and priest, psalmist and historian alike look back to the Red Sea and Mt Sinai, and when Jesus talked with Moses and Elijah on the mountain of Transfiguration, their subject was his 'exodos'—so the Greek for 'departure' (Lk. 9:31)—which he was to accomplish at Jerusalem ; so inwoven was that event into the texture of God's dealings with men. The Exodus is for the OT and Judaism what the life, death and resurrection of Christ are for the NT and Christianity. And for Christians, what Jesus brought to fulfilment was the purpose of the Exodus.

b Gen. 1–12 describe the human situation and give an explanation of man's predicament, why he finds himself neither as God intended him to be nor as he himself fain would be. The rest of the Bible tells how God dealt with that situation. And whether the election of Israel took place with the call of Abraham, as one strand of the tradition suggests, or with the events of the Exodus, as the other appears to imply, the Exodus in fact represented a new beginning, since the effective knowledge of God had apparently been forgotten in Egypt.

c Modern scholarship increasingly emphasises the 'election' of Israel. With the events of the Exodus and Mt Sinai something new took place, which constituted a break. It becomes more and more difficult now to believe that the monotheism of the 8th cent. prophets could have evolved naturally from polytheism, as was formerly supposed, and we are driven more and more to postulate on the one hand some divine thrusting-in of revelation by which the Hebrews were pointed from one plane of apprehension to a higher, and, on the other, some great personality to interpret the thrusting-in. In other words, we are being driven back to take seriously what the Hebrews said in our book—that God entered into a covenant with their forefathers at Sinai, which determined not only their relation to him, but also the form of their society. Their emphasis, unique in the ancient world, upon justice and righteousness, derived from the character of the God who revealed himself there, and not from growing insight into what was humanly desirable. Any theology of the OT which is to be written will have to be a covenant-theology. In the same way, it is no longer possible to dismiss Moses as little more than a figure of legend. Legend and saga do still attach to him, and like all great heroes he has drawn to himself much that originally had no connection with him. But of his mediation to his people of the God revealed to him himself on Sinai, and that he laid the foundations of the social, ceremonial and legal systems of Israel, of these there can now no longer be any reasonable doubt. The more our knowledge of the ancient East grows, the more the need appears for some great interpreter of a revelation such as he. **17**

The three sources J, E and P reappear in the book. **d** (For the explanation of these and other symbols used in this article see §§137*a*, 143*c*). But it should be noticed that another mark of more recent scholarship is the disposition to treat P with much more respect, and to regard it as a source from which valuable historical information can be derived. It can no longer be looked on as a largely idealistic exilic and post-exilic projection-back. In many places it is now seen to be based upon sources that are quite old and to make use of ancient tradition. Even if in some cases the priestly editors have used such material in wrong contexts, it is still clear that, for example on the Tabernacle, we can gather not a little from their account which has real historical value.

Divisions—The book falls into three parts : (i) **e** 1–12:36, the distress in Egypt, the call and sending of Moses, and the wonders that attested them ; (ii) 12:37–18, the passage of the Red Sea and certain events in the wilderness. The latter are probably wrongly placed here and should come later in the wanderings ; (iii) 19–40, the making of the covenant at Sinai-Horeb, and the construction and furnishings of the Tabernacle.

The Date of the Exodus—It is difficult to bring **f** all the pieces of evidence, internal and external, into harmony. Two chief dates are suggested : (i) *c.*1440 B.C., and (ii) *c.*1250 B.C. (i) depends upon 1 Kg. 6:1, which states that Solomon began to build the temple in the fourth year of his reign, 'in the 480th year after the people of Israel came out of the land of Egypt.' This fourth year would be *c.*962, which would make the Exodus *c.*1440. The Pharaoh of the Oppression would then be Thuthmosis III, who died *c.*1436. Thuthmosis was a great builder, and among the building-labourers depicted on the tomb of his vizier who superintended many of his works are Semitic foreigners. This would harmonise with the picture in 1:7ff. The 1440 date, which would bring the Hebrews into Palestine *c.*1400, allowing for the traditional 40 years in the wilderness, would also enable them to be identified with the Ḫabiru, see §87. This identification is, however, doubtful. And against the 1440 date two other important objections can be brought : (*a*) So far as is known, Thuthmosis's building activities were confined to Upper Egypt, while the Biblical tradition represents the Hebrews as dwelling in the Delta ; (*b*) Num. 20:14, 16ff. represents Moses as asking the king of Edom for permission to pass through his territory. But Nelson Glueck (*The Other Side of the Jordan* (1940), 27) has shown that from about 1900 B.C. until the beginning of the 13th cent., there is no evidence of settled civilisation in Edom. If the Exodus had taken place about 1440, Moses would have found only roaming Bedouin tribes to oppose his passage. But by the 13th cent., the kingdom was again organised and fortified.

This latter fact lends considerable support to view **g** (ii), that the Exodus took place about 1250. It starts from the notice in 1:11. See the notes there, where the main evidence is set down. This date of *c.*1250 would

176g also fit in with the inscription on the *stele* of Merenptah, the successor of Rameses II, which gives evidence that by the fifth year of his reign, *c.*1229, Israel was already in Palestine. 'The people of Israel is desolate, it has no offspring. Palestine has become a widow for Egypt (that is, has lost the power which protected it).' It also harmonises with the archaeological evidence that some of the cities which the Book of Joshua represents the Israelites as capturing at the time of the conquest, for example, Debir and Lachish, were in fact destroyed shortly before 1200—provided, of course, it can be established that these cities fell to the Israelites who came out of Egypt.

h The chief objection to the 1250 date is that it does not agree with 1 Kg. 6:1. On the other hand, the figure of 480 there may well be artificial, twelve generations of 40 years each. While it cannot be asserted with certainty that the Exodus took place *c.*1250, that date suits the bulk of the evidence better than any other, and has strong support, especially from Glueck's discoveries.

(A) Israel in Egypt (I–XII 36)

176a **I 1–5** P, **6** J, **7** P ('they multiplied and grew exceedingly strong' J). **The Sons of Israel**—The purpose of the first six books of the OT is to tell the way in which God fulfilled his promise to the patriarchs recorded in Gen. 12:7, 13:15, and settled their descendants in the land of Canaan, under Joshua. The summary here points both backwards and forwards. The 'sons of Israel' (1), the twelve sons of Jacob, whose story has been told in Gen. 29–50, now become, in the person of their 'descendants' (7), the nation of Israel. And henceforth the OT deals with the nation. The emphasis is on the amazing increase of the family (7, cf. 9 and 20), an increase which is divinely ordained and preserved. It not only fulfils the promise to Abraham, Gen. 12:2, 17:6, and to Jacob, Gen. 35:11, but it also makes the conquest of Canaan possible. With the phrasing in 7 cf. Gen. 1:28. It is certain that in fact a large part of the Israelites did not go down into Egypt, but remained in Canaan, and so were without experience of the slavery there and the deliverance under Moses—see also on ch. 34. It is also clear that the stories in Genesis and Exodus were originally unconnected. But in view of such promises as Gen. 15:13f., 46:4, 50:24 the editors of the Pentateuch stress the solidarity of the patriarchs' descendants with the Israelites who came up from Egypt. With the list of the sons (2–4) cf. Gen. 35:23–6. In both lists the principle of grouping is the same: the sons of the wives precede those of the concubines. See also Gen. 30:4–13. In **5** 'seventy' is a round number, traditional, cf. Gen. 46:8–27, Dt. 10:22. LXX here and in Gen. 46:27 (cf. Dt. 10:22, LXX[A]) reads 'seventy-five,' probably on the basis of Num. 26. This is followed by Ac. 7:14. Those added are the grandsons and great-grandsons of Joseph.

b **6,** from J, continues the last J verse in Gen. 50:14, cf. 50:26 (E), and leads on to the J passage beginning at 8. **7.** 'Note the accumulation of the synonyms' (Hertz): the writer wishes to emphasise the rapidity of the increase, a multiplying which far exceeded the natural. A divine factor is entering in, whose power is going to be demonstrated at once in the struggle with Pharaoh. **The land**: Gen. 47:11 (P) settles Jacob in the 'land of Rameses,' which Gen. 47:4 (J) calls the 'land of Goshen.' It is identified with the Wâdī Ṭumilât, a narrow valley between 30 and 40 miles long which stretches eastwards from the eastmost branch of the Nile to the present Lake Timsâḥ, on which Ismailiyeh stands.

c **8–12** J, **13–14a** (to 'service') P, **14b** (to 'field') J, **14c** P. **Measures to Check the Growth of Israel**—The repression was designed to conserve the Hebrews as an economic asset while at the same time preventing such increase in their numbers as might make them potentially dangerous to Egypt. The 'new king'—new probably not in the sense of the founder of a dynasty, but as the inaugurator of a new policy towards the Hebrews—was most probably Rameses II, the strong third ruler of the XIX dynasty. See also Introduction. Rameses' 'shrewdness' (10) was to treat the Hebrews like prisoners-of-war, and virtually enslave them, setting them to forced labour under Egyptian overseers, the 'taskmasters' of 11. Such a policy would serve all the ends which he had in view. The Hebrews' spirit would be broken—for the slave mentality which was created, see 2:14, 5:21—the loss of energy and the heavy mortality due to the *corvée*, as well as the reduced standard of living, would hinder increase. Forced labour, often by prisoners-of-war or conquered peoples (cf. 1 Kg. 9:15ff.) was the general method by which in antiquity royal or public buildings were erected. The building was for the state—Pharaoh is not yet the personal title of the ruler but 'a synonym for public authority' (IB). The 'store cities' (11) were used for storing food against famine, and perhaps arms also, for they were strategically placed for campaigns against Syria. LXX suggests that they were fortified. They may also have been centres of trade. There is now fairly general agreement about their identification. Pithom (Pi-Tum, 'dwelling of Tum') is the present Tell er-Raṭâbeh in Wâdī Ṭumilât. Rameses II undertook work upon it. Raamses has been identified by Montet (RB 39 (1930), 1–28) with the ancient Avaris, Ṣân el-Ḥagar. The capital of the Hyksos, the 'Rulers from Foreign Countries', Asiatics who dominated Egypt from *c.*1720 to 1580 B.C., it was destroyed after their expulsion by Aḥmosis I (1570–1546) and apparently left desolate. The capital was moved to Upper Egypt, to Thebes. Rameses II, however, rebuilt it completely, and made it his main residence, with the name House of Rameses. This agrees with the picture in Exod. 2, where the Pharaoh's court is not far from where the Hebrews were living in the land of Goshen. In the XXI dynasty its name was changed to Tanis. See also W. F. Albright, 'Exploring in Sinai with the University of California African Expedition', BASOR 109 (Feb. 1948), 15. Herodotus (ii, 158) mentions Pithom as on a canal built by Pharaoh Neco (610–594 B.C.) to join the Nile to the Red Sea.

d The Pharaoh's scheme failed, however. 'Spread abroad' in **12** is literally 'breaking beyond limits', while the 'dread', a strong word, cf. Num. 21:5, 22:3—though it may here mean rather 'had a loathing for'—affords the hint that what is about to follow is more than an ordinary clash between two peoples. An uncanny, supernatural and irresistible factor is to enter in as well. The 'work in the field' (14) would be the gathering of straw and stubble for the making of the bricks, and it might include other public works, like the making of canals or labour at irrigation; cf. Dt. 11:10. Egyptian drawings which are extant show Semitic labourers at building and field works; see §175*f*. The mud of the Black Nile was used for making both bricks and mortar. On the passage Buber (*Moses* (1946), 34) says: '"and as they oppress him the more so does he increase and spread forth" is not chronicle but poesy; and the same is indicated by well-weighed repetitions, like the rhyming reiteration "with rigour" or the fivefold repeated and hammered "servitude, bondage" in the same two verses. Here the ignominy has obviously been raised to a theme of folksong, as prelude to the story of the Exodus, ever enchanting the audience; the story which is constructed round the recurrent leitmotif that the God of Israel has liberated his people from the "servitude" of Egypt in order to take them into his own "service".'

e **15–22** E? (**20b** J). **The Order to Kill the Male Children**—The two measures to be mentioned, the destruction of the male children at their birth by the midwives, and the casting of them into the Nile, appear to conflict with the policy described in the last section, which was to prevent too great an increase

176e amongst the Hebrews, while at the same time maintaining them in sufficient numbers to be a useful labour force. Of course, the edicts here mentioned could have been withdrawn at any time, once their purpose was achieved. But the explanation is probably rather that here we have to do with a different tradition, and that this story connects more with the birth of Moses motif which is to follow than with the hard labour which has gone before. 'The unsophisticated tone of the story is to be noted. The Pharaoh is called *the king of Egypt*, and is little more than the headman of a village in which Egyptians and Israelites live side by side. His plan for dealing with the alien population is naïve in the extreme, and he himself interviews the midwives' (C. A. Simpson). According to Josephus (Ant. II, ix, 2) the midwives were Egyptian; according to the Massoretic punctuation they were Israelites. But Pharaoh would hardly have entrusted *Hebrew* women with an order which they would have been most unlikely to fulfil. That there were only two midwives suggests either that the names of only two were handed down in tradition, or, more probably, that the Hebrew community was in fact small. E. O. James (*The Old Testament in the Light of Anthropology* (1935), 24) estimates that the nomad population supported by the Wâdī Ṭumilât about a century ago was 4,000. But contrast 12:37, and see notes there. **16.** upon the birthstool: lit., 'upon the two stones', is generally taken to mean stones upon which women in labour sat or knelt, a custom vouched for elsewhere. (LXX, Vulg., Syr. are different, perhaps because the word was unknown to them.)

f The midwives however refused to obey Pharaoh, no doubt partly through professional honour, which they held higher than state policy, but also because, as the story wants to suggest, they 'feared God' (21, cf. Gen. 20:11, 42:18). 'The expression "fearing God" in Scripture is used in connection with heathens to denote the feeling which humanises man's dealings with foreigners, even where national interests are supposed to be at stake' (Hertz). 'In pure human sympathy the narrator sees a proof of true religion which he does not deny even to the national enemy, the Egyptians' (Beer). The midwives' excuse (19) is substantiated amongst primitive peoples—with them birth is generally easier than with more civilised folk. (In **19b** we should perhaps read for 'vigorous', 'like wild beasts'.) The purpose of God remains thus undefeated (20). **21** is perhaps a gloss. As Beer points out, having children would interfere with the midwives' professional duties: the glossator has taken it that they were Hebrews, and therefore due a recompense from God. (For children as a blessing from God, see Ps. 128:3.) Assuming, however, that they were Egyptians, we have in 21 the first hint, to be developed almost immediately, that the God of the Hebrews has power over the Egyptians also. In **22** is a further and more sweeping measure of the Pharaoh, which serves as a bridge to the story of Moses. Now it is no longer just the midwives, but the whole population of Egypt, who are set against God's people.

177a **II 1-4** E **Birth and Parentage of Moses**—Probably by the time that Moses' story was composed formally, his parentage had been forgotten. And tendencies have been at work both to harmonise varying accounts of it, and to magnify the hero himself. Here Amram's wife is 'a daughter of Levi' (1), or, as LXX reads, 'one of the daughters of Levi', and therefore his aunt, the sister of his father Kohath; cf. 6:14–20, Num. 26:59 P. But, since Levi is the grandson of Jacob, the descent here is difficult to harmonise with the 400, or 430, years of the sojourn in Egypt, Gen. 15:3; Exod. 12:40f. And there is a further difficulty. In **2** it appears to be implied that Moses was the *eldest* child of Amram and Jochebed, since the term employed, 'conceived and bore', is only used of a first child, cf. Gen. 4:1, 17 and 38:2f.; Hos. 1:3. But in **4** Moses has a sister, unnamed certainly, old enough to watch over him, and in 7:7 his brother Aaron is three years older than

himself. The facts that in 15:20 Miriam is called 'the 17
sister of Aaron', and that in Num. 12 she sides with Aaron against Moses, have given rise to the suggestion that she and Aaron were the children of Amram by a former marriage. On the other hand, the interest of the narrator here is centred upon Moses, so that he may have telescoped his beginning. A further possibility is suggested by 4:14, where Aaron is called 'the Levite'. It may be, as has been said already, that by the time the tradition took shape, Moses' parentage had in fact been forgotten, but, in order to magnify him, and to make him on every side of their life the father of his people, he was attached to the house of Levi on both sides. In **2** 'goodly' means, probably, healthy or vigorous, likely to survive—see also Ac. 7:20; Heb. 11:23, 'beautiful'. The 'basket made of bulrushes' (3) was a kind of chest or boat (cf. Isa. 18:2; Job 9:26) made of papyrus strips woven or bound together and then rendered watertight by being plastered over with bitumen and pitch. Bitumen was imported from the Dead Sea (cf. Gen. 14:10) and also, from an early period, from the district between Tyre and Safed, north-west of the Sea of Galilee (cf. W. J. Perry, *The Growth of Civilisation* (Pelican Books 1937), 112). A. S. Yahuda (*The Accuracy of the Bible* (1934), 68) says that such chests served as housing for images of the gods dedicated to temples: 'The mother had devised a means for saving her child which was peculiarly conformable to Egyptian conditions. . . . Her hope was that the princess would, at the first glance, suppose it (the chest in which Moses lay) to be a chest containing the image of a god, that had fallen from a boat into the river and drifted ashore, and that she would have it rescued forthwith.' Similar stories are told about the birth and exposure of many heroes. That of Sargon of Agade (see B. W. Rogers, *Cuneiform Parallels to the Old Testament* (1912), 153) is often thought to have influenced the composition of the Moses story. But, however much the latter may have been coloured by legend, there can be little doubt about Moses' origin in Egypt, since the Hebrews would hardly have invented so close a connection between their deliverer and their oppressors.

5-10 E **Moses Found and Adopted**—Tradition b
gives names to Pharaoh's daughter—Tharmuth (Jub. 47:5), Thermouthis (Jos. Ant. II, ix, 5), Batja (Rabbinic), Merris (Eusebius, *Praep. Ev.*, ix, 27). The last of these recalls an inscription on the temple at Abydos in Egypt giving the names of the 59 daughters of Rameses II, one of which is Meri. **5.** The ark would be hidden from the 'maidens' who were walking up and down the river-bank to ensure the princess's privacy, but visible to her herself from the water. The 'maid' attending her is in the water. The humanity of the princess is even more daring than that of the midwives, since the order she disobeys is that of her own father. Note the implied contrast between the bloodthirsty tyrant and his kind daughter. Women, those just mentioned, Jochebed and the midwives, Miriam and Pharaoh's daughter, are made to play a large part in this cycle of stories.

Two motifs appear in **5-10**: (*a*) Moses had to be c
made completely one of his own people—and 'in ancient Hebrew as in current Arabic thinking, ethnic solidarity is established by the suckling of the infant' (IB); (*b*) as the future deliverer, Moses had to be one to whom the Pharaoh would listen. And one who was himself a complete slave would hardly have delivered slaves. Ac. 7:22 says that 'Moses was instructed in all the wisdom of the Egyptians.' **10. he became her son** means that she adopted him. Weaning would take place at about 3 or 4 years of age, cf. 2 Mac. 7:27.

The name Moses appears to be Egyptian, cf. d
Thuthmosis, child of Thut, or, as Sethe, Thut is born (ZDMG 80 (1926), 50), Aḥmosis, Rameses, etc. To it the princess may have joined the name of a god, which the Hebrew tradition dropped as pagan. The etymology suggested is popular, based on assonance with the Hebrew root *māshāh*, to draw forth. The

d form is, however, active, and may covertly suggest Moses as the one who draws forth (Buber). Yahuda holds that *sheh* is a common Egyptian word meaning 'pond, lake', and that Mu-sheh simply means 'the child of the Nile' (op. cit., 66).

e **11-15a** J **Flight to Midian**—Though brought up in the court, and so exempt from the hardships of his fellow-Hebrews, Moses knew that he was one of them. A Hebrew he had remained at heart. Ac. 7:23 particularises 'grown up' (11) as 40 years of age; cf. Jub. 48:1, 42 years. The 'Egyptian' would be one of the taskmasters of 1:11 and 3:7. His lashing of the Hebrew caused Moses' feelings of oneness with his people to come to active expression; see here Heb. 11:24ff. The complaint in **14,** suggesting that the years of oppression had made the Hebrews look to self-interest only, gives a foretaste of an attitude of his people towards him that Moses was to experience later; cf. 16:2, Num. 14:2. Josephus (*Ant.* II, x, 11, cf. Num. 12:1) gives a different tradition about the reason for his flight: after he had led a campaign against the Ethiopians and married a daughter of their king, Pharaoh became jealous of him. For other political offenders who sought refuge in flight, see 1 Sam. 21ff.; 1 Kg. 11:17ff., 26ff.; Jer. 26:20ff. Also, in the romantic story of Sinuhe, the hero, to save his life, had to leave Egypt, and spend ten years among the Bedouin.

f This incident sets the keynote for much of what is to follow. Moses intervenes against the Egyptian's oppression—the same is to be God's reason for freeing Israel from Egypt; cf. 3:7, 9. Moses tries to restore harmony in his people—God will have Israel to be a society in which each is a brother to his neighbour. If Moses' first attempt misfired, and he needed still to learn self-control, more prudence and patience, none the less, when the task is given him by God, as it is in 3:10, he will carry it through to a successful end.

g **15b-22** J **Moses in Midian**—According to Gen. 25:1-6, Midian was the son of Abraham by Keturah. The Midianites and the Hebrews were thus of kindred stock. Biblical references suggest that, with the Amalekites and the 'children of the east', the Midianites lived to the E., SE., and S. of Palestine. Here they are shepherds, in Gen. 37:28 they are caravan traders, and in Jg. 6-8 raiders. Isa. 60:6 speaks of their camels, and Albright holds that Jg. 6-8 contains the first record of the extensive use of camels in the east. Midian would lie outside of Pharaoh's jurisdiction. Phythian-Adams thinks of it as 'that region of the present Northern Hejaz which lies to the east of the Gulf of Akaba and the mountains of ancient Edom' (*The Call of Israel* (1934), 123). Others prefer the eastern part of the Sinai peninsula, as the traditional location of Mt Sinai demands. See further on 16:1. As the Midianites were a large people, different branches of them probably occupied different districts, and as Bedouin they would move about seeking pasture.

h At this new beginning of his life, Moses once again sets himself on the side of the oppressed, helping these girls, unknown foreigners as they were, to get their rights at risk to himself. Like Jacob, Gen. 29, he sits down by a well. The young women, who, according to Burckhardt, still tend the flocks in the Sinai peninsula, had filled the troughs, which were probably of stone, when male shepherds came and drove them away, and started to use the water for their own sheep. The question in **18** suggests that this was a common, if not a daily, occurrence. Moses intervened, not only driving the intruders off, but helping the girls with the hard work of drawing water (lit., 'he actually drew water for us'). The name of their father, 'the priest of Midian' (16), or, as Onkelos and Rashi, 'the chief', is not given in the Hebrew there, but LXX calls him Iothor. 'Reuel' (18), meaning 'friend of God', is probably a gloss, due to a misunderstanding of Num. 10:29 by a scribe who did not think about 3:1. The exact interpretation of Num. 10:29 is not certain, but Hobab appears to be the name of Moses' father- 177h
in-law (cf. Jg. 4:11, also 1:16), and Reuel Hobab's father. Had the name been original here, its natural place would have been in 16 or 21, and not 18. In view of the hostility between Israel and Midian from the time of Gideon, and of the legislation in Num. 25:6-9 P, the connection of Moses and his work with the Midianites must have its basis in actual fact. Zipporah (21) means 'little bird'; cf. Jg. 6-8, where the Midianite chiefs are 'Raven' and 'Wolf'. Gershom (22) is another popular etymology, 'a foreigner (*gēr*) there (*shām*)'; cf. LXX, Gersam. Probably the word is to be connected rather with *geresh*, sprout, or *geresh*, drive away, the one driven away. Jg. 18:30 states that the priests of Dan were descended from Gershom.

II 23-III Moses' Call and his Return to Egypt, 178a
First Account. 23a J, **23b-25** P, **III 1** E, **2-4a** J, **4b** E, **5** J, **6** E, **7-8** J, **9-14** E (**9a** J ?), **15** Rje.

II 23-25 Transition to the Call and Commission—'Many days' (23) can hardly refer to the 67 years of Rameses' reign, but either to Moses' exile in Midian, or, as what immediately follows suggests, the oppression of the Israelites. The former harmonises with the notice in 7:7 P, where Moses is 80 years of age when he appears before Pharaoh. On the other hand, in 4:20, 25 J, Gershom is still young. J therefore did not think of Moses as staying a long time in Midian. 'Many' is probably a redactorial attempt to harmonise the two varying traditions.

23b-25 are P's sequel to 1:14. Not only had the b
death of the king removed the obstacle to Moses' return, but the long oppression would have made the Hebrews more ready now to welcome a deliverer. Also, in the East the death of a king was often the signal for his subjects to rise in rebellion to better their conditions; cf. 1 Kg. 12:4. The Hebrews 'groaned' and 'cried' (23) because the change of the throne had brought no alleviation of their misery. But God took cognisance of their condition—'knew' (25) has, as the sequel shows, the Hebrew sense of 'enter into relationship with', or, as LXX renders, 'made himself known to them'. For the covenant with Abraham, see Gen. 15:18, 17:1-14; with Isaac, Gen. 26:2-4; with Jacob, Gen. 28:13ff. 6:4f. also represents God's remembrance of his covenant with the patriarchs as the motive for the deliverance from Egypt. **24. remembered**: 'Not that He had forgotten it (the covenant), but that now the opportunity had come for the fulfilment of His merciful purposes' (Hertz).

III 1-6 The Burning Bush—Like Amos later c
(Am. 7:15), Moses is taken from being a shepherd to the work of a prophet. At the beginning of the summer, the grass in the lower pastures begins to be burnt up, and the Bedouin go to the mountain slopes. 'The mountain of God' (1), that is, the sacred mountain, was so called either because the Midianites already regarded it as sacred, as the dwelling-place of deity, or else, and more probably, by anticipation, since the law was to be given upon it later. It is sometimes called Horeb (E, D), sometimes Sinai (J, P), the names appearing to be interchangeable. Some think that Horeb refers to the range and Sinai to the peak; others the opposite. Heinisch holds that there is much to be said for the conjecture of Šanda (*Moses und der Pentateuch* (1924), 37, 359) that Horeb represents the Midianite name for the mountain and Sinai the one used by the Canaanites and the Amorite population of the peninsula. It is thus called Horeb here, since Moses is among the Midianites. Dt., Heinisch holds, avoids the name Sinai, since it suggested the Babylonian moon-god Sin. But the word is more likely to be connected with *seneh*, a thorn-bush. For the location of Horeb-Sinai, see on 16:1. In **2** 'the angel of the Lord' is, as 4 and 7 show, Yahweh himself, in so far as he reveals himself. The phrase may be a reverential gloss here, but there are similar alternations of 'the angel of the Lord' and 'the

178c Lord', e.g. Gen. 16:7, 13, 21:17 ; Jg. 6:11. Fire is a common form in which deity manifests itself ; cf. Gen. 15:17 ; Exod. 13:21, 19:16, 18, 20:18, 24:17 ; Jg. 6:21 ; Ezek. 1:27, also 1 Tim. 6:16. It is the least material of the elements, and when it shoots up, it seems to make a link between earth and heaven. The 'bush' (2), mentioned again only in Dt. 33:16, can hardly be identified. Nor is it worth while to seek rational explanations of the miracle. Some consider it an electric phenomenon due to volcanic activity.

d Like Samuel (1 Sam. 3), Moses responded immediately when God called to him. The removing of the sandals before entering a holy place is still done by the Samaritans at the holy place on Mt Gerizim, and by Mohammedans when they visit a mosque. Also, the OT priests performed their duties barefoot. The motive may have been to avoid pollution of a sacred place. Or the custom may have been due to the fact that people once went barefoot normally, and in the cult the conservative usage of olden times was maintained (Heinisch). **5.** Moses is later to go up to God (19:3), but first he has to make experience of his own paltriness (Heinisch). **6. Moses hid his face :** in awe and fear ; cf. 1 Kg. 19:13 ; Is. 6:2. This is E's parallel to J's removal of the sandals.

e The God to whom Moses is to introduce his people is no new God, but the one who had been worshipped by the ancestors of the race (6). In the Pentateuch there is the attempt to harmonise two different traditions about the origin of Yahwism, the one which saw its beginning in the call of Abraham, the other which regarded the Exodus complex of events as the start. Whatever the origin of Israel's call was in actual fact, it is clear that E is here insisting that the God who confronted Moses in the foreign land of Midian is the God of the forefathers, of whom, presumably, he had heard in Egypt. (In 6 'your father' may be meant collectively, 'your fathers', or it may be taken, as the Midrash suggests, literally, referring to Amram). There is no break between past and present, neither in respect of God's faithfulness to his covenant, nor of the nation's experience of his saving power. It has been argued that the God who revealed himself to Moses at the Bush was a new God, the God, in fact, of the Kenite clan of the Midianites, to which Jethro belonged. On this see ch. XVIII.

f **7-10** God now reveals the meaning of the vision and the audition at the Bush, and declares his purpose. Just as Moses had gone into action when he saw oppression (2:11–14, 16f.), so now it is the 'affliction of his people' that moves God to intervene and 'come down'—for the last expression cf. Gen. 11:5 ; also Exod. 19:8, 'descended'. Moses would thus find his own outlook and impulses justified and powerfully reinforced. But there is more than that. Right at the very creation of the national life, and as the reason for the coming into being of this new stage in God's dealings with Israel, and so with mankind, is set the concern for justice and the hatred of oppression which runs through the whole of the OT.

g **8** Canaan was 'broad', that is, extensive, in comparison with Goshen, though it is in fact quite small. With the description of it in the verse, cf. Gen. 15:18–21 ; Lev. 20:24 ; Num. 13:27–29 ; Dt. 26:9, 15 ; Jer. 11:5, 32:22 ; Ezek. 20:15. 'Honey' perhaps includes not only honey from bees, but, like the Arabic *dibs*, grape-juice boiled down into a kind of syrup. For a similar list of the peoples of Palestine to be dispossessed, cf. 17, 13:5, 23:23, 28, 32:2, 34:11 ; Gen. 15:19–21, etc. Canaanite and Amorite are general terms for the existing stock, and are often interchangeable. Where there is a distinction, the Canaanites are represented as inhabiting the coastlands and the Jordan valley, while the Amorites are those on the higher country east and west of Jordan. The power and extent of the Hittite empire, the home of which was Asia Minor and Syria, has now been revealed by archaeology. Those mentioned here, cf. Gen. 23:3, 5 ; Num. 13:29, probably represent pockets from an invading army that 1
stayed on, for the main body of the Hittites were never conquered by Israel. The Perizzites appear from Jos. 17:15 to have been a people living in central Palestine. But some think that the word is not properly a tribal name, but denotes 'country-folk, peasantry' ; cf. Dt. 3:5 ; 1 Sam. 6:8, where p^{e}rāzî has that meaning. The Hivites were an unimportant people inhabiting the country round Shechem (Gen. 34:2) and Gibeon (Jos. 9:7, 11:19). The Jebusites maintained themselves in Jerusalem until they were conquered by David (2 Sam. 5:6–9).

11-12 Moses' First Difficulty—In contrast with his 17
former impulsiveness (2:11–15), Moses now shrinks from the task laid upon him. In Egypt he was one of the royal household, but in Midian only a shepherd and a mere fugitive. For his shrinking cf. Jeremiah (1:6) and Gideon (Jg. 6:15). But, as with these two, God gives the assurance of his continuing presence. The same words of support as in 12*a* are spoken to his successor Joshua (Jos. 1:5). The 'sign' (12) is a promise and a pledge rather than a token. It is an event which would come to pass only in the future, cf. 1 Sam. 2:34 ; Isa. 7:14. It would call forth faith in Moses, and that faith, in the future, would give him courage to go to Egypt and confront Pharaoh. Faith is to be the mainspring of Moses' whole action henceforth.

13-15 Moses' Second Difficulty—In early religion b
it was thought necessary to know the deity's name before cultic relations could be entered upon with him—and such relations Moses wished to establish. At the same time, the 'name' was regarded as indicative of character. The Israelites' question is thus a very practical one It is equivalent to, 'who, of what nature, with what power, is this God?' And unless Moses can answer the question, he will be unable to convince his fellow Hebrews that an objective reality lay behind the experience given him at the Bush. According to Egyptian ideas, each god had several names. But his real name he kept a secret. Thus it would not be enough for Moses simply to say, 'the God of the fathers' or 'the God of the Hebrews'.

The name Yahweh is connected with the Hebrew c
root *hāyāh* or *hāway*, to be. Yahweh is thus, 'he who is', or 'he who will be'. (MT transposes the divine 1st person, *'ehyeh '^{a}sher 'ehyeh*, into the 3rd.) The root Yau appears in personal and place names in Babylonia, and in the Tell el-Amarna letters. But whether there is any connection between it and the Biblical name is disputed. Also, in the Bible there are the contracted forms Yahu, Yo, Yau and Yah. G. R. Driver has argued (*Old Testament Essays* (1927), 23) that these are the most ancient, but others deny this. As to the exact meaning of the name Yahweh there is still no agreement. The conception of God throughout the OT rules out any idea of abstract, metaphysical being in the sense of the Greeks. Four main views are held today. (*a*) The original meaning of the root letters is *to fall* or *to blow* : Yahweh is thus 'he who falls', or, causative, 'he who causes (the Lightning) to fall', or else 'the blower' or, again causative, 'he who causes (the wind) to blow'. It is true that Yahweh is associated with nature phenomena in different parts of the OT, e.g. Exod. 15:10, 19:6 ; 2 Sam. 22:11, etc. On the other hand, whatever he was originally, in the records as we have them now, he is no nature god, but the Lord of nature. (*b*) 'He who causes to be', the Creator. So recently Albright, who denies that such a conception is too advanced for the time of Moses, and adduces parallels from Babylon, Egypt and Canaan. (*c*) 'He who will be what he will be', the 'living' God, the God who will guide history, and who will reveal himself to his people continuously in their ever changing experience. He promises to be with Moses : so will he be with them. And, since he is in himself changeless, and faithful to his nature, they will find him there in every situation, and adequate

9c to it. ' God sets his signature to it that he will remain true to himself in his disposition, his purposes and his promises' (Baentsch). (*d*) Some hold that the name developed from an exclamation or an ejaculation used in the cult. Buber quotes Duhm : ' possibly the name is in some degree only an extension of the word *hû'*, meaning ' He ', as God is called by other Arabic tribes at the time of religious revival—the one, the Un-Nameable '. ' The dervish cry, " Ya-Hu ",' says Buber, ' is interpreted as " O He ". It is the God himself who unfolds his name as the one who is and will be present, not merely some time and some where but in every now and in every here. . . . The exclamation was its hidden form ; the verb is its revelation.' See also W. A. L. Elmslie, *How Came our Faith?* (1948), 120, Auerbach, *Moses* (1953), 47. Recently R. A. Barclay has asked (' The Origin of the Name " YHWH " ' (*Transactions of Glasgow University Oriental Society* XV (1955), 44–7), whether there may be a connection between the original form of the name and the sacred syllable of the Aryans, the *om*, used in invocation of their deities. ' A Moses at the court of a Pharaoh may once have heard the mystic syllable, or a Moses at a Midianite priest's may have heard from the Midianite traders of the Mitanni word, which was uttered before the gods were mentioned but which was not the name of a god '.

d After the Exile, for motives of reverence based upon Exod. 20:7 and Lev. 24:16, the Jews ceased to pronounce the Tetragrammaton, YHWH. When it occurred, they read *'Adhônai*, Lord. Later, the Massoretes attached the vowels of this word to the consonants of the unpronounceable Name. This gave rise to the medieval form Jehovah, and the true pronunciation was lost. But, partly on the basis of Greek transcriptions, and partly on the analogy of other names derived from verbs, scholars are now fairly well agreed that the original form was Yahweh. **15.** ' remembered ' : so as to be called upon in the cult.

e **16-17 J Moses' Message to the Elders**—In 15, E represents the message as to be passed on to the whole people, but here J restricts its communication to the ' elders ', the heads of families and clans, or their representatives. These originally managed all the affairs of the community, as a kind of aristocracy. And when the control of military affairs passed to the king, as it did increasingly from David onwards, the elders retained certain powers in the administration of justice.

f **18-22 The First Announcement of the Plagues. 18 J, 19ff.** E—Sacrifice (18) was the natural response to the divine revelation. And that it should take place at a considerable distance away in the wilderness—' three days' journey ' is a round figure, cf. Gen. 30:36, Num. 10:33—was equally natural. They wished to sacrifice, if not in the country where Yahweh had revealed himself, at a shrine there, at least in the direction of it. The ' wilderness ' would be the limestone plateau between Egypt and Palestine now called et-Tih. That the Israelites say that Yahweh has met with ' us ' (18) means that they realise that what happened at the Bush was not a revelation that concerned Moses alone. It was more than something personal. It was given to him only in so far as he was the chosen leader of his people. In general God speaks to us in order that we may speak to others. Note that in 6:11 P, full release from Egypt is demanded.

g The stage is now set for the clash between the God of the Hebrews and Pharaoh. If it was natural for the Hebrews now to want to sacrifice, it was extremely unlikely that the king would allow the journey. And that not on religious grounds, for the God of the Hebrews, as a national god, would not worry the Egyptians, but on political grounds, for Pharaoh could very well suspect that, once these slaves were out of Egypt, they would not return. So the curtain is lifted off the immediate future for Moses, both to warn him, and to give him courage to endure. On the spoiling of the Egyptians (21f.) see also 12:36. It is difficult to see why the subject is introduced here, unless the 179g
reason is to show that, in distinction from the malignant attitude of Egypt's ruler to the Hebrews, which is to be the theme of chs. 5ff., the Egyptian people regarded them kindly, cf. 1:15ff., 2:6. If we could presume an older form of the tradition which expected that the request to go away for sacrifice would be granted, then the ' spoiling ' could have been a temporary borrowing of adornments for a feast, which would be returned at the end of it. The Hebrews as slaves would have few adornments of their own. There may also be a link in thought with the command in Dt. 15:12ff. which says that when a Hebrew slave leaves his master, he is to be generously endowed from his master's property. Wis. 10:17 calls this spoiling ' a reward of their toils ' (cf. Jub. 48:18), and Philo (*Vit. Mos.* i, 141f.) says that the Hebrews did not take away in avarice or covetousness, but (1) they were receiving a bare wage for all their time of service, (2) they were retaliating for their enslavement, and (3) in war, the victors take the enemy's goods : the Egyptians had begun the hostilities, and now that Israel was victorious, they were avenging themselves according to the laws of the victors. Hertz maintains that ' spoil ' is a wrong rendering, and should be ' save ', ' i.e. clear the name, and vindicate the humanity of, the Egyptians. Bitter memories and associations would have clung to the word ' Egyptians ' in the minds of the Israelites, as the hereditary oppressors and enslavers of Israel. A friendly parting, and generous gifts, however, would banish that feeling.' **22b.** Read ' and of her in whose house she sojourns ', that is, as a slave or a servant ; cf. Job 19:15, RVm. If RSV text is kept, by ' her who sojourns ' would probably be meant an Egyptian woman staying as a visitor with a Hebrew. While J makes the Hebrews dwell apart in Goshen, E makes them live among the Egyptians.

IV 1-9 J Moses' Third Difficulty—Moses still 180a
fears that his people may not listen to him or believe in the revelation that has been given him. (' They ' in 1 are surely the Hebrews, in view of the following ' the Lord ', and not Pharaoh and the Egyptians.) When he asks Yahweh's advice what he is to do, he is ' endowed with supernatural powers like a divine king ' (E. O. James, *The Nature and Function of Priesthood* (1955), 71), and told to perform three signs. The fact that the Egyptian magicians could do the first sign, the rod which turned into a serpent and back again into a rod (2–5)—Egypt was renowned as a land where magic with snakes was performed—would convince his people that he has the help of some kind of supernatural power at any rate. In the same way, since leprosy was regarded as being sent by deity, and was rarely curable, though the physicians of Egypt did claim to be able to cure it, its coming and going would again prove that Moses had divine power at his disposal.

Note differences due to different sources. In b
7:8–13 P, Moses performs the first sign before Pharaoh, evidently to move him rather than to convince Moses' own people. In 7:14–25 E and P, the last sign (9) becomes the first plague. In J Moses' rod is simply his shepherd's staff—' in your hand ' (2) : in E (17) it is apparently something given him by God, and in 20 it is called ' the rod of God '. In 17 the rod is brought into connection with all the signs, but J connects it only with the first. It may be that originally the signs of 17 referred to the plagues. In P (7:8–13) the rod is Aaron's. Quite clearly the rod was an element in the oldest tradition, since it is present in all the sources. At the beginning of 5 there appears to be an omission. We should have expected something like ' and Yahweh said to him, Thus shalt thou do, that they may believe '.

10–16 J, 17 E Moses' Fourth Difficulty—Though c
the people may believe him because of his wonder-working endowments, Moses still objects to the commission which is being laid upon him on the ground now that he is not a ready speaker, either by

180c nature (cf. Jer. 1:6) or by special endowment. Yahweh overrules the objection. He can and will render Moses eloquent. 'He who gives the office will also give the equipment.' With 'I will be with your mouth' (12) cf. Jer. 1:9, 15:19. The fulfilment of the promise is referred to in Ac. 7:22. It is to be noticed, however, that in the J narratives of the plagues, Moses speaks for himself. Unless therefore **13-16** are from E, as Smend, Eissfeldt, Simpson, etc. hold, they would appear to be secondary, a supposition confirmed by the use of the term 'the Levite' in **14** : 'to tell Moses to what tribe his own brother (or half-brother) belonged would be quite superfluous' (McNeile). The term must here denote profession—the priests were Levites—and not descent. The verses were perhaps inserted to authenticate the later practice of the priests in giving 'tôrôth' —in Dt. 33:10 ff. and Lev. 10:11 the Levites are not confined to performing the rites of the cult, but they teach as well. Or the words in 14, 'he is coming out . . . glad in his heart', may be intended to compose the hostility which developed later between prophet and priest—the suggestion being that both have their parts to play in mediating divine revelation. None the less, **15** suggests that the writer regarded the prophet as the more immediate and authoritative channel.

d **18** E Moses obtains permission from Jethro, as the head of the clan into which he has married, to return to Egypt. The fact that he says nothing about Yahweh's appearance to him could be an argument against the Kenite hypothesis—see on c. 18—for had Yahweh been Jethro's God also, it would have been natural for Moses to say to his father-in-law that the reason for his wishing to go away was a command from that God. Unless 'kinsmen' (18) means 'relatives', then this verse agrees with E's earlier representation of the Hebrews as few in number, 1:15–21.

e **19-20a** J These verses are J's continuation of 2:22. Only one son is mentioned there, cf. 4:25. The plural 'sons' here is probably due to a desire to harmonise with 18:2–4, and is probably not original. On 'the rod of God' in 20*b*, see on 4:1–9.

f **21-23** J **The Death of the First-born Threatened** —These verses serve as the transition from the account of Moses' call to that of his work in Egypt, the plagues. The words, 'when you go back to Egypt' (21) connect the passage with Egypt and the journey to it. But they properly belong to the call, and form its conclusion, reminding Moses (21f.) of what he has already been forewarned in 3:19. That its present position is redactorial is apparent also from 21*a* ; no mention has yet been made of miracles to be done to convince Pharaoh—the signs in 4:1–9 are to be worked to convince Moses' own people.

g **21-23** raise the great, and still unanswered, question, how are the omniscient and omnipotent working of God and the freewill of man to be reconciled? (Expressions such as 'God hardened Pharaoh's heart', or 'Pharaoh's heart was hardened', or 'Pharaoh hardened his heart', occur nineteen times in the subsequent narrative.) We today do not attribute results to the *immediate* action of God. But to the Hebrew mind it was so important that God should be regarded as in sole control, and the doctrine of his omnipotence had so to be safeguarded, that some of them, at any rate, did not hesitate to take the risk of the theological problem involved here. The practical point is, the more we refuse to listen to God's commands, the more incapable we become of obeying them, until the point is reached when it might seem as if God himself had hardened our hearts, so that we are unable to obey. But in fact our hearts are hardened only because we ourselves have first hardened them. Or, to put it in another way, we raise our barriers to God's call. Therefore, conversely, the call causes the barriers. If the call had not come, our hearts would not be so hard; cf. Jn 15:22, 'if I had not come and spoken to them, they would not have sin'.

h **22 Israel is my first-born son**; cf. Hos. 11:1— The words point forward to the election of Israel, 18
ch. 19. 'The prophetic intuition which saw Yahweh's love for Israel as a father's for his first-born son became one of the grand commonplaces of Hebrew religion' (Harford). For the corollary of God's fatherhood, see Isa. 63:16, 64:8.

25-26 J **Circumcision**—The incident continues i
20*a*. But its significance is far from clear. In 24 the phrase 'sought to kill him' is 'an anthropomorphic way of saying that Moses fell suddenly into serious illness' (Hertz). But it is an attack from the quarter from which it was least to be expected, namely Yahweh, who has just laid his commission upon Moses. Zipporah attributes it to the neglect of the rite of circumcision. But who is uncircumcised? Moses? Their son Gershom? Is it even Eliezer, who is mentioned first in 18:4 (so Gispen). If it is one, or both, of the sons, Yahweh's anger at the omission of the rite is appeased by its performance now. If it is Moses who is uncircumcised, then the child's circumcision is counted as equivalent to his. Some, e.g. Gressmann, Beer, etc., conclude that what we have here is the modification of an older story which referred to Moses' and Zipporah's bridal night. Arabic words similar to those in the Hebrew for 'father-in-law' and 'bridegroom' mean 'circumciser' and 'circumcised'. So it is conjectured that the Midianites performed circumcision not until before marriage. Moses had therefore neglected the Hebrew prescription of infant circumcision, which is quite probable, since a stranger would conform to the customs of the people who had received him. But now that he is to be the Hebrews' deliverer at the behest of Yahweh, he must fulfil Yahweh's law. The customs of the Midianites must give place to those already divinely ordained (Gen. 17:9ff.) for the Hebrews. **25. feet** : probably a euphemism.

27-28 E, **29-31** J **Moses' Introduction to his** j
Kinsmen.

27 the mountain of God: Horeb. **29-31** give the fulfilment of the commands in 3:16 and 4:2–9.

V 1-VI 1 (**1, 2** E, **3** J, **4** uncertain, the rest J). **Fruit-** 18
less appeal to Pharaoh—V 1-9. In 1, 'feast' (*ḥagh*) denotes a pilgrimage to a shrine followed by a feast there. It is the same word as the Arabic *Ḥaj*, the pilgrimage to Mecca. Under the Ramesside dynasty private complaints, even of slaves, could be made directly to the Pharaoh. But the king had no intention of complying in this case. His question (2) is contemptuous. A polytheist himself, he does not deny Yahweh's existence. Only, he has never heard of him. And for the religious feelings of his slaves he has no consideration. (His attitude to Yahweh is soon to be very different, 8:8, 28, 9:28, 10:16f.) That the 'pestilence' (3) might spread to his own people he possibly did not consider. Living as the Israelites did in Goshen, the entrance to Egypt for invading armies or border raiders, they were particularly exposed to the dangers of war ('with the sword', 3). It was a common ancient belief that such things as pestilence and war followed the neglect of cultic obligations. **4.** Pharaoh regards Moses and Aaron as agitators who encourage the workpeople to be idle. (In **5** Meek (*American Translation*) emends 'are now many' into 'are lazy as it is', which fits well with 'idle' in 8 and 17.) So the king's reply is, longer hours and harder work. The slaves are no longer to have straw supplied to them, but they are to cut the stubble and chop it for themselves, while at the same time maintaining the old rate of production. Chopped straw was sometimes used to bind the Nile mud from which the bricks were made closer together, sometimes sand was used. The bricks were made in a frame or mould, then left to dry in the sun. Some think that the straw was used to prevent the bricks from sticking to the mould.

10-14 Distinguish between the 'taskmasters', who b
were Egyptians, and the 'foremen of the people', who were Israelites, chosen by their fellows as a kind of shop-steward. The latter had to see that the

181b quota of bricks was made, absentees accounted for, etc. And on them fell any communal penalties.

c **15-19** Direct appeal to the monarch himself is fruitless. He does not deal with the reasonable grounds for the complaint, but says that the Hebrews are making religion an excuse for a holiday, and reiterates his previous order in 7. In the last clause of **16**, read with LXX, Syr., ' and thou shalt be guilty of a wrong against thy people '—the Hebrews were Pharaoh's subjects.

d **V 20-VI 1** The foremen, faced with an impossible situation, not unnaturally turn on Moses and Aaron. It is Moses' demand for leave to go on a pilgrimage that has brought them into bad odour with the king and as good as effected their destruction (21). Moses gives no answer, but as elsewhere (cf. 17:4, 32:11–13 ; Dt. 9:26–9), turns to Yahweh in prayer. He does not understand God's ways. But he is reassured. 'The confidence that help will be given in the darkest hour of need is well expressed in the Jewish proverb, " When the tale of bricks is doubled, then comes Moses " ' (McNeile). **VI 1. by a strong hand** : whose hand, Yahweh's or Pharaoh's, is not clear. In 3:19 the ' mighty hand ' is the former's, and so it could be here, cf. Ac. 13:17. But it could also mean ' with violence on the part of Pharaoh ', cf. 12:39, ' they were thrust out of Egypt '.

e **VI 2-9** P **Second Account of Moses' Call**—The section 6:2 to 7:7 is not a continuation of the narrative covered by 3–4:1, but a parallel and supplementary account from a different source, namely, P. There are variations between the accounts. For example, the Priestly editors think of the revelation to Moses and his call as taking place in Egypt, and not in Midian, as in ch. 3. Here (9) the people refuse to listen to Moses, contrast 4:31. In 4:16, 30 Aaron is Moses' spokesman with the people, in 7:1f. he is Moses' spokesman with Pharaoh. The Priestly writers also think of the name Yahweh as revealed now for the first time, though it is in fact frequently used in the earlier sources before this point. They do, however, like the older writers (3:6, 15f.) stress the identity of Yahweh with the God of the patriarchs. In **3**, *mg.* El Shaddai is preferable. El, the characteristic Canaanite name for the high god, is found in the Râs Shamra tablets, and the most probable derivation of the word Shaddai is from the Akkadian *shadu*, mountain, hence ' the mountain God '. Like the discoveries at Nuzu (see §86*c*), this appellation confirms the Biblical tradition of the connection of the patriarchs with Mesopotamia. (For various other suggested derivations, see McNeile, 40.) The term occurs again in Gen. 17:1, 28:3, 35:11, 48:3, all P ; 43:14 E ; 49:25 LXX ; Ezek. 10:5. Shaddai alone is found forty times, especially in Job. By the time of P its original significance had been forgotten.

f **4 Covenant**—P conceives of God as dealing with mankind by means of a series of covenants ; with Noah, Gen. 9:8ff. ; with Abraham, Gen. 17:1f., 7f. ; and with the people of Israel, Exod. 19ff. Two main views are held today about the origin and nature of the Biblical covenants. Pedersen (*Israel I–II* (1926)), thinks of the Bedouin institution. By it two or more parties, in order to establish peaceable relationships between themselves, entered into solemn obligations, with terms agreed upon and ratified by sacrifice. By means of this covenant, the contracting parties became in a sense one—a kind of blood-brotherhood was established. Between this secular covenant, however, and those of the Bible there is this difference, that the latter are not for the mutual advantage of each of the parties contracting. While God bound himself in the covenant with Abraham to multiply Abraham's seed and give them the land of Canaan, and while he binds himself now to redeem the people, he himself gains nothing from these actions. All the advantage is on the side of Israel, who on its part has nothing to contribute but its grateful obedience. Between the Bedouin covenants and those of the Bible there is thus a considerable difference, and in consequence G. E. Mendenhall, ' Covenant Forms in Israelite Tradition ', BA 17 (1954), 50–76, thinks rather of the suzerainty treaties which were common in western Asia in the 2nd millennium B.C. He draws attention to six respects in which they show parallels with the Biblical covenants. (*a*) They begin with mention by name of the superior who contracts with his vassal, cf. Exod. 20:1–2 ; Jos. 24:2. (*b*) The great king tells of his benevolent deeds towards his vassal, cf. Exod. 20:2 ; Jos. 24:2–13. (*c*) In the vassal's obligations there is a prohibition against entering into relations with other powers. In the case of the Mosaic covenant, this becomes a prohibition against entering into relationships with other gods, cf. Exod. 20:3. (*d*) The treaty was to be deposited in a sanctuary and publicly rehearsed from time to time, cf. Exod. 25:16, 21f. ; Dt. 31:9–13 ; Jos. 24:26 ; 1 Kg. 8:9. (*e*) Witnesses are invoked, cf. Jos. 24:22. (*f*) Blessings and curses are invoked upon those who keep or break the treaty, cf. Exod. 23:20–2 ; Lev. 26 ; Dt. 27f. ; Jos. 8:34. Mendenhall's explanation seems better to fit the Biblical data. On an extra-Biblical use from the first third of the 14th cent. B.C. of the Hebrew word for a ' covenant ', see W. F. Albright, ' The Hebrew Expression for " Making a Covenant " in pre-Israelite Documents ', BASOR 121 (Feb. 1951), 21f. **6. redeem** : this is the first occurrence in the OT of the thought of God as redeemer. See also 15:13, and Ps. 74:2 ; Isa. 41:14, etc. The word means ' to deliver ', or ' to resume a claim upon ' ; both senses apply here. **8.** The oath to Abraham is referred to in Gen. 24:7.

VI 10-13 and **28-30, VII 1-7 The Commission to Moses and Aaron**—**11.** Moses demands full release for his people, not just the three days' pilgrimage of 3:18 J and 5:1 E. **12 uncircumcised lips** : For similar expressions, see Jer. 6:10, RSVn, the ear, Lev. 26:41 ; Ezek. 44:7, 9, the heart. The figure is generally used of moral or religious defects, but here it is purely physical, the inability to speak well or convincingly, cf. 4:10*b*, ' slow of speech and of tongue '. **28-30** with **VII 1-7** continue 6:2–13. 28–30 repeat 2–12, taking up the narrative interrupted by 14–25, see below. **VII 1.** Moses is to be ' as God to Pharaoh ', that is, he will be in possession of God's authority as he deals with Pharaoh. In 4:16 he is to be as God to Aaron. A prophet is God's spokesman. Whatever the derivation of the word *nābhî'*, prophet, the emphasis is upon speaking, not on prediction. The prophet is ' a man whose organ of speech was thought to be at the disposal of deity. Through the mouth of the prophet, God might announce his will and purpose—might become articulate ' (S. H. Blank, HUCA 15 (1940), 21f.). In **2** ' you ' is emphatic, as ' I ' is in **3**. In 2*a* LXX adds ' to him ', that is to Aaron. **5.** ' The hardness of Pharaoh's heart serves to the glory of God : since the Egyptians realise, when they cannot keep the Israelites any more, the power of Yahweh and the powerlessness of their own gods' (Heinisch). **7.** The age assigned to Moses is too high to be probable, and the figures are schematic, based on forty years, or a generation, in Egypt (cf. Ac. 7:23), a generation in Midian (cf. Ac. 7:30) to be followed by a further generation in the wilderness (cf. Num. 14:33 ; Dt. 2:7 ; Ac. 13:18). g

VI 14-27 The Tribe and Family of Moses—Into the section just noticed has been worked a genealogical list, which is secondary. The motive of the insertion is P's interest in Aaron, Moses' ' prophet ' (7:1). In **14b-16a** (cf. Gen. 46:8–11), Jacob's two eldest sons, Reuben and Simeon, are mentioned only to introduce his third son Levi, with whose descendants the rest of the list deals, since Moses and Aaron were of the tribe of Levi, see on 2:1. A parallel list of the sons of Levi is given in Num. 3, cf. Num. 26:52–61. The line of interest runs from Levi through Kohath and Amram to Moses and Aaron. The list is carried on to include Korah's sons, probably because in later times the Korahites acted as gate-keepers in the Temple (1 Chr. h

181h 9:19, 26:1–9), and the Priestly writers were interested in all that concerned the Temple. That the list does not carry on through the descendants of Moses but through those of Aaron may be due to the fact that tradition (Jg. 18:30) represented the former as heretical. While the list may more or less represent the Levitical families in their relationships after the Exile, the presence of what are most probably Egyptian names, Putiel and Phinehas, and the fact that a marriage such as Amram's with his aunt was forbidden by the later legislation of Lev. 18:12, suggest that we are here in touch with ancient tradition. **14. fathers' houses** : clans. **16.** 'generations' : times, or priority, of birth.

182a **VII 8-13** P **The Sign of Aaron's Rod**—This section goes with 6:2–7:7 rather than with the plagues which follow, because it tells of the dealings of Moses and Aaron with Pharaoh following upon Yahweh's command in 6:10–12 and 7:1–6, and comes from the same hand.

b In 4:1–5, Moses is to perform a similar sign to his own people. In P here the rod is Aaron's, and the action is done to support Moses and Aaron in their demands upon Pharaoh. The word for 'serpent', *tannîn*, here and in vv. 10 and 12 is different from the word used in 4:13 and in 15 below. *Tannîn* is any large reptile, or sea- or river-monster, cf. Gen. 1:21 ; Dt. 32:33, snake, Ps. 74:13, 91:13 ; Ezek. 29:3, 32:2, crocodile. Here the crocodile, which was the symbol of Egypt, may be intended. *Nāḥāsh* in 4:3 is the ordinary serpent. **11f.** The magicians of Egypt are successful in imitating Aaron's action—in them reside the powers of the gods of Egypt, as does the power of the Hebrews' God in Aaron. But the swallowing-up of the Egyptians' rods by Aaron's rod made no impression upon Pharaoh. His 'heart was hardened' (13)—see on 4:21. Jewish tradition (cf. 2 Tim. 3:8), preserved the names of the Egyptian magicians—Jannes and Jambres—and there was an apocryphal book about them. In the lore of magic, there is no record of rods being turned into serpents. But to this day in Egypt, charmers turn snakes into rods, either by pressure on their necks, which renders them rigid, or by sleight of hand, the substitution from a pocket or a fold of the garment of actual rods for snakes, done when the performer has distracted his audience's attention.

c **VII 14-XII 36 The Ten Plagues**—(*a*) The fact that all the three strands, J, E and P, tell of plagues, makes the conclusion inevitable that, however much the account as we have it now has been embellished by the dramatic imagination of later ages, and the miraculous element heightened—we already notice a heightening in E, while in P the wonders are multiplied very greatly—still, the departure from Egypt was accompanied by 'signs and wonders'. 'The traditions have a firm foothold in real events' (Harford).

d (*b*) The plagues are divided thus amongst the sources :

	J	E	P
1	Nile smitten	Nile turned to blood	Nile turned to blood
2	Frogs	——	Frogs
3	——	——	Lice
4	Flies	——	——
5	Murrain	——	——
6	——	——	Boils
7	Hail	Hail	——
8	Locusts	Locusts	——
9	Darkness	Darkness	——
10	First-born	First-born	First-born

The third and fourth plagues, both insect plagues, are possibly duplicates, from J and P, of what was originally one and the same plague. And the same is true of the fifth and sixth, murrain J, boils P—see analysis. Ps. 78:44–51 gives a list of seven plagues corresponding to those of J. Ps. 105:26–36 also seems to give a seven, or perhaps an eight, series.

(*c*) Each source has characteristic formulae and 18
ways of doing the miracles. See CB or Cent. B.

(*d*) The main points of difference between the f
sources are : in J the plagues come about directly from Yahweh after Moses has announced them, in E they come when Moses stretches out his rod or his hand, in P Aaron is the speaker, and it is he who stretches out the rod. P also introduces the magicians of Egypt in competition with Aaron. In J the Hebrews are living apart by themselves in Goshen, but in E they are dwelling amongst the Egyptians. Also, each source has a term of its own for 'plague'.

(*e*) Each plague, except the last, has a basis in g
natural phenomena or diseases which occur in Egypt, either annually or at intervals, between July of one year and April of the next. At the same time, the plagues are regarded as miraculous, even by the Egyptians, partly because of their unusual severity, partly because they come and go as announced beforehand by Moses. What is of importance, however, is not their natural basis, but the connection which the faith of Israel made between them and God. In these, in part, ordinary events, the Israelites saw the hand of God active on their behalf. What we have here is fact plus interpretation. And that remained characteristic of Hebrew thought, especially in the prophets with their interpretation of history (cf. Isa. 10:5–15), and in the Deuteronomic historians (cf. 2 Kg. 17:7–23). 'The faith of the OT can be understood only when we see the influence which the history exercised upon the fashioning of the faith, and, conversely, the OT history will be fully understood only when we push our analysis to the point where the forces exerted by faith are recognised as factors in the forming of the history and are taken into account' (A. Weiser, *Glaube und Geschichte im Alten Testament* (1931), 2f.).

(*f*) Drama, a characteristic of J, and dramatic h
progress, are apparent in the story. 'The first four plagues produce annoyance and distress ; the next four inflict serious damage to property and person ; the ninth is mysterious and terrifying. Moses, at first courteous, becomes more and more outspoken ; Pharaoh, at first indifferent, shows an increasing disposition to temporise and to yield ; his magicians confess their impotence at the third plague and are unable to appear at the sixth ; his courtiers advise surrender at the eighth' (*A Catholic Commentary on Holy Scripture*).

VII 14-24 (**14-15a** to 'meet him' J ; **15b** E ; **16-17a** J ; i
17b, 'with the rod . . . hand', E ; **17c-18** J ; **19-20a**, 'commanded', P ; **20b** to 'servants' E ; **20c-21ab** J ; **21c-22** P ; **23** E ; **24** J) **The First Plague : Water turned into Blood**—In order that Pharaoh may begin to recognise the power of Yahweh (17), Moses and Aaron go to meet him at the Nile bank. Why he is there is not stated. It may have been to bathe. Or, more probably, to worship the river-god. In any case, Moses meets him at the river upon which Egypt depends for its very existence. Without the inundations of the Nile Egypt would be desert. And this river, which sustains the life of Egypt, Moses is about to threaten. As a result of the smiting—notice how P magnifies the miracle to include all the waters of Egypt—the Nile turned red, the water became undrinkable, and the fish, a staple article of Egyptian diet, died. Normally, in June or July, at the inundation, the Nile water becomes dirty red, through the soil carried down, then for a short time green, due to the presence of vegetable matter, then again red, and finally back to white. During this stage it is called by the natives the Red Nile. But normally the water remains drinkable, and the fish do not die. It is the intensification of the natural phenomena to include these unwonted happenings that constitutes the miracle. P makes the magicians of Egypt do the same miracle. But the representation is artificial, since P already (19) thinks of *all* the waters as contaminated.

15. the rod (E) is brought into connection with the j
rod given to Moses in 4:3 J. **17b.** 'I', that is,

182j Yahweh (cf. 25), but in 20 it is Moses who strikes. The variation in person could be due to the conflation of the different sources, but there is also truth in what Heinish says: 'since the prophet is commissioned by Yahweh, what God says often passes over into what the prophet says, and *vice versa*'. **19. rivers**: the Nile and its arms. **20. he lifted up**: not as by implication from 19 P, Aaron, but, since this is from E, Moses.

k **VII 25-VIII 15** (**25** J, **8:1-4** J, **5-7** P, **8-15a**, to 'his heart', J, **15b** P) **The Second Plague: Frogs from the Nile**—Frogs accompany the inundation of the Nile, though only on occasion are they so numerous as to be a plague. What constitutes the miracle here is their numbers, the fact that they are not brought into contact with the Nile flood but come and disappear at Moses' behest, and that they are everywhere in the land. Why Pharaoh should begin to be impressed by this second plague when he was unmoved by the first is not stated. Perhaps the reason is that, as the saga was recounted orally, at every fresh blow the Egyptians had to give a little, and gradually be brought to realise that 'there is no one like the Lord our God' (10). That the frogs died at the time appointed was a sign to Pharaoh not only of the power of Yahweh, but also of Moses' authority as his spokesman. But when Pharaoh saw that 'the respite had come' (so better in 15)—the respite promised in 11—he 'hardened his heart', as had been foretold in 4:21ff. **VIII 3 ovens**: earthenware stoves. **12. gathered**: piled.

l **VIII 16-19** P **The Third Plague: Gnats**—Egypt, especially the Delta, suffers from mosquitoes more or less all the year round, but they are at their worst during and just after the inundation, while the fields are still flooded, and rise from their breeding-grounds like clouds of dust. The ancients believed that they were self-generated (cf. Verg. *Geo.* iv, 197–209 for the same belief about bees). In actual fact the eggs and larvae develop in the standing water. The miracle here then may be that the mosquitoes arise from the dry ground. This may also be the reason why, this time, the magicians are unable to imitate. Notice, as the next step in the unfolding of the clash between Yahweh and Pharaoh, that the magicians now admit that there is divine power over which they have no disposal at work in Moses and Aaron.

183a **20-32** J **The Fourth Plague: Flies**—This plague looks like J's version of the previous plague, P. The kind of fly is not specified. The Hebrew word, which occurs again only in the sequel here and in Ps. 78:45 and 105:31, in allusion to this plague, comes from a root meaning 'to mix'. 'It expresses the idea either of incessant involved motion in a dense swarm, or more probably a large number of varieties of insect' (McNeile). LXX renders 'dog-fly' and Vulg. 'flies of every kind'. Since ordinary flies are in such numbers in Egypt as to be a pest—Isaiah (7:18, perhaps also 18:1) characterises the land by means of them—the miracle here probably lies in the fact that the Israelites who dwelt apart in the land of Goshen were exempt. The drama heightens. Moses is much more forthright with Pharaoh than hitherto: 'let my people go' (20), and Pharaoh is now ready to meet his demand in part at any rate. The Hebrews may now offer the sacrifice (5:1) that has caused all the trouble, although they may not make the three days' journey into the wilderness (3:18, 5:3). They are to sacrifice 'within the land' (25). Moses' refusal of this condition (26) was an excuse based on the fact that the Hebrews sacrificed animals such as cows, sheep and goats, that were sacred to the Egyptians. If such were offered on Egyptian soil, there would be the danger of a popular riot; cf. Herod. ii, 38, 41, 42, 46. Pharaoh recognises the force of the argument, and makes a further concession (28), which of course, as always when the danger is over, he withdraws. As in 8:8, he acknowledges the power of Yahweh (28*b*). **23 division**: so better than Heb. 'set redemption'.

b **IX 1-7** J **The Fifth Plague: Rinderpest**—Cattle plagues are rare in Egypt, though severe when they do 183b occur. The mention of camels is, in spite of Gen. 12:16, 24:10 ff., etc., an anachronism, for there is evidence that the camel was not yet domesticated in Egypt in the 13th cent. B.C. As in the previous plague, the Hebrews are again spared. Since cattle belonging to the Egyptians are mentioned subsequently (19, 21, 11:5, 12:29, 13:5), 'all' in 6, if it is not just folklore exaggeration, is to be taken either as 'a very large number'—Hertz compares the phrase, '*all* the world knows'—or as meaning that while the animals at pasture, 'in the field' (3), were killed, those still in the farmyard escaped. In the Delta cattle are taken to pasture and kept there from January to April.

8-12 P **The Sixth Plague: Boils**—Diseases of c the skin are common in Egypt; cf. Dt. 28:27. The particular disease here is not stated. Some have thought of leprosy, and others of the Nile-scab, small red blisters which often break out in summer. Notice that the magicians are now not only powerless, as at 8:18 (also P), but are themselves infected with the plague. The fact that the cattle are infected suggests that this sixth plague is P's parallel to J's fifth plague. Gressmann, however, thinks that in the original form of the incident, the soot thrown towards heaven was intended to bring on thick darkness. So he holds that this plague is P's parallel rather to the ninth, J and E. **8, 10** 'ashes': rather, soot.

13-35 (**13-21** J; **22-23a**, to 'heaven', E; **23b** J; d **24a**, to 'midst of the hail', E; **24b-30** J; **31-32** E?; **33-34** J; **35ab** E; **35c** R) **The Seventh Plague: Hailstones**—This plague and the two which follow have in common that the trouble comes from above. So they are symbolically brought on by Moses' raising his hand towards heaven, 22, 10:21 and, by inference, 10:12. Hailstorms, with thunder and lightning, are not common in Egypt, but they do occur sometimes in the early months of the year. January or February would seem to be suggested here, since barley is in the ear then and flax buds (31), while the wheat and spelt are not yet up (32). Flax was used for making linen, especially for garments for the priests. Spelt, Heb. *kussemeth*, only again Isa. 28:25 and Ezek. 4:9, may be vetch, as Jerome takes it to be.

Into the announcement of the plague (13, 17–18) e are worked verses designed to explain why God continued to allow Pharaoh, who had already twice broken his word—the frogs and the flies—to live, when he could have destroyed him at any time. The reason is (16) that Pharaoh may be shown God's power (cf. v. 14), and that God's 'name may be declared throughout all the earth' (cf. Rom. 9:17). **20** suggests, as a further stage in the drama, that there is now division in the court circles of Egypt due to the plagues, a division which is about to turn into active opposition to the royal policy (10:7). And although in the sequel Pharaoh again hardens his heart, even already he is willing to concede Moses' demand, since 'I will let you go' (29) seems to mean allowing the people to go for ever rather than a temporary absence. But it is a concession made because of his anguish, and not through any fear of God, as Moses is well aware (30). **14. all my plagues upon your heart**: 'all' suggests that 14–16 are editorial, since only one plague is dealt with here. 'Upon your heart' is not clear. Read with Baentsch 'upon you'. **24.** 'fire': that is, lightning. **25.** See last sentence of notes on ch. 11. **31f.** break the connection. They were probably inserted to explain why the locusts of the next plague could still find something to eat after the devastation of the hail. 'Are late in coming up': Heb. concealed; that is, still in the ground, unsprouted.

X 1-20 (**1-11** J (**1bc-2** Rd); **12-13a**, to 'Egypt', E; f **13b** J; **14a** E; **14b** 'and rested' to **15a** 'darkened', J; **15b**, to 'left', E; **15c-19** J; **20** E) **The Eighth Plague: Locusts**—For vivid descriptions of locusts, see Jl 2, and Driver in *Joel*, CB, and Sir G. A. Smith, *The Book of the Twelve Prophets*, ii, 398ff. They attack Egypt only infrequently, but travellers

183f tell of clouds of them brought up by the wind, then carried away again when the wind changes. Another new feature appears with this plague. Pharaoh's courtiers, terrified by this fresh threat, and losing patience because of all the disasters that have already fallen upon the land, demand that the king grant the Hebrews' request. Pharaoh makes a partial concession. The men, whose presence alone was necessary at the feast (cf. 23:17, 34:23; Dt. 15:16) may go, but they only. After the plague he humbles himself as after that of hail (9:27). But once again, the danger over, he hardens his heart.

1bc-2 is an expansion in the style of D ; cf. Dt. 4:9, 6:7. **Made sport of** : ' an anthropomorphism which is not consistent with the higher Christian conceptions of God ' (McNeile). **10.** Pharaoh's words are, of course, ironical. **13.** For the wind as Yahweh's instrument in J again, see 14:21 ; Num. 11:31. **17.** death : since the locusts' devastations would lead to famine.

g **21-29** (**21-23** E ; **24-26** J ; **27** E ; **28-29** J) **The Ninth Plague : Darkness**—The Khamsin, a hot wind from the desert containing an immense quantity of particles of sand which darken the atmosphere, blows intermittently in Egypt in March and April, and sometimes into May. It usually lasts only three or four days, but since it occurs within a period of fifty days, it takes its name from the Arabic *khamsin*, fifty. The miraculous element here lies in the timing—the darkness comes at Moses' command. As well, ' what causes terror for the Egyptians in the plague described here is the fact that in the darkness they saw evil spirits at work which brought all kinds of illnesses, and death itself, amongst them ' (Kees, quoted by Beer). As a result of the darkness, Pharaoh makes a concession which is more generous than that of vv. 8–11 : *all* the people may go (24). But he is not yet completely conquered, since the flocks and the herds must be left behind. On the other hand, as he shrinks in stature, Moses grows. He is not only insistent that the Hebrews' cattle go with them, but he demands that the Pharaoh must go further and actually himself provide other cattle for sacrificial victims, since, Moses says, until they reach the place of sacrifice, they do not know how many animals will be needed ! (For an offering, one of each kind would have been enough —is Moses now mocking the powerlessness of Pharaoh?) **21. a darkness to be felt** : lit., so that one may feel darkness. The sand and dust particles would make the atmosphere sensible to the touch and the skin. For the fearsomeness of this time of darkness, see Wis. 17:1–18:4, 23. As in 8:22, 9:26 (cf. 9:4), and 18:18, the part of Egypt where the Hebrews lived was exempt. 25. sacrifices : Heb. *z^ebhāḥîm*, the general sacrifices, part of which was burnt upon the altar for the deity to receive as his share, while part was eaten by the worshippers to symbolise their communion with him and with one another. Burnt offerings, *'ôlôth*, were completely consumed upon the altar. **28. never see my face again** : Moses does see Pharaoh again, 11:4–8. Evidently 11:4–8 were originally part of this section, and the insertion 11:1–3 of material from E has broken the connection.

184a **XI** (**1-3** E ; **4-8** J ; **9-10** Rp) **The Tenth Plague, its Announcement : Death of the First-born**—**1-3,** the continuation of 10:27 E, break the sequence, while **4-8** follow immediately upon 10:29, and give the end of the final interview with Pharaoh. Moses announces to Pharaoh that Yahweh will slay the first-born of the Egyptians. ' Each night, according to Egyptian mythology, the sun fought and overcame the snake, Apophis, who symbolised the hostile darkness. As a god, Pharaoh was an incarnation of the sun, and the hostile darkness was his enemy also. The force of Moses' announcement is that the night is at hand when the customary victory, on which the existence of Egypt depends, will not take place ' (IB, summarising H. and H. A. Frankfort, in *Intellectual Adventure of Ancient Man*, 24). As a result of this final stroke, Pharaoh will ' drive ' the Hebrews ' away completely '. 18

2-3a See on 3:21f., 12:35f. **3b** adds another reason why the Egyptians granted the Hebrews' request—the prestige now accruing to Moses, due to the wonders he had done and the sufferings he had brought upon Egypt. **5.** The grinding of the daily corn for making bread was the most menial of tasks, often done by slaves or prisoners-of-war ; cf. Jg. 16:21 ; Isa. 47:2. The first-born of the cattle ; see 9:6. **7. growl** : lit., whet his tongue, a proverbial expression ; cf. Jos. 10:21, ; Jdt. 11:19. **8.** Pharaoh's courtiers no longer try to move him, as in 10:7, but, disregarding him, address themselves directly to Moses. **9-10** are editorial and summarise. **10** does not refer to the death of the first-born, which comes first in 13:29ff., but to the previous plagues. We may notice that this plague is the first threat to human life, in spite of 9:25, where ' man ' has nothing to support it in the context.

XII 1-13 P **Rules for the Passover, First Series**— b
Three rites are made to derive their origin from the Exodus, the Passover, the Feast of Unleavened Bread, and the Dedication of the First-born to Yahweh.

On the history of the Passover, see §213*b*. c
' Passover is universally recognised to have been a ritual observance native to the Hebrews, practised by them before the settlement in Canaan ' (Welch, *Prophet and Priest in Old Israel* (1936), 39f.). It may have been a lunar feast, intended to promote the increase of flocks and herds. But under the influence of the Exodus, its character was completely changed ; see especially on v. 23. In the Biblical tradition, it is brought into close connection with the feast for which Moses asked permission to make a three days' journey into the wilderness, 5:3, 8:27. But originally the two were distinct. Passover was a family festival, celebrated in the home, while the other was a community act, and required pilgrimage (*ḥagh*) to a shrine. ' Throughout the entire OT the technical term of *ḥagh* is never applied to Passover ' (Welch, op. cit., 40).

The clash between Yahweh and Pharaoh, now d
hastening to its climax, is interrupted by the Priestly narrators, who wish to give rules for the celebration of the Passover and the Feast of Unleavened Bread which will be valid for all time, and to stress the connection of these feasts with the tenth plague and the deliverance from Egypt. There may be an historical kernel here. It is possible that the Hebrews took advantage of an epidemic affecting Egyptian children to make their escape. But a popular and dramatic motif is also at work. At the beginning, Pharaoh did not spare the first-born of Israel ; now, when Egypt is at its wits' end because of the plagues (10:7), Israel's God will not spare those who, represented by their monarch, have not only opposed him, but so often broken their promises to him. So the first-born of Egypt must now be killed ; cf. 4:23. ' The origins of the Paschal ritual are wrapped in obscurity, but as Frazer says, " the one thing that looms clear through the haze of this weird tradition is the memory of a great massacre of the first-born " ' (James, op. cit., 157).

The Exodus is so much the constitutive event for e
Israel that it is represented as inaugurating a new calendar, from which all the subsequent national history was to be dated (2). The Hebrews had two systems of reckoning the year, one which made it begin in the autumn, at the end of the harvest (cf. 23:16, 34:22), another, as here, which made it begin in the spring, when the first ripe ears of corn appeared. The Babylonian year also began in the spring. But whether the change in the Hebrew way of reckoning was made under Babylonian influence is not apparent. The present verse may be an attempt to give the sanction of antiquity to what was in fact an exilic or post-exilic innovation. By J and E (13:4, 23:18, 34:18) and D (16:1) the first month is called *Abib*, the month of growing corn, March–April. In certain post-exilic writings (Neh. 2:1, ; Est. 3:7) it is called by its Babylonian name of Nisan. But the Priestly editors

184e avoid names for the months, and prefer to call them 'first, second', etc. See further art. *Times*, etc.

f In 2, 'you' means the whole people, not just Moses and Aaron. The 'congregation' (3) is P's regular designation of Israel as an organised religious community, which was led by the elders (16:22), a projection backwards of the post-exilic age, when the nation became a church.

g The Passover is to be a family festival. 'Even when in post-exilic times it was celebrated in Jerusalem and the victims were slain in the Temple (i.e. until A.D. 70) and the blood was offered at the altar by the priests, small groups of ten to twenty of the pilgrims assembled for the sacred communal meal with its prescribed ingredients and procedures' (James, op. cit., 160). 'The original unit from which the community grows (die Urzelle der Gemeinde) is for P—and here he preserves what is primitive—the family, the house, the tent-community' (Beer). In the early period, too, the officiant is the head of the household. 'The *pesach* was the one rite which needed no priest, no temple, no altar' (R. K. Yerkes, *Sacrifice in Greek and Roman Religion and Early Judaism* (1953), 85). Only, practical considerations were to be taken into account (4). Women, children, the aged and the infirm would eat less than the normal adult male. According to later usage, the minimum for a household was ten (Jos. B.J., ix, 33). Why the victim, a lamb or a kid—for the Heb. word includes both sheep and goats, hence RVm (cf. 5:5)—was to be selected on the tenth day (3), though not eaten till the 14th, is not given. Perhaps it had to be examined, or in some way made 'holy'. 'Both the Athenian Bouphonia and the Magnesian bull festival had the same requirement' (Yerkes, op. cit., 84). **6. In the evening**: lit., 'between the two evenings', a technical expression of P, the exact meaning of which is uncertain. The Pharisees and the Talmud held that the time meant was from about 3 p.m., when the heat of the sun begins to lessen, until sunset. The Sadducees, the Samaritans and the Ḳaraites, the 8th cent. A.D. sect, believed the words to signify 'from sunset to darkness'. Dt. 16:6 orders the sacrifices to take place at sunset. The fact that all the heads of the household slew the victim at the same time gave the feast a communal as well as a family character. **7.** The original purpose of the sprinkling of the blood on the doorposts and the lintel, a usage found in ancient Babylon and in Palestine of the present day, and which may go back to palaeolithic times, was to ward off the attacks of spirits and demons; see further on 21ff. The flesh was to be roasted (8f.), possibly as the quickest way of cooking it. It was not to be eaten raw, because the eating of the blood, in which the life-force was thought to reside, was forbidden; see Lev. 7:26f., 17:10 ff. But the prohibition against boiling is less easy to understand, since sacrifices of which the worshippers partook —and Passover was one of them—were generally boiled (cf. Lev. 6:28; Num. 6:19; 1 Sam. 2:15, etc.), and Dt. (16:7) does in fact prescribe boiling for the Passover lamb. Beer suggests a primitive survival, roasting being the oldest form, since nomads would not always have water available. The oldest form of sacrificial participation among the Arabs was eating the flesh raw (Holzinger). 'The prohibition forbidding the eating of the flesh raw is evidence that originally the flesh was eaten raw, the purpose of the sacred meal being that of imbibing sacramentally the inherent vitality of the victim, as in the Arabic camel sacrifice described by Nilus in the 5th cent. A.D.' (James, op. cit., 157).

h **8.** The unleavened cakes (Heb., plural) were a kind of biscuit which could be baked quickly. In Dt. 16:3 they are called 'the bread of affliction' and brought into relation with the hardness of the bondage in Egypt. Originally they were independent of Passover; see below on *Mazzoth*.

i **8.** The 'bitter herbs' were, according to the Mishnah, lettuce, chicory, pepperwort, snakeroot, and dandelion (*Pesahim*, 2:6, Danby). These suggest a festival held 184i in spring, almost certainly originally independent of Passover. But the term for 'bitter herbs' (Heb. *m^erōrîm*), was connected with the Egyptians' making of the lives of the Hebrews bitter, the same root as in 1:14 (*y^emār^erû*). Of the food, nothing was to be left over till the morning; cf. Dt. 16:4, also Passover, and Lev. 7:15. The motive was to avoid the profanation of flesh which was sacred, and burning was the simplest way of disposal. Those who partook were to eat 'in haste', better 'in trepidation' (11). Their robes were to be fastened as for a journey, and they were to have their sandals already on as for a journey, instead of lying at the door, where they were normally left upon coming into a house. According to *Pes.* 9:5, this eating in trepidation belonged only to the first celebration—the text belongs to the historicising of the primitive rite. But 'eating "on the run" and the removal of every trace of a meal suggest early nomadic or agricultural days when proximity of enemies frequently gave little opportunity for eating and necessitated removal of all traces of the performance in order to make pursuit more difficult' (Yerkes, op. cit., 86). The whole proceedings were a 'passover' to Yahweh. The term is explained in **13.** The root *pāsaḥ* in the sense of to 'pass over' is otherwise unknown. It may be connected with *pāsaḥ*, to limp, 1 Kg. 18:21, 26, or with Akkadian *pasāḫu*, to be soothed (see Driver's Appendix, CB). **12.** The fact that the gods of Egypt are powerless to protect their own devotees shows that they have no power over against Yahweh.

14-20 P Mazzoth, or the Feast of Unleavened 185a **Cakes**—Originally the Feast of Unleavened Cakes was an agricultural festival, in celebration of the beginning of the barley harvest. It was to last seven days. **14.** 'This day' is not the 14th of Nisan, Passover, but the 15th, the first day of Mazzoth, which ran till the 21st. Originally Mazzoth was distinct from Passover, the latter being pastoral and the former agricultural. But they are now attached together in the tradition. When the two festivals became one is not known, but it was certainly after the time when the celebration of Passover was transferred to the sanctuary, for from the beginning Mazzoth was a pilgrimage feast (*ḥagh*) and Passover was not, see §184*c*. The union was no doubt due to the fact that both festivals were celebrated at approximately the same time, and that *mazzoth* had been connected with Passover (8). '*Mazzoth* belong to the daily food of the nomad or the semi-nomad. But at this festival they are prescribed as the only food' (Beer). The eating of them, and the assembly, when work ceased, on the 1st and 7th days, are what gives the festival its special character. **15.** Leaven was prohibited either as something which produced corruption or as an antique survival, the relic of a time when it was not in use. No sacrifice offered at the altar might contain it, 23:18 E, 34:25 J; Lev. 2:11 P. But in Lev. 7:13 leavened bread is offered. For leaven as signifying corruption, see Mt. 16:5ff.; 1 Cor. 5:7; Gal. 5:9 (AV, RV). Violation of the prohibition against the eating of leaven at Mazzoth involved being 'cut off' (15:19), a common formula of P meaning excommunication; cf. Ezr. 10:8. In **16** 'assembly' means at a sanctuary. That is, P is legislating not for the immediate present, the Exodus, when no sanctuary was available, but for future generations, as 17 says. **17-20** repeat, and are almost certainly from another hand. 17 looks back on the Exodus as a thing of the past. **19.** The 'sojourner' too is forbidden to eat what is leavened, since there was to be no leaven in the land: **in your houses** (19) is a standing phrase of P for 'throughout the land'.

XII 21-28 (21-27 J, 28 P) Rules for the Passover, b **Second Series. The Passover in Egypt**—This section does not represent the carrying-out of the rules given in 1–14, but is an independent account, from J, of the institution of the feast. It omits nearly all of the actions prescribed in 1–14, but adds other details, the

185b hyssop, the basin, the confinement to the house. Its interest is in the manipulation of the blood. And it allows us to see how the pre-Mosaic feast was transformed and adapted to the Yahweh faith. Originally the feast had been one to propitiate a destructive demon, the 'destroyer' (24). Yahweh is not substituted for the demon, but 'it is expressly stated that Yahweh shall deliver Israel from its fear of the destroyer. . . . Instead of being the night of the destroyer's power, it has become the night of Yahweh's power : as such it is a night much to be remembered in Israel, because then its God came down to deliver his own. . . . The character of the rite was changed precisely because the character of the deity who was recognised in it had become different. Certain obstinate features of the old ritual were continued. . . . The daubing of door-post and lintel with the protective blood had its significance as long as the destroyer was central in the thought of the people, but it was hopelessly incongruent with the thought of the advent of Him who came to redeem Israel from Egypt. So it was supplied with the lame interpretation that when Yahweh went abroad through the land of Egypt, He should by its presence be able to distinguish the homes of the Israelites' (Welch, op. cit., 90 f.). **22a.** Hyssop is a species of marjoram growing in walls and rocks (1 Kg. 4:33), and was used in purification rites (Lev. 14:4–6 ; Num. 19:6, 18 ; Ps. 51:7). Its twigs are pliant, adapted for sprinkling. 'in the basin' : LXX, 'by the threshold'. The lamb was probably slaughtered at the threshold, where there may have been a special hollow to catch the blood. IB quotes reports of H. Oort on Armenian miniatures which depict the slaying in this manner. **22b.** To leave the protected house would have been dangerous : one could be attacked by the demon-destroyer. **24** is possibly an addition. J's account probably concluded with 27*b*, 'and the people bowed their heads and worshipped'—'in acknowledgment of the promise of protection and deliverance given in vv. 21–23' (Driver). **25-27a** are a duplication, reminiscent of the style of D, from which they may come. They are didactic, and stress the historical meaning of the Passover, and its perpetual obligation. The command in 26f. is still observed today. 'The youngest child present asks the questions, which are answered by a recitation of the events that culminated in the original institution of the Passover' (Hertz). The questions are : 'Why do we eat only unleavened bread ? Why do we eat bitter herbs ? Why do we dip the vegetables twice ? Why do we preserve a certain posture ?' The feast is a reminder both to the Jewish community and the Christian church that they owe their existence not to themselves, but to a mighty and gracious act of God.

c **29-32** J **Death of the First-born of Egypt**—These verses are the sequel to the threat made in 11:4f., J. Epidemics are frequent in Egypt in the spring. The miraculous element in this tenth plague lies in the facts that only the children of the Egyptians suffered, and that of them only the first-born were affected. (Originally, was it only the first-born of Pharaoh himself who was slain ?) According to 10:28, Pharaoh had resolved not to see Moses again. But it is not necessary to think of a different strand of the tradition now. Pharaoh's anguish as to what had happened could easily have led him to the change of conduct. **31b.** Does Pharaoh still think of only a temporary absence, as against 31*a* ?

d **33-36** (**33f.** J, **35f.** E) **The Departure**—The people of Egypt were now eager to make into a state order what was originally a request on the part of state slaves (5:3), the refusal of which by their sovereign had led on, through the annoyances and disasters of the first nine plagues, to this culminating disaster of the tenth. **34** (and **39,** also J) give the traditional explanation of the *Mazzoth* festival : the Israelites had not time to leaven their dough because of the haste with which they were expelled, a view different from that of 1–20. **35f.** show that the instructions given in 3:21f. 18
and 11:2–3*a* had already been carried out.

(B) From Egypt to Sinai (XII 37-XVIII)

e **XII 37-39** J **The Exodus**—On Rameses, see 1:11 note. Succoth, about 30 miles from Rameses. 13:17 notes that the Israelites did not travel by 'the way of the land of the Philistines', which was the main road to Canaan parallel to the sea-coast. It was too well guarded by Egyptian troops. They went southwards, and came to Succoth, the present Tell el-Maskhûṭah, in the Wâdī Ṭumilât (BASOR (1948) 109). Their numbers, 600,000 (cf. Num. 11:21), are impossible : a total population of between two and three millions would be implied. Had they been so many, they could easily have risen in revolt against Pharaoh, since at the battle of Kadesh, where Rameses II brought up his whole force against the Hittites, he had only about 20,000 men. Nor does the number square with 23:29, which implies that the Israelites were not numerous enough to populate Canaan all at once. In spite of Num. 1:46 P and 26:51 P, 600,000 is an ideal figure, arrived at by *Gematria*, the use of the consonants for numbers. The value of the consonants in the Hebrew words for 'the children of Israel' gives 603 × 1,000 = 603,000, which is roughly 600,000 (Beer). **38. the mixed multitude** : it consisted probably of connections by marriage (cf. Lev. 42:10), and other Semitic minorities, perhaps slaves also, living on the frontier land. Flinders Petrie reckons that the Heb. *'eleph* means here not thousands, but families, and reckons those who went out as about 5,500 (*Egypt and Israel* (1925), 42ff.). But his view has won little acceptance.

f **40-42** (**40f.** P, **42** addition ?) **The Length of the Sojourn in Egypt**—The length of the sojourn is given here as 430 years ; cf. the 400 years in Gen. 15:13 ; Ac. 7:6 ; Jos. Ant. II, ix, 1, B.J. v. 9. This figure cannot be brought into agreement with other P passages such as 6:16, 18, 21 ; Num. 14:1, 26:7–9 ; Lev. 10:4, which represent Moses as being in the fourth generation from the sons of Jacob—unless, of course, P here represents a generation as 100 years ; cf. Gen. 15, where cf. 13 with 16. LXX, Sam. read here, 'in the land of Egypt and in the land of Canaan', i.e. from the time of Abraham's entry into Canaan until the Exodus, a clear attempt to lessen the difficulty. **42.** Possibly an addition. **A night of watching to the Lord,** i.e. a night when Yahweh kept vigil over his people. Therefore his people were in their turn to observe the festival for ever.

g **43-50** P **Further Rules for the Passover**—The question at issue here is, under what conditions were non-Israelites to eat the Passover. The section is probably due to the mention of the 'mixed multitude' in 38. 'That nationality and religion were one in antiquity is especially clear in connection with the high occasions of public life, the festivals' (Beer). The general rule (43) is that no foreigner (*nēkher*, member of a foreign community who worships another god, and who is in Israel as, perhaps, a trader) is to partake. This regulation is further defined in 45: the 'foreign settler' (so render *tôshābh* rather than 'sojourner'), who was perhaps one who enjoyed the protection of an Israelite, is debarred, unless, presumably, he accepted the condition of circumcision imposed upon the stranger (*gēr*) in 48. Nor is the hired servant to partake : his residence would probably be temporary, and he could not therefore be reckoned as belonging to the family. A 'foreigner' (*gēr*, referring perhaps especially to the native Canaanite population) could eat, provided he let himself become a technical Israelite ; cf. Gen. 17:12f. **46f.** break the unity of the narrative, but they are inserted to reinforce the unity of those who celebrate the feast. Though families may club together, the one lamb must be eaten in the one house ; no part of it is to be taken away by those who join the household where the feast was

5g celebrated ; no bone of the lamb was to be broken, unity again ; and no Israelite was to fail to eat. It is uniformity expressing solidarity. **51** is repeated from 41 to conclude the section.

6a **XIII (1-2 P ; 3-16 J**, with additions from D ; **17-19** E ; **20** P ? ; **21-22** J) **The Setting-apart of the First-born to Yahweh**—P (1f.) gives here a summary statement of the law which he sets forth more fully in Num. 3:11–13, 40–45, 18:15–18. It is a law noticed by all the strands. But they vary in the details of its application. Here, P, *all* the first-born are to be set apart to Yahweh. In J (12f., 34:19f.) and E (22:29f.) only the first-born *males* are dedicated. Of them, the first-born of men are ransomed, the firstlings of clean animals, which could be offered in sacrifice, were to be killed, the ass, as an unclean animal which could not therefore be offered in sacrifice, was either to be redeemed with a lamb, which was of less value than an ass, or killed. In D (Dt. 15:10–23) all male firstlings that were unblemished were to be offered in sacrifice at the central sanctuary, and the flesh eaten by the offerer and his household. In P (Num. 18:15–18) the first-born of men and unclean beasts were to be redeemed, those of clean beasts sacrificed. But in P the flesh falls not to the offerer, but to the priests. According to Num. 3:11–13, 40–51, at the census in the wilderness, the Levites were taken by Yahweh in place of the first-born of the rest of the tribes. The origin of the custom of sacrificing the first-born is not known. But it was a widely adopted usage among Semitic peoples, and the bodies of children discovered in the foundations of many Canaanite buildings are no doubt due to it. The child-offering was thought to give strength or permanence to the building. J and P however, in line with the denaturalising, historicising tendencies of the OT, give it an historic ground. For J (13:15) it is a commemoration of the slaying of the first-born of Egypt, while P (Num. 3:13, 8:17) says that on that occasion Yahweh consecrated as his own all the first-born of Israel.

b **3-10** J **Laws for Mazzoth**—These verses are, with editorial additions from a Deuteronomic redactor, J's version of the *Mazzoth* regulations already given by P (12:14–20), with certain variations. The main points of difference between the two accounts are these. The month is here called by its old Canaanite name of Abib (cf. 23:15, 34:18 ; Dt. 16:1), a designation which P avoids, preferring ‘ the first month ’ ; cf. 12:2 (q.v.), 18. For J the chief day of the feast, the *hagh*, is the seventh (6), and not the first (12:14). There is no mention here of a ‘ holy assembly ’ with ceasing of work. On **5**, cf. 3:8, 6:8. **8.** The children are to be taught the meaning of the observance ; cf. 12:26f., 13:14, also Jos. 4:6f. **9.** The clause, ‘ the law of the Lord may be in your mouth ’, is a later addition, unsuitable to the context, which is the deliverance from Egypt. **A sign upon your hand** : like a man's signet ring. **A memorial between your eyes** : many primitive races tattoo or brand a mark upon the body in symbol of their devotion to their god. But it is figurative here, and for Israel the eating of the unleavened bread is to be the equivalent. Later, under the influence of Dt. 6:8 and 11:18, the passages Exod. 13:1–10, 11:1–6 ; Dt. 6:4–9, 11:13–21 were written on small scrolls of parchment and put in cases and bound with leather straps to the brow and the left arm. They were the *Tephillîn*, the Prayers, the phylacteries of Mt. 23:5. ‘ These four sections have been chosen in preference to all the other passages of the Torah, because they embrace the acceptance of the Kingdom of Heaven, the unity of the Creator, and the Exodus from Egypt—fundamental doctrines of Judaism (*Sefer ha-Chinuth*, quoted Hertz).

c **11-16** (J, with additions from a Deuteronomic redactor) **The Law of the First-born**—As with Passover (12:27) and Mazzoth (13:3, 8), the consecration of the first-born is brought into connection with the tenth plague and the deliverance from Egypt. But the details of the motivation are somewhat confused. 186c
12:11ff. connect Passover with the smiting of the first-born of the Egyptians, while 12:27 connects it with the sparing of Israel. Mazzoth is generally linked with the bringing-forth from Egypt, 12:17, 13:8f. The setting-apart of the first-born commemorates the slaying of the first-born of the Egyptians, 13:15.

12 The first half of the verse gives the general regulation : every first-born is the property of Yahweh. d
Set apart : lit. cause to pass over, Heb. *he‘ebhîr* : it is the word used also for sacrificing children to Molech, 2 Kg. 16:3 ; Ezek. 20:31, etc. Since the Canaanite practice, resorted to on occasion certainly, was abhorrent to Israel, it is unlikely that the term was borrowed from them. The usages of the two peoples were quite different. Though in Israel the first-born were to be set apart to Yahweh as his, they were not to be given to him by sacrifice, but they were to be ‘ ransomed ’ from him, a term which could suggest that they were sacrificed in theory, though not in actual fact. **13.** The ass, which seems to be the one unclean household animal, could not be sacrificed, because it was unclean. If it was not redeemed with a lamb, its neck was to be broken—that would not involve the shedding of blood, and therefore not sacrifice. The price of the redemption of the first-born of human beings, which is not stated here, was later fixed at 5 shekels, Num. 18:15f., P.

17-20 (**17-19** E, **20** P) **The Route of the Exodus**— e
The main caravan and military road from Egypt, the ‘ way of the land of the Philistines ’, led from Memphis via Pelusium and el-‘Arîsh to Gaza, running practically parallel to the Mediterranean coast, after passing the frontier-post of Zilu. This road, though the shortest to Canaan, was not only too strongly fortified for the Israelites to have had hope of passing through by it, but the route would have brought them immediately face to face with the Canaanites, who were much better armed than they. Especially, the Canaanites knew the use of chariots, which the Israelites did not. Also, they had to get used to the idea that they were free men, and lose their slave-mentality. So they turned southwards to the Wâdī Ṭumilât and to Succoth, and then by ‘ the way of the wilderness ’ towards the Red Sea (but see below).

The older and common identification of the waters f
through which the Israelites passed dry-shod must now be given up. The present Red Sea is not in question. The Heb. *Yam Sûph* is ‘ the sea of Reeds ’, the Papyrus Sea. And not only are there no reeds by the Red Sea, but excavations have made it clear that Pi-Hahiroth (14:1) is to be located not far from the modern Qanṭarah. ‘ The crossing of the sea was made at a point not far from Rameses. Since the Suez Canal was constructed, the topography of the district between the Gulf of Suez and Lake Menzaleh on the Mediterranean has been changed somewhat, and at least one lake, the former Lake Balah, has disappeared. The Reed Sea which the Israelites crossed was probably in this area, perhaps at a southern extension of the present Lake Menzaleh ’ (WBA (1957), 62). ‘ Geological investigation carried out to the north of Suez and archaeological information from various ruined sites suggest that, at the time of the Exodus, the Bitter Lakes were linked to the Gulf of Suez. There were consequently shallows; and this throws light upon the Biblical reference to “ a strong east wind ” which sufficed to divide the waters ’ (GAB (1956), 48).

18 equipped for battle : uncertain. Perhaps read *ḥophshîm*, ‘ free ’, for *ḥamūshîm*, ‘ equipped for battle ’. **19.** See Gen. 50:25. **20.** P's usual formula for the stages of the journey. **Etham**, also Num. 33:8, was probably another border fortress. Chetan (Etham) in Egyptian means fortress or castle. The presence of a fortress would explain why the Israelites turned back, 14:1.

21f. J **The Pillar of Cloud and Fire**—The section g
takes up the theme of God's leading of 13:17, the pillar being the symbol of his presence. For fire as a manifestation of the nearness of the divine, see on

186g 3:2, cf. 19:16, 18, 20:18, 24:17. All the strands contain the tradition of the fiery presence, though in different forms. In J, the pillar goes before the people, cloud by day and fire by night, to guide them ; cf. 14:19*b*, 24, also Ps. 78:14. E speaks only of the cloud, and does not make it lead, but come down from time to time to the door of the Tent of Meeting, when Yahweh speaks with Moses, 33:9f., Num. 11:25 ; also Ps. 99:7. In P the fiery cloud, not spoken of as a pillar, rests on the Tent of Meeting after it is erected, and, when the march is to be resumed, rises above it ; cf. 40:34–38 ; Num. 9:15–22 ; also Ps. 105:39. In all probability, the symbolism has a natural basis in the attested custom of the Bedouin of carrying a brazier before an army or a caravan on the march. According to Heinisch, this was done not to show the way, but to honour important persons. Here the human custom is transformed. It is used to show that Yahweh, who has taken this people to himself, will lead them and protect them and reveal himself to them.

187a **XIV 1-4** P **The Crossing of the Reed Sea**—Aimé-Giron has identified Baal-Zephon with the Greek Daphne, the modern Tell Defneh south-east of Tanis ; see 1:11. Pi-Hahiroth is then near Qanṭarah. And Migdol (Jer. 44:1, 46:14 ; Ezek. 29:10, 30:6) is the present Tell el-Ḥeir, 12 km. south of Pelusium. Albright considers Pi-Hahiroth (lit. mouth of the canals), to be a popular Semitic etymology of an Egyptian *Pi-Ḥ-r-t, 'Temple of the goddess Ḥ-r-t' (BASOR 109 (1948), 16). The actual reason for the change in the direction of the march was probably a garrison fortress, see on 13:20. But P's characteristic standpoint comes out in 4 ; the deviation, and the action of the Egyptians, is divinely motivated ; there must be an occasion for a final demonstration to Pharaoh of the power of Yahweh.

b **5-9** (**5-7** J ; **8** P ; **9**?) **Pharaoh's Pursuit**—The Israelites fled. And Pharaoh, informed perhaps by the commandant of the Etham fortress that they were trying to make a complete getaway from Egypt, and not just going on a three days' pilgrimage, reflects, with his ministers, upon the valuable slave-labour they would lose. He therefore changes his mind. And they go after the fugitives, the use of chariots indicating the need which they felt for speed. 'The horse and wheeled vehicles were introduced to Egypt by the Hyksos' (W. J. Perry, *The Growth of Civilisation* (1937, Pelican), 149). The Egyptian chariot carried two men, the driver of the chariot and the fighter. **8.** 'defiantly' : cf. AV, 'with a strong hand'. The Heb. phrase occurs again in Num. 33:3 P, where RSV renders 'triumphantly'. In view of 7:4, 13:21f., cf. 6:1, we should rather render 'under mighty protection', i.e. of Yahweh. **9. all his horses . . . army** come after 'by the sea' in MT, and are most probably a gloss.

c **10-20** (**10a,** to 'fear', J ; **10b** E ; **11-14** J ; **15a,** to 'me', E ; **15b** P ; **16a,** to 'rod', E ; **16b-18** P ; **19a** E ; **19b** J ; **20a** E ; **20b** J) **The People are Afraid : Yahweh's Reassurance**—The Israelites fell into panic when they saw Egypt (so MT) marching after them—the sea before them, the Egyptian fortress behind them, and Pharaoh's army on the flank—only a miracle could save them. (The verse is an argument against the number of 600,000 in 12:37.) Although the occasion of the incident mentioned in 12 is not given in the present text, Moses had already had to experience murmurings from the people (5:20f.) and he was to meet with many similar complaints in the future (16:2f., 17:3 ; Num. 11:4f., 14:1ff., 16:12ff., 20:2ff., 21:4f.). In contrast with the people who had yet to learn what faith meant is set the leader who had already learned to trust. That Yahweh will fight for the Israelites, of that Moses is certain (14). All that the people have to do is to stand firm. The phrases belong to the ideology of the Holy War ; cf. G. von Rad, *Studies in Deuteronomy* (Eng. tr., 1952), 47f. Moses' prayer (15) is implied, though not mentioned. But Syr. inserts before 15 'and Moses cried to Yahweh'. The answer is, the people are to go forward. 'There is a time for prayer and a time for action. The time for 18
action has come' (*Abing. Comm.*). In 19f. the conflation of the sources is apparent. In J, the 'pillar of cloud' takes over the function of E's 'angel of God'. In **20b** the text is uncertain. RSV, **and the night passed,** follows LXX. The Heb. is 'and it lit up the night'. RSV is more in accord with Jos. 24:7 E, 'he (God) put darkness between you and the Egyptians'.

21-31 (**21a,** to 'sea' P, **21b,** to 'dry land' J, **21c-** d
23 P, **24-25** J, **26-27a,** to 'the sea' P, **27b** J, **28a** P, **28b** J, **29** P, **30** J, **31** R) **The Crossing of the Sea**—For the Hebrews, the Exodus was the great constitutive event of their history, 'parallel to the "ab urbe condita" in Rome and the "anno domini" of the Christian era' (John Marsh, *The Fulness of Time* (1952), 42). The remembrance and the wonder of it echo through the whole of the OT ; see e.g. Dt. 26:3, 5–8 ; 1 Kg. 8:16, 21, 51, 53 ; Isa. 11:16 ; Jer. 2:6f., 22:25 ; Hos. 2:15, 11:1 ; Am. 2:10, 3:1 ; Mic. 6:1–4 ; Ps. 77:11ff., 136:12–15, cf. 135, etc.

That the Hebrews saw in the Exodus God's act led, e
as time went on, to the heightening of the miraculous accompaniments of the divine work. In the oldest strand of the tradition, the crossing is made possible by a natural event, an east wind, which is nevertheless seen by faith as sent by Yahweh—'the Lord drove' etc. (21). The next oldest strand, E, brings Moses' magic rod into connection with the dividing of the waters (16). The latest, P, makes the divided waters a wall (22). 'In P there is no thought of any wind : the waters divide automatically at the signal given by Moses' (Driver). 'But this is not to be taken as the difference between one "miraculous" and one "natural" explanation of the phenomenal experience of Israel at the Sea of Reeds. On the contrary, the early narrative of J is quite explicit that "this was the Lord's doing" : *the Lord* caused the sea to go back by a strong east wind. . . . The unit of understanding, in the earlier and the later narrative (i.e. P) alike, is not simply the events that occur in this world of "phenomena" ; it is God acting in and through these phenomena. . . . Indeed, the Bible gives us no clue to any judgement upon history that does not have God's activity as its conditioning ground' (Marsh, op. cit., 45). Even the Egyptians are made to recognise the hand of Yahweh, although too late (25 and 27).

It would appear that the Egyptians followed when f
there was light enough to see. According to Ps. 77:17–19 there was also torrential rain, with thunder and lightning. With **27** cf. Dt. 11:4 ; Ps. 78:53 ; Heb. 11:29. **28.** Was Pharaoh himself drowned? It is not so stated, and he need not have been, for he need not even have been present. 6 could mean only that he ordered the pursuit. In 10 the word 'Pharaoh' could denote 'Egypt'. 17f. need not imply more than that Yahweh will get glory over Pharaoh by destroying his army, while 15:4, 19 do not suggest that Pharaoh himself joined in the pursuit over the sea. **31.** The first result of the deliverance was that the Israelites gained a conviction of Yahweh's power and of Moses' authority. For the Exodus as the type of future deliverance, see Isa. 43:1f., 16–19 and 51:9–11 ; also Lk. 9:30, where 'departure' is lit. 'Exodos'. For a discussion of the location of the passage of the sea, see on 13:17ff.

XV 1-21 The Songs of Moses and Miriam—While g
the Song of Miriam (21) is fairly generally accepted as contemporary with the event which it celebrates, the Song of Moses (1–18) is usually regarded as later, and even very much later. The reasons are that, while 1–11 certainly celebrate the Exodus, 13–16 seem to suggest that the wilderness wanderings and the settlement in Canaan are things of the past. 17, too, is usually taken as referring to the Temple built in the time of Solomon. A selection of the dates proposed for the time of composition is as follows : in the earliest days after the settlement (Kittel), the time of David and Solomon (Driver, Sellin), the deuteronomic period before the fall of the Southern Kingdom

7g (Baentsch), the exilic or post-exilic period, generally on grounds of linguistic affinities with Jeremiah and some of the Psalms (Bennett, Harford, Lagrange, McNeile), shortly after the return (Holzinger), the second half of the fifth century (Pfeiffer). Albright, however, argues that, on the basis of the Canaanite literature discovered at Ugarit, 'there is no longer the slightest valid reason for dating the Song of Miriam (i.e. of Moses) after the 13th cent. B.C.' (*The Archaeology of Palestine* (Penguin, 1949), 233); 'the literary genre of the triumphal poem, celebrating military victory, was then at the climax of its popularity in ancient times' (ibid., 232). He denies also that 17 refers to the Temple at Jerusalem, since the Canaanite epic, composed before 1400 B.C., speaks of Baal's house as 'on the mountain of his inheritance'. A possible explanation is that the old, and perhaps contemporary, material in 2–10 has had a later hymn celebrating the conquest joined to it, for use in the cult. 'In Israel, as among the Arabs, it became the custom to add new verses to old poems' (George Adam Smith, *The Early Poetry of Israel in its Physical and Social Aspects* (1910), 51). That the Song had a place in the cult seems certain. Weiser thinks it was composed for the enthronement festival of Yahweh celebrated at the national festival of the renewal of the covenant. Beer suggests that it was a 'Passover cantata composed for, and presented on the occasion of, the great celebration of the feast in Jerusalem attending the reformation of Josiah', while Schmidt thinks it was sung on one day of the great harvest and New Year festival. Whatever the hymn's date, its vividness, fire and vigour make it one of the grandest specimens of Hebrew poetry. (But for a very different judgment, see Pfeiffer, *Introduction to the OT*, 281.)

h The motif of the song is given in 1*b*, joy at the destruction of the Egyptian army and gratitude to Yahweh who brought the miracle about. 2–5 expand that theme. 6–10 give it a fuller and more vivid treatment—Yahweh is the mighty, irresistible man of war, controlling nature and disposing over men as he will. 11–12 are the climax, the song of praise to Yahweh, whose action has shown him to be incomparable.

i **1** 'his rider': better, 'chariot' or 'charioteer', since the Egyptians did not ride on horses at this time. **2.** 'the Lord': Heb., *Yah*, a contracted form Yahweh; cf. 17:16; Isa. 12:2, which quotes the present verse, 26:4, 38:11, and late Psalms, where it is generally found in the call *Hallelu-Yah*. 'Salvation': 'deliverance'. 'My father's God': the expression suggests Yahweh's faithfulness (Beer). **3.** 'man of war': cf. Ps. 24:8; Isa. 42:13. **5.** 'cover': better 'covered'—the words describe the chariots as they sank, not what they are now from the point of view of the singer. **6.** 'thy right hand': cf. Isa. 51:9; Ps. 118:15f. 'Shatters': 'shattered'. **7.** Again render the verbs as pasts. **8.** 'the deeps': probably the fountains which, in the mythology, connected the sea with the primeval waters under it. **9.** 'destroy': 'dispossess', 'oust them my hand' (G. A. Smith). 'Sank': 'the word is onomatopoeic (in Arabic it is used of gurgling water) . . . *Gurgled* is better; yet *sank* itself somewhat echoes the sound intended' (G. A. Smith). **11.** The reality of other gods is not denied, cf. Ps. 58:1, 86:8, but Yahweh's **holiness,** that is, his majesty and incomparable power, set him apart from them, which is the root-meaning of the word. Also implied is the dangerous quality of Yahweh.

j **13-17** The verbs should be taken as aorists—'didst lead', etc. 14–16. The description is idealised in retrospect. Edom in fact refused the Israelites passage through their territory, Num. 20:14–21. But there is evidence that the conquest was quicker and the subjugation of the Canaanites more complete than used to be supposed a short time ago. For another vivid description of the entry into Palestine and the terror which it occasioned, see Ps. 68. 19. A redactorial addition.

k **20 E The Song of Miriam**—For Miriam as 'sister of Aaron' see on 2:1. She is nowhere else called 'the
prophetess'. The fact that this song is so short and 187k
impromptu is proof of its genuineness. Women also met returning warriors with song and dance in 1 Sam. 18:6–8. See also the story of Jephthah's daughter, Jg. 11:34. On the whole subject of the dancing of Israelites at victory feasts, see W. O. E. Oesterley, *The Sacred Dance in Israel* (1923), 159–176).

**XV 22-27 (22-25a J, 25b E, 26 R, 27 J) Journey 188a
from Elim to Marah**—Now begins the Journey in the Wilderness. The 'wilderness' is not desert, but, as opposed to the cultivated land, steppe country in which, the hot season apart, herds find pasture enough. The Wilderness of Shur, mentioned again in Gen. 16:7, 20:1, 25:18; 1 Sam. 15:7, 27:8 and called in Num. 33:6ff. Etham, lay to the east of the present Suez Canal. Since the location of Mt Sinai is debated (see below) the route taken by the Israelites cannot be plotted out for certain. But if Sinai is identified, as traditionally, with Jebel Mûsā, at the southern end of the Sinai peninsula, then they went along the road used by the Egyptians to the copper and turquoise mines of Sinai which they worked. (It is probable that the Egyptians were the discoverers of the use of copper. 'Thus came about . . . one of the most important events in the world's history, the invention of the copper chisel' (W. J. Perry, op. cit., 50).) Marah would then be, most probably, the modern 'Ain Ḥawârah, and Elim the Wâdī Gharandel. The name Elim, 'terebinths', points to an oasis.

24 The Israelites make their leader responsible for their plight; cf. 14:11. **He proved them**: the meaning is not clear. The root of 'proved' is *nsh*, which suggests a connection with Massah of 17:1–7 rather than with Marah; see on 17:1–7. **25.** Lesseps is quoted as mentioning a kind of barberry which grows in the desert and has the properties of the bush shown to Moses. **26** seems to imply a lawgiving, or at least, the giving of laws, before Sinai. The present text tries to harmonise by putting the hearkening into the future.

XVI Manna and Quails—'The analysis is extra- b
ordinarily difficult' (Eissfeldt). The following is only tentative: **1-3** P, **4-5** (**5b** an addition) J, **6-13a,** to 'covered the camp', **P** with additions, **13b-15** J, **16-26** P? (Eiss., L and J), **27-30** J, **31-36** P (Eiss. L and J).

1 The Location of Sinai. Since Byzantine times c
Christian tradition has identified Mt Sinai with the granite range of mountains in the south-central part of the peninsula of Sinai. On this range there are three peaks, within 25 miles of one another, Jebel Serbal (6,759 ft.), Jebel Mûsā (7,519 ft.) and Jebel Katherina (8,551 ft.). The Jebel Mûsā, that is, the 'mountain of Moses', is the peak traditionally associated with Sinai-Horeb and the Lawgiving. But the identification is not universally accepted. Wellhausen, for example, held that according to the older sources, J and E, the Israelites went direct from Egypt to Kadesh Barnea (see map at end); the mount of the Lawgiving was therefore to be sought in that region, and P's journeys in the southern part of the Sinai peninsula were a later construction. Others identify the mountain with the volcano Hala el-Bedr, which rises on the eastern slope of a range called Tadras, in Arabia, east of the Red Sea (see Phythian-Adams, *The Call of Israel*, especially 152f., 211f.). Some again argue for the plateau of Petra in Mt Seir, for Serbal, and, in view of the inscriptions found there, for Serâbîṭ el-Khâdim.

The chief reasons for discounting the traditional d
identification are (*a*) that the description of the mountain in Exod. 19 is widely thought to point to a volcano, but there are no volcanoes in the Sinai peninsula; (*b*) that the Sinai peninsula lay within the jurisdiction of the Pharaoh, and that therefore the fugitive Israelites would avoid it; (*c*) that Jethro's clan of the Midianites lived east of the Gulf of 'Aqaba, and not in the south of the Sinai peninsula.

It is by no means certain, however, that 19:16–19, e
20:18 describe a volcano in eruption. For one thing, there is no mention of ashes, which would have been

188e expected had a volcano been in question. Nor was there apparently any danger from being in the vicinity of the mountain ; the people drew near to it, and Moses went into the cloud. The danger was from the presence of Yahweh on it. Again, the natural phenomena described, thunder, lightning, cloud, and darkness, better suit those of a storm. The words in 18*b*, 'and the whole mountain quaked greatly', could be a gloss which has come in from 16*b*, where 'the people trembled' : for the verb used, the same in both cases, is, except in 18*b*, always applied to persons. It is also argued, in favour of the traditional interpretation, that Egyptian troops were stationed in the Sinai peninsula only when the mines were in operation, that is, in winter and spring. They would therefore have left by the month on which the Israelites are represented as leaving Egypt. Also, the more recent archaeological identifications of the places mentioned in ch. 15, and those to be mentioned in 16, seem to lend support to the traditional location. On the location of the Midianites, see on 2:15. North of Jebel Mûsā is the plain er-Râḥa, which could have afforded camping-ground, and there are several streams in the neighbourhood.

f **2-36 Manna and Quails**—In 2 notice that, as is usual with P, Aaron shares the responsibility with Moses. Leaving Elim, the Israelites moved parallel to the coast and came to the Wilderness of Sin. If the Dophkah of Num. 33:10–12 is to be identified, as the etymology of the Hebrew word—*dāphakh*, to beat or knock—suggests, with the Egyptian mining centre of Serābîṭ el-Khâdim, then the Wilderness of Sin is the place on the edge of the Sinai plateau today called Debbet er-Ramleh. The Sinai peninsula is barren, and the Israelites could not have subsisted on what they might have foraged. So, all that had been hard in Egypt forgotten now, they idealise the past. And, in worse straits now than those of 15:24, they once again complain ; see also 14:11ff. The promise of 'bread from heaven' (4) is, in 5, brought into connection with the law of the Sabbath, to be given in 22–29. On 4f. should follow 9–12, since the communication to the people in 6–8 depends upon Yahweh's word in 12. In 7 'glory' is apparently to be taken in the sense of Yahweh's greatness as shown in the provision of the manna, but in 10 it is the fire in the cloud which is the symbol of Yahweh's presence. In 9, 'before the Lord' implies a sanctuary, or the Tent of Meeting. There is displacement then here, since there is as yet no sanctuary or Tent. In 10 'wilderness' (*midhbār*) should probably be 'sanctuary' (*miḳdāsh*) or 'Tent' (*mishkān*), for, since they were in the wilderness, they could hardly be directed to look towards it. MT will be due to a corrector who, after the displacement, realised that no sanctuary or Tent was yet in existence.

g **13-21 The Appearance of the Manna and the Quails**—'Flesh' has already been mentioned in 8 and 12 : the quails take the place of the flesh which the Israelites now missed, remembering the 'fleshpots of Egypt' (3). Verse 13*a* is from P. But in J's account in Num. 11 the quails come after the manna, when the people are tired of the latter. In spring quails migrate in great numbers from Africa to the north, and some come over the Sinai peninsula, although not many, owing to the sparseness of the feeding there. The miracle here consists in the large numbers in which they come. They fly low, and when they come to the ground, exhausted, they are easy to catch. On the manna (13*b*–15), F. S. Bodenheimer writes : 'Two closely related species of scale insects produce the manna by excretion . . . This manna is none other than the well-known honeydew excretion of so many plant lice and scale insects. . . . Rapid evaporation due to the dry air of the desert quickly changes the drops into sticky solids. These manna pieces later turn a whitish, yellowish or brownish colour. . . . We must make one thing clear about the Biblical report. All the statements about manna in the early formations of Scripture, the Elohim or Yahweh codes, agree closely with our observations. However, many commentaries on the Priestly code, which were added hundreds of years later and which are based on conjectures or on misrepresentation of oral tradition, show definite divergencies' ('The Manna of Sinai', BA 10 (1947), 4). 188

15a What is it ?—The Hebrew *man hû'* is once again a popular etymology, manna being *mān* in Hebrew, and *man hû'* taken as meaning 'what' (*man*) (is) 'this' (*hû'*) ? But *man* in the meaning of 'what ?' is Aramaic rather than Hebrew. It has been conjectured that *mān* is the corruption of an Egyptian word for a plant with which the Israelites were already familiar : *mān hû'* would then be a statement—'this is *mān* !' i.e. 'this is what we are already familiar with as *mān*'. But Bodenheimer says that *man* is the common Arabic name for plant lice. The words in 15*b* are then quite intelligible, since the substance was hitherto unknown to the Israelites. h

15-21 Directions for Gathering the Manna—Each was to gather only what he needed. 'An easy explanation can be offered for the worms and stinking decay of the manna which was collected in excess of need. The manna grains are eagerly collected by ants, and in a primitive tent there is little protection against them. The worms can be called ants, while the addition of stinking decay is a later misinterpretation and interpolation. The Bible knows a special word for ant (n^{e}*mālāh*), but in this place it uses the general word for worms and vermin (*tôlā'*). However, a personal experience may explain this. When I asked our nomad guide for the name of the many manna-collecting ants, he called them *dudi*, which corresponds to the Hebrew *tôla'ath*. When I asked him if they might be called *nimleh* (n^{e}*mālāh*), he answered that it was possible. Since he knew both designations, he had used the more general one. This was almost certainly the procedure of the oral tradition. Because the late redactors of the Priestly code did not properly understand the situation they added the misleading interpolation' (Bodenheimer, ibid., 5). **Omer** (18) is found only here. It is 'perhaps an old word handed down in the story' (Driver). See §34*l* ; Kennedy (DB) gives its capacity as 6½ pints. 'One steady man may collect over a kilogram a day at the peak of the season. This certainly does not allow for the 'bread' or daily food of the wandering Israelites. However we must note that *leḥem* does not have an original meaning of bread, but of food in general. Otherwise it could not have come to mean 'meat' in Arabic. All in all, the nutritive value of these few kilograms of manna could not have been important enough to deserve a recording in Israel's history. There must have been a special quality to justify its inclusion in the chronicle. The special quality was its sweetness. A chemical analysis reveals that this type of manna contains a mixture of three basic sugars with pectin. One who has wandered with nomads in the desert knows that sweetness is their highest culinaric dream. At the time in which the Israelites wandered in the desert, neither sugar-beet nor sugar-cane was known. Sweet dates had only a limited productivity and may have been unknown or almost unknown in the desert. Therefore, the sudden discovery of a source of pure and attractive sweetness would have been an exciting event' (Bodenheimer, ibid., 2f.). **21. melted when the sun grew hot** : 'we must regard the melting as a late and mistaken interpolation. The ants begin to collect the manna only when the temperature of the soil surpasses 21° C. (70° F.). In most of the wadis at the time of our visit the rays of the sun usually accomplished this about 8.30 a.m.' (ibid. 6). i

22-30 The Institution of the Sabbath—The origin of the Sabbath is here connected with the provision of the manna ; cf. v. 5. Since the Sabbath is to be a day of rest, the necessary manna is to be gathered on the previous day, and the additional quantity gathered for it will not corrupt. 28 is a gloss by an editor who assumed that the Sabbath law of 20:8ff. 189

9a had been already promulgated. The connecting of the Sabbath here with the giving of the manna is another instance of the tendency at work in Israel's faith to *historicise*, that is, to connect rites and usages which were quite primitive with the people's experience, for the observance of the Sabbath was in all probability, pre-Mosaic. What now happens is that an old custom is given an historical context in the Yahweh faith. On the Sabbath, see further on 20:8ff., 35:2f.

b **31-36 The Memorial Pot of Manna**—The continuation of 13*b* to 21. The children of Israel continued to enjoy the provision of manna after they left Sinai, Num. 11:6ff., both as they circuited Edom, Num. 21:5, and in east Jordan, Jos. 5:10–12. There it ceased, at Gilgal, where they ate for the first time the produce of Canaan. Heb. 9:4 calls the urn 'golden'. The 'Testimony' (34) was the Ark (cf. 25:16, 21, 27:21, etc.), which later contained the stone tables of the Decalogue. P regularly uses the 'Testimony' for the Decalogue. According to 1 Kg. 8:9 the pot was not in the Ark at the time of Solomon. If one was made in the desert, what happened to it we do not know. It may have been lost when the Ark was captured by the Philistines, 1 Sam. 4.

31 coriander seed: about the size of a peppercorn. Num. 11:7 says that its colour is that of bdellium, that is, pale yellowish. wafers: according to Num. 11:8 the taste of the manna was 'like the taste of cakes baked with oil'. **36.** a later note. An *ephah*, or bath, is about 8 imperial gallons or 36–44 litres (Lauterbach, art. 'Weights and Measures', in JE, vol. x). See also §§34–7.

c **XVII 1-7 (1a P, 1b-2 J, 3** (? J or E), **4-6** E?, **7a,** to 'Massah' and **c,** 'because... or not', J, **7b** E) **Water from the Rock**—On reaching Rephidim, the modern Wâdī Refâyid, about 8 miles south of Jebel Mûsã, the Israelites again suffered affliction, this time from thirst. Once more they find fault with Moses (cf. 5:20 f., 14:10 ff., 16:2f.), and doubt the power of Yahweh to lead them. Moses is commanded to strike the rock with his rod, and water will gush forth.

d Two variants of the one incident are fused together here, the one which calls the place Massah, Proof, and the other Meribah, Contention (7). A third water story is given in Num. 20:2–13. There the place is called Meribah, and it is brought into connection with Kadesh (cf. Ezek. 48:28), and not Rephidim. It is probable that all the water stories, Marah-Massah (15:22–27), Massah-Meribah (17:1–7) and Meribah-Kadesh (Num. 20:2–13), are variants of the one incident, and that it should be placed at a much later stage in the wanderings; see on the next section. Horeb (6) could be a later addition by a scribe who remembered the Mt Hor of Num. 20. On the other hand, the Blessing of Moses, which is ancient, seems to imply that Massah and Meribah are different places (Dt. 33). Also, those who are put to the test differ in the accounts. In 15 and Deuteronomy it is Yahweh who tests Israel, while here it is Israel who tests Yahweh. Any certainty is impossible, but on balance the stories look like variants of the same incident. **5. thy rod**: 'The rod which could make the waters of the Nile undrinkable for the Egyptians (7:17) could produce water to satisfy the thirst of the Israelites' (Hertz).

e **8-16** E **Battle with the Amalekites**—This incident is wrongly placed, and ought to come amongst the latest in the book. Not only is Joshua mentioned, and that for the first time, without introduction, as if he were already well known (see on 10), but the Amalekites are generally represented as living well to the north of Sinai, and not to the south as here. Num. 13:29, 14:25, 43:45 places them in the Negeb, while Gen. 14:7 brings them into connection with Kadesh. While it is not impossible to suppose that a raiding-party, or a party seeking pasture on the higher ground, might have penetrated as far as the neighbourhood of Sinai, it is more likely that the present incident reflects a fight for the possession of Kadesh, and so should come after the departure from Sinai.

Moses' action (11) is most likely not prayer. Nor is 189f
the uplifted rod, the rod of 4:17, a kind of banner, the sight of which would encourage the fighters, though 15 might so suggest. Like the symbolic actions of the prophets, it was an action designed to secure the desired victory. (For the assuming of a physical attitude or position to ensure a desired result, see also 1 Kg. 17:21, 18:42. For the effective uttered curse, see Num. 22:6.) Bentzen (*Introduction to the OT* (Eng. tr., 1948), I, 139), brings 16, which he calls a conjuring song, comparing Jos. 10:12–13 and 2 Kg. 13:17, into connection with the lifting-up of Moses' hands. Translating with the Swedish Authorised Version, 'Surely with (my) hand (raised) to the throne of Yahweh (I swear): war has Yahweh against Amalek from generation to generation', he goes on: 'here the conjuror mobilised the war-power of Yahweh against the hated neighbour'. (In 16 RSV adopts the reading *nēs*, banner, cf. AV, *nissi*, my banner, for the *kēs* of the MT which is otherwise unknown, but is taken as another form of *kissē'*, throne.)

8 Amalek: called in Num. 24:20 the 'first of the g
nations'. Dt. 25:18 says that on the occasion dealt with here, Amalek cut off from the rear of Israel all who were faint and weary. **10. Joshua**: called in Num. 13:8 Hoshea, and in Exod. 33:11 Moses' 'servant . . . a young man'. **Hur**: again only 24:14. Josephus (Ant. III, ii, 4) calls him the husband of Miriam, the Talmud the son of Miriam and Caleb. He has been connected, because of his name, with the Horites, or Hurrians, who were a dominant people in the Middle East in the 2nd millennium B.C., and of whom knowledge has come from the excavations at Nuzu (see §86*c*). **14.** write: it is now known that the art of writing was well developed by the time of the Exodus. 'Accordingly, we should accept the tradition that even before the occupation of Canaan both commandments of the religious law (34:28) and historical records were written down' (Geo Widengren, *Literary and Psychological Aspects of the Hebrew Prophets* (1948), 62).

15 If the incident is connected with Kadesh, then we have here an aetiological story explaining the name of the Kadesh altar or shrine. That an altar was built means that the victory was regarded as having been given by Yahweh, as indeed is suggested also by the quite passive role assigned to Moses. **16.** For the continuing hostility between Israel and Amalek, see Num. 24:20; Dt. 25:17–19; 1 Sam. 15, 27:8, 30. 1 Chr. 4:41–43 says that the Amalekites were finally destroyed in the time of Hezekiah.

XVIII 1-12 (1a, to 'Midian' J, **1b,** to 'father in law' 190a
E, **1c,** 'heard' J, **1d,** to 'his people' E, **1e-5a,** to 'encamped' (except 'Moses' father in law', **2,** and 'Moses' father in law . . . with his sons and his wife', **5,** E) J, **5b-6a,** to 'coming to you' E, **6b** J, **7-8a,** to 'sake' E, **8b** J, **9a,** to 'Israel' (except 'Jethro' J) E, **9b-10** J, **11-12** (except 'Jethro' J) E. The analysis of 18 given here is Eissfeldt's) **Jethro meets Moses**—The chapter is displaced. According to 17:1, 8, the Israelites are now at Rephidim, which they leave only at 19:2. But 5 locates them as already at 'the mountain of God', that is, Horeb-Sinai. Further, the organisation of justice described in 13ff. would require longer time than would be allowed by a temporary camping-place on the march. The judges would need instruction, if not indeed written prescriptions such as the Decalogue or, better, the Book of the Covenant, to which they could refer. Further, Dt. 1:3–18 places this appointment of judges after Israel has 'stayed long enough at this mountain' (5), i.e. Horeb. After Horeb must have been its original setting. The reason for the ante-dating here may be that a later editor took it as offensive that a Midianite priest should offer sacrifice at Sinai *after* God had revealed himself there to Israel, and do so, moreover, when there was now a consecrated priest of Israel's own, namely Aaron.

2-4 attempt to harmonise 5 and 2:22, 4:20, 24–26, b
where Moses has only one son (see on 4:20), and

190b Zipporah apparently goes with Moses to Egypt. According to later tradition, Aaron had demanded that Zipporah should be sent back to her father. In 4 Eliezer is another popular etymology. **10–12** are one of the foundations of the Kenite hypothesis (see also on 4:18), according to which Yahweh was originally the God of the Kenites, who revealed himself to Moses at the Bush, and after triumphantly delivering the Israelites from Egypt, entered into covenant relationship with them as their God. **12** is taken to be Jethro, the Kenite priest of Yahweh, initiating Aaron and the elders into the Yahweh cult. According to Beer, the meal here is parallel to the covenant sacrifices in 24:4–8. For a discussion of the hypothesis, see the larger commentaries or H. H. Rowley, *The Rediscovery of the OT* (1945), ch. 5). Rowley accepts the hypothesis, but points out that 'whatever the worship of Yahweh may have meant to the Kenites, from the days of Moses it meant something richer and deeper to Israel. He (Moses) was more than a transmitter from Kenites to Israelites. He was a medium of divine revelation. Kenite worship of Yahweh was not based on any historical experience of His choice of the Kenites, confirmed in a great deliverance achieved before the Kenites had begun to worship Him, or based on the solemn and willing pledge of the Kenites to choose and serve Him Who had first chosen and notably served them. All this meant inevitably that there was a new quality in the Yahwism of Israel' (85).

c **13-27** (**13-14a,** to 'people' E, **14b** J, **15-16a,** to 'neighbour' J, **16b-18** E, **19-20** J, **21** (except 'able men, such as fear God' J) E, **22-23** (except 'and God so command you' J) E, **25a,** to 'people' J, **25b-27** E) **Appointment of Judges**—If the Kenite hypothesis is correct, and the religion of Israel derived from an outside source, so also, it is represented here, do the beginnings of her system for the administration of justice. And in the ancient world religion and law were always most closely connected. Jethro advises that Moses should depart from the Bedouin custom whereby the military and religious leader was also the judge and legislator, and delegate some part of his functions. Moses was to represent the people before God, that is, to act only in cases which required resort to the sacred lot and, on the basis of decisions given thereby, show the people what God's will was (19f.). Decision in lesser matters was to be delegated to a new body.

d Of J's account, only a few words have been preserved. E supplements it in three respects: (*a*) It gives the reason for Jethro's advice—Moses will soon be worn out if he does not delegate authority (18); cf. Moses' own complaint in the parallel in Num. 11:11–14. (*b*) It lays down the organisation and functions of the new judiciaries: men were to be appointed as 'rulers of thousands, of hundreds, of fifties, and of tens' (21). The meaning is not, however, clear. Was each Israelite to be under *four* magistrates? The divisions represent the later division of the people for military purposes, and it is extremely doubtful if such a division existed as early as the Mosaic period. These men, who, according to Num. 11:16, 24f., numbered seventy, were to take over the ordinary routine judicial work where decisions could be given easily on the basis of statute or precedent. Cases not so provided for were still to be brought to Moses, who would, as 19 (J) suggests, seek an oracle for their decision. (*c*) E's account also gives an additional motive for the new institution: it would save the people delay; cf. 2 Sam. 15:1–6. 'Go to their places in peace' (23*b*): 'return quickly to their houses satisfied, without having to stand all day before Moses (v. 14)' (Driver). While sacred and civil law were not distinguished in Israel any more than in the rest of the ancient East, where all law was regarded as divine, this incident marks the differentiation between them which obtained later. But the passage safeguards the divine quality of all law in two ways: (*a*) 'the civil judges receive their authority from Moses, the
sacral head' (IB); (*b*) the words in 23, 'and God so command you', are a veto against any inference that 19[0e]
Israel's legal arrangements were simply taken over from Midian. Even if Midianite practice lay at their basis, they had also the sanction of Yahweh. **16, 20. Statutes and decisions:** the former (*ḥuḳḳîm*) were directions already laid down and permanent, the latter (*tôrôth*) were directions in particular cases, especially difficult cases (25), which would serve as precedents for the future. The mention of the 'statutes' suggests that this chapter has been displaced; see introductory paragraph.

(C) Israel at Sinai (XIX-XL)

Chs. 19–24 may be called, along with Gen. 3, the 191
most important chapters of the OT. Man fell (Gen. 3). But God wanted him back. And the method which he chose was to take one people from all the peoples into a special relationship with himself. In Exod. 19–24 he offers, and Israel accepts, that relationship. 'This was the most important moment in its (Israel's) history until the hour when Pilate confronted it with the decision whether it wished to choose Jesus as its king, or the murderer Barabbas' (Heinisch).

XIX (**1-2a,** to 'wilderness', P, **2b-3a,** to 'God', E, b
3b-6 Rd ?, **7-8** E, **9a,** to 'ever', J, **9b** R, **10** E, **11a** E?, **11b** to **13a,** to 'shot', J, **13b-14** E, **15** J?, **16**?, **17** E, **18** J, **19** E, **20-22** J, **23-24a** Rje, **24b-25** J) **The Revelation of God**—The chapter is highly composite. The sources have been so woven together and glosses added that it is impossible to form from the text any clear picture of what actually took place. Nor is there any certainty about the source analysis. What is given is no more than very tentative. Many details remain doubtful, and lack of space precludes discussion.

The note about the time and place come from P, c
and it is the continuation of P's itinerary in 17:1. The verses are not a unity. Originally the text ran probably thus: 2*a* 'and they (omit 'when' with Hebrew) set out from Rephidim and came into the wilderness of Sinai. 1, on the third new moon after the people had gone forth from the land of Egypt, on that day they came into the wilderness of Sinai'. 'They encamped in the wilderness' 2*a*, is omitted by LXX, and the words were probably added to connect with 2*b*. In 1, RSV rendering, 'on the third new moon', avoids the difficulty in the usual rendering, 'in the third month'. If the latter is kept, then in 'on that day' (1) a note of the exact day must have been dropped out, presumably because it conflicted with the later tradition that the giving of the Law took place fifty days after Passover (Dillmann).

1 the wilderness of Sinai: the plain er-Râḥa, north-west of Jebel Mûsā.

E's narrative tells that when Israel was encamped d
before the mountain (2*a*)—the promise of 3:12 is now fulfilled—Moses went up to God (3*a*). Omitting 7–8, which are displaced and should probably come after the giving of the Decalogue, Yahweh bids Moses go to the people and command them to consecrate themselves for two days, wash their garments (10), and be ready on the third day (11*a*). When the trumpet sounds, they are to come up the mountain (13*a*). Moses carries out the command (14). Then in 16 is described how on the morning of the third day there were thunders etc., and a loud trumpet-blast, so that the people trembled. Then, as the sound of the trumpet grew louder, Moses spoke and God answered
him (19). J's account is as follows. Yahweh (9*a*) e
says to Moses that he is coming to him in a thick cloud, and that he will speak to him in the hearing of the people. Sinai was wrapped in smoke because Yahweh descended upon it (18). Moses is called to the top of the mountain, only to be bidden go down again and warn the people not to break through to Yahweh to gaze. The priests are also to consecrate themselves (20–22). 11*b*–13*a* follow here, though 13*a* may be a gloss by a redactor who did not understand 12 as

191e death at the hands of Yahweh, cf. 24. Moses is also to bring up Aaron, but not to allow the priests and the people to break through. He obeys (24*b*–25). 23 R points back to 12.

f Into the combined narrative of JE has been worked, probably by a Deuteronomic redactor, though Eissfeldt, Beer, etc. think it is from E, one of the most beautiful passages of the OT, 3*b*–6, stating the method and purpose of Israel's election. 'It is the classic passage in the OT on the nature and aim of the theocratic covenant' (Dillmann). Yahweh, the Lord of all the earth, proposes to take the children of Israel into a special and intimate relationship with himself. They were to be his 'own possession' among all peoples; cf. Dt. 7:6, 14:2, 26:18. But the election involved also obligation; Israel was to be a 'kingdom of priests' (cf. Isa. 61:6), and a 'holy nation'. 'Holy' here has more than just its original sense of 'set apart'. As the priests stand nearer to the godhead than the people, so Israel stands nearer than the other nations. But as the priests have to be characterised by morality and piety, so the Israelites have to observe the commandments which Yahweh will give them, and so be a 'holy people' (Heinisch). Implied also in the notion of priesthood is the task of bringing the other nations to God. The motive of Israel for entering into the offered covenant relationship was to be gratitude. With 'eagles' wings' (4) cf. Dt. 32:11. Past deliverance and present guidance should give the elected people confidence for the future; see also on 3:13ff. The power which brought them from Egypt is offered to them now for ever. But the offer is conditional—Israel must obey God and keep his covenant (5).

g **5** 'all the earth is mine': implicit monotheism; see also on 20:3. **6.** 'kingdom of priests': 'since according to Dt. 33:8–10 the priest is custodian of the Torah or teaching, the ideal in 6 runs parallel to Jer. 31:34' (Beer). **10.** Only those in a state of ritual purity might approach deity. **Consecrate**: by bathing or washing the body, and avoiding anything that would cause uncleanness. For washing of garments cf. Lev. 11:24ff, 39f.; for changing of garments for purification cf. Gen. 35:2; for sexual intercourse as making ritually unclean cf. Lev. 15:16ff.; for abstention from the same cf. 1 Sam. 21:4. **13.** Since the man who has touched the mountain has acquired 'holiness', he is dangerous, and it would be fraught with peril to touch him; cf. 22 and 1 Sam. 6:19; 2 Sam. 6:6f.—'Trumpet' (Hebrew *yōbhēl*), a different word from that used in **16** and **19**, where it is *shôphār*. **21f.**, J: in 16, E, the people are trembling, with no disposition to break through. **22.** The fact that the priests, whose duty it is to come near to God, are also to consecrate themselves and not break through, expresses the uniqueness of the occasion.

h **XX 1-17 The Decalogue.** E expanded—The Decalogue (or Ten Words, so called in Dt. 4:13 and 10:4, and in Exod. 34:28, where the expression may be redactional), stands at the head of the law codes of the OT. But it is not itself a code. 'It is not a social instrument concerned with details; it is a comprehensive epitome seeking to set forth the inner meaning and purposes of all actual laws' (Abingdon Commentary). Hence its position, since in actual fact its insertion here breaks the clear original connection between 19:17 and 20:18.

i Three different methods of dividing the Decalogue are current: (*a*) Jewish tradition, ancient (cf. Targum of Pseudo-Jonathan) and modern, regard 2 as the first word, and 'deduce from it the positive precept, "to believe in the existence of God"' (Hirsch). Verses 3 and 4 are then combined as the 2nd Commandment. (*b*) The numbering adopted in this commentary, which derives from Philo, Josephus, and the Greek Church through Calvin. (*c*) The Roman Church and Luther, following Augustine, join verses 3 and 4 as the first Word, and divide v. 17, the 10th Commandment of (*b*). Another form of the Decalogue is found in Dt. 5:6–21. It has variations from the 191i
form here, the chief being the humanitarian motive for the observance of the Sabbath, and the reversed order of 'wife' and 'house' in the 10th. In the latter, the Nash papyrus, which generally supports the Exodus version, reads as Deuteronomy. Both lists have had expansions, hortatory and explanatory, added to them, and it is altogether likely that in the original form all the commandments were brief, consisting of a single clause: 'you shall not make yourself a graven image', 'honour your father and your mother', etc. It is also possible that all were formulated negatively: 'do no work on the Sabbath', 'do no wrong to your father or your mother', etc. That such a kernel may well come from Moses is increasingly maintained at the present day. Rowley has argued convincingly against the priority of the so-called Ritual Decalogue in 34:10–26, which, on the former evolutionary view of OT religion, was held to be earlier than Exod. 20 and Dt. 5, and possibly Mosaic, as the others were not. Yahwism, Rowley argues, came into Israel in two ways. Those tribes which were never in Egypt took it over from the Kenites, the clan to whom Jethro belonged, and at a lower level than the others, who had experienced the events of the Exodus and Sinai, and the creative personality of Moses. The Ritual Decalogue, which is from J, preserves the tradition of Judah derived from the Kenites, while Exod. 26 and Dt. 5 reflect the more ethical level attained in the wilderness (*The Rediscovery of the Old Testament* (1945), 85f.).

The preface (2) cannot be separated from what 192a
follows; it is because of the deliverance from Egypt that the people ought to obey the Commandments. God's saving action is everything. All Israel's subsequent history, and the creation of the Church, are due to God's gracious action then. See also on 6:4 for the formula itself.

3 The **First Word** forbids the worship of other b
gods than Yahweh. He only is to have veneration amongst his people. This is monolatry, which leads logically to monotheism. And what we have here, even at this early stage, may be called practical monotheism, since other gods, although their existence is admitted, do not come into the question or count. Albright indeed maintains that Moses had already attained to speculative monotheism. 'If . . . the term "monotheist" means one who teaches the existence of only one God, the creator of everything, the source of justice, who is equally powerful in Egypt, in the desert, and in Palestine, who has no sexuality and mythology, who is human in form but cannot be seen by human eye and cannot be represented in any form—the founder of Yahwism was certainly a monotheist' (FSAC, 207; cf. *The Archaeology of Palestine* (Pelican, 1949), 163, ARI, 96). On the other hand, while the exact meaning of this First Word is not certain—the Hebrew is literally, 'there shall not be to thee other gods over my face'—G. E. Wright points out that such a verse as Exod. 15:11, 'who is like unto thee among the gods, O Yahweh', 'is almost identical with that used by good polytheists to honour their deities. A seal found at Hamath in Syria bears an inscription in which there are the words: "Who can rival thee, O Lady of E-anna!" The Babylonian god Marduk has this said about him: "Lord, thou art exalted; who can rival thee? Marduk, among the gods as many as are called by name, thou art exalted!" Similar passages in the OT, therefore, if examined outside their total context, could easily be taken as evidence of polytheism as well as of henotheism.' ('How did Early Israel Differ from her Neighbours', BA 6 (1943), 14) These were interpreted monotheistically by the 5th cent., but how much earlier than than is uncertain. Wright's own view is that 'whether between the 13th and the 9th cent. there were a few men in Israel who actually believed that no other gods existed but Yahweh, is something we do not surely know. It is certain, however, that there were

192b those who held that Israel must not worship anyone or anything but Yahweh and him alone, and that this God of Israel was all-powerful on earth, even in Egypt with all its might, splendor, and great gods of hoary antiquity' (ibid., 14f.).

c 'The first commandment is religiously and psychologically necessary, for God as the supreme object of love and worship must be a single being; there can be no competitors for this exalted position' (Otto J. Baab, *The Theology of the Old Testament* (1949), 52).

d 4–6 The **Second Word** forbids the making and worship of a graven image, a *pesel*, properly a carved image, of wood or stone, but here used for all images, including those of Yahweh. The reason for the command is given in Dt. 4:15: 'since you saw no form on the day that the Lord spoke to you at Horeb'. Yahweh is spiritual being, and must not be represented by anything material. By *pesel* was thought a human form, so the lawgiver, or the amplifier, adds the equivalent of 'any form whatsoever'. **in heaven above**: the sun, the moon, the host of heaven, as in Babylonia and Egypt, also 2 Kg. 21:3f.; Jer. 8:2, etc. Birds also, such as the ibis and the phoenix, would be excluded. **in the earth beneath**: gods were given human and animal forms, or combinations of both, especially in Egypt. **in the water under the earth**: here the sea. There were fish-gods in Syria and Philistia, and Egypt held the crocodile as holy. For those who fall away to the worship of other gods, or lead others to worship them, Dt. 13 lays down the death penalty; cf. Num. 25.

e To reinforce the Second Word, 5*b* speaks of Yahweh as a 'jealous' God, one who will tolerate no encroachment on his sole right to his people's worship, whether through reverence given to other gods (cf. 34:14), or, as here, to an image. (But 5f. suggest that he reacts in jealousy not only against idolatry, but also against disobedience of any kind on the part of his people.) Penalty falls, as commonly in the ancient world, not only on the individual offender, but on his kindred as well; cf. Jos. 7:10 ff.; 2 Sam. 21; Isa. 14:21. This theory of retribution, strongly insisted upon by Deuteronomy, and attested by much in human experience, was seen in the course of time not to cover all the facts, and led to the equally one-sided individualism of Ezekiel (18), and to the discussions in the post-exilic period such as Job, Wisdom, Sirach, etc. 5f. are Deuteronomic. If the difference in the numbers—the *third* and *fourth* generation of them that hate, but *thousands* of them that love—is not just parallelism, then it could be meant that the grace of God lies deeper than his anger. For similar statements about the nature of God, which seem to constitute an OT creed, see 34:6f.; Num. 14:18; Neh. 9:17; Ps. 86:15, 103:8–10, 145:8f.; Jl 2:13.

f The Second Word is commonly adduced against the Mosaic origin of the Decalogue, since clearly what it regards as images were widely used in the post-Mosaic period, the ephod (Jg. 8:27, 17:4f.), the teraphim (Jg. 18:14ff.), the brazen serpent (Num. 21:8f.; 2 Kg. 18:4), Jeroboam's calves of gold (1 Kg. 12:28ff.), and of the last no criticism is recorded until the time of Hosea. On the other hand, the fact that a commandment is not observed does not mean that it is not in existence. It is also argued that such objects were in no sense idols to begin with—Jeroboam's bull images represented Yahweh's empty throne, and not him himself; and that when they came to be regarded as idolatrous, they were done away with (Eichrodt, *Theologie des Alten Testaments*, i, 44f.). It is also noteworthy that no figures of *Yahweh* have been found in excavations, though plenty are dug up of those of the Canaanite mother-goddess, in houses that are undoubtedly Israelite, evidence of a widespread syncretism. 'Most of the people of Israel apparently thought that Yahweh was simply not honored in that way' (G. E. Wright, op. cit., 16).

g 7 The **Third Word.** For the significance of the 'name', see on 3:13. The commandment does not
prohibit the taking of oaths. It rules out any misuse 192
of God's name as in perjury, making vows and not keeping them, etc., and any use of it in spells and magic. Since 'being' and 'name' belong together, misuse of the name is an offence against God's holiness. To avoid any possible breach of the Commandment, the Jews in the post-exilic period ceased to pronounce God's name, and used substitutes like the Eternal, the Most High, the Place, the Name. See also on 3:13. **hold guiltless**: leave unpunished; cf. 34:7; 1 Kg. 2:9.

8–11 The **Fourth Word** enjoins the keeping of the h
seventh day as a holy day, that is, as a festival when sacrifice was offered, and the community ceased from work. The term Sabbath is thus connected with the Hebrew root for 'to rest', *shābhath*. But the original meaning of the word, which is also found in the Babylonian, is disputed. The observation of the phases of the moon, and so the institution of the week, is very old. After the destruction of the Temple in A.D. 70, it was the observance of the Sabbath, together with circumcision, which bound Jews together and separated them off from Gentiles. **10a.** By 'manservant', 'maidservant', understand slaves. Dt. (5:15) gives a different and, characteristically, more humanitarian motive for the observance of the Sabbath: 'thou shalt remember that thou wast a slave in Egypt, and Yahweh thy God brought thee out'; cf. Exod. 23:12. Here the motive is the example of God at creation, Gen. 2:1–3. Man is to follow God's example.

It is alleged that the Fourth Word cannot be i
Mosaic; such a rest from labour would be impossible for nomads with flocks and herds to tend. But Bedouin do other work, such as shearing, weaving, making of clothes and tents, which could stop on the Sabbath. Again, it is argued that, since Sabbath observance became so marked a feature of Jewish life only after the Exile, the real development of it derived from Babylon. But there are striking differences between the Babylonian *šapattu* and the Jewish Sabbath. The former is the day of the full moon, the 15th of the month, and the festal days of the 1st, 7th, and 28th were not called *šapattu*. Also, there is nothing said about stopping work on these days, and that is what is characteristic of the Jewish institution. If in the Assyrian period certain work was forbidden on the 7th, 14th, 21st, and 28th days, the prescription concerned only certain people who stood in close relations with the gods, such as the king and the priests; and the reason for the stoppage was that these days were unlucky. It is much more probable that the Sabbath, like the new-moon festival, was ancient in Israel, and is now, at Sinai, given a new interpretation; see on 16:23ff. This does not mean, of course, that the observance of the Sabbath may not have become much stricter in the post-exilic period. On the Sabbath, see further, as well as 16:23ff., 34:21.

12 The **Fifth Word** enjoins respect for parents. 193
The importance which the Israelites attached to this obligation is shown by the position which this Word occupies. Duty towards parents is the most binding obligation after duty towards God, and partakes of the nature of piety. The commandment is addressed not only to young children, but also, and perhaps rather, to those of any age who have parents. Especially are old and weak parents to be respected and cared for. For the authority of parents over children, see Num. 30:3ff.; Neh. 5:5, which probably shows the power of a father to sell children into slavery; also Exod. 21:7ff. For the penalties which attached to the disregard of the commandment, see 21:17; Lev. 20:9; Dt. 21:18ff., 27:16. **that your days may be long**: 'the first commandment with a promise', Eph. 6:2. **You** refers both to the individual and the nation—a sound national life depends upon a sound family life.

13, 14, 15 The **Sixth, Seventh,** and **Eighth** b
Words uphold the three pillars upon which society rests, the sacredness of human life, the sanctity of

3b marriage, and the right to possess property. The Sixth refers to murder, not to killing in war (cf. Dt. 20:1ff.), or capital punishment (cf. Exod. 21:12f.). Both of these the OT sanctions unequivocally. For Jesus' extension of it, see Mt. 5:21–6. The Seventh Word refers to sin with another man's wife; cf. Lev. 18:20. For the penalty for breach of this commandment, namely, death, see Lev. 20:10 and Dt. 22:22. For Jesus' teaching on it, see Mt. 5:27f. For penalties for stealing, see 21:16, 22:1.

c **16** The **Ninth Word** prohibits perjury in the law-courts. It could be extended to include injuring a person's good name by making false statements about him generally. For penalties, see Dt. 19:16–21.

d **17** The **Tenth Word** is generally taken as referring not to an overt act, as do the rest of the commandments, but to an inward feeling or disposition. If so, it might be thought to be a later addition to the Decalogue. On the other hand, it is argued that 'the commandment, "thou shalt not covet", is concerned not so much with the secret desires of the heart, but with the outward manifestations of them, and really means, "thou shalt not attempt to acquire"' (Kennett, *The Church in Israel* (1933), 143). The latter view could find support from Mk 10:19, 'do not defraud', which most take as referring to the 10th Commandment. The verse could however equally well apply to the 9th Commandment. The 'house' clause was possibly added later, after the settlement. Probably the whole has been expanded from a simple prohibition, 'do not defraud', to 'do not covet'.

e What makes the Decalogue unique is not its ethical prescriptions, since these were already paralleled in the world around. The following special features are, however, to be noted:

(*a*) Outside Israel polytheism was the rule, with the result that a quite different character is given here to the concept of sin. In Babylonia and Egypt fear of demons, magic, etc. bulked largely, and sin was often the neglect of rituals due to irrational and generally malevolent powers. In Israel, demons and the like are put aside, and a moral God who binds men to himself enjoins a moral life upon them.

(*b*) If Israel abandoned the commandments, Yahweh might abandon her. The election meant that there was no natural or necessary connection between God and his people, as many other races held.

(*c*) The form in which the Decalogue is couched, the apodictic form, is almost unique to Israel. The common form of Sumerian law is what is called casuistic: 'If a man do . . . then . . .', or, 'whoever does . . .'; cf. 21:12 etc. But here, with apodictic law, we have a direct, categorical command in the 2nd person singular, implying that each individual is made responsible. Further, the fact that the commands are given by God gives them a new sanction. They are no longer grounded only in common law, as the casuistically formulated are, but in the will of God.

f **18-21** E **The Impression upon the People**—These verses resume the account of the theophany at Sinai interrupted at 19:19, the last E verse. It was dangerous to see or to hear God. So the people, in fear and trembling at the thunderings and lightnings, beg Moses to act as intermediary for them. **20. to prove you**: to see if you will really be loyal and keep his commandments; cf. 16:4.

g **22-26** E **Laws of Worship**—These laws open what is called 'the Book of the Covenant', which ends at 23:19. For its provenance, date, etc., see especially Henri Cazelles, *Études sur le code de l'Alliance* (1946).

h **22b** is a redactorial addition. In **23** 'to be with me', cf. 20:3, 'before me', means 'in my cult' (Cazelles). Cazelles also says that Vincent is inclined to believe that during the whole course of the Bronze Ages II and III (*c.*2000–1200 B.C.) all the Canaanite idols representing deities were gold- or silver-plated. **24-26. the altar**: (*a*) Altars were to be of the simplest construction, either of earth (cf. 2 Kg. 5:17), or, if of stone, then of unhewn stone (cf. Jos. 8:30 ff.; 1 Kg. 18:31). **193h**
The reason was, to allow the blood to drain into the ground. Altars of coarse brick with a coating of mud have been found at Mari (*Syria* 21 (1940), 10). P's altar in 27:1–8 constitutes a departure from the more primitive practice here, and Ezekiel's altar (43:13–17) could not have been built without tools. It was also to have steps. (*b*) Altars are here to be built at any place where the divine presence manifests itself; cf. 17:15; Gen. 35:6f.; Jos. 8:30 ff. Contrast the one altar of Dt. 12:8–14. Martin Noth has shown, however, that in the time of the amphictyony there was a central shrine to which the tribes resorted for common sacrifice and the ordering of the national life. There was thus precedent for the later single sanctuary. (*c*) Sacrifice is not yet here restricted to the priesthood, which was not yet in existence, but heads of families and clans are to approach the altar (12); cf. Jg. 21:4. (*d*) Of the sacrifices mentioned—cereal offerings are not included (Holzinger)—the burnt-offering (*'ôlāh*, that which goes up) was completely consumed upon the altar. The root *'lh* has a sacrificial sense in other Semitic languages, such as Canaanite and Akkadian. But it is never found as a substantive in them. Thus, 'the *'ôlāh* has then every appearance of being a native Israelite tradition coming from the patriarchs' (Cazelles). The meaning of 'peace offerings' (*shelāmîm*) is disputed. The term has its parallels in the Akkadian and the Râs Shamra texts. Some think of it as a sacrifice with the intention of obtaining peace from God, taking *shillēm* in the sense of 'paying what is due'. Others, with more probability, regard it as a feast of communion, in which the relations with God remained friendly (*shālôm*, peace), where the deity receives his share through what was burnt upon the altar, while the rest was given back to the offerers to make a feast with. 'From the 'šlm' (i.e. the shelāmîm) the deity receives the portion of honour that is his. The remainder serves as a joyous meal for the offerers. Fellowship at table binds the spirits together. The 'šlm' establishes communion between God and the offerers and between the offerers themselves' (Beer). **25. tool**: Hebrew 'sword'. 'The Talmud explains the prohibition as follows: "Iron shortens life, whilst the altar prolongs it. The sword, or weapon of iron, is the symbol of strife; whereas the altar is the symbol of reconciliation and peace between God and man, and between man and his fellow"' (Hertz). **steps**: when, later, altars with steps were constructed, and only the priests could offer sacrifice, a special priestly dress that would conserve decency was designed; cf. 28:42f.

XXI 1 E **The Ordinances or Judgments,** the **194a**
mishpāṭîm, the heading of a fresh collection, 21:2–22:17—An ordinance or judgment is 'properly a decision given in an individual case, and then established as a precedent for similar cases' (Driver, DB iii, 66). The *mishpāṭîm* are in casuistic form.

2-11 E **The Laws concerning Slavery**; cf. Lev. **b**
25:39–55; Dt. 15:12–18—**2-6. Release of Hebrew Male Slaves.** The term 'Hebrew' is here equivalent in practice to the later term Israelite, though it might include kindred tribes who had joined in the Exodus; see on 12:38. But it seems also to keep something of its original meaning, in which it did not denote a race or people, but a social status, usually one of dependence. An Israelite might be enslaved (*a*) through being sold by his or her father (cf. 7; Neh. 5:5); (*b*) through selling himself because of poverty (cf. Lev. 25:39); (*c*) for having committed theft (cf. 22:1); or (*d*) because he had become insolvent (2 Kg. 4:1; Am. 2:6, 8:6). After six years' servitude he was to be set free, and, as Heinisch says, the *status quo ante* was restored. If at the time when he became a slave he was already married, his wife was set free with him (3). But if he was only given a wife while he was a slave, the wife and her children remained the property of the master; the mother's relationship to the family was regarded as closer than the father's, a very primi-

194b tive survival. According to Codex Ḥammurabi (CH) 117, a debtor could sell his wife and his children into servitude, but they were to be set free after three years. **5-7** treat of the case of a slave who refuses to be set free, who prefers 'slavery with economic freedom to freedom with economic insecurity' (I. Mendelsohn, 'Slavery in the Ancient Near East', BA 9 (1946), 78), who also quotes evidence from Nuzu of Ḥabiru who sold themselves because they were unable to find employment. Such a man became a slave in perpetuity. He is brought to God (6)—RVm 'judges' is less likely—where he might solemnly make the asseveration contained in **5.** 'To God' generally means 'to a sanctuary'. But the significance of the ritual, which is that the slave is now brought into a very close relationship with the family, suggests that the 'door' and the 'doorpost' are those of the home of the master. It may be that a special sanctity attached to them (cf. 12:7, 22f.), or because the images of the household gods were kept there. Menes (*Die vorexilische Gesetze Israels* (1928), 27) sees in the clause a laicising of the act, inspired by the desire to abolish the local sanctuaries—the solemn act would retain its publicity but lose its religious character. **6. bore his ears**: the ear is the organ of obedience (Baentsch). **7-11. Female Hebrew Slaves.** The evidence from Nuzu (see Mendelsohn, *sup.*) makes clear that there were two kinds of sale of children. There was (*a*) unconditional sale, where the parents sold the child absolutely and outright. And there was (*b*) conditional sale, by which the child was adopted into the purchaser's family. **7** deals with unconditional sale. The Deuteronomic legislation, however (15:12–17), gives the female slave the same right to freedom as the man. **8-11** is a fragment dealing with conditional sale. In this case, 'the condition that the girl is to be adopted is fundamental' (Mendelsohn). The purchaser of the girl buys with the intention of marrying her himself. If, however, he does not do so—'has dealt unfaithfully with her' (8)—he may not sell her like a slave bought unconditionally, but must either let her be redeemed (bought back by her father) (8), or give her as wife to one of his sons, with the full status of daughter-in-law (9). If, again, he does marry her, but then takes another wife, he must treat her as before (10). The consequence of a breach of these provisions is given in **11.**

c **12-17** E **Capital offences**—The general principle is laid down in **12**; cf. Gen. 9:6; also Lev. 24:17; Num. 35:30 f. In the earliest times, the avenging of murder was a private affair, laid on the next of kin; cf. Num. 35:19, 21, 27 P, 'the avenger of blood', Dt. 19:12; 2 Sam. 14:11. But murder had public consequences (cf. Dt. 19:13), and Löhr (*Asylwesen* (1930), 35) may be right in thinking that already here the community is thought of as the instrument of punishment. **13-14**: as in CH (206f.) and the Hittite Law (HL) (1:1–5), a distinction is made between intentional and unintentional homicide; cf. also Num. 35:9–34; Dt. 19:1–13. **13. but God . . . hand** means, if he killed accidentally, without premeditation. In that case, the slayer had the right of asylum in a sanctuary ('my altar' 14), till his case was judged, or till the anger of the avenger of blood had cooled, when compensation might be arranged. Later legislation restricted the right of asylum to certain fixed cities; cf. Num. 35:13ff.; Dt. 4:41ff.; Jos. 20. **15** and **17** belong together; cf. LXX. The prescription follows from the high respect for parents enjoined in 20:12. With **15** cf. Dt. 21:18–22; with cursing Lev. 20:9. The curse was thought to have real effect. But in view of Dt. 27:6 and the other codes of the ancient East, the expression 'curses' here should probably be extended to mean 'behave in an unfilial manner'. Sumerian law enacted that a son who so behaved was to be put out of the household or sold or disinherited. CH (195) enacted that a son who lifted his hand against his parents was to have his hands cut off. **16. kidnapping**; cf. Dt. 24:7, where it is limited to the kidnapping of an Israelite. CH 19
(214) also prohibits the offence, and HL (1:19–21) judges it more severely than murder.

18-32 E **Non-capital Offences—18-27. Bodily** d
Injuries caused by Human Beings. Dillmann and others transpose 23–25 to follow 18–19. The dislocation is due to the occurrence of 'eye and tooth' in 26f. 18–19 treat of injuries inflicted in a quarrel. In CH the aggressor has to take an oath that he did not intend to kill, and also compensate the injured party for his loss of time. In the Hittite parallel, a third party has to be paid to work for the injured man. **18. fist**: so LXX. Only again Isa. 58:4. Others suggest 'spade' or 'cudgel'. **19. loss of time**: Hebrew 'residence': either his loss of time or his enforced residence at home. **23-25** state the *lex talionis*; cf. Lev. 24:19f.; Dt. 19:21; also Gen. 4:23, a principle of justice widespread in early societies, effecting fit punishment and at the same time imposing limits upon vengeance. CH (198ff.) provides for a monetary compensation when the injury is done to a social inferior, while HL imposes a fine in all cases. **30** also provides for a fine ('ransom'), cf. Jos., *Ant.* IV, viii, 35, 'unless he that is maimed will accept money instead of it (sc. the corresponding member).' **22. Miscarriage as the Result of a Quarrel.** For the last clause read with Budde: 'and he shall pay for the miscarriage'. If the woman died, presumably the *lex talionis* would apply in some form. In Dt. 25:11 the case is somewhat different. There the woman's miscarriage is due to her intervention in the quarrel. But here it could be caused by, say, excitement, or the man's bumping into her. **20-21, 26-27.** 'The laws governing the corporal injury of slaves shows the effect of resting on two irreconcilable postulates, i.e. that the slave is a human being, and that he is another man's property' (*Abing. Comm.*). Even a slight loss, such as of a tooth, sets him free. If, however, he lingers a day or so and then dies, his owner is considered to have suffered loss enough, through having the slave's services no longer, and is quit. The punishment levied upon the owner if the slave died at once is not stated. According to CH and HL, injury to a slave by an outsider required compensation to be made to the owner.

28-32 E **Injuries to Men due to Animals**—The e
regulations are clear. The ox is perhaps taken as the type of all animals, as the most dangerous. Its flesh was not to be eaten, since it had incurred a blood-guiltiness taboo. **30** allows the owner to compromise for a fine, 'ransom', stipulated either by the family of the man gored, or by the judges. **32.** 'thirty pieces of silver': probably his value in the slave market.

33-34 E **Injuries due to Pits etc.**—Pits, that is, f
wells and cisterns, are often still left uncovered in Palestine. When an animal dies through falling into one of them, the carcass becomes the offender's property after he makes restitution of the value of the animal. He could use the hide and perhaps, at this early period, the meat also. Dt. 14:21 forbids the eating by Israelites of anything that dies of itself, but allows it to be given to resident aliens or strangers. Lev. 17:15f. makes the prohibition against eating such flesh absolute. Parallel cases are similarly decided in CH and HL.

35-36 E **Injuries by Cattle to Cattle**—'This g
represents a more advanced civilisation than that of the Bedouin, where the living animal is exchanged for the dead' (Heinisch).

XXII 1-6 E **Theft, Burglary, and Damage—1,** 195
3b, and **4.** Add to references given in RSV 2 Sam. 12:4–6. Cazelles cites from Jaussen (*Coutumes des Arabes au pays de Moab* (1908)) that four-fold restitution is still the compensation for sheep, and even for asses, stolen, amongst tribes united by the tie of Ben-'ameh, that is, tribes who consider themselves cousins. **2-3a** are an insertion dealing not with restitution, but with a thief who breaks in by night. They may originally

5a have been connected with the group 21:12ff. (Jepsen, Menes). The killing of one who breaks in by night is allowed, probably since the householder does not know whether the intruder intends burglary or murder. But with burglary by daylight identification is possible —a small community where everyone knows everyone else is presumed—and so information is to be laid before the judges. The case of a householder killing a burglar by daylight would fall under 21:13. **2. bloodguilt for him** : blood vengeance which would fall upon the slayer.

b **5-6** E **Damage to Fields**—As against the emendation proposed by Driver and others, ' if a man cause a field or a vineyard to be burnt, and let the burning spread, and it burn in another man's field ', HL supports MT, and Cazelles says that Arabs designate by the term *krm*, vineyard, a field cultivated with particular care. To meet the difficulty that the carelessness in **5** is more heavily punished—' from the best in his own field '—than that in **6**, where the damage is more severe, read, following LXX, Sam., after ' in another man's field ', ' he shall make restitution from his own field according to its produce ; but if it eat the whole of his (the others's) field, he (the offender) shall make restitution from the best, etc.' **6.** thorns : the undergrowth brushwood in the field, or the field's thorn hedges ; cf. Isa. 5:5.

c **7-13** E **Deposits—7-9.** Heinisch points out that tenders of cattle must often be from home, and therefore deposit their property with a neighbour. **8. shall come near to God** : in Nuzu, ' divine images were used in deciding cases where contradictory claims led to a deadlock. . . . The ordeal-oath before the gods is a common feature of the Nuzu trials ' (Cyrus H. Gordon, ' Biblical Customs and the Nuzu Tablets ', BA 3 (1940), 11). **8. to show** : how the innocence or guilt is demonstrated is not said. LXX, Vulg. think of an oath, as is prescribed in **11,** which the guilty party would be afraid to take. Other possibilities are the ordeal (Num. 5), the Urim and Thummim (so Daube ; cf. 1 Sam. 14:41ff.), or an oracle. By any of these the guilty party would be condemned of God (9). **9** extends the principle laid down in **8** to take in all cases of breach of trust or suspected misappropriation. **This is it**, i.e. the thing which has been lost, and is claimed to be found in the possession of another.

d **10-13 Animals Injured or Lost**—The principle is the same as for goods deposited, 7ff. The person in whose care the animal has been put must attest on oath that he has not misappropriated it to himself, a usage still followed by the Arabs, according to Burckhardt and Doughty. **11b** should probably be read : ' and the owner shall accept the dead (or hurt) animal, and he (the other) shall not make restitution '. In **10,** ' driven away ' is a dittograph of the previous word, and is to be omitted : the case of the animal stolen is dealt with in **12.** CH also prescribes restitution for a stolen animal, and gives exemption for one torn by wild beasts. For the usage that the shepherd should produce evidence of what had been torn, see Gen. 31:39 ; Am. 3:12. The fragments would prove that the shepherd had been on the alert ; cf. 1 Sam. 17:34f.

e **14-15** E **Compensation for Injury to an Animal Borrowed**—The Hebrew has simply ' if a man borrow ', without object. But the context (cf. Syr.), makes clear that an animal is meant. **15.** RSV seems to mean that if the borrowed animal was in its owner's charge, then the borrower was not required to pay compensation ; the responsibility rested with the owner (15*a*). If the owner hired it, however (15*b*), he should have reckoned with the possibility of injury when he fixed the price of the hire. But *śākhîr* (hire) usually has a reference to persons, and not to things. So some render **15b** : ' if a hired servant (caused the injury), it comes on his hire ', i.e. compensation is taken from his wages. But Cazelles, on the basis of HL 76, renders, ' if it is a hirer, he shall receive his hire price ', that is, when a contract was made subject
to payment and not gratis, the hirer shall receive his 195e
money, but that only.

16-17 E **Seduction of Virgins**—The unmarried f
daughter is regarded as her father's property. If she is violated, he will have difficulty in getting a husband for her. So, even in the case where he refuses to allow the seducer to marry her, compensation has to be paid equivalent to the ' marriage present ' (*mōhar*). The *mōhar* is mentioned only here and in Gen. 34:12 and 1 Sam. 18:25, but it is well known amongst the Arabs, the Canaanites and the Mesopotamians. It was paid by the bridegroom to the father of the bride at the time of the betrothal. In Dt. 22:28f., where the case is rape, not seduction, the compensation is fixed at 50 shekels. Assyrian law exacted a compensation of three times the *mōhar*, while in Moab the case was treated exactly as here (Jaussen). For the seduction of a girl who is betrothed, which is equivalent to adultery, see Dt. 22:23ff.

18-31 E **Miscellaneous Ordinances—18-20.** g
Three Capital Offences. (i) Magic, which is the attempt to control the higher powers, was rife in the ancient world, especially in Babylon and Assyria, and CH and Assyrian law also prescribe the death penalty for it. cf. also Lev. 20:6, 27. Eight forms of magic are given in Dt. 18:10 ff. Other OT references to it are Isa. 2:6 and Ezek. 13:18. (ii) Bestiality was also common in the ancient Orient. Herodotus (ii, 46) attests it for the Egyptians, and HL makes it a capital offence, except where a horse or a mule was concerned. Lev. 18:23–25 attests it for the Canaanites. (iii) Yahweh alone is to be worshipped (20). Omit ' save to the Lord only '. **Utterly destroyed** : put to the ban. By the ' ban ' (*ḥerem*) people and things were made over to Yahweh, men and women being put to death, with or without their cattle also. See Dt. 13:12–18 ; 1 Sam. 15. ' Devoted ' would better bring out the religious significance of the act.

21-27 Admonitions concerning Care for Others— h
22-24. The Widow and the Orphan. The suggested order of Mayer-Lambert (*Revue des Études Juives* 36 (1898), 203) is better. He rejects 21*b*, as having come in from 22:9, and then arranges 21*a*, 23*b*, 22, 23*a*, 24. Consideration for the widow and the orphan, and for the resident alien, is constantly enjoined in the OT, e.g. Lev. 19:33f. ; Dt. 1:16, 10:18, 14:29, 16:11–14, etc. ; Isa. 1:17 ; Jer. 7:6. In the NT, see Jas 1:27. **23f.** ' What is uniquely stressed here is the immediate and dynamic role the God of Israel plays in this concern for and accomplishment of justice ' (*Abing. Comm.*) ; see notes on 3:7–10.
24. An application of the *lex talionis*. **25-27. Lending** i
on Interest. ' The lending of business capital on terms offering good chances of repayment was not in question ' (A. J. Carlyle, in *Property : its Rights and Duties*, 100). What is prohibited in this early code is the exploitation of people's needs. No interest is to be taken from a fellow-member of the community, though it might be taken from a foreigner, Dt. 23:19f. **25b. and you shall not exact** etc. is probably an explanatory gloss on ' creditor '. The kindly spirit which the Israelite was to show to his fellow Israelite is further exemplified in **26f.** The ' garment ', a large square of cloth, is the upper garment, in which the peasant also slept. Amos (2:8) complains about the breach of this injunction.

28-31 Religious Laws—28. Blasphemy was pun- j
ished by death, Lev. 24:15f. **29a.** The Hebrew is : ' thy fulness and thy trickling thou shalt not delay '. RSV follows LXX. But some (Heinisch, Cazelles, etc.) connect ' fulness ' with wine (cf. Num. 18:27), and ' trickling ' with oil. In any case, what is referred to is the offering of the first-fruits, later fixed at a tenth of the yield, Dt. 14:22ff., 26:1–15. Tithing is the acknowledgment that the land and its produce are God's. **29b.** The cases of child sacrifice attested for Israel are only on extraordinary occasions. So, although it is not stated, the principle of redemption already laid down in 13:12ff. is to be understood here.

195j **30. eighth day** : cf. Lev. 22:26 H. **31.** The pronouns, plural in Hebrew instead of singular, as in the preceding verses (see AV), make it possible that 31 is a later addition. The prohibition is connected with the taboo against eating of the blood. In the case of a torn beast, the blood would not be properly drained. The ' dogs ' are the shepherd's dogs.

196a **XXIII 1-3** E **Truthfulness and Impartiality**—These prescriptions, like those in 6-9, are in apodictic form, and their standpoint is ethical rather than juridical, to create the correct attitude in the matters; cf. Lev. 19:15–18. In **1b** by ' join hands ' some formal gesture may be meant rather than simply a metaphor; cf. Job 9:33. **2** warns against being influenced by a majority, both to do evil in general, and specifically in testifying in a court of law. For ' is a suit ' (2), some follow LXX and read ' with a multitude ' (*rōbh* for *rîbh*). In **3** ' great ' (*gādhōl*) is generally read for ' poor ' (*wᵉdhāl*), since, it is held, a prohibition against showing partiality to a poor man is superfluous. Cazelles, though leaving the text as it stands, suggests that the verb might have the meaning attested in Arabic, ' to shed blood with impunity '. The poor man would then be the man of little consequence whose inconvenient testimony could thus easily be put out of the way.

b **4-5 Assistance to Animals**—An insertion, in casuistic formulation. The spirit of the commands connects them with 22:21–27. ' These two injunctions breathe a spirit unusual in the OT (cf., however, Lev. 19:17–18) and remind one of Mt. 5:44 ' (Driver). ' Moral and social responsibility transcend personal enmity ' (*Abing. Comm.*).

c **6-9 Further Counsels on Justice**—Parallel with honesty in bearing witness (1–3) goes equity in administering justice. **6. your poor** : with the pronoun only again in Dt. 15:11 (so Hebrew), points to the community. ' The sense of community is to transcend social differences ' (Heinisch). Cazelles, however, takes ' your poor ' as ' the protégé of the man addressed by the legislator '. **7b.** LXX renders ' you will not acquit '. But MT can stand. The wicked are reminded, as in Prov. 15:3, that there is also a God who sees and judges. **8.** Taking of bribes was common; see Isa. 1:23; Am. 5:12; Mic. 3:11; Ps. 15:5, 26:10; Prov. 17:8, 23; Dt. 27:25; 1 Sam. 8:3, etc. **Officials**: lit., ' open-eyed ', found only here. ' A bribe blinds the witnesses who saw ' (Cazelles) : ' a bribe makes the blind to see ' (Heinisch). **9.** cf. 22:21. **heart** : outlook, condition. The verse is the root of the OT.

d **10-19 Laws on Worship**—These connect with the other cultic prescriptions in 20:24–26, 22:29–30. **10-11.** The custom of letting the land lie fallow every seventh year is attested amongst other peoples also. According to Lev. 25:4, the reason was religious, the acknowledgment of God's ownership of the soil by the renouncing of the use of it every seventh year. Here the motive is rather humanitarian—' that the poor of your people may eat ' (10). In the seventh year the poor man would be in the worst case of all. The rich could lay up provision against it, and the slave was cared for by his master. But the poor man, if he were an agricultural labourer, was done out of even his livelihood. Hence that which came up self-sown was reserved for him. In the later usage (cf. Lev. 25:2–7), the fallow year is represented as to be observed in the same year throughout the country. **12,** with its mention of the Sabbath, which all observe simultaneously, could suggest that the same is meant here. Deuteronomy omits the law, and Lev. 26:34f. and 2 Chr. 36:21 suggest that the provision was not strictly observed in the pre-exilic period. Neh. 10:31 and 1 Mac. 6:49, 53 point to post-exilic observance. In Dt. 15:2 and Neh. 10:31 release of debtors and slaves was connected with the fallow year; cf. 21:2. **12. the Sabbath** : cf. 20:8–11. **The son of your handmaid** : either the home-born slave, whose parents were also slaves (Driver), or the son of a concubine (Bertholet, Baentsch). **13a** would come more naturally at the end of the Book of the Covenant, 19
or of one of the smaller collections of which it is made up.

14-17 Three Annual Pilgrimages—See notes on e
ch. 12 and §§37*f*, 115*a*, 238*d*. As well as the Sabbath, three pilgrimage feasts are to be observed : (*a*) **15,** the feast of Unleavened Bread, or Mazzoth, with which was connected Passover, see ch. 12 and the notes there; (*b*) **16a,** the feast of the harvest, or the feast of weeks (34:22), seven weeks and a day later, hence Pentecost (*pentekonta*=50=7×7, + 1). This feast was not historicised in the OT, but was later, in the Maccabaean period, connected with the giving of the law; (*c*) **16b,** the feast of the ingathering, which took place in the seventh month, Sept.–Oct., at the end of the old economic year. (On the reckoning of the year, see on 12:2.) The threshing was then over, and the grapes and olives gathered. Grapes and olives were important as the main sources of fat used in cooking and for oil for the lamps. In Lev. 23:34; Dt. 16:13 and in later writings generally the name of this festival is ' the festival of Tabernacles, or Booths ', explained in Lev. 23:43 as commemorating the fact that the Israelites dwelt in ' booths ' after they left Egypt. Originally, it is probable, the ' booths ' were the tents made of branches in which the peasants slept in the fields as they gathered the harvest. For fuller accounts of these festivals, see Lev. 23:4–21, 33–44; Dt. 16:1–17. **17. appear before me** : the regular formula for pilgrimage to a shrine, as here.

18-19 cf. 34:25f. On **18a,** see on 12:8. In 34:25 J, f
the sacrifice of **18** is defined as the Passover, but here the prescription is probably general. **18b. the fat of my feast** : i.e. the fat portions, as the best part of the animals, which were to be burnt upon the altar. Keeping them overnight would mean that they were no longer fresh, and so unworthy to be offered. **19a. the first of the first fruits** are either the first ripe or the choicest. **19b.** The significance of this prohibition has now been made clear by the Râs Shamra texts. According to the *Birth of the Gods*, i, 14, a kid was cooked in its mother's milk to procure the fertility of the fields, which were sprinkled with the substance which resulted. In this case, a Canaanite practice is rejected, no doubt because it savoured of magic; see on 22:18.

20-33 (**20-22a,** to ' say ', E; **22b-24** J, **25f.** E, **27** J; g
28 E; **29-31a,** to ' Euphrates ', J; **31b-33** E; so Eissfeldt) **Appendix to the Book of the Covenant**—The Holiness Code and D both close with a similar hortatory epilogue; cf. Lev. 26; Dt. 28. But the verses here are not in their proper place. There is no reference at all in them to the Book of the Covenant, or to keeping the commandments contained in it. Moreover, the blessing promised is connected with commandments still to be given. The whole context suggests that the original position of this passage was the departure from Sinai, and on the way to Canaan. Israel is to obey the angel (20, see on 3:2), who is Yahweh's ambassador, though he is not distinguished from him : ' my name is in him '. With **20f.** cf. 32:34, 33:14. (For J, the pillar of cloud is Israel's guide.) **23.** For the list of peoples, see on 3:8. Blessings will follow loyalty to the divine leading, **25f.** Yahweh will help his people to conquer Canaan, though the conquest will be gradual (27–30; cf. Jg. 1:19, and contrast the Book of Joshua). And (31) the boundaries of the nation are to be what they became in fact under David and Solomon (1 Kg. 4:21). For similar promises, see Gen. 15:18; Dt. 11:24, and for the restored nation, Isa. 27:12. **24. pillars** : the standing stones which were a regular feature of a Canaanite shrine. **27. terror** : ' the climax of the Holy War is that terror sent by God . . . comes upon the enemy, a numinous panic in which they act blindly and accomplish their own destruction; cf. Jos. 10:10; Jg. 4:15; 1 Sam. 7:10, etc.' (von Rad, op. cit., 47f.). **28. hornet** : cf. Dt. 7:20; Jos. 24:12; Wis. 12:8. Garstang's suggestion that the Egyptians

6g are meant has not been generally accepted. Probably the word is to be taken literally, as some plague that would come upon the Canaanites.

h **XXIV** (**1-2** J, **3-8** E, **9-11** J, **12-15a** E, **15b-18a** P (?), **18b** E) **The Covenant: The Ratification of the Covenant**—According to the present text, the ratification takes place in two stages. In **3-8** E, the people accept the covenant and Moses ratifies it. In **9-11** J, it is ratified by Moses and the elders at a sacrificial meal. The two accounts, now combined, were originally independent traditions. The present text suggests that 'the appearance of God gives those who accompany Moses the certainty that God and the people belong together, and that God will protect Israel as his people' (Heinisch). In J's narrative (1–2, 9–11), Moses, with Aaron and two of Aaron's sons (cf. 6:23, 28:1; Lev. 10:1ff.) and the elders are commanded to come up to the mountain of the Lord, though in fact 'Moses alone' (2) is to go to the top: the others remain only some distance up, to worship, in preparation for the vision of the God of Israel in 9–11. They appear to have gone up later (9f.) for they too see the vision. God's glory is not seen directly, but between it and them was the bright blue of a heaven now cleared of the clouds which had covered the mountain at 19:18 and 20:18. With the description cf. Ezek. 1:26. The chief men, lit. corner stones, were not harmed, though ordinarily it was fatal to see God; cf. 33:20; Gen. 16:13. They then ratify the covenant by a sacrificial meal in which it was supposed that Yahweh joined, whether on the mountain top or when they came down is not
i stated. In E's account, Moses, taking up the people's request in 20:19 that he should be God's spokesman to them, came and told the people all the words of the Lord (3—omit 3*a* 'all the ordinances'; cf. 3*b*). The people promise obedience. Then follows E's account of the ratification, by sacrifice and the sprinkling of blood. With 'the altar' (4) cf. 20:24; for the 'pillars', see on 23:24; for the 'burnt offering' etc. (5), see on 20:24. It is not yet priests who offer, but young men (5). In **8** the 'blood of the covenant' means the blood which ratifies the covenant; cf. Zech. 9:11. With it, however, Moses acts as priest. Half of it was thrown over the altar (6), as representing God, the other half over the people (8), as the other contracting party. Heb. 9:19 represents the book (7, also by implication 4) as sprinkled also. (From the 'book' of **7** comes the name of the 'Book of the Covenant' given to the collection of laws in 20:23–23:33. Moses then (12–15*a*, 18*b*) goes up the mountain again, apparently taking Joshua with him, cf. 32:17. 'Moses' servant' (13) is Joshua's regular title, cf. 33:11; Num. 11:28; Jos. 1:1. Moses then receives the two tables of stone, generally taken as having the Decalogue written upon them. In **12** the meaning of 'with the law and the commandment' is not apparent, and the words are probably a later addition. **15b-18a** is perhaps P's account of the events described by J and E in ch. 19. In P the cloud regularly conceals the glory or presence of God: here the fire of the glory (cf. Zech. 2:5) breaks through the cloud, so that the people can see it. In 11 J the elders see it.

7a **XXV-XXXI** P **The Tabernacle**—As is pointed out below, the Tabernacle and the Ark have affinities with the portable tent-shrines in use among the Arabs. 'We must suppose that the portable red-leather tent was one of the oldest motifs of Semitic religion. Thus it goes without saying that the Tabernacle and the Ark have historical connections with their Semitic past' (Frank M. Cross, Jr., 'The Tabernacle', BA 10 (1947), 46-68). The construction of the Tabernacle in the wilderness can therefore no longer be regarded as a fiction of the later Priestly writers. (And indeed it is increasingly recognised that much in P is based on sound ancient tradition, see §175*d*.) That some tent-shrine of the nature here described, though much less elaborate, was in use in the wilderness can be taken as certain. A later element does, however, enter into the description of the Tabernacle here,
namely the influence of the Canaanite temple. The 197a
division into two, the Holy Place and the Most Holy Place, derive from the temple—and not from the tent-motif, and Cross points out that the *ḳ^{e}rāshîm* framework—see on 26:15–30—which converts the tent into a portable temple, seems to have had Canaanite connections. 'Apparently the *qerashim* framework has historical connections with the abode of deity in Canaanite mythology'. At Ugarit, 'the *q-r-sh* refers to the throne room of El'. Phoenician influence also is traceable in some of the Tabernacle furnishings.

The Tabernacle has thus two sources of origin, b
which the Priestly writers do not completely harmonise. Galling (128ff.) holds that by separating out all the desert characteristics in the description and leaving the rest aside as later elaboration, we can arrive at the Mosaic tent, a simple tent structure of an outer covering draped over poles. He thus rejects the *ḳ^{e}rāshîm* framework, the division into Holy Place and Most Holy Place, and the bulk of the furnishings here described. Cross brings evidence in support of the view that the account of the Tabernacle given here reflects the Davidic tent, and not the Temple of Solomon, as is often supposed, though he admits that some influence of the Temple on the Priestly account is undeniable. 'The Priestly sources are describing the culminating development of the Tabernacle institution'. In any case we may be sure that some structure characteristically Semitic was made in the wilderness as a Tent of Meeting (29:42f., 25:22, 30:36), where God met with and spoke to his people, and where he 'tabernacled' with them. Cross says that the word for the sanctuary (*mishkān*) meant originally a 'tent'. In P it is restricted to the Tabernacle. And the corresponding verb *škn*, Cross argues, is also restricted to the idea of God's 'tabernacling' at the Tent. God does not 'dwell' (*yāshabh*) in the Tabernacle—he 'dwells' in heaven—but he 'settles impermanently' upon it. 'So P solves the problem of the divine immanence and transcendence. The one cosmic God could not be confined in any shrine. At the same time he had to be present with his people. The bridge is effected by the idea of his "tabernacling"' (Cross).

XXV 1-9 P **Provision of Materials** (cf. 35:20–29)— c
For the sanctuary by means of which God may 'tabernacle' with his people, 'dwell in their midst' (8), Moses is to collect 'contributions'—so rather than 'offerings' (2). The Hebrew word *t^{e}rûmāh* means something 'taken off' from a larger mass (Driver), as e.g. the part of a sacrifice given to the priest, Lev. 7:14, the first-fruits, Num. 15:19–21, the temple area, Ezek. 45:1, 48:8, etc. Willingness on the part of the contributors is stressed again in connection with the second Temple, Ezr. 1:6, 2:68, 3:5, 7:15, 8:28. The gold, silver, and bronze were for the vessels, the gilding of the Ark, etc. The blue (violet), the purple (purple-red) and the scarlet were for the curtains. Blue and purple dyes were got from shellfish, scarlet from a species of cochineal. Fabric of goats'-hair was spun by the women 35:26, and served as a first covering over the curtains of the Dwelling, 26:7. The skins formed the second and third coverings, 26:14. The word translated 'goatskins' (5) is uncertain. Some think of a sea-animal of the kind of the dolphin found in the Red Sea. Cross says that the most reasonable suggestion is that of Bondi, who connects the Hebrew word *taḥash* with an Egyptian root meaning 'to stretch or treat leather'. 'This would suggest that the mysterious *tahash* skins were actually an imported (?) specially finished leather'. Acacia wood (5) was needed for the framework, 26:15ff. LXX omits 6, and the verse is a later addition. Onyx (7) is uncertain. For the Hebrew *shōham* beryl, chrysoprase and malachite are variously suggested. For the ephod and the breastplate, see on 28:6–30. The 'sanctuary' (8) from the root *ḳdš*, holy; the 'tabernacle' (or Dwelling) (9), from root *škn*, see §197*b*, at end. **9. I show you concerning the pattern:** the cultic

197c arrangements of Israel as well as the laws of its life are given it by God.

d **10-22** P **The Ark**—Amongst certain Arabic tribes objects similar to the Ark survive; see especially Cross, loc. cit. In time of war they accompanied the tribe into battle and guided it in its wanderings; cf. Num. 10:35f. In peace, they stood near the chief's tent. Some of them contained sacred stones (*betyls*), or were thought of as the dwelling-place of Allah. They were thus places of worship, and rallying-points for the tribes. This fits in with what we know of the Ark in Israel. And if the Kenite hypothesis is correct (see on ch. 18), the institution may have been taken over from the Midianites. Called the 'Ark of Elohim' (so often in Joshua) and the 'Ark of Yahweh' (so often in 1 Sam.), in the JE tradition it is the symbol of God's presence with his people—cf. 1 Sam. 4:7: 'the gods are come into the camp'—and the throne upon which he rested invisibly. In D (10:1–5, also 16 here), the Ark is the receptacle for the two tables of stone. Eerdmans (*The Religion of Israel* (E.T., 1947), 42) says that the historical value of 16 has been doubted, 'as it seemed improbable that tablets of law would have been hidden in a chest. Yet there must have been made some receptacle for transporting them when the people were moving'. The name which resulted, the 'Ark of the Covenant', suggests that 'the Ark became rather a memorial of the once-for-all concluded alliance between Jahweh and Israel, than the instrument of the divine presence' (Harford). In P it becomes the most sacred object in the whole appurtenance of the nation's worship, and, as the 'Ark of the Testimony', set up in the Most Holy Place, the place where God meets with his people (22). It thus takes over the function of E's Tent of Meeting, 33:7–11. In size about 3¾ by 2¼ by 2¼ ft., the Ark was a casket of acacia wood overlaid inside and outside with gold, with a moulding, which may have run round the top, for the cover to fit into, or which may have been a cable-mounting going round the middle; cf. LXX. It was also to have gold rings and gold poles. For a different tradition from that in 15, see Num. 4:6. The point here is that Yahweh is represented as not bound to any particular place, but his Presence goes with his people. When the Ark was finally put in the Holy of Holies, its poles could be seen from the Holy Place, 1 Kg. 8:8. The 'mercy seat' (17) was a cover, a slab of pure gold. It was the place of propitiation, and became the most sacred object in all the holy place. On the day of Atonement the culminating rite was the sprinkling of the mercy seat with the blood, atoning for the sins of the people, Lev. 16:2, 13–16. Its special sanctity was due to its being the throne of Yahweh who sat on the cherubim (1 Sam. 4:4), and there met and spoke with his people

e (22). On the two ends of the mercy seat were two 'cherubim' (18–21). 'A number of scholars have thought that they (the cherubim) were the great winged bulls which were so popular in Mesopotamia. But a check of the art of Palestine and Syria shows that such monsters are practically non-existent in this area. A process of elimination shows that the cherub can have been only one thing: a winged sphinx, that is, a winged lion with a human head. This is the most popular winged being in Phoenician art. It is to be found on artistic objects uncovered in almost every excavation in this area; and it is the only being which could possibly be the cherub' (WBA, 141). Their religious significance, Wright says, is something which is rather vague. 'Apparently in the religion of Israel as in other Near Eastern religions such winged beings were thought to be assistants who aided a god in getting from place to place'. But clearly they are here the throne for Yahweh's invisible presence, like Jeroboam's bulls; cf. Ezek. 1:5. The making of them shows that the Decalogue (20:4–6) did not intend to prohibit the making of all images, but only such as were objects of worship.

198a **23-30** P **The Table of Showbread** (cf. 37:10–16)—We now pass to the description of the furniture of the holy place. Anciently it was believed that a god needed food, and that he consumed what was set before him, e.g. the story of Bel and the Dragon, and the cakes kneaded for the queen of heaven in Jer. 7:18, 44:19. Here the usage is spiritualised, and 'bread of the presence'—also called 'holy bread', 1 Sam. 21:4, 6; 'continual bread', Num. 4:7 P; and 'bread of setting out', 1 Chr. 9:32, 23:29; 2 Chr. 13:11; Neh. 10:34—is regarded as something like the first fruits, an acknowledgment that daily bread comes by the bounty of Yahweh. Some, however, think that it is rather a symbol of the presence of Yahweh. For its preparation and mode of offering see Lev. 24:5–9. On the 'moulding of gold' (24), see on 11. Josephus (Ant. III, vi, 6) says: 'It was hollowed out on each side to a depth of about three inches, a spiral border running round the upper and lower portion of the body of the table' (Thackeray's translation (1930), 381). See also Driver *in loco.* The 'frame' (25) can be seen on the Arch of Titus. It is a golden rail going round the legs about half-way up, to give additional strength. The 'plates' or salvers (29) were for carrying the loaves of the presence to and from the table, the 'dishes' (cf. 1 Mac. 1:22) were cups containing the incense which was put on the loaves and then burnt (Lev. 24:7). Nowhere is it said in the rest of the OT that an offering of wine was part of the ritual of the presence bread.

31-40 P **The Lampstand** (cf. 37:17–24)—The lampstand represented on the Arch of Titus had been made, like the table, by Judas Maccabaeus after the pollution of the Temple by Antiochus Epiphanes (1 Mac. 4:49), no doubt on the model of the previous furnishings. But in Mosaic times it would be much simpler, although the number of seven for the branches—the six mentioned with the addition of the central shaft—is apparently early. Albright has found at Tell Beit Mirsim terra-cotta lamps dating from 900 B.C. pinched in seven places to hold seven wicks. With the candlestick here, from a massive central stem three 'branches' bent outward and upward on either side, on the top of each of which was placed a lamp (37). The ornamentation provided by the 'cups' is not altogether clear. Each cup consisted of a calyx ('capital') and corolla ('flower') of almond blossom (31, 33). Each of the six branches had three such cups (33), and the stem itself had apparently four (34). But Kennedy (DB iv (1902), 664a) thinks that two of the latter were in the base and two in the upper part of the stem itself, and that the stem had in addition three cups without petals ('a capital of one piece', 35) where the branches joined it. The 'lamps', probably of terra-cotta, were to be fixed on ('set up', 37) with their wicks facing north, to give light in front of the lampstand. The exact significance of 'snuffers' (38) is uncertain. They may have been for trimming the wicks, or they may have been tweezers for drawing the wicks up. b

XXVI P **The Tabernacle**—The Tabernacle is to be 30 cubits long and 10 cubits wide and 10 cubits high (45 × 15 × 15 ft.). It is to have two chambers, the outer, or Holy Place, 30 × 15 × 15 ft., and the main part of the shrine, the Most Holy Place, or Holy of Holies, 15 × 15 × 15 ft. This inner chamber is separated from the outer by a curtain. The Ark was to be placed in the Holy of Holies, the Table of the Presence Bread, the Altar of Incense, and the Lampstand, in the Holy Place. The whole structure was to be a framework covered with various materials. c

1-14 P **The Coverings** (cf. 36:8–19)—For the covering seen from the inside, ten 'curtains' or panels were to be prepared of richly coloured material decorated apparently with cherubim woven in. Out of these were to be made—how, is not stated—two large curtains, each of five panels (3), which in turn were to be joined together by means of 'loops' and 'clasps' of gold (4–6), a method of joining still used in the East (Heinisch). They could thus be taken apart for d d travelling. These curtains were spread over the framework 'as a pall is thrown over a coffin' (Kennedy). Over them was to be placed a second covering made of eleven panels of goats'-hair cloth, such as is still used by the Bedouin (7ff.). They are to be joined together in the same way as the panels of the first covering, although this time each curtain consists of eleven panels, and the clasps are of bronze (11). This covering was two cubits longer than the inner one, and would just reach to the ground, according to the specifications in 15–30. It would protect the inner curtain and the foot of the framework from damage by the weather (13). The sixth breadth was to be doubled over in front (9), ' covering the pillars at the door of the Tent and entirely excluding the light of day. This secures that the dwelling shall be in perfect darkness ' (Kennedy). 12 is then a gloss, for there is nothing left over to hang down the back. Two further coverings are added (14) for protection against the weather, a practice also adopted by the Romans. The one is of rams' skin. For RSV ' tanned ', AV and RV ' dyed red ', that is, with madder, should probably be retained, since we now have evidence from the Bedouin that ' the portable red leather tent was one of the oldest motifs of Semitic religion ' (Frank M. Cross, Jr.). On ' goatskins ' (14), see note on 25:5.

e **15-30** P **The Framework** (cf. 36:20–34)—A. R. S. Kennedy's rendering (DB) of the Hebrew *ḳ^{e}rāshîm*, AV ' boards ', by ' framework ' has been justified by the evidence from Râs Shamra. ' The *qerashim* framework had historical connections with the abode of deity in Canaanite mythology. . . . There is no need to assume with most modern scholars (most recently Galling) that the Tabernacle framework is the fiction of later writers who wished to make the Tabernacle conform more closely in structure with the Temple ' (Frank M. Cross, Jr.). The frames were to be ten cubits high (15 ft.) and a cubit and a half in breadth (2 ft. 3 in.)—that is, each frame had two uprights (' tenons ' 17) joined to each other by cross-rails. The coverings would thus show through. There were to be 48 frames in all, 20 for each side and 8 for the back (18, 20, 22), making the Tabernacle 45 ft. long by 15 ft. wide by 15 ft. high. The frames were to stand in bases of silver (18–22), each upright fitting into a socket. 23f. are obscure. Kennedy thinks of the ' frames for the corners of the tabernacle in the rear ' as a kind of buttress. If RSV is adopted for 24, ' separate beneath, but joined at the top ', what is meant seems to be a buttress—there is a space between the two frames in the rear and the wall of the Tabernacle at its foot, but they are joined at the top. But ' separate ' really means ' twins ', which Kennedy takes as signifying that these corner frames were to be made double, that is, to consist of two ordinary frames braced together for the sake of strength. They terminate just under the uppermost of the bars about to be described.

f **26-30** P **The Bars** (cf. 36:31–33)—The whole framework is further strengthened by bars, which passed through gold rings and ran horizontally along the two sides and the back. Since it is said that the middle bar ran along the whole length of the wall, the presumption is that the two above it and below it did not, and only ran along part of the wall.

g **31-37** P **Veil, Contents and Screen** (cf. 36:35ff., 40:20, 22, 24)—The chamber so formed was to be divided into the Holy Place in front, 20 by 10 cubits, and the Most Holy Place (AV : Holy of Holies) at the back, 10 by 10 cubits. The means of division was an embroidered veil (31ff.), which hung from golden hooks fixed at the top of the four pillars of acacia wood. The pillars were gilded and set in bases of silver. The ' mercy seat ' (see on 25:17) was to be set in the Ark in the Most Holy Place, and outside the veil were to be put the candlestick on the south side and the table on the north. For the entrance a screen was to be made (36f.), similar in material to the veil and similarly hung.

XXVII P **The Altar and Court—1-8 The Altar ;** 198h
cf. 38:1–7. An altar is to be constructed, that is, for burnt offerings. Since it is called *the*, i.e. the one, altar (1), the passage is at variance not only with 20:14, but also with 30:1. 30:1 must therefore derive from a later strand of P. This altar is called the ' altar of burnt offering ' in 30:28 and 31:9, and the ' bronze altar ' in 38:30 and 39:39. A frame of acacia wood (1, ' boards ' 8) was overlaid with bronze. The ' horns ' (2), projections at each of the corners, were regarded as the most sacred part of the altar, why is not known. The blood of the sin offering was applied to them (29:12), fugitives grasped them (1 Kg. 1:50, 2:28). Their use was taken over by Israel from the Canaanites, but their origin is not known. If they are to be connected with the Oriental idea of the bull as the symbol of strength, then in Israel they could have represented Yahweh's power. The vessels of the altar were to be of bronze (3). The ' ashes ' (3) are literally ' its fat ', the fat of the sacrifice which ran down and mixed with the ashes. The lower part of the altar was surrounded by a bronze grating, coming half-way up the altar, and supporting a ledge upon which the priests stood to offer sacrifice (4f.). Rings and poles were also to be prepared to allow the altar to be carried. How this altar was to be used is not clear. If the fire were set inside, the acacia framework would be burnt up ! On the other hand, the hollow may have been filled with earth and stones, and the fire kindled on them. If this were so, then this altar would be brought more into conformity with the regulations in 20:24. Probably the Priestly writer is projecting the stationary altar of Solomon's Temple back to the days of the wilderness, without taking into account the practical details required for an altar that had to be moved about.

9-19 The Court (cf. 38:9–20)—Round the Taber- 199a
nacle was to be a court, 150 ft. long and 75 ft. broad. It was enclosed by means of hangings of linen 7½ ft. long, which hung from silver hooks attached to pillars of wood. The pillars were set in sockets of silver and had ' fillets ' (11, 17) of silver, probably a band of silver running round at the base. The entrance, which faced east, was closed by a screen, 30 ft. long, of embroidered linen (16). For the lack of symmetry which is involved in the description of the pillars, see the larger commentaries.

20f. The command to provide oil for the lampstand b
is out of order here, and comes from Lev. 24:2–4. It has probably been set here by a later editor, to mark the transition to the chapters which follow (28f.) on the duties of the priesthood, since the care of the lamps was part of the priests' duty (21).

XXVIII-XXIX P **The Priesthood**—Having des- c
cribed the Tabernacle and its furnishings, the writer now comes to its personnel. **XXVIII. The Priestly Dress.** In **1-5** the priestly office is assigned to Aaron and his descendants. (For the development of the priesthood, see §§113*f*, 115*e*, 116*d*, 117*e*, 118*bc*.) Aaron is the prototype of the later high priests. His superiority over the rest of the priesthood is shown by the distinction made between his garments and those of his sons (1–39, 40–43). The description of his vestments, and of the high priest's function, corresponds with that given in Sir. 45:6–22 (Aaron), 50:1–21 (Simon).

6-12 The Ephod (cf. 39:2–7)—The ephod was an old d
cultic vestment in Israel. Samuel wore it at Shiloh (1 Sam. 2:18f.), as did David when he brought up the Ark (2 Sam. 6:14f.). A similar garment was also in use in Egypt. It encircled the body, but its position is not certain. Some think of it as worn above the waist, as a kind of waistcoat, others as below, a sort of apron or kilt ; see here Driver, 312. If we read in 7 with LXX and Sam. ' it shall have two shoulder straps joined (to it) : at its two edges shall it be joined ', then it hangs from the shoulders. But the meaning of the latter half of the verse is not clear. 39:4 suggests that the edges are the top edges, to which the shoulder straps are attached. But the

199d phrase might mean the sewing-up of the linen cloth, or its pieces, at the sides. Lev. 8:7 suggests that the 'skilfully woven band' (8) was a girdle to hold the ephod close to the body. For 'materials' RV gives 'of the same piece', that is, the girdle was permanently attached. To the shoulder straps were attached two stones with the names of the sons of Israel upon them (9ff.), to remind Yahweh of his people; cf. the stones of the breastplate (17–21, 29).

e **13-29 The Ḥōshen**—This, the 'breastplate of judgment' (15), was a bag 8 or 9 inches square (16). Its name derives from the fact that the Urim and Thummim (see §116*f*) were placed within it. (See 30 below) The identification of the twelve stones in 17–20 is not in every case certain. Their purpose is given in 29. For two other lists of precious stones which show close resemblances to this one, see Ezek. 28:13 and Rev. 21:19–20. The fastenings of the bag are carefully described, but the details are not all clear. Two cords of gold, already mentioned in **14,** pass through two rings of gold attached to the pouch (23f.), and are fastened on to the shoulder pieces of the ephod by means of two settings of filigree, or rosettes (13f., 25). **26-28** are omitted in LXX. If they are not just a secondary account of what has just been described, and so to be omitted, we have to think of two further rings of gold attached to the *lower* inside corners (' at the two ends' 26) of the bag, through which a cord of blue passes to two other golden rings in the ephod. **29-30** show the priest as having a double function. He represents the people before God (cf. 12), and he declares to the people the will of God which he has disclosed to him by the Urim and Thummim, the sacred lot.

f **31-35 The Violet Robe** (cf. 39:22–26)—This robe, which was always worn with the ephod, and under it, was of the royal colour. It was like a pullover, without sleeves, and put on over the head. It was decorated with pomegranates in variously coloured embroidery, and with bells of gold. As for the bells, their original function was probably to drive away evil spirits—which were supposed to haunt the threshold especially—from the holy place or person. Their purpose here is not apparent. In **43,** 'lest they . . . die', it is not clear who are meant, though the obvious implication is that contact with the presence of Yahweh, or with those who have been in that presence, is dangerous. In Sir. 45:1–12 the sound of the bells is 'for a memorial for (i.e. to remind God of) the children of his people'.

g **36-39 The Golden Diadem, the Turban, and the Coat** (cf. 39:27–29)—The turban of the high priest was of fine linen (39), to which was attached, by means of a cord of blue (37), a plate or diadem of pure gold, engraved with the words 'holy to the Lord'. The special consecration of the high priest to Yahweh is thus indicated, as is also the fact that he, as the chief priest, bears the final responsibility for any ritual error which might occur in connection with the people's offerings (38). Aaron is also to have a coat, a long tunic, something like a cassock, made of linen, with checks on it, and a girdle or sash (39). His sons, the lesser priests, were to have tunics, sashes, caps, and linen breeches. Omit 41, a later addition, which breaks the connection. **42f.,** see on 20:26.

h **XXIX** P **The Consecration of the Priests, and the Daily Burnt Offering** (cf. Lev. 8, where the instructions given here are carried out. The section presupposes Lev. 1–7)—**1-36a. The Consecration of the Priests.** After the exile the priesthood was restricted to the members of the tribe of Levi, as is here represented. But the monopoly is a later development. In the pre-exilic period, there were priests from other lines—Joshua (Jos. 33:4), Micah (Jg. 17:5), Abinadab (1 Sam. 7:1), David (2 Sam. 8:18), Nathan (1 Kg. 4:5).

i Materials are to be provided for the sacrifices and brought to the Tabernacle (1–3). The three kinds of cakes are for the *minḥāh* or meal offering (see on Lev. 2 and 6) which accompanied the installation offering, the bullock is for the sin offering (10–14), the one ram is for the whole burnt offering, and the other is for the sacrifice of consecration (19–21). Then follow the details of the consecration in two main acts (*a*) preparation, and (*b*) sacrifice. (*a*) Aaron and his sons, that is, the ordinary priests, are prepared in three stages. First (4) they wash, for ritual purity (cf. Lev. 8:6), which suggests a washing of the whole body, as distinct from the daily washing of hands and feet before service; see 30:19f. Second, they are invested with the garments described in 28:5–6, 8–9, special attention being paid to the investiture of Aaron; cf. Lev. 8:7–9. Third, Aaron is anointed with oil (7). For the ingredients of the oil, see 30:22–33. Only Aaron, the high priest, is anointed here; cf. Lev. 16:32, 21:10. But in other strata of P the ordinary priests also are anointed; cf. 28:41, 30:30, 40:15. In **9,** 'ordains' is lit. 'fill the hands of': the expression probably refers to the custom of placing some sacred object in the hands of a person ordained—cf. today a Bible—as a symbol of his office. The second main act is (*b*) sacrifice. (i) The Sin Offering (see on Lev. 4, for Aaron and his sons (10–14; cf. Lev. 8:14–17)). By laying their hands upon it, Aaron and his sons denote it as their sacrifice. 'Some sort of identification of subject and object was ceremoniously expressed' (Yerkes, op. cit., 135). There is probably also the idea of confession of sin—they deserve the death which the animal is about to suffer. Moses himself has to kill the bullock (11), since Aaron and his sons are not yet priests, but still laymen. On the 'horns of the altar' (12), see on 27:2. On the 'base of the altar', see on Lev. 8:25. For the sacrificial parts (13) see Lev. 3:4, 4:1f. In **13,** the 'appendage of the liver': a finger-shaped lobe of the liver. The size, shape, configuration, and bends of this upper lobe were all of significance in divination. Hepatoscopy, or examination of the liver for purposes of divination, was widespread in the ancient world. Israel rejected it. Hence the prescription to burn the appendage. Of a sin offering nothing was eaten. But when the sin offering was for others than the priests, the priests were allowed to eat what was not burnt upon the altar, Lev. 5:13, 6:26. But here there is still no proper priesthood. **14. dung**: rather, offal. (ii) The Burnt Offering (15–18); cf. Lev. 8:22–29. See on 20:24. One ram is burnt on the altar, signifying the complete devotion of the life of the priest to Yahweh. (iii) The Installation Offering (19–25); cf. Lev. 8:22–29. The second ram, the 'ram of ordination' (22) is offered as a peace offering (28), the offering of communion. **20.** 'The priest must have consecrated ears to listen at all times to God's holy voice, consecrated hands continually to do holy works, and consecrated feet always to walk in holy ways' (Dillmann, in McNeile). **21** is a later addition. For similar rites in connection with a healed leper see Lev. 14:14ff., 25ff. **22f.** The fat and the kidneys to be burnt upon the altar are the same parts as those designated for the peace offering in Lev. 3:3–5. The ceremony of 'waving' (24) meant that some parts of the sacrifice were swung or elevated towards the altar, signifying that they were given to God, and then swung back again, indicating that they were given back by God to the priests, for them to eat. Only, since there are as yet no regular priests here, Moses is to burn these parts upon the altar. **27-30.** Two parenthetical notes. In **27,** the Hebrew word for 'wave offering' is *t^{e}nûphāh*, distinct from *t^{e}rûmāh* (25:2). In the *t^{e}nûphāh*, the portion waved is given back to the priests, as their fee. But the term is sometimes used more loosely, as an offering in general, e.g. 24, where the portion is not given back, but burnt, and 35:22. **29-30** deal with the installation of Aaron's successors, and should perhaps follow **35. 31-34** continue **26**; cf. Lev. 8:31f. A sacrificial meal goes along with the peace offering. Nowhere else in P is a *peace offering* said to make atonement. There is nothing corresponding to this in Lev. 8; atonement has already been made by the sin-offering; the command that no stranger, that is, no layman, should

91 participate, is superfluous—therefore the verse is probably a later addition. The ceremony of installation was to last for seven days (35–36*a*). Lev. 8:33 adds that the priests 'shall not go from the door of the tent of meeting for seven days'.

j **36b-37 The Offering for the Altar**—For seven days also the altar was to be cleansed. It had been constructed by human hands and from ordinary materials. It had therefore to be 'un-sinned' (Driver). Holiness is here regarded as something contagious. Any unauthorised person (read 'whoever' rather than 'whatever' in 37) who touches the altar becomes 'holy', that is, at the disposal of the deity, even to the extent of losing his life; cf. 2 Sam. 6:6. See also Ezek. 46:20f. This regulation has nothing to do with the installation of the priesthood, and is a later addition.

k **38-42 The Daily Burnt Offering**—This section breaks the connection between **37** and **43,** and has been inserted from Num. 28:3–8. Burnt offering in the evening as well as in the morning was the post-exilic usage. But in pre-exilic times the burnt offering was made only in the morning, 2 Kg. 16:15; see also Ezek. 46:13–15. In the evening a cereal offering, the *minḥāh,* was made. The regulation here makes the *minḥāh* a subordinate offering. **39. in the evening**: see on 12:6. **40. a tenth measure,** that is, of an ephah. An ephah was probably about a bushel, and an hin about a gallon and a half. Lauterbach (JE, x) sets an ephah as 36·44 litres, and an hin as 6·074 litres.

l **43-46** Conclusion to chs. 25–29. **43-44** continue **37.** 'There' and 'it' (43) then referred originally to the altar. **45-46,** reminiscent of CH in style, indicate the purpose of the Exodus, 'that I may dwell among them'.

0a **XXX-XXXI** P **Supplementary Regulations**—After the solemn close of the regulations given in **25-29,** it is surprising to find others. These two chapters show themselves to be later priestly additions. For all its importance, the altar of incense is here mentioned for the first time. Nor is it mentioned in Lev. 16, where incense is offered in censers. Also, in certain passages (e.g. 27–29, Lev. 1–3, 5–6, etc.), the altar of burnt offering is spoken of as *the* altar, implying that there was only one altar. Further, Lev. 16 knows nothing of the annual rite of atonement mentioned in 30:10. There are similar indications of lateness in the rest of the prescriptions in the two chapters.

b **XXX 1-10** P **The Altar of Incense** (cf. 37:25–28, 40:26)—The offering of incense goes back to prehistoric times, and incense altars are common in Mesopotamia in the third millennium B.C., and in Canaan from 1100 B.C. on. Albright thinks that the use of them was pre-exilic in Israel, but that they had been frowned upon by the prophets. According to 1 Kg. 6:22, 7:48, Solomon made one, the golden altar; cf. Exod. 39:38, 40:5, 26; Num. 4:11. This may have been one of his innovations (Landersdorfer). On the other hand, the *Kings* passage may be late, and dependent upon our passage here—so Kennedy (Cent. B., *Kings,* in loco). The fact that there is no mention of any such altar in Ezekiel suggests that its use was a post-exilic development, and that this passage is therefore late. The altar was to be made of the same materials as the table, with a similar moulding at the top (1–3), and with similar rings and poles (4–5). It was to be set in the Holy Place, before the veil (6). Incense was to be burnt upon it morning and evening (7–8). No other offering was to be made upon it, and no other incense used than that to be prescribed in 34ff. ('unholy'). An annual rite of atonement was to be made upon it (10); see introduction to 30–31. **6. before the mercy seat**: probably a later addition, leading to the misunderstanding in Heb. 9:4 that the altar stood within the Holy of Holies.

c **11-16 The Ransom Money or Poll Tax** (cf. 38:24–31)—It was believed to be dangerous to take a census; cf. 2 Sam. 24. See Driver's note here for a similar belief amongst other peoples. Therefore a ransom for their lives of half a shekel was to be exacted from everyone from the age of twenty years upwards, rich and poor alike (12–15). The tax was to be paid in the 'shekel of the sanctuary' (13), the sacred shekel (cf. Lev. 27:25), which was possibly Phoenician money. In Phoenician money the shekel weighed 224 grains, 6 grains more than a British half-crown (Driver). The parenthesis in **13** gives the equivalent of the shekel in Babylonian terms. *Gērāh,* cf. Lev. 27:25; Num. 3:47, 18:16; Ezek. 45:12, is the Bab. *girû.* This contribution was to be used for the upkeep of the sanctuary. But it is not a Mosaic institution. It may have originated with Nehemiah. In Neh. 10:32 the people resolve to pay one-third of a shekel. This whole Exodus passage is therefore late. 200c

17-21 The Bronze Laver (cf. 38:8, 40:30)—Unlike the previous descriptions, no details are given about the form or the size of the laver (basin), in which the priests are to wash their hands and feet before entering the tent or performing their sacred duties. The verses are, again, a later addition, for the prescriptions should have followed the law of the altar, 27:1–8; cf. the order in 38:1–8. In 38:8 the laver is constructed from the mirrors of the women who served the Temple. According to 1 Kg. 7:21ff., 38ff., Solomon's Temple had ten basins and a 'molten sea', a larger tank. d

22-33 The Anointing Oil (cf. 37:29*a*)—The mention of the altar of incense and the laver, and the fact that not only Aaron but his sons as well are to be anointed (contrast 29:7), show the passage to be a later addition. Unction is in use for religious purposes such as consecration from the earliest times, and also for healing and adornment. Four ingredients are to be used. Myrrh was a gum from Arabia. Cinnamon came probably from the far East, China. The aromatic cane was imported from India. Cassia is akin to cinnamon bark, and came also from the far East. Sabaean, i.e. African, merchants would import them. **31-33** restrict the use of the oil to the priests. The oil is not to be made up for ordinary use. Breach of these regulations entails excommunication. e

34-38 The Incense (cf. 37:29*b*)—The word *ḳeṭōreth,* incense, meant originally something which went up from the sacrifice, by means of which the deity participated in the offering (see the transferred use in Ps. 141:2). Later it was restricted to manufactured incense. Four ingredients are specified here; stacte (lit. a drop), perhaps some form of myrrh oil; onycha, parts of a shellfish found in the Red Sea; galbanum, a resin; and frankincense, a fragrant gum resin; salt was added. The mixture was to be ground, and part of it placed in the censer, or on the altar of incense. With 37f. cf. 32f. f

XXXI 1-11 P **Bezalel and Oholiab** (cf. 35:30–36:3)—The section is again late, as is shown by the inclusion of the incense altar and the laver in the list of the furnishings to be made (7–11). Bezalel, possibly meaning 'in the shadow of God' has his genealogy given in 1 Chr. 2:18–20, 50, where he is said to be a Calebite. Caleb, originally a separate clan (cf. 1 Sam. 30:14) was later absorbed by Judah, hence here 'of the tribe of Judah'. Oholiab, meaning apparently 'father's tent', is perhaps a foreign word. These men are chosen by God and filled with his spirit. For the spirit as a divine energy equipping men with practical wisdom or skill, see Gen. 41:38; Dt. 34:9; Jg. 3:10; 1 Sam. 11:6; Isa. 42:1. **10. finely worked garments**: the sense is doubtful. RVm, 'garments of service' follows LXX, Sam., Syr., Targ. Galling connects the Hebrew root *ś-r-d* with a Babylonian word *serdu,* and renders 'the prescribed garments'. g

12-17 P (**12b-14a,** possibly H). **The Sabbath**—These verses 'may in some sense be regarded as the *locus classicus* on Sabbath observance in the OT' (McNeile). The day is to be hallowed in perpetuity as a reminder of what God does for Israel (13; cf. Ezek. 20:12), and of the covenant relationship between h

200h them (16). It is a day of solemn rest from work (14f.; cf. 20:8ff; Dt. 5:12ff.). It also commemorates the creation (17; cf. 20:11; Gen. 2:3). The strongest penalties are attached to breaking it (14; cf. Num. 15:32–36 P). In **12** read 'that men may know': 'the weekly rest-day is the sacrament in time, linking God and his world in mutual remembrance, and revealing the invisible God to an unbelieving world' (Harford).

i **18a** P, **18b** E **The Tables of Stone**—This verse points forward to chs. 32–34 by its mention of 'the two tables of the testimony, tables of stone, written with the finger of God'; cf. 34:1, 4.

201a **XXXII-XXXIV** These chapters, which are composite in their literary structure, come between the giving of the instructions for the making of the Tabernacle and their being carried out. They deal with the covenant relationship, in particular with the question how it would stand with that bond if the people on their side failed to fulfil its obligations, and, as here, broke one of the commandments. No explicit answer is given. But the suggestion seems to be that because of the zeal of Moses for Yahweh and his faithfulness to him (32:30–34), and also because of his power as intercessor (32:11–14), God will continue to lead his people, though in a less immediate way ('my angel', 32:34, 'my presence', 33:12). Thus no solution is offered for the general problem of apostasy, or for such a case as Jeroboam's calves, though these were possibly in mind when this episode was composed. On the other hand, what Moses, one single man, effects for his people leads out into the doctrine of the Remnant.

b **XXXII** (**1-8** E, expanded **9-14, 15-24** E, **25-29** J, **30-34** E (?Rje), **35** E) **The Golden Calf**—The calf was not originally thought of as an image of Yahweh, but, like the cherubim, the throne on which he was invisibly present; see on 25:18. Against Jeroboam's bull-images (1 Kg. 12:28–33) there was no protest that we know of before the time of Hosea (8:5f.). The present narrative may then be late, and ante-dated to the time of the Exodus. As Bennett says, 'the part assigned to Aaron is puzzling; Aaron is usually connected with the Ark and its priesthood at Shiloh and Jerusalem, and not with Bethel. It is possible—the idea is of course a mere conjecture—that at one time there was an image of Yahweh in the form of a Calf in the Temple, and its construction was attributed to Aaron, the connection being regarded as honourable both to him and to the image. The present narrative takes a different view, but does its best to excuse him; he acted under compulsion, hardly knowing what he did, verses 22–24'.

c **1-6** The Making of the Calf. While Moses is away from them on the mount (24:18*b*), the people want 'gods' to be leaders whom they could see; cf. Ac. 7:40f. Aaron consents to their demand, thus abandoning the principle of charismatic leadership for something more immediately apprehensible (cf. 1 Sam. 8:5), and makes a calf of gold from the people's earrings, like the Egyptian Apis or the Canaanite Baal. **4. these are your gods**: only one image is made here, so the plural probably has Jeroboam's images at Dan and Bethel in mind. The graving-tool was probably used on the bull after it was cast. **6. play**: possibly a euphemism for immoral practices which came in from the Canaanite cult; cf. Num.
d 25:1–9; 1 Kg. 14:24; Am. 2:7. In **7-10**, Yahweh, after telling Moses what has happened, declares his intention of destroying his people (cf. Am. 9:8), though he will make a great people of Moses, who has had no part in the apostasy. But Moses intercedes. He reminds Yahweh of the Exodus (11), of what the Egyptians might say (12), of the covenant with the forefathers (13; cf. Gen. 12:2). So Yahweh relents.
e **12. the mountains**: the Sinai peninsula. Moses then discovers the image and breaks it up (15–20), an action which would follow more dramatically on **6.** To the third clause of **18** LXX adds 'and of wine';
one has to think of the Canaanite fertility cults. As 20
well as destroying the calf, Moses also broke the tables of stone—'not of uncontrolled passion, but of righteous indignation. . . . The greatest punishment a people can suffer is to lose God's law. cf. Am. viii, 11, 12' (J. C. Connell, *The New Bible Commentary*). **20. drink it**: cf. Num. 5:24. Moses also reproaches Aaron, whose answers are weak—the people were evil (23), he only threw the gold into the fire, and the calf came
out! (24). The Levites then intervene—an aetiological f
story which is not particularly in place here. Since they, and they alone, apparently had remained faithful, and had even disregarded the closest natural ties in their loyalty, they are ordained to the priesthood (25–29); but contrast Num. 8:5–22. In **30-34** Moses intercedes for the people, and proclaims his own readiness to die on their behalf; cf. Num. 11:15.

25 had broken loose: from their loyalty and obed- g
ence to Yahweh. **32.** thy book: cf. Ps. 69:28; Isa. 4:3; Mal. 3:16. **34** 'Behold, my angel shall go before you'; omit as a gloss which has come in from 33:2. The phrase anticipates 33:12ff.

XXXIII-XXXIV 5b-9 (**1** J; **2** R; **3-4a** J; **4b-5** R; h
6-11 E; **12-23** J; **34**: **5b-9** J) **The Promise of God's Presence**—The order in **33f.** has been very much disturbed. The rearrangement given is only tentative.

Yahweh bids the people leave for Canaan, though i
he himself refuses to go with them (1 and 3). **2** is an interpolation, as **12** shows. For the 'angel' see 23:20f. When the people heard this, they were dismayed, and put off their ornaments (4 and 6). **5** is probably an explanatory gloss, since the action in **4** appears to be a spontaneous reaction to the 'evil tidings'. On **7-11** see below. **17** presupposes **12,** though it is then impossible to tell what 'this very thing' (17) is. Then Moses, assured of Yahweh's favour, asks to be told whom Yahweh will send with him, and also to be shown his 'ways', his 'method of working' (McNeile) (12f.). 34:9 should probably follow here. In response to this request, Yahweh promises that his 'presence', lit. his face, will go with them (14–16). The Presence is Yahweh less immediately apprehensible.

Moses then makes a further request, to see God's j
glory, the full manifestation of himself (18). God agrees to let his 'goodness', that is, his goodliness, his beauty (LXX 'my glory'), pass before Moses, and to reveal new depths of meaning in his name (see on 3:14), explained in **19b**; cf. 34:6f. Only, Moses cannot see his face and remain alive (20); contrast 24:11 and Dt. 34:10. So Moses is put in a cleft of a rock where he is to see, not Yahweh's glory, but his 'back', 'the afterglow which he leaves behind him, but which may suggest what the full brilliancy of his presence must be' (Driver) (21f.). The promised revelation is then given in 34:5*b*–9. With 34:6f. cf. 20:5; Num. 14:18; Dt. 5:9. At the end Moses worships and prays for the people (8f.).

XXXIII 7-11 E **The Tent of Meeting**—These k
verses interrupt the narrative, and have no connection with the context, though, as Dillmann says, the implication of the present text is that the ornaments of **4ff.** would be used for the construction or decoration of the Tent. The Tent here is equated with P's Tabernacle or Tent. But it was clearly not so originally. This Tent stood outside the camp (cf. Num. 11:26f., 12:4), while P's Tent stood at its centre. This Tent is portable, since Moses, with perhaps Joshua, carried and pitched it (7), but P's Tent needed wagons and Levites for its transportation (Num. 4). The minister of this Tent is the Ephraimite Joshua, not the Levites who alone could enter P's Tent (Num. 3:5–10). This is an oracle tent, not a ceremonial one. On the basis of Num. 9:15, 17:7f., where it is called the 'tent of testimony', some think that the Ark was housed within it. It is generally assumed that **7-11** are all that have survived of E's account of the Tent or Tabernacle, the rest being omitted because the final editors preferred P's (chs. 25–27).

1k **11.** face to face : cf. Dt. 34:10. as a man speaks to his friend : cf. Num. 17:7f.

l **XXXIV,** omitting **5b-9,** see last chapter. **1-5a** and **10-28** J, **29ff.** P—In these verses are preserved some part at any rate of J's account of the covenant laws. Originally in J they followed on the descent of Yahweh upon Sinai described in **19.** But when E's account of the laws (20:23–23:19) was preferred by the compilers, these of J were set here, and, through the insertion of the clauses in **1** and **4** mentioning the *first* tables, the present incident was given the appearance of a *renewal* of the covenant broken by the sin of the Golden Calf. The laws in **10-28,** which have probably been expanded from an original ten to thirteen, are sometimes called the 'ritual decalogue' as opposed to the 'ethical decalogue' of ch. 20, since they are on a more primitive level and are concerned with cultic requirements. But on the relationship of the two, see §191*i*. The following is the parallel of the laws in J and E. 14*a* || 20:3 ; 17 || 20:4, 23:13 ; 18 || 23:15 ; 19–20*a* || 22:30 ; 20*b* || 22:29*b* ; 20*c* || 25:15 ; 21 || 23:12 ; 22*ab* || 23:16*ab* ; 23 || 23:17 ; 25*ab* || 23:18*ab* ; 26*ab* || 23:19*ab*.

m **XXXIV 29-35** P **The Shining of Moses' Face**—As Moses came down from the mountain, his face shone with the reflection of the divine glory. The word for 'shone' occurs only in this passage. It is connected with the word for 'horn' in the sense of 'ray' ; cf. Hab. 3:4. Jerome rendered literally, 'horned' ; hence the frequent representation in art of Moses with two horns. Moses wore a veil. The reason is not stated, but apparently it would be because the people could not bear the brightness. For Paul's different interpretation, see 2 C. 3:7–18.

2a **XXXV-XL** P **The Carrying-out of the Cult Ordinances**—These chapters follow on chs. **25-31,** and are from a later hand of the Priestly School. While for the greater part they repeat chs. **25-31** almost verbally, with only the necessary changes of person and tense, they show variations from them in order, as well as certain additions. LXX too gives a different order from the Hebrew text, and has omissions, of which the most significant is the altar of incense. Apparently the Hebrew text existed in different recensions at the time when the LXX text was made, and had not yet reached a final form. For the relations in detail between chs. 25–31 and chs. 35–40, see Driver, 376ff., or McNeile, 224f. The latter includes a comparison with the LXX also. For the description of Solomon's Temple, see 1 Kg. 6–8 ; for Ezekiel's ideal Temple, see Ezek. 40–48.

b **XXXV 1-3** The description of the construction of the Tent is preceded by a repetition of the law of the Sabbath, summarising 31:12–17. The kindling of a fire on the Sabbath is not anywhere else forbidden in the OT, though it is implied in 16:23. Driver says that the command is 'placed here apparently as a reminder to the Israelites that the Sabbath must not be broken even for sacred purposes'. Galling takes 'the fires' to mean those necessary for the purpose of working metals. But the words, 'in all your habitations', suggest rather a general prohibition of work, as does also 16:23, where household fires are clearly meant.

c **4-19** ; cf. 25:2–7. The people are invited to make freewill offerings of the materials needed (4–9), and skilled craftsmen amongst them are given the opportunity of assisting in the work (10–19). There is no corresponding invitation in chs. **25-31** to that given to the craftsmen. The 'veil of the screen' (12), that is, the veil which served as a screen in front of the Holy of Holies (cf. 39:34, 40:21 ; Num. 4:5) and the 'screen for the door' (15), are put in the order in which they were to be made, and not together, as in 36:35ff. The 'cords' (18 ; cf. 39:40 ; Num. 3:26, 37, 4:26–32) are not explicitly mentioned in 27:19.

d **20-29 The Presentation of the Offerings**—On 'offering' (22), see on 25:2. **22.** brooches : the word elsewhere means a 'hook'—for the jaw, Ezek. 29:4, or for the nose, 2 Kg. 19:28. armlets : uncertain, perhaps 'necklaces'. **23** breaks into the metal 202d
offerings of **22** and **24** and would better follow **24.**

30-XXXVI 1, cf. 31:1–11. Moses tells the people e
of the divine appointment of Bezalel and Oholiab.

XXXVI 2-7 The Liberality of the People—They f
brought more than enough, and had to be stopped. The picture clearly reflects a wealthier age than that of the wanderings in the wilderness. **2.** Come : in the Priestly sense of draw near to offer himself for the work.

8-38 The Dwelling—8-19. The making of the g
curtains of the dwelling ; cf. 26:1–14, 20–34 ; **20-34** : the wooden framework ; cf. 26:15–34 ; **35-38** : the veil and the screen ; cf. 26:31f., 36f. **38.** The capitals and fillets are not mentioned in 26:37. There is a gradation in the gilding. The pillars at the entrance of the court have only silver gilding on the capitals (cf. 38:19) ; those at the entrance to the Tent have gold gilding on the capitals only (cf. 36:38) ; but those at the entrance of the Most Holy Place are entirely gilt with gold (36 ; cf. 26:32).

XXXVII The Furnishings of the Tent—1-9, the h
Ark (cf. 25:10–20). **10-16,** the Table (cf. 25:23–29). **17-24,** the Lampstand (cf. 25:31–39). **25-28,** the Altar of Incense (cf. 30:1–5, but omitted by LXX). **29,** the Anointing Oil and the Incense (cf. 30:22–25, 34–36). **1.** Bezalel made the Ark : contrast Dt. 10:3.

XXXVIII Altar, Laver, and Court—1-7. The i
Altar of Burnt Offering ; cf. 27:1–8. **2.** bronze : according to Num. 16:36–40, the bronze covering was not made till later. **8a.** The Laver ; cf. 30:17. **8b** is a gloss, since it presupposes the erection of the Tent, which is complete only in **40.** 'Ministering women' are mentioned again only in 1 Sam. 2:22. What their duties were is uncertain. They may have been menial, such as cleaning. Others think of singing and dancing. At a later period they could have been conceivably the temple prostitutes. The word for 'ministering' is the same as that applied to the service of the Levites in Num. 4:23 (RVm). **9-20.** The Court ; cf. 27:9–19. There are slight variations in the order and wording of the two passages. In **15,** 'on this hand . . . court', not in 25:15, is a gloss. **21-31,** giving the metals used, is a later addition to the narrative : (*a*) the Levites (21) were only separated off for their duties in Num. 3 ; (*b*) **25f.** presuppose the census, although according to Num. 1:1f. that was not taken until after the Tabernacle was completed ; (*c*) the rest of the account stresses that the Tabernacle was made from the freewill offerings ; cf. especially 36:2–7. But here there is a misunderstanding of 30:11–16, where the money derived from the poll-tax was to be used for the 'service', that is, for the upkeep, of the Tent ; (*d*) in **24, 29,** the Hebrew word for 'offering' is *tᵉnûphāh* (see on 35:22), the gift of dedication, corresponding with the view that the poll-tax was used in the building of the Tabernacle, and not *tᵉrûmāh,* as in 25:3, 30:13. **21.** testimony : cf. 25:16. **Ithamar** : cf. 6:23 ; Num. 4:28, 33, 7:8. These passages put him in charge of the Dwelling. **24.** talents : cf. 25:30. **26.** *beḳa'*, the shekel of the sanctuary ; cf. 30:13. On the number of the males, 603,550, see on 12:37.

XXXIX The Vestments for the Priests—1-31 j
(cf. 28). **1a.** to 'holy place', may be a fragment of a complete account of what was made of the woven fabrics, and **1b** may be the real beginning of the section. **3,** telling how the gold was worked in, has no parallel in 28:6. In **24** the 'fine twined linen' is not in the instructions of the Hebrew text of 28:33. The 'holy crown' of **30** is not mentioned in 28:36. There are also abridgments here.

32-43 When the work was finished—the 'workers' k
are the people of Israel (32, 42)—the Tabernacle and all its furnishings, which are again listed very much as in 35:11–19, are brought to Moses. He, seeing that the divine instructions had been carried out, blessed them. Notice how the motive of obedience is stressed in the chapter : 'as the Lord had commanded Moses'

202k occurs seven times (1, 5, 7, 21, 26, 29, 31). Is the seven significant?

l **XL The Erection of the Tent**—Moses is instructed to set up the Tent and its furnishings (2–8), to anoint and consecrate them (9–11), and to robe and anoint the priests (12–15). Most of the instructions have already been given in 25:1–31. In **17,** he carries out the instructions (16:33). **17,** the second year, i.e. the second year after leaving Egypt. Notice the further sevenfold ' as the Lord commanded Moses ', **19, 21, 23, 25, 27, 29, 32.** Then (34–38) the cloud (see on 13:21f.) covered the Tent, and filled the Dwelling. In this way the thought of the unapproachable (ch. 35) and transcendent God was harmonised with the idea of his continual presence with his people. These verses are the fulfilment of the promise in 29:43, 45f., which carry us back to the purpose of the Exodus.

Bibliography—Commentaries: B. Baentsch, HKAT (1903); G. Beer, HAT (1939); F. M. Th. Böhl, *Tekst en Uitleg* (1928); A. Dillmann and V. Ryssel, KEH (1897); S. R. Driver, CB (1911); W. H. Gispen, *Korte Verklaring* (1932, 1938); H. Gressmann, SAT (1922); P. Heinisch, HSATes (1934); H. Holzinger, KHC (1900); A. H. McNeile, WC (1917); J. C. Rylaarsdam and J. E. Park, IB (1952); S. L. Browne (in *A New Commentary on Holy Scripture*, ed. C. Gore, H. L. Goudge and A. Guillaume, 1928); G. Harford (in Peake's *Commentary on the Bible*, 1928); J. H. Hertz, *Pentateuch and Haftorahs* ii (1930); J. F. McLaughlin (in *The Abingdon Bible Commentary*, 1929); S. Michelet, S. Mowinckel and N. Messel, *Det Gamle Testamente* i (1929–30); E. Power (in *A Catholic Commentary on Holy Scripture*, 1953).

Other Literature: W. F. Albright, *From the Stone Age to Christianity* (2nd ed. 1946); M. Buber, *Moses* (1946); O. Eissfeldt, *Hexateuchsynopse* (1922); K. Galling, *Die Erwählungstraditionen Israels* (1928); H. H. Rowley, *From Joseph to Joshua* (1950); A. Šanda, *Moses und der Pentateuch* (1924); E. Sellin, *Mose und seine Bedeutung für die isr.-jüd. Religionsgeschichte* (1922); C. A. Simpson, *The Early Traditions of Israel* (1948); P. Volz, *Mose und sein Werk* (2nd ed. 1932).

LEVITICUS

By N. H. Snaith

203a **Name**—Leviticus is an English transcription of the Latin (Vulg.) name of the book, itself derived from the Greek (LXX) name. LXX calls the book 'Levitical (book)', because of its contents. The Hebrew title is *Wayyiḳra* ('and he called'), this being the first word of the book in Hebrew; it is the normal Hebrew way of naming a book. This is 'the Third Book of Moses', i.e. the third book of the Pentateuch.

b **Contents**—It can be divided into five sections. The first (1–7) contains the Law of Sacrifice, the first part of which (1:1–6:7) is mainly addressed to the people and gives details of the various types of sacrifice and the different rituals. The second part (6:8–7:38) is addressed almost wholly to the priests, and deals with their sacrifices and with their share of the offerings of the people. The second section (8–10) describes the inauguration of the worship. It gives an account of the consecration of Aaron and his sons, details of Aaron's first offerings, the fate of Nadab and Abihu who sought to establish themselves as legitimate priests, and it ends with further directions to the priests concerning the disposal of offerings. The third section (11–16) contains the Law of Purification. It deals with ritual uncleanness caused by eating animals that are ritually unclean, and gives lists of such creatures. It deals with uncleanness caused by contact with dead creatures, with uncleanness after childbirth, from leprosy and from 'issues', and it ends with details of the main features of the Day of Atonement, that climax of all ceremonial cleansing. The fourth section (17–26) contains the Law of Holiness, where the emphasis is on God's Holiness and on the necessity that his people Israel shall also be holy. These laws deal with every phase of human life and they are an early model of that mixture of exhortation and detailed pattern of behaviour with which modern readers are familiar in the *Manual of Discipline* of the Dead Sea Scrolls. The section includes a list of sacred days and seasons (23) and details concerning the sabbatical year and the year of Jubilee. The fifth section (27) resumes the style and pattern of the third section, and deals with vows and tithes and their commutation.

c **The Law of Holiness**—This is the name given by Klostermann in 1877 to chapters **17-26,** because of the prominence given to the idea of Holiness. This 'Holiness Code' is usually referred to as H, and in style and matter it is distinct from the rest of the book, which belongs to the Priestly stratum (P) of tradition. The emphases on holiness, on 'I am Yahweh', and on the idea of the land as polluted by sin, provide close contact with Ezekiel; the interest in sacrifices, the duties of the priests and the ecclesiastical calendar show affinities with P, and the emphasis on morality connects the H-tradition with the D-tradition. But the style and language are different. Further, there are different strata in H. At one time scholars thought in terms of a first editor who used existing codes, introduced exhortatory discourses and impressed on the whole of his work the character of holiness which makes the whole section distinctive. They then inferred the existence of a second editor who incorporated H into the rest of the book and was responsible for those elements which show affinity with P. On the basis of this literary analysis, H is between D and P, but is most closely related to Ezekiel, 203c
so that its date is between 600 and 570 B.C., the last days of the first Temple and the first days of the Babylonian Exile. But these dates refer only to the H element. There are many traces of earlier material, and many traces of later (mostly P) material.

I-VII The Law of Sacrifices—There are five main 204a
types: Burnt Offering (1), Cereal Offering (2), Sacrifice of Peace Offering (3), Sin Offering (4:1–5:13), Guilt Offering (5:14–6:7). The section concludes with details mostly for the instruction of the priests.

I 1-2 This is the usual P introduction. The term b
'offering' (Heb. *ḳorbān*: RV 'oblation') is here used comprehensively of 'that which is brought near', and can thus be used of any offering, even of the Passover Lamb (Num. 9:7, 13). It has also a limited, technical meaning, a gift brought or dedicated (Mk 7:11) for use in the Temple, as against the Holy-gift, which was for the maintenance of the priesthood. All sacrificial animals were domesticated. No wild animal could be brought. Jewish tradition says that this is because it costs nothing.

3-17 The Burnt Offering—RSV has retained the c
rendering of AV and RV, but the term 'Whole Offering' is better. Other offerings also were burnt; the essential feature of this offering is that the *whole* animal was burnt on the altar, including even the entrails. The Hebrew name signifies 'that which goes up' in smoke. Normally the whole-offering was a bull, or a ram or a he-goat. In early times it could be a human being (Jg. 11:31; Gen. 22:2), the firstborn being the most costly of all such offerings (Mic. 6:7), offered only in cases of extreme necessity: cf. 2 Kg. 3:27, where the Hebrew author recognises the efficacy of the Moabite king's last desperate resource. The purpose of the whole-offering is to declare the worshipper's devotion and submission, and in the last resort to bespeak God's intervention. It was to secure at-onement (4), but not specifically to remove sin. The tent of meeting in P is a shrine in the centre of the camp. It is E's tent of meeting, which was outside the camp, remodelled to be the prototype of the central shrine of the Jerusalem Temple, partly of Solomon's Temple, and partly of the Second Temple. Thus P's tent of meeting is Solomon's Temple in embryo with its two sections, the inner part being separated off by the 'second veil', and it is also the Holy of Holies of the Second Temple, within the Court of the Tabernacle, P's prototype of the Court of the Priests which was beyond the Gate of Nicanor. The general confusion is increased by the use of the term Holy of Holies in connection with Solomon's Temple. The main type of whole-offering was a *bull* (not 'bullock', as in AV and RV, which mostly in modern speech means a castrated animal). It was brought to the opening of the tent of meeting, i.e. the Gate of Nicanor of the Second Temple. The offerer placed his hand firmly (so Targum) on the head of the animal. This rite of 'laying on of hands' varied in its significance, and could signify responsibility, sharing, substitution, etc., but in all cases it implied transference, whether of guilt, holiness, identification, though in this particular case it probably was a declaration of

204e the offerer that it was his offering. The blood was drawn off and thrown against the altar, once at the north-east corner to cover the north and east sides, and once at the south-west corner. The primary reason for thus disposing of the blood is that it is taboo, too sacred and too dangerous for the ordinary man to handle. The animal was cut into pieces without any bones being broken, and laid on the altar so that the fire passed between the pieces (Gen. 15:10), thus symbolising the making of the covenant between God and man. The offering was ' whole ' because it was wholly burnt on the altar ; it was a ' fire-offering ' because it was burnt ; it was a *pleasing odour* because it was intended to be well pleasing to God. This phrase is an ancient survival, used frequently in P and elsewhere (Gen. 8:21, J) ; cf. the ' goodly odour ' (*eresha tabu*) offered to the Babylonian gods by the Babylonian Noah when he reached land after the flood. The phrase ' sweet savour ' is due to LXX. The old English ' savour ' included smell as well as taste. Religious phraseology is full of such outgrown anthropomorphisms, but let us hope there are new interpretations. **10-13.** An alternative offering is a ram or a he-goat, not necessarily because it is less expensive, but because it was so from ancient times, the shepherd's offering as against the bull which is the herdsman's offering. **14-17.** A concession to the poor : two small birds. This concern for the poor is thus not confined to Deuteronomy. It is here embedded in the Temple ritual. From ancient times the poor man was permitted to bring two turtle-doves or pigeons (not necessarily young). The rabbis pointed out : it is the bringing that counts, not the value of what is brought. The head of the bird was wrenched off and thrown on to the altar. The blood was drained off at the side of the altar, there not being enough to collect and throw. The crop and its contents (so AVm, RV ; RSV follows AV, RVm and LXX ' feathers ') were torn out and thrown down on the ashes to the east (in front) of the altar. The bird was torn apart, though not completely, and wholly burnt.

d **II The Cereal Offering**—AV called it ' meat ', 17th-cent. English for ' food ' in general. RV called it ' meal ', but ' grain-offering ' is probably best. The term included all offerings of grain, but it has a particular post-exilic reference to the grain-offering which accompanied every whole(burnt)-offering, and these two, with the specified drink-offering (7:1–11 ; Exod. 29:38–41), provided a complete meal for the Deity, meat and bread and wine. The Hebrew word *minḥah* etymologically means ' gift, tribute '. It is commonly held that before the exile the term was used of any gift offering, whether animal or grain, but that after the exile it signified only grain-offerings.

e **1-3** The offering could be of uncooked grain, not necessarily ' fine flour ' (RV and RSV), but coarse meal, similar to the ' grits ' served at every meal in the south of the United States. Oil was added as the normal condiment, but the frankincense was special. This was incense of high quality. It was white, like the manna (Exod. 16:14 ; Num. 11:8). The priest took a handful of the grits and all the frankincense, and this was food for God, burnt on the altar as a ' memorial portion ' (token) of the whole grain-offering. The remainder went to the priests. It was ' a most holy gift ', lit. ' a holy-gift of holy-gifts '. Holy-gifts (Hebrew *ḳodhāshîm*) were allocated to the priesthood and could be taken out of the sanctuary and eaten by the families and dependents of the priests, but a ' holy-gift of holy-gifts ' could not be taken out of the sanctuary, and if it was eatable, it could be eaten there and only by the priests themselves. Here, ' sanctuary ' means in the Court of the Priests, within the Gate of Nicanor. **4-10.** The grain-offering could be of cooked grain, in which case it had to be baked, and either unleavened cakes mixed with oil or wafers spread with oil. Tradition says there had to be ten. The cakes were pierced, i.e. with a hole in the middle ; the wafers were thin cakes, probably round. The cakes could be baked on a griddle or baked in a deep pan with a cover, cf. a casserole. **11-13.** Further details. No leaven and no honey were allowed, because of the fermentation, which was regarded as being ceremonially unclean. The Hebrew word could be used both of grape-syrup (Gen. 43:11 ; Ezek. 27:17, modern Arabic *dibs*) and of bee-honey. This *dibs* was used by the Canaanites, Babylonians, and Egyptians in religious rites. Leaven was held to be corrupt, cf. Mt. 16:11 ; Lk. 12:1 ; 1. C. 5:7, 8. The idea is found among the Romans and the word was used by the Rabbis as a metaphor for evil (' Leaven ', HDB iii, 90). Salt was essential to all sacrifices (Ezek. 43:24, 47:11 ; also Mk 9:49 in some MSS). It began as necessary to a proper meal, but it is an emblem of fidelity in the near East and it became ' the salt of the covenant ' (' Salt ', HDB iv, 355).

f **14-16** The first-fruits mentioned here (*bikkûrîm*) consisted of grain only, fresh grain in the ear roasted, and then ground. According to the Mishnah (Bikk. i, 3) this class of first-fruits comprised seven types only : wheat, barley, grapes, figs, pomegranates, olive oil, and honey. This was honey from the comb. All other first-fruits were technically known as *rē'shîth*, and included the leaven and the honey (*dibs*) of **12**, which could be brought as first-fruits but not to the altar. The theory of first-fruits is that all increase of every kind belongs to God, whether of man or field or fold. A token, the first and the best, is to be brought to the shrine and presented to God—not ' given ' because it is his already. God accepts this as representing the whole and permits man to use the rest.

g **III The Sacrifice of Peace Offering**—A more accurate name is ' slain-offering ', but the usual rendering is ' sacrifice ', or more fully, ' sacrifice of peace offering '. The word *zebhaḥ* originally meant ' slaughter ', and in earliest times all slaughter was also a sacrifice in that the blood and presumably the fat were given to the god. With the introduction of the One Central Sanctuary (Dt. 12:20–28), a distinction had to be made between slaughter for food and slaughter for a sacred meal. The word *shᵉlāmîm* is rendered ' peace ' because of the rendering of LXX and Vulg. in 1 and 2 Sam., 1 and 2 Kg., and Prov., but the Hebrew means more than ' peace '. It means ' health, prosperity ', cf. Isa. 53:5. The usual opinion is that this sacrifice was a shared meal, shared by God and man to promote unity and communion. This theory is based on the theory that the origin of religion is to be found in totemism. It is more likely that the animal was regarded as sacred food and the people ate the holy food (ate the god) and so found new strength and vigour. The blood was poured out at the altar, the fat was burnt on the altar, both these rites being followed whatever the sacrifice and whatever its purpose. Certain parts of the flesh were the perquisite of the priests (7:32–36), but all the rest was eaten by the worshipper. **9.** the fat tail entire (AV ' the whole rump ') is the broad fat tail of a species of Palestinian sheep, esteemed a great delicacy (Isa. 9:24) and so heavy that it needed support in a little wicker cart on wheels attached to the sheep. See illustration in JE xi, 50. ' All fat is the Lord's ' (**16**) and it is ' food offered by fire to the Lord ' (**11**). This is because both the blood and the fat were regarded as specially containing the life of the animal and so were taboo, RS 379.

h **IV 1-V 13 The Sin Offering**—This sacrifice was not known before the exile except in the form of fines, 2 Kg. 12:16. The animal did not go to the altar and was in no sense a gift to God. The blood was drawn off into bowls as usual ; some of it was used for sprinkling-rites, and the rest was poured out at the base of the altar. The blood was still taboo and so had to be given to God, but at the same time it was in some sense ' sin ', and could not therefore be poured on to the sides of the altar. The internal fat, as always, was burned on the altar. If the sin-offering was on behalf of the priest himself or on behalf of the com-h munity as a whole, thus including the priest, the flesh was taken away ' outside the camp ' and destroyed by fire. If the sin-offering was on behalf of any person or group which did not include the priests, then the flesh was eaten that same day by the priests within the holy place. The essential element was that the flesh, which had become ' sin ', should be taken away, destroyed. When the sin is got rid of, it is no longer between God and the sinner. The sin-offering is thus a means by which the sin of man is ' taken away '. The cleansing ceremony included sprinkling the blood seven times before the Lord in front of the Veil and smearing the horns of the altar of incense. This altar was a post-exilic innovation and according to P was within the Tabernacle in front of the Veil which shrouded off the Ark. There was no altar of incense in Solomon's Temple, and the altar of burnt-offering was outside the temple in the outer court. In the Second Temple it was within the innermost court, in front of the Holy of Holies. The ' seven ' is the sacred seven, found in all areas where in early times there was Mesopotamian influence. Its origin is in the Mesopotamian cult of the seven stars, i.e. sun, moon, and the five planets known to antiquity. The horns of the altar were the most sacred parts of the altar, a survival from ancient times when the high god was represented by a bull, symbol of life and generative power. The high god of Canaan, Il, is regularly referred to in the Ugarit (Râs Shamra) texts as Shor-Il (the bull-El), and the deity was worshipped at Bethel and at Dan in the form of a bull.

i **IV 2** forms the general statement. This offering has to do with sins done unwittingly, accidental errors, mostly in ritual matters, brought later to the doer's knowledge. Some maintain that there is no such thing as unconscious sin. If sin is described as a deliberate, conscious action, then obviously there can be so such thing as unconscious sin. But a man can do wrong without knowing it, and probably the most serious offences are those which arise unconsciously out of self-centredness. But the offences mentioned here are ritual offences.

3-12 The Sin Offering of the High Priest—According to Levitical theory a high priest can bring guilt on the people in his representative capacity through carelessness in ritual. ' The anointed priest ' (**3**) is Aaron's successor (6:22), the high priest of post-exilic times (21:10). Behind all these regulations there lies the conviction that repentance is not enough. Something must be done and must be seen to be done. The ritual is not to please God, who requires only repentance and faith, but for's man sake so that the repentance shall be real and not submerged in a wave of undefined sentiment. **6.** The detail ' in front of the veil ' is not found in Exod. 29:12. Similarly ' the altar of fragrant incense ' is an addition (cf. Exod. 27–29). It is evident that there are different strata in P.

j **13-21 The Sin Offering for the whole Congregation**—The offering is, as before, a young bull, traditionally three years old. In this case, the elders of the congregation, who appear only here in P, lay their hands on the head of the beast. The animal thus becomes the sin, and is removed and destroyed, since the priests, as part of the community, cannot eat their own sin.

k **22-35 The Sin Offering for the Ruler and for the ordinary Israelite**—The ruler's sin-offering is a he-goat, and that for the ordinary individual is a female goat or an ewe lamb. According to Num. 15:27 the goat must be a yearling. The phrase used for the he-goat (**23**) is literally ' a hairy one of goats ', a phrase used regularly for the sin-offering in Leviticus and Ezekiel, and elsewhere only in Gen. 37:31. Possibly some particular breed of goats is intended.

l **V 1-6 Details of Sin-offering Offences**—With one exception, these are all actions done unwittingly and afterwards brought to the notice of the offender. The exception is deliberately keeping silence when put on oath as a witness. It is a sin committed, so to speak, 204l
negatively, by doing nothing ; cf. 6:1–7. Our Lord had to speak at the Trial when he was put on oath, Mt. 26:63. **1.** ' He shall bear his iniquity ', i.e. he shall bear the consequences. The Hebrew words for ' sin ' can be used both for the act itself and for its consequences. See Gen. 4:13, where all VSS rightly agree in translating by ' punishment ', but the same word is used there as here. **2.** ' beast ' means wild animal, and ' cattle ' means domesticated animal. **5** demands open confession in addition to the sin-offering itself. **6.** The reference to ' guilt-offering ' is most strange, since here we are concerned with sin-offerings ; cf. 14:13 where the same anomaly is found, and 5:7 where LXX has made a ' correction ' and has substituted ' sin-offering '. The explanation is that the word is used in an earlier pre-P technical sense, just as the corresponding verb has an early non-technical meaning of ' liable to pay '. Read therefore ' he shall bring what he is liable to pay to the Lord '.

m **7-13 Concessions for the Poor**—This is the usual concession whereby the offender may bring two turtle-doves or pigeons, one for a whole-offering and the other for a sin-offering, the extra bird probably being an acknowledgment of gratefulness for the concession. The priest wrenches the head backwards, but does not wring it off, as before (1:15). There is a further concession in the case of extreme poverty (**11-13**), seven pints of flour, but without oil or frankincense, because it is not reckoned as a grain-offering. A handful of the flour goes to the altar as a token, probably not for the rest of the flour, but for the second bird (the normal whole-offering). The remainder of the flour, as LXX says, goes to the priest to be eaten. This is not because it is a grain-offering, but because it is a sin-offering and must be got rid of.

n **V 14-VI 7 The Guilt Offering**—These are different from the sin-offerings because they have to do with offences where damage has been done and can usually be assessed. They are compensation payments and in most cases one-fifth is added to the assessment.

o **V 14-16 Errors concerning Holy-gifts**—RSV excellently translates ' breaches of faith ', which is much better than the indefinite ' trespass '. The errors are unwitting infringements of the rights of the priests, who therefore suffer loss. They are concerned not with holy gifts in general, but with the Holy-gifts (*ḳᵒdhāshîm*) which were allocated to the maintenance of the priesthood. Thus the added one-fifth had to be given to the priest. **14.** Ancient tradition said that ' the shekel of the sanctuary ' was twice the weight of the ordinary shekel, but see A. R. S. Kennedy, ' Money ', HDB iii, 432. It was the old traditional shekel of 224 grains (an English silver half-crown weighs 218 grains), and not the later post-exilic shekel of 168–173 grains, the normal post-exilic currency. In NT times all Temple dues had to be changed into this holy currency, not so much because it was Jewish and nationalistic, but because it was the ancient unchanging shekel.

p **17-19** This is the case of a possible transgression of the regulations. The man does not know whether he has offended or not. The offence, if any, is not known, so that the damage cannot be assessed and no fifth can be added. It was called by later Jews the *'āshām tālûy* (suspended guilt-offering), and in the last days of the Temple men of scrupulous conscience would bring such a guilt-offering daily ; cf. Job 1:5 and its similar offerings of whole-offerings.

q **VI 1-7** (Heb. 5:20–26)—This section comes nearest to associating Temple sin- and guilt-offerings with conscious acts. It concerns cheating or robbing a kinsman (not ' neighbour ') by not doing what ought to be done, e.g. by not restoring a deposit, or by not returning what has been found, i.e. stealing by finding. The sin is negative rather than positive, and in some cases would never have been known unless the offender declared it. They are all clear cases for guilt-offerings and compensation because the owner has suffered loss.

204r **VI 8-VII 38** (Heb. 6:1–7:38). **Detailed Instructions for the Priests**—This section gives instructions as to what the priests are to do with offerings and sacrifices which have been handed over to them. **6:8-13** does not infer that there was to be one burnt (whole) offering each day and that in the morning. The instructions concern duties at the altar in the early morning, the clearing-away of the ashes and the fat which had been smouldering overnight, and the rekindling of the fire with wood so that it never went out. This symbol of the everburning fire is common to many religions, cf. the Vestal fire at Rome. There were probably offerings both morning and evening in pre-exilic times, 2 Kg. 16:15 and, for the evening offering, 1 Kg. 18:29, 36. Jewish writers make the most of ' he shall take up ' (10), since the same word *hērîm* is used of ' taking up ' the so-called ' heave-offering ' (*t^{e}rûmāh*). They found here the justification for the ' heave-offering of ashes ', the late ceremony whereby the priest took a handful of the ashes and laid it aside as a memorial of yesterday's whole-offering. The priest who had the morning duty of clearing away the overnight fat-and-ashes, wore special clothes, washable linen robe and drawers. These were worn only when in immediate contact with the altar, because when he has removed the ashes and placed them beside the altar, he changes into his ordinary sacred garments and then removes the ashes to a ' clean ' place (not a defiled rubbish heap) outside the camp.

s **VI 14-23 The Daily Cereal Offering**—The first section contains general instructions for all grain-offerings, whilst the second section (**19-23**) deals with the regular grain-offerings which the High Priest offered daily. The phrase ' on the day when he is anointed ' (**20**) must be a mistaken gloss, since the word ' regular ' is used in **20b** and it is ' decreed for ever ' (**22**). The confusion was probably caused by the custom whereby every priest at his installation offered a grain-offering of similar quantity, once and for all and without dividing it. These grain-offerings are wholly consumed on the altar. There is no token to be taken, and they are not ' holy-gifts ' because they do not go to the maintenance of the priests. They are the priest's own gift.

t **24-30 The Ritual of the Sin Offering**—The animal was to be slaughtered in the usual place, to the north of the altar, and it had to be eaten by the priests in the inner courts : it was ' most holy ' (a holy-gift of holy gifts). The sin-offering is taboo, and whatever touches it is taboo, lit. ' shall be holy ' (**27**). Garments which are touched must be washed, earthenware pots must be smashed because the holiness will be absorbed, and bronze pots must be scoured. The blood is used for de-sinning, but is not holy in that it can be thrown against the sides of the altar. This blood approaches what Sir J. G. Frazer called ' an exact taboo ' (EBrit. 9th ed., xxiii, 18), in which ideas of sacredness and uncleanness are indistinguishable.

u **VII 1-38 Supplementary Regulations**—In the case of the guilt-offering, the blood is thrown against the altar, since it is not sin-blood as in the case of the sin-offering. It is normally sacred blood and is treated like the blood of the whole-offering and of the slain-offering. The fat, as usual, goes to the altar, but the priests alone eat the flesh within the court (it is a holy-gift of holy-gifts). Jewish tradition interprets **7-8** to mean that the priest received as his perquisite the hides of sin-offerings, guilt-offerings, whole-offerings, but not of slain-offerings (peace-offerings) which went to the offerer, who also received the major part of the flesh. **11-18** deals with the three types of slain(peace)-offerings : thank-offerings, vows and freewill-offerings. The thank-offering, which was for well-being and good is the only offering, according to the Rabbis, which will still be teaching its lesson in the Day of Messiah. It was accompanied by three types of unleavened grain confections : ' pierced ' cakes mixed with oil, thin flat round cakes (wafers) smeared with oil, cakes mixed with oil, and also by leavened cakes. Tradition says there were ten items in each group, and the levy for 20
the priest was one item from each group. All the remainder of the cakes was eaten by the worshippers, and the flesh also, that of the thanksgiving sacrifice wholly on the first day, but the other two types on either the first or the second day. **19-21.** All who eat sacred meals must be ritually clean. The penalty for infringement is outlawry. **22-27** re-emphasise the importance of not eating the fat and the blood, which are taboo. **28-36** give details of the disposal of the flesh of the slain(peace)-offerings. The share of the priest steadily increases through the centuries. In 1 Sam. 9:24 it was the thigh and the fat-tail; in Dt. 18:3 it was the shoulder, the two cheeks and the maw ; here and in Exod. 29:37f. it is the breast and the right thigh. For ' wave offering ' (**30**) read ' special contribution ', and for ' offering ' (usually rendered ' heave-offering ') read ' levy ' : cf. G. R. Driver, ' Three technical terms in the Pentateuch ', JSS i (1956), 100–103. The rendering ' portion ' in the sense of ' measured portion ' (**35**) is sound ; the renderings of AV (' portion of the anointing ') and RV (' anointing-portion ') rest on a false etymology and are in any case meaningless in the context. **37f.** is a general conclusion to the whole section.

VIII-IX The Consecration and Installation of the 20
Priests—This section is the carrying-out of the instructions of Exod. 29, but there are additions, the assembly of the people and the references to Urim and Thummim. All the necessary people and objects are first assembled, Aaron and his sons, various objects and the people. In modern times the unleavened bread consists of round flat cakes, 12 inches in diameter and ¼ inch thick.

VIII 5-9 The Cleansing and Investment of Aaron b
the High Priest—After all are ritually cleansed, Moses as officiating priest deals first with Aaron and invests him with the high-priestly garments. The tunic was long-sleeved and of the finest linen. The sash (girdle) was 48 ft. long ; the robe was blue with a hole for the head and reaching down to the feet (so Josephus, but others say it was shorter than the tunic). The ephod was then bound tightly on him with lacing : ' skilfully woven ' is due to a mistaken etymology. The ephod of early times was probably little more than a linen cloth (2 Sam. 6:20), but this post-exilic ephod was much more elaborate. It was woven from many colours (Exod. 28:6), had shoulder-pieces and a tightly fitting belt. S. R. Driver, *Exodus* (CB), 312f., discusses four types of ephod, none of which was an image, since even that of Jg. 8:27 may have been made from the purple raiment of the kings of Midian. The general opinion is that the high priest's ephod was some kind of waistcoat with a belt round the bottom of it. But it may have been a pair of elaborately woven breeches which took the place of the long linen drawers of Exod. 28:42, and this would account for there being no mention of breeches in this chapter. The belt was thus round the top of the ephod with shoulder-straps attached to it. The breastpiece was attached to the shoulder-straps and the waistband. The Urim and Thummim (Exod. 28:30) were placed in pouches in the breastpiece. It is not known what these were, but they were used in ancient times in the casting of the sacred lot. Three answers could be given : Yes, No, and neutral. Urim and Thummim were probably two discs, black (say) on one side and white or yellow on the other, and perhaps if two blacks came up, the answer was No, and so forth. If the words are Hebrew words, they apparently mean ' Lights and Perfections ', or, changing the vowels of the first word, ' Curses and Perfections ' (No and Yes). The basis of the theory of divination by lot is the assumption that all events are caused by a personal agency. If therefore an event can be staged in which it is obvious that there has been no human agency involved, then there must be a non-human agency at work. If the event takes place on sacred premises or by the manipulation or through the medium of a sacred person, then the author of the event must be

205b the numen of the place. This is the theory of the sacred lot, of divination by the liver (hepatoscopy), by dreams, or in ecstasy or any other means by which a man ceases to be in control of his own actions. The Canaanite prophet (*nābhî'*) was of this type, as he whirled in frenzied abandon uttering strange noises, and such behaviour was contagious, 1 Sam. 10:9–13. Here also is basis of the glossolalia, that speaking with tongues which has survived from antiquity. The turban is said to have been 24 ft. long, wound round Aaron's head. On it there was a golden flower. RSV has 'plate' following the usual translation, but LXX has *petalon* and the Hebrew word actually does mean 'flower'. This flower was engraved as if on a seal with 'Holiness to the Lord'. The engraving was in 'holy' characters, Exod. 28:36–37. 'Holy' characters probably refers to the ancient script which is to be seen in the Siloam Inscription (J. Finegan, *Light from the Ancient Past* (1946), 158, Plate 69). This was the regular Hebrew script before the introduction of the square characters. The 'holy crown' was a diadem after the Persian model as worn by Persian kings, S. R. Driver, *Exodus* (CB), 309. This diadem was a blue silk scarf speckled with white and two inches wide, and it was tied round the base of the tall hat which they wore, fastened so that the ends hung down behind, Xenophon, *Cyropaedia*, viii, 3, 13.

c **10-12** The oil was specially prepared, Exod. 30:22–33. The use of the oil and of the diadem suggests royal status, for here it is only the high priest who is anointed and not his sons. This agrees with Exod. 29:7, but elsewhere it is said that the ordinary priests also were anointed, Exod. 40:15; Num. 3:3, etc. Possibly this was a comparatively late development, later than the custom of anointing the high priest, which itself appears to be post-exilic. Previously the hand of the priest was filled, presumably with his first offering as priest, but after the exile the high priest was virtually the ruler of a theocratic state. Further, everything he was to touch was anointed. The installation of a new high priest evidently marked the beginning of a new era, since everything was cleansed and everything was reconsecrated. Compare the laws which permitted the homicide to leave the city of refuge and return home safely only at the death of the high priest, Num. 35:26–32. **13.** Ordinary priests were invested with tunic, sash, and headdress.

d **14-29 The Offerings**—There were three offerings to be made on behalf of the high priest in connection with his installation: a sin-offering, a whole-offering, and 'the ram of ordination'. **14-17.** The sin-offering for the new high priest was a bull, the costliest of all sin-offerings, Exod. 29:10–14. The usual smearing of the altar with the blood of the sin-offering takes place, but there is the additional phrase 'and purified the altar'. The Hebrew word is 'sinned'. Chapman and Streane (*Leviticus* (CB), 46) refer to the English phrase 'to stone plums', whereby we mean 'to de-stone' them. Sin could penetrate even a material object, so that it had to be decontaminated as if from poisonous gas. It is not easy for us to understand how the altar could be thus unclean, or how atonement could be made for it, but the object of all the ceremonies is evidently to make a perfectly clean and new start and to remove every possible taint of sin and unseemliness. **18-21.** There were two rams to be offered, the first a whole burnt offering with the normal rites, but the second (22–29) was the ram of ordination (Exod. 29:19–26) with its unique ritual. Three purposes are served: the hallowing of the priests; a whole-offering on behalf of the priests; a shared meal, truly shared by God and the priests. The priests are hallowed by blood being placed on the tip of the right ear, right thumb and right big toe. S. R. Driver, (*Exodus* (CB), 319) explains that these are the organs of hearing, handling and walking. An alternative suggestion is that they are the extremities and signify complete sanctification of the body. The whole-offering for the priests consists of the fat (which in any case goes to the altar), the right thigh (normally a 'levy' which goes 205d
to the officiating priest), and **26** one item from each of the three kinds of cakes in the basket. All this is placed on the hands of Aaron and his sons who treat them as a 'special contribution' (RSV 'wave offering'). The right thigh becomes a token for the whole beast and the three cakes a token accompanying grain-offering, and thus we get these parts of the bull making a whole-offering, whilst the rest of the animal and the rest of the cakes are eaten by the priests. We thus get a truly shared meal, shared by God and the priests, and this is eaten by the priests after they have been sprinkled with the anointing-oil and the cleansing-blood. Everything therefore is done to secure the removal of every slightest suggestion of uncleanness. Everything is done to ensure holiness and at-onement between God and the priests. Further, the priests stay for seven days at the opening of the tent of meeting, where they have eaten the ram. Once more, we have the sacred 'seven', the time of insecurity and danger from evil influences: cf. van Gennep, *Les Rites de passage* (1909) and N. H. Snaith, *The Jewish New Year Festival* (1947), 117. There were seven days of birth (circumcision on the eight day), seven days of marriage (Gen. 29:27; read 'seven' instead of 'week') and seven days of mourning for the dead (Gen. 50:10). This is why the seven-day period is found regularly in Hebrew rite and custom, sometimes with holy negative (taboo) associations and regularly with cleansing-rites.

IX The actual installation takes place on the octave, e
because it is the first day after the seven days, the first day of Aaron's life as high priest. He makes a new beginning of worship: first a bull-calf for his own sin-offering, then a whole-offering for himself. Next a sin-offering for the people, and then the way is clear for the whole-offering for the people and the slain-(shared)-offering. There are two variations from the normal ritual. The first is in connection with his own whole(burnt)-offering: **13** instead of him placing all the pieces at one time on the altar, they are handed to him piece by piece by the assistant priests. Possibly this is because of the impressiveness of the ceremony, but it may be that, since this is the first time that Aaron touches the holy flesh, he must perform the rites gradually and carefully, lest the holiness be too strong for him. Compare the initiation ceremonies of the Larakia tribe of northern Australia, where the old man rubs the holy *bidu-bidu* stick through his own armpit and then across his stomach, lest the strong magic enter the boy's body and cause him to swell up, B. Spencer, *Native Tribes of the Northern Territory of Australia* (1914), 155. The other variation from the normal is in the 'peace offering', where both the breasts and the right thigh are treated as special contributions (RSV 'wave offerings'). This means that both go to the priesthood as a whole. Normally the breast is a special contribution and so belongs to the whole priesthood, and the thigh is a levy and belongs to the officiating priest. The variation is due to the piece-by-piece ceremony which makes this the one ceremony in which the officiating priest coincides with the whole priesthood. There is thus no need to assume, as some scholars do, that 'the right thigh' is an interpolation in **21**. **22-24.** The glory of the Lord appears to the people. This is the luminous splendour of his Presence, as though the Glory is his 'body'. This manifestation takes place on special occasions, particularly at the inauguration of worship, Exod. 40:34–38 P and 1 Kg. 8:10–11. See also Ezek. 10:3–4, where God departs from his Temple in order to travel away over the deserts to where his people are and are in need of him by the river Chebar. The Glory of the Lord is the later Shekinah of Jewish theology. The word is often used in the Targums to stand not so much for the Glory as for the centre of this radiance; cf. Mt. 17:5, 'a bright cloud overshadowed them; and a voice from the cloud'; also, Ac. 1:9, 'and a cloud took him out of their sight'.

205e The sudden miraculous burning of the whole-offering is an addition to the story, since it had already been burnt (15). Compare the similar addition in 2 Chr. 7:1 (cf. 1 Kg. 8) and also in 1 Chr. 21:26 (cf. 2 Sam. 24:25). Other examples of such a spontaneous kindling of the altar fire are Jg. 6:21 (Gideon) and 1 Kg. 18:18 (Elijah on Mount Carmel). These are special demonstrations of divine power. Usually such manifestations are connected with the setting-up of a new form of worship.

206a **X The Duties of the Priesthood**—This chapter deals with four important matters concerning the priesthood. The first matter deals with who is and who is not to perform priestly duties, i.e. those specific priestly duties which are concerned with the altar, privileges and duties which in the post-exilic period were reserved for the Aaronite priesthood alone. The other matters concern the proper observance of these priestly duties.

b **1-3 The Sin of Nadab and Abihu**—Nadab was Aaron's oldest son and Abihu was his second son, Exod. 6:23. They had precedence over their brethren because they were chosen in addition to the seventy to approach nearer to God than the remainder of the people at Sinai, Exod. 24:1, 9–11. Possibly, as Bertholet suggested, this story is an echo of a struggle on the part of northern priests to establish themselves at Jerusalem. It may well be that it is an echo of the attempt to establish southern priests at Jerusalem. We know that Josiah brought to Jerusalem all the priests of the local shrines in Judah, but that these priests were not permitted to approach the altar, but only to eat unleavened bread with their brother-priests, 2 Kg. 23:8–9. The true post-exilic priesthood was traced back to Aaron through his two younger sons, Eleazar and Ithamar. In later times (1 Chr. 5:34) the Zadokites traced their descent back through Eleazar and the Aaronites back through Ithamar. The post-exilic priests of P were called 'the sons of Aaron', but only eight of the twenty-four courses were Aaronites and they were, as we have seen, descended from the youngest of Aaron's four sons. In much of Hebrew tradition God is represented as choosing the younger in preference to the older, Abel before Cain, Jacob before Esau, David before his brothers, Joseph before his ten older brothers, Dt. 7:7, 9:5; 1 Sam. 16:7 and in the NT, 1 C. 1:25–29, where this tradition is given a theological reference: 'the Lord sees not as man sees' and 'God chose what is low and despised in the world . . . so that no human being might boast in the presence of God'. But here we have another factor at work, the historical basis on which such theological explanations were built. The Zadokites were the original Jerusalem priesthood. H. H. Rowley, *Zadok and Nehushtan*, JBL lviii (1939), 113–141, showed that Zadok was the Jebusite priest when David captured the city and that the bronze serpent, Nehushtan, was the original Jerusalem fetish. When the Zadokites were carried off to Babylon, the Aaronites probably intruded from Bethel, R. H. Kennett, 'The Origin of the Aaronite Priesthood', JTS vi (1905), 161–186. Zech. 3:1–10 is thus a declaration that the priests who were taken away to an unclean land may return to be legitimate priests once more in Jerusalem, N. H. Snaith, 'Worship' in *Record and Revelation*, ed. H. W. Robinson (1938), 263–267. We thus have an aetiological story to explain why the priesthood descended through Eleazar and Ithamar and not through Nadab and Abihu. Their crime was not that they omitted to take fire from the altar, nor that they used wrongly compounded incense. They had no business to do it at all. This is why it was 'unholy' fire; cf. the late story of king Uzziah (2 Chr. 26:16–21) which reflects a struggle between the king (? post-exilic civil leader) and the priest, because it is certain that the king offered sacrifice in early times, cf. Solomon, 1 Kg. 8:64.

c **4-11 Prohibitions**—The prohibition here against mourning is absolute, as in 21:10, where it concerns the high priest. The strictness here, which includes the two surviving sons of Aaron, is probably because of the 20
special circumstances. The more extreme mourning customs (21:5) are not mentioned here, but only the baring of the head to let the hair hang free and the tearing of clothes. **8-11** concerns alcohol. The tradition that Nadab and Abihu were drunk is doubtless due to the juxtaposition of the two paragraphs. The prohibition against alcohol applies only when they are due to enter the tent of meeting, i.e. the sanctuary. 'Strong drink' is also mentioned (though not in Ezek. 44:21). The reference is to a beer brewed from dates or from barley. It has been suggested that the prohibition was due to association with Canaanite cults, cf. the Nazirites and their vows, but similar rules existed at Rome, where the Flamen Dialis (the priest of Jupiter) was not permitted even to walk under a vine. The reason for the Hebrew prohibition is the necessity of maintaining Habdalah, that separation between holy and unholy, clean and unclean, which is the essence of Judaism.

12-15 Priestly Dues—The distinction is between d
what is 'holy' and what is 'most holy'. Holy-gifts (*ḳ^{o}dhāshîm*) may be taken out from the Holy place and eaten by the families of the priests. But gifts that are 'most holy' (*ḳōdhesh ḳ^{o}dhāshîm*) must be eaten only by the priests themselves and only in the Holy place.

16-20 The Importance of eating the Sin Offering e
—The special events of the installation day are involved. The priests had not eaten the flesh of the people's sin-offering (9:15), but had treated it 'like the first sin-offering', i.e. the calf 'which was for (Aaron) himself' (9:8). This was correct for the first sin-offering, since the priest could not get rid of his own sin in this way. The rule of 6:30 is: if the blood is brought into the tent of meeting, the flesh must be burnt and not eaten. The problem arose because of two doubts: were the two sin-offerings treated in every respect in the same way (9:15)? which altar was it whose horns were smeared with blood (9:9)? If a sin-offering was not for the priest, then the rule of 4:34 was followed and the horns of the outside altar (i.e. of burnt-offering) were smeared with the blood and the flesh was eaten. If the sin-offering was for the priest or for the community, as including the priest, then the horns of the inside altar (i.e. of incense, inside the tent of meeting) were smeared and the flesh was burnt. Was the second sin-offering on behalf of the community as a whole including the priests (in which case Aaron was right)? or was it on behalf of the community as against the priests, since the first sin offering was for the priests only (in which case Moses was right)?

XI-XV Ritual Cleanness and Uncleanness— 20
Animals (11), Childbirth (12), Skin diseases (13–14:32), fungus in houses (14:33–57), 'Issues' (15). This section has nothing to do with ethical matters, but with ritual cleanness and uncleanness. 'Holy' is that which has to do with God, and everything that belongs to God is 'holy'. Uncleanness has to do partly with the preservation of society and partly with the other world of spirits and taboos. The Hebrews acted on the theory that God is concerned with every aspect of life and with the whole of it, and this led them to bring all these primitive laws, based on early natural religion, within their religious system. Thus rules which, as a sanitary necessity, involved exclusion from the community, also involved exclusion from worshipping God within the post-exilic religious community. Being cut off from the people involved also being cut off from God. There is often uncertainty concerning a taboo as to whether the taboo arises from sacredness or from the opposite. Some animals were unclean (taboo) because they were sacred to other gods, some because they were repulsive in looks or in habits. It is said, possibly correctly, that the British dislike of horsemeat as human food is due to the fact that the horse was sacred to Odin and was made taboo therefore for Christians. All blood was taboo, and all fat. All issues of blood are always unclean and all running sores are unclean, partly because of un-

07a pleasantness, partly because of contagion, partly because blood is ' the life ' and too powerful for ordinary
b mortals. **11:1-8** deals with unclean animals. Clean animals are those which have a parted foot (e.g. rabbit) or a cloven hoof (e.g. cow) and also chew the cud. Both conditions must be fulfilled. Uncleanness does not necessarily mean there is anything edibly harmful in the flesh. They may be good to eat, and some of them undoubtedly are ; but they are taboo. The theoretical classification is unlikely to be original. The actual reasons may vary from case to case, and are unknown. **11:9-12** deals with unclean fish. J. G. Frazer (EBrit. 9th ed., xxiii, 18) says that in some parts of the world all fish is taboo. Among the Hebrews the taboo was limited to whatever had neither fins nor
c scales, whether fresh-water or salt-water fish. **11:13-19** deals with unclean birds ; cf. Dt. 14:11–18. The prohibited birds seem to be birds of prey and carrion birds, mostly vultures and owls. The species are difficult to identify and the English versions vary considerably. **13** are all vultures ; **14** deals with the kite and all species of falcons ; **15** refers to ravens (or carrion crows) ; **16** deals with owls and all hawks ; **17** deals with owls ; **18** with two more owls and the osprey ; **19** includes the stork (or heron), all cor-
d morants, the hoopoe and the bat. **11:20-23** concerns creatures that swarm or teem. RSV calls them ' winged insects that go on all fours ', but this must mean winged creatures which also creep. All such are taboo unless their legs are jointed so that they can leap. Some locusts may be eaten (22), and RVm is right in describing them as four types of locusts not certainly identified. Locusts are mentioned as edible in Mt. 3:4, but the Rabbis prohibited all locusts as food because it was difficult to identify the various species. **24-28** says that uncleanness lasts till sundown, that touching unclean animals incurs uncleanness and that (27) animals that walk on their paws (? dogs and
e cats) are unclean. **29-38** refers to small animals that breed freely. Some of these are earthbound, but most of them can climb about the house and are liable to fall on to things or into uncovered vessels. Once more the species are difficult to identify with certainty. Mostly they include all kinds of lizards and geckos. Whatever their bodies fall into is unclean till sundown ; water into which they fall is unclean and carries uncleanness with it, unless it is water from a spring or a cistern. **39-40** says that even clean animals are unclean if they die from natural causes. **41-43.** All earthbound creatures that breed freely, crawl on their bellies or have more than four feet are unclean and may not be eaten. **44-45.** The reason is that God is holy and he requires that his people shall be holy. Holiness includes ritual cleanness. This holy God is the God who brought them out of Egypt, and all the laws in this chapter, elsewhere in Leviticus, and even the Ten Commandments, are based on this. The basis of all conduct is religious rather than ethical ; it is based not on the fact that God is moral, but on the fact that he is their Saviour. This is why it is unfortunate when Exod. 20:2 is omitted in the recitation of the Ten Commandments. Further, in **46-47** the aim of all these regulations is to make the distinction plain. This Judaistic theory of Habdalah is made to explain the mystery of taboos, just as in Gen. 1 it is used to describe the process of Creation : this is always by ' dividing between ', making a Habdalah.

f **XII Childbirth**—Taboos on women in childbed are common among primitive peoples, and these rules are survivals. The custom also is common of observing a longer period for girls than for boys, it being held that the birth of a girl is more dangerous than that of a boy. Circumcision takes place on the eighth day, the first day after the seven days of birth. Nothing is said here about an association between circumcision and the covenant, Gen. 17. The rite, practised in many parts of the world, was originally a puberty rite and very ancient since a flint-knife was used, Exod. 4:25. Some scholars see a departure from strict rule in Lk. 2:21–39,
as if Mary appeared at the Temple before the forty 207f
days were completed. This is not said : verse 22 is separate and tells what happened at the end of the forty days. This period is intended to cover the time of the discharge (hence the taboo) and it is assumed that the period of discharge is doubly long in case of a girl. The prescribed offerings at purification consist of a yearling lamb for a whole-offering and a turtle-dove or a pigeon for a sin-offering. The sin-offering is not brought because of moral sin, but because of the blood taboo. It is a matter of ritual uncleanness and not of moral fault. **8.** The usual concession to the poor is made, and the Mother of Jesus availed herself of this, Lk. 2:24.

XIII Skin Diseases—Affections of the skin, whether g
a mark, a scab or a blotch, have to be reported to the priest in case they are more than skin deep. The classical signs of leprosy for which the priest must look are white hairs and an infiltrated lesion, i.e. an infection involving deeper layers of skin than the epidermis. Most of the cases cited are not true leprosy according to modern terminology. In the case of **3,** the diagnosis is certain : it is leprosy. **4-6** is an infection such as impetigo, not serious enough for segregation if it clears within two weeks. **9-11** are true leprosy beyond doubt, but not **12-13**, since leprosy does not affect the whole body in this way. It is probably leucoderma, but if it ulcerates later and raw flesh appears, it is true leprosy after all. **16.** If the sore heals again, it cannot be leprosy. In **18-20** the two classical signs of leprosy appear in a boil. If the infection spreads, but the two signs do not appear, it is smallpox or some similar disease. **24** may indicate leprosy if the signs appear, **28** otherwise it is an ordinary tropical sore or perhaps erysipelas. **27.** If it continues to spread, it is to be treated as leprosy. **29-31** seem to indicate ringworm. **31-34** may be impetigo, **40-41** deal with two types of alopecia, and **42f.** may be either leprosy or a type of ringworm called favus. **45f.** The leper must wear torn clothes, let his hair hang loose ' as though dead ' (Josephus, Ant. III, xi, 3), and cry ' Unclean, unclean ' that others may avoid him.

47-49 deals with ' leprosy ' in clothes. It concerns rot h
and mould in garments, whether made of wool or linen or skin. Everything depends on the affected part being reddish or greenish in colour and on this discoloration spreading. A double seven days' isolation is demanded. **48.** The phrase ' warp or woof ' does not make sense in this context, since one could scarcely be infected without the other. RVm suggests ' woven or knitted ', indicating two ways of making the garment, but ' yarn or piece ' is best.

XIV Cleansing Leper and House—**1-32** deals with i
the leper and **33-53** with the house. The leper is dealt with ' outside the camp ' because he is still isolated. If the priest is satisfied that the man is cured, then the leper's friends are to provide two small birds, traditionally sparrows, some cedarwood, marjoram and scarlet thread. Killing over running water is a widespread custom, Frazer, *The Golden Bough* 3rd ed., iii, 15f., 101f. The cedarwood (traditionally a foot long) was bound with the marjoram by means of the scarlet thread into a brush which was dipped in the blood of the bird, and the blood sprinkled seven times over the man. The living bird was dipped in the blood and released to fly away into the open country. This, like the running water, is symbolic of the removal of uncleanness. Cedarwood is said to have healing properties and marjoram (hyssop) makes a good sprinkler, being bushy. **9b.** In the days of the second Temple, the second bathing took place in a chamber in the NW. corner of the Court near the Gate of Nicanor. The double hair-cutting is similar to that which belongs to the Nazirite cleansing (Num. 6), but this rite is an illustration of the danger of supposing that the same rite always involves the same principle, The Nazirite's hair was the sign of consecration, but the leper's hair is unclean. The hair is in each case the sign of a taboo, but a taboo can work two ways. It can be a

207i taboo to God and away from man (Nazirite), or a taboo away from both God and man (leper). The cleansed man must bring on the eighth day (the first day of his new life) two male lambs and one ewe lamb, with grain and oil. One of the male lambs is to be a guilt-offering, but not with the usual rites, It is similar to the case of the Nazirite whose taboo-period was interrupted (Num. 6:12). There was no restitution and no fifth added. Here also the blood of the guilt-offering was sprinkled on the leper. This was not normal in the case of a guilt-offering, nor was the touching of ear, thumb, and toe. Presumably the ancient cleansing rite could not be brought within the rigid scheme of the P-sacrificial system. It was partly like the true sin-offering and partly like the true guilt-offering, and they called it the latter because it approximated most closely to it. **13.** In NT times 'the holy place' was the Court of the Priests, and **14** the leper put his head, his hand, and his foot through the Gate of Nicanor, the limit beyond which the non-priest could not penetrate. **33-53** is concerned with fungus growth (leprosaria) in houses. The analogy with leprosy is the colour of the patches and the 'below the surface'; these are the two classical signs of leprosy. If, after the customary seven days' isolation, the patch is bigger, the infected stones are to be taken away and all the daub inside the house to be scraped off. If this does not cure the trouble, the whole house is to be taken down and removed to the 'unclean' rubbish heap.

j **XV 'Issues'**—This chapter is concerned with discharges from the sexual organs. **1-15** and **25-30** deal with abnormal discharges, and both require a seven-day quarantine, bathing- and washing-rites, and a sin-offering and a whole-offering. **16-18** deals with the discharge of semen, whether in sexual intercourse or not, and **19-24** deals with normal menstruation. In these two cases washing and bathing is demanded, but no offerings. There are undoubtedly sanitary reasons for all these restrictions, but at root there are the taboos which have to do with things that contain life, i.e. blood and semen. In **31** RSV has 'separate', which is probably right, though the nazirite word is used and not the normal *habdalah* word. The ancient versions were puzzled and read 'advise, warn'.

208a **XVI The Day of Atonement**—This chapter logically follows chapter 10 and gives details as to how and in what attire the true priest shall approach God. He is to enter the holiest place only at one time, on the Day of Atonement, the tenth day of the seventh month (29). He is to wear the linen garments in which the officiating priest comes into close contact with the altar (6:10), but with the notable addition peculiar to the high priest, the linen turban on which was fastened the golden flower with the diadem and the inscription 'Holy to the Lord'. This marked him out as Israel's special representative (8:9 and Exod. 28:36–39).

b **2** The 'mercy seat' was the covering of the Ark of the testimony, a slab of gold, 4 ft. by 2½ ft., and on it there were two cherubim facing each other, whose outstretched wings reached inwards to cover the Ark. These cherubim were quite different from the giant guardian figures of Solomon's Temple, 1 Kg. 7:23–28. 'Mercy seat' is Coverdale's translation and it is due to the religious use of the Hebrew root k-p-r (atone, make propitiation). Wyclif's word was 'propitiatory', based on the Latin. It is probable that the Hebrew word (*kappōreth*) has its original meaning 'covering', though this rendering is now scarcely satisfactory in view of all the interpretative renderings. For 'drew near' (1) it is better to follow the ancient versions (cf. Num. 3:4) and read 'offered illicit fire' (10:1).

c **6-10** Aaron must first present and offer a bull as his own sin-offering, since he must not otherwise come near and enter the holiest place. He must then present the two goats, both as sin offerings, one 'for the Lord' and normal, the other 'for Azazel' and unique to this ceremony. **11-14** describe the ceremony of cleansing the innermost shrine of Israel, the mercy 208
seat itself. He must first slaughter the bull so as to make available the blood for the de-sinning rite. By means of the censer, the glowing wood from the altar-fire and the incense, he must then create the cloud which shall shroud the Presence of God, without which not even Aaron dare appear before the second veil. The full ritual for the Day of Atonement as it was observed in the last days of the Temple is to be found in the Talmudic tract *Yoma*. **15-19.** Aaron now can act as intermediary for the people and he repeats the cleansing-rites on their behalf. This section is far from clear, because P's plans are modelled partly on the Second Temple with its Holy of Holies (within the Court of the Priests beyond the Gate of Nicanor) and partly on Solomon's Temple which had no Holy of Holies, but simply the two divisions, the House and the inner Shrine. **18.** Thus the Mishnah (Yoma v, 5) takes the altar to refer to the golden altar of incense which, according to P, was within the Tabernacle but outside the second veil, but it is more likely that the reference is to the altar of whole-offering which in Solomon's Temple was outside the whole building and in the Second Temple was within the Court of the Priests in front of the Holy of Holies. The confusion is caused by an editor who confused the two Temples (cf. 1 Kg. 8), or who held that the Second Temple was largely a replica of the First Temple, so that sometimes 'the holy place' means the Court of the Priests of the Second Temple (i.e. everything within the Gate of Nicanor) and sometimes it refers to an inner section of the Holy of Holies which the P-writer assumed to be divided into two sections on the analogy of the two divisions of Solomon's Temple.

20-22 The live Goat for Azazel—Having thus isolated d
the sin of the people from all holy things, Aaron now proceeds to get rid of their sin altogether. He puts both hands on the head of the live goat, recites over it all the sins of the people of Israel and thus transfers their sins to the goat. The goat is then sent away and is lost in the wilderness. There was a man waiting in order to follow the goat and see that it was successfully lost. In the time of the Second Temple this man was usually a non-Israelite. The goat is the scapegoat, familiar to all students of primitive religion. It is a common idea that evil can be transferred, both in the sense of misfortunes and also of moral evil. Further, the custom of public scapegoats is well attested, J. G. Frazer, *The Golden Bough* (1923, abridged ed.), 546–587, and examples are cited from all parts of the world. According to Hebrew tradition, as preserved in the Mishnah, *Yoma* vi, 8, the goat was driven to a rocky terrace twelve miles east of Jerusalem, identified as the modern Bet Hudedun (ZDPV 3, 214–219), and was driven over these jagged rocks to perish over the precipice. For a discussion of the significance of the rite, see Chapman and Streane, *Leviticus* (CB), 185–189, but G. R. Driver, 'Three technical terms in the Pentateuch', JSS i (1956), 97f., shows that the 11th cent. Jewish commentator Rashi was right when he understood Azazel to refer to the place to which the goat was sent. It means 'jagged rocks, precipice', and only later did the word come to refer to a desert demon. Azazel was said to be the tenth in order of the Fallen Angels (1 Enoch vi, 7) who were 'the chiefs of tens'. It was Azazel who was held mostly to have led men astray because he taught men the art of working in metals, the use of antimony for the beautifying of eyelids, and the use of all kinds of costly stones. Through these arts men learned idolatry and fornication. But in spite of all this, the Rabbis were very clear that the goat was in no sense a gift to Azazel. Rabbi Eliezer declared that the goat was not a gift to Semjaza (Sammael), the chief of the Fallen Angels, nor a bribe to him not to make their offerings void or falsely to accuse Israel. It was not a sacrifice, since it was not slaughtered. It was sent away by God's command. God chooses the goat that is sent away to Azazel. Plainly and simply God himself is

8d providing a means of getting rid of Israel's sin. **23-28.** With the final washings and cleansings all taint of sin is removed and a new beginning is made. **29-34.** The Day of Atonement is the great penitential day, the climax of the ten penitential days which began with the first day of the tenth month, Tishri. It is a 'sabbath of solemn rest' (31), a day of extraordinary and ultimate taboos (Hebrew *shabbath shabbāthôn*). It is not the regular weekly Sabbath. The word Sabbath originally meant 'come to rest' and so marked the end of a period. Later it came to mean 'rest-day' in the sense of 'taboo-day' and ultimately this rest-day was the seventh day, but there are survivals, such as here, of the earlier Sabbath, see N. H. Snaith, *The Jewish New Year Festival* (1947), 96–130, where the whole question of the origin and the development of the Sabbath is discussed.

9a **XVII-XXVI The Holiness Code:** see §203*c*. **XVII 1-9** concerns the slaughter of domesticated animals. They must all be brought to the Temple and slain there as slain-offerings (RSV 'sacrifices of peace offerings'). The passage is confused because of the word 'sacrifices' (5*a*); the word should be translated more generally: 'animals that are slaughtered'. Further 'open field' means 'in the country' as against 'at Jerusalem'. In the old days the Israelite slaughtered his animal at home, poured the blood over a stone, or took the animal to the local shrine and poured out the blood there. But with the establishment of the One Sanctuary in Jerusalem, this local killing becomes a survival of heathen cults, sacrifices to the spirits of the countryside (2 Kg. 23:8, where read 'high places of the satyrs'). The section is thus
b against worship at the local sanctuaries. **10-14.** The prohibition against local slaughter leads to a prohibition against eating blood under all circumstances. The life of the flesh is in the blood, and all blood was to be drained out before the flesh was eaten. The purpose of blood (11) is to make atonement. This is why even the burnt(whole)-offering makes atonement for the worshipper (1:3). But only the blood of domestic animals may be used at the altar. The blood of wild animals is to be drained off into the ground and covered (13). **15-16.** The prohibition against blood is not as strict here as in Dt. 14:21. There no Israelite may eat any animal that dies a natural death, i.e. is not deliberately slaughtered. Here such eating is not absolutely prohibited except so far as the blood of the animal may still be in it. The penalty for eating such an animal is light: the eater is unclean till sundown and must wash his clothes and bathe himself.

10a **XVIII Immoral Behaviour**—The chapter opens with a general warning against Egyptian and Canaanite customs. Israel's God has his own customs, and his people must observe them. It is not easy to decide whether the chapter is concerned with sexual intercourse within or outside marriage, since it deals with a society which allowed more than one wife and also admitted concubinage. The general statement is in **6**, 'uncover nakedness' being a euphemism for sexual intercourse. Some scholars have found here four groups each of five prohibitions: **6:10**, kinship of the first degree, **11-15**, of the second degree, **16-19**, through marriage, **20-23**, purity outside the family. A better approach is to recognise that the whole system depends upon what is 'one flesh'. There are three categories of this: husband and wife, persons born of the same womb, persons from the same thigh (same source of
b semen). **18** prohibits the taking of two sisters as wives. This has nothing to do with any ecclesiastical law concerning the deceased wife's sister. The fact that polygamy does not bring happiness in the home is shown by the existence of the word 'rival' to
c describe the other wife, cf. 1 Sam. 1:6. **16** apparently prohibits the levirate marriage (Dt. 25:5–10), the means whereby the widow was provided for and whereby also the deceased man's rights and property were preserved for his own family. But there is every evidence that the levirate marriage system prevailed.

21 is generally interpreted as referring to a ceremony 210d
whereby children were passed through fire, possibly burning them as whole-offerings. But it is curious that the prohibition here occurs among sexual matters. The ancient versions have 'cause to serve' (Sam.), 'serve' (LXX), 'cause to lie down for sexual intercourse' (Syr.), whilst other Greek Versions have 'compel by force'. MT has *Molech*, intended to be the name of a false god. Possibly the reference is to dedicating children to a Canaanite god or in a mixed Canaanite-Yahweh cult for purposes of temple prostitution. **24-30.** In any case, all these customs are declared to be Canaanite practices, because of which the land was made to 'vomit out' its inhabitants. What happened before can happen again.

XIX Miscellaneous Matters—Each section finishes 211a
with the regular refrain (? response) 'I am the Lord (your God)', which has already appeared in chapter 18. Perhaps **5-8** (repetition of 7:15–18) and **19** and **20-22** are later additions. **1-4** is a rudimentary code of laws, b
and may be an original basis of the Ten Commandments of Exod. 20:1–17, an indication of the extreme antiquity of some elements in P. Molten images are prohibited in Exod. 20:4, whilst Dt. 5:8 is against images hewn from wood or stone. **9-10** concerns leaving unharvested the corners of fields and the gleanings. It is said that the original idea of leaving the corners (23:22; Dt. 24:19–21) unreaped was to keep the corn-spirit alive. The rule also includes c
(9*b*) 'fallen grapes' lost in the vintage, but according to the Mishnah the reference is to individual grapes as against bunches, so that it means any single grape that has fallen or any single grape on the vine that is not part of a bunch. All these gleanings are for the poor and the resident alien, two of the depressed classes in ancient Israel.

11-16 is a continuation of the early code in 1–4. Men d
must not cheat or lie, nor must they swear oaths they do not intend to keep. The man hired by the day (13) must receive his day's wage that same day (Dt. 24:14; Mt. 20:9). The deaf must be treated with consideration, and no man may put obstacles in the way of the blind. There must be strict, impartial justice, no gossip, and no plotting against the life of a fellow-countryman. In **17-18** we get behind actions to motives. No man must nurse hatred against another, but must go and talk the matter out with him (Mt. 18:15–17). No man must bear any grudge against his neighbour, but shall love him as himself. This is the second commandment of Jesus, Mt. 22:39; Mk12:31; Lk. 10:27. According to Paul, all the rest can be summed up in this, Rom. 13:9; Gal. 5:14, and it is 'the royal law' of Jas 2:8. In Leviticus the neighbour is a fellow-Israelite, and possibly the 'stranger' (resident alien). In Lk. 10:36 it is clear that 'neighbour' includes national enemies. The Jew is neighbour to the Samaritan. The Briton is neighbour to the Russian, the Egyptian, the Jamaican.

19 The principle of separation and distinction (*Hab-* e
dalah) is to be extended to the smallest details: no mixture of domestic animals, no mixture of seed, not even a garment may be of mixed material. Dt. 22:5, 9–11 goes still further. It is possible that these rules are survivals of ancient magic taboos, but here they are part of the Habdalah system (Gen. 1:11f.).

20-22 prohibits sexual intercourse with a slave-girl f
who is the property of another man. It is not a case of 'betrothal' (RSV) but of assignment. She has not been bought from her owner, nor has he set her free. It is not a case of adultery, else both would be put to death. The woman is not a free agent, so no punishment attaches to her. The man must bring a guilt offering, because he has done damage to property, but there is no compensation laid down, because the damage was not held to be assessable. Instead of 'an enquiry shall be held' (RSV), AV ('she shall be scourged') follows Jewish tradition, and RV has 'they shall be punished'.

23-25 Newly planted Trees—The tree and its fruit g

211g are taboo for three years, lit. ' treat as uncircumcised '. The tree is in the nursery, so to speak, being born, and is not a proper tree until the fourth year : cf. a baby boy who is not a separate entity till the eighth day. The fruit of the fourth year is holy ; the fourth year is a first-fruits year (so Sam., which is right). ' An offering of praise ' (RSV) follows MT, but is wrong.

h **26-37** contains miscellaneous precepts. 26 prohibits eating flesh with the blood, a curious reference in this context. LXX has ' on the mountains ', a prohibition against eating sacred meals at any hill-shrine except Mount Zion. ' Augury ' includes hydromancy (Gen. 44:5) ; ' witchcraft ' refers to necromancy. 27 possibly prohibits the offering of hair to the dead to maintain their life in the spirit-world, since 28 has that purpose, partly that the flowing blood may keep the ghosts alive, and partly that the tattoo-memorial may preserve their memory. To honour the old and stand in their presence is a feature of ancient cultures : Egyptians, Spartans, and the father-god cults of Australian aborigines. The insistence upon fair treatment of aliens (33) is found elsewhere, Exod. 22:21, 23:9 ; Dt. 10:9. It is earlier than Deuteronomy. The reason given throughout is that the God who commands these things is their Saviour from Egypt, Exod. 20:2.

i **XX** deals for the most part with the penalties for the crimes mentioned in 18. **1-5** is a fuller form of protest against the Molech-cult (18:21). There is nothing here about ' passing the children through the fire '. LXX knows nothing of such a cult, and has ' to the ruler '. **2** prescribes stoning to death as the penalty, but **3** apparently belongs to another stratum of tradition. **21** states the penalty as childlessness. This is the usual interpretation, because of Gen. 15:2, but the word means ' stripped ' not necessarily of children. The word is used of Jeconiah (Jer. 22:30) who certainly had children (1 Chr. 3:17ff.). LXX has ' outlawed ', and Syr. ' proscribed '. The word evidently means disgraced, stripped of honour, of property, ostracised in some other way than being ' cut off from kinsfolk '. In **26** we get the twist in the idea of Holiness which completely altered the significance of the word. It should mean ' separated *to* ' God, because ' holy ' is what belongs to God, and that is what it meant in Hebrew religion. Judaism insists upon ' separation *from* ' things and other peoples, a logical sequence, but not, from the Christian point of view, a religious one.

212a **XXI Special Taboos involving the Priest**—The special holiness of the priests demands special taboos. The ordinary priest must have nothing to do with any dead person who is not of close kin : i.e. mother, father, son, daughter, brother, and virgin sister. If the sister is married she is her husband's close kin. **4.** According to RSV he must not approach even his wife's dead body. This appears plainly in AVm and RVm. MT is certainly difficult, but it is unlikely that the reference here is to the wife. She is not usually mentioned at all (Exod. 20:10). Probably four or five letters have been omitted by haplography and we should read (4) ' he shall not defile himself for (a sister) who is married to her husband '. This follows naturally on **3** and makes good sense. In Ezek. 44:26 contact with next of kin involves a seven-day taboo
b from the holy service. **5.** ' make tonsures ' RSV is misleading. This has nothing to do with the tonsure of the Roman priest. The custom prohibited here is a mourning-custom, at one time allowed (Isa. 22:12 ; Am. 8:10 ; Mic. 1:16), but later prohibited for all Israelites (Lev. 19:27f.). The references elsewhere to the custom (Jer. 9:26, 25:23, 49:32) are all to Arab tribes ; this confirms the testimony of Herodotus.

c **6.** Not ' bread ', but ' food '. The word *leḥem* refers to the staple food of the country. The Arabic equivalent means ' flesh, meat ', and the Hebrew word can be used of honey (1 Sam. 14:24) and goat's milk (Prov. 27:27) ; cf. the word ' corn ', which means ' cereal ' in Britain, but ' maize ' in North America. **9.** This
burning with fire is the most serious of all penalties 212
(20:14), and is equal to the fate of the man who has intercourse with both a woman and her mother.
16-24. The priest must have no physical defects what- d
ever. ' A mutilated face ' (RSV) is usually understood to mean ' slit nostrils, or ear or lip ', but in 22:23 the second word (RSV ' limb too long ') is rendered ' a limb too long ' and the contrast is with what is stunted. Probably, therefore, the end of this verse should be
' undergrown or overgrown '. **20.** The word can e
scarcely mean ' hunchback ', because the word certainly means ' twisted ' and in cognate languages, it is associated with eyebrows. It means ' misshapen eyebrows '. The next word (RSV ' dwarf ', AVm ' too slender ') means ' thin ' like a thin film. Since we are dealing with eyes in this part of the verse, understand ' a cataract ' (film over the eye). The next phrase ' with a defect in his sight ' is a guess. In cognate languages the word means ' moisten '. Understand, therefore, a discharge from the eye. **22.** The descendant of a priest may enter ' the holy place ' (the Court of the Priests of the Second Temple) and eat there ' holy gifts of holy gifts ', but he may not function at the altar.

XXII Further Details concerning Offerings—By f
' holy things ' is meant ' Holy gifts ', offerings presented by the Israelites and allocated to the maintenance of the priests. **2.** The phrase ' keep away from ' is not clear. It does not mean ' keep away from ' absolutely, but only in such circumstances as would cause them to defile the offerings. If the priest is ritually unclean, he must not touch them, whether for any length of time (leper, ' issue ') or for a short period (till sundown).
10-16. Holy gifts are to be eaten by the priests and g
their families. The man who lodges with a priest and the hired servant are ' outsiders '. It is a mistake to use the term ' layman '. If an outsider eats a holy gift by mistake, he must restore the full value plus one-fifth, as in the case of a guilt-offering. **17-25** prohibits any animal with a blemish, except that an overgrown or a stunted animal may be offered as a freewill offering (23). Otherwise no blemish or mutilation is tolerated, and this applies whatever the source from which the animal is obtained, whether home-bred or acquired from a foreigner. The seven-day period of birth must be observed, and thus no animal may be offered until it has, so to speak, a life of its own, Exod. 22:30. In any case ' mother and child ' must not be killed on the same day. In Dt. 22:6 this rule is extended to include a bird and her eggs. This extension in Deuteronomy is an indication of the fact, more generally recognised today than formerly, that there are early elements in P. **29** deals with the thank-offering, i.e. a particular type of slain-offering, distinguished from other types, not basically because of what happens to them after they are offered, but because of the motive behind the offering. This particular type of slain-offering (RSV ' sacrifice ') must be eaten the same day, and in this it differs from other slain-offerings, those which arise out of vows or are freewill offerings. These latter two types may be eaten on the second day (7:16), but the slain-offering which is a thank-offering must be eaten on the day it is slaughtered.

XXIII Feasts and Festivals—The term ' appointed 213a
feasts ' (RV ' set feasts ', RVm ' appointed seasons ') is a general term to include all religious occasions, the Sabbath, the three ' feasts ' (Pilgrimages, Unleavened Bread, Weeks, Booths) and the other festivals, such as Passover, Trumpets, and the Day of Atonement.
4-8 The Passover is to be observed on the fourteenth b
day of the first month (Nisan) according to the post-exilic calendar, which is the ancient Mesopotamian calendar of Nippur. The lamb is to be slain ' between the two evenings ' (RSV ' in the evening '). The word has occasioned much discussion through the centuries. It probably means ' between sunset and dark ', a shorter period of time in Palestine than in Britain. The word *pesaḥ* (Passover) means ' limp, hop over ', though there is an Akkadian root which

3b means 'placate, be soothed'. See Exod. 12:1–14; Dt. 16:1–8. The Passover was never a harvest festival, as Wellhausen and W. Robertson Smith suggested. It was a seasonal apotropaic festival, that is, a protective rite against the power of evil spirits. There was an ancient Arabian custom of sprinkling every tent with blood, and in the Athenian spring festival of Anthesteria the doors of houses were smeared with pitch. But the Hebrews took this ancient rite and they reinterpreted to tell the story of the rescue from Egypt and those mighty acts of salvation which God wrought for them when he saved them and made them into a nation, his own special people. See N. H. Snaith, *The Jewish New Year Festival* (1947), 13–23.

c **6-8 Unleavened Bread**—cf. Exod. 12:15ff. This feast began on the fifteenth day of the first month. It lasted for seven days, the normal sacred period. The first and seventh days were 'holy convocations', a day on which no regular work is to be done. With the introduction of the One Sanctuary, the Passover (essentially a home festival) had to be observed at Jerusalem in a room which became technically 'home' (Mk 14:12–16); the tendency was to run the two sacred occasions into one. Thus Passover tends to be called 'Unleavened Bread' and lasts for seven days.

d **9-14 The 'Waving' of the Omer**—The first sheaf of the new harvest is a 'special contribution' (RSV etc. 'wave offering'), and it was to be made on 'the morrow after the sabbath' (11). The phrase has occasioned much dispute, and it is important because it is the day which fixes the observance of the Feast of Weeks (Pentecost). The Sadducees maintained that 'sabbath' here means the seventh day of the week, so that 'the morrow after the sabbath' is always the first day of the week (Sunday). The Pharisees contended that it means the day following the first day of Unleavened Bread, which was a sabbath, though not the weekly sabbath. The special sheaf was therefore always to be offered on the 16th, whatever day of the week it happened to be. In the first century A.D. the interpretation of the Pharisees was followed, as is clear from the Mishnah: see G. B. Gray, *Sacrifice in the Old Testament* (1925), 326–328. For the use of the term 'sabbath' in a wider sense than of the seventh day, see N. H. Snaith, *The Jewish New Year Festival* (1947), 111–130.

e **15-21 The Counting of the Omer (Sheaf)** (cf. Exod. 34:22; Dt. 16:10)—The whole harvest period is fifty days, counted by the waving of the sheaf, Dt. 16:9. This harvest period was 'closed' (Dt. 16:8, read 'closing ceremony' for RSV 'solemn assembly') by what originally was a one-day feast, thus marking the end of the cereal harvest period, J. Wellhausen, *Prolegomena to the History of Israel* (1885, Eng. trans.), 86. Pentecost ultimately became the festival of first-fruits. There is confusion in **20** because 'the two lambs' are not 'holy gifts' (RSV 'holy'). Vulg. tries to correct by omitting the reference to 'holy-gift', which refers only to 'the bread of the first fruits'.

f **23-25 The Feast of Trumpets**—The pre-exilic autumnal feast was held at the beginning of the year on the night of the harvest full-moon. With the change of calendar this New-Year feast fell on the 15th of the 7th month, a ridiculous date. Ultimately, part of the feast gravitated to the 1st of the 7th month, part to the 10th, but the main part of the feast with the all-night illuminations necessarily clung to the bright night of the harvest full-moon and became the post-exilic Feast of Tabernacles, N. H. Snaith, *The Jewish New Year Festival* (1947), 131–149. The remembrance of trumpet-blowing is a feature of modern Jewish ritual, and the traditional reasons, as drawn up by Rabbi Saadya (10th cent. A.D.), are to be found in the Jewish Prayer-books.

g **26-32 The Day of Atonement**—This is the modern Yom Kippur, a day of self-mortification and abasement. It is said that this rite is the last rite abandoned by the modern Jew who grows slack in his observance of Jewish customs. The day is a holy convocation, i.e. no regular work is to be done and everybody must be present. The day is a 'sabbath' (32), the word here being a survival of the original meaning of the term, a taboo-day. Also **(32)** 'evening to evening' is the Jewish system of reckoning the day, Gen. 1:5, etc. 213g

33-36 The Feast of Tabernacles (cf. Num. 28:7–11; h
Dt. 16:13–15; Ezr. 3:4)—This began, according to the post-exilic calendar, on the 15th of the 7th month, and lasted for the customary seven days. Like all harvest festivals, it was a pilgrimage (cf. the Muslim *ḥajj*). A harvest festival must be a pilgrimage, because the essence of it is the offering of first-fruits at the shrine. The eighth day (36) is an addition to the original seven. It was a 'closing festival' (RSV 'solemn assembly'). According to Dt. 16:8, this closing festival was on the seventh day, and the eighth day is a later custom; cf. Num. 29:35; Neh. 8:18; Jn 7:37, and 2 Chr. 7:9, but not 1 Kg. 8:66 unless here we have the transition from one custom to the other. **37-38** is the closing summary, so that **39-43** are definitely a later addition. There are two customs involved. One is the carrying of the fruit of 'goodly trees'. The word 'goodly' (Hebrew *hādhār*) is strange. It can mean 'swelling', and hence the rounded fruit of trees, e.g. citrous fruits, as indeed was the custom (the *'ethrôgh*). The 'branches of palm trees and boughs of leafy trees' are traditionally the *lûlābh*, a bundle of myrtle, willow and palm, Josephus, Ant. III, x, 4. The other custom is that of 'camping out', living in booths (43). The Hebrew *sukkôth*, from which word the feast is named, means 'intertwining', and so the booths were made of the intertwined boughs of leafy trees. It is an ancient custom, reinterpreted, as were many borrowed customs, to speak of the salvation which God wrought for Israel when he brought them out of Egypt, through the desert and into the Rest of Canaan.

XXIV 1-4 concerns the maintenance of the Lamp, 214a
Exod. 27:20f., 25:31f. Did the lamp burn continually? Or was it kindled regularly? This section is concerned with Aaron's duty to keep the lamp burning from dusk to dawn. Possibly 2 is an ancient instruction belonging to the days when there was one lamp, 1 Sam. 3:3. Later, there were ten lamps, 1 Kg. 7:49, but 4 refers to the candlestick with its seven lights, as shown on the Arch of Titus. Instead of 'continually' (4), LXX and Sam. have 'till the morning'.

5-9 deals with the showbread; cf. Exod. 25:30, 37:10ff.; b
Num. 4:47. The showbread (the term is due to Tindale in Heb. 9:2, following Luther) consisted of 12 cakes each containing about 14 pints of flour. They were therefore very large loaves, since $\frac{3}{4}$ pint of flour weighs approximately half a pound. They were set out in two rows, and were placed on the table in the Presence of the Lord. Hence the Hebrew name 'the Bread of the Presence'. The custom of placing bread before the deity was widespread in ancient times, and the twelve loaves were known in Assyria; cf. EB, 4116. This involves an association with the twelve signs of the zodiac, but the number twelve was interpreted by the Jews as referring to the twelve tribes. Josephus, *Ant.* III, vi, 6 says the loaves were made of unleavened bread, and the Talmud (*b Men.* 76*b*) says that the flour was eleven times sifted. The loaves were eaten, half by the outgoing priests and half by the incoming priests (*b Suk.* 56*a*).

10-22 This section deals with blasphemy, and is a c
P-insertion into H. Into the history of the cited case an excursus on the *lex talionis* has been inserted (17–22). The penalty is stoning to death, and the case cited is that of a half-caste Danite whose father was an Egyptian. The principle of *lex talionis* was repudiated by Jesus in Mt. 5:38. Such a law is regarded by many as the minimum for the maintenance of society, but it is not the optimum. Many rabbis knew this, and the story is told with approval of the judge who rightly fined the guilty man and then paid the fine himself;

214c thus they contrasted *din* (strict justice) with *ṣᵉdhāḳāh* (righteousness), showing that they knew of a 'righteousness which exceeds that of the scribes'. The *lex talionis* is common in that ancient Amorite law on which early Hebrew law was founded, and much in this section finds a parallel in the Code of Ḥammurabi : human life for human life (116, 210, 219, 229), tooth for tooth (200), eye for eye (196) ox for ox (263), sheep for sheep (263), goods for goods (232).

215a **XXV Sabbath Years and the Year of Jubilee**—The idea of the Sabbath rest is extended to years and still further to seven times seven years, whereby the 50th year was a 'closing sabbath'.

b **1-7** The land is to keep its sabbath in the seventh year ; no pruning, no sowing, no first-fruits, no proper harvest. Everything is to be left free for all, as and when they take it. Probably here we have an ancient fallowing custom, standardised by the religious authorities. The custom of fallowing was practised by the Hebrews in ancient times, Hos. 10:12 ; Jer. 4:3 ; Prov. 13:23, all of which reflect the pre-exilic legislation of Exod. 23:11, where the purpose is clearly stated to be for the poor. But here we have a universal fallow year, the same year throughout the country. This would have its obvious difficulties, and Lev. 26:35 admits that the custom was not followed in pre-exilic times, cf. also 2 Chr. 36:21. Possibly the seventh-year fallowing was observed, but only as the seventh year for each particular plot of land. Josephus says that the general seventh year with its simultaneous fallowing was observed in the time of Alexander the Great (Jos. Ant. XI, viii, 6) by both Jews and Samaritans, in the time of the Hasmonaeans (Jos. Ant. XIII, viii, 1 ; cf. also 1 Mac. 6:49, 53) and in the time of the Herods (Jos. Ant. XIX, xvi, 2). Tacitus (*Hist.* v, 4) ascribes the custom to laziness.

c **8-55 The Year of Jubilee**—This began on the 10th of the 7th month, the old New-Year Day. It is difficult to see how a second fallow year did not lead forthwith to a famine. Perhaps this part of the jubilee legislation was priestly theorising and never a practical policy. On the other hand, Hebrew has a word (*sāphiaḥ*) for that which grows of itself in the first year and another word (*sāḥīsh*) for that which grows of itself in the second year, 2 Kg. 19:29 ; Isa. 37:30. The jubilee involved general freedom throughout the country, and once again this does not seem to have been known in pre-exilic times. **10.** Every man returned to his home and clan, and all land reverted to the original owner or his heirs, a custom expressly designed to prevent 'adding field to field till there was no place left'. The value of property was influenced by this reversion, the purchase price being regulated by the number of years still to run before the next jubilee. What was being sold was actually the number of crops yet to be harvested. The word 'jubilee' comes through Vulg. *jubilaeus* and is from the Hebrew *yōbhēl*, meaning 'ram'. It was the Year of the Ram, i.e. of the blowing of the ram's horn. **18-22.** There is confusion here. Was the jubilee the 50th year, or the 49th ? According to 10, the jubilee was the 50th year, and this is involved in the 'ninth year' of 22, but 'when you sow in the 8th year' suggests that the jubilee was the 49th year, unless here the year is counted from the spring and not from the 10th of the 7th month (autumn). According to **11,** they were not allowed to sow in the 50th year, which would be an 8th year. Possibly there was actually no fallowing in the 50th year, except in the mind of a redactor.
24-34 deals with details of the administration of the
d general rule laid down in 23. **29-34** is concerned with houses which pass out of the owner's possession. Everything here depends on whether the house is in a walled town or not. The owner who sells a house which is in a walled town, has the right to buy it back within one year from the date of the sale. Otherwise the house becomes the absolute property of the buyer. In an unwalled village the right of redemption never
lapsed, and the house in any case reverts to the original 21
owner or his heirs at jubilee. The jubilee reversion laws are evidently agricultural laws, and it was realised that they could not be applied in an urban community. Houses belonging to Levites in their allocated cities are counted as non-urban. In **33** RSV is right in following Vulg. and inserting a negative. RV and AVm ('if one of the Levites redeem') make sense if we assume the meaning to be : Any Levite in the city may redeem the house (presumably sold to a non-Levite), but at the jubilee it reverts to the original Levite owner. The idea that the purchaser was a non-Levite seems to be involved in 33*b*. Presumably he was a refugee homicide who would have to live somewhere in the Levitical city. **34.** The open country round a Levite town cannot be sold, so the problem of redemption does not arise. 'Fields of common land' is 'open fields of *mighrāsh* (where cattle are *driven*)' in Hebrew.
35-38 contain a digression dealing with the problem of e
the pauper Israelite. The poor Israelite must be maintained (RSV). The Hebrew means 'strengthened'. This probably means 'set on his feet again', and since the next verse refers to taking interest, the intention is that he shall have money lent to him in order that he may make himself independent. Meanwhile he is to live in the midst of his fellow-Israelites as a resident alien or as a temporary resident, i.e. without any civic rights. He must not be exploited in any way, and no interest of any type must be charged on the loan. 'Interest' (36) means deducting the interest from the capital advanced. 'Increase' (36) means adding the accrued interest to the sum to be repaid. This applies whether the loan is in money or in food. The reason given for this generous treatment is the regularly inculcated one : the God who commands these things is the God who was their saviour out of Egypt and who gave them the land of Canaan. 'Freely ye have received, freely give'.
39-46 Hebrew Slaves—The problem of the debtor f
who sells himself and his services to his creditor comes under the general jubilee legislation, because he must be released in the year of jubilee, both he and his family. The debtor is to have the status of a hired man or a resident alien. He is not to be treated as a slave, nor can he be sold by his creditor. The word translated 'harshness' is that used in Exod. 1 of the slavery in Egypt ; it is used elsewhere only in Ezek. 34:4. But the main emphasis in this section concerns the Hebrew ownership of slaves. He may possess his fellow Hebrews, but only the males. These he must not treat harshly and he cannot resell them. But he may purchase both male and female foreigners, even resident aliens and settlers provided they have been born in the country. These become the owner's absolute property and he can leave them by will to his heirs and successors.
47-55 deals with the poor Israelite who has sold him- g
self to a resident alien or to a settler who has become wealthy. The fixed element here is that he becomes automatically free in the year of jubilee equally with the man who has sold himself to one of his own nationals. Meanwhile, he can be redeemed at any time by a near kinsman, or he may redeem himself, if he becomes rich enough. Apparently this right of redemption does not apply in the previous case, where the owner is an Israelite. The price is to be regulated according to the number of years before the next jubilee, as in the case of redeemable property, but the period is to be reckoned at the rate of the wages of an ordinary hired man. In the case of a field, it is the number of crops that is being bought ; in the case of a man it is the years of future service. Once more there is the provision against the harsh treatment of a slave (53). The man, whoever he is, Israelite or foreigner, must be treated with proper consideration. The reason is that the Israelites are God's slaves. He has treated them with kindness and he expects all slaves in his land to be treated with similar kindness.

6a **XXVI The Final Exhortation**—This chapter closes the Law of Holiness, and makes clear that, in spite of all minutiae of regulations, the aim of the writer is full and true consecration to God, manifested in true worship and upright living. **1.** The prohibition is against idols generally. specified as carved images, standing stones and figured stones. The standing stone was a legitimate religious object in early days. It marked the scene of a theophany (Bethel, Gen. 28:18), particularly in the E-tradition, according to which Moses himself set up twelve such stone pillars, Exod. 24:4. In Hos. 10:1 such pillars are as sacred as altars, and the threatened destruction applies equally to both. The prohibition first appears in Dt. 16:22 and they are condemned in 1 Kg. 14:23 etc., and the prohibition is renewed here in H.

b **3-13 The Reward of Obedience** (cf. Dt. 28:1–11)—The promise is of abundant prosperity and of a fruitfulness that belongs to the land of dreams. The seasonal rains will fall regularly, the former rain (October–November) and the latter rain (March–April), those that softened the ground baked hard by the summer drought, and those that strengthened and filled the growing grain in the spring. The threshing will last till the vintage, from Pentecost through to Tabernacles. The vintage will last till the sowing in November. There will be no wild beasts and no war on Israelite territory. Israel's enemies will flee and even a small company of Israelites will defeat large armies of foreigners. There will be so much grain that last year's carry-over of grain will have to be removed to make way for the storage of the new grain. Israel will be free men, able to walk erect, not bowed down and submissive under the yoke of slavery.

c **14-20 The First Penalty** (cf. Dt. 28:15ff.)—The penalty for the disregard of these commands is panic, wasting diseases and burning fevers. They will be conquered by their enemies, browbeaten and hunted down till they keep on fleeing even when the pursuit has ceased. If Israel still persists in stubbornness, these terrors will come upon them sevenfold till their stubborn pride is broken.

d **21-26 The Second Penalty**—Here distresses multiply with more plagues and still greater disasters. Wild beasts will ravage the country, as did indeed happen when the Northern Kingdom was partially depopulated after the Assyrian invasion of 722 B.C., 2 Kg. 17:25. There will be wars in which they will be besieged and in their cities will pestilences break out. There will be such shortage of food that all the baking for ten households can be done in one oven, and what food there is will lack nourishment. Food will be rationed and meagre.

e **27-39 The Third Penalty** is complete desolation. They will be driven to eat their own children, Lam. 4:10. All the shrines (RSV 'high places') will be destroyed, and the 'incense altars' (RSV, correctly, not 'sun-images') will be cut down. All these will be desecrated with rotting corpses thrown down on the rotting idol-logs. The devastation will be so great that even their enemies will be appalled. The people will be exiled and the land will enjoy (receive satisfaction) for all the sabbaths which were denied it during the Israelite occupation. Even exile will not be the sum-total of disaster, for even there the exile will know the extremes of terror and wasting disease. 'My soul' (30) is a fulsome way of saying 'I', common in Isa. 40–55, and indeed a characteristic of that author's style.

f **40-46 The Door is still open**—In spite of all the catalogue of disasters, the door is still open. The offer of salvation still remains. The condition of restoration is confession of sin and an earnest desire to amend their ways. Then God will remember the covenant with their fathers of ancient time. He who brought them out of Egypt will still be their God, and he will repeat the mighty deliverance of former days. 216f
What he did once, he can and will do again.

XXVII Commutation of Vows—We return to the g
P-tradition with its emphasis on the exact fulfilment of details, but associated with a deliberate relaxation of restrictions in favour of the poor. In the old days such a vow could involve human sacrifice, and from this there was no relief, cf. Jephthah's daughter, Jg. 11:34–40. But according to later custom, almost everything could be redeemed at a price. The price of redemption for a full-grown man between the ages of 20 and 60 was fifty silver shekels, Temple currency, i.e. the ancient silver shekel of 224 grains, roughly the weight of the pre-1914 English half-crown. Thus, according to pre-1914 standards, the value of a grown man was £6 5s.; a grown woman was estimated at £3 2s. 6d.; a youth between the ages of 5 and 20 at £2 10s.; a girl of the same age at £1 5s.; a child less than 5 years old at 12s. 6d. for a boy and 7s. 6d. for a girl. Over 60 years of age, the assessment was £1 17s. 6d. for a man and £1 5s. for a woman. But if the man was too poor to pay this standard rate, then the priest must exercise his discretion. Here again we have evidence that the care for the poor inculcated in Deuteronomy is as clear here in Leviticus as there, and further, in Leviticus definite legislation is introduced in order to put the humanitarian principles into practice. When a beast is vowed, that same beast must be given. No other will do as a substitute, neither better nor worse, and no commutation is allowed. This applies to clean beasts. If the beast that is vowed is an unclean beast, then the priest must assess its value, and if the man wishes to redeem it, he must pay the priest's estimate and add the usual one-fifth.

14-15. Similar rules of redemption apply to houses h
that are vowed. They can be redeemed at the priest's valuation, together with the addition of the one-fifth. Presumably, in the case both of unclean animals and houses, if there is no redemption the priest sells the animal or house at the proper valuation.

16-25 The vowing of land and its redemption is i
complicated by the jubilee system. The rate of the valuation is to be a silver shekel for each homer (eleven bushels) of barley that is needed to sow the field. If the land is valued at the year of jubilee then fifty shekels for every homer is the price. If the owner redeems the land, then the price he pays depends on the length of time that must elapse before the next jubilee, and he must then add the customary one-fifth. If he does not redeem the property or if he sells it, then at jubilee the land becomes the property of the priests. If a man buys a field and then vows it, at jubilee it reverts to the original owner.

26-29 No firstlings of clean animals may be vowed j
because they belong to God in any case under the firstlings law. But the firstlings of unclean beasts can be vowed and redeemed with the addition of the customary one-fifth. But objects can be 'devoted' (Hebrew *ḥerem*), i.e. irredeemably vowed. Such objects are holy-gifts of holy-gifts, and must not go out of the sanctuary.

30-33 Commutation of Tithes—The tithe of produce k
from land and trees can be redeemed with the customary addition of the one-fifth, but not the tithe of flock and herd. Every tenth animal to pass under the counting-rod belongs to God, that animal and no other, and if any change is made, then both belong to him.

Bibliography—Commentaries: B. Baentsch, HKAT (1903); A. Bertholet, KHC (1901); A. T. Chapman and A. W. Streane, CB (1914); A. Dillmann, KEH, 3rd ed. rev. by V. Ryssel (1897); A. R. S. Kennedy, Cent.B; N. Micklem, IB (1953).

Other Literature: Articles in EB, HDB, and IB; F. Steiner, *Taboo* (1956).

NUMBERS

By N. H. SNAITH

217a **Name**—The Hebrew name of the book is taken from the first significant word (the fourth) in the book, *bemidhbar* (in the desert of). LXX gave it a descriptive title, and it is this title, translated into Latin in Vulg., and again translated into English, which gives the English title. It is the ' Fourth Book of Moses ', and is invariably the fourth book in all Bibles.

b **Contents**—The book can be divided into three sections according to the setting of the events recorded. 1:1–12:16 is at Sinai ; 13:1–21:35 is in Paran ; 22:1–36:13 is in Moab. The first section tells of the census and the temporary sojourn in the wilderness of Sinai and concludes with details of the journey from Sinai to Paran. The second section tells the story of the spies, the Rebellion of Korah, Dathan, and Abiram, and includes various laws and minor incidents, ending with the journey into the Plains of Moab. The third section tells the story of Balaam and Balak, gives the account of a second census, includes various laws and incidents, and especially gives an account of the war with Midian.

c **Sources**—According to the customary literary analysis, the sources of Numbers are J, E, and P (see §143*c*). Approximately three-quarters of the book is P. It is not easy to distinguish between J and E, and it is plain that P is composite. Different generations have contributed and the traditions have solidified at different periods. Some commentators find as many as nine different strands in the P-material, but it is better to think of P as a broad tradition, bound together by common interests and, for the most part, by a common vocabulary and style, but with many minor differences and points of view depending on varying times and places. The two strands, J and E, provide us with ancient stories and sagas which have come down from the earlier days of the Canaanite occupation and from the actual time of the wanderings in the desert. P's interest lies in the origin of the people of God, and especially in the origin of their institutions. The interest focuses on the Temple and the priesthood and there is the ever-present tendency to read back into the days of Moses the institutions of post-exilic times.

218a **I 1–X 10** This is the first section of the book. It is all from the P-tradition, and it tells the whole story of the sojourn in the wilderness of Sinai.

b **I 1-46 The First Census**—Moses takes a census of the whole of the fighting-men of Israel. He counts all the men who are over twenty years of age and are fit for military service. The Levites are counted separately since, according to P, they were a sacred tribe from the beginning at Sinai. Moses and Aaron are to do the counting, assisted by one leader from each tribe. The names of the leaders are given again three times in Numbers (2:3ff., 7:12ff., 10:14ff.), but never again anywhere except possibly for two in Ruth 4:20. The names are partly characteristic of early times and partly characteristic of later times. The list is therefore of comparatively late compilation, and may in part depend upon ancient traditions. The numbering of the men is to be ' by families, by fathers' houses ' (RSV). It is better to read ' clans ' for ' families '. It is difficult to be sure of the exact significance of the words used for the various units of Hebrew tribal organisation, since the different traditions vary in their use of the terms, each from each, and each within 218
itself, but the pattern is fixed by Jos. 7:16–18, with the twelve tribes, each composed of various clans (RSV ' families '), each clan composed of several ' fathers' houses ', and each ' father's house ' composed of individuals. **5-15.** The order of the tribes in this list is unusual, but in **20-42** the actual census order is the same as in the second census (Num. 26), except that there Manasseh precedes Ephraim. In the list of assistant enumerators, the main tribes come first, the full Leah tribes, the full Rachel tribes, and then the four concubine tribes, Dan, Asher, Gad, and Naphtali. In the actual census list, Gad comes third, following Simeon. The numbers of the tribes are fantastic and incredible. The total number of fighting-men is 603,550, so that presumably the number of all the Israelites was in the region of two million. The tribes are represented as all keeping close company, and able to be summoned by the blowing of two trumpets (10:2). When they were so summoned, they all gathered at the entrance to the tent of meeting. Further, a horde of people of such a size as this could not maintain itself in the country between Egypt and Canaan for any period of time whatever. When on the march, they would constitute a column twenty-two miles long, marching fifty abreast with one yard between each rank. Some editions of RSV contain two errors in **43** : the true reading is ' Naphtali ' and ' 53,400 '. RSV uses the word ' clans ' (16) for the AV and RV ' thousands '. This latter may well be correct ; cf. the old English ' hundred ' for a small village community of approximately that population.

47-54 The Duties of the Levites—The Levites c
are not numbered with the rest. Possibly this is because the census is a military one ; possibly it is because the Levites are separated from the rest of the people and this separation in holiness must be maintained. Another reason may be that since they belonged especially to God, it is a sin to number them, cf. 2 Sam. 24, where David's numbering of the people is regarded as an offence against God. In this case, 3:14–38 belongs to another tradition. The duties of the Levites are carefully described. They are to care for the Tabernacle, carry it during the journeys, care for it, pitch their tents round it, and generally act both as its servants and as its guards, protecting it against contact with the unconsecrated and the unconsecrated against contact with it. The primitive idea of the ' wrath ' (53) against common contact is preserved, 2 Sam. 6:6–8, and often in P, 8:19, 16:46, etc. The idea still prevails among devout people who hold that only those who have been consecrated according to fixed formulae and a particular succession may approach a holy place. For ' wrath ', see C. H. Dodd, *The Epistle to the Romans*, 20–24, Moffatt *NT Comm.* (1932).

II 1-34 The Positions of the Tribes in Camp—The d
order is that of Num. 26, if the points of the compass are taken in the order : south, east, west, north. Roughly the tradition of ancestry is maintained ; east and south are the full Leah tribes with Gad (concubine tribe) taking the place of Levi (as in 1:24) : to the west, the three Rachel tribes : to the north, the remaining three concubine tribes. There is no

218d geographical distribution, and no relation with any known state of affairs apart from the traditions of origin. **2.** 'Standard'. LXX has *tagma* (company, division) and some prefer this. The etymological evidence for 'standard' is not strong, and the VSS do not support it. If 'standard' is correct, then each group of tribes had a standard and each father's house an ensign. Arabic evidence is mixed (see C. M. Doughty, *Arabia Deserta* (1888), i, 221, 414). The numbers given here are those of the census of the previous chapter.

e **III 1-4 Aaron and his Sons**—This paragraph fixes the descent of the legitimate priesthood through Eleazar and Ithamar only, the two younger sons of Aaron. For the story of Nadab and Abihu, see Lev. 10:1–3. It is not said there that they had no children, but cf. 1 Chr. 24:2 which is based on this verse.

f **5-10 The Levites are Servants of the Priests**—Aaron and his sons are to be sacrificing priests, and the Levites are 'wholly given' (9) to them. In early times any Israelite could be a priest (Jg. 17:5), though Micah knew it was better to have a Levite as priest (Jg. 17:10, 18:4), and it was this Levite who became the Danite priest of Dan in the far north (Jg. 18:19). There is no evidence that the House of Eli, the ancient priests of the Ark from Egypt, were Levites (1 Sam. 2:27–36), and Samuel was not a Levite (1 Sam. 1:1) until later tradition made him so (1 Chr. 6:28; 1 Sam. 8:2), neither was Obed-edom (2 Sam. 6:10) nor David's sons (2 Sam. 8:18, 20:26). According to 1 Kg. 12:31 all priests should be Levites, and this is the theory of Deuteronomy where the phrase is 'the priests, the Levites'. The change comes in Ezek. 44:10–31, where the Levites are degraded, being charged with having gone astray after idols. Henceforth they are 'ministers' and are not permitted to come near either 'holy-gifts' or 'holy-gifts of holy gifts' (most holy), Lev. 10:12–15. This is the position here, except that the distinction between priests and Levites is traced back to Sinai, being the work of Moses, and further, the position of the Levites is one of honour and there is no suggestion that they have been downgraded.

g **11-13** (cf. 40–51) **The Levites are Substitutes for Israel's First-born**—Here is another tradition of the origin of Levites, possibly from H (13*b*: 'I am the Lord', cf. Lev. 18:6 etc.). In any case the explanations are secondary. The first-born are God's because he slew the first-born of Egypt, and the Levites are his as a substitute. The first-born are God's primarily because all increase of every kind is his, whether of field or fold or family. The idea of substitution is taken still further in 3:44, where cattle of the Levites are the equivalent of the cattle of the Israelites, but here the original idea is followed, that all cattle fundamentally are God's.

h **14-39 The Numbering of the Levites and their Duties**—There were three clans, Gershon, Kohath, and Merari. The Gershonites are responsible for all coverings and hangings, but not for the screen which, according to P, was between the holy place and the holy of holies, elsewhere called 'the veil' (Exod. 26:31), 'the veil of the sanctuary' (Lev. 4:6), or 'the veil of the testimony' (Lev. 24:3). The Kohathites are responsible for the sacred utensils and the Merarites for all posts and sockets. The confusion between the two temples is manifest here, and in 38 LXX omits 'before the tabernacle on the east'. Again, were there two altars or only one? MT has the plural in 31, but Syr. and the Targum Onkelos have the singular. It is generally assumed that the theory of a portable temple (P's tabernacle) is post-exilic and modelled on the Second Temple, but it is more likely that the Tabernacle was originally a portable Solomon's Temple and that the traditions were edited on the basis of the Second Temple.

i **40-51 The First-born of the Israelites**—There were 22,273 male first-born Israelites over one month old, and there were 22,000 Levites. The number of the 218i
first-born does not agree with the census figures of chapter 1, which, assuming an average family of ten, are approximately five times too large. The overplus of first-born (over the number of Levites) is redeemed at five shekels (about 12 shillings at pre-1914 standards) per head. The shekel is the ancient coin of 224 grains, 'the shekel of the sanctuary', and not the post-exilic shekel of 173·3 grains.

IV 1-20 The Kohathites—This was the most j
favoured clan of Levites. Their duty was to carry the 'most holy things' (Hebrew *ḳōdhesh ḳᵒdhāshîm*), the things which never went out of the Holy Place, the Court of the Priests of the Second Temple. These utensils were packed by the priests and carried by the Kohathites. The limits of age for active service are here from 30 to 60; in 8:23–26 the age limits are 25 to 50 with limited service after that age; but according to the Chronicler the lower limit from the time of David onwards was 20 years old with no upper limit. Evidently the age limit varied. **3.** The word used for 'service' is the same as the word used in chapter 1 for military service. The utensils were all wrapped in *taḥash*-skin, except for the ark which had an additional wrapping of blue cloth. RSV translates *taḥash*-skin as 'goatskin'. It was probably some marine animal such as a porpoise, or dolphin. **13.** The Rabbis say that the altar-fire never went out: it lay beneath the cloth like a lion during the journeys, covered with a large copper vessel. **16.** Eleazar had general charge of the Kohathites, but special charge of the holy material as distinguished from the holy furniture. The phrase 'continual cereal offering' is strange. It may be the grain-offering which accompanied the burnt-offering and was offered twice each day (Exod. 29:38–40), but it is more likely to be the 'regular cereal offering' (Lev. 6:19) offered, half in the morning and half in the evening, by 'the priest who is anointed to succeed' Aaron.

21-33 The Gershonites and the Merarites—These k
two clans are under the general charge of Ithamar, and they are to carry the less sacred items of the holy furniture. The Gershonites carry all hangings and covers, and the Merarites all posts, sockets, frames, pegs, and ropes. **25.** RSV has translated *taḥash*-skin here by 'sheepskin'. The rendering should be as in v. 12, 'porpoise'. The usual 'badgers' skins' of AV is even less defensible.

34-49 The Census of Levites—The total number l
between the ages of 30 and 50 is 8,580. In view of the 22,000 of 3:39, this number is very high even for modern times with our much greater expectation of life.

V 1-4 Exclusion of Unclean Persons—All lepers 219a
(Lev. 13), all who have any kind of discharge from their sexual organs (Lev. 15), and all who are unclean through contact with the dead are to be excluded from the community. The penalty here is much stricter than in Leviticus, where only the leper is excluded from the camp (Lev. 13:46). The strictness has been explained on the grounds that the regulations apply to a military camp, but this is unlikely because of the reference to women (3). Further, the seclusion of women during menstruation was observed among eastern Jews in the Middle Ages, Maimonides, *Moreh Nebuchim*, iii, 47.

5-10 Supplement to Lev. 6:1-7 (MT 5:20–26)— b
This section deals with a complication arising out of the offences mentioned in Lev. 6:1–7, denial of the receipt of a deposit, 'stealing by finding', and similar cases of voluntary confession. Normally there was to be restitution to the man who had suffered damage with the addition of one-fifth of the value, in addition to the ram for the guilt-offering. This ram is here called 'the ram of atonement (i.e. propitiation)', thereby signifying that a wrong done against a man is also a wrong done against God, and the offender must get right with God in addition to giving full restitution to his victim. The complication concerns the death of

219b the victim. In this case the six-fifths are to go to the priest as God's representative. The so-called guilt-offering is properly a restitution-offering, as RSV makes clear, since 'restitution for wrong' (8) is *'āshām* (the word for 'guilt-offering') in MT. Such a restitution is a *t^erûmāh* (RV 'heave offering': RSV the general term 'offering'), for every *t^erûmāh* (levy) belongs to the officiating priest.

c **11-31 The Ordeal of Jealousy**—These regulations deal with cases where adultery cannot be proved. The woman is pregnant and the husband thinks he is not the father of the child. The husband is to bring his wife to the priest, who brings her forward and sets her 'before the Lord' (16): in the Second Temple, the woman stood in the Gate of Nicanor, but according to the Mishnah (*Sotah* ix, 9) the whole ceremony was abolished by Johanan ben Zaccai soon after A.D. 50. **19.** The woman has to drink the 'water of bitterness that brings the curse', i.e. the water of ordeal (or dispute) which may carry a curse. The ancient belief was that in case of guilt, the potion would cause a miscarriage. But if the woman was not guilty, the potion would have no deleterious effects and the woman would bear the child normally. For details of similar customs, see E. B. Tylor, 'Ordeal', EBrit., 9th ed., xvii. Trial by ordeal is well attested in Britain down through the Middle Ages. Suspected witches were flung into deep water, men had to hold red-hot iron bars, accused persons had to drink poison. In earliest times, the damage was thought to be done magically by the water itself, but here (21) God is thought to be acting through the ancient rite. The water, said to have been taken from the holy laver, contained holy dust from the floor of the Tabernacle and the writing of the curse was washed into it off the scroll. The unbinding of the woman's hair was a traditional sign of shame, and the Mishnah (*Sotah* i, 6) adds that she was to be clothed in black and that her breast was to be bared. The penalty of the curse was 'miscarriage or abortion' (21*b*, 27*b*: RSV follows the Hebrew literally), the two terms depending upon the period that has elapsed since conception.

d **14.** The phrase is used 'if the spirit of jealousy comes upon' the husband. Here is a characteristic use of the Hebrew word *rûaḥ* (spirit, wind, breath). The word is used of the storm wind, not of a gentle breeze. When it is used psychologically, it is used, as here, of overpowering, dominant emotions, those tides of passion which carry a man headlong. The idea of a more-than-human power is never far away, and sometimes the word signifies that Spirit which belongs to God as contrasted with the flesh that belongs to man (cf. N. H. Snaith, 'The Spirit of God in Jewish Thought', in *The Doctrine of the Holy Spirit* (1937), 11–37).

e The offering required is a cereal (grain) offering without oil or frankincense, since it is not an offering which goes to the altar. It has two names (15*b*), 'cereal offering of jealousy' and 'cereal offering of remembrance, bringing iniquity to remembrance'. The significance of the first is plain. The explanation of the second is to be found in the idea what when God remembers, he acts. God remembered Noah (Gen. 8:1) and forthwith caused the flood to subside. He remembered Abraham (Gen. 19:29) and Rachel (Gen. 30:22). He can 'remember' for good, but he also remembers for harm and to punish sin, 1 Kg. 17:18. This is what happens here, and the rite brings guilt to remembrance in the sense that if the woman is guilty, the punishment follows immediately.

f **VI 1-21 The Law of the Nazirite**—The Nazirite was an ancient institution in Israel. Samson was a Nazirite (Jg. 13:5). There were Nazirites in the time of Amos (Amos 2:11), in the 2nd cent. B.C. (1 Mac. 3:49), and in the last days of the Second Temple (Jos. Ant. XIX, vi, 1). According to this chapter there were three restrictions: nothing to do with wine (3), with any product of the grape-vine, or with any fermented liquor; unshorn hair on the head (5); no contact with a corpse (6). The taboos for a Nazirite 219 probably varied through the centuries, but at all times there was a taboo on hair. Indeed the use of the word *nazir* of the unclipped vine (Lev. 25:5, 11) indicates the paramount importance of this taboo. Note also the emphasis on the hair in vv. 7, 9, 18. This is in accordance with the belief that the hair of all sacred persons is taboo; it had either to be shaved clean (priests in ancient Egypt, Buddhist priests), or to be allowed to grow untouched, as in old Israel. Letting the hair grow long is parallel to the proper custom of priests and kings (hence the *nēzer*, the origin of the crown), but the difference is that the Nazirite's hair must 'hang loose' (RSV 'grow long' is inadequate: similarly AV and RV), Lev. 10:6, 21:10. This custom of letting the hair hang loose is associated with special taboos: in the case of the priest, in mourning for the dead; in the case of volunteers for a holy war (Jg. 5:2, where the Hebrew appears to mean 'for the loosing of the long locks in Israel', RSV being an interpretation). The connection is plainly seen in 6-9, where it is clear that contact with the dead is the one thing which can nullify a Nazirite vow. The sacred hair is defiled, and the Nazirite must shave off all his hair, shave again after the seven-day taboo period (§203*h*), and start again.

The abstinence (3–4) is secondary. It concerns g wine and beer, coarse wine and strong beer, and also any produce of the vine, grape juice, grapes fresh or dried, and even the pips and the skins. cf. the taboos of the priest during his period of ministration (Lev. 10:9), restrictions in ancient India, the Rechabites, and in Islam. The Rechabites apparently abjured the vine as part of their protest against the cults of Canaan and their agricultural background, treating the vine as the emblem of the new and treacherous Canaanite environment as against the old nomadic life of Israel's halcyon days. But this can scarcely be the reason for the other taboos. It is known that among some peoples, the drinking of alcohol was regarded as a means of securing divine revelation, on the theory that what a man said when he was not in control of his tongue was the word of some other personal agency in control of him. If such practices were connected by the Hebrews with heathen divination, then this would secure their prohibition with the strictest care on specially sacred occasions and for specially sacred people. **18.** Which fire is it in which the hair was burnt? It was 'the fire which is under the sacrifice of the peace offering', i.e. the slain-offering of which only the blood and the fat were burnt on the altar. The Targum and Rashi both realised that this could not be the regular altar fire, because the peace-offering was never burnt on the altar of burnt(whole)-offering. They therefore assumed that the hair was burnt in the fire on which the flesh of the peace-offering was being boiled, to be eaten later by priest and Nazirite. This is important, because it means that the hair was not a gift to God, and there is no clear indication that such 'sacred hair' was ever regarded as an offering to God. Such was clearly the purpose of the growing of hair among other peoples, and Philo of Alexandria interpreted the custom in this way. He seems to have thought that the hair was burnt on the altar, as representative of the whole man. But the phrase is definitely not the usual phrase 'on the whole burnt offering', and the 'peace offering', which was never burnt on the altar, is especially mentioned. The conclusion of the ceremonies which mark the completion of the vow is in 20. The priest takes one cake and one wafer out of the basket (15), places them on the hand of the man (it is the man's offering), and then takes them as a special contribution (Hebrew *t^enûphāh*: RSV 'wave offering') together with the breast of the peace-offering (the usual *t^enûphāh*) and the thigh (Hebrew *t^erûmāh*: RSV 'offering', better 'levy'). These are all 'holy gifts' and can be eaten by the priest's families as well as by the priest, and can also be taken out of the holy place. At the conclusion

9g of all these ceremonies the Nazirite is free to drink wine. This was permissive, but it is natural to suppose that the Nazirite and his friends would definitely drink wine at the sacred meal, when they ate the peace offering, and so mark the close of the taboo period.

h **22-27 The Priestly Blessing**—This is the blessing pronounced by the Aaronic priesthood of post-exilic days, but it is doubtless of high antiquity and is partially quoted in Ps. 4:6 and 67:1. The use of this blessing by the high priest is described in Sir. 50:20f. According to the Mishnah (*Tamid* vii, 2) this blessing was pronounced every morning in the Temple at the time of the morning sacrifice and the Sacred Name was used. The high priest is said to have lifted his hands no higher than the golden flower on his head-dress. In the synagogues, both in the morning service and at other times, the Sacred Name was not used, but the word *Adonai* (Lord) was used instead. The suggestion that the three occurrences of the Sacred Name is a basis for a doctrine of the Trinity is without foundation. **25.** 'make his face to shine' is a metaphor either from the lighting of the dawn (2 Sam. 2:32) or from the lightnings lighting up the world (Ps. 77:18, 97:4). In any case it expresses the joy of inward delight arising from good favours bestowed. **26.** May God look favourably upon us and give us peace and health and prosperity.

i **VII The Offerings of the Tribal Leaders**—The reference is back to Exod. 40:1, the setting-up of the Tabernacle, and to Exod. 40:10, the setting-up of the altar and its utensils. The leaders brought their *Corbans* (3: 'offerings'), the term being used here not only in the general sense of 'that which is brought near' (offering), but in the particular sense of an offering for the maintenance and use of Temple property within the holy place (as against 'holy-gifts' which were for the personnel). These offerings are the covered wagons and the oxen necessary for the transport of the Tabernacle. They were for the use of the Gershonites, who had to carry the screens and the coverings, and of the Merarites who had to carry the posts and frames, etc. There were no wagons and oxen allocated to the Kohathites who had to carry the altar and its accompaniments themselves. There was one wagon from every two leaders, and one ox from every leader, and these were allocated, two wagons and four oxen to the Gershonites, and four wagons and eight oxen to the Merarites.

j **9-88 Dedication Gifts for the Altar**—Each leader's gifts were identical with all the others. They took the form of the necessary materials for the regular sacrifices: a silver plate and a silver basin both full of flour for the cereal offerings: a gold dish full of incense, and domestic animals for the three types of animal offerings—the burnt(whole)-offering: a young bull, a ram and a yearling male lamb; the sin-offering: a male goat; the 'peace (slain) offering': two oxen, five rams, five male goats, and five yearling male lambs. **13.** The word 'plate' does not sufficiently represent the Hebrew, since the Arabic equivalent means 'deep' and the Syriac equivalent is used of the calyx of a flower and of an acorn cup. 'Dish' is more suitable. Also, the RSV 'basin' was a bowl used for tossing blood against the altar. **14.** The word 'dish' is inadequate; 'spoon' (RV) is better, but 'cup' better still. The same word is used of the hollow of the hand. It was probably a smaller dish than the 'silver plate' of 13, though both types of dishes were used in the incense ritual, Exod. 25:29. Jewish commentators made much of the numbers, using the method of Gematria: for instance, the word for 'incense' has a numerical value of 613 (according to what is known as the Method of Permutation), and this is the number of the precepts of the Law according to the traditions of the scribes. See Rashi's commentary on Numbers, and also J. H. Hertz, *The Pentateuch and Haftorahs* (1936), iv, 72–75.

89 is a fragment referring back to Exod. 25:22. RSV 219k
rightly substitutes 'with the Lord' for Hebrew 'with him'. The last phrase strictly is 'and he said to him', with the actual speech missing. The VSS smooth this out and make the verse a general statement to the effect that since all was now in order, God spoke plainly and clearly to Moses.

VIII 1-4 The Setting-up of the Menorah—The l
Menorah is the seven-branched candlestick which is a favourite symbol of Israel to this day. According to Jos. Ant. III, vi, 7, the seven lamps represent the sun, moon, and the five planets known to antiquity. This explanation is sound, since this is how the 'seven' became the sacred number in ancient Mesopotamia: see §203*h*. But Josephus reinterpreted this to make it declare the creative activity of God. The lampstand (candlestick) is described in Exod. 25:31–40. RSV 'set up' (3, fixed) is correct. AV and RV are not correct with 'lightest', because these lights burned continually (Exod. 30:7). The Menorah was so placed on the south side of the holy place that the seven lamps shone across over the table of the shewbread which was on the opposite (north) side. For 'from its base to its flowers' (RSV), read 'including stem and flowers' (4).

5-22 The Purification of the Levites—The Levites m
are to be separated from the people and ritually cleansed. **7.** They are sprinkled with 'water of expiation' (lit. 'sin-water', i.e. water used to de-sin). They are to be shaved from head to foot. Reference is usually made to Herodotus ii, 37 who says that Egyptian priests shaved the whole of their bodies every other day 'so that no lice or any other foul thing may be upon them when they minister to the gods.' But for the Levites the complete shaving comes at their original purification and it is similar to that of the Nazirites, the idea being that the whole growth of hair, new from the dedication, shall continue untouched and holy. There are three differences in the purification ceremonies between priests and Levites: priests are sanctified, wholly washed and given new clothes: Levites are cleansed, sprinkled and their clothes washed. **10.** The people laid their hands on the Levites to indicate that they, the people, are offering them. **11.** The Levites are then offered as a *t^{e}nûphāh* (RSV 'wave-offering'), i.e. a 'special contribution' (see §204*a*). This is the verse which makes the translation 'wave-offering' in the highest degree unlikely. The 'special contribution' always went for the use of the officiating priest, and this is why the Levites are a *t^{e}nûphāh*. They are given to God and by him to Aaron and his sons to minister to them, cf. 3:5–13, and once more the association with the first-born is emphasised. 'The people of Israel' occurs five times in 19: Jewish exegesis says this indicates the love which God bears towards the bearers of the name 'Israel'. The 'plague' is the fatal blow (*negheph*) which, according to P, falls upon all who rouse the anger of God (19). We are here once more in the primitive world of amoral taboo. **23-26.** The age-limit for full levitical service is from 25 to 50 years old. In Num. 4:3 it was 30 to 50, but in 1 Chr. 23:24 it was from 20 with no upper limit. The easiest solution is that the age varied. The Jews explain the differences by saying that from 25 to 30 they were being initiated into the lighter duties; further here, whilst they retire from the full service, they performed light duties (26), said to involve closing the gates and assisting in the choral singing. Rabbi Hertz said: 'A superannuated life need not be a useless life'.

IX 1-14 The Second Passover—The Mishnah n
directs that all who are unable to keep the first normal Passover must keep the second. According to tradition, the problem arose on the first Passover after the Exodus, when men who had been involved with a funeral were ritually unclean and could not eat the Passover. Moses consults the oracle and the rule concerning a supplementary Passover is established. A Passover in the second month is described in 2 Chr.

219n 30:1–27. It is said that there had been no observance of Passover for a long time, and Hezekiah was not able to get the priests consecrated in time, nor had enough sanctified people been able to gather at Jerusalem by the fourteenth of the first month. **9-14.** The same rules apply to the second Passover as to the first. The phrase 'in the evening' (RSV) is strictly 'between the two evenings': see §213*h*. In the 1st cent. A.D. the phrase meant between about 3 p.m. to about 5 p.m., i.e. between the time of the evening sacrifice and sunset.

o **15-23 The Fiery Cloud**—According to P, the Tabernacle was in the middle of the camp, and the cloud rested on the Tabernacle (Exod. 40:36, 38; Num. 10:11) or on the tent (Exod. 40:35). By day the fire was not apparent, but only from sunset to dawn. In J (Exod. 13:22) the cloud goes ahead of the people as guide, but in P the cloud is not a guide, but the sign of the Presence of God within his people Israel. If the cloud remained low over the Tabernacle all day, the people did not break camp. Sometimes the cloud remained 'many days' (19), 'a few days' (20), but whatever the period, whether (22) 'two days, a month, or a longer time' (RV, AV 'year' is unsound: RSV is right, the time is indefinite, but long), all the movements of the people were at the direct command of God through the cloud. When the cloud lifted, they moved; when the cloud stayed, so did they.

p **X 1-10 The Silver Trumpets**—These trumpets were in use in the Second Temple. They were straight, about 18 inches long and with flared ends: see the representations on the Arch of Titus. They were used mostly on sacred occasions, and are often mentioned in the work of the Chronicler. Their secular use is mentioned twice only, 2 Kg. 11:14; Hos. 5:8. In the post-exilic period they were blown on joyful occasions, the regular festivals, the beginnings of months, and over all whole-offerings and slain-offerings. They were blown 'for remembrance' before God, i.e. to secure immediate action. They are to be distinguished from the ram's horn (*shôphār*) which was curled and from the similar *yôbhēl* (cf. jubilee year). For the explanation of 'God remembering', see §219*e*. According to P, these trumpets were used in the desert to summon the whole congregation of Israel and to tell the various groups when to set out from their camping-place. Traditionally there were two types of trumpet-blast, described in 7 as 'blowing' and 'sounding an alarm'. The alarm (t^{e}*rûʿāh*) consisted of a rapid succession of three sharp notes, and the 'blowing' (t^{e}*ḳîʿāh*) equalled the length of three 'alarms', which is sometimes interpreted to mean the three notes of one 'alarm' and sometimes the nine notes of three 'alarms'. The alarm is the sign to break camp; the blast (blowing) is the sign for assembly.

220a **X 11-XII 16 The Journey from Sinai to Paran**—This is the second section of the book. The first subsection (10:11–28) is from the P-tradition. The rest is JE. The framework is P, so that the general outline is first a journey from Sinai to Paran (10:12), a long sojourn in Paran, with a short stay at Kadesh (20:1) on the way to the Plains of Moab (22:1). They had been at Sinai for ten days short of a year (Exod. 19:1). According to P, most of the forty years were spent in Paran. But the JE tradition thinks in terms of Kadesh as the place of the long stay (Exod. 16:1). Num. 13:26 is an assimilation, placing Kadesh in the wilderness of Paran. Thus we have three traditions concerning the sojourn at Kadesh. According to P, the people stayed there for a short while at the end of the journeying; according to JE, most of the forty years was spent at Kadesh; according to D, they spent eleven days in journeying from Horeb to Kadesh (Dt. 1) and spent a short while there at the beginning of the journeying. The easiest solution is to think of Kadesh as situated in the north-west of the Wilderness of Paran, with Paran as signifying generally the whole area north of the Sinai Peninsula, south of the Negeb proper and west of the rift which links the Jordan Valley with the 220
Gulf of ʿAqaba.

b **X 13-28**—The companies of the tribes and Levites set out partly according to the prearranged plan. According to 2:17, the three Levite clans marched together in the middle of the column, the east and south contingents in front of them, and the west and north behind them. But here (17) the east lead the way, followed by the Gershonites and the Merarites; then the south contingent set out and after them (21) the Kohathites marched carrying the specially holy furniture. This had the advantage of securing that at the next stopping-place the tabernacle was set up before the Kohathites arrived with the holy things.

c **29-32 Moses and Hobab**—The name of Moses' father-in-law varies in the different traditions. Here (J), the name is Hobab and there is evidence in the ancient versions that this name was originally in Jg. 1:16 as it still is in Jg. 4:11. He is called a Kenite in these passages, but in the E-tradition he is Jethro the Midianite (Exod. 3:1, 4:18f.). In Exod. 2:18 (J) his name is Reuel, a Midianite, but the general opinion is that 'Hobab' was suppressed here in order to conform to other passages. Reuel is perhaps a clan name. There are two traditions: one, that Jethro the Midianite did not accompany the Israelites (Exod. 18:27, E), and the other, that Hobab the Kenite did accompany them. This latter is apparently the J-tradition, supported by Jg. 1:16 and even Jg. 4:11. The term 'Midianite' in 29 will thus be due to a JE assimilation. If the E-tradition belongs to the Northern tribes, and the J-tradition belongs to Judah, then both traditions are sound. The father-in-law of Moses did not accompany the Joseph tribes who crossed the Jordan under Joshua, but there were Kenites in those elements of Judah who seeped in from the south. For this solution of the problems of the settlement in Canaan, see C. F. Burney, *Israel's Settlement in Canaan* (1918). **30, 31.** If Hobab had indeed left the Israelites to go home, then Sinai can scarcely have been in the Sinai Peninsula, but must have been north of the Gulf of ʿAqaba. Hobab was to be their guide, the man who knew the desert and could lead them by a route which would pass through the oases.

d **33-36 The First Stage**—The first stage was a three-day journey from Mount Sinai. There is a Jewish tradition which says that the Ark miraculously did the journey in one day to show how eager God was to lead the people into the Promised Land. Here (33) is the only place where Sinai-Horeb is called 'the mount of the Lord'; probably the 'God' of the original E-tradition has been harmonised with the J-tradition. The whole section shows much editing, because 'the ark of the covenant of the Lord' is a D-phrase, and 34 is definitely P, because in JE the cloud leads the people, just as in JE the Ark precedes the people. The recurrence of the phrase 'three days' journey' is difficult, because the Ark can scarcely have travelled three days ahead, unless, perchance, this really is intended and *tûr* (RSV 'seek out') is used in the sense of 'go on ahead and spy out' as in the story of the spies, Num. 13. Most commentators either follow Syr. and read 'one day's journey' or omit as an accidental repetition. **35** and **36** contain two very ancient sayings dating back to the time when Yahweh was the God of a militant people, i.e. the time of the Book of Jashar (Jos. 10:13; 2 Sam. 1:18), the epic of the wars of Canaan and the victories of David. **35.** The first saying refers to the desert journeys and to God clearing the way for the advancing Israelites (Num. 32:21). The second saying (36) envisages a settled abode in Canaan with the Ark going out to battle, 1 Sam. 4:3. In Ps. 68:1, 7 the Ark is associated with the march through the desert and the rout of the Amorite kings. In Ps. 132:8 the second saying is associated with the final resting-place of the Ark on Mount Zion: cf. Rashi, who preserves the interpretation of Menachem ben Seruk who

0d associates the *shûbhāh* (' return ') of **36** with the *shûbhāh* (' rest and tranquility ') of Isa. 30:15.

e **XI 1-3 The Fire of Taberah**—The people complain of their misfortunes. RV has gone astray through not realising that the Hebrew *ra'* can mean misfortune as well as moral evil (? cf. Mt. 6:13). The fire of Yahweh sweeps through the camp and does damage in the outskirts, but Moses intercedes and the destruction ceases. The story is aetiological, told to account for the name Taberah (burning). Commentators explain the phenomenon by lightning or some other electrical discharge, but it is better to leave the story as it is. These early stories cannot necessarily be explained in terms of normal, or even abnormal, physical or natural agents.

f **4-35 The People tire of Manna**—Other elements have been inserted into the quail story : the appointment of the 70 elders (16–17) and the story of Eldad and Medad (24-30). The people crave for a change from the manna, nothing to eat and nothing to see but the manna. But if the people had flocks (Exod. 12:32, 38, 17:3 ; Num. 32:1), how should they lack fresh meat? The difficulty is faced by Rashi, who turns to the ancient Midrash and refers to 11:1 and the word translated ' complained ', which in Jg. 14:4 is rendered ' seek an occasion (pretext) '. We have a story here which is independent of the main tradition and thinks of the Israelites as not having flocks and herds in the wilderness. The mention of plenty of food in Egypt is a regular feature of their behaviour when things went wrong (Exod. 14:12, 16:3, 17:3), even though the food there consisted of fish and vegetables, but no flesh. The flesh-pots are indeed mentioned in Exod. 16:3, the E-story of the quails, with which this account has much in common. Fish was the staple diet of the poor in Egypt, and Herodotus (ii, 125) mentions radishes, leeks and onions as supplied to the workers on the pyramids. If the manna tasted like butter-cakes kneaded with olive-oil, it is not surprising that the Israelites longed for a change of diet to include the sharp tang of onions and garlic. The manna (**7-9**) was about the size of a peppercorn (so Exod. 16:31, but Exod. 16:13 says it was in small flakes), greyish-white or yellowish, with a sweet, spicy flavour and looking like gum-resin. The plant known as *Tamarix gallica* exudes such a resinous substance in June and July during the night, and it is melted by the heat of the sun. But how could this be ground or pounded, unless it was used as a condiment or as a medicine with other food? **6.** ' Our strength is dried up ' (RSV) is not very good : read ' nothing at all to whet our appetite '. **10a** continues from **4-6** and presumably the anger is due to complaints about the manna. For Moses these complaints are the last straw, the climax of difficulty that made his task too great for him. God deals with both problems. He solves the immediate problem by providing the quails, and the fundamental problem by the appointment of the 70. In the E-tradition (Exod. 18:5–27) Jethro suggests the appointment of assistants to Moses, and the number 70 is. mentioned in Exod. 24:1. God promises to take some of the ' spirit ' (17) from Moses, as though it is a quantitative semi-material stuff, and
g put it on the 70. The expression 'some of the spirit' is a survival of early mana-ideas. The 70 elders are chosen (24–30), taken outside the camp where the tent is (E-tradition, not P), and there the spirit rests on them and they ' prophesy '. This is the strange prophetic frenzy of 1 Sam. 19:20–24, men seized with strange power and madly whirling. But, more strangely still, two of the 70, detained in camp perhaps because of temporary ritual uncleanness, were also seized with this same strange frenzy. Joshua is disturbed lest anyone shall rival Moses in any sort of God-given manifestation of power. In the E-tradition, Joshua is the attendant always on duty at the Tent. **29.** Moses' famous reply declares that the power of God in the lives of men and women cannot be limited by time and place nor by the performance of
any set ceremony. God gives the power of the Spirit 220g
to whom and when and where he wills. The story of the craving for fresh meat is taken up again in 18–20 from 13. The people will get their meat, but it will mean meat, meat, meat, for a whole month till they vomit meat through nose and mouth. Moses asks, with some justification, where he is to find fresh meat for 600,000 foot-soldiers apart from the rest of the community. God's answer is given in 31-35. The wind gets up at sunset and brings quails with it. Travellers speak of huge masses of the common quail which suddenly appear at the time of migration, returning to Palestine ' by myriads in a single night '. This occurs in March and the southward migration is in September. **31.** RSV says that the Israelites found them 3 feet deep (' about two cubits ') on the ground, but an ancient interpretation of MT is that they flew 3 feet off the ground and so were easily netted. Each man gathered at least a hundred bushels and the Israelites spread them out round the camp to dry them in the sun, as the ancient Egyptians are said to have done. But in **33** we seem to merge into another story, because instead of a whole month of eating quails (18–20), the people die in great numbers before they can chew the flesh. And the story becomes aetiological and explains the name of the place (34).

XII The Uniqueness of Moses—The purpose of the h
story is to emphasise the supremacy of Moses, cf. Dt. 34:1–12. He is greater than any prophet, because God spoke to him face to face, not in visions and dreams. The uniqueness of Moses is demonstrated not only by the severe punishment meted out to Miriam, but by the instantaneous cure on the intercession of Moses. Tradition varies concerning the identity of the ' Cushite woman ' whom Moses had married. The ancient Versions understood ' Cushite ' to mean Ethiopian, and there are many legends concerning Tharbis, the daughter of Kikanos king of the Ethiopians. Modern writers tend to think of the Cassites, east of Babylonia, or, with better justification, of Kusi in North Arabia, mentioned by Esarhaddon of Assyria. Perhaps the reference is to Cushan, Hab. 3:7. In this case, the reference may be to Zipporah, who was certainly a North Arabian, being a Midianite (Exod. 2:16–21) or a Kenite (Jg. 1:16, 4:11). There is a Rabbinic tradition that ' Cushite ' means ' fair of appearance ', this being an interpretation by Gematria, the counting of the value of letters, since the two expressions in Hebrew both add up to the same number. **3.** The statement that Moses was ' very meek ' does not mean that he was patient under human maltreatment and unresisting. The word refers to humbleness before God, Zeph. 2:3. **4.** The sudden action of God brings us within the same realm as the anger of Taberah (11:1–3), and the same is true of the sudden departure of the cloud which left Miriam a leper, white as snow (9) ; cf. Uzzah in 2 Sam. 6:7. **6-8** are in oracular, poetic form. The reference to God speaking in ' dark speech ' (Hebrew ' riddle ') suggests that the dark, enigmatic sayings are a cloak to cover the naked Word of God, which only Moses is able to hear. In **6,** RSV rightly is emending on the basis of Vulg., since the Hebrew means ' if the Lord is your prophet ', which can scarcely be correct. **14.** To spit in the face is a grave insult (Dt. 25:9), but there is no record of it causing uncleanness for a seven-day period. In any case, though Miriam be clean in the sight of man, she still must observe the seven-day isolation which the law demands.

XIII 1-XXI 35 covers the period spent, according to 221a
P, in the Wilderness of Paran. Some of these chapters are interwoven from the three traditions, J, E, P, and this gives rise to discrepancies in the stories.

XIII gives the story of the spying itself and the reports b
of the spies. 1-17*a* gives the names of the spies, one from each tribe. The list is from P. 17*b*-20 is from JE and they are to spy out the Negeb. The area is further defined in 22-24 which is also from JE. They go as far north as Hebron, i.e. only some 60 miles

221b from Kadesh, which is where the people were encamped, according to JE. The JE report is given in 26*b*-31 : the land is fertile, but the inhabitants are strong, and their cities well defended. Caleb alone protests and says that the Israelites are well able to conquer the country. This report is continued in 32*b* and 33. Interwoven with this is the P-report. According to this, the whole country was explored, as far as the entrance to Hamath, the farthest ideal limit of the country. In 25-26*a* the spies return after 40 days, but they return to Paran, which is where the people were encamped, according to P. Their report (32*a*) is unfavourable : it is a bad country, one that ' devours its inhabitants '. **20.** The time of the first ripe grapes is the end of July. **22.** ' The descendants of Anak ' are the giants of ancient Hebrew tradition who inhabited the Hebron area. The later D-tradition (Dt. 9:2) makes their habitat more general : see also Dt. 1:28, 2:10. According to Jos. 11: 21–22 they were scattered all over the hill-country of Palestine, and some still survived after the time of Joshua in the Philistine country. The word *Anak*
c means ' (long) neck '. Zoan is the ancient Avaris, and the Tanis of classical times. It was the capital of the Hyksos kings, and later the home of the great Rameses II in the 13th cent. B.C. It is commonly identified with the Rameses of Exod. 1:11, the scene of the hard labour of the Israelite slaves, ' the fields of Zoan ' of Ps. 78:12, 43 ; most scholars identify the site as being near Ṣân el-Ḥagar in the NE. of the Delta : GAB (1956), 40, 45, 165, esp. map 7, p. 43. **23.** The Wâdī Eshcol has not certainly been identified, but it was near Hebron and is possibly the Wâdī Iskahil, to the north-west of Hebron. The name means ' cluster (of grapes) '. **25.** The Amalekites were semi-nomads
d who ranged south of the Negeb. The Hittites were by no means comparable with the other somewhat small tribes mentioned here. There was once a great Hittite Empire which at its height (14th cent. B.C.) covered most of Asia Minor as far west as Ankara, as far east as the Tigris and as far south as near Damascus. They were thrusting westwards towards the Aegean Sea and southwards towards Egypt, and were strong enough to halt the Egyptian advance into Syria. They captured Babylon *c.*1600 B.C. See GAB, 152 ; C. W. Ceram, *Narrow Pass, Black Mountain* (1956, Eng. trans.), a popular account of the great Hittite Empire and the discovery and decipherment of their strange script. The Jebusites were a local tribe, and the
e original inhabitants of Jerusalem. The ' Amorites ' in D is a general name for the Canaanites as a whole, more particularly the two kingdoms east of Jordan which the Israelites overwhelmed, Sihon king of the Amorites and Og king of Bashan. Actually the Amorites were a great people who spread all over the Mesopotamian valley. They were Semites who advanced along the Fertile Crescent *c.*2000 B.C., and when the third dynasty of Ur fell about this time, they occupied first one and then another of the cities of Mesopotamia. Mari fell to them *c.*1950 B.C., and by *c.*1750 B.C. the Amorite kings were in control of the whole area from Syria through to Babylonia. The most famous of these Amorite kings was Ḥammurabi (died *c.*1686 B.C.), possibly a contemporary
f of Abraham. **33.** ' The sons of Anak ' are here identified with the Nephilim, the legendary giants and demi-gods of Gen. 6:3. The name is of uncertain origin, but *n^{e}phîlā'* is the Aramaic name of Orion, the giant of the sky. For ' and so we seemed to them ', read, with change of vowels only, ' we looked like gnats to them '.
g **XIV 1-10a The People are discouraged**—This section is mostly P, but the Priestly editor seems to have embodied elements from JE in vv. 3–4 and 8–9. When the people hear the adverse report of the majority of the spies, they murmur and want to return to Egypt. Their attitude here is thus a repetition of their attitude at Baal-zephon when they saw the Egyptian army behind them (Exod. 14), in the wilderness of Sin when the food was short (Exod. 16), and
in the valley of Rephidim when the water was short 22
(Exod. 17). On every occasion when they received a check they wished they had never left Egypt. This time they propose to elect a new leader who shall lead them back to Egypt. Moses and Aaron passionately intercede with the people, whilst Joshua and Caleb plead directly with them, and only just escape being stoned to death. **9.** The Hebrew *leḥem* refers to the staple food of the country. In modern English, ' they are our meat '. ' Their protection ' is lit. ' their shadow ', one of the most familiar figures of speech in OT for protection, a metaphor drawn from the need to shelter from the heat of the sun, under branches (Jg. 9:15), or wings (Ps. 17:8), or rock (Isa. 32:2). There is general agreement that the reference is to divine protection ; some say the meaning is the Yahweh has withdrawn his protection from them (cf. Dt. 32:8), and others that the gods of Canaan are henceforth powerless to aid their peoples.
10b-25 is wholly from JE. Note that the chief char- h
acters are now Moses and Caleb. The additions of Aaron and Joshua belong to the P-tradition. Yahweh intervenes in exasperation and he proposes to destroy this wayward, vacillating people who do not trust in him. He proposes to destroy them with pestilence and raise up from Moses a greater and more faithful people. This actually is what God has done in history more than once : he rejected Israel and chose Judah (Ps. 78:67–68), he rejected Judah and chose ' the children of the captivity ' (Ezr. 4:1–3), and, as Christians maintain, he rejected the Jews and chose the new Israel in Christ. Moses intercedes for the people. Moses and Samuel are the two great intercessors for Israel, Sir. 46:16 ; Ps. 99:6. God who brought his people out of Egypt cannot abandon them now. What if the Egyptians tell the Canaanites? All the nations who have heard of the rescue from Egypt will say that Yahweh could not perform what he had promised, and that is why he killed them all in the wilderness. Yahweh is (18) ' slow to anger ', full of forbearance, and he is characterised by his steadfast love for his people Israel : cf. the Jewish prayer ' With abounding love . . .', ed. S. Singer, *The Authorised Jewish Prayer Book*, p. 39. But at the same time the price of iniquity and rebellion (not ' transgression ' RSV, 19) must be paid to the third and fourth generations. God therefore pardons the people, but the rebels must pay the price of their rebellion and die in the desert. Only Caleb shall enter the Promised Land, since he alone was faithful to God and trusted in him. **11.** The ' believe in ' of St John is a literal rendering of this Hebrew phrase. It is the ' trust,
have faith ' of Paul. **18.** One of the important elements i
in the OT idea of God is his forbearance. The right and proper thing to happen is the immediate punishment of sin, and this is what is described on occasion in terms of the sudden blazing-forth of the anger of God. But God is full of forbearance and he is always holding up the punishment. The punishment of sin in this world is certain and it is by groups since we are all bound in one bundle of life. **25** should read not ' by the way to the Red Sea ', but ' by the way of the Red Sea ', i.e. by the Red Sea caravan route ; cf. Exod. 13:17–18.
26-38 The P-variant of 10b-25—Aaron is now in- j
cluded as well as Moses, and Joshua as well as Caleb. Apparently Eleazar (32:28) is also permitted to be a survivor. This is involved in 29, where it is all those who were numbered from 20 years upwards who were to fall in the wilderness. This excludes all the children and young men and women and all the Levites, who were not numbered from 20 years old upwards. These children are to be ' shepherds ' (RV ' wanderers ' is due to Jewish exegesis) in the desert for forty years. Every day of the forty days which the spies spent in spying must be paid for by one year wandering in the desert. The ten rebel spies died immediately by ' the plague ' (RV : RSV has ' a plague '). Jewish exegesis insists here on the definite article of the Hebrew, because

21j it was the particular plague which they deserved. They based their exegesis on Isa. 57:4 and said that the tongues of the spies grew long and extended right down to their navels, and that worms came from their tongues into their navels. **27.** The 'wicked congregation' was held by the Jews to refer to the ten spies who 'caused the Israelites to murmur': the same form of the verb was read as in v. 36. Thus the word 'congregation' must include at least ten, and it is from this passage that the necessary quorum of ten for the synagogue is deduced; see Talmud *b Meg.* 23*b*.

k **39-45 The People repent, but too late**—This is a JE account of a first and unsuccessful attack on Canaan. It was from the south up through the Negeb. The people resolve to show their repentance by attacking after all, but this is now contrary to the will of God who has condemned them to forty years of wandering, and this price must be paid. They 'presumed' (recklessly insisted) on advancing into the hill-country without the Presence of God (the Ark) and without Moses, with the result that they were routed and pursued as far as Hormah, a former Canaanite royal city (Jos. 12:14), and possibly the modern Tell el-Mishash, ESE. of Beersheba. **40**: the phrase 'went up to the heights of the hill country' is difficult. Either omit as accidental intrusion, or read 'towards'. For the story of this abortive attack, see Dt. 1:41–45 and possibly there is a reminiscence of it in Exod. 17:8–16. It is probable that the tribe of Judah did actually enter Canaan from the south, and did not partake in the long march round the desert after the sojourn in Kadesh (JE), but this story here does not appear to have anything to do with that.

2a **XV** contains a miscellany of rules and regulations, all of them drawn from P. The first section (1–16) is concerned with the quantities of flour, wine and oil to be offered with the various animal offerings. 17–21 is concerned with first-fruits and 22–31 with sin-offerings, i.e. propitiatory gifts for unwitting errors. 32–36 concerns Sabbath laws and 37–41 deal with the custom of wearing tassels on the corners of outer garments. The various items are introduced in different ways and probably belong to different periods. Possibly the last section (tassels) has affinities with H.

b **1-16** These rules apply to all animal sacrifices, whether for a burnt(whole)-offering in which everything was consumed on the altar, or for a 'sacrifice', i.e. a slain-offering of which only the blood and the fat went to the altar and the flesh was eaten by the worshipper and by the priests. Some of these slain-offerings were in fulfilment of vows, some were freewill gifts, and others were the regular appointed offerings at the statutory services, cf. Lev. 2. These rules are to be observed when the people have conquered Canaan (2). This is obvious because the grain gifts are those of an agricultural people and not of nomads such as the Israelites were before they entered Canaan. This gives support to the opinion of Amos (5:25) and of Jeremiah (7:22) that there were none of these offerings in the wilderness. Whatever sacrifices there were in the wilderness, they certainly did not include such grain-offerings as are listed in this section. Every animal sacrifice is to be accompanied by its proper grain- and drink-offerings together with the specified quantity of olive-oil. The quantities here are less than those listed in Ezek. 46; not much less for a lamb (one-tenth as against one-sixth in the case of grain and one-fourth as against one-third for oil and wine), but considerably less for rams and bulls (two-tenths as against a whole ephah of grain and one-third and one-half as against a whole hin of wine and oil). An ephah is roughly a bushel, so that one-tenth is roughly seven pints. A hin is about twelve pints, so that one-quarter is about three pints. Resident aliens (RSV 'the stranger who sojourns with you') must comply with these regulations equally with the native-born Israelite.

c **17-21 The Law of the Ḥallāh** ('cake', 20)—It concerns the first of the 'dough' (RSV 'coarse meal', 20); so LXX and EVV, correctly. The offering, which is a 'heave-offering' (RV, but better 'contribution'), must be a cake (*ḥallāh*) cut off from the dough of the first ground flour, fresh from the threshing-floor. According to tradition, the minimum quantity was one-twenty-fourth for the housewife and one-forty-eighth for the professional baker. Originally the *ḥallāh* went to the priest, but in modern times it is thrown into the fire. The priest (Cohen) is prevented from observing the laws of priestly purity in the modern world and must not therefore eat a holy gift. 222c

22-31 The sin-offering is for the unwitting non-observance of commandments. It includes the omission of ritual actions which should have been performed on behalf of the whole community and unwitting errors which involve the individual only. Ancient Jewish tradition refers this section to unintentional idolatry, but later commentators assumed a wider reference. Once again, resident aliens must comply equally with native-born Israelites. The man who sins wilfully, knowing what he is doing, has no remedy in the cultus with its sacrifices. He has broken the covenant and therefore cannot avail himself of the provisions and the mercies of the covenant. He has reviled Yahweh, despised his word, and must be 'utterly cut off' to bear the punishment of his own iniquity. The forbearance, characteristic of the whole system, is withdrawn and God has provided in the ritual no means of interposing between a man and the consequences of his actions. d

32-36 The Sabbath Law—Here is an illustration of deliberate sin ('with a high hand') and its consequences. The man knew well enough that he ought not to have been gathering sticks on the Sabbath. A difficulty arises over v. 34, because it is stated plainly in Exod. 31:14f. and 35:2 that the offender is to be put to death. The traditional Jewish explanation is that the manner of the death was not fixed, and that here it is definitely stated that he must be put to death by stoning. e

37-41 The Tassels—The custom is ancient and is shown on ancient Asiatic monuments. The tassels were originally probably amulets, and may have had something to do originally with the four legs of an animal's skin. The Israelites adopted the custom and it came for them to have a new and different significance. The tassel was to have a bluish-purple thread worked into it, to be a reminder of the law and of the necessity laid upon them to observe it. Once more the explanation is associated with the God who brought them out of Egypt. The blue-purple dye was made from a certain mollusc, the chalazon, found on the Phoenician coast, but even in Mishnaic times this dye was scarce, so that it was permitted to use a thread of white wool. The numerical value of the Hebrew word (*ṣîṣîth*) is 600, and this with 8 threads and 5 knots makes 613, the number of the commandments involved in the traditions of the elders. The custom has changed during the centuries. There came a time (13th cent.) when the Jews no longer wore tassels on the corners of their outer garments, but wore instead an under-garment (the Arba Kanfos), which consisted of a rectangular piece of cloth, three feet by one foot, with a hole in the middle so that it could be passed over the head, and the tassels on the four corners. The modern Tallith is a mantle of wool or silk worn during worship in the daytime, and is a variant of the under-garment of medieval times. The translations of AV and RV are 'fringes', and these are the 'fringes' (RSV, 'borders' in AV and RV) of Mt. 23:5. f

XVI Revolts against Moses—This chapter contains three interwoven accounts of two rebellions against the authority of Moses and Aaron. One revolt is that of Dathan and Abiram (JE). These were two Reubenites, who, possibly looking back to a time when Reuben was the leader of the sons of Jacob (Gen. 37:22, E), disputed the civil leadership with Moses. These two rebelled against Moses and refused 223a

223a to come to him when he summoned them (1*b*, 2*a*, 12–15). They brought up the old complaint of the Israelites when in trouble, that they had been much better off in Egypt, and that if Moses had left them alone all would have been well (13). The phrase 'a land flowing with milk and honey' is even made by them to refer to Egypt. They aver that Moses has not fulfilled his promises to them, but that instead he has made himself a prince over them. Whereupon (25–34) Moses goes down to them, orders everybody else to move away from the dwellings of Dathan and Abiram (omit 'Korah' in 27), and they and all theirs are swallowed up alive. The second revolt is that of

b Korah. This is a P-tradition, but there are two variants of the story. The first is found in 3–7, 18–24, 35, 41–50. Here the revolt of Korah is based on the claim that every Israelite is holy, and may therefore approach Yahweh. This rebellion is against Moses and Aaron. The second variant is found in 8–11, 36–40, and it is a revolt of Levites led by Korah against Moses and Aaron. They demand priestly recognition and claim that they have the right, equally with Moses and Aaron, of offering incense. This offering incense is regarded in later time (2 Chr. 26:16–19) as the special and unique function of the priest. Both variants agree in the sequel. Korah and his company are burnt up by the fire which flares out from the sacred altar. 36–40 gives an account of the disposal of the censers of Korah and his company. They had been offered to Yahweh and were therefore holy, in spite of the fact that the men who offered them had no right to do so. Eleazar therefore takes the bronze of the censers and beats them out into a bronze covering for the altar. There for ever the bronze is to remain as a perpetual reminder than none but the Aaronic priests shall ever approach the altar. That this is a variant account is shown also by the fact that it is a secondary account of the origin of the bronze covering of the altar. According to Exod. 27:2 (P) the altar had this bronze covering from the beginning. **2** (1 in MT). The word translated 'took' is difficult, and the word 'men' has been supplied (following Ibn Ezra) in order to make sense. Various suggestions and emendations have been made, but the best suggestion is that of G. R. Driver, who holds that the word does not mean 'take' at all, but that it is another root which means 'were insolent'. **15.** '**taken one ass**': cf. Samuel's defence in 1 Sam. 8:11–17. **22.** The phrase 'God of the spirits of all flesh' is a P-phrase, found only here and 27:16. It shows the advanced ideas of P, wherein Yahweh is indeed the God of Israel and has his covenant established with them, but is also the maker of all men, on whom 'all flesh' (i.e. all human beings) are dependent for every breath they draw, **Ps.** 104:29. In MT, ch. 17 begins at 16:36.

c **41-50** is the sequel of the first P-variant, and it tells the story of what happened next day. The people grumbled at the slaughter of Korah and his company, whereupon Yahweh descends in the cloud of his glory to destroy this rebel people. Moses bids Aaron rush with his lighted censer to intercede (interpose) between the people and the wrath of God. Aaron stands between the living and the dead, but not till 14,700 have died.

d **XVII 1-13** (MT 17:18–28). **Aaron's Rod that budded**—The tribe of Levi is to be pre-eminently the tribe of Yahweh. This chapter is from the P-tradition, with the last two verses detached from the story of the rebellion of Korah to form an introduction to ch. 18. Moses bade the tribes produce one rod each, the staff which the ancient tribal leaders carried. The Heb. word *maṭṭeh* means both 'staff' and 'tribe'. All twelve rods were deposited in the Tent with Aaron's rod (for Levi) 'among them'. The Rabbis translated this 'in the midst of them' in order to preclude the statement that Aaron's rod budded because it was nearest the divine Presence on the edge of the rods. In the morning Aaron's rod had not only budded, but blossomed and produced 22 almonds. It was the sign of God's choice and a warning for all who in the future were minded to rebel.

XVIII Duties and Dues of Levites and Priests— 22 The important element in this chapter is the extent of the dues demanded for the Levites. They are greater than those which are allocated to them in Dt. 14:22–29. There, the Levites and the other depressed classes receive the tithe of the third year, whilst the Israelites eat the tithes of the other two years locally at a feast; here the Levites alone are to receive the tithes every year. In Lev. 27:30–33 a tithe of cattle is added to what is mentioned here. The list in Ezek. 44:28–31 grants to the priests substantially the same dues as here. It is in other parts of the P-tradition that larger demands are made (Lev. 5:16, 7:8, 22:14, 24:5–9), though these may well be included in the general terms of v. 19. Cf. the general and comprehensive terms of Ezek. 44:30, 'every offering of all kinds from your offerings'. It is evident that the demands made by the post-exilic priesthood and Levite community were much greater than in pre-exilic times, and in later Judaism (cf. the Mishnah) these demands were greater still.

1-7 Duties of the Levites—They are to 'bear b iniquity in connection with the sanctuary', i.e. to accept full responsibility for it and incur the whole blame if anything goes wrong. Similarly the Aaronite priests are to accept full responsibility for the duties of the sanctuary and the altar. The Levites are a gift, given first to God and by him to the priests. And to the priests God freely gives the privilege of priestly service. **4.** The phrase 'no one else' is inadequate, and the 'stranger' of AV and RV is as misleading as the rendering 'layman', which has too technical a modern meaning. 'No unauthorised person' is best.

The explanation is offered here (2) of the name c 'levite' that it is connected with the root *lāwāh* (join). A similar explanation, of assonance rather than of etymology, is provided in Gen. 29:34, where the explanation is that Leah is 'joined' to her husband now that she has borne him a third son, whose name is therefore Levi. The name Levi is an ancient tribal name. It is difficult to accept the suggestion that the name originally means 'joined to Yahweh'. The explanation of Gen. 29:34 is against this. Whilst, on the one hand, the word is found in the Minaean inscriptions at El 'Ola, apparently referring to some kind of cult official, yet among the Hebrews it was not necessary for a man to be a levite in order to be a priest. Eli was not a levite, neither was Samuel until later tradition made him one. The Levites were never priests at Jerusalem, but were priests at local southern shrines. Levi the tribe was probably destroyed together with Simeon (Gen. 49:7), and both tribes attached themselves to Judah. The Levites as 'given' (*n^ethûnîm*) are to be distinguished from the Nethinim, mentioned in the Chronicler's history and distinguished there from both priests and levites. They were said by him to have been instituted by David as a serving-class, 1 Chr. 9:2, etc. See N. H. Snaith, 'Worship', *Record and Revelation* (1938, ed. H. W. Robinson), 262–7.

8-20 The Priests' Dues—**8a** is not clear in RSV. d It means: to you I give charge of all the levies (AV, RV 'heave-offerings') made to me for holy gifts. These are the allotted portion, a perpetual due to the Aaronite priesthood. These dues consist of all that is presented, but not burned on the altar. It includes all 'most holy things' (holy gifts of holy gifts), i.e. that which is never to be removed from the holy place, and is to be eaten there by none other than the priests. The reference to anointing, found in AV and RV, is due to mistaken identification with the root (same consonants) 'anoint'. The priestly dues include also all offerings (*ḳorbān* in the general sense of the word), specified as cereal-offerings, sin-offerings and guilt-offerings. These all are to be eaten

4d only by the priests. It includes the contribution from the gifts of the people, i.e. all their ' special contributions ' (RSV, ' wave offerings ') from their sacrifices (slain-offerings). These are ' holy gifts ' and may be eaten by the priests' households. The use of the word ' gift ' (11) is strange and rare. We would expect a reference to the so-called peace-offerings, but these are rightly called ' gifts ' because they are not sacrificial offerings in the sense that they are burnt on the altar. Only the blood and the fat go to the altar, and the rest is eaten by the people, apart from the special contribution and the levy which go to the priests.
e Further, all first-fruits belong to the Levites, the best (lit. ' fat ') of oil and wine and grain, 12–13. The two types are mentioned, both first-fruits (*rē'shîth*) and first-ripe fruits (*bikkûrîm*). In later time the *bikkûrîm* consisted of seven types of first fruits : wheat, barley, vines, fig-trees, pomegranates, oil and date-honey (i.e. not comb-honey, but the Arabic *dibs*) (§204*f*). **14.** All grain first-fruits are *ḥerem*. This word when used of human beings or in the context of a holy war involves death and complete destruction. Here the word means ' irredeemably dedicated ' in contrast to living creatures, the conditions of whose redemption are given in succeeding verses, 15–20. The first-born of man must be redeemed and so also the first-born of all unclean animals, and the price is twelve shillings per head according to pre-1914 standards. Here is an example of the way in which in ritual the same thing can be done, but for different reasons. The first-born of unclean animals must be redeemed because they are unclean : they cannot go to the altar and they cannot be eaten by the priests. The first-born of men must be redeemed because of the developed humanitarian ideas of the passing years. Apparently the first-born of man could be sacrificed, though exceptionally, as late as Mic. 6:7, but in later times such offerings were wholly prohibited and the payment of a ransom price was compulsory. The first-born of all domesticated beasts are not redeemable, because they can be eaten by the priests. The blood and the fat, as usual, go to the altar, and the flesh to the priests. All this is because the priests have no share in the land. Their share is God himself. This allocation of holy gifts is called ' a covenant of salt ' (19). Opinion varies as to the exact significance of this phrase, but the idea of a firm bond is certain, cf. Arabic *malacha* (to salt) and *milchat* (treaty). Possibly the idea is that of a common meal, but it is more likely that the association is with the preservative value of salt.

f **21-32 The Tithe and the Tithe of the Tithe**—In return for performing the service of the tent of meeting and so enabling the Israelites to avoid the deadliness of holiness for those who are unauthorised, the Levites are to be given every tithe. But another reason is given in 23–24 ; it is a compensation to them because they, like the priests, have no share in the inheritance of the land. This does not take account of the cities of refuge which were given to them ; §230*h*. But the Levites themselves must tithe what they receive as tithes, and this is to go to the priests. This tithe is to be reckoned in the same way as the ordinary tithe, just as is done with the grain from the threshing-floor and the full yield of the winepress. It is best to omit ' to the Levites ' (30), following Vulg.

g **XIX Purification from Uncleanness by touching the Dead**—This section is from the P-tradition, and the chapter begins with the rite of the Red Heifer. Those who wish to allegorise can point out that God provides the remedy even before men realise the need for it.

h **1-10 The Red Heifer**—This rite was recognised by the Jews as being the most puzzling in Scripture, so much so that even King Solomon gave up in despair. Jewish exegetes emphasise the paradox : ' it cleanses the defiled, and defiles the clean ', the reference being to the fact that everyone who had anything to do with the water of purification became unclean. The explanation is to be found in the (to moderns) confused 224h
realm of taboo, which gives rise to the curious situation whereby the verb *ḥāṭā'* can mean both ' sin ' and ' de-sin '. According to the Mishnah, the rite of the Red Heifer was performed only seven times, once by Moses, once by Ezra, and five times since Ezra. The English Versions, followed by RSV, have established the animal as a heifer, but there is nothing in MT to warrant this. The animal was a red cow, and Jewish tradition is that the animal had to be at least two years old and might be as much as five years old Possibly the translators, who followed LXX (but not Vulg.), were influenced by the condition imposed that the animal had to be one that had never known a yoke, cf. the phrase ' untrained heifer ', Hos. 10:11. The red colour has been said to be due to its being the colour of blood, since blood has cleansing, atoning power. This may well be correct, since the Romans sacrificed red puppies and red-haired men in order to scatter their ashes on the threshing-floor, and this was said to be because of the red colour of the ripened corn. Both are cases of ' mimetic magic ' originally. One Jewish explanation is that it needed a red cow to atone for the sin of the golden calf. The cow was taken outside the camp, slaughtered in front of the priest, who sprinkled the blood with his forefinger seven times ' toward the front of the tent of meeting '. In the time of the Second Temple, the priest stood on the Mount of Olives across the valley to the east of the Temple, and he placed himself so that he was able to look straight through the East Gate of the Temple and through the Gate of Nicanor. The whole animal was then burnt, and this included the skin, the flesh, the blood and the faecal matter. The cedarwood, the marjoram and the scarlet thread (cf. Lev. 14) were cast into the burning fire. Later the ashes were gathered together, and kept in a ritually clean place outside the camp ready to be used to make ' the water for impurity ' (9). AV and RV have ' water of separation ', which depends on ancient Jewish exegesis (Ibn Ezra), but Rashi explained it as ' water of sprinkling '. RSV concludes 9 with ' for the removal of sin '. MT has ' it is a sin offering ', but all translators are unjustifiably careful to avoid this, on the ground that the cow was not slain in front of the altar. The cow is definitely a sin-offering in the true meaning of the word : it is an animal that is offered in order to be the means of getting rid of sin. To say that an offering cannot be a sin-offering unless it is slain in front of the altar is to misunderstand the essential meaning of the rite. Nevertheless, the RSV is a correct interpretation, though it would be better to read : ' it is an offering for the removal of sin '.

11-13 Touching a dead Body—This entails ritual i
uncleanness, a common idea in ancient times throughout the world, and not wholly absent even in modern times, however we may imagine ourselves to be emancipated from ancient superstitions. Instances are cited, from American Indians, Zulus, Tibetans, ancient classical times, Mesopotamians and Aztecs. Sometimes the dominant fear is that of corruption, sometimes it is the influence of demons, since death is the supreme triumph of the king of demons ; sometimes (according to Frazer) it is the fear of the spirits of the dead. Almost everywhere the rite of washing is involved. Among the Hebrews the usual seven-day period was involved, with necessary washings with the ' water for impurity ', i.e. water with the ashes of the red heifer thrown into it. The washing on the third day is not usual. Neglect to fulfil these rites involves the penalty ' cut off from Israel '. This may well have been intended by the priestly writers to involve death, but this would not be allowed by the civil power.

14-22 contains further details concerning unclean- j
ness through contact with the dead. The rules apply to any slightest contact, to anything that is within the tent or house in which the man dies, and even to skeletons accidentally exhumed, and to graves. **It was**

224j in order to warn passers-by that all graves were whitened, Mt. 23:27.

225a **XX Events at Kadesh**—This chapter is mostly drawn from J and E, but with editorial traces of P. According to JE, thirty-eight years have passed, and two of the three leaders are to die. Miriam dies at Kadesh and Aaron dies near by on Mount Hor (P), the Moserah of the E-tradition, possibly the Jebel Madûrah, NE. of Kadesh and a day's march from the Dead Sea.

b **2-13 The Waters of Meribah**—The story is based mostly on Exod. 17:1–7, where the people contend with Moses because there is no water. The difficulties concern the condemnation of Moses and Aaron (12). How did they fail to trust in God and so fail to demonstrate his holiness to the people? One suggestion is that the words of v. 10 (' You rebels ', etc.) were rash (Ps. 106:32f.). Another is that Moses was bidden to speak to the rock (8 : but note that he is told to take the rod), but that he struck the rock. Yet another is that he was bidden to strike once, and he struck it twice. But probably the actual sin of Moses and Aaron has been lost, perhaps deliberately lost, in the editing. In Dt. 1:37 the reason given is not the disobedience of Moses, but the disobedience of the people. The mystery remains, and its solution must be a matter of conjecture. There are two aetiological assonances in the paragraph : Kadesh and ' sanctify ' in vv. 12 and 13 ; Meribah and ' contend ' in v. 13.

c **14-21** explain why it was that the Israelites got so near to Canaan, and then turned back to go round the Edomite country and enter Canaan across Jordan. The sending of the angel (16) is an element of the E-tradition, Exod. 14:19 etc. ' The King's Highway ' (17) is not a well-kept highway, nor even a road as well defined as the ancient Roman roads. It was probably the well-known through-route which formed the regular caravan route from Egypt through to the country east of Jordan. The enmity between Israel (Jacob) and Edom (Esau) is found in the earliest traditions of the twin sons of Isaac and Rebekah.

d **22-29 The Death of Aaron**—And so the Israelites set off on towards Canaan, and got as far as Mount Hor, on the Edomite border, before they turned south (21:4) to go round the Edomite territory. **24.** Once again we find the unexplained reference to Aaron's rebellion at Meribah. Aaron is stripped of his holy garments and Eleazar is invested with them, and the Israelites mourned for him for thirty days. Aaron is the peacemaker of Israelite history. The great Hillel made each man to be a ' disciple of Aaron, loving peace and pursuing peace, loving his fellowmen and bringing them near the Torah ' (so J. H. Hertz, *The Pentateuch and Haftorahs* (1936), iv, 212). The phrase ' gathered to his people ' is strictly ' gathered to his father's kin ', the phrase thus being a parallel to ' gathered to his fathers '.

e **XXI The Victory at Hormah**—It is difficult to see how, if the people as a whole gained this victory in the Negeb, they abandoned what they had gained and turned away south so as to encircle Edom. Arad is the modern Tell 'Arâd, 17 miles south of Hebron. The easiest solution is that this JE-story tells the tale of Judah's advance into the Negeb, generally admitted to have been a successful venture separate from that of the Joseph tribes. There is a tradition in Jg. 1 that Judah and Simeon acted independently, though it is said there that they set out from Jericho. ' Atharim ' (1) is a proper name. The rendering ' of the spies ' (AV) is due to Sam. and other VSS (not LXX). The site is unknown, unless the word is a miswritten *Hattᵉmārîm*, the city of palms (Jg. 1:16), where Arad also is mentioned, in which case the site is Hazazon-tamar, the modern 'Ain el-'Arûs, immediately south of the Dead Sea. Hormah is mentioned in 14:45, and is the modern Tell el-Mishash, ESE. of Beer-sheba.

f **4-9 The Bronze Serpent** (JE)—The people object to turning back. The way is long, and both food and water are short. The penalty for disloyal grumbling is the plague of venomous serpents (*sᵉrāphîm*) and many 22
of the people die of snakebite. The same word is used of the Seraphim of Isa. 6:1, but these are personifications of the lightnings, God's harbingers, his messengers. Here the *sᵉrāphîm* may be associated with snake-demons, since the jinn of the desert are usually of serpent form (RS, 2nd ed., 168), though these jinn are those that inhabit healing-waters. Moses is bidden make a bronze serpent, and whoever looked to it was healed of the poisonous bite. Tradition associated this with the bronze serpent which Hezekiah destroyed (2 Kg. 18:4). It is generally agreed that the serpent which Hezekiah destroyed was the original Jebusite fetish, taken over after the time of David and incorporated into Yahweh worship by means of its alliance with this story, H. H. Rowley, ' Zadok and Nehushtan ', JBL 58 (1939), 113–41. The first allegorising of the story is found in Wis. 16:7 (' For he that turned himself toward it was not saved because of what he saw, but because of thee, the Saviour of all '), and then in 1 C. 10:9 and Jn 3:14.

10-16 On to Pisgah—This is a composite account, g
partly from P (**10-11a**) and partly from JE. It brings the people practically to the end of their journeying. Two ancient songs are embodied (**14-15** and **17-18a**), of which certainly the first and probably the second also come from the ancient saga, the Book of the Wars of Yahweh, associated with the invasion of Canaan. It is better to divide 14–15 differently and read ' Waheb in Suphah and the gorges : Arnon and the watershed of the gorges ', and perhaps ' slopes down ' for ' extends '. Waheb (LXX has Zohob or Zahab) and Suphah are unknown. The Song of Israel (17–18*a*) was sung every third Sabbath in conjunction with the Song of the Sea (Exod. 15:1–19), see Talmud, *bRH* 31*a* and *j Meg.* iii. Possibly in this song we have the relic of an ancient custom whereby when water was found in the desert, there was a formal opening of the well by the chiefs who opened it with their official staffs. Some of the sites mentioned in these verses have been tentatively identified : Oboth ('Ain el-Weiba), Iye-abarim (Mahay), Bamoth (Khirbet el-Qweizîyeh), Pisgah (Râs es-Siâghah), the first two of which are S. and SE. of the Dead Sea, and the latter two farther north. The Valley of Zered is the Wâdī el-Ḥesā which runs into the SE. end of the Dead Sea, and the Arnon runs into the Dead Sea from the east.

21-32 The Defeat of the two Amorite Kings, h
Sihon and Og—The defeat of these two Amorite kings forms one of the great feats of the Days of Old, and is one of the favourite themes of later days. Sihon's territory was between the Arnon and the Jabbok, and from the Jordan on the west out into the desert to the east. RSV (24) has Jazer, a place name, following LXX, but it is better to follow MT : ' as far as the frontier of Ammon, because that was rough ground ', i.e. the boundary was ill-defined. This was indeed disputed territory, Jg. 11:12–28, not only between Israel and Ammon, but also between Ammon and Moab (cf. 26). The ' ballad singers ' of 27 is good ; for ' the lords ' (28), follow LXX and read ' it swallowed up '. 30 is difficult and uncertain ; RSV partly follows LXX and partly retains the consonants of MT. Site identifications are : Jazer (Khirbet Jazzir, near the modern es-Salṭ), Heshbon (Ḥesbân), Dibon (Dhībân), Mâdebā (so now), and Edrei (Der'ā, away to the north, ESE. Sea of Galilee). At Dibon, the Moabite Stone was found, King Mesha of Moab's own account of his revolt from Israel in the time of Ahab (GAB, 80). At Mâdebā a 6th cent. A.D. mosaic map was found in the floor of an ancient church (GAB, 61).

XXII-XXXVI is the third main section of the book, 22
and gives an account of what happened on the high ground of Moab to the north of the Dead Sea and east of the Jordan.

XXII 2-XXIV The Story of Balaam—There are b
variations in the story difficult to reconcile, probably

6b because it is a combined JE narrative. There is the variation between ' elders ' and ' princes '. If Balaam went with the princes (22:21), why was he riding his she-ass accompanied only by two menservants (22:22)? If God indeed told Balaam to go with the princes of Moab, then why was he angry with Balaam (22:22)? The story of the ass is a variant of the previous paragraph (cf. 22:20, 35).

Balak, son of Zippor, king of Moab, is full of fear at the hordes of Israelites who have come up from Egypt and are encamped on his northern border. The mention of Midian (4) is strange. Probably it ought to be ' Moab ', with the reference to ' the elders of Midian ' an insertion in 7. The changes may be due to a scribe who remembered 31:8 where Balaam is slain with the five kings of Midian. This belongs to another stream of tradition which makes Balaam an enemy of Israel, a tradition which developed greatly in post-Biblical times, instead of the friend of Israel as in Num. 22–24. Pethor (5) is identified as the ancient Pituru on the Euphrates, 20 miles S. of Carchemish and 50 miles off the great bend where the river turns east. This is actually in the land of Amaw. Here MT reads ' his people ' (AV and RV), which some VSS (not LXX) have read as the more familiar ' Ammon ', thus introducing an additional source of confusion into a story already so confused that modern orthodox Jewish exegesis accounts for all the discrepancies by assuming that they are the sudden changes of a dream. **6.** All curses and blessings were thought in ancient time to have a power in themselves of coming true (Gen. 27:37), but Balaam's blessings and curses were held to have more inherent power than the normal.

c **XXII 22-35 Balaam's Ass**—This paragraph is not a sequel to the former, since here Balaam is going contrary to God's will and apparently without any escort other than his own two menservants. Possibly this small escort indicates a much shorter journey than that from the Euphrates and we have here part of the other tradition which links Balaam with Midian. The ass sees ' the angel of the Lord ' (notice the difference : it is not ' God ') standing in the track with a drawn sword, and she turns aside to the open country beside the track. The next time, the angel stands in a sunken way between the walls of the vineyards. The princes of Balak reappear in **35b**. Kiriath-huzoth has not been identified : it means ' city of streets '. **36-40.** Balak comes to meet Balaam, and reproves him for his hesitation and delay. The translation ' sacrificed ' (40) is misleading. The verb is used in the ancient sense of slaughter for food. Balak is acting as host and seeing to it that his guests are fed.

d **XXII 41-XXIII 12 Balak's first Attempt to secure an Oracle against Israel**—Balak prepares seven altars and, according to LXX, Balak alone offers the sacrifices (cf. end of 6). Balaam turned away ' quickly ' (**3**: so LXX ; MT has ' to a bare height ', RSV) to meet God. Balaam utters his first oracle (7–10) ; he cannot curse Israel, because God declares otherwise. **10**: for ' fourth part ' read ' dust '.

e **XXIII 13-24 Balak's second Attempt to secure an Oracle against Israel**—The same ritual of altars and burnt-offerings is followed, with Balaam retiring and then returning to utter his oracle. The field of Zophim (i.e. watchers) is some unidentified location near to the top of Mount Pisgah. For ' repent ' (19) it is better to read ' change his mind ', which is the earlier significance of the word. The ' misfortune ' and ' trouble ' (21) of RSV is better than the translations ' iniquity ' and ' perverseness ' of AV and RV. In **22b** read ' He (God) is to them as the curved horns of the wild ox '. **23** is difficult ; the meaning probably is : there is no need of any magic arts of divination in Israel, because God declares his will and manifests his saving work ' at the proper time ' (Rashi : ' when it is required ').

f **XXIII 25-XXIV 9 Balak's third and last Attempt to secure an Oracle against Israel**—The same ritual of altars and burnt-offerings is followed, but this time 226f
Balaam does not retire before he utters his oracle, which now is wholly and emphatically a blessing on Israel. For ' whose eye is opened ' (3, and later 15) read ' grim '. Instead of ' valleys ' (6) read ' palms '. For 8*b*, see 23:22. Instead of 8*d*, read ' smash their limbs ', following Syr.

XXIV 10-19 An additional Oracle for Israel—Balak g
reproves Balaam because his oracles have been unfavourable to him and wholly favourable to Israel. Balaam replies by saying that all along he has declared that he can and will speak nothing but the word which is given him by God. He concludes with an additional, unsolicited oracle telling of the future glory of Israel. **16**: for ' eyes uncovered ', read ' staring eyes '. **17.** The star traditionally is that of David, and hence becomes the star of Messiah. The leader of the last Jewish revolt against the Romans, that in the time of the Emperor Hadrian, was Bar Cozeba, but he changed his name to Bar Cochba (son of the star) as a sign of his messianic claims. He died in A.D. 135, and after his death the Romans created a non-Jewish city in Jerusalem and called it Aelia Capitolina. Cf. Mt. 2:2 and Rev. 22:16. For ' sceptre ' read ' comet '. Instead of ' Sheth ' it is better to follow RV and read ' tumult '. **19**: for ' cities ', read ' Ar ', the well-known Ar of Moab (21:28).

20-25 Oracles against surrounding Nations— h
They deal with Amalek, the Kenites and with an invasion of the Kittim. 22*b* is difficult. There is no record of Assyria deporting the Kenites. It could be a statement concerning a near-certainty which never actually happened, such as the expected capture of Babylon by the Medes, Jer. 51:11 etc. An alternative rendering is ' how long shall I look upon thy dwelling?'
23-24. This oracle is difficult. LXX has no mention i
of ships, but refers to men attacking from the direction of Kittim. Kittim is the ancient Kition in Cyprus. In Dan. 11:30 the reference is undoubtedly to the Romans, and so the Douay Version here, following Vulg., has ' and they shall come in galleys from Italy '. 1 Mac. 1:1 and 8:5 refer to Macedonia. Everything depends on the date of the oracle. If the oracle is 8th or 7th cent. B.C., the invaders may be Cypriots. If the oracle is early enough (13th cent.), it may refer to the sea-people who overran Ugarit. Possibly the oracle is late and may refer to Alexander overthrowing Persia, because we have the strange reference to Asshur and Eber. The Targum suggests that ' Eber ' means beyond the Euphrates, and so means roughly Assyria and the farther east.

XXV The Affair of Baal-peor—There are two 227a
interwoven stories here, one concerning the seduction of the Israelites by the Moabite women, and the other concerning intercourse with Midianite women. The first story is a combined JE-narrative, and concerns the worship of Baal-peor and intercourse with Moabite women. The second story is from the P-tradition. It deals with the immoral and blatant behaviour of the Simeonite Zimri and the Midianite woman Cozbi, followed by the vengeance of Phinehas. The two stories have a combined conclusion in 16–18.

1-5 Baal-peor—This is the local god of Peor, who b
may have been identified by the Moabites with their national god, Chemosh. The site has been identified with Khirbet esh-Sheikh-Jayil, north of Mt Nebo. Shittim means ' the acacia trees ' and was the last stopping-place of the Israelites before they entered Canaan, Num. 33:49. It was from there that Joshua sent out his spies, Jos. 2:1. The Moabite women invited the Israelite men to their sacred feasts. It is misleading to say ' sacrifices ' (2) because the story depends upon recognising that these were sacred meals, whereat the ' slain-offerings ' were eaten, and where often great licence was present, 1 Sam. 1:13. The penalty is given in RSV as ' hang them in the sun ' (4), but the verb probably means ' fling down ' (RS, 2nd ed., 398), and so ' fling them down a cliff in broad daylight ' ; cf. 2 Sam. 21:6, 9, 13. Part of the

227b adverse tradition concerning Balaam is that this misbehaviour was following his advice.

c **6-16 The Vengeance of Phinehas**—The Simeonite leader Zimri openly and brazenly took the woman into his tent and into the alcove, the inner part of the vaulted tent which was the women's quarters. Phinehas seized a spear, rushed into the alcove and pinned them both to the ground. Thus he stays the plague, though 24,000 died. Paul (1 C. 10:8) gives the figure as 23,000. The reward is the covenant of perpetual priesthood. Read 'my covenant as a reward' for 'my covenant of peace' (12). This is the Zadokite priesthood, the only priesthood allowed in Ezek. 40–48. See also Ezr. 7:1–5. The post-exilic priesthood was two-thirds Zadokite and one-third Aaronite. The Zadokites traced their descent back through Eleazar and Phinehas, and the Aaronites through Ithamar. **11.** Both in Greek and in Hebrew the same word is used for 'jealous' and 'zealous'. **13.** 'made atonement for' has become a difficult phrase. The original English was 'to make an at-one-ment', i.e. to reconcile, but the word 'atonement' and the invented verb 'atone' have come to have other and wider meanings in modern English theological terminology. It is best to avoid the term 'atonement' and to use 'reconciliation' in these passages. The Heb. root *k-p-r* originally appears to have meant 'cover', and was used in a religious sense to mean the covering of sin so as to hide it away, take it away, with the result that reconciliation could take place.

d **XXVI The Second Census**—This is from the P-tradition. The first census took place at the beginning of the wandering in the desert; this takes place at the end. Eleazar takes the place of Aaron, now dead. Once more it is a military list: men of twenty years and upwards capable of bearing arms. This time the names of the clans are given, and these are based on the lists in Gen. 46:8–28 of the descendants of Jacob who went down to Egypt. Some of the variations are probably textual corruptions. The chief difference is in the names of the sons of Benjamin. Here Becher is a son of Ephraim (35) and Ard and Naaman are grandsons instead of sons. A comparison of the numbers with those given in ch. 1 shows chiefly a great decrease in the tribe of Simeon, from 59,300 to 22,200 (the smallest), and a large increase in Manasseh, from 32,200 to 52,700.

e **57-62 The Census of the Levites**—The three sons of Levi are as elsewhere: Gershon, Kohath and Merari, and these are the main castes of Levites. In **58** there are given five other levitical families, but the relationship of these to the previous five is not given. These relations vary from list to list. The first four are always grandsons of Levi. In Num. 3 Korah is not mentioned at all, but in 16 he is a great-grandson of Levi and a son of Kohath. The descent of Libni varies: sometimes a son of Merari (1 Chr. 6:20) and sometimes of Gershon (Num. 3:18). The Levites have increased by 10,000. The conclusion (63–65) points out that only two men appear in both census lists, Caleb and Joshua.

f **XXVII 1-11 The Daughters of Zelophehad** (P) —This is the traditional case-law which determines what happens to the property of a man who dies without an heir. One of the fundamental principles of Hebrew society was that landed property shall not pass away from the family. It must continue with the tribe to which it originally belonged. The importance of this is seen in the regulations concerning the Year of Release (Lev. 25), which ensured that landed property reverted to the family in the fiftieth year. It is seen also in the establishment of the so-called Levirate marriage, Dt. 25:5–10, and in the right of redemption on the part of the relative, Jer. 32:6–15. But none of these regulations concerned the destination of the estate of a man who left no sons. The case of the daughters of Zelophehad is the test case. Their father's death was natural. He was an ordinary plain sinner, and was not involved in the desperate and
dreadful sin of Korah and his company. The decision 22
ultimately declared by Moses was: The daughters are to inherit as if they were sons. If the man leaves neither son nor daughter, the property goes to his brother, and failing him to the nearest male kin. The problem is not entirely solved, and a further point is raised by the Gileadites in Num. 36.

12-23 Joshua, Successor to Moses—This also is g
from the P-tradition. Moses is permitted to see the land from afar, but not to enter it. He prays for a successor to be appointed, who is to be their leader in war (17), in all the fighting that lies ahead. Joshua is appointed. **16.** 'God of the spirits of all flesh', i.e. of all mankind, is a late phrase, see 16:22 (§223*b*). The figure of 'sheep without a shepherd' is found also in 1 Kg. 22:17 in Micaiah's vision of Israel after the death of Ahab. **18.** 'The spirit' is that more-than-human power which enables a man to do that which, as a man, he is unable to do. This is the 'mana' of primitive religion. Joshua is already possessed of the 'spirit', so that the laying-on of the hands of Moses is an official commission, publicly investing him with some of the authority of Moses. But he does not absolutely succeed Moses, for God does not speak directly to Joshua as he did to Moses. Eleazar the priest is to seek the will of God on his behalf, and the priest is to use the sacred lot in order to determine the will of God.

XXVIII-XXIX The Offerings on Holy-days— 22
These two chapters are from the P-tradition and specify the actual animals required and the quantities of cereals and liquids needed. The details of the performance of the rites are given elsewhere (e.g. Lev. 1–7). For specified animals and quantities, cf. Lev. 23:5–36, to which much of these chapters is a parallel. The regulations concerning the daily offering varied through the years. Pre-exilic custom in Ahaz's time demanded a morning burnt(whole)-offering and an evening cereal-offering, 2 Kg. 16:15, and in 1 Kg. 18:29 and 36 the evening offering is twice called a *minḥāh* (cereal-offering). But it is not certain that *minḥāh* always had this limited meaning, since the word primarily means 'gift, tribute'. Ezek. 46:13–15 is satisfied with a whole-offering each morning, accompanied by its appropriate cereal-offering. Cf. also Neh. 10:33. Here in Num. 28 we have two whole-offerings daily, with the cereal-offering subsidiary to the whole-offering and the drink-offering supplementing both. **9-10.** On the Sabbath the offerings are doubled. **11-15.** The new-month day. For these days and for all the seven days of the Feast of Unleavened Bread, the statutory offerings are the same, together with one he-goat for a sin-offering, both for these days and all other special days in the list.
16. Passover is mentioned, but no details of special b
offerings are given. The passover lamb was not a Temple sacrifice, since the whole ceremony essentially belonged to the home, and had nothing to do with temple or altar (though in the last days of the Temple the actual slaughtering of the lamb was in the Temple, and the blood was passed up to be thrown at the foot
of the altar). **26.** 'the day of the first fruits' is the c
first day of the Feast of Weeks, the actual Pentecost
of later times. **Chapter 29** deals with the sacrifices of d
the seventh month, the sacred month of the Jewish ecclesiastical calendar. It contains the three sacred occasions into which the pre-exilic Feast of Ingathering was broken. On the first day (the Festival of Trumpets) and on the tenth day (Yom Kippur, Day of Atonement) the offerings consist of one bull (as against two for other special days), one ram and one yearling ram with the same cereal- and drink-offerings as before, together with the usual goat for the sin-offering. These are also the prescribed offerings for the last (eighth) day of Tabernacles, but for the intermediate days, two rams and fourteen yearling rams are offered every day together with the sin-offering (a goat), but the number of bulls varies, from thirteen on the first day to seven on the last, i.e. one bull less each day. These

228d regular public sacrifices are the basis of the sacrificial system, and all vows, freewill-offerings, shared(slain)-offerings are in addition.

e **XXX Vows made by Women**—The theory is that a man is responsible for his own conduct, but a woman is not unless she is a widow or has been divorced. The father is responsible if the woman is not married, the husband if she is married. The man responsible must register his disapproval immediately he hears of the vow. If then he says nothing, the vow stands : he is giving tacit approval. If he declares later that the vow is void (15), then he is deemed to have broken the vow and he must bear the consequences. The objection must be made on the day when he first hears of the vow. This is the only passage where women's vows are dealt with. Other passages deal with vows in general, Lev. 5:4, Num. 6, Dt. 23:21–23. Two types of vows are envisaged : first, a vow to give something to God ; second, a pledge of abstinence. This latter is involved in the phrase ' any binding oath ', since the idea of abstinence is found for this root (' bind ') in Mishnaic Hebrew, Biblical Aramaic (Dan. 6:8) and in Syriac. See also ' to afflict herself ' (13), a phrase which usually means ' fasting '.

229a **XXXI The Massacre of Midian** (P)—Moses, now near death, orders the Israelites to destroy Midian because the Midianite women led the Israelite men astray (25:1–16), with the result that 24,000 men died of the plague. The interweaving of the Baal-peor apostasy and the Midianite plague (ch. 25) is here carried a step farther, and Balaam is held responsible for the Baal-peor apostasy (16). The story is similar to some of the late stories in Chronicles, where the priests take the lead, go out to battle with all the sacred vessels and trumpets of the Sanctuary, and win a complete victory without losing a man, 2 Chr. 20:13–30. Phinehas is in charge of the expedition, perhaps because he was the hero of 25:6–9. Each tribe furnished a thousand men, so that the expedition was evident to all as the action of the whole people. Moses is angry when he hears that they have saved all the women alive because it was the women who led Israel astray in the first instance. He commands that only young virgins shall be kept alive. This involves the complete extinction of Midian as a people. Kill every male of whatever age and every woman who is not a virgin. The victorious Israelites are to stay without the camp for seven days, de-sin themselves on the seventh day, and thus rid themselves of the uncleanness which is involved in contact with a dead body. Everything which will stand fire is to be passed through fire to be cleansed. RSV assumes that these metals shall also be passed through the water for ritual purification (19:9), but the Heb. does not necessarily demand this. It says that there shall also be cleansing with this special water, and that this applies to all objects which cannot be cleansed with fire.

b **25-31 The Division of Booty captured in War**—The precedent is here established, one-half to members of the fighting-force and one-half to the whole people. In 1 Sam. 30:24–25 this rule is said to have been established by David. But here there are additional regulations and all these concern the rights of the priests, and of the Levites. There is to be a levy ' for the Lord ' : one in five hundred from the army for the priests, and one in fifty from the people for the Levites. Muslim custom was to take one-fifth of all the booty, and this fifth belonged to God, to the prophet, to widows and orphans and to the poor generally, *Quran* 8:42.

c **32-47** gives the list of animals and women who survived the massacre, and it gives the totals which were levied for priests and levites, including the women.

d **48-54** Some maintain that every officer and man plundered for himself and took what he could carry, and that this was private booty and did not come into the common stock and is mentioned in 22. But this is not necessarily the case, because the booty mentioned in 42–47 as belonging to the common stock refers only to living creatures, women and animals. 229d
It may well be that ornaments and suchlike did not come into the common stock, and so were not subject to levies for priests and Levites. In this case this paragraph means that the officers were so grateful at not losing a man that they voluntarily surrendered all their private booty and gave it to the Lord, a weight of some 600 lb. of gold.

XXXII 1-32 Reuben and Gad settle east of Jordan—Reuben and Gad wish to settle in the good cattle country east of Jordan. Moses is angry at this request. To him it is the old apostasy which prevented the advance from Paran (Num. 13–15). The result of the old apostasy was that only the two faithful spies were permitted to enter the land out of all who were 20 years old and over. What is to happen now? Another sinful brood of men has grown up in place of their fathers. But Reuben and Gad never intended to desert the other tribes. They will build walled towns for their families and folds for their flocks, and then the fighting-men will lead the van of the invading Israelites till the whole land is conquered. 230a

33-42 List of Towns built by Gad and Reuben— b
Verse 33 is a summary to include not only the Gadite and Reubenite towns but also the Manassite settlements created later in a west–east migration across Jordan. Most of the sites have been identified. Dibon is the modern Dhībân, 4 m. N. of the Arnon ; Ataroth is the modern 'Aṭṭārûs, 8 m. NW. of Dhībân ; Aroer is SE. of Dhībân close by the Arnon. Jazer is the modern Khirbet Jazzir, 15 m. N. of Heshbon ; Jogbehah is the modern Jubeihât, NW. of 'Ammân. Beth-nimrah is possibly Tell Bleibil, 10 m. NW. of Heshbon. Heshbon is 16 m. E. of the mouth of the Jordan where it enters the Dead Sea, and Elealeh is the modern El-'Âl, NE. of Heshbon ; Kiriathaim is 4 m. NW. of Dibon. Nebo is 8 m. E. of the mouth of the Jordan ; Baal-meon is 5 m. S. of Nebo, and Sibmah is probably 3 m. E. of Nebo. **41.** For ' their encampments ' (there is no antecedent in Heb.), read ' the encampments of Ham ', 25 m. E. of Jordan and ESE. of the Sea of Galilee. Jair captured the encampments of Ham and called them the encampments of Jair.

XXXIII From Egypt to Canaan—The list of stop- c
ping-places is composite, some from the JE-tradition, some from the P-tradition, and some from an unknown source. **5-15** is dependent on Exod. 12:37–19:2 except for the unidentified Dophkah and Alush (12–14). **16-36** is largely independent. **37-38** is dependent on 20:22–29. The section **37-49** envisages the march from Kadesh through Edomite territory to the Jordan. For ' Punon ' (43) read ' Pinon ' with the ancient VSS ; it is in northern Edom.

50-56 First destroy all Idols, and then allot the d
Land—' High places ' is the traditional name for the hill-shrines of Canaan. These were taken to be localisations of the great Mount Zaphon (' North '), the distant inaccessible home of the gods. Then the land is to be allotted according to need, but all the Canaanite population is to be driven out lest they contaminate the people of God. All the evidence is that this last did not take place, but that the Hebrews largely intermarried with the Canaanites and took over in large measure their culture and pursuits.

XXXIV 1-15 The Boundaries of Canaan—This is e
P's ideal allocation. The southern boundary runs from the south end of the Dead Sea to where the modern Wâdī el-'Arîsh enters the Mediterranean. The farthest south is Kadesh. There is considerable difference of opinion concerning the northern boundary, since none of the places (Mount Hor, Lebo-hamath, etc.) are certainly identified. Some hold that the ideal border was close to the Lebanon ; others say it was much farther south. On the east the Jordan was the boundary from the Sea of Galilee to the Dead Sea, but all other boundaries are largely conjectural. The ideal nature of the boundaries shows itself in the statement that the Mediterranean is the western boundary all the way from the Wâdī el-'Arîsh as far

230e north as well beyond Carmel. The coast-lands actually were never Israelite territory. The southern part was Philistine, and away in the north the Phoenicians were in control.

f **16-29** gives the names of the princes of the tribes who were responsible for the allocation of the tribal territories.

g **XXXV The Cities of the Levites**—The Levites had no share in the allocation of the country by lot. They were therefore to have cities granted to them out of the lots of the tribes. Each property consisted of a square of about 207 acres with the city in the middle of it. There were to be 48 such cities, of which 6 were to be cities of refuge. It is possible that the 6 cities of refuge are historical, but the 48 levitical cities look like an ideal put forward by a later enthusiastic ecclesiastic. There is no historical evidence that the scheme was ever put into practice.

h **9-15 The Cities of Refuge**—3 of these 6 cities were east of the Jordan and 3 were west of the Jordan. In old Israel the next-of-kin had the duty of exacting vengeance for the death of his kinsman. This involved the slaying of the homicide. Evidently in early times no distinction was made between accidental death and murder. This law seeks to introduce modifications, and to distinguish between accidental and deliberate killing. If the homicide could reach a city of refuge, he could be assured of a fair trial.

i **16-34 The Trial of the Homicide**—What is murder? Striking with any sort of lethal weapon in the hand; stabbing in hatred; lying in ambush, or even striking and killing with a blow of the hand in enmity: all this is murder, and the next-of-kin must kill the homicide when he meets him. In all other cases (accidental death, and death by misadventure) the homicide is safe till the death of the high-priest provided he stays within the city of refuge. If the next-of-kin meets him 23
outside the city, he may kill him. At the death of the high-priest the homicide may return home. Evidently it was not yet possible to take the right of execution for murder out of the hands of the individual. Nor was it possible entirely to deny the right of vengeance even in the case of accidental death. Further, one witness is not enough on a capital charge. Also, no money payment may be accepted for a murderer or a homicide. These laws admit of no relief. The murderer must die, because unavenged blood that has been shed pollutes the land and the land cannot be cleansed except by the blood of the murderer.

XXXVI Zelophehad's Daughters again—The law j
concerning heiresses (Num. 27:1–11) did not entirely clear away the difficulty. If the daughters inherit by their own right, what happens if they marry outside the tribe? If they marry outside their tribe, the tribe loses the property, since it is only purchased land which reverts to the owner at the Year of Release. The answer is the obvious one. The heiresses are free to marry where they will, but only within their father's tribe. In this way the land is retained within the tribe. The five daughters of Zelophehad married their cousins and all was well.

Bibliography—COMMENTARIES: B. Baentsch, HKAT (1903); L. E. Binns, WC (1927); A. Dillmann, KEH (2nd ed. 1886); T. E. Espin, Speaker's Bible (1871); G. B. Gray, ICC (1903); H. Holzinger, KHC (1903); A. R. S. Kennedy (Cent.B); A. H. McNeile, CB (1911); J. Marsh and A. G. Butzer, IB (1953); R. A. Watson, Ex.B (1894).

OTHER LITERATURE: Articles in EB, GAB, HDB and IB; G. A. Smith, *Historical Geography of the Holy Land.*

DEUTERONOMY

By G. HENTON DAVIES

231a **Name**—Deuteronomy is the English form of the Gr. *Deuteronomion* (it does not occur in classical Gr., Vulg. *Deuteronomium*), taken from the LXX rendering of Dt. 17:18, where 'a copy of this law' is in Gr. inaccurately translated 'this repetition of the law', this *Deuteronomion*. In post-biblical Heb. the book is known by its first two Heb. words: These (are the) words, or simply, Words, etc.

Place in the Canon—It occurs in the Heb. and in modern Bibles as the fifth book of the Hebrew Law, i.e. the Pentateuch, the five books of Moses, the first five books of the OT.

Contents—Israel has arrived in the Plains of Moab and is about to enter the promised land. At this point Moses now delivers a series of addresses to Israel, and it is these with various additions and appendices which make up the book. The record covers a period of forty days only (cf. 1:3 and Jos. 4:19). The speeches are in turn made up of reminiscences, sacred stories, anticipatory legislation, preached law, songs, blessings, appeals, warnings and threats, and some historical traditions and notices.

First Address 1:1-4:43—1:1–5 are introduction; 1:6–3:29 speak of the journey from Horeb to Jordan; 4:1–40 contain practical and theocentric exhortations and 4:41–3 provide for new cities of refuge.

Second Address 4:44-28:68—4:44–9 are an introduction; 5:1–11:32 set forth the divine commandments and covenant; 12:1–26:19 set forth the laws, and chs. 27f. various traditions and ceremonies concerning these laws.

Third Address 29:1-30:20—The choice for Israel.

Appendices 31:1-34:12—Ch. 31 is mainly concerned with Moses' final arrangements for Israel; 31:30–32:47 The Song of Moses; 32:48–52 speak of his approaching end; 33:1–29 The Blessing of Moses, and 34:1–12 his death and burial.

b **The Appraisal of the Book**—The approach to Dt. must reckon among other things with the following facts:

(*a*) The account of itself given in the book. (i) The speeches and laws are not spoken by God, as is normally the case in the other law books, where God speaks to Moses, etc., but they are spoken directly by Moses to Israel. This in spite of the tradition that he was not a speaker (Exod. 4:10–17). (ii) The occasion is the eve of the entry into Canaan, and the scene the border of the land. (iii) It is stated at Dt. 31:9 that this law was delivered later to the priests, the sons of Levi. (iv) Verses in the book reveal a standpoint west of Jordan, i.e. in the land (cf. 1:1, 3:11), and a time long after the days of Moses (Dt. 34:10–12).

(*b*) Style—The characteristic preaching style is uniform throughout the book, and is marked by a variety of distinctive words and phrases showing affinity with the E stratum of the Pentateuch, and with such prophets as Hosea and especially Jeremiah. There are also distinctive theological features in reference to God, Israel, the single sanctuary and the diagnosis of idolatry, etc.

(*c*) The Tradition concerning the Book—2 Kg. 22f. relate that a law book was discovered during the renovation of the Temple in Jerusalem in the reign of Josiah. Early Christian fathers identified this book as Dt.

The Critical Appraisal—The scientific appraisal of Dt. began with the work of De Wette who claimed that the main part of D (see §137*a*) had been composed shortly before its discovery in Josiah's reign, i.e. 621. This thesis soon prompted such questions as: How much of our present D was discovered? What was the relation between D and Josiah's reform? What were the real character and purpose of the book? One hundred and fifty years of investigation have yielded many theories, but the main result and tendency of the discussion can be fairly stated. 231c

Minority opinions apart, as e.g. those which separate the book from Josiah's reform, it is true to say that more scholars have seen the book as the origin of the reform than as the deposit from the reform, and a book which underwent more than one later revision. The D of the reform may have been only chs. 12–26 and 28, but more probably as much as 4:44–30:20. That 621 is the 'publication' date of D is still the most widely held view, and the composition date cannot be very far from the days of Josiah. The linguistic and conceptual similarities with the 8th-cent. prophets, and especially with Jeremiah, point to a composition date some time after the 'bookless' reform of Hezekiah, or in the reign of Manasseh. But behind these dates there lies a long history of transmission and interpretation of really ancient material in the book.

The credit for new insights into D goes back to Adam Welch who traced material in D to the early monarchy and even earlier. Welch's view of the early character of typical D material has proved substantially sound, but has remained to some extent neglected because it was combined with a doubtful interpretation of Dt. 12:1–7. It is on Welch's lines that the most important work on D has continued, even leading some to think of D as the foundation document of Solomon's Temple, or even as the law book laid up by Samuel at Mizpah (1 Sam. 10:25). It is thus probable that the real future of the study of D lies along these lines. First, there is the long history of priestly transmission by which early material, with no doubt Mosaic utterance as the original oral nucleus, supplemented by traditions and usages from Shechem, were handed on and expanded in northern circles. D material may thus be dated from the days of Moses to those of Manasseh. Secondly, a date of composition or editing possibly in prophetic circles such as Isaiah's disciples, but more probably priestly circles, as Dt. 31:9 suggests. Von Rad has shown that such priestly circles would not be those of Jerusalem but were from the north. D may well be the work of a single Levitical preacher who was either the founder of the well-known style or its outstanding exponent. Thirdly, there is the publication or appearance date of 621 in Jerusalem, with the adding of further material such as the Appendices soon after. D may no longer be conceived as a point on a date line, but as a stream of material, whose source is Moses, whose course was through some sanctuary like Shechem, and whose outlet, after diversion from the north, was the Temple at Jerusalem. d

This conception of D as a stream rather than a gusher involves the modification of the so-called comparative dating of D as after J and E and as before P. Rather is D the tradition of an independent use and e

231e theology existing in a northern sanctuary. The differences between D and other law codes are thus not those of chronological development but of geographical apartness, illustrating what happened at different sanctuaries, and are not to be judged in the light of some conception of unilinear development. [For a different view, see §69c.—H.H.R.]

Again it is more profitable to think of D as the first book of the material which extends from Dt. to 2 Kg. than as the last book of the Pentateuch. Just as Gen. to Num. is the P ' Bible ', so Dt. to 2 Kg. is the D ' Bible ', and Dt. itself is the introduction to this D ' Bible '. Thus Dt. has to be interpreted in the light of the period covered by the so-called D ' Bible '. In turn this view has solved the problem of the two introductions which now stand at the beginning of Dt., viz. chs. 1–4 and 5–11. The latter is the introduction to Dt. proper, whereas 1–4 is the introduction to the D ' Bible ' or History. These illustrations from the study of D show the interesting possibilities for further study of the place and aim of the work.

f **Teaching**—S. R. Driver's summary of the religious principles of the book remains basic. He emphasises the book's teaching concerning the solity and spirituality of the Lord, the holiness of Israel, the one sanctuary, the one priesthood and with reservation the one law book. Then there must be added G. E. Wright's valuable account of the book as the exposition of the gospel of Israel's faith set in the framework of the divine law as the revealed order for Israel's society. Among other things he also emphasises the ' theology of inheritance ' which underlies much of the book. Von Rad had previously emphasised the sacral traditions and homiletical interpretations. Also he drew special attention to the traditions concerning the Ark and the Name of God from the amphictyonic sanctuary at Shechem, and the revival of the theology of the Holy War from ancient Israel in the days of Josiah.

g Yet the purpose and character of the book are best seen as the attempt to relate the Mosaic faith of Israel to the new life in Canaan. What happens to the little community of Israel, divinely redeemed and covenanted by God, when it enters the way of the world? Dt. is thus concerned to show what problems arise when simple faith meets complex living conditions. It is thus the evaluation of a social, military and political transition from nomadism to agriculture in the light of a theistic faith. Religion and progress set the problem. Dt. shows that the immediate if temporary cost of progress is idolatry. Dt. is supremely the book of the diagnosis and evaluation of idolatry, and it is that because it is also completely theocentric as 10:12–22 show. Placed at the head of the D ' Bible ' the book thus offers a retrospect of the centuries covered by the D History in the form of an anticipatory prospect of those same centuries on the eve of the settlement in Canaan. Dt. is thus a judgment on Israel's history in Canaan in the form of a sermonic anticipation of that history, or an evaluation of Israel's history in the guise of a sermonic sketch of a new order of life and society.

h It follows that its warnings and prohibitions are in fact the mirror of the bitter experiences of the evils of Canaan, its promises and demands largely the benefits of the settlement in Canaan. The book thus aims at showing how Israel's covenant faith, born in the desert, is yet compatible with and possible in the more advanced and wealthier life in Canaan. This is the real meaning and relevance of the ' crossing to inherit the land ' theme of the book. It will thus be seen that Dt. did for Israel in the new life in Canaan what still remains to be done for the Christian faith as it crosses over into the industrial and atomic age. In that sense it is not merely an exposition of Israel's faith and so on, but in the position it faces, the solution it applies, and the method in which this solution is applied, the book is both a parallel and an example to the Christian preacher in his contemporary tasks. So finally it is not enough to say that Dt. is preached law, or an exposition of Israel's faith, or the revelation of a revealed order of society. The book is not only a period piece, 23
for its aim is to redeem and safeguard the contemporary Israel to which it is addressed. Dt. is not merely a story, it is a saving story. Likewise it is not merely in its law a revealed order, it is saving law, law designed through obedience to convey life and blessing. Dt. is *Heilsgeschichte* (sacred story) in the framework of *Heilsgesetz* (sacred law), saving story in the context of saving law. Words from this book succoured Jesus in his temptations on the eve of his ministry, as it can succour us on the threshold of this new age. 10:12–22 are the quintessence of that theocentric faith, and 8:12–14, 17–18 are the precise revelation for the welfare state.

I 1-5 A Preface to the Book—These verses transmit 23
traditions of the occasion and the scene of the words of Moses. The occasion is the end of the wilderness wanderings after Moses' victories over the kings Sihon and Og. **3**, probably a note introduced by the Priestly editor, gives the occasion as the first day of the eleventh month of the fortieth year following the departure from Egypt, six months after Aaron's death (Num. 33:38). The scene is thus the wilderness beyond Jordan in the Arabah in the land of Moab. But the place names in 1*b* and the route of the journey in 2 are most naturally understood not of places in Moab, but as fragments of Israel's desert itinerary belonging to a separate tradition.

1 The words are not the contents of Exod.-Num., but of Dt. **All Israel,** a D description conveying a theological and cultic ideal; **beyond the Jordan,** that is, the verse depicts the standpoint of somebody west of Jordan in Canaan itself. The Arabah is the deep cleft in which Jordan flows and the area of the Dead Sea and southwards. Suph, probably Gulf of 'Aqaba; Paran is the wilderness of Sinai corresponding to et-Tih, but is unknown; Tophel uncertain; Laban and Di-zahab unknown; Hazeroth according to Num. 11:35, 33:17, a wilderness station.

2 Horeb (E, D) or Sinai (J, P) is commonly identified with Jebel Mûsā, though some would locate Horeb in the neighbourhood of Kadesh Barnea ('Ain Qedeis) or on the eastern shore of the Gulf of 'Aqaba. Modern travellers have taken about eleven days to journey from Jebel Mûsā to 'Ain Qedeis. The route here described is the most easterly from the Sinai peninsula. **5. undertook to explain:** took upon himself to expound or explain. What follows is at least an exposition or commentary. **this law:** that is, the revelation of the will of the Lord contained in the book. The word is one of the principal key words of the book.

I 6-III 29—This first part of Moses' first speech b
recalls the principal events of the sacred story of Israel's days in the desert. All Israel is reminded of what God has done for them, of their own failures, and of Moses' intercession on their behalf.

I 6-8 Departure and Entry—Whereas Exod. 33:1–6 (almost certainly) depict Israel's departure from the mount as an expulsion, this verse describes how God bids Israel leave Horeb in order to possess the promised land, though the Heb. idiom may suggest more than merely that Israel had been at the mount long enough. **The LORD** (i.e. capitals to show the Heb. has YHWH). **10. your God:** D's frequent use of the possessive pronouns, ' our ', ' thy ', ' your ', portrays the confident and ardent bond of the covenant which binds the Lord and Israel. He is our God and we are the people of his pasture (Ps. 95:7). The usage may be rooted in patriarchal religion, as Albright suggests.

7 Amorites: so E and D for pre-Israelite inhabitants of hill country east and west of Jordan. **lowland:** the Shephelah, the foothills between the Judaean ' hill country ' and the maritime plain; **South:** the Negeb—southern extension of Palestine; **Canaanites:** inhabitants of the northern sea coast. The Euphrates is the border of the promised land. Compare the extent of the territory, no doubt reflecting the Davidic empire, with the extent of the land promised in e.g. Gen. 13:14–17. God having given life to Abraham

2b and his wife, and out of that life built up his people Israel, has now provided for that people a land, the promised land. Here are the foundation themes of the Hexateuch.

c **9-18 Moses organises Israel**—Exod. 18:13–27 relates how Jethro provided the plan for the organising of Israel before the covenant at Sinai. D does not mention Jethro, and appears to put the event after the covenant and just prior to the departure. It is the founder-leader Moses, who, too much burdened by all the problems of Israel's life, puts into operation this plan of delegated judicial function, reserving the hardest cases for himself. **10. Multitude:** an obvious proof of divine blessing; **15. heads of your tribes . . . officers:** there are several ranks of officials from head men to officers, organisers. Officials and people alike are charged with the several responsibilities and the plan is put into operation at Horeb.

d **19-46 Rebellion and Rejection**—These verses recapitulate the stories of Num. 13, 14, 21:1–3. In D the people propose the mission of the spies and Moses assents, and the spies bring back a good report. In P, Num. 13:1–3, God proposes the mission, and though the spies bring back a good report of the land yet ten of the twelve advise the people not to advance into Canaan. Only Caleb and Joshua urge the attack on the land. The story in D is not meant to be a historical record, but an illustration in a sermon. The real point is not even disobedience but murmuring and rebellion as the proof of a lack of faith. Israel refuses to trust their king, and cannot believe he will accomplish his purpose for them. So their doubt transforms the Exodus into an act of God's wrath designed for their destruction, melts their courage and their faith and changes the people and cities of the land into unconquerable and impregnable forces. The Anakim are known as a tribal name from Egyptian Execration texts of the early 2nd millennium. They were apparently a tribe of tall people in the Hebron area. Thus though Moses reminds them that God is their Warrior Guide, the doubt of the people leads to their doom, and only a remnant, Caleb and Joshua, of the men of that generation were allowed to enter the land. Not even Moses entered.

At first sight it might appear that Moses was unfairly treated, for he had endeavoured to dispel the doubt of the people. Moses is elsewhere condemned for having infringed the honour of God (Num. 20:11–12 (P); cf. Dt. 32:50–2). Yet the passage is revealing in showing how the life and fortunes of Israel are vested in Moses so that their fate is his fate. Wright sees in this passage the germ of the ideas of Isa. 53, and there is of course a parallel in Exod. 32:32, where intercession is made with life as well as words.

The people's attempt to save the situation is itself contrary to the will of God. Their doom is confirmed in the abortive attempt to invade the land, and in their enforced sojourn at Kadesh.

e **II 1-25 On the Way to the Promised Land**—In his sermon the preacher now recollects some features of Israel's journey, which illustrate how the Lord, who has promised Canaan to Israel, has also made other territorial allocations, and these must be respected by Israel.

The varying traditions of the place of the 38 or 40 years' sojourn, in JE in and about Kadesh, in D between Kadesh and the south of Mt Seir, in P in the desert of Paran, could probably be reconciled if the traditions were more detailed. Not so easy to explain, however, is P's route in Num. 33, whereby Israel passes from Kadesh on the north side of Mt Seir through Punon, where D like E takes them on the south side of Mt Seir and along the eastern border of Moab. So D makes Israel depart from 'Aqaba, from Elath, probably known later as Ezion Geber, through Wâdī Yitm.

3 Turn northward: as Israel embraces a second opportunity to enter the land, they are to respect the territories they pass. The Lord has given Mt Seir to Edom (5), Ar to the Moabite sons of Lot (9), and the
land of Ammon to the Ammonite sons of Lot (19). 232a
This conception of divine allocation is in the Song of Moses described as the work of El Elyon (Dt. 32:8), a pre-Israelite God of Jerusalem, so that the conception may be a part of Canaanite theology, inherited by Israel, or paralleled in Israel by the thought of the Lord's allocations of territory (cf. 2:5, 12, 19, 3:20, etc. and the words 'inheritance' (previous references), 'portion' or 'share' (Dt. 12:9, 18:1), 'region' or 'lot' (Dt. 3:4, etc.)).

9 Ar, uncertain. The antiquarian notices in 10–12 f
and 20–3 relate how the Moabites had displaced the Emim (similar to Anakim), how the Edomites displaced the Horites (who were not cave-dwellers, but representatives of the Hurrian people who lived after 1600 B.C. in the country of Mitanni along the route of Abraham's journey from Ur to Haran), how the Ammonites displaced the Zamzummim, and how the Philistines from Crete displaced the Avvim. All these earlier peoples apart from Horites were Rephaim (also shades of the dead in Sheol) who were probably an early race of giants in Palestine.

These earlier displacements prepare us now for the beginning of Israel's military action in conquering certain Transjordan kings, whose misfortune it is to live in the territory divinely allocated to Israel.

II 26-III 11 Sihon and Og—Sihon refuses Israel's 233a
request for peaceful transit, and in the attempt to prevent Israel's passage, loses his life and his kingdom. All the inhabitants were put to the ban, that is, utterly destroyed as a sacrifice to the Lord, and their land from Arnon to Jabbok became Israel's possession. The ban (utter destruction, 2:34 and 3:6) is one of the features of The Holy War (see espec. 20:10–18). Next the same fate befell Og, king of Bashan and northern Gilead. These kingdoms, like Moab and Edom, were probably founded in the 13th cent. following the interval after the break up of the city-state system of Amarna days.

II 26 Kedemoth: a Levitical city in Reuben (Jos. b
13:18) near the upper reaches of Arnon. **Heshbon:** Sihon's capital about 16 miles east of Jordan, half-way between Arnon and Jabbok. **32. Jahaz:** probably between Dibon and Medeba; **36. the city in the valley** could of course be Ar. Gilead is on both sides of the Jabbok. **III 1.** Bashan was famous for its pastures, cattle and oak forests. **4.** Argob is some region of Bashan. Israel's double victory gave them control of Transjordan from under Hermon to Arnon. Og was a survivor of the Rephaim and his height is shown by the length of his bedstead of iron (11), possibly a sarcophagus of basalt, which was 9 × 4 cubits of a man, i.e. full cubits, something like 13½ ft. × 6 ft.

III 12-22 Moses assigns Transjordan to the Two and a Half Tribes—To the Reubenites and Gadites he gave the area between Arnon and Jabbok, which includes the part of Gilead south of Jabbok. To the half-tribe of Manasseh and its leading clan Machir he gave northern Gilead and Bashan. 14–17 repeat the information of 12f. and are probably a later insertion, for by Num. 32:41 Jair's work was done in Gilead and not as here in Bashan. **14.** Jair was probably a descendant of Manasseh, and Geshur and Maacah two Aramaean tribes on the western border of Bashan (cf. Jos. 12:5, 13:11 and 1 Chr. 2:23). **17. From Chinnereth . . . Salt Sea** describes the length of Jordan from the Sea of Galilee to the northern end of the Dead Sea overlooked by Pisgah from the east.

18 I commanded you means, of course, these tribes, and not all Israel. They are bidden to assist in the conquest of Canaan before settling with their families in Transjordan. God's plan and their efforts will achieve God's purpose, the rest or peace of Israel in Canaan. God's activity in Transjordan will be the prototype and assurance of God's victory in Canaan.

23-29 Moses' Last Request—In the many stories of c
the meetings of the Lord and Moses, the latter had made many requests of his God. He had on the day

233c of his call enquired into the mystery of the name of God (Exod. 3:13). At the height of the crisis in Sinai, he had prayed to be vouchsafed a vision of the glory of God (33:18), and now when the work of his lifetime was almost complete he asked that he might complete his work and enter and view the promised land. Instead of his name God gave Moses what is apparently a circumlocution—I am what I am—and instead of his Glory God revealed his Goodness—his Back (33:23). So now to enter is forbidden, but to behold is granted. Moses is too much bound with the doomed Israel of the desert to avoid their fate. But to him is this extra grace given that he may see afar off the end of his mission, whilst Joshua brings about the possession of the land.

28 Charge Joshua: command, that is, commission or appoint.

29 Beth-peor: uncertain. It lies in one of the valleys debouching into the Jordan plain, where Israel was encamped, where Moses made the speeches and where at last he died.

d **IV 1-40—And now:** these words introduce the second part of the sermon, and show how the preacher has turned from the past to the present, from the illustrations to the tasks, from the story to the moral. Israel must now work out her salvation with fear and trembling. The chapter is essentially a unity, and belongs integrally to 1–3, and together 1–4 are, as we have seen, the introduction not merely to Deuteronomy but to the whole Deuteronomic history. So 4:25–31 are not a later addition, but an essential part of such an introduction.

1-8 The Mark of Israel: Statutes and Ordinances—D uses these words and, frequently, this phrase, as synonyms for the divinely revealed law; **teach:** that I am about to teach you. The stories of 1–3 are saving stories which are to be told, the laws likewise are saving laws which need to be taught, and learnt and obeyed. Saving laws when kept confer life, and life is the proof of God's blessing. To add to or to take from the law is forbidden, but this prohibition is probably a metaphor of exact and complete fulfilment, rather than a definition of the quantity of the law. The context stresses not the exact identity or quantity but the fulfilling of the law. Of that obedience the incident at Baal Peor (Num. 25) is now quoted as an illustration. Idolatry is not only disobedience but death, but true worship is covenant and life.

The ground for obedience to the law is the uniqueness of Israel among the nations, and this uniqueness is threefold: (*a*) Israel possesses a divinely revealed law; (*b*) Israel's law is more righteous than any other law; (*c*) Israel enjoys the nearness of God, a nearness which is manifested in the hearing of prayer.

e **9-14 Teaching**—These verses begin with the word 'only' which is a Heb. restrictive particle to isolate the essential point. If laws are to be remembered and performed, then salvation stories must be remembered and told, especially to the children. This is how the life and soul of Israel are maintained. Israel lives on and by its gospel.

At once the preacher turns back to the central theme of his gospel: Horeb with all its glory of fire and darkness and cloud—a condescending Presence, invisible as to form, but luminous in spoken revelation—the assembled people knit by covenant and life to their God—the ten commandments, given at Sinai, embraced by the people, the law of Israel's life in Canaan and for ever. How rich the passage is too in its devotional diction; for it speaks of the gathered people, the hearing of the word, the lifelong lessons for themselves and their children in godly fear or reverence, the drawing near to God and standing to wait upon him.

15-24 One Form of Idolatry—For D to think of his God is soon to recall the alternative—the worship of somebody or something other than their God. At Horeb they saw no form, therefore they must never worship anything that can be seen. All likenesses of all things, human, animal, bird, fish and heavenly body are excluded. Even if a divine providence has 23
allocated underling gods to other nations, Israel is for God. Here again, no doubt, is a trace of that Canaanite High God theology, for the thought is really inconsistent with the main tenor of the passage. God is a burning fire which seeks out and destroys the alternative, for he is a jealous God who brooks no rival.

25-31 The Consequence of Idolatry—These verses, f
for so long and by so many considered to be an exilic interpolation, rather express the logical consequences of the D point of view. As life goes on in the richer land of Canaan, idolatry and the corruption of sin will result in their exile from the promised land. Many will die, but a small remnant will be dispersed among the lands, where idolatry, at first their free choice, will become their unavoidable fate. But in time this fate will set up another chain reaction. The tribulation of exile will incline the sufferers towards God, will promote obedience and the discovery that God is merciful and stands by his covenant. God has created Israel, so that there ever remains within them a nucleus of imperishable life which can be revived. God is faithful.

32-40 The Theocentric Art—The preacher moves on g
piling up his arguments. 31 with its 'for' gives the ground of his confidence—the nature of God. 32 begins with another 'for' which is not so much parallel to the 'for' of 31 as explicative of 31. God is a merciful, faithful, remembering God, and this is true because he condescended to reveal himself at Horeb, and previous to that had rescued them from Egypt. The God who speaks and saves is the true God. Revelation and redemption show that Yahweh is God. But still the proofs of God's mercy come. God taught from heaven and out of the fire at Horeb. God loved the patriarchs and chose their descendants, rescued them from Egypt, and settled them in Canaan. Here are the themes of Israel's gospel. They have taken centuries to fulfil, only heaven and earth last long enough to witness the unfolding of the story. So Israel must consider that there is none beside God. It is idle to discuss the significance of these words in terms of a monotheistic concept, or of the influence of the second Isaiah and so on. Here rather is an expression of Israel's art, her theocentric faith, which revels in her God. This theocentric art underlies many parts of the OT and comes to clear expression in several places.

41-43 Three Cities of Refuge beyond Jordan—A historical note of Moses' action and not a report of his words. The verses are an appendix; see 19:1–13.

44-49 Second Preface—These verses are another 234
preface before the main portion of D, in which the following material is identified as from Moses (44f.), and in which the place and the occasion of the words of Moses are described in detail greater than that of the first preface in 1:1-5.

V 1-XI 32—What is represented as a second and the principal speech of Moses and as introductory to the laws of 12–26, really consists of a series of probably separate sermons in which a number of familiar themes recur. The Levitical preacher constantly seeks to bring his congregation to a double vantage point. He bids them remember who they are and to recall the covenant mercies of God to them. He thus takes them back to Horeb, or brings Horeb to them. Thus ch. 5 is a foundation chapter recollecting and recapitulating the faith of God's people. But the Levitical preacher continually calls to his congregation, which in fact is at worship in some shrine in Canaan, to go back to that moment when the people were about to enter the God-promised and God-given land. This crossing theme—or entering theme—is a constant feature of the sermons. So the preacher is occupied with Israel and its faith as it is about to enter Canaan. What happens to Israel when it enters the way of the world? What happens to the country cousins when they come up to town? What happens to the covenanted Israel of Horeb when it seeks to live its

234a life as God's people in the new, unfamiliar land which flows with milk and honey?

b **V 1-21 The Ten Commandments**—At a time which is ostensibly that of 4:44–9, but which was probably an occasion of the renewal of the covenant by Israel at an amphictyonic shrine, there is the story of the giving of the Ten Commandments. The preacher's identity is veiled in the name of Moses, and the assembly is described as the Israel of Horeb. Of course according to 1:35–9, and 2:14, that Israel of Horeb was dead, but in this passage that Israel is still alive. For some commentators this means that the author of the first speech must be different from the author of the second speech. But it seems better to suppose that each generation of Israel is thought of as Israel, and to realise that a preacher could claim that though the Israel of Horeb was dead, yet the covenant of Horeb was made with each contemporary Israel. But such a view carries with it the idea of an actual service of renewal in which the words would be appropriate.

In 6 God himself speaks and gives the revelation of the Ten Commandments in an address which is singular, though the context of the chapter is plural. The historical sections are mainly plural, and the hortatory mainly singular, but such differences do not permit the idea of separate sources. Israel is the one people of God composed of many Israelites and the speaker oscillates from singular to plural according to his mood, his purpose and the warmth of his utterance.

c **6 I am the Lord your God who . . .**: Vischer has finely described these divine utterances couched in the first person as the Auto-Kerygma of the OT. 'I am Yahweh thy God' is probably the most comprehensive clause of scripture, and as such the preacher lays it upon the souls of his hearers. The self-predication continues in the English relative clause which describes the divine deliverance from Egypt. So sacred story is the prelude to sacred law, for the divine Saviour and the divine Lawgiver are one and the same person. The purpose of the Exodus and of the lawgiving is also one—it is to save Israel. For God who has delivered Israel must needs now direct Israel's way so as to preserve his saved community. *Heilsgeschichte* and *Heilsgesetz* belong together as of grace.

Only specially D points will be noticed in what follows, as the exegesis of the Decalogue belongs to Exod. 20:1–17.

d **9b-10** almost certainly contain a part of a credal confession which was of ancient usage in Israel's worship.

The fourth commandmant varies from the Exod. version. D has 'keep' instead of 'remember', and there are unimportant additions in 12*b* and 14. Whereas P in Exod. 20:11 links the Sabbath with the creation according to his theories, D in 5:15 links the Sabbath with the Exodus. D's treatment illustrates his historical and humanitarian interests, and connects the first four commandments, concerned as they are with Israel's duty to God, with the remainder which directs Israel's duty to itself.

In 5:15 there is again the well-known phrase 'a mighty hand and an outstretched arm'. This may be a metaphor of the divine activity, but in view of Dt. 34:10–12, the phrase may be an incognito for Moses himself. Indeed one wonders whether Moses did not himself coin the phrase to describe his own role in the Exod. story. It is possible then that this traditional phrase represents some words and thoughts of Moses himself.

There are additional words in D's version of the fifth commandment, but commandments 6–9 are virtually the same, except that D has a different word (meaning 'vain') for 'false' in the ninth commandment. In the tenth commandment D not only promotes the wife to the first place, but places her in a class by herself (cf. 21:10–14, 22:13ff., 24:1ff.).

e **22-33**—This passage is based on Exod. 20:18–21. The Exod. passage probably describes a section of the people who were unfamiliar with the Mount, and who would not go near it, whereas that section of the people 234e
described in Exod. 19:21 had to be restrained from walking on the Mount as was their custom. The comparison of those two Exod. traditions suggests the confluence at Horeb of two different groups of people. But in D the condition is used to emphasise the unique position of Moses in the covenant-making at Horeb (cf. Gal. 3:19; 1 Tim. 2:5; Heb. 8:6, 9:15, 12:24).

VI 1-3 Transition—5:31 has prepared the way for further teaching. The preacher turns from the revelation in the past to the duty in the future before them. The God-centred life of Israel at Horeb is to be maintained in Canaan.

4-19 Israel's Faith and Duty—These verses begin f
with a call to obedience and a promise as the reward of that obedience which introduce the *Sh^{e}ma'*, the 'Hear, O Israel', the basic Israelite confession of faith. The words 'the Lord our God is one Lord' represent four Heb. words which may be translated as RVm in four different ways. The words either emphasise the unity of the Lord (the Lord is single and is the single object of Israel's devotion) or may also declare the uniqueness of the Lord, who is the exclusive object of Israel's devotion. It is not really possible to tell whether it is the idea of unity in God or the uniqueness of God over against other deities, which is the dominant thought of this creed; though the first is more likely, those ideas are to some extent controlled by a monotheistic interest, so that it is practically equivalent to the first commandment, but a first commandment restated in the light of Israel's experience of Canaanite deity.

In 5 Israel is bidden to love this Lord completely, g
the Lord who has previously shown them his election love by redeeming Israel from Egypt. For God is lovable and can transform even the inability to love into the capacity to love God. Love in this divinely orientated dimension is also charged with reverence and awe, for such love inevitably takes on something of the character of the person who is loved. It was thus some unknown Levitical preacher who canonised in scripture the idea of love to God, and whose insight was crowned by the Lord Christ himself who made it also the first law of his kingdom.

with all your heart means, of course, the whole mind and will; **the soul** is the vital self—the man himself; and **with all your might** is a metaphor of the superlative, completely. Israel must possess herself of these words by meditation, by instruction of the children, and by wearing them in prayer and by hanging them on their door posts and gates. These last two instructions are the origin of the *t^{e}phillîn* (frontlets) and *m^{e}zûzāh* of later times. The instructions may have been intended metaphorically at first, but were later fulfilled ritually, but when the change took place is not known. The Jews wrote 6:4–9, 11:13–21 and Exod. 13:1–10, 11–16 on small scrolls secreted in small containers and worn on the person or attached to the dwelling as directed.

10-15 The Faith and the Transition—Now Israel h
is warned lest settlement in the land with all ensuing benefits will cause her to forget God. The warning, of course, conveys the grim fact that this is exactly what Israel did do in Canaan. But see ch. 8 for a fuller treatment of the same theme, that increasing prosperity can mean idolatry.

16-19 Recurrent Problem of Massah—The preacher adduces a historical illustration based on Exod. 17:1–7. The reference could be either to a doubt concerning God's sovereign provision, or more characteristically, concerning the reality of God's Presence with Israel (Exod. 17:7).

20-25 Scripture Lesson—The meaning of the laws is to be found in the story of Israel's deliverance from Egypt. God rules and preserves his people through his laws. It is by obedience to these laws that Israel has maintained her life in Canaan, and that obedience is Israel's righteousness, or rather vindication or justifica-

234h tion. Thus in an embryonic catechetical form the faith and duty of Israel before God was transmitted to each generation.

235a **VII Israelites and their Neighbours**—The Levitical preacher returns to his transition theme and takes his hearers back in imagination to the eve of their entry into the promised land. He instructs his people in the duties proper to that situation. They are to destroy their idolatrous neighbours, to have no dealings of any kind such as commerce or matrimony, and they are to destroy the shrines and their contents.

The command to destroy utterly, that is to put to the ban, the different peoples of Canaan seems at first to be a blot upon the humanitarian outlook of D. This command is given in order to prevent idolatry. Now for D idolatry can only have one outcome and that is the destruction of Israel. It is through idolatry and only through idolatry that Israel can destroy itself and thus bring to naught God's purpose for Israel. The choice before D then was either to live with these peoples of Canaan, which would inevitably bring about idolatry and so the death of Israel, or to destroy these peoples and so remove the greatest cause of idolatry. It is more evil to be idolatrous than to slay these peoples. Thus the real meaning of idolatry for D begins to be clear for us, even though many moral difficulties in the command remain.

b It must however be remembered that the preacher was only laying down what he considered to be the ideal policy, namely, extermination. In actual fact he was preaching to people who had long settled in the land, had long lived with these groups and had frequently been idolatrous. His words show the situation confronting him. He bids his hearers exterminate idolatry. That is what had not happened. He then bids his hearers to make no covenants or marriages with them. That is what in fact did happen. So D faces the problem of Israel's contemporary idolatry.

Accordingly his second solution is the destruction of Canaanite altars with their accompanying stone and wooden (*'ashērāh*) symbols of deity and images. The sanctuaries are the centres of holiness, blessing and life for the Canaanites, and to destroy them is to destroy the life and body of Canaanite religion.

c **6-16 Israel the People of God—6** begins with the word ' For '. This word gives the reason for the cruel commands just laid down, but the word is also used in liturgical contexts to introduce short credal statements (cf. Ps. 95, 100). What is at stake is nothing other than the status of Israel as God's people, and Israel's function in the world. The fate of Israel's neighbours in Canaan must be subordinated to that first consideration. Exod. 19:5f. is the primary passage. In D Israel's holiness, that is her kinship with God, that she belongs to God, is mentioned. Israel is God's own special possession or property. As in Exod. it is noteworthy how at the very point of the closest association of the Lord and Israel, D's horizon broadens to ' all peoples . . . of the earth '. D's horizon does not often broaden, but the concentration upon a specially selected Israel requires the larger context.

Israel owes this status to God's grace alone. A jumble of sentences sets this forth. First God loved Israel (8) and so he set his love on Israel and chose Israel (7). It was nothing to do with the size or significance of Israel. Then secondly God had sworn an oath to the patriarchs and therefore had redeemed Israel from Egypt. Thirdly God by nature is a covenant keeping God and so having selected his people cannot but sustain them. In 9 ' know therefore ', as in Ps. 100, is simply a variant for ' because '. So God's sovereign love manifests itself in action, and that action is the oath to the fathers, the Exodus from Egypt, and the maintenance of covenant with a loyal Israel.

d **12-16**—The preacher now turns to a catalogue of benefits which will be the rewards of obedience. In the form of promises uttered on the eve of entry he sets forth his own experience of Israel's life in Canaan when she has been faithful to God. The worship confers material benefits. That is his faith and his experience. The promises in D always reflect the actual benefits of Canaan, just as the prohibitions in D reflect the sins that Israel actually committed after entry into Canaan. 235d
17-26 The Reassurance—Israel may be few and therefore afraid. This thought is certainly an ancient traditional motif and may have a Mosaic basis. Israel however is not to fear. Israel will see that God will do in Canaan what he did in Egypt, and more if necessary. For the hornet will complete the destruction. So to the Holy War are added natural pestilences. In 22f. the gradualness and the completeness are linked, the gradualness being a concession to the continuing existence of those Canaanites who would persist in living in Canaan (cf., e.g., Jos. 13:13, 15:63, 16:10, etc.). Sanctuaries, kings, idols, people all must be destroyed. The abomination in 25–6 is of course that which is ritually tabu. The word expresses the hatred and the loathing for idolatry and all its works. An idolatrous image is like a snake in the house—loathsome and dangerous.

VIII 1-6 The Divine Discipline—This chapter is e
one of the most important chapters in Dt., and indeed in the Bible, because it points the way to a final analysis of idolatry. The chapter begins with the call to obey, and continues with a command that Israel should remember her pilgrimage—forty years long—in the wilderness. That pilgrimage with all its hardships was the discipline imposed by God on Israel so that he might discover whether Israel was set on obedience or not. But the grace that imposed the discipline yet supplied the means to endure the discipline. The means was the manna, that food, unknown to later Israel, which yet became the classic emblem of providence. Manna is actually those portions of sap sucked from certain trees by certain insects, which are superfluous to the needs of these insects and are then passed through their bodies and appear as this strange substance. Thus God provided for Israel.

From the discipline of hunger and the discovery of manna Israel learnt not that man does not live by bread, i.e. material means as opposed to spiritual, which is the LXX sense of the antithesis and appears to be followed by our Lord, but that man lives by everything that comes out of God's mouth, that is, his commands and words which convey all the benefits of life, material and physical. Man is utterly dependent on God for guidance, nourishment, raiment, health and his spiritual education. Material sustenance no less than spiritual comes from God, but it is not sufficient by itself. Man depends on God for everything.

7-18. The first six verses thus establish the principle f
which regulates the chapter. If out of the discipline came also the manna, now God's providing grace becomes yet more abundant, for he also provides a lovely land of water and grain and fruits and metals. Such bountiful provision will enable Israelites to enjoy a higher standard of living through food, housing, possessions and cash. Truly, life in Canaan is to be Israel's welfare state but it brings its problem. In her new affluence will Israel still recognise that she lives by everything that comes from God, or will her prosperity lead her to pride, to forgetfulness of God and worse ? Is Israel to attribute her good fortune to God, which is true worship, or to herself, which is, as G. E. Wright says, virtually self-deification ? The words (17), ' My power and the might of my hand have gotten me this wealth ', show that the speaker is envisaging an alternative to God.

In this way, even if he does not explicitly achieve g
it, the Levitical preacher points the way to the final analysis of idolatry. In modern parlance there are three possibilities. There is first the view that man depends upon God for everything including the welfare state with all its knowledge and achievements, for God sustains his covenant, his relationship with Israel and with all mankind, at all stages of man's

35g pilgrimage (cf. 18). There is secondly the danger that Israel will abandon the true God, and will serve other gods. That is the continuing idolatrous alternative to which many in Israel and in the modern world turn. There is however the third possibility. If man does not worship the true God, and reaches the stage when he is too cultured or educated to worship idols and other gods, he then is inclined to promote himself to the divine vacancy. Thus in 17 and 18 the preacher stands on the threshold of the final analysis of idolatry. In 17 it is man, in 18 it is God. Man worships either God or himself. If it so happens that he has worshipped an idol or other gods, then those idols or other gods are simply projections of his own emotions and characteristics like Mars, Venus and Baal. Idolatry in any form is ultimately man's self-deification, and apparently in the wonderful blessings of a welfare state, man is more than ordinarily prone to it.

10 is the origin of the custom of grace at meals. In turn saying grace is one way in which man blesses his God. Blessing is a two-way traffic in Israel. God blesses man, but it is also man's privilege to bless God (Ps. 103:1).

19f. Israel, who displaces nations punished for their idolatry, will herself be destroyed if she chooses idolatry rather than life, for worship of the true God is life, but idolatry is death.

36a **IX 1-6 The Divine Purpose**—In 7:7 the preacher pointed out that God had not chosen Israel because of Israel's weight of numbers, but because of his grace. Similarly there is no ground for God's action in any fancied righteousness of Israel. So the preacher continues to find the springs of God's action in his nature or in his obligations. The preacher thinks of Israel on the eve of the entry into Canaan, and that entry takes place so that God's bond with their founding fathers may be fulfilled. At the same time it is true that Israel's possession of the land will mean the expulsion of the present occupants. But this fate these occupants have themselves deserved. As God works out his righteous and covenanted purposes for Israel in Canaan, Israel might think that such favours were due to their own merits. In fact such favours, seen from above, are covenant favours, but, seen from below, they serve also to punish the Canaanites for their wickedness. So the preacher is concerned to show the many-sidedness of God's purpose, and how lesser themes are congruous within the divine purpose itself. In spite of being stiff-necked the current Israel will accordingly possess the land by virtue of God's undertakings beyond their particular horizon.

b **7-29.** Can the leopard change his spots? Israel is and always has been stiff-necked. Of this there is the ancient, the classic and decisive illustration. At Horeb, after their deliverance from Egypt, after the great covenant service at the sacred mount, Israel made and chose the golden calf. Israel's behaviour at Horeb was like that of Judas at the Last Supper. Moses is in retreat upon the mountain, alone with God, preoccupied with the Ten Commandments, immortal code for so much of the human race. Israel, free of their leader, is at idolatrous play at the foot of the mountain, on or near the altar where they had sworn the covenant. God, who had begun with Adam, and then begun again with Noah, and then again with Abraham, now ponders yet a new beginning in Moses. So Moses came in haste and anger down the Mount. The tables of the law were smashed, and the golden calf was smashed and ground, but God's oath with the fathers was not broken. In fasting intercession Moses prays for his people, for his brother, and moves God to remember the bond with the fathers, to guard the honour of his own reputation, and to realise that Israel is God's own people.

c It has been said that such intercessory activity reveals the post-exilic stamp of these narratives. But it must be pointed out that intercession is so characteristic and constant an activity of Israel's kings, prophets, priests and leaders, and is also central to Moses' work in all parts of the traditions concerning him (Exod. 32:11-14, 236c
31-2, 33:12-16; Num, 14:13-19), that it is surely true to say that Moses was an intercessor. At the same time the D account is not so profound as Exod. 32:32, where intercessory prayer becomes embraced within an act of intercessory sacrifice.

It is remarkable that in 1-7*a*, which is exhortation, Israel is addressed in the singular, but in the historical retrospects the plural is resumed. This could mean different sources, unless the varying material brings about the varying style.

22-23 Further illustrations of Israel's wickedness.

Taberah: cf. Num. 11:1-3; Massah: cf. Exod. 17:1-7 (JE and/or P); Num. 20:10-13; Kibroth-hattaavah: cf. Num. 11:31-4.

X 1-11 The Ark—The preacher now tells the story d
of the second pair of stones and of the Ark, the box of Shittim wood in which they were deposited. JE preserves no story of the Ark, but such a story was probably in the Exod. traditions in the first place.

Then suddenly there come 6-7—a fragment of Israel's subsequent itinerary. Here it interrupts the narrative. In P Aaron died at Mount Hor on the border of Edom. Here he is said to have died at Moserah, and Eleazar succeeded him.

'At that time' (1) refers of course not to Jotbathah (7), but to Horeb (1-5); cf. Exod. 32:25-9. The Levites have four functions, three to God, and one, to bless in (with) his name, to men. 8 gives a glimpse of the position of the Levites contemporary with the preacher.

11. This verse like Exod. 33:1 sets a severe problem, e
for it may be interpreted in two ways. In one way it is a verse of promise. Israel has been long enough at Horeb. It is time for them to make their way to the promised land. But in another way the verse describes an expulsion. The Israel who has danced to the calf may no longer stay at Horeb. This second view is clearly the view taken in Exod. 33:1-6, where the people grieve to hear the news and strip themselves of their ornaments. This is more natural than to suppose that 33:1 is to be detached from the following verses, and is not the news that made the people mourn. Read as an expulsion the narrative becomes clearer. Israel was ordered out of Sinai. Before they left, God made provision for them. Instead of his living voice from the mount, the tables of stone; instead of the sanctuary at the mount, the Ark, a travelling sanctuary for their journeys; and instead of the covenant mediator Moses, the Levite priests. So righteousness expels, and grace contrives a way.

12-22 The Theocentric Life—And now, Israel: f
these words bring us to the practical conclusion of the matter. By a question similar to that in Mic. 6:8 the author sets forth Israel's simple but complete duty in familiar D phraseology. Israel's life must be directed towards God, to fear him because he is a king, to walk in his way because he is covenant-keeping, to love him because he is their Redeemer, and to worship him wholeheartedly.

Perhaps behind this passage and Mic. 6:8 there lies a brief catechism, and this with the credal elements in 14f. suggest a priestly origin for the material. On the other hand 16, which is similar to Jer. 4:4, could be prophetic, and there are phrases in 17ff. which remind us of both laws and prophecy. Perhaps the whole passage is a summary of priestly forms and ideas of teaching. In addition to the references to God's election grace (15), to his impartiality (17), to his providing care (18), and to his blessing in increasing Israel (22), there are dominantly in the passage verses which speak of the work of God (14), of the sublimity of God (17), and the solity of God (21), verses which direct the worshipper to God and illustrate Israel's theocentric art in life and worship. **14. heaven of heavens** is of course a superlative for the most 'heavenly' heavens. **15. Yet** is the limiting particle, which brings into the foreground God's loving delight through covenant in the fathers and in Israel, as the

236f chief historical event. The phrases in **17, God of gods** and **Lord of lords**, express the superlative once more—the ' godness ' of God—his sublimity and supremacy. **18. The sojourner:** the resident alien with rights and obligations, yet often oppressed. Israel were resident aliens in Egypt, and the memory of that plus God's own example instructs them in the treatment of such unfortunates. **20 Cleave:** expresses an ardent love; and **21, your praise,** means preferably the sole object of your praise.

g **XI 1-25** These verses appear to be a recapitulation, and probably a separate sermon, which leads up to the decisive act of choice in 26–32. ' Therefore ' in 1, 8 and 18 are interpretations of the simple Heb. word for ' and ', and so there is not necessarily any logical sequence involved in the ' therefores ' of these verses. **1 keep his charge** is a phrase reminiscent of P, but that shows, not that the phrase is an interpretation from P, but that we are in priestly circles.

In 2 **discipline** (chastisement in AV) is probably the object of ' know ye ' or ' consider this day '. **this day** shows in any case that the preacher is addressing his own congregation under the guise of the Israel of Horeb, his own Israel which will presently face the alternatives of the covenant in 26–32. 2–6 recapitulate the traditional and theocentric phraseology.

h It is however not only God's mercies and judgments in the past which are to prompt Israel's love and obedience, which will in turn bring long life. For 10 and 31 give a future ground for present obedience for this Israel of Horeb. God is going to give them a new land, which, unlike Egypt, which can only be cultivated by hard toil and irrigation, is a land in which God delights, which he regularly waters with the first rain (in October–November), and the latter rain (in March–April), and where he causes the crops to grow. Idolatry then would cut at Israel's food supply.

The verses not merely express God's and Israel's delight in this land, but show how God was now conceived to be the Lord of nature and to have taken over functions previously attributed to the fertility gods of Canaan. Whereas we should find it difficult to believe that obedience to God inevitably means good crops, yet the principle that is here expressed in agricultural terms, namely that righteousness has its reward, is not to be discarded.

The preacher reiterates that his words are vital for life, for education, for prosperity, and that Israel's obedience is the necessary precondition of the conquest of the land, a land which stretches from Sinai to Lebanon, and from the Mediterranean to the Euphrates—limits reminiscent of the Davidic empire (1:6–8).

i **26-32 The Choice for Israel**—Israel is called upon to choose between God, obedience and blessing, and other gods and idolatry and curse. The passage which must be read in conjunction with ch. 27 (cf. Jos. 8:30–35) dramatises the choice into a ceremony at Gerizim. Unfortunately these verses seem to imply a double locality, one at Gilgal near Jericho, the other at Shechem, near to which was the oak (not plain) of Moreh. This second location would suggest a Gilgal near Shechem, and not the more famous Gilgal near Jericho. Putting the blessing and the curse on the respective hills (29) is scarcely a figurative expression, but refers rather to the utterance of blessings and curses from these hills.

237a **XII 1** has a typical identifying title, and since there is no similar title again until 29:1, it would appear that 12–28 is a unity. It is not really possible to offer a neat classification of the legal material of these chapters, but it is possible in some degree to distinguish the ancient laws and the more recent commentary or homiletical expansion, and to observe too how the principles of Israel's covenantal religion have impinged upon the legal material. Worship of course is the initial theme.

2ff. The Law of the Sanctuary—It is remarkable how the great law codes of the OT are concerned 237a almost invariably in the first instance with the law of the sanctuary or of the altar (cf. Exod. 20:24, 25:8; Lev. 17:4; Dt. 12; Ezek. 40). First the sanctuaries of the land with their altars, i.e. places where sacrifices are offered, stone pillars, symbols of gods, and possibly of the king of Canaan's pantheon, and the *'ashērim*, i.e. trees or poles or the like, emblems of Asherah the mother goddess in Canaan, must be destroyed. Note how the laws of this chapter have the forms of direct commands or prohibitions, i.e. they are apodictic laws. This type is peculiar to Israel, in contrast with the ' if ', or case laws, characteristic of much in the OT and of Israel's neighbours.

5 By contrast Israel must seek out the divinely b appointed place of God's habitation, and that place is to be the scene of sacrifice, offerings, communal meals and rejoicings. It is clear that the preacher has one sanctuary in mind, probably to be identified with that sanctuary where the Ark was kept, i.e. Shiloh and later Jerusalem. **habitation** may represent a Heb. noun occurring here only in the OT, and then it is in apposition to ' unto the place ' (AV). It is however better to read this Heb. word as a verb: ' to tabernacle it ', to put his name there, make his tabernacle or habitation there. The word is *shākhan* and it is used of God's dwelling or tabernacling in the sanctuary. Thus in the P document of the Jerusalem priests there is portrayed the tabernacling Presence of the glory of God. The D equivalent is ' to put his name there '. At first sight these appear to be two different conceptions, but it is possible that they find their reconciliation in the Ark. Certainly the Ark is spoken of in terms of glory (1 Sam. 4:21f.) and of the name (2 Sam. 6:2). This is not to say that the presence of the Ark exhausts the cultic reference of the glory and the name, but the Ark is at the centre of both conceptions even if glory and name have gained further and richer associations through the increasing influence of the shrines. To put the name there could mean that the tetragrammaton was inscribed somewhere on or in the shrine, or that the shrine was the place where it was uttered in prayer and blessing. The Heb. phrase is too concrete to admit simply of a metaphorical expression, and the best solution in view of 2 Sam. 6:2 is that the designated sanctuary is really the Ark sanctuary.

8-14 Whereas in 1, 9 the preacher sees his Israel as c at the point of entry, now in **8** he sees them as the Israel of Canaan, called upon to give up their irregular habits of sacrifice and service. Canaan is the resting-place of Israel (cf. Ps. 95:11) and their inheritance from God, an inheritance in trust for all generations of Israel.

Levite in Dt. means priest. The P document distinguishes between priests who were certain descendants of Aaron and ministered at the central altar, and Levites who did not. Here of course (12) the Levite is the family chaplain, hitherto minister of sacrifice and teaching, but hereafter of teaching alone.

15-28 provide, in the new circumstances of the central shrine, for the non-ritual slaughter and consumption of meat, on condition that the blood is poured to the ground, and that the prescribed offerings are offered and eaten before God in the sanctuary. The repetition of the relaxations show how widespread were the practices which the lawgiver is opposing and how increasingly affluent Israelites were becoming. **29-31.** These verses warn the Israelites against the dangers of syncretism and its idolatrous practices, such as infant sacrifice. The one sanctuary will be devoted to one form of worship precisely.

XIII Idolatrous Tempters—Dt. is among other d things the book of the diagnosis of idolatry. The preacher's way of thought and life is so centred on his God that he inevitably possesses one of the keenest senses for idolatry in the OT. Here in this chapter, which in the Heb. begins with what is 12:32 in the English, three idolatrous possibilities are considered. A similar

7d case is found in 17:2–7, a variant of, rather than a portion misplaced from, ch. 13.

1-5 The problem here is one of reality. A prophet or dreamer gives a sign or wonder, which here clearly means a prediction of an extraordinary event, and in due course his sign comes to pass. The prophet has thus passed the test, for his prediction is fulfilled. He is a true prophet, and his word is truth. But if this same person then invites his fellows to follow other gods, he is no true prophet. He is a preacher who preaches truth and death. The only explanation is that God has given him his message of truth, and his idolatrous invitation is his own bright idea. Thus God has given him a true sign to test their love for God. As soon as this true prophet contemplates idolatry, then Israel is to follow him no more. He is to be destroyed. If idolatry is death, then the tempter to idolatry is as good as dead, and must be destroyed, so that Israel may burn out the horror from her midst.

6-11. When even a kinsman or bosom friend who can be relied upon to seek what is good and never makes any suggestions which are not wholesome and desirable, proposes other gods, then friendship and kinship end. There must be no mercy. The hand of the person enticed as first witness shall throw the first stone. Stoning as in the case of Naboth, 1 Kg. 21.13, means that one stands a little way off and thus risks neither pollution nor piteous persuasion (cf. Exod. 19:13).

12-18 Similarly if it is proved that some 'base fellows' have of set purpose seduced a city into idolatry—other gods—then such a city, in which death is already at work through idolatry, must be destroyed. All its life, human and animal, must be destroyed and the city must never be built again. No article from the banned, i.e. devoted, i.e. doomed, city, is even to touch the hand. Guarded thus from the abomination (14), which is the repulsive and repugnant antithesis of what is pleasing and holy, God is able to resume and maintain his sworn covenant with Israel.

The three cases thus considered have the legal form of case-law—'if', cf. vv. 1, 6, 12, which is customary throughout the laws of the ancient Near East.

18 shows again the hortatory framework in which the ancient laws were set.

a **XIV 1-2 Dt. is Preached Law**—Israel, who are sons to the God of Israel and his holy and elect possession, must not compromise their religious observances with pagan customs though widespread and familiar. Bodily disfigurement whether as token of grief or of the bond with the dead is forbidden. The preaching context implies that such customs will impair their status with their God.

3-21 Permissible and Prohibited Foods—In these verses D preserves what is probably a northern, Levitical variant of food laws known to us in the Jerusalem use preserved in P in Lev. 11:2–23. Permitted animals, fish and birds are listed, and the forbidden exceptions stated. The forbidden are the abominable, the repugnant. The grounds for the choice are lost to us, but difference from the previous or neighbouring inhabitants of the land, remnants of totemism, natural repugnance and so on have played their part. Boiling a kid in its mother's milk was a religious practice known in Israel's Canaanite and polytheistic context, and hence forbidden to Israel. Milk and meat foods are thus to be separated.

b **22-29 The Earth is the Lord's, but Israel has a Life Interest**—Israel must devote the first fruits of the produce of the soil and the firstlings of the animals for consumption at a sanctuary feast. For transport convenience an alternative method is permitted. The law here differs from that in P (Num. 18:21–32), where the tithe is for the Levites and a tenth of it for the Aaronite priests. Yet there is an approach to this law in Dt. 18:4. The two customs probably reflect the northern and Jerusalem (P) usages. Sanctuary feasts meant feasting, revelry and strong drink, but at once the limit is imposed. Such feasts must also instil reverence.

28f. A triennial tithe is to be collected and distributed 238b
to the family chaplain, the resident alien and other unfortunates. Amos probably mentions this tithe (4:4), so that this law again is fairly old and probably distinctively northern. At least there is no equivalent in the Jerusalem laws.

XV 1-11 The Lord's Release—The preacher quotes c
an ancient law that every seventh year there shall be a release. The second clause of 2 may continue the law, or probably 2f. may be the explanation of the ancient law. Every seventh year Israelite debtors may have their debts cancelled. The reason is that it is the Lord's release, i.e. the release is God's will. Thus Israelite creditors fulfil all righteousness and thus Israelite poor are succoured. Israelites may lend to foreigners as distinct from resident aliens and may recover their loans at the appointed time, the seventh year, but they may not borrow from foreigners. Foreign control implies the shadow of idolatry. In the preacher's expansion, 4–11, he is careful to add, 4f., that obedience to God's law will prevent poverty. Yet in 11 it is stated as a matter of fact that the poor were always with Israel. They must be succoured even if the proximity of the seventh year meant lenders might forfeit their loan. Then the preacher penetrates to the inner springs of motive.

12-18 Release of Slaves—12 gives the ancient law d
for the release of slaves who have served six years. 13–18 give the expansion. Israel, enslaved in Egypt, was released, so Israelite slaves, men and women equally (cf. Jer. 34:9–11 and contrast Exod. 21:2–11), may depart, and must be set up, to begin a new life. Provision is also made for such slaves as desire to remain, and then they remain permanently. The cost of maintenance was half the cost of labour.

19-23 Firstlings—19 is the old law and 20–3 the expansion. Firstlings of flocks and herds belong to the Lord in token that all life is his, and so firstlings must be used for feasts at the central shrine, provided they are without blemish, and the blood has been properly manipulated. Imperfect firstlings may be consumed at home. (Cf. parallels Exod. 13:11–16, 22:29f., 34:19f.; Lev. 27:26f.; Num. 18:15–18.)

XVI 1-17 The Festal Calendar (cf. Exod. 12f., e
23, 34; Lev. 23; Num. 28f.).

1-8 Passover—Every year Israelites are to celebrate three pilgrimage feasts at the central shrine. The first was Passover-Abib-Nisan (March-April), originally a feast in which firstlings were sacrificed, but which gained unique significance from Moses, who linked it with the liberation from Egypt. After the settlement in Canaan Passover was linked with the feast of unleavened bread, clearly of agricultural and Canaanite origin, and the Egyptian reference. The unleavened bread became the bread of affliction in memory of the bondage in Egypt. Jewish Passover became Easter in Christianity.

9-12 Weeks—Seven weeks later, on the fiftieth day, hence Pentecost, the feast of weeks, of harvest, of first fruits, was celebrated by a pilgrimage, a festival, an offering and great rejoicing. The feast celebrates the Lord of harvest; but, later and successively, in Judaism the feast of the lawgiving at Horeb, and in Christianity the festival of the Holy Spirit.

13-15 Tabernacles—In the autumn, Sept.–Oct., the feast of Tabernacles, or booths, was celebrated. Originally a festival of the wine harvest it becomes associated with the 'booths', or tents, of the Exodus from Egypt. It lasted for seven days and was marked with exceptional rejoicing.

The three feasts are kept to the Lord. That is the theocentric axis of the feasts.

16 Three times a year the manhood of Israel must come, not 'to appear before the Lord' but 'to see the face of the Lord', and in coming must bring their gifts. 'To see the face' may be a figure of worship, but it may imply that something, e.g. the Ark, was seen, i.e. shown, on these occasions.

XVI 18-XVIII 22—These laws are mainly devoted f

238f to the officers in Israel's life and cult: judges, kings, priests and prophets, with some laws on worship, 16:21–17:7.

XVI 18-20 Judges—18 is a command to Israel to appoint judges and officers. The judicial system is the gift of God. **19f.**, commonly taken as apodictic laws addressed to the people, could also be precise commands to the judges themselves. Indeed 16:19–17:7 may include several directions addressed to the judges.

21-22 Symbols of Worship—Israelites are forbidden to plant or erect symbols of worship which are really Canaanite. In these verses we have probably very ancient apodictic law. One altar is not necessarily implied. The law could refer to the days when Israelites had many altars, and the law thus appears in this context, because it was the duty of the local officers to prevent the appearance of these Canaanite symbols in the districts in their charge.

g **XVII 1 The Blemished Sacrifice**—We must suppose either another law unrelated to its context, or a law whose operation involved the judges. If a dispute arose as to whether an animal were blemished or not, who decided between people and priests? The law of the blemished animal may have to be explained by its context.

2-7 The Idolater—Again it would appear the judges were involved, especially if 4f. are directly addressed to judges. The judges must test the accusation, hear the witnesses, (condemn the guilty) and bring the condemned to the gates for execution.

8-13. In contrast with the foregoing section, there now appears a central judicial and priestly court. Here is centralisation law for cases too hard for local decision. Since a judge was involved nationally in judicial and cultic cases, presumably he was also involved locally in cultic cases as instanced in the verses above. The main emphasis is on civic offences, and decisions of this court were final. 16:21–17:7 and 17:8–13 probably thus transmit old apodictic law and later Deuteronomic centralisation law, respectively.

h **14-20 The King**—This passage concerning the king, and indeed the sole passage concerning the king in the Pentateuchal laws, is not really law at all, but an exhortation and indeed a warning. The effect of the passage is to regulate the monarchy, and to prevent further Solomons. The king featured in this passage is clearly Solomon, and so the law probably belongs to the early days of divided monarchy. Noteworthy is the king's duty to be conversant with this law, i.e. D, which is in the charge of the Levitical priests. Reading the law, etc., was probably part of the king's duty in public worship. The connection of the law with the Levitical priests is important for the transmission and editing of D.

239a **XVIII 1-8 The Priests**—The priests are to own no lands, but their living is to come from the Lord through reserving certain portions of the sacrifices for them.

The opening words, literally, 'There shall not be to the priests, the Levites all the tribe of Levi', may be interpreted in two ways. The words after Levites may be supplementary to the foregoing, so that the AV brings out the sense by inserting 'and' after 'Levites', 'and all the tribe of Levi'. On this view the tribe of Levi is more than all the priests the Levites, who are the sacrificing priests, as Levites then are the teaching priests. It is difficult to justify this from the grammar: 'all the tribe of Levi' no less than 'Levites' is in apposition to 'priests'. It is an assumption that D by Levites means teaching priests, and by priests—the Levites—means the ministers of the altar. **6** shows that Levites—not Levitical priests—may give up country posts and minister to the Lord at the central sanctuary with full rights (but cf. 2 Kg. 23:9). **8** suggests that the priests had some private income if not property.

b **9-22 The Prophet**—Whereas the peoples of Canaan employ devious magical means to coerce their deities into giving knowledge and benefit, Israel must bear a blameless attitude to the Lord. The means include the
ordeal of passing through fire, possibly child sacrifice, 23
and divination.

In contrast the Lord will give Israel a succession of prophets; the word 'prophet' is singular collective, and means many prophets, just as the 'false prophet' of 20ff. is also singular collective. **16** shows that the prophet is to mediate God to Israel, his Presence, his words and his authority.

20-22 show how Israelites were taught to distinguish between true and false prophecy (cf. 13:1–5).

XIX 1-10 Accidental Slaying—Israel, having c
already appointed three cities of refuge in Transjordan districts (4:41–3), are now instructed to appoint three, and if necessary six, more cities of refuge. To these cities, and, presumably to the altars in these cities, people who accidentally killed others could flee and be safe from the rights of blood revenge, while their innocence of murder was established. The regulations though given again in the form of preaching are very ancient and probably pre-monarchic.

11-13 Murder—Cities of refuge provided no asylum for murderers, who, when their guilt was proved, were to be handed over to the avenger of blood, that is the kinsman of the deceased whose responsibility it was to exact a life for a life.

14 Theft—Law and preaching (AV order) here combine to denounce falsification of boundaries (Isa. 5:8).

15-21 Witnesses—Two or three witnesses are d
necessary for proof of guilt. Disputes must be settled at the sanctuary before priests and judges. Here again old laws which presuppose local sanctuaries rather than a single sanctuary are probably assumed.

21 is not to be understood, as it is commonly done, as a permission for general vengeance. The words make the punishment fit the crime, and limit the punishment to the exact equivalent of the injury. An eye, but no more than an eye, for an eye, and not the death of one man for wounding another (Gen. 4:23).

XX 1-20 Holy War—1–9 War. Dt. has the follow- e
ing passages concerning the Holy War: 20:1–20, 21:10–14, 23:10–14, 24:5, 25:17–19. These passages contain old laws of varying dates, which have been reinterpreted and expounded and indeed humanised by D. **1-9** concern war itself. Israel must not fear, because the Lord is with them. This in earlier days would be a reference to the Ark, though a general reference would develop. There follows an exhortation by the (chief) priest, and directions by the (recruiting) officers stating which individuals may be released from military service. **6. has not enjoyed:** lit. profaned, i.e. made common. A vineyard became free for use in its fifth year (Lev. 19:23–5).

10-18 The Siege of Cities—To distant cities the options of peace with servitude or destruction must be given. Near, i.e. Canaanite, cities, must be destroyed forthwith, lest they tempt Israel to idolatry. In **17 utterly destroy** are the words which describe that feature of the Holy War known as the ban. The ban involves total destruction as a sacrifice to God. **19f.** In war fruit trees must not be cut down. Another kindly provision in D.

XXI 1-9 Expiation for a Murder by an Unknown f
Person—Obviously a very ancient community law, perhaps coming from the Canaanites in which a city nearest to the place where a murdered person has been found, purges any possible responsibility for the crime. The elders must go to an uncultivated valley where there is a running brook, and there before priests kill a heifer which has never even been yoked, wash their hands over the heifer and protest their innocence. Perhaps the heifer was a substitute for the murderer. The communal and indeed quasi-magical character of the rite is obvious.

10-14 Women Prisoners of War—Another regulation of the Holy War giving the conditions in which an Israelite warrior may marry a woman captive, and then, later, if he wills not to keep her as a wife or slave, must release her. But first she must spend the first

239f month mourning her parents. Possibly the shaving of her head and the nail paring marked the day of entry into her captor's house, as new hair and longer nails would show that the month was ending. Another law showing humanitarian motives.

A number of case laws, generally without expansion, now follow in rapid succession.

g **15-17 Law of Inheritance**—First-born sons, even if by hated wives, must be guaranteed inheritance, i.e. a double portion or share, lit. mouthful, cf. handful, Gen. 43:34. **18-21.** The stubborn and rebellious son, who will not honour his parents, is to be slain by stoning at the hands of the men of the city. **23f.** The body of a criminal who has been executed for his crime may be exposed for further shame by hanging, but only until night. Such hanging carries with it a divine curse, and so the body must be buried before nightfall lest the Promised Land be polluted.

h **XXII 1-12 Some Miscellaneous Laws—1-4.** Israelites must take the initiative and not hold back in restoring lost property to its rightful owner, or in helping to raise up fallen animals. Thus they show love to their fellows. **5** is one of a series continuing in 9–11, whereby mixture of garments, seed, animals and materials are prohibited. They are obviously ancient laws, the neglect of which brought religious risk of some kind, for a mixed crop became holy, or forfeited to the sanctuary. **6** limits protection to the mother bird but not to the eggs or young in the nest. **8** prescribes parapets for the flat roofs, lest anyone fall over. The law is retrospective and not anticipatory. Bitter experiences in Canaan taught Israel the necessity of this law. The laws in 5, 6f., 8 and 10 are peculiar to Dt. **12** implies decoration only, but the parallel in Num. 15:37–41 explains the tassels as emblems of God's commandments.

i **13-30 Laws concerning Sexual Matters**—13–29 contain five case laws, the first in **13-21** relating to unfaithfulness in a bride. If a husband brings a charge against his wife which is proved to be false, then he is to be whipped, fined, and must never divorce his wife. The guilty bride is to be stoned. The absence of the tokens of virginity do not necessarily prove such an accusation, for there may be other causes, so the risk of injustice was evident. **22** provides that adultery must be punished by the death of the parties. **23-9** legislate for seduction: first of a betrothed maiden with her consent (in a city), an offence punishable by the death of both parties; secondly of a betrothed maiden against her will (in the country), then the man dies; and thirdly, of an unbetrothed maiden, in which case the man must pay a dowry to the girl's father, marry the girl and never divorce her. **30** prohibits marriage with a wife of one's father. There were a number of such laws which were obviously ancient. Perhaps only this one is quoted in Dt. because the conduct here prohibited carried with it the right of inheritance.

j **XXIII 1-8 Cultic Disqualification**—1, 2, 3, 7, 8 are a series of ancient apodictic laws which control membership of the sacred assembly. Eunuchs, bastards as physically imperfect or tainted, Ammonites or Moabites as ancient enemies, are excluded. Edomites and Egyptians newly settled in Israel and their children are also excluded, but the children of the third generation have the right of entry.

9-14 These laws providing for camp sanitation are part of the rules of Holy War. It is not health which is the acknowledged motive, though that is scarcely absent, but the Presence of Israel's God in camp. Therefore the camp itself must be holy and not be polluted.

k **15-16** A runaway slave is not to be returned to his owner. Possibly foreign slaves are meant, because Heb. nationality is not stated as it is in 15:12. **17f.** As the Heb. words show it is cultic prostitutes of both sexes which are here forbidden. 'Dog' is used in reference to the male. **19f.** Israelites may not charge interest on loans to fellow Israelites, though they may do so to foreigners. **19** has parallels in Exod. 22:25 239k
and Lev. 25:35–7, but **20** is peculiar to Dt. **21-3.** Vows, because they are virtually oaths, and oaths invoke God, must be fulfilled. **24f.** Israelites may pick and eat grapes and grain, but may not remove any from a neighbour's vineyard, or cut grain with a sickle. Thus robbery was prevented.

XXIV 1-4 (cf. Jer. 3:1). The first husband of a 240a
twice-divorced woman may not remarry her after her second divorce. Although it was easy for men to obtain a divorce in the ancient Near East, it is clear that the old case law here quoted required that a man had to have a reason for his divorce, then he had to write or have written a form of words of dismissal, place this written document in her hand and then formally dismiss her. The context does not necessarily require that the case had to go before officials, or that the document had to be obtained from them, but it may be implied. 'Some unseemly thing' (cf. 14), lit. 'the nakedness of a thing', is indefinite. Second marriage obviously was thought to defile a woman, i.e. render her tabu as far as her first husband was concerned.

The English versions do not properly render the sense of 1–4. The four verses are an example of case or common law, 1–3 expressing the condition, if or when, and the apodosis then . . . first beginning only in 4. There are some expanding clauses at the end of 4, otherwise the law is ancient and traditional.

5. The newly wed husband shall be free of military or other public service for the first year of his marriage. Obviously an ancient law of Holy War.

6 The first of three laws (10–13) relating to pledges. This law, peculiar to D, forbids the taking of a millstone for security. This law shows concern for the poor because daily grinding of grain meant the family's food supply.

7 (cf. Exod. 21:16). Man stealers must be executed. Note the last clause, the D formula to follow sentence of death.

8f. A typical D exhortation to recollect certain ancient prescriptions concerning leprosy (cf. Lev. 13f.). Behaviour in a plague of leprosy is intended.

10-13 Pledges—A creditor may not enter a debtor's b
house to choose his pledge. He must accept what is brought out to him. This requirement is peculiar to D, but the next, that the pledge, if a garment, usually outer garment, must be returned before nightfall, is found in Exod. 22:26f. Such behaviour is right conduct acceptable to God.

14f. The poor wage-earner, Israelite or alien, must receive his pay the day he earns it. So Israel's laws protected those without means of redress.

16 The necessity for such a law asserting individual culpability for crime is interesting. It is not a law formulated on the basis of the prophetical principle in Jer. 31:29, or Ezek. 18, but is earlier as 2 Kg. 14:6 shows.

17f. Though the text is a little uncertain, the three classes of needy, resident aliens, orphans, widows, are specially protected against injustice.

19-22 The last sheaf in the grain fields and the gleanings of olives and grapes must be for the use of the poor. Gleaning of olives peculiar to D, and the gleaning laws (Lev. 19:9f.) of H (cf. §203*c*), appear to be more developed. Perhaps the reference to the last sheaf is not a reference to gleaning at all, but originally implied some animistic practice in reference to the tutelary spirit of the field. The reference in the context however clearly means the relief of poverty. 22 is again D expansion like so many clauses in the foregoing miscellaneous laws.

XXV 1-3 Case law, 1 being the condition, 2 the c
decision, and 3 further details of the punishment. **deserves to be beaten,** lit. son of strokes. Note the safeguards: punishment is to be administered only after trial and sentence, in the presence of the court, in accordance with the crime, and with an upper limit of punishment. **be degraded,** lit. seem light, i.e. be dishonoured by excessive punishment.

240c **4** A law of kindness to animals which is peculiar to D. The labourer is worthy of his hire ; cf. 1 C. 9:9 and 1 Tim. 5:18.

5-10 These verses legislate for the so-called Levirate marriage (cf. Lat. *levir*, husband's brother). If one of brothers living together dies leaving a childless widow, then a brother of the deceased must marry the widow to raise up children to his dead brother. If he refuses privately and publicly, the widow has the right of humiliating him publicly for the refusal. The law, which is very ancient (cf. Gen. 38), shows the importance of the family unit.

d **11-12** A wife intervening in a certain way in a struggle between her husband and another man must have her hand cut off. The penalty is thus mutilation ; cf. 19:21.

13-16 Commercial honesty requires just weights and measures, i.e. not greater weights when you purchase, and smaller weights when you sell, but standard weights. In Lev. 19:35f. Israel must use just weights because the Lord brought them out of Egypt, and in order that they may live long and not be an abomination to God.

17-19 Israel is bidden to remember the treacherous conduct of the people of Amalek in the desert days. They picked off Israelite stragglers and did not fear God. These verses have more the form of an exhortation than a law, and thus really describe Israel's traditional attitude to this enemy. There is no exact parallel in the references to Amalek (cf. Exod. 17:8–15 and other references in 1 Sam 14:48, 15:2f., 27:8f., 28:18, 30:1–20 ; 2 Sam. 8:12 and 1 Chr. 4:43), which corresponds to the charges against Amalek in this context.

e **XXVI** This chapter forms a fitting end to the laws of D, for it records two ceremonies which are suffused with D's warmth and point of view, rounded off with a call to obedience set within the context of the covenant faith and status of Israel.

1-11 The Presentation of the First Fruits—This is a very early law, so early that it probably antedates the laws of tithing (cf. 14:22f. and 18:4), which represent later developments. But the law has been expressed in the D phraseology, 1–5*a*, and put as an introduction to the credal confession in 5*b*–10. So the rite includes the choice of first fruits, unless the very first fruits are intended, their removal to the central shrine, an affirmation of the possession of the Promised Land to the sanctuary priest who then deposits the basket before the Lord. The visiting Israelite must then testify with prescribed words, i.e. recite a creed, before the Lord. The creed is virtually an Israelite 'Apostles' Creed' because it summarises Israel's sacred history. The 'wandering Aramean' (or, as AV and RV have, 'Syrian ready to perish'—presumably because of the famine and that in the very land where his descendants are so blessed) was the patriarch Jacob, who went down to Egypt and became a nation, whom the Egyptians later oppressed. Then God did two great things. He rescued his people from Egypt with many miracles and led them into the land of Canaan. In token of which the Israelite now brings the first of the fruit to God. Then in contrast with 4, the worshipper is himself to deposit the offering, prostrate himself and then rejoice, that is, probably eat and drink with his family before God. Like 6:20–5, 5*b*–10 here contain a historical credo, which is a summary of the themes of the Hexateuch, and almost certainly represents one of the earliest worshipping formulae of the Israelite family. It is the combination of rite and creed which is so striking, for it thus sets the pattern for Israel's feasts. In these verses history is being added to harvest festival, Israel's gospel is being joined with harvest to explain the harvest and to bring the harvest within the orbit of Israel's historical faith. Christian Harvest Festival Services must likewise follow this pattern and relate the Christian Gospel to the Christian view of nature, for there is no comparable parallel in the NT.

12-15 Words for use with the third-year tithe (14:28f.). 24
Every third year the tithe of produce must not be taken to the central sanctuary but given to the local poor. When this has been completed, the donor must at the sanctuary solemnly state that he has so distributed the tithe, and kept the laws of the tithe in general. The sacred character of the tithe has been maintained even though it was to be given not to God but to the poor. The affirmation ends with a prayer that God will (therefore) bless his people in the promised land. The cultic conduct of the rite suggests that what they did for their brethren was as if they had done it to their God (cf. Mt. 25:40). The two rites thus exemplify Israel's worship and piety in terms of faith and obedience.

16-19 are the conclusion to chs. 5–26. 'This day' ostensibly refers to the times of entry into the land, but again is a reference to the recurrent annual day of worship on which the covenant was renewed. This final exhortation thus set forth Israel's duty, and reminded them how earlier in, or in virtue of, this service they had once again taken God as their God and vowed their obedience. Similarly through some declaration God had taken them for his own people, promising to them a superior status among the peoples, and designating them as a people holy and belonging to himself. These verses offer in part a parallel to the cultic oracle of Ps. 95:7*b*–11.

XXVII, XXVIII It appears clear that 26:16–19 g
preserve features of an actual service of covenant worship. 27:1–8 contain instructions for the celebration of a service on the day of Israel's first entry into the promised land. 9f. appear to resume the 'this day' theme of 26:16–19, while 27:11–26 contain directions for a great service of blessing and cursing at Shechem. Ch. 28 then continues the speech of Moses from ch. 26—a speech recapitulating the blessings and curses implicit in the covenant religion. Though there appears to be a variety of passages, it seems also to be clear that it is a liturgical theme which accounts for the present position of these passages. But this liturgical theme has a double strand. First of all there are the rubrics and feature of the annually recurrent service of covenant, probably at Shechem, which is to be traced through 26:16–19, 27:9f., 11–26 and 28, and there is, secondly, the tradition of a service which was held at (?) Ebal on the day when Israel first set foot in Palestine. This is to be traced partly in 11:26–32 and then in 27:1–8, though these passages have been much worked over in the interests of the permanent service at Shechem.

XXVII 1-8 At the Edge of the Land—As Abraham 24
entered the promised land and laid claim to it by the erection of altars, so Israel is to enter and then, on the very same day of the crossing, to erect whitewashed stones on which the law of D is to be written. This is an Egyptian method of writing. 4 is the repetition of this command with the added information that the stones are to be erected at Mt Ebal. There too an altar to the Lord is to be erected, an altar of undressed stones, on which sacrifices are to be offered. Here is a piece of very ancient tradition which virtually contradicts the idea of the central sanctuary, and which probably preserves a tradition concerning the afternoon and evening of Israel's first day in Canaan. Unfortunately the place is uncertain. 4, which repeats 2, places the scene at Mt Ebal, and this points to Ebal and Gerizim, nearly 20 miles from the crossing-place near Jericho. It is unlikely that they reached Shechem the day they crossed over. The course of events in the Book of Jos. requires a very much longer time. It follows then that either 4 is a later addition to repeat 2 in the interests of Shechem, or Ebal in 4 really stands for an Ebal at or near Gilgal. It is extraordinary that the stones of law and the altar were erected on Ebal, which by 27:13 is the mount of curse. Late in the first day then, and on the very edge of the land, Israel erects the stones written with the laws, and then erects an altar. These are Israel's first acts in Canaan,

1a acts which put revelation first and sacrificial worship second. These are the earnest of Israel's settlement in the land, and these are the tokens of Israel's life in Canaan and of Israel's legacy to the world. This first day and night Israel proclaimed the revelation, a revelation of the will and law of her king, and then too Israel raised an altar. Israel's first meal in Palestine was around the altar, where she worshipped her God and rejoiced before him.

9f. contain a rubric for Israel's silence and in the silence for the recognition of Israel's status as the Lord's people. These verses are thus the continuation of 26:16–19, and probably the fulfilment of 18f.

b **11-26 At Shechem**—This passage resumes the account of the annual covenant ceremony, and provides for the division of Israel for liturgical purposes. At Shechem six tribes including Levi are to stand on Gerizim to bless Israel, and the other six upon Mt Ebal for the curse. Then the Levites who are on the mount of blessing are to announce the curses. There are difficulties in both the genealogical (cf. Gen. 35:22–6) and the geographical explanations of the choice of the tribes. Israel is styled the people as in E (e.g. Exod. 24:3), while the Levites appear as a tribe in 12, and as priests in 14. It may be that only representatives of the tribes were stationed on the mountains, to embody the blessing or the curse, and the people stood between with the ' cursing ' Levites at their head or in some other position. Otherwise all the tribes are divided and set on the hills, in symbolic station, and answer antiphonally to the Levites. 12f. would suggest blessings as well as curses, but only curses follow. The ritual is fragmentary. It has been suggested that the six blessings of 28:3–6 and the six cursings of 28:16–19 may belong here, but in the present state of the text no solution is certain. The Levites are to testify the twelve curses with a high, possibly intoned, voice. The curses are generally single-sentence statements beginning with the Heb. passive participle for cursed. The people's response is consistently, Amen, i.e. truly, assuredly. The curses refer to misconduct in worship, in family, social and sexual life.

c **XXVIII** This chapter continues the direct address of 26, possibly through 27:9f., setting forth the blessings which attend the keeping of covenant, and the curses which follow the breaking of covenant. Yet the connection is not simply that obedience brings reward, and that unfealty brings punishment. The connection is more existential than that. Covenant conditions life, and indeed is life. To keep the covenant is to be within the covenant, and the content of the covenant is life and well-being. To break the covenant is to abandon it, and live outside covenant, that is to die. Life inheres in covenant, and death outside it. The covenant gives life and life is manifested in its blessings. Outside the covenant comes the curse, and the curse is an instalment of death. The curse may thus warn the transgressor to return into the life of the covenant, though it will increase and become death for those who persist in their transgression. Covenant is universal blessing, and covenant breaking, which is virtually idolatry, is universal frustration and chaos and eventually death. As suggested above, original liturgical elements may be present, in 3–6, blessings, and in 16–19, curses, but the rest of the chapter shows the usual signs of D's preaching and expanding style. The chapter offers a parallel to Lev. 26 though the chapters are independent of each other, and it was almost certainly part of the original corpus which was read and caused such great distress to Josiah king of Judah (cf. 2 Kg. 22:13 and Jer. 11:3).

d **1** gives the condition and **2** states the reward of obedience. Israel's covenant promotion will be manifested in the quickening, abundance and security of her life in all its parts. Apart from the fourth and expanded blessing the other five blessings have a rhythmic three accented form.

7-14 D now expands Israel's well-being in universal blessing, but at the centre is the affirmation of Israel's 241d peculiar status and title before God and mankind (9f.). The word holiness is not merely an ethical quality but expresses also the principle of kinship in covenant, i.e. belonging to God. Heaven as God's treasury is conceived as a reservoir of water. **Head** and **going up** in 13 are images of prosperity, but **tail** and **decline** are images of misfortune. The unswerving path is true worship, and deviation is idolatry.

15-68 The Curses—15-19 are an almost perfect parallel e
in form and order to the blessings of 3–6. The fourth blessing becomes the third curse, and 18 shows in Heb. and Gr. that the extra clause of v. 4 is probably an addition. **20** shows that idolatry stands at the entry to the way of death. All manner of calamities follow in all walks of life. It is not necessary to suppose exilic or post-exilic expansions. What is here described is well within the pre-exilic experience of Israel and Judah. 35 and 41 may be added or out of place, and many regard 26–37, 48–57 and 58–68 as later expansions. But logical considerations are really subservient to other considerations. It is no argument that the horrors are more than the blessings. Abundance of horror is necessary to enforce or frighten people into obedience. It is true that horror is more listened to than blessing, so that the sermon offers us what is virtually a crescendo of curses, which eventually puts Israel back into Egypt.

XXIX-XXX Again the Covenant—29:1 is in Heb. 242a
28:69, and could thus be the subscription to the covenant in the main part of the book. On the other hand 29:1 is more probably the heading to chs. 29–30 and the words of the covenant in v. 1 are a reference to the sacred story of 2–8, and the ceremony of the Moab covenant that follows. The verse is thus an editorial note identifying the beginning of **Moses' third address.** But the liturgical interest is again dominant. The recapitulation of the sacred story is the prelude to a solemn charge (10–14) and warning (16–29), followed by the alternative of repentance and restored national life, all in a quasi-narrative form. Then the preacher defines the nearness and inwardness of God's word before coming finally to the moment of decision and to the choice of true worship or idolatry. These chapters then contain an address appropriate to services of covenant renewal and may indeed belong to the occasion described in 31:9–13.

XXIX 2-9 is preaching, recital. Note how the b
preacher begins by referring to the Lord, but in 5f. the preacher falls, as so often in the OT, into the divine first person, culminating in what Vischer has so graphically described as Auto-kerygma, ' I am the Lord your God ', the sovereign sentence of all scripture. The clue to the transition lies partly in 4, where it is claimed that worship (this day) conveys vision and understanding.

10-15 identifies the worshipping community in their own right as individuals (10f.), as the covenanted worshipping Israel (13), whether present or absent (14), and as the descendants of the patriarchs (13f.).

16-29 recounts Israel's experience of the idolatry c
prevalent in the nations through which Israel passed, and warns against the fallacy that a context of covenant automatically affords personal salvation to anyone without his own personal participation in the service. Such a person would be destroyed, as indeed would the entire nation if it proved to be idolatrous. A desolated territory is the proof of a broken covenant, for it is like the destruction of Sodom and Gomorrah, whose downfall was due to sin. Idolatry, divine anger, curse, dispersion and exile are the links in the chain of destruction. 29 contrasts the future, which is hidden and belongs to God, with what is known and has taken place, namely the past, and with the present as offering the opportunity of obedience.

XXX 1-10 Restoration after Repentance—An d
Israel in exile that repents will receive mercy from God and will be restored to its own land. Further God will himself assist the restoration, for having

242d restored them to the land, he will then dispose the heart of Israelites and their children that they will love their God. Thus further disobedience will be prevented. God's curses will fall upon Israel's foes, and an obedient Israel will enjoy prosperity. But all this depends on the initial act of repentance. **Restore your fortunes** means a complete reversal of fortunes in the reconstitution of Israel's life in all its aspects, spiritual and material, and the phrase probably goes back to a piece of ritual which portrayed such a change of fortune (for the same phrase cf., e.g., Ps. 53:6, 85:1, 126:1 ; Hos. 6:11, etc.). The passage could have been written in late pre-exilic times, for it is not necessarily exilic or later.

e **11-14** The preacher reinforces his appeal with the thought of the relevance and nearness of God's word. Like God himself (cf. 4:7), his word is given to the people in the covenant service, and it is given to them that they may fulfil it. If sacrificial worship is limited to one altar, nevertheless the possession of the word in the heart of the worshipper creates the conditions for universal and spiritual worship.

15-20 Peroration—This last exhortation sets before the people the final choice of obedience (16) or idolatry (17). That is the choice before Israel, and indeed before all—the everlasting choice. Heaven and earth are summoned to witness that the choice has been given to Israel. The issues are clear and the responsibility is now Israel's and Israel's alone. God or idols, his way or their way, and their choice is a decision fraught with the destiny of life or death.

f **XXXI-XXXIV** These chapters contain a series of appendices of varied contents from various sources which complete the Book of Dt., set the book in the general framework and theme of the Pentateuch as a whole, and afford links to the Book of Jos. which follows. Editorial intervention and activity are thus inevitably traced in these chapters.

XXXI 1-8 The Immediate Future: The First Arrangement—LXX takes 1 as 'finished speaking', i.e. in reference to what has preceded. The reference is surely to words already spoken to Moses which he now proceeds to address to his people (e.g. 3:26-8 or even 31:14-23). Moses at the age of 120 years, possibly a detail from P, has spanned three generations, and he now makes a number of arrangements for Israel's future after his death. The first is that Joshua, who is mentioned as somebody well known (Exod. 32:17, 33:11), is to take over the leadership, in order to achieve the conquest of Canaan. That the Lord accompanies Israel at their head is probably a reference to the Ark.

g **9-13 The Second Arrangement**—Moses writes the law of D, entrusting it to the care of the religious and civic authorities, and ordains that every seventh feast of Tabernacles, that is, the Tabernacles which falls in the Sabbatical Year (15:1-11) shall be dedicated to this law. The reading of the law at the central sanctuary is enjoined, when all Israel comes to appear, i.e. see the face of God. 'You shall read' in 11 is singular, and may be a reference to the actual person who performs the reading. This is better than to suppose that the original reference was to Joshua. 12 may be a recapitulation of 11 loosely expressed, though it may mean that all those Israelites, who have not gone to the central sanctuary, must also hear the law read.

h **14-23 The Call of Joshua**—14f. are not really a parallel to 1-8 as is often claimed, but rather the presupposition of 1-8. It may well be that 14-15 and 23 once stood before 1-8, but in order to become the introduction to the Song in ch. 32 they may have been removed, but in any case expanded. As they stand, 14-23 clearly are both the background of 1-8 and lead up to the Song. 14-15 and 23 are strongly reminiscent of E. **Present yourselves** is of taking up a station, here, for worship. Tent of meeting (revelation) and pillar of cloud are the emblems of the Tabernacling Presence, revealed and veiled in the cloud. 23 also promises the continuing Presence. 24
16-22 are an editorial introduction to the Song, 22 being resumed in 30. It contains features not characteristic of D ; cf. vv. 17 and 20. The introduction describes the Song as God's prevenient explanation of the situation that will arise in Israel after the settlement. After Moses' death Israel will become idolatrous and will incur God's wrath manifested in many evils. Israel's explanation of these evils will be God's absence. The Song is given as the true explanation, as showing God's prevenient warning and plea to his people. **Purposes** in 21 is *yēṣer*, moulding, imagination, distortion—sometimes good, sometimes neutral, and sometimes of the evil imagination in rebellion against God.

24-27 The Third Arrangement, whereby the book i
of the Law is to be placed beside the Ark as a witness against Israel—The similarity between the words for Law (*Tôrāh*) and Song (*Shîrāh*), and that both Law and Song are to witness against Israel, have led some to suppose that 24-30 once referred to the Song only, but it is better to regard 24-7 or perhaps only 24-26*a*, or perhaps 24-28*a*, as what is left of a command associating the Law with the Ark. The first word of 26 is in Heb. an Infinitive Absolute used as an Imperative, and that may be a pointer to the great age of the tradition. **28f.** 'these words' cannot refer to the Law but must refer to the Song. The chapter is thus in considerable disorder, but the simplest explanation on the whole is to see the chapter as presenting Moses' three plans for his people expanded by an editorial introduction to the Song, whereby the Editor showed that the Song was also a part of Moses' last words to his people. The traditions concerning the written Law and the written Song have become confused.

XXXII 1-47 The Song of Moses is a unity depicting 24
the faithfulness of God and the wickedness and folly of Israel. The Song is didactic, but strong, enthusiastic and sustained. There is a vivid and diverse imagery and also a keen insight into the character and being of God. **7f.** show that the conquest of Canaan is in the days of old, so that the period of composition must be considerably later than Joshua. Even the end of the Judges period, which would suit the military and syncretistic position of the Song, is probably too early. Thus the days of the Syrian wars (*c.* 800 B.C.), or the Assyrian invasion (*c.* 700 B.C.), about 630 B.C., or an exilic and even an early post-exilic date, have all been suggested. No firm decision is possible, but it is probable that it comes after Elijah and before the end of Judah. The metre of the Song is generally 3:3, i.e. each line is divided into two parts, the second part being a parallel to or a balance of the first part, and each part consisting generally of three accented words or groups of words.

1-3 Introduction—Heaven and earth are summoned b
to listen to the speaker's words, for the majesty of the theme demands a supreme audience. In 2 'my teaching' is literally 'my taking', something received, my message, and it is gentle, refreshing and abundant. The first word of 3, 'for', gives the ground for the previous exhortation which is the proclamation of the name, the glory, the character of the Lord. **4-6** is the theme contrasting the enduring faithfulness of God and the treachery of his people. 'The Rock' is a Semitic and Heb. figure of the stability and durability of God. His ways are judgment. He is consistently just and right. 5*a* is corrupt, and the verse may once have had three parts as a variation of the metre.

7-14 shows God's choice of Israel, and his gift to them c
of the land and all its richness. 7 shows that many generations separate the singer from the settlement in Canaan, and the reference to Most High, Elyon, El Elyon, points to a time later than David. El Elyon was the pre-Davidic god of Jerusalem who later became identified with Yahweh, and who brought with him patterns of thought, worship and ritual into the new syncretism of Israel's religion in David's days. Thus the Most High's division of the lands according

3c to the gods may well reflect some old Canaanite theology which passed into Israel and to Yahweh through the syncretism. In 8 the number of the sons of god, or the angels of god, follows LXX, for Heb. has Israel. This Gr. reading has been confirmed from the Heb. MS of Dt. discovered in Cave 4 of the DSS. Thus under Elyon the gods and peoples have their appointed places, and because Canaanite ideas have now been transferred to Yahweh, the high God, i.e. Yahweh, reserves Israel for himself. The Lord alone is Israel's leader, and idolatry should have been excluded in the transition to the agricultural life of Canaan. In 14 again there is an extra half-line. The LXX and Samaritan add a clause (' and Jacob ate and
d was full ') though that may not be necessary. **15-18.** Israel's new agricultural prosperity led to increasing idolatry with new gods and new forms of worship. Jeshurun is Upright or Honest, so the word is obviously used here ironically. Demons, *shēdhîm*, an Akkadian loan word for lesser deities, in fact non-existent deities with whom Israel's fathers had not been acquainted rather than had dreaded. **19-25** portrays the divine judgment described as spurning, hiding of the face, vexation and catastrophes of various kinds. Israel provokes God by means of no-gods, so God will employ peoples that are without God and without hope in the world to rouse Israel. Fire is an appropriate figure for jealousy. 24f. list the evils of 23. **26f.** Yet God stayed the fullness of his judgment, for the dispersion and destruction of Israel would have led Israel's enemies to suppose that Israel's fate was their triumph. Thus God does in the last resort what best suits his will.
e **28-33.** The interpretation depends on the reference of the pronouns. ' They ' in 28f. and ' them ' in 30 probably refer to Israel rather than Israel's foes ; ' their ' in 31–2 refers to Israel's foes, but there is no certainty regarding 28–30. The gods of the peoples cannot compare with Israel's God. It must be he who is responsible for this débâcle, for Israel's enemies are to be classed with the people of Sodom and Gomorrah, who are like the fruits of that region, bitter and poisonous. **34-43** describe God's judgment on Israel's foes. God has sealed up the knowledge of the wickedness of his enemies in his treasuries. ' Vengeance ' does not mean angry revenge but is the appropriate divine attitude : his vengeance spells punishment for the wicked but deliverance for the oppressed. In vindicating his people and reconstituting them there naturally arises the two sides of the theocentric faith of Israel. There is negatively the taunting question concerning Israel's false and now forsaken deities. ' Where are their gods . . . ? ' The disappearance of these false deities leaves the way open for Israel's God to proclaim himself, and to describe himself. God, so to speak, predicates himself. Here again is Auto-kerygma, God's proclamation and description of himself. ' I kill and make alive ' expresses the totality of his power and action. All events go back to the Lord's action. ' Lifting the hand ' in 40 is the sign of the oath, and ' as Yahweh lives ' the most frequent formula of the oath. The Lord takes an oath by himself, for there is no greater than God by whom he may swear his oath. 41f. are the judgment of God depicted in the possible figures of warfare. 43 is a conclusion summoning the people of the earth to praise God and giving the reasons for the summons in God's vindication of his people, and because he has made atonement, i.e. expiation, for the land of his people (so Gr. but Heb. ' his land, his people '). The Heb. word for expiation, *kipper*, is a sacrificial term, used here with God as the subject of the verb to show how God effects forgiveness and clears guilt away from his land and people. **44-7** probably combines an editorial conclusion to the Song (44), and also a conclusion to the Law (45–7) with more characteristic D phraseology. Hoshea is a mistake in the Heb. of 44 for Joshua.

f **48-52 The Last Arrangement**—God bids Moses ascend Nebo in order to view the promised land and to die on the mount. This passage is probably an 243f
expanded parallel or variant of P's account in Num. 27:12–14. ' The day ' of 48 is of course that of 1:3, and cf. Num. 33:50, 36:13. ' Abarim ' in 49 means ' regions beyond ', and suggests the story was told from west of Jordan. P's story of Aaron's death is in Num. 20:22–9. Moses' sin is described in 51 in terms of P's story in Num. 20:11f., and cf. Dt. 1:37, 3:23–9.

XXXIII The Blessing of Moses—The introduction, 244a
1–5, is followed by the blessings bestowed on eleven of Israel's twelve tribes (6–25), followed by a conclusion. The blessing depicts the conquest as in the past, but the song is nevertheless very ancient and must belong to Israel's history when that was still tribal. Joseph has eminence, Judah is in difficulty, Dan has migrated, so that it is most likely that the poem dates from the late Judges period, or the end of the 11th cent. B.C. This is confirmed by the increasing knowledge of Canaanite poetry, and by the claim that the orthography of the poem is probably not later than the 10th cent. The tendency is to date the poem earlier than the previously suggested dates, namely, Jeroboam I or II. The blessings of Moses are comparable to the oracles of Jacob in Gen. 49. They both represent a kind of last testament—Jacob's more from a family point of view, and that of Moses at least in a cultic context. There are thus similarities concerning the location and endowment of the clans, but there are also difficulties. Since 2 depicts a journey by God, and 5 speaks of the assembly of the tribes, it is possible that the clue to the poem is the idea of a procession to or in the Temple. As the tribes pass by they hear the oracles of blessing concerning themselves, so that the occasion is a kind of cultic review of Israel. Even in the days of the early kings tribal groups were maintained, and these would persist to a later date in cultic institutions.

1 is an editorial link to ascribe the blessing to Moses. b
The blessing is Moses' last testament to his people, though of course the poem is of unknown authorship. **2-5** is the prologue or setting of the blessings. 2 is often interpreted as the passage of a thunderstorm across the sky, or of the rising sun, accompanied by the heavenly host, unless of course ' ten thousands of holy ones ' in 2 is corrupt for Meribah-Kadesh as a geographical parallel to the previous clause. ' Flaming fire ' in 2*e* is a guess, but probably some part of the divine retinue is meant. 3. ' his people ' is Gr. for Heb. ' peoples '. Some take ' all those consecrated ' as referring to gods, showing that Israel in possessing the gods holds the leadership, but the procession theme is better, the reference being either to priests almost at the head of the procession or to specially consecrated warriors, who followed or fell in, but hardly reclined or sat, behind the religious emblems at the head of the procession. 4–5 are taken of the lawgiving at Sinai, but if the procession interpretation is right, the verses might simply refer to the Law being carried along, followed by the king leading the tribes as they follow in turn. The tribes must have been gathered in identifiable groups as in an assembly, or successively as in a procession.

6 First comes Reuben, but the introductory rubric, cf. 7*a*, is missing. Reuben is not well represented, because of the danger of extinction, or because of distance from the sanctuary, and the men had to stay to defend their homes. Simeon is not mentioned in the blessing of Moses at all.

7 A prayer for Judah, who is oppressed by enemies. c
Perhaps this prayer implies that Judah was not even present. **8-11** is the blessing of Levi where his double priestly office is described. They are to teach and to sacrifice, though their teaching function is more emphasised. Thummim (Yes) and Urim (No) are the priestly dice or lots used for sacred decisions and advice. The reference to Massah and Meribah is obscure, because Exod. 17:1–7 and Num. 20:2–13, which are the Massah and Meribah narratives, contain no reference to Levi. On the other hand 9 appears to refer to Exod. 32:26, and it may be that the geography

244c of Meribah, and its possible identity with Kadesh, will supply the clue. It has been claimed that 11 alone is the original blessing of Levi and it is more reminiscent of the Levi of Gen. 49. **12** pictures the favoured position of Benjamin whose territory contained the sanctuary of Jerusalem. It is hardly a reference to Benjamin tabernacled between the Lord's shoulders which, even as a figure of divine protection, is meaningless. **13-17.** The longest blessing is spoken to Joseph and the half-tribes of Ephraim and Manasseh. Like Gen. 49 this oracle speaks of Joseph's agricultural wealth, and of his primacy among his brethren. Here is added Joseph's military power and dominion.

d In 13 'the deep' is Tehom—the mythical monster of Babylonian mythology known as Tiamat. The personification lingers in the word 'couch' or 'crouch'. 16. 'bush' is *seneh*, so some read 'who dwelt or tented on Sinai'. 16 summarises 13–15 and depicts the Lord as the giver of all good. 17. Joseph's military might is likened to the goring horns of a bull, and the final clauses mark the end of the passing by of the representatives of these tribes. **18** addresses words of congratulation to Zebulun for their access to the sea or trading ventures, and to Issachar for the location of their homes in some of the cities in or near the plain. **19** however praises them as rich and righteous in sacrifice, and so possibly this cultic meaning should also control 18. Zebulun is then congratulated on its place in the procession and Issachar on its tents of pilgrimage, or possibly of Tabernacles. **20.** Gad was the strongest tribe in Transjordan with a vast territory planned of course for Gad by God. The last two lines of **21** may belong to 4f., unless it has a military reference to Gad assisting Israel in the conquest of the mainland. From **22** it is clear that Dan has migrated from the SW. to the northern position. **23-5.** Naphtali's position, E. of the sea of Galilee, is a very fertile one, so too was Asher's territory—all this northern region being famous for its olives. **26-9** is the conclusion praising Israel's incomparable Lord, the God of Jeshurun. Like the Canaanite Baal, the Lord, no less, is the glorious rider of the clouds. God is Israel's refuge and their support, and the donor of Israel's land. 27 is a short line, and 28 means apartness, either as purity or security. The good fortune of Israel in 29 is couched in heroic rather than religious terms. 244

XXXIV The Death of Moses—The final appendix relates the last scene of all, a triple account of the death of Moses. JE, 1*b*–5*a*, 6, 10 ; D, 11–12 ; and P, 1*a*, 5*b*, 7–9. P's account of the death of Moses would naturally come at the end of Num., but it is here accommodated to the traditions of D. 'Plain of Moab' is the eastern plain in the Jordan valley. 'Nebo' is P and Pisgah E. From the mount there was visible the land with Dan in the north, the Mediterranean on the west, the Negeb in the south, and from Jericho below to the southern end of the Dead Sea (Zoar). **6.** He was buried, but his grave is unknown. Where he preached (3:29, 4:46), there too he was buried. Moses' life force remained fresh and vigorous. Joshua had been formally instituted into office (Num. 27:18–23 (P)) and thus participated to some extent in the executive capacity and authority of Moses himself. But even so Moses remains as the greatest of Israel's prophets (Num. 12:6–8), unique in his standing before God. He was a spiritually endowed leader, with prophetic, priestly and ruling functions. He is the lawgiver and the revealer of God's will and power to Israel. He remains the covenant-maker, the mediator and the founder of Israel, and the originator of the originality of Israel. e

Bibliography—COMMENTARIES : H. Cunliffe-Jones, Torch Comm. (1951) ; S. R. Driver, ICC (2nd ed. 1896) ; J. Reider, *Deuteronomy* (2nd ed. 1948) ; G. Adam Smith, CB (1918) ; G. E. Wright, IB ii (1953).

OTHER LITERATURE : H. H. Rowley, 'The Prophet Jeremiah and the Book of Deuteronomy', *Studies in OT Prophecy* (1950) ; P. W. Skehan, 'A Fragment of the Song of Moses (Dt. 32) from Qumrân', BASOR 136 (1954), 12–15, 'The Structure of the Song of Moses', CBQ 13 (1951), 153–63.

G. von Rad, *Studies in Deuteronomy* (1948) ; A. C. Welch, *The Code of Deuteronomy* (1924), *Deuteronomy : the Framework to the Code* (1932).

THE HISTORICAL BOOKS OF THE OLD TESTAMENT

By G. W. ANDERSON

45a **Introductory**—The OT contains no scientific history in the modern sense of the term. It provides a wide range of material which the modern historian can use, together with the extra-biblical evidence, in writing a history of Israel ; but the books which are commonly classed as historical vary considerably in their general character as literature as well as in the diverse elements of which they are composed. In the arrangement found in the English versions (following LXX and Vulg.) these books are grouped together (Jos.–Est.) as a continuous block of narrative writing between the Pentateuch and the Poetical Books (Job, Ps., Prov.). In the Heb. Bible, however, they are divided between the second and third sections of the Canon. Jos., Jg., 1, 2 Sam., 1, 2 Kg. form the first group in the prophetic Canon, the Former Prophets. The other books are included in the Hagiographa : Ru. and Est. in the Megilloth ; and Ezr., Neh., and 1, 2 Chr., in that order, as the final items in the entire collection. This earlier arrangement, which probably reflects the order in which the books came to be recognised as canonical, has the advantage of separating works which differ considerably in their character and purpose, but also has the demerit of reversing the original order of Ezr.-Neh. and 1, 2 Chr.

b For reasons which will appear in the course of the discussion, it will be appropriate to consider the books in the following order : first, the Former Prophets ; second, 1, 2 Chr., Ezr., Neh. ; and, finally, Ru. and Est.

46a **The Former Prophets**—These books survey the story of Israel's life in Canaan from the Conquest to the Exile. Jos. describes the Conquest (1–12), the division of the land (13–22), and the farewell speeches and death of Joshua (23–4). Jg. begins with an account of various local operations against the Canaanites (1:1–2:5), continues with a long central section which is mainly concerned with the exploits of the Judges (2:6–16:31), and ends with a double appendix (17–21) containing the stories of Micah and the Danites (17f.) and of the outrage at Gibeah and its sequels (19–21). 1, 2 Sam. tell of the transition from the Judges to the monarchy during the ministry of Samuel (1 Sam. 1–12), of the reign of Saul and the success and subsequent outlawry of David (1 Sam. 13–31), of David's reign at Hebron and his establishment as king of all Israel (2 Sam. 1–8), and of the intrigues and struggle for power at the court (2 Sam. 9–20), ending with an appendix of narratives, lists, and poems (2 Sam. 21–4). The story of David's court reaches its climax in Solomon's accession (1 Kg. 1–2). The remainder of 1, 2 Kg. describes Solomon's reign (1 Kg. 3–11), the Disruption and the history of the two kingdoms to the fall of Samaria (1 Kg. 12–2 Kg. 17), and the history of Judah thereafter to the fall of Jerusalem (2 Kg. 18–25).

b In all of these books there is ample evidence of composite authorship. In some ways this evidence resembles the data on which is based the documentary hypothesis of the composition of the Pentateuch. The two main critical questions which arise are (*a*) whether, and to what extent, the main Pentateuchal sources are continued in the Former Prophets, and (*b*) whether the Deuteronomic element in these books represents but one of a number of stages of editorial activity or was the decisive and constitutive influence which gave shape and purpose to the entire compilation. 246b

(*a*) In the narratives in Jos. 1–12 there are signs of a conflation of sources, as may be seen if we compare 3:1f. with 4:10f., 4:8, 20 with 4:9, and 8:3 with 8:12, or try to reconstruct from 6 the preparations for the fall of Jericho. Various elements have been assigned to the sources L, J, and E, but the analyses differ greatly in detail ; and it is probably safer simply to recognise the presence of varying strands of pre-Deuteronomic material. The importance of the aetiological motive in these stories has been emphasised by Alt and his school. There is little trace of the influence of P ; but the framework of the narratives is Deuteronomic (1 *passim*, 2:10f., 4:21–4, 8:30–5, etc.). c

Jos. 13–22 contains many lists, the presence of which, together with some traits of a Priestly character, has suggested that P is the dominant element in this part of the book. There are, however, sundry short notices which indicate the piecemeal nature of the Conquest and thus contrast with the general impression given by 1–12. These notices are certainly old and have often been assigned to J. But even the lists may well contain ancient material. Alt has contended that 15 goes back to Josiah's reign and that the rest of 13–19 is pre-monarchic. There are also some Deuteronomic sections. Jos. 23 is Deuteronomic ; and Deuteronomic features also appear in 24, though the bulk of it has usually been assigned to E. d

Jg. 1:1–2:5 is mostly ancient material, sometimes attributed to J (or L). 2:6–16:31 consists of narratives set in a Deuteronomic framework and with a Deuteronomic preface (2:6–3:6). There are signs that the narratives are composite. But there is considerable difference of opinion about the analysis into J (or L and J) and E ; and some scholars reject the view that these sources exist here. The framework interprets the stories in terms of the Deuteronomic principle that apostasy leads to disaster and repentance brings deliverance. It presents the crises as the result of *national* apostasy, whereas the narratives give them a merely regional setting. Further, it supplies chronological data which are generally regarded as artificial (contrast the chronological data given for the Minor Judges in 3:31, 10:1f., 3–5, 12:8–10, 11f., 13–15) and unreliable. This chronological scheme is continued into 1 Sam., but does not appear in Jg. 17–21. The stories in these latter chapters contain very old material (which has been assigned to L and J) with some later modifications (possibly akin to P). Because of the absence of the framework and of other Deuteronomic features, it has usually been held that this appendix was not present in the Deuteronomic edition of Jg. But the implied criticism of the sanctuary of Dan in 17f. and of Saul's tribe, Benjamin, in 19–21, would have been congenial to a Deuteronomic writer. e

In 1 and 2 Sam. signs of composite authorship are f

246f particularly evident in 1 Sam. 8–12, where at least two (and possibly three) accounts of the origin of the monarchy appear, one treating it as a gift of God to his people (1 Sam. 9:1–10:16, 11:1–11, 15), the other critical of it (8, 10:17–27, 12). Other duplicate narratives occur (e.g. 1 Sam. 2:31–6 and 3:11–14, 13:7*b*–14 and 15, 16:14–23 and 17:55–8, 21:10–15 and 27:5–12, 24 and 26). As in Jos. and Jg., some scholars have found here L, J, and E; but some of the material assigned to E has been thought by others to be Deuteronomic. Against this kind of analysis, however, it is argued that much of the material is derived from sources relating to persons or institutions, thus: S (7th cent.), stories about Samuel (1 Sam. 1–3, 15:1–16:13); A (10th cent.), stories about the Ark (1 Sam. 4:1–7:1; 2 Sam. 6); D (7th cent.), a source critical of the monarchy (1 Sam. 7:2–8:22, 10:17–27, 12; 2 Sam. 7); M (10th cent.), a source favourable to the monarchy (1 Sam. 9:1–10:16, 11:1–11, 15, and most of 1 Sam. 13–2 Sam. 6); C (10th cent.), the history of David's court (2 Sam. 9–20 with the conclusion in 1 Kg. 1f.); and various minor additions.

g In 1, 2 Kg. some of the sources are named in the text: the Book of the Acts of Solomon (1 Kg. 11:41), the Book of the Chronicles of the Kings of Israel (1 Kg. 14:19 etc.), the Book of the Chronicles of the Kings of Judah (1 Kg. 14:29 etc.). But clearly there were others. As noted above, 1 Kg. 1f. is the conclusion of the history of David's court. The story of Solomon's reign contains archival and annalistic elements (e.g. 1 Kg. 4:1–19, 27f., 5:6–11, 9:10–14, 15–28, 10:11f., 14–29, 11:14–25), some at least of which may have come from the Book of the Acts of Solomon. There are also entertaining or edifying tales drawn from popular tradition (3:3–15, 16–28, 10:1–10, 13). The account of Solomon's building-enterprises contains technical details, possibly taken from Temple records. In 1 Kg. 8, which records the dedication of the Temple, the Deuteronomic element is prominent. It also appears sporadically throughout these chapters, notably in 11:1–13. But both here and elsewhere in 1, 2 Kg. the attempt to trace a continuation of the earlier Pentateuchal sources seems questionable. In the remainder of 1, 2 Kg. it is probable that the Books of the Chronicles of the Kings of Israel and Judah (not to be identified with the canonical Books of Chronicles) have provided the bulk of the less detailed records of the acts and policies of the kings. Some passages relating to the Temple (e.g. 2 Kg. 11:4ff., 12:4ff., 22:3ff.) may have been taken from records preserved there. The stories about Ahab in 1 Kg. 20 (except vv. 35–43), 22 have been attributed to a hypothetical 'Acts of Ahab'. Ahab is there (especially in 20) presented more favourably than elsewhere. Whatever the character of this source, it was probably nearly contemporary with Ahab. The doings of Elijah (1 Kg. 17–19, 21; 2 Kg. 1) and of Elisha (2 Kg. 2–10, 13:14–19, 20f.) were no doubt transmitted, at first orally and later in writing, in prophetic circles in the north. Other material which may have been derived from prophetic sources is found in 1 Kg. 14 and 2 Kg. 18:17–20:19 (= Isa. 36–9). 1 Kg. 13 may be a sanctuary tradition from Bethel refurbished in the interests of edification. Throughout 1 Kg. 12–2 Kg. 25 short Deuteronomic passages frequently occur. There are also a few longer passages, such as 2 Kg. 17:7–23, 21:1–18, 24:8–25:30, which narrate or comment on events in terms of Deuteronomic teaching. Finally, as in Jg., there is a framework which provides both a chronological scheme and religious judgments on the reigns.

h Critical opinion has varied so widely that it is impossible to state concisely and fairly the balance of scholarly opinion. The case for the existence of sources which may be equated with the Pentateuchal J and E is strongest in Jos.; but throughout Jos.–2 Kg. scholars differ widely about the passages which they ascribe to these sources. On the other hand, the Deuteronomic passages are for the most part unmistakable. Further, whereas in Gen.–Num. the framework is P, in Jos.–2 Kg. the framework (most obviously in Jg. and Kg.) is provided by D. It is, therefore, safest to regard these books as a compilation of earlier material from various sources made by a Deuteronomic writer or writers. There are, it is true, passages akin to P; but these (except, perhaps, in Jos.) are relatively few and unimportant. 24

(*b*) It has usually been held, particularly by those who find the earlier Pentateuchal sources in Jos.–2 Kg., that at least Jos., Jg., and 1, 2 Sam. existed in a pre-Deuteronomic form, were edited by D, and subsequently revised and expanded. But it is doubtful whether the evidence is sufficient for so detailed a reconstruction. Far more probable is the view, which has been cogently presented by M. Noth, that in Jos.–2 Kg. we have a historical corpus which was first given substantially its present shape by a Deuteronomic writer. The term Hexateuch has often been used to describe Gen.–Jos. as a complete literary whole; but Noth holds that the Pentateuchal sources, J, E, and P, are not found after the end of Num., and that the code of D and its hortatory preface have been incorporated in a great Deuteronomic history, spanning the period from the Conquest to the Exile. This seems the most likely view; but it should be added that in 1, 2 Kg. there are signs of more than one phase of the Deuteronomic authorship (1 Kg. 8:18, 11:36; 2 Kg. 8:19, 22, 22:20; cf. 2 Kg. 23:29f., 25:8ff.). i

Thus we have in Jos.–2 Kg. a selective historical work which is intended not only to provide historical information but to exemplify Deuteronomic teaching. Because it is selective, much important material has been omitted. Many reigns (e.g. that of Omri) are only briefly recorded; others (e.g. those of Ahab and Josiah) are recounted at considerable length because of their religious importance. Among Solomon's achievements the building of the Temple takes pride of place. But the selection has preserved for us a wide range of material: stories of the saga type, folk tales, prophetic traditions, annalistic and archival records, and the Deuteronomist's own interpretative comments and narratives. j

The value of the historical record varies. The main features of Joshua's campaigns are probably correctly outlined; but the gradual character of the Conquest and settlement is obscured in Jos. 1–12, though it is implied by Jg. 1 and by occasional references in Jos. 13–22. Jg. reflects vividly both the conditions of the period after the settlement and also the development towards monarchy; but the artificial chronological scheme imposed on the narratives by the Deuteronomic historian is misleading. 1, 2 Sam. contain much valuable material about the transition from the judges to the monarchy, and in some of the passages of later origin a penetrating criticism of what the monarchy subsequently became. But their supreme historical and literary treasure is the Court History, which is in all probability the work of one who had personal knowledge of the events which he described. Here we have passed from the realm of tradition and saga to historical and biographical writing of a remarkably objective character about events and persons of decisive importance in the development of Israel's life. The obvious parallel to this in 1, 2 Kg. is the sequence of narratives about the house of Omri and the prophets Elijah and Elisha (1 Kg. 17–2 Kg. 10). As we have seen, these are of diverse origin; but again we have a series of critical situations described with insight and literary power. These chapters contribute richly to our knowledge of the political, social, and religious history of the Northern Kingdom in the 9th cent. The closing sections of 2 Kg., describing the great reform and the closing decades of the kingdom of Judah, provide an illuminating picture of events of far-reaching importance. k

Two features in 1, 2 Kg. call for special comment: (1) Though the chronological data do not reveal the artificial features which appear in the framework of Jg., l

246l the synchronisms between the reigns of the kings of Israel and Judah raise complicated problems. (2) The Deuteronomic outlook, which doubtless greatly influenced the selection of material from the available sources, is evident in both the implicit and the explicit judgments on persons and events. The building of the Temple is presented as the great glory of Solomon's reign; and when he is criticised it is for religious infidelity. The religious policy of Jeroboam I is condemned by Deuteronomic standards (1 Kg. 12:25–33). A similar indictment is advanced to account for the fall of the Northern Kingdom (2 Kg. 17:7–18). Further, the apportioning of praise and blame to the kings of both Ephraim and Judah is governed by the Deuteronomic hostility to syncretism and by the law of the single sanctuary.

m Thus in the Former Prophets we have a historical corpus in which are preserved data and documents of great interest and importance. But the selection and presentation of the material has been influenced by a religious aim: to show the operation of God's will in the history of his people, the fulfilment of his promises and warnings in their prosperity and affliction.

247a **The Chronicler's History**—1, 2 Chr., Ezr., and Neh. form a comprehensive though sometimes disjointed history from Adam to the 5th (or perhaps 4th) cent. B.C. Strictly the history begins at the end of Saul's reign. 1 Chr. 1–9 contain genealogical tables; and 10–29 take the story on from the death of Saul to the death of David. Solomon's reign is surveyed in 2 Chr. 1–9, and the remainder of the history up to the return from exile in 10–36. Ezr., Neh. focus attention mainly on three phases in the life of the returned community: the rebuilding of the Temple under Zerubbabel and Jeshua (Ezr. 1–6); the work of Ezra (Ezr. 7–10); and the achievements of Nehemiah (Neh. 1–13). The account of Nehemiah's work falls into two parts: the repair of the city wall (1–7) and other incidents during his double governorship, prefaced by a description of the public reading of the Law under Ezra's supervision and a celebration of the Feast of Tabernacles (8–13).

b It was noted above (§245*a*) that in the Hebrew Bible Ezr.-Neh. precede 1, 2 Chr. Presumably this indicates the order in which the books were admitted to the Canon. The overlap of a verse or two (2 Chr. 36:22–3 = Ezr. 1:1–3*a*) points to the original continuity.

c The entire work covers a longer period than the Former Prophets; but it does so selectively and from a somewhat different point of view. Clearly Sam. and Kg. have been used as sources for the appropriate periods; but no use has been made of the narrative of David's reign at Hebron (2 Sam. 1–4) or of the Court History (2 Sam. 9–1 Kg. 2); and the history of the Northern Kingdom is referred to only incidentally. Additional material is included, notably in the genealogies and lists, in passages which reflect an interest in the Temple, and in the whole of Ezr.-Neh.

d In 1, 2 Chr. there are references to 'the Book of the Kings of Judah and Israel' (2 Chr. 16:11 etc.), 'the Book of the Kings of Israel' (2 Chr. 20:34), 'the Commentary on the Book of the Kings' (2 Chr. 24:27), 'the Book of the Kings of Israel and Judah' (2 Chr. 27:7 etc.), and 'the Chronicles of the Kings of Israel' (2 Chr. 33:18). All these titles, however, may refer to the same source. There are also frequent references to what appear to be prophetic sources, e.g. 'the Chronicles of Samuel the seer', 'the Chronicles of Nathan the prophet', 'the Chronicles of Gad the seer' (1 Chr. 29:29), 'the history of Nathan the prophet', 'the prophecy of Ahijah the Shilonite', 'the visions of Iddo the seer' (2 Chr. 9:29), 'the chronicles of Shemaiah the prophet and of Iddo the seer' (2 Chr. 12:15), 'the chronicles of Jehu the son of Hanani, which are recorded in the Book of the Kings of Israel' (2 Chr. 20:34), 'the vision of Isaiah the prophet the son of Amoz, in the Book of the Kings of Judah and Israel' (2 Chr. 32:32). Again, it is unlikely that each of these titles refers to a separate source. Some, at least, may be identified with portions 247d of Sam. and Kg. The Chronicler's account of the reigns of David and Solomon is clearly derived from these books; but in the later period (2 Chr. 10–36) he gives additional information not found there. Probably he used an expanded edition of 1, 2 Kg.

In Ezr.-Neh. parts of the narrative are autobiographical. e Neh. 1:1–7, 73*a* and some passages in Neh. 11–13 probably come from a personal journal written by Nehemiah himself. If the autobiographical passages in Ezr. 7–10, Neh. 8–9 go back to Ezr., they have been more extensively edited. Other sources incorporated in this part of the Chronicler's history are difficult to evaluate and interpret. The lists of names and other documents quoted are not always in context. The most bewildering collocation of documents and narratives is in Ezr. 4–6, most of which is in Aramaic. In this short passage there are references to the reigns of Cyrus, Darius I, Xerxes I, and Artaxerxes I, and to the rebuilding of the Temple, the walls, and the city of Jerusalem, in an order which is neither logical nor chronological.

It is generally held that there is a homogeneity of f editorial method and style which justifies us in treating this work with its varied ingredients as one, though there may have been more than one recension of it. Probably the 4th cent. is a reasonable period to which to assign the definitive editorial work; but there is considerable variety of theory about the dating and the number and extent of the editorial processes.

What we know of the use made by the Chronicler of g Sam. and Kg., and what we can readily infer about his use of other sources, suggests that reconstructing from his narrative the actual course of events will not always be easy. Two outstanding historical problems are raised by his history. The first is the early history of the returned community, on which the contemporary evidence of Hag. and Zech. is not easily reconciled with that of the early chapters of Ezr. The second is the date of Ezra's coming to Jerusalem, which the Chronicler appears to place before Nehemiah's arrival. On both internal and external evidence, many scholars have held that a later date is more probable, 397 B.C. being the year most commonly suggested. On these and other questions of detail, reference should be made to the discussions in the commentaries. For our present purpose we may note two general principles. On the one hand the Chronicler's selective and confusing use of his sources should not lead us to underestimate their value. Though great skill and caution are needed in their interpretation, the documents and lists which he cites need not simply be written off as late fabrications. On the other hand, this is highly interpretative history writing. If, like the Deuteronomistic historian, the Chronicler uses history as a vehicle of religious teaching, he is more prone to impose his ideas on the narrative than simply to elicit the lessons conveyed by the events.

His general interpretation of the history has much in h common with the Pentateuchal source P; and some of his favourite themes resemble those found there. There is the same cultic and liturgical interest, but with this difference, that the Levitical order is more prominent. The central theme is the establishment and re-establishment in the land of Israel of the holy community, and the right ordering of its life and worship. Judah, its capital, its royal house, and its sanctuary are exalted at the expense of the Northern Kingdom, which, both in the genealogical lists and in the narrative, is given a subordinate position. This undoubtedly reflects the opposition in Judah in the Chronicler's own day to the Samaritan community and its claims. Some of the important developments in that mounting hostility are recorded in Ezr.-Neh. Presumably it is this rivalry which has led the Chronicler to lay so much emphasis in his narrative on the pre-eminence of the tribe, dynasty and city of David. It is all the more remarkable that he seems to make no reference to any hope of the restoration of David's house.

248a **Ruth and Esther**—In these two books it may be said that we have examples of historical fiction ; but the statement calls for both qualification and discrimination. It is unlikely that either is a purely imaginative construction set against a particular historical background ; and of the two it is probable that Ru. is closer to authentic historical record. It has also been claimed that both were produced as the instruments of religious propaganda, though it has been a common complaint against Est. that it is lacking in religious content.

b It is usually held that the classical style and diction of **Ruth** are the result of the conscious artistry of a post-exilic writer ; and although a pre-exilic date is not absolutely impossible, it is less likely. Granted a post-exilic date, then, it is tempting to find in the story a reflection of developments in the religion of that period. Many scholars have been quick to succumb to the temptation. The idyll of the magnanimity, courage, and devotion of the Moabitess is usually taken to be a counterblast to the hostility of Ezra and Nehemiah to marriages with foreign women. But this, the prevailing interpretation of the book, is not convincing. It has been observed that Ruth, though a foreigner, had become a worshipper of Israel's God and that this would blunt the point of any intended thrust at the policy of Ezra and Nehemiah. Surely the commanding position of the Davidic house in the tradition and hopes of Israel provided sufficient motive for the telling of this tale, in which, moreover, some of the basic virtues inculcated by Israel's religious teachers are so effectively set forth.

c **Esther** tells of a plot to massacre Jews throughout the Persian Empire, which was foiled by the adroit and courageous intervention of Esther, and of the celebration of this deliverance at the feast of Purim. The historical inaccuracies which the book contains amply justify the description of it as fiction. King Ahasuerus is Xerxes I (485–465 B.C.), in whose reign a survivor of the deportation of 597 B.C. (Mordecai is so described) could hardly have taken an active hand in events. Further, the records of the king's reign say nothing of Vashti or Esther. On the other hand, it is probably wrong (but cf. §331*f*) to try to identify the main characters with deities (Mordecai=Marduk, Esther=Ishtar, Vashti=Mashti, Haman=Human). The writer means to tell a story about the doings of Jews under Persian rule. He may have had some historical basis for his tale ; but he has departed considerably from strict historical truth.

d It is difficult to resist the conclusion that part at least of his purpose was to commend (or, as R. H. Pfeiffer held, to introduce) the feast of Purim. For the vexed question of the meaning of the name of this feast and the source from which the Jews borrowed it, cf. §§331*fg*, 334*i*. Whether or not we accept Pfeiffer's view that it was introduced in the reign of John Hyrcanus (135–104 B.C.) as a nationalistic festival, its character as presented to us here agrees well with the nationalist spirit which pervades Est. and also with the nationalism which flourished in the Judaism of the 2nd cent. B.C., the period to which the composition of the book is assigned. Further, it is characteristic of the OT that, in commending this feast, for which there is no warrant in the Pentateuchal legislation, the author associates it with a historic setting.

Conclusion—Basic to any understanding of the historical books of the OT is the Israelite faith that Yahweh had revealed himself and continued to reveal himself in historical events. This presupposition underlies not only the literature surveyed above, but much else in the OT. It is the central message in the Pentateuch ; it is the motive of much of the praise and supplication in the Psalter ; and it is the very staple of the prophetic teaching in its classical form. Only when we remember the existence of this faith can we rightly appraise and interpret the varied literature which we have surveyed. e

Much that has been said above may have seemed to suggest that this selective, interpretative writing of history is a singularly distorting mirror of the past. But the supremely important fact is that the record has been set down in order to make plain the purposes of God rather than the policies of nations and their rulers. The great glory of Israel, in the eyes of the writers, is not any achievement of its own, but the fact that it is the chosen people of Yahweh. That is why successes are the triumphs not of kings and heroes but of Yahweh, and defeats and reverses are presented as the just punishment of apostasy and as remedial discipline. Even the darkest pages of the record convey the sense of the continuing divine purpose. f

Bibliography—In addition to the relevant parts of the standard Introductions to the OT and the literature on the separate books (see commentaries), see the following : R. C. Dentan (ed.), *The Idea of History in the Ancient Near East* (1955) ; O. Eissfeldt, *Geschichtsschreibung im AT* (1948) ; J. Hempel, *AT und Geschichte* (1930) ; E. Jacob, *La tradition historique en Israël* (1946) ; C. R. North, *The OT Interpretation of History* (1946) ; M. Noth, *Überlieferungsgeschichtliche Studien* (1943) ; G. Östborn, *Yahweh's Words and Deeds* (1952) ; A. Weiser, *Glaube und Geschichte im AT*, BWANT iv, 4 (1931).

JOSHUA

By H. G. MAY

249a **Date and Authorship of the Book of Joshua**—The division of the OT into the Law (Genesis to Deuteronomy), the Prophets (the Former Prophets—Joshua, Judges, Samuel, Kings, and the Latter Prophets—Isaiah, Jeremiah, Ezekiel and the twelve so-called minor prophets), and the Hagiographa or Writings (the remaining canonical books) has unfortunately suggested a false discontinuity between Deuteronomy and Joshua. Rather than speak of Genesis to Deuteronomy as the Pentateuch, one should consider the first six books of the OT together as a Hexateuch. Although OT scholars are not unanimous on the subject, the same four basic sources which occur in the Pentateuch may be traced at least as far as through the book of Joshua.

b If this is true, in its present form the book of Joshua must be dated to about the time of the completion of the Pentateuch. Just when this was is a matter of difference of opinion, some scholars presuming that the Pentateuch was completed as early as the time of Ezra (458 or 398), while others would date it later than Ezra. In any case, it was probably not much after 400 B.C. at the latest that the books of the Hexateuch had taken the form in which we now have them. Whatever one's views may be regarding the sources and date of the book of Joshua, it is generally agreed that the book is composite, and that it must certainly come from a long time after Joshua. Hints of later origin are found in the recurrent phrase 'to this day' (4:9, 5:9, 6:25, 7:26, etc.) or in the reference to a source book, 'The Book of Jashar' (10:12, 13), which also had in it David's lament over Saul and Jonathan (2 Sam. 1:17, 18). There is a presumption of the Temple at Jerusalem existing or having existed (6:19, 24, 9:27, 22:19), and the exile is apparently an accomplished fact (23:12, 13).

c Not only does the book of Joshua have to be seen in its associations with the Pentateuch, but it also must be viewed in special relationship to the books of Deuteronomy, Judges, Samuel and Kings. One might, indeed, call Deuteronomy, Joshua, Judges, Samuel and Kings a Deuteronomic Pentateuch; all have been subjected to Deuteronomic (D) revision or revisions. In other words, there existed a Deuteronomic corpus of literature which began with a series of addresses by Moses, recapitulating the journeys from Mt Horeb and the conquest of Transjordan, giving the laws and statutes the Israelites were to observe in Canaan, and reaffirming the covenant; it continued with the account of the death of Moses, the conquest of Canaan, the rule of the Judges, the formation of the monarchy, and the history of the united and divided monarchies. This Deuteronomic corpus, which had used the relevant parts of the JE history, may have been consciously regarded as a continuation of it, but was nevertheless a unified composition. It was composed obviously after the reformation of Josiah in 621, perhaps in more than one stage, and its final date may have been during the exile or just after the return from exile.

d Some details of the Deuteronomic message in the book of Joshua are as follows. The Lord had given Israel the land, and therefore no enemy could withstand her if Israel was faithful to him and obeyed the law of Moses (1:3–9, 22:4, 5, 23:6, 7). There are many references to the law, and it is in keeping with this that the Deuteronomist stresses Joshua as Moses' successor, who reaffirmed the law at Shechem (see (1:5, 16, 4:14, 8:30–35, etc.). The Canaanites' hearts melted in fear because of the wonders the Lord had wrought even before the Israelites had struck a blow in the promised land (2:10, 11, 5:1). This is e
consonant with the Lord being really responsible for the conquest of the land, as the conquest of Jericho or the defeat of the kings at Gibeon, accompanied by the miraculous, dramatically illustrates (see 6:2–5, 10:11–13). We have here the 'Holy War' concept, recalling the legislation in Deuteronomy 20. 'The Lord fought for Israel' (10:14, 42), and it was he who drove out the great and strong nations before Israel (3:10, 9:24, 23:5–10). The completeness of the conquest is stressed, particularly in the summaries (10:28–43, 11:20–23). Joshua 'left none remaining, but utterly destroyed all that breathed', we are told (10:40; cf. 11:14). The Deuteronomist may be responsible for the picture of the conquest completed in two major campaigns (11:16–21), although it is recognised that the conquest was actually not as complete as it was in theory.

As one might expect, the Deuteronomist makes f
much of the role of the Levitical priests in relation to the Ark, and the Ark is called the Ark of the Covenant of the Lord, consonant with the Deuteronomic concern for the Covenant (3:2–4, 6–9, 4:11, 8:33). The didactic purposes are illustrated in the memorials which are to serve for teaching purposes to the descendants of Israel (4:21–24), and educational interests are also reflected in the picture of the reading of the law before all Israel, including children and foreigners (8:35). God's miraculous acts in history were so that all peoples might know that his hand is mighty and that Israel might fear him (4:23, 24), and the universal rule of God is affirmed (2:10, 11).

The extent of the Priestly source (P) in Joshua is g
uncertain, depending in part on whether the detailed geographical lists in chs. 13–19 belong to P. The D materials in these chapters are not such as to indicate whether they were originally accompanied by geographical lists (see 14:6–14; 21:43–45), although the earlier sources were apparently acquainted with a tradition that the tribal allotments were 'by towns' (18:9). More recently some scholars have described chs. 13–21 as essentially a D edition. However, it is certain that P writes with the geographical lists in mind, and in favour of the fact that they were inserted by P rather than D is the characteristic P phrase, 'according to their families' in the lists, found also in P more than 50 times in Numbers, often in associations recalling the diction of the lists. The use of the phrase 'fathers' house' to represent a technical tribal division is characteristic of P, occurring some 40 times in Numbers alone. P, rather than D, is responsible for listing the Levitical cities in ch. 21. It is more than probable, however, that P did not invent the geographical lists, but is relying on early source materials; the lists of border cities may ultimately

249g go back as early as the time of Solomon, and the lists of cities within the tribes to the seventh century or earlier.

h John Bright ('The Book of Joshua', IB ii (1953), 542–6), following the lead of Martin Noth (*Das Buch Josua*, HAT (1938), xiv–xv), argues that there is no reason to assign the bulk of chs. 13–19 to P, for there is no real P document here, but only a few P glosses. Noth himself denies that Joshua contains any of the Pentateuchal sources, save for D, and would, in fact, find JEP only in Genesis to Numbers, reckoning Deuteronomy to Kings a single literary unit. Bright more plausibly recognises P material in Joshua, although ascribing the geographical lists to the Deuteronomic edition.

i The P source concern for the details of the allotment of the land, the appointment of the cities of refuge, and the Levitical cities is consonant with the character of P in the Pentateuch. P introduces the allotment of the land at Shiloh, the predecessor of the Jerusalem sanctuary (18:1, 19:51 ; it has been suggested that 18:1 is misplaced, and that it should introduce the allotment narrative, placing all of the allotment at Shiloh, rather than part of it at Gilgal). Naturally it is this source which makes Eleazar, the grandson of Aaron, the colleague of Joshua in the allotment (14:1*b*, 17:4, 19:51). Characteristically P presents the Israelite community as a 'congregation', an ecclesiastical conception ; this appears particularly in the story of Gibeon's deception (9:15, 18, 27) and of the conflict between the Cisjordan and Transjordan tribes (22:12, 16, 18, 20, 30). The prerogatives of the sanctuary are maintained (6:19 ; see also 9:21). It is the P source which narrates the celebration of the Passover at Gilgal shortly after the Jordan crossing (5:10–12), and which gives the date for the crossing as the tenth day of the first month in the calendrical style of the P source (4:19 ; see Exod. 12:1–20).

j The quite complete confusion in OT scholarship in the differentiation between the J and the E sources in Joshua exemplifies the difficulty in making such a distinction. W. Rudolph (*Der Elohist von Exodus bis Joshua*, BZAW 68 (1938), 164–253) finds no E material at all in Joshua 1–12, but rather J material. Noth finds neither J nor E, but interprets the pre-Deuteronomic materials as aetiological legends preserved at Gilgal and two locally preserved legends from the south and the north (10 and 9:1–9), these all dating between the division of the monarchy and the time of Ahab. Compare also the aetiological-legend views of Alt and Möhlenbrink. S. R. Driver, C. R. North, A. Weiser and J. Bright find a composite JE, without trying to disentangle them, and this is the conclusion to which we are forced and which has been adopted in this commentary. But A. Bentzen is probably also correct in not denying that there are some values in the aetiological and hero-legend theories, or in the cult-motif or cult-lyric approach of G. von Rad, for this may show us the ultimate origins of certain materials in JE.

250a **The Joshua of History and the Story of Joshua**—It is seemingly as difficult to determine the role of Joshua in history as the role of Moses. Both figures are inextricably bound up in the whole complicated problem of the nature and date of the Exodus. See the general introductory article, *History of Israel : Pre-Exilic*, for a discussion of the history of this period, and, more particularly, the rich collection of data and creative interpretation in H. H. Rowley's volume, *From Joseph to Joshua* (1950). The relationship of the *Ḫabiru* (*Ḫapiru*) of the Amarna correspondence to the Hebrew conquest under Joshua is more obscure than ever, and it is difficult to maintain with any assurance the position of T. J. Meek that Joshua led the northern tribes into Canaan in the Amarna period in the early 14th century and conquered northern Canaan, including Hazor (T. J. Meek, *Hebrew Origins* (Revised
b Ed., 1950), 18–29). Hazor's fall was clearly in the following century (see on 11:1). It has been suggested (Rowley) that there were invasions from both the **25**
north and the south in the Amarna period, with the Joseph tribes then going down into Egypt to come out the following century under Moses, Joshua taking over after his death and conquering the central highlands. It may be that the Hazor excavations point to a larger role for Joshua than some hypotheses have presumed. Whereas the presence of aetiological and cult legends in the book of Joshua and much idealisation of the conquest cannot be denied, there lies behind the narrative a Joshua who provided significant leadership in the conquest of Canaan after the death of Moses.

Among the later accretions of the tradition are probably the following : (1) The conquest divided into just two major campaigns. (2) The conquest of some cities by Joshua which were actually conquered after his death, as is evident from Judges, ch. 1. (3) The presence of the Ark and the tent of meeting. (4) The role and largely the nature of the priesthood as described. (5) Shiloh as a central sanctuary in this period. (6) The role of the Transjordan tribes in the conquest of Cisjordan. (7) The division of the land among the tribes at one time and by lot. (8) The covenant at Shechem before the conquest. (9) The assignment of the Levitic cities at the time of Joshua. (10) The selection of the six cities of refuge during Joshua's lifetime. Although the last two items post-dated Joshua's age, they are not an invention of the authors of the sources of the book of Joshua. Exodus 21:13, 14 (E) reflects the appointment of a place of refuge ; specific cities of refuge, with the number not specified, may have been an early institution. Originally the local sanctuary may have served as place of asylum. It has been suggested that the Deuteronomic reform of Josiah may be the earliest time that the six cities of refuge were appointed, after the abolition of the local sanctuaries. **c**

The Contents of the Book of Joshua—After the death of Moses Joshua succeeded to the leadership of Israel and made plans for crossing into Canaan from the camp at Shittim. He first sent spies to Jericho, who were aided by Rahab and who brought back a report favourable to the Israelites (1–2). Moving camp to the edge of the Jordan, the Israelites crossed over, the waters of the Jordan stopping as soon as the feet of the priests bearing the Ark touched the water. Twelve stones were set up to commemorate the event, and camp was established at Gilgal, north-east of Jericho (3–4). The Israelites were circumcised at Gilgal and the Passover was celebrated (5:1–12). **d**

The first two cities to be taken were Jericho and Ai. With instructions from the Lord to make a *ḥerem* or utter destruction of Jericho, the city fell when the Israelites marched around it the thirteenth time in procession, led by the priests bearing the Ark, and only Rahab and her household were spared (6). Because of Achan's sin in keeping some of the spoil of the city for himself, the first attack on Ai met with failure, and the sin was expiated from Israel by the burning and stoning of Achan and his household (7). The second attempt on Ai resulted in the devotion of the city and the hanging of its king (8:1–29). Then at Shechem Joshua built an altar and made a copy of the law, and the covenant was reaffirmed (8:30–35). **e**

Through a ruse the Gibeonites, who represented a tetrapolis comprising Gibeon, Chephirah, Beeroth and Kiriath-jearim, secured a treaty from Joshua and the Israelites (9). In reprisal against this defection to the invaders, Jerusalem led a coalition of cities of southern Canaan (Jerusalem, Hebron, Jarmuth, Lachish, Eglon) against Gibeon, which asked and secured the aid of Joshua ; the Israelites defeated the coalition, its kings were slain, and Makkedah, Libnah, Lachish, Eglon, Debir and Hebron were put to the sword, presumably resulting in the conquest of south Canaan (10). A coalition of Canaanite cities in the north was led by Hazor, in close association with Madon, Shimron, and Achshaph ; it was defeated **f**

0f by Joshua at the waters of Merom, giving Joshua north Canaan (11). The defeated kings of Canaan are listed (12).

g The conquest completed, the division of the land among the tribes followed (13–21). First the territory of the three Transjordan tribes, Reuben, Gad and half of the tribe of Manasseh, was delimited (13). Then the distribution of the land in Cisjordan by lot was made, preceded by explanatory materials and giving an inheritance to Caleb (14). The first tribe to receive its allotment at Gilgal was Judah (15), followed by the Joseph tribes, Ephraim and Manasseh (16, 17). The rest of the land was surveyed to determine the allotments of the remaining seven tribes, Benjamin, Simeon, Zebulun, Issachar, Asher, Naphtali and Dan, the lots being drawn at Shiloh (18, 19). The allotment concluded with the appointment of the cities of refuge (20) and the Levitical cities (21). The Transjordan tribes returned to their allotment, building an altar on the west side of the Jordan River to indicate their integral relationship with the rest of Israel (22). Joshua made two farewell addresses and was buried at Timnath-serah in the hill-country of Ephraim (23, 24).

1a **I 1-18 Introduction to the Story of the Conquest of Canaan**—The consistent Deuteronomic character of the diction and ideology of this chapter hardly needs detailed exposition; compare Dt. 1:29, 30, 3:18–20, 5:32, 7:21, 11:24, 25, 31, 20:3, 29:9, 31:6, 23, etc. A comparison of 1:1 with 13:1 and 23:1 suggests the main framework of the Deuteronomist's arrangement of his materials (i.e., 'after the death of Moses', 'Joshua was old and advanced in years', 'a long time afterwards'). Note how the Lord's speech in 1:1–9 is balanced by Joshua's words in ch. 23.

b **1-9 The Commission of Joshua**—Moses, the servant of the Lord, was dead (Dt. 34:5). Before his death Joshua had been commissioned by the Lord (Dt. 31:14–22). Moses is many times called 'the servant of the Lord' in the book of Joshua. Joshua is designated the 'minister' of Moses in Exod. 24:13, 33:11; Num. 11:28 (JE); it has reference to him as personal assistant, and not to cultic service, although the term is often used of priests and Levites. In **2** delete with LXX the explanatory gloss 'to the people of Israel', and in **4** with LXX and Vulg. 'all the land of the Hittites'. The latter has special reference to north Syria; compare the Assyrian designation of Syria as 'Hittite land'. **3-5** echo Dt. 11:24, 25*a*. 'The wilderness' is that of the north-east part of the Sinai peninsula, east of the Brook of Egypt (Wâdī el-'Arîsh). 'The Great Sea', also called the Western Sea, is the Mediterranean. Compare the ideal limits of the Promised Land in Num. 34:1–12; Ezek. 47:13–20; cf. Gen. 15:18. **7.** 'All the law', not in LXX, is an insertion influenced by v. 8. 'Have good success'—the Hebrew word carries also a connotation of wisdom. 'The book of the law' is the Deuteronomic law; see 2 Kg. 22:3–10 for the story of its 'recovery'. Compare meditation on the law day and night in Ps. 1:2; cf. Ps. 119:97.

c **10-11 Command to prepare for the Crossing**—For the appointment of the 'officers' see Dt. 1:15, 16:18; cf. 20:5; the term is translated 'foremen' in Exod. 5:6, 10, etc., and its literal meaning is 'scribes', not applicable here. 'Within three days'—see 2:22, 3:2.

d **12-18 Commitment of the Transjordan Tribes**—The insistence of the narrative on the participation of all twelve tribes in the conquest of all of Canaan is an expression of the ideal unity of the tribes on both sides of the Jordan, perhaps to ease certain real cultural and political conflicts between the two areas (see Jos. 22:10–34; Jg. 12:1–6, 21:5–14). **14.** The Transjordan soldiers, 'men of valour', were to lead the other tribes. 'Beyond the Jordan' is a technical geographical term, referring to the territory east of the Jordan, from the viewpoint of one living west of the Jordan; compare the designation 'Beyond the River'
(Akkadian Ebir-nari), the name of a province of the 251d
Persian empire, west of the Euphrates, which one might render 'Trans-Euphrates' (Ezr. 5:3, 6, etc.). 'Armed'—compare the rendering 'equipped for battle' in Exod. 13:18; it does not necessarily mean, as some suggest, 'in battle array'; see Jg. 7:11.

II 1-24 The Mission of the Spies—We may be e
certain that the Canaanites of Jericho would have held a different evaluation of Rahab, the Tokyo Rose of Jericho, from that of the author of Heb. 11:31 or of Jas 2:25. In Mt. 1:5, if the same person is intended, she is represented as the wife of Salmon and the mother of Boaz, but this is hardly credible. Jewish tradition makes Joshua her husband. She and her household were apparently accepted within the Israelite community (see 6:25).

We cannot know why Rahab agreed to assist the f
Hebrews, if the tale is historical. The present account makes her acknowledge the God of Israel and Israel's claim to Canaan. If Jericho's defences were considerably less than they are pictured, which is very probable, she may have realised the inevitability of its fall and have wanted to save herself and her family. It has been suggested that she was perhaps a cultic personage, a sacred prostitute. Compare also the theory that 'the house of Rahab' (*bêth-rāḥābh*) originally referred to a house of prostitution, 'the house on the square' (*bêth r^e ḥôbh*—see Ezek. 16:24, 31); see Noth.

This chapter, in contrast with the following two g
chapters, seems to be a literary unit, belonging to one of the two early sources in Joshua; it is often identified as J. The hand of the Deuteronomist, however, is evident in vv. 10, 11.

1-7 The Spies hidden by Rahab—**1.** They had left h
the camp at Shittim, which is probably to be located with Glueck at Tell el-Ḥammâm, on the south side of Wâdī el-Kefrein, guarding the approaches to the Plains of Moab. Shittim is the same as Abel-shittim, a name meaning 'Acacia Stream', not 'Acacia Meadow', as formerly held (Num. 33:49). Jericho is Tell es-Sulṭân, north-west of the modern village of Jericho. 'Especially Jericho' may be an interpretative gloss, or else may be out of place and we should transpose and read 'went to Jericho and came' etc. (cf. LXX). The word rendered 'harlot' (*zônāh*) at times may be used to designate a cult prostitute (Gen. 38:21, 22; Ezek. 16:16, 17; Hos. 4:12, 14, 9:1; Mic. 1:7. **2.** Canaan had no over-all government, and the king of Jericho was a city kinglet; there were numerous city kings, such as those mentioned in chs. 10–12 or those whose letters appear in the Amarna correspondence. **6.** Flax was cultivated in Palestine and Egypt; see Prov. 31:13; Isa. 19:9; Hos. 2:5, 9. The stalks were dried on the flat roof. The woody fibre of the bark provided the flax fibre woven into linen.

8-14 Rahab's Request—**11.** Rahab confessed that i
Yahweh 'is he who is God in heaven above and on the earth beneath'; these words are a reflection of the Deuteronomist's credo put in the mouth of Moses in Dt. 4:39. **12-14.** Rahab required that the spies swear by the God whom she had just acknowledged, the God of the spies. 'Kindly' (12, 14) is too weak a word to represent adequately the Hebrew *ḥesedh*, which has overtones of loyalty and commitment, and is often, as here, associated with faithfulness; compare Prov. 3:2, where the two words here rendered 'kindly and faithfully' (14) appear as 'loyalty and faithfulness'. The 'sure sign' (12) is probably the oath in v. 14; it involves acceptance of sentence against themselves if the spies break their part of the agreement; they will, however, not be responsible if Rahab does not keep their secret (see 17, 20). Placing a curse on oneself was a common type of oath; see Ru. 1:17; 1 Kg. 2:23, 20:10; Job 31; Ps. 7:3–5.

15-21 The Escape of the Spies—**15.** Rahab's home j
was 'built into the city wall', more literally, 'in the wall of the city wall'. Before the recent excavations it was thought that Rahab's house was built over the

251j gap between an outer and inner city wall which were about twelve to fifteen feet apart, and which had been uncovered by the archaeologists. It is now evident that the walls previously ascribed to Joshua's time belong to an earlier date and are the walls of two different periods of occupation. **16.** ' The hills ' would be the area of the rough and desolate ridge (Jebel Qurunṭul) to the west of Jericho. ' Three days ' would give the spies time to get back conveniently before the crossing of the Jordan ; see 1:10. One might conjecture whether originally the ' scarlet cord ' (18, 21) was a sign of the house of a prostitute, used here in the story to indicate the house to be spared ; note, however, the use of a scarlet thread as a distinguishing mark in Gen. 38:30 and the figure of the scarlet thread in Ca. 4:3.

252a **III 1-V 1 Crossing the Jordan**—This section of Joshua is composed of all four sources, J, E, D, P, intertwined in a mosaic, resulting in duplication of events and inconsistencies in detail. This can be seen from the following brief analysis. In 3:17, 4:1 the crossing has been completed, but in 4:4, 5, 10 the people have not as yet crossed. Note in 4:1 ' all the nation had finished passing over ', and 4:11 ' all the people had finished passing over '. The twelve stones taken from the Jordan were placed at Gilgal (4:3, 8, 20), and were placed ' in the midst (middle) of the Jordan ' (4:9). Twice Joshua gave orders to select the twelve men who were to take up the twelve stones (3:12, 4:2). The Deuteronomic historian has obviously here combined two accounts, and his own contribution may be seen largely in the speeches which have a homiletic or exhortative function (3:2–4, 6–9, 4:14, 21–24 ; also 4:11*b*–12, 5:1 belong to D). The numerical and chronological data in 4:13, 19 belong to P, and also 4:16 (see below) and the related vv. 13, 17. It is thought by some that 3:8, 15 represent the priests standing at the brink of the river, while 3:13, 17, 4:3 in the middle of the river, and that 3:13 implies the waters were stopped just above the fording-place, while 3:16 a considerable distance off, but this is by no means clear.

b **III 1-13 Preliminaries to the Crossing**—**1.** From Shittim to the fords of the Jordan is about ten miles. The Israelites ' lodged there before they passed over ', i.e. they crossed over the next day, and this is also the implication of Joshua's words in v. 5. **2.** The three-day wait is to be linked with the three-day wait in 1:10. ' The Ark of the covenant ' (3, 6, 8, etc.) appears in connection with the story of the crossing of the Jordan here and in the conquest of Jericho and Ai in Jos. 3–7, and in one passage in the appendix to the book of Judges, in an explanatory gloss (Jg. 20:27*b*, 28*a*—see G. F. Moore, *Judges* (ICC, 1895), 433–4). The absence of dependable reference to the Ark in the period of the Judges is notable, and its appearance in Joshua is not in passages which encourage confidence in its existence at this time ; see
c the analysis of Jos. 6 below. It may be that the Ark was an institution adopted by the Hebrews after they entered Canaan. Historically it seems to have been primarily a part of a temple-centred cultus. It may indeed have had the form of a miniature temple decorated with cherubs, in exterior appearance not unlike certain incense altars found in the excavations (see H. G. May, ' The Ark—a Miniature Temple ', AJSL 52 (1936), 215ff.). With the expression ' ark of the covenant ' in 3:3, 6, 8, etc. contrast ' ark of the testimony ' in 4:16, exclusively a P phrase. The significance of the story of the entrance into Canaan is dramatised in part by the role given to the Ark.
d **3.** ' The Levitical priests ' is a characteristic D expression (Dt. 17:9, 18, 18:1, 24:8, 27:9, etc.). In Ezekiel's legislation a sharp distinction is made between the Zadokite priests (the Jerusalem priesthood descended from Zadok) and the Levites, the non-Jerusalemite priests, demoted to the position of Temple servants (Ezek. 44:9–31). The P Code makes a similar distinction between the Aaronite priests and the Levites, with the Levites assigned to the work of 25
service and bearing burdens in the tent of meeting, the Kohathite Levites having special charge of the Ark (Num. 4). No such division of the priesthood is envisaged by the Deuteronomist. **4.** The distance e
of two thousand cubits would be about three thousand feet, the ordinary or shorter cubit measuring about $17\frac{1}{2}$ inches. This distance apparently became later part of the precedent for the Sabbath Day's journey (see Acts 1:12) of two thousand cubits, as it appears, for instance, in the Zadokite Fragments, XI, 5 : ' Let no man go after beasts to pasture them (on the Sabbath) outside his city for more than two thousand cubits '. Part of the precedent for the Sabbath Day's journey was the interpretation of Num. 35:5, where the district of a Levitical city extended two thousand cubits from the wall on each side. The distance between the Ark and the people was symbolic of the sanctity of the Ark. **5.** The assurance of wonders (see also 7) recalls f
the promise made before the crossing of the Red Sea (Exod. 14:13). In **8** ' in the Jordan ' is correct, not ' at the Jordan ', as some suggest. **10.** The wonders of God attest his greatness and his nature as ' the living God ' (see Dt. 5:26 ; 1 Sam. 17:26 ; Hos. 1:10, etc.). The Hivites seem to have been in central Palestine, but the name may be a mistake for Horites (Hurrians). The Horites had a kingdom, the kingdom of Mitanni, in northern Mesopotamia in the second half of the second millennium when the Hittite kingdom was flourishing in Asia Minor. The Girgashites may be identical with the Qaraqisha of the Hittite records. Sihon was king of the Amorite kingdom in Transjordan (Num. 21:21ff.), but the Amorites played a much larger role than just this in the ancient Near East. The Jebusites were the inhabitants of Jerusalem at the time of the Judges and its capture by David, when the city was called Jebus (Jg. 1:21, 19:10 ; 2 Sam. 5:6–8).

14-17 The Waters of the Jordan cut off and the g
People cross over—These verses continue the narrative from v. 6. **14.** ' Of the covenant ' is here a later addition, as shown by the Hebrew construction. **15.** It is around the end of April that the Jordan overflows its banks as a result of the melting of the snows in the Lebanon mountains. **15b** emphasises the spectacular quality of the miracle. **16.** Adam (=Adamah) is to be located at modern Tell ed-Dâmîyeh and Zarethan at Tell es-Sa'idîyeh. The former is about 25 miles north of the Dead Sea, here designated as the Sea of the Arabah or the Salt Sea. Contrast AV ' very far from the city Adam ' and RSV ' far off, at Adam, the city ' ; the latter corresponds to the Hebrew consonantal text, and is correct as over against the versions and MT. Perhaps as the Israelites were h
preparing to cross, an earthquake caused the banks of the Jordan to collapse. An Arab historian, Nuwairi, reports that in December of the year 1267 a mound which overlooked the river on the west fell into the Jordan and dammed it up so that the water ceased to flow down for about 16 hours. A similar occurrence took place in 1909. More recently, in 1927, the high west bank collapsed below the ford Jisr ed-Dâmîyeh, which is about half a mile from Adam, and dammed the river, cutting off the water from the river-bed below it for $21\frac{1}{2}$ hours.

IV 1-10a The Twelve Stones set up—4-7 is pro- i
bably to be linked with 3:12, representing one source telling of the selection of the twelve men and the instruction given to them, while 1–3 comes from another source which is obviously linked with the immediately preceding verses. Note also that the instructions to answer the question, ' What do these stones mean to you ? ' in 6, 7 are duplicated in 21–24 (D), reflecting variant sources. Compare the instructions to answer the children's (sons') questions in Exod. 12:26, 13:14 (JE) ; Dt. 6:20, 29:22 ; Jos. 22:24. In **3** and **8** ' lay (laid) them down ' may better be rendered ' placed them ' or ' set them down '. The text does not specify that they were laid down on

2i the ground ; compare ' set up ' in 9, 20. **5.** ' Each of you a stone upon his shoulder ' may intend to suggest the considerable size of the stones. Memorial stones are mentioned elsewhere in the Biblical narrative (Gen. 28:18, 31:45–49 ; Jos. 7:26, 8:29, 24:26). Alignments of standing stones or single pillars, found by archaeologists, may sometimes have been memorials. A passage in the Ugaritic Daniel (Aqht) epic may illustrate a memorial stele (I:27, II:16) ; see also 2 Sam. 18:18.

j **10b-19 The Completion of the Crossing**—The continuing presence of the Ark in the middle of the Jordan apparently was related to the stoppage of the waters, for when the priests carrying the Ark lifted their feet from the Jordan, the waters returned, as they had receded at the moment the priests' feet touched the brink of the river. If the Ark had stayed in the midst of the Jordan while the people passed over (9), how could ' the ark of the Lord and the priests pass over before the people ' (11) ? To solve this, some change ' before ' to ' behind ', and some insert 15–16 between 11*a* and 11*b*. **13.** ' The plains of Jericho ', irrigated by the perennial waters of Wâdî Qelt, provided a strong contrast with their desert surroundings. **19.** The P source gives the exact date for the entrance into the promised land, using a calendar system introduced by the Hebrews in the Neo-Babylonian period. Ezekiel saw his vision of the new Jerusalem on the same tenth day of the first month (Ezek. 40:1). The day of atonement came on the tenth day of the seventh month (Lev. 23:26, 25:9) ; it has been suggested that calendar shifts resulted in the equinoxes falling on the tenth of the first and the
k seventh months. Gilgal was formerly located at Khirbet en-Nitleh, three miles south-east of ancient Jericho, where there is a supposed pool called, probably only in most recent times, Birket Jiljûlieh. The name Jiljûlieh, reminiscent of Gilgal, has also been associated by the local Arabs with Khirbet el-Mefjir, a mile and a quarter north-east of Jericho. The topographical data in the literary records support the latter location. Excavations in the area of Khirbet en-Nitleh have disclosed nothing earlier than the 4th cent. A.D. On the other hand, at Khirbet el-Mefjir exploratory excavation has revealed occupation in Early Iron I–II period, *c.*1200–600, or perhaps a little earlier, which suits the biblical data (see J. Muilenburg, ' The Site of Ancient Gilgal ', BASOR 140 (1955), 11–27). The name Gilgal probably means ' a (stone) circle ', and has reference to sacred stones of the sort mentioned above. There were two other sites in Palestine which bore the name Gilgal, both mentioned in Joshua (12:23, 15:7).

IV 20-V 1 The Stones set up at Gilgal—20. Compare 9, the duplicate sources giving the impression that the stones were set up twice ; this verse relates to 1–3, 8, which may have preceded 20 in the original source from which they have been taken. **23.** The crossing of the Jordan is compared with the Red Sea crossing, as in 2:10, also D. **V 1.** With this picture of the Amorites in Transjordan and the Canaanites in Cisjordan compare Num. 13:29 ; Jos. 11-3, where Canaanites, Amorites and others dwell in Cisjordan. The gentilic terms are used quite indefinitely here, but perhaps with some reference to Sihon's kingdom in Transjordan. ' They had crossed over ' is with a number of Hebrew MSS, while MT and VSS have ' we were passed (crossed) over ' (AV).

3a **V 2-VII 1 The Conquest of Jericho**—The main narrative portions here come from the older sources, in which evidences of duplication will be noted below. 5:4–7 most clearly reveals the hand of the Deuteronomist, while 5:10 and probably 5:11, 12, 6:19, 7:1 belong to the Priestly editor.

b **V 2-9 The Circumcision**—Although bronze and copper had long been in use by this time, flint instruments were used for the circumcision rite ; so Zipporah had used a flint to circumcise Moses' son (Exod. 4:25). Perhaps a natural conservatism in ritual practice
dictated the use of flints in circumcision. Circum- 253b
cision was a token of the covenant, and was traced by the Israelites back to Abraham (Gen. 17:9–14, 21:4). It was observed by the Israelites in Egypt, and there, as here, it is represented as a prerequisite for a celebrant of the passover (Exod. 12:43–48). Circumcision was an ancient Semitic institution, not limited to the Hebrews. A sixth-dynasty Egyptian tomb relief depicts a boy being circumcised, perhaps with a flint knife (Pritchard, ANEP, No. 629). Two prisoners of a Canaanite king on a 12th cent. Megiddo ivory are circumcised (G. Loud, *The Megiddo Ivories* (1939), Pl. 4, 2*a*, *b*). Circumcision was perhaps originally a puberty rite.

2 ' The second time ', omitted by LXX, may be a c
gloss, or possibly a D insertion into 2–3 (JE). Gibeath-haaraloth, ' the hill of the foreskins ', may have been a place in the Gilgal vicinity where it was later customary to perform the rite of circumcision in connection with the Gilgal sanctuary. **4-7.** The Deuteronomist explains why the people had to be circumcised at this time and were not already circumcised. The reason for the forty years in the wilderness (**6**) is given in more detail by D in Dt. 1:19–46 ; see
also Num. 13, 14. **9.** The name Gilgal is explained d
by a folk etymology, but this is an implausible explanation since it was the name of more than one town. The ' reproach of Egypt ' is perhaps the uncleanness of a foreign country (see Hos. 9:3). The LXX refers to the flint knives as later put by Joshua at Timnath-serah and buried with him in his tomb there (Jos. 21:40, 24:30).

10-12 The Celebration of the Passover—10. The e
chronology is from P (see Exod. 12:1–20). The passover event has been prepared for by the chronological data in 4:19 ; this is four days later. **11.** ' On the morrow ', i.e. on the 15th (see Num. 33:3). This would be the first of the seven days of the feast of unleavened bread (see Exod. 12:16 ; Lev. 23:5–8). **12.** ' On the morrow ' here might be either the 15th or the 16th. The manna ceased five or six days after the Israelites had entered the promised land ; this has been taken to be in conflict with Exod. 16:35 (P), which affirms that the people ate manna till they came ' to the border of the land of Canaan '.

13-15 The Appearance of the Commander of the f
Lord's Army to Joshua—The man with the drawn sword, not distinguishable in appearance from a human (compare Gen. 18:1ff., 19:1ff.), was the commander of the Lord's army. It was the same messenger (angel) who appeared to Balaam and his ass (Num. 22:23–25). Yahweh was king, and like a human king had his army commander-in-chief, and also his army of horses and chariots, the latter best illustrated in 2 Kg. 6:17 ; see also 2 Sam. 24:15–17 ;
2 Kg. 2:11. The expression ' Lord of hosts ' (*Yahweh* g
Ṣ^ebhā'ôth), i.e. ' Lord of Armies ', may have reference to both the Lord's own armies (see Gen. 32:1, 2) and the armies of Israel. Originally the phrase may have been a title of the Israelite God, meaning ' He brings into existence the armies [of Israel] ', as Albright has suggested. Moses had removed his sandals at the burning bush (Exod. 3:5), and so did Joshua as he stood on ground made holy (taboo) by the presence of the Lord's messenger who was an ' extension of the Lord's person ' (see A. R. Johnson, *The One and the Many in the Israelite Conception of God* (1942)). **14.** Joshua's question to the Lord's messenger is not answered in the present form of the narrative, but the answer may have been in the original sources. The messenger's words are perhaps to be rendered ' No, for I am the commander of the army of the Lord. Now I have come . . .', and they may have originally included the reason for his coming (cf. 2 Sam. 14:15).

VI 1-VII 1 The Fall of Jericho—A few years ago h
an outstanding archaeologist stated that there could be no doubt that it was the fourth city level (City D) at Jericho (Tell es-Sulṭân) which was captured by

253h the invading Israelites and devoted to destruction, the date of its fall being narrowed to between 1385 and 1250. Garstang had earlier dated its destruction to about 1400 B.C. Double city walls presumably destroyed by an earthquake were pointed out; layers of burnt brick and grey ash, pockets of charcoal, charred roof beams, and carbonised grain and food were taken as mute evidence of the accuracy of the
i Biblical tale. But more recent excavations have necessitated a revision of these conclusions. The Middle Bronze Age occupation came to an end perhaps after the expulsion of the Hyksos from Egypt in 1580, and to this period must be dated the city which earlier had been ascribed to Joshua. Little evidence of a Late Bronze Age (1550–1200) city was found; there were the remains of the foundations of a wall and a contemporary floor a little more than a yard square on which was a small oven and a 14th cent. juglet. A so-called 'Middle Building' found by Garstang belongs to the second part of the Late Bronze Age, perhaps contemporary with the Late Bronze tombs, the date of which is uncertain, with suggestions ranging from 1350 to the late 13th cent. Kathleen Kenyon, director of more recent excavations, has affirmed that present evidence points to the middle of the 14th cent. for the end of the Late Bronze occupation, but that there might have been a later settlement. It may be that Joshua's Jericho was not much more than a fort above the spring. See Kathleen Kenyon, 'Excavations at Jericho, 1954', PEQ 86 (1954), 61.

j This section has a complicated structure. 6:1 seems to stand by itself and 7:1 may belong to P. 6:27 is obviously D; see 1:5, 3:7, 4:14. The destruction of the city is told twice (21, 24), as also the rescue of Rahab (22–23, 25). It seems probable that the earliest form of the narrative made no reference to the priests or the Ark. In *4a* 'and seven priests shall bear seven trumpets of rams' horns before the ark' seems to interrupt the context, for one would expect the orders for the seventh day to follow directly v. 3. If this is so, 'the priests blowing the trumpets' would also seem due to expansion (*4c*), for it belongs to *4a*. Also, one can see by comparing 11 with *14a*, *15a* how the Ark may not have been in the earliest account, for the comparison shows that 11 may have begun 'And they marched around the city . . .'

k **VI 1-7 Instructions for the Conquest of the City —1.** Jericho was shut up not because it was as yet under siege, but in anticipation of attack by Israel. 'From within and from without' is interpreted at the end of the verse to mean that both exit and entrance were barred. **4.** The miraculous aspects of the number seven appear often in the OT. Note here the seven horns, the seven priests, the seven days, and the sevenfold circuit of the walls. The trumpets of rams' horns should be contrasted with the silver trumpets (Num. 10:1–10). The rams' horn (*shôphār*) was used to give signals (Jg. 7:8, 16, 20; 1 Sam. 13:3; Jer. 4:5, 19), at a royal coronation (1 Kg. 1:34, 39), and on religious occasions (Lev. 25:9; Ps. 81:3).

l **VI 8-VII 1 March around Jericho and Destruction of the City**—The tradition of the march around the city may reflect sacred processions around the city of Jerusalem (see Ps. 48). The shouts (*t^erû'āh*, 5, 20; see also 10, 16) recall the cultic shouts in the Psalms (27:6, 33:3, 47:5, 89:15), as well as the use of the same Hebrew term as a war-cry (Job 39:25; Jer. 20:16; Amos 1:14, 2:2). The camp (11, 14) was of course at Gilgal. After marching around the city once a day for six days, the Israelites on the seventh day encircled Jericho seven times. At the command from Joshua (16), rather than at the sound of the trumpets (5), the people shouted, and the city walls fell down flat.

m **VI 17** All who were in the city were 'devoted to the Lord for destruction'. The city was made a *ḥerem*, a Hebrew term used to designate complete destruction or sacred use, and therefore prohibition from profane **253**
use; compare Akkad. *ḫarāmu*, seclude, ritually separate, or the Arabic cognate meaning prohibited,
sacred. Mesha, king of Moab (see 2 Kg. 3:4), around **n**
839, tells in the Moabite Stone how he took the city of Nebo from Israel, slaying everything, including seven thousand men, boys, women, girls and female slaves, 'for I had devoted them to destruction to Ashtar-Chemosh'. For the orders thus to devote to destruction the cities of Canaan, see Dt. 20:16–18. Here in Joshua the silver and gold and vessels of bronze and iron were set apart for sacred use, to go into the treasury of the Lord. See Lev. 27:28, where a devoted thing (*ḥerem*), which might include man, beast or field, cannot be sold or redeemed, and is most sacred to the Lord. According to Num. 18:14 'every devoted thing in Israel' is to belong to Aaron and his sons. Israel itself would become a *ḥerem* if it disobeyed the Lord's commands (18); compare Isa. 43:28, where the same word is used. With this account compare the ban of destruction against Amalek in 1 Sam. 15.
18. Very possibly one should read 'lest you covet them **o**
and' with LXX and in accord with 7:21, rather than 'lest when you have devoted them'. **19.** 'The treasury of the Lord' (compare 24) is written from the vantage-point of the later Temple at Jerusalem (see 9:21). The allusion to vessels of iron would also reflect a time later than Joshua, for iron did not come into significant usage until after 1200. Note similarly that **26** belongs to a time at least as late as the ninth century, for it is a *post eventum* prophecy (see 1 Kg. 16:34). The man here cursed is Hiel the Bethelite. **VII 1** is an editorial insertion (P?), which on one hand goes with what precedes, relating to the fall of Jericho, and on the other prepares the reader for the story of the attack on Ai. Compare 7:10–12, written as though it were the first time the reason for the defeat appeared in the narrative. The genealogy of Achan suggests the P source. In 1 Chr. 2:7 Achan appears as Achar, the troubler (Heb. *'Ôkhēr*) of Israel, perhaps an attempt to extend the pun element in Jos. 7:25, 26. The LXX reads Achar throughout the Joshua narrative.

VII 2-VIII 35 The Attack on Ai and the Covenant **25**
at Shechem—Archaeologically Ai presents as difficult problems as does Jericho. It has been located at modern et-Tell, a mound about one and a half miles east of Bethel, at a point where two routes from Jericho into the highlands converged. Although the Israelites may have gone up in this direction and attacked and destroyed Bethel, yet Ai, if correctly located here, was not occupied at this time. Perhaps the story of an Israelite attack on Bethel has become confused with a legend of Ai's fall at some earlier date.
The excavations at et-Tell show that it was a flourish- **b**
ing city in the third millennium, but that it was destroyed around 2200 and not reoccupied except for a little settlement there around 1000. The city was thus a 'heap of ruins' (Heb. *tel*) not only at the time of the writer (8:28), but also at the time of Joshua! The story may be in part an explanation of the name Ai, meaning 'ruins'. Bethel is mentioned in connection with the battle in 8:17 (although not in LXX), and there is archaeological evidence of a disastrous destruction of Bethel in the 13th century. The Late Bronze Age city of Bethel passed through two chief phases, the 15th to 14th centuries and the 14th to 13th centuries. At the end of the latter phase there was one of the most spectacular evidences of great conflagration found at any site in Palestine, perhaps the result of Israelite destruction of the city. The city which replaced it was much poorer and without the usual Canaanite religious symbols (see J. L. Kelso, 'Excavations at Bethel', BA 19 (1956), 36–42).

Deuteronomic terms can be found here and there **c**
in this section, and probably 8:30–35 is entirely D (see Dt. 11:29 and ch. 27). The composite character of the earlier sources may be seen in the twofold

254c burning of Ai (8:19, 28), the twofold setting of the ambush (8:9, 12), and the duplicate start for Ai (8:3, 10). While 7:15 anticipates the burning of Achan, in 7:25 it is both stoning and burning, the stoning an addition or from a different tradition or source; v. 25 has suffered from expansion. There is a suggestion of P in the genealogy of Achan (7:18; cf. 7:1). The Achan story is an aetiological legend to explain a heap of stones in the Valley of Achor; note 'to this day' twice in 7:26. In 15:7 the Valley of Achor marks the boundary of Judah. Compare the heap of stones in Gen. 31:46–54. In both instances the stones may have had some significance as a boundary mark.

d **VII 2-5 The Defeat of Israel—2.** The reference to Beth-aven is perhaps to be omitted with LXX, or its appearance here may be due to a conflation of variant readings. Bethel and Beth-aven are the same town, and Beth-aven is a substitute for Bethel in Hos. 4:15, 5:8, 10:5. The consonantal text may be vocalised Beth-on, perhaps an original alternate name for Bethel, vocalised as Beth-aven (' house of wickedness ') to express contempt for the city. The tradition of the Judaean origin of Achan may be due to the fact that he was thought to be buried in the Valley of Achor on Judah's boundary. **3.** It was a long, hard, uphill trek from Gilgal to Ai, from around 900 ft. below sea-level at Gilgal to about 2,600 ft. above sea-level at Ai. Hence the suggestion that the whole people should not toil up there. **5.** The location of Shebarim is unknown; the word may mean ' quarries ', and perhaps should be so rendered here.

e **6-15 Joshua's Prayer and the Lord's Answer—** Here, as often in the OT, defeat is taken as a sign of the wrath of the Lord because of the sin of the people. Israel as a whole participated in the guilt of one of its members; when one sinned, Israel sinned. The Ark of the Lord had not been with Israel as it attacked Ai, for the Lord was not with Israel; compare the attack on the hill-country of Judah without the Ark in Num. 14:44, 45, there as here (2) after spies had been sent out. Perhaps this Joshua incident is deliberately reminiscent of that in Numbers.

f **6.** Tearing the clothes and putting dust on the head were conventional signs of mourning (1 Sam. 4:12; 2 Sam. 1:2, etc.). **7.** When faced with difficulties and trials, Israel often wished it had remained behind and did not want to go forward (Exod. 14:11–12); Num. 14:1–3, 20:3, etc.). **9.** ' The Canaanites and ' may be an interpretative gloss on ' all the inhabitants of the land '. The purpose of Israel's existence was to glorify the great name of the Lord; it was through Israel that the Lord would glorify himself (Lev. 10:3; Isa. 26:15, 44:23, 49:3, etc.). The exile resulted in the profanation of the name of the Lord (Ezek. 36:20–23, 39:7). 'To cut off our name' was to annihilate, since the essence of a person or people was somehow involved in the name of the person or people (see Dt. 7:24, 9:14, 12:3; Ps. 9:5, 83:4).

g **14.** The Lord ordered that the guilty person was to be discovered by means of the sacred lots. ' The tribe which the Lord takes ' means the tribe selected by lot (see 1 Sam. 10:20, 21; and 14:38–42). The people were to be ' sanctified ', i.e. purified, so that they could approach the deity for the casting of lots. The division of the community was into tribes, families (i.e. clans), and households (i.e. families, literally ' houses '; compare ' fathers' houses ' in Num. 1:2–4, 18, etc.). The Hebrew terms for the divisions of the community were used quite loosely; compare the present wide use of the term ' family '. **15.** The penalty for the sin was to be burning, and involved the destruction of the guilty one, his household, and his property, including his livestock. Compare Num. 16:25–33 and Num. 16:35. In Num. 16:22 (P) the cry of Moses, ' Shall one man sin, and wilt thou be angry with all the congregation ', represents an individual-responsibility emphasis comparable to that in Ezek. 18 and in contrast with that in the Joshua narrative 254g
and the earlier sources in Num. 16.

**16-26 Discovery of Achan's Guilt; His Con- h
fession and Punishment—17.** The plural ' families ' occurs in a few Hebrew manuscripts (see LXX), otherwise it is ' family '; the Syriac ' tribe ' interprets what is meant. For ' man by man ' we should perhaps read ' by households ', in accord with v. 14 and with some manuscripts, Syr., Vulg. **19.** Achan was exhorted to render praise to the Lord and give glory to him, for he had sinned, and although he must be punished, he should give to God the honour due to him. God was to be praised also because it is he who uncovered the culprit. **21.** Achan had taken ' a beautiful mantle from Shinar ', i.e. from Babylonia, doubtless prized
as an imported garment of great value. The shekel i
weighed around 11·4 grams. A series of eight-shekel weights from Lachish averaged 0·402 oz., or 11·389 grams per shekel, and a ' royal ' shekel from Gezer weighed 11·14 grams. Shekel here does not refer to coins, for coins did not begin to appear in Palestine until the 5th cent. ' Bar of gold ' is literally ' tongue of gold ', doubtless suggesting its shape; compare Akkad. *lišân ḫurâṣi*, ' tongue of gold ', especially in a Neo-Babylonian inscription where we read, ' One tongue of gold, one mina its weight '.

24. ' The valley of Achor ' could better be rendered j
' the plain of Achor '. As Noth, Cross and others have shown, it is to be identified with the Buqe'ah, a small plain in the northern part of the wilderness of Judah south-east of Jerusalem and north-east of Bethlehem, just west of the jagged hills that fall away to Khirbet Qumrân and the Dead Sea. (See F. M. Cross and J. T. Milik, ' Explorations in the Judaean Buqe'ah ', BASOR (1956), 5ff.). **25.** For burning as a penalty, see Gen. 38:24; Lev. 20:14, 21:9. The burning is anticipated in 15, but the stoning may be introduced to explain a heap of stones on the Judaean side of the boundary between Judah and Benjamin in the plain of Achor. ' Brings trouble ' is formed from the same Hebrew root as Achor, interpreted to mean ' trouble ' See Hos. 2:15, where in the picture of the future restoration as a kind of second Exodus the Lord promises to make the plain of Achor (trouble) a door
of hope. In the excavations at Tell el-'Ajjûl (Beth- k
eglaim) Sir Flinders Petrie found bones of men and animals crushed together along with gold earrings and scarabs, and the metal of gold, silver and copper objects found with them had been fused by fire. He suggested that this might represent an Achan-like punishment, but this is most uncertain (F. Petrie, *Ancient Gaza*, ii (1932), 6,7).

VIII 1-29 The Conquest of Ai—The account reflects l
the usual all-over D editing, beginning with a speech of the Lord in vv. 1–2. The earlier dual sources are also in evidence. The ambush is set twice (3–9 and 10–13), with a variant number in the ambush (30,000 in v. 3 and 5,000 in v. 12); 9*b* parallels 13*b*, telling of Joshua spending the night (in the latter instance after he had arisen early in the morning! see 10*a*). In the present arrangement the 5,000 is made to appear as a second, independent setting of an ambush.

1-2. The D character of Yahweh's words may be seen m
by comparing the phraseology and ideology of Dt. 3:2, 3. **3.** This attack involved the whole army, in contrast with the first attempt (7:2–5). The 30,000 obviously are the men of military age, the total band of Israelites (see 4:13 for 40,000 among the Transjordan tribes alone). It is curious that much later at the time of David all the chosen men of Israel, i.e. those of military age, numbered only 30,000 (2 Sam. 6:1). **6.** ' So we will flee from them ' may be dittography from the end of 5, identical in the Hebrew, and is omitted by LXX. The end of **9** and **13** may originally have been identical; ' among the people ' is the same in the Hebrew as ' in the valley ' save for the omission of one letter; i.e. *'m*, people; and *'mq*, valley.
10. ' People ', as often elsewhere refers to the armed n
forces; in 8:1, 3, 11, 10:7, 11:7, the phrase

254n ' fighting men ' is literally ' people of battle '. **11.** In the morning Joshua placed the main force of his army north of the city of Ai, separated from Ai by a ravine or valley, but in full sight of the city. The preceding night (9) the ambush had been placed west of Ai, between Ai and Bethel, at a point where it would be invisible from the city of Ai. **15.** ' Beaten ' occurs only here in this form in the Hebrew, and many emend to ' smitten ' by changing one letter. ' The wilderness ' is the rugged territory between Ai and the Jordan valley. **17.** ' Or Bethel ' is lacking in the LXX and may be a gloss, and the latter part of the verse implies that only one city had been mentioned. **18.** Presumably Joshua's outstretched javelin originally was thought to have effected the victory of Israel, even as the outstretched rod of Moses caused the plagues of Egypt (Exod. 7:19, 8:16, etc.), or as the uplifted hands of Moses, holding the rod, caused victory over the Amalekites (Exod. 17:8–12), and v. 26 increases this impression. In its present context the outstretched
o hand is interpreted as a signal. **28.** ' A heap of ruins ' is in the Hebrew *tel*, the equivalent of the modern name of the site, et-Tell, i.e. the mound. This is the designation of mounds containing buried cities ; so the site of Gibeah is today called Tell el-Fûl, Lachish Tell ed-Duweir, Mizpah Tell en-Naṣbeh, etc. **29.** The body of the king of Ai was taken down at sundown in accord with the law in Dt. 21:23 ; contrast the procedure earlier in 2 Sam. 21:10.

p **30-36 The Covenant at Shechem**—This is a duplicate of the incident in Jos. 24. In its present form the account here belongs to D, and is taken as the fulfilment of the commands of Moses in Dt. 11:29, 27:1–26. **30.** Read Mt Gerizim after the Samaritan text of Dt. 27:4, rather than Mt Ebal. Mt Gerizim (Jebel eṭ-Ṭûr) above Shechem was the ancient sanctuary site of Israel. The Samaritans there built a temple which was destroyed by John Hyrcanus in 128 B.C. (see Jn 4:20, 21 ; Jos. Ant., xii, 1). Mt Gerizim is on the south side of the valley in which Shechem lies, and Mt Ebal (Jebel Eslamîyeh) on the north side. **31.** ' Altar of unhewn stones ', see Exod. 20:25. **32.** The law was perhaps not to be written on the stones of the altar, as the text seems to imply, but on separate stones, plastered over, as apparently also in Dt. 27:2, 3. **33.** The sojourner and the home-born are the alien (proselyte ?) and the native Israelite, both equal under the law ; see Num. 9:14 ; Dt. 1:16, 27:19, 31:12, etc.

255a **IX 1-X 43 The Conquest of South Canaan**—There are two main themes here, the treaty secured with the Israelites by the Gibeonites through a ruse, and the defeat of the coalition of Canaanite kings of the south. The two are related, for the coalition was established more immediately for the purpose of punishing Gibeon for consorting with the enemy. This section of the book (9–11) is introduced by D in 9:1, 2, describing how the kings of the entire extent of Canaan gathered together with one accord to fight against Joshua and Israel, a situation hardly supported by either the older sources incorporated in the narrative or by the probable historical situation. There are other D passages here, particularly 9:9*b*, 10, 10:8, 12*a*. There is some evidence of P (9:15*b*, 17–21) ; note the P reference to the leaders of the congregation in 15*b*, 18, 21, and to the congregation in 18, 21, 27. The penalty is twice imposed on the Gibeonites for their deception (31, 27).

b **IX 1-27 The Covenant with the Gibeonites**—The story of the Gibeonites is told for two primary purposes, to provide a motivation for the coalition of the kings and to explain the later position of the Gibeonites as temple servants at Jerusalem (27). **1-2.** Beyond the Jordan here means west of the Jordan ; see 5:2 where it is defined. The lowland, better rendered as a geographical term, the Shephelah, is the foothills between the hill-country of Judah and the coastal plain. Such geographical notations are typical of D ; see 10:40, 11:2, 16, 12:8.

3-15 The Deception by the Gibeonites—In an 25
earlier source 3 followed 8:29 ; the context has been interrupted by the Shechem covenant in 8:30–35, and the introduction in 9:1, 2. **3.** Gibeon is modern el-Jîb, 5½ miles NW. by N. of Jerusalem, definitely identified through inscriptions found by James B. Pritchard's excavations. **4.** ' they on their part acted with cunning ' may imply some clever strategy also on the part of Ai or Jericho in the earlier tradition. ' Made ready provisions ' is with a number of versions ; the Hebrew is most obscure ; compare AV, ' as if they had been ambassadors '. Goatskins were used as wineskins ; see Job 32:19 ; Mt. 9:17. **10.** See on 2:10, from the same D source and in much the same phraseology. **15.** The expression ' leaders of the congregation ' may be due to late priestly editing of the narrative, for it is a characteristic phrase of P (Exod. 16:22 ; Num. 4:34 ; 16:2, etc.) ; see also the reference to the ' congregation ' in 18–21, 27. That it reflects pre-monarchial usage is most dubious.

16-27 The Discovery of the Deception and its d
Penalty—**17.** ' Their cities ', i.e. the cities of the Gibeonites. Besides Gibeon, the Gibeonite ' tetrapolis ' included Chephirah (Tell Kefîreh, west-south-west of Gibeon), Beeroth (Râs eṭ-Ṭaḥûneh, north-east of Gibeon), and Kiriath-jearim (Tell el-Azhar, south-west of Gibeon). Each of these was about 5 miles distant from Gibeon. They may have formed a Horite alliance in this limited area. They occupied a strategic position in the central highlands, and their defection to the Israelites would have been regarded as serious by their fellow Canaanites. Although this alliance is mentioned in a later source (P ?), the tradition of their association may be very early. Note, however, that in the subsequent narrative of this war Gibeon alone appears.

The Gibeonites were penalised by being made e
hewers of wood and drawers of water for all the congregation (21), slaves, hewers of wood and drawers of water for the house of my God (23), hewers of wood and drawers of water for the congregation and for the altar of the Lord, in the place which he should choose (27). This may represent variant sources (23 JE, 27*b* D, 21, 27 P ?), and 23 might imply the sanctuary at Gilgal or Jerusalem (see 6:19, 24), 27*b* more certainly means the sanctuary at Jerusalem, being a favourite D expression (see Dt. 12:5, 26:2, etc.), and 21 and 27*a* may be phrased to avoid distinctly implying a non-Jerusalemite sanctuary site. The story is told to explain how it came about that Gibeonites served as menials in the later Temple service. Com- f
pare the later tradition of the Nethinim, the Temple slaves, reportedly given by David for the service of the Levites (Ezr. 8:20), or the sons of Solomon's servants and the Nethinim of Neh. 7:57–60, or the similar service by the Midianites in Num. 31:47. The Gibeonite temple slaves perhaps first functioned at the great high place at Gibeon at the time of Solomon, and moved to Jerusalem after the building of the Temple there (see 1 Kg. 3:4). **24-25.** This is the language of D ; see the words of Rahab in 2:9–11 ; cf. Dt. 7:1, 2.

X 1-43 The Defeat of the Coalition of Southern g
Canaanite Kings—Jg. 1:1–20 contains the story of the conquest of southern Canaan after the death of Joshua. Not only is this seemingly inconsistent with the account in Jos. 10, but the book of Joshua itself does not present a clearly consistent picture of events. 10:33 indicates the annihilation of the people of Gezer, but 16:10 notes that the Canaanites continued to dwell in Gezer ; Jos. 15:17 tells of Othniel's conquest of Debir apparently during Joshua's lifetime, and Jg. 1:13 places it after the death of Joshua, while Jos. 10:38 accredits the conquest of Debir to Joshua. Jos. 10:41 suggests Gaza was taken by Joshua, in contrast with Jos. 13:2, 3 ; according to Jg. 1:18 Gaza was taken after the death of Joshua by Judah. In Jos. 10:36 Hebron is captured by Joshua, but in Jg. 1:20 apparently after the death of Joshua. It has

5g been argued that both Jos. 10 and Jg. 1:1–20 are historical, and that the work of Joshua had to be done over in the following generation.

h Ch. 10 discloses at points the editing of D, but the earlier sources predominate.

i **1-5 The Coalition against Gibeon**—Adoni-zedek bore a name similar in formation to that of his great predecessor, Melchizedek, and the names may mean respectively 'My Lord is righteousness', and 'My king is righteousness', or perhaps the second element in the name may be that of a Canaanite deity, Zedek. If Adoni-zedek belongs to the 13th cent., we may also place among his predecessors Abdi-ḫeba, king of Jerusalem in the 14th cent., whose letters are among the Amarna correspondence (ANET, 487–9). The four cities in alliance with Jerusalem (el-Quds) were Hebron (el-Khalîl, 20 miles south of Jerusalem), Jarmuth (Khirbet Yarmûk, 16 miles west-south-west of Jerusalem), Lachish (Tell ed-Duweir, 27 miles south-west of Jerusalem), and Eglon (Tell el-Ḥesī, 8 miles beyond Lachish). Three of the five cities were in the Shephelah, and Hebron and Jerusalem in the hill country.

j **6-15 The Defeat of the Kings**—There may be two traditions reflected in this chapter, one concerning the fight of Joshua against the five kings, and the other concerning a struggle against numerous cities in south Canaan. **10, 11.** These verses may be duplicates from the earlier sources ; one verse refers to pursuit as far as Azekah and Makkedah, and the other omits Makkedah ; one has 'the ascent of Beth-horon' (10) and the other 'the descent of Beth-Horon' (11, so the Hebrew, RSV emends or interprets). The ascent of Beth-horon leads from Lower Beth Horon (Beit 'Ûr et-Taḥtā) to Upper Beth Horon (Beit 'Ûr el-Fōqā), the latter about 2½ miles south-east of the former. The chase led from Gibeon to Upper Beth-horon to Lower Beth-horon, and thence into the valley of Aijalon (Wâdī Selmân), and then south-west to Azekah (Tell ez-Zakarîyah), about 18 miles from Lower Beth-horon. 'The great stones from heaven' were the hailstones ; compare Exod. 9:23, 24. The tradition of the destruction by hailstones may be in contrast with that preserved in the ancient poem in 12*b*, 13, which suggests that the major destruction was at the hands of Israel.

k **12b-13.** The implication of the poem is that the sun stood still in the east and the moon in the west. The Deuteronomist makes the poem the words of Joshua, but the poem itself is non-committal as to the speaker. 'The Book of Jashar' is also quoted in 2 Sam. 1:18, and in the LXX of 1 Kg. 8:53. It was apparently a collection of poems. Compare the Book of the Wars of the Lord (Num. 21:14). The poem is interpreted to mean that the sun delayed its setting for a whole day, and that it was in the zenith of the heavens rather than the east when it stood still. **15.** The return to Gilgal is obviously out of place here, interrupting the narrative of the defeat of the coalition of kings. **21** places the camp at Makkedah, but LXX omits 'to the camp'.

l **16-27 The Slaughter of the Kings at Makkedah**—The relation of this to the preceding is uncertain. In an earlier source this might have followed 10, or it may be, as some think, a later addition, an aetiological tale associated with the pile of stones at Makkedah (see 27). **24.** The chiefs with their feet on the necks of the conquered kings is reminiscent of the numerous Egyptian and Mesopotamian representations of the prostrate foe under the foot of the victorious king. **27.** The bodies were taken down in the evening, as in the case of the king of Ai (8:29), where a cairn of stones also marked the place of burial.

m **28-39 The Conquest of the South Canaan Cities**—The Deuteronomist seems to be responsible for these verses in their present form. The conventionalised phraseology of the description of the conquests suggests that we have here not so much a historical record as the writer's endeavour to emphasise the complete conquest of the land. It is this passage 255m
which is in primary conflict with the account of the capture of the cities of south Canaan in Jg. 1:1–20 (see also Jos. 15:14–19). Joshua was presumably carrying out the orders in the legislation in Dt. 20:16–18. Joshua moved from north to south, which may have been the opposite direction of the conquest of Judah, as some scholars think who maintain that the attack on Judah came from the south, from the direction of Kadesh-barnea. **29.** Libnah (Tell eṣ-Ṣafī ?) is five miles west of Azekah, and along with Azekah was one of the sites investigated by Bliss and Macalister in 1898–1900, but lack of careful records of the excavations makes it impossible to relate the excavation to the Biblical narrative of the conquest.

31. The excavations at Lachish have produced a n
pottery bowl which had Egyptian writing on it referring to the 'year four', which some think belongs to the reign of Merneptah. If this is the 4th year of Merneptah it would be 1231, and the suggestion is that not long after this Lachish fell to the Israelites. Olga Tufnell thinks that the fall of Lachish may have occurred after 1200 B.C., rather than before, in view of a Rameses III scarab in disturbed Bronze Age debris near the palace citadel (Olga Tufnell, *et al.*, *Lachish* iii (1953), 46). **33.** Gezer (Tell Jezer) itself was not to become Israelite until the days of Solomon (16:10 ; 1 Kg. 9:16). **34.** Eglon (Tell el-Ḥesī ?) was excavated by Sir Flinders Petrie in 1890. **38.** The excavations at Debir (Tell Beit Mirsim) showed the third last city there belonged to the Late Bronze Age, and the pottery and a scarab indicate the city was still occupied at the time of Rameses II (1299–1232). Its destruction was in the second half of the 13th cent.

40-43 Summary of the Conquest of South o
Canaan—The Deuteronomist, having in mind the promise to Moses, represents the conquest as complete. **41.** Kadesh-barnea is probably 'Ain Qedeis or Khirbet el-Qudeirât, about 65 miles south of Gaza. The country of Goshen is here a region in the south of Judah, not to be confused with Goshen a district in Egypt. **42.** This illustrates the theory of the divine right of conquest and the Hebrew belief that the conquest of Canaan was not due to their own strength, but to Yahweh's power ; see Dt. 9:1–5 ; Jg. 7:2 ; Ps. 44:1–3.

XI 1-XII 24 The Conquest of North Canaan— 256a
The basic narrative in 11:1–9 was taken by the Deuteronomist from the earlier sources which provided the main materials for the narrative of the conquest. The summaries in 11:10–23 and 12:1–24 reflect his view of the conquest of Canaan and are the fulfilment of the Deuteronomic promises in ch. 1, thus bringing to a fine literary—if not always historical—conclusion the story of Israel's possession of the promised land.

XI 1-5 The Conquest of the North—There may b
be here a dual tradition, i.e. of a coalition of four kings under Jabin's leadership (1), and a coalition that included all north Canaan (2–5*a*). Israel's conquest of Hazor may form the main historical kernel of the narrative. Jabin of Hazor belongs more properly to the story of the conquest than in the period of the Judges at the time of Deborah (Jg. 4:2, 7, 23). Hazor is to be located at Tell el-Qedah, about 10 miles north of the Sea of Galilee, south-west of Lake Huleh. It is mentioned in records of the Egyptian kings Thuthmosis III, Amenhotep II, Seti I, and in
four Amarna letters. Beginning in 1955, Yigael Yadin c
excavated at the site, both on the mound proper and on the adjoining rectangular enclosure which had been interpreted as a Hyksos camp. In one area on the mound there were at least seven Iron Age strata beginning with the period of the Judges, the latest probably built after Tiglath-pileser's conquests in 732 B.C. Four of these strata were uncovered, the next to the last showing evidences of terrific destruction by fire, perhaps at the hands of Tiglath-pileser III. In the so-called camp area there was discovered a well-built city, with Mycenaean pottery present, dated

256c to the last part of the Late Bronze Age in the 13th cent. Although there is no proof that this was the city destroyed by Joshua, it corresponds with the general period of the destruction of Canaanite cities in the south. It is obvious that Hazor was a very large city at this time, for the tell covers more than 25 acres, not including the adjoining fortified enclosure of about 3,250 by 2,200 feet. Madon is Qarn Haṭṭîn, about 5 miles west of the Sea of Galilee. Shimron is perhaps to be located at Tell Semunîyeh, about 15 miles to the south-west of Madon and 5 miles west of Nazareth, Achshaph may have been situated at Tell Kisân on the coastal plain, 6 miles south-east of Acco.

d **2, 3.** The term 'Arabah' is used at times to designate the Jordan Valley, or part of the Jordan Valley, or the continuation of the depression below the Dead Sea. One of the names of the Dead Sea is 'the Sea of the Arabah'. Here the Arabah refers probably to the Jordan Valley. 'Chinneroth' may here be the Sea of Chinneroth (the Sea of Galilee), although it is also the name of a town, modern Tell el-ʿOreimeh near the north-west shore of the Sea of Galilee. The term 'Naphoth-dor' is uncertain; it may refer to the coastal plain south of Mt Carmel, the town of Dor being located there at modern eṭ-Ṭanṭûrah. With 'the land of Mizpah' compare 'the valley of Mizpah' in 8.

e **5.** The waters of Merom may be identified with Wâdī Meirôn, which goes from the town of Merom (Meirôn) south-east to the Sea of Galilee. **8.** The coalition was defeated and chased as far as Great Sidon, the same Hebrew rendered 'Sidon the Great' in 19:28, and has reference to the greater area controlled by Sidon, extending southward to the Līṭânī River; the conquest is represented as reaching the northern boundary of Israel. Sidon (Ṣaidā) was an important seaport about 40 miles beyond Merom, while Misrephoth-maim (Khirbet el-Musheirefeh) is about 20 miles toward the west of Merom. The valley of Mizpah may be in the general region of Mt Hermon. The place of the battle and the route of the flight suggests a north Galilee campaign. **10-14.** 'The cities that stood on their mounds' is more literally 'the cities that stood on their tells, i.e. on hills formed by the ruins of earlier cities (13). Compare Jer. 30:18: 'The city shall be rebuilt upon its mound, and the palace shall stand where it used to be'.

f **16-23 Summary of the Conquest of Canaan** (D) —Compare 10:40–42, where some of the same geographical terms appear. **16.** The Arabah here is primarily the Jordan valley. **17.** Mt Halak is Jebel Halâq, about 25 miles south of Beersheba, near the south-east border of Judah, where it approaches the borders of Edom, i.e. Seir. Only later did Edom's borders extend west of the Arabah, and this passage may reflect the later situation. Baal-gad was in the far north of Israel's territory; perhaps at present-day Ḥaṣbaiya, a little more than 11 miles north of Dan, although the Mizpah of vv. 3, 8 has been located here by some scholars. **21, 22.** The defeat of the Anakim is given special attention; their expulsion is here attributed to Joshua, but in 15:13, 14; Jg. 1:20 to Caleb. The tradition reckoned them giants (Dt. 2:10) dwelling in south Canaan, particularly in the vicinity of Hebron, which was captured by Caleb. Their location here in the Philistine cities of Gath, Gaza and Ashdod may imply a belief that Goliath, Ishbi-benob, and other huge Philistines were descended from them (1 Sam. 17:4; 2 Sam. 21:15–22). Anab is Khirbet ʿAnâb, less than 5 miles south of Debir.

g **XII 1-24 List of conquered Canaanite Kings**— This is in essence an additional D summary. **1-6.** This recapitulates the conquest of Sihon and Og in Transjordan as told by the Deuteronomist in Dt. 2:26–3:11, based on the story in Num. 21. **1.** The Arnon River (Wâdī el-Môjib) flows into the Dead Sea from the east, and it formed the southern boundary of both the kingdom of Sihon and the tribe of Reuben, and was the southern border of Israel's territory in 25
Transjordan. 'The Arabah eastward' has reference to the territory east of the Jordan. **2.** Heshbon (Ḥesbân) was Sihon's capital, near the centre of his kingdom. Aroer is at ʿArâʿir, about 15 miles east of the Dead Sea. The Jabbok River (Nahr ez-Zerkâ) h
flows into the Jordan from central Transjordan. The southern extension of the River Jabbok marked the western boundary of the Ammonites, who dwelt thus in eastern Transjordan. 'Half of Gilead' is South Gilead; the River Jabbok formed the boundary between South Gilead and North Gilead, with its southern extension the boundary between South Gilead and Ammon. **3.** Beth-jeshimoth (Tell el-ʿAzeimeh) was near the north end of the Dead Sea, and Mt Pisgah (Râs es-Siâghah) to the east was a part of the Abarim range of mountains, just to the west of Mt Nebo (Jebel Nebā). **4.** For the Rephaim at Ashtaroth and Karnaim see Gen. 14:5, 15:20; compare the Anakim in 11:21, 22. Ashtaroth (Tell ʿAshtarah) and Edrei (Derʿā) were 20 to 25 miles east of the Sea of Galilee. **5.** Geshur and Maacah were territories east of the Jordan above the sea of Galilee.

7-23 The Kings conquered by Joshua in Cisjordan i
—The list contains some places not mentioned in the preceding account of Joshua's conquests. In 9–13*a* the cities are listed in the order in which they are mentioned in chs. 6–10. **14.** The destruction of Hormah (Tell el-Mishash?) appears in Jg. 1:17, and possibly is presumed in Num. 21:3, both after and before Joshua's time. For Arad (Tell ʿArâd) see Num. 21:1, 33:40; Jg. 1:16. These cities were in the Negeb. **15.** Adullam (Tell esh-Sheikh Madhkûr) was in the Shephelah; see 15:35. **16.** The cities beginning with Bethel were north of Jeruṣalem, in central and north Canaan. **17.** Tappuah is apparently different from that in 16:8, 17:7, 8. Hepher is possibly Tell Ibshâr on the plain of Sharon. **18.** Aphek (Râs el-ʿAin) was also on the plain of Sharon. Lasharon may be a corruption, the text reading originally 'Aphek which belonged to Sharon', to distinguish this Aphek from other places of the same name; compare 'Jokneam in Carmel' in 22. **20.** In Shimron-meron 'meron' may be a gloss, with some versions. **21, 22.** Taanach (Tell Taʿannak), Megiddo (Tell el-Mutesellim), Kedesh (Tell Abû Qedeis?), and Jokneam (Tell Qeimûn) are on the south side of the Plain of Esdraelon (Plain of Megiddo). **23.** 'The king of Goiim in Galilee' is one possible emendation of a corrupt text; there may have been here a reference to Gilgal (Jiljûlieh) north of Aphek on the edge of Sharon. **24.** Tirzah (Tell el-Fârʿah) seven miles north-east of Shechem was later to be the capital of Israel (1 Kg 14:17, 15:21, etc.). If 'King of Lasharon' in 18 is an error, there were originally only 30 kings in this list, rather than 31.

XIII 1-XIX 51 The Tribal Allotments—The earlier 25
narrative may have reported little more than that Joshua before his death allotted to the tribes their territories, and its basic elements may be found in 13:1, 7, 18:2–11. This has been elaborated by D and P, the latter perhaps responsible for the insertion of the detailed boundary designations and the list of tribal cities. This does not mean that P invented its geographical data out of whole cloth, but they may be based on earlier geographical lists of tribal borders and cities preserved in priestly circles. These lists in their earlier contexts very possibly had no setting in the age of Joshua. F. M. Cross, Jr. and G. E. Wright date the boundary lists to 'the time of the pre-monarchic tribal league' and the lists of tribal cities (province list in Jos. 15) in the reign of Jehoshaphat (JBL 75 (1956), 202ff.). P's introduction to the allotment is in 14:1*b*–4, while 1*a* and 5 may come from introductions of earlier accounts of the allotment. Since 14:3 refers back to 13:15–23, this is also perhaps P. P introduces Eleazar as Joshua's colleague in the assignment of the territory; see 14:16, 17:4.

XIII 1-7 Joshua directed to make the Allotment b

257b **to the Cisjordan Tribes—2-6** is D, somewhat out of context, listing not the unconquered parts of the tribal territories, but the region of the Philistines, the Geshurites, the Avvim, and the Phoenicians. The Geshurites usually refers to the people of Geshur, which is in northern Transjordan (12:5, 13:11), but here and in 1 Sam. 27:8 to a people in south Palestine, apparently between Philistia and the Shihor. Shihor is perhaps here Wâdî el-'Arîsh, which is also called 'the brook of Egypt'. The Avvim 'lived in villages as far as Gaza' (Dt. 2:23). Mearah (Mogheiriyeh?) is north of Sidon, and Aphek (Afqâ, south-east of Gebal) is also in Phoenician territory. The Phoenicians are here and often elsewhere called Sidonians. 'From Baal-gad below Mt Hermon to the entrance to Hamath' is the territory between the Lebanon and the Anti-Lebanon ranges; the entrance to Hamath was the later northernmost boundary of the Hebrew kingdoms in their furthest expansions (1 Kg. 8:65; 2 Kg. 14:25). Hamath (Ḥamâ) was an important city of north Syria on the Orontes River.

c **8-13 The Territory of the Transjordan Tribes**—See 12:1–6 for details. **8** must be emended with RSV to include the half-tribe of Manasseh in Transjordan. **9.** Dibon (Dhîbân), the capital of Moab, has been recently investigated by the American Schools of Oriental Research. It was at Dibon where the famous Moabite Stone was found in 1868. **11.** The territory of Geshur and Maacah, Aramaean kingdoms, was perhaps first incorporated into Israel at the time of David, who took a wife from Geshur (2 Sam. 3:3, 10:6, 8, 13:37). **14** largely duplicates 33, and the Hebrew construction and 33 support the omission here of 'the offerings by fire to'; so also LXX, which omits 33.

d **15-32 The Boundaries of Reuben, Gad and Manasseh**—Reuben included the southern part of Sihon's territory, from the Arnon on the south and including Heshbon and Mephaath (Tell el-Jâwah?) in the north. Gad's inheritance was comprised of the rest of the territory of Sihon to the Jabbok River, and also a section of North Gilead of decreasing width extending from Mahanaim (Tell er-Reheil?), just north of the Jabbok and about 20 miles from the Jordan, to the Sea of Chinnereth. The eastern half of North Gilead and the territory north of the Yarmuk River belonged to the half of the tribe of Manasseh. **21.** In Num. 31:8 Evi, Rekem, Zur, Hur and Reba are called five kings of Midian. **25.** 'Half the land of the Ammonites' refers to the territory west of the north-south extension of the Jabbok.

e **XIV 1-XIX 51 The Allotment to the Cisjordan Tribes**—There were apparently three traditions of the manner of the allotment: (1) an older tradition, in which the people of Israel allotted the land (14:1*a*, 5; see 19:49, 50); (2) a Deuteronomic view, perhaps based on an earlier tradition, that it was done by Joshua alone (14:6, 18:2–10; see also 13:7); (3) and a Priestly view that it was done by Eleazar the priest, Joshua, and the heads of the fathers' houses (14:1*b*, 19:51*a*). The tradition of a formal allotment of the land presumes a more closely knit organisation of the tribes in the early period than is historically probable. We may contrast the manner in which Dan acquired its new territory in Jg., ch. 18, or the stories of the conquest in Jg. 1:1–21, suggesting much less concerted action among the tribes in the conquest.

f **XIV 1-5 Allotment to the Nine and One-half Tribes explained**—Eleazar the Priest (1) was the son of Aaron and the chief of the Levites, succeeding Aaron in the high priesthood (Num. 3:32, 20:25–28). **4** anticipates the allotment of the Levitical cities in ch. 21.

g **6-15 The Inheritance of Caleb**—The Calebites were perhaps a non-Israelite group which was assimilated into Judah and dwelt in the Hebron area at the time of the writer (see 14, 'to this day'). **6.** Caleb is here a Kenizzite, a descendant of Kenaz, an Edomite people (Gen. 36:11). Because the Kenizzites dwelt within Judah, Caleb is reckoned a Judaean in Num. 13:6, 34:19. **7.** If Joshua was 40 years old then, and the conquest began 38 years later (Dt. 2:14—or 40 years, Jos. 15:6), and Joshua was now 85 years old (10), the conquest of Transjordan and Cisjordan is reckoned by the Deuteronomist to have taken 7 years (or 5 years). **9.** In the words of Joshua, Caleb was given 'the land on which your foot has trodden', reflecting the phraseology of Moses' (Yahweh's) promise to Caleb in Dt. 1:36; cf. Num. 13, 14). **15.** Kiriath-arba is interpreted to mean 'Town of Arba' (see also 15:13, 21:11), with Arba a legendary hero of the Anakim; literally, however, it means 'town of four', i.e. perhaps a city of four quarters or a tetrapolis.

h **XV 1-63 Allotment for the Tribe of Judah**—The south, east, north and west boundaries of Judah are described in turn (2–12); Caleb's portion within Judah is again noted (13–19); a list of Judaean cities in the Negeb, the Shephelah and coastal plain, the hill-country, and the wilderness of Judah is given (20–32, 33–47, 48–60, 61–62); and special mention is made of the Jebusites and Jerusalem (63). The four parts to this chapter may ultimately represent variant sources. The boundary list and the list of towns belonging to Judah may have been added by the Priestly writer from two earlier sources. Similar lists of towns within Benjamin (18, 21–28), Simeon (19:2–9) and Dan (19:40–46) are given, and such lists may be as early in origin as and come from the time of Solomon or Josiah, when all of Benjamin could be counted within the larger Judaean territory.

i **1-12** The southern border of Judah here corresponds to the southern border of the promised land as in Num. 34:3–5 (P). It led from the lower end of the Dead Sea south-west for about 55 miles, past the Ascent of Akrabbim ('Scorpions' Ascent', Naqb eṣ-Ṣafa), and along the Wilderness of Zin on the border of Edom (see on 11:16, 17), and then it turned north-west from Kadesh-barnea to the nearby Hazar-addar (corrupted in 3 to 'Hezron up to Addar', but see Num. 34:4) and Azmon, and along the brook of Egypt (see 13:3) to the Mediterranean. Hazar-addar is probably Khirbet el-Qudeirât (if the latter is not Kadesh-barnea) and Azmon is Qeṣeimeh. The Dead Sea formed the east border. **6.** The stone of Bohan the son of Reuben on the north boundary may be Ḥajar el-Aṣbaḥ. **7.** Gilgal here does not seem to be the Gilgal of the earlier Joshua narrative at Khirbet el-Mefjer, which with Jericho lay within Benjamin. **8.** This irregular northern border passed just south of Jerusalem, just below the junction of the Kidron valley and the valley of Hinnom. **9.** The Kidron valley was between Jerusalem and the Mt of Olives, and the valley of Hinnon west and south of the city.

j 'The spring of the waters of Nephtoah' is perhaps to be read, without change of consonants in the Hebrew text, 'the spring of Merneptah', named after the Egyptian Pharaoh of the XIX dynasty who had attacked Canaan and Israel; it may be located at 'Ain Liftâ, west-north-west of Jerusalem. **10.** Mt Seir is obviously not Edom, but a ridge west of Kiriath-jearim on which is the village of Saris, reminiscent of the name Seir. **11.** The northern boundary came out at the Mediterranean a few miles south of Joppa, after passing Jabneel (Yebna). The west border is the Mediterranean, the Great Sea.

k **13-19 Caleb's Inheritance**—In Jg. 1:9–15 it is Judah rather than Caleb who conquered Hebron, and who went up against the inhabitants of Debir; otherwise there is largely verbatim similarity in the two passages, which come from a common early source with the Judges' account perhaps more original. **19.** The 'springs' (Heb. *gullôth*) have been associated with the ground wells at Debir (Tell Beit Mirsim) or are cisterns or reservoirs perhaps to be sought in Sel ed-Dilbe south-west of Hebron. The importance of cisterns in the Negeb has been dramatically illustrated by recent explorations there.

257l **20-62 Cities of Judah**—In this list of Judaean towns there are 11 districts. The list originally had 12 districts, perhaps provinces of the kingdom of Judah. From the Negeb (21–32) the list moves to the north Shephelah (33–36), to the south Shephelah (37–41), to the central Shephelah (42–44), to Philistia (45–47), to the most southerly hill-country (48–51), to the south hill-country around Hebron (52–54), to the eastern edge of the south hill-country, south-east of Hebron (55–57), to the hill-country around Beth-zur (58–59). At this point the LXX adds another district, originally in the Hebrew text, in the north hill-country of Judah around Bethlehem, listing 11 towns. Of the 2 remaining districts (the 11th and 12th of the original list), one includes the edge of the northernmost part of the hill-country of Judah and western Benjamin (60; cf. 18:25–28), and the other includes eastern Benjamin and north-eastern Judah (61–62; cf. 18:21–24). Recently identified sites in the wilderness of Judah (**61**) are Middin (Khirbet Abû Tabaq), Secacah (Khirbet es-Samrah), and Nibshan (Khirbet el-Maqâri) in the Buqeʿah; see F. M. Cross, 'A Footnote to Biblical History', BA 19 (1956), 12ff. There are discrepancies in the list, as when 21–32 contain 36, not 29 cities; among other corrections, Hazor and Ithnan should be one city, namely Hazar-ithnan, and Ain and Rimmon are also one city, En-rimmon, while Hazor-hadattah and Heshmon should be omitted, and Biziothiah should be corrected as in LXX to 'her villages' (literally, 'daughters'). So also in 33–36 there are 15, not 14 towns, and perhaps Tappuah should be omitted, as in the LXX. Iim in 29 may be a corruption of Ezem (cf. Jos. 19:3). Cross and Wright regard 45–47 as an editor's addition, while Alt and Noth relate the territory of Dan in 19:41–46 to these verses as the 5th district here. If the former suggestion is accepted, Jos. 18:21–25 may be presumed to have belonged to this list, a district in the eastern half of Benjamin, to complete the total of 12 districts. The 11th district is given but 2 cities (60), but some have seen in 18:25–28 the more complete list of cities of this district.

m **XVI 1-XVII 18 The Allotment of the Joseph Tribes**—16:1–10. This chapter, which is in considerable disorder, is concerned with the southernmost of the Joseph tribes, Ephraim. In 16:1–3 the southern boundary of the Joseph tribes is given, from the Jordan to the Mediterranean; this is the southern border of Ephraim, and it belongs to 5–6*a* where the southern border is not given, and where Beth-horon and Ataroth-addar belong on the south, not the east, for the east border is given in 7. Since Bethel is Luz, 'from Bethel to Luz' (2) can hardly be correct (see 18:13). Both upper Beth-horon and lower Beth-horon (5, 3) are on the south border; compare the northern border of Benjamin in 18:12, 13. The northern border is confused in 6*b* and 8; it went from Taanath-shiloh (Khirbet Taʿnah) to Michmethath (Khirbet Makhneh el-Fôqa) to Tappuah (Sheikh Abû Zarad), and along the brook Kanah (Wâdî Qânah) to the Mediterranean. The eastern boundary went from Taanath-shiloh southward beside Janoah (Khirbet Yanûn) to Ataroth (Tell Mazâr), and to Naarah (Khirbet ʿAujā Taḥtā, north of Jericho), not reaching the Jordan. The Archites (2) are unknown to us, save that Hushai, David's counsellor, was an Archite (2 Sam. 15:32). The Japhletites (3) are otherwise unknown; any association with Japhlet of 1 Chr. 7:32 is improbable. **9, 10.** These two verses do not seem to have been a part of the original list. Gezer did not come under Hebrew domination until the time of Solomon (1 Kg. 9:15–22). Gezer should have been mentioned on the south border of Ephraim.

n **XVII 1-13 The Allotment of Manasseh—1-6.** Allotment among the Clans of Manasseh. **1.** The allotment of Transjordan territory to half the tribe of Manasseh is told in terms of the allotment of Gilead and Bashan to Machir, the first-born of Manasseh (see 13:29–31. In Num. 26:30–32 (P) these six 'male descendants' (literally 'sons') of Manasseh are called 25'
the sons of Gilead and grandsons of Machir. **3.** This is almost verbatim with Num. 26:33 (P). The five daughters of Zelophehad, the son of Hepher, received five portions, and the five male descendants of Manasseh, apart from Hepher who was dead, received five portions. This makes the ten portions of v. 5. The five daughters of Zelophehad also appear in Num. 27:1–11 in an inheritance case, in a story told obviously in part as a precedent for the Joshua story here. See also Num. 36:1-12 (P).

7-13 The Boundaries of Manasseh—7, 8. The o
north–south extent of Manasseh's territory was from the border of Asher to Michmethath, which was on Ephraim's border at the latter's most northerly point, and to En-Tappuah or Tappuah a lower point on Ephraim's border to the south-west of Michmethath (see 16:6*b*, 8). **8, 9** follow of course the northern border of Ephraim, which formed the southern border of Manasseh. The second sentence of 9*b* is obscure and corrupt in the Hebrew. The northern border of Manasseh adjoined that of Zebulun, as well as Asher. **11.** 'The third' is the third city mentioned, i.e. Dor, which is Naphath-dor, perhaps to distinguish it from En-dor, if the RSV conjecture of the meaning of the obscure text is correct (see 11:2). Placing Dor within Asher is strange in the light of 19:26, where Asher's boundary only touches Carmel (Mt Carmel) north of Dor. Vv. **12, 13** are identical with Jg. 1:27, 28; see also Jos. 16:10.

14-18 The Protest of the Joseph Tribe against p
a single Allotment—Vv. 14, 15 and 16–18 may come from duplicate earlier sources, added here at the end of the allotments to the Joseph tribes, Ephraim and Manasseh. **14, 15** (see also 16:1, 18:5) may imply an earlier tradition of a single lot for both tribes. **15, 18.** The Joseph tribe is told to clear the forests of the hill-country; this is probably not a reference to the Transjordan 'forest of Ephraim' of 2 Sam. 18:6.

XVIII 1-XIX 51 The Allotment to Seven Tribes q
at Shiloh—1-10. The survey of the remaining territory. The account begins with a P introduction (1). From the earlier source or sources comes a second introduction (2–10), describing how Joshua sent 21 men, 3 from each of the remaining 7 tribes, to explore and report on the land, providing a plan of partition for the as yet unassigned territory into 7 areas. Then Joshua cast lots to determine what should belong to whom. The historical role of Shiloh in this period is very ambiguous. Originally Gilgal alone and not Shiloh was mentioned in 9, 10 (also in 8), as the expression 'in the camp' shows, for Gilgal was the place of the camp (see 10:15, 43. etc.; cf. 14:6). Likewise Gilgal suits better the reference to Judah in the south and Joseph in the north in 5.

11-20 The Boundaries of Benjamin—Benjamin lay r
between Ephraim and Judah. For its northern boundary (12, 13), see the southern boundary of Ephraim in 16:1, 2, 5. Near lower Beth-horon the boundary turned south (14, 'goes in another direction') to Kiriath-baal or Kiriath-jearim (Tell el-Azhar) to form the western border. From this point the boundary turned east to form the southern border, which would be identical with the eastern portion of Judah's northern border (15–19; see 15:5–9). Beth-aven in 12 is probably a misrepresentation of the name Bethel; see on 7-2.

21-26 The Cities of Benjamin—This city list is s
divided into two parts, with 12 and 14 cities respectively in each, and they may have been taken from the original list of Judaean districts; see on 15:20–62. Those in the first part (21–24) are in eastern Benjamin from a district now missing in Jos. 15:20–62, although compare the 12th district in 15:61, 62. Those in the second part (25–28) should be compared with the 11th division of Judah in 15:60. Both Ephraim and Benjamin claimed Bethel (22, 18:13), but Benjamin's claim may be primary, Ephraim's control of Bethel perhaps beginning with its establishment as sanctuary

s centre for the kingdom of Israel (1 Kg. 12:29). Benjamin may historically have preceded the other tribes into Canaan; see J. Muilenburg, 'The Birth of Benjamin', JBL 75 (1956), 194–201.

t **XIX 1-9 The Allotment for Simeon**—Simeon lay in the south of Canaan, within Judah's territory. Fifteen cities, rather than the designated total of thirteen, are given in 2–6. In 7 only three are listed, instead of the given total of four, En-rimmon (Khirbet Umm er-Ramamîn) being one and not two towns (contrast AV; see 15:32; Neh. 11:29). Instead of Ether probably read Athach (1 Sam. 30:30); Ether was in the Shephelah of Judah (15:42), and Athach in the Negeb; a scribe has copied an *r* instead of a *k*.

u **10-16 The Allotment for Zebulun**—A list of border cities and a list of cities within Zebulun have apparently been confused, and just how the total of twelve is to be secured is a mystery. Most are not really border cities, and from Jg. 1:30 we learn that from two of them, Kitron (instead of Kattath) and Nahalal, the Zebulunites did not drive out the Canaanites. The description begins with the southern border, which extended west of Sarid (Tell Shadûd) to just east of Jokneam (Tell Qeimûn), and then east of Sarid (i.e. 'in the other direction eastward toward the sunrise') to Chisloth-tabor (Iksâl) and Daberath (Debûriyeh), below Mt Tabor. The eastern boundary is difficult to determine, or to square with the boundary of Naphtali in 19:34. Japhia (Yâfa) and Gath-hepher (Khirbet ez-Zûrra') are in Zebulun, near the east border, but the former is west of Daberath and the latter north-west, while Rimmon (Rummâneh) is about three miles north of Gath-hepher, and hardly on the border (13). The lower part of the western boundary seems to be described in 14, from Hannathon (Tell el-Bedeiwîyeh) following the valley of Iphtah-el (Wâdī el-Melek) and then cutting south toward Jokneam. Or is the western boundary missing? The northern boundary is also obscure, for 19:27 seems to imply that Zebulun's north-west corner was near Neiel and 19:34 that its north-east corner was near Hukkok, making the north border about five miles north of Rimmon, and it is difficult to get this from this passage.

v **17-23 The Allotment for Issachar**—Here the city list only is given, the sixteen cities including three border cities only. Tabor is probably the same as Daberath (13), which is ascribed to Issachar in 21:28. The original list of border cities has perhaps dropped out, leaving only the fragment in 22*a*. Probably Chesulloth is the same as Chisloth-tabor of 12. We may presume that Chesulloth was near its north-west corner, Jezreel at its south-west corner, and Beth-shemesh (el-'Abeidiyeh, near the southern end of the Sea of Galilee), at its north-east corner.

w **24-31 The Allotment for Asher**—The twenty-two cities in the original list cannot be recovered, nor the exact boundary lines. In 29 read 'Mahalab, Achzib' as in RSV (cf. LXX), instead of 'from the coast to Achzib' (emending the Hebrew; cf. LXX and Jg. 1:31). Asher's western border was at the sea, and its eastern border touched Zebulun and continued further north alongside Naphtali, its territory extending north beyond Rehob, Hammon and Kanah to the border of Sidon the Great (see on 11:8). In 30 read Acco (Tell el-Fukhkhâr), as in LXX and Jg. 1:31, instead of Umma. **25, 26a** and **28a** seem to be names from a list of Asher's cities, rather than from a list of its border towns.

x **32-39 The Allotment for Naphtali**—A border list has here also been confused with the addition of names from a list of cities belonging to Naphtali, although there has been added in 35–38 a list of sixteen (not nineteen) fortified cities of Naphtali. Heleph (33) is unknown, and from Jg. 4:11 it would appear that 'the oak of Zaanannim' (read 'Elon-bezaanannim'?) was near Kedesh, north-west of Lake Huleh. Jabneel (Yemmâ) and Lakkum (Khirbet el-Manṣûrah) are near the lower end of the Sea of Galilee. From this
south-east corner the southern boundary ran westward 257x
to Aznoth-tabor (Umm Jebeil), near Mt Tabor, adjoining the boundary of Issachar. The western boundary went northward from Aznoth-tabor to Hukkok (Yaqûq), near Zebulun's north-east corner and opposite the northern end of the sea of Galilee. The west and north boundaries of Zebulun adjoined Naphtali, and 'touching Zebulun at the south' (34) refers to the northern boundary of Zebulun where the west boundary of Naphtali makes a right-angle turn near Hukkok toward the west to meet the border of Asher. North of Zebulun Asher adjoined Naphtali on the west.

40-48 The Allotment for Dan—There is here no y
pretence of listing boundaries (although 46 has been taken as a boundary fragment), and only the cities of the area are given. Alt maintained that the list of Danite towns in 41–46 belonged originally with the southern-province (Judaean district) city lists of Jos. 15:21–62. Note that in 15:33 Zorah and Eshtaol are credited to Judah, and in 15:45 Ekron also. The area is bordered by Judah, Benjamin, Ephraim and the Mediterranean. The story of the migration of the tribe of Dan from its location here near the coast (see Jg. 5:17) to north Canaan is told in Jg. 18, where the conquered city is called Laish, rather than Leshem, a variant form of the name.

49-51 Conclusion of the Allotment—There are z
really two conclusions here: the first in 49, 50 from the earlier source, which adds that Joshua was given Timnath-serah (Khirbet Tibneh) as an inheritance (cf. 15:13, 24:30), and the second in 51 from the Priestly source, which notes the role of Eleazar and the location at Shiloh.

XX 1-XXI 45 Cities of Refuge and Levitical 258a
Cities—Both chapters are largely from the P source, although there is some D material (see especially 21:43–45). That P provided the framework for the story of the selection of the Levitical cities is indicated by their selection by Eleazar and Joshua (21:1). Some scholars deny the historicity of the appointment of the Levitical cities, and some date the list of Levitical cities as early as the reign of David. It does seem to imply a kind of organisation of the priesthood more probable for a later period, perhaps the time of Josiah.
The function and role of the high-priest (20:6) and b
the designation of the community as the 'congregation' (20:6, 9) reflect the late Priestly view, although the concept of the cities of refuge may itself be earlier. The earlier sources had presumed no inheritance for the Levites (13:14, 33; Num. 18:20; Dt. 10:9), and this may be in contradistinction to the earlier view. The P source anticipates this narrative of the selection of the Levitical cities in Num. 35:1–8; Jos. 14:4. The former reference is the best witness of the priestly character of ch. 21, for ch. 21 is regarded as the fulfilment of Num. 35:1–8.

XX 1-6 The Function of the Cities of Refuge—**2.** c
'Of which I spoke to you through Moses' is a reference to Num. 35:9ff. (P). **3-6.** These verses have been enlarged by an editor on the basis of the law in Num. 35 or Dt. 19, vv. 4, 5 being absent in the LXX. The LXX also omits 'unwittingly' in 3 and omits 6*b* as well, having no reference to the high priest. It is very likely that in the earliest period a person might find asylum at any sanctuary, any altar serving for this purpose, and Exod. 21:13 and 1 Kg. 1:50, 2:28–34 may imply this. The six cities eventually selected as places of asylum were perhaps originally all significant sanctuary centres. **4.** 'The entrance of the gate of the city' was the open place (see RSV 'square' in Ezr. 8:1) just inside the city gate where the judges sat (Ru. 4:1, 2; Am. 5:10, 15). The ancient custom of blood feuds, which made a place for the 'avenger of blood', did not distinguish between homicide and unintentional slaying, and the legislation tried to provide for this distinction. **6.** The office of the high-priest belongs to the post-exilic period, preceded in the pre-exilic period by that of the chief priest.

258d **7-9 The Six Cities of Refuge**—West of the Jordan, from north to south, they were : Kedesh (Tell Qades) in Galilee, Shechem (Tell Balâṭah) in the hill-country of Ephraim, and Hebron or Kiriath-arba (el-Khalîl) in the hill-country of Judah. East of the Jordan, from south to north, they were : Bezer (Umm el-'Amad ? east of Mt Nebo) in Reuben's territory, Ramoth (Tell Ramîth) in North Gilead, and Golan (Saḥem el-Jolân) in Bashan, east of the Sea of Galilee. The hill-country of Ephraim here designates the district of Samaria, including Manasseh as well as Ephraim, for Shechem was in Manasseh. **7.** ' In the hill country of Naphtali ' may be a secondary addition by a scribe who erroneously took Ephraim and Judah as references to tribal territories.

e **XXI 1-42 The Levitical Cities**—For discussion of this list, see W. F. Albright, ' The List of Levitic Cities ', *Louis Ginzberg Jubilee Volume* (1945), 49ff. It is to be expected that the Aaronites would be given by P cities in Judah, Simeon and Benjamin, because they were the only full-fledged priests and should have their possessions around Jerusalem. The rest of the Levites in the priestly organisation from the time of Ezekiel were regarded as little more than Temple servants, and P naturally assigns to them cities in the territory that had once belonged to the kingdom of Israel. The P source distinction between the Aaronites and Levites is presumed in this arrangement, and this must be recognised regardless of the question of the antiquity of the institution of Levitical cities.

f The list of Levitical cities occurs again in 1 Chr. 6:54–81, and divergencies between the two may be due largely to scribal errors. Originally, as Albright has demonstrated, Shechem and Hebron, two cities of refuge, were not in the list of Levitical cities. There were originally four Levitical cities in each tribe. Judah and Simeon together should have eight, but the addition of Hebron made nine (13–16). That Shechem is an addition in 20–22 can be shown by the fact that it was in Manasseh, not Ephraim as presumed here. The addition of Shechem might seem to demand five in 20–22, rather than the four now listed, but Jokmeam has dropped out from the list of Ephraimite cities ; it is preserved in 1 Chr. 6:68, where by a scribal error Kibzaim is missing. In other words, Ephraim's four Levitical cities were originally Gezer, Kibzaim, Jokmeam, and Beth-horon. In Naphtali only three cities are now listed (32), but originally this part of the list contained Hammon, now missing but found in 1 Chr. 6·76. Manasseh is counted as one tribe and therefore as containing four Levitical cities, two in Transjordan and two in Cisjordan (25, 27). Incidentally, these corruptions occurred in the list as it was in the source used by P, for P reckoned Hebron and Shechem as among the Levitical cities, since in the P source in Num. 35:6 the Levitical cities are regarded apparently as the six cities of refuge, plus forty-two more.

g **1-3 The Setting of the Allotment at Shiloh**—The heads of the fathers' houses of the Levites came to Eleazar and Joshua at Shiloh ; see 14:1*b*, 18:1, 19:51. **4-8.** The Plan of Allotment. Gershon, Kohath and Merari were sons of Levi. Kohath had three sons, one of whom was the ancestor of Aaron (Exod. 6:16–25; Num. 3:17–32, 26:57–59). Hence the distinction here between those Kohathites who were descendants of Aaron (and so true priests), and the rest of the Kohathites. There were thus four groups to be assigned cities, i.e. the Aaronite Kohathites (4), the rest of the Kohathites (5), the Gershonites (6), and the Merarites (7). **9-19.** Cities for the Aaronitic Kohathites. Vv. **11-12** may be an editorial expansion, reconciling the giving of Hebron to the Aaronitic Kohathites in view of the fact that it had been earlier given to Caleb (14:14–15). In **16** read Ashan (Khirbet 'Asan) for Ain with 1 Chr. 6:59. In **18** perhaps read Alemeth with 1 Chr. 6:60 for Almon.

h **20-26 Cities for the Rest of the Kohathites**—Two Gathrimmon's are mentioned, one in Dan (24) and one in Manasseh (25), but the latter is probably 25
an error by dittography for Ibleam (Tell Bel'ameh), with the LXX and 1 Chr. 6:70 (Bileam). **27-33.** Cities for the Gershonites : For Be-eshterah (27) read with Syr. and 1 Chr. 6:71 Ashtaroth (Tell 'Ashtarah). Jarmuth (29) is Remeth of 19:21, and 1 Chr. 6:73 has Ramoth ; read Remeth here (Kôkab el-Hawa ?). **34-40.** Cities for the Merarites : All but four of their twelve cities were located in Transjordan. **41-42**
Summary of the Allotment of the Levitical Cities. i
Num. 35:4, 5, defines the extent of the pasture-lands to be a thousand cubits on each side of the city, each city with its property forming a square 2,000 cubits on each side.

43-45 Deuteronomic Conclusion—This originally j
was apparently the conclusion to the allotment of tribal territory, and was not written to follow the allotment of the Levitical cities. Compare the P conclusion in 19:51 (see also 19:41, 50).

XXII 1-XXIV 33 The Last Days of Joshua—In 2
22:7ff. the P source relates the story of the return of the Transjordan tribes to their territory and their conflict with the Cisjordan tribes for the purposes of stressing the rights of the Transjordan tribes in the congregation of Israel and to emphasise the fact that the Jerusalem sanctuary was the single shrine for all Israel. This is preceded by the D account of Joshua's address to the Transjordan tribes and their return home (1–6). Chs. 23 and 24 give the impression of two occasions on which Joshua's ' last ' words were spoken to the same group of people. This may represent two D recensions, although it may also be sermonic admonitions to the Israelites, in ch. 24 using materials from an earlier source. 24:28–31 recalls the D introduction to the story of the Judges in Jg. 2:6–9, v. 31 and Jg. 2:7 being nearly identical. The hand of P seems to be evident in v. 33, in view of the role of Eleazar in the P materials earlier in the book.

XXII 1-6 The Return of the Transjordan Tribes b
—According to the beginning of the Deuteronomic account of Joshua's conquest, Joshua had promised the men of the Transjordan tribes that they would return to their possessions after they had helped their fellow-tribesmen conquer Cisjordan (1:12–18). This is the fulfilment of that promise, and it follows naturally after 21:43–45, which also emphasises the promise of the Lord. **5** reflects the phraseology of Dt. 6:5–7, from the same source.

7-34 The Return of the Transjordan Tribes and c
the Altar Incident—The dual sources result in two blessings (6*a*, 7*b*) and two returns (6*b*, 9). **10, 11.** The location of the altar was on the west side of the Jordan, as the RSV translation implies, in which ' at the frontier of the land of Canaan ' interprets the Hebrew text, as did the LXX ; contrast AV ' over against the land of Canaan '. See also RSV ' on the side that belongs to the people of Israel ' in contrast with AV ' at the passage of the children of Israel '. RSV ' side ' is a common meaning of the Hebrew word rendered inaccurately in AV as ' passage '. The Transjordan tribes built ' an altar of great size ', more literally ' an altar great to sight '. This altar is reckoned a violation of the single-sanctuary law (see Dt. 12:5–14), the ideal of both P and D. With the threatened intertribal warfare here compare Jg. 20:1–48, where the tribes fight against Benjamin, or Jg. 21:10, in which the ' assembly ' (correct RSV ' congregation ') of Israel sends an army against Jabesh-gilead. The assembly was gathered ' at Shiloh ' ; contrast Jg. 20:1 where the people of Israel gather at Mizpah.

13-20 The Protest of the People of Israel— d
Phinehas led the delegation to the Transjordan tribes, for he was known for his stand against pagan practices ; see Num. 25:6–9 (P) and Ps. 106:28–31. **14.** The ten chiefs represent the ten tribes who had their inheritance in Cisjordan, while Phinehas would represent the tribe of Levi. **17.** The reference to Peor would come naturally to Phinehas (see Num. 25:1–16 ; cf. Num. 31:16 ; Hos. 9:10), who was presumably the spokes-

d man for the ten chiefs. The plague in punishment for the sin at Peor caused the death of 24,000 (Num. 25:9), and was stopped by the action of Phinehas.
e **19.** The sin of the Transjordan tribes would, in the words of the people of Israel, ' make us rebels ' (changing the vocalisation of MT which reads as does AV ' rebel against us '). This verse suggests that Cisjordan, because the tabernacle (i.e. as the prototype of the Temple) was there, was more truly Israel's land than Transjordan ; note that in Ezek. 48 the new allotment of all the twelve tribes is made west of the Jordan.

f **21-23 The Excuse of the Transjordan Tribes**—The drastic curse on themselves that the Transjordan tribes risk if they have been guilty reflects the author's view of the vital importance of the single-sanctuary (22–23), as does the denial of the sacrificial function of the altar built by the Transjordan tribes (26–27). The altar was to be a ' witness ' that the Transjordan tribes had a portion in the Lord and his sanctuary. Compare the stone as a witness in 24:26, 27 and the heap of stones in Gen. 31:48. The altar was given the name ' Witness ' ; in MT the name ' Witness ' is missing, but the explanation discloses the nature of the missing name ; see also Syr.

g **XXIII 1-16 The First Farewell Address of Joshua—4-7.** The conquest was as yet incomplete (see 13:1), and the Israelites must not assimilate the religion of the Canaanites remaining in the land, nor should they intermarry with them, and so take over also their gods (see Dt. 7:3). ' The book of the law of Moses ' is mentioned also in 1:6, 8, where there is the same admonition not to turn from it to the right hand or to the left (see also 22:5). **9.** ' No man has been able to stand before you ' is a fulfilment of 1:5, 10:8 ; see also 21:44. **10.** ' One man of you puts to flight a thousand ' ; compare Lev. 26:8. **11.** ' Love the Lord your God ' ; see 22:5. **13.** The threat of exile also occurs in Dt. 6:15, 8:20, etc. The fate of the Canaanites would become Israel's fate. **14-16.** God both rewards and punishes. See Dt. 28:15–68 for a long list of the ' evil things ' the Lord would bring on Israel for disobeying his commandments and statutes.

h **XXIV 1-28 The Second Farewell Address of Joshua and the Covenant at Shechem**—This chapter contains what not only appears to duplicate or parallel ch. 23, but its account of the covenant at Shechem seems to duplicate the Deuteronomic story of the consummation of the covenant in 8:30–35. Of course it may be that the sources of D indicated two covenant events at Shechem. While ch. 23 presents a setting when Joshua was old and advanced in years and so suggests a farewell address (see 13:1), 24:1–27 does not explicitly state that the address was at the end of Joshua's career, and so some have presumed that this address is out of place here. It is also pointed out that the account of Joshua's death and burial is to be found in the introduction to the Deuteronomic book of Judges (Jg. 2:6–9), which seems to make the account of his death and burial here in 24:29–31
i superfluous. The allusion to Shechem as a gathering-place of Israel is unique here in the Deuteronomist, who avoids specific mention of it in 8:20–35 and also in Dt. 11:29, 27:1–26, which anticipates 8:20–35. There is enough to suggest at least the possibility that ch. 24 is by a secondary Deuteronomic hand. This, however, does not mean that the covenant at Shechem after the conquest is less historical than the covenant in 8:20–35. It may, indeed, be more historical. The associations of Shechem with covenant-making may even be pre-Israelite, for the Canaanites worshipped there El-berith or Baal-berith (' El of the covenant ' or ' Baal of the Covenant ') ; see Jg. 9:4, 46.

1. Shechem (Tell Balâṭah) may have been a more 259j
important early Israelite sanctuary than our sources evidence, for they are edited or reported with an anti-Israelite (in the sense of the ten northern tribes) and anti-Samaritan bias.

**2-13 Joshua's Description of the Lord's Pro- k
vidence in the Past—3.** The call and migrations of Abraham are narrated in Gen. 12. For Nahor, Abraham's brother, see Gen. 11:26. **4.** The hill-country of Seir is the highlands west of the Arabah, south-west of the Dead Sea. For Jacob's descent to Egypt see Gen. 47. **6-7.** See Exod. 14, 15. The darkness placed by the Lord between the Egyptians and the Israelites reflects the tradition that the pillar of cloud took its place between them (Exod. 14:19, 20). **8-10** recapitulate the conquest east of the Jordan. **9-10.** For the Balaam incident see Num. 22–24. **12.** The hornet must be symbolic for the action or terror of the Lord which drove out the Canaanites. The two kings of the Amorites were Sihon and Og, but they are out of place here in the description of the Cisjordan conquests. Instead of two the LXX has twelve kings of the Amorites, taken obviously as the kings of Cisjordan. **13.** Compare Dt. 6:10, 11.

14-15 Joshua's Exhortation to Choose the Lord l
—The covenant was to be made by the free choice of Israel, who must choose between the Lord and the gods worshipped by their ancestors in Mesopotamia and Egypt, or by the Amorites (Canaanites) in Canaan. ' In sincerity ', i.e. completely, whole-heartedly, single-mindedly. Joshua made his choice
first. **16-18 The People's Choice.** They elected to m
serve the Lord, crediting him with their rescue from Egypt, their safe sojourn to Canaan, and the conquest
of the land. **19-28 Consummation of the Covenant.** n
The statutes and ordinances (25) were the details of the covenant. Jacob's disposal of pagan gods at the Shechem sanctuary (Gen. 35:2–4) has a parallel perhaps in Israel's rejection of pagan gods at Shechem in this chapter. **26.** The story of Jacob setting up the stone at Bethel (Gen. 28:10–22), also associated with the covenant, may have furnished the inspiration for the story of Joshua's action. The sacred oak-tree at Shechem was associated in tradition with Abraham and Jacob (Gen. 12:6, 35:4). **27.** The stone was a ' witness ' to the covenant for it had ' heard ' the words of the Lord. Nature is often pictured responding to the Lord and with human qualities and senses ; see Ezek. 36:1, 4 ; Mic. 6:1, 2.

29-31 The Death and Burial of Joshua—Joshua o
was buried, at the age of one hundred and ten years, at Timnath-serah (Khirbet-Tibneh) in the hill-country of Ephraim (see 19:50 ; Jg. 2:9). **31** prepares the way for the time after the death of Joshua and the elders of his generation when Israel apostasised, as in
the stories of the Judges. **32 The Burial of the** p
Bones of Joseph. Joseph's bones had been brought back by Israel when it left Egypt, as Joseph had ordered before his death (Gen. 50:25 ; Exod. 13:19). They were now buried at Shechem in ground bought by Jacob from the sons of Hamor (Gen. 33:19). ' A piece of money ', Hebrew *ḳ^{e}śîṭāh*, is of uncertain weight. **33.** Death and burial of Eleazar. The location of Gibeah of Phinehas in Ephraim is unknown.

Bibliography—COMMENTARIES : P. J. Boyer, RV for Schools (1902) ; J. Bright, IB (1953) ; G. A. Cooke, CB (1918) ; H. Holzinger, KHC (1901) ; M. Noth, HAT, 2nd ed. (1953) ; H. W. Robinson, Cent.B.

OTHER LITERATURE : J. Garstang, *Joshua–Judges* (1931) ; H. H. Rowley, *From Joseph to Joshua* (1950) ; W. Rudolph, *Der Elohist von Exodus bis Joshua* (1938).

JUDGES

By J. N. SCHOFIELD

260a **Place in Canon**—It is important to recognise that in the Heb. Bible the book of Jg. is a prophetical work. It belongs to the second of the three main divisions of that Bible, the Prophets, consisting of the Former Prophets, Isa., Jer., Ezek. and the Book of the Twelve. The Former Prophets include Jos., Jg., Sam. and Kg. We shall therefore expect to find in the book not historical records but prophetical teaching and, as in the other prophetical works, the use of history to illustrate and reveal the character and work of Israel's God. In the present form of the book the stories used by the religious editors have their chronological setting between the death of Joshua (1:1, 2:8) and the foundation of the monarchy (18:1, 19:1) as related in the books of Sam., and the book has thus a natural chronological position among the Former Prophets. In the Gk. versions of the OT as in the RSV, the book of Ru. follows Jg. because its setting is in the same period, 'In the days when the judges ruled' (1:1), but in the Heb. Bible Ru. belongs to the third division —the Writings—as one of five Megilloth or Scrolls designed to be read at a festival.

b **Relationship to Joshua**—Despite the fact that Jg. 1:1 dates the contents of the book after the death of Joshua, as Jos. 1:1 dates the book of Jos. after the death of Moses, it is clear that Jg. is not a sequel to Jos., but that the two books are parallel narratives. In Jg. 1:16 the tribes are still at Jericho, 'the city of Palms'; and in 2:1 Gilgal is the headquarters as in Jos. 4:19 and 14:6, but the tribes had moved to Shiloh in Jos. 18:1, and to Shechem in 24:1. Both books give accounts of the settlement of the Israelite tribes in Palestine: in Jos. the dominant tradition is of a rapid conquest by all Israel acting together under Joshua, but there is evidence of another tradition of a partial and gradual conquest: Geshur and Maacath were not occupied by Israel (13:13), Caleb and Othniel took Hebron and Debir (15:14, 17), Jerusalem remained in the hands of Jebusites (15:63), Gezer was not captured (16:10) nor the line of cities from Beth-shan westward to the Mediterranean (17:11–13), Joseph was crowded by Canaanites (17:14–18), and Dan also until he found territory in the north (19:47). A similar tradition to this latter one is seen in Jg. 1–3, and it is not till the end of Jg. that Dan makes good his position in the north (18:29). Parallels between Jos. and Jg. are given in the footnotes in RSV (Jg. 1–2). In Jg. 4 Barak and Deborah are credited with victory over Jabin, king of Hazor, who, according to Jos. 11, was defeated by Joshua. Many scholars regard the connection between Jos. and Jg. as closer, and believe it is possible to trace through both books the same documents, cycles of oral traditions, or the work of the same schools of writers as have been isolated as elements in the composition of the Pentateuch—L, J, E, D, P—but on this there is not agreement among scholars.

c **The relationship with Samuel** is also close. In 1 Sam. 4:18 after the death of Eli we read 'He had judged Israel forty years', a phrase comparable to the conclusion of the accounts of many of the judges. Samuel is also said to have judged Israel (1 Sam. 7:15), so that Eli and Samuel may be thought of as the last of the judges. Further, the reference to Philistines as
well as Ammonites in the introduction to the rise of 2
Jephthah (Jg. 10:6ff.) would fit more closely to the story of the rise of Saul, and it has been suggested that these verses in Jg. 10 were originally the introduction to Saul's defeat of Ammonites and Philistines (1 Sam. 11, 13), and that Samuel's speech (1 Sam. 12) originally concluded the book of Jg. (cf. S. A. Cook, *Notes on OT History*). The final story in Jg. concerns the Benjaminites from whom Saul sprang, Jabesh Gilead delivered by Saul (1 Sam. 11), and the festival at Shiloh, whither Hannah came to pray for the birth of a son.

Contents—There are **three sections: 1:1-2:5** d
describes the conquest as gradual, and incompletely made by individual tribes; though containing old traditions it has been inserted between Jos. 24 and Jg. 2:6 by an editor who probably added 1:1, 8f., 2:1*b*–5*a*. **The main portion, 2:6-16:31,** gives an account of thirteen judges (using the word in the wider sense of ruler or leader). Of these stories six are set in an editorial framework, reiterating the prophetic teaching that apostasy brings the wrath of God, who sends human enemies to punish Israel, but when she repents and cries for help he delivers her by a human leader. Most scholars regard this framework as due to the Deuteronomic school of writers during or after the Babylonian exile (586 to 516 B.C.); C. F. Burney regarded it as pre-Deuteronomic from a northern writer (E_2). **Chs. 17-21, the third section,** are usually regarded as an appendix. No judges are mentioned by name; the stories reflect pre-monarchical conditions and show considerable antipathy to the northern sanctuary of Dan and to the tribe of Benjamin; the interests are clearly Levitical, and are dated during the lifetime of grandsons of Moses (18:30) and Aaron (20:28). The editorial hand (D or E_2) is not found by commentators in this section.

Composition—The usual theory (cf. Budde, *Die* e
Bücher Richter und Samuel (1890)) is that a *pre-Deuteronomic* editor collected hero stories and poems from north (E) and south (J) Palestine, and harmonised or collated them, giving local leaders a national character, and producing a religious book showing that unfaithfulness to God brought evil on the nation; later a *Deuteronomic* editor emphasised the cycle of sin–punishment–repentance–deliverance and omitted sections that did not serve his purpose (chs. 1, 9, 17–21) or were too scandalous (ch. 16) and probably concluded the book with 1 Sam. 12 (omitting 1 Sam. 1–6); later still a *post-Deuteronomic* editor expanded this expurgated edition by bringing back the omitted sections and adding short notices of 'minor' judges to produce a book of the *Twelve Judges of Israel*. The weaknesses of this theory are shown by Eissfeldt (*Einleitung in das AT* (2nd ed. 1956)). Editorial alterations and glosses make it difficult confidently to trace stages in the growth of the book. A clue to editorial activities can be seen in the alternating use of 'Israel' and 'people of Israel' (cf. 6:1–6), referred to in the following commentary as evidence of the work of 'singular' and 'plural' editors respectively; attention is also drawn to evidences for the activity of a Levitical editor or glossator.

Chronology—Much ingenuity has been used to har- f

30f monise the chronology of the book with 1 Kg. 6:1, which states that the fourth year of Solomon corresponded to the four hundred and eightieth year after the exodus from Egypt. The total number of years of oppression and peace given in the book of Jg. is 410, to which must be added 40 years in the wilderness, the generation of Joshua's contemporaries, 40 years of Eli, the years of Samuel and Saul, and 40 years of David and 4 of Solomon. The most elaborate recent attempt to work out a chronological scheme was made by J. Garstang (*Joshua-Judges* (1931)) who finds a correlation with Egyptian history.

1a **I 1-II 5 First Introduction: Israel's Settlement in Western Palestine** is represented as effected by the tribes acting in pairs or singly, and as incomplete. Cities, main lines of fortifications running across the country from E. to W., as well as the wide fertile valleys remained in native hands. The narrative used an old account, usually regarded as belonging to the J tradition, found in a different form in the book of Jos. The purpose of the editor and a reason why he gives an altered version of the original source are seen in 2:2: namely, that failure to capture the whole country was due to disobedience to God's command and resulted in heathen worship and lack of peace; so the editor changes the statement that Israel 'could not' cast out the natives to the fact that she 'did not', because he believed that all things were possible to those who obey God. This summary of the story of the settlement is not a unity; there are contradictions (cf. 8 with 21), and differences in vocabulary which are often obscured because the RSV is not consistent in its translation of Heb. words. Probably the phrase 'people (Heb. 'sons') of Israel' is an indication of the hand of the editor. The summary was prefixed to an earlier book of Jg. which began at 2:6 with a repetition of the closing verses of Jos. 24; it is parallel in form to the opening of the book of Jos.: 'After the death of Moses' is balanced by 'After the death of Joshua' in 1:1; but in 2:6 Joshua is still alive, his death being recorded in 2:8.

b **I 1-10** The sacred oracle is consulted (cf. 1 Sam. 14:37ff.), Judah is chosen to open the attack and obtains the assistance of Simeon to conquer the territory already allotted to them by Joshua. Judah's portion is detailed in Jos. 15:1–12, Simeon's portion being within Judah's. Possibly Gen. 34 (cf. 34:30) may be the story of the destruction of the tribe of Simeon at Shechem, after which the remnant fled south, amalgamating with Judah. Judah and Simeon are here represented as individuals, but clearly the tribes are meant, and in **8f.** 'men (Heb. 'sons') of Judah' is used. The campaign resulted in the defeat of the inhabitants of Bezek and the capture of Jerusalem and Hebron. The account of the victory at Bezek is confused and has probably been altered: the result is given before the battle (4); the name of Adonibezek (5) appears to mean 'Lord of a small pebble, or little stone idol' and is probably a deliberate alteration, by a play on sounds loved by Jewish writers, of Adonizedek, 'My lord is Zedek or righteousness', the name of the king of Jerusalem in Jos. 10:1; 'in Bezek' has then been added or changed from Gibeon, and the story is another account of the defeat of the allies of the king of Jerusalem recorded in a ballad in Israel's

c national poetry book (Jos. 10:13). **8, 9.** The maimed king was carried by his followers into Jerusalem, where he died before the city was stormed by the men of Judah. Bezek, modern Ibzîk, 11 miles SW. of Beisân (1 Sam. 11:8), would not fit the context, which requires a site in the south. 'Canaanites' is used as a general term for the inhabitants of Palestine, and for lowlanders as distinct from the Amorites of the hill country; Egypt called all West Syria and Palestine Canaan, and the Tell el-Amarna tablets used the word for the Phoenician coastland. 'Perizzites' were dwellers in unwalled towns and were found near Shechem (Jos. 11:3; Gen. 34:30) and in the south (Gen. 13:7). 8 conflicts with 21, but agrees with
Jos. 15:63 in linking Jerusalem with Judah and not 261c
with Benjamin. The city was captured by David the Judaean (2 Sam. 5) but the statement in 21 may reflect a tradition that Saul, the Benjaminite, and his men had previously been allowed in the city. In Jos. 18:16, 28 the city is assigned to Benjamin. In contradiction to 8 it is related in Jos. 15:63 that Judah could not drive out the Jebusites, and in Jg. 19 it is still in their hands. **9** is a summary of Judah's further fighting in the hills east and west of Jerusalem, in the Negeb, the drier land south of Hebron, and in the lowland or Shephelah, where the Judaean hills run out into the maritime plain (cf. SHG (1896), 201ff.). 8 and 9 are probably editorial. Judah then attacked Hebron, defeating the three Anakim leaders previously met by the spies (Num. 13:22) and driven out of Hebron by Caleb (1:20; Jos. 15:14). 1 Chr. 2 shows that Calebite elements were included in Judah, and the traditions of the two groups were interwoven.

11-20 contains the story of the **conquest of the south:** 262a
Debir was captured by Othniel, Zephath by Judah and Simeon, and the Philistine cities of Gaza, Ashkelon and Ekron by Judah. **11.** 'They went' (Heb. 'He went') refers to Judah, but the parallel Jos. 15:15 has 'he went up' referring to Caleb, and is geographically less accurate. Debir is Tell Beit Mirsim, 13 miles SSW. of Hebron. It was excavated by Albright (AASOR I–III, XIIf. XVII, XXIf.), who dates this destruction about 1200 B.C. The other names for the city, Kiriath-sepher, the book-city, and Kiriath-sannah (Jos. 15:49), city-of-palm-leaf, a writing material, both suggest a scribal guild city. **13.** The city was captured by Caleb's brother (cf. Jos. 15:17 where it is not mentioned that he was younger) Othniel, who married his niece, Caleb's daughter, whom he *urged* (so read in 14) successfully to obtain the valuable heritage of some otherwise unknown springs. **16-17** are probably another account of the attempted invasion from the south, related as a successful attack on the Canaanite king of Arad in Num. 21, as a defeat by Amalekites and Canaanites in Num. 14:44f., and by Amorites in
Dt. 1:44. Here **16f.**, possibly an editorial comment b
(cf. 'people (Heb. 'sons') of Judah'), makes the point of entry Jericho, 'the city of Palms' (cf. 3:13), and pictures the attack on Arad as made from the north and not from the south. Jericho is Tell es-Sulṭân, dug by Garstang (PEQ (1951–5), AAA (1931–1936)) and Kathleen Kenyon (M. Wheeler, *Walls of Jericho* (1956)). **16.** The Hebrew is corrupt; probably we should read 'And the descendants of Hobab the Kenite (cf. 4:11) . . . and settled with the Amalekites (cf. Num. 24:20f.; 1 Sam. 15:6). Hobab is represented as having acceded to Moses' request (cf. Num. 10:32) and as accompanying Israel in the wilderness wanderings as far as Jericho, but then remaining nomadic. Moses' father-in-law is Hobab the Kenite (4:11), but elsewhere he is a Midianite, named variously Reuel (Exod. 2:18), Jethro (Exod. 3:1), and Hobab the son of Reuel (Num. 10:29). 'Kenites', descendants of Cain, lived in the Negeb (1 Sam. 27:10, 30:29, friendly to Judah), in the hills of Ephraim (1 Sam. 15:6), and farther north (Jg. 5:24). 'Arad' is probably Tell 'Arâd, 17 miles S. of Hebron. 'Hormah' is here derived from the Hebrew *ḥāram* = to destroy utterly by devoting to the deity; like 'Hermon' it
may originally have denoted a Holy Place. **18, 19.** c
'Gaza', on the Egyptian border (PEF (1923, 1927)), 'Ashkelon', 17 miles N. of Gaza on the coast (PEF (1921–3)), and 'Ekron' (Qaṭrā), about 18 miles NE. of Ashkelon in the Vale of Sorek, were Philistine cities in the maritime plain, from which Judah did not drive out the inhabitants (3:1–3) because of their iron chariots (cf. Jos. 17:16; Jg. 4:3). The LXX removes the contradiction by reading, 'Judah did not take'. **19b.** Heb. 'not . . . to drive out' omitting 'was able' (RSV 'could') which is found in the phrase when used in Jos. (cf. 17:12). RSV has here supplied 'could', but it was probably omitted intentionally by the editor of this chapter (as in 21, cf. Jos. 15:63;

262c and 27, cf. Jos. 17:11f.). The introduction of iron is dated about 1200 B.C. by Albright (*The Archaeology of Palestine* (1949), 110). **21.** 'Jebusites' are not known outside the OT, but the name 'Araunah the Jebusite' (2 Sam. 24:16) suggests a connection with Hittite-Mitanni people; Benjaminites are mentioned as a tribe at Mari in NE. Mesopotamia in the 18th cent. B.C. (cf. ET 66 (1954–5), 250ff.).

d **22-34** relates the **conquest of the central and northern hill country**. The house of Joseph was composed of the two tribes of Ephraim and Manasseh, but here it is differentiated from them and regarded as a group who obediently destroyed the previous inhabitants, the Lord being with them (a different phrase from that in 19). Both Bethel and Jerusalem, according to the editorial addition in 8, were new cities completely free of the contagion of the old heathen inhabitants. The capture of Bethel is not mentioned in the book of Jos. but its king is among those conquered (Jos. 12:16); the details of Joseph's portion are given in Jos. 16f. 'Bethel' is Beitîn, about 12 miles N. of Jerusalem on the hills E. of the road to Shechem (Nâblus); it was excavated in 1934 (BASOR 55 (1934), 56 (1934), 137 (1954); BA 19 (1956), 36ff.). 'Luz', cf. Gen. 28:19. 'Hittites', §86*d*. The two sections of Joseph, Manasseh and Ephraim *did not* (not 'could not' as Jos. 17:12f.) drive out the Canaanites. Manasseh infiltrated into the line of fortresses from Bethshan, Taanach, Megiddo, to Dor, which controlled the passes over the Carmel hills; Ephraim settled among the Canaanites in Gezer. The Canaanites insisted on remaining and Manasseh made no real attempt (Heb. 'certainly did not'; not as RSV 'did not utterly') to drive them out. The emphasis is on the fact that even when Israel grew strong in the time of Solomon no effort was made to drive out the Canaanites; they were reduced to forced labour (1 Kg. 9:15ff.). 'Bethshan' is Beisân in the Jordan valley (A. Rowe and G. M. Fitzgerald, *Bethshan* (3 vols. 1930–40)); Taanach lies 17 miles W. of Bethshan (cf. ZDPV (1928), 169ff.); 'Dor' was on the coast (cf. *Bull. Brit. School of Arch.* (1924–7)); 'Megiddo' is Tell el-Mutesellim, 5 miles W. of Taanach (cf. *Megiddo* I (1939), II (1948); and cf. references in BA 13 (1950), 28f.), and is out of place in the list, as is also 'Ibleam'. 'Ephraim', the other section of the Joseph tribe, had its portion south of Manasseh and north of Benjamin on the central hill country. Its SW. point was 'Gezer', the modern Tell Jezer on a spur of the Judaean foothills 18 miles WNW. of Jerusalem. It was given as a wedding present to Solomon by the king of Egypt (1 Kg. 9:16) (Macalister, *The Excavations of Gezer*, 3 vols. (1912); PEF (Jan. 1935)). Both Thuthmosis III (1501–1447) and Merneptah (*c.* 1225) captured it, and a letter at Tell el-Amarna records an appeal for aid from its king Yapahi; another king, Horam, was defeated by
e Joshua (Jos. 10:33). **30.** Zebulun's territory was north of Manasseh and probably included Carmel (Dt. 33:18f.), where Baal Zebul, Lord of the High Place, was worshipped (2 Kg. 1). The towns mentioned are not certainly identified: 'Kitron' may be Tell Qurdâneh in the plain south of Acre; 'Nahalol' may be Tell en-Naḥl or Ma'lûl 3½ miles W. of Nazareth. **31.** Asher also did not drive out the Canaanite inhabitants but dwelt among them in the coastal strip farther north (Jos. 19:24ff.; Jg. 5:17). Asher is mentioned by the Egyptian kings Seti I (*c.* 1313) and Rameses II (*c.* 1292) as settled in W. Galilee; if this was before the Israelite invasion under Joshua it would suggest that not all the tribes were in bondage in Egypt. 'Acco' is the modern 'Akkā, at the N. of the bay of Acre, but the ancient site was probably farther E.; 'Sidon' is Ṣaidā, about 25 miles S. of Beirût; 'Achzib' is probably Ez-Zîb 9 miles N. of 'Akkā. In Isa. 65:11 Asher is treated as the name of a god of Fortune. **33.** Naphtali like Asher dwelt among the Canaanites, occupying land N. of Zebulun, between Asher and the Jordan (Jos. 19:32f.), but the towns mentioned suggest
that, like Dan, the tribe originally settled in the south 262
of the central hill country (cf. Dt. 33:23); 'Bethshemesh' would then be 'Ain Shems on the railway line from Jerusalem to Lydda, and 'Beth-Anath' may have been in the same neighbourhood (cf. Anathoth). Both names suggest heathen worship: the former meaning House of the Sun, and the latter House of Anath, a Canaanite goddess of love and war (ARI 74–7) worshipped by Jews at Yeb in the 5th cent. B.C. (A. E. Cowley, *Aramaic Papyri of the 5th Cent. B.C.* (1923)). Zebulun and Naphtali are mentioned as settled in the north in Isa. 9:1 and the foreign element in the territory is indicated by the phrase 'Galilee (circle) of the Gentiles'. **34.** Dan attempted to settle in the fertile lowlands of the SW. (cf. the story of Samson, Jg. 13:2, 25) but was driven out and migrated to the north (Jos. 19:47). **35.** 'Harheres' (Hill of the Sun, Heres = Shemesh) may be in the neighbourhood of Bethshemesh; 'Aijalon' is the modern Yâlō about 7 miles NNE. of 'Ain Shems on the edge of the Shephelah. It is suggested that after Dan had been driven out by Amorites (or Canaanites), who had themselves been driven from the coastal plain by Philistines, the Joseph tribes subjugated the land. **36.** For 'Amorites' some versions read 'Edomites', and treat the verse as indicating where the boundary between Israel and Edom ran (cf. Num. 34:3ff.; Jos. 15:1ff.) but it is not possible to trace it from this verse.

II 1-5 concludes the summary of the conquest; it f
has no parallel in the book of Jos., was probably not in the original source but composed by the editor who added ch. 1, to emphasise the belief that disobedience to God's command brings apostasy and foreign oppression, although it did not, and could not, break God's covenant with his people. The angel of the Lord is mentioned in 6:11f., 21f. and 13:15, perhaps indicating the same editorial activity there. Palestine is thought of as conquered from Gilgal (so Jos. 4:19, 9:6, 10:15, 43, 14:6). In Jos. 18:1 the next move was to Shiloh, but in Jg. 20:18, 26, 21:2 Bethel was the next headquarters and there the Ark was kept. Later there was considerable rivalry between Jerusalem and Bethel, and the LXX here suggests that an original Bethel has been changed to Bochim (using the name from the Oak of Weeping in that locality, Gen. 35:8). The angel whose guidance was promised (Exod. 23:20, 32:34, 33:2) still went up with the people until the Ark found its resting-place at Bethel and sacrifices began. In Jos. 8:30ff. the first sacrifices were offered at Shechem between Ebal and Gerizim, cf. Dt. 11:29, 27:1ff.; in Jos. 18:1 the tent of meeting was set up at Shiloh. **3.** 'Adversaries' follows some versions; the Heb. has 'sides' as in Num. 33:55; Jos. 23:13, to which this may be an abbreviated reference.

II 6-III 6 Another Introduction to the History 263
of the Judges, setting forth the historian's attitude that inevitably sin brings punishment, and disaster is the proof of previous sin—an attitude rejected by Jesus (Jn 9:3). This attitude, stated in 2:11–16, is crystallised into a stereotyped framework for each judge (cf. 3:7–9*a*, 11*a*). **6-9** is in Jos. 24:28–31 with alterations which show the editor's hand (cf. 6, 'the people [sons] of Israel went . . .'). The element common to both accounts uses the Deuteronomic 'outlive' (Heb. 'prolong days') suggesting that the editor wrote after the first Deuteronomists and probably not before the return from exile in 520 B.C. **7** changes 'known all the work of the Lord' (Jos. 24:31) to 'seen all the great work' as in Dt. with emphasis on the acts of the Lord at Horeb rather than at the Exodus, for all the earlier generation died before the invasion of Palestine. **10.** 'Know the Lord' reflects prophetic influence and means, 'to have experience of intimacy' with him. The rest of the section is not homogeneous. **11-19** represents punishment as through neighbouring nations as in the remainder of the book; **2:20-3:6** regards the enemy as original inhabitants of the land as in Jg. 1, and the

263a purpose of this remnant is not to punish Israel but to prove it religiously (2:22, 3:4) or teach the art of war without any express religious purpose (3:1f.). There have been successive amplifications in the style of the secondary Deuteronomists, who were responsible for the books of Kg. in their present form and for additions to Dt., and it is no longer possible to isolate the introduction to the earliest book of Jg. Perhaps the use of 'Israel' as distinct from 'people of Israel' may be a clue. **13.** 'Baals' are those who possess rights (it was a common name for husbands). Like Elohim it was a general name for 'god' and is seen in Baal-Hermon and Baal-Berith (8:33). In the OT the plural may be used to include all the various baals or it may be an expression of contempt. At Râs Shamra Baal was the youthful god of vegetation (ARI 73ff.). Ashtaroth, also a plural as a general term for all goddesses, was the consort of Baal and one of the many names for the mother-goddess or the goddess of fertility in the ancient world (ARI 74ff.). **17.** 'played the harlot' is used in the prophetic books of the worship of deities other than Yahweh and referred to actual sexual rites of the fertility cults. **3:3.** 'Baal-Hermon' is probably the same as Baal-Gad (Jos. 13:5) and is Bâniyâs, known in the NT as Caesarea Philippi, near the sources of the Jordan. 'Entrance of Hamath', mentioned often as the northern limit of Israel (1 Kg. 8:65), is probably the southern end of the valley between the Lebanon and the Anti-Lebanon leading up to Hamath in Syria. 'Lords of the Philistines', cf. 1 Sam. 5:8. **5.** 'Hivites', probably Horites or Hurrians now known from Mari and Râs Shamra. **6.** Intermarriage is forbidden in Dt. 7:3 as part of the nationalistic movement seen also in Neh. and protested against in Ru.

b **III 7-11 Othniel,** the first judge, was Caleb's brother settled in the south (1:13). The story relates a deliverance from the oppression of a king of Mesopotamia (Heb. Aram, or Syria, of the two rivers) in the north. More probably it was an account of a repulsion of an Edomite invasion into the south, Edom having been misread as Aram and 'of the two rivers' added identifying the king with a Kassite leader (cf. Gen. 10:8) of NW. Mesopotamia. But Cushan was also a tribal name of S. Palestine where Othniel settled (Hab. 3:7); *rishathaim*, the double sinner, is a typical Hebrew play on words. **7.** 'asheroth', an unusual plural (2 Chr. 19:3, 33:3) of Asherah, a Canaanite goddess whose cult object was a wooden post or grove set up near altars (ARI 77f.). **10.** 'The Spirit of the Lord' came also on other judges (6:34, 13:25). In Hebrew thought man was open to the invasion of spirit forces for good or bad, and any abnormal human activity was ascribed to the power of spirit forces acting within him. **11.** 40 years denotes a complete generation, multiples of 40 occur often in the chronology.

c **12-30 Ehud,** a Benjaminite, and left-handed like other members of the tribe (20:16; 1 Chr. 12:2), wearing his weapon unnoticed on his right side, delivered central Palestine from Moabite oppression. Traces of the older setting can be seen in the use of 'Israel' in 12, 13, 30, but the editor has added his framework and modified the story. **13.** The greatness of the oppression is emphasised by reference to Ammon and Amalek, who are not again mentioned, and the capture of Jericho. Ehud is not stated to have judged Israel, but the land had rest for two generations, so severe was the defeat of Moab. Amalek, a traditional foe of Israel, was a bedouin tribe in the south (Num. 13:29; Dt. 25:17f.; 1 Sam. 27:8) but may also have spread to central Palestine (5:14 RSV*n*, 12:15; 1 Sam. 15). 'City of palms' (1:16): even though the city remained unbuilt (1 Kg. 16:34) the massive ruins would be a stronghold dominating the Jordan ford and surrounding country. **15.** 'Gera' was a Benjaminite name (Gen. 46:21; 2 Sam. 16:5) and here probably refers to Ehud's clan. **16.** 'Cubit': the Heb. word occurs only here in the OT and possibly indicates the shorter cubit of 13½ in.; the intention is clearly to indicate the fatness of Eglon. **18.** The 263c
tribute would be paid in kind (2 Kg. 3:4) as Jehu's to Shalmaneser III shown in the Assyrian Obelisk (ANET 281) and it would be carried by a train of bearers. **19a** does not fit between **18** and **19b**; it is connected with **26** and may be part of the original escape story. 'The sculptured stones' (Heb. 'graven images') may be sculptured boundary stones or a circle of carved standing stones or *maṣṣēbhôth* which gave to the place the name Gilgal or circle. **22.** 'The dirt came out' should probably be omitted as a mistaken repetition of words at the beginning of **23** where the meaning of the word translated 'vestibule' is not known. **25.** For description of ancient wooden keys cf. DB ii, 836. **28.** The fords were seized to prevent the raiders escaping or being reinforced.

31 Shamgar—There is neither introduction nor con- d
clusion nor a note of the length of the time of the oppression, nor of the rest that followed the deliverance. In some versions the verse appears after 16:31 introduced by 'And there arose after Samson'; it was not in its present position when the editor wrote 4:1 referring back to Ehud, and it shows no sign of the editor's hand. The name clearly comes from 5:6 where it is parallel to Jael and has been treated as the name of another deliverer; the act of deliverance being similar to that of Shammah the son of Agee, also against the Philistines (2 Sam. 23:11). The name is comparable to Sangar king of Carchemish in the 9th cent. B.C. The Heb. word for 'oxgoad' occurs here only (DB i, 49). 'Anath' is the name of a Canaanite goddess (ARI 74).

IV 1-V 31 Deborah—The chapters place side by 264a
side a prose and a poetic account of the same event, and a comparison of them throws light on the use of poetic sources by OT prose historians (cf. H. M. Chadwick, *Growth of Literature* III, where it is used to illustrate the feminine provenance of much Hebrew poetry). The structure of the poem suggests that this ballad was almost contemporary with the event (*Archaeology of Palestine* (1954), 231; cf. Burney, 158ff.); the prose is much later, differs in many ways noted below, and combines with the ballad another story which related the defeat of a confederacy of northern kings under Jabin king of Hazor by the waters of Merom (Jos. 11:1–9). For the saga of Israel's invasion, the first victory over the dreaded iron chariots was as important as the capture of the first fortified city, Jericho.

IV 1-14 Deborah's Strategy—**1-3** reveals the edi- b
torial framework. 'Jabin', unmentioned in the poem, is called king of Canaan, not king of Hazor as in v. 17 and Jos. 11:1; the modern Tell el-Qedaḥ, 4 miles W. of the S. end of Lake Huleh (Garstang, AAA 14 (1927), 35–42; cf. BA 19 (1956), 2ff.). 'Sisera', in the poem the kingly leader of the Canaanites, is here Jabin's army commander, stationed at 'Harosheth-ha-goiim', probably Tell el-Harbaj where the plain of Acre enters Esdraelon. Its predominant Canaanite population is indicated by Ha-goiim, 'of the Gentiles'.

4-10 Deborah and Barak—'Prophetess' (Heb. 'a c
woman, a prophetess'): like Miriam (Exod. 15:20), Huldah (2 Kg. 22:14), the anonymous one (Isa. 8:3), and Noadiah the opponent of Nehemiah (Neh. 6:14), none of whom is treated as a judge, though Miriam was a leader (Mic. 6:4) and sang another ballad; the others were on the staff of the Temple at Jerusalem. In 5:7 Deborah is 'a mother in Israel'. **5** is editorial, not in the poem, and shows a lack of knowledge of Palestine which may suggest that the editorial work was done in Babylonia. Palm trees do not grow on the hills near Bethel; the Deborah of the poem may have sat under a palm in Esdraelon, but the Deborah whose tree was near Bethel was Rebekah's nurse who was buried under an oak (Gen. 35:8). 'Ramah' is er-Râm, 5 miles N. of Jerusalem. (Bethel, cf. 1:23.)
6. Barak lived 7 miles NNW. of Hazor at Kedesh, Tell d
Qades, a hill fortress known to the Egyptians. **7.** The rallying-place is to be Mount Tabor, an isolated,

264d conspicuous, dome-shaped hill, rising 1,300 ft. from the NE. end of Esdraelon, whose wooded slopes would give Israel a refuge from Sisera's chariots. The poem does not mention Tabor nor limit the troops to men of Naphtali and Zebulun: there Ephraim, Benjamin, and Issachar are included. 'River Kishon', a wadi or river bed swollen to a river in the rainy seasons only, crosses Esdraelon between the Megiddo hills and Tabor. On dry ground the chariots would give Sisera superiority over the Israelite infantry, but after a heavy thunderstorm the plain becomes a quagmire, useless for manoeuvring chariots, which could not be withdrawn westward across the swollen Kishon, and the charioteers, forced to dismount, would be no match for the fierce tribesmen. **11.** Not in the poem, is based on the story of Jabin's defeat at Merom (Jos. 11:7), also in the north of Palestine, probably Jebel Meirôn, 5 miles W. of Kedesh in Naphtali. An oak of Zaanannim is mentioned in Naphtali (Jos. 19:33), but such a location of Jael's tent would involve a flight of 40 miles for Sisera to a place 12 miles beyond the gates of Jabin's fortified city of Hazor. The verse is intended to explain why a Kenite who should be dwelling in the south was found so far north.

e **12-23 The Defeat of Sisera**—'Harosheth', like Tabor, is E. of the Kishon; **16** suggests that Sisera's forces remained on the E. and were caught by Israel in the narrow pass between the river and Harosheth, but 5:19 suggests that they assembled W. of the Kishon at Tanaach, crossed the river to meet Israel and were swept away as they tried to retreat back across it after the thunderstorm. **17,** like 11, is an addition by the editor showing lack of knowledge of bedouin life; the poem knows nothing of peace between Jael and Jabin, which would make Jael's action the blackest treachery for a bedouin, the murder of a guest; there is no treachery in the poem. **18ff.**, cf. 5:25ff. Here Jael invites him into her tent, covers him with a rug (only here in Heb.), opens a skin of milk and, after giving him a drink, covers him up again and stands guard. None of this is in the poem. **21.** The 'hammer' and 'tent-peg' are treated as two separate weapons; in 5:26 poetic parallelism uses an abstract word from another root meaning 'to hammer' as a synonym for 'tent-peg' (cf. Mt. 21 where through a similar misunderstanding Jesus is represented as riding two animals). **21.** 'From weariness': RSV amends the difficult Heb. (cf. Burney, *ad loc.*); there is no sleeping Sisera in the poem.

f **V 1-31 Deborah's Song** contains many rare words and unusual grammatical forms reflecting poetic usage and northern dialect, influenced more strongly than classical Heb. by Aramaic. **2** states the occasion of the song 'When real leaders offered themselves freely'; the Hebrew is not clear and may refer to the bedouin custom of wearing the hair long and flowing during the period of vow or consecration for war (cf. Samson). **4-5,** the theophany, pictures the Lord as marching to his people's help from his dwelling-place in Sinai in the south, and revealing his presence by a violent thunderstorm (cf. Dt. 33; Hab. 3). 'Quaked' follows the versions instead of the Heb. 'flowed down'. 'Yon Sinai' or 'This is Sinai' spoils the parallelism and rhythm and is probably a marginal addition. (W. F. Albright (BASOR 62 (1936), 30) takes the view that the verse should be translated 'the one of Sinai', the pronoun being the equivalent of the Arabic *dhû*.) **7.** 'peasantry' (as 11): in Hab. 3:14 the same root is translated as 'warriors' and here the meaning may be the same. 'You arose' treats the Heb. as a dialect form of the 2nd feminine singular instead of a 1st singular. In 1 she is the singer, in 3 the 1st person is used, in 12 she is addressed or addresses herself. **8a.** Probably (reading *ḥārāshîm*, 'smiths', for *ḥ*[a]*dhāshîm*, here translated 'new gods') a reference to lack of skilled smiths or armourers (cf. 8*b* and 1 Sam. 13:19). **9.** The parallelism suggests that both Shamgar and Jael were leaders before Deborah, but were unable to help an oppressed people. **10.** The three classes of people addressed are unidentifiable; 264 possibly the first two denote the rich and 'you who walk by the way' are the poor, and it means 'rich and poor alike'; 'a tawny ass' was probably of a rare reddish-grey colour and its owner wealthy; 'rich carpets': the Heb. word denotes a measure of width or length and may refer to people clothed with particular garments. **11.** 'Musicians' is also doubtful; RSV g
follows the LXX and treats as a musical term; it may mean 'divide into bands' (Prov. 30:27) and so 'Above the noise of groups among the watering places' or, if the word comes from the same Heb. root as 'arrows', 'Away from the sound of the archers'. 'Triumphs' are the righteous or loyal acts of the Lord which show that he fulfils his obligations to the covenant and so gives victory to his people. **13.** RSV amends the difficult Heb. and makes 'the people of the Lord' the subject of 11*b*; perhaps it means, 'Then let a remnant, even a people, have dominion for the nobles; Let the Lord have dominion for me against the mighty'. **14.** Heb. 'From Ephraim whose root is in Amalek' (3:13): RSV changes 'their root' to a verb, and Amalek to *'ēmeḳ* = valley. 'Following you, Benjamin' was probably the Benjamin battle-cry (Hos. 5:8): 'Behind thee, Benjamin' may mean 'We are with thee, Benjamin' or 'Look to your rear, Benjamin'. 'Machir' for Manasseh (1:27); Machir was the son of Manasseh who settled in Gilead, E. of Jordan (Jos. 17:1; Num. 26:29); perhaps the settlement took place after the time of Deborah. 'Marshal's staff', Heb. 'scribal staff', may refer to one who kept the records. Zebulun is mentioned again (18) as showing outstanding bravery. **15.** Heb. 'My prince in Issachar': in 15*b* for the second 'Issachar' perhaps read 'Naphtali'. **18.** Barak's h
tribe (4:6). Reuben's reputation for indecision is seen in Gen. 49:4. Shepherd boys in modern Palestine still call their flocks by notes on flutes home-made from pieces of iron-piping. **17.** Gilead is probably the tribe of Gad settled in S. Gilead in E. Jordan (Jos. 13:24; Dt. 3:12). Dan neither in its location in the south (Jos. 19:41) nor in the north (Jg. 18:29) was on the coast; the reference may be to fishing-boats on the lake. **18.** 'Heights of the field': either poetic for the fiercest places of the battle or it may suggest that the fighting was carried beyond the Kishon into the hills round Taanach and Megiddo. No mention is made of the southern tribes Judah and Simeon nor of the priestly tribe Levi. **19.** 'Kings of Canaan' suggests an alliance of the city rulers or chieftains against Israel and may account for the prose editor linking it with the story of the confederacy under Jabin. **20.** Heb. 'From Heaven they fought; the stars in their highways fought against Sisera'. A similar expression of supernatural support for Israel is found in the poetic quotation in Jos. 10:13. **21.** 'Onrushing' explains the Heb. word as from an Arabic word 'to advance' or 'be bold in attack' instead of the usual Heb. root 'to be in front', and hence to be 'eastward' or 'old in time'. **22.** 'Then horses' hoofs hammered; from the galloping, galloping of those mighty ones' (cf. Jer. 8:16 where the word here translated 'mighty ones' is used of horses—RSV 'stallions'). **23.** Nothing is known of Meroz; the line is long and has probably been altered or corrupted.
24-7. The contrasting pictures of the victorious Jael i
and the anxious waiting mother of the slain Sisera are vividly drawn and show the feminine interest of the poem. **25.** By poetic hyperbole the poet says Jael would no more have given her enemy water than milk or curds in a dish fit for nobles; instead she felled him, as he stood at the door of her tent, with a tent peg used like a workman's hammer. **26.** 'Struck a blow', Heb. 'hammered' (as 22): 'crushed' only here in OT, apparently meaning 'utterly destroy'. **27.** 'Between her legs he bowed, he fell, he lay down; Between her legs he bowed, he fell; Where he bowed down there he fell, violently handled'. There was no sleeping Sisera, but an Amazonian woman astride her

4i battered foe. **28.** In contrast Sisera's mother anxiously awaits his return while her princesses or ladies-in-waiting—ironically called ' wise '—cheer her with visions of his victory and the booty he is bringing. **30.** ' Maiden ' : Heb. ' womb ' used on the Moabite stone for the temple slave girls in the Yahweh temple on Mt Nebo ; the same root provides the common Heb. word for the ' mercy ' of God. **30.** ' My neck as spoil ' amends the Heb. ' necks of spoil ' ; some versions read ' his neck as spoil '. **31.** So may all the enemies of the Lord and his people perish, ignominiously slain by a woman. ' Forty years ', clearly an addition to the original ballad, denoting a whole generation.

5a **VI 1-VIII 28 Gideon**—It is clear that, as in Jg. 4, two different stories have been combined, but there is also much evidence of editorial additions, often obscured in RSV by inconsistency in translation of singulars and plurals.

VI 1-10 Introduction—The editorial ' people of Israel ' used as a plural is seen in 1, 2, 6, and has been added to an earlier introduction that used ' Israel ' as a singular in 2*a*, 3, 4*b*, 6*a* and stated the historical facts ; the distinction between the two introductions is clear in a comparison of 6*a* with 6*b*. **1.** ' Midian ' is regarded as a wandering bedouin tribe linked with the east (Gen. 25:6), with Moab (Num. 22:4, 7), with S. Palestine (Exod. 3:1), and is confused with Ishmael (8:24 ; Gen. 37:25ff.). **3.** ' Would come up ' : the tense is frequentative, ' used to come '. The description of the weight of the oppression is increased by the addition here and in 33 of other invaders : Amalek (3:13) and the people of the East (used for Arab tribes E. of Jordan so far as the Euphrates, Jer. 49:28 ; Ezek. 25:4) ; it is also increased by the extension of the area invaded to Gaza on the southern border, so that all Palestine is involved and not the central part only as elsewhere in the story. **8.** ' Prophet ' (Heb. ' a man, a prophet ', cf. 4:4) : no other prophet is mentioned in Jg., but often in the Chronicler God's messenger is an anonymous prophet and the use here may be a clue to the milieu from which the verses came. ' House of bondage ' : so Dt. 5:6 ; Jer. 34:13. ' Brought out ' : as in Dt., which avoids ' brought up ' to describe the Exodus, a term used in the liturgy of the golden calf (Exod. 32:4 ; 1 Kg. 12:28 ; Neh. 9:18) and in southern writers ; here both phrases occur (cf. 2:1).

b **11-24 Gideon's Call**—The story fits with the earlier introduction that used ' Israel ', for Gideon has no knowledge of the religious reason for Midian's oppression emphasised by the plural editor. He is called to deliver Israel by the angel of the Lord (2:1), who accepts his offering as a sign of his call and who becomes the Lord himself in 14, 16, 23. **11.** ' Ophrah ' : between Shechem and Jezreel, but the site has not been identified. ' Abiezrite ' : part of the Machir clan of Manasseh (Num. 26:30, RSV Jezer ; 1 Chr. 7:18). ' Wine press ' : usually two rock-hewn troughs; in the larger upper one grapes were trampled and the juice drained into the lower one ; wheat was thrashed on an exposed, elevated, wind-swept floor ; here it has to be done secretly because of Midian. **13.** ' Recounted ' : as required of fathers in the family religion of Israel (Dt. 6:20ff.). **15.** The word ' sir ' (13) is here vocalised differently in Heb. to suggest that Gideon had recognised his divine visitor as the Lord. **16.** ' I will be with thee ' : reminiscent of the story of the revelation of the divine name to Moses
c (Exod. 3:12 ; cf. Jos. 1:5). **18.** ' Present ' : translated ' tribute ' (3:15) ; it can mean an ordinary gift but in priestly language and in Ezek. it is a technical term for the sacrificial meal offering ; the fact that an *ephah* (about 45 lb.) of flour was brought with the food also suggests a sacrifice ; a tenth of an ephah was the usual offering (Num. 5:15) ; an ephah was offered with a whole bullock (Ezek. 45:24). **20.** ' Angel of God ' (Heb. ' The God ') instead of ' angel of the Lord ' shows the hand of a late Levitical glossator whose work is seen especially in Chr., and who here makes 265c
the action more miraculous ; ' This rock ' (Heb. ' yonder crag ') is contrasted with the rock (21) which was near enough for the angel to touch. From this glossator came also the second sign (36–40). The prophets and Dt. condemned worship under green trees and on high hills, but archaeology gives ample evidence for such worship and for the use of rock altars and cup-holes cut in the rock (J. N. Schofield, *The Religious Background of the Bible* (1944), 46ff.). **22.** ' Face to face ' : as Moses saw the Lord (Exod. 33:11). This story ends with the building of an altar, and may have been the story told at Ophrah of the theophany causing the foundation of that holy place and commemorating the ' day of Midian ' (Isa. 9:4).

25-35 is a parallel distinct story also involving the d
building of an altar ; it is linked more closely with the religious introduction, the first act of deliverance being the overthrow of Baal worship. The name of the deliverer is Jerubbaal (32, cf. 7:1, 8:29, 35, 9:1) and this form of the story was known to the historians (1 Sam. 12:11 ; 2 Sam. 11:21, where the name is changed to Jerubbesheth, where *besheth* = shame) ; Gideon is not used outside Jg. 6–8. Baal is treated as different from the Lord as in Hos. (2:16) although Jeremiah still uses ' baal ' of the Lord (31:32, translated ' husband ', RSV) ; the story here illustrates the impotence of Baal. **25.** ' Second bull ' : the Heb. is corrupt and probably we should read ' ten men and the fatted calf of thy father ' (cf. 27) ; the change to ' second ' may presuppose that one was offered in 24. **26.** ' Asherah ', see 3:7. **31.** ' You ' is emphatic. **33-5.** The destruction of Baal worship opened the way for the defeat of the invaders by the spirit-filled deliverer. **33.** ' Vale of Jezreel ' : where the plain of Esdraelon narrows eastward to the Jordan N. of Gilboa. **34.** ' Took possession ' : Heb. ' Clothed itself in Gideon ' (1 Chr. 12:18 ; 2 Chr. 24:20). **35** relates the calling to arms of the northern tribes who are again called out (7:23f.) with Ephraim ; but 8:2 suggests that the defeat of Midian was the work of Gideon's own clan of Abiezer ; perhaps the 300 were Abiezrites. **36-40** (cf. note on 20). Testing God by asking for a sign was forbidden (Dt. 6:16) but the Lord urged Ahaz to do it (Isa. 7:10) ; Jesus regarded such a suggestion as coming from the devil (Lk. 4:12). Gideon's second test was the more difficult because naturally the woollen fleece would absorb moisture and be wet even when the ground was dry.

VII 1-8 The Testing—300 lapped water out of e
cupped hands ' as a dog laps ' ; the rest knelt down and put their mouths to the water. The 300 may have been more alert or, in view of the night attack, knew the locality better ; the banks of 'Ain Jālûd (SHG 397f.), which is probably the spring of Harod (= trembling), are still infested with leeches and no-one knowing the place would put his mouth down to the water. **1.** ' Moreh ' : the oracle-giver ; there was a tree of Moreh near Shechem (Gen. 12:6 ; Dt. 11:30). **3.** ' Fearful ' : in accordance with the law (Dt. 20:8). ' And Gideon tested them ' (Heb. ' and depart from Mt Gilead ') : RSV amends the difficult Heb. ; ' depart ' occurs only here in this sense, and Gilead is in E. Jordan and reference to it is out of place here ; possibly originally the reading was ' and leap away from Mt Galud '. **8.** RSV alters the ungrammatical Heb. ' victuals ' to ' jars ' (cf. 16).
9-14. A further sign, again evidence of the hand of f
the late glossator (cf. 6:20) who used ' the God ' (14). The opening words are the same as 6:25 and the section may originally have followed the mobilisation of Abiezer (6:34). **15-20.** The night attack. The night was divided into three watches and at the beginning of the second (10 p.m.) the attack was launched. It is difficult to see how all the actions were performed simultaneously ; possibly the blowing of trumpets or horns is an addition from the priestly glossator (cf. Jos. 6), regarded as a ritual act heralding God's intervention, or the use of jars, torches, and trumpets

265f may be due to combining two different stories. **21.** ' Ran ' : probably read ' awoke '. **22.** The places on the line of flight have not been identified ; ' border ' means ' bank ' and suggests the edge of a wadi leading down to the Jordan. **23.** ' Men of Israel ' : as in 20:17, the phrase comes from a later glossator who regarded all the northern tribes as involved in the pursuit.

g **VII 24-VIII 3 Ephraim's Intervention**—The story is comparable to Ephraim's attitude to Jephthah (12:1) and differs from the story in 8:4–27 ; the names of the Midianite leaders are different ; they are Oreb and Zeeb here, 7:25, but Zebah and Zalmunna in 8:5 ; in 7:25 Gideon is already beyond Jordan, but he crosses it in 8:4. The first account is referred to in Isa. 10:26 ; Ps. 83:11 (Heb. 12) knows both. **24.** ' Bethbarah ' is unknown. **25.** ' Oreb ' and ' Zeeb ' mean ' Raven ' and ' Wolf '. **VIII 2.** Ephraim's gleaning had achieved more than all the harvesting of Gideon's men, for to Ephraim had fallen the honour of killing Midian's leaders. Gideon's ' soft answer ' was more effective than Jephthah's treatment of Ephraim.

h **4-21 The Second Account**—Gideon crossed the Jordan with his 300 men (but cf. 7:23), pursuing the Midianite leaders, here called kings, Zebah and Zalmunna (' Sacrifice ' and ' Shelter-withheld '). He is refused aid by Succoth and Penuel, cities that have not heard of any victory over Midian ; after defeating the 15,000 Midianites who remained from the original 135,000 (figures that suggest the hand of the later idealising editor), he took his vengeance on Succoth and Penuel and slew the two Midianite kings because they had killed his brothers at Tabor. The beginning of the story is missing, a new motive for the fighting is introduced : not the call of God (6:12) nor the overthrow of Baal (6:25), but blood revenge for the slaughter of his brothers. **5.** ' Succoth ' : probably Tell el-Aḥṣâṣ, 2 miles N. of the Wâdī Zerkâ and E. of the Jordan. **6.** ' Officials ' : Heb. ' princes '. The reply shows they did not expect him to be suc-
i cessful. **7.** ' Flail ' : trample your flesh on thorns as corn is trampled on the threshing-floor. **8.** ' Penuel ' is unidentified **10.** ' Karkar ' : probably in the Wâdī Sirḥân, about 150 miles SE. of Succoth. For the phrase ' who drew sword ' cf. 20:15 in a story added by the plural editor and also using large numbers. **11.** ' Nobah ' : unidentified ; Num. 32:42 says it was previously called Kenath. ' Jogbehah ' : a fortified city with a sheepfold (Num. 32:35f.), possibly el-Jubeihât between 'Ammân and Wâdī Zerkâ. ' Off its guard ' : like Laish (18:27), over-confident. **14.** ' Wrote down ' : the writer believed that writing was in common use at this early period (cf. G. R. Driver, *Semitic Writing* (1948)) ; the art of writing was known at a much earlier date but was mainly used for documents and as an aid to memory. **21.** Crescents were worn as amulets (Isa. 3:18).

j **22-27 Gideon's Rejection of Kingship**—**22.** ' Men of Israel ' (cf. 7:23) shows a late writer with the same theory of Israel's theocracy as in 1 Sam. ; all Gideon's sons ruled over Shechem (9:2). **27.** ' Ephod ', here not the apron worn by priests (Exod. 28) but some idol (cf. 18:18). ' Played the harlot ', cf. 2:17.

28-35 Conclusion—The plural editor's framework is clear in 28, 33f. ; what remains of the singular compiler's conclusion may be in 35, and possibly in 30–2 (cf. 12:14) which may however have been his introduction to the story of Abimelech. **33.** ' Baal-Berith ' : the covenant god (cf. 9:46, El-Berith) of Shechem (31). At Shechem, perhaps in front of the ' Lord of the covenant ' identified as Yahweh, Jacob renewed his allegiance to God (Gen. 35:4), Joshua made a covenant (Jos. 24:25 ; cf. Dt. 27), and Rehoboam went to be crowned as king of all Israel (1 Kg. 12:1).

266a **IX Abimelech**—The story appears to be part of the singular compiler's history of pre-monarchical Israel (cf. 9:22), and there is no evidence of the religious
framework of the plural editor ; the moral is supplied 26
by the glossator who used ' men of Israel ' (Heb. ' man of Israel '), 55ff. The reference in the plural editor's summary (8:34) to the ingratitude of the people of Israel suggests that originally the story contained an account of Israelite, as apart from Canaanite, action in Shechem ; possibly Israelites and Canaanites combined to destroy the sons of Gideon. Traditions of Shechem, like those of Bethel, were probably altered by writers from the rival religious centre at Jerusalem and are difficult to reconstruct. Shechem itself had a long history, being mentioned in Egyptian execration texts of the 19th cent. B.C. Excavations show it to have been strongly fortified, covering nearly 14 acres, with a massive temple (80 ft. × 60 ft. with 17-ft. walls). In the Tell el-Amarna letters its king Labayu was a rebel leader against Egypt with influence as far as Gezer and Taanach. In a letter he quoted a proverb about ants which, when smitten, bite the hand that smites, and we are reminded of Jotham's fable. There is evidence of Israelite occupation from the 11th cent. B.C. Jacob buried there his idols (Gen. 35:4), and bought a site for an altar (Gen. 33:19f. ; cf. David's purchase at Jerusalem, 2 Sam. 24:21). The enmity between Israel and Canaanites there is related in Gen. 34, but after the Exodus Joshua did not have to capture the city (cf. Dt. 11 and 27), and Joseph's bones were buried there (Jos. 24:32). Jacob claimed to have captured it (Gen. 48:22, RSV ' mountain slope ') by sword and bow, but probably Joshua's invading troops found it occupied by a mixed population including friendly Israelites. In Jacob's time (Gen. 34) its chief was Hamor = ' ass ' ; at Mari the ass was connected with covenant making and it is noteworthy that the god of Shechem was Lord of the Covenant.

1-6. Abimelech becomes king through the influence b
of the Canaanite kinsmen of his mother, the concubine (9:31) or maidservant (9:18), and murders all but one of his half-brothers, the sons of Jerubbaal (Gideon). **2.** ' Citizens ' (Heb. ' baals ') : owners, used in the plural section of 20:5 of the citizens of Gibeah. ' Bone and flesh ' expresses kinship (cf. Gen. 2:23 where it is used of marriage). **5.** ' One stone ' (cf. 18) : probably to remove blood revenge by giving the killing the form of a sacrifice (cf. 1 Sam. 14:33) or a legal execution at an official place. **6.** ' Beth-millo ' : the filled-up place, perhaps the tower (46) ; there was a similar place at Jerusalem. ' Pillar ' (Heb. ' siege works ', cf. Isa. 29:3) : a deliberate alteration to avoid calling Joshua's stone a pillar (Jos. 24:26).

7-25 Jotham's Fable is in poetic form. The trees, c
wanting a king, offered the crown to the olive, the fig-tree, and the vine ; but all were too busy serving the community to waste their time waving their branches over their fellows ; finally they chose the useless bramble bush, a dangerous choice, for conflict would bring conflagration and all would perish in the forest fire. If Shechem was as lacking in loyalty to Abimelech as to Gideon, then king and people would perish together. **21.** ' Beer ' : not mentioned elsewhere ; it means ' well ' and was clearly a known place remote from Shechem. **22.** ' Ruled ' : acted as prince over Israel, not king of Shechem (6) ; the verse assumes that all the men of Shechem were Israelites. **23.** ' Evil spirit ' : as there is only one God, both good and evil, from a human standpoint, must come from him (1 Sam. 16:14 ; 1 Kg. 22:22 ; Isa. 45:7) and no theology of the OT is satisfactory which does not find a place for evil within the purposes of God, who aids the unjust as well as the just (Mt. 5:45). **25.** ' Against him ' : perhaps meaning against his interests.

26-41 The Revolt of Gaal—a tantalising fragment of d
Shechem tradition difficult to relate to 23–5 where the anarchy is caused by God, as in the religious framework of the plural editor ; here revolt is given as a fact of history, as in the singular compiler's collection of stories. Gaal, a new leader, boastfully challenges the

266d absent Abimelech at the annual vintage feast, but Zebul the city governor remains loyal and Gaal is driven out. **28.** Heb. is difficult; RSV changes an imperative 'serve ye' to a perfect. The meaning seems to be 'Who is Abimelech compared with our ancestor Shechem that we should serve him? Is he not the son of Jerubbaal, and Zebul is his officer; serve ye the descendants of Hamor the father of Shechem (Gen. 34); why indeed should we serve him?' **29.** 'I would say' (Heb. 'he said'): the sequel shows that Gaal had not spoken to Abimelech. **31.** 'Arumah' (41): the versions translate as an adverb, 'craftily'. 'Stirring up' amends a late Heb. construction found also in 1 Chr. 20:1 where RSV translates 'besieged'; the context shows Gaal was in the city, not besieging it. **37.** 'Diviners' Oak': perhaps the oracle oak (Gen. 12:6); divination in its various forms was forbidden (Dt. 18:10; Lev. 19:26; cf. Jer. 27:9; Mic. 5:12). **38.** Gaal's loud mouth, his only weapon, was silent at the approach of danger.

e **42-57 The Destruction of Shechem and Abimelech**—There is confusion; the rebellion was already over before the attack on the city (41); perhaps the story continues 9:25, or it may be a late addition from a different source ('the men' (42), 'his men' (43) both translate the Heb. 'people' used by a late glossator, cf. Burney, p. 449). **45.** 'Sowed it with salt': symbolic of complete destruction (Dt. 29:23) or of a sacrifice to God (Ezek. 43:24). **46.** 'Stronghold' (1 Sam. 13:6, RSV 'tombs'): perhaps an underground crypt. El-berith, cf. 8:33. **50.** 'Thebez' may be Ṭūbâṣ, an important town between Shechem and Bethshan; no reason is given here for Abimelech's attack. **53.** 'Upper millstone': the smaller of the two stones turned by women and riding on the lower stone to crush corn; usually about 18 in. in diameter and 3 in. thick. **55.** The writer who added the moral assumed that Abimelech died leading a band of Israelites (cf. 45, 'the people'). The whole story owes its present form to the late glossator; 8:33f. may be the remains of the plural framework to an earlier form of the story.

f **X 1-5 Tola and Jair**—The historical singular compiler continues the stories of Israel's early leaders by two notices comparable to that about Shamgar (3:31). The present story of Abimelech does not show him as a deliverer of Israel, but originally the attack on Shechem and Thebez may have been thus represented. In Gen. 46:13 Tola and Puah (RSV Puvah) are sons of Issachar (Num. 26:23 (RSV Puvah); 1 Chr. 7:1ff.). The name Dodo appears in 2 Sam. 23:9, but in the Moabite stone (lines 10–13) it is used in connection with a cult object. **2.** 'Shamir' is unknown; LXX reads 'Samaria' though this was not built till the reign of Omri (1 Kg. 16:24). The 23 years of his judgeship suggests a genuine tradition rather than a symbolic number. **3, 4.** 'Jair the Gileadite' appears to be the same as Jair the son of Manasseh (Num. 32:41) who founded the Havvoth (tent villages) of Jair (Dt. 3:14; 1 Kg. 4:13). 'Asses': a sign of importance (5:10, 12:14); 'cities': so the versions, for Heb. 'she-asses'. A Deuteronomic tradition located the cities in Bashan, not Gilead (Dt. 3:14; Jos. 13:30).

267a **X 6-XII 7 Jephthah**—The main story is an account of the defeat, by Israelites settled E. of the Jordan, of an invasion by Ammonites. Many alterations and additions have been made both to the introduction (10:6–18), and to the original story, which has been used for the threefold purpose of asserting the right of Israel to land E. of the Jordan, of giving the historical origin of an annual women's festival, and of condemning the treatment by Ephraim, the parent tribe safely settled on the central hills in Palestine, of her offspring in Transjordan.

b **X 6-18 Introduction**—The hand of the plural editor is clear but additions have been made by piling up phrases (cf. 6, 11f.); **7.** The oppressors are the Philistines and the Ammonites, in that order as though the words are an introduction to the stories of Samson and of Jephthah, and yet there is also the usual plural introduction to Samson (13:1). It is possible that the plural editor has used here an older introduction, which originally introduced the accounts of the defeat of the Philistines by Samuel (1 Sam. 7) and of Ammon in Transjordan by Saul (1 Sam. 11) (S. A. Cook, *Notes on OT History*), and applied it to the stories of Jephthah and Samson. Traces of the singular compiler are also seen (7) in the anger of the Lord, (9) the distress of Israel, and (16) the preparation for the Lord's intervention, but neither writer has integrated the story into his scheme (cf. the new beginnings in 11:1 and 4); **8.** 'that year' has no antecedent in the present introduction, and is followed by 'eighteen years'; the oppression is limited to Transjordan in 8 but in the next verse extended to Palestine and even to the southern tribe of Judah. **11.** 'Did I not deliver': not in Heb. Many versions omit 'from', reading 'Did not Egypt . . . oppress you'. Clearly the text has received additions. 'Amorites' (cf. 1:7): introduced surprisingly in 1 Sam. 7:14. **12.** 'Maonites': inhabitants of Ma'în, 18 miles ESE. of Petra, and enemies of Israel under Uzziah (2 Chr. 26:7, RSV Meunites).

XI 1-11 Gilead calls Jephthah—The situation is c
different from 10:17 but 10:18 attempts to link the two by an action comparable to 1:1. The story is connected with that of Abimelech by the fact that Jephthah is also the son of a harlot, but, unlike Abimelech, he was driven out by his stepbrothers and became the leader of a band of outlaws in the land of Tob (= good), mentioned as allied with Ammon in the reign of David (2 Sam. 10:6). **1.** 'Gilead': the district is treated as the name of the father, as often in the work of late priestly glossators. **11.** Jephthah is unwilling to accept the word of the elders of Gilead and insists on an oath being taken before the Lord at the sanctuary at Mizpah. The name means 'Watchtower' and the site cannot be identified. **12-28.** An embassy is sent to Ammon. Ammon claimed that when Israel invaded Palestine all southern Transjordan between the Arnon, which flows W. into the Dead Sea, and the Jabbok, the modern Wâdī Zerkâ about 50 miles farther N., had been seized by Israel. Jephthah replied that neither Edom nor Moab, who were then settled in Transjordan, had been molested, but that the land N. of the Arnon was then held by Sihon king of the Amorites and was captured by Israel from him and not from Ammon. This agrees with the harmonising addition to Dt. 2:37 (as a sign of a different hand, note the change to 'thou' in Heb. there; RSV has 'you'); the historical traditions referred to are found in Num. 20f., Dt. 2 and Jer. 48f., but there is no mention in those traditions of an embassy to Moab; in Dt. 23:3ff. Ammon and Moab are both condemned for their treatment of Israel at that time. The old ballad quoted in Num. 21:27ff. (cf. Jer. 48:45ff.) states that Sihon had captured the land from Moab, and Ammon had no possible claim to it. The stress in the traditions and in the ballad on Moab has caused a similar stress in the words put into the mouth of Jephthah's messengers, and has probably caused a glossator to add 'Chemosh'—the name of Moab's god—to 'your god' (24). **23b.** Probably not a question but the statement: as the Lord dispossessed the Amorites you (emphatic and sarcastic) indeed would dispossess the Lord's people; **25.** as Balak failed against Israel (Num. 22–4) so you will. **26.** Jephthah's final argument is that Israel has had 300 years of undisputed possession of the land, approximately the total figures for oppressions and rest in the previous narratives in Jg. 'Heshbon': probably Tell Ḥesbân, 20 miles E. of the Jordan opposite Jericho. 'Aroer': probably 'Arâ'ir on the N. bank of the Arnon.

29-40 Jephthah's Vow—**29** does not fit well with d
11; Jephthah was already at Mizpah; perhaps the meaning is that he passed through Gilead and Manasseh to raise an army, returned to Mizpah and, having

267d made his vow in the sanctuary there (cf. 11), went out to meet the Ammonites (32). In 12:2 it is stated that Ephraim was asked to send troops ; the plural editor says the Israelite army was already in camp at Mizpah before the call of Jephthah (10:17) ; much of 29 may be from a later glossator. **30.** Jephthah vows to make a human sacrifice to the Lord as an incentive to the Lord to give him victory (cf. 2 Kg. 3:26f.). This is different from the normal sacrifice of eight-day-old firstborn sons commanded in Exod. 22:29, accepted as a command from God by Ezekiel (20:26), condemned by Jeremiah (7:31), but continued in the post-exilic period (Isa. 57:5) ; this was an extraordinary sacrifice for a particular purpose (cf. 2 Kg. 16:3, 17:17 ; Mic. 6:7). Here the vow is not regarded as contrary to the worship of the Lord, for it achieved its purpose ; **33.** 'Aroer' : probably another city E. of 'Ammân (Rabbath Ammon, Jos. 13:25) ; 'Minnith' (cf. Ezek. 27:17, RSV*n*) : the site is unknown. 'Abel-keramim', 'Meadow of vineyards' : not identified. **34.** His daughter led the women singers who greeted the victor, as Miriam had led the singers who celebrated the deliverance from Egypt (Exod. 15:20) ; it was women singers who praised David (1 Sam. 18:6) and Jg. 5 is a woman's song. 'His only child' : the tragedy was that the leader of the women whom first he met was his only child. The Heb. is very emphatic, 'And she only, an only child ; he had not, apart from her, son or daughter'. **39.** 'Custom' : not the usual Heb. word but meaning 'statute' or 'ordinance' ; both the word and the verse division are intended to support the Jewish interpretation that she became the cause of an ordinance forbidding child sacrifice. **40.** 'Year by Year' : the virgins' festival (cf. Burney, pp. 332f.), was probably connected with the Tammuz cult (cf. Ezek. 8:14), and is here de-mythologised by being given a historical origin.

e **XII 1-6 War with Ephraim**—The story comes from a milieu hostile to Ephraim, perhaps from Reubenites who eventually were driven out of Transjordan and, after the Exile, are found in south Palestine. From the taunt (4) it appears that Ephraim claimed possession of the land of Gilead and regarded the men of Gilead as intruders into the portion of the Ephraimite tribe of Manasseh. **1.** 'Zaphon' (Heb. 'northward'): the site is unknown ; Jos. 13:27 mentions a Zaphon in the Jordan valley in this region. **5.** Jephthah interposed his army between the Ephraimites and the Jordan, cutting off their line of retreat. **6.** 'Shibboleth' (= 'ear of corn') : the test turned on a dialectical difference in the pronunciation of a sibilant, an interesting proof that there were differences in the Heb. of north and south Palestine, some of which survive in the OT, and similar differences were still present in the 1st cent. A.D. (Mt. 26:73). **6.** 'Forty-two thousand' : the large number suggests that the story (or this verse) comes from the same milieu as Jg. 20.

f **8-13** 'Ibzan, Elon, Abdon' : three further notices comparable to 3:31 and 10:1–5 not expanded by the plural editor, but taken by the singular compiler from early traditions or annals of northern Palestine. **8.** 'Bethlehem' : possibly the town in Judah, but there was a town of the same name, modern Beit Laḥm, 7 miles WNW. of Nazareth in Galilee (Jos. 19:15). **11.** 'Elon' : a son of Zebulun of the same name is mentioned in Gen. 46:14. **13.** 'Pirathon' : possibly Far'âtā 6 miles WSW. of Shechem. Ibzan and Abdon, like Jair, were remembered for the size and importance of their family.

268a **XIII 1-XVI 31 Samson**—The story is connected with that of Jephthah by the fact that both have mythical elements behind them—perhaps at a very remote distance—and their form has been influenced by mythology. Samson has clear links with a solar myth. His name Samson (Heb. *Shimshôn*) is connected with Shemesh = 'sun' : the names of many places in the area in which the stories are set show their connection with sun-cult ; the strength lying in his locks is that of the sun in its rays ; the fighting with a lion is found in Babylonian solar myths ; the eruption of a spring to restore his life, the lifting up of the gates of Gaza when he rose as a strong man from his bridal chamber (Ps. 19:5), and probably the name Delilah —all these elements in the story can be paralleled in solar myths. But the story as it is told in the OT is far removed from any such origin. It belongs to the youth of a nation ; the incredible feats of strength and prowess of national heroes against impossible odds. The religious motive is also clear : God can use a consecrated person, however crude he may be, in fighting the enemies of his people, but when the vow is broken and the man 'plays the harlot', he is delivered to his enemies and is found 'eyeless in Gaza, at the mill with slaves' ; repentance and prayer bring back the divine aid so that in his death he slays more of the enemy than he had killed in his life.

b **XIII 1-25 The Call of Samson**—Like other OT heroes, Samson is God's gift to a barren woman, chosen from his conception, dedicated from his birth to deliver his people. **1** shows the plural framework. 'Philistines' were the remnant of the Cretan civilisation who, attempting to enter Egypt from Asia Minor through Palestine and by sea, were driven out of Egypt by Rameses III at the beginning of the 12th cent. B.C. (cf. *Chambers's Ency.*, new ed., s.v.). **2.** 'Zorah' : probably modern Ṣar'ah by the vale of Sorek 14 miles W. of Jerusalem. 'Tribe' (Heb. 'clan') : part of a tribe (cf. 18:2) ; the Danites had been reduced by Philistine pressure (1:34). **3-5.** 'The angel of the Lord', cf. 2:1. **5.** 'Nazirite' (Heb. 'consecrated') : Num. 6 gives the laws for a temporary Nazirite vow which includes abstention from all products of grapes, allowing the hair to grow uncut, and avoiding contact with dead bodies. The abstention from wine is recognised as a characteristic of a Nazirite in Am. 2:11f., and Samuel's consecration symbol was uncut hair (1 Sam. 1:11 ; cf. Ac. 21:17ff.). Here Samson's mother has to abstain from wine during pregnancy, but Samson appears to know no such prohibition (cf. 14:10 where the Hebrew word for 'feast' suggests a drinking-bout ; he also appears to have had considerable contact with dead Philistines, as well as eating honey from the body of a dead lion). 'Begin to deliver' recognises that the story of Samson begins the long struggle against the Philistines culminating in David's independence. **6.** 'Man of God, Angel of

c God' (Heb. 'The God', so also 8, 9 ; cf. 6:20) : the angel of God (9) becomes the angel of the Lord again in 13, and God himself in 22. 'The God' occurs also in Samson's final prayer (16:28) and, if the word denotes the hand of a glossator, stress is there laid on Samson's return to God, and here in 6–14 a second divine visit is added. **15.** 'Manoah', like Gideon, offers to prepare food for his guest. Here the food is refused but the present is accepted explicitly as a burnt offering. **17.** 'Manoah', like Jacob (Gen. 32:29) and Moses (Exod. 3:13), asks the name of the divine visitor, but it is not given to them, it is 'too wonderful' for them, for in primitive thought knowledge of God's name would have given power over him. **19.** Here Manoah himself offers the sacrifice, and the angel ascends in the flame from the rock altar (cf. 6:21). **22.** 'Seen God' : for the idea of the danger of seeing God, cf. Gen. 32:30 ; Moses could speak with the Lord face to face (Exod. 33:11), and Israel did at the day of the assembly (Dt. 5:4, but this statement is modified later ; cf. 5:5). The woman's common sense overcomes her husband's fear. **26.** 'Stir him' (Heb. 'disquiet') : Samson's superhuman activities are ascribed to the work of the spirit of the Lord. 'Mahaneh-dan ('camp of Dan') is located at a different site in 18:12. 'Eshtaol' : perhaps Eshwā' about 2 miles NE. of Zorah.

d **XIV Samson's Marriage Feast**—Samson's weakness was for Philistine women. The first lived at Timnah, the modern Tibneh, 4 miles SW. of Zorah

68d across the vale of Sorek. It is a border city of Judah (Jos. 15:10), a city of Dan (Jos. 19:43), but here is occupied by Philistines. It was captured from Judah in the time of Ahaz (2 Chr. 28:18). **2.** ' Get her for me ' : the arrangements and settlement of the bridal price were to be made by the parents. The story shows peaceful coexistence between the Danites and Philistines with Samson breaking the ban on intermarriage (cf. 3:6). **3.** ' Uncircumcised ' : the usual epithet applied to the Philistines (cf. 15:18) as though they alone of Israel's neighbours were uncircumcised. Circumcision did not become a distinctive mark of the Jew until it became a rite practised on eight-day-old males during or after the Exile. ' Get her ' : in Heb. there is a strong emphasis in this rough command to his father. **4ff.** in its present form represents Samson's father and mother, under protest, going down to Timnah with him to make the necessary arrangements, but **7** suggests that Samson was alone. Then the three returned home and later (8f.) all went down again to take her, and later Samson and his father went down to the wedding-feast (10). Possibly the story has been expanded ; the removal of ' to take her ' (8) would make the account more smooth. **8.** ' Swarm of bees ' : bees would only nest there if the carcass had dried, but there was an ancient belief that bees bred from rotting animal matter (cf. Burney, p. 359).

e **10-20 The Wedding Feast—12.** ' Garment ' : a large piece of linen either for a garment or a sleeping-wrap, mentioned as part of female clothing (Isa. 3:23) and as made by the ideal housewife (Prov. 31:24). **14.** The Heb. couplet is more compact :

> From the eater went food,
> From strong went sweet.

Similar riddles lay behind some of the wisdom literature and gave rise to sayings that used numbers in Prov. 6:16ff., 30:7ff. and in the prophecies of Amos 1. **16.** ' Only ' should be ' Surely '. **18.** ' Before the sun went down ' should probably, with a small emendation of the Heb., be ' before he entered the bridal chamber ' ; the Philistines waited till the marriage was about to be consummated, at the end of the festivities, before triumphing over Samson ; he, in anger, went home without entering the bridal chamber. **19a** may be a later addition to the story (Ashkelon is about 23 miles from Timnah) ; if so then here and in 15:14 the attributing of his superhuman strength to the Spirit of the Lord was not part of the original story.

f **XV Samson's Revenge**—The story of the foxes is usually regarded as evidence linking Samson with solar myths. In early belief red blight on ripening wheat was caused by the hot sun on dew-damped corn, and in ancient Rome an annual ceremony of hunting foxes, with lighted torches tied to their tails, took place in the Circus during the April festival of Cerealia, apparently to prevent the Sun-god from sending the burning blight on the growing corn. Similar Semitic folklore may have influenced the form in which this story of Samson was told. **3.** ' I shall be blameless ' : the Heb. tenses suggest the translation ' I am quits with the Philistines for I am just about to do them evil ' ; his plan was sufficiently worked out to make him think of himself as already avenged on his enemies. **8.** ' Hip and thigh ' (Heb. ' leg on thigh ') is probably a wrestling term for an action in which an opponent was thrown head-first over a protruded leg and thigh. The phrase is used here to denote a complete slaughter. Neither Etam nor Lehi are identified.

g **9-20 The Betrayal and Escape of Samson—11.** The Philistine domination was so strong that the Judaeans preferred to hand over a fellow Israelite rather than risk reprisals (cf. 14:4). **13.** ' New ropes ', cf. 16:10. **14.** A vivid description of the uselessness of even new ropes against the power of the Spirit of the Lord. **15.** ' Fresh ', and so not brittle. **16.** Samson's two lines of poetry have the same repetitive parallelism as Deborah's song, by which the first half of one line 268g
is repeated as the first half of the next line, and the story is carried forward by the second half of the lines. A similar device is found in the poetry of Râs Shamra (Ugarit). The first line contains characteristic play on vowels and consonants, and with a slight change should probably be translated :

> With a red ass's jawbone, I have reddened them red ;
> With a red ass's jawbone, I have smitten a thousand.

17. ' Ramath-lehi ' : the meaning of the name, as of h
En-hakkore (19), is derived from popular play on sounds, not philology ; ' *rāmath* ', meaning ' hill ', is here connected with a Heb. root meaning ' to throw ' ; ' *haḳḳōrē* ', ' the caller ', is used in Heb. for the partridge. **19.** This verse uses ' God ' instead of ' the Lord ' and may be from a late glossator who added this miraculous divine intervention. **20.** The form used by the singular compiler. The words occur in a slightly different form in 16:31, and suggest that ch. 16 has been added by a glossator.

XVI Samson and Delilah—A clear picture of the i
stages by which playing with temptation leads inevitably to the sin which breaks man's fellowship with God. Like the similar picture in Gen. 3 it must have been drawn by a great religious teacher of Israel with a keen insight into human nature and a sound knowledge of the basic truths lying behind psychology. In Gen. 3 sin led to the spiritual death of being driven out from the presence of the Lord ; here it leads to physical death because the Lord had left Samson (16:20). However primitive the material used in the stories, in their present form they reflect a developed theology. **1.** ' Gaza ', cf. 1:18 ; it is about 38 miles from Hebron ; Samson's connection with Hebron and the reason why he is made to carry the gates this distance is not clear, but it may give a clue to the milieu of the story-teller, who may have not been aware of the distance between the two towns ; the woman is an unnamed harlot and the men of Gaza are not thought of as Philistines. **4.** ' Sorek ', cf. 13:2. ' Delilah ' : possibly the name was intended to suggest a devotee of a foreign goddess and so a sacred prostitute, and to symbolise the dangers of such a liaison (3:6), or in popular etymology to play on the
Heb. word *laylāh* (night). **5.** ' Eleven hundred ' : j
calculated as about £150 from each of the five Philistine lords. **7.** ' Seven fresh bowstrings ' : seven is a sacred number linked with the taking of oaths. **9.** Delilah's shout tests Samson's explanation of the secret of his strength without revealing her treachery or the presence of the Philistine ambush. **13.** Samson's third answer gets nearer the truth. **15** ' Heart ' : in Heb. the seat of the intellect rather than the emotions ; the same word is translated ' mind ' in 17. **19.** ' Had him shave ' (Heb. ' She shaved '). **20.** ' And he did not know ' : the most tragic sentence in the story, as **22** is the most dramatically exciting with its promise of renewed strength, through the return of the symbol of consecration, unperceived by his captors. **23.** ' Dagon ' (cf. ARI, 74) : a Semitic god known from inscriptions and from Râs Shamra. Originally a corn god, he is mentioned as the god of Ashdod (1 Sam. 5) and in later Jewish thought was regarded as a merman, half-man and half-fish, probably because of a connection with the Heb. word for ' fish '. **24.** The k
Philistine victory song was four lines of two beats in each, rhyming like the song of Lamech by the use of pronominal suffixes :

> He has given, the God of us,
> Into our hands the enemy of us ;
> Ravager of the land of us,
> Multiplier of the slain of us.

26. ' Pillars ' : archaeological remains suggest that supporting a deep balcony were wooden pillars which could be slipped off their stone bases, killing in their

268k collapse those underneath as well as many in the crowded balcony. **28.** ' One of my two eyes ' : the character seen in the early boyish pranks appears again in the grim humour of his dying jest. **30.** Though the strength returns, the curse of sin remains and Samson can triumph only by his own death.

269a **XVII-XXI** contain two supplements from Levitical traditions of the pre-monarchical period ; the first concerns the origin of the Levitical priesthood at Dan, and the second relates to strife between Benjamin and the other Israelite tribes over the treatment of a Levitical sojourner. The second story is used as a link to the Levitical account of the last judge, Samuel.

b **XVII-XVIII The Foundation of the Sanctuary at Dan and its Priesthood**—There is evidence that two versions of the story have been combined. The name of Micah is spelt differently in 17:1–4 from its form in the remainder of the story ; the sacred objects differ, there being one graven image in 18:30f. (cf. 17:4*c*), a graven image and a molten image in 17:3, 4, an ephod and teraphim in 17:5, all four in 18:14, 17f., and three in 18:20 ; the Levite is variously described as a youth, a man, a priest. **17:1-4** has become disarranged ; probably read (2) ' about which you took an oath and said in my hearing, I consecrate the silver to the Lord ', etc. (cf. 3). The effect of the oath was to put a curse on anyone using the stolen silver for any other purpose than that for which it had been consecrated, and the words were spoken in the hearing of the son whom his mother suspected of the theft. **3.** ' Graven image ' : the Heb. denotes a carved image but the word is also used of a cast or molten image ; if the word was used here in the wider sense, ' molten image ' may have been added because the context required this meaning ;

c **4c.** that there was only one image is suggested by ' it '. Graven images were forbidden in the decalogue (Exod. 20:4 ; Dt. 5:8) ; the duodecalogue (Dt. 27:15) forbids both molten and graven images ; ' molten image ' is often applied to the golden calf and the addition here may be from a southern writer who identified Micah's image with the calf of Dan (1 Kg. 12:29). **5.** ' Ephod ' (8:27) : with the teraphim was used for divination. ' Teraphim ' were small enough to be put in a camel's saddle-bag (Gen. 31:34), but large enough to deceive Saul's men (1 Sam. 19:13). They may have been human skulls, and the name connected with ' rephaim ' or ghosts of the dead. Miss Kenyon found evidence of some such strange use of human skulls at Jericho (PEQ (1953), 86ff. ; BA 16 (1953), 53f.). ' One of his sons ' : so David's sons were priests (2 Sam. 8:18) and Jeroboam made non-Levitical priests (1 Kg. 12:31) ; the later writer in 6 explains this ecclesiastical irregularity. Micah is

d happier with the ministrations of a Levite (13). **7.** ' Of the family of Judah ' : Levi (Gen. 49:5ff.) was a secular tribe condemned with Simeon for an outrage comparable to the treachery at Shechem (Gen. 34) ; but a priestly tribe (Dt. 33:8ff.) that has to overcome considerable opposition ; the tribe is also spoken of as set aside because of faithfulness to the Lord (Exod. 32:25ff.) against the bull worshippers. It is possible that the Levitical survivors from the Shechem disaster, with Simeon (1:3), became absorbed in Judah, but, perhaps through kinship with Moses or Aaron, acquired a priestly function, which was officially recognised by David when the Ark became the symbol of the presence of the Lord at Jerusalem (cf. Dt. 10) ; that they fought against their brethren in the north whose symbol was the bull ; and at the division of the kingdom Jeroboam was not willing to use Levites as priests (clearly there are conflicting traditions ; for another point of view cf. ARI 109ff.). ' And he sojourned there ' : a man of Judah would not be likely to be a sojourner, in the technical Heb. use of the word as ' a resident alien ', in Bethlehem of Judah ; the Heb. here probably should be read, ' and he was (the son of) Gershom ' (18:30). **8.** He was setting out to find a place where he could sell his priestly services and sojourn.

XVIII 1. ' In those days ' : the glossator who wishes 269
to explain Dan's lawlessness picks up the words in the text to which his gloss is attached. **3.** ' Recognised the voice ' : the Danite spies, living among Judaeans (15:9ff.), recognised the dialect or the priestly intonation of the Levite. **7.** ' Laish ', called Leshem (Jos. 19:47), is probably Tell el-Qâḍī near Bâniyâs, NW. of Lake Huleh. ' Sidonians ' : Laish was isolated, cut off from Sidon on the west by the Lebanon, and from Syria (reading Aram for *'ādhām*, ' man ') by the Hermon range.

11-26 Capture of the Image and of Laish—**12.** f
' Kiriath-jearim ', probably the mound above Abū Ghôsh (Enab), about 9 miles from Jerusalem on the main Lydda road. **14-20.** The priest, who had been befriended by Micah, gladly assisted in the theft of the image and the means of divination so that he might become priest of a tribe rather than of one family. It is of interest that the Danites are represented as not possessing an image of their own. **21-6.** Micah calls his household to arms, attempting to recover the spoil ; pathetically he cries ' You have taken my god and my priest, what have I left ? ' ; but wisely he decides that his life is of more value than either god or priest, and goes home. **27-31.** Laish is destroyed and the sanctuary of Dan established. The writer has nothing but contempt for Dan and its image : made from a small part of the dedicated sum (17:4) which had been consecrated only because it had been stolen ; plundered from Micah through the treachery of its priest ; set up in a brutally captured city. **28.** ' Beth-Rehob ', cf. 1:31. **30.** ' Moses ' : g
in the Heb. an ' n ' has been added above the line to change Moses to Manasseh, to suggest, perhaps, the wicked king of Judah (2 Kg. 21), rather than such a priest as the grandson of Moses. The verse, if ancient, is interesting as linking Moses with the North and the golden calf of Dan, instead of with the Ark and Jerusalem in accordance with the dominant tradition. Jeremiah, from Anathoth, uses the Mosaic tradition (Jer. 15:1) but Ezekiel from Jerusalem does not (Ezek. 14:14). ' The captivity of the land ' : if this is the same as the date in **31** it would appear to refer to the destruction of Shiloh by the Philistines (1 Sam. 4) ; but Shiloh appears to have remained a holy place until after the captivity of the South in 586 B.C. (Jer. 41:5), and Jer. 7:12ff. suggests a recent disaster. The captivity of the land may refer to the destruction of the north by Tiglath-pileser in 734 B.C. (2 Kg. 15:20, RSV Pul) or the Assyrian capture of Samaria in 721 B.C. (2 Kg. 17:6). The date of the destruction of Dan is not known. The note of date is probably an inference from 1 Kg. 12:29 that Jeroboam put an image at Dan.

XIX-XXI The Outrage at Gibeah shows more 270
clearly than chs. 17–18 marks of the lateness of the story in its present form by the use of ' congregation ' and ' assemble ' (20:1), and the large numbers of men involved. The story has probably been added, after the completion of the work of the singular compiler, by the plural editor whose work was completed by late glossators. That the original story belonged to the traditions of the North is suggested by Hosea's reference to the ' days of Gibeah ' (9:9, 10:9). There is contact between Jg. 19 and Gen. 19, the story of the outrage at Sodom ; and the final defeat (20) resembles Joshua's strategy at Ai (Jos. 8) ; the mode of assembling the tribes is similar to that of Saul (1 Sam. 11:7), perhaps a form of oath or covenant (Gen. 15 ; Jer. 34:18). The link between this story and Saul the Benjaminite king at Gibeah, rescuing the men of Jabesh-gilead (still a fortified place (1 Sam. 11) though destroyed by Israel (21:11)), is clear, and the story ends at Shiloh where 1 Sam. begins.

XIX The wickedness of Gibeah is aggravated by the b
fact that it was perpetrated against a man who was both a Levite and a sojourner, and so doubly protected by law. **1.** ' A concubine ' : Heb. ' a woman (or wife), a concubine ', a construction comparable to

0b ' a man, a Levite ' (1) and ' a woman, a prophetess ' (4:4). **2.** ' Angry ', following some versions ; the Heb. construction is unusual. **3.** ' Speak kindly ' (Heb. ' to her heart ') : cf. Hos. 2:14, in a similar situation. **10.** ' Jebus ' (1 Chr. 11:4f.) was not an ancient name for Jerusalem, but derived from the name used for the pre-Israelite inhabitants. The story ignores the accounts in 1:8. **12.** ' Gibeah ' : Tell el-Fûl on the ridge N. of Jerusalem (ASOR (1924)). **16.** It is emphasised that the old man was a sojourner in Gibeah, an Ephraimite and not a Benjaminite, to show up more clearly the badness of the natives (cf. Gen. 19 where the hospitable Lot was also a sojourner and Lk. 4:25ff. where the widow of Zarephath too was not an Israelite). The attitude to Ephraim is different

c from that in 8 and 12. **22.** ' Base fellows ' : Heb. ' sons of Belial ', which may mean ' utterly worthless ' or, as here, low, never moving higher in any way (cf. Ps. 41:8). ' Know him ' : used of the sex act (Gen. 4:1) and here of homosexuality. When used of ' knowing the Lord ' (2:10), it probably retains the nuance of closest intimacy or fellowship, not intellectual apprehension. **23.** ' Vile ' : often used of sex crimes which were not the ' done thing ' (2 Sam. 13:12 ; cf. Gen. 34:7 and Dt. 22:21) ; the ' vile man ' is one who is regarded as a godless man (Ps. 14:1). **30.** The LXX inserts, ' And he commanded the men whom he sent out saying, Thus shall ye say to all the men of Israel, " Has such a thing as this happened from the day when the children of Israel came up from the land of Egypt until today ; pay attention, take counsel, and speak " .'

d **XX The Outrage avenged—1.** Dan to Beersheba is the limit of Palestine given often in the historical books ; the larger limit was ' From the entering in of Hamath to the river of Egypt '. Here Transjordan is explicitly included : a much bigger assembly than against Sisera. ' Congregation ' : this word marks the narrative in its present form as coming through a post-exilic priestly or Levitical milieu. ' Mizpah ' : Tell en-Naṣbeh, about 7 miles north of Jerusalem, on the left of the main road (Badé, *Bull. of Pacific School of Relig.* (1926) ; PEF (1927, 1930, 1931)) ; it was a religious centre for Israel under Samuel (1 Sam. 7:5, 16, 10:17) and became the civic centre during the Exile (Jer. 40:6, 41:3). **2.** ' The assembly of the people of God ' : the description of Israel as ' an assembly ' is a favourite one in Dt. ; this verse uses ' the God ' and appears to be a gloss duplicating v. 1. **13.** ' Put away evil ' : a common phrase in Dt. (cf. 22:21). **16.** ' Seven hundred ' : the picked marksmen were probably the contingent from Gibeah. **18a** in Heb. reads ' And they arose and went up to Bethel to inquire of God ; and the people of Israel said . . .' ; the first clause probably comes from the same hand as 26 reflecting the belief that Bethel, not Mizpah, was

e the place where the oracle was consulted. **19.** ' People of Israel ' probably reveals the hand of the plural editor in contrast to ' men of Israel ' in 20 which may denote the remains of the original narrative (Heb. has a singular collective ' man of Israel ', construed with a singular verb). The relationship is not clear between this account and that of the singular compiler, whose hand may possibly be seen in the use of ' Israel ' (cf. 10, 13, 21 (RSV ' Israelites '), 29, 31, 35). **26.** ' And came to Bethel ' has probably been added (cf. 23), as well as the statement in 27 that the Ark of the God, ministered to by Phinehas, was there. **270e**
27. ' Covenant ' is the Deuteronomic name for the ten words or decalogue delivered at Horeb (Dt. 5 ; and 29:1) ; the Ark was the Ark of the Covenant because it contained these ten words. **33.** ' Baal-tamar ' : a village near Gibeah, but unidentified. ' West of Geba ' : the Heb. is not clear ; Geba is about three miles NE. of Tell el-Fûl. **40.** ' The whole of the city ' : as in Dt. 13:16, where, as here, it should be translated ' the holocaust of the city ' went up. The contacts between the singular portions of this chapter (Benjamin is here singular) and Dt. 13 suggest that the singular compiler was a Deuteronomist who regarded the destruction of Gibeah as an application of the law of Dt. 13:12ff. **43.** ' Nohah ', if intended as a proper name, is not known ; in 1 Chr. 8:2 it is a Benjaminite name. **45.** ' Rimmon ' : probably Rammûn, 12 miles N. of Tell el-Fûl and about 3 miles E. of Bethel. ' Gidom ' is unknown and the reading may be incorrect. It is difficult to reconstruct the lines of attack and flight.

XXI The Saving of the Tribe of Benjamin— f
Benjamin had been treated as idolaters and cut off by oath from intermarriage. To find wives for the 600 surviving, forgiven, Benjaminite warriors, it was decided to destroy Jabesh-gilead, a city in Transjordan that had given no help in the holy war, and give them its 400 virgins as wives. The remaining men were allowed to take Israelite girls from the vineyard booths during the fertility rites at the feast at the end of the vine harvest. **2** is another addition making Bethel, not Mizpah, the holy place. **4.** The altar was thus thought of as built at Mizpah. **5.** ' A great oath ' : Heb. ' *the* great oath ', perhaps previously mentioned in the original account. **8.** ' Jabesh-gilead ' : E. of the Jordan, but not identified. It was still a fortified city in the time of Saul (1 Sam 11:1) and its inhabitants
remained loyal to him (1 Sam. 31:8ff.). **12.** ' Shiloh ' g
(cf. 18:31) : it is difficult to understand why the centre should here be Shiloh instead of Mizpah or Bethel, and why it was necessary here (cf. Jos. 21:2, 22:9) and in 19 to define its location as though its site was not known. **19.** ' Yearly feast ' : as in 1 Sam. 1:3, probably the origin of the feast of Booths or Tabernacles, later given a historical setting as a memorial of the wilderness wanderings (J. N. Schofield, *Religious Background of the Bible* (1944), 169f.). **25.** The closing verse makes clear the purpose of the singular compiler. Under the God-given leader, Joshua, and the generation that followed him, Israel served the Lord faithfully (2:7) ; afterwards apostasy led to defeat and oppression by outside nations, who were defeated by deliverers raised up by God ; intermarriage (3:5f.) brought more disasters, even to the chosen leaders, and internecine strife until God gave the nation a king, and every man ceased to do what was right in his own eyes.

Bibliography—COMMENTARIES : C. F. Burney, *The Book of Judges* (1930) ; G. A. Cooke, CB (1913) ; H. W. Hertzberg, ATD (1953) ; G. F. Moore, ICC (1895) ; B. Ubach, *La Biblia* 5 (Montserrat Bible (1953)).

OTHER LITERATURE : O. Eissfeldt, *Die Quellen des Richterbuches* (1925) ; J. Garstang, *Joshua-Judges* (1931) ; C. A. Simpson, *Composition of the Book of Judges* (1957).

RUTH

By A. S. HERBERT

271a The story of the book is set in the period of the Judges (1:1), and this appears to be the reason for transferring the book from its original place in the Hebrew Bible to its present position in the versions. In the former it is the second of the Megilloth, and is prescribed for reading as part of the Jewish liturgy of Pentecost, the harvest festival that celebrates the giving and receiving of the Law. Both in subject matter and in style it is a book unsurpassed in its charm, ' the loveliest little epic and idyllic whole that tradition has given us ' (Goethe). The high literary quality of the original is perhaps best reflected in the AV.

b There is no evidence in the book or elsewhere which will determine **the author.** The statement in the Talmud (Baba Bathra 14*b* : ' Samuel wrote his own book and Judges and Ruth ') is supported neither by evidence nor probability. Even the date of composition is difficult to determine, and suggestions vary from the time of David to the 4th cent. B.C. Clearly the book as we now have it cannot be earlier than the days of David since it contains his genealogy (4:17, 18–22). The opening sentence of the book (1:1) suggests that the time of the Judges was somewhat remote. The property transaction and proposed marriage of Ruth in 4:1–12 includes a note (4:7) which suggests that the customs were unknown or imperfectly remembered, and that they needed to be explained. The passage appears to refer the reader to the story in Gen. 38 and the law in Dt. 25:5–10. There are important differences between what is required by tradition and law and what is practised in Ru., but the references to the sandal and to Tamar appear to be something well known, though imperfectly understood. This would be appropriate to the post-exilic era, since presumably the deuteronomic law was practised in the reign of King Josiah. Certain linguistic features of the book are more easily explained by a post-exilic date than by an earlier period. The word for ' therefore ' is Aramaic (and appears in the OT only otherwise in Job 30:24 ; Dan. 2:6, 9, 4:27 (twice); while other words (' to confirm ') show Aramaic influence and appear otherwise only in later books of the OT. Some further support for a late date is suggested from its appearance in the Hebrew Bible among the writings. Tentatively we may suggest a date in the 4th cent., perhaps soon after the great reforming work of Ezra.

c This late date in no way impugns **the antiquity** or **the authenticity** of the material. We may see that both are necessary for the author's purpose. The book concludes with the statement (4:17) that the fruit of this marriage was Obed, the grandfather of David, and this is followed by a genealogy (4:18–22) which appears in an expanded form in 1 Chr. 2:3–18. There is no necessity to suppose that the genealogy is a later addition to the book. To the modern reader it may seem an anticlimax, but it may well serve to emphasise the whole purpose of the book. At the least it is the telling of a well-known story, which may have existed in oral form (cf. J. M. Myers, *The Linguistic and Literary Form of the Book of Ruth* (1955)), and derive from pre-exilic days. What the writer has done is to use this well-known and often repeated story and give it a point. He has effected this (1) by drawing atten- **271**
tion to the connection between this story and Israel's Messianic hope, 4:17, 18–22 ; (2) by gently underlining the Moabite background of Ruth (1:22, 2:2, 6, 21, etc.); (3) by emphasising the divine intention that is fulfilled in the literary climax of the story, 4:13–18. Perhaps also it is deliberately intended, that the action of Boaz ' goes beyond ' the tradition suggested by the Judah and Tamar story and what is required by the law of Dt. 25:5–10. It is by such fulfillings of the Law that Judaism is saved from becoming a legalistic religion, and that Israel enters into the divine purpose.

It would appear then that Ru. is **a parable**, and a **d**
worthy forerunner of the parables of Jesus. Its purpose will be to awaken the people of God to their high privilege and responsibility. They have received the great revelation of God which must be kept free from the contaminations and dilutions of paganism, yet must be available for all, even a Moabite woman. From the 4th cent. B.C. the Jewish community was almost compelled, by the pressure of history, to become exclusive. We read of the vigorous and, to us, fanatical attempts to maintain the purity of Judaism in Ezr. 10 and Neh. 13:25–7. It would be only too easy for such religious zeal to become arrogant and hostile to Gentiles. But the very exclusiveness of Israel's monotheism has as a necessary correlative the compulsion to receive the Gentiles into the community of Israel (cf. Isa. 2:3f., 45:22f.). It is probable that the book of Jon. also belongs to this same period and is akin to Ru., both as a literary type and in its purpose.

It should be added that **other interpretations** of **e**
the book of Ru. have been suggested, e.g. a polemic against the work of Nehemiah and Ezra, an entertaining story, a story to inculcate such virtues as disinterested kindness or the fulfilment of the requirements of levirate marriage. None of these seem to do justice to the book as we have it. It does not speak the language of polemic, and its treatment of levirate marriage is incidental to the story. It is unquestionably an ' entertaining story ', but so are some of the stories told by Jesus. The ' point ' in the story is in the Moabite ancestry of David, the fact that a Moabitess recognised the claim of Israel's God and was fully received into the commonwealth of Israel.

I 1-22 The Coming of Ruth the Moabitess with **272**
Naomi to Bethlehem—During the Judges period a Bethlehemite family, Elimelech, his wife Naomi, and their two sons Mahlon and Chilion, were compelled by famine to leave their home and migrate to Moab. Then Elimelech died, and the two sons married Moabite women, Orpah and Ruth. After ten years the sons also died and the three women were left widows and childless.

2. Elimelech means either ' My God is King ' or **b**
' Melek is God ' (cf. Elijah ' Jahu is God '). The name is known from pre-Israelite Canaanite sources. The remaining names in 2 and 4 are of doubtful origin. Apparently Naomi means ' my sweet one ', Mahlon ' weakness ', Chilion ' pining ', Orpah ' stiff necked ', and Ruth ' friend '. Ephrath is a district associated with Bethlehem (cf. Gen. 35:19, 48:7 ; 1 Sam. 17:12 ; Mic. 5:2). **3.** It is consistent with the

272b relatively late date of the book that Naomi invokes Yahweh's blessing in Moab ; in earlier days, Yahweh's sovereignty was thought of as not extending beyond Israel (cf. Jg. 11:24 ; 1 Sam. 26:19). 'deal kindly' hardly does justice to the Hebrew ; a nearer approximation would be 'keep faith'. **11-13.** The law of Dt. 25:5–10 requires the brother of the dead man to marry the childless widow, and the first son would be reckoned as the dead man's heir. But there is no such near kinsman for Orpah and Ruth. Note that what we would call 'misfortune' is regarded by the biblical writer as the direct working of God. **15-17.** A magnificent utterance in which religious devotion and human love are compounded. **17.** 'May the Lord . . .' is the conventional form of the solemn oath, originally accompanied by a symbolic action describing an injury. **20.** Do not call me Naomi (my sweet one), call me Mara (bitter). The phrasing of 20f. is so similar to Job 27:2, even to its use of 'the Almighty' (Shaddai) as the name of God, as to suggest that the book of Ru. also had its origin among the wisdom writers of Israel. **22.** Barley harvest, i.e. April. Barley was the first of the crops to be cut.

c **II The Meeting of Ruth and Boaz—1. kinsman** (cf. 3:1) ; the word used here does not suggest the obligation of the word in 20, 'one of our nearest kin'; 'man of wealth', a term also translated 'man of valour'. It suggests that vigour or energy that leads to mastery in any sphere of life, cf. 3:11, 'a woman of worth'. The meaning of the name Boaz is doubtful, although it includes the element *'az*—'strong'. **2.** cf. Dt. 24:19 ; Lev. 19:9f., 23:22. **3.** 'she happened', but unknown to her Providence was directing her steps. **7.** 'without resting even for a moment', a very probable emendation with help of ancient versions of a text that has suffered in transmission. MT, 'Her dwelling at the house is short'. **12.** 'under whose wings . . .'; cf. Ps. 36:7, 57:2, 91:4. **13.** 'comforted me and spoken kindly to', cf. Isa. 40:1, 2. 'spoken kindly to' is literally 'spoken upon the heart of'. **16.** 'bundles', i.e. the bound sheaves. **17 ephah**, a measure corresponding to our bushel ; $\frac{1}{10}$ homer. **18.** 'she showed'. MT reads 'her mother saw'. **20. one of our nearest kin.** The Hebrew word *gô'ēl* emphasises not only relationship but the responsibility of the kinsman for the needy members of the family ; Naomi describes him as the legal guardian of their rights. So 3:9, He is the one who reclaims, cf. Lev. 25:25ff., 47ff.

d **III Naomi's Plan for Boaz and Ruth—2.** Boaz is a relative ; he may act as the reclaimer of their rights. Winnowing was done in the late afternoon when the breeze sprang up. The threshing-floor would be an exposed site, open to the breeze. **9.** 'spread your skirt', a symbolic action proclaiming the invitation to marry. 'Next of kin' (cf. 2:20), in fact Boaz was not ; cf. 12. **10.** 'Kindness'. Hardly adequate, perhaps we should translate 'You have made good your (family) loyalty in this last action more than formerly'. For she has not merely sought remarriage, but the one kind of marriage that should perpetuate the family name. **11. my fellow townsmen** : lit. 'all the gate of my people'. In the gateway of the town wall the affairs of the town were administered ; cf. 4:1, 11. **15.** 'six measures' : there is no word in the Hebrew for measure and we are left to infer what it was. Perhaps 6 omers or $\frac{6}{10}$ of an ephah ; cf. Exod. 16:36. **16.** 'How did you fare?' correctly represents the Hebrew 'Who art thou?'; so, literally, in RV.

IV Ruth's Marriage—Boaz, who clearly intends to marry Ruth, must first deal with the nearer relative upon whom the responsibility falls of (*a*) keeping the property in the family and (*b*) of raising up an heir to Elimelech by marrying Ruth. He is willing to redeem the property but not on terms that will alienate it from his own family. **1.** 'A friend'. The Hebrew has a word corresponding to our 'so-and-so'. Apparently the name of the true next of kin had not been preserved. **2. ten men of the elders of the city** : the elders exercised the functions of a modern Justice of the Peace, or magistrate ; cf. Dt. 19:12, 21:2–4, 25:7–9. 'is selling' : i.e. has resolved to sell. The idiomatic English corresponds here to a Hebrew perfect. **4.** 'I thought' : perhaps more definitely 'I promised' (lit. 'said'). 'tell you' : the Hebrew is more picturesque, 'uncover your ear', i.e. draw aside the long hair that covers the ear, so as to whisper, cf. 1 Sam. 9:15. **redeem** : the verb is the same root as that for 'next of kin', 4:1 ; for a similar situation affecting property cf. Jer. 32:7–9. **5. you are also buying Ruth** : a small emendation supported by the ancient versions gives this undoubtedly correct meaning. But this act goes beyond the strict requirement of the law ; Lev. 25 and Dt. 25:5ff. The property should be redeemed by the next of kin. The law only requires the brother of the dead man to marry the widow. The story of Gen. 38 shows that the father of the dead man, who refused to allow the legal fulfilment of the levirate marriage, was responsible for fulfilling the purpose of the law of Dt. 25:5ff. But that hardly fits the present case. The obligation on the next of kin is moral rather than legal. But, as the story shows, popular feeling supported Boaz in his generous interpretation. **7.** Apparently a reference to the law preserved in Dt. 25:8–10 although the parallel is not exact. The statement that this was the custom in former times indicates the late date of the book of Ru., unless this verse be regarded as an explanatory gloss. But **9**, which recognises the right of a widow to inherit, also suggests a date after the Pentateuch was complete ; cf. Jdt. 8:7, 16:21f. 272e

f **11f.** The greatest blessing that can be invoked on a woman is given to Ruth the Moabitess. **14f.** The sentence is ambiguous. It may mean that the child is to be regarded as the kinsman redeemer ; but more probably we should place a full stop at 'next of kin' and regard this as a reference to Boaz. Then begin the new sentence, 'May his [the child's] name . . .' **18f.** Naomi adopts the child as her own to replace the dead. **18-22.** If the view suggested in the introduction be correct, the genealogy is essential to the story and not to be regarded as a later addition, although it may be of independent origin.

Bibliography—COMMENTARIES : A. Bertholet, KHC (1898) ; G. A. Cooke, CB (1913) ; M. Haller, HAT (1940) ; P. Joüon, *Commentaire philologique et exégétique* (2nd ed. 1953) ; A. R. S. Kennedy, *The Book of Ruth : Heb. Text* (1928) ; G. A. F. Knight, *Torch* (1950) ; C. Lattey, *Westminster Version of the Sacred Scriptures* (1935) ; W. Nowack, HKAT (1902) ; W. Rudolph, KAT (1939) ; G. W. Thatcher, Cent.B.

OTHER LITERATURE : J. H. Myers, *The Linguistic and Literary Form of the Book of Ruth* (1955) ; E. Robertson, 'The Plot of the Book of Ruth', BJRL 32 (1950), 207–28 ; H. H. Rowley, *The Servant of the Lord* (1951), 161–86.

I AND II SAMUEL

By L. H. BROCKINGTON

273a **Introduction**—The two books of Sam. were originally a single book and were written as such in Heb. MSS. In LXX the book was divided into two parts before the great uncial MSS were written (first half of the 4th cent.), and from there the division ultimately passed over to Heb. where the earliest instance of it is from the middle of the 15th cent., not very long before the printing of the Heb. text began (1477). The ascription to Samuel was made partly because the early chapters are about him and partly because of the strong Jewish tradition that much of the OT was written by prophets.

b **The first book** begins with the story of Samuel (1–7), then goes on to deal with the institution of the monarchy and the relations between Samuel and Saul (8–15) and finally tells the story of Saul, David and Jonathan, of gradual estrangement on the one hand and growing affection on the other (16–31). **The second book** is concerned entirely with David's reign, telling of his military successes, his family, his friends and the loyalties and disloyalties that showed themselves. Between them the two books cover the history of the last 'judge', Samuel, and the first two kings, Saul and David. Broadly speaking, therefore, the books tell of **the beginnings of the Hebrew monarchy**. It is not history as we know it, with careful marshalling of all the facts and the presentation of them in chronological or logical sequence, but rather a series of kaleidoscopic pictures of incidents, for the most part personal, in the lives of the principal characters. The reader soon notices that there are **two traditions apparent** in much of what is recorded in the first book. In one narrative Samuel is represented as a seer who is consulted by men about their problems, however trivial, such as the finding of lost asses. He is commissioned by God to anoint Saul as king. Elsewhere (8, 10:17–27*a*, 12) another picture altogether is found in which Samuel is a national figure, a 'judge', ruler of the people but near the end of his life so that his sons begin to relieve him of some of the administration. The people clamour for a king, but Samuel is at first unwilling to accede to their request because it is in effect an act of rebellion against their heavenly king, Yahweh. Further, there are two portraits of David: one, that of a shepherd lad, lovable but inexperienced, and the other of a man of parts, a warrior and a member of Saul's court. Several incidents seem to be twice recorded, e.g. Saul's attempt to kill David (18:10–16 and 19:8–10) and David's sparing of Saul's life (24 and 26). These and other details of the two traditions are noted in the commentary.

c The question arises as to how far these traditions may be regarded as continuations of the J and E stories in the Pentateuch (§136*f*). No certain answer can be given because the narratives as recorded in Sam. do not bear many of the distinctive features of those early narratives. There are traits here and there that are reminiscent of J and E but they are inconclusive. It remains an open question whether the narratives continue those of the Pentateuch (and Jos. and Jg.) or whether by coincidence the same phenomenon of parallel narratives occurs in Sam. independently. A further question hangs on it, namely, whether J and E were planned to take the story as far as David or not. 273

The twofold narrative virtually ends with 1 Sam. 2 Sam. shows practically nothing of it. One feature in 2 Sam., however, is noteworthy: chs. 9 to 20 tell the story of various court intrigues and other episodes of David's reign in a manner that sets them apart as brilliant story-telling. From beginning to end of these chapters a strong personal interest is maintained, stronger than that in the rest of 1 and 2 Sam. We read of Mephibosheth and Ziba, Uriah and Bathsheba, Amnon and Tamar, Absalom, Shimei and many others who stand out vividly as living characters. The chapters are commonly called the **Court History of David** and tell, among other things, of attempts to secure succession to the throne. They include 1 Kg. 1 and 2 and close with the statement that 'the kingdom was established in the hand of Solomon'. The limits of the narrative, however, are not clearly defined. There are incidents recorded earlier in 2 Sam. which anticipate the 'Court History'. But it is generally agreed that at least 2 Sam. 9–20 and 1 Kg. 1, 2 were written as a single narrative unit. The date of writing is uncertain. If it can be shown to be an eye-witness account, as many think, then its date will fall within easily fixed limits; but need it be so regarded? Good historical writing frequently and inevitably draws on imagination as well as on ascertainable fact and still remains true in spirit. d

The date of composition of the whole work (1 and 2 Sam.) must be placed as late as, or later than, the writing of the anti-monarchic story of the anointing of Saul, possibly in the 8th cent. The final story was subjected to some slight editing by a member of the Deuteronomic school. 1 Kg. 1 and 2, continuing the 'Court History', were probably included in Sam. originally and became attached to Kg. when the story of Solomon was told. e

The historian to whom we owe 1 and 2 Sam. as a completed book probably had the following material to draw on: two traditions of the life of Samuel and the part he played in the institution of the monarchy, two traditions of the introduction of David to Saul and of their subsequent relationship, stories of the early years of David, both as outlaw and as king, the 'Court History', and in addition access to lists of officers and heroes. Some of these were almost certainly written down already, but some of them may still have been held in memory as sacred traditions of highly revered heroes of Israel's prime. f

A note must be added about differences between the Heb. and Gr. of Sam. Often LXX has a reading that is to be much preferred to the Heb. (cf. 1 Sam. 14:41; 2 Sam. 11:22–5). Discoveries in the Qumrân caves have shown that the Qumrân community used a Heb. text of Sam. in which a number of readings agree more closely with the text underlying LXX than with the MT. g

74a **THE FIRST BOOK OF SAMUEL**

Part I I-VII Samuel
Samuel, who plays a leading part in the first half of 1 Sam., appears in two distinct roles, that of seer or visionary (*rō'eh*), whose activities were probably limited to his own neighbourhood or only as far as his fame might spread, and that of judge (*shôphēṭ*) of all Israel, the last of the leaders whose stories are now found in the book of Jg. The role of seer probably belongs to an earlier tradition than that of judge and shows Samuel as a willing agent in the institution of the monarchy which he saw to be Israel's only effective way of maintaining her independence against the growing power of the Philistines. The later tradition presents Samuel himself as the one who effectively suppressed the Philistines and who agreed unwillingly to the people's request for a king. It is to this later tradition that 1 Sam. 1–7 belongs; it is unlikely that so elaborate a tradition of birth and earlier childhood would be told of a purely local figure.

b **I 1, 2 Samuel's Parents,** Elkanah and Hannah—**1.** Ramathaim-Zophim as it stands here is to be regarded as a compound proper name, but perhaps the two parts should be separated and read as 'from Ramathaim, a Zuphite'. Later on in this verse Elkanah is called 'son of Zuph' and in 9:5ff. we learn that there is a Ramah (meaning height or hill, and of which Ramathaim is the dual form) in the land of Zuph. Zuph lies between Joppa and Shiloh.

c **3-8 The Annual Family Visit to Shiloh**—With the attention shown to Hannah, the childless wife, we may compare that shown to Rachel. Childlessness was a reproach to a woman in Israel (Gen. 30:1). **3.** Shiloh, 20 miles north of Jerusalem, was an important sanctuary in early Israel (see R. Brinker, *The Influence of Sanctuaries in Early Israel* (1946)), and was at this time the home of the Ark. After the capture of the Ark (1 Sam. 4:11) the sanctuary ceased to be used. The Philistines may have destroyed it after capturing the Ark; at all events we know it to have been destroyed at some time (Jer. 7:12, 14) and its priests to have settled at Nob (1 Sam. 21:1; 22:11). 'Year by year': an annual visit was probably the custom in early times but later on three visits were to be required (Exod. 34:18–24). **4.** 'Portions': there is evidence elsewhere that families shared in the sacrificial meal (Dt. 12:18; 14:22–9; 15:19–23). In v. 5, RSV follows LXX. The rendering of the Syriac 'because he loved Hannah he gave her a double portion' would give an immediate reason for the spiteful treatment of Hannah by Peninnah.

d **9-11 Hannah's Vow**—However strongly Elkanah might claim to be worth ten sons (8), only the birth of a son could adequately console Hannah. She vowed that she would dedicate her son, if she had one, to Yahweh. The unshaved head is reminiscent of the Nazirite vow (Num. 6:1ff.; cf. also Samson, Jg. 13) although it is only one of the three requisite observances. **12-18.** Eli, mistakenly thinking her to be drunk, is convinced by Hannah's sincerity and gives her his blessing. In those days blessing was no mere formality; to give a blessing involved the exercise of all one's power for good in the interest of the person to be blessed. Words uttered were never mere words, they not only expressed, but also carried in them, something of the personal power or vitality of the one who spoke them (see J. Pedersen, *Israel I–II* (1926), 182ff.).

e **19, 20 The prayer granted,** Hannah named her son Samuel. The name, in the narrative, is interpreted as meaning 'I have asked him of the Lord' but this interpretation belongs, etymologically, to the name Saul. It is almost impossible to connect the meaning 'asked' to the name Samuel except perhaps by assonance. It has therefore been suggested that the etymology, and probably the whole birth story with it, has been displaced from Saul to Samuel in the course of compilation or transmission.
21-28 Hannah presents the Boy at Shiloh—After weaning the boy, at a very much later age than is 274e
usual nowadays, Hannah took him with her when she resumed the annual visit to Shiloh. Although the boy himself was to be given to Yahweh she took with her the materials for an offering, probably that customary for the redemption of a first-born son (Exod. 13:13; 34:20). **24.** 'Three-year-old bull': the preference for LXX instead of the three bulls of Heb. is because v. 25 implies one only and in Gen. 15:9 a three-year-old heifer is mentioned as a sacrificial victim. 'And the child was young': this is obvious from the context; it is possibly to be rendered 'and she brought him, awake, into the house of the Lord at Shiloh'. **28.** The phrases 'I have lent him' and 'he is lent' continue the assumed etymology of the name. The last phrase of the verse brings Elkanah into the picture (see 2:11). LXX omits, and in 2:11*a* reads 'and she left him there before the Lord and went home to Ramah'.

II 1-10 Hannah's Song—Although attributed to her, f
there is only one line that is even remotely relevant to Hannah's situation, i.e. 'the barren has borne seven'. The opening verse of the song celebrates a triumph over enemies through the help of Yahweh. There follows a hymn of praise to Yahweh who controls human lives and fortunes, and the song ends with an affirmation that Yahweh will give strength to the king, his anointed one. It is a royal psalm, similar in some respects to Ps. 2. The Magnificat (Lk. 1:46ff.) has phrases reminiscent of some of the phrases of this song. In **5** it is possible to derive the verb from an Arabic cognate and instead of 'have ceased to hunger' read 'are well-nourished again'. **10. Anointed:** This is the word that was ultimately anglicised to 'Messiah'. It was the practice to anoint the head with oil in token of consecration to kingly (or priestly or prophetic) office (9:16; 10:1). The idea of God's anointed and the sanctity of his person runs like a thread through the stories of Saul and David (1 Sam. 2:35, 12:3, 5; 16:6, 24:6, 10; 26:9, 11, 16, 23; 2 Sam. 1:14, 16; 19:21; 22:51; 23:1) and may be one of the reasons for the compiler's choice of the poem.
11, 18-21, 26. Short summary statements about Samuel's residence in Shiloh and his acceptability to God and to Eli. They are interspersed in material relating to Eli's sons. They serve to set in contrast the rightness of Samuel's behaviour and the wrongness of that of Eli's sons. **18.** 'linen ephod': a garment worn round the waist during ceremonial duties and acts. It is not certain what connection it had, if any at all, with the Ephod to which was attached the pouch containing the Urim and Thummim (see on v. 28, and on 14:41).

12-17, 22-25, 27-36. Three paragraphs dealing with g
the lawless and irresponsible behaviour of Eli's sons. The first and third paragraphs are concerned with their behaviour during the performance of their priestly duties. The second paragraph, as the text now stands, deals with their irregular sexual practices, possibly in the interests of a debased form of worship. If, however, 22*b* is omitted with LXX, then all reference to sexual practice is removed and the paragraph becomes an immediate sequel to 12–17 and shows Eli's disapproval of his sons' performance of their duties. The ritual fault of which they are accused is that of valuing their own share of the sacrificial victim more highly than that due to God. Two stages in the misappropriation of the sacrificial meat seem to be mentioned. **13.** The priests appear to demand as their share, not such parts as the worshipper voluntarily sets aside for them, but such parts as they or their servants choose from the pot as the flesh was cooking. **15.** They apparently lay claim to some of the raw flesh, presumably so that they could have it cooked in their own way. Their right to some of the flesh was not in question. Priests were entitled to their 'dues'. In Lev. 7:34 these are specified as the breast and the thigh after they have been manipulated as special offerings, and in Dt. 18:3 as the 'shoulder,

274g the two cheeks, and the stomach'. These differences may well imply different customs according to local tradition; that at Shiloh need not be expected to have conformed to either. **22.** 'women who served at the entrance'; cf. Exod. 38:8, 'the ministering women who ministered at the door of the tent of meeting'. **24.** or, 'it is no good report that I hear men spreading among the people of the Lord'. **27-36** anticipate the downfall of the Eliad priestly line in favour of the Zadokite line whose official priesthood was inaugurated under Solomon (1 Kg. 2:26f., 35). The passage therefore reflects the same background as the narrative in 1 Kg. 2, probably Deuteronomic. On the other hand, one would expect that when the doom on the house of Eli was first announced Samuel would have been the obvious man to take Eli's place; if we omit 35*b* as a gloss in favour of the Zadokite priesthood, 35*a* would then certainly refer to Samuel. **28. wear an ephod before me:** the same phrase occurs in 14:3 and in LXX of 22:18 and might also be translated 'carry an ephod before me'. It is difficult to decide whether this ephod is to be identified in kind with that which Samuel wore (2:18) or with an earlier form of the one to which the pouch for the Urim and Thummim was attached. If the second alternative is right, as it may well be, it was a symbol of the priestly function of oracle-giving. If that is so, this verse sets out the principal duties of the Eliad priesthood, altar service and oracle-giving, and mentions also what their dues were to be (cf. Lev. 2:3, 10).

275a **III 1-18 The Revelation to Samuel**—These verses probably describe what is technically known as an 'incubation-oracle'. The devotee spends the night in the sanctuary in expectation of a divine revelation. Ps. 17:15 may refer to such an experience. Normally the person would remain awake, but sleep need not be regarded as invalidating the experience, especially in the case of one so young. **1.** 'rare': it would be true to say that in any age in Israel the revelation of the word of God was rare or precious, but the mention of it here enhances the significance of the revelation to the young Samuel. **3** implies that the night vigil was almost at an end, dawn was near but the lamp was still burning. 'Ark of God', see §§114*de*, 197*d*. **12.** 'all that I have spoken': probably the prophecy in 2:30ff.

b **III 19-IV 1a.** Samuel is recognised as a prophet throughout Israel and is represented by the writer as the ruler of all Israel. This may be regarded as the introduction to the story of Samuel's success over the Philistines in 7:3ff. **20.** 'From Dan to Beersheba': see on Jg. 20:1 (cf. also 2 Sam. 3:10). **21.** 'again': suggesting that 1-18 describes the first, and inaugural, vision of a series. The obvious repetition in this verse may be due to the use of more than one source or tradition in the writing of the book.

c **IV 1b-VII 2 The Adventures of the Ark**—In this story the Ark is first introduced as 'the Ark of the covenant of the Lord of hosts' and then as 'the Ark of the covenant of God'. Two things are indicated: (1) The use of the word 'covenant' in the title is a Deuteronomic trait suggesting subsequent editing by a member of that school, and (2) the alternation from Yahweh to God implies two sources for the material, but no clear separation can be made.

d **IV 1b-21 Battle breaks out between the Israelites and the Philistines:** the Israelites are utterly defeated, the Ark captured and Eli's two sons killed. The national disaster is symbolised by the name Ichabod given to Eli's grandson born on the day the news was brought. **1. Ebenezer** or 'a stone (called) help': probably situated in the land of Zuph some 12 miles inland from Joppa. This reference anticipates 7:12. **Aphek** bears the meaning 'enclosure' or 'stronghold', which probably accounts for its frequent occurrence as a proper name. At least four are recorded: (1) mentioned here, near Mizpah; (2) on the northern frontier of Sidonian territory, east of Byblos (Jos. 13:4); (3) that of Jos. 12:18 and

1 Kg. 20:26, 30 which is variously identified, either 275
in the plain of Sharon near Jezreel, or east of the Sea of Galilee; and (4) in the territory of Asher (Jos. 19:30; Jg. 1:31). They may all have had their origin in battle encampments (see on 29:1). **4.** 'Enthroned on the cherubim': the phrase occurs again in 2 Sam. 6:2; 1 Chr. 13:6; Ps. 80:1, 99:1. (On cherubim see Gen. 3:24; Exod. 25:22.) **5.** 'A mighty shout': in Ps. 47:5 the same word is used of the acclamation of God as king. Here it is the acclamation given to the Ark as the symbol of the presence of the sovereign God. **8.** 'smote the Egyptians': the Exodus is already the central and formative experience of Israel's history as God's people. Even Philistines are made to echo it. **10.** 'thirty thousand': in v. 2 we read that four thousand fell on the first day. The figures probably come from the lively imagination of the historian. **12.** The torn clothes and earth on the head were signs of mourning and betokened the bad news he bore; the messenger from the battle of Gilboa was similarly dishevelled (2 Sam. 1:2). **18.** 'judged Israel forty years': this is in line with the chronological scheme of the book of Jg. and is here added by the same (Deuteronomic) editor whose work may also be seen in 13:1; 2 Sam. 2:10*a*-11, 5:4, 5. LXX has 'twenty' in harmony with Jg. 13:1, where we read that the Philistines dominated Israel for forty years, of which twenty would be those of Samson (Jg. 15:20) and twenty those of Eli. **21. Ichabod:** meaning 'there is no glory' or 'the glory is not'. Glory here means that in which Israel boasted or gloried and is only dimly anticipatory of the use of 'glory' in Ezekiel and later writers to connote the conception of God's presence on earth.

V The Philistines in Distress on Account of the e
Ark—1-5. Dagon, the Philistine god, falls from his pedestal in the presence of the Ark. **1.** 'Ashdod': one of the five Philistine cities, the other four being Gath, Ekron, Gaza and Ashkelon (6:17). **2.** 'Dagon': a corn-god (Jg. 16:23). **3, 4.** 'face-downward': or, perhaps better, 'forward'. 'threshold': another possible meaning is plinth or pedestal (Ezek. 9:3). **5.** 'do not tread on': because the place would have been made sacred (taboo) by this calamity; cf. the somewhat similar practice mentioned in Zeph. 1:9.

6-12. Disease breaks out in Ashdod and the lords of f
the Philistines (see on Jg. 3:3) decide to try sending the Ark first to Gath and then to Ekron. The latter place was the home of the god Baal-zebub (2 Kg. 1:2). Disaster fell on Gath, and the people of Ekron refused to receive the Ark. Why did they thus send it round? Was it to see if one or other of the chief Philistine cities would prove acceptable to Yahweh, or was it in the hope that the gods of Gath or Ekron might prove stronger than Yahweh?

VI The Ark is returned to Israel with compensa- g
tory gifts in the form of gold tokens of the disasters suffered by the Philistines.

1-9. Preparations for removal of the Ark with proper compensatory offerings and due precautions. At the end of v. 1 LXX adds 'and their land swarmed with mice'. Whether this may be regarded as original or not, it does at least prepare the way for the gold token mice mentioned later (4). **3. Guilt offering** or 'gift in compensation': this is not a guilt offering in the Levitical sense of the term (see Lev. 5:15, 16) by way of restitution, it is rather a gift made on the principle of sympathetic magic; the plague was of boils (and mice) and the gift intended to secure its removal was of the same kind. If the plague was bubonic plague the mice may be regarded as its carriers. Some think that two traditions are mingled here, one telling of gold tumours and the other of gold mice. **7. A new cart and two milch cows:** by using a cart and animals not previously used for profane work they would avoid uncleanness or taboo and at the same time ensure that the animals had no tendency to follow paths already familiar to them. The way they took would be conceived as being

5g directed by Yahweh. Implicit also is the recognition that only the first and best are suitable for divine use. **9.** 'Beth-shemesh' was the first Israelite town of any importance on the main road to Israel from Ekron along the valley of Sorek, and lies about 15 miles west of Jerusalem. It may have been a border town. If the Ark went there it would clearly be Yahweh's will that it return to Israel.

h **10-16.** The Ark travels to Beth-shemesh and halts on the estate of a man named Joshua. The Israelites offer a sacrifice, using the cows for victims and the cart for fuel. **14.** 'A great stone' to serve as an altar; this reflects a time before the rule of a central sanctuary. Exod. 20:24 permitted the building and use of an altar at any place where God recorded his name, as he did on this occasion when the Ark halted at Joshua's field. **15** is an editorial addition made to ensure that the Ark was handled only by those qualified to do so, the Levites. The stone now serves the purpose of a base for the Ark and the sacrifices are to be understood as being made on an altar in the proper way. 15*b* therefore does not mean that a second sacrifice was made. **17, 18.** The five gold tumours and mice represent one for each of the five Philistine cities and their lords. The great stone was a local landmark.

i **VI 19-VII 2.** Disaster falls on the men of Beth-shemesh, so the Ark is removed to Kiriath-jearim where it remained for some considerable time. **19.** It is unlikely that all the men of Beth-shemesh looked into the Ark; LXX may therefore be right in limiting the incident to 'the sons of Jeconiah among the men of Beth-shemesh'. **21.** Kiriath-jearim was one of the Gibeonite cities (Jos. 9:17) and lay north-east of Beth-shemesh. It may be presumed that Shiloh was in ruins (see on 1:3), that a new home had to be found for the Ark, and that Kiriath-jearim was chosen as being an ancient sanctuary. Its former name was Baalah (Jos. 15:9). 'The house of Abinadab on the hill' (7:1): nothing further is known of Abinadab or of Eleazar, but both were names in frequent use. That of Eleazar is reminiscent of Aaron's son and may have been used here on that account. 'On the hill' translates the Heb. word Gibeah, and for this reason some scholars have attempted to identify it with Gibeon, the sanctuary which was of considerable importance at the beginning of Solomon's reign. **2.** 'Some twenty years' more closely defines the 'long time' and is probably due to a Deuteronomic editor (see 4:18). This verse closes the account of the Ark but it also prepares the way for the following narratives by mentioning the yearning for Yahweh.

j **VII 3-17 Samuel's Judgeship—3, 4.** Samuel urges the people to put away their idols if they really intend to return to Yahweh. This reform is in the spirit of Deuteronomy and is probably to be regarded as an anticipation of it. 'Baals and Ashtaroth', see §88*cd*. **5-11.** The Philistines are defeated by divine agency while Samuel leads the people in proper worship to Yahweh. The point of view in this narrative is that if the people offer Yahweh true worship and obedience he will fight on their behalf. The same point of view may be seen in a series of stories running through chs. 7, 8, 10:17ff., 12 and 15, and together they constitute a single and late narrative of the inauguration of kingship in Israel. In it divine disapproval of the monarchy is strongly expressed because it means neglect of the kingship of Yahweh. Its literary affinities are with the E narrative of the Pentateuch. **5.** Mizpah was the centre of Israel's activities in pre-monarchic days (see Jg. 20 and 21). It lay about 5 miles north-west of Jerusalem. **6.** 'Drew water and poured it out': if this was a drink offering of water it is a unique instance in the OT (2 Sam. 23:16f. being altogether different); the normal drink offering was of wine or of the blood of sacrificial victims. In view of the confession made at the end of the verse it has been suggested that the pouring out of water was symbolic of the shedding of sin. **9.** 'Sucking lamb . . . as a whole burnt offering' is unique as a description of the victim which is usually a young animal 'without blemish'. **11.** 'Beth-car' is unknown. 275j

k **12-14.** The end of the Philistine war is marked by the erection of a stone called 'stone of help'. The earlier references (4:1 and 5:1) to Ebenezer are anachronisms. **14.** 'From Ekron to Gath': there is no evidence that Israel ever did recover actual Philistine territory. Ideally, Israel regarded the whole of southern Palestine as her territory (Jos. 15:45-7; Jg. 1:18). The Amorites were pre-Israelite inhabitants of Canaan. **15-17.** A summary statement of Samuel's authority as judge and of the places in which he exercised it, Bethel, Gilgal, Mizpah and Ramah, all ancient sanctuaries.

276a **Part II VIII-XV Samuel and Saul**

Within these chapters two traditions of the institution of the monarchy are embedded; one reflects an attitude favourable to the monarchy and is to be found in 9:1–10:16; 10:27*b*–11:15; chs. 13, 14, and the other an unfavourable attitude found in ch. 8; 10:17–27*a*; 12:1–25; ch. 15.

b **VIII 1-9.** Samuel's sons, not of the same calibre as their father, provide the occasion for a request for a king which is shown to be rejection, not of Samuel and his sons only, but of Yahweh himself. **2.** 'Beer-sheba': it is not clear why so southerly a centre was chosen. Josephus says that Samuel appointed one son in Bethel and the other in Beersheba (Ant. VI, iii, 2).

c **10-18.** Samuel outlines the kind of overbearing behaviour typical of oriental despotism, cf. Dt. 17:14–17. 'Thousands . . . fifties': in 22:7 the divisions are given as thousands and hundreds and in Exod. 18:21, 25 as thousands, hundreds, fifties and tens.

d **19-22.** Yahweh grants permission for the appointment of a king in response to the people's request. The last sentence of 22 is inconclusive; one would expect action to be taken, rather than a return home. The immediate sequel to ch. 8 is 10:17–27*a* where, at an assembly at Mizpah, Saul is chosen by lot, and Samuel made a deposition of the rights and duties of kingship before Yahweh. A summons to meet him at Mizpah would have fitted better with 10:17; probably the insertion by the final writer of the intervening narrative caused 22*b* to be so worded.

e The unfavourable attitude to kingship shown in this chapter is similar to that expressed by Hosea and may have come from circles familiar with Hosea's point of view. No one in Samuel's day could have had experience of monarchy in Israel. On the other hand, there were kings among the Canaanite tribes and such behaviour may well have been common knowledge based on experience of kings in general. The fact remains, however, that this attitude is characteristic of one tradition in 1 Sam. and that another and different tradition begins at ch. 9 which is favourable to the monarchy. Attempts to identify these two traditions as continuations of the J and E documents are not conclusive, though they have many things in common with J and E.

f **IX 1-27.** Saul, sent by his father to look for lost asses, is introduced by his servant to Samuel. Samuel, previously warned by Yahweh that the future king is to visit him, seizes the opportunity and entertains Saul. In this chapter there is no hint that to choose a king is rebellion against God, nor is there any recognition of the defeat of the Philistines by Samuel (ch. 7). Samuel plays a leading part, but only as a local seer with a wide reputation and not as judge of all Israel. **1.** Abiel is called Ner in 1 Chr. 8:33 (see also 1 Sam. 14:51). **2.** Saul means 'asked for', which makes it plausible that the birth story now attached to Samuel was once told of Saul. The lost asses provide the means whereby Saul and Samuel are brought together. **4.** Shalisha and Shaalim are not identifiable with any certainty. There is a Baal-shalisha mentioned in 2 Kg. 4:42. **5.** Zuph was Samuel's native place (1:1). Saul had now passed again from Benjamite to Ephraimite territory. **9,** which properly introduces

276f 11 where seer is mentioned for the first time otherwise, has attracted much discussion on account of the use of two words, **seer** (*rō'eh*) and **prophet** (*nābhī'*). All that can be said with certainty is that the note recognises a change in terminology. Seer and prophet are virtually identified; the word 'seer' was falling into disuse and 'prophet' becoming popular. Though here used virtually as synonyms the words do suggest different characteristics. *Rō'eh* refers to the visionary element in the prophetic phenomenon whereas *nābhī'*, from a root meaning 'to utter', seems to refer to the prophetic utterance of God's word. It is, of course, possible that a change was taking place in Samuel's time in the nature as well as in the name of the phenomenon which we know as prophecy. In some respects the two traditions about Samuel echo the change. The man to whom Saul appeals about lost asses was essentially a visionary, but the man who stood before the assembled elders of Israel and warned them of the inherent evils of monarchy was a spokesman of God. **12. High place** or 'hill shrine'. Places of sacrifice were often on the hill summit above the town and the hilltop would become a sanctuary. In this story the town is the unit for sacrificial purposes. In 20:6, 28f. the family is the unit.

g **13. Bless . . . afterward . . . eat:** sacrifice and slaughter for food were originally a single process, i.e. there was no slaughter for food that was not at the same time a sacrifice. The sacrificial acts would first be performed and then the remainder would be eaten at a common meal. Samuel officiates: he is priest as well as seer. **16.** 'Anoint': with oil as a token of consecration to the kingship. In the OT the ceremony of anointing was limited to kings (cf. 2:10, 10:1), priests (Exod. 28:41) and prophets (one passage only, 1 Kg. 19:16). 'The Philistines': in this earlier narrative the Philistines were regarded as so serious a menace to the existence of Israel as to be the primary reason for the election of a king. **20.** 'All that is desirable': the monarchy, compared with which the asses are of no importance. **21.** 'Least of the tribes': such self-depreciation was natural and proper, cf. Gideon's answer in Jg. 6:15. **24.** Samuel, presiding at the feast, could show honour to Saul by the way in which he received him and set before him the choicest pieces of food. The term 'upper portion' is obscure. The Targum, with a change of one Heb. consonant, renders 'fat tail'. This would give a more precise meaning, the fat tail being a delicacy, but according to the law (Exod. 29:22; Lev. 3:9, 7:3, 8:25, 9:19) it was included among the parts to be burnt in sacrifice and thus offered to God.

277a **X 1-7.** Samuel anoints Saul privately and tells him to regard subsequent incidents as signs; he will be told that the asses are found, and will then meet three men from whom he will receive homage, At Gibeah he will fall in with a band of prophets in whose company the spirit of God will come upon him and he will behave with prophetic frenzy. Then he is to do whatever opportunity offers. This last sign is significant for it will clearly be the act that brings Saul to public notice as the natural leader in time of crisis.

1. 'Kiss': presumably on the cheek and as a sign of homage, cf. Ps. 2:11. 'Anoint', see 9:16. **2.** 'Rachel's tomb': a well-known landmark (Gen. 35:19; Jer. 31:15). Saul, as a Benjamite, was a descendant of Rachel. **3. Oak of Tabor:** in primitive religion trees were often regarded as sacred and as the home of, or representing, the deity. This tree, mentioned only here, may have been on an ancient sacred site. The three men were perhaps carrying sacrificial victims with the proper bread and wine offerings, but the quantity is generous unless the men were part of a larger company. Josephus mentions only one kid (Ant. VI, iv, 2). Why they should give Saul two loaves is not clear. It was probably quite an ordinary thing to do, perhaps as a sign of hospitality, but to Saul, after his interview with Samuel, it would appear to be a token of homage to the future king. **5. Gibeath-elohim** meaning 'hill of God' is called simply 'Gibeah, hill', in ch. 10 and elsewhere, while in 11:4 it is called 'Gibeah of Saul'. It is probably to be distinguished from Geba (modern Jeba') in 13:3 although the similarity of name led to some confusion in 1 Sam. 13. They are situated just north of Jerusalem and are about 3 miles apart. **Garrison of the Philistines:** garrison is the most likely meaning of the Heb. word here. Literally it means 'something set up' and could also mean a 'prefect' and even a 'pillar' (Gen. 19:26). A prefect, however, would have a body of soldiers under him so that there would be a garrison in any case. A Philistine garrison at Gibeah, so far within Israelite territory, shows how strong a hold they had on the country. Its overthrow would be the first sign of a bid for independence. Here at Gibeah Saul is to meet the prophets and be possessed by the spirit. **Band of prophets:** it is a long step from the behaviour of these men when possessed by the spirit to that of men like Isaiah, Jeremiah or Ezekiel. There was clearly a development in the nature and behaviour of the prophets which probably went hand in hand with a developing social structure and moral conscience. A development can also be seen in the Heb. idea of the spirit of God; in early times prophecy was but one of many ways in which possession by the spirit showed itself; often its effect was seen in the performance of extraordinary feats of strength, but in later times prophecy and the spirit were very closely, and almost exclusively, associated. **7. Whatever your hand finds to do:** in the circumstances described in 5*a* this can be no other than the overthrow of the enemy garrison at Gibeah, an act which would be readily understood by the people as a mark of effective leadership. The reference to Gibeah in Hos. 9:9, 10:9, could be taken to imply that Saul was in fact made king at Gibeah, which would be a natural sequel to his overthrow of the garrison there. Another interpretation, however, is that the appeal for help from Jabesh-Gilead (ch. 11) was what Saul's hand found to do; v. 8 is a link in this sequence. **Signs:** often in the OT signs are everyday events taken up into God's plan and thereby becoming organic elements in revelation and providence.

8. An editorial verse to link the story of Saul's anointing, 10:1–7, with that of his institution as king at Gilgal, 11:15, and further with that of Samuel's visit to Gilgal in 13:7*b*–15*a*. It is clear from 11:15 and 13:7–15 that Gilgal, according to one line of early tradition, was the place of institution. We may thus have to reckon with another early tradition in which Gibeah was the place of institution. There were many Gilgals, the name meaning '(stone-)circle'. b

9-13. Saul becomes a changed man under access of the spirit of God, and the proverb is coined, 'Is Saul also among the prophets?' This byword occurs again in 19:24. Possibly the question, 'And who is their father?' is another byword; as used here it expresses surprise that Saul, well known, should consort with men of no known ancestry. Frenzied behaviour must have been about the only thing in common between Saul and the prophets; such behaviour was scarcely distinguishable from that of a madman (2 Kg. 9:11). c

14-16. Saul, questioned by his uncle, keeps his own counsel. This small section rounds off the story of the lost asses which began at 9:1, but it appears to be fragmentary in that it does not record Saul's homecoming, nor does it say why Saul is questioned by his uncle and not his father. The uncle may be Ner, father of Abner. Josephus says 'he was of all his relatives the one whom he loved the best' (Ant. VI, iv, 3). d

17-27a. Samuel convenes the people at Mizpah; **Saul is chosen by lot and acclaimed king.** Samuel then registers the 'rights and duties of the kingship' and dismisses the assembly. This is a continuation of ch. 8. **17.** 'Mizpah': it was here that Samuel e

77e assembled the people for the defeat of the Philistines (7:5). Now he assembles them for the election of a king. **19.** 'Rejected your God': see 8:7. 'Thousands': in Num. 1:16 the word is rendered 'clans' and this would be better here to go with tribes. **25-7** may be editorial, linking up with ch. 11 which belongs to the other tradition. Saul goes home to Gibeah where he hears news of the plight of Jabesh-gilead (11:4). 'Worthless fellows' (27) or 'scoundrels'; the fact that they brought no present suggests that others did do so. 'But he held his peace': LXX 'but after a month': this involves the change of one consonant in Heb. and would then serve to introduce ch. 11.

f **XI 1-15 Relief of Jabesh-gilead and Renewal of Saul's Sovereignty at Gilgal**—As the narrative now stands this event is intended to be the working out of the injunction to 'do whatever your hand finds to do' (10:7), but, in view of the Philistine menace and the tradition (Hos. 9:9) of a beginning of the evils of monarchy at Gibeah, it is unlikely that Saul was made king at Gilgal after an exploit east of the Jordan against the Ammonites. On the other hand there is a very strong tradition that such was the case and we must suppose that two lines of tradition have come together in the pro-monarchic account, the one recognising the Jabesh-gilead incident as the initial event and the other the overthrow of the Philistine garrison.

g **1.** On Ammonites see Gen. 19:38; Jg. 10:17. Nahash (meaning 'serpent') was probably their king. Jabesh-gilead is in the Jabesh (mod. Yabis) valley which runs into the Jordan valley from the east. Apart from Jg. 21 Jabesh-gilead is known only in connection with this incident (31:11ff.; 2 Sam. 2:4ff.). **2.** 'Gouge out all your right eyes', thus causing a defect that would disqualify for high position. **3.** 'Give us seven days': to us it seems extremely unlikely that any aggressor would give seven days' respite. On the other hand we may think that Nahash granted the respite in the confidence that, because the Israelites were virtually in servitude to the Philistines, the men of Jabesh-gilead could expect no help from them.

h **6. The spirit of God came mightily upon Saul:** possession by the spirit was not a permanent condition. This instance is similar to those in Jg. in which Othniel (3:10), Gideon (6:34), Jephthah (11:29) and Samson (13:25, 14:6, 19, 15:14) were enabled to do noteworthy or superhuman deeds. **8.** Bezek lies opposite Jabesh-gilead on the west side of the Jordan some 10 miles inland.

12-14 are perhaps to be regarded as editorial (cf. 10:8), linking this account with that in 10:17ff. where Saul was elected at Mizpah but some scoundrels withheld their allegiance (10:27). 'Renew the kingdom': a unique phrase but showing editorial recognition that Saul had already been made king at Mizpah (10:17ff.), but was now about to be made king at Gilgal.

78a **XII Samuel's Farewell**—This continues the narrative which left off at 10:24 with the acclamation of Saul at Mizpah, and it is to be presumed that the people are thought to be still assembled at Mizpah.

1-5. Samuel elicits from the people a solemn testimony of his integrity. **3.** 'To blind my eyes with it', so as not to see the intended wrong. For 'to blind' LXX has 'as much as a pair of sandals', which is supported by Sir. 46:19. It gives a more concrete picture than the present form of the Heb. and is reminiscent of Am. 2:6, 8:6, where a pair of sandals is the paltry thing for which an Israelite of that day would even sell a fellow-Israelite.

b **6-18.** Samuel rehearses some of Yahweh's providential acts to Israel showing thereby how kingship implies rejection of him, but promising Yahweh's help if they and their king obey him. **7.** 'Saving deeds': literally 'righteousnesses'; it is one of the marks of Israelite religious genius that the term for righteousness when used to describe a trait of God's character holds in it also what God does in his righteousness for his 278b
people. **9.** 'Sisera': Jg. 4 and 5. **10.** 'The Baals and the Ashtaroth', cf. 7:4. Jerubbaal, Jg. 6–8; Barak, Jg. 4 and 5 (Heb. has Bedan who is otherwise unknown. In form it suggests Abdon (Jg. 12:13) but he is only a minor judge. The inclusion of Sisera in 9 is strong support for LXX 'Barak'). **11. Samuel, the last of the judges:** two ancient versions (one form of LXX and Syr.) have 'Samson', which brings the list nearer to the sequence of judges in Jg. **12.** Nahash: mention of him here is evidence of the strength of the tradition that the Jabesh-gilead incident was strongly embedded in the tradition of the institution of the monarchy.

16-18. The people are brought to a mood of submission by a signal act by Yahweh, rain at wheat harvest being practically unheard of.

19-25. A closing exhortation to sincere worship of c
God. **22.** 'For his great name's sake': the honour of Yahweh's name was a familiar theme of the prophets; the name was enriched by the deliverance of Israel from Egypt, cf. 2 Sam. 7:23.

XIII, XIV Overthrow of the Philistine Garrison d
at Gibeah and Defeat of the Philistine Forces at Michmash—This may well be what was anticipated when Samuel said, 'do whatsoever your hand finds to do' (10:7), although in the present form of the narrative the Jabesh-gilead incident is what next follows.

XIII 1. Introduction to the reign of Saul; a redactional notice similar to those in the books of Kg. The numbers are missing from the Heb. text while the whole verse is lacking in LXX.

2-4. Jonathan overthrows the Philistine garrison. e
Jonathan's emergence is unheralded; the implication so far has been that Saul is still comparatively young. **2.** 'Three thousand': but in 15 Saul has only six hundred men with him. The two numbers cannot be reconciled and probably offer further evidence of the welding of different traditions in the narrative. 'Gibeah of Benjamin': the similarity of names seems to have led to some confusion. We must probably understand Jonathan to be at Geba and the Philistine garrison at Gibeah of Benjamin which is to be identified with Gibeath-elohim (10:5) and Gibeah of Saul (11:4). 'Sent home': after the assembly at Gilgal which had welcomed him on his return from Jabesh-gilead (11:15). **3.** Geba should probably be Gibeah, as implied by LXX. **Let the Hebrews hear is a** surprisingly empty message, indeed the whole verse seems to be in some disorder for it is naïve to say simply that the Philistines heard about the overthrow of their garrison. For 'Let the Hebrews hear' LXX has 'the servants have revolted', 'servants' being a misreading of 'Hebrews'. This points to a possible reconstruction of the verse as follows: 'When Jonathan routed the Philistine garrison at Gibeah the report went out among the Philistines, "The Hebrews have revolted". Saul caused a trumpet to be sounded through the whole land.' **4.** 'At Gilgal': this is probably an addition by the compiler. The people had been sent home (2) but are found to be assembled again at Gilgal in vv. 8–15*a*.

5-7. A note about the disposition of the opposing parties, with a concluding reference to Saul at Gilgal in readiness for the following episode. Beth-aven was close to Bethel and may have been the original name of Ai.

8-15a. Samuel makes the **first rejection of Saul:** f
a second is recorded after the battle with the Amalekites (ch. 15). Saul, tired of waiting for Samuel, defies his spiritual power and offers sacrifice in his absence. Samuel regards this as an act of rebellion against God and solemnly rebukes Saul telling him that he will not now be the founder of a dynasty; God will appoint someone else to follow him on the throne.

It is not easy to determine the place occupied by this episode in the Samuel-Saul traditions. There is a similar declaration of rejection in ch. 15. The

278f affinities of the latter are almost certainly with the later tradition. The anti-monarchic spirit of the present episode is against identifying it too closely with the earlier tradition. Moreover, a Gilgal episode is out of place against a background of conflict with the Philistines at Michmash. It seems therefore to be a later expansion of the earlier tradition and is heralded by 10:8 and 13:4, 7.

g When Saul offered sacrifices he was flouting Samuel's orders (10:8) and undermining thereby the foundations of theocracy, for Samuel regarded himself as God's agent in this matter. In general, it was quite legitimate for a ruler to preside at sacrifices. **12.** ' Entreated the favour of the Lord ' by sacrifice or by prayer, cf. Mal. 1:9. The Heb. phrase still shows the older anthropomorphic idea of smoothing the distorted face of an angry god. **13.** ' Would have established your kingdom ' by founding a dynasty. **14.** ' A man after his own heart ' : David, thus anticipating 16:12f. **15.** Why did Samuel go to Gibeah? There is no obvious reason. LXX has, ' Then Samuel arose and departed from Gilgal, and the rest of the people went up after Saul, to overtake the men of war, and when they had come from Gilgal to Gibeah of Benjamin . . .' Gibeah of Benjamin should probably be Geba (see on vv. 2 and 3) as in 16 : Jonathan had gained control of it (3).

15b-18. The disposition of the Israelite and Philistine troops.

h **19-23 Philistine Monopoly of Blacksmiths**—Excavations have shown that the Philistines possessed iron and it may be assumed that they had learnt how to work it before they migrated from their northern home. They seem to have held a monopoly of it in Palestine and to have guarded the secrets of its production and use. This passage shows that the Israelites lagged far behind the Philistines in the use of iron. **21** is obscure : the value of the pim appears to have been two-thirds of a shekel ; the translation ' a third of a shekel ' rests on a slight emendation of the Heb. Saul and Jonathan had weapons ; the pride of the Israelite historian could not endure the thought that Israel's leaders fell short of the Philistines in any respect.

279a **XIV A further Exploit of Jonathan against a Philistine Garrison**—The garrison was probably in Michmash from which place the Philistines had sent out their troops in three companies (13:17, 18). The Philistines suffer defeat at Michmash. Two background incidents are recorded : (i) Jonathan refreshes himself with honey in ignorance of his father's oath and thus puts himself in the wrong, and (ii) the people thoughtlessly slaughter looted animals without proper handling of the blood.

b **1-5.** Jonathan and his armour-bearer set out. **2.** ' The pomegranate tree which is at Migron ' : the tree was obviously a landmark and probably sacred but if it was at Gibeah why is it also described as being at Migron? The place mentioned in Isa. 10:28 is too far away. By a change of vowel the word could be translated ' threshing-floor ' giving good sense. **3.** ' Wearing an ephod ' : see on 2:28. The ephod was used in seeking oracles (see on 18). Ahijah is known only from this narrative. **4.** ' Rocky crag ', literally ' tooth '. They may have been needle-shaped. There is no certainty about locating the rocks or the defile on which they looked down. *Bozez* means ' shining ' and *Seneh* ' (blackberry-)bush '. The next verse implies that the rocks afforded shelter from observers both in Michmash and Geba.

c **6-15.** The plan of assault outlined by Jonathan is successfully carried out. **6.** ' Uncircumcised ' was a common derogatory nickname for the Philistines in Israel (Jg. 14:3). **9** offers a further example of how ordinary happenings are used as signs to determine actions which may in themselves be unconnected with the sign (cf. 10:3ff.). **14.** ' Acre of land ', literally ' yoke of land ', seems to be a contraction for a familiar term of land measurement and may mean what a pair of oxen would plough in a given time, perhaps a normal working day. 279c

16-23. Saul, seeing the enemy panic, at first uncertain what to do, numbers the people and begins to seek an oracle from God through the priest, but then decides on quick action to take advantage of the initial success. **18.** ' Ark of God ' : it is very unlikely that Ahijah had the Ark with him ; it was at Kiriath-jearim in charge of Eleazar (7:1). It is probably an error for ephod ; according to v. 3 Ahijah was carrying an ephod. This is supported by LXX, ' " Bring the ephod near ", for it was he who carried the ephod at that time before Israel '. **21.** The Hebrews who were among the Philistines were there either as mercenaries, probably coerced, or as refugees in the same manner as David and his men at a later time (ch. 29), or they may have been simply caught up in the Philistine advance. In any case their presence is evidence of the strength of Philistine domination. **22.** ' Hid themselves ', cf. 13:6, 14:11. d

24-30. Saul adjures the people not to eat until evening and until the enemy is defeated, but Jonathan, ignorant of the adjuration, eats some honey and is refreshed. Noteworthy are (i) the strict abstention of warriors while in battle ; they must pursue their duty without deviation, consecrated to their task, and (ii) that Jonathan allowed himself to criticise his father's command while at the same time accepting it as binding. **24** apparently gives two (alternative?) limits to the duration of the injunction, evening or the end of battle in Saul's favour. There is some confusion of text in 25f. Neither Heb. nor LXX give sense as they stand, moreover it may be noted that the word for ' forest ' in 25 and that for ' honeycomb ' in 26 are identical in Heb. An alternative reconstruction might be : ' Now there was a honeycomb on the ground in the open country. When the people came to the honeycomb the honey ran freely (or, the bees had left it) but no one put his hand to his mouth . . .' e

31-35. After a successful battle the people are faint and fall upon the enemy's cattle, slaughter it and eat. We must imagine that it is already evening, or that the people feel that victory is assured and are no longer tied by the adjuration. They incur guilt, however, in failing to observe the long-standing custom of draining the blood and thereby symbolically ensuring that the life of the animals is maintained (cf. Lev. 17:11, 14 ; Dt. 12:16 ; Gen. 9:4). To expiate the guilt Saul offered animals on behalf of the people in the proper way on an altar built for the purpose. **31.** The incident is placed on the same day as that on which Jonathan had incurred guilt by eating honey, but it does not naturally follow that incident, and in fact v. 36 should follow on 30 without a break. It is probably misplaced here. **32.** ' Ate them with the blood ' : it was customary in early Israel to make a sacrifice of any domestic animal slaughtered for food. In all cases the blood was regarded as belonging to Yahweh. The life was in it and must be returned to its source to ensure its renewal and the continuation of the species. The blood should have been allowed to drain from the animal into the ground and thus constitute a drink offering to Yahweh. **33.** ' A great stone ' as an improvised altar (cf. 6:14). f

36-42. Saul desires to press home his first success but is advised by the priest to consult God. Failure to receive an answer is taken to be a sign of guilt and they proceed to discover the identity of the guilty man, Jonathan, by use of the Urim and Thummim. The priest (37) was probably Ahijah who had the ephod (14:3) and with it, presumably, the Urim and Thummim. **37.** ' Inquired of God ' : the grammatical form of the Heb. phrase implies that the inquiry was made by some kind of manipulation of an object (such as Urim and Thummim). **41** has become the key verse for any discussion of the use of Urim and Thummim. It will be seen from RSV*n* that the translation follows the Vulg. supported by LXX. The shorter Heb. text is due to error known as homoeoteleuton whereby the g

9g scribe's eye ran from a word in one line (Israel in this case) to the same word in a lower line. This is the only place in OT where the actual use of Urim and Thummim is mentioned. We know nothing about the form, shape, size, colour or markings, or whether there were two objects, one called Urim and the other Thummim, or one object of which the markings on one face were 'Urim' and the other 'Thummim'. It may be significant that Urim begins with the first letter of the Heb. alphabet and Thummim with the last. One thing is clear, it served to indicate one of two parties.

h **43-46.** The soldiers are unwilling that Jonathan should die and they ransom him from the death penalty. Since the soldiers would firmly believe that God required the death of the offender it is unlikely that they would expect to 'ransom' Jonathan for anything less than a life and the implication cannot be resisted that they chose one of their own number to die for him. Philistine power was now checked for a time, but it was destined to rise again towards the end of Saul's reign and bring disaster on him and Jonathan.

i **47-51. Summaries of Saul's Enemies and of his Family**—How this section came to be placed here is not clear. Perhaps the writer felt that with Philistine power subdued the time had come for some kind of reflection on Saul's reign; moreover, the closing years of Saul's reign became so animated and charged with personal interest that summaries of this kind would be intrusive. The further 'rejection' of Saul in ch. 15 makes a summary at this point all the more suitable; ch. 15 itself closes the first part of the story of Saul.

j **47f. Saul's Successes over Enemies**—The same nations are listed in a similar summary for David's reign in 2 Sam. 8:1–12. Zobah was one of the Syrian states situated east of Lebanon between Hamath in the north and Damascus in the south. 'Put them to the worse': RV 'vexed them'; LXX 'was victorious' (connecting the Heb., perhaps rightly, with an Arabic cognate). The Amalekites are mentioned separately on account of the story to be told in ch. 15.

k **49-51 Saul's Family**—Ishvi is called Eshbaal in 1 Chr. 8:33 and is probably to be identified with Ishbosheth, 2 Sam. 2:8. Ishvi may be a contraction of Ishyahu which would be changed to Ishbaal at a time when Yahweh was called Baal, 'lord', and subsequently to Ishbosheth when baalism was strongly condemned by the prophets. (Bosheth means 'shame'.) Abinadab (31:2) is missing from this list. **51** should probably be read, with one slight change in Heb., as 'Kish, Saul's father and Ner, Abner's father, were sons of Abiel'.

l **52** is a proper sequel to 46 showing what steps Saul took to hold the Philistines at arm's length and also serves, indirectly, to introduce the David-Saul stories, David being one such valiant man.

m **XV War with the Amalekites: Rejection of Saul —1-3.** Samuel commands Saul to attack the Amalekites without mercy to punish them for their behaviour to Israel during the Exodus (Exod. 17:8–16; Dt. 25:17–19). The chapter belongs to the anti-monarchic tradition; Samuel is in authority over Saul and the story is told for the purpose of showing up Saul's failure to obey fully. The Amalekites were predatory Arabs living in the south (cf. 30:1–20 where they make raids on Philistine territory), and Saul undoubtedly had to make punitive expeditions against them. If we ask why an enemy so remote was made a test of Saul's obedience we must answer that Samuel himself had already (ch. 7) driven the Philistines from Israelite territory and the writer is able to link Saul's story with that of the Exodus by picking up the threat made after the battle of Rephidim that God would utterly blot out the remembrance of Amalek (Exod. 17:14). A common attitude towards the Amalekites binds this narrative with those in Exod. 17:8–16 and Dt. 25:17–19. The meaning of utterly destroy is to put under sacred ban (*ḥerem*) to Yahweh and ensure that no
human (profane) use whatever is made of it (see 279m
§253*mn*).

4-9. Saul carries out his commission in all but two n
respects, he spares Agag and he keeps some of the best cattle. **4.** The numbers seem astronomical: for the Philistine campaign we are told of three thousand (13:2), but of only six hundred in 13:15. The separate mention of Judah is in line with all we know of the loose connection of Judah with the other tribes in the Israelite confederacy. Telaim was near Ziph (23:14) but of unknown site. Kenites, see §90*f*. **8.** Agag: one of the same name is mentioned in Num. 24:7 but the identity is not certain.

10-16. Samuel comes to remonstrate with Saul. o
12. Carmel is not the mountain of that name but a town in the south of Judah (Jos. 15:55). The erection of a monument was a typical act of an oriental king. The first rejection is recorded as having taken place at Gilgal (13:8–15).

17-23. To meet Saul's claim that he has obeyed and p
defeated the Amalekites and will now sacrifice the animals (apparently a last-minute excuse) taken by the people, Samuel declares that sacrifice without full obedience is of no value, that Saul's disobedience is a rejection of God's word and that therefore God has rejected Saul from being king. **22f.** offer a terse summary of the prophetic attitude to sacrifice, and, like much of the prophetic material, is in poetic diction. **23.** 'Divination', see on Num. 22:7. 'Iniquity and idolatry': LXX has 'iniquity (sin) of idolatry' which is better. The word rendered 'idolatry' is *t^erāphîm*, rendered 'household gods' in Gen. 31:19 and 'image' in 1 Sam. 19:13. The context here shows that some kind of divinatory practice is meant and this is supported by the use of the word in Hos. 3:4 and Ezek. 21:21.

24-31. Saul, full of remorse, pleads for pardon and q
begs Samuel to go with him and share in the sacrifice. Samuel at first refuses. Later he relents and goes with Saul, but not until his torn robe, the result of Saul's importunity, has been made a symbol of the tearing of the kingdom from Saul to give to another (David). **29.** 'Glory of Israel' is a unique expression; the word for glory is different from that in Ichabod (4:21) and in the phrase 'the glory of Yahweh'. The contrast between God and man in terms of moral integrity became one of Israel's most significant contributions to religion (cf. Num. 23:19, etc.).

32f. Samuel himself kills Agag. r

34f. Both men go home and there is complete estrangement between them.

Part III XVI-XXXI Saul and David 280a

XVI 1-XVIII 5 The Introduction of David—This is a composite narrative: in one tradition David is a shepherd boy and in the other an accomplished young warrior and musician.

XVI 1-13 The Anointing of David—This intro- b
duction to the story of David shows no strong literary affinities and may be an editorial paragraph written when the composite tradition was put together. It follows closely upon ch. 15. Saul has been rejected as king and Samuel now designates his successor. The reference to Samuel's grief in v. 1 links with 15:35. But there remains little doubt in a reader's mind, after reading the subsequent account, that, no matter what tradition about David is preferred, his rise to power came about through his own prowess and that this anointing ceremony is an idealised picture. The continuing narrative (16:14ff.) knows nothing of it. It serves, however, to link closely together the leadership of Samuel on the one hand and that of David on the other. Both were charismatic leaders, the one spiritual, the other temporal.

1. 'Jesse the Bethlehemite': David therefore belonged to Judah. Saul had come from the tribe of Benjamin. Herein lies a cleavage within Israel which intensified as time went on; Judah on the one hand and Benjamin with the remaining tribes on the other.

280b Judah had always been a tribe apart. Bethlehem came to occupy a unique place in religious life. It was Samuel's prerogative to offer sacrifice so that if he came with a heifer (2), the proper animal for sacrifice (Gen. 15:9 ; Dt. 21:3ff.), his reason for coming was obvious and suspicions would be allayed. **4.** 'Trembling', i.e. deferential (Gen. 42:28 ; 1 Sam. 13:7). **6-9.** The names of David's three oldest brothers are given also in 17:13 and 1 Chr. 2:13, but in 1 Chr. 2:13 Shammah is given as Shimea. (Eliab is also called Elihu in 1 Chr. 27:18, and Shammah is also called Shimea(h) in 2 Sam. 13:3 and 1 Chr. 20:7 and Shimei in 2 Sam. 21:21.) **13.** The name 'David' is unique in the OT. The coming of the Spirit upon him endowed him with power to do those tasks that would fall to him as Saul's successor. As will be seen from v. 14 there is an implicit recognition that possession by the Spirit was not just a mark of God's favour but was virtually limited to leaders of the people—kings and prophets. **14-23.** Saul, rejected by God, loses the influence of the Spirit of Yahweh and finds himself tormented by an evil spirit. On the advice of his servants he finds a musician who can soothe him. The musician, David, is also a warrior. This is a different picture of David from that in ch. 17 where he is a shepherd. These two traditions, of which that of shepherd is the simpler and older, may be thought to continue the two lines of tradition already discerned in the story of the institution of the monarchy. **14.** 'An evil spirit from the Lord': the Hebrews had a limited understanding of mental phenomena and of mental disorders. One thing they knew—unusual effects have unusual causes. In prophetic frenzy it was a spirit from God that induced the prophet so to act and when Saul behaved in a similar manner it was natural to think of a similar cause. Though at this time his mad behaviour was not in any way allied to prophetic frenzy it was equally natural to ascribe it to an evil spirit. It was God who had endowed Saul with power to reign, but it was now also God who brought these mad fits upon him. The power for good was withdrawn from him and a power for evil took its place : God had complete control over human life. **19.** 'Who is with the sheep' : this must be regarded as a harmonising phrase to link this section with ch. 17 as well as with 16:1-13. **22.** 'Remain in my service' : cf. 14:52.

c **XVII David and Goliath**—Chs. 17 and 18 seem originally to have existed in two different forms, a longer one represented by the present Heb. text and by some LXX MSS (notably the Alexandrian Codex), and a shorter one represented by the Vatican MS of LXX. This latter omits 17:12-31, 41, 50; 17:55-18:5, 10, 11, 17-19. Each version offers an account that is complete in itself, although the shorter one minimises the differences between the two traditions about David.

d **1-11.** The background of the story is of war between Philistines and Israelites : both armies have taken up their positions and the Philistine champion utters his defiance and challenges Israel. **12-18.** David, apparently not hitherto known to the narrator of this episode and therefore given his family background (cf. 16:6-10), is sent by his father to visit his brothers at the front. **19-27.** He hears this challenge and utters his scorn of the champion, at the same time showing some interest in the promise of Saul's daughter to the man who should kill the Philistine. **28-30.** His oldest brother attempts to hold him back by anger and rebuke. **31-40.** But news of David's scorn reaches Saul, to whom David introduces himself as a shepherd, one who had fearlessly wrestled with lions or bears. Unable to wear Saul's armour, he goes out with only his sling. These latter ten verses are possibly secondary to the main story of the chapter for later on (55) Saul shows no knowledge of David. They may be an editorial attempt to link this story with that in 16:14-23 where David is already in Saul's service. **41-51a.** After an exchange of defiant words in which David affirms his loyalty to Yahweh, he strikes Goliath down and despatches him with his own sword. **51b-53.** The Philistines take it as a sign of Israelite superiority and flee with the Israelites in pursuit. **54.** Goliath's head is taken to Jerusalem, but David retains his armour. Another tradition was that the sword was deposited in the sanctuary at Nob and remained there until David claimed it on his flight from Saul (21:9). **55-8.** Finally, Saul makes inquiries about David's father as if he had never heard of him. 28

e **4.** 'Champion' : literally 'a man of between', i.e. ready to challenge one of the enemy's men in single combat between the lines. According to 2 Sam. 21:22 Goliath was one of the four descendants of the Rephaim in Gath (cf. Jos. 12:4, 13:12). Details about these fights in single combat were liable to confusion in tradition. According to 2 Sam. 21:19 it was Elhanan who killed Goliath, whereas in 1 Chr. 20:5 Elhanan is said to have slain Lahmi, brother of Goliath. If we take the cubit to be from the elbow to the finger tips, Goliath was considerably more than nine feet tall. The weight of his armour was several hundredweights (see on Weights and Measures). V. 15 can only be properly understood as an editorial addition to harmonise with 16:21. **25.** 'Free in Israel', i.e. without taxes or dues. **39.** 'And David girded his sword' : LXX, preferably, 'and he (Saul) fastened his sword on David'. The reference to Jerusalem in 54 was written at a time when the Israelites had been in Jerusalem long enough for it to seem no anachronism.

XVIII David's Relations with Saul and Jonathan 28
—**1-5.** David and Jonathan make a bond of friendship. The two friends, as part of their compact, exchange clothing (4) so that each wore something that represented the personality of his friend. This may have been the only outward sign of their covenant together, although the phrase in Heb. for making a covenant (3) bears the marks of the original practice of shedding blood to bind the parties together in its life force.

b **6-29.** The beginnings of Saul's envy of David. **6-9.** The women chant in David's honour. Their song shows that David was steadily usurping the honour and prestige which should belong to the king alone. **8.** 'What more can he have but the kingdom ?' or, 'even the kingdom will yet be his'.

c **10-16.** Saul, thwarted in his mad attempt to kill David, sends him out on campaign. In 19:8-10 a similar attempt on David's life is recorded, probably a second tradition. 'Went out and came in' on military campaigns.

d **17-19.** Saul promises to give his daughter Merab to David but then gives her to another man. This may be a sequel to the promise made in general terms in 17:25. In any case the narrative is compressed, for there must be an interval between the promise (17) and the discovery that Merab has been given to Adriel (19). It is probably to be thought that the interval was filled with campaigns against the Philistines. Saul obviously desired the Philistine danger to prevent the marriage. In 2 Sam. 21:8 Adriel is called son of Barzillai. Meholah is perhaps to be identified with Abel-Meholah in Jg. 7:22 ; 1 Kg. 19:16.

e **20-29.** David, in love with Michal, is offered her at the price of a hundred Philistines. Saul's expectation is that the price was out of David's reach and that he would fall in the attempt. **27.** 'Two hundred' : LXX has 'one hundred' evidently to harmonise. These two accounts, 17-19 and 20-9, are sometimes regarded as doublets of a single incident : both tell of David's prospect of marrying a daughter of Saul, and both speak of the Philistines as a possible means of preventing the marriage.

f **XVIII 30-XIX 7.** David becomes Saul's most successful general in skirmishes with the Philistines. Saul, his envy roused, tries to persuade his men, Jonathan among them, to put David to death. Jonathan eloquently pleads David's cause and he is reinstated. **8-10.** A further victory by David becomes the occasion

1f for a renewed outburst of Saul's madness and he again tries to take David's life (cf. 18:10–16).

g **11-17.** David's wife Michal is loyal to him and covers up his escape. The 'image' which she put in the bed is that known as *t^{e}rāphîm*; see on 15:23. This passage might imply that the object was a lifelike, life-size image, but in view of the uncertain meaning of the word here rendered 'pillow' we cannot be sure just what Michal did put on the bed. Did the magic element that clung to the teraphim act as a scare and discourage further pursuit? If so, the figures need not be thought to be life-size.

h **18-24.** An episode in the flight of David told to account for the proverb 'Is Saul also among the prophets?' There is another account of its origin in 10:9–13, which is woven into the earlier account of the monarchy. The affinities of the present story are with the later narrative. Samuel occupies a leading position and his home is at Ramah; David seeks refuge with him because it was he who had designated him as Saul's successor (16:1–13). It is to be noted that in the earlier story Samuel is distinguished from the prophets and does not join them in their prophetic frenzy; here he is one of them, at the head of them. The proverb must have been much used in Saul's day and became firmly embedded in every tradition about him so that it had to be accounted for by anyone who wrote up a history of Saul's reign. It may have been that his behaviour in some of his mad fits was at times indistinguishable from that of the dervish-like prophets when they were stimulated by music and dancing. 'Ramah', cf. 7:17, 15:34, 16:13. 'Naioth' is uncertain: it seems to be a proper name and occurs only in this context. It may in origin be a name describing the kind of settlement occupied by companies of prophets. 2 Kg. 6:1ff. offers evidence of such a settlement though it does not use this name for it. 'Secu' is not known.

i **XX 1-42 Jonathan proves his loyalty to David** by his willingness to discover what Saul's feeling about David was and by communicating it to David and assisting him in his flight. **5.** 'New moon': for the importance of the new moon see 2 Kg. 4:23; Isa. 1:13; Hos. 2:11 and Am. 8:5. This passage may be thought to imply that Saul held a regular court beginning on the first day of the new moon. **6.** 'A yearly sacrifice there for all the family' indicates that an annual family festival was customary and that the head of the family could command the attendance of other members (29). The family was one of the units for sacrificial purposes, as the town was another (9:12).

j **14. Loyal love**: Heb. *ḥesedh* (see §251*i*). Love and loyalty are of the very essence of any relationship based on a personal covenant; in Heb. these two aspects are bound together in the single word *ḥesedh.* Here it is described as 'loyal love of the Lord' perhaps for two reasons, first that the covenant was made binding in the presence of the Lord, and second, there could be no greater *ḥesedh* than that shown by Yahweh. **16.** Though the house of Saul must inevitably be counted David's enemies when he becomes king, Jonathan is not to be counted among them; he is to be reckoned as belonging to David's house. **25.** 'Sat opposite' is based on conjecture, but it is just possible that the Heb. word, based on a Syr. cognate, could mean 'was present'. **26.** 'He is not clean': ritual uncleanness lasted till evening of the day on which it was contracted; cf. Lev. 15:16; Dt. 23:10, 11. **30f.** Saul denounces Jonathan's disloyalty to his own family; he was breaking the strongest bond known to the Hebrews. The significance of Jonathan's utter loyalty to David probably lies in the strong link that it forged between David and the royal house. David was steadily drawing to himself the forces that would eventually carry him to the throne. He was, as it were, gathering to his own person the unseen forces of royalty. Not only so, but his attachment to Jonathan, public as it was, would build up a strong expectation in the people that David would succeed
to the throne. This was acknowledged by Jonathan, 281j
implicitly in 14–16 and explicitly in 23:17, and also by Saul himself in 24:20.

XXI 1-9. David, in his flight, reaches Nob and k
persuades Ahimelech to let him have the Showbread and the sword of Goliath. He is seen there by Doeg, chief of Saul's herdsmen. Nob was situated between Jerusalem and Anathoth. The priests from Shiloh seem to have settled there after the loss of Shiloh; Ahimelech was a great-grandson of Eli (22:9, 14:3). He met David trembling, i.e. deferentially. **4.** 'Holy bread', also called 'bread of the Presence' (6), consisted of twelve cakes set out in two rows (Lev. 24:5ff.). 'Kept themselves from women', this being one of the conditions for approaching holy things (Exod. 19:15). **5.** 'The vessels of the young men are holy': vessels is a euphemism. The verse is based on the Heb. practice of abstention from sexual intercourse during military campaigns. The story of David and Uriah hinges on this practice (2 Sam. 11:11). **6.** 'Hot bread', i.e. newly baked. **7. Doeg the Edomite** is here described as the chief of Saul's herdsmen. When he is mentioned in 22:9 he is called 'Doeg the Edomite who stood by the servants of Saul'. This difference of designation suggests that the two passages come from different lines of tradition, which may account for the fact that the present passage is not completely welded into the narrative. Doeg is said to be 'detained before the Lord', apparently performing some kind of ceremonial act within the precincts. Jer. 36:5, where the same verb is used, shows that the restraint could also prevent a man from entering the sanctuary. Doeg, as a servant of Saul, although he was an Edomite, would doubtless worship in the same way as his master, or as his Heb. companions in service did. There is no record that the sword of Goliath (9) had been deposited at Nob. In 17:54 it is recorded that David put Goliath's armour in his own tent. At some time it had evidently been dedicated to God. 'Ephod': it is very unlikely that this was the garment called 'ephod' (see §199*d*), it is much more likely to have been something in the nature of an image.

10-15. David flees to Gath where Achish was king, l
but discovering that the men there knew about him and could repeat the song of the Hebrew women (18:7) he conceals his identity by pretending to be mad, and apparently does not stay there. The narrative clearly intends us to draw the conclusion that he did not stay, although in 27:1f. he goes to Achish as one well known and sure of a welcome. It has been suggested that this story became current among those who felt that a future king of Israel could not stoop so low as to seek refuge with the Philistines. **11.** The description of David as king of the land is an anachronism that would be easily made by the historian.

XXII 1-5 Three Details connected with David's 282a
Flight—1, 2. David establishes a centre at **Adullam** in the Shephelah (Jos. 15:35). There he is joined by his family and by men who for various reasons were outlaws like himself until the company was four hundred strong. **3, 4.** He places his parents under the protection of the king of Moab. This is not unnatural if the book of Ru. is right in making Ruth the Moabitess a great-grandmother of David. **5.** On the advice of Gad the prophet David moves from Adullam into Judaean territory, to the forest of Hereth. There are two difficulties here that make it probable that the verse is an editorial addition due to misunderstanding. First, Adullam is in Judah so that David would not go from there into the land of Judah, and second it is strange to find Gad entering into David's life at this point and not Samuel. We do not come across him otherwise until 2 Sam. 24:11. It is, of course, possible that 'stronghold' in this verse is not Adullam but some place outside Judah.

6-23. A sequel to 21:7. Saul challenges the loyalty b
of his followers where David is concerned, whereupon

282b Doeg reports what he saw at Nob. Saul causes the priests to be summoned and after inquiry has them put to death. There was one survivor, Abiathar son of Ahimelech, who escaped to David. **6.** ' Tamarisk tree ', cf. on 10:3. ' On the height ', or, ' at Ramah '. **7.** ' You Benjaminites ': in appealing to his own tribesmen in this way Saul is anticipating the cleavage which ultimately led to the disruption of the kingdom ; cf. the cry of revolt raised by Sheba, 2 Sam. 20:1. ' Thousands and hundreds ', cf. 8:12. ' To lie in wait ' (8 and 13) is not well suited to the context ; LXX has ' enemy ' ; this may give a truer meaning to the Heb. word which could mean ' intriguer ' (from an Arabic cognate). The Edomite (18), although apparently a Yahweh worshipper (21:7), had no compunction in doing what the Israelites shrank from. Eighty-five makes a fair-sized priestly community. ' Wore the linen ephod ' : but there is no certain evidence that it was the regular priestly garment (see on 2:18). LXX^B omits linen and if that is right the reference may then be taken to mean the ephod used for divinatory purposes (2:28). The pronoun in 19 must refer to Saul and we are to understand that Nob ceased to exist or to be used as a sanctuary. Abiathar (20) is now the sole survivor of the house of Eli, which had evidently moved from Shiloh to Nob (21:1). Abiathar carried the ephod with him (23:6).

c **XXIII-XXVII Incidents during David's Outlawry**—Within these chapters there are two stories of how David spared Saul's life after finding him in his power, 24:1–7 and 26:6–12. They probably represent two different traditions in existence concerning these years in the same way as there are two traditions about the earlier times.

Ch. 23 illustrates the way in which Philistine power pressed upon the Israelites at that time. The chapter opens with a report to David that the Philistines are raiding Keilah and closes with a report to Saul, as he pursued David, that they were raiding territory in Judah.

d **XXIII 1-5 David rescues Keilah from the Philistine Raiders**—Keilah is in the Shephelah. **2.** ' Inquired of the Lord ', see on 14:37. Abiathar was probably already with David so that his services as priest could be used. **6-14. David consults God about Saul's threat** to catch him in Keilah. The ephod was used on this occasion. Clearly it was more than merely a garment ; it was an instrument for seeking God's will. It may be noted that questions are put which require answer ' yes ' or ' no '. **15-18. Jonathan comes to David** to pledge loyalty to one whom he declares to be the future king. With fine dramatic force the writer tells his readers about this visit immediately after he has said that Saul sought for David in vain. Moreover, Jonathan's acceptance of David as king-designate has a noble dignity of its own (see also on 20:30). His hope to be next to David in the kingdom (17) was, of course, unfulfilled because of his death. **18.** ' Covenant ': this overlooks the fact that they had already made a covenant (18:3), and doubtless belongs to another tradition. **19-24a. The men of Ziph betray David** to Saul as the people of Keilah had threatened to do (12). Jeshimon is the wilderness of Judah lying to the south of the Judaean hills : the wilderness of Ziph lies farther south still. Horesh and Hachilah remain unidentified. **24b-29.** Saul, in pursuit of David, is informed of Philistine raids on his own territory and gives up the pursuit. The wilderness of Maon is simply that part of the Judaean wilderness that lies round Maon. The Arabah is the name given to the Jordan valley both above and below the Dead Sea.

e **XXIV David spares Saul's Life—1-7.** Saul retires within a cave and unwittingly puts himself within David's reach. David refuses to do any injury to the person of the Lord's anointed (see §274*f* on 2:10) but cuts off the skirt of his robe as a token. To have injured Saul would have meant laying himself open to God's vengeance. **8-15.** David reveals himself to Saul and shows him the token strip of cloth. 28 He goes on to try to convince Saul that his life was perfectly safe as far as David was concerned. In the reference to the pursuit of a dead dog or a (solitary) flea we may probably see allusion to a popular proverb of that day. After using one proverb (13) and acknowledging it as such it is quite likely that the writer might use a further one unacknowledged. **16-22.** Saul, apparently moved to generosity of spirit through David's loyalty to his king, gives David his blessing, assuring him that he would succeed to the throne and begging him to spare the survivors of his house. Implicit here is the recognition of the powerful influence of God on the course of events. David, honouring Saul as God's anointed king, will not injure his person and lay himself open to reprisal from God ; in that way he holds himself aloof from anything that would invalidate him from holding the sovereignty. Saul, knowing David to be God's appointed successor to himself, gives him a royal blessing.

XXV David, Nabal and Abigail—This incident, f though it does not materially further the cause of David, yet illumines the story of David by its rich personal interest and by the way in which it helps to raise him above the ordinary level of life. Particularly noteworthy is Abigail's plea for avoidance of bloodshed. The story puts into striking relief the churlishness of Nabal, whose name means ' churl ', and the noble loyalty of Abigail towards David.

1a. Notice of the death of Samuel. This occurs again g in 28:3. There it is a natural introduction to the story of the witch of Endor ; here it seems to have been inserted because Saul's blessing of David as future king could be regarded as closing the work of Samuel. Moreover, while Saul is a ' rejected ' king and David still an outlaw, it serves to keep Samuel before the reader as the one who was the true head of the community until the monarchy had been well established.

1b-8. David sends men to Nabal at shearing time h soliciting a gift, in effect to provide sustenance for himself and his men. **1.** Paran lies so far to the south, towards the Sinai peninsula, that LXX ' Maon ' is probably right (see 23:24). **2.** Carmel means ' garden land ' ; it is therefore natural that there should be more than one place bearing the name. This one lies some 15 miles west of the Dead Sea. ' Shearing his sheep ' : sheep were as much valued for their wool as their meat (2 Kg. 3:4) and shearing time was of such importance that it was celebrated as a festival (see also 2 Sam. 13:23). David may have laid claim to some of the wool as well as the food provided for the feast (8, 11). **3.** ' Calebite ': Hebron and the territory to the south had been allotted to Caleb.

9-13. David's request is rejected and he prepares to i use force. **10.** ' Nowadays ' reads like a typical dissatisfaction with the age in which one lives, but it may also reflect the conditions of Saul's reign ; he may well have been faced with disaffection as David was to be later. **13.** ' Remained with the baggage '; in 30:7–25 it is recognised that such people play their part and are entitled to their share of the spoil. The numbers are the same here as those given in ch. 30. Six hundred seems to have been a ' round number ' for military units, cf. Exod. 14:7 ; Jg. 3:31, 18:16, 17, 20:47 ; 1 Sam. 13:15, 14:2, 23:13, 27:2, 30:9, 10 ; 2 Sam. 15:18.

14-17, 18-22. Nabal's men consult their mistress j Abigail who takes David a present, meeting him as he is on his way to carry out an oath he has made against Nabal.

23-31. Abigail cleverly and tactfully pleads with David not to commit bloodshed so that, when he comes to the sovereignty, he may suffer no self-reproach for it. When she refers to David as ' bound in the bundle of the living in the care of the Lord ' (29), Abigail is expressing the normal Heb. notion of sovereignty as something directly ordained and protected by God. It is probably significant that this

2j recognition of David's ultimate accession is made by a Calebite; the Calebites had close associations with Judah. **32-5.** David expresses gratitude to her.

k **36-38.** Next morning, when his drunkenness had worn off, Abigail tells Nabal what she has done and the news brought on what we might diagnose as a stroke from which he died ten days later. To the Heb. mind his death, coming suddenly, could appear only as the punishment of God for his unco-operative attitude towards David. **39-42.** David sees the hand of the Lord in Nabal's death and takes Abigail to be his own wife.

l **43, 44 Summary of David's other Marriages**—Michal had been faithful to David while he remained in Judah, but when he became an outlaw her loyalty apparently ended. It is to be remembered, however, that when David was back again as king in Hebron there was nothing to prevent him asking for her to be returned to him, 2 Sam. 3:13f. In this later passage Palti's name is given as Paltiel.

m **XXVI David spares Saul's Life**—This is a second story of how Saul comes within David's reach and suffers no harm. The first is in ch. 24. Both stories begin with a betrayal of David's hiding-place by Ziphites. They may represent divergent traditions of a single occasion.

1-5. The Ziphites betray David to Saul (cf. 23:19ff.). Saul comes against him with a picked army but David engages in counter-espionage and learns where Saul's tent was. Abner was mentioned as Saul's commander-in-chief in 14:50.

n **6-12.** David and Abishai go to Saul's camp and carry away the spear and water jug from beside Saul. David declares to Abishai that no man can strike the Lord's anointed with impunity (cf. 24:10). **6.** 'Ahimelech the Hittite': no other mention is made of him. On Hittites see §86*d*. Uriah was also a Hittite (2 Sam. 11:3). 'Joab's brother Abishai the son of Zeruiah': Zeruiah was sister to David and there was a third brother, Asahel, 2 Sam. 2:18. It is probably on account of their close connection with David that their mother's name is given instead of their father's which is more usual. 2 Sam. 2:32 mentions their father's grave at Bethlehem. Joab became commander-in-chief and then finally supported Adonijah's cause against Solomon. Abishai became chief of the Thirty, 2 Sam. 23:18f., of whom Asahel was one.

13-16. David taunts Abner with his failure to prevent access to Saul, a failure all the more reprehensible because Saul is the Lord's anointed.

o **17-20.** David, speaking to Saul, who appears and speaks when he hears David's voice, disclaims knowledge of any fault for which he could be pursued and asks that if God is angry and has turned Saul against him then a sacrifice should be made, but if men have wronged him and incited Saul against him then they should be put under a curse. **19.** 'Go, serve other gods', i.e. be banished from his own land and from the territory in which Yahweh is worshipped (see 2 Kg. 5:17). This anticipates the stay in Philistine territory, 27:1ff.

21-25. David explains to Saul why he did not touch him, i.e. he was held back by reverence for the sanctity of the anointed king and he expresses the hope that his life may be similarly held in reverence. Saul then gives David his blessing.

3a **XXVII David among the Philistines—1-4.** In order to be right out of Saul's reach David crosses over to Philistine territory thus giving truth to his own statement (26:19) that he had been banished from his own country and from the worship of Yahweh. He is received by Achish in such a way as to suggest previous acquaintance, see 21:10–15. Achish is also mentioned in 1 Kg. 2:39ff. The principal Philistine cities each had its own ruler for whom the OT uses a word (*seren*) found in no other connection and possibly therefore a loan word from the Philistine language.

b **5-7.** Achish assigned Ziklag to David. In Jos. 15:31 Ziklag is reckoned as Judahite territory, and in Jos. 19:5 as Simeonite (cf. also Neh. 11:28). It was probably a town on the eastern fringe of Philistine territory which David would naturally annex to Judah when he became king (6*b*). 283b

8-12. David raids local Bedouin tribes but conceals it from Achish by claiming to have raided Israelite territory, thus building up a false trust in his fidelity to Achish and his enmity to his own people. 'Geshurites': Geshur lies to the north of the Sinai peninsula, Jos. 13:2. 'Girzites' occur only here; there may be some confusion of text, a variant reading is Gezrites, i.e. people of Gezer; some MSS of LXX omit altogether. 'Amalekites', see 15:2. 'Negeb' (10) is the name given to the district to the south of the Judaean hills and extending to the desert. It is repeated here in designating different parts of it. For Jerahmeelites see 1 Chr. 2:9, 25ff. and for Kenites §90*f*. c

XXVIII-XXXI War with the Philistines and the Death of Saul and Jonathan—XXVIII 1-25 Saul consults the Witch of Endor—After briefly mentioning that the Philistines were gathering for war with Israel and that David went with the Philistine armies in Achish's company the narrative begins to prepare the way for the account of Saul's death by showing graphically what a lonely and deserted man Saul had become, deserted even by God. Samuel was dead, dreams and the oracle-giving Urim and even the prophets were silent, and Saul resorted to necromancy only to hear Samuel's returning shade pronounce Saul's almost immediate end. d

3a repeats 25:1 but is probably a necessary introduction here to the story of Saul's visit to Endor; 3*b* anticipates 9 and may be editorial. In any case the whole of 3 breaks the sequence between 2 and 4. Dream, Urim and the prophets (6) were the three normal ways in which the will of God was sought and revelation received. For direct revelation through dream cf. 3:2–9 and 1 Kg. 3:5ff.; for oracle given by manipulation of the Urim by a priest cf. 14:41. **7.** 'medium' or 'a woman who controls a ghost (familiar spirit)'; cf. Isa. 8:19. It is clear from the context that necromancy is meant by this. There is no record of Saul's having prohibited the practice of necromancy or other 'black' arts, but it is the kind of thing that one might expect Samuel to have inspired in Saul and it is fully in keeping with the purer Yahwism of the prophets. **13.** 'A god', i.e. a supernatural figure. **15-19.** Samuel expresses anger at this resort to necromancy, repeats previous denunciations and rejections of Saul and adds that on the very next day Saul and his sons would fall before the Philistines. There is no hint of a survivor: the narrator has steadily dethroned Saul and prepared the way for David's succession. **20-5.** At all this Saul is cast into utter despair and can only with difficulty be persuaded to eat.

XXIX. David is not allowed to remain with the Philistine armies. The Philistine commanders become aware of David and his men in their ranks and, in spite of all the pleas of Achish who shows a strong loyalty to David, they insist that he should withdraw and go home. They recall the song of the women (18:7, 21:11) in which David is ascribed ten times the honour given to Saul. In 28:4 the Philistines are said to be at Shunem and the Israelites at Gilboa, here (1) they are at Aphek and Jezreel respectively. They are probably not contradictory statements but represent a different geographical point of view. The fountain in Jezreel probably lay at the foot of Mt Gilboa and Aphek was a common enough name to expect to meet with anywhere (see on 4:1); indeed the word means 'enclosure' or 'stronghold' and may have been given to the place after the Philistines gathered there. 'Lords of the Philistines', see 5:8; Jg. 3:3. **9.** 'As an angel of God': a proverbial saying, cf. 2 Sam. 14:20, 19:27. e

XXX. David defeats the Amalekite marauders who had raided Ziklag in his absence. A ruling is made con- f

283f cerning the dividing of spoil between combatants and non-combatants. **1.** 'Negeb', see 27:10. **2.** 'Killed no one': so that the captives could be sold in the slave market. **11, 13.** They had a young Egyptian slave with them which suggests that Egypt was their natural market (cf. Gen. 37:28, 36). **6.** 'Strengthened himself in the Lord': asserting David's continuing faith in Yahweh in spite of his declaration (26:19) that to be outlawed meant worshipping other gods. **7-10.** It is very properly followed by the notice that on this occasion he inquired of Yahweh by means of the Ephod handled by Abiathar (cf. 23:6, 9). In vv. 9, 10 the same figures are given for combatants and non-combatants as are given in 25:13. The brook Besor: a wadi S. of Gaza, possibly Wâdī Ghazzeh. **14.** 'Cherethites': this seems to be a name for a section of the Philistines or for a people closely connected with them. 16*b* mentions Philistines and not Cherethites, so they are virtual synonyms. In Zeph. 2:5 and Ezek. 25:16 LXX has Cretans for Cherethites. Crete and other islands or coastlands in the Aegean sea may have been the original home of the Philistines (see §89*b*). David later had Cherethites (and Pelethites) in his bodyguard, 2 Sam. 8:18. **17.** 'Four hundred': that so many fled on camels creates an impression of an immense host. The exact detail of number and the mention of camels look as though the author intended to make mention of them again elsewhere. **21-5** are of special interest in showing us a law in the making. Although it is stated in Num. 31:27 and applied in Jos. 22:8, this narrative clearly shows that this was a new situation for which David had to lay down a rule that then became binding for all time, namely that those who remain with the baggage shall share equally with those who fight. **26-31.** David woos the men of Judah by sending them presents. The places named are all in the Negeb but not all identified. For Racal (29) LXX has Carmel, the place from which Abigail came.

g **XXXI The Battle of Gilboa; Death of Saul—2.** 'The sons of Saul', see 14:49, and for Abinadab, 1 Chr. 8:33. Saul's armour-bearer was no more willing to kill Saul (4) than David had been and for the same reason, Saul was Yahweh's anointed. V. 7 shows that at the death of Saul the Philistines virtually ruled the whole of the territory occupied by Israelites. Only David, in the south, was independent of them. The valley is that of Jezreel. **9.** 'Their idols': this is probably a later alteration of 'their gods'. The announcement may have taken the form of a parade of trophies. 'Ashtaroth' is plural of Ashtoreth (cf. §295*i*): but a temple would probably be in honour of one deity only and we should probably read Ashtoreth as implied by LXX.

h **11-13.** The men of Jabesh-gilead, in gratitude (see ch. 11), fetch the bodies of Saul and his sons and give them proper burial. There is no evidence that the Hebrews burned their dead instead of burial; another possible translation of the phrase at the end of 12 is 'they anointed them with spices' i.e. ready for burial. 'Tamarisk tree', cf. 10:3, 22:6.

THE SECOND BOOK OF SAMUEL

Part I I-VIII David's Kingship

284a **I-IV Dual Monarchy and Civil War—I 1-16.** News of the deaths of Saul and Jonathan reaches David at Ziklag: his grief finds immediate outlet in harsh treatment of the Amalekite news-bearer. A comparison of this account with that given in 1 Sam. 31 reveals several differences: here an Amalekite kills Saul, there the armour-bearer is unwilling to do so and Saul dies by his own hand; here there are chariots and horsemen close by, there mention is made of archers only; here Saul is seized by 'anguish', there he is badly wounded; here one of David's young men kills the Amalekite, in 2 Sam. 4:10 it is implied that David himself did so. There are therefore 2
two traditions of the death of Saul. It is not possible to separate them completely: a tentative division is this: earlier tradition (J?) 1 Sam. 31; 2 Sam. 1:1–4, 11, 12; later tradition (E?) 2 Sam. 1:6–10, 13–16; v. 5 forms a connecting link looking forward to 6–10 and yet by referring to Jonathan looking back to 1–4. Another view is that the divergences are embellishments by the same narrator; the Amalekite's claim to have killed Saul and David's claim (4:10) to have killed the messenger being due to rhetorical exaggeration (Pfeiffer, *Introduction to the OT*, 350f.). **8.** 'An Amalekite': so far north as Gilboa? Probably there are two reasons for his appearance in this later tradition. First, there was so strong a reverence for the person of the anointed king that it was unthinkable that an Israelite should kill him (1 Sam. 31:4). Second, since this belongs probably to the same tradition as that which told of Saul's rejection because he did not entirely annihilate the Amalekites (1 Sam. 15) the narrator may have felt a sense of 'poetic justice' in Saul's death at the hands of an Amalekite. **10.** The crown and the armlet were the royal insignia; there is no other reference to the armlet (but see 2 Kg. 11:12). **14.** 'The Lord's anointed', see 1 Sam. 24:6, 26:11.

17-27 David's Lament over Saul and Jonathan— b
18. 'It should be taught'; as will be seen from the mg. Heb., has here a word normally translated 'bow'; if we assume the root *ḳāshāh* we might translate 'he said that, grim though it was, it should be taught'. 'Jashar', see Jos. 10:13. 21*a* is difficult; another possibility would be to translate:

> Let no dew fall upon the mountains in Gilboa,
> Nor rain upon you, O treacherous fields.

21. 'Not anointed with oil': not cleaned or cared for; oil would preserve the leather fittings.

II 1-4a David becomes King over Judah in c
Hebron—1. 'After this' is an opening phrase used several times in 2 Sam. to link a new section of narrative to what has gone before, when it does not follow closely on the preceding verses. It occurs also in 8:1, 10:1, 13:1, and 15:1. 'Inquired of the Lord', see on 1 Sam. 14:41. Hebron was an ancient city of southern Palestine formerly known as Kiriath-arba, Jos. 15:13. Its history goes back to the time of Abraham, Gen. 13:18, and before the capture of Jerusalem it was the natural Judahite centre.

4b-7. David sends an embassy to the people of Jabesh- d
gilead commending their loyalty to Saul (1 Sam. 31:11, 12) and extending his favour towards them as he now becomes king. The section appears to be fragmentary; there is no statement of how the people of Jabesh-gilead received the embassy or responded to David's appeal.

8-11. Ishbosheth, the sole survivor of Saul's sons, is e
proclaimed king of Israel at Mahanaim, east of the Jordan. On the name Ishbosheth see 1 Sam. 14:49. Abner, a cousin of Saul, was commander-in-chief of the army (1 Sam. 14:50) and at first played a leading part in trying to hold the kingdom for Saul's house, but later betrayed it into the hands of David (3:6ff.). The proclamation had to take place east of Jordan because the Philistines controlled the west. There is a dramatic element in the placing of this immediately after the notice of David's embassy to Jabesh-gilead. Gilead is mentioned as one of the districts over which Ishbosheth became king and one wonders whether David's messengers were embarrassed. Ashurites, i.e. the people of Assyria, but it is unlikely that Ishbosheth became king over them. We might read Geshurites with Peshitta and Vulg. (Geshur being adjacent territory, east of the Galilean lakes, and not to be confused with the Arabian Geshur, 1 Sam. 27:8), or read Ashrites with the Targum. **10.** 'Two years': this figure gives some difficulty for we are to assume that it was more than five years before the Israelites were prepared to accept David's sovereignty. That David was king

4e 'over Judah' for seven and a half years is repeated in 5:5.

f **12-32 Civil War—12-17. The First Incident**—a single combat encounter between twelve warriors from either side at Gibeon resulting in victory for David's men. Single-handed combat seems to have been a practice in those days, e.g. Goliath and David. **18-23.** Events take a new turn when David's three nephews set off in pursuit of Abner ; one of them, Asahel, outstrips his brothers and gains on Abner. Abner kills him and thus creates a blood feud whose outcome is told in 3:26–30. **22.** 'Lift up my face to your brother Joab' : because of the blood-feud ; it would fall to Joab to avenge Asahel. **23.** 'With the butt of his spear', or, 'with a backthrust of his spear'. **24-8.** Joab and Abishai continue the pursuit but Abner is reinforced by Benjamites and, thus strengthened, appeals for a break in hostilities. Joab realises Abner's stronger position and agrees to do so although he says he had been confident that hostilities would have ended by morning anyhow. **24.** Ammah and Giah were local landmarks ; the words bear the meanings 'aqueduct' and 'gusher' respectively and may be features in the local waterways. **29-32.** Both combatant armies return to their headquarters. Arabah is the name given to the Jordan valley.

g **III-IV The End of the House of Saul—III 1.** A summary notice that the civil war was protracted : it is not in contradiction to 2:28 for it refers to the whole period and not the subsequent period.

2-5. David's family born in Hebron. For those born in Jerusalem, see 5:13–15. Amnon was killed by Absalom for his outrage on Tamar, 13:1ff. Nothing is known of Chileab who would become the oldest after Amnon's death, unless he had died young ; LXX gives his name as Delaiah and 1 Chr. 3:1 as Daniel. Absalom rebelled against his father, 2 Sam. 15–18. Nothing further is known of his mother than is recorded here. Her father's name, Talmai, is the same as that of one of the giants, Jg. 1:10. Geshur is probably the Syrian state of that name, see on 2:9. Adonijah attempted to secure the succession in place of Solomon, 1 Kg. 1. Shephatiah occurs as a proper name in Jer. 38:1, but we know nothing further of this son. Ithream is probably the same as Jerimoth (2 Chr. 11:18) whose daughter became the wife of Rehoboam.

h **6-11.** An accusation of Abner by Ishbosheth concerning his father's concubine Rizpah becomes the occasion of Abner's decision to further David's cause. Rizpah : see 21:8ff. To hold her may have given Abner some claim to be Saul's successor, cf. 16:21 ; 1 Kg. 2:13ff. **8.** The term 'dog's head' is not found elsewhere but is obviously contemptuous ; the words 'of Judah' suggest suspicion of treachery and if that is so Abner dramatically makes it true. 'From Dan to Beersheba', 1 Sam. 3:20.

i **12-16.** Abner sends to David to negotiate, claiming that the whole land is under his control. David is willing to enter into agreement on condition that Abner brings with him David's former wife Michal, daughter of Saul, who had been given to Paltiel (cf. 1 Sam. 25:44). This would renew David's connection with the house of Saul and smooth the path to sovereignty. **14.** David's direct appeal to Ishbosheth for the return of Michal may come from a different tradition from that of vv. 12, 13, or it may simply mean that his dealings with Abner were secret and that he could ask for Michal openly. **17-19.** Abner confers with those in Israel and Benjamin whom he knew to be ready to see David on the throne—apparently a not inconsiderable number. **20, 21.** Abner then comes to David leading a deputation and an agreement is reached.

j **22-25.** Joab hears of Abner's visit and of the success of his mission—'he has gone in peace'—and is suspicious. Joab has double reason to distrust Abner, first because of the blood feud between them (2:18–23) and second for jealousy of Abner's influence on David.

24. 'So that he is gone' : LXX adds 'in peace', 284j
cf. 23.

26-30. Joab recalls Abner and kills him as he comes, k
unsuspecting, into Hebron. David, when he hears of it, disclaims any part or interest in the deed and lays a curse on Joab. **26.** 'The cistern of Sirah', north of Hebron : water supply was so urgent a necessity in southern Palestine that cisterns might well become landmarks. **29.** 'Holds a spindle', i.e. fit only for women's work. Abishai is mentioned in 30 because he played a part in the story in 2:18.

31-39. David publicly laments the death of Abner, a l
great man, who died as a victim of wicked men's might. He then gives expression to a feeling of weakness, anointed prince though he is, when confronted with these cruel nephews of his, the sons of Zeruiah. His genuine sympathy for Abner arouses the admiration of the people. In his own interests he is careful to make his behaviour towards the remnant of Saul's kingdom as correct as possible. **34** means that Abner's death was like that of a man of lowest rank. A warrior would have been able to defend himself, or would have been in fetters as a prisoner-of-war. **35.** It was customary to fast during mourning, 1 Sam. 31:13 ; 2 Sam. 12:20f.

IV The Murder of Ishbosheth—1-3. Ishbosheth's m
courage failed him after Abner's death ; so did that of his followers, two of whom are introduced here to prepare for the story to follow. **2.** Rimmon is here a personal name but is also the same as that of one of the gods worshipped at Damascus. Beeroth ('wells') is named in Jos. 9:17 as one of the Gibeonite cities, hence the point of emphasising that it belongs to Benjamin. **3.** Gittaim obviously lay outside Benjamite territory at this time but was later included (see Neh. 11:33).

4. A parenthetical reference to Mephibosheth who is n
the subject of the story in 9:1ff. There seems no reason for its inclusion at this point.

5-12. Rechab and Baanah murder Ishbosheth and carry his head to David at Hebron expecting a reward. David, maintaining his correct attitude towards the house of Saul, orders the men to be killed as he had killed the man who brought news of the death of Saul (1:15).

V-VII Jerusalem becomes the Capital of the 285a
Hebrew Kingdom—V. The capture of Jerusalem and defeat of the Philistines. **1-5.** David becomes king over all Israel and his accession is ratified by solemn covenant. **4, 5** are part of the Deuteronomic framework, cf. 2:10, 11. **6-10.** David captures and occupies Jerusalem. 'Jebusites' : Jerusalem was originally called Jebus (Jg. 19:10). The allusion to David's actual attack on the city is obscure. Another way of translating 6*b* is : 'You will not come in except after getting rid of the blind and the lame', which serves as a better introduction to David's command to attack the blind and lame. The meaning is that they deemed Jerusalem to be so impregnable that it could easily be held against attack. **8. Get up the water shaft to attack :** in later times there were certainly two water shafts, the Siloam tunnel and Warren's shaft, which could have given a raider entrance into the city, but there is no certain evidence that either of these or a similar shaft was in existence in David's day. Moreover, the verb normally means 'touch', 'reach' or 'strike' and not 'go up'. LXX has 'dagger' instead of water shaft : if we accept this it allows the translation : 'let him stab the lame and blind, who are hated by David's soul, with his dagger'. **9. Stronghold :** following Josephus the tradition has been to identify this with the SW. hill but scholars are now of the opinion that it was on the east hill above Gihon. 'The Millo', literally the 'filling', could refer to a dam, rampart or earthwork. LXX, 'the citadel'. It was not a line of fortification but rather one particular part of the fortifications from which David could begin his building.

11, 12. David's increasing power attracted the atten- b

285b tion of Hiram of Tyre who sent expert craftsmen to help David in his building. This may belong to a later part of his reign when the Philistines were subdued. The semi-nomad Israelites were probably glad to enlist the technical help of the Phoenicians.

c **13-16.** The family born to David in Jerusalem (cf. 3:2–5 for the Hebron family); the list also occurs in 1 Chr. 3:5, 6; 14:4–6. Of the eleven sons mentioned here, only Solomon and Nathan occur outside these lists, Solomon as king, and Nathan in the genealogy of Jesus in Lk. 3:31. 1 Chr. adds Nogah and a second Eliphelet.

d **17-21. Battle with the Philistines** in the valley of Rephaim, south of Jerusalem, at Baal-perazim, i.e. the place of bursting forth. It is difficult to arrange the events of this chapter chronologically. The capture of Jerusalem, a strategic move, was likely to be one of David's earliest tasks, but, unless he felt in need of it as a base for the Philistine war, and there is no evidence that he used it as such, it would more naturally follow the subjugation of the Philistines. Some think that if Ishbosheth did only reign two years (2:10) then the Philistine war could be placed in the period before David became king of all Israel. **17.** The stronghold is probably Adullam, as implied in 23:13f.

e **22-25.** A further account of fighting with the Philistines in the valley of Rephaim. There is a difference of outlook shown in the narration here. When David inquires of Yahweh he is told to wait until he hears the sound of marching in the balsam trees, i.e. until God himself joins battle and puts the Philistines into panic, then David is to press home the advantage thus gained. In all probability the incidents told in 21:15ff. and 23:8ff. belong to this campaign in the valley of Rephaim.

f **VI Removal of the Ark to Jerusalem**—It had remained in Abinadab's house at Kiriath-jearim in the charge of Eleazar, 1 Sam. 7:1. Its removal to Jerusalem was doubtless designed to draw all Israelite loyalty towards Jerusalem and establish the chief sanctuary there.

1-5. David takes thirty thousand picked men and fetches the Ark from Kiriath-jearim (here called Baale-judah; cf. Jos. 15:9–10 where it is called Baalah, and Jos. 15:60 where it is called Kiriath-baal). They carry it on a new cart (see on 1 Sam. 6:7) driven by Uzzah and Ahio, sons of Abinadab, and celebrate its removal with dances and song. Two questions arise: (1) Why is not Eleazar mentioned? (but Uzzah could be a short form of it), and (2) Is Ahio a proper name, as rendered by RSV, or does it here mean 'his brother' and conceal a reference to Eleazar or even, as some have suggested, to Zadok?

g **6-11.** At a certain threshing-floor Uzzah accidentally violates the sanctity of the Ark and instantly perishes. The incident roused both David's anger and fear, and being unwilling to proceed farther, he lodged the Ark with Obed-edom the Gittite. This incident reflects the belief that had developed among the Israelites that contact with holiness was fatal unless the proper conditions existed and the proper safeguards maintained. (For the Heb. idea of holiness see §191*fg*.) The name Obed-edom suggests (i) that Edom here is the name of a god since Obed means servant or worshipper, and (ii) that being a Gittite and therefore a Philistine, he had attached himself to David in his Ziklag days and had now settled in Judah. Were non-Israelites felt to be immune from the effect of Yahweh's holiness? Compare the tradition that it was an Amalekite who slew Saul. **6.** Nacon, here treated as a proper name, could also be translated 'a certain', i.e. 'a certain threshing-floor'.

h **12-15.** There being no further disaster, David begins to move the Ark to Jerusalem, making sacrifices of an ox and a fatling (or buffalo) at every six paces. The dancing was probably the traditional way of honouring a god among such people as the Canaanites, for example, and may well have had movements in it that might offend at a purer level of Yahweh-worship. The linen ephod was probably the same kind of garment as the boy Samuel wore (1 Sam. 2:18). 28[6h]

i **16-19.** The Ark is brought into the City of David while Michal looked on from a window and despised David for his dancing. After sacrifices have been made David distributed food to the people and dismissed them. Michal's scorn may have been aroused either by David's dance movements, or his dress, or both together.

j **20-23.** David comes home ready to bless his family so that they may share in his elation only to find Michal waiting to scold him. David declares himself to be ready to receive even more scorn if it be earned in the service of Yahweh. Michal remained childless, possibly because David withheld intercourse from her, but also, apparently, in the judgment of the narrator, as punishment for despising David as he honoured Yahweh.

28[7a] **VII A Temple is planned and a Promise is made to David**—This chapter stands apart from the main narrative both in its literary nature and in its strong theological interest. The prophet Nathan is a leading figure and it is regarded as natural to consult God through him. No mention is made of priest or ephod. There is no clear evidence of date of composition or literary affinities.

b **1-3.** David consults Nathan about a temple and is encouraged to build one. Nathan more nearly resembles the 8th-cent. prophets than he does prophetic leaders like Moses, Deborah and Samuel: in him religion and ethics are more prominent than politics.

c **4-17.** In a night vision Nathan receives revelation that David may not build a temple but is to be given a promise that his house would continue and enjoy God's favour for all time. This is the first mention of the promise that was to become fundamental, cf. 23:5; Ps. 89:28f.; Isa. 55:3, etc. There is a play on the Heb. word 'house' which can also mean 'temple' and 'family'.

d **18-29.** David makes a prayer of gratitude to God for the promise and for the initial acts of grace shown to the nation in the Exodus and the Settlement. **23.** 'Making himself a name': this conception of the great name (1 Sam. 12:22) achieved by Yahweh through the events of the Exodus plays a large part in subsequent thought (cf. Isa. 63:12, 14; Jer. 32:20; Ezek. 20:9). 'A nation and its gods': this is a comprehensive statement to include both Canaanites and Philistines—the pre-Israelite occupiers of the land.

e **VIII.** A collection of summary statements intended to round off an account of David's reign. **1. Defeat of the Philistines.** 'After this', see on 2:1. 'Methegh-ammah', an unknown place. The name may mean 'The Aqueduct Dam' or something of that sort; *methegh* normally means bridle, and *'ammāh* may mean canal, aqueduct, cf. 'hill of Ammah' in 2:24. **2. Moab.** No mention is made otherwise of a campaign against Moab. David's friendship with the king of Moab, 1 Sam. 22:3–5, makes such a campaign unlikely. The callous method of dividing the people to be killed or spared may be a relic of a well-known custom for dividing land or prisoners; it is not mentioned in the parallel in 1 Chr. 18:2.

f **3-8. Syria.** The name Hadad-ezer means 'Hadad (Canaanitish storm-god) is help'. He is called son of Rehob, but since a place Beth-rehob is mentioned in 10:6, shortened to Rehob in 10:8, one wonders if Hadad-ezer was a Rehobite. 'Restore his power' or, 'renew (restore) his monument of victory'. **6.** 'Aram of Damascus' means that district of Syria (Aram) of which Damascus was the chief city. The garrisons would probably guarantee trading rights. **8.** Betah and Berothai are named Tibhath and Cun in 1 Chr. 18:8.

g **9-12.** The king of Hamath, one of the Syrian states, sends tribute of silver, gold and bronze; this leads on to another list of peoples from whom precious metals had come. **10.** 'Joram': it is strange to find a *Ya*-bearing name among Syrians, unless it be a g Hebraised form of Hadad-ram for which there is evidence in the *Ieddouran* of LXX and Hadoram of 1 Chr. 18:10. **13, 14.** Edomites in subjection.

h **15-18. David's Officers of State**—' Recorder ' was the highest civil office ; a modern equivalent might be ' secretary of state '. **17.** This is the first mention of Zadok who was to become the head of the line of legitimate priests. There appears to be an error in the mention of Ahimelech son of Abiathar : it should be Abiathar son of Ahimelech, cf. 1 Sam. 22:20, 30:7. Abiathar was David's priest, 15:24ff., but the name of Ahimelech may have crept in by reminiscence of the part he played in the incident in 1 Sam. 21:1–9. Seraiah is called Sheva in 20:25 and Shavsha in 1 Chr. 18:16. ' Secretary ', literally ' scribe ' (the word is so translated in Ps. 45:1), was probably assistant to the recorder. Benaiah (18) supported Solomon against Adonijah and was appointed commander-in-chief (1 Kg. 1:32–8, 2:34f.). ' Cherethites ', see 1 Sam. 30:14. ' Pelethites ' : possibly so pronounced for assonance with Cherethites and to be identified with *Pelishti*, i.e. Philistine. They were foreign bodyguards. ' David's sons were priests ' : they were days when any man might still be consecrated as priest (Jg. 17:5). In 20:26 we learn that Ira the Jairite was David's priest. Evidently he had personal priests as well as public ones.

a **Part II IX-XX The ' Court History ' of David**

These chapters, together with 1 Kg. 1 and 2, form a single narrative and tell the stories of several court intrigues and of attempts to undermine and overthrow David's authority so as to secure the throne or the right of succession to it. They end : ' So the kingdom was established in the hand of Solomon '. The chapters are widely recognised as the most vividly written narrative of the OT. It bears the marks of a true account, some think that of an eye-witness, and it is remarkable for its interest in persons, its psychological insight and dramatic ability. Continental scholars are accustomed to call it the story of the succession to David's throne. The eye-witness, if it is by one, might be Jonathan son of Abiathar, or Ahimaaz son of Zadok, for only they, apart from the woman, could know where they hid (17:17–21). Ahimaaz is the more favoured of the two because 18:19–32 is thought to contain his own reminiscence. Another view is that Abiathar wrote it. There is no absolute certainty about its limits : 2 Sam. 9–20 and 1 Kg. 1, 2 form a historical unit, but it is possible that some of the earlier stories in 1 and 2 Sam. were written by the same narrator.

b **IX Mephibosheth and Ziba—1-13.** David, for Jonathan's sake, makes Mephibosheth, Jonathan's son, a retainer in his household and commits Saul's property to Ziba, a servant of Saul, to manage on behalf of Mephibosheth. **1.** ' Of the house of Saul ' : this must be an editorial phrase for David did it for Jonathan's sake, not for Saul's : as an oriental monarch it would not be in his interests to care for the welfare of Saul's family. In point of fact Saul's family suffered their inevitable fate at the hands of the Gibeonites, 21:1–9, an incident which may have taken place before the present one and is not now in chronological order. By putting Mephibosheth under his own personal patronage he was not only preventing reprisals against him as a member of Saul's family but was also guarding against the outbreak of pro-Saul feeling centred in Mephibosheth, crippled and unfit to reign though he was. The story of Ziba is continued in 16:1–4, 19:17, 29. The reference to his fifteen sons and twenty servants (10) paves the way for the story of his ambition. **6.** Mephibosheth : in 1 Chr. 8:34, 9:40, the name is given as Meribbaal which may be the original form, cf. on 1 Sam. 14:49. The note in 4:4 as to how Mephibosheth was crippled would be more fitting in this chapter than in its present place. **12.** The mention of Mica seems to prepare the way for some other mention of him by the writer, or, alternatively, shows that at the time the narrative was 287b
written Mica was a well-known figure because it was through him that there were any descendants of Saul alive at all, 1 Chr. 8:34ff., 9:40.

X-XII Campaigns against the Ammonites leading up to David's Marriage with Bathsheba and the Birth of Solomon—The section begins with the characteristic ' After this ', cf. 2:1, 8:1, 13:1 and 15:1. c

X. Successful war with the Ammonites and their allies the Syrians. 1-5. Hanun, king of the Ammonites, affronts David by his shameful treatment of David's messengers. It was natural for David to make overtures to the Ammonites whom Saul had defeated in the affair of Jabesh-gilead, 1 Sam. 11:1–11. The reference to Nahash's loyalty to David hints at a possible friendship with David while Saul was still alive. **4.** The treatment deprived the men of their manly appearance and exposed them to mockery. To shave the whole beard, on the other hand, was a sign of mourning, Isa. 15:2.

6-8. The Ammonites coerce four Syrian states to join d
them. Two of these, Beth-rehob and Zobah, have already been mentioned, 8:3–7, a passage which may be an anticipation of this incident. **9-14.** Joab divides his forces to attack the allies simultaneously : the strategy is successful. **15-19.** The defeated Syrians get reinforcements from Syrian states beyond Euphrates and muster at Helam (east of Jordan). David defeats the reinforced armies and thus breaks the alliance between Ammonites and Syrians. **16.** Some difficulty is felt about the phrase ' beyond Euphrates ' which does not make clear which side of the river is meant, moreover it is improbable that Hadadezer controlled so vast a territory as is implied. The section (15–19) may be an editorial expansion.

XI-XII David's Adultery with Bathsheba and its Sequel—XI 1. Prologue giving the background ; e
war with the Ammonites, Joab besieging Rabbah and David remaining in Jerusalem. The epilogue is found in 12:26–31. **2-5.** David satisfies his lust for Bathsheba. Bathsheba means ' daughter of oath '. 1 Chr. 3:5 has Bathshua. ' Eliam ' : in 1 Chr. 3:5 the two parts of the name are inverted to give Ammiel. Uriah the Hittite is listed in 23:39 as one of David's heroes. He was probably a member of David's foreign troops. It is noteworthy that, though a Hittite (see 1 Sam. 26:6, and §86*d*), he has a *Ya*-bearing name. Bathsheba's simple message ' I am with child ' forced David to take some action to avoid shame and perhaps reprisal.

6-13. David attempts to conceal his action by giving f
Uriah leave to visit his wife, but his soldierly bearing spoils the plan. **8.** ' Wash your feet ' : a comprehensive phrase enlarged by Uriah's own words in 11, ' to eat and drink, and to lie with my wife '. ' A present ' : a token of the special favour and attention of the king intended to make Uriah feel under an obligation to do as the king wished. **11** shows that intercourse was forbidden to soldiers on campaign, cf. 1 Sam. 21:5. **14-21.** As a last resort David arranges for Uriah, who maintained his correct bearing throughout, to meet his death in battle. The narrator's art is at a high level as he portrays Joab instructing the messenger to introduce Uriah's death incidentally and in such manner as to allay David's anger. Abimelech the son of Jerubbesheth, see Jg. 9:50–7 : here is a further example of the avoidance of Baal in proper names (see on 1 Sam. 14:49).

22-25. The messenger reports to David. This inter- g
view does not follow the pattern of Joab's instructions : the LXX version of it does do so and may therefore represent an earlier form.

XI 26-XII 6. David makes Bathsheba his wife and Yahweh sends Nathan to stir David's conscience with his famous parable. The parable elicits from David the expected judgment on himself.

XII 7-15a. Nathan points out to David that he h
stands self-condemned and that what he has done is unworthy of a prince who owes so much to Yahweh.

287h The punishment from God will be twofold : as Uriah died by the sword so David will suffer by the sword for the rest of his days, and at the same time he will lose the child of his adultery. **8.** 'Your master's wives': it is not recorded that David did take Saul's wives, but it was not an unknown practice ; see 16:22 and 1 Kg. 2:17.

i **15b-23.** A poignant narrative showing David's anxiety over the child while still alive and his unexpected behaviour in refusing to observe the customary rites of mourning when he was dead. **24, 25.** Solomon is born and called also Jedidiah which means 'beloved of Yahweh'. The name occurs only here.
26-31. The narrative now returns to the theme of its opening verse (11:1). Joab reports to David that he has made a token capture of the 'city of waters' and invites David to come and take the whole city of Rabbah. The city of waters must clearly mean the source of water supply for the large city; 'Rabbah' itself means 'large'. It is likely therefore that 'royal city' in 26 is a copyist's error for 'city of waters'. In 30 for 'their king' LXX by a change of pronunciation has Milcom, the name by which the Israelites knew the Ammonite god, 1 Kg. 11:5. A talent was heavy for an ordinary crown.

288a **XIII, XIV Amnon's Incest** : the incident involved three of David's children, Absalom, Amnon and Tamar. **XIII 1-6.** Amnon, desperately in love with Tamar, follows his cousin's advice and feigns illness so that David shall let Tamar wait on him. Tamar was Absalom's full-sister and half-sister to Amnon. Jonadab is mentioned only here ; his father Shimeah is called Shammah in 1 Sam. 16:9. **6.** 'Make a couple of cakes': translation obscures the fact that 'make' and 'cake' come from the same root in Heb., *l-b-b*, from which comes the word 'heart', *lĕbhābh*. In Ca. 4:9 the verb is translated 'you have ravished my heart'. We may suppose that the cakes were heart-shaped and were intended to bewitch Amnon to full health ; secretly Amnon would expect them to intensify passion and enable him to take her by surprise.

b **7-14.** Amnon's plan partially succeeds and he finally takes her by force. **15-19.** Complete revulsion now comes over Amnon and he has her removed from his room. **18.** The 'long robe with sleeves' was a distinctive garment—Jacob gave Joseph such a garment as a mark of his affection for him, Gen. 37:3. Tamar made the outward signs of mourning for the loss of her maidenhood.

c **20-29.** Absalom shelters Tamar and harbours enmity towards Amnon, and then (23-9) finally secures the death of Amnon. On the significance of the sheep-shearing occasion see 1 Sam. 25:2-4. Absalom must have known that David would refuse to go in person but that he would allow his eldest son to go for him. Only on important matters of state would the king leave his capital city.

d **30-33.** Report reaches David, first that all his sons have been killed, but then Jonadab corrects the report and tells him that Amnon alone is dead. This is heavy enough news, for Amnon was the eldest son and would be expected to succeed his father.
34-36. The king's sons return and the whole court goes into mourning for Amnon. **37-9.** Absalom flees to the home of his mother's family at Geshur (cf. 3:3). David gradually accustomed himself to the loss of Amnon and began to long for Absalom's return.

e **XIV Joab secures Absalom's Return—1-3.** He instructs a 'wise woman' to present an acted parable to the king. For mourning customs see Gen. 37:34 ; Jos. 7:6 ; 1 Sam. 4:12 ; 2 Sam. 1:2. **4-7.** The woman presents her case as nearly parallel to David's as she can and pleads for the life of the one who killed his brother. **8-11.** The king is on the point of dismissing her, but she presses her plea, and, while not overlooking the fact of blood feud, is able to get the king to agree to exercise his royal prerogative and absolve the feud.

f **12-17.** Now that the parable has elicited the king's judgment the woman goes on to relate her tale to the 28
situation in the royal house and urges David to recall Absalom. Vv. 15-17 seem to belong more to the woman's own story than to its application to the king's family. Their natural place would be between vv. 7 and 8, but the author may have made the woman press her own case here to draw away the king's resentment. **18-20.** David has a glimmer of suspicion and learns that the incident has been arranged by Joab. 'Like the angel of God', cf. 1 Sam. 29:9. **21-4.** Joab is instructed to arrange for Absalom's return, but he must not live in the royal palace.

25-27. A description of Absalom and details about his g
family. The description of his long hair is intended to prepare for 18:9 where Absalom's head is caught in a tree as he rides under it ; but in 18:9-15 there is no mention of his hair at all. This passage may be secondary and editorial. Here he is said to have three sons, but 18:18 says he had no sons. There is also uncertainty about his daughter's name. Here she bears the same name as his sister, Tamar, but in 1 Kg. 15:1f. we learn that the mother of Rehoboam's son Abijah was Maacah, daughter of Abishalom (Absalom). Actually Maacah was the name of Absalom's mother. LXX, harmonising with 1 Kg. 15:1f., adds here 'and she became the wife of Rehoboam, son of Solomon, and bore him Abiathar'. **28-33.** Absalom, probably already meditating rebellion, begins to chafe at his exclusion from the king's presence, and, by the ruse of setting fire to Joab's barley field, gets him to arrange his reconciliation with David.

XV-XIX Absalom's Rebellion—XV 1-6. Absalom h
woos the loyalty of such Israelites as had cases at law for which they could get no hearing. Justice in those days depended entirely on the ruler's capacity to exercise it. David in his later years seems to have become neglectful and thus to leave room for disaffection. The raising of an escort of fifty men was not in itself an act of rebellion but Absalom would have no kingly authority without such support (1 Sam. 8:11). The fact that no particular tribe is mentioned in v. 2 suggests that Absalom from the beginning intended his rebellion to include all Israel.

7-12. Four years later Absalom, ready to rebel openly i
against his father, seeks permission to visit Hebron. Absalom pleaded having a vow to fulfil : vows were regarded with awe in Israel and obstacles to their fulfilment could not be brooked. Hebron was still an important city and a natural place from which to challenge the authority of the king in the new capital. That the rebellion began there indicates clearly that all Israel, including Judah, was expected to take part ; later rebellions, Sheba, 2 Sam. 20, and Jeroboam, 1 Kg. 12:12ff., were of the northern tribes against Judah. **8.** For Geshur, see 13:37. **12.** Ahithophel the Gilonite held an almost legendary reputation for counsel. If his son Eliam (23:34) can be identified with Bathsheba's father (11:3) then he was Bathsheba's grandfather and might be all the more willing to join a rebellion against David on his granddaughter's account.

13-18. David, alarmed at the news of the rebellion, j
leaves Jerusalem with his foreign troops. **16.** 'Ten concubines', see 16:21. **17.** 'At the last house': on the road out of Jerusalem. On Cherethites and Pelethites see 8:18 and 1 Sam. 30:14. Gittites, cf. 6:10. 'Six hundred', see note on 1 Sam. 25:13. V. 18 prepares for the next part of the narrative and suggests some kind of mustering or review of troops.

There now follows, 15:19-16:14, a series of personal encounters with David mainly showing that there were a number of men upon whom he could rely, but showing at the same time, in the incident of Shimei, that there was strong emotional support for Absalom engendered by ill-feeling towards David.

19-23. David, moved by the loyalty of the Gittites, in k
spite of their very recent adhesion to the Israelite cause, suggests to their leader Ittai that he should remain behind with them and not jeopardise their

8k safety. Ittai reaffirms his loyalty. In 18:2 he is given charge of a third of David's troops. **19.** 'Stay with the king': to speak thus of Absalom David must have been in a mood of utter despair.

l **24-29.** The priests, represented by Zadok, bring the Ark from the city to join David. This was an appropriate gesture for the Ark was primarily a palladium. David seems now to have more confidence than when he received Ittai, for he sends Zadok and Abiathar, with their two sons, back to the city to act as spies; they are to take the Ark with them. It is clearly intended that the Ark should not henceforth leave Jerusalem. The fact that Zadok's name stands first and that Abiathar is introduced incidentally in v. 24 (RSV has altered the order of the Heb.) indicates some disorder in the text, perhaps due to a desire to ensure that the Ark was properly handled by Levites with Zadok at their head. Elsewhere in the story of David Abiathar is the first of the priests. For Zadok, see on 8:17.

m **30f.** David is in dismay at hearing of **Ahithophel's defection** to Absalom. The covering of the head is to be understood as a sign of mourning, but, if an Arabic cognate be followed, it could be translated 'with his head uncovered'. The uncovered head, being exceptional, was the more likely to be a sign of mourning and is forbidden to priests (Lev. 10:6, 21:10; Ezek. 24:17). These two verses introduce the next personal encounter.

32-37. David meets Hushai his friend and sends him back to Jerusalem to feign allegiance to Absalom and confound Ahithophel's counsel. **32.** 'Archite', see Jos. 16:2. **37.** 'Friend', see Gen. 26:26; 1 Kg. 4:5.

9a **XVI 1-4. Ziba (ch. 9) now meets David**, bringing with him supplies for David's followers and asses for David and his family. It transpires that Mephibosheth is entertaining the hope, a forlorn one, that the civil war might enable him to regain his father's kingdom. David dispossesses Mephibosheth and hands the property to Ziba (but see also 19:24–30, 21:1–14).

b **5-8. Shimei, a Benjamite** and a member of Saul's house, now takes advantage of David's situation to curse him for the destruction of the house of Saul (21:1–14) and predicts the success of Absalom. Shimei is called son of Gera: there is a Gera listed among the sons of Benjamin in Gen. 46:21, and Ehud (Jg. 3:15) is the son of Gera the Benjamite. Thus Gera is an established Benjamite name, but there is no evidence of a Gera among Saul's immediate family. There are sequels in 19:16–23 and 1 Kg. 2:8f., 36–46.

c **9-14.** David feels that God may have inspired Shimei's cursing and that some good may eventually come of it, so he refuses to let Abishai behead him. If David's own son felt able to rebel, how much more might a Benjamite feel able to!

15-19. Hushai, to mislead Absalom, plays on the theme of kingship as being a divinely appointed office which thus demands men's utter loyalty. This is very much like the idea of the Lord's anointed which ran like a thread through the story of David's dealings with Saul. Absalom's taunt about Hushai's friendship with David can thus be brushed aside with the remark that the son, chosen by God, deserves the loyalty once given to the father.

d **20-23.** Ahithophel advises Absalom to demonstrate his assumption of royal power and prerogative by intercourse with his father's concubines (see on 12:8).

XVII 1-4. Ahithophel outlines a further plan; it is that he, Ahithophel, with twelve thousand men, should make a surprise attack on David while he is weary after marching, strike him down and lead the rest of the people home.

e **5-14.** Absalom seeks Hushai's approval of the plan. He condemns it on the grounds that, first, David would not be found encamping with the rest of his followers, and second, he and his men were doughty warriors and at the first hint of trouble Ahithophel's men would panic. Absalom should muster every available
Israelite and lead them in person; their overwhelming 289e
numbers would ensure the total annihilation of David and his men. The plan met with approval. **14.** The narrator adds that God controls history.

15-20. David's priest-spies, Zadok and Abiathar, pass f
on the news of this counsel but disaster nearly overtakes their sons who are forced to hide in a well. This is the kind of detail that suggests an eye-witness account. **21f.** They carry the news to David who promptly acts on it and crosses the Jordan. **23.** Ahithophel commits suicide.

24-26. The respective positions of David and g
Absalom on the east of the Jordan. It was at Mahanaim that Ishbosheth became king. Abigal is said to be the daughter of Nahash, but she was the daughter of Jesse, 1 Chr. 2:16; Nahash must have crept in by error from v. 27. **27-9.** A further personal encounter: Shobi, Machir and Barzillai bring necessities. Shobi evidently belonged to the royal house of the Ammonites who were tributary to David (chs. 10–12). Machir is mentioned in 9:4 as the one in whose house Mephibosheth had settled. It is significant that a staunch adherent of the house of Saul should now offer help to David. Nothing more is known of Barzillai than is given in the sequel in 19:31–40. As a Gileadite his loyalty might be expected to have been pledged to the house of Saul because of the Jabesh-gilead incident. Even those least expected now rally to David's help.

XVIII 1-5 Preparations for Battle—David divided h
his men into three under the leadership of Joab, Abishai and Ittai. They persuaded him not to accompany them and they were charged to spare Absalom. **6-8.** Absalom's adherents are defeated with the loss of twenty thousand men. 'Forest' here means rough land strewn with boulders and dotted about with trees.

9-15 Death of Absalom—Joab, told of Absalom's i
plight in the tree, decides, despite David's charge (5) and the urgent remonstrance of his informant, that Absalom must die and himself strikes the first blow. **16f.** Joab stops the fighting. They bury Absalom and pile a great heap of stones over the grave: it might be to serve as a monument, or it might be a relic of primitive custom to ward off evils consequent upon such tragedy. **18.** The mention of the heap of stones reminded the writer that Absalom, having no son (but cf. 14:27), had erected a monument for himself that his name might be remembered.

19-33. The writer's dramatic interest shows clearly in j
this account of how the news reached David. Ahimaaz volunteers to carry it but is discouraged by Joab on the grounds that, being a good man and thus raising hope of good tidings, he ought not to carry bad news. A Cushite is sent, but Ahimaaz goes too (19–23). The two runners are seen and recognised as news-bearers because each is alone. Ahimaaz's approach is hailed with joy; his news was expected to be good (24–7). He announces the result of the battle but holds in suspense the news of Absalom's death, which the Cushite then gives (28–33).

XIX 1-43. In his grief for Absalom David delays his k
return to Jerusalem; the tension that exists between Israel and Judah is revealed as men from each seek to persuade him to return. The delay becomes the occasion for a number of personal matters to be arranged between David and certain men who have played their part in the unfolding of events.

When the Israelites, i.e. the non-Judah tribes, show l
their dismay at David's delay (8*b*–10) David hears of it and appeals to the Judahites, through Zadok and Abiathar, not to be last in restoring him. Amasa is specifically included in the appeal (13) and promised office as commander-in-chief. That had been his position under Absalom and the offer would placate the Judahite elements among Absalom's followers. Shimei and Ziba, both Benjamites, come and offer to accompany David (16–23). Abishai still desires Shimei to be punished (cf. 16:9) but David swore to

289l protect him. Mephibosheth follows his servant, Ziba, and complains of Ziba's treatment of him. Since their last appearance in the narrative, Mephibosheth had neglected his personal appearance, while Ziba had done all he could to implement David's assignment of Saul's property to him. The gesture now made by Mephibosheth (30) was only a way of showing his satisfaction at the king's decision. Barzillai the Gileadite, representing the trans-Jordanian tribes of Israel, now pledged his help but asked to be relieved from the journey to Jerusalem and for Chimham to go instead (37). Chimham was probably Barzillai's son ; a note to that effect may have dropped out of the text. Nevertheless, there were some Israelites who felt slighted by the Judahites and claim to have ten shares in David (41–3). 'Ten' is traditional, see 1 Kg. 11:30f., 35f., but only one tribe is mentioned over against them. 'In David also we have more than you' : the reading of LXX is probably to be preferred, 'and what is more, we are senior to you'. It is widely recognised that Judah was a late-comer into the Israelite confederacy.

m **XX Revolt of Sheba and Death of Amasa—1-13.**
The dissentient elements among the Israelite tribes eventually find expression in the cry of revolt raised by Sheba, son of Bichri, a Benjamite. The same cry is found in 1 Kg. 12:16. After settling his affairs in Jerusalem, David turns his attention to this fresh menace and orders Amasa to raise the Judaean army. Amasa had been appointed commander-in-chief in place of Joab, but it looks as if David's confidence in him was misplaced, for he was so long about the task that David had to send Abishai and Joab with the Cherethites and Pelethites to suppress the revolt. They meet Amasa whom Joab kills treacherously. In v. 8, instead of 'as he went forward, it fell out' it is possible to translate 'he swaggered stupidly as he went forward'. The murder was probably an act of spite for his displacement of Joab as commander. The following verses 10*a*–13 suggest that the men made an example of Amasa as a usurper.

n **14-22.** Sheba, pursued by Abishai and Joab, seeks
shelter in Abel-beth-Maacah. Led by a 'wise woman' who excused her treachery by an appeal to a popular tradition about Abel, the people throw Sheba's head to his pursuers outside the city.
23-25. David's officers. See also 8:15–18 and 1 Chr. 18:14–17. 'Adoram was in charge of the forced labour' is mentioned again in 1 Kg. 12:18, where his death was the first act of a further revolt. 'David's priest', see on 8:18.

Part III XXI-XXIV Six Appendices to the Story of David

290a (1) **XXI 1-14.** David surrenders seven of Saul's sons
to the Gibeonites to resolve a blood-feud on account of which the land was suffering famine. The story is not in its proper chronological position. The vengeance on Saul's sons and the burial of Saul and Jonathan belong to the early years of David's reign. **1.** 'Because he put the Gibeonites to death' : it is not known what this refers to. It has been suggested that Nob may have belonged to the Gibeonites and the reference is to the incident in 1 Sam. 22:17ff. **10-14** seem to introduce another thread into the story, namely that of the proper burial of the remains of Saul and Jonathan. It is closely interwoven with the burial of the seven victims of the Gibeonite revenge.

b (2) **XXI 15-22.** A summary statement of the deaths
of four Philistine giants. **15.** 'War again', in the early years of David's reign, perhaps following that described in 5:17–21 or 22–5. **16.** 'Ish-bi-be-nob' is not mentioned elsewhere, but the text is uncertain. 'Giants' : this is the same Heb. word as Rephaim in Gen. 14:5 (q.v.). **17.** 'Lamp of Israel', see 1 Kg. 11:36 ; a token of the continuance of the royal line. 2 Sam. 14:7 has a similar figure. **18.** 'Gob' is an unknown place, but the tradition is uncertain ; LXX has Gath (cf. v. 20) and 1 Chr. 20:4 has Gezer. **19.** 'Elhanan son of Jaareoregim' : 1 Chr. 20:5
has Elhanan son of Jair, i.e. it omits *oregim* probably 2
rightly for it is a dittograph of '*ōr^e^gîm*, 'weavers', at the end of the verse. This alternate tradition about Goliath naturally arouses speculation on the relation of Elhanan and David. **21.** 'Jonathan the son of Shimei' : another son, Jonadab, is mentioned in 13:3.

(3) **XXII 1-51.** The Song of David. This is said to c
have been sung after victory over his enemies and over Saul. Apart from a few small differences it is identical with Ps. 18. It has two parts.

Part I 2-31 A Thanksgiving—2-4. Declaration of trust in God.
5, 6. Distress of the author, expressed in terms of a stay in Sheol.
7-16. God descends to rescue the psalmist and to demonstrate his saving power. This description is reminiscent of (i) the theophanies elsewhere recorded in the OT, cf. Ps. 97:2–5, and (ii) the mythological conception of the descent of a god to the underworld, e.g. the descent of Ishtar. 'Cherub', see Gen. 3:24, etc.
17-20. God rescues the psalmist and sets him in freedom.
21-25. God's intervention is recognised as the reward given to a faithful servant.
26-31. A description of God's character as one who rewards men according to their character and desert ; he is utterly trustworthy.

There is nothing in this first part that specifically relates to David's circumstances.

Part II 32-51 A Royal Thanksgiving—32-43. d
The psalmist, a warrior and leader, probably a king, describes the way God has instructed him in the art of war and then assured him victory over his enemies.
35. 'Bronze bow', probably bronze-tipped : an all-bronze bow would lack the necessary resilience.
44-46. The psalmist's success won him also the submission of other nations.
47-51. An ascription of praise to God who gives triumphs to his king, 'to David, and his descendants for ever'.

The last verse makes it almost certain that this second part is a royal thanksgiving by one of the kings of the Davidic dynasty. The Psalm may be read as a fitting epilogue to David's story and was probably inserted for that purpose.

(4) **XXIII 1-7 David's Last Words**—This is a brief e
hymn of praise to God for his favour to David with whom he has made an everlasting covenant (7:15f.) and who stands in sharp contrast to scoundrels who come to no good. There is a similarity between this hymn and some of the Wisdom writings, and it may be a late composition. **1.** 'Sweet psalmist' : the first clear record of the tradition about David that was to endear him to later ages more than anything else ; cf. ben Sira's praise of him, Sir. 47:1–11. **4.** 'Makes grass to sprout', or, 'to sparkle', which is a better parallel. The text of 7 is difficult : with slight change it could be translated :

> Or a man touch them except with an iron tool,
> or the shaft of a spear ;
> and they must be destroyed with fire.

(5) **XXIII 8-39 David's Heroes : the Three and** f
the Thirty—(i) **8-12.** the Three : Josheb-basshebeth, Eleazar and Shammah. The first has an unfamiliar name for which 1 Chr. 11:11 has Jashobeam a Hachmonite. LXX has a form which implies an original Ishbosheth (Ishbaal) which is the best form of proper name.

(ii) **13-17.** An exploit of three of the Thirty. There is nothing to show whether these three were the Three just mentioned or not ; probably they were. The dignity, courage and nobility portrayed by the incident rightly make it one of the better known in the OT. **16.** 'Poured it out', as a drink offering to God.

(iii) **18-39.** The Thirty. Thirty is obviously a round

290f number, for v. 39 says there were thirty-seven. Some of them appear elsewhere and are well known, Abishai (1 Sam. 26:6), Benaiah (2 Sam. 8:18), Asahel (2:18), Uriah (11:3, 6). Some of the names may have suffered corruption during transmission, for example, in 32 we ought to accept the reading of 1 Chr. 11:34 (supported by LXX here), 'Hashem the Gizonite', instead of 'the sons of Jashen', and 'Jonathan, Shammah' should probably be 'Jonathan son of Shammah'; cf. 1 Chr. 11:34.

g **(6) XXIV 1-25.** The census and its consequences. **1-9.** David takes a census against the advice of Joab. **1.** 'Again the anger of the Lord': this implies an earlier occasion of anger, probably 21:1–14 where famine is reported. 'Incited David': the same verb is used in 1 Sam. 26:19; that God incited David to act reflects the natural Heb. attribution to God of the control of human affairs. To the Chronicler it seemed wrong and he wrote: 'Satan . . . incited David', 1 Chr. 21:1. 'Dan to Beersheba' (2), 3:10. The places listed in 5ff. indicate the extent of David's kingdom: eastward to Aroer in Moabite territory, northward to Kadesh on the Orontes and north-westward to Tyre and Sidon on the Phoenician coast. Joab's objection to the census (3) was probably dictated by fear of levies and taxes.

10-14. The prophet Gad comes to offer David, now full of regret, a choice of three calamities as punishment. Gad is mentioned elsewhere in 1 Sam. 22:5; 1 Chr. 21:9ff.; 2 Chr. 29:25, and has won a place in tradition as seer, historian and inspirer of the establishment of Levitical choirs in the temple. 290g

15-17. God sends three days' pestilence, but when the destroying angel reaches Jerusalem he orders him to stop. He stops at the threshing-floor of Araunah the Jebusite. The floor would be in a prominent position to catch the wind for winnowing purposes. **18-25.** Acting on Gad's instructions, David buys the threshing-floor and offers sacrifices on it, using the oxen and threshing instruments which had belonged to Araunah. The sacrifices are said to be intended to avert the plague, but the angel had already ceased his destructive work, and they really inaugurate sacrifices of all kinds at Jerusalem, for the story is to be regarded as an aetiological one. In 1 Chr. 22:1 and 2 Chr. 3:1 the threshing-floor became the starting-point of Solomon's Temple. h

Bibliography—COMMENTARIES: K. Budde, KHC (1902); P. Dhorme, EBib. (1910); S. R. Driver, *Notes on the Hebrew Text of the Books of Samuel* (2nd ed. 1913); H. W. Hertzberg, ATD (1956); A. R. S. Kennedy, Cent.B; H. P. Smith, ICC (1899).

OTHER LITERATURE: H. Cazelles, 'David's Monarchy and the Gibeonite Claim', PEQ 87 (1955), 165–75; I. Mendelsohn, 'Samuel's Denunciation of Kingship in the Light of the Akkadian Documents from Ugarit', BASOR 143 (1956), 17–22.

I AND II KINGS

By J. MAUCHLINE

291a **Introduction**—The books of Kg. are a record of the history of Israel from the death of king David to the fall of Jerusalem in 586, with a postlude concerning Gedaliah and the release in 561 of Jehoiachin (see §308*f*). In the Babylonian Talmud *Baba Bathra*, 15*a*, it is said that 'Jeremiah wrote his own book, the book of Kings and Lamentations'; it is true at least that 2 Kg. 24:18–25:21 is paralleled in Jer. 39:1, 2, 4–10 and 52, and that 2 Kg. 25:22–6 is a short form of a narrative of which a much fuller form is contained in Jer. 39:11–43:7.

b **I Sources**—The main sources used in the compilation of the books of Kg. appear to have been these: (*a*) the book of the acts of Solomon and records of the Jerusalem Temple; (*b*) the annals, or official chronicles, of the kings of Israel and Judah, or historical records based on them; (*c*) biographies of Elijah (1 Kg. 17–19, 21; 2 Kg. 1:2–17) and Elisha (2 Kg. 2, 4:1–6:23, 8:1–15, 13:14–21) and Isaiah (2 Kg. 18:17–19:35); and (*d*) excerpts from a popular history of Israel (e.g. 1 Kg. 20, 22:1–38) and of Judah (e.g. 2 Kg. 12, 16, 22f.).

The student of the period has also available to him for comparative study 1 and 2 Chr. and Isa. 36–9, as well as Egyptian, Assyrian and Babylonian records (cf. e.g. ANET), and the results of modern archaeological investigation; for the last-named field of study, reference may be made to: FSAC, ARI, APB, WBA and the Pelican Book by W. F. Albright, *The Archaeology of Palestine* (1949).

c **II Method**—One of the most notable features of the style of writing of the books of Kg. is that the record of a king's reign is normally, but not unvaryingly, presented within an editorial framework, which is in two parts:

(*a*) An Introduction, consisting of (i) a dating of the king's year of accession, not in terms of a pivotal date of the kind A.U.C., A.H. and A.D., for none was available, but by means of a cross-reference to, or a so-called synchronism with, the current reign of the king of the neighbouring kingdom, Israel or Judah as the case might be; (ii) his age at his accession; (iii) the length of his reign; (iv) his mother's name, and (v) a judgment upon him in terms of his fidelity to Yahweh and, in particular, of his attitude to the worship at the hill shrines or local altars. (ii) and (iv) are commonly omitted in the case of the kings of Israel and there is no occasion for (i) in the case of the kings of Judah after the fall of Samaria in 721 B.C. The kings of Israel are consistently condemned for their infidelity, which is described as following Jeroboam the son of Nebat who made Israel sin (by setting up the calves at Bethel and Dan, cf. 1 Kg. 12:28ff.); even the reforming Jehu does not escape condemnation (cf. 2 Kg. 10:29f.). In the case of the kings of Judah, Hezekiah (2 Kg. 18:3–5) and Josiah (2 Kg. 22:2–23:25*a*) are unconditionally commended, a group, consisting of Asa (1 Kg. 15:11–14), Jehoshaphat (1 Kg. 22:43), Jehoash (2 Kg. 12:2f.), Amaziah (2 Kg. 14:3f.), Uzziah (2 Kg. 15:3f.) and Jotham (2 Kg. 15:34f.) receive limited commendation, and the others are condemned because they did what was wrong in the eyes of Yahweh; David is commonly referred to as the ideal king, by comparison with whom his successors are measured. The limited commenda- 29
tion is given to kings who showed fidelity to Yahweh but who did not remove the hill shrines. That judgment is in terms of a demand for the one legitimate sanctuary which, whenever it may have been formulated, was not made authoritative until the Josianic reformation of 621 B.C. (cf. 2 Kg. 22f.).

(*b*) An obituary notice, which cites the annals for further information about the king's military campaigns and his achievements, makes an occasional comment, gives formal notice of the king's death and place of burial, and states the name and relationship of his successor.

Thus the historical record as presented is set within d
an editorial framework; it is clear that what is presented was intended to be something quite different from the official annals or even the popular histories which seem to have been available; it is a religious history. That being the purpose in view, a careful selection of the available material was made. Considerable space is given to the reigns of Ahab and Jehu, for example, because these reigns were important from the point of view of Israel's religious faith and practice; on the other hand, great kings like Omri and Uzziah (Azariah) receive very scant notice. The point of view of the editor (or editors) is shown in several ways:

(*a*) He judged the importance of a king's reign not e
in terms of imperial expansion, economic wealth or material benefit, but in terms of the king's fidelity to Yahweh, on the ground that only what he did or did not do in that sphere was of fundamental importance in the life of his people. Much more space is given to the life and work of Elijah and Elisha than to any two kings; they, indeed, are described as the real defences of Israel (2 Kg. 2:12, 13:14). Elijah is portrayed as a great figure, austere and uncompromising and wholly dedicated to preserving the life of Israel against the assault of foreign cult and alien custom; Elisha, a prophet of a different mould, an ecstatic in association with the prophetic schools or fraternities, a man around whom legends gathered, was set for the rise and fall of kingdoms, so that R. H. Pfeiffer is justified in describing him as at once a more historical and a more legendary character than his predecessor Elijah (IOT, 406).

(*b*) In the condemnation he passes on the kings who f
were guilty of infidelity to Yahweh, the editor expressed the twofold demand, that Yahweh alone should be worshipped so that all idolatrous practices and foreign cults must be eradicated, and that that worship should be offered at the central shrine which Yahweh has chosen, so that the hill-shrines must be destroyed. In view of the fact that these were among the main objectives of the Josianic reformation, and that they are characteristic of the book of Dt. (e.g. 12:1–7), it has been concluded that the books of Kg. were edited after 621 B.C. and the style of editing has been named Deuteronomic.

(*c*) Another characteristic of the editor, which g
amplifies his entitlement to the epithet 'Deuteronomic', is his belief in the doctrine that those who are faithful to Yahweh prosper, while the unfaithful suffer penalty. Here is to be found the explanation of the fact that

1g Solomon's polygamy and apostasy are referred to the very end of his reign (1 Kg. 11:4) and his loss of territory is recounted in the same chapter (14ff.), that Jehu's loss of empire is minimised (2 Kg. 10:32f.), that the devastation of Judah by Sennacherib in the time of king Hezekiah is not mentioned at all while the remarkable deliverance of Jerusalem from the besieging Assyrians is duly noted (2 Kg. 18–20), and that the prosperity of the reign of Manasseh is not recorded. In other words, the editor believed that prosperity was a sign of the blessing which Yahweh bestowed upon his faithful servants, but he obviously found difficulty in making the historical record conform to the doctrine. Now this doctrine is expressed frequently in Dt. (cf. e.g. 6:1–3, 10–15, 7:9–11, etc.) and it is explicitly stated in 1 Kg. 2:2–4; the books of Kg. constitute a Deuteronomic presentation of the history of Israel, and the view has been developed that they are the final part of a much more comprehensive work (cf. §138*e*). The possibility is that the editing was done in the main soon after 621 B.C., before the Exile, but certain sections were probably added at a later date (cf. John Skinner, Cent.B, 18–23).

h **III Chronology**—The method of dating reigns, mentioned in II above, may fall into error at two points: in the length of the reign as stated and in the synchronism. Of these two details, the former was the earlier, the latter being derivative from it. Incidental statements in the commentary draw attention to the fact that the chronological scheme has serious faults, and that the situation is complicated by the occasionally discordant evidence from LXX, especially LXX^{L}. The sum of the reigns in Israel from Jehu to the fall of Samaria is 135 years, in Judah 158. Menahem paid tribute to Tiglath-pileser in 738 B.C., presumably at the beginning of his reign (2 Kg. 15:19); he reigned 10 years, then Pekahiah 2, Pekah 20 and Hoshea 9, a total of 41 years to be accommodated in the period 738–721 B.C., i.e. an excess of 23 years in the roll of the reigns as stated. Again, it seems clear that part of Jotham's reign in Judah (2 Kg. 15:33) should be reckoned as overlapping with that period of Azariah's reign when he acted as regent (2 Kg. 15:5). The subject is complicated and cannot be handled in the space available here; see J. Skinner, Cent.B, 38–47; Oesterley and Robinson, *History of Israel*, I, 454–64; W. F. Albright, 'A Third Revision of the Early Chronology of Western Asia', BASOR 88 (1942), 28–36, 'The Chronology of the Divided Monarchy of Israel', BASOR 100 (1945), 16–22; E. R. Thiele, 'The Chronology of the Kings of Israel and Judah', JNES 3 (1944), 137–86).

i **The Greek Version**—The differences between the Heb. and Gr. texts of Kg. are considerable. Note in particular the transposition in LXX of 1 Kg. 20 and 22, the long insertions after 1 Kg. 2:35 (35*a*, *b–o*) and 2:46 (46*a*, *b–l*)—most of the inserted material is to be found in Heb. at various places within chs. 3–11—the insertion after 1 Kg. 12:24 of an account of Jeroboam's career, and the omission of 14:14–20. There are, of course, many smaller differences, of word or phrase, and there are many cases mentioned in the commentary in which LXX, sometimes LXX^{L}, seems to preserve a better text than MT (see J. Skinner, op. cit., 33–8).

THE FIRST BOOK OF KINGS

2a The first two chapters of 1 Kg. are a sequel to 2 Sam. 11–20. Their style is vivid and there is a wealth of detail which supports the view that they are derived from more or less contemporary documents. The weakness of the aged David now gave scope for intrigue, his imminent death gave an occasion. The claim of the first-born to the succession was doubtless strong but not universally recognised; a king might nominate his successor; there might be the popular choice of a leader who had commended himself. In other words, there were as yet no determinative precedents for the succession. 292a

I 1-4. It is clear that Abishag was provided for the king, not simply as a nurse, but as a paramour (cf. 2:17); the king did not respond. Now the prevalent belief was that the vitality and welfare of the community was bound up with the vitality of the king; it must, therefore, suffer under a king who had become so weak as David (cf. A. R. Johnson, *The Vitality of the Individual in the Thought of Ancient Israel* (1949); J. G. Frazer, *The Golden Bough* (abr. ed. 1923), 264ff.).

Shunem, the home of Abishag, was near Jezreel (cf. Jos. 19:18). For the relation of the Shunammite woman with the Shulammite of the Song of Solomon, see §410*c*; and E. J. Goodspeed, 'The Shulammite', AJSL 50 (1934), 102ff.; H. H. Rowley, 'The Meaning of the Shulammite', AJSL 56 (1939), 84ff.

5-10 On the assumption that Chileab had died, b
Adonijah was the eldest surviving son of David (cf. 2 Sam. 13:28f., 18:14, 3:3). He gathered support; he had personal attractiveness; he doubtless believed that resolute action on his part would carry the day. Joab the commander of the national militia was on his side, and Abiathar, sole representative now of the priests of Nob (1 Sam. 22:18–23). The fact that others, including Solomon, were not summoned to his aid shows Adonijah's knowledge or suspicion that Solomon was the centre of a court intrigue to make him David's successor. It is noteworthy that Adonijah, like Absalom before him (cf. 2 Sam. 15:10), found support in Judah (9), but no act of rebellion was involved if David had made no proclamation about the succession. Zadok (8) may have been a priest of the Aaronic line of Eleazar (cf. 1 Chr. 24:3) installed as priest by Saul after the destruction of the priests of Nob, who were of the line of Ithamar; but another possibility is that he belonged to the old Jebusite priesthood of Jerusalem and may have been the priest-king there when David occupied the city (cf. H. H. Rowley, *The Re-discovery of the OT* (1945), 52; A. R. Johnson, *Sacral Kingship in Ancient Israel* (1955), 46, *n.* 1).

En-rogel (9) is a spring on the south side of Jerusalem. The significance of the Serpent's Stone or Stone of Zoheleth (AV) is debated; it may be a symbol of a serpent cult which was later introduced into the Jerusalem Temple, but G. R. Driver has argued for its meaning as 'the rolling stone' ('Hebrew Notes', ZAW 52 (1934), 51).

11-14 give the first hint that a promise of the succession c
for Solomon had been made to Bathsheba, and Nathan plans with her to provoke the king now to make a public proclamation of it. It seems neither necessary nor right to take the view that Nathan's action was a confidence trick played on an old king's failing memory. **29f.** The plan succeeded and Solomon was anointed king at Gihon and was publicly acclaimed (**32-5**). **39** states that Zadok alone anointed Solomon, whereas **34** says that Nathan was associated with him. For Cherethites and Pelethites, see the comment on 2 Sam. 8:18. **41ff.** Solomon having now been anointed, the assembly at En-rogel became a rebellious one; it had to be dissolved. Adonijah was treated with clemency by Solomon (**50-3**), undertook to be loyal to the throne and withdrew into private life.

II 1-46 Death of David; Solomon secures him- d
self on the Throne—Apart from a few verses which may be editorial insertions (e.g. 10–12, 27), this chapter comes from the same source as ch. 1 (LXX has additions after 35 and 46). **3-4** may be a deuteronomic interruption, but they express a conviction that David probably shared (cf. 1:1–4). But that conviction did not make David neglect to give Solomon some practical advice for securing dynastic stability. **4-9.** He recommended that the family of Barzillai should be kept as royal pensioners (cf. 2 Sam. 17:27ff., 19:31ff.), that the masterful trouble-maker Joab (cf. 1:7) should be destroyed (2 Sam. 3:22–7, 18:11–13, 20:8ff.), to take away the blood-guilt which lay like a curse on the

292d house of David (**5**, reading with RSV ' my loins ' and ' my feet '), and that the unreliable Shimei (2 Sam. 16:5ff., 19:18ff.) should likewise be eliminated.

e David's advice to Solomon was not disregarded. That Adonijah who expected the kingship (15) should have sought Abishag in marriage (cf. 1:3) is difficult to understand. It was a most temerarious action, since it constituted a claim to the throne (cf. 2 Sam. 3:7, 12:8, 16:21f. ; W. Robertson Smith, *Kinship and Marriage in Early Arabia*² (1895), 104ff.). Is it conceivable that Bathsheba saw nothing sinister in it and was willing to support it? Could Adonijah himself possibly have entertained the hope that Solomon could not resist the entreaty of the queen-mother (for the position of the queen-mother, cf. 15:13 ; 2 Sam. 10:13 ; Jer. 13:18, 29:2) and that, married to Abishag and supported by Joab and by the legitimate priest Abiathar (so, rightly, RSV in 22), he could even now make Solomon's position precarious, if not untenable? Solomon, at least, had no hesitation in defining his attitude to Adonijah's action ; his response to Bathsheba was sharp (22) and his sentence against Adonijah was immediate (23–5).

f He proceeded now to deal with Abiathar and Joab, who had been two of Adonijah's foremost supporters. The former was removed from priestly office (26) and rusticated to Anathoth, a village a few miles north of Jerusalem (cf. Jos. 21:18 ; Jer. 1:1, 32:7) ; **27** seems to be an editorial addition to support the legitimacy of the Zadokite priesthood. **28ff.** With Joab Solomon took the extreme course of violating sanctuary, maintaining (31–3) that no blood-guilt would rest on David's house because of his death since he had slain two innocent men and that the blood-guilt that lay on David's house for the death of Abner and Amasa had now been removed.

g **36-46.** Shimei, instructed to remain under surveillance in Jerusalem, had occasion to leave the city ; but a visit to a Philistine city could easily be construed as having a sinister motive ; he was put to death and the curse he had laid on David's house was annulled (cf. 2 Sam. 16:5–10).

Solomon's position was now secure. If Zadok had been priest of the pre-David Jebusite shrine (see 292*b*), it was now possible that the old order in Israel might be changed and a centralised state with a subordinate priesthood replace the old amphictyonic order.

293a **III-XI.** These chapters give an account of Solomon's reign. The main sources used appear to be : (*a*) royal annals (cf. 4:3, 11:41, etc.), from which 4:1–28 and 9:10–28 may be extracts, while 10:14–29 is, at least partly, from the same source ; (*b*) narrative sources, of which several may have been available ; (*c*) deuteronomic supplements and editorial connectives and expansions. Solomon is presented as a monarch who was so devoted to God's service that he greatly prospered ; only in the final chapter is there any evidence that the glory of his reign was not maintained unimpaired.

b **III 1-IV 34** deal with Solomon's wisdom and describe his national and domestic economy. It was argued by Winckler (KAT³ (1903), 236 ; cf. Knudtzon, *Die El-Amarna Tafeln* (1907–15), 55) that since, according to a statement in the Tell el-Amarna Letters, no daughter of a Pharaoh could marry a foreigner, the ref. in 3:1 must be to Muṣri, north of the Taurus mountains, and not to Egypt (Miṣraim) ; but that argument cannot be pressed. By Solomon's day the greatness of Egypt had passed away and a marriage alliance with Solomon may have seemed to a Pharaoh of the XXI Dynasty a very wise move.

c **III 3.** The high places were the elevated platforms or altars which had been the Canaanite sanctuaries ; they were used by the Israelites, whether in the worship of Yahweh or of Baal ; cf. ARI, 105f., 202. To ' burn incense ' may be correct because it is now known that the use of incense in this way went back to early times ; cf. ARI, 145f., 215, *n.* 58 ; M. Burrows, *What mean these Stones?* (1941), §35 ; but the meaning of the original verb could be ' to make offerings by fire '. 293c

4. Gibeon, an important town 6 miles NW. of Jerusalem, had taken the place of Nob as the chief sanctuary (cf. Jos. 9, 10:1–15). Solomon, be it noted, offered sacrifices at Gibeon and later at Jerusalem beside the Tent containing the Ark (15). The first should not be interpreted as an act of private worship and the second as an act in public assembly with an official feast ; probably the double ceremony was meant to comprehend the whole population, Canaanite and Israelite, within the significance of the act (cf. 2 Chr. 1:3).

5. A dream was recognised as a mode of divine communication, which might readily be experienced by a d
worshipper at a sanctuary (see 9:2 ; cf. Gen. 28:2, 31:11, 32:22ff., etc.). It was only long after Solomon's time that dreams came to be regarded as an uncertain means of divine guidance (cf. Jer. 23:23ff.).

9. In his dream at Gibeon Solomon asked for wisdom. He felt himself to be young and inexperienced (cf. Jer. 1:6) ; he, therefore, asked for wisdom that he might be enabled to discern right from wrong and to administer justice. The request pleased God who promised that riches and honour would be added to him (13). The wisdom intended was practical wisdom, knowledge of men and affairs, even astuteness, excellently illustrated in the story of the two women (16–28) but also, if less commendably, in the advice given Solomon by David (2:5–9).

How old Solomon was at this time is not known ; some MSS of LXX at 2:12 say he was twelve years of age ; Josephus (Ant. VIII, vii, 8) says fourteen.

IV 1-6 provides a list of Solomon's chief officers of e
state (cf. 2 Sam. 8:15ff.). The functions of some of the officers are uncertain. Elihoreph and Ahiah (3) may have been secretaries or adjutants-general ; Jehoshaphat (3) was not a recorder or annalist but secretary-of-state ; Ahishar (6) was royal chamberlain. The position with regard to the priests is not clear ; probably 4*b* is an interpolation, being absent in LXX of 2:46*h* although in its text here ; with its reinstatement of Abiathar it cannot be a later addition (cf. §292*g*).

7-19. According to 22f., 27f. a heavy provision of f
food was required daily for the royal household and of fodder for the royal stables. To ensure an efficient supply the land was divided into twelve districts with a local official in charge of each ; for a plan of these districts, see G. E. Wright and F. V. Filson, *The Westminster Smaller Bible Atlas* (1947), Plate V ; W. F Albright, ' The Administrative Divisions of Israel and Judah ', JPOS 5 (1925), 17ff., and ARI, 140f. To some extent this system of districts cut across the old tribal divisions and consolidated the new order with its centralised government and highly organised administration, but the boundary lines cannot be traced with accuracy to show how much this was so. Judah seems to be reckoned apart (19 ; so RSV, following LXX ; for a possible reason, cf. WBA, 130) ; but if reduplication took place between Ben Geber in Ramoth-gilead (13) and Geber son of Uri in the land of Gilead (19), the officer for Judah, who is named with a distinctive title, would be No. 12 (cf. W. F. Albright, ' The Administrative Divisions of Israel and Judah ', JPOS 5 (1925), 26ff.).

20-28. The ideal extent of Solomon's empire (20., 24f.) g
was from the Euphrates (' the river ' in 21 and 24 ; Tiphsah (24) was an important crossing in its middle reach) to the Mediterranean Sea, and from Dan in north Galilee to Beersheba (25) or the border of Egypt (21). The population was large (20) ; the amount of tribute from subject peoples Solomon received gave them a high standard of living (21) but they had to bear at least some of the burden of the cost of the court and the administration as well as of the king's ambitious building programme (26). 2 Chr. 9:25 mentions 4,000 (not 40,000) chariot horses in stalls, probably rightly; ; the 12,000 (26) were probably horses for mounted troops, not horsemen. ' On

3g this side of the river ' (24) means west of the Euphrates ; it may have been a name for the area.

h **29-34.** Solomon encouraged literary activity and a cultivation of the arts. He himself became famous as a man of wisdom without peer (the men named in 31 are unknown now) ; he had also the ability to express his wisdom in proverb and maxim, drawing lessons from the open book of nature (cf. Jg. 9 ; 2 Kg. 14:9 ; Prov. 30:15ff.), and was a lyric poet as well (32f.). It is not to be wondered at that Hiram of Tyre sent an embassy to bear greetings to David's successor (5:1).

i **V Commercial Alliance between Solomon and Hiram**—The first step towards this alliance was a friendly greeting from Hiram (i.e. Ahiram) to Solomon upon the latter's accession (1f. ; cf. 2 Sam. 5:11) ; the LXX reading that Hiram sent messengers to anoint Solomon implies an overlordship over Israel which is not otherwise supported (cf. 1 Kg. 9:11, 14). Tyre was built on a rocky islet a little off shore, 40 miles north of Carmel ; a great trading centre, it was difficult of capture (cf. Isa. 23 ; Ezek. 27), but from the time of Alexander the Great it was united with the mainland by a causeway.

In reply to Hiram Solomon said that he now proposed to fulfil in Yahweh's name the promise given to David that his son would build the Temple in Jerusalem (3–5 ; cf. 2 Sam. 7 ; 1 Chr. 22:8, 28:2 ; Dt. 12:9f., 25:19). The word translated ' adversary ' in 4 is in the original ' satan ' ; it refers to a hostile human agent in this context (for Satan as the prosecuting counsel of the heavenly court, cf. Zech. 3:1f. ; Job 1:6–12).

j Phoenician skilled workmen were to superintend Israelite labourers in Lebanon in felling cedar and fir timber for the Temple, to have it taken down to the sea and floated by raft to an Israelite port, from which its transport to Jerusalem was to be undertaken by the Israelites. The Israelite labour force for this purpose was 30,000, working in relays (9, 13f.). In return Solomon was to provide Hiram annually with 220,000 bushels of wheat and 1,800 gallons of oil (LXX, 180,000 gallons).
13-18 show that another Israelite labour force, 150,000 strong, was engaged in quarrying and porterage work in Palestine, Phoenicians serving as masons and stone-dressers. The men of Gebal (18) must be assumed to have been famous as workers in stone ; but LXX reads a verbal form for ' the men of Gebal ' and this has suggested the reading ' and dressed them ' (i.e. the stones). The number of overseers means 1 for every 50 men (LXX gives the number as 3,600 ; cf. 9:23) ; at the end of 18 LXX adds ' for three years '.

k The annual provision of grain and oil for Hiram (11), together with the very heavy provision that was required annually (381,350 bushels of grain ; cf. 4:22) for Solomon's household, must have meant a very heavy national burden, so that the king was on occasion financially embarrassed (9:11, 14), and a heavy service for the peasantry. Again, forced labour for the building of the Temple might be rendered willingly to some extent, but scarcely for the king's grandiose building scheme (7 ; 9:15).

4a **VI The Temple and its Furnishings—1** means that the Temple in Jerusalem, the house of Yahweh among his people, was founded twelve (LXX, eleven) generations after the Exodus (cf. 1 Chr. 5:29ff. ; for the date of the Exodus, see §§175*f–h*). The separate chronological statement in 37f. has cast doubt on the authenticity of **1** but without adequate reason. **2-10** are concerned with the main Temple building (cf. e.g. Mishnah Tractate Middoth ; A. Parrot, *The Temple of Jerusalem* (1956) ; G. A. Smith, *Jerusalem* (1907) ; G. E. Wright, ' Solomon's Temple Resurrected ', BA 4 (1941), 17ff. The Temple was built on a platform (RSV, structure, 5), which covered the inequalities of the site. Rectangular in shape, it had three chambers, the porch or vestibule which projected in front of the main building over its whole width, the nave or holy place, and the inner shrine or most holy place. A temple of the 9th cent. B.C., discovered at Tell Tainat (cf. illustration in BA 5 (1942), 21 ; GAB, 71), shows that the Jerusalem Temple was built to a Phoenician model, although the use to which the inner shrine of Solomon's Temple was put was distinctive ; the extensive use of cedar in temple construction can now be paralleled in the same area. 294a

4-6. The structure which surrounded the Temple b
proper on three sides (not the east) and rose to half its height, had three storeys, containing chambers which were smallest on the lowest storey and largest on the highest and were so built that their supporting beams were not imbedded in the walls of the main building but rested on revetments (RSV, offsets ; for plan, see BA 4 (1941), 22). This detail and the prohibition of stone-dressing on the site were out of respect for the holiness of the Temple.

7-22. The windows (4) were set high in the walls and c
were precursors of clerestory windows ; they are sometimes termed Tyrian and are to be distinguished from the lattice type ; and they widened towards the outside (RSV, recessed frames). The beams and planks (9) probably were the roof beams and the coffering or panelling. The amount of cedar used for internal furnishing (15f., 18, etc.) must have made an interior both magnificent and fragrant. Doors in the form of a pentagon (31) presumably had apex tops. The amount of gold overlay (21f.) is remarkable, and in the case of the floor (30) incredible ; the pure gold mentioned in 20f. was probably red gold.

23-28. The cherubim (cf. 29, 32, 35) were winged d
figures which had the body of a lion and a human head (for illustration, see BA 4 (1941), 24 ; W. F. Albright, *The Archaeology of Palestine* (1949), Plates 16, 18, 24). They served as the pedestal of the invisible divine throne (lion and bull figures have been found in the Near East similarly used). 2 Sam. 22:11 and Ps. 18:10 imply that they could be thought of as conveying the divine throne on a journey ; but Gen. 3:24 presents them rather as guardians of the shrine (cf. BA 1 (1938), 1–3). Thus it is an old mode that is used, as is the case with the representation of gourds, palm-trees and open flowers (18, 29, 35).

VII 1-12 Solomon's Buildings other than the e
Temple—The whole building programme required twenty years for its completion (1 ; cf. 9:10).
2-5. The plan of the House of the Forest of Lebanon is obscure. If the phrase ' fifteen in a row ' (3) refers to the forty-five cedar pillars, we must, with LXX, read *three* rows (so RSV ; Heb. four). If it refers to the side-chambers, it may be assumed that the building as a whole rested on four rows of pillars which at once served as bearers and provided an open-air colonnade and shelter at ground level ; the central chamber, resting on the two inner rows, was flanked by side-chambers built in three storeys and receiving light from windows set at the end of the rows of fifteen chambers. In this case the forty-five chambers would be those on one side, which is all an observer could see at a time. If there was such a colonnade at ground level, the name of the house becomes intelligible. This house was larger than the Temple (cf. 10:17 and Isa. 22:8) and was used as a store.

The Hall of Pillars (6) probably stretched across the f
front of the House of the Forest of Lebanon ; the porch in front of it is difficult to understand ; even as a covered porch or shelter it is a strange adjunct to a Hall of Pillars which was, presumably, covered.

The Throne Room (7) was a Hall of Judgment ; Solomon's own palace and the house of Pharaoh's daughter were in a separate court, and were private residences.

The massive blocks which were used in the foundation of these buildings in stone (10) were trimmed with saws, proving that it was the native limestone which was used ; it is easy to work but quickly hardens with exposure to the atmosphere. The whole building complex was surrounded by an outer wall (12).

294g **13-51 Vessels and Furnishing for the Temple**—A Phoenician craftsman had to be hired for the bronze-work, the Israelites lacking the skill. The text of **15-22** is seriously confused but the rendering given in RSV would receive wide support. The two bronze pillars had ornamentation of lattice- or net-work and chain-work, as well as an extensive use of a pomegranate motif. Other examples have been found in the Near East of such pillars standing in front of temples (cf. Herodotus ii, 44 ; BA 4 (1941), 21 ; A. Parrot, *The Jerusalem Temple,* 14). Probably by Solomon's time they had become a conventional mode, but their original significance has been disputed. Standing stones, sun pillars, fire pillars, ornamental torches—these suggestions and others have been made ; but the ornamentation supports the view that they were formalised representations of the tree of life (cf. note on *asherah,* §296*h*).

h **21.** The most plausible explanation of their names is that they were the initial words of dynastic oracles and signified : Jachin, ' The Lord *will establish* his throne for ever ' ; and Boaz, ' *In the strength* of the Lord the king will rejoice ' (cf. R. B. Y. Scott, ' The Pillars Jachin and Boaz ', JBL 58 (1939), 143ff. ; ARI 139).

23-26 The bronze sea was a large bowl of over 16,000 gallons capacity, mounted on twelve bearer oxen. It may have been put to practical use (so 2 Chr. 4:6) but it was undoubtedly an old traditional cult object and probably represented the great deep and, in consequence, the primeval struggle between God and Tehom (cf. ARI, 148f. ; S. R. Driver, *The Book of Genesis,* WC, 27ff. ; J. Skinner, *I & II Kings,* Cent.B, 127).

i **27-39** describe the **mobile lavers or basins** (cf. C. F. Burney, *Notes on the Hebrew Text of the Books of Kings,* 91 ; GAB, 70 ; A. Parrot, op. cit., 35). The stand or trolley itself had a top which was six feet square ; the basin was fitted into a bronze collar which rested on the top of the four corner stays of the trolley (34–8). The capacity of the basins being 400 gallons, and the overall height of the trolleys probably as much as eight feet, the trolleys must have been very ponderous to handle.

j The bronze casting was done in the Jordan valley, ' in the clay ground ' (RSV) or, rather, in the earthen foundries (46). Much evidence of copper smelting has been found recently around ancient Ezion-geber (cf. WBA, 134f. ; N. Glueck, *The Other Side of the Jordan,* 50ff., 89ff. ; BASOR 79 (1940), 2ff.). The vessels and furnishings described in **48-50** were, presumably, not made of gold, but were overlaid with it. For the significance of ' the bread of the Presence ' (48), cf. §214*b*.

k **VIII The Dedication of the Temple—1-13** describe how the Ark of the covenant was brought to Jerusalem, **14-61** give Solomon's address to the people and prayer of dedication, **62-6** tell of the sacrifices which were offered on the occasion.

The chapter shows many marks of later expansion and editing. The first part gives stylistic evidence of priestly expansion, ' the priests and the Levites ' (5) is a late distinction of priestly office, and to put the autumn festival in the seventh month is a post-exilic way of reckoning ; in the first five verses LXX has a shorter and, apparently, purer text than MT. The second part has been much subjected to Deuteronomic editing, and parts of it (e.g. 44–53) may be post-exilic.

l **1.** From the city of David which lay on the ridge to the south, the Ark was brought up to Mount Zion ; the occasion was an autumn festival, so that the city must have been thronged. This festival when the Temple was dedicated was presumably that which followed almost a year after the completion of the building. The Ark was placed in the inner shrine. **8.** The fact that the bearer staves were not removed (Exod. 25:15) and projected against the curtain gave the people ground of assurance that it was there. **11.** When the Ark had been set in place, the mystery of the Godhead settled upon the house (cf. Exod. 33:9 ; 294
Ezek. 43:1–5). **12-13** (reconstructed with the help of LXX) give what may have been Solomon's prayer of dedication. It celebrates the Creator God who dwells among men in the darkness of impenetrable mystery, so that the darkness of the inner shrine in the exalted house Solomon has made for him is a fitting abode. For the phrase ' exalted house ' or ' princely house ', see G. R. Driver, *Canaanite Myths and Legends* (1956), 44f., 50f., 78f. ; C. H. Gordon, *Ugaritic Manual* (1955), iii, 261 (594) ; cf. W. F. Albright, ' Zabûl Yam and Thâpiṭ Nahar in the Combat between Baal and the Sea ', JPOS 16 (1936), 17f.

Solomon, having built the Temple, has fulfilled the m
promise given by God to his father David (2 Sam. 7:12ff.). Therefore, in his prayer he celebrates the God who keeps covenant with his people and is faithful to his promises (23–4). In this new house, where his name will be (cf. Gen. 32:29), he will meet with his people and his presence will be among them ; and in it the people will make their prayers to God, whatever may be their need (31–53).

54-61 The benediction speaks of the God of all the earth, beside whom there is no other—a theological outlook that developed in Israel much later than Solomon's day. It is said that the sacrifices Solomon offered were so many that the bronze altar was not sufficient, and he had to consecrate the middle of the court in front of the house ; but there is no evidence of a bronze altar in Solomon's Temple. **63.** For peace-offerings in which offerers shared, see §204*g*.

IX Solomon's Labour Force and Treaty with 29
Hiram—1-9 describe the second appearance of the Lord to Solomon (cf. 3:5) and the promise made to him. **6-9** is a later Deuteronomic addition addressed, not to Solomon, but to the whole people. In **8** ' this house will become a heap of ruins ' (RSV) should be read instead of ' this house is high ' (AV), which is unintelligible.

10-14 inform us about the commercial relationship b
between Hiram and Solomon. Solomon did not surrender to the Phoenician the twenty cities in Galilee because he had fallen behind with his payments in kind (cf. 5:11), but sold them for one hundred and twenty talents of gold to relieve his financial embarrassment. When A. R. S. Kennedy (DB iii, 150) gave a gold talent (14) the value of £6,150 sterling, he referred to its intrinsic value assessable by weight ; that valuation would require to be at least doubled today, but the purchasing power of a talent cannot be assessed.

The name Cabul (13) may mean ' good-for-nothing ' ; LXX supports the meaning ' borderland ' ; the name is still used for a place near Akko (cf. GAB, Maps 11, 17 ; Jos. 19:27).

15-23 give details about Solomon's compulsory labour c
service (cf. 5:13ff.). The Millo may have been a defensive tower of the old Jebusite city but was more likely an earthwork (cf. WBA, 130) or an embankment which provided a level road from the city of David on Ophel to the Temple area. Hazor was an important town in North Galilee (cf. e.g. Jos. 4:2, 19:36 ; 2 Kg. 15:29) ; Megiddo (for description see WBA, 130) dominated the famous pass of Mt Carmel, and Gezer controlled an important approach from the coast to Jerusalem. Gezer until now had remained Canaanite, uncaptured by Israelites or Philistines. Lower Beth-horon was on the northerly route from Jerusalem to Jaffa ; Baalath is unknown ; Tamar may have been a city of Judah (cf. Ezek. 47:19) or, less probably, Tadmor, a city 150 miles NE. of Damascus. That only the non-Israelites were involved in compulsory service (22) is contradicted elsewhere (cf. 5:13, 11:28).

24-28. Solomon, in offering sacrifices (25) was exer- d
cising his office as chief priest and as representative of the people (cf. 2 Sam. 24:25). For his trade by sea (26–8) he employed Phoenician sailors. The location of Ophir is disputed: on the African coast opposite Madagascar, on the western shore of the Red Sea at its southern end (the ancient Punt or Put) or, most

d probably, on the Arabian shore of the Persian gulf where there was a gold-producing area.

e **X Solomon's Wealth and Magnificence**—The Queen of Sheba may have been the most illustrious of the visitors to Solomon's court at Jerusalem. According to later writers (Pliny, for example), Sheba was in South Arabia, but Gen. 25:2 and Job 1:15, 6:19 imply that in Solomon's time the Sabaeans lived in North Arabia and had not yet expanded southwards, so that they were neighbours of Israel. The queen's visit may have been for commercial purposes as much as for the pleasure of seeing Solomon's splendour and listening to his wisdom. For the value of her gift (10), see the note on 9:14. In **5** 'the burnt-offerings which he offered' is a possible translation, but it is inapt; read rather 'the pomp of his procession to the house of the Lord'. In **8** the RSV reading 'Happy are your wives!' is to be sustained.

f **11f.**, **22** give information about **Solomon's maritime trade**; ships of Tarshish were such as were capable of making the long journey to Tartessus in Spain or were heavy ore-carrying vessels (see the note on §424*h*); for Ophir see the note on 9:26. The gold that was brought back was used for Temple furnishings (cf. 6:20–2, 28–32, 7:48–50), for large shields and for bucklers (16f., 21; cf. 2 Sam. 15:18), and for drinking-cups and other vessels. Silver was not highly valued as a precious metal (21, 27) and was probably a means of exchange; the ivory was used for inlay work (18–20) and the almug wood for musical instruments and other purposes (11f.). Almug wood cannot be confidently identified; it must have been fine and close-grained; pine, North African thyina and Indian sandalwood have all been proposed.

g **28-29** deal with Solomon's trade in horses and chariots which may have been a royal monopoly. RSV is right in reading Kue (28), a town in Cilicia, as against 'linen yarn' (AV) or 'drove' (RV). It is probable that for Egypt (Miṣraim) in 28 we should read Muṣri, a district in Asia Minor. 29 implies that it was not an exchange trade operated by Solomon between Asia Minor and Egypt, but that the horses and chariots purchased by him from these two places were sold to the Hittites and the Syrians, the former at this period being in the neighbourhood of Damascus.

Solomon's total revenue is estimated at 666 talents of gold (14; see 9:14). The first phrase in 15 should be read as 'besides the tolls levied by the customs officers' (so LXX); this probably refers to dues levied upon goods in transit.

h **XI Solomon's Sin and the Defection of his subject Peoples**—The view that it was late in his reign that Solomon gave himself to the worship of other gods and that, in consequence, there arose defection against his rule in Edom, Syria and at home, represents later Deuteronomic editing of the historical record. **9-13.** It is also affirmed that Solomon kept his empire intact until his death, not by his own wisdom or power, but because God deferred, for David's sake, the punishment which his unfaithfulness warranted.

i **3.** The fact that Solomon had so many wives and paramours is not incredible; the laws against such conduct (e.g. Dt. 7:1–4, 17:17; Exod. 34:11–16) are much later in date. These marriages were political alliances and testify to Solomon's power and influence. David in a small way had followed the same policy (2 Sam. 3:2–5, 15:16, 20:3). The worship offered in temples built to foreign gods was a courtesy worship, but it tended to develop religious syncretism (e.g. Exod. 34:16; Dt. 7:3f.). **7.** Molech (sometimes Moloch; Milcom is a by-form) is an artificial modification of Malik (king; cf. ARI, 162), being given derogatively the vowels of the Hebrew word *bōsheth* (shame); this is also the explanation of the form Ashtoreth (5) of which Ashtart was the proper form (Ishtar and Astarte are common variants of it); Ashtoreth was a goddess associated with Baal and, at least in later times, had a famous temple at Sidon.

j **14-25** describe the **defection of Edom and Syria**. A prince of the royal house of Edom had escaped to Egypt when David devastated his country; he was now married, with a house of his own. **18**, because of its reference to Midian, south-east of Ezion-geber, and Paran, might seem to refer to a separate Midianite defection. But an escape route from Edom to Egypt via Ezion-geber and Paran is not unlikely and the former place might be attributed to Midian. **25**, as far as the name Solomon, goes closely with what precedes;–if LXX is wholly followed, **25b** gives the rendering 'this is the mischief Hadad wrought; he was indignant against (*or* hemmed in; so Syr.) Israel and became king over Edom', and these words may be fittingly read after **22**.

23-25a. Rezon, a vassal of Hadad-ezer of Zobah, had also found refuge in Egypt until David captured Damascus and subjugated Syria, when he returned and eventually became king of Damascus, to be a thorn in the flesh of Solomon (cf. 1 Sam. 22:2; 2 Sam. 8:3ff., 10).

26-40. The encounter of Ahijah (1 Kg. 2:26) with k
Jeroboam, and his symbolic representation to him of the coming division of the kingdom (this is done by Shemaiah, according to LXX 12:24*o*) is the earliest recorded example of the type of action which is not only symbolic but is believed to be in some degree efficacious in bringing about what it symbolises. **32-9** is an obvious Deuteronomic expansion (cf. 4–7, 12 f.).

26 gives the name of Jeroboam's mother as Zeruah, l
i.e. leprous, while LXX says she was a harlot (12, 24*b*); each may be intended as disparaging. **36.** That David is to continue to have a lamp or a hearth in Jerusalem means that he is to have a home there so that his name is not cut off.

It is notable that LXX, in 12:24*a–z*, offers much m
more information about Jeroboam's background and early days, saying that Jeroboam, an Ephraimite, built and fortified Sareira, gathered 300 chariots and rebelled against Solomon, and was forced to flee to Egypt. Eventually he returns after Solomon's death, gathers all Israel to Shechem and is designated king of the ten tribes by Shemaiah.

It is debatable whether this story of Jeroboam is at n
some points modelled on that of Hadad mentioned above; it is not debatable that Egypt seems to have been willing to give asylum to any Israelite insurrectionary who gave evidence of faction and division in Solomon's kingdom.

History of the Divided Kingdom
(1 Kg. XII-2 Kg. XVII)

1 Kg. XII 1-XIV 20—Jeroboam I of Israel 296a
XII 1-20 The Revolt of the Northern Tribes (*c.* 925 B.C.)—**3** states that Jeroboam returned from Egypt soon after Solomon's death; **20** defers his return to a later date and is supported by LXX (cf. 12:24*d–f*). The national assembly before which Rehoboam appeared in order to be acclaimed took place at Shechem, the place to which Jacob came on his return from Haran (Gen. 33:18), and at which the national assembly was held in the days of Joshua and the Israelite amphictyony was enlarged (Jos. 8:30 ff., 24:1), and where the first Israelite king exercised rule, albeit precariously (Jg. 9:6); it was, therefore, a place of ancient traditions in Israel.

The demands presented to the King at Shechem proved that the principle of hereditary monarchy could not be taken for granted. The people had no intention of having a second Solomon, with his resplendent court, his demands for taxes and labour service, and his horde of administrative minions. They demanded relief. His senior advisers warned Rehoboam to adopt a conciliatory attitude or he would do irreparable harm; his own contemporaries bade him put down any insubordination at once or he would invite complete disorder. He took the latter way and split

296a the kingdom in two. It is interesting to note that some people of the north remained loyal to David's house (17), but the death of Adoram (18) showed Rehoboam that the people were in earnest about their demands. In **21-4** Shemaiah appears as a moderating influence, restraining the king from violent reactions to the situation (but cf. 14:25–30 ; 2 Chr. 12:15).

b **25-33** describe various incidents in Jeroboam's reign. **25** may mean that he was forced to leave Shechem on the occasion of Shishak's invasion (14:25f.) and cross the Jordan to build Penuel as a temporary refuge ; but the verb ' went out ' suggests a military campaign, and in that case Penuel may have been a forward defensive post against invaders from the east of Jordan and a control post for the trade routes there.

The golden calves may have been set up at Bethel and Dan because Jeroboam had quarrelled with the priests at Shechem and that may have induced his general recruitment of priests (31 ; cf. E. Robertson, ' Investigations into the OT Problem : The Results ', BJRL 32 (1949), 30) ; Bethel had a place in Israelite tradition (cf. 1 Sam. 8:18, 20:26 ; cf. BASOR, 55–7), and Dan was doubtless geographically necessary and may have meant more for the tribes north of Jezreel than we know.

c The golden calves must have been an ancient and familiar mode (cf. Exod. 32:4, 8 ; Gen. 49:24 ; Dt. 33:17), or they would never have served to take the place, either of the serpent symbol at Jerusalem (cf. H. H. Rowley, ' Zadok and Nehushtan ', JBL 58 (1939), 113–41) or of the Ark, and to keep the people from resorting to the Jerusalem Temple. W. F. Albright has maintained that such bulls or calves served as a pedestal or throne for an image of a god, and were not themselves images to be worshipped (FSAC, 229 ; cf. WBA, 148) ; but they must have been popularly esteemed as images in the context of fertility cults in Palestine ; indeed, it is said that Jeroboam commended them to his people as gods (28). Shrines on hill tops (30) had been in use long before Jeroboam's time, although the Jerusalem Temple may have diminished their importance and' their use ; for the reference to the Levites, see Jg. 17:7ff. The feast of the eighth month which Jeroboam instituted presumably corresponded to that of the seventh in Judah (cf. 8:2), agricultural seasons being later in the north (but cf. Montgomery and Gehman, ICC, *in loco*). Jeroboam was, therefore, not a wicked innovator ; rather he revived or continued old practices ; his condemnation reflects a much later standpoint.

d **XIII The Man of God from Judah**—The interest of the chapter obviously centres upon this man of God ; the old prophet of Bethel (11–32) has a subsidiary role to play. Montgomery describes the story as ' the first extensive case of midrash in the historical books ' (ICC, *in loco*). The reference in the story to Josiah's destruction of Bethel (which actually took place *c.* 621 B.C.) and to the cities of Samaria (Samaria was not built till the time of Omri ; cf. 16:24) is evidence of composition at a time much later than that of Jeroboam (2, 32) ; communication by angelic messenger belongs to an early period of Israel's religious thought (cf. e.g. Gen. 18 ; Jg. 6:11ff.) or to a much later period (cf. Ezek. and Zech. 1–8) ; the mechanical, unethical relationship of the prophet to his message, as exemplified in the second part of the story, is indicative of an immature outlook. The withering of Jeroboam's arm (4), the ruin of the altar (5), the subsequent healing of the arm again (6), and the unnatural act of the lion in refraining from devouring the dead man of God and his ass (24f., 28) are represented as miraculous happenings. There is a strong temptation to consider the temporary withering of the king's arm as due to muscular spasm or nervous rigidity caused by shock as he realised that he had attempted to arrest a man of God ; but it is futile to attempt to give a naturalistic or rational explanation of the features of the story mentioned above ; they are part of an old story that was handed down, probably 29
over a long period (cf. 2 Kg. 23:16), and are tokens of its ethos.

e **1-6**. Jeroboam took what appeared to him to be justifiable action in restraining a disturbing influence, but it is construed in the story as presumption ; he asked for pardon and suffered no permanent hurt. The man of God, having fulfilled his commission at Bethel, did not delay even to accept hospitality ; he was under marching orders. It required downright deceit to turn him aside (18). The old prophet of Bethel was either used by a lying spirit (cf. 1 Kg. 22:20f.) or deliberately seduced the man of God because of the threat he had made against the sanctuary of Bethel ; his conduct is not subjected to moral judgment ; he is but a subsidiary instrument in the action. It was the old prophet who gave the man of God decent burial, but in Bethel, far away from his own people in Judah (29f.), and asked that he himself, when the time came, should be buried beside him, being now convinced of the authenticity of the word which the man of God had spoken against Bethel (31f.).

f **XIV 1-18 The Sickness and Death of Jeroboam's Son, Abijah**—According to LXX (12:24*g*–*n*) the incident took place before Jeroboam's accession, his wife did not disguise herself and the prophet was not blind. The narrative in MT puts the incident late in Jeroboam's reign, long after the encounter of Ahijah with Jeroboam (11:29ff.) ; Ahijah is now aged. **5** says that Jeroboam's wife disguised herself to deceive the prophet ; therefore, he was probably not totally blind but had poor eyesight owing to his age. A gift for a prophet was quite normal (cf. 1 Sam. 9:8) ; the word rendered ' cakes ' signifies ' spots ' and may mean here ' currants ' or ' raisins ' ; the honey was carried in a narrow-necked flask.

g **12** gives the original answer of the prophet ; its sequel is in 17. **7-11** is a Deuteronomic expansion, intimating that the destruction of the house of Jeroboam the unfaithful is now imminent, while **13-16**, also Deuteronomic, describes Abijah as the only member of Jeroboam's house who deserves decent burial. Tirzah (17) was the capital of Israel at a later period (15:21, 16:15ff., etc.). In 14 a full stop may be put at ' Jeroboam ' ; then read ' So much for the time being ' (lit. ' this (for) today '). ' What more after this ? ' (following LXX). The phrase ' bond and free ' (10) may mean ' under the protection of the family or not ', but its significance is uncertain. **19-20** is an obituary notice typical of the book (see §291*c*).

h **21-31 Rehoboam of Judah**—(For **21-4** and **29-31**, which are an editorial framework, see §291*c*). The king's Ammonite mother, who was the ruling lady in the royal household, must have encouraged the worship of foreign gods. Stone pillars and asherim or wooden posts were commonly found beside the altar at Canaanite sanctuaries ; the former were abodes of deity and represented the god Baal, the latter symbolised the tree of life and represented the goddess Asherah or Astarte. Asherah as a proper name is found in Jg. 3:7 ; the corresponding word in Ugaritic means goddess or may be a proper name, Asherah, wife of Baal, and Asherah of the Sea, wife of El, being named (cf. R. Dussaud, *Découvertes de Ras Shamra* (1937), 71f., 77 ; J. A. Montgomery and Z. S. Harris, *The Ras Shamra Mythical Texts* (1935) ; G. R. Driver, *Canaanite Myths and Legends* (1956) ; ARI, 74–9).
25f. refers briefly to the Egyptian invasion of Palestine under the Pharaoh Shishak (Sheshonq I). A record of the campaign has been found in the temple of Amon at Karnak (ANET, 242f., 263) ; it mentions the capture of many towns in Judah, and a number in Israel, such as Megiddo, Taanach, Shunem and Bethshan. Jeroboam may have called in Egyptian help to obstruct Rehoboam's attempts to regain lost territory ; that would account for the mention of Israelite towns in the campaign ; but the location of these towns and the hint of tribute payment by Israel

296h afterwards make it possible that Shishak took advantage of weakness in the divided kingdom to extend his own dominions ; but subsequent history shows no trace of effective domination.

297a **XV 1-32—The reigns of Abijam (1-8) and Asa (9-24) of Judah, and Nadab (25-32) of Israel:** Albright's dates for them are 915–913, 913–873 and 901–900 respectively (see §291*h*). Much of the chapter has been taken by the Deuteronomic editor from the royal annals. Abishalom (2, 10) is probably David's son Absalom. The fact that this might well make Maacah older than Rehoboam has raised the question whether Abijam (Abijah in 2 Chr. 11:20 ff., 13:1, etc.) and Asa, being brothers, may have been grandsons and not sons of Maacah (so Jos. Ant. VIII, x, 1 ; but cf. **9** and 2 Chr. 11:20ff.). But Maacah in **2** must be the queen-mother, Rehoboam's widow ; she may have retained influence at court in the reign of Abijam's son, Asa (8), so that ' mother ' in **10** means ' grandmother '. Abijam is condemned but the dynasty remained in power for David's sake ; for ' a lamp in Jerusalem ', see 11:36 ; the last phrase of **5** may be additional (cf. LXX) ; **6** is a mistaken repetition of 14:30 (so LXX[BL]).

b **11ff.** Asa is commended for his religious reforms. The worship at the local shrines, which was not essentially idolatrous and was condemned only in terms of the later reformation of Josiah, remained ; his father's idols he removed, and the sacred prostitutes who practised immoral fertility rites at the Canaanite shrines, as well as an indecent symbol which the queen-mother had made for Asherah (cf. 1 Kg. 14:23). **15** is unintelligible here ; what it says is intelligible and in order at 7:51.

c **16-22.** The action of Baasha of Israel in occupying the border town of Ramah in Judah must have laid a stranglehold on Jerusalem. Syrian help called in by Judah meant the impoverishment of Jerusalem (18 ; cf. 14:26) and the invasion and plunder by Syria of North Israel and the area around the Sea of Galilee (20). The fact that Asa built two forts with the stones and timber of Ramah (22) shows his fear of further trouble. **18.** In the name Ben-hadad, Hadad was the storm-god, to be equated with Baal ; in Tabrimmon (i.e. Rimmon is good) Rimmon was the Assyrian storm-god (cf. R. Dussaud, *Les Religions des Hittites et des Hourrites, des Phéniciens et des Syriens* (1945), 389ff. ; A. Dupont-Sommer, *Les Araméens* (1949), 107ff.).

At **25** the narrative goes back to take up the history of the Northern Kingdom from the death of Jeroboam. Gibbethon (cf. Jos. 19:44, 21:23) must have taken the place of Gezer as a strongpoint on the border of the Philistine country. **27** gives evidence of aggressive activity by the Philistines, and Nadab was caught between their stout resistance and Baasha's attack on him. Baasha then eliminated the house of Jeroboam, probably not in an excess of religious zeal, but in order to secure dynastic stability.

d **XV 33-XVI 34 deals with the reigns of Baasha, Elah, Zimri and Omri, kings of Israel,** and gives an introduction to that of Ahab ; it reveals a time of great insecurity when dynastic changes were frequent, with the consequent extermination of the fallen royal houses. The house of Baasha, like that of Jeroboam (14:7, 9–11) was condemned for its wickedness and blotted out. For Tirzah (15:33) see 14:17, 15:21, 16:15ff. It is notable how Baasha, who destroyed the house of Jeroboam (15:29) and so fulfilled a sentence pronounced against it (14:7, 9–11), is himself condemned for doing it (7).

e Baasha's successor, Elah, had reigned briefly when he was killed in an insurrection led by an army officer named Zimri (9f.), who exterminated the house of Baasha (11-13) ; but the army regarded him as a usurper and nominated their captain king (16). They left Gibbethon (cf. 15:27) which they had been besieging and captured the capital Tirzah, Zimri perishing in his blazing palace (18). **Omri,** when he had overcome the stubborn resistance of a certain Tibni (21f.), moved his capital to Samaria, a strong defensible hill position and a potential centre of trade (24). This is all that is said of a great king who conquered Moab (see Stone of Mesha ; ANET, 320 f. ; WBA, 155f.) and made such a name for himself that Assyrian records for the next hundred and fifty years name Israel the land of Omri.

f Omri is condemned for his sins (25f.) ; his successor **Ahab** made the situation in Israel much worse by marrying **Jezebel,** daughter of the king of Sidon. For her he built in Samaria a temple for the Phoenician Baal, Melkart. The term ' baal ' can mean ' husband ' or master, or a local god ; here it is used as a proper name to designate a national god. What Ahab introduced was a clash of cultures, in which Melkart might rival Yahweh of Israel and Phoenician customs and practices might contend with Israelite.

g **34** implies that Jericho, which had been laid under a curse in Joshua's day (Jos. 6:26), may have been reoccupied sporadically thereafter (2 Sam. 10:5 ; Jg. 3:13) but was not rebuilt as a city until Ahab's day. The deaths of two men at its rebuilding may be regarded as foundation sacrifices (of which evidence has been found at Gezer, Taanach and elsewhere ; see ARI, 162–4) or they may have been fatal accidents which were later regarded as such sacrifices in fulfilment of the ancient curse.

h **XVII-XIX A Cycle of Elijah Stories, derived from a Life of Elijah**—There is a notable absence of Deuteronomic editing in them ; that fact, taken together with the absence of any denunciation of Jeroboam's golden calves and Elijah's complaint that the altars of the Northern Kingdom had been destroyed so that Yahweh could not be worshipped as he ought to be (19:14), are arguments for a date, not only before the Deuteronomic reformation, but also before Amos and Hosea.

The stories have a miraculous element in them. It is a misguided procedure to attach other vowels to the word rendered ' ravens ' (17:6) and make it ' merchants ', or ' Arabs ', or to look for a natural explanation of the continuing adequacy of the supply of meal and oil (17:16) or to argue that the woman's child did not die but fell into a coma (17:17) ; in the form of the stories before us these are miraculous events and their like can be paralleled in the case of Elisha and others.

i One other general point must be noted. There had never been a real conflict between the naturalistic fertility cult of the local baals and the ethical worship of Yahweh. But this age saw a conflict between Melkart, the national Baal of Phoenicia, and Yahweh, God of Israel ; it was a conflict of two cultures which were at important points disparate. Melkart worship was established in Samaria (16:32f.) and Phoenician culture threatened to envelop Israelite culture.

j **XVII 1-16.** In 17:1 we should read not ' who was of the inhabitants of Gilead ' (AV) but ' who was of Tishbe in Gilead ' (RSV, following LXX) ; this is to distinguish his place from Tishbe in Galilee. Presumably Elijah was commanded to hide himself by the Cherith, east of the Jordan, in order to escape from Ahab. The wonderful thing is that predatory birds like the ravens should have fed him ; no less wonderful was it that a Phoenician woman should feed him, feed him even before her own son when her provision was exhausted (12). Zarephath (Sarepta in Lk. 4:26 (AV) ; Sarafend today) lay 7 or 8 miles south of Sidon.

k In **18** the woman, who interpreted the death of her son as a punishment, says that it was Elijah who had brought her sin to remembrance (or to light) ; without his visit she might have escaped the penalty. **21** illustrates the belief that the life-force was so strong in such a man of God as the prophet that he could breathe some of its abundant energy into the dead child and bring him back to life (cf. 2 Kg. 4:34f. ; Ac. 20:10).

298a **XVIII 1-19 Elijah's Meeting with Ahab—3b and 4,** probably interjected verses, imply that Jezebel took

10

298a such forceful action to establish the worship of the Phoenician Melkart in Israel that she persecuted the prophets of Yahweh (cf. 13), and **30** implies that she destroyed his altars; but Obadiah, Ahab's chamberlain, and possibly others, offered effective resistance and saved alive in secret cave refuges a hundred prophets of Yahweh. The fact that the land was searched for grass in the third year of the drought, that the horses and the mules might be saved, shows that it was a period of inadequate rainfall, not of absolute drought.

b **9-14**. Elijah's commission to Obadiah to inform the king of his return elicited an answer which reveals the deep enmity of the king against the elusive prophet. **17**. The question: 'Who is the real troubler of Israel?' introduces the great contest on Mt Carmel. The number of the prophets of Baal and Asherah (here the name of a goddess; cf. 14:23, 15:13), mentioned in 19, shows the size of Jezebel's domestic establishment. 'The Lord of Hosts': In the original Hebrew the word 'hosts' can mean in the singular army, warfare, or host (e.g. of heaven). 1 Sam. 17:45 indicates that the primary meaning of the name 'Lord of hosts' was God of the armies of Israel. When later the majesty and transcendence of God were emphasised in the religious thought of Israel, the name came to be understood as God of the heavenly hosts (cf. 1 Kg. 22:19; Ps. 102:20f., 148:2), signifying the God, not only of angels (cf. 1 Kg. 22:19, etc.) but of the sun, moon and stars (cf. 2 Kg. 17:16, 21:3, 5); and Gen. 2:1 may imply that it could mean God of all in heaven and earth.

c **20-46**. The time for the people's choice between Yahweh and Baal had now come (see §297*i*); they must cease to vacillate between the two (21); Mt Carmel was a sacred place both for the Phoenicians and the Israelites (cf. SHG 25 (1931), 381ff.: Otto Eissfeldt, *Der Gott Karmel* (1953)), and one that stirred memories (Jg. 5:21; cf. Isa. 9:4). The prophets of Baal, having offered their sacrifices, indulged in their ecstatic excesses to no effect (28); the derisive taunts of Elijah (27) doubtless roused them to greater frenzy, but in vain. If **31** and **32a,** which contradict **30,** are regarded as a later addition, Elijah's repair of Yahweh's altar (30) was in itself an act of defiance of Jezebel and of Baal. In his preparations he poured water over the altar three times (32–5). That act might be interpreted as aimed at accentuating the effect of the expected answer by fire from Yahweh who had revealed himself to Israel among the fires of Sinai (Exod. 19:16–18; cf. Gen. 15:9–11, 17; Jg. 6, 21, etc.), but the pouring of water on the altar and the subsequent ritual prostration of Elijah (probably crouching in such a way as to represent a cloud) at the top of Carmel (42) constitute an acted prayer for rain. The answer which came was twofold; fire destroyed the altar and everything on it (38) and there was heard the sound of a coming rainstorm (41f.). The fact that lightning was often described as the fire of God (cf. e.g. Gen. 19:24; Exod. 24:17; Lev. 10:2; Num. 11:1, 16:35), and the form of the narrative of Elijah's experiences at Horeb (especially 19:11f.), support the view that the fire here was a natural phenomenon, presumably lightning.

d **XIX Elijah's Journey to Horeb; his Call to Elisha**—Especially if we read in **3**, as we probably should, 'Then he was afraid' (RSV) instead of 'When he saw that' (AV, RV), it appears that Elijah fled the land of Israel in fear because Jezebel threatened his life.

If he had merely wanted to escape, he could have returned to the Cherith. But the great day of Carmel having left the people unmoved, and the prophets of Yahweh, such as Obadiah's hundred (18:4), being still in hiding, Elijah felt alone and unsupported. He needed encouragement for his faith (cf. 10, 14); so he turned to Judah and the southern wilderness. A day's journey out from Beersheba he came near to despair; but the wonderful sustenance he received as he sat under the broom bush there reminded him of his 298 experience at Zarephath (17:8–16) and renewed his courage and his will to endure. **7** may, although it need not, imply that his intention from the start was to go to Horeb (Sinai), where God had revealed himself to Moses and had given him the law (for that was his special dwelling-place; cf. Jg. 5:4; Ps. 68:8; Hab. 3:3), and to seek renewal of his faith there.

9b-11a, which anticipate **13-14,** are a repetitive inter- e polation and ruin the whole dramatic effect. Wrapping his cloak over his head, Elijah awaited God's word, for man cannot look upon God and live (cf. Gen. 32:30; Exod. 3:6, 33:20, etc.). Earthquake, wind and fire, each a wonder of the Lord, he experienced, but none had the message he needed. Then came the sound of a faint whisper and he learned that not by the wonders of nature is God's will known or is a people won to faithfulness and loyalty, but by the voice which speaks to the conscience, illumines the mind and strengthens the purpose.

15-16. Elijah was commissioned to anoint Jehu king f of Israel, Hazael king of Syria, and Elisha as his own successor, and was told that a judgment would fall upon the unfaithful in Israel more terrible than that of the prophets of Baal on Carmel. Those who escaped the Syrian sword and the fanatic purges of Jehu would perish at the hands of Elisha. Hazael was actually anointed by a messenger of Elisha (2 Kg. 8:7–15); Ahab was followed by Ahaziah and Jehoram before Jehu became king (2 Kg. 9:1–13), and Elijah remained active yet awhile (2 Kg. 1:2–17).

For the casting of the prophetic mantle upon Elisha g as a sign of his call to prophetic office, and, probably, of the transference to him of prophetic power, see 2 Kg. 1:8.

XX Ahab at War with Syria—For Ahab's part in 299 the coalition of Syrian princes who fought against Shalmaneser II of Assyria at Qarqar, near Hamath in Syria, see §95*f*.

From the time of Baasha (1 Kg. 15:20) the possession of the area east and north-east of the Sea of Galilee had been disputed; possession of it gave control of important trade routes. It has often been noted that Ahab is said in this chapter to have received guidance from prophets in his campaigns and did not show opposition to them; but his opposition was directed particularly against Elijah. Nevertheless, it may be that this chapter and 22 came from a source different from that to which 17–19 belong.

3 may be Benhadad's call to Ahab for complete sub- b mission on humiliating terms, which he accepted (4), and **5** may be the demand that he submit forthwith. But it may rather be that Ahab's words of submission (4) were typically oriental in their excessive politeness and that he handed over his gold and silver only (so 7, LXX), so that, on the second occasion, Benhadad demanded his wives and children as signs of complete surrender, and Ahab refused to comply.

13-21. The plan of campaign advised by the prophet c is obscure. The attendants of the district governors had to leave the city, presumably to create a diversion and to split the Syrian forces (17); thereafter, Ahab was to lead out his main force and attack the Syrian armour (21). The plan worked effectively. Possibly 21 should be read before 20.

The Syrians reorganised their forces, appointed different company commanders (24) and tried to choose favourable circumstances of battle (23), but again the Israelites triumphed. The number of Syrians killed (30) is obviously greatly exaggerated; compare the 7,000 Israelites mentioned in 15.

30b-34. A shrewd piece of diplomacy by Benhadad's officers induced Ahab to spare their king's life. Ahab showed this unwonted clemency either in order to establish profitable trade relations with Damascus (34) or to have Syria as an active defence against Assyria. But the alliance with Syria which resulted had all the dangers of the one formerly made with Phoenicia.

9d **35-43** is, in some respects, a grim story; and the prophet who appears in it has a parallel in 13:11–19. He contrived to look like a man wounded in battle; then he appeared before the king in disguise and confessed to a serious dereliction of duty so that an enemy escaped. The king condemned him at once without mercy. The prophet then removed his disguise and the king perceived the fitness of the prophet's sentence upon himself for sparing Benhadad's life.

For the sons of the prophets (35), i.e. the prophetic fraternities, cf. 2 Kg. 4:38ff., 6:1ff.; they were attached to sanctuaries and lived in communities, and are now commonly termed cultic prophets (see 414*a–c*).

e **XXI Naboth's Vineyard**—The LXX places ch. 21 before 20 and this arrangement brings together chs. 20 and 22 which seem to belong to the same source. Ch. 21 with its emphasis upon the place of Elijah in the community seems to have association with chs. 17–19 although it is doubtful if it comes from the same source. It is concerned with Ahab's appropriation of Naboth's vineyard and the sequel to that act. **2-4**. Ahab offered a fair deal to Naboth; there was no thought of summary expropriation of him; but Naboth refused to surrender a portion of his family inheritance, honouring the Israelite tradition that land is held in trust from the Lord and is not to be alienated from the family. The king took it in bad grace and sulked, but there is no sign that he proposed compulsory acquisition; he knew the strength of the Israelite tradition in such matters.

f **5-14**. In the estimation of Jezebel, Naboth's act was one of gross insubordination and she had no compunction about handling him. Presumably Ahab must have connived at the use of his name and of the royal seal in the letter Jezebel sent to the elders and nobles of the city to celebrate a fast as a sign of mourning for a crime that had been committed. Naboth was arraigned before his peers in Jezreel, was accused of blasphemy and treason by two witnesses (Dt. 17:6), who had been suborned, and was stoned to death together with his sons (2 Kg. 9:26). It is evidence of Jezebel's power that the elders and the nobles, who were privy to the plot, conspired with her. **15, 16**. Ahab did not shrink from going down from Samaria to his country residence at Jezreel to take possession of the vineyard, although LXX says Ahab tore his clothes and put on sackcloth (cf. 27) before he went, which, if true, makes the king still more despicable.

g **17-20a**. It was an obvious occasion for an intervention by Elijah; the rights of a free citizen had been ruthlessly overridden, an innocent man had been put to death. The penalty to be announced by the prophet was that of an ignominious death for Ahab, and **23** announces a shameful end for Jezebel without decent burial. **20b-22** and **24-6** contain later Deuteronomic additions to the narrative, saying that the whole house of Ahab will be cut off, none being buried, while **25-6** read like an obituary notice for the king, reciting not his merits but his demerits.

h **27-29**, a separate section, speaks of remorse on Ahab's part, and, in consequence, the postponement of the penalty upon him and his house (cf. 11:12); it may have been the later incidence of the fall of the house of Ahab (cf. 2 Kg. 9:25ff.) which gave rise to the belief that it was postponed because of the sign of grace in Ahab's remorse.

i **XXII is a continuation of 20** and probably comes from the same source. **1-40** give a narrative concerning the circumstances of Ahab's death. He called the attention of his courtiers to the fact that Ramoth-gilead had not yet been ceded to him by Syria, although three years had now elapsed since their peace treaty (20:34). Jehoshaphat, his son-in-law (2 Kg. 8:18), submissively promised Ahab full support (**4**) but asked for prophetic guidance concerning the chance of victory. The 400 who were consulted at first (cf. 20:35) prophesied success for the two kings (6) and symbolically represented their message in order to reinforce it (11). Meanwhile Micaiah had been
summoned for consultation and was given the hint 299i
to behave himself and to agree with the other prophets (13). His first word to Ahab (15) was dutifully acquiescent, but the king, unconvinced, consulted him a second time. His answer on this occasion was two-fold: he foretold the death of Ahab and the scattering of his people (17), and described a vision of the heavenly council in which it was resolved to deceive the 400 prophets (23). The record of this vision raises acute theological problems. The 400 are exempt from blame; they were enticed, unwitting instruments in a heavenly plan. That it should be said that God enticed Ahab to his doom and used prophets for the purpose, is evidence of immature theology and an unethical conception of prophecy. The exigencies of a monotheistic faith had made the one God the author of both good and evil in such a way that men ceased, in such a case as the one here, to be moral agents and became unwitting and, hence, inculpable instruments.

24-37. Micaiah was rebuked and cast into prison. j
But Ahab disguised himself for battle, hoping to escape his doom, and sent Jehoshaphat into the fray in his royal robes that he might draw the enemy after him (30). Jehoshaphat escaped death (33); Ahab was mortally wounded by a random shot (34). In **38** probably read ' and they washed out the chariot by the pool of Samaria where the harlots washed, and the dogs licked up his blood ', etc. (cf. 21:19). For the ivory house (39), cf. J. W. Crowfoot and G. M. Crowfoot, *Early Ivories from Samaria* (1938): for the commendation of Jehoshaphat of Judah (41–6), cf. 1 Kg. 15:11–14. **47-50** tell of a projected enterprise in maritime trade from Ezion-geber on the Red Sea (cf. 1 Kg. 9:26–8, 10:22).

The accession of Ahaziah in the seventeenth year of k
Jehoshaphat (51) is against the normal chronology of Kg. (cf. 16:29, 22:41) which would make it the twenty-fourth year (so LXX).

THE SECOND BOOK OF KINGS

I 1-II 25 The Last Days of Elijah; Elisha succeeds him—These chapters may come from the 300a
same source as 1 Kg. 17–19 and 21, but the first chapter gives a representation of Elijah so bloodthirsty and crude as to make such a view unlikely, if not untenable, and that is supported by the distinctive spelling of the name Elijah here.

I 1 is a separate fragment which stands here in b
isolation; an account of the revolt of Moab is given in ch. 3.

2-17a. The fact that Ahaziah inquired of Baal-zebub of Ekron rather than of Yahweh of Israel was either a plain act of unfaithfulness to, or disregard of, Yahweh, or a proof that he feared an unfavourable reply if he had sent to Yahweh's prophet, Elijah. In **2** ' lay sick ' (RSV) should be rendered as ' was injured '; the lattice window projected from the wall, like an oriel window of today; it had a wooden fretwork, glass being as yet unknown. It is now accepted that Baal-zebub, god of flies, is a derogatory form of the original Baal-zebul, god of the high-place or lofty dwelling; the name is found in the Râs Shamra Tablets (cf. R. Dussaud, *Les Découvertes de Ras Shamra et l'AT* (1937), 69, 79; and refs. in G. R. Driver, *Canaanite Myths and Legends* (1956); cf. also Mt. 10:25). Baal-zebul was, therefore, not a local god of Ekron, but the god of life of Syria, so that to consult him was an act analogous to the service Ahab rendered to Melkart.

In records of premonarchic Israel references are c
found to divine intermediaries, i.e. angels of the Lord (3), and in documents of the exilic and post-exilic period, but at this period the common form of expression is: ' The word of the Lord came to so-and-so '.

9-17a presumably represents an attempt to arrest and, d
probably, to silence Elijah. The fact that the prophet destroyed the first two companies of soldiers, who were

300d merely instruments of the king's will, seems to indicate that the passage is a later legendary addition in which the greatness of the prophet is compromised by the adulation of much smaller minds.

18 should precede **17**; it lacks the usual statement concerning the king's burial. For the chronology of **18**, see the note on 1 Kg. 22:51, and contrast 2 Kg. 3:1.

e **II 1-25 Elisha succeeds Elijah**—This chapter is part of a collection of traditions concerning Elisha which is continued in chs. 4–6, 8:1–15, 13:14–21. Skinner is right in saying that 'Elisha's work touched life at much lower levels than that of his great predecessor' (Cent.B on *Kings, in loco*); the parallels to be found in the stories concerning the two prophets give the impression that Elisha lived in a reflected glory and had a derivative distinction.

f **1-18.** Aware that his end was near, Elijah paid farewell visits to the prophetic communities at Gilgal, Bethel and Jericho (1-5). (The Gilgal referred to here was a place some seven miles north of Bethel; for the prophetic communities see 1 Kg. 20:35.) The two prophets then crossed the Jordan, its waters being driven back miraculously so that a passage was provided (8); and from his departing leader Elisha asked a double portion of his prophetic power (9), i.e. the portion of the first-born, so that he might be his successor in office. The fact that his request would be granted only if he had a vision of Elijah's translation implies that spiritual gifts can be transmitted only to those who are fit to receive them (10–12); he had the vision, received the gift and picked up Elijah's cloak that had fallen from him (13). The prophetic community at Jericho were sceptical about Elijah's translation, and had search made for him, but in vain (15–18).

g While this story concerning Elijah is thought of in association with those of 1 Kg. 17–19 and 21, there are some notable features, e.g. the relation of Elijah to the prophetic communities is mentioned only here, and in 1 Kg. 19:15f., 19–21 Elisha is already chosen as his successor. The present narrative has the character of an introduction to the Elisha stories rather than a conclusion to those about Elijah.

h Admittedly, the chariot and horses of fire (11) belonged originally to the sun god (cf. Hab. 3:8; Ps. 68:17); here it is said that the God who revealed himself in the mysterious element of fire at Carmel translated Elijah in a chariot of the same element. In 12 it is this chariot which is described as the true defence of Israel. In due course the expectation arose that Elijah would return and 'restore all things' before the advent of the Messiah (cf. Mal. 4:5; Mt. 11:14, 17:10–12).

i **19-22** and **23-5** give two signs of the spiritual power that had come upon Elisha. The first tells how, by the use of purifying salt (cf. Lev. 2:13, etc.) he made sweet the waters of the spring at Jericho (named 'Ain es-Sulṭân today and located beside the ruins of the old city) so that it ceased to cause miscarriages (so RSV; not 'barren land', as AV); the other tells how a group of children who had grossly insulted the prophet suffered a grim penalty. The first we might now believe to be explicable on psychological grounds, i.e. in the belief that the waters had been purified; the second offends our moral sense and is an example of an interpretation of a dire calamity in a way characteristic of the times or is a bit of later legendary lore.

j **III Jehoram of Israel and the Rebellion of Moab** —In **1-3** the king is condemned for his religious apostasy but in extenuation it is admitted that he removed the 'pillar of Baal' (2) which was either a sacred stone beside the altar or an image representing Baal (cf. Dhorme, *L'Évolution religieuse d'Israël* I (1937), 161ff.).

k **4-27.** For the rebellion of Moab there is important evidence in the Mesha Stele (or Moabite Stone); it says that Moab was subject to Israel all the reign of Omri and half the days of Ahab, forty years in all (cf. WBA, 155f.; W. F. Albright, *The Archaeology of Palestine*, 132, 134). But it would require more than the reigns of Omri and Ahab to make up the tale of forty years. Rebellion at the beginning of a king's reign, as is indicated here (5) is the likeliest eventuality. Tribute payments, which had been very heavy (4), were discontinued. Jehoshaphat, who was subject to Israel, agreed to join Jehoram in war against Moab; Edom, which was tributary to Judah, was also impressed into service, her troops being incorporated in Jehoram's army on his journey south (9). When lack of water threatened disaster, it was the faithful Jehoshaphat who asked for prophetic guidance (11) and who commended Elisha (12). Elisha condemns Jehoram's approach to him as insincere and hypocritical (13, but cf. 2) and answers for the sake of Jehoshaphat. That he used music as a stimulant to prophetic utterance like an ecstatic makes Elisha a prophet of a more primitive type than Elijah (cf. 1 Kg. 18:20–40). He promised water would come without their knowing anything of wind or rain, and they were to dig trenches for it. A sudden cloudburst has been suggested as the explanation of what happened, or the draining of water into the trenches from the mountains of Edom; the red sandstone of the area (Edom means 'red'), might be part explanation for the circumstance described in 22–3. The water in the trenches appeared to the Moabite sentries as blood in the morning sun; that suggested a fracas in the Israelite camp; the Moabites attacked and were defeated. The prophet had given stern orders for the destruction of Moab (18–19) (contrast Dt. 20:19f.); these were carried out. In **25** before 'till only its stones' (RSV) there should be inserted the words 'and they harried Moab' (so LXX). That the king of Moab should have attempted an outbreak from encirclement by attacking the Edomites, who were presumably the least inclined to give battle, was a likely procedure but the original Heb. cannot give that meaning; probably it was an attempted breakthrough to Aram or Syria (the names Edom and Aram being very much alike in Heb.). Foiled in that effort, the king of Moab, in desperate extremity, resorted to human sacrifice (cf. Jg. 11:29f.; 2 Kg. 16:3). Great wrath fell upon Israel (27); that means that the fortunes of battle suddenly changed, either because the Moabites regained their courage in the confidence that Chemosh would accept their sacrifice or the Israelites became afraid when they saw the desperate measures adopted by the Moabites; the alternatives are not mutually exclusive.

IV 1-VI 23 Incidents in the Life of Elisha 301

IV 1-7 The miraculous Amplification of a Widow's oil Supply—The widow of a prophet was about to see her two children made slaves for debt—a legitimate demand on the part of the creditor (cf. Exod. 21:7; Lev. 25:39; Isa. 50:1, etc.). She appealed to Elisha and, upon obeying his instructions, found her oil supply so enlarged that she could not only discharge the debt but had an ample reserve for the use of herself and her sons. The story might be interpreted as a pictorial representation of the fact that Elisha started for the widow an unfailing stream of neighbourly generosity and kindness, but in form the story describes a miraculous provision.

8-37 The Lady of Shunem and her Son—Shunem b
was about 5 miles from Jezreel and 20 from Carmel (25). In the house of the lady of Shunem a special guest chamber had been built for Elisha on the roof (10). The prophet, wishing to recompense his benefactor, asked her what he could do for her but she professed to be content with her lot (11–13; cf. 2 Sam. 19:36f.). At Gehazi's suggestion he promised her a son (14–16); in **16** 'when the time comes round' means 'at this time next year'. The child born in due course died later of sunstroke. Pacifying her husband's anxious inquiry (in 23 read 'all is well' instead of 'it will be well', RSV), she went to Elisha and blamed him for her tragic sorrow (28). Gehazi was

1b sent home in haste (29) to lay the prophet's staff on the child, since it was believed to be charged with vitalising power; but the child did not revive (31). Then Elisha came and bent over the child, breathing into him, and the child revived (32–7). The story, which has a parallel in 1 Kg. 17:17ff., illustrates the Heb. belief in that communication of power by direct or indirect contact which is generally known as extension of personality (cf. A. R. Johnson, *The Vitality of the Individual in the Thought of Ancient Israel* (1949).

c **38-41 Death in the Pot**—In a time of famine, when food was very short, some colocynths had been gathered to help to provide food for a prophetic community, either because they were mistaken for something else or because the need was so great that risks had to be taken. Colocynths can act as a strong purgative and an irritant, and, taken in large quantities, are poisonous. The meal added to the cooking pot at the prophet's instruction may well have served as a counteractive agent so that the result was wonderful to the prophets but need not be described as miraculous.

d **42-44.** An offering of first fruits is miraculously multiplied to provide food for a hundred men, probably prophets. (For the location of Baal-shalisha in Ephraim, see Map 8 at end.) First fruits would normally be offered to a priest but prophets and priests were associated at many shrines (cf. A. R. Johnson, *The Cultic Prophet in Ancient Israel* (1944)).

e **V 1-27 The Healing of Naaman and the Sequel—1-7** is the first movement in the story. Naaman, a successful and honoured Syrian general, informed by a Heb. slave-girl about the prophet Elisha, is sent to Israel by his king to be cured of his leprosy, and is given a letter of introduction to the king of Israel. The latter, having suffered much from Syrian raiders, regards the letter, not as a diplomatic note, but as peremptory and offensive in tone.

8-14. Elisha intervened to say he would see Naaman (8). His aloof attitude incensed Naaman (10–12), whose servants tactfully advised him to follow the prophet's instructions because, if they proved ineffective, it was the prophet who would lose face. He accepted the advice and was cured of his malady.

f **15-19** has several notable features: Naaman's confession of faith in Yahweh as God alone (15), his request for a load of earth that he might worship Yahweh on his own soil (17), and his plea for forgiveness for the formal worship which he must still offer to Rimmon (18). For Rimmon see note on 1 Kg. 15:18. The meaning of 19*a* is that Elisha bade Naaman farewell. **20-27** illustrates the opportunism and self-interest of Gehazi. Elisha might refuse a gift (15–16) but he saw no reason why he should not reap some benefit from Naaman's sense of indebtedness. The story he concocted gave himself no appearance of astuteness or cupidity and elicited a generous response. He tried to cover up his tracks but failed (24–5); he was severely censured by Elisha and the leprosy of Naaman was laid upon him and his posterity. In 24 ' the hill ' (Heb. Ophel) must refer to Samaria here, and not to the hill on which the old city of Jerusalem stood, its usual connotation.

g **VI 1-7 The Axe-head that floated**—The first part of this section gives evidence both of the expansion of the prophetic communities which necessitated an enlarged settlement for them by the Jordan, and of Elisha's close association with them. **6.** The act of throwing a piece of wood upon the water to make the submerged axe-head float is essentially an example of mimetic magic; in this Elisha appears simply as a wonder-worker or shaman.

h **8-23 Warfare in two Kinds**—The king of Syria found that all his military plans against Israel were miscarrying (8–10); he suspected treachery but his staff told him that Elisha had supernatural gifts that enabled him to penetrate the secrets of the human mind and so to reveal the king's plans to his own master in Israel (12). The attempt of the Syrians to capture Elisha in Dothan, a town some 10 miles north 301h
of Samaria (13f.), is contrasted with the action of the unseen auxiliaries of Elisha and the power of God in him by which he struck the Syrians blind (15–17) and enticed them into Samaria (18f.). The king of Israel was ready to destroy them there but was restrained by the prophet. In **22** the question in RSV (Would you slay . . .?) cannot be the right rendering. We must follow either LXX[L] and read the question: ' Would you slay those whom you have *not* taken captive . . .? ' or the Targum and read: ' You may slay . . . bow, but set bread . . .' The king of Israel was not entitled to put to death men whom he had not captured. So the Syrians were spared (23) and this act of clemency inaugurated a period of peaceful relations between the two countries.

VI 24-VII 20 Elisha during the Siege of Samaria i
—This section is probably not from the same source as the preceding sections, but from the historical source to which 1 Kg. 20 and 22 belong; or Skinner may be right in believing that ' a chapter of political history may have been utilised as the basis of a prophetic biography ' (Cent.B, 306). **25-30.** The severity of the conditions in the city during the siege is shown by the excessive cost of anything edible, and by the desperate expedient of the women who conspired to sacrifice their own children to allay their unendurable pangs of hunger. Some commentators suggest that dove's dung may have been the name of a herb, but there is no known support for the suggestion. The appeal of one of the women to the king revealed to him the desperate extremity of the besieged people and gave him greater cause than he had known for the sackcloth he was wearing (30). **31.** The king blamed Elisha for the situation because he had advocated resistance in the faith that God would deliver the city (33); he now lost patience and decided to kill him (**31-3**; read ' king ' for ' messenger ' in 33 and, possibly, 32). **7:1.** The prophet promised immediate alleviation of conditions in the city and a supply of decent food again; whether prices remained still abnormally high cannot be determined.

VII 3-20 The Four Lepers of Samaria—3-8. Four j
lepers, living in isolation outside the gate of Samaria and facing certain death there from hunger, and aware that no less certain death would befall them if they attempted to enter the city, decided to take the chance of escaping with their lives by going over to the Syrians. They found the enemy camp empty, the Syrians having interpreted a noise which they heard as the arrival of auxiliaries for the Hebrews. They therefore satisfied their hunger and then looted some of the tents (for the possibility that in **6** Muṣri, a district in Asia Minor, should be read for Egypt, i.e. Misraim, cf. 1 Kg. 10:28). **9-10.** But on reflection, they saw their conduct as selfish enjoyment of the Syrian flight, and returned and reported their discovery in Samaria. The king suspected a Syrian stratagem to entice the Israelites out of the city so that its capture would be made easy (11–12); but he was persuaded to let a reconnaissance party be sent out. Horses and men alike would perish in the city in any case if the siege continued, so that there was no reason why the risk should not be taken. They found the camp empty and followed the trail of the retreating Syrians as far as the Jordan (13-15). For 16–20, see vv. 1–2; the king's officer perished for distrusting the word of Elisha.

VIII 1-15 continues the Elisha Narratives in Sequence to IV 1-VI 23—1-6. The Shunammite 302a
woman (cf. 4:1–37), who is now a widow, after an absence of seven years from the country to avoid the rigours of a famine of which Elisha had foretold her, has returned to find her property appropriated and gets instant redress when she appeals to the king for help. The fact that, when she appealed to the king, he was listening to Gehazi giving a recital of Elisha's wonderful doings, may mean that his hostility towards the prophet had ceased (cf. 6:31–3); but it may also

802a mean that he was looking for an opening for renewed opposition.

b **7-15** describes an interview between Elisha and Hazael. The Benhadad mentioned here was probably the same king as opposed Ahab (cf. 1 Kg. 20:1); Hazael was probably his army commander. That Benhadad inquired of Elisha in Damascus concerning his chance of recovery from his illness, assumes a period of peaceful relations between Israel and Syria and shows that Elisha's renown was known in that city. Elisha's reply (10) may have been unexceptionable in intent, meaning that the king would not die of his illness but would die in another way; but that is not explicitly stated. How Hazael received the news is not hinted at; whether a look that suggested ambitions about to be realised by Hazael induced the prophet's trance experience that followed, we are unable to say. **11** describes the prophet's fixed stare and rigid attitude that arose from spiritual tension within him; the personal reference in 'until he was ashamed' is probably to the prophet, but it was a state of embarrassment rather than of shame which ensued. In vision Elisha foresaw Hazael as the scourge of Israel (12). If Hazael had had no ambitions for kingly power before this, the intimation now made to him (13) must have given him strong provocation. 15 does not say that the king died at Hazael's hands, but it seems to leave it to be inferred. Hazael certainly started a new dynasty; he was not the legitimate successor; his name appears without patronymic; in the Berlin Inscription he is named 'the son of a nobody' (ANET, 280).

c **16-19** makes clear that the marriage of Jehoram to Ahab's daughter Athaliah introduced the apostate ways of Ahab's Israel into Judah. The fact that, nonetheless, Jehoram's reign was prosperous is attributed to the merit of good king David and to the promise given to him that his line would not be extinguished in Jerusalem (19) (cf. 1 Kg. 11:9–13); 23f. is from the hand of the same compiler as 16–19. **20-2** records a successful revolt by Edom. **21** in RSV describes a victory by Jehoram (or Joram) and the subsequent, unexplained panic and flight of his army; that is unlikely. Either Jehoram and his army broke out of encirclement and escaped complete disaster, or the text in its original form told explicitly of an Edomite victory. The loss of Edom to Judah must have lost her the trade by the Red Sea route and, possibly, tolls from caravan traffic.

d **25-29.** Ahaziah, who succeeded Jehoram of Judah, reigned briefly and imitated his father's ways. **28f.** is in effect introductory to chs. 9–10. Ahaziah, ally of Joram of Israel in battle against Syria, visited him as he lay at Jezreel recovering from his wounds. The death of Ahaziah is mentioned incidentally (**9:27f.**) in the story of Jehu's rebellion, so that the compiler's normal scheme of reference to the beginning and the end of reigns is here disordered.

e **IX-X The Revolution of Jehu**—These chapters are from the same source as 1 Kg. 20, 22 and 2 Kg. 6:24–7:20. They give a graphic objective account of the events that brought about the destruction of the house of Ahab, apart from **9:7-10** (especially 9) and 10:28–31 which bear marks of Deuteronomic editing (contrast 10:30 with Hos. 1:4). The narrative leaves it to be inferred that Jehu had popular support, but that probably expressed the desire for political and social freedom more than religious zeal (cf. 1 Kg. 21).

f **IX 1-10.** Elisha may or may not have provoked Hazael to regicide (cf. 8:10–15); he certainly had Jehu anointed king when the reigning king Joram was still alive (9:1–3, 14). Jehu was an army officer; but the movement he led was not a military uprising but a political and social revolution instigated by Elisha, which was a sequel to the work of Elijah. The aim of it was the extermination of the apostate house of Ahab (cf. 7–10). For the phrase (AV, 8) 'shut up and left', see 1 Kg. 14:10.

g **11-13.** When Jehu's fellow-officers learned the nature of the prophet's errand, they acclaimed Jehu and gave him whole-hearted support, thus giving evidence of popular hostility against Ahab's house. In 11 the term 'mad fellow' means that the prophet messenger showed in his demeanour and actions some of the signs of the primitive ecstatic type. In 13 'bare steps' is as likely a rendering as any of an uncertain text. 30...

Jehu depended upon speed and secrecy for the success of his *coup d'état* (15). **16-29** describes in a vigorous and graphic narrative the deaths of Jehoram and Ahaziah. Jehu left Ramoth-gilead in haste for Jezreel where the two kings were (cf. 8:28, 29). Two messengers were sent out from the city in turn to inquire what news the riders brought from the battle-field; Jehu detained them. The style of riding now having revealed Jehu's identity, the two kings went out to meet him unsuspectingly, and the meeting took place fittingly at the property of Naboth (cf. 1 Kg. 21:17ff.). Jehu's attitude at once revealed his rebellious intentions (22f.); Joram, attempting to escape, was shot dead and was flung upon Naboth's land, to lie unburied (25f.). Ahaziah reached Beth-haggan where he was wounded but escaped capture, and eventually he arrived at Megiddo, where he died (27f.). Beth-haggan is the modern Jenîn, 7 miles south of Jezreel; Ibleam is somewhat farther south; Megiddo is on Mt Carmel to the north-west (see GAB, Map 17). 29 is a separate fragment which interrupts the flow of the narrative.

30-37 describes the ignominious End of Jezebel h —'Is it peace?' (contrast the use of the phrase in 17–19, 22) is a direct challenge to Jehu; the stinging epithet Zimri (31; cf. 1 Kg. 16:10) was flung at him by Jezebel defiantly; she faced the issue with all her weapons in use (30). The eunuchs who appeared at her window were either traitorous or were curious about the cause of the din on the street. Jezebel in her death was treated with contempt (33). Jehu took it all imperturbably (34) but at least he ordered decent burial for her. He gave the instruction too late (35–7; cf. 1 Kg. 21:23).

X Jehu now turned his Attention to Samaria— i He could feel secure on the throne only if he had destroyed all the members of the royal house and so obviated blood revenge. He challenged the city fathers of Samaria to put the most likely member of Ahab's house on the throne and contest the issue; they declined the challenge and pledged their loyalty to Jehu (1–5). His next letter to the city fathers demanded the death of the 70 members of the royal house, and it was obeyed (6–7). His act of stacking the heads of the slain at the gate of Jezreel and claiming that it had been done by supernatural intervention in fulfilment of a prophecy (cf. 1 Kg. 21:21) represents a code of conduct against which our moral sense strongly rebels.

The subsequent slaughter of a group of Judaean princes who were on, or returning from (AV, RSV respectively), a visit to their relatives of Ahab's house shows the blood-lust that possessed Jehu (12–14). Beth-eked may be a place-name or may mean simply 'meeting-place'; in the latter case a well-known meeting-place was probably in mind.

15-16 describes the alliance between Jehu and Jeho- j nadab. The latter seems to have become well known by this time as a strong nationalist and an advocate of the old ways; the Rechabites, related to the Kenites originally (cf. 1 Chr. 2:55), exalted the austere life of the wilderness as a protest against the luxuries and indulgences of an agricultural and commercial civilisation (cf. Jer. 35). **18-27.** Jehu's final act was the extermination of the prophets, priests and worshippers of Baal in Samaria. He enticed them into the temple of Baal by sheer deceit, and induced their priests to proclaim a festival and supplied them with festal dress (20-2; cf. Gen. 35:2; Exod. 19:10). He himself offered sacrifices to give a semblance of sincerity to his invitation (24f.); he had ensured that all who were invited came and he

302j let none escape (19, 24). Temple, prophets, priests and worshippers were destroyed, a disgusting holocaust arranged by guile and subterfuge.

k **32f.** makes it quite plain that, with the extinction of the house of Ahab, the alliance of Israel with Judah and Phoenicia ceased and Israel's power to hold Syria in check came to an end. Jehu seems to have lost control of all land east of the Jordan and thus suffered the economic loss of the trade routes in that area. The Black Obelisk of Shalmaneser III represents Jehu as paying tribute to Assyria (ANET, 281).

303a **XI-XIII In these Chapters the Scene is changed to Judah—11:1-20** tells of the revolution in that kingdom comparable to the one under Jehu's leadership in the north ; but whereas the latter was inspired directly by prophetic influence, the former was directed by Jehoiada the priest. The record runs smoothly, but two factors raise the question of its unity : (*a*) the sudden reference to the people in **13**, the preceding verses speaking only of Jehoiada and the Temple-palace guards ; (*b*) the brief reference to the death of Athaliah in **20** when it is already described in **13-16.** It may be that **13-18a** come from a different source from the rest of the chapter, but, if so, this source was used because it preserved a more circumstantial account than the other of the queen's death and of the eradication of Baal worship. We may assume that during her reign she exercised a rigid control, so that the people supported the palace revolution ; likewise, we cannot separate the political aspect of the movement (4–12) from the religious (15–18*a*) ; these were inextricably interrelated. **13-18a,** therefore, is complementary to the rest of the chapter and amplifies the narrative.

b **1-3** tells how Athaliah, the only survivor of Ahab's house, secured the throne of Judah for herself, when her son Ahaziah died, by destroying the male members of the royal house. But an infant son of the late king, named Joash, was saved from death by his aunt Jehosheba, wife of the priest Jehoiada (cf. 2 Chr. 22:11), and was hidden away securely in the priests' quarters. Queen Athaliah had reigned only six years when a *coup d'état*, carefully planned by Jehoiada and the Temple-palace guards, was successfully carried out. **5-7** are not wholly intelligible, **6** probably being parenthetical ; but the plan clearly was that the young prince should be acclaimed king in the Temple on an appointed Sabbath, at the time when the guards were being changed and both incoming and outgoing companies could easily be concentrated in the Temple for maximum security while the palace was left untended (8–9). The spears and shields of David may have been issued to the company leaders as symbols of rightful authority for the coronation ceremony (10). The meaning of the testimony (12) is not clear ; it may signify the law, so that it represented the covenant obligation of an anointed ruler (cf. 17) and the crown his regal power ; many scholars, by a minor change, would read ' bracelets ' or ' ornaments ' in place of ' testimony ' (cf. 2 Sam. 1, 10). **14** implies that there was a special place in the Temple for the coronation ceremony, ' by the pillar ' (RSV) or, more likely, ' on the platform ' (or dais). **14-16** tells how Athaliah, hearing the noise, rushed into the Temple and quickly recognised what had happened ; she was carefully removed from the Temple by the undignified route of the horse gate (cf. 19) and put to death in the palace. **17-18a** expresses the religious side of the revolution, and the renewal of the covenant. The final act seems to have been the enthronement of the king in the palace (19). The Carites or Carians (4, 19) were foreign mercenaries, named also Cherethites or Cretans (cf. 2 Sam. 20:23) : 2 Chr. 23:1–21 substitutes Levites for such foreign servitors. Mattan (' gift ', 18) is an abbreviated form of Mattan-Baal.

c **XII Joash and the Repairs of the Jerusalem Temple—11:21** should follow **12:1.** The young king during his minority was under the tutelage of the
priest Jehoiada (2). In his maturity he resisted foreign 303c
cultural influences (2, reading probably ' as ' for ' because ') but local Baal worship continued (3). In **4-16** is a record of Temple repairs which were urgently required. Whereas the upkeep of the Temple buildings was a royal responsibility, there is here an organised attempt to meet the cost of heavy repairs from Temple revenue derived from assessed dues and voluntary gifts. The difficult phrase set in parenthesis in **4** in RSV has been interpreted by G. R. Driver as meaning ' the money from the persons assessed with him ' ; but that is not the main difficulty of verses **4-7.** The form of **4-5** in RSV implies that the priests were to gather the assessed dues (cf. Lev. 27:2ff.) and the voluntary gifts from their own acquaintances—a most unlikely procedure. Note that on the later occasion described in verses **6-8,** when the priests are forbidden to take any more money from their acquaintances, there follow the words ' but hand it over for the repair of the house ', in which the word ' it ' has no clear reference. The meaning of the Hebrew word which is rendered in RSV as ' acquaintances ' is uncertain ; G. R. Driver considers that the word means ' private property '. If we accept that, **5** will mean that the dues and freewill-offerings are to be devoted *in toto* to the repairs of the Temple and that priests are to provide for their maintenance from their own resources, and **7** will mean that they are no longer to use the income from their private property for their own maintenance but to devote it to the repair work.

By the twenty-third year of the reign of Jehoash d
no repairs had been carried out (6). As a penalty the king demands that the priests are to use the income from their personal property (cf. 5) only for the repairs. **7-8.** The priests rebelled and refused to handle the Temple moneys at all or to have charge of the repairs.

9-12 describes the arrangement now made. A box e
was placed in the Temple by a pillar (so some Gr. MSS ; RSV, altar) for offerings ; the box was emptied, as need arose, by a palace official and the high priest, and the money (i.e. uncoined silver and gold) was melted into ingots, counted, and handed over to the overseers to pay the wages of the tradesmen and the cost of materials. The priests had defaulted badly ; they were relieved of any responsibility for the repairs ; by contrast the overseers are commended (15). The retention of the services of the so-called high priest (10, cf. 2) is notable ; it may be due to later editing.

17-18 tells of a remarkable extension of Syrian power f
at this period (cf. 2 Kg. 10:32, 13:3). The capture of Gath on the coastal plain must have meant that Israel had become largely a subject province. Even Jehoash, king of Judah, had to exhaust his resources to buy impunity. It may have been this national crisis in Judah which provoked rebellion against Jehoash (19–21) ; 2 Chr. 24:25f. gives a more specific reason for it. It was another palace plot, but it is notable that Amaziah, son of Jehoash, succeeded his father (and, in due course, suffered a similar fate ; cf. 14:19). In 20 the meaning of ' the house of Millo that goes down to Silla ' is quite uncertain.

XIII is a Continuation of X—1-9. Jehoahaz of g
Israel : 3 confirms the fact of Syrian dominance of Palestine evidenced in 12:17f. ; 7 describes the serious reduction in man-power of military age in Israel. 4–6 are quite contradictory to 3 and 7, speaking of God's mercy to Israel, of a deliverer unnamed, and of the resumption of peaceful conditions again. These verses are to be taken in close association with **23** and with 14:27 ; the words ' until now ' in **23** suggest that they came from an Israelite editor after the fall of Samaria in 721 ; but **24f.** makes it clear that Israel's recovery of power did not begin until the reign of Jehoahaz, so that the mention of a deliverer here is a proleptic reference to Jeroboam II (14:27).

10-25 Jehoash of Israel—Thirty-seventh year (10) h

803h is not in agreement with 1; it should be thirty-ninth. **12-13** is a normal form of obituary notice for the king, yet it is followed in **14-21** by the final part of the history of Elisha and in **22, 24f.** by an extract from the annals of Israel, both of which should have a place within the editorial framework of the reign. In addition, a second obituary notice for Jehoash (or Joash) is given in 14:15f., following the record of a conflict between Amaziah and Jehoash (**14:8-14**). Skinner's theory (Cent.B *in loco*) seems sound; he submits that 14:8–14 originally followed 13:25 as part of the record of Jehoash's reign and after it came the obituary notice of 14:15f.; but it was later transferred to its present context, the obituary notice with it. The notice now included at 13:12–13 is a later editorial insertion to make good the resultant lack.

i **14-21 Elisha's Death**—Jehoahaz recognised Elisha as the only true defence of Israel. The prophet had sympathy with the king and joined him in a final act of defiance against Syria. He laid his hands over those of the king as he set his bow to shoot an arrow of victory eastward against Syria in an act regarded at once as symbolic and efficacious; he thus tried to transfer to the king some of his own indomitable spirit (15–17) (cf. the idea of extension of personality as in A. R. Johnson, *The One and the Many in the Israelite Conception of God* (1942)). For Aphek, cf. 1 Kg. 20:26. The fact that he beat the ground only three times with the arrows (18–19) showed that only a modicum of the prophet's zeal had possessed the king. So great a spirit as Elisha's could not easily be extinguished; 20–1 contains a tradition showing that even after his death some life-force remained in his body (see A. R. Johnson, *The Vitality of the Individual in the Thought of Ancient Israel* (1949)).

j For **22-5** see note under **1-9**. The occasion of the improvement of Israel's position was the death of Hazael of Syria and the preoccupations of his successor, Benhadad, in making his position secure; but it may also have been the aggressive movement of Assyria westward in 803 under Ramman-Nirari III and the consequent breaking of Syrian power.

804a **XIV 1-22 Amaziah of Judah**—He reigned twenty-nine years, it is said (2); but if, beginning in the second year of king Joash of Israel (13:10), he reigned that time, he must have died in the fifteenth year of Jeroboam II; but 15:1 says that his successor Azariah began to reign in the twenty-seventh year of that monarch. There is thus a discrepancy of twelve years between the chronological scheme represented by 13:10 and 14:2, 17, 23 on the one hand, and 15:1, 8 on the other (see §291*h*). The high-places were not removed (4; cf. note on 12:1–3). The fact that Amaziah destroyed his father's assassins but not their children (6) seems to indicate a departure from the thought of the family as the essential social unit; the law quoted is Dt. 24:16.

b Since Joram's campaign (8:20–2) Edom had been independent; Amaziah's campaign against it was probably for control of trade routes and of the Red Sea port of Elath. The Valley of Salt (cf. 2 Sam. 8:13) was the area south of the Dead Sea. Sela (rock) suggests Petra, 'the rose-red city half as old as time', which lay midway between the Dead Sea and the Gulf of 'Aqaba; this identification is now supported, although the application of the name Joktheel to it is not known.

8-14 Amaziah and Jehoash—At this time Amaziah, elated by his success over Edom (10), either sought freedom from vassalage to Israel or challenged Jehoash to battle, according to the interpretation we put on his words (8). Jehoash tried to humour him with a little parable and told him not to try and pick a quarrel. But battle was joined and Amaziah suffered inglorious defeat and loss.

c **15-22** is substantially editorial. **22** seems strangely out of place. Either Azariah occupied Elath during Amaziah's reign and, possibly, won popular favour thereby; or it was one of the first acts of his own reign, Amaziah having lost it to Edom (cf. WBA, 160). We must assume that Azariah is an erroneous form of the more common Uzziah, or that the former was a throne-name (cf. A. M. Honeyman, 'The Evidence for Regnal Names among the Hebrews', JBL 67 (1948), 13–25).

d **23-29.** Jeroboam II was one of the most illustrious and successful kings of Israel. The power which Assyria in his time exercised over Syria gave him the opportunity to extend his empire northwards and eastwards to rival Solomon's (25, 28). In **25** 'the entrance of Hamath' (RSV) should be read as the place-name Lebo of Hamath, i.e. in the area of Hamath on the Orontes in Syria. The Jonah, son of Amittai (25), may be the prophet under whose name the book of Jon. was later written. Gath-hepher was near Nazareth (cf. Jos. 19:13). For the phrase 'bond or free' (26) see the note on 1 Kg. 14:10; for **26f.** cf. 13:4–6, 23; in **28** for 'which had belonged to Judah' (RSV), read 'in Yadi', Yadi being a district in northern Syria (cf. G. A. Cooke, *A Textbook of North Semitic Inscriptions* (1903), 163f.).

e **XV 1-7 Azariah of Judah**—Much light is shed upon the period covered by chs. 15–16 in the inscriptions of Tiglath-pileser III (cf. ANET, 282–4). Azariah's was a long and successful reign. The record of it here is extremely meagre in spite of the commendatory judgment passed on him (4). His death as a leper was regarded as a punishment; the crime mentioned in 2 Chr. 26:16–21 is that he offered sacrifice. 2 Chr. gives information about his military organisation and campaigns and about the economic development of Judah during his reign. **5** implies that as a leper Azariah lived in quarantine, 'in a separate house' (RSV), or 'in freedom at home'. For the name Azariah see note on 14:22; and for twenty-seventh year (1) see note on 14:2.

f **8-12 Zechariah of Israel**—With him Israel entered upon a period of great uncertainty and conflict when no king reigned securely, few reigned long and fewer still died a natural death. To reconcile **8** with 14:23, twenty-seventh year would need to be read; in terms of 15:1 the difference is still greater: twenty-three years (see §291*h*). For **12** cf. 10:30.

g **13-16 Shallum**—A usurper (10, reading 'at Ibleam' (RSV) instead of 'before the people' as AV), he reigned one month, being ousted by a rival claimant for power, Menahem (14), who had occupied the old capital Tirzah (cf. 1 Kg. 14:17, 15:21, etc.). He conquered the towns in its neighbourhood which supported Shallum (16); for Tiphsah, known as a town on the Euphrates, read probably Tappuah, which was a town on the border of Ephraim and Manasseh (Jos. 16:8, 17:7).

h **17-22 Menahem**—His reign was notable for the direct intervention of Assyria in Israel. Pul, known in the Babylonian inscriptions, was a personal name, Tiglath-pileser was the throne-name. Menahem paid tribute as a subject and as a protégé of Assyria (19). A poll-tax of 50 shekels which produced 1,000 talents meant 60,000 'wealthy men', i.e. men of social standing. For the value of a talent of silver, see §35*a*; but that is intrinsic value estimated by weight; purchasing power of silver at this period cannot be estimated.

i **23-26 Pekahiah**—After two years he was destroyed by his army commander Pekah (25). Argob and Ariah (25) should be transferred (see RSV) to **29**, the latter being read as Havvoth-jair (cf. 1 Kg. 4:13).

j **27-31 Pekah**—A reign of twenty years is impossible chronologically (see §291*h*). **37**, 16:5ff. and Isa. 7 show Pekah as conspiring with Syria to rebel against Assyria and attempting to coerce Judah to join them (735–734 B.C.). The Assyrian invasion of North Galilee (29; cf. 1 Kg. 15:20) was the result; probably Gala'za should be read in place of Gilead. **30** implies that Hoshea usurped the throne; Assyrian records make him a nominee, which may mean that he willingly submitted. The dating by reference to a

304j king of Judah in 30 is abnormal ; the date agrees with 27 but not with 17:1.

32-38. The upper gate, mentioned in the brief record of Jotham's reign in Judah, probably means that referred to in Jer. 20:2 (see note in J. Skinner, Cent.B, 366). 2 Chr. 27 shows that Jotham continued the constructive and successful policy of his father.

305a **XVI Ahaz of Judah** (cf. 2 Chr. 28)—Chronologically speaking, the seventeenth year of 16:1 agrees with the twentieth of 15:27, but see note on 15:27. In **2** Ahaz is said to have been twenty years old when he began to reign and reigned sixteen years. 18:2 makes Hezekiah twenty-five at the beginning of his reign, which would make his father a boy of eleven years when his son Hezekiah was born. There is error somewhere in these figures.

3-4. Only Manasseh is more severely condemned than Ahaz. The latter not only encouraged Canaanite modes of worship but revived in Judah the rite of child sacrifice (cf. ARI, 162). It had been intermittently resorted to among the Israelites in extremity (cf. Jg. 11:34ff.) and was known among the surrounding peoples (3:27, 17:31), but it seems to have become rife in the closing years of the kingdom (17:17, 21:6, 23:10, etc.).

b **5-9** is concerned with the Syro-Ephraimitic invasion (cf. 14:29, 37 ; 2 Chr. 28:1–15 ; Isa. 7) ; see the note on 14:27–31. **6.** Judah's predicament enabled Edom to regain possession of Elath (cf. 14:22) ; Aram (Syria) is an error for the similar name Edom (see 6*n*) since Syria could not regain what it had never possessed and since the last clause of 6 obviously refers to the Edomites) ; and it forced Ahaz to appeal to Assyria for help and to incur the condemnation of the prophet Isaiah (Isa. 7). To gain this help he had to surrender Jerusalem's treasures ; and when it came, North Galilee was devastated (15:29), and Damascus was captured in 732 B.C.

c **10-16 A new Altar in the Temple**—It is said that Ahaz ordered for the Temple an altar on the model of one he had seen in Damascus. This was probably an Assyrian type and the installation of one in Jerusalem may have been obligatory. That Ahaz could issue such an instruction shows the authority he exercised in the Temple. Whereas the priest normally offered the royal sacrifices (15), the king himself offered the sacrifices at the consecration of the new altar (13–14). The rest of **14** is uncertain ; it seems to describe the transference of an existing bronze altar to a position on the north side of the new altar ; the latter was to take the place of the old (15) which was to be reserved for the use of the king when he wanted to obtain an oracle (lit. to examine the entrails of animals) ; for alternative explanations of what took place, cf. J. Skinner (Cent.B) and N. H. Snaith (IB) *in loco*.

d **17** illustrates Ahaz's desperate need for bronze to enable him to pay the tribute to Assyria. Trolleys, laver, the sea and its oxen bearers were all cut down. In **18** not ' the covered way for the Sabbath ' but ' the audience chamber ' ; it and the special royal entrance were demolished, presumably because of valuable furnishing.

e **XVII Hoshea of Israel**—15:30 implies that Hoshea was the leader of a pro-Assyrian party. **3-5** might indicate that later he himself rebelled against Assyria, so that Shalmaneser IV made Israel tributary (3) ; thereafter Hoshea defaulted in tribute payments and was imprisoned (4) ; finally Shalmaneser invaded Israel and captured Samaria after a siege of three years. The fall of Samaria was not later than 721 B.C. ; the siege must have begun in 723 ; and Shalmaneser IV came to his throne in 727 ; therefore, the interval of time for two, possibly three, invasions of Israel in his reign is very short. Skinner (Cent.B, *in loco*) proposes that Shalmaneser made one campaign westwards, as the Assyrian records say ; that 3 records an act of submission on Hoshea's part before Shalmaneser had reached Israel ; that 4 refers to an imprisonment of Hoshea (probably not in Israel) because of his treachery,
and 5 the subsequent (and only) invasion of Israel. 305e
There is much to be said for this view.

6. Halah was a district near Haran in northern Meso- f
potamia, and the Habor was a tributary of the upper course of the Euphrates. So or Sewe (4) is doubtfully identified with Shabaka, the first king of the XXV Dynasty. The Sargon Inscription says that 27,290 Israelites were removed to captivity (cf. ANET, 284), a number in sharp contrast with the 60,000 men of wealth mentioned in 15:19f. It has been calculated that not more than one in twenty was taken captive (H. G. May, BA 6 (1943), 57f.).

7-23 A Reflection on the Fall of the Northern g
Kingdom—The editor considered this event as a punishment for unfaithfulness to Yahweh (12–15), the worship of Baal and Asherah like the Canaanites and of the host of heaven like the Assyrians (16), and the practice of divination and sorcery and of child sacrifice (17). In **9** read ' spoke ' for ' did secretly ', and in **17** ' acted deceitfully ' for ' sold themselves '.

24-41 The Samaritans—Foreign settlers, trans- h
planted, according to Sargon's Annals, for the same reason as the Israelites were transplanted to Assyria, were settled in Israel ; they came from Babylonia (Cuth or Kuthah was an ancient city there) and from three cities in Syria, unless Sepharvaim is to be identified with Sippar in Babylonia (in which case it might have been expected earlier in the list). A plague of lions (25–8) compelled the settlers to be trained in the service of Yahweh, but (29–34) they maintained the service of their own native gods at the same time. **30-1.** For Succoth-benoth, Montgomery has proposed the ' androgynous deity, Marduk-Banit ' (ICC, *in loco*). Nergal was a well-known Babylonian god, the name Ashima is found in Am. 8:14 and in one of the Elephantine papyri ; of Nibhaz and Tartak, the former is unknown while the latter may be the goddess Atargatis (see Montgomery, op. cit.) ; Adrammelech and Anammelech are for Adad-melekh and Anu-melekh, Adad being the storm-god and Anu the heaven-god worshipped over a wide area (cf. ARI, 163). **29** contains the only mention of the Samaritans by name in the OT.

RSV rightly makes a break in **34, 34b-41** referring not to the foreign settlers but to the Israelites, and being a continuation of **7-23.**

XVIII-XX Hezekiah and Israel (cf. 2 Chr. 29–32) 306a
—**18-25** give the history of Judah after the fall of the Northern Kingdom. Of **18-20, 18:17-20:19** comes from a biography of the prophet Isaiah, similar to those of Elijah and Elisha ; it was incorporated in Isa. 36–9 from Kg. (cf. S. R. Driver, *Introduction to the Literature of the OT*[9], 226f.).

XVIII 1-8 Hezekiah's Reform and Conquest of b
Philistine Territory—The latter was undoubtedly an act of defiance of Assyria subsequent to Sargon's campaign of 711 B.C., and the reform of religious practice was a correlated act of independence. **3.** Hezekiah is notably commended by the editor (cf. 23:25) ; for Asherah, see note on 1 Kg. 14:23. **4.** Nehushtan was traditionally the bronze serpent of the wilderness period (cf. Num. 21:9) ; but it is now known that the serpent symbol was common in Palestine as a fertility symbol (cf. APB, 87ff.) ; for the view that the serpent was the sacred symbol of the old Jebusite shrine in Jerusalem under Zadok, cf. H. H. Rowley, ' Zadok and Nehushtan ', JBL 58 (1939), 137.

There was a general revolt against Assyria towards c
the end of the 8th cent. B.C. (cf. 2 Kg. 20:2ff. ; Isa. 36–7). The narrative in Kg. is in three parts :

(*a*) **XVIII 13-16** Probably an excerpt from the annals. Sennacherib devastates Judah and Hezekiah surrenders and pays heavy indemnity. In **13** ' fourteenth year ' is clearly in error, twenty-fourth may be right. This section is closely parallel with the Assyrian record which puts the surrender of Jerusalem after the victory over Egypt at Eltekeh (cf. ANET, 287f.).

(*b*) **XVIII 17-XIX 9a** From the prophetic source (see above). It describes an attempt by Sennacherib

306c to gain occupation of Jerusalem by a mixture of threat and cajolery. Hezekiah stands firm, Isaiah supporting him and saying that the danger will quickly disappear.

(*c*) **XIX 9b-35** Hezekiah receives a threatening letter demanding surrender. He refuses to comply; Isaiah again supports him. **36f.** reports an outbreak of plague in the Assyrian camp, Sennacherib's withdrawal from Judah, and his subsequent assassination in Nineveh.

d As for the interpretation of these narratives:

(i) (*b*) and (*c*) cannot be taken as records of what happened before the surrender of Jerusalem (cf. (*a*)), because each states clearly that Hezekiah did not surrender—unless (*b*) and (*c*) refer to a different and earlier occasion than (*a*).

(ii) (*b*) and (*c*) would fit in excellently after the surrender of Jerusalem (*a*) and before the battle of Eltekeh, giving evidence of Sennacherib's anxiety to occupy Jerusalem before engaging the strength of Egypt; but the Assyrian record is against that order of events (see above). It remains possible that some time after Eltekeh, Tirhakah advanced into Palestine and caused the situation described in (*b*) and (*c*). In this case (*c*) might be a parallel narrative to (*b*) or describes an accentuation of Sennacherib's anxiety.

e **XVIII 17-XIX 9a** Three high-ranking Assyrian officers demanded the surrender of Jerusalem; the Tartan was the commander-in-chief, the Rab-shakeh the chief of staff (or chief butler), and the Rab-saris the chief of the eunuchs. The challenge of the Assyrians was fourfold: Jerusalem had not the power to resist; Yahweh could not save it; Egyptian help could not be relied on; Sennacherib's conquering career was ordained by God (19–25). They appealed to the people of Jerusalem not to be duped by their leaders; their fate was inescapable (28–35). For the conduit from the Virgin's Spring (17), cf. Isa. 7:3; in **20** follow the rendering in RSV. Aramaic at this time was the language of commerce and diplomacy while Hebrew was commonly spoken (26). For Hamath, Sepharvaim and Ivvah (34), see 17:24; Arpad was near Aleppo; Hena was a town in Syria, site now unknown. Before the final question in **34**, LXX[L] and OL, insert: 'Where are the gods of the land of Samaria?' This gives a proper setting for the final question.

Hezekiah consulted Isaiah who told him (19:6–7) that a rumour of trouble would induce Sennacherib to leave Jerusalem; the reference could be to the danger implicit in the arrival of Tirhakah in Palestine or to trouble at home from Assyria's immediate neighbours, especially Babylon. **35** gives a different reason for Sennacherib's departure, and Herodotus ii, 141 attributes it to the damage done to the Assyrian shields and bowstrings by mice—a pointer to bubonic plague.

19:8-9a provides a disjointed and truncated ending to this part of the narrative, but the arrival of Tirhakah made Sennacherib anxious to capture Jerusalem.

f **XIX 9b-35. 9b-20** is continued in **32-5**, while **21-31** is separate. On this occasion Isaiah came forward to tell Hezekiah that Sennacherib would depart without threatening the city (cf. 6–7). **34** speaks of God as now saving his people, not judging them.

For Libnah, see 8:22; for Gozan, 17:6; for Hamath, Ivvah (or Avva) and Sepharvaim, 17:24; and for Arpad and Hena, 18:34. In **13** read after Arpad, 'the king of Lair, Sepharvaim, Hena or Ivvah?'; Lair was a town on the border of Elam (cf. G. R. Driver, *Aramaic Documents*, 21, *n*. 2). Haran (cf. Gen. 11:31, etc.) was a trading centre in northern Mesopotamia; Rezeph was west of Haran, on the road to Palmyra; Eden (i.e. Beth-eden) was a small kingdom on the Euphrates south of Haran, and Telassar was probably one of its cities.

g **21-28** is a taunt-song composed possibly after the power of Yahweh had been revealed in the deliverance of Jerusalem. It contrasts the spectacular and transitory might of Assyria (23f.) with the overruling purpose and invincible power of Yahweh (25–7; cf.
Isa. 10:5–11, 44:28, 45:1), and intimates that Senna- **30**
cherib will be sent away in shame and ignominy. The Dead Sea Scroll Isaiah A in 37:27f. gives a better text for part of **27-8** here but does not alter the sense. **29-31.** But Jerusalem and Judah will not escape suffering. The sign given in confirmation of the message (cf. Exod. 3:12; Isa. 7:11, etc.) says that in the current year the people would have for food only what had grown from fallen kernels (cf. Lev. 25:5, 11), and in the following year whatever corn should grow of itself; only after that would normal agricultural operations be resumed.

According to **35-7** the Assyrian army was devastated by plague (cf. 2 Sam. 24:15f.). That Sennacherib died a violent death is confirmed in Eusebius, *Chronicles* i, 25–9 (cf. ANET, 288). Nineveh, capital of Assyria, fell in 612 B.C. Ararat (Assy. Urartu) is Armenia; the god Nisroch is not known.

XX 1-11 deals with Hezekiah's illness and **12-19** with **h**
the embassy of Merodach-baladan for which the king's illness provided an occasion (12). Merodach-baladan (Berodach erroneously in 12, MT) was the ruler of a small principality in lower Mesopotamia who took advantage of Sargon's accession to the throne of Assyria in 721 to seize Babylon, which he held until 710. The date of his embassy is commonly given as 711 B.C., when Sargon threatened his rule, and that would be suitable if Hezekiah died *c*. 696; but the chronology of the period is difficult, and the end of Hezekiah's reign is sometimes reckoned as 687, which would make the embassy *c*. 702, preparatory to revolt against Assyria (cf. BASOR 100 (1945), 22). **7** shows that the curative value of a fig plaster for draining boils and ulcers was known; the rendering of **7b** in RSV (following LXX and Syr.) is preferable to that of AV in view of the terms of 8.

In **8-11** alternative signs are offered: that the shadow should go forward ten steps or degrees, meaning that the shadow of the declining sun would be lengthened with preternatural acceleration, or that it should go back that amount, a phenomenon reversing the order of nature. The parallel account in Isa. 38:7–9, in which the prophet offers the latter sign only, is probably an earlier form of the story. Sun-dials were known at the time in Babylonia, but the word used here refers to a series of steps which Ahaz may have found conveniently set for reckoning the time of day by the shadow cast by the sun upon them, or which he had made for the purpose.

12-19 describes an occasion when Merodach Baladan **i**
(Marduk-apal-idinni) sought the aid of Hezekiah. The king showed him all his resources and armaments, and Isaiah made a typical rebuke against confidence in foreign alliances for safety and security (14f.). The statement about captivity to Babylon (17–18) may be a Deuteronomic addition, referring to the captivity of the 6th cent., or it may indicate Isaiah's view that Merodach-baladan, who sought Hezekiah's help now, might turn against him tomorrow.

The final paragraph is longer than usual and refers particularly to the tunnel made from the Virgin's Spring to the Pool of Siloam to ensure the water supply of the city in the event of siege. The tunnel has been found and the famous Siloam inscription which was found on the wall of it says that the excavators worked from both ends and contrived to converge in middle course. The length of the tunnel is over 1,700 ft. (cf. GAB, 84; W. F. Albright, *The Archaeology of Israel*, 135; S. R. Driver, *Notes on the Hebrew Text of the Books of Samuel*, pp. xv f. and Pl. II).

XXI The Reigns of Manasseh and Amon—1-18 **307**
deals with Manasseh who reigned for fifty-five years (696–641 B.C. are the dates commonly given, but Albright allots to him forty-five years, 687–642 (in BASOR 100 (1945), 22)). His reign witnessed a reaction from the reforming ways of Hezekiah; the local sanctuaries were rebuilt (3); Baal worship was resumed with vigour, altars being built even within the

307a Jerusalem Temple (4). The star worship which had a vogue (5) was doubtless due to the fact that Judah was subject to Assyria during Manasseh's reign ; Assyria under Esarhaddon (681–669) and Ashurbanipal (669–626) rose to great power and ruled even Egypt from 671 to 652. Manasseh's name actually appears on two Assyrian lists of tributary princes, one telling how he was one of a group summoned to Nineveh to learn their overlord's demands in connection with new building operations in his capital (ANET, 291, 294). This may give the clue to the interpretation of 2 Chr. 33:11–13, which relates how Manasseh was taken captive to Nineveh and later restored to his throne.

b The religious retrogression of Manasseh's reign had several aspects. Child sacrifice was practised (6) ; that had been done in the time of Ahaz (16:3) but otherwise it had been resorted to in Israel only in extreme emergency (cf. Jg. 11:31 ; 1 Kg. 16:34) ; for the abolition of the practice, cf. 23:10. The observation of signs and omens was also practised, and soothsayers and wizards were active, so that conditions are likened to those that had existed under Ahab (6 ; cf. Dt. 18:10 f.). In 7 Asherah is the goddess for whom a graven image is said to have been made, and is not in this context the wooden post commonly found beside a Canaanite altar.

In 13 the plummet and the measuring-line are presumably not to be used for building but to show how Jerusalem is about to fall as Samaria had already fallen (cf. Am. 7:8). The innocent blood which Manasseh shed (16) was probably of members of the prophetic party who must have protested vigorously against his reactionary ways.

c Amon (19–26) reigned briefly, followed the policy of his father, and was assassinated by some of his supporters, probably not in religious protest, but in political intrigue which may have been intended as a gesture of independence against Assyria.

The whole chapter is generally recognised as showing signs of later Deuteronomic revision, but the two courts (5) need not refer to the second Temple (thus indicating a late revision) but signify the court between the Temple and the palace (cf. 1 Kg. 6:36).

For royal burial in the garden of Uzzah (18, 26), cf. 23:30, 24:6.

d **XXII 1-XXIII 30** This section tells of **the discovery of a law-book** during the execution of repair-work in the Temple at Jerusalem, the resultant consternation on the part of king Josiah when he saw how disobedient he and his people had been to the demands of the law as expressed in that book, the covenant of loyalty and obedience to Yahweh that was made by them, and the national movement of reform which ensued. The law-book has commonly been identified with the kernel of our book of Dt. (Dt. chs. 12–26, 28), although that identification has been called in question recently from several points of view (see §231*d*). But if it can be maintained, it is probable that the book, incorporating much material very much older than the date of its composition, was written during the reactionary and oppressive reign of Manasseh by the so-called prophetic party which suffered persecution (21:16). But such a reformation as Josiah led would have constituted a dangerous act of rebellion in Manasseh's reign when the power of Assyria was dominant in Palestine and dictated the pattern of life. But with the death of Ashurbanipal in 626 the decline of that great empire was accelerated, and the rise of the Medes and Babylonians and the predatory raids of Scythians and Cimmerians caused a confused situation in the plain of the Tigris-Euphrates, which gave Assyria no respite to heed any show of independence by a tributary state like distant Judah and brought about her eclipse with the fall of her capital city Nineveh in 612 B.C.

The upkeep of the Temple fabric was at first a charge upon the royal exchequer, but in the reign of Jehoash the practice was used of inviting public donations for the purpose (12:4–16). Evidently that practice still continued in Josiah's reign (4–6). In **9** the servants 307d did not empty out the money, but melted it down, i.e. cast it into ingots.

e The book which was found is named, in the first reference to it, *the* book of the law (8), although Shaphan reports to the king about 'a book' (10). But since, for instance, the Burning Bush is called '*the* bush' on the first occasion when it is referred to (Exod. 3:2), it is probably a Heb. mode of speech not paralleled in English, so that in **8** we should read 'a book of the law'. The fact that Huldah, a prophetess, was consulted (14) and not Jeremiah probably means that the latter had not yet come to an accepted place as a prophet in the community.

f **XXIII 1-3 describes the great public assembly in Jerusalem** at which the book of the law was read and the king, standing by the pillar (or, more probably, upon the platform), pledged his own obedience and loyalty to the Lord, and the people joined with him.

g **4-15 The Reformation in Terms of the Demands of the Book**—It was substantially corrective of the religious practices which had been encouraged or tolerated in Judah in the idolatrous days of Manasseh (cf. 2 Kg. 21:3–7) ; and the reference in 5 to the worship of the heavenly bodies and the host of heaven makes that aspect clear, since such worship in Judah betokens Assyrian influence. The reformation had a fourfold aim :

(*a*) It cleansed the Jerusalem Temple of alien accretions and expelled the idol-priests who officiated in the worship of Baal, Asherah (cf. 1 Kg. 14:23) and the host of heaven (cf. Dt. 4:19, 16:21f., 17:2–7). The dust of the Asherah image, when it was burned, was cast on the graves of the common people to desecrate it (4–6) ; for the place of cult prostitutes in such worship, cf. 1 Kg. 14:24 ; Dt. 23:17. In 4 read 'the deputy high-priest' (so Targ.) in place of 'the priests of the second order' (RSV), and in 5 read 'planets' in place of 'constellations'. The word used for idol-priests, *k*[e]*mārîm* (5), was used in Syria, Egypt and elsewhere as a normal word for 'priests' but it has a contemptuous flavour here (cf. Hos. 10:5 ; Zeph. 1:4) ; appointed by the king, they were presumably not members of a priestly family. In 8*b* read 'the high places of the satyrs' in place of the unintelligible 'the high places of the gates' (cf. Lev. 17:7 ; 2 Chr. 11:15). 8f. tells how the priests of the local shrines were brought to Jerusalem, but, although they were given their maintenance, they were not allowed to officiate at the altar (cf. Dt. 18:1–2, 6–8).

(*b*) It thus cleared away religious abuses in the neighbourhood of Jerusalem also. Topheth (10), where human sacrifice by fire was made, lay south of the city ; for the form of the word (similar to Molech), see the note on 1 Kg. 11:7. Its original form and meaning (hearth ?) are uncertain. Sun worship and roof altars (11f.) were foreign modes, imported from Assyria, while the altars to the gods of neighbouring peoples (13) were in the first instance attributable to Solomon's marriage alliances. In 13 read 'mount of olives' for 'mount of corruption'.

(*c*) It desecrated the local sanctuaries throughout the land (8), so that Jerusalem was left as the only legitimate place of worship (cf. Dt. 12:2f., 11–14). Mention is made particularly of the desecration (4) and destruction (15f.) of Bethel.

(*d*) It abolished wizards and mediums, teraphim (cf. Gen. 31:19ff. ; Jg. 17f. ; 1 Sam. 19:13ff., etc.) and idols (24), and made clear that Yahweh alone is God (cf. Dt. 18:10 f.).

The close parallelism between these aspects of the reform and the regulations of Dt. has been indicated in references.

16-20 is a later addition. 16 assumes the continued h existence of the altar which is said in 15 to have been broken to pieces, and the treatment of the priests of the local shrines as given in 20 is in sharp contrast with that expressed in 4.

In spite of the high commendation of Josiah (**25**

307h the wrath of the Lord did not abate against Judah (26f.). The occasion of the king's death is left in doubt in 29. It is now known that Neco was on his way to bolster up Assyria as a buffer state against Babylon after the fall of Nineveh in 612 B.C. (ANET, 303ff. ; WBA, 174). Josiah may have thought the occasion propitious for gaining some territory in Esdraelon from Assyria or for obstructing Neco's ambition to regain control of Syria and Palestine ; and the fuller record in 2 Chr. 35:20–5 says he sought battle against a Pharaoh who was anxious to avoid combat. Whatever is uncertain, it is not in doubt that Josiah perished at Megiddo (609 B.C.).

308a **XXIII 31-XXV 30 The Decline and Fall of Judah**
XXIII 31-35 Jehoahaz, who came to the throne now, was probably a popular choice or was supported by a strong faction, as he was younger than Eliakim (31, 36). He was soon deposed by Neco and was taken as a prisoner first to Riblah on the Orontes and then to Egypt, where he died (33f.). Eliakim was then made king as a nominee of Egypt and paid tribute (35 ; in 33 probably 'ten talents of gold' should be read) ; the change of his name to Jehoiakim ('Yahu will establish') was probably intended as a conciliatory gesture. For Jehoahaz and Jehoiakim, see Jer. 22:11–23.

b **XXIII 36-XXIV 7 Jehoiakim** ruled as an underling of Pharaoh Neco until the latter's defeat by Nebuchadnezzar at Carchemish in 605. The fruits of that victory could not be wholly gathered by Nebuchadnezzar because he was called home to become king of Assyria upon the death of his father. Jehoiakim remained a willing subject of Babylon for three years (**24:1**) ; a defeat of Nebuchadnezzar at the hands of Egypt in 601 B.C. may have encouraged Jehoiakim to rebel (cf. WBA, 176). And if 2 Chr. 36:5 is right in saying that the bands of Chaldaeans, Syrians, Moabites and Ammonites (**2**), that were sent as punitive raiders against him, were forced to withdraw, that must have been still greater encouragement ; he died before the Babylonian invading army arrived. **3-4** make idolatrous Manasseh the cause of all Judah's sufferings ; Jer. 22:13–23 condemns Jehoiakim as another Manasseh. In **5** there is the last reference in Kg. to the royal chronicles.

c **XXIV 8-17 Jehoiachin and the Surrender of Jerusalem**—He was but three months on the throne when he had to surrender Jerusalem to the Babylonians (12) and, together with his household and court officials, was taken prisoner (597 B.C.). 15–16 are the continuation of 12. The potential leaders of the community were removed ; but the 7,000 men of substance (rather than 'valour') and the 1,000 craftsmen and artisans constitute a number much in excess of the 3,023 given by Jeremiah (52:28). 13–14 is a later addition. It says that Nebuchadnezzar removed all the treasures of the Temple, but 25:15ff. shows, and Jer. 27:18ff. confirms, that it was but partial plundering that was done on this occasion. The two verses together seem rather to fit the destruction of Jerusalem in 586 (cf. 25:11–21). A son of Josiah, Mattaniah, now ruled Judah as the agent of Babylon ; the name Zedekiah he may have assumed as a throne-name (cf. Azariah—Uzziah in 15:1).

d **XXIV 18-XXV 21 Zedekiah and the Destruction of Jerusalem**—There is scant evidence here of Zedekiah's feeble vacillations, but he must have lacked experienced and wise advisers ; for fuller information, see Jer. 27ff. (cf. 2 Chr. 36:11–23). Zedekiah rebelled in the ninth year of his reign ; Jer. 51:59ff. may well mean that he had threatened rebellion five years earlier and had been called to account. After a siege of eighteen months (read 'siege-towers', not 'siege-works' in 1) the city walls were breached and the city was captured and completely destroyed (4, 8–10). In **9** 'every great house' (RSV) is very doubtful ; G. R. Driver has suggested 'all the household of Gedaliah'. An attempt on the part of Zedekiah and his household guard to escape across the Jordan was foiled (4–7) ; having seen the death of his sons, he was taken as a captive to Babylon. The leading officials of the city were put to death at the Babylonian headquarters at Riblah in the Orontes valley (18–21) and the whole population was removed except for the poorest (11–12), the purpose being to make Judah an agricultural community without potential political leaders ; in 11 we may read 'engineers' or 'skilled workers' in place of 'multitude' (RSV) in terms of Jer. 52:15. Confirmation of the two Babylonian invasions at this time has been found in clear evidence of destruction at two excavated sites in particular, Debir and Lachish (see W. F. Albright, *The Excavation of Tell Beit Mirsim, Vol. III : The Iron Age*, AASOR 21-2 (1943), 68 ; H. Torczyner, *The Lachish Letters, Lachish I* (1938) ; Olga Tufnell, *Lachish III : The Iron Age* (1953) ; WBA, 175f.).

XXV 22-26 Gedaliah and the Mizpah Débâcle e
(cf. Jer. 39–40). Gedaliah was a member of one of the moderate, stable families of Jerusalem to which Jeremiah owed much (cf. Jer. 22:12, 26:24). The seal 'Belonging to Gedaliah who is over the House', which was discovered at Lachish, probably belongs to this man (cf. S. H. Hooke, 'A Scarab and Sealing from Tell Duweir', PEF (Oct. 1935), 195–7). **23.** He gained the support of some leaders of local resistance to Babylon (cf. Jer. 40:7) and advised peaceful acceptance by them of the existing situation (24). A revolt instigated by Ishmael, a prince of the Davidic line, caused the death, not only of Gedaliah and some of his supporters, but of some Babylonians as well (25). The result was that the remaining supporters of Gedaliah sought an asylum in Egypt (for a more circumstantial account, cf. Jer. 39:11–43:7).

27-30 The Release of Jehoiachin, after thirty-seven f
years in prison, as soon as Evil-merodach, Nebuchadnezzar's successor, came to the Assyrian throne in 562 B.C. This was interpreted as an act of favour to the Jews and a sign of God's care for the Davidic house. Evidence is now available that Jehoiachin was regarded as the rightful king of Judah and was kept as a hostage in Babylon for the good behaviour of his countrymen. Three stamped jar-handles have been discovered in southern Palestine, bearing the words, 'Belonging to Eliakim, steward of Yaukin', which indicate that during Zedekiah's rule the royal estates were administered for Jehoiachin so that his interests were conserved. In addition, tablets have been discovered in Babylon which detail payments of rations of oil and grain by the government to captives and skilled workmen during the period 595–570 B.C., and mention is made of Yaukin and five sons (cf. BA 5 (1942), 49ff. ; JBL 51 (1932), 77–106 ; WBA, 177f.). The importance of Jehoiachin is further illustrated by the fact that the chronological references in the book of Ezek. have reference to that monarch's reign.

Bibliography—COMMENTARIES : W. E. Barnes, CB (1908) ; I. Benzinger, KHC (1899) ; O. Eissfeldt, HSAT (4th ed. 1923) ; F. W. Farrar, Ex.B (1893–4) ; R. Kittel, HKAT (1902) ; J. A. Montgomery and H. S. Gehman, ICC (1951) ; M. Rehm, Ech.B (1949) ; J. Skinner, Cent.B ; N. H. Snaith, R. W. Sockman and R. Calkins, IB (1954) ; R. de Vaux, Jer.B (1949).

OTHER LITERATURE : C. F. Burney, *Notes on the Hebrew Text of the Books of Kings* (1903) ; Articles on Israel, Judah, Kings, Temple, etc. in EB, ERE and HDB.

I AND II CHRONICLES

By A. S. HERBERT

309a **Title and Place in the Canon**—Originally our two books of Chr., together with Ezr. and Neh., formed one book. It appears to owe its title, in the English and German versions, to Jerome's comment (Prologus Galeatus) that it might well be called ' the chronicle of the whole of sacred history '. It is in fact an equivalent to the Heb. title ' The matters of the days '. The Gr. title, Paraleipomena, ' Things omitted (of the kings of Judah) ', is followed in the Vulg. Its position in the Christian canon, following 1 and 2 Kg., derives from the LXX order. In the Heb. canon it is the last book in the OT and follows Ezr. and Neh. This position as the last book in the Heb. scriptures appears to be referred to by Jesus Christ in Mt. 23:35 ; Lk. 11:51 (cf. 2 Chr. 24:20–2), as we might say ' from beginning to end of the Bible '. It seems that the closing part of the original book (Ezr.-Neh.) was included in the scriptures because it told the story of the Jewish people in the days of the Exile not otherwise recorded ; we can only assume that the remainder of the book (our 1 and 2 Chr.) was subsequently added because its teaching proved effective in building up the life of the Jewish community.

b **Characteristic Features**—Its position in the canon may prepare us to recognise this as a ' teacher's book ' ; i.e. it is consciously making use of known material and giving an interpretation of that material to meet the needs of the people of God. The date of writing and the manner of presentation confirm this.

Date—(*a*) Its use of the material in Kg., its reference to the Edict of Cyrus in 2 Chr. 36:22f., and its continuation into the story of Ezr. and Neh. demands a date not earlier than 400 B.C. (*b*) The genealogy of the Davidic line in 1 Chr. 3:19–24 takes us to at least six generations after Zerubbabel, i.e. about 350 B.C. The ancient versions at 3:21f. increase this to eleven generations, and would thus date the book not earlier than 250 B.C. This evidence from the versions must not be pressed, but we may confidently accept *c.* 300 B.C. as the time of writing. Such a date is supported by the language. The Heb. is late post-exilic in style, is affected by Aram., and contains Persian words (' darics ' in 1 Chr. 29:7). Its ecclesiastical and theological interests support such a dating. According to Rabbinic tradition, Chr. was begun by Ezra and concluded by Nehemiah. While this tradition cannot be accepted at its face value, there can be no doubt but that Chr. represents the piety and devotion of the community that owed so much to the work of these two men.

c When we observe the manner in which the Chronicler uses his *Sources* (where we can check them), we can gain a clear idea of the teaching he is giving. (*a*) Gen.-Jos. are the main sources of the material in 1 Chr. 1–9. (*b*) Sam. and Kg. are the main sources of the material in 1 Chr. 10–2 Chr. 36 and in most instances these sources are quoted literally. (*c*) Traditions, written or oral (probably in the main, oral) from sources referred to, as in 1 Chr. 29:29, 2 Chr. 9:29, 12:15, 13:22, 20:34, 26:22, 32:32 (a notable feature of these is their association with prophets), and 1 Chr. 9:1 ; 2 Chr. 16:11, 24:27, 25:26, 33:18f., 35:27, 36:8. (These, from the material quoted, cannot be our books of Kg. since they contain matter not written there.) In addition there is *midrash* (' story ' or ' commentary '), 2 Chr. 13:22, 24:27. The term occurs only in these two passages and nowhere else in the OT (but cf. Sir. 51:23), and its precise significance is not easy to determine. Etymologically it means ' enquiry ' or ' work ' in the sense of a scholar's study in some field of scholarship, and that appears to be the meaning in Chr. The term in this sense is appropriate to much of the material in this book not found in the earlier canonical books. The term is used in later Judaism to describe a learned use of biblical material for the edification of the faithful, and in that later sense it would be an appropriate term for the whole of Chr. 309c

It is evident that **the framework of the book** is provided by the earlier canonical material, but it includes much of a novel character. Where that material differs from Sam. and Kg., we should be inclined to follow the account preserved in the earlier books. Yet it would be a mistake to assume that all the material peculiar to Chr. is lacking in historical reliability. Each passage must be examined independently. When, however, we observe the manner in which the Chronicler uses the material from Sam. and Kg., we can recognise that he is writing of these early days in terms of conditions in Judaea in the 4th cent. B.C. The writer's assumption is that the history of his people has special meaning for his own time. This is not peculiar to Chr., but it is strikingly presented in this book. Thus we note the virtual ignoring of the history of the Northern Kingdom (politically much the more important until its downfall in the 8th cent. B.C.) and the additional material in the account of David, associating with that king the Temple appointments which are largely those of the period after Ezra. Chr., then, contains a great deal of historical material, but it is not the purpose of the book to present us with a history. That, as it says, is preserved in ' the books of the kings of Israel and Judah '. Its purpose is to give an interpretation of that history. Its purpose is religious, and for that purpose the traditions of the past are used to convey the message. We may add that the effectiveness of that teaching and its worth is demonstrated by the survival of the book in spite of its obvious contradictions of earlier scripture. It is evident that neither the Jewish community nor the Church assessed the book primarily on the ground of its historicity. **The purpose and teaching** of the book may be recognised by observing (*a*) what from its known sources it selects, (*b*) what it omits, (*c*) what it modifies and (*d*) what it adds. Thus (*a*) it selects the material relating to the deeds of the Judaean kings as they directly affect the life of the people of God, especially in their relation to Yahweh, with particular reference to the Jerusalem shrine. (*b*) Notable omissions are those from the history of Saul, the personal life of David and the history of the Israelite kings. These events have no direct bearing on the life of the sacred community. (*c*) An example of modification is that at 1 Chr. 21:1–22:1 which is clearly derived from 2 Sam. 24. The census is instigated by the Satan instead of Yahweh ; the angel is a more transcendent figure ; the elders share in David's penitential mourning ; the price paid for the threshing-floor is very much greater ; fire from heaven comes upon the altar ; and it is noted that this was

309e the site of the Jerusalem Temple. The modifications show the theological insight of post-exilic days, and the story is specially related for post-exilic Judaism to the all-important matter of the Temple. (*d*) Examples of additional material may be found in 1 Chr. 15–16, the ceremony of conveying the Ark to Zion, and chs. 22–9, David's preparations for the Temple and its service. The function of the messianic prince (David), in the worship of Israel centred on the Temple, is unmistakable. This, for the Chronicler, was the all-important feature of God's choice of David and, presumably, of him that should come of the Davidic line.

f In the compilation of the book of Chr. **two main influences** can be recognised, the Deuteronomic and the Priestly schools (see §137*a*). The Deuteronomic influence, with its doctrine of righteous retribution, may be observed especially in its treatment of history; thus the unusually long reign of Manasseh in spite of his great wickedness receives in Chronicles an 'explanation'—he repented and humbled himself (not in 2 Kg. 21). No less obvious is the Priestly interest in the cultus throughout the book, and the particular interest in the Levitical order. It is possible that the book as we have it is a priestly (or, more precisely, Levitical) revision of an originally Deuteronomic work, in the light of the establishment of the Priestly work under Ezra. This would suggest a 5th cent. B.C. date for the original. But it should be noted that arguments based on inconsistency between D and P must be used with some caution. An ancient writer did not conform to our literary standards. The book of Dt. retained its place in the Torah in spite of its inconsistency with the teaching of the Priestly School even on important cultic matters. While the forms of post-exilic Judaism were shaped by the teaching of the Priestly School, the characteristic teaching of Dt. on the sole rule of God in the fulfilment of his righteous and gracious purpose was an ineradicable element in Jewish thought. It is, however, very probable that 1 Chr. 1–9 was originally independent of the rest of the book. It may have been added later; or it may have been deliberately attached to the main work by the author(s) as an introduction. For while the modern reader finds these genealogies tedious, and the long list of names meaningless, to the man whose delight is in the law of the Lord, who treasured the records of ancient Israel, each name is meaningful, directing his mind to the mighty acts of God.

310a It is **the holy community**, brought into being by God and maintained by him through all the vicissitudes of history, its worship centred on the Jerusalem Temple and ordered from the beginning of the Kingdom that interests the Chronicler. This is the true Israel. The division of the kingdom at the beginning of Rehoboam's reign is more than a political severance. It is rebellion against the divinely chosen Davidic dynasty and the forsaking of the one place in which the legitimate worship of Israel may be offered. The northern tribes have separated from the covenant of Israel and are therefore rejected as Yahweh's people. Israel finds its historical expression in Judah and Benjamin and in those from the northern tribes who come 'to Jerusalem to sacrifice to the Lord, the God of their fathers' (2 Chr. 11:16). It was this religious community, rather than any political achievement of the pre-exilic kingdom, that had astonishingly survived the shattering experience of invasion and exile. Judah had, in fact, proved the enduring element in Israel. The Northern Kingdom had collapsed and, as an entity, had disappeared from history. But in the Chronicler's own day an attempt was being made, beginning apparently in the 4th cent. B.C., to revive the 'Northern' community with a centre of worship and temple in deliberate opposition to that of Jerusalem. The movement was all the more dangerous since it was based on the same Torah, under the leadership of a genuinely Aaronic priesthood and associated with a sacred place whose antiquity in Israelite tradition could be speciously presented as superior to that of Jerusalem. The rebellion of Jeroboam the son of Nebat had been repeated in the rise of the Samaritan community (the *Shômᵉrônîm*) which called themselves the Guardians of the Law (*Shômᵉrîm*). It may be too much to say that Chr. is a piece of anti-Samaritan polemic, but it can hardly be doubted that it has that movement in mind. The total impression left by the book is that there is one legitimate Aaronic priesthood and Levitical order, one legitimate holy place divinely chosen, the Jerusalem Temple; there alone true sacrifice may be offered, and this, with its great liturgical collection, the Psalter, was intimately bound up with the divinely appointed Davidic dynasty. It may be that 2 Chr. 11:13–17, 13:3–20, 25:6–10 reflect this anti-Samaritan feeling. 310

More important, however, is the positive teaching of the book on **the holiness of the Lord's people** and the Jerusalem Temple with its ordinances. History had demonstrated that the Lord's people were in fact narrowed down to those for whom Jerusalem, the Temple and the Davidic line were central to their loyalty. To deny this was apostasy. Not to know this was heathenism. For these were of Yahweh's choosing, and through their media his people acknowledged his rule. Yet it is an important element of the Jewish faith, as reflected in this book, that the apostate might return and the heathen acknowledge the one true God, the sole ruler of all history who is known in his dealings with his chosen people. All historical success or failure are the direct product of Divine reward for loyalty to the Torah or punishment for apostasy. Those great institutions of post-exilic Judaism, the ritual and religious practices, the Temple, the organisation of Priestly and Levitical courses, the celebration of the Feasts, notably Passover, the role of the messianic prince, all receive full and detailed treatment; and the understanding of these, characteristic of post-exilic Judaism, is traced back to pre-exilic days; the history of the People of God is presented so as to demonstrate the insight of the Levitical teachers of the Torah. It has been described as 'the first apology of Judaism'. b

The fact that the book is written in Heb. while the normal language of the ordinary people was Aram., and that it contains so many incidental references meaningful only to the scholar (but for him full of significance), suggests that the book was written for the (Levitical) teacher rather than for the general public.

Historically, such a presentation of Israel's history is anachronistic. It appears that the convention of writing differs greatly from what is acceptable to us. The modern western writer would say that what was explicit in that post-exilic Judaism was implicit in the beginning. Yet the actual course of Israel's history, and, most of all, the sovereign acts of God in that history, were necessary for its culminating expression. No less does the Christian assert that the whole of the OT points to Jesus Christ and his Church, not because the OT explicitly refers to him, but because what it has to say comes to its fulfilment in him. The modes of expression of the 20th cent. A.D. western Christian and the 3rd cent. B.C. Jew may be different, but their insight and purpose are strikingly similar. If at times the latter appears to be forcing the events of history into too narrow a mould, this may be because his categories of expression are inadequate. The faith that is expressed is one with the faith of the Church as declared by its noblest exponents. All history is ruled by the one God who manifests his rule in the life and history of his people, and this is known most truly in the response of worship. The events of history are never merely of social, military or political importance; there is a further dimension—the sovereign will of the redeeming God—the neglect of which can only bring confusion to thought and disaster to life. In humbly accepting this dimension comes welfare and renewal of life. c

0c There are four clearly marked divisions in Chr.: (i) 1 Chr. 1–9 Genealogical Lists, summarising the history from Adam to David. (ii) 1 Chr. 10–29 The history of David, which occupies nearly a third of the total book of Chr. or nearly a quarter of Chr.-Ezr. Neh. (iii) 2 Chr. 1–9 The history of Solomon. (iv) 2 Chr. 10–36 The history of the kings of Judah to the Exile with a brief note, 2 Chr. 36:22f., of the return to Jerusalem in the reign of Cyrus.

THE FIRST BOOK OF CHRONICLES

d **Part I I-IX**
Genealogies—It will be noted that particular attention is given to the tribe of Levi (ch. 6), Judah (chs. 2 and 4:1–22), Benjamin (ch. 8); and to the descendants of David (ch. 3). Ch. 1 presents in genealogical form the nations and peoples known to the OT writers. The stage is set for the appearance of Israel. The Israelite tribes are presented in an order that suggests a definite plan. For the order is not that of seniority in the family of Israel, nor in the order in which they are named in 1 Chr. 2:1f. Both the order and the attention given to the various tribes may be intended to suggest (*a*) that Israel is really comprised by Judah and Benjamin (cf. 2 Chr. 11:12*b*), (*b*) that the Levitical priesthood is at the centre of Israel's real life (cf. 2 Chr. 11:12f.) and (*c*) that the house of David is the Lord's peculiar gift to Judah.

e **I 1-II 2 The Genealogy of the Nations**—The purpose of this introduction is to call to mind Yahweh's sovereignty over all mankind, and at the same time to remind the Jewish community that they are the people of his choice. The lists are wholly taken from Gen. 1–36. The terse manner of presentation shows that the readers are assumed to know Gen. There are some minor variations from the names in Gen., easily explicable from the similarities between certain Heb. letters. Thus the Heb. equivalents for 'd' and 'r' are similar, cf. v. 6 'Diphath' for Gen. 10:3 'Riphath'; but in v. 7 'Rodanim' (Rhodians) represents the original form in Gen. 10:4 instead of 'Dodanim'. Again the Heb. letters for 'w' and 'y' (often used to represent 'o', 'u' and 'e', 'i' respectively) are sometimes confused: so v. 22 'Ebal' (Gen. Obal) and v. 36 'Zephi' (Gen. Zepho). **17.** After 'Aram' insert 'and the sons of Aram' and for 'Meshech' read 'Mash' (cf. Gen. 10:23). **51f. chiefs Timna, Aliah,** etc.: read 'chiefs of Timna, Aliah, etc.'

11a **II 3-VIII 40 The Tribes of Israel**
II 3-55 The Tribe of Judah
III The Davidic Line—High importance was attached by the Chronicler to the preservation of that genealogy. There are minor variations between this list and those to be educed from Kg. and Lk. 2, and these may indicate different traditions of reckoning the intermarriages within the royal family.

IV 1-23 Further Judahite Genealogies, fragmentary in character—The lack of relationship within this section, and between this and ch. 3, suggests the intention of the Chronicler to preserve whatever had survived.

24-43 The Tribe of Simeon—The notes are very fragmentary and have all the appearance of ancient traditions. The Simeonite clans preserved the semi-nomadic life to a relatively late date.

V 1-10 The Tribe of Reuben
11-17 The Tribe of Gad, situated north of Reuben in the trans-Jordanic district of Gilead—The paucity and somewhat confused information about these three trans-Jordanic tribes reflects the conditions of the Chronicler's day, since as the result of the Assyrian and Babylonian invasions, these tribes had largely disintegrated. 17 explicitly refers to the days before the Assyrian invasion, and the verb 'enrolled by genealogies' suggests that it is the Chronicler's note on these ancient traditions.

b **18-22 The Wars of the Trans-Jordanic Tribes**—This may be a fuller account of the note to v. 10, but 311b
more probably refers to a long period of border warfare against Arabian incursions.

23-24 The half Tribe of Manasseh (cf. 7:14ff.)
25-26 The Apostasy of the Trans-Jordanic Tribes—We do not need to suppose that there was a wholesale deportation, but that, as the result of the invasion and the removal of their leader, they lost their political and ethnic identity. **26.** The Chronicler supposed that there were two Assyrian kings, perhaps by a misunderstanding of 2 Kg. 15:19, 25. In fact Pul was the name by which the Assyrian king ruled over Babylonia.

VI 1-81 (MT, 5:27–6:66) **The Tribe of Levi and** c
the Levitical Cities—The purpose of this chapter is clear. It is to record the legitimacy of the Zadokite priesthood and Levitical order as they existed in the Chronicler's day. An essential element of this legitimacy in the post-exilic days was that of physical descent. What we should describe as historical continuity is presented by the Chronicler (and by the post-exilic Priestly School) as physical descent.

1-15 The Priestly line from Levi through Aaron down to the Exile.

16-48 Levitical Genealogies—27. After 'Elkanah his son' we should probably add, as v. 28 requires, 'Samuel his son'. We note that Samuel is accorded Levitical ancestors, although this would not seem probable from 1 Sam. 1:11. But the account in 1 Sam. shows that he exercised cultic functions and was therefore a Levite. The Chronicler naturally infers Levitical descent. **48, 49.** The explicit distinction between Levitical and Priestly functions. To the priests belong exclusively the sacrifice, the service of the sanctuary (Num. 18:5) and the expiation of Israel's sins (Lev. 4f.).

50-53 repeats vv. 4–8, i.e. to the time of David, presumably because, although the Levitical cities about to be named were allotted in the time of Joshua, they were thought of as possessed in the days of David.

54-81 The Levitical Cities—The passage is based on Jos. 21:1–42.

VII 1-40 Further tribal Genealogies—1-5 Issa- d
char. 6-12. Benjamin. But the genealogy of Benjamin appears in ch. 8. It is possible that originally the genealogy of Zebulun was given here, but if so some Benjamite names were subsequently added; cf. Num. 26:38–41. The list however is at variance with ch. 8 and occurs when we might reasonably expect Zebulun to occur. Again in v. 12*b* we may have a fragment of a Danite genealogy, otherwise absent. In Gen. 46:23 Hushim is given as the son of Dan and, apparently with a changed order of consonants, Shuham in Num. 26:42. **12.** We should read 'The sons of Dan: his son Hushim, one' (in place of 'by the sons of Ir, Hushim the sons of Aher'). **13. Naphtali**: cf. Gen. 46:24, Num. 26:48f. As a tribal entity Naphtali appears to have dwindled to insignificance after the Judges period. **14-19. Manasseh:** the text has suffered. RSV follows LXX in v. 14. But we should omit 'Asriel' as a dittograph of the following words. The name appears as the son of Gilead in Num. 26:31. **15*a*.** Read 'And Machir took a wife, and the name of his wife was Maacah'; cf. 16. **20-7. Ephraim**: cf. Num. 26:35–7. 21 preserves an ancient tradition which almost certainly belongs to the Judges or Samuel period. It was apparently not originally connected with vv. 22ff. **28f. The Josephite territory. 30-40. Asher.**

VIII 1-40. Benjamin: cf. Num. 26:38–41. **3. 'Gera, Abihud':** read Gera the father of Ehud.

IX 1a is an appendix to chs. 2–8 corresponding to 2:1*a*. The Chronicler refers to his sources which are manifestly not our 1 and 2 Kg.

IX 1b-34 The Inhabitants of Jerusalem—There e
is a close relationship between vv. 1–17 and Neh. 11:1–19, but there are some notable divergences. The correspondence (allowing for orthographical divergences) is greatest for the priests and Levites. The

311e most notable difference is the inclusion in Chr. (v. 3) of Ephraim and Manasseh. It is reasonable to infer that in both places use was made of the same list. In Neh. the list represents those who dwelt in Jerusalem as the result of Nehemiah's repopulation policy. It may be the Chronicler's intention to suggest that the same families were represented, though in greater numbers and with some additions (especially Ephraimites and Manassites) in the days immediately before the Exile. It would emphasise the continuity between the pre-exilic and post-exilic community. **35-44. The family of Saul:** a repetition of 8:29–38 in order to introduce the account of Saul's death.

f **Part II X-XXIX**

The History of David—The history of Israel, as Yahweh's people whose worship is centred on the Jerusalem shrine, begins with David. It was only in that situation that the divine revelation to Moses—the Torah—could be put into practice. That, for the Chronicler, was what really mattered. There was no need to repeat the story of the Mosaic period, since the whole of the life of Judaism in his day was governed by that. The intervening period could be ignored as irrelevant to his purpose. Saul could not be ignored because he was Yahweh's anointed, but he was unfaithful (10:13) and so was rejected. It was David who put into effect the will of God revealed to Moses. Nothing could more clearly indicate that the Chronicler was not writing a new history of Israel. His purpose is to teach the sovereignty of God, the necessity of loyal obedience and trust, and the supreme importance of worship.

X 1-14 The Rejection of Saul (cf. 1 Sam. 31:1–13)—**6. 'all his house'**, where Sam. reads 'all his men'. The modification indicates the Chronicler's point of view. **10. house of their gods,** when Sam. has 'house of Ashtaroth', i.e. Astarte. **his head in the temple of Dagon** perhaps originally is the text of Sam. **12. buried:** Chr. omits the burning of 1 Sam. 31:12, either as a simple abbreviation or perhaps because such a practice was, in the Torah, confined to grave sexual offences (Lev. 20:14, 21:9). **13f.** The Chronicler's comment; but cf. 1 Sam. 28:6.

g **XI 1-47 David the anointed King over all Israel** (cf. 2 Sam. 5:1–10, 23:8–39)—Immediately after Saul's death, he is recognised as king by *all* Israel. All account of his struggle for power is omitted, as not germane to the Chronicler's purpose. A brief reference to the seven and a half years as king in the South appears in 3:4. **3. made a covenant:** Chr. draws attention to this all-important and distinctive feature of Israelite monarchy. The king is responsible before Yahweh for his people's welfare. **4. Jebus:** apparently an alternative name (cf. Jg. 19:10 f.) for Jerusalem based on the name of its inhabitants, the Jebusites. But the name Jerusalem (Urusalim) is known from the Amarna letters *c.* 1400 B.C. **10.** Peculiar to Chr. **13b.** The name Shammah has been omitted, see 2 Sam. 23:11. **15. cave:** the Heb. word for 'cave' so much resembles that for 'stronghold' as to suggest that the latter word originally was here also. The point is, not that David was in hiding, but that he was in a strong position. **17-19.** One of the few 'human' touches remaining in the Chronicler's account. It is an example of David's nobility of soul that he should spontaneously recognise that a gift so costly could be given to none other than Yahweh. **20f.** The text is in some confusion and RSV has corrected (with Syr. support), but at end of 20 we should probably read 'and he had a name (i.e. reputation) among the thirty'. **22. ariels:** the word possibly means 'hero' or 'champion' (ET 40 (1928–9), 237, followed by Rudolph). **26-41a.** Cf. 2 Sam. 23:24–39*a*. **41b. Zabad:** not in our text of Sam., but it may have been in the list in the Chronicler's day. **42-7.** A list from an unknown source. The mention of a Moabite in 46 is a mark of its antiquity.

312a **XII 1-22 David's Supporters at Ziklag**—The Chronicler's account differs considerably from 1 Sam. 22:1ff., 27:1ff. There he was joined by some four to six hundred men drawn from his own clan and from the ranks of the disaffected. Here it is a mighty army from Benjamin, Gad, Judah and Manasseh, the finest men of Israel. The list may well recall the names of those who were adherents of David and became prominent families under the monarchy. **8. like the faces of lions:** the word for 'lions' is very similar to 'ariel' in 11:22. Perhaps the text originally read 'like the faces of heroes'. **18** is a passage of some importance. The divinely chosen king is recognised by the spirit-quickened mind. And the spirit clothed itself with Amasai (cf. Jg. 6:34). Then follows a fragment of an ancient blessing. *Peace* is always an inadequate translation of the Heb. term, which means rather 'total well-being', appropriate to the man in whom the divine blessing dwells. **For your God helps you:** the Heb. perfect is to be understood as a prophetic perfect. **22. like an army of God:** in prosaic English 'a mighty army'.

23-40 The Troops who came to David at Hebron (cf. 2 Sam. 5:1; 1 Chr. 11:1–3)—It is usually assumed that this list is a fabrication of the Chronicler's, who thus with quite artificial numbers exaggerated the occasion. Certainly an army of some 400,000 did not come to Hebron. It may even be doubtful whether the tribes in the extreme north knew anything about David at this time. Yet the numbers, though doubtless exaggerated, are strange. Judah provides less than 2 per cent of the whole, and is even less than Simeon. Ephraim provides less than 6 per cent and is less than Zebulun. Zadok (v. 28) is specifically referred to as a warrior (so the context requires us to understand the phrase 'mighty in valour', although the term itself is of much more general application, 'man of unusual power'). A curious note is attached to the tribes of Issachar (v. 32) which may mean that they were skilled in astrological lore, or simply that they were quick to seize the opportunity when it offered. All this suggests that the list is of ancient origin, perhaps from the early days of David's rule; and that, though the numbers must be regarded as unreliable, the list may represent the militia available to David for his campaigns.

XIII The Removal of the Ark from Kiriath-jearim (2 Sam. 6:1–11)—This event is made to precede the events of 2 Sam. 5:11–25; from the Chronicler's point of view it is an event of primary importance. The point is made clear in vv. **1-4** (peculiar to Chr.) where also we have the introduction of priests and Levites. **5. from the Shihor** (the Wâdī el-'Arîsh): the ideal southern boundary of Israel's land; **the entrance of Hamath:** the northern boundary. **6-14.** See notes on 2 Sam. 6:1–11. **14. in his house:** probably 'in *its* house'. This replaces 'the Gittite' of 2 Sam. 6:11 which the Chronicler apparently regarded as unseemly for so holy an object. The house was probably a tent (cf. 15:1). b

XIV David in Jerusalem (cf. 2 Sam. 5:11–25)—Having placed the removal of the Ark from Kiriath-jearim at the beginning of David's reign, the Chronicler now transfers the previous events in his source, to follow and so to fill up the three months' interval. For these verses, see commentary on Sam. The Chronicler adds (v. 12) that David had the Philistine idols burned, in accordance with Dt. 7:5, 25, etc., a post-Davidic law. **17** is the Chronicler's addition.

XV, XVI The Bringing of the Ark to Jerusalem c —In Chr. the account is considerably expanded from the account in 2 Sam. 6:12–20: 15:1–24, 16:37–42 have no parallel in Sam.; 16:7–36 is an addition. What was undoubtedly a religious, but also an important political action in Sam., has become a matter of great liturgical significance. It furnishes the occasion for the appointment of the guilds of Levitical singers and musicians, and their functions. The

2c failure of the first attempt in ch. 13 is attributed to the fact that the Ark had not been carried by the Levites.

d **XV 1.** A remarkable feature of this passage, which is explicit in this verse and 16:37–9 (cf. 21:29 ; 2 Chr. 1:3f.), is the separation of the Ark and the Tabernacle. This meant that the worship of the Lord was celebrated in two places—an obvious breach of the Law in post-exilic days. No explanation for the retention (in the Chronicler's view) of the Tabernacle at Gibeon is offered. **3. assembled:** the word is commonly used in the sense of a properly constituted religious assembly. **12. Sanctify yourselves:** this would involve the washing of the garments and body, abstinence from sexual relationships and from wine (cf. Exod. 19:10–15, 30:19 ; Lev. 10:9). **13a.** The Heb. word corresponding to 'Because at the first time' is an unusual contraction, and there is no word to correspond to 'carry'. The meaning of the verse appears to be 'Because you were not there (or 'with us') the first time, the Lord our God broke forth upon us. For we had not inquired of him in the ordained manner.' **17.** Here we have the historical situation in which, as the Chronicler describes it, the guilds of musicians and singers for Temple worship were appointed ; cf. 6:31ff. **18.** RSV rightly omits 'Ben' (= son of) with LXX (cf. v. 20 and 16:5). **gatekeepers:** these exercised a liturgical function and apparently retained in the post-exilic cultus something of the earlier functions suggested by Ps. 24:7–10, when the victorious divine king, Yahweh, in solemn procession, entered the Temple ; cf. also Ps. 118:19, 20 ; Isa. 26:2. Note that Obed-edom is henceforward described as a Levite and (16:38) given a Levitical ancestry. **20 f. Alamoth-Sheminith:** both words occur in the titles of some Psalms (cf. Ps. 46:1, 6:1), and are clearly of some musical significance. They are commonly supposed to indicate soprano (women's voices) and bass (an octave lower?) respectively. But they may refer to modes (as our use of Dorian, Lydian, Phrygian mode) and may therefore be Gentilic names. The suggestions 'Elamite' and 'Shimyonite' (from Shimron, Jos. 11:1, later Shimyon) have been offered. But our knowledge of Israel's music is too scanty to give any certainty. **21. to lead:** the verb appears also in Psalm titles (cf. Ps. 4, 'To the choirmaster'), but the meaning is unknown. **22.** The Heb. of this verse is obscure and the rendering is suggested by LXX. MT may refer to carrying the Ark. **24. blow the trumpets:** cf. Num. 10:1–10. The trumpet was a straight silver instrument and is not to be confused with the horn of v. 28. In post-exilic days it was an important instrument associated with the liturgy of festal days. **25-16:3.** cf. 2 Sam. 6:12–19. Surprisingly Chr. omits the sequel with the punishment that befell Michal, probably because it describes David's dancing in terms that would appear unseemly.

e **XVI 4-6. The permanent appointment of the Levitical service for the Ark. 4. to invoke:** better 'to celebrate' by repeating the divine Name, or to sing the appropriate Psalms to accompany the memorial offering ; cf. titles of Ps. 38, 70. **to thank:** or 'to confess' or 'utter the doxology', and so in **7. 7-36.** This hymn consists of Ps. 96:1*b*–13*a*, 105:1–15, 106:1, 47, 48. The verses that have been chosen are appropriate to the occasion. With the coming of the Ark to Jerusalem, the Lord has triumphantly fulfilled his purpose declared to Moses, manifested his sovereignty over the nations and established his dwelling-place in the midst of his people. It is the beginning of a new era in the life of the people of God, as it is the fulfilment of that which was promised to Moses. (For notes on these verses, cf. the commentary on the Psalms referred to.) **12b.** The Heb. text is the same as in Ps. 105:5*b*. The Heb. for 'wonders' and 'miracles' suggests, by its frequent use in connection with the plagues of Egypt, our word 'portent'. A good illustration of its meaning is to be found in Jl 2:30f. (MT, 3:3f.). **25b.** MT as in Ps. 96:4*b*. RSV in the Ps. gives a verbal translation and in Chr. a good interpretation. **27b. joy:** Ps. 96:6*b* has 'beauty'. Chr. here uses an Aram. word (only elsewhere in Neh. 8:10) ; **place,** instead of 'sanctuary', is apparently deliberate since the Temple is not yet built. A similar alteration is given at v. 29. **30 f.** transposes the clauses of Ps. 96:10 f. **35. Say also** is added to Ps. 106:47. The Psalm as a whole is a confession of sin and acknowledgment of divine judgment. That is hardly appropriate here. The beginning and end of the Psalm are quoted, an acknowledgment of the fulfilment of God's saving purpose. We may note that the use of the closing verse makes it evident that this section of the Psalter (Book IV) was complete with its doxology by this date. Further the use of the indicative in Chr., replacing the jussive of the Ps., emphasises the part played by the congregation. **37-43.** Further duties of priests and Levites continuing vv. 4–6. **41. For his steadfast love endures forever** should be in quotation marks as a reference to the liturgy ; cf. v. 34*b*, Ps. 136. 312e

XVII How David's Purpose to build the Temple was to be fulfilled—The chapter is based on 2 Sam. 7:1–29 with slight modifications. The text of this chapter of Chr. is a valuable check on the MT ; cf. 2 Sam. 7. David proposes to build a permanent dwelling for the Ark of the Covenant, but Nathan, while at first approving, receives a word of God to say that this task is to be left to his successor. The chapter emphasises the divine purpose in establishing the Davidic dynasty. **4. You shall not build . . . :** better 'It is not you who shall build . . .' **5b.** MT is defective. LXX suggests 'but I was in a curtained tent'. RSV is based on the Targum. **10b. Moreover I declare to you:** MT has suffered and all EVV emend ; read with LXX using the consonants of MT 'But I will make you great.' **17b.** MT is corrupt and gives no meaning ; lit. 'thou dost see me as a row of men upwards'. **18. according to thine own heart:** i.e. according to thy purpose. The heart is, in Heb. thought, the seat of intellection and volition. **21. other:** so LXX and Vulg. The Heb. for 'other' and 'one' differ only in the last consonants (*r* and *d*) and these could easily be confused. **24. and thy name will be established:** the verb 'established' is an addition to 2 Sam. 7:26. We should translate 'Let it (the 'word' of v. 23) be established, that thy name be great for ever.' 313a

XVIII 1-17 David's Wars (see notes on 2 Sam. 8 b which Chr. largely reproduces)—**1. Gath and her villages:** this is either the original text of 2 Sam. 8:1 or an attempt to correct the text of Sam. where RSV translates the Heb. 'bridle of the mother' to make a most improbable proper name. **2.** Chr. omits the difficult middle part of the verse in Sam. **3. Hadadezer:** this is the correct form of the name and signifies 'Hadad (the supreme God of Syria) is ('my' or 'our') help'. **monument** as a sign of victory. It is not clear from the sentence whether it was David or Hadadezer who was the victorious king. Probably the Chronicler meant David. **10. Hadoram:** this would seem to be the Syrian form (abbreviated from Hadadram) of which Joram in 2 Sam. 8:10 is a Hebraised modification, replacing the name of the Syrian god Hadad with that of Yahweh ('Jo'). **17. David's sons were chief officials:** This is a deliberate alteration of 2 Sam. 8:18 to conform with post-exilic requirements.

XIX The War with Ammon and Syria (cf. 2 Sam. c 10)—The variations from the text of Sam. are few and usually designed to glorify David.

XX 1-3 The Conquest of Ammon (cf. 2 Sam. 11:1, 12:26, 30 f.)—The remarkable feature of the Chronicler's account is the omission of the story of David, Bathsheba and Uriah. **2. their king** (MT *Malkām*) : should probably be read as Milcom the Ammonite god. **3.** RSV seems to represent the original meaning of the verse in Sam., but it is difficult to imagine that if this were original to Chr. it would

313c have been altered by a later scribe to MT. The difference between 'And we set' and 'And he cut them to pieces' is small in Heb., and it would appear that Chr. reproduces a corrupt text of Sam.

4-8 Exploits against the Philistines (cf. 2 Sam. 21:18–22). **5. Elhanan . . . slew Lahmi the brother of Goliath:** thus the Chronicler emends the text of Sam. to avoid the inconsistency of the earlier book.

d **XXI, XXII 1 The Census, the Plague and the Choice of the Temple Site** (cf. 2 Sam. 24:1–25)—The variations between the story in Chr. and that in Sam. serve to show clearly the Chronicler's theological interests. It should be said that the variations have led some to suggest a source other than 2 Sam. 24, or a development of that account intermediate between Sam. and Chr. But in spite of the divergences and abbreviations, the identity of language between these two chapters appear to make such a hypothesis unnecessary. The most striking differences are (*a*) the appearance of the Satan, v. 1, (*b*) the numbers, v. 5, (*c*) the omission of Levi and Benjamin from the census, v. 6, (*d*) the appearance of the angel 'between earth and heaven', v. 16, (*e*) the association of the elders with David in the penitential mourning, v. 16, (*f*) the greatly increased price paid for the threshing-floor, v. 25, (*g*) the coming of fire from heaven upon the altar, (*h*) the recognition by David that this is the site of the Temple (vv. 28ff.). The Chronicler has used the ancient story for his own purpose. While in Sam. we are told of the wrath of God that was responsible for a mysterious plague, and how that wrath was appeased, in Chr. David was tested and failed, but the consequences of his failure led him to penitence and thus he receives the great revelation concerning the site of the Temple. The story in other words is the dramatic prelude to the chapters that follow.

e **XXI 1 Satan:** literary 'an adversary'. There are three occasions in the OT at which this term is used of a supernatural being. In Job (1:6, 2:2) and Zech. (3:1f.) the word is used with the definite article, and is clearly not a proper name but a common noun, i.e. 'the (supernatural) adversary'; cf. Num. 22:22, 32 where the angel of the Lord is a 'satan' (RSV 'adversary' and 'to withstand'). Here the word is used without the article and is probably to be rendered as a proper name. Yet even here he is not presented as the devil of later Jewish and Christian teaching, and there seems no need to suppose the influence of Persian thought in this passage. His function is little more than to test David; will he trust wholly in God, or will he, like other kings, put his confidence in military strength? Furthermore, the Chronicler and his readers would be clearly aware that the term was replacing and therefore in some sense interpreting the phrase in Sam., 'the anger of the Lord'. **to number Israel:** the attitude to the census in Chr. is different from that in Sam. In the earlier book it reflects a common attitude of mind which regards a census as impious *per se*, perhaps infringing upon a sphere of knowledge only proper to the deity, and so the breaking of a taboo. But the taking of a census in the time of the Chronicler had divine authority; cf. Num. 1:2, 26:2 (P). David's action is therefore represented as being done without reference to God and for self-glorification; cf. Prov. 14:28. It is the sin of self-assertion and mistrust. **6.** The Levites could not be numbered for military purposes; cf. Num. 1:49. The reason for Benjamin's omission is not given; it may be because the 'tabernacle of the Lord' was in Benjamite territory. The verse is added by the Chronicler. **16b. David and the Elders:** in the king's sin all Israel is involved, just as in the king's obedience all Israel is blessed. Yet in **17** David recognises his own guilt. The Chronicler emphasises the inevitable paradox of social solidarity and individual responsibility. **18** and **20.** The part played by the angel of the Lord is peculiar to Chr. and characteristic of post-exilic Judaism. Some would suggest Persian influence, 31
but it might well be a development of early Israelite thought. **23. wheat for a cereal offering:** an addition by the Chronicler (cf. Lev. 2:1ff.). **25. six hundred shekels of gold:** added by the Chronicler to emphasise the value of the Temple site. The silver of Sam. has become gold in Chr. and the fifty of Sam. has become twelve (? to correspond to the twelve tribes) times fifty in Chr. **28** continues in 22:1. **29f.** is in parenthesis. **30. afraid** is quite inadequate as a translation of the Heb. He was 'terrified' or 'struck with terror'

XXII 2-29 The Preparations for the Temple-building and the Cultus—The whole of this section 31
is the Chronicler's addition to the reign of David. It is represented as the climax of David's rule, and all that precedes is but the necessary preliminary. He had been anointed by God to acquire the land for the Lord's people in order that they might worship him at Jerusalem. The Chronicler would apparently present David as, like Moses, having to leave to his successor the completion of his work.

2-19 The Preparation for Building and the Commission to Solomon—2. aliens: these were foreigners who were permanently resident in Israel and under Israelite protection, and in that respect their political condition resembles that of the Israelite tribes in their earlier period in Egypt. They had no political rights and could therefore be levied for hewing stone. **3.** It should be noted that iron was a somewhat rare commodity in the ancient world. **9. Solomon, and I will give peace:** a word-play; in Heb. *Sh*^{e}*lōmōh* = Solomon, *Shālôm* = peace. Etymologically Solomon's name is connected with that of the deity whose name is preserved in Jerusalem. **10b. He shall be my son . . . :** a repetition of the covenant with David (2 Sam. 7:13, 14*a*). **14. With great pains:** the Heb. word probably means 'In spite of all my troubles' and apparently refers to the wars in which he was involved. In this and the following verses the Chronicler speaks with characteristic hyperbole.

XXIII 1-32 The Courses and Duties of the Levites—In this and the following chapters, the b
Chronicler ascribes to David the organisation of the Temple-service that in fact only came into effect from the 4th cent. B.C. Superficially, then, his description is completely unhistorical, although very valuable evidence for a study of post-exilic Judaism. But this superficial judgment does the Chronicler an injustice, for he is not using our forms of expression and he is not writing as a historian. It is, moreover, undoubtedly true that the king, throughout the monarchy period, was the essential person in the cultus and is directly responsible for its maintenance and organisation. It would appear that in pre-exilic days the priesthood was an adjunct to the king, and that for the important occasions in the Israelite cultus it is the king who is the important figure. Through him Israel comes to God, and through him the divine blessing becomes operative in Israel's life. Whatever their particular occasion, many of the Psalms are royal liturgies. The account of Solomon (even allowing for Deuteronomic interpretations) and even more of Ahaz (2 Kg. 16:10ff.), Manasseh (2 Kg. 21:3–9 and Josiah (2 Kg. 23:1–25), makes it evident that the Davidic king controls and even modifies the cultus, and that the priests are subordinate to him (cf. A. R. Johnson, *Sacral Kingship in Ancient Israel* (1955)). Two further points need to be remembered. The first is the Heb. manner of speech and thought, whereby the acts of all his successors are expressed in terms of the founder of the dynasty. In a very real sense David lives on in his descendants; their life is an extension of his. The second is the continuity, however many the modifications, of the post-exilic cultus with that of the monarchical period. For those who take cultic action seriously, it is safe to say that no completely new practice would be allowable, just as no cultic act which had proved its worth

4b in the worship of Yahweh could be abandoned. The Chronicler, then, manifests a genuine sense of history, although his mode of expression would expose him to the criticism of a modern historian.

c **1f.** These verses anticipate ch. 28, and the intervening chapters appear as David's last words. The Chronicler ignores the struggle for the monarchy in 1 Kg. 5ff. **3-5. The numbers and offices of the Levites. 3. were numbered :** this was according to divine requirement (Num. 4) and in no sense a contradiction of 1 Chr. 21. **thirty years old :** cf. Num. 4:3,23,30, 35. The age of admission to the ministry varies ; cf. v. 24, Ezr. 3:8, where it is given as twenty, Num. 8:24f., where it is twenty-five. The variation may reflect an actual conflict between theory and practice. **9.** There is some confusion in this verse. The simplest solution is to omit 9*a*. **10. Zina :** a scribal error for Ziza ; cf. v. 11. **22. their kinsmen . . . married them :** in order to maintain the family of their father Eleazar.

d **XXIV 1-19 The Courses of the Priests—2. Nadab and Abihu died :** cf. Lev. 10:1f. ; Num. 3:4. **5. Officers of the Sanctuary :** perhaps better, in accordance with Heb. grammar, ' sacred office '.
20-31. Another list of Levites which differs at some points from 23:13–23 and is probably an addition to the original text of Chr. reflecting later conditions.
XXV 1-31 The Courses of the Singers and Musicians—The interest shown by the Chronicler in the musical guilds has suggested that he belonged to one of the guilds. It should be remembered, however, that the singing and music were not for ornamental purposes. The correct chanting of the liturgy and the correct mode and accompaniment is no less important for ritual efficacy than the correct performance of the sacrifice. The uttered word, like the acted word, if divinely sanctioned, has power to effect the divine purpose of forgiveness and salvation. It may well be that it is to these singers and musicians that we owe the preservation of the Psalter, the collection of those liturgies and prayers that had proved effective. The singers in Chr. occupy the place of the cultic prophets of pre-exilic days ; cf. v. 1. They no longer utter spontaneous prophetic words, but they must receive inspiration rightly to discharge their function. Apparently one might even utter a prophetic oracle ; cf. 2 Chr. 20:14ff., and the Psalter gives evidence of similar phenomena (cf. Ps. 81:5*c* ff.). **4. Hananiah . . . Mahazioth :** seven of these names cannot be proper names but the words can be rendered, with very slight emendation, as part of an ancient lament :

> Be gracious to me, O Lord, be gracious to me.
> Thou art my God ; I magnify thee, I exalt thee.
> Thou art my help when I dwell in trouble.
> I wither away ; set thou me free.
> Thou art my refuge.

The appearance of these words as proper names in vv. 23–31 would suggest (*a*) that the misunderstanding was earlier than the Chronicler's time and (*b*) that he is making use, however artificially, of earlier lists in compiling this chapter. The essential point is the twenty-four courses.

e **XXVI 1-32 Other Levitical Officials—1–19.** The courses of the gatekeepers. **20–8.** Temple treasurers. **29–32.** Officials to function outside the Temple precincts. **5. for God blessed him :** i.e. Obed-edom. This appears to be a deliberate reference to 13:14, and would seem to suggest that in pre-exilic days, before the validity of the Levitical order was expressed in terms of *physical* descent from Levi, Levite was a cultic term. It further suggests that the story of 2 Sam. 6:6–7 was associated with a Yahweh-shrine (at Perez-uzzah ?) and was preserved by the guardians of the shrine. **18. parbar :** probably from a Persian word meaning ' court ' or ' colonnade '. **20. of the Levites, Ahijah :** the Heb. can hardly be so translated. We should read with LXX ' And the Levites their brothers ', i.e. fellow-Levites. The
difference in Heb. is very slight. **29. outside duties :** 314e
i.e. matters external to the Temple service, though hardly what we should call secular duties, since the work of the judges was intimately related to the Torah ; cf. Dt. 17:8ff., etc. It is possible moreover that ' officers ' would be responsible for civil administration in the state ruled by the High Priest of post-exilic days.

XXVII 1-34 Military and civic Officials (cf. f
11:10 ff.)—The list and the numbers are of course artificial. The Chronicler is presenting an impressionistic picture of military and civic forces under the ideal king. Obviously the economy of the land could not support either the numbers of the army or the dislocation caused by their monthly courses. In prosaic terms : ' The king's state was magnificent and secure.' **4.** we should probably restore with 11:12 and 2 Sam. 23:9 ' Eleazar son of Dodai the Ahohite . . .' **33. the king's friend :** a recognised term in oriental monarchies. It is something more than a title of honour and signified more than companionship. His functions are not explained in the OT, but he would seem to be one who would share in a peculiarly intimate way the king's mind and purpose in order to transmit them to others in time of peace, or to act for the king in time of war. It was a position of great responsibility and honour ; cf. 2 Sam. 15:37, 16:16ff.

XXVIII 1-XXIX 19 David's final Address—He g
gives his charge to his officers to fulfil his plan for the Temple (1–8), commits the plan to Solomon (9–21), challenges the assembly by his own example to a like liberality (29:1–5). The assembly makes free-will offering (6–9) and David makes his final confession of faith (10–19). There is no suggestion in this section of the weakness of the aged David and the intrigues for the succession as portrayed in 1 Kg. 1:1–11. This section follows on 22:19.

XXVIII 2. my brethren and my people : whatever 315a
may have been the intentions of individual kings towards absolutism, this is at the heart of the teaching on monarchy in the OT. He occupies a unique position in Israel, religiously as well as politically, and may even be called Yahweh's son (cf. v. 6), but he is a human and not a deified being, *primus inter pares* (cf. Dt. 17:15, 20 ; 1 Sam. 30:23 ; 2 Sam. 19:12). There is nothing in contemporary oriental conceptions of monarchy to prepare us for Israel's conception. **I had it in my heart :** i.e. it was my purpose. **the footstool of our God :** a term variously used of the whole earth (Isa. 66:1), of the Ark (Ps. 99:5, 132:7), but here apparently of the Temple ; cf. Isa. 60:13 where the thought is the same although the word is not used. **4f.** The Divine election is fundamental to the Davidic dynasty; cf. 2 Sam. 7:8ff., but as it relates to individual kings it was always conditioned by their response (cf. v. 7, 9*c*). It is part of this election that the king should observe the Torah (cf. 2 Kg. 11:12 ; Ps. 132:11f.). The Chronicler relates that specifically to the building and maintenance of Yahweh's Temple (v. 10). **11-19.** The plan is a divine revelation, with the suggestion that the Jerusalem Temple corresponds to a heavenly temple. The Heb. of v. 19 suggests that the divine plan was communicated to David and it was ' upon him to consider ' the detailed working out of the plan. **12. he had in mind :** lit. ' it was by the spirit with him.' The use of *rûaḥ* as meaning ' mind ' is unusual but not unique in later Heb. writings. But it is unique in Chr. It is possible that the phrase should be translated ' By the spirit that was with him '. This would accord with v. 19, which should read ' all this according to an edict from the hand of Yahweh ; it is my part to consider all the workings of the plan.'
XXIX 1. whom alone God has chosen : ' whom ' is a correction of MT ' one ', and ' alone ' should therefore be omitted. **palace :** a word used only here and in v. 19 for the Temple. It is normally used for a fortress (RSV ' capitol ' in Est. 1:2, 5) ; cf. Neh. 2:8, 7:2. **5. consecrating himself :** MT ' to fill his hand '. The phrase is otherwise used in the OT in the consecration to the priesthood ; cf. Exod. 28:41, etc.

315a A similar term is used in Akkadian of instituting the king. It is improbable that a term so closely related to the priestly office would be used by the Chronicler in this vague metaphorical sense. It seems better to translate in a literal and non-technical sense ' Who is willing freely to fill his hand (sc. with gifts) for the Lord today ? ' (cf. v. 9). **11-19.** The prayer is undoubtedly based on liturgical prayers in use in the Chronicler's day. Many of the phrases appear in prayers still in use in the synagogue.

b **20-22a. The solemn preparation for the accession of the new king. 22b-25. Solomon's accession. 26-30. Summary of David's reign. 29. The Chronicles of Samuel, etc.** Three separate sources seem to be referred to, of which we only know of 1 and 2 Sam. But since Nathan and Gad appear in Sam. and Kg., it is probable that the Chronicler has no more than these biblical sources in mind.

THE SECOND BOOK OF CHRONICLES

c **Part III (2 Chr. I-IX) The Reign of Solomon**

I 1-13 The Sacrifice at Gibeon—1-5. These verses are the Chronicler's expansion of 2 Kg. 3:4. But what in Kg. is described as a customary procedure (' used to offer ') is here described as a single act together with the whole assembly, necessitated by the fact that the tent of meeting and the bronze altar (1 Chr. 16:39f.) were there. No reference is made in Kg. to the bronze altar of Bezalel in Gibeon, although there was at Gibeon, as at every high place, an altar. It is the presence of these holy objects which, for the Chronicler, necessitates and justifies Solomon's sacrifice at the high place. **7-13.** See notes on 1 Kg. 3:5-15. **14-17. Solomon's might:** see notes on 1 Kg. 10:26-9. It is not clear why Chr. transfers this excerpt from Kg. to this place in the narrative, since the remainder of 1 Kg. 10 appears at 2 Chr. 9. It is possible that he felt that some specific reference to Solomon's wealth should follow the vision of vv. 7-12. **15.** Chr. characteristically adds ' gold ' to the account in Kg.

d **II 1-18 Preparation for Building the Temple**—See notes on 1 Kg. 5. The numbers in Chr. vary slightly from those in Kg., and in Chr. it is explicitly stated that the labourers were non-Israelites (v. 17). **5. for our God is greater than all gods :** is quite appropriate to the Chronicler but not in a communication sent to the Tyrian king. It is not in Kg. **8. algum** (Kg. almug) : possibly a species of juniper (the word appears in the Râs Shamra tablets as *'lmg'* ; the spelling in Kg. is to be preferred). **10.** Characteristically Chr. has increased the amount of provisions. **13. Huram-abi:** RSV correctly reads this as the full name (cf. 4:16), which is abbreviated in 4:10 to Huram. **14. of the daughters of Dan:** cf. 1 Kg. 7:14, ' widow of the tribe of Naphtali '. The reason for the variation in Chr. can only be conjectured. It has been suggested that it is an attempt to harmonise the Solomon story with that of Exod. 31 where (v. 6) Oholiab of the tribe of Dan is the skilled craftsman for the tabernacle (cf. also Exod. 35:34).

III 1-V 1 The Building of the Temple and its Furnishing—See notes on 1 Kg. 6:1-28, 7:15-51. The account follows that of Kg. but additions and modifications are made to accord with the post-exilic Temple.

e **III 1** It is explicitly stated that the Temple was built on the threshing-floor of Ornan. The site is identified with the scene of Abraham's sacrifice of Isaac ; cf. Gen. 22:2 (not otherwise in the OT). **6. setting of precious stones :** not mentioned in Kg., but it seems to be a heightening of the account in 1 Kg. 5:17, ' costly stones ', where, however, the adjective refers to the cost of preparation. The Heb. adjective is the same, though used in Chr. in our sense of precious stones. **Parvaim:** this is apparently a place name, but the form corresponds to no known gold-producing district. The context makes it clear that what is referred to is ' gold of best quality ' (so Vulg.). The amount 31
of gold in this and the following verses is characteristic of the Chronicler's hyperbole ; the six hundred talents of v. 8 (at least 27,000 lb., and probably more than twice that amount) is not in the Kg. account. **9a.** MT has suffered in transmission and RSV gives, with LXX support, the probable meaning. Each nail weighing one shekel supported fifty shekels of gold. **10. of wood :** MT has a word which suggests molten images, although the word occurs only here. It seems unlikely that Chr. would have replaced ' olive wood ' in 1 Kg. 6:32 by such a term. RSV, following LXX, supposes some accidental duplication of consonants. **14.** Kg. does not speak of a veil. It is introduced in accordance with Exod. 26:31ff., and probably existed in the post-exilic Temple. **16. like a necklace :** MT ' in the inner sanctuary ', which is obviously impossible. RSV, by transposing the consonants for ' inner sanctuary ' (*d^{e}bhîr*), reads ' necklace ' (*rābhîdh*). **4:1ff.** The variations between this and 1 Kg. 7:23ff. reflect the conditions of the Chronicler's day. **17. in the clay ground :** should probably be read ' at the ford of Adamah '.

V 2-VII 10 The Dedication of the Temple (see f
notes on 1 Kg. 8:1-66)—Most of the material from Kg. is used and the variations indicate the Chronicler's point of view. **5:4. the Levites took up the ark,** instead of the priests in 1 Kg. 8:3, in accordance with 1 Chr. 15:2. **5. the priests and the Levites :** RSV is probably right in introducing the conjunction (with good support from the ancient versions) ; its absence in MT by contrast with its presence in 1 Kg. 8:4 is very difficult to understand, since the Chronicler always recognises the distinction between the two. **9. from the holy place :** RSV has emended MT (' from the ark ') with the support of LXX and 1 Kg. 8:8. **11ff.** The Chronicler has considerably expanded the account in 1 Kg. 8:10 f. On this Dedication Day the whole priestly and Levitical order was present, and they join in the hymn of praise, using the familiar words of the liturgy. **VI 16. in my law :** a characteristic addition by the Chronicler. **41f.** Chr. gives his own conclusion to Solomon's prayer from Ps. 132:8f. The liturgical character of this pre-exilic Psalm makes it singularly appropriate in this setting. Chr. probably preserves something of the original purpose of the Psalm by quoting it in connection with the dedicating of the Temple where, in pre-exilic days, the Ark was the visible symbol of Yahweh's presence. **Saints :** the Heb. word is etymologically connected with that for ' steadfast love ', and suggests those who are steadfast and loyal. It is quite unconnected with the word for saints in Dan. 7:18. The rendering of **42b** ' thy steadfast love ' involves a slight emendation and correctly gives the meaning (cf. Isa. 55:3). **VII 1-3.** Not in 1 Kg. It is emphasised that it is Yahweh himself who hallows the Temple. The assembly makes the liturgical responses in v. 3. **5.** The high numbers of animals sacrificed are taken from 1 Kg. 8:63. **6.** Added by Chr. **8. the feast :** sc. of Tabernacles.

11-22 The Divine Answer to Solomon's Prayer (cf. 1 Kg. 9:1-9)—Vv. 13-15 have been added by Chr. and refer back to Solomon's prayer.

VIII 1-18 Various Undertakings of Solomon g
(cf. 1 Kg. 9:10-26)—**2** is in striking contrast to 1 Kg. 9:11. The Chronicler ' corrects ' what must have seemed to him a mistake in Kg. While the account in Kg. is *historically* correct, that in Chr. represents what was appropriate to the Solomon of tradition. His statement may well represent the official teaching of his day. **11** appears to be an attempt to minimise the impropriety (in the Chronicler's day) of Solomon's marriage with an Egyptian princess. In the 10th cent. it appeared as an outstanding diplomatic achievement, but in the 4th cent. it was an offence against strict Jewish sentiment. Further, it was contrary to the Law for a woman to be in regular contact with a holy place (cf. Lev. 12:1ff., 15:19ff.).

6a **IX 1-31 Solomon's Wisdom and Wealth** (cf. 1 Kg. 10:1–29, 11:41–3)—Chr. omits from the narrative of Kg. the account of Solomon's idolatry and the growing resentment against his oppressive rule. **7. Your wives:** RSV emends here and in 1 Kg. 10:8, in both places with support from ancient versions. The difference in Heb. is slight and the emendation is in accord with ancient usage. **21. For the king's ships went to Tarshish:** this is a misunderstanding by Chr. of the phrase in 1 Kg. 10:22. Tarshish is Tartessus in Spain, and, as the conclusion of the verse shows, the merchandise was brought from the East. The term 'ships of Tarshish' was a conventional term for large ships capable of sailing a long distance. (For a different view, cf. §424*h*.) **29.** Cf. 1 Chr. 29:29. In the book of Kg. Nathan appears at the beginning of Solomon's reign (1 Kg. 1) and Ahijah at the end (1 Kg. 11:29ff.). Iddo is not known outside Chr., although there appears to have been a tradition that this was the name of the unnamed prophet in 1 Kg. 13. It is possible that Chr. is referring to some written teaching material bearing these names.

b **Part IV (2 Chr. X-XXXVI) The History of Judah from Rehoboam to the Edict of Cyrus**—The most striking difference between Kg. and Chr. in this section is the omission in the latter of almost every reference to the Northern Kingdom. The explanation for this is given in 2 Chr. 13:5ff. A notable addition by the Chronicler is the frequent mention of prophets and Levites in the Southern Kingdom. The latter reflect the conditions of post-exilic Judaism. It is not possible to say with certainty whether the introduction of a series of prophets into the narrative preserves a tradition not recorded in Kg., or is a method of teaching. The function of these prophets is to warn the people of God against seeking help from any source apart from Yahweh, to encourage them to fulfil his law and to rebuke their disobedience. They appear as the fulfilment of the promise in Dt. 18:15 ff.

X 1-XII 15 The Reign of Rehoboam (cf. 1 Kg. 12:1–24, 14:21–9)—1 Kg. 14:22–4 is omitted by Chr. To the account in Kg. is added 2 Chr. 11:5–23, (*a*) Rehoboam's cities of defence, (*b*) the immigration to Judah of the priests and Levites from the apostate Northern Kingdom, and (*c*) an account of the family of Rehoboam. We can recognise (*b*) as the Chronicler's characteristic teaching, but (*a*) and (*c*) may well rest on good tradition.

11:5. he built cities for defence: i.e. he fortified existing towns apparently against Egyptian attack. **17. They strengthened the Kingdom:** because they kept the people loyal to Yahweh. **12:2.** The reason for the invasion of Shishak (more correctly Sheshonq) is added by Chr. The Sukkim are now known as foreign troops in Egyptian service. **5-8** is an addition to the account in Kg. The prophet's rebuke is followed by penitence and an easing of the disaster. **7.** Some deliverance, perhaps 'deliverance in a short while'; cf. Ezr. 9:8 where the same Heb. word is translated 'a brief moment'.

c **XIII 1-XIV 1a The Reign of Abijah**—Vv. 3–20 have no parallel in Kg. and have been derived from 'the story of the prophet Iddo', v. 22. Nothing is known of this source, and the contents of the chapter make it clear that we have here teaching material, perhaps earlier than the date of Chr. That there was hostility between the two kingdoms during the reign of Abijah (Abijam) is attested by 1 Kg. 15:7. It is possible that some tradition of a battle at Zemaraim had persisted into the Chronicler's day, and that it included the tactical note in v. 13. On the basis of this, the Chronicler develops his teaching. The Northern Kingdom was apostate because (*a*) it had broken away from the Davidic line, and (*b*) its worship was corrupt and invalid. Its downfall was therefore certain. But that downfall was brought about by direct divine agency (v. 15*b*) and not by the superior military might of Abijah. The 'moral' of the story is 316c
made clear in v. 18.

13:1. Abijah: in 1 Kg. 15:1 'Abijam', which is probably original, but it was very early modified to Abijah. **2. Micaiah:** read with LXX, Syr. and 11:20 'Maacah'. **5. a covenant of salt:** cf. Num. 18:19, i.e. a perpetual covenant. **7. scoundrels:** RSV correctly translates 'sons of Belial'. Belial is not a proper name in OT but a term meaning 'wickedness'. So 'sons of wickedness', 'wicked men'. This description of the northern tribes seems hardly justified in view of ch. 10, and still less in view of the account in Kg. But in the Chronicler's view, whatever may be the human justification, nothing could excuse the revolt against the Davidic line and the consequent religious apostasy. **young:** not in age, since he was forty-one at his accession, but in experience. **irresolute:** lit. 'soft of heart'. But in Heb. usage the heart is the seat of volition and understanding. Vv. **8-12** may well reflect the Samaritan schism of the 4th cent. B.C.

XIV 1b-XVI 14 The Reign of Asa (cf. 1 Kg. 15:8, d
11–23)—While the account in Kg. is used by Chr., it has been considerably expanded and modified. The material in 14:9–15, 15:1–15, 16:7–10, 12*b* has no parallel in Kg. and presents the characteristic teaching of Chr. on the necessity for trust in Yahweh alone. The argument is that for the first thirty-five years of his reign Asa was loyal to Yahweh and enjoyed success, but then he began to rely on human help (and Syrian help at that!) and became weak. The closing six years present a picture of progressive deterioration. **XIV 1b-8.** Ten years of peace during which a religious reform took place and various defence measures were undertaken. The corruption of religion with which Asa had to deal seems hardly to accord with the Chronicler's portrayal of the previous reign, but is entirely in accord with 1 Kg. 15:3, 12. **5. incense altars:** cf. 2 Chr. 34:4, where the word is used in connection with altars of the Baals; cf. also Lev. 26:30; Isa. 17:8, 27:9; Ezek. 6:4, 6. The rendering 'sun images' in AVm and RV is incorrect. **9-15.** The defeat of Zerah the Ethiopian is attributed directly to Yahweh at the prayer of Asa. This might be regarded as an illustration of the prayer in Ps. 20:6, 7. There seems to be no justification for identifying Zerah the Ethiopian (Cushite) with the Pharaoh Osorkon I. The story probably reflects (and characteristically magnifies) a raid from the Arabian desert. **14. the fear of the Lord:** cf. 17:10, 19:7, 20:29. The Heb. word used indicates a dread sent by God, such as is suggested by our word panic (etymologically a groundless fear induced by Pan). The term appears in Gen. 31:42, 53 as a proper name. **XV 1-19. Asa's religious reforms, inspired by Azariah.** The account appears as an expansion of 1 Kg. 15:11–15, and as such forms an excellent example of the Chronicler's teaching method. The point of the story is made in vv. 12–15. The argument is that in the period of the Judges (vv. 3–6) Israel was without a priest to teach (*mōreh*) and without a law to be taught (*Tôrāh*), and from this ensued anarchy and distress. But now that Law is known, and in observance of it is true welfare. Asa appears as a forerunner of Hezekiah, as that king does of Josiah. **16. Maacah his mother:** probably (cf. 11:20) his grandmother who continued in power as queen mother after the death of Abijah. **abominable image:** some particularly offensive object, doubtless associated with the fertility rites, so obnoxious to Israelite thought as to produce shuddering horror. **17** is in direct contradiction with 14:3, unless we take the words 'out of Israel' to mean exclusively the Northern Kingdom. This appears to have been the intention of Chr. in order to assimilate the account in Kg. to his own. **XVI 1-10.** The war with Israel (vv. 1–6; cf. 1 Kg. 15:16–22) introduces the account of Asa's defection and the rebuke of Hanani (vv. 7–10)—the Chronicler's teaching material. The strength of the people of God lies in absolute reliance on and obedience to Yahweh

316d (v. 9). This defection of Asa and his condemnation is added by Chr. and related to his dropsical condition of 1 Kg. 15:23. So in the concluding note, **11-14**, the disease is magnified and the ' moral ' is underlined. Asa sought medical help instead of seeking Yahweh to discover the cause of his illness. There seems no need to suppose that Chr. objects to doctors as such, but to Asa's action in this particular situation ; cf. Sir. 38:9–15.

317a **XVII 1-XX 37 The Reign of Jehoshaphat**—In this section, while the material in 1 Kg. 15:24, 22:1–35, 41–50 has been used, most of the account is new. The king's piety is in Chr. greatly magnified and, in consequence, so is his prosperity, but his alliance with the Northern Kingdom is condemned on religious grounds. It seems that the whole section in Chr. is related to the name of the king (= Yahweh judges) and this is particularly evident in 19:4–11 (cf. Jl 3:2 for a similar word-play). **XVII 1-6** gives a brief survey of Jehoshaphat's strength and prosperity which are directly related to his piety. V. 6*b* can hardly be reconciled with 20:33 ; but the latter verse is taken directly from the source 1 Kg. 22:43, while 17:6 is part of the Chronicler's reflection. **7-9** tells of Jehoshaphat's promotion of the teaching ministry of the Levites and is a necessary precondition for 19:4–11. The account corresponds to conditions in the 4th cent. B.C. It is to be noted that similar activity is ascribed to Nehemiah in Neh. 8:9ff. **10-19**. The king's wealth and military might are described in terms appropriate to his piety. It is made clear that his security was not the product of his own might but of the divinely inspired 'dread' (cf. 14:14). **XVIII 1-34** reproduces the account in 1 Kg. 22:1–35 with little variation (see notes *ad loc.*) and serves to introduce the Chronicler's teaching in **XIX 1-3**, for from the marriage relationship of 18:1 and the associated political alliance with the Northern Kingdom nothing but evil could come. **4-11**. It is to be assumed that this represents Jehoshaphat's return to piety as a consequence of the prophet's rebuke. It tells of the king's reform of the kingdom's judicial system, in which the requirements of Dt. 16:18–20, 17:8–13 are put into effect. It is to be noted that here, as elsewhere in OT, the right administration of justice is integrally

b related to the will of God. **XX 1-30** is another example of the Chronicler's teaching. It tells of an invasion from the desert from which the Judaeans were saved solely by a divine act in answer to the king's prayer, and without any human intervention. It seems hardly likely that this is a retelling of the story in 2 Kg. 3:4ff., since apart from the mention of Moab and Edom there are no points of resemblance. It is of course quite possible that a tradition existed of some invasion from the desert which was repelled ; but we have no independent evidence. The Chronicler's interest is didactic. **1. Meunites :** this is undoubtedly the correct reading and is supported by LXX ; they came from a district of Edom. **2. Edom :** there is constant confusion between this and Aram (= Syria). The correction has some support from ancient versions and from v. 10 (Mt Seir). **5. before the new court :** appropriate to the post-exilic Temple but not to Solomon's Temple. **7. Abraham thy friend :** cf. Isa. 41:8 ; Jas 2:23. The meaning is ' Abraham who loved thee '. **9. the sword, judgment :** the footnote ' the sword of judgment ' is to be preferred ; cf. Num. 20:14–21 ; Dt. 2:4f., 9, 19. **14. Jahaziel :** not otherwise known and the meaning of his name ' God gives visions ' is almost too apt. But we note that the prophetic word comes from a Levite and that this happens ' in the assembly '. For the Chronicler, the Temple singer is the successor of the cult prophet. **16. Ziz . . . Jeruel :** neither place is known, although the latter may have stood originally in Gen. 22:14, where it would, by its apparent meaning ' God sees ', well fit the story. **17. victory :** RSV correctly interprets here the word normally translated ' salvation '. **20. Believe . . . be established :** Chr. makes use of the saying of Isa. 7:9, which may, in order to convey the assonance, be rendered ' Be firm . . . and be confirmed in your faith'. **21** reflects the Chronicler's love for the liturgy. It is based on Ps. 96:9 and 136:1. **22f.** The ambush is clearly of a superhuman character and we should render ' And the men of Ammon ' not ' For . . .' **31-7**. The narrative now continues that of 1 Kg. 22:41–5, 48, 49. But the account in 35–7 completely changes the meaning of 1 Kg. 22:48f. The destruction of the fleet in Chr. is interpreted as the punishment for the alliance with Ahaziah of Israel.

c **XXI 1-20 The Reign of Jehoram** (cf. 1 Kg. 22:50 ; 2 Kg. 8:7–24)—But Chr. has added considerably to the narrative of Kg. Thus vv. 2–4, 11–19 are peculiar to Chr. ; and notes are added to the material taken from Kg. in order to emphasise the religious judgment on his rule ; cf. v. 10*b* and the note in v. 20 ' he departed with no one's regret.' It would seem that the doom pronounced on Jehoshaphat in 19:2 is actualised in his son, whose life was corrupted by his marriage to ' the daughter of Ahab ' (and so cf. 22:3). **2-4**. In these verses, the Chronicler has preserved historical information from a tradition current, perhaps, among the descendants of David. It will be observed that in these verses the reason for the assassination is not given and it is reasonable to infer that a political conspiracy lies behind the story. The Chronicler has made use of this story, together with the material from Kg., in order to pronounce a religious judgment (v. 13), and to suggest that they were seeking to maintain pure religion in opposition to Jehoram. **2.** The appearance of Azariah twice in the list of brothers is unlikely. In MT there is a slight difference in spelling (Azariah . . . Azariahu) ; it has been suggested that for the second we should read ' Uzziah ' (a later king of this name was also called Azariah ; cf. 2 Kg. 14:21 ; 2 Chr. 26:1). In vv. 2 and 4 RSV reads ' Judah ', in v. 2 with some MSS support, but in v. 4 with none. It is better to retain ' Israel ' in both instances ; cf. 11:3, 12:6, 28:19. The Chronicler thinks of the Judaeans as, religiously, Israel. **11. unfaithfulness :** i.e. marital infidelity, a particularly obnoxious sin in Israelite thought, and used because Israel is thought of as Yahweh's wife. **12-15. A letter from Elijah.** The date of this event (cf. 2 Kg. 2 and 3:1), the improbability of this prophet of the North thus communicating with a Judaean king, and the style of the letter suggest that this is the Chronicler's teaching rather than history. Such conduct as that of Jehoram deserves and receives a Divine rebuke. The doom is worked out in vv. 16–19 and in ch. 22 almost to the extinguishing of the ' lamp ' of David (v. 7). **17. Jehoahaz** is simply another form of Ahaziah, a compound of *'āḥaz* (grasped) and the Divine name.

d **XXII 1-9 The Reign of Ahaziah** (cf. 2 Kg. 8:25–9, 9:21–7)—The account in Chr. is abbreviated and modified. It is possible that vv. 7–9 are based on a tradition other than Kg. **1. The inhabitants of Jerusalem.** No reason is given for the prominence of the people in this accession, and the statement has no parallel in 2 Kg. 8:25. It is reminiscent of 2 Kg. 21:24*b*, 23:30*b* (= 2 Chr. 33:25, 36:1). Since Ahaziah was the only survivor of Jehoram's sons, there would seem to be no other choice. Perhaps in the Chronicler's mind the solemn act was necessary in view of the doom pronounced in 21:14 and still to be worked out in Ahaziah (22:7) in order to prepare the way, however precariously, for the coming of Joash whose birth occurred during his father's reign of one year. **2. forty-two :** this is an error for twenty-two (2 Kg. 8:26) since his father was only forty at his death (2 Chr. 21:20). **4f.** The evil influence of the association with the house of Ahab begun under Jehoshaphat (18:1) is worked out to its end. **7-9.** The account differs in important details from 2 Kg. 9:16–27.

e **XXII 10-XXIII 21 Athaliah the Usurper** (cf. 2 Kg.

7e 11:1–20)—**11.** Chr. adds to the account in Kg. that Jehoshabeath (Jehosheba) was married to Jehoiada the priest. **XXIII 1-11.** Chr. modifies the account of Kg. to make the Levites and priests take the leading role instead of the royal guards (foreigners), since the presence of the latter in the Temple court would be quite intolerable to his thought (v. 6). The whole action as described in Chr. is an ecclesiastical one, and for an ecclesiastical purpose.

f **XXIV 1-27 The Reign of Joash** (cf. 2 Kg. 12:1–21) —The account in Kg. is used in Chr., but the differences in presentation are characteristic of the Chronicler's method of teaching. The Temple is renovated, not because of priestly neglect (Kg.) but because the adherents of Athaliah 'had broken into the house of God' and committed sacrilege. The land suffered from a Syrian invasion and Hazael of Syria had to be bought off by means of the Temple ornaments and treasures (Kg.), but in Chr. the invasion is the result of the apostasy of Joash. The king was assassinated in a palace conspiracy (Kg.), but this is described in Chr. as the killing of the severely wounded king, apparently on the field of battle, as a just avenging of the murder of Zechariah. We have here a clear example of the Chronicler's teaching method (or that current in his day). In 2 Kg. 12 we have the story of a pious king who was assassinated. In Chr. the story is modified so as to account for this assassination. **2** introduces the first modification; cf. Kg. 12:2. The king was pious while Jehoiada lived. **3** (not in Kg.). The priest stands *in loco parentis* to the
8a king. **4-14. The restoration of the Temple.** **5.** The money is collected by levying a tax on the whole community while in 2 Kg. 12:4 it is obtained from those who come to the Temple. The Levites (who do not appear in Kg.) were dilatory, but there is no mention of twenty-three years. **6.** The tax is that of Exod. 30:14–16, 38:25f., a half-shekel from each male. **7.** Not in Kg., but Chr. omits the statement in Kg. that the money had been appropriated by the priests. **9.** Not in Kg. **14** differs completely from 2 Kg. 12:13f. Clearly the Chronicler thought it offensive that this 'holy' money should be used for the workmen's wages. **And they offered burnt offerings . . . :** i.e. the service of God in the Temple was completely restored; cf. Exod. 29:38ff. It is this which makes the remainder of the chapter so tragic. **15-22. The death of Jehoiada and the apostasy of Joash** (no parallel in Kg.). The Chronicler introduces this to account for the events in 23ff. **16. among the kings:** in contrast to the king (v. 25). **17ff.** The apostasy of the people, wilfully persisted in, led to the tragedy of v. 21f. (this passage is referred to in Mt. 23:35; Lk. 11:51, qq.v.), the sins of murder, sacrilege and base ingratitude. **22. kindness:** Heb. *ḥesedh*, 'constant love'. **23f.** The Syrian invasion is in punishment for the apostasy, and divinely ordered. This is not suggested in Kg. **25-7. The death of Joash:** this is directly related to the murder of Zechariah and is at the hands of men of mixed marriages (not in Kg.). **27. Commentary (midrash) on the book of Kg.:** this seems to refer to some, otherwise unknown, teaching material to which the Chronicler had access.

b **XXV 1-28 The Reign of Amaziah** (cf. 2 Kg. 14:1–20) —The Chronicler has added to and modified the narrative in Kg. **1-4** = 2 Kg. 14:1–6. **5-10. Preparation for war:** not in Kg. It contains the Chronicler's warning against trusting to armaments and condemnation of the use of Israelite troops, characteristically given by a prophet. **11f. Victory over Edom:** cf. 2 Kg. 14:7; but the details of v. 12 appear to derive from some tradition, perhaps a variant of that in 2 Sam. 8:13. **13.** A consequence of v. 10. **14-16.** Not in Kg. but an example of the Chronicler's teaching on apostasy. The verses prepare for **17-24** (= 2 Kg. 14:8–14), **the Israelite victory over Judah.** **20** is the Chronicler's addition exposing the folly of idolatry;
cf. v. 14. **25-8** (2 Kg. 14:17–20). **The assassination** 318b
of Amaziah: this is by Chr. (not Kg.) connected with the king's apostasy.

XXVI 1-23 The Reign of Uzziah (cf. 2 Kg. 14:21– c
15:7)—The account of Uzziah (Azariah) in Kg. is very brief, and is all included in vv. 1–4, 20, 21, except his tolerance of worship on the high places. The account of his prosperity and military successes (vv. 5–10) appears to rest on a good tradition. The account of his army (vv. 11–15) must be regarded as hyperbole, but there is archaeological evidence to suggest that Uzziah was a much more important king than Kg. would suggest. The Chronicler's interest in these accounts is shown at vv. 7 and 15; he was supported by the power of God. Chr. then proceeds to explain why Uzziah became a leper (16–19). He failed to recognise his dependence on God and presumptuously tried to usurp the priestly functions at the altar. **5. Zechariah** is not otherwise known. Presumably he was a priest or Levite and may be the same person referred to in Isa. 8:2. **6. Gath:** this one-time Philistine city disappears from history after this period, and this fact supports Chr. It does not appear in the list of Philistine cities in Am. 1:6–8. **Jabneh:** later known as Jamnia; cf. 1 Mac. 4:15, etc., the chief centre of Jewish scholarship after A.D. 70. **22. Isaiah . . . wrote:** this clearly does not refer to our book of Isa., but appears to mean that part of the teaching material which Chr. is using.

XXVII 1-9 Reign of Jotham (cf. 2 Kg. 15:33–8) d
—Chr. adds the material in vv. 4–6 which concludes with the Chronicler's comment. The reference to an Ammonite war during this reign may reflect the disturbed conditions induced by the Syro-Ephraimite coalition against Judah; cf. 2 Kg. 15:37.

XXVIII 1-27 The Reign of Ahaz (cf. 2 Kg. 16)— e
The Chronicler has largely rewritten the narrative of Kg., apparently in order to emphasise the wickedness of Ahaz, and to relate the disasters of his reign to the divine judgment. Vv. 8–15 are an addition. **3. burned his sons,** where Kg. has 'son'. **5-7.** While using the material of Kg. (*a*) makes invasion a consequence of apostasy and (*b*) speaks of two invasions. **8-15** is a remarkable passage in Chr. in that it presents the Northern Kingdom in a position of moral superiority. It is a finely told story on the theme 'Be merciful if you would obtain mercy'; cf. Mt. 5:7. It is one of the finest stories in Chr., and the more remarkable in view of contemporary feeling against the Samaritans; cf. Lk. 10:25–37. **20.** There seems no evidence of an Assyrian invasion of Judah at this time, and it is better to regard this statement as an emphatic way of saying that reliance on Assyria could only lead to disaster; cf. Isa. 8:8. **22. this same king Ahaz:** Heb. is even more laconic, 'that was king Ahaz!' **23. the gods of Damascus:** the Kg. account suggests what is in every way probable, that Ahaz was acknowledging (with other states) the gods of his Assyrian overlord. He might well have inferred that the Assyrian gods were more potent than the gods of the Syrian states conquered by Assyria. **24. he shut up the doors of the house of the Lord:** the account in Kg. would lead us to suppose that Ahaz replaced Yahweh worship in the Temple with the cult of the Assyrian deities. **27** appears to conflict with 2 Kg. 16:20.

XXIX 1-33 The Reign of Hezekiah (cf. 2 Kg. f
18:2f., 4, 13–35, 19:1–4, 14–19, 35–7, 20:1–21)—The Chronicler uses the material from Kg. somewhat freely, adds considerably and may have used another tradition of the events. **3-30** (not in Kg.). The reopening and resanctifying of the Temple is a reversal of the policy of Ahaz in 28:24. **3. in the first month:** i.e. Nisan. **5. filth:** an offensive term expressing the utmost abhorrence (cf. Lev. 20:21, 'impurity'). The context suggests that the term is used here for the pagan cult objects referred to in 2 Kg. 16:10 ff., or 2 Chr. 28:23. **10.** A renewal of the covenant is necessary after the apostasy of Ahaz. **12.** A remarkable

318f feature of this section is the prominence accorded to the Levites; cf. vv. 4, 34. Undoubtedly this is appropriate to a Levitical author, but it is hardly likely that he invented it. It may be a recollection of the priestly compliance with Ahaz in 2 Kg. 16:11, 16. **20-4.** After the cleansing of the Temple comes the solemn reconciliation of the Kingdom, the sanctuary (and its officials) and the people; cf. Lev. 4. **25-30** continues with a solemn act of worship culminating in the burnt offering in which the people are received by God. **31-6.** The sacrifices symbolise the restoration of communion and the thank offerings the gratitude. **36. for the thing happened suddenly:** i.e. the whole matter was carried out at the beginning of Hezekiah's reign. Not a moment was wasted on man's side and God was immediately responsive to the national penitence.

g **XXX 1-27 The great Passover** (not in Kg.)—The significance of this account seems to be that Israel has been born again. It is a dramatic re-presentation of the first Passover at the Exodus. It is to be for all Israel, although only a few responded from the northern tribes. But for all who celebrated this Passover a full reconciliation was effected. It is clear that what is described in this chapter is not a historical event, but a remarkably irenical hope in the Chronicler's day, especially apparent in the 'whosoever will' of vv. 1–9, and the willingness to recognise the validity in spite of irregularities of the non-Judaean celebration in vv. 18–19. It seems clear that we must read this chapter against the background of the Samaritan schism of the 4th cent. B.C. It could scarcely have been contemplated in 727 B.C. during the period of Assyrian invasion (cf. 2 Kg. 18:1ff.). It is to be noted that the Samaritans celebrated Passover in a manner different from the Jews (cf. 2 Chr. 30:18f.). Apparently Chr. has ascribed to Hezekiah an action recorded of Josiah (35:1–19; cf. 2 Kg. 23:21–3), but made that of Hezekiah wider in scope and longer in duration.

XXXI 1-21 The Organisation and Provision for Temple Officials—Apart from v. 1 (cf. 2 Kg. 18:4) the chapter is peculiar to Chr. The action is necessary after the apostasy of Ahaz.

319a **XXXII 1-23 The Invasion of Sennacherib** (cf. 2 Kg. 18:13–19:37)—The variations between Kg. and Chr. are considerable. Vv. 2–8 have no parallel in Kg. and some of the factual material may come from an oral tradition not otherwise preserved. The Chronicler has used the material to show how the people who trust in God will be delivered from the gravest of threats. **3f.** These rather obscure verses appear to be a reference to the diverting of the waters of the Gihon. If that is so, we have here a variant, in exaggerated form, of the account in 2 Kg. 20:20; 2 Chr. 32:30 (cf. Isa. 22:9–11). **4. the brook that flowed through the land:** no such brook is known. But if we render this as 'the brook that flowed through the earth' and understand *stopped* as meaning prevented access by the enemy and secured the supply for Jerusalem, we may recognise that as referring to the Siloam tunnel and reservoir. (For a full description of the tunnel, and the Heb. inscription, cf. S. R. Driver, *Notes on the Hebrew Text of Samuel*, viii ff.; also G. E. Wright, *Biblical Archaeology*, 167ff.). **24-6.** These three verses summarise 2 Kg. 20:1–19, but nothing is said about the Babylonian embassy in this section; a passing reference is made in v. 31. **29 cities:** this seems inappropriate to the context; the addition of one letter would give the word for 'herd' (*'ᵃdhārîm* for *'ārîm*). **32. the vision of Isaiah** is obviously not our book of Isa., but it may refer to the fact that 2 Kg. 18:17–20:21 is substantially reproduced in Isa. 36:2–39:8.

b **XXXIII 1-20 The Reign of Manasseh** (cf. 2 Kg. 21:1–18)—The remarkable feature of this section is the additional material in vv. 11–17, and the considerable modification introduced in vv. 18f. Nothing of this appears in Kg., and the unqualified condemnation of the apostate Manasseh in 2 Kg. 21:10 ff. and 31
by his contemporary Jeremiah (15:4) raises doubts about the historical probability of his repentance and restoration to divine favour. It has been suggested that the account has been added in order to justify the long reign of Manasseh which, on the Chronicler's view, could only be the result of divine approval. That seems to be an over-simplification of the facts. This is the Chronicler's teaching material. But he gives his teaching by making use of traditions (written or oral). The Assyrian inscriptions tell us that Manasseh, with other subject kings, was responsible for the production and transport of building material to Nineveh under Esarhaddon, and that Ashurbanipal required Manasseh, with other kings, to bring tribute and march with him against the Egyptian rebels. The tradition of his going to pay homage to his overlord may well have persisted in Jerusalem circles. This has been heightened, in the telling, to make him go as a captive—an appropriate punishment—although it is not likely that he went to Babylon. In post-exilic Jewry, Babylon was *par excellence* the place of captivity. The treatment of captives in v. 11 was all too well known among the Jews, and has been applied to Manasseh. The reference to his building operations may also rest on a tradition. This has furnished the Chronicler with the material for his lesson, that even the wickedest of men, if he repent, will receive God's forgiveness; cf. Ezek. 18:27. The Chronicler is not writing a history, he is using his material to teach a lesson. **20. in his house:** we should read with LXX 'in the garden of his house'.

21-25 The Reign of Amon (cf. 2 Kg. 21:19–24)— c
The only important variation from the account in Kg. is at v. 23, which the Chronicler's account of Manasseh makes necessary.

XXXIV 1-XXXV 27 The Reign of Josiah—Cf. d
2 Kg. 22:1–23:30, which forms the basis for the story in Chr. There are, however, important differences. In both, the main emphasis is on the reform of the cultus. But while in Kg. that reform begins in the eighteenth year of the reign, and as the result of finding 'the book of the law' in the course of repairs to the Temple fabric, Chr. describes a reform, extending to the old Northern Kingdom, deliberately undertaken in the twelfth year of the reign, and moreover the piety of the king was already apparent when he was only sixteen (v. 3); i.e. the material of 2 Kg. 23:6, 16, 19f. is brought forward. Then followed (vv. 8–13) the repair of the Temple (characteristically under Levite oversight, v. 12) and the discovery of 'the book of the law of the Lord' (14:18) which, as the Chronicler would naturally suppose, was the whole Pentateuch. The narrative then follows that of Kg. **18. And Shaphan read it:** RSV by omitting one word in the Heb. sentence has missed the point of the sentence. He read '*in it*'. The Chronicler would not suppose that the whole Pentateuch was read at one session. In the Kg. account, 'it', referring as it apparently does to the Deuteronomic Code, could be so read.

XXXV 1-19 The Passover—It may be noted that this part of Chr. begins 1 Esd., i.e. a Gr. translation independent of, and apparently earlier than, the present LXX of Chr., Ezr. and Neh. It continues v. 19 with two further verses (1 Esd. 1:23, 24) which may have been in the original text of Chr. The account in Chr. is much fuller than that in Kg., and more magnificent. **20-4. The death of Josiah:** again the account in Kg. is expanded and modified. 2 Kg. 23:29 tells us that Josiah 'went to meet' Neco, and the latter apparently had him assassinated. 2 Chr. 35:20 describes Josiah as going to fight Neco, refusing to listen to the divine warning communicated by the Egyptian king, with the result that he was killed in battle. The Chronicler was apparently influenced in his interpretation by the untimely death, despite the prophetic promise, of so good a king. Perhaps he wished to convey the teaching of Ezek. 18:26. Also to this story is added the statement (v. 25) which associated

319d Lam. with Jeremiah. The closing verses are very much weaker than 2 Kg. 23:25, 28.

e **XXXVI 1-4 The Reign of Jehoahaz** (see notes on 2 Kg. 23:30–4).

5-6 The Reign of Jehoiakim (see notes on 2 Kg. 23:36f., 24:1)—**7** is an addition to the narrative in Kg.

9f. The Reign of Jehoiachin (see notes on 2 Kg. 24:8–17)—**9. eight years old:** we should emend, with good support from the ancient versions, 'eighteen'; so 2 Kg. 24:8.

11-21 The Reign of Zedekiah; the Destruction of Jerusalem (see notes on 2 Kg. 24:18–20, 25:1–7, 13–15; cf. also Jer. 37–39:8, 52:1–27)—**20 f.** The Captivity is regarded as the fulfilment of Jer. 25:9–12.

22f. The Decree of Cyrus permitting a Return—These verses, a doublet of Ezr. 1:1–3*a*, were added to Chr. after it had been separated from Ezr. It was obviously inappropriate that the last book of the Bible should end in the gloom of v. 21. So the book closes with a note of hope.

Bibliography—Commentaries: W. H. Bennett, Ex.B (1894); I. Benzinger, KHC (1901); H. Cazelles, Jer.B (1954); E. L. Curtiss and A. A. Madsen, ICC (1910); E. Dhorme, La Bible (Bibliothèque de la Pléiade) (1956); W. A. L. Elmslie, CB (1916); K. Galling, ATD (1954); J. Goettsberger, HSATes (1939); R. Kittel, HAT (1902); L. Marchal, La Sainte Bible (ed. Clamer) (1949); M. Rehm, Ech.B (1949); J. W. Rothstein and J. Hänel, KAT (1927); W. Rudolph, HAT (1955); I. W. Slotki, Soncino Bible (1951).

Other Literature: G. Gerleman, *Studies in the Septuagint: 2 Chronicles* (1946); M. Noth, *Überlieferungsgeschichtliche Studien* I (1943); G. von Rad, *Das Geschichtsbild der chronistischen Werkes* (1930); W. Schlögel, *Die Bücher der Chronik* (1911); C. C. Torrey, *Ezra Studies* (1910), *The Chronicler's History of Israel* (1954).

A. M. Brunet, 'Le Chroniste et ses Sources', RB 60 (1953), 481–508, 61 (1954), 349–86; G. von Rad, 'Die levitische Predigt in den Bücher der Chronik', in *Festschrift Procksch* (1934).

Dictionary Articles: F. Brown, HDB; E. Mangenot, *Supplément au Dictionnaire de la Bible* (1947); W. R. Smith and S. A. Cook, EBrit., 11th ed. (1910); W. R. Smith and S. R. Driver, EBrit., 10th ed. (1899).

EZRA AND NEHEMIAH

BY L. E. BROWNE

320a In our English Bibles Ezr. and Neh. follow directly after the two books of Chr., where they originally belonged. Actually there can be little doubt that they all formed one continuous work covering the whole period from Adam to the time when it was written, shortly before the invasion of Alexander the Great. The earliest part of the story is summarised in genealogies, for the writer's great interest was in David, and so it is with David that the real history begins. The last part of the history, dealing with the work of Ezra, takes us up to the early years of the century that began with 400 B.C.; after which the end of the book, up to Alexander's time, is completed with lists and genealogies of names. In broad outline the whole work shows the ecclesiastical outlook which must have been characteristic of the 4th cent., an outlook which is also reflected in the Priestly Code (P) of the Pentateuch. The purpose of writing it was no doubt to further the particular views of the author (whom we call the Chronicler) and of the priests of the period, rather than to write new history. Indeed as the greater part of it covered the same ground as Sam. and Kg., there was no move for a long time to bring it within the canon of Holy Scripture. The need at first was felt for the inclusion of the chapters dealing with the post-exilic period, and it was in this way that the chapters which we call Ezr. and Neh. started their separate existence, sometimes as one book, and sometimes (as in our Bibles) as two. The second part of the OT canon, the so-called Prophets, i.e. Jos., Jg., Sam., Kg., and all our prophets except Dan., was closed before Ezr.-Neh. was admitted, so that this post-exilic history was included in the Writings, but it comes in the Heb. Bible before Chr. which must have been included later.

b Between the writing of the work Chr.-Ezr.-Neh., and the inclusion of Ezr.-Neh. in the Heb. canon, lies a long and complicated **literary history**. When dealing with the literary history of the Pentateuch we have nothing to go upon except the internal evidence of our present text. We may be able to frame fairly satisfactory theories of the various strands and earlier editions before the Pentateuch was completed, but we have no direct evidence for these earlier stages. In the case of Ezr.-Neh. we are more fortunate, for in addition to the Heb. and Aram. text from which the Ezr. and Neh. of our OT are translated, we have another work in Gr. which is translated into English in our Apoc. under the title of 1 Esd. We shall presently see that 1 Esd. is neither the child nor the parent of our Ezr. and Neh., but a cousin. Although all the problems of the relationship between the two texts have not yet been solved, the general picture is now fairly clear, and we are able to reconstruct with some measure of confidence the contents and order of the book as it originally left the Chronicler's hands.

c The first thing to remember is this. The present form of both our recensions does not date earlier than the 3rd cent., and probably not earlier than the 2nd cent., B.C. This seems to follow from the fact that Dan., written mid 2nd cent., occupies a place in the Writings earlier than either Ezr.-Neh. or Chr. We are working on the theory that the original book was written before the time of Alexander the Great. Thus, between the writing of the book and the appearance of the texts we know, there took place one of the greatest upheavals that Western Asia has known. We are so apt to think of the advantages of the spread and unification of culture that followed in the wake of the Greek forces, that we are inclined to forget the awful destruction, not only of property but also of traditions, that resulted both from the armed conflict and also from the 'civilising' policy of the conquerors. One of the small marks of this upheaval is seen in the fact that for some years there was no agreement in Syria and Palestine as to how the years were to be reckoned.

d Bearing this fact in mind, we need not be surprised to find that neither Ezr.-Neh. nor 1 Esd. has its material arranged in chronological order. These two recensions differ in order from one another, and both must differ from the order of the original book. The people responsible for the rearrangement of the material did not know the order of the kings of Persia. We find exactly the same ignorance of Persian history in the book of Dan. Probably all the official records, which were formerly ready at hand for any author or scribe in Jerusalem to use, had been destroyed or scattered. On the other hand it is almost inconceivable that anyone writing a history within the Persian Empire (as Palestine was), so long as that Empire lasted, could have been ignorant of the order of the kings.

e K. Galling has a theory that there were two distinct stages, by different authors, in the production of the whole of Chr.-Ezr.-Neh. His first Chronicler he would put about or soon after 300 B.C., and the second Chronicler about the end of the 3rd cent. B.C. That there were some additions to the text in the 3rd or 2nd cent. B.C. is probable, but the date he ascribes for the first Chronicler is simply due to the assumption that the Chronicler did not know the order of the Persian kings. Our judgment on this matter must follow our reconstruction of the original work of the Chronicler.

f Let us, then, compare **the contents and order of our two recensions**. The first thing we notice is that 1 Esd. does not tell any part of the story of Nehemiah. There is a possibility, favoured by Rudolph, that the editor of this recension was particularly interested in the Temple and in Ezra the priest, but had no interest in the political and social reformer Nehemiah. If so, we have an interesting sidelight on the two opposing parties in pre-Christian Judaism, for the author of Sir. takes exactly the opposite viewpoint: he praises Nehemiah highly (49:13), but never so much as mentions Ezra. However, most commentators are agreed that 1 Esd. owes its present form to sheer accident, particularly as the words 'and they were gathered together', the closing words of our text of 1 Esd., are the opening words of a sentence in the Gr. (not in the Heb.) of Neh. 8:13.

g The contents of 1 Esd. in relation to our Ezr. and Neh. can be summarised as follows:

20g 1 Esd. 1 = 2 Chr. 35:1–36:21. Josiah's passover and death. The end of the kingdom and a homily thereon.

1 Esd. 2:1–15 = Ezr. 1. Cyrus. The return of Sheshbazzar.

1 Esd. 2:16–30 = Ezr. 4:7–24. Complaint to Artaxerxes against building the walls of Jerusalem.

1 Esd. 3:1–5:6. No parallel. Story of the Three Guardsmen. Darius authorises the building of the Temple.

1 Esd. 5:7–73 = Ezr. 2:1–4:5. List of returned exiles. Foundations of the Temple laid. Adversaries offered help in building the Temple, and being refused hindered the work.

1 Esd. 6:1–9:36 = Ezr. 5–10. The Temple built in Darius's reign. The story of Ezra.

1 Esd. 9:37–55 = Neh. 7:73–8:13*a*. Continuation of story of Ezra.

21a It is quite clear that a writer who knew the order of the Persian kings could not have arranged his material in the order of either of our two recensions. In order to understand the original order we have to understand **our author.**

He was no historian in the modern sense. He recounts such details as the number of silver bowls of a second sort, and this gives an impression of accuracy. Similarly he came across certain lists of names which he found useful to suggest the large number of returned exiles, but he did not verify whether they fitted the occasion. Thus in Ezr. 2:1–67 there is a list of exiles who returned at different times under different leaders, inserted here to represent the caravan led by Sheshbazzar. The same list (with merely textual variations) is introducd in Neh. 7:6–69 as representing the families in Nehemiah's time.

b Another example of his disregard of history is shown by his linking up the chief characters of the post-exilic period with characters who lived at the time of the fall of Jerusalem. Zerubbabel, the man chiefly responsible for rebuilding the Temple, who appears to have been hailed as Messiah by the contemporary prophets Haggai and Zechariah, is made out to be a grandson of the king Jehoiachin or Jeconiah who went into captivity in 597 B.C. (see Hag. 1:1 ; Ezr. 5:2 ; 1 Chr. 3:17–19. In this last passage Zerubbabel is the nephew instead of the son of Shealtiel). Jeshua the son of Jozadak (Ezr. 5:2), the high priest in Zerubbabel's time, is said in 1 Esd. 5:5 to be the grandson of Seraiah. This links up with 1 Chr. 6:14 in which Jehozadak the son of Seraiah was the high priest who went into captivity in 586. However unlikely these two identifications are, they are at least chronologically possible. But the Chronicler's last achievement is distinctly impossible, for he makes this same Seraiah the father of Ezra, and in Ezr. 7:1–5 gives a full genealogy so as to show that Ezra's father was the Seraiah of Nebuchadnezzar's time, 1 Chr. 6:4–5. At the lowest estimate the interval between Seraiah and Ezra would have been 130 years, and on the critical view of Ezra's date it would be over 180 years.

c **Certain parts of Ezr. are written in Aram.** instead of Heb. and it is generally agreed that the best explanation is that these parts were copied from an earlier book. Probably at any time after the Exile the Jews were bilingual, but the tendency would be to use Heb. for religious books. Nehemiah's objection to the children of mixed marriages who could only speak Ashdodite (a dialect of Aram.) and not Heb., indicates that in 430 B.C. Heb. was still very much alive (Neh. 13:24). The Aram. portions of Ezr. are so short that they would only be a very small part of a book, and the question arises, Why did not the Chronicler use the rest of the information that the book contained? His habit in the earlier part of his work was to use all the information about the kingdom of Judah that he could get from Kg. Let us first see the contents of these Aram. passages. They are :

(1) Ezr. 5:1–6:18. The story of the building of the 321c
Temple in the reign of Darius. Tattenai the Governor Beyond the River asked for the authority, and being told that the work was authorised by Cyrus sent a letter inquiring whether this was true. In due course the truth was confirmed, and the Temple was completed and dedicated.

(2) Ezr. 4:5. A fragment of an accusation against the Jews in the reign of Xerxes.

(3) Ezr. 4:6–23. Objection raised against the Jews for building the city walls. Artaxerxes, on receiving the complaint, made inquiry, and found that the Jews were notoriously rebellious. He therefore ordered the building to stop, and this was forcibly carried out.

(4) Ezr. 7:12–26. Authority given by Artaxerxes to Ezra for the improvement of the Temple and its services, and to enforce the Jewish law, also granting him certain supplies.

It is clear that all this material is intended to show d
how accusations against the Jews were dealt with by the Persian authorities. In (1) the detractors were immediately rebuffed. Although the building of the walls was stopped in (3) it seems to be balanced by the full favour shown to Ezra in (4) by Artaxerxes, who was thought to be the same king. This does not read like fragments of a book. It is a complete memorandum written with a very definite purpose. It may well have been notes prepared for an advocate at some later time, say after the death of Artaxerxes II in 358, when the Jews were asking some favour at court, to show that their loyalty had always been recognised. One might wonder why the story of Nehemiah was not introduced as an answer to (3). The probability is that when Nehemiah was made Governor he got permission to do repairs to some buildings, but not for full-scale fortifications of the city (see Neh. 2:8). Now, if the Aram. memorandum was to serve a legal purpose, it would have to be more or less true, or, shall we say, not demonstrably false, or else it would defeat its own object.

If then we accept the Aram. memorandum as ' not e
demonstrably false ' we shall have to look at its contents again. Most scholars, except Torrey, would be willing to accept (4) Ezr. 7:12–26 as substantially true. Evidence will be given later to show that (3) Ezr. 4:6–23 relates to a true incident that occurred shortly before the arrival of Nehemiah. But (1) Ezr. 5:1–6:18 needs closer attention. It begins with a statement, that we readily accept, that the Temple was built by Zerubbabel and Jeshua at the instigation of Haggai and Zechariah, beginning in the second year of Darius, because we know it from the books of Hag. and Zech. Answering a complaint by the Persian Governor Beyond the River, the Jewish elders replied that the work was authorised by Cyrus in the first year of his reign, that Cyrus handed over to a certain man named Sheshbazzar, whom he made Governor, all the sacred vessels which Nebuchadnezzar had taken from the Temple, and that the said Sheshbazzar had brought the vessels and had laid the foundation of the Temple. Hitherto scholars have entirely rejected this story (1) because Haggai says that the Jews had done nothing to restore the Temple, and (2) because there is no evidence of any considerable return of exiles before the time when Haggai appealed to ' the people of the land '. But if we look carefully at what is said in Ezr. 5 there is not really any contradiction. We know from Cyrus's cylinder that he sent the gods back to their lands. As the Jews had no idols to be returned, it would be reasonable to return the sacred vessels by the hands of the Governor. It would also be reasonable for him to order the Governor to inaugurate the Temple. There is no suggestion in the story that Sheshbazzar was a Jew. Any normally efficient oriental official could be counted on to carry out his orders to the letter : we should expect him to hand over the vessels to the chief priests, and to arrange for a formal foundation-stone laying in the next week.

321e The statement in 5:16 that the said Sheshbazzar laid the foundation of the Temple, and that it had been in building for the last eighteen years, and was still not completed, can have been perfectly true. No-one would have supposed that the last clause implied that any further stones beyond the foundation stone had ever been laid. Haggai was certainly justified in saying that the Jews had done nothing. Ezr. 6 goes considerably further in saying that Cyrus specified the plan of the building, and authorised the cost to be paid from the treasury. Obviously it is not a real copy of the decree, and obviously its flattery of the generosity of Cyrus would only cause a smile of amusement when the Jewish orator proclaimed it in the court of one of Cyrus's later successors.

f When the Chronicler came to use this Aram. memorandum he found himself in an obvious difficulty. From Zech. 4:9 he knew that Zerubbabel had begun the work on the Temple, and was expected to finish it. From the Aram. memorandum (Ezr. 5:2) he knew that the prime movers (in the reign of Darius) were Zerubbabel and Jeshua. Yet from the same Aram. source he learnt that Sheshbazzar had laid the foundation in Cyrus's time, and he could get no further information about this event, or even about who Sheshbazzar was. So he jumped to the conclusion that Sheshbazzar and Zerubbabel were the same person. It was a wrong conclusion as is shown plainly by Ezr. 5:9, 14, where the elders, who must have included Zerubbabel, referred to Sheshbazzar as 'one whose name was Sheshbazzar whom Cyrus had made Governor' (see Rudolph, p. 18).

g There are two other sources used by the Chronicler. The easiest to deal with is the **story of Nehemiah**, who was a Jew who managed to get himself appointed as Governor of Judah with the purpose of rebuilding the city of Jerusalem and carrying out social reforms. The record is vividly written in the first person, and bears the stamp of being genuine autobiographical material. The date of his arrival in Jerusalem is given as the twentieth year of Artaxerxes, and this is agreed by all to mean 445 B.C., the king being Artaxerxes I, Longimanus. As Nehemiah's work was only indirectly concerned with religious matters, the Chronicler seems to have interfered with his Memoirs much less than with any of his other sources.

h **The Ezr. sources** are a much more complicated matter. The part that is in the first person may well be a genuine work of Ezra, but the rest is the work of the Chronicler himself. Ezra's work was not merely religious, or perhaps we should say ecclesiastical, but also took what we should nowadays call a distinctly party line. His general attitude was certainly such as appealed to the Chronicler, and there is reason to think that the Chronicler, in the parts he wrote himself, may have overemphasised those characteristics which he himself admired. The result is that, even to those of us who try to sympathise with Ezra's work, he appears rather like a dummy. One author, C. C. Torrey, had this feeling so acutely that he could only believe that Ezra was a creation of the Chronicler. Most writers would probably agree that Ezra was not quite so artificial as the Chronicler made out, and that he actually played a great part in the history, and probably in the literary activities, of the Jews. It seems probable that the Ezr. source did not indicate which Artaxerxes it was in whose reign Ezra came, and that the Chronicler, as well as later copyists or editors of the book, took it to be Artaxerxes I. There is now very strong evidence that it was actually Artaxerxes II, Mnemon. This evidence will be given in the commentary.

322a It is now time to set out what we believe to have been **the original order** of the book as it left the Chronicler's hands, and how it reached the curious and impossible orders that we find in our two recensions. With one exception this order is due to the brilliant scholarship of Torrey, and also to him is due the recognition that certain verses, at present only found in the 1 Esd. text, are genuine parts of the original work. The one departure from Torrey's scheme concerns Ezr. 4:6–23. His argument for his placing of this passage is not conclusive, and it is therefore placed in its natural chronological position. This, then, is the order of the original work :

a	1 & 2 Chr.	Cyrus
b	Ezr. 1	
c	1 Esd. 4:47–56	
d	1 Esd. 4:62–5:6	
e	Ezr. 2:1–4:5, 24	
f	Ezr. 5:1–6:22	Darius
g	Ezr. 7:1–8:36	Artaxerxes without specifying whether I or II
h	Neh. 7:70–8:18	
i	Ezr. 9:1–10:44	
j	Neh. 9:1–10:39	
k	Ezr. 4:6–23	
l	Neh. 1:1–7:69	
m	Neh. 11:1–13:31	

The first stage of corruption was when a scribe b
copying the MS came to Neh. 7:70 and saw what was written about the generosity of the heads of houses, which he thought he had previously copied in Ezr. 2:68–3:1. So he omitted the whole of *h* and proceeded to copy *i*. When he came to *j* he found that it presupposed the reading of the law which he had omitted. So he omitted *j* also, and later on inserted *h* and *j* (both of which had, by interpolation, the name of Nehemiah in them) into the Neh. story after *l*, thus :

a	1 & 2 Chr.	*i*	Ezr. 9:1–10:44
b	Ezr. 1	*k*	Ezr. 4:6–23
c	1 Esd. 4:47–56	*l*	Neh. 1:1–7:69
d	1 Esd. 4:62–5:6	*h*	Neh. 7:70–8:18
e	Ezr. 2:1–4:5, 24	*j*	Neh. 9:1–10:39
f	Ezr. 5:1–6:22	*m*	Neh. 11:1–13:31
g	Ezr. 7:1–8:36		

A later editor decided to interpolate the story of the c
Three Guardsmen, 1 Esd. 3:1–4:42 (*N*). He added a few connecting verses 1 Esd. 4:43–6 (*O*), and 4:57–61 (*P*). He made some verbal changes, which will be noticed later, and he moved Ezr. 4:6–23 (*k*) earlier as an introduction to his interpolated story, thus :

a	1 & 2 Chr.	*e*	Ezr. 2:1–4:5, 24
b	Ezr. 1	*f*	Ezr. 5:1–6:22
k	Ezr. 4:6–23	*g*	Ezr. 7:1–8:36
N	1 Esd. 3:1–4:42	*i*	Ezr. 9:1–10:44
O	1 Esd. 4:43–6	*l*	Neh. 1:1–7:69
c	1 Esd. 4:47–56	*h*	Neh. 7:70–8:18
P	1 Esd. 4:57–61	*j*	Neh. 9:1–10:39
d	1 Esd. 4:62–5:6	*m*	Neh. 11:1–13:31

Then the history of the text divides. In one recen- d
sion the story of the Three Guardsmen (*N*) and the adjoining verses *O*, *c*, *P*, *d* were rejected. Ezr. 4:6–23 (*k*) was seen to be impossible where it now stood, so it was pushed a little later after Ezr. 4:5 (*e*). This is our Heb. and Aram. text of Ezr. and Neh. of the OT :

a	1 & 2 Chr.
b	Ezr. 1
e, k	Ezr. 2:1–4:24
f, g, i	Ezr. 5:1–10:44
l, h, j, m	Neh. 1:1–13:31

There is a Gr. translation of this work in the LXX, but it is not translated separately into English.

In the other recension the Ezra stories found em- e
bedded in the Neh. story (*h* and probably *j*) were put after *i*. It was from this Heb. and Aram. text that the Gr. translation was made which is the original of our 1 Esd. After it was translated into Gr. it was accidentally mutilated at both ends, so that only two chapters of *a* and nothing of *j* appear, thus :

22e

a	2 Chr. 35:1–36:21	=	1 Esd. 1
b	Ezr. 1	=	1 Esd. 2:1–15
k	Ezr. 4:7–24	=	1 Esd. 2:16–30
N, O, c, P, d	1 Esd. 3:1–5:6	=	1 Esd. 3:1–5:6
e	Ezr. 2:1–4:5	=	1 Esd. 5:7–73
f, g, i	Ezr. 5–10	=	1 Esd. 6:1–9:36
h	Neh. 7:73–8:13*a*	=	1 Esd. 9:37–55

It should perhaps be added that the book in the Apoc. called 2 Esd. has nothing to do with Ezr. and Neh.

f This reconstruction of the steps by which the original order of the book was changed is so satisfactory that it has in the main been accepted. This means that there is now no reason to say that the Chronicler did not know the order of the Persian kings, and therefore no reason to date him later than Alexander. He must, however, have lived some time after Ezra to have regarded him as contemporary with Nehemiah. A date just before Alexander, suggested by the mention of the high priest Jaddua, may therefore be confidently accepted.

3a **Ezr. I 1** (= 2 Chr. XXXVI 22). Jeremiah at different times (25:12, 29:10) had said that the exile would last 70 years, a round figure for a long time. Zechariah (1:12 and 7:5) said that it was fulfilled (586–520=66). The Chronicler copied this statement, but referred it to the supposed building in 537 B.C. (49 years).

b **2-4** is the Chronicler's idea of the sort of thing that Cyrus would have said in the special decree relating to Israel. His general decree, applicable to all captive peoples, is preserved on a clay cylinder (see §100*a*). The Chronicler had no evidence for anything that happened in Cyrus's reign beyond what he read in the Aram. memorandum (see above, §321*c*). We may be certain that some formalities were carried out as a result of Cyrus's decree, such as authority to the Babylonian officials to issue passports for Jews to Judah, and a Governor may have been appointed with orders to cancel other restrictions laid down by the previous régime. But we may be certain that there was no large return of exiles at that time, and no serious effort on the part of the local Jews to restore the Temple.

c **1 Esd. IV 47-56, IV 62-V 6.** The following is a suggestion of how the Chronicler's book originally continued after Ezr. 1:11, mainly based on the **reconstruction of the text** given in C. C. Torrey's *Ezra Studies*, pp. 125ff. and 132ff. The few places where this original text differed from the text of 1 Esd. are shown in italics, and the references to notes are explained in §323*d*.

'Then *Cyrus* [1] the king wrote letters for him to all the treasurers and governors and generals and satraps, that they should give escort to him and all who were going up with him to build Jerusalem. And he wrote letters to all the governors in Coelesyria and Phoenicia and to those in Lebanon, to bring cedar timber [2] from Lebanon to Jerusalem, and to help him build the city. And he wrote for all the Jews who were going up from his kingdom to Judaea, in the interest of their freedom, that no officer or satrap or governor or treasurer should forcibly enter their doors; that all the country which they would occupy should be theirs without tribute; that the Idumaeans should give up the villages of the Jews which they held; that twenty talents a year should be given for the building of the temple until it was completed, and an additional ten talents a year for burnt offerings to be offered on the altar every day, *as the Lord had commanded them*; [3] and that all who came from Babylonia to build the city should have their freedom, they and their children and all the priests who came. He wrote also concerning their support and the priests' garments in which they were to minister. He wrote that the support for the Levites should be provided until the day when the temple should be finished and Jerusalem built. He wrote that land and wages should be provided for all who guarded the city. And they 323c
praised the God of their fathers, because he had given them release and permission to go up and build Jerusalem and the temple which is called by his name; and they feasted, with music and rejoicing, for seven days.

'After this the heads of fathers' houses were chosen to go up, according to their tribes, with their wives and sons and daughters, and their menservants and maidservants, and their cattle. And *Cyrus* [1] sent with them a thousand horsemen to take them back to Jerusalem in safety. *And all their brethren playing upon musical instruments of drums and cymbals, sent them on their way as they went up.* [4]

'These are the names of the men who went up, according to their fathers' houses in the tribes, over their groups: the priests, the sons of Phinehas, son of Aaron; Jeshua the son of Jozadak, son of Seraiah, and *with him arose* [5] Zerubbabel, the son of Shealtiel, of the house of David, of the lineage of Phares, of the tribe of Judah, *in the second year of Cyrus* [1] *king of Persia, in the month Nisan, on the first day of the month.* [6]

How the original text came to be altered—[1] In each of these three places 1 Esd. changed 'Cyrus' to 'Darius' so as to link up with the interpolated story of the Three Guardsmen. For the same purpose the words 'rose up and kissed him' were added in 1 Esd. 4:47, and the words 'who spake wise words before' were added in 5:6. [2] In Ezr. 3:7 the Chronicler says that it was Cyrus who granted the wood. [3] The Gr. text of 1 Esd. has 'as they have a commandment seventeen to offer' through misreading an abbreviation of the sacred name 'Yahweh' as the Heb. numeral letters for 17. [4] The music obviously belongs here, and was not, as in 1 Esd. 5:2, by command of the king. [5] The Gr. clause 'Joakim the son of' is a misreading of the original Heb. words 'and there arose with him'. [6] With the text as thus restored we get the date of the first return from the Exile, which, with his fondness for dates, the Chronicler would never have omitted. d

Ezr. II 1-67 is a list of returned exiles, which must have been composed, as v. **2** shows, after the time of Nehemiah. The Chronicler found it, and inserted it here to give the impression of the vast caravan that returned in the second year of Cyrus, and followed it by a few verses **68-70** in which he speaks of the generosity of the leaders, and of the safe arrival of the caravan. He used the list again when he came to the story of Nehemiah (Neh. 7:1–69), and rounded it off there by a few verses 70–3 in which he spoke again of the generosity of the leaders, especially Nehemiah himself, and the safe arrival of his caravan. e

III. The Chronicler knew from his Aram. source (5:1) that the **Temple** had actually been built by Zerubbabel and Jeshua in the reign of Darius. The Aram. source had learnt this fact from Hag. and Zech., and the Chronicler also probably knew these two books. But as the Chronicler supposed that the Temple building had begun as soon as the exiles had returned, he brought Zerubbabel and Jeshua in at that earlier date, and he must have supposed that Sheshbazzar and Zerubbabel were the same person. Actually it is most unlikely that a Jew had two names, both Babylonian. **1** says it was the seventh month when they erected the altar, i.e. six months after the date of the return (1st day of Nisan, 537 B.C.) which we have now restored from 1 Esd. 5:6. **6** should be translated 'From the first day of the seventh month they began to offer burnt offerings to the Lord. Now the Temple of the Lord was not yet begun', as Batten has shown that the word does not necessarily mean laying a foundation. There need, then, be no contradiction with the statement in Ezr. 5:16 that Sheshbazzar laid the foundation (see §321*e*). f

8 in our Heb. text says that **Zerubbabel, Jeshua and the rest of the priests and Levites, who had returned, began.** A few words have dropped out, and can be g

323h supplied from 1 Esd. 5:57, ' they began, and laid the foundation of the Temple of God on the new moon of the second month of the second year of their coming to Judah and Jerusalem.'

10-13. It is better to translate ' When the builders built the Temple ' instead of ' laid the foundation '. The word implies more than foundation stones (and presumably the same applies to the lost Heb. of 1 Esd. 5:57). There would be no occasion for weeping until the people saw the small scale of the rising building. This incident does not come in the Aram. source, but was enlarged by the Chronicler from Hag. 2:3, where it refers to the building in Darius's reign.

324a **IV 1-5.** The mutual hatred of **Jews and Samaritans** began in the days of the kingdom. It got worse after the Exile, and reached its climax in the time of Alexander the Great when the Samaritans built a temple on Mt Gerizim. In spite of the venom of this passage, it has behind it the history of a genuine attempt on the part of Samaritans to bring about a spiritual rapprochement with the Jews (see §100*b*).

b **6-24** is misplaced from its original position before Neh. 1. For the commentary see §328*a*. Before the intrusion of this passage the text of 4:5, 24 probably ran as follows : (Heb.) ' And hired counsellors against them to frustrate their purpose all the days of Cyrus king of Persia. Then ceased the work of the house of God which is at Jerusalem, and it ceased until the reign of Darius king of Persia '. (Aram.) ' Now in the second year of Darius, Haggai and Zechariah . . .'

c **V 1.** The language changes to Aram., and we are now in the reign of Darius I. It is possible that the extract from the Aram. memorandum does not begin till v. **6**, the first five verses being written by the Chronicler, who will have learnt the name of Iddo from Zech. 1:1. The ' we ' in the Aram. text of **4** was carelessly copied by the Chronicler or a scribe from **10**.

d After the Samaritan offer of help had been rejected, some of them stirred up trouble, and ch. 5 shows how they did it by getting Persian officials to question the authority to build. There is no doubt that Cyrus had given permission, just as he had returned captured idols, and, as this was easily proved, the work was allowed to continue. The Chronicler put his story 4:1–5 earlier so as to explain the long delay since (as he supposed) the work had begun in the reign of Cyrus.

e **3.** Tattenai (Ushtani in the contract tablets) was satrap of the combined satrapies of Babylonia and Beyond the River. The latter meant the West of Euphrates, and included Phoenicia, Syria, Palestine, Cyprus and part of Arabia. From the time of Darius the two satrapies were separated. The word translated ' structure ' in RSV here and in **9** is not the word used for city walls. It occurs in the description of the Jewish temple at Elephantine (Batten, ad loc.).

f **7-17.** The actual words of this document were presumably composed by the author of the Aram. memorandum. Thus Solomon is described as a great king of Israel, and the cause of Nebuchadnezzar's victory over Jerusalem was the wrath of the God of heaven against his people Israel. It was easy for this later writer to make the slip (15) of saying that the vessels were to be put by Sheshbazzar in the Temple, although it was not yet built. But, as explained above, the purpose of the memorandum necessitated its being substantially true. The letter probably correctly reflects the friendly attitude of Tattenai, who did not stop the work during his inquiries (see **5, 8, 16**) as if (as Rothstein says in his *Juden und Samaritaner*, p. 44) ' he had personally convinced himself of the groundlessness of the charges '.

g **VI 1-12** may also be regarded as substantially true. Whatever exaggerations it contained would be regarded by any Persian court or officials as pardonable flattery of Cyrus for his generosity. Ecbatana, the Median capital, was the summer residence of the Persian kings. **10** correctly reflects the words in Cyrus's cylinder that the gods of the nations should intercede with Bel and Nebo for the long life of the king.

13-18 are still written in Aram. **16-18** are almost certainly by the hand of the Chronicler, as they show so plainly his ecclesiastical interests. **13-15** may be from the Aram. memorandum. The words ' God of Israel ' sound as if they were written for non-Jews, but the words ' and Artaxerxes king of Persia ' are an obvious addition by a copyist in the post-Alexandrine period. It is generally supposed that the original reading of **18** must have been ' the service of the house of God which is in Jerusalem ' instead of ' the service of God which is in Jerusalem ', but in 1:2 we get the sentence ' He is the God who is in Jerusalem ', and in 7:15 ' the God of Israel whose dwelling is in Jerusalem'. In all three cases the author may have had non-Jewish readers in mind. But the Brooklyn Aramaic Papyrus 12 has ' Yahu the God who dwells in Yeb the fortress '. At the end of **18** we should probably add with 1 Esd. 7:8 ' and the porters were at every gate ' as in 2 Chr. 8:14, 23:18, 19, 35:15. 32

19-22. These verses reflect the spirit of separateness which prevailed from Nehemiah onwards. Cf. the language of Neh. 13:29–31. It follows closely the pattern described more fully in 2 Chr. 35:11–15. The killing of the animals was performed by the Levites because the priests were offering the burnt offerings. The expression ' king of Assyria ' has caused trouble. Some have taken it as meaning Syria. Galling attributes the passage to a late writer who had Antiochus III in mind. Probably the Jews did not like to call Darius ' the Great King ' or ' the king of Armies ', and used other names for preference. In Ezr. 1:2 Cyrus is called ' king of Persia ', a title which is now known to have been used as early as Cyrus (see Rudolph, p. 3*n*). In Neh. 13:6 Artaxerxes is called ' king of Babylon ', and in Ezr. 7:1 ' king of Persia '. i

VII 1. Here we come to **the story of Ezra**, and the commentary will follow what we believe to have been the Chronicler's order, viz. Ezr. chs. 7–8, Neh. 7:70–8:18, Ezr. chs. 9–10, Neh. chs. 9–10. All this is in Heb. except the decree of Artaxerxes, Ezr. 7:12–26, which is in Aram. The parts written in the first person, Ezr. 7:27–8, and 8–9, are so vividly written that they appear to be by Ezra himself. We cannot be so certain how much of the remainder of the story is from Ezra, and how much the work of the Chronicler. 32

As has already been explained, the Chronicler, and those that followed him in dislocating the text, thought that both Nehemiah and Ezra had worked in the reign of Artaxerxes I. No-one doubts that Nehemiah came in the reign of Artaxerxes I, but the opinion of scholars in the last forty years has turned steadily towards the opinion that Ezra came a generation later in the reign of Artaxerxes II. The suggestion (Rudolph, p. xxiv) that Ezra came during Nehemiah's absence on furlough is sufficiently answered by the story of Tobiah's appropriation of the tithe-room (Neh. 13:4–9). It is impossible to imagine such a thing happening when Ezra was near at hand. b

The chief arguments in favour of **the later date of Ezra** are : c

(1) The general impression that each of these two men was an autocratic ruler in his time.

(2) From the lists of high priests in Neh. 12:11 and 22 we see that Jonathan was the same as Johanan, and was the grandson of Eliashib. Now Nehemiah was contemporary with Eliashib (Neh. 3:1) and Ezra was contemporary with Johanan (Ezr. 10:6) who is there described as son of Eliashib. Thus Ezra would be one or two generations later than Nehemiah.

(3) Confirming the last argument, the Elephantine papyrus (Sachau's 1 and 2) dated 408 B.C. shows that the high priest in Jerusalem was Johanan.

(4) Neh. 12:25, 26 gives a list of porters in the days of Joiakim (high priest after Jeshua), Nehemiah and Ezra.

(5) The list of people who had returned from exile (Ezr. 2:2 ; Neh. 7:7) begins with the names of those who led the parties. The first three names are Zerubbabel, Jeshua and Nehemiah ; the next is Seraiah or Azariah, and among the other names there is no

25c mention of Ezra. The Chronicler in Ezr. 7:1 gives an impossible pedigree of Ezra, taken from 2 Chr. 6:4–14, making him the son and grandson respectively of Seraiah and Azariah, who lived in the time of Nebuchadnezzar. But it is quite likely that these were the actual names of his father and grandfather, and that one or both of them led the next return party after Nehemiah. The seventh year of Artaxerxes II (Ezr. 7:8) would be 397 B.C., but as there is no mention of the year of Ezra's coming in the Aram. memorandum, this date is by no means certain, and it was more probably about 400 B.C.

d Considerable attention has been given to **the title given to Ezra** in the Aram. memorandum, **Ezr. 7:12.** 'Ezra the priest, the scribe of the law of the God of heaven'. We owe to Eduard Meyer, and later to Schaeder, the discovery that this was an official appointment at the Persian court, making Ezra a Commissary for the religious affairs of all the Jews (see Eissfeldt, *Einleitung* [2], p. 688; Rudolph, p. 73). The comparison, however, with the head of subject races under later governments is not really parallel. Under the Abbasid Caliphs at any rate the responsible authority was the head of the community; e.g. the Nestorian Catholicos, as head of the church, was responsible not only for the enforcement of Christian family law, but also for the collection of taxes from Christians. A further, and very probable, suggestion comes from Galling. We know from Josephus that in the reign of Artaxerxes II the high priest Johanan murdered his brother Jeshua, and that, although the Governor Bagoas punished the Jews by a penal tax on each lamb sacrificed, which would have the effect of reducing the size of the pilgrim crowds, he apparently did not depose Johanan. Bagoas would naturally report the matter to the satrap of the province Beyond the River, and through him to Artaxerxes II. Now Galling's suggestion is that Ezra was an official at the Persian court as Minister for Jewish religious affairs in the provinces of Babylonia and Elam. When the news reached the king he decided, after consultation with Ezra, to send him on a special mission to Palestine to make inquiries and put things right, which is fairly accurately stated in **7-14** 'to make inquiries about Judah and Jerusalem according to the law of your God'.

e We know from the Elephantine papyri that Bagohi (= Bagoses or Bagoas) was Governor of Judah in 410 and in 407 B.C. Artaxerxes II came to the throne in 404. We may provisionally place the Temple murder and the mission of Ezra round about 400 B.C. A year or two before that, through the loss of Egypt, Palestine had become a border state of the Persian Empire, and the internal security of border states is always an important concern to a government.

f **12-20,** the part of the decree addressed to Ezra, seems on the face of it reasonably accurate, and so would fulfil the purpose of the Aram. memorandum of providing evidence of the goodwill of the Persian king towards the Jews. **7:21-4,** though still in Aram. purports to be directions to treasurers to provide apparently unlimited supplies for Ezra. Even if he travelled in great style as a Minister of State, it is doubtful if he would need such great sums, and it is probable that what originally stood there has been greatly exaggerated. **7:25, 26** turns again to address Ezra, and gives him legal powers, no doubt intended to be exercised over Jews in the province Beyond the River, and not over all the inhabitants. This has become much more probable since it has been learnt that Ezra was a Government official.

g **27-28.** Ezra's narrative in the first person begins. It is then interrupted (8:1–14) by one of the Chronicler's lists of names, and is resumed in 8:15 by Ezra's account of his journey.

VIII 15. The words 'and the priests' have been questioned; but they must stand, as the foregoing list contains the names of priests. It must simply mean that he found no Levites who were not priests.

17. The place Casiphia. The word 'place' is used 325h
frequently in the sense of 'holy place' or 'sanctuary', and so must be taken here. As 'Shushan the fortress' means obviously 'the fortress in Shushan', and 'Yeb the fortress' in the papyri means 'the fortress in Yeb', so 'Casiphia the place' means 'the sanctuary at Casiphia'. Where but in a sanctuary would one expect to find Levites and temple slaves? 'The leading man' (RV 'chief') should be translated 'chief priest'. In this verse the Heb. consonants, instead of 'Nethinim' (Temple servants), read *n*[e]*thûnîm*, and the Gr. and Syr. versions suggest that this word meant 'who were present' (see Rudolph, p. 80). The sentence can then be translated, 'And I sent them to Iddo, the chief priest at the temple in Casiphia, telling them what to say to Iddo and his brethren who were in the temple at Casiphia, to send us ministers for the house of our God.' Presumably 'Casiphia' or Silvertown was a Heb. corruption of Ctesiphon. The suggestion that the Jews had a temple there was made soon after the discovery of the Jewish temple at Elephantine (JTS 17 (1915–16), 400f.). But, as there is no mention of any priests coming from Casiphia, they probably had no animal sacrifices there.

21-36. The opening verses of this section give a very i
human touch, suggesting that Ezra was not quite so inhuman as the great divorce described in chs. 9, 10 has led many to think. **24** seems to mean twelve Levites in addition to the twelve priests. This clumsy addition, and the gross exaggerations of the following verses, shows the hand of a later editor. 'The fourth day' (**33**), i.e. of the fifth month, cf. 7:9.

For **Ezr. IX-X**, see §326*c*.

Neh. VII 70. Having related in Ezr. 8 the enormous 326a
wealth brought by the returned exiles and handed over in the Temple, and having recorded the help given by satraps and governors (Ezr. 8:36), it seemed natural to the Chronicler to mention the amounts contributed locally by the Governor and the heads of houses. This is all due to the Chronicler. He thought that Ezra and Nehemiah were contemporary, and therefore much money was needed for the building programme. Since we know that Ezra came later there remains no reason for such expenditure, and if the Governor in Ezra's time was Bagoas he was not likely to subscribe. The bringing together of the Ezr. and Neh. narratives has resulted in Nehemiah's name being introduced, presumably by copyists, in Neh. 8:9 and 10:2 and 1 Esd. 5:40, but in every case there are differences in the Heb. and Gr. texts; and Ezra's name has been introduced into Neh. 12:36.

VIII. The suggestion that Ezra was sent to Judah to b
inquire into and settle the internal disturbances within Israel makes it all the more likely that he would begin by **teaching the people the law**, not a new law, but the existing law (Ezr. 7:14). This law, as we shall see presently, was Deuteronomy. **9.** Its contents were so unknown that the people wept when they heard its curses for the first time. So slack had observances become that the people did not know about the Feast of Booths, though the suggestion by the Chronicler that the feast had not been observed since the days of Joshua (**17**) is absurd, and he had already contradicted it himself in 2 Chr. 5:3, 7:8, and Ezr. 3:4. The Chronicler, however, has not edited this chapter much. He has not even put the feast on the fifteenth day of the month as required by P. It is only in the last two verses that he shows his hand, when he says that the whole congregation consisted of returned exiles, and that there was a solemn assembly (as in P) on the eighth day of the feast.

Ezr. IX. The narrative is now continued in Ezr. 9. c
'After these things had been done', i.e. after the reading of the Law, and the Feast of Tabernacles, a deputation of important people came and complained to Ezra about **mixed marriages.** Occasional mixed marriages had caused trouble some thirty years earlier in the time of Nehemiah. But from the zeal with which Ezra devoted himself to this matter above all

326c else it is not difficult to see that he realised that it was the root cause of the trouble which had finally resulted in the murder of Jeshua by his brother Johanan the high priest. Josephus tells us that Bagoas the Governor had offered to make Jeshua high priest. It was bad enough that a heathen Governor should dare to interfere in so sacred an affair, but one is bound to ask, Why did Bagoas make this offer? and, in view of Ezr. 9–10, the obvious answer is that Bagoas wanted to induce Jeshua to arrange an alliance by marriage, probably of a daughter of Bagoas with a son of Jeshua. This may sound very conjectural, but how else can we explain the fact that Ezra not only condoned the murder but actually went into Johanan's house and spent the night there (Ezr. 10:6) when he was distraught with the affair of the mixed marriages? It seemed that nothing less than the death of Jeshua could have prevented a heathen woman from being the wife of the high priest.

d **2.** 'The officials and chief men' are somewhat vague terms, but allow for the possibility that members of the high-priestly family were involved, as one of Johanan's brothers had been thirty years earlier (Neh. 13:28). **4.** 'Returned exiles', from the context does not refer to those who had just returned with Ezra. So also in Ezr. 10:6. Rudolph (p. 86) says that, ever since the return of the first exiles, the term 'the Captivity' was the honourable title of the Palestinian community.

e **9.** 'to give us a protection in Judaea and Jerusalem'. The word (translated 'wall' in RV) is used for a wall or fence, such as a partition wall in the temple courts, or a fence round a flock. It does not mean city walls, and so does not directly refer to Nehemiah's wall, as is sufficiently shown by the mention of Judaea. The best explanation of the expression is seen from Ezek. 22:30 where the same word is used, 'And I sought for a man among them who should build up the wall and stand in the breach before me for the land; but I found none.' The reference here then will clearly be to the favour shown to Israel by Artaxerxes II in sending Ezra.

f **11-12.** The direct quotations come from Dt. 7:1, 3 and 23:6. But nowhere in the Pentateuch or the Prophets is Israel called an unclean land. The nearest parallel, where the same Heb. word for 'unclean' is used, is Lam. 1:17, 'Yahweh has commanded for Jacob "Let her enemies be round about her": Jerusalem has become unclean in the middle of them', which is obviously intended as a contrast to Ps. 125:2, 'Jerusalem, the hills are round about her: Yahweh is round about his people'.

g **X 6-17.** In v. **6** 'where he spent the night' is the correct reading, restored from 1 Esd. 9:2. The Heb. text, differing only in one letter, has 'and he went there'. **9.** 'ninth month': Ezra had arrived in the fifth month (Ezr. 7:9) and read the Law in the seventh month (Neh. 8:2). These dates help to confirm the order of the chapters as here restored. **16.** 'Ezra the priest selected men' is the correct reading from 1 Esd. 9:16. The Heb. text, by the duplication of one consonant, became unintelligible.

h **18-44.** The Heb. of **44** is unintelligible. Read with 1 Esd. 9:36 'All these had married foreign women, and they put them away with their children'. **19.** Previously only the priests had promised to divorce their wives. It has generally been regarded as somewhat of an anticlimax that, after all this fuss, only 111 offenders should be found. But it is quite possible that it was their status (see Ezr. 9:2) rather than their numbers that created the problem.

i **Neh. IX-X.** The narrative is now carried on in Neh. 9–10. In Ezr. 10:17 we read that the last investigations of the Mixed Marriage Commission were completed by the 1st day of the 1st month. The Commission had heard representatives from different towns on different days. Now we read (**9:1**) that some three weeks later, on the 24th day of the same month, there was a **solemn assembly of Israelites**, in which they made an act of repentance as the wholesale divorce 32
was confirmed. Anyone reading the book of Neh. in the order in which it stands in our Bibles sees at once the difficulty of the sudden change from the very great gladness of Neh. 8 to the fasting and sackcloth of Neh. 9. It is only the rearrangement of the chapters that makes sense of the story.

IX 2-6. The proceedings began with the solemn j
repudiation of foreigners—a general confirmation of the divorces already arranged individually—and a confession. Reading of the Law and worship followed. Levites stood on the platform to interpret the Heb. reading into Aram., and also (5) to lead the responses in the worship. The names of the Levites correspond in part with those who signed the Covenant (Neh. 10:9–13) and with those who had interpreted at the first reading of the Law (Neh. 8:7). In **5-6** there is a slight dislocation of the text, some words having dropped out. Before **6** RSV adds from the Gr. the words 'And Ezra said', but this emendation still leaves the Levites commanding the people to bless the Lord from everlasting to everlasting. We should read, 'The Levites . . . said, "Stand up and bless the Lord your God"; *and Ezra said*, "*Blessed art thou O Lord our God* from everlasting to everlasting, and blessed be thy glorious name, etc."' (see Torrey, pp. 280f., and cf. 1 Chr. 29:10). The words in italics were accidentally omitted by a scribe's attention slipping from 'your God' to 'our God'. The Greek translators added 'and Ezra said' to make sense, but unfortunately added the words in the wrong place.

IX 6-37. The prayer or psalm that follows has no k
special connection with the Ezra story, and is simply inserted here by the Chronicler. It is most unlikely that Ezra, an official of the Persian court, would have emphasised the distressed state of the Jews under their foreign masters, which could so easily be taken as an instigation to revolt. The general pattern of the prayer is what is familiar in Ps. 78, 105 and 106. Like them this prayer shows a knowledge of the ancient history, which probably implies a knowledge of the Pentateuch itself. The reference to God's 'spirit' and 'good spirit' in **20** and **30** seems to point rather to Isa. 63:11, 14 than to Num. 11:25. The mention of the Assyrians as their oppressors of old would suggest that the prayer was originally written by a Samaritan, which would also account for the likeness to Isa. 63 (see Welch, *Post-Exilic Judaism*, 26–33, and L. E. Browne, *Early Judaism*, 70–86). The general probability is that it was written during the 4th cent., and the author may well have been a contemporary with the Chronicler. There is nothing to suggest a date later than Alexander.

X. The Covenant forms a suitable conclusion to Ezra's 327
work. He had dealt with the question of mixed marriages, in accordance with the policy that had been developing ever since the time of Zerubbabel to keep Israel separate from her neighbours. There can be no doubt that this policy was also concerned with the Temple murder which had resulted from the interference of the foreigner Bagoas. But beyond that, Ezra had to put the whole of the organised religion on a firm basis, and this is what the Covenant was aimed at.

The Law Book—Wellhausen's idea that the law book b
which Ezra brought to Jerusalem was the completed Pentateuch rounded off so nicely the theory of the sources that it was readily accepted. Others felt that the theory was better supported by supposing that Ezra the priest was the author of the Priestly Code, and that it was this strand P, before being combined with the earlier strands, which Ezra brought. The evidence of the text is, however, perfectly clear. Both the celebration of the Feast of Booths, and the terms of the Covenant, follow D, or the combined earlier codes JED quite closely. There are a few additions by a later hand which give details taken from the later P, but they betray themselves as additions, and in any case do not bring the Ezra narratives into con-

327b formity with P or with the completed Pentateuch. The details are as follows :

c **The Feast of Booths** (Neh. 8)—The feast was held on the 2nd day of the 7th month (8:14). JED do not give the date at all, but the 7th month was probably traditional, cf. Jeroboam's heretical feast in the 8th month 'which he had devised of his own heart' (1 Kg. 12:33). P consistently has the 15th day of the 7th month (Lev. 23:34 ; Num. 29:12 ; cf. Ezek. 45:25). On the 1st day of the feast P orders blowing of trumpets and a holy convocation (Lev. 23:24), but there is no mention of either of these in D or in Neh. 8. We have already seen the prominence of the reading of the Law in Neh. 8:2–18 : this is in accordance with Dt. 31:11, but it is not mentioned in P. The rejoicing and the command not to mourn is emphasised in Neh. 8. This is found in Dt. 16:14–15 and also in H (Lev. 23:40) but not in P proper. Gifts for the poor in Neh. 8:10 follow the prescription of Dt. 16:14, 31:12, to provide for the stranger, the fatherless and the widow, but P again is silent. Similarly P has nothing to say about women and children taking part in the feast, which is specially mentioned in Neh. 8:2–3 and also in Dt. 16:14, 31:12. H alone (Lev. 23:43) makes the feast a memorial of the Exodus. But the most impressive fact of all is that P directs that the 10th day of the 7th month be kept as a day of fasting for the Day of Atonement (Lev. 23:27–32 ; Num. 29:7–11). There is no mention of the Day of Atonement in D, and our story of the Feast of Tabernacles leaves no room for it at all. In all this long catalogue Neh. 8 follows D and contradicts P. There is only one single item in which P is followed, the solemn assembly on the 8th day (Lev. 23:36 ; Num. 29:35 ; Neh. 8:18). Here we have no hesitation whatever in seeing the hand of the Chronicler, for he made exactly the same addition when he copied 1 Kg. 8:66 in 2 Chr. 7:9. It is difficult to imagine any circumstances in which this account of the Feast of Booths could have been written if either P or the whole Pentateuch had been known and in use in Jerusalem at the time.

d **The Covenant**—When we turn to the terms of Ezra's covenant in **10** the dependence solely on the earlier codes is not evident at first sight (1) because some of the commands are found in all the codes, and (2) because of two considerable additions by the Chronicler. The first of these is 10:33. The previous verse had mentioned the Temple tax, so this added verse gives a list of the purposes for which the Temple tax was used, viz. the showbread, the continual cereal offering, the continual burnt offering and sin offerings. These are found in P (Exod. 29:38–42 ; Lev. 7:37, 24:5f.) but nowhere in JED. Now in the actual covenant it was not necessary to specify what the Temple tax was used for, but the Chronicler added this information for the benefit of his readers, who would include many outside Palestine who had never seen a sacrifice. The other addition by the Chronicler is vv. 37–9, ending with the words 'the gate-keepers and singers'. The previous verses had recorded the different kinds of first-fruits, and concluded with the words 'to bring to the house of our God, to the priests who minister in the house of our God'. Vv. 37–9 begin again, repeating the first-fruit of trees, and giving 'coarse meal and contributions' (RV 'dough and heave offerings') as a further explanation of the first-fruits of the ground already mentioned. The addition also describes how the Levites receive the tithe for themselves and then tithe it again. The actual names 'coarse meal and heave offerings' only come elsewhere in P (Num. 15:20) and Ezek. 44:30.

e Apart from these two additions, the evidence is as follows : Neh. 10:20 against mixed marriages corresponds to Dt. 7:3, and has no parallel in P ; Neh. 10:31, sabbath trading is forbidden in all codes, and so is the command to forgo the 7th year (Neh. 10:31 ; E in Exod. 23:11 ; D in Dt. 15:1–11 ; P in Lev. 25:1–7). But the command to forgo all debts in the 7th year only comes in Dt. 15:2. Finally the Temple tax of one-third of a shekel is peculiar to Neh. 10:32. In the earlier codes there is no mention of such a tax, and in P it had risen to half a shekel. As taxes are so rarely reduced, this is pretty good evidence that the Covenant of Ezra depended mainly on the earlier codes, and that P was not yet known. 327e

Ezr. IV 6-23. We come now to an Aram. section, which stands in different places in our two recensions, and is out of place in both. **6** is a fragment of a complaint against the people of Judah and Jerusalem in the days of Xerxes. **7-23** is a story from the Aram. source of **resistance to the building of the city walls** of Jerusalem in the reign of Artaxerxes. The text of the first few verses is in confusion. In **7** the senders of the letter are Mithredath and Tabeel, probably a Persian official and a Samaritan in Samaria. Bishlam is not a proper name, and is perhaps a corruption of 'against Jerusalem'. Perhaps these men made the first complaint, which was then taken up by the higher officials mentioned in **8**. It looks as if the Chronicler has abbreviated his source. To the Chronicler again is due the slander that the Samaritans were heathen deportees, as in 4:2. But here he says the king responsible was Osnappar, i.e. Ashur-banipal. In 4:2 it was Esar-haddon, whereas in 2 Kg. 17 it was probably intended to be Shalmaneser. It seems clear that the authorities in Samaria, seeing the Jews engaged in fortifying Jerusalem, suspected an intention to rebel. As soon as it was reported to Artaxerxes the work on the walls was stopped at once. It was probably the author of the Aram. memorandum who made the mistake of saying that it was the Jews who had returned to Jerusalem who were doing the work. Exiles had been coming back from time to time in the course of nearly a century : there is no reason to suppose that they formed a distinct community in Jerusalem. 328a

The occasion for this abortive attempt to build the walls was just before Nehemiah's mission in 445. It was 446 B.C. when he heard the news of the destruction of the gates and walls (Neh. 1:3, 2:3, 13). Trito-Isaiah in numerous places had spoken of the restoration of old ruins, with special reference to the walls and gates of Jerusalem (e.g. Isa. 49:16, 17, 58:12, 60:10, 61:4, 62:5–7 ; see *Early Judaism*, pp. 124f.). Galling (p. 12) connects these events with the rebellion of the satrap Megabyzos in 448 B.C. If Trito-Isaiah had preached about 450 B.C. the Jews in Jerusalem might well have seized the opportunity of the unrest during the rebellion of Megabyzos to start quietly on the defences of the city. Their work was stopped forcibly, although, as they had shown no actual signs of revolt, and had not helped in the rebellion, Artaxerxes added the saving clause (Ezr. 4:21) 'until a decree is made by me'. Later on, Galling thinks, Artaxerxes, desiring to bind to himself by an act of friendship those provinces that had not taken part in the rebellion, approved of the building of the walls of Jerusalem. This is possible, though it is not supported by Nehemiah's narrative, and it is doubtful whether he did in so many words authorise the building of the walls. What he may have done was to appoint for the Jews a Governor of their own race, and to discontinue the authority over Jerusalem previously held by the Governor of Samaria. But see also §101*c*. b

20. Galling understands the 'mighty kings' to have been those of Assyria, Babylonia and Persia who received tribute from the Jews. More probably the Aram. writer wished to give the idea that Artaxerxes had been impressed by the record of the great kings of Israel and Judah who ruled over a great area and collected taxes from subject races (see Rudolph, p. 45). c

Neh. I. We come now to **the story of Nehemiah,** which undoubtedly follows an account by Nehemiah himself, and consequently has not been the field of such critical battles as have been waged over all the other parts of Ezr. and Neh. However, the critical work which has now restored the credibility of Ezr. 4:7–23 has provided a badly needed introduction to the Nehemiah narrative. d

328e **1.** The date is incomplete, and as far as it goes it disagrees with 2:1. If Nehemiah approached the king in Nisan (the spring) of the 20th year of Artaxerxes, he could not have received the bad news in December of the same year (Chislev). The simplest explanation is that the original reading in **1** was 'in the month Chislev *in the 19th year of Artaxerxes the king*' and that the words in italics were accidentally omitted. A later scribe supplied '20th year' from 2:1 but did not give the name of the king. It will have been 446 B.C. when Nehemiah heard the bad news from his brother Hanani and others, and some three months later in 445 when he saw the king. 'Susa the capital' (RV, Shushan the palace) should be 'the fortress in Susa'. The word is an Assyrian loan-word, and is used also for the fortress at Ecbatana (Ezr. 6:2) and the fortress close to the Temple in Jerusalem (Neh. 2:8, 7:2). 'The fortress in Susa' comes once in Dan. and repeatedly in Est. The state of the city described in **3** reflects a recent disaster. In each of the four places in chs. 1 and 2 where the state of the walls and gates is mentioned the city and walls are described by a participle 'are lying in ruins' while the gates are described by a perfect tense 'have been burnt'. It is this fact which has established the accuracy of the report given in Ezr. 4:7–23. Previously commentators had been puzzled as to why Nehemiah showed such grief over something that happened 140 years before. The Chronicler has composed an appropriate prayer, reflecting the ideas of Dt. 30:1–4, and put it into the Nehemiah narrative, **5-11**. The last verse, 'give success to thy servant today, and grant him mercy in the sight of this man', looks as if it was originally intended to stand after 2:4 'so I prayed to the God of heaven'.

f **II 1-8.** 'Now I had not been sad in his presence': probably translate 'and I was not out of favour with him'. Some commentators, with a small emendation, read 'and I had not previously been sad'. Nehemiah's fear is easily understood, seeing that so recently Artaxerxes I had ordered repairs to the walls to be stopped. The presence of the queen (6) added both to his anxiety and to his hopes, for the ladies of the court had great influence over Artaxerxes I. Eight years before, the queen had forced her husband to execute an Egyptian rebel out of personal revenge, although he had surrendered to the Persian general Megabyzos under the promise that his life would be spared. On the other hand, when Megabyzos rebelled against Artaxerxes, he owed his life to the intercession of the king's mother and sister (Eduard Meyer in EBrit., 14th ed., ii, 448; Rudolph, p. 107). Nehemiah said nothing about fortifying the city, but played on the sympathy of the king and queen by talking of the state of disrepair of the family graves. If Artaxerxes I was a good Zoroastrian he would have hated the idea of the earth being polluted by burying corpses in it; but he was an easy-going if capricious ruler, and his chief object after the recent rebellions must have been to keep the Israelites quiet. It is difficult to make out exactly what Nehemiah got permission to do. The casual way wood for the city walls is introduced, between that required for repairs to the Temple fortress and for Nehemiah's own house, suggests some small repairs near those two buildings. But the document may have been so worded as to give Nehemiah full authority to build walls and set up gates. There is nothing said here about his appointment as Governor of Judah, but we learn from 5:14 that this appointment dated from the 20th year of the king. Probably it was by virtue of his Governorship that he was able to defy Sanballat.

g **9-10.** The satrap of the province Beyond the River would have various grades of sub-satrap or governor under him. It seems pretty clear that Sanballat held one of these minor posts as Governor of Samaria, and in the absence of a separate Governor of Judah exercised authority over Judah. Sanballat's opposition was therefore purely political. Although he had a Babylonian name, his sons, whom we know of from 32
the Elephantine papyri, had Jewish names showing them to be worshippers of Yahweh. So also had Tobiah, whose name means 'Yahweh is good'. He may have been Ammonite on his mother's side; or he may have held a Persian official position in Ammon.

11-16. The city of Jerusalem in NT times was h
bounded on the east by the Kidron Valley and on the south by the Valley of Hinnom. In ancient times this valley 'Ge Hinnom' was used for human sacrifices, and afterwards as a refuse dump. As an abhorred spot it gave its name to Gehenna, the place of torment for the wicked. This refuse dump was approached from the SE. corner of the city through the Dung Gate. From this gate, in a direction slightly west of north, the city was divided by the Tyropoeon Valley. Recent research has made it probable that in Nehemiah's time the city did not extend west of the Tyropoeon Valley. Nehemiah's night journey began at the Valley Gate some 500 yards from the Dung Gate. In NT times this Valley Gate was west of the Dung Gate, and therefore near the head of the Valley of Hinnom. But if the newer view of Nehemiah's Jerusalem is correct, the Valley Gate will have been towards the head of the Tyropoeon Valley. Beginning at the Valley Gate Nehemiah inspected the walls from the outside, but soon after leaving the Dung Gate he had to follow the inside of the wall. His night journey did not include the north and west walls (on the older view) or the north wall (on the newer view). Those parts were more easily visible from the streets, and Nehemiah could have seen them on his first day in the city without exciting suspicion. But we must remember too that the parts which he inspected by night were the most important as being more liable to surprise attack: an enemy clambering up the sides of the Kidron Valley, where the slope is about 1 in 2, might not be seen till quite close.

17-20. The day after his inspection Nehemiah called i
together the leaders, and they agreed to start work immediately. The opposition of Sanballat and Tobiah began at once by their spreading rumours that the Jews were planning rebellion. With them also appears a man named Geshem, one of an Arab tribe which had recently occupied the land of Edom, which came to be known as Idumaea. Geshem was presumably the Governor of Idumaea.

III. Work must have begun simultaneously on **the** 329
gates and the walls: either without the other was useless. Response to Nehemiah's appeal was universal. The only slight sign of resistance comes in **5** where we are told that the gentry of Tekoa objected to doing labourers' work, but evidently they repented, for we find the Tekoites doing another portion of the wall as well (**27**). The catalogue of the work starts with the Sheep Gate, north of the Temple area, and then goes counter-clockwise round the city till it comes back to the Sheep Gate again.

IV 1-5. The opposition of Sanballat and Tobiah is b
parallel with 2:19–20, and like it is probably the Chronicler's work. **6** would have followed directly after 2:18. 'Will they sacrifice?' should be translated 'Will they begin?'; cf. the Urdu idiom '*bismillah karna*' (literally 'to do in the name of God') which means 'to sacrifice' or 'to begin' since all important undertakings were inaugurated by sacrifice.

6-23. V. **10** means 'The Jews were saying'. The c
difficulty of the Tekoites was widely felt, and in practice the heavy work had to be left to those accustomed to it, cf. **14, 17**. Vv. **12, 13** with slight emendation read 'Now when the Jews who lived near them came and told us again and again (lit. 'ten times') all the evil intentions they were plotting against us, I set spearmen in open places in the space behind the wall, and stationed the people . . .' (Rudolph, p. 126). It is clear from ch. 3 that many of the workers lived in the country, and came in daily to the work. They were thus able to bring word of the enemies' plans. But later on (**22**) Nehemiah decided that this

29c was too dangerous, and that master and slave alike must stay in the city. **23.** ' each kept his weapon in his hand ' is a rather free emendation of an impossible text. A simpler emendation is ' each had his weapon all the time '.

d **V** interrupts the story of the walls to tell of certain **social reforms.** It is part of Nehemiah's memoirs, and he has inserted it here because of the problem of rich and poor which had already been referred to in ch. 4. V. **2** should read (adding one letter that has dropped out) ' We are obliged to give our sons and daughters in pledge that we may buy corn that we may eat and live.' **5** voices the complaint of the poor that they are Israelites as much as those that oppress and enslave them. This problem did not arise because of the emergency of the building work, but it was made more evident when the physical weakness of the labourers was seen. It is probable that some of the Jews who had returned from Babylon in the last 80 or 90 years, with wealth earned by trade, were forming a new aristocracy, encroaching on the land of small-holders as in the 8th cent. The reference to interest or usury in **7ff.** is difficult, especially as it seems at first sight from **10** that Nehemiah himself had lent money at interest. But it may be that it is not interest that is in question, but the pledge or security on the loan. Both Rudolph and Galling understand that in **10** Nehemiah is offering to renounce the whole debt, and not merely the interest on it.

e **14-19.** Nehemiah did not avail himself of his right to charge various expenses to the community, as previous governors had done. There may have been no separate Governors of Judah since Sheshbazzar and Zerubbabel, and the Governors of Samaria would probably, like Sanballat, have no interest in the welfare of the Jews. In **17** omit with LXX$^{BA\aleph}$ the words ' and officials ', and with LXX$^{A\aleph}$ the word translated ' besides ', thus, ' And the hundred and fifty Jews, who had come unto us from the Gentiles who lived in our neighbourhood, were (entertained) at my table ' (Batten, p. 246). Nehemiah is quoting this fact, not in order to boast, but to encourage other Jews to care for their poorer Jewish brethren.

f **VI.** The story of the building of the walls is continued after the digression about Nehemiah's social reforms. Although Nehemiah himself gave this account, and inserted it in this position, he included later stages of his work for social reform. Thus the sentence in 5:16 ' I acquired no land ' referred to the whole period of his office. It was not the sort of thing that he would or could have done while the urgent work of repairs was in hand.

g The Samaritan leaders and their friends, having found that neither mockery, nor surprise attacks, were of any avail, tried (1) to lure Nehemiah to an out-of-the-way place where he could be quietly disposed of, (2) spreading rumours of plots of rebellion, and (3) friendly advice to hide from threatened assassination. It is interesting to note the political use to which ' prophets ' were put. We sometimes forget that the proportion of prophets who were concerned with promoting true religion was small. The rest were not necessarily followers of false gods, but, as mere politicians or flatterers of kings, they were rightly described as ' false prophets '. The wall was finished in 52 days in October 445, so short a time that some source used by Josephus made it 852 days. But the foundations of the wall still stood, and it only needed repairs. It was only the gates that had to be made afresh.

h The result was amazing. **16** should be rendered ' And when all our enemies heard it, and all the heathen who lived round about us saw it, they [the Samaritans] fell greatly in their eyes [i.e. the eyes of the heathen], and they [probably the heathen] perceived that the work had been accomplished with the help of our God.' No emendation of the text is needed. It is a triumphal statement of the reversion of the fortunes of the Samaritans, who had so long lorded it over
others, and now were defeated by the God whom they 329h
professed to serve.

VII 1-5. As soon as the walls and gates were finished, i
regular gate-keepers were appointed, and control of the city was handed over to Nehemiah's brother (1:1) and to Hananiah the governor of the castle by the Temple. The singers and Levites were accidentally added from vv. 43–5 where they are connected with the gate-keepers of the Temple courts. Nehemiah then saw that there were not enough people to defend the city, and houses needed to be built. The suggestion has been made that this expression means that families needed to be raised up ; but that cannot be done in a day, and one naturally thinks of Nehemiah's request (2:5) for permission to build the city. So he called the leaders and people together (**5**) not ' to be enrolled by genealogy ' as the Heb. says, but ' for conference ' as the Gr. has it. Nehemiah's memoirs continue in ch. 11, where we read the result of their consultation.

6-69 is not part of Nehemiah's memoirs. It is the j
same list as in Ezr. 2, and was inserted here by the Chronicler, who added the introductory words, ' And I found the book of the genealogy of them that came up at the first, and I found written in it : ' It was probably a later scribe who, seeing this word ' genealogy ', altered the verb ' to consult together ' in the first part of the verse into ' to be enrolled by genealogy ', a change only involving a single letter.

VIII-X. For the commentary, see §§326*b*, *i–k*, 327*a*.

XI 1-2. The result of the conference was that all the 330a
leaders decided to live in Jerusalem (instead of ' lived in Jerusalem ' translate ' came to live in Jerusalem '), and of the rest of the people one-tenth, drawn by lot, moved from the villages into the city. Some won general approval by volunteering to move in.

3-19 bears close resemblance to 1 Chr. 9:2–34. This b
seems to be a genuine list which the Chronicler found amongst the archives, but it has suffered a good deal in transmission, and the version in Neh. is considerably the shorter. One omission, that of Ephraim and Manasseh in Neh. 11:4 (cf. 1 Chr. 9:3), is intentional on the part of the Chronicler, who could not believe that Northerners were allowed in Jerusalem after Nehemiah had expelled Sanballat and his confederates with the words ' You have no portion, or right, or memorial in Jerusalem ' (Neh. 2:20). **Neh. XII 1-26** is a further list inserted by the Chronicler. Attention has already been drawn to the important list of high priests, extending from the time of Zerubbabel to the advent of Alexander the Great in **10, 11** ; and the chronological succession of Jeshua, Nehemiah and Ezra in **26.** Perhaps the earliest reference to antiphonal singing of two halves of the choir is to be seen in **9,** ' And Bakbukiah and Unno their brethren stood opposite them in the service '. Cf. Ezr. 3:11 and Ps. 118:2–4, where it may be that only the choir and congregation were singing alternately. ' And ' must be added after ' Unno '. The word rendered ' service ' properly means ' guards ', and seems scarcely applicable to the singers. We should perhaps change *sh* into *z* and read ' psalms '.

XII 27-43. Here we are again in Nehemiah's memoirs, c
as is indicated by the first person in **31.** The two processions round the city at the **dedication of the walls** are of interest. So long as the city in Nehemiah's time was thought to include the western hill, no sense could be made of it. Whatever place was chosen for the start of the procession, the directions ' right ' and ' left ' seemed wrong. But if the western wall went up the west side of the Tyropoeon Valley, with the Valley Gate near the top of the valley, it becomes perfectly clear. It should be remembered that in Heb. as in Arabic ' right ' means south, and ' left ' means north, as if one stood facing the sunrise. The processions, having formed up in the Temple area, moved out south-west for not more than one or two hundred yards to reach the Valley Gate. Then they divided. The first moved ' right ', i.e. southwards, to the Dung Gate, then turned sharp north to the Fountain Gate,

330c and the Stairs of the City of David, and entered the Temple area again on the east side by the Water Gate. The other procession moved from the Valley Gate 'left', i.e. northwards, as far as the Broad Wall which goes due west to the Corner Gate (see 2 Chr. 26:9), and then north and east to the Old Gate, the Fish Gate, the Tower of Hananel, the Tower of the Hundred and the Sheep Gate, and so to the Gate of the Guard which was presumably on the north side of the Temple area. Thus the two processions between them traversed practically the whole of the wall, and both started and finished at the Temple.

d **XII 44-XIII 3.** A section added by the Chronicler, apparently intended to show how well the ordinances of the Temple were carried out in the whole post-exilic period. He describes this period as 'the days of Zerubbabel and of Nehemiah', these being either the only Governors of Judah whose names he knew, or the only Jewish ones. The text is not quite sound, and in particular **46**, which probably meant to say that the singing-guilds of David and of Asaph carried out their duties as laid down by their founders. The Chronicler added **13:1-3** as an introduction to the Tobiah story. By the words 'on that day' he presumably was thinking of the service in connection with the dedication of the walls, but the same expression in **44** seems to cover the state of affairs in the whole post-exilic period. The quotation is from Dt. 23:3–5 with some abbreviations. The passage seemed appropriate as Tobiah was said to be an Ammonite.

e **XIII 4-31.** From **6** onwards, where Nehemiah speaks in the first person, we have the memoirs of Nehemiah. Vv. **4** and **5**, however, have apparently been worked over by the Chronicler, if they are not entirely due to him. The result has been to present the commentators with a pretty problem. Batten is quite clear that the Eliashib who let Tobiah occupy **the tithe-room** was the high priest. Rudolph and Galling are equally certain that he was not. There is truth in both contentions. When Nehemiah wrote **7** in his memoirs, and referred to Eliashib without any further qualification, he obviously meant the high priest, as he states unequivocally in **28**. Eliashib the high priest was an old man, at least in his late seventies, in 433 B.C., if he was the grandson of Jeshua the high priest in 520. Under those circumstances Tobiah could easily have arranged to occupy the vacant room, through an intermediary, without the feeble old high priest discovering who the intended tenant was. No particular blame attached to Eliashib, and Nehemiah does not rebuke him. When, however, the Chronicler came to write or rewrite the introduction to the story, he could not believe that the high priest could be responsible for such an act of sacrilege as allowing a heathen to have living quarters in the Temple. Yet, thought the Chronicler, if this Eliashib was not the high priest, how could he have had authority to give the room to Tobiah? So he described him as 'Eliashib the priest who had been appointed over the chambers of the house of our God'. Then, to explain why the priest should want to do this favour to Tobiah, the Chronicler added, 'who was connected with Tobiah', thinking no doubt of a connection by marriage. The idea that the high priest could have been appointed over the rooms was too absurd, but as an explanation by the Chronicler with reference to an ordinary priest it is easily understood. We need then have no further difficulty in believing that the event happened in the high priesthood of Eliashib, and that no other person of the same name was involved. The things that seemed to make it impossible were written nearly a hundred years later by the Chronicler who could not visualise the situation.

f The abuse of the tithe-room followed its disuse because tithes had been neglected. The result was that the Levites had had to return to the land to earn their living. Nehemiah restored the practice of tithing, **10-14**. The observance of the sabbath was one of the great difficulties for Jews in the Diaspora, and here (**15-22**) we see how Nehemiah faced the problem of sabbath trading with foreigners in Jerusalem itself. Nehemiah concerned himself with the case of mixed marriages with women of Ashdod (**23-7**). The Chronicler, with his text from Dt. 23 in mind, added Ammon and Moab, but failed to notice that the only foreign language the children spoke was that of Ashdod (see 321*c*). The other mixed marriage that he dealt with was that of a son of the future high priest Joiada (Jehoiada). This son was presumably not Jehohanan, who later on succeeded his father as high priest. It might have been Jeshua, who was afterwards murdered (see §326*c*), or a younger brother. It is clear that Nehemiah only dealt with a few special cases of mixed marriage, and did not take up the problem in the wholesale way that Ezra did later on.

Bibliography—Commentaries: L. W. Batten, ICC (1913); T. Witton Davies, Cent.B; K. Galling, ATD (1954); W. Rudolph, HAT (1949).

Other Literature: L. E. Browne, *Early Judaism* (1920); C. C. Torrey, *Ezra Studies* (1910); A. C. Welch, *Post-Exilic Judaism* (1935).

ESTHER

By L. E. BROWNE

331a The Book of Esther occupies the same place in sacred scripture as the villainous rogue in a story or play which has been written with a moral purpose. In the whole book there is **no mention of God or religion,** and no noble character. Even Esther, who in some sense is the heroine of the story in that she risks her life to save the Jews from destruction, is expressly said to have done so only after Mordecai had threatened that she herself would not escape the massacre. Gentile and Jew alike are represented in the story as actuated by the basest motives of pride, greed and cruelty. If the book fills any useful place in the Bible it is as a picture of unredeemed humanity.

b The explanation why the book was written and accepted by the Jews, and why its manuscripts exceed in number those of any other book of the Bible, and are often magnificently illuminated and encased in silver and gold of exquisite workmanship, is simply that it began in connection with a heathen carnival, and has never lost its purely secular character.

c Internal evidence has led all modern scholars to date the book **between 150 and 100 B.C.,** after the persecution of Antiochus Epiphanes. The Hebrew is undoubtedly late. The Persian Empire is given a halo of romance which indicates that it had long ceased to exist. The references to proselytes to Judaism (8:17, 9:27) suggest a date in the Graeco-Roman period. The last verse of the Greek version of Esther, which is one of the additions not found in the Hebrew text (see Ad. Est. 11:1 in our English Apocrypha) reads as follows, 'In the fourth year of the reign of Ptolemy and Cleopatra, Dositheus, who said that he was a priest and Levite, and Ptolemy his son, brought the foregoing letter concerning Purim, which they said was [genuine], and that Lysimachus, the son of Ptolemy, one of the inhabitants of Jerusalem, had interpreted it.' If this note is true, it means that a Greek translation of Esther was brought to Egypt in 114 B.C. when Ptolemy VIII (Lathyrus) and his wife Cleopatra reigned in Egypt. A less likely date is 178 B.C., when Ptolemy VI (Philometor) was king, but his marriage to a lady named Cleopatra was at a later time. The evidence from reference to forcible proselytising points to a date later than 128 B.C. for the composition of Esther (see §334*d*). Josephus (c.Ap. i, 8) quotes the Greek Esther in A.D. 90. Purim is first referred to, though not by name, in 2 Mac. 15:36, where the fourteenth day of the month Adar is called the Day of Mordecai. There is no other early reference to the book.

d From the apologetic tone of the note quoted above from Ad. Est. 11:1, it is clear that there were considerable doubts about the book when it was introduced into Egypt. The Egyptian Jews may have taken kindly to a day of carnival, but were probably put off by the irreligious tone of the book. For this reason large additions were made in the Greek translation of Esther, with the object of adding the name of God, and making the book ostensibly religious. These additions are found in the Apocrypha in the AV and RV, but do not concern us in this commentary. They add nothing to the understanding of the original book. No Hebrew or Aramaic texts of Esther contain these additions; and the best the Hebrew scribes could do to bring God into the book is seen in three 331d
manuscripts which have the initial or final letters of successive words in 1:20, 5:4, 5:13, 7:7 written large so as to show the divine name YHWH as an acrostic.

The story is set in the city of Susa in the reign of e
Akhashwerosh, king of Persia and Media. This name is now proved to refer to Xerxes, who reigned over Media as well as Persia. The book correctly states that his empire extended from India to Ethiopia, a fact which may well have been remembered long afterwards, especially by someone living in the East, but in other matters the author is inaccurate, for instance in regard to the number of provinces (see §332*a*). Xerxes' wife was named Amestris, and not either Vashti or Esther. The statement in Est. 1:19 and 8:5 that the laws of Persia were unalterable is also found in Dan. 6:9, 13. It is not attested by any other early evidence, and seems most unlikely. The most probable suggestion is that it was invented by the author of Daniel to form an essential part of his dramatic story, and afterwards copied by the author of Esther.

It is therefore agreed by all modern scholars that f
Esther was written long after the time of Xerxes as **a novel,** with no historical basis, but set for the author's purposes in a time long past. It is pretty clear that the author's purpose was to provide an historical origin for the feast of Purim, which the Jews living somewhere in the East had adopted as a secular carnival. This feast and its mythology are now recognised as being of Babylonian origin. Mordecai represents Marduk, the chief Babylonian God. His cousin Esther represents Ishtar, the chief Babylonian Goddess, who was the cousin of Marduk. Other names are not so obvious, but there was an Elamite God Humman or Humban, and an Elamite Goddess Mashti. These names may lie behind Haman and Vashti. One may well imagine that the Babylonian festival enacted a struggle between the Babylonian gods on the one hand and the Elamite gods on the other.

With the rise of the Persian Empire, and the exten- g
sion of the Zoroastrian religion westwards until it was accepted by the royal court in the time of Darius, the original mythology of the festival must have been forgotten. It may have come to represent some other conflict, such as that between the old religion of Iraq and the new Zoroastrianism, or that between the Persians and their foreign Magian priests (see J. H. Moulton, *Early Zoroastrianism*, Lecture VI). Thus it seems useless to speculate on the interpretation of the festival as it was understood when the Jews first took part in it. Whatever it was, they changed it into a conflict between Jews and Gentiles. One of the difficulties in tracing continuity of the festival is its date; the Jewish feast is a fortnight before the vernal equinox when the Persians and Babylonians would have celebrated their New Year rejoicings.

We now have to consider the circumstances under h
which a Jewish author would have composed the book. It would have no meaning unless there was such feeling of Gentiles against the Jews as to make a pogrom, or indiscriminate massacre of Jews, a dreaded possibility. There is no real parallel in the persecution of Antiochus Epiphanes, which was against the Jewish

331h religion rather than against their persons. Notice the difference between 1 Mac. 1:50, which provides the death penalty for those Jews who disobeyed the commandment of Antiochus Epiphanes to abandon their religion, and Est. 3:13 which orders the destruction of all Jews, men, women and children. Esther presupposes a condition such as we have known in modern times in which the Jews have become unpopular and hated, either for economic reasons, or because, owing to peculiar food laws, etc., they did not mix socially with others. Now it is difficult to imagine that such a lawless pogrom could be allowed to break out to any large extent in Palestine, Syria or Egypt, which would be within reasonable distance of a strong seat of government.

i There is one district which would apparently supply the necessary conditions, and that is **the province of Persis,** north-east of the Persian Gulf. After the death of Alexander the Great Persis became part of the Seleucid Empire. That empire had varied fortunes and at one time lost control of Babylonia, Susiana and Persis ; but the vigorous king Antiochus Epiphanes, whom we know mostly as the persecutor of the Jewish faith, restored his authority over these provinces. At his death, however, in 163 B.C., the Seleucid Empire began to break up ; the Parthians came in and conquered Media and northern Babylonia, while Mesene, Elymais (Susiana) and Persis secured their independence. Of these three it was Persis that gained real independence of spirit from Seleucid and Greek influence. The coins of Persis show that they regarded themselves as the inheritors of the Achaemenian traditions, and the upholders of Zoroastrianism and the Fire-cult. They had to acknowledge the political suzerainty of Parthia, but it was in Persis alone that Zoroastrianism was supreme, and the sacred writings of Zoroastrianism were preserved. Everywhere else the religion of Zoroaster degenerated, and when, in the 3rd cent. A.D., the Sassanian Empire was founded, it was from Persis that the new empire received the restored religion of Zoroaster (EBrit., 14th ed., xvii, 577, 611–612). When, in the Sassanian Empire, the Zoroastrian religion comes out into the clear light of history, it appears as fanatically persecuting. It would not be surprising if the position of Jews living in Persis among such zealous Zoroastrians was exceedingly difficult ; and the danger of an uprising of the population against the Jews would be much greater when there was no strong government in Antioch to keep the peace. If the Book of Esther was written in Persis between 150 and 100 B.C., we can well understand how the scene was set in the old Persian capital of Susa, and the might and magnificence of Xerxes' empire was proclaimed. It would also be easy to understand the memory of certain details of Xerxes' times and inaccurate information about other things that had changed in a period not far short of 400 years.

332a **I 1-4** The Hebrew text of Esther, like that of Joshua, Judges and Ruth, begins with the words, 'Now it came to pass'. The author asks that it be taken as real history. We take it to be an unhistorical work, and can see in it many signs of the novel or folk-tale ; but that gives no excuse for Haller to begin his translation with the words, 'Es war einmal', 'Once upon a time', as if the author was consciously writing a fairy tale.

The author, who gives the number of satrapies, both here and in 9:30, as 127, was only slightly enlarging on the 120 of Dan. 6:2. The actual number, as we know from contemporary inscriptions, varied from 21 to 29. Herodotus gave the number as 20. Whether Daniel's additon of 100 was an accidental clerical error, or a deliberate exaggeration, does not much matter. Either is easily understood after so long an interval. It is now established from the inscriptions that Akhashwerosh, the Hebrew name for the king, means the one whom we know by the Greek name of Xerxes, who reigned from 485 to 465 B.C. Elsewhere in the OT his name only occurs once, in the 332a
fragment preserved in Ezr. 4:6. The curious expression 'Shushan the palace' (RSV incorrectly 'Susa the capital'), meaning the palace or fortress in Shushan or Susa, is borrowed from Neh. 1:1 and Dan. 8:2. It is not probable that our author, even though he made Xerxes entertain his guests for 180 days, intended to represent the whole army as guests. Commentators therefore agree in adding a word to make it read '*the officers of* the army of Persia and Media'.

5-8 This great feast was followed by one week's b
entertainment to all the inhabitants of Susa. Some words seem to have dropped out in the account of the decorations of the mosaic-paved court in the park surrounding the palace, but it is sufficient for us to know that the author intended it to be as beautiful as a fabulously wealthy oriental king could make it. The remark that there was no compulsion in drinking can only be understood as a humorous touch, as if to say, 'So far from the guests asking whether the drinks were rationed, there was so much provided that the guests might wonder whether they were ordered to drink a gallon each.'

9-12 The ancient Persians did not seclude their c
women, a custom only introduced by Islam many centuries later. No explanation is given for the separate feast for the ladies in the palace, but, after the reference to the heavy drinking at the king's feast, one would guess that the ladies felt it was no place for them. Nor is any reason given for Vashti's refusal to obey the king's command to come and show off her beauty to the assembly. As it is definitely stated that the king was merry with wine, we are irresistibly reminded of Salome performing a very questionable dance at Herod's birthday party. Only, if that is intended here, Vashti's refusal was fully justified, and it has for the reader the unhappy effect of removing so early from the stage the only character who commands his respect.

13-22 The king in his wrath took counsel with 'the d
wise men who knew the times', an expression which clearly refers to magicians and astrologers. The author, writing in the 2nd cent. B.C., certainly had the Magians in mind. These were people of non-Aryan stock, famed of old in Media for their magical powers, who became the priests of Zoroastrianism. In the reign of Cambyses a Magian plot placed on the Persian throne a pretender whom they declared to be Cambyses' son, who was in fact dead. The Magians were so powerful politically that they were only suppressed by a massacre in which great numbers of them were slain, including the usurper. The day was kept afterwards as a festival called the Magophonia, and the suggestion has been made that a boisterous festival was already observed on that date, and gave opportunity for the massacre (Louis H. Gray in ERE v, 874). It is possible that the memory of this massacre helped to put the Jews in fear of a pogrom against them. In view of the high position the Magians held as priests of Zoroastrianism, it is not surprising to find them in our story playing the important political part of urging the deposition of Queen Vashti. That a king should divorce his wife for disobedience is what one would expect, but to advertise the fact throughout the kingdom in order to put all wives in fear of their husbands sounds more like a novel than history. In accordance with the author's ideas of the former glories of the Persian Empire, he has the edict sent out in many languages in order that every husband should be encouraged to be master of his own house. What else this surprising edict is supposed to have contained we shall never know, as the last clause about 'talking in the speech of his people' is corrupt and untranslatable.

II The king, on the advice of his servants, agrees to e
take another wife in place of Vashti, and to have suitable candidates brought from all over the kingdom. Mordecai, who now enters the story, is said to have

32e been a grandson of Kish of the tribe of Benjamin. Either he or his grandfather was carried away captive by Nebuchadnezzar in 597. As Xerxes reigned from 485 to 465 it is just possible that Mordecai's grandfather was led away captive as a child, and that Mordecai flourished in Xerxes' reign. In that case Mordecai could easily be the exile of Ezr. 2:2 who returned with Zerubbabel. Our author may also have been so completely ignorant of history as to have believed that this Kish was the same as Saul's father, and that Haman the Agagite was a close relative of Saul's arch-enemy Agag the Amalekite. The appearance of the name of Mordecai in Ezr. 2:2 and Neh. 7:7 is evidence that at any rate as early as Alexander's time (when Ezr. was written) this was a name that a Jew living in Iraq might bear, and thus rather weakens the argument for a Babylonian myth behind the Esther story.

f Esther is introduced as an orphaned cousin of Mordecai, brought up by him as a daughter. She was very beautiful, and was accepted without question amongst the other damsels sent up to the palace. Readers of Ezr.–Neh. are surprised that Mordecai should have desired his ward to marry a heathen. But the fact is that mixed marriages were never so strongly objected to by the Jews as they were by their political and religious leaders. Nehemiah and Ezra were concerned with the future political fortunes of Israel. A man like Mordecai only thought of personal advancement. Mordecai warned Esther not to speak of her relationship to him, or of her being a Jewess, presumably because the Jews were hated. As he lived in Susa, it must have been well known that he was a Jew. In 2:19, 21 it says that Mordecai was sitting at the king's gate, and in 2:11 that he walked every day in front of the women's quarters. It is easiest to suppose that he obtained a post as porter in the palace, but the difficulty remains as to how he could communicate with Esther (2:22). The same verse says that the plot against the king's life 'was made known' to Mordecai, a passive verb suggesting that he was informed by someone else. This is possible if he held some official position, however humble. Otherwise we must suppose that he chanced to overhear the plotters whispering together as he loitered by the gate. He somehow got the news to Esther, and she told the king, and mentioned the name of Mordecai as connected with the discovery. The name 'Mordecai' meant nothing to the king, and, having ordered the plotters to be executed, he forgot all about the incident.

33a **III** This chapter begins with the sudden and unexplained promotion of Haman, who has not been mentioned before. One Greek version, the Lucianic, tries to remove this lack by identifying him with Memucan, the spokesman of the committee of wise men in 1:16. This is no doubt only a later attempt to remove a difficulty. The names Haman and Hammedatha can be explained as Persian (or Babylonian) names, and commentators through the ages may have been too ready to assume that 'Agagite' means a descendant of Agag. Anyhow, the Greek translators did not understand 'Agagite'. Generally they omitted the word, but occasionally wrote 'Bougaios' instead.

b The reason why Mordecai refused to do obeisance to Haman, though not explicitly stated, is evident from the whole tone of the book: Haman, the enemy of the Jews, was typical of all Gentiles, only fit for destruction. The Jews, like other peoples striving for nationhood, often tended to selfish nationalism, which reached its lowest depths in this book, but at other times outshone all other nations in the breadth of their universalistic vision of the salvation of all mankind. Pressed by the king's servants for the reason for his conduct, Mordecai eventually told them that he was a Jew, perhaps pretending that he was obeying the Second Commandment. Haman's reaction was to resolve to take vengeance on the whole race of the Jews, and to slay them all with Mordecai. Reading 333b
between the lines it is easy to see what he did: he took counsel with magicians, who cast lots in some way to discover his lucky day. **7** as it stands in the Hebrew is unintelligible, but fortunately in this place the Greek version has preserved some words that have dropped out of the text, though, influenced by the date of Purim, the Greek has 'the 14th day' instead of 'the 13th day' which it must have been. Thus v. 7 originally read, 'In the first month, which is the month of Nisan, in the 12th year (of the reign) of king Xerxes, they cast 'pur', i.e. the lot, before Haman, for every day and every month, and the lot fell on the 13th day of the 12th month, i.e. the month of Adar.'

If the theory is correct that Purim was a heathen c
carnival before this time, the oracle told Haman to use the occasion of the carnival for a massacre of the Jews. Armed with this encouragement he went straight to the king and asked for permission to exterminate the Jews as their manners and customs did not fit in with those of ordinary people. Not only was permission given, but action was taken at once, orders being sent on the 13th day of the first month to every province for a massacre eleven months later. To arrange so far ahead, and to promote publicity by sending out the decree in every language, are obvious signs that we are not dealing with real facts of history. **9, 11.** The financial arrangements are not quite clear, but presumably mean that Haman undertook to pay 10,000 talents from the booty into the royal treasury, but that the king declined the gift, and allowed Haman to use the money as he liked, i.e. in payment to the actual murderers, and in largesse to the people.

IV With so much publicity it is no wonder that the d
Jews throughout the kingdom were alarmed and dismayed. But the emphatic way in which this chapter opens, literally translated 'As for Mordecai, he learnt everything that had happened', indicates that somehow he secured full information of the plans, including (as we see in 8) a copy of the actual decree. It is not quite clear whether the author means that Esther knew nothing of the plan. In any case she might have been ignorant of the details. Mordecai made a show of his fasting and mourning, even going as far as he dared towards the entrance of the palace, in order to attract Esther's attention. He succeeded in this, and sent her a message that she must at all costs see the king and pray for the Jews. It seems to be assumed that the secret of her own Jewish birth was still kept. Dramatically the author uses an old Persian custom, known to Herodotus, that anyone who dared to approach the king unsummoned would be put to death unless immediately pardoned by the king. Conveniently the author forgot the fact, also recorded by Herodotus, that a suppliant might send a letter to the king asking for an interview. Esther's heroism in risking her life for her people is somewhat lessened by the fact that she refused to do so until Mordecai warned her that otherwise she would be massacred with the rest of the Jews. It must be supposed that Mordecai knew that the secret of her birth could not be kept indefinitely. The nearest approach to anything bordering on religion in this book is the mention in this chapter of fasting, sackcloth and ashes, and the hope of 'deliverance from another quarter' (14). Mordecai, having now attained his object of persuading Esther to plead with the king, put off his sackcloth, and returned to his usual position in the gate of the palace.

V This is the most dramatic chapter of the book, in e
which the reader is kept in ever-growing suspense, while Esther delays making her request, and Haman rises to greater heights of overweening pride and hatred of Mordecai, as the wheels of fate prepare for his sudden fall. One is reminded somewhat of the suspense in the story of Joseph, but there the effect is far greater because Joseph had good reason for his

333e delay in making himself known : he must have all his brothers present. In this case the delay was only of story-telling value, and in fact might have resulted in disaster if for any reason the king had not come to dinner the second time.

f **VI** If our author had, as seems probable, passed beyond the stage in which religion and God had any meaning for him, it seems he was still conscious of an unseen Fate ordering the affairs of men. It was such a Fate that decreed that the king should have a sleepless night, just at the appropriate moment, and that he should ask to be entertained by having the *Chronicle of Memorable Deeds* read before him. In this he heard the story of how his life had been saved by the intervention of Mordecai. Recalling the forgotten incident, the king was surprised to learn that no reward had been given to Mordecai, and sent the servants to fetch any official who was at hand. The author had by now forgotten that it was in the middle of the night, and so arranged for Haman to arrive at that very moment to ask that Mordecai should be hanged on his gallows. The poetic justice by which Haman had to bestow on Mordecai the honours which he had envisaged for himself, is a kind of mental torture preliminary to his execution which the next chapter brings. Haman, having carried out the king's orders and sent Mordecai forth on his procession through the city, returned home in deep depression to his not too sympathetic wife and friends. In such a state of gloom he might have forgotten his dinner with the queen had not the servants come to call for him.

g **VII** At the second dinner given by Esther to the king and to Haman, Esther at once answered the king's question. She said she was pleading for her life and for that of her people, who were all to be exterminated. Humbly she said that if they had only been enslaved she would have made no complaint, but—and here the text is corrupt and untranslatable. The RSV may well be right in suggesting that it originally said that the death of so many of his subjects would have been a serious loss to the king. The king was amazed, as if he had never heard of the decree. But if we read ch. 3 carefully we notice (i) that Haman in making his original request to annihilate a certain people had not said that they were the Jews, (ii) that the decree, which does mention the Jews by name, was composed by Haman and sealed by him with the king's seal, but had not been seen by the king, and (iii) that we are probably meant to suppose that neither the king nor Haman was aware that Esther was a Jewess.

h As soon then as Haman heard Esther's words, accusing him of being the author of the plot, he knew that there was little hope for him if Esther was a Jewess. His alarm was sufficient confession of guilt, and the king could be in no doubt about it. Yet the king was in considerable difficulty : he could scarcely condemn Haman for carrying out orders which bore his royal seal. It may have been intentional to make the king such a fool that he forgot the name of the man who saved his life, that he ordered the destruction of a subject people without enquiring who they were, and that he married a woman without enquiring about her family. It is certainly in keeping with such a character that he needed a breath of fresh air to collect his scattered wits, and therefore strolled out into the garden. Again Fate comes in and plays the right card, so that when the king returns and finds Haman prostrate before the queen, his instant death can be ordered for attempted assault upon her majesty, which was high-treason. One of the chamberlains was ready to point out the gallows all ready in Haman's garden, and the suggestion to use it for Haman himself was readily adopted.

334a **VIII 1-2** Not only was Haman executed, but, as he was condemned for high-treason, his house and fortune were confiscated, and given to Esther. When the queen explained Mordecai's relationship to herself, he was given the honourable position that Haman had held.

3-8 Esther now with greater confidence asked a 334
new favour of the king, viz. that the decree ordering the extermination of the Jews should be repealed. The author, as we have already seen, had learnt from the Book of Daniel that the laws of the Medes and Persians could never be repealed. Consequently he wrote that the king gave Esther and Mordecai permission to make any new decree they liked concerning the Jews (so RSV and RVm), and Mordecai now held the royal seal with which it could be authorised.

9-17 Thereupon Mordecai ordered the secretaries c
to prepare a new edict, to be issued at once in the name of the king, and sent with all speed to the ends of the kingdom. The speed, with the help of the best of the noble horses of Persia that were in the royal studs, was only for literary effect. There was no need for it, as this was still only the third month, and the day of danger was nearly nine months ahead. The edict could not cancel the order for the attack on the Jews, but authorised the Jews to annihilate any armed force that rose against them on that one particular day, the 13th of the twelfth month. **11.** 'Armed force' (RSV) is the correct translation of this verse and not 'all the power of the people' (RV). The words 'with their children and women' probably means that an attack on the Jewish women and children would justify retaliation just as much as an attack on Jewish men. Probably it did not mean to authorise the Jews to murder Persian women and children, though either interpretation is grammatically possible. The Jews were, however, clearly given permission to plunder the goods of those whom they slew, though 9:10 says they did not actually do so.

The author gives no indication how the Jews, who d
recently were a small frightened minority, were expected to disarm and slay the Persian army. He just describes the position of honour of Mordecai, and the rejoicing throughout the kingdom, as if the Jews were in the majority. **17.** A very unpleasant feature appears that many heathen became Jews out of fear. This verse helps us to date the book, as it must certainly be based on the policy of John Hyrcanus and his son Aristobulus (135–104 B.C.), who forcibly 'converted' the people of Samaria, Idumaea and Galilee. Hyrcanus's attack on Idumaea took place after the death of Antiochus VII (Sidetes), which was in 128 B.C. (Jos. Ant. XIII, ix, 1).

IX 1-10 The method by which the Jews were supposed e
to have gained the mastery was that on the morning of the 13th day of Adar they gathered together, and, as soon as any armed men appeared, the Jews attacked first. The soldiers dared not stand against the Jews because it was known that Mordecai the Jew held the highest position in the kingdom next to the king. Especially was this true of all governors and officials, as they knew that they only held their posts by the favour of Mordecai. These officials therefore either ordered the disarming of the army or gave legal approval to their 'execution' by the Jews. The whole situation is of course quite impossible, and the eight and a half months' warning makes it even more impossible, because the disarming of the soldiers would have taken place before the 13th of Adar, and if they had had no arms they would not have been so foolish as to attack the Jews.

11-19 In Susa alone 500 Persians were reported as f
having been killed, and the king supposed that equally large numbers had perished throughout the kingdom. Yet he did not seem moved at this tragedy, and asked Esther what else she would like. In response she humbly asked that the Jews might be allowed to continue the slaughter for another day, and also that the ten sons of Haman might also be hanged. Here the author made a careless slip, as the sons of Haman had already been slain (9:10), unless it means that their dead bodies were to be hanged on Haman's gallows. The king immediately granted Esther's request, and in Susa a further 300 men were killed on the 14th day of Adar. This further day's slaughter

334f only took place in Susa, and not in the rest of the country.

g The slaughter of 75,000 men in one day by the Jews, who were everywhere only a small minority, is an impossible exaggeration. When in A.D. 1258 Hulagu sacked Baghdad it is true that he slaughtered between 800,000 and 1,000,000 persons, but then the Mongol army of 100,000 men was five times greater than the Caliph's army, and the slaughter occupied a whole week. The mention of the second day's slaughter in Susa is put into the story to explain why there was a difference of usage as to a festival of one day or two. The real reason of course is that when the date of a festival had to be determined by the appearance of the new moon, different places might be found to be observing the festival on different days. The festival was therefore extended to two days, so that all the people would at some part of the time be celebrating the occasion simultaneously.

h **20-32** The story now being ended, the moral is drawn. It is that Jews everywhere should keep this feast of Purim. **31** seems to suggest a day or days of fasting before the two days of rejoicing, merry-making and mutual gifts, although no date for the fasting is mentioned. Later Jews kept the 13th day of Adar as a fast-day, and the 14th and 15th as days of rejoicing. The fast would be in commemoration of the original fast ordered by Queen Esther in 4:3.

i One modern author (Pfeiffer, *Introd. to the OT*, 745) goes so far in his criticism as to suppose that there was no previous heathen carnival which the Jews copied, and no historical occasion whatever for the festival of Purim; in other words that every word of the book is pure invention for the very purpose of inducing the Jews to keep a feast that they had never heard of before. An almost complete answer to this suggestion is that the only way such a new feast could be ordained would be through the organised authorities of church and state in Jerusalem. Yet 334i according to ch. 9 the order was issued by Esther and Mordecai, who were Jews, but held no priestly office, and indeed only held their civil power by the authority of a heathen king. The sort of Jew who would produce such an ultra-nationalist book as this, and encourage hatred of foreigners, would not be likely to make his favourite feast of Purim dependent upon the fact that at one time Jerusalem was subject to the king of Persia.

X This final chapter begins with a statement, thrown j in apart from any context, that Xerxes levied *tribute* on the land and the islands. The Greek translators were undoubtedly right in taking this word in the sense of 'tribute', and have been followed by the English versions, in spite of the fact that elsewhere in the OT it always means a gang of slaves or forced labourers. It is used for 'tribute' in the later Talmudic Hebrew. The author probably meant that the wealth of the whole Persian Empire, both the mainland and its outer territories, rolled in for the benefit of the Jews, regarding it as a fulfilment of the prophecy of Isa. 60:5, 9, which spoke of Jews returning from all countries, including the 'islands', i.e. the Mediterranean coastlands, bringing with them silver and gold, the wealth of the nations, as an offering to the house of the Lord at Jerusalem. It is a fitting ending to the book, for the author is only carrying to its logical conclusion Third Isaiah's hope of the subjugation of the Gentiles to the Jews. In this spirit the author of Esther offered the Jews as their hero a man who overcame the enemies of his race, and raised himself and all the Jews to wealth and prosperity by the destruction and impoverishment of the Gentiles.

Bibliography—M. Haller, HAT (1940); L. B. Paton, ICC (1908); D. C. Siegfried, HKAT (1901).

HEBREW WISDOM

BY J. C. RYLAARSDAM

335a Wisdom represents a distinct category in Israel's legacy, comparable to Prophecy, Law, History, and Psalmody. While related in various ways to all of these it is differentiated both by its spirit and in its literary form. Job, Prov., and Ec. are the wisdom books in the canon. In the Apoc. Wis. and Sir. represent this tradition. Its influence is also clearly evident in the Ps. and in later literature including Tob., Jdt., Bar., 4 Mac., the Pirḳē Abôth, and, in the NT, in the Parables and Jas. Many of the earlier books of the OT contain references that can serve as clues to the origin of the movement and its early history in Israel. Notable among these are Solomon's reputation for wisdom (1 Kg. 3, 4:29–34), allusions to the wise as a class giving leadership in Israel (Isa. 29:14 ; Jer. 8:8f., 9:23, 18:18), proverbs and other wisdom materials (e.g. Jg. 9:7ff. ; 1 Sam. 24:14 ; and Ezek. 12:22, 18:2), and the frequent and variable use of the word *māshāl*, the chief term for the basic literary unit in the wisdom literature.

b **Background**—Besides alluding to the wise in Israel, the OT also gives evidence that ancient Israel was aware of the existence among other nations of leaders called 'wise' or 'wise men': in Egypt (Gen. 41:8, 39 ; Exod. 7:11 ; Isa. 19:11f.), in Canaan (Jg. 5:29), in Phoenicia (Ezek. 28:2, 6 ; Zech. 9:2), in Edom (Ob. 1:8), in Babylon (Jer. 50:35, 51:57 ; Dan. 2:12ff., 4:6, 18, 5:8, 15), and, indeed, among all the nations (Jer. 10:7). These sages are the aides and counsellors of kings, intimates of the court who are often equated with magicians, astrologers, sorcerers, and other purveyors of oracles. They are implicitly or explicitly denounced as proud and as servants of alien gods and powers who stand under the judgment of the Lord of Israel. In the role they play they are comparable to the 'wise women' in Israel (2 Sam. 2:14, 20:16), to such 'counsellors' as Ahithophel (2 Sam. 15:12ff.), and, in some respects at least, to the 'wise' cited in Isaiah and Jeremiah (cf. Isa. 29:14 ; Jer. 8:9, 9:23, 18:18), though there are also 'scribes' who inquire in the 'law' (Jer. 8:8).

Prov. and the rest of the wisdom literature hardly give one the impression that their wise are oracle mongers or the custodians of occult powers. In these books they are very sober teachers, practical in their concerns and rationalistic in spirit. In contrast to the rest of the OT they look at life from an anthropocentric viewpoint and, in the early stages of the movement, their overt concern with cultic matters is minimal. What is the historical connection between these very different kinds of 'wise'? This is a part of the problem of the origin of the wisdom movement.

c Outside Israel, especially in Egypt, the situation is similar. The recovery of a large body of Egyptian didactic material, beginning with the Proverbs of Duauf in 1858, has made it increasingly evident that in Egypt there was a class of teachers whose purpose and function closely resembles that of the *ḥ^{a}khāmîm*, or wise men, who wrote Prov. in Israel. The awareness of this resemblance was greatly intensified by the discovery, in 1926, that a late document of this Egyptian movement, The Wisdom of Amen-em-opet, was utilised as a source in Prov. 22:17–23:11 (cf. §397*a*). The work of these Egyptian schoolmasters dates back to a time before the middle of the 3rd 33
millennium B.C. and continued for fifteen centuries or more. Throughout it shows the same practical concerns and the same indifference to cultic matters that characterises the oldest section of Prov. Both movements flourished in court circles where the magicians, astrologers, and similar cult-oriented 'wise' were also located. But there is a sharp difference. The 'counsellor' and the king as possessor of divine wisdom may constitute some sort of bridge between the two (cf. 1 Kg. 4:29–34). *The Wisdom of Aḥiḳar*, an Aramaic collection of proverbs that is of Mesopotamian origin, is likewise comparable in form and spirit to Prov.

Some scholars, among them Bentzen and Engnell, have spoken of the wisdom movement and its literature as 'an offshoot of the cultus'. Considering the prudential character of Prov. and the analytical tendencies in Job and Ec., to speak only of the situation in Israel, it is obvious that this hypothetical bifurcation must lie in a distant past. No other part of the OT shows so little interest in cultic matters as wisdom. Nevertheless, there is considerable evidence for some sort of relationship in origin, as the apparently double use of the term 'wise' seems to imply. This is reinforced by a similar range given the term *māshāl* in the OT.

The *māshāl* is the proverb, in its simplest form a d
couplet in which the two lines are parallel to each other, either antithetically or synthetically. The oldest sections in Prov. consist almost entirely of this simple unit and all subsequent wisdom literature probably involves either an elaboration of this form or mixing of it with other forms. A *māshāl* is a 'comparison'; the word is derived from the verb meaning 'to become like' (Ps. 28:1, 49:12(13), 143:7 ; Isa. 14:10) or 'to be comparable with' (Isa. 46:5). In the OT it is used of proverbs (Ezek. 16:44, 18:2f.). It is also used of didactic and historical poems (Job 27:1, 29:1 ; Ps. 49:4(5), 78:2). A *māshāl* may further be a 'taunt song' (Isa. 14:4ff. ; Mic. 2:4f. ; Hab. 2:6ff.) ; or a 'by word' (Dt. 28:37 ; Ps. 44:14, 69:11f. ; Ezek. 14:8, et al.), both of which embody something of the force of a curse. Finally, it is used of the ecstatic prophetic visions of Balaam (Num. 24:3, 15) in which the word of the seer is a 'likeness' of the destiny of Israel that tends to its realisation. In Ezek. 17:2ff., 20:45–9 (Heb. 21:1–5), 24:3ff., we have three instances in which in a very similar way the word is used to describe 'allegories'. Considering the propensity of Ezek. for the 'acted parable' (cf. Ezek. 4:1ff.), it is not impossible that symbolic action may have been a part of a *māshāl* of this sort. The *māshāl* or 'likeness' was, therefore, an authoritative word which helped to effect what is said. Since, as noted, Ezekiel also uses the term of a folk proverb, his book may enshrine a witness to its development from a magical spell characterised by homoeopathic action to a simple literary simile. It seems quite probable, therefore, that some of the roots of Israel's (and Near Eastern) wisdom lie in ancient cultic patterns. It does not follow, however, that this lineal development expressed in literary form accounts for Israel's wisdom movement in all respects. Many other factors con-

5d tributed to its growth and about most of these it is still impossible to give a specific description.

e The relation of Solomon to the wisdom movement is analogous to that of David to psalmody. Both were founders and patrons. Further, just as the phrase 'a Psalm of David' refers to a recognised genre of religious poetry, so that the phrase 'proverbs of Solomon' is synonymous with the literary forms characteristic of wisdom. There is still no agreement on the precise role Solomon personally had in the development of wisdom; however, in general, much more weight is given to it than in the recent past.

As in Egypt and elsewhere, in Israel wisdom originally flourished at the court. This is clear not only from the references in Kg. but also from the contents and spirit of the wisdom literature. On their practical and prudential side books like Prov. and Sir. provide guidance for those who move in polite society. Great importance is attached to the observance of the proper forms that apply to a given situation. Characteristically, ostentation and loudness are shunned, but taste and elegance are appreciated. A premium is placed on reserve, self-control, and propriety. In Israel, more than elsewhere, compassion for the poor is inculcated; yet they are normally outside the circles of the sages. Respect for constituted authority is virtually accepted as absolute, giving wisdom literature a more conservative cast than any other part of the OT. Whether because of the prophetic spirit or because of the destruction of Jerusalem and the court in 586, the wisdom movement in Israel exhibits a 'levelling' tendency not so noticeable outside. While originally nurtured at the court, the teachings of the sages were made applicable to ever larger sectors of society. The emphasis upon industry and, especially, upon the nobility of manual work, decried in the Egyptian materials as incompatible with wisdom, afford the most striking example of this (cf., however, Sir. 38:24ff. for a note of dissent).

f As the monarch who introduced the oriental court in Israel, and who had close cultural and economic relations with both Egypt and Phoenicia, Solomon may well have established a school of wisdom. He was himself, by virtue of his kingship, the one through whom divine counsel and wisdom were, in principle, mediated to men. The account of his judicial insight (1 Kg. 3:16ff.) and of his utterance of proverbs and fables (1 Kg. 4:29ff.) seems to indicate that he personally exhibited some of the attributes of his office. As M. Noth has pointed out (VT, Suppl. III, 225ff.), the fact that Solomon is reported to have made his request of God for wisdom while sacrificing at Gibeon (1 Kg. 3:3ff.), probably indicates that the tradition reaches back into the pre-deuteronomic era.

The type of circle Solomon may have sponsored must have stood in close relation to the *sōphᵉrîm*, the scribes (Ps. 45:2) who were distinguished not only by the fact that they could write but probably also knew foreign languages. The writing down and copying of wisdom teaching was apparently an established practice in the time of Hezekiah (Prov. 25:1) and may have begun earlier. In Egypt the sayings of the wise were handed down in the form of 'copy books' for pupils over many centuries and something comparable probably took place in Israel. Eissfeldt and other historians of literature have pointed to a difference between the popular folk proverbs (*Sprüchenweisheit*), represented by scattered bits in the prophetic and historical books, and the professional 'sentences' (*Weisheitsspruch*) produced by the wisdom school proper. There is evidence that the latter appropriated the legacy of the former in what must have been a gradual process. The difference, as diagnosed by literary criticism, is a matter of form.

g The similarity in spirit, content, form, and method between wisdom in Egypt and Israel, already mentioned, illustrates the close relations throughout between Israel's sages and the outside world. Writing at the beginning of the 2nd cent. B.C., Jesus ben Sirach still speaks of his travel and his exchange of 335g
ideas with foreign cultures (51:13). For the early period the connections point to Egypt. This is clear not simply from such striking superficial similarities as the common use of the term 'my son' to address a pupil, but, in a deeper sense, from the fact that in the wisdom of both the themes and the way in which they are treated are similar. It was once common to look for Greek influence in the later stages of Israel's wisdom movement, including Ec. This is now qualified by the recognition that such influences, in so far as they are discernible at all, entered indirectly through Phoenicia. For example the oft-repeated phrase 'under the sun' appears in Phoenician inscriptions of the 5th cent. B.C.; and it is probably through these that the Greek phrase ὑφ' ἡλίῳ influenced Hebrew usage. There are growing indications, also, that in the earlier period Canaanite culture performed a similar mediating role. Direct Greek influence is more palpable in such later items as Wis., produced in a Hellenistic cultural environment.

Outlook—Before examining the separate units of the 336a
wisdom literature or dealing with the amplification and, gradually, the alteration of its literary forms, it seems appropriate to consider the general spirit and outlook of the movement that produced it. There is a consistency about this even more persistent, perhaps, than developments in form and subject-matter might lead one to suppose.

The basic outlook of the movement is anthropocentric. It is preoccupied, in its central thrust, with the human situation and with human destiny. It takes God and the meaning of God for human existence very seriously; but it does so in the context of its concern to understand and deal with the human problem. The outlook of the OT as a whole is theocentric; its starting-point is the action of God and the call to man to relate himself in faith and obedience to this action. In so far as wisdom bears witness to this divine action its testimony is a by-product of its struggle with the human situation in the course of which it recovers an awareness of Israel's heritage of faith. The speeches of the Lord in Job (38–41) offer one illustration of this.

The anthropocentric outlook of wisdom can be b
illustrated in several ways. First of all, it is the fundamental reason for its lack of interest in history, specifically in the history of Israel. The canonical wisdom books ignore this history completely. There are no references to the stories of the patriarchs, the enslavement and the exodus from Egypt, the wandering in the wilderness, Sinai, or the inheritance of Canaan. Nor, despite the patronage of Solomon, is there any interest in Israel's history under the house of David. It must be remembered that in Israel these historical traditions constituted the themes of faith. The preoccupation with them in history, prophecy, and the law was not for the sake of an antiquarian or scientific concern, or as a way of inculcating patriotism, but for the sake of the testimony of faith. The OT interest in history rests on the assumption that God has acted in it. It seems inconceivable that the sages did not know these historical traditions of Israel; rather, they failed to use them because the action of God was not their focal concern; or, in so far as it was a concern, it was not located in the national history. Wisdom differs from the rest of the OT in the sense that it does not seriously affirm the historicity of revelation. Later wisdom books such as Wis. and Sir. do make use of Israel's history. But even there its role is secondary and illustrative rather than primary. For example, in his praise of 'famous men' (44–50) Jesus ben Sirach not only finds an outlet for his own national pride but, in his delineation of the great figures of Israel's history, provides us with examples of men who were wise and prudent. Similarly, in Wis. 10–19 the work of the Spirit is illustrated by a rehearsal of Israel's history; but the disclosure of Wisdom and the Spirit is not integrally a part of the history. It seems

336b to stand outside it. In the earlier wisdom literature the revealing action of God is equated with the forms of creation and the tendency is to define God in terms of a series of structures and laws man must seek to discover, understand, and adjust himself to for his own advantage. In the later stages this is supplemented by God's special gifts in Wisdom, Word, Law, or Spirit ; and of these Israel is usually the special beneficiary. Nevertheless, a concern with the possibilities of human life in relation to them seems to continue to outweigh a commitment of life to God in faith, apart from calculable resources.

c This anthropocentric outlook of the wisdom movement with its non-historical view of revelation also helps to explain its individualism. In Prov. progress in wisdom depends upon the native gifts of the individual pupil, the skill of his teachers, and his personal effort, rather than upon the fact that he is an Israelite. Further, the vindication of the values inculcated is accomplished by an appeal to reason and the empirical facts of general human experience rather than by reference to a particular confessional or cultic tradition. This is also largely true of the criticism of accepted values in Job and Ec. It is not to be denied that the ethical values in Prov. reflect in a measure the serious moral outlook inculcated in Israel. And theologically, especially in Job, one encounters echoes both of Israel's experience of suffering and of its confession of the God who is the living Lord. But the particularism of the Covenant with Israel remains in the background ; the explicit utterance of the books is in the arena of universal human experience, a fact which helps to account for their persistent appeal throughout the centuries to those who stand outside synagogue and church and to whom the language of biblical faith may have become unintelligible. It must be noted that the individualism and universalism in Israel's wisdom are parts of the same whole, in contrast to the communal particularity of her covenant faith rooted in a revelation in history. In its later stages the wisdom movement is assimilated into the communal traditions so that it exhibits more of the features of the particular institutions of Israel and increasingly tends to speak in their name. But this ' nationalisation of wisdom ' still does not fully overcome its anthropocentricity. The Temple cultus and, especially, the Law (Sir. 24; Bar. 4) tend to become the substance of the Covenant, not simply its instruments and symbols. The legacy of Israel became the primary resource in man's ongoing quest for wisdom, so that law and wisdom coalesce to form the rabbinic tradition that produced the Talmud. Job may offer an exception to this.

d In moving away from the OT emphasis upon God's revelation in history and in its tendency to displace faith in the immediate operation of the action of God by man's understanding of his situation and of his utilisation of the resources at his disposal, the wisdom movement set out in the direction of a kind of conceptualism. It seems fair to raise the question whether at least one of the roots of the Gnosticism on the margins of later Judaism and early Christianity is not located in wisdom. Knowledge and understanding become antecedent to faith. Revelation is expressed in terms of inherited values, general principles, or existential awareness rather than as the freedom of God's action affirmed in faith. The conservatism bred by wisdom's setting in society is reinforced by its ideological orientation. The projections relating to life and its meaning tend to be made on the basis of the measurable possibilities. The notions of grace and forgiveness as transforming and redemptive factors in the human situation are almost wholly absent in the canonical wisdom. There is an anthropocentric concern with human obligation. In a book such as Prov. the neglect of an opportunity involves an irretrievable forfeiture of life in an ultimate sense. It is significant that prayers are lacking in the older wisdom writings and that literary analysts view the occurrence of prayers in Sir. as a sign that the movement had begun 33
to import literary forms from outside. In the canonical records of wisdom, at least, every experience of the limitations of human power generates protest or resignation, a feature not wholly lacking even in Prov.

Viewed as a stage in the history of religious development the wisdom movement plays an extremely important role in the transition from the OT to the NT. This becomes clear when one examines the difference between them in terms of the eschatological outlook of each. In the OT the redeeming work of God, expressed in the call of Israel and in its inheritance of the land of promise, is to attain its goal on earth in the universal rule of God in history. Israel constituted the first instalment of the work of God. Particularly in the Deuteronomic re-formation of the meaning of the Covenant, the progressive advancement of the goal of the divine purpose is the sound responsibility of Israel. For its task God has not only made Israel an elect community but equipped it with the Law. In the proper utilisation of this resource Israel will not only insure its own survival and prosperity, as Dt. emphasises, but contribute to the realisation of the promise to Abraham (Gen. 12:3), interpreted as the material transformation of history into the kingdom of God. This historical and evolutionary view of the divine purpose and its realisation was expressed in the so-called doctrine of rewards, which assume both that history is morally controlled and that the moral forms that insure its true direction are available to man. e

The sages presupposed this view of history and accepted the doctrine of rewards. Their work as scholars and teachers was really a quest for the true forms of the moral order. Books like Prov. and Sir. are optimistic in the sense that they believe these are discoverable and effective. Job and Ec. criticise this optimism and its assumption in a variety of ways. Both recognise that, to the human eye, the law of moral rewards is not vindicated in human affairs. And for both, since justice is not maintained in life, there arises the question whether history lacks moral substance or content. Even if the reality of the moral order is not denied outright, there is a growing awareness of the inscrutability of the ways of God and a despair about the availability of the forms by which men can achieve their true destiny. Koheleth (see §400*a*) seems to land in a cul-de-sac of rational scepticism; while avoiding a thorough-going nihilism, all values are relativised, history loses its meaning, and faith in the eschatological purpose of God is destroyed. In Job the crisis does not end in such scepticism, but in faith. The criticism of God and his ways is matched in its intensity by Job's cry for him. The flight from God alternates strongly with the yearning to meet him. The drama, accordingly, reaches its climax in the theophany (38–41). (The ' speeches of the Lord ', sometimes considered spurious, must very probably be considered an integral part of the drama.) In this confrontation by God the breakdown and surrender of Job is complete and final ; but it is accompanied by the generation of his faith in the adequacy of God. Henceforth Job is ready to trust God for the meaning and significance of his exercise of moral responsibility. Rather than attempt to assess the ' ways of God ' he is prepared to live and work as a faithful servant who simply confesses that the justice of God is as great as his power, but that both pass human comprehension. f

Job therefore marks the break of a calculable relationship between man's moral responsibility and action and the course of history itself. The crisis occasioned by ' the doctrine of rewards ' is surmounted in a recovery of the meaning of faith for life. Nevertheless, the accomplishment of the divine purpose in the form of an historical actuality remains an object of hope to be realised in time. Thus in a profound way Job serves as a charter for the Jewish eschatological outlook that has been remarkably consistent ever since. Whether the author intended it so or not, the figure g

6g of Job serves as a mirror for the career of Israel in both its literal history and its faith. In referring the meaning of man's service to God in faith Job leads toward the recovery of a theocentric point of view. Paradoxically, it both prepares the way for and represents an alternative to the NT affirmation that, for faith, the realisation of the purpose of God in history is no longer primarily a matter of steadfast hope, but of present actuality. The affirmation of the historicity of revelation, by-passed in wisdom, is not recovered in Job as it is in the NT. While, in so far as its genetic antecedents are concerned, the NT eschatology owes a great deal to Jewish apocalypticism and, in terms of some of its characteristic forms, to such Hellenistic notions of the immortality of the soul as one encounters in Wis., the recovery of faith in Job contributes to it most of all.

7a **The Literature**—Considering the limitations of space, it is not possible to present a detailed analysis of each of the wisdom books. Moreover, fuller treatments of some of them can be found elsewhere in this commentary. Here we shall attempt to note some features about each item that seem of particular significance in a consideration of its role in the wisdom movement as a whole and the place it occupies in the entire corpus of this literature.

b **Proverbs**—The core of Prov. consists of collections of sentences of wisdom produced by the professional sages (chs. 10–22:16, 25–9). These ' proverbs ' consist of couplets in which the lines stand in parallel relation to each other. This represents the primary literary form of wisdom and, as such, is of great value in the literary analysis of the more complex and mixed products of later writings in the wisdom tradition. These basic collections were prepared by combining earlier collections (25:1) and, probably, by drawing on current oral resources. While the product of several centuries of activity, in all likelihood beginning with Solomon, the sentences are remarkably consistent both in form and spirit. They assume that man lives in a world that has been created by God and that constitutes a moral order. It is believed that by diligent search and self-discipline man can obtain a knowledge of his world and a character that will enable him to realise his true destiny. Wisdom as man's understanding is the source and means of ' life '.

In addition to the main collections, Prov. contains several other sections. Among these the ' thirty chapters ' (22:17–24:22) is modelled on and in part utilises The Wisdom of Amen-em-opet. As such it is of great significance in the study of the relation between Israel's wisdom and that of other peoples. By far the most important supplementary section, however, is in chs. 1–9. It treats wisdom not only as a human achievement but as a universal reality, the work of God that precedes his creation of the world. This divine Wisdom is presented as a person who calls men and seeks to help them in their search for knowledge and as such constitutes a type of divine activity in behalf of men. This personal divine Wisdom must probably be considered a personification rather than an ontological reality in Prov., though there is no complete unanimity on the question. However, it marks the beginning of a development which is of immense importance for the historical understanding both of NT Christology and of Gnosticism. The individual-universal focus of the wisdom movement is illustrated by the fact that the divine action in Wisdom is unrelated to the historical faith of Israel, or to its forms.

c **Job**—The crucial significance of Job for our understanding of the role of the wisdom movement in the development of OT eschatology has been dealt with above. In the ' speeches of the Lord ' (38–41) the book breaks with the ' doctrine of rewards ' as presupposed in Prov. and deepens Israel's understanding of its affirmation of the moral order of existence.

The prose preface and conclusion of the book is usually considered older than the poem itself and seems to reflect the pre-critical notions about human virtue and reward that are under attack in the dialogue. 337c
The story, with its references to ' the land of Uz ' and ' the sons of the east ', seems to reflect the reputation for wisdom enjoyed by Edom and the nomadic regions beyond. In the LXX, which designates Job as king of Edom, the additions to 42:17 seem consciously to elaborate this connection.

The dialogue reveals the spiritual crisis which represents the main issue of the book. The speeches of Job challenge the conventional views about the relation between virtue and reward defended by the friends. But equally distinctive is their quality of immediacy and personal involvement in the questions at stake, so that the dialogue is something much more than a theoretical discussion of theodicy or of the meaning of suffering ; almost inadvertently it lays bare the whole human situation. In both the speeches of Job and the Lord the didactic gives way to the confessional mood. In terms of objective logic it can be shown that the latter represents no rational solution for the problem of the dialogue, a fact which has contributed much to whatever doubts about its authenticity have been raised. But the profundity of the ' answer ' seems to consist precisely in the fact that it goes beyond logic in transforming the ' problem ' as such.

With respect to literary form Job exhibits little evidence of the primary *māshāl* of Prov. The dialogue style appears elsewhere in wisdom, as, for example, in the Egyptian *Dispute over Suicide* (ANET, 405) or the Babylonian fables and the *Dialogue about Human Misery* (ANET, 438ff.). L. Köhler thinks the form is derived from judicial speech, while Bentzen speaks of it as a dramatised form of the psalm of lament. Actually there are other cult-related forms beside the lament embedded in the poem : the hymn, the confession, the oath, and the theophany. This need not mean that the book came out of the cult, as has been suggested. More probably Job shows a pioneer effort, and a very able one, on the part of a thinker and poet in the wisdom movement to adopt cultic literary forms for his own purpose. This became a very common tendency in the wisdom movement, as both the wisdom psalms and Sir. show, and was the manner by which it permeated Judaism as a whole. The distinctive thing in Job is the imagination and artistic skill with which the adaptation proceeds.

Ecclesiastes—In Ec. the issue is fundamentally the d
same as it was in Job ; i.e. it is impossible to document the moral authority of God by an empirical examination of what happens in history. Whereas Job questions the availability of the moral norm Koheleth seems to be sceptical about the action of God itself. He remains a rationalist and a sceptic ; while strict logic should perhaps have driven him to nihilism, he seems to end up as an agnostic relativist. The book comes from a later era than Job, probably as late as the 3rd cent. The traces of Greek influence, once taken very seriously, must probably be discounted. Traces of the same mood are not infrequent in either Egypt or Babylonia. Yet, as in the case of Job, it seems plausible to locate the real basis for the work in the inner dynamics of Israel's own wisdom movement, making all outside influences peripheral.

While secondary elements are minimal, the book is a collection of separate sayings or units rather than a continuous narrative. Some of these units, especially in chs. 7, 9, 10, seem to consist of a quotation of a couplet from Prov. plus a critical commentary on it. These unrelated instances of critical reaction can remind us that the author's view of life remains largely implicit and lacks a systematic structure.

Ecclesiasticus—The Wisdom of Jesus the Son of e
Sirach, which is the other title of this book, was probably written at the very beginning of the 2nd cent. Its basic literary form is similar to Prov., though, as in some of the younger portions of that book, the simple couplet tends to expand to the proportion of a paragraph. Further, as in Job, forms originally at home in

337e the cultus are adopted for literary service. Notable among these are the hymn and prayer (39:12ff., 42:15ff., 51:1ff.). Prayers are conspicuously lacking in the early stages of the wisdom movement and their incorporation contributes especially to the breakdown of the separation between wisdom and psalmody. In its general outlook and spirit Sir. is also comparable to Prov. The crisis documented in Job and Ec. has hardly touched its author, who seems to feel that God's reward of virtue is a matter capable of historical demonstration. As already noted, the natural heritage is singled out as a special resource for wisdom though the basic notions of revelation and faith that inform it are not fully understood. The treatment of Israel's great leaders as ' heroes ', in striking contrast to the absence of the heroic element in the OT, illustrates a continuing anthropocentric tendency.

f **The Wisdom of Solomon**—This book was probably written in the Jewish colony in Egypt and contains many Hellenistic influences. In the wisdom movement it constitutes a resolution of the issues left open by the sceptical criticism of Ec. Chs. 2 and 3 are virtually a direct refutation of that book ; and this is accomplished by means of an appeal to the belief in the immortality of the soul, a novel feature in Judaism and obviously imported from the Greeks. Another novelty is the equation of wisdom with the universal spirit that is ' the breath of the power of God ' (7:25) that permeates all things. The second half of the book reviews all biblical history as the story of the guidance and protection of this universal wisdom-spirit of which Israel was the special beneficiary. This preoccupation with Israel's history in its latter half has often raised questions about the unity of the book. It must be noted, however, that the review is essentially for the sake of illustrating the meaning and role of wisdom as defined at the beginning. Furthermore a similar recital of history occurs in some non-cultic psalms which may emanate from wisdom circles, notably the didactic Ps. 78, designated as a *māshāl*, and also the
poems of praise in Ps. 105 and 106. The latter of **33**
these particularly carries a strong undertone of admonition.

Wider Influences—We have already seen that in its **33**
forms and themes the influence of the wisdom movement is discernible in the Psalter. Mowinckel, who calls the sages the last collectors of psalms, a point well illustrated by the character of Ps. 1, thinks all non-cultic psalms reflect some wisdom influences. Just as a wisdom book like Sir. copied the hymn and prayer forms of the Psalter, the latter learns to incorporate couplets of wisdom (cf. Ps. 31:23 (Heb. 24),
34:5ff., 37). Others, among them Ps. 1, 49, 78, 127, **b**
exhibit much of the vocabulary of wisdom. Similar influences are present also in the Psalms of Solomon. Further, the apocryphal book of Bar., which Ringgren has described as a liturgy for a day of repentance, incorporates a poem (3:9–4:4) that equates wisdom and the Law. Finally, the rabbis of the Talmud are also called sages or *ḥ^{a}khāmîm* and in both its spirit and style preserve something of the wisdom sentence, while in the NT the divine Wisdom becomes a facet of Christology and in the parables of Jesus the *māshāl* continues its very ancient role as an authority-bearing word (cf. Mt. 7:29).

Bibliography—W. Baumgartner, *Israelitische und altorientalische Weisheit* (1933), 'The Wisdom Literature', OTMS, 210–37 ; H. Duesberg, *Les scribes inspirées*, 2 vols. (1938–9) ; J. Fichtner, *Die altorientalische Weisheit* . . . (1933) ; A. H. Godbey, ' The Hebrew Māšāl ', AJSL 39 (1922–3) ; P. Humbert, *Recherches sur les sources égyptiennes de la littérature sapientiale d'Israël* (1928) ; O. S. Rankin, *Israel's Wisdom Literature* . . . (1936) ; H. Ringgren, *Word and Wisdom* (1947) ; J. C. Rylaarsdam, *Revelation in Jewish Wisdom Literature* (1946) ; VT, Suppl. III—the entire volume is important, but for this study two articles merit special attention : A. R. Johnson, ' Māshāl ', 162ff., and S. Mowinckel, ' Psalms and Wisdom ', 205ff.

JOB

By W. A. IRWIN

339a Of the greatness of the Book of Job it is unnecessary to speak at length. Every informed person recognises that it is one of the classics of our heritage. Its phrases and couplets have become familiar as everyday sayings : ' the eyelids of the dawn ', ' the morning stars sang together and all the sons of God shouted for joy ' ; ' days swifter than a weaver's shuttle and spent without hope ', and very many of similar effectiveness. The literary skill of its authors, their deep feeling of the essential poetry of nature, animate and inanimate, the glory of the heavens above, the mystery of the cycling seasons, the might of crocodile and hippopotamus, the impatient energy of the war-horse, the vignettes of ancient life, the deep understanding of human motivation—its wisdom and its foolishness—and most of all the exaltation and universal appeal of their theme and the profound insights which one at least of them brings to it : all these and much else combined in one brief document from the ancient world suffice to establish it as one of the high achievements of the human spirit.

b The content of that theme, it is usual to explain, is the problem of suffering : why do the righteous endure so much of frustration and pain, while in a world allegedly ruled by a God of right, the wicked not infrequently ' have more than heart can wish ' : more simply, ethics and welfare commonly go diverse ways that cross if at all only incidentally. The book would then be a theodicy, a defence of the ways of God to man. Again it is said that the Prologue concentrates on the questions of disinterested goodness, and some feel that the issue persists further. All this is doubtless true, within its proper limits. Certainly Job's friends berate him for his wickedness, real or imputed. Yet the point is scarcely worth pursuing ; for the concern of the great author of the Dialogue, at least, is deeper and wider. We understand it only if we recognise that its theme is not ethical good and evil in relation to human recompense, but rather the total of human pain and woe. Why is it that we must all endure loss and pain, frustration and despair, and finally leering through our happiest moments is the grim spectre that soon or late will overtake us, every one :

> ' Come he slow or come he fast,
> It is but death that comes at last.'

The book thus takes its place alongside the Greek tragedies (cf. D. B. MacDonald, ' The Original Form of the Legend of Job ', JBL 14 (1895), 66)—it is the tragedy innate in life of which it speaks—and it holds an honoured place in the succession of similar literature all the way to Hardy and Dostoievsky and Eugene O'Neill. It is not irrelevant to note that long before Aeschylus—or our Book of Job, whichever was earlier—the problem had engaged the best thought of evolving human speculation ; it was the theme of *The Songs of the Harper*, of *The Dialogue With One's Own Soul*, in ancient Egypt ; and of *Adapa*, and of *Gilgamesh*, not to speak of the commonly cited theodicies of early Babylonia (cf. Steinmann, *Le livre de Job*). Great as these authors were, profound as has been the thought devoted to the problem through these forty centuries, it will become apparent, it is hoped, that the poet-thinker to whom we are indebted for the Book of 339b Job penetrated deeper and rose higher than any other.

c The locale of the story as given in the Prologue has raised questions whether the book is really Hebrew in its origin. This doubt has been enhanced by consideration of the language it employs. Its Hebrew has many unique words, considerable Aramaic influence, and not a little Arabic. Consequently suggestions have been offered that the book was originally written in Arabic, or in Edomite, and translated into Hebrew. That would, however, be very strange : that the most profound intellectual book of the OT, one too that is saturated with exalted concepts of the transcendence and righteousness of God, was written by someone in regions which, at the time in which we must place the book, had attained only a meagre culture, if indeed they were not still in essential barbarism ! In all the ancient East there was but one people that could by any reasonable possibility have produced such an author ; and that people was Israel (but see Pfeiffer, ' Edomite Wisdom ', ZATW 44 (1926), 13–24). It is best to understand the peculiarities of the book's language, not as translation Hebrew, or the tongue of a related people, but rather as a Hebrew dialect different from that of Jerusalem, which was standard for most of our OT.

d A date is difficult to assign. There are no historical allusions on which to hang it ; 15:19 has been cited for this purpose, but clearly without basis. The same is to be said of the invocation of Job's patriarchal life. We have no evidence other than the level of religious thinking ; and this is always a tenuous clue. Still it is probably safe to say that the book could have been written only after Judaism attained somewhat mature stature, that is some time after the exile. If we say approximately the 4th cent. B.C. we shall probably not be far wrong. And in that vagueness the matter must rest.

e More than in any other book of the OT an understanding of Job is dependent upon its analysis. The book falls into five distinct parts : (*a*) the Prologue, chs. 1–2 ; (*b*) the Dialogue, 3–31 ; (*c*) the Speeches of Elihu, 32–7 ; (*d*) the Speeches of Yahweh (with Job's brief rejoinders), 38–42:6 ; and (*e*) the Epilogue, 42:7–17. The first and the last of these are mainly in prose, the others mainly in poetry. These facts are obvious ; but the interrelations of the parts are a matter of opinion : scholarly, well-considered and keenly debated opinion, but still opinion. It is almost universally agreed that (*c*) is not the work of the original author. Rather less, but still very high, is an agreement to deny the Epilogue to the original author. Much less unanimity attaches to denial of the Prologue, but such is the course taken in this discussion. Scholars are somewhat evenly divided in regard to the Yahweh speeches. Some reject 40–42:7 and find the original conclusion of the discussion in Yahweh's first speech (in whole or in part) ; a few reject the section as a whole. Again this latter is the course followed here, arguments for which and for similar deletions will be given in discussion of the several parts. This leaves the Dialogue as the original Book of Job. But here again

339e considerable paring must be done. Practically everyone recognises that ch. 28 is of secondary origin. The unusual character of chs. 24–6, the confusion of 27, and the disparate mood of 29–31 conduce to the view that the Dialogue proper comes to an inconclusive end in ch. 27 with tattered fragments of its original structure, and its original ending completely lost. In addition to this mutilation, the text of the Dialogue is poorly preserved in not a few places. Notably bad is ch. 17, all of which as far as the last three verses is practically unintelligible; but others have suffered likewise in considerable measure.

f No more than in the analysis of other biblical books does this mean that the rejected parts are negligible. On the contrary they all possess high interest and great worth. But the problem of the interpreter of the book is to discover, so far as possible, the quality and thought of the original author, that is, of the Dialogue, and in the light of this to investigate the contributions of the others. The task, challenging enough in its essence, is doubly difficult in the disordered and incomplete condition in which the great poem has come down to us. Interest in the literary forms in vogue through the ancient East has inevitably turned to the Book of Job, and here as elsewhere there have been identified types of lament, complaint, prayer, and the like, so familiar to students of Israel's literature (cf. Westermann, *Der Aufbau des Buches Hiob*; Fohrer, VT 7 (1957), 107–11). However, no engrossment in formal features may obscure the basic reality that the concern of the authors of the book far transcended limits and guides of rules for writing, which instead they used only as tools for their high purpose. The essential matter in a study of the Book of Job is the thought and its movement, therein presented; on this the real divisions of the book depend.

340a **I-II The Prologue**—It is widely recognised that these chapters preserve an ancient, popular story; and certainly the marks of folk-tale are abundant: the idyllic life of this wealthy sheikh and his family, the traditionally perfect numbers of his belongings and his family—seven, three, five—the use of supra-normal forces in development of the plot (the interference of the Satan), but most of all the reiterated episodes and repetition of identical phrases in relating them.

b There is little to indicate its origin or date. Parallels in Babylonian literature (and mention of Job in Ezek. 14:14, 20) indicate no more for our purpose than the prevalence through the ancient world of a tale of a righteous sufferer. This old story, then, as it circulated in Israel, was employed here as introducing the problem that engrosses the Dialogue. That it was not the composition of the author of the latter is shown by a number of considerations. Of some value, though admittedly slight as evidence, is the prevalence of the proper name Yahweh (the LORD) throughout the story, a name that occurs only once in the Dialogue and then in an apparently secondary insertion (12:9). A comparable comment relates to the Dialogue's ignoring essential features of the Prologue, such as the source of Job's misfortunes being in the Satan's interference. Determinative evidence, however, lies in the facts that the two sections treat diverse themes, and that the character of Job and his attitude to his sufferings is quite different in them, with no explanation given or development indicated, so that they are really contradictory. The Prologue investigates the question of disinterested piety, but the Dialogue, as mentioned, is concerned with human tragedy: the two are related but not intimately. The completely patient and ideally devout sufferer of the Prologue becomes in ch. 3, with no indication whatever of any reason for the change, a complaining invalid who already, before the friends sting him into acute realisation of his plight, resents the injustice of God's dealing with him (3:26). Against the enforced conclusion it may be urged that lacking the introduction we possess in the Prologue, the poem would be abrupt and its allusions meaningless. True, it would for *us*. But the tale was so well known in the ancient world 340b that the author could well presume on this familiarity, and begin with Job's complaint. It was as though with a wave of his hand he said to his audience, 'You know that story about suffering Job? Well, this is what Job really said'. (But see Kautzsch, *Das sogenannte Volksbuch von Hiob* (1900).)

I 1-5 The Idyllic and Exemplary Life of Job— c The name Job in its Hebrew form is apparently derived from the verb 'to be an enemy'. But speculation on this is futile; the name is so old that we cannot know what was its original connotation. It occurs as the name of one of the desert immigrants in the Beni Hassan relief of the 19th cent. B.C. The land of Uz is not well known. It is mentioned in only one other passage in OT (Jer. 25:20) in a list of countries that goes from Judah to Egypt, then Philistine territories, and Edom, Moab, Ammon, and so northward. This might imply a southern location, a view mildly supported by the fact that the personal name Uz is given as Edomite in Gen. 36:28 (=1 Chr. 1:42). But Uz is presented as a son of Aram also in Gen. 10:23, as a son of Shem in 1 Chr. 1:17, a son of Nahor in Gen. 22:21 where he is apparently also uncle of Aram. These relations, it is freely recognised, are really ethnic: the writers are telling that Uz was peopled by real or quasi Aramaeans. Hence we would naturally expect to find it in the north. **3** equates it, in some more or less indefinite way, with the habitat of the people of the East (better, the people of Kedem). These are mentioned eleven times in OT, and their land, or mountain, three times. Some of these occurrences shed no light on our problem, some indicate only that the land was not a great distance from Israel, and like Moab and Ammon bordered on Arabia. But Num. 23:11 implies, just as the cited references to Uz, that the region was Aramaean. Also Gen. 29:1 has Jacob arrive there on his journey northward to upper Mesopotamia, and Jer. 49:28 associates it with Hazor as having been ravaged by Nebuchadnezzar. All this harmonises with Egyptian evidence that Kedem was east of the Lebanons; the biblical evidence would be satisfied by the view that it was east of the southern Lebanons. **5.** We are not told Job's ritual of sanctifying his sons, but the term is frequent in the ritual legislation. Along with the burnt offerings here and in 42:8 this is all we have in the book relevant to the author's support of Jewish ritual. Mention of burnt offering instead of sin offering is to be noted, but not too much may be deduced from it. The verses succeed well in their objective of presenting Job as a meticulously proper and, doubtless, sincere, religious man.

6-22 The First Affliction of Job—With this picture d of the heavenly court cf. 1 Kg. 22:19–22. The sons of God are in no way to be confused with NT and Christian concepts of divine sonship; cf. instead Gen. 6:1–4. Israel believed in an order of semi-divine beings lower than God—not unlike later concepts of angels and archangels. It is notable that here the Satan is in good standing among these, his one fault is a liking for unpleasant questions; he is the adversary (RSV*n*), an attitude that later steadily deteriorated into the essence of all badness. He does not charge Job with hidden crimes, as do the friends later, but only suggests that his piety is self-centred. **15.** 'Sabeans', in Hebrew the same name as that of the country of the queen who made her famous visit to Solomon (1 Kg. 9), but apparently the author does not think of this kingdom but of nomadic Arabs. So, too, 'Chaldaeans', **17**, are not to be confused with the kingdom of Nebuchadnezzar (2 Kg. 24, etc.); they are rather the desert tribe from which the settled Chaldaeans of Babylonia came. It is tempting to relate these facts to the historic situation of the author, but this is precarious. **16.** 'The fire of God' is lightning. Note the cumulative force of the disasters, leaving Job not a moment to adjust himself to each. Even so, his piety was unshaken.

0d **20.** He performed the usual rites of mourning, but expressed only gratitude to God that he had so long enjoyed good things.

e **II 1-10 The Second Affliction of Job**—God's reference to Job's trial is appended in folk-tale fashion (see above) to a verbatim repetition of his former commendation of him. **4.** ' Skin for skin ', apparently a proverbial saying, is here expressive of the Satan's basic charge that Job's piety is one of calculated commercialism. He had, as it were, bartered his belongings and family for his life ; that would be the final test : touch himself. **6.** So the second affliction is permitted to include anything short of death. **7.** It is futile to seek to identify Job's disease. The Hebrews had meagre medical knowledge ; their names for diseases are sweeping generalities ; *sh^{e}ḥîn*, ' sores ', apparently denoted any skin eruption. **9-10.** A final bitterness was his wife's failure to understand that life must be of mixed quality ; LXX has a much longer rebuke by Job. D. B. MacDonald argued (op. cit. 63–71) that in the original folk-tale the friends came to commiserate Job, with expressions of indignation against God. (Cf., too, Buhl, *Zur Vorgeschichte des Buches Hiob*, and Cheyne, *Job and Solomon.*) It may be ; certainly their role in the Dialogue may not be regarded as original ; it is the creation of the great poet-author. **11.** ' Teman ' is mentioned several times as a famous district, or city, of Edom, and commonly is used as a poetic synonym for the entire land. The site, if actually a city, has not been identified with certainty. ' Eliphaz ' seems to have been a familiar Edomite name ; cf. Gen 36:15. ' Bildad ' is supposed to have come from Shuhu, a region on the middle Euphrates ; his name is perhaps a corruption of Bel-Hadad, the god Hadad is Baal. The land of ' Naamah ' is unknown ; the name means pleasant. The friends on their arrival performed rites of mourning ; however the folk-tale features of the account continue with the seven-day silence on the ground beside Job.

1a **III-V Job and Eliphaz**—The skill of the author is manifest in this introduction of his theme ; setting out to discuss one of the most profound problems that have perplexed human speculation, he begins—with a very sick man and his entirely natural complaints ! Job curses the day of his birth with an implication, becoming specific in 10, that he wishes he had never been born. But since it happened, then why could he not have died at birth and now be in the peace and rest of the underworld ? Why must people live and endure trouble ? For his suffering is persistent, and without reason ! The curse is reminiscent of Jer. 20:14–18 ; apparently the writer knew his Bible, or what was soon to become Bible ! In **4–9** the Hebrew is in some confusion, though not such as to obscure the thought. The irregular occurrence of tristich lines, the unintelligibility of the phrase at the end of 5, and the vacillating movement of thought from day to night all point toward additions and corruptions. God's not seeking the day, **4**, and its not being numbered among days or months, **6**, are poetic and exaggerated wishes for its non-existence. **8** alludes to an aspect of the magical concepts of the time, and as well to its mythology. The Leviathan concept was derived from Canaanite religious thought (cf. Pritchard, ANET (1955), 138). The name becomes a frequent term in OT for the monster whom God overcame at or before creation. The superb phrases in **9**, ' the stars of its dawn ' and ' the eyelids of the morning ' already reveal our author's literary resource and quicken further expectation. Better sense is secured by placing **16** between **12** and **13**. ' Who rebuilt ruins ', **14**, is an error ; the thought is rather of great men of the long past whose buildings at the time of the writer were ruins. So, too, the Egyptian *Songs of the Harper* (Pritchard, op. cit. 467), express the transience of all things human. The ' untimely birth ' was ' hidden ' doubtless through some sense of shame ; cf. Ec. 6:3, which seems to evidence a practice of hurriedly burying still-born children in the night. 341a
The quality of this great poem is perhaps indicated by the fact that the translation of **17** (AV) is taken over verbatim into the metre of Tennyson's *Maud.* The tenses of **26** in RSV are surely wrong. The first three Hebrew verbs are inconclusive, but the fourth carries the entire sequence into the past. Further, this is demanded by Eliphaz's rebuke of Job's ' vexation ', 5:2, which otherwise is a baseless charge. Surely the author did not so soon forget what he had said. Read, ' I was not at ease nor quiet ; I had no rest, but trouble came ', an allusion to the belief that the gods, or God, might be stirred to jealousy if a mere human were too happy. Two points in Job's speech it is important to note ; they become motifs on which the Dialogue develops. Job's wistful turning to death and the underworld for release seems but a sick man's gloom. And so the author doubtless intended, but also he meant to use it in a way that will presently become significant. It is easier to recognise the development, under the sting of the friends' comments, of Job's arraignment of the divine government of the world ; this is a famous feature of the poem. The former was no more unique than this latter ; it had been voiced both in the *Songs of the Harper* and in the Babylonian *Dialogue with a Servant* (Pritchard, op. cit., 437–8, 467).

In view of the dignity accorded to age in the Orient, b
it is probable the writer presents Eliphaz as the eldest of the friends. He speaks with consideration, dignity, and authority, and as we shall see, with some claim of scholarship (5:27). He begins in strict courtesy, if the text in **4:2** is correct, but LXX has him strike hard at the very first. In any case, his courtesy, if actual, immediately degenerates into innuendo. Is he praising or condemning Job in **5**? Does he encourage him in **7**, or insinuate that he is now seen to be less than innocent ? The overtone of **6** is lost in translation, for the word rendered ' confidence ' also means stupidity with more than a dash of culpability. (Cf. Fullerton, ' Double Entendre in the First Speech of Eliphaz ', JBL 48 (1929), 320–74) Even such poor cloak for his charges is dropped in **8ff.**, for it is apparent that Job is the cultivator of evil, and the lion whose teeth are smashed. Allusion to the death of Job's family as the scattering of whelps, **11**, is a callous brutality. It is odd to have Eliphaz enforce his position with a ghost story, **12-17**. In quite modern mood, the grisly apparition made his hair stand on end ! Yet the ghostly revelation wears thin ; any ignorant person of the street might also have told that mortal man cannot be pure by divine standards. But that is scarcely the point. Eliphaz still indulges in innuendo: he implies that Job had paraded himself as of more than God-like righteousness ; how absurd, for man is weak and transient ! **4:21.** ' Wisdom ' means more than the modern word ; here we might paraphrase, man dies without ever approximating an understanding of the mystery of his being. The sequence of thought is from **4:21** to **5:2** ; we are to see other evidence that some person, or persons, with marked poetic skill, added one or more lines to the original poem.

Still short of the blunt charges which later in the c
discussion he is to hurl against Job, Eliphaz makes clear his meaning that Job has been guilty of ' vexation ' ; the allusion is to Job's querulous outburst against the divine government in 3:26. In this he puts himself in the class with senseless and depraved fools, whose undoing Eliphaz has witnessed, **5:3-5.** The text is dubious in **3** and **5** ; ' I cursed ' is surely wrong ; the point is not Eliphaz's share in their undoing, but rather that there is a moral order in the universe. Probably read ' Suddenly his dwelling rotted away '. **5b** is even more nonsensical in Heb. than in English ; the stich is a marginal comment or a corruption, perhaps both ; ignore it. **6** continues the line of thought : over against the ' vexation ' felt by ' fools ' in the presence of loss, there is a rational

341c explanation for it. But this explanation is blurred, and is inherently contradictory in the present text and translation of **7** ; with slight change of vowels only, read, ' But man begets trouble '. So Eliphaz argues, trouble is not in the nature of things, **6**, but man creates it himself—a profound insight into a partial answer which, however, Eliphaz wants accepted as final. **7b** says literally ' and the sons of Resheph fly high '. Resheph was a Canaanite god of pestilence, hence the name became a common noun for something burning (like fever). RSV *may* be correct, but the truth is we do not know just what the line means. But Eliphaz is a practical religious man. He has shown, so he believes, that Job erred in his refusal to accept humbly his proper role as a frail and transient mortal, and so has brought trouble on himself ; now what is he to do about it ? Repent and abase himself before the might, **9-11**, and wisdom, **12-14**, of transcendent God ! The catalogue of divine attributes is almost certainly expanded ; then too the translation of **15a** is based—probably correctly—on emendation of a corrupt text. **17-26** portray the good fortune of the accepted penitent—again probably with some additions to the original. And Eliphaz rounds out his oration with an effort at authentication : he and his friends have arrived at these views by careful study : as ' wise men ' they have ' searched ' it ; Job should give attention.

d Of the exaltation and general soundness of this theology there can be not a doubt. Yet the author clearly holds it up for criticism. One might comment that from such lofty levels of religious thought he sets out in search of richer truth. The friends are the voice of the orthodoxy of the day ; Job speaks the mind of the author ; and it will become clear in the sequel, he can be scathing toward this current thinking. Here, he treats it with mild ridicule ; he makes its exponent a pompous platitudinarian, uttering with pious unction commonly accepted trivialities, or at best sweeping generalisations which betray their superficiality in their failure to come to grips with actual facts. Yet it will appear that his real objection to Eliphaz's position lies in its almost Calvinistic or Islamic stress on the transcendence of God. The entire emphasis is that God is exalted, and man is a mean creature. Job affirms, and is to reiterate, that however mean may be man's estate, at least he has cosmic rights that not even God may with impunity transgress. Little wonder Eliphaz recognised this, even in its incipience, to be ' vexation '. Our concern will be to see how far the poet succeeds in integrating this into a real faith in the goodness of God.

342a **VI-VIII Job and Bildad**—Job admits the charge of ' vexation ' but claims there is extenuation ; even the wild ass brays when it is uncomfortable, and tasteless things occasion revulsion. Reverting to his obsession with the underworld, he wishes that God would grant him a violent death ; that would be an occasion of joy. **6:10c** is a gloss that confuses the thought, which is purely of Job's eagerness to end his sufferings. Still, his mind runs on, **11-13**, to a touch of self-pity and a suggestion of further ' vexation ', which becomes explicit in ch. 7.

b **14ff.** He addresses the friends in a touching expression of disappointment ; they have been reminiscent of the too familiar tragedy hidden in the all-encompassing desert. Their ' kindness ' is like an intermittent desert stream—dry when most needed, a source of death for those who trust it. **18** is to be transferred to follow **20** ; the expectant caravans, in anxious consternation, turn their course toward the next pool or stream, but perish in the blighting heat before they can reach it.

While deeply hurt by his friends' unwarranted desertion, **22-3**, Job is still irenic and tractable ; the mood of **24-30** leaves no recourse but to adjudge **27** an intrusion by someone who did not understand the movement of thought. **25-6** are difficult, but a clue to their meaning is provided by the fact that ' forceful ' is a completely unsupported meaning of the Hebrew word which rather is consistently in the area of 34
difficulty or sickness. Translate :

' Why did honest words displease,
  and how should one accept reproof from you ?
Did you suppose that you were reproving mere
  words,
and that the utterance of a desperate man was
  only wind ? '

28-30 are also difficult, in particular the force of the verb translated ' turn ' ; probably it has here instead its frequent adverbial force, and means only ' again '. Job implores their gracious attention, for he is honest. ' Once again (attend) ', he says, ' take no offence. Once again, please, for only so can I be cleared of these charges. Has my utterance offended you ? Has it lacked sufficient reason in the deep suffering I endure ? '

VII. The skill of the writer is to be recognised once c
more in his universalising of Job's suffering, **1-2**. The thought advances, not by logical process but through deep emotion. Job is cut to the quick by the friends' desertion and callous misunderstanding. Stung by the strictures of Eliphaz, he realises that he shares in universal human tragedy. This development is of the essence of the poem ; Job's thinking is in constant movement, away from the naïve theology with which he had begun, not essentially different from that of the friends. Here we set out on the real pilgrimage of Job's thought and religious quest. (For a different view, cf. Kraeling, *The Book of the Ways of God* (1938), and Baumgärtel, *Der Hiobdialog* (1933), who hold that this changed mood is evidence of secondary origin.) Still the universal is explicit in the particular. Job is in complete despair. Who has not endured black periods that seemed best voiced in the words of **6** ? The sketch of his illness brings Job easily to his obsession with death and Sheol, **7-10**, here serving, however, to crystallise his questioning into resentment : man is so frail and transient, specifically Job himself is physically so much less than the forces of Nature, why does God in his might afflict him ? It is almost as if he charges a grim divine sport in watching human pain. But death will bring relief, and escape from the almighty tormentor. **14** appears to be an allusion to Eliphaz's ghost story (4:12–17) and would lead to a supposition that the resentment here expressed is against the friends. But use of the singular pronoun (in the Hebrew) indicates the object is God, who, perhaps we may say, is charged with ultimate responsibility for the grisly apparition. In **17-18**, in words reminiscent of, and perhaps actually suggested by Ps. 8:4, Job voices a thought the reverse of the psalmist's ; God's daily concern with man is for the sake of persecuting him. There is a serious problem in the seeming admission of sin in **20**. There is no conditional particle in the original ; its use is merely the translator's effort to escape the dilemma of the Hebrew which says flatly, ' I have sinned '. Another and more probable course is to regard this entire line (to ' watcher of men ') as an intrusion. ' Burden ' in **20c** may be right, though we expect rather something like ' target ', to parallel **20b**.

Thus in his second speech Job has clarified the issue that is to engage our thought through the remainder of the Dialogue : if God is so mighty, then why man's miserable estate ? And in the process of clarification, he has thrown down his challenge to orthodox dogma. The friends take it up ; the argument has begun.

VIII. Indeed, Bildad, less facile than the first speaker, d
blunderingly injects the note of personal animosity that is to become steadily more prominent through further exchanges. Taking his suggestion from Job's pained questioning, 6:26, he avers that merely to imply less than justice on the part of God is the essence of windy talk. Completely devoid of the restraint of finer feeling he charges boldly that the reason for all Job's

2d trouble lies in the sin of his children, as yet barely cold in their graves ; God gave them what they richly deserved ! How brutal can be the *odium theologicum* ! But if Job himself will seek God—and now we are ready for a résumé of Eliphaz's ponderous platitudes—he will emerge from this time of suffering greater than before—in what way greater he does not specify. True, this is conditioned on Job's being ' pure and upright ', but 20-1 imply that he so adjudged Job.

e Eliphaz had sought authentication in special revelation, Bildad turns to the authority of ancient sages, quoting, it is clear, from some collection of proverbs since lost. (For the vogue of such teaching from the nature of plants, cf. 1 Kg. 4:33.) It is not certain how far the quotation extends ; probably, however, only through **11-12** ; the rest being Bildad's application. Interpretation of the passage is clear down to **13** ; but **14-18** contain serious corruptions, such that the total sense is lost. It is apparent that **13** concludes the account of the fate of the ' godless ' ; if, as our present text reads, **14-18** continue this theme, then **20-2** are not at all a logical conclusion of Bildad's argument, as we expect, but an abrupt introduction of a different theme. Further, the character of **14**, and its smooth rendering of a word that does not exist in Hebrew, the absurdity of **15**, the lack of sequence into **16-17**—strange to have this ' godless ' one thriving under the sun and sending out roots—and the pure nonsense of **19a** all combine to show inescapably that we must look below the surface if we are to understand what Bildad was urging. (See ' The First Speech of Bildad ', ZATW 51 (1933), 205–16) It is hopeless to attempt a full restoration of the text, but enough becomes apparent on careful study to give us the line of thought. **14** is not a relative clause describing the ' godless ', as the Hebrew makes it (obscured in RSV) ; instead the relative particle is evidently a corruption, as LXX, Vulg. indicate, of the word for ' upright '. Here is our indispensable clue. **12-13** told of the nemesis of the wicked, symbolised in a swamp plant, growing with every advantage of heat and water ; **14** introduces the contrast : it is something about the ' upright '. And **16** shows that the figure of a plant is continued, the upright is like some other sort of plant which **17** indicates to be some hardy growth of the desert, that remains green under the blighting sun and with little sustenance but stones. It is subject, too, to violence, **18a**, probably the teeth of a grazing camel. We can afford to ignore the corrupt **18b**, unless we wish to conjecture that it said, ' Is cut off without a trace '. The pure nonsense of **19a** is dissolved by recognising one word—and we can be even approximately confident of no more—the character of the Hebrew word and the parallelism of **19b** indicate that joy stands for an original ' from the (or ' his ') root '. Then all becomes obvious. Bildad says that the upright, in contrast to the ' godless ' with their apparent advantages, are like the desert plants, which endure every hardship, even to apparently complete destruction. But they can't be killed ; they grow again from the root ! **20-2** are a true summary ; they give a specific statement of the contrast of ' blameless ' and ' evildoers ' with which the speech has concerned itself. The friends are much less naïve in their theory of reward and retribution than is commonly supposed. They recognise that innocent and wicked alike suffer ; the difference comes in the sequel. The author of the Dialogue was not shadow-boxing or feinting. He meant to treat his opponents with complete fairness, even generosity, and then defeat them on their own ground.

43a **IX-XI Job and Zophar**—Job is still in tractable mood ; he admits Bildad's contention, but points out that it is all aside from the issue. As though harking back to Eliphaz's emphasis, the question for him is how a mere mortal can be right (RSV, ' just ') with God ; the word, commonly rendered ' righteous ', is forensic ; how can one establish his ' rightness' with God ? Indeed the forensic phraseology continues, for ' contend ' is the term for legal procedure : in such cosmic court of law, God is unanswerable. 343a

b **IX 3.** ' Once in a thousand times ', literally ' one out of a thousand ', is probably a proverbial or current phrase ; cf. 33:23. As though to emphasise his agreement with Bildad's theology, Job outdoes him in portrayal of the divine transcendence. It is again probable that the catalogue is amplified by some devout Jew who found here a congenial opening ; but such additions, if actual, do not alter the thought. **9.** The ' Bear ', ' Orion ' and the ' Pleiades ', cf. 38:32, are not literal translations, but our western equivalents ; the probable meanings are the Lion, the Fool, and the Fat One—in any case they indicate that the Hebrews, not less than the Greeks on whom we are dependent, had their astral mythology. **11b.** ' Moves on ' represents a word, *ḥālaph*, used often in the dialogue with its connotation not entirely clear. ' Rahab ', **13b**, is a frequent OT name for the primeval monster overthrown at creation, like Tiamat in the Babylonian epic ; her ' helpers ' were her fellow-monsters in the fight. How small man's might in presence of a God who triumphed over such mythological beings ! **15.** ' Innocent ' should be ' in the right ', the same word as in *2b*. **16** is badly confused through neglect of the Hebrew tenses, which are a perfect, followed by its equivalent, and by two imperfects ; translate, ' Although I called and he answered me (i.e. in Job's happier days), I do not believe that (now) he will listen to my voice '. **17.** Even God has betrayed him, has unjustly persecuted him, yet **19b**, he cannot be summoned for examination. In **20a** it is probable that ' my mouth ' is merely the well-recognised usage of the relative part of the organism standing for the entire personality (e.g. Ps. 27:8, ' my voice I cry '), hence probably, ' Though I am in the right, he will hold me guilty ; though I am blameless, he will put me in the wrong '. **21** is difficult, perhaps corrupt ; ' I am blameless ' may be wrongly repeated from **20** ; ' regard not ' is literally ' do not know ', and perhaps this is the meaning : he is so disfigured by disease that he cannot recognise himself. In any case, the thought of **20-4** is a clear indictment of the callous amorality of the divine government of the world. With **25-6** cf. 7:6. **26** is one more example of the poet's vivid use of common incidents and objects. **29** is almost certainly intruded ; it does not speak of future condemnation, but of present guilt, which Job consistently denies. Further the thought moves smoothly from 28 to 30, the hopelessness of escape from the divine tormentor. Now naturally, then, the figure of the ' umpire ', **33**, enters the discussion, a mysterious figure upon whom much of the developing thought of the Dialogue is to depend. But true to his method, the poet here barely introduces him : the sick Job is too distraught to hold long to any one idea except his suffering and his desire for release. But the thought will come up again, and with each return something further and greater will be added.

In **35b** and **10:1a** the text is confused ; but the movement of thought is clear : if God would only give Job some respite, he would utter freely his charges. c **10:2-3.** He actually goes on to this : why should God take pleasure, as it seems, in tormenting his own creature ? **4-7.** He ought to be at least as moral as man ; will he not remember his status as creator ? And in this mood and vein of thinking, Job's tortured mind runs on freely to an amazing admission. How naturally the poet brings him to it ! God made him by biological processes—the ancient shape of the concept is quaint—and so brought to completion, what ? It is almost incredible to find the complaining Job admitting life's good things, **12.** The author has tricked him into it—no, rather, with his keen understanding of the human mind, he lets Job babble on until he must have checked himself, in astonishment, asking, What is this I have said ? For this allegedly

343c persecuting God has surrounded Job constantly with love and care! The poet does not deny—he does not at any time deny the reality of Job's suffering, but here he has him admit this is not the whole of life's story. It would not be false to his thought to say that the pessimist who flatters himself on his honest realism, is just as false as the starry-eyed optimist; life consists of neither good nor bad, but an amazing mixture of both. Any true appraisal, and any sound approach to its problem demands full recognition of each. **12** and **13** belong together; the 'things' are the kindness and love of **12**. 'Yet' should be deleted; the Hebrew is merely 'and'.

d In this astonishingly realistic way the author has brought Job to the crisis of his dilemma, and an insight which is to prove determinative in his spiritual pilgrimage. Precisely here the direction of the Dialogue changes its course. However, the poet understands too much to perpetrate the error of a sudden transformation in Job; the sufferer has caught one hasty glimpse of truth; it will bring about great things, but he is still sick in body and mind, and cannot withstand his obsession. The speech concludes with the now familiar thoughts of the divine persecutor, Job's longing for death, and the inevitability of the underworld. Of this latter no significant use is made here, but its interweaving through Job's thought is to be noted. Something will come of it presently. The text is confused in **15-17**, though doubtless the movement of thought is accurately preserved. **22** is in worse condition than its deceptively smooth rendering might indicate; the words rendered 'chaos' mean 'no order'. So the underworld is a place where laws of nature are lacking, and one can depend on nothing at all! **21** has also hidden relevance; its words contain clear allusion to the famous phrase 'the land of no-return', found in the Babylonian poem of 'Ishtar's Descent into the Underworld' (Pritchard, op. cit. 106–9). Our poet, then, like every great writer, was conversant with the literature of his time.

e **XI**. With Zophar's speech we are introduced to the last of the friends. It is of interest that, in this first cycle of speeches at least, they are not pale puppets, but possess vivid personality. Eliphaz is polite and deferential, but brutal in his pompous orthodoxy; Bildad is brusque and outspoken, but essentially kindly. On the other hand, Zophar is hot-headed, loses his temper, and converts the argument into the wrangle that it continues to the end. Eliphaz stressed the transcendence of God; also he is mildly mystical; his authority is in supernatural revelation, which then he examines in the light of human experience. But Bildad relies on the accumulated wisdom of the past and bolsters his argument with quotation from it. Zophar is a rationalist; he depends on human reason. It is a devout reason, however, at best a learning of the wisdom of God. **6**. He is impressed with the divine 'secrets of wisdom' and their 'practical expression' (not 'understanding'). **7-9**. There are 'deep things of God'; the Almighty is beyond man's intellectual grasp. **11-12**. 'Worthless men' and 'stupid man' merit only contempt. **12**. There is as much hope for their intelligence as for a wild ass to be born human. The divine wisdom, so inaccessible for man, is available through revelation, **5-6**. Still, apparently, this is a rational universe, and must be understood rationally. Job's error has been his superficiality; he has 'been full of talk' and uttered 'babble'. **13**. So then, he should 'set his heart aright', and make submission to God; the result will be, as the others had stated, security and well-being beyond his dreams.

The alleged quotation from Job's words, **11:4**, is at best no more than a garbled version of his defence (cf. too 33:9). **11b** is a famous difficulty, with numerous solutions proposed. Recourse to interrogative mood, as RSV, is highly dubious. Rather we should probably, with Gersonides, take the last words as a relative clause, and translate, 'He sees the man of iniquity, who will not consider' (Lassen, *The Commentary of Levi ben Gerson* (1946), *ad loc.*). RSV's 34
rendering of **20c** is to be regarded with great caution; the passage does not at all refer to Job's desire for death, but probably says rather, 'Their hope is an expiring breath'.

Since the Dialogue began with a speech by Job, it f
is best to consider that with Zophar's the first cycle comes to an end, a view that is supported by the change which the discussion undergoes as it moves into chapters 12–14 and the sequel. The first cycle is important for its presentation of the orthodox position in the varying facets of the friends' speeches; in the sequel they have nothing of significance to add. It is a worthy and exalted interpretation of religious faith that they give us, although the poet is clearly holding it up for criticism and as a foil for the presentation of his own deeper insights. The inadequacy of Eliphaz's notable survey of religious faith we have already noted. Bildad and Zophar fall foul of the same strictures, but in addition it is evident that the writer wants us to recognise that all three alike have been strict traditionalists, debarred by their piety from looking with open eyes at what they profess. We shall soon see that he makes this charge specific.

The major significance of the cycle, however, has been the movement of Job's thought. Beginning in essential agreement with orthodox theology, he has been driven by the wrong thinking of the friends and by the relentless logic of facts to realise the universality of human woe, its seeming meaninglessness, and hence the indifference if not immorality of a transcendent God. His indignation leads him to wish for a personal encounter with his great adversary, whom he might confront with human standards of right and wrong. But alas, there is no umpire to stand between the two! Then, giving vent to his pain, he stumbles soon on a profound insight: that in addition to its suffering, life is rich in happiness; and this as well must be attributed to God.

XII-XIV The Beginning of Job's Hope—Elsewhere 34
Job has adequately presented his point in a speech of one or two chapters, a procedure that holds to the end, for the long section, chs. 27–31, is no exception, as we shall there point out. Suspicions of the originality of this speech's continuance through three chapters. 12–14, are accordingly valid. And examination of the content of 12 reveals that it is in large measure composed of trite phrases related to the emphasis of the friends, rather than of Job. There can be no doubt, however, that vv. 1–3 are valid, how much more it is difficult to say, though probably the lengthy recital of the great works of God, 7–25, had some original basis, if brief. Job, then, retorts in scathing repudiation of the friends' assumed deeper understanding; as in ch. 9, he seems also to have affirmed his agreement with their words, claiming only that they are platitudes, **3b**. Most translations, including RSV, gloss over the textual difficulties of vv. **4** and **5**, the former of which suffices to raise suspicion, and the latter approximates nonsense; **6** is irrelevant, if indeed it says anything rational.

But with **XIII** Job's argument takes up, in clarity, b
force, and not a little personal resentment, **4-12**. Typical of the poet's method, the thought presented lightly in 9:35–10:2 is now resumed and becomes central in Job's musing. He would argue his case in person before the Almighty. In contrast to his own sincerity and concern, the friends make a pretence of religious thinking: in **7**, they speak falsely for God. **10**. 'in secret', i.e. in the secret of their own consciousnesses, they show him favours. The far-reaching implications of the passage are too little realised. Job charges that the friends employ pious phrases which they have never critically examined, because that seems the orthodox thing to do. They show favours to God by adoptihg toward him a deferential restraint that would never be tolerated in secular thinking, to that extent an inferior method of thought. The passage is

4b the Magna Charta of religious freedom in its age-long struggle against the strangling effects of a false traditionalism. It is a liberalism that is magnificently exemplified by the poet himself. **11a.** ' Majesty ' is an inadequate translation. The Heb. word is an infinitive of the verb used in the phrase, ' show partiality ' ; clearly the writer is saying, You show favours to God ; he will show you special attention, but it will be a terrifying experience.

c It is pertinent to point out what has perhaps become evident already, that Job's speeches are developing a certain pattern. Along with some direct reply to the friends, and considerable exposition of his preoccupation with his suffering, there occurs a brief but highly important passage in which his thought takes a leap forward. The idea is never developed to its full implications ; as we have noted, it is typical of the author's skill that he has this sick man merely grasp momentarily at some redemptive thought, then abandon it, overcome by his obsessive complaining ; but presently he takes it up again and carries it a little further. These brief insights are the links in Job's progress toward the ultimate solution which the writer is in process of exploring. Such a ' clue ' passage is **13:15-16.** Already familiar with our author's methods, it scarcely calls for comment that Job's argument moves so naturally into the passage we hardly realise its significance. And admittedly it is difficult. RSV's translation is only one of several possible. It is well to speak first of **16a** ; ' this ' represents the Hebrew masculine pronoun. To translate it so is possible, though unusual. The word is strengthened with a Hebrew emphatic particle ; in **16b** the word order imparts comparable emphasis to ' before him '. Such parallelism implies that in both clauses the 3rd personal pronoun means the same ; apparently the verse should be translated, ' He himself will be my salvation, for a godless man does not come before him '. But a little examination discloses that **15a** is likewise dubiously translated. When Job declares unequivocally in **16** that he is to find ' salvation ' (whether through ' him ' or ' this '), it is strange to have him here profess complete hopelessness. Here again RSV's translation is possible ; but hope is very frequently mentioned in the Dialogue, and consistently by another word, whereas the verb occurring here is used with the meaning to delay ; so correctly RSV in 14:14*b*. Something similar relates to the word rendered ' Behold '. It is probable that the correct translation of the verse is, ' Though he may slay me, I will not delay ; but I will argue my ways to his face '. Consistent with his developing thought, Job wishes to meet God face to face and argue his rights. It would be a desperate action, **13-14,** but even if his life were forfeit, he would persist. Yet no such result will ensue ; God himself will be his surety and will save him, for he will recognise Job's sincerity and justice, since ' a godless man ' does not press into the presence of his Almighty judge.

The thought is so astonishing that one may well question whether the meaning has been correctly grasped. A look backward, and then forward, will provide corroboration. From the rebellious, resentful Job of chs. 9–10, this seems an impossible development ; but it is a natural, if bold, advance from his thought in 10:12–13. Equally it is clearly an anticipation of the great insights of this same speech as it develops, notably **14:13-17.** Here are the great steps of the advancing solution ; and indeed much is implied in ch. 13 prior to these verses, for quite apparently the God who is not satisfied with the dishonest arguments of the friends, is in some way a just God, the antithesis of the tyrant of 9:13–10:3.

d **19a.** ' Who is there ' is a too literal translation ; rather ' Would that he would argue with me . . . only grant two things '. **18b.** ' I know that I shall be vindicated ' can scarcely be correct ; rather, ' I know that I am in the right ' ; he is confident that his case is ineluctable. He sketches it in **23-7.** Sequence
of thought and poetic structure indicate that **28** should 344d
be removed to follow **14:2.** In **14:1** Job returns to that universal aspect of his problem that had engaged him likewise midway in his reply to Eliphaz (7:1ff.) ; but true to the poet's method, he now carries it much farther than in that preliminary comment. When we recognise that **4** is an interruption by some pious commentator, it becomes apparent that the chapter moves on in consistent development of the theme of man's tragedy, his transience, and ultimate doom of extinction. The flat denial of persistence beyond death has, very naturally, led some interpreters to acceptance of this as the author's final conviction. But such is merely to confess failure to grasp the poet's methods. Indeed he immediately belies this view—with a mere wish, it is true, **13** ; yet for him, man's deepest longings are challenges to exploration of possibility.

Still it is a pale hope as yet ; merely the familiar e
concept of Sheol, but there to be preserved in some vague waiting for an uncertain change. But it is hope ! And as such it merits full examination as the opposite of Job's black mood through most of his previous speeches. Such waiting in the underworld is again reminiscent of the chthonic literature of the ancient East. Thus Ishtar waited until the messenger from the high gods secured her release. Indeed the parallel carries farther ; God's postulated concern for imprisoned Job is like a sublimation of the gods' disturbance over the detainment of Ishtar. Also the word translated ' release ', **14c,** is a noun from the verb rendered ' sprout again ' in 7—another concession to the ' fertility ' thinking of the ancient world. It is of interest, too, that the word translated ' cover over ', **17b,** really means ' plaster over ', obviously an allusion to the clay ' envelopes ' in which Babylonian tablets were preserved.

Job held and exploited his dawning hope through vv. **13-17,** altogether the longest sustained brightness in his utterances as yet. But as we fully expect, in **18-22** he fell back then into his besetting gloom : the hope of man is not that of a tree, but is like inanimate nature where wear and erosion are eternal. The hope of man perishes.

XV-XVII The Second Argument of Eliphaz and 345a
Job—Eliphaz runs true to type ; his emphasis on man's inherent sinfulness, **15:14-16,** reads almost like a quotation from his former speech. Yet his is no mechanical repetition; he meets new situations with intelligence, though like all of us, intelligence directed by basic convictions. His veiled and polite accusations have given way to forthright charges ; it is Job's iniquity that impels him to such shocking utterance, **2-5.** He has abandoned, too, his recourse to special revelation ; instead he is here one with his associates in citation of tradition. How astonishingly the author has sketched the debate between traditionalism and liberalism from that day to our own ! **4.** Because Job has defied dogma to think independently about religious questions, he is an enemy of the faith. How absurd to follow one's petty intelligence against the hoary authority of the ages, **7-10** !

V. **11** introduces us to the textual uncertainties of the b
chapter. Brief examination reveals that **11b** has little relevance to **11a.** It is probable that a simple omission has occurred, and with it an erroneous division of words ; presumably the original **11b** said, ' and for you an irrational matter '—alluding to Job's charges of the divine misgovernment. Similar problems are a major concern in the study of the rest of the chapter. RSV gives plausible rendering but, with only a few notes of the underlying uncertainties, glosses over a text that in nearly half its extent leaves one questioning its validity. Yet it would seem that little is actually lost. The movement of thought is apparently correctly outlined. Eliphaz spends himself in delineating the unhappy fate of the wicked. **16.** The relevance of his tirade is that Job, in his bold thinking, is ' abominable and corrupt, a man who drinks iniquity like water ' ; hence nothing but unrelieved disaster awaits him.

345c **XVI.** Dubious text continues through Job's speech. Careful study reveals that omissions have almost certainly occurred, and that some words are corrupted. Yet through ch. 16 the meaning is in general clear, the worst uncertainty, unfortunately, occurring at the high point of the speech. However, 'join words together against you', **4b**, should read 'make a din over you with words'. Our major astonishment is to find Job, after his venture of hope in chs. 13–14, here submerging himself largely in utterances more akin to his initial complaints. We must presume the poet is concerned to depict the ruinous effects of unfeeling reproof upon a dawning hope and faith. The blunt denunciations of Eliphaz have thrown Job back into self-justification and all the unhappy results that follow in its train. Yet the author is fully in control, for soon he leads this rambling indignation back to the insights that have already proved so enriching for the tortured Job. **19.** Denied understanding and sympathy which he had a right to expect from Eliphaz and the others, Job turns for vindication to the mysterious figure of his 'witness in heaven'. One somewhat naturally presumes he is speaking of God; and several interpreters have given us the notion of God pleading with himself on behalf of Job. But we may dismiss this with the comment that however much or little it may have meaning today, the idea was unknown to our author. Mowinckel is certainly correct in repudiating this exposition ('Hiobs go'el und Zeuge in Himmel', BZAW 41 (1925), 207–12). In reality a first step in identification is simple and certain. The 'witness' is no other than the 'umpire' of 9:33, the yet strange figure of Job's intermediary. It is one more of the complex threads the author is interweaving for a solution of his intricate problem. The 'witness' in the present passage is much more than the former 'umpire', but he is still a puzzling figure; it is best to attempt no identification until more is available on which to base it.

d Yet it would appear we have more here than usual translation provides (RSV, AV, RV). JV points in the direction of richer possibilities, rendering 'friends' (of RSV) as 'inward thoughts', and 'scorn me' as 'my intercessors'. In the latter it is almost certainly right. The same word occurs in 33:23, where JV, in full consistency, renders it as 'intercessor', but RSV as 'mediator'. In the context it cannot be other than a term for the intermediary, hence presumably here also. With slight paraphrase of the passage, its most probable meaning comes out thus:

> 'My mediator is my friend;
> unto God my eye has poured out tears (formerly, though in vain; but now)
> he (the mediator) will plead for a man (i.e. myself) as a human being (pleads) for his friend.'

In **22** Job does more than merely reiterate his obsession with the idea of death; he replies specifically to the trite assurances of the friends that repentance will bring him restoration of health and fortune. Rather the situation is that the end is hurrying on; then what of vindication? It cannot occur here, time is too short; the only hope lies beyond death. With such insight we then recognise that **18** had said the same; earth is not to cover his dead body, but it is to lie unburied while his restless cries still go up to God, for he has a witness and mediator there to plead for him. The wishful thinking of ch. 14 is strengthening into a conviction; there is something beyond death! In passing it must be noted that **22b** is again an allusion, perhaps even clearer than in 10:21, to the chthonic literature of the author's time. In the famous Babylonian poem, it will be recalled, Ishtar 'set her ear' to 'go to the land of No-return'.

e **XVII.** In ch. 17 we are once more plunged, in regard to the Hebrew text, into perplexity. V. **1** gives no more than hints of what it originally meant; **2** may be correct; the following verses provide relatively acceptable Hebrew, but so irrelevant that only by a *tour de force* can they be interpreted. The effort to extract sense, or to find some advance of Job's thought, does not reward the toil entailed. But from **13** onward, suddenly we are again in the clear; and the chapter concludes on a note harmonious with the end of ch. 16. It seems probable that originally it was entirely concerned with this theme. **17:1**, in its mention of 'graves', evidently continued—whatever its other, now corrupted, words may stand for—the ideas of 16:22. And at **13** Job is still contemplating his prospective and imminent descent into the underworld, a contingency described with poetic richness and variety. Having perhaps gone down there, where will his hope be? Pure despair, we would comment. But no! By a trick of words not unlike Job's stumble on his great insight in ch. 10, he here affirms hope in death: if he and his hope together descend into the dust (**16b** is not a question), it will be with him beyond the bars of Sheol; more prosaically, he will still have hope when death has supposedly ended all. 34

XVIII-XIX The Second Argument of Bildad and Job—'Hunt for words', **18:2**, rests on dubious text; quite possibly instead 'How long until you put an end to (mere) words?' Bildad begins with brief but contemptuous dismissal of Job's attitudes. **4bc** is striking in its enunciation of something like an incipient concept of natural law—does Job suppose the order of the universe is to be altered just for him! Then the thought moves into a sustained affirmation of the unhappy fate of the wicked. Relevance to Job's immediately preceding speech is not at once apparent, though one might hold that in his complaint, so Bildad charges, he has overlooked the one essential point, that he is getting just what a wicked man, such as he, richly deserves. And doubtless this is the thought; but careful examination provides richer pertinence. **13** and **14**, in their emphasis on the terrors of death, are clearly a reply to Job's interest in the underworld: it will be a place, not of rest and confident waiting, but of horror! The 'king of terrors', **14**, is the grisly figure of death, into whose horrible presence Job will be hurried. Indeed, RSV's 'is brought' glosses over a feature of the text that is perhaps significant. The verb is feminine! It says, 'and she will make him stride along to the king of terrors'. A tempting explanation is that we have here one more, and still more pointed, allusion to the chthonic literature, already more than once cited. In *Ishtar's Descent*, Ereshkigal, the goddess of the underworld, brought the imprisoned and now dishonoured Ishtar to judgment before her throne. 'The first-born of death' (Heb. *māweth*), a forceful metaphor, is perhaps to be associated with Mot, the Canaanite god of death. Indeed it is probable that, with very slight emendation, the line should be read, 'Mot devours (his) first-born with disease'. **19.** The claim of eradication of posterity is aimed at Job's dawning hope of survival beyond death; Bildad says he has not even the normal basis for it, through posterity, with his characteristic bluntness providing one more heartless allusion to the disaster to Job's family (cf. 8:4). In this mood of quoting himself Bildad invokes again, **16**, a figurative reference to plant life, just as in 8:11–19. 'At his day', **20**, is surely to be read, by a different division of the consonants, 'at him'. 'They of the west', and 'of the east' may be correct; but equally the meaning may be 'later generations', and 'earlier' (sc. now in Sheol). 34

XIX. These taunts and rebukes call forth from Job the most sustained and ordered defence of his position yet offered; also they impel him to a moving plea for sympathy and understanding from the friends. One cannot but be stirred by the appeal, **21-2**, that climaxes his tale of woe. Even the retort with which he begins is less bitter than hitherto. Apparently the unmitigated hopelessness that Bildad pictures as his fate, has evoked in Job a sense of awful loneliness; b

b **6-12.** God is against him. **10b.** Even his hope that had fluttered to a dubious dawning in recent speeches, God tears away. **13-19.** His normal and most intimate associates turn away or ignore him.

c **24.** Mention of inscribing words on rock with use of lead raises acute difficulty. Tablets of lead were used widely in Roman times, but we have no knowledge of them in the earlier Orient. Metal was inserted in depressions in rock carvings by the Achaemenid kings (Cameron, *Persepolis Treasury Tablets* (1948)), but it was the precious metals that were so used. A ‘ house of lead ’ is mentioned in an Assyrian inscription as some sort of depository for an inscribed boundary stone (Olmstead, *History of Assyria* (1923), 169). But none of this provides the illumination we require. The situation must not now be pressed beyond a serious suspicion that the text is corrupted ; though evidently it did speak of some permanent record of Job's sufferings.

d At **25** we come to one of the great enunciations of the Dialogue. But unfortunately after **25a** the text becomes uncertain. Of **25b** little more may be said than that it *may* be right and we must seek to expound it as though it were. **26a** is completely irrational ; even if the original reading is only slightly obscured, yet it cannot be restored. Happily **26b** commends itself, and thus provides an index of the movement of thought. **27** may in general be accepted, except that **c** is apparently a gloss. **28-9** give no relevant idea ; whether corrupt, or composed entirely of glosses, we cannot draw them into the advance of thought.

e Here we find the third, and unfortunately final, appearance in the Dialogue of the intermediary, though he is mentioned again in the first speech of Elihu (33:23). Many serious questions as to his function will remain unanswered—did the author invoke him again in the later part of the Dialogue which now is lost?—but at least his nature and function are at last indicated, thanks to the illumination provided in the Râs Shamra literature. **25a** is so nearly a quotation of a passage there—‘ So I knew that alive was Puissant Baal ’ (Pritchard, op. cit., 140) —that it is inescapable our author is writing in full consciousness of the pervasive ancient speculation about the chthonic tragedy. This is the meaning of his several allusions to it, already pointed out. His engrossment, too, with the nature and inevitability of Sheol, which, we saw, expressed itself in the very beginning of Job's utterances, is clearly of a piece with this thread of his theme with which the poet is weaving his integrated solution of the human predicament. The ‘ redeemer ’, **25a** (not Redeemer, Heb. *gō'ēl*, the normal word for the next of kin, responsible for requital of wrong done the family), patently corresponds to the messenger of the gods who was instrumental in release of the dead god of life. Then with sudden comprehension we realise that this well-known drama is the model for much else in this justly famous chapter. **6b**, Job's capture, **7**, his cry for help, **8**, his confinement in darkness, **9-10**, the nakedness and despair to which he was subjected, **11-12**, the enmity of his great jailer and the organised troops of besetting minions—why, here is precisely the plight of Ishtar admitted through the seven great gates of Arallu, progressively stripped of her clothing until, conducted by infernal demons, she stands naked in the presence of raging Ereshkigal! (Pritchard, op. cit., 106–9). But this is not the end. If we avoid the temptation to make figures of speech ‘ go on all fours ’, it will become apparent that Job's personal estrangement, **13-19**, especially his wife's revulsion, **17a**, corresponds in a free way to the baneful results of Ishtar's confinement.

f Job, then, accepts Bildad's warnings of the terrors of the underworld, but insists on his own view of them. He is consistent with his claims and speculations in chs. 16–17, but in answer to Bildad, carries them farther. It is as though he were already enduring the horrors of that dingy abode ; not yet dead, he is experiencing the meaning of death. But, he insists,
that is not all ; the hope he had claimed, 17:16, is real. 346f
It is more : it is a certainty ! For, just as the messenger of the gods secured deliverance for Ishtar, and as Baal though dead was alive, so Job's ‘ redeemer ’ lives. It is precarious to attempt interpretation of **25b** ; it is entirely good Hebrew, but suspicions of its accuracy are well based. **26a** we can profitably ignore; tempting suggestions for emendation of the quite impossible Hebrew are numerous, but not convincing. The direction of thought is indicated by **26b**, where the text fortunately is irreproachable, though less than lucid. ‘ Without my flesh ’ is highly debatable. As the note in RSV indicates, it could also be translated, ‘ from my flesh ’ ; is Job saying, ‘ as a disembodied personality ’, or ‘ from the vantage-point of my body ’, i.e. before death ? An answer is possible only from consideration of the total and direction of the author's evolving thought. What we have seen already leaves no doubt that RSV is right ; Job affirms his conviction that after death he will see God. However, ‘ on my side ’, **27a**, while a possible translation, is highly improbable ; rather, ‘ for myself ’. And ‘ not another ’, **27b**, is surely wrong ; read, ‘ not (an unfriendly) stranger ’ ; i.e. God, when seen, will not be hostile. The living ‘ redeemer ’ will in some unstated way effect reconciliation. In his after-death existence, for which he had consistently longed and which he had increasingly affirmed, Job will realise his desire to meet God but will not find him a stern antagonist. This falls short of a conviction of the grace of God. Job has made remarkable progress, but we must not demand too much ; there are yet things to be said. Equally it is evident that the ‘ redemptive ’ role of the intermediary in this crucial passage is left vague. In some way he intervenes for Job's reconciliation to God ; but how ?

XX-XXI The Second Argument of Zophar and 347a
Job—Zophar had an advantage over us. He lived in the same thought-world as Job and understood him immediately, not by some complicated process of interpretation such as we must invoke. The word translated ‘ thoughts ’, **20:2**, occurs elsewhere only in Eliphaz's story of the ghost, 4:13, and since ‘ answer ’ here is really ‘ bring back ’, it is as if he said, ‘ That sort of talk merely gives me, once again, the creeps ’ ! **2b** is of doubtful text ; and evidence from LXX indicates that **3b** was approximately, ‘ and a wind lacking intelligence answers me ’. **6a**, ‘ height ’, is very uncertain ; ‘ physical power ’ is an equally plausible guess. **7-9** allude to 7:8–10 and 14:2 ; more remotely **10-11** re-echo 14:21–2. One might paraphrase the inference ; ‘ You were right in your previous utterances, before this nonsense about hope in the underworld took hold of you. Wicked folk—like yourself—die and they are dead ! ’ **14-15** give a vivid description of acute indigestion ; apparently the ancient world too had experience of ‘ sour stomach ’. **16** speaks of death by snakebite ; the existence of poisonous serpents in ancient Palestine is abundantly testified by the OT. **17** has one more light allusion to chthonic literature ; the Râs Shamra tablets speak of the heavens raining oil and the valleys flowing with honey through the mythical revival of the god's resurrection (Pritchard, op. cit., 140). Again Zophar's thought is best realised through paraphrase : ‘ There'll be no Elysian fields for you ! ’ Perhaps this area of thought is not far from **23c** likewise, for in the Canaanite myth the gods rain blessings, but here terrors. The seemingly barren turn which Zophar here gives to the discussion, continuing then through subsequent speeches of the friends, is apparently the author's way of telling that they have reached the limit of their theological resources. Their conservatism can now do no more than threaten the questioner with dire disaster.

Here the second cycle comes to an end, if we are b
correct in regarding Job as the initiator of each new round in the argument. The friends, as we were prepared to believe, have given us little ; their finished and final theology had been presented in their

347b first speeches. For the poet, orthodoxy does not change ; it claims to possess the truth once delivered to the saints, in which there can be no shadow of changing. Human crises, then, call not for its enlargement but its application. Consequently they had told Job that his proper course was dictated in terms of repentance and reconciliation. In this second cycle they have merely moved to ever more overt expostulations of Job's badness and the evil that his incorrigibility would bring, the poet employing this for subtle advance and for development of Job's thought.

Along this line, the astonishing gains of the first cycle are exploited. Setting out from his new insight in ch. 10 that God's relation with his creatures reveals 'steadfast love' and 'providence', Job seized upon wistful hope ; perhaps life's blackest spectre, death itself, might hold some promise of a better day. The underworld could, perhaps, then probably represent only an interval, beyond which was reconciliation and restoration. In this saving experience the mysterious intermediary was to play a central role ; he would be the witness in heaven, the 'redeemer' through whom in some mysterious way Job after death would see God and find him 'not a stranger'. But the discussion is not yet ended ; the poet has still to carry his thought to some insight transcending these too vague premises. The third cycle lures us with undefined promise.

c **XXI**. Job's speech in ch. 21 is at first glance puzzling. Here is none of the characteristic structure that has become familiar : a picture of his suffering and of God's mysterious ways with him, a central passage that advances the growing faith and hope, and a conclusion that appears to abandon the hard-won insight. Instead, after its brief personal retort, **2-6**, the chapter is one consistent exposition of the theme, the wicked never meet with the overthrow which the friends in monotonous reiteration claim ; right to the grave they enjoy advantages over other men. Job's course here is not to be confused with his denial of cosmic justice presented so cogently in chs. 9–10 ; he is not abandoning the painful gain of all the intervening search. He is speaking here relevant to his new-won insights, and is preparing the ground for a further leap forward. Over against the superficial platitudes of the friends, the obvious fact is that moral retribution does not come in this world. Where then, if at all ? He has been groping for hope through descent into Sheol. Now the way is open for full exploitation of this possibility.

Only a few details call for comment. 'How often', **17**, governs the entire passage to **20**. In **19** there is no 'You say' ; that is merely the translators' effort to give sense when the original meaning has been overlooked ; read, 'How often does God store up trouble for his sons, or requite him evil ? How often do his eyes look on disaster, and he himself drink of the Almighty's rage ?' Probably, too, **21** should read : 'But (instead) how great is his pleasure in his house after him ! And the total of his months is secure.' Apparently, too, the meaning of **31-3** is obscured ; not 'Who' but the desiderative force of the pronoun : 'Would that someone might tell him to his face where he is going, and requite him what he does ! But he is carried to his burial, and ceremonial watch is kept over his tomb.' In **33** those who go before and after are the funeral procession.

348a **XXII-XXIV The Third Argument of Eliphaz and Job**—In a sense, Eliphaz's third speech declares the bankruptcy of the friends' case ; for it has recourse to charges of unethical conduct for which there is not a scintilla of evidence. It seems to be orthodoxy run to earth ; or, rather, its implications carried to their conclusion. When dogmas are absolute and not subject to appraisal through empirical fact, if facts disagree, they must be adjusted to the dogma ! Yet the speech is not lacking in interest—and difficulty. **22:2.** 'Man' represents a less usual Hebrew word ; though not the one used in Eliphaz's first speech, 4:17, it seems to carry some deprecation, as though 'mere man'. **2b** is ambiguous, but apparently means, 'No, but a prudent man can be profitable to him (i.e. to God).' In **3** the transcendence of God is set forth in ultimate terms reminiscent of Milton, 'On His Blindness' :

> 'God doth not need
> Either man's work or his own gifts . . .
> . . . . His state
> Is kingly.'

5 is adversative to **4** : not for your piety but for your great wickedness, does God reprove you. The verbs in **6**, **7**, and **9** are 'imperfect' : this conduct was habitual. Similar is the thought of **8** ; Job practised or tolerated class privilege.

b Yet major interest inheres in **12-20**. Reverting to his favourite theme of the transcendence of God, Eliphaz charges Job with scepticism ; his questioning is forcing him into disbelief. As is not uncommon in such rebukes, Eliphaz is not concerned to be accurate, but attributes to Job what can nowhere be found in his speeches. But this would not worry Eliphaz ; doubtless he would reply that such was the gist of all Job's utterance. **13a** should read, as is demonstrated by the sequel, 'How can one know God ?'—so there it is bluntly ! Job has rejected traditional dogmas, when he insists that religious faith is beset with acute problems demanding answer. For Eliphaz this is equivalent to denying all valid knowledge of God ; he goes on, **15-17**, to charge that such infidelity is a very old story. It is of the utmost interest to have this testimony to the existence of far-reaching critical thought in Israel. We are prone to suppose that tradition sufficed for Hebrew thinking, and that no-one ever questioned basic dogmas. Enough evidence is available to show that the situation was far other. And while Eliphaz has here exaggerated, and distorted Job's actual intent, yet in a large way he is right ; Job's questionings are intimately related to those of the unbeliever ; the difference being not in their source and character, but in their outcome. Job is in process of struggle toward an answer of faith that conforms with the evidence ; for the others, first impressions are final : we cannot know God ! How intimately related this is to the view of Koheleth (Ec. 3:11), and as well, of the modern atheistic humanist. Indeed it is close, too, to theologies that claim God is 'totally other', which surely means he is unknowable. Their strange feature is that such quality is a ground of religious faith ! However, for Eliphaz there is no such problem ; he is quite certain he has valid knowledge. It comes through revelation and tradition, but clearly the intellect has no part in it ; he merely accepts, he is almost gullible in his eagerness to believe, hence, as is usual in such temper, he grasps avidly at mere superstition and mental vagaries, 4:12–21.

Eliphaz's peroration, **21-30**, is in essence a reaffirmation of his advice in 5:17–27. We may here ignore it, noting only the interesting point, **24-5**, that he distinguishes between material and religious values.

c **XXIII**. Job turns immediately to Eliphaz's central charge. It is as though he said, 'Far from denying a knowledge of God, I am seeking it earnestly ; but it is a different sort of knowledge and hard to attain'. There is basis for uncertainty as to the text of some verses. LXX seems to have omitted **14** (a consideration that is not conclusive) ; **8-9** seem to break the structure of the chapter. But even so, the thought is beyond dispute. Job's persistent desire to confront God recurs, but with astonishing advance. **6-7**. Here is no longer the mighty and overwhelming adversary, but one whom Job could approach with firm confidence in his justice and goodness. Such faith gives insight into the present suffering ; God is testing Job, and will purify him like gold in the furnace. The reaction which his moments of insight have always prefaced is also on a higher level. No longer does he fall back into gloom ; he speaks only

48c of the inscrutable purposes of God, and apparently his transcendence, before which Job bows in godly fear. **15** is too strong in RSV ; it would have been better to have used the translation employed in 22:10 for essentially the same Hebrew words, and have said, ' Therefore I am overwhelmed because of him, and I fear him '. Also ' is unchangeable ' in **13** is doubtful. Literally it says, ' in one ' ; but probably the text is corrupted from ' has chosen '. There is no sound basis for interpreting Job as terrified before a mighty and irresponsible God, but only as overcome with devout awe of God's exaltation and his sovereign will.

d **XXIV.** This is a terrible chapter, next to impossible to arrange into any rational content or movement of thought. **2-4** seem to deal with some class of rapacious oppressors, but connection with v. 1 is not clear ; similar is **9**, which apparently interrupts an account of unidentified wretched poor, **5-11** (**12?**). Then **13-17** tell about city ruffians ; perhaps the theme continues through **20**, though this latter is so corrupt that RSV is no more than a guess at the meaning. Likewise the rendering of **22-4** is misleading in its lucidity ; the Hebrew is obscure in the extreme. **25a** is in the main a duplicate of 9:24*c*, and both are apparently explanatory ejaculations by some unknown reader. If **12** is correctly preserved, it declares its secondary origin, for the Dialogue does not move in the atmosphere of city life ; the same would apply to **20** if the reading of RSV could be established.

Such discussion is probably more than the chapter merits ; for if there is any fragment of it that originated in the speech of Job, he would be a bold expositor who would undertake to identify it. In any case we have arrived at a circumstance that will become still clearer in chs. 25–7 ; significant development of the Dialogue has come to an end. So much the higher, then, is the importance of ch. 23. In its clear expression of confident hope we have for all practical purposes the culmination of Job's argument with his friends. An attempt at grasping the full significance of the Dialogue we postpone, however, until all evidence is before us.

49a **XXV-XXVII Concluding Fragments of the Dialogue**—A glance at ch. 25 tells that something unusual has occurred. Bildad's speeches have run through normal-length chapters ; here we have only six verses ; and they say little that is relevant. Their stress on the transcendence of God re-echoes Eliphaz. Completely lacking is the personal vituperation which has become a feature of most of the friends' speeches. If one will, he may claim that the author is expressing the triumph of Job ; he had talked the friends into a position where they can only stammer out a few irrelevant platitudes ! It is ingenious, but scarcely cogent. Rather the conclusion is inescapable that we deal with a tattered manuscript ; at this point only fragments could be assembled, and the editors did the best they could in putting them together. But that best is not good enough ; it is not even certain that the chapter contains anything from a speech of Bildad. One Hebrew manuscript reads in v. 1, ' Then Job answered ' ; it is certainly wrong. This is no speech of Job's, but it looks suspiciously like a collection of platitudes thrown together to supply the lack of Bildad's speech. Further comment is unnecessary.

b But in ch. 26 we move definitely into a genuine utterance of Job. The Heb. of v. **2** has a fine assonance such as our author loves ; the stinging rebuke of the friends is also in part. Yet such early confidence is soon disabused ; for from v. **5** onward the chapter is disturbingly strange to what we have learned of Job's thought and utterance. It is a cosmological poem, possessed of distinct literary merits ; but by this time Job is too engrossed in his discovery of hope and faith to turn aside to such alluring, though completely irrelevant, discussion. Perhaps we shall not be far wrong if we conclude that only the beginning of Job's speech came into the hands of the assemblers of our book, and they filled it out with this striking excerpt,
justified in that it is not unlike the cosmic theme of 349b
the first of Yahweh's speeches in ch. 38. Probably **5** should say, ' The shades beneath the waters tremble, their inhabitants (i.e. of the waters) also '. While the full relevance of the word rendered ' shades ' is not known, it is apparent that here we have a concept related to the belief that after his cosmic victory over rebellious forces, Yahweh confined them under the sea. **6** is similar to Prov. 15:11. Abaddon is mentioned seven times in the Bible (one of these in the NT : Rev. 9:11), three of these occurrences being in Job, here and 28:22, 31:12. The facts conduce to the conclusion that the occurrence of the word here is support for the view that these verses are not original. **7** and **8** are of great interest as revealing a cosmic theory diverse from that of Gen. 1 where the earth floats on the primeval deep, and the upper waters are held back by the ' firmament '. A similar comment relates to **10**, which clearly speaks of the horizon ; beyond it is the realm of darkness. ' The moon ', **9**, should probably be more literally, ' his throne '. ' The pillars of heaven ' were a widespread concept ; they supported the sky. The whole description relates to God's work in creation, as becomes clear in **12**. On ' Rahab ' see 9:13. **13.** ' The fleeing serpent ' has become familiar to us from the Râs Shamra literature (Pritchard, op. cit., 138) ; cf. Isa. 27:1 where it is associated with the Leviathan concept. **14** is magnificent in its literary quality, and also in its theology.

A glance at **27:1** reveals that something is wrong. e
Never hitherto has a speech been introduced in these terms, and only in 29:1 do they occur again. There is no logical reason for the innovation ; rather it is one more indication of the confused condition of these fragments. However, we need not argue the case, for it is freely recognised that some part of the otherwise lost third speech of Zophar is contained in this chapter. It is a plausible view of vv. **13-23** ; some would claim also **7-12** (J. M. P. Smith in *The Complete Bible*). It is possible that the remainder, **2-6**, is really a part of a speech of Job ; but this is not very convincing—it lacks ' the feel ' of the utterances of Job with which we have become familiar. However that may be, the broken nature of the text in these chapters leaves us without suitable context to which these verses might serve as reply. We can only pass over them with the comment that denial of any wrong-doing adequate to explain his suffering is consistent with Job's position elsewhere. **7** is of very doubtful flavour, whether attributed to Job or Zophar. **12** cannot be from one of the friends, although **13ff.** are very similar to what they have said in previous speeches ; but here they lack the relevance that might provide some contribution to the movement of thought.

XXVIII The Source of Wisdom—With few excep- 350a
tions, students of the Book of Job agree that ch. 28 is a separate poem of different authorship. Though thus unrelated to the great theme with which we have so long been engrossed, it possesses worth of its own. Quest for the source of wisdom was a favourite topic of the ' wise men ' ; cf. Ps. 111:10 ; Prov. 1:7, 20 ff., 3:19–20, 8:1–36. Reference to ancient mining, **1-11**, is also of peculiar interest ; for though man had searched for minerals for thousands of years before the time of this author, and ' mining ' of flint is attested from the Stone Ages (J. H. Breasted, *Ancient Times* (1914), 32), literary descriptions of the industry are meagre. A first problem of the chapter is its text.
3a is clearly confused ; in what way do men ' put an b
end to darkness ' in their search for ore ? Probably instead, ' There in utmost and extreme darkness ', (the miner) searches for ore in gloom and murk. **4** is highly misleading ; it seems to imply descent into a deep shaft by a ' swinging ' or ' hanging ' basket or car. Obviously all this is false to ancient mining. It is doubtful that any was done by shafts, but rather through tunnels or drifts. The Hebrew word conforms with this, for it means literally a ' stream-bed '. The hanging and swinging, then, does not refer to the

350b miners, but to the tunnel : it turns deviously in a region (underground) that man's foot does not frequent. **6** speaks of 'lapis-lazuli flecked with gold'. **7** and **8** still are concerned with the underground 'path' followed by the miner. **9.** 'Flinty rock'; better, 'quartz vein'. **10.** 'Channels' is another word for a river, here obviously again the mine drifts. Where the writer learned about mining and smelting is not apparent. There were, and are, no mines in Palestine proper, though copper ore was found in the land of Edom and smelted at Elath at the head of the Gulf of 'Aqaba (Glueck, *The River of Jordan* (1946), 146). But for gold, silver, or lapis-lazuli he would have been compelled to go much farther. Probably he did not know the industry at all at first hand, but, just as is common today, spoke out of 'general knowledge'.

c The thought of the chapter, presented with effective sense of problem, is thus that wisdom is not secured by methods which provide material treasures, nor yet in exchange for those material things, however precious. It cannot be found even by intensive search through 'the land of the living'. It is a spiritual quality; its origin is with God himself and it is found only through 'the fear of the Lord', i.e. devout religious experience.

Wisdom in the Bible, it deserves remark, is by no means identical with the modern connotation of the word. Rather it corresponds to the total of the finer things of life, intellectual, aesthetic, and religious. We hear it said at times that the chapter is pessimistic : such wisdom is beyond man's attainment, and can be secured only by special divine intervention. But surely this is to miss the point. We have here an expression of the pervasive thinking of the Orient, which speculated on the mystery of civilisation, and found its essence in a divine quality implanted in man (Irwin, *The OT : Keystone of Human Culture* (1952), 72, 99ff.) ; man is made of, and for, better things, and he is restless until he finds rest in them.

351a **XXIX-XXXI The Present Conclusion of the Dialogue**—Again Job takes 'up his discourse'; and again the strangeness of the phrase gives the reader pause. Equally unexpected is the fact that here Job is a city-dweller (**29:7ff., 30:28, 31:32**) and apparently surrounded by numerous people (so throughout), features which, to say the least, are not obvious in the Dialogue. The idyllic picture of his former life, here ascribed to Job, while not entirely foreign to the story given in the Prologue, has no parallel in the Dialogue, but at the most only casual reference. This theme occupies **2-10**, **21-5**, and perhaps **18-20**, though it is apparent that **21** forms a natural sequel to **10**. **11-17** are very like an Egyptian epitaph, and probably bear some actual relationship. The picture of Job's primacy in a city council, drawn so unmistakably in **20-5**, goes far beyond even what the Prologue claims for him. Details call for no discussion; the place of the gateway in the life of the ancient oriental city, the various marks of respect for an elder or superior, the figure of the 'unrighteous' as a beast of prey carrying off his victim in his teeth—all this is familiar.

b **XXX** begins suitably as the counterpart of 29, and certainly **9ff.** carry on somewhat consistently with the theme. But **2-8** can be defended only on the theory that they describe the menial state of the group who, in contrast to their former respect for him, now revile Job. But this is not very convincing; the extreme terms of disdain go far beyond anything the Dialogue has given us reason to regard as fitting; cf. 16:10, 19:13–19. Rather the verses resemble the description in 24:5–8, 10–11. They seem to have been in some way intruded into the original structure of the chapter. On the other hand the description of Job's suffering, **11-23**, has numerous parallels in the Dialogue. With **9-10** cf. 19:13–19; with **12a** cf. 10:17*c*; with **12b** cf. 19:12*c*; with **14a** cf. 16:10*c*, 16; with **15b** cf. 19:7*b*, 9*a*; with **16a** cf. 16:14; with **16b** cf. 7:3*b*; with **17** cf. 7:4; with **18** cf. 16:12*b*; with **19** cf. 9:31; with **20** cf. 19:7; with **21** cf. 13:24*b*, 19:11; with **22** cf. 9:17*a*; with **23** cf. 10:21, 16:22; with **25** cf. 22:6–7, 9; with **26** cf. 22:11; with **27b** cf. 7:3; with **28, 30** cf. 7:5. Even at such length the list is probably not complete; besides it is of varying relevance and significance. But it is impressive and revealing. While recurrence of familiar ideas is common in the Dialogue, yet it cannot be established that there is there redundancy on the scale here manifest. Under examination it becomes increasingly dubious that we have here that obsession with his persecution and suffering which certainly is a feature of the Dialogue; it is far overdone. Rather one can only with difficulty resist the conclusion that some reader of the Dialogue has compounded this passage out of phrases and suggestions occurring there. If so, it is to his credit; he pays silent tribute to one of the greatest literary achievements of the ancient world, But his sincere admiration must not blind us to his activity. However, the most serious obstacle to our ascribing the chapter to the great author of the Dialogue is that it harmonises not with the development of Job's thinking, but only with moods and utterances from which he had steadily moved away. Specifically, it has no place whatever in the exalted insights and dawning faith portrayed clearly in his latest genuine utterances, those in chs. 19 and 23. If this chapter is genuine, then all the author has toilfully built up goes for nothing. We may only conclude that 30, like 29, is further testimony to the disordered and tattered condition of the manuscript from which our Book of Job has descended, testimony that was unmistakable in chs. 25–7, but must be recognised as continuing into this alleged final speech.

V. **24** is highly dubious; the text is certainly corrupt. c
25 is similar to 31:16f. **28.** 'Blackened', while accurate, scarcely indicates the sense, which is 'in black garments, indicative of mourning': he is a black figure, but not because of sunburn. He is a 'brother of jackals and of ostriches' in the sense that he is an outcast from the civilised community. His skin turns black (a different word from that in 28) through disease; the burning in his bones, **30b**, implies intense fever bringing a deep flush to the skin. **XXXI** is a sort of antithesis to ch. 22; there Eliphaz had given a catalogue of Job's alleged iniquities; here Job denies by implication a still more comprehensive list. It is possible, though not very evident, that the connection of the two is deliberate and of intent. Some of the ethical ideals presented in this negative fashion are of notable elevation, as for example, **13-15**, the expression of the basic brotherhood of high and low alike, and the deep sense of social responsibility, **16-21a, 29-32**. Remarkable, also, is the standard of sex ethics in **1**, transcending, as it does, outward act and finding ultimate norm and sanction in a person's thinking; it is comparable with the exacting demand made by Jesus, Mt. 5:28. Less astonishing, though by no means negligible, is the further treatment of the theme in **9-12**, which gives, however, the normal ethics of the ancient world, distinguished mainly in its mention of Abaddon as the limit of passion's sequel. **29.** Consideration for one's enemy also deserves comment, for the ancient world normally prescribed for him only hatred; again the chapter gives an anticipation of Jesus' teaching (Mt. 5:44). **26-8** seem to speak of worship of the heavenly bodies, although we know too little about its ritual and about Hebrew modes and implications of kissing to assume a certainty.

It will be observed that the conditional sentences in d
29ff. are incomplete; RSV has met the situation by the use of a dash after **34**, a device on which one can only comment 'Perhaps'. It is more probable that we are to understand the oath formula, and that each protasis is really a strong negative; i.e. 'I have never rejoiced at the ruin—' etc. It becomes, then, probable that the usage begins at **24,** and that **28** is

351d not the apodosis, but merely a marginal comment by some reader. **35-7** seems to be the conclusion, whether original or not, of the chapter; hence the true conditional sentence in **38-40** is probably a later addition, a conclusion enhanced by the observation that the verses seem to make Job primarily a farmer, instead of a cattleman, which he is clearly in the Prologue, and probably also in the Dialogue. **39.** 'Payment' is that which was due to his tenant-farmers, who are also apparently meant by 'owners', really masters, i.e. those in charge. **35b.** 'Here is my signature', is very difficult: really, 'Here is my mark'. But in the ancient East business and legal documents were not signed; they carried names of the witnesses, who then in case of dispute would be called to testify orally to the terms of the agreement. Our modern understanding of the phrase is totally foreign to ancient usage, so much so indeed as to call into question its correctness. One is impelled to the guess that a slight omission in spelling of the word has occurred, and that the author's meaning, whoever he may have been, was, 'Here is my desire, that the Almighty would answer me'. Even so, it is apparent that **35c** is the logical sequel of **35a.** The verse is highly reminiscent of Job's repeated wish for a meeting with God; also 35*c* alludes to the obscure 19:23–4 though in their present uncertain form these mention the writing of Job's case, not God's.

At point after point we have been forced to the suspicion, if not the definite conviction, that in these chapters, 29–31, there is nothing that originally belonged to the Dialogue, but only some rather clear allusion to parts of it. Further, the writer (or writers), anticipated the long misunderstanding of the great poet by failing to recognise the advance of Job's thought, supposing instead that his position is properly represented by scattered references to utterances which in the advance of the Dialogue he abandons.

352a **XXXII-XXXIII The First Speech of Elihu**—Happily we are here in accord with the great mass of scholarly opinion when we proceed on the conviction that this speech, as well as the three that immediately follow, contains nothing that had a place in the original Book of Job. It is, however, a conclusion which possesses an overlooked, but highly valuable, implication to be employed in the study of the book. Of this presently.

Elihu is a 'Buzite', i.e. of the tribe of Buz. In Gen. 22:21 the latter is named as a second son of Nahor, Abraham's brother; the first son was Uz. Doubtless in these facts we have the author's motivation; as Job was of 'the land of Uz', it seemed appropriate to maintain the archaic flavour by introducing a descendant of the parallel line of Aramaeans. In Jer. 25:23 Buz appears with Dedan and Tema, hence evidently Arabian. Elihu's clan (RSV 'family'), Ram, is unknown, although it is tempting to associate it with an ancestor of David (Ru. 4:19), who in 1 Chr. 2:9 is mentioned as a brother of Jerahmeel, and in v. 25 as his eldest son. Both relationships would again indicate Arabic connections. But the reading, Aram, in one manuscript of LXX (MS C) is attractive.

b **32:2-5.** The prose introduction to the speech gives the main content of the chapter. Elihu is younger than the others; he had deferred to them, but in the now apparent failure of the friends to silence Job, he can wait no longer. The poetic speech adds the colourful item that he is full of words like a wine-skin ready to burst, **18-19**; he must speak, but he will show no partiality, an assurance that will call for attention in a moment. Elihu's claim that he can succeed where the others have failed excites immediate interest, such that we turn eagerly to his argument, After some preliminary declaration, **33:1-3**, of his sincerity, and, **4-6**, of his humanity not less than Job's, he moves, **9-11**, into rebuke of Job's claims of integrity and charges of divine persecution. On the contrary, he claims, God in his supremacy warns man through dreams, **12-18**, and chastens him through suffering, **19-24**; his purpose is benign, he would restrain man by these means 'from going down into the Pit'. At the height of his crisis there may be with him 'an angel, a mediator' who will graciously tell the sufferer 'what is right for him (to do?)', and thus recovery will ensue, bringing with it devout thankfulness and confession. The speech ends with intimation of more to be said on the subject; and actually the three following chapters are given as further speeches of Elihu, but this we must examine as we proceed. 352b

Briefly, then, Elihu advances the idea of the disciplinary purpose and function of suffering; and everyone who has suffered, or has with insight observed affliction, will be stirred to affirmative response. Suffering is not blind; it is frequently the minister of God's grace to us. Elihu, whoever he may have been, had a real contribution to make to the discussion. The friends, with all their pompous and argumentative orthodoxy, had only remotely come in sight of this great truth. Indeed, apart from the solution which the author of the Dialogue was working out (which remains yet to be fully assessed) here in Elihu's contribution we find the one real insight as yet in the book into an understanding of human woe. c

Yet the significance and relevance of the speech go considerably beyond this. Reverting to **32:21-2**, it becomes apparent that the writer is referring to Job's charges against the friends in 13:8–10, with the same concluding play on the verb (to lift up); for a literal rendering is 'I will not lift up a man's face . . . my maker would soon lift me up'. Given this clue, further facts fall into place. Every careful student of the book is impressed with the similarity of **15** to 4:13; apart from its third member, which is not in 4:13, and apart from the first word in each, the two passages are essentially identical. This has led some commentators to reject **15b,** as a mere quotation from ch. 4, and to retain **15c** as the original second member of the verse. But this is to miss the point; it *is* a quotation! The writer here is referring in this direct fashion to Eliphaz's first speech. Further examination reveals this: **4** is reminiscent of 10:8–12; **6a** refers to 9:32, and **6b** to 10:9*a* (it is relevant to our findings elsewhere to note that the pinching off of a piece of clay to make man is an allusion to the passage in the Gilgamesh Epic where Aruru so made Engidu; cf. Pritchard, op cit., 74); **7a** is an adaptation of 9:34*b* and of 13:21*b*, while **7b** (which should probably read 'My hand will not be heavy upon you') is similar to 13:21*a*, so that **7** and 13:21 are almost duplicates; **9** re-echoes the wrong charge which we noted in 8:6, but is justified by the wording of 9:15*a*, 16:17, and the claim in 10:6–7. **10b** is almost a quotation of 13:24*b*, and **11** of 13:27*ab*. **13b** refers to 9:16 and 19:7; the verb 'contend', **13a,** is the one used normally of Job's argument with God (9:2, 10:2). The terror inspired by the dream in the night, **16b,** is a reminiscence of 7:14. The soul's descent to the Pit, **18, 22, 24, 28,** is an allusion to Job's obsession with death and the underworld, except only that he commonly uses the name Sheol; but cf. 17:14. V. **19a** has the same idea as 7:3–4, 13, and **19b** seems to refer to 7:15; **20** perhaps alludes to 3:24*a*, and **21** to 19:20*a*. d

This is something more than the heterogeneous, though rich, allusions disclosed in ch. 30. While the parallels are to some extent scattered, yet in a rough way the thought of ch. 33 follows the advance of the Dialogue. The quotations and near-quotations are symbolic of the close use the present writer is making of it. Further, at v. **22** his survey has arrived at that anticipation of the near approach of death which was Job's foreboding in 19:23–7, then to our astonishment he introduces, right there, the intermediary, who was likewise the notable feature of this famous passage in the Dialogue, there to serve in some not too clear way in Job's reconciliation and restoration to divine favour. At that point the Dialogue left him, but here his function is carried farther. He is the gracious minister of rebuke and guidance, leading the sufferer to joyous e

352e restoration. And the sketch ends with the recovered invalid in an act of worship (apparently in the shrine), declaring his thanksgiving and confession. It merits comment that this is, as well, the ending of the so-called Babylonian Job, the poem known from its first line as 'I will praise the Lord of Wisdom' (Pritchard, op. cit., 434–7). We have thus one more testimony to the familiarity of these writers with the literature of their time. But a conclusion still more relevant to our purpose is inescapable. This man who wrote the first speech of Elihu knew and used the Dialogue in its original complete form, before the manuscript became torn and defective in the way in which to our immense loss we now have all that is extant from it. So far as present-day relevance is concerned, he was the last man so to see and use it. And his invoking of the intermediary and his sketch of the ending of the drama, both corresponding, as they do, with the direction of movement in the Dialogue and the conclusion toward which it was apparently tending, demonstrate that he has actually left us notes of the now lost course of the Dialogue beyond what we call ch. 23. It is a thrilling disclosure—until disillusionment steals upon us!

f Alas, the notes are too brief, leaving still many unanswered questions as to the function of the intermediary and much besides. But enough is evident to support cogently the view to which the actual course of the Dialogue has impelled us, and to provide basis for an estimate of the solution the author had reached for the profound problem in which he was engrossed. It is notable that the sketch we are examining has not the slightest hint of any appearing of Yahweh, in the whirlwind or otherwise, to speak to Job—objective evidence, once again, of just the sort we have needed as to the conclusion of the original poem; it is evidence from silence, but still of considerable cogency. Apparently neither the speeches of Yahweh nor any part of them had a place in the original poem. And this carries obvious implication for the history of our Book of Job: the Yahweh speeches—and presumably the Epilogue also—were added subsequent to the insertion of the Elihu speeches.

Yet it must be recognised that the author of chs. 32–3 was no mere copyist. He followed the Dialogue, it is true, but he had his own views to express. And these were not confined to his important emphasis on the disciplinary function of suffering. Three times in ch. 33 he expresses a hope of deliverance from 'going down into the Pit'. It is a striking contrast to the fact that from his first speech onward, Job had steadily anticipated his descent to Sheol, and in the course of his developing thought had found in that experience the course and means of his salvation. The contrast here is so striking as to deny accident; the writer is with full intent reproving Job's attitude. For him salvation is being saved from 'the Pit', which as it would work out meant prolongation of life; salvation from premature death. He wants none of Job's mystic musings; he prefers physical life. His emphasis contributes unintentional support to the interpretation to which we have been led. Some important element in the Dialogue's answer to the problem of human woe lies in a hope of survival of physical death.

353a **XXXIV-XXXVII The Further Speeches of Elihu** —Ch. 34 also has quotations. **7** takes up Eliphaz's charge in 15:16*b*. And **3** is approximately the same sort of repetition of 12:11, a fact which may not be significant, for we saw reason to believe that most of ch. 12 is secondary; besides, this saying is very like a popular proverb. **5** summarises Job's claim, though it is less than a quotation. **9a** is dependent on 22:2. **14** is modestly reminiscent of 12:10, and **23** apparently refers to Job's wish to meet God. However, it is apparent that the situation is very different from that in ch. 33. Also the thought lacks the depth of the previous speech; it is merely a recapitulation of what the friends had reiterated: the transcendence of God, man's lowly estate, and the justice of the divine rule, specifically his infliction of suffering is because of human wickedness. Thus it is apparent that the chapter does not at all continue 33, as the ending of that chapter would imply. Further, the boldness of this writer toward the wise, **2-4**, is in striking contrast to the laboured deference manifest in the first speech. It seems the best course to conclude that here we have a second writer who, under the name of Elihu, pays his tribute to the intellectual stimulus of the Dialogue, and undertakes, though very unsuccessfully, to supply it with an orthodox conclusion.

35:2b seems to allude to 9:2, and back of that to 4:17; b **3** is apparently suggested by 34:9, but it is more heavily dependent on 15:3; **7** echoes 10:15. But again the allusions are of little significance; the writer had *some* knowledge of the Dialogue. **5** seems irrelevant, but it sets the scene for the question in **6**: the lofty heavens and clouds are a symbol of God. The abruptness of **12** is resolved by recognising that it refers to **9**, with **10-11** the development of a subsidiary thought. **11** is the most striking element in the chapter; it is of a piece with the pervasive ancient speculation on the essential difference between man and animals. The answer, just as here, was that it inheres in possession of 'wisdom', a gift of God. However, as a contribution to the argument or a development of chs. 32–3, or even 34, this chapter is very thin. Again we meet the current dogma of the exaltation of God. One may hold what he will as to a relationship with 34; certainly there is nothing, except the name of Elihu, on which to base a cogent case for unity.

The diverse introduction of the speaker in **36:1** may c have an implication similar to that pointed out as relevant to 27:1 and 29:1. More cogent is the mood immediately apparent in **2-3**; we are led to suppose that this is a man of some training and ability. 'I have something' is over-translation, doubtless influenced by an *a priori* theory of the unity of these chapters; Heb. merely says, 'there is something'. The text of the chapter, notably of **16-19** and **27-33** is bad; RSV, in common with the practice of translators, obscures real difficulties under a deceptive lucidity. The most to be said is that in general it gives the best guess possible. However, the exalted insight offered in **15a** is highly dubious; perhaps the words mean no more than '*in* their affliction' and 'gives them guidance *in* adversity', which then surely accords with the sequel in **16**. **21** is logically difficult; **a** warns against turning to iniquity, but **b** states the choice has already been made. Perhaps the meaning is, 'Do not actually turn to the practice of iniquity although you have already chosen it'. More attractive is the rendering of *The Complete Bible*: 'Because for this you were tried by suffering'. **31a**. 'He judges', although an accurate rendering, is surely wrong; rather, 'he nourishes'. **30** also is perplexing; what is one to understand by 'covering the roots of the sea'? And 'lightning' is really 'light'. Probably again we are to recognise corruption of the text, with then the original providing, 'Behold, he spreads his mist about him, and covers the tops of the mountains'. 'These', **31a**, would then be the clouds, **28, 29**, and the mist.

The thought of the chapter may be summarised: **5-7**, God rules with discernment and justice; **8-15**, he employs suffering for disciplinary purposes; **16-21**, but Job has rejected the divine guidance; **22-33**, yet God is great. It will be noted that this writer reaffirms the view of the first Elihu speech as to the benign purpose of suffering; but he is far below the insight of the other; rather he employs the idea merely to emphasise the view of the friends, **7, 11**, that devout submission is the way to material blessings.

Ch. **37** makes no claim to be a new speech, but rather d to continue 36. And certainly the opening verses are consistent with this; **7** seems a digression, but probably the connection lies in the idea of knowing God's work; however, the meaning of **7a** is quite uncertain. Some

53d interpret it of winter's interruption, **6**, of man's activity, when in the mighty phenomena of nature he will recognise the work of God. It is possible, but not beyond question. In any case, the account of winter continues : **8**, then beasts hibernate ; **9-12**, then come storms and cold—all expressive of various purposes of God. The fresh beginning in **14** may imply a new author ; the content is of slightly differing mood, it is much like the survey of Nature's wonders given in ch. 38. **20** is of uncertain meaning, and probably of corrupt text. The chapter is obviously superior to much that precedes ; yet its contribution to the discussion is practically nil.

To summarise, then, in regard to the Elihu speeches : their context indicates diversity of authorship, apparently these items, chs. 32–3, 34, 35, and 36–7, the last probably somewhat expanded by a later commentator. Of these four additions to the book, the first is by a wide margin the most important. It gives priceless information about the course of the Dialogue, but as well its author was a man of marked ability, with something of significance to offer relevant to human frustration. The other three are of meagre ability, though as a literary man the last rises to some importance ; but the thinking of all alike is devoid of insight or originality. They have some familiarity with the Dialogue, but of a general sort such that they never supplement the high contribution of the first speech.

54a **XXXVIII-XXXIX The First Speech of Yahweh**—Whatever is to be our judgment as to the origin or the unity of the Yahweh speeches, their presence at this point in the book is a dramatic triumph. On the background of the polemic confusion of the Dialogue and its present lack of culmination—and it is difficult to believe that the author so far forgot reality as to have the orthodox friends convinced by Job—and in the light of Job's insistent desire to meet and argue with God, it is not less than genius to have Yahweh here appear in the whirlwind and overawe Job with revelations of his exalted might. Further, both speeches contain passages of great impressiveness and the first, chs. 38 and 39, is throughout of superb literary quality.

b This does not necessarily require that it is of unified authorship. Indeed there is some evidence to the contrary : most notable, perhaps, is the shift from a cosmic theme to animate Nature at **38:39**, though it is striking, too, that redundancies occur, as 'light' in **39:19-21**, but taken up again in **24** ; storms in **25-7**, and again in **34-8**. It is difficult, as well, to evade the conclusion that **38:15** is intruded ; such moralising has little place in a catalogue of Nature's wonders. Though v. **39** is more relevant to its context, it is likewise suggestive of interpretative glossing, also the comment on the raven, **38:41**, has no context, forward or back ; but perhaps the solution here is of a different sort ; if **a** might be deleted, then **b** and **c** fit admirably into the sketch of the lion's needs. The magnificent poem on the war-horse, **39:19-25**, by its very excellence sets itself apart from the effective but less than comparable notes on lion, wild ass, and others. Probably, too, on the same ground we are to isolate the passage on the hawk and eagle, **39:26-30**. The description of the ostrich, **39:13-18**, raises questions of a different sort. The theme of the chapter as a whole is the wonder of God's work as seen in wild creatures, but most of these verses give rather the stupidity of the ostrich. The only part of the account that will fit the purport of the chapter is **18** ; and it is significant that in the Hexapla the passage as a whole is marked with an asterisk ; it was not in Origen's Hebrew Bible ! Yet the total of all such comments cannot obscure the fact that the speech as a whole is magnificent literature. It is eloquent testimony to Israel's sense of the wonder of Nature ; it is Hebrew 'Nature poetry' on a high level, and like the best of Wordsworth, it takes its exaltation from the fact that its author (or authors) felt in Nature :

'a sense sublime 354b
Of something far more deeply interfused
Whose dwelling is the light of setting suns,
And the round ocean and the living air.'

The impressive sketch of creation, **38:4-7**, is not at c all in accord with prevalent ancient theories, such as we find in Gen. 1. It is rather an imaginative sublimation of building done by man. The formation of the sea is ascribed to a different phenomenon : it was a sort of birth. As the fluid around the foetus is released at birth, so the ocean came into being by cosmic birth ; it was clothed with clouds and darkness. But surely the figure of the new-born child ends here, for we must not be tempted to say that the sea was then shut up in a cosmic play-yard ! However, it is difficult to resist commenting to the point of tedium on the magnificence of the poetic concepts and literary presentation in passage after passage through the chapter. A bold metaphor, consistent with the genius of the entire poem, meets us in **13-14**. Dawn comes up over the hills like a traveller who has slept in the open, wrapped in his blanket from which in the morning he shakes out the insects and crawling things that have crept in for warmth. **14** is not well understood, and unfortunately RSV has perpetuated the confusion. It should not have said 'changed', but 'turned' or 'turned over'. Also, in **b** emendation is unnecessary ; the text is good. 'It' in **13a** is the dawn, but in **b** the earth. It is the earth that is 'turned over', i.e. into rounded hillocks. As one looks down across a rolling landscape with darkness still filling its depressions, it appears as though stamped out with an immense seal. Changing the figure, it is like the folds of a garment 'standing out' above the concealed body. For Hebrew thought, the mysterious depths of the sea lay close to the doors of the underworld, **16-17** ; cf. Jon. 2:5–6 ; and indeed our modern knowledge of the immense depressions in the lowest parts of the Pacific, with their earthquake and eruption, is not remote from such mythical theory. The idea of cosmic storehouses, **22-4**, was widely held (1 Enoch 18:1, 41:3–5, 60:14–22 ; cf. R. H. Charles, *The Book of Enoch* (1893) ; the references are said to be dependent on the present passage, but still they are valid evidence). For hail as an instrument of divine intervention, see Exod. 9:18–34 ; Jos. 10:11 ; Isa. 30:30, etc. The sense of wonder in the mystery and majesty of nature expressed through these verses is not minimised even if we discount **29-30** on the ground of Palestine's relative unfamiliarity with freezing temperatures. For **31-2** cf. on 9:9. The 'Mazzaroth' have not been identified ; they are tentatively equated with the 'Mazzaloth', 2 Kg. 23:5, or variously supposed to be the Zodiac or part of it, or again the Morning, or Evening, Star. **33.** 'The ordinances of the heavens' provide evidence even clearer than 18:4 of a growing sense of fixed order in the natural world.

Turning to animate nature, **38:39-39:30**, the author d expresses still the same deep sense of wonder ; once again mystery, order, and power, beyond man's intelligence or interference. For the 'wild ass' cf. on 6:5 ; he seems to this writer, and correctly, the very essence and symbol of the freedom of the great spaces. Clearly some species of wild cattle was extant in the ancient world ; it is referred to several times in the OT, and frequently in cuneiform literature. Though reputed for size and strength it was almost certainly not comparable with modern breeds, but it derived repute from its horns ; cf. Num. 23:22, 24:8 ; Dt. 33:17 ; Ps. 22:21, 92:10. 'Clothe his neck with strength', **19b**, is a very dubious translation. There is some effort of late to equate the word (for 'strength') with an Arabic term for mane. Perhaps ; but in fact it is the normal Hebrew word for thunder, except here in fem. It merits serious consideration that with the literary boldness characteristic of this striking poem, the author likens the arched neck of the war-horse to

354d the bow in the stormy heavens, and so says, 'Do you clothe his neck with *thunder*?' This section, like that on the hawk and eagle, **26-30**, is so amazing in its keen observation and vivid portrayal as to beggar comment.

355a **XL-XLII The Second Speech of Yahweh, the Responses of Job, and the Epilogue**—Apart from the particle rendered 'it', **40:2b**, this speech begins with no indication that, as in our present book, it is a second speech. And while 'it' may mean the total of the questions in chs. 38–9, as many believe, the view is not very impressive. The verse is highly obscure, and its translation quite uncertain; since it is of no great importance in the total, one can afford to dismiss it with the comment that RSV *may* be as near correct as can readily be attained. **6** is identical with 38:3; **8** is a somewhat good allusion to the temper of the Dialogue. Then with **9** thought turns to continuation of the recital of divine might in Nature, as in chs. 38–9, but almost immediately, **11-14**, is diverted into a relatively brief comment on its exercise in abasing the proud and wicked. **13b** becomes intelligible when it is recalled that 'face' was sometimes a sort of synonym of personal presence: 'Bind *themselves* in the lower depths'. The rest of chs. 40–1

b is occupied with two Nature poems. 'Behemoth' is really the plural of the word for domestic animals, but here a sort of plural of majesty: The Beast! The original is commonly supposed to have been the hippopotamus, but certainly the description is not exact. The huge and stiff tail, **17**, is anything but characteristic; not less is it false that mountains give him his food, **20**. But we must admit that **21-4** are more apt. If the hippopotamus is really intended, then apparently we are compelled to conclude that the writer knew it only by remote hearsay, or else has deliberately incorporated certain foreign, but colourful, embellishments. [For the view that Behemoth is the crocodile and Leviathan the whale, cf. G. R. Driver, in *Studi orientalistici in onore di Giorgio Levi della Vida*, i (1956), 234ff.—H.H.R.]

c For Leviathan as a mythological idea see on 3:8. The concept is at hand here, even though common interpretation may be correct that the author is referring to the crocodile; its might, its ferocity, and generally terrifying character were such as to lead to its identification as the mythical monster of pristine times. **41:1.** 'Draw out' means, obviously, draw out of the water, like a fish; but the relevance of **1b** is not clear. Driver-Gray favour the theory that **1b** and **2b** have been interchanged, and thus **1b** refers to what might be done after capture: the creature might perhaps be led about with a rope tied around its lower jaw. **8.** 'Think of the battle' is odd. But all that can be done is to accept the usual interpretation that it refers to the fierce reaction of 'leviathan' if handled. **10b-11** is difficult through its shift from 3rd person to 1st. However, twenty-seven Hebrew MSS and some of Targum read 3rd in **10b**; also the first pronoun in **11** is read as 3rd person by LXX. Every Hebraist will understand how the present reading could have come about through haplography. It is best to read 3rd person consistently, except 'mine', **11b.** RSV, through its effort to retain the present (corrupt?) text has gone far astray; read:

> 'Who can confront him and come off safe?
> Under all the heavens he (supremely) is mine';

i.e. he is the greatest of 'my' creatures.
13. 'Outer garment', literally 'the surface of his clothing', apparently refers to the belief that the creature had scales, an idea developed more fully, **15-17**, after the interruption of **14**. The details of description in **15-17** are heightened by poetic imagination—better, by poetic imagery and exaggeration—it is not necessary to suppose that mythological elements are drawn in. 'Doors of his face', **14a**, is a literalism; read, 'his mouth'; in **14b** read 'Round about, his teeth are a terror'. **18b.** 'Eyelids of the dawn' is perhaps quoted from 3:9, unless we are to 355 accept the less probable assumption that in both it merely indicates a popular phrase of the time. Not much smoke comes from a boiling pot, **20**! Nor does Heb. say 'burning'. Probably we have the same word as in **19b**; read, 'like blown sparks in bulrushes'—a smouldering fire in damp rushes would give quantities of smoke. **25b.** 'Crashing' is really breakers, the immense waves raised in the river by his movement. **27.** 'Iron' and 'bronze' clearly refer to weapons of attack. His 'underparts like sharp potsherds', **30a**, naturally suggests the threshing-sled, **30b**; better, he is like a threshing-sled spread out (or, set out) on the mud. **31b.** The 'pot of ointment' (properly, omit 'a pot of') alludes to the cream-like froth of the river water stirred violently. So too **32.** The vigour of this description is apparent; it transcends far the account of behemoth, and is comparable only with that of the war-horse, though of much greater bulk.

The replies of Job are unimpressive; whether that d reveals skill or incompetence of the author will be variously answered by interpreters. Notwithstanding the repeated longing throughout the Dialogue to confront God, when now the movement brings him to it, Job is overwhelmed and can only ejaculate a few unimportant platitudes. His complete surrender and humiliation has provoked comment by students of the Prometheus drama that the tortured Hebrew is a figure far inferior to the Greek god who could not be broken with thirty thousand years of acute agony. It is a charge difficult to counter; the reverent piety of **42:5** merits respect; but it must be borne steadily in mind that fortitude and courage are virtues of the highest order, and the submissive Job is not notable for them. If something had happened to show that his demand for divine justice was in any way erroneous, then obviously he would have been right in abandoning it; lacking that, his attitude in these replies may be adjudged nothing other than craven. The Greek went deeper than this Hebrew! (Irwin, 'Job and Prometheus', JR 29 (1950), 90–108). Yet the contrast here with the defiant Job, in hardihood ready to risk all in his demand for justice, 13:14–15, is so absolute as to raise questions. Even his deepening understanding of the ways of God, revealed through further development of the Dialogue, is remote from the surrender presented here. At the culmination of his quest in ch. 23 he still holds to his hope to meet God, and to his conviction of his own innocence, although his defiance is softened with growing faith and insight. To expect us to leap lightly from that stance to his being crushed by a recital of the mighty works of God is to put too heavy a strain on our credulity. These replies cannot be by the author of the Dialogue.

It is apparent that **42:2-6** is in confusion; **3a, 4a** are intruded under the influence of 38:3. With their removal, the utterance of Job becomes lucid if not convincing.

One feature of the **Epilogue** merits praise. It e recognises that Job is the hero of the Dialogue; he is the one who has spoken right. This is the more notable and welcome by contrast with the Elihu speeches. Yet it is odd to have this commendation immediately after the severe rebuke implied in the Yahweh speeches.

The cultic procedure of **8** is reminiscent of 1:4; but elsewhere it is foreign to the mood of the book, as is also intercessory prayer, **8, 10.** 'Restore the fortunes' is a very common phrase in the OT, though normally with national relevance; cf. Dt. 30:3; Jer. 29:14, 31:23; Ezek. 39:25; Am. 9:14, etc. It is odd, by our thought, to have his relatives now sympathising with his suffering, **11**, rather than congratulating him on his recovery. 'A piece of money' is really a kesitah, the name of some unfamiliar Hebraic weight. It is mentioned besides only in Gen. 33:19 and Jos. 24:32, both referring to Jacob's purchase of a field near Shechem for one hundred

55e kesitahs. Apparently it was then of considerable value. **12.** Job's new prosperity is exactly double the former ; cf. 1:3. But it is then strange that his second family is only the same as the one he had lost. Does the writer invoke a belief in survival beyond death, and so intimate lightly that Job's family, likewise, was doubled? **15.** The daughters' names are apparently meant as testimony to their attractiveness. The meaning of Keren-happuch is clearest, literally 'Horn of Antimony', about equivalent to 'Bright-Eyes', a happy name for a little girl. With their inheritance among their brothers—unusual in the ancient world—cf. 1:4*b*. The long subsequent life of Job, **16**, is one further item by which the writer seeks to heighten the patriarchal mood of his story. 'Full of days', **17**, fails to carry the thought : literally 'satisfied with days', i.e. he lived till he had all of life he wanted, and could die without bitterness or regret.

f The Epilogue provides an idyllic ending to Job's trials ; but as a serious answer to the great issue of the book it is open to precisely the charge of complete falsity which Job had hurled against the orthodoxy of his time. Life comes out this way only exceptionally; illness and despair do not inevitably terminate in long years of complete happiness. Such a story provides no answer to our human predicament. The author of the Dialogue was too penetrating and too honest ever to have offended his readers with these superficialities. Further, there is no adequate reason for seeking to affiliate the story with the Yahweh speeches, or with any other part of the book, though its closest affinities are with the Prologue. Instead we must boldly face the conclusion that here is still one more ancient writer who was stirred by the greatness of the Dialogue—but he was the weakest of the entire succession.

g The literary exaltation of the great bulk of the Yahweh speeches needs no further praise. In this regard they make a superb contribution to the total of the book. Yet, after one enjoys all this to the full, questions will obtrude themselves. What do the two speeches say? In particular what do they offer as relevant to the development of the theme of the book? And were they written by the author of the Dialogue?

h Almost unanimously, interpreters of the book have found here the culmination of the debate and the author's answer to its problem. Probably the most cogent presentation is that of G. B. Gray (ICC (1921), lviii–lxiii). The charges made by the friends, he believes, are here implicitly dismissed through their being ignored. The condemnation of Job in 38:2 and 40:2 is 'of Job's criticism of God's ways, not as they actually were, but as they would have been' if the penal theory of suffering were true. The speeches also rebuke a claim 'persistently maintained by the friends and only half abandoned by Job himself . . . to an extent of acquaintance with God's ways which it is the purpose of the speech to show that man did not possess. . . .' Similar is the view of Robert Gordis, which merits citation as typical of the entire effort to defend the originality of these speeches : there is order and harmony in the natural world, which man cannot comprehend ; no more can he understand the moral world, but must face 'the mystery with a courage born of faith in the essential rightness of things' (Gordis, 'The Conflict of Tradition and Experience (The Book of Job)' in *Great Moral Dilemmas*, R. M. MacIver, ed., 155–78. Cf. Burrows, 'The Voice from the Whirlwind', JBL 47 (1928), 116–32, and his survey of other views). Gray confessed 'some subtlety' in his reasoning. His criticism of Budde's effort to defend the Elihu speeches provides the best additional comment on this entire sort of interpretation : 'it may be doubted whether a doctrine which, however true and profound in the abstract, is so little developed by the poet himself, can have formed the main idea of his work' (ibid., lxiv). All this attitude to the Yahweh speeches is patently eisegesis (i.e. gives **355h**
the commentator's own interpretation). Were it not for their place in the book and the consequent implication that they *must* say something profound relative to the book's theme, no-one would for a moment suppose that they speak of anything other than the might and knowledge of God. Save for 38:15, the originality of which we saw reason to doubt, and 40:10–14, there is no concern anywhere with God's righteousness or with his justice. The devout Muslim ejaculation well sums up the total of the four chapters : *Allah Akbar!* Still more relevant is the fact which all these interpreters overlook, in whole or in part, that the speeches say only what the friends had reiterated time and again (so D. B. MacDonald, op. cit., 66 ; and Stevenson, *The Poem of Job* (1947), although he accepts this as evidence of the originality of the section). Their entire content might be regarded as an expansion of Eliphaz's devout expostulations in 5:9–16 except that Eliphaz actually voices more of the just government of God than do these chapters. They are, too, a sort of footnote on Zophar's awed piety expressed in 11:7–9. More than that, Job himself had voiced in brief their entire theological content, in 9:4–12. What possible rationality can there be in belabouring him here with a view which he has already made fully clear that he holds?

We have seen, too, how the author of the Dialogue **i**
sets up the orthodox position of the friends only to point out its inadequacy ; and he has Job grope his way forward from their theology into some higher faith and hope. If we invoke here Gray's reminder that we should recognise what the speeches omit, the crucial relevance of these considerations becomes evident. For they omit any and all reference to the painful gains of Job's tortured pilgrimage of faith; they ignore the function of the intermediary, whatever it was ; they are oblivious of the insight of the great poet of the Dialogue that final answer must in some way take account of death as transition, through which, having been tested, one comes out like purified gold. Briefly, the point of the matter is that to accept these speeches as original is to nullify the entire Dialogue and to adjudge the friends victors in the debate. The ideas here evolved had been their basic emphasis throughout.

So then our questions answer themselves. There is **j**
some tendency to analyse the speeches and find the second, with its lengthy descriptions of Behemoth and Leviathan, foreign to the mood of the first, In all probability this is sound. But it falls into minor significance in view of the conclusion to which we are compelled, that both alike ignore the progress of thought in the Dialogue, and that their place in the book is nothing more than further testimony to the greatness of the original author who inspired numbers of lesser, if thoughtful, men to discussion of his high theme. The speeches of Yahweh possess much that is of high worth, yet they lack the profound insight into human nature and the grasp of its most poignant problem which makes of the Dialogue one of the great classics of our literary heritage. (But cf. Fullerton, 'The Original Conclusion to the Book of Job', ZATW 42 (1924), 116–36, who thinks the author of the Dialogue had no solution of the problem to offer, and was merely poking fun at those who thought they had.)

Conclusion—There is no occasion to reiterate con- **356a**
clusions as to the origins of our Book of Job to which our detailed study has led us. But it is apparent that the 'solution' offered by the book is equally diverse. The Prologue was concerned to affirm that disinterested piety is a reality, but also it seemed to hold that human woe is not a matter for a theodicy at all, for it takes its rise, not in the will of God, but in the machinations of the Satan. On the other hand, the Epilogue means that if only the sufferer has the toughness to endure, all will come out right in the end. In the clamorous reiteration of divine sovereignty in the other sections, it is a relief to find one, the first

356a speech of Elihu, which has something incisive to offer : that suffering comes to warn and recall the sufferer.

b The basic fact for an understanding of the Dialogue is that Job is represented, not in a theological position, but in a spiritual pilgrimage away from uncritical, current orthodoxy toward a faith and hope deep grounded in experience : hope that there is meaning in life's devious pattern, and faith that God is good and 'his tender mercies are over all his works'. A notable advance was the realisation that life is a mottled fabric ; it has much of evil, but also great moments of joy and exaltation. Life's tragedy is in part answered by life's bounty beyond the richest deserts of the best of men.

c In some way which even at the end we cannot fully delineate, the intermediary plays an indispensable role in Job's healing. It became steadily clearer through our study that the figure is intimately related to the mythical sufferer whose passion was central in the chthonic literature which our author was fond of citing in varying definiteness. In some way through his pain and death and restoration, or rather through the profound reality which the pagan myth vaguely apprehended—that is, through the healing and redemptive forces operative for those who will give them free course—Job was restored to well-being and reconciliation. So much is clear. Unfortunately the incompleteness of the Dialogue and the brevity of the notes in ch. 33 leave us with less than full elucidation of the work of the intermediary. Perhaps it was never really clarified. For we must recall that Paul's somewhat copious treatment of the comparable role of Jesus Christ in the Christian doctrine of salvation left the core of the matter so indefinite that to this very day it provides ground for theological disputation. In 16:19–21 the intermediary in some way plays a part as intercessor with God, and perhaps in 19:25–7 also, in so far as it is possible there to trace the movement of thought. But 33:23–6 seem to attest a function toward both God and man. In both, however, his role apparently is entirely persuasive ; sacramental intercession cannot be discerned.

d Yet the entire context of the concept is such as to preclude flat denial. The cultus of the dying god must be recognised as nothing less than the profound sacrament of the ancient world : a god laid down his life that through death life might arise triumphant, and suffering and sorrow give place to joy. The recurrent allusions to this range of thought presented 356d by the Dialogue permit no other conclusion than that the author intended some such meaning by the figure of the living 'redeemer' through whom the sufferer should see God as one not estranged from him. As in the myth the sufferer is a god, so in the Dialogue the intermediary is more than human. This is obvious even in 9:33 ; in chs. 16 and 19 he has already taken on quasi-divine qualities. Much as our evidence lacks of final clarity, we shall probably not err seriously if we hold the ultimate answer which the Dialogue offers to life's grim enigma to be that suffering is in the nature of things—God himself suffers. In that sense it is sacramental, and through it we enter most truly into communion with him. Pain instinctively repels—that is its function. Yet we must not see in it a mark or symbol of our fallen estate, nor yet condign punishment by a righteous or indignant God. Difficult as the thought is for us to apprehend, suffering is our privilege ; it is an opportunity ; by it we may participate in life's purest and deepest and become fellow-citizens with the saints in light. Through it—and the point we are making is that such citation of St Paul is not eisegesis, but true interpretation of the Dialogue—through it 'we share in his sufferings becoming like him in death'.

Bibliography—COMMENTARIES : C. J. Ball, *The Book of Job : a revised text and version* (1922) ; K. Budde, HKAT (1913) ; M. Buttenwieser, *The Book of Job* (1922) ; A. B. Davidson, CB (1884), rev. ed. by H. C. O. Lanchester (1951) ; P. Dhorme, *Le Livre de Job* (1926) ; S. R. Driver and G. B. Gray, ICC (1921) ; B. Duhm, KHC (1897) ; G. Hölscher, HAT (1952) ; M. Jastrow, *The Book of Job* (1920) ; E. G. Kraeling, *The Book of the Ways of God* (1938) ; A. L. Lassen, *The Commentary of Levi ben Gerson (Gersonides) on the book of Job* (1946) ; A. S. Peake, Cent.B (1905) ; J. Steinmann, *Le livre de Job* (1956) ; W. B. Stevenson, *Critical Notes on the Hebrew Text of the Poem of Job* (1951) ; F. Stier, *Das Buch Ijjob* (1954) ; S. Terrien, IB iii (1954).

OTHER LITERATURE : F. Baumgärtel, *Der Hiobdialog : Aufriss und Deutung* (1933) ; J. B. Pritchard, ANET (2nd ed. 1955) ; W. B. Stevenson, *The Poem of Job* (1947) ; C. Westermann, *Der Aufbau des Buches Hiob* (1956).

THE PSALMS

By G. W. ANDERSON

357a **The Structure and Growth of the Psalter**—Modern study of the prophetic books of the OT has shown that they are for the most part collections of smaller collections of units of material, partly oracular and partly narrative. In a rather different way Ps. is also a collection of collections, some at least of which may be discerned behind the present formal arrangement of the contents, which is generally held to be a deliberate imitation of the five-fold division of the books attributed to Moses. The five books of Ps. are: I, 1–41; II, 42–72; III, 73–89; IV, 90–106; V, 107–50. Each of them ends with a doxology (41:13, 72:18f., 89:52, 106:48, 150:6), with the probable exception of V, where the closing words of 150 do not offer a satisfactory parallel to the other doxologies.

b Varied as are the contents of Book I, nearly all the pss. in it have two characteristics in common: they use the divine name 'Yahweh' (Lord), and their superscriptions contain the expression 'of David'. The exceptions are 1, 2, 33, which are not ascribed to David. Of these, 1 seems to be a prologue to Ps., 33 is perhaps a later addition, and 2, which is a Royal Psalm, is probably a Davidic ps. which has lost its title (cf. commentary). Thus 2–32, 34–41 form a Davidic Yahwistic collection.

c By contrast, the name 'Yahweh' is generally avoided in 42–83, and instead the word 'Elohim' is used. This difference is particularly noteworthy in 53 and 70, which are in other respects exactly identical with 14 and 40:13–17. Clearly the change of divine name is no accident. Within this Elohistic collection three main subdivisions are evident. 42–9 are 'of the Sons of Korah'; 51–65, 68–71 are 'of David'; and 50, 73–83 are 'of Asaph'. 72, which is 'of Solomon' is followed by the statement that 'the prayers of David, the son of Jesse, are ended', and is evidently the conclusion of a Davidic block, which probably consisted of at least 51–72, though MT does not label 66, 67 as 'of David'. The removal of this block to follow the Yahwistic Davidic pss. in Book I would link 50 with the other Asaphite pss., 73–83. A further indication of deliberate arrangement may be found in the fact that 42–5 and 52–5 are headed 'A Maskil', and are followed by others differently designated in slightly irregular groups.

d The Elohistic collection, 42–83, is followed by an appendix of Yahwistic pss. (84–9), of which 84, 85, 87, 88 are 'of the Sons of Korah', 86 is 'of David', 89 is 'of Ethan the Ezrahite'. Had these originally formed part of the Elohistic collection, the name Yahweh would doubtless have been replaced by Elohim.

e In Books IV–V the outlines of earlier groupings are not so easily discerned. 93–9 (or 100) are pss. of Yahweh's kingship (cf. 47); 105, 106, 111–17, 135, 146–50 are Hallelujah pss. (cf. on 113); 120–34 are 'Songs of Ascents' or 'Pilgrim' pss.; 101, 103, 108–10, 122, 124, 131, 133, 138–45 are designated 'of David'.

f The very nature of the pss. makes it impossible for us now to trace the history of these collections or the process by which they were combined. Nor is there any precise evidence to enable us to date the completion of the entire collection; but although a generation ago some critics assigned many pss. to the 2nd cent. B.C. 357f
or even later, it is probable that the collection was complete by the beginning of that century.

The Superscriptions and Technical Terms in 358a
Ps.—The great majority of the pss. have superscriptions. These vary considerably in extent and in character; and the divergences between them in MT and LXX indicate that they represent a singularly insecure textual tradition. They present other difficulties. It is perhaps no exaggeration to say that where their meaning is clear, we have reason to doubt their reliability, and that where they might provide us with valuable data about the history and use of various pss., their interpretation is debated or obscure. Those which are straightforward but unreliable are the historical notices which assign individual pss. to particular occasions. These are discussed below in the commentary on the pss. to which they are prefixed. The remainder seem to indicate the authors or origin of the pss., their character, the tunes or musical instruments appropriate to them, and the cultic actions for which some pss. were intended. But there is so much uncertainty about the interpretation of most of these terms that even a general classification can be offered only with considerable reserve.

Terms which seem to indicate the authorship or source of b
the pss. Of these the most frequent is *l^{e}dhāwîdh*, which is traditionally rendered 'of David', but which can also mean 'for David' or 'about David'. The fact that this expression is sometimes combined with an allusion to some incident in David's life (e.g. 3, 51) suggests that at least at some stage in the transmission of Ps. it was taken to indicate authorship. But these historical allusions are seldom if ever particularly appropriate and sometimes improbable (see the commentary), and although it is harder to demonstrate conclusively that David did not write many of the pss. than some scholars have assumed, the tradition that he wrote them (if the term *l^{e}dhāwîdh* is to be taken in this sense) is not prima facie very reliable. Possibly the term indicated authorship in a somewhat looser sense. If the corpus of legal tradition was ascribed to Moses and much of the Wisdom literature attributed to Solomon, it is possible that David's reputation as a poet and musician attracted pss. to his name, and thus by such a process of accumulation a 'Davidic' collection grew up around a nucleus of authentically Davidic pss. This interpretation accords with the attribution of other pss. to collections associated with Asaph, the Sons of Korah, and the choirmaster (see below *c, d*). It has, however, also been suggested that *l^{e}dhāwîdh* means 'for' or 'about David', that 'David' means 'the king', and that 'Davidic' pss. were associated with rituals in which the king took part. On any view it should be recognised that there was some inconsistency in the use of this term (as a comparison of MT and LXX shows). It is also possible that it was understood in different senses at different times.

The term 'of the Sons of Korah' is prefixed to 42 c
and 43, 44–9, 84, 85, 87, 88. 1 Chr. 6:31ff. (cf. 2 Chr. 20:19) suggests that a Levitical guild of temple singers traced its descent from Korah, Levi's

358c great-grandson (Num. 16). Similarly Asaph, to whom 50, 73–83 are ascribed, is mentioned in 1 Chr. 6:39, 15:17, 19, 16:5 as a musical functionary. It is generally held that 'of the sons of Korah' and 'of Asaph' indicate pss. derived from collections associated with Levitical guilds or choirs. 88, a Korahite ps., is also 'of Heman the Ezrahite' (1 Chr. 6:33); and 89 is 'of Ethan the Ezrahite' (1 Chr. 6:44). A comparison of 1 Chr. 2:6 with 1 Kg. 4:31 suggests that there may have been some confusion in the traditions about persons bearing these names. 'To Jeduthun' (39) seems to be a similar personal reference (cf. 2 Chr. 5:12); but 'according to Jeduthun' (62, 77) is probably a musical direction. The ascription of 90 to Moses and of 72, 127 to Solomon may have been suggested by features in the contents of these pss. (see commentary).

d The term 'to the choirmaster' appears in the superscription of 55 pss. (cf. Hab. 3:19). This interpretation of the Heb., which has been widely accepted, suggests that these pss. belonged to a choirmaster's collection. If so, then there must have been considerable overlapping in the contents of the collections, for many of these pss. are also 'of David'. The rendering in LXX, 'unto the end', suggests not only a different interpretation but a different form of the word. Two modern suggestions (both of which presuppose vowel changes) are that it refers to the musical rendering and that it is a cultic term meaning 'for propitiation'.

e *Terms which seem to describe the character of the pss.* Some of these are quite clear: 'A Song' (e.g. 30), 'A Psalm' (e.g. 3), 'A Song of Praise' (145), 'A Prayer' (e.g. 17). The meaning of others is elusive and it may well be that some should not be included under this head. 'Maskil' (e.g. 32 and cf. 47:7, RSV*n*) has often been taken to be a meditative or didactic poem; but this does not really describe the varied contents of the pss. so headed. The term may mean 'acting wisely or skilfully' or 'giving insight', which some interpret as 'a skilful song' and others in a cultic sense. 'Shiggaion' (7; cf. Hab. 3:1) is a quite obscure term; the supposed root meaning 'to err', 'to go astray' has been interpreted in musical and cultic senses, of irregular rhythm, or of a connection with the sin-offering. A parallel with an Akkadian word meaning 'lament' has also been suggested. 'Miktam' (e.g. 16), another obscure term, has been understood in various senses, e.g. 'secret prayer', 'expiatory song'.

f *Terms which refer to instruments or tunes.* This is a field which has been fertile in conjectures but barren in assured results; and again we must note that if certain interpretations are sound some of these terms should be included in the list of cultic terms. 'With stringed instruments' (e.g. 4) is self-explanatory and certain. 'For the flutes' is the most likely rendering of a phrase which occurs only in 5. 'According to the Sheminith' (6, 12), may refer to an eight-stringed instrument. 'According to the Gittith' (e.g. 8) may refer to a melody associated with the vintage or may contain an allusion to some association with Gath. 'According to Do Not Destroy' (e.g. 57; MT has simply 'do not destroy') perhaps refers to the song mentioned in Isa. 65:8. 'According to Alamoth' (46) may indicate a tune or instruments (cf. 1 Chr. 15:20) or women's voices. There is a similarity between this phrase and 'according to Muth-labben' (9), and also 'for ever' in 48:14 (see commentary). We may make our choice between guessing that 'according to Muth-labben' (9), 'according to Lilies' (45, 69), 'according to Shushan Eduth' (60), 'according to Shoshannim Eduth' (80; RSV 'according to Lilies. A Testimony'), 'according to the Hind of the Dawn' (22), 'according to Mahalath' (53, 88), 'according to the Dove on Far-off Terebinths' (56) are names of tunes and speculating more adventurously about their possible allusions to cultic usage; in the present state of our knowledge we cannot hope for certainty or even any high degree of probability.

Terms which indicate cultic or choral use. 'For the 358g
thank offering' (100) may indicate a ps. to accompany that sacrificial act (but see commentary). 'For the memorial offering' (38, 70) may indicate the offering mentioned in Lev. 2:2, 9, 16. 'Leannoth' may be a direction for antiphonal rendering. 'A Song at the dedication of the Temple' (30) and 'A Song for the Sabbath' (92) also fall into this class (see commentary). The 'Songs of Ascents' (120–34) are perhaps best included here, though the term has sometimes been taken to refer to the literary form of these pss. or to the going up or return of the Exiles from Babylonia. According to the Mishnah the Levites used to sing on 15 steps leading from the Court of the Women to the Court of the Israelites; and these steps correspond to the 15 Songs of Ascents. But the most likely view is that these pss. were intended for use when worshippers came up to the sanctuary at Jerusalem to join in the worship of the great festivals.

The term 'Selah' occurs 71 times in Ps. (92 times h
in LXX), almost exclusively in Books I–III, and 3 times in Hab. It has been explained in many different ways: as a pause, an instrumental interlude, or the lifting up of the voices, as an abbreviation of some musical direction, and as an indication that a refrain should be sung. In 9:16 it is accompanied by the word 'Higgaion' (cf. 92:3, where the word 'Higgaion' is rendered 'melody'), variously interpreted as 'meditation', 'murmuring music', or 'resounding music'.

The Dating and Classification of the Psalms— 359a
Those parts of the titles which allude to incidents in David's life exemplify an attitude to the interpretation of the Ps. which survived even among those scholars who rejected the Davidic authorship of all or most of the Ps., viz. the attempt to associate individual pss. with specific persons and events. Thus 72 and 110 have been related to persons and events in the Hellenistic age, 46 to the raising of the Assyrian siege of Jerusalem in 701 B.C.; 74 to the fall of Jerusalem in 586 B.C. or to the desecration of the Temple by Antiochus Epiphanes. While the possibility of making equations of this sort should not be entirely excluded, the very nature of worship makes it unlikely that the precise historical setting of a liturgical composition will matter as much as it would, for example, in the interpretation of a prophetic oracle. Hymns and prayers are applicable above all not to specific historical situations but to those which occur repeatedly in the experience of the worshipping community and of the individual. For this reason questions of date will seldom be raised in the following commentary. There is seldom anything like adequate evidence to enable us to do more than assign any given ps. to a general period.

The application of form criticism to the OT docu- b
ments has nowhere been more effective than in the study of Ps. The pioneer worker in this sphere was Gunkel, who sought to supplement analytical literary criticism, and the attempt to date books or parts of books, by the study of literary forms (*Gattungen*) and of their setting in life (*Sitz im Leben*), and the attempt to trace their history. Of the literary types which he recognised in Ps. only the most important can be mentioned here.

First and simplest is the *Hymn*, which is a summons c
to worship Yahweh for his greatness and goodness. Its character can be seen in massive simplicity in 100 and again in 145–50.

The second is the *Communal Lament* (*Klagelied des* d
Volkes). Its occasion was some situation of national affliction, such as a drought, or a reverse in war, when it would be appropriate to hold a day of fasting, penitence and prayer. In such a lament the community's plight is described and Yahweh's help is besought, usually with some reference to his past goodness. Examples are 44, 74, 79, 80.

The third main type is the *Royal Psalm*. Pss. of this e
type had often been interpreted in Messianic or

359e Christological terms or applied to some historical ruler, e.g. of the Maccabaean period. But Gunkel maintained that they must refer to Israelite kings of the pre-exilic period, and interpreted them in terms of the religious status and functions of the monarchy. Such pss. were appropriate to special occasions such as the king's accession (2, 110) or wedding (45) or to the beginning of a campaign (20) or the celebration of a victory (18).

f The fourth type is the *Individual Lament* (*Klagelied des Einzelnen*), in which a worshipper appeals to Yahweh to deliver him from affliction. In some pss. of this type there is a confession of sin, in others a profession of innocence. Often the prayer for help passes over into an assurance that it will be given and into thanksgiving or a vow of some kind. In the descriptions of the worshipper's plight two themes recur frequently. Sometimes he is described as a sick man, and on occasion we hear that he is, as it were, in death's clutches, and almost overwhelmed by the destructive waters of the underworld. At other times we hear of malicious enemies who gloat over his misfortunes, who are depicted in military terms as attacking him, or in forensic terms as having brought false accusations against him, or as hunting the Psalmist as if he were a beast. The identification of these enemies presents difficult problems (see §360*d*). Pss. of this type are more numerous than any other. As examples we may note 3, 5, 6, 7, 42f., 51.

g The last of the main types is the *Individual Song of Thanksgiving* (*Danklied des Einzelnen*). Pss. of this type were doubtless intended to accompany an offering made in gratitude for some benefit received. They describe the affliction which had befallen the worshipper, his prayer to Yahweh for succour, and the way in which his need had been met. Such a ps., uttered in the sanctuary, was a public testimony to Yahweh's power and will to help those who trusted in him; and accordingly we often find that in giving thanks the worshipper exhorts his hearers to take to heart the lessons of his own experience. Instances of this type are 30, 32, 34, 62, 116, and, outside Ps., Isa. 38:10–20; Jon. 2:2–9. There are obvious points of contact with the Individual Laments, particularly in the descriptions of the worshipper's plight, where the themes noted in *f* recur.

h Other types recognised by Gunkel include *Wisdom Poems*, *Torah Liturgies*, *Pilgrimage Songs*, *Communal Songs of Thanksgiving* and *Liturgies* (i.e. a combination of different types in one complex whole).

i The work of classification carried out by Gunkel and continued on similar lines by other scholars has as its background the literatures of the ancient Near East. Since Gunkel's day the publication of the Ugaritic poetical texts from Râs Shamra has made important additions to the comparative material which was already available from Egypt and Mesopotamia; and it is evident that in structure and phraseology Hebrew psalmody has much in common with these literatures. There are also important resemblances in religious content. Here again we move into a highly debatable field of study. But no serious examination of the religion of Ps. can afford to neglect the problems which these similarities raise. The most important of these questions are touched on in §360.

360a **The Religion of the Psalter**—In his discussion of the literary types Gunkel not only classified them according to form, but assigned to each a particular setting in life. For the most part these were originally cultic, but he held that most of the poems in Ps. were imitations of the types which had been used in cultic situations, and that these poems were not themselves intended for cultic use but were produced in pietistic circles in which the cultic legacy became the expression of a supposedly more spiritual worship. But since one of the most noteworthy features in recent OT study has been an emphasis on the vital part played by the cult in OT religion and on its positive value, it is not surprising that others have not been satisfied with this position. Attempts have been made to recreate the 360a
actual cultic situations in which, it is claimed, the main types of pss. were used. The field of cultic practice is seen, not as a graveyard of lifeless forms but as an arena of life-and-death struggles, of exhilarating triumphs, in which, in high moments, the presence and power of Yahweh were realised. On some of the points to be mentioned below there is still considerable disagreement among scholars; but the increasing scepticism about the late dating of pss. which was at one time fashionable and the corresponding readiness to allow that many pss. may be pre-exilic have lent support to the view that Ps. provides useful evidence about the rich cultic life of ancient Israel.

Among the Hymns there is an important and dis- b
tinctive group known as the pss. of Yahweh's enthronement: 47, 93, 95–100. These celebrate the kingship of Yahweh, his triumph over his enemies, and his coming as Judge. They have been interpreted as referring to some signal historical manifestation of Yahweh's power, or as predicting his final, decisive advent at the end of time to inaugurate a completely new order. But, chiefly through the work of the Norwegian scholar Mowinckel, these pss. are often now understood in cultic terms, and related to the New Year festival (cf. §132*k*). On this interpretation these and other pss. are treated as the liturgical texts for that festival, in which Yahweh's creative and redemptive work was celebrated, his triumph over the power of chaos, his subjugation of the nations and their rulers, who were the enemies of his people, and his renewal of the covenant bond between himself and Israel. These great themes were presented not only in the language of liturgy but in ritual drama: the Ark, the symbol of Yahweh's presence (cf. §131*q*), was carried in solemn procession to the Temple (cf. on 24); and he was hailed as King over all. This theory has been and still is criticised as being based on misleading analogies from other religions; and there are still those who would interpret the Enthronement pss. in terms of history or of eschatology. But in its general outline it has been fairly widely accepted and further elaborated or modified in various ways. It was an important part of Mowinckel's original theory that the themes of the festival provide the framework of the later eschatological hope. More recently it has been argued, notably by A. R. Johnson, that the festival itself included an element of eschatological expectation. Particular attention has also been devoted to the part which the king may have played in the ritual drama. Elsewhere in the ancient Near East important cultic functions were performed by kings (cf. §132*l–n*); and it has been maintained that some pss. record ritual acts and experiences of the Davidic king, son and Messiah of Yahweh, who in his own person summed up the life of the nation (see especially the commentary on 2, 18, 89), and that, at a critical point in the ritual he was assailed by the powers of chaos and death, but was succoured by Yahweh and given the assurance of victory over all his enemies. Some of the suggestions advanced are highly debatable; but on any reasonable interpretation of the Royal Psalms it is clear that the kings of Israel played a significant part in pre-exilic worship.

In the Individual Laments, and in the Individual c
Songs of Thanksgiving, some important points call for comment. First we may note that it has not always been taken for granted that the subject of these pss. (the 'I') is in fact an individual. It used to be widely assumed that 'I' commonly represented the nation or the worshipping community, and that the descriptions of illness and of attacks by enemies referred to national calamities. This view is now generally abandoned; but it is possible that sometimes the 'I' is the king or other representative speaking on behalf of the nation.

The 'enemies' who are frequently mentioned in d
these pss. have been variously identified. One view is that they represent apostate Jews who persecuted the

360d faithful in the post-exilic period. They have also been identified with foreign enemies, in which case the 'I' must be the leader of the community. Mowinckel has offered an interesting but much criticised interpretation of the phrase 'workers of evil' by which the enemies are often described. He maintains that the 'evil' is not simply moral evil but the spells which sorcerers have used to bring misery and affliction on the 'humble', who, in such pss., seek the divine aid to counteract these malign acts. Yet another view, which is probably appropriate to some of the pss., is that the enemies are men who have sought to bring about the Psalmist's undoing by false accusations. Thereupon the accused person resorted to the sanctuary that his name might be cleared, possibly by some act of divination or by some form of ordeal. It is probably unwise to look for any single explanation of the terms used.

e We have already noted (§359*f*) that in the Individual Laments the prayer for help is often followed by what looks like an anticipation of the divine deliverance. Sometimes a mournful plea is followed by jubilant thanksgiving. It has been thought that such abrupt transitions may point to the communication of a reassuring oracle to the worshipper.

f A number of other pss. contain oracular material of different kinds (e.g. 2:7ff., 50:5ff., 95:7*b*ff.). In all probability these are to be attributed to cultic prophets (cf. §133*d*) who formed part of the sanctuary staff. The idea that there was a sharp line of demarcation or a perennial conflict between prophet and priest cannot reasonably be maintained ; and as we must recognise that the sanctuaries and their liturgies contributed to the prophetic literature, we must similarly allow for the presence of prophetic influence in the worship of which Ps. was the expression.

g Suggested lines of interpretation such as have been mentioned above help us to understand the pss. in their original and native setting, recreating for us the colour and movement of the worship of ancient Israel. The many points of contact with the literature and thought of Israel's neighbours are important and illuminating ; but Ps. remains an essentially Israelite collection, celebrating the God who brought his people out of Egypt, made a covenant with them, and gave them his Law, brought them into the land which he had promised to their fathers, raised up David and his house to rule over them, established his sanctuary in Jerusalem, and made himself known not only in deliverances but also in chastisements. It is an epitome of Israel's religion ; and so varied are its contents that any attempt to summarise or systematise its teaching is likely to fail ; but some of its most noteworthy features call for comment here.

h First, there is the extraordinary objectivity of its praise. In simplicity, dignity and directness pss. like 93, 96, 100 or 150 are still models of their kind.

i Second, there is the implicit faith of the laments. The language in which they express human need and affliction is often passionate and almost rebellious ; but the underlying conviction is that God is ready to hear and to deliver. Even in 88, in which no flicker of hope appears, the Psalmist has still been impelled to lay his need before God.

j Third, there is the awareness of the moral obligations which are imposed in worship. This is evident both in passages like 15, 24:3f. and in pss. like 19 and 119 which describe the Law as a precious gift of God to his people.

k Fourth, there is the note of joy which appears in the thanksgivings, and which seems to have been one of the essential elements in Israelite worship.

l Finally, we may mention two features which are often felt to present difficulty in the modern Christian use of Ps. The first is the violent denunciation of enemies and the invoking of vengeance on them. The outstanding example is 137:7–9. It is obviously foolish to attempt by some form of mental gymnastics to reconcile such passages with the command to love your enemies. But it is well to remember that it was 360l natural for those who suffered because of their allegiance to the God of Israel to think of those who maltreated them as his enemies. The presence of similar violent outbursts in Jer. is a reminder that even a sensitive and dedicated spirit may yield temporarily to such feelings.

m The second is the presence of passages such as 6:5 which deny the meaning or worth of any existence beyond death. A bare existence there may be, but it is shadowy and joyless because death means separation from Yahweh. Such a belief was held in Israel. Some passages which seem to counterbalance this outlook do not in fact do so. Frequently the sore affliction of the Psalmist is described in terms of death. Though he has not in fact died, he is in some measure in the power of death ; and consequently deliverance means that he is 'saved from death', 'brought up from Sheol', or the like (cf. Jon. 2:2–9). But this clearly does not mean a real victory over death in our sense. Nevertheless there are passages in Ps. which seem to rise above the belief that this earthly life is all (see commentary on 16, 49, 73). In them the Psalmist realises that the communion with God which he enjoys in this present life outweighs the afflictions he has to endure and is a possession of which death itself cannot deprive him. This, perhaps, is the supreme message of Ps., that to know God, to praise him, and to obey him is life indeed.

361a **Book I—Pss. I-XLI**

I. This ps., which has no title or superscription, is probably an introduction to the entire Psalter, summing up the faith in God's righteousness and the ideal of piety to which it bears witness. It is a reflective poem rather than a psalm for use in public worship. Its teaching about the reward of the righteous and the punishment of the wicked echoes a theme which runs through Deuteronomic and Wisdom teaching. Its emphasis on the written Law, which is also reminiscent of the Deuteronomic tradition, is characteristic of late Jewish piety. Its witness to the divine ordering of human affairs is central to all OT teaching. The ps. may be divided thus : 1–3, the well-being of the righteous ; 4–5, the ruin of the wicked ; 6, the contrast explained by the divine ordering of human life. **1. Blessed:** better, 'Happy' (cf. 112:1, 128:2 ; Mt. 5:3ff.). The three clauses in this verse are probably intended to express a climax : doing what wicked men advocate, persisting in the habits of the sinful, associating with those who deride religion. The ideal of separation from the wicked and godless is prominent in post-exilic Judaism. **2.** The positive aspect of piety. **Delight** in the Law is another mark of post-exilic piety (cf. 119, *passim*), which did not regard its requirements as a burden. For the ideal of the study of the Law, cf. Jos. 1:8. **3.** cf. Jer. 17:8. The **streams** are artificial channels for irrigation. **he prospers:** cf. Jos. 1:8. **4f. the chaff,** to which the wicked are likened, is often used figuratively in descriptions of judgment. Here the point is perhaps simply the insecurity of the wicked. The **judgment** referred to may be, but is probably not, the last judgment but rather the dispensation of divine judgment in this life. **6. knows:** not simply 'takes cognisance of', but 'takes an active interest in'. Like many other OT passages, the ps. seems to take a naïve view of reward and punishment in this life. But underlying it is the passionate faith in God's righteous control of the world.

II. A Royal Psalm. Possibly a superscription 'Of David' was lost when Ps. 1 was prefixed to the whole collection. The situation presupposed is the accession of a king and the widespread revolt of vassals which commonly took place in the Ancient East at the beginning of a new reign. But the king rules by divine decree as Yahweh's son. The rebels are admonished to submit to Yahweh's power. The reference has often been taken to be to the future reign of the b

61b Messiah ; and the mention of universal dominion has been said to be inappropriate to any historical Israelite king. On the prevalent modern cultic interpretation of the Psalter, the accession is taken to be that of a historical king. The occasion may be either the actual accession or a re-enactment of it as part of the ritual of the autumnal festival. Some argue that the references to widespread revolt and world-wide dominion are purely conventional features characteristic of ancient oriental court style : but if the anointed kings of David's line were thought of as sons and vicegerents of Yahweh (cf. 89:19–29), the phraseology needs little further explanation. The heirs of the covenant promises made to David cannot be thought of merely as the petty rulers of an insignificant state. **1-3.** Without preamble (which is understandable if the ps. formed part of a larger liturgical whole) the international uprising is described. **2. anointed :** the word from which ' Messiah ' is derived. The term ' Messiah ' is applied by some scholars not only to the ideal king of the future but also to the reigning king considered as a present channel of divine blessing. **saying :** not in the Heb., but appropriately supplied. **4-6.** The revolt is certain to fail, because the king in Jerusalem is established by the power of the heavenly King. The thought of God's choice of the royal house and of Jerusalem is emphasised. The vividly human terms in which Yahweh's reaction is presented are characteristic even of those parts of the OT which make most of the unique and exalted character of God (e.g. Isa. 40–55). **6.** The response to the rebellious outburst in 3. There is strong emphasis on ' I ', reinforced by ' *my* king ', ' *my* holy hill '. The rebels have to deal not only with Israel and her earthly king but also with the heavenly King who supports them. **7-9.** The king speaks, quoting the divine oracle by which his position is guaranteed. His special relationship to Yahweh as his ' son ' (cf. 2 Sam. 7:14*a*) dates from his accession, as the word ' today ' shows. Thus he is son, not by nature, but by adoption, in virtue of Yahweh's choice of him to be his anointed. On the other hand, ' today ' does not have the emphasis which AV, RV, RSV seem to accord it. The emphasis is again on ' I ' : ' *I myself* have begotten you today '. **10-12.** An appeal for timely submission by the rebels. As in the preceding sections, it is Yahweh's authority and power which must be acknowledged. **11/12. with trembling kiss his feet :** the phrase rendered ' Kiss the son ' in RV (AV, ' Son ') and ' Worship in purity ' in RVm is linguistically difficult. LXX has ' Receive instruction '. RSV adopts the suggestion that some letters in 11 belong to 12 (hence the omission of ' rejoice ' from 11), a simple change in Heb., giving a smooth sense. **12. Blessed :** better, ' happy ' (cf. 1:1).

c **III.** An individual lament. The suggestion in the superscription that the occasion is Absalom's revolt has nothing to commend it other than the quite general reference to enemies. The peculiarly poignant nature of David's experience is not reflected here. But this may well be the prayer of a king or other leader of the community, who is beset by numerous enemies and who prays not only on his own behalf but for his people's well-being (8). Some, however, think that the plight of an ordinary individual is described in metaphors drawn from war or revolt (1, 6). The former is the more likely view. As in other laments, the description of need and the prayer for help are interwoven with the assurance and even the anticipation of divine intervention : the Psalmist's enemies threaten (1–2), Yahweh's protection is sure (3–4), the Psalmist is confident when threatened (5–6), prayer for help (7), blessing on the people (8). **2. help :** the same word as **deliverance** in 8. **6. people :** Heb. *'am* here probably has a military significance, ' fighting men ' (cf. Num. 20:20) ; but some take it to refer to Israelites, thus making the Psalmist's enemies his own countrymen. **7. Arise :** a characteristic appeal in the laments, probably echoing the ancient invocation
associated with the Ark (Num. 10:35). **8. Deliver-** 361c
ance : the Heb. can also mean ' victory '.

IV. For the superscription see §358*bdf*. The ps. is an d
individual lament, but one in which the note of trust in Yahweh is prominent. Hence it may be classed as a ps. of confidence. The worshipper seeks the help of God which he has experienced in the past (1). He then turns to his opponents, contrasting his security with the ineffective power on which they rely (2–5), and advises them to reflect, to sacrifice to Yahweh, and to trust him (4–5). Finally he renews his prayer and reaffirms his own trust in Yahweh (6–8). The ps. has been traditionally taken as the sequel to 3 in the context of Absalom's revolt. The language used does not indicate clearly either the nature of the Psalmist's difficulty or the identity of his adversaries. He has been thought of as a ruler beset by foreign enemies, as an exponent of faith when dearth was driving his countrymen to apostasy, as one falsely accused, or as one whose plight leads others to doubt his righteousness or God's will to help. The last two suggestions seem the most likely. What is unmistakable is the spirit of humble assurance and serene faith which the ps. expresses. **1. God of my right :** i.e. Vindicator of my cause. **Thou hast given me room :** a reference to past deliverance. **2. O men :** probably means ' men of standing '. **vain words,** ' lies ', taken by some to refer to false gods, by others to false accusations. **3. godly :** the word *ḥāsîdh* is frequent in the Psalter. It is connected with ' steadfast love ' (*ḥesedh*), and probably means ' one who shows devotion (to God) ' rather than ' one who experiences God's steadfast love ' (cf. note on 5:7). **4. Be angry :** or, ' Stand in awe ', as AV, RV. **7.** The joy which is God's gift is greater than the joy over an abundant harvest. (For the comparison see Isa. 9:3.)

V. For the superscription see §358*bdf*. An individual 362a
lament by one who is assailed by ruthless enemies. It is classed by Schmidt and others as a prayer of one falsely accused. The Psalmist approaches Yahweh with prayer and sacrifice, seeking his help (1–3). He knows that Yahweh hates evildoers but he worships with reverent confidence (4–7). He prays that he may be safely guided, that his enemies may be punished, and that all the faithful may enjoy Yahweh's blessing (8–12). By contrast with 4, the enemies are here described in some detail. **3. prepare a sacrifice :** ' set in order ' ; the verb is used of preparing a sacrifice (Lev. 1:8), but also of presenting a case or argument (Job 23:4, 32:14, 33:5, 37:19). Hence AV and RV supply ' my prayer ' as object of the verb. If ' prepare a sacrifice ' is the meaning intended, the object of the sacrifice may be the granting of a divine revelation (hence ' watch '). **4-7.** The description of the enemies and of the Psalmist's own purpose has affinities with the liturgies of approach to the sanctuary (cf. 15, 24:3–6). **5. evildoers.** On the meaning of the term see §360*d*. **7. steadfast love :** Heb. *ḥesedh* (cf. note on 4:3). The term denotes primarily loyalty such as the terms of the covenant require, but it also has an emotional content and goes beyond the purely legal sense of obligation. **fear :** awe and reverence rather than terror. **9.** A vivid description of the false accusers, reflecting the Hebrew belief in the potency for good or ill of the spoken word. **10.** This imprecation, like many others in Ps. and in Jer., is redeemed from mere spitefulness by the thought that the evildoers are not only hostile to the Psalmist but rebels against Yahweh. **transgressions :** the term denotes rebellion against a personal authority. **11.** Well expresses the joy which in OT is the normal accompaniment of right religion. **thy name :** ' thy nature as revealed to man '.

VI. For the superscription see §358*bdf*. An individual b
lament, containing the characteristic features : (*a*) description of the sufferer's plight, (*b*) appeal for succour, (*c*) assurance that God will hear and answer. In 1–3 and 4–7 (*a*) and (*b*) are blended. (*c*) is triumphantly expressed in 8–10. Mowinckel holds that the

362b appeal was accompanied by an offering, that a temple prophet then gave an oracle assuring the worshipper of divine help and restoration and that 8–10 is the worshipper's response. The suffering is described in terms of sickness and of the hostility of enemies. According to Mowinckel the potent curses of the 'evildoers' had brought sickness on the Psalmist. But it may be that the description of almost mortal sickness is used simply of dire affliction. The enemies may have been the cause of the affliction or they may have added to the Psalmist's suffering by attributing it to God. This is one of the seven Penitential Psalms of Christian usage, the others being 32, 38, 51, 102, 130, 143. **1.** The negatives refer particularly to 'in thy anger', 'in thy wrath', rather than to the verbs 'rebuke', 'chasten'. Possibly the Psalmist recognises a divine discipline in his affliction while pleading for deliverance (cf. 38:1). **2. my bones:** my physical frame; but here, as often, the physical is associated with psychological experience. **3. my soul:** this rendering suggests the dualism of body and soul which is foreign to OT thought. Heb. *nephesh* has a very wide range of meaning. 'my being' would be better here. **how long:** a characteristic question and appeal in the laments. **4. steadfast love:** cf. commentary on 5:7. **5.** In some laments the ravages of disease and the onslaught of death are used to describe dire affliction and the diminished vitality which it brings, though the affliction need not actually have taken the form of illness. But here it seems that the Psalmist feels that he will go to Sheol, the abode of the dead, and this will mean one fewer worshipper of Yahweh in the land of the living (cf. the very human plea in Job 7:21*c*). The thought that Sheol is in some sense outside Yahweh's domain is found elsewhere (e.g. 30:9, 88:10ff.) but is by no means universal (e.g. 139:8; Am. 9:2). **8. workers of evil:** see §360*d*.

c **VII. Shiggaion:** see §358*e*. The historical reference in the superscription is obscure. No Benjamite named Cush is referred to elsewhere; but there may be a muddled recollection of 2 Sam. 16:5ff., 18:21ff. The ps. is an individual lament by one falsely accused, who turns to Yahweh for succour (1–2), solemnly professing his innocence (3–5), appealing to Yahweh as Judge (6–9) in whose righteous dispensation he has confidence (10–11); then, after a vivid description of the fate of the wicked (12–16), the ps. ends on a note of thanksgiving (17). Some have thought that the ps. is composite, mainly because 6–9 seem to refer to an international and even eschatological judgment which is inappropriate to the personal and individual character of the ps. But this conclusion is unnecessary, particularly if one thinks of the ps. not simply as a private prayer but as having its place in the public cult in which the thought of Yahweh as Judge of all was prominent. The situation has sometimes been explained in terms of 1 Kg. 8:31–2. If this is sound, 3–5 will be the oath of innocence; and we must allow for the possibility that some part of the ps. (e.g. 11–16) is chanted by a member or members of the sanctuary staff, as a reply to the worshipper's prayer. **1. pursuers:** a trifling change in the Heb. would give the singular, which would accord with 'rend' and 'dragging' in 2 and also with the language of 4ff.; but such variation of singular and plural is common in Heb. **3-5.** The Psalmist turns from the threat to his safety to the allegations of his guilt, protesting his innocence by invoking a curse on himself if he is guilty (cf. Job 31). **5. soul:** cf. commentary on 6:3. **6.** Note the realistic appeals for divine intervention, 'Arise . . . lift thyself up . . . awake . . . take thy seat' (or, as Heb., 'return'), which are reminiscent of the ancient formula associated with the Ark (Num. 10:35–6). **8. judge me:** probably means 'vindicate'; cf. 'judge the widow and the orphan'. **10.** Perhaps we should render, 'My intercession is towards God'. **12.** Text and interpretation are very difficult. The RSV rendering is obtained by tacitly omitting a phrase and assuming a tacit change of subject in Heb. Other (and preferable) renderings 362 are (*a*) 'If he (the evildoer) does not repent, but whets his sword, bends his bow and aims it, (13) against himself he has prepared', etc., or (*b*) 'he will surely whet his sword again; he has bent his bow and aimed it, (13) but it is against himself that he has prepared', etc. To the belief in God's intervention in judgment 12–16 adds the complementary idea that evil is self-destructive.

VIII. For the superscription see §358*bdf*. A superb d
example of the hymn, setting forth the greatness of Yahweh the Creator. It begins (1*a*) and ends (9) with an ascription of praise. The dignity conferred by God on man, who might otherwise seem to be dwarfed by the immensity of the heavens, is described in 3–8. The relation of 1*b*, 2 to the rest of the ps. depends on the view taken of its somewhat elusive sense (see below). This is not primarily a poem about nature, but a celebration of the majesty of God and man's honoured position as his vicegerent. What moves the Psalmist is not merely the wonder of the night sky, but the concern which its Creator has for mankind. **1. name:** manifested nature (cf. commentary on 5:11). **1b-2.** The form and meaning of the verb rendered 'is chanted' have evoked much speculation. The older rendering 'hast set' is impossible unless the text is modified. The present rendering plausibly ascribes the form to a verb meaning to sing or chant antiphonally. AV and RV take 2*a* with 2*bc*, implying that the praise of children or of humble believers is used by God to confound his enemies. But RSV connects 2*a* with 1*b*, probably rightly. 2*bc* then refers to God's action against his enemies, probably in creating the firmament which kept the destructive waters at bay (cf. Gen. 1:6–8, a transformed counterpart of the ancient myth about the overthrow of the chaos monster). **3.** Note again the parallel to the creation story in Gen. 1. **4. man . . . son of man:** the emphasis is on the frailty of man; **art mindful . . . visitest:** the expressions denote active care (cf. note on 1:6). **5. God:** perhaps the capital letter is misleading. Though Yahweh is the supreme and incomparable Being, the Israelite believed in the existence of other divine beings (cf. especially Gen. 6:2 and Ps. 82:1, 6), to whom man is here likened. 'Little less than divine' is perhaps a better rendering. AV 'a little lower than the angels', which is derived from LXX, Vulg., though no doubt influenced by theological considerations, is near the mark. On the other hand Gen. 1:26 may be held to support RSV. **6-8.** Note, again, the similarity to Gen. 1:26–8. The ps. illustrates the way in which ancient mythological and cosmological ideas are used and transcended in OT thought. Further, it presents the true dignity of man as derived from God. Above all, it sets its picture of nature and of man within a framework of praise to God.

IX, X. These two pss. are combined into one in four 363a
Heb. MSS, LXX and the Vulg. Ps. 10 has no superscription (for 9 see §358*bdf*) and an acrostic scheme runs through both. Further, there are striking similarities of language and content. Hence the two are commonly treated as one ps. Against this it has been argued that the acrostic scheme is imperfect and that 9 gives thanks for the overthrow of national enemies and 10 laments the arrogant success of the wicked in Israel. But at many points there is doubt about the text, and it may be that textual corruption or editorial revision have broken the acrostic scheme. The interchange of confident thanksgiving with pleading and lament is found in other pss.; and the alleged discrepancy in the description of the enemies can be disposed of. The ps. is best taken as a lament which includes (as laments often do) elements of thanksgiving and confidence in which past experiences of deliverance are recalled or future ones anticipated. If it is the lament of an individual, then the references to God's judgment on nations probably belong to its liturgical setting in the cult (cf. note on Ps. 7). If it

363a is a communal lament, the people represented by the king or other leader pray for deliverance from foreign enemies. The latter seems more likely. It has been suggested that 10:1ff. may refer to foreign occupation rather than Israelite evildoers; and we may compare Hab. 1, where the identification of the wicked also presents a problem. But it is hazardous to try to identify the precise situation. The combined Ps. 9, 10 may be analysed thus: 9:1–4, thanksgiving for past succour; 5–8, Yahweh's judgment on the nations; 9, 10, Yahweh, help of the oppressed; 11, 12, thanksgiving; 13, 14, prayer for succour; 15, 16, Yahweh's judgment on the nations; 17–20, prayer for divine intervention; 10:1–11, lament over the arrogance of the enemy; 12–15, prayer for divine intervention; 16–18, assurance of a righteous outcome. **9:12, he who avenges blood:** Yahweh. **afflicted:** a common term in Ps., often taken to denote a special class in the community, but meaning simply victims of oppression or affliction, sometimes with the suggestion of humility and piety. **13. gates of death:** dire distress is described as coming near to the realm of death. The phrase presents a powerful contrast with the following verse. **14. daughter of Zion:** Jerusalem. **16. Higgaion:** this word is rendered 'melody' in 92:3. What may be the same word in a slightly different form is rendered 'meditation' in 19:14. The cognate verb means 'to moan', 'to make a low sound' and 'to meditate' (cf. 1:2). Here the noun may be a musical direction. For **Selah**, see §358*h*. **17. Sheol:** the abode of the dead.

b **X 1.** Such complaints of seeming divine inaction are common in the laments. **4.** What the wicked denies is not the existence of God but his effectiveness and concern, as indicated in 11, 13 (cf. 14:1). **17. the meek:** Heb. almost identical with the word rendered 'afflicted' in 9:12, 10:12.

c **XI.** For the superscription see §358*bd*. This ps. is variously described as a prayer of the falsely accused, as a ps. of trust, and as a lament uttered by a national leader on behalf of the nation in time of invasion. Strictly it is not a prayer. Yahweh is not addressed. In 1–3 we learn that friends are urging the Psalmist to flee to the hills from his enemies who are preparing attack. The reply in 4–7 (anticipated in 1*a*) is that Yahweh the righteous Judge is the refuge and support of the righteous. The descriptions of the preparations of the wicked and of the judgments of God are vivid and colourful. Highly coloured pictures are not always clear; and it is perhaps pointless to try to define exactly the nature of the Psalmist's danger. What is manifest is his unquestioning faith. Whatever may be the appearance, or indeed the reality, of human power arrayed against the righteous, he knows that the last word is with Yahweh.

d **XII.** For the superscription see §358*bdf*. The ps. is classified as a liturgy, consisting, 1–4, of a lament over the arrogance of the wicked, 5, a reassuring divine reply which may have been uttered by a priest or sanctuary prophet, and, 6–8, an answering assertion of confidence in Yahweh's promises and protecting power. The general tenor makes it probable that the ps. contains the prayer of a group rather than of an individual. The statement that 'there is no longer any that is godly' suggests that the wicked are not foreigners but Israelites. As in other similar pss. the wicked are characterised as proud and deceitful. The situation may be similar to that described in Mal. 3:13ff.; the success of unscrupulous lying and overbearing conduct seems to put piety at a discount, but the faithful can count on Yahweh's succour. **1. godly:** cf. on 4:3. **2. lies:** Mowinckel and others have taken this to refer at least in part to false religion or magic. **5. poor:** cf. on 9:12. **6.** There is doubt about the text of the latter part of the verse.

e **XIII.** For the superscription see §358*bd*. An individual lament. The Psalmist bewails his lot (1f.), appeals for succour (3f.), and joyfully declares his confidence in God. We can hardly hope to identify the Psalmist's enemy or define the affliction referred to. But the 363e
point of the ps. is that it is to Yahweh that he appeals and in Yahweh's help that he trusts. **1.** This very direct and seemingly almost irreverent type of appeal to God is common in both communal and individual laments, and is found in startlingly frank forms in Jer. **hide thy face:** indicating displeasure or neglect. **2. bear pain:** the textual change based on Syr. (see note in RSV) seems unnecessary. The Heb. word in MT can mean 'sorrows' as Prov. 27:9 and Sir. 30:21 show, though its normal meaning, 'counsels', is not impossible here. The Psalmist's difficulties keep him thinking anxiously how to overcome them. **3. lighten mine eyes:** 'restore my vital powers'; affliction has drained the Psalmist of strength and brought him, as it seems, within sight of death (cf. on 6:5.). **4.** The Psalmist's discomfiture will encourage the wicked. **5f.** The Psalmist rejoices confidently even before he experiences deliverance.

XIV. For the superscription see §358*bd*. The text of f
this ps. recurs in Ps. 53, where, among other changes, the name of Yahweh is replaced by Elohim (God). The ps. had been included in two collections which were embodied in the Psalter. There are three main parts: 1–3, impiety and corruption are prevalent; 4–6, Yahweh will intervene to discomfit the wicked; 7, a prayer for deliverance. The evildoers may be either foreigners who oppress Israel, or the godless within the nation who oppress the righteous. 7 may, but need not, tell in favour of the former view. **1. Fool:** Heb. *nābhāl*. The translation is misleading. One who is by normal standards anything but a fool may yet be a *nābhāl* if he wantonly disregards the claims of God and man; cf. 1 Sam. 25:25; Isa. 32:5f. (Note that the words 'wise' and 'wisdom' are similarly not confined to the intellectual sphere but include sound religion and morals.) 'Churl' is perhaps the least unsatisfactory rendering. Mgr Knox's rendering here, 'reckless hearts', is admirable. **There is no God:** a denial not of God's existence but of his effective concern for human affairs. The *nābhāl* acts as if God were not a power to be reckoned with. **2. act wisely:** sound religion, as well as sound sense, is meant. The three verses numbered 5–7, which appear in PBV between 3 and 4 (8), are derived from LXX and Vulg. (cf. Rom. 3:13–18). **4. who eat up . . . bread:** better, perhaps, 'eating my people they eat bread', i.e. they thrive on their oppression of God's people. **my people:** Israel, or the faithful in Israel. **5f.** The differences between Pss. 14 and 53 are most marked at this point, and raise textual problems too complicated for discussion here. The general sense is that in spite of their recklessness the evildoers will be confronted by God's power. **7. restores the fortunes:** AV, RV 'bringeth back the captivity' is misleading. RSV gives the correct sense (cf. Job 42:10). The Psalmist hopes not only for a punitive judgment on the wicked but for the restoration of the life of God's people.

XV. A liturgy of approach, summing up the qualities 364a
required in those who would enter the precincts of the sanctuary (cf. 24:3–6). It is not to be thought of simply as a didactic poem, but as, in all probability, an antiphonal chant. A procession of worshippers, approaching the precincts, ask the questions in 1 and are answered from within, by a member or members of the sanctuary staff. **1. sojourn in thy tent** is an apt rendering of the sense: the worshippers are guests of Yahweh; 'tent' recalls the precursor of the Temple (2 Sam. 7:6). **2-5.** The strongly ethical qualities required are characteristic of Israel's religion. Nothing is said of ritual purification. Obedience to God and righteousness in dealings with men are the necessary conditions (cf. Isa. 1:16f.; Jer. 7:22f.; Hos. 6:6; Am. 5:24; Mic. 6:8). **2** gives a general description which the following verses amplify: integrity of life, righteousness in action, sincerity in speech. **3.** The righteous man avoids the malicious or careless gossip which disrupts common life. **4. a**

364a **reprobate is despised:** some think that this shows lack of concern for the sinner ; but the point is probably that the righteous man judges men by moral and religious standards irrespective of other conditions such as power and wealth. In a society where the reprobate is honoured it is likely to go ill with those who 'fear the Lord'. **5.** He does not exploit another's affliction, either by lending on interest or by perverting justice for reward. Laws against usury occur in Exod. 22:25 ; Lev. 25:36 ; Dt. 23:19f. The ps. ends with an assertion of the unshakeable security of the faithful worshipper of Yahweh.

b **XVI.** For the superscription see §358*be*. This is an individual ps. of confidence, in which everything else is subordinated to the thought that life in God is the Psalmist's supreme good. Although it is not certain that there is any explicit reference to either immortality or resurrection, the experience of communion with God as the supreme satisfaction and faith in God as a sure succour in adversity form part of the OT preparation for the hope of life after death (cf. 73:25f.). The Psalmist appeals to Yahweh, whom alone he owns as God (1–4). Yahweh is his Benefactor, Guide and Helper (5–8). Therefore he looks forward to the future with glad confidence (9–11). **2b.** Text uncertain. RSV gives the probable sense. **3.** Text again uncertain. RSV tacitly presupposes a slight emendation. Widely differing suggestions have been made, e.g. 'holy ones' (saints) is taken to refer to other gods : 'As for the holy ones who are in the land, and the lofty ones, I have no pleasure in them', an interpretation which connects 3 with 4. **4a.** Obscure Heb. has again given rise to several conjectures, one of which RSV adopts. **4b. libations of blood:** either in the literal sense, or as offered by the hands of guilty men. **5f. cup** has the sense of 'lot', 'fate', 'destiny', here in a good, but often in a bad, sense (e.g. Ps. 11:6 ; Isa. 51:17, 22 ; Jer. 25:15ff. ; Ezek. 23:31ff.). Otherwise the figure in these verses is from the allocation of land. **8. at my right hand:** as a protector (cf. 73:23). **9. heart . . . soul:** (Heb. 'glory') . . . **body . . . me** (Heb. 'my *nephesh*') : not different parts of the human constitution, but all indicating the Psalmist's whole being. **10. Sheol . . . Pit:** against the view that the Psalmist believes in a full life after death it is pointed out that 'death' and similar terms are frequently used to express diminished vitality or sore affliction. To be restored to life or preserved from Sheol and the like is to be re-established in vigour and prosperity. The Psalmist's meaning will then be that Yahweh delivers him from present affliction and will enable him to live to a good old age. On the other side, however, it is claimed that the Psalmist does not speak of present affliction, and therefore that he means that when he dies he will not descend to Sheol but will live a full life with Yahweh. Even if the latter view is rejected, the Psalmist holds that communion with God is the supreme good ; and this is a central element in the final biblical view of life after death. **godly one:** cf. on 4:3.

c **XVII.** An individual lament (the superscription describes it as a prayer) by one beset by enemies. The Psalmist appeals to Yahweh to maintain his cause (1f.), and protests his innocence (3–5). He then renews his appeal for divine help (6–9), and goes on to describe the ruthless machinations of his adversaries (10–12). A final appeal for Yahweh's intervention leads to a contrast between the lot of the wicked and the Psalmist's hope of satisfaction in the presence of Yahweh (13–15). **1f.** The language is in part forensic. **3f.** RSV presupposes a slight change in the pointing and punctuation of the Heb. **7. Steadfast love:** cf. on 5:7. **8. apple:** i.e. 'pupil' ; cf. Dt. 32:10. **10. They close their hearts to pity:** lit., 'their fat they have shut'. The reference may be to the midriff, thought of as a seat of the feelings. A slight emendation gives 'the fat of their hearts they have shut', i.e. they are insensitive. **11a.** RSV presupposes a slight emendation. MT has 'Our steps they have now surrounded me (us)'. Another slight change would give 'Their steps now surround me'. **14.** Text and interpretation are uncertain. RSV takes the verse as an imprecation on the wicked and their descendants, continuing the appeal in 13 for Yahweh's intervention ; and the word translated 'what thou hast stored up for them' is taken to mean punishment. AV, RV treat the verse as a contrast to 15 : the wicked enjoy material prosperity now ('thy hid treasure' instead of 'what thou hast stored up') and pass it on to their descendants ; but the Psalmist's reward is the presence of Yahweh. **15. when I awake:** a difficult expression, which has been taken to mean (*a*) morning by morning, (*b*) after the night of affliction, (*c*) after the sleep of death. But there is probably a reference back to 'by night' (3). The worshipper has come to the sanctuary to plead his case in Yahweh's presence, to spend a night there, and to submit to the divine scrutiny. He confidently expects, his innocence having been acknowledged, to experience the manifestation of Yahweh's presence. 364c

XVIII. To the choirmaster: see §358*d*. This ps. is also found in 2 Sam. 22 with some textual variations. d
In both places the superscription states that the ps. was written by David when he had been delivered from Saul and his other enemies. Against Davidic authorship it has been argued that the profession of innocence in 20–4 is inappropriate in content and expressed in Deuteronomic language. But there are also archaic features in the poem. The reference to 'David and his descendants' (50) points to use by a Davidic king. The ps. is one of thanksgiving for deliverance. The view that it is not a unity is an unwarranted inference from its varied contents. 1–3 : the king celebrates the greatness of Yahweh, his deliverer. 4–6 : he describes his plight and his deliverance. 7–15 : the theophany is depicted in characteristic language. 16–19 : the king is delivered from his enemies. 20–30 : he professes his own righteousness and fidelity but confesses his utter dependence on the fidelity of Yahweh. 31–45 : he celebrates Yahweh's might by which the king is enabled to triumph over his enemies. 46–50 : in thankfulness he extols Yahweh, the living God. The ps. has a rich mythological background : the subjection of the cosmic sea and the triumph over death. Granted this, there are two main lines of interpretation. (*a*) Some hold that the ps. celebrates an actual historical deliverance which is described in terms of Yahweh's primeval triumph over the sea. (*b*) Others maintain that it refers to the conflict and suffering undergone by the king in the cult, when he encountered his enemies in the ritual drama of the New Year festival but was delivered (and, with him, the nation) by the mighty intervention of Yahweh. **1.** Not in 2 Sam. 22. **4. cords:** 2 Sam. 22:5 has 'waves', which perhaps ought to be read here. **7ff.** Many features in the description resemble the account of the theophany on Sinai (Exod. 19:16ff. ; cf. Hab. 3). **10. cherub:** a mythical, hybrid creature (cf. Gen. 3:24 ; Exod. 25:17–22 ; Ps. 99:1), here thought of as Yahweh's mount, in other passages as supporter of his throne. **13. Most High:** Heb. 'Elyon', probably the title of a deity worshipped in pre-Davidic times and transferred to Yahweh. **15. channels of the sea:** so 2 Sam. 22:16 ; but Heb. here has 'channels of (the) waters'. **20-4.** These verses express the strongly ethical character of the Israelite ideal of kingship. **25. loyal:** Heb. *ḥāsîdh*, as in 4:3 etc. **26. perverse:** A. R. Johnson suggests 'Thou dost prove ready to wrestle' (cf. Gen. 30:8), an attractive rendering. **29. crush:** implies a slight change in pointing. Johnson takes the word rendered 'troop' in the sense 'division', 'fence', which gives good parallelism with the following line. **35. help:** assuming the word found in 2 Sam. 22:36 ; lit. 'thy answer' : when Yahweh answers prayer, he succours. Heb. here has 'lowliness'. **50.** Here the king is called the 'anointed' or 'Messiah' of Yahweh. Note that in the super-

4d scription David is also called 'servant'. This verse refers to the covenant pledge to David and his house (cf. 2 Sam. 7; Isa. 55:3f.).

5a **XIX.** For the superscription see §358*bd*. 1–6 is a hymn celebrating the manifestation of God's power in nature. 7–14 is a poem in praise of the Law, ending with a prayer (12–14) for pardon and guidance. The former has obvious affinities with 8 and 104, the latter with 119. Differences in content, style and metre are said to indicate that the two parts were of independent origin. One may wonder why two such different poems should have been combined. One answer is that the author of the poem on the Law used an older hymn (or a fragment of one) about the heavens and the sun as an appropriate prologue to his own verses. But the unity of the ps. has been defended, on the grounds that the combination in one poem of the two ideas (the testimony of nature to the majesty of God and the testimony of the Law to his will) is by no means unthinkable and that there are parallels in Babylonian hymns to the sun god (cf. ANET, pp. 387ff.). **1-4b.** By day and by night the heavens are constantly bearing witness to the majesty and power of God. **1. firmament:** cf. on Gen. 1:6ff. **3f.** Though their message is not heard or expressed in words, it is none the less eloquent. **4ab. voice:** Heb. 'line'. RSV reverts to the reading of LXX, Syr., Vulg., which was followed by AV (which, however, renders the whole verse somewhat differently). The Heb. has been understood in the sense of 'measuring line', indicating the extent of occupation or possession; but some word meaning 'sound' or 'voice' is required to give a parallel to 'words'. **4c-6.** The Psalmist now turns to the most conspicuous of the heavenly bodies, likening the progress of the sun across the sky to a bridegroom coming out from the bridal tent, or canopy, and a champion exulting in his strength. These lines have been likened to the Babylonian conception of the sun god Shamash, who, after crossing the sky, entered a tent in the sea where his bride dwelt; and some have made the easy (in Heb.) but unnecessary change of 'in them' to 'in the sea'. Granted the likeness, we may also note the difference, that this is not a hymn to the sun god but to Israel's Creator God, and that the sun is not a deity here but one of the works of that God. **7-11.** In these verses we note both the joy in the Law and the variety of terms applied to it which reappear in 119. Here the Law is not a burden but a means of entering into the will of Yahweh and of being enlightened and upheld by him. Note how the name Yahweh (Lord) is repeated, so that the idea of a personal link with him is conveyed. To know and to do his will is more precious to the Psalmist than earthly rewards. **9. the fear of the Lord:** here 'fear' means 'religion'. **12-14.** Contemplation of the excellence of the Law moves the Psalmist to humble penitence and supplication. **12.** Sins of ignorance and inadvertence are meant. **13. presumptuous sins:** better, 'arrogant men'. **14. transgression:** better, 'rebellion' or 'apostasy'. The word indicates revolt against personal authority.

b **XX.** For the superscription see §358*bd*. A Royal Psalm containing a liturgical prayer for the king at the beginning of a campaign, when he offered sacrifices (5) and sought the help of Yahweh. The prayers offered on the king's behalf in 1–5 are followed by an assurance, presumably uttered by a priest or sanctuary prophet, that they will be granted (6–8, a passage which is strongly reminiscent of the certainty of being heard in the laments); and finally the whole assembly invokes Yahweh's aid (9). Some cultic act may have taken place between 5 and 6. **1. name:** the word 'name' means an active power. **protect you:** Heb. 'set you up on high' (beyond reach of attack). **5. set up our banners:** celebrating the victory. **7.** The faith in God rather than in human resources, which appears so often in OT, is expressed here in terms strongly reminiscent of Isa. 31:1, 3. **name:**
cf. on 1. **9.** A slight change in the Heb. accents gives 365b
'O Lord, help the King . . .'.

XXI. For the superscription see §358*bd*. A fitting c
sequel to 20, being a Royal Psalm containing thanksgiving for blessings granted to the king (1–7), an oracle predicting the king's future triumph over his enemies (8–12), and a final ascription of praise to Yahweh. **1, 7:** note how the account of the king's blessings is prefaced by a statement of his exultation not in his own but in Yahweh's strength and concluded by a declaration of his trust in Yahweh, which is the condition of the divine help. **3. a crown of fine gold:** this has led some to conclude that the ps. was used in the ritual of the king's coronation or of an annual celebration of his accession. **4.** cf. 1 Kg. 3:11. **for ever and ever** is not to be taken literally. **9.** Attempts have been made to emend the text; but perhaps this is simply a compressed comparison: 'You will make them as (the fuel which is consumed in) a blazing oven'.

XXII. For the superscription see §358*bdf*. In this d
great ps. a sufferer brings his need before God (1f., 6–8, 12–21), remembers the ground of his confidence (3–5, 9–11), anticipates his deliverance and summons others to praise Yahweh (22–6), and foresees the universal worship of Israel's God (27–31). The varied contents, and, in particular, the sharp contrast between 1–21 and 22–31, have led some to suppose that two pss. have been combined; but sudden changes from urgent supplication to grateful assurance are common in laments. In form this is an individual lament. The Psalmist describes his affliction in terms of dire sickness (14f.) and of the ridicule (6–8) and active hostility (12f., 16–18) of enemies. The description of the suffering is reminiscent of Isa. 52:13–53:12 both in its variety and in some details. The ps. has been thought of as the prayer of the community or of its representative, e.g. a king who prays for succour at a time of national reverses. Again, it is thought to belong to the ritual passion and restoration of the king in the cult; having been humiliated and attacked by the power of death the king is restored to vitality at dawn and summons the people to worship. A very different view is that the varied description of suffering suggests that the ps. was used when those who were afflicted in different ways were gathered at the Temple. It is, perhaps, safest to hold that this is the prayer of an afflicted private individual. It is not clear whether he is a sick man over whom his enemies gloat or one who has been the object of hostility and malice and so has been robbed of his vitality. Two features which are common in such pss. are missing here: a profession of the Psalmist's innocence and imprecations on his opponents. The striking appositeness of parts of the ps. to the passion narratives in the Gospels and the fact that Jesus quoted it on the Cross, as well as the long tradition of Christological exegesis, make it natural for the Christian reader to find here an anticipation of the NT. But the anticipation is not a historical prediction. The ps. gives memorable expression to an experience which is described in varying ways in other passages: an experience of the utter desolation of soul which suffering can bring. But out of that experience comes the triumphant assurance of divine deliverance. When Jesus made the words of the ps. his own, he bore witness to the presence of the divine deliverer in the very experience of desolation and affliction. **1.** cf. Mt. 27:46; Mk 15:34. **3. enthroned:** the phrase is reminiscent of 'enthroned upon the cherubim' (99:1). Israel's praises form a throne for the invisible Yahweh. LXX has 'Thou art enthroned in the sanctuary, O Praise of Israel'. **6.** cf. Isa. 41:14, 49:7, 53:3. **7f.** cf. Mt. 27:39ff. **12f.** Bashan, which lay east of the Jordan and north of the Jabbok, was rich in pasture-land and famous for its cattle. Some think that Sumerian and Babylonian texts show that these animal forms represent not human but demonic adversaries. **14f.** This description of extreme physical infirmity (fever?) exemplifies

365d the idea that to have lost one's vitality is to have come already, in some measure, under the dominion of death. **18.** cf. Jn 19:23f. **20. my life:** see RSV*n*. The same Heb. word is used in the same sense in 35:17. **sword:** the next three lines show that this need not be taken literally. **21. my afflicted soul:** see RSV*n*. The change of text is unnecessary. 'From the horns of the wild oxen thou hast answered me'. The abrupt change from petition ('save me') to confident assertion leads on to the second part of the ps. **24.** Affliction does not necessarily indicate God's displeasure. **24, 26. afflicted:** cf. on 9:12. **26. shall eat:** referring to the sacrificial meal. **27-31.** From the thankfulness for his deliverance the Psalmist's thought continues to dwell on Yahweh's greatness and on his world-wide sway. **29. Yea, to him:** Heb. is obscure; RSV represents a reasonable emendation. **all who go down to the dust:** some have seen here the thought that the dead will join in worship (contrast 6:5), but probably the phrase simply means 'all mortal men'. Even so, the ps. ends with a spacious vision of the spread of Yahweh's praise in every land and in every age.

366a **XXIII.** Two pictures are presented in this ps.: the Shepherd caring for his sheep (1–4) and the Host supplying the needs of his guest (5f.). It is a ps. of trust in which the emphasis lies wholly on the goodness of Yahweh; the varied needs and afflictions of the Psalmist are not the subject of petitions, but are incidentally described as he tells of Yahweh's unfailing care. The implication that he does experience affliction is important. The presence and favour of Yahweh bring comfort and strength in suffering, not immunity from it. **1. shepherd:** commonly applied in the OT and other ancient oriental sources to a ruler (cf. Ezek. 34); hence the idea of authority is combined with that of care. **3. soul:** better, 'life' (RSV*n*), or 'vitality'. **paths of righteousness:** not conduct which is morally right but tracks which are right and safe. **for his name's sake:** in all his dealings Yahweh is true to his own revealed character. This is the Psalmist's ultimate security. **4. the shadow of death:** better, 'deep darkness' (RSV*n*). The gloomy glen through which the sheep are led represents not only the danger of death but any sore affliction. **thy rod and thy staff:** the iron-tipped club used as a weapon, and the staff for support and for guiding the sheep. **5.** The figure changes. To one who is pursued by ruthless enemies Yahweh, as Host, gives hospitality and asylum. **6.** The thought of pursuit by enemies gives place to the idea that Yahweh's steadfast goodness now follows the Psalmist throughout his life. **mercy:** 'steadfast love' (cf. on 5:7).

b **XXIV.** A hymn which celebrates Yahweh's creating and controlling power in nature (1f.) is followed by a Torah-liturgy or liturgy of approach (cf. on 15), describing the character required in those who would worship at Yahweh's sanctuary (3–6). The ps. reaches its climax in an antiphonal song at the Temple gates (7–10), in which those who seek admission answer the challenging questions of those who are within. The whole forms a processional liturgy used on some festal occasion when the Ark, the symbol of Yahweh's presence, was carried up to the sanctuary. The allusion in 1f. to Yahweh as Lord of nature who controls the tumultuous waters and the celebration of him as King and Victor in 7–10 have, not unnaturally, suggested that the occasion was the autumnal festival. There are striking parallels in Isaiah's vision (Isa. 6); the song of the seraphim echoes 1; Isaiah's confession of unworthiness matches 3–6; and the thought of the exalted majesty of Yahweh the King is common to both passages. The superscription in the LXX and the references in the Talmud show that in the second Temple the ps. was used on the first day of the week. **2. the seas . . . the rivers:** the underground waters; cf. Gen. 1:7, 9; Exod. 20:4. Note that 'he' at the beginning of this verse is emphatic: '*he*, and no other'. **6a. generation:** the Heb. may mean 'lot'. **6b.** Heb. has 'thy face, O Jacob' (see RSV*n*). The 36
change, based on LXX, is widely accepted. The reference is to seeking the manifestation of the divine presence in the Temple. **7-10.** Those who carry or accompany the Ark seek admission to the Temple for the warrior King, Yahweh of hosts (cf. 1 Sam. 4:4).

XXV. An individual lament in slightly irregular c
acrostic form. First the Psalmist prays for help against enemies (1–3), for guidance (4f.), and for forgiveness (6f.). Then he describes Yahweh's care for the sinful and the humble (8–10). After another plea for pardon (11), he outlines the blessedness of those who fear Yahweh (12–15). Finally, he again appeals for deliverance (16–21), ending with a prayer for Israel. Both the Psalmist's afflictions and his opponents are described in such general terms that they are not easily identified. The ps. is noteworthy for its forthright confession of sin and for its emphasis on divine guidance and instruction. In the latter feature some have seen influence from Wisdom teaching and from the post-exilic devotion to the Law, and have accordingly dated it late. But Wisdom is not necessarily late; and the direction mentioned in the ps. is the personal guidance of God, there being no explicit allusion to the written Law. **5. Lead me in thy truth:** i.e. 'by thy faithfulness'. **6. steadfast love:** cf. on 5:7. **7. transgressions:** or, 'rebellions'. **8.** The thought of Yahweh's concern for sinners is noteworthy. **14. friendship:** the Heb. means 'secret counsel' (Am. 3:7), 'council' (Jer. 23:18), and, as here, 'intimate friendship' (cf. Prov. 3:32). It is important to notice that this boon is mentioned in addition to material blessings. **fear:** 'revere', 'serve with awe'. **17.** The rendering of RSV (cf. RVm) represents a slight change in the grouping and vocalising of the Heb. consonants, which is almost certainly correct. **22.** Falls outside the alphabetical scheme, and is often held to be a later addition to the ps. to give it a national application.

XXVI. Commonly classed as an individual lament. d
The dominant features, however, are the appeal for, and the certainty of, deliverance, and the Psalmist's profession of innocence. **1-3.** The Psalmist appeals for vindication and professes himself ready to submit his life to divine scrutiny. The opening verb (AV, RV, 'Judge me') has been taken as evidence that the Psalmist had been unjustly accused by his enemies. The use of the Heb. verb 'to judge' in the sense 'to vindicate' illustrates the fact that Yahweh's action as Judge is often to be equated with his action as Deliverer. **4-7.** Enlarging on the theme of 3, the Psalmist describes his avoidance of evil and his practice of piety. Possibly, however, 6f. refers to ritual acts on this occasion, by which the worshipper effectively declares his innocence and is thus enabled to join confidently in the worship of the sanctuary. **8-12.** The Psalmist renews his appeal. Presumably the description of sinners and their fate is a side glance at his enemies (false accusers?). **8. the place where thy glory dwells:** the place where (as the resting-place of the Ark) Yahweh's presence was manifested (cf. 1 Kg. 8:11).

XXVII. This ps. falls into three well-defined parts: e
(*a*) a confession of faith in Yahweh's protection (1–6), (*b*) a plea for deliverance from malicious enemies (7–12), and (*c*) an assertion of faith and a word of encouragement (13f.). Because of the marked contrast between (*a*) and (*b*), and the fact that the prayer for help follows the expression of confident trust, it is widely held that there are two independent pss. here, viz. (*a*) a ps. of confidence (or of thanksgiving?) and (*b*) + (*c*) an individual lament by one unjustly accused. It must be admitted that (*a*) and (*b*) + (*c*) could each stand alone as independent pss.; but this makes it difficult to understand why they should have been combined if they were originally separate. Further, the contrast between (*a*) and (*b*) should not be exaggerated. There are hints in (*a*) of the situation from which in (*b*) the Psalmist asks to be delivered (2f.). The ps. may therefore be taken as a unity,

366e (*a*) being an assertion of trust which prepares for the plea for help in (*b*), and which is echoed in 13. 14 may be an oracle addressed to the worshipper by a priest or temple prophet. **1. light:** practically a synonym of salvation. **2. uttering slanders against me:** Heb. ' to eat up my flesh ' (cf. 7:2, 17:12). The interpretation offered in RSV has a possible parallel in the Aram. phrase in Dan. 3:8, 6:24. But the Heb. may simply mean ' to destroy me utterly '. **4.** cf. 23:6. **8.** Heb. has : ' To thee my heart has said, Seek ye my face ; Thy face, Yahweh, I (will) seek ', the interpretation of which is highly problematic. RSV (1) assumes that ' Seek ye my face ' is a parenthetical quotation by the Psalmist of Yahweh's command, and (2) alters the word order and adds ' Thou hast said ' to make plain the assumed sequence of thought. **10a.** A vivid expression for loneliness and isolation (cf. Isa. 49:15). **13a.** Heb. ' Unless I had believed . . .' is difficult. RSV solves the problem by dropping the doubtful word ' unless ' ; AV, RV add ' I had fainted '. RSV is preferable.

f **XXVIII.** An individual lament. The Psalmist implores Yahweh to hear him (1f.), and asks that he may not be destroyed with the wicked, who deserve their fate (3–5). He then gives thanks for the succour of which he is assured (6f.). The ps. ends with a prayer for king and people (8f.). This closing prayer has been taken to indicate that the individual who speaks in the ps. is the king. But this, though possible, is not certain. It may be that the sufferer makes his plea before God in the presence of king and congregation. The nature of the Psalmist's need is difficult to determine. He does not actually say that the wicked are oppressing him personally, but only that they are in danger of destruction because of their wickedness and that he fears that he may share their fate. **2. thy most holy sanctuary:** the Holy of Holies, the inmost shrine of the Temple. **6f.** Possibly a reassuring oracle preceded this utterance. **8. anointed:** most naturally interpreted as a reference to the king. Other suggestions are the high priest and the people as God's chosen.

367a **XXIX.** A hymn celebrating the manifestation of Yahweh as King. The heavenly beings are summoned to render to Yahweh the glory due to him (1f.). The theophany is described in terms of thunderstorm and earthquake : Yahweh's voice sounds forth across the waters, shatters the cedars, and makes Lebanon and Hermon (Sirion) leap like calves, sends forth lightning flashes, and shakes the wilderness of Kadesh, bringing terror to nature, while in his Temple the cry of ' Glory ' resounds (3–9). The ps. ends with the acclaim of Yahweh the King, triumphant over the waters of chaos, who can bestow well-being on his people (10f.). With its vivid and vigorous eloquence this ps. is one of the literary masterpieces of the Psalter. It has been called ' The Psalm of the Seven Thunders ', because of the sevenfold occurrence of the ' voice of Yahweh ', representing peals of thunder. The subtly varied parallelism and metrical pattern have been compared with the structure of Canaanite poetry as known to us from the Ugaritic texts ; and it has been suggested that it is an Israelite adaptation of a Canaanite hymn to Baal-Hadad, the storm god. In all probability it comes from the early monarchy, possibly 10th cent. ; and quite apart from the emphatic repetition of the name 'Yahweh', the similarities to other pss. which celebrate the kingship of Yahweh and to the descriptions of the theophany, and the link with the Sinai tradition in 8, stamp the ps. in its present form as Israelite. The superscription in LXX assigns it to the last day of the Feast of Tabernacles (in the Talmud and in later use it is associated with the Feast of Weeks; it also belongs to the Sabbath liturgy) ; and since it celebrates Yahweh's kingship and his control of nature, it has been argued that it was used in the pre-exilic celebration of the autumnal festival. **1. heavenly beings:** the Heb. ' sons of gods ' (RSV*n*) means ' beings who share the divine nature '. The phrase reflects the belief in a heavenly assembly (cf. Job 1:6, 2:1 ; Ps. 82:1), composed of superhuman beings who were subject to Yahweh. **2. in holy array:** cf. 96:9 (=1 Chr. 16:29). Ugaritic evidence suggests the translation ' when he appears in holiness '. **3. voice:** the Heb. word can be used of thunder, as in Job 28:26, 38:25. **6. Sirion:** Hermon (cf. Dt. 3:9). **9ab.** Another interpretation is ' The voice of the Lord makes hinds to calve and causes the birth of kids in haste '. **10. flood:** the reference is to the cosmic deep, by which life would be engulfed if it were not controlled by Yahweh. 367a

XXX. An individual thanksgiving, apparently for recovery from illness. The Psalmist thanks Yahweh for delivering him from death (1–3). He summons others to join him in thanksgiving (4f.). Then he repeats his own story in great detail. Before his affliction he was secure and self-confident. Then came his affliction, which drove him to appeal to Yahweh, who heard him and restored him. The ps. ends with renewed thanksgiving (6–12). The superscription is awkwardly expressed in Heb : ' A Psalm, a Song at the dedication of the House, of David '. Presumably the words ' a Song at the dedication of the House ' are a later insertion into the original title, ' A Psalm of David '. The ' dedication ' referred to is probably the purification of the Temple by Judas Maccabaeus (1 Mac. 4:42ff. ; cf. Jn 10:22). Thus what was individual in origin was applied to a national deliverance. **1. drawn:** from the depths of Sheol ; i.e. the sore distress by which the Psalmist was afflicted. **3. Sheol . . . the Pit:** the ebbing of vitality, as in a serious illness, is in a measure an experience of death. **4.** The Psalmist has presumably come to the sanctuary to offer his thanks, and he calls on other worshippers to join with him. On ' saints ', see on 4:3. **5. tarry:** the Heb. means ' lodge '. ' Weeping may come in to lodge at even ; but in the morning there is a shout of joy '. **7. thou . . . mountain:** the exact text and sense are elusive. **9.** cf. 6:5, 88:10–12, 115:17. **12.** my soul : Heb. ' glory ' ; cf. 7:5. b

XXXI. For the superscription see §358*bd*. This is an individual lament in which trust and thanksgiving are prominent. It illustrates the marked changes of mood which such laments often display, and which should not too readily be assumed to indicate composite authorship. In 1–8 the Psalmist professes his trust in Yahweh (the request for help appears in 3–5 and thanksgiving in 7f.). In 9–18 he pleads for help, describing his sore plight (the element of trust is present in 14f.). Finally he gives thanks for deliverance and exhorts others to trust Yahweh. The terms in which the Psalmist's need is described suggest, on the whole, that his plight is caused by the malice of enemies ; see, especially, 7*b*, 8, 13, 18, 20. The ps. has therefore been interpreted as the prayer of one falsely accused who seeks asylum and divine acquittal in the sanctuary ; and some assume that an oracle vindicating the worshipper was uttered between 18 and 19. At all events 23f. imply that the sanctuary is the setting. **4. net:** cf. 9:15, 25:15. The adversaries are likened to hunters. **5a.** cf. Lk. 23:46. **6a. Thou hatest:** this reading (cf. RSV*n*) gives a better contrast to 6*b*. **7. steadfast love:** cf. on 5:7 (so below, vv. 16, 21). **8. a broad place:** deliverance means freedom from cramping conditions. **9.** cf. on 6:2, 3. **10.** In support of reading ' misery ' rather than ' iniquity ' (see RSV*n*) it is argued that the ps. contains no other suggestion of a sense of sin. **11-13.** The similarity to Jeremiah's experience is striking. See especially Jer. 20:10. **11. horror:** One of a number of suggestions made to avoid the awkwardness of MT (see RSV*n*). **23. saints:** cf. on 4:3. c

XXXII. For the superscription see §358*be*. In Christian liturgical tradition this is one of the Penitential Psalms ; but it is in fact an individual thanksgiving. It tells of distress which persisted until the Psalmist acknowledged his sin, and of the forgiveness which followed d

367d penitence and confession, and concludes with exhortations to accept divine discipline and so enjoy the security of the faithful. The didactic element in the closing verses is thought to indicate affinity with the Wisdom literature. **1f.** The happy state of the forgiven man. On ' blessed ' see on 1:1. The words rendered ' transgression ', ' sin ', ' iniquity ' describe sin respectively as rebellion, missing the way or the mark, and crookedness. The three verbs ' forgive ' (bear, lift), ' cover ' and ' impute ' (reckoning a debt) are characteristic OT ways of expressing forgiveness. But the threefold statement is probably made to emphasise the reality of the experience rather than to bring out shades of meaning. **3f.** The Psalmist's distress while his sin remained unconfessed. This is usually interpreted as a description of illness which the Psalmist regarded as punishment for his sin. It may, however, refer to an experience of physical distress which accompanied the sense of Yahweh's displeasure. **5.** Recognition and open confession lead to forgiveness. **6f.** Others are exhorted to pray in time of need to Yahweh, the source of deliverance and security. **6. godly:** see on 4:3. **at a time of distress:** if this suggested modification of the Heb. is correct, the sense may be that affliction should be regarded as a pointer to sin and should make the afflicted person turn to penitent prayer, a point of view expressed by Job's friends. If the Heb. is rendered ' at a time when thou mayest be found ' we may compare 69:13 ; Isa. 55:6. **great waters:** affliction, calamity. **8f.** An exhortation (in the manner of Wisdom teaching) to willing obedience, which may be addressed by the Psalmist to his fellow worshippers or may be spoken by Yahweh, more probably the latter. **10f.** A concluding statement of the contrasted lot of the wicked and the faithful, and an exhortation to joyful worship. **steadfast love:** cf. note on 5:7.

e **XXXIII.** A hymn celebrating the greatness of Yahweh as Lord of nature and history. It begins with an exhortation to jubilant worship (1–3). The righteous constancy of Yahweh's purpose (4f.), his creative power (6–9), his sovereign ordering of history (10–17), and his special care for his own (18f.) are described. Finally comes a profession of faith in him (20–2). The contents are appropriate to the autumnal festival. **3. new song:** cf. 40:3, 96:1, 98:1, 149:1. **4-9.** The thought of the creative power of the divine word (4, 6, 9) is reminiscent of Gen. 1. ' Breath of his mouth ' (6) is synonymous with ' his word '. **5. steadfast love:** cf. on 5:7. **7.** The reference is to the gathering of waters above the firmament and in the subterranean deeps (Gen. 1:7). RSV ' as in a bottle ' presupposes a different vocalisation of the Heb. consonants from ' as an heap ' (AV, RV).

f **XXXIV.** An individual thanksgiving in acrostic form. The superscription refers to 1 Sam. 21:10–15 (where, however, the Philistine king is called Achish and not Abimelech, as here), but is not particularly appropriate. In 1–10 the Psalmist invites others to praise and thank Yahweh because of his unfailing goodness to those who trust him. Then in 11–22 he offers instruction, very much in the style of the Wisdom teachers, about the nature and rewards of the good life. **2. afflicted:** cf. on 9:12, and note ' poor man ' (v. 6, below). **4-6.** Here the Psalmist records the experience which prompted his own thanksgiving. The text assumed by RSV in 5 is probably correct. **7. The angel:** probably here thought of as a representative or commander of a heavenly army (cf. Jos. 5:14). **8. happy:** cf. on 1:1. **11. the fear of the Lord:** the OT ideal of piety—reverent obedience to Yahweh. **17f.** This thought that the righteous can and do experience affliction shows that the ps. does not simply proclaim a naïve belief in immediate material rewards for righteousness.

368a **XXXV.** An individual lament by one who has been unjustly attacked by enemies. It consists mainly in appeals for help and descriptions of the Psalmist's plight, and has little of the elements of thanksgiving and confidence. There are three main parts (1–10, 36
11–18, 19–28), each of which includes a cry to Yahweh for succour. **1-10.** The Psalmist asks Yahweh to take up his cause, and invokes punishment on those who have maliciously assailed him. The climax is a promise of praise and thanksgiving (9f.). There is a blend here of terms from law (' contend '), warfare (' fight ', ' shield ', ' buckler ', ' spear ', ' javelin '), and hunting (' net ', ' pit ') ; but it seems likely that the Psalmist's enemies are false accusers (cf. 11, 15, 20) against whose charges the Psalmist protests his innocence (' without cause ', 7). **3. javelin:** AV, RV take the Heb. word as a verb, ' stop (the way) '. It is often taken as a noun and rendered ' battleaxe '. **7. pit:** is rightly transposed. **9f. soul . . . bones:** cf. on 6:2f. **11-18.** Here the appeal for help, linked with a promise of thanksgiving, is the climax of an account of the treacherous enmity of men whom the Psalmist had befriended in their affliction. **13. I prayed . . . bosom:** the meaning is disputed. Another interpretation is that the Psalmist says that his prayer will (or asks that it may) return to his bosom, i.e. bring blessing to himself (cf. AV, RV). **15. cripples whom I knew not:** or, perhaps, ' smiting me unawares '. **16a.** Heb. is obscure and possibly corrupt. **19-28.** Further appeals for punishment on the enemies and vindication of the Psalmist, and a prayer that he and his friends may have cause to praise Yahweh.

XXXVI. For the superscription see §358*bd*. This ps. b
has often been thought to be composite. It begins with a description of the impious arrogance of the wicked (1–4). This is followed by a hymn of praise to Yahweh for his goodness (5–9), leading to a prayer for continued protection (10–12). The contrast between 1–4 and the rest of the ps. is admittedly sharp ; but it is perhaps so pointed as to be intentional and original. The unity of the ps. may be defended on the ground that the worshipper, turning to Yahweh for succour from the wicked (11), first describes them and their ways and then celebrates the certainty of Yahweh's succour. **1. Transgression speaks . . . in his heart:** there is some difficulty about the text. RSV adopts the likely correction (' his ' for ' my '). As elsewhere, ' transgression ' means ' rebellion '. ' Speaks ' represents the Heb. word used of divine utterance to and through a prophet. Possibly the sense is that instead of the voice of Yahweh the voice of rebellion is heard in the heart of the wicked. **2.** There is doubt about the text and interpretation. **5. steadfast love:** cf. on 5:7 ; so in vv. 7, 10. **6. mountains of God:** lofty mountains. **7-9.** The life-giving blessings which flow from Yahweh are here described in language which is derived at least in part from the sanctuary, its sacrificial worship, and the manifestation there of Yahweh's presence. ' Light ' and ' life ' are synonymous. Hence ' see light ' should not be taken in the sense of mental illumination, but as denoting the experience of a full, free and satisfying life.

XXXVII. A ps. which is acrostic in form and c
strongly didactic in content. It is not a cultic lyric but a Wisdom poem containing reflections on the problem of the success of the wicked and the affliction of the righteous. The firmly held Israelite belief in the righteousness of Yahweh was not easily reconciled with the facts of individual experience. Job is the outstanding example of an attempt to grapple with this problem ; but it is raised in Ec., in parts of the prophetic literature, and elsewhere in Ps. (cf. 49, 73). The solution offered in this ps. is that the seeming injustice of life is only temporary. Before long the righteous will be rewarded and the wicked punished. The righteous should, therefore, continue to trust and serve Yahweh patiently and not be bitter and discontented because of the prosperity of the wicked. Much in this ps. resembles parts of Prov., both in content and in the loose construction of thought. There are four main sections : exhortations to patient

8c trust (1–11) ; the transient prosperity of the wicked (12–20) ; the lasting blessedness of the righteous (21–31) ; the contrasted outcome for the wicked and the righteous (32–40). In some ways the ps. may seem to offer a superficial solution to the problem which it raises, and one which, within the limits of this life, does not really stand the test of experience ; but it voices a strong faith in the sovereign righteousness of God even in the face of events which challenge it. **11a.** cf. Mt. 5:5 ; and see on 9:12. **20. the glory of the pastures :** the transient prosperity of the wicked is compared to the short-lived flowers in the fields in the brief Palestinian spring.

d **XXXVIII.** For the superscription see §358*bg*. This ps., which in Christian liturgical usage is one of the Penitential Psalms, is an individual lament by one who is suffering in body, and is conscious of sin, who is forsaken by friends and threatened by enemies. The appeals for Yahweh's help are in 1 (with which cf. 6:1), 15f., 21f. The remainder of the ps. describes the Psalmist's plight in poignant language. Apart from the confession of sin (4f., 18), the ps. is reminiscent of Job's condition. **19a. without cause :** the slight change (see RSV*n*) is supported by the parallel with ' wrongfully '.

e **XXXIX.** For the superscription see §358*b–d*. This ps. is not easily classified. It contains elements of lament and confession, but the experience of affliction has led not only to appeals for deliverance but also to reflections on the brevity of human life. In its reflective character it has affinities with pss. such as 73, and in its subject-matter it recalls 90. No hope is expressed of a life beyond death ; but, since it is not merely a negative assessment of life but a prayer to God, ' trust and hope are breathed from amidst its plaintive chords '. **1-3.** Sorely tried, the Psalmist has refrained from complaint in the presence of the wicked, lest his words should do harm (cf. 73:15) ; but his distress has increased, and now he must lay his complaint before Yahweh. **4-6.** The awareness that his own life may be nearing its end moves him to pray for understanding of the brevity of human existence. With 6 cf. Lk. 12:20. **7-11.** He prays for deliverance from his sins and their results. It is Yahweh that has chastened him ; and it is only to Yahweh that he turns for help. **8. transgressions :** ' rebellions '. **fool :** see note on 14:1. **12f.** The transience of human existence is now the ground of the Psalmist's appeal. His life on earth is like that of an alien residing in a land not his own, who is dependent on the goodwill of the ruler (cf. Exod. 22:21 ; Lev. 19:33f.) ; and he prays for relief before his sojourn ends (Job 10:20f.). **13. Look away from me :** cf. Job 7:19, 14:6 ; and contrast Ps. 13:1, 80:3, etc. The Psalmist shrinks from the searching look of Yahweh's displeasure.

f **XL.** For the superscription see §358*bd*. In 1–10 the Psalmist gives thanks for deliverance from affliction. 13–17 is an appeal for help against enemies. Accordingly these are commonly regarded as two separate pss., and the fact that 13–17 reappears later as Ps. 70 is advanced in support of this view. There is some difficulty about 11f., which, if the ps. is not a unity, is perhaps best taken as a connecting link inserted by whoever joined the two parts. But a case can be made for the original unity of the ps., if we think of the worshipper recalling with thankfulness past deliverance as he prepares to seek Yahweh's help in his present need. **1-3.** The Psalmist recalls his past experience of divine deliverance. His affliction is described in terms of a descent into the underworld (cf. 69:2, 14) from which Yahweh rescued him. It is perhaps not necessary to emend to ' *desolate* pit '. Heb. ' pit of tumult ' may well refer to the tumultuous waters of the underworld. The Psalmist's deliverance moves him to thanksgiving and others to awe and trust. **4f.** The happiness of those who so trust Yahweh and render to him loyal obedience. **4. Blessed :** cf. on 1:1. **5. us :** the plural suggests both that the Psalmist is in the presence of other worshippers and also that he links his own deliverance with the historic deliverance 368f
of Israel. **6-8.** The Psalmist offers Yahweh the response of whole-hearted obedience. These verses present textual and metrical difficulties ; but the main problem is the interpretation of the apparent denial that Yahweh desires sacrifice, with which should be compared both the prophetic sayings in 1 Sam. 15:22 ; Isa. 1:10ff. ; Jer. 7:21ff. ; Hos. 6:6 ; Am. 5:21ff. ; Mic. 6:8, and also similar passages in Ps. (50:9ff., 51:16f., 69:30f.). Such a denial is extraordinary in a collection of poems used in the cult. Probably the point is that Yahweh does not want sacrifice and offering apart from the obedience of the heart. Since the implied question which these verses answer is ' How can gratitude for Yahweh's goodness best be shown ? ' Mic. 6:6–8 is the best parallel. **7f.** as here translated seems to mean that the Psalmist's devotion is recorded in a heavenly book. Another rendering is ' it is prescribed for me ' ; i.e. Yahweh's requirements are recorded in written form. The reference may be to Dt. With 8 cf. Dt. 6:6 ; Jer. 31:33. **9-10.** The Psalmist has openly acknowledged Yahweh's goodness. **10. steadfast love :** cf. on 5:7. **11-12.** He now appeals for a continuation of Yahweh's goodness in his present trials and admits his sin. **11. Do not thou . . . let thy steadfast love . . . ever preserve me :** or, ' Thou wilt not . . . thy steadfast love . . . will ever preserve me : '. **13-15.** A plea for help and for the discomfiture of his enemies. **16f.** A prayer for all the faithful and for the Psalmist in his special need.

g **XLI.** For the superscription see §358*bd*. The central part of this ps. (4–10) is in the form of an individual lament. The worshipper has been afflicted by illness and by malicious enemies and false friends who gloated over his distress. This is preceded (1–3) by a description of the compassionate and righteous man who is delivered from his afflictions by Yahweh. The didactic tone of the verses accords with a fairly common feature in thanksgivings, when the worshipper publicly acknowledges the blessings he has received so that others may share his thankfulness and emulate his faith and integrity (cf. 34, *passim*). Since the lament (4–10) begins with ' As for me, I said ', it seems natural to interpret 1–3 as the utterance (addressed partly to other worshippers and partly to Yahweh) of one who has been delivered, and 4–10 as a recollection of his supplication in a crisis which is now passed. 11f. is thanksgiving for the deliverance and restoration which Yahweh has granted. 13 does not belong to the ps. but is a doxology rounding off Book I. **1. Blessed :** cf. on 1:1. The corresponding verb is used here in 2 (' is called blessed '). **4b.** There is no necessary contradiction between this and 12*a*, any more than there is in ' Grant . . . to thy *faithful* people pardon and peace, that they may be cleansed from all their sins '. **5b.** The obliteration of the name means the extinction of the personality. **6. empty words :** words which do not have the strength of truth. **8. has fastened :** Heb. ' is poured out '. **9. my bosom friend :** Heb. ' the man of my peace (*shālôm*) ', i.e. one bound to him by the most sacred ties of friendship (cf. 1 Sam. 18:3). The expression may be collective, denoting a circle of friends. **who ate of my bread :** hospitality and the sharing of a meal created a bond of union. **10b.** This seemingly vindictive sentiment is found elsewhere in Ps. and also in Jer. (e.g. Jer. 11:20, 18:21–3). To understand it we need to remember that those who were afflicted by malicious enemies had some reason for thinking of their own discomfiture as a blow against righteousness, of their enemies as God's enemies, and of their triumph as his.

Book II—Pss. XLII-LXXII

369a **XLII-XLIII.** For the superscription of 42 see §358*c–e*. 43 has no superscription. This is one of a number of features which suggest that these two pss. form one poem. The theme is the same ; 43:2 echoes 42:9, a refrain occurs in 42:5, 11, 43:5. The ps. is an individual lament, in which the Psalmist prays that he may again

369a have that access to the sanctuary which is now denied him but which he formerly enjoyed ; he speaks of enemies who oppress and taunt him. 42:6 refers to the region of Mt Hermon and the headwaters of the Jordan as the place of his exile ; and conjectures have been made about historical situations which might be appropriate (e.g. Jehoiachin on his way into exile in 597, or the High Priest Onias III). But the ps. does not provide sufficient evidence to link it with specific historical events or persons. Even the geographical data have been questioned. Some would emend 42:6 so as to eliminate the geographical names, and others would regard them as symbolic of distance from the Temple or as designations of the underworld (see below). But historical and geographical uncertainties cannot obscure the beauty and power of this prayer, with its passionate longing for the joys of the sanctuary and its robust faith and hope. **42:1-5.** The Psalmist laments his separation from the sanctuary and longs for restoration. He takes comfort in the memory of his former joy in the festival worship at the Temple, and looks forward with hope. **1. As a hart longs :** the verb is feminine ; and a Ugaritic parallel supports the suggestion that 'hind' should be read. **2. behold the face of God :** i.e. experience the presence of God in the Temple. The Heb. is pointed to give the sense 'appear before God' (hence AV, RV), doubtless to avoid the suggestion that man can see God. **4.** There is some doubt about the text ; but the general picture of joyous worship is sufficiently clear. **6-11.** He describes his present plight, making his plea to God, and again stirs up his hope. **6f. Jordan . . . Hermon . . . Mizar :** one of the sources of Jordan is on the lower slopes of Hermon. Hermon is plural in Heb., possibly referring to more than one peak. Mizar is unknown ; but attempts have been made to identify it with a place in the vicinity. 7 should not simply be interpreted in terms of streams in spate on the nothern hill slopes. The language resembles that used elsewhere of the chaos waters which threaten to engulf the afflicted. To emend the geographical names out of the text is too drastic. It may be that in his need the noise of the mountain streams suggested to him the tumult of the waters of chaos. **7. cataracts :** in OT only here and in 2 Sam. 5:8, where it means 'water shaft'. **8. steadfast love :** see note on 5:7. There are metrical and textual difficulties here. One suggestion is : 'By day I watch for Yahweh, and for his steadfast love by night. I sing within me a prayer to the God of my life'. **43:1-5.** He prays for vindication against his enemies and restoration to the privilege of worship at the sanctuary.

b **XLIV.** For the superscription see §358*c–e*. A communal lament used when Israel had suffered military reverses. 1–3. The mighty deeds which God wrought for Israel in settling them in Canaan are recalled. 4–8. These past victories are the ground of present confidence. 9–16. Then comes the lament proper : a description of the defeat and humiliation which Israel has suffered ; 17–22 a plea that Israel has been faithful to God ; 23–6 an appeal for speedy deliverance. 4, 6 suggest that part at least of the ps. was uttered by a leader, who may have been a religious leader (priest or high priest) speaking on behalf of the worshipping congregation, but is much more likely to have been a king or other similar military figure. Some of the Christian Fathers, Calvin and many moderns have related the ps. to the Maccabaean period, but it seems likely that the Psalter was complete by that time ; and earlier periods are at least as appropriate to the situation described : e.g. (*a*) the aftermath of the rebellion against Artaxerxes Ochus, *c.* 350 (of which relatively little is known) ; (*b*) the crisis following Josiah's death at Megiddo (particularly appropriate to 17, 20) ; (*c*) Sennacherib's invasion in Hezekiah's reign. Of these, (*b*) seems the most probable ; the possibility that the ps. comes from the Northern Kingdom should not be ruled out. There is, in fact, little evidence to support a definite conclusion ; and it should be remembered that such pss. 36
would not be used only on one occasion and that they might be adapted to suit different situations. 2 Chr. 20:4ff. describes an appropriate setting for such a ps. as this. **1-3.** The great national traditions of the Conquest were handed down from father to son and remembered at the great festal occasions (cf. Dt. 6:20 ; Jos. 4:6, 21). **3** reflects the Deuteronomic view of the Conquest (cf. Dt. 4:37f., 7:7f., 9:4, 6). **11.** May refer to the Exile or to prisoners of war or refugees. **12.** cf. Isa. 50:1*bc*. **19. in the place of jackals :** i.e. the wilderness. The somewhat compressed phraseology may mean either that the country has been reduced to waste or that fugitives have had to flee to the wilderness. **deep darkness :** cf. note on 23:4. **26. steadfast love :** cf. note on 5:7.

XLV. For the superscription see §358*c–f*. This is c
a Royal Psalm, written for the marriage of a king to a foreign princess. Various attempts have been made to identify the king : Solomon, Ahab, Joram, Jeroboam. Ahab has been a particularly popular candidate because of the reference to 'daughter (see RSV*n*) of Tyre' in 12, and because of the fame of Samaria's ivory palaces (cf. 8*b*). But no such identification can be more than a possibility. Some moderns would associate the ps. with the supposed annual celebration of the sacred marriage ; but there is nothing in the diction and content (except 6, on one interpretation) to suggest such a setting. Doubtless the ps. owes its place in the canon to the view that it celebrates the marriage of the Messianic King with his bride Israel, a view which some modern scholars have advocated. A finely expressed Christological interpretation is to be found in Charles Wesley's hymn, 'My heart is full of Christ, and longs Its glorious matter to declare!' After an introductory word (1) in which the poet speaks with enthusiasm of the inspiring power of his theme, he addresses the king (2–9), praising his beauty and eloquence, wishing him victory in the cause of right, celebrating his just rule, and describing the brilliance of his royal array and of his entourage. He then turns to the queen (10–12) bidding her forget her country and kin and yield herself to the king. He describes her bridal attire and her escort (13–15). Finally comes a promise to the king of the continuance of his line and the everlasting glory of his name (16f.). **4b.** RSV adopts a simple emendation ; an even simpler change gives 'for the cause of truth and meekness and right'. **6. Your divine throne :** cf. RSV*n*. A much disputed phrase. The rendering 'Your (thy) throne, O God' may be taken to support the Christological interpretation or the view that the Hebrew kings were regarded as divine, or (by a somewhat strained exegesis) as a parenthetical address to God. Though the term 'god' (= divine being) could be applied to persons inferior to Yahweh but superior to ordinary men, the direct address of the king as 'god' is unusual. RSV text and note offer two plausible ways of interpreting the phrase. Probably the best rendering is, 'Your throne is like that of God, for ever' (cf. the promise in 2 Sam. 7:16). **7b. God, your God :** here as elsewhere in the Elohistic collection, 'God' (Elohim) has been substituted for 'Yahweh'. The original was no doubt 'Yahweh, your God'. **8. ivory palaces :** palaces inlaid with ivory. **9. gold of Ophir :** cf. 1 Kg. 9:28, 10:11, 22:48. The location of Ophir is uncertain, but was most probably in SW. Arabia or in Somaliland. **12. people of Tyre :** a legitimate rendering of the Heb. 'daughter of Tyre'. **13.** RSV takes the opening words with 12 (contrast AV, RV). Text, metre and interpretation are difficult.

XLVI. For the superscription see §358*cdf*. The d
structure is threefold : (*a*) 1–3, (*b*) 4–7, (*c*) 8–11. It is generally thought that the refrain which follows 6 and 10 should also follow 3, thus giving a symmetrical poem. It is difficult to assign the ps. to any literary category. It contains elements of the hymn and of the ps. of confidence. It speaks of the security which God

9d gives to Israel and to Jerusalem in the upheavals of the natural order (*a*) and in the assaults of the nations (*b*), and describes the triumph and exaltation of Yahweh (*c*). Various historical situations have been suggested as providing the background, the invasion of Judah by Sennacherib in 701 B.C. being the most favoured. Some features, notably the thought in (*c*) of a universal peace, have suggested that the ps. is an eschatological prophecy. But in all probability it is to be understood in mythological and cultic terms and to be associated with the celebration of the kingship of Yahweh at the autumnal festival. Thus, in (*a*) the security which God provides is related to his triumph over the primeval deep and the elemental forces of nature, in (*b*) there follows the thought of the widespread upheaval of the nations, a frequent theme in the hymns of Yahweh's kingship, and finally in (*c*) we must probably assume a dramatic presentation of the events described in 9. On any view the ps. is a vigorous and moving expression of the OT faith in the power of God as the ultimate succour of his people. Luther's *Ein feste Burg* is its most memorable paraphrase. **4. a river :** some would compare the thought of a life-giving stream which was to flow from the Temple (Ezek. 47:1ff.), others interpret as a symbol of the divine presence (cf. Isa. 8:6, 33:21), or as a current of the cosmic deep, cf. on 72:8. **Most High :** probably a title of the pre-Israelite god of Jerusalem, cf. 47:2. **5. right early :** or, ' at break of dawn '. **6b.** cf. 29:3–9.

e **XLVII.** For the superscription see §358*cd*. A hymn of the kingship of Yahweh, and, as such, closely connected with 93, 95–100. It has been interpreted as celebrating a historical victory and as predicting the future manifestation of Yahweh's lordship. But it is probably rightly associated with the cultic celebration of Yahweh's kingship in the autumnal festival. The worshippers are summoned to worship the God who is Lord of all, who has chosen and exalted Israel, and who has now gone up (i.e. ascended Mt Zion to the Temple) (1–6). Again there is the call to worship the King of the whole earth to whom the leaders of all nations own allegiance (7–10). **2. Most High :** cf. note on 46:4. **5.** Probably refers to the processional progress of the Ark (the outward token of Yahweh's presence) up the Temple hill ; cf. 24:7–10. **7. with a psalm :** on this term (cf. RSV*n*) see §358*e*. **8. God reigns :** the Heb. has been understood in a future (eschatological) sense (so Vulg.) or as a present, referring to Yahweh's constant exercise of sovereignty (cf. 2) ; or as a perfect, ' God (Yahweh) has become king ', referring to the cultic enthronement of Yahweh. The third of these is particularly appropriate to the cultic interpretation of this and other pss., but the second is also possible on that interpretation. **10. shields :** i.e. ' rulers '.

0a **XLVIII.** For the superscription see §358*c*. A hymn celebrating the glories of Zion and the majesty and power of Yahweh the King. Like 46, 47 this ps. has been taken to refer to a historical deliverance interpreted eschatologically. But in all probability it should be understood in cultic terms similar to those suggested above for 46 and 47. **1-3.** A summons to praise God and a description of Jerusalem, the appropriate setting for his worship. **2. His holy mountain:** these words are in 1 in Heb. (cf. AV, RV), but belong in metre and sense to what follows. **in the far north :** better, ' the recesses of the North (Zaphon) '. The Temple hill is given the name of the holy mountain, which is known to us from the Râs Shamra texts (cf. Isa. 14:13). **4-8.** By Yahweh's power the assembled nations have been overthrown. Since 8 says that the worshippers have witnessed this in Jerusalem, it seems likely that the reference is to a symbolic representation of Yahweh's victory. **7.** Should perhaps be rendered ' As the east wind shatters the ships of Tarshish '. **ships of Tarshish :** cf. 1 Kg. 10:22 (cf. §424*h*). **9-14.** The presentation of Yahweh's steadfast love moves the worshippers to joyful and confident praise as they move in procession through Zion. **9. thought on :** Heb. ' made like ', probably referring to the 370a
visible enactment of Yahweh's saving deeds. **11. judgments :** acts of deliverance. **14. our guide for ever :** the meaning of the last two words is disputed. They may be part of a musical direction wrongly included here. Another suggestion is that they mean ' against Death '. In the Ugaritic mythology Mot (Death) is engaged in conflict with Baal ; and so here Death may be represented by Israel's enemies whom Yahweh overthrows.

XLIX. For the superscription see §358*cd*. This is a b
Wisdom poem on the transience of earthly prosperity, which has affinities with 37 and 73. The Psalmist contemplates the prosperity of the wicked, at whose hands he has himself suffered persecution. Whereas the author of 37 takes comfort in the thought that in this life the righteous will in time be rewarded and the wicked brought low, this Psalmist looks to death as the experience which comes to all, which wealth cannot buy off, and beyond which no earthly advantages can be taken. The question then arises whether he finds only the somewhat bleak comfort that death is the great leveller. The answer to this depends on the interpretation of 15. Some have unjustifiably regarded the verse as an interpolation. Some take it to refer to divine deliverance from affliction in this life, or from premature death, others hold that it expresses a genuine hope of life beyond death for the righteous. It seems clear that 15 is an antithesis to 8 : the wealth of the wicked cannot ransom them from death ; but God will (in some sense) ransom the Psalmist. Since, however, the Psalmist emphasises in 10 that the experience of death comes to all alike, 15 probably means that when that experience comes to the Psalmist, God will take him to himself. If ' ransom ' in 15 referred only to deliverances wrought in this life, the Psalmist would be in no better case than the unrighteous rich, since, like them, he would ultimately be consigned to the gloom of Sheol. The ps. consists of an impressive prologue (1–4) followed by two sections (5–12, 13–20), each ending with the same refrain. **1-4.** In diction characteristic of Wisdom writings, the Psalmist summons men of all classes to listen to his teaching. **4. proverb :** this word has a variety of meanings. Here it seems to denote instruction which has been received, like a prophetic oracle, by inspiration. **my riddle :** the problem which is the subject of the ps. **5-12.** The Psalmist presents his problem : the prosperity and arrogance of the wicked at whose hands he has suffered. But death awaits them and wealth can neither buy it off nor accompany them to the grave. **7.** The reading adopted in RSV is preferable to that in AV, RV. **9. see the Pit :** experience death. **10. wise . . . fool . . . stupid :** this contrast, instead of that between the righteous or godly and the wicked, is in keeping with the usage of the Wisdom writers. ' Fool ' here means the obstinate and self-willed. **11. Their graves :** this reading (cf. RSV*n*), which entails only a slight change in the Heb., is preferable to MT. **13-20.** The Psalmist contrasts the lot of the unrighteous rich with his own, describing in grim language how they are herded to Sheol, and returning to the theme that earthly wealth and glory must be left behind. At several points MT is difficult and probably corrupt ; and a number of plausible changes have been adopted in RSV. **15.** The interpretation of this verse has been discussed above. If the view there adopted is sound, ' receive ' is used in a sense similar to that in Gen. 5:24 ; 2 Kg. 2:3ff.

L. For the superscription see §358*c*. This ps. com- c
bines a description of a theophany ending in a summons to worship (1–6) with prophetic oracles describing the nature of the worship (7–15) and denouncing wrongdoers (16–21). It ends with a solemn warning (22f.). It is probably best understood, not as a didactic imitation of prophetic speech, but as associated with the cultic renewal of the covenant, the implications of which are made plain in oracles uttered by a prophet

370c or prophets attached to the sanctuary. 7ff. resembles some of the great anti-cultic passages in the prophets (Isa. 1:10ff. ; Jer. 7:21ff. ; Am. 5:21ff. ; Mic. 6:6ff.) ; cf. note on 40:6–8. **2.** The reference to Zion, rather than Sinai, is noteworthy in a context which refers to the covenant and the divine requirements. **3.** Fire and tempest are among the familiar natural accompaniments of the theophany. **4.** The purpose of the theophany here is primarily that God may arraign his people ; cf. Mic. 6:1ff. **5. faithful ones :** cf. note on 4:3. **14a.** The reference is probably not to the actual thanksgiving sacrifices (Lev. 7:12), but to the spiritual offering of thanksgiving (cf. 23*a*).

d **LI.** An individual lament expressing penitence for grievous sin. It is the fourth of the Penitential Psalms in Christian liturgical usage. The superscription connects it with David's repentance for his adultery with Bathsheba but this connection cannot easily be maintained. 18f. which speaks of the restoration of Zion is incompatible with it, but is commonly regarded as a later addition. The specific statement of 4*a* is said (perhaps somewhat unnaturally) not to apply to David's sin. The attitude to sacrifice in 16f. suggests the later prophetic teaching ; and the thought and language of 10–12 resemble parts of Jer. and Ezek. In fact the ps. makes no unmistakable reference to any specific sin, but is nevertheless a profoundly personal expression of penitence and a movingly direct appeal to God for forgiveness and restoration. **1f.** The Psalmist prays for mercy and cleansing. He appeals to God's covenant faithfulness ('steadfast love' ; cf. on 5:7) and compassion ('mercy' ; N.B. the verb 'have mercy' is from another root, meaning 'to be gracious'). On 'transgression', 'sin', 'iniquity', see note on 32:1f. **3-5.** He acknowledges his sin, which he sees as a defiance of God. God's judgment on him is justified. He is conscious not only that he has committed wrong acts but that his nature is sinful. 5 should not be understood to mean that marital relations are sinful, or that the Psalmist is excusing his acts on the ground that he inherited a sinful nature. He is expressing forcefully his awareness that he has always been prone to sin. **6-12.** The Psalmist's awareness of the inwardness of evil is matched by his sense of the inward righteousness which God requires. He now prays for inward cleansing and forgiveness, for the gladness that comes from reconciliation, and for such a change in himself as may issue in steadfast allegiance to God. **7. hyssop :** was used in the ritual for cleansing lepers (Num. 19:6). This and other terms of purification are used figuratively here. **8.** The reference to broken bones is sometimes taken to indicate that the Psalmist had been moved to penitence by an illness which he regarded as punishment for his sin. It is more likely that the words simply express the physical accompaniment of the crushing sense of guilt, i.e. not that illness moved him to penitence, but that the sense of separation from God robbed him of physical vitality. **10. right :** or, 'steadfast'. **11. holy spirit :** the term occurs in the OT only here and in Isa. 63:10f. **13-17.** The outcome of restoration will be that the Psalmist will seek to turn others to God, will sing to God in thanksgiving, and will make the offering, not of an animal sacrifice but of a broken and contrite heart. **14. bloodguiltiness :** Heb. 'bloods', variously understood as guilt of murder, any sin for which death was an appropriate punishment, death (i.e. as a result of the illness from which some think that the Psalmist was suffering), or (by a slight change in Heb.) silence. **16.** cf. 40:6, 50:8. **18f.** A prayer for the restoration of Zion and for ritual worship there, added, perhaps, during the Exile, or just before Nehemiah's time.

371a **LII.** The historical reference in the superscription is not appropriate to the contents of the ps. Doeg's fault was not that he lied (3f.) but that he told the truth maliciously. The ps. is not easily classified. 1–7 is a denunciation of an evildoer, reminiscent of prophetic passages such as Isa. 22:15ff. 8f. is a thanksgiving for blessings received or expected. 37
Probably the most natural interpretation is that it is in some sort an individual lament, in which the Psalmist, being oppressed by a powerful enemy who trusts in his wealth and attains his ends by falsehood, finds in God's righteousness the assurance that the oppressor will be brought low and his own welfare secured. **1b.** RSV adopts a plausible emendation. For 'godly' see note on 4:3. **5-7.** The assurance of the ultimate downfall of the wicked is reminiscent of 37. **6. see, and fear :** cf. 40:3. **8.** cf. 1:3, 92:12ff. **steadfast love :** cf. on 5:7.

LIII. For the superscription see §358*bdef.* For the b
text see commentary on Ps. 14.

LIV. For the superscription see §358*bdef.* The c
historical reference (to 1 Sam. 23:19) is no more appropriate to this ps. than to many others which speak of oppression by enemies. The ps. is an individual lament. **1f.** The Psalmist appeals for divine succour. **1. by thy name :** note the use of 'name' as an active power (cf. on 20:1,7). **3.** He is threatened by ruthless and godless enemies. **4f.** He professes his faith that God will uphold him. **6f.** He vows that he will bring a freewill offering in thankfulness for his deliverance. The Psalmist's desire to see the overthrow of his enemies should not simply be ascribed to vindictiveness. For him their triumph would be the triumph of evil.

LV. For the superscription see §358*bdef.* This ps. dis- d
plays some of the characteristics of an individual lament ; but there are serious difficulties of text and interpretation. Attempts have been made to resolve some of these by treating the ps. as composite ; but it is probably better to regard it as a unity, even if uncertainties remain on some points. **1-2.** The Psalmist appeals to God for help. **3-5.** He describes his plight and the assaults of his enemies. **6-8.** He longs to escape from the turmoil and find peace in solitude. **9-11.** Invoking God's punishment on his enemies he speaks of civic strife. Some think that 10 alludes to a state of siege. **12-15.** The Psalmist now laments the cruel treachery of an intimate friend, and goes on to invoke destruction on his enemies. There is no need to assume any contradiction between the references to enemies in general and those to the perfidious friend. **15b.** cf. Num. 16:30ff. **15c.** The conjecture adopted in RSV is unnecessary. The Heb. means that evil is in their homes and in their midst (or, within them). **16-19.** An expression of confidence. **19. they keep no law :** Heb. 'who have no changes', which has been variously interpreted as 'who have no vicissitudes of fortune', 'who do not change (for the better)', 'who receive no retribution (for the wrong they have done)', 'who own no mutual obligations'. **20f.** The Psalmist returns to his friend's treachery. **22.** A word of comfort and assurance. **23.** Finally the Psalmist expresses both his conviction that retribution will overtake the wicked and also his own trust in God.

LVI. For the superscription see §358*bdef.* The his- e
torical reference is to 1 Sam. 21, but has no special bearing on the content of the ps. This is an individual lament by one who is threatened by powerful adversaries. In 1f. he pleads for deliverance from his persecutors. 3f. is an assertion of confidence in God's help. In 5–7 he again describes his plight and prays for punishment on his enemies. His certainty that God will act on his behalf is again expressed in 8–11 ; and finally comes thanksgiving for deliverance (12f.). Some have thought that the enemies are national enemies and the worshipper a representative leader or that the 'I' should be understood collectively. The reference to 'the peoples' (7) might seem to support this ; but 6 suggests private hostility. **7a.** The text is uncertain. **8bc.** His tears are not to be casually forgotten but treasured up and noted in the divine record (cf. Mal. 3:16). **13.** Deliverance means that the Psalmist is transferred from the sphere of death to the sphere of life.

71f **LVII**. For the superscription see §358*bdef*. The historical reference to 1 Sam. 22–4 is not particularly appropriate. The ps. contains a lament (1–6) and a thanksgiving (7–11); or, if 5 and 11 are treated as a refrain, it might be divided thus: 1–5, 6–11. It is probably unnecessary to adopt the theory of composite authorship which some scholars have advanced. In content and language the ps. resembles 56. The Psalmist turns to God for refuge from the assaults of his enemies. The note of confidence in God predominates, both in the lament and in the thanksgiving. It is difficult to reach any sure conclusion about the character of the enemies. **6.** The enemies have been described (4) as lions; here they are hunters and the Psalmist is their intended prey. **10. steadfast love:** cf. on 5:7.

g **LVIII**. For the superscription see §358*bdef*. This ps. combines some of the characteristics of the lament with those of the prophetic denunciations of evil. The denunciation of evil begins, however, in the divine realm. It is probable that 1f. reflects the belief that subordinate divine beings have some responsibility for the ordering of the world (cf. 82), and are ultimately responsible for the wickedness which is rampant on earth. 3–5 is a highly coloured and forthright condemnation of wicked men. In 6–9 the Psalmist invokes God's just punishment on the wicked in a comprehensive sevenfold execration. The ps. ends (10f.) with a grim picture of the rejoicing of the righteous over the downfall of the wicked and a triumphant assertion (balancing 1f.) of the supreme lordship of God. Clearly the ps. is concerned not so much with the affliction of any individual as with the corruption of society by tyrannous rule. **1. you gods:** this implies a slight vowel change in the word which AV renders 'O congregation' and RV 'in silence'. **7b.** MT is obscure. RSV adopts a reasonable conjecture. **9.** MT is difficult and perhaps corrupt.

h **LIX**. For the superscription see §358*bdef*. The historical reference is to 1 Sam. 19:8ff.; but some features of the ps. are inappropriate (6, 8, 11, 13, 14). It is an individual lament, probably by a private person unjustly assailed by enemies, though a case can be made for the view that the Psalmist is a representative of the community speaking on its behalf. **1f.** Appeal for deliverance from cruel enemies. **3-4a.** Though threatened in this way the Psalmist is innocent. **4b-5.** Plea for divine intervention. **6f.** A vivid picture of his adversaries, who are like scavenger dogs in an eastern city, prowling through the streets after dark. **7b.** The textual change adopted in RSV seems unnecessary. 'Swords are in their lips' expresses the destructive power of the spoken word. **8-10.** The Psalmist's confidence in Yahweh. **8.** From the mention of 'nations' here and in 5 some have argued that national elements have been interpolated into an individual ps. or that the Psalmist is a national leader and the enemies foreign assailants of Israel. Others maintain that the Psalmist is using the traditional language of the cult in which Yahweh manifested himself as Lord of the unruly nations. **9. I will sing praises:** cf. RSV*n*. The change seems unnecessary. **10. steadfast love:** cf. on 5:7. **11-13.** He prays that the enemies may be destroyed gradually, so that Israel may not quickly forget the lesson of these events. Here again the communal element is present. **14f.** Echoes the description of the enemies in 6f. Some scholars would delete 14 and insert 15 after 6. **16f.** A final vow of thanksgiving arising from the Psalmist's assurance of succour. 17 echoes 9f.

372a **LX**. For the superscription see §358*bdef*. The historical reference is to 2 Sam. 8:1 (but cf. 2 Sam. 8:13), but the situation described there does not correspond to the experience of national disaster presupposed by this ps. This is a national lament (cf. 44) which includes an oracle (6–8). The latter may well be an earlier composition quoted in this context, and therefore cannot easily be used to determine the situation or date of the ps. For this the rest of the ps. offers little help. 9 is taken to mean either that an attack 372a
on Edom is planned (the reverse mentioned in 1ff. might then be that referred to in 2 Kg. 8:20ff.) or that some of the survivors of the national disaster intend to flee to Edom for safety (this might refer to the aftermath of the fall of Jerusalem in 586 B.C., though Edom would not have been a particularly suitable place of refuge then). No certain conclusion can be established; but on the whole it seems safest to assume that the ps. refers to military operations in Edom at a time which the incompleteness of the historical records prevents us from identifying. **1-5.** The plight of the nation is described, with an appeal for help. Characteristically, the reverses are attributed to divine displeasure. **3b.** cf. 75:8; Isa. 51:17, 21f.; Jer. 25:15ff. **4** is perhaps better taken ironically: 'Thou hast set up . . . that they might flee from the bow'. This is in keeping with the reproachful tone of this part of the lament. **6-8.** This oracle is the response to the appeal 'answer us' (5), spoken, perhaps, by a cultic prophet. It seems to be a poetical description of the extent of the territory promised to Israel and of part of the sphere of influence (Moab, Edom, Philistia) which existed in David's time. The union of north and south is presupposed. Shechem was an important centre in the north; the Vale of Succoth was east of Jordan, as were Gilead and Manasseh; Ephraim was the strongest tribe in the north. **8. my wash basin:** i.e. degraded to menial service. There may be a reference to the Dead Sea, west of Moab. **I cast my shoe:** in token of possession (Ru. 4:7). **9-12.** For the meaning of these verses see above.

LXI. For the superscription see §358*bdef*. An individual lament; and probably also a Royal Psalm. In time of need the Psalmist turns to God for succour (1–4), which he feels has been already granted (5). There follows a prayer that the king may enjoy length of life and that his reign may be blessed (6f.). Finally the Psalmist vows to live a life of thanksgiving (8). **2a. from the end of the earth:** the inference that this shows that the Psalmist is in exile is unnecessary. It is probably poetical language expressing the sense of distance from God which affliction has brought. **2b. the rock that is higher than I:** or 'the rock that is too high for me' (to reach in my own strength). **4.** He longs to be Yahweh's guest in the sanctuary (cf. 23:6). **6f.** Variously interpreted as an intercession for the king included in or inserted into the prayer of a private individual, as showing that the ps. was uttered on the king's behalf by a substitute, and, most naturally, that the king prays for himself in the third person. **7. steadfast love:** cf. on 5:7. **8.** A vow would normally be paid once for all; but the Psalmist's vow is that he will live a life of daily thanksgiving. b

LXII. For the superscription see §358*b–d*. An individual ps. of confidence expressing the steadfast trust in God of one who is beset by treacherous adversaries. He begins with a profession of utter faith in God's help (1f.) and in that alone. (Note the occurrence in 1, 2, 4, 5, 6 of the words 'alone', 'only', which represent the same Heb. word. It is rendered by 'but' in 9*a*.) His quiet trust ('my soul waits in silence') contrasts with the anguished appeals in some other pss. Then he turns to his enemies and rebukes them for their envious malice (3f.). The word 'eminence' (4) may well indicate that the Psalmist was a leading member of the community. A repetition of the profession of faith (5–7) leads to an exhortation (addressed to the congregation in the sanctuary?) to trust in God: human power and earthly resources are as nothing (9f.). Finally, in a style reminiscent of Wisdom ('once . . . twice' gives emphasis, cf. Prov. 6:16, 30:15, 18, 21, 29; Am. 1:3, 6, 9, 11, 13, 2:1, 4, 6), he imparts a divine revelation about God's power, love and retributive justice (11f.). c

LXIII. The superscription, which refers the ps. to a time when David was in the wilderness of Judah, 2 Sam. 15-17, was probably suggested by 1*d* ('in a d

12

372d dry and weary land '). This is an individual lament by one who seeks the comfort of God's presence in the sanctuary. **1-4.** These verses are a blend of longing (cf. 42:1ff.), confidence, and thanksgiving. **1bc. soul . . . flesh:** i.e. the entire being. **1d. a dry and weary land :** a figurative expression for the sense of deprivation which affliction brings (cf. commentary on 61:2). **2.** The Psalmist resorts to the Temple where, in the past, he has experienced God's presence. **3. steadfast love :** cf. on 5:7. **5-8.** The assurance of divine succour brings to the Psalmist complete satisfaction and security. **7b. in the shadow of thy wings :** cf. 17:8, 61:4*b*. The phrase may be an allusion to the overshadowing wings of the cherubim in the holy of holies. **9f.** The Psalmist's enemies are marked out for destruction. It is impossible to determine who these enemies were. **9. into the depths of the earth :** i.e. to Sheol. **11.** The king and all his righteous subjects will be blessed ; but the treacherous will be silenced. This reference to the king suggests that he is the worshipper who speaks in this ps. Some, however, hold that the Psalmist is a private individual who ends his prayer with an appropriate reference to the king as the leading figure in the Temple worship. **who swear by him :** i.e. either ' by God ' or ' by the king '. For the oath by royalty cf. Gen. 42:15f. ; 1 Sam. 17:55, 25:26 ; 2 Sam. 11:11, 15:21.

e **LXIV.** For the superscription see §358*bd*. An individual lament. The Psalmist appeals to God to save him from his enemies (1f.), who plot against him secretly and feel secure in their secrecy (3–6). He is convinced that God will foil their plots and bring them to destruction and that men will learn from this example (7–9). He prays that the righteous may find joy and security in God (10). **3f.** The language used here expresses the destructive power of the spoken word (cf. on 59:7). Possibly the malign spells of sorcerers are referred to (cf. §360*d*). **6.** Heb. is obscure and possibly corrupt, but there is no generally agreed reconstruction. **7.** God's arrow should perhaps be understood in terms of 3*b*, i.e. it is his word of judgment. **8.** Heb. is obscure. RSV represents a slight change ; but perhaps some words have been omitted.

f **LXV.** For the superscription see §358*bd*. A national ps. of thanksgiving. The people approach Yahweh to praise him and to pay the vows which they have made to the God who forgives their sins and grants the blessings of his house (1–4). He has intervened to save them ; he controls all nature and all nations, and all men witness the tokens of his might (5–8). Refreshed by abundant rain, the land is radiant in its beauty, and a bountiful harvest is in store (9–13). Attempts have been made to associate the ps. with specific historical situations. It may be that it is a thanksgiving for the end of a drought and the averting of a threatened famine. At all events it seems best to regard it as a festival hymn. Some features resemble the liturgies of the autumnal festival, with which some scholars associate it. But since it seems that the rains have recently come and that the corn is still in the fields, the beginning of the barley harvest would be more appropriate (Lev. 23:10–14). **1. is due to :** AV, RV ' waiteth ', a doubtful rendering. RSV presupposes a vowel change suggested by LXX, Syr. **4. Blessed :** cf. on 1:1. **whom thou dost choose :** the members of the chosen nation. **5. dread deeds :** God's mighty acts on his people's behalf. **6f.** The theme of creation appears here ; the mountains have been established (cf. 18:7, 46:2) and the chaos waters quelled (cf. 46:2f.). **8. outgoings of the morning and evening :** farthest east and farthest west. **9. river of God :** the waters above the firmament which come down as rain. **11. the tracks of thy chariot :** some have supposed that this refers to the wagon on which the Ark was transported and that it was taken over the fields to bestow fertility. But the thought may be the more general one that Yahweh has been traversing the land.

373a **LXVI.** For the superscription see §358*d*. This ps. falls into two parts. 1–12 is a hymn celebrating God's 37
deliverance of his people (or, more precisely, a hymn in praise of God's majesty (1–7) leading to a communal thanksgiving (8–12)). There are allusions to the crossing of the Red Sea and the Jordan (6) and also to a recent deliverance (9–12). 13–20 is the thanksgiving of an individual who now pays his vows to God because his prayer has been answered. The most natural interpretation is that in the latter part of the ps. the king (or other national leader) speaks. Other views are (*a*) that a private individual used 1–12 as a solemn prelude to his own prayer and (*b*) that two separate compositions were combined by a later editor. **16.** In the pss. of thanksgiving the congregation is often invited to consider the deliverance which the worshipper has experienced. **20. steadfast love :** cf. on 5:7.

LXVII. For the superscription see §358*df*. Classifica- b
tion of the ps. has presented difficulties. It is mostly a prayer for divine blessing so that all nations may recognise God's goodness and power. But in 6 it is stated that the blessing of a good harvest has been bestowed. The ps. ends (see below on 6f.) with a renewed prayer for blessing. The thanksgiving for harvest would be appropriate at the autumnal festival, a time at which it was also natural to look forward to the coming year and pray for the continued well-being of the nation. The theme of God's universal dominion is also appropriate to the worship at that festival. **1b.** Note the similarity to Num. 6:24ff. **6f. has blessed us :** in both verses the rendering should be ' may (God) bless us '.

LXVIII. For the superscription see §358*bd*. Inter- c
pretations of this ps. have varied widely. It has been regarded as a cento of disconnected lyrics and even as a list of opening lines of pss. The problem of interpretation is further complicated by the many difficulties in the text. But the alleged lack of unity or sequence is probably to be explained by the fact that the ps. is the accompaniment of a solemn festival procession and ritual action to various aspects of which its several parts were related. Many features point to the autumnal festival and the celebration of Yahweh's kingship as the appropriate setting. Numerous parallels to the Ugaritic texts have been traced in the ps. ; and accordingly a date early in the monarchic period has been suggested. **1-3.** The opening words should be rendered ' (when) God arises, his enemies are scattered, and those who hate him flee before him '. So, too, perhaps, with the verbs in 2, 3. The similarity to Num. 10:35 suggests that the Ark is being carried in procession, symbolising the presence of the mighty God who puts all his enemies to flight. **4-6.** A call to worship Yahweh and a short hymn in his praise. In 4*b* read ' lift up a song for him who rides through the deserts ' (cf. 7ff.). The emendation in RSV suggested by a Ugaritic parallel is unnecessary, since the Exodus tradition, to which the reference to deserts is appropriate, reappears later (7ff.). Active concern for the oppressed (5f.) is one of the central features in the OT conception of Yahweh. **6. to prosperity :** the Heb. has been interpreted in the light of Ugaritic to mean ' skilfully ' or ' with jubilant songs '. **7.** A blend of the familiar Exodus tradition with the thought of the giving of rain (cf. Jg. 5:4f.), which was an important element in the autumnal festival. **11-14.** Elsewhere in the pss. of the autumnal festival the thought of God's control of the waters is combined with that of victory over the nations. So here there is a spirited description of the sequel to Yahweh's mighty victory : the crowd of women bearing the glad tidings, the hostile kings in headlong rout, the apportioning of the booty. **13a.** cf. Jg. 5:16. The phrase may mean ' lie down between the saddle bags ', acting like an obstinate or lazy beast of burden. **13bc.** Sometimes taken to be a figurative expression for Israel (the dove) returning laden with booty ; but may be a straightforward reference to an item of spoil. **14.** Either, the fallen kings were like snow on the hillside, or, a snow-storm

3c discomfited the enemy. The location of Zalmon is uncertain. **15-18**. The procession now approaches Mt Zion, and the high hills of Bashan are asked why they look enviously at the hill which Yahweh has chosen, which he now ascends as a conqueror. **19-23**. The worshippers celebrate Israel's Saviour God, who has rescued the nation from death and has quelled its enemies. **22**. The enemies cannot hope to escape Yahweh (cf. Am. 9:3). **24-7**. A description of the procession as Yahweh enters the sanctuary. **26b. O ye who are of Israel's fountain:** lit. 'from Israel's fountain'. The point may be that Yahweh has ascended the Temple hill from Gihon (1 Kg. 1:33–5) at its foot. **28-31**. The details of text and interpretation in this section are difficult; but the general sense is that the nations are to bring tribute to Yahweh and own his supreme authority. **30a. the beasts that dwell among the reeds:** a pictorial expression for Egypt. The word rendered 'beasts' may be singular or collective; and the reference is probably to the crocodile or the hippopotamus, or both. **30b**. The foreign kings with their peoples. **30cd**. Those who sought booty in war will now themselves be subjected. **32-5**. A final hymn, celebrating the majesty of Yahweh.

d **LXIX**. For the superscription see §358*bdf*. An individual lament. **1-3**. An appeal for help, in which the Psalmist uses the familiar and varied language of the laments to describe his plight: the mire, the floods of the cosmic sea, the ebbing of physical vitality. **1. up to my neck:** AV, RV 'soul'; Heb. *nephesh*, of which 'neck' or 'gullet' seems to have been the original meaning. **4f**. His enemies are many and powerful. Though their accusations are false he admits his sin. **4ef**. May be a statement or (as RSV) a question. **6-8**. His suffering may undermine the faith of others, since it is his loyalty to God which has brought persecution on him. 8 suggests that his enemies are his countrymen. **9-12**. He enlarges on the character of his religious fidelity and the contempt it has earned him. **13-18**. He now prays again for deliverance, echoing the language of 1–3 in his description of the danger by which he is threatened. 'mire', 'deep waters', 'flood', 'deep pit' all allude to the dark horror of the power of chaos and death. **16. steadfast love:** see on 5:7. **mercy:** compassion. **19-21**. He pleads that his enemies are relentless and that he is friendless. **22-8**. A comprehensive imprecation on his persecutors, marked by an intensity which recalls Jeremiah's outbursts of fury against his enemies. **28. The book of the living:** Yahweh was thought to have a book in which were recorded the names of those who were alive, and from which their names were blotted out at death (cf. Exod. 32:32; Isa. 4:3, 56:5) **29**. A brief word of appeal, in which the Psalmist remembers his own present plight. **30-7**. A concluding song of thanksgiving, anticipating deliverance. The Psalmist realises that true gratitude matters more than animal sacrifice (cf. 40:6, 50:7ff., 51:15–17). He summons all nature to join in a hymn of praise to Yahweh, who will restore the land and give it to the faithful as their inheritance. This closing section has been thought to be a liturgical addition to the original ps. to adapt it to communal use. This theory is unnecessary. If, however, these verses belong to the original form of the ps. it must be post-exilic.

e **LXX**. cf. commentary on 40:13–17. For the superscription see §358*bdg*.

f **LXXI**. An individual lament. The Psalmist is an old man (9, 18), who is in sore straits because of the assaults of enemies and possibly because of other afflictions; but with his prayers for deliverance he expresses his unshaken faith, strengthened by long experience, and still praises God for goodness received and hoped for. Several parts of the ps. resemble passages in other pss. It is, however, questionable whether we can speak of direct borrowing. The Psalmist is steeped in the traditional language of this type of psalmody. **1-3**. A plea for deliverance and support (cf. 31:1-3). **3b. a strong fortress:** 31:2 and the LXX here suggest that this is the correct 373f
reading. **4-6**. The appeal is renewed; and the Psalmist passes to a retrospect of his lifelong trust and to a word of praise. 5f. resembles 22:9f., but the word rendered 'took' (6*b*) is different; and there is some doubt about its meaning. **7-11**. His sufferings have been regarded by others as an instance of God's chastisement; and they think that he is defenceless; but he makes his prayer to the God in whom he trusts. **12-16**. A further prayer for help, linked with imprecations on his enemies and promises of thanksgiving. **17-21**. He looks back again over his lifelong experience of God's goodness and prays that he may be preserved to proclaim God's greatness to others. **20c. from the depths of the earth:** from the deeps of the earth (the subterranean chaos waters), i.e. from the dominion of death. **22-4**. The Psalmist vows to offer to God a song of thanksgiving.

LXXII. A Royal Psalm. The superscription was pre- g
sumably suggested by various features which seemed to refer to Solomon (1, 8, 10, 15). The description of general well-being also accords with the tradition about the brilliance of Solomon's reign. In both Jewish and Christian tradition the ps. has been interpreted as Messianic. Some modern commentators have attempted to identify the king mentioned in the ps. with a kown ruler or historical person. But there is nothing in the ps. to enable us to associate it with any specific king. It is a prayer for divine blessing on a ruling king and his people, and would have been appropriate at a king's enthronement. It illustrates admirably the ancient Israelite conception of the king as the channel of divine blessing for his people. Of fundamental importance are his relationship to Yahweh and his maintenance of justice among his people. Since the ps. expresses an ideal of kingship which was embodied in the later Messianic expectation it has an important place in the development of that hope. It should be noted that some contemporary scholars apply the term 'Messianic' to the person and function of the reigning king. On that view this is a Messianic ps. **1-4**. A prayer that the king may maintain justice and defend the oppressed, that the whole nation may enjoy well-being. **1. the king . . . the royal son:** synonymous, parallel expressions. **justice . . . righteousness:** these are given special prominence in the divine gifts to be bestowed on the king. This emphasis on the maintenance of order and equity is characteristic of the Israelite ideal. **2. thy poor:** cf. on 9:12. The Heb. may also be rendered 'thy humble ones'. The OT ideal of justice emphasises compassion for the afflicted and the active vindication of their cause; cf. 4. **3. prosperity:** AV, RV 'peace'. The Heb. denotes all-round well-being and harmony. **5-7**. A prayer for a long and prosperous reign. **5**. Such hyperbolic language was common in descriptions of royal personages and in greetings addressed to them. **6**. cf. Hos. 6:3. **7. peace:** the word rendered 'prosperity' in 3. **8-11**. A prayer for world-wide dominion. **8. from sea to sea:** the earth was thought of as surrounded by water. **the River:** commonly identified with the Euphrates, but may refer to a stream from the cosmic sea; cf. on 46:4. **9. his foes:** Heb. 'the desert dwellers', or 'animals of the wilderness'. The thought of the dominion of the ideal king over the animal kingdom is found elsewhere (Isa. 11:6ff.); but parallelism here suggests 'enemies'. **10. Tarshish:** Tartessus in Spain. **the isles:** the islands and coasts of the Mediterranean. **Sheba:** in Southern Arabia. **Seba:** in Northern Arabia. **12-14**. The king's justice and mercy are the conditions of his world-wide dominion. **15-17**. A prayer for material prosperity during the king's reign and for his everlasting and world-wide renown. **16**. There is some difficulty about the text, vocabulary and syntax. RSV gives the general sense. **17ab. his name . . . his fame:** the same expression in Heb. **17cd**. cf. Gen. 12:3, 18:18, 22:18, 26:4. May his prosperity be such that all men may pray for a like

373g blessing on themselves. **18f.** Probably not part of the ps. but a benediction to close Book II. **20.** This note must be a survival from a time when a collection of 'Davidic' pss. was followed by others (cf. §357*a–c*).

374a **Book III—Pss. LXXIII-LXXXIX**

LXXIII. In its theme this ps. has obvious affinities with 37, 49; and it is usually classed as a didactic ps. from Wisdom circles. This is the most natural interpretation, though attempts have been made to claim for it a royal and festal character. The Psalmist grapples with the problem of the prosperity of the wicked, which is a challenge to his faith in the righteousness of God. Only when he comes into God's presence in the sanctuary does he realise how precarious and impermanent is the supposed security of the rich and how great is the privilege he enjoys of communion with God, an experience which outweighs the afflictions and sorrows of this life and which death cannot destroy. **1.** The Psalmist begins with an assertion of the faith which he regained after the inner conflict which he is about to describe. Perhaps he is quoting a proverbial saying which experience seems to disprove. In 1*b* MT may be retained (see RSV*n*): the slight emendation adopted by RSV is unnecessary. **2f.** he tells how his faith was almost destroyed. **4-12.** The prosperity of the wicked: vigour of body, freedom from affliction, confidence in themselves, the trust and regard of others, ample wealth. **4.** RSV presupposes a change in the division of the Heb. consonants. **7a.** Following LXX and Syr., some would read 'their iniquity comes forth from within them'. **7b.** RSV presupposes a slight emendation. The sense may be 'The imaginations of their hearts (minds) overflow (in evil actions)'. **9.** A vivid picture of the defiant arrogance of the wealthy. **10.** A difficult verse, rather freely emended in RSV. Less drastic changes give the sense 'Therefore the people resort to them, and water in abundance is drained by them', i.e. people are impressed by their confidence and drink in what they say. **11.** This is the careless boast of the *nābhāl*; cf. on 14:1. **13-20.** The Psalmist was tempted to regret his fidelity; and his perplexity was not dispelled until in the sanctuary he realised the fate of the wicked. **15.** Had he expressed his doubts openly he would have weakened the faith of others. **17f.** In the sanctuary he realised the insecurity of the wicked and the certainty of their fall. **20.** A difficult verse. Instead of the emendation of 'Lord' to 'They say' presupposed by RSV, we may read 'they are gone'. If 'Lord' is retained, we must render 20*b*, 'when thou arousest thyself thou shalt despise their image': i.e. when God comes in judgment, the unreality of their power will be evident. **21-6.** The Psalmist repents of his envy and doubt, and realises that in communion with God he enjoys the supreme good and the ultimate security. **24.** A much disputed verse. The Heb. does not suggest life beyond death as strongly as EVV. For 'to glory' we should perhaps render 'gloriously' or 'with honour'; and some think that only deliverance and blessing in this life are meant. But (*a*) 'afterward' seems to be a parallel to 'their end' (17), the ultimate fate of the wicked; (*b*) 'receive' may well be used in the special sense of being taken from earthly life to another (cf. on 49:15); (*c*) whatever may be the precise interpretation of this verse, the context (23, 25f.) describes an experience of God's presence which is fulness of life in spite of affliction and weakness, and which the Psalmist appears to hold that nothing can break. **27f.** The Psalmist sums up his convictions about the fate of the wicked and the high privilege of knowing God's presence in worship.

b **LXXIV.** For the superscription see §358*ce*. A communal lament describing a grievous national catastrophe: Yahweh seems to have abandoned his people; and enemies have desecrated and set fire to the Temple. Commentators usually associate the ps. either with the fall of Jerusalem in 586 B.C. or with the profanation of the Temple by Antiochus Epiphanes in 168 B.C. The description of the destruction wrought by the enemy accords better with the former. Moreover, some features in the ps. resemble parts of Lam. It is a moving expression of the people's anguish and also of a stubborn faith which defied the hard facts of experience. **1-3.** A plea to God to lay aside his wrath against his people and to be mindful of the plight of Jerusalem. **4-8.** A description of the havoc wrought by the enemy. **4a. Thy holy place:** 'meeting place' rather than 'assembly' (RV) or 'congregations' (AV). **4b.** A much disputed line. The 'signs' have been identified with the heathen religious symbols introduced into the Temple area by Antiochus; but the word may refer to military symbols (cf. Num. 2:2). **5.** Obscure and perhaps textually corrupt. The Heb. may be rendered: 'They (he) became known as one who lifts axes upwards in a thicket of trees'. Attempts to improve on this are guesswork; but as in 6 the reference is to the destruction of the woodwork of the Temple by the invaders. This accords better with 586 than with 168 B.C. **8. meeting places:** the Heb. word is rendered 'holy place' in 4. The translation 'synagogues' (AV, RV), which would make the date 586 impossible, is neither necessary nor probable. Presumably sacred sites other than the Temple are referred to. **9-11.** In spiritual desolation Israel pleads for divine help. **9. our signs:** the following clauses make it unlikely that this means military symbols. The reference is more probably to indications of God's presence and impending action than to institutions such as Sabbath, sacrifice, etc. **no longer any prophet:** appropriate to the Maccabaean age (cf. 1 Mac. 4:46, 9:27, 14:41), but also to 586 B.C. (cf. Lam. 2:9; Ezek. 7:26). **11.** For the picture implied cf. Exod. 4:6ff. The hand when inactive is in the folds of the garment, from which it is withdrawn when the time for action has come. RSV presupposes a slightly altered text; but perhaps MT may be rendered 'Why drawest thou back thy hand, even thy right hand? From the midst of thy bosom (pluck it forth and) consume.' **12-17.** There is a sudden change of mood, a common feature in laments. This hymnic passage recalls God's triumph over the primeval chaos monster, controlling the waters, and bringing order into the realm of nature. The theme and imagery may be paralleled in Babylonian and Ugaritic mythology and elsewhere in the OT (cf. 89:9–12; Isa. 51:9–11). There may also be a reference to the dividing of the Red Sea at the Exodus; but this is not explicit. **14. the heads of Leviathan:** the seven-headed monster Lotan is mentioned in the Ugaritic texts as in conflict with Baal. **for the creatures of the wilderness:** or, perhaps, 'for the sharks of the sea'. **15.** This description of God's power over the desert and water may be an allusion to the giving of water in the wilderness and the dividing of Jordan. **16f.** cf. Gen. 1:3–5, 16–18, 8:22. 'Luminaries' here represents a sing. in Heb. Presumably the moon is meant. **18-23.** The appeal is renewed. **18b. impious:** Heb. *nābhāl*, so in 22; cf. on 14:1, and see also Sir. 50:26. **19. thy dove:** i.e. Israel.

LXXV. For the superscription see §358*cdf*. An opening word of thanksgiving (1) is followed by a divine oracle about impending judgment (2f.). A leader of the worshipping congregation then utters words of warning to the arrogant: God alone is Judge and his judgment is sure (4–8, but note that, as in RSV, the divine oracle may be 2–5 and the admonitory speech 6–8). Finally there is a word of thanksgiving, presumably uttered by the congregational leader (9f.). Attempts have been made to link the ps. with specific historical events (for which there is insufficient evidence), or to interpret it eschatologically (to which some of its features are appropriate); but it is probably best understood in a cultic setting (in which an eschatological element may be present). Mowinckel associates it with the enthronement festival, in which the theme c

4c of the stabilisation of the earth (3) and the execution of judgment (2, 7) were prominent. **1b**. RSV presupposes an emendation of the difficult MT. Another possibility is ' and they that call on thy name tell of thy wondrous works '. **3**. The earth is thought of as supported by pillars, which, because of God's victory over the powers of chaos, remain fixed. **5. lift up your horn :** be arrogant. **8**. The figure of the cup representing appointed lot or destiny is common (cf. 60:3 ; Isa. 51:17ff. ; Jer. 25:15ff.). **10. horns :** as often, symbol of strength. **he will :** MT has ' I will ', which may stand if 9f. is spoken by the leader of the community.

5a **LXXVI**. For the superscription see §358*cdf*. The ps. celebrates the majesty and power of the God who glorifies and safeguards Zion by dwelling there and making his presence known. It has affinities with 46, 48. Interpretations of it are (*a*) historical, linking it with specific past events (e.g. David's victories or the siege of Jerusalem in 701), (*b*) eschatological, and (*c*) cultic. (*c*) seems most likely ; but it is well to remember the close links between eschatology and the cult. **1-3**. God is known in Judah and Jerusalem (Judah and Israel are synonyms in 1 and similarly Salem and Zion in 2). **2b, 3a**. The first word of 3 should probably be transferred to the end of 2 with a slight change of pointing : ' his dwelling place in Zion he has set. He broke ' etc. **3. flashing arrows :** incendiary arrows used to set fire to a besieged stronghold. **4-6**. God has overthrown the enemies and paralysed them. It is possible that here and in 3 a symbolic ritual conflict is meant. **4. everlasting mountains :** a widely accepted emendation. But MT ' mountains of prey ' may perhaps stand with a change of line division : ' Glorious art thou, (and) majestic. On the mountains of prey (5) they are despoiled. The stout-hearted slumber their sleep ' (i.e. the sleep of death). **6. rider :** Heb. ' chariot ', which should be retained. **lay stunned :** the verb describes a deep sleep supernaturally induced. **7-9**. God's judgment, irresistible and awe-inspiring, yet exalting the oppressed. **9. oppressed :** cf. on 9:12. **10-12**. Tribute to the all-victorious, righteous God. **10a**. This may mean that even the violent acts of the wicked are taken up into the divine purpose, or that the suppression of the wicked will redound to God's praise, or that the demonstration of God's power in judgment will make even the wicked praise him. **10b**. God makes the remnants of human wrath into an ornament for himself.

b **LXXVII**. For the superscription see §358*cd*. The ps. begins with a lament over present distress which is contrasted sadly with past blessing (1–10). The Psalmist then takes courage in the remembrance of God's mighty acts of deliverance for his people (11–15), and celebrates the majestic manifestation of power and his triumph over the forces of destruction (16–20). There is a marked change of rhythm at 16, and in 11–20 the style is hymnic, contrasting with the lament in the opening verses. It is impossible to discover from the lament the nature of the affliction or whether the Psalmist is a representative person bewailing the people's plight or one whose individual distress is here presented in the context of communal worship and the national cult traditions. The reference to ' the sons of Jacob and Joseph ' may indicate northern origin. **5. I remember :** transferred from 6, probably rightly. **6. I commune . . . and search my spirit :** plausible emendations based on VSS. **10**. A difficult verse which has been variously rendered and interpreted. AV, RV have in 10*b* ' (But I will remember) the years of the right hand of the Most High '. But the word rendered ' years ' probably means ' to change '. We may render as RSV or ' This is my weakness : (to think) that the right hand of the Most High could change '. The former is the more probable. The Psalmist reaches the point of despair before the dramatic change which comes in 11. **14f**. An allusion to the Exodus. **16-20**. Here the thought of God's triumph over the cosmic deep is blended with the traditional features of the theophany (as at Sinai ; cf. Hab. 3 *passim*), and the memory of the crossing of the Red Sea. **16. the deep :** the plur. of the word in Gen. 1:2. 375b

LXXVIII. For the superscription see §358*ce*. This ps. is a didactic poem applying the lessons of Israel's history. As such it may well have had an important place in ritual usage, perhaps at the renewal of the Covenant (there is evidence of similar use of a historical recital in the Manual of Discipline from Qumrân). It has been argued that the retrospect ends with David's reign and says nothing of the disruption of the kingdom, and that therefore the ps. should be dated before 930 B.C. But the spirit of 59ff. makes it highly unlikely that the ps. would have been used in the undivided kingdom. It reflects the Deuteronomic exaltation of Zion and probably comes from the period after the return from Exile. **1-8**. An introduction in characteristic Wisdom style. **2. parable :** cf. on ' proverb ' in 49:4. **5. testimony . . . law :** if the ps. is late, the reference of both words is to the written Law. **9-31**. In spite of God's goodness, Israel disobeyed and rebelled in the wilderness. He chastised them but also provided water and food. **9**. The reference is not clear. If it is to Num. 14:1ff., then the Ephraimites were not alone at fault. If it is to some later incident, we cannot now identify it. Some regard the verse as a later addition. The Heb. is difficult and RSV omits one word. **12. Zoan :** Tanis, a city in the eastern part of the Delta. **20**. RSV omits ' Behold ' before ' He smote '. **25. angels:** Heb. ' mighty ones ', probably rightly interpreted by RSV (following LXX, Vulg., Syr.) ; cf. Wis. 16:20. **32-9**. In spite of his discipline and chastisement they continued in their disobedience ; yet God was unwearying in his compassion. **40-55**. Israel's sin was all the more grievous because of the wonders which God had wrought in Egypt. The fact that the Psalmist mentions the plagues *after* the wilderness wanderings is no more surprising than that he speaks of the giving of water (20) before the manna and quails (23ff.), thus reversing the order of the Pentateuchal narratives. In 44ff. only six (or perhaps seven) plagues are mentioned ; and the order differs from that in Exod. The plagues mentioned are those described in the J source, a fact which might be used in support of an early date. **43. Zoan :** cf. on 12. **48. hail :** another reading is ' pestilence ', referring to the murrain. **51. Ham :** cf. Gen. 10:6. **54. mountain :** the hill country of Canaan, or, specifically, Mt Zion. **56-66**. Israel's infidelity in Canaan moved God to punish them by forsaking Shiloh, allowing the Ark to be captured, and giving the people up to their enemies ; but once again he had mercy on them. **60. Shiloh :** for a time the temple at Shiloh was the resting-place of the Ark (1 Sam. 3:3). The place appears to have been destroyed by the Philistines (cf. Jer. 7:12), at the time when the Ark was captured (1 Sam. 4). The new resting-place of the Ark was Jerusalem. **61. power . . . glory :** both words refer to the Ark. **62-6**. This refers to the Philistine domination of Israel, and to subsequent victories over the Philistines. **67-72**. God's rejection of Ephraim and choice of Judah, Jerusalem, and David. The Deuteronomic theme of election is present here. c

LXXIX. For the superscription see §358*c*. A national lament. The situation is similar to that presupposed in 74 : invasion, the destruction of Jerusalem and the desecration of the Temple. Like 74, this ps. has been assigned to 586 B.C. and to the Maccabaean period. The former is the more probable (see on 74). In later Jewish usage 79 and 137 were prescribed for use on the 9th of Ab, commemorating the destruction of the Temple in 586 B.C. and A.D. 70. **1-4**. Lamentation over the horrors of invasion. **2. saints :** cf. on 4:3 ; ' the godly '. **3**. Quoted in 1 Mac. 7:17. **5-13**. A plea to God to intervene. **5**. A recognition that the calamity is a divine judgment. **8. iniquities of our** d

12*a*

875d **forefathers:** or, 'former iniquities'. **12f.** cf. 6. Such imprecations are common in the laments. Though Israel's affliction is seen as divine punishment, it is also regarded as the malice of cruel enemies who themselves merit doom.

876a **LXXX.** For the superscription see §358*cdf*. A national lament with a refrain (3, 7, 19 ; note also the echo of it in 14) which was presumably sung by the whole congregation in response to the leader or choir by whom the remaining parts were sung. The ps. begins with a plea for God's help (1–3), followed by a description of the divine displeasure, which is the cause of Israel's affliction (4–7). Israel is a vine, planted by God in the land, but now at the mercy of wild beasts (8–13). The ps. closes with a prayer for renewed divine favour (14–19). The reference to Ephraim, Benjamin and Manasseh (2) suggests that the ps. describes the afflictions of the Northern Kingdom. The superscription in LXX contains the phrase 'concerning the Assyrian', which may point to the Assyrian invasions. The situation might be that after the fall of Samaria ; or, since only the tribes in the centre of Palestine are mentioned, the period between 734 and 721, when the northern parts of the Northern Kingdom had been absorbed into the Assyrian Empire. **1. Joseph:** as father of Ephraim fitly represents the tribes of the centre and north. **enthroned upon the cherubim:** the cherubim were thought of as the supporters of God's throne (cf. on 18:10). It has been argued that, since there were representations of cherubim in Solomon's Temple, the ps. must be southern. But there is no reason to suppose that the figures, the phrase, or the idea were exclusively Judaean. **2. Benjamin:** this tribe is sometimes, as here, connected with the north, and sometimes with Judah (1 Kg. 12:21, 23). **3. let thy face shine:** cf. Num. 6:24–6. **4. how long wilt thou be angry . . .?** Behind the seemingly naïve anthropopathism lies the thought that the calamity is a divine judgment. **5. in full measure:** this no doubt gives the sense, though the exact meaning of the Heb. is uncertain. **8.** The thought of Israel as a vine or a vineyard occurs several times in the prophets (Isa. 5:1–7, 27:2–6 ; Jer. 2:21, 12:10ff. ; Hos. 10:1), and reappears in the NT. **11. sea . . . River:** usually understood of the Mediterranean and the Euphrates, the ideal boundaries of Israel, realised in the reigns of David and Solomon ; but may refer to the cosmic deep which was thought to encompass the earth, 'the River' being one of its currents (cf. on 72:8). **13. boar:** the ferocious unclean beast represents Israel's enemies. The occurrence of the refrain at this point would make the ps. more symmetrical. Some think that 14 indicates that it did once appear here but that the text is now defective. **15.** RSV deletes the closing words of this verse as an intrusion from 17. **stock:** Heb. uncertain ; some change to 'garden'. **17. the man of thy right hand:** the reference may be to Benjamin ('son of the right hand'), but it is more probably to the king (cf. 110:1), possibly Hoshea (2 Kg. 17:1–6). **the son of man:** parallelism suggests that this means 'man'. It is unlikely that the expression is used in the special sense (Dan. 7:13ff.). **18. never:** nothing in the Heb. corresponds to this.

b **LXXXI.** For the superscription see §358*cdf*. It has been suggested that the two parts of the ps. (1–5*a*, 5*b*–16) do not form a natural unity ; but there is no reason for separating the opening hymnic summons to worship from the prophetic oracle (cf. 95). The ps. is classed as a prophetic liturgy. Clearly it is associated with one of the great festivals. Passover has been suggested ; but Tabernacles, with which the ps. is connected in Jewish tradition, is much more likely. The reference to Joseph (5) probably indicates northern origin and consequently a date before 721. In the festival God speaks to his people, presumably through a sanctuary prophet, reminding them of their deliverance from Egypt and appealing for their obedience. Presumably this was linked with a renewal of the Covenant. **1f.** Clearly the festival is a joyous one, as Tabernacles was. **3. trumpet:** the ram's horn, to be sounded, according to the Mishnah, on New Year's Day. **new moon . . . full moon . . . our feast day:** often explained as the first day of Tishri (New Year's Day), and the fifteenth day of Tishri (the first day of Tabernacles). But it may be that in the pre-exilic period the month and the New Year began with the full moon, that the Heb. words here rendered 'new moon', 'full moon' both refer to that day. **5ab.** Linking the festival with the Exodus tradition. **5c. I hear a voice I had not known:** a difficult line, which probably refers to the experience in which the prophet received the oracle he is about to utter. **6.** The deliverance of Israel from Egyptian bondage. **7b.** Probably the theophany at Sinai. **7c.** cf. Exod. 17:7. Note the close parallel here and in later verses with 95:7*d*–11. **9f.** cf. Exod. 20:2–5. The reminiscence of the Decalogue is significant: the distinctive Hebrew tradition had established itself in what was a nature festival. **15. fate:** Heb. 'time', i.e. in this context 'bad time'.

c **LXXXII.** For the superscription see §358*c*. In this ps. God takes his seat as judge (1), and arraigns those who are guilty of unjust judgment (2–4). There follow a description of their ignorance and a divine prediction of their downfall (5–7). The ps. ends with a prayer that God will judge the whole earth (8). The main problem of interpretation is whether the unjust judges are human (cf. Jn 10:34ff.) or superhuman beings. The latter is the more likely, since it gives the more natural meaning to 6f. The picture is that of a divine assembly (cf. 58 ; Job 1:6ff., 2:1ff), presided over by Yahweh, and composed of superhuman beings who are subordinate to him. The idea was no doubt derived from the Canaanite pantheon, but modified in such a way as to preserve the uniqueness of Yahweh. It is implied here that these beings have exercised jurisdiction over men ; and they are condemned for their perversion of justice. (The activities of the Satan in Job offer a partial parallel ; cf. also the references in the NT to demonic powers.) Thus this faded survival of pantheism is used as a partial explanation of the harsh experiences of life, which can be overcome only by the intervention of the supreme Judge of all the earth (8). The ps. may have formed part of the liturgy of the New Year festival in which the thought of Yahweh's judgment was prominent. **1. God:** doubtless 'Yahweh' was the original reading. **divine council:** cf. 89:6f. ; 1 Kg. 22:19. **the gods:** cf. on 6f. **5ab.** For the ignorance of the heavenly beings cf. 1 C. 2:8. **5c.** The misconduct of the heavenly beings threatens to bring about a return of chaos. **6f.** The persons addressed partake of the divine nature, and so are addressed as 'gods' and 'sons of the Most High' (cf. Gen. 6:2 ; Job 1:6, 38:7), but are not in themselves immortal, by contrast with Yahweh who has life in himself and is the giver of life.

d **LXXXIII.** For the superscription see §358*c*. A communal lament, beginning with an appeal for God's intervention (1) against enemies who have allied themselves against Israel (2–8) and continuing with a violent and comprehensive imprecation (9–18). The ps. has been understood as purely cultic, with no reference to any specific historical situation ; but the references to particular nations make it probable that some actual historical crisis is described, though, of course, the prayer would be offered in the sanctuary in the setting of the cult. Attempts to identify it have varied from the time of Saul to the Maccabaean age. If, as seems likely, Assyria (8) really means Assyria, the period will be one in which she was a power to reckon with, but not overwhelmingly powerful. Significantly, Syria is not mentioned. The age of Jeroboam II and Uzziah would suit these conditions ; but we do not know of any hostile alliance corresponding to all the details mentioned. **3. protected ones:** AV, RV 'hidden ones'. The idea is presumably of something prized and therefore protected. **4b.** The obliteration of the name means utter extinction. **6. Edom:** south of

3d the Dead Sea. **Ishmaelites:** desert tribes (cf. Gen. 25:16–18). **Moab:** east of the Dead Sea. **Hagrites:** in Gilead, east of Jordan, in the Hauran (cf. 1 Chr. 5: 10, 19). **7. Gebal:** just south of the Dead Sea. **Ammon:** east of Jordan and north of Moab. **Amalek:** desert tribes (cf. Exod. 17:8–16 etc.). **Philistia:** the coastal plain between Joppa and Gaza. **Tyre:** the Phoenician port. **8. Assyria:** probably the real Assyria ; but if the ps. is late the name may stand for some other world power hostile to the Jews. **children of Lot:** Moabites and Ammonites (Gen. 19:37f.). **9-12.** A prayer that the allies may suffer the fate of those overthrown by Deborah and Barak (Jg. 4f.), and by Gideon (Jg. 7f.). **13-18.** A prayer that the allies may be scattered and destroyed. **13. whirling dust:** the word may refer to the dried calyx of a kind of thistle, blown about by the wind (cf. Isa. 17:13). **16, 18.** In spite of the prayer for destruction of Israel's enemies, there is here the positive hope that they may come to acknowledge Israel's God.

e **LXXXIV.** For the superscription see §358*cdf.* A hymn celebrating the joys of worship at the Temple. This ps. has affinities with the songs of Zion (e.g. 48) and the Pilgrim Psalms (120–34), and it is a complement to 42, 43 ; but it has its own distinctive and individual quality. It expresses both the eager longing of the pilgrim who goes up to Jerusalem to worship and also the satisfaction and security which are his in the Temple courts. What some pss. say of the glories of the sanctuary and others of the satisfaction of communion with God, this ps. expresses with memorable freshness and grace. The occasion to which the ps. relates may well have been the autumnal festival. The period of its composition is clearly that of the monarchy (9). **1f.** The Psalmist's longing for the Temple courts. **2. soul . . . heart . . . flesh:** i.e. the whole being. **the living God:** who has life in himself and is the Giver of life (cf. on 82:6f.). **3f.** The happiness of those who dwell in the Temple. The Psalmist envies the birds who nest in the Temple precincts, and the privilege which the priests enjoy of being there constantly and joining in worship. **4. Blessed:** cf. on 1:1. **5-7.** the happiness of those who make pilgrimage to the Temple. **5b. to Zion:** has been added (see RSV*n*). Heb. is 'who have highways in their hearts', which may mean 'who are bent on pilgrimage'. **6. the valley of Baca:** this rendering is better than 'valley of weeping' (LXX, RV). The location of the valley is unknown. Baca may mean 'balsam tree', which grows in dry soil. The point at all events seems to be that the valley is arid but seems to the expectant pilgrims to be well watered, since at the coming festival they will offer their prayers for rain. **a place of springs:** Heb. 'a spring'. **early rain:** the rain which was expected in the months immediately following the autumnal festival. **7a.** Their strength, drawn from God, is constantly renewed (cf. Isa. 40:31). **7b.** This is probably the best interpretation of the consonantal text, referring to the manifestation of God's presence in the sanctuary. **8f.** A prayer for the king, appropriate at the autumnal festival. **9. our shield:** rightly taken not as a vocative, referring to God, but as the object of the verb, referring to the king, as the parallelism with 'thine anointed' suggests. For 'shield' = 'king' cf. 47:10. **10-12.** The blessedness of worship at the sanctuary. **10. elsewhere:** not in Heb. Possibly the word rendered 'I would rather' belongs to this line and should be altered to 'in my own chamber' or the like. The next line would then read '(Better) to be a doorkeeper' etc. **11. sun:** better 'battlement' (cf. Isa. 54:12, where 'sun' is used = 'pinnacle') or 'buckler'.

7a **LXXXV.** For the superscription see §358*cd.* A communal lament, which begins with a retrospective appeal to Yahweh's mighty acts on his people's behalf (1–3), continues with a plea for help in present need (4–7), and ends with a promise (uttered by a cultic prophet?) of restoration and blessing (8–13). The 377a
ps. is commonly assigned to the time immediately after the return from Exile, when a great deliverance had been followed by adverse conditions (cf. Hag. 1:6). It has also been associated with the autumnal festival and assigned to the pre-exilic period. On the whole the later date is more likely. The cultic setting effectively links the somewhat disparate elements. **1. restore the fortunes:** a better rendering than 'bring back the captivity of', hence there is not *necessarily* any reference to the return. **2. iniquity . . . sin:** cf. on 32:1f. **4-7.** These verses imply that the national affliction is a punishment for sin. **7. steadfast love:** cf. on 5:7. **8.** The prayer of the congregation is followed by the voice of the cultic prophet or priest, who thus introduces the promise of blessing. **peace:** well-being and harmony. **saints:** cf. on 4:3. **to those who turn to him in their hearts:** this is one of a number of emendations suggested for the MT (see RSV*n*), which is somewhat abrupt. **9.** When Yahweh's glory is in the land its whole life is renewed. The Temple was the place where his glory was supremely manifested. **10-13.** A moving poetical description of the renewal of material and spiritual well-being, of harmony between man and God and of nature bountifully supplying man's need. **13.** The meaning is somewhat elusive, but seems to be that righteousness is the herald of Yahweh's coming and marks out the path in which he treads. Righteousness is not simply ethical, but the vindicating action of God.

LXXXVI. An individual lament, consisting mainly b
of appeals to Yahweh for deliverance, and saying relatively little of the worshipper's plight. In the opening petitions for help the Psalmist bases his plea not only on his need but on his own faith and devotion and on Yahweh's goodness and constancy (1–7). The central section combines confession of Yahweh's greatness (8–10) with a prayer for guidance (11) and thanksgiving for the expected succour (12f.). In the closing verses the Psalmist speaks of his bitter foes, and prays again for deliverance. **1. poor:** cf. on 9:12. **2. godly:** cf. on 4:3. **3. Thou art my God:** transferred by RSV from 2. **5. steadfast love:** cf. on 5:7. **8. the gods:** the existence of divine beings other than Yahweh is not denied ; but his incomparable supremacy is maintained (cf. 10*b*). **9.** The breadth of the Psalmist's outlook is comparable with that of Deutero-Isaiah. **13. the depths of Sheol:** dire affliction in which the sufferer feels himself to be already within death's domain. **16. the son of thine handmaid:** i.e. thy servant.

LXXXVII. For the superscription see §358*c.* A c
song of Zion, beginning with a hymnic celebration of the glories of the city, the foundation and the special delight of Yahweh (1–3), after which God speaks, claiming the nations as his own in his register of the peoples (4), a thought which the Psalmist repeats: men from other lands may be reckoned citizens of Zion (5f.). Finally we catch a glimpse of the joyful worshippers celebrating the holy city (7). Various attempts have been made to rearrange the metrical lines ; but there is no firm ground for any such reconstruction. It is better to try to make sense of the ps. as it stands. The concise and allusive style raises problems of interpretation, the most important of which is the point of the reference to other countries. Some hold that it is the Jews born in the Diaspora who are said to be citizens of Jerusalem, others that the reference is to Gentile nations. The former view (which probably involves dating the ps. in the Persian period) is less likely, because the territories mentioned (other than Egypt and Babylon) are not specially appropriate. The thought is, rather, that the supremacy of Zion is such that men of all nations may be reckoned as her citizens. This is a spiritualised form of the idea of Yahweh's triumph over the peoples of the earth. If this interpretation is sound it is a striking fact that among the nations mentioned are some at whose hands Israel had suffered much (cf. Isa. 19:19–25). **2. the**

377c **gates of Zion:** the gates, as a specially important part, stand for the whole city. This verse expresses the supremacy of Zion to which Dt. gave formal, legal expression. **3. are spoken:** or, with a change of vowels, 'he speaks'. **4. Rahab:** Egypt (cf. Isa. 30:7). The name denoted the chaos monster (89:10; Isa. 51:9f.), and was applied to Egypt, possibly because of the fusion of the Exodus tradition with the mythical idea of the destruction of the primeval dragon. **Ethiopia:** the regions around the Upper Nile. **This one:** either any of the entire nations just mentioned, or any individual member of them may be recorded as enjoying citizenship of Zion. **5. And of Zion it shall be said:** or, following LXX, '"Mother Zion", shall each one say'. **6.** Yahweh is thought of as having a register of all nations. **7. say:** added in RSV (cf. RV). The Heb. is abrupt and somewhat enigmatic. Perhaps the meaning is that the citizens of Zion celebrate her with song and dance, the second line being the theme or first line of their song. 'Springs' = sources of blessing.

d **LXXXVIII.** For the superscription see §358*c–g*. An individual lament by one who has long suffered grievously. He has been near to death through sore sickness and his friends have forsaken him. Other laments express or imply the assurance that God will intervene; but no such confidence finds a place here. We hear of the Psalmist's past and present affliction and of the future which he fears; but his faith is expressed simply in the fact that he turns to God in his need. Yet he feels that God's wrath is engulfing him; and if death should befall him there is only the bleak prospect of Sheol, where God's goodness cannot be known and where his praise is not uttered. The ps. contains three appeals to God, each followed by a description of the Psalmist's anguish: 1f.+3–9*a*; 9*b*+10–12; 13+14–18. The ending is abrupt; and it has been surmised that a less sombre sequel has been lost; but this is speculation. As it stands the ps. is the utterance of one who in unrelieved anguish 'cleaves to God most passionately when God seems to have withdrawn himself most completely'. **1.** RSV emends the slightly incoherent MT. **3-6.** cf. note on 6:5. **5a. like one forsaken:** Heb. means 'free'; but the sense is obscure, and no satisfactory suggestion has been offered. **5cd.** Note the emphatic assertion that the dead are beyond God's care (cf. 10–12). **7a.** Though the Psalmist attributes his sufferings to God's wrath, the ps. contains no confession of sin. **7b. thy waves:** cf. 42:7. **8.** His friends turn from him, either because of the repulsive nature of his illness or because his afflictions mark him as a man under divine displeasure. **10-12.** cf. on 6:5. **11. steadfast love:** cf. note on 5:7. **Abaddon:** a synonym for Sheol, 'place of destruction'. **18b.** Heb. 'my companions (are) darkness'. The meaning may be that in place of friendship he has only darkness.

e **LXXXIX.** For the superscription see §358*ce*. The interpretation of this ps. depends in large measure on whether or not it is regarded as a unity and on the view adopted of the situation in which it was (or its several parts were) used. After an overture which formulates the theme of the ps. as the steadfast love of Yahweh as seen in his covenant with the Davidic line (1–4), there follow three main sections: a hymn of praise of Yahweh, the Victor over the powers of chaos, the Lord of nature, and the God of Israel (5–18); a detailed recital of the covenant made with David and his house (19–37); a lament over the affliction and humiliation which the king is now suffering and a prayer to Yahweh to remember the covenant and deliver his servant (38–57). Some scholars have divided the ps. into two or even three independent compositions. But in conception it is a unity, as it probably was in liturgical usage. It is a Royal Psalm invoking Yahweh's help for the reigning king in a situation which some regard as historical

and others as cultic. If it is historical, we must 37
associate the ps. with some grievous military reverse: the disasters from the death of Josiah to the destruction of Jerusalem have been suggested. If it is cultic, the king is suffering a ritual humiliation, in which he appears as the suffering servant of Yahweh, who delivers him from his enemies. The appropriate setting would be the autumnal festival. It should be added that considerable evidence of Canaanite borrowing has been found in the ps.; and although it has usually been dated near or after the end of the monarchy, a 10th-cent. date has been suggested for at least part of it. **1. steadfast love:** cf. note on 5:7. **2.** The changes tacitly adopted in RSV seem unnecessary. We may render, 'For I acknowledge that steadfast love will be built up for ever; in the heavens thou wilt establish thy faithfulness'. **3f.** The allusion is to the occasion described in 2 Sam. 7. **3. Thou hast said:** in Heb. the divine speech begins abruptly without these words. **5-7.** For the divine assembly see on 82 and cf. the references there given. **9f.** The reference is to the subjugation of the cosmic deep and the chaos monster, here called Rahab (cf. 87:4; Isa. 51:9). **12. Tabor and Hermon:** the mention of these northern mountains has been taken as evidence that this part of the ps. originated in N. Israel. **14.** The maintenance by Yahweh's might of order in the natural world is matched by his righteous government. **15-18.** Here the thought passes to the special place in Yahweh's purpose of Israel and the royal house, thus forming a transition to 19–37 (but see below on 18). **15. the festal shout:** the glad acclamation of Yahweh in the festival. **18.** In RSV this is a reference to the earthly king (for the meaning of 'shield' cf. on 84:9). But it is also possible to translate, 'Surely *Yahweh* is our Shield, surely the Holy One of Israel is our king'. **19. thy faithful one:** cf. on 4:3. The reference is to Nathan or David (2 Sam. 7). Another reading is plural. **crown:** Heb. 'help'. The change is unnecessary. Render, 'I have bestowed help upon'. **25.** cf. on 72:8. **26.** cf. 2 Sam. 7:14. **29-33.** cf. 2 Sam. 7:13–16. **37.** The change in RSV is unnecessary. Render, 'As the moon which is established forever, a faithful witness in the sky'. **38-45.** In this description of the king's humiliation it is noteworthy that it is attributed ultimately to the will of Yahweh and that there is no suggestion that it has come about because of the king's infidelity and sin. **44.** RSV emends the text slightly. MT may be rendered, 'Thou hast brought his lustre to an end' (made him to cease from his lustre). **45.** If the ps. is referred to a specific historical situation this would apply appropriately to Jehoiachin (2 Kg. 24:8ff.). **47.** RSV slightly emends the difficult and perhaps corrupt Heb. **51.** RSV adopts a plausible emendation. MT seems impossible. **52.** A liturgical conclusion to Book III.

Book IV—Pss. XC–CVI 37
XC. The attribution of this ps. to Moses arose perhaps from the thought that it expresses the prayer of the generation that wandered in the wilderness and died without entering the promised land. In spite of suggestions that it embodies two independent poems, it is a unity, and is best classified as a communal lament. The occasion may have been a fast day during a prolonged period of distress, such as drought and bad harvests. But the ps. rises above the immediate need and expresses in moving language the transience of human existence and the enduring life of God. There are two main sections: 1–12, the contrast between the everlasting God and mortal man; 13–17, a plea for the renewal of God's favour and blessing. The ps. is memorably paraphrased in Isaac Watts's 'O God, our help in ages past'. **1f.** In all the changes of human life, God abides, the sure home (or refuge) of his people, who was before the world itself had been formed. **3.** cf. Gen. 3:19. **5a.** Difficult, and perhaps textually corrupt. MT has 'Thou dost sweep

378a them away; (they are) a sleep'. A suggested emendation is 'Thou doest plant them year by year', which gives consistency of metaphor in 5f. **7f.** The affliction is ascribed to God's wrath at Israel's sin. **10c.** their **span:** a slight emendation of MT 'their pride', which, however, may stand. **11. and thy wrath according to the fear of thee:** this line has been variously interpreted, and by some emended. The best interpretation of MT is '(Who understands . . .) thy wrath against sin in such a way as to show thee the reverence which is thy due?' **14. in the morning:** speedily. **steadfast love:** cf. on 5:7. **15.** The nature of the distress is not described, only its long duration.

b **XCI.** A ps. of trust. Though it has often been regarded as a didactic poem, it is best understood as a liturgical composition reaching its climax in a divine oracle (14–16) in which God (through a priest or cultic prophet) promises the worshipper protection and blessing. In 1–15 RSV adopts slight changes, so that the whole is addressed to the worshipper who comes to the sanctuary seeking protection; but in MT there is a change of person in 2 and 9*a* (see the exposition below), which suggests that the worshipper may at these points have made a profession of faith in response to the words of assurance addressed to him in 1, 3–8, 9*b*–13, by a priest or choir. The ps. reflects the insecurity of life and health and the fear of malign unseen powers, by which men were oppressed in the ancient world; but over against them it sets the security of those who trust in the Almighty. **1f.** Several different renderings (sometimes with minor emendations) have been proposed. RSV presupposes a change of vowels in the first verb of 2, making it third instead of first person. If in 1*b* we render 'shall abide' and in 2*a* retain the 'I will say' of MT, 2 may be taken as the worshipper's affirmation in response to the assurance given him in 1. **1. shelter . . . shadow:** though there may be an allusion to the sanctuary, the meaning is primarily the divine protection. **3. the snare of the fowler:** either hidden dangers in general or the secret malice of enemies. **pestilence:** LXX suggests a change of vowels to give 'word', referring to false accusations, or, possibly, the spells of sorcerers. **4. buckler:** the precise meaning of the Heb. is unknown; but clearly it denotes protection of some kind. **5.** This has sometimes been understood of surprise attacks by night and open warfare by day; but it probably refers to unseen demonic powers (cf. Lilith, the night demon, Isa. 34:14) which cause illness. The 'arrow that flies by day' may, however, be the sun's rays. **9.** RSV emends to avoid change of persons. MT may be rendered, 'For *thou*, O Lord, art my refuge!' (spoken by the worshipper), 'You have made the Most High your habitation' (addressed to the worshipper). **11f.** Quoted in Mt. 4:6; Lk. 4:10f. Belief in angels existed in early Israel, but developed considerably in the post-exilic period; but this is insufficient evidence for dating the ps. after the Exile. The idea of protection by subordinate divine beings is found in Babylonian literature. **13. adder:** or, cobra. **14. name:** cf. on 5:11.

c **XCII.** This ps. combines the characteristics of a hymn and an individual ps. of thanksgiving. The worshipper, having been delivered from affliction, comes to the sanctuary to give thanks for what God has done for him. According to the Mishnah it was used in the Temple as a Sabbath ps. (cf. the superscription). Thus an individual ps. had been adopted for congregational use (cf. the paraphrase of it by Watts in 'Sweet is the work, my God, my King'). We may analyse the contents thus: 1–3, To give praise and thanks to Yahweh is good. 4–11, His mighty works are seen in the punishment of the wicked and the deliverance of the godly. 12–15, The righteous enjoy lifelong well-being. **1. Most High:** cf. 91:1. **2. steadfast love:** cf. on 5:7. **in the morning . . . by night:** probably refers to the statutory times of worship (cf. Exod. 29:38–42). **3. to the music of:** 378c
RSV expands the Heb. somewhat. **6. The dull man:** the word rendered 'stupid' in 73:22, where it also refers to a failure to appreciate the working of God's providence. **stupid:** rendered 'fool' in 49:10, 94:8, q.v. **7-9.** The temporary prosperity of the wicked is admitted; but it is emphasised that it is only temporary; cf. 37. **10.** The figurative language refers to the renewal of well-being. The reference to oil has suggested to some that the Psalmist, having been ill, has been cleansed and healed according to the regulations of Lev. 14:15–18. The form and meaning of the verb rendered 'poured oil over me' are uncertain. **11. the downfall of my enemies:** RSV adds 'the downfall of'. The word rendered 'enemies' is uncertain, but is represented by 'enemies' in VSS. **the doom of:** an addition by RSV. **12.** cf. 1:3, 52:8.

XCIII. This ps., 47, 95–100 are the enthronement d
pss. *par excellence*; cf. note on 47. This short but magnificent hymn sets forth vividly some of the central themes associated in the New Year festival with the kingship of Yahweh: Yahweh's royal state (1*ab*); the establishment of the natural order by his power (1*c*, 2), because he has quelled the tumult of the chaos waters (3f.); the certainty of his decrees (5). **1. The lord reigns:** cf. note on 47:8. The emphasis is on the subject. It is *Yahweh* and no other who is (has become) king. The description of Yahweh's regal splendour is drawn from the ceremonial arraying and arming of earthly kings. **1c.** cf. 24:2. **3f.** The tumult of the chaos waters represents the forces by which life might be engulfed if Yahweh did not exercise his sovereignty. **4b.** RSV adopts a slight and plausible emendation. But MT may be rendered, 'Above the sound of many waters, the mighty breakers of the sea, mighty on high is Yahweh'. **5.** From the power of the conquering creator the hymn passes to the thought that his will as revealed to his people is utterly dependable, and that the Temple is forever graced by holiness.

XCIV. Two literary types appear to be combined e
in this ps.: (*a*) a national lament (1–15), which may be analysed into the lament proper in which Yahweh is asked to intervene because the wicked triumph in Israel (1–7), an admonition in Wisdom style to the wicked (8–11), and a blessing on the righteous (12–15): (*b*) an individual lament in which confidence and thanksgiving are present (16–23). Some have concluded that (*a*) and (*b*) are independent compositions; but the situation of the afflicted individual resembles that of the afflicted community (cf. 5f., 20f.), and we may suppose that the worshipper is presenting his own affliction as part of his people's need and resting his hope of relief on the conviction that 'the Lord will not forsake his people' (14). The wicked are probably to be identified not with foreign oppressors but with ruthless Israelite rulers. The description of this injustice recalls the prophetic protests against social wrong. **1. God of vengeance:** to the modern reader the phrase suggests an unpleasant vindictiveness; but, as the parallel with 'judge of the earth' (2) indicates, it expresses God's activity in maintaining justice and order in the community. **4.** cf. 31:18, 73:9f. **7.** This denial that God concerns himself with the human scene is referred to elsewhere (e.g. 10:11, 59:7; cf. on 14:1). **8.** This seems to imply that the oppressors are not foreigners. **dullest . . . fools:** cf. note on 92:6. **10.** The thought that God instructs the nations is noteworthy. **12a.** The thought of divine chastisement as an educative process is also found in Prov. (e.g. 3:11f.) and in parts of Job (e.g. 5:17). **12b. law:** probably referring to the written Law rather than to religious truth in general. **15.** A difficult and much disputed verse. RSV departs slightly from MT by substituting 'the righteous' for 'righteousness'. MT may mean 'for unto righteousness shall (the administration of) justice return'. **17. the land of silence:** i.e. Sheol (cf. 115:17).

378e 18. **steadfast love :** cf. on 5:7. 20. **wicked rulers :** lit. ' the throne of destruction '.

f **XCV.** Here a hymn (1–7*b*) is followed by a prophetic warning (7*c*–11) ; but there is no need to assume that two distinct poems have been artificially combined. In structure and content this ps. offers a remarkable parallel to 81, and, like it, is probably to be associated with the autumnal festival. It celebrates the kingship of Yahweh, his triumphs in creation (though the mythological background is not emphasised), and his care for his people Israel, whom he brought into being ; and it recalls the disobedience and obduracy of the wilderness generation as a warning to the worshippers who are now summoned to obedience. The vivid and forceful diction is matched by the effectiveness of the contrast between the two parts of the ps. The resounding praise of those who worship Yahweh is answered by the searching message of the prophetic voice. 2. **come into his presence :** presumably this indicates the movement of a festal procession. 3. **King above all gods :** the thought of heavenly beings over whom Yahweh is supreme is here implied but not obtruded (cf. notes on 58, 82, 96:4f, 97:7, 9). Note the association of this thought with the reference to creation which follows. **4f.** The whole extent of the created world belongs and is subject to Yahweh, its Creator. 6. **O come :** not the same verb as in 1. Here we might translate ' enter '. Perhaps at this point the worshippers move into the Temple court. **our Maker :** the point is the creation not of mankind but of Israel as a nation, as 7 shows. **7c.** This rendering is to be preferred to AV (' Today, if you will hear his voice '). ' Today ' is emphasised. Presumably a priest or cultic prophet makes this appeal. Note the change of person from ' his ' to ' me ', ' my ' (9), ' I ', ' my ' (10f.). 8. **Meribah . . . Massah :** cf. Exod. 17:1–7 ; Num. 20:1–13. 9. **tested . . . put me to the proof :** the divine deliverance which they had experienced left them still prone to complain, to doubt God's power, and to ask for fresh demonstrations of it, instead of relying quietly on his providence. 10. **I loathed :** a forceful expression. 11. **my rest :** the immediate historical reference is to the promised land (cf. Dt. 12:9) ; but presumably the intended application for those who hear this prophetic warning is that unbelief and disobedience may bring a like punishment on them (cf. Heb. 3:7–11).

379a **XCVI.** A hymn, containing a general exhortation to praise Yahweh and extol his mighty deeds (1–6), a summons to the nations to acknowledge him and bring offerings to him (7–9), and an acclamation of Yahweh as universal Sovereign and Judge. In 1 Chr. 16:23–33 this ps. appears (with slight omissions and changes) together with parts of 105, 106, and is associated with David's removal of the Ark to Jerusalem. The superscription in LXX assigns the ps. to David but gives as the occasion ' When the house (i.e. the Temple) was being built after the captivity '. Like other of the pss. of Yahweh's kingship, this has been associated with the situation after the return from Exile. Again, the emphasis on the thought of Yahweh's coming as the Judge has suggested an eschatological interpretation. But the main features of the ps. are best understood in terms of the celebration of the Kingship of Yahweh at the autumnal festival. 1. **a new song :** cf. 33:3, 40:3, 98:1, 144:9, 149:1 ; Isa. 42:10. **4b.** cf. note on 95:3. 5. **idols :** a contemptuous term, probably denoting the ineffectiveness of the other gods. 9. **in holy array :** cf. on 29:2. 10. **The Lord reigns :** this rendering and ' The Lord has become King ' (or ' has assumed his kingship ') are both possible. The Old Latin Version adds ' from the tree ', which by some of the Latin Fathers is applied to the victory of Christ's death. Hence the line ' Regnavit a ligno Deus ' in the hymn ' Vexilla regis '. **the world is established :** the sovereignty and triumph of Yahweh ensure the stability and order of nature (cf. 93:1). **11f.** The whole of nature is exhorted to acclaim Yahweh's coming as Judge. For the thought of such rejoicing cf. 65:8, 13, 98:7–9 ; Isa. 55:12. 13. When Yahweh comes as Judge it is to establish righteousness. Hence, as Judge he is also Saviour ; and his advent is welcomed with jubilation.

b **XCVII.** A hymn celebrating the kingship of Yahweh. It opens with a description of Yahweh's advent in cloud, lightning flash, and earthquake ; his righteousness and glory are manifested to all (1–6). He has triumphed over other deities and put their worshippers to shame (7–9). The righteous may well rejoice in the care he has for them (10–12). In LXX there is a superscription : ' of (to ? for ?) David, when his land was restored ' ; and accordingly the return from Exile has been taken as the occasion of the ps. It has also been understood as wholly eschatological or as having at least an eschatological element. Its most appropriate setting is the autumnal festival (cf. note on 96). 1. **The Lord reigns :** cf. on 96:10. **coastlands :** the word is rendered ' isles ' in 72:10 (q.v.). 2. **righteousness and justice :** cf. 89:14. Note how the awe-inspiring accompaniments of the theophany are associated with these moral qualities. 7. **worthless idols :** cf. on 96:5. **all gods :** LXX has ' angels ' ; cf. on 82 and on 95:3. 8. cf. 48:11. **daughters of Judah :** cities of Judah. 9. **most high :** Heb. *'Elyôn*, which appears to have been a Jerusalemite title of the deity (cf. Gen. 14:18). **10a.** RSV presupposes slight changes of vowels and consonants (cf. RSV*n*) to give a better balance of clauses. **10b. saints :** cf. on 4:3. 11. **light dawns :** this reading is commonly accepted ; but MT ' is sown ' should probably be retained as harder but not impossible. ' Light ' means ' well-being '.

c **XCVIII.** A hymn celebrating the kingship of Yahweh : 1–3, a summons to praise Yahweh for his signal acts of deliverance ; 4–6, let all the earth hail him as King ; 7–9, let all nature rejoice at his coming to judge the world. Like 96, 97, it has been associated with the return from Exile and has been thought to reflect the literary and theological influence of Deutero-Isaiah. Alternatively it has been interpreted eschatologically, as celebrating in anticipation Yahweh's final advent as Judge. But its general character is best explained in terms of the autumnal festival, though here, as in other hymns of Yahweh's kingship, we may recognise features which become part of the eschatological hope. There are some striking similarities in thought and diction to the Magnificat, to which this ps. is an alternative in Evening Prayer in BCP. 1. **a new song :** cf. note on 96:1. 2. **vindication :** or ' righteousness ', which in OT frequently means ' vindicating action '. 3. **steadfast love :** cf. note on 5:7. **5f.** cf. 81:1–3. **7-9.** cf. 96:11–13. 9. **righteousness . . . equity :** the moral emphasis is characteristic. As 97:10 makes clear the moral conditions which Yahweh requires from his worshippers ; so here it is evident that his manifestation as King is profoundly moral and not merely a demonstration of power (cf. on 96:13).

d **XCIX.** A hymn of the kingship of Yahweh, resembling 96, 97, 98, and yet with its own distinctive features, notably the specific persons and events in Israel's past history (6f.). All nations are summoned to praise Yahweh, who rules over all (1–3). His rule is just and righteous (4f.) ; and his goodness has been shown in his past dealings with Israel both in mercy and in chastisement (6–9). As in 96, 97, 98, nothing in this ps. is a sufficiently explicit reference to contemporary events to justify a precise dating, though it has been assigned to the time immediately after the return from Exile. An eschatological import has often been found in the opening verses. However this may be, the appropriate setting, as for 96, 97, 98, is the great autumnal festival. 1. **The Lord reigns :** cf. note on 96:10. **He sits enthroned upon the cherubim :** cf. note on 80:1. **3f. Holy is he ! Mighty King, lover of justice :** MT has ' Holy is he (or it) ! The king's strength loveth justice '. The Heb. is somewhat

79d unusual; but if retained is best taken to mean that, though powerful, the universal King chooses to rule according to right. RSV adopts one of a number of suggested changes. Another, which involves transferring the first word of 4 to the end of 3, is 'Holy is it (i.e. the name) and mighty. Loving justice thou hast' etc. **5. his footstool:** i.e. the Temple, as in Isa. 60:13 (also applied to the Ark in 1 Chr. 28:2, the earth in Isa. 66:1, and Jerusalem in Lam. 2:1). **6.** Commonly taken as linking Moses and Aaron as priests and Samuel as a representative of the prophets (' those who called upon his name' referring to the intercessory function of the prophets). But perhaps Moses is meant to stand alone, the priestly and prophetic orders being represented by Aaron and Samuel respectively. **They cried to the Lord:** cf. Exod. 17:11f., 32:30–2; Num. 11:10f.; 1 Sam. 7:8f., 12:16–18; Sir. 46:16f. **7. the pillar of cloud:** cf. Exod. 33:9; Num. 12:5. **8. forgiving . . . avenger:** the reference has passed over to Israel, and is not simply to Moses, Aaron, and Samuel. The combination of mercy and chastisement is characteristic.

e **C.** It is uncertain whether the superscription means 'A Psalm for the thank-offering' or 'A Psalm of thanksgiving'. If, as seems likely, it was suggested by the word in 4, then the latter alternative is preferable. But, in either event, the superscription does not aptly describe the ps., which is a hymn, which in vigorous, dignified language summons God's people to worship and sets forth the ground of worship in the nature and activity of God. Those who hold that the kingship of Yahweh was celebrated at the autumnal festival usually associate this ps. with it; but, while it would be entirely appropriate in such a context, it contains no specific reference to Yahweh's kingship, and its contents do not themselves suggest any specific festival. It well exemplifies the joyful character of much Hebrew worship. **1. lands:** Heb. has sing. (cf. RSV*n*). Some interpret as 'the whole land of Israel', which accords with 3; others as 'the whole earth', which accords with the universal perspective of 93, 95–9. **2. serve:** referring to liturgical worship. **come into his presence:** cf. on 95:2. **3a.** Yahweh alone is God; cf. Dt. 4:35, 39. **3b. and we are his:** this is to be preferred to the alternative reading (RSV*n*), both as less repetitious and as leading forward to the thought of the next line. **4.** An invitation to the worshippers to move into the sacred precincts. **thanksgiving:** parallelism and the general sense of the ps. both suggest that this (and not 'a thank offering') is the correct rendering. **5. steadfast love:** cf. on 5:7.

80a **CI.** A Royal Psalm, expressing the code of conduct and of government of an Israelite ruler in Jerusalem (8). In 1–4 he states the moral and religious standards by which his own life will be ordered; in 5–8 he outlines the measures he will take to ensure that his subordinates are men of integrity and piety. The ps. is usually thought to have been used in some ceremony such as that of the king's accession, when it would be appropriate that he should solemnly profess his resolve to maintain such standards. But it has also been suggested that this ps. was associated with a ritual act in which the king, undergoing symbolic humiliation, pleaded his own and his people's righteousness. On this interpretation the verbs which appear in RSV as futures must be rendered as presents; and 2*b* is an appeal for deliverance from the experience of humiliation. The former seems the more likely view. On either view the ps. is important for its emphasis on the moral elements in the Hebrew ideal of kingly rule. **1. loyalty:** the Heb. is usually rendered 'steadfast love' in RSV (cf. note on 5:7). **2b.** Often emended to 'Let truth come unto me', on the ground that MT is abrupt. But the interjection of such a prayer does not seem unnatural, even if the interpretation mentioned above is not accepted. **3b.** RSV emends slightly. MT may be rendered, 'I hate the doing of deeds that swerve'; but the sense is uncertain.
4. Perverseness of heart: or, 'a crooked heart'. 380a
I will know nothing of evil: or, 'I will not acknowledge an evil person'. **8.** This seems to refer to the daily dispensation of justice by the king (cf. 2 Sam. 15:1–6).

CII. The superscription gives a more accurate b
account of this ps. than the traditional Christian inclusion of it among the Penitential Psalms, since it includes no expression of penitence. Nevertheless, the varied content makes it at first sight difficult to classify. In 1f. the Psalmist appeals for Yahweh's intervention to deliver him from the plight which he describes in 3–11; drained of physical vitality, and railed at by enemies who gloat over his sufferings, he is keenly aware of the transience of his life. In 12–22 there follows a hymnic passage, celebrating the power and compassion of Yahweh, and invoking his will to restore his city and his people. The theme of the transience of life reappears in 23–8; but it is subordinated to the thought of the enduring and unchanging being of God and his lasting goodness to his servants. 12–22 has sometimes been treated as a separate ps.; but this is unnecessary. Elsewhere in the laments the mighty deeds of Yahweh in nature and in history and his care for his people are recalled (e.g. 77:11ff.); but here the need of the individual is related to the hope that the people will be delivered from the affliction (presumably the Exile) which has now befallen them. **3-11.** These verses resemble some of Job's complaints. **12b. thy name:** lit. 'thy remembrance'. **15.** Here, and in 21f., there is an international outlook combined (as in Deutero-Isa.) with the plea for deliverance. **26.** cf. Isa. 51:6. The thought that the natural order will pass away seldom appears in the OT. **27. thou art the same:** Heb. 'thou art he', i.e. the self-existent One.

CIII. Alike in literary quality and in religious c
content this is one of the supreme treasures of the Psalter. It is an individual thanksgiving in which thankfulness for the blessings received by the worshipper (1–5) leads to praise of Yahweh for his fatherly goodness to his people Israel (6–14). The transience of human life on earth is contrasted with Yahweh's enduring faithfulness from generation to generation (15–18). The Psalmist calls upon the higher powers and the whole natural order to praise Yahweh and ends as he began, with a summons to himself (19–22). There is a significant change from the singular in 1–5, where the worshipper records his own blessings, to the plural in 6–14, where Yahweh's goodness to Israel is recorded. This doubtless reflects the use of the ps. in congregational worship; and it may be that 6ff. is a choral response to the individual thanksgiving. **1. my soul . . . all that is within me:** i.e. 'myself . . . my whole self'. **3f.** The individual's experience of forgiveness and of material blessings corresponds to the experience of the nation (7–10). **4. redeems your life from the Pit:** this refers not to resurrection but to deliverance from illness. **steadfast love:** cf. on 5:7. **mercy:** compassion. **5a.** MT has 'Who satisfies your ornament with good'. Possibly the word rendered 'ornament' had an alternative meaning, such as 'prime' or 'soul'. LXX has 'desire', 'longing'. **5b. the eagle's:** or, 'the vulture's' (cf. Isa. 40:31). **6. vindication:** 'righteousness', in the sense of help. **8.** cf. Exod. 34:6. **9.** Render, 'nor will he be wroth forever'. **11. fear:** 'revere'. **12. transgressions:** 'rebellions'. **13.** The thought of the fatherly love of God for Israel is fairly common in the OT. See especially Isa. 1:2; Hos. 11:1f.; Mal. 1:6. **pities:** 'has compassion'. The root is the same as in 'mercy' (4) and 'merciful' (8). **14. we are dust:** cf. Gen. 2:7. **15. man:** the Heb. expresses the frailty of man. With the language and thought of this and the following verses cf. Isa. 40:6–8. It is a striking fact that though in some of the laments the thought of man's ephemeral existence deepens the sense of affliction, here it seems to emphasise the Psalmist's joyful confidence in the

380c enduring goodness of God. **17.** No hope of personal immortality is expressed in this ps., only the thought of the unswerving faithfulness of God to successive generations of his people. **20f.** For the belief in supernatural beings subordinate to Yahweh cf. on 8:5 and 82.

d **CIV.** A magnificent hymn celebrating the power and wisdom of Yahweh as displayed in the wonder and variety of his creation; first the splendour of Yahweh's heavenly abode, the realm in which he lives and moves and whose resources are at his command (1*b*–4); then the earth, brought into being and maintained in due order by Yahweh's mastery over the chaos waters (5–9); next the furnishing of the means of life for plants, animals and men (10–18), and the regulating by sun and moon of the seasons and the activity of animals and men (19–23), and last the mighty sea, with its teeming life and its monster, Leviathan (24–6): all are utterly dependent upon Yahweh, whose gifts sustain the life bestowed by his spirit (27–30); to him in his might and awesome majesty the Psalmist renders joyful praise (31–5). There is a close, but not exact, resemblance to the creation narrative in Gen. 1. This, however, need not indicate that either passage is dependent on the other: both give memorable and individual expression to material drawn from Israel's faith and worship. Moreover, this ps. does not for the most part describe the initial acts of creation but the created order as the worshipper now witnesses it. Many parallels to the ps. have been cited from other literatures. The most striking of these is the Egyptian 'Hymn to Aton' (the disk of the sun), from the time of the so-called heretic Pharaoh, Akhenaton (14th cent. B.C.). It is improbable that the ps. is directly dependent on the Egyptian text; and whether or not there is direct or indirect dependence, the ps. expresses the distinctive Israelite conception of God, who is not, as in the Egyptian hymn, equated with the sun's disk but is creator of the sun, as of the whole natural order. The ps. is also noteworthy because of the picture which it gives of the dependence of all living things on Yahweh. The individual note in 1*a*, 33–5 has led some to regard it as the hymn or thanksgiving of an individual, whose personal reasons for gratitude are overshadowed by the majesty of Yahweh's creative work which he celebrates. There is, however, much that is reminiscent of the great themes of the New Year festival; and the suggestion that it belonged to that liturgy is at least plausible. **1. clothed with honour and majesty:** cf. 93:1. **2a.** cf. the description of the theophany in Hab. 3:4. See also 1 Tim. 6:16. **2b.** cf. Isa. 40:22. **3a.** The thought is of the waters which are above the firmament (cf. Gen. 1:7), on which Yahweh's house rests as the earth rests on the lower waters. **3bc.** cf. 18:10. There is an interesting Ugaritic parallel to the thought of Yahweh riding on the clouds (cf. on 68:4). **4.** Yahweh uses the forces of nature to carry out his purposes. The renderings of RSV, RV are to be preferred to PBV, AV. But it should be noted that the use of the second person in 2–5 in RSV represents the third person in MT (so in 5*a*). **5.** For the thought of the firm establishment of the earth on its foundations cf. Job 38:6. **6-9.** The encroaching waters are restrained and held in check by Yahweh's authority (cf. Gen. 1:2, 9f.). **13. thy lofty abode:** the word is rendered 'chambers' in 3. MT has 'his', not 'thy'; and the verbal forms referring to God in 10–13 may be rendered by the third person, as in PBV, AV, RV. **14. Thou dost cause:** or, 'who causes'. **19. Thou:** MT has 'He'. With this verse cf. Gen. 1:14. **24. In wisdom:** for the thought of God's creative wisdom cf. Prov. 3:19, 8:22ff. **26. ships:** some would emend to 'dragons', or the like, as more appropriate in a list of living things. **Leviathan:** cf. note on 74:14. **28-30.** Here the thought of the dependence of all living things on God is vividly expressed. Note the conception of the Spirit (or breath) of God as a life-giving agent (cf. Gen. 1:2).

32. There is a reminiscence here of the awe-inspiring 38
features of the theophanies (cf. Exod. 19:18). **35.** After his hymn of praise for the excellence of Yahweh's creation, the Psalmist utters what Kirkpatrick calls 'a solemn prayer for the restoration of the harmony of creation by the banishment from it of "all things that cause stumbling, and them that do iniquity"'.

CV. This poetical survey of Israel's religious history 381
is to be classed as a hymn. In 1 Chr. 16:8–22 the first 15 verses are quoted along with 96, 106:47f. in the story of the installation of the Ark in the Jerusalem sanctuary; and this suggestion that it was appropriately used in the cult accords with the contents of the ps., which is not simply a factual record of historical events but a selective and interpretative retrospect addressed to the covenant congregation. In pss. such as 95 we may see how the events of the past were used in Israelite worship; but here and in 78, 106, 107, 136 we have more extended surveys. **1-6.** An exhortation to worship, recalling Yahweh's mighty deeds, and addressing the congregation as heirs of Abraham and Jacob. **6. his chosen ones:** some MSS have the singular, which is preferable. **7-15.** Yahweh's covenant with the patriarchs: his promise that their descendants would inherit the land (cf. Gen. 12:7, 13:14ff., 15:18, 17:2ff., 24:7, 26:3, 28:13ff.). Emphasis is laid on their comparative insignificance in order to bring out the fact that the fulfilment of the promise was a work of God. **14.** cf. Gen. 12:10ff., 20, 26. **15. anointed ones:** i.e. as set apart by God for himself. **prophets:** cf. Gen. 20:7. The word, like 'anointed ones', presumably expresses their special relationship to God. **16-23.** The Joseph story and the migration to Egypt (cf. Gen. 37, 39ff.). **18a.** MT 'His feet they afflicted with fetters'. **18b.** MT '(into) iron his soul (*nephesh*) entered'; i.e. 'his person was put into fetters'; but some think that *nephesh* here means 'neck'. **22. to instruct:** this emendation gives better parallelism than MT. **23. Ham:** cf. Gen. 10:6. **24-36.** The Egyptian oppression and the plagues. This account, not unnaturally, varies in order and in detail from the narrative of Exod. 1–12. **28. they rebelled:** MT 'they did not rebel' is difficult unless 'they' means Moses and Aaron, which is unnatural. Some retain the negative and change the verb to 'observed'. **37-42.** The Exodus and wilderness wanderings (cf. Exod. 12ff.). **43-5.** The ps. returns to the thought of the covenant and to the duty of obedience.

CVI. This ps., like 105, surveys the past history of b
Israel, but with a different emphasis. In 105 the record is one of Yahweh's mighty acts, wise providence and sure promises. Here the emphasis is on the repeated ingratitude and apostasy of Israel; and the interpretation of the history resembles that of Jg. The communal lament or confession in 6–47 (cf. Neh. 9:5–37) is introduced by an exhortation to praise (1f.), a blessing on the righteous (3), and a prayer for succour, uttered presumably by the leader of the congregation (4f.). Some have regarded these opening verses as a separate ps., but they may be a preparation for the great act of congregational confession. At a solemn renewal of the covenant it would be appropriate to recall both Yahweh's promises and acts of deliverance and also to acknowledge the people's repeated faithlessness. The seeming allusions to exile and dispersion in 27, 47 have led most scholars to assign the ps. to the post-exilic period. **1. steadfast love:** cf. note on 5:7. **3. Blessed:** cf. note on 1:1. **6-12.** Rebellion at the Red Sea. Whereas in some prophetic passages (e.g. Jer. 2:1ff.) the Exodus period is presented as a time of religious bliss and fidelity, Israel's unfaithfulness is here represented as having begun even then. This agrees with the Pentateuchal narratives, and also with the survey in Ezek. 20, with which this ps. should be compared. **7d.** RSV omits 'at the sea', probably rightly. **13-15.** Rebellion in the wilderness (cf. Exod. 15:22ff., 16:2ff., 17:2ff.; Num. 11:4). **16-18.** Rebellion of Dathan and Abiram (cf. Num. 16). **19-23.** Rebellion in the making of the

81b golden calf (cf. Exod. 32). **19. Horeb:** Deuteronomic name for the mount of God. **20. the glory of God:** Heb. ' their glory '. According to Rabbinic tradition the reading should be ' his glory ' or ' my glory '. **23.** cf. Exod. 32:10ff. ; Num. 14:11ff. ; Dt. 9:25f. **24-7.** Rebellion in the refusal to enter Canaan (cf. Num. 13f.). **26. he raised his hand and swore:** Heb. ' he raised his hand ', i.e. he took a solemn oath. **27.** The resemblance to Ezek. 20:23 is striking, and lends support to the otherwise plausible emendation adopted by RSV. **28-31.** Rebellion in Moab (cf. Num. 25). **28a. attached themselves to:** ' became worshippers of '. **28b. sacrifices offered to the dead:** Heb. ' sacrifices of the dead ', which may mean sacrifices offered to a lifeless idol. **32f.** Rebellion at Meribah (cf. Num. 20:1–13). **34-9.** Rebellion in Canaan, in fraternising with the inhabitants of the land and adopting their religion. The view that Israel ought to have exterminated the Canaanites is Deuteronomic, like much else in the thought and diction of the ps. (cf. Dt. 7:2ff.). **37f.** Human sacrifice seems to have occurred at times when alien religious influence was strong in Israel (cf. Ezek. 16:20f.). The word rendered ' demons ' is found only here and in Dt. 32:17. **40-6.** The severity and the goodness of Yahweh. The thought of disciplinary chastisement resembles the presentation of Israel's history in Jg. ; and that may be the period referred to here ; but many commentators hold that there is at least an implied allusion to the Exile. **47.** A final prayer for succour. **48.** This closing doxology is probably intended as a conclusion to Book IV.

82a **Book V—Pss. CVII-CL**

CVII. This beautiful ps. consists of a communal thanksgiving (1–32) and a hymn praising God for his gracious acts (33–43). It is unnecessary to assume composite authorship, since the latter part is a quite appropriate sequel to what precedes. The thanksgiving has a double refrain (6+8, 13+15, 19+21, 28+31), each occurrence of which seems to mark a section of the thanksgiving ; and each section is appropriate to a particular group of those who have experienced Yahweh's succour. The hymnic conclusion then sums up the whole. **1-3.** Summons to thanksgiving. **1. steadfast love:** cf. on 5:7. **3. from the south:** Heb. ' from the sea '. RSV accepts a simple and probable emendation. **4-9.** The first group of ' redeemed ' : those who have made perilous journeys in the wilderness. **4. Some wandered:** MT ' They wandered '. **10-16.** The second group : those who have been released from bondage. **10, 14. darkness, gloom:** Here, as often, metaphorically used of sore affliction (cf. note on 23:4). **12. Their hearts were bowed down:** MT ' And he subdued their hearts '. **16.** cf. Isa. 45:2. **17-22.** The third group : those who have been restored to health. **17. sick:** some such emendation (see RSV*n*) seems to be required by parallelism. **20. he sent forth his word:** note the idea of the word as an active power (cf. 147:15, 18). **22. sacrifices of thanksgiving:** for the regulations for the thank-offering see Lev. 7:11–15, 22:29f. **23-32.** The fourth group : seafarers saved from peril of shipwreck. **25. the waves of the sea:** MT ' its waves ' ; so in 29. **33-41.** The power of Yahweh as shown in his compassion for men in their need and in his punishment of the wicked. **39-41.** Some would change the order to 40, 39, 41 ; but this is unnecessary. If we take the verses as they stand, 39 describes the affliction of the righteous, 40 the humiliation of their oppressors, and 41 the restoration of the righteous. But note that 40 appears in Job 12:21*a*, 24*b*, from which it may be an insertion. **42.** cf. Job 22:19. **43.** cf. Hos. 14:9.

b **CVIII.** Here 57:7–11 and 60:5–12 are combined (6 is the connecting verse). For exegetical details see the commentary on these passages. We can only speculate on the reasons for the union of the two passages. Note that whereas in 60 vv. 5–12 follow a lament, they are here preceded by a hymn of praise. 382b

c **CIX.** For the superscription see §358*bd*. In this individual lament there are appeals for succour against malicious enemies in 1–5, 20–5 (including a description of the Psalmist's pitiful plight) and 26–9, and a vow of praise and thanksgiving for the expected deliverance. A problem is raised by the comprehensive imprecation, 6–19, which seems at first sight to be the Psalmist's prayer. But in the rest of the ps. he speaks of his enemies in the plural, whereas here the singular is used. It has been suggested that he is speaking of them collectively, or of an outstanding individual among them. A more likely view is that in 6–19 the Psalmist is quoting the ' words of hate ' (3) which his enemies level against him. Such imprecations, like blessings, were believed to have an inherent energy by which they could accomplish what they described. In 20 the Psalmist prays that this malign assault on him may be warded off and turned back ; and in his isolation and anguish he puts himself in God's hands. **4b.** RSV adopts a reasonable emendation of difficult Heb. **6. an accuser:** Heb. *śāṭān* ; but the picture is that of a human court and the reference is not (as in AV) to Satan (cf. Job 1:6ff., 2:1ff. ; Zech. 3:1). **8. seize his goods:** ' take his office ' is also a possible rendering. **10b.** If the Heb. ' and may they seek out of their desolate places ' is retained, some phrase such as ' their bread ' must be supplied. **13.** Note the connection between the extinction of the family and the obliteration of the name. **23. at evening:** Heb. ' when it is stretched out '. **26. steadfast love.:** cf. note on 5:7. The word is rendered ' kindness ' in 16. **28a.** Heb. expresses strong antithesis between ' them ' and ' thou '. Against Yahweh's blessings the most potent imprecations of the Psalmist's enemies will not avail. **28b.** MT ' when they arise, they shall be put to shame '. **29-31.** Note the echo of 19 in 29 and of 6f. in 31. The Psalmist has moved from the hostile atmosphere of his enemies' maledictions to the certainty of Yahweh's succour.

d **CX.** Both the text and the general interpretation of this Royal Psalm have been much disputed. The traditional Christian interpretation is Christological and Messianic. Some modern critics have found in it an acrostic on the name Simon (Simeon) and have related it to Simon the Maccabee ; but the acrostic is incomplete and the theory far-fetched. In all probability it refers to a king of pre-exilic Judah. It begins with an oracle of Yahweh delivered, presumably, by a priest or cultic prophet, assuring the king of lofty status and of the subjugation of his enemies (1). A promise that Yahweh will extend his dominion and a description of how his people will render willing service led up to a second oracle in which the king is confirmed by a divine oath in the status of priest in the ancient Jerusalemite line which went back to Melchizedek (2–4). The ps. closes with another picture of God-given triumph over the king's enemies (5–7). In this ps. the religious status of the royal house is expressed at least as emphatically as in 2. Part of the traditional background may well be David's victorious entry into Jerusalem. The reference to Melchizedek implies an appropriation of the pre-Davidic religious traditions of the city ; and there seem to be allusions to a wider background of myth and ritual ; but uncertainties about text and interpretation make it unwise to attempt to define this too precisely. But it is clear that however exalted the status of the Hebrew kings, they were utterly dependent on Yahweh, who was the source of their authority and the guarantor of their security. The most probable suggestions for the occasion at which the ps. would be used are (*a*) the king's accession or enthronement and (*b*) a part of the ritual of the autumnal festival. **1. The Lord says:** lit. ' utterance (or oracle) of the Lord '. Note that ' LORD ' represents the divine name ' Yahweh ', whereas ' lord ' is the common noun, referring to the king. **sit at my right hand:** implying both honour and delegated authority. **thy footstool:** cf. Jos.

382d 10:24. **2.** If the occasion was the king's enthronement, the reference to his sceptre would be particularly appropriate : the meaning is that Yahweh extends the king's dominion. Perhaps 'from Zion' should be taken with 'Rule'. **3.** The most disputed verse in the ps. As rendered in RSV it describes the young warriors who rally to the king and who are as fresh as morning dew. It has also been translated (with a slight change of vowel points) : 'Your people offer themselves freely on the day of your birth on the holy mountains (or, 'in sacred splendour' ; see RSV*n*) from the womb of the dawn. You have the dew (i.e. 'freshness') with which I have begotten you'. This will then refer to the declaration at the king's accession that he is son of Yahweh (cf. on 2:7) or to the renewal of the king's life in the autumnal festival. Some have found in the language an allusion to the divine king's birth of the dawn goddess. But this seems to be unduly fanciful, though there may well be some mythological colouring in the language (e.g. 'on the holy mountains' ; cf. on 48:2). **4.** The priestly functions of the king (cf. 1 Kg. 8:14, 54ff., 62f., 9:25) are here associated with Melchizedek (cf. Gen. 14:18). This doubtless indicates a fusion of Hebraic usage with the ancient cultic traditions of Jerusalem. **5-7.** In this description of the destruction of the king's enemies RSV takes the tenses as futures, describing coming victories, but they may be rendered as perfects describing symbolic victories enacted in the cult (cf. on 46). **7.** An abrupt conclusion, which may describe the warrior Yahweh refreshing himself as he pursues his enemies. Or there may be a tacit change of subject ; some think that there is an allusion to some sacramental act by the king at the spring Gihon (cf. 1 Kg. 1:38-40), others that this is simply a description of how he refreshes himself by the wayside when pursuing his enemies. **lift up his head :** the attitude of victorious confidence.

e **CXI.** This ps. blends the characteristics of hymn and thanksgiving ; and although sung by an individual is corporate in its reference. It celebrates the greatness and goodness of Yahweh and his care for his people, and ends with an implicit appeal for the reverence and obedience which are the true wisdom. There is little development of the theme. In form it is an acrostic. **4-6.** The references seem to be to the providential events of the Exodus and the wilderness wanderings. **10.** cf. Job 28:28 ; Prov. 1:7, 9:10. 'Fear' means the reverence of true religion (cf. note on 19:9).

f **CXII.** In its acrostic structure and in its language this ps. resembles 111, and might well be taken as a commentary on 111:10. It is a didactic poem celebrating the well-being of the righteous (cf. 1, 15) in the manner of the Wisdom writings. **3b. righteousness :** not to be limited to morality. It is the true covenant relationship with Yahweh, with all its attendant blessings, material and spiritual. **4a. Light . . . darkness :** i.e. 'Well-being . . . affliction'. **4b. The Lord :** not in Heb. (see RSV*n*). Another rendering (omitting one letter) is 'Gracious and merciful is the righteous'. Note the parallel with 111:4*b*. **9c. his horn is exalted :** cf. on 75:5. The meaning here is that the righteous is strong and secure.

383a **CXIII.** This and the following five pss. form a group known as the *Hallel* (*Praise*, because of the recurring exhortation *Hallᵉlû Yāh*, 'Praise the Lord') or the *Egyptian Hallel*, to distinguish it from 146-50, which are also known as the *Hallel*. The title the *Great Hallel* is applied to 120-36, to 135-6, or to 136 alone. The present group is used at the three great festivals, the Feast of Dedication and the New Moons, but not at the New Year and the Day of Atonement. At Passover, 113-14 precede and 115-18 follow the meal (cf. Mt. 26:30). The present ps. is a hymn : 1 summons to worship ; 2-4 set forth the praise of Yahweh ; 5-9 give reasons for praising him and end with a shout of praise. The two reasons mentioned are, characteristically, Yahweh's exalted greatness and his gracious condescension. **6. looks far down :** a better rendering than 'humbleth himself' (AV, RV). 383 **7. the ash heap :** a haunt of the afflicted outcast (cf. Job 2:8 ; Lam. 4:5). This and the following verses are reminiscent of 1 Sam. 2:8, 5 and of Isa. 52:1-2, 54:1ff. (cf. the Magnificat). The reversal of human fortune by divine intervention is a favourite theme in keeping with the Exodus deliverance. The heavenly King is also the compassionate Saviour.

b **CXIV.** A hymn celebrating the wonder of the Exodus and the entry into Canaan. The poetical language may have been influenced by the theme of the quelling of the forces of nature in the myth of creation ; but the thought is chiefly of Israel's historical deliverance. **1. A people of strange language :** the hostility of the oppressor is emphasised by the unfamiliar speech (cf. Isa. 28:11). **2. Judah became his sanctuary :** presupposes the pre-eminence of the Temple at Jerusalem. 'Israel' probably means the chosen people rather than the Northern Kingdom ; and it may be that Judah is here equated with the chosen people. **3.** The crossing of the Red Sea and of Jordan are here brought together. **4.** The earthquake at Sinai may be referred to ; but there is probably a blend here of Israel's national traditions with the myth of God's triumph at creation over the unruly forces of chaos. **8.** A reference to the events of the wilderness wanderings (cf. Exod. 17:6 ; Num. 20:8ff.).

c **CXV.** In LXX, Vulg. this ps. is combined with 114, but it is undoubtedly an independent poem. It is not easy to classify it, except as a liturgy in which various elements are combined and some form of antiphonal rendering seems to have been used. Its opening lines (1f.) recall the form of the communal lament and ascribe glory to Yahweh at a time when enemies deny his effectiveness. In 3-8, a hymnic passage, his worshippers reply by deriding the impotence of idols. The antiphonal element is evident in 9-11, an exhortation to trust Yahweh, followed by an assurance of, and prayer for, blessing (12-15) and a hymn of praise (16-18). **1. steadfast love :** cf. note on 5:7. **2.** The question implies a doubt about the effectiveness of Israel's God (cf. note on 14:1). **3-8.** The scornful description of the idols is reminiscent of Isa. 40:18-20, 44:9-20, 46:6f. **9-11.** Each of these verses is clearly antiphonal, the second line being a response to the first. 'House of Aaron' refers to the priests, 'Israel' to the congregation, and 'You who fear the Lord' to both together, rather than, as some have suggested, a third group of worshippers such as proselytes or Levites (cf. 22:23, 118:2-4, 135:19f.). **17. silence :** i.e. Sheol, the abode of the dead. Though still in some sense existing, the dead are thought of here as cut off from communication with Yahweh and from the privilege of praising him (cf. 6:5, 30:9, 88:4, 5, 10-12, 94:17 ; and contrast 139:8 ; Am. 9:2).

d **CXVI.** A beautiful example of the individual thanksgiving, in which the worshipper, who has been delivered from serious illness, comes to the sanctuary in the presence of other worshippers to acknowledge by thanksgiving and thank-offering what Yahweh has done for him. The LXX unjustifiably divides the ps. into 1-9, 10-19. **1f.** Thanksgiving for Yahweh's answer to prayer. The opening words in Heb. are awkward : 'I love because (that) Yahweh hears'. **3-4.** The worshipper's illness and his prayer for recovery. Here, as elsewhere, the lowering of vitality is represented as an experience of the power of death : in some measure the afflicted person has come within the dominion of Sheol. **4. called on the name :** i.e. invoked the power. **5-11.** The divine succour. **6. simple :** here, as in 19:7, in a good sense. **7. rest :** peace and security based on trust (cf. Isa. 28:12). **10.** RSV gives a plausible interpretation of a difficult verse. **12-19.** The worshipper's thank-offering and vows. **13. the cup of salvation :** a libation of wine. The expression may be compared with 'the cup of wrath' (Isa. 51:17, 22). **15.** Yahweh does not readily permit the death of his saints. On 'saints' see 4:3. **16. the son of thy handmaid :** cf. note on 86:16.

83e **CXVII.** A hymn inviting all mankind to worship. Brief as it is, it exemplifies the simple, dignified and objective character of Israelite worship as reflected throughout the Psalter. It also effectively combines the thought of God's ' steadfast love ' (cf. on 5:7) and ' faithfulness ' to Israel with that of his universal dominion and with the hope that all nations will join in his worship. In a number of MSS the ps. is appended to 116 or prefixed to 118 ; and some commentators have adopted one or other of these arrangements, both of which are inappropriate.

84a **CXVIII.** The dominant themes of this ps. are praise and thanksgiving ; but its structure is complex. After an antiphonal hymnic opening (1–4) there is an individual song of thanksgiving (5–21), followed by a passage which is clearly an antiphonal accompaniment to a procession, and which concludes with an echo of the individual thanksgiving and of the opening words of praise. Neither the complex structure nor the alternating congregational and individual passages points to composite authorship. This is a liturgy of thanksgiving in which the ' I ' is the leader of the community, in all probability the king. But since the life of the community was summed up in its head, his danger and his deliverance have been theirs, and in giving thanks for himself he speaks on their behalf. There is thus nothing incongruous in the setting of communal praise in which the solo voice is heard. If this is a thanksgiving for the deliverance from the actual hazards of war (10–14), it is useless to speculate about the historical occasion which prompted it ; for the ps. does not supply the evidence for such an identification. According to the Talmud it was used at the Feast of Tabernacles (cf. on 27) ; and it has been suggested that the autumnal festival was in fact its original setting and that the military language in 10–14 refers not to actual war but to symbolic ritual combat. **1. steadfast love :** cf. note on 5:7. **2-4. Israel . . . the house of Aaron . . . those who fear the Lord :** cf. on 115:9–11. **5b. and set me free :** Heb. ' in (with) a broad place ' (cf. 18:19). **8f.** These words are an epitome of a leading theme in the teaching of Isaiah. **12. they blazed :** if MT (see RSV*n*) is retained the meaning is that the ferocity of the attack died away like the blaze of a thorn-bush. **13. I was pushed hard :** if MT is retained (see RSV*n*) ' thou didst push me hard ' must be addressed to the leader of the enemy, who, on the cultic interpretation mentioned above, would be one of the participators in the ritual combat. **15. victory :** or, ' salvation '. **17f.** On the cultic interpretation this means that the powers of the underworld were not allowed to overwhelm the king. Passages such as this are taken to indicate that in the ritual of the autumnal festival the anointed of Yahweh was also his suffering servant. **19f.** Here the king approaches the entrance to the temple court (cf. 24:7–10), leading the procession of worshippers (' righteous ' in 20 is plural). His righteousness has been sustained by Yahweh ; and his people, being in a real sense one with him, share in it. **22-5.** Probably sung by the congregation or by a choir. The experience of deliverance which is the subject of the thanksgiving is here described in a metaphor from building, ' the chief cornerstone ' being the bondstone, which links two walls at right angles (the expression is given a Christological interpretation in the NT ; cf. Mt. 21:42 ; Mk 12:10 ; Lk. 20:17 ; Ac. 4:11 ; Eph. 2:20 ; 1 Pet. 2:7). **25. Save us :** Heb. ' Save, pray ', the ejaculation which appears in Mt. 21:9 etc. as ' Hosanna '. **26.** A greeting to the king and those who now enter the temple courts with him (cf. Mt. 23:39 ; Mk 11:9, etc.). **27b. light :** i.e. ' deliverance ', ' well-being '. **27cd. Bind . . . altar :** this rendering is to be preferred to AV, RV At the Feast of Tabernacles the worshippers encircled the altar, carrying branches of palm, myrtle, and willow. Some such usage seems to be referred to here. The ' horns ' were the protuberances on the four corners of the altar.

CXIX. This, the longest ps., is also the most elaborate 384b
in structure. Each of its 22 sections corresponds to one of the letters of the Heb. alphabet and each line in a section begins with the appropriate letter (cf. Lam. 3, §493*a*). It is a eulogy of the Law, which it describes in a variety of ways : ' law ', ' testimonies ', ' ways ', ' precepts ', ' statutes ', ' word ' (two terms in Heb.). In form it combines several literary forms, such as the blessing (1–3), the hymn (13f.), and the thanksgiving (7) ; but the requirements of the acrostic pattern have prevented any parallel development of structure and thought. There is no sustained argument, but a succession of brief utterances, reminiscent of Prov. In substance it is the antithesis of the attitude to the Law as ' a yoke . . . which neither our fathers nor we have been able to bear ' (Ac. 15:10) ; here the Law is a gracious gift of God to his people, in the knowledge and practice of which they may find fullness of life. But the wonders of the Law are not allowed to obscure the glory of the Giver : throughout the ps. there is a deep sense of God's greatness and of man's dependence on him. It is akin to 1 and 19:7–14, particularly the latter, in which several of the characteristic words for the Law are also used These pss. give a vivid impression of the delight in the Law which was a mark of a noble tradition of Jewish piety, for which the Law was neither a wearisome burden nor simply a reference book to be consulted in time of need but a constant source of refreshment and of life, a means of communion with God. The content of the ps. suggests a post-exilic date. **1-3**, cf. 1:1f. **9.** This concern about the moral guidance of the young is characteristic of Prov. and of the Wisdom literature generally. **14.** In spite of the Wisdom teaching that piety leads to prosperity, wisdom and goodness are prized above worldly success (cf. 127, 19:10 ; Prov. 3:13–15). **19. a sojourner :** cf. note on 39:12. **21-3.** The mention of ' the insolent ' is reminiscent of passages in the laments ; cf. the references below to the Psalmist's affliction (25, 28, 51, 61, 67, 71, 83, 85, 87, 143, 150, 161). **33. to the end :** or, ' as a reward '. **41. steadfast love :** cf. on 5:7. **45. at liberty :** Heb. ' in a broad place ' ; cf. note on 118:5. **71.** The thought seems to be that the Psalmist's sin was followed by suffering (cf. 67), which led to amendment of life. **83a.** The picture is of a wine-skin hung up indoors which is shrivelled and blackened by the smoke from the fire. The Psalmist's suffering has had a similar distorting effect on him. **153ff.** In the latter part of the ps. the references to the Psalmist's affliction become more frequent and urgent. This and other expressions of deep feeling indicate that the ps. is no merely artificial literary exercise. We may compare the acrostic compositions in Lam. 1–4.

CXX. For the superscription see §358*g*. This is an c
individual lament by one who is assailed by enemies ; but it is difficult to define his situation more precisely. If 5 really refers to foreign lands then he is an exile from the land of Israel. But it is more probable (see below) that the geographical names in 5 are simply pejorative references to his enemies, and that he has been falsely accused by fellow-countrymen. On this interpretation it is rather difficult to understand why the ps. is included in the ' Songs of Ascents ' : possibly the seeming reference to exile in 5 was taken to indicate a longing to return to the sanctuary in Jerusalem. **1f.** An appeal for Yahweh's help. **3f.** The Psalmist addresses his enemies. Their own barbed shafts will return upon them, and they will be consumed as by fire. **4. A warrior's sharp arrows :** i.e. arrows which are meant to kill. **coals of the broom tree :** charcoal made from broom gives intense heat for a long time. **5-7.** The Psalmist laments his situation among enemies. **5. Meshech . . . Kedar :** the former (cf. Gen. 10:2 ; Ezek. 32:26f.) was near the Black Sea ; the latter (cf. Gen. 25:13) is applied to Arab tribes living to the east of Israel. Clearly no precise geographical location is intended ; and it is probable that these words simply indicate the

384c hostile character of those amongst whom the Psalmist lives.

d **CXXI.** For the superscription see §358*g*. There are several different views of the character and use of this ps. In form it is a dialogue ; but we are not told who the speakers are (cf. 91). Is the worshipper communing with his own soul ; is he given a word of assurance by another as he makes the pilgrimage up to Jerusalem ; or does a priest at the sanctuary invoke the divine protection on the pilgrim who, having worshipped at the sanctuary, is about to return home? There is not sufficient evidence to enable us to decide. Indeed, apart from the superscription there is no specific reference to festival or sanctuary. But such uncertainties do not obscure the faith which the ps. expresses : faith in Yahweh, the Creator and Sustainer of all, the Protector of Israel, the constant Guide and Guard of the individual Israelite. By contrast with the tension and anguish of many of the laments there is here a sense of deep peace and unshakeable confidence in the power and goodness of Yahweh. **1. the hills :** opinions differ whether these are the hills of Jerusalem, hills on which the sanctuary of the gods stood, or dangerous hills on the pilgrim's journey. At all events the point is that Yahweh is the source of the Psalmist's security. ' Whence ' is an interrogative and not a relative pronoun as in the familiar metrical version of the ps. **3ff.** A priest or some other person responds to the worshipper's profession of faith with words of assurance. Some editors have suggested changing ' your ' and ' you ' in these verses to ' my ', ' me ' and ' I ', thus eliminating the element of dialogue. This is arbitrary and unnecessary. **5. shade :** cf. Isa. 32:2. **right hand :** the appropriate place for a protector (cf. 16:8) ; or, if ' shade ' is taken literally, this may mean ' the south '. **6.** Sunstroke is an obvious danger in a hot climate. The belief that the moon can harm appears in many different regions.

e **CXXII.** For the superscription see §358*bg*. This is one of the songs of Zion. It begins by referring to Jerusalem, the longed-for goal of the pilgrim (1f.), the centre of national worship and the seat of the royal house of David (3–5). Then the Psalmist exhorts others to bless the holy city and himself does so (6–9). The reference to thanksgiving in 4 makes it likely that the ps. was used at the Feast of Tabernacles. The three main themes are the joy of pilgrimage, the unity of national worship at the central sanctuary and the peace (well-being) which is appropriate to Jerusalem. 4 is generally taken to be a reference to the law of the central sanctuary (Dt. 12), and thus to put the ps. at the end of the 7th cent. or later. But the presence of the Ark in Jerusalem made its sanctuary pre-eminent even in earlier times. **3b.** The meaning is uncertain ; and may be either that the city is compactly built or that those who resort thither are united. **4.** cf. Dt. 16:16f. **5. were set :** the Heb. need not mean that the monarchy is a thing of the past. **for judgment :** referring, perhaps, not only to the judicial functions of the monarchy but to the dispensing of judgment at sanctuaries (cf. Isa. 2:2–4). **6-9.** There is a play here on the Heb. *shālôm* (peace, well-being) and the name 'Jerusalem', in which the same root occurs ; and there is probably a similar intentional assonance in the Heb. for ' pray ', ' prosper ', ' security '.

385a **CXXIII.** For the superscription see §358*g*. This is a lament which in 1 is individual and in 2 and 4 communal. The leader of the community offers prayers at a time (after the Exile?) when the people are treated with contempt by those who rule over them. It is sometimes said that this lament expresses no certainty that Yahweh will hear his people's prayer ; but 2 expresses with memorable and beautiful simplicity an enduring faith and hope in time of trial.

b **CXXIV.** For the superscription see §358*bg*. This short but powerful ps. is a communal song of thanksgiving, which seems to have been intended for use when the nation had been signally delivered from its enemies. On linguistic grounds it has often been assigned to the post-exilic period. The vivid language used in 3–7 to describe the danger recalls the descriptions of distress in other laments (' swallowed up ', ' swept away ', ' torrent ', ' raging waters ', ' prey ', ' snare of the fowlers '). Unlike the inhabitants of Jerusalem in 701 B.C. (cf. Isa. 22), they thankfully ascribe their deliverance to Yahweh. **8.** cf. 121:2.

c **CXXV.** For the superscription see §358*g*. This is a national ps. of confidence which culminates in a prayer for continued divine protection. It is unnecessary to conclude from 3, as has often been done, that Israel was actually under foreign domination at the time. The security which Yahweh gives to those who trust him is expressed in a vivid simile (1f.). He will not allow their faith to be so sorely tested that despair leads to sin (3). The ps. ends with a prayer.

d **CXXVI.** For the superscription see §358*g*. This superficially simple ps. presents subtle problems. As rendered in RSV it contains a retrospect to a past deliverance (1–3), followed by a prayer for a new act of restoration (4–6). The old rendering of 1*a*, 4*a* (see RSV*n*) naturally suggested that the deliverance was the return from the Babylonian Exile, though on this interpretation the appeal for a second return (4*a*) is unnatural. But ' restore the fortunes ' is the true rendering of the expression (cf. Job 42:10). Even so, reference to the immediate post-exilic period can still be maintained : ' restored the fortunes ' in 1*a* being a reference to the return and ' restore the fortunes ' in 4*a* the prayer of those who still had great difficulties to face (as Hag. shows). But the reference may be neither to this nor to any other specific historical situation. The references to water (4) and to sowing and reaping suggest a connection with the autumnal festival (see below), when men looked forward to the rains and to renewed fertility and blessing in the agricultural year which was just beginning. 1–3, as rendered by RSV, would then refer to the experience of previous years. But the tenses in 1–3 may be futures, looking forward to the fulfilment of the prayer of 4*a*. The ps. is best taken as part of a festal liturgy. **4. water-courses in the Negeb :** the Negeb or south is arid ; but the water-courses which have become dry in summer are filled again by the autumn rains. **5f.** It has been suggested that this refers to the custom of weeping for the dead fertility god at the time of sowing, and subsequently rejoicing over his resurrection. But perhaps it is only some proverbial expression that underlies these verses.

e **CXXVII.** For the superscription see §358*g*. The attribution to Solomon may have been suggested by the supposed allusions in 2 ('his beloved') to Solomon's name Jedidiah (' beloved of Yahweh ', 2 Sam. 12:25), and to the revelation to him in a dream (1 Kg. 3:5). Perhaps ' the house ' (1) suggested the Temple. There is also a certain appropriateness in the character of the ps. which consists of typical Wisdom utterances. Most commentators hold that there are two independent parts : 1f., human enterprise cannot succeed without Yahweh's help ; 3–5, a flourishing family, with its attendant blessings, is a gift from Yahweh. But the desire to separate the two parts is simply a manifestation of the occupational disease of commentators. The ps. is a perfectly plausible unity. Like some other Wisdom pss. it might be a meditation ; but its presence in the Songs of Ascents suggests that it may have been used on festal occasions when the blessing of Yahweh was sought, e.g. the autumnal festival with its concern for well-being in the coming year. It expresses with great emphasis one of the main themes of OT religion : the dependence of every human enterprise on Yahweh's favour and blessing. **2.** This description of feverish, restless activity suggests that in some ways the ancient East resembled the modern West. **for he gives :** or (see RSV*n*), ' so (i.e. ' in like measure ') he gives '. **3-5.** The thought that children are a mark of God's blessing is common in the OT. For the converse cf., for example, 1 Sam. 1:5. Here vigorous sons are

385e described as weapons on which a man may rely. **5. in the gate:** the place where local disputes were discussed and settled (cf. Ru. 4:1f.).

f **CXXVIII.** For the superscription see §358*g*. This is a Wisdom ps. in the form of a blessing on the pious, and, like 127, would be appropriate for festal use. 5 suggests that the setting is the Temple at Jerusalem; and 6 gives the whole a national reference. The benefits described are the due reward of labour, a happy and prosperous family life, a well-ordered and flourishing national life. **1. Blessed:** cf. on 1:1. **3. within your house:** the women's apartment was the farthest from the entrance. **6. peace:** harmony and well-being.

g **CXXIX.** For the superscription see §358*g*. The ps. consists of a communal song of thanksgiving (1–4) followed by an imprecation or a prediction of disaster on Israel's enemies. The worshipping congregation looks back over a long period (from the oppression in Egypt onwards) during which Israelites had often been sorely afflicted by enemies but never forsaken by Yahweh. The righteousness of Yahweh is the pledge of Israel's survival and of his enemies' discomfiture. **4. the cords:** either of the animals which pull the plough or, by a change in the metaphor, of the yoke imposed on Israel. **6f.** The reference is to self-sown grass growing in crevices on the housetop. **8.** Such blessings were vehicles of power, intended to promote well-being.

386a **CXXX.** For the superscription see §358*g*. This is a penitential individual lament. In Christian liturgical usage it is one of the seven penitential pss.; and it was memorably paraphrased by Luther. The worshipper turns to God in his deep affliction (1f.), acknowledging his sinfulness, yet confident of forgiveness (3f.) and waiting patiently yet eagerly (5f.); then he turns to the assembled worshippers and speaks of the certainty that Yahweh will redeem his people from sin (7f.). The references to Israel in 7f. have led some commentators to conclude that the 'I' of the ps. is the nation; but the above interpretation seems more natural. **1. the depths:** the reference is to the waters of the great deep (cf. on 42:7). **4. that thou mayest be feared:** this means not terror but devout awe and reverence. **6.** This simple yet effective figure may be compared with others in the Songs of Ascents (e.g. 123:2, 125:2, 131:2). **7. steadfast love:** cf. note on 5:7. **8. he:** the emphasis lies on this word.

b **CXXXI.** For the superscription see §358*bg*. This is a ps. of confidence, expressing beautifully the attitude of patient trust in Yahweh, and ending, like 130, with an exhortation to the congregation. It is one of the neglected gems of Ps., expressing a type of piety not always credited to OT religion.

c **CXXXII.** For the superscription see §358*g*. Three elements are prominent in this ps.: the Davidic royal house, the Ark and the sanctuary at Jerusalem. It is a Royal Psalm for processional use; and it commemorates David's bringing of the Ark to Jerusalem and Yahweh's promise to dwell in Zion and to maintain David's descendants there (cf. 89). The references to David's descendants make it certain that the ps. was used in the time of the monarchy. There are two main parts: 1–10, a prayer to Yahweh to show favour to the royal house because of David's solicitude for the Ark; 11–18, the divine promise of a blessing to David's house and to Zion. **1.** A reference to 2 Sam. 7:1–3. **5. the Mighty one of Jacob:** cf. Gen. 49:24; Isa. 1:24, 49:26, 60:16. **6. Ephrathah:** i.e. Bethlehem. **fields of Jaar:** Kiriath-jearim, where the Ark rested after its return from Philistine territory (1 Sam. 7:1) until David took it up to Jerusalem (2 Sam. 6). Some who emphasise the dramatic character of this ps. hold that at this point the search for the Ark was re-enacted before it was carried in triumph to the sanctuary. **7. footstool:** here variously interpreted as parallel to 'dwelling-place' (i.e. the Temple) and as the Ark. **8.** cf. Num. 10:35f. **9. saints:** cf. note on 4:3. **10. anointed one:** i.e. the king. **11ff.** This part of the ps. may have been chanted by a priest or cultic prophet. For its substance 386c
cf. 2 Sam. 7:5ff. **17. a horn to sprout . . . a lamp:** indicating the continuing vigour and prosperity of the dynasty.

d **CXXXIII.** For the superscription see §358*g*. This is a Wisdom ps., sometimes taken to refer to the blessedness of family unity, but possibly referring to the unity of the covenant community in the celebration of one of the great festivals. On the former interpretation it might well have been composed at a time when the old social order was breaking up. On the latter interpretation it would be particularly appropriate for cultic use. **2.** A reference to the anointing of the high priest (cf. Exod. 30:23ff.). The figure is more in accordance with ancient oriental taste than with that of the modern West. **3.** The figure changes. The reference to the dew of Hermon coming down on the mountains of Zion seems geographically absurd, unless dew of Hermon is a proverbial expression. But some would change Zion to a word meaning 'parched ground' or to 'Ijon' (cf. 1 Kg. 15:20), a place SW. of Hermon, which might suggest that this is a northern ps. associated with the sanctuary of Dan.

e **CXXXIV.** For the superscription see §358*g*. An exhortation to the priests to praise Yahweh (1f.), followed by a blessing (3), which may be the response of the priests. The allusion to nocturnal worship is commonly taken to point to the celebration of the Feast of Tabernacles. **2. lift up your hands:** the appropriate posture of blessing.

f **CXXXV.** This hymn was probably intended for antiphonal rendering, at least in its opening and closing sections. It begins with an exhortation to worship (1–4), leading to a recital of Yahweh's mighty acts in creation (5–7) and in the Exodus, the wilderness wandering and the conquest (8–12). After a brief hymnic interlude (13f.) and a passage deriding the ineffectiveness of idols (15–18), the ps. closes with a further summons to bless Yahweh. There are so many echoes of other parts of the OT that it is generally regarded as a late composition. **3. for he is gracious:** or, 'for it is pleasant'. **11.** cf. Num. 21:21ff., 33ff. **14. vindicate:** i.e. 'judge' in the positive and redemptive sense. **15-18.** cf. 115:4–8. **19f.** cf. on 115:9–11.

g **CXXXVI.** This is a hymn in which the note of thanksgiving is heard throughout. Its most obvious formal characteristic is the recurrence of the words 'for his steadfast love endures for ever' in the second half of each verse. Clearly it was rendered antiphonally. As in 135, the main themes are Yahweh's works in creation and his acts of deliverance in Israel's early history. In all probability it was intended for use at one of the great festivals. In Jewish liturgical use it is known as 'the Great Hallel' (cf. on 113). The main sections are: 1–3, invitation to worship; 4–9, Yahweh's acts in creation; 10–22, Yahweh's deliverance of Israel; 23–5, Yahweh, Saviour of Israel and Sustainer of all; 26, closing word of praise. **1. steadfast love:** cf. note on 5:7. **5-9.** There are interesting resemblances here to the account of creation in Gen. 1. **6.** The earth is thought of as resting on the subterranean deep (cf. 24:2). **10-22.** This description of Exodus, wilderness wandering, and settlement should be compared with 135:8–12. **23f.** Presumably this is a general reference to Israel's misfortunes after the settlement, or particularly to the Exile.

387a **CXXXVII.** This ps. is often classified as an imprecation or ritual curse; but it is better to treat it as a lament, which is the most natural description of 1–6. 7ff. is admittedly an imprecation; but this is an element which occurs elsewhere in laments (cf., for example, 55:15). After describing the bitterness of exile in which the Jews had no heart to sing the songs of Zion (1–3), the Psalmist professes undying devotion to the Holy City (4–6). But the thought of Jerusalem recalls the horrors of the siege and the malice of the Edomites; and the ps. ends with a violent imprecation

387a on Babylon. The Exile is over ; and 1–4 is a vivid commemoration of past events and emotions. As in other pss. the events of the Exodus are vividly and perhaps dramatically recalled, so here the miseries of the Exile are the subject of a prayer which may well have been used at a fast such as that mentioned in Zech. 7:3. The melancholy beauty of 1–3 contrasts pointedly with the vindictive fury of 8f. **1. waters :** canals used for irrigation. **2. willows :** a kind of poplar is meant. **4.** The foreign land is unclean (cf. Am. 7:17) ; and the songs appropriate to the Temple could not be sung there. **5f.** This passionate expression of loyalty to Jerusalem ranks this ps. with the other 'Songs of Zion' (e.g. 84, 122). **7.** When Jerusalem fell, the Edomites took advantage of Judah's plight, hence the bitter hatred of Edom which runs through much post-exilic literature (Isa. 34 ; Lam. 4:21f. ; Ezek. 25:12ff. ; Ob. 10). **8. daughter of Babylon :** i.e. Babylon. When Cyrus captured the city he did not destroy it. Hence this imprecation is consistent with a date after the return. **9.** The antithesis of these bitter words is found in Jer. 29:7.

b **CXXXVIII.** For the superscription see §358*b*. An individual thanksgiving by one who has been delivered from affliction. Here the note of thankfulness and praise predominates over the recollection of the worshipper's need. There are three main parts : 1–3, thanksgiving for Yahweh's mercy to the worshipper ; 4–6, a hymnic passage describing the universal homage which will be paid to Yahweh ; 7f., an expression of trust in Yahweh's continuing care. **1. before the gods :** Yahweh is thought of as supreme in a heavenly assembly of divine beings (cf. note on 82). **2b. steadfast love :** cf. note on 5:7. **2cd.** The emendation adopted by RSV seems to be necessary. **4-6.** For this movement of thought from individual deliverance to universal worship cf. 22:27–31. **6.** cf. the thought of 113:5–9. **7-8.** These verses have been appropriately compared with 23.

c **CXXXIX.** For the superscription see §358*bd*. There are wide differences of opinion about the literary classification of this ps. Though it has hymnic elements it is most appropriately classed with the laments. The worshipper speaks of 'the wicked' who are his own and God's enemies (19–22). The prayer that God will scrutinise the worshipper's life (23f. ; cf. 1–12) is another feature of the laments, particularly when the worshipper is the object of malicious accusations (e.g. 7:3–5). But its intensely individual and personal character puts this ps. in a class by itself. In depth and range of thought and in the sense of intimate communion with God it is one of the treasures of Ps. Attempts have been made to suggest a cultic situation ; but it is doubtful if adequate evidence is available and if any such reconstruction is appropriate to this highly individual meditative ps. The thought is developed in three sections : 1–6, God's unerring and inescapable knowledge of the Psalmist ; 7–12, God's inescapable presence ; 13–18, the wonder of God's creative work. These are followed by an imprecation on the wicked (19–22) and a prayer that God will search the Psalmist's own heart (23f.). **7. thy Spirit . . . thy presence :** the expressions are synonymous. **8. in Sheol :** even in the underworld man will encounter God's active presence. This presents a notable contrast to assertions found elsewhere that to be in Sheol is to be separated from Yahweh (cf. 6:5). **13. inward parts :** the seat of the emotions. **14.** RSV translates a widely accepted but perhaps unnecessary emendation of the difficult Heb. **15. in the depths of the earth :** this is sometimes taken to be a poetical expression for the womb ; but perhaps it expresses the ancient idea of Mother Earth and of the creation of man from the dust (Gen. 2:7). **16.** A difficult verse. RSV adds 'as yet' and 'for me' to MT ; but is probably right (as against AV, RV) in the view that it is not the members of the body, but the days of the Psalmist's life that were recorded. The idea that a man's life is known to God beforehand and in some sense predetermined by him appears elsewhere 387c in the OT (cf. Isa. 49:1 ; Jer. 1:5) ; but is never systematically presented in such a way as to undermine human responsibility. For the idea that Yahweh has a register of the living cf. 69:28 ; Exod. 32:32f. ; Isa. 56:5. **18. When I awake :** this is difficult to fit into the context. Perhaps we should render as RSV*n*. The preceding passage has dealt with the mysterious processes of God's creative power. When the Psalmist comes to the end of his meditation on much that might baffle him, he is still conscious of the presence of God. **19-22.** It is unnecessary to press too far the contrast between these and the preceding verses. If we hesitate to make 21 our own, we should nevertheless recognise that for the Psalmist the experience of communion with God was not an escape from life in this world. He knew that there is a conflict between good and evil, that God is not neutral in that struggle, and that we are not called upon to be neutral either. **23f.** The Psalmist's final prayer is that his own life may be tested by the divine scrutiny. **the way everlasting :** possibly 'the (good) old way' (see RSV*n*) ; but more probably the enduring way of life and peace.

CXL. For the superscription see §358*bd*. In this d individual lament (with which 64 should be compared), the malice and ruthlessness of the Psalmist's enemies are described in a variety of ways. In 1–3 they are malicious plotters, stirring up strife by spiteful speech. In 4f. they are like hunters who try to snare him. He turns momentarily in 6–8 to an expression of his confidence in God, and again to imprecations on his enemies in 9–11, where they are described as slanderers. The ps. ends with a renewed assertion of God's righteous dispensation (12f.), in which, presumably, the Psalmist anticipates his own deliverance. Though the language is vivid and forceful it does not give us a clear picture of the Psalmist's situation.

CXLI. For the superscription see §358*b*. This e individual lament presents a sharp contrast to 140. The Psalmist prays to be delivered from evil as well as from the assaults of enemies. There are connections with the language and thought of the Wisdom literature. Unfortunately the text is probably corrupt in places, as is indicated by RSV*n*. **1f.** The Psalmist prays that his worship may be acceptable to Yahweh. The 'evening sacrifice' is the cereal offering made every day (cf. Exod. 29:39–41). **3f.** A prayer to be preserved in speech, thought and action from the evil which is prevalent in society. **5-7.** The Psalmist prefers the chastisement of the righteous to the hospitality of the wicked (oil was used in anointing the guests at banquets). He looks for condign punishment on evil-doers. The exact form and meaning of the text are, however, difficult to establish. **8-10.** Again the Psalmist turns to God, praying for his own deliverance.

CXLII. For the superscription see §358*be*. With the f reference to David in the cave cf. 57 and 1 Sam. 22, 24. This is an individual lament by one who is in sore straits. Enemies assail him ; and in his danger he implores the help of Yahweh. The appeal in 1–3*b*, followed by a reference to the plots of his enemies (3*c*–4), is renewed in 5–7, where we note the anticipation of deliverance and of thanksgiving for it. **3b. thou knowest my way :** cf. on 1:6. 'Thou' is emphatic. **4. I look to the right :** a protector would stand on the right ; cf. 16:8, 121:5. **7. prison :** probably a figurative expression for the Psalmist's distress.

CXLIII. For the superscription see §358*b*. In 388a Christian liturgical usage this is the last of the seven Penitential Psalms. It is an individual lament in which the worshipper recognises that his affliction is a punishment for sin. This note is already sounded in the opening appeal (1f.). It is followed by a description of the crushing cruelty of his enemies (3f.). Then he recalls God's past goodness (5f.) and pleads for speedy succour (7f.). His prayer passes over into a plea that he may be enabled to do God's will (9f.),

388a but ends with a request for deliverance and for the destruction of his enemies. **1f.** Note that here Yahweh's righteousness is his readiness to succour. It does not mean a strict morality with no place for mercy. The Psalmist recognises (2) that by such an impersonal test no man could be acquitted (cf. 130:3). **3.** Already the sufferer is experiencing the gloom of the realm of the dead (cf. 7 below) ; but his language does not enable us to determine the nature of his enemy's action. **7c.** To see Yahweh's face is to receive blessing and renewed vitality. **8. steadfast love:** cf. note on 5:7.

b **CXLIV.** For the superscription see §358*b*. It has been pointed out that this ps. begins on an individual note but ends with a communal reference. There is, however, no need to dispute its essential unity, as many scholars have done. It is a Royal Psalm. In the prayers of the king individual and communal concerns are intimately related. The similarities between this and other pss. need not be the result of direct borrowing but of sharing in a common liturgical tradition. In 1f. the king acknowledges thankfully that he owes his military success to Yahweh. In sharp contrast there follows (3f.) a confession of the frailty of man, followed by an appeal that Yahweh will manifest his presence and power amid the familiar accompaniments of a theophany, for the king is hard pressed by his enemies (5–8). Deliverance is anticipated in the vow of thanksgiving which follows (9–11); and the ps. ends with a prayer for national well-being. **3.** cf. 8:4. **5f.** cf. 18:7–15. **7.** Though it appears that the king is threatened by enemies, the familiar figure of the underground waters is used to express dire distress. It may be that the conflict referred to is symbolically enacted in the cult. **9. a new song:** the phrase is familiar from the pss. of Yahweh's kingship (e.g. 96·1). **10. David his servant:** i.e. the king. **12-15.** This closing prayer looks to the dissemination throughout the entire national life of the blessing bestowed on the king.

c **CXLV.** For the superscription see §358*be*. This is a hymn in which a solo voice is heard. It is a remarkably successful composition within the limits of the acrostic form. After the opening words of praise (1–3), the singer recalls Yahweh's mighty acts in history (4–7) and his condescension, compassion, and faithfulness (8f.). He then looks to all Yahweh's creatures to praise him (10–13*b*). There follows a description (sung by choir or congregation ?) of Yahweh's universal goodness (13*c*–20) ; and the ps. ends with an ascription of praise. On linguistic grounds it is usually regarded as late ; and it well illustrates Judaism's spacious conception of God's universal and enduring dominion and of his unfailing goodness to all men. **8.** cf. Exod. 34:6. **10b.** saints : cf. on 4:3. **13cd.** See RSV*n*. Without these lines a letter is missing from the acrostic.

d **CXLVI.** This is the first of the five Hallelujah Psalms with which Ps. ends, all of which are hymns. Running through it is a strong note of trust in Yahweh. **1f.** Opening ascription of praise. **3f.** The transience of human power and glory. **5-9.** Yahweh, the God of Jacob and the Creator of all, is a mighty help in time of need. These verses express the characteristic concern of Yahweh for the oppressed and defenceless. **10.** A closing ascription of praise.

e **CXLVII.** This hymn falls into three parts : 1–6, praise to Yahweh for his mighty works in nature and history ; 7–11, praise to Yahweh who sustains the natural order ; 12–20, praise to Yahweh who cares for his people and makes their land fruitful. **2.** This probably refers to the rebuilding of Jerusalem after the Exile and to the return of the exiles. **4.** To give a name is to have authority over the person or thing so named (cf. Gen. 2:19f.). **14. peace:** 'well-being', 'prosperity'. **15.** The idea of the creative word of God recalls Gen. 1. In 19 the reference is to the revelation of God's will in his Law.

f **CXLVIII.** In this hymn all nature and all men are summoned to worship Yahweh. It offers an interesting parallel to the Songs of the Three Holy Children (The Benedicite). A summons to the heavenly host and the heavenly bodies (1–4) is followed by a statement of the reason for their praise (5f.). Then all earthly things are exhorted to praise God (7–12) ; and again a reason is given—his sovereign greatness and his goodness to Israel (13f.). **2.** For the thought of the heavenly host cf. 82. Note that they are not independent beings but creatures of Yahweh (5). **4b.** cf. Gen. 1:6f. **7.** The reference is to the mythical monsters associated with the cosmic deep under the earth. **14. has raised up a horn:** 'has given success and prosperity'.

g **CXLIX.** This hymn, which is called a 'new song' (cf. 96:1, 98:1), has a markedly martial character. Some interpreters have associated it with some historical campaign, others with the eschatological triumph of God's cause, and others again with a symbolic cultic representation of the overthrow of the enemies of Yahweh and of Israel. On the whole the third interpretation seems the soundest (cf. on 46). The appropriate occasion would be the autumnal festival, with which the expression 'a new song' is associated. **1. faithful:** cf. note on 4:3. **5. on their couches:** probably the couches are those on which the worshippers recline at the festival. **9. the judgment written:** probably the reference is to a heavenly book in which Yahweh's decrees are recorded (cf. Job 13:26 ; Isa. 65:6).

h **CL.** This final hymn fitly concludes Ps. Its thought is all of Yahweh's praise, to be offered in his earthly sanctuary and in heaven for all that he has done. Every instrument is to be used to his glory ; and all are to join in the song. Kirkpatrick aptly quotes Maclaren's words : 'The Psalm is more than an artistic close of the Psalter ; it is a prophecy of the last result of the devout life'.

Bibliography—COMMENTARIES : W. E. Barnes, WC (1931) ; M. Buttenwieser (1938) ; J. Calès (1936) ; H. Gunkel, HKAT (1926) ; A. F. Kirkpatrick, CB (1902) ; H. J. Kraus, BK (1960) ; E. A. Leslie (1949) ; W. O. E. Oesterley (1939) ; E. Podechard (1949) ; A. Weiser, ATD[5] (1959).

OTHER LITERATURE : H. Gunkel and J. Begrich, *Einleitung in die Psalmen* (1933) ; G. S. Gunn, *God in the Psalms* (1956) ; A. R. Johnson, *Sacral Kingship in Ancient Israel* (1955) ; S. Mowinckel, *Psalmenstudien I–VI* (1921–4) ; W. O. E. Oesterley, *A Fresh Approach to the Psalms* (1937) ; T. H. Robinson, *The Poetry of the OT* (1947) ; D. C. Simpson (ed.), *The Psalmists* (1926) ; N. H. Snaith, *Studies in the Psalter* (1934) ; A. C. Welch, *The Psalter in Life, Worship and History* (1926).

THE PROVERBS

By J. C. RYLAARSDAM

389a **Setting**—Prov. constitutes the earliest documentary deposit of Israel's Wisdom Movement now extant. There are, to be sure, older bits of recorded wisdom, folk wisdom in such forms as fables and riddles (e.g. Jg. 9:9–21, 14:18). But their survival is not by design. Prov., in contrast, is a most carefully planned and assiduously polished achievement of a highly self-conscious and professional literary and cultural movement in Israel (cf. §§335–8). The sages of Israel who composed Prov. worked with a sense of responsibility and purpose, for they felt that their ' words ' were an indispensable means for the fulfilment of human life. There is a note of urgency about their educational
b mission. The Heb. word for ' proverb ', *māshāl*, means ' comparison ' or ' parable ', a definition illustrated by the similes, both implicit and explicit, in the parallelistic structure of the sayings. However, the root from which *māshāl* derives has the basic meaning of ' to rule ' and ' to have authority '. Thus, a ' proverb ' is an authoritative word. This helps to explain the fact that the prophetic oracle of Balaam is also called a *māshāl* (cf. Num. 23:7, 18, 24:3, 15; RSV ' discourse '). In many ways the sages make clear in Prov. that their words establish a standard. The authority consists not only in the tested quality of the pronouncements but is also displayed in and certified by the literary style of their work. The terseness, the economy of words, assonance, and the accent of rhythm all figure in this close bond between form and reality as assumed in Prov.

390a **General Features**—Though the book is a composite of several documents, probably spanning some centuries, it has certain general characteristics:

(*a*) It omits any clear references to Israel's national history and to her faith and religious institutions, which were closely bound up with this history. Such great themes as the deliverance from slavery, the wandering in the wilderness, the inheritance of Canaan, the establishment of the monarchy, and the Exile, are never mentioned. Nor are the great festivals or Jerusalem and its Temple. Solomon and Hezekiah are kings mentioned by name, but there is no account of their work; there is only the implication that under their rule the Wisdom Movement flourished. The saying that the wicked will be cut off from the land (2:22; cf. 10:30) very probably reflects the Deuteronomic vocabulary and Israel's religious interpretation of its place in history, but it is only a reflection. God is named as the Lord but is not related to the particularism of the Covenant. Egypt's sages would have noted some strange elements in Prov., but would not, one feels, have found the work basically alien.

b (*b*) In all its sections, with the probable exception of The Words of Agur (30:1–14), the book is optimistic. That is, it assumes and insists that men can know the way to ' life ' or ' the fear of the Lord ' and can follow it. The doctrine of rewards, stressed in Dt., that those who obey God will have ' peace ', is fully endorsed. The only difference is that in Prov. not the Law of Moses but the words of the wise are the form for obedience. In this optimism, relying only on the teachings of the wise, Prov. is unique in Israel's wisdom literature.

c (*c*) Like the other canonical wisdom books (Job, Ec., Ca.), but in sharp contrast to nearly all of the 390c
rest of the OT, Prov. has an anthropological focus. It looks at man *qua* man, rather than in the light of God. The human will, rather than the redeeming action of God, is the decisive factor in a man's destiny. The action of God has taken place in creation and, with the exception of chs. 1–9, where the divine Wisdom pleads with men, the current role of God is a rather static one; he is a righteous judge. The forgiveness of God plays a slight role (cf. 28:13). The way of knowledge rather than the life of faith is dominant in the Wisdom Movement. Hence, beginning in Prov. (30:1–14), doubt about man's adequate capacity for knowledge tends to issue in despair. All recognition about the uncertainty of life and man's inability to control the future leads to a sombre outlook (cf. e.g. 27:1).

(*d*) Every part of the book bears the mark of foreign d
influences upon Israel's Wisdom Movement. The close connection between the first part of the Thirty Sayings (cf. 22:17–24:22) with Egyptian wisdom, discovered with the publication of *The Instruction of Amen-em-opet*, is only a special instance, as the work of scholars such as Gressmann, Humbert, and Oesterley has made clear. The forms of literary art, the subject-matter, and the social and moral ideals overlap at many points. But since the distinctivenesss of Prov. is as apparent as its similarity when comparison is made with foreign traditions, it would seem much more appropriate to say that here also, as elsewhere, Israel has shown her capacity for assimilation. The work is creative rather than imitative.

(*e*) Though it makes no overt references to Israel's e
national life and religious institutions, Prov. exhibits the Hebraic spirit. Its vocabulary is often Deuteronomic, a fact which led Oesterley to a comparison of Dt. and Amen-em-opet. The spirit of the Ps. and the prophets is reflected in the contrast of the ' righteous ' and the ' wicked ' set alongside the contrast of the ' wise ' and the ' fool '. Significantly, too, in this context, Prov. shows a popularising tendency. The words of the wise are for all, rather than for a special class of official servants as in Egypt. Further, manual labour and agriculture are idealised.

Literary Analysis and Date—The book of Prov., 391a
as we now have it, is the result of a long process of growth. This process was continuous and cumulative. In its present form, the book seems to contain at least eight documentary units; but some of these, notably the earliest, had a long history before attaining their present form. In 25:1 a prefatory note speaks of the copying out of the sayings that follow, an instance of what was happening right along. Solomon himself may personally have been a sage. In any case, he is the patron of the Wisdom Movement and there is every reason to suppose that it was launched at his court. His close associations with the Egyptian court may have encouraged this; it has, however, also been suggested that there was a tradition of Canaanite wisdom on which to draw. Sayings were composed or borrowed, orally transmitted, and written down in ever growing collections. It is doubtful whether any b
collection was written down in Solomon's day as we now have it, but there may be embedded in it some

391b remnants of documents from the Solomonic era. If the cultural and literary activity that produced Prov. began in the era of Solomon, when did it end? In all likelihood well before the publication of Sir. about the end of the 3rd cent. B.C., a book which carries on the tradition of Prov. More probably Prov. was substantially complete before the work of Ezra had made the completed Mosaic Code the official 'Law' of Judaism. This would help to explain why in Prov., unlike Sir. (cf. 24:23ff.), the sages can repeatedly refer to their Sayings as 'law' and 'teaching' (*tôrāh*) without ever referring to Moses. In all probability, therefore, Prov. is a distillate of five centuries in the life of Israel's Wisdom Movement.

392a The documentary units, as designated in this commentary, are listed here with brief explanations; additional introductory remarks for the sections are found in the commentary.

(1) Discourses in Praise of Wisdom (I-IX)—Probably the youngest part of the book. The literary form is complex: exhortations outweigh pronouncements; there are many lengthy pericopes with continuous themes; both prophetic (1:20ff.) and hymn (8:22ff.) styles appear. There is considerable speculative interest; wisdom is the primordial creation of God and is set over against 'the loose woman'.

b **(2) Proverbs of Solomon (X-XXII 16)**—Probably the earliest collection consisting of couplets which are antithetic parallels in chs. 10–15, more often synthetic thereafter.

c **(3) Thirty Sayings (XXII 17-XXIV 22)**—A work whose paragraph-length 'chapters' were apparently suggested by the Egyptian *Instruction of Amen-em-opet.* The first part (22:17–23:11) uses Amen-em-opet as a source.

(3a) A Supplement to the Thirty Sayings (XXIV 23-4)

(4) The Hezekian Collection (XXV-XXIX)—Couplets and quatrains. Antithetic parallelism is rare. Spirit and form most closely resemble 10–22:17; of early origin.

d **(5) Four Appendices (XXX-XXXI)**—

(*a*) **The Words of Agur** (30:1–14). See commentary.

(*b*) **Numerical Sayings** (30:15–33); lack inner unity.

(*c*) **The Instruction of Lemuel** (31:1–9). See commentary.

(*d*) **An Acrostic on the Virtuous Wife** (31:10–31)

393a **First Section I-IX Discourses in Praise of Wisdom**

I 1 Inclusive Superscription (cf. 10:1, 25:1)—**Proverbs of Solomon** may be a synonym for the sentences of ethical wisdom typical of this book. The word for proverb, *māshāl*, is also used of taunts (Dt. 28:37; Ps. 44:15; Mic. 2:4), poets and poems (Num. 21:27–30; Ps. 49:4 (Heb. 5)), and riddles or allegories (Ezek. 17:2, 20:49 (Heb. 21:5)).

2-6 Purpose and Value of Book—The Egyptian *Instruction of Amen-em-opet* (ANET, 421) has an analogous statement of purpose (cf. Prov. 22:17–21). The goal is to know wisdom; i.e. to have one's character express life as it truly is. **Instruction** (Heb. *mûsār*) is the authoritative discipline (cf. 3:11, 12, 6:23, 13:1, etc.) by means of which the goal is to be won. Parents, teachers, God exercise the discipline. **2-3.** Adherence to accepted standards, the fulfilment of duty, and consistency of life—**righteousness, justice, and equity**—constitute the public results of this discipline in wisdom. **4.** The simple and inexperienced must become subtle; the young, perceptive. **5.** Trained adults can deepen their **learning,** a subjective quality (cf. 9:9), as well as the thing taught (Dt. 32:2); **skill,** tactical capacity (24:6; Job 37:12), is available for the discerning. **6. Figure:** lit. 'satire', 'taunt' (cf. Hab. 2:6f.). The term *māshāl* applies to all three others.

b **7 The Motto of the Wisdom Movement** (cf. 9:10; Job 28:28; Sir. 1:14)—God is Creator (Gen. 1:1); 393b man is his creature. This basic relation is **the beginning** that both prompts and controls man's quest for wisdom. The fear of the Lord is not simply a point of departure for knowledge, but its substance (cf. 4:7) or its most important part (cf. Dt. 33:21). This knowledge is a personal possession of wisdom relating man to God (cf. 2:5). In contrast, Walther Zimmerli, *Zur Struktur der alttestamentlichen Weisheit*, ZATW 51, 177ff., denies this Creator-creature relationship as the real point of departure for the sages. In a very careful argument he develops the thesis that the wise are individualistic and strictly anthropocentric when they ask what makes for human happiness. The issue is both important and complex. The **fools** (Heb. *'^{e}wîlîm*, lit. 'fat ones') are a class opposite to the wise (10:14, 11:29, 12:15f., etc.); in rejecting the discipline of wisdom they deny their creator (Ps. 53:1).

8-19 Parable on the Way of Sinners—As in Egypt, c
the sage addresses the pupil as **my son** (8, 10). He builds on the father's discipline (Heb. *mûsār*) and the mother's guidance (Heb. *tôrath*). Like fools, **sinners** do not fear God (23:17); they are the opposite of the righteous (13:21). The appeal of the boastful swashbuckling bandits to the spirit of an adventurous youth serves the sage to illustrate the universal temptation of the way of sinners (Ps. 1:1). Omit final clause **v. 10** (cf. 15). Delete v. 16 (= Isa. 59:7*a*). **15.** Resist temptation. **17-19.** No bird is caught in a net set in its presence; sinners themselves set the trap that devours them.

20-33 Wisdom's Call to Repentance—Elsewhere d
the personified Wisdom acts as a hostess (9:1–12) or as a primordial divine being (8:22ff.). Here she preaches a sermon reminiscent of Israel's prophets (cf. 8:1ff.). **20f.** She goes where the crowds are, at the head of the roaring (street). **21a.** The LXX reading of τειχέων does not fit the sequence (cf. 8:2f.). The scorner (cf. Ps. 1:1), here equated with the simple and the fool (*k^{e}sîl*), resists wisdom more actively (19:25, 21:11). Contentious (22:10), he hides the issues in figures of satire (cf. 1:6). **23.** To those who heed, Wisdom offers herself in her spirit and words. The rejection of both **reproof** and **counsel**, the gift of wisdom (21:30; Job 12:13), introduces the *quid pro quo* of divine judgment marked (26) by the **'I also'** (*gam correlativum*) of prophetic style (cf. Jer. 4:12, 7:11; Hos. 4:6). **26f.** Wisdom, endowed here with divine authority, will mock the scorner in panic and laugh at the fool; her unheeded appeal will be matched by their futile search. **29. The fear of the Lord** now is a synonym for knowledge, counsel, and reproof. **31f.** The fools destroy themselves; the vengeance of Wisdom is without passion, like an inexorable law (Gal. 6:7). **33.** Security, the realisation of man's possibilities, a preoccupation of the sages (W. Zimmerli, op. cit., 194), is available to whoever will heed Wisdom.

II Five Fruits of Wisdom—1-4 comprise a protasis e
with a conclusion in five parts, 5–8, 9–11, 12–15, 16–19, 20–2. The first of these exhibits a theocentric preoccupation in contrast to the general anthropological orientation. This has led many exegetes to the conclusion that it is a later insertion (cf. C. H. Toy, *The Book of Proverbs* (1908), 34).

1-4. The quest for wisdom demands both a receptive and expectant attitude, an attentiveness of sense (**ear**) and reason (**heart**), and an active search. Like the treasure hidden in a field, or the pearl of great price (Mt. 13:44f.), its acquisition requires the sacrifice of everything else. The pure in heart alone can win her. The **commandments** of the sage are a new synonym for wisdom and the means to it; in form they cannot be equated with the laws of Israel's covenant, and their warrant is human experience, not the word of God.

5-8. The highest gift of wisdom is **the knowledge of God,** a living relationship of faithfulness and trust with the source of wisdom (cf. Hos. 4:1, 6:6). Here God does what sages do elsewhere (1:23); **he stores up sound wisdom.** It is almost impossible to decide

393e whether God is synonymous with wisdom in its fullest sense or whether he is the living God who acts ; the metaphors here show the influence of the rest of the OT. The Heb. *tûshiyyāh* (sound wisdom, cf. 3:21, 8:14–16) carries the notion of efficiency, that which facilitates results.

f **9-11.** As a second gift the persistent prayer and search for wisdom offers the integration of one's life. Desire and duty will coalesce. Wisdom will inform the mind (**heart**) and the whole personality (**soul**) will find knowledge attractive ; hence, a man can keep going straight on **every good path** (LXX κατορθώσεις (cf. 9:15) preserves parallelism). **Discretion,** the action ruled by understanding, will become 'second nature'.

12-15. Thirdly, wisdom delivers from evil men ; it conquers the temptation of their way. The doctrine of the two ways, prominent in later Judaism, postulates two classes of men, each rather immutable, **the way of evil** and the way of righteousness (8:20). The former leads to **darkness** and death (4:19, 20:20 ; Job 3:4, 5, 6) ; those who subvert the accepted values travel it. The latter leads to light and life (4:13, 18).

g **16-19.** The wise will also be safe from **the loose woman.** Chs. 5, 6:20–35, 7, 9:13–18, all concern this woman. She is the antithesis of wisdom, the embodiment of evil. **Her paths** are not **the paths of life,** but death (**18f.**). Since she is set over against the personified Wisdom some interpreters see in her an allegorical figure, Folly (e.g. M. Friedländer, *Griechische Philosophie im AT* (1904), 68–76). They make the telling point that no single immoral person would represent an adequate counterpart to Wisdom. Others contend that the sages are describing a concrete person of flesh and blood, but disagree on the identity. Gemser (*Sprüche Salomos* (1937)), e.g., renders the phrase **loose woman** (lit. 'strange woman'), *eines anderen Weib*, considering her the wife of an Israelite who was away from home (7:19). Gustav Boström (*Proverbiastudien* (1935)), however, insists she is a foreigner who has broken the marriage vows made before her own god. She is now in the service of an alien cult (7:14f.), tempting Israelites to apostasy as well as immorality. The term *'elōhîm* can, however, refer to the God of Israel (cf. 3:4, 25:2, 30:9).

20-22. Finally, those who receive wisdom **will inhabit the land.** Palestine is intended (cf. 10:30) ; the promise and the way are Deuteronomic (Dt. 4:10, 5:16, 33, 6:18, et al.). **Men of integrity,** *tāmîm*, perfect, a characteristic liturgical term (Lev., Ps., Ezek.) of Israel's cultus, used here to show completeness of character. **Wicked** are nearly always set over against **upright** or righteous ; fools against wise, a fact that makes H. Gunkel conclude that the former is closer to the religious outlook of OT (cf. 'Vergeltung', RGG v (1927)). The vocabulary of **20-2** strongly reflects the particular faith of Israel.

h **III 1-12 Six Forms of Wisdom with Rewards**—**2.** The term 'abundant welfare' (Heb. *shālôm*), often translated 'peace', denotes the most comprehensive form of well-being of which a long life is one part. The faithful disciple will enjoy an increase of both. The commandments of the sage are the cumulative voice of experience which for Prov. give an adequate account of the will and character of God, an assumption challenged in Job and Ec.

3. In **loyalty** (*ḥesedh*) and **faithfulness** (*'emeth*), as in **teaching** (*tôrāh*), the characteristic vocabulary of Israel's faith is subtly altered in an anthropocentric setting. They refer to relations between men ; **loyalty,** mercy, and kindness to the helpless (16:6, 20:28 ; 1 Kg. 20:31 ; Hos. 4:1), **faithfulness,** reliability. **The tablet of your heart** (cf. Jer. 17:1), indelibly a part of human character. **4.** The reward : **God and man** will have a good opinion of you ('understanding' in the objective sense, cf. Neh. 8:8).

5f. The Lord will give success (**make straight your paths,** cf. 11:5) to all who take him into account and count on him (**trust in,** Heb. *'el*, 'to' ; cf. Ps. 56:4, 86:2 ; Jer. 7:4). 393h

6. The fear of the Lord prevents a dangerous subjectivism (**7f. flesh,** following LXX, signifies the whole life ; cf. 4:22). i

9, 10. The belief that the payment of tithes and other prescribed offerings was a prerequisite for good yields was typical of late Judaism (Mal. 3:8–10) ; earlier the offerings were joyful acts of thanksgiving (Dt. 26:1–11). The *do ut des* tendency is here evident. This sort of cultic piety is also found in the Egyptian sages, but the vocabulary of Prov. reflects the Jewish scene. For **with plenty** LXX reads 'with corn' (σίτου), preferable as a parallel to **wine.**

11f. The **Lord's discipline** (Heb. *mûsār*, cf. 1:2–6 *supra*) denotes misfortune that seems to deny the doctrine that 'peace' is the reward of those following the teaching of the sages. The issue of theodicy, to become acute in Job and Ec., is here implied (cf. Rylaarsdam, *Revelation in Jewish Wisdom Literature* (1946), 59f.). As in Job 5:18f., suffering is a token of the love of God and has a morally purgative function (cf. Job. 1–2, 42:7–17 where it is explained as probationary). In LXX, **12b** 'and he (the Lord) scourges (strikes) the son . . .', maintaining a parallelism with the preceding line (cf. Gemser, op. cit., 20 ; also Job 5:18*b*). The patient acceptance of reproof is rewarded by the deepening awareness of one's filial relation to God who is the author of all disaster and whose purpose it serves.

13-20 The Happiness of the Wise—The NT beatitudes (Mt. 5:3ff.) stand in the legacy of the sages. In the OT the beatitude with its initial term *'ash^erê* (happy, blessed) is found mostly in Prov. (cf. 8:34, 16:20, 20:7, 28:14, 29:18) and in Ps. (cf. 1:1 et al). As a literary form it is both a pronouncement and an admonition ; a summons lies beneath its blessing. In v. **13,** where it introduces an exposition on the incomparability of wisdom, it is also a call to seek it. Wisdom yields more than silver, gold, or corals (for **jewels,** cf. Job 28:18 ; Lam. 4:7), because she offers long life, honour, and peace (cf. 3:2). **18.** Then, in praise of Wisdom, the poet invokes a metaphor of mythological import : Wisdom **is a tree of life.** j

In recent years, the liturgical patterns of the ancient Near East have stressed that the tree is a cult symbol representing both deity and king ; both king and tree exhibit and mediate the life of the god (cf., e.g., S. H. Hooke, *The Labyrinth* (1935), 213ff. and I. Engnell, *Studies in Divine Kingship* (1943), 26ff.). The web of concepts and interrelationships entailed in this ritual pattern has indubitably given OT writers a rich array of metaphors even though there is a wide difference of opinion about the degree to which the fabric of the ritual pattern remained intact in Israel and about the literal significance assigned to each symbol (cf., e.g., Geo Widengren, *The King and the Tree of Life in Ancient Near Eastern Religion* (1953) and S. Mowinckel, *He That Cometh* (1957)). The sages, in using mythological terms, may have hinted at a more profound source of wisdom than was once thought. As **a tree of life,** Wisdom may connote an intimate aspect of the life and work of deity (cf. Gen. 3:22). This makes the transition to vv. **19f.,** anticipating 8:22ff., quite natural. By Wisdom God created, and **by his knowledge** (20) he supplies the earth with water and rain. The unity of deity is strictly maintained ; Wisdom is personified, not hypostatised. k

In **21-6,** the pupil is encouraged further in his search. **Sound wisdom** (cf. 2:7) insures against failure, fear, and panic. Neither darkness (Ps. 91:5f.) nor dreams (Job 7:13–15) will trouble him.

27-35 On social Obligation—Six negative prescriptions are reinforced by four antithetical parallels to provide a motivation for their observance. The rejection of quarrelling (cf. 13:10, 15:18, 17:14, 18:6, 18) and violence (4:17, 10:6, 13:2, 16:29, 21:7) is a feature of all wisdom materials (cf. *Amen-em-opet,* l

393l ANET, op. cit., 422, and the Egyptian distinction between the 'hot' and 'silent' man). The two classes of men (cf. 2:12–15 *supra*) are separated on this basis.

m **IV 1-9 Wisdom, a father's Bequest**—The taste for wisdom is a father's noblest legacy; the pursuit of understanding is the highest mark of filial respect, an ingrained quality of Jewish character (cf. Exod. 20:12) to which the sage appeals. In a father's place before his pupils he plays the role of Solomon and tells of his own boyhood, **tender, the only one** (in sense of 'precious', cf. LXX 'beloved') **in the sight of my mother**; i.e. 'in care of' (Gen. 17:18). Instead some manuscripts read 'among the sons of . . .' (cf. 1 Chr. 3:5). Solomon's mother pinned her hopes on him (1 Kg. 1:11ff.). His choice of wisdom (1 Kg. 3:3–14) he credits to David.

The text of vv. **4-7** is redundant and uncertain. **4b. and live,** lacking in LXX, probably a homiletical gloss. **5b.** MT **get wisdom; get insight,** lacking in LXX^{B}, follows immediately: redundant, anticipating v. **7.** Eliminate 5*b* and transpose vv. **6** and **7.**

n The father commends wisdom as a bride (cf. 7:4; Wis. 6:12ff.; Sir. 14:20ff.). As for a good wife (18:22, 19:14, 31:10ff.), no bride price is too high for her. **get wisdom:** to acquire (Heb. *ḳānāh*), often in sense of purchase (Gen. 47:22, 50:13; Exod. 21:2). Once purchased, faithfulness to her is a man's security. **6. Do not forsake her, and she will keep you.** As with a good wife, those who love, protect, and embrace wisdom will receive her honour and crown (cf. Ca. 3:11). **8. Prize her highly:** root meaning of Heb. term 'to weave'; probably an act of protective endearment parallel to **embrace.**
10-19. The 'two ways' are compared as darkness and light: the **way of wisdom** (**11**) and the **way of the wicked** (19). Ps. 1:6 offers an analogy, though there the **Law of the Lord** keeps a man on the right way; here wisdom, the words of the sage. Long life and prosperity are the rewards of both, but the explicit equation of the Law and wisdom is first recorded by Jesus ben Sirach (Sir. 24). Wisdom gives a man freedom of pace (Job 18:7), yet prevents him from stumbling. Wisdom is life; in contrast to Gen. 3:22 and Job 28, both are attainable by man. **13.** But the pilgrim must keep his eye on the guide, not relaxing his grip on discipline lest he fall into **the path of the wicked** (14). G. Kuhn, *Beiträge zur Erklärung des solomonischen Spruchbuches* (1931), 12, reads **16a:** 'they find no rest' (Heb. *y^{e}sha'an^{e}nû* for *yishnû*) to be rid of a tautology. Relying on Syr. he also alters reading of **16b** 'unless they have played the fool'; i.e. 'sinned.' **19.** The **deep darkness** points to the supernatural darkness of chaos (cf. Exod. 10:22f.; Dt. 28:29), in contrast to the dawning light of righteousness, though neither metaphor has attained a full eschatological meaning. Transpose vv. 18 and 19.

o **20-27.** Wisdom must not only guide; it must become a life principle resident in the heart. The words of the sage are not simply a practical device to give a man success. **22.** They are a **healing to all his flesh;** i.e. his whole life (cf. 3:8) will be permeated by them. The words of wisdom are **life** (cf. 8:35): life is breath (Gen. 2:7), blood (Dt. 12:23), and the span of human existence in its totality (3:2; Ps. 34:13); in Prov. it also becomes a spiritual reality in which man can participate but in which not all do. So here (cf. 3:18, 22, 8:35; Ps. 16:11). Wisdom is this life; and through discipline it must possess man's heart, the source of his purposes. **23.** The Heb. for **springs** does not refer to fountains; it is used of borders (Job 16:3, 17:18), the outskirts of a city (Ezek. 48:30), and of an escape (Ps. 68:21). A slightly different form (Mic. 5:1) is used to refer to place of origin, as here. As a man thinks in his heart so is he (cf. AV 23:7). 'It is the heart which brings up its lord as one who hears or as one who does not hear. The life, prosperity, and health of a man is his heart' (*The Instruction of . . . Ptah-hotep*, ANET (1950), 414). **25.** The **eyes** 393o
as a gate to the heart had to be guarded almost as carefully as the heart itself (cf. Job 31:1), a concern alive in NT (Mt. 6:22f., 18:9; Lk. 11:34). **27. To the right or left:** a Deuteronomic phrase (Dt. 5:32, 17:11, 28:14) found only here in Prov.

V Beware the strange Woman—The chapter continues the warning against 'the other woman' (cf. 394a
2:16ff.). Who is she? What does she represent? We cannot be certain that the author's first intention is to warn against adultery (Gemser, op. cit., 27) or sexual licentiousness (Toy, op. cit., 101); as in the entire Wisdom Movement, in Israel and abroad, the author's views on both are presupposed and obvious; does he utilise them here to attack some heresy or alien cult? Beyond 1–9 Prov. gives rather scant attention to either adultery or immorality (22:14, 23:26–8, 29:3, 30:20, 31:3). The prophets described heresy and apostasy as adultery (cf. Jer. 2:1–12; Ezek. 16, 23; Hos. 1–3). The 'other' (Heb. (*zārāh*) is the stranger, who does not belong: in family (Ps. 109:11), to nation (Hos. 7:9, 8:7, et al.), in cult (Exod. 30:9; Num. 3:4). Boström (op. cit., 32ff.), following Oort, insists the woman is a foreigner; rejecting the allegorical interpretations (e.g. Friedländer, Reitzenstein, Diettrich), he nevertheless feels the author's concerns are ideological and cultic rather than simply ethical. The Egyptian *Instruction of Ani* says 'Be on thy guard against a woman from abroad' (ANET, 420).

1-6. Text of v. **2** is corrupt, as the metaphor of lips b
guarding knowledge indicates. LXX reads 'That you may keep a good design I commend to you the knowledge of my lips', connecting with v. **3.** The woman speaks (cf. Job 29:29; Am. 7:16) with the sweetness of honey; those taken in experience her deceit (lit. 'the end of her', i.e. in its effect on them). **Wormwood,** symbol of suffering (Am. 5:7, 6:12), and judgment (Rev. 8:10f.; in Arabic the root includes a word for 'curse'). For sweetness, bitterness, and sharpness (lit. 'sword of two mouths'). **5.** Her victims go to death with her, missing rewards of life. **Sheol,** a synonym for **death**; both evil here; i.e. untimely and as punishment. **6.** The seductiveness of the woman is greater because she has no course of her own, the undisciplined freedom of licence.

7-14. To encourage a sober resolve in his pupil the sage c
conjures up a vivid picture of the outcome of a misspent life, including a pathetic soliloquy. **8.** The woman occupies a house (cf. 2:18, 7:8, 9:13ff.), whereas some illicit cults did not (Isa. 65:3f., 66:17). Those who go near it risk loss of **honour** ('majestic splendour', cf. Job 39:20; Ps. 45:4, 104:1), **years** ('life', cf. Job 36:11; Ps. 31:10), **strength** (ability? cf. 24:10; Job 30:2), and the fruits of their **labours** at the hands of an **alien** (Heb. *nokhrî*): foreigner; i.e. non-Israelite (Jg. 19:12), of another family (Gen. 31:15) unknown or unfamiliar (Job 19:15; Ps. 69:9). The exhaustion (**consumed**) of physical power makes the plaint pathetic; the past cannot be revoked (cf. Ec.). **The assembled congregation** (lit. 'assembly and congregation': as synonyms), terms significant in Israel's cultus.
15-23. The monitory inhibiting tone gives way for a moment to an affirmative note pervaded by romantic enthusiasm. The aesthetic motif dominates the moral. Vv. **15-19** stand apart; they seem to demand a simple literal interpretation. Like Ca. they eulogise marriage in terms of sensuous enjoyment (cf. especially **19b: be infatuated,** lit. intoxication. Cf. Isa. 28:7). **Cistern, well, springs, fountain:** all metaphors for **wife** (cf. Dt. 33:28; Ps. 68:26; Ca. 4:12, 15; Isa. 51:1?). Cf. Gen. 3:20, woman as source of life. With v. **20** the interlude is over. The sage again warns against **the adventurers** (lit. 'alien').

VI 1-19. The discourse on the evil woman is inter- d
rupted by four paragraphs: **1-5,** on suretyship; **6-11,** on sloth; **12-15,** on subversion; and **16-19,** on seven sins. More specific and briefer than most discourses in chs. 1–9, they nevertheless exhibit their

394d characteristic essay style, in contrast to the aphoristic parallelisms of chs. 10ff., but similar to Sir.

1-5 Abrogate Surety Commitments—It is unwise to undertake obligations for others (11:15, 17:18, 22:26) ; once caught by the snare of your own promise (**2**), every effort must be made to terminate the guaranty; the collection of debt is not the real issue. The cancellation of the sponsorship apparently requires the consent of **your neighbour** who is **a stranger** in the sense that he is not of the sponsor's family and, hence, free to make his own plans though they implicate the surety. Like a gazelle or bird, you must get out of this trap : **importune your neighbour** (Heb. ' act boisterously ' ; cf. Ps. 138:3*n*, difficult to reconcile with ' humble yourself ' ; LXX ' do not relax ' = **hasten**). The obligation, sealed by clasping hands (lit. for **1b** ' clasped your palm for a stranger ' ; cf. 17:18, 22:26), is here probably for debt ; other forms existed (cf. Gen. 43:9 ; cf. the Lord, Ps. 119:122). Sir. 29:14–20 warns of the risks in suretyship and admonishes the beneficiaries to be responsible. In case of loans, the creditor had no legal protection (Exod. 22:25–7 ; Sir. 29:1–13) ; likewise here, it seems.

e **6-11 Sloth breeds Poverty**—Industry and forethought rank high on the sage's list of virtues. On a strongly individualistic basis human misfortune is considered avoidable. So, **poverty** is due to sloth (10:4, 13:18, 20:13, 23:21, 24:34, 28:19). **The ant** (cf. 30:24 ; 1 Kg. 5:13) illustrates the virtue of industry (12:11, 24, 27, 14:23). In Egypt the sages deprecated physical work (e.g. *The Instruction of Duauf*) ; in Israel they honour it (cf. Sir. 38:24–39:11 for a qualifying view). The rhetorical questions put to the **sluggard** are followed by an ironical taunt well known (cf. 24:33f.). Like **an armed man** (lit. ' man with a shield ') poverty, once admitted, is irresistible.

12-15. Subversion : talebearing, misrepresentation, illicit charges and plots (cf. 16:27–30). In the Babylonian Code of Ḥammurabi the punishment for a charge falsely made was given to the one who made it (cf. Exod. 23:1). The gestures of eye, feet, and finger are sly attempts at hiding the discord being fomented. Heb. *b^e^lîyya'al*, **worthless**, is synonymous with death in Ps. 18:4 (cf. 2 C. 6:15).

f **16-19 Seven Sins**—Seven, a *complete* list (cf. 24:16, 26:16, 25). **Six things—seven,** characteristic poetic device (cf. 30:18, 21, 24, 29 ; Am. 1:3, 6, 9, et al.). The first five illustrate the OT tendency to ' personify ' members of the body, giving each an individuality of its own. For interpretations of this phenomenon, see an essay by H. W. Robinson, ' Hebrew Psychology ', in *The People and the Book*, ed. by A. S. Peake ; also A. R. Johnson, *The Vitality of the Individual in the Thought of Ancient Israel* (1949). The use of the eye to convey arrogance seems to have been common (21:9 ; Ps. 18:28, 131:1 ; Isa. 10:12 ; cf. also 30:17). The **lying tongue** and **the hands that shed innocent blood :** in traditional sections of the Semitic world today, notably on the peninsula of Arabia, the Koranic custom of punishing a wrongdoer in his offending members is still exercised (e.g. amputating a finger or fingers from the hand of a thief). Matter (means) and spirit (will) can never be discretely separated ; physical proximity incurs guilt or blessing, as the case may be.

g **20-35 The Defence against Adultery**—This section, like ch. 5, commends wisdom as the antidote to the appeal of the alien woman. But to keep him safe, a man must keep alive the parental discipline. Almost in paraphrase of Dt. 6:4–7 he gives it a role comparable to the Law of the covenant ; guide on the road, guard at night, teacher who **will talk with you** (cf. Job 12:8, evoke true thoughts). In **23a commandment** and **law** still refer to parental maxims but, again, like the Law, are equated with **lamp** and **light** (cf. Ps. 119:105) and as **way of life** (cf. 13:9, 20:20, 24:20), **the reproofs** also function as the Law (Dt. 5:30).

26. This teaching protects from **the evil woman** (LXX ' neighbour's wife ' ; Kittel, in loc., *zārāh*, ' strange ' ; parallel to **adventuress :** i.e. *nokhriyyāh*, ' alien ' ; cf. V *supra*) ; but it must rule the **heart** and evil desire must not rise (cf. Mt. 5:27–30). 394g

The text of **26** is uncertain. Kittel proposes an emendation which yields ' For a harlot desires even a crust of bread ' (i.e. everything), leading to a parallel rather than a contrast in the next line (cf. also Gemser, op. cit., 32, and 23:27).

The doom of a man who **commits adultery** (32*b*) with **his neighbour's wife** (29*b*) is inevitable and sure (27f.) ; the only unambiguous reference to adultery in chs. 1–9. The adulterer is a thief in the worst way ; all theft demands restitution (**sevenfold,** if taken literally, is higher than legal demands cited in OT ; cf. Exod. 22:1–9) ; but a man's wife is his most valuable possession (legislation respecting daughters and wives is best interpreted on property principles) ; besides, she is an extension of his own life and a part of that psychic unity, the family (cf. J. Pedersen, *Israel, Its Life and Culture, I–II* (1926), 60ff.). Hence, he not only invokes the laws : **jealousy makes a man kill** (slightly emended reading of **34a,** cf. Kittel, in loc.), the same bond that makes the Lord fight for his people (Isa. 42:13, 63:15 ; Zech. 1:14, 8:2). h

VII The Shield of Wisdom—In realistic tableaux the fourth section (cf. 2:16–19, 5, 6:20–35) sketches the lures of **the loose woman** which only those armed with wisdom can withstand. Though she is the antithesis of Wisdom (4f.) and the embodiment of Folly (9:13), the irresistible conclusion is that the author talks about a flesh-and-blood person. His concern is with morality, though possibly with an alien cult (cf. *supra* 2:16–19 and Boström, op. cit.). 6:20–35 concentrated on the dreadful fate of the adulterer ; here, the seductiveness of the temptation to which he yields. i

1-5. The preface corresponds closely to 6:20–4, also disclosing affinities with Dt. As in Arabic, the Heb. for **the apple** of the eye is ' little man ' (cf. Dt. 32:10 ; ' daughter ' in Lam. 2:18). Like the words of the Law (Exod. 13:9 ; Dt. 6:8, 11:18), the words of the sage, like an amulet, must be bound on the fingers as a ' sign ' to remind and protect. The Jewish phylacteries serve such a purpose ; so the ring (Jer. 22:24 ; Hag. 2:23). Wisdom must be the wife of your youth (5:18), the bride to whom you remain faithful (for **sister** as bride, cf. Job 17:14 ; Ca. 4:9f., 12, 5:12 ; Tob. 7:15) ; let her be **your intimate** (lit. ' kinswoman ' ; cf. Ru. 2:1, 3:2). In communion with Wisdom (cf. 3:3, on the table of your heart) you are safe from the folly of **the loose woman.** Note the close analogy with 5:15ff., a reminder that symbol and fact reinforce one another in the discourses.

6-9. Through the trellis of his window the sage (LXX, the woman) looks down into the street to watch evening strollers. More than the prophets (Isa. 2:18 ; Hab. 2:1) the sages observed people as the source of their understanding of life. A youth goes to the woman's door ; his course is premeditated (cf. Sir. 7:9), **a young man without sense** who does not take thought. j

10-12. The woman meets him wearing the garment of a harlot (**dressed,** cf. Gen. 38:14f. ; Ps. 73:6), wily of heart, i.e. on her guard, suspicious as well as abandoned. She is restless (for **wayward,** Heb. *sōḥāreth* for *sōrāreth*, for sake of parallelism).

13-20. The invitation of the woman and the description of her luxurious home must be seen as an imaginative portrayal of actual scenes in the author's experience. The seduction of the youth apparently begins in the street : **with impudent face** (lit. ' she makes bold her face ') she connects her solicitation with a tale about a sacrificial feast. The offering of meat or meal at a shrine, in payment of a vow or for some other occasion, entailed the eating of some of it at home, often in festal manner (cf. 1 C. 8:1–10, 10:14–28). The eating of flesh in Israel was originally perhaps

394j always an aspect of a sacrificial act (cf. Dt. 12:1–19 for a relaxing tendency). Vow offerings were to be eaten on the day of the sacrifice (Lev. 7:16). Boström, op. cit., 110ff., uses these verses to illustrate his thesis that the woman was not an ordinary adulteress but the devotee of a foreign sexual cult designed to promote fertility ; the youth is solicited for the completion of rites related to the vow. His seduction causes death because it is apostasy. The hypothesis must probably remain conjecture for want of evidence in Prov. to confirm it.

21-27. The youth without sense becomes a victim ; as **an ox to the slaughter** (cf. Isa. 53:7f.), the embodiment of stupidity. The Heb. for **entrails,** liver (cf. Lam. 2:11), as seat of life. The house of the adulteress is the way to Sheol (2:18, 5:5, 9:18) ; there is a curious vagueness about the manner of the youth's death.

k **VIII 1-21 The Invitation of Wisdom**—As in 1:20–33 Wisdom is a preacher. There she utters prophetic judgment against the scorners and calls to repentance ; here she is an evangelist offering men her gifts. Denunciation and taunting scorn are exchanged for a tender pleading. Her call to life stands in dramatic contrast to the invitation to death given by **the loose woman** (2:16–19, 5, 6:20–35, 7). The sages frequently eulogise Wisdom as the source and mediator of all that is good for man (Job 28 ; Wis. 6–9 ; Sir. 1:1–2). Here, as in 1:20–33 and Sir. 24, they offer their praise of Wisdom by letting her speak for herself. There is no hint that the invitation is for Jews only, nor that they have special access to Wisdom. (For a discussion of the relations between Israel's Wisdom Movement and her election faith, cf. Rylaarsdam, op. cit., 18–46.)

1-3. Wisdom goes out ‘ to the highways and hedges ’ (Lk. 14:23). The initiative of God, through Wisdom, on behalf of men in 1–9 is lacking in the rest of the book. In **in the paths** RSV wisely adopts LXX reading (cf. 1:21f.). For the sake of the parallelistic structure R. Kittel (BH in loc.) suggests ‘ she calls ’ for **in front of the town** (3*a*) ; the form of the calling was a rhythmic chant (cf. 1:20).

l **4-21 Wisdom speaks for Herself**—She addresses men ; as an expression of the action of God this is her special function (**31** ; Sir. 24:1–7). Without her, men are simple ; frequently (14:7, 18:2, 23:9, 24:7, 27:22) the sages assume fools to be incorrigible. Here the rescue of the callow and unformed is perhaps envisaged (4f.). Wisdom speaks **noble things** (lit. ‘ princely ’), i.e. truth, righteousness, and what is upright and straight, free from everything wicked, twisted, and perverse : the doctrine of the two ways (cf. 2:16–19 *supra*) ; **9.** Wisdom is pure light, but only those illumined by her know it.

16f. By me kings reign : In Israel, as in Egypt, the king was the patron of wisdom ; and adroit royal decisions (1 Kg. 3:16ff.) were admired. But there is a deeper meaning to the statement that rulers govern by Wisdom. In the ancient Near East kingship is established by the gods in the initial cosmological ordering of existence. The king is the sign and embodiment of the authority of the deity ; he has access to his wisdom and shares in his counsels. The wisdom by which **princes rule** is an eternal and divine quality. The king was wise as son of God. Ḫammurabi of Babylon, son of Sin, declares himself ‘ god among kings, acquainted with wisdom ’ (ANET (1950), 165). As ‘ sun of Babylon ’, i.e. as a god, he ‘ has made the four quarters of the world subservient ’ ; it is by virtue of his station that he is ‘ the one who plumbed the depth of wisdom ’. His law code exhibits the divine wisdom resident in him. Wisdom as the counsel of deity was traditionally—also in Israel—available only to persons occupying special offices ; e.g. prince, priest, prophet (cf. P. A. H. de Boer, ‘ The Counsellor,’ VT *Supplement* III, 42ff.). **15f.** echo the ancient notions of divine kingship and its relation to divine Wisdom. It accentuates the recommendations of Wisdom which in this chapter seeks to illumine all men. In synergistic 394l manner, wisdom is found by those who seek her (cf. Mt. 7:7) ; in some later traditions wisdom is not to be found (Job 28 ; Enoch 42). Those who forsake all else to seek wisdom will have as a by-product the wealth they forsake (cf. Mt. 6:33). **13** breaks the discourse and is probably misplaced.

22-31 The Descent of Wisdom—The reason for the m transcendent value and power of Wisdom, just recited, is now given : she is antecedent to all creatures, the first act of the Lord. To wisdom belongs the primacy and excellence of the first-born (cf. 1:7 ; Gen. 49:3 ; Job 15:7–9, 40:19 ; Col. 1:15 ; Rev. 3:11). Wisdom is the Alpha (cf. Rev. 22:13) ; **22** closes with the Heb. word *'āẓ* (**of old,** lit. ‘ then ’) which frequently has a meaning simultaneously primeval and eschatological (Ps. 76:8, 89:19, 93:2, 96:12, ‘ when once ’ ; Isa. 44:8, 45:21, 48:5, 7, 8 ; Jer. 17:12, ‘ from the beginning ’ ; cf. also Ps. 2:5, ‘ then ’, at the decisive moment). Wisdom is, indeed, an expression of the creative action of God, not an eternal existence ; yet she is the decisive act in which the meaning of all God's creative acts is disclosed. The identification of this Wisdom with the Word of God (Λόγος), with the Law (Sir. 24:23), Spirit (Exod. 28:3 ; Job 32:8 ; Wis. 1:7, 9:17, 11:20), and with Christ (1 C. 1:24, 30) always includes this element of the decisive action of God. A generation ago scholars explained Wisdom as here presented primarily with reference to hellenising influences (cf., e.g., Toy, op. cit., 172) ; while this must not be discounted entirely, there is today an increased awareness that the figure of primeval Wisdom represents an aspect and phase of Israel's assimilation of the mythology and cultic patterns of the ancient Near East. The Lord's creation of Wisdom (cf. Gen. 14:19, 22 ; Dt. 32:6 ; Ps. 139:13 for other examples where Heb. verb *ḳānāh* means ‘ create ’) indicates that Israel's faith is not compromised by the assimilative process.

24-26. As primal creature, Wisdom is prior to the n physical world. The series **when there were no** and **Before** adopts the style of the Creation epic of Babylon *Enūma Eliš* (ANET (1950), 60f. ; cf. Gen. 2:5f.), to stress the distinctiveness of Wisdom. **I was brought forth** must be understood as a synonym for **created** (22). The point is, Wisdom was **set up** (cf. Ps. 2:6) ; she **was there** before the Lord had done anything else. In OT it is impossible to separate logical from chronological priority ; both are present here.

Therefore, **27-31,** Wisdom was present when God made the cosmos and **his inhabited world.** The order of creating is roughly parallel to Gen. 1:6–10. **30.** That Wisdom participated as **a master workman** is disputed ; many scholars prefer the slightly different reading found in Aquila's version, meaning ‘ nursling ’ (cf. Lam. 4:5) because it comports with the following portrayal of Wisdom as a child at play, the delight of the Creator at his work (cf. 3:19f.) ; God made the cosmos for Wisdom, and with Wisdom as pattern. This affirmative view of material existence corresponds to Gen. 1, ‘ it was good ’.

32-36. Having described her title, Wisdom renews the o invitation in the form of a double beatitude : **Happy are those . . .** (cf. 3:13). Drop **33** altogether (so LXX) or place it after **34.** The appeal ends with a sharp challenge. The issue is **life** or **death.** The search for Wisdom is the decisive matter. Man's choice with respect to her sums up the either-or of the doctrine of the two ways. Jesus' concluding parable in the Sermon on the Mount (Mt. 7:24–7), with the typical phrase ‘ everyone who hears these words of mine ’, duplicates this antithesis. The invitation of Wisdom is the call of God.

IX 1-6, 13-18 Lady Wisdom and Dame Folly— p There are two influences in the world, two ways, and two invitations. Separated by an extraneous unit (7-12), these two are symbolised by the two women, Wisdom and Folly. While the discourses on **the loose woman** elsewhere (2:16–19, 5, 6:20–35, 7) may be

394p primarily realistic, here the **foolish woman** is symbolic of a type view and action antithetical to the way of Wisdom.
1-6. As elsewhere (1:20–33, 8:1–21), Wisdom is personified as a good woman inviting mankind. Here she invites men to the banquet of life. She **has built her house:** some (e.g. Toy, op. cit., 184) feel that this has no cosmic implications; the metaphor applies to an everyday house. Others, notably Boström (op. cit., 1–14), hold that the **house** of Wisdom is the cosmos whose creation she attended as model (cf. 8:22ff.). The Pseudo-Clementine Homilies (XIII, XVII, XVIII) report that the cosmos rests on seven pillars, while in rabbinic tradition the number was either twelve or seven (J. Scheftelowitz, *Altpalästinensisches Bauernglaube* (1925), 28). Only palatial homes and temples had pillars. A temple or a palace was a structure of cosmic significance and its pillars may sometimes have had a symbolic meaning. Boström (op. cit., 13) thinks that Wisdom displaces the alien feminine deity, Ishtar, the 'queen of heaven' and that the **seven pillars** are the Babylonian planetary deities, a suggestion perhaps too full of imponderable factors. Meat and wine mark a feast: and in OT a feast is a sacrifice as well. But Wisdom, as hostess, offers the gift of life to men (cf. Isa. 55:1–3; Jn 6:35). **4-16.** Both Wisdom and Folly invite the **simple**, the uninformed. Wisdom calls **leave simpleness, and live:** LXX, by translating the Heb. for **live** by ζήσεσθε, implies this means participation in true life, not continuity of physical existence.

q **13-18.** k^{e}sîlûth, Folly, a fem. noun derived from the Heb. root 'to be or become stupid' personifies the antithesis of the universal Wisdom. **Woman** can be dropped. Folly is loud (7:11), a brawler (20:1) without shame in her seduction. Like Wisdom she also calls men. But she prepares no banquet; her house is chaos, and her invitation is a wanton solicitation. Instead of the meat and wine of life she offers the water and bread of death: the sin of fornication or adultery is probably indicated by the proverb, **Stolen waters . . .** (cf. 5:15, 7:18, 30:20; Sir. 23:17), though the particular sin is a symbol of the call of evil in general; the way of death. **He does not know,** i.e. the simple one, untaught by Wisdom (7:24–7), whom she seduces. For the sages ignorance is fatal; Wisdom is the only hedge against death. **The depths of Sheol** (lit. 'the deepest parts'), to intensify the contrast with the fullness of life in Wisdom.

r **7-12.** These verses are related to the two parables they separate only by the fact that like them, they emphasise the contrast between Wisdom and Folly as a constant state of affairs; as there are two ways, so there are two classes of people in the world and each excludes the other. Once a man has made his choice there is no further hope of conversion. Separation of the sheep from the goats (Mt. 25:32ff.) begins here and now. Unlike the simple (4, 6) the **scoffer** and **wicked man** are men who have made their choice; they are conscious opponents of Wisdom. **7.** To attempt to discipline them is to incur abuse (cf. 3:35, 6:33, 11:2, 12:16; Jer. 13:26) and *reproach* (instead of **injury**; Heb. 'his blemish'; i.e. incur apostasy). Leave the **scoffer** alone (cf. Ps. 1:1). The **righteous** and **wise** embody a hunger for teaching and correction (1:5, 14:6, 19:25, 21:11; Mt. 13:12) that will make them ever wiser. **11. By me** lacks a clear antecedent; Kuhn (op. cit., 18) suggests *by her*; i.e. **fear of the Lord.** The point of **12** seems to be that both the reward of wisdom and the punishment of the scoffer will come to each individual according to his desert and are inescapable. This individualisation of life is a feature of the Wisdom Movement.

395a **Second Section X-XXII 16 The Proverbs of Solomon**

The primary collection of aphoristic sentences. Probably the oldest portion of the book: see §392*b*. The entire section consists of simple units of two lines 39
in parallel relation to each other. Each unit is complete in itself. There is rarely a logical continuity of thought holding successive units together. Rhyme, other types of assonance, catch words and similar devices influenced the arrangement of the units; but these can rarely be reproduced in translation.

The plan for this commentary proposes the interpretation of paragraphs; verse-by-verse annotation would require a larger scale. Besides, in this section, one frequently meets several two-line units that deal with the same subject in substantially the same way, though not standing together. To avoid repetition there will be brief philological notes relating to the rendering of the text and to illumine obscurities. In addition, in connection with some chapters, there will be more comprehensive notes on some subject, or subjects, touched on in a given chapter but probably also raised in other chapters of the section.

X 6. After **blessings** LXX adds *kuriou*, of the b
Lord. **6b = 11b**; probably misplaced here due to loss of original line. **7. will rot:** Toy proposes 'will be cursed'; but see Sir. 41:11. **8.** The implication is that he walks safely because of heeding commands: antithesis of **b. 9.** In the parallelistic structure **be found out** is hardly antithetical to 'walks securely'; emend to 'suffer harm' (cf. 11:15, 13:20). **11b = 6b.** For **conceals violence** Kuhn (op. cit., 20) proposes 'a cup of vinegar', removing illogical metaphor and stressing parallelism. **16b. To sin**; i.e. to death, the opposite of **life.** Heb. word for sin means 'to miss the mark' (cf. **2b**, 11:19*a*). **17a.** Read Heb. for **path** as active participle 'a traveller to life is he who heeds instruction'. **18a.** LXX, 'Righteous lips conceal hatred, but . . .', recommended reading, for antithetical parallelism. **23.** The stupid take satisfaction in **wrong** (evil deeds, often unchastity); the understanding in wisdom. **26.** A conclusion with two comparisons, cf. Baal and 'Anat II, lines 6ff., 28ff. (cf. C. H. Gordon, *Ugaritic Literature* (1949), 45). **28a.** For **ends in gladness,** 'springs up'. **32a.** Read, **The lips of the righteous** *utter* (lit. 'cause to bubble up').

The Righteous—In Prov. the righteous oppose the c
wicked. These two classes of men are analogous to the wise and foolish, respectively, yet distinct from them (cf. 2:15–19 *supra*). In the Ps. and elsewhere in OT the righteous are often equated with the poor and oppressed crying for deliverance. Especially in NT, the reward of righteousness is not expected in this life (cf. Mt. 6:2–4). This is not so in Prov. The deliverance of the righteous is swift and sure (11:8, 21, 12:13). He will enjoy success, wealth, and honour in this life. He avoids hunger (10:3, 24, 13:25), prospers (12:28, 13:21), and escapes trouble (12:21). He becomes wealthy (15:6). By the grace of God (14:9) the righteous will rule over the wicked (14:9, 21:18, 29:16), and all men rejoice in their triumph (11:10, 14:34, 21:21, 28:12, 29:2). Aided by prayer (15:29) the righteous gain the life they desire (11:23, 30, 10:24). Like the trees in a well-watered garden (cf. Ps. 1:3) their **root will never be moved** (12:3, 12), their house stands (12:7), and their light does not go out (13:9). The righteous endure **forever** (10:25, 30. Heb. *'ôlām*, in sense of absolute finality). They are an influence for good that is effective after their lifetime (10:6f., 21:26). They are thoughtful of the poor (29:7) and of animals (12:10). For the sages the tongue is a treacherous instrument (cf. ch. 11 below), but in the righteous speech and thought are a source of life and blessing (10:11, 20, 21, 32, 11:9, 12:5, 13:5, 15:28). The righteous walk the way of life; the wicked the way of death.

XI 1b. Just weight: lit. 'a complete stone', d
primitive measure of weight (cf. 20:10, 23). **3b. Crookedness:** probably refers to speech (cf. 15:4). **4a. The day of wrath:** the day of God's final judgment (cf. Ezek. 7:19; Zeph. 1:15, 18), here synonymous with death (cf. Job 21:30). **7. Heb. text,**

395d basis of RSV, is very dubious ; it lacks antithetical parallelism. LXX reading, 'When the righteous man dies his hope does not perish, but the boasting of the wicked perishes', is preferable. Hope of righteous at death need not imply future life ; simply durability of his works and his memory. **8. Instead,** the wicked does not suffer in behalf of righteous ; the law of justice works in behalf of both, delivering one and destroying the other. **12. Remains silent:** if there is nothing helpful to say. **15.** On suretyship cf. 6:1–5 above. **16.** An antithesis between men and women does not occur elsewhere, nor is it meaningful here. In LXX two stichoi stand between **a** and **b:** 'a gracious woman gets honour, but a throne of dishonour is a woman hating uprightness ; the estate of sluggards declines ; but the industrious attain wealth.' This reading is very probably true to the original Heb., now corrupt. **19.** Perhaps 'he who establishes righteousness', parallel with **b** (cf. Gemser, op. cit., 44 ; Job 31:14). **21a. Be assured:** lit. 'hand to hand' (cf. 16:5) ; the metaphor has reference to the gesture of clasping hands as a sign of an agreement, specifically when a man becomes surety for another (cf. 6:1–5 above). **24.** Cf. Lk. 6:38. **25b.** BH chooses reading of Syr., 'but who curses will be cursed'. **27a.** LXX reads 'He who devises good . . .' **29.** Lacks parallelistic structure, perhaps indicating misplaced stichoi. For wind as a metaphor for nothingness cf. Ec. 1:14, 5:15 ; Isa. 2618, 41:19. **30a.** Perhaps (with LXX) 'righteousness' for **righteous. 31.** Intimates punishment is even more sure than reward ; a wholly latent notion in Prov. that leads to serious discussions about theodicy in later stages of Wisdom Movement. Cf. 1 Pet. 4:18 for quotation of v. 4 from LXX.

e **Speech**—The spoken word was the primary medium of the sages and the ordering of human life their chief concern. Quite naturally, because of this, the instruments of speech—tongue, lips, and mouth—were of central importance. It is the **mouth of God** (2:6) that is the source of wisdom. The sages impart Wisdom by their mouth (4:5, 5:7, 7:24, 10:31) ; and in the gate where they sit the fool does not open his mouth (24:7). **The tongue of the wise** (15:2) gives knowledge ; and **the lips of a king** are inspired (16:10). Speech plays a decisive role whether for good or ill : words are **deep waters** (18:4), and they can be destructive **sword thrusts** or the means of **healing** (12:18). In fools and scoffers speech is the means of destruction, including their own (6:12, 10:6, 14, 11:9, 11, 13, 12:6, 22:14). As with other parts of the body playing an active role, there is a tendency to personify the organs of speech. The tongue may be a **tree of life** (15:4). Death and life are **in the power of the tongue** (18:21). The proper use of the mouth yields good fruit (8:20, 12:14, 13:2). A man's word puts him under obligation (6:7). Therefore, and because it has so many consequences, restraint in speech is inculcated (10:19, 11:12, 15:28, 17:28, 21:23). Fools use their gift of speech indiscreetly (10:14, 15:2) or with evil intent (6:12, 11:11, 13, 17:4). Like the scoffer who uses it, **the perverse tongue will be cut off** (10:31).

f **XII 1. Stupid:** i.e. brutish (cf. 30:2). **2. Evil devices:** the Heb. term for this sometimes has a good meaning (cf. 1:4, 2:11, 3:21, 5:2, 8:12, 14:17), sometimes evil (10:23, 21:27, 24:8, 9). **3. The root** hints at the frequent tree metaphor. **4. Good wife:** lit. efficient, capable (cf. 31:10–31) ; **crown,** an ornament or wreath. **5. The counsels:** lit. 'tactics' ; a naval metaphor (cf. 1:5, 11:14). **6.** Heb. ends the verse **delivers 'them'** ; for sake of parallel read **lie in wait** for 'the perfect'. **8.** LXX gives 'dull-minded' for **of perverse mind,** a closer parallel with good sense. **9.** To restore parallelism BH proposes 'who has bread' for **who works for himself. 10b.** Note the keen irony. **12.** MT text is impossible to interpret. For the range of proposed reconstructions see Toy, op. cit., 249f., and Gemser, op. cit., 46. BH, in loc., proposes 'The foundation of evil men will be destroyed, but the root of the righteous is permanent'. **13. Is ensnared** follows LXX : Heb., 'in the transgression of his lips is a snare of an evil man'. **16.** The fool makes known his arrogance (cf. LXX). **26a.** RSV gives a reconstruction proposed by Toy (op. cit., 258), LXX : 'the righteous takes thought for his neighbour'. **27.** No real parallelism, probably indicating misplaced stichoi. For other proposals for reconstruction cf. Toy, op. cit., 258. **28b.** MT contains two words meaning way or path. By emending second *n^e^thîbhāh* to *tô'ēbhāh* (error, abomination) we arrive at RSV reading. 395f

g **The Diligent Man**—The sages advocate 'the strenuous life'. The diligent man is one whose hand is *sharp,* i.e. gripping the tool it employs. The sluggard is the slack man, one whose hand is open and limp because unemployed. The two are contrasted (10:4, 12:24, 27, 13:4). Hunger and poverty (10:4, 12:27, 13:4, 19:15, 21:5, 24:30–4), slavery (12:24) and an evil reputation (10:26) are the lot of the lazy. The slack man is no better than the destroyer (18:9). But the diligent are sure to attain wealth (10:4, 12:27, 13:4, 21:5), authority (12:24), and, in the case of the ideal woman, a fair name (31:27). Toil and effort bring results ; mere talk ends in want (14:23). The rewards of diligence comprise, in part, the 'good life' as the sages define it ; and their appeal to diligence rests on the assumption that it lies within man's capacity to attain this as his goal. The Wisdom Literature subsequent to Prov. is more complicated in its treatment of the relation between human effort and human destiny.

h **XIII 1a. Hears** is lacking in Heb. ; LXX suggests it did appear there originally. Gemser (op. cit., 48) prefers emendation of extant Heb. text (*'āhēbh* for *'ābh*), to read 'a wise son loves instruction' (cf. 12:1). **2a.** Heb. not clear : the intent is to contrast speech with violence. LXX : 'the good man eats of the fruits of righteousness'. **5b. Acts shamefully:** Heb. 'odiously' ; or, 'causes that which is odious'. But cf. 19:26. **6. Upright,** in sense of perfect (*tām*), blameless (29:10). **8b.** Heb. repeats last half of **1b.** RSV reconstruction, suggested by the principle of parallelism, features disadvantages of food (cf. 14:20, 19:47, 30:14). BH, also activated by parallelism, proposes (less probably), 'a poor man values a gerah' (cf. §35*b*) ; i.e. poverty breeds calculation. **9. Rejoices** : the flame burns brightly, in contrast to **put out.** Textual emendation (cf. BH, in loc.) seems superfluous. **10b. Take advice:** lit. 'counsel together'. **13b. Rewarded:** LXX renders Heb. as 'be safe', the real antithesis to first clause. **19.** Two unrelated stichoi, cf. 12*b*, 29:27*b*. **23. Fallow ground** may refer to land given its sabbatical rest, from which poor might eat (Exod. 23:10f. ; Lev. 25:1–7) or to marginal land left for use of poor. Heb. text is very difficult ; but point seems to be that man's injustice thwarts bounty of nature.

XIV 1. Wisdom: here plural (cf. 1:20). The term 'women' (RSV*n*) may have entered Heb. text under the influence of personification of Wisdom as a wise woman. For possible cosmological connotations of **house** of Wisdom, cf. 9:1 above. **2a.** Heb. has 'in his uprightness' ; i.e. one who is true to himself. Less probably, the way of the Lord. **3a.** Heb. 'shoot of pride' ; i.e. the boastful speech of a fool is the growth that brings on his destruction (cf. Isa. 11:1). **4a.** Heb. 'a manger is clean (empty)' ; the cleanliness is due to a lack of fodder caused by absence of oxen. **7b.** RSV gives a reconstruction that lacks parallelism. LXX, 'but wise lips are instruments of perception'. Better still, 'but hasten to associate with wise lips' (cf. BH, and Kuhn, op. cit., 32). **9a.** Heb. may have read 'Fools scoff at offence'. **11b.** For **flourish** LXX has 'stand' (cf. 12:7). **13.** A mood more characteristic of Ec. unless we interpret **laughter** and **joy** as malicious (cf. 10:23*a* ; Ezek. 35:15). **14b.** Lit. 'from upon him' or 'from himself' which 396a

396a LXX interprets ' from his thoughts '. **16b. Throws off restraint,** as an act of arrogance. **17b.** A possible emendation of Heb. would give ' is quiet ' (*y^esha'^anān* for *yishshānē'*). **27a.** LXX says ' the command of the Lord ' (cf. 13:14).

b **29. Slow to anger** (lit. ' long of nostrils ' : this chapter contrasts the quick-tempered (**17,** lit. ' short of nostrils ') with the man of controlled temper as fool and wise, respectively. This is typical of Prov. A wise man is **slow to anger** (15:18, 16:32, 25:15, **patience** ; cf. 25:28). Egypt's sages spoke of the ' hot ' and the ' silent ' man. Possibly in relation to this a common word for anger in Prov. is ' heat ' (*ḥēmāh*, cf. 15:1, 18, 16:14, 19:19, 21:14, 22:4, 27:4, 29:22) ; for the opposite, ' cool ', cf. 17:27. To remain silent under provocation is a virtue (cf. ch. 11). Having attained control of temper, a man must put his virtue to active use : a soft answer (15:1), the secret gift (21:14), and the quenching of social turmoil (29:8). The highest expression of self-control is to feed the man who hates you (25:21). The prudent avoid the short-tempered (22:24) for they stir up trouble (29:22). Only jealousy matches a short temper for evil (27:4). Wrath belongs to God (24:18). **31. A poor man :** God is Lord of poor as well as of powerful ; he is **Maker** of both (cf. 22:2). The attitude of Prov. to the poor is somewhat ambivalent. On one hand poverty is often seen as a result of irresponsibility and laziness (cf. ch. 12 above), justifying scorn. On the other hand, as here, the common humanity of all men under God is recognised ; and this demands responsibility toward the poor. Poverty is the ruin of the fool (10:15) ; it deprives him of friends (19:4), invites hatred (19:7), subjects him to the rich (22:7), and makes him defenceless (28:15). But a poor man with character is preferable to a wealthy one lacking it (19:1, 22, 28:11). Respect for, and care of, the poor is a mark of character and a duty (19:17, 21:17, 22:9, 29:14) which is rewarded by God. To hurt the poor or take advantage of them is wicked (22:16, 22, 28:8, 29:7). Most foolish of all are the poor who hurt their own kind (28:3). Wealth is no end in itself ; and poverty is not the final evil (15:16, 16:8, 17:1).

c **XV 1. Harsh word :** lit. ' a word that hurts '. **3b. Keeping watch,** to look after the good as against the evil (cf. Gen. 31:9). **4a.** Lit. 'the healing of the tongue'. **5b. Prudent,** i.e. he *becomes* shrewd through correction. **6b.** Toy (op. cit., 304) emends Heb. for **trouble befalls** to ' is cut off ', improving parallelism with **a. 8. Abomination,** a common word in Prov., usually with reference to the Lord. But cf. also 8:7, 13:19, 16:12, 24:9, 29:27. For **sacrifice** and **prayer** cf. 15:29, 21:3, 27, 28:9. It is difficult to estimate to what extent sayings such as these betoken a living relationship with Israel's cultus and faith. **11.** Cf. Job 26:6 ; Ps. 139:8. That God penetrated Sheol was the highest mark of his majesty. Nevertheless, Sheol could not respond to him (cf. Ps. 6:5 ; Isa. 38:18). **19a.** Probably ' like a thorn hedge ' for **overgrown with thorns** (cf. Gemser, op. cit., 52). **20b. Foolish man,** cf. 21:20*b* for identical Heb. phrase : lit. ' a fool of a man ' (cf. Gen. 16:12). **23a. Apt answer.** Heb. for ' answer ' includes notion of correspondence as well as response. Hence, **apt.** There is joy for both speakers and hearers. **25b. The widow's** landmark (cf. 22:28, 23:10) ; the sanctity of the hereditary boundary of lands (Dt. 19:14) is used as a metaphor for the rights of the weak. Amen-em-opet, ' Nor encroach on the boundaries of a widow ' (ANET, 422).

d **The Lord**—Prov. uses Israel's personal name for God almost exclusively and without exception in this section (on 14:9 cf. above). In chs. 15–16 the term Lord occurs 19 times, a very heavy concentration (cf. esp. 16:1–9). Ec. does not use Lord at all ; in Job God predominates. Does this mean that Prov. stands closer to Israel's religious tradition ? Or is the use of ' the name ' simply a device, a metaphor for the laws of life described by the sages ? And, is the Lord ' the 396d
God who acts ' ? There are no clear references either to Israel's history in which this action occurred for the establishment of faith or to the national cultus in which it was celebrated. The historical deeds of God's mercy are lacking (cf. Rylaarsdam, op. cit., 26ff.). Nevertheless, Lord is not simply a synonym for law. His eyes are everywhere (15:3, 11), he hears prayer (15:29), inspires speech (16:1, 20:12), weighs man's intentions (16:2, 17:3, 21:2), and guides men (16:9, 20:24). Significantly, thinking is supremely the human instrument of the divine action (21:1) ; and God decides in the lot (16:33). The power of ' the name ', always important in Israel (Gen. 32:29 ; Exod. 3:13–15), may be alluded to in 18:10. The Lord has a purpose (19:21), but everything has its own purpose (16:4). The view of deity is strongly immanent and providence has a quasi-mechanical quality.

XVI 1. Plans rests on a military metaphor : ' rank ', e
' battle lines '. Implicit seems our notion of ' analysis ', or the patterns of thought. **3a. Commit,** lit. ' roll ' (cf. Ps. 22:9, 37:5) ; i.e. cast your burden upon God (cf. Ps. 55:23). Analogously, in Amen-em-opet ; ' Sit thou down at the hands of the god ' (ANET, 424). **4a.** MT reads ' for his (God's) purpose ', but the second clause scarcely permits that. **6. Loyalty and faithfulness,** characteristic qualities of God (cf., e.g., Ps. 25:10), are here human virtues that represent **fear of the Lord. 10a. Inspired decisions :** lit. ' a divine oracle ' ; note the exalted view of a monarch (cf. vv. **12-15**). **11. Just balance,** a favourite theme of prophets and Egyptian sages (cf. Amen-em-opet, xvi ; ANET, 423). **18.** Lit. ' before crushing : pride ; and before stumbling : a haughty spirit '. The verse illustrates translation difficulty due to frequent omission of verbs in Heb. **27a. Plots evil,** lit. ' digs evil ' ; an unusual use of Heb. word. Slight textual emendation (*Kûr* for *Kôreh*) yields ' a worthless man is a furnace of evil ', which is completed by the following clause. **28b. Whisperer,** one who slanders (cf. 18:8, 26:20, 22).
31. A hoary head : cf. 20:29. The sages, both in Israel and elsewhere, pay great respect to age. This is true of the OT as a whole, but the outlook of the Wisdom Movement accentuates the emphasis. Wisdom is the result of a cumulative process of study, discovery, and experience ; in a profound sense only the more aged can claim it. The parents are the teachers of youth and the judges of their proficiency (10:1, 15:5, 20, 17:21, 25). Their discipline is both severe (13:24, 24:13f.) and final. Strength is the glory of youth (20:29), but the discipline of wisdom is preferable to the warrior's prowess (16:32). However, as between age and youth, each is the glory of the other (17:6).

XVII 1b. Feasting, lit. ' sacrifices ' ; i.e. the sacri- f
ficial meat occasioning a feast (1 Sam. 9:12f.). **2b.** Lit. ' in midst of brothers '. The reference is probably to the son of a slave woman, home born (Gen. 15:2f.), the son of the same father as **the brothers.** Such preference for the wise slave-son is still common in Arab society today. **7a. Fine :** LXX has ' upright ', which is balanced by **false speech. 8.** Must very probably be understood in an ironical sense. Bribery was roundly condemned in Israel (Dt. 10:17, 16:19 ; 1 Sam. 8:3) ; virtue is indicated by its rejection (v. **23** ; Ps. 15:5 ; Prov. 6:35 ; Isa. 45:13). Occasionally the word is used of a shrewd political gift or ' present ' (1 Kg. 15:19 ; 2 Kg. 16:8). **10b.** The legal maximum was forty (Dt. 25:3). **14a.** Probably like the opening of a dam. **19b. Who makes his door high** ; probably means to speak with pride. For door as a synonym for mouth, cf. Mic. 7:5.

Forgiveness—For this section the word **forgives** g
occurs only once in RSV (cf. v. 9 above). The Heb. root from which it comes is *kāsāh,* ' to cover '. The same term is translated with other English words ; e.g. ' conceal ' (10:6, 11, 18), ' keep hidden ' (11:13), and ' ignore ' (12:16). Thus, in 17:9 ' forgiveness ' connotes the covering up of wrong for the sake of the

396g common good. It means not 'repeating' (cf. also 11:13, 20:19). The Heb. *kipper*, 'to cover', or 'to propitiate', also occurs: as 'ransom' (13:8, 21:18), as 'appease' (16:14), and in 16:6 as 'atoned for' by loyalty and faithfulness. Whose? The terms 'loyalty' and 'faithfulness' frequently refer to God's character but here very probably connote human qualities. The covering and overcoming of iniquity is a human transaction, whether by the one forgiven or by his fellows. There is no clear hint of a forgiving action by the Lord, nor is sin clearly specified as an offence against him. The verb *sālaḥ*, 'pardon', always used of the forgiving action of God in OT, does not occur. Nor does the verb *rāḥam*, 'to have compassion', which also often has God as subject (cf. 28:13, in passive voice). The fact that the divine pardon and mercy are inoperative seems to inhibit deep forgiveness and compassion in the human scene as well. Forgiveness is suppression of evil only.

h **XVIII 1. Estranged:** from his own (cf. 16:28, 17:9, 19:4). LXX says 'seeks pretexts to be estranged', but this requires further emendation of Heb. text and is unnecessary. **2.** The fool's inability to learn is here complicated by aggressive self-assertion. **4b. Fountain** elsewhere always occurs with life (cf. 10:11, 13:14, 14:27, 16:22); so LXX. **5a. Partial:** lit. 'to raise up'; i.e. taking by the hand one who comes to do obeisance. **6a. Bring:** Heb. 'come'; LXX 'bring him'. **8a. Delicious morsels:** lit. 'things greedily swallowed'; cf. doublet 26:22. **10a. Name of the Lord,** the sacred name, very common in OT as symbol of God's character; only here in Prov. (cf. 30:9). Perhaps used with **tower** to stress divine power. **11b. Protecting him** follows LXX. Heb. 'in his imagination'; i.e. he *thinks* it will keep him safe; probably in ironical sense. **14.** Cf. 17:22. **16a. Gift:** not an endowment of character, but a present (cf. 19:6). The word is not that for 'bribe' (cf. 17:8 above). **19a.** RSV follows LXX. With slight emendation (*w* for *p*) Heb. 'an offended brother is like a strong city' (paralleled in **b**); i.e. inaccessible. **21b.** For **love it** LXX has 'control it'. See §395*e*. 18:23–19:2 missing in LXX.

i **22. He who finds a wife:** A good wife is a greater gift than wealth (12:4) but is less subject to human planning (19:14). This element of uncertainty and the importance of the issue help to account for the piety expressed (cf. 19:14). A man unfortunate in his wife is to be pitied above all others (12:4, 19:13, 21:9, 22:14). It must be noted that a good wife (or the opposite) is assessed in terms of the effect upon her husband; this is characteristic of Heb. society throughout: a woman's role is fulfilled in service to her husband and her family. Yet she is honoured (11:16, 31:10ff.) and there is no greater sin than to fail a mother in respect or to cause her shame (10:1, 15:20, 19:26, 20:20). Character and devotion, not superficial seductiveness, are the qualities of a good woman (11:22, 31:10ff.). In the *Instruction of Ani* the father admonishes his son to care for his mother because she bore him and cared for him in infancy (vii, 18ff.; ANET, 420); further, he is told not to interfere in his wife's supervision of her household once she has proved her efficiency (ix, 1ff.; ANET, 421). The *Instruction of Ptah-hotep* contains similar guidance (325ff.; ANET, 413).

j **XIX 1.** Cf. 28:6, originally probably identical. 'In his ways' more probable than **in speech**; also perhaps 'rich' for **fool. 2a. Man** rests on Heb. *nephesh*, which here more probably means 'zeal'; cf. Rom. 10:2: 'zeal without knowledge'. **7c.** RSV presents this as continuous with **a, b.** It is more probably the last of four additional lines in LXX: 'a good understanding is near those who know it, and a sensible man will find it; he who does many evil things will fulfil evil, and he who runs after words will not slip away.' **9.** Cf. v. **5. 15a. Deep sleep:** LXX has 'effeminacy'; more probably 'causes roof to fall' (cf. Ec. 10:18); not only hunger but also ruin of house is the end of sloth. **20b. For the future:** lit. 'at your end'. Syr. by transposition of letters has 'for your way'. **22a. What is desired:** LXX 'fruit'; i.e. loyalty is its own reward. **b.** For **liar** Gemser (op. cit., 60) proposes 'cruel man' (cf. 11:17). **24.** Too lazy to eat (cf. 26:15). **25.** The **scoffer** is not improved (cf. 9:7ff.) but the chastisement serves as a lesson to the simple. **27. My son:** only occurrence in this section; Toy (op. cit., 380), following LXX, prefers eliminating it. If interpreted as intending irony (only !), RSV rendering of Heb. is meaningful. **28b. Devours:** perhaps 'pours out' (cf. 15:28). **29a. is ready:** LXX has 'robs' which is completed in **b.** 396j

k **Wealth**—In this section of Prov. the value and function of wealth and riches are weighed as nowhere else in the OT. Israel anticipated the realisation of life's ultimate purpose within history, which enhanced the importance assigned to all material and human values, including wealth. In the Wisdom Literature this outlook is transformed by the Wisdom of Solomon (Rylaarsdam, op. cit., 95ff.). Riches in any material form are not a goal of life even though they are among its rewards, a distinction not easily observed. The goal of life is wisdom, described by such synonyms as 'Life' and 'the fear of the Lord'(22:4). Wealth is a more or less certain by-product of the discipline that leads to wisdom (10:22) and as such the sages seem frequently to invoke it as an incentive in lieu of the goal itself (12:27, 14:23, 21:17, 22:4). This was analogous to Deuteronomy but also similar to Egyptian wisdom. Since it is an incentive rather than a goal the sages can face the fact of the transiency of riches (11:4, 28, 23:4). They can, and do, condemn the passion for wealth as an end in itself (10:2, 11:16, 13:11, 15:27, 20:2, 22:16); and they do remember that God the Creator, rather than wealth, is the norm for all mankind (22:2), a fact which makes care for the poor a duty (14:21, 19:17, 21:13, 22:16).

l **XX 1. Astray:** Heb. root also means 'to reel'; so here. **2a.** Cf. 19:12*a*. **6a.** Syr. and Lat. read 'Many a man is called faithful'; the saying expresses impatience with cant. **9.** The sinfulness and impurity of all is axiomatic (cf. 'Solomon's Prayer', 1 Kg. 8:46), probably reflecting Deuteronomic influences. In LXX vv. **20-2** follow v. **9.** Thus **10** comes immediately after **22** and illustrates its point. **10a.** Lit. 'a stone and a stone, a measure and a measure': expressive idiom difficult to translate. **12.** Moral: man in his powers must serve the purpose of God (cf. 16:4 and note on 1:17 *supra*). **14.** Typical of an oriental bazaar to this day. **16.** Cf. 6:1ff., 27:13. **20. Utter darkness:** lit. the 'pupil of darkness'; the very centre, referring to the eye. The **lamp:** he will perish leaving no family to continue his name (cf. 13:9; 1 Kg. 15:4; Ps. 132:17). **21.** Cf. 13:11. **22.** God will recompense Israel for its undeserved sufferings (cf. Dt. 32:36; Heb. 10:30); the notion is here applied to the social relationships of individuals. **23.** Cf. v. **10. 24.** A hint of the issue that becomes acute in Job (cf. 16:33, 18:18); in wisdom, unlike the rest of OT, God's initiative and obscurity tend to become a problem rather than a basis of comfort. **27a.** BH, followed by Gemser (op. cit., 61), proposes 'The Lord protects the spirit of man' (cf. 24:12*b*; Job 7:20*a*), making God the **searcher** ('taster') of men.

m **The King**—Though in Israel the sages, at least in the later stages of the Wisdom Movement, were not as closely co-ordinated with the life of the court as was the case in Egypt, they exalt the authority and office of the ruler. On earth nothing is more dreadful than the king's wrath, nothing more desirable than his favour (19:12, 20:2). The king is the ready and creative instrument of God (21:1) who speaks the word of God among men (16:10, cf. note in loc.) and deserves obedience no less than God (24:21). As vicegerent of God he winnows evil and pronounces judgment on the wicked (20:8, 26) and rewards the righteous and pure (16:13, 22:11). That a prince

396m may be untrue to his office is recognised (17:7) but he is expected to exhibit the character that will exalt it (20:28) and the hereditary station of its occupant (19:10). Sociologically speaking, the Wisdom Movement is a very conservative force.

n **XXI 1a. A stream of water:** lit. 'canals of water', the man-made channels of an irrigation system. The metaphor often carries the notion of prosperity (Job 29:6; Ps. 1:3, 65:9). **2b. Weighs** or 'measures' (16:2, 24:12). God's 'weighing of men in a balance', in the Egyptian manner, is not directly indicated. **4.** Both RSV and Heb. make little sense. Probably two unrelated clauses whose complements are lost. **Lamp:** so LXX; Heb. 'ploughing' more plausible. **6b. Fleeting:** lit. a 'driven vapour'. **9.** Repeated in 25:24. The **corner** may indicate a small room apart (cf. 2 Kg. 4:10; Jdt. 8:5). **12a.** Lit. 'a righteous one'; probably God (cf. Job 34:17), in view of the result. **14a. Averts:** perhaps 'covers' (*kpr* for *kph*); cf. §396*g*). **16b. The dead:** lit. 'shades'; i.e. he will suffer an early death (cf. 10:21; Ps. 55:23). **17b. Oil:** the use of it was favoured in the refined circles of the sages (27:9; Ec. 9:8). **18.** More commonly the righteous 'covers' the sins of the wicked (cf. §396*g*). **20a.** LXX: 'precious treasure will rest on the mouth of a sage'; i.e. it would be wasted on a fool; or, less probably, the fool is too loquacious to acquire such treasure. **22.** The sage is mightier than the warrior (cf. 16:32, 24:5). The Egyptian sages made similar comparisons: 'Greater is the respect of the mild man than the strong' (*Ptah-hotep*, 320 (ANET, 413); cf. *Instruction for King Men-Ka-Re*, 32 (ANET, 415)). **25.** i.e. he dies of want (cf. 19:24). **30.** Man cannot hoodwink the Lord (cf. 20:24). His purposes transcend those of men. **31** similarly underscores the finality and inscrutability of the divine decision (cf. 16:1, 2, 9, 33, 19:14, 21, 20:24; and Lord, ch. 15 *supra*).

o **XXII 1. Favour:** acceptance by men (cf. 13:15). The Heb. word, *ḥēn*, also means 'charm' and 'beauty' in Prov. (11:16, 22:11). **4a. And,** an emendation making the fear of the Lord the source of gifts cited in **b. 6a. He should go:** lit. 'in accordance with his way' which can be interpreted to mean his natural endowments (cf. Toy, op cit., 415), but more probably the way his mentors intend for him. **8b. Will fail:** plausibly, 'will smite him' (cf. BH, in loc.; Gemser, op. cit., 64); i.e. he will suffer for his own deeds. **11a.** LXX reads 'The Lord loves . . .' Following **11a** it inserts 'and his favour is to all who are blameless'. **11b** should perhaps be rendered 'gracious lips have the king's favour'. **14a. Loose woman:** lit. 'stranger' (cf. 2:16:19 *supra*).

397a **Third Section XXII 17-XXIV 22 Thirty Sayings**

This collection differs from the preceding most obviously in the fact that, for the most part, it consists of longer units and is introduced by a ten-line preface (**17-21**), similar to the First Section (cf. 1:2–6). It likewise uses the appellation 'my son' (23:15, 19, 26, 24:13, 21) for a pupil, which does not occur in the Second Section (on 19:27 cf. above). The really distinctive character of the section became apparent with the first publication of the Egyptian papyrus of *The Instruction of Amen-em-opet* by Sir Ernest A. Wallis Budge (*Facsimiles of Egyptian Hieratic Papyri in the British Museum*, Second Series (1923). This disclosed a close relationship between 22:17–23:11 and Amen-em-opet. The Egyptian document is virtually paraphrased by the Heb. writer who apparently used it as one of his sources in the compilation of an anthology of his own. This anthology reportedly consisted of **thirty sayings** (22:20), a plan which was itself adopted from the 'thirty chapters' of Amen-em-opet (ch. 30; ANET, 424). In his commentary published in 1873, Delitzsch drew attention to a break at the end of 23:11. This, as it turned out, is the point at which the compiler ended the utilisation of Amen-em-opet as his primary source. The fact that this section is directly dependent on Egyptian sources but is, nevertheless, in general spirit and content so similar to Prov. as a whole, reminds us of the strongly international character of the Wisdom Movement and should warn us against overstating the significance of apparently distinctively Israelite aspects of any part of Prov. (e.g. the use of Lord, or of the antithesis 'wicked'—'righteous'). 397a

XXII 17-21 Preface—The first three lines of ch. 1 of Amen-em-opet are followed closely in **17, 18a. Words of the wise** (**17**) should be lifted out as a superscription for the section (cf. LXX). After **hear** (**17**) add 'my words' (cf. LXX). Read 'to know' (LXX) for **my knowledge. 18b.** Read 'They are fixed as a peg on thy lips' (cf. Amen-em-opet, ch. 1, line 8), to stress the virtue of restraint and self-control in speech. **19b.** For **even to you:** 'His ways' (cf. LXX[NA]); in Egyptian wisdom 'the way of God' corresponds to 'the fear of God' (cf. 8:32). On **thirty** (**20**) cf. Amen-em-opet, ch. 30. The word **written** occurs only here in Prov.; it must be related to the compiler's dependence on Egyptian and possibly other documents and points to the likelihood that collections of wisdom had a separate existence as documents. How one arrives at thirty sayings is disputed. Is 23:12 a 'saying'? Or should it be combined with **13f.**? Similarly 23:19 and **20f.**? Are 24:8f. one or two 'sayings'? Should this Preface count as one of the thirty as a similar introduction in Amen-em-opet does? It is probably impossible to give a definite answer to such questions. b

22-23 The Poor—Cf. Amen-em-opet, ch. 2. The emphasis upon the Lord as the avenger of the poor is typical of OT (Exod. 22:21–4).

24-25 The 'hot' Man—Cf. Amen-em-opet, ch. 9, and note 14:29 *supra*.

26-27 Suretyships—Cf. 6:1ff. No parallel in Amen-em-opet. **why** rests on a dittograph in Heb. Read 'your bed will be taken from under you'.

28 The Landmark—Cf. 23:10f.; Dt. 19:14; Amen-em-opet, ch. 6.

29 The 'ready scribe'—Cf. Ps. 45:2; Ezek. 7:6; Amen-em-opet, ch. 30; **stand before kings:** i.e. be in their employ. **c** is probably an explanatory gloss.

XXIII 1-3 Table Manners—Cf. Amen-em-opet, ch. 23; also, Ptah-hotep, 'Thou shouldst gaze at what is before thee' (ANET, 412); Sir. 31:12–33:13 indicates the growth of interest in the matter in Israel's later Wisdom Movement. **3a = 6b.** It is difficult to determine whether self-control or suspicion of the host provides the motive for the instruction; W. O. E. Oesterley (*Book of Proverbs* (1929), 199) cites *Pirkē Abôth* 2:3 in support of the latter view. c

4-5 Transiency of Riches—Cf. 'Wealth', ch. 19 *supra*; Amen-em-opet, ch. 9. The Egyptian and Hebrew view agree closely, but the purpose of the Lord, with all its mystery, displaces Egyptian 'Fate and Fortune'. In **flying like an eagle** Heb. sage has substituted for 'geese' of Amen-em-opet.

6-8 The Calculating Host—These lines are related to ch. 11 of Amen-em-opet but its concentration on the attitude of a **stingy** (or 'evil intentioned') host is distinct. The Heb. text is very difficult. **6a.** omitting **bread,** read 'Do not eat with a man of evil purpose' (lit. 'evil eye'). **7a.** Probably 'For it is like a storm in his throat (soul) and like bitterness in his gullet' (cf. Amen-em-opet, ch. 11, and Oesterley, op. cit., 201).

9 Silence before a Fool—Cf. Amen-em-opet, ch. 21: 'Spread not thy words . . .'; Prov. 9:7. d

10-11 The Landmark—Cf. 22:28; on basis of Amen-em-opet, ch. 6, **ancient** (*'ôlām*) should perhaps be read as 'widow' (*'almānāh*). Close dependence upon Amen-em-opet ends here.

12. Cf. 17:22.

13-14 Discipline—Cf. 13:24, 19:18, 22:15; Words of Aḥikar: 'If I smite thee, my son, thou wilt not die . . .' (Aram. version 82; ANET, 428).

15-16 A Wise Son—Cf. 10:1*a*.

397d **17-18 Fear of the Lord**—Zeal for God rather than envy of the wicked is basis for hope. **18a.** Read LXX, ' If you guard it **surely** . . .'
20-21 Gluttony and Drunkenness—Cf. Dt. 21:20 ; vv. **29ff.**
22-25 Filial Piety—V. **23** is probably extraneous to this unit.
26-28 The Strange Woman—Heb. has *zônāh* for ' harlot ', but LXX reads ' stranger ' (*zārāh*, cf. 2:16–19 *supra*) ; Heb. for **adventuress :** ' foreigner ' (2:16).
29-35 The Drunkard—A six-fold rhetorical question introduces this warning against drunkenness. **30.** ' Mixed wine ', lit. a drink or libation produced by mixing (cf. Isa. 65:11). **31c** is related to Ca. 7:10 (9) ; it should probably be excised ; otherwise its parallel, ' gliding over lips and teeth ', should be added (Gemser, op. cit., 68). The description of the inebriate's stupor (**33-5**) is highly realistic, heightened by use of second person. **34b.** LXX, ' Like a steersman in a great storm ', seems more probable. **35.** The words of the drunkard and on regaining consciousness.
e **XXIV 1-2.** Avoid evil companions, cf. 23:17f. ; Ps. 1:1.
3-7 The Vitality of Wisdom—These verses may have been intended as two separate units (**3-4, 5-7**) but there is a continuous theme : all accomplishment is by wisdom. The **house** is symbolic of the goal of a creative enterprise, here a human activity (cf. 3:19, 8:21, 14:1). Cf. 16:23, 21:22 on v. **5.** The nautical term, ' tactics ', is given as **wise guidance.** LXX for **6a,** ' war is made by tactics ' ; brains, rather than brawn, are important.
8-9. The devising of folly : probably the ' scheme of a fool ' ; in Prov. the word ' devise ' (*zimmāh*) invariably has an evil meaning. Note strong term, **abomination,** applied to **scoffer** (cf. 9:7f. *supra*).
10-12 Moral Courage—**Faint,** relax (cf. 18:9) ; i.e. do nothing to help in the **adversity** which strikes one's neighbours. **11b.** Read ' Do not hold yourself back from ' for **hold back** (cf. LXX) ; those to be reserved are probably victims of social and moral injustice (7:22, 9:18, 14:25). The excuse of ignorance of what was happening is rejected, either because it is untrue, or, if true, because it shows a lack of responsibility. God, who protects the one who failed to help, knows it ; so should he. The profundity and nobility of this unit is impressive.
f **13-14.** Honey as a symbol for wisdom (cf. 2:10, 16:24). **14a** gives Heb. text as it now stands ; authorities agree this is an abbreviation of the original (cf. Gemser, op. cit., 68 : ' so knowledge is sweet to your heart and wisdom good for your soul ').
15-16. The security of the righteous should deter one from attacking them. **In 15a, as a wicked man** is a redundancy that may be excised as a gloss. The words for **dwelling, home** refer to a shepherd's abode and a place of sleeping respectively.
17-18. The notion, still prevalent in the Near East, that God will take away from man what he delights in most, seems to be operative in this unit ; to rejoice at an enemy's discomfiture may cause God to turn **his anger from him.** There may be the implication that it will then strike those who were too gleeful.
19-20. Evil has no future (cf. 1, 13:9, 14). Statements such as this seem to indicate that the issues raised in Job and Ec. are already latent.
21-22. Cf. ' King ', ch. 20 *supra.* By using the LXX reading for **22b** it becomes necessary to interpret **from them** as referring to the punitive action of God and king. The Heb. is ' their disaster ' and refers to **disaster** that may befall those with whom one is told not to associate (cf. RSV*n*).
g **23-25 A Supplement**—Similar to Third Section in style. V. **23** shows they were added to **Thirty Sayings.** **23-26. Partiality :** lit. ' paying attention to faces ' (cf. 10:34, 28:21). **26.** A **right answer** : i.e. tells the truth. **kisses the lips :** i.e. like a true friend. **27. For you** (Heb. *lākh*) should probably be pointed to read ' go ' and introduce **b :** i.e. ' go thereafter and build your house ' ; meaning, found a family. 397g
30-34 The Sluggard's Field—Cf. §395*g*. The precept is recast as a personal experience and becomes a parable (cf. 1 Kg. 4:33).

XXV-XXIX Fourth Section 398a

The title of this section offers the best evidence for the view that the Wisdom Movement in Israel, beginning with Solomon, constitutes a long process with a continuous history (see §391). R. B. Y. Scott (' Solomon and the Beginnings of Wisdom ', VT *Supplements*, III, 262ff.) takes the view that in the era of Hezekiah Israel's sages began their first real interchange with the legacy of wisdom in Egypt. The section has two parts, 25:2–27:22 and 28:1–29:33, separated by a discourse on a grazing economy (27:23–7).
First Part—The sayings consist of couplets and b
quatrains, some of which are combined to treat a selected topic. The antithetic parallelism, so common in chs. 10–15, is rare.
XXV 2-7b. About kings. Two couplets (**2, 3**) and two quatrains (**4f., 6f.**). **4b. Material :** this word is introduced by RSV because refining *per se* does not produce a vessel (but cf. Exod. 32:24). Read ' and the smith brings forth a vessel '. LXX, ' and it will be wholly purified ', is too tautological and destroys analogy in **5b.** The word ' king ' rather than any continuing idea holds the units together (on ' King ', cf. ch. 20 *supra*).
7c-10. As it stands this unit cautions against public legal suits, a common feature of later Judaism as well as in NT (Mt. 5:25). It is possible, however, that **court** should be read ' multitude ' ; a warning to a young nobleman against gossiping to the masses (cf. Amen-em-opet, ch. 24) ; but **9f.** makes this unlikely.
11-12. Two couplets united by **gold** and by relating the word in ' its circumstance ' (**fitly**) to the speech of the wise reprover. The setting of silver probably refers to an ' engraved ' (Num. 33:52) receptacle.
13-14. Cold : plural ' coolnesses ' ; probably refer- c
ring to snow-fed mountain streams. In sharp contrast, to describe the boaster, the promising clouds that give no rain. **13c** may be a gloss.
15-20. Unrelated couplets : some stand together because of identical words (cf., e.g., **16f.,** ' lest you be sated ' and ' lest he become weary '). **19.** Omit **trust in** ; read ' like ' **a faithless man . . . 20a,** a dittograph for **19b.** Omit and compare **a** to **c** as given in RSV. LXX has additional couplet : ' as moth a garment and worm wood, so distress mars the spirit of a man '.
21-22. Bread and **water** are lacking in LXX and are not needed. The Lord rewards the placating of an enemy (cf. Rom. 12:20f.).
23-24. Cf. 19:13, 21:9.
26. The ' slipping ' (Heb. *māṭ*) of the righteous man may refer to his being overpowered by the wicked. More probably, however, what is here meant is his yielding to the temptations they present (cf. Oesterley, op. cit., 229, and Ps. 17:5).
27. Cf. v. **16.** RSV has wisely chosen LXX reading (cf. footnote in loc.).
28. On self-control, cf. ch. 14.
XXVI 1-12 Portrait of a Fool—A series of eleven d
couplets, broken by v. **2,** dealing with the fool but not interrelated by an organic theme. V. **1** is one of the frequent metaphors in Prov. with a rural flavour (cf. 25:13).
2. A curse that is causeless : the saying refutes the widely held view that merely by its utterance a curse was effective. For a similar view cf. ' What men's lips curse God does not curse ' (Words of Aḥiḳar, 151 ; ANET, 429 ; cf. also Num. 23:8). **3.** Cf. 14:3, 22:15. The possibility of a fool becoming wise is left open ; in any case, the beating has exemplary value (cf. 19:25, 21:11). **4, 5.** Two sayings about answering the fool

398d paradoxically related to each other (cf. Sir. 13:10). The wise are consistent in refusing to treat with fools on their own level ; on the other hand, they are bound to refute them and refute their foolishness. Both aspects are here brought together. **6.** Much depends on a messenger for he bears an oral communication (cf. 13:17, 25:13). **7.** i.e. the fool's ability to repeat a saying does him no more good than a lame man's legs. **8.** A stone must be laid in a sling, not *bound.* **9.** Cf. v. **7** ; not a thorn piercing the palm ; but, probably, a cone from a thorn bush, ludicrous in hand of a drunken man. **12.** Ironical relief for the fool !

e **13-16 Portrait of a Sluggard**—Four independent couplets (cf. 6:6–11, 24:30–4). **13.** A variant of 22:13. **14.** The net effect of the motion of both is to leave things unchanged (cf. 6:9f.) ! **15.** Cf. 19:24. **16.** Cf. v. **12** ; lack of discernment is the greatest price claimed by sloth.

17-28. Abuses of Speech (cf. ch. 11 *supra*)—**17.** For ears, LXX has ' tail ' ; **passing** can be deleted. **18f.** To deceive one's neighbour, even in jest, is to play with his confidence : a ' practical joker ' who lacks sensitiveness and taste offends. **20f.** On slander, cf. 10:18, 11:13, 16:28, 18:8, 20:19 (cf. Sir. 28:10ff., which seems to combine elements from both couplets). Instead of **charcoal,** LXX has ' bellows ' (cf. Sir. 8:3 ; Jas 3:5f.). **22.** Cf. 18:8. **23.** ' Silver plated clay ' as a metaphor for insincerity. **24-6.** RSV apparently follows suggestion of BH to read **dissembles with his lips** (lit. ' tries to act like a stranger ') instead of ' dissembles himself ' (i.e. hides his real intentions) of Heb. text ; **25f.**, however, would seem to favour latter. **28a. Hates its victims :** LXX, ' hates truth '. Gemser (op. cit., 74) emends to ' hates its owner ' ; i.e. hurts the one who uses it, which continues the pattern of **27.**

f **XXVII 1-22.** Various aphorisms ; couplets, except for **15f.**

1. Do not boast : i.e. about what you will be or do. Uncertainty about human life and the future often carries a sombre note (cf. Isa. 56:12 ; Sir. 18:25f. ; Lk. 12:16–21 ; Jas 4:13ff.). In Amen-em-opet (xix, 10) we find the thought that the future may bring improvement : ' Do not spend the night fearful of tomorrow. At daybreak what is the morrow like ' (cf. Mt. 6:34 ; Lk. 12:22ff.). **2. Another . . . a stranger :** outsider and foreigner (*zār, nokhrî* ; cf. 2:16) ; here, one disinterested. **3.** Cf. Sir. 22:15. **5.** BH proposes ' enmity ' for **love** ; not necessary. An ironical comment on **love** that fails to express itself in any action, whether of praise or blame. **6b. profuse :** Toy (op. cit., 483) suggests ' perverse ' ; Gemser (op. cit., 75), ' crooked '. **8.** The word for **strays** often has meaning of a fugitive's flight ; **home:** lit. ' his place '. The saying seeks to evoke a deplorable picture. **9a. perfume :** the word also means incense (Ca. 3:6) ; for **b**, the LXX reading used by RSV has little meaning in relation to **a**, but all improvements require radical emendation ; Toy (op. cit., 485) suggests ' sweetness of counsel strengthens a soul '. **10.** Cf. 17:17 ; **b** is extraneous to **a, c. 11.** Cf. 23:15 ; Ps. 119:41f. The reproach may concern the pupil's ability. **12.** Cf. 22:3. **13.** Cf. 20:16 ; the point in **a** seems to be that the pledge to a stranger is no basis for excuses (cf. Dt. 24:10–13 ; Am. 2:8). **14c.** Lit. ' It will be counted to him as cursing ' ; i.e. because he makes a show of it. **b** can be omitted. **15f.** Cf. 19:13 ; point of **16** is that the woman's way will never change. **17b.** Lit. ' sharpens the face of his companion ' ; i.e. influences his behaviour (cf. 13:20). **19b.** RSV stresses the notion that in heart a man can discover his real nature ; included also is the notion that a man's mind is the source of another man's knowledge of him. **20.** Cf. 30:15f. ; the eye is the seat of desire (Job 31:1 ; Ec. 1:8, 2:10, 4:8 ; 1 Jn 2:16). **21b. His praise :** what men say about him (cf. LXX). **22.** Omit **b.**

g **23-27 The Economy of the Herdsman**—Cf. Isa. 28:23–9 for an analogous poem on agriculture. In **24b** the negative particle should probably take the place of the interrogative (cf. LXX) ; and for **crown** read ' treasure ', synonymous with **riches** in **a** ; viz. ' nor is there treasure from generation to generation '. **27b** can be omitted (cf. LXX).

h **Second Part XXVIIIf.**—These two chapters consist mostly of couplets, predominantly in the antithetic style typical of chs. 10ff.

XXVIII 1. Wicked and **righteous** both appear in singular in LXX. **2a** follows MT text ; reminiscent of Northern Kingdom of Israel (Hos. 7:16, 8:4). LXX : ' Through the sins of the wicked quarrels arise '. Reconstruction of **b** with aid of Gk. : ' but a perspicacious man extinguishes them '. **3a.** LXX has ' wicked ' for **poor** (*rāshā'* for *rāsh*). **4.** Their apostasy itself constitutes the ' praise '. **Law :** i.e. *tôrāh*, the words of parents and teachers (vv. **7, 9**), which may, however, include the laws of the covenant (cf. 28:18). **5a. Evil men :** perhaps ' men of evil ' (*rōa'*) ; i.e. evil by nature. **6.** Cf. ' Poverty ', ch. 14 *supra.* **7.** Makes specific the call to honour parents (cf. 10:1, 23:20, 27:11, 29:3) ; Words of Aḥiḳar, ' My son has been a false witness against me ' (138 ; ANET, 429). **8.** On **interest**, cf. Exod. 22:25 ; Dt. 23:19f. ; Ps. 15:5. **9.** Religious sanctions are applied to the pupils of the wise. **10.** Cf. 26:27. **c** is probably not originally **a** part of this saying, but remnant of another (cf. LXX). **12.** Cf. 29:2. **13.** Repentance through confession of sin and amendment of life as the condition for divine mercy is typical of OT (cf. Ps. 32:3–5 ; Isa. 1:16–18 ; Hos. 14:2–4). The assumption that the confession here is made to God and that mercy is shown by him is not unshakeable inasmuch as Prov. has no other references to mercy (cf. §396*g*). **14. Fears :** lit. ' dreads ', ' lives in awe ' (*m^ephaḥēdh*) ; Lord does not occur in text, but **b** furthers the view that the implied reference is to God. **17.** Cf. 13:21. **19.** Cf. 12:11 ; Amen-em-opet, viii, 17f., ' Plow in the fields that thou mayest find thy needs, that thou mayest receive bread of thy own threshing floor '. **20. Hastens :** i.e. procures riches by evil means ; hence, punishable (cf. 11:21, 16:5, 17:5, 19:5, 9). **22. Miserly :** lit. ' evil of eye ' ; i.e. with evil intent. But cf. 22:9, 23:6. **24. Or his mother** may be an addition. **28.** Cf. v. **12.**

i **XXIX 1b.** Cf. Dt. 10:16 ; Jer. 7:26, 17:23, 19:15 for this metaphor for stubbornness. **2a.** MT text : ' When righteous increase ' ; RSV emendation is justified by parallelism (*bir^edhôth* for *bir^ebhôth*). **4b. Gifts :** unlike 19:6, the Heb. word here is *t^erûmôth*, normally used for cultic offerings. For parallel with **a** it should probably be emended as *tarmîth*, ' treachery '. **8a. Aflame** refers to the incitement of turbulence. **9.** Avoid arguments with a fool ; they settle nothing ; the verse is a further application of the general principle in Prov. that one must avoid dealing with fools on a common level. **10b.** Instead of reading **wicked** for ' upright ' (RSV) Gemser (op. cit., 78) proposes ' seek out ' (*y^ebhaḳ^erû*) for **seek** (*y^ebhaḳ^eshû*) ; i.e. the upright seek out the blameless for their mutual good (cf. Ezek. 34:11). **11.** Cf. §395*j*. **12.** Cf. Sir. 10:2. **13.** Cf. 22:2 ; **the Lord gives light** ; i.e. the righteous will outlast them. **18.** Prophecy : misleading ; the word is ' vision ' (*ḥāzôn*) and, along with ' word ' and ' utterance ', is used of prophetic oracles. It is probably more closely related than either of the others to general notions of cultic divination, including dream visions, in which the self-conscious participation of the agent in the oracle is recessive. Perhaps for this reason it is prominent in Dan. ; cf. also Job 4:13, 7:14, 33:15 ; Ps. 89:19 ; Mic. 3:6. Here the term can be identified with Israel's prophecy no more closely than law (**b**) should be with the Code of the Covenant. **21b.** Dubious : LXX, ' he who lives in luxury from childhood will be a servant, and in the end will come to grief '. **24b.** Cf. Lev. 5:1 ; Jg. 17:1–4. **Partner** (*hôlēḳ*), one who shares in the loot. Since he does not confess the effect of the curse will fall

98i upon him. **26.** Cf. ' as for justice, the great reward of god ' (Amen-em-opet, ch. 20).

9a **Fifth Section XXX-XXXI Four Appendices**
This section consists of four independent units or collections : (1) The Words of Agur (30:1–14) ; (2) Numerical Sayings (30:15–33) ; (3) The Instruction of Lemuel (31:1–9) ; and (4) An Acrostic on the Virtuous Wife (31:10–31). The first two of these are apparently composite ; the others, unitary.

b **XXX 1-14 The Words of Agur**—The best defence for so delimiting this appendix is the fact that this much of ch. 30 stands by itself in the LXX, before 24:23ff. There is no evidence of a single theme. The form of the piece is oracular, similar to the oracles of Balaam (cf. especially Num. 24:3ff., 15ff.) ; but its spirit and substance stand close to the book of Job, notably to the speeches of Job and the Lord and to ch. 28.

c **1. Massa :** if a proper name, points to non-Israelite aspects (Gen. 25:14). Agur and Jakeh do not occur as proper names in Israel, though their discovery in Sabaean-Minaean inscriptions is reported. Beginning with the Lat. version there has been a persistent tendency to render the names as common nouns. Saadia was the first to read the Heb. for Massa as *māshāl*. The fact that this term occupies an analogous location in the oracles of Balaam speaks in its favour. For **b,** LXX has ' these things says the man to those who trust in God and I cease ', which also eliminates proper names. Ever since Cocceius, attempts have been made to emend and read the Heb. text itself on this principle ; following this tradition, Gemser (op. cit., 78) offers ' oracle of the man who wearied himself with God, wearied himself and triumphed ' (cf. Gen. 32:25). A fully satisfactory solution seems impossible. **2f. Surely :** perhaps ' when ', followed by LXX for **3a,** ' Then God taught me ' ; i.e. the point may be that when he was **too stupid to be a man** God taught him. **4.** Cf. Job 26:8 ; Isa. 40:12ff. ; Am. 4:13. **5.** Cf. Dt. 12:32 ; Ps. 18:30. **7-9.** On **8c** cf. Mt. 6:11 ; Lk. 11:3. **11-14.** There are those : lit. ' a generation ' (cf. Mt. 11:16 et al. in Synoptic Gospels) ; four deadly sins : filial disrespect, hypocrisy, pride, cruelty.

d **15-33 Numerical Sayings**—Vv. **17, 20** are exceptions. **15a** is misplaced here, perhaps a remnant of a lost *saying*. **17.** Cf. Gen. 9:20–7. **18f.** Awe before the ' mysteries ' of natural process. For **the high seas** Heb. idiom has ' the heart of the sea '. **21-3.** The four examples seem to sum up the sages' distaste for the arrogance of the *nouveaux riches*. **24-8.** On the **ant** cf. 6:6–8. The small **lizard** is still frequently found in the interior of houses in Iraq : a quick creature, it runs up walls and along joists, and is quite harmless.

XXXI 1-9. The Instruction of Lemuel—That the Heb. for Massa must be interpreted as a tribal or place name (cf. 30:1) is here reinforced by the fact that the words are described as the teaching of his mother (cf. 1:8). Lemuel may be thought of as a chieftain of NW. Arabia, probably in the region near Edom ; ' the sons of the east ' were as famous for wisdom as Egypt (cf. 1 Kg. 5:10 (4:30)). Teman and the land of Job are also in the region of Edom (Job 2:11, 5:10, 18f. ; Jer. 49:7 ; Lam. 4:21). The genealogies in Kg. regularly cite the name of the king's mother ; her role at court was one of great influence. **2a. My vows :** cf. 1 Sam. 1:11. **3.** In oriental history, throughout, the harem is the cause of effeminacy and dissoluteness ; women destroy the king's prowess as a warrior (cf. Dt. 17:17 ; Sir. 47:12–22, on Solomon). **4-7.** Wine is for convicts at their execution (Mk 15:23), to dull their pain ; and for the poor, to bear their troubles. Kings must have clear minds, to maintain power and to judge for the poor and helpless (cf. Ps. 72 ; and §396*m*). 399e

10-31 An Acrostic on the Virtuous Wife—The acrostic is quite common in Heb. poetry (cf. Ps. 9–10, 25, 34, 37, 111, 112, 119, 145 ; Lam. 1–4 ; Nah. 1:2–10). The good wife is here defined in terms of her role as ' home-economist '. Initiative, inventive ingenuity, and industry characterise her life as a far-sighted manager. In her function as householder she claims a degree of independence consonant with her capabilities (cf. v. **11**). It is to be noted that this sort of career is praised in the context of a society in which the *individual* legal rights of a wife were very slight ; she is, therefore, presented as motivated by eagerness for the ' name ' and reputation of her husband and family (cf. vv. **12, 21, 23, 28, 31**) rather than by a desire for ' personal self-realisation ' (cf. §396*i*). **21b. Scarlet :** perhaps ' double ' (*sh*^{e}*nāyim* for *shānîm*) ; scarlet was for royalty or the very rich (2 Sam. 1:24 ; Jer. 4:30). **31b. in the gates :** where her husband and sons display them or speak about them. f

Bibliography—Commentaries : B. Gemser, HAT (1937) ; C. T. Fritsch, IB iv (1955) ; W. O. E. Oesterley, WC (1929) ; T. T. Perowne, CB (1899) ; J. van der Ploeg, *De Boeken van het OT* (1952) ; C. H. Toy, ICC (1899) ; H. Wiesmann, HSATes (1923).

Other Literature : W. Baumgartner, ' Wisdom Literature ', OTMS (1951) ; G. Boström, *Proverbia-studien* (1935) ; P. Humbert, *Recherches sur les sources égyptiennes de la littérature sapientiale d'Israël* (1929) ; M. Noth and D. W. Thomas, eds., *Wisdom in Israel and in the Ancient Near East* (VT *Supplement* III) (1955) ; H. Ranston, *OT Wisdom Books* (1930) ; J. C. Rylaarsdam, *Revelation in Jewish Wisdom Literature* (1946).

ECCLESIASTES

By E. T. RYDER

400a **Title**—The name 'Ecclesiastes' derives by way of the Vulg. from the Gr. Ἐκκλησιαστής as found in the LXX, and is an interpretation of the Heb. *ḳōheleth*, a feminine singular participial form, peculiar to Ec., which is connected with the noun *ḳāhāl*, 'assembly'. Its precise connotation remains a problem. H. L. Ginsberg's proposal that it is a misrendering in Heb. of the Aram. *ḳāhlā'*, 'the Convoker', rests on the theory of an Aram. original for Ec. (see §401*b*). The more usual explanations of the term follow the line that it refers *either* to one who takes part in or addresses an assembly, hence Jer. *concionator*, EVV : preacher, E. H. Plumptre : debater, *or* to one who for purposes of instruction gathers people together in an assembly or collects sayings in the sense of persons 'represented by their opinions' (A. L. Williams, H. Ranston). The occurrence of *ḳôheleth* with the Art. at 12:8 (cf. 7:27, emended text) would suggest its being a designation rather than a proper name ; and the otherwise incongruous feminine termination would further support its being a title (GK, 122*qr*), possibly intensive in force (W. Wright, *Arabic Grammar*[3], 233 Rem.*c*), and thereby indicating pre-eminence (cf. RVm 'the great orator') rather than, according to some, its standing for the feminine *ḥokhmāh*, 'wisdom', whether personified (cf. Prov. 8f.) or as represented by Solomon. Such considerations together with other data in the book (cf. 12:9f.) serve to portray Koheleth as one who assembled and conducted his classes with great distinction, imparting to them as also to a wider public (whom he sought to reach by his attractiveness, yet withal integrity, as a writer) practical wisdom carefully selected and arranged from the gnomic sources available to him.

b **Authorship**—The superscription (1:1) identifies Koheleth with Solomon (cf. also 1:12, 2:4–10). That this is fictive is suggested (*a*) by 1 Kg. 8:1 where the use of the verb *ḳāhal*, 'assemble', in connection with Solomon may have prompted the term *ḳōheleth* ; (*b*) by literary convention in OT Wisdom books (cf. Prov., Ca., in which, however, unlike Ec., the name of Solomon is actually used) ; and (*c*) by comparison with Egyptian formal types where royal authorship is similarly assumed (cf. P. Humbert). Moreover it is mostly admitted that Solomon could not have been the author of Ec. on grounds of content, treatment, and language which all indicate a period not earlier than the Hellenistic age. The author also, incongruously for Solomon, refers to a number of royal predecessors in Jerusalem (1:16, 2:9), writes in the vein of subject rather than of ruler (3:16, 4:1), hints at anarchy in the contemporary scene (4:13–16, 10:16–20), and in the epilogue (12:9–14) is not referred to as a king. F. Dornseiff has argued that the book was pseudepigraphically written as an address by Solomon from beyond the grave.

Unity—The presence in Ec. of contradictions, inconsistencies, and sudden changes of subject has given rise to widely differing opinion regarding its structure and unity.

c 1. Those who consider it a single literary entity, in its entirety (e.g. C. Cornill, G. Wildeboer) or with some editorial modification (e.g. A. L. Williams, H. Odeberg, H. Ranston, H. W. Hertzberg), variously explain its disorder and incoherence as being due to **40**
such factors as : Koheleth's changing moods with their alternation of doubt and faith, or the presence of dialectic whether in monologue or dialogue form, or displacement of sheets of the original work, or death preventing the author from making systematic disposal of his material.

2. Of those who have denied the unity of the book **d**
the most thorough-going was C. Siegfried who discerned in it an initial composition in pessimistic vein 'divorced from Judaism and influenced mainly by Stoicism' which was subsequently and successively worked over by eight other hands. Although this analysis was too radical to gain acceptance, A. H. McNeile, variously followed by G. A. Barton and E. Podechard, assigned about a fourth of the verses in Ec. to two different glossators, a *ḥākhām* (i.e. a wise man who contributed proverbial material in support of wisdom, e.g. 4:5, 9–12, 9:17–10:3) and a *ḥāsîdh* (i.e. a devout Jew concerned for the orthodox doctrine of retribution, e.g. 2:26*ab*, 8:2*b*, 3*ab*, 5, 6*a*, 11–13).

3. Differently, K. Galling, subjecting Ec. to formal **e**
analysis, discerned in it, excluding the epilogues (12:9–11, 12–14), thirty-seven independent poetical sentences of varying length. He thus conceived of Koheleth both as a poet who composed each unit quite unrelatedly and as his own editor who assembled his poems without any progressive thematic arrangement. Accordingly Ec. has, as it were, an autobiographic unity, being a sort of scrap-book collection of contradictory meditations on identical themes and taking in quotations from the lore of the wise for purposes of comment and refutation.

4. It has also been urged that the solution to the **f**
literary problem of Ec. lies along ideological lines. The fact that the book is unique in the OT for the blending in it of a religious with a secular outlook would account for its manifest contradictions, and since it is therefore a psychological unity there is no need to look for interpolations. Such a view based on more recent study of Koheleth's characteristic ideas and terminology is in varying degree apparent in the writings, for example, of J.-H. Blieffert and H. L. Ginsberg, and of R. Gordis who contends that 'the book emerges as a literary unit, the spiritual testament of a single, complex, richly endowed personality'.

5. Each of the above methods of approach has **g**
contributed to a truer appraisal of the structure and character of Ec., and from consideration of them the following points may be noted : (*a*) The impress of a strongly individualistic mind imparts an overall unity to the book which presents a loosely connected account of Koheleth's wisdom. (*b*) In it the oscillation between an inherited religious faith and a spirit of critical inquiry which may owe much to environmental factors tends to conflict and contradiction. (*c*) The teaching as recorded not only exhibits this but also is in keeping with the pedagogic method of the time. Thus as a unit of instruction the poetical sentence is employed, varying in length according to the theme and intention of the author. It need not be linked with what precedes or with what follows, but, when it is, connection may be effected by, e.g., a mnemonic device quite as legitimately as by a logical sequence.

400g (*d*) Whilst conceding this, however, a certain amount of interpolative editorial activity should not be discounted. On a cautious estimate this would include beside the superscription (1:1) and epilogues (12:9–11, 12–14) possibly such expressions of orthodox sentiment as 3:17, 8:11–13, 11:9*c*, 12:1*a*. The recent discovery of a Koheleth scroll from Qumrân (4QKoh), which, although fragmentary, according to J. Muilenburg supports the literary order of our present book and is reckoned to be not later than 150 B.C. (see §401*c*), would appear to reduce the margin of time previously thought possible for editorial activity and rearrangement of the material, and to that extent diminishes the likelihood of any considerable alteration to the author's original draft. Two recent attempts to discover a plan in Ec. may be noted: (1) H. L. Ginsberg discerns four main divisions in 1:2–12:8: (A) 1:2–2:26—All is zero (vanity) and man's only plus (profit) is in using his goods, (B) 3:1–4:3—All happenings are foreordained, but never fully foreseeable, (A^1) 4:4–6:9 and (B^1) 6:10–12:8 are complementary to A and B. (2) O. S. Rankin proposes a threefold arrangement: (*a*) 1:2–4:3—Koheleth's world outlook, (*b*) 4:4–9:16—The wise man's response to life's contingencies, (*c*) 10:4–12:7—Koheleth's final words to his disciples.

h **Thought**—The essential thought of Ec. has been most diversely assessed. H. Odeberg, e.g., as against J. Pedersen who impressively demonstrated Koheleth's scepticism, described Koheleth's aim as being to induce a desire for and participation in the better life, by exposing in no uncertain terms the vacuity and unreality of man's ordinary life in the world. 1. There is little doubt that Koheleth's teaching is away from the central OT emphasis on personal religion. Nowhere is the name Yahweh employed, and the idea of the hand of God at work in the history of his people, and with it the Messianic hope, is absent from the book. Unlike the prophet who makes known the divine word and the psalmist who praises God for his wonders in creation, Koheleth in his rationalism seeks through wisdom to understand the nature of reality (e.g. 1:13, 7:23ff., 8:16ff.) and views natural processes as one oppressed by their mechanical and monotonous regularity (1:5ff.). Sharing with the author of Job (e.g. 38ff.) the thought of God's transcendence, he travels much farther in the direction of a thoroughgoing determinism (e.g. 1:9, 6:10, 7:13). His teaching concerning contraries or opposites (3:1–9) underlines his fatalism with its limitation of man's freedom (3:11, 15). 2. Regarding man's life, Koheleth's thought is clouded over by the certainty of Sheol beyond which he cannot see (e.g. 3:19–21, 9:4ff., 10). Obsessed by the inevitability of death and the darkness of the grave, he focuses attention on the enjoyment of life so long as it is granted and rejoices in the light of the sun (e.g. 11:7–9). The possession of life's goods and the capacity to enjoy them are the gift of God (e.g. 2:24f., 3:13, 8:15). Even so, no satisfaction is to be won in any sphere of human activity—material, intellectual, or moral (e.g. 2:4–11, 8:16ff., 9:2). Herein consist his fatalism and pessimism, having their roots in his determinism, which all underlie his indictment of life as illusory and meaningless, on the note of which Koheleth's teaching begins and ends (1:2, 12:8). 3. A distinction appears to be made between theoretical and practical wisdom. On the one hand, the recognition of wisdom as inadequate for understanding life's meaning and the divine purpose leads to agnosticism (8:16f., with which contrast Job 28, especially v. 28). On the other hand, wisdom has a limited value for the conduct of daily life (e.g. 2:13f., 9:13–16), and notably in regard to the avoidance of extremes (e.g. 7:16, 8:2–6). 4. The value of Koheleth's teaching is generally seen as negative rather than positive. Without any hope in the triumph of righteousness in this world or of compensation for its injustices in the hereafter he does not share the virile optimism of the OT and NT, yet in his forthright pessimism he takes with them a
realistic view of the problem of mortality and suffering, **400h**
demonstrating the need for the hope realised only in the gospel of Christ. Because for him the mystery of life is dark, the urgency of the present is great—an important emphasis (cf. Eph. 5:16), although for Koheleth it involved divorcing the present from the past and future. By turning away from those values (ready to hand in Israel's faith) which alone lead to a true knowledge of God, Koheleth testifies to the bankruptcy of an intellectual quest which is limited to material ends.

Affinities and Influences—1. Jewish. (*a*) It has been **401a**
generally held that Ec. was known to and used by Ben Sira (*c.* 180 B.C.) on account of correspondences between Sir. and Ec. in language and thought, where of the two Koheleth shows originality; and although the priority of Ec. has been denied by R. H. Pfeiffer, and the matter is regarded as still open by C. C. Forman, the evidence of 4QKoh (see §400*g*) as to date would appear to support the majority view. (*b*) In Wis. (*c.* 100–50 B.C.), especially 2:1–9 (which should here be considered in the larger context of 1:16–2:11), whilst most commentators have perceived a deliberate rebuttal of Koheleth's denial of a future life and his advocacy of present enjoyment, a small number (e.g. J. A. F. Gregg, E. Podechard, A. L. Williams) regard this polemic as inapplicable to the teaching of Ec. (*c*) Koheleth's affinities with the Pharisees, Sadducees, and Essenes have been discussed (e.g. by E. Podechard, H. Odeberg) but without any firm conclusions. In this connection the fact that Ec. was in use at Qumrân—in the traditions of which there appear to have been heterodox elements and of which the community according to the majority of scholars was Essene, although C. Rabin has put up a case for its having been Pharisaic—may prove significant. 2. Foreign. (*a*) Similarities to Greek thought in Ec. have suggested indebtedness on Koheleth's part to Heraclitus (e.g. O. Pfleiderer) or to Aristotle, Zeno, and Epicurus (e.g. T. Tyler, cf. also E. H. Plumptre), but this has been otherwise explained or else discounted (e.g. G. A. Barton), A. Lods pertinently observing that 'the Jewish sage does not move in a world of abstract principles, but in the world of everyday occurrences'. H. Ranston examined the possibility of a connection with early Greek Wisdom literature, and concluded that Koheleth, as a result of contact with those well versed in such material, employed Theognis as the main source of his foreign aphorisms. Whilst H. W. Hertzberg would concede at least an indirect knowledge of Theognis to Koheleth, K. Galling is not convinced by the parallels adduced, J. Pedersen is sceptical of any direct Greek influence, and C. C. Forman pronounces H. Ranston's findings 'untenable'. (*b*) Parallels to Ec. have also been sought in other literary sources of the ancient Near East. Thus, e.g., S. Langdon considered that the cycle of Babylonian Wisdom literature to which the *Dialogue of Pessimism* (9th cent. B.C. or earlier) belonged influenced Koheleth's thought, and G. A. Barton noted a similar indebtedness in 9:7–9 to the *Gilgamesh Epic* (*c.* 2000 B.C.). Likewise in the matter of Egyptian gnomic sources P. Humbert pointed to resemblances of form and content apparent in Ec. which are indicative of borrowing, e.g. passages on the theme of death and enjoyment (e.g. 2:24, 9:7–9, 11:7–9) are strongly reminiscent of the funerary *Song of the Harpist* (*c.* 3400 B.C.), and 12:3–7, dealing with the effect of declining years on the human frame, may be an echo of a section in *The Instruction of Ptahhotep* (3rd millennium B.C.). Even here, however, there is no instance of contact so close as that between Prov. 22:17–24:34 and the *Wisdom of Amen-em-ope*. (*c*) With regard to Koheleth's thought, his determinism has been explained, independently of Stoicism, as reflecting in the sphere of religion the absolutism characteristic of the contemporary political scene or, according to O. S. Rankin, as more probably due to Mesopotamian belief in stellar influences on human destiny. C. C. Forman maintains that although Koheleth's pessimism

401a (wherein lies his distinctive contribution as a thinker) has much in common with that of Egypt, Babylonia, and Assyria, the only satisfactory clue to its origin is to be found within the Hebrew tradition, in connection with which he cites especially the myths of Gen. 2, 3, 11 (belonging to R. H. Pfeiffer's *S Document*) and the book of Job. (*d*) On balance it seems reasonable to conclude, at the present stage of the discussion, that Koheleth in his quest for gnomic material drew from the common stock of international wisdom sayings current throughout the ancient Near East, and that what he found both in form and content he freely adapted with a high degree of creative skill to suit his purpose. That Egyptian influence may in this respect be found to preponderate (e.g. P. Humbert, W. Baumgartner, K. Galling) would be due to contacts during the Ptolemaic period. That also, even though he drew—and perhaps primarily—on native Hebrew sources, e.g. for his pessimism, Koheleth's unashamed scepticism, his occasional philosophical manner of setting forth a problem, his appeal to individual reason, and his world secular outlook may well have been stimulated through the invasion of the Near East by the Hellenistic spirit which together with its culture became rapidly and popularly widespread.

b **Language**—With its admixture of late Heb. akin to that of the Mishnah (*c*. A.D. 200) and Aram., Ec. presents a linguistic phenomenon. Its Aramaisms, noted increasingly since Grotius (A.D. 1644), have been examined as a basis for the theory—tentatively advanced in 1922 by F. C. Burkitt, and yet more recently developed and reinforced by F. Zimmermann, C. C. Torrey, and H. L. Ginsberg—that an Aram. original underlies the present Heb. rendering of the book. This translation hypothesis has been impressively combated by R. Gordis, who maintains that the linguistic peculiarities of Ec. are to be accounted for by the fact that it is the product of one whose Heb. was influenced both by the Aram. which he normally used and by the nature of the ideas he sought to express. That a number of sections (e.g. 1:2–8, 3:2–8, 7:1–11, 10:1–3, 6–20, 11:8–12:8) are written in poetry, if not the whole of Ec. (cf., e.g., H. W. Hertzberg for whom ' it passes without question that Koheleth is a poetical book '), would further conflict with its being a translation. M. J. Dahood has urged that Ec. was written in Heb. (Koheleth as a sophisticated writer naturally using the language of the schools) *but* in Phoenician orthography and under ' heavy Canaanite-Phoenician literary influence '. The scroll fragments of the book (4QKoh), in the opinion of J. Muilenburg, lend some slight support to this (although R. Gordis has strongly disputed Phoenician influence), and at the same time make more likely a Heb. than an Aram. original. The presence or otherwise of Graecisms has also come under discussion, but even here the two thought possible by O. Eissfeldt (*la'ªśôth ṭôbh* = εὖ πράττειν, ' do well for oneself ', RV : do good, RVm : get good, RSV : enjoy themselves, 3:12 ; and *miḳreh* = τύχη, ' chance ', RSV : fate, 2:14, 3:19, 9:2f.) have not passed unchallenged.

c **Date**—Consideration of affinities and language (see §401*ab*) causes most scholars to assign Ec. to the Greek period, and to regard Ben Sira's date (*c*. 180 B.C.) as the lowest possible limit for its composition, which would accord with its lack of any Maccabaean indications. Passages such as 4:13–16, 8:2–5, 9:13–16, 10:6f., 16f., of which possible underlying historical situations have been very fully explored (cf., e.g., G. A. Barton, H. W. Hertzberg) with a view to pinpointing the time of writing, are found to be primarily illustrative and too vague to furnish any positive clue. The recent evidence of the Qumrân fragments (4QKoh) suggests a time well prior to 150 B.C. unless they are unusually close to the original autograph. Some time in the second half of the 3rd cent. B.C. when Hellenistic influences were well under way would, therefore, seem the most likely period for the book's composition.

Place of Writing—Familiarity with Egyptian wisdom 40 and such allusions as are found in Ec. at 11:1, 5, 12:5f., 12 have been thought by some (e.g. E. H. Plumptre, E. Sellin, P. Humbert) to point to Aexandria as its place of origin. M. J. Dahood inclines to the view, on the ground of historical and social indications in the book, that Koheleth resided in a Phoenician city. The prevailing opinion, however, is that Ec., whilst being of Palestinian origin, was most probably written in Jerusalem (cf., e.g., A. H. McNeile, G. A. Barton, A. L. Williams, H. Odeberg, O. S. Rankin, R. Gordis). In favour of this, and quite apart from textual allusions, are (*a*) the natural likelihood of Jerusalem as being the traditional locus of the Wisdom school, (*b*) the language of the book, and (*c*) its apparently having been regarded as scriptural from a relatively early date (see §401*e*). The most recent support for a Palestinian setting is provided by H. W. Hertzberg who, after examining upwards of a score of passages in Ec.—relating to a wide variety of geographical considerations as well as references to Jerusalem and the Temple (1:1, 16, 2:7, 9, 5:1–7, 8:10), finally points to 9:2 as having, in the light of data from Qumrân, possibly a bearing on Essene (and *ipso facto* Palestinian) practice and so as underlining the rest of his evidence.

Canonicity—Fourth in order of the Five Rolls (Heb. e *m^{e}ghillôth*) in the third division of the Heb. Bible, Ec. was appointed to be read in the synagogues on the third day of the Feast of Tabernacles. Aided mainly by the identification of its pseudonym Koheleth with the name of Solomon, but also by the fact (*a*) of its popularity, (*b*) of certain orthodox corrections (see §400*c*), and that (*c*) 1:3, 12:13f. were regarded by the rabbis as revelational, it received canonical status, after much controversy—being favoured by the school of Hillel but opposed by the school of Shammai, as a result of the discussions of the Synod of Jamnia (*c*. A.D. 100). H. E. Ryle's statement that ' it is everywhere implied in these discussions, that the book was already in the number of the Scriptures, and, according to a Talmudic story, it was quoted as Scripture by Simon ben Shetach in the reign of Alexander Jannaeus (105–79 B.C.) ' is of particular interest in view of J. Muilenburg's conclusion regarding 4QKoh, ' In any event we must reckon with the possibility that (Koheleth) had attained canonical status, or something approaching it, in the Essene community by the middle of the second century B.C.'

Hebrew Text—The fragments of the Koheleth Scroll f from Qumrân present a text centuries older than the MT and very close in time to the original. In them have been noted (*a*) orthographical variants in 5:14, 17, 6:4–8, 7:5f., 8, and (*b*) textual variants in 5:14f., 6:3f., 6, 7:2, 4, 6f., 19, of which some may preserve the original reading.

I 1 Superscription—The Preacher (Heb. *ḳôheleth*) g is identified with Solomon (cf. §400*b*), a literary convention maintained as far as 2:12.

2-11 Preface—Koheleth inveighs against the aimless repetitiveness of human activity and natural processes, the ineffectualness of which is expressed by his cardinal term ' vanity '. **2. Vanity** (Heb. *hebhel*) occurs 40 times in Ec. and some 35 times elsewhere in the OT. Its root meaning is ' vapour ', ' breath ', suggestive of evanescence, vacuity, illusion, ' unreality ', cf. F. C. Burkitt, ' bubble ', H. L. Ginsberg, ' zero '. From other OT usage W. E. Staples concludes that, having to do with cultic mysteries, it has in Ec. the idea of that which is humanly incomprehensible. **Vanity of vanities** is the Heb. superlative (cf. ' Song of Songs '), i.e. ' sheer unreality ', or, possibly, ' utter incomprehensibility ', cf. 12:8 which, however, does not repeat the phrase. **3-8** in poetical form amplify 2. **3. gain:** a commercial term peculiar to Ec., ' surplus ', ' profit'. **toil:** possibly ' hard-earned income ', cf. H. L. Ginsberg for verb and noun = ' earn ', ' earning '. **under the sun:** peculiar in the OT to Ec. but found in Phoenician and Elamite

401g inscriptions; is not now regarded as due to Greek influence. **5. hastens:** lit. 'pants', suggesting breathless, hurried, or laboured movement. For the steeds of the sun to which the verb might apply cf. 2 Kg. 23:11. The OT has no other reference to the sun as presumably suffering from strain and there may here be a contact with the Egyptian idea of the sun showing signs of age, cf. O. S. Rankin. **7.** That the level of the sea is not affected by all the water flowing into it appears particularly meaningless to the author. **9-11.** Novelty is an illusion induced by the shortness of man's memory. **9** refers to the repetition of event and action. **10.** What is thought to be new is in fact quite old. **11.** The thought possibly connects with that of 3:11.

402a **I 12-II 26 Koheleth's Inquiry and Conclusion**—In the guise of Solomon, renowned for his wisdom and riches, Koheleth assesses the value of life as revealed by (*a*) intellectual inquiry (12–18), (*b*) luxurious pleasure-seeking (2:1–11), both of which lead nowhere. Further pondering (after abandoning his kingly role) shows (*c*) that wisdom has no ultimate advantage over folly (2:12–17), and (*d*) that the best course is to take what enjoyment one can out of life as it is, although this too is vanity (2:18–26).

b (*a*) **I 12-18. 12. have been king:** since Solomon was king to the end of his life Koheleth cannot have been Solomon. F. Delitzsch proposed that Solomon was 'resuscitated by the author of the book'. The first person may here indicate employment of the I-form characteristic of the royal admonitions in Egyptian Wisdom literature, according to which the king imparts instruction on relinquishing his throne, cf. K. Galling. H. L. Ginsberg's interpretation of 'king' as 'property-holder' (Heb. *melekh* as *mōlēkh*) is ingenious but unlikely. **13a.** An exhaustive inquiry by means of the wisdom for which he was noted, cf. 1:17, 7:25, 8:9, 16. **13b. unhappy business** is one of Koheleth's characteristic phrases, rendered 'bad venture' in 5:14. The noun means 'occupation', 'task', and the verb, 'occupied, worried by' (K-B). **14. striving after wind**, cf. RVm and Hos. 12:1, is another characteristic phrase, suggesting futile, aimless activity. 'Wind' (Heb. *rûaḥ*) also means 'spirit', and W. E. Staples would take the last clause as, 'everything is incomprehensible, yet the spirit drives one on'. **15.** A proverb, emphasising the foregoing and underlining Koheleth's pessimistic determinism. **what is lacking** may refer to deficit in accounts. **16.** Cf. §400*b*. Koheleth is concerned more with literary effect than with historical accuracy. **17.** In the Wisdom literature 'folly' is the antithesis of 'wisdom', and 'madness' possibly here connotes mental deviation rather than irrational behaviour. **18.** A proverb to illustrate what has just been stated, stressing the frustration and suffering arising from 'much wisdom'.

c (*b*) **II 1-11. 1.** The next experiment is with pleasure or enjoyment to see whether it is a wholly satisfying good. **enjoy yourself:** lit. 'look upon (in the sense of 'experience') good', cf. Ps. 34:8. **3. to cheer:** a forced rendering of the Heb. *māshakh*, 'draw', 'drag', which is better taken according to Aram. and Arab. usage, and so without emendation, as 'to sustain', cf. G. R. Driver. **5. parks:** Heb. *pardēsîm*, only elsewhere Neh. 2:8; Ca. 4:13, and a Persian loan-word, though found in Akkadian, whence παράδεισος (e.g. Lk. 23:43), and so 'paradise'. **7. and had slaves . . . house:** i.e. 'even though I had house-born slaves (e.g. Gen. 17:12). **8. treasure:** Heb. *s^eghullāh*, 'valued property', 'peculiar treasure', cf. RV. The word has reference (*a*) to Israel as Yahweh's chosen people (e.g. Exod. 19:5), and (*b*) to '(private) property' (K-B), cf., e.g., 1 Chr. 29:3f., 'gold of Ophir', being here used for the royal perquisite of fiscal control. **many concubines, man's delight:** although the Heb. is uncertain the pleasures of the harem appear to be intended. LXX, Syr., 'cupbearers, male and female'. The sense of the passage as a whole is well summed up by H. L. Ginsberg, 'I acquired a large fortune, and had the good sense to apply it to the gratification of my desires. *And that was all I ever did get out of it.*' 402c

d (*c*) **12-17.** The advantage of wisdom over folly is cancelled out by death, since the same end awaits both wise man and fool. **12b** raises the question as to whether men in general are intended or the king's successor, which the closely similar expression in 18 would appear to support together with the fact of Koheleth's preference for the more general term for man (Heb. *hā'ādhām*) rather than for the more particular (Heb. *hā'îsh*). **he has already done:** so Vulg., Syr., but RV as MT, 'hath been already done'. The point is that the king's successor could not act differently. Some would transfer this part of the verse to follow 11*b* as suiting better the context of the previous section (e.g. C. Siegfried). **13f.** have the appearance of two proverbial utterances introduced by 'then I saw that' and concluded by 'and yet I perceived . . .' **fate** (Heb. *miḳreh*, 'contingency', 'chance', 'fortune') here signifies the mere occurrence of death, of which the assonance of the phrase may be illustrated by, e.g., 'one hap happens'.

e (*d*) **18-26.** The thought of 12*b* is developed with regard to the character of the one who will succeed to and so gain without effort the inheritance so hardly won by toil and wisdom, an inevitability the unfairness of which causes Koheleth to despair (18–23). It follows that the best course is to seek present enjoyment, which is the gift of God and dependent on his favour (24–6). **21. skill** or 'proficiency' (Heb. *kishrôn*): cf. 4:4, 5:11 ('gain', i.e. as accruing from skill), and its verbal use in 10:10, 'succeed', and 11:6, 'prosper'. Although found in late Heb. and Aram., the root occurs also in earlier Akkadian and Ugaritic sources, where it has mythological associations, cf. its use in Ps. 68:6. **22. strain,** lit. 'the striving of his heart', probably refers to mental exertion. **25. apart from him:** cf. RSV*n*. **have enjoyment:** from a Semitic root 'experience', 'feel', having the same consonants as the root 'hasten', cf. RVm. LXX, Syr. 'drink', R. Gordis, 'refrain'. **26. the man who pleases him,** lit. 'who is good before him', and **the sinner** (cf. 7:26) are possibly here not to be taken in an ethical sense, for which elsewhere Koheleth employs 'the righteous' and 'the wicked' (e.g. 7:15), but rather as denoting the one who finds and the one who misses the enjoyment alluded to in 24f. (cf., e.g., G. A. Barton, R. Gordis as against H. Odeberg). On such an interpretation there is no thought of moral retribution in the verse and this would preclude its being the addition of a devout glossator (Heb. *ḥāsîdh*, cf. §400*d*). O. S. Rankin here notes a very close affinity with Egyptian Wisdom teaching which would further support its authenticity.

f **III 1-15 The Futility of Human Endeavour**—The list of times and seasons (1–8) in a poem of contraries and related in thought to 1:2–11 is probably best understood in the light of what follows, viz. that all human activity is of no avail since everything is predetermined, and that in face of life's inevitabilities it is for men to wrest what enjoyment they can in the present (9–15). **1. season:** 'fixed moment', 'appointed hour'. **time:** 'occurrence'. For this terminology cf. H. W. Robinson, *Inspiration and Revelation in the OT* (1946), 106–22. The controlling thought appears to be that every occurrence is ordained by God so that everything happens when it must happen, and not the opportunist notion that there is an appropriate time when men should carry out certain actions. **matter:** a late meaning of the Heb. *ḥēpheṣ*, 'delight', having here the sense of 'occupation', 'activity', 'business', but cf. H. L. Ginsberg, 'phenomenon'. **5.** According to the Midrash, *Eccles. R.*, the casting away and the gathering together of stones refers to participation in and abstention from marital conjunction, an interpretation which would accord with the second member of the

402f verse and is on the whole to be preferred to alternative explanations, cf., e.g., A. L. Williams. **9.** appears to imply that since man is devoid of freedom he wins nothing from the round of activities just listed. **10.** Cf. 1:13 for thought and language. **11.** A most discussed and crucial verse. **made,** Heb. *'āśāh,* ' do ', ' make ', is identical with ' done ' at the end of the verse and may have that meaning here, cf. H. L. Ginsberg, ' made happen '. **beautiful,** ' right ', ' well-arranged ' (K-B), may correspond to ' good ' in Gen. 1:4, 12, 25, 31, cf. Sir. 39:16, 33, although the ' time ' thought is present here. But the crux is **eternity,** Heb. *h'lm,* vocalised as *hā'ôlām.* As vocalised it is rendered as (*a*) ' the world ', a post-biblical usage. So Vulg., AV, RV and many (e.g. T. K. Cheyne, V. Zapletal). R. Gordis interprets as ' the love of the world '. As (*b*) ' eternity ', cf. LXX, RVm, it is taken (i) with a temporal reference (e.g. A. H. McNeile), for which cf. H. W. Robinson, op. cit., 122, ' The point seems to be the permanence or continuity of God's work (of which man is conscious, 3:14) in contrast with the transitory beauty of the time-content ' ; or (ii) in a spiritual sense, as referring to the divine in man, cf. Gen. 1:26f. (e.g. G. Wildeboer). With different vocalisation two of a number of alternatives may be noted as having a special bearing on the rest of the verse which concerns man's inability to comprehend God's activity in its totality : (*a*) *hā'elem,* ' ignorance ', ' forgetfulness ' (cf. G. A. Barton, O. S. Rankin), and (*b*) *he'āmāl* (also transposing *l* and *m*), ' toil ', ' striving '—a common term in Ec., which is adopted by H. L. Ginsberg. If (*a*) be adopted it would link the thought with that of 1:11, which concerns the faultiness of man's memory. **12f.** Cf. 2:24–6. **enjoy themselves:** lit. ' do good ', cf. §401*b*. The underlying determinism is amplified in **14f.** The **fear** which God thus instils is of a different order from ' the fear of Yahweh ' (Job 28:28 ; Prov. 1:7, 9:10). **15ab.** Some have here discerned the influence of the Stoic cyclic doctrine or of a simpler form of it in Hesiod (cf. H. Ranston). For the thought cf. 1:9. The idea that everything is determined by God appears to be extended to include past, present, and future. This becomes clearer if **God seeks what has been driven away,** with its awkward grammar and two verbal forms, be rendered ' God claims it (*scil.* each moment, present and future), as it passes on ' (so G. R. Driver).

g **16-22 Men are but Beasts**—They display no moral superiority and share the same destiny. **16.** Lack of justice and righteousness characterise those in authority, a thought to which Koheleth returns (e.g. 4:1, 8:9). The Heb. is dramatically terse—' there wickedness ', and repeated for emphasis. **17.** The hand of the devout glossator is here suspected by many on account of the thought and its disturbance of the connection between 16 and 18. **19f.** Cf. Ps. 49:12–20. **breath** (Heb. *rûaḥ*) : cf. 1:14, ' wind ', and ' spirit ' (21 below). **one place:** i.e. the dust, but probably Sheol in 6:6. **from the dust:** cf. Gen. 2:7, 3:19. **21** is rendered by AV, RVm as a statement, but the RSV, RV follow the ancient versions in taking it as a question. This suits the context and thought of Koheleth, who in asserting a common fate for men and cattle appears to challenge the view, attributed (e.g. by O. S. Rankin) to Mesopotamian astral religion, that the spirit of man ascends to heaven at death. Nor does this conflict with 12:7, where the spirit, i.e. the life principle, is said to return to God as the body to dust, there being no idea of the continuance of personality. **22.** Since knowledge of the hereafter is beyond human grasp, enjoyment of the present is advocated.

h **IV 1-3 Tyranny**—The opening theme corresponds to the injustice of the preceding section and is also followed, but in a different connection, by the thought of death. **1. oppressions:** cf. Job 35:9 ; Am. 3:9. Koheleth is moved by the plight of the oppressed. **no one to comfort them** may be repeated for emphasis, but its second occurrence in juxtaposition to the ' oppressors ' is regarded by some as curious, and G. R. Driver has proposed a slight change, in the vocalisation only, of the verbal form to read, ' and there was none avenging himself on them '. **2f.** The thought of such tyranny causes Koheleth to envy the dead who have escaped from it, and even more the unborn who have not experienced it, cf. 6:3 ; Job 3:1–16. Difference of context may be sufficient to explain the apparent contradiction between 2 and 9:4.

4-12 The Merit of Co-operation—It is possible to i understand these verses as dealing with the advantage of co-operation (9–12) over rivalry (4, with two gnomic sayings, 5f.) and solitary self-seeking (7f.). **4.** Koheleth discerns in the competitive spirit (Heb. *ḳin'āh,* ' ardour ', ' zeal ', ' jealousy ', but here possibly ' rivalry ', cf. 9:6 ; Isa. 11:13) the mainspring of industry and craftsmanship (cf. on ' skill ', 2:21). Perhaps the ruthlessness implied in such competition provides a link with the tyranny of the previous section. A. L. Williams here follows, as against the RVm and RSV, the AV and RV which suggest that the proficiency is the cause of envy. **5f.** are two proverbs seemingly parenthetically introduced to reinforce the argument to the effect that whilst it is suicidal to be lazy there is much to be said for tranquillity as opposed to feverish competition which leads nowhere, cf. R. Gordis. **folds his hands** is indicative of idleness, cf. our ' twiddles his thumbs ', and for the expression elsewhere, Prov. 6:10, 24:33. **eats his own flesh** suggests either living off his relations or bringing about his undoing, but for a different connection cf. Isa. 9:20, 49:26. **handful . . . hands full** may have the force of a *little* tranquillity . . . a *lot* of worry, but cf. R. Gordis, ' Better a handful acquired with ease than two hands full gained through toil '. **7f.** A singular instance of futility (cf. ' vanity ', introducing as well as concluding the thought) is that of the man, all alone in the world, who with his insatiable yearning for riches never pauses to ask for whom he is thus wearing himself out, cf. Sir. 14:4. **a person who has no one:** lit. ' there is one and not a second ', which in effect is ' take the case of a bachelor who is all alone '. **9-12.** A series of proverbs, possibly resulting from Koheleth's researches (e.g. 12:9), on the subject of co-operation, and lacking the concluding ' vanity ' formula. **9.** The ' good reward ' concerns the mutual help under consideration. **12a. prevail:** an Aram. verb meaning ' overpower ', suggesting here an assailant such as a brigand. **12b. a threefold cord:** i.e. a rope with three strands and so extra strong, implying perhaps, to strengthen the argument, that three are better even than two.

13-16 A Parable concerning Wisdom versus j **Folly**—The interpretation of this passage is problematic on account of (*a*) confusion of pronouns and terseness of expression, (*b*) uncertainty of connection between 13 and 14, (*c*) the mention in 15 of a ' second youth ', cf. RSV*n*, and (*d*) the possibility of some historical allusion about which there can be no positive conclusion. It seems best regarded as a parable, where wisdom and folly are contrasted with reference to a poor youth who through his wisdom ascends the throne, in which case as with certain NT parables ' we need seek for no correspondence in historical facts ', C. H. Dodd, *The Parables of the Kingdom* (1936), 151. W. A. Irwin, identifying the ' second youth ' with the youth of 13, considers that folly accompanied by wealth and power is here set over against wisdom minus such assets, the theme being the supremacy of wisdom. Differently, C. C. Torrey distinguishes between the two youths and attractively suggests that if 10:16f. (which he thinks originally belonged to the present context but were accidentally omitted by a scribe who, later realising his mistake, inserted them between 10:15 and 18) be restored to supply the connection between 4:13 and 14, it becomes clear that the first youth was weak and unworthy and the second wise and acceptable to his subjects. ' The second ' has alternatively been explained as referring to the youth's

2j status, cf. O. S. Rankin. **16**, suggesting the vanity of popularity, has frequently been taken as supplying the main theme of the passage, and A. L. Williams regards ' those who come later ' as those at the end of the procession.

V 1-20 = MT, VSS **IV 17-V 19**

3a **V 1-7 Sage Advice on Worship**, comprising a series of gnomic sayings concerning the approach to worship (1), prayer (2f.), and vows (4–7). **1**. Do not go to the Temple (or possibly, the synagogue) thoughtlessly. **to listen:** i.e. either to hear the law expounded or to obey (e.g. 1 Sam. 15:22). **2f.** Cf. Sir. 7:14 ; Mt. 6:7. Prayer is to be uttered with care and brevity, having regard to God's remote sovereignty, counsel which is backed up by a proverb to the effect that just as over-concern brings on dreams so loquacity results in fatuous utterance. **4-7.** Vows are not to be lightly undertaken, and are to be promptly fulfilled ; cf. Dt. 23:21–3 ; Sir. 18:22f. According to the Talmud their evasion was not uncommonly sought in later Judaism. **into sin:** i.e. into incurring the penalty of sin. **before the messenger** (Heb. *mal'ākh*, ' angel ', cf. RSV*n*) : a term used in the OT *inter alia* of the priest (Mal. 2:7), may here have reference to the Temple official charged with registering vows and collecting dues, although A. L. Williams considers that the Angel of Justice is intended. The LXX has ' before God ' which could mean ' at the sanctuary ' (cf. Exod. 21:6). To say that it was a **mistake** or inadvertent sin (e.g. Lev. 4:2) would be particularly thin in the case of a vow which involves solemn deliberation. For **7a**, the text of which is uncertain, read RSV*n*. **fear God**, cf. on 3:14, is probably in the nature of a *caveat* rather than an exhortation to godly fear, and some regard it as the conclusion to 6.

b **V 8-VI 6 Observations on Wealth**—The greed for wealth underlies the rapacity of state officials (8, 9), its acquisition fails to satisfy and multiplies cares (10–12), and its loss has tragic consequences (13–17). Wealth and possessions and power to enjoy them are God's gifts and have value in this life (18–20), yet it were better to be still-born than, having such resources, to be denied the gift of enjoying them (6:1–6). **5:8f.** It is hardly surprising that oppression and injustice flourish in a province, when, from top to bottom of its hierarchy of officialdom, each watches the one below him to grasp his pickings of the revenue, the most senior receiving the lion's share. **higher ones** need not be ' an impersonal allusion to the king ' (G. A. Barton), nor a plural of majesty signifying God (cf. BDB). **9** is perplexing and for alternatives cf. also RV, RVm. As it stands (RSV) the value of the king in maintaining agriculture appears to be indicated (cf. G. A. Barton), suggesting a somewhat unusually favourable view of the monarchy on Koheleth's part. The rendering of the RSV*n* (cf. A. L. Williams, H. Odeberg, O. S. Rankin) seems to provide the best connection with 8, implying that cultivated land *ipso facto* has a king over it, and so is subject to taxation. **10-12. nor he who loves wealth, with gain:** possibly (cf. A. L. Williams, and differently R. Gordis), ' he who loves wealth (has) no (i.e., to him, appreciable) increase ' (a word indicating income from produce). **11. gain:** a different word—cf. on 2:21, hence R. Gordis, ' what value is there in the owner's superior ability, except that he has more to look upon ? ' **13-17. a bad venture:** cf. on 1:13, pointing to some kind of calamity. **15** seems to apply to the father (although R. Gordis here discerns a chiastic arrangement of the father in 14, 17 and of the son in 15, 16) in terms reminiscent of Job 1:21 but with a different purport, cf. Sir. 40:1. **16. grievous** : from a root = ' be sick, ill ' and emphatic by repetition from 13. **17** concerns either the luckless man's parsimony in hoarding the wealth that was lost or the remainder of his tragic life. The LXX is generally preferred as against the MT, cf. RSV*n*. **18-20.** From the failure to enjoy wealth instanced in 8–17 Koheleth

403b turns to emphasise the power to enjoy it as God's gift along with the toil that is involved. The recipient of this gift will have no time for brooding because **God keeps him occupied:** the verb so rendered (cf. RV ' answereth ') has the support of LXX, Vulg. and agrees with the usage in 1:13, 3:10. **6:1-6.** The inability to enjoy life's good things is an acute problem and of this instances are now given. **2.** What a man is not given power to **enjoy** a stranger (in the absence presumably of an heir) **enjoys**, lit. ' eats ', cf. Isa. 3:10 ; Jer. 15:16. **3.** A still-born child (cf. 4:3 ; Job 3:16 ; Ps. 58:8) is better off than a man who fails to enjoy his blessings which include a large progeny (e.g. Ps. 127:3–5) and longevity (e.g. Dt. 11:21). **and also has no burial:** death without burial was viewed with abhorrence (e.g. 2 Kg. 9:30–7 ; Isa. 14:19 ; Jer. 22:19), the more so if none of a man's family would undertake this pious obligation (cf. Tob. 1:17, 2:4–7). But the words do not connect and may therefore be in the nature of an aside or transposed from 5. Alternatively the Heb. (lit. ' burial has not been to him ') might imply that the man still has some years in front of him (cf. 6). With a slight vowel change in the negative particle R. Gordis proposes, ' even if he have an elaborate funeral '. **4-6.** The still-born child has the advantage of repose (cf. Job 3:13) denied to the other, for of what advantage is longevity, however prolonged, without the gift of enjoyment ? **the one place:** i.e. Sheol.

7-9 A Proverbial Pendant—These verses, gnomic c in character, are usually included with the foregoing, 7 being regarded as a gloss which breaks the connection between 6 and 8 (e.g. A. H. McNeile, O. S. Rankin). If, however, the satisfaction of desire is the underlying thought they may have a loose kind of unity. **8.** Cf. 2:14–16 where wise man and fool have a common fate. K. Galling would render, ' What advantage has the wise man over the fool, the intelligent poor man over him who lives thoughtlessly ? ' **9.** What one can see and is therefore within one's grasp is preferable to unrealistic yearning after the unattainable.

10-12 Man's Helplessness—Cf. 3:9–15. **10.** For d the determinism cf. 1:9, 3:15. **has already been named:** lit. ' its name has already been called ', i.e. it has already been called into being. **10b.** Cf., e.g., Job 9:1–24. **11.** Words are worse than useless considering man's ignorance. **12. passes like a shadow:** lit. ' makes like a shadow '. The meaning is uncertain but cf. 1 Chr. 29:15 ; Job 8:9 ; Ps. 144:4.

VII 1-14 Proverbs concerning the Way of e **Wisdom**—Although man is ignorant of what is good (6:12), there is good of a relative kind after which the wise man will strive, e.g. a sober attitude to life (1–7), and equanimity (8–14). **1a. name,** Heb. *shēm*—as standing for the personality (or the thing itself, 6:10)—here connotes ' reputation ' (cf. Prov. 22:1 ; Zeph. 3:19), and the comparison with **ointment** (Heb. *shemen*) which was highly esteemed offers a play on words, cf. Ca. 1:3. Reputation, associated with the end of a man's life, may provide the link with 1*b* which re-echoes 4:2f., 6:4–6. **2.** The sober outlook of the wise accords more with funeral ceremonies than (wedding) festivities, each of which lasted a week (e.g. Gen. 50:10, 29:27). **feasting:** 4QKoh reads ' mirth ', possibly because of its occurrence in 4, cf. Millar Burrows, *More Light on the Dead Sea Scrolls* (1958), 144. **3.** Thoughtful sadness is preferable to levity, ' for by a serious outlook the understanding is improved ', cf. C. D. Ginsburg. **5a** suggests the classroom of the sage (e.g. Prov. 13:1). **5b.** Cf. the ' idle songs ' of Am. 6:5. **6.** Here again is word-play, burning **thorns** (Heb. *sîrîm*) under a **pot** (Heb. *sîr*) being noisy rather than serviceable for fuel. **this also is vanity** is regarded (e.g. by A. L. Williams, H. Odeberg) as belonging to 7, which should read, ' This also is vanity, that oppression makes . . .' A. H. McNeile follows F. Delitzsch in regarding **7** as the second half of a *māshāl*, the lost first half having

403e resembled Prov. 16:8, cf. also K. Galling, O. S. Rankin. That some words may have fallen out of the text at this point appears to be supported by a corresponding break in the lines of 4Q Koh, concerning which J. Muilenburg notes that 'the reading here is extremely obscure . . . the letters in the first line (7:7) do not correspond to MT at all'. As it stands 7 would accord with the sentiments of 5:8f. An alternative rendering of the verse on the basis of comparison with the VSS and cognate languages is proposed by G. R. Driver, viz. 'slander driveth a wise man mad, and it (*scil.* a false accusation) destroys a (or his) stout heart'. **8** is possibly an echo of 1*b*. **thing** as 'word' could here refer to control of speech. **10** appears to conflict with 1:11 but if concentration on the present is implied the thought would accord with, e.g., 2:24. **11.** Wisdom combined with means is an asset, cf. also 12, 19, and for its association with poverty cf. 4:13f., 6:8, 9:15f. **those who see the sun**, i.e. the living, cf. 6:5. **12a.** The Heb. reads tersely, 'in the shadow of wisdom, in the shadow of money'. For wisdom as a shade or protection cf. Sir. 14:27*a*, and for the shadow as evanescent cf. 6:12. **12b.** Wisdom quickens life in its different aspects. **13.** For the determinism cf. 1:15*a*, 3:15, 6:10. **14. so that man may not find out anything that will be after him:** 'after him' in the sense of 'in the future' with reference to man occurs in 3:22, 6:12 (cf. also 9:3). Symmachus renders the clause, 'in such wise that no man may find any fault with him', i.e. with reference to God who is the subject of the main clause; and this makes excellent sense. F. C. Burkitt considered that this would be the meaning of the Heb. if it were read as Syriac (Eastern Aram.) in which 'to find out after' = 'to find fault with', thinking it to be an over-literal translation from an Aram. original. It is not unlikely, however, that this Aram. idiom gained currency in the schools where it became a part of the language that was used, in which case Symm. may here be representing the original thought, cf. G. R. Driver.

f **15-18 Concerning the Way of Moderation**—Consideration of prosperity and adversity in the preceding deterministic setting leads to the advocacy of a middle course. **15.** The problem of the suffering of the innocent and the prosperity of the wicked is touched upon (cf. 8:14). Koheleth's experience brings him to a reversal of the view underlying, e.g., Ps. 1. **16.** He looks with disfavour on extremes of piety and wisdom. **why should you destroy yourself?** or 'bring about your own undoing?': cf. also H. Odeberg following A. L. Williams, 'lest thou lose thy senses'. Some have here seen a reference to the pietistic zeal of the *ḥ^{a}sîdhîm*, which the probable date of Ec. now makes unlikely. **17.** The opposite extremes are to be shunned since they too can bring disaster. **18.** 'this' and 'that' are perhaps intentionally vague and therefore not to be particularised with reference to the alternates in 15–17, the language here indicating that Koheleth is advocating an attitude of compromise, cf. 8:2–5. **shall come forth from them all** is possibly best understood in the light of Mishnaic usage of the verb 'come forth' = 'fulfil an obligation', hence, 'the one who fears God will carry out his obligations to them all (*scil.* 'to all men', 'to both', or 'in every respect').

g **19-22 A Proverbial Pendant**, consisting of citations more or less complementary to the above theme—**19.** Wisdom as a source of strength is depicted in terms of Hellenistic local government with its city councils of 'ten chief men' (δεκάπρωτοι). **20.** That no-one is free from sin (cf. 1 Kg. 8:46), by context underlines the reasonableness of compromise. **21f.** The censorious way in which men talk about each other's failings offers an example of a sin to which all are prone. 'heart' is here 'conscience'.

h **23-29 An Inquiry and the Result**—Koheleth's quest for reality, which appears unattainable (23f.), involves the search for wisdom and 'the *rationale* of things' (A. L. Williams), which has to do, obversely as it seems, with the hypothesis that 'wickedness is 4
folly and foolishness is madness' (25) as exemplified in the case of the prostitute (26). The result of this investigation, repeatedly made (27), has not been successful, although it has shown a truly worthy man to be extremely rare, a category in which women are out of the running (28). There can be only one conclusion, viz. that God has made men straightforward and they have deviated. **23. all this** provides a link between what has been stated and what is now to be propounded. **24.** For the unattainableness of wisdom cf. 8:16f.; Job 28:12–22. **25a. the sum of things:** a late Heb. and Aram. term, 'reckoning', 'account', so 27, cf. 29, 'devices', 9:10, 'thought', Sir. 42:3, 'keeping accounts'. Cf. 'add up' in current usage. **25b** amounts to a description of wisdom by contraries. **26a.** The example *par excellence* of wickedness and folly, cf. Prov. 5:3–6, 7:5–27. **26b.** Cf. 2:26. **28.** Koheleth's opinion of women may be connected with 'the moral independence of women not being distinctly recognised' in the OT, cf. C. H. Toy, *Proverbs* (1899), 103. **29** in thought as well as language is integral to the passage and is not to be regarded as a glossator's protest (cf. O. S. Rankin) against Koheleth's specious arguments ('devices').

VIII 1-9 The Wise Man and Superior Authority 40
—Koheleth reflects upon the harsh arbitrariness of higher authority (9). Gifted with acumen, a gracious courtliness, and an accommodating spirit (1), the wise man, true to his oath of loyalty, is well fitted for the service of a monarch who is liable to act on the merest whim, and whose authority and judgment may not be called in question (2–4). He has equanimity and also knows when and how to meet a given situation, even though he shares the common human limitation of not knowing the future (5–7). Further limitation is seen in the fact that no man is ruler over the spirit, death, war, and evil (8). W. A. Irwin (but cf. R. Gordis, O. S. Rankin) against most commentators regards 2–9 as a unity on a single theme, centering in the king and his court. The clue to the passage, which (as indicated above) may well include 1 by way of introduction, lies in 9, but in the course of his reflections upon monarchical despotism, Koheleth, as 6–8 suggest, touching again upon man's lack of foreknowledge (cf. 3:22, 6:12), appears to develop his theme away from absolutism in the direction of determinism. **1. interpretation:** i.e. the 'solution' (Heb. *pesher*, in Rabbinical usage 'compromise') of a problem (e.g. Dan. 5:16f.). **2f.** Cf. RSV*n*. The MT begins 3 with 'be not dismayed' (cf. RV), but the RSV here follows the LXX. **your sacred oath:** lit. 'oath of God', possibly in the sense of 'an oath of loyalty to the king made before God', although it has been otherwise explained as either a divine oath of support for the king, or, as applied in the Ptolemaic period, an oath sworn to the king regarded as divine—after the manner of Egyptian belief. **be not dismayed:** i.e. if obedience involves inner conflict over a moral issue, but cf. RV where the rendering would accord with 10:4. **5. command:** presumably, of the king (cf. 2). **time and way:** perhaps 'the right moment and procedure'. **6. man's trouble**, cf. 6:1, is elaborated in 7. **8. no man has power:** i.e. 'no man is ruler' (Heb. *shallîṭ*, 'ruler', at 10:5, cf. also C. D. Ginsburg), apparently implying—not even the king! **to retain the spirit** (Heb. *rûaḥ*, cf. on 1:14, 3:19, 21), here in all likelihood referring to the life principle in the sense of holding the life force (indefinitely) within oneself (cf. the parallel, 'death'), although some would render 'wind', and W. A. Irwin 'the (king's) anger' (cf. RV, RSV at 10:4). **day of death:** W. A. Irwin, 'day of execution', although OT usage would seem to favour natural death (e.g. Jg. 13:7; 1 Sam. 15:35, cf. especially Gen. 27:2, 'I know not the day of my death'). **war** may here be viewed 'as sweeping aside all attempts to evade its consequences' (O. S. Rankin), but for **discharge** from war in the narrower sense cf. Dt. 20:5–8. Finally,

404a no man can escape from the moral evil of which he has become a victim.

b **10-17 The Absence of a Moral Purpose** in human affairs as Koheleth views them (10–14), compels him to reiterate the desirability of enjoying life whilst it lasts (15), and to comment on the futility of wisdom (16f.). **10.** The confusion in the MT of this perplexing verse is hinted at in the RVm. Two points of special difficulty relate to (*a*) **praised** (LXX, Aq.), in the MT a unique form of the verb ' forget ' (cf. RV), and (*b*) **they had done such things** which can also mean ' they had done right ' (RV), 10*a* referring to the wicked and 10*b* to the righteous. Of attempts at a solution two quite different ones may be noted. K. Galling (who sees Egyptian influence in the regarding of a burial-place as sacred rather than unclean) would render, ' And so I saw that wicked men were brought to the grave at a holy place, but they who had done what was right had to withdraw and be forgotten in the city '. G. R. Driver proposes, ' and then I have seen wicked men, approaching (' buried ' with transposition of consonants and change of vowels) and entering the holy place, walk about and boast (so many Heb. MSS and the chief VSS) in the city that they have done right '. **11-13** according to A. L. Williams ' form some of the strongest evidence ', on account of their orthodoxy, for the devout glossator, a view shared by many. **13. like a shadow:** cf. 6:12. **14.** For the thought cf. also, e.g., Job 9:22, 21:7 ; Ps. 73:3 ; Jer. 12:1. **15.** Cf. 3:12f., 5:18–20. **16a.** Cf. 1:13. **16b** makes a better connection if transposed to 17*b* (so O. S. Rankin, but cf. R. Gordis, who would place it after ' then I saw ' in 17*a*) reading ' However much man may toil in seeking (though neither day nor night one's eyes see sleep), he will not . . .'

c **IX 1-12 Man's Common Fate**—The sense of futility which characterises the foregoing section, well connected by 1, here leads to consideration of the common fate of righteous and wicked—death with all its despair (2–6). Again there is the injunction to enjoy life to the full (7–10). But even as in 10 the thought of death recurs, Koheleth, caught in the toils of his determinism, pauses to consider men as the victims of ' time and chance ' (11f.). **1. examining it** is based on H. Grätz's emendation of an obscure word in the MT rendered ' declare ' (AV) in the sense of ' make clear '. **love or hate** appears to refer to God by whom human actions are predetermined. **vanity** (cf. LXX, Symm., Vulg., Syr.), but MT reads ' everything ' (cf. RSV*n*) as the first word of 2. The phrase is ambiguous but may mean ' everything in their sight is vanity ' (cf. E. Podechard). **2a. the evil:** cf. RSV*n*. **2b.** It is uncertain as to which is preferable : the one ' who swears ' or the one ' who shuns an oath '. For the possibility of a link with Essene practice cf. §401*ad*. **3a** may have superlative force as ' the supreme misfortune '. **3d.** The Heb. is vigorous, ' and thereafter—off to the dead ! ' **4.** The despised cur (cf. 1 Sam. 24:14) and the king of beasts (cf. Gen. 49:9f.) are here used with telling effect. **5.** The consciousness of death appears to be a doubtful advantage over the unconsciousness of the dead ! **7-9.** Cf. 3:12f., 5:18–20, 8:15. The theme is here elaborated in terms reminiscent of other ancient Wisdom literature (cf. §401*a*), but in a way characteristic of Koheleth, e.g. the implied determinism of 7*c*. **10a** may, in the light of the preceding context, concern thoroughgoing participation in enjoyment (e.g. G. A. Barton), but toil may more probably be intended since Koheleth elsewhere associates it with pleasure (e.g. 2:10, 24), and it is also mentioned in 9 and implied in 10*b*. **Sheol,** only here in Ec., is the destination of all men and characterised by the absence of mental activity. **11f.** That men are frustrated in life as well as by death pertains to man's common fate. There is no guarantee that competence and industry will receive their deserts. **chance,** ' contingency ', ' occurrence ', is found in the OT only here and, coupled with ' evil ', at 1 Kg. 5:4 (MT, 5:18), H. Odeberg renders ' adverse 404c
fate '. The unknown hour of doom strikes suddenly and men are ensnared.

13-16 A Parable concerning a Poor Wise Man— d
Koheleth here cites an example, in narrative form, of applied wisdom (13–15), possibly to amplify 11, but mainly intended to illustrate and underline the pronouncement in 16*a*. The narrative interest is in consequence of secondary importance, and its insufficiency of detail makes historical identification (for various attempts cf., e.g., G. A. Barton) wellnigh impossible. In certain aspects it recalls 2 Sam. 20:15–22, concerning which C. H. H. Wright observes that Koheleth ' has substituted ' a poor man ' in place of ' a wise woman ', because the anecdote corresponds better thus with the sentiment of v. 11, which it was intended to illustrate '. **13. great,** with vowel change and transposition of consonants in the Heb., would yield ' remarkable ' (G. R. Driver). **15f.** According to some (e.g. A. H. McNeile, H. W. Hertzberg, H. L. Ginsberg) 16*b* contradicts 15*b* which accordingly should read, ' and he by his wisdom would (or could) have delivered the city. Yet no one remembered (to make use of) that poor man.' The traditional rendering defended by others (e.g. G. A. Barton, A. L. Williams, R. Gordis), is supported by 13, by the use of ' found ' in 15*a*, and by the correspondence of thought with 11, to the effect that there is no relation between a man's worth and the treatment he receives. The conclusion of the matter is that ' wisdom is better than might ' which implies that the poor wise man did in fact save the city as the story relates.

IX 17-X 20 Proverbs concerning Wise Men and e
Fools, including observations on those who rule (10:4–7, 16–20)—**17. The words of the wise,** so 12:11*a*. **heard in quiet,** according to the parallel, suggests the quiet speaking of the wise, although the silent attention accorded them may be intended. **ruler** (Heb. *môshēl*, so 10:4), alternatively ' speaker (or maker) of proverbs ' (e.g. E. Podechard, and cf. Num. 21:27 ; Ezek. 16:44). The phrase is interpreted as ' arch-fool ', cf. R. Gordis, ' the ranting of the king of fools '. H. Odeberg, following A. L. Williams who takes his cue from the Targ., sees in the verse as a whole a reference to the conduct of prayer. **18a.** Cf. 9:13–16. **18b. sinner:** possibly ' blunderer ', or with some Heb. MSS, Syr. ' sin ' (or ' blunder '), which would suit the parallelism. **10:1a. make . . . odour:** read with the MT (cf. RVm), ' make a compounder's unguent(s) to stink (and) ferment ', cf. G. R. Driver. **2.** Cf. 2:14 : the reference here is apparently to the moral bent of the personality. **3b.** I.e., ' his behaviour shows him to be a fool ', or ' he calls everyone a fool ', or ' everyone says he is a fool '. **4-7** may, a propos of ' wise men and fools ', reflect the advice given to candidates for government service in the schools of the wise. **4.** In effect perhaps, ' do not resign your post, for equanimity will obviate serious mistakes '. **5. as it were,** etc. : ' a sort of oversight ', possibly with a touch of irony. **6f.** Cf. Prov. 19:10. The promotion of the unworthy to the detriment of the nobility (' the rich '), characteristic of despotism, has suggested *inter alia* to some the reign of Ptolemy Philopator (222–205 B.C.). **8-11** concern wisdom in the sense of ' safety first ', the kind of prudence and forethought needed in occupations where dangers may arise. **8f.** The verbs are best rendered hypothetically, ' may fall ' etc. Snakes are prone to nest in loose stone walls. **10a. whet the edge:** ' edge ' is impossible. With very slight change of the Heb. read ' sharpen it beforehand ' (cf., e.g., C. D. Ginsburg, G. R. Driver). **10b. succeed:** cf. on 2:21. **11.** The function of the snake-charmer (lit. ' the owner of the tongue ', probably because he muttered incantations, as, e.g., in India today, where snake-charmers are employed not only to entertain but also to lure away and capture poisonous snakes) being to divert the snake from its victim, it is of no avail if the snake has already bitten before the snake-charmer can get into

404e action. **12-15** return more explicitly to the subject of wise men and fools. **12a. win him favour:** i.e. 'command approval'. **12b. consume him:** lit. 'swallow', i.e. 'bring about his undoing'. **14f.** are obscure. Some would connect 14*a* with 15, regarding 14*b* as a misplaced Koheleth fragment (cf. 3:22, 6:12, 7:14). As 14 stands it would seem to mean that although no-one can hope to solve the problem of human destiny, the fool holds forth at length on the subject. **15.** The exertions of a fool tire him out either (*a*) because he does not know the way to his destination, or (*b*) so that he does not get to his destination, i.e. he never accomplishes anything. **16-20** appear to be a return to the theme of 4–7 and have at most but a tenuous unity. **16f.** Cf. on 4:13–16. **child** (Heb. *na'ar*, 'boy', 'lad', 'youth', 'servant'), if it here means 'servant' (cf. 7), would be an appropriate parallel to 'son of free men' in 17, but however it be taken 16 as a whole alludes to irresponsible government. **17. son of free men:** only here in the OT but found in Aram. form in North Syrian inscriptions and in the late Heb. of the Mishnah, and signifies 'noble descent'. **strength:** i.e. with 'self-control' (K-B). **18f.** consist of two gnomic sayings, which may illustrate 16, relating to the ruin caused by neglect and the extravagance resulting from over-lavish feasting. **answers:** 'provides', the nuance here being 'for all of which money has to be provided'. **20.** It is not safe even in complete privacy to malign those in authority. **in your thought:** better for sense and parallelism, 'in your resting-place' (the Heb. consonants *yd'* representing two distinct verbs, 'know' and 'be at rest'), cf. G. R. Driver.

405a **XI 1-8 A Call to Venture** with prudence and foresight upon a full and active life (1f.), rejoicing in it whilst it lasts (7f.), for even though everything is predestined by God whose ways are hidden (3, 5), there is no place for indecision and lack of enterprise (4, 6). There is no agreed interpretation of **1f.** which seem closely connected in thought, 1 suggesting that no venture is lost, and 2 implying that one should play for safety by distributing one's assets. Thus they have been taken as referring to (*a*) the practice of charity, of which there is an echo in an Arabic proverb (cf., e.g., G. A. Barton), and (*b*) overseas trade (cf., e.g., A. L. Williams), which on the whole is preferable since it accords well with the tenor of both verses and strains the meaning less of the verb rendered 'cast' (Heb. *shallaḥ*, 'send off, away'), although departing from the agricultural bearing of much in the rest of the passage. Some have discerned in 1 an allusion to the sowing of seed in the moist alluvium of the Nile, and O. S. Rankin notes the practice of flinging baskets filled with seedlings into the sea and rivers at the end of the Adonis festival, observing that 'the casting of bread upon waters appears to be the means of obtaining a rich return'. By taking 'for' in both verses as 'yet', H. W. Hertzberg regards them as indicating the uncertainty of human undertakings. **3f.** There is no halting natural processes (A. H. NcNeile's suggestion of rhabdomancy, cf. Hos. 4:12, with reference to the tree falling to rest in the direction from which it has been blown, appears unnecessarily to introduce the human element), and the farmer who waits for ideal weather conditions will never begin his work. **5f.** Even though, like the embryonic development of human life, the creative activity of God is a mystery, one should not therefore refrain from sowing both early and late, simply because one does not know how either or both sowings will turn out. **5a.** Lit. 'what is the way of the spirit (i.e. *rûaḥ* as the life force) with (so many Heb. MSS against the MT 'as') the bones (i.e. the embryo) in the womb'. **6a. morning . . . evening** are variously understood—literally, or as from morning till night (i.e. continually), or as from youth to old age, or as above (i.e. early or late in the season) which well suits the context. **7f.** Life must be enjoyed to the full under the compulsion of the shadow of death, even as (3–6) husbandry must go on in spite of man's inability to control the weather and his ignorance of God's methods in creation. And so to the concluding theme of:

b **XI 9-XII 8 Carpe Diem**—Youth pre-eminently is the time for rejoicing and making the most of life (11:9–12:1) until old age, portrayed under different figures of speech, comes on (12:2–5) followed by death and what it signifies (6–8). **9c.** R. Gordis disputes the view of many that this is a devout gloss, rendering 'but' by 'and' and apparently relating 'judgment' to the duty of youthful enjoyment. **10c. dawn of life** (the Heb. also means 'black hair', cf., e.g., H. W. Hertzberg—as against the white hair of old age), i.e. youth or early prime, 'vanity' standing here possibly for its transience. **12:1a. your Creator,** so all the VSS, is uniquely written as a plural in the MT, and has been explained as a 'plural of majesty' or as a Mishnaic trait (R. Gordis). Some regard it as having been but slightly altered from a similar word meaning 'cistern', which would here have the force of 'your wife', cf. Prov. 5:15–18, and accord with Koheleth's thought, cf. 9:9. K. Galling proposes 'your grave' as being appropriate to the context. The hand of the orthodox glossator is suspected by O. S. Rankin, who also thinks that 'before' in 1*b*, 2*a*, 6*a* is governed by 'Rejoice' in 11:9*a*. **2-6** form an allegory on the approach of old age and death, in which have been variously discerned anatomical allusions, storm phenomena, the onset of nightfall, the gloom in a house of mourning, and the 'seven days of death' (i.e. the wintry conditions prior to the Palestinian spring), none of which is consistently carried through. **2.** Old age is incipient death, warmth and light giving place to cold and darkness, and, as in winter, storm following storm without any brightness. Rabbinical exegesis explains the luminaries mentioned as parts of the head. **3.** In the great house which has fallen on evil days the doddering menservants, decrepit masters, depleted women-servants (e.g. Exod. 11:5), and enfeebled mistresses (i.e. those who have ceased—for 'dimmed', cf. G. R. Driver—to look through the lattices) are similarly interpreted as arms, legs, teeth, and eyes. **4** appears to concern the onset of deafness rather than mourning at the approach of death. **one rises up at the voice of a bird** would accord with this if emended as 'and the sound of the bird is silent' (cf. E. Podechard), although as it stands it hints at the old man's sleep being early disturbed. Alternatively, some have seen a reference to his childish treble, rendering, 'he shall approach to the voice of a bird'. **daughters of song:** i.e. 'songbirds', cf. G. R. Driver. **5a.** Any kind of ascent and movement abroad are unnerving to the aged and infirm. **5b.** The interpretation depends on the way in which the nouns are to be understood, and (in relation to them) the verbs (partly owing to textual uncertainty) are to be read. No proposal has proved free from objection, and of the many offered three of the more distinctive attempts at a solution are here given. The 'almond tree' (*amygdalus communis*) is noteworthy for its early blossom which appears white and its edible nuts, the 'grasshopper' (or locust) as devouring (2 Chr. 7:13) and as an article of diet (Lev. 11:22), and the caper-berry ('desire') as a condiment and (though this is much disputed) as an aphrodisiac. H. W. Hertzberg (cf. also K. Galling) discerns a reference to the spring with the almond in blossom, the grasshopper loaded with food, and the caper bursting into bloom as contrasted with the dying old man. Others (e.g. A. H. McNeile, E. Podechard) consider the old man's failing appetite to be intended since he can no longer digest such delicacies as almonds and grasshoppers nor be tempted by caper sauce. A further possibility lies in regarding the almond blossom as standing for the old man's white head, and the dragging of the grasshopper as indicating lowered sexual vitality, which the caper-berry is no longer able to stimulate (cf. R. Gordis). **5c. eternal home:** i.e. the grave. The use of the

05b expression only here in the OT has been thought to reflect Egyptian influence, although also found in Aram., Arabic, and Punic sources, cf. P. Humbert. In anticipation of employment, professional mourners are ghoulishly in evidence, cf. Jer. 9:17–22. **6.** Death is now figuratively portrayed, although the number of metaphors (from four down to one) employed is debated. There appear, perhaps most naturally according to parallelism and meaning, to be two : a golden lamp bowl suspended by a silver cord, and a pitcher with the spindle whereby it is lowered and raised at the well. The light goes out and the water supply is cut off, graphically signifying that life (for which light and water are common enough symbols) has ceased. **7.** Cf. on 3:21. **8.** Cf. on 1:2. Opinion is divided as to whether this verse concludes the foregoing or introduces the closing section.

c **9-14 Appendices**—(*a*) 9–11 in praise of Koheleth and in the third person are from the hand of one who valued his teaching. **9a. Besides** etc., or ' In addition to the fact that Koheleth was a sage ' (Heb. *ḥākhām*, ' wise '—an adjective used as a noun and often in a technical sense), i.e. one who taught wisdom professionally in the schools. **also taught** etc. is taken as meaning (*a*) that Koheleth published for a wider public than the classroom, hence the present book, or (*b*) that having written the foregoing he then went on to write for popular consumption. **9b** relates to Koheleth's methods of research and writing. If with the LXX the third verb be taken as a noun, the clause will read, ' and he pondered and sought out the ordering of many proverbs ', cf. G. R. Driver. ' Proverbs ' here include maxims, reflections, parables, and allegory as found in the book. **10. uprightly :** for such professional integrity cf. Sir. 37:23. **11. collected sayings :** the RV ' masters of assemblies ' appears to have come by way of Rabbinical exegesis, and may well be close to the meaning here if the expression is taken as being parallel to ' The sayings of the wise ' and so to refer to such utterances. The phrase seemingly is nowhere used of literary collections. G. R. Driver emphasises that it is the *words* that sway assemblies. Hence he would render the verse, ' The words of the wise are like goads or like nails driven home ; they are the rulers of assemblies, given of one shepherd.' Such utterances were devised to stimulate and to stick in people's minds. **by one Shepherd** suggests a common source and, according to OT usage, that God is here intended, cf. Gen. 49:24 ; Ps. 23:1, 80:1 (MT, 80:2). (*b*) **12-14** begin with a warning and end with an injunction to fear God, and have all the indications of a writer concerned to uphold the traditional view of divine judgment. O. S. Rankin's surmise that he wrote ' several generations ' after the time of the writer of the first epilogue is apparently now ruled out by the evidence of 4QKoh. **12a. My son :** cf. Prov. 1:8, 10, 15. **beyond these** concerns either the sayings of the wise (11), or the contents of Ec., or ' books ' and ' study ' (12*b*, cf. A. H. McNeile, A. L. Williams). The verse generally may be taken as a corrective against Koheleth's heterodoxy or as a caution regarding the voluminous non-Israelite literature such as was available in the great library of Alexandria, cf. E. H. Plumptre. **13f.** recall 3:17, 11:9*b*. **this is the whole duty of man :** lit. ' this is every man ', i.e. ' this befits every man '. **14.** The searching nature of the divine judgment is emphasised as the concluding word. 405c

Bibliography—Commentaries : G. A. Barton, ICC (1908) ; K. Galling, HAT (1940) ; C. D. Ginsburg, *Coheleth, commonly called the book of Ecclesiastes* (1861) ; H. W. Hertzberg, KAT (1932) ; G. Kuhn, *Erklärung des Buches Koheleth*, BZAW 43 (1926) ; G. C. Martin, Cent.B (1908) ; H. Odeberg, *Qohæleth* (1929) ; E. H. Plumptre, CB (1881) ; E. Podechard, EBib. (1912) ; O. S. Rankin, IB (1956) ; C. Siegfried, HKAT (1898) ; G. Wildeboer, KHC (1898) ; A. L. Williams, CB (1922).

Other Literature : W. Baumgartner, ' Die israelitische Weisheitsliteratur ', ThRs (NF) 5 (1933), 259–88, *Israelitische und altorientalische Weisheit* (1933), ' The Wisdom Literature ', OTMS (1951), 210–37 ; H.-J. Blieffert, *Weltanschauung und Gottesglaube im Buch Kohelet* (1938) ; M. J. Dahood, ' Canaanite-Phoenician Influence in Qoheleth ', Bi. 33 (1952), 30–52, 191–221 ; F. Dornseiff, ' Das Buch Prediger ', ZDMG 89 (1935), 243–9 ; G. R. Driver, ' Problems and Solutions ', VT 4 (1954), 225–45 ; A.-M. Dubarle, *Les Sages d'Israël* (1946) ; H. Duesberg, *Les Scribes Inspirés* II (1939) ; C. C. Forman, ' The Pessimism of Ecclesiastes ', JSS 3 (1958), 336–43 ; K. Galling, ' Kohelet-Studien ', ZATW 50 (1932), 276–99, ' Stand und Aufgabe der Kohelet-Forschung ', ThRs (NF) 6 (1934), 355–74 ; H. L. Ginsberg, *Studies in Koheleth* (1950), ' Supplementary Studies in Koheleth ', PAAJ 21 (1952), 35–62, ' The Structure and Contents of the Book of Koheleth ', VT Suppl. 3 (1955), 138–49 ; R. Gordis, ' Koheleth—Hebrew or Aramaic ? ', JBL 71 (1952), 93–109, *Koheleth—The Man and his World* (2nd ed. 1955), ' Was Koheleth a Phoenician ? ', JBL 74 (1955), 103–14 ; P. Humbert, *Recherches sur les sources égyptiennes de la littérature sapientale d'Israël* (1929) ; A. H. McNeile, *An Introduction to Ecclesiastes* (1904) ; J. Muilenburg, ' A Qoheleth Scroll from Qumrân ', BASOR 135 (1954), 20–8 ; J. Pedersen, ' Scepticisme israélite ', RHPR 10 (1930), 317–70 ; O. S. Rankin, *Israel's Wisdom Literature* (1936) ; H. Ranston, *Ecclesiastes and the Early Greek Wisdom Literature* (1925), *The OT Wisdom Books* (1930).

THE SONG OF SOLOMON

By A. S. HERBERT

406a Within the third section of the Heb. Bible, Ca. is the first of the Festal Megilloth, and was appointed to be read at the Passover. The meaning of the title, ' The Song of Songs ', which is given in the first verse of the book, is that it is the loveliest song, as Holy of Holies means the most holy. It is further associated with the name Solomon, an apparent reference to 1 Kg. 4:32. There is nothing to determine when this title was given, although the form of the relative pronoun in 1:1 would suggest a date other than that of the poems (cf. 3:7 (AV), ' Behold his litter which is Solomon's ', where the relative is that used elsewhere in the book). The book was already part of the second canon by the 1st cent. A.D., although even at that date there was some uneasiness felt by certain Jewish scholars about its inclusion. The vigorous defence of the book as part of the Sacred Scriptures by Rabbi Akiba at the Council of Jamnia—' all the ages are not worth the day on which the Song of Songs was given to Israel ; for all the writings are holy, but the Song of Songs is the Holy of Holies ' (Mishnah, *Yadaim* 3:5)—may be regarded as the definitive word. As part of the Jewish Palestinian canon it passes without further question into the Christian canon.

b **Date and Authorship**—There is nothing in the book which would suggest Solomon's authorship. The name Solomon appears at 1:5, 3:7, 9, 11, 8:11, 12, but is used in a manner which indicates that he was not the author. The language of the book is even more decisive. The book contains many words which show the influence of Aram. This can hardly determine the date, since in certain parts of the country, notably the North, Heb. was influenced by Aram. at an early date. It is not, however, the language of Judah and certainly not that of the court. More decisive is the occurrence of a Persian word at 4:13 (' orchard ') occurring elsewhere only at Neh. 2:8 ; Ec. 2:5, and a Gr. word at 3:9 (' palanquin '). The presence of these Hebraised Persian and Gr. words indicates that the book can hardly be earlier than 300 B.C. (It should be noted that the presence of another Gr. loan-word has been suspected at 4:4 (' arsenal '), but the word is better explained from a Semitic root to mean ' course of masonry ' ; cf. A. M. Honeyman, JTS 50 (1949), 51f.) The contents of the poems can hardly be expected to provide evidence of date ; it is not the nature of such poetry to make allusions to historical situations or to political conditions. The most that can be said is that they come from a time when Solomon has become, in popular imagination, the type of magnificence. The 3rd cent. B.C. would be the appropriate chronological setting for the book as we have it. The scenes described in the book, like the language, suggest the North rather than Judaea as the place of origin.

c We have no means of determining the author. Many would suggest that the book is a compilation of previously existing and largely traditional poems. The similarity of language, especially the use of unusual words throughout the poems, and the fairly clear evidence of progression of thought towards a climax in ch. 8 (however the poems are interpreted) strongly suggest unity of authorship. The poet may well have used traditional material, but he has shaped
it to his own ends. Granting the conventions of the **406**
East, and estimating the lyrical quality of the poems by those standards, we can recognise a poet sensitive both to the beauties of the natural world and to the wonder and mystery of human love. Rarely has nature's awakening been more exquisitely portrayed than in 2:11–13 ; while the description of love in 8:6f. could only have come from one whose own experience of love was so profound as to quicken his poetic genius to its highest expression. It is the work of a poet who would convey the beauty and the mystery of human love.

Now the deepest of all human emotions cannot be **d**
treated in abstraction ; it is a relationship. The poet therefore has presented love through the medium of a youth and maiden in an appropriate setting, the countryside. He has essayed the profoundly difficult task of conveying the emotions both of the youth and of the maiden and has done so with rare artistry and insight. So finely and sensitively indeed has the poet portrayed the maiden's feelings, that we might even conjecture that the poet was a woman. But the important fact to remember is, that it is a poet whose words we read, and that must determine our interpretation.

Nature of the Book—The presence of Ca. in our **e**
English Bible between Ec. and Isa., or in a Heb. Bible between Job and Ru. well illustrates the rich variety in the biblical material. The liturgical association with Passover will occasion some surprise ; for there seems to be no obvious connection in thought between the solemn and joyful celebration of God's salvation of his people and the uninhibited erotic poetry of Ca. We may wonder how this book became part of the Canon of Sacred Scripture ; it occasions less surprise to learn that passages from it were being sung, even at the beginning of the Christian era, at banquets (Tosephta, *Sanhedrin* 12; Bab. Talm., *Sanhedrin* 101*a*).

Superficially at least, it is a collection, or a cycle, **f**
of love songs expressed with a boldness of language that is startling to our Western ears. The uninhibited expression of human love which these poems express had led many, both Jews and Christians, to look for some meaning concealed beneath the imagery of the poetry, such as would make it more appropriate to its setting in the Bible. Such an interpretation is indicated by the chapter headings in the AV ; its ancestry can be traced to the Mishnah (*Ta'anith* 4:8), the teaching of Akiba and the early Fathers of the Church. Until comparatively recent days it was the prevailing mode of interpretation. It was assumed that Ca. was an *allegory* and was written as such. But within the realm of allegorical interpretation there was wide divergence ; at times the treatment of particular passages transgressed the bounds of good taste. As **an allegory** it has been regarded as treating of God's dealings with his beloved people, Israel ; of Christ and his church ; of the divine Logos and the faithful soul. Moreover, within each of these main lines of interpretation there was wide divergence in the treatment of particular passages. There can be no doubt but that this book has formed the vehicle of genuine piety and religious teaching of the best

406f kind, as, for example, in the eighty sermons on the first two chapters by St Bernard of Clairvaux. But the ingenuity required and the diversity of results raise doubts about this mode of interpretation. A great deal too much has to be read into the text. There is nothing in the poems which suggests that they are allegories; and where in other parts of the OT, as in Jer., Ezek. and Hos., nuptial language is used, the metaphorical or parabolic nature of the language is made clear. The language of the book has been adapted to teaching otherwise derived; that teaching is not contained within the book. It is to be noted that no such use of the book is to be found in the NT, even if it be admitted that Rom. 8:35 has been influenced by Ca. 8:6: 'love is strong as death.'

g From the various, and at times fantastic, forms of allegorical interpretation we return to the obvious and literal meaning of the text; it is a collection of love poems. It is true that this raises theological difficulties as to the fitness of such a collection to be within the covers of the Bible. But the difficulty is not of our making and an honest recognition of the facts may lead the way to a solution. If it be granted that love between a man and a woman with a desire for an indissoluble union has its proper place within the divine ordering of the world, and the OT entirely supports that belief, then there is nothing inappropriate in a book directed to that end being included in the Bible. Natural love, freed from its sinful perversions and sensuality, is recognised in the Bible to be the least inadequate type of the love of man for God, and of God for man. The same Heb. verb and noun is used for human and divine love. Our difficulty appears to derive from (*a*) the boldness of the language in the poems which we could not and should not imitate, and (*b*) the fact that we belong to a society in which the debased coinage of sensuality threatens to devalue the pure gold of love.

h As early as the close of the 4th cent. A.D. this literal understanding of Ca. was advocated by Theodore of Mopsuestia, who accepted its association with Solomon. His views were condemned by the Council of Constantinople (A.D. 553). It would appear from the language of some of the Fathers even before his time that he was not alone in advancing this view, and similar views have been advanced since his time. The understanding of Ca. as a collection of love poems has commanded wide acceptance in the present century and has led to various attempts to define more precisely the literary form and the origin of Ca.

i Parallels have been noted between Ca. and poems called *waṣfs*, or descriptive poems sung in Syria in the seven days of celebration at rural weddings, and it is suggested that 6:10, 13–7:5 belongs to the bride's sword dance. Undoubtedly such poems would have a long tradition behind them. In the nature of the case we should expect to find similarities of expression. It is, however, going beyond the evidence to argue that Ca. is a collection of material derived from pre-Christian Palestinian rural weddings. It is rather more probable that wedding-songs would derive from previously existing love-poetry. Nevertheless the comparison is valuable. For while formally there may exist a similarity between the language of Ca. and that of the nuptial songs sung at such rural weddings, (*a*) not all of the poems would fit into this category, and (*b*) where the resemblances are closest it is rather in form than in language. It would be reasonable to suppose that the poet had used, at times, the form; but his language has lifted it far above common usage.

j Again the attempt has been made to present Ca. as **a drama** with three main characters, Solomon, the maiden and her rustic lover, and various subsidiary characters. The details vary in this mode of interpretation; but briefly we are to see the royal lover seeking to win the maiden for his royal harem, while she yearns for her true love. The attractions of the court fail to win her, and she is finally reunited with her lover. This explanation requires much ingenuity 406j in assigning the poems to the characters, and more in providing stage directions. We find it difficult to associate the romantic and generous king of such a drama with the despotic monarch of 1 Kg. But, more seriously, there is no evidence that secular drama existed anywhere in the Semitic world. To suppose that Ca. is a drama seems to suggest the appearance of an art form with neither ancestry nor posterity; as such it would have no place in the life of a people.

More recently attention has been drawn to the many k parallels between the expressions of Ca. and the fertility cult-myths of the ancient Semitic and Egyptian world. Ca. may then be seen as poems relating to a religious drama or series of cultic acts celebrating the marriage of the divine lovers. Such fertility cults were widespread in Western Asia in ancient times; they are referred to in the OT (Jer. 7:18, 44:17f.), and were popular in the Graeco-Roman world. The cult involved a representation of the divine lovers (e.g. Ishtar and Tammuz), and a sacred marriage. The purpose was to promote the fertility of flocks and crops, and it was accompanied by gross and licentious rites. It is evident, when we study the parallels, that there is a great similarity of language between Ca. and such poetry as has survived from such cults. Yet when we recall the vigorous condemnation of such rituals in the OT we may find it difficult to accept the suggestion that Ca., as a collection of such ritual words, or the deposit of a fertility-cult liturgy, could have been acceptable to post-exilic Judaism. For the Jews of that time lived in a world in which such practices were common. The Christian has adopted the pagan occasion of Easter; he has not adopted the pagan cults and recitals associated with that time of the year. We are led therefore to look again at the similarities of language and to ask whether they are not in fact inevitable, granting the view that Ca. is celebrating the experience of love. Varied and considerable though the language of love may be, it is none the less limited. Moreover, the ritual language that would describe the acts of the divine lovers must inevitably draw on the language of human love which, in the experience of man, is prior.

We return, then, to the simplest form of the **literal** l **interpretation.** Ca. is a series of poems celebrating the love of a man and a woman. We may find in these poems a progression leading to love's consummation in marriage, and the depth and intensity of love itself is acknowledged. We shall not look for any particular man and woman whose love is being described. Rather we shall hear the words of a great poet who has chosen this medium for presenting the simplicity and the greatness, the gentleness and strength of love. The scenes he describes did not necessarily exist as he speaks of them; neither did the people he referred to have objective reality. We may draw an illustration from the work of Shakespeare. There never was an historical Prince of Denmark like the Hamlet of the play, but Hamlet lives in every land and in every age. So the poet of Ca. is not describing people and scenes as does a reporter. He is, in a poetically heightened form of the language and art forms of his day, conveying his insight.

Viewed in this light, what is the **religious signi-** m **ficance** of Ca.? And what is its place in the canon? It is part of the glory of Israel's faith that it saw human life in all its aspects as having a full and rightful place in the divine purpose. Human love and marriage are part of God's will for man (Gen. 1:27f., 2:24; Ps. 45:11f.); through love's fulfilment in marriage human nature reaches the greatest heights of earthly experience. The horrors of man's perversion of love must be continually challenged by its true expression as God gave it to man, and as it is celebrated in Ca. Further, the love that is declared here could have meaning only in a lifelong, monogamous partnership. If love between a man and a woman is seen in those terms, then, and not otherwise, may it be

406m appropriately used of the love of man for God, and of God for his people. It is notorious that the Christians, writing Gr., could not use the ordinary word for love in their religious vocabulary, because its associations made it unfit for such usage. In Heb. the same word is used for the love of God as for human love, for it belongs to the life of man as God created him.

n **The Form of the Book**—Ca. consists of a series of poems. If we accept unity of authorship, it is reasonable to expect some progression of thought, although in the view of many the book consists of a collection of unconnected love poems. It is possible however to trace a movement of thought from courtship to marriage in the mind of the poet, although it is not suggested that the progress of an actual courtship is being described. Some of the poems are in the form of reveries, some in dialogue form ; two are dream fantasies (3:1–5, 5:2–8) and one (8:6f.) a reflection on the nature of love. The most appropriate term for these poems is idylls. At certain points a refrain occurs (cf. 2:7, 3:5, 8:4). This may be intended to lessen for awhile the emotional tension. We cannot always be confident where the individual poems begin and end, and therefore of the number of poems contained in the book. It will appear that we have distinguished some nineteen poems, but some of the divisions are perhaps arbitrary.

407a **I 1** is the original title of the book : 'Solomon's loveliest song'. It would seem however to be no part of the original collection, and may have been added because of Solomon's traditional association with the song collections (cf. 1 Kg. 4:32).

2-4 The Maiden remembers her Lover—The original (cf. RSV*n*) 'he' and 'his' should be restored in **2a.** She remembers him, and so vivid is the memory that she then thinks of him as present and addresses him thereafter in the second person. It is not unusual in love poetry to address the object of love directly, even in solitude. **2b. love:** i.e. 'caresses'. **3. your name:** the name in Heb. thought is so integral to the person that in English idiom this means 'you yourself'. **oil poured out:** the translation of MT is difficult since the name is normally masculine and the verb here is feminine. It is possible that the apparent verb *tûraḳ* represents an otherwise unknown place-name from whence some perfumed oil was obtained, and we should render 'Turaq-oil'. A small emendation would give 'cosmetic oil', and a word from the same root occurs at 5:13, 'spices'. But the general meaning is clear ; the lover is loved by all. **4. The King . . . :** on the dramatic theory, this verse describes the maiden taken by Solomon into his harem, and greeted by the ladies of the court. It may simply be that the lover is a king to his beloved. She looks forward eagerly to the wedding-day, when she will go to the home he has prepared escorted by her accompanying maidens. **rightly** in English is ambiguous. It means here 'uprightly'.

b **5f. The rustic Charms of the Maiden**—The poem is in the form of a soliloquy. She reflects on her ruddy sunburnt countenance, and, by contrast, the fair complexion of the ladies of Jerusalem whose faces are never exposed to the sun. The contrast is a common theme of Arabic love poetry. **5. very dark** and **6 swarthy** are two forms of the same verbal root in Heb., as we might say, 'dark' and 'darkened'. Dark she may be like the black tents of the bedouin tribe (Gen. 25:13, etc.), whose very name suggests the thought of darkness of hue (*ḳdr*, 'to be dark'). Yet for her lover, her colouring will bring to mind all the rich splendour of the curtains in the royal palace. **6. were angry with** means literally 'snorted against' (the cognate noun occurs at Job 39:20 ; Jer. 8:16). There is no need to conjecture some reason for her brothers' anger. The verb simply describes the rough manner in which her brothers sent her about her work of guarding the family vineyard. There is a fine contrast in her status merely as a member of the family, and her newly discovered worth (8:8f.) when she is sought in marriage. **but my own vineyard:** 407
some would delete this clause on metrical grounds ; but its excision seems unnecessary. It makes a fitting climax, if we suppose a swift transition in the spirit of Ca. from a literal to a metaphorical usage (cf. 8:12). The meaning may be either that she has not taken care of her beauty (that would be in the mood of the poem), or that she has given her heart to her lover. The second meaning would prepare us for the following poem.

7f. The Maiden seeks her Lover—In spite of the c
paragraphing of the RSV, it seems better to take these verses together in view of the obvious community of terms. In form it is a lover's dialogue in which first the maiden, then the lover speaks. But it may be simply the poetic way of expressing the longing of the maiden for her lover, and her confidence that they will meet. The motif of seeking and finding appears again in the reverie of 2:8ff. and the dream of 3:1ff. Those who interpret Ca. in terms of cult-poems draw attention to the occurrence of the same motif in the Tammuz liturgies. Allegorically it may serve to express the quest for God. **one who wanders:** the translation 'that is veiled' (so RSV*n*, AVm and RV) is based on a simple emendation of MT with good support from the versions.

I 9-II 7 Lovers' Dialogue—In a series of impres- d
sionistic similes and metaphors each dwells on the other's charms. The terms are those appropriate to an oriental setting. They are not intended as pictorial likenesses, but as mental impressions. **9-11.** The pure-bred mare of the royal stables, richly bedecked for ceremonial use, evokes wonder and admiration. The same comparison appears in old Egyptian and modern Arabic love poetry. So the bridegroom looks to his bride. He sees with the eyes of love far more than does the casual beholder in the beauty of the maiden and her carefully treasured ornaments. Would that she might be arrayed with gold and silver! **ornaments:** apparently strings of beads. The word is rare, and occurs only in the latest books and in a metaphorical sense : 1 Chr. 17:17 (generations) and Est. 2:12, 15 (turn) ; in these passages the events are described as beads or knots on an unbroken string. So in Ca. the word refers either to necklaces or strings of jewels woven into the hair and hanging in loops on either side of the cheeks. **12-14.** She returns the compliment. He is to her like a great king, magnificent and splendid. In his presence, she feels the pleasurable emotions such as are evoked by perfumes. **couch:** either a low seat going round a table or a round table. If the latter we should translate 'at his table'. **nard:** an aromatic grass native to Palestine. **myrrh:** a resinous gum from a shrub, much used for incense and perfume. **henna blossoms:** sweetly scented flowers found only at Engedi by the Dead Sea (the scent is that of chypre). **15f.** First the lover then the maiden with a brief cry of delight acknowledges the beauty of the other. **16b, 17.** Then together they speak with longing of their rustic bower, the shepherd's booth of leafy branches. But the woods referred to, cedar and pine (or Phoenician juniper), carry with them an overtone of meaning. Such woods are used in the panelling of palaces.

II 1f. First the maiden speaks in words of modest e
self-depreciation ; then the lover takes up her words and charmingly transforms them into a word of praise. In **2:1** neither **rose** nor **lily** is a literal translation of the Heb. ; but the former, certainly, is an excellent transposition into English idiom. The 'rose' is in fact the autumn crocus (cf. Isa. 35:1) or meadow saffron ; while the 'lily' is the anemone coronaria, or scarlet anemone (cf. 5:13). Both are common wild flowers in Palestine. We recall the use made by our Lord of this second flower in Mt. 6:28ff. The appropriate English metaphors are common wild flowers, the wild rose and the wood anemone. **2.** So the lover appropriately replies that her beauty is indeed like a wood anemone—among brambles.

407e For him, there is only one who evokes his love. **3.** Not to be outdone in this lovely contest of endearment, she replies that he excels in beauty like an apple-tree covered with blossom among the common trees of the forest. Her thoughts go on to recall the pleasures of resting in the shade of an apple-tree and enjoying its fruit ; metaphor and actuality intermingle.

f **4-7.** The picture changes. The thought of the closing words of 3 lead her thought on to the marriage day. **4. banqueting house :** lit. ' house of wine '. It may simply be a reference to the home where the marriage is to take place, or, as the following words may suggest, to the marriage chamber itself. With charming candour, she speaks of the intensity of their love : his like a strong army overcoming her, so that she was languishing with love for him. Hence her cry for raisins and apples, traditionally associated with love. **6.** With simple naturalness she longs for the consummation of their love in marriage. The day-dream closes with a refrain repeated at 3:5 and 8:4. The reiteration of the refrain has suggested the use of these poems in a dramatic setting : but the sentiments expressed in the preceding poems and the brevity of the whole hardly justify this interpretation. It seems better to regard them as expressing a natural climax in the movement of thought. The mind of the reader is briefly taken from the lovers. The emotions expressed in the previous verses could so easily lead to mere eroticism ; they are rescued from any such perversion by the very words of the refrain. A genuine and pure love needs no false or artificial stimulus ; let the final expression of love be spontaneous and natural. The **daughters of Jerusalem** are little more than imaginary figures, but perhaps representing the more artificial life of the city by contrast with the simplicity of the rural lovers. The adjuration by gazelles and hinds is strange, and outside Ca. unparalleled. It appears to signify : ' By all that is lovely and free ! ' (Delitzsch).

408a **8-14 The Springtide of Love**—It is the maiden who speaks describing the coming of her lover and recalling his words to her. It is one of the most beautiful lyrics in the book, and expresses both the unfeigned longing of the maiden for her lover and a response to the joyous awakening of springtime—an appropriate setting for love. The opening phrases, describing in brilliant hyperbole the coming of her lover, suggest that the remainder of v. **9** and the lover's words are emotion remembered, if not in tranquillity, certainly in solitude. **8.** Render perhaps better ' Hark ! my lover ! Behold he is coming.' **9. stag** is too heavy a word for the Heb. which represents a young ibex ; ' hart ' would be better. The words convey the idea of fleetness and eager movement. We may note that **9c** is also used of the man seeking wisdom in Sir. 14:23. The **window** is no more than an opening in the wall, protected by the **lattice**. **11. winter** is the rainy season after which for six months rain is infrequent (cf. 1 Sam. 12:16f.). This word for winter occurs only here in MT, but is known from Akkadian and Arabic usage. The rainy season has ended, the heavy clouds sweep away over the horizon and then (12f.) the spring comes, when the ground almost bursts into a wealth of colourful flowers. ' singing ' : it is not certain whether the Heb. means ' singing ' or ' pruning ' (cf. RVm). In favour of ' pruning ' is (*a*) the use of the cognate verb in Isa. 5:6 ; (*b*) the oldest versions so translate it ; and (*c*) when the word appears elsewhere it is used of the human voice accompanied with a musical instrument. But (*a*) the season appears to be too early for pruning ; (*b*) the noun is not otherwise used for pruning ; and (*c*) while the line does not specifically mention bird songs (' of birds ' is an addition in AV and RV), it seems somewhat pedantic to suppose that there is anything inappropriate in all animate creation joining in the song of happiness. **13. puts forth :** this can hardly be the meaning of the Heb. verb, which appears to be connected with the noun for ' wheat '. We should possibly translate ' has begun to redden '. This is the 408a
first crop which appears before the leaf ; it is followed by a later second crop. **13. are in blossom** (only here, v. 15 and 7:12, 13) : the word suggests something round and may mean ' are in bud '. **15** is difficult and seems unrelated to its context. Its position may be accounted for by the occurrence of the unusual word ' in blossom (or bud) '. It may be a fragment of a vineyard watcher's song. The verb ' catch ' is 2nd plural masculine, itself an intrusion. And if the meaning is that by ' foxes ' (or jackals, as in Ps. 63:10) is meant young men and by ' vineyards ' the maiden's charms, it seems quite out of place at this point.

16f. The Maiden speaks of her Lover—It seems b
most appropriate to regard this as a soliloquy. The opening words describe the complete reciprocity of true love. We may further observe that such a sentiment makes anything other than monogamy meaningless. Love goes beyond and so fulfils the law. **17** (cf. 4:6) may refer either to the evening, with which the final clause is most commonly associated (although the phrase has no precise parallel), or to the morning, which would better suit the second clause. If the second is the correct interpretation, then ' turn ' would be imaginatively addressed to the lover : let him leave the flocks he has watched through the night and come to her with the swiftness of a gazelle. **rugged** is a guess, connecting MT *bether* with a verb meaning ' to cut in pieces '. The word is otherwise unknown but may be the same as *Bithron* (2 Sam. 2:29, AV and RV, but RSV ' forenoon '). It may be better to regard the word as a proper noun and render ' the mountains of Bether '.

III 1-5 A Dream of Love—There can be little doubt c
that vv. **1-4** are the narration of a dream. **5** has suggested to many that the dream was told by the bride to her companions. But this refrain appears at 2:7 and 8:4 ; while the ' daughters of Jerusalem ' are appealed to at 1:5, 3:11, 5:8, 16. It is probable that they have no objective reality, but are conjured up in the mind of the speaker as the poet presents her. In **1-4** we have a sensitive presentation of natural love. The thought of the bridegroom (e.g. in 2:16ff.) creates desire for him. Desire finds expression in dreams of seeking and finding. **1. by night** is ambiguous. The noun is plural and conveys the entirely natural thought that night after night her longing was reflected in her dreams. The repetition of **I sought** is in keeping with this. It would be pedantic to object that precisely the same dreams would not come each night. This is poetry, not a literal description for analysis. **I called him . . .'** is not in MT ; it appears in LXX and OL, but not in Vulg. It seems more reasonable to suppose that it was added from 5:6 by the Gr. translators than that it was omitted by MT. The omission of this line from RSV leaves precisely that sense of incompleteness and sadness that the theme of the poem requires. We may render :

Nightly on my bed I sought
Him whom my soul loves
I sought him and found him not.

2. We should think of **the city** as a small country town with its narrow ' streets ' and wider spaces of intersection (**the squares**). The repetition of ' my soul loves ' from v. 1 and so also in vv. 3 and 4 well portrays the emotional content of the poem. The soul (*nephesh*) is the totality of psychic life. In love there is a sharing of ' soul '.

6-11 The Coming of the Bridegroom—Again we d
have a passage of magnificent hyperbole, effectively answering the wistful longing of the previous poem. The transition of mood is swift, almost violent, yet singularly appropriate to the rapidly changing moods of love. The coming of the bridegroom is described in terms of a royal wedding procession as imagined by a country dweller. It seems unnecessary to find in these verses a description of the historical Solomon's

408d wedding procession. It is intended to be an imaginative picture. We do not need therefore to suppose that the poem is a speech of the bride, or of a spectator; or that a group of women are addressed in v. 11. The poem is a descriptive piece; this is how the bridegroom appears to the bride: not even Solomon in all his glory appeared like her lover. A similar reflection on the bride's beauty occurs at 6:10, 8:5.

e **6. What is this coming up . . . perfumed . . .:** the interrogative is normally translated 'who?'; the pronoun and verbs are feminine. This has led to the interpretation of the verse as referring to a woman in the palanquin. But this is inappropriate to the poem, which is describing the splendour of the man (Solomon or the bridegroom). It would strike a false note even on a dramatic interpretation. The interrogative may be used as in Gen. 33:8, where RSV translates the literal 'Who for thee the camp?' as 'What do you mean by all this company?' So here, 'what' expresses astonishment. The feminine demonstrative will then represent the neuter (a normal usage in Heb. grammar), but we should prefer 'What is this . . .' as both more literal and appropriate to something which commands the whole attention. The 'column of smoke' will be dust raised by the procession. The bridegroom is appropriately (in the East) perfumed; cf. Ps. 45:8. **7f.** The description of the bridegroom's attendants is not to be taken literally, but rather as hyperbole. They are a veritable Solomon's bodyguard! **9. Solomon** here appears to be a later addition from v. 7. Its inclusion spoils the metre. 'The King': i.e. the bridegroom. **palanquin:** a Gr. loan-word in Heb., just as the English word was received from India through Portuguese. The same word appears in the Mishnah (*Sota* IX, 14) as a bridal litter. **10. back:** the word occurs only here; its meaning is 'that which supports', i.e. that upon which one leans. **it was lovingly wrought:** the word translated 'lovingly' appears in this place to be a quite different word meaning 'leather'; we may render: 'within it was covered with leather'. **11. daughters of Zion** is unusual, but possibly to avoid repetition. Possibly it should be omitted with 'Solomon' and so read: 'Go forth and see the king.' **his mother crowned him** is quite obscure and no parallel can be found either in an accession ceremony or in a marriage. A crowning by a priest at a wedding is known in Christian usage. It can only be supposed that this refers to a custom otherwise unknown.

409a **IV 1-7 The Bride's Beauty as seen by the Bridegroom,** cf. 6:4–10, 7:6–9—The form of the poem is that of a *wasf*, a descriptive poem used in marriage ceremonies. It is in such poems that the canons of taste of the Western and Eastern worlds differ. Such a poem ill suits the task of the allegorist. It is better to see it as the work of a poet, making use of conventional forms but using them with fine artistry. To the Bridegroom she is wholly lovely.

1. behind your veil: older Jewish commentators, AV and RVm, translated as 'locks of hair'. But the word appears at Isa. 47:2, which supports the translation 'veil'. In Ca. the veil is part of the bridal attire. **flock of goats** (cf. 6:5*b*): the image is that of a flock of black goats winding down the mountain slopes. **moving down:** the word occurs only here and at 6:5; but its meaning is known from Arabic. **2** describes her gleaming white and evenly matched teeth. There is an untranslatable word-play in the Heb. words translated 'all of which' and 'bereaved', the first words in the Heb. stichoi; we might roughly render: 'Bears each her twins, barren is none.' **3. your mouth:** 'your speech'. **cheeks:** the Heb. word properly means 'temples', as in Jg. 4:21f., 5:26, but the simile and context suggest 'cheeks'. **4. arsenal:** better '(masonry laid) in courses' (Honeyman, JTS 50 (1949), 51f.). The whole simile is strange to us, but natural to an inhabitant of the land. He speaks of her firm and finely shaped neck encircled with rows of necklaces (cf. 1:10*b*). The general intent of these verses is to celebrate with (to 409 him) appropriate imagery the perfection of her feminine beauty. **6** probably means that he looks to the consummation of their love in marriage. It is expressed in discreetly veiled language, the latter half of the verse referring to the bride's person; cf. 12ff. This is love's natural expression by contrast with 2:7; and it corresponds to the bride's longing in 2:17. It is a natural climax of thought leading to the rapturous cry of v. **7**: 'You are in every way perfect.'

IV 8-V 1 The Bridegroom pleads with the Bride b —The passionate longing of the preceding poem accentuates the fact that they are not yet united. The present poem expresses the sense of separation, but leads to a mood of confident expectation at the nearness of their marriage. The place-names in **4:8** are chosen to suggest distance and inaccessibility, while, being separated from the beloved, the lover imagines all sorts of dangers threatening her. But the thought of her faithfulness and answering love leaves him with confident joy. **8. Amana** and **Hermon** (the snow-capped) are peaks in the Anti-Lebanon range; **Senir** is an alternative name for Hermon (Dt. 3:8f.). They represent to the country dweller the limits of inaccessibility and peril. It seems unnecessary to suppose that the maiden was in fact in all these places, or in danger from actual lions and leopards. It is normal for a lover to use hyperbole. **Come** represents, with the ancient versions, a revocalising of the Heb. consonants. But MT could be translated as it stands:

With me from Lebanon, my bride
With me from Lebanon do thou come.

Depart: this rendering appears to be based on a slight emendation of MT, but it is unnecessary. The verb appears at Isa. 57:9, 'journeyed'; so here 'make your way' or 'descend'. **9. You have ravished my heart** renders a demonstrative verb from the noun 'heart'. It could also be rendered 'You have quickened my heart'. **10. my sister, my bride:** the phrase occurs only in this poem, 4:10, 12, 5:1, and a corresponding term 'brother' in 8:1. But sister and brother are recognised terms in Egyptian love poems. They appear to be used to emphasise the sense of psychic nearness, and tenderness. They are already in thought 'one flesh'. **your love:** i.e. your caresses. **11. distil nectar** is a somewhat free, but perhaps justified, rendering of the Heb. 'drop honey from the honeycomb' (cf. Prov. 5:3), a charming way of describing the sweetness of her words. Haupt renders 'From thy lips virgin honey is dropping.' **12. garden . . . garden:** the c second occurrence is an emendation, with the ancient versions, of MT 'spring' (AV and RV). The two words, *gan*, 'garden', *gal*, 'spring', are similar. A similar word appears at Jos. 15:19; Jg. 1:15. The more usual word *gal* means 'waves of the sea' and this has possibly been the cause of the emendation. On the other hand the repetition of 'locked' is in favour of an original 'garden'. The meaning is in either case clear; she is chaste and modest and belongs only to her bridegroom. **13f.** simply gathers together the names of aromatic and sweet-smelling plants reaching a true (oriental) climax in cool running water, to do justice to the charms of the bride. In Sir. 24:15 Wisdom is similarly described. **orchard:** Heb. *pardēs* is a Persian loan-word; cf. English paradise. **16.** The response of the bride is, by the poet, appropriately interjected into the bridegroom's rhapsody.

V 1. The Heb. verbs may be construed as 'perfects of confidence', i.e. 'I know I shall come, etc.', and this is further reflected in his invitation to the wedding-feast. **lovers** is, in English, ambiguous and might suggest an invitation to all who are in love to join the wedding-feast. The word means 'beloved ones', but this is hardly English usage. We may render: 'Eat, O companions, and drink: drink deeply, O

409c friends'. The closing phrase could be translated 'drink deeply of caresses', but this is improbable because of the requirements of Heb. parallelism.

d **V 2-VI 3 The Bride's Dreams and Reveries**—This appears to be a single poem, with sub-divisions, leading to its climax in 6:2f. We may recognise the following stages: **2-8**, a dream of seeking; **9**, reflection induced by v. 8; **10-16**, the charms of the Bridegroom; **6:1**, reflection induced by 5:16; **6:2f.**, rapture of the Bride.

The details are somewhat obscure. The appeal to the 'daughters of Jerusalem', and the questions at **5:9** and **6:1** seem intrusive. It is improbable that such intimate thoughts (especially 6:2f.) would be declared to a group of women who are at best acquaintances, and apparently strangers. The whole may be a soliloquy produced by the dream, and the daughters of Jerusalem may then be the product of the bride's imagination. We need to recall that the whole is the work of the poet, not of a reporter, and the introduction of the proud beauties of Jerusalem (cf. Isa. 3:16), serves to emphasise the natural charm of the rustic maiden. The whole expresses the most intimate feelings of the bride on the eve of the wedding.

e **2-8.** So vivid and realistic was the dream that she seemed to be awake. **3.** She hears him at the door, but cannot move for reasons that seem quite reasonable in the dream however unconvincing in fact. **4. heart:** the word used represents the seat of strong emotion; cf. AV. The same word is used in Jer. 31:20 and, in Gr., in Phil. 2:1. **5.** Then she arose to welcome him and she is suddenly perfumed as a bride in the nuptial chamber. **6.** But he has vanished; in a moment she is wandering through the town in search of him but is violently prevented. It is a most penetrating description of a dream of longing, entirely appropriate to the setting. **6. spoke:** some would translate as from another Heb. verb, 'turned away', and this would suit the context. **8** gives the reason for the dream: 'languishing because of love am I'. **9.** She imagines or perhaps recalls the disdainful comments of other women. **10ff.** give a description of the bridegroom as the bride sees him, a fitting response to 4:9–15.

f **12. fitly set:** MT appears to mean 'sitting by a full-flowing stream'. The iridescent plumage of doves, gleaming as though bathed in milk and against the background of pure running water, suggests the irises and the whites of the eyes. **13.** She likens his perfumed beard to beds of balsam shrubs, his lips to scarlet anemones and his breath to fragrant myrrh. **14.** The comparison is rather mental than physical. As bejewelled gold and ivory appeal to the aesthetic sense, so does her lover's appearance. **14b.** Render: 'His body is a sheet of ivory, with sapphires decked.' The word for 'sheet of' (RSV **work**) occurs only here; the cognate verb means 'to be smooth'. **16.** 'His speech' is literally 'his palate', MT *ḥikkô*. The same word appears at 7:9 (Heb. 10), RSV 'kisses'. Unless we emend to *ḥinnô*, we should translate the same in both places. 'His kisses' would well suit the context here. **16. He is altogether desirable**; cf. 4:7. 6:1. An imagined or recollected comment: 'Where is this paragon of beauty fit for so fair a maiden?' and it leads to the rapturous cry of 2f. which describes with charming allusiveness the union of bride and bridegroom; cf. 4:12f., 5:1. Again, nothing but a monogamous union will satisfy the sentiments expressed. Each belongs wholly to the other.

410a **VI 4-10 The Bridegroom speaks of the Uniqueness of the Bride**—As he thinks of her charms, he is filled with a wonder that is akin to awe. She is incomparable; and such love makes a king's harem seem cheap and shoddy.

4. Tirzah, whose name suggests 'city of delight', was the old Israelite capital (1 Kg. 14:16). The use of the name offers no clue to the date of the poem; it is used because of its 'choice' name. An English poet might have said: 'You are lovely as Beaulieu'. The name has the further advantage of avoiding the hated name of Samaria, Such beauty is all-conquering. Genuine love is compounded of desire and humility. The closing words (cf. also 10*c*) may seem to us excessively harsh; yet we also speak of a lover being 'smitten' with his beloved's charms. Moreover, both in Semitic and Greek religion the goddess of love is associated also with war, and in English 'captivate' and 'capture' are closely connected. **5b-7.** The poem takes up and almost repeats 4:1*c*–3. **8f.** presents a fine contrast between the luxury of the oriental king, with its poverty in real love, and the true wealth of these 'twain become one flesh'. The ladies of the royal harem might well envy the rustic bride. **10** is the climax of the lover's praise. Let all the world see and wonder at her who rivals the dawn, the sun and the moon.

11f. Surprised by Love—The poem effectively describes the way in which into the quiet tenor of her life, love came and so she was caught up into the joy of marriage. **12** is difficult: **in a chariot beside my prince** gives good sense although it involves a slight emendation. Emendations are also required for AV and RV, the former being suggested by the ancient versions and perhaps referring to 2 Sam. 6:3. But the suggestion that the bride is thought of as the Ark of God is hardly probable. **my fancy:** hardly adequate to the Heb. 'my soul'. It seems best to regard the 'chariot beside my prince' as poetic hyperbole. Surprised, but fully consenting (my soul set me), she prepares for her wedding-day. b

VI 13-VII 9 In Praise of the Bride—The poem is in form a sword-dance *waṣf*. But the expressions used, although uninhibited by our canons of taste, are not a report of the normal coarse comments of a crowd watching the bride dancing and, as she dances, exposing her charms. The language, though frank, is too choice for that. But if such a dance formed a normal part of wedding festivities then the poet has made use of that form and made it part of the bridegroom's sincere appreciation of his bride's beauties. **6:13** (Heb. **7:1**). 'return': it is possible that this has replaced a similar-sounding Heb. verb, 'Turn round (in the dance)'. **Shulammite** is difficult. It has been understood as (*a*) the maiden of Sholem, i.e. Shunem (1 Kg. 1:3f.), (*b*) a feminine form of Solomon (Heb.: *Šh^elômōh*), (*c*) a Hebraised form of the goddess Shulmānītu. As for (*a*), nothing in the recorded story of Abishag suits the context except her beauty. It is moreover highly improbable that one who had been a member of the royal harem would have had any chance of being united to a rustic lover. Neither is there any evidence that she became a type figure for feminine beauty. As for (*c*), it seems virtually impossible that the name of a pagan goddess would have been used in this connection at so late a stage in the argument, although it is attractive from the cult-myth point of view. The context seems to favour (*b*). She is 'Solomoness' to her 'Solomon'. 'a dance before two armies': the introduction of 'before' is hardly justified by the Heb. We should perhaps render 'camp dance' or 'dance of Mahanaim', the second alternative being a reference to a recognised, but now unknown, mode of dancing. The dance is normally in the OT a ritual act. **7:1.** Since in the dance the feet are most obvious the account of the bride's charms move from the feet to the head. **queenly maiden** is rather too heavy for the Heb.: better, 'prince's daughter'. Most of the points of comparison are obvious; but it is a poet's, not a reporter's, description. Jewels, the rounded bowl brimming with wine, the heap of wheat, are aesthetically satisfying images rather than physical descriptions. **4. like a tower of Lebanon** seems to us grotesque. But such a tower seen from a distance, sharply cut against the sky, may well have seemed fitting to associate with the sharp aquilinity of the nose seen in profile. **5. tresses:** the word otherwise means watering-troughs (Gen. 30:38, 41; Exod. 2:16). The root meaning is c d

410d 'running' (of water), so probably here 'flowing locks'. **6.** A cry of sheer delight interrupting quite naturally the description of the bride. It could hardly have been said by any other than the bridegroom. The rendering in **6b** involves a small vowel change and a division of the last word in MT. Both find support in ancient versions. **7. palm tree** (Heb. *Tāmār*) : a favourite term of comparison because of the slender swaying gracefulness ; it is used as a feminine name in 2 Sam. 13:1, 14:27. **8** speaks of the bridegroom embracing the bride in the consummation of love. **9.** The closing simile involves a slight emendation of MT which might be rendered 'as it goes gliding smoothly, glides smoothly o'er lips and teeth.'

e **10-13 The Bride responds to her Husband**—Drawn to him with answering rapture, she proclaims herself his as he is hers. The precise meaning of the following verses is not easy to determine. They may be referring in veiled language to love's consummation and so correspond to **8f.** Alternatively she may be recalling scenes and objects associated with love (cf. 2:10, 13, 15, 4:13, 6:11). Some would see here a description of the *hieros gamos* (sacred marriage) in the vineyards (emending 'villages' (*k^{e}phārîm*) to vineyards (*k^{e}rāmîm*)). If the view be correct that we have in Ca. the work of a poet, rather than a description of an actual marriage, the first suggestion may well be the most satisfactory, and indeed necessary in the movement of the cycle of poems. **13.** 'mandrakes' : a plant of the *solanum* family, which might well be rendered, in close conformity with the Heb., 'love apples'.

f **VIII 1-4 A Love Song of the Bride**—The opening verse seems to respond to 4:8–5:1 ; while 3f. echo 2:6, 7. The poem expresses the bride's longing for the bridegroom, and that she may enjoy his company continually without reproach. It seems out of place here and might well follow 4:16. **5.** A brief interjection in which the bridegroom speaks in playful terms to his bride. He refers back to 3:6 and 6:10, but skilfully combining them. Now they are no longer alone, but together.

g **6f. The Bride's Hymn to Love**—It is remarkable that this, one of the profoundest utterances of the poem, is set in the mouth of the woman. For a moment we stand apart from the movement of the poem and reflect on the real nature of love that so completely unites man and woman. It is strongly demanding and inexorable as death itself. Like a forest fire it cannot be extinguished nor swept away. It is more precious than all riches. **6. set me as a seal** (cf. Gen. 38:18) : the seal was worn on a cord round the neck, or carried as a ring on the finger. **jealousy :** perhaps 'passion'. The word must be translated sometimes as 'zeal' as at Isa. 9:7(6), sometimes as 'jealousy' as at Isa. 11:13. **a most vehement flame :** lit. 'a flame of Yah'. **7b** so exalts love as to make it impossible to think of it merely in physical and emotional terms. Love in the OT can never be mere lust. But this profound conception of love is in the poet's mind from the beginning. It is in these terms that we should understand its emotional manifestations.

h **8-15 Reflections after Marriage**—The poem is in the form of a dialogue between the newly married couple : **8-10**, the bride ; **11-13**, the bridegroom ; **14**, the bride. After the preceding poem this appears as anticlimax. Part of the difficulty arises from treating **8f.** as the brothers seeking a good bride-price ; that would certainly be out of place at the close of this book. Some would see this section as fragmentary in character, or as a clear example of the view that Ca. is a collection of originally independent poems. That 410 again would make the compiler singularly maladroit. The same difficulty obtains if we regard these verses as a later addition. We may, however, read them as reflective dialogue. The profound exposition of love in **6f.** has been made in words. What this means in the man/woman relationship must now be stated. In **8-13** the bride recalls the proper care which her brothers had exercised as she grew from childhood to adolescence. If she guard her virginity (if she is a wall), they will give her a silver crown ; if she shows evidence of flightiness (a door), they will bar the way with a cedar plank. It was all unnecessary. **10.** She rejoices in the pure life she brings to her husband when, having come to maturity, she was married. Thus she brought to her husband true welfare (peace) in the intimacies of home life. **peace :** the Heb. *shālôm* picks up the names Solomon and Shulammite. It is that profound sense of well-being with its accompaniments of happiness in the home and success in life's undertakings which plays so great a part in the OT. It is therefore both the basis and the outcome of a marriage in which there is mutual love and trust. It is an insight into the OT way of thinking that this is especially dependent on the woman in marriage (cf. Prov. 31:10–31). **11-13.** The term is skilfully taken up by the husband. Solomon, whose very name suggested true welfare, failed. His mistake lay in supposing that love can be quantitatively measured. Solomon had his harem and it brought confusion (Baal-hamon means 'lord or possessor of tumult'). The husband had his one, and had *shālôm.* **13** is obscure. It may be that the husband is proudly introducing the newly married wife to his friends, but that interpretation suits rather the English than the Heb. It is possible that the opening clause refers to 2:10ff., and that would suit the closing appeal. It would seem that this last clause, 'cause me to hear thy voice' (cf. Vulg.), is the important one, and the appeal to which she lovingly responds in v. **14.** Skilfully the words of longing (2:9, 17, 4:6) are combined. The longing finds fulfilment in the home.

Bibliography—COMMENTARIES : K. Budde, KHC (1898) ; D. Buzy, *Le Cantique des Cantiques* (1949) ; F. Delitzsch, *The Song of Songs and Ecclesiastes* (1877) ; J. Fischer, Ech.B (1949) ; R. Gordis, *The Song of Songs* (1954) ; A. Harper, CB (1902) ; P. Joüon, *Le Cantique des Cantiques* (1909) ; G. A. F. Knight, Torch Commentaries (1955) ; G. Kuhn, *Erklärung des HL.s* (1926) ; S. M. Lehrman, Soncino Bible (1946) ; G. C. Martin, Cent.B (1908) ; A. Miller, HSATes (1927) ; W. O. E. Oesterley, WC (1929) ; H. Ringgren, ATD (1958) ; P. P. Saydon, in *Catholic Commentary on Holy Scripture* (1953) ; G. Siegfried, HKAT (1898) ; W. Staerk, SAT (1911).

OTHER LITERATURE : W. W. Cannon, *The Song of Songs edited as a Dramatic Poem* (1913) ; T. K. Cheyne, EB, 681–95 ; P. Haupt, 'The Book of Canticles', AJSL 18 (1902), 1923–4, 19 (1902), 1–32 ; M. Jastrow, *The Song of Songs* (1921) ; T. J. Meek, 'Canticles and the Tammuz Cult', AJSL 39 (1922–3), 1–14, 'Babylonian Parallels to the Song of Songs', JBL 43 (1924), 245–52 ; H. W. Robinson, E.Brit. (1947 ed.), 767–70 ; J. W. Rothstein, DB (1902), 589–97 ; H. H. Rowley, *The Servant of the Lord* (1952), 187–234 ; W. H. Schoff (ed.), *The Song of Songs : A Symposium* (1924) ; D. R. Scott, *Pessimism and Love* (1915) ; L. Waterman, 'The Role of Solomon in the Song of Songs', JBL 44 (1925), 171–87.

OLD TESTAMENT PROPHECY

By J. Muilenburg

411a **Introduction**—The Hebrew prophets tower head and shoulder over their contemporaries both in ancient Israel and in the ancient Near East. Kings, priests, sages and psalmists have their distinctive place in the life and religion of Israel, but none rise to the stature of the prophets or continue to exert so major an influence in subsequent history. Whether we view them in the light of the phenomenology of religion or in the context of human culture or in the frame of the history of literature, they occupy a position in the thought and faith of mankind unmatched by any other single group. They belong to their own times, but are not confined by them; they are in many ways typical members of their race, yet they often transcend the characteristic features of their Semitic cultural heritage and environment. They address themselves to the needs and crises of the ancient world of men in which they lived, but their words continue to stir the conscience of men, to call them to responsibility, to assert the claims of the divine imperative.

b **Hebrew Terminology for Prophet**—But what precisely is a prophet and what was his peculiar function in the religion of Israel? For an answer to these questions we may turn first to the linguistic explanations which have been offered for the meaning of *nābhî'*, the Heb. word for prophet. It was formerly held that the word is derived from the verb *nābha'*, *bubble forth, pour out* (sc. words. cf *nāṭaph*, which is used in a somewhat similar sense in Ezek. 21:2; Am. 7:16; Mic. 2:11), and was said to describe the ecstatic character of inspiration. This view has been now quite generally abandoned. Others have sought to derive the word from an Arab. root meaning *announce*. The prophet was said to be 'one who is in the state of announcing a message which has been given him' (Alfred Guillaume, *Prophecy and Divination* (1938), 112). W. F. Albright calls attention to the common Akkad. verb *naвû*, *to call*, and refers to the Code of Ḥammurabi where the verbal adjective has the meaning of *called* (FSAC, 231). This explanation has much to commend it, for the prophet's sense of vocation is lodged deep in his self-consciousness, and his call continues to influence his life and message throughout his ministries. Yet T. J. Meek, on the basis of the same Akkad. root, says the word means not only *to call*, but also *to call out* or *to speak*. He therefore interprets the meaning of the word as *speaker* or *spokesman* and calls to witness the rendering of the LXX προφήτης (*Hebrew Origins*, 2nd ed., 15f.). Meek, as others before him, supports his contention by reference to Yahweh's words to Moses in Exod. 7:1–2 (P): 'See, I make you as God to Pharaoh; and Aaron your brother shall be your prophet. You shall speak all that I command you; and Aaron your brother shall tell Pharaoh to let the people of Israel go out of his land' (cf. Exod. 4:16; Dt. 18:18; Jer. 1:7, 15:16, 19). The word *nābhî'* is a denominative in Heb. as is clear from its *niph'al* and *hithpā'ēl* forms: *to act the part of a prophet*, which very probably indicates an ecstatic state or condition. The best clue to the meaning of the word is the Akkad. *nabû*, but its precise denotation is not certain.

c Two other names are closely associated with *nābhî'*: *rō'eh* and *ḥōzeh*. The *locus classicus* for the former is 1 Sam. 9:9: 'Formerly in Israel when a man went to inquire of God, he said, Come, let us go to the seer (*rō'eh*), for the prophet of today was formerly called a seer.' The verse by itself simply identifies prophet and seer, but the context suggests that the latter may have been a clairvoyant (cf. vv. 11, 18–20; 10:2). Partly on this basis G. Hölscher, and others following him, believed that the seer received his supernatural knowledge through dreams, night visions, or the dreamy state between sleeping and waking (*Die Profeten* (1914), 125f.). Albright suggests that he may have been an 'offshoot of the general class of diviners, which originated in Mesopotamia and spread in all directions as early as the middle of the second millennium B.C.' (FSAC, 159; cf. Guillaume, op. cit., 109, 124). Yet the *nābhî'* was also a *rō'eh*. The terminology of seeing is frequently applied to him, not least of all the Qal participle *rō'eh*, and it is extended to prophetic auditions as well (A. R. Johnson, *The Cultic Prophet in Ancient Israel* (1944), 13). Moreover the prophet is at times identified with the seer, as in Isa. 30:10 and in Chr., which may be archaising, however. It would seem hazardous, then, to differentiate too sharply between seer and prophet. Similarly, the word *ḥōzeh*, also rendered seer, is practically synonymous with *rō'eh* (cf. Isa. 30:10), and later OT usage again makes it precarious to differentiate between them (Isa. 30:10; Am. 7:12; Mic. 3:7, etc.). It is probable that the former is Aramaic in origin, the latter Arabic (G. R. Driver, *Problems of Hebrew Verbal System* (1936), 98ff.; Johnson, op. cit., 14; H. H. Rowley, 'The Nature of Prophecy in the Light of Recent Study', HTR 38 (1945), 10). The fluidity of Heb. speech is illustrated in the foregoing usage. The words may at one time have borne differing denotations, but the present OT text does not permit hard and fast distinctions.

d **Near Eastern Prophecy**—There were prophets in other lands of the ancient Near East and indeed long before Israel appeared on the historical horizon. J. H. Breasted has written, perhaps in somewhat exaggerated terms, about prophets among the ancient Egyptians, men of high ethical ideals and often of genuine compassion (*The Dawn of Conscience* (1939), 154–60, 183–93, 200–5). Guillaume has described Mesopotamian prophecy; the *bārû* was both priest and prophet, 'inasmuch as he was servant of the gods . . . and an interpreter and foreteller of the purpose of the gods' (Guillaume, op. cit., 40f.; compare with this the more extreme view expressed by A. Haldar in *Associations of Cult Prophets Among the Ancient Semites* (1945)). Hölscher (*Die Propheten* (1914), 140f.) has sought to explain the origins of prophecy as it is manifested in the earlier period of Israel's religion by its presence in Asia Minor and Syria at a much earlier time. That there were prophets in Canaan is corroborated both by the OT and by extrabiblical records. Tyrian prophets were present in the court of Ahab and Jezebel (1 Kg. 18:19, 40; 2 Kg. 10:19), and Jeremiah condemns the prophets of his day for prophesying by Baal (Jer. 2:8). The well-known story of Wenamon from Byblos in Phoenicia at the beginning of the 11th cent. B.C. describes an ecstatic

411d trance of one of the noble pages: 'Now while he was making offerings to one of his gods, the god seized one of his youths and made him possessed.' The oracular utterance follows (J. B. Pritchard, ANET, 26). It is probable that the immediate origins of Israelite prophecy are to be traced to a Canaanite milieu. 'The whole institution belonged to Canaan, and was closely connected with Canaanite culture' (J. Pedersen, *Israel III–IV* (1940), 111). Its earliest manifestations are like those in Canaan (1 Sam. 10:10–11, 19:23–4), and it is significant that they appear chiefly in the Northern Kingdom, which was more open to influences from Canaan than was the kingdom of Judah.

e **Prophecy in Israel**—Yet Israelite prophecy advanced in a direction quite different from that of her neighbours. The prophetic impulse was destined to come to terms with what was unique in Israelite faith, and the result was a radical transformation of its character and content. 'In the course of time Israel brought forth a specially Israelite type of prophet, produced by the friction between the two cultures' (Pedersen, ibid.). How are we to explain this change? First of all we must look to the historical experience of Israel in the redemptive event of the Exodus from Egypt, the hour of her election to be the people of Yahweh, and in the momentous events associated with Sinai—the covenant relationship and the giving of the Torah, especially the Mosaic decalogue (Exod. 20:1–17). These events were remembered and made present in the celebrations of the old Shechemite amphictyony. They are the firm foundation upon which Israel's faith was erected, the very soul which animated its existence, and it was the prophets above all others who sought to perpetuate them and to interpret their implications for the people of Yahweh. The God of Israel was no Canaanite Baal, although the temptation to identify the two persisted for centuries; rather he was the Lord of history who had made himself known in a series of unique events, had made his demands upon his people, had given them a great mission, and directed them to their unique destiny. The conflict between Yahweh and Baal is vividly presented in the prophetic activity of Elijah, and more than a century later in the ministry of Hosea. The influence of the religion of Moses and of the apodictic commands of the Elohistic decalogue can be discerned behind their urgent insistence upon the uniqueness of Israel's God. Moreover, the historical consciousness of the prophets and their awareness of the activity and persistence of Yahweh's will and purpose in history inevitably raised the issue of its realisation and fulfilment. There is justification, therefore, for the assertion that the prophets were eschatologists, more especially if the word may be employed in a flexible sense.

412a **The Israelite Prophet**—We may achieve a firmer grasp in our understanding of the nature of the Israelite prophet and of his message by examining some of the expressions which are used to describe him. In the early period he is frequently called a **man of God**, an *'îsh 'elōhîm* (1 Sam. 9:6–10; 1 Kg. 12:22; 13:1; 2 Kg. 1:9–13, 4–8), which does not mean that he is a godly man but rather that he is psychically related to Yahweh and is an extension of the divine holiness (2 Kg. 4:9). Thus he shares in the power and mystery of a supernatural order. As a man of God, he receives the charisma of the *rûaḥ* or Spirit of Yahweh. The vitality of the divine revelation and activity extends itself into his life and work (1 Sam. 10:6–10; Isa. 61:1; Ezek. 2:2, 3:12, 14, 11:1; Mic. 3:8). It was only natural that he should be feared because of his strange endowment (1 Kg. 22:24–7). On the other hand, men would repair to him in times of distress or need for help or counsel (2 Kg. 1:2–4, 4:18–37, 5:3ff., 19:5ff.). As Pedersen says, 'There was strength in visiting a man of God and being near him' (op. cit., 120). King and peasant alike recognise his great authority and strange power.

b The prophet is also a **messenger** (Hag. 1:13). He is the herald who has received a report or a disclosure 412b from Yahweh. The basic literary form and cast of his speech and its most characteristic expressions are therefore those of the messenger's report or 'news' (M. Buber and F. Rosenzweig, 'Die Sprache der Botschaft', *Die Schrift und ihre Verdeutschung* (1936), 55–75). This explains the emphasis we encounter everywhere on *proclamation* and the urgency of hearing. Second Isaiah characteristically brings this prophetic motif to its climax in his proclamation of good tidings (40:9–10, 52:7–10). Perhaps the form and terminology of the messenger's report is to be explained by its provenance from ancient court language. In Mari on the Middle Euphrates, in the 18th cent. B.C., messengers were sent from a god to the king Zimri-lim with a report whose phraseology and style remind one of the prophetic oracles of the OT (M. Noth, *History and the Word of God in the OT*, BJRL 32 (1950), 194–206; A. Lods, in *Studies of OT Prophecy*, 103–10; L. Köhler, *Deuterojesaja stilkritisch untersucht* (1923), 102ff.). The prophet is **Yahweh's herald** and the style and form of his speech is especially appropriate since Yahweh had revealed himself as king from the time of the covenant (G. E. Wright, 'The Terminology of OT Religion and its Significance', JNES 1 (1942), 404–14; G. E. Mendenhall, *Law and Covenant in Israel and the Ancient Near East* (1955), 24–50). It was his task to declare to Israel what Yahweh is doing and is about to do. The word of Yahweh has come to him, and he therefore begins his oracles with 'Thus Yahweh says' (or 'has said') or 'Yahweh said to me', or 'Thus Yahweh made me see', and he calls upon Israel, 'Hear this word which Yahweh has spoken against you' (Am. 3:1). The prophet, it should be noted, speaks of the future as well as of the present. The notion commonly held in the past that the prophets did not predict or foretell events is contradicted by every prophet whose words have been preserved. Sometimes the word of God is related to imminent events, sometimes to the distant future, and this word he reveals to the prophets. It is Second Isaiah, again, who draws the theological inference of this predictive activity of the prophets, and indeed makes it the basis for his proclamation of the uniqueness and oneness of God (cf. 41:4, 26–9, 43:8–13, 45:1–13; cf. also H. Gunkel, 'The prophet received superhuman knowledge of the future. If we are to understand aright the prophet, even of the highest type, we must always first ask, what event of the immediate future did he come forth to predict?' ('The Secret Experiences of the Prophets', *Expositor*, 9th series, II (1924), 30)).

Other terms are used to describe the prophet. He c
is **Yahweh's servant** (2 Kg. 21:10; Isa. 20:3; Am. 3:7); it is Yahweh's way of dealing with his people that he makes his will known through his servants the prophets. In this respect as in so many others the prophet is an Israelite *kat' exochēn*, for Israel is called from the beginning to serve Yahweh (C. Lindhagen, *The Servant Motif in the OT* (1950), 82ff.) and Second Isaiah is thus able to gather the whole of the election-covenant tradition from the beginning into his great portrait of the Servant of the Lord. Again, the prophet is a **watchman** who takes his post on the watch-tower that he may warn Israel of the approach of danger and to sound the signal (Isa. 21:11–12; Ezek. 3:17, 33:2–7; Hab. 2:1). Further, he is an **assayer** or **tester**, a term which is applied to Jeremiah whose task it is to separate the dross from the precious metal (6:27; cf. 9:7, 15:19). More especially it was his function to serve as the **intercessor** for Israel. The Elohist carries back this tradition to Abraham (Gen. 20:7), who as 'prophet' prays for the life of Abimelech. But already in the early period, during Samuel's prophetic ministry, we hear of his many intercessions (1 Sam. 7:5, 12:19–25, 15:11). Amos (7:1–6), Jeremiah (7:16, 11:14, 15:1) and Ezekiel (14:14–20) pray to Yahweh on behalf of Israel, and Second Isaiah brings his poem on the Servant of the Lord to a

412c climax in the intercessory motif (Isa. 53:12). Jeremiah, in his denunciation of the 'false' prophets says: 'If they are prophets, and if the word of Yahweh is with them, then let them intercede with Yahweh of hosts' (27:18). This, in short, is the authentic mark of the true prophet. Finally, the prophet is said to stand **in the council of Yahweh** (H. W. Robinson, *Inspiration and Revelation in the OT* (1946), 167ff.). He has listened to Yahweh's announcement of an impending event, and has been obedient to the command to go and proclaim to Israel what he has heard (1 Kg. 22:19; Isa. 6:1ff., 40:1–11; Jer. 23:18–22).

d Yet nowhere in the OT do we receive so clear an insight into the nature of prophecy as in the prophetic calls (Isa. 6; Jer. 1:4–10; Ezek. 1:4–3:15) (cf. H. H. Rowley, 'The Nature of Prophecy in the Light of Recent Study', HTR 38 (1945), 24). We have already seen that the word *nābhî'* has been explained as *one who is called*. What is so impressive about the prophetic experience is that it continues to influence the prophet throughout his career; Yahweh's act of election means that he is with the prophet to watch over his word to perform it (Jer. 1:12). The content of Isaiah's call keeps authenticating itself through the years of his ministry. He had seen the King high and lifted up, the One seated on the throne with the seraphim singing their trisagion of praise, and in the many national and international events of his age he continues to proclaim the reality of the divine sovereignty and holiness. Significantly Isaiah's key words are echoed again in the 'eschatological drama' of Second Isaiah at the close of the Semitic age and the rise of Persia. In Jeremiah's call in the ominous year 626 B.C. we have a concise and vivid reflection of what it means to be a prophet. All of the first-person verbs which Yahweh uses penetrate deeply into the mystery of the relation between prophet and God. Already at the beginning we hear Jeremiah travailing with the word of Yahweh, and it seems to have continued in one way or another to the end of his life.

The prophet, then, is **Yahweh's representative** to his covenant people Israel. He has been sent on a great commission. He is to proclaim Yahweh's word. He is not simply another man. He is more! Yahweh's Spirit (*rûaḥ*) and Word (*dābhār*) have entered into him. So dynamic and intimate is the relationship that he can use the first-personal pronoun 'I' of himself or Yahweh interchangeably in the same context. At other times he must subordinate his own human thinking to that of Yahweh. We see this in its most moving expression in the confessions of Jeremiah, and it is all the more remarkable because he is the most subjective of all the prophets. Yet the Word masters him (12:5, 15:19–20). But the prophet is also the representative of Israel before Yahweh. As he represents Yahweh in his oracles and some of his symbolic prophecies, he also represents Israel in his prayers and intercessions, in his suffering and distress, and in other of his symbolic acts. Yahweh's name is upon him (Jer. 15:16), and his children sometimes bear names which give concrete content to his message (Isa. 7:3, 8:1–4; Hos. 1:4–6, 8). Thus the living and dynamic power of Yahweh's word is extended into the prophet's life and into the relationship of father and son.

e **Prophecy and History**—The word which Yahweh reveals to his servants the prophets is not a timeless truth universal in validity and relevant to every historical situation. To view it in this manner is not only to do violence to the OT itself but also to destroy the uniqueness of the revelation. For the word of Yahweh is spoken in concrete historical times and is relevant to those times. It may indeed be relevant to other historical situations, but is meant first of all for the period in which it was addressed to Israel by the prophet. A knowledge of the historical background and environment is therefore essential to an understanding of what the prophet has to proclaim.
Prophecy and history are thus intimately related; 412e
word issues in event for the event is the realisation of the purpose of the word. Hence the Heb. *dābhār* can be used for both.

Prophecy arose in the turbulent and chaotic period f
of the Philistine domination over the Palestinian corridor, and the activity of the early prophetic guilds and of Samuel is to be understood in the light of the conditions prevailing at the time. In the 9th cent. B.C. the smaller powers are compelled to come to terms with the new situation created among the nations by the rise of Assyria under Ashurnazirpal II (883–859 B.C.) and his successor Shalmaneser III (858–824). It is against the background of Phoenician mercantile power and political diplomacy, of Aramaean commercial interests and military pressure, and of the politics of the Omri dynasty that we are to read the accounts of the prophetic activity of Elijah, Elisha, and Micaiah. The pro-Phoenician policies of Ahab and Jezebel were responsible for the life-and-death struggle between Baal and Yahweh, and we cannot simply isolate the political and international events from their religious implications, nor indeed the religious ideology of Phoenicia and Israel from its political effects. A century later Amos, the shepherd of Tekoa, is confronted with the social and economic conditions growing out of the expanding economy of the reign of Jeroboam II (786–746 B.C.). Hosea prophesies during the stormy years of the decline and fall of the Northern Kingdom, and his words concerning the kingdom and the covenant are to be understood in the light of the anarchic conditions prevailing at the time. Isaiah of Jerusalem in the south proclaims his oracles during the period of Assyrian aggression and domination from the accession of Tiglath Pileser III in 744 B.C. to the invasion of Sennacherib about 705 B.C., while Micah, his contemporary, addresses himself to the shocking social conditions existing among the poor and dispossessed. During the fateful years from the death of Ashurbanipal (*c.* 631 B.C.) to the destruction of Jerusalem in 586 many figures appeared on the prophetic horizon, among them men like Zephaniah, Nahum, Habakkuk, Jeremiah and Ezekiel, who prophesied among the exiles in Babylonia from 593–571 B.C. Second Isaiah in his profoundly moving poems addresses his words to the period of the decline and fall of Babylonia and the rise of Persia, and his theology gains in pertinence and profundity by a recognition of the nature of the vast historical and theological issues involved in what was happening in the world of the Near East including Asia Minor during the 6th cent. B.C. It is clear, then, that history gives to prophecy an immediacy of historical relevance. Yet the prophetic perspective is by no means limited to the particular events of the times. On the contrary it is comprehended in the light of the mighty acts of God in the history of the chosen people, and it is from the standpoint of the covenant relationship at Sinai that the prophets discern the divine will and intention. The prophets are not merely politicians or statesmen or ethical idealists or social reformers. They would have disclaimed such tributes. They are messengers and spokesmen called by Yahweh to bring Israel back to true community with him. Moreover, the Deuteronomic prophetic historians were able to interpret the meaning of Israel's history in wider contexts of faith in the great Deuteronomic work of 1 and 2 Kg. which unfolds the drama of more than four centuries of history from the point of view of the dynamic and efficacious power of the Word of Yahweh spoken by the prophets (G. von Rad, *Studies in Deuteronomy*, 78ff.).

The Literary Character of Prophecy—The pro- 413a
phets of Israel were primarily speakers. They delivered their oracles and sermons by word of mouth, and their original oral character is stamped indelibly upon them in their terminology, literary style and atmosphere. However we may explain the consummate art with which many of the prophetic utterances

418a are composed, particularly exemplified in their firm structure and in the recurrence of key words at strategic points, the dominant impression they leave upon us is of words spoken and addressed to a living body of men. Yet it is possible to exaggerate the place of oral tradition in Israel's prophecy. (For a critique of the Swedish traditio-historical scholars, who stress the presence and extent of oral tradition in the OT, see G. Widengren, *Literary and Psychological Aspects of the Hebrew Prophets* (1948).) On occasion we are told that the prophets did put their words into writing (Isa. 8:1–4, 30:8 ; Ezek. 43:11–12). But it must be admitted that these are exceptional cases as the contexts plainly show. In the case of Jeremiah, we have an important account where the prophet is commanded by Yahweh to write all the words he had spoken from the time of his call to the year 605 B.C., the fateful year of the Battle of Carchemish, and later when the scroll was burned by Jehoiakim he is commanded to make a new record of his prophecies and to add to them (Jer. 36:2, 28). Again this may be admitted to be exceptional (E. Nielsen, *Oral Tradition* (1954)). But the general situation is sufficiently clear : the prophets were not primarily literary men but speakers. Whether Ezekiel transcribed any of his prophecies is debatable though the possibility must not be excluded. Similarly, the question of the original character of Second Isaiah's poetic compositions cannot be answered with absolute confidence. They appear to be so meticulously wrought, however, that at some point they may have assumed literary form.

b How, then, were the oracles and sermons of the prophets preserved? The most plausible explanation is that they were treasured in the memories of the prophet's disciples. It is well known that the Oriental memory is very retentive, and the traditions may have been preserved in this way for some time. The next stage would be the collection into small compilations of the prophet's words, either by his disciples or by those who remembered the traditions associated with him ; later, probably in the exilic and post-exilic periods, these would be assembled into what is substantially the present form of the prophetic books. It need not be assumed that the period of oral transmission lasted to the time of the Exile or that it was only then that the oral traditions were first put into writing. It is unlikely that the prophets themselves compiled their utterances, although the possibility cannot be dismissed, least of all in the case of Jeremiah. The argument for the activity of the disciples in the transmission of the tradition is that so much of the secondary material shows affinities with the message of the particular prophet. The Deuteronomic material in Jer., for example, need not be late, but simply an almost contemporary tradition from those who sought to preserve the prophet's words in their own style and manner. This, too, may explain a number of the passages in Ezek., although here the style of the supposed editors is so close to Ezekiel's style that it is difficult to decide. The best illustration of the work of disciples is to be found in Third Isaiah (Isa. 56–66), which has many striking relationships to Second Isaiah, yet cannot belong to him, since it represents a somewhat later stage in literary and theological development. 418b

c A substantial part of OT prophecy is in poetic form. Now rhythmic utterance characterises a large part of the OT, even passages which are printed as prose in our translations, so that it is often difficult to draw the line between prose and poetry. Yet the presence of poetry in large portions of the prophetic books cannot be denied. We encounter the same use of parallelism in the prophets as in the poetic books, and it is often employed with a high degree of versatility. The metre can usually be identified without difficulty ; frequently the prophet employs the 3′3′ metre, or the 3′2′, the lamentation or *ķînāh* metre, sometimes also the ancient 2′2′. That the lines fall into certain fixed units is clear ; these are usually styled 'strophes'. They need not be of the same length ; more often than not they vary in the number of lines. When refrains are present, there is no question as to their scope (Isa. 9:8–10:4 ; 5:24–9 ; Am. 4:4–11). The ancient Hebrew was very sensitive to sound ; therefore assonance plays an important role in Hebrew literary style. It may take the form of alliteration or of paronomasia or of repetition of the same word. Here again we recognise the oral character of Hebrew prophecy. The first word is always 'Hear !', not 'Read !' The value of stylistic and form analysis is that it often provides a hermeneutical key for discerning what is central in the prophet's thought.

d The first task for the student of the OT is to determine the limits of a literary composition. Failure to identify the extent of the literary units opens the way to confusion and misinterpretation. The second task is to define the literary type. The study of literary forms and types has been greatly advanced in recent decades, thanks to the pioneering work of Hermann Gunkel and his disciples ('Die israelitische Literatur', *Die Kultur der Gegenwart* I, vii, 53–112, and *Genesis* (5th ed. 1922) ; also Introduction to H. Schmidt, *Die grossen Propheten*, xxxvi–lxxii). OT prophecy as a whole belongs to the literature of revelation. Its general character is determined by the conviction that God has communicated his word

LITERARY FORMS OF PROPHETIC LITERATURE

Narrative Legends : 1 Sam. 9:1–10:16 ; 1 Kg. 11:29–39, 12:33–13:32, 17:1–24 ; 2 Kg. 1:2–17
Narrative Autobiography : Isa. 6 ; Jer. 1:4–10 ; Hos. 3:1–4
Narrative Biography : Jer. 26–9, 32–45 ; Am. 7:10–17
Sermon : Dt. 8 ; Jer. 7:1–8:3 ; Ezek. 20
Vision : Jer. 1:11–12, 13–14 ; Ezek. 1:1–28*a* (with accompanying audition 1:28*b*–3:15) ; Am. 7:1–3, 4–6, 7–9, 8:1–3, 9:1–2
Invective : Isa. 3:9*c*–12 ; Hab. 2:6*b*–17
Threat : Isa. 13:6–16
Invective and threat : Isa. 5:8–25 ; Jer. 7:16–20 ; Hos. 7:8–16, 10:9–15 ; Am. 1:3–2:16, 6:1–7 ; Zeph. 2:8–11, 3:1–8. Compare also Ezekiel's use of the invective and threat in the '*because . . . therefore*' *style* (Ezek. 13:2*b*–15, 25:3*b*–7, 8–11, 12–14, 15–17
Judicial proceeding : Isa. 3:13–15, 41:1–42:4, 43:8–13, 50:8–9 ; Jer. 2:5*b*–13 ; Dan. 7:9ff. ; Hos. 2:2–13 ; Mic. 6:1–8
Exhortation : Am. 5:4–5 ; Zeph. 2:3
Confession : Isa. 50:4–9, 53:1–9 ; Jer. 11:18–12:6, 15:10–21, 18:18–23, 20:7–18
Dirge : Isa. 14:4*b*–21 ; Am. 5:2
Lament : Ezek. 19:1–14, 27:3*b*–9, 26–36 ; Hos. 6:1–3
Apology : Jer. 26:12*b*–15 ; Am. 7:14–15 ; Mic. 3:8
Liturgy : Isa. 33 ; Jer. 14:1–15:4 ; Jl 1–2 ; Mic. 7
Mocking Song : Isa. 37:22–9, 46
Satire : Isa. 44:9–20
Letter : Jer. 19:1–23, 24–32
Hymn : Isa. 42:10–13 (cf. Ps. 47, 93, 96–9), 44:23
Allegory : Ezek. 17:2–24, 19:2–14, 23:2–35
Herald's report : Isa. 40:10–11, 52:7–10
Prophetic or priestly torah : Isa. 1:10–17, 58:1–8 ; Hos. 6:6 ; Mal. 1:10
Torah in casuistic style : Hag. 2:12–14 ; cf. Mal. 1:1–14, 2:10–17
Proverb : 1 Sam. 10:12 ; 1 Kg. 20:11 ; Jer. 31:29 (Ezek. 18:2)

413d (*dābhār*) to the prophet. It is therefore often described as oracular. The most distinguishing feature is its oracular style. This may assume various guises and literary forms, however, in accordance with the literary conventions of oracular utterances in Israel and the ancient Near East. The most characteristic beginning is *kōh 'āmar Yahweh*, thus Yahweh says; the most characteristic ending *nᵉ'ûm Yahweh*, oracle or utterance of Yahweh, or *'āmar Yahweh*, says Yahweh (cf. Am. 1:3–2:16). Many of the earliest oracles were very brief, often a single sentence (1 Kg. 21:19); others, however, were more extended. It is widely held that the literary units of the pre-exilic prophets were all relatively short. Whether this view can be extended to Jeremiah, Ezekiel and Second Isaiah is questionable, however. In the early period the prophet receives the oracle and announces what he has received, but in later times he tends to identify himself with what he has heard, to participate in the revelation by interjecting his own response or even by beseeching Yahweh to alter his word. At times he even enters into a dialogue with Yahweh, as in Amos' visions (7:1–9) or Jeremiah's call (1:4–10) or the prologue in the heavenly council of Isa. 40:1–11.

e As to the specific literary form and types employed by the prophets, the OT contains an almost bewildering variety. Each has its formal terminology, the words characteristic of the type; moreover, the same motifs tend to recur within the same literary form. When the type has been recognised one must determine its situation in life, its *Sitz im Leben*, and then bring it into relation with other representatives of the same type in the OT or in the literature of the ancient Near East. The outline at the foot of the previous page is meant merely to suggest some of the literary forms represented in the prophetic literature; their significance may be grasped only when their particular function in Israel's life and in the prophet's message and situation is understood.

414a **The Prophets and the Cult**—Among the most noteworthy changes in the study of Israelite prophecy in recent decades is the sharp reversal of point of view regarding the relationship of the prophet to the cult. It was formerly believed that the prophets and the priests were ranged against each other in sharp antagonism. The prophet opposed the cult and all its works, so it was supposed, and sought thus to purge Israelite faith of all that interfered with the immediacy of relationship between man and God. Along with this emphasis went a serious neglect of the priestly literature of the OT and a low estimate of its value. Into the historic origins of this distortion of the biblical representation we need not here enter. A strong impetus was given to a fresh evaluation of the biblical records by the publication in 1914 of Gustav Hölscher's book, *Die Profeten*. He discerned the historical origins of Hebrew prophecy in the prophetic movements and prophetic associations of the Canaanites and maintained that Israel also took over the cults of Canaan. As in the worship of Baal, the early prophetic enthusiasts in Israel attached themselves to the ancient sanctuaries together with the priests. Sanctuaries such as Ramah, Gibeah, Jericho, Gilgal, Bethel and doubtless others possessed prophetic guilds, and even though their personnel wandered through the country at times, their centre of operations was in all likelihood the local sanctuary.

b Hölscher did not extend his theory of cultic prophecy to the canonical prophets. But in the year 1923 Sigmund Mowinckel, in the third of his studies on the Psalter, maintained that the canonical prophets were also to be understood as belonging in general to such cultic associations (*Psalmenstudien III: Kultprophetie und prophetische Psalmen*). Prophet and priest are engaged in a common task of communicating to the people 'information in religious matters from a divine source'; they both seek to mediate the directions of the deity to the community. Indeed, the sacramental, i.e. the prophetic, is present in every cult (ibid., 4–5). Mowinckel contends that the psalms 414b
are all cultic compositions, and then calls attention to the fact that they contain a considerable number of divine oracles in the characteristic style of the old prophets, answers which are given to the suppliant, whether the king or some other petitioner (see Ps. 20, 21, 60, 72, 75, 110, etc.). For a detailed discussion of the prophetic character of the form, situation and content of many of the psalms, see H. Gunkel, *Einleitung in die Psalmen* (1933), Section 9, 'Das Prophetische in den Psalmen'. In 1944 Aubrey R. Johnson subjected the theory of the presence of the cultic prophet in ancient Israel to an independent scrutiny. Following Mowinckel he holds that the prophets as well as the priests were revealers of the divine word and will: 'as regards the Jerusalem Temple, the *nābhî'* or "prophet" originally filled a cultic role of at least equal, if not greater, importance (than the priest)' (A. R. Johnson, *The Cultic Prophet in Ancient Israel*). The priest and prophet were not only representatives of the people; both are spokesmen of Yahweh, and both were 'consulted for the sake of securing oracular guidance' (G. von Rad, *Studies in Deuteronomy* (1953)). Like Mowinckel he recognises the presence of oracular elements in the Psalter. Elijah and Elisha and other early prophets were 'cultic specialists' and were consulted by the people to give Torah or cultic direction and guidance. The frequent association of priests and prophets (Isa. 28:7; Jer. 4:9, 8:10; Hos. 4:4–5; Mic. 3:11; Zeph. 3:4, etc.) speaks for itself, and the dominant role of intercession played by the prophets confirms the view that their function was to offer prayer as well as to give the divine oracle. Indeed Johnson goes so far as to affirm that there is abundant evidence to show that there were prophets who 'belonged to the cultic personnel of the different sanctuaries in as real a sense as did the priests'. With the decline of the authority and prestige of the prophets following the destruction of Jerusalem they became members of the Temple choir. Johnson supports his contentions with an impressive array of evidence and has given the deathblow to the old view of the prophets as opponents of the cultus as an institution. Alfred Haldar in his *Associations of the Cult Prophets among the Ancient Semites* defends a more radical position than Johnson's. Arguing from a comparison with the Sumerian, Akkadian and Ugaritic texts, he holds that the king was at the head of associations of cult prophets, that the canonical prophets belonged to such groups, and that their prophecies are to be understood in general against the background of the ideology of the sacral kingship. For a discussion of Haldar's view, see N. Porteous, 'The Basis of the Ethical Teaching of the Prophets', *Studies in OT Prophecy*, 143–56. H. H. Rowley has issued a warning against exalting the prophet at the expense of the priest: 'To think of prophets only in terms of the best and priests only in terms of the worst is unwise. There were good prophets and good priests, and while there was undoubtedly a difference of emphasis between them, they were all exponents of the same religion' ('Ritual and the Hebrew Prophets', JSS (1956), 360).

The following important conclusions may be c
drawn from the foregoing sketch: (1) the early prophets were cultic and were probably associated with sanctuaries where they performed tasks similar to those of the priests; (2) the distinction between priest and prophet must not be exaggerated since they shared a common work in their oracular direction; it is important to remember, however, that there were different kinds of prophets; (3) that the prophets were deeply concerned over the cult and its practices is certain; not only the priestly Ezekiel but also Jeremiah is constantly occupied with matters pertaining to the purity of Yahweh worship (Jer. 7:15, 26). The severe indictment of the cult (Isa. 1:10–17; Jer. 7:21–3; Am. 5:21–4) must not be interpreted as a rejection of the cult *per se*, but of the gross abuses

414c and corruptions which had come to be associated with it ; (4) whether the canonical prophets belonged to the personnel of the cultus is less certain. H. H. Rowley comments as follows : ' If there were cultic prophets who had a defined place in the ritual of the shrines, and who shared with the priests in the services which took place there as officials of the cultus, it is impossible to suppose that the major canonical prophets exercised their ministry in this way ' (ibid., 342ff.). But this is not intended to suggest that they did not concern themselves with cultic matters. It may be an exaggeration to speak of the ' solitary prophets ', but nowhere do we receive the impression that they belonged to such cultic organisations as Haldar suggests.

415a **The Prophetic Experience**—The prophets of Israel were aware that the unseen world had impinged upon their consciousness, that they were endowed with unusual psychic powers, and that they had been ' inspired ' to prophesy. This awareness manifests itself in so many different ways throughout the course of Hebrew prophecy, however, that it is difficult to comprehend it under any single psychological category. Yet the term *ecstasy* has been frequently employed by scholars to describe the nature of the prophetic experience. It cannot be said to be altogether satisfactory, however, both because of the wide range of meaning it is meant to cover and because the term in psychological literature is generally applied to an advanced stage of mysticism. In *The Religious Consciousness* (J. B. Pratt, 394), ecstasy is described as the mystic state *par excellence.* The attempt to draw parallels between the experience of the prophets and the medieval mystics is hazardous. Now it is doubtful whether the prophets were mystics in any precise meaning of that often ill-defined word. That they felt themselves to be in intimate communion with Yahweh and believed that his ' life-soul ' (*nephesh*) had somehow extended itself into their own lives, or that the dynamic power of his word lived on in their words, or that his revelatory power enabled them to perform remarkable acts is true. But nowhere do we have a clear instance where the consciousness of the prophet is so lost in the divine consciousness that his own personality is effaced, or where the separation between the human and divine is really overcome. As Coleridge said long ago, the prophets of Israel are not ' superhuman ventriloquists '. Nevertheless, the term ecstasy has been so commonly employed in the discussion of the prophetic experience that we shall employ it in lieu of a better word.

b Our earliest historical contact with the prophets appears in the account of the beginnings of the monarchy. Samuel describes to Saul the various events that are to befall him on his return to Gibeah. At Gibeath-elohim, he will meet a band (lit. ' string ') of prophets coming down from the high place, prophesying (*mithnabb*^{e}*'îm*). The *rûaḥ* of Yahweh will come mightily upon him and he will prophesy and be turned into another man (1 Sam. 10:5f.). All this comes to pass, to the manifest surprise of the people. Later, on the occasion of Saul's jealousy of David after the slaying of Goliath, an evil spirit from God rushes upon him and he ' prophesied ' (RSV ' raved ') within his house (1 Sam. 18:10). In the next chapter we see Samuel standing at the head of a prophetic band. The *rûaḥ* of Yahweh falls upon Saul's messengers and they prophesy. It is clear from these contexts that the early communal groups are subject to abnormal or ' ecstatic ' behaviour. There is no record here of any giving of oracles ; the ' ecstasy ' itself was doubtless regarded as a demonstration of the work of Yahweh. The ecstatic condition makes it possible for the prophets to perform all kinds of unusual acts. G. Widengren explains all of these acts as falling within the department of parapsychic faculties. He offers a useful classification of the different kinds of actions represented among the earlier prophets, among them far-hearing (1 Kg. 18:41 ; 2 Kg. 6:12, 32f.) ; far-seeing (2 Kg. 5:26, 415b
8:10ff.) ; rain-making (1 Sam. 7:7, 12:16ff. ; 1 Kg. 17:1, 18:42ff.) ; production of food (1 Kg. 17:14 ; 2 Kg. 4:1ff., 42ff.) ; healing of sickness (1 Kg. 13:6 ; 2 Kg. 5:11, 14) ; raising from the dead (1 Kg. 17:21 ; 2 Kg. 4:33f.). The hand of Yahweh falls on Elijah and he runs before Ahab's chariot all the way from Carmel to Jezreel (1 Kg. 18:46). Elisha calls a minstrel and, as he plays, the divine power enables him to utter an oracle to the king of Israel (2 Kg. 3:15ff.). The same prophet orders Joash to shoot arrows through an open window, and the shooting is said to be a portent of what is to happen in the war against Syria (2 Kg. 13:14–19). Yahweh's word through the prophet has power over life and death (1 Kg. 17:21 ; 2 Kg. 1:16). It is to be observed that in many instances the prophetic act is preceded by prayer or by the command of Yahweh ; thus they are relieved from the coercions of magic. It will also be noticed that the prophets now deliver oracles ; indeed they are often consulted for a word from Yahweh (2 Kg. 3:11, 5:9ff. ; Isa. 37:2ff.). In all of these actions and many more like them prophet and people recognised the activity of God. They know that something from without has entered into the prophet, and that his works are not his but Yahweh's. But the conditions under which they perform their acts vary as greatly as the acts themselves ; sometimes the prophet serves as court consultant, at other times he is located at some cultic centre ; in other instances he is consulted in his own home, as in the case of Elisha and Ezekiel. He may customarily have performed his acts on festival days, but surely not always. The one thing that remains constant is that he is possessed of a power not himself that invades his *nephesh*, masters it, and makes it a vehicle for the accomplishment of Yahweh's will.

But the question now arises whether the canonical c
prophets—men like Amos, Isaiah, Jeremiah and Second Isaiah—also had experiences similar to those of the early prophets. A sharp line has sometimes been drawn between the former and the latter on this basis. Now it is clear that they all had remarkable experiences. Isaiah has a number of unusual sensations during his vision : he not only sees Yahweh high and lifted up, but hears the singing of the seraphim, senses that the house is filled with smoke, feels the burning coal sear his lips, and is filled with dismay by what he hears. Jeremiah feels the touch of Yahweh's fingers on his lips (Jer. 1:9). His description of the terrible anguish which overcomes him is almost a perfect description of an ' ecstatic ' state :

' My anguish, my anguish ! I writhe in pain !
 Oh, the walls of my heart !
My heart is beating wildly ;
 I cannot keep silent ;
for I hear the sound of the trumpet,
 the alarm of war.' (Jer. 4:19)

Hananiah dies at the word of Yahweh through Jeremiah (28:17), and while Ezekiel is prophesying Pelatiah also dies (11:13). Yahweh can take such full possession of the prophet's consciousness that he speaks his divine ' I ' through him. Again, we hear Jeremiah crying that he is so filled with the divine fury that he is exhausted from ' holding it in ' (6:11). Finally, we may refer again to the prophets' consciousness of being present in the divine council (1 Kg. 22:19 ; Isa. 6, 40:1–11 ; Jer. 23:18, 22). It is clear then that we cannot differentiate between the earlier and later prophets solely on the basis of ecstasy.

Yet there are distinctions. Ecstatic experiences d
seem to be much more common in the early period, although there are instances as in the case of Nathan where no such abnormal state is suggested (2 Sam. 12:1–4 ; cf. however 7:4). The action of the divine *rûaḥ* is frequent among the early ' ecstatics ' ; it

415d almost seems to be studiously avoided by the canonical prophets. Mowinckel points out that in Amos, Zephaniah, Nahum, Habakkuk and Jeremiah the mention of Yahweh's *rûaḥ* is absent, and that the single reference to it in Mic. 3:8 is a gloss (S. Mowinckel, 'The "Spirit" and the "Word" in the Pre-exilic Prophets', JBL 53 (1934), 199–227). Not until the time of Ezekiel does it become the medium of prophetic inspiration (Ezek. 11:5), 'but as a rule it is purely a motive principle'. He attributes this situation to 'the repudiation of popular *nebhî'ism* in general by the reforming prophets'. 'On the whole,' he says, 'little remains of the ecstatic element, apart from that which is the sound psychological substratum and core of religious ecstasy: the all-predominating, all-exclusive consciousness of having been called by Yahweh to deliver a religious and moral message'. Such a statement may minimise the ecstatic element in the canonical prophets; yet the paucity of reference to the *rûaḥ* of Yahweh cannot be regarded as accidental.

e Nevertheless it is questionable whether primary stress should be laid upon these ecstatic experiences. Certainly many of the prophetic utterances cannot be said to be the result of ecstatic trance. To identify the experiences of Amos of Tekoa, Hosea, Isaiah, Jeremiah and Ezekiel as ecstasy does not, after all, describe what is most significant in them. This is not to deny the presence of ecstasy in their lives; it is rather to say that an independent examination of the central experiences, such as those of the call, may prove more fruitful to our understanding and appreciation of their work. After all, it is not the medium of revelation that is of the first importance but the revelation itself, the content of the words that were revealed. What is of supreme moment is that the prophets and the people believed that God was making himself known. Jeremiah in one of his confessions says, 'Thy words were found' (Jer. 15:16), and with this all the prophets would surely have agreed.

416a The *dābhār* of Yahweh *came* to the prophets, and in the *dābhār* the vitality and power of the One who speaks was transmitted. For 'behind the words stands the whole of the soul which created it' (Pedersen, *Israel I–II* (1926), 167). The word therefore triumphed over the old magical religion as we recognise already in the Elisha stories where the magical elements lie so much on the surface. It is victorious over all the hostile forces in history which oppose it. We see clearly how the word of Yahweh affects historical events in the Elijah stories (1 Kg. 17:1, 8, 24, 18:1, 21:17; 2 Kg. 1) and in the vivid description of the imminent fall of Israel in Isa. 9:8–21, in which all the minutely detailed events follow upon the opening line: *The Lord has sent a word against Jacob, and it will light upon Israel.* In the Deuteronomic history of 1 and 2 Kg., the word of Yahweh through the prophets determines the movement of events from Solomon to the fall of Jerusalem in 586 B.C. 'This Deuteronomic theology of history, the theology of the word finding certain fulfilment in history, and on that account the creative word in history, may be described in respect of its origin, as pertaining to the old prophecy' (G. von Rad, *Studies in Deuteronomy*, 83). The compelling drive and vitality of Yahweh's *dābhār* exerts a profound effect in the prophetic ministry and experience (Isa. 1:2, 6:8, 8:11; Ezek. 3:1ff.; Am. 3:8; Mic. 6:1f.), of Jeremiah above all, for whom it was like a blazing fire or a hammer which crushes rocks (Jer. 20:9, 23:29; cf. also 1:5ff., 15:16). In Second Isaiah the word of God achieves its greatest depth and widest range, for here it is a power which controls the whole of nature and history, an active and self-validating reality; it will accomplish Yahweh's purpose and succeed in performing the mission upon which it was sent.

b **Symbolic Acts**—The word which goes forth from Yahweh is directed to what he is about to do and finds fulfilment in the event. The prophet as his mediator lives in such psychical relationship with 416b Yahweh's word which has come to him and identifies himself with the event with such intensity that he often describes it as having already happened. Not infrequently he 'dramatises' the event by acting it out symbolically before the people. Thus it is somehow realised, made actual and present. The act is more than a vivid illustration; it is instrumental in bringing the event to pass. It is full of portent, and as such it is impressed with the divine purpose and activity. So Ahijah the prophet of Shiloh tears his new garment into twelve pieces and gives ten of them to Jeroboam, who is destined to become king of the ten northern tribes (1 Kg. 11:29–40). The arrows which Joash shoots at the behest of Elisha 'symbolise' the imminent engagements with Syria (2 Kg. 13:14–19). Isaiah walks through the streets of Jerusalem for three years 'naked and barefoot'; thus he becomes 'a sign and a portent' against Egypt and Ethiopia (20:3–4). Jeremiah is commanded to buy a linen loin cloth, wear it on his loins, then go to the Euphrates where he is to bury it, and after many days return to recover it in its spoiled condition. Yahweh explains the strange act: 'Even so will I spoil the pride of Judah and the great pride of Jerusalem' (13:1–9). Jeremiah resorts to other symbolic actions (19:1–2*a*, 10–11*a*, 14–15, 27:1–3, 12, 28:10–11, 32:6–15, 43:8–13, 51:59–64). But it is in the Book of Ezekiel where we meet the largest number of such prophetic 'symbols': e.g. of Jerusalem under siege (4:1–3, 7), of years of exile (4:4–8), of the fate of the city (5:1–17), of exile and siege (12:1–20). Even the death of his wife is a portent (*môphēth*). He may not grieve for her, any more than Yahweh will grieve the loss of his sanctuary: 'You shall do as I have done.' Again the meaning of the event is succinctly described, 'Thus shall Ezekiel be a portent to you; according to all that he has done you shall do' (24:22–4).

Several conclusions emerge from an examination c of these and many other symbolic acts: (1) While they are related to magic and betray affinities with similar actions among other Near Eastern peoples, they are invariably transformed by being performed at the command of Yahweh; the forms of mimetic magic are clearly present in the principle behind the acts that 'like produces like', but the mechanical and coercive aspects are overcome by the purpose of Yahweh. (2) These actions are *continuous with the word of Yahweh*; they are Yahweh's word in action, 'acts in miniature of the purpose of Yahweh'; *Yahweh, word* and *event* are paralleled by *prophet, word* and *event*, and the two are united by the driving-power of revelation and by Yahweh's use of the prophet as his mediator. (3) It is not always clear whether the acts were carried out in vision or in actuality; it is often easier to assume the latter, but we must be on our guard against introducing modern mentality into ancient ways of acting and thinking. The prophet was a holy 'man of God' and was strange even to his contemporaries. (4) The prophet can take the part of Yahweh because Yahweh projects his will and purpose into him, and he can take the part of Israel because he *is* Israel. Thus Hosea represents Yahweh in his domestic experience while Gomer represents faithless Israel; on the other hand Ezekiel represents Israel in his symbols of siege and exile. (5) These acts are more than dramatic illustrations; they are in part realisations of what is to happen and indeed were thought to contribute to their realisation. (6) The ancient Hebrew makes no such hard and fast distinction between physical and spiritual as modern man does. They are integral parts of one and the same event. As H. W. Robinson has remarked, 'Just as Hebrew psychology ascribed psychical qualities to the physical organs and made the body an essential part of human personality, so Hebrew philosophy (if the term may be allowed) ascribed metaphysical significance to events in the external world, and made them (as symbols) parts

416c of a larger world of reality ' (' Prophetic Symbolism ', *OT Essays* (1927)).

417a **The Prophetic Faith**—The faith which undergirds, sustains and pervades all that the Hebrew prophets have to proclaim is that Yahweh has revealed himself to them and through them to Israel, his chosen and covenanted people. In the unique events of the sacred history he has made his will and purpose known. In the Exodus from Egypt he entered into history to set apart for himself a people, he took the initiative in their behalf that they might serve him, he chose them as the instrument for the fulfilment of his purpose. In the sojourn through the desert he was their Leader, and continued to lead them on their way through history by manifesting himself in great and mighty acts. At Sinai he entered into covenant relationship with them so that henceforth they might belong to him and he to them. There he gave them the guidance and direction of his Torah so that they might know the way they were to walk. In the decalogue (Exod. 20:1–17) he demanded an exclusive allegiance, forbade the making of visual images to represent him, for he, Yahweh, their God, was invisible and reigned invisibly over their destiny. He gave them the good land of Palestine as his heritage, but it was not to be exploited or corrupted by injustice, unrighteousness or apostasy to other gods. In time he raised up David to be king over them that he might be his chosen and covenanted servant, a righteous ruler over his people Israel.

It is against this background of election-covenant faith that the prophets present themselves to their people. The revelation which comes to them is revelation of what God has done, is now doing and yet will do. It is not man's discovery, but God's gift ; not man's intuitive genius, but God's gracious action. When the prophets speak of Yahweh's righteousness (*ṣᵉdhāḳāh*) or justice (*mishpāṭ*), or steadfast love (*ḥesedh*), they do not refer to ethical principles or ideals or norms but to the ways of the divine activity in history. They are not concerned with promulgating a doctrine of monotheism, whether philosophical or ethical ; rather they are intent upon proclaiming the uniqueness of his holiness and righteousness, the exclusiveness of his sovereignty, his sole direction of the course of history from beginning to end, the triumphant power of his word which will not return to him empty.

b Yahweh is Israel's King, and therefore all earthly and temporal powers are subservient to his lordship. All the relativities of history—whether political or social or economic or religious—are subject to his righteous reign. Therefore the prophets can face the kings of their time with a fortitude sustained by their faith in the kingship of Yahweh. Samuel pronounces the divine judgment upon Saul ; Nathan condemns the adultery of David at the height of his power ; Elijah calls Ahab the enemy of the people ; Amos sounds the knell of doom upon the house of Jeroboam. Yahweh as Israel's King is also Judge, and the prophets are sent to announce his righteous judgments. As King, Yahweh is exalted in holiness (Isa. 6), but his holiness is made known in justice and righteousness (Isa. 5:16). As King, Yahweh determines the destiny of Israel ; even her repeated apostasies and persistent waywardness cannot abrogate the covenant. As he alone initiated the covenant, so he alone can bring about its end. He is not only Israel's Judge, but also her Redeemer.

c The prophets call Israel to repentance. In season and out they cry, ' Return, O Israel ! ' The people go after other gods, the fertility gods of Canaan and the astral gods of Assyria, but the prophets plead with them to turn about, to walk after Yahweh their leader and King. The terminology of sin in the prophetic books is rich and varied. Before the divine tribunal Israel is guilty. The many judgment scenes reflect the depth of Israel's guilt. Sin for Amos is social injustice, exploitation, callousness and heedlessness to the needs of the poor or those who have none to plead their case. To Hosea it is infidelity, whoredom, 417
gross and inveterate waywardness. To Isaiah it is rebellion, pride or *hybris*, self-exaltation, living as though Yahweh were not King. For Jeremiah it is backsliding, apostasy, ingrained and deep-dyed corruption. Ezekiel views it as profaneness, stubbornness, insensateness, *hybris* and gross whoredom. Second Isaiah stresses Israel's blindness. To be sure, all of the prophets employ various terms and do not confine themselves to a fixed terminology. Yet in all of them, even in Amos, the cry of repentance is either heard or clearly implied. Yahweh does not will the destruction of Israel, though the sound of judgment is constantly heard ; his will is that she turn and be healed.

The prophets were not only agents of doom. They d
also were heralds of hope and redemption. Again and again they hold out promises of a better future. History as the sphere of God's redemptive activity moved on toward a denouement, when Yahweh's holy and righteous will would be realised, his purposes fulfilled and his sovereignty established in the earth. Thus Isaiah can look forward to a time when the dark night would be broken by the light of a new dawn, an age of plenty and an age of peace. For a child will be born who will be the Prince of Peace, the government will be upon his shoulder, and he will reign with justice and righteousness. The constant repetition of the motif of peace in this and other oracles is a poignant expression of universal longing for a time when nations will learn war no more. Jeremiah speaks of the new covenant which Yahweh will engrave on the hearts of men, when all men will know him with that knowledge which is born of the grace of forgiveness. Ezekiel, too, speaks of the new covenant, and of the cleansing fountains of renewal and quickening, of the new spirit which will animate men's minds so that they will serve Yahweh and obey him in the bonds of a new relation. In the Servant passages of Second Isaiah we receive a matchless portrait of Israel's election-covenant past, of all the central events from the call of Abraham to Cyrus—or rather, from the creation of the world to the time of redemption—which point to Israel's unique mission in the world as Yahweh's Servant. All the streams of covenant faith converge in the eschatological drama of the prophet of the Exile. The portrait of the Servant is drawn with myriad colours, and the materials which are employed are many and diverse, but it culminates in the incandescent words of Isa. 52:12–53:12, where the confessional lament (53:1–9) is surrounded by words of the Servant's vindication and exaltation and by his vicarious atonement, his work of justification and his intercession for the transgressors.

Bibliography—W. F. Albright, *From the Stone Age to Christianity* (1940) ; H. Birkeland, *Zum hebräischen Traditionswesen* (1938) ; M. Buber, *The Prophetic Faith* (1949) ; O. Eissfeldt, ' The Prophetic Literature ', OTMS (1951), 115–61, *Einleitung in das AT* (2nd ed. 1956) ; G. Fohrer, *Die symbolischen Handlungen der Propheten* (1953) ; O. Grether, *Name and Wort Gottes im AT* (1934) ; A. Guillaume, *Prophecy and Divination among the Hebrews and other Semites* (1938) ; H. Gunkel, Introduction to Hans Schmidt, *Die grossen Propheten* (1915), xxxvi–lxxii, ' The Secret Experiences of the Prophets ', *Expositor*, 9th series, 1 (1924), 356–66, 427–35, 2 (1924), 23–32 ; A. Haldar, *Associations of Cult Prophets among the Ancient Semites* (1945) ; J. Hempel, *Worte der Propheten* (1949) ; G. Hölscher, *Die Propheten* (1914) ; A. R. Johnson, *The One and the Many in the Israelite Conception of God* (1942), *The Cultic Prophet in Ancient Israel* (1944) ; J. Lindblom, *Die literarische Gattung der Prophetischen Literatur* (1924) ; A. Lods, *Israel from its Beginnings to the Middle of the Eighth Century* (1932) ; T. J. Meek, *Hebrew Origins* (2nd ed. 1950) ; J. Morgenstern, *Amos Studies* I (1941) ; S. Mowinckel, *Psalmenstudien III. Kultprophetie und prophetische Psalmen* (1923), ' The " Spirit " and the

" Word " in the Pre-exilic Prophets ', JBL 53 (1934), 199–227, *Prophecy and Tradition* (1946) ; J. Pedersen, *Israel I–II* (1926), *III–IV* (1940) ; N. W. Porteous, ' Prophecy ', *Record and Revelation*, ed. by H. W. Robinson (1938), ' The Basis of the Ethical Teaching of the Prophets ', *Studies in OT Prophecy*, ed. by H. H. Rowley (1950) ; G. von Rad, *Studies in Deuteronomy* (1953) ; H. W. Robinson, ' Prophetic Symbolism ', *OT Essays* (1927), 1–17, ' The Hebrew Conception of Corporate Personality ', *Werden und Wesen des ATs*, BZAW 66 (1936), *Inspiration and Revelation in the OT* (1946) ; T. H. Robinson, *Prophecy and the Prophets* (1923) ; H. H. Rowley, ' The Nature of Prophecy in the Light of Recent Study ', HTR 38 (1945), 1–38, ' Ritual and the Hebrew Prophets ', JSS 1 (1956), 338–60 ; R. B. Y. Scott, *The Relevance of the Prophets* (1944) ; G. Widengren, *Literary and Psychological Aspects of the Hebrew Prophets* (1948).

APOCALYPTIC LITERATURE

By H. H. ROWLEY

418a Each of the Testaments contains a great apocalyptic work. In the OT the book of Dan., though it stands amongst the Prophets in our Bibles, has a special character which differentiates it from the other prophetical works. The prophets spoke to their own generation and declared to men God's word to them in their contemporary situation. They saw through the events of their day to their inevitable issue, if the misguided policies they denounced were persisted in. It is true that they also sometimes spoke of the more distant future, not causally connected with the present, when the purposes of God should be perfectly realised. Most of these passages have commonly been held by scholars to be secondary, though there is less disposition today to eliminate them as later additions, and the present writer favours the utmost caution in such later ascription. Despite such caution, it remains true that by and large the prophets delivered God's message to their own generation, through oracles dealing with current conditions and policies.

b **The book of Dan.** has quite another character. The stories of the first half of the book are told about one who was faithful to his own religion in a heathen country and who cleverly interpreted dreams and mysteries, but who never engaged in a prophetic ministry by public proclamation. The interpretation of Nebuchadnezzar's dream was not charged with a message to the king, but was an unfolding of future events, culminating in a time long after Nebuchadnezzar's. The second half of the book records Daniel's visions in the 6th cent., but all primarily concerned with things that should happen much later, with a culmination in the 2nd cent. B.C. Modern scholarship dates the composition of the work, at least in its present form, in the 2nd cent., and finds that the author's purpose was to deliver a message to his contemporaries ; but this does not affect the wide difference between the form of this book and the form of the prophetic books in general.

c **The book of Revelation** again has a similar form. It unfolds in visions the future course of events. That it stands apart from all the other books of the NT is clear to every reader, though again there are passages elsewhere in the NT, and especially in Mk 13 and its parallels, which share something of the same character. It is quite unlike the prophetic books of the OT, and finds its closest links within the Bible with the book of Dan. That is why so many writers down the centuries have studied these two books together. The NT book is called the Revelation or the Apocalypse, and this literary genre is known as apocalyptic.

In the intertestamental period many other works of the same general character were written, though in some the apocalyptic element is found in sections only. The two biblical apocalypses are incomparably greater than any of the others. Nevertheless, it is important to realise that they belong to a whole category of literature, and should be studied in relation to the other books of this period.

d **The Rise of Apocalyptic**—In spite of what has been said above, it should be recognised that apocalyptic is the child of prophecy. Reference has been made to the passages in the prophetic books dealing with the far horizons of time. These passages are often called eschatological passages, because they deal with the end 418 to which it was believed history would lead when the purpose of God reached its climax. Eschatology is to be distinguished from apocalyptic, though all apocalyptic literature had an eschatological interest. The apocalyptists believed that the end was near in their own days, and indicated the course of events that they thought would lead to the great dénouement of history, and the signs of the end. No more than the prophets did they think this climax would arise out of history by any natural evolution. They were persuaded that it could only come about by the direct intervention of God in history. This was not a new conception to the Jew. He believed that God had intervened in history before, in the Exodus and in other critical moments of the history of his own people. God was believed to be always in control of history, and an actor on the stage of history. He was never thought to be the sole actor, and all that happened was not ascribed to him. But in the divine intervention that was looked for to inaugurate the end of history, he was conceived of as the sole significant actor. In the passages in the prophets dealing with the Golden Age—often called the messianic passages, because many of them speak of the divinely raised up leader who should rule in those days—it is important to note that the fundamental character of that age would be the perfect reflection of the will of God in human affairs, and universal submission to his law in a society in which perfect justice would be administered and economic well-being would be achieved. The Golden Age was always conceived to be a Kingdom of God. It was this side of prophecy which its child, apocalyptic, took up and developed.

While the extent of this element in the prophetic e books varies, there is one section of the book of Isa., which is believed to be of independent origin, in which we find a development which goes a long way towards the stage reached by apocalyptic. Many writers call this section, Isa. 24–7, an apocalyptic section. While the present writer would not go so far as this, he recognises many of the elements which mark apocalyptic, and finds here an important forerunner of apocalyptic.

It is not seldom said that one of the marks of f apocalyptic is **pseudonymity**. It is true that many of these writings are pseudonymous. Isa. 24–7 cannot be called pseudonymous. These chapters have been attached to the book of Isa., but there is no internal evidence that the author wrote in the name of Isaiah, any more than there is that other non-Isaianic parts of the book of Isa., which have no apocalyptic character, were written in the name of Isaiah, and were therefore pseudonymous. The great NT Apocalypse was not pseudonymous. It claims to have been written by one named John, and there is no reason to dispute this claim, even though the identification of the particular John may be uncertain. The book of Dan. is not, strictly speaking, pseudonymous. The first part of the book is, rather, anonymous, consisting of stories about Daniel, with no indication of their author. Dan. 7, which in several respects marks a transition within the book of Dan., begins anonymously, writing of Daniel in the third person, and passes over to the use of the

418f first person, which marks the later chapters. This transition to pseudonymity may have been the author's way of indicating community of authorship for the stories and the visions, and so far from being an attempt to mislead his readers as to the identity of the author, may have been his way of telling them who the author was. It has to be remembered that title-pages were unknown, and that we do not know the name of the author of any book of the OT in the form it now has. Once the second part of the book of Dan. had been given this pseudonymous character to show that its author was the author of the by now well-known Aramaic stories about Daniel, other apocalyptic writers imitated this feature without the same reason, and pseudonymity became a common—though not universal—mark of apocalyptic literature, until the author of the NT Apocalypse boldly broke with it and gave his own name.

419a **The non-canonical Apocalyptic Books**—It is impossible here to offer more than brief notes on the chief writings of the apocalyptists of the period that spanned the years between the completion of the book of Dan. in its present form and the end of the first Christian century. The precise dating of several of these works is not agreed, but this is not material for our purpose. A new interest has been given to their study by the discovery of the Dead Sea Scrolls, which by the broad consensus of scholarly opinion fall within the limits of our period. Some of the non-biblical texts from Qumrân show affinities with previously known works, and there is little doubt that the Zadokite Work emanated from the sect of the Scrolls. How far others of the works came from the same sect is less certain, and we should be cautious about attributing to the sect works which do not express the characteristic ideas it cherished. The fact that fragments of a work have been found in the Qumrân caves does not of itself establish that it was composed by a member of the sect. The Qumrân sectaries were not the only Jews interested in apocalyptic, and they may well have kept copies of the writings of others which touched certain sides of their interests, but which do not relate to the discipline, history, or characteristic dreams or expectations of the sectaries.

b **1 Enoch**, or the Ethiopic Enoch—Following Charles many scholars have divided this book into various sections, which are ascribed to dates ranging from the pre-Maccabaean period to 64 B.C. Charles's reasons for assigning the Apocalypse of Weeks (93:1–10, 91:12–17) to a pre-Maccabaean date are not always self-consistent (cf. the present writer's *Relevance of Apocalyptic*, 2nd ed., 78ff) and it is more likely that it should be placed slightly later. Frey disputes Charles's dates for some of the other sections, and holds that all the principal sections of this work come from the 2nd cent. B.C., either from the time of Antiochus Epiphanes or shortly after his death. In the section contained in chs. 6–36 we find the expectation of a great world judgment, when the fallen angels, demons, and men should receive the recompense of their works, with the Golden Age following the judgment. There is no thought of the Messiah as the head of the kingdom, though this does not mean that the idea was rejected, but merely that the person of the leader was not in the focus of the writer's thought. Sheol is conceived of as divided into sections, where men
c would be separated according to their deserts. The Apocalypse of Weeks divides history into ten periods, of which the seventh is the age of apostasy, the eighth an age of righteousness, the ninth the age of the destruction of the wicked, and the tenth the age of enduring bliss. The rest of chs. 91–104 depict a time of apostasy and idolatry, with the promise of eternal torment for the wicked and of lasting joy for the righteous. Chs. 83–90 review the history of Israel under the symbolism of sheep, until one sheep develops a powerful horn against a Gentile attack, and achieves a victory which involves the destruction of the foe, to be followed by the resurrection of the righteous and the ushering in of the kingdom of God. The horned 419c
sheep is to be identified with the Maccabees, and a white bull, who should be the leader of the coming kingdom, is conceived of as the Messiah, though the term is not used of him. Chs. 37–71 are known as the Similitudes of Enoch and are of particular interest because of the figure of the Son of Man found here. Many scholars find Christian interpolations in this section, and it is further disputed whether the Son of Man is a transcendental figure or not. T. W. Manson argued that the Son of Man here is a collective concept, pre-existing in the mind of God, but to be realised, like the Son of Man of Dan. 7, in the saints. The Anointed One, or Messiah, is found in these chapters, but it is not clear whether he is a human leader, and Messel believes this is again a collective symbol.

The book of Jubilees—This work is not strictly d
apocalyptic or pseudonymous, but is in some sense a revised Pentateuch. It is cast in the form of a vision of Moses, but does not claim to have been written by him, and it has a strong calendrical interest. History is divided into Jubilees, and the calendar of this work differed from the calendar current at the time. According to this calendar the year consisted of 364 days, so that all festivals fell on the same day of the week each year. From the Zadokite work it is clear that the Qumrân sect valued this book and shared its calendar, and Mlle Jaubert has argued that this may throw light on the disagreement between the Synoptic Gospels and the Fourth Gospel as to the date of the Passover in our Lord's Passion Week. We need not ascribe the authorship of Jubilees to a member of the sect, and this calendar, which was older than the book of Jubilees, may have been followed by others beside the sectaries, including our Lord, who then would celebrate Passover on the Tuesday night. This date is not contradicted by Synoptic evidence, Mlle Jaubert argues, and is supported by patristic tradition, and it leaves more room for the succession of events that spanned the period from the Last Supper to the Crucifixion. The unwillingness of Jews to enter the praetorium lest they should be unable to eat the Passover then refers to the official, as against the sectarian, Passover.

The book of Jubilees almost certainly comes from the middle of the 2nd cent., though some have disputed this date. Its background would seem to be the Maccabaean age, when the observance of the Sabbath was prohibited by Antiochus, when the Jewish food laws were forcibly violated, when circumcision was illegal, and when idolatry was practised even in the Temple. All of these things seem to be in the mind of the author.

The author of this book looked for a gradual coming of the kingdom, with the gradual lengthening of men's days until they reached a thousand years. There is no mention of a resurrection of the dead. The descendants of Levi are promised ecclesiastical and civil power, but Judah is promised the throne. It would therefore seem that the king is thought of as subordinate to the priest—an idea we shall meet again.

The Zadokite Work—In 1910 Schechter published 420a
two fragments which had been found in medieval manuscripts in the Cairo Genizah. In part they overlapped and in part they supplemented one another, so that it was known that they belonged to a single work, though the two manuscripts differed in age. It was at once thought that the composition of the work must have taken place many centuries before the writing of these manuscripts, and by some writers it was placed in the 2nd cent. B.C., while others put it somewhat later. The fact that fragments of the same work dating from not later than the 1st cent. A.D. have been found in the Qumrân caves confirms the antiquity of the work.

It recounts how the sect from which it emanated, b
who were called the Covenanters of Damascus, came into being 390 years after the destruction of Jerusalem, but groped in darkness for twenty years until one

420b called the Teacher of Righteousness was raised up to lead them. Little reliance can be placed on the 390 years, and if it were approximately accurate, as the present writer thinks likely, that is but an accident. The sect is almost certainly the Qumrân sect, though there are differences between its way of life as reflected here, and that reflected in some other texts from Qumrân. This may be because a different point in the history of the sect is reflected here. The text tells of the migration of the covenanters to Damascus, but several scholars believe that by Damascus Qumrân is meant. Since the archaeological evidence points to the fact that the Qumrân centre of the sect was built in the last third of the 2nd cent., this would carry the existence of the sect into that century. If the migration to Qumrân were under the leadership of the Teacher of Righteousness, his work must have gone back to that century. If, as interpreters before the discovery of the Scrolls thought, the migration was under a later leader, called the Star, the work of the Teacher would be carried back still earlier in the 2nd cent., while if Damascus really means Damascus, the migration thither would have to be placed before the building of Qumrân, and we should be pushed back still earlier in the 2nd cent. for the work of the Teacher.

c The composition of this work lay within forty years of the death of the Teacher, since this date was looked forward to as significant. On the other hand, it lay after the composition of Jubilees, since there is a reference to that work. There is a reference to a book of Hagu, which was highly valued by the sect, and in a Dead Sea Scrolls fragment there is a further reference to this work as valued by the Qumrân sect.

d The book reflects a period of evil, during which a Remnant should preserve their faithfulness, and it speaks of a period from the gathering in of the Teacher to the coming of the Messiah, when all the wicked should be destroyed, including those covenanters who were faithless, and the faithful should be granted eternal life. The Messiah is here called the Messiah of Aaron and Israel, an expression that occasioned much speculation until the Dead Sea Scrolls were discovered, when references to the Messiahs were found. It now became probable that the Zadokite Work looked for two Messiahs, a priestly and a lay. That this was not a new idea has been said above. It should be remembered that Messiah simply meant anointed, and there is nothing surprising in the sect looking for a priestly and a civil leader in the Golden Age. That Aaron is put before Israel probably indicates the precedence of the priestly leader.

e The sect clearly had an interest in the Zadokite priesthood, and one of its names for itself was the Sons of Zadok. It is certain that we are not to identify them with the Sadducees of the NT, and today it is common to find here the beginnings of the Essenes, though we should not expect their practices at this time to agree in all things with those of the 1st cent. A.D., when we find references to the Essenes in the writings of Philo, Pliny, and Josephus.

f **The Dead Sea Scrolls**—It will be convenient here to look briefly at other Qumrân scrolls, though their relative and actual datings are not by any means agreed. There are certain texts which mention the Teacher of Righteousness, and contain some allusions to the conflicts in which he figured and to his sufferings and those of members of the Sect at the hands of enemies, both Jewish and foreign. These are the commentaries on biblical texts, in which contemporary events are read into the passage interpreted, and the text is rather applied to a contemporary situation than expounded for itself. There are fragments of several of these commentaries, including **commentaries on Nah., Mic., Isa.** and **Ps. 37,** but the longest of them, containing most references to the Teacher, is that on the first two chapters of **the book of Hab**. It would seem probable that all of the texts which mention the Teacher of Righteousness were composed within a few years of his death, 42
when their allusions would be understood. In several of the texts he does not figure at all.

The Manual of Discipline describes the way of life g
of the sect, and gives expression to many of their principal ideas. The organisation of the sect is not our concern here, and this is not strictly an apocalyptic text, though there is a passage in which the characteristic dualism of apocalyptic, and its hope of the destruction of evil and the triumph of good, find expression. It may be noted that references have been found to the ritual washings of the sect, and these have been brought into association with NT baptism, and also to the meals of the sect, which have been brought into association with the NT Lord's Supper. There is no clear evidence of a rite of initiation by water, and the meals appear to be the daily meals. The sect acknowledged priestly leadership, and each group of members was under the direction of one who was armed with authority over them, and each member had a definitely regulated place in meetings and must not speak out of turn. The members brought their belongings to the sect, and this has been connected with the practice of the early Jerusalem church. There are two columns of a related text, in which the book of Hagu (here called Hagi) is mentioned, and a **Scroll of Benedictions,** where we find it clearly laid down that in what has been believed to be the Messianic Banquet, the priestly leader is to take precedence over the Messiah. Finally, mention should be made of a **Testimonies Scroll,** in which a number of OT texts of a messianic character are collected together. These are Dt. 5:28f. (Heb. 25f.), 18:18f. ; Num. 24:15–17 ; Dt. 33:8–11 ; Jos. 6:26. It will be noted that nothing from Isa. 53 figures here.

The Manual of Discipline ends with a Psalm, and a h
collection of similar **Psalms** has been found. Many writers believe these were composed by the Teacher of Righteousness, but this is only conjecture. They may have been used liturgically by the sect, but this we cannot know. They reflect the sufferings of the sect—or of the Teacher—and their piety and aspirations. There are, however, apocalyptic elements where the future judgment is described.

There is a Genesis Apocryphon, of which a few columns have been published. This is a sort of paraphrase of the book of Gen. in Aramaic, and it has something of the character of the book of Jubilees. There is nothing apocalyptic here, and nothing that reflects the peculiar ideas or practices of the sect, and there is no reason to ascribe its composition to one of the sectaries.

Of more relevance here is the text called **The War** i
of the Sons of Light against the Sons of Darkness. This describes a war, which opens against the Kittim of Assyria, in which also the Kittim of Egypt take part, and tells how victory will be finally achieved by the faithful Jews after seven campaigns. There will then follow thirty-three years of war against the other nations of the earth in succession, until final victory is won. The text then returns to the war against the Kittim, and describes the organisation, equipment, and tactics to be employed. It would appear that behind this text is a historical situation, which lay somewhere in the seven years of battle against the Kittim, and that the author believed this was the beginning of an apocalyptic era of battle, which should inaugurate the kingdom of God.

The Testaments of the Twelve Patriarchs—It has 421
commonly been thought that this was a pre-Christian text which later received Christian interpolations, and to the present writer this seems the most probable view, though a Dutch scholar, de Jonge, has argued that it was of post-Christian origin. Fragments of a Testament of Levi, probably older than the Testament of Levi contained in the Testaments, have been found in the Qumrân caves.

In the Testaments there are references to the Messiah, which have been held to show that these

421a Testaments came from circles that looked for a Levitical Messiah, rather than a Davidic. There are also references to a Davidic Messiah, however, and it would seem that the thought was of a priestly leader alongside a civil leader, with the civil subordinate to the priestly. We find also the expectation of the resurrection of the righteous to receive the reward of everlasting happiness in the New Jerusalem.

b We must pass over certain sections of the Jewish **Sibylline Oracles**, dating from the 2nd cent. B.C., which present apocalyptic ideas, and the **Psalms of Solomon**, dating from the middle of the 1st cent. B.C., in two of which the thought is of the Davidic Messiah and the kingdom over which he should reign. Here we have simply a development of OT ideas, with little that goes fundamentally beyond what can be found in the OT.

c **The Assumption of Moses**—This was probably written during the lifetime of our Lord, and it surveys Jewish history down to the Seleucid era, and then on through the Hasmonaean period to an insolent king, who is probably Herod the Great. The following chapter describes a period of persecution which would well fit the time of Antiochus Epiphanes, and many think this chapter has been misplaced and should stand earlier. Then a mysterious figure, Taxo, appears. He exhorts his sons to withdraw with him to a cave, there to die rather than be disloyal to their faith, and from their death we pass to the expected intervention of God in history and the establishment of His kingdom. This appears to be conceived as a supramundane kingdom, rather than one established on earth. Numerous attempts have been made to identify Taxo with a historical character, but none is really successful. One such attempt has identified him with the Teacher of Righteousness, and has claimed to find in the name Taxo a truncated Greek rendering of one of the titles of the Teacher.

d **2 Enoch**, or the Slavonic Enoch—A second work cast in the form of a vision of Enoch has come down to us in Slavonic. It is commonly dated in the 1st cent. of our era, but some have argued that it really dates from several centuries later. In this work we have the idea of a period of rest, following 6,000 years of history, and lasting for 1,000 years, after which time should come to an end. If the 1st-cent. dating is correct, this is the first expression of a millennium, in the sense of a 1,000-year period, known to us. Unlike most of the apocalyptic works, this does not appear to have a background of crisis, or to contemplate a time of distress and conflict preceding the inauguration of the period of rest and bliss.

e **The Life of Adam and Eve**—This work has come down in two forms, one in Latin and one in Greek. It contemplates the coming of the Messiah, the Son of God, after 5,500 years, but some believe this to be a Christian interpolation. It looks for a judgment of fire, followed by a resurrection of all flesh.

f **4 Ezra** (= 2 Esd. 3–14)—This work is generally believed to come from the latter part of the first Christian century, and it exhibits features which have led many scholars to set aside some passages as secondary, while others have thought the author depended on diverse traditions which he did not fully integrate. It is cast in the form of seven visions, in the fifth of which Daniel's vision of Dan. 7 is reinterpreted. The visions all have to do with the end of the present age and the coming of a day of judgment, with the establishment of the kingdom of the Messiah, but it is hard to find a common pattern in them. In the third vision the Messiah is to have a reign of 600 years, and then to die, and all men with him. After seven years of complete silence the resurrection of all men for judgment should take place.

g **The Apocalypse of Baruch**—The relation of this work to 4 Ezra is uncertain, but it is probably dependent on 4 Ezra, and may belong to the end of the 1st cent. or the beginning of the 2nd. It depicts the disasters which will precede the dawn of the messianic age, and sets forth the thought of four world empires, 421g
of which the fourth, which is doubtless the Roman, is harsh and cruel, and destined to be followed by the rule of the Messiah.

The Ascension of Isaiah is a Christian apocalyptic h
work, with a general structure similar to that of the book of Dan., recounting stories about Isaiah, followed by a vision of Isaiah, and setting forth the coming of Christ as revealed to the prophet. Joseph and Mary are here mentioned by name, and the Crucifixion figures. Antichrist is to be identified with Nero in this work. **The Apocalypse of Abraham** is believed to have been written not long after the destruction of Jerusalem, when the author believed the end was imminent, and the heathen should be destroyed and God's Elect should come with power. Finally, **the Testament of Abraham** is an apocalyptic work which has no background of crisis, and which thinks of seven ages and a threefold judgment. Of the NT Apocalypse it is unnecessary to write here, since it is dealt with in its proper place in this commentary.

The enduring Value of Apocalyptic—That apoca- i
lyptic contributed to the development of thought in the intertestamental period is clear from the brief notes given above. Its sharp **dualism**, while it has its roots in the OT, goes beyond what is there found. The world is divided into the good and the bad, and in the transcendental world evil is personified in Belial, or Beliar, or Mastema (the last of these names being found in the book of Jubilees and in the Zadokite Work). Many of the works, though not all, think of a time of persecution and suffering which should precede the great deliverance, and reflect a background of crisis, so that apocalyptic has sometimes been described as 'tracts for hard times'. Their purpose was to keep alive hope in God, and to remind men that while God is not the sole actor on the stage of history, he is in final control of all. What matters is less the detail of the expectations, which differ so widely and could not all be accurate forecasts of the future, as the religious message which is valid for all generations, that when there is least ground for hope in contemporary conditions, faith in God may fortify men's hearts.

This is reinforced by the thought on **the future** j
life. There is again great variety in the ideas found in this literature. Some think of a resurrection of the good to life on earth, while others think of a blissful hereafter. Inspiring all is the confidence that loyalty to God will lead to enduring joy beyond the trials of the present, and that that joy will be found in what can only be described as the Kingdom of God. Whether in this world or beyond, its bliss will be found in the triumph of God's will, for only in a world in which his will is perfectly done can the righteous find their joy perfected.

Characteristic of these works, though found in k
differing form and in varying measure, is the recognition that the Golden Age will not come of itself, but that it will be **God's gift**. This belongs to the message of the OT, but here it is given a greater focus of interest. This does not mean that all that happens in the human sphere is meaningless. For the apocalyptists believed that in obedience to the will of God and in loyalty to him men might serve his purpose, and that the only worthwhile way for man is to link himself with God and with the divine purpose, even though it entailed anguish and distress.

Inherent in this is the thought of the **final judg-** l
ment, which figures so much in apocalyptic. The apocalyptists had no place for the sentimentality which supposes that God in his love would confer a common bliss on all in the Hereafter. It recognised that fundamentally bliss was not an extraneous prize to be handed out, but that it lay in obedience to God in a world that was obedient, and that therefore it could not be given to men who despised the will of God and set themselves up against Him. In the day of judgment men would be found to be what they had chosen

421l to be, and if they had elected to hate the will of God they would be found to hate it, and therefore could not have a place in a kingdom which perfectly reflected his will.

m The ideas on the **Messiah** found in these works are again most varied, but through all their varieties their authors cherished the hope, born of the OT, that in the kingdom there would be a divinely raised up leader, or leaders, who would be the instrument of the divine purpose.

n Christianity was born in a world in which all these ideas—and only a small selection of them can here be noted—were current. They formed an important part of the background of the NT. Not a few of them were taken up into the NT, often refashioned and shedding the varying and sometimes extravagant and fantastic forms they have in the apocalyptic writings, yet in their essential meaning not dissimilar. These writings can be read as a confused jumble of inconsistent dreams and forecasts; but they can also be read as works that sought to convey a spiritual message, in which there were enduringly valid elements. This is not to say that here we find the Christian message anticipated. For while there are apocalyptic elements in the NT, its faith is more than apocalyptic. The NT speaks of One in whom God entered into history, to redeem by suffering and to lift men into a union with himself whereby they might be taken up into the fellowship and purpose of God. If its writers shared with the apocalyptists the hope of a future millennium, they also cherished a faith in the Person and Work of One who suffered under Pontius Pilate, which had no counterpart in the writings of the apocalyptists of the intertestamental period, but which is taken up into the great Apocalypse of the NT.

Bibliography—J. Bloch, *On the Apocalyptic in Judaism*, JQR Monographs, No. 2 (1952); W. Bousset, *Die Religion des Judentums im späthellenistischen Zeitalter*, 3rd ed., rev. by H. Gressmann, HNT 21 (1926); M. Burrows, ** *The Dead Sea Scrolls* (1956), ** *More Light on the Dead Sea Scrolls* (1958); R. H. Charles, *A Critical History of the Doctrine of a Future Life* (1913); R. H. Charles (ed.), *The Apocrypha and Pseudepigrapha of the OT*, 2 vols. (1913); E. de Faye, *Les apocalypses juives* (1892); J. B. Frey, 'Apocalyptique', in Pirot's *Supplément au Dictionnaire de la Bible*, i (1928), 326–54, * 'Apocryphes de l'AT', ibid., 354–459, 'La vie de l'au delà dans les conceptions juives au temps de Jésus-Christ', *Biblica* 13 (1932), 129–68; T. H. Gaster, *The Scriptures of the Dead Sea Sect* (1957); Mlle A. Jaubert, *La Date de la Cène* (1957); M. de Jonge, *The Testaments of the Twelve Patriarchs* (1953); E. Kautzsch (ed.), *Apocryphen und Pseudepigraphen des ATs*, 2 vols. (1900); J. Klausner, *The Messianic Idea in Israel* (1956); T. W. Manson, 'The Son of Man in Daniel, Enoch and the Gospels', in BJRL 32 (1949–50), 171–93; N. Messel, *Die Einheitlichkeit der jüdischen Eschatologie*, BZAW 30 (1915), *Der Menschensohn in der Bilderreden des Henoch*, BZAW 35 (1922); C. V. Pilcher, *The Hereafter in Jewish and Christian Thought* (1940); F. C. Porter, *The Messages of the Apocalyptical Writers* (1905); C. Rabin, *The Zadokite Documents* (2nd ed. 1958); H. H. Rowley, * *The Relevance of Apocalyptic* (2nd ed. 1947), ** *The Zadokite Fragments and the Dead Sea Scrolls* (1952), *Jewish Apocalyptic and the Dead Sea Scrolls* (1957); K. Stendahl, *The Scrolls and the NT* (1958); C. C. Torrey, *The Apocryphal Literature* (1945); P. Volz, *Die Eschatologie der jüdischen Gemeinde im nt.lichen Zeitalter* (1934).

Note—The literature in this field is immense, and for fuller bibliographies on apocalyptic in general, the reader is referred to the works above with prefixed *, while for literature on the Dead Sea Scrolls fuller bibliographies will be found in those with prefixed **.

ISAIAH—I

By J. Bright

422a Our knowledge of the life of Isaiah is scanty, and is derived almost entirely from chs. 1–39 of the book that bears his name. Called to the prophetic office (6:1) in the year of Uzziah's death (*c.*742), he was presumably born some two decades previously. His boyhood thus coincided with the ministry of Amos. He seems to have spent his whole life in Jerusalem. From the ease with which he had access to the king it would appear that he was of good family, if not a member of the court itself. We know (7:3, 8:3) that he was married and had at least two sons, both of whom bore names symbolical of major features in his message. The older of these was apparently a child in 735, while the younger was born perhaps a year later. Isaiah's career extended over half a century, through the reigns of Jotham and Ahaz, and at least until near the end of that of Hezekiah (*d.*687/6). The tradition that he was martyred under the apostate Manasseh, while possibly correct, is late and unsupported. In the course of his life he gathered a group of disciples about him (8:16), who presumably preserved his sayings and carried on his work after him.

b Reconstruction of Isaiah's career is rendered more difficult by the nature of the book itself. Leaving aside 40–66, which is of later date, the book is by no means the creation of the prophet's pen. Though he reduced certain of his oracles to writing (8:16, 30:8), his book, like those of other prophets, came into being through a long process of transmission and collection. The prophets normally delivered their oracles publicly; these were heard, remembered, passed on orally for a longer or shorter period, and finally written down. As time passed small collections of the prophet's sayings, drawn together by common theme or by catchword, began to form. These small collections were gradually assembled into ever larger collections, until ultimately the Isaiah book as we know it took shape. The book is thus somewhat in the nature of an anthology of the prophet's remembered preaching, together with a few incidents from his life. This means that, except within narrow limits, one may not look for chronological or logical order in it: adjacent units may come from widely separated dates and deal with entirely distinct subjects. One must begin by isolating the smallest units of tradition and studying them individually, and then, from the mosaic of the whole, seek to reconstruct the message and career of the prophet. Moreover, even in 1–39 one must continually confront the question of genuineness. Since the process of collection went on long after Isaiah's death, it is only to be expected that some of the material in these chapters should represent the Isaiah tradition as carried forward in later prophetic circles. 1–39 falls into certain clear divisions: 1–12, 13–23, 24–27, 28–33, 34f., 36–39. The last of these is a historical narrative, also found in Kg., which tells of incidents in Isaiah's life and contains oracles of his the basic genuineness of which need not be questioned. Save for 24–27 and 34f., which are of much later date, all the other divisions contain, in varying degree, genuine oracles of Isaiah together with material of later origin. Critical problems will be discussed *ad loc.* There is today, however, a growing consensus that earlier critics, whether because of preconceived notions of the development of Israel's religion, or because of 422b insufficient appreciation of the process by which the prophetic books were collected, were frequently too hasty in declaring passages non-Isaianic, and that a greater degree of caution is required in this regard. It is, further, probable that there has been a tendency to place the admittedly post-Isaianic portions of 1–39 in many instances *too* late.

c However he is evaluated, Isaiah is one of the towering figures of the OT. He came to his work in a time of grave emergency for Israel. Uzziah's death marked the end of the last great period of wealth and national glory that she was ever to know; soon the Assyrian tide would roll over the land, engulfing the northern state altogether and reducing Judah to helpless subservience. This was a national humiliation, and more. With the acknowledgment of Assyrian overlordship, and the attendant recognition of Assyria's gods, the theological foundations of the monarchy—Yahweh's eternal choice of Zion and David (2 Sam. 7)—were thrown into question. In addition, though it is unlikely that social and moral decay had advanced as far in Judah as it had in the north, there is evidence that the nation was in no very healthy condition internally. The greed of the wealthy dispossessed the poor and, the courts being venal, the poor had no redress (5:8–10, 10:1–4; Mic. 2:1f., 3:1–3). Luxury and indulgence walked side by side with hopeless poverty. Worse, the national religion had become a hollow and external thing which tolerated these abuses without protest and, demanding only lavish ritual, fostered the delusion of unconditional national security based on the promises of God (1:10–20; Mic. 3:9–11). It was a nation ill fitted to withstand the crisis that was upon it. That it did so was in no small part due to the labours of Isaiah and those likeminded with him.

d Isaiah's message was, on the one hand, a powerful reaffirmation of Yahweh's promises to David; on the other hand, Isaiah informed this national dogma with an awareness of the moral obligations of the ancient covenant which had made Israel a people (5:1–7). His inaugural vision shows him overwhelmed with a sense of the awful holiness of Yahweh whose throne was on Zion, and equally with a sense of the depth of the national sin. This sin he must denounce; and denounce it he did, with an eloquence rarely matched in Hebrew literature. Yet he did this (6:9ff.) in full awareness that he would not be heeded. The nation with blind eyes and deaf ears was marching headlong to judgment; only a remnant would return (10:22f.). Judgment came soon enough in the form of the Assyrians. And for a whole generation Isaiah, though seldom listened to, asked the ear of the king, counselling repentance and trust in the promises of Yahweh. Thus in 735 when Ahaz, threatened by the anti-Assyrian coalition (7), considered an appeal to Tiglath-pileser for aid, Isaiah begged him to take no such step, but to trust in the very theology he affirmed in his official cult. Ahaz did not listen, and Isaiah, writing down his words as a witness (8:16–18), was forced to yield. From that moment Judah was a vassal of Assyria. Yet later (*c.*714–11), when Hezekiah toyed with the notion of revolt in reliance upon Egypt, Isaiah coun-

422d selled against it (chs. 18, 20), and for identical reasons: Yahweh, and Yahweh alone, will save the nation—trust in him! Perhaps his word was heeded, for the revolt was dropped. It is possible that Isaiah's voice, like Micah's (cf. Jer. 26:18f.), encouraged Hezekiah in his efforts at reform. Later (705–1), when rebellion was made, again in alliance with Egypt, Isaiah denounced it bitterly (28:7–22, 30:1–7, 31:1–3) and predicted for it nothing but disaster. His advice refused, he again recorded his words as a witness (30:8). To him the whole thing was nothing but rebellion against God, and it ought to be given up (1:2–9). Throughout his life his motto remained 'in returning and rest you shall be saved; in quietness and trust shall be your strength' (30:15). Assyria is Yahweh's tool to do his work; that work done, she will be cast aside and broken—but by Yahweh, and Yahweh alone (10:5–34).

e But Isaiah's message was not wholly one of doom. Assured as he was of the judgment, he did not at any time believe that the nation would be utterly destroyed. The promises of God to David, and the purposes of God in history, are after all sure! No doubt only a remnant will escape—but still a remnant! All his life Isaiah entertained the hope, repeatedly frustrated (e.g. 22:1–14), that the calamities through which the nation was passing would serve as a purge, a refiner's furnace in which its sin would be burned away, leaving a repentant and purified people who would trust in Yahweh and obey him (1:24–26, 10:20f.). So it was that in the hour of Jerusalem's extremity (for the chronological problem, cf. §446), when Sennacherib's army ringed its walls, it was Isaiah who almost alone had the incredible faith to tell his king that the city would never be taken: Yahweh would defend it for his own sake and for David's sake (37:33–35). The Assyrian in his pride has blasphemed God and will now himself feel the judgment. How much this confidence of Isaiah's, vindicated as it was by events, contributed to the later conceit of the inviolability of Zion cannot be said. But we may be sure that Isaiah would have repudiated such a dogma, as Jeremiah did, for to him deliverance was always conditional on repentance and trust.

f Coupled with the expectation of a purified remnant, and given classical form by Isaiah and those who perpetuated his teachings, is the notion of the coming King of the line of David, the Messiah (9:2–7, 11:1–9). This hope was a transmutation of the national dogma of the promises of Yahweh to David, as this was regularly reaffirmed in the cult and glorified in the popular imagination. With Isaiah this hope was given a moral content doubtless too often lacking in its popular expression, and elevated far above the monarchy as it presently existed. There will come a prince of David's line who will set up his beneficent and righteous rule, governing as no Davidide had ever governed, as Yahweh's charismatic vicegerent. To him and to his people will all the promises be given. With this, the future hope of Israel was given a form that it would never lose. The power of this hope cannot be overestimated. Through the centuries tenaciously clung to, often flaring up and as often befooled, it was a hope—so Christians affirm—that went a-begging till 'in the fulness of time' there came one of the house and lineage of David who is called the Christ (Messiah), the Son of the Living God.

423a **I 1-31 Yahweh's Case against his People**—The chapter is a collection of oracles, or fragments of oracles, uttered at various periods in Isaiah's ministry. As elsewhere in the prophetic books, the material has been brought together on the basis of common theme or, in some cases (e.g. 9f.), catchword. The theme here is the sin of Judah and the punishment which it has brought, or will surely bring. Yahweh himself appears both as accuser of his people and as the judge who brings indictment against them. The chapter furnishes a brilliant introduction to the entire message of Isaiah.

1 An editorial heading which perhaps originally introduced a shorter collection of oracles addressed to 'Judah and Jerusalem' (cf. 2:1, 3:1, etc.), but which now serves as the title of the entire book. 423a

2-9 Judah's Rebellion and its Dire Consequences—The oracle is best dated in 701, when (cf. 36:1; 2 Kg. 18:13–16) the Assyrians, to punish Hezekiah for his rebellion, invaded the land, took and destroyed all its fortified cities save Jerusalem itself, where they shut Hezekiah up, forcing him to surrender and beg for terms. Judah, ravaged by the invader (7) is likened to a man fearfully beaten and wounded who can endure no more (6). Isaiah, who had consistently branded the rebellion, and the Egyptian alliance which supported it, as a sin against Yahweh (e.g. 30:1–7, 31:1–3), here seems (5) to counsel that it be given up. b

Heaven and earth are called on to witness Yahweh's case against his people. He has reared them as his children, but they have rebelled against him. In relying on their own strength, and on Egyptian help, they have rejected Yahweh's explicit word and refused to trust in him. This was not to display the intelligence of a farm-animal, which at least knows who feeds it. The prophet indignantly reproaches the people for the sin through which they have forsaken and despised their God. And how they have paid for it! The body politic is from head to foot nothing but bruises and festering wounds, for which there is neither treatment nor cure. Why go on with it any longer? Give up the mad folly! The whole land has been ravaged; Zion only is left, pitiful and frail. Had it not been for the mercy of God, the nation would have joined Sodom and Gomorrah in oblivion.

4. offspring: better 'family', 'brood' (Mt. 3:7); they themselves are the evildoers. The fourfold address, 'nation', 'people', 'family', 'sons' concentrates progressively on the family relationship between God and his people. The last clause (lit. 'they are estranged backward') is awkward and may be corrupt; LXX omits. **5 why:** many read 'on what' (i.e. on what part of the body, since bruises are already everywhere). But this is unnatural: one giving a beating would not trouble to select only untouched spots. **7. as overthrown by aliens:** perhaps 'aliens' mistakenly repeats the same word in the previous line, and we should read 'like the overthrow of Sodom' (cf. 13:19; Am. 4:11, etc.). **8. daughter of Zion:** better 'daughter Zion', Jerusalem personified as a maiden (cf. 37:22). **booth:** a watchman's hut, lonely and frail. **9. survivors:** AV, RV read 'remnant'; but the word here (*śārîdh*) is not Isaiah's characteristic word for 'remnant' (*sh*[e]*'ār*). Isaiah did not regard the survivors of 701 as the purified remnant of Israel. c

10-20 The Worthlessness of Empty Ritual—A distinct oracle begins in 10, which is linked to the foregoing by the catchwords 'Sodom', 'Gomorrah' (cf. 9); 18–20, though formally separate, furnishes a splendid conclusion to 10–17, and so may be treated together with it. No exact date can be assigned; but one gains the impression, otherwise than in the case of 2–9, of a time before calamity had overtaken the nation (cf. 20), perhaps rather early in Isaiah's ministry. The theme is one thoroughly characteristic of the pre-exilic prophets: that lavish sacrifice without righteous conduct is worthless, indeed offensive, in the eyes of God (cf. Am. 5:21–24; Hos. 6:6; Mic. 6:6–8; Jer. 7:21–23). This does not mean, however, that the prophets were hostile to the cult as such and would have abolished it if they could. Note (15) that Isaiah likewise condemns empty prayer. It was ritual divorced from morality that the prophets hated. Yet it must be said that the cult was never to them the central feature of religion, but rather faithfulness to Yahweh and obedience to his covenant law. d

Isaiah perhaps spoke these words on a feast-day when the Temple was thronged with worshippers. He calls upon the rulers and people of Jerusalem (Sodom and

423d Gomorrah) to hear the word of their God. What good, he demands, are all these sacrifices? God is weary of them. He has never demanded this lavish worship and can endure it no more. Let them pray as long and as loudly as they wish, but God neither sees nor hears. All he sees are the cruel wrongs which they have visited on their fellows, and which stain their hands as if with blood. Until they wash themselves internally by a turning from wrongdoing to justice, especially to the weak and helpless, their worship will never be acceptable. In 18–20 it is as if Yahweh, the Judge, hails the people before his bench and invites them to state whatever case they may have. EVV render 18 as a gracious promise or invitation, which is unlikely in the context. The words can be understood as high sarcasm (your sins are scarlet, but naturally all this mummery will make them white!), or as an indignant question (will this make them white?). Or, perhaps (Scott), the Judge is thought of as summing up the case as they would have stated it, only in 19f. to give his verdict. No! Such hypocrisy will get no hearing! The alternative before the accused is plain: obedience to the divine will, or destruction by the sword.

e **10. teaching:** Heb. *tôrāh* ('law': AV, RV). No law code is referred to; the word is used in its primary sense—the authoritative instruction given by priest or prophet (cf. 'word'). **11.** On the various types of sacrifice cf. Lev. 1ff. **I have had enough:** lit. 'I am sated, surfeited'. The notion of sacrifice as food for the god was common among the ancient pagans, but not proper to Israel's faith (Ps. 50:13), though it persisted in the popular mind. **fed beasts:** beasts fattened for sacrifice. **12ff.** The text presents difficulties. LXX reads 'fasting' for 'iniquity', and puts this word and the next with 14; perhaps they are a marginal note. Perhaps read: 'When you come to see my face (i.e. to worship me), who has required this of you? Trample my courts—do it no more! To bring offerings is worthless(ness); incense is an abomination to me. New moon and sabbath, the calling of assemblies, I cannot endure. (Fasting and solemn assembly), your new moons and set feasts. . . .' **14. my soul:** here as an emphatic first person 'my very being' or the like. **17. correct oppression:** better 'set right (i.e. restrain) the oppressor'. **defend, plead for:** forensic terms better rendered 'do justice by', 'champion the cause of'. **18. let us reason together:** again forensic, 'let us argue the case together'.

424a **21-26 Corrupt Jerusalem and Yahweh's Purifying Judgment**—The section is in two parts: an elegy over the corrupt city (21–23), and an oracle (24–26) telling how Yahweh will purge her and restore her. The date is uncertain; but the notion of a purifying judgment is one of the characteristic features of Isaiah's preaching. How like a harlot this city has become! Once noted for justice and faithfulness, her virtue is now counterfeit, like impure metal or wine that has been diluted with water. And what crooks her rulers are! Every one of them can be bought; no longer do they dispense justice, nor can the poor and the helpless even get a hearing. But Yahweh, the Sovereign Lord, will intervene in behalf of these helpless ones and avenge. He will hurl this adulterated metal into the hot furnace of trial and burn all the refuse away. Then, and only then, will good days like those of David return (cf. 2 Sam. 8:15), and Jerusalem become what she ought to be. It must not be forgotten that the Messianic hope had its ultimate origin in the idealisation of David and the belief in the eternal covenant made with his house (2 Sam. 7; Ps. 89).

b **22. dross:** better, silver mixed with dross or a glaze of lead-oxide which looks like silver. The national character is 'not sterling'. **23. gifts:** here, of course, bribes. Mention of the widow and the orphan (cf. 17) is thoroughly characteristic of OT law and prophetic preaching, in which the God of the covenant is thought of as intervening to safeguard the rights of those too weak to help themselves (e.g. Exod. 22:22; Dt. 10:18, 14:29; Jer. 7:6). **24. vent my wrath:** better: 'comfort myself', 'ease myself'. Yahweh is like one who has suffered an insult and demands satisfaction of the offender. **25. as with lye** (*kabbôr*) is awkward in the context; we should probably read (*bakkûr*) 'in the furnace'. **26. faithful:** the word also means 'enduring', 'established', and is possibly a play upon the promise to David of an enduring house (2 Sam. 7:16; Ps. 89:37).

424b

c **27f.** The passage is probably a later addition. It employs words rarely or never instanced in the utterances of Isaiah, while the sharp division between the righteous and the sinners is characteristic of later literature. Israel will be 'redeemed' (i.e. 'ransomed'), presumably from exile and slavery (cf. 35:10, 51:11), by 'justice' and 'righteousness'—which here seem to refer to Yahweh's mighty acts of deliverance rather than to any ethical qualities of Israel itself. The sinners and apostate, however, will be destroyed.

d **29-31 Against Pagan Worship**—The passage is a fragment. Some would deny it to Isaiah, but without sufficient reason. Just what cult is referred to is uncertain; but it is probably some form of the fertility cult which, as we know, was practised on the hilltops and under great trees (e.g. Hos. 4:13; 2 Kg. 16:4; Jer. 2:20). Since this cult was prevalent at all periods of Israel's history, there is no reason to regard the passage as late; it would fit especially well in the reign of Ahaz. The prophet declares that the people will be grievously disappointed in the gods of fertility after whom they have run. As their sacred trees shed and their gardens wither in the heat of summer (symbolising the death of the god of fertility), so will they be who in their nameless rites have felt—so they thought—the surge of divine energy; they are tinder dry, and their idolatrous deeds will provide the spark to destroy them in a blazing inferno.

e **II 1-5 Yahweh's Universal Reign of Peace**—This famous passage is repeated with minor variations in Mic. 4:1–3. Since it sits loosely in context in both books it is difficult to say in which it is original; possibly it was brought into both from a common source. Many scholars regard it as post-exilic. This judgment, however, seems to rest chiefly on the assumption that the passage contains ideas not proper to 8th cent. thought. This is questionable. The idea of an at least supranational triumph of Yahweh is quite old, being implicit in the notion of the Day of Yahweh and explicit in a number of pre-exilic Psalms (e.g. Ps. 2, 72), while the thought of an eternal reign of peace is to be found in 9:2–7, 11:1–9 (does Jer. 8:8 play upon the thought of 3?). Yahweh's sacred truce was a central feature of the primitive concept of covenant; here that truce is extended to include the nations of the world. While caution is demanded, objective reasons for denying the passage an 8th cent. date are lacking. Possibly it represents traditional material cherished among the disciples of both Isaiah and Micah, and so brought into the books of both. The title (1) was probably originally the heading of a longer complex of oracles (cf. 3:1, 5:3) into which the present passage has been inserted; 5 (in expanded form in Mic. 4:5) here serves as a transition to what follows.

f 'In the latter days' the Temple mountain, the seat of Yahweh's rule, will be elevated above all other mountains. All the peoples of the world will stream to it in order to hear Yahweh's teaching (law) and to learn how to walk in obedience to him. Yahweh will arbitrate all quarrels. Since his law is obeyed everywhere, peace is universal; weapons, no longer needed, are beaten into useful tools. And (so Mic. 4:4) all fear is banished from earth. It is a beautiful vision; but, be it noted, peace rests in no human programme, but in obedience to the divine law.

2. in the latter days: sometimes signifying simply 'in the remote future' (Gen. 49:1; Num. 24:14), the expression here denotes the effective goal of history,

424f the triumph of God's rule. **4. judge, decide:** i.e. adjudicate, arbitrate.

g **6-22 The Coming Day of Yahweh**—The section is a thematic unit, but confusion in the text is obvious to any who attempt to trace a sequence of thought through it. A refrain is repeated in 10, 19 and 21, and another in 9, 11, 17 (cf. 5:15), both with slight variations. Further, 9–11 and 12–17 repeat the same theme, as do 18f. and 20f. It is possible that two similar poems, or two recensions of the same poem, have been worked together in the course of transmission. But efforts to disentangle them are most uncertain, and it is better to treat the section as it stands. It fits best in Isaiah's earliest period before the wealth and strength which Uzziah had brought to the land had faded away.

Yahweh has rejected Judah for her sin (6–8). This rests at bottom on the alliances which she has made with foreigners. These have brought great wealth and military strength, but also a self-sufficient pride and the absorption of foreign ways: divination, magic and idolatry. And in these things men trust (cf. Mic. 5:10–15). But (9–11) that will not long continue. Mortal men, brought low, will flee in terror before Yahweh; all their pride will be humbled and Yahweh alone exalted 'in that day'. This theme is repeated in 12–17. 'That day' is the Day of Yahweh, the day of his judgment (cf. Am. 5:18–20) before which nothing can stand. Isaiah singles out the bravest, strongest things of nature and of human ingenuity to enforce his point: mighty trees and lofty mountains, strong towers and tall ships—all are nothing before God. As for idols (18f., 20f.), men will throw them away and run scuttling for some burrow in which to hide in that awful day when Yahweh comes to judge. 22, lacking in LXX, provides an editorial transition to ch. 3.

h **6. diviners:** the word is lacking in MT, but is reasonably inferred from the context. Sorcery and divination had at all periods been forbidden in Israel (Exod. 20:7, 22:18; 1 Sam. 28:3, 9, etc.). **they strike hands with foreigners:** seemingly in concluding bargains. But the meaning is uncertain; some (cf. K-B) suggest 'they abound with (i.e. have an excess of) foreigners'. The prophets were opposed to foreign alliances because they were an entering wedge for foreign customs and gods. **7.** Wealth and armaments are censured, not for themselves, but because men were led to trust in them rather than in God. **9. forgive them not:** probably corrupt. 1QIs[a] omits the words together with 10. **16. ships of Tarshish:** a type of ocean-going ship developed by the Phoenicians for carrying cargo from their copper-refineries in Sardinia and Spain to the homeland (*tarshîsh* means 'refinery'). Solomon had a fleet of such ships plying out of the refinery port of Ezion-geber on the Gulf of ʿAqaba (1 Kg. 10:22). Attempts to revive this trade were made by Jehoshaphat (1 Kg. 22:48) and, presumably, Uzziah (2 Kg. 14:22). **beautiful craft** is the correct translation (cf. K-B).

425a **III 1-15 Rapacious Rulers and the Collapse of Society**—The section falls into three parts (1–7 8–12, 13–15) which may originally have been independent, but which have the common theme of Yahweh's judgment on a corrupt society. While it is hazardous to argue that 4 and 12 allude to the youth of Ahaz at his accession (2 Kg. 16:2), the picture of social disintegration presented here fits best in the reign of that king. A date not far from 734 would suit.

In 1–7 there is a graphic picture of the fate of a society whose leaders are unworthy of their trust. Yet when Yahweh removes them like the rotten boards they are—as remove them he will—there is nothing to forestall collapse, for there is lacking in society any sense of social responsibility, any religious faith, upon which a new structure might be built. Society, leaderless, will fall a prey to upstarts who will rule with utter wilfulness. Complete anarchy will ensue, with everyone crowding his neighbour, and insulting his betters. Then men will be glad to seize upon anyone who has so much as a coat to his back (i.e. who is of good family and who has salvaged something of his position) and make him ruler, so that someone may take responsibility and restore order. But no-one will have the job! 'Jerusalem has stumbled, Judah has fallen'; and it is clear (8–12) that her leaders are at fault. By word and deed they have defied their God; their sin is as blatant as Sodom's, and they do not trouble to hide it. Such leaders, incompetent and rapacious, are misleaders who bring the nation to ruin. But (13–15) Yahweh has taken note of all this. It is none other than he who rises in court to espouse the cause of the wronged and indict the wrongdoers. What do you mean, he demands, despoiling the poor, grinding the helpless like grain in the mill? The accused give no answer; indeed none could be given, for in Hebrew theology to mistreat the weaker brother was to violate covenant law and come automatically under judgment.

1. the whole . . . water: probably a gloss; 'stay and staff' refers to those listed in 2f. Along with soldiers, judges, nobles, one notes (professional) prophets (cf. Mic. 3:5), diviners and other representatives of popular superstition: these are pillars of society upon whom the people have leaned. **4. babes:** better, 'caprice', 'wilfulness'. **6.** Possibly read, 'Yea, a man will take hold of his brother in whose father's house is a mantle saying, Come, you shall be our ruler'. **10f.** Perhaps an interpolation in the manner of later wisdom Psalms (e.g. Ps. 1). Though the thought is not impossible in the pre-exilic period, the verses fit poorly in the context. **12.** One might read, 'my people—its exactors (tax-gatherers) are gleaning (it), usurers (*nôshîm*) rule over it'; the reading of EVV is possible but questionable. **13. his people** is preferable (so LXX; cf. 14) to MT ('peoples'), unless Yahweh is thought of as standing in the heavenly court to judge the nations—and there, surprisingly, indicting his own people! b

III 16-IV 1 The Fine Ladies of Jerusalem and their Doom—The passage is of uncertain date, though the picture of luxury and ease which it presents, with war only a threat, argues for a time rather early in Isaiah's ministry. The material is related thematically to what has gone before. In 2:7, 15–17, etc. Isaiah has assailed the things in which men take pride—armaments and wealth, strong fortifications and great ships—and has pronounced their doom. Here he turns upon the well-to-do ladies of Jerusalem, vain and affected, who think only of their luxuries and little feminine affairs. Like Amos (cf. Am. 4:1–3), he knew that women, through their ceaseless demands on their menfolk for material things, share fully in the sins of the social order (13–15), even though they may have had no direct hand in them. He addresses these ladies in rough, even indelicate, language. He observes them with scorn as they walk haughtily, chin in air, with affected, mincing gait, jingling their ornamental ankle-chains and immodestly ogling the men as they go. Yahweh loathes these creatures—and will make them loathsome with scabrous sores. No more sweet perfume, but a sickening stench; no more fine girdles, well-groomed hair and costly clothing, but a rope about the waist and the shaved head and sackcloth of mourning. Their men will die in battle, and they will be left alone to weep. Men will be so scarce that they will fight over those that are left, so far forgetting their pride as to offer to support themselves if only the disgrace of their spinsterhood and childlessness be removed. The catalogue of articles of feminine attire and adornment in 18–23 is probably an insertion; it is in prose and interrupts the connection between 17 and 24. The fact, however, that 25f. address not the women, but Jerusalem itself, does not mean that these verses are an insertion; such a shift of address is characteristic of Hebrew poetic style. c

16. mincing: the chains which connected the anklets forced the wearer to take short steps. **17. secret** d

425d **parts :** the word does not elsewhere have this force ; perhaps read ' foreheads ' (i.e. their hair will be shaved off). **18-23.** See the larger commentaries and lexicons for the details. Many of the words are of uncertain meaning. **24. instead of beauty, shame** follows 1QIs^{a}. But the text is possibly damaged.

e **IV 2-6 The Purged and Purified Zion of the Future**—The passage no doubt owes its position in part to the catchword ' daughters of Zion ' (4). It declares that ' in that day ' (i.e. that future day when Yahweh shall have brought his purposes for Israel to fruition) the vegetation and produce of the land will flourish amazingly and will be a source of pride and glory to the survivors of Israel. All who are left alive in Jerusalem will be called holy : i.e. consecrated to Yahweh, and both ritually and morally pure. This will be when Yahweh has purged the filth and the blood of Jerusalem by a ' wind of judgment ' and ' a wind of burning ' (i.e. by catastrophe). Then over Zion and its holy assemblies the glory of Yahweh will be like a great pavilion symbolising, like the pillar of cloud and of fire of the Exodus (Exod. 13:21f.), Yahweh's presence with his people which protects them from all harm.

f The passage is regarded as post-exilic by perhaps the majority of scholars (others delete only 5f.). The reasons given are its prosy style, and a vocabulary and ideas allegedly of a time later than Isaiah's. The style is prosy, but since parallelisms may be detected in every verse, it is probable that a metrical basis has been overlaid and obscured in transmission. While there are words not found elsewhere in Isaiah (' branch ', ' create ' : cf. below), the vocabulary is not necessarily a post-exilic one ; practically all of the words are attested as early as Isaiah, or earlier, most of them elsewhere in the genuine utterances of Isaiah himself. Nor are the ideas expressed necessarily late. The passage speaks of a purge out of which a purified remnant will emerge—a thoroughly Isaianic notion (e.g. 1:24–26). There is no hint of an exile or a destruction of Jerusalem. The notion of the Glory of Yahweh, the pillar of cloud and fire, is present in the older Pentateuchal narratives (JE), and was certainly well known in Judah in the 8th cent. It is true that Isaiah does not elsewhere apply the epithet ' holy ' to individuals, but the ideal of a holy people —and the present passage speaks of the ideal to be realised ' in that day '—is incontestably pre-exilic (cf. Exod. 19:5f. ; Dt. 7:6 ; 14:2, 21). While one cannot prove that the passage comes from Isaiah, there is little reason to relegate it to a post-exilic date. It is somewhat akin to 37:30–32, the genuineness of which ought not to be doubted ; perhaps, like that oracle, it comes from late in Isaiah's ministry.

g **2. The Branch of the Lord :** the word ' branch ' (*ṣemaḥ*) is not the same as that used in 11:1. Though later a technical term for the Messiah (Jer. 23:5 ; Zech. 3:8, 6:12), it here means no more than ' growth, vegetation ' (cf. ' the fruit of the land '). The fact that the word has a technical messianic connotation in Jer. and Zech. argues that it must have had some connection with notions of future hope prior to that time. Perhaps this passage supplies some of that background ; if so, it must be presumed to be of pre-exilic date. **3. recorded for life :** i.e. listed as living, as in a census book. Since life and death are in God's hands, the names of those who are to live are listed in his book. **4. spirit of judgment . . . of burning :** cf. 11:2 ; 28:6. The word for ' spirit ' can also mean ' wind '—and so probably here (cf. Jer. 4:11f.). **5f. create** (*bārā'*) **:** the word is not characteristic of Isaiah ; LXX reads ' and he will come ' (*ûbhā'*). The text may be corrupt. 5*b*, 6*a* are likewise uncertain, but RSV gets the sense. Of course, ' heat ', ' storm and rain ' are not to be taken literally : the Glory of Yahweh like some great canopy will protect Jerusalem from all adversity.

426a **V 1-7 The Song of the Vineyard : a Parable**—Isaiah here conveys his message in a manner both striking and unique. The passage is a poem in the form of a parable, the interpretation of which is reserved to the very end, and which is introduced (1–4) in the guise of a popular ballad such as a minstrel might sing at a feast. Probably the prophet actually sang it at a vintage festival. In the midst of glad rejoicing, as vintage songs are heard on all hands, the prophet steps forward as if to sing one of his own. By thus disguising his intent, he possibly gained a more ready hearing than he might otherwise have had. His technique closely parallels that of Amos (Am. 1–2) and of Nathan in his rebuke of David (2 Sam. 12:1–12). The date is uncertain, but the tone of the passage, which suggests a time of peace with calamity lying yet in the future, argues for Isaiah's earliest period, perhaps before the crisis of 735–3.

The prophet begins to sing, as if on behalf of a dear ' friend ', a song about the ' friend's ' vineyard. It was a good vineyard, well located on a sunny, fertile hill. Every care had been lavished on it : the ground had been well turned, the stones removed, and the very best type of vines planted. More, a hedge and a wall had been built around it (5), a watchtower constructed to guard against thieves, and a wine-vat hewed out of the rock to receive the pressed-out juice. It was, in short, a permanent investment from which, naturally, the owner expected the best possible crop. Imagine, then, his dismay when, instead of fine grapes he found only evil-smelling, bitter, wild grapes ! Speaking for his ' friend ', the prophet challenges his hearers to render judgment. Could anything more have been done for that vineyard ? Was the owner in any way at fault ? Obviously not ! What, then, can be done with such a vineyard except to give it up ? Cut down its hedge, overturn its walls, let the cattle trample it and nibble the leaves, let thorns and briers choke it ! As the song moves to its end, it becomes obvious that Isaiah is not talking of a mere vineyard of some friend of his. Yet he does not reveal his hand till the very end, not even when his ' friend ' orders the clouds to withhold their rain, for a man might possibly pronounce such a curse (2 Sam. 1:21). It is only at the end that, with all the force of a blow in the face, or of a Nathan crying, ' Thou art the man ', he drops the mask. The vineyard is Israel ! God has bestowed on Israel his grace and loving care, and has expected the fruit of justice and rectitude—only to get the foul fruit of injustice and oppression. It is Israel that is to be given to the thorns and briers ; God will remove all defence of her, care for her no more, leave her to her fate.

1. The precise force of the verse is obscure. ' My b
beloved ' clearly refers to Yahweh. Yet it is surprising, to say the least, that Isaiah should refer to his God in such intimate terms, even in a parable. Nor is what follows by any stretch of the imagination a ' love song '. Perhaps both words (*yᵉdhîdh, dôdh*) are to be taken in the weakened sense of ' friend ' : ' now hear me sing for my friend my friend's song about his vineyard '. The word (*dôdh*) pointed differently (*dāwîdh*) is the name David, while *yᵉdhîdh* occurs in the name of Solomon (Jedidiah), 2 Sam. 12:25. The words may, therefore, conceal allusions to the official cult that escape us. On the other hand, Isaiah may simply have begun with words from a well-known song. **7.** There is a word-play here that cannot be brought into English : ' and he looked for *mishpāṭ* and behold *miśpāḥ*, for *ṣᵉdhāḳāh* and behold *ṣᵉʿāḳāh* '.

8-30 Denunciation of various Sins and An- c
nouncement of the Divine Judgment—This section consists of a series of ' woes ' with attendant threats of doom (8–24), followed by an announcement of the final divine judgment (25–30). The text has suffered considerable disturbance in transmission. A relationship to 9:8–10:4 is evident ; cf. the introductory ' woe ' (8, 11, 18, etc., and 10:1), and the concluding refrain (25, 9:12, 17, 21, 10:4). It is possible that 9:8–10:4 once stood in juxtaposition to 8–24 with 25–30 as its conclusion, and that this in turn led into 9:1–7 (cf. 30

426c and 8:21f.) ; then, when 6:1–8:18 was inserted, 9:8–10:4 was torn from its original position. But one cannot be sure. A date in the earlier years of Isaiah's ministry is likely.

d **8-10.** The first 'woe' addresses greedy landgrabbers who amass property and crowd small farmers from their holdings at such a rate that one would think they wanted the land all to themselves. It is implied that this was often enough accomplished by unethical means (cf. Mic. 2:1–2, 9) ; no doubt the incident of Naboth (1 Kg. 21) was re-enacted more than once. Well, they will have a solitude they had not bargained for: that of desolation, with their fine houses abandoned and the land yielding far less than the seed put into it. **10 acres:** lit. 'yokes', a yoke being what a pair of oxen could plough in a day. **bath:** a liquid measure of *c.* 5 imperial gals., a very small yield. **ephah:** a dry measure of about a bushel, or $\frac{1}{10}$ of a homer. The crop would thus equal only a tenth of the seed put in.

e **11-13.** The second 'woe' is upon carousers who begin their drinking in the morning and keep it up till late at night, when they are sodden drunk. They care for nothing save self-indulgence and have no eye for the working of God in events. Because they have no knowledge of God (cf. Hos. 4:1, 6) their end will be exile, where they will all die of hunger and thirst.

f **14-17.** 14 (which does not continue 13) and 17 may be the conclusion of a third 'woe', the beginning of which has been lost. 15f. repeats with variations the refrain of 2:9, 11, 17, and may be an intrusion from another context (14 leads well into 17). On the other hand, the entire section may have been displaced from 2:6–22 or from some lost section similar to it. In 14, 17, Sheol is depicted, like some monster, opening wide its maw to swallow the city down, after which sheep graze among the ruins. When all human pride has been humbled (15f.), Yahweh will be exalted and will 'show himself holy' (i.e. exhibit his character as God) in justice and righteousness. These are qualities which belong to the essential nature of Israel's God. **14. its appetite:** perhaps 'throat', as occasionally in Ugaritic. 14*b* reads : 'and her splendour and her noisy crowd shall go down . . .' ; 'Jerusalem' is supplied by RSV.

g **18-24.** A series of four further 'woes' ; but possibly the word 'woe' should be added also at the beginning of 19 and 23, making the total six. Woe to those who are tied to their sin as if harnessed, and haul its consequences after them like oxen pulling a cart ! (Woe to) those sceptics who mockingly demand that Yahweh prove himself by his mighty acts, but who do not believe that he can or will ! This is not atheism, but a denial of God's moral rule (cf. Jer. 17:15 ; Zeph. 1:12 ; Ps. 10:3–6). Woe to those who have 'advanced' beyond moral distinctions, who call good bad and bad good, and think it makes no difference ! Woe to those who self-sufficiently order their own lives and plot the course of state (cf. 28:14–22) without reference to God ! Woe to these 'heroes' of the winecups who, unafraid of the strongest drink, valiantly challenge any quantity of it to get the better of them ! Naturally they are not the sort who would shrink back from doing a favour for a crony—at a price. (Woe to them) for this perversion of justice ! They have despised the covenant law and shown contempt of court before Israel's God. Woe to them indeed ! They will be like stubble in the fire, or like a plant rotten to the root whose blossom turns to dust.

h **25-30.** It is generally agreed that this section belongs with 9:8–10:4. Since the formula of 9:12, 17, 21, 10:4 is repeated in 25 (which does not continue 24), it is probable that this verse represents the conclusion of a further strophe like those of 9:8–10:4, the beginning of which has been lost. It seems to refer to an earthquake. It is further probable that 26ff., where the formula does not recur, supplied the original conclusion of 9:8–10:4, announcing the final blow of Yahweh's avenging hand. Or possibly 26ff. originally formed the conclusion of 9:8–21 before 10:1–4 (which refers to Judah) was added to that section. If so, 42
it was first spoken of the northern state ; but in its present context it has been adapted to refer to Judah.

Israel's sins have provoked stroke after stroke (9:8–10:4) from the hand of Yahweh, but after each a fresh stroke has been announced. Now comes the final blow. It comes in the form of the Assyrian army. Yahweh gives the signal, whistles for it (cf. 7:18), and it comes hurrying to do his bidding in perfect battle array, awesome in the perfection of its equipment. It leaps on Israel like a lion on its prey, and no-one can save her.

30 The verse fits poorly in context, and is similar to 8:21f., of which it may be a misplaced variant, connected to the preceding by the catchword 'growl'. It is possible that 8:21–9:7 once stood here and, like 9:8–10:4, was displaced.

VI 1-13 The Inaugural Vision—We have here 42
Isaiah's own account of the experience through which he received his call to the prophetic office. Other prophets (e.g. Jer. 1) have recorded similar experiences, but none so breathtakingly majestic as this. Isaiah's call came in the year of Uzziah's death (742), but, as 1 indicates, the present account was not written down until later. It need not, however, have been very much later, nor is there reason to suppose that the account has been coloured by the prophet's later disillusioning experience. Nor should any inference be drawn from the reference to Uzziah's death, as if anxiety over the passing of that able king played a part in the experience, for it is not certain that Uzziah, long ailing, had actually died at the time ; the reference merely supplies the date. Were the words of Isaiah arranged chronologically we should expect this chapter to stand at the beginning of the book. Probably it begins a collection (6:1–8:18), partly in autobiographical style, which records Isaiah's experiences down to the Aramaean-Ephraimite crisis (735–733), and which circulated separately for a time.

The setting is the Temple, probably on some festal b
occasion when the kingship of Yahweh was cultically affirmed (Ps. 24:7–10, 47, 93, 97–99), and his eternal choice of Zion and David celebrated (e.g. 2 Sam. 7 ; Ps. 89). As the service progressed and the songs of massed choirs rang through the sanctuary, Isaiah, gazing toward the portals of the *Debir*, where stood Yahweh's throne, seized with emotion, saw the visible scene replaced by a vision of Yahweh the king. There he was enthroned, with the seraph attendants about him hiding their faces that they might not behold his glory. The swirling incense-smoke which filled the Temple became the train of Yahweh's robes, the antiphonal shouts of the choirs the voices of the seraphs praising the God who is thrice holy, exalted, utterly unapproachable, whose glory fills all the earth. Isaiah was seized with terror at what he saw. A sinful man of a sinful people, he had penetrated the heavenly court and gazed on God face to face—a thing no man could do and live (Exod. 33:20). He cannot join the song of praise, nor have his people a right to do so. But then one of the seraphs flew to him, not to kill him but to touch his lips with a hot coal taken from the altar, thereby symbolically purging his sin. Thus purified, he could stand in the divine presence without fear. And as he stood on the outskirts of the heavenly company, he heard the voice of God himself speaking : Who will go for us and take our word to this people ? And Isaiah in simple, unquestioning obedience, said, 'Here am I ; send me'. With that he became a prophet, a messenger of God's heavenly council to men (cf. Jer. 23:18, 22). In a private oracle (9f.) he is told what he is to do : he is to speak again and again a word which will be heard but never understood. Indeed, the only effect of his preaching will be to stultify his hearers and render hearing impossible. And how long, he asks, is this to go on ? Till the end ! Till the land is left empty and desolate ! Nay, even if a tenth of the people are left (Judah ?) and think themselves a saved 'remnant', they too will

7b have again to face the fires of catastrophe. On 13 see below. Isaiah certainly believed, or came to believe, that a purified remnant would be spared. But it is hazardous to read such a notion from this verse, so uncertain is the text. Isaiah began his ministry with full awareness that, in the immediate view at least, he would fail.

c **2. above him:** i.e. about the seated King. **seraphim:** though the word at times denotes 'flying, fiery serpents' (14:29, 30:6; Num. 21:6ff.), and though an image of a brazen serpent was presumably to be seen in the Temple at this time (2 Kg. 18:4), there is no reason to think of the seraphim as serpentine in form. They were Yahweh's attendants, guardians of his sanctuary, conceived as winged creatures who stood upright, partly human in form. **covered his feet:** a euphemism. **7. forgiven**: 'covered over, atoned for'; the word is a technical term for the expiatory effect of sacrifice. **9.** The sense is: (Scott) 'go on hearing, but do not understand (since you choose not to); go on seeing, but perceive nothing (since you will to be blind)'. **10** expresses not the purpose but the result of Isaiah's preaching. **13.** There is no agreement either on the text or its meaning. The translation 'felled' is a guess; and the word rendered 'stump' elsewhere means a sacred 'pillar' or 'stele'. W. F. Albright, following 1QIs[a] with very slight changes (cf. VT Supp. 4 (1957), 254f.), suggests: '... like the terebinth goddess and the oak of Asherah, cast out with the stelae of the high place' (cf. S. Iwry, JBL 76 (1957), 225–32). The final clause is lacking in LXX, but probably through error. Yet the words are so cryptic that it is dangerous to read a 'remnant' doctrine from them.

d **VII 1-9 A Warning to Ahaz; the Sign of Shear-jashub**—7:1–8:18 tells of Isaiah's actions and words in connection with the crisis of 735–733. For further details, cf. 2 Kg. 16:5–9, 15:29f. An attempt was made to force Ahaz to join an anti-Assyrian coalition, which probably included (2 Chr. 28:16–18) Edomites and Philistines as well as Israel and the state of Damascus. Indeed (6), the confederates intended to depose Ahaz and replace him with a king amenable to their designs. The heading in 1 is based on 2 Kg. 16:5. The incident actually took place (2f.) as news came that the enemy was moving against Jerusalem. The royal court ('the house of David'), terrified at the intelligence, saw no course save to send tribute to the Assyrians and implore aid. As Ahaz was inspecting his water supply in preparation for the siege, Isaiah, accompanied by his son, whose name embodied a warning to the king, met him and urged him to take no such step. Let the king but keep calm and not fear. Rezin and Pekah are burnt-out faggots, incapable of carrying out the mischief they intend. Their plans are the plans of little men, not of Yahweh, and will come to naught. Let the king have faith, for if he refuses to trust in Yahweh and his promises (2 Sam. 7:16; Ps. 132:11f., etc.) neither he nor the nation will stand. 9*b* is thoroughly characteristic of Isaiah's political advice throughout his career.

e **2. is in league:** lit. 'rests upon', i.e. Aramaean forces have already encamped on Ephraimite soil (cf. 19). **3. Shear-jashub:** the name may have a hopeful ('a remnant will return') or a threatening sense ('only a remnant will return'). Both are developed in 10:20–23, but it is probable that the latter is intended here. The lad was undoubtedly taken along because his name would convey to the king a warning of the disaster his policy entailed. Since he was a child old enough to walk, the name was given earlier, no doubt on some occasion of which the king was well aware. Features fundamental to the thinking of Isaiah are implicit in it: the nation will be left only a remnant —but still a remnant, which will turn to its God. **Fuller's Field:** the Rabshakeh stood here many years later to deliver his taunting speech (36:2). **6. son of Tabeel:** Bêt Ṭâb'el is known from contemporary inscriptions (W. F. Albright, BASOR 140 (1955), 34f.) as an Aramaean land in northern Transjordan. 427e
Ben Tabeel was thus a prince of that land, possibly even a son of Uzziah or Jotham by an Aramaean princess (cf. Absalom). **8b.** The sentence is not in accord with the facts, and would, in any case, be cold comfort to Ahaz. Possibly it should be read, 'Yet six, nay five, years more . . .' and placed after 9*a* (Kissane). **9b** contains a word-play which may be paraphrased: 'if you will not stand firm, trusting in Yahweh's faithfulness, you will not be confirmed in your position'.

10-17 The Sign of Immanuel—This incident 428a
probably took place only a few days after the foregoing, before Ahaz had publicly committed himself to his policy. Isaiah presented himself before the king and his court and offered him a sign as proof that the word which he had spoken was true. It is an index both of Isaiah's personal boldness and his unshakeable faith in his God that no limit is placed on the sign which may be chosen. Ahaz, however, evades the offer with pious cant; he does not doubt Yahweh and therefore will not put him to the test. It is probable that Ahaz did in fact believe in the possibility of such a sign but that, having already chosen his course, he did not wish to be embarrassed. His refusal provoked Isaiah to anger: the king has exhausted both his patience and God's. A sign will be given him whether he wishes it or not.

The sign itself has provoked endless debate; see the larger commentaries for adequate discussion. It must be remembered that Isaiah is addressing the royal court, which feared for its safety before the approaching foe and for the permanence of the Davidic dynasty (6). The promises to David (cf. 2 Sam. 7, 23:1–7; Ps. 89), the theological foundations of the state, were being put to the test. Isaiah's words, which are loaded with cultic overtones, are reminiscent of a dynastic oracle. Indicating a young woman, possibly among the company present, certainly known to them, he declares that she is pregnant and will soon bear a son who will be named Immanuel ('God is with us'). Probably the young woman was one of the wives of the king. If so, Isaiah's words are an announcement of the birth of a royal son with a name suggestive of the promise of dynastic permanency. This remarkable child will be nurtured on curds and honey (see below) the more quickly to reach the age of minimal discernment. Before he does this—a few years at most —Aram and Ephraim will be destroyed. The sign thus consists both in the birth of the child and his name, which symbolises the promises made to David. Isaiah says in effect: let the king take the language of his official cult seriously! He has repeated its promises, no doubt piously enough, but he lacks any real faith in them, as his conduct shows. Let Immanuel be the sign that Yahweh is powerful to preserve the dynasty and faithful to his promises! But since Ahaz has already refused the sign, it is to him also a sign of calamity. He will indeed be saved from Rezin and Pekah, but at the price of a disaster unparalleled since the schism of the state on the death of Solomon, namely subservience to Assyria. Is the passage Messianic? It is not a direct prediction of Christ, or even of a scion of David's line who would rule his people in justice and peace (9:2–7, 11:1–5). But it is expressive of the hope once reposed in the promises to David. Since the Christian affirms that this hope, and all the hope of Israel, found its ultimate fulfilment in Christ, he may say that this prophecy too points onward to him.

14. a young woman is correct; 'virgin' derives from b
LXX. An *'almāh* is a young woman of marriageable age, whether virgin or not. Heb. has 'the' young woman, which possibly indicates a specific young woman known to the court, or a class of woman (the king had many *'alāmôth*: Ca. 6:8). Isaiah's words are reminiscent of a birth oracle (Gen. 16:11f.; Jg. 13:3–5; Lk. 1:31–33); almost identical words (*hl ġlmt tld bn*) occur in the Râs Shamra texts announcing the birth of a god or prince. **Immanuel:** the name

428b plays on words frequently recurring in passages relating to the Covenant with David (2 Sam. 23:5), and perhaps on some cultic response as well (cf. Ps. 46:7, 11). **15. when he knows:** more naturally, 'that he may know'. **to refuse the evil and choose the good:** not the age of moral responsibility, but the first beginnings of teachability. **curds and honey:** does this imply a diet of plenty or privation? Curds (or milk) and honey were a delicacy to the nomad (Gen. 18:8; Jg. 5:25, etc.), and are often used to describe luxury and plenty (Exod. 3:8, 17; Dt. 32:13f.; Job 20:17f.); in certain Babylonian rituals they have a cultic significance; in the myths of Ugarit they are a part of the description of the fruitfulness of the earth when Baal comes alive; and certain Greek myths know of the divine child preserved alive, when abandoned, on milk and honey. Probably the sense here is that the promised child will be nurtured (through a period of distress?) on the 'food of the gods', the better to know 'good' from 'evil'.

c **18-25 The Dire Consequences of Ahaz' Policy**—The section consists of four oracles (18f., 20, 21f., 23–25), each introduced with 'in that day'. It is distinct from the foregoing, but carries forward the thought of 17 and belongs to the same period. Since the anti-Assyrian coalition probably hoped for Egyptian help—as Hoshea later did (2 Kg. 17:4)—Ahaz' policy will turn Israel into a battle-ground (cf. Hos. 7:11, 9:3). The opposing armies will come like swarms of insects and settle down all over the land. In appealing to Tiglath-pileser, Ahaz has tried to shave with a 'hired razor'; now he will be shaved with the same razor—and thoroughly! In 21f. there is a play, probably sarcastic, on 15. In that sad day a man will be lucky to keep alive a cow and a couple of sheep. Such will be the 'abundance' of milk that he can eat curds. 'Truly curds and honey (the food of paradise indeed!) will every one eat who is left in the land'. Fine vineyards will become impenetrable thickets into which one goes armed (for protection or hunting). Once cultivated hillsides will become brier patches where only cattle roam.

20. the hair of the feet: a euphemism (cf. 6:2).

d **VIII 1-4 The Sign of Maher-shalal-hash-baz**—Isaiah is told to take a large tablet and write on it conspicuously the cryptic words: Maher-shalal-hash-baz ('the spoil hastens, the plunder comes quickly'). This he does in the presence of two witnesses, one of whom, Uriah, was the chief priest (2 Kg. 16:10–16). Presumably he explained to them the meaning of what he did, so that when the prophecy came true they could testify that Isaiah had made it. He then had relations with his wife ('the prophetess') and begot a son who was given the same cryptic name, for before he should learn to utter his first words Damascus and Samaria would be despoiled. The name thus embodies a threat for Judah's foes. Since the child was born before Tiglath-pileser's invasions of 733/2, the sign must have been given at least a year sooner.

1. common characters: so the words ('stylus of a man') are usually understood. But since the tablet was meant to be read it is difficult to see why Isaiah must be told to write it in the common script. Perhaps 'with bold strokes' would better catch the idea.

e **5-15 Further Words of Isaiah during the Aramaean-Ephraimite Crisis**—The passage falls into three parts: 5–8*a*(8*b*), (8*b*)9–10, 11–15. It dates at least for the most part to the same period as the foregoing.

5-8a(b). Contrast is made between the gently flowing waters of Shiloah and the mighty flood of 'the River' (Euphrates). The waters of Shiloah probably refer to the conduit leading from the spring of Gihon before Hezekiah's tunnel was dug (cf. 7:3). Since Gihon seems to have played a part in the coronation of kings (1 Kg. 1:33f.), it may be that Shiloah carried associations with the theology of the Davidic dynasty. Since this people will not trust in Yahweh's promises to David, because they seem so small, and in fear have chosen to rely on Assyria, Assyria will roll down like the Euphrates in flood and will sweep them all away. 42

8b. Unless 'its outspread wings' denotes the extreme limits of the flood, we have the figure of a large bird whose wings cover the land. This could carry a hostile sense (Jer. 48:40). If so, 8*b* may be taken with 8*a*, and 'O Immanuel' understood as an apostrophe to the (yet unborn?) child of 7:14. But outstretched wings more naturally indicate protection (cf. Ps. 17:8, 91:4), in which event 8*b* goes with 9f. and 'O Immanuel' is to be read as in 10*c*; 8*b*–10 then form a fragment of a liturgical poem, the beginning of which is lost.

8b-10. Though not a continuation of the foregoing, f
there is no reason to regard this as a late insertion. It is in the spirit of 7:3–9, and is a bit of a liturgy (cf. Ps. 46) affirming the faith which the people should have felt, but did not. God is with us, his wings protecting us—so it was affirmed in the cult. The nations may take up arms against Zion, but no plan they make will succeed (cf. Ps. 2)—for God is with us!

9 Be broken: read with LXX (*deʿû*) 'know' (cf. 'give ear').

11-15. Isaiah has felt compulsion from God not to g
acquiesce in the national policy. He has, apparently, also urged others (the verbs in 12f. are plural) to adopt a similar position. Take a stand against this drift! Do not be afraid of this move to dethrone Ahaz (7:6), and go about in a panic crying 'conspiracy'! Rather count Yahweh the conspirator, for it is his doing, and fear him alone. He will be the stone on which both houses of Israel will stumble, and a trap to take Jerusalem too. Many (but not all) will stumble into that trap and be taken. In thus calling his hearers to separate themselves from the national policy in obedience to God, Isaiah began, in effect, to call out a faithful 'remnant'.

11. with his strong hand: not necessarily through an ecstatic experience, but certainly by the compulsion of the divine word (e.g. Am. 3:8; Jer. 20:7–9).

13. regard as holy: a better connection with 12 is gained by reading (*takshîrû*) 'count him the conspirator'. **14. sanctuary:** probably an incorrect dittography of 'snare' (*môkēsh*) in the next line.

16-18 Isaiah's temporary Withdrawal from 42
Public Ministry—The date is 734/3. Seeing that his words have not been heeded, Isaiah resolves to say no more. Writing down a record of what he has said, he hands it over sealed to his disciples who will witness, when the time comes, that he has said it. For his own part, he will wait with that complete trust which he had so notably failed to awaken in Ahaz and his court for the fulfilment of his words, for the action of Yahweh, who now hides his face in anger from his people. Meanwhile he and his sons, by their portentous names (cf. 7:3, 8:1) and by their very presence, will be living reminders from Yahweh of his word. Exactly what Isaiah wrote is unknown, but probably the memoirs of 6:1–8:18, of which this section is the conclusion. Thus, probably, was made the first step in that long process which was ultimately to give us the Isaiah book. We cannot trace the part that Isaiah's disciples played in this, or in the perpetuation of the prophetic spirit, but it was undoubtedly great. Perhaps the Deuteronomic reformation was one of its fruits.

16. Read 'I will bind up the testimony'.

19-20 A Fragment on Necromancy—The b
passage has no demonstrable connection either with what precedes or what follows; furthermore, the text is so obscure that one can make little of it. Necromancy, essentially an attempt to manage the divine powers for egotistical ends, had at all periods been regarded as incompatible with Israel's faith. Yet it had always been practised, though at times more or less *sub rosa*. 19*b* can be rendered as RSV or, better, as the continuation of the discourse of 19*a*: 'should

429b not a people consult their *'elōhîm* (' departed spirits ', cf. 1 Sam. 28:13), should they not on behalf of the living consult the dead ? ' 20 can be understood (RSV) : Get back to the teaching of Yahweh ! People who talk like this will have no dawn of hope. But possibly 20*a* is a marginal note meaning ' this has reference to the teaching and the testimony ' (of 16), while 20*c* (lit. ' which has no dawn ') may be a mutilated beginning of what follows. The remaining words of 20 would then be the prophet's shocked comment on 19 : ' truly, that is what they say ! '

c **VIII 21-IX 7 Light shines in the Darkness : the Messianic King**—The section consists of three originally separate parts which have been juxtaposed with rare dramatic effect (cf. A. Alt, *Festschrift A. Bertholet* (1950), 29–49). The text of 8:21–9:1 is extremely obscure ; but one sees a picture of black darkness (8:21f.), balanced by one of brilliant light (9:2–7), with a skilful transition between (9:1). Objective reasons for denying 9:2–7 to Isaiah do not exist, though some believe it to be later. The passage presupposes the existence of the monarchy, and fits well in the thought of the prophet. 9:1 is to be dated after the Assyrian invasions of 733/2 (see below) ; but since there is no hint of the fall of Samaria (722/1), it probably lies before that event.

d **8:21-22a.** A fragment with verbal similarities to 5:30*bc*, itself a fragment and possibly a variant of 22*a*. Perhaps read : ' . . . which has no dawn. And they will pass through it hard pressed and hungry, and (when they are hungry) they will break out in anger and curse their king and their God. And they will turn their faces upward, and gaze on the earth—and behold (5:30*bc*) darkness and distress ; and the light is darkened by its clouds '. This is a picture of the embittered despair of the survivors of the Assyrian invasion, who curse their king for leading them to this plight and their God for not saving them from it.

e **8:22bc-9:1.** It is possible (Kissane) that 22*bc* begins the transition piece ; with one small change (*m*e*'ôphēph* for the otherwise unknown *m*e*'ûph* ; cf. 1QIs[a] in 23) one could read : ' But behold, distress and darkness are flown, trouble and gloom are driven away '. 9:1 seems to indicate the area ravaged by Tiglath-pileser III in 733 (2 Kg. 15:29). Possibly (Alt) ' the way of the sea, the land beyond the Jordan, Galilee of the nations ' corresponds to the three provinces into which the Assyrians divided this territory : Dor, Gilead and Megiddo. This region, so bitterly humiliated, will ' in the latter time ' be glorified. This prepares, in the present context, for what follows.

f **9:2-7.** This passage is of the greatest importance for understanding the Messianic hope of Israel. It follows the pattern of a dynastic oracle, celebrating probably not the birth, as many think, but the accession of a king who, on the day of his enthronement, was hailed as the (adopted) son begotten of Yahweh (Ps. 2:7). Its various motifs find parallels in the Royal Psalms (e.g. Ps. 2, 21, 72, 89, 110, 132). The theological basis of the monarchy in Judah was the eternal covenant with David (e.g. 2 Sam. 7, 23:1–7 ; Ps. 89) ; at the accession of each new king the promises to David were reaffirmed. Lively hope was engendered of the coming of a king who would make the dynastic ideal actual. From this hope the Messianic expectation developed. It is the ideal Davidide (not this Ahaz !) who is here hailed. The tenses are perfects, for Isaiah uses the language of a dynastic oracle spoken at the king's accession ; but in the present context they are ' prophetic perfect ' affirming the certainty of something hoped for. A bright light shines into the darkness ; there is joy as at a harvest festival, or as when victorious warriors divide the spoil. The oppressor's yoke is broken as in Gideon's day (Jg. 6–8), the gory debris of the battlefield disposed of. For a new Davidide has come to the throne, hailed this day as Yahweh's ' son '. He has received the great ceremonial names bestowed on the king at his accession. He will sit on David's throne ruling his domain in justice and righteousness. There will be no end to that rule ; Yahweh will see to it. This is, to be sure, not a prediction of Christ in the direct sense, but of a great and good king who should come to deliver his people. But the Christian is within his rights in reading this passage as the Christmas lesson, for it found no other fulfilment than in Jesus who is called Christ (Messiah) and ' King of the Jews '. 429f

g **3.** Better : ' Thou hast multiplied the exultation (*haggîlāh* for *haggôi lō'*), increased the joy '. **4.** Perhaps (*môṭath* for *maṭṭēh*) : ' . . . the bar (i.e. the yoke) of his shoulder, the rod of his driver . . .' **6.** Emphasis should fall on ' child ', ' son ', not on ' to us ' : ' for *a child* is born to us, *a son* is given to us '. **Mighty God :** grammatical construction indicates the reading ' God of a hero ' (i.e. godlike hero, endowed with divine power) ; the king is not hailed as divine or identified with God. The names stress the wisdom, the might, the fatherly care, and the beneficent harmony of the king's rule. Pharaohs of the Middle Kingdom were given five ' great names ' on their accession ; perhaps the relics of a fifth lie in the superfluous two letters in the Hebrew at the beginning of 7. **7.** Deleting these letters (*lm*) as surmised, or as a dittography, the verse begins, ' Great is the dominion . . .'

430a **IX 8-X 4 The Outstretched Hand of Yahweh's Wrath**—The section should be studied in connection with 5:8–29. It is generally agreed that 5:25–29 forms its conclusion, though possibly this conclusion originally followed 9:8–21. Since the tenses in these strophes are for the most part perfects, it is probable that they describe disasters which have already overtaken northern Israel, while 5:26–29 predicts the crowning blow, the Assyrian invasion. In 10:1–4 there is a ' woe ' of the type of those in 5:8–24, but with the refrain of the preceding strophes ; it seems to address evildoers in Judah, and may have been placed here when the original peroration was detached, thus applying the lessons of the foregoing to the southern state as well. The date is before the Assyrian invasion of 733, which 5:26–29 announces.

b **IX 8-12.** Yahweh has sent his power-laden word against Israel. It falls devastatingly on Ephraim, arrogantly sure of its ability to recover from any reverse however bad. Aramaeans and Philistines have invaded the northern state. Since Israel was allied with Damascus against Judah in 735/4, this may refer to a prior effort on the part of Damascus to force Israel into alliance against Assyria. Menahem (2 Kg. 15:19f.) had given tribute to Assyria in 738 ; possibly Aramaeans and Philistines were behind the revolution (737) which overthrew his house and placed the anti-Assyrian Pekah on the throne. Israel has suffered this, but there is more to come. **10.** Possibly a proverb : we have suffered a reverse (the tribute given by Menahem ?), but we will come back stronger than before. **11. adversaries :** cf. RSV*n*. Read : ' their adversaries (i.e. Rezin) ' ; ' Rezin ' is a correct gloss. The verbs of 11 are perfects and refer to past events.

c **13-17.** Since the foregoing brought no repentance, Yahweh has slaughtered in Israel small and great, leaving widows and orphans everywhere. What is referred to is uncertain. Since the Assyrian invasion seems yet in the future, possibly one of the numerous civil wars, often brutal and bloody (2 Kg. 15:16), which rent Israel at the time is intended. Israel's leaders are misleaders who bring their followers to ruin. But Yahweh has no compassion on the slain and on the bereaved, for the whole nation is godless and wicked. Even so, there is more to come.

d **14. head and tail, palm branch and reed :** all classes, high and low. **15f.** commonly regarded as an insertion. But, though 15 may be an erroneous explanation of 14 (though possibly an example of the prophet's mordant humour), 16 (cf. 3:12) is required before 17. **17. folly :** moral folly, impiety.

18-21. Evil has broken out in Israel like a forest fire which, catching first in the underbrush, sends all

430d the mighty trees up in smoke. Anarchy reigns; brother turns on brother, and they tear at one another like so many cannibals. Sectional jealousies flare, and the north takes up arms against the south. This refers to the civil wars in Israel between 745 and 737 (2 Kg. 15:8–26), and to the coalition against Judah in 735/4. But even this is not the end. Probably one should read 5:25–29 at this point.

18. The tenses again are perfects, describing what godlessness has already done in Israel. **20. his neighbour's flesh:** Heb. 'the flesh of his arm' (cf. RSV*n*). A simpler emendation (*zar'ô* for *z*^{e}*rō'ô*) would give 'the flesh of his offspring' (cf. 2 Kg. 6:24–31).

e **X 1-4** This strophe seems to be addressed to Judah; the prophet wishes to show her that she too is under condemnation. Woe to these crooked judges and rulers who keep issuing unjust decrees designed to deprive the helpless of their rights, so that they may the better rob them! What will they do in the day of Yahweh's judgment, when the foe comes like a storm from afar? Having forfeited Yahweh's protection, to whom will they turn? What will become of their wealth? Nothing for them but the lot of a prisoner, if they have not already fallen on the field of battle!

1b. Perhaps (H. L. Ginsberg, JBL 69 (1950), 54) read: 'and documents of oppression they keep writing'. **4a.** An uncertain text; RSV probably gets the sense.

f **5-34 'Be not afraid of the Assyrians'**—A complex of Isaiah's utterances drawn together about the theme of the arrogance of Assyria, its punishment, and the deliverance of Judah. A date in the reign of Sennacherib (705–681) is indicated; most scholars believe that the invasion of 701 supplies the background. But since (cf. below) some of the material might be held to reflect circumstances after that event, and since Isaiah's attitude here is in some respects in marked contrast to that which he is known to have exhibited then (e.g. 1:2–9, 28:14–22, 30:1–17, 31:1–3), it is possible that at least parts of the section refer to a second invasion of Sennacherib later in his reign (cf. §446).

g **5-19.** It is possible that two poems on the same theme have been woven together here. The Assyrian boast is given twice with identical introductions (8–11, 13f.), and the ruin of that tyrant is described (16–19) under two rather incompatible figures: a raging fire and a wasting sickness (cf. below). Assyria serves a function in Yahweh's economy: she is the rod of his judgment wherewith he disciplines godless nations, here specifically Judah. Assyria, however, does not see herself in that light at all. Indeed, she boasts (8–11) of her might, and holds states and rulers together with their gods in contempt. None of these gods, not even Samaria's, could save their lands. How, then, does Jerusalem imagine that Yahweh can save her? The answer is that Yahweh is using Assyria for his purposes; when he is done, her pride will be punished. 13f. repeats the boast. The Assyrian credits his victories to his own strength and cunning. He has deported peoples, incorporated their lands, looted their wealth with the ease of a man robbing a bird's nest—and no-one dares utter the smallest chirp of protest. But what folly! This is like a tool getting the notion that it controls the man who uses it. This is *hybris* which Yahweh will punish. A wasting disease will gnaw at the vitals of Assyria; she will be like a forest through which a fire has raged, leaving so few trees that a child could count them.

h **5.** cf. RSV*n*. By a transposition of words we might read: 'Ah, Assyria! The rod of my anger, the staff of my fury, it is in their hand!' **6.** The words 'spoil' (*shālāl*), 'plunder' (*baz*) may play on the name Maher-shalal-hash-baz (8:1–4; cf. the play on Shear-jashub, 20–23). **8.** The Assyrian ruler was known as the King of Kings; many of his officers were vassal kings ruling territories far larger than Judah. **9.** Calno, Carchemish and Arpad were in
northern Syria, Hamath in central Syria. All the 430
places mentioned had been overrun by Tiglath-pileser III or Sargon II, some more than once. Damascus fell to the former in 732, Samaria to the latter in 722/1. The words here remind us of 36:19, 37:12f. **10.** The text is hopelessly corrupt; probably a line is lost. Possibly read (cf. Kissane): 'As my hand has reached to these kingdoms and their idols (will the idols of Judah succeed?), or will they protect Jerusalem?' **13c.** Uncertain; RSV gets a tolerable sense. **16. his stout warriors:** better 'his fat limbs'. **under his glory:** perhaps (*k*^{e}*bhēdhô* for *k*^{e}*bhôdhô*) 'beneath his liver'. The figure is of a once-healthy man consumed by a wasting disease; 16 is continued in 18*bc*. **18. The Lord will destroy:** 'it (i.e. the disease) will destroy'; 'the Lord' is not in Heb. **a sick man wastes away:** very uncertain, but the context demands something of the kind.

20-23. The passage seems to lie after 701 for, although 431a
Judah had been a dependency of Assyria since 734, not before 701 had she felt the blow of Assyrian military force. In that year (cf. §446) Hezekiah surrendered to Sennacherib, acceded to his demands and became once more his unwilling vassal. The national policy was again orientated toward 'him that smote them'. Isaiah here looks for the day when the nation will no longer depend on Assyria or any earthly power, but will trust in Yahweh—as he had always begged them to do. There follows a play on the name Shearjashub (cf. 7:3), both the threatening and hopeful connotations of which are developed. A repentant remnant will return to 'the mighty God'. But it will be only a remnant. Were the seed of Israel as numerous as promised to the Patriarchs (cf. Gen. 22:17, 32:12), only a repentant few will survive the judgment which Yahweh has decreed.

21. The mighty God: the word is that applied to the Davidic prince to come (9:6); it is not impossible that he (the 'godlike hero') is intended here as the ruler of the remnant.

24-27ab. Isaiah consoles his people as they groan under b
a bondage to Assyria severe enough to be compared with the Egyptian bondage of long ago. This, too, fits best after 701 when the Assyrians had both handed over large portions of Judah to her neighbours and laid on her a brutal tribute. Let Zion not fear this taskmaster! Very shortly now, and the time of wrath will be over; Yahweh will brandish his whip over the Assyrians and drive them as he once drove Midian before Gideon (Jg. 6–8). It will be a deliverance worthy to be compared with the Exodus—a miracle of Yahweh's power. Then Judah will be freed from the yoke of oppression. Cf. the language of 26f. with 9:4; the passage, like the preceding, has Messianic overtones.

27c-34. A graphic picture is drawn of the onward c
march of the Assyrian army as it burst into the land from the north with terrific force. One can almost feel the panic that was abroad, and see the roads clogged with refugees as village after village took to flight. The tide rolls up to the very walls of Jerusalem. Then, when all seems lost, Yahweh intervenes like some mighty woodsman felling trees, and brings the invader low. Read alone, the passage might be construed to mean that it is Judah that will be cut down (cf. 2:12f.); but in the present context the opposite seems to be intended. Some have objected that the Assyrians did not in fact march on Jerusalem from this direction. But we know few details of their actual movements. Samaria was an Assyrian province, and contingents could well have moved directly on Jerusalem from there while the main army marched down the coast. Yet the picture may be merely an imaginative one, describing the route the Assyrians were expected to take.

27c. With less change read: 'he has come up from d
the direction of Samaria'. **28-32.** The places, so far as known, lie in a line from north to south. **Aiath:**

431d Ai (*et-Tell*), east of Bethel, or Khirbet Haiyân near by. **Michmash:** *c.* 2½ miles to the south, north of the pass of the same name (1 Sam. 14:1–5). **Geba:** opposite Michmash, south of the pass. **Ramah . . . Gibeah:** *c.* 5 and 3 miles north of Jerusalem respectively. **Anathoth:** Jeremiah's home (Jer. 1:1), scarcely 2½ miles north of the capital. **Nob:** (cf. 1 Sam. 21:1), probably on Mt Scopus overlooking the city.

e **XI 1-9 The Just Reign of the Ideal King**—Like 9:2–7, this oracle celebrates the coming of a scion of the line of David who would exhibit all the qualities a king was ideally supposed to have. Endowed with Yahweh's spirit, he will rule as Yahweh's representative. The charismatic gifts are described (2) in three pairs, the first stressing wisdom, the second right resolution and the ability to act upon it, and the third piety. With these gifts the king will rule wisely and well (cf. Ps. 72:1f.). Not relying on appearances or hearsay, he will espouse the cause of the weak and destroy the wicked who oppress them. A time of idyllic, Eden-like peace will ensue. Wild animals become tame, all violence ceases, for the whole earth is filled with the knowledge of Yahweh. No doubt godly people hoped that each succeeding Davidide would make this picture actual. It was in this hope, tenacious yet repeatedly befooled, that the Messianic expectation of Israel had its roots. Some argue from v. 1 that the Davidic dynasty has been destroyed and that the passage, therefore, cannot be Isaiah's. But the text scarcely requires such an inference; it may mean only that a new twig will grow from the tree of David. There is no hint of a return from exile or of a re-establishment of the dynasty. An 8th cent. date is quite possible.

3a. The translation is free; the clause is probably a variant of the preceding one. **4. smite the earth:** probably (*'ārîṣ*) 'smite the tyrant'. **6. and the fatling together:** possibly (cf. 1QIsa) 'shall fatten together'.

f **10-16 Prophecies of the Future Restoration of Israel**—The section, consisting of a short oracle (10) and a longer one (11–16) both with the introduction 'in that day', is apparently post-exilic. A world-wide dispersion of Israel is presupposed (11f.), while the motif of the highway of the New Exodus (15f.) is a feature of 40–55 (cf. 19:23; Zech. 10:10f.). But it is entirely possible that some of the material is older. 13f. states merely that the schism of the nation (cf. 7:17) will be healed and that a united Israel will again recover the empire held by David; this could well be pre-exilic. The date of 10 will depend on its interpretation. In any avent, the section illustrates the way in which Isaiah's words were treasured and expanded in subsequent generations. The 'root of Jesse' will stand like a standard about which all the nations rally. This 'root', in 1 the Davidic dynasty, is probably in 10 a technical term for the Messiah. Yet this is far from certain; and the notion of a Davidic king ruling the nations of the world is not in itself a late one (cf. Ps. 18:43–45, 72:8–11, etc.). Yahweh will give the signal, and the remnant of his people will be gathered from the four corners of the earth and, once more united, will subdue the surrounding peoples. Yahweh will dry up the Egyptian sea and 'cleave' the Euphrates so that men can cross it dryshod. Then there will be a highway for the exiles returning from Mesopotamia, like the Exodus highway from Egypt.

g **11. extend—a second time:** 'extend' is not in Heb.; probably (*śe'ēth* for *shēnîth*) read: 'The Lord will again raise his hand'. There is no necessary implication that a return from exile has already taken place; 'again' refers back to Yahweh's first deliverance in the Exodus. **Pathros:** Upper Egypt. **Elam:** east of Babylonia. **Shinar:** Babylonia. **Hamath:** cf. 10:9. **the sea:** the Mediterranean. **15. utterly destroy:** probably 'dry up' (LXX). **the sea of Egypt:** the 'Reed Sea' of the Exodus, possibly an arm of Lake Menzaleh; the exact site was probably no longer remembered. **with his scorching wind:** uncertain; possibly (Scott), 'he will cleave the sea with his wind (breath)'; cf. Exod. 14:21. 431g

XII 1-6 Songs of Thanksgiving—As Israel sang a song on the occasion of the Exodus (Exod. 15:1–18), so the announcement of the new Exodus calls for hymns of praise. The first great division of the book is therefore concluded with two brief psalms (1f., 4–6), both introduced by the rubric, 'and you will say in that day (cf. 25:9*a*, 26:1*a*). In 3 a promise serves as a transition between the two parts and as a liturgical introduction to the second. The date and origin of these psalms is unknown, but the phraseology is reminiscent of certain of those of the Psalter (cf. 2*b*; Exod. 15:2; Ps. 118:14). 'In that day' (i.e. of the new Exodus) 'I' (Israel, or any Israelite) will praise Yahweh, who has put aside his wrath and comforted his people (cf. 40:1); he is my salvation, and I will trust and joy in him. When water is drawn from the wells of Yahweh's life-giving deliverance, then praise Yahweh before the nations for his mighty acts. h

XIII-XXIII These chapters consist for the most part of oracles directed at foreign nations. Similar collections are to be found in other prophetic books (e.g. Jer. 46–51; Ezek. 25–32). Much of this is hard to date since it represents a type of oracle uttered by prophets of Israel from the beginning of their activity onward. Some of it is certainly Isaiah's; some is equally obviously much later. Much of it no doubt represents traditional material handed down in prophetic circles from Isaiah's time and before until a date well after the exile. Most of these poems have the designation 'burden', '(doom) oracle' (13:1, 14:28, 15:1, etc.). 432a

XIII 1-XIV 23 The Doom of Babylon—The historical circumstances here are those of a time much later than Isaiah's. Babylon, in the 8th cent. struggling vainly, like Judah, for its independence from Assyria, is here the proud tyrant who rules the earth. The exile of Judah is presupposed (14:1–4*a*). The fact that Babylon is threatened by the Medes (13:17–22) may argue for a date soon after the death of Nebuchadnezzar (562), before Cyrus the Persian ascended to power (*c.* 550). The section is, however, not an original unit. After an editorial heading (13:1), there is a poem describing the awful Day of Yahweh (13:2–16), complete in itself and having no necessary connection with the overthrow of Babylon by the Medes (13:17–22). 14:1–4*a* is a prose transition leading into 14:4*b*–21, a taunt song celebrating the downfall of a tyrant. This poem does not mention Babylon and might apply to any tyrant; it swarms with mythological allusions of timeless antiquity. Only in its prose introduction and conclusion (14:3–4*a*, 22f.) is it applied to Babylon. Thus while the piece as a whole must date to the mid-6th cent., much of its material is of traditional character and presumably much older. It cannot be proved that any part goes back to Isaiah himself; but the possibility exists that pre-exilic material, some of it perhaps originally spoken of Assyria, has here been reapplied to Babylon. It is at least remarkable that there is no full-length doom oracle on Assyria in the collection. b

XIII 1-16 The Day of Yahweh's Judgment—The poem recalls certain words of Isaiah (cf. vv. 2, 5 and 5:26; vv. 6, 11 and 2:11f.); but it also has parallels in prophetic literature both before and after the exile (e.g. Zeph. 1:14–18; Jer. 6:24, 30:5–7*a*; Jl 1:15, 2:1–11). The Day of Yahweh in the popular hope was the day of Yahweh's vengeance on the foes of Israel and the establishment of his kingly rule. Here the judgment is conceived of in world-wide proportions. Yahweh has mustered his forces (2–5), a great host drawn from the ends of the earth, to execute his wrath. They are 'consecrated' (i.e. ritually prepared) for battle. The day is near (6–8)! Men wail and their courage fails. It is a day (9–13) of cruel slaughter on earth and cataclysms in heaven; it brings punish- c

432c ment to the wicked and arrogant tyrant. When it is over, human beings will be scarcer than gold. Those attracted or brought captive to the tyrant's capital (in the context Babylon, but perhaps not originally so) will flee each man to his home. All caught there will be killed, their infants dashed in pieces (cf. Ps. 137:8f.), their women ravished (14–16).

d **2. the gates of the nobles:** uncertain; perhaps (*pith*^{e}*hû*) read, 'open (the gates) you nobles' (or, 'volunteers'?). **8. their faces will be aflame:** apparently with dismay or feverish excitement. **12. Ophir:** probably on the east coast of Africa, approximately Somaliland, whence Solomon's ships brought gold (1 Kg. 9:28, 10:11). The location is irrelevant here; the expression is proverbial.

e **17-22 The Overthrow of Babylon by the Medes**—The preceding poem of Yahweh's judgment is here applied to Babylon, and the agent of vengeance identified with the Medes. The Medes will come against Babylon, irresistibly and pitilessly, refusing to be bought off. Babylon will join Sodom and Gomorrah in oblivion, never to be inhabited again. It will be a place accursed, its ruins the haunt of wild beasts and demons, where not even nomads pitch their tents. And the time is close! Babylon was not in fact taken by the Medes, but by Cyrus (539), who had brought the Medes under his rule. Nor did Cyrus harm the city; it suffered a partial destruction at the hands of Darius I, but was still inhabited in the days of Alexander the Great. This poem, like the preceding one, swarms with conventional expressions characteristic of this type of literature.

f **17. Medes:** an Indo-Aryan people who first appeared in NE. Iran in the 9th cent. Subsequently a strong kingdom, they co-operated with Babylon in the overthrow of Assyria (616–610), after which they further enlarged their holdings in Iran, Armenia and Asia Minor. They were taken over by Cyrus *c.* 550. **18a.** The text is uncertain. **19. Chaldeans:** an Aramaean people who had infiltrated southern Babylonia since *c.* the 11th cent., and who had become the dominant element in the population there. Independence from Assyria, sought by Merodach-baladan in the 8th cent., was gained (626) by Nabopolassar, father of Nebuchadnezzar and founder of the neo-Babylonian empire. Cf. 19*b* and Am. 4:11; Jer. 50:40. **21f.** The language is conventional (cf. 34:11–15; Jer. 50:39f., 51:37; in Zeph. 2:14f. the same language is used of Assyria). The creatures named include both animals and demons (e.g. 'satyrs', probably demons in the form of goats). In popular superstition, ruins were haunted by uncanny monsters, so that people were afraid to go there.

g **XIV 1-4a.** A prose transition piece. The fall of Babylon means that Yahweh has compassion on Israel and will again (cf. 11:11) choose her, as he once did in Egypt, and bring her home. Many foreigners will join her as proselytes (cf. 56:1–8; Zech. 8:20–22); less large-heartedly, the nations will convey Israel to her land and, their roles reversed, Israel will use her erstwhile oppressors as slaves (cf. 60:10, 14, 61:5, etc.). Then, when Israel has been given rest from hard bondage (cf. Exod. 1:14), she will lift up this taunt song (*māshāl*) against Babylon.

h **4b-21 The Downfall of the Tyrant**—This poem, a mocking dirge celebrating the overthrow of the tyrant who has terrorised the world, is one of rare beauty and dramatic power. In the context (4*a*, 22) the tyrant is Babylon; but there is nothing in the poem itself to indicate this. In view of its numerous mythological allusions, there is every likelihood that the composer of 13:1–14:23 has taken over a much older poem, handed down in prophetic circles, and applied it to Babylon. The possibility that it originally referred to Assyria deserves consideration. 'How still the oppressor has become! How the insolent raging has ceased!' The whole earth (4*b*–8) breathes a sigh of relief. The tyrant who has rained blow after blow on the peoples, and persecuted them unrelent- ingly, is now broken. A song of joy rises as if the very 43
trees of the forest rejoice that the woodsman comes no more with his axe. The poet then (9–11) pictures Sheol bestirring itself at the tyrant's coming. The shades of the great kings of the past rise from their ghostly thrones to greet him, asking how it is that one so mighty should come to such an end. Yet there he is, weak in death as any mortal, his pomp and power ended, his bed and coverlet worms and maggots. The poet then (12–15) addresses the tyrant in the language of myth, likening him to that lesser deity who tried to storm heaven and make himself king of the gods. So has been the tyrant's self-deifying pride; he would be higher than the stars, equal to the Most High (Elyon). But he receives his reward—hurled down to the recesses of the Pit. There (16–21) he will be an object of amazement. Can this really be the great tyrant who terrorised the earth? Where other kings lie in state in their tombs, he is cast out unburied like the bloodstained garments of the slain, like a corpse trampled underfoot in battle. No honourable burial for him, for he has been the ruin of his people! Let his line be utterly cut off, lest it rise to begin its tyranny again.

9. Sheol: the underworld (not 'Hell'), where all i
alike go, there to pursue a shadowy existence, a pale reflection of their lives on earth (cf. Job 3:13–19; Ezek. 32:18–32, etc.). **12-15. Day Star son of Dawn:** Helal ben Shahar, a figure known from the Râs Shamra texts, where Shahar is god of the dawn. **the mount of assembly in the far north:** known from the Râs Shamra texts and elsewhere as the home of the gods (cf. Ezek. 28:14; Ps. 48:2; Exod. 15:17). We have here an adaptation of the Canaanite form of a myth, widespread in the ancient world, in which a lesser deity—here the morning star—aspires to make himself the chief god, only to be hurled down to earth. **19. like a loathed untimely birth:** the context demands something of the kind; MT ('a loathed branch', i.e. scion? cf. 11:1) is hardly correct. **clothed with the slain:** better '(like) the garments of the slain'. **the stones of the Pit:** the meaning is uncertain. If the text is correct it seems to refer to the common grave on the battlefield into which corpses were dumped and covered with stones (cf. 2 Sam. 18:17). Others see a reference to the stone tombs in which wealthy persons were buried; if so, the clause should be read with 20*a*. The sense is that the tyrant will be cast out unburied like an abortive birth (?), or the bloody garments of the slain, or a corpse trampled on the field of battle. **21. with cities:** perhaps delete as a textual variant.

22f. A prose conclusion by the same hand as j
1–4*a*, applying the preceding poem to Babylon. Yahweh will sweep Babylon as with a broom, leaving neither relic nor remnant. Its dykes and canals neglected, it will become a swamp, a haunt of wild creatures.

24-27 Yahweh's Purpose to destroy Assyria 433
—This brief oracle is undoubtedly Isaiah's. It refers to the same situation as 10:5–34, with which it may originally have stood in connection. It cannot be proved that, before the addition of 1–4*a*, 22f., it served to apply the poem of 4–21 to Assyria, but the thought is worthy of consideration. Yahweh has a purpose and it will stand, namely, to break Assyria on the soil of Palestine, thus making it clear to all that he had done it. The deliverance of Judan thus accomplished becomes an event of world-wide import, since all the world is subject to Assyria. And since Yahweh has decided upon this, no-one can prevent it.

25b. Cf. 9:4, 10:27. It is unnecessary to regard 25*b* as a gloss; the language is conventional. **26.** Cf. 5:25, 9:12, 17, 21, 10:4.

28-32 A Warning to the Philistines—The b
occasion for this oracle is disputed. It is dated in the year of Ahaz' death. Owing to confusion in the Biblical data (cf. 2 Kg. 16:1f, 18:1, 9f., 13) dates ranging from 727 to 715 have been suggested for this

433b event. For reasons that cannot be discussed here, the last is far the most likely. But the superscription merely supplies the date; the death of Ahaz is not the reason for the Philistines' rejoicing, for Ahaz had never been in a position to oppress them. Both Philistia and Judah were vassals of Assyria; and the enemy with whom the Philistines are threatened (31) is clearly Assyria. It has been assumed, therefore, that the Philistines were rejoicing over the death of an Assyrian king. And, since the death of no Assyrian king can plausibly be connected with that of Ahaz, some have supposed that the superscription is incorrect. But the 'serpent's root' (29) probably refers to the Assyrian nation rather than to a particular king (the same word is used of the Philistines in 30). The passage may have its background in the troubles which Sargon II (721–705) experienced in the early years of his reign, especially in Babylon where Merodach-baladan succeeded in establishing his independence for over ten years. Sargon, busy elsewhere, had little time to devote to Palestine, and this might have encouraged the belief that Assyrian power was breaking. In 711 Sargon had to deal with a revolt centering in Ashdod, which had been brewing for some years and which relied upon the support of the Egyptians. Probably encouraged by the death of Ahaz, who had been a loyal vassal of Assyria, an attempt was made by the Philistines to draw Judah, as well as Edom and Moab, into the rebellion; 32*a* is possibly a reference to their ambassadors. Isaiah bitterly opposed this plot (ch. 20), which was crushed in 711. So viewed, the present passage dates to 715/14, just as the plot began to hatch. Isaiah tells the Philistines not to rejoice that the rod that smote them seems to be broken. It is not. A worse horror will come from the oppressor's 'root', and it will destroy the Philistines 'root' and remnant. As for the ambassadors, let them take back the message that Judah will have no part of it. Yahweh has founded Zion, and there will his afflicted people find refuge. This is a word characteristic of Isaiah's message throughout his life (cf. 7:9, 28:16, 30:15, etc.).

29. flying serpent: a mythical creature (cf. 30:6). **30. first-born of the poor:** better (*b^{e}khārî*), 'the poor shall feed in my pasture'. **31. no straggler in his ranks:** perhaps read, 'and none can measure (*môdhēdh* for *bôdhēdh*, cf. 1QIs^a) its columns (*'ammûdhāw*)'.

c **XV 1-XVI 14 The Doom of Moab**—These chapters are a dirge describing how Moab has been overwhelmed by some great disaster. Resemblances to the longer collection in Jer. 48 are so numerous that there can be little doubt that the two are parallel recensions of the same material. What occasion is described is uncertain. The archaic flavour of the poem makes it unlikely that it is of post-exilic origin, as some have held. It has been argued from 16:13f. that Isaiah took over an older poem and used it as a threat to Moab in the days of the invasions of Sargon or Sennacherib. Most of those who take this position think that the poem originally referred to the conquest of Moab by Jeroboam II (cf. 2 Kg. 14:25; Am. 6:14). The fact that refugees on Edomite soil (15:7, 16:1–5) appeal to Judah for sanctuary argues for a strong king in that country who would be in a position to help them; and this would fit Uzziah, in whose control Edom was (cf. 2 Kg. 14:7, 22). On the other hand, the attractive suggestion has been advanced (W. F. Albright, JBL 61 (1942), 119) that both this poem and Jer. 48 refer to an irruption of Arab tribes into the Transjordanian lands *c.* 650, which ended Moab's existence as a strong autonomous state. If so, the poem was composed after the time of Isaiah and before that of Jeremiah and, because of its popularity and uncertain origin, found its way into the books of both prophets.

d **XV 1-9.** Calamity has overwhelmed Moab with catastrophic suddenness. In every city there is mourning, till it seems that the very land itself cries out in anguish. The refugees are a sight to tear the heart.
They clog the roads, carrying their pitiful possessions 433d
on their backs, weeping as they go. The streams having been stopped up, they find no water. With nowhere left to go, they flee across the 'Brook of the Willows' southward into Edom. Behind them the land howls in agony and the watercourses run with blood. Yet even this is not the end; worse yet awaits the fugitives.

1. because: read 'yea' on both occasions. On the places mentioned in these verses, cf. the atlases and commentaries. Many of them are of uncertain location. **Kir:** also Kir-hareseth and Kir-heres (16:7, 11). **2. Dibon:** Dhībân, north of the Arnon, where was found (1868) the Moabite (Mesha') Stone telling of that king's victory over Israel (cf. 2 Kg. 3:4f.). **4. The armed men of Moab cry aloud:** probably (cf. LXX), 'the loins of Moab tremble'. **6f. Nimrim:** probably Wâdī en-Numeirah, which flows into the Dead Sea near its southern end. **Brook of the Willows** (*'^{a}rābhîm*): probably Wâdī el-Ḥesā (Brook Zered), the boundary between Moab and Edom (cf. 'Brook of the Arabah', Am. 6:14). **9. Dibon:** Heb. 'Dimon'; the correction adopted by RSV is questionable. **for the remnant of the land:** perhaps, 'and for the remnant of Edom——' (a word is missing).

XVI 1-5. From Edom the Moabite fugitives send e
tribute to the king of Judah, begging him for sanctuary until the trouble has passed. If this be not a request (4*a*) for admission into Judah itself, it must be assumed that Judah at the time controlled Edom and could give the refugees asylum there. The language of 5 is reminiscent of the hopes attached to the line of David (cf. 9:7; Ps. 89:19–37). But Moabite diplomats would certainly have known of these formulae; they are depicted as flattering the king of Judah by voicing the conviction that the hopes of his dynasty will be realised—or have actually been realised in him.

1 They have sent lambs: Moab once yielded tribute of sheep and wool to Israel (cf. 2 Kg. 3:4). **2** places the fugitives at the fords of the Arnon, far to the north; it interrupts the connection between 1 and 3, and is possibly displaced from the preceding chapter. **3. grant justice:** 'arbitrate for us', 'decide in our favour'.

6-12. Moab's plea is rejected. Her past arro- f
gance is well known, her present wheedling insincere. The lament is then resumed. The famous vineyards of the eastern highlands, whose wine once laid kings low, and which sprawl like one great vine from the Dead Sea to the desert, are now ruined. The poet, deeply moved, enters into the grief of the ravished land whence peaceful harvest and joyful song have fled, his heart responding to its anguish like a lyre to the touch of the musician. But Moab is doomed; all her prayers to her gods on all her high places cannot save her.

6 his boasts: 'his idle talk'. **7. raisin cakes:** cakes of pressed grapes, a great delicacy, used at religious festivals (Hos. 3:1). **8b** might be read, 'whose (grape-laden) branches struck down (in intoxication) the lords of the nations' (cf. 28:1). **9. the weeping of Jazer:** possibly 'weeping' (*b^{e}khî*) is an error for a word (*mbk*) meaning 'fountain' (cf. G. M. Landes, BASOR 144 (1956), 30–37: 'I weep for you, fountain of Jazer——'. **battle shout:** properly (cf. 10) 'vintage shout'; the only vintage shout will be the battle-cry of invading armies. But Jer. 48:32 reads 'destroyer' (*shôdhēdh*). **11. my soul:** lit. 'my bowels', i.e. the seat of the emotions.

13f. An application of the foregoing poem to a new g
crisis which is about to overtake Moab. If the poem is older than Isaiah, these words could come from the prophet himself; but it is dangerous to insist upon it, for the poem is possibly later (cf. above). 'Like the years of a hireling' means that the time is to be precisely three years: a hireling works for the stipulated period, neither more nor less (cf. 21:16).

XVII 1-14 A Complex of Oracles on various 434a
Subjects—The chapter has the heading 'an oracle concerning Damascus'; but this applies only to

434a 1–3, where both Damascus and northern Israel are addressed. Following this are three brief oracles (4–6, 7f., 9–11), each introduced with the words 'in that day', the first of which is closely linked to 1–3 and likewise addressed to northern Israel. The chapter closes with a further oracle (12–14) addressed to an unnamed power, almost certainly Assyria.

b **1-3 Doom of the Aramaean-Ephraimite Confederacy**—This oracle, like 7:1–8:18, falls in 735/4 when Rezin and Pekah joined forces to coerce Judah into alliance against Assyria. It is predicted that Damascus will soon become a ruin, as will all the cities of her domain; flocks will graze where once they stood. The two confederate nations will meet an identical fate.

2. Her cities will be deserted for ever: a plausible correction (cf. RSV*n*); no Aroer (so Heb.) is known in Syria or northern Israel.

c **4-6 The Fate of Ephraim**—The date is approximately that of the preceding. The might of the northern state will be brought low like that of a once robust man who wastes away with hunger or disease. It will be as when grain is reaped and only gleanings are left; or as when the olive crop is harvested by beating the tree with sticks: a few olives may remain on the most inaccessible branches, but no more. So Israel will be left a remnant.

5. the Valley of Rephaim: just SW. of Jerusalem; Isaiah and his hearers must often have seen harvesters at work there.

d **7f. A Turning from Idolatry**—This brief fragment, which declares that 'in that day' (i.e. after the judgment has fallen) men will no longer trust in the pagan cult objects which their hands have made, but in Yahweh alone, has no original connection with its context. Many scholars regard it as a late insertion. While this is quite possibly so, caution is in order. In language and thought the passage is not unlike 10:20f., 22:11; the word for 'men' (*hā'ādhām*) is used similarly in 2:9, 11, 17, 20. Possibly this is an Isaianic fragment from another context.

8. Asherim: symbols of Asherah, goddess of the fertility cult, made of wood (Jg. 6:25f.; 1 Kg. 15:13) and apparently erected beside the altar in Canaanite shrines.

e **9-11 A People doomed because of Idolatry**—The passage is frequently taken as the continuation of 1–6, directed to northern Israel. But it could as well be a separate oracle addressing Judah (cf. 1:29–31). The people are censured for turning from Yahweh to the practice of the fertility cult. They have planted 'gardens of Adonis', which apparently consisted of seedlings stimulated to forced growth in pots or baskets, and which were intended by sympathetic magic to bring to life the dead god of vegetation. Such plantings naturally withered as quickly as they grew. And so will Israel's hopes wither. In the day of Yahweh's judgment cities will be deserted like those haunted ruins left by the Amorites who were driven out before Israel. Yahweh alone can save; false gods cannot.

9. RSV emends after LXX and gets a good sense. But the reading is uncertain in detail. **10. pleasant plants:** 'plantings of the desirable one' (*na'amān*). This word occurs both as a proper name and as an appellation in the Râs Shamra texts (cf. 2 Kg. 5:1ff.). Here it is a name for the vegetation god who annually died and rose again (cf. 'alien god'). Adonis, Baal, Tammuz, etc., were all gods of this type.

f **12-14 An Oracle against Assyria**—Though the foe in question is not named, it is almost certainly Assyria. The prophet hears the approach of the enemy army, composed of the many subject peoples of the Assyrian empire, as if it were the roaring of a storm-tossed sea. But at Yahweh's rebuke it is dispersed like chaff blown from a high threshing-floor, or like dust driven by the wind. In the evening there is sheer terror. But suddenly, before morning, it is gone. Such is the fate of those who despoil God's people. There is no reason to deny the passage to Isaiah, as some have done; it fits in the context of 14:24–27 and 10:24–34, and may be assumed to refer to the same situation (cf. 37:22–29, 33–35, 36). Usually placed in 701, it may refer to a later invasion *c.* 688 (cf. §446). 434f

13a. a mistaken repetition of 12*b*.

XVIII 1-7 Oracle to the Ethiopian Ambassadors —Ambassadors of the XXV (Ethiopian) Dynasty of Egypt have come to Jerusalem, undoubtedly in an attempt to draw Hezekiah into alliance against Assyria. Since this dynasty seized power *c.* 715, the passage must date after that time; but since its rulers meddled continually in Palestinian affairs as long as the dynasty endured, it is difficult to be sure which occasion is in question here. Hezekiah was in alliance with Shabako (710/9–696/5) in 701 (cf. 30:1–7, 31:1–3), and apparently (37:9) Tirhakah (690/89–*c.* 664) at a later date (cf. §446). Still earlier (cf. ch. 20), an effort had been made to get Judah to join in a revolt centering in Ashdod, which was crushed by Sargon II in 711. The fact that Isaiah's tone is mild—as it was not later—and that the Ethiopians seem to be a novel sight arousing curiosity, plus the fact that they are said (2) to be a greatly feared, conquering people, all perhaps favour an early date (*c.* 714) soon after the Ethiopian conquest of Egypt and before their reverses at the hands of Assyria. But assurance is impossible. Isaiah addresses the ambassadors who have come so far—these tall men with glossy skins—and he bids them take a message home to those who sent them. The world is to await the signal which Yahweh will give. This word (4–6) has come to him in a private oracle. While the nations are busily plotting, Yahweh superintends the scene, hovering over it like the shimmering heat of summer, dazzling bright, or like the high, fleecy clouds which bring the dew. As these hasten the harvest, so Yahweh quietly works. Then, in his time, just as the grape is ripening, he will lop off the branches of this vine (Assyria) with the pruning-hook of his judgment. Assyrian corpses will be left to feed the carrion-birds and the beasts. Then the Ethiopians will bring tribute to Yahweh. g

1. whirring wings: presumably a reference to the swarming insect life of the Nile valley. But the meaning is uncertain. **7.** Possibly, but by no means certainly, a later addition.

XIX 1-25 Oracles concerning Egypt—Though its various parts hang together about the common theme 'Egypt', the chapter is not an original unit. It falls into two parts, the first of which (1–15) is poetry, the second (16–25) prose. But even these two parts are composite. The latter consists of five brief oracles (16f., 18, 19–22, 23, 24f.), each with the introduction 'in that day'; and 5–10, which has a different theme from the rest of 1–15, may have come from an originally separate poem. 435a

1-15 Doom Oracle against Egypt—The situation reflected in the passage is uncertain. Some believe it to be post-exilic. But while this is possible, there is little compelling evidence for it. A plausible background can be found in circumstances of Isaiah's lifetime. One might regard 2f. as a description of the internal chaos into which Egypt had fallen prior to the invasion of Piankhi (*c.* 716/15?), in which event 4 would refer to the conquering Ethiopian dynasty. On the other hand, if 2f. is predictive, as seems likely, the disintegration of Egypt is in the future, and 4 then refers to the Assyrians. It is true that Assyria did not conquer Egypt until after Isaiah's death; but that Isaiah expected this imminently is clear (cf. ch. 20). Yahweh comes to Egypt riding on a cloud. The gods of Egypt tremble at his presence. Egypt is thrown into turmoil, her leaders rendered incapable of intelligent action. Frantically they consult their idols and their diviners—but in vain; Egypt is delivered into the hand of a 'hard master'. Then follows (5–10) a picture of a disaster attendant upon the drying-up of the Nile. Vegetation is parched, the b

435b fishermen cannot ply their trade, the textile industry languishes. In 11–15 the thought of 1–4 is resumed. Pharaoh's counsellors are taunted with their inability to solve the national problem. How can they call themselves wise? If they were wise they would tell Pharaoh of Yahweh's purposes. But they can't. It is as if Yahweh has mixed for Egypt a stupefying drink, causing her to reel in confusion like a drunken man. There is nothing that she can do to save herself.

c **1.** The concept of the god riding on the storm-cloud (cf. Ps. 18:10f, 104:3) is an old one and not peculiar to Israel (in the Râs Shamra texts Baal is called the 'cloud rider'). It became associated with Yahweh's coming to judge (cf. Nah. 1:3; Dan. 7:13). **5. the Nile:** Heb. 'the sea', i.e. the underground sea from which fresh-water streams were supposed to spring. **7a. bare places:** probably an Egyptian word (cf. K-B) signifying some sort of grass or rush. Read: 'the rushes by the Nile, by the brink of the Nile——'. **9.** With two slight changes (cf. K-B) read: 'The workers in flax are dismayed, the carders and weavers grow pale'. **10. the pillars of the land:** lit. 'its "pillars"'; but the word is a technical term (cf. K-B) meaning 'its weavers (?)'. **11. Zoan:** Tanis in the NE. of the Delta, the Egyptian capital under the Hyksos rulers, the XIX Dynasty, and at other times; the Raamses (House of Rameses) of Exod. 1:11. **13. Memphis:** one of Egypt's great cities and at various times the capital; near Cairo. **cornerstones:** chiefs (cf. 1 Sam. 14:38), probably of the various 'nomes', or districts. **15b.** Cf. 9:14.

d **16-25 Further Oracles concerning Egypt**—This section is generally conceded to be post-exilic, although the ambiguity of the allusions in it makes exact dating impossible. The first oracle (16f.) is threatening in tone: 'in that day' the Egyptians will tremble like women before Judah and Judah's God, for they will realise that he is the source of their chastisement. In its present context, however, it prepares the way for the next oracle (18), which states that five cities in Egypt will speak Hebrew and worship Yahweh, one of which will be the City of the Sun (probably Heliopolis). Then it is declared (19–22) that there will be an altar to Yahweh in the middle of Egypt and a pillar (*maṣṣēbhāh*) to him at the frontier. The Egyptians will cry to Yahweh, and he will deliver them; he will reveal himself to them, and they will offer their sacrifices to him. He will treat them, not as in the Exodus days, but as he treats his own people, chastening in order to heal and forgive. Then (23) a highway will connect Egypt and Assyria, allowing free intercourse between them. And Israel (24f.) will be a full partner with them, all of them the people of Yahweh and a blessing to the world. Few passages of wider sympathy are to be found in the entire OT.

It has been suggested that the altar (19) refers to a temple to Yahweh built *c.* 160 at Leontopolis by the exiled high priest Onias IV. It has further been suggested that the City of the Sun (18)—some would read 'City of the Lion'—is also Leontopolis. This is unlikely. Not only is there the statement of Josephus (Ant. XIII, iii, 1) that Onias called upon this passage as support for his action; by the 2nd cent. there were far more Jews in Egypt than could be accommodated in five towns. Furthermore, most of these Jews had become Greek speaking—which is why the LXX translation was made. Jews had settled in Egypt as early as the 6th cent. (cf. Jer. 43f.), and almost certainly sooner. A Jewish military colony at Elephantine in Upper Egypt had a temple to Yahweh with a syncretistic cult as early as 525. Though the Deuteronomic law forbade worship at any place save Jerusalem (Dt. 12:13f., etc.), and the erection of pillars anywhere (Dt. 16:22), Jews in Egypt were either ignorant of this or unconcerned by it. Whether the pillar at the border refers to Elephantine or some other place cannot be said. Nor can the five cities be identified. While the passage is post-exilic, it
should not be placed too late. A date in the Persian 435d
or early Hellenistic period is probably best.

e **18. City of the Sun:** another Heb. reading (*heres* for *ḥeres*) is 'city of destruction', which is probably an alteration by Palestinian Jews expressing disapproval of a cult of Yahweh in Egypt. LXX ('city of righteousness') probably reflects the feelings of Greek-speaking Jews in Egypt. **23. Assyria:** not the Assyrian empire, but its successor power in Mesopotamia, whether Persia (cf. Ezr. 6:22) or the Seleucids.

f **XX 1-6 An Acted and Spoken Prophecy against Egypt**—This incident is known from Sargon's inscriptions. The date is 711. Three years previously (cf. 3) a revolt had broken out in Ashdod supported by the hope of aid from the XXV (Ethiopian) Dynasty. Efforts were made to get Judah, Moab and Edom to join in. In protest, Isaiah removed his sandals and outer garments and for three years went about Jerusalem half clad, symbolising the fate of Egypt and all who trust in her. In 711, as Sargon's forces marched, he put this acted prophecy into words: as he had worn the garb of a captive, so will the Egyptians be made captives and deported. Then those who trusted her will see what a frail help she is. Such, in fact, she proved to be. The Assyrians took Ashdod and allied towns and treated them with great severity. Egypt not only failed to send help; she even cravenly surrendered the rebel leader, who had fled to her for sanctuary. Perhaps partly because of Isaiah's advice Judah seems not to have joined the rebellion, at least not overtly, for she was not molested. The XXV Dynasty was in fact overthrown when Assyria invaded Egypt; but this was nearly fifty years later.

g **1. the commander in chief:** the Tartan (*turtanu*); cf. 2 Kg. 18:17. **Sargon,** mentioned only here in the OT, had captured Samaria in 721. **2. sackcloth:** a symbol of mourning (cf. 37:1f.), and perhaps also the customary garb of the prophet (cf. 2 Kg. 1:8; Zech. 13:4). Isaiah was not literally 'naked'; he was clad in a loincloth or undergarment. **6. this coastland:** Philistia (cf. Jer. 47:4).

436a **XXI 1-10 The Fall of Babylon**—Because of its cryptic language, its disjointed—even ejaculatory—style, and because the text is obscure at certain crucial points, few passages in the book are more difficult to interpret than this. The prophet tells how a 'stern vision' has come to him, rushing upon him like a storm wind from the desert. What this vision is we are not told at first save in the enigmatic words (2*a*), 'the plunderer plunders, the destroyer destroys', but it is clear that it brought the intimation that Babylon has fallen. The thought leaves the prophet unmanned; his mind reels, he is 'too distraught to listen, too dismayed to look'. The vision brings to his mind flashes of the actual scene: he hears the rallying-cry of attacking Elamites and Medes (2*b*); he sees a feast suddenly interrupted (5). He then tells (6–9) how the vision was confirmed to him. He is to watch; and when he sees riders coming—as come they assuredly will—he will know that Babylon has fallen. And this he tells (10) to his 'threshed and winnowed' people.

b The passage is usually referred to the conquest of Babylon by Cyrus in 539. So viewed, Elamites and Medes are contingents in Cyrus' army, which is 'the plunderer', 'the destroyer'; the riders who are seen with mind's eye are likewise the approaching Persians, while it is in Babylon that the feast is interrupted by the foe's coming. But this interpretation, though plausible, presents certain difficulties. It is certainly strange that a Hebrew prophet in 539 should find the fall of Babylon news too terrible to contemplate. To explain this out of the prophet's subjectivity, or the stress of ecstasy, is unconvincing. Further, since the prophet seems to be at a distance from Babylon, the riders of 6–9 might best be explained as the messengers who would bring news to Palestine of Babylon's fall. Moreover, the text creates the impression that Elamites and Medes act, not as mere army contingents,

436b but as independent and allied powers. Finally, a banquet in Babylon overtaken by surprise is difficult to understand if invading forces were actually moving upon that city at the time.

c The passage requires a time when there was a concerted operation by Elamites and Medes involving Babylon, when that city was taken, and when news of this would come as a terrible blow to Jews. It is, therefore, worth asking if the 'destroyer' is not Assyria, against whom Babylon is in rebellion, and if Elamites and Medes have not come to the aid of Babylon with some initial success. The prophet, however, knows that this is illusory, and is distraught. Judah, herself involved, has high hopes of good news. But the prophet must bring bad news. So interpreted, the 'hard vision' comes to the prophet while a rebellion in Babylon in which Judah has a stake is going well. Its gist is: 'the plunderer (Assyria) is going to plunder, the destroyer is going to destroy'. In his mind (2*b*) he hears his people cheering the coalition on: 'Advance, Elam! Close in, Media!' And victory seems in sight, for there is celebration (5), perhaps in Babylon, but quite as probably in Jerusalem (cf. 22:13). But the prophet knows better. He cries to the celebrants: Get ready to fight! You will have to! For when messengers come they will bring news that Babylon has gone under. Poor 'threshed and winnowed' Judah (10), you are in for it now!

d If this interpretation be correct, in what historical situation would it best fit? Sargon's defeat of Merodach-baladan's rebellion (*c.* 710) has been suggested, as has Sennacherib's defeat of that same individual in 703. Merodach-baladan had Elamite backing on both occasions. But in 710 Judah was not, apparently, involved; and although she was involved in 703 (cf. ch. 39), the rebellion was rather quickly and easily crushed. A more attractive suggestion would be to find the background in events of 691–689. After Sennacherib's campaign in the west in 701, he found Babylon in uproar. His own son, who was viceroy there, was taken prisoner and murdered. In 691 a coalition of Babylonians, Elamites and various groups from the Iranian highlands administered him a stinging defeat at Khalule on the Tigris. It is possible that at this time (cf. §446) Tirhakah of Egypt (cf. 37:9) stirred up trouble in the west, and that Judah, pinning her hopes on the success of the Babylonian cause, was drawn in. But in 689 Sennacherib took Babylon, ravaged it and carried the statue of Marduk to Assyria (cf. 9*b*). This would have left Judah to face the wrath of Assyria virtually alone. One might also think of 652–648, when Ashurbanipal faced revolt on the part of Shamash-shum-ukin, his brother and viceroy in Babylon, who was backed by Elamites and Medes. At the same time Arab tribes ravaged Transjordania. Though the revolt was crushed, and Babylon sacked, the security of Assyria was seriously endangered. While we do not know that Judah was involved, it is possible that she was (cf. 2 Chr. 33:11). There is some evidence of unrest in Palestine at this time (cf. Ezr. 4:10), and it is probable that Psammetichus I (663–609), himself newly free of Assyria, was behind it. While dogmatism is impossible, either of the two last-mentioned dates seems preferable to one in 539. Isaianic authorship thus remains within the realm of the possible; but it ought not to be insisted upon.

e **1. the wilderness of the sea:** Some see a reference to the 'Sea Land' of southern Babylonia, the home of Merodach-baladan. But the text (cf. LXX, 1QIs[a]) is suspicious and probably corrupt. **2. all the sighing she has caused I bring to an end:** lit. 'all her sighing' or 'all sighing'. One might read (Gray): 'bring all (her) sighing to an end'. The ambiguity of this verse helps to make the interpretation of the whole passage uncertain. For adequate discussion, see the larger commentaries. **lay siege:** this can be the meaning; or simply, 'take hostile action', 'vex', 'harass', etc. **5. oil the shield:** i.e. get ready to fight. Shields were made of leather, or wood covered with leather, and had leather straps; oiling was necessary to keep this equipment in proper shape. **6. a watchman:** the prophet himself (cf. 8f.; Hab. 2:1). 436e

11f. Oracle on Edom—The oracle is so cryptic that one cannot be sure to what circumstance it was spoken. No original connection with the preceding poem may be assumed. Yet if the date of 652–648 (cf. above) be selected for 1–10, it is tempting to think of the Arab irruption of *c.* 650 which laid waste all the Transjordanian lands. The passage is not a 'doom oracle'. Edom calls as if to a night watchman, 'Guard, what of the night (i.e. of trouble)?' The enigmatic answer could mean: respite is coming, followed by new trouble; or, there will be respite for some, trouble for others; or, respite is coming, but trouble is not yet over. The seer invites the inquirers to come back again; he is not yet sure of the future. f

11. Dumah: an Ishmaelite clan (Gen. 25:14); but here (cf. Seir) clearly Edom (so LXX).

13-17 Oracle on Dedan and Kedar—Once again it is impossible to be sure of the circumstances in question. It is, however, once more tempting to think of the Arab incursions of *c.* 650 and (16f.) Ashurbanipal's reaction against them. Caravans of Dedanites (a N. Arabian tribe, near Edom: cf. Jer. 49:8; Ezek. 25:13) are seen fleeing from the foe. The people of Tema (Teimā, *c.* 250 miles SE. of Edom) are commanded to bring them food and water. The statement (16f.) that Kedar (a powerful N. Arabian tribe: cf. 42:11, 60:7) will be destroyed in exactly a year suggests that she is the cause of the trouble. g

13 in Arabia: better, 'in the steppe'. **thickets:** presumably such scrub growth as might be found in the desert. But the word may mean 'stony ground'. **16.** Cf. 16:14; 1QIs[a] reads 'three years' as there.

XXII 1-14 The Inexcusable Sin of Jerusalem—The occasion of this prophecy, far the bitterest that we have from the lips of Isaiah, is disputed. It fits best, however, in 701 when Sennacherib, having received the surrender of Hezekiah and imposed tribute upon him (cf. 2 Kg. 18:13–16), lifted the siege of Jerusalem and withdrew. Since the people had certainly expected far worse, this was the occasion for wild rejoicing (1-2*a*, 13). Isaiah, however, is shocked; he can see no reason for revelry (2*b*–4) for, after all, Judah's army has disgraced itself. Its slain met no honourable death in battle but were cut down in full flight, while those captured had been executed or led away into slavery. Sennacherib tells us that certain of Hezekiah's troops deserted him; some such shameful incident may be alluded to here. Isaiah, weeping bitterly over the nation's agony, cannot join in the merriment. Some have held that (3, 5–8*a*) he was oppressed by a vision of calamity which he saw yet in store for his people. But these verses probably refer to the events just experienced. It has been a day of Yahweh's judgment. The assaulting forces—archers, chariotry, infantry—recruited from the various peoples of Assyria's far-flung empire, ringed Jerusalem round and made ready for the attack. The helplessness of the city was evident to all. But did the people then turn to their God (8*b*–11)? They did not! They made ready their weapons; they put the walls in repair, tearing down houses in the city to find the materials; they saw to their water supply in anticipation of siege. But they gave not a thought to the God whose judgment it was, and whose purpose had brought it to pass. Through that very judgment (12–14) Yahweh was calling them to penitence. And now—feasting, drinking, and telling themselves fatalistically that since life is short they might as well! And this, says Isaiah, is unforgivable sin. It is a capital crime against God requiring the life of those who have committed it. h

1 valley of vision: the title is taken from 5; what valley is meant is uncertain. **3.** Transposing two clauses and reading 'your mighty ones' (*'ammîṣayikh,* i

436i cf. LXX) for 'you who were found' (*nimṣā'ayikh*), read : 'All your chieftains fled together, far off they fled ; all your mighty ones were taken together, without bow (i.e. without resistance ?) were taken.' **5a.** Read : 'Truly it was a day of discomfiture—from the LORD God of hosts.' The rest of the verse is obscure ; reference to various contingents in the Assyrian army (Koa, Shoa ? cf. Ezek. 23:23) may be concealed in the corrupted text ; cf. 6. **6. with chariots and horsemen :** with slight changes (*'arām* for *'ādhām*), 'Aram (Syria) mounted horsemen' or 'with Aramaean chariots and horsemen.' **8. the house of the forest :** built by Solomon and so called because of the cedar pillars that supported its roof ; it was used as an armoury (1 Kg. 7:2, 10:17). **9b.** Transpose to the beginning of 11 ; reference here is probably to the digging of the Siloam tunnel (2 Kg. 20:20 ; 2 Chr. 32:3f., 30).

437a **15-25 An Oracle against an Ambitious Politician**—The prophets now and then uttered oracles which were in effect solemn curses upon individuals who had opposed them and their word (e.g. Am. 7:16f. ; Jer. 20:1–6, 28:12–17). Isaiah here turns upon one Shebna and, although a high royal official, addresses him with a scathing contempt scarcely appropriate to the meanest lackey. The reasons for this are not altogether clear. The fact that Shebna was preparing a tomb for himself, apparently among those of the nobility, may indicate that he was an upstart ambitious to gain position for himself and his family. The fact that his father's name is not given also suggests that he was of ignoble origin—though there is no reason to assume that he was a foreigner. But such fine scorn must have been provoked by something more than mere vulgar ambition. Possibly there were personal reasons of which we know nothing ; possibly Shebna (cf. 21*b*) had misused his office. It is even more likely that he had, as a member of the king's cabinet, favoured the alliance with Egypt which Isaiah had opposed. In any event, taking his stand apparently beside the tomb which Shebna was preparing, Isaiah announced that worthy's downfall. Yahweh will hurl him from his high office as one hurls a ball into a wide open space where there is nothing to stop it, and there he will die. What good will his fine tomb do him then? Shebna is a disgrace to the royal court. He will be replaced by Eliakim ben Hilkiah, who will hold office worthily as a father to the people—and no doubt influence the king's policy for good. Eliakim will be secure in his position, like a peg driven into the wall, and a credit to his father's house.

This prophecy was only partly fulfilled. Eliakim did indeed (36:3, 37:2) replace Shebna as the officer 'over the house' ; but Shebna, far from being disgraced, continued to function as the king's secretary-of-state, a position in the cabinet but little, if any, inferior to the one he had previously held (cf. 1 Kg. 4:3 ; Jer. 36:12). The present incident is thus to be placed before the events of chs. 36f., which are usually dated in 701, but which (cf. §446) may lie *c.* 688. In 24f. we have a later addition, whether by Isaiah or another cannot be said, describing how Eliakim in turn procured his downfall through nepotism. The secure peg of his position was overloaded and crashed to the ground.

b **15. this steward :** the title is known as that of an official ; the feminine occurs (1 Kg. 1:2, 4) as that of a personal attendant of the king. Is there an overtone of sarcasm here : 'this servant' ? **over the household :** the title (*'al habbayith*) of one who was master of the king's establishment and property (1 Kg. 4:6), and also the chief cabinet minister. **17f. O you strong man :** 'O man'. Probably contemptuous ('Mister', 'Mr Man' !). **whirl you round and round :** better, 'wind you up tightly (into a ball)'. **wide land :** if this means that Shebna is to be exiled, 19–23 must be regarded as an adjustment of the oracle when Shebna was merely demoted ; but exile is not necessarily implied. **your splendid chariots :** 437b chariots were reserved for persons of rank, and no doubt Shebna was proud of those at his disposal ; but some would read 'your splendid tomb' (*ḳibhrath kᵉbhôdhekhā*). **22. on his shoulder the key :** the key, carried slung from the shoulder, was the symbol of the major-domo's authority to admit or deny access to the king (cf. Mt. 16:19 ; Rev. 3:7).

XXIII 1-18 Oracles concerning Tyre—The chapter c falls into two parts : a poem describing the destruction of Tyre at the hands of an invader (1–14), and a later supplement (15–18), mostly in prose, announcing its ultimate restoration.

1-14. This poem has been assigned to dates ranging d from the Assyrian period to the capture of the city by Alexander the Great (332). The fact that 13 seems to be a gloss applying the prophecy to the thirteen-year siege by Nebuchadnezzar (585–573) probably indicates that the piece is older and originally referred to an invasion by Assyria. The tone of the poem, a graphic description of the shock occasioned by the fall of Tyre, the great merchant city, from her long-favoured position, fits best with this assumption. The great period of Phoenician commercial and colonial expansion fell between the 10th and the 8th cent., and was brought to an end when the homeland was overrun by Assyria and overseas ventures began to feel increasing competition by the Greeks. But which of the many Assyrian invasions is in question here cannot be said with assurance. In 701 Tyre, with other Phoenician cities, was involved in the general unrest, and was dealt with severely by Sennacherib ; its king fled overseas to Cyprus (cf. 12). Though Tyre was not then taken or destroyed, a Hebrew prophet might well have expected it to be. Later, a reader (13) who knew that the prophecy had not been literally fulfilled, applied it to Nebuchadnezzar's siege. It cannot be proved that the poem is Isaiah's, but neither its date nor its sentiment forbids it. The text is unusually difficult.

Let the Tarshish ships howl ! As they come from Cyprus they learn that Tyre is destroyed and that they no longer have a haven. The proud merchant people, long enriched by their lucrative trade, are struck dumb with dismay. Egypt, too, linked for centuries to the Phoenicians by trade, is appalled at the news. Can this really be the proud and ancient city whose far-flung interests have led her sons to settle beyond the seas ? Who can have done this to Tyre, the mother of colonies ? Yahweh did it, who has purposed to bring all human pride low (cf. 2:12ff.). His judgment is like a Nile flood which nothing can restrain ; at his command the Phoenicians (Canaan) are destroyed. Their days of glory are done. Let them flee to Cyprus —but even there they will find no escape.

1. Tyre is laid waste : Heb. 'it is ——'. With e slight changes read : 'The Tarshish ships (cf. 2:16) howl, for their home port is destroyed ; coming from the land of Cyprus it is revealed to them.' But some read 1*a* as 14. **2f.** The text is corrupt, but RSV gets the sense. Egypt and the Phoenician cities had been linked by mutual trade since the dawn of history. **Shihor :** the Nile (cf. Jer. 2:18). **4.** Since Sidon is addressed, we should probably regard 'the stronghold of the sea' as a gloss. It is as if the sea disowns her children (the Phoenicians). **8. bestower of crowns :** probably a reference to Tyre's colonies governed (at first) by rulers appointed by her. **10.** Very uncertain. Perhaps read : 'He (i.e. Yahweh, cf. 9, 11) has passed over your land like the Nile (in flood)'. The word rendered 'restraint' properly means (cf. K-B) a puberty girdle. Perhaps there is a somewhat indelicate word-play (cf. 'daughter Tarshish'). **13.** The text is again corrupt ; see the larger commentaries. The words, 'the land of the Chaldeans. This is the people ; it was not Assyria', indicate a gloss which seeks to say that the prophecy really is to be fulfilled by the Babylonians, not the Assyrians (Scott).

15-18. The piece seems to be a post-exilic addition, f

14

437f like 19:16–25. ' In that day ' (i.e. when she has been destroyed) Tyre will sink from importance for seventy years. Then it will be with her as it says in ' the song of the harlot ', a fragment of which is quoted (16) ; she will go back to her old profession, plying her trade with all the nations of the earth. She will not, however, use her wealth for herself, but will devote it to Yahweh for the support of his people (cf. 60:4–14). The prophecy is frequently referred to the interval between the capture of Tyre by Alexander and its recovery under the Ptolemies. This is possible, but not certain. The ' seventy years ' may be taken from the traditional duration of the Exile (Jer. 25:11f., 29:10 ; Zech. 1:12), and thus represent a round number. The writer is contemptuous of Tyre, but he expects, in some way, her conversion to Yahwism.

438a **XXIV-XXVII The Judgment of the World and the Deliverance of God's People**—These chapters are a collection of eschatological prophecies, psalms and prayers, originally independent of one another, which have been brought together by an unknown author to form a unified composition. It is often but inaccurately called the ' Isaiah Apocalypse '. It is true that some features of apocalyptic literature are present here : e.g. universal judgment, the eschatological banquet, the imprisonment of members of the heavenly host, the resurrection of the dead. But characteristic motifs of apocalyptic—pseudonymity, the use of visions and cryptic numbers, world powers symbolised by fearsome beasts, the reinterpretation of earlier prophecies, tendencies toward dualism, etc. —are conspicuously absent. Some have held that the basis of the section is a connected ' apocalypse ' (24:1–23, 25:6–8, 26:20f., 27:1, 12f.), into which various psalms and prayers have been interpolated. But it is probable that the various pericopes were originally independent and that unity was given the section by its author who, often with telling skill, wove the parts together into an articulated whole. Since much of the material is traditional in character, it is difficult to say which parts the author borrowed and which are original with him. The section, as its style, diction and thought indicate, is certainly post-exilic. Yet it should not be given too late a date, e.g. in the Maccabean period. None of the numerous attempts which have been made to relate it to particular historical circumstances have carried conviction.

b **XXIV 1-20 The Judgment of the World**—This section may, for the sake of convenience, be treated in two parts. The first of these(1–13) consists of an oracle, begun in 1–3 and resumed in 13, describing the coming judgment, into which (4–12) has been worked an eschatological poem (or fragments) depicting the desolated earth. The second part (14–20) introduces a shout of joy over expected deliverance which the prophet cannot share (14–16), after which (17–20) the picture of judgment is resumed.

c **1-13.** An oracle (1–3) announces the judgment of God, fearful and imminent. The earth will be emptied out, laid waste, and its inhabitants scattered. No-one, high or low, will escape ; the judgment is decreed by Yahweh, and all must face it. In 4–12 the material has been taken from a poem describing the ruined earth and (10–12) a ruined city. The tenses are perfects. The earth languishes under a curse. It has been polluted by its inhabitants, who have transgressed the laws of God and violated the ' everlasting covenant ' made with Noah, forbidding bloodshed (Gen. 9:5f., 11, 16). So the earth, cursed as it was before the Flood, suffers for its guilt. Few indeed are left. All joy is ended, merry feasts with wine and song are no more. The proud, evil city is in ruins, its gates battered down, its houses shut and barred. It is idle to speculate what city is meant. Probably a poem describing the ruin of some enemy city is here applied to the judgment of the world powers who have oppressed God's people ; 13, a brief oracle, supplies this application, ' Thus it shall be——'

1. Begin : ' behold the Lord is about to empty out the earth——'. **twist its surface :** i.e. distort it, as an earthquake would. **2. As with the people—priest :** cf. Hos. 4:9. **10. the city of chaos :** ' the city of *tōhû* ' (cf. Gen. 1:2) ; probably a description of, not an epithet for, the city : i.e. ' the wasted city '. **13.** Cf. 17:6. 438c

14-20. The awful picture of judgment is interrupted by a shout of joy (14–16*a*), as those who have survived sing praises to Yahweh. The prophet in his mind hears the glad song ringing from one end of the earth to the other (cf. 42:10–12, 44:23, etc.). But, oppressed as he is with the fearful judgment yet to come, he answers the joyous cry with a sigh of woe (16*b*). Whereupon (17–20) the grim picture of wrath is resumed. Terror, the pit and the snare are upon the earth, and there is no escape. The judgment comes like a great new Deluge (18*b* ; cf. 5), or like a mighty earthquake that rocks the earth on its foundations. The earth rolls like a drunken man, sways like a flimsy watchman's hut in a high wind. Its crime lies heavy upon it ; it falls, no more to rise (cf. Am. 5:2). d

14f. Perhaps : ' These (i.e. the redeemed) lift up their voice, they sing for the majesty of Yahweh, they shout from the west, they exult (Procksch) in the east (lit. ' the lights '), they give glory to Yahweh on the coasts of the sea ——'. **16. the Righteous One :** i.e. God. But the ' righteous ' (i.e. vindicated) people, Israel, may be intended (cf. 26:2). **I pine away :** lit. ' leanness to me ', in contrast to ' glory (honour) to the righteous ' one. **17f.** Cf. Jer. 48:43f. **windows of heaven :** cf. Gen. 7:11, 8:2. **19** uses powerful word-plays incapable of exact translation : ' shattered-shivered is the earth, rent-riven is the earth, shaken-staggered is the earth '.

XXIV 21-XXVI 6 Prophecies of Yahweh's Triumph interspersed with Songs of Praise—Following hard upon the foregoing there comes a section consisting of three oracles (24:21–23, 25:6–8, 10–12) telling of the triumph of Yahweh's rule, each answered by a hymn of thanksgiving (25:1–5, 9, 26:1–6). e

XXIV 21-23 The Enthronement of Yahweh on Mt Zion—This oracle leads from the foregoing into the hymn which follows. It builds on the myth of the struggle of the high god against a rebellion in heaven, which in Judaism would have been interpreted as Yahweh's conflict with rebellious angels and their earthly minions. ' On that day ' (i.e. the day of judgment just described) Yahweh will punish his foes celestial and terrestrial, casting them into the pit where they await final judgment (cf. 2 Pet. 2:4 ; Rev. 20:1–3). Then, as sun and moon pale before him (cf. 60:19 ; Rev. 21:23), Yahweh mounts his kingly throne in Zion, manifesting his glory before the elders of his people. This is the fruition of covenant theology. As the seventy elders at Sinai beheld the glory of Yahweh (Exod. 24:9f.) and entered into covenant with him to be his vassals, so in the end the elders of Israel will gather about the throne and see the glory of the King of the universe. f

21. in heaven : lit. ' in the height ' ; in the myth the mountain of the gods in the far north (cf. 14:12–15 ; Ezek. 28:11–19), but here, of course, heaven. Identified with the heavenly bodies (e.g. 40:26), the ' host of heaven ' at times became objects of worship (e.g. Dt. 4:19 ; 2 Kg. 17:16, 21:3, 5, etc.). **23. will reign :** better, ' is king ', ' has mounted the throne '.

XXV 1-5 A Psalm of Thanksgiving—The description of Yahweh's enthronement is followed appropriately by a hymn praising him for his redeeming acts. This hymn originally (2) celebrated the fall of some enemy city, though which one cannot be said (cf. 10–12 ; Ps. 60:9, 108:10) ; in the present context it hails the final victory of Yahweh, conceived of as having already taken place. Yahweh has carried out his marvellous purposes, formed of old and sure. He has brought low the power of his foes ; strong nations stand in awe of him. He has been a mighty fortress to his ' poor ' and ' needy ' people, against whom the g

438g blast of the tyrant has blown like a howling storm or a scorching wind. As clouds cut the searing heat, so has Yahweh stilled the exulting of the foe.

2. the palace of the aliens is a city no more: perhaps (*zēdhîm* for *zārîm* : LXX ; *m^{e}'ôrār* for *mē'îr* : Kissane) read : 'the palace of the insolent ones is razed'. **4. a storm against a wall:** read (*kōr* for *kîr*), 'a winter storm'. **5. aliens:** 'insolent', as in 2.

h **6-8 The Eschatological Banquet**—The thought of 24:21–23 is resumed. There Yahweh has taken his throne on Mt Zion ; here on the same mountain there is spread the coronation feast of the King (cf. 1 Kg. 1:9, 25). His rule now being triumphant, 'all peoples' are bidden. All will be joy, for Yahweh will take the veil of mourning from the face of the world. Death, who swallows up men in the grave, will himself be swallowed up (i.e. abolished). God will wipe away all tears, and the reproach of his people, who have suffered so much, he will remove. The notion of the abolition of death found here is a novel one in the OT ; but the first clause of 8 is not to be omitted as an insertion (e.g. Duhm). The language is of very ancient origin, possibly deriving ultimately from the myth of Baal's victory over Mot (Heb. *mōth*, *māweth*, means 'death'), god of death and the underworld, whereby fertility was (annually) restored to the earth. The present passage, however, is in no sense mythological. Death is not personified. Nor have we to do with a cyclic restoration of nature, but with the abolition of the curse of death at the issue of history (cf. Gen. 3:19, 22f.). There is no mention of resurrection (but cf. 26:19) or heaven here ; but the NT plays upon this passage in describing the present and future victory of the risen Christ over the 'last enemy' (1 C. 15:26, 54 ; Rev. 21:4). The notion of the great sacrificial feast is frequently linked with that of the Day of Yahweh (cf. Zeph. 1:7 ; Ezek. 39:17–20) ; cf. also the marriage supper of the Lamb (Rev. 19:9, 17f. ; cf. Mt. 22:1–14 ; Lk. 14:15–24), and the words of the Lord's Supper (Mt. 26:29 ; Mk 14:25 ; Lk. 22:18 ; 1 C. 11:26) pointing forward to the victory of Christ's kingdom.

i **9 A Hymn of Praise**—Like 24:21–23, 25:6–8 is followed by a hymn. We have waited for Yahweh's salvation ; now let us rejoice in it. The words 'it will be said on that day' are the nexus with which the author links the hymn, which he quotes, to the preceding oracle.

j **10-12 The Overthrow of 'Moab'**—Mention of a specific enemy, Moab, is surprising in the context, but there is no reason to emend the word. The poet has taken over a traditional doom oracle on Moab (cf. chs. 15f. ; Jer. 48, etc.) and used it to express the fate of Yahweh's foes in general. It is doubtful if any particular outrage on the part of the Moabites is in his mind. The figure employed is somewhat obscure, and not too elegant. Moab will be trodden down like straw in a dung-pit. He struggles to get out, flailing his arms as one trying to swim, but to no avail. **12** illustrates the conventional nature of the material ; cf. 26:5.

439a **XXVI 1-6 A further Hymn of Thanksgiving and Praise**—The psalm is a liturgy for a triumphal procession (cf. Ps. 24). The words 'in that day' (1*a*) link it to the preceding piece. It begins with praise of Zion's strength, whose defence is Yahweh. Then comes the call to open the gates that the victorious, vindicated nation, trusting in God and guarded by him, may enter. Then follows the call to rely forever on Yahweh the everlasting rock ; he has humbled the proud enemy city so that the feet of his 'poor' and 'needy' people (cf. 25:4) trample it.

1. Cf. 60:18 ; Ps. 48:13f. **salvation:** i.e. deliverance, protection. **2.** Cf. Ps. 118:19f. ; Rev. 22:14. **righteous:** i.e. 'vindicated through victory' (cf. 24:16). **3.** Probably read : 'steadfast of purpose, thou dost guard her peace (welfare), because she trusts in thee' (Scott). **4. an everlasting rock:** lit. 'a rock of ages'. **5.** Cf. 25:2, 12.

439b **7-19 A Prayer of Entreaty and Trust**—This piece carries forward the thought of the preceding hymn without break. But since it is cast in the form of a psalm of entreaty, such as was recited in solemn assembly in time of calamity (cf. Ps. 44, 60, 74), it is better to treat it separately. The opening cry of complaint (cf. Ps. 60:1ff., 74:1) is missing, but in 7 we have the accompanying assertion of confidence in Yahweh's justice. The community protests (8f.) its loyalty to Yahweh : it has eagerly awaited the time when his law will be supreme and all people will learn righteousness. The wicked, however, will not do so (10f.) ; even under optimum conditions they will continue to do evil. They will, therefore, find no favour. May they, to their own confusion, see the uplifted hand of Yahweh which they had always refused to see ! In 12-15 the people again voice their trust in Yahweh, who will bring them peace. They have had many lords, but they acknowledge none but Yahweh. These tyrants die, never to rise again, but Israel will receive the promised enlargement and vindication. 16–18 returns to the national distress. Israel has laboured like a woman in childbirth, but nothing has come of her agony. How can the hoped-for enlargement ever be ? 19 gives the answer : God will cause his dew to fall upon the dead bodies of his loyal ones and, unlike the other dead (14), they will awake and sing for joy. The verse affirms the resurrection of the righteous only, and is the earliest mention of a resurrection in the Bible. In Dan. 12:2, a later passage, the apostates too are resurrected for punishment. But some see here only the resurrection of the nation (cf. Ezek. 37).

c **8. thy memorial name:** lit. 'thy name and thy remembrance', i.e. the sacred name by which Yahweh was solemnly invoked. The two words are virtually synonymous (cf. Exod. 3:15 ; Ps. 135:13). The name stands for the essential nature ; Yahweh's name is known and remembered in his mighty acts. **9a.** Read : 'With my soul I yearn—with my spirit—I seek thee'. As often in the Psalms, the first person singular stands for the worshipping congregation. **soul** does not have its present-day connotation, but rather signifies the life, the totality of the being, the desires, etc. **10.** Perhaps (Marti) the negative has been lost by haplography, and we should read : 'The wicked will be shown no favour——'. **11c.** Perhaps read (LXX) : 'let fire consume thy adversaries'. **12.** The sense is probably : Lord, do thou give us peace, for thou hast rewarded us as our deeds deserved. **13. other lords:** primarily earthly lords (cf. 14), though the gods of the earthly overlords may also be intended. **15.** Some see here an allusion to an enlargement of Jewish territory but, if so, the circumstances cannot be identified. It is probable that traditional material celebrating Yahweh's vindication of his people (cf. 9:3) is here quoted as a hope for the future. **16.** The text is very difficult. Possibly we should read : 'O Yahweh, in the stress of thy punishment we cried out ; thy chastisement has pressed hard upon us'. **18. have not fallen:** i.e. been overthrown. But some (RVm) read 'have not been born' (i.e. the land is still depopulated). **19.** Perhaps (LXX, 1QIs^{a}) : 'they who dwell in the dust will awake and sing for joy'. But possibly 19*a* should be read as a petition : 'let thy dead live, etc.' **dew of light:** either the dew of the heavenly regions of light (cf. Ps. 104:2), or the 'dew of the dawn' (or, the 'glistening dew') which gives life to vegetation.

d **XXVI 20-XXVII 13 Assurance and Encouragement for Israel**—The concluding section of the prophecy consists of an oracle in response to the foregoing psalm of entreaty, calling upon Yahweh's people to take shelter till the judgment has passed (26:20–27:1), a poem describing Yahweh's care for his 'vineyard' (27:2–6), a reflection on the meaning of Israel's suffering (27:7–11), and two brief oracles (27:12f.) announcing her ingathering.

e **XXVI 20-XXVII 1 Hide until the Judgment has**

439e **passed !**—The prophet comforts his people with the thought of the imminence of the judgment. It is coming soon, and it will be terrible—but brief. Hide and wait till it has passed ! Yahweh will judge this blood-stained world, guilty thousands of times over of the sin of Cain, and from him no crime will be hid. 'In that day' he will slay Leviathan—a mythical monster which here stands as a symbol for Yahweh's foes celestial and terrestrial—and thus put a final end to all the powers of chaos and evil.

f **XXVI 21 is coming:** 'is about to come'. **disclose the blood—slain:** crimes long hidden will be revealed. The blood of the slain was thought to cry out of the ground for vengeance (cf. Gen. 4:8–12, 37:26).

XXVII 1. One monster, not three, is in question. The verse has a close parallel in the myths of Râs Shamra (I AB, 1:1) : 'Because (when) you smote Lotan (Leviathan) the writhing serpent, destroyed the twisting serpent, the accursed one (?) with seven heads' (cf. C. H. Gordon, *Ugaritic Literature* (1949), 38f.). In Ps. 74:13f. Leviathan is many-headed. The monster appears elsewhere as Leviathan (Ps. 104:26), the Dragon (51:9 ; Ps. 74:13 ; Job 7:12, etc.), Rahab (51:9 ; Ps. 89:10 ; Job 26:12), the Serpent (Am. 9:3), or simply Sea (51:10 ; Hab. 3:8 ; Job 26:12, etc.). Egypt is on occasion called Rahab (30:7 ; cf. Ezek. 29:3, 32:2), but there is no allusion to any specific historical power here. The myth tells how the god slew, or imprisoned, the chaos monster in order to create the world. Projected, as here, into the realm of eschatology, this becomes a symbol for Yahweh's final triumph over all rebel powers (cf. 24:21f.) and the establishment of his kingly rule.

g **XXVII 2-6 A Song of Yahweh's Vineyard**—With the words 'in that day' a poem, perhaps very ancient, telling of Yahweh's loving care for Israel, is given an eschatological frame of reference. The poem develops the motif of 5:1–7, but in reverse direction, for here Yahweh is highly pleased with his vineyard and guards it tenderly from all harm. Let foes (thorns and briers) attack it, and he will trample them and burn them if they do not surrender. So Israel will in days to come flourish like a great vine and fill the earth with fruit.

2. Perhaps the opening formula originally read, 'In that day shall this song be sung' (cf. 26:1), or the like. **a pleasant vineyard:** the reading is well supported and probably correct ; MT reads 'a vineyard of wine'. **4. I have no wrath:** i.e. against Israel. The line goes with 3. **set out against them:** perhaps, 'tread on them'. **6.** As in 5:7, the identity of the vineyard is revealed only at the end.

h **7-11 A Reflection on the Meaning of Israel's Suffering**—This passage is possibly fragmentary, and is so exceedingly obscure that confident interpretation is impossible. The poet's mind seems to flash back from 'that day' (1, 2, 6) to Israel in her present suffering. He asks if Israel has been smitten as severely as her oppressors have been. It is implied that she has not. This thought is carried forward in 10f. The 'fortified city', symbolic of Israel's foes (cf. below), is vacated like an abandoned camp where cattle lie and nibble the branches which, in turn, are gathered and burned. These are people without understanding upon whom Yahweh will have no pity. But Israel is not so (8f.). Yahweh made his case against her and executed the sentence of exile. But Israel may yet expiate her sins if only she will put away idolatry and return to her God.

8. Measure by measure, by exile: very uncertain. Perhaps read, 'by driving her out, sending her away, thou didst argue thy case with her'. **east wind:** the sirocco, a searing wind from the desert, often used to describe the divine judgment (cf. Jer. 4:11f., 18:17 ; Hos. 31:15). **9. by this:** i.e. on these terms. They are stated in 9*b*. **10. the fortified city:** in this context hardly Jerusalem, as some think, but probably the enemy city of 24:10, 25:2, 26:5, identification of which is impossible.

i **12f. The Ingathering of Israel**—The prophecy ends with two brief oracles introduced with 'in that day'. Yahweh will thresh his harvest (cf. Jl 3:13 ; Mt. 13:39 ; Rev. 14:15) from the Euphrates to the Egyptian frontier—i.e. throughout the ideal bounds of Israel (Gen. 15:18)—separating his loyal people from the heathen. A great trumpet will sound (cf. Mt. 24:31 ; 1 C. 15:52 ; 1 Thess. 4:16), calling Jews wandering beyond those ideal bounds to worship Yahweh on Mt Zion. 439i

12. the Brook of Egypt: the Wâdī el-'Arîsh, *c.* 50 miles SW. of Gaza. **13. those who were lost:** the word (*hā 'ôbhedhîm*) is used in the ancient cultic confession of Dt. 26:5 : 'a wandering Aramean (*'arammî 'ōbhēdh*) was my father'.

XXVIII-XXXIII The basic material of these chapters is Isaiah's and relates for the most part to the Assyrian crisis in the reign of Hezekiah. Certain portions, however, cannot be dated with assurance, while others appear to be post-Isaianic (cf. below). The material is arranged, somewhat artificially perhaps, in a series of complexes each introduced by the word *hôi* ('Woe ! Alas !') : cf. 28:1, 29:1, 15, 30:1, 31:1, 33:1. 440a

XXVIII 1-29 The first 'Woe' Complex: the Dissolute and Unbelieving Nobles—The section falls into three parts : 1–13, 14–22 and 23–29. The first of these is itself composite. 1–4, pronouncing doom on the proud and besotted nobles of Samaria, must have been first uttered before the last siege of that city (726/5 or earlier), But it is here used as a prelude to 7–13, which addresses the equally drunken and incorrigible nobles of Judah, and which was apparently spoken as rebellion against Assyria broke out after the death of Sargon (705). This general date also suits 14–22 ; 23–29 cannot be dated exactly, but may have been uttered at about the same time. On 5f., usually regarded as an insertion, see below. b

1-13 The Drunkards who guide the National Policy—The section begins with the quotation of an oracle uttered before the fall of Samaria (1–4). Woe to the drunken princes of Ephraim ! Their proud city, set on its tall hill and encircled by walls, is like the faded garland on a reveller's head. Yahweh will send (and now has sent) his agent, Assyria, who comes with hurricane force, snatches off the proud crown and tramples it under foot. Ephraim is gobbled up like a choice bit of fruit. The oracle of hope in 5f. (cf. below) is used here as a transition. 'In that day' Yahweh himself—not a drunkard's garland or strong city walls—will be the glorious crown of the remnant of his people (Judah). He will impart justice to the judges and give strength to repel the foe. So the ideal. But what a 'remnant' (7f.) ! All drunk ! The prophet too drunk to give an oracle, the priest too befuddled to give *tôrāh* ! They have turned the sacrificial feast into a sickening debauch. But when Isaiah rebukes them they mock him (9f.). Who does he think we are ? Does he take us for children that he stands over us like a schoolmaster monotonously repeating the lesson ? Isaiah is infuriated (11–13). Very well, since you will not hear Yahweh's lesson spelled out in plain Hebrew, it will be taught you in Assyrian ! Yahweh has told you often enough that your true hope is to trust in him, but you would not listen. So now the lesson will begin indeed—and it will be one at which you will fail ! c

1. Perhaps (Kissane), with a transposition, begin: 'Woe to the proud crown of the drunkards of Ephraim, they who are overcome with wine !' **2. with violence:** lit. 'with the hand' ; cf. 'underfoot' (3). **4. first-ripe fig:** ripe before the normal season (late summer), a great delicacy (cf. Mic. 7:1 ; Jer. 24:2). **5f.** seems to fit poorly in context ; a promise to the remnant seems strange between a threat to Israel and a threat to Judah. Most scholars regard this as a later addition, and this may be correct. But the theology is certainly Isaianic. 1–13 combines words of Isaiah uttered at different dates, and he may well have uttered these, though no doubt originally in another context. d

440d Placed where they are, they provide a powerful contrast between the prophetic ideal of the remnant and the actual ' remnant ', Judah ; they lead into 7 (' these too ——'). **10. precept upon precept — line upon line :** the Hebrew cannot be translated ; it would be better simply to transliterate : *ṣaw lāṣāw ṣaw lāṣāw ḳaw lāḳāw ḳaw lāḳāw.* Perhaps this mimics the babble of babies or, better, a class repeating the lesson by rote after the schoolmaster. **here a little, there a little :** either ' a little at a time ' or (Procksch) the teacher calling on his pupils, ' the little one here, the little one there '. **11. strange :** lit. ' stammering ' ; so Assyrian speech would sound to Hebrews. **12** is characteristic of Isaiah's political advice : Israel's only hope is to trust Yahweh and refrain from foreign entanglements (cf. v. 16, 7:9, 30:15, etc.).

e **14-22 The Covenant with ' Death '**—This oracle follows hard on the foregoing. Isaiah addresses the nobles who have scouted his advice and made treaty with Egypt, invoking the names of pagan gods and looking to them for protection. Listen, you scoffers ! You think your treaty, and the gods in whose names it has been made, will save you when the Assyrian tide rolls through the land ? You should have known what the true refuge is—the building which Yahweh has founded on Zion, whose cornerstone is faith and which is erected in justice and righteousness (16–17*a*) —and you should have trusted in that, for it will endure. As for your flimsy shelter, the Assyrian will come like a boiling flood, and will sweep it away. Your covenant with ' Death ' will not help you, and the divine word will be one of doom which it will be sheer terror to hear. You have worked yourselves and your country into a trap from which you cannot extricate yourselves (20). Yahweh will indeed rise to act as he did for David but—how strange !—against you. Now stop your scoffing lest you be bound by your folly past all escaping. For the decree of Yahweh is destruction !

f **15. death — Sheol :** ' death ' (Heb. *môth*) is also the name of the Canaanite god of the underworld and infertility. Since the pact was with Egypt, reference is probably to Egyptian deities of similar character (Osiris ? Seth ?) in whose name the pact was sealed ; cf. ' lies ', ' falsehood ', which are prophetic terms for false gods. Of course, the words are Isaiah's, not the plotter's own. **overwhelming scourge :** ' overwhelming flood ' (cf. K-B) ; so also in 18. **16-17a. a tested stone :** ' a *bōḥan* stone '. The word (cf. K-B) is Egyptian and denotes a type of hard stone suitable for carving. It is the cornerstone of Yahweh's building, and bears the inscription, ' he who believes (trusts) will not be alarmed ' (cf. 12, 7:9, 30:15). The building has been variously interpreted as the future remnant, the Temple, the monarchy, Yahweh himself, the Messiah, etc. However understood, the relationship of God and people, founded upon trust, is the central idea. The NT frequently plays on this passage (cf. Rom. 9:33, 10:11 ; 1 Pet. 2:6f.). **20.** A proverb for an intolerable situation which no expedient can remedy. **21.** Reference is to David's victory over the Philistines (2 Sam. 5:20, 25, reading ' Gibeon ' for ' Geba ' with 1 Chr. 14:11f., 16).

g **23-29 The Farmer and his Crops : a Parable**—The prophet here speaks in the style of a contemporary wisdom teacher. The meaning of the parable is not wholly clear because of obscurities in the text, and because no interpretation is appended. Does the ploughman, when he has turned and harrowed his land, go on doing it over and over ? No, when he has prepared the soil, he puts in the various kinds of seed, each in the place best suited for it. And this wisdom he has from God. Too, different grains are threshed differently. Dill and cummin are not threshed by driving a sledge over them, but are beaten out with sticks. Bread grain must be ground ; the farmer does not, therefore, go on endlessly driving his cart over it, for this separates it but does not grind it. And this too is God-given wisdom. The meaning seems to be that, in the realm of history, 440g
Yahweh also acts purposively and as suits the occasion. He does not behave haphazardly, nor always in the same way. He does not plough aimlessly, but to put in a crop (i.e. to work a purpose) ; and he does not handle every crop alike (i.e. he deals with each situation as his purpose requires). The inference is that Israel ought to show as much sense as the farmer. Some situations call for resistance, some for passive submission. Let the national policy conform to the circumstances and the divine purpose, and not stubbornly press on in one single course which can lead only to ruin.

25. in rows—in its proper place : two obscure h
words, possibly the result of dittography. **28.** Very uncertain. The first line is probably not a question (cf. RV) ; ' with his horses ' (*ûphārāshāw*) is unlikely, for horses were not used for this work. Reading (*ûph^{e}rāśô*), ' he spreads it out ' (separates it ?), translate : ' Bread grain is ground. Surely he does not go on threshing it forever. When he drives his cart-wheel over it, he separates it but does not grind it.'

XXIX 1-14 The second ' Woe ' Complex : 441a
Yahweh's Marvellous Work with Jerusalem—The section consists of three oracles : 1–8, 9–12, 13f. all of which relate to the Assyrian crisis in the reign of Hezekiah. In 1–8 a prophecy of doom is dramatically turned into one of hope. But it is unnecessary to regard the hopeful portion as a later insertion, for it is known that when Jerusalem was placed under siege Isaiah declared that the city would not be taken (cf. 37:6f., 21–29, 33–35). The passage is in this respect similar to 10:5–34, 14:24–27, etc. It is usually dated in 701 but, since a message of hope accords ill with Isaiah's known attitude on that occasion (cf. 1:2–9, 28:14–22, etc.), at least parts of it may relate to a later invasion of Sennacherib *c.* 688 (cf. §446).

1-8 The Distress and Deliverance of Ariel— b
Interpretation is complicated by obscurities in 5f. Some take 5*c*–6 as a continuation of the threat to Jerusalem, and therefore regard 5*ab* as misplaced from before 7. This last seems to be correct. But the hopeful message probably begins in 5c (' and in an instant, suddenly——'), and is continued in 6, 5*ab*, 7f. The prophet addresses a dirge (1–4) to Jerusalem, here called Ariel. There is a play (cf. below) on the meanings of that word (mountain of God, the great altar ; and denizen of the underworld, a shade), and perhaps also on the pre-Israelite name of the city. Ah, Ariel, city against which David once fought ! Let the yearly feasts come round a little while longer, and Yahweh will bring distress on Ariel. She will be like Jebusite Jerusalem which David once besieged ; she will be like an Ariel, a ghost, roused by a necromancer and feebly muttering and whispering from the dust. But then, in an instant, Yahweh will intervene in mercy, with storm, earthquake and fire (5*c*–6), and the foes of Ariel will be like driven chaff (5*ab*), or like a nightmare that passes. An empty dream, too, is the enemy's hope of feasting on Jerusalem.

1f. Ariel : here a name for Jerusalem. The word c
derives (ARI (3rd ed. 1953), 151ff.) from the Akkadian *arallu*, which has the dual meaning of ' the underworld ' and ' the mountain of the gods ' (i.e., the cosmic mountain where the gods are born and reared). Its Hebrew form is properly *har'ēl* (cf. Ezek. 43:15), ' the mountain of God '. It suggests the great altar of the Temple, built on a Canaanite pattern derived ultimately from Mesopotamia, where the stepped temple tower symbolised the cosmic mountain. The word also means ' denizen of the underworld ', ' a shade ' : ' and she (you) shall be to me like an Ariel —a ghost ' (2, cf. 4). It is just possible, too, that there is a further play on the pre-Israelite name of Jerusalem, Uru-salimu, with El (God) substituted for the name of the Canaanite deity Shalim. **where David encamped :** better, ' against which ——'. **yet I will distress :** better (RV), ' then (after a few

441c years) I will distress ——'. **3. round about:** lit. 'like a ball' (cf. 22:18), 'like a circle'. Better (LXX) read, 'like David' (*kᵉdhāwîdh* for *kaddûr*). **5. your foes** (*ṣārāyikh*) is preferable to MT (*zārāyikh*) 'your strangers'; 1QIsᵃ reads (*zēdhāyikh*) 'your insolent ones' (cf. 'ruthless').

d **9-12. The Spiritual Stupor of the People**—The thought is that of 6:9f. The people have stupefied themselves spiritually till they are like men who are too drunk to see what they are doing. This, too, is God's doing; for when men stultify their moral senses, it is God's judgment upon them that those moral senses be lost. It is as if Yahweh had drenched them with a deep sleep, so that the prophetic word is a sealed book to them: the educated man won't read it, and the ignorant can't.

9. RSV is probably correct, but a word play (cf. RV) is possible: 'Tarry long (in your drink) and be stupefied; take your pleasure and be blind.' **10.** Omit 'the prophets', 'the seers' as incorrect glosses. **11f.** 11*b*–12 is possibly, but not certainly, a prose expansion.

e **13f. Empty, Formal Religion rebuked**—Isaiah once more addresses the leaders who, trusting in their own cleverness, think to save the nation through alliance with Egypt. They call on Yahweh, to be sure, but only in an empty, formal manner (cf. 1:10–15); their hearts are far from him, their religion a hollow thing repeated by rote. So Yahweh must show himself again, as in the ancient days (cf. 10:24–27), as the one who *acts* toward his people—to judge, but also to rescue. He will act in such a way as to bring all their wisdom to confusion (cf. 1 C. 1:18f.).

13. Perhaps (LXX, Mt. 15:9) read (*wᵉthōhû* for *wattᵉhî*), 'and vain is their fear of me (i.e. their religion), a human commandment learned (by rote)'.

f **15-24 The third 'Woe' Complex: Doom on the Conspirators, with Hopeful Forecasts**—In 15 woe is pronounced (cf. 28:14f., 30:1f., 31:1) on those who make treaty with Egypt thinking that what they do is hidden from Yahweh. In 16 this is sharply rebuked: is the creature to deny his Creator and cast aspersions on his intelligence? Then follow two closely linked oracles (17–21, 22–24) describing the coming transformation and redemption of society. In a very little while the land will be transformed; those who had been deaf and blind (cf. 9f.) will hear Yahweh's word and see his work. Then the 'meek' and the 'poor' (i.e. Yahweh's loyal and oppressed people) will joy in their God, for ruthless injustice will be ended. Yahweh who redeemed Abraham will once more act (22–24), and when his people see this they will revere him and fear him. Even the errant and rebellious will come to right understanding.

While 15 is certainly Isaianic, 16 and 17–24 are probably later. It is true that Isaiah hoped for the purification and redemption of his people, but the language here is reminiscent of that of later literature (cf. 16 and 45:9f.; cf. 17–22 and 35:2, 5, 41:8, 17, 19, 42:16, etc.). But too late a date need not be assumed: 16 is probably based on a traditional saying, as is 17 (cf. 32:15), while the rest plays on stock prophetic ideas (cf. 21 and Am. 5:10, 12). The verses illustrate how Isaianic ideas were further developed among his later disciples.

g **16. You turn things upside down:** a guess; probably some words have been lost. **17.** The meaning could be that things will be reversed: Lebanon will become garden land, garden land a forest (i.e. the exalted will be humbled, and vice versa). But (cf. 32:15) the clauses are probably synonymous: what is now forest will become garden land, and what is now garden land will be thought no better than a forest. **21. by a word:** either by a false accusation, or (RV) 'in his cause'. **reproves in the gate:** i.e. calls injustice to account (cf. Am. 5:10, 12). The elders administered justice in the city gate. **with an empty plea:** i.e. with specious arguments deny redress to the innocent (Scott). **22. concerning:** read (*'ēl* for *'el*) 'the God of'. **23. his children:** probably a correct gloss on 'he': 'when he (i.e. his children) sees . . .' 441

442 **XXX 1-33 The fourth 'Woe' Complex: further Utterances concerning the Assyrian Crisis, with appended Oracles**—The basis of the section is a 'woe' against the alliance with Egypt (1–7). To this has been attached a summation of Isaiah's witness in the matter and an account of his written testament (8–17). Then follows a description of the future blessedness of the people (18–26), and a further oracle telling of the overthrow of Assyria (27–33). For discussion of date and critical problems, see below.

1-7 Woe to the Rebels who make League with Egypt—The oracle does not end with 5 (cf. below), but extends through 7. Like 28:14–22, 29:15, 31:1–3, it relates to the years just after the death of Sargon (705) when rebellion was being plotted against Assyria in alliance with Egypt. It was apparently uttered (2) just as the ambassadors of Judah set out on their mission. As elsewhere, Isaiah denounces this alliance. The plan was made without reference to God, and it has added to this the sin of invoking Egyptian gods (cf. below). It will, therefore, fail. Though Pharaoh seems both strong and receptive to the idea, Egypt is a people who cannot help. That caravan toiling down through the heat of the Negeb, laden with gifts, has been sent in vain, for Egypt's help is worthless. She is Rahab, the chaos monster, whose end is destruction. b

1. make a league: perhaps lit. 'pour out a libation', i.e. to Egyptian deities in sealing the treaty (cf. 28:15). **not of my spirit:** not inspired by me. **4. his officials . . . envoys:** i.e. Pharaoh's. **Zoan:** near the NE. frontier of Egypt (cf. 19:11). **Hanes:** the later Heracleopolis Magna, S. of Memphis, near the Fayum. Some have inferred that these places mark the limits of the Pharaoh's domain. If so, we have to do with one of the weak Pharaohs of the XXIII or XXIV Dynasties (e.g. Bocchoris (*c.* 716/15–710), who controlled parts of the Delta and little more, and the present passage must date in Sargon's reign, *c.* 715–711 (cf. ch. 20). But apparently the meaning is that, as the ambassadors set out from Jerusalem, news has come that Pharaoh's officials are waiting at Zoan on the frontier, while special messengers from his court have been reported at Hanes. The Pharaoh is almost certainly Shabaka of the XXV (Ethiopian) Dynasty (710/9–696/5; but cf. §85*d*), and the date *c.* 705–703. **6** seems by its title to begin a new section. But what follows is not a 'doom oracle' (cf. the series in chs. 13–23), specifically not against 'beasts of the Negeb'; the thought of the preceding is carried forward. Read probably (Scott) 'in the heat of' (*baḥᵃmath*) for 'beasts of' (*bahᵃmôth*), and 'they carry' (*yiśśᵉ'û*) for 'oracle' (*maśśā'*) as in 6*c*. The verse then begins: 'They carry through the heat of the Negeb, through a land of trouble . . .' **7. Rahab who sits still:** better (Gunkel) read (*hammoshbāth* for *hēm shebheth*), 'Rahab who is subdued'. On Rahab cf. §439*f*. c

8-17 A Summation of the Prophet's Witness, and a Written Testament—The passage is undoubtedly directed against Judah's policy in the years between 705 and 701. As once before (cf. 8:16–18) in the crisis of 735–733, so again, his advice having once more been flouted, Isaiah records what he has said as a witness for the future. Just what he wrote is unknown, but it was certainly (cf. Jer. 36) a representative selection of his utterances on the subject, possibly the nucleus of the oracles against the alliance with Egypt now found in chs. 28–31. The section consists of a private oracle to Isaiah (8–11), and two further oracles pronouncing the doom (12–14, 15–17). A written witness was needed so that Yahweh's word might be vindicated after the event. The people had never heeded the divine teaching, but had asked of their prophets only favourable oracles. They had told Isaiah to 'get out of the way' and stop prating about the Holy One of Israel. It is in the name of that very d

442d Holy One that Isaiah gives his rejoinder (12, 15). Because this people have despised his word and trusted in force and deceit, they have piled up a tale of guilt which is like a bulging wall about to crash down on them. It will smash them like a clay pot, leaving not the smallest sherd intact (12–14). Their only hope (15) is trust in Yahweh (cf. 7:9, 28:16). This was no call to inactivity, but to faith in Yahweh's purpose and deed ; it involved ' returning ' to him in penitence, ' rest ' from this restless plotting, quietness of mind and utter trust. But the people put trust in arms and alliances : ' we will speed on horses . . . ride on swift steeds '. Well, speed you shall—in pell-mell flight—and your pursuers will speed faster! However many you are, you will not stand ; you will be left like a lonely beacon on a hill. One is reminded once more of the ominous note in the name of Isaiah's son Shear-jashub (7:3, 10:22f.) : only a remnant will come back.

e **8. tablet :** a wooden writing-tablet. **book :** a papyrus or leather scroll. Presumably the prophet is to use one or the other. **9. lying sons :** i.e. who claim sonship but deny it in their actions (cf. 1:2). **10. illusions :** the people do not actually ask to be deceived, but only to hear ' smooth things ' (cf. Am. 2:12 ; Mic. 2:6). **12. oppression and perverseness :** i.e. force and deceit (Scott) ; or perhaps (*'iḳḳēsh* for *'ôshek*) ' crookedness and deceit '. **14. to take fire :** better ' to rake together, poke, bank ' (cf. K-B). **to dip up . . . cistern :** perhaps ' to splash water (into a vessel) from a shallow ditch or pond ' (cf. P. Reymond, VT, vii (1957), 202–7). **17b.** Perhaps (Kissane) read ' at the threat of five a myriad shall flee '.

f **18-26 Future Restoration and Blessing**—The passage is usually, and probably correctly, regarded as a later expansion of Isaiah's thought. This is not because of the sharp transition at 18—which in view of the manner in which the prophetic books were collected is not surprising—nor because Isaiah held no hope of the restoration of his people, but because (cf. 29:16–24) the passage both in language and thought contains many reminiscences of later literature (cf. 60:19f., 65:17–25). Except for 18, the whole is in prose and might almost be regarded as a commentary developing the thought of that verse. The felicity of Yahweh's rule as described here, based in obedience and issuing in material plenty, is thoroughly characteristic. Yahweh will wait till his time and then show mercy, for he is just and will not disappoint those who wait for him. No weeping then, for Yahweh's answer anticipates the cry of his people. Though he leads them through grievous times, he will be their teacher, pointing them to the right way whenever they are tempted to stray. Then they will get rid of their idols, and God will give them plenteous rain and good crops, so much so that even the work animals will eat provender of the best grain. Nature itself will be transfigured ; the moon will shine like the sun, and the sun will be seven times bright.

g **19. will answer :** lit. ' has (already) answered '. **20. your Teacher :** MT reads plural, but with singular verb. Most scholars take it to refer to God, and this is probably correct (cf. 2:3, 28:26; Ps. 25:8, 94:10, 12, etc.), though 20 hardly means that God will be seen with the physical eye. Some, however, read plural (cf. 1QIs^a) and take it as meaning teachers of the law. **25b** apparently refers to the day of Yahweh's judgment on the world. But the clause (Scott) may be displaced from the next section (q.v.). **26. as the light of seven days :** i.e. seven days' light in one. Some omit with LXX.

443a **27-33 Yahweh's mighty Intervention**—The drive of the passage is for the most part clear, but the text in places exhibits such disarray that little can be made of it. In particular, 29 seems incongruous in the context, as does the mention of timbrels and lyres in 32. Though RSV prints 29–33 as prose, it is probable that metre has been obscured by textual corruption. It has been plausibly suggested (Scott) that this corrup- 443a
tion is due in good part to the intrusion of a second poem into the text. This poem, consisting of 25*b*, 29 and some words from 32, may once have been written on the margin and then mechanically copied into the text at various places. Once this has been set aside, the remainder is a very consistent piece telling of Yahweh's judgment on Assyria, similar in tone to 10:24–34, 14:24–27, 29:5–8, etc., and presumably directed to the same circumstances. Yahweh comes from afar with awful might to the aid of his people (cf. Hab. 3:3–15 ; Jg. 5:4f., 20f. ; Ps. 18:7–15). His wrath is like a consuming fire or a river in flood. With his bridle he deliberately drives Assyria on to destruction ; with his brandished arm and chastening rod he strikes her. He has a hearth ready for his sacrifice, prepared for a king (Sennacherib !) ; with his flaming breath he will light it. The second poem (25*b*, 29, 32*b*) is one of joy. It reads (cf. Scott) : ' In the day of the great slaughter, when the towers fall, you shall have a song as in the night when a pilgrim feast is hallowed ; and gladness of heart, as when one sets out to the sound of the flute to go to the mountain of Yahweh, with timbrels and lyres and whirling dances (*m^{e}ḥôlôth* for *milḥ^{a}môth*) to the Rock of Israel '. This poem, if in context, belongs at the end.

27. the name : to the Semite the name manifests the b
character ; the character of Yahweh is disclosed in his mighty acts. **in thick rising smoke** is questionable. Perhaps read ' burning is his anger and grievous his burden (of judgment) '. **28. sift . . . sieve :** also questionable. Perhaps read (cf. K-B), ' to jerk the nations with the yoke of destruction '. **32.** Very obscure ; cf. the larger commentaries. Removing the intruded words (cf. above), the verse may originally have read : ' And every stroke shall be by his chastising rod, which Yahweh will lay upon him ; battling with brandished arm (?) he will fight with them '. **33.** Read : ' for ready long ago is his burning place (Tophet) ; it too is prepared for a king . . . ' The verse plays upon the name of the spot in the Valley of Hinnom where children were made ' to pass through the fire ' to Molech (2 Kg. 23:10 ; Jer. 7:31f., etc.). Molech (Malk) ' the king ', is the appellation of a pagan god. Yahweh's Tophet is also ready for a king—the king of Assyria.

XXXI 1-XXXII 20 The fifth ' Woe ' Complex. c
Further Oracles of Condemnation, Warning and Hope—As in the case of the preceding sections, the basic element of this collection is a woe pronounced against the Egyptian alliance which stands (cf. 29:1–8) in dramatic contrast to a word of hope (31:1–9). To this has been appended, perhaps rather artificially, further oracles of warning and hope of uncertain date, some of them possibly—but not certainly—later than Isaiah.

XXXI 1-9 The Folly of Reliance on Egypt ; d
Yahweh's Defence of Zion—1-3, a companion piece to 30:1–7, belongs to the years between 705 and 701. 4-9 was spoken as Isaiah became convinced that Yahweh would not let Zion fall (cf. 29:5–8, 37:21–35, etc.) ; usually dated in 701, it may refer to a later invasion *c.* 688 (cf. §446). 6f. interrupts the thought and is an intrusion, though very possibly Isaianic (cf. 2:20), from another context. 4f. presents serious difficulties not evident in RSV. The words ' fight upon ' would more naturally be rendered ' fight against ' (cf. 29:7) ; this would have Yahweh first attacking (4), then defending (5), Jerusalem. But such an abrupt shift is unlikely, while the sense of 4-9 is that Jerusalem will be defended. One may omit (Scott) ' to fight ' as a dittograph of ' of hosts ' ; or one may regard the words ' so the Lord . . . like birds hovering ' as an intrusion, thus retaining only the figure of the lion who refuses to be scared off his prey ; or one may accept the rendition of RSV as a possible, if not the most natural, one : Yahweh will ' wage war on ' Mt Zion. For further discussion see the larger commentaries.

443d Woe to those who have sent to Egypt for help! They put their trust in horses and chariots because this is the sort of power that they can understand. But they do not look to Yahweh or consult his will. Yet, says Isaiah with sarcasm, ' he too is wise ', perhaps as wise as you—wise enough, at any rate, to bring disaster! And he does not go back on his word! He has forbidden this course and, since you have taken it, he will rise against you and the Egyptians who help you. Who do you think the Egyptians are—God? No, they are men; and their horses are nothing but flesh. Yahweh is God and will have his way. Yet he does not purpose to let the Assyrians have Jerusalem. Like a lion growling over his prey, undaunted by the shouts of the shepherds who try to frighten him away, so Yahweh will defend Jerusalem. Then, says the insertion (6f.), you will return to Yahweh and throw your idols away. The Assyrian will fall (7f.) by no human sword, but before Yahweh. His army will break in panic and flee.

e **5. he will spare:** lit. ' passing over ' (AV), of the same root as ' Passover ' and possibly containing an allusion to the Exodus deliverance. **8. and he shall flee from the sword:** another reading (cf. 1QIs[a]) is, ' and he will flee, but not from the sword (of man) '. **9a.** Hopelessly obscure and never satisfactorily explained. The sense apparently is that the Assyrian army, officers and men alike, break in panic and flee. **fire . . . furnace:** cf. 29:1f., 30:33.

f **XXXII 1-8 Just Rulers and a rightly ordered Society**—The passage is capable of two interpretations. Read as in EVV, it is a prediction that a just king will one day rule with a transforming effect on society. It would thus fall in a class with the other Messianic passages of the book (9:1–7, 11:1–9), but with the figure of the Messianic king much less clear and definite than elsewhere. So viewed, 6-8 might be regarded as an addition in the style of wisdom literature. But the sense is probably hypothetical rather than predictive. If a righteous king and princes were in power (or when . . .), then rulers would be protectors of the people and a source of blessing to them. The moral blindness that plagues the land would be removed. The voluble, inconsiderate complainant would learn restraint, while he who hesitates to speak up because of timidity would no longer fear to do so. No more would the impious knave be called noble, for each would be seen for what he is. After all, the knave can be told by his deeds, and so can the man of nobility. The former is godless, callous, dishonest, ready to take unjust advantage of the weak; the latter is known by his noble deeds. So understood, it is unnecessary to regard 6-8 as an addition, for the whole passage is in the style of the wisdom teaching (cf. Prov. 13–15, 16:10–15, 20:8, 26, 28, 25:5, etc.). But this is not in itself sufficient reason to deny it to Isaiah. No idea expressed here is inconsonant with his theology; and he has elsewhere (28:23–29) cast his message in the form of wisdom teaching. Wisdom teaching in Israel was far older than Isaiah, while the tradition (Prov. 25:1) that it enjoyed a renaissance under Hezekiah should not be dismissed cavalierly. On the other hand, it must be admitted that positive evidence of Isaianic authorship is lacking. While nothing forbids this, the passage could represent the moral instruction of later disciples. The question of authorship and date must, therefore, be left open.

g **1f.** Better translated, ' When a king reigns in righteousness, and princes rule in justice, then each (of them) will be . . . '; or, ' If a king were to reign in righteousness . . . then each would be . . . ', and read ' would ' for ' will ' through 5. No particular king is envisioned, but a hypothetical—and desired—situation. **3. eyes . . . not be closed:** contrast 6:10, 29:9. **5ff. fool:** not merely a stupid person, but one who is impious and knavish, and whose conduct breaches public morality and the law of Yahweh.

9-14 Warning to the Complacent Women of Judah—The passage is somewhat parallel to 3:16–4:1, and may come from the earliest period of Isaiah's ministry. The prophet addresses the women, joyous and careless, perhaps at a vintage feast, and calls on them to hear. In a little more than a year they will not be rejoicing, for vintage and harvest will have failed. They will put on sackcloth and mourn for the lovely fields and fine vineyards now growing up in thorns, and for the happy homes of the joyous city among whose deserted ruins the flocks graze. 444a

10b. Translate (cf. Scott), ' for the vintage will have failed, and the fruit harvest will not come '. **12.** The text is confused; MT begins, ' on the breasts they (masc.) are mourning '. Possibly ' on the breasts ' is a variant of ' on the loins ' (11), and 12 should read, ' mourn (*s^ephōdhāh*) for the pleasant fields, the fruitful vine '. **13f. the joyful city:** Jerusalem; cf. the same words in 22:2. **the hill** (*'ōphel*): the hill S. of the Temple area on which the original city was built.

15-20 The Transforming Outpouring of the Spirit of Yahweh—In its present position the passage continues, and reverses, 9–14. While this connection may not be original, the passage is a typical prophetic description of the ideal order to come. It is possible that (cf. 29:17–24, with which there are verbal similarities) it represents a development of conventional prophetic motifs in the school of Isaiah. But one ought to be very cautious in denying it to the prophet himself, for the ideas are for the most part characteristically his (cf. 17 and 30:15, etc.; also 11:1–9). The date, therefore, must be left an open question. In that future day, Yahweh will pour out his spirit on the earth (cf. 44:3; Jl 2:28f.; Ac. 2, etc.). Nature will be transformed (cf. 35:1f., 7, 55:13, etc.), and justice and righteousness will reign everywhere. As a result, peace and confident trust in Yahweh will obtain. Happy are those who see the day—who plant beside abundant streams and let their stock run free, unafraid of drought, wild beast or robber. b

15. Cf. 29:17. The steppe will become tilled land, and what is now tilled land will bear luxuriant growth. **19.** RSV gets the approximate sense, though the verse may be an intrusion from another context. But perhaps read, ' And when the forest comes crashing down, and the city is utterly laid low, happy are ye——'.

XXXIII 1-24 The sixth ' Woe ': Judah's Present Distress and Future Deliverance—The chapter forms a connected discourse in which prophetic oracles are interspersed with entreaty (2), lamentation (7–9), and dialogue of a liturgical type (14–16). Though it may never itself have been used as such, the piece may have been patterned on liturgies of entreaty such as were recited in the Temple (cf. Ps. 12, 20, 60, 85). The situation presupposed is uncertain. A foe is reproached for attacking and plundering without excuse (1) and in violation of treaty (7f.). If the poem be Isaiah's, some action of Assyria must be in question, such as a demand for unconditional surrender after Hezekiah's submission in 701. But, though such a thing may have happened, we have no record of an Assyrian attack in violation of treaty. Because of stylistic features not otherwise found in Isaiah, the passage is usually—and probably correctly—regarded as of later date. On the other hand, to relate it as some have done to some incident in the Maccabaean wars (e.g. the perfidy of Lysias and the destruction of the Temple fortress in 162) is most precarious. It is doubtful if any part of the prophetic canon is so late. The date of the passage must be left unsettled. Whether it contains a nucleus of Isaiah's words, which have been expanded with conventional material and applied to a later situation, likewise cannot be determined with assurance. Though the chapter is a connected discourse, it may for the sake of convenience be treated in three parts: 1–6, 7–16 and 17–24. c

1-6. The section begins with a woe on the oppressor d

444d who has destroyed and played false without the slightest provocation. In the end he will taste his own medicine. Then follows a prayer of entreaty : Yahweh, have pity on us and be our defence continually, saving us in time of trouble. An oracle then gives assurance that he will indeed do this. The nations will flee before him, and great spoil will be gathered. Yahweh, who dwells on high, will fill Zion with justice and righteousness, deliverance, wisdom and knowledge ; and these gifts will be her treasure.

1. Cf. the same words in 21:2. **2. Be our arm every morning :** i.e. be our strength and defence continually. **6.** The text is uncertain. Perhaps for ' your times ' read ' her store ' (*ᵃthîdhôthehā*), and transpose the first two lines ; 6 then continues 5 : ' — abundant deliverance, wisdom and knowledge ; and faithfulness will be her store, the fear of Yahweh—that will be her treasure.'

e **7-16.** The envoys of Jerusalem make lament. The foe has broken treaty, scorned those who were its witnesses, and shown regard for no man. Travel is unsafe, the roads are deserted (cf. Jg. 5:6) and nature itself languishes. 10–13 is an answering oracle. Yahweh will arise and intervene ; his fiery breath will consume the foe and his plans as if thorns or stubble. People far and near will see what Yahweh has done and acknowledge his might. Then comes (14–16) a liturgical dialogue (cf. Ps. 15, 24:3–5) describing the terror of sinners in Zion. Who can abide the fire of Yahweh's wrath ? Only those who are upright in all things and despise evil in thought, word and deed. Such will dwell as if in an impregnable fortress amply provisioned.

7. the valiant ones : the meaning of the word (*'er'ellām*) is uncertain. Perhaps it should be taken as a plural of Ariel (*'ᵃrî'ēlîm*) and understood as ' men of Jerusalem ' (cf. 29:1f.). If so, ' peace ' (*shālôm*) may conceal (Kissane) the name Salem (cf. Gen. 14:18 ; Ps. 76:2). **8.** Read : ' He has voided the covenant, despised the witnesses ; he has regard for no man '. Possibly transpose 8*a* and 8*b*. **11. your breath is a fire :** with a slight change, ' my breath like a fire will consume you '. **13.** Possibly (cf. 1QIs[a]) read verbs as prophetic perfects : ' those far off hear—those near acknowledge '. **14. can dwell :** i.e. sojourn as a client or guest (cf. Ps. 15:1).

f **17-24.** The concluding section is a promise. Though its general sense is clear, the text is in places exceedingly obscure. In that glad future the people will see their king in his splendour, ruling a wide domain. Then they will muse on the terror now forever passed. Where are the foreign tax-gatherers and officials now ? Where the arrogant tyrants bawling their orders in a tongue no-one could understand (cf. 28:11) ? All gone ! Instead, Zion stands securely, a tent which nothing can uproot. The land will be watered by broad streams upon which no hostile ship can come, for Yahweh the judge, ruler and king is its defence. Victory will be Israel's, and the most helpless of her people will share in the spoil. Sickness, too, will be ended, for sin will be forgiven (cf. Ps. 103:3 ; Mt. 9:2).

g **17. the king in his beauty :** cf. Ps. 45:2. This is probably not Yahweh (AV), but the ideal future king who reigns as his vicegerent. **18. counted the towers :** apparently for taxation, or to decide which ought to be razed. The text may be incorrect, but of the many emendations proposed (' precious things ', ' captives ', etc.) none is convincing. **20.** The figure is possibly drawn from the tent shrine which was the predecessor of the Temple. **21a** is exceedingly difficult cf. the larger commentaries. Perhaps omit ' in majesty ' as a dittograph of the same word (' stately ') in the next line, and point ' Yahweh ' to read ' there will be ' (*yihyeh*) ; then begin the verse, ' But there shall be for us a place of rivers, streams broad and wide—'. **23a** seems to continue the figure of the hostile ship (21) interrupted by 22, and to describe its helplessness to attack. But the translation is most uncertain. **23b.** Perhaps (*ḥillēḳ 'iwwēr*, or the like) read : ' Then shall the blind divide much spoil, and the lame take the prey '. The meaning is not merely that spoil will be so abundant that even cripples will arrive in time to share in it ; ' blind ' and ' lame ' are probably terms for Yahweh's abused and disheartened people (cf. 35:5f., 42:16 ; Jer. 31:8, etc.). 444g

XXXIV-XXXV The two chapters, probably from the same hand, constitute a sort of diptych : an Inferno followed by a Paradiso. They ought to be studied in connection with chs. 40–66, with which they are closely related both in style and idea. Some (Torrey) have even argued that they are the work of Second Isaiah himself ; but it would be safer to regard them as coming from the circle of that great prophet. They may date to the late 6th, or the 5th cent. 445a

XXXIV 1-17 Dies Irae : a Vision of Yahweh's Judgment—Since the chapter tells of vengeance on Edom, most commentators are at pains to describe the history of enmity between Judah and that country, and to deplore the fierce hatred of the neighbour exhibited here. But this is rather to miss the point of the passage, and to show misunderstanding of the vivid imagery in which it is cast. True, it is a fearful passage. And hatred of Edom was certainly intensified when, as Judah went down before the Babylonians, Edom gave her a stab in the back (cf. Ob. 10–16 ; Ezek. 35), and later occupied much of her land. But the passage is not a mere hymn of hate against a neighbour. The judgment on Edom appears as an aspect of the Day of Yahweh ; Edom here seems to stand—like Babylon in the NT—as a type of the enemies of God's people (cf. 63:1–6). The present passage was quite possibly selected from a store of similar poems (cf. ch. 13) as a fitting expression of the theme. The theme is the day of judgment—a fearful enough theme, but one treated here in possibly the only terms available to an OT poet. One ought to keep the opposite picture of ch. 35 in mind as one reads. God's intervention has ever these two sides in biblical theology, and the two are held in the same balance, though expressed in different terms, in NT no less than in Old (cf. Mt. 25:46, etc.). It may be added that the picture here is no more lurid—perhaps less so—than many a conventional Christian description of Hell. b

The chapter consists of two movements. 1-8 tells of the outpouring of Yahweh's fury. The judgment is announced and all peoples are summoned to hear the sentence, which is one of total destruction. Yahweh in his rage has put all the nations of the world under the ban. There will be a fearful slaughter ; the stench of rotting corpses will ascend to heaven, and the mountains will run with blood till they appear to melt. The heavens will be rolled up like a scroll, and the stars will fall like sere leaves from a great tree (cf. Rev. 6:12–17). The judgment falls with fury on ' Edom ' ; it is described in terms of a great sacrificial feast (cf. 25:6 ; Zeph. 1:7 ; Jer. 46:10 ; Ezek. 39:17–20). Yahweh's sword descends from the skies on the victims and slaughters them great and small till it is gorged with blood, smeared with fat—till the very ground is soaked. It is the great day of Yahweh's vengeance, and it is terrible. When it is done there is naught but ruin (9–17). Streams are turned to pitch, the soil to brimstone, and smoke ascends forever as from some Sodom destroyed a thousand times over. Yahweh measures ' Edom ' with the line and plummet of chaos, and men call it by the mocking name ' No Kingdom There '. Its fortresses, overgrown with thistles, are given over to wild creatures, and to the hideous demons which, as everyone knows, are wont to inhabit ruins. This is written in the book of Yahweh ; ' Edom ' has been allotted to them as their ' promised land ', and they will possess it forever. c

1. all that comes from it : i.e. all mankind. **2. he has doomed them :** lit. ' he has put them under the ban ' (cf. Jos. 6:17, 21) ; so also in 5. **3. shall** d

445d **flow:** lit. 'shall melt'. **4.** 1QIs[a] begins: 'and the valleys shall be split open, and all the host of heaven shall wither'. **6. Bozrah:** a chief city of Edom (cf. 63:1; Jer. 49:13), today Buṣeirah. **8. the cause of Zion:** perhaps better rendered (Torrey), 'the Champion (i.e. the one espousing the cause) of Zion', i.e. Yahweh. **11.** Many of the creatures named in this and the following verses are of uncertain identity; see the larger commentaries. **confusion—chaos:** the words are used to describe primeval chaos (Gen. 1:2). Since line and plummet are builder's tools, the sense seems to be that Yahweh will carefully build—destruction! **13ff.** Cf. 13:21f. **14. wild beasts—hyenas:** probably demons of some sort are meant: cf. 'satyr' (a demon in goat form), and 'night hag' (Lilith). The last, a figure borrowed from Babylonian belief, appears in later Rabbinical tales where, in female form, she is the deceiver of Adam. **15f.** Perhaps end 15 and begin 16 (Torrey), '—each one seeks her mate. From the book of Yahweh their names are read'. **the book of the Lord:** cf. Mal. 3:16; Dan. 12:1.

e **XXXV 1-10 The Redemption of Israel**—A description of Yahweh's salvation, in brilliant contrast to the foregoing, and again cast in terms proper to the OT mind. Prominent in the chapter is the transformation of nature, and the highway along which God leads his people home to Zion (cf. 40:3f., 42:16, 43:19, 48:20f., 49:10f.). As his judgment has burned and seared and ruined, so his redemption causes the desert to blossom. His people see his glory, the visible sign of his accompanying presence, as in the Exodus of old (cf. 40:5). Let the despondent take courage, for soon the God of Israel will come to rescue his own. Then eyes long blind will see, deaf ears will be opened, the lame will leap and the dumb sing for joy, for Yahweh's crippled people will be whole again. Before them will lie the highway of the new Exodus through a desert now flowing with streams. It is the Holy Way from which the unclean and depraved are excluded, and along which no robber or wild beast is found. On it the people, ransomed from bondage, will march safely to Zion with songs of joy which know no end. The NT saw the hope of new Exodus fulfilled in Christ (cf. Heb. 12:18–24; Jn 6:48–51; 1 C. 10:1–4).

f **1. Lebanon — Carmel — Sharon:** all noted for luxuriant vegetation; cf. 33:9. **2. weak:** lit. 'drooping'. **feeble:** lit. 'stumbling'. **4b.** One could read (Torrey): 'Behold your God will requite; the recompense of God will come; he himself will come to your rescue'. **5f.** Cf. 42:7, 16, 49:9, 61:1f.; Mt. 11:5. Though the words are intended literally, a purely literal interpretation scarcely satisfies these passages. **7b.** The text is possibly mutilated here. **8b.** Cf. the larger commentaries for discussion. One might regard 'and fools' and 'and he is for them' (corrupt and omitted by RSV) as a mistaken reduplication, and read, 'The unclean and fools (i.e. depraved) will not pass over it; those walking the way will not stray'. **9. ravenous:** the word elsewhere means 'robber'. Perhaps (Kissane) two lines have been scrambled, and we should read: 'no robber shall come up upon it, nor wild beast be found there'.

446a **XXXVI-XXXIX** These chapters repeat 2 Kg. 18:13–20:19, to which place in the commentary the reader is referred. Our task here is merely to outline the historical problem of chs. 36f. as this relates to Isaiah's preaching, and to deal with one passage (38:9–20) not included in Kg.

With minor verbal differences 36f. are identical with 2 Kg. 18:13–19:37, save that the account of 2 Kg. 18:14–16, which should follow 36:1, is omitted. These verses tell us that Hezekiah, his land ravaged by the Assyrians, sued for terms and surrendered. This is corroborated by Sennacherib's inscription describing his action in 701 against a coalition including Tyre, Ashkelon, Ekron and other states, in which Hezekiah was a ringleader. Sennacherib tells us that he moved down the coast and, having wreaked vengeance on Ashkelon and its towns, turned upon Ekron. The people of that city appealed to the Pharaoh (Shabaka, 710/9–696/5) for aid. But when an Egyptian army advanced, it was met and defeated by Sennacherib, who then reduced Ekron and its dependencies at his leisure. Turning then on Hezekiah, Sennacherib ravaged forty-six of his towns (cf. 36:1) and placed Jerusalem under siege. Hezekiah, deserted by certain of his troops, surrendered. Sennacherib, having given large portions of Judahite territory to kings who had remained loyal, laid on Hezekiah an increased annual tribute, which Hezekiah's envoys subsequently delivered to Nineveh. It is thus clear that the defence of Jerusalem in 36f. took place after an initial capitulation. It is usually assumed that Sennacherib, regretting his leniency, demanded unconditional surrender, and that Hezekiah, preferring to die rather than to accede, and assured by Isaiah that Jerusalem would not be taken, refused. Thus the events of 36f. likewise fall in 701. The appearance of Tirhakah (37:9), who became co-regent only in 690/89 and Pharaoh in 685/4, is regarded as a harmless anachronism ascribing to him the position he subsequently occupied.

This explanation, however, involves difficulties. b
2 Kg. 18:13–16 does not harmonise well with the remainder of the narrative. Hezekiah is addressed as a rebel (36:4–20, 37:10–13) and called upon to surrender, although (2 Kg. 18:14f.) he had presumably already done so. He is chided for relying on Egypt (36:5f.) when, according to Sennacherib, the Egyptians had already been beaten—no doubt one reason for his surrender. The people are told (36:16f.) to expect deportation, although Hezekiah had been required to deliver—and did subsequently deliver—increased tribute to Nineveh. Are the two sets of terms compatible? Or is a mere reduction of Hezekiah's territory compatible with intention to deport him? Further, 37:7, 37f. imply that Sennacherib was murdered soon after (and the account was written after that event), although it was twenty years from 701 until this actually took place (681). Nor can the appearance of Tirhakah in 701 be regarded as a harmless anachronism. Tirhakah indeed became co-regent to his brother Shabataka, the successor of Shabaka, in 690/89; but recently published inscriptions (cf. W. F. Albright, BASOR 130 (1953), 8–11; 141 (1956), 23–26) show that he was but twenty years old at the time, and thus not over nine or ten in 701. The reference in 37:9 is therefore unhistorical unless the whole account refers to a later occasion. But the essential historicity of 36f. is not to be denied. There is nothing intrinsically improbable in it (cf. the tradition of Herodotus, repeated by Josephus, that Sennacherib's army was overrun by a plague of mice at the border of Egypt); and some marvellous deliverance of Jerusalem must be assumed, if only to explain the later dogma of the inviolability of Zion.

This raises the question if Isaiah's oracles regarding c
the Assyrian crisis are not better understood under the assumption of two invasions by Sennacherib. In 37:5–7, 22–35, calm in the assurance that Zion will be saved, he urges Hezekiah to have no fear. A similar confidence is to be seen in 10:24–27, 14:24–27, 17:12–14, 29:5–8, 30:27–33, 31:4–9. But in other places (e.g. 28:1–22, 30:1–7, 31:1–3, cf. 22:1–14) he has naught but censure for the national policy, and predictions of dire calamity. In 1:2–9, which dates to 701, he even seems to counsel surrender (1:5). While certainty is impossible, it may be (Albright, ibid.) that Kg. has telescoped the accounts of two separate invasions, and that the date of 2 Kg. 18:13; Isa. 36:1 (701), applies only to 2 Kg. 18:14–16 (not in Isa.), the campaign of which Sennacherib also tells us. It is known that after 701 Sennacherib faced further trouble in Babylon, culminating (691) in a serious defeat at the hands of a coalition of Babylonians, Elamites and others; only in 689 did he succeed in quelling the revolt. It is possible that during these

446c years rebellion flared again in the west backed by Tirhakah, and that Hezekiah was once more drawn in. If so, Sennacherib must have moved against it *c.* 688; the marvellous deliverance of Jerusalem may well have taken place then. The death of Hezekiah soon after (687/6) would have saved him from further reprisals. To the objection that Sennacherib tells us of no such campaign, it may be answered that we have virtually no information of that king's reign after 689 at all.

d **XXXVIII 9-20 The Psalm of Hezekiah**—The psalm is a liturgical composition designed for the use of an individual who, after deliverance from serious trouble, presents his thank-offering before Yahweh. Like similar pieces (cf. Ps. 56–60) it falls into two parts: a description of the plight of the sufferer (10–15), and his praise to God upon deliverance (16–20). As in the Psalter, the title (9) is not an original part of the poem, which was probably taken from a collection of psalms as suitable for the occasion (cf. Jon. 2). The king tells of his despair. He had thought that he would die in the prime of life and go down to Sheol, where there is neither fellowship with God nor with any living being (cf. 18; Ps. 88:5, 115:17). It was as if his life had been struck like a shepherd's tent and carried away, rolled up like a weaver's web and cut by God from the loom. He cried out through the long nights, but there was no apparent answer. His plaint was like the twittering of a sparrow, or the moaning of a dove, so piteous it was. He called on his God for rescue—but what was the use? It was God himself who had done it. Through the sleepless hours he tossed in bitterness of spirit. But still his trust was in Yahweh, to whom he cried for deliverance. And his prayer was answered! Now he knows that this bitterness was for his good. Yahweh has both held him back from the grave and forgiven his sins. How good it is! Now he can praise his God, as he could not had he gone down to Sheol. But he is alive! And praise God he can, and will. Yes, he will tell his children of God's faithfulness, and all the days of his life sing glad songs of thanks in the Temple. 446d

e **9. a writing:** probably 'Miktam' (for *mikhtābh*), the title of certain psalms (Ps. 16, 56–60) **12f. loom:** 'thrum', the threads which attach the web to the loom. **bring me to an end:** or possibly, 'deliver me up (to my torments)'. The text in this and the succeeding verses is very obscure. **14c.** Like a debtor led to jail, he appeals to Yahweh—to the creditor himself—to be his security (cf. Job 17:3). **15a.** Better: 'what can I say that he should speak to me? For it is he who did it'; or perhaps, 'What can I speak or say to him——'. **16.** The text is obscure and all translations conjectural; that of Kissane involves the fewest emendations: 'O Lord, with thee are the days of my life; thine alone is the life of my spirit——'.

Bibliography—Commentaries: G. H. Box, *The Book of Isaiah* (1908); T. K. Cheyne, *The Prophecies of Isaiah* (5th ed. 1889); F. Delitzsch, *Biblical Commentary on the Prophecies of Isaiah* (Eng. tr. of 4th ed. 1889); B. Duhm, HKAT (4th ed. 1922); G. B. Gray, ICC (1912), chs. 1–27 only; V. Herntrich, ATD (1950), chs. 1–12 only; E. J. Kissane, *The Book of Isaiah* i (1941); E. König, *Das Buch Jesaja* (1926); K. Marti, KHC 1900); O. Procksch, KAT (1930); R. B. Y. Scott, IB (1956); J. Skinner, CB (rev. ed. 1915); I. W. Slotki, Soncino Bible (1949); G. A. Smith, Ex.B (rev. ed. 1927); G. W. Wade, WC (2nd ed. 1929); O. C. Whitehouse, Cent.B (1905–9); J. Ziegler, Ech.B (1948).

Other Literature—H. Birkeland, *Zum hebräischen Traditionswesen* (1938); C. Boutflower, *The Book of Isaiah in the Light of Assyrian Monuments* (1930); S. R. Driver, *Isaiah: His Life and Times* (2nd ed. 1893); R. H. Kennett, *The Composition of the Book of Isaiah* (1910); S. Mowinckel, 'Die Komposition des Jesajabuches, Kap. 1–39', *Acta Orientalia* 11 (1933), 267–92, *Prophecy and Tradition* (1946); J. Steinmann, *Le prophète Isaïe* (1950).

ISAIAH—II AND III

BY DOUGLAS R. JONES

447a The gain of 19th-cent. scholarship was to discover the secret of the *difference* between the various sections of the book of Isa. First, 40–66 was distinguished from the earlier chapters, on the ground of internal evidence, literary style and theological ideas. It belongs to the period of the Exile and after, and contemplates release. The Exile is '*presupposed* and only the *release* from it is *predicted*' (S. R. Driver). A further distinction was necessitated, by more prolonged investigation, between 40–55 and 56–66. The former section belongs to the time of Cyrus, immediately before the release (538), while the latter betrays a Palestinian background and is later. The homogeneity and individual character of 40–55 have led to its ascription mainly to a single mind, the unknown poet-prophet of the Exile, usually called Second Isaiah. There has been little agreement that a single mind was responsible for Third Isaiah.

b More recent scholarship has rediscovered, without denying the validity of previous analytical work, the significant *cohesion* of the whole Isaianic corpus of prophecies. The signs of unity are to be explained not by unity of authorship but by the unceasing work of a school of disciples from the time of the 8th-cent. Isaiah of Jerusalem down to the period following the rebuilding of the Temple (520–516). Second Isaiah was the most distinguished representative of this school. 56–66 also is the work of a post-exilic prophet or prophets of the same school, in Palestine. The commentary will attempt to show the relation of Second Isaiah's prophetic work to the existing prophetic material held in trust by the school, and the way the later prophets of 56–66 reinterpret his work and sometimes transform it in the light of their own situation. There is no longer profit in peeling away 'interpolations' and 'unauthentic' passages. We are dealing with the living witness of a remarkable school which produced at least two and possibly three towering personalities, but also others whose humbler contributions nevertheless share the same inspiration.

c On disputed points the standpoint of this commentary is as follows:

(1) 40–66 is a collection of oracles originally delivered *orally*, rather than a sustained literary composition. While, therefore, the units show the unity of their common origin, there is also an apparent inconsequence in their arrangement, *considered as sustained composition.*

d (2) On the other hand only *traces* of the oracle-forms, clear in 1 Isa. and Jer., can be discerned. 'The dissolution of the prophetic types' begins with 2 Isa. (Gressmann). This is partly due to the character of the message, which was generally not that of the 'reproach' or 'threat'; and partly to the probable circumstances of its delivery. There is much to be said for the view that, denied the Temple and the market-place, the exilic prophet found his congregation in the sabbath assembly (Volz). He may even have composed laments or confessions or acts of faith for congregational use. This becomes clearer in 3 Isa. and will be suggested in the commentary. But it does not follow that this was the exclusive mode of preaching.

e (3) Oracles which had an independent origin did not come together haphazardly. The study of their arrangement is vitally important to the understanding of their meaning. If there was a 'literary revolution 447
in Israel and perhaps in the Near East generally towards the end of the 7th century' (Sidney Smith), its influence is to be discerned in the *arrangement* of the oracles. The use made of 2 Isa. by 3 Isa. shows that 2 Isa. must have attained its present form shortly after the return (538) and well before 520. The arrangement must therefore be due either to the prophet himself or a close disciple. Isaiah of Jerusalem arranged for the setting down of a nucleus of his oracles, Jeremiah (ch. 36) did more. Second Isaiah may well have committed his work to writing in a more complete way, either in part or in whole, sometimes remembering his very words, sometimes summarising, perhaps even sometimes composing afresh. There is evidence that his work is, in fact, two collections viz: (*a*) 40–8 and (*b*) 49–55. In (*a*) there is mention of Cyrus and Babylon: in (*b*) there is not. In (*a*) repeated appeal to prophecy from history: in (*b*) none explicitly, though the theme is under the surface. In (*a*) Israel is the 'servant' frequently and explicitly: in (*b*) the term is confined to the 'Servant Songs'. In (*a*) Jacob-Israel is the name of the redeemed community: in (*b*) Jerusalem-Zion. If 40–8 represents the arrangement of the prophet and 49-55 that of his disciples, this may be the truth in the otherwise unacceptable theory of some that this latter section was composed in Jerusalem (Kosters, Kittel, Procksch, Levy). Others think that 49–55 is slightly later, but still in Babylon looking forward to the liberation and return. However it may be, the *arrangement* is significant for the interpretation of the oracles, not least of the 'Servant Songs'. The principles of arrangement will be discussed in the commentary.

(4) All 40–55 belong to the period of the rise of f
Cyrus and the months before the liberation. 56–66 belong variously to the year before the rebuilding of the Temple and a few years after, i.e. ±520. A greatly later date is nowhere *demanded.*

(5) Consistently with the principles set forth above, g
the 'Servant Songs' (42:1–4, 49:1–6, 50:4–9, 52:13–53:12—a delimitation first made by Duhm and followed by many, but not by all) are interpreted strictly in the light of the total teaching of Isaiah. It is not easy to free the mind from the influence of interpretations based on their more or less strict isolation. For a comprehensive survey of the bewildering variety of interpretations and formidable mass of literature, the reader is referred to the book of C. R. North and the essays of H. H. Rowley listed in the bibliography.

On the place of these prophecies in the theology of the OT see §126*h*. The outstanding effect of the discovery of two MSS of Isa. among the Dead Sea Scrolls is to vindicate the general antiquity and reliability of the Massoretic text. The more important and complete MS (1QIs[a]) offers a large number of variant readings, but usually MT is to be preferred. RSV adopts only six such readings where they depart from MT in chs. 40–66, and not all scholars would agree on all of these. The other MS (1QIs[b]) contains a much less complete text of chs. 10–66 and is closer to MT. Together, these MSS, perhaps a thousand

47g years older than the medieval MSS on which we have hitherto depended, show that, by the beginning of the Christian era, the text of the prophets was already substantially standardised. Our present, traditional text of Isa. has been shown to be, in the main, the best we have. For a description of these MSS and a cautious estimate of their importance, see Millar Burrows, *The Dead Sea Scrolls*, 19–22, 303–15.

SECOND ISAIAH

48a **(A) XL-XLVIII Grounds of Faith in the divine Plan of Salvation**

XL 1-11 Prologue—Though not exhausting the prophet's themes, this passage expresses his central message which is an announcement of the imminence of salvation for exiled Israel. The cohesion of its content, subsequent theme and variation and the use made of it by a disciple in 62:10–12 suggest that it is the deliberate and definitive introduction to the prophecies that follow.

1-2. The double imperative, characteristic of this prophet, expresses the intensity of feeling which is also apparent in 2 (cf. Hos. 2:14). The prophet speaks, according to divine bidding, to the holy people in exile (Jerusalem is here a theological, not a geographical term) announcing that her hard service (cf. RSV*n*) is at an end. The suggestion that the punishment has outstripped the crime is strange and unique. It is possible to translate : ' double by reason of all her sins ' or ' by the number of ' (BDB 90*b*), i.e. ' according to '. The punishment proceeds from Yahweh (cf. 1:25), just as he is also the source of comfort (cf. 51:12). For a similar association of judgment and mercy cf. 54:7. **3-5.** The **voice** is either a poetical equivalent for ' Thus saith the Lord ', or, more concretely, the voice of a member of Yahweh's heavenly council (cf. 1 Kg. 22 ; Job 1 ; Isa. 6). It emphasises that the message is not the prophet's own word, but *given* ; and it introduces the primary theme of a highway for Yahweh. The return from exile is in some sense a return of Yahweh himself, bringing his flock with him (11), and involves a theophany (5, 9 ; cf. 52:7–9). This imagery, in part suggested by the cult, becomes the material for further, figurative, interpretation in 3 Isa. where the **way** is the way of life (57:14) or the way of worshippers making pilgrimage to Zion (62:10). The return is a revelation of the **glory** of Yahweh. This is a central motif, though the word ' glory ' is used hereafter in 2 Isa. only in the sense of ' honour '. Here it is equivalent to ' revelation ' (cf. the centrality of ' glory ' in 6:3, though it is not otherwise prominent in 1–39), and is a key word. The editor of the collected prophecies so understood this theme to be *the* theme that he brought the book to an end on the same note (66:18–19, 23). **All flesh** is all mankind (49:26, 66:16, 23f.) with a suggestion of its weakness over against the creator (31:3). **Together** is a characteristic word of the Isaianic corpus and seems here to indicate the unity of mankind in the day of fulfilment. Fulfilment must come because the word of God is self-fulfilling (5 ; cf. 44:26, 55:10–11).

b **6-8.** The voice now addresses the prophet who speaks of the transience and weakness of ' all flesh '. His occasional utterances on his own account are few and marked by remarkable self-effacement ; cf. 48:16. The impossible will happen because **the word of our God** knows no transience or weakness. Thus the contrast *implied* in 5 is made explicit. **9-11.** The revelation of Yahweh is announced by a **herald**. The RSV has correctly observed that the Heb. word is fem. and is in apposition to Zion. The herald must be understood to be the true Zion (the servant of later oracles) who announces the return to the cities of Judah ; that is, Israel, considered from the point of view of a special *function*, has a mission to all Israel. This is a conception with which the prophet's hearers must come to terms again and again ; cf. 49:1–6. 448b
The command **fear not** is much used by 2 Isa. and, as frequently in the stories of the patriarchs, is part of the preparation for theophany. **His arm :** the ' arm ' is a symbol of strength and the arm of Yahweh a symbol of deliverance (cf. Exod. 6:6, 15:16 ; Isa. 5:25). The image is that of Yahweh returning with the reward of his labour with him (cf. Isa. 49:4 ; Jer. 31:16), not that of returning with booty taken in war (cf. Gen. 15:1). The image of the shepherd feeding his flock is verbally close to Ezek. 34:12. Much will be made later of the thought that Yahweh *carries* his people ; cf. 46:3. There are thus three images in two verses : the mighty deliverer, the workman with his reward, the shepherd with his flock. Isaiah's thought is from beginning to end pictorial.

12-31 First Ground of Faith : the incomparable c
Power of the sovereign Creator—If it be asked who can achieve the impossible, the answer is : He who created the world, before whom the idol-gods are nothing. The prophet appeals to the empirical facts of the universe and history. In fact this is apologetic.

12. He employs a familiar form of the ' hymn of praise ', beginning with the question, Who ? (as frequently in 40–66).

13. The Spirit of the Lord is the prime mover in creation (Gen. 1:2 ; Job 33:4, Ps. 104:30), but also he who brings the things of man to naught (6–8) and therefore also he who directs the course of history. **His counsellor :** lit. ' the man of his counsel or plan '. Yahweh's purpose is sovereign.

15-17. The nations include the mightiest nations of the earth. **The isles** are the far coastlands. **Lebanon** was famed for its magnificent forests and in 2:13 is therefore a symbol of human pride and achievement. In true proportion, all are as **nothing and emptiness** (unreality).

18-20. God is strictly incomparable so that no image d
or idol of him is possible ; yet he is also personal will (13). Cf. the guarded way Ezekiel hazards a comparison when he speaks of ' the likeness as the appearance of a man ' (Ezek. 1:26). Most scholars insert 41:6–7 between 19 and 20. This is intrinsically plausible since the passage seems to break the sense in 41 and to complete the sense when inserted in 40. On the other hand the reader must be prepared for inconsequential passages in a book which is a collection of summary oracles rather than a sustained literary composition, and reason will be given for leaving 41:6–7 (q.v.) where it is. This passage anticipates the more scathing and detailed ridicule of idols in 44:9–20. **20a.** The rendering is wholly uncertain.

21-26. The sovereign creator, incomparable power and e
sole source of renewal and strength, is identified with Yahweh, the holy one—an identification which Israel ought to have been able to make. **Have you not known . . . from the beginning ?** A few thousand Jews, utterly subject and powerless in mighty Babylon, are challenged to realise what they have always known. The cosmology implied in the description of 22f. is best understood by reference to a diagram such as that in *Clarendon Bible*, vi, 20. **22. It is he who . . . :** there follows in the Heb. a string of participles characteristic of the ' hymn of praise '. The prophet is powerfully drawing out the implications of Israelite worship. **21.** Notice the threefold negative question and in **24** the threefold ' scarcely ', repetitions typical of this prophet's style, deepening the intensity of his conviction.

27 echoes a strong feeling among the exiles that f
Yahweh overlooked their fate and that justice miscarried without his attention ; cf. 42:1–4, 49:14 and also 8:17. This is the first reference to Jacob-Israel, characteristic of 40–8. **28-31.** The prophet's answer is to make the first connection of creation and eternity in respect of God. Yahweh is both **Creator** and **Everlasting God.** That means he is lord both of the universe and of *time*. Strictly, God is not defined as

448f timeless in the usual sense of the word ' eternal '. This is not eternity conceived as pure simultaneity and opposed to duration. On the other hand the prophet certainly understands God to be superior to the limitations of both time and space. A similar phrase in Gen. 21:33 means rather ' God of antiquity ', i.e. lord of the time that stretches back to the beginning. The full scope and implication of the conception in **28** is unique in the OT. **31.** Such is God and therefore the source of renewal and vigour in those who wait for the Lord ; cf. 8:17, 49:23, 51:5, where the expression means : those who wait expectantly for the fulfilment of prophecy. Here, those who wait patiently, wait for him to reverse their fortune and bring salvation (cf. the Psalms where the meaning is those who wait *upon* Yahweh in prayer).

449a **XLI 1-20 Second Ground of Faith : the divine Control of History**—The power of Yahweh has been demonstrated ; the question now is his will and plan. The prophet draws attention to what he has done before in history as an earnest and ground of hope that he will so act again.

1-4 The Call of Abraham—1. The far coastlands and peoples are called to listen, because the call of Abraham took place on the stage of wider history and so also will the new call and journey take place. **Renew their strength :** not a corruption as most scholars think, but a deliberate linking of the oracle with the preceding verse. The prophet or his disciple who thus arranged the oracle suggests, by this connection, that the foreigners who draw near to Yahweh may share in the renewal of strength. The sharing of blessing with the nations is to be a notable theme of 40–66. **For judgment :** i.e. the right which Jacob-Israel complains has been disregarded (40:27) and is the function of the ' servant ' to bring forth to the nations (42:1, 4). **2. Who stirred up one from the East ? :** the question implies an unassailable fact to which appeal can be made, a certainty of history which can be made the basis of the interpretation of contemporary events. The one from the East must therefore be Abraham, and this is supported (*a*) by the parallel question of **4 : Who has performed and done this, calling the generations from the beginning ?** and (*b*) by **8-10** as interpreted below. If it is then asked why only the *military* activity of Abraham in Gen. 14 is referred to, the answer is that it is just that military activity of Abraham which provides the pattern of the activity of Cyrus. Hence some can see here a reference to the early victories of Cyrus and especially in ' by paths his feet do not tread ' (N.B. present tense as against RSV), a reference to the speed of his march from Halys Pass to Sardis. Such a reference to Cyrus in the mind of the prophet is not excluded by the primary reference to Abraham. In the parallel passages 45:1, 13, Cyrus alone is in mind. In **8** the servant is in mind ; the well-known call of Abraham is appealed to as a ground of faith in Yahweh to call again. Hence in **4**, in what will be a familiar self-predication, Yahweh declares that he is **the last** as well as **the first.** He is in supreme control of all history and will perform his will now, even as he achieved it at the very beginning of Heb. history. **2. whom victory meets at every step :** although this is the most straightforward translation of the Heb., 42:6 and 45:13 suggest that the RV may still be right, viz : ' whom he called in righteousness '.

b **5-7.** The unexpected reversion to the theme of idols serves to contrast the pitiable weakness of the heathen over against him who is the First and the Last. They try to achieve permanence by ' fastening an idol with nails '. **Take courage, encourages** and **fasten** in 6 and 7, and **I took** in 9 and **hold** in 13 are all forms of the same Heb. verb which means ' grow firm ', ' strengthen '. The conclusion seems inescapable that this arrangement of the oracles is as early as any, that the prophet or his disciple wished by the association of this catchword to contrast the strength which is illusory with the strength to be found in Yahweh's right hand. 44[9]

c **8-10.** This is the first passage to refer to the **servant** and explicitly to identify him with Jacob-Israel ; and, being first in a carefully arranged collection of oracles, it is significant. Not only is Jacob explicitly described as **the seed of Abraham, my friend,** but the passage seems to be directly based on Gen. 26:24 : ' And the Lord appeared to him (Isaac) the same night and said, " I am the God of Abraham your father : fear not, for I am with you and will bless you and multiply your descendants for my servant Abraham's sake." ' Notice (*a*) Jacob-Israel is now the fulfilment of this promise—the offspring (seed) of Abraham ; (*b*) he is also now ' my servant ' as Abraham was ; (*c*) **Fear not, for I am with you** is not only verbally identical, but we have already seen this command to be the accompaniment of a theophany (cf. 40:9, as in Gen. 26:24). Abraham the servant is probably therefore the source of the conception of Israel as the servant and the source also of the strong individualising of the idea of the servant to be found later ; cf. also Ps. 105:6, 42, which may have influenced 2 Isa. (see on 48:20–2). **9.** Though immediately said of Abraham, the phrasing is clearly determined by the prophet's thought of the contemporary servant taken **from the ends of the earth** and called **from its farthest corners.**

d **11-13.** The metre (*ḳînāh* or lament) would suggest that this is a separate oracle. **13** provides its connection with 8–10. This is the familiar prophetic principle that although nations, all unknowing, may administer Yahweh's punishment of his people, they in their turn must suffer judgment.

e **14-16.** A separate oracle, as shown by the abrupt change from 2nd pers. sing. masc. in previous oracle to fem. in this. Its purpose is to contrast the weakness of Jacob-Israel (**you worm Jacob**) with the startling reversal of fortune that is to take place. She is to become a **threshing sledge,** i.e. an instrument of the judgment indicated in 11–13. The term ' worm ' is not here a depreciatory description implying a moral criticism, but rather a deliberate contrast with the ruthless threshing-sledge (cf. Am. 1:3). That which ordinarily is crushed will crush. The chastised is to chastise. **Your redeemer is the holy one of Israel :** the first occurrence of a characteristic description of Yahweh as Israel's *gō'ēl,* i.e. the near kinsman who rescues in time of need (cf. Ru. 3:11–12, 4:1–6 ; Job 19:25).

f **17-20 Yahweh's wonderful Provision**—The prophet now uses the theme of the desert become fertile (cf. 44:3). This is the reverse of the process often described in the Day of the Lord imagery. Both processes are described in Ps. 107, the judgment in 33 and the salvation in 35 ; and significantly Ps. 107:35 corresponds verbally with 18*c* here. The growth of noble trees also signifies the reversal of the process of judgment, since the Day of the Lord is frequently symbolised by the felling of trees ; cf. Isa. 2, and see on 40:16. The prophet is not therefore thinking of the miraculous way through the desert (Volz), but of the fulfilment of the historical redemption grounded in the example of Abraham (1–4). Thus he uses already familiar imagery to describe the prosperity, fertility and blessing that is to come. **17. The poor and needy** in 1 Isa. are those who are oppressed by the rich and powerful in society. In 2 Isa. they are the Israel of promise nationally afflicted. **19.** The trees cannot be certainly identified. **20.** The fulfilment of Yahweh's plan in history, seen and recognised, will provide a solid ground of conviction. Because the prophet has declared it beforehand, it will be recognised as the work of Yahweh who has thus revealed his mind. This is to be a familiar theme ; cf. 41:23, 26, 43:10, 45:3, 6, 49:23, 26, 52:6. **20** links with the new theme of 21ff.

g **21-29 Third Ground of Faith : Appeal to the Fulfilment of Prophecy**—The far-coasts and peoples of 41:1, i.e. all non-Israelites, are now challenged to

9g disputation. The setting is suggested by ordinary legal procedure. If history is the sphere of Yahweh's redemptive activity, prophecy is his mind, revealed in advance that its fulfilment may prove the prophet's claim. Let those who worship other gods show the same insight into events and produce the same examples of prophecy made and fulfilled. Their inability reveals their nothingness. Again a major theme ; cf. 42:8f., 43:9, 16–19, 44:6–8, 45:9–13, 20f., 46:9–11, 48:3ff. (characteristic of the first complex of oracles in chs. 40–8).
22. Tell us the former things, contrasted here with **what is to happen, the things to come** and **what is to come hereafter,** elsewhere summed up as ' new things ' (42:9, 43:19, 48:6). The former things must be interpreted according to their context and may vary in precise meaning. In general the ' former things ' are all the events of the first dispensation from the beginning (creation) until the new dispensation. This becomes clear in the eschatological interpretation offered by a disciple of the prophet in 65:16f. where the dividing line is the new creation, i.e. of the new heavens and the new earth. But in 40–8 the prophet is more narrowly concerned with the new redemptive act of the Return and Cyrus's part in it. In this context the more precise meaning is indicated by the concrete example of 25–9, which clearly echoes 41:1–4.
h **25. One from the north :** both Abraham and Cyrus came immediately from the north, mediately from the east. Gen. 26:24 (see on 8–10) is followed by the notice that ' he built an altar there and called upon the name of the Lord '. So here : **he shall call upon my name,** although in the Cyrus Cylinder (ANET, 315f.), Cyrus reveals perfect loyalty to Marduk. Restored Israel will of course worship at the rebuilt altar in Zion. **26. Who declared it from the beginning ?** may then refer to such a foreshadowing of the return of Israel and of the role of Cyrus in the migration of Abraham, or more generally to the oracles predicting the fall of Babylon, 13:17ff. and 21:2ff. (C. R. North), or both. In any case this kind of preoccupation with the word of God in history is plain in the handling of the oracles of Isaiah of Jerusalem by his long line of disciples. In the end of the Southern Kingdom, they see the fulfilment of prophecies of judgment. There remain the prophecies of salvation (the ' new things ') to be fulfilled. In principle therefore the distinction has been long understood in Isaianic circles. The Heb. of 26 does not contain the word ' it '. **Who declared from the beginning, that we might know, and from beforetime, that we might say, ' He is right ' ?** may therefore be a pointer to the activity of the school of Isaiah within the now collected oracles 1–39, as they discern prophecy and fulfilment within the old dispensation. This came to an end in 586. Here then is ground of faith in ' the things to come '. They are now living ' between the times'. **27.** RSV translation involves conjectural emendation and is uncertain though probably near to the sense.
50a **XLII 1-25 The Role of Israel the Servant—1-4 (the first ' servant poem ').** His royal function to guarantee judgment among the nations. This is the first of four poems usually marked out for separate consideration as ' the Servant Songs ' (see §447*g*). But the poem only in fact gathers together what the reader has already learned. **1. Behold my servant :** he who was addressed in 41:8–10 is now *presented* to the nations who have come together for judgment (41:1). That this is *righteous* Israel, fulfilling the royal *function* of giving judgment, is intelligible in the light of the distinction implied in 40:9–11. **my servant :** cf. 41:8. **whom I uphold :** cf. 41:10. **my chosen :** cf. 41:8. **I have put my spirit upon him :** cf. 11:2. The spirit is the royal endowment which alone enables the royal guardian of justice to ' judge the poor with righteousness and decide with equity for the meek of the earth '. As the ideal king is to Israel, so will Israel be to the nations ; cf. 2:4.

2. He will not cry nor lift up his voice or make it heard in the street : some interpret as contrasting the quiet, humble ' servant ' with proud Cyrus receiving noisy acclamation, and suggest that the prophet became disillusioned with one who kept loyal to Marduk. They contrast the servant poems with the Cyrus oracles to the extent that ' a fixed point here seems to have been reached in the matter of interpretation—namely, the conception of the Servant Songs as a correction of the Cyrus poems ' (Hempel). But the word ' cry ' indicates the plea of a plaintiff for justice and the image is of a person pleading publicly without securing hearing or vindication. The translation could be ' One will not cry . . . ', in which case the meaning is that royal Israel will judge with perfect righteousness. Or else it means that Israel herself will never again have reason to make the complaint voiced in 40:27. **4. The coastlands wait for his law :** better ' instruction '. Judgment and law comprehend all the divine requirements ; cf. 2:4. The servant Israel is to be the great spiritual teacher of mankind. 450b
5-9. Amplification of the role of the servant and renewed appeal to prophecy. **5** alludes to the now familiar theme of the creator and reaffirms his power to achieve his will. **6. I have called you in righteousness :** the language of 41:2 now firmly applied to Israel. **I have taken you by the hand :** cf. 41:10, 13. All the echoes of 1–6 prove that the prophet or his disciple, in arranging the oracles in this way, understood the servant to be Israel. **and kept you :** cf. 49:8. **I have given you as a covenant to the people, a light to the nations :** lit. ' a covenant of people ' (cf. 49:8). ' People ' must refer to gentiles rather than to Israel, while ' covenant ' suggests the permanence and reliability of Israel's coming relationship with and service to the nations. The text and meaning are not certain. The verbs in 6 trace the steps of Israel's covenant history and reach a climax in 7. **to open the eyes that are blind :** The prophet subsequently develops the image in various ways (in 16 of the helpless, in 18f. of the unperceptive). Here the thought develops the idea of the light to the gentiles. The servant will not only be light to them but will also open their eyes to see. **to bring out the prisoners :** again a figure of the liberation which the servant will procure for all nations, a liberation of which his own is the precursor. Hence the same language is used of the release from Babylon in 22 and 49:9. **8. I am the Lord, that is my name.** These words, so trite in English, conceal the whole power of revelation. The name Yahweh (probably a form of the verb ' to be ', §179*c*) is the clue to the sovereign personality revealed at Sinai. To be addressed by him in the first person and to know his name is at once to believe that the impossible is possible and his will to be fulfilled. **my glory :** in the sense of ' honour '. c
9. The former things (see on 41:22) are here the prophecies of the past which have been fulfilled, especially those which form the study of the Isaianic school within 1–39, relating to the Day of the Lord as partially fulfilled in 586.
10-13 A new Song—An interlude of praise, such as often occurs, like the sound of bells suddenly breaking forth upon the air. As in the enthronement psalms (cf. 96:1, 98:1, 149:1), there is a new song for a new king, so now a new song for the ' new things ' which Yahweh will bring to pass. **Kedar** and **Sela :** deliberately obscure. Even obscure and distant desert tribes and villages will join in the universal praise. The hymn ends in a bold anthropomorphic picture of Yahweh as a warrior. **like a man of war :** cf. Exod. 15:3. The ' new things ' will be of the order of the events of the Exodus. **A mighty man :** conversely the prince of 9:5 was described as ' a mighty god ', and, as there, ' the zeal of the Lord of hosts will do this ' (9:7), so here he stirs up his zeal (better than RSV ' fury '). d
14-17 Yahweh's Silence to be broken—Yahweh e

450e himself now speaks and the image is the equally bold and anthropomorphic one of a woman in childbirth. The highest hebraic conception of God permits these metaphors, since God is personal will rather than pure, changeless being. The silence of God is not therefore inactivity and disregard (40:27), but deliberate restraint until the time for action has come. **15.** Imagery which in itself suggests judgment is here used of *the way* which is to be created for the redeemed; cf. 40:4. Perhaps it is used because it is also suggestive of the miraculous creation of a way through the Red Sea. However that may be, the present allusion is to Babylon. The blind are the helpless exiles who see no way out of their darkness (as the disciple responsible for 59:9f. clearly understood). But they will be given light and the rough places will be turned into level ground; cf. 40:4. **16. These are the things I will do.** The Heb. 'word' can certainly mean 'thing' or 'event', but probably the reference here is to *prophetic words* which will be performed; cf. 40:5, 44:26, 55:10–11. **17.** As a result the idolaters will be shamed.

f **18-25 The paradoxical Character of the Servant**—The servant of this passage is often contrasted with the righteous servant of the four 'servant songs'. But this is to overlook his paradoxical character strongly asserted in **19** by fourfold repetition. The one who is blind and deaf is '*my* servant', 'my messenger whom I send' and 'my apostle' (this for RSV 'my dedicated one' involves slight conjectural emendation but serves to complete a chiasmus; RSV is plausible). His blindness is not that of *moral* obtuseness but, as 20f. shows, of lack of insight into Yahweh's purpose. **20. Many things** have happened—not different from the 'former things'—but their meaning has been missed. **21.** And all this is the plan or 'pleasure' of Yahweh which may be discerned in the Isaianic prophecies. **To magnify his law and make it glorious** is to fulfil it; for the 'law' here is the divine instruction to the prophet as in 1:10, 8:16. They are blind and deaf in respect of that to which they ought to be witnesses (43:9, 44:8). But *they are to become* the blind who see and the deaf who hear of 43:8. And if their condition has been one of imprisonment, subjection (22) and darkness (42:7), their understanding of prophecy ought to have taught them that even this was in the divine plan (24), a proper chastisement for Israel's sin and disobedience. **25** refers to the events leading to the fall of Jerusalem—Israel has been blind to the nature of that judgment. The servant will fulfil his mission *in so far as he now sees and hears.*

451a **XLIII-XLIV 5 Justly punished but freely redeemed**

1-3 The divine Protection—Although the disaster of 597–586 was a punishment, yet, in so far as it was a human predicament, Yahweh remained with his people. Judgment and mercy are one. The creator (1*ab*) who sends his creatures through the waters and fires of judgment (2) is also the redeemer in closest relationship with his people (1*d*). The idea of the water of judgment, through which Israel has to pass, is that of 8:7f., 28:2; and just as there (8:8) the prophet is able to declare 'Immanuel', i.e. 'With-us-God', so now the same assurance is expressed, but from Yahweh himself, '*With-thee-I*'. The 'I' of course is filled with all the power of the being of Yahweh (cf. 41:4), as is strongly suggested in the divine self-predication of 3*a*.

b **3c-7 The Role of the Nations**—The role of Babylon in Israel's judgment was obvious. The other great world-area for Israel was Egypt. **Egypt, Ethiopia and Seba** may be taken to represent all Africa known to Israel in OT times. Possibly the thought is of their expected conquest by Cyrus: they are to be given up in exchange for Israel. In any case, 11:10ff. is in mind and the prophet at once introduces the theme of the great *ingathering* (5f.) from the four corners of the earth; cf. 11:12. It will be the function of these nations to bring back the scattered Israelites (cf. 49:12, 66:20), i.e. all whom Yahweh created for his glory (cf. 11:10). (N.B. 11:16 also speaks of 'a *highway* from Assyria for the remnant which is left of his people'.) 451

8-13. The blind and deaf servant of 42:19 now has eyes to see and ears to hear and therefore is prepared as a witness (10) to the divine plan in so far as, already revealed in prophecy, it has been fulfilled and seen (the 'former things', 9). The idea of witness to the fulfilment of prophecy is marked in 1 Isa.: it is explicit in 8:2, 18 and implicit everywhere. The motive is always that the fulfilment may be recognised as Yahweh's work and he may be acknowledged, as clearly in 10*c* here. **Believe** has all the overtones of the teaching of Isaiah of Jerusalem; cf. 7:9, 28:16. The general picture implied by **9ff.** is the court of justice and disputation as in 41:21ff. But the object of the demonstration is not merely to bring mental conviction or to show the divine hand in history: it leads to the apprehension of *God in himself*. Thus (*a*) **know** involves apprehension by and through the whole personality. This is true knowledge. (*b*) **believe me** means 'stand fast in me'. This is faith. (*c*) All is summed up in the pregnant **I am he**—which is no otiose repetition but the very heart of the matter. Whoever knows him, knows all that there is to know. (*d*) **10d.** This is the *eternal* God of 40:28, q.v., the Alpha and Omega of 41:4. (*e*) **11a** only points the inner logic that this is full monotheistic faith. (*f*) **Besides me there is no saviour**—i.e. (as in 43:3) the content of the word 'God' is given in all that is known in his redeeming (and revelatory) activity. These verses thus contain all the central mysteries of the biblical doctrine of revelation and response. c

14-21 The new Exodus—14. The general sense is certainly that of RSV but the Heb. text is difficult. **Lamentations** represents a widely supported emendation. Perhaps the rendering **break down** goes too far beyond the literal meaning of the word 'cause to go down'. If that is so, it is plausible to render 'nobles' for **bars** and to think of their descent to *Sheol* as in 14:9–11. There also the kings of the nations are consigned to Sheol and the pomp of Babylon is 'brought down'. This would give added point to the description of Yahweh as **your king.** Otherwise, of course, the 'bars' are the bars of imprisonment. **16.** The God who will send to Babylon is the God who has already led his people from a bondage to freedom. The **way in the sea** refers to the passage of the Red Sea. The order of the Heb. emphasises the word 'way'. As then a way was made through the water, so now through the desert (40:3, 43:19) and mighty obstacles will be overcome (17). **18.** Here, plainly, the Exodus is included within the 'former things' (cf. on 41:22), and the 'new thing' is the new Exodus, now unfolding before their eyes (19). **Remember not:** future anamnesis or remembrance will not be (as in the Passover; cf. 52:12) of the escape from Egypt, but of the new act of redemption. Better: 'You shall not remember'. **20.** Water in the desert was one of the great gifts of the period of the wandering through the desert. So now his provision will be bountiful (cf. 41:18f.). The change from the 2nd to the 3rd person **20b** and **21** is entirely characteristic and no indication of a gloss. d

22-28. This section is probably to be understood as a deliberate contrast with 1:10–15. There assiduous worship is envisaged and, because Israel was sinful, was unacceptable. Here, no sacrifice is offered (nor could be in exile; cf. 3 Isa.) but Israel remains sinful. In 1:13 'bring no more'—and here 'you have not brought'. Sacrifice did not then avail to atone for sin or avert judgment; neither will it merit redemption now. The sin is the same; and to deal with it there is free grace and forgiveness. **25. For my own sake** indicates not self-concern but unmerited grace, a necessity of the divine character. The complementary truth is in 45:4. **26. Put me in remem-** e

51e **brance ; let us argue together :** cf. the legal encounter of 1:18. But this does not lead to self-justification, as RSV would suggest ; for ' set forth your case ' (a single word in Heb.) as in 21 means ' recite ' (the praise of Yahweh, i.e. his mighty works). The recitation amounts therefore to a *credo* and act of faith ; whereupon Israel will be ' justified ' or pronounced ' right with God '. **27.** The inner meaning of the Exile and its proper cause is Israel's sin. The frequent reference to Jacob and the parallelism suggest that **your first father** is Jacob, the typical Israelite. The **mediators** are kings, priests and prophets. The whole body is sick ; cf. 1:5f. **28. The princes of the sanctuary :** the whole verse is parallel to 27 and there is chiasmus, so that ' our first father ' is further explained as Jacob-Israel and ' your mediators ' are ' the princes of the sanctuary '. The terms are unusual.

f **XLIV 1-5 A new Spirit and Blessing for all Believers—1f.** The creator, who has also elected Israel to be his servant, addresses him as **Jeshurun,** probably a diminutive from a word meaning ' upright ' (cf. Dt. 32:15, 33:5, 26), i.e. a poetic name for Israel under her ideal character. The theme of the desert made fertile (41:17–20, 43:20) is here used figuratively of the spiritual growth and blessing of Israel. As water makes dry ground fertile, the spirit will recreate Israel (cf. Ezek. 36:26f., 30, 37) and bless her offspring. Fruitful ' seed ' was the first part of the promise to Abraham ; the second that in him ' all the families of the earth will bless themselves ' (Gen. 12:3). And the fulfilment of this seems adumbrated in **5.** The language of this verse would be somewhat otiose used of Israelites, even if apostate ; it most naturally refers to proselytes and is an expression of the universalism which is to gather momentum in the oracles to come ; cf. Ps. 87:4f. The sign on the hand may be a tattoo or a sign bound on the hand as in Exod. 13:16 ; Dt. 6:8f., 11:18. The interpretation above is by no means invalidated by passages in which the subservience of the gentiles is set forth, e.g. 45:14.

52a **6-23 The Incomparability of the one God—6-8** repeat what we have already learned about the one God in terms of uncompromising monotheism. Thus **6b,** the Alpha and Omega ; cf. 41:4. **7a,** his incomparability ; cf. 40:18, 25. **7b,** the lord of history whose mind is revealed in prophecy ; cf. 41:21ff., 42:9, 43:9, 16–19. **8b,** exclusive monotheism; cf. 43:11, and Israel's function to witness ; cf. 43:12. All this is brought together in a passage of classical clarity to contrast the more vividly with the passage that follows on the ludicrous absurdity of idols (9–20). *7b* in RSV represents an entirely convincing and generally accepted conjectural emendation. The Heb. is unintelligible. There is some relationship, difficult to define, between this chapter and Dt. 32. In common are ' rock ' and ' Eloah ' (an early, singular form of the term for ' God ', which in later poetry is an archaism) ; cf. Dt. 32:15 where the two terms are also in parallelism. Similarly 43:11f. seems to echo Dt. 32:10, 12, 16, 39. This in no way removes the stamp of originality which is everywhere apparent.

b **9-20.** This is the most sustained exposition in 2 Isa. of the meaninglessness of idols and amplifies the briefer passages, 40:19, 41:6f., 42:17. In each case the contrast is made between the one incomparable God who is creator and these makeshifts of credulous men. The setting here is therefore entirely suitable and deliberately introduced by 6–8. The darkness of ignorance is to be seen all the blacker against the light of truth. Theories of displacement miss the point. It is possible that, despite RSV, the passage is poetry, although the special vocabulary may have been the cause of a certain disturbance of normal poetical form. Should grammatical peculiarities point to the hand of a disciple, that disciple correctly expresses the teaching of the master.

9. their witnesses neither see nor know : in contrast to Israel (41:20), the witnesses of 43:10 who see the true nature of events and know Yahweh. 452b
Emendation is indefensible. **12.** RSV is dependent for ' fashions it ' on a conjectural emendation. **13. in a house :** i.e. in a domestic shrine or a temple. **18. shut :** lit. ' smeared '.

21-22. Exhortation to the servant to turn to c
Yahweh : in contrast to the strange loyalty shown by men to their false gods, the servant is exhorted to a single-minded loyalty to Yahweh. The second **my servant** in the Heb. of **21** is more emphatic than the first—almost ' a servant of *mine* '. **21. Remember these :** ' remember ' so easily takes on a cultic sense (make remembrance of) that ' these ' cannot refer to the idols of 9–20. Rather it refers to the preceding oracles and shows that the passage is a deliberate concluding exhortation and a link with what is to come. **22** is a quite remarkable anticipation of the NT. **return to me** is Heb. for μετανοεῖτε or ' repent ', and the motive, **for I have redeemed you,** implies prevenient, redeeming love. **23** is a characteristic interlude of praise ; cf. 42:10–13, 49:13, 55:12. **and will be glorified in Israel** ; cf. 49:3, 60:19, 21, 61:3.

XLIV 24-XLV The Programme and the Agent d
of Salvation

24-28 The Programme of Salvation—The passage begins with now familiar language descriptive of the creator, for it is he who is author of the *new* creation. That is the first ground of faith. **25** contrasts the diviners, whose efforts to interpret history are shown to be foolish, with the servant or messenger of Yahweh who has true insight into the plan of God ; cf. 45:20ff. That the plan of God, as set forth in the word of his servant, is surely confirmed (26) is the second ground of faith. In this confidence the programme of Yahweh's redemptive acts is set forth (26*b*–28). Notice that the servant Israel is endowed with the prophetic gift : there is a word of *Israel* to mankind, which of course is spoken by individual messengers. To change to the plural ' servants ', even with the support of LXX and Targ., is to miss the point. **27.** Similar poetic imagery has been used to signify the making of a way for the redeemed (cf. 42:15) ; and that is the meaning here. It has nothing to do with the diverting of the course of the Euphrates and Cyrus's capture of Babylon. **28a. my shepherd :** figuratively in OT usage a ' ruler '. Here the word echoes 40:11 and attempts to discover a different meaning are unnecessary. **28b** is often regarded as an addition. Certainly the Heb. ' and saying ' seems clumsy and the Temple is not again mentioned in 2 Isa. But these are precarious grounds for rejection. For if not by the prophet himself, the line is introduced by a disciple to complete the programme which is incomplete without it. And whether it is by the unknown, inspired Second Isaiah or the no more unknown but no less inspired disciple makes no difference to its importance. The language both anticipates 45:13 and echoes 14:32 and 28:16.

XLV 1-7 The Role of Cyrus—As in Ezek. 34 a
Yahweh is the good shepherd who nevertheless appoints royal shepherds to rule in his name, so in 2 Isa. it is Yahweh who ' comes with might and his own arm rules for him ' (40:10), yet who anoints one who shall act in his name. The term **messiah** is nowhere in the OT a technical term in the sense of later Judaism and Christianity : this is the only occurrence of the term in Isa., and nowhere else in the OT is it applied to anyone outside the covenant community. Its primary use is of one who acts in Yahweh's name and by his authority, whether king or priest or prophet. Its figurative force here is obvious, and its boldness becomes apparent. **To Cyrus** has been regarded by some as an identifying gloss which ruins the poetry and radically alters the interpretation—a ' fact beyond question ' (Torrey). But the **Thus says the Lord** is anacrusis and outside the rhythm. Then it will be observed that the first *three* lines of the Heb. begin each of them with *two* words prefaced with *lāmedh.*

452e Triads and repetitions are marked characteristics of the style of 2 Isa. It is therefore a ' fact beyond question ' that the word ' to Cyrus ' belongs to the very first form of this poem.

f **1a** is naturally in the language of 41:2, and the oracle as a whole is mainly a combination of familiar themes. **2a :** cf. 40:10. **3b** is the motive of 41:20, **I call you by your name :** cf. 42:6, 43:1. Language applied to Abraham and Israel is now applied to Cyrus with the implication of close relationship between God and his anointed agent. The monotheism of **5** is that which has been already presented as the great ground for understanding all events as part of Yahweh's plan. But as always, there is new with the old. Cyrus is the one for whom doors and gates (1*c*, 2*b*) are opened, i.e. whose career of triumph Yahweh permits, who also is given the treasures of Babylon (**darkness** as in 19). The levelling of ' rough places ' (RSV ' mountains ', following LXX and 1QIs[a]) is a figure of the way Yahweh expedites his progress. Three motives are given for the triumphant appearance of Cyrus : (i) that Cyrus might know that **It is I, the Lord** (3*b*). This was not fulfilled. Cyrus remained a worshipper of Bel-Marduk, and his liberal provision for Israel was made expressly in the name of Marduk. **Though you do not know me** (4*b*) remained true. (ii) For Israel's sake (4*a*)—the complement of 43:25. (iii) That the peoples from E. to W. might know the only God (6). **7** adds participial clauses which declare the power of Yahweh in new and daring contrasts. There can be no rival power of evil. The sovereignty of the universal creator is absolute : dualism is unthinkable. He is finally responsible for good and evil, whatever philosophical distinctions, unnecessary to the Heb. mind, may subsequently be demanded. **I make weal and create woe :** the Heb. has ' peace ' (or ' harmony ') and ' evil '. 1QIs[a] has the obvious and unimaginative ' good ' for ' peace '. MT is to be preferred. It does not follow that the prophet is here attacking any particular dualism : he is in his own way drawing out the implications of his doctrine. **8** is another interlude of praise ; cf. 42:10–13, 43:23, 49:13, etc.

g **9-13.** The inflexible purpose of the creator is not to be questioned. The difficulty felt by some in the designation of Cyrus as ' my shepherd ', ' my anointed one ' was apparently felt by contemporaries of the prophet. **9.** RSV **potter :** an emendation, but undoubtedly right ; cf. RV, which does what it can with MT. **no handles :** Heb. ' hands '. RSV is right and provides an interesting basis for the interpretation in Rom. 9:20f. **10. Woe :** better ' Shame on . . .' The form of the earlier ' reproach ', but without the denunciatory content. This is apparent in that the ' reproach ' is not direct ; the figurative element (the clay and the child) involves an indirect approach to the understanding, as almost always in 2 Isa. **11b.** RSV here takes refuge in an emendation which has the effect of omitting the word ' things to come '. This is precarious. Render : ' In respect of things to come, will you question me about my children ? ' It is for them neither to question nor to dictate the divine purpose to use Cyrus (cf. 42:5f.) to rebuild Jerusalem and free the exiles. **13. not for price or reward :** superficially contradicting 43:3f. But the emphasis here, as of the whole passage, is on the plan and act of Yahweh. It is he who gives salvation for neither price nor reward : it is free, unmerited grace ; cf. 55:1.

h **14ff.** The programme of salvation having been stated and the role of Cyrus set forth and defended, there follows a collection of oracles without sustained logical connection, although it is not difficult to see the reason for their present position. The whole collection is cemented together by a refrain which summarised 44:6f. : **I am the Lord and there is no other.** It occurs six times in 5, 6, 15, 18, 21, 22 and the arrangement is such that a climax is reached in the image of the universal worship of Yahweh in 23. **14f.** The homage of the nations ; cf. 43:3. **in chains :** this may refer to their coming defeat at the hands of Cyrus (43:3). But the activity of Cyrus is but part of the wider scheme of universal salvation : therefore when they pay tribute, they must pay tribute to the holy people through whom they will come to the recognition of the only God. This is a central, not a peripheral theme, as shown by its commanding importance in ch. 60. If on the other hand the ' chains ' mean that the enchained are *Israel's* subject peoples, that is but a familiar theme of the cult as in Ps. 2, 110. **15** is probably still the speech of the nations. The particularity of Yahweh's identity as God of Israel hides his universality. He has hidden himself in the silence of Israel and the darkness of Babylon.
16-17 is the familiar contrast between idol-worshippers shamed (cf. 24f., 41:11, 42:17, 44:9, 11) and Israel saved with **everlasting salvation.** This is a consequence of the character of God himself (40:28) and characterises his devotion (54:8), and his covenant (55:3).

18-23. The hiddenness of God himself to the nations is contrasted with the *openness* of his word spoken. **i**
19. It is probably an error to interpret ' in a land of darkness ' as parallel to ' in secret '. Rather : ' I did not speak secretly in a land of darkness ', i.e. he spoke openly to Israel in Babylon (cf. 42:7). In fact he speaks *righteousness* (19*c*) ; and as he says in 23: **from my mouth has gone forth in righteousness a word that shall not return,** anticipating the expansion of this theme in 55:11. This leads naturally to a reassertion of the conviction that the word has been spoken by the prophets throughout the first dispensation (21*b*), and therefore to a renewed call to the representatives of foreign gods to declare the mind of God in disputation (20). This is the theme of the fulfilment of prophecy. Those who are called to disputation are more precisely defined here as **you survivors of the nations** (i.e. those who escape judgment ; cf. 66:19) and as **those who carry about their wooden idols.** No doubt religious processions, witnessed in Babylon, determined the language : but Isaiah in consequence contrasts elsewhere the God, who, so far from being carried, himself *carried* his people ; cf. 40:11, 46:3. Here the context requires the single point that these gods cannot save (20*c*) and leads to the classical expression of 21*d* : **a righteous God and a saviour.** **8** and **21d** are the first of a set of expressions in which righteousness and salvation are associated closely together (46:13, 51:5f.). God is righteous because he is the source of all rightness and wills to set right that which is wrong. A righteousness of God therefore *goes forth* : this is God's redemptive activity : the great word has become in 2 Isaiah's handling of it fundamentally soteriological, in fact close in meaning to salvation. ' Salvation is, so to speak, the clothing, the manifestation of Jehovah's righteousness ' (A. B. Davidson). (N.B. This is exactly the meaning of righteousness in Rom. 3:21ff. and is no doubt the background to St Paul's thought. All is on the widest scale of the purpose of the universal God.) **22.** Therefore the chapter comes to an end with an invitation to the nations to accept salvation. Righteousness has gone forth from his mouth, i.e. the whole prophetic word which bears witness to it ; and the final image is of universal worship (23*c*) in terms which St Paul found apt to use of the universal worship of the ascended Christ (Phil. 2:10f.).

XLVI-XLVII On Babylon—Salvation for Zion : Judgment on Babylon—The arrangement is clear. **453**
46:1f. draws attention to the gods (Babylonian) who are carried. In contrast (3–13), Yahweh carries his people and saves them. 47 sings of the humiliation of Babylon at the hands of Yahweh. This in itself is an expansion of the theme of 45:20, 24f., and indeed 45:24f. is the link between what precedes and what follows.

XLVI The gods who are carried and the God who carries—This chapter echoes in every verse now familiar themes, but in a total combination of freshness.

3a **1f.** The striking picture of 45:20 is here made more precise. The gods whose processions Israel has seen in Babylon are identified as Bel, originally the god of Nippur, father of the gods, now identified with Marduk; and Nebo, son of Bel-Marduk, god of wisdom and one of the favourite gods, patron of Nebuchadrezzar and Nabonidus. If the prophet here, as in 42:17 and 44:9–20, identifies the gods with their idols, that is not because he is naïve or incapable of understanding the better side of polytheism, but because he cannot acknowledge that these gods have any other meaning than that of lifeless idols.

b **3-13** is an address to Israel in which that which we have already learned is harnessed to point the sharpest contrast between belief and superstition. (*a*) **3-4.** Yahweh carries his people from birth to old age. **From birth . . . to the womb** ; cf. 44:2, 24 (48:8, 49:1, 5). The image of Israel as a man brought up by Yahweh is that of 1:2 and summarises his relationship with his people throughout the saving history. (*b*) **5-7.** The incomparability of Yahweh ; cf. 40:12–20. **6.** cf. 44:10, 15, 17. The vanity of trying to make a god of *permanence* ; cf. 41:7. **7. They lift it upon their shoulders, they carry it** shows how this is a dominant motif in the prophet's mind ; cf. 45:20, 46:1, 3. (*c*) **8-13.** Yahweh's purpose stands and is vindicated by prophecy ; cf. 41:21-9, 42:8f., 43:9, 16–19, 44:6–8, 45:20f. The **former things** here are all the predicted events of the first dispensation, especially those that form the special preoccupation of the Isaiah school (see on 41:22, 26). **10. My counsel shall stand** (cf. 40:8, 44:26, 48:14) in contrast with all other counsel (8:10). **11. Bird of prey :** in parallelism with **man of my counsel,** i.e. man of destiny, i.e. Cyrus. A not inapt description of the career of Cyrus. Israel is addressed (8) as **you transgressors :** this characteristic prophetic word for sin as personal rebellion against God (cf. 1:2) does not in 2 Isa. necessarily indicate a direct judgment or denunciation. Elsewhere (43:25, 27, 50:1) the prophet makes clear that rebellion was the inner cause of the judgment of 597–586. In 48:8 ' a rebel from birth ' perfectly exemplifies his use of the conception. The term in 2 Isa. implies not denunciation but *confession,* as explicitly in 53:5, 8, 12. The Israel of the first dispensation is a rebel, and of course the Israel whom the prophet addresses is the same Israel. That rebellion and its consequences are all written in the plan of Yahweh. These three themes are thus combined to show that, as against the no-gods, Yahweh will accomplish his purpose of salvation : and this is the subject of the concluding exhortation.

c **12-13.** There is a deliberate play on the word **far from . . . not far off.** Righteousness has the soteriological meaning defined in the note on 45:21*d*. Thus the contrast is between the silence of exile and judgment and the word of salvation that is now being spoken. There is possibly also a sense in which the spatial distance of exile is regarded as a symbol of separation from Yahweh. Zion is regularly associated with righteousness and salvation (1:26f. and the new Jerusalem 60:17f.) : hence **I will put salvation in Zion** (13*b*). The RSV rendering of ' righteousness ' here by ' deliverance ' achieves only half of its meaning, and disguises the importance of this passage as part of the conceptual background of Rom. 3:21ff. The phrase **far from righteousness** is thus seen to have special meaning in a context of oracles proclaiming the nearness of God's righteousness in the sense of his saving activity. This exhortation is, in a single sentence, the gospel of the OT according to Isaiah : comparable in principle to Mk 1:15.

d **XLVII The Humiliation of Babylon**—In 46:1f. the gods that cannot save go into captivity : in 47 the city of Babylon itself is humbled in the varied imagery of a powerful taunt-song (in the usual *ḳînāh* rhythm ; cf. 13, 14, where however there is little to be found in common). Although the special theme demands a special vocabulary, it is not necessary to separate the song from the oracles of 2 Isa. It is carefully and 453d
significantly placed in its present position ; moreover 9ff. are closely related to 44:9–20. The main points are (*a*) 1–4 : humiliation as a result of divine vengeance ; (*b*) 5–7 : Babylon, having been commissioned with the task of chastising Israel, has overstepped her commission. (*c*) 8–11 : Babylon merits destruction because she has put herself in the place of God (8*b*, 10*c*) ; cf. the charge against Tyre and Egypt (Ezek. 28:1–10, 29:3, 31:10) and also in respect of Babylon, Isa. 14:12ff. (*d*) 12–15 : Her mentors cannot save : only Yahweh is saviour. These principles of divine judgment amongst the nations are those of Heb. prophecy generally.

1. Virgin daughter implies youth and beauty unsullied by hard experience ; but it need not necessarily mean unconquered (unravished), since the expression is widely used of many nations. So also *widowed* Jerusalem sits upon the ground (3:26 ; cf. 52:1f.). **2a.** Her task shall now be that, not of the delicate princess, but of the female slave. **2b.** The robes of privilege are to be laid aside. **pass through the rivers :** an accepted figure of judgment ; cf. 43:2. **5. darkness :** i.e. Babylon's own imprisonment. For Israel, darkness *is* Babylon ; cf. 42:7, 45:19. **7. for ever :** that is a command which can be given only by Yahweh, the everlasting God, 40:28. **8. I am and there is no-one besides me :** in the language of 2 Isa. this is a pregnant divine self-predication ; cf. the six-times-repeated affirmation in 45. The image has now quietly changed : Babylon is proud mother with husband and children. The change is easy for the Heb. mind which does not aim at one consistent image : the unifying factor is in the meaning ; cf. Isa. 3:25–4:1 ; Lam. **11** implies the twofold principle of atonement as it becomes clear in OT and NT, viz. (*a*) that sins must be atoned and (*b*) no atonement is possible except *God* provide the means. **12f.** The Chaldaeans were renowned in the ancient world for soothsaying and astrology. **13. Your many counsels :** i.e. conflicting and useless, and contrasted with the single counsel of Yahweh ; cf. 44:26, 46:11. **15b :** the ultimate truth about Babylon. Yahweh alone is saviour ; cf. 43:3, 45:15, 20, 46:4, 7. e

XLVIII Exhortation to hear the News of Salvation—The final chapter of the first complex of the prophecies of 2 Isa. is a set of oracles arranged here by reason of their aptness for a concluding exhortation. Their original independence fully explains any differences such as some scholars have seen within the chapter. On the other hand they are carefully woven together by means of the repeated exhortation to hear (1, 12, 14, 16), and as a whole form an expansion of the invitation of 46:12. Familiar themes are used but in a new connection. Thus predominant is the theme of the fulfilment of prophecy ; but it is not here a ground of faith (as earlier) so much as a demonstration of Israel's deafness to God's word and a reason for urgent response and action now. f

1ff. The key to the interpretation of the chapter is given in the opening verses with their marked contrast between Israel's profession (1f.) and practice (5ff.) and real character (4, 8), thus pointing to the true nature of redemption as unmerited grace (9, 11). **From the loins of Judah** (a generally accepted emendation) : but descent is no substitute for obedience (cf. Lk. 3:8). **Swear by the name of the Lord . . . confess the God of Israel** (i.e. make remembrance of ; cf. 43:18) all suggest assiduous cultic observance (cf. 1:10–17). But this is not in truth or righteousness. There follow a series of remarkably severe descriptions of Israel (4f., 7f., 18f.). This is an amplification of 46:13. The essential principle to grasp is that the Israel of the past and present is one Israel. This is the conception which has been aptly called that of ' corporate personality ' (Wheeler Robinson)—and ' such a psychical whole has an extension in time as well as space, so that the mystic bond which unites society may be conceived retrospectively g

453g as regards its ancestors and prospectively with regard to future generations' (A. R. Johnson). There is therefore no contradiction in addressing Israel at one moment a rebel, at another chastened, at another the Lord's righteous servant. By this principle the prophet is able to address the Israel he knows, about to return to Jerusalem forgiven, and yet to describe her as a rebel from birth and to speak of her sin as that which merited the judgment of exile. **3.** Thus the **former things** are the prophecies which reach back to the beginning of the Isaianic corpus and especially Isaiah of Jerusalem's prediction of the Day of the Lord and the preoccupation with this theme that is to be discerned in the final arrangement of chs. 1–39, but also, possibly, in a general way all the prophecies of the old dispensation (**of old**). **I made them known:** i.e. by prophets and, of course, especially by the Isaiah school of prophets. **Suddenly they came to pass:** such a general fulfilment was the fall of Jerusalem, widely recognised as the partial fulfilment of the Day of the Lord in so far as that was to be a day of judgment on Israel. **5.** And the reason for prediction was that the events should be recognised as Yahweh's work. The idolatry is clearly that of pre-exilic Israel. **6.** The **new things** are the new prophecies of salvation, **hidden things**, not before known or heard (repeated with emphasis in 7, 8), a distinction now crystallised in the difference between chs. 1–39 and 40–55. It can be said of Israel that she has not listened to her prophets, i.e. **from of old your ear has not been opened (8a)**; this is the same as calling her a rebel from birth **(8b)**; cf. 46:8.

h **9-11** implies the inevitability of judgment upon a sinful people; and the difficult v. **10** seems to mean that the refining process of defeat and exile, **the furnace of affliction** (a term used of the Egyptian bondage; cf. Dt. 4:20), has produced dross, not silver (cf. 1:25). There is still no inherent worth which Israel possesses of herself which should merit redemption. Deserved punishment would have been complete destruction (cf. 40:1); the motive of salvation is the sheer unmerited love of Yahweh (cf. 43:25).

i **14-16** begins with a command to assemble which, being addressed to the Israel who in 1 is challenged by the profession of her cult, and not rhetorically to the far coasts and peoples (e.g. 41:1, 43:9, 45:20), must be understood literally of the assembly of the congregation of Israel in exile. (Volz envisages the prophet addressing the sabbath assembly and thinks that most of the oracles belong to this setting.) This is a Cyrus oracle. **The Lord loves him**, i.e. Cyrus; cf. 44:28, 45:1, 46:11. **on Babylon**, cf. 45:1ff. **16** is the only certain reference to the prophet himself apart from 40:6, and is marked by a reticence which amounts to obscurity. **From the first I have not spoken secretly** (cf. 45:19), i.e. the prophet claims to have spoken openly. **From the time that it came to pass I am there**, i.e. interpreting the 'former things', the fact of the fall of Jerusalem and the Exile, in the light of prophecy. **And now the Lord God has sent me**, i.e. to proclaim the new things. **And his Spirit** is awkward as subject or object, but is best taken in the light of 40:13 as practically equivalent to the counsel of Yahweh in process of fulfilment.

j **17-19** is a plaintive expression of sorrow that Israel has by sin interrupted the fulfilment of the covenant promise.

20-21 concludes the chapter with the direct and final command to leave Babylon. The imagery of 21 is that of the exodus and the language verbally related to Ps. 105:41ff. **The Lord has redeemed his servant Jacob** would appear to be an adaptation of Ps. 105:42 and to indicate that the prophet is using this psalm. **22** concludes the whole section 40–8; cf. 57:21.

454a **(B) XLIX-LV The Paradox of present Humiliation and the divine Plan of Salvation**

XLIX-L The Paradox of the universal Role of the Servant and the Forsakenness of Israel—This section begins and ends with the self-declaration of the servant (49:1–6, 50:4–9) and is rounded off with a pronouncement on the consequences of belief and unbelief (50:10f.) In between occur the passages 49:15ff., 20ff., 50:1–3 which deal with Israel's complaint of forsakenness and anticipate the picture of the widowed mother Zion in 54:1–6. 49:7 and 50:4–9 anticipate the suffering servant of 53 and hint at the positive virtue hidden in suffering and humiliation. 49 receives remarkable reinterpretation in 60, q.v. 60 belongs to the period shortly after the rebuilding of the Temple, 520–516: the complex of oracles represented in 49 must therefore have been in its present form within a few years of their utterance, and the interpretation of the servant of 1–6 given by the juxtaposition of 7–13 must go back to the circle of the prophet, if not to the prophet himself.

b **XLIX 1-6 The Restorer of Israel and Light to the Gentiles** (the second of 'the Servant Songs')—In 40–8 the dialectic presents a servant at once righteous and a rebel. The first 'Servant Song', 42:1–4, represents one side of this dialectic. In 49–55 the dialectic presents an *Israel* with a mission to *Israel* (already hinted in 40:9–11) and, beyond Israel, to mankind. The three 'Servant Songs', 49:1–6, 50:4–9 and 52:13–53:12, all raise this problem. How central it is is shown by the fact that in 49–55 the term 'servant' is not used of Israel outside these poems in the way so familiar in chs. 40–8. The 'servant' is now Israel in respect of this startling function of mission. The difficulty for the modern mind is overcome by realising the oneness of Israel in time as well as space (see on 48:1ff.). It is the Israel of history, promise and judgment to whom Israel (the 'servant') has his mission, i.e. the Israel that fulfils the function for which he is destined. This somewhat mystical distinction became stereotyped in the circumstances of restoration into a distinction between the pious and the faithless; cf. 65 (and cf. 50:10f.). It cannot be overemphasised that 5f., which have often provided the main ground for the interpretation of the servant as an individual by many scholars, are the very heart of the prophet's insight into the mission of *Israel* and the place where we see how this prophet surpassed all previous prophecy.

c **1.** The call from the womb; cf. 44:2, 24, 46:3, all of *Israel*. **2.** The word of God—entrusted to Israel as to a prophet; cf. 48:6, 51:16 which echoes this passage, and especially 44:26. The hiddenness is that of preparation and protection in readiness for mission. **3.** The explicit identification of **my servant** with Israel is to be accepted. Deletion of *Israel* on the score of one inferior MS is indefensible. **glorified:** cf. 44:23, also of Israel. **4b.** This is the proper trust, exemplified in the servant, which was noticeably lacking in questioning Israel; cf. 40:27. **5.** As clear a definition of Israel's election for service as is to be found anywhere. **6. to raise up the tribes of Israel**, i.e. to restore Israel to the corporate identity of the days of promise (the twelve tribes) before that identity was destroyed in the judgment of the end of her history. The return from Babylon is not simply the first step in making Israel what she *was*; the new dispensation involves a greater commission: **a light to the nations**; cf. 42:6. **my salvation:** cf. 46:13. **7** now presents the paradox that this involves—that of present humiliation and this divine plan of salvation to be realised through Israel. These three lines contain a whole set of verbal connections with 53 which may be taken as an expansion and fuller interpretation of this verse.

d **8-12** interpret 1–6 in terms of the familiar themes of 40–8. It is 'a typical Deutero-Isaianic oracle on the deliverance of Israel'. Thus 8*b* = 42:6*b*. **9.** The prisoners and darkness of exile: cf. 42:7, 45:19. **10.** The theme of the desolate places becoming fertile: cf. 41:18, 43:19f. **11.** The 'way': cf. 40:3. **12.** The 'ingathering'; cf. 43:5f. **Syene** (modern Aswân)—a plausible emendation. **13** is an interlude

454d of praise like 42:10–13, 44:23, 55:12, with an ending reminiscent of 40:1, 41:17; cf. 52:9.

e **14-21.** But all this is too great a miracle in the face of Israel's present humiliation. In **14** Zion voices her complaint of forgottenness in the form of a lament and response such as is common in the psalms. **15ff.** is Yahweh's answer in the bold image of the one whose love is more constant than that of a mother for her child. This is followed by the image of **19b-21** of Israel as the wife of Yahweh with many children (cf. 54:1ff.). As so often, the unifying factor is the theme and there is what seems to the modern mind a strange mixture of metaphors. Thus **16** may be an image of the lover who tattoos upon the palms of his hands either the name or a representation of beloved Zion (16*b*). **17. The builders** (cf. 44:26, 28, 45:13) a great ingathering—are like a bride's jewels—on Yahweh! **19a,** despite the apparent lack of a verb, demands no emendation. Two complementary reasons are given for the bridal rejoicing of 18*b*: (*a*) for *once* (what your eyes saw was) **your desolate places**; (*b*) for *now* **you will be too narrow for your inhabitants. 21.** The answer to the question of 21*a* is Yahweh; cf. 54:1ff. There are three states—barren, divorced and widowed (all descriptive of the exile) with three corresponding questions. The threefold **these** represent the repopulated Zion. The same three metaphors are present in 54:1, 4, 6.

f **22-23.** The theme of the great ingathering (cf. 11:10, 43:6) and the part of kings (and queens) in serving vindicated Israel; cf. 45:14. **23c** gives the familiar motive (cf. 45:3), and for the meaning of **wait for me** see on 40:31.

24-26. The spoiler spoiled: a characteristic reversal involved in judgment; cf. on 47:5–7. **24** is the question of 14 in another form. On the power of Yahweh to save see on 45:15, 21*d*.

g **L 1-3 No final Separation**—Israel was exiled and **put away** (49:21) but Yahweh, her husband, has not taken the unalterable decision of divorce (cf. Dt. 24:1, 3). Notice that present Israel is addressed as the children of **your mother.** Nor has Yahweh *creditors,* as though, having sold his children into slavery in order to pay his debts (cf. 52:3; Exod. 21:7; 2 Kg. 4:1), he were now in the power of his creditors (Babylon). On the contrary the 'selling' and the 'separation' were free, responsible acts of Yahweh (1*c*), and with equal freedom he will redeem (2*b*). **2c** is the imagery, partly controlled by the traditional imagery of the Exodus, of the way through the wilderness; cf. 42:15, 43:16. **3.** Equally Yahweh is responsible for the dark clouds of judgment.

h **4-9 The Prophet expresses the proper Response of faithful Israel** (the third 'Servant Song')—In contrast to the doubt and questioning expressed in 49:14, 25, here is the response of faith to the impossibility of the plan of salvation. The poem declares the prophetic function of Israel in relation to that plan, despite present humiliation. **4. the tongue of those who are taught,** i.e. as the disciples of Isaiah had been taught (cf. 8:16) and had continued to declare his teaching from the 8th cent. to this day, witnessing especially to prophecy and fulfilment. All good Israelites are to be disciples of Yahweh (54:13). **4b** is difficult: the weary are those without the divine strength (40:29) and the source of strength is the divine word entrusted to the servant. **4c** is the imagery of inspiration. The double emphasis on the open ear contrasts with the deafness of 42:19; cf. 43:8. The servant is deaf *qua* the Israel elected for service and, as a result of his failure in that service, deserving the chastisement of exile; but alert and hearing *qua* the Israel who now responds to the yet greater commission to be a light to the gentiles. 'Those who are taught' are thus essentially those who have insight into the divine mind as revealed in prophecy and fulfilled in event. **5b-6. I was not rebellious:** this obedience contrasts with the characteristic sin of the Israel of history. The faithful learned to accept the chastisement as no miscarriage of justice but 454h
rather a just act of the redeemer of Israel; cf. 42:24, 43:28, 47:6*b*, 48:9, 51:17. Submission to suffering of this kind may well owe its *description* to the known experience of Jeremiah or, less probably, to the submission of the king in the Babylonian New Year Festival, when the high priest of Marduk pulled his ears and smote his cheeks. What is important is that *Israel's* experience is here the issue, characteristically expressed in terms of individual suffering. The true meaning is plain in 51:23. **7.** The confidence that Yahweh will **help** echoes the promise to help repeatedly made by Yahweh in 41:10, 13, 14, 44:2 and 49:5 (1QIs[a]). It is also the *Israel* who puts her trust in Yahweh (as against idols) who shall not be ashamed; cf. 41:11, 42:17, 45:24, 49:23. **8a** is precisely the thought of 46:13 (also in 1st person but certainly of Israel) while the **who will contend with me?** is reminiscent of 41:11, 21, and especially 49:25. The legal terminology of 8–9*a* is also that of the repeated appeal for decision in 40–8 (otherwise the challenge to disputation on the question of prediction is absent from 49–55). **9b** (cf. 51:6–8) is a new expression of the thought of the vanity of all human pretension, as in 40:6–8. This then is the song of faith sung by those who have learned the meaning of Israel's tragic history through prophecy, who have the ears to hear, submit with understanding to the humiliation of the Exile and wait expectantly for the new divine act of redemption which they know to be near. It is not unlikely that it was composed to be sung by faithful exiles as an act of trust and belief, and that its intensely individual character was encouraged by the use for which it was intended. Each exile would embody in himself the experience of Israel; cf. the 'I' of the Psalms. By uttering the song in the assembly, he would identify himself with 'the servant' (cf. on 48:14–16).

10-11. Is it fanciful to suppose that these verses, which i
set forth the varying consequences of belief and unbelief, are addressed *from* the assembly to the generality of Israel whether in exile or later in Jerusalem? However it may be, they are now the warning climax of 49–50. Those who walk by the light of the fire of their own kindling will find it a fire of judgment.

LI 1-LII 12 The great Summons to hear and to awake—50:10f., as understood above, forms an 455a
apt transition to a set of oracles which are collected together on the basis of their common character of urgent exhortation to awake and hear. This is apparent not only in the repeated **Hearken** (51:1, 4, 7, 21; cf. 52:8), and in the characteristically doubled **Look to, look to** (51:1f.), **Awake, awake** (51:9, 52:1), **I, I** (51:12), **Rouse yourself, rouse yourself** (51:17), **Depart, depart** (52:11), but also in the sense of imminent redemption, reaching a climax in the announcement of the herald (52:7) and the theophany (8–10). 52:7 means precisely: 'The kingdom of God is at hand' (Mt. 3:2; Mk 1:15).

1-3. The address is to those who will **pursue deliverance,** i.e. 'righteousness' in the sense of redemption, b
as in 5. The exhortation that follows implies a kind of thought familiar in the preceding oracles. The holy people extends in time as well as space: there is therefore a relationship between the present Israel and the Israel of history; cf. on 48. All are from one rock or from one quarry. It is true that 'rock' is usually a metaphor for Yahweh himself (see on 44:8); but he is a rash interpreter who would confine 2 Isa. to uniformity of imagery. The thought is clearly that of looking to the fundamental character of Israel from the beginning as the elect people or servant of God, i.e. as he was in the divine intention before rebellion led to temporary rejection. This receives confirmation by the next line with its reference to Abraham and Sarah as the mother and father of the people to whom the promise of seed and land was made. Now there is to be a new beginning on the yonder side of the judgment: hence **3a** echoing 40:1 and implying the

455b situation to which the comfort answers. This is exactly the thought underlying 41:2, 8. **3bc** is the now familiar theme of the desert made fertile, with language of joy and psalm akin to 12:1, 3, 35:10 and anticipating the last chapters of the Isaianic prophecies.

c **4-8**. Righteousness and salvation are imminent and will be for ever. Words and thoughts so often found in other connections in these prophecies are here gathered together to create an overwhelming sense of urgency. **4b. a law will go forth,** i.e. in the sense of the divine instruction, as in 42:3 ; cf. 2:3. Both 2:1–4 and 42:1–4 combine instruction and judgment as offered to the gentiles and provide the conceptual background to this passage. **5.** Notice that the righteousness of God is near in the sense of his redeeming activity, as in 46:13, and, as there, is associated with 'salvation'. On the waiting expectantly see on 40:31 and 42:4. **6** expresses the same thought, though with a variation of imagery, as 40:6–8 ; cf. 50:9*b*. Salvation and righteousness are eternal because of the character of God himself ; cf. 40:28. **7.** To **know righteousness** is to have insight into the saving plan of Yahweh. **in whose heart is my law:** cf. Jer. 31:33. **Fear not the reproach of men:** the familiar command of 40:9, 41:10, 13f., etc., combined with a word for 'men' which, as shown by its association with flesh in 12, carries the suggestion of the inherent weakness of humanity over against God.

d **9-11** is a daring address to Yahweh, using ancient mythological language of the East which originally told of creation and is here descriptive of the Exodus. The thought is : Let the new Exodus begin. **Rahab, the dragon, the sea, the great deep** are all expressions for the original chaos. The hebraic genius habitually interpreted these myths historically, and that is the case here : the historical interpretation in terms of the Exodus, as shown by 10*b*, forces the imagery into the primary theme of the prophet. The Magnificat recognises the fulfilment of 9. **11** is deliberately taken from 35:10 : *it is prophecy quoted as about to be fulfilled.* Those who would excise this verse sadly miss the point.

e **12-14** begins with a divine self-predication which thus presents Yahweh in all the power of his being (cf. 41:4 and see note on 42:8) to **comfort** (cf. 40:1) ; and so throws into greater relief the vanity of human resources (cf. 40:6–8). For he is the creator (cf. 40:12ff.). **13. The fury of the oppressor** has already disappeared, by anticipation. And Zion shall once again be **my people** (cf. 40:1). **16** clearly echoes 49:2 and once again vividly presents the image of an Israel who is God's prophet and to whom God's words are committed. This is no doubt the instruction to the gentiles ; cf. 4 and the parallelism of 2:3.

f **17-23**. Suffering Jerusalem is bidden to awake to the end of her suffering, which is described in the image of **the cup of his wrath, the bowl of staggering** (a familiar symbol of prophetic eschatology (cf. Ps. 60:3, 75:8 ; Hab. 2:16 ; Zech. 12:2 ; Rev. 14:10, 16:19) indicating punishment and divine retribution). This cup is given by Yahweh to Israel to drink, i.e. Israel is punished *by him* ; cf. the insistence that the events of 597–586 are a just act of God, 42:24, 43:28, 47:6*b*, 48:10. It is because the destruction of Jerusalem is in mind that the wording of Lam. 2:19 is used in **20.** The prophet sees these events over again as though witnessing them. **22f.** But now Yahweh will give the cup to Israel's tormentors in a great reversal typical of the prophetic understanding of judgment and salvation ; cf. the spoiler spoiled, 47:5–7, 49:24–6. The paradox of present humiliation and the divine plan of salvation is again apparent.

g **LII 1-2. Reversal of Zion's Humiliation**—As in the taunt-song of 47 the 'virgin daughter of Babylon' was driven to sit upon the ground stripped of her regal dignity, so now **the captive daughter of Zion** is to awake and put on the robes of her new dignity (cf. 49:18). Babylon now a queen will become a slave : Zion now a slave will become a queen. **Uncircumcised and unclean:** as earlier used of the Philistines, symbolises the enemies of Israel who would destroy her. Now of course the Babylonians are the uncircumcised (Volz). Thus the conception does not contradict the universalism of Isaiah and the role of Israel to be a light to the gentiles. There may also be the thought here of the festal procession to Zion, in which case cf. the holy way to Zion in 35:8 over which the unclean shall not pass. **2. O captive Jerusalem:** a widely held emendation which is undoubtedly right. The objection that the repetition of 'captive' does not make good Heb. style does not stand. 455g

3-6 The Freedom of Redemption—This passage is easily misunderstood since **you were sold for nothing** superficially seems to mean 'your tragedy was undeserved', and that is clean contrary to the repeated teaching of 2 Isa. that the exile was a deliberate and just, divine act ; cf. 51:17. The meaning must be determined by 50:1. Yahweh is under no obligation to Babylon : he neither paid Babylon nor was he in Babylon's debt. He retained the sovereign freedom of God : and with the same freedom he will redeem Israel, i.e. without money. The same freedom has marked his dealings with Israel throughout her history and notably at the beginning. **4.** The Egyptian bondage and the Assyrian oppression are the great examples. It is not a matter of money but of grace (the expression 'for nothing' is a derivative from this word 'grace', and word-play would be characteristic —a good translation would be 'gratis'). **5.** The motive of redemption is not in the merit of Israel but in the necessity of the divine character (name). **6. They shall know that it is I:** rather 'that I am he'—again the self-predication which tells of the sovereign freedom of God. He is the God who speaks, whose word is revelation (40:5) and, as in 40:8f., is heralded by the messenger. Thus 3–6 reveals correspondences with the thought of 2 Isa. more significant than those difficulties of metre or style which lead some scholars to regard the passage as an intrusion. h

7-12 The Herald's Announcement of the Coming of Yahweh—The climax of the section is reached in the heralding of Yahweh's saving act before the world. The one **who brings good tidings** is not Zion, as in 40:9, for here the masculine is used and he speaks to Zion without suggestion that in some sense he is Zion. This may well be because the whole image is presented in terms of the theophany of the New Year festival in so far as that festival probably had a counterpart in the Israelite cult and determined the language of the so-called enthronement psalms ; for this passage is verbally dependent not only on Isa. 40:1–10, but also on Ps. 98. **7. upon the mountains:** cf. 40:9. **your God reigns:** the central affirmation of the enthronement festival. It was *cultically* expressed in Ps. 47:8, 93:1, 97:1, 99:1 ; in so far as the monarchy failed it became an *eschatological hope* (a transformation which may already have influenced the psalms) ; it was now to become *historical actuality*. This is the king who, at his epiphany, is seen (6, 33:5f.) ; wherefore (**8b**) **eye to eye they see the return of the Lord to Zion** ; cf. 40:5; Ps. 98:3. The return of the Lord to Zion : i.e. as in the old festal processions ; as also after judgment (cf. Ezek. 43:15) ; and by further application as he brings his people from Babylon (cf. 12*b*, 40:10). i

9a. Cf. 49:13, Ps. 98:4. **9b.** Cf. 49:13, 51:3, but also 40:1. **10. his holy arm,** cf. Ps. 98:1 ; Isa. 40:10 and the prayer of 51:9, to which this is the answer. **before the eyes of all the nations,** cf. Ps. 98:2. And then 10*b* = Ps. 98:3. Here then is the true *recognition* of the kingship of Yahweh and the coming of the kingdom (sovereign rule) of God in the OT. j

But the prophet's thought is not determined by the imagery. Rather does his thought determine the imagery, which he changes as he wills. In **11** and **12a**

55j the thought is again of the new Exodus and the Passover. The priests shall bear the vessels as then (Exod. 12:35), but there will be no need of the haste which marked the eating of the first Passover (Exod. 12:11) **for the LORD will go before you** = Exod. 14:19. **And the God of Israel will be your rearguard:** in both Jos. 6:9, 13 and Num. 10:35 this was said of the Ark. But whereas the Ark was guarded, now God himself will be Israel's guard; cf. 40:10, 58:8.

6a **LII 13-LIII 12 The Paradox of present Humiliation and the divine Plan of Salvation resolved in the Work of the righteous Servant** (the fourth 'Servant Song')—So far three strands of thought have been pursued separately: (*a*) the sin of Israel (cf. on 42:4, 43:25-7, esp. 46:8, 48:8) leading to punishment at Yahweh's hand; (*b*) the suffering involved for the whole people (cf. 49:7, 50:6, 51:23) including the righteous; and (*c*) the role of the righteous servant in relation to the plan of salvation (cf. 42:1–4, 49:1–6, 50:4–9). There has been a partial connection of (*a*) and (*b*) and of (*b*) and (*c*), but now for the first time all three are brought together in the image of a righteous servant who shares the suffering and in so doing bears the cause of that suffering, viz the sin of the people. Thus the prophet penetrates to the mystery of vicarious suffering—the righteous servant suffers for the sin of the many. There is a solitariness about this passage, but that is because *familiar* themes and problems for a moment have a new dimension in depth, not because it is alien to its context. The individualism of the imagery (cf. 46:3f., 47:1–3, 5, 7f., 54:1–8) and its sustained character (i.e. as more than an allusive metaphor) is but the inspired development of a prophetic mode natural to this prophet. The unusual proportion of words (46 in all) not otherwise found in 2 Isa. only answers to the unusualness of the subject. Above all though the prophet describes the role of the servant Israel in intensely individual terms, yet the characteristics of *Israel's* 'personality' and situation in turn influence the image so that it is neither a consistent individual image nor a plain account of Israel's divine role but a compound of both—cf. 54:1–10. That is why interpretations which expound the passage in terms of an individual servant *only* or as consistent allegory of Israel *only* cannot be satisfactory. Neither imagery nor form is homogeneous. That is why it is not sufficient to think in terms of a psalm of thanksgiving (Begrich) or the funeral dirge with confession of sins (Mowinckel) or any other form as more than a mere suggestive framework of thought. If it is the prophetic remodelling of a liturgical composition (Engnell), the liturgical form has largely disintegrated under the pressure of the thought. The primary determinative of interpretation must be the echoes of the prophet's thought throughout his oracles. It will be seen that the richness and flexibility of the conception of the 'servant' from 41 onwards is such as to permit the epoch-making turn given to the conception in 53 (see on 41:8–10, 48:1ff., 49:1–6). There is evidence that the language of certain psalms has both assisted and influenced the expression, and a verbal relation to a passage in Jeremiah suggests that, as in 50:4–9, that prophet came inevitably to mind. The cultic background is the same as that of 52:7, and with the same important qualification. But there is no single key of interpretation, not because it has not yet been found, but because there are plainly several keys.

b **13. Behold,** in 2 Isa., introduces something which is as yet present only in prophetic vision or insight, cf. 40:10, 43:19, 47:14, 49:12, though it is none the less certain and real. Yahweh announces the triumph of the servant in language used of the Day of the Lord; cf. 2:13ff. and cf. 6:1—**exalted and lifted up,** i.e. an astonishing reversal from humiliation to a share in the dignity of Yahweh himself. This imagery is cosmic and means that Yahweh thinks of his servant in relation to the nations who become the subject of
14. 'Many' superficially suggests the community over 456b
against the individual, but both **15** and esp. 53:12 show, in the light of OT usage, that the nations are the many, i.e. the nations over against Israel. The nations, represented by their kings (15) are appalled at the magnitude of the transformation from an extreme of humiliation (14*b*) to a dignity comparable with that of God himself in his Day (13). The language used of their response in 14f. is suggested by the role of the nations in the cult. What is cultically expressed in the psalms and has become an eschatological hope is now about to be seen as historical actuality. *All this is the implication of 'Your God reigns'* (52:7) *and the psalm background is the same.* Thus comparison may be made with Ps. 2:7, 10, 46:7, 47:8, 48:5f., 96:3, 98:2f. There is now no mere cultic recitation (**that which has not been told them:** for the Heb. word see on 43:26, where it means 'recite the mighty works' of God; and for the cultic use cf. Ps. 2:7, 48:14), there is no myth (**that which they have not heard**) attached to some dramatic symbolism or representation in the cult. Rather there is the act of God in history to be *seen*; cf. Ps. 48:6, 9. So far the thought is that with which we have been made familiar. It is the paradox of humiliation and salvation, the salvation now considered as present by prophetic anticipation. A hint of that which is to come may be contained in the word 'startle' (15) which if the Heb. is retained should be rendered 'sprinkle' (cf. Lev. 4:6, etc.)—a cultic term which would suggest the servant's mediatorial and atoning role; cf. 53:10. In our uncertainty it is better to keep to the Heb. which, despite many contrary opinions, ought not to be excluded on grammatical grounds and in fact anticipates the central theme of the song.

LIII 1. Who has believed what we have heard?: c
In view of the repeated command to hearken in the preceding chapters, this must be reckoned the right translation. The matter heard is *the kerygma of salvation* and the revelation of **the arm of the Lord** is the decisive event to which all previous prophecies point; cf. 40:10, 48:14, 51:5, 9, but especially 52:10. The expression here is, like 52:10, indebted to Ps. 98:1 (a psalm which we have shown to be directly in the prophet's mind), where the revelation of Yahweh's righteousness is 'in the sight of the nations'. It is then the nations who speak in 2ff., but this will include all who are recipients of the divine grace thus mediated, Israel *qua* the rebel as well as the gentiles. This identification is important in view of the great emphasis on 'our' throughout the succeeding verses:
the reader ought to know who 'we' are! There d
follows a prophetic anticipation of the confession of sin and faith which will be made when, salvation having arrived, it is accepted by those for whom it is intended. It will be a *fact,* not a doctrinal theory, that this salvation will have come to Jew and Gentile alike through an Israel which has drunk the dregs of the cup of suffering and *in so doing has become the righteous servant that he was intended to be when Yahweh first called Abraham.* **2b.** To the recipients of salvation, the appearance of Israel is such as to *hide* her true mission. If the servant in 42:1–4 was given in royal categories, in 49 and 50 in prophetic categories (Lindblom), here the image is of a man of sorrows, subject to the two greatest misfortunes which could befall an Israelite, viz to fall victim to sickness and to fall foul of justice. **4b.** He is acquainted with sickness and stricken, a word which may possibly, though not certainly, imply leprosy. Whatever the picture, he was **smitten by God.** This was accepted by Jew and Gentile alike and is part of the firm teaching of the prophet; cf. 42:24, 43:28, 47:6*b*, 48:9, 51:17. But now in respect of the Israel that has recovered his identity as the servant of God, this chastisement *is no longer pure punishment.* When the light has flooded upon the gentiles as a result of his suffering, that suffering is recognised as **the chastisement that made us**

456d **whole,** or, in a paraphrase which admirably expresses the sense : 'that leads to our peace'. Here the confession of sin and of faith ends.

e **7** and **8b** are so verbally close to Jer. 11:19 that the suffering of that prophet must have influenced the expression here. Now the reality of which the individual suffering is the image, viz the end of Israel as a kingdom and her exile to 'the land of darkness' (45:19), leads the prophet to speak of the death of the servant. **8a** is difficult. Most satisfactory is : 'From protection and right . . .' Paradoxically it is the servant who is to guarantee judgment to the peoples (42:1–4). **9.** Because the servant's grave is in Babylon, it is among those (nations) who are both wicked and rich, although these two terms are not semantically equivalent (Mowinckel). Notice however the parallel-

f ism of Ps. 52:7. **10.** The servant's suffering is spoken of in terms of a guilt-offering, possibly because that was the only sacrifice which involved a satisfaction rendered to justice. The whole verse is difficult. The compounding of the individual image with the reality of which it is the image, now enables the prophet to speak of the resurrection of the servant. Israel died but will live again. The divine intention revealed in the call of Abraham, frustrated by Israel's sin and punishment, will be fulfilled in the righteous servant. Moreover, concerned more with the reality than with the consistency of a literary portrait, the prophet slips insensibly from the past to the future tense. Although he began with prophetic anticipation of the time when the salvation would have arrived, he now looks forward, from his own standpoint shortly before 538, to the resurrection of Israel (Ezek. 37:1–14 ; Hos. 6:2), and speaks in terms not strictly applicable to an individual at all. **He shall see his offspring,** i.e. literally 'he shall see *seed*' : the theological importance of the promise of 'seed' to Abraham is recognised by 2 Isa. (41:8, 43:5, 44:3, 48:19). The meaning is that the promise made to Abraham will

g now be fulfilled ; cf. especially 54:3. **11. he shall see the fruit of the travail of his soul and be satisfied :** this verse is a textual crux and its solution is entirely uncertain. RSV extorts the above rendering from an unwilling Heb. The missing object of the verb 'see' is probably 'light', as in LXX, now supported by 1QIs[a] and 1QIs[b]. Better : 'After his travail, he shall see light, he shall be satisfied with his knowledge ; righteous himself, my servant shall make many to be accounted righteous'. **I will divide him a portion with the great and he shall divide the spoil with the strong :** 'the great', i.e. the 'many' of 52:14f., and 53:12*c*. **The strong :** usually of the nations ; in Isa. 8:7 and Zech. 8:22, combined with 'many'. This implies the national vindication of Israel and the tribute of the nations, as previously in 2 Isa. and more plainly in 3 Isa. **12bc** returns to the essentially new insight of this prophecy ; a principle and a doctrine only partially true of the empirical Israel, even the most faithful Israel that there was. For atonement at such a depth depends on the righteousness of the servant (**11b**). The passage therefore remained an enigma within Judaism, only intelligible when changed out of recognition (see Targ.) ; intelligible only in the light of the Christian revelation of a truly righteous servant in whom the mysteries of vicarious suffering are witnessed fact.

457a **LIV The Servant's Heritage**—The reason for the position of this section after 53 is plain, despite the perplexity of commentators. The issue of the servant's sacrifice shall be the justification of 'the many' (53:11*b*), but also he himself shall live again to witness the fulfilment of the ancient promise of 'seed' (53:10*b*) and to receive 'a portion' (53:12) as one of the great nations of the earth. This portion is now defined. 54 describes the portion or heritage of the servant in two of its aspects : (*a*) the 'seed' (1–10) and (*b*) the new Jerusalem (11–17) ; and, as if to make this quite plain, ends **This is the heritage of the servants of the Lord** (plural because the prophet thinks of those who will inherit the work of the servant). Both parts are shot through with a repeated emphasis on the *permanence* of this heritage as founded in the indestructible love of God (8*b*, 10, 14, 15ff.). Since this section will have been placed here by a disciple of the prophet, if not by the prophet himself (see §447*e*), it is a powerful support of the interpretation of 53 given above.

b **1-10** Humiliation for ever overcome by the unshakeable love of Yahweh—Israel's humiliation (end of kingdom and exile) is here given under the allegorical picture of a barren woman (1) ; separated from her husband (6) ; and indeed widowed (4*b*). The three metaphors are also those of 49:21. Once again it is the theme, not a consistent image, which provides the unifying factor. She will rejoice as Yahweh's wife with many children. **1. O barren one who did not bear** is verbally reminiscent of Gen. 11:30, and therefore at once suggests Sarah and her barrenness ; cf. 51:2. **2.** The tent of the mother of Israel is the sign of her station ; cf. Gen. 24:67. As barren Sarah became the mother of Israel, so then will this childless, separated, bereaved woman (Israel punished) become the mother of a new Israel. As the pilgrimage from the east was repeated (41:2ff.), so also will be the miracle of the multiplication of the seed to the barren. Significantly St Paul thinks of Sarah when he quotes 1 in Gal. 4:27. Characteristically the application breaks through the image in **3. Your descendants will possess the nations :** RV has 'seed' and this shows the verbal link with 53:10 (RSV 'offspring') ; RSV disguises, by its varied renderings, both this link and the allusion to the promise of 'seed' to Abraham and therefore obscures the treatment of the theme by St Paul. **4.** Cf. 45:17. **4b. The shame of your youth** need not be pressed to mean only the Egyptian bondage ; rather those aspects of early history which seem to belie the fulfilment of the promise. **widowhood :** the exile. **5** connects the theme of Yahweh the husband (cf. Hos. 1–2) with the more usual emphasis of 2 Isa. on Yahweh the creator. **5b. God of the whole earth :** by reason of its uniqueness c an *emphatic* assertion of transcendent monotheism : only otherwise so expressed in Gen. 24:3. The prophet now places Israel's tragedy in proper *proportion* as he exhausts the resources of his language to emphasise the permanence of the new dispensation. **7.** Though the fall of the kingdom and the exile seem like **overflowing wrath** (paronomasia in the Heb.), that is temporary. **9.** The new covenant relationship will be unbreakable like the covenant made with Noah after the flood. The **steadfast love** or 'devotion' (8) is the inner bond of the **covenant of peace** (**10**), which is also the 'everlasting covenant' of 55:3. **not be removed :** an expression already applied to Zion and creation in the cult and therefore familiar, as in Ps. 46:5, 93:1, 96:10, 104:5. The thought is : 'you sing that the mountains and hills are unshakeable. I tell you that they may be removed, but my covenant, like my word (40:8), shall never be removed' ; cf. Mk 13:31.

d **11-17 The new Jerusalem**—The 'portion' of the servant is further described in terms of rebuilt Zion (cf. 44:28, 45:13*b*). That the oracle is addressed to Israel before the Return, like all the oracles of 40–55, is shown by the address of **11a :** it is before the 'comfort' of 40:1 has been realised. The Temple is neither explicitly excluded nor explicitly included : Zion without a Temple was unthinkable before the vision of the New Jerusalem of Rev. 21:18–22, a passage based on this ('And I saw no temple in the city'). **13.** In this city of the new covenant, all (**your sons,** as RSV, is right rather than 'builders' which is sometimes suggested on the basis of a repointing of the Heb.) shall be disciples of Yahweh himself ; cf. 8:16, 50:4 and Jer. 31:34. **14.** That Zion (**you**) will be established in righteousness is but the fulfilment of what Jerusalem was meant to be from the days of Melchizedek (King-righteousness, Gen. 14) until the present. Her kings were meant to be the embodiment

57d of righteousness and Zion 'the city of righteousness' (1:27); cf. 9:6 which is close to 14*a*. Also close to the thought of the prophet is the prophecy of 28:16 now about to be fulfilled *like this*. **17.** Zion will be safe from attack and calumny.

The elements in this picture are (*a*) glorious beauty (11f.), (*b*) direct relationship with God (13), (*c*) the city of righteousness (14), (*d*) absolute security (15–17).

e **LV Final Invitation**—In the light of the great salvation truths which have been proclaimed and the visions of glory through humiliation, 55 represents the invitation to share in the boons of the new covenant. It is addressed in the first instance not exactly to Jews or Gentiles but to **everyone who thirsts**. That the 'life' offered (3*a*) is to be shared by gentiles is shown by 5 and by 44:1–5, which clearly anticipates this theme.

f **1.** The waters are those which mark the new epoch and are a sign of the blessing and fertility of the holy seed (cf. 44:3). It has been a repeated emphasis that Yahweh *gave* Israel into the hand of Babylon and freely redeemed her; cf. 48:10, 50:1, 52:3. As unpurchasable as redemption itself are the benefits thereof. The imagery gains point from the preciousness of water sold in the streets. The divine bounty will go beyond the bread and water of the wilderness to the wine and milk of the promised land. **2b-3** echoes the oft-repeated call to **hearken**. Those who have ears to hear will find *life*. **that your soul may live:** the soul here is a pregnant periphrasis for the 'person', frequently associated with the verb 'live', and means 'your whole being' (A. R. Johnson). To live is to live with full vitality. Life is life with all its fulness—the eternal life of the NT—whose source is the 'living God' of Ps. 42:3, where, strikingly, the same metaphor of thirst and water is used; cf. also **seek the Lord** which, in Am. 5:4*b*, 14 is to *live*. **The everlasting covenant** is the 'covenant of peace' of 54:10 and, like all that is permanent, derives its indestructibility from 'the everlasting God' (40:28; cf. 45:17, q.v.). **Sure love for David:** this phrase occurs also in 2 Chr. 6:42; that is, in two works from which the hope of a restoration of the monarchy is otherwise conspicuously absent. This is an act of faith: somehow the promise made to David (2 Sam. 7:8–16) will be fulfilled in Israel. **4.** As David was a witness (4) of Yahweh in his kingship and rule (cf. Israel's role as witness in 43:10, 44:8), so shall Israel be *vis-à-vis* the nations (5; cf. Ps. 18:43). The earlier passages show that this is the *spiritual* vocation of Israel, not the military. The nations shall come to Zion (cf. 42:6, but especially 49:7ff.) in fulfilment of the classical
g image of 2:2–4. **6.** The nearness of Yahweh is of course the imminence of salvation, as throughout the prophecies, but especially 51:5, 46:13, etc.—not a comfortable nearness in prayer as the warning of **7a** shows. The return to Zion along the 'way' of 40:3 must also be a return to the way of Yahweh, i.e. the way of *life*—and that is the life of the redeemed and forgiven. The freedom of the exiles is, in the first instance, physical release: but it is altogether in keeping with the prophet's emphasis on the sin of Israel that it should involve the deeper freedom from sin and guilt and that this should form a climax to the whole collection of oracles. **7b.** There is play on the word **return** in the whole Isaianic corpus. It is 'return' but also 'turning again'; i.e., in fact, 'conversion'; cf. 1:27, 7:3, 35:10, 51:11, 59:20, and 44:22, which is an exact summary of this passage:
h 'return, *for I have redeemed you*'. **10f.** is anticipated by 45:23, and is one of the great grounds of prophetic certainty; cf. 40:5, 8, 44:26, 46:10f., 50:4. The word of God is filled with the power of God himself; and is therefore self-fulfilling. This is certainly more than metaphor, though less than hypostasis. **11. that which I purpose** (lit. 'please'): the word of God and the plan of God are one. There is an intense concern with the *purpose* of the sovereign Lord; cf. 44:28, 46:10, 48:14f., 53:10. **12f.** reverts
finally to the theme of the new Exodus. Forgiveness 457h
is not purely inward but has its outward expression in return and restoration. **Joy:** as 51:11. On the sympathetic rejoicing of creation, cf. 44:23, 49:13. **shall clap their hands:** as Ps. 98:8 (a psalm much in the prophet's mind; cf. on 52:10, 14). **The memorial** (name): cf. 48:19, i.e. of the holy seed. **sign:** i.e. the desert made fertile for all to see, a *standing* witness. There is a last play on words: the everlasting covenant is (in Heb.) **cut**: but that the name and sign may be also everlasting they shall not be cut (off).

THIRD ISAIAH

LVI 1-8 The right Worship of the universal 458a
Temple—The third part of the Isaianic corpus opens on a new note of the institutional and moralistic, but, as the first verses suggest, on the foundation of the teaching of 2 Isa. The latter is the gospel of salvation: here are the problems of the redeemed community when the return has taken place (538) and probably when the Temple has been rebuilt (520–516).
1. The *language* is that of 2 Isa. but the slight change b
of usage betrays a change of meaning. Justice is to be *kept*; righteousness *done*. **1b** reads like a quotation from 2 Isa. (cf. 46:13, 51:5) suggested by 1*a*, but it introduces a conception outside the scope of this chapter. **Justice** here means all the divine requirements, including those of the cult (cf. 2 Kg. 17:26f.). The prophet begins with a demand for *obedience*. **2.** A primary mark of the true Israelite is obedience to the Sabbath law, now given a new prominence in contemporary priestly history and, no doubt, of special importance in conditions of exile, as providing one of the remaining ways of observing the law of Moses; cf. 58:13; Dt. 5:12; Neh. 13:17f.; Ezek. 20:12ff.
3-8. The Place of Proselytes and Eunuchs—This c
is the application to concrete situations of the universalist principles set forth by 2 Isa. in 44:5, 45:14, 33, 55:5. The eunuch presented a special problem because by the law of Dt. 23:1 he is expressly excluded from the cult community. Significantly **3** takes the form of a prophetic *tôrāh* or instruction; cf. 1:10–17, 58:9*b*–14. The complaint is that he will not contribute offspring to the community of God: the answer is that to hold fast to the covenant (with special emphasis on Sabbath observance) is the one thing needful; and that, whereas a man's name is normally perpetuated in his children, the eunuch's fidelity will be a monument and an everlasting name better than sons and daughters.

6. The question of foreigners in the Temple service is difficult. **to minister** is a technical term of priestly duty. Until the Exile foreigners had an important place as attendants in the Temple. Ezekiel seems to have objected to the presence of *uncircumcised* foreigners in the Temple (44:7) and to have required their replacement by Jews. The prophet here lays down conditions which should enable certain foreigners to serve the Temple. To **hold fast the covenant** will include such conditions as entitled a foreigner to be regarded as a proselyte and this, as later, may well have included circumcision. If these are the Nethinim (RSV 'temple servants'; cf. 1 Chr. 9:2) this provision marks the conversion of the uncircumcised foreigners that they were into the 'order' that they became (Ezr. 8:15–20). **7.** the concluding announcement is but the working out of the inner logic of 2:1–4, 40–55; cf. 60:1–14, 66:18f. The significant label **house of prayer** will be seen to be characteristic of this prophet's use of such descriptive titles. It is in the manner of 'prophetic symbolism'; not now in order to achieve that which it symbolises, but rather to declare the perfect realisation of that which it describes; cf. 58:12, 60:14, 17f., 61:6, 62:4, 12. **8** implies that the fulfilment of 11:12, 43:5 is as yet partial. The return from the Exile itself is only part of the great ingathering of the dispersed.

458d **LVI 9-LVII 13 The Unrighteousness of false Worship**—This denunciation, in the manner of classical prophecy, should cause no surprise. The Israelites who remained in Judah (the majority) throughout the period of the Exile were the same people (or their children) who had occasioned the prophetic criticism of Jeremiah and Ezekiel. They were not miraculously changed by the fall of Jerusalem, still less by the return of a proportion of the exiles. Ancient Canaanite country superstitions, dormant but alive, broke out afresh in a time of social disintegration like that of the end of the kingdom. And now, after the return, the same practices are carried on without apology or protest (56:10) either in **clefts of the rocks** (57:5) or **behind closed doors** (57:8). There is no need to look for any other period (pre-exilic, exilic or the period of Ezra-Nehemiah) than that which is the general background of the rest of the oracles. The descent from the mount of transfiguration (chs. 40–55) to the plain below (post-exilic Judaea) reveals a familiar condition of spiritual and moral degradation.

e **9**. Not actual wild beasts ravaging Judah, but a figure for nations like Edom who are a constant threat during these years of Judah's weakness. **10**. The watchmen are probably prophets (cf. Isa. 21:6ff., 62:6 ; Ezek. 3:17, 33:7), false prophets, who encourage the practices to be described. **dumb dogs:** it is the essential task of the prophet to *speak*, indeed to roar like a lion (cf. Am. 1:2) or sound like a trumpet (58:1), but those who connive at the practices of the people can be silent. **11**. The insatiable self-concern of those who are not genuinely concerned with the flock ; cf. the shepherds of Ezek. 34:3, 10. **11b** may be an early comment : if so, it is a true one. **12**. Possibly the prophet quotes a fragment of a drinking-song. **12b**. There is no reference to the Day of the Lord in 2 Isa., as so frequently in 1–39. There are several in 56–66. Accordingly this may be a covert reference to the contemporary obliviousness to judgment in a blind concern with the immediate today and tomorrow.

f **LVII 1f**. The indifference of the wicked to righteousness is shown by their unconcern at the death of the righteous. They do not understand that in the bed of the grave they are in peace. Already there is an appearance of two *classes* of men in Judah, implicit in the post-exilic situation described above, increasingly obvious in the oracles that follow ; cf. 57:13, 65:8–10. **3**. For apostasy as adultery cf. Jer. 3 ; Ezek. 16 ; Hos. 1–3. **offspring:** i.e. 'seed', but here as in **4** the reference is to the wicked *as distinguished from the righteous* ; whereas in 1:4 and 41:8 the reference is to the whole people. **4**. The answer is : 'against the righteous'. And once again the **rebels** are the wicked as distinguished from the righteous, rather than Israel as a whole ; cf. 1:2, 43:25, 46:8, 50:1. **5**. The reference is to the familiar Canaanite nature cult and to child sacrifice ; cf. 2 Kg. 23:10 ; Jer. 7:31, 19:5 ; Ezek. 20:28, 31, 23:39. **under the clefts of the rocks,** cf. 2:21, i.e. in the place where men will flee in the day of judgment ; *this* is what the wicked now do ! **6**. cf. Ps. 16:5, where Yahweh is the portion and the lot. The passion of **they, they** suggests some superstitious practice in the place of faith in Yahweh, described by means of word-play. But the allusion in the uncertain Heb. is so far unexplained. **6b**. The terms are those of sacrificial gifts normally offered to Yahweh, but they are wrongly devoted. **7. upon a high and lofty mountain:** sacred prostitution at mountain shrines instead of pure worship on 'my holy mountain' (56:7) ; cf. Jer. 2:20ff., 3:2 ; Ezek.
g 16:28 ; Hos. 4:13. **8**. This is what happens behind doors on which the Shema' ought to be written—in spirit if not as later in fact ; cf. Exod. 13:9 ; Dt. 6:9, 11:20. Whether the later mezuzah and phylactery then existed or not, the passages which gave rise to them were in the mind of the prophet. 'This is your kind of symbol (memorial)'. If the writing was on the doorpost, the rift between profession and practice was blatant. **nakedness:** perhaps 'love' but uncertain. **9b**. As so often, religious compromise and political intrigue went hand in hand. **to Sheol:** i.e. to consult the gods of the underworld. **10**. A play on 'way' which in 2 Isa. is the manner of salvation. Already in 35:8 (cf. 57:14ff.) it is a way of life ; here the long journey after false gods. **11. Have** h
not I held my peace, even for a long time ? cf. 42:14, where the meaning is Yahweh's restraint as he waits but prepares to save his people. Here it is his restraint in punishment. The resultant misunderstanding is not as in 43 of his will to save but of his purpose to punish. **12**. Accordingly the wicked cease to fear him. His speech, when he breaks silence, will be judgment. **13. collection of idols:** interpretation of one Heb. word which is as yet unexplained. **When you cry:** it is Yahweh alone who responds to the sincere cry and saves ; cf. 5:29, 42:22, 43:13, 44:17, 20, 46:7, 47:14, 50:2 ; Exod. 3:7, 9. **13b**. The now familiar contrast between the wicked and the righteous. The *form* of the pronouncement is that of 40:31 ; but the meaning is different. The trust is that of instant obedience ; the inheritance not that of the holy land at the end of a migration (exodus) or return (538), but the spiritual inheritance ; cf. 60:21, 61:7, 63:18, 65:9.

LVII 14-LVIII 14 The true 'Way' of Life—As there have already occurred a number of contrasts between the way of the wicked and the way of the faithful, so now this whole section is set in contrast with 56:9–57:13. 459a

LVII 14-20 The Way of humble Piety—The deliberate transformation of the concepts of 2 Isa. to make them applicable to a different situation, here becomes transparent. 14 directly echoes 40:3 which is regarded in the manner of a text to be interpreted. Thus the language of 14 is *literally* appropriate only in the sense of 40. But it is yet highly appropriate *figuratively* to the way of the obedient and faithful believer. The obstructions are now moral and spiritual. **15a**. The transcendent majesty of God and the power of the creator of all life (16*b*) are not here the ground of his power to save, but the source of wonder at his condescension to **the contrite and humble spirit** (cf. 61:1 ; Ps. 51:1), and the ground of hope in his power to revive a new and vital relationship with himself (15*bc*). The association of **heart** and **spirit** is typical of a language which penetrates to the centre of the mystery of the relationship between God and man. The heart is the centre of his self-consciousness : his spirit that which moves him, i.e. that through which what we call the *will* finds expression. And this spirit is to be in accord with the spirit of Yahweh himself. **16b. From me proceeds the spirit**. This is the language and the thought of Ps. 51. This is the mystery of personal religion. **17ff**. But the very clarity of the distinction between the wicked and the righteous at once raises the problem of the suffering of the righteous, to be dealt with more fully in 59, but adumbrated here. Suffering is the fatherly discipline of God : he will heal and **requite him with comfort** (18*b*). In 40–55 comfort is that of restoration—the great redemptive act ; here it is the comfort of forgiveness for sin. The 'leading' of **18b** is the life of obedience : the 'requital' the reward of reconciliation. **18c** is difficult. The **fruit of the lips** is either joy and thanksgiving, or words—i.e. the pronouncement that follows. **21** is an integral part and climax of the passage here, not an editor's quotation to mark the end of a collection of oracles as in 48:22.

LVIII 1-9a The Fast of righteous Conduct—The b
problem of the *justice* of God's dealings with men has been raised (57:17ff.) and lies behind this chapter. **3**. It is an answer to the question : **Why have we fasted and thou seest not ?** Probably the fasts are those which commemorated the fall of Jerusalem and for which the five laments of the book of Lam. had

459b been earlier composed. (There are strong indications that both 2 Isa. and 3 Isa. were acquainted with Lam.) The evidence of the prophet Haggai proves the poverty and dispiritedness of the community *c*. 520. Here the prophet answers the question in a classical way; cf. Mt. 25:31ff., 6:16–18, 9:14f.; Mk 4:2; Lk. 5:33–5, 18:11f. It is not *necessary* to suppose that the Temple has been rebuilt: but it is *easier* to assume that the remaining building problem is the walls (12).

c **2. Yet they seek me daily:** in the spirit of Isa. 1:12ff. and Am. 4:4f. the people are assiduous in worship. Again not necessary but easier to suppose the worship of the Temple. **2c** supports this. **2b** is the conception of righteousness characteristic of this prophet and very different from that of 2 Isa.; see on 56:1. **3.** In 2 Isa. the complaint is that Yahweh has not seen their affliction (40:27); here that he has not responded to their fast. **3b.** Better 'You pursue your own business (RSV*n*) and press your own occupations'. **4.** This does not mean that fasting makes them quarrelsome, but that the only discipline that God discerns in their lives is the discipline they exercise in their business activity, involving competition, 'strife and contention'. **5.** The outward motions and assiduous practice of the rules of fasting are no substitute for obedience. **5b. a day acceptable to the Lord:** a clear play on the word 'day' which in Isa. 2; Am. 5, and throughout 1–39, is the 'day of the Lord', since what follows is not a *day* but a condition of obedience. In Am. (5:21) the feast-day is to be a day of judgment: here the fast-day is to be realised in the prayer of a sincere heart. In 49:8 the 'time of favour' is 'the day of salvation'. **6.** There follows a list of the kind of actions appropriate to those who fast truly. **8f. Light** is now the light of healing and the presence of Yahweh is not the coming of the redeemer to save (40:9f., 52:6) but rather his presence vouchsafed in response to sincere prayer.

d **9b-14.** The theme of this section is now completed with two laws of the spiritual life. In 56:3f. the prophet used that *form* of the law which is an unconditional imperative (apodeictic); here he uses the *form* of case-law (casuistical). This is typical of the spirit of 3 Isa. (1) **9b.** The specific items laid down are those of 6 and 7 with the addition of not **pointing of the finger** (a gesture of contempt) and **speaking wickedness** (slander); and the reward is again the shining of the light of the faithful, now explained as unbroken guidance and spiritual food (11*a*), strength (**bones** stand for the whole man, as in Ps. 51:8, in respect of his basic stability) and vitality (11*bc*). All this will be matched by the outward restoration of the walls and ruins of Jerusalem. **12.** When this is complete, the faithful will receive an *appropriate name* declaring the realisation of that which it describes; cf. on 56:7. (2) **13f.** The 'law' of sabbath observance, having the form of law but the character of a prophetic comment; cf. the imperative of the law in Exod. 20:8; Dt. 5:12. **my holy day:** as Zion is the holy *place* (56:7, 57:13), so the sabbath is holy *time* and, for those who can receive it, a **delight** and **exaltation** (cf. Dt. 32:13, 33:29) whereby the (spiritual) heritage of Jacob is appropriated (14*b*; cf. 1:19f., 57:13, which seem to be in mind).

e **LIX The great Problem of Faith**—The conditions implied by this chapter are those of 58 and the problem raised by them the same problem of faith. In 58 it was raised in respect of the disappointing results of public fast-days: here in respect of the more general situation, i.e. the unchecked progress of injustice. There has been bloodshed (3*a*, 7*a*), lying (3*b*), and perversion of the legal processes (4*a*, 9*a*, 14). Probably all these are connected and innocent men have wrongfully been put to death while the faithful have been powerless to counteract lying witnesses and corrupt judges. The chapter takes the *form* of a community lament, involving confession on behalf of the *whole* community (12–15), together with the Lord's response (15*b*–20) which corresponds to the familiar priestly oracle in God's name, expressing '*the certainty of* 459e
hearing'. We have here, in the disillusionment which followed the return from exile, the source of that intense preoccupation with the problem of suffering which characterises much post-exilic literature.

1-8 is the prophetic word which interprets the delay f
in the realisation of the mighty promises of 2 Isa. **1a** directly echoes 50:2. But whereas in 2 Isa. God saves in his mighty act of the redemption of his people, here he saves from the power of injustice. **2.** Sin is essentially that which separates man from God: present relationship. **3.** Some think that **blood** here is the blood of sacrificial offerings. But the form and context of the passage support the interpretation above. (Note—hands-fingers are defiled with blood-iniquity; lips-tongue speak lies-wickedness.) Moral and social, not ritual, offences are in question. **5.** Evil plottings under the apt figures of the snake and spider's web. **6.** 'The profits arising from injustice are as unsubstantial as a spider's web' (Kissane). **7b-8.** Four Heb. words for 'way', indicative that this is a central feature of the ethics of the Bible (cf. ch. 35).

9-15a. The lament of the community follows the g
prophetic word. **9b** is directly reminiscent of Am. 5:18f.—light-darkness, brightness-gloom. Now as then men look for the day of the Lord and find it darkness rather than light. Now as then 'justice' and 'righteousness' are the divine requirement which is wanting. 'Righteousness' here lacks the soteriological meaning that it bears in Isa. 40–55 (cf. 12, 14). It is 'rightness' in human relationships according to the ultimate norm of rightness in Yahweh himself. **10. among those in full vigour:** the best solution of a verse that defies certain translation. **11-13.** Because this is a 'general confession' it lacks the particularity of individual confession, but also it can be expressed in terms which might seem descriptive of the wicked rather than the faithful. The community of the faithful confess to the sins of the whole community, including those sins of which they are more victims than perpetrators (cf. 13).

15b-17. It was to be the task of the servant to inter- h
vene for the transgressors (cf. 53:12; RSV conceals the fact that the same Heb. word is used). For the magnitude and depth of the work of the servant, see §456*a*. But here the man to intervene is one who can secure justice from miscarrying in the situations envisaged above. The complete unresponsiveness of men leads to the intervention of God himself (16*b*–18)—expressed in the prophetic *perfect* of certainty, though the prophet's confidence is in his *future* saving activity. This is the 'certainty of hearing'. This last turn in the poem is characteristic of the lament in the Psalter. The striking imagery of God the warrior who fights for perfect righteousness (cf. 42:13, 49:25, 52:10; Exod. 15:3) is the classical type of Wis. 5:17–23; Eph. 6:14–16; 1 Th. 5:8. **18.** Perfect justice will be done and (a 2 Isaianic touch) the far peoples will benefit. **19.** The imaginative picture of the universal recognition of the name and glory (cf. 35:2) of God is also 2 Isaianic, but the prophet betrays his special standpoint when he adds that the redeemer will come to Zion **to those in Jacob who turn from transgression** (cf. 1:27, 35:10, 51:11). **19a** is virtually a quotation from Ps. 102:15, also a lament. **21** is in the nature of an extended comment on the certainty of the oracle as the word of God, such as is frequent in the Isaianic collection; cf. 31:2, 34:16, 37:26, 40:8, 44:26, 45:19, 48:16, 49:2, 55:10f. But its reference to the primary inspiration of the spirit stamps it with the standpoint of the latest prophet in the school; cf. especially 61:1ff. (q.v.). Thus this chapter has a rounded completeness not to be disturbed.

LX The new Jerusalem—This picture of the new 460a
Jerusalem is not, as might be expected, commentary on 54:11–17: it is rather complementary to it, so that, while the 2 Isaianic passage provides the imagery for Rev. 21:18–22, this passage provides the imagery

460a for Rev. 21:23–6. The passage mainly used in the working out of its theme is 49 and there are either verbal allusions to or quotations from 49:1, 3, 5, 6, 7, 8, 10, 12, 14, 18, 22. It is not unlikely that the New Year covenant liturgy (Volz) provided the conceptual background for this nexus of images, e.g. the theophany in terms of light and glory, the predication of the divine name (16*b*, 22 ; cf. 9*c*), the recital of the acts of God (6*b*). **Arise** is originally a cultic direction. The reason for the position of 60 here is that it provides an exposition of 59:16 (note the centrality of the Name (9) and the Glory (1f.) and the part of the gentile nations). Its relation to 49 discloses the main theme which is **the coming of the nations to Zion, the centre of revelation** (light-glory-name) (1–3) ; bringing back the Jews of the dispersion (4, 9) ; offering their wealth (5*b*–7) ; building the walls and beautifying the Temple (10–14). The result is glory and prosperity for Zion. In this and the chapters that follow, the themes are those of 40–55 and turn away from the institutional issues and the perplexities of 56–9. On the other hand when the redeemer comes to Zion, it is always now **to those who have turned from transgression** (59:20).

b **1.** Zion is here pictured as a woman prostrate upon the ground, bidden to arise. This is preparatory to revelation. **your light,** as in 58:8, is parallel to **the glory of the Lord.** This is the reinterpretation of 40:5 ; cf. 19*c*, 20*b*. **2. Darkness** and **thick darkness** are also the frequent language of revelation ; cf. especially Exod. 20:21 ; Ps. 97:2. **3.** The coming of nations and kings is of course the theme of the classical 2:2–4, but it is also close to 49:7, 23 and **4a** close to 49:18*a*, while **4b** is close to the thought of 49:22f. But while 49 thinks primarily of the return from Babylon, here the theme of the great ingathering is used of the dispersion generally.

c **5b-7.** The nations contribute their wealth and pay homage—the idea is, in principle, in 45:14. As the queen of Sheba gave gifts to Solomon (cf. 1 Kg. 10:2), so shall her successor join with the pastoral tribes of N. Arabia in paying tribute. Foreigners **shall proclaim the praise of the Lord,** i.e. recite his mighty acts which are worthy of praise (cf. 43:21), and shall themselves be an acceptable offering (note the liturgical language of 7*b* ; cf. 56:7), and assist in the beautifying of the Temple (evidently now standing; for it is difficult to imagine the prophet silent about this vital part of restoration if it were still in ruins : he is not silent about the walls (10)). **9. The ships of Tarshish** in 2:16 are symbolic of human pride as being the finest and most distant-sailing ships ; cf. Ps. 48:8 ; Ezek. 27:49 ; Jon. 1:3, 4:2. It is the function of the best ships to be used in the service of
d the holy people. **10.** But in the event, strangers did not build the walls, except that Artaxerxes gave permission. **10b** is a familiar collocation of judgment and mercy ; cf. 54:7, and cf. 42:25 with 43:1f., 43:27f. with 44:1ff., 57:17 with 18ff. **11** seems to echo 45:1. But whereas the opening of gates was to Cyrus the sign of god-given military triumph, here the gates of Jerusalem are continuously open for their tribute. Nehemiah kept the gates closed. This prophecy is true only of the heavenly city ; cf. Rev. 21:24–7. **13.** As Lebanon had contributed to Solomon's Temple, so shall it contribute again (cf. Ezr. 3:7). The attitude of respect, even of subjection (cf. 16, with which cf. 49:23) is suggested by the cult (cf. Ps. 2:8–11, 49:7, 23, 99:5, and 132:7). The significant name, descriptive of Zion when all the prophecies relating to her have been fulfilled, is **the city of the Lord** (cf. Ps. 48).

e **15.** The image of the forsaken wife, suggested by 49:14. **A joy from age to age :** Zion is 'the joy of the whole earth' ; cf. 24:11 ; Ps. 48:3. So she was celebrated in the liturgy. **16b** practically=49:26. **17b-18 :** further significant names descriptive of the realised quality of the new Jerusalem embodying great concepts of 2 Isa.—**Peace-Righteousness, Salvation-Praise** (mighty works). **19-22.** Cosmological imagery to express the marvel of the divine 460e
glory in Jerusalem. God is light and in him is no darkness at all. **days of mourning :** the end of grief is symbol of the joy of redemption ; cf. 35:10, 51:11, 57:18, 61:2, 3, 65:18f., 66:10 ; Rev. 21:4. **22. righteous :** i.e. 'participating in salvation' (Volz). **22b** is a clear ending to the oracle (cf. 57:21, 58:14, 59:20f.).

LXI Inspired Proclamation of the Fullness of Time—Beginning and ending in the 1st person, 461a
this passage presents the heart of the prophet's message. The sudden introduction of an intensely personal note and the language are characteristic of 2 Isa., but the differences are more important. Thus (*a*) while in 50:4–9 the servant speaks out of full implication in the sufferings of the time and the passage expresses faithful Israel's *response* to redemption, here the prophet announces redemption (of its kind) and himself has no part except to state his inspiration ; (*b*) the *content*, while in similar terms, is different (see notes below) ; (*c*) **10-11** (in the 1st person) is more in the nature of an interlude of praise after the manner of a psalmist than a resumption of the prophet's own word of 1ff. This abrupt introduction of the personal corresponds to the spontaneity of inspiration. We are to think not of the prophet's call but of his spirit-moved intervention at the cultic assembly (the place of prophets in the cult is hardly now in dispute). If this is so, what was the reason for his intervention? As in 58 he used the fast-day to demonstrate the true nature of fasting, so here he uses the year of Jubilee (**liberty to the captives** ; cf. Lev. 25:10) to proclaim the true nature of release or redemption.

1. He is **sent** (i.e. he is an apostle) to the **afflicted** b
(i.e. 'poor' in the sense of 'pious') and **broken-hearted** ; cf. Ps. 51:9 ; Isa. 57:15. **The opening of the prison** is an interpretation. If this is the meaning, it is figurative of those who are prisoners of fate and wait for divine freedom. Otherwise 'opening of *the eyes*', i.e. to see the redemptive work of God (cf. Lk. 4:18). This language, so like that used by 2 Isa. of release from Babylon, is here used of a more general release from the difficulties and injustices of post-exilic life. **2. The year of the Lord's favour** and **the day of vengeance** are one. The day of the Lord always had this twofold aspect. 586 was recognised as the fulfilment of one aspect : 538 as another. But still the enemies of Israel remained and Israel's meagre life in Judaea did not look like divine favour. Hence the perplexity which breathes through 3 Isa. That this preaching is of an eschatological character in the limited sense that the day of favour and vengeance is an ideal event of the future (though within history) is shown by the interpretation of this day given in 63. **Comfort** is not now the divine word for powerless exiles (40:1) but for the sorrowful dispirited of post-exilic Judah in their disappointing homeland. **3.** Those who receive the word will, in contrast, merit the significant title **Oaks of righteousness** (cf. on 56:7), the oak being a symbol of strength and stability. **4** is a description of the work of restoration yet to be done, revealing the grounds of prevalent disillusionment. There is not a hint of the Temple, presumably because it was rebuilt (520–516). **5f.** 56:6f. dealt with a disputed c
question on ministerial orders. In 60 foreigners will build walls, bring back the dispersed and provide wealth. But here the question is of the general role of aliens in respect of Israel's function as an elect people. As a priest is to Israel and is released from ordinary toil to concentrate on priestly functions, so shall Israel be to the nations, which shall release her from manual toil for her priestly function in relation to the whole world (cf. Exod. 19:6 ; 1 Pet. 2:9). **You shall eat** even as the priests were given their portion. **You shall glory :** so 1QIs[a] and some VSS. Others follow LXX and render 'beautify yourselves'. **6.** Israel shall have significant descriptive names ; cf. on 56:7. **7.** RSV is the best that can be

61d done with difficult Heb. **8f.** Yahweh now speaks in a way typical of the psalms and therefore of the cult, and gives a promise of blessing (of seed) based upon an eternal covenant (55:3, 59:21). It begins with self-predication : ' I am Yahweh who love . . .' **10f.** The prophet is the mouthpiece of Zion. The thanksgiving is in personal terms in order that the individual may express his own share in Israel's gratitude, thus prophetically anticipating the blessing. **garments of salvation** and the **robe of righteousness :** in contrast to the garments of vengeance (58:17*c*) and mantle of fury (zeal) worn by Yahweh himself. **11** is a variation of the concluding note of certainty at the end of each of these sections ; see on 60:22.

e **LXII Prophetic Intercession for Redemption and the Worship of the Redeemed**—This prophet, who has given directions on certain aspects of Temple worship (56:1–8), declared the true fast (58) and proclaimed the true nature of the year of release (61), now exhorts his people to worship (10ff.) on the ground of their new relationship with Yahweh (4ff., 12). It is the prophet who speaks, rather than Yahweh (as some have thought), as is shown by 4 ; and the placing of this oracle after 61 probably indicates that it was so understood by those who collected the oracles. 1–9 speak of the importunate prayer of the prophet and his assistants for the fulfilment of the divine promises relating to Zion. The intensity of expression and the ceaseless prayer are evidence of considerable stress in the post-exilic community. It is probable that the men of the Isaiah circle found the salvation words of 2 Isa. thrown in their teeth.

f **1f.** The prophet **will not keep silent**, i.e. will not cease that work of intercession (cf. 6f.) which is the great *godward* function of the prophet, until righteousness and salvation are fully realised fact and the nations witness the glorious fulfilment (**2**). As there was a new song for a new redemptive act (see on 42:10), so there shall be **a new name** for the people of the new Jerusalem, not a name symbolic and instrumental of what *shall* be but descriptive of what *is* ; cf. on 56:7. **4.** The names **Forsaken** and **Desolate,** which link up the present complaints of the people and previous prophecy (49:14, 54:1, 6, 60:15) shall be replaced by new names, **My delight is in her** (cf. Manasseh's mother in 2 Kg. 21:1) and **Married** (cf. 54:1), the one for Israel and the other for the land (as the parallelism shows), both descriptive of the new relationship with Yahweh. This, the new covenantal marriage, will be the final fulfilment of the bold thought of 2 Isa and Hos. 1–3. **5. Your sons,** to the western mind, seems an intolerable mixture of metaphor ; but the reality it betokens presses the poet beyond logical limits (cf. 49:18, 61:10). **6.** The prophet still speaks. The **watchmen** are the disciples of the prophet who will speak his message to all Jerusalem. They will be no more silent than the prophet himself. (For the prophet as watchman see on 56:10 ; others think they are the men who guard the safety of Zion or angelic guardians.) Likewise those **who put the Lord in remembrance,** whose intercession will be unceasing, giving Yahweh no rest until the prophecies relating to Zion have been fulfilled.

g **8f.** The divine promise, of which Yahweh is put in remembrance, in the form of an oath which expresses the great power of his word (cf. especially 45:23, 54:9), and which introduces a word of great solemnity and urgency. It is also Yahweh's answer to the intercession, promising freedom from enemy despoliation (nations like Edom continuously took advantage of the weakness of Judah-Jerusalem) and freedom to eat the fruits of her labour and bring them to a joyous harvest thanksgiving (9). The power of the divine word is further enhanced by the reference to the **right hand** and **mighty arm** (cf. 40:10, 41:10, 51:9, 52:10, 53:1) and by the strong oath-form of the Heb. in 8*bc*, concealed in RSV : ' Surely (or Verily) I will not . . .'

10-12. Exhortation to worship in terms of 40:1–10. 461b
The original meaning of 40:1–10 is lost in a quite new application to the pilgrims coming through the ever-open gates to worship at Zion. The way (cf. 40:3) is now the way of pilgrimage to Zion : **11b** is directly parallel to 40:9*c* but the address is not now to the cities but to the **daughter** of Zion as she comes to worship. **11c** = 40:10*b*. But then **12** is unique to 3 Isa. in the use of significant designations : the **holy people** (cf. Exod. 19:6) and the **redeemed of the Lord** (cf. 35:9f., where the meaning is similar). **Sought out, a city not forsaken,** which are the answer a people engaged in prayer learn to their problem, express the central biblical principle of redemption.

LXIII 1-6 The Day of Vengeance and the Year 462a
of Redemption—It ought to be no problem that this passage occurs with crag-like abruptness. We are not presented with a sustained literary composition. But it is easy to see the reason for its position here, once 59, 61, 62 were in position. In 61:2 the prophet announced the day of vengeance and the year of redemption of 63:4. This then is an anticipatory *picture* of that day of vengeance. It is what Yahweh swore to do (62:8f.). He is seen coming from Edom, whose special importance was that they were predatory on Israel's desperate weakness and therefore specially hated (cf. 21:11f., 34:1–17 ; Ps. 137:7 ; Jer. 49:7–22 ; Lam. 4:21–2 ; Ezek. 25:12–14 ; Ob. 1–21 ; Mal. 1:2–5). Furthermore the eponymous ancestor of Edom was Esau and therefore they stand over against the elect children of Jacob as those Yahweh has rejected (Rom. 9:13). They are therefore a specially significant type of the enemies of Israel.

1f. The picture is the more vivid by reason of the b
double question and answer : (*a*) **Who is this?** It is Yahweh the warrior (cf. 42:13, 25, 59:17ff.), not simply the coldly impartial judge, but one whose word is the embodiment of righteousness (in the soteriological sense of 2 Isa.) and who is **mighty to save** (cf. 43:3 ; cf. the implied doubt of 59:1) (RSV ' announcing vindication ' is misleading). (*b*) **Why is the apparel red?** (2). **3.** There follows the classical image of ' the great wine press of the wrath of God ' (Rev. 14:19–20). As Yahweh alone secures justice within Israel (59:16) and arms himself with righteousness, salvation and vengeance, so, as hinted in 59:18, he will give requital to the nations. And as there he acted alone because ' there was no man ' (59:16), so here **no-one was with me** (3), **there was none to help** (5). As there (59:16) his own arm brought victory, so 5*b* is in almost identical terms. All this is eschatological in the sense that present hopes and faith are projected on to the screen of a single future day.

LXIII 7-LXIV 12 The Prophet's Intercession— c
As 63:1–6 owed its position to its more complete explication of 61:2, so this long prayer is the intercession of the prophet and his assistants as described in 62. We may guess that this was the subject and summary of the prophet's unceasing prayer, as it was also uttered by the remembrancers (62:6f.). That it includes praise, historical retrospect, lament and confession as well as intercession is natural and right : true intercession never stood alone. This is the more meaningful if the intercession was designed also to be the vehicle of the prayers of the community. The dating of the section depends on the interpretation of 63:18 and 64:9f. But the first is a crux and the second could mean any time from 586–520. But it seems unlikely to belong to the early exile (Volz) and everywhere to suggest the same Palestinian background as the surrounding chapters. Determinative must therefore be the view of the Isaianic circle who understood the passage to express the content of the prophetic intercession of 62.

7-14. Remembrance of the mighty works of God. d
7. I will recount : in Heb. the same word as ' put

462d in remembrance' (62:6)—concealed in RSV. **Praises** and **steadfast love** (devotion) both here refer to the saving deeds of God. **8f.** The appeal is to election. **He became their saviour:** cf. the striking emphasis on this in 43:3, 59:1, 63:1, etc. **9** is difficult. RSV is possible; but equally possible is LXX: 'Neither envoy nor messenger but his own Presence saved them'. **10. his holy spirit:** the spirit is a term which expresses above all the directing will of God who, being spirit and not flesh (31:3), is the source and guide of the 'will' of man. It is *holy* spirit just as his mountain (11:9, 56:7, etc.), city (52:1), arm (52:10), day (58:13), courts (62:9), people (62:12, 63:18), house (64:11) are holy to him. Rebellion, being essentially a wilful act, is resistance to his holy spirit; cf. 11*c*, 14. **11-14.** The recital of the first great act of redemption at the Exodus as the proof of his power and earnest of his saving action now.

e **15-19 Appeal and Lament—15.** Cf. 57:15 and see on 66:1f. **16.** In 8 the appeal was to election and covenant relationship; here the ground of confidence is the fatherhood of God (repeated; cf. 64:8)—'though we may not look like brothers of the great Abraham and Jacob!' **17. Return,** i.e. turn again. **18.** RSV is a literal rendering of a line probably in confusion. The most plausible solution short of emendation is: 'It is only a short time ago that our enemies dispossessed thy holy people' (Bewer).

f **LXIV 1-5 Prayer for Theophany and divine Intervention—1.** For the divine action from heaven to earth cf. Exod. 3:7f. The trembling of the mountains is a usual feature of divine self-disclosure (Exod. 19; Ps. 18:7; Hab. 3:6). **2.** Fire also regularly accompanies a theophany; cf. Exod. 19:18; Isa. 66:15ff.; Heb. 12:18. **4.** Cf. 1 C. 2:9, to which, with the help of LXX, some adjust the Heb. **4b** is a pervasive theme of 2 Isa. **5a.** Read 'O that thou wouldst meet . . .' thus echoing 1 and making an excellent climax to the prayer.

g **5b-7 Confession—7. There is no-one:** see on 59:11–13. Note the absence of a strong sense of the division of the community into two classes. This is truly prophetic in its apprehension of the involvement of the whole body in sinfulness. Yet even as this (especially 6) is the confession which must be made, the prophet and each who makes this prayer his own calls and **takes hold** of God in importunate prayer; cf. Gen. 32:26.

h **8-11 Final Appeal—9.** When Yahweh *remembers* sin, he punishes. This is a dynamic word. **10f.** A description of the consequences of the Babylonian conquest. These lasted long and it is easy to think of the period from the return to the rebuilding of the Temple (520) as the background here. There is no need to think of the abortive attempt to rebuild the Temple in 537 or of a supposed burning down of the Second Temple in 485. **12.** The restraint and silence of Yahweh contrasted with the prophet's refusal to keep silence (62:1, 6f.; cf. 42:14, which also may be in mind). 'He said he would break his silence and cry out. Why does he delay?'

463a **LXV-LXVI 16** is a collection of oracles with marked similarities, gathered together in two sections of identical pattern to provide an answer to the prayer of 64.

LXV Yahweh's Answer to Prayer—65 has little inherently in common with the intercession of 63:7–64 or indeed with 60–63:6; for all those chapters are concerned with Israel's situation *vis-à-vis* the nations. The *brief* answer to the prophetic intercession is given in 62:8f. and is that Yahweh will give Israel freedom from her predatory enemies (e.g. Edom). And it is with external enemies that the long intercession is primarily concerned as the evil from which deliverance is sought (e.g. 63:18). The confession of 64:5*b* ff. is therefore a confession of the community evoked by her external situation. (The confession evoked by her internal condition is given in 59.) But now in 65 (and 66) Israel is clearly divided into two classes, the wicked and the pious, and the divine answer is not so much freedom for Israel as a people, as judgment upon the wicked and blessing for the faithful. This reverts to the theme of 56:9–57:13; see especially on 57:1. The section is crowned with a vivid image of the new Jerusalem for the faithful (originally independent). The section is, as a whole, originally independent of 64 and it is vain to seek for complete homogeneity or even for a national liturgy in 63:7–65:25 (Bentzen). On the other hand, certain features of 65 made it a suitable passage to place here, thus giving it the place of an answer to 64. The familiar connection of lament and oracular response in the psalms provided the pattern, and the emphasis upon answer to importunate prayer (65:1, 10, 12*b*, 19, 24) provided a strong link. **6. I will not keep silent** is a *catchword* which links with the significant emphasis on this word in 62:1, 6f., and above all 64:12. Indeed here is Yahweh's answer to the specific question of 64:12; cf. 57:11*c*. There is the same dependence upon 2 Isa., together with freedom of interpretation, which marks every part of 3 Isa.

1. RSV is misleading. Rather: 'I let myself be found'. For the cultic significance of **seek** cf. 58:2. **Here am I:** theophany is at the heart of both the cult and the eschatology based upon it; cf. 40:9, 66:18, etc. **2.** Cf. Rom. 10:21. Yahweh has been as unceasing in solicitation as the prophet in intercession. **3-7.** The items of unacceptable cult practice. See on 56:9–57:13 for the way in which superstitious practices survived. But the list here has little in common with the earlier. That is because the concern there was with the sexual cult of 'the harlot': here the concern is with more general cult practice—incense (3), consultation of the dead (4), the eating of unclean sacrificial flesh (**abominable things**) including the forbidden swine's flesh. **6f.** The Lord's silence will be broken in judgment. b

8-10. The wheat and the tares: because there are good as well as evil in Israel, Israel will not utterly be destroyed. But that is not to say that the whole will be saved for the sake of the few righteous, as in Gen. 18:20–33, or even in Isa. 53. There will be a separating of the good from the evil and the evil will be destroyed. **8. For my servants' sake:** the servants themselves alone shall prosper (9*b*, 13–15). The plural **servants** distinguishes this conception radically from that of 'the servant' in 2 Isa. The mystery of the servant (Israel fulfilling her divinely given commission) who suffers for Israel (the rebel from birth) is entirely absent. The servants are simply the faithful as distinct from the wicked. **9b** shows just how far reinterpretation can go: **my chosen** and **my servants** are together in the parallelism so familiar in 2 Isa. but now in the plural and in the sense defined above. They will have 'seed' ('descendants'; cf. on 44:3, 53:10) and land, two great elements of the promise made to Abraham. **10. Sharon:** symbol of rich pasture and prosperity. **The valley of Achor:** where Joshua entered and where a *new* beginning shall be made; cf. Hos. 2:15. **11. Fortune,** i.e. Gad, **Destiny,** i.e. Meni, both gods of fate and found separately and together in inscriptions. c

13-16 draws out yet more sharply the distinction between 8–10 and 11f., the lot of the faithful and of the wicked. **15. a different name,** cf. the new name of 62:2. **16. God of truth,** i.e. Amen. All other instances of this word are liturgical. The faithfulness of God and the truthfulness of men will answer to one another. **The former troubles,** perhaps originally what is described in 63:18, 64:10f. But the juxtaposition of 17–25 gives it the meaning of 'the former things'. d

17-25 The new Creation—The eschatological note is revealed in the proclamation of **new heavens and a new earth.** *These* now are the 'new things' of 42:9, 43:18f., etc., to be contrasted with the 'former e

463e things' which are all the times of the first dispensation before the dawning of the new age. In other words this is the eschatological reinterpretation of 42:9 and 43:18f., etc. What 2 Isa. understood of new redemptive acts (release from Babylon), 3 Isa. understands of a new creation. Life in the new Jerusalem will be characterised by joy (18), the end of mourning (19), freedom from sickness and the universal gift of old age (20), individual property and independence (21f.), perfect communion with God (24), and perfect fulfilment of the messianic picture of harmony in 11:6–9 (with however no hint of Messiah). Indeed **25** is a condensed form of 11:6–9.

464a **LXVI A further Answer to Prayer**—Although this section has less homogeneity than the previous one, it derives cohesion from its pattern. Thus **1f.** corresponds to 65:8–10. These are they whom the Lord will answer. **3f.** corresponds to 65:11f., **4bc** =65:12*bc*, **5** corresponds to 65:13–16, sharply distinguishing between the brethren, **7-9** speaks of the birth of the new land (corresponding to 65:17), and so leads to **10f.**, which corresponds to 65:18ff.—rejoicing over the new Jerusalem. Then **12-14,** the picture of prosperity, corresponds to the idyllic picture of 65:20–5. This correspondence cannot be accidental and means that the prophet has significantly arranged his material to provide a fresh enforcement of the themes of 65. Within this general framework each oracle has its own character and point.

b **1f.** The correspondence noted above (65:8–10), provides the clue to the central point of this passage which has been misunderstood by modern commentators. The question is not primarily whether Yahweh needs a temple. The theme is the marvellous condescension of the transcendent creator to the humble man. *The greatness of God is illustrated by his independence of a temple.* The inner meaning of **1b** is 'Where is the house that could possibly be the throne of God, seeing his throne is the heavens; where the sanctuary for his feet when the whole earth is his footstool?' Yet it is *this* God who looks to the humble man, thus answering the cry of 63:15 'Look down from heaven and see, from thy holy and glorious habitation' (and 64:8). This is the thought of 57:15f. It tells us neither that the Temple was still in ruins nor that it was standing; cf. Ps. 11:4 for the truth that Yahweh is in his temple, yet his throne is in heaven, and cf. 2 Sam. 7:4ff.; 1 Kg. 8:27ff.

c **3f.** Here in contrast is the description of the worship of the apostates; cf. 65:11. The correspondence is close—first the pagan superstition, then the divine destiny which in 65:11 is a play on the word Destiny and in **4** is changed to **affliction,** with the rest of the verse almost identical. Since in 65:11 the impious are **those who forget my holy mountain,** the probability is that the Temple is standing and that pagan cults are practised in the old sanctuaries, where they offer what would be legitimate in the Temple. Such offering is wicked and false. A slaughtered ox is no better than murder—and so on (3). **5** is set here because of its verbal link with 2*b*, **You who tremble at his word**, but also because it corresponds to the vivid distinction between 'the servants' and their **brethren** in 65:13–16. **6. A voice from the temple** supports the view taken on other grounds that the Temple was standing.

d **7-9. The birth of the new age,** but without birth-pangs, so unexpected and swift will salvation be. This is the birth of the new land and nation (**8**), i.e. the new Israel—eschatological in the sense that it involves the end of the old dispensation and a new creation (65:17), but it is still within history, not the end of history.

10f. 'appropriate **joy**', cf. 65:18; but here the image is used of Jerusalem the mother of us all. **11. from the abundance of her glory:** on the basis of cognate Ugaritic, render 'from her bountiful breast'. **12-14.** A picture of the glorious life of the new Jerusalem in general correspondence with
65:20–5, but developing the theme of Jerusalem the 464d
mother. **14. servants:** characteristic (seven times) of 65.

15f. Final comment, leading from 14*b*, on Yahweh's e
coming in judgment. The fire of theophany. Both the announcement of his coming and the familiar fire-imagery correspond to the prayer of 64:1f. **17** is a fragment which is set here as a further identification of **those slain by the Lord (16).** It speaks of lustrations before cultic practices in gardens, and the difficult Heb. probably indicates some mystery rites in which initiates act under a leader, **the one in the midst**; cf. Ezek. 8:11. **Abomination** is probably an irresistible play on 'creeping things'. Add 57:5–10, 65:3–7 and 66:3f. for a complete account of these post-exilic Judaean cult practices.

18-24 Universal Recognition of the Glory of f
God—This section lies outside the pattern common to 65 and 66 and is probably set here as a climax to the body of prophecies 56–66, perhaps to 40–66 or even to the whole Isaianic corpus 1–66. Despite RSV and most commentators, it is in 'unexceptionable verse' (Rowley), once it is recognised that the list of nations in **19** is an identifying gloss of a kind familiar in the early chapters of Isaiah (especially 7–9), and that the list of animals in **20** is likewise a prosaic comment on the means of transport to Jerusalem. For a convenient setting forth of the passage in its verse form see H. H. Rowley, *The Biblical Doctrine of Election* (1950), 82. This is the final picture of all nations that survive the judgment acknowledging the glory of God and bringing the dispersed people of Israel to the holy mountain that the vision of 40:5 might be fulfilled.

18. The Heb. is defective. RSV represents one g
conjectural solution. Another (Duhm) is to transfer **their works and their thoughts** to the previous line and read 'I am coming' for Heb. 'it is coming'. This is a safe emendation since it is Yahweh who gathers the peoples in 56:8 (cf. 11:22, 43:5). **18** is the divine intention. **19** *then proceeds to show how this will be accomplished* (it is not successive in time). Those who survive the judgment on the nearer nations (cf. the typical picture in 63:1–6) will be sent to the far-off nations who have not yet seen the glory of God. This glory is itself destruction to some, salvation to others. As survivors of judgment (*a gentile remnant*), they will in themselves be a sign of judgment. The list of nations is suggested by Ezek. 27:10–15, 38:2, 39:1. **20.** These gentiles will then bring back the dispersed of Israel to Zion (**all your brethren from all the nations**) and this will be their priestly task and offering. It is not that they will bring their cereals with them: the returned Israelites will themselves constitute their offering. **21** draws out the full universalist implications of this doctrine. **Some of them,** i.e. of the gentiles, as in 19, shall be privileged with Temple service (cf. 56:6). **22** declares the permanence of the holy *seed* as a feature of the new creation. **23** verbally echoes 40:5 to show its complete fulfilment and joins Jew and gentile together in the
common humanity of **all flesh**. See on 40:5. **24** is a h
characteristic warning which the modern mind finds inconsistent with the foregoing universalism and attributes to a redactor. But the difficulty was not felt by Jesus (Mk 9:47–9) or the author of Revelation (11:9f.). This is no doubt an imaginative picture of the valley of Hinnom (Gehenna) (cf. Jer. 7:31f.), where later the fires were continually burning to consume Jerusalem's refuse. The idea of a judgment outside Jerusalem is derived from the cultic conflict with the nations (cf. 8:9f., 10:12, 17:4f.; Ezek. 38; Zech. 12:1–9). The choice between the way of life and the way of death has to be made ever anew. Widest hope and universalist expectation are accompanied with severest warning.

Bibliography—COMMENTARIES: J. Levy, *Deutero-Isaiah* (1925); J. Muilenburg, IB v (1956); C. R. North,

Torch Commentary (1952); C. C. Torrey, *The Second Isaiah* (1928).

OTHER LITERATURE: K. Elliger, *Die Einheit des Tritojesaia* (1928), *Deuterojesaia in seinem Verhältnis zu Tritojesaia* (1933); L. Glahn and L. Köhler, *Der Prophet der Heimkehr* (1934); J. Lindblom, *The Servant Songs in Deutero-Isaiah* (1951); C. Lindhagen, *The Servant Motif in the OT* (1950); S. Mowinckel, *He that Cometh* (1956); C. R. North, *The Suffering Servant in Deutero-Isaiah* (2nd ed. 1956), 'The "former things" and the "new things" in Deutero-Isaiah', *Studies in OT Prophecy* (ed. H. H. Rowley) (1950); J. van der Ploeg, *Les Chants du Serviteur de Jahvé* (1936); L. G. Rignell, *A Study of Isaiah Chapters 40–55* (1956); H. Ringgren, *The Messiah in the OT* (1956); H. W. Robinson, *The Cross of the Servant* (1926), republished in *The Cross in the OT* (1955); H. H. Rowley, *The Servant of the Lord* (1952); S. Smith, *Isaiah Chapters 40–55* (1944); H. W. Wolff, *Jesaia 53 im Urchristentum* (1950).

See end of preceding article for literature on the whole book of Isaiah.

JEREMIAH

By JOHN PATERSON

465a **Life and Times of Jeremiah**—The second half of the 7th cent. B.C. was no less fateful and historically significant than the first half of the present century. Great events were taking place, and great men arose to meet the challenge of the hour. The brutal empire of Assyria with its hot, greedy, snatching appetite had passed its zenith and was moving towards final dissolution. Roving bands of Scythian invaders poured down from the northern mountains and through the last quarter of the century spread havoc and terror from Armenia to Egypt. There seems no reason to doubt the historical accounts of these invasions by those marauding hordes who, though untrained in the technical arts of war, spread fear and dread by sheer force of numbers and unbridled ferocity. Strangely enough, though the terror was felt in Judah she remained unvisited and unscathed. By a gradual process of erosion the imperial structure of Assyria was reduced to the point of collapse. In 612 B.C. 'the bloody city, full of lies and booty' (Nah. 3:1), was swept away. Into the vacuum thus created stepped the new Babylon to occupy the imperium for another century when it would yield before the conquering Cyrus.

It was a period full of history and world-shaking events. It was a period, too, when great men were not lacking. Nebuchadrezzar and Neco were great rulers of men and they shaped history: around them they gathered great military commanders of stature and quality. All these have vanished with the empires they served and ruled, but still, in lonely splendour, stands Jeremiah, the prophet of Judah's decline and fall.

b In such a period Jeremiah was born (*c.* 650 B.C.). In such a time he was called to be 'a prophet to the nations' (1:5). Born in Anathoth (modern 'Anâtâ), just three miles north-east of Jerusalem, he was the son of Hilkiah—not to be confused with Hilkiah, the priest who found the book of the Law—and heir to an ample spiritual heritage. For Anathoth was the village to which Abiathar, high priest of David, was relegated on the accession of Solomon (1 Kg. 2:26, 27). If, as seems probable, Jeremiah stood in that ancient line of succession he was heir to no mean tradition. His father may have officiated in the Temple at Jerusalem but more probably he was priest at Anathoth.

c His call came in 627 B.C., and it is recorded in his own words (1:1–10). The story impresses us with its naturalness and simplicity. The awe-inspiring accompaniments of Isaiah's vision (Isa. 6) or the overpowering glory that came to Ezekiel (Ezek. 1) are not here. Everything here is inward and in line with that close fellowship and communion with God that seem to be his all through his life. Here we see the inner working of the soul: his heart lies before us like an open book. In this matter of the prophetic consciousness none tells us more than Jeremiah. And if there be here a shrinking reluctance to accept the great responsibility shall we not say that this is due to his innate nobility of character? For a man's true humility is the inverted image of his real nobility. Jeremiah stood in the great succession of Amos, Hosea, and Isaiah, and if they failed to stem the flowing tide of evil in Israel how could a lad so young carry a load so heavy? This shrinking reluctance characterises the prophet's whole ministry, and it is to be noted, as 465c
Hertzberg has pointed out, that in no other prophet does the pronoun 'I' enter so much as in the case of Jeremiah. For while he will not forget that he is called of God he cannot but remember that he is one with his people. Thus his emotions are in constant conflict with his prophetic vocation, and the heart struggles with the head (9:1, 12:1, 15:18). There is something similar to this in Hosea but in that case Hosea sets the struggle within the heart of God himself: here it is the heart of Jeremiah that is riven. For while the other great prophets seem to stand somewhat aloof and hurl down the words of judgment, Jeremiah seems to stand between men and God and gather to his own bosom the shafts of the divine indignation. He is not only God's messenger: he is the people's representative. None is so mighty or continuous in intercession and none other shows as clearly how the ministry of intercession is integral to the prophetic vocation. For friends and enemies alike he prays (15:11, 18:20; cf. 17:16, 29:7). It breaks his heart when prayer for the people is banned by God's wrath (7:16, 11:14, 14:11). His love for the people constrains him constantly to seek earnestly for the grounds of judgment (5:4, 6:9, 9:7), and his sympathy is stirred when he sees the judgment to be just (14:18, 8:18, 9:1). Even at the risk of being charged with treason he will seek to save a few (21:1–10). Like Bunyan's Evangelist he pleaded with men, and his plea was in agony of soul and sore travail of spirit. Those fervent pleas involve many a tender similitude drawn from the world of Nature and human life, and at times they are reinforced with symbolic actions not lacking in dramatic features and imaginative colour. When these fail he will have recourse to pen and ink (30:2, 36:1f.), and when the penknife assails the pen he will write again and add more words (36:32). For the aim of the prophet and his heart's desire is that Israel may be saved.

Chs. 2–6 are usually assigned to the prophet's early d
ministry. Duhm would assign 2–4 to Anathoth and 5–6 to Jerusalem but this division seems unnecessary. No immediate reaction to these early oracles is recorded. The raids of rampaging Scythians must have filled men's minds with anxious foreboding but Judah was unvisited. Jeremiah thus seemed a false prophet—such must have been the popular opinion—and he seems at this time to have retired with confusion of face. It probably raised serious questions in his sensitive mind and perhaps he felt, as he felt later, deceived or 'enticed' by God (20:7). We need not wonder that for the next few years he remained silent, and we hear no more of the prophet until the reformation of Josiah. It may be, as Skinner suggests, that some of the undated oracles fall into this period, but of that we cannot be certain.

Jeremiah played no active part in the introduction e
of the book of the Law. That may be due to his youth or it may be that he was not yet recognised as a prophet: his earlier prophecies had not been fulfilled. But Jeremiah could not remain indifferent to such a movement. What part he played in the reformation is not quite clear, and opinion is divided on the question. Duhm, Cornill, Marti, Welch, Hyatt and

465e others would deny any participation on the part of Jeremiah. The text of 11:1–8, 18–12:6 is not altogether clear and may have suffered expansion at the hands of later editors. The question has been thoroughly discussed by Skinner, Rowley (*Studies in OT Prophecy*, 157–74), and Eissfeldt (*OT and Modern Study*, 153, ed. by H. H. Rowley), who hold that the arguments against Jeremiah's active participation in the movement cannot stand. This view seems most reasonable and is generally accepted by most scholars. The record seems to indicate that Jeremiah did engage in a preaching mission to further the reform but his favourable attitude did not last long, and he soon found himself in opposition to the movement (8:8). It is not difficult to understand this change of attitude. If the book of the Law was some form or part of the book of Deuteronomy we can understand how the prophet would readily respond to the prophetic ideals codified therein. Its monotheism, its denunciation of idolatry, its warm humanitarianism and its demand for a life motivated by love to God could not fail in its appeal. But it is a sad fact of human experience that when ideals are codified they are apt to lose the vitalising, quickening spirit, and the articulation of fine theories in daily life may often lead to unexpected and disastrous results. The intention was noble but the execution was faulty and the results were inadequate. For it is easy to tear down heathen altars but difficult to change the heathen heart. Centralisation of worship is not equivalent to regeneration of spirit. A spiritual vacuum was created and the human heart cannot abide a vacuum. A hierarchy was created in Jerusalem that proceeded to lord it over men's souls while the Temple became a fetish that obscured the Lord of the Temple and removed the thought of a righteous God far from the minds of men. Hindsight is easier than foresight and, as Skinner remarks, a woman may become engaged to a man before she discovers she cannot marry him. Jeremiah soon came to see the shallowness of the movement and that it healed the wound of 'my people' all too lightly. The fallow ground must be broken up and the heart circumcised. Deep and drastic surgery was required in the realm of the spirit. Such seems to have been the prophet's reaction to the reform, and it seems more reasonable to read the matter this way than to credit Jeremiah with the mature wisdom that could 'see the end of a thing in the beginning thereof'. He accepted the reform on the principle that half a loaf is better than no bread. This interpretation explains the fury and rage of his kinsmen at Anathoth: their own kinsman was seeking and helping to put them out of business and was on the side of those who had ousted their ancestor Abiathar. The fierce words of 12:3 are the measure of his suffering, which was sharpened to an intolerable point of agony. A man of sorrows and acquainted with grief, he goes his lonely way: this also is of the divine appointing and Jeremiah will bear it.

466a Again there seems to be a period of silence during the later years of Josiah's reign, but when the good king fell at Megiddo (609 B.C.) a new and different situation arose. From this point things move downwards at a rapid rate towards final catastrophe. Egypt was in the ascendant for the moment and the popular choice of Jehoahaz as king was set aside by the Egyptian overlord in favour of his elder brother, Eliakim, whose name was changed to Jehoiakim. This monarch seemed to regard himself as a second Solomon, and engaged in lavish building enterprises with the use of forced labour (22:13–19). To this period belongs the Temple speech, recorded in chs. 7 and 26. Here Jeremiah provoked a hostile reaction which almost cost him his life: his fellow prophet Uriah did not fare as well (26:20f.). About this same time Jeremiah engaged in the symbolic action of breaking an earthen flask 'at the entry of the Potsherd Gate' (19:2), and added words of interpretation in the court of the Lord's house (19:4), whereupon he received, for the first time, physical mistreatment at the hands of Pashhur (20:1). This led to the fiercest of all the prophetic outbursts (20:7) wherein he bitterly assails God and feels he has been 'enticed' by him. The scorn and contumely of friend and foe weighed heavily upon him and it was more than he could bear. Here he seems to be fighting not only against men but against God himself: *Jeremia contra mundum et Deum.* Nevertheless the pressure of the divine is ineluctable and the prophet knows himself gripped and held by a power he cannot escape (29:9). The prophet is learning more and more that the meeting-place of God and man is in the solitudes of the human soul and that true religion consists in inward fellowship with God. The Battle of Carchemish (605 B.C.) again prompted the prophet to speak, and to this period belongs ch. 25 with its oracles against the nations. The 'northerner' is now clearly identified and the prophet sees the judgment of God in the events of history. This time there is no mistake and this time there will be no reprieve. The prophet sees to the centre of things and he sees clearly.

b In the hostile atmosphere of Jerusalem Jeremiah dare not speak freely, and at this time he dictates to Baruch the prophecies made through the preceding twenty-three years (36). Great commotion ensues on the reading of these to the public, and the matter is reported to the king. There can be few more striking scenes than this incident of the pen and the penknife as the jaunty monarch slits the scroll and burns it in the fire. But the pen is mightier than the penknife: the scroll was rewritten 'and many similar words were added to them' (36:32).

c Some time elapsed after Carchemish before stability returned and Jehoiakim took the oath of loyalty to his overlord. But in the fourth year he broke his oath (2 Kg. 24:1). Because Nebuchadrezzar could not personally attend to the matter he instigated the neighbouring peoples to attack Judah (12:7–17). Before the Babylonian king could give personal attention to the revolt Jehoiakim was dead: ch. 35 may refer to this period of the siege. 15:10–21 also may belong here and again we see the prophet perplexed. To him comes the challenge of God and renewed experience of deliverance and protection. To be a 'tester' of the people one must submit himself to most searching self-examination. For only the pure in heart see God.

d In 597 B.C. came the first captivity, and the flower of the nation was deported with Jehoiachin (Coniah) and the queen mother. Jeremiah gives the number of captives as 3,023 (52:28). Mattaniah, whose name was changed to Zedekiah, was set upon the throne to be Judah's last king. Those who were left in control plumed themselves on the fact that they had not been deported, but the prophet's words on the two baskets of figs must surely have deflated their ego: 'bad figs, very bad' were they and the best had gone to Babylon (24). The letter to the exiles (29), with its amazing combination of vision and common sense, sought to lay a cool hand on the fevered brows of the fanatics there. Again in the fourth year of Zedekiah, when revolt seemed ready to break out, Jeremiah performed another symbolic action (28) and spoke a decisive word against the smooth-speaking nationalistic prophets to whom the whole situation was as a sealed book while they cried 'Peace, Peace'. The shallowness of the false prophets was made clear in the lurid light of the last days of the kingdom.

e But Jeremiah did not succeed in his second attempt to arrest the madness of the pro-Egyptian party. In 589 B.C. the rebellion broke out that was to bring an end of Judah's line of kings. The city was surrounded and the siege was pressed. Through all this time the prophet counsels submission to Nebuchadrezzar 'the servant of God' (25:9): to fight against Babylon is to fight against God. The approach of Hophra's army might cause a brief interruption of the siege but its doom was fixed and sure (37). During

466e this interval occurred the shameful incident of the slaves released and again enslaved (34:8f.), and at the same time Jeremiah was arrested as he sought to leave the city in connection with family business (37:12f.). In prison the prophet did not cease to urge desertion to the foe (37:21) and the military clamoured for his death. But for the compassion of Ebedmelech he would have perished most miserably (38:1–13). The king sought his counsel but was too weak to follow it (38:24f.). The faith of the prophet was here demonstrated by the transaction recorded in ch. 32 where he buys the ancestral field from his cousin.

f The city fell in 586 B.C. Zedekiah's sons were slain before his eyes and he himself blinded and carried to Babylon. Jeremiah gives the number of deportees as 832 but this seems an underestimate.

Gedaliah was appointed governor and Jeremiah remained with him. The omens seemed auspicious but mutual jealousies muddied the situation. Gedaliah was slain and panic seized the survivors. Against the prophet's counsel (42) they fled to Egypt (43) and settled at Tahpanhes. Thither they carried Jeremiah and Baruch and there revived the idolatrous worship of the Queen of Heaven. The prophet was unsparing in his denunciations of their idolatry and his prophecies of righteous judgment (44:24f.). Here the curtain falls and the prophet is lost in Egyptian darkness. Tradition has it that he was stoned to death by the infuriated mob : Cornill thinks that the last chapter in the book which we now have is a pale substitution for the story of his tragic end. There is no real reason to think so. The last word we hear from the prophet is a word of thanks to his faithful Baruch (45:5).

467a **Jeremiah as Prophet**—Our interest here lies not in any new theological ideas expressed by the prophet but rather in his personality. For here we see revelation at work. The heart of the prophet is laid bare before us in all its conflicts and tensions. ' The book of Jeremiah ', says A. B. Davidson, ' does not so much set before us religious truth as present a religious personality. Prophecy had taught its truths : its last effort was to reveal itself in a life ' (HDB ii, 576). In typical Hebrew fashion the word was made flesh : in Jeremiah personally we see the real intention of the divine heart. Thus Cornill writes : ' In Jeremiah we have the purest and highest consummation of the prophecy of Israel and of the religion of the Old Testament. After him One only could come, who was greater than he ' (*The Prophets of Israel*, 98). It is not to be wondered at that when men sought to explain the personality of Jesus they thought of Jeremiah (Mt. 16:14). No prophet reminds us more of Christ, and at times none is more unlike Christ. It is this so human element that intrigues us.

b Jeremiah is the spiritual heir of Hosea and is pre-eminently the prophet of repentance and personal religion. Reference has been made to his early training but we learn more from his own words. We can perceive that he was a lovable personality with a great capacity for affection. He shrinks from publicity, and his place as a younger son in his home made him more naturally a follower than a leader. In that home he had leisure to behold the wonders of Nature and like St Francis he loved the birds and knew them well (8:7 12:9, 17:11, 22:23, 48:28). The simple innocent joys of life were forbidden to him (16:1f.) but he observed them all with sympathetic eyes. Nothing human was alien to him. The almond tree putting forth its blossom, the iron pot boiling over, the farmer clearing the ground (4:3), the debtor and creditor with their mutual hatred (15:10), all these he sees *sub specie aeternitatis*, for all were revelations of God. The happy wedding songs, the tinkling timbrels of the dancing virgins, the loud laments of the mourners, and the silent rumble of the millstones (25:10)—all these he heard and they spoke to him of God. He notes with interest, tinged with pain, how father, mother and children so skilfully divide the labour as they go about to worship the Queen of Heaven (7:18). He knows the robber lurking by the way (3:2) and how the 467b traveller hastens on the road (13:16). What a sacrifice it must have been to a spirit so large in love that he should not be permitted to know those common joys of home and family ! But this was of the divine appointing and Jeremiah will bear the cross.

All this and more must be borne in mind as we c think of the cost of his prophetic service. The strain and tension of his life lie just in this, that he loved the land wherein were so many beautiful things, and he loved God who had given that land to Israel. His piercing laments for land and people are the expression of his vast abiding love. As with Hosea there is only one sin here, the sin of infidelity that has spat in the face of God and done despite to his grace (2:25f., 6:15f.). It may be difficult to gauge the agony of a Hosea or Jeremiah but it is only those who have stood in the counsel of God who know that he is most wonderfully kind and, at the same time, a consuming fire. Jeremiah's doctrine of sin is the direct outcome of his knowledge of God and his profound acquaintance with the human heart. The human heart he knew well from his own encounters with the High and Holy One : ' it is desperately corrupt ' (17:9). Even in the choicest spirits the gold must be passed through the fire to smelt away the dross and man's spirit must be ' stabbed broad awake '. Here the divine revelation comes through the channels of human experience, and the prophet knew that his experience could be the experience of every mother's son in Israel.

The prophet's most significant contribution lies in d the area of religious thought. His life of conflict and tension made him conscious of resources in God which a man might not otherwise discover. Out of weakness he was made strong : he fought his doubts and gathered strength. He reaches heights of spiritual vision that are rarely equalled elsewhere in the OT and in him we reach the peak points of OT piety. The Temple speech (chs. 7, 26) shows how he came to see clearly that mechanical and material relations can never take the place of relations personal and spiritual. The prophet need not be understood as rejecting the cult in religion : even the ' saints ' require and employ ' sensible signs ' in the life of the spirit. The letter to the exiles (29) contains so much that is novel and unprecedented—the thought of prayer for enemies, the idea that ' the unclean land ' can be the sphere of revelation, and that God can reveal himself to individual men and women—that the prophet must himself have been surprised by the words he wrote. He builded better than he knew. And surely that is more so in the matter of the New Covenant (31:31f.). Here it took ages for men to comprehend the greatness of this seminal thought and to learn that neither Jerusalem nor Samaria mattered as much as men thought, that ' God is spirit and those who worship him must worship in spirit and truth ' (Jn 4:24). It is the glory of the prophet that he allows us to see this spiritual growth within himself and that he reveals the essence of religion. That thought had to wait for its fuller explication. And on that night in which the Lord of Glory was betrayed he reached his hand across the centuries to greet his great predecessor as he said, ' This cup is the New Covenant in my blood '. Jeremiah may be late in coming to his own but the final recognition is full and ample.

Jeremiah as Poet—No prophet surpasses Jeremiah e in poetic skill. Nahum may stand near him in excellence but Jeremiah excels him in the variety of his muse. The richness of poetic fancy that meets us in the opening oracles is sustained throughout. There is here an effortless ease that marks the born poet : he sings because he must.

All his pictures are striking and some are really memorable, as, for example, his description of Death in 9:21, 22 :

Death has come up through our windows,
Has entered our palaces,

467e Cutting off from the streets the children,
And young men from the squares.
And the corpses of men lie fallen
Like dung on the open field,
Like sheaves behind the reaper
With none to gather.

'That belongs to the masterpieces of poetry' (Cornill). Mark the pathos of the poet's lament for Rachel and her little ones :

Hark ! in Ramah is heard lamentation,
Weeping most bitter !
Rachel for her children weeping,
Refusing to be comforted
(Thus says the Lord)
Refrain thy voice from weeping
And thine eyes from tears
For reward there is for thy travail—
They return from the enemy's land. (31:16, 17)

His high poetic power is wedded to his capacity as a moral analyst and his ability to get inside the soul of man. Strongly emotional as he is he never fails to control the poetic medium. The text may at times fail to reveal his artistry by reason of the fact that many prosaic minds have worked upon the text in the course of its transmission. But not all the blundering efforts of pedestrian scribes can obscure the beauty of his poetry or make his music mute.

Hebrew poetry is essentially lyrical : the poet sings with his eye on the subject :

When I go forth to the field
Lo ! there the slain of the sword :
When I enter the city
Lo ! there the horrors of famine. (14:18)

That is brief and compact, full of thrills and horrors. And where may we find anything like this to express intensity of pain ?

My bowels, my bowels ! O mine anguish !
O walls of my heart !
My heart is in storm within me,
I cannot keep still :
For I hear the trumpet's sound,
The uproar of war. (4:19)

That reaches the heart with a veritable stab of pain. Grosser natures cannot be so moved. Here indeed we witness

The desperate tides of the whole world's great anguish
Forced through the channels of a single heart.

For Jeremiah climbed heights where lesser men dared not follow and he sounded depths we cannot fathom. Rhetorical adornment he avoids by a natural reserve : he will not embellish the holy word of God with the tawdry tinsel of human art :

O that my head were waters,
and mine eyes a fount of tears !
That day and night I might weep
for my people slain. (9:1)

468a Here, too, we find a warm tender sympathy with Nature, an interest akin to that of Tennyson and Burns. To the Hebrew Nature was the garment of God, half concealing and half revealing the divine being. To Jeremiah every bush was aflame with God. He knows the great and terrible wilderness and he loves the land where men live and labour. He knows the sorrow on the sea (49:23) and the roaring sirocco that blasts the sown-land (23:19). The proud cedars of Lebanon draw his admiration (22:7, 23), and the first bloom of spring reveals the glory of God (1:11).

As he looked into the heart of the glowing sunset he 468a
trembled at the thought of the coming darkness (13:16). The wild beasts find a friend in him and he marks the lordly lion as he rises from his lair (4:7) and the lurking panther that seeks his prey (5:6). Birds also he notes in their coming and going, and what a pathos lies in these words :

I looked—and, behold, no man was there,
And all the birds of heaven were flown. (4:25)

A world without birds was as 'the abomination of desolation' to Jeremiah. For these birds were the divine remembrancers.

No less does he find joy in 'the still sad music of b
humanity'. What agony for the prophet to proclaim doom on little children ! For Jeremiah loved 'those little ones' as did the Saviour himself. The voice of the bridegroom and the bride sound often in his ears, and he finds deep satisfaction in the sound of the rolling millstones and the light of the cottage lamp. For in these elemental things is man's deepest joy and the loss of them is the supreme tragedy. Happy days will come again when the dancers go forth with glee on Samaria's hills (31:4, 5). These things are always with him and with deft touches he reveals their presence, the maids returning with pitchers empty (14:3), the joy of the festal dance (31:4), or Jehoiakim limned with a single stroke (23:13). At times this dramatic power is sustained with a series of literary vignettes and his pictures shine like facets of a diamond.

All is 'simple, sensuous, passionate', as poetry c
should be (Milton). The enemy as a storm-cloud (4:13), God's messengers as fishers and hunters (16:16), the bird-catchers filling their baskets with birds (5:26)—all these simple and sensuous things are here. Here, too, is the bride with her ornaments (2:32)—surely she will not forget her sash—and the black-visaged Moor (13:23), the war-charger that thunders into battle (8:6), the fresh-watered gardens (31:12), the balm of Gilead (8:22) and the broken cisterns that hold no water but which 'my people' love—all these are here and much more. This is life and this is the poetry of life's simplicities. Thus the poet speaks home to the hearts of men.

The Book of Jeremiah—The book as we now have d
it is a collection made by various hands and it may not have assumed its final form before the post-exilic period. The main sources of the book are clear as is the case with most prophetic writings. Here we have three main groups of material. First we have the oracles of the prophet, the messages given by God for delivery, usually prefaced with the words 'Thus says the Lord' or sealed with the formula 'oracle of Yahweh'. The second group is composed of narratives about the prophet in the third person, while the third group consists of narratives in the first person. The oracular poetry is found mainly in the earlier part of the book. To this group we assign 1:15–3:5, 3:19–6:30, 8:4–10:25, 11:15–12:17, 13:15–27, 14:1–10, 14:17–17:18, 18:13–23, 20:7–18, 21:11–14, 22:6–23:40, 25:30–6, 30:4–31:32, 46:1–51:58 (in part). Included in these sections are the 'Confessions' and reflections of the prophet. Frequently short prose pieces are found within these sections and these may have been originally in poetic form. Duhm would accept only oracles in poetic form but this seems arbitrary and unreasonable. The second group is not properly a biography of the prophet but forms rather the 'Passion Story' of Jeremiah. It is the story of what he suffered through fidelity to his prophetic vocation. This narrative is generally attributed to Baruch and to this group may be assigned 19:1–20:6, 21:1–10, 26, 28, 29, 30:1–3, 33, 34, 36–45, 51:59–64. Concerning the third group of material there is a large difference of opinion. This is frequently referred to as the Deuteronomic source : Mowinckel would question whether it is a literary source in the proper sense of that term. The passages involved here are 1:1–14, 3:6–18, 7:1–8:3,

468d 11:1–14, 13:1–14, 14:11–16, 17:19–27, 18:1–12, 22:1–5, 24, 25:1–29, 27, 31:23–40, 32, 35. (Reference should be made to the Introductions by Oesterley & Robinson, Pfeiffer, Bentzen.)

e Regarding this third source none can fail to perceive the apparent influence of the Deuteronomic writers. Here we seem to have a consistent theme developed in stereotyped monotonous style. The theme may be varied with such forms as 'give heed to these words or destruction will come upon you' or 'Judah and Jerusalem are doomed because they have not hearkened to the words of Yahweh'. There is little interest in Jeremiah personally or the occasions on which he spoke but merely a sustained emphasis on this theme. Some scholars see in this material a genuine Jeremianic core: Mowinckel suggests that these words were originally in the third person and that a Deuteronomic editor has changed them to addresses in the first person. This seems highly improbable. It seems wiser here to agree with Oesterley & Robinson who hold that this was the regular style of prose from the 8th cent. B.C. onwards and that it was not created by Jeremiah or Deuteronomy but inherited. This was the language of liturgy and the temple service (Weiser). And such speech tends to have a cast-iron quality as can be observed in all liturgical literature. The prophet, reared in such surroundings, would find it a suitable and natural speech. It is true that the language of the poetical pieces is vivid and colourful, and it may well be that those narratives in the course of tradition were modified in some degree by pedestrian members of the various schools of prophetic tradition. There seems no real reason for the undue scepticism of Mowinckel and Hyatt: we may still regard these narratives or sermons as containing a genuine tradition concerning the prophet.

These are the three main groups lying behind our present book of Jer. All of them contain material that is later than the prophet and some of the material may date around the beginning of the 4th cent. B.C. There are sections which must be denied to Jeremiah. 50:1–51:58 is generally so regarded while 52 is a historical addendum from the book of Kg. (2 Kg. 24:18–25:21, 27–30). 10:1–16, 23:34–40, 33:14–26 are interpolated from a later period. Smaller interpolations are found throughout and are pointed out as they occur.

f The structure of the book is easily discerned. In its composition chronology is not generally followed: the arrangement is frequently according to subject-matter. The book may be divided thus:

I Chs. 1–25:13 Prophecies of doom against Jerusalem and Judah (with few minor exceptions). There are signs of chronological order, chs. 1–6 referring to the reign of Josiah, chs. 7–20 to the time of Jehoiakim, chs. 21–4 to the later monarchy.

II 25:15–38, 46–51 Oracles against the Nations.

III 26–36 Prophecies of salvation for Israel and Judah. (27–9 concern Jewish captivity, 30f. northern Israel, 32 deals with Palestine while 34:1–7 is a conditional prophecy to Zedekiah.)

IV 37–45 The Passion Story of Jeremiah by the scribe Baruch.

g **The Greek Version**—The LXX is about one-eighth shorter than the MT. The main difference here is the position of the Oracles against the Nations which in MT appear as chs. 46–51. In the LXX they follow immediately after 25:13*a*. The individual oracles in this collection are set in different order in MT and LXX. Notable omissions in the LXX are 29:16–20, 33:14–26, 39:4–13, 52:28–30. In some instances the LXX seems to offer a better text (e.g. 25:1–12) but no claim may be made for its general superiority. Where variations occur each must be judged on its merits. As in the case of other OT books the translation seems to be the work of two different hands: the division seems to lie between chs. 28 and 29.

469a **I 1-3 Title**—This probably referred originally only to the first chapter and was later expanded to cover the 469a
whole book. With the help of the LXX we may assume the original here read 'the word of the Lord which came to Jeremiah, the son of Hilkiah, in the days of Josiah, the son of Amon, king of Judah, in the thirteenth year of his reign'. V. 3 is added by a later hand. We learn that Jeremiah began to prophesy in the year 626 B.C. and that he prophesied until the fall of Jerusalem in 586 B.C. The book, however, contains prophecies beyond the latter date. Jeremiah's father was a priest descended probably from Abiathar, high priest of David, who carried the ephod before Israel's beloved king and was deposed by Solomon on his accession (1 Kg. 2:26). It is not said that Jeremiah held the office of priest. The family resided at Anathoth (modern ʽAnâtā). Hilkiah means 'the Lord is my portion' but the meaning of the prophet's name is uncertain: it may mean 'the Lord exalts'. **2.** 'thirteenth year': for this T. C. Gordon (ET 44, 562–5) would read 'twenty-third' but the MT affords no ground for this (cf. 25:3). Hyatt assumes that this is the date of the prophet's birth but such an assumption is unwarranted.

4-10 The Call of the Prophet—Here Jeremiah tells b
in his own words how God called him to be a 'prophet to the nations'. The call is the one event in a prophet's life that becomes regulative and determinative of all his activity. Amos, Hosea, Isaiah, Ezekiel all ground their ministries on such a decisive encounter with God. Paul knew the same experience and its decisive quality (Gal. 1:15). To each it comes in different form but always in the form of an irresistible constraint. Here the profound spiritual experience is expressed through inadequate physical media, and we are presented with an elevated idea, suffused with intense emotion, entering into consciousness in dramatic form and uttering itself in poetic language. The experience is a real experience, as real as the bread he eats or the water he drinks. 'The secret of the Lord is with them that fear him' (Ps. 25:14, AV). The prophets know God and are known of him. The terms used here emphasise the inner nature of this experience. This event in the prophet's life had its origin in the eternal counsels of God: before Jeremiah was born he was a thought in the mind of God. Moreover the word 'know' in Hebrew has a large affective content: to the Hebrew the heart is the organ of intellection. The word 'know' is almost equivalent to 'elect' or 'love' (cf. Am. 3:2). And the word 'consecrated' has here its original meaning, 'set apart'. Jeremiah is a predestined man. Israel may seem politically insignificant but God's purpose is for the world and Jeremiah shall speak his word 'to the nations'. Duhm would read this 'to my nation' but the text is clear and the prophet's ministry confirms the text. The prophet trembles before such a lofty call: unlike Isaiah (6:8) but like Moses (Exod. 4:10) he shrinks from this awful responsibility. The Greek renders better: 'I am too young'. The prophet was probably about 20 years of age: he was God's chosen vessel and God will use him for his purpose. **9.** 'Grace specialises' (M. Henry): with Isaiah grace was cleansing, with Jeremiah it is empowering. And the work the prophet is called to do is of both destructive and constructive nature. Perhaps we should omit 'to destroy and to overthrow': LXX omits 'to overthrow'.

11-19 Two Visions—The two visions recorded here c
may suggest a continued reluctance on the part of the prophet and the need of a reinforcing experience. Mowinckel thinks these were earlier visions that predisposed the prophet to the Call Vision. More probably, however, the prophet set them here as confirmations of his call. To a mind attuned to the divine it was not difficult to see God in commonplace things (cf. chs. 18, 32). **11.** There is a play on words here: *shāḳēdh* (branch of almond tree) and *shōḳēdh* (waking) would sound alike to the Hebrew (cf. Am. 8:1 where *ḳayiṣ* (summer fruit) and *ḳēṣ* (end) sound alike).

469c To Jeremiah the sight of the almond tree waking from its winter sleep suggests that the living God is about to strike into the national life with decisive action. Men shall soon know that God is not dead but fearfully alive and is moving to fulfil his purpose. Nature is a parable of God's working. **13-19.** The second vision is more difficult. Here for the first time we have mention of the mysterious north. What Jeremiah intended by this is not clear: probably in the manner of the prophets he desires to stir a sense of uneasiness by the suggestion of the weird and the uncanny. The RSV, following a suggestion of G. R. Driver (JQR 28, 77) reads *ûphānûy* (turned away from) for *ûphānāw* (its face), and the thought seems to be of a caldron in the north tilted towards the south and about to spill its boiling contents in that direction. Duhm's suggestion, 'its face turned toward the north', has support from the LXX but the RSV seems preferable. Both suggestions involve minimal changes in the text. It may be the prophet had the Scythians in mind, but whoever they may be the prophet regards them as the instrument of God's purpose. And the ground of the coming judgment is none other than Israel's infidelity and apostasy. The prophet is encouraged to speak boldly and to stand firm, for God is with him.

d **II 1-III 5**—Here we have some of the prophet's earliest preaching. The whole section to the close of ch. 6 represents his activity immediately after his call. The preaching consists of a historical retrospect revealing the wondrous fellowship with God that Israel enjoyed in the days of her youth. Not that Jeremiah commends the desert life for its own sake, for the desert was harsh and cruel, and Israel looked for something better from her God. Palestine was 'the Promised Land' to which the wandering tribes finally came. What Jeremiah recalls is the faith and simple trust that once was Israel's when she walked with God and trusted in his grace and power. It may be, as Engnell suggests, that the desert ideal is grossly overrated and born of romantic notions; in ch. 35 Jeremiah might seem to agree with such a view. But it is not the desert as desert the prophet glorifies but rather the faith of their fathers which was revealed in the desert and may be Israel's again. It is the sorrow of God and his servant the prophet that the original bond which bound them to God has been sullied and broken. This is the surpassingly wonderful thing, and it is without precedent. Look where one will, north, south, east or west, such faithless apostasy is without parallel. How comes it that a people could be so foolish and so lacking in gratitude? Here Jeremiah reflects the puzzled bewilderment of Hosea. Will it ever be possible to recapture the ancient spirit that animated Israel then, and will it ever be possible to renew that fellowship and communion with God?

e **II 1-3 Halcyon Days**—The prophet to the nations begins with Jerusalem, the head and front of all offending. He begins with a picture of what she once was. For history is judgment and the prophet will speak to the heart. 'Devotion' is a rich word with manifold meaning: it may mean, *inter alia*, God's love to man, man's love to God, man's love to his fellow man, the love of a servant for his master, or of master for servant. Here it means Israel's response to her redeemer God for his grace and righteousness. 'Holy' (3) has its original sense of separateness, 'a peculiar people', God's very own. And God responded to their devotion by defending and upholding them.

f **4-13 Sorrow's Crown of Sorrow**—Duhm denies these verses to Jeremiah but without adequate reason. The regular poetic metre (*Ḳînāh*) is absent here but the thoughts expressed are worthy of the prophet. Moreover Jeremiah was deeply interested in northern Israel (4) though it was now gone into exile. 'Worthlessness' signifies the exhalation or vapour from a man's mouth: it is the same word as is used by Ecclesiastes and there translated 'vanity' (*hebhel*: cf. Jas 4:14). So unsubstantial are these gods, and the people are become like them. For when people lose the sense of history they lose the sense of gratitude (6): they lose hold on character as they lose hold on God. **10.** Kittim (Cyprus) and Kedar (a Syrian desert tribe) put them to shame, for these remain loyal to their heathen gods. Surely no such apostasy has ever been witnessed elsewhere. Israel has exchanged her 'glory' for an empty shadow. **13.** By a homely simile he shows the utter folly of hewing out cisterns that easily crack and let the flat stagnant water ooze away while they neglect the fresh water that springs from flowing fountains. The Hebrew 'thinks with the eye' and none could miss the meaning of this word (cf. Isa. 55:1; Jn 4:13, 7:37). 469f

14-28. Vv. 14-17 interrupt the connection between 13 and 18 and may be due to displacement or be a later addition. The words in 17, 'when he led you in the way', are not found in the LXX. The root cause of the decadence of Israel, who is no slave, but a son, is not political but religious. And neither Assyria nor Egypt can avail to help. Only the Lord who redeemed them at the first can save them now. Here Jeremiah stands as the prophet of repentance. In **19**, 'apostasy' (*meshûbhāh*), we meet a word that recurs often throughout these oracles: the word 'fear' is the word used for the God of Isaac (*Paḥadh Yiṣḥāḳ*, Gen. 31:42). It is a fearful thing to fall into the hands of the living God. And here the prophet reveals the ugly nature of Baal worship. Israel has been set free to serve her God, that in that service she might find perfect freedom, but now she has thrown off all restraint. There is here an element of malice aforethought: it was deliberate apostasy. God had given the law for a fence and protection but Israel has run wild like a young camel in her heat. There may be here a reminiscence of Isaiah's parable of the Lord's vineyard (Isa. 5:1f.). It was not so in her youth—but now! 'how art thou turned to a foul smelling thing, an alien vine' (reading in **21**, with Duhm, *lesōriyyāh gephen*). Sin is ingrained in the national life and no remedy of men's devising can erase the record of their evil-doing. In **24** the 'wild ass' should perhaps be rendered 'heifer'. Sensuality of life has followed upon political corruption and all the result of the prophet's preaching seems to be a hardening of the nation's heart. The moral urge to higher life is wholly lost: he who is filthy will be filthy still. They see the better and approve the worse. Man-made deities, however many they be, are but so many nonentities, 'nothings', but all the 'nothings' in the world are not equal to the One. **16.** Read with Cornill and Duhm 'have shaved' for 'have broken' (BH). 470a

29-37 Israel has no Ground for Complaint—The misfortunes that have befallen her are sent by God and are proofs of his providence and love: they are intended to recall men to the right way. The past leading of God guarantees his power still to guide, but Israel shuns God as a waste howling wilderness, so strange has he become to her. The union once forged in happier days is now dissolved and Yahweh is disowned. The thing seems inconceivable, as inconceivable as that a bride should forget her wedding finery. Nevertheless, the solid sad fact is there for all to see. Israel has forgotten her redeemer God, and to such mastery of evil has she attained that even the experts in immorality are her pupils (33). The prophet is amazed and ponders further the evil results of this apostasy. Brazen social injustice and political opportunism are the inevitable result when a nation loses its spiritual vision and ceases to walk with God. **34.** 'on your skirts': the Versions here read 'on your hands'. **35.** 'I have not sinned': no pious Hebrew speaks thus. Contrast Ps. 51:4; 1 Sam. 7:6; 2 Sam. 12:13. b

III 1-5 Israel's Infidelity—The introductory formula seems to have fallen out of the text and only the word 'saying' remains. By an illustration from their own law the prophet makes clear that the people c

470c are imperilling their status before God. The reference here is usually taken to be to Dt. 24:1–4 but it may be questioned whether Dt. was yet published. The reference may be to Israelite practice from an earlier period. The question is not of divorce but of adultery. If in such a relatively simple matter as is here introduced there be pollution of the land—MT is to be preferred here to LXX which reads 'woman' for 'land'—how much more in the case where infidelity has been carried on at a higher level, and in most brazen fashion the bride of God has lavished her love on all comers, sitting by the wayside like a robber Arab. Little wonder is it that the heavens have refused the shower and the clouds withheld their rain! With a brow of brass and a heart of stone they think to cozen God with endearing terms and treat his indignation as a transient passion. Their light and easy words are grossly belied by their actions. **1.** LXX reads 'Shall she return to him?' The word 'return' (*shûbh*) occurs eight times in 3:1–4:4. It may mean 'turn to' (repent) or 'turn from' (apostatise). **2.** The word 'Arab' occurs only here and in Isa. 13:20. **3.** For 'harlot's brow' we might better read 'brow of brass' (BH, cf. Isa. 48:4).

d **6-18 An Instructive Comparison**—This oracle plainly does not belong here: it interrupts the connection between 3:5 and 3:19. It may well be Jeremianic, for Jeremiah's interest in North Israel was unceasing: 'ethnologically Benjamin belonged to Israel and Anathoth was in the territory of Benjamin' (Skinner). Here in contrast to usual practice 'Israel' is confined to northern ten tribes. These passed into exile in 721 B.C. Their cup of iniquity was full, and Yahweh brought the covenant relation to an end or suspended it. He gave 'a decree of divorce'. But the prophet harbours undying hope and envisions undreamed-of revelations of grace. Meantime he will enforce a lesson. Judah saw all this and took it not to heart. Judah went the same way and went farther. Judah is more guilty than Israel for she has spurned the lessons of history, and history is the channel of God's revelation. Now the prophet addresses a word of hope to these exiles: God's hot indignation is overpast and grace remains for the penitent. **14-18** seem to be a later addition to this intrusion and we are presented with a glowing vision of the exiles, Israel and Judah, returned and reunited under good kings in Jerusalem which becomes the centre of a purified religious life. No more will the outward material symbol of the Ark be asked for or required, for God himself will be a living presence in Jerusalem. These five verses may rest on a word of the prophet but they represent a contraction of his thought as expressed in vv. 6–13 and in chs. 30, 31. **6.** 'that faithless one Israel': lit. 'that apostasy Israel', as if Israel were apostasy incarnate. **12.** 'look on you in anger': lit. 'let my face fall upon you' (cf. Gen. 4:6).

e **III 19-IV 4 The Way of Repentance**—This is the natural continuation of 3:5. There is a certain obscurity about 19 but it is best understood as the expression of a deep desire. What place will God give to Israel among the nations? Surely none other than the goodliest heritage, 'the heritage of the beauty of the beauties of the nations' (cf. Ezek. 20:6; Dan. 8:9, 11:16, 41). For this gift the Lord expected gratitude but Israel—the surviving Judah—turned her back on God and became unfaithful. In a passage full of tender emotion the prophet represents the people confessing their sin. On the bare heights, the scene of her idolatry, is found the place of her penitence, and like sweet music of silver chimes comes the swift response of God summoning her to complete moral renewal with full purpose of heart. The question asked in 3:1 here finds its answer: God will take back his bride and she shall be his own. Israel's joy shall be full and she will bring joy to the world (cf. Gen. 12:3; Ps. 72:17). But this repentance must be no outward thing like circumcision in the flesh: it must be deep set in the spirit and issue in life purged
and purified. Else surely his wrath shall be kindled 470e
against them.

IV 5-31 The Alarm of War—The first verse of this 471a
oracle should probably be omitted: the prophet in dramatic style breaks right into his oracle. 'Oracle' may seem a pale term for what follows, for here we have lyric poetry of the highest order, animated description of martial scenes yet to be and a wealth of emotion that breaks the bounds of regular speech. The prophet as poet here makes things live before our eyes, and in his short staccato-like strophes rouses our sympathetic excitement. The dramatic element is the more wonderful in that it is spontaneous and unstudied. The tender words of contrite hearts which the prophet had dreamed to hear (3:21–5) are not heard, and now nothing awaits the sin of Judah but the judgment of her God. In the dramatic overture (5–8), where imperative piled upon imperative gives the sense of panic and haste, the evil from the north gives the first sign of its appearing. It will mean destruction to the last man. It may come in the form of wild Scythian marauders or in the embattled array of mighty Babylon, but the final source and origin of this evil is not in the north. It is in God. These earthly hosts are but the agents of his judgment. Judah had not seen war for wellnigh eighty years, when Sennacherib came down 'like a wolf on the fold'. Men had been lulled into a false sense of security. Their false prophets and their foolish rulers had never ceased telling them that God could not do this to them. But they failed to discern the signs of the times: they failed to perceive the real nature of their God. With swift strokes the onrush of the foe is described, horses swifter than vultures, unending masses of men, chariots like the whirlwind. V. 14 is omitted by many commentators but in the swift emotional rush of the prophet's mind this appeal seems not unnatural. Ruin draws nigh, the siege is set, the city encircled, and Judah is about to reap the harvest of her sin. All this comes of rebellion against God. This also is the cross of Jeremiah, and in words of matchless beauty his agony is revealed (19–22). 'My tents' shows how completely the prophet felt himself bound up with his people. Their sorrow is his sorrow. In 23–31 is a marvellous description of chaos returned: the ancient *tōhû wābhōhû* (Gen. 1:2) appears once more and a new creation must be devised. Many scholars would deny these lines to Jeremiah but it seems difficult to credit such imaginative power to any other than the impassioned man of Anathoth. A heaven without light and cities without inhabitants, the birds of the air all gone—that is not the world God intended for man, but it is the world man has brought about. No meretricious arts (cf. 2 Kg. 9:30; Ezek. 23:40) or cajolery will avail to turn away the devouring foe. These wild men from the north love not beauty: they love blood. This is no soft evening zephyr but the fierce wind of God's anger. All that is left them is their eyes to weep with.

10. For 'I said' read with Arabic version 'they (the false prophets) will say'. **13.** 'Eagles', better 'vultures'. **14.** Probably an interpolation. **19.** 'my anguish', lit. 'my bowels': the bowels were the seat of emotion in Hebrew psychology. **28b.** Read better with LXX: 'I have spoken and will not repent; I have purposed and will not turn back from it'. **29.** 'all the cities': read with LXX and Targ. 'all the land'. **29b.** Erbt, with aid of LXX, would read 'they enter caverns, hide in the thickets'.

V 1-9 Corruption unbounded—Duhm would refer b
this poem to Jeremiah's first visit to Jerusalem, and suggests that the impression made on his mind was similar to that made on the mind of Luther when he visited Rome. This is somewhat fanciful. Anathoth was but three miles from Jerusalem and the prophet must frequently have visited the city before his call. Skinner cautiously suggests that it should be dated after the Reformation when the prophet was forced to leave home on account of the hostility of his kinsmen.

471b This seems doubtful. Such a state of affairs as is here described is hardly likely to have prevailed immediately after Josiah's reform. These chapters (1–6) seem to belong to his earliest preaching. In this chapter the element of reflection is obvious. Social sins are emphasised and the sorry state of public life in Jerusalem is revealed. Not one righteous man can be found, no, not one. The prophet sees the justice of the coming judgment. The people are incorrigible : they know not the ethic of their God. The multiplied imperatives, ' run ', ' look ', ' take note ', ' search ', reveal the urgency of the situation. One righteous man might save the city but such cannot be found (cf. Gen. 18:16–33). The ' man in the street ' and the ' higher-ups ' are alike godless, and the sacred name is used only in empty oaths. The reference in v. 8 may be to religious prostitution and the Baal orgies. All discipline and restraint have been cast to the wind. Chastisement does not produce penitence : hard faces are but the outward sign of hard hearts. They refuse to change. In vivid similes (cf. Hab. 1:8) the impending attack is foreshadowed. No forgiveness is possible to ' a nation such as this ' (9), a phrase that conveys the deepest sense of alienation and rejection. Once they were ' my people ' but now they are so full of pride and bread and inordinate lust. *Corruptio optimi pessima.* The Lord will surely react in hot indignation and require it at their hands.

c **10-19 A consuming Fire**—The invader is summoned to execute judgment. The vineyard of the Lord's planting shall be rudely despoiled by the invaders, for it is no more the Lord's to guard and keep. The foolish folk who thought little of God and his Word, who set aside his messengers (Jeremiah and Zephaniah) with contempt, shall learn that ' it is a fearful thing to fall into the hands of the living God ' (Heb. 10:31), and that his Word is ' as a hammer which breaks the rock in pieces ' (23:29). They shall learn that their God is a consuming fire, and ' who can endure the day of his coming, and who can stand when he appears ' (Mal. 3:2) ? The enemy is at the gates, a great and ancient people : to the Hebrew antiquity made a nation more imposing and unknown speech heightened the sense of terror. Four times we read ' they shall eat up ' whereby emphasis is laid upon those hot, greedy, snatching appetites that will devour and swallow Judah. **10.** ' make . . . end ' : probably an addition. **11.** ' the house of Judah ' seems to be an addition. **12.** LXX reads ' the Lord their God ' : the metre seems to require this. **15.** LXX has accidentally omitted the words ' it is an enduring . . . ancient nation '. **16.** Rudolph and Volz read ' their mouth '.

d **20-31 Wickedness in Excelsis**—Senseless and foolish is this people, unable to understand the omnipotence of her God who set bounds to the raging sea (cf. Job 38–41 ; Ps. 19:1). The unfailing recurrence of seedtime and harvest, the rain that God sends to water the earth and make it fruitful (Dt. 11:10–12), these silent remembrancers of his grace and power should have evoked gratitude and saved them from apostasy. Little wonder is it that social injustice prevails and that life has become unduly hard for widows and little children. But God is concerned with man's relation to his fellows : justice is a glowing passion in him. Total corruption and decay, spiritual wickedness in high places, prophets false and priests delinquent, and a general satisfaction with things as they are—as God lives and reigns there can only be one end to this. The last verse drives home that solemn truth and nails it down.

e **VI 1-8 Disaster impends**—Ch. 4 proclaimed the coming of war, ch. 5 justified its coming, and ch. 6 adds to this justification with particular severity toward Jerusalem. The seat and centre of God's rule has become wholly corrupt. The Benjamites were Jeremiah's kinsmen, and as country folk might well be better than the city-dwellers : they had already fled to Jerusalem and are now summoned again to flee, for
evil impends from the north. Set up signs southward 471e
to direct the fleeing feet as they seek the caves and holes of the desert. Vv. 4–6*a* are spoken by the enemy and reveal the hot lust of destruction. Those foreign warriors are thirsting to attack and neither the heat of day nor darkness of night will daunt them. The trees are cut down (cf. Dt. 20:19, 20), the siege engines are ready, and Jerusalem is ripe for destruction. But God would fain save his people—if Israel would but receive instruction. For the Lord ' hates putting away ' (Mal. 2:16). **2.** Better translate : ' Is the daughter of Zion like a luxuriant pasture That shepherds come to her with their flocks.' **4.** Lit. ' sanctify war ' : the Hebrew regarded war as religious service. ' Beth-hacherem ' : three miles NE. of Tekoa, which was twelve miles south of Jerusalem. **6.** For ' this is the city which must be punished ' LXX reads ' ah, city of falsehood '. **7.** According to the Rabbis the middle letter of ' well ' (*bôr*) is the middle letter of the OT.

9-15 Is there no Hope ?—The prophet lingers on the f
thought of possible repentance. Has he searched with absolute thoroughness ? He will search again ' the remnant of Israel ' (Judah) with all the carefulness of a gleaner gleaning the last hidden grapes on the outermost bough. But all is vain : the previous judgment is confirmed. Deaf ears will not hear, and God's word is outrightly condemned. Here the prophet finds his first experience of rejection. A holy indignation fills his mind and he becomes one with God in judgment. It is characteristic of the prophet that he should think of the helpless victims, the young children in the streets and the very aged. Sin taints and infects all : it spawns an awful issue. Corruption is deep and total. Prophet and priest alike are false and the lust of gain pervades the whole community. Surely the righteous God will require it at their hands. **11.** ' Pour out ' : read with LXX ' I will pour out '. **Vv. 12-15**, repeated from 8:10–12.

16-21 Plea upon Plea—The only hope for the people 472a
is in repentance and return (*Shûbh*). The lessons of history and the admonitions of the prophets they wilfully set aside. The nations around are called upon to witness the just judgment of God : that judgment is the inevitable result of Israel's evil ways. Nor need they try to cozen and flatter God and turn aside his anger with lavish sacrifices. These will not be given for the nation's soul. There remains nothing but a fearful looking forward to judgment. **16.** This verse is not to be understood in the sense of Mt. 11:29. Material well-being and security depend on obedience to God. ' Your souls ' here simply means ' yourselves '. **17.** ' I set ' : verb here expresses repeated action. **18.** ' Know, O congregation ' : read ' know of a surety ' (BH). **20.** ' Sheba ', in South Arabia ; ' A distant land ', probably India.

22-30 The fearful Foe—This section turns back to b
4:5f., 5:15 f., 6:1–8. The prophet cannot get the thought out of his mind : it haunts him continually. A certain amount of uncertainty surrounds the identity of the foe—Scythian or Chaldaean ? The description is probably composite, and features from both are introduced to heighten and intensify the fearful nature of the impending blow. The encircling bands of wild warriors are about to overpower the daughter of Zion : terror fills every heart within the city. A similar scene is described in Isa. 5:26–9 and there it seems to be regarded with a certain objective admiration by that prophet. Jeremiah cannot stand aloof, for Zion's sorrow is his sorrow and there is no sorrow like it. But God will justify his ways to his servant. His prophet is set as a tester and as a man tests metals so will the prophet test his people. A thoroughgoing testing and assaying is applied but only base metal appears. They are wholly bad and rejected of God.

Here we come to the close of the early ministry of Jeremiah. The prophet is filled with despair. His devoted service seems in vain. Bowed down under the weight of Judah's sin the prophet seems to retire for a time. Now comes the period of reaction and

72b reflection. The prophet shall yet be found to be ' an iron pillar ' and strong as ' a fortified city '. **22-6,** repeated in 50:41–3. **25.** Perhaps better read ' For there is the sword of the enemy, Terror on every side '.

c **VII 1-15 The Temple Speech**—The date, as we learn from 26:1, is 608 B.C. and the occasion was probably the harvest festival. The political situation was full of uncertainty : good king Josiah was gone and Jehoiakim was on the throne. Assyria had come to an end and relations with Egypt were not friendly. It was a time of anxiety and the main question in men's minds was the question of security. About 100 years earlier Isaiah had proclaimed that the Temple would not fall before the attack of Sennacherib (701 B.C.). Now that faith had hardened to a dogma and men believed in the inviolability of Zion. Here was the guarantee of security. But Jeremiah rudely shatters this belief and seeks to awaken the people to reality. The speech is not in poetic form and it may well be that it has been expanded by a circle of disciples under the influence of Deuteronomy. Duhm would reject it as non-Jeremianic but there is no real reason for this. While we may not hear the actual voice of the prophet in these words there is no reason to doubt its essential authenticity. The prophet calls for repentance : the unrighteous shall not inherit the kingdom of God. God's promises are morally conditioned and true religion does not consist of slogans concerning an edifice, however lofty and imposing that edifice may be (cf. Mk 13:1), but is expressed in visiting the widow and caring for the under-privileged. National security hangs on obedience to God's holy law. This they have trampled underfoot : they have transgressed his commandments and think to remain his people. They pride themselves on Election but forget the accompanying responsibilities. They were once set free to serve God's purpose, but they abused their freedom and now moral anarchy prevails. They have made God's house a den of robbers. But God will sacrifice his house and his people : the destruction of Shiloh (*c.* 1050 B.C.) and the captivity of Ephraim are standing evidences of his uncompromising righteousness. Their judgment shall be as that of Ephraim. **2.** For ' gate ' 26:1 reads ' court '. The prophet probably stood in the gate between inner and outer court. **3, 7.** For ' I will let you dwell ' read with LXX and Vulg. ' I will dwell with you '. **11.** ' Den of robbers ', first words of sentence for emphasis.

d **16-20 The Queen of Heaven**—No more may the prophet pray for this people. Their panic now finds expression in the practice of gross heathen rites : this particular rite may have been the special concern of women. Ch. 44 indicates the practice was general, and it may be compared with worship of the Virgin. This worship of Ishtar was probably first introduced by Manasseh and reintroduced after the death of Josiah. There is a certain irony in the description of men, women and children all going about these ceremonies with feverish zeal and total forgetfulness of the fact that Israel's God is a jealous God. No prayer of the prophet can avert the judgment. **16.** ' I do not hear you ' : read better ' I will not listen to you '. **18.** ' To provoke me to anger ' : The Hebrew regards as purpose what we regard as result or consequence.

e **21-28 Obedience better than Sacrifice**—Sacrifices are in vain and the people might as well eat them themselves : they cannot prevail with God. Here Jeremiah reaches to the foundations : did God command sacrifice in the beginning (cf. Am. 5:21–4 ; Hos. 6:6, 8:13 ; Isa. 1:10–12) ? Religion in the beginning was simple fellowship and devotion to God (cf. 2:1f.) but now it has been overlaid with rites and ceremonies of alien origin. The original demand for simple obedience has been forgotten. The summons to repentance given by prophet after prophet has been disregarded. Life in the Promised Land has been a steady process of degeneration (2:2f.). The prophet recalls these things to the people but they give no 472e heed. Two cannot walk together unless they be agreed (Am. 3:3). **22.** Clearly the Pentateuch in its present form was unknown to Jeremiah. **24-8.** These verses may be a later addition.

VII 29-VIII 3 Lament and Mourn—Lamentation f is heard on the bare heights, for lamentable things have been wrought. God's holy house has been defiled by heathen usages. It is characteristic of the prophet that he singles out the absence of the bride and the bridegroom as signs of absolute desolation. The time will come, too, when the bones of the idolatrous worshippers will be disinterred by robber hordes and exposed to the natural elements which they worshipped with such ardour. In that day, so fearful will it be, death will be preferred to life. **31.** The reference here is probably to the heathen rites introduced by Manasseh (2 Kg. 21:2–9 ; Mic. 6:6–8), which customs were wholly repugnant to the mind of Yahweh. The meaning of Topheth is uncertain. It may mean ' fireplace ' (*tephath* ; the vowels have been changed to suggest the Hebrew word for ' shame ' (*bōsheth*). Hinnom may be the name of a former owner : its location is probably the Wâdī er-Rabâbi. From such practices it came to be synonymous with Hell. **8:3.** The sentence should end with the words ' evil family ' : the rest is added. **33.** This was a fearful punishment : the unburied dead find no rest.

VIII 4-9 Consider the Fowls of the Air—The 473a conduct of Judah was wholly unnatural. When one goes off the way one must surely seek return to the proper path. But Judah has refused to return. The sense of moral discernment has been blunted and atrophied. The birds by God-implanted instinct choose their path (cf. Isa. 1:3) but man refuses to obey the ordinance of God implanted in his bosom. Like a heedless war-charger they rush along their senseless way. Vain is their boast of wisdom, for that wisdom is based on corrupt readings and crooked interpretations which have evacuated the divine demand of its real significance. Their wise men have been just too clever, and their pretended wisdom, which does not rest on God's word, will ultimately be revealed as sheer folly. **4.** ' You shall say to them ' : omit with LXX. **4-6.** The word ' *shûbh* ' (turn) occurs here six times. In **5** ' perpetual backsliding ' regards the nation as a total mass of apostasy. **8.** The reference is to Dt. or more probably the falsified additions to Dt. The prophet had the authority of God's spirit : the scribe's authority rested on the written letter (cf. Mt. 5:17). Rites may not be exalted above right and ritual must not obscure the ethical. Even the Devil can quote Scripture. **9d.** Read better ' What benefit will their wisdom be to them ? '

10-17 Judgment on Leaders and Led—10–12 seem b to be loose repetition of 6:13–15 and are mainly absent from LXX. The connection between 9 and 13 is easy and natural : we may thus regard 10–12 as added here. By their fruits men shall be known, and if there be only withered leaves upon the vine when the Lord visits his vineyard then the vine will be cut down and cast away (cf. Lk. 13:7). Destruction is sure and no flight to fenced cities will avail (cf. 4:5). The snorting of the battle-charger is in their ears : serpents are about to bite and no charmer's art will turn aside their stroke. **13.** MT is quite obscure and various renderings have been suggested. With LXX omit the words ' what I gave them . . . them '. **14.** In imagination the prophet hears the cry of the distressed. **17.** With LXX we should read the last word of 17 with strange form of first word in **18** : ' they shall bite you beyond power to heal '. Skinner omits the verse as entirely unsuitable here.

VIII 18-IX 1 Too Little and too Late—Incalcul- c able is the pain of the prophet's bewildered heart. This section may refer to some divine visitation, such as famine, which has come upon the land. ' Here we are not in the region of revelation but of human sympathy ' (Rudolph). God speaks to his people in

473c such visitations (cf. Am. 4:6f.) yet his people do not return. Throughout, in the imagination of the prophet, is heard the cry of distress : religion becomes interrogative. Where is God ? Jeremiah gives expression to his heart of love in this passionate outburst of 9:1. Here he shares and bears the nation's sorrow. **18.** Read ' my pain rises within me, my heart faints '. **19c.** Later addition of prosaic scribe. **20.** Harvest was from April to June : if it failed there was still the fruit harvest to come. If that failed there was disaster. ' saved ' : reference is to physical deliverance. **21.** ' wound ' : literally, breach (*shebher* : Am. 6:6). **22.** ' balm ', probably mastic, the resin of the mastic tree, used for medicinal purposes. ' Why does not the fresh flesh come up upon her ' ? the fresh layer of skin that covers a wound. **9:1.** This is 8:23 in MT : a most unfortunate chapter division in the English versions.

d **IX 2-22 The Wages of Sin**—The prophet's despondency increases from 6:10f. through this chapter and ch. 15, and reaches a climax in ch. 20. He would fain escape his task as assayer (6:27). He is sick of men's sins. He exhausts vocabulary as he seeks to set forth the total corruption of the people. Conspicuous here are sins of the tongue, slander, falsehood, deceit, untruthfulness. There is a vast weight of weariness in the longing of the prophet to escape from it all. A wayside khan in the inhospitable desert would be a welcome change from this sin-sodden society where the religious sense seems wholly dead (1–6). But Yahweh will sift them and his holy righteous wrath will be revealed against this ungodly folk (7–9). Let loud laments arise on mountain and plain for destruction draws nigh. **12-16** seem to be an addition : it interrupts the poetic flow. These verses may be the sombre reflections of a later copyist. In 17–22 we hear the summons to the mourning-women (mentioned only here in the OT) who ' keen ' the dirge in which the people join. A mighty dirge it must be for it is taught by Yahweh himself and befits the greatness of the coming disaster. In a verse of surpassing beauty (21) we see the Grim Reaper silently and surely mowing the grim harvest of the doomed. The gladness of children in the street is stilled and young men vanish from the squares. None shall escape the Strong Man armed. **4.** ' supplanter ' : a play on the word ' Jacob '. ' Every brother acts as Jacob '. **7c.** Volz reads (with Targ. and LXX) ' What shall I do because of their wickedness ? ' **10.** Note the prophet's love of birds and beasts. **17.** Syr. and LXX omit ' Consider '. **18.** The cry of anguish is set in lines of two beats, thus giving a staccato effect. **22a.** Omit with LXX.

e **23-26 The Ground of Glory**—This oracle may have been misplaced but there is no reason to deny it to Jeremiah. Riches, fame, power—none of these give ground for man's glorying. ' Man's chief end is to glorify God and to enjoy him for ever ' (Westminster Shorter Catechism). **25f.** may be a detached oracle. Circumcision and uncircumcision are nothing, says Paul, and the only valid circumcision is of the heart (4:4). **26.** ' cut . . . hair ' : reference is to some desert tribes in Arabia who shaved their heads as a religious act.

f **X 1-16 The Folly of Idolatry**—There is general agreement that this section does not belong here. Like 9:23–6 it breaks the connection between 9:22 and 10:17. It appears to be addressed to Jewish exiles and finds points of contact with the Letter of Jeremiah. Throughout these chapters the prophet is dealing with a complete apostasy already present while in these verses such apostasy seems only to be contemplated. The LXX omits a considerable portion of the text (6, 8, 10) and shows confusion in the order of the verses (9 follows 5, while 11, in Aramaic, is clearly late). Let Israel not learn heathen ways, for they are false ways (cf. 1 Jn 5:21), false and empty as the idols they manufacture so laboriously (cf. Isa. 40:19f.). These are just ' nothings ' ; insubstantial as scarecrows in a field they are but the work of man's hands, put together with hammer and nails. They 473f cannot do a thing. They cannot carry but must be carried. What a travesty of deity ! Israel's God is different far, great and greatly to be feared. Possessed of surpassing wisdom he is the true and only God, Incomparable and Unique. None may abide the day of his coming. His greatness and power are evidenced in Creation (cf. Rom. 1:18f.) : he rules through all natural phenomena. What folly to put one's trust in one's own handiwork ! The folly of idolatry shall be exposed and Israel's God shall appear as Lord of all. **1.** Israel's religion is one of reverential awe (*yir'ath Yahweh*) : heathen religion is full of fear and anxious dismay. **2.** ' the way ' : the Hebrew views religion in concrete and definite fashion (cf. 2:23 ; Ac. 18:26, 19:9, 23). ' the signs of the heavens ' : probably the extraordinary phenomena which the heathen attributed to demons. **6.** ' thy name ' : the divine revelation. **7.** ' this is thy due ' : a late Aramaic phrase. **12-16.** Note how ridicule of idols is conjoined with enthusiasm for Israel's God.

17-26 Prepare to flee the City—Yahweh is about 474a to hurl them forth and away. In 19 we hear the voice of the people or the land. Bereft of home and children through the folly of their shepherds (rulers) the flock is scattered. The enemy is on his way and soon Judah will be a desolation. Man cannot walk alone or direct his course unaided. O Lord, in wrath remember mercy ! But let full measure of wrath fall on Israel's foes. **17.** Verse begins with form of verb ' *'āsaph* ' and 9:22 ended with similar form. Oracles were often assembled on this recurrence of similar words. ' Bundle ' : word occurs only here in OT and meaning is uncertain. **23.** Reference here is not to human feebleness but to moral and spiritual incapacity. **24.** LXX reads ' correct us '. ' In just measure ' (Luther, *mit Massen*) : let not wrath exceed due bounds. **25.** Recurs in Ps. 79:6 and can hardly be from Jeremiah, who constantly regards the foe as Yahweh's agent to execute judgment.

XI 1-XII 6 Proclamation of the Covenant— b Here we enter an area of uncertainty. Hyatt rightly remarks ' it is difficult to interpret correctly '. Duhm and Cornill regard 11:1–14 as unhistorical though Giesebrecht, Budde and Rothstein do not follow this view. Most commentators (e.g. G. A. Smith, Skinner, Peake) regard the passage as referring to Jeremiah's advocacy of the Josianic reform. Rudolph and Volz hold that a genuine tradition is present here though Volz would date the section in the reign of Jehoiakim. The question is fully discussed in Skinner, *Prophecy and Religion*, and in *Studies in OT Prophecy* (ed. H. H. Rowley), 157–74, and reference should be made to these works (cf. §465*e*).

XI 1-8 Proclaim this Covenant—The prophet is c commanded to proclaim a curse (cf. Dt. 27:26) on all who fail to keep the terms of ' this covenant '. The expression ' this covenant ' would most naturally refer to Dt. and is usually understood in this sense. Welch, Volz, Rudolph and others take the reference to be to the covenant at Sinai. Vv. 4, 5 might seem to lend support to this interpretation but it seems wiser, with Erbt, to regard these verses as an editorial expansion. The main weight seems to rest on ' this covenant ' which seems to imply something present and actually before the community. Support is given this interpretation by the fact that vv. 7, 8 are absent from the LXX save for the words ' they did them not '. Let the people observe the terms of this covenant and a right relation between the nation and its God will be established. Nothing is known from elsewhere about a preaching mission of Jeremiah on behalf of ' this covenant ' but such activity does not seem unreasonable : it was probably such activity that stirred the hostility of his kinsfolk. ' It seems quite credible that Jeremiah should have undertaken the role here assigned to him ' (Peake). **4.** ' iron furnace ' : not made of iron but a furnace in which iron was smelted (cf. Dt. 4:20 ; 1 Kg. 8:51).

474d **9-17 Reaction and Revolt**—The reference here seems to be to the reaction after Josiah's death at Megiddo. Here is studied and deliberate revolt and undoing of the work of the reformation. Judah has reverted to the inveterate evil example of her forefathers and forsaken the covenant so recently established. Vv. 11–14 seem to be an addition setting forth the ramifications of Baal worship and its complete futility. God will not listen to the cry of this apostate people nor hearken to the prophet's intercession for them. V. 15 is the natural sequel to v. 10 ; sacrifices and offerings will not avert the merited doom. Once an olive tree, beautiful and fair as those in the Temple court or on the Mount of Olives, there is now no beauty in this folk : God will blast and consume them in hot indignation. **9.** ' forefathers ', i.e. ' first fathers, ancestors ' : ' fathers ', i.e. fathers of the generation addressed by the prophet. **13.** ' altars you have set up to shame ' (*bōsheth=Baal*) : omitted by LXX. **14.** ' when they call ' : Targ. reads ' when thou callest '. **15, 16** : MT is confused and RSV has followed LXX in the main. For ' can you then exult ' LXX reads better, ' Can you escape by these ? ' **17.** Probably a late addition.

e **XI 18-XII 6 Jeremiah's Life endangered**—This section is introduced rather abruptly and it may be well, with Cornill, to read 12:1–6 before 11:18. The general sense, however, is clear enough. It must have seemed a monstrous thing to the descendants of Abiathar that their ecclesiastical status should be reduced in favour of the sons of Zadok, and that one of their own kin should be consenting to such an act. That surely was ' the most unkindest cut of all ' and it awakened fierce resentment. Both Jesus and Jeremiah had to learn by experience that a prophet is not without honour save in his own country. A man's foes may be those of his own household. The resentment appears to have been mutual—and here Jeremiah differs from Jesus (1 Pet. 2:23)—and the prophet utters wild whirling words of vengeance. We need not condone such words but perhaps we should judge them less as personal resentment and more as zeal for his divine vocation (cf. Ps. 139:19–22). Here again in these ' Confessions of Jeremiah ' religion passes into the interrogative mood and the prophet seeks to understand ' the reason o' the cause and the wherefore o' the why '. Here for the first time in this book is raised the question, Why do the wicked prosper and the innocent suffer ? ' My God, my God, why ? ' It may not be always possible to see to the other side of sorrow or catch a glimpse of the gospel that God hides within our suffering. ' What I do thou knowest not now, but thou shalt know hereafter.' ' Here we see through a glass, darkly ', and must walk by faith. Meantime the prophet will utter his hot dusty questionings. He will learn this is only the beginning and more is yet to come. If racing with footmen has wearied him how will he keep up with horses ? And if in a land of peace he ' falls on his face ' how will he do among the twining thickets of Jordan's jungle ? **4b.** LXX reads better ' all the herbs of the field '. **4e.** LXX reads ' because they said, God will not see our ways '. **5.** ' fall down ' : literally, ' fall flat on your belly '. The jungle of Jordan, thick with rank undergrowth and haunted by wild beasts, was visible from Anathoth. **11:19.** ' with its fruit ', literally ' with its bread '. Perhaps we should read ' with its sap ' (*lēḥô* for *laḥmô*). Targ. renders ' let us put poison in his food '. **12:3.** ' thou seest me '—omitted by LXX.

f **XII 7-17 Yahweh and His Heritage**—This section seems to refer to the events described in 2 Kg. 24:1, 2 when in his fourth year Jehoiakim rebelled against his overlord and Nebuchadrezzar sent the neighbouring peoples, Moab, Ammon, Syria, to chastise him· and bring him to heel. These peoples proceeded to make havoc of the land but not Jerusalem itself. Jeremiah is stirred by reason of the stupidity of the officials in the capital. The word ' heritage ' (*naḥ^a^lāh*) recurs frequently here, for Jeremiah delights in the beauteous 474f
land and is moved to profound sorrow by its desolation. As the text lies before us Jeremiah, in unique style, sets the lamentation in the mouth of Yahweh himself. For the heritage was Yahweh's gift to his people.

The lament opens with Yahweh's declaration that he has abandoned his people to the ravages of her foes, for they have turned like a lion upon him. Love has given place to hate. Like birds of prey attacking a gaily plumaged bird these nations beset Judah—and this at Yahweh's instigation. The repeated word ' desolation ' reveals the immense sorrow in the heart of God and the tragedy that none can understand his purpose. All their labour will be without return or profit because of his fierce anger (cf. Ps. 122:1). If vv. 14–17 are from Jeremiah they reveal a violent surge of emotion in which mercy strives with judgment and grace finally triumphs. These enemies, too, may be finally saved if they will but hearken and repent with full purpose of heart : if not, judgment for them will be complete and final. **7.** ' my house ', usually means the Temple, here ' the land ' (cf. Hos. 8:1, 9:16). **9b.** This may be read positively ' the birds of prey are round about her '. **9c.** LXX and Vulg. read ' Assemble ye wild beasts, and come to devour '. **11b, 12** break the metre here and may be regarded as glosses. Yahweh is here referred to in the third person though he is the speaker. **16a.** LXX reads ' the way ' for ' ways '. **17.** ' will not listen ' : LXX reads ' will not turn back '.

XIII 1-11 Parable of the Waistcloth—This section 475a
has been interpreted variously and it seems difficult to take it literally. Did Jeremiah journey twice to the Euphrates and twice return simply to prove the elementary fact that dirt spoils fine linen ? The journey from Jerusalem to Babylon—over 1,000 kilometres—took Ezra 100 days (Ezr. 7:9) under conditions more favourable than obtained in Jeremiah's time when wars and rumours of wars made travel dangerous and difficult. Mowinckel thinks we have here a visionary experience such as we meet with in Ezek. More probable is the interpretation that sees in ' Perath ' not the Euphrates but rather the Wâdī Fârah, a little stream near Anathoth. This stream is mentioned in Jos. 18:23 (Parah, with definite article). This interpretation seems to be that of Aquila's Greek version.

As to the meaning of this symbolic action many have interpreted it in relation to the Babylonian exile but this does not seem probable : Judah was purged and cleansed by that experience (Isa. 40:1f.). The reference seems rather to the heathen influences that had infiltrated Israel's religion and corrupted it. The people who had been ' holy to the Lord ' (2:3) and bound in closest intimacy with him had become paganised and polluted by association with heathen culture and heathen folk. Israel is the waistcloth of God, the girdle such as priests wore close to their person, but now it has become sullied, marred, and ' good for nothing '. The salt has lost its savour and is only fit to be trodden under foot of men. God's purpose in the election of Israel seems nullified. Such seems to be the meaning of this acted parable. **3.** ' a second time ' : omitted by LXX. **4.** Read with Aquila ' to Fara ' (*eis Pharan*). **10a.** ' who stubbornly follow their own heart ' : omitted by LXX. **11a.** Syro-Hexaplar omits ' the whole house of Israel and '.

12-14 The Wine Jars—This seemingly incongruous b
paragraph seems to be based on a common roisterers' saying. The prophet uses it to make his point. He takes their own ribald expression and gives it a new turn. Yahweh will fill them with his fury and make them to drink the cup of his wrath : there shall be no end to his fury. No mercy will mingle with judgment. The accumulation of verbs in 14*b* expresses the hot indignation of offended majesty. **12a.** Read with LXX ' to this people ' instead of ' to them '. LXX also omits ' Thus says . . . Israel '. **12c.** Read with LXX ' and if they say to you '.

475c **15-17 Take Warning**—Let them cease from arrogance and self-trust. Let them give glory to God before final darkness falls and they are lost in the gathering gloom : it is not in man that walketh to direct his steps. Let them take heed lest they come to know the surpassing sorrow of a people carried away (cf. Am. 1:6, 9). **17c.** LXX omits ' will weep bitterly and '.

d **18-19 For the King**—Let the king (Jehoiachin) and the queen mother descend low, for the crown is gone from the royal heads. Captivity has come and escape there is none. **18a.** Read with LXX ' Say ye '.

e **20-27 The Woes of Jerusalem**—This oracle is addressed to Jerusalem and may be dated in the reign of Jehoiakim just after the king of Babylon had defeated Pharaoh Neco (605 B.C.). The capital has failed to function satisfactorily and has not fulfilled its responsibilities to the people. The former friends, united with them in a common hatred of Assyria, are now become their overlords, and they are in terror. All this comes of their sins and they are about to receive the due reward of their deeds. So inured to sin are they that change seems impossible : the winds of God will sweep them away as chaff. They have forgotten Yahweh and put their trust in vanities. How manifold and multifarious are their sins ! Can they ever be made clean ? **20.** Insert with LXX ' O Jerusalem '. **21.** MT is difficult : perhaps we should render ' What will you say, O Jerusalem, when they visit you, they whom you were wont to count as friends ? ' **25.** Better with LXX ' this is your lot and the reward of your infidelity towards me '. **27.** With LXX read ' on the hills and in the field '. **27c.** Jeremiah will not give up hope.

f **XIV-XV 9 The great Drought**—The original heading here was probably ' Concerning the Drought '. The section consists of several small poems and dialogues between the prophet and God. From 13 we may infer it belongs to the early years of Jeremiah's ministry. In 1–6 the drought is described realistically in a gradual crescendo, (*a*) in the city, (*b*) in the open country, (*c*) in the forest and desert. In 7–9 is set forth the people's prayer at a solemn assembly—why should Yahweh act as if he were a total stranger with no interest in the people ? Surely Yahweh and his folk belong together. In strict accord with ritual practice comes the prophetic oracle (10–16) in which Yahweh disowns them, denies their prayer and refuses help because of their long-continued waywardness. The prophet is forbidden to intercede further : no offerings or sacrifice can avert the coming doom. Yet though Yahweh forbids intercession he cannot restrain the prophet's heart of love as he seeks to excuse the people on the ground that they have been misled by false prophets. But Yahweh will hold both prophets and people alike guilty : their wickedness shall be returned upon their own heads in terrible destruction. In 17–19 the prophet gives rein to his grief and, through his tears, paints the completeness of disaster both within and without the city. Death is everywhere : leaders and led will perish for lack of knowledge. In 19–22 comes a stormier and more clamorous prayer of the people where all that is sacred is invoked, God's throne of glory, his name, his covenant. But all to no avail (15:1–4). The day of grace is gone by and only death remains. Israel's greatest intercessors, Moses and Samuel (Exod. 32:11f. ; Num. 14:13f. ; 1 Sam. 7:9 ; Ps. 99:6), could not turn back the judgment. Yahweh dismisses his people to death by the sword, famine, pestilence. In 5–9 we have the prophet's lament for this people who have wearied God beyond the point of repentance. The glory has departed and thick black night descends. **3.** The water in the city being exhausted they seek it farther south. **3c.** Omitted in LXX and should be omitted here. **5, 6.** The hind is most graceful and tender of animals, the wild ass the most intractable and toughest animal of the desert. **9.** ' confused ' : LXX reads ' asleep '. **10a.** Quoted from Hos. 8:13. **12b.** Pronoun ' I ' is emphatic in Hebrew. **13.** Here Jeremiah gets his first insight into real nature of false prophets. **15:4.** This seems a scribal addition. Jeremiah believed the present generation was responsible for the coming disaster. **8b.** MT is confused : Volz reads ' I bring upon her young men the spoiler at noonday '. Rudolph renders ' I bring on them the destroying nation, the robber at noonday '. 475f

XV 10-21 The Prophet's Lament and Yahweh's Rebuke—Here without a doubt we have the genuine words of Jeremiah and an intimate dialogue between him and his God. Here the soul of the prophet is laid bare. How reluctantly he entered upon this vocation and with what expense of spirit it was discharged ! The constant enmity of those whose highest welfare he sought wears him down (6:9f.) and consumes his spirit until he would fain give up (9:2). There is no sorrow like his sorrow, for his sorrow is the distress of love spurned and spat upon (*hinc illae lacrimae*). All his efforts have met with contumely and cursing. Borrowing and lending may ' dull the edge of husbandry ' and lead to loss of friends (10) but Jeremiah had not so involved himself with his fellows though they treat him as if he had (cf. Job 6:22). Rather he had laboured beyond his strength and gone to all lengths to help save them. 13, 14 are misplaced here and rightly appear in 17:3, 4. In 15 we see love exhausted and giving place to a prayer for vengeance : the prophet is human and the precious has to be sifted from the vile if he would be God's true spokesman. Why should it be that he who loved God's word and sustained himself thereon (cf. Ezek. 3:1 ; Jn 4:32), he who was chosen by God—why should such a load of suffering be laid upon him ? Has Yahweh misled him and will he prove as false as the wadi whose waters have dried up and disappointed unto death the weary traveller (cf. Job 6:15f.) ? Yahweh's answer is a rebuke and an encouragement (cf. Jn 21). Jeremiah must repent, change his mind and mood, if he would stand fast in the service of God. He must speak only things that are right and sound as God gives him to speak : the reward of service is more service. So will Yahweh uphold his servant. The words here (20) are reminiscent of those spoken at his call : 21 is probably an addition. **11.** MT is obscure and the RSV follows the LXX. Jeremiah is the first man in OT to pray for enemies (cf. 29:7). **12.** MT is again obscure : perhaps we should read ' I have broken iron and brass ', i.e. spared no effort to help his enemies. Bewer suggests the meaning ' Can I do the impossible ? my task is beyond human strength '. The first words of **15a,** ' O Lord, thou knowest ', seem to have stood originally at the close of this verse. **15.** ' forbearance ', i.e. towards the prophet's enemies. **16.** The LXX offers a more satisfying reading : ' Know that for thee I have borne reproach from those that despise thy words : consume them, but let thy word be to me a joy and a delight to my heart.' **18b.** Most of the versions, from motives of reverence, seek to modify this expression. But Jeremiah's prayers, like those of Luther, were ' half-battles '. 476a

XVI 1-XVII 18 Jeremiah's Life a Prophecy of Doom—This section is closely connected with 11:1–14 and may be dated about 606 B.C. Jeremiah's life itself constitutes a symbol of judgment : vv. 1–9 are commentary on 15:17. In a land where custom had the force of law it seemed unnatural that a man of the prophet's age should remain unmarried. In this respect Jeremiah resembles Jesus and Paul. This must have been a real deprivation to a nature of such vast affection : surely none was more qualified than he to rejoice with those who rejoice and to weep with those who wept. The high calling entails sacrifice. Stranger, too, it seemed that he should refuse the last sad offices to the dead and to the mourners, but these actions are purposeful. They are a *memento mori.* Why beget children when they must fall so soon to death ? The dead will soon be so numerous that there b

76b shall be none left to bury them. All life in the pleasant land is about to be quenched by the Great Reaper. Nor need we ask why : their infidelity to God and the faithlessness of their fathers shall bring exile upon them and service in an alien land. There they shall find no favour (cf. 1 Sam. 26:19). 14, 15 recur in 23:7, 8 and are misplaced here. 16–18 continue the threat of 9–13. What the main army (the fishers) fails to finish the clean-up troops (the hunters) will complete and none shall escape. In 19, 20 we have an upsurge of hope which may be out of place here but there is no reason to deny the verses to Jeremiah. 21 seems very like Ezekiel and may be regarded as a later addition. 17:1–4 show how deep-seated and indelible is the sin of Judah (cf. Job 19:24), and how Yahweh's righteous wrath burns with inextinguishable judgment. In sundry counsels, after the fashion of the sages, is set forth the folly of self-trust and the security of him who trusts in God (cf. Ps. 1:3, 4), the corruption of the human heart, and the transience of ill-gotten gains. As a bird that usurps another's nest and is later deserted by her alien brood so shall stolen wealth take wings and fly away. 13, 14 are hardly to be ascribed to Jeremiah but to a later writer who gloried in the cult, but 16–18 are certainly authentic words of the prophet. Like Isaiah (5:19) Jeremiah had to endure scorn for the delay in the Word's arrival and fruition. It was a grief to the prophet to proclaim it, but come it must, the evil day. Yahweh knows that his servant spoke the given word. Let Yahweh remember his servant in the evil day and let judgment fall on the prophet's persecutors. **2.** ' in this place ', not Anathoth but Jerusalem or Judah. **7.** It was customary at such times for friends to provide food and drink for the mourners whose own food was rendered unclean by the presence of death (HDB iii, 453ff.). **9.** For ' deceitful ' LXX reads ' deep ', i.e. inscrutable. **10-13.** Reason is given in the form of the *lex talionis* : foreign gods they served and to the land of these gods they will go in exile. **13d.** Read with LXX ' they will show you no favour '. **17:1-4.** Omitted by LXX (apparently inadvertently). **5a** should be omitted with LXX. **13.** ' earth ' is here equivalent to ' dust ' (cf. Job 14:8) : the contrast is between those written in the ' dust ' and those written ' in the book of life ' (Isa. 4:3 ; Exod. 32:32 ; Mal. 3:16).

c **19-27 Remember the Sabbath Day**—Most scholars are agreed that this section is not from Jeremiah. It is akin to the post-exilic mood and practice represented in Neh. 13:15–22. It seems difficult to believe that Jeremiah, the prophet of spiritual religion, would stake the fate of his people on the observance of an outward rite. Amos pleads for the Sabbath (Am. 8:5) but he does so on the ground of social and religious concern : the writer here has no such motivation but is pleading merely for a legal institution. Jesus' treatment of the Sabbath (Mk 2:27) is in accord with that of Amos and would have delighted the heart of Jeremiah. The mood here is that of Malachi or Nehemiah and the style, with its detailed list of sacrifices, reveals the post-exilic scribe. **23.** ' their neck ' : LXX adds ' more than their fathers'.

d **XVIII 1-12 A Visit to the Potter**—Duhm would deny this section to Jeremiah on the ground that it is trivial. But such criticism is too drastic and overlooks the fact that the most familiar and commonplace things may become channels of revelation (cf. 1:11ff.). ' The eye brings with it what it sees '. Omar Khayyam paid a similar visit to the Potter's House and came back with a gospel of despair : Jeremiah found there a gospel of hope. To Omar men were clay in the hands of the Potter, subject to his imperious whims. In Isa. 29:16, 45:9, 64:8 and Rom. 9:21 the same figure is used to emphasise the almightiness of God before whom man is as nothing. Erbt views the oracle from his viewpoint and sees in it a threat while Cornill sees a promise. Jeremiah visited the Potter's House on the south side of the city and returned with a gospel other than Omar's. To Omar life was all whirring wheels but behind the wheels Jeremiah saw a Person who had a 476d
purpose of love. For he will make and remake ' vessels meet ' for his use : God is the great mender of men. Cornill would excise 5–12 as a later insertion : it may have been worked over by a Deuteronomist but it bears the genuine Jeremianic ring. Moreover these verses convey a clear logical thought and the meaning is clear. History depends on the response men make to the will of God (7–10) : ' in his will is our peace '. His omnipotence is not arbitrary ; Judah may yet return and be saved by repentance (11). But to the divine demand Judah will not accede. Here we have the philosophy of history and the theology of evangelism. **3.** ' at his wheel ', lit. ' the two wheels ', connected by a wooden rod, the lower being turned with the foot while the clay rested on the upper stone (cf. Sir. 38:29, 30).

13-17 Wickedness without Parallel—Judah's e
failure to respond aright is incomprehensible. In 2:32 the prophet illustrates and emphasises this with a human illustration : in 8:7 he draws a parallel from animal life, and here he draws on the realm of Nature. The text may be uncertain but the sense is clear. Nature is constant, Judah is fickle. The people have left the king's highway and wandered in illicit paths to the amazement and horror of all. When men see the judgment of God they will signify by apotropaic gestures their prayer that such a fate may never overtake them. God will turn his back upon his people in a gesture of repudiation and scatter them before their foes. **14.** MT is difficult ; read with Cornill ' Does the white snow flow away from the rock of Sirion (Hermon) ? '

18-23 Plot against Jeremiah—In their wilful way- 477a
wardness his enemies threaten the life of the prophet. There is something subtle in their approach. It is better here to follow the Syr. and render 18*b*, ' Come, let us smite him with his own tongue and let us pay careful attention to all his words.' Like the authorities who sought to take Jesus they seek ' to entrap him in his talk ' (Mk 12:13). Jeremiah had uttered quite a few words against priests, prophets and sages (4:9, 8:8, 9) and the rough times of Jehoiakim favoured those who would make reprisals against him and call him to account. He would be condemned out of his own mouth. The prayer of vengeance, most passionate of such utterances (11:20, 12:3, 15:15, 17:14–18, 20:4–6), is clear evidence of the fearful stress and strain imposed by his vocation which left him alone and without friends—alone with God. Cornill, Duhm and Peake would reject these verses as impossible on the lips of the prophet, but he was human, like Christ, yet so unlike at times. A great gulf divides these words from those of Lk. 23:34.

XIX 1-XX 6 First Mistreatment of Jeremiah— b
This section is linked to the preceding through the use of the word ' Potter '. Here, too, begin the memoirs of Baruch. The section consists of two separate incidents which may be divided in different ways. 3–9 seem to be addressed to ' the kings of Judah and the inhabitants of Jerusalem ', while in v. 1 the audience seem to consist of elders and senior priests. The unusual style of the LXX in 3–9 would indicate that we have here a later insertion and most commentators regard it so. 2*a* seems to find its continuation in 10. In the first incident the prophet is bidden to take an earthen flask and go down to the Potsherd Gate. There he is to break the vessel in symbolic fashion (cf. Isa. 20 ; Ezek. *passim* ; Ac. 21:10f.) and announce that thus shall Yahweh smash city and people. Jerusalem shall become unclean as Topheth itself. These words Jeremiah repeats in the Temple court (14, 15). Pashhur—not the same as in 21:1, 28:1—the priest takes disciplinary action against the prophet who receives corporal punishment for the first time. The prophet was set in the stocks at the Temple gate on the north side. Jeremiah fiercely resents this action, not as an affront to himself but to the majesty of the God whose word he declares. Doom, terrifying and com-

477b plete, is foretold for Pashhur and his friends with burial in an unclean land (cf. Am. 7:10–17). Pashhur seems to have gone with the first captivity, for by 594 B.C. his office is in other hands (29:25). Babylon is here mentioned for the first time as the place of exile. **2.** ' Potsherd Gate ' : name otherwise unknown. Perhaps so called because broken pottery was dumped there or because potters worked in that vicinity. It should probably be identified with the Dung Gate (Neh. 2:13, 3:13, 12:31). **4.** ' blood of innocents ' : the reference is probably to Manasseh (2 Kg. 24:4). **7.** ' make void ', lit. ' empty out ' as from a flask (*bakbûk*, v. 1). **5, 7, 11c** are repeated from 7:31–3. **20:1.** ' chief officer ', the official entrusted with maintenance of proper order in the Temple precincts and with discipline of disturbing elements (29:26). **2.** ' upper Benjamin Gate ', a Temple gate on the N. side to be distinguished from the city Gate of Benjamin. **3.** There seems to be a play on words here but it is not clear. The bold bad Pashhur will be dominated, haunted by terror, and named from his dominant emotion. LXX omits ' on every side ', probably correctly.

c **XX 7-18 Out of the Depths**—Here we come to one of the most impressive and most revealing passages in all prophetic literature. Here the soul of Jeremiah is disclosed in its bleakest, blackest hour. The forces of evil are in the ascendant and God's messenger is treated with contumely and scorned. In a time of comparative peace such prophecies of doom seemed irrelevant to the contemporary situation. Pashhur's action seemed to be approved by the populace and the steady contempt and scorn of his fellows was a grievous burden to the sensitive spirit of the prophet. To the Semite life without honour was not worthy of the name, for honour was a main constitutent element of the soul (Job 29:1f.). Hence those fierce outbursts, and this is the fiercest of all, ' near to blasphemy ' (Bewer). Yahweh has ' deceived ' his prophet, taken advantage of his youth : the word ' deceived '—used again in 10—has almost a technical meaning in this connection. It is used of a young man seducing a maiden (Exod. 22:16), of Yahweh's deceiving false prophets (1 Kg. 22:19–23). Ezekiel uses it of a prophet being ' deceived ' or ' enticed ' to his own ruin and made the victim of divine vindictiveness (Ezek. 14:9). Has Yahweh so dealt with his servant Jeremiah ? Yahweh has overpowered him and now Jeremiah is assailed on every side and threatened with destruction. But if through weakness of the flesh he would leave off his high vocation he could not do so and keep the peace with his own conscience. The divine pressure is irresistible and he has no capacity to withstand. He is helpless in the grip of God—' I am helpless '. No words could make clearer that Jeremiah is a prophet not of his own choosing. ' So help me, God, I can do no other '. His enemies may lie in wait to trap him in his talk but God will defend his own and will return the wickedness of the wicked on their own heads. There is no need to excise v. 13 for it accords with the strongly emotional character of the prophet. Nor is it difficult to understand the upsurge of depression in 14–18. The wish that first found expression in 15:10 (cf. 12:5) returns here with overwhelming power. Jeremiah, like his greater Lord, is ' exceeding sorrowful, even unto death ' (Mk 14:33). In wild, whirling words he curses the day of his birth (cf. Job 3:1f.) and wishes his mother's womb had been his grave. This is the measure of his sorrow. But such bleak, black hours are but milestones on man's journey to the nearer presence of God. The Hosanna is reached finally through great whirlwinds of doubt. It is significant that here no divine rebuke or exhortation is given (cf. 15:18). Why does the prophet record these awful moments ? Firstly, to ' cleanse the bosom of his perilous stuff ' and find relief. And secondly, to comfort those who must pass through the same deep waters. ' Jeremiah was forsaken by all, and now he loses his last support—his own self ' (Volz). But when man yields his self the soul becomes receptive of God's word, and strength is perfected in weakness. The metal has been assayed and tested, the dross consumed, and the chosen vessel stands ready for the Master's use. Jeremiah's pain is turned to peace which the world cannot give and cannot take away. 477

d **XXI 1-10 An anxious Inquiry**—This section takes us down to 588 B.C. when the siege of the city was just beginning and the Jews were still able to sally forth and engage the foe outside the city walls. The reason for its appearance here is due to the recurrence of the name Pashhur though this is not the man who mishandled Jeremiah. The literary material seems frequently to have been assembled on this principle of recurring words (cf. Isa. 1:1–9, 10–17 where *Sodom and Gomorrah* occur in each oracle). There is no reason to think (with Ewald) that this story is a duplicate of 37:3–10, and less reason to think (with Duhm) that both incidents are fictitious. In a prolonged siege various inquiries of this kind would be made. 37:3–10 seems to come at a more advanced stage, after the diversion caused by Hophra, when men looked again for a repetition of the wondrous deliverance of 701 B.C. The inquiry is addressed not to the false prophets whose falseness had been exposed : it is directed to Jeremiah. And to the anxious inquiry he gives a straight answer. The mighty God who delivered them at the Exodus will not save them now. Rather he will fight against them : sword, famine and pestilence will devour them and Nebuchadrezzar will burn the city. For Nebuchadrezzar is God's agent and to fight against him is to fight against God. Desertion to the Chaldaeans is the way of wisdom: only so shall men save their lives. 11, 12 may belong to an earlier period when there was yet hope. 13, 14 are difficult but they may contain a reference to the response made by the authorities to Jeremiah's word. They still believed in the inviolability of Zion and indulged in boastful wishful thinking. **8.** 'the way of life . . . death ' : occurs first here in OT and is meant literally. **11, 12** form a parallel to 22:1–7. **12.** ' in the morning ' : that is, every morning, continually (cf. Am. 4:4). **14a**, lacking in LXX. **14b.** Volz would read ' I will kindle a blazing fire ' (*bō'ᵃrāh* for *bᵉya'rāh*) : there was no forest in Jerusalem.

478 **XXII 1-XXIII 8 A Mirror for Magistrates**—Here we have a series of oracles concerning the kings of Judah, under five of whom the prophet exercised his ministry. The oracles have been set together by an editor and have been expanded in the process.

XXII 1-9 Righteousness and Royalty—These verses are an expansion of 21:11, 12 and are addressed to the royal house of Judah. They may probably be dated in the early years of Jehoiakim and were probably delivered on a feast day when the people were assembled at the palace gates. There justice was dispensed and decisions given. Jeremiah is commanded to address king and judges in the presence of those seeking justice. Such a plea was timely in the days of Jehoiakim. Righteousness alone can uphold the dynasty (cf. 17:25) : let judgment be just and let not the cry of the needy go unregarded. So shall the royal estate maintain its dignity and splendour, but, if not, the royal house will become a ruin (cf. 17:25). When the prophet sees his words disregarded he pronounces judgment. The palace may be beautiful as the crest of Lebanon and as Gilead for strength, but Yahweh will cause it to be destroyed for its infidelity, and the destruction will be astounding and without parallel (cf. 1 Kg. 9:8, 9 ; Dt. 29:24, 25). **3.** ' the oppressor ' : LXX reads ' his oppressor '. **6.** One part of the palace was called ' the house of the forest of Lebanon ' for its rows of cedar pillars and beams (cf. 1 Kg. 7:2–5 ; Isa. 22:8).

b **XXII 10-XXIII 4 Concerning the Kings**—Here we have oracles addressed to individual kings. 10–12 concern Jehoahaz, fourth son of Josiah, who was chosen by the people to succeed his father but was set aside by the Egyptian overlord in favour of his elder brother

478b Eliakim (Jehoiakim). Shallum may have been his name before his accession : he may have been the popular choice because the people knew well the character of his elder brother. Josiah was dead and gone : weep not for him but weep for Shallum whose fate is harder far. For he must go into exile for life : never more shall he see his homeland.

c **XXII 13-19 Concerning Jehoiakim**—This king was Jeremiah's worst enemy. As a monarch he was cruel and despotic. He had an inordinate passion for fine buildings and like a veritable Pharaoh he built with lavish splendour. This he did in spite of the impoverished state of the country and the high tribute he had to pay to Egypt. His buildings were raised on forced labour and founded on injustice. Cedars and vermilion adorned his chambers and there was no limit to his devouring egoism. No true son of his father was this man, for violence prevailed and the cry of the needy was unheard. But true religion ' is to visit orphans and widows in their affliction ' (Jas 1:27). Jehoiakim did not have such religion: his life was full of unholy deeds and greedy violence. So we have this most mordant judgment on this conscienceless king. Unhonoured and unsung he shall die : none shall lament his going and the customary lamentations will not be heard (cf. 1 Kg. 13:30). Ignominious burial shall be his and his body shall be cast out like the carcass of an ass. The record in 1 Kg. 24:6 and 2 Chr. 36:8 does not support this prophecy. But it is possible, and even probable, that though his body was buried it was later disinterred and dishonoured by the Chaldaeans. Such practices were common enough in those rough times. **14.** ' windows ': perhaps better ' window ' such as Ahab had (2 Kg. 9:30). This seems to have been Egyptian style ; at this window the monarch made royal appearances.

d **XXII 20-30 Concerning Jehoiachin**—Preceding the oracle on the king we have a short word to Jerusalem (20–3). This word would seem to date from 597 B.C. The high mountains, so often the scene of joy and festivity, become now the scene of woeful cries. It is too late now to think of repentance : their long-continued unfaithfulness and disobedience must now end in judgment. The word ' lovers ' may signify the Baalim or the nations allied with Judah but the parallelism here seems to indicate the reference is to their own rulers. Friends and lovers alike are swept away and the lofty ones are brought low and abased with painful abasement. **20.** Lebanon to the north, Bashan to the north-east, and Abarim, of which Mt Nebo was part, to the south-east. For Jehoiachin we have here two brief oracles apparently spoken at different times. **24-7** indicates the captivity is still future, while in **28-30** it has taken place. The signet ring signifies a most intimate personal possession guarded with extreme care (Hag. 2:23): nevertheless though Jehoiachin were as close to God as that it would not avail. God's purpose marches on though the authorities in Jerusalem might imagine that the Chaldaean would be satisfied with the death of Jehoiakim and cease from further hostilities. Nor would God intervene in miraculous fashion to deliver them. The decree has gone forth and Coniah and the queen mother will go into exile and see their own land again no more for ever. In 28–30 there is deep pathos and we mark the prophet's sorrow for the fate of the untried prince (cf. 13:18). The situation is real and tragic. The folk did not realise the gravity of the impending doom and the light optimism of the false prophets spoke of a speedy return (ch. 28). The prophet will certify that their hope is vain. No son of Jehoiachin will sit upon the throne of his fathers. And ' if they do these things in a green tree, what shall be done in the dry ? ' (Lk. 23:31, AV).

In 1939 E. F. Weidner published a few of 300 tablets found in the Hanging Gardens of Babylon, and these tablets list the rations allotted to certain groups of people. One dated in the year 592 B.C. lists the rations apportioned to ' Yaukin and five royal princes ' (ANET, p. 308). It would appear that Yaukin (Jehoiachin) was regarded as the true king of Judah and that he was being held as hostage for the good behaviour of the Judaeans. This seems confirmed by the discovery of three jar-handles (1928–30) in Palestine wherein Eliakim (Zedekiah) is referred to as ' the steward of Yaukin ', and this is interpreted to mean that Eliakim (Zedekiah) was regarded as regent in the absence of the true king Jehoiachin. Moreover the framework of the book of Ezek. seems to be provided with a series of dates reckoned by the captivity of Jehoiachin. Furthermore it is worthy of note that the line of Messiah in Mt. 1:11–12 is traced through Jehoiachin and not through Zedekiah. No son of Jehoiachin sat upon the throne of David, but in 1 Chr. 3:17 seven sons of Jehoiachin are named : the eldest was Shealtiel, father of Zerubbabel. 478d

XXIII 1-8. Here we should expect an oracle on Zedekiah. Probably that is what we have here and v. 6 would suggest that. But the prophet here branches out beyond the immediate present. The rulers, hitherto, have been like wolves devouring the flock : their evil deeds will now be recompensed to them. V. 3 seems to imply a wide dispersion and appears to be a late addition. V. 4 introduces a more comforting word and the assurance of a new king, a real king—' he shall reign as king '—who shall be no weakling like Zedekiah who belies his name, but a ' righteous Branch ' (*ṣemaḥ ṣaddîḳ*)—there is a play on the word *ṣedheḳ* which is the first part of the name Zedekiah (the Lord is righteous). When that king comes there will be a deliverance far more wonderful than the redemption from Egypt. His name will be Yahweh Ṣidhḳenu (the Lord is our righteousness). e

7, 8 = 16:14, 15 : a post-exilic addition.

9-40 Concerning the Prophets—The kings and prophets are naturally associated as leaders of the community : the priests, as third main group, receive only passing mention here (11). Preceding these oracles we have a brief lament by the prophet who, having been brought up in a godly home, must have been amazed beyond measure as he looked upon ' spiritual wickedness in high places '. This lament must belong to his early ministry (cf. 5:1f., 9:1f.). The general corruption of the community and the prevailing state of moral anarchy fills his mind with consternation and even affects him in his physical frame. The land, too, seems infected and tainted with the blight of man's sin, while the thought of the judgment the prophet must announce causes him to quail. Judgment must come upon all. The slippery ways—and how well he knew them on the mountain heights around his home !—in which they walk with such vigour will be enveloped in thick darkness and they shall perish. V. 13 begins the series of oracles on the prophets. The prophets of Samaria seduced their people from their main loyalty but the behaviour of the Jerusalem prophets is no less disgusting than the Baal orgies of the Northern Kingdom. Immoral and false they have made the Holy City even as Sodom and Gomorrah. Those who should have brought blessing to the land have fostered and encouraged ungodliness. Judgment shall surely overtake them. Can the blind lead the blind ? Let none listen to them for the word of God is not in them. Their words are born of wishful thinking and shallow optimism as they cry ' All will be well ' and promise immunity to hardened sinners. Vv. 19, 20 recur in 30:23, 24 and are interpolated here. If these prophets but knew anything of the nature of God and his demands they would not heal the hurt of the people so lightly. If they had stood in close fellowship with him, in his intimate council (*sôdh*), then they would have spoken his word (22 ; cf. Am. 3:7f.). They do not possess the commission of the Great King : their mission is unauthorised of God. ' By their fruits shall ye know them ': they turn neither themselves nor others to righteousness. Religion without morality is worthless. ' To proclaim good things to impenitent sinners is decisive proof that 479a

479a they are not true prophets of the Lord' (Bewer).
b **Vv. 23, 24** are somewhat difficult and various interpretations have been offered. The words contain a rebuke to the prophets who think so lightly and speak so glibly of God. They think of him as their next-door neighbour on whom they can call at will for any service. They forget that he is the high God, glorious in holiness, exalted in righteousness, whose eyes see to the ends of the earth and from whom nothing is hid (cf. Ps. 11:4, 138:6, 139; Am. 9:2; Job 34:22). They thought he was altogether as one of themselves but he is God and not man, the Holy One of Israel. If moral laxity is the first feature in these prophets the second defect lies in the origin of their oracles. It is tempting to read 'I have dreamed' (25) three times as in 7:4. But Jeremiah scorns their dreams. These prophets enjoyed the adulation of the populace: vain and pompous they strutted around and finally came up—with a dream! 'The mountains labour and a mouse is born'. Yahweh's word is not a dream and it may seem commonplace beside the fanatical outpourings of these ecstatics. But a dream is one thing and the Word of God is another thing, and let them not confuse things that differ. For the difference is the difference between chaff and whole grain, between the substantial and the insubstantial, between false and true. The Word is dynamic, 'sharper than a two-edged sword'. They speak from the teeth, not from the heart, nor by the Spirit. Their only fruit is to cause the name of God to be forgotten. Furthermore, there is no originality in them: they plagiarise and steal oracles one from another and masquerade under false colours. These Pharisees are Sadducees as well. But God's Word is unique and 'mighty to the pulling down of strongholds' (1 C. 10:4; Am. 7:10; Hos. 6:5). It is known by its effects. It made Jeremiah a man of iron. 'What beggarly characters these must have been with whom God's greatest servants had to contend as they sought access to the people' (Volz). **V. 33** appears to belong to the final period of the siege. The false prophets are gone or are become dumb. Jeremiah is the man to whom they turn. 'What is the burden (*maśśā'*) of the Lord? Has God a word for us? 'Burden' is from the root *nāśā'*, meaning to lift up, probably derived here from the fact that when inquiry was made of the priest or prophet he 'lifted up' his voice and gave the response or oracle (*maśśā'*). Here the response is a final word of doom; 'you are the burden (*maśśā'*) and I will cast you off', says the Lord. Most scholars judge this to be the last word in these oracles.

c What follows in vv. 34–40 is a very late addition made by some quibbling scribe or rabbi on the danger of using the word 'burden' instead of the term 'word' (*dābhār*) of the Lord. 'We have here a piece of Talmudic learning which says really nothing' (Rudolph). It must be later than Zechariah or Malachi, for *Maśśā'* is used by both these prophets (Zech. 9:1, 12:1; Mal. 1:1), and is one of the latest additions in the OT. It may have value in showing the subtle refinements wrought by later scribes of whom we hear much in the NT. 'These verses', says Volz, 'are wholly without value and are a clumsy misunderstanding of the prophet.'

d **XXIV 1-10 Two Baskets of Figs**—The Jews left behind in Jerusalem in the captivity of 597 B.C. regarded themselves with self-satisfaction. The evil ones had been carried away but they who were left in the city were spared because of their own excellence. They were 'the flesh in the pot' while the exiles were but the offscourings (Ezek. 11:3). So they thought. But the prophet thought otherwise. The best elements of the people were in Babylon and the future lay with them. Erbt has suggested that in its original form the distinction here drawn had reference to the exiles (good) in Babylon and the motley crowd (bad) who fled to Egypt after the fall of the city. This is highly improbable. Hyatt would regard the chapter as a literary production from about 550 B.C. but this is quite unwarranted. There is no reason to doubt the genuineness of the passage. For the form of this vision we may compare Am. 8:1ff. which may have influenced Jeremiah here. 479

The section should be read in close connection with 3:6f. and 13:1–11. The latter passage may be dated shortly before 598 B.C. In the present chapter God speaks directly to the prophet and clarifies his servant's mind as to the real situation. For the false prophets were busy encouraging the people's false estimate of themselves and the situation. Jeremiah's view has advanced since 598 B.C. and he now sees clearly—or Yahweh makes him see clearly—where the future lies. It may be that this developed view is due to the effectiveness of Ezekiel's ministry among the exiles and that Jeremiah was aware of the change for the better. And the change that has come about is due to divine grace. God gives them a new heart and they sorrow with a godly sorrow unto repentance (cf. 32:39; Ezek. 11:19, 36:26). Jeremiah's own words to the exiles (ch. 29) had borne fruit and they had come to a fuller understanding of God and his purpose. They shall 'return' with their whole heart and they shall be his people. Not so shall it be with the wicked. Those ungodly people who remain in Jerusalem and whose wickedness is vividly portrayed by Ezekiel (chs. 8, 22, 23) shall bring upon themselves a divine judgment that shall astound the nations by its magnitude. Destruction, utter and complete, shall be the portion of those empty boasters in Jerusalem. **1.** 'placed before the temple': Cornill and Rothstein would reject this phrase on the ground that none would offer such a vile sacrifice, but cf. Mal. 1:13f. Also on the ground that the word for 'temple' (*hêkhāl*) used here is not used elsewhere on the lips of Jeremiah. It occurs on the lips of the people in 7:4. **5.** 'Thus says the Lord . . . Israel' seems to be an addition. Yahweh here addresses the people directly. **8.** 'those who dwell . . . Egypt': there was a Jewish colony at Syene before 525 B.C. and its worship was largely pagan. The reference here is probably to those carried away with Jehoahaz in 608 B.C. or to political exiles of the pro-Egyptian party who dared not abide the coming of Nebuchadrezzar. e

XXV 1-14 Retrospect and Summary—The date of this section is given precisely in the MT though the reference to Nebuchadrezzar's accession year is lacking in the LXX. 605 B.C. was a decisive year in world history, for after the battle of Carchemish in that year the leadership passed into the hands of the new Babylonians. Egypt retreated within its own borders never again to exercise real power in Palestine and Syria. To the prophet these international events were not simply happenings but part and parcel of Yahweh's purpose: Yahweh is Lord of History. Thus we should expect a 'prophet to the nations' to speak of those wider movements. The section here appears to have undergone considerable editorial expansion and the Versions here offer a much smoother text. In 1–7 the prophet seems to be summarising his twenty-three years' ministry and there is reason to believe that here we have the foreword to the original scroll (ch. 36) which Jeremiah dictated to Baruch in this same year. That scroll contained 'all the words that I have spoken to you against Israel and Judah and all the nations, from the day I spoke to you, from the days of Josiah until to-day' (36:2). 'This book' (13*a*) would then refer to all that had preceded and would include the main contents of chs. 1–24, though not exclusively: certain sections in these chapters are dated later than 605 B.C. This seems the most reasonable interpretation of the section and is accepted by most commentators. Here we have the prophet's final appeal at that stage of history (605 B.C.) when decisive events were in the making. Here he rehearses what he has said and done. Following the lead of the Versions we would omit the last clause of v. 3 together with v. 4 while in v. 5 we find the sum and substance of the prophet's preaching. But that preaching had 480

480a fallen on deaf ears. Continued disobedience to God is now bringing disaster: the foe from the north is at hand. In v. 9 the LXX omits the words 'and for N. my servant' and seems right in so doing. For the prophets were not wont to be too definite but preferred to suggest the weird and unknown: this indefiniteness heightens tension and terror (cf. 4:6; Am. 1:4). The destruction will be complete. No more will be heard the sound of the turning millstones as the housewife grinds the daily bread for her household: no more will the oil-lamp be lit to signify the presence of life within the house (cf. 7:34, 16:9). The light shall be put out and the house will be dead. As in the holy wars of old when Israel put everything 'under the ban' (*ḥērem*: Dt. 13:15; 1 Sam. 15:3) so will God utterly destroy them. The land shall become a waste and the people shall be thralls among the nations—here we follow LXX, Peake, Weiser, Skinner, Volz—for 70 years. It seems highly improbable that Jeremiah would blunt the edge of this threat by the words of v. 12, and it should be omitted. The prophet is here concerned with the fate of Judah alone and he sets a sheer stark choice before the people—life with obedience or death by disobedience to God.

b **V. 13** must be read with LXX, 'I will bring upon that land (Judah) all these words which I have uttered against it, everything written in this book.' In 13*b* the words 'which Jeremiah prophesied against all the nations' seem unusual in a passage where the prophet is speaking in the first person. In the LXX they stand as the superscription of a new section containing the oracles against the nations (MT 46–51). The order of the oracles in the MT text differs from that of the LXX: under this superscription the LXX begins with the oracle against Elam (MT 49:34f.), and after going through all the oracles it returns and resumes at v. 15 of the present chapter. It would appear that in some Hebrew versions—not the original—these oracles against the nations were inserted at this point and v. 13*b* formed the superscription as in LXX. **V. 14** is lacking in the LXX and may have been interpolated at a later time. As to why these oracles were inserted here it is difficult to understand. The position seems unnatural in view of vv. 15–38 which would naturally precede, and not follow, the oracles against the nations. In the MT they have been relegated to the end of the book (46–51).

c **15-29 The Cup of Wrath**—This section tells of the prophet's summons to handle the wine-cup of the divine wrath and administer it to the nations. This peculiar thought may derive from ancient ordeal procedures (Num. 5:11f.; Ps. 75:8; Hab. 2:16; Ezek. 23:31f.; Isa. 51:17f.; Lam. 4:21). Here is the vision of the judgment of God in dramatic form. There is nothing eschatological here, simply the conviction of Jeremiah that Yahweh controls the destinies of the nations: he holds the whole world in his hands. The section seems to have undergone editorial expansion, for while in 17 the judgment is not regarded as world-wide but upon 'the nations to whom the Lord sent me', in v. 26 it seems to be upon all the inhabitants of the earth. In v. 18 Jerusalem is regarded as destroyed 'as at this day'. The list of nations reads somewhat monotonously but the long catalogue adds tension to the narrative. Vv. 17–26 are generally considered to be a late addition as they break the connection between 16 and 27. One might wonder what knowledge Jeremiah was likely to have of Phoenician colonies along the Mediterranean Sea or how much he knew of Elam. The vague expression 'all the kings of' (20, 22, 24, 25, 26) arouses suspicion in the minds of most commentators, and these references are generally rejected. Strangely enough Damascus is not mentioned in this list though it occurs in 49:23f. Vv. 27–9 read rather strangely, for here the possibility that some may refuse to drink is considered, while in 17 we are told they have drunk. Weiser sees no real contradiction but only an emphasis on the divine authority. Rudolph would reject 29 on the ground that the sentiment expressed is that of 480c later Judaism and was not in the mind of Jeremiah. Weiser would regard it as worthy of the prophet and regard it as a solemn warning that Yahweh who did not spare his holy city, the seat and centre of revelation, will much less spare them. **20.** 'the remnant of Ashdod': this city had been destroyed about 25 years earlier by Psammetichus after a siege of 29 years. It seems to have revived later (Neh. 13:23). **26.** 'Babylon': Hebrew *Shēshakh*, a cipher (*Atbash*) form in which the last letter of the alphabet is interchanged with first, second last with second, and so on.

30-38 Universal Lamentation—This also is an d editorial expansion and belongs to later Judaism. V. 30 recalls Am. 1:2 and Jl 3:16 though here Zion yields place to high heaven. The picture of the warrior here is mingled with that of the crimsoned grape-treader (Isa. 63:1f.), and the huzzas of the grape-treader mingle with the shouts of the armed man and resound to earth's end. Yahweh draws near to judge the nations and slay the wicked. The slaughter will be endless and bodies shall cover the ground like dung. Kings and their peoples shall be sacrificial victims for the conqueror and none shall escape. There shall be weeping and wailing as the pastures are despoiled and the shepherds (rulers) slain. For the sword of the conqueror is the sword of the Lord. **38cd.** Read with BH 'because of the devouring sword and the fierce anger of Yahweh'.

XXVI-XXXVI. With ch. 26 we begin a new section 481a which is mainly characterised by a note of hope. 26–9 may seem to deal with other matters but they form a unity within the main section and accord with the writer's main intention, as is clear from 27:22 and 29:10–14. In 26 we have Baruch's account of the Temple speech (7:1ff.) with special reference to the judicial acquittal of the prophet and his public recognition as a true prophet—denied implicitly by priests and prophets of the Temple (26:10f.)—who speaks the true word of God. This is Baruch's first narrative of the prophet though 19:1–20:6 precedes it in our present text. In chs. 27, 28 we see him in conflict with false prophets where his standing as a true prophet is further established and recognised. This also is recognised in 29:15f. where Jeremiah's position seems to be acknowledged by the Temple officials. In these chapters we have 'good words, comforting words' (Zech. 1:13) of the prophet as recorded by Baruch.

XXVI 1-24 The Temple Speech and its Sequel— b This is the same incident as recorded in 7:1–8:3. The speech is here given in summary form but the sequel is detailed. The date is in the period between Jehoahaz' deposition and the formal coronation of Jehoiakim. The occasion may have been the harvest festival. The word came 'to Jeremiah'—insert these words from OL and Syr. versions—and he is bidden to declare the whole truth without reservation: neither sympathy with the people nor thought of personal danger may minish the word he is given to speak. A faint hope ('it may be') is expressed that it may prove effective and that the people will give heed and turn from their evil ways. If not, Jerusalem will become as Shiloh. The response was immediate and it was fraught with great danger to the prophet's life. For nothing so aroused the fanaticism of the people as a threat against the Temple (7:4). Such an utterance exposed a man to the charge of blasphemy, the penalty for which was death (Exod. 22:28; Lev. 24:10f.; 1 Kg. 21:13; Mt. 26:60f.; Ac. 6:13f.). The commotion spread and Jeremiah might have been lynched there and then by the mob—as was Stephen (Ac. 6:13f.)—but for the timely arrival of the responsible authorities. Here reason began to prevail. The princes (members of the royal household) and other high officials were obviously impressed by the sincerity of a man who was willing to risk his life in the discharge of his prophetic function. Jeremiah's defence is simply that he is carrying out the divine command

481b (cf. Am. 3:8), and further states that the judgment may yet be turned away by repentance. An appeal to conscience (14) accompanies the caution that the shedding of innocent blood will only aggravate their iniquity and demand requital (cf. 2 Sam. 21:1f. ; 1 Kg. 21:19 ; 2 Kg. 9:36). Like Pilate (Lk. 23:22) the authorities found no fault worthy of death. And in this case the decision lay with these authorities and not with priests and prophets. The Hebrews in that old time were wise enough not to entrust such mischievous powers to ecclesiastics. The decision of the competent authorities was aided by some wise old greybeards from the country who cited the similar prophecy of Micah and its issue in the reform of Hezekiah (2 Kg. 18:4f.). Here we see the prophet standing in a living vital tradition and how that tradition saved his life on this occasion. We note also that the prophet, armed only with the Word of God, was able to withstand the power of priests and prophets intensified by hatred and fanaticism. Yahweh was mindful of his servant and made him ' a fortified city ' (1:18). The final outcome was that Jeremiah was permitted to go free (24) under the protection of Ahikam, father of Gedaliah (39:14) and one of the deputation who waited upon Huldah the prophetess in the days of Josiah's reformation (2 Kg. 22:14).

c To indicate the grave danger in which Jeremiah stood Baruch tells us of another prophet who spoke similarly and paid for his boldness with his life (20–3). It is interesting to note that there were other faithful prophets of whom we know nothing save for these few details here. It may be that Uriah attacked the king personally and was guilty of *lèse-majesté* but of that we have no knowledge. Extradited from Egypt he was put to death by Jehoiakim—the only recorded case of execution of a prophet in the OT. It may be, too, that Baruch intends a contrast between Jeremiah who stood his ground and Uriah who ran away to Egypt. **6.** ' a curse for all nations ' : such utter destruction as people will invoke on their enemies—a complete contrast to Gen. 12:13. **8b.** ' all the people ' should probably be deleted as repetition from *8a* (BH). **10.** ' the New Gate ', probably the Benjamin Gate (20:2). **18.** ' Jerusalem ', written fully only this once in Jeremiah and only five times so in the whole OT. **22.** ' Elnathan ' : one of the princes and probably father-in-law of Jehoiakim (2 Kg. 24:8).

d **XXVII-XXIX.** These three chapters seem to have formed a unit though they are from different sources—Jeremiah himself and Baruch's memoirs. They are characterised by certain stylistic peculiarities which may have been imposed upon them at a later date : (*a*) Here the name of the king of Babylon appears in the form Nebuchadnezzar though the more usual form Nebuchadrezzar appears in 29:21. (*b*) Names compounded with Yahweh have the short form *-yah* rather than the normal *-yahu* (*Yirmᵉyāh* appears instead of *Yirmᵉyāhû*). (*c*) The phrase ' the prophet ' is attached to the name Jeremiah much more frequently than elsewhere in the book. There may be reason for this in that he is dealing with false prophets. These chapters are a specific application of the general charges of ch. 23. The divergences in the LXX are more considerable than usual and in view of the diffuse style of the MT the LXX may be closer to the original, though one might judge the original message was more concise than that represented by the LXX text.

e **XXVII 1-11 Counsels of Rebellion** — Pharaoh Neco died in 594 B.C. and was succeeded by Psammetichus II (594–589 B.C.), and as usually happened at a change of dynasty thoughts of rebellion began to rise in the minds of subject peoples. Envoys of Edom, Ammon, Tyre and Sidon seem to have foregathered at Jerusalem to discuss the possibility of casting off the yoke of Babylon. The date is 593 B.C. and the first verse—absent in LXX—must have contained the phrase ' the fourth year of Zedekiah '. Such a scheme could not succeed without the help of Egypt, and at this moment Psammetichus was engaged in war with Ethiopia. At such a juncture the prophet intervenes with the word of the Lord and reinforces that word with the symbolic action of wearing a yoke on his neck. The message is given to eye and ear. How far the prophet's words were effective in dissuading the plotters—Zedekiah himself may have been rather reluctant towards the proposals—is not clear, but they combined with the situation to render the plot abortive. To those kings, through their envoys, is given the message grounded not on the political situation but on the word of Almighty God, that only in submission to Babylon is their peace and welfare secure (cf. 29:7). To hearken to their prophets and diviners is to invite destruction upon themselves. **3.** For ' envoys ' read with LXX ' their envoys '. **5.** Hebrew has no word for ' universe '. ' Man and beast ' or ' heaven and earth ' are the Hebrew equivalent. These phrases express total lordship. **6a.** ' my servant ' : LXX and some Hebrew MSS change this, for dogmatic reasons, to ' to serve him '. **7.** not in LXX and quite unsuitable here.

f **12-22 Counsel to Zedekiah**—Here the same message is given to Judah's king. Was he vacillating in this matter ? Let him hearken to the word of the Lord and give no heed to those prophets who are not commissioned by the Almighty. To priests and people he addresses like words and denounces the shallow optimism of those prophets. If they be real prophets let them become mighty and instant in prayer to God that he may turn from his purpose which he has revealed to his servant Jeremiah. There is no contradiction between 18 and 19, for the divine judgment may be averted by repentance. The last clause of 22 is omitted by the LXX : it is doubtful that Jeremiah should have been greatly concerned for the Temple vessels. Volz would omit 19–22 but this is unnecessary. **17.** Omitted by LXX : it interrupts the connection between 16 and 18. **20.** ' nobles ' : a word of Aramaic origin, frequent in Nehemiah, and probably indicating a late date.

482a **XXVIII 1-17 A decisive Encounter**—We must read the first verse as in LXX and date this section ' in the fourth year of Zedekiah '. Inasmuch as the narrative is in the third person we may take it to be from Baruch's memoirs. The words ' to me ' (v. 1) may have been added or they more probably represent a short form of ' to Jeremiah ' (' *'el* J.'). The chapter follows naturally on ch. 27. Jeremiah with the yoke on his neck and his prophecy of doom must have been an offence and provocation to the war-party, and Hananiah intervenes with a prophecy of another kind. With great assurance he puts a two-year limit on his prophecy : fanatics are always in a hurry. It is to be noted that the Temple vessels are named ahead of the king (Coniah) and it may be symptomatic of popular taste that his substitution by another would be contemplated with equanimity. The prophecy of Hananiah finds a large reception, and even Jeremiah, with no less ardent patriotism, breathes a solemn ' Amen '. But something here gives him pause and that something is the history of prophecy. ' It hath not been so wrought heretofore in Israel.' Prophecy had been of doom and judgment : here was something new and unprecedented. Only time could tell. Caution was in place at this point but Hananiah eschews caution. Hananiah repeats his words with ecstatic energy and confirms them by breaking the yoke on Jeremiah's neck. He is in the ascendant ' and Jeremiah went his way ' (11). This last word has caused difficulty to Peake and Cornill : the latter strikes it out altogether. Did Jeremiah falter in his prophetic certainty ? Surely the matter is not so difficult. Hesitation and caution are natural here, and more than once we see the prophet exercise similar caution (32:8, 42:2f.). How could Jeremiah hope to get a hearing amid such seething excitement ? A ' cooling-off ' period was required lest faith should fall into fanaticism. Jeremiah will return at the right

32a moment with the right word, and, like Hananiah, he will date it. That word will be condemnation for Hananiah and a judgment on all he stood for. 'And H. died . . . that same year.'

b Here we have one of the great interviews in Scripture and large questions are involved. H. was no common impostor like Bishop Blougram. He was conscientious —but his conscience was not fully illumined. He thought too much of divine favour, too little of divine judgment, too much of Israel's privilege and too little of Israel's responsibility. He did not take all the facts into account: he was deceived by his own heart. How may we distinguish between Hananiah and Jeremiah? how do we recognise the truth? We may not say that the seat of authority in religion is *quod semper, quod ubique, quod ab omnibus creditur*. The voice of the people is not the voice of God. The true prophet, like Jeremiah, may often find himself in a minority of one (cf. 1 Kg. 22). Perhaps we may say that the spirits of the prophets are subject to the prophets, that the inspired speaker can only be discerned by the inspired hearer, and that the *testimonium internum Spiritus Sancti* will here be our guide. **11.** Here the LXX omits both 'Nebuchadnezzar' and 'within two years'. **16b** is omitted by LXX and was probably added here by a later hand in view of Dt. 13:6 (cf. Dt. 18:20).

c **XXIX 1-32 The Letter to the Exiles**—This is a unique document in the OT and the first of its kind. It may be dated shortly after 598 B.C. and is closely connected with chs. 27 and 28. Ch. 28 deals with the situation in Jerusalem while ch. 29 speaks to the circumstances in Babylon. The object of the diplomatic mission mentioned in v. 3 is not stated but among its personnel were two friends of Jeremiah, Elasah, brother of Ahikam (26:24), and Gemariah (36:10). These conveyed this letter which reveals the most amazing combination of vision and commonsense. For the exiles, incited by their prophets, were refusing to settle down: their only thought was of speedy return to the homeland. Their hatred of Babylon led to riots which resulted in the summary 'taking-off' of two of their most prominent and rabid prophets (22). Here Jeremiah lays a cool hand on hot heads lest by their rashness they should all perish in a pogrom in Babylon. All this is easily understood. Deuteronomy had made it impossible for a good Jew to live in an alien land. If Jerusalem be the only place where worship of Yahweh is possible, and if all life's activities such as building, planting, marrying and begetting children be associated with the religious cult, how could they escape a feeling of total frustration? For the cult was impossible in Babylon: only in Jerusalem could Yahweh be worshipped. Here Jeremiah writes to say that the world is God's world and God is not limited to Jerusalem and its Temple. Prayer is possible in Babylon (7) and the man who prayed for his enemies (18:20) gives them the unique injunction to pray for Babylon. That was a 'hard saying' for the Jews and it is without parallel in the OT. God, too, has a plan and a purpose that embraces the Jews in Babylon and his plan is for good and not for evil. The vision may tarry—70 years it may tarry —but it will be fulfilled. And God can be found, or rather 'lets himself be found', in Babylon: the 'unclean land' becomes the sphere of revelation (12). Here Jeremiah is the Founder of Foreign Missions as he is also the father of true prayer. And here they built their synagogue to be a house of prayer and study of his word. He is gracious, and beyond the iron discipline which they undergo lies the restoration (14). **7.** 'the city': LXX reads 'the land'. **8, 9.** Many commentators regard these as added: others would set them after 15.

d **15** renews the attack on the false prophets. Most MS authorities agree with LXX in omitting **16-20** which plainly interrupt the connection with **21.** Evidently these prophets were inciting such trouble in Babylon that they were summarily executed. It is
interesting to note they were morally bad, Sadducees 482d
as well as Pharisees. Interesting is the sequel to this letter. Clearly the 'grapevine' functioned freely between Babylon and Jerusalem. Letters of complaint were sent to the authorities—better with LXX the singular 'supervisor'—at Jerusalem asking that Jeremiah be rendered ineffective, his mouth closed, and his pen taken from him. Evidently there was a supervising official in Jerusalem who had control over the prophets though to what extent we cannot clearly discern. Jeremiah's reputation must have been heightened by the incident recorded in the previous chapter and the 'supervisor' was not inclined to accede to the request of the prophets in Babylon. Rather Jeremiah was permitted to send an answer to that request and in another letter he pronounces a ban upon Shemaiah that he should not see any good from the Lord. And again we cannot but wonder at the sheer common sense of this visionary.

XXX-XXXI Jeremiah and Israel — Regarding 483a
these chapters there is considerable variety of critical opinion: few commentators accept them as wholly from Jeremiah. Both Volz and Rudolph are convinced of their general authenticity and we may follow them. Volz likens this little 'book' to a medieval triptych. In the left panel we see the tumult of peoples that normally found place upon dynastic changes and we see the penitent Jacob bowed beneath the strokes of ill fortune. Here also appears the Comforter bringing to Jacob the message of approaching release. In the centre is the main picture in two parts, Yahweh's meeting with Israel in the wilderness and greeting the Prodigal with boundless mercy: close by is the crowd of returning exiles straining eagerly toward the homeland. The right panel combines both past and future, Rachel weeping for her children and Ephraim crushed and broken, with the New Covenant made between Yahweh and his banished ones brought home. The OT contains no real dramas but all the elements of drama are here in the swift alternation of scenes and change of speakers. The recurring use of *shûbh* (return) in its various senses (cf. 3:6–18) and *yesha'* (salvation) reveals the prophet's spiritual insight and poetical skill. Throughout there runs a connected thought, and a fulness of emotion is revealed in many a tender detail. The sections of the 'book' divide at 30:32 and 31:13. The date of it may be quite early: perhaps we should think of that period in the reign of Josiah when the king was asserting his authority in the north after the fall of Assyria (612 B.C.). The words 'and Judah' (3, 4) may be regarded as an addition: the prophet had already spoken to Judah and its exiles and his concern here is with Israel. Vv. 5–7 reveal the usual situation that emerged when one monarch gave place to another. Panic and fear are on every side and Jacob cannot escape involvement. It is the time of distress preceding release. Let Jacob wait for the salvation of the Lord. Vv. 8, 9 may be regarded as a gloss and no part of the original. Let Jacob have no fear, for Yahweh will deal with things and order them to a righteous end. Suffering there will be but it shall be in just measure for chastening: the heathen oppressors will be consumed by his wrath. Here (12) the prophet turns to assert the deserved nature of the suffering of Israel, for the prophet will not allow them to forget the ground of judgment. Even in this glad song the prophet will hold before the exiles the moral demands of their righteous God. Their guilt is great and their sin flagrant and only the divine mercy can save them. Vv. 16, 17 should be omitted: the reference to Zion is out of place here. Israel shall be restored and things shall again be as once they were in the heyday of the kingdom. The shouts of joy and songs of praise shall greet the renewing mercy of God. Life shall be free and ample for young and old. No longer shall they suffer under foreign rule but from their own midst shall come their king. 30:22–31:1 is rightly omitted by the LXX: v. 22 appears in its

483a right place at 31:33 while vv. 23, 24 are repeated from 23:19, 20. **6a.** A common figure of extreme distress (cf. 4:31, 6:24, 22:23): men behave thus because of their great anguish. **9.** For the ideal ruler cf. 23:5; Hos. 3:5; Ezek. 34:23, 37:24f. **10, 11** recur in 46:27, 28 with better text: here omitted by LXX. **14c** should be deleted as doublet of 15*b*.

b **XXXI 2-30 Good Tidings**—The day is at hand for the exile's return and here the prophet's words take on tints and colours. The word 'wilderness' recalls the wondrous mercy of God in days of old (2:2f.; Hos. 2:14), and in the wilderness of exile God finds the survivors and brings them home. Life again in all its glow and colour shall be on Samaria's hills and with glad response men will answer the call to go up to the house of God. Again we hear (7–9) the glad 'hosannas' of worn men and weary women and children. For they now behold the salvation of the Lord. From the north and the far parts of the earth they come, blind, broken, labouring: tears mingle with cries of joy as God gently leads them like a shepherd and reveals a father's love to his first-born. This is a matter for the world to know. The Lord hath redeemed his people and waits to bless them with all natural abundance. The maidens dance and merriment fills the hearts of young and old. Mourning has taken flight and joy abides. In one of those swift changes (15–20) the prophet passes from the present to the past. The exiles are not yet here though their coming is assured. Near Anathoth at Ramah was the tomb of mother Rachel and the prophet hears her endless weeping for her children. Refrain thine eyes from tears! they are coming home and love's labour will not be lost. Ephraim, too, weeps for sorrow at his sin and pleads for restoration. God responds to the prayer of the penitent and Rachel's tears are dried away. Now let the exiles set their heart to the highway (21, 22). Here Israel is addressed as daughter and the prophet emphasises the need of moral steadfastness, for he knows well that repentance all too often is but superficial.

c The meaning of v. 22 is not clear and volumes have been written on these words. The most probable explanation seems to be that here we have a grammatical gloss wherein the copyist is indicating that the masculine (son) has been changed to the feminine (daughter) in vv. 20, 21, 22 (Bewer). Both Rudolph and Volz omit vv. 23–30 and they are questioned by most commentators. The blessed hope expressed throughout this 'book' stirred many minds and later writers lingered on the subject. But Jeremiah here is concerned with Ephraim. In 27–30 we seem to have reminiscences of his call (1:10) and the assurance that Yahweh is 'wakeful' (*shōḳēdh*) over his word to perform it. The positive aspects (to build and to plant) are here emphasised. And part of the future salvation will be that men will not any more have reason to doubt the justice of God in the matter of moral retribution. **3c.** 'one of Jeremiah's immortal sentences' (Bewer): LXX and Vulg. read 'with loving kindness have I drawn thee'. **5d.** LXX reads 'and shall give praise' or, more specifically, 'celebrate the vintage festival' (*hillûlîm*). The difference here is infinitesimal (the difference between *Hē* and *Ḥēth* in Hebrew). **7.** For 'for the chief of the nations' read 'on the top of the mountains' (BH). **26.** Looks like a marginal gloss of a copyist.

31-34 The New Covenant—The genuineness of this passage has been much questioned, and most strenuously by Duhm who at first accepted it as from Jeremiah but later resiled from that opinion and regarded it as the composition of a late Jewish legalist. The passage has been subjected to most thorough and penetrating analysis by both Cornill and Skinner, and there seems no adequate reason to doubt the authorship of Jeremiah. The old covenant had been annulled by Israel's disobedience, for a covenant is a mutual agreement between two parties that remains in force only so long as both parties abide by the terms of the agreement. Israel had been unfaithful. Josiah had sought to 48 reform matters but the reformation was ineffective. It dealt only with external organisation and what was required was inward regeneration. The golden age cannot be built on leaden instincts: 'circumcision of the heart' is required (4:4). Religion must be internalised and spiritualised. The prophet knew from his experience of communion with God that such experience could be the portion of every mother's son in Israel. 'Would that all the Lord's people were prophets' (Num. 11:29). Jeremiah had to use the thought-forms of his own time and could only express his idea 'in an antithesis between the external law written in a book or on tablets of stone and the dictates of the inward moral sense informed by true knowledge of God' (Peake). Phrases like 'born anew' and 'a new creation' were not then in use but this is precisely what the prophet has in mind. 'Knowledge of God' in the OT is equivalent to 'faith' in the NT and the issue of such faith or knowledge of God is a sound morality: the tree is known by its fruits. Man's will becomes one with the will of God and man's meat and drink is to do that will. And he does so in grateful response to what a forgiving God has done for him. In this view Jeremiah and Paul are one (Rom. 12:1). Religion is no longer bound to priest or Temple or land: its character is both individual and universal. Jeremiah thinks here only of his own nation but this seminal thought was to find its fuller expression in the NT (Lk. 22:20; Heb. 8:6, 13, 10:16f.). **32.** For *bāʿaltî* (I was a husband) LXX and Syr. read *gāʿaltî* (I abhorred or spurned), but the text here seems to be supported by 3:14 where *bāʿaltî* is used similarly. In **35-7** the everlasting mercy is proclaimed by Yahweh himself. In the exalted style of the hymn he speaks to assure Israel that his love and mercy are fixed, firm, and lasting as the stars and the heavens. **38-40** are out of place here. Jeremiah had little or no concern for the dimensions of Jerusalem in the present or future.

XXXII 1-15 The Redemption of the Land—This 484 chapter is clearly a piece of prophetic history. By the act recorded here Jeremiah demonstrated his unswerving faith in God. The record here has been largely amplified and almost all commentators are agreed that later writers have filled out the original. The date is clearly indicated and the passage is to be read in close conjunction with 37:11f. The first five verses may be regarded as editorial—note the reference to 'Jeremiah the prophet'. Here as frequently (1:11 f.) the word of God is suggested to the prophet through a commonplace mundane thing, and here, too, we note something of the process of revelation (8). This was God's leading and it was confirmed. Such an act as this seemed contrary to reason for the land was in the hands of the Chaldaeans. The inference is that Jeremiah paid the full fair price: there was no regular currency and money was weighed. Both Livy (xxvi, 11) and Florus (ii, 6), the Roman historians, record how when Hannibal was at the gates of Rome the site on which his camp was set was exposed for public sale in the Roman market-place and brought full price: such faith had Rome in itself! But Judah was weak and about to be swallowed up by the Chaldaeans, and Judah had no faith in anything! But the prophet had faith and was willing to venture his substance to testify to his faith in God. In a sense he was 'on the spot' for if he had refused how could he expect others to believe his prophecies? Jeremiah had faith in the purpose of God and he bought the field. The process of sale described here, like all legal processes, is somewhat involved, but archaeological discovery has shown that it was the custom to place a pillow-shaped clay tablet inside a clay envelope on the outside of which was written the contents of the enclosed tablet. Thus one did not require to break the envelope to get to the sealed tablet unless the exterior writing had become illegible. There were thus two copies, one sealed and one open. Everything here is in legal order and the documents are com-

484a mitted to Baruch (whose full name is here given) for safe keeping in an earthen jar. **5.** LXX omits the words ' until I visit . . . succeed '. **7.** These regulations were designed to keep property within the family (Lev. 25:25f. ; Ru. 3:9–13, 4:1–12). **11.** LXX omits ' sealed deed ' but has it in **14.** MT is to be preferred here.

b **16-44 The Prayer of Jeremiah**—This section, too, has been expanded and is interesting for the light it sheds on Jewish liturgy in the synagogue The turgid phrases are reminiscent of Dt. and the real prayer seems to be in 17*a*, 24, 25. Jeremiah seems unable to grasp the full meaning of the word that has come to him : it seems so unreasonable in the circumstances. But in 26–44 we have the answer—in 26 we should read with LXX ' unto me ' for ' unto Jeremiah ' —and the answer is fourfold : (*a*) Yahweh, not the Chaldaean, is Lord of History (27), (*b*) judgment is certain and it will be upon sinners, (*c*) the judgment will not be annihilation, but after it normal life shall return (43), (*d*) the preceding destruction is the guarantee of restoration (42). In v. 40 we have a strong echo of the New Covenant of 31:31ff., and here is the note of hope for Judah's land. Objection has been raised to the pedestrian nature of this hope in that it centres on real estate transactions. But Jeremiah was making no wild eschatological flights : he had his feet firm on the ground and dealt with solid realities. **30b.** Omitted by LXX. **39.** ' one heart . . . way ' : LXX reads ' another heart . . . another way '. The difference in consonantal text is infinitesimal. MT is to be preferred, meaning singleness of heart and unwavering devotion. **41.** ' with all my heart . . . soul ' : only here used of God.

c **XXXIII Words of Hope**—Here we have a continuation of the prophecies of weal, and here, too, we have again the question of the genuineness of these words. Vatke, Stade, Cornill and Duhm reject the chapter *in toto*, while other commentators would allow a Jeremianic nucleus in 1–13 (Hyatt would accept vv. 4, 5). Regarding 14–26 almost all scholars reject this section, which is absent from LXX and must have been absent from the original from which LXX translation was made. Between the two sections one can discern unmistakable difference. In 1–13 the outlook is hopeful to a degree approaching the idyllic (12, 13) while in 14–26 an atmosphere of despair and scepticism appears, an atmosphere similar to that found in the book of Mal. Behind these verses we sense a fading of faith and a spirit of questioning as to the purpose of God. The vision tarries and men are weary of waiting, doubting whether it shall ever be accomplished.

d **XXXIII 1-13.** Against the background of the besieged city the writer promises (*a*) that the city will be restored and rebuilt, (*b*) that sin, which has brought this ruin upon them, shall be removed, (*c*) that Jerusalem shall be exalted and draw the wondering admiration of all the world because of the great things God hath done. The waste places shall be restored and idyllic peace shall prevail. This writer breathes the spirit of Apocalyptic : the revelation is given in answer to prayer and it concerns mysteries (3). The Jeremianic nucleus may be no more than v. 10, which rests on 32:43, and v. 11, which recalls 16:9, 25:10 in the form of promise. **10.** The fall of Jerusalem is here presupposed.

e **14-26.** These verses belong to a period long after the fall of the city and they speak of a period of disillusionment. The words of hope and promise spoken by Jeremiah have not come to pass and men were beginning to doubt the reality of Israel's election (24). It may be, as Volz suggests, that many were ready to discard their whole religious heritage and become as other nations. To comfort the former and admonish the latter this late writer speaks these words. He, too, draws from Jeremiah's book, and from 23:5 he forms his vision of the restored kingdom and a king reigning in righteousness (14–16). Beside him shall be the Levitical priesthood : Church and State will work hand in hand (cf. Zech. 6:13). In 19f. there is a 484e slightly polemical element and the writer becomes ' the defender of the faith '. 31:35–7 here afford him a suitable text. As firm and sure as natural law, so stands the purpose of God toward Israel. The mercy of the Lord endureth for ever. **18.** Note the Dt. phrase ' the Levitical priests '. **21c.** This may also be read, as Bewer suggests, ' that they should not minister to me '.

XXXIV 1-7 A Word to Zedekiah—The incident f related here seems to have taken place during the interruption of the siege by the approach of Hophra's army. Only Jerusalem, Lachish and Azekah remained unsubdued. The prophet is commanded to speak a word to the king, and it seems to be a word of promise. That promise was not realised and vv. 4. 5 raise a problem of interpretation. LXX omits the last words of 4, ' you shall not die by the sword ', and in place of these words Volz would read ' if you will not hearken to my voice '. The promise must be conditional and perhaps we should read ' Obey the voice of God, so shall you not die by the sword ' (cf. 38:17f.). **7.** Lachish, modern Tell ed-Duweir, 23 miles SW. of Jerusalem. Azekah, modern Tell ez-Zakarîyah, 11 miles N. of Lachish (cf. Torczyner, *Lachish Letters*, 79, 83, 84).

8-22 A dishonest Deal—In old Israel when a man g could not meet his debts he could discharge them by service to his creditor. He and his family might submit to slavery for a period of time—six years according to Hebrew law (Exod. 21:2 ; Dt. 15·12). The present instance, however, seems to be a special act in a general emergency. In the stress of the siege it would not be possible to maintain large domestic establishments and there may have been need of fighting-men. The act was not motivated by strictly religious considerations. It was carried through under the leadership of the king and with solemn religious ceremony (15, 18). But no sooner was it carried through than the doers of it repented of their sudden generosity and the freed slaves were re-enslaved. Vv. 13, 14 seem to be irrelevant here and the narrative proceeds more smoothly if we pass directly from 13*a* to 15. What they did pleased God but what they did thereafter was a profanation of his holy name (used in the covenant), and Yahweh will not hold them guiltless. He will proclaim liberty to them liberty to be destroyed and die. As they had passed between the two halves of the victim (Gen. 15:10) and repeated the formula, ' God do so to us and more also if we keep not the terms of this covenant ' (cf. 1 Sam. 11:7), so shall it be done unto them. For treachery to their fellowmen and for disloyalty to God their own bodies shall be devoured by carrion beasts and birds (20). King and kingdom will be desolated and destroyed. **8.** ' liberty ' (*d^erôr*) : this word is not found in earliest legislation nor in Dt. It occurs in Lev. 25:10 (Year of Jubilee) ; Isa. 61:1 ; Ezek. 46:17.

XXXV Jeremiah and the Rechabites—This inci- 485a dent may be dated about 598 B.C. The community (they had no ' house ') of the Rechabites traced their origin to Jonadab ben Rechab (1 Chr. 2:55), who espoused the cause of Jehu in the bloody purge of the house of Omri (2 Kg. 10:15f.). They were fanatical devotees of Yahweh and the nomad life, and they obeyed their father's command to build no house, plant no vines, sow no seed, all of which acts marked the sedentary agricultural life. They were characterised by a hatred of Baal religion and very zealous for Yahweh of Hosts. They opposed culture on the ground that it implied a forsaking of Yahweh and a departure from wilderness ways and ideals. Thus they associated religion with an external form and bound Yahweh to a particular form of social organisation—the nomad life. For all the ills of life, social, political, religious, they had one simple cure—retreat to the desert and a tent in the wilderness. The movement was built on a protest against civilisation and it was wholly lacking in creative power. But they were faithful to a human

485a command. Jeremiah applauds their fidelity but does not approve their asceticism. The prophet did not believe that religion is opposed to culture but rather that religion is the mother of culture. To Jeremiah Yahweh is dynamic and he ' will become what he will become '. He reveals himself in the busy city streets as he did in the wilderness. He will be sufficient for all the emerging situations of life : his quickening spirit is not limited by time or space. The incident is an object lesson and its meaning none could miss. The Rechabites will not lose their reward. But how shall Israel, who has refused to hearken to the voice of her God, escape just retribution ? **4.** ' Keeper of the threshold ' : an important official whose duty it was to see that none entered the Temple in an unclean state (cf. Ps. 15).

b **XXXVI The Pen and the Penknife**—Jeremiah is instructed to write down all his prophecies of the last twenty-three years and read them in public. It may be that what the isolated oracle did not achieve the collected group will effect and produce repentance in the people. The prophet summons a professional scribe (Baruch) who may also have been a secret disciple. There is no reason to think with Mowinckel that Jeremiah could not write. It seems very probable that he here dictated from written memoirs, for it is hard to believe he could recall all he had said through twenty-three years. The story sheds an interesting light on the process of literary composition : we learn how paper and ink (18, 23) and the scribe's knife were part of the equipment. Volz would set v. 9 between 4 and 5 and this improves the story. The ' disbarring ' of the prophet from the Temple (5) may have been the result of Temple police activities following the incident recorded in chs. 20–21:6. The fast (9) may have been proclaimed in view of a threatened drought rather than because of a political crisis. The impression made by the reading on the first two groups, the general public and the princes, appears to have been considerable. The princes were scared and deemed it wise to communicate the matter to the king. After careful investigation they assured themselves this was a prophetic word from God (17) and before reporting to the king they requested Jeremiah and Baruch to go into hiding. The king ordered the scroll to be read before him and surely there can be no greater contrast than that of the king and his father Josiah. When the latter heard the words of ' the book of the Law ' (2 Kg. 22) he was awed and moved to religious reformation : when it was read to Jehoiakim he treated the matter with levity and tossed it into the fire, slitting the columns three or four at a time. Some there sought
c to restrain him (25) but in vain. The arrest of Jeremiah and Baruch was ordered but ' they hid themselves ' (reading with LXX). As to what the scroll contained there is much question ; ' all the words that I have spoken to you against Israel and Judah and all the nations ' is the description given in v. 2. The fact that it was read three times in one day might indicate it was not unduly long, while v. 23 might convey the impression of a fairly large scroll. The final triumph, however, was not with the penknife. The prophet returned with another word of doom for king and people (27). And a new scroll was written on a larger scale (32). **2.** For ' Israel ' LXX reads Jerusalem : but the MT is to be preferred. **15.** ' Read it ' : LXX reads ' read it again '. **16.** With LXX omit the words ' to Baruch '. **18.** LXX and Syr. read ' Jeremiah dictated '.

d **XXXVII 1-10 A Request from the King**—The narrative here is similar to that of 21:1–10 and may have occurred a short time later Vv. 1, 2 seem an editorial insertion indicating the general background of this and succeeding chapters. During the temporary lifting of the siege Zedekiah sends officers to the prophet, thinking still that there might be a wondrous repetition of the deliverance of 701 B.C. (Isa. 37 ; 2 Kg. 19:20f.). But the word of the Lord stands firm and his purpose is fixed. This is not a question of
Chaldaean might but of the will of God, and with 485
characteristic Hebrew hyperbole the prophet repeats the word of doom. **1.** LXX omits ' Coniah, the son of '. **3.** Jehucal was no friend of Jeremiah (38:1).

11-21 Jeremiah Arrested—During the interval of e
the interrupted siege Jeremiah undertakes a journey to Anathoth, probably to complete the business recorded in 32. At the gate he is arrested as a deserter : the message of 21:8–10 might well justify this action. The prophet repudiates the charge and is brought before the princes, not those of 36:12 who were sympathetic to him, but a new group of upstarts who had taken the place of those deported in 598 B.C. This group hated Jeremiah for his attitude and apparent defeatism, as also for the stinging rebuke he had administered to them in the shameful act of the ' release ' (34:17). The prophet was cast into an improvised prison—the regular prisons were overfilled with would-be deserters—and from this damp and dangerous cell he is summoned secretly by the king who desires to know the divine intention. Zedekiah seems to have thought the Lord was as fickle and unstable as himself. Doom is again proclaimed. Jeremiah can do no other, let false prophets speak as they may. To a plea for himself so unjustly treated—who could doubt his patriotism ?—the king accedes by sending him to the court of the guard and allotting him a small daily portion of food.

XXXVIII 1-13 Bonds and Imprisonment—Here f
we see the princes in their evil machinations. Gedaliah is not the later governor (40, 41) but may be the son of Pashhur mentioned in 20:1–3. He was little likely to be well disposed towards Jeremiah. The princes could not but take notice of the prophet's words and from the viewpoint of the military they were justified. The king weakly accedes to their request and Jeremiah is cast into a miry cistern : these bad men were restrained by a superstitious dread from killing outright a man of God. From his sorry plight the prophet was rescued by the compassionate intervention of Ebed-melech. After this laborious rescue the princes seem to trouble the prophet no more ' and he remained in the court of the guard '. **9.** LXX reads ' thou hast acted wrongly in what thou hast done to slay this man ' but the MT is to be preferred. The eunuch was hardly likely to speak so directly to the king. Eunuchs, normally associated with the harem, frequently attained to high position (cf. Gen. 37:36, 40:2, 7 ; Est. 1:10 ; Dan. 1:3). They were mostly foreigners and excluded from the congregation by law (Dt. 23:1).

14-28 Interview with the King—Zedekiah again g
seeks a secret meeting with Jeremiah and promises immunity for anything the prophet may say. The word of doom is again announced and surrender is advised. The king expresses fear that if he surrenders he may be mishandled by those Jews who have already deserted to the Chaldaeans and who were fiercely opposed to his policies. In vision the prophet sees the final scene and in the haunting *Ḳînāh* rhythm he hears the women sing (22). V 23 is probably no part of the original and should be omitted, save for the words ' and this city shall be burned with fire '. Secrecy is enjoined upon Jeremiah ; let none know what has transpired except that the prophet asked for alleviation of his harsh punishment. But the princes discover the meeting and inquire : Jeremiah reveals only his petition and conceals the rest. Serious questions arise in connection with this incident and Duhm discusses them at length in his commentary. It is clear that if Jeremiah had told all he would have provoked a bloody purge within the city and made the end far more terrible. He did not conceal things with a thought of his own safety (cf. Gen. 12:10f.) but for the safety of the people. Is such action justifiable ? Must the truth be always spoken (cf. Jeanie Deans in Scott's *Heart of Midlothian*) ? Is it possible that, as here, love for others may constrain to silence and yet allow us ' to truth it in love ' (Eph. 4:15) ? Jeremiah was of all men a true man and we can say that here ' truth '

5g was regulated and dominated by love. **24-8.** This section, as Volz and Bewer suggest, belongs originally after the interview in 37:17–21.

6a **XXXIX 1-14 Fall of the City**—This section is rather confused textually and vv. 4–13 are missing in the LXX. Vv. 1, 2 intervene between 38:28*b* and 39:3 and may be regarded as an insertion. They refer to a period long past and are irrelevant here. By their removal we get a well-connected sentence, as in RSV, and the narrative reads smoothly. Vv. 4–10 are an abridgment of 52:7–16. The genuineness of 11–13 is questioned by many : according to 52:12 Nebuzaradan did not reach Jerusalem until a month later. V. 14 would connect naturally with v. 3. Baruch's primary interest is in the fortunes of Jeremiah and this story seems reasonable enough. The Babylonian authorities must have known from the deserters the attitude of the prophet. The story is given in fuller detail in 40:1–6. **3.** Nergal-sharezer, prince of Sin-magir, later became king Neriglissar. **4.** Arabah : i.e. the Jordan valley.

b **15-18 Promise to Ebedmelech**—The prophet does not forget his friends (cf. 45:5). The good deed of this coloured eunuch is commended as an act of faith. The princes, whose plan he had baulked, shall not wreak vengeance upon him : in the ensuing tumult he shall be secure. He stands in sheer contrast to Zedekiah whose one thought was to save his own life. Ebedmelech was saved by faith and for lack of that faith Jerusalem fell and Zedekiah perished.

c **XL 1-6 Jeremiah Released**—The opening words here seem out of place as no oracle is involved. The section is somewhat confused and there is something strange in the theological reflections of the captain of the guard (2*b*, 3 ; cf. Gen. 26:20). The first clause of v. 5 seems corrupt and is lacking in LXX. After the fall of the city Jeremiah seems, according to this version, to have been swept away with the captives and is found in the train of prisoners halted at Ramah. It may be that Gedaliah's hand moved in this matter and prompted the discovery. The prophet is offered choice of location and he decides to abide with the 'remnant'. Perhaps he was influenced thereto by his faith expressed in 32:15.

d **7-16 The Colony at Mizpah**—A new rallying-point for the remnant was set up at Mizpah under Gedaliah, son of Ahikam. To this place gathered the remnants of the Jewish forces and Gedaliah seems to have been empowered by the king of Babylon to grant amnesty to all such. Let them accept the situation and let them have no fear of the Chaldaean officials appointed to supervise (2 Kg. 25:24). The governor himself will serve and vouch for them—the word 'stand' has both meanings here—to the Chaldaeans. Let them each go about their lawful tasks and vocations. The Jews who had fled across the Jordan now returned and fair harvests greeted their arrival. It is a tribute to the humane methods of warfare employed by the Chaldaeans that the fruit trees were standing with fruit ready to harvest. But an evil fate seemed to dog the steps of the young community. The jealousy of the king of Ammon was aroused and he found a ready tool in Ishmael, who was remotely connected with the line of David. Gedaliah rebuffed the warnings of Johanan ben Kareah and perhaps therein revealed the nobility of his character. Perhaps he was too trusting and should have taken some preventive action when so much was at stake. It is to be noted that Jeremiah does not appear in this or the next section.

e **XLI 1-3 Murder of Gedaliah**—The suspicions of Johanan were soon confirmed. The governor was foully slain in his house and his Jewish guests with him and the Chaldaean supervisors. Thus in two short months what had seemed a new beginning came to a sad end. **1.** 'one of the chief . . . king' : omit with LXX and 2 Kg. 25:25. **3b.** 'soldiers' : omit with LXX. The murder would hardly have taken place in the presence of Chaldaean soldiers. Only the supervisory officials were involved.

4-18 Treachery and Confusion—Johanan's worst 486f
fears (40:15) were soon confirmed. The removal of Gedaliah's wise head and guiding hand plunged the community into confusion. Murder followed murder. Eighty pilgrims coming from the north to worship at Jerusalem were treacherously lured to destruction. These pilgrims were not ignorant of the fall of Jerusalem—the signs of mourning were upon their persons—but it seems that worship and sacrifice were still possible in the ruined Temple. The schism between Jew and Samaritan had not yet taken place. In v. 6 we should perhaps read with LXX, 'as they were going along and weeping'. The pilgrims might well suspect such a display of emotion on the part of Ishmael. At the elevated town of Mizpah they would get their first view of the desolated city and they were moved to tears (cf. Lk. 19:41). In a most shameful violation of the law of hospitality they were lured into the city by a feigned invitation from Gedaliah and most foully slaughtered, save for ten who offered to disclose the hiding-place of stores of food. Why Ishmael did this dastardly deed is not told. The cistern, so necessary to the defence of the city and set there by Asa (1 Kg. 15:22), was defiled by this senseless act. With a train of captives, 'all the remnant', Ishmael and his ten men set off across the Jordan to Ammon. It is another mark of the Chaldaean humane methods that they had left the royal princesses, related to Ishmael, in charge of Gedaliah. The reaction of Johanan was swift and energetic. At Gibeon they came upon Ishmael, slew two of his men, rescued the captives, but Ishmael escaped. The location of Geruth Chimham is not known : probably we should read (BH) 'the sheepfolds of Chimham', Chimham being a son of Barzillai (2 Sam. 19:37–40). Panic had seized the group and they were minded to flee down to Egypt. They feared what the Chaldaeans might do : Gedaliah was now more missed than ever.

XLII 1-XLIII 7 The Search for Guidance—The g
thoroughly scared community turned to Jeremiah and asked that he should seek guidance from God for them. The prophet, once despised and rejected, is now their main resource and refuge. They solemnly pledge themselves to follow whatever directions may be given and to obey the voice of God. But it seems from the sequel that their minds were already made up. Jeremiah does not have a word ready and must wait for it: this delay may have been damaging. In ten days the prophet received the word, a sane word that should have saved the group from their insane folly. Let them abide in the land and have no fear of the king of Babylon. A constructive future is possible (10) and the Chaldaeans had already acted humanely. The prophet evidently discerned their real intentions and amplified his oracle with stern and solemn warnings. He stood against the people as 'an iron wall'. Let them not add folly to folly : the end of such conduct is distress and death. In Egypt where they think to 'live' they shall 'die' (17). Had they not solemnly pledged themselves to follow the divine direction? In swift and violent reaction (43:1–7) they spurned the prophet's word. It marched not with their own resolve. Panic had stolen away their wits and even Johanan succumbed to the panic. They will not declare the word of God a lie but they deny the source of the word. It is of Baruch and not from God. Perhaps that is why Baruch says three times, 'Thus says the Lord' (9, 15, 18). They will not listen. To Egypt they will go and to Egypt they went. But all Hebrew history shows that the 'going down' to Egypt was not only a physical descent but a moral descent as well. **43:7.** Tahpanhes (Daphne or Defenneh ; cf. 2:16) : probably there was a Jewish colony already there.

XLIII 8-13 A symbolic Prophecy—Duhm regards h
this section as unhistorical but this judgment is not generally accepted. There are textual difficulties but RSV gives a clear rendering. An almost magical power was attributed to words : they were alive and 'ran'

486h to fulfilment. More so was that the case with symbolic action (cf. H. W. Robinson, *Revelation and Redemption*, pp. xxxii ff.). Here the prophet not only proclaims the future but creates the event. The word enters by eye and ear. They thought to flee from Nebuchadrezzar but he shall overtake them in Egypt. He shall conquer it—this event took place in 582 B.C. and Josephus reports that those Jews were carried to Babylon (Ant. X, ix, 7). The Josephus story has been questioned, but an inscription of Nebuchadrezzar shows that he defeated Amasis in 568 B.C. but did not conquer Egypt. **9.** ' Pharaoh's palace ' : not a royal residence but rather a kind of ' Government House '. **10.** ' I have hid ' : read with LXX and Syr. ' thou hast buried '. ' Royal canopy '—the word occurs only here in OT. **12b.** A vivid simile rightly rendered by RSV. **13.** The temple at Heliopolis was world-famed. An avenue of obelisks stood in front of it, of which ' Cleopatra's needle ' was one. Others are now in Paris, Rome and Constantinople. Only one remains in place.

487a **XLIV Contumacy and Apostasy**—Here we have Jeremiah's last prophecy and a most interesting view of the community in Egypt. The chapter seems unduly diffuse and may have been expanded. Here we see how things developed. Events had proved too much for the group and the force of ' brute facts ' drove them to superstition. We have here two views of history, that of the community and that of the prophet. Both had passed through the same dreadful experience and they emerged with different conclusions on the matter. To the bewildered community the Reformation of Josiah seemed all a mistake : those new-fangled ways of worship brought only disaster. Better now to return to the *status quo ante* (cf. 7:17) and resume the old forms of worship. No date is assigned to this event but it would seem as if the Jews in Egypt had assembled for some solemn event connected with heathen worship. Migdol and Memphis were near to Tahpanhes but Pathros was far to the south near Syene, where a Jewish colony with largely pagan worship existed (Cowley, *Aramaic Papyri of 5th Cent. B.C.*). The prophet seeks to dissuade the group from their purpose and in so doing states his view of history. Judah's destruction was due to her apostasy. The movement here may have been led by the royal princesses (Skinner) and Jeremiah was unable to prevail against this ' fanatical chorus of shrieking women and womanish men ' (Volz). In vain does he proclaim the inevitable end of all this. In v. 15 the voice of Baruch becomes more audible as he tells of the defiant contumacious group. The women were more assertive than the men and RSV has rightly added (with the Syr.) at v. 19 the words, ' and the women said '. Their husbands were involved with them for without their husbands they could not vow (Num. 30:4-17). 20–3 seems interpolated. In 25f. the prophet ironically, like Amos (4:4f.), bids them perform their vows and assures them no Jew will be left alive in Egypt (26). Yahweh is still ' wakeful ' (1:12, 31:28) and will not allow their sinful act to go unpunished (27). For a sign the prophet announces that the king of Egypt will share the same fate as Zedekiah, and Babylon will prevail. According to Herodotus (li, 161–3, 169) this was fulfilled by the murder of Pharaoh in 570 B.C. Thus was made clear whose word was true (28). Here we see nothing but darkness and the setting sun, but in the east the sun was rising and in Babylon a new community was being shaped and moulded to be the real people of God. **9.** ' The wickedness of their wives ' : read with LXX ' the wickedness of your princes '. **14.** ' except some fugitives ' : this may be an addition in view of 14*a*.

b **XLV A Word for Baruch**—The prophet does not forget his friends and, like Ebedmelech (39:15 f.), Baruch receives a word from the prophet. Many commentators question the date given but Cornill's arguments seem decisive for its retention. One can understand the anxiety of Baruch after reading the scroll of doom (36) and enduring the persecution of the 48 brutal Jehoiakim. Was this the reward of his faithful service? Like the disciples of Jesus Baruch asks ' What then shall we receive ? ' (Mt. 19:27). Here Baruch reveals his own soul and here Jeremiah reveals himself not only as prophet to the nations but as a father-in-God skilled to guide and comfort the troubled soul. It was a time of suffering for God himself who must destroy his own creation (4, 5) : can the servant be greater than his master ? In the world we shall have tribulation but God will keep and protect his own. Personal ambition must be renounced but the way of sacrificial service will lead to the full life. God will watch over Baruch, and Baruch will not lose his reward. **4.** Omit the words ' Thus shall you say to him ' (BH). **4b.** ' that is, the whole land ' : omitted by LXX : read with BH ' I will smite the whole earth '.

XLVI 1-LI 58 Oracles against the Nations—This c collection has been the subject of great debate and many scholars deny it to Jeremiah. But in spite of large dissenting opinion we should probably hold with Cornill that a fair proportion of this material comes from Jeremiah. There is almost unanimous agreement as to the non-Jeremianic origin of 50:1–51:58. It seems best to consider each oracle by itself. Jeremiah was called to be a prophet to the nations and he represents the universal God.

XLVI 1-12 The battle of Carchemish (modern d Jerâbish) made a deep impression on the ancient world. Jeremiah could not remain unmoved by this decisive event. The poem falls into two parts, 3–6 and 7–12. In the first part the commanders exhort the troops to action (3, 4) while in 5, 6, by swift transitions, the poet describes the result—defeat, flight and death on the banks of the Euphrates. In 7–12 the scene moves back in time to show the initial preparations of the Egyptian army, proud, boastful, imperious. They will conquer the world. Again the poet speaks (7, 8) and the Pharaoh addresses his troops (9), but the poet tells us that the Pharaoh has failed to reckon with the Great King, the Lord of Hosts. The Lord has prepared a sacrifice and the Egyptians shall be the victims. This is the Day of the Lord and his will shall be revealed. Egypt shall be shamed and her inglorious end will shock all peoples. **1.** Lacking in LXX **8.** With LXX omit ' cities and '. **10.** ' the sword ' : read with LXX ' his sword ' (i.e. the Lord's sword). **11.** According to Herodotus (ii, 84) Egypt was ' full of physicians '.

According to the four new tablets of the Babylonian e Chronicle, whose discovery was announced in 1956 by D. J. Wiseman of the British Museum, the Egyptian army was totally annihilated at Carchemish in 605 B.C. Earlier British excavations at the site of the ancient city had suggested this. More surprising, however, is the information that in 601 B.C. Nebuchadrezzar was heavily defeated by Egypt. This may explain the readiness of Jehoiakim to revolt in 598 B.C. On this occasion Nebuchadrezzar captured the city and took Jehoiachin prisoner to Babylon. These new discoveries confirm the biblical story in 2 Kg. 24:10–12 and help to set the chronology on a firmer basis.

13-28 The date of this poem may be the same as that of the foregoing or it may date from Jeremiah's residence in Egypt. It may be a prophecy of the later conquest of Egypt by Nebuchadrezzar in 568 B.C. The battle here is waged on the Egyptian border and the report reaches Migdol, Memphis and Tahpanhes : ruin advances upon them all. Their bull gods cannot deliver them : a mighty monarch advances against them and they shall be wholly wasted. Pharaoh shall be revealed in his true character as one who failed to discern the signs of the times (17) : the mercenary soldiers, well fed but useless for war, melt away and return to their own land. With swiftly changing figures that may offend our modern taste, the weakness and effeminacy of Egypt is set forth and the ruthless power of the invaders portrayed. The end of all is

487e the destruction of Egypt. **25-8** may be a later addition: here a future is promised to Egypt (cf. Ezek. 29:13f.) and Jacob is promised restoration after due affliction. **15.** RSV follows LXX and renders MT rightly. **17.** There is a play on words here but the meaning is not clear (cf. Isa. 30:7).

f **XLVII Against Philistia**—There is no reason to doubt the genuineness of this oracle. In v. 1 the LXX has only 'Concerning Philistia' and this is probably correct, the rest being added. The event referred to here may be the overthrow of Gaza by Neco on his retreat from Carchemish though the reference in Herodotus (ii, 159) has been questioned. The historian says that Neco destroyed 'Kadytis, a city of Syria', and Kadytis is generally identified with Gaza. The invader here is from the north and like a raging flood, a familiar feature in Palestine, he floods the land: his rushing horses and rolling chariots strike panic to the hearts of all. No more shall Philistia succour Phoenicia: the end has come and all its great Goliaths (Anakim) are laid low (5). To the pathetic cry of the crushed (6) comes the reply that the sword shall not rest, for it is the sword of the Lord and it executes his charge. No reason is given for the punishment of Philistia nor is there any hatred expressed in the poem. **4.** Caphtor: usually identified with Crete though others locate it in the delta coast of Egypt (cf. Am. 9:7; Dt. 2:23).

488a **XLVIII Concerning Moab** (For the numerous geographical references, see *Westminster Historical Atlas to the Bible*, by Wright and Filson; also Rudolph, pp. 245-7)—From south to north we might expect the order of these oracles to be Edom, Moab, Ammon; the words 'you also' in 48:7*c* might suggest that the oracle on Edom came before that on Moab. This oracle is rather lengthy and has received considerable expansion but a genuine Jeremianic core is admitted by most commentators. The destruction of Moab, city by city, is announced and she is warned to flee. She deemed herself impregnable and trusted in her gathered power, but Chemosh, her god, is helpless as his people in face of the overflowing scourge. Their cry of distress reaches far down, down to Zoar at the south-east corner of the Dead Sea. The bloodthirsty v. **10**, favourite of Pope Gregory VII, is not from Jeremiah (cf. Jg. 5:23). **9.** LXX reads (probably correctly): 'set up a monument (gravestone) for Moab, for she shall be completely ruined.'

b **11-20.** Here Moab is referred to in masculine form while the previous section used feminine forms. Moab, famous for its wine, has not been disciplined and developed by the vicissitudes of war: its character has remained static, unenriched by the dynamic movements of history. It needs shaking up, 'tilting'. The proud boasts of this self-centred people are proved hollow before the shattering events that they now witness. Their false trust shall be destroyed as was the false confidence of Israel (cf. Am. 5:5). **17-20** form a lament for Moab fallen. **18.** 'on the parched ground': Syr. reads 'in filth'.

c **21-27.** These prose sections are to be regarded as later additions: this oracle seems to have become a general depository for Israel's hatred of Moab. Whom the gods would destroy they first make mad. Moab is drunk with the cup of Yahweh (25:15). Once they 'clapped their hands' (LXX) at Israel's misfortune but now they themselves are become a derision. The biter has been bitten and his scorn returned upon him.

d **28-39.** Proud and arrogant Moab has been, far-flung and spreading like a vine, but no more will she joy with the joy of harvest. Worship has ceased for Chemosh is undone: Moab is a mourning people. Echoes are here of Isa. 15 and 16 but the writer has used his source with considerable freedom.

e **40-47.** Like a vulture the enemy swoops down. Moab is wasted. All this is of Yahweh's appointing. **45-7** are lacking in LXX. There will be a future for Moab; this promise Cornill holds to be from the prophet.

f **XLIX 1-6 Concerning Ammon**—The weight of critical opinion is against the genuineness of this 488f oracle. Gad had lived in Gilead from the days of Moses (Num. 32:34f.; Jos. 13:24f.) but after the deportation of 733 B.C. Ammon had encroached upon and occupied that territory (cf. Am. 1:13). **2** is reminiscent of Zeph. 2:9 but is here mere wishful thinking as Israel was also doomed to exile at this time. Ammon was a city state and as Amman it later formed part of the Decapolis in NT times. It was well watered and its situation seemed to render it impregnable. But it shall surely fall and its false confidence in material might will be revealed. **3.** For 'Ai is laid waste' read with BH 'the spoiler is come up'. No town of this name is known in Ammon. **6** is lacking in LXX.

7-22 Concerning Edom—We have here probably an g expansion of a Jeremianic nucleus. Edom lay south of the Dead Sea and, with Moab, was a near neighbour of Israel. It seems reasonable that Jeremiah should utter oracles concerning these near neighbours. Panic had seized upon the Edomites despite their vaunted wisdom (Job 2:11, 15:18; 1 Kg. 5:10). The neighbouring Dedanites are warned to flee for thorough destruction is about to come upon Esau's land (8, 9). V. 10 with its strangely compassionate note stands in contrast to the inveterate hatred of Israel towards Edom (cf. Am. 1:11, 9:12; Ezek. 25:12-14, 35; Isa. 34:5f., 63:1; Ob.; Jl 3:19; Ps. 137:7). The present passage is closely related to the book of Ob. which constitutes a real 'Hymn of Hate'. Of vv. 12-22 probably only the last verse is from Jeremiah. The thought of Israel's undeserved punishment (12) is alien to the prophet's mind. Here it is 'the nations' rather than Nebuchadrezzar who are called to make war (14). Here, too, their trust in the impregnability of their mountain height proved false (cf. Ob. 4): they are overthrown like Sodom and Gomorrah. The Edomites were later driven out of their land by the Nabataeans: the Herods were Edomites. **19-21** appear more relevantly in 50:44-6.

23-27 Concerning Damascus—This is rejected by h Cornill, Köberle and others: the contents scarcely harmonise with the title. Vv. 26, 27 are probably added. The cities here mentioned are not named in 25:18f. Hamath (Ḥamā) was 110 miles north of Damascus while Arpad (Tell-Erfâd) was 10 miles north of Aleppo. Damascus enjoyed a reputation for splendour which is reflected in the modern names of the city, 'Paradise' and 'Pearl of the Orient'.

28-33 Against desert Tribes—In 25:23, 24 the i desert tribes mentioned are Dedan, Buz, Tema. Josephus quotes Berossus to show that Nebuchadrezzar waged war in Arabia but no confirmation of this statement is available. Kedar (Gen. 25:13), famous for its archers (Isa. 21:16f.), was in the desert east of Palestine, and Hazor may be the name for villages in which semi-nomads dwelt. They, too, shall lose their all and none shall be left. For v. 32 see 9:26, 25:13.

34-39 Concerning Elam—This oracle is dated in the j beginning of Zedekiah's reign and is too vague to allow us to learn anything of Elam, situated near Babylon and north-east of the Persian Gulf. The Elamites were famed as bowmen but their bow shall be broken. Elam was destroyed by Assyria in 640 B.C. (cf. Ezek. 32:24f.) and later formed part of the Persian empire. V. 36 is reminiscent of Ezekiel and should probably be omitted. The LXX retains the last verse though it omitted 48:47 and 49:6. **38.** 'I will set my throne in Elam': probably, with aid of LXX, we should read, 'I will make the throne of Elam desolate' (BH).

L 1-LI 58 Oracle against Babylon—This oracle is 489a almost universally denied to Jeremiah. It is characterised by frequent repetitions—the approach of destruction is announced eleven times, the capture of the city nine times, and Israel's return seven times. The view of Babylon as an arrogant militarism is opposed to Jeremiah's view of Nebuchadrezzar, 'my servant', the agent of Yahweh (cf. 29:7f.). If there be in this

489a 'long and monotonous oracle' (H. W. Robinson) a genuine nucleus of Jeremianic material it seems impossible to discern it. In parts it resembles Ezek. and Deutero-Isaiah but the closest resemblance is to Isa. (chs. 13, 14). The date of these chapters cannot be before 550 B.C. and this present oracle is still later.

b **L 1-20**. The repetitions begin in v. 1—LXX omits *2b, g, h*—where doom is pronounced on Babylon and its gods, Bel and Marduk. The foe 'out of the north' may be Media but more probably these vague terms are intended simply to suggest the weird and uncanny. Babylon's fall shall initiate Israel's return—probably 'Judah' was added here and Israel represents the whole people—which Jeremiah anticipated (3:12, 30:1f.). The people who had been misled by their leaders shall return to their true habitation and rest in the Lord. Foreigners in Babylon are counselled to flee (8) for Babylon is about to fall to the nations. Babylon itself, still sitting in arrogant ease, is warned of her doom (11–13) and the foe is summoned to sack the city (14–16). Great nations, Assyria and Babylon, had preyed upon Yahweh's flock but the Good Shepherd of Israel will take vengeance on the oppressors and lead a people, restored and forgiven, back to the old homesteads.

c **21-28**. There is here a play upon words. Merathaim is *nar Marratim*, the southern point of Babylon's border, while Pekod (Pukudu ; cf. Ezek. 23:23) is to the east. Hebrew vocalised the first term to read 'double defiance' and the second to read 'punishment', the one term denoting the character of Babylon and the other indicating its final fate. The smasher of nations shall be smashed : she is trapped like a wild beast in a snare, and Yahweh hath done it. Her strong men ('bulls') will be slain, and the exiles freed shall carry the glad message to Zion. **28**. 'vengeance for his temple' : according to 7:14 the Temple was destroyed because of Israel's sin.

d **29-41**. A renewed call for Babylon's destruction. Neither military might nor the wisdom of seers will avail against the Holy One of Israel (this term of Isaiah's occurs only this once in Jeremiah). The 'ban' is to be applied and total destruction made of the proud land. **38**. For 'drought' read 'sword' (BH). The five-times-repeated 'sword' is very emphatic.

e **41-46**. The first two verses are an almost exact reproduction of 6:22–4, while 44–6 are repeated from 49:19–21. Babylon is the very soul of arrogance, 'the Atheist of the OT and the Antichrist of the NT' (G. A. Smith), but the sound of her fall will reverberate throughout the nations. The preceding sections declared Yahweh's intention to destroy : here we are assured that he has the power to bring it to pass.

f **LI 1-19**. The destroyers are summoned to execute the will of God and assurance is given that Yahweh will not forsake his people or leave them 'widowed'. Babylon, glorious in her power, who seduced the nations, is sick unto death ; no human medicaments or potions can heal her. For all her wealth and might she is doomed : the invaders are at her gates. Israel shall see her vindication. **15-19** repeat 10:12–16. **1**. Chaldaea is here represented by a cipher, as is also Babylon in 41. This literary device (*Atbash*) consists in substituting the last letter for the first of the alphabet, the second last for the second, and so on.

g **20-26**. The might of Babylon is great and it has been used as Yahweh's instrument, but it lifted haughty hands against his Temple to provoke his avenging wrath. The state, that seemed massive and mighty as a mountain, shall be laid low by his avenging fury.

h **27-44**. Babylon cannot stand against Yahweh. The report of her fall spreads like a forest fire. Memories are stirred and the exiles recall how the mighty king swallowed them up as the great fish swallowed Jonah. Let Yahweh remember Israel ! Yahweh is mindful of his own, and soon 'the ultimate decency of things' shall be shown. Babylon will drink the cup of his wrath and sleep an endless sleep. On this assurance follows the 'taunt-song' (41–3). Like Jonah Israel will be delivered from the devouring monster. **27**. Ararat, Minni, Ashkenaz : peoples conquered by the Medes. Ararat is roughly Armenia. The Minni (Manneans) and Ashkenaz (Scythians) lived around Lake Urmia. **44b-49a :** lacking in LXX. 489h

45-58 Let Israel hope in the Lord—The final event may linger yet awhile and rumours may disturb the waiting folk. But Yahweh is 'wakeful' to fulfil his word. The slain of Israel shall be avenged and the dishonour done to the Temple by alien rites shall be purged away. The lofty city shall be brought low Already its crashing fall may be heard. This is Yahweh's doing : he alone hath wrought it. i

59-64 An Appendix to the Oracle—According to this the written oracle was weighted and sunk in the Euphrates. There is no record elsewhere of a visit by Zedekiah to Babylon and many scholars judge this section to be unhistorical. Budde, Cornill and Driver uphold its historic value : the mention of Seraiah, own brother to Baruch, would seem to support this position. The oracle carried to Babylon need not be identified with the two preceding chapters (which would be highly dangerous reading in Babylon). The LXX calls Seraiah 'the commissary of tribute' and says he went 'from Zedekiah'. This symbolic action, which has the marks of history, emphasised in striking form the word, 'Thus shall Babylon sink to rise no more'. j

LII Historical Appendix—This is reproduced mainly from 2 Kg. 24:18–25:30 (except for 25:22–6). It is appended here as 2 Kg. 18–20 is appended to the end of Isaiah (36–9), though with less obvious reason, for it tells nothing of Jeremiah. It may have been added to show the fulfilment of his prophecies. k

We here call attention only to more or less significant divergences in the narrative as given here and in Kg. The general exposition will be found in the commentary to Kg. **4-16** are also found in abbreviated form in 39:1–10, while 10, 11 are slightly shortened in Kg. We have additional information as to the slaughter of all the princes and as to the fact that Zedekiah spent the rest of his days in prison. **12** reads 'tenth day' where Kg. has 'seventh day'. In **15** we should, with Kg., probably omit 'the poorest of the people'. **17-23** are abbreviated in Kg. Where **25** reads 'seven' Kg. reads 'five'. **28-30** are lacking both in Kg. and LXX : the editor seems to have had a separate source here. The precise figures given would suggest authenticity though they seem rather low and vary considerably from the 10,000 of 2 Kg. 24:14. The first deportation took place under Jehoiachin (597 B.C.), the second, of those in Jerusalem, in 586 B.C., while the third, of which we have no other reliable report, occurred in

582–581 B.C. **31-34**. Jehoiachin languished long in confinement but his position was eased at the accession of Amel Marduk in 561 B.C. The occasion may have been a general amnesty or it may have been only a special favour to the king. It is good that the book should end on this note of modified joy : it was a sign and token of the general release so soon to come for all the exiles. l

Bibliography—COMMENTARIES : J. Bewer, Annotated Bible (1954) ; L. E. Binns, WC (1919) ; A. Condamin, EBib. 12 (1936) ; C. H. Cornill, *Das Buch Jeremia* (1905) ; S. R. Driver, *The Book of the Prophet Jeremiah* (1906) ; B. Duhm, KHC (1901) ; F. Giesebrecht, HKAT (1907) ; J. P. Hyatt and S. R. Hopper, IB v (1956) ; E. Leslie, *Jeremiah* (trans. and int. 1954) ; S. Mowinckel, *De Senere Profeter*, Det Gamle Testamente 3 (1944) ; A. S. Peake, Cent.B (1910–12) ; W. Rudolph, HAT 12 (1947) ; A. W. Streane, CB (1913) ; P. Volz, KAT 10 (1928) ; A. Weiser, ATD (1952–5).

GENERAL : W. Erbt, *Jeremia und seine Zeit* (1902) ; J. R. Gillies, *Jeremiah : the Man and his Message* (1907) ; H. W. Hertzberg, *Prophet und Gott* (1923) ; S. Mowinckel, *Zur Komposition des Buches Jeremia* (1914) ; H. W. Robinson, *The Cross in the OT* (1955) ; J. Skinner, *Prophecy and Religion* (7th ed. 1951) ; G. A. Smith, *Jeremiah* (4th ed. 1951) ; J. Steinmann, *Le Prophète Jérémie* (1952) ; A. C. Welch, *Jeremiah* (1951).

LAMENTATIONS

By A. S. HERBERT

490a The importance of this small collection of poems becomes apparent when we study it against its **historical background.** These poems arose within, and were composed for, a people who had suffered irretrievable calamity. Their land had suffered the full horrors of invasion from the Babylonian armies, and was defenceless against the border raids from Edomite tribes. Their capital city, Jerusalem, had been captured, looted and destroyed ; the king and the royal household, the nobles and the priests, everyone in fact who was capable of exercising influence and might therefore be a centre of disaffection against the Empire, had been taken into exile or had fled for safety to Egypt. It needs little imagination to recognise that for those left in Judah as for those taken into exile, there was no political future. It is true that the land with much diminished borders was set under the governorship of the Judaean, Gedaliah, but the crazy ambition of Ishmael of the Davidic line destroyed even that alleviation (cf. 2 Kg. 25:22–6 ; Jer. 40, 41). The words of Ezekiel had been utterly fulfilled (cf. Ezek. 7). But for this people the disaster was even more terrible, it was the total collapse of their religious faith and hope. For the city was the place that Yahweh had chosen (Dt. 12:5, etc.). Moreover, since the great reformation of King Josiah, Jerusalem and the Temple were the unique centres of the religion of Yahweh's people (2 Kg. 23), where alone the sacred rites might be performed. The conclusion was inescapable ; either Yahweh had been defeated by the deities of the invading armies, or he had abandoned his ancient people. When the invading armies had withdrawn after the land had been ' pacified ', the majority would come to the bitter conclusion that Yahweh had ' no power to deliver ' (Isa. 50:2). For them, since men must worship some god, the way of common sense would be to come to terms with the deities of the invader, or the old divinities of the land (cf. Jer. 7:18, 44:17ff.). There were some, however, who remembered the words of the prophets, and would see in these events the fulfilment of Yahweh's judgment on his people ; ' The Lord has rejected and forsaken the generation of his wrath ' (Jer. 7:29). The former point of view is a disillusioned attempt to find some alleviation of a hopeless situation. But, however ' natural ', it is hopeless. It is the abandonment of all that made this people distinctive, and the result could only be their absorption into the life of their neighbours. It is the end of Israel. The second reaction is much more painful, yet in it are the seeds of hope. It is an interpretation of the events of history in personal terms, the judgment of God. It is the recognition that however tragic and grievous are these events, Yahweh is still the sovereign lord of his people. It means, moreover, that the grace of penitence has begun to work in men's hearts. The acknowledgment of divine judgment is also self-criticism, even though that may seem to be too late. History was to show that among those who refused the ' easy way out ', and accepted the pain and grief of this disaster as the Lord's punishment, there was a future even more wonderful than they had known under David or Solomon. For the God whose judgment they acknowledged was he whom they had first known as having ' seen the affliction of my people ' and as having known (i.e. entered into and 490a
experienced) their sufferings (Exod. 3:7).

It was from such circles that these five laments b
arose. Traditionally these poems have been associated with Jeremiah (*Baba Bathra* 15*a*), and this association is reflected in the ancient versions of the Bible as in our English versions. No such connection is suggested by its title or position in the Heb. Bible, where it appears among ' The Writings ', has the title ' How ' (the first word of the book), and is the first of the Megilloth (see §57*d*). Neither the style nor the contents suggest Jeremianic authorship, and if we rightly understand the purpose of these laments as penitential liturgies, the association with the prophet is even less probable. It is not likely that Jeremiah would have used such words as we find in 2:9*c*, 4:17 or 5:7. Apparently the tradition arose from a mistaken interpretation of 2 Chr. 35:25 and the assumption that 4:20 referred to Josiah. The suggestion however that these poems come from the time of Antiochus Epiphanes or later (cf. A. Duff in Peake's Commentary, 1st ed. and literature quoted there) is hardly convincing, and has received little support. The association of these poems with what we know of the conditions in Judah during the period 586–540 B.C. may be regarded as reasonably sure. The probable chronological order is 2 and 4 (soon after 586 B.C.), 5, 1, 3 (later post-exilic dates for 3 and 5 have been suggested, but the grounds are inevitably subjective). The contents and emotional feeling of 2 and 4 seem to be especially closely related to the disasters of the fall of Jerusalem. All the poems reflect an immediate experience of conditions in the land of Judah. It is probable that the laments were composed by more than one poet.

They are not, however, poems expressing the c
sorrows and distress of an individual poet. They have their setting in the life of the people of the land. Jewish liturgical tradition, in appointing this book to be read on the commemoration of the destruction of the Temple, the Fast of the 9th of Ab, may well be true to their original purpose. Evidently at an early date after 586 B.C. the practice arose among the worshippers of Yahweh to come to mourn over the ruined Temple (Jer. 41:5f.) and such appointed Fast-days continued into the post-exilic age (Zech. 7:3ff., 8:18f.). The most natural setting for these laments is such an occasion of mourning over the ruined city and shrine. There is evidently a close connection between these poems and such Psalms as 77, 79, 102. They belong to the category of liturgical poetry which may be described as communal laments. However truly they express genuinely emotional distress, the contents of these poems suggest that they were composed for the surviving community of Yahweh's loyal ones.

This is made even clearer by the obvious features of d
these poems, their **poetic form** and their acrostic character. Basically, the poetic form is that of the *Ḳînāh* or 3:2 metre. (For a discussion of the forms of Heb. poetry, see §72*a* ; and T. H. Robinson, *The Poetry of the OT.*) This form coupled with a masterly choice of language has an almost hypnotic effect comparable to the effect of Chopin's *Marche Funèbre*. It is characteristic of the dirge in 2 Sam.

490d 1:19–27 ; Am. 5:16f. These dirges were of a ritual character and were normally uttered by a professionally trained class of women, Jer. 9:17ff. It was thus used by prophets in order to stimulate sorrow for a predicted disaster (i.e. national death) and so heartfelt penitence and return to the God who will restore to life (cf. Jer. 9:16f., 22, 18ff. ; Am. 5:2). It should be noticed that the first word of Lam. 1, 2, 4 is the characteristic first word of the dirge.

The next feature is the acrostic form of the first four poems. (The last poem is not alphabetic but it has the same number of verses, 22, as there are letters in the Heb. alphabet.) There are, however, variations among the four. Thus chs. 1, 2 and 4 have a stanza to each letter, but the letter is used only at the beginning of the stanza. In ch. 3 the three stichoi (balanced couplets) of each stanza begin with the proper letter as in Ps. 119. Again ch. 4 differs from 1–3 in having two instead of three lines to the stanza. Further the order of the Heb. letters varies as between ch. 1 and chs. 2–4 ; the sixteenth (*'Ayin*) and seventeenth (*Pē*) letters in 1 (cf. Ps. 119) are reversed in chs. 2–4. No obvious reason for the variation in alphabetic order has been suggested. This acrostic form appears highly artificial, 'scholastic and rather petty' ; yet there is nothing artificial about the contents. It may be that what appears superficially as artificial is rather a strict and disciplined form comparable to a Bach fugue. In part the acrostic form may be for mnemonic purposes to lead the congregation through these prayers of lament and penitence to the hope of restoration. They may even have been composed in this form to express the ritual requirement of completeness, as we might say 'from A to Z' or in terms of the Heb. alphabet 'from Aleph to Taw' ; we might compare the saying in Rev. 1:8 'I am the Alpha and Omega' (cf. Rev. 21:6, 22, 13).

491a We would see these poems then as composed during those dark and seemingly hopeless years 586–540 B.C. by shrine priests or prophets who had escaped the wholesale deportations of 597 and 586. They were composed for a disillusioned and despairing people who gathered at the ruined shrine, where once in magnificent ritual the divine blessing had been sought and found, to mourn the vanished glory and the ruined altar. Their thoughts were led through sorrow to repentance and thus to the rebirth of the ancient hope : 'For the Lord will not cast off for ever' and his 'throne endures to all generations', and 'his mercies never come to an end'.

b **I The First Lament—1-11.** The leader speaks in the name of the community, describing the disasters that have befallen Yahweh's people and Jerusalem. It is a lament with, at its centre (5), a confession of sin and acknowledgment of divine judgment. **12-22.** Zion speaks, through the lips of the leader, uttering her grief, accepts the divine judgment (17) as right (18ff.) and concludes with a prayer for requital against her exultant enemies. The whole is an alphabetic acrostic in twenty-two stanzas, normally three lines to a stanza in *Ḳînāh* (3:2) measure.

c **1. How** (so 2:1, 4:1 ; cf. 2 Sam. 1:25 ; Isa. 1:21 ; Jer. 48:17, etc.). The word is commonly used to introduce a dirge for the dead. It should be treated as an exclamation and introduce the whole stanza :

O how ! She sits solitary, the city once full of people
She has become like a widow. Once great among the nations
She was princess among the cities ; she has become a slave.

2. Cf. Jer. 22:22, 30:14 ; Ezek. 2:3, 22ff., a reference to vain political alliances. **4.** The background of this whole verse is the cultus to which the people used to come, in which the priests and virgins performed their ritual acts. Deprived of all this, Zion knows only bitterness. **5. transgressions:** better 'rebellions' against Yahweh's rule. **6.** Cf. 2 Sam. 1:19. **7. bitterness:** the word occurs again only in 3:19, and 491c
Isa. 58:7, and appears to mean the condition of being outcast, or homeless. The margin 'wandering' is to be preferred. (*d*) 'The adversaries mock as they see her because of her downfall.' **8f.** The realism of these verses (cf. Ezek. 16), though offensive to Western sentiment, well represents the experience of shameful humiliation. Jerusalem is as a woman taken in adultery. **10.** Everything associated with the covenant relationship and its renewal has been profaned.

12. With this verse begins the lament of Jerusalem. d
The opening words, although they can hardly be a translation of the Heb., represent the general sense of the verse. The Heb. MSS suggest that the text is uncertain. The suggestion (Löhr) 'Therefore all ye that pass by, look and see' is probably the most satisfactory and makes good use of the Heb. consonants. **13.** 'he made it descend' : this reading has good support from the LXX, and involves little consonantal change. The text 'and he has mastered me' seems hardly appropriate to the verse. **14.** A difficult verse to translate, as the EVV show. A possible translation with slight emendations would be :

He has kept watch over my rebellions ;
In his hand they are entwining ;
They have come up upon my neck,
He has caused my strength to fail . . .

The meaning would seem to be : 'God has taken my acts of rebellion and placed them around my neck as a necklace, which instead of adorning (and perhaps giving magical strength), weighs me down and weakens me' ; cf. 5:5 ; Isa. 52:2. **15.** The collapse of Judah's army before the enemy which is described as Yahweh's people summoned to the sacrificial banquet. **16. courage** is the Heb. *nephesh*, the life force, commonly translated 'soul'. **17.** Apparently a rubric, with comment, introducing the next phase of the liturgy. To stretch out the hands is the normal attitude of supplication, the palms open to receive the gift from God.

18f. Confession of Guilt—19. my lovers: prob- e
ably the expected allies. The alteration of metre (2:2) in the first four lines emphasises the sense of desolation. Jerusalem was abandoned by man and God.

20-22 Prayer for divine Action—The prayer for vengeance offends us who have not suffered the horrors of invasion. But the terminology is conventional (cf. Ps. 69, 109), and fundamentally a prayer that the Lord will vindicate his elect. Jerusalem has sinned, and suffered the consequences. There is no attempt to evade that. But in a morally ordered world, a like fate should attend all evil-doing when it is brought before the divine judge. It should be noted that from the same period comes another way of dealing with iniquity (Isa. 53). And the Servant Songs should be read in the context of the Law, and the 'Imprecatory' Psalms. **20. my soul:** Heb. 'my bowels', characteristically the seat of emotion (cf. 2:11). Possibly the last line should read 'in the house there is death'. **21. bring thou** represents a slight emendation of the MT (see note 'thou hast brought'), but the latter might be retained in the sense of an utterance of faith whose fulfilment is confidently expected. The Day of the Lord will certainly come, because it is already determined by God. **22.** The background is that of the law-court in which God, the judge, will give sentence and effect it. The sentiments may repel but that should not obscure for us the hope that is expressed, based on the faith in him who comes to the help of the oppressed and sets right what is manifestly wrong. That faith receives finer expression elsewhere, but it was the same faith, not primarily in the triumph of the Jewish people, but in the sovereignty of God.

II The Second Lament—If, as we believe, this f
lament was composed soon after the fall of Jerusalem, it is remarkable in its refusal to recognise any other agency than Yahweh as the bringer of disaster. Thus

491f from the beginning the afflicted people are led to a confession of guilt, and an appeal for help. Everything in the poem fits the historical situation of the period soon after 586 B.C. The fact that there are affinities in this poem with both Ezekiel and the Psalter may suggest (as is inherently probable) that both the prophet and the poet are so familiar with the Psalms as unconsciously to use the familiar phrases. In verses 1, 2, 5, 18, 19 we find the word *'ᵃdhōnay* used for 'Yahweh' ('Lord' for 'LORD'). In each case however there is good Heb. evidence that 'Yahweh' was original. Later Jewish sentiment, for motives of reverence, in their reading aloud always used *'ᵃdhōnay* for the proper name, and sometimes this has replaced the proper name in the written text.

In spite of the intense emotional tone of this poem, evoked by the dreadful scenes of material damage and human suffering, the lament seems to have a definite structure appropriate to its liturgical use. **1-10** describes the destruction of Jerusalem as the work of Yahweh. **11-17.** The leader expresses his own distress at the suffering of the inhabitants. **18f.** summons to Zion to pray to the Lord. **20-2.** The supplication.

492a **1.** As in the first lament, **How** is the opening cry of a dirge. The glory of God has departed from Zion, and the city is now under a thick cloud. The Temple and the Ark have been destroyed, and God has taken no action. **2. Kingdom:** we ought perhaps to read with the LXX 'her King and her rulers'. **in dishonour** is hardly adequate. The Heb. word means 'profane' and this is the appropriate word for the Davidic king who was the divinely appointed mediator for the blessing; cf. Isa. 11:1ff. The king was much more than a political figure; he was the psychic centre of Israel's life, Lam. 4:20. The verb is used to describe the preparation of the altar, sacred objects, or the name of God. **3. right hand:** the strong power to help and save which God has displayed in Israel's history; cf. Ps. 16:8, 11, 77:4. **4.** The metre in this verse is in some confusion, and it is doubtful whether 'set' can qualify 'right hand'. The verse may have read originally:

He has bent his bow like an enemy, taking his stand like a foe;
He has slain all delight of the eyes in the tent of the daughter of Zion;
He has poured out his fury like fire . . .

5. The closing words of this verse might be rendered, to reproduce the Heb. assonance, 'mourning and moaning' or 'moaning and groaning'. **6** is difficult, especially the word translated **like that of a garden.** The addition of one letter to this word would give the meaning: 'He has broken down his booth (tabernacle) like a thief'. In this as the following verse the lament describes the end of all those cultic activities through which Israel was wont to know the renewal of life; and this has been brought about by him who is the 'Renewer of life'; cf. Ps. 74. **7.** Where once the solemn assembly gathered for the appointed feasts and uttered the ritual cry, the profane enemy came with violence and shouting. **9. ruined and broken:** these are variants and one of the verbs should be omitted. With the removal of the king to an unholy land, the divine direction (the law) can no more be given; and the (cultic) prophets can no longer receive an authentic vision when the sanctuary has been destroyed. **10** describes the depth of mourning and desolation.

b **11-17 The Lament of the Leader**—While this undoubtedly expresses his own grief, something more may be intended, and is suggested by its inclusion in the whole lament. If, as it seems, he is taking over the sacred functions of the king, he may be both representing the people's distress to Yahweh and Yahweh's grief over his stricken people; the divine judgment on his people and (17) their acceptance. These verses would then be more in the nature of a divine oracle expressing Yahweh's grief over the fate of 'my people'. 492b Such 'oracles' occur in the Psalter; cf. Ps. 81:6ff. The strong emotional terms of 11 have their parallel in Hos. 11:8. It seems difficult to account in any other way for the distinction between the speaker and the people in vv. 13-17. The speaker has become, like the prophets, the mouthpiece of Yahweh.

11. my heart, lit. 'my liver'. Although the Akkadian equivalent is commonly used in a psychical sense, this is the only certain occasion of its use in Heb. It is probable, however, that the word 'glory' in (RV) Gen. 49:6; Ps. 7:5(6), 16:9, 30:12(13), 57:8(9), 108:1(2) should be read as 'liver'. The consonants in Heb. are identical and in RSV the assumption is made that 'liver' was original to the passages, and that it was used in a metaphorical sense ('spirit' or 'soul'). It is normal in biblical usage to speak of various parts of the body as centres of, and identical with, psychical conditions. **12.** It is possible that 'and wine' should be omitted from this line. **13.** There can be no comparison with Jerusalem, for no other place could claim to be Yahweh's dwelling-place and have fallen so low. **vast as the sea is your ruin:** the appropriateness of this phrase might escape us. But the Sea is the sentient being that represents the hostility to the living God. In popular Semitic thought, the sea threatened the sovereignty of the gods and was only overcome after a great combat. Echoes of this popular belief appear elsewhere; cf. Ps. 74:13. So Zion has been broken as the sea-monster was broken in the Canaanite myth. **14.** The language of this verse, in Heb., closely resembles Ezek. 13:15f., 22:28 and should be translated:

Your prophets observed for you—vanity and whitewash;
They did not lay bare your iniquity—to restore your well-being;
They observed for you oracles—vanity and dispersion.

That is to say that they prophesied 'Peace' when there was no 'peace'; they were 'taking the Lord's name in vain' (Exod. 20:7), created an illusion of fair security, instead of leading the people to genuine repentance, and so made judgment inevitable. **15.** Cf. Ps. 50:2; Ezek. 16:14. And for the same theme against Tyre, cf. Ezek. 27:25, 28:12. **The perfection of beauty** truly belonged to Zion but only as it is the habitation of Yahweh. **16f.** Here, as in chs. 3 and 4 and apparently also in Ps. 9, 10, *Pē* precedes *'Ayin.* The resemblances in 16 to Ps. 25:21, 35:16 and in 17 to Lev. 26:14ff.; Dt. 28:15ff., make evident the liturgical setting of the lament, for all these passages are related to the pre-exilic Jerusalem liturgies. **16. destroyed:** better 'swallowed her up'.

18f. The Call to Prayer—18. A difficult verse but c RSV gives the correct meaning. **19.** The verse appears to have a couplet too many. This may however be deliberate. There are three conventional calls to prayer applied to a particular situation. Jerusalem, the mother, pleads for her helpless babes.

20-22 The Supplication—The dreadful horrors of a d city first starved into submission and then given over to the sword, are described. The prophets are the regular order of shrine prophets. All this is recognised as a terrible replacement of the appointed feast-day that should renew the covenant relationship, and a fulfilment of the unheeded word of Jeremiah (6:25).

III The Third Lament—Probably the latest in 493a date, but apparently before the new hope stirred by the new conditions under the Persian Empire. The fact that there is no reference to the restored Temple make a 5th-cent. date less likely. A date that would suit the feeling of disillusionment and deferred hope would be about 540 B.C. The immediate horrors of ch. 2 have become less, but there is no obvious sign of a restoration. In form it is remarkable, in that in each stanza the three lines all begin with the same letter. So vv. 1, 2, 3 begin with *'Āleph,* 4, 5, 6 with

493a *Bēth* and so to the end of the lament. The fact that it contains many quotations from, or echoes of, the Psalter and Jer. is also to be noted. Most remarkable is the use of the first person singular in vv. 1–24, 48–66. The very particularity of many of these phrases prompts the question 'Who is the poet?'; cf. vv. 1–6, 16–18, 52–4. On the other hand 40–7 use the first person plural. Yet v. 48 (singular) is the closing line of a plural stanza and, with the remaining verses, forms part of 'our' prayer. This might be explained by supposing that the lament is a compilation from previously existing lament psalms by a poet who was greatly influenced by Jeremiah. Yet the notable acrostic character of the whole would make it necessary so much to modify the earlier material that such an explanation appears over-ingenious. Further both the inclusion of this lament with the other four, and vv. 40–7, would lead us to suppose that this is a community lament. Further, as we enumerate the afflictions described in the lament we feel that they are too many to have befallen an individual, but are quite appropriate to a community. We meet the same problem in many of the Pss. which are expressed in the form of an individual lament, where again there is a rapid transition from singular to plural (cf. Ps. 44:4f., 75:1, 9, 106:4–6, 118), and the same description of an individual's affliction in terms appropriate to a community. It would be reasonable, therefore, to think of this lament as offered by the leader in the midst of the community on their behalf. He is organically related to them, and seeks to lead them into the same religious apprehension of the affliction that he shares with them, that they might also share his faith. The leader of the community is not merely a pious individual, but one in whose soul this afflicted people comes to focus, and through him they will find again the 'steadfast love' and 'faithfulness' of God. It is perhaps for that very reason that so much of this lament reads like a catena of phrases from the Pss., i.e. familiar liturgical phrases. Although the Servant Songs of Isa. go beyond the lament and come from another environment, there is a relationship of suffering in terms of Israel's faith.

b The lament may be conveniently divided: **1:18**, the lament of the leader on behalf of the community. **19-39**, confession of faith and hope. **40-57**, prayer of the community. **58-66**, confession of faith and hope.

1. the man: the Heb. word used here suggests 'the strong man' who has been brought into weakness. **6.** We need to remember that there was at this time no doctrine of the resurrection. The dead went to Sheol, the place of darkness, the antithesis of the living God; cf. Ps. 38:4–6, 10–12. **7-9.** Against this description of actual experience we can set the vigour of the prophetic hope in Isa. 40:3–5. **14. peoples:** this, as against the RV (my people), is very probably the correct reading and has good support in Heb. MSS. If it is accepted it strengthens the suggestion that the 'I' is the whole people. **17. my soul is bereft:** a repointing of the Heb. consonants gives this translation and has the support of some ancient versions.

c **19. bitterness:** cf. 1:7. **Remember:** it is probable that we should read 'I remember' with LXX. The prayer to God has not yet begun. **22. The steadfast love:** one of the great words of OT vocabulary, and the translation well represents the meaning, for it includes both the love which was at the heart of the covenant relationship and the determination (on God's side) to maintain the covenant. This with the following verses is a recall to Israel's ancient faith generated in the great work of salvation from Egypt. The reading of this verse involves the omission of the AV word 'because' and a slight emendation with support of some ancient versions. **25-7.** Each of the three lines begins with the same word, 'Good'. **31-9.** A great confession of faith which leads to genuine penitence. **33. willingly:** lit. 'from his heart'—the heart in Heb. thought is the centre especially of the will. **36. not approve:** lit. 'not see'. 'To see' is not to be thought of in our rather passive sense, but in the active sense of receiving into the personality; cf. 2 Kg. 10:16; Jer. 29:38. Characteristically, Yahweh will not 'see with approval' oppression or injustice. **38.** For Israel there can be only one sovereign power in the world; cf. Isa. 45:7.

d **41.** Only the man of clean hands and pure heart may approach God. Only God can make them clean and pure. So the hands, i.e. the ritual act, and the heart, i.e. the inner life, must be lifted to him in prayer. **42. We have transgressed and rebelled:** both verbs express rebellion. **thou hast not forgiven:** the fact of affliction shows that the amnesty has not been granted. It is this theological approach to disaster that leads Israel to a deeper repentance; hence the transition from v. 54 to v. 55. **56.** It may be better to punctuate and translate the verse: 'Thou hast heard my cry; close not thine ear to my respite [i.e. plea for respite]', omitting the last word in the Heb. as, originally, a variant: 'salvation'. **57ff.** Cf. Ps. 69. **58-63.** The oppressed and afflicted pleads his cause before the righteous Judge to whom he looks not only to pass sentence but to effect it in order that right may prevail. 'Will not God vindicate his elect . . . ?' Lk. 18:7. **65. the curse** is the calamity divinely brought upon an evil-doer.

e **IV The Fourth Lament**—Again in this lament we are very close to the ruin and disaster that befell Jerusalem at the hands of the invaders. It is similar to ch. 2 in its acrostic form, but has only two lines to each letter. Again we find a special condemnation of the shrine prophets and priests (13) and the horrors of the siege (10). But a particular point of interest is the singling out of what appears to be the greatest of all disasters, the loss of the Davidic king (20), the very centre of Israel's life, specially equipped by Yahweh for his task. However badly most of these kings had fulfilled this divine commission, the blessing once and for all given to David was a permanent element in the life of this people, and seems to have been permanently enshrined in the ritual recitals. (For a full treatment of this subject, cf. A. R. Johnson, *Sacral Kingship in Ancient Israel.*) We may again read this as a recital at the ruined shrine. It begins with a description of the national tragedy, **1-12**, and an acknowledgment of guilt, **13-15**; this leads to a religious evaluation of the disaster, **16-20**, and an expectation of divine action against Edom, **21-2**.

f **1.** The verse is clearly inspired by the sight of the burned and looted Temple. **is changed** is just possible. It may be a misunderstanding for a Heb. word meaning 'old' (*yāshān* for MT *yishnē*). So: 'How is the ancient gold become dim, that fine gold'. **2** suggests a fine insight. The fine gold of the Temple is the people of God. **3.** It is difficult to see why Zion is described as cruel and failing in maternal love. Perhaps originally it was 'daughters', and so referring to the mothers (cf. vv. 4 and 10). **6. chastisement:** the Heb. word means both the iniquity and the chastisement that follows on iniquity. Similarly **punishment** and sin. The fate of the 'cities of the valley' (Gen. 18, 19) was perpetuated in Israel's thought, perhaps forming part of a ritual curse. **no hand being laid on it** should be translated 'no hand whirled about her', and appears to mean that no human hand 'whirled' the curse around her head; cf. 2 Sam. 3:29. It was a direct act of God. **7-10.** Better to be killed in battle and so to descend to Sheol as a warrior than to die in this weakened and deformed condition when they will be unrecognisable. **10.** The word for 'compassionate' emphasises the word for mothers, being cognate with the word for 'womb'.

g **11f.** It is quite incredible that a people's God should destroy his own habitation. **13.** The real sin and iniquity (v. 6) lay in those who were the recognised mediators of the divine revelation, and should have exalted Yahweh's righteousness; so **14f.** the holy ones become unclean as lepers. The lines in **15** are

493g unusually long and the words **men cried at them** and **men said among the nations** may be explanatory glosses. **16.** They suffer the fate of Cain. **17** appears to refer to Egypt, stigmatised more than a century before as a broken reed, Isa. 36:6. **18-20.** The relentless pursuit of the besieged by the Babylonian armies reaches its climax in the capture of Zedekiah; cf. 2 Kg. 25:1–7; Jer. 39:1–9. **20.** This is more than a political disaster. The king was more than the head of the state; he was the person in whom all the psychic life of Israel was centred and through him in his cultic capacity, the blessing and protection of Yahweh was mediated. **21f.** Various Edomite tribes had taken advantage of Judah's stricken condition and, after invasion, were granted Judaean territory. Their ancient kinship with Israel makes their gloating the more heinous. We note the same horror at Edomite action in Ps. 137:7; Isa. 63:1–6; Jer. 49:7ff.; Ezek. 35; Ob. 10–15.

h **V A Prayer for God's Help in Time of Need**—This poem differs from the other four in that (*a*) it is not acrostic although it has twenty-two verses, and (*b*) it is not in the *Ḳinah* (3:2) rhythm; predominantly it is in the 3:3 metre. It is evidently a congregational prayer, rather than a lament by the leader for and in the presence of the congregation. The obvious parallels between v. 21 and Ps. 80:3, 7, 19 and Jer. 31:18 and the somewhat striking phrase 'Renew our days as of old', may help us to recognise the setting of the prayer. It is clear from Ps. 80 and Jer. that a congregational prayer for restoration formed a normal part of the cult liturgy. It is possible that such a prayer formed part of the national act of penitence at the new year. But the proper place for that was at the national shrine. When that was destroyed, the normal ritual actions could not be performed; and in any case how can such a prayer be offered when the Temple is in ruins and the place is forsaken by Yahweh (cf. Jer. 12:7–11). The prayer therefore includes a petition for a divine restoration of his people and their ritual through which they may seek a renewal of the covenant relationship.

The exiled period seems the more natural historical setting, probably (v. 7) a generation after the destruction of Jerusalem and certainly before the rebuilding of the Temple (v. 18). The people are living in conditions of poverty and hardship, and see no hope of recovery. They cannot protect themselves against bandit raids; all their energies are spent in keeping alive. The memory of the horrors of invasion torment them, and the whole social structure has been destroyed. Yet when everything denies hope, the real hope remains. v. 19. And in that hope, as history has demonstrated, there was renewal of life.

i **1. Remember:** this is a word having greater significance than we usually associate with it. We should understand, 'Remember, and let that determine action'. 'Behold' and 'see' are probably variants. **2. Our inheritance:** the alienation of a family's inheritance had a religious significance; cf. 1 Kg. 21:3. **4.** It is normal in many parts of the world today for spring water and wood from the forest to be free for the peasant. A charge on these would be a heavy imposition. **5.** The words for **yoke** and **on** are spelt with the same consonants in Heb. One of these, omitted by haplography, has been restored in RSV. **6.** The reference to Assyria is difficult since the Empire had been destroyed in the previous century and was in any case not, like Egypt, a potential ally; and unless the prayer belongs to a much later period it is not likely that it is used as a metaphorical term for the enemy of the people of God. It may be a striking way of saying 'We have looked to the ends of the earth for help'. Or it may, if v. 7 is a logical sequence, be a reference to the confused statesmanship in Judah of the 8th cent. B.C. which was condemned by the prophets. **7** is not a contradiction of Jer. 31:29 and Ezek. 18:2, but is complementary; cf. v. 16. What is morally and spiritually disastrous is to say that present evil is solely the result of the sins of the fathers. **8. slaves rule over us** probably refers to the minor colonial and civil servants of the Babylonian Empire. **9.** 'the sword in the wilderness': a reference to desert marauders to whose attacks this land is always liable unless it is well policed. Vv. 9–18 describe the total breakdown of the ordered conditions of life that prevailed under strong local government. The Judaean province was of no economic importance to the Babylonian Empire, and provided that it could not become a centre for insurrection, the condition of its inhabitants could be ignored.

j **19-22.** This, as the climax of the prayer in which the desperate conditions have been described with utmost realism, is one of the great utterances of faith in the Bible. It takes its place with Ps. 22; Hab. 3:17–19 and Rom. 8:35–9. **20** and **22** should be read in the light of Ps. 74 and 79. The Rabbis directed that when Lam. was read aloud, **21** should be read again after **22.** Similar directions were given for the closing passages of Ec., Isa. and Mal.

This book presents us with first-hand evidence of a people who have suffered the worst horrors of material destruction, physical suffering and religious despair. It shows also that among them were those who had found the source of hope and renewal of life in the midst of despair and death and exercised their pastoral office to bring a dying people to the living God.

Bibliography—COMMENTARIES: W. F. Adeney, Ex.B (1901); S. Goldman, Soncino Books of the Bible (1946); M. Haller, HAT (1940); M. Löhr, HKAT (1907); F. Nötscher, Ech.B (1947); A. S. Peake, Cent.B; W. Rudolph, KAT (1939); A. W. Streane, CB (1913); A. Tony, Bible du Centenaire (1947).

OTHER LITERATURE: N. K. Gottwald, *Studies in the Book of Lamentations* (1954); G. B. Gray, *The Forms of Hebrew Poetry* (1915), 87–120; T. H. Robinson, *The Poetry of the OT* (1947), 205–16.

Articles in Dict. de la Bible, Supplément (A. Gélin); EB (T. K. Cheyne); EBrit., 11th ed. (C. J. Ball); EBrit., 13th ed. (T. H. Robinson); HDB (J. A. Selbie).

EZEKIEL

By J. MUILENBURG

494a Among all the figures who make their appearance in the history of ancient Israel, there is none perhaps more alien to the mood and temper of Western culture than the prophet Ezekiel. At least so it has been in past generations. His personality was said to betray signs of acute abnormality. His visions seemed strange and other-worldly; his apparent harshness and exaggeration repelled not a few of his readers; his imagery was often obscure or unintelligible. His literary style was prolix and repetitive, his protracted narratives of harlotry revolting, his answer to the vexing problems of theodicy too neat and simple to be convincing. Perhaps contemporary response to the prophet will prove to be otherwise: modern psychiatry, with its somewhat more sympathetic attitude to abnormality; contemporary art and literary criticism; present-day preoccupation with symbols; the realism of current fiction and drama; and the theology of recent decades with its stress upon the divine transcendence and 'otherness'—all these suggest that Ezekiel may yet come into his own as one of the greatest of all Israel's prophets.

To understand a writer one must enter into his world of thought and imagination, to sit where he sat, and, indeed, to think his thoughts after him.

Wer den Dichter will verstehen
Muss in Dichters Lande gehen.

Of no-one is this more true than of Ezekiel.

b **Composition of the Book**—Our understanding of Ezekiel as a person and of his prophetic thought will depend in no small measure upon our view of the composition of the prophecy which bears his name. In striking contrast to the other great prophetic corpuses (Isaiah, Jeremiah, and the Book of the Twelve), the dominant impression which one gains from reading the book is one of striking homogeneity. Indeed, until recent decades the prophecy has been generally held to be a literary unity. The same person was present throughout; the same style pervaded the oracles and visions; the same historical background was reflected from beginning to end; and essentially the same theology controlled the thought throughout. Diversity there was, to be sure, but no greater than one would expect from such a person as the book describes Ezekiel to have been or from such temporal circumstances as he is reported to have confronted in the shattering years of exile, national destruction, and the demolition of the ancient Solomonic Temple. So strong was this impression of unity that the book became a bulwark for historical criticism, for here, it was said, we have a literary monument of whose date and literary unity we may be confident. Consequently, other OT literary strata were dated by the fixed point of Ezekiel.

The unity of the book was further reflected in the apparent orderliness of its composition. After an elaborate theophany (1:1–28*a*) there follow oracles of doom against Jerusalem and Judah (chs. 2–24), judgments against the foreign nations (25–32), and assurances and promises of future restoration, both of the nation and its inhabitants and of the Temple and its community (chs. 33–9, 40–8). Moreover the book contained a number of dates, which with few excep- 494b
tions followed a chronological sequence. The date of 26:1, on the first day of the . . . month of the eleventh (MT) or twelfth (LXX[A]) year is later than 29:1, the twelfth day of the tenth month of the tenth year, but this is easily explained by the natural desire to include all the anti-Egyptian oracles together. 32:1 similarly is later than 32:17, but in 32:1 we should probably read with LXX and Syr. 'the eleventh year' (see Carl Gordon Howie, *The Date and Composition of Ezekiel* (1950), 39). It may be observed here that most scholars now recognise that only materials immediately following a date belong to the context and that other materials were inserted later.

But in more recent times the foregoing position has c
been subjected to heavy assault by many critics. Instead of a unified work by a single author, there is now presented to us a heterogeneity of materials from different writers and from different times. Many phenomena, to which scholars of the previous period did less than justice, now began to create problems of great difficulty. Not only was the text notoriously corrupt, as had always been recognised, but it became apparent that the orderly sequence was not as clear as had been supposed. Attention was called to many duplications, contradictions, inconsistencies, and such differences in terminology as would make it difficult to believe that we have to do with one and the same mind. The history of modern critical study has been sketched by many critics, e.g. Otto Eissfeldt, *Einleitung in das AT* (1st ed. 1934), 412–16, (2nd ed. 1956), 446–51; Howie, op cit., *passim*; H. G. May, IB vi (1956), 41–5; H. H. Rowley, 'The Book of Ezekiel and Modern Study', BJRL 36 (1953–4), 146–63. Notable among recent contributions is Gustav Hölscher's *Hesekiel: Der Dichter und das Buch* (1924). Following essentially the same principles as employed by B. Duhm in his commentary on Jeremiah (*Das Buch Jeremia übersetzt* (1903)), Hölscher contended that Ezekiel was primarily a poet and that of the 1,273 verses in the prophecy only 170 were in actuality of his authorship. Following a different methodology W. A. Irwin in *The Problem of Ezekiel* (1943) rescued some 261 verses 'genuine in whole or in part'. C. C. Torrey had long maintained that the book was a product of the Greek period, and in 1930 his book appeared under the title, *Pseudo-Ezekiel and the Original Prophecy*, in which he sought to demonstrate that *Ezekiel* was a pseudepigraph, purporting to come from the time of Manasseh (2 Kg. 21:2–16), but in reality written in 230 B.C., a view which he supported by its historical reflections and linguistic usage. To Volkmar Herntrich the key to the problem lay in the prophet's locale. While the prophecy consistently represents Ezekiel's ministry as carried on in Babylonia, his oracles are directed for the most part to Jerusalem, whither he was carried by the Spirit of Yahweh. Herntrich reaches the conclusion that in the original form of the book the whole of the prophet's ministry was in Jerusalem, and that the Babylonian setting was achieved through the work of an editor or editors. Torrey had already taken the same position. A number of scholars have been influenced by these results (Bertholet, I. G. Matthews, Pfeiffer, May).

494c More recently Georg Fohrer has written a critical commentary on the book, and comes to essentially conservative conclusions ; with the exception of twenty-four relatively short passages, the book is
d assigned to Ezekiel. Indications are not wanting that current investigations are moving in the same direction. That the book passed through a long and complicated literary history can scarcely be questioned, and that it represents a compilation of traditions of great diversity is apparent. But the weight of evidence seems to fall in favour of a view not greatly unlike that held by scholars of previous generations. The considerable disagreement in the results achieved by recent scholars does not inspire confidence in their validity. While the presence of expansions and supplements may well be admitted, even here the difficulty is that the passages are so similar in style and content that absolute certainty concerning their secondary character is excluded. H. G. May states the situation admirably : ' One of the most impressive aspects of the book, despite the opinion of some scholars, is its considerable homogeneity . . . Despite obvious evidence of later glosses and emendations, one person was largely responsible for the present form of the book, and it is often futile to depend upon literary criteria to isolate the work of Ezekiel ' (IB vi, 45). But if appeal is made to diversity of thought, the situation is quite as precarious, since differing historical situations would naturally elicit different responses ; moreover the presence of different literary types might explain in part the differences in terminology. Ezekiel spoke to the concrete needs of his people, and it is too much to ask that he should be logically self-consistent. Our conclusion, then, is that the book as a whole comes from him, that while there are expansions here and there throughout the book and perhaps numerous glosses, even these represent essentially the prophet's own point of view. Like the disciples of Second Isaiah (Isa. 56–66), the redactors stand in close relation with their master's teaching. Indeed it is not too much to say that the tradition which finds its classical expression in Ezek. perpetuated itself for many decades and even centuries.

495a **Ezekiel the Man**—Ezekiel was the son of a priest by the name of Buzi and was himself a priest. He was deported to Babylonia in the exile of 597 B.C. (1:1, 33:21, 40:1), and lived in the community of Tel-Abib on the banks of the river Chebar (3:15). It was there that he was called to be a prophet. In an extraordinary vision he sees the glory of Yahweh seated on a throne chariot, and the vision is followed by an audition in which he receives his commission. He lived in his own house, and the elders among the exiles came to him from time to time to inquire for a word from Yahweh (8:1, 14:1). He was a married man. On the eve of Jerusalem's destruction his wife dies, for the prophet a symbol of great portent. His prophetic career falls into two periods, from 593 B.C. to the fall of the city and from that event to 571 B.C., the date of his last oracle (29:17). Psychologically Ezekiel presents problems of great difficulty. His ecstatic transports and symbolic prophecies are very strange. They have been accounted for in various ways—by catalepsy, schizophrenia, Freudian presuppositions, etc. But most of these diagnoses fail to point out that this ' abnormality ' is consistent with his theology : his awareness of the divine transcendence, his conviction concerning the absolute holiness of God, and his experience as priest in the Temple. The comment of W. F. Albright is relevant here : ' Ezekiel was one of the greatest spiritual figures of all time, in spite of his tendency to psychic abnormality—a tendency which he shares with many other spiritual leaders of mankind. A certain ' abnormality ' is required to divert a man's thoughts and his emotional experiences from the common treadmill of human thinking and feeling ' (FSAC, 248f.).

b Ezekiel is the most many-sided and versatile personality in the history of Israel's religion ; in him are combined in unique fashion the activities and interests 495b
of the prophet, priest, pastor or ' watchman ', apocalyptist, theologian, ' architect ' of the new Temple, and the organiser of the ecclesiastical community. Like his prophetic predecessors, he comes with a message of divine judgment upon Israel, and in passionate utterances he inveighs against her sins, which for him are primarily apostasy and infidelity, pollution and profaneness, idolatry and ' bloodshed ', a term which includes within it all manner of ethical and ritual transgression. But he is also a priest in the cast of his mind, literary style, and thought. He shows such intimate familiarity with the Temple and its cult and has such an inward sense of its meaning that one is disposed to think of him as rather mature, even at the time of his call. His mind is saturated with priestly tradition ; he appeals again and again to the binding authority of the Torah. He is overborne by his sense of the awful holiness of Yahweh, and feels himself and his people involved in the absolute Either-Or of the holy and the profane, the sacred and the common, the clean and the unclean. Much of his theology is priestly in character, and is closely related to the Holiness (Lev. 17–27) and Priestly Codes (e.g. Exod. 25–40 ; Lev. 1–16). But he is also a poet, gifted with a spacious imagination, which sometimes borders on the bizarre, an appreciation of symbols, and a fondness for allusions (cf. 19:2–14, 23:32–4, 24:3*c*–5, 27:3*b*–9*a*, 25–36, 28:2*b*–23, 31:2*b*–9). He employs the *ḳînāh* or ' lamentation ' metre with dexterity and versatility. Later in his career he is called to be a watchman over the house of Israel. The harshness of his earlier judgments is qualified by his strong sense of personal responsibility, by his hopes for a new age, and by his faith in the unmerited grace of Yahweh. Again, Ezekiel appears as a theologian, the thinker who finds himself confronted with the grave problems of theodicy and destiny. He has sometimes been called ' the father of c
apocalyptic '. Prophecy and apocalypse belong to the same stream of thought and faith, though the latter is more dualistic with its strong sense of the cleavage between this world and the world of the Beyond. His visions are akin to those of the great apocalyptic seers (Daniel, Enoch, 4 Ezra). He is fond of allegory, and represents historical figures in the guise of birds, animals, and trees. The transcendent world is peopled with angels, and the angelic guide, so characteristic a feature of the apocalypses, is also present in his book. As ' architect ' of the future Temple and organiser of the Temple cult for the new age, he was destined to exert a profound influence upon later centuries.

Literary Style and Form—The man is reflected in d
his style. His literary versatility and the diversity of his literary forms reflect a man of wide-ranging interests and extraordinary knowledge, of varying mood and temper, of many emotional and intellectual facets. He is heir to a long literary tradition, of which he avails himself, but always with independence and creative imagination. Historical events are bodied forth in great symbols ; like a true poet he has a sense of ' far-off things ', of the uncharted areas of experience, of a transcendent world of reality impinging upon the world of the Here and Now. His rhetorical habit is well illustrated by his frequent use of questions to open an oracle (8:6, 12, 17, 12:22, 15:2–4, 18:2, 20:3–4, 23:36, 31:2, 18, 32:19, 37:3) or by his exclamation *Behold, I am against you* . . . (5:8, 13:8, 20, 21:3, 26:3, 29:3, 10, 30:22, 34:10, 35:3, 38:3, 39:1). His employment of the *sword* motif shows a profound awareness of the ranges and nuances of this ominous symbol. He uses ancient myths, like the chaos-dragon conflict, or the world tree, or the primeval man (*Urmensch*) in the garden of God, or the river of life (47:1ff.), or the storm, and many others. Similarly, he has memories of old folk-tales (e.g. chs. 16, 23), which he recasts and elaborates to suit his theological design. His most commonly used literary form is the invective and threat, which he presents in the oft-repeated *because*

495d . . . *therefore* style (cf. the classical *Woe . . . therefore* of his predecessors, which he also uses. See 25:3–7, 8–11, 12–14, 15–17, 28:2–10, 36:2–6). His laments are among the most powerful of his contributions to literature (19:1–14, 26:17*b*–18, 27:3*b*–9*b*, 26–36, 32:12*b*–15). The allegory is congenial to him (17:2–24, 19:2–14, 23:2–35, 36–48). He quotes popular proverbs (12:22*b*, 18:2*b*, 16:44*b*), and develops old fables into allegories (17:3ff., 19:2ff.). The traditions of both priestly and prophetic Torah obviously lie behind much of his work. Like most writers, he has his lapses, but at his best he has few who rival him in imaginative power and range.

496a **Theology**—The opening theophany which culminates in the vision of the glory of Yahweh seated on the throne above the firmament provides the best general context for an understanding of Ezek. Through the use of many strange and mysterious symbols it gives superb expression to the reality of the divine transcendence, the basis of Ezekiel's theology. Yahweh is not merely 'high and lifted up', as in Isa.; he is exalted above all creation, enthroned in supernal majesty above his universe, whom no words can adequately describe. Yet he is so intensely present, so intensely real, so sovereign over the world of history and nature that the prophet exhausts the resources of his spacious imagination to proclaim to Israel what he has seen and heard. God is God, and man man. God alone is holy, and man is not holy unless God perform within him his work of 'making holy'. Yet he mediates his power and will through the agency of his Spirit; Ezekiel falls prostrate before the presence of the glory, but it is the Spirit which raises him and enables him to hear. Through the Spirit, too, he receives his inspiration, and through it he is borne in ecstasy to Jerusalem and its Temple. Here Ezekiel stands in striking contrast to the pre-exilic literary prophets, who, with the exception of Micah (3:8), do not appeal to the Spirit as the source of their inspiration, but to the Word of God. To be sure Ezekiel, too, knows the power of the divine word; indeed at times he surpasses his predecessors in proclaiming its great power (cf. 37:4–10). Above all, the power of the Word comes to expression in the frequently repeated line: *and (that) they may know that I am Yahweh.* This great asseveration appears some 54 times, always at the climax of the oracle. The purpose and end of revelation is that men may 'know' Yahweh. This knowledge is never a recognition of divine attributes, but always a proclamation of his activity. His act is witness to his divine sovereignty. Yahweh is sovereign in Word and Deed; to hear his word is to acknowledge his sovereignty in the concrete event of history. Yet Ezekiel also bears witness to Yahweh's revelation in Israel's history from its earliest beginnings to its culmination in the new age. He recalls ancient myths of the *Urzeit* and *Endzeit* and elaborates them at considerable length; his visions of the glory—i.e. Yahweh's self-manifestation—are shrouded in an aura of theophanic symbolism. But Israel's history, between beginning and end, is also described symbolically, in allegories and folk-tales, perhaps in order to do justice to the transcendent ranges behind the immediacy of concrete times.

b The first half of the prophecy is dominated by the message of judgment. Jerusalem has sinned grievously, and its sin is inveterate, reaching back to the very beginnings of its history. Its origins are pagan (16:3, 45); already in Egypt Israel feasted on 'detestable things' and worshipped the idols of Egypt (20:7–8*b*). Jerusalem's 'whoredoms' obsess her; her whole history is one of rank infidelity. Despite all that Yahweh does for her, she persists in her rebellions in a brazen and callous way, completely unmindful of her holy calling and covenantal bond and heedless of all his promptings. She disobeys the divine laws and statutes, profanes holy things, above all the Temple, where his glory dwelt in the Holy of Holies. She has outraged the divine honour, desecrated the Sabbath (20:12–24, 22:8, 23:38), and indulged in **496** every kind of uncleanness and defilement (chs. 16, 23). She has entered into foreign alliances and engaged in international intrigues (23:12–21). False prophets and prophetesses misguide her (13:1–14:11). Ezekiel associates ethical and ritual sins; perhaps he would not draw the line of separation as sharply as modern men. For him it is the profanation of Yahweh's holiness which is the most heinous of all crimes, but under profanation he would surely include both moral and ritual transgressions. Every immoral act is a violation of God's holiness and disobedience to his law.

Punishment is inevitable; there is no alternative but destruction. When Yahweh commands the angelic destroyers to defile the Temple and to slay the inhabitants of the city, Ezekiel intercedes, but his intercession is of no avail. Even if Noah, Daniel, and Job, venerable righteous men of the past, were within the city, they would deliver only themselves, but the people would still perish (contrast Gen. 18:22–33).

The problems of theodicy do not seem to have **c** greatly perplexed the mind of the prophet. To be sure, he was confronted with them, as was Jeremiah, but his overwhelming sense of the reality of God, of his righteousness and holiness, and of the absolute justice of his ways prevent him from feeling the acuteness of the dilemmas. When the proverb about the sour grapes is quoted to him (18:2*b*), his answer is categorical and immediate: the lives of all men belong to Yahweh, of father as well as son; the one who sins will die. Then he proceeds to apply his doctrine casuistically to various instances (ch. 18). Yet Ezekiel is more the pastor and watchman over Israel than the casuist in such situations. His words are designed to give comfort and hope to the individual and to demonstrate that Yahweh desires only repentance and obedience. When the exiles come to him in despair before the heaviness of the divine judgment and ask, 'How, then, can we live?' he faces the alternatives of life and death in a remarkable way. Man lives by righteousness, he dies through sin. The issue of life or death is the issue of righteousness or iniquity. Men therefore must choose between the two, and the open door to the choice is repentance (33:10–20). On another occasion the exiles come in great disillusionment and recite another proverb: 'The days grow long, and every vision comes to naught' (12:22). In characteristic fashion he rejects the complaint and cancels it with Yahweh's word: 'The days are at hand, and the fulfilment of every vision.' The exiles are to live by Yahweh's word; Yahweh speaks his word and will perform it (12:24–5). It is clear that the questions of God's righteous sovereignty in history come for the most part from the second period of the prophet's ministry. The destruction of the Temple and of Jerusalem obviously filled the minds of the exiles with great perplexity, although there were those who were too quick to place an optimistic construction on all that had happened and failed to see that they were themselves under the same judgment as their brothers in Jerusalem.

The dominant theme of the final portion of the book **d** (33–48) is restoration and renewal. Yahweh is to institute a radical reversal in the life of his people. The nation is to rise from its death and destruction, as is vividly portrayed in the vision of the valley of dry bones (37:1–14); Israel and Judah are to become united into one kingdom ((37:15–23); and Yahweh's servant, David, will reign over them. The meaning is not that David will return, but rather that the line of David will be restored, and the king will be Yahweh's prince for ever (37:24–7). In a very moving chapter Yahweh is portrayed as the good Shepherd who cares for his sheep, who performs the functions of the perfectly righteous ruler, searches for the lost in the dark ravines, and finds for them fresh pasture. The contrast between the past and the future is present everywhere in chs. 33–7; indeed old things have passed

496d away, all things become new : a new nation and a new people, a new return after the manner of the Exodus, a new land made supernaturally fertile through the abundance of the divine blessings ; but above all Israel will be sprinkled with clear waters of regeneration, she will be given a new heart disposed to obey Yahweh and to serve him, and a new spirit which will motivate her unique relationship to Yahweh. Yahweh will establish a new covenant, a covenant of peace and well-being, which will stand forever. The old covenant words now have fresh content : You shall be my people, and I will be your God.

In the new age the life of the community will be centred about the Temple. The glory of Yahweh will return to dwell among his people. The corruptions of the old Solomonic sanctuary will be removed, and the new edifice will express to the last detail of its construction the reality of Yahweh's holiness. Nothing common or unclean must be allowed to enter into the Temple or come into contact with it. The priests are his holy ministers, and are to perform their holy functions according to clearly defined rules. The Levites, because of their past connection with the high-places, are assigned menial tasks ; only the Zadokite priests will have full status. Great stress is laid upon rites of expiation and atonement, notably the sin and trespass offerings (42:13, 43:18–25, 44:29, 45:17–25). In this way the danger of pollution through sin, even unwitting violation of the ceremonial requirements, is removed. The name of the new city is appropriately given at the close of what is to Ezekiel the climax of his prophecies : **Yahweh is there.**

e **The Text**—The text of Ezek. is notoriously corrupt, and the translator is frequently forced to conjectural emendations (see the notes in RSV). This corruption seems to have been present at a very early period, since the LXX obviously attempts to correct and improve upon the original Heb. text. While the latter can from time to time be of some assistance, it must be used with caution because of its 'popular' nature and theological *Tendenz*. The Chester Beatty papyri contain portions of 11:25–17:21, and the John H. Scheide papyri, from the end of the 2nd or the beginning of the 3rd cent., most of 19:12–39:29.

497a **I 1-3 Superscription**—The book opens with **1** an introduction to the vision, **2** an explanation of the enigmatic 'thirtieth year', and **3** a general introduction in the manner of other prophetic books. Its composite character is shown by the shift from the first to the third person and by the two chronological and local references. No completely satisfactory explanation has been offered for the meaning of the thirtieth year. The prophet is among the exiles who were carried into captivity in Babylonia by Nebuchadrezzar in 597 B.C. They are living near the river Chebar (Akkad. *nār kabari*, 'the great river'), the canal which leaves the Euphrates above Babylon, passes through Nippur, and returns to the Euphrates near Uruk (bib. Erech). It is the modern Shaṭṭ en-Nil, known from two inscriptions from the 5th cent. B.C. There, on 28 July 593 B.C., far removed from Jerusalem and its Temple cult, **the heavens were opened** (cf. Isa. 63:19 ; Mk 1:10 ; Jn 1:51 ; Ac. 7:56, 10:11 ; Rev. 4:1), and the prophet saw **a vision of God** (reading the singular with LXX; cf. 1:26–8, 8:4, 40:2). He was a priest, as the literary style and theology of the book amply confirm. In Chaldaea, the neo-Babylonian kingdom, the hand or power of God fell upon him (cf. Elijah in 1 Kg. 18:46 and Isaiah in Isa. 8:11).

b **I 4-III 15 Vision and Audition**—Like Isaiah (6:1–13) and Jeremiah (1:4–10), Ezekiel is sent to proclaim the Word of God to Israel. While his call resembles those of his predecessors in some respects, the differences are noteworthy. These may be explained by his cultural and social situation in exile, by his priestly office and his separation from the Temple cult, and by the peculiarities of his temperament. Like Daniel (8:1ff.) and Paul (2 C. 12:1–4), he is transported to another world. Visions are not uncommon in the 497b book, but the emphasis always falls on the word spoken. Thus the vision culminates in call and commission (1:28*b*–3:15). The sources of the imagery may be traced largely to OT passages, usually betraying foreign influence, and to Canaanite (Phoenician) and Babylonian motifs.

I 4-28a The Vision—Despite additions the composition is well ordered : two divisions of three sections each. Each division opens with **I saw** (4, 15), and the keyword of each section is **likeness** (Heb. *d^{e}mûth*, cf. 5, 10, 13, 16, 22, 26). The terminology of comparison is profuse throughout. God cannot be directly portrayed ; he can only be compared (cf. Isa. 40:18). The prophet experiences a theophany of grandiose and awesome proportions. An atmosphere of strangeness and mystery pervades the whole ; not until the final verse do we learn that it is a vision of the glory of God. c

4-14 A Storm Theophany—The opening words connect well with 1, 'vision of God'. Ezekiel sees a storm from the north, the direction from which Yahweh is coming to the exiles. Storm theophanies are not infrequent in the OT (Job 38:1, 40:6 ; Ps. 18:9ff., 29 ; Zech. 9:14 ; cf. also Exod. 19:16 (E)). Out of a vast cloud (Exod. 19:16 ; Ps. 18:11–12, 97:2 ; Isa. 19:1 ; Exod. 24:15 (P)), with fire flashing within it (Exod. 9:24 ; cf. 14:24) and at its centre intense light like gleaming brass, there emerges something that looks like four living creatures, later identified as cherubim (ch. 10). Each has four faces—of a man, a lion, an ox, and an eagle—and four wings. Two wings cover the body, two move forward as the spirit impels them (cf. Isa. 6:2). d

15-28a The Throne Chariot—The stress upon the movement of the creatures is accentuated by the wheels, of gleaming chrysolite, with hubs 'full of eyes round about' (18), wheels within wheels, which also move at the spirit's impulse. Two features of the vision now become clear : its cosmic range and the throne chariot. Over the heads of the creatures and their outspread wings is the firmament or platform of the chariot (Heb. *rāḳîaʿ* ; cf. Gen. 1:6–8 ; Ps. 19:2), shining like crystal or ice. The sound of their advance is like that of many waters (Heb. *mayim rabbîm*, Ps. 93:4 ; cf. Dan. 7:2 ; Rev. 1:15), like the thunder of El Shaddai, possibly originally 'god of the mountain(s)' (cf. Exod. 6:2 (P)), and of tumult (cf. Jer. 11:16). Above the firmament the prophet sees the **likeness of a throne,** like lapis lazuli (cf. Exod. 24:10 (P)), and seated upon it a form like that of a human being. His reticence before the divine mystery culminates here, as the imagery of light and fire, so characteristic of theophanies, also reaches its climax (Ps. 97:3–4 ; Dan. 7:9–10 ; Hab. 3:4). The final line is intense in its terseness : *such was the appearance* (*d^{e}mûth*) *of the likeness of the glory of the Lord*. Glory (*kābhôdh*) is the *terminus technicus* for the divine self-manifestation (Exod. 16:10, 24:16–17 (P), 33:18 (J), 40:34 (P) ; Isa. 6:3, 40:5). The influence of the experience pervades the entire prophecy (3:12, 23, 8:4, 9:3, 10:4, 18, 11:22, 43:2–5, 44:4). e

I 28b-III 15 Call and Commission—The theophany introduces the call (cf. Exod. 3:2–4:26 (JE) ; Isa. 6). The prophet is overwhelmed by what he has seen and falls prostrate. But then he hears a voice speaking. f

II 1. He is addressed by the title **Son of man,** i.e. 'man' or 'mortal man' (Smith-Goodspeed rendering), which expresses his sense of remoteness and finitude before the transcendence of the mystery of the divine glory (cf. also Job 25:6 ; Ps. 8:4). The title occurs some 87 times in Ezek., relatively seldom elsewhere in the OT. He is commanded to stand on his feet to hear what Yahweh has to speak (cf. Dan. 10:11 ; Ac. 26:16). **2.** The spirit enters him to give him vitality and power to obey ; **3** again he hears the voice addressing him and giving him his commission, which begins **4** with the oracular words,

497f **Thus says Yahweh.** Such terminology may have its ultimate provenance, so far as form is concerned, in the oracles sent to the kings of the ancient Near East, notably at Mari (see Martin Noth, ' History and the Word of God in the OT ', BJRL 32 (1949–50), 194–266). Whatever the consequences, the prophet is to make known the royal edict of Yahweh to his rebellious people. Their words may be harsh, but he must not fear them ; **6** he may suffer **briers and thorns** and the sharp sting of **scorpions,** but he must bear them ; their looks may be full of disdain and contempt, but he must not be terrified by them. Whether they hear or refuse to hear, they will be compelled to acknowledge that a prophet of Yahweh has been among them.

g **II 8-III 3 The Scroll of Judgment**—Ezekiel is commanded to hear and not to be rebellious, to open his mouth, and to eat what is offered him. The vision is introduced as in 1:4, 15. **9.** A hand is stretched out to him ; contrast the very personal words to Jeremiah (Jer. 1:9). In the hand was a scroll, either of papyrus or leather. Yahweh unrolls it before Ezekiel, who sees to his surprise that it is written on both sides, with words of lamentation, mourning and woe. Ezekiel eats the scroll, i.e. he appropriates its contents to himself, makes them his own, and identifies himself with them. The taste was sweet as honey, as Yahweh's words are to those who welcome or accept them (cf. Ps. 19:10, 119:103). Rev. 10:8–10 and 2 Esd. 14:38–41 have been influenced by this vision.

h **III 4-9 A Mission to the Obdurate**—The prophet's commission is elaborated. He is sent to the house of Israel with Yahweh's words. But it will be a grievous burden (cf. Isa. 6:9*b*–13). If he had been sent to a foreign people of heavy and unintelligible speech, as the Assyrians were, for example (Isa. 33:19), he would not have understood them nor they Ezekiel ; yet they would have listened. So great would be the power of Yahweh's word that they would have sensed it. With the house of Israel it is otherwise. They will not listen to the prophet because they are *not willing* to listen to Yahweh. Instead of hard and heavy speech they have what is worse, a hard forehead and stubborn heart. Against such opposition the prophet is to be well armed. Yahweh will equip him with a forehead of adamant (cf. Jer. 1:18 ; Zech. 7:12). He will not be dismayed (cf. Isa. 50:7).

10-11 A Final Charge—Ezekiel must listen intently, take to heart, receive within himself all the words which Yahweh will speak to him. Then, thus armed, he must go to the exiles, and proclaim to them the divine oracle. This is the distinctiveness of his mission.

i **12-15 The Vision Ended**—The call of the prophet is over. He has witnessed the great theophany and heard the momentous words addressed to him. Now the Spirit lifts him up (cf. 2:2), and simultaneously the glory arises (reading *b^e^rûm* for *bārûkh*) from its place. He sees no more, but behind him hears the sound of wings (1:24), like a great earthquake (1 Kg. 19:11f.). In great perturbation of spirit, with the power of Yahweh strong upon him, he comes to the exiles at their home in Tel-Abib (cf. Akkad. *til abûbi*, related to *abûbu*, ' deluge ' ; Heb. ' mound of green barley ears '). There he sits overwhelmed for seven days.

j **17-21 A Watchman for Israel**—The passage belongs to the second period of Ezekiel's ministry (see 33:1–9, the parallel recension, for further detail). Ezekiel is appointed God's watchman, responsible for sounding the warning of imminent danger. Four situations are envisaged : (1) if Yahweh has spoken his word to the prophet and he fails to report it to the wicked, then the wicked will die, but he is responsible ; (2) if he sounds the alarm but the wicked do not repent, then he is absolved of further responsibility ; (3) if he fails to warn the righteous who has fallen into sin, then again he bears the consequences ; and (4) if he warns the latter and he repents, then both prophet and penitent will live.

k **22-27 The Prophet Restrained**—In ecstasy Ezekiel hears Yahweh instructing him to enter the plain that he may speak with him. The region is not the same as in the vision (cf. 8:4, 37:1). The prophet obeys, sees the glory standing, and falls prostrate as in 1:28*b*. Again, as in 2:1, the Spirit sets him on his feet, and Yahweh decrees for him a time of silence and apparent inactivity. He is to be confined to his house and restrained from rebuking rebellious Israel. Yet, when Yahweh chooses to speak, he will open the prophet's mouth that he may proclaim again the divine oracles. The passage is notoriously difficult in this context. Some scholars suggest that it means no more than that the prophet's activity was confined to his home (cf. 8:1). Others, more plausibly perhaps, transfer it to 24:25–7 (Fohrer ; cf. Pfeiffer, Bertholet). In view of the commission of 1:28*b*–3:15 and of the commands to prophesy in the succeeding chapters, it is hard to think of a protracted period of silence at this time. Ezekiel's dumbness has sometimes been explained as catalepsy or schizophrenia, but these and similar views are now generally rejected. More than any other prophet Ezekiel is overwhelmed by the power and awe-inspiring majesty of God.

498a **IV-V Symbols of Siege and Exile**—By means of a series of symbolic signs Ezekiel portrays the coming siege of Jerusalem and the exile of its people. Other leaders and prophets of Israel resorted to the same means for making Yahweh's imminent actions known : Moses (Exod. 9:8–12), Joshua (Jos. 8:18–26), Ahijah (1 Kg. 11:23–9), Elisha (2 Kg. 13:13–19), Isaiah (8:1–4, 20), Jeremiah (13:1–11, 16:1–9, 19:1–11, 27:1–12). These symbolic prophecies have their origin in the principle of mimetic magic that *like produces like*, but they are relieved from being purely magical because they are expressions of a divine personal will and purpose. They are certainly much more than mere illustrations or child's play. They are performed by a ' man of God ', through whom and, indeed, in whom God is revealing what he is about to do. The acts are in psychical relation to the events to which they point. They are performances in miniature of Yahweh's mighty acts in history. The prophet is therefore a mediator between Yahweh and Israel, a mediator of both word and event (see H. Wheeler Robinson, ' Prophetic Symbolism ', *OT Essays* (1927), 1–17).

b **III 16, IV 1-3, 7 Symbol of a City under Siege**—Upon a tile of unburned brick, Ezekiel outlines a plan of a city under siege. Such representations are familiar in the Babylonian monuments (see ANEP, Nos. 100, 129–32). **3.** The iron plate, customarily used in baking, is a barrier between Yahweh and Jerusalem (cf. Isa. 59:2). Yahweh is determined to destroy the city and bares his arm against it for conquest (cf. Isa. 52:10 ; Jer. 21:5). Here again Ezekiel is playing the role of Yahweh. What the prophet is doing, that Yahweh will do.

c **IV 4-8 Symbol of the Years of Exile**—The prophet re-enacts the years of punishment in exile of Israel and Judah. For 390 days he is to lie on his left side, for 40 days on his right, signifying thereby the Northern and Southern Kingdoms respectively. The LXX reads 190 years for 390, but neither number satisfies the historical data. A literal execution of the command seems hard to accept ; yet there may have been ways of interpreting it which have not been disclosed (cf. Isa. 20). We must remember that throughout his prophecy Ezekiel intensifies all that he sees and hears and performs ; a mere visionary experience would hardly have the force of a dramatic act. The external sign is a manifestation of a future event.

d **9-17 Symbols of Exile and Siege**—Two originally distinct symbolic acts have been combined : the one concerned with unclean food to be eaten in exile (9, 12–15), the other with rations in time of siege (10f., 16f.). 9*b* is a transition from the symbol of the years of exile.

9, 12-15. The prophet is commanded to make bread out of a mixture of grains and vegetables. Such a

498d mixture was not unclean as has sometimes been supposed (Bertholet). The bread is to be baked in the sight of the exiles, presumably on heated stones or on an iron plate (cf. 4:1–3). For fuel the prophet must use human excrement. Such uncleanness is an offence to a man of Ezekiel's priestly sensibilities (cf. Dt. 23:13f.). He protests that from youth up he has never defiled himself, i.e. broken the dietary laws (14; cf. Exod. 22:31; Lev. 11:39, 17:15, 19:7f.; Dt. 14:21; Isa. 65:4; see also Ac. 10:4). Yahweh then permits him to use animal excrement instead. This is still used as fuel in parts of the Near East today.

10f., 16f. The prophet must carefully weigh his food and measure his drink: twenty shekels, about eight ounces, of food a day and a sixth of a hin, about a quart, of water. This is symbolic of the rationing restrictions of Jerusalem under siege. Yahweh will break the staff of bread (5:16, 14:13; Lev. 26:26; Ps. 105:16). Men will eat their meagre rations in fear and dismay and waste away under their punishment.

e **V 1-17 Symbol of the Fate of the City**—The chapter contains a symbolic act (1–4) and a conclusion to all the symbols of ch. 4. The composition shows signs of expansion (2*d*, 3–4).

1-2c The Symbol of the Razor—Cf. Isa. 7:20. Ezekiel is commanded to shave off his hair and beard and to divide it into three parts by weighing it on scales. One part is to be burned with fire, another to be cut up with a sword a third to be scattered to the winds. A man's hair was his dignity; it was therefore a disgrace to cut it off (cf. 2 Sam. 10:4–5). The final act is the most terrible of all. The editorial expansion of 3–4 is reminiscent of Isa. 6:11–13.

f **5-17 This is Jerusalem**—After the opening oracular formula, the meaning of the symbols is succinctly stated: **This is Jerusalem.** Yahweh had made Jerusalem the centre of the nations (cf. 38:12, 'the centre of the earth'). Mohammed speaks of Jerusalem in the same way, and the idea was later developed in apocalyptic, rabbinic, and Christian literature. Pindar and Euripides speak of Delphi as the navel of the earth and Livy calls Rome the *umbilicus orbis terrarum.* The judgments against the city are given in the rhetorical manner of a repeated *because . . . therefore* (or *Behold*), the favourite device of Ezek. already referred to in §495*b*. The cardinal sins of Israel are disobedience and rebellion on the one hand, and the defiling of the sanctuary on the other. The threats are vehement in their intensity. The anthropomorphic self-asseverations show the unrelenting severity of God's purpose against his people: **8** 'I, even I, am against you'; **9** 'I will do with you what I have never yet done'; **10** 'I will scatter you to all the winds'; **11** 'I will cut you down, mine eye will not spare, and I will have no pity'; **13** 'I will vent my fury upon them and satisfy myself'. The thought of the Temple's defilement inspires Yahweh's terrible oath. It is noteworthy that the threats reach their greatest pitch of intensity and startling concreteness in 16–17. While they are awkwardly attached to their context, this characteristic feature of the prophet's style may well argue for their originality. How shall we explain the vehemence of the language in this chapter? The reason seems clear: the prophet has such a profound sense of the holy, of the awfulness and sublimity of the divine majesty, of his overpowering glory, and of the authority and sacredness of the Torah that disobedience, profanation, and rebellion fill him with utter outrage.

g **VI 1-14 The Doom of the Idols**—Externally the chapter is unified by the presence of such keywords as **idols** and **sword,** and especially by the recurring line, **You (they) shall know that I am Yahweh** (7, 10, 13, 14), but closer inspection shows that 8–10 come from a later period than 1–7, that 13–14 go with 1–7, and that 11–12 are an independent unit.

h **1-7, 13-14 Hear, O Mountains**—In characteristically rhetorical manner, the prophet is to address the mountains of Israel (cf. Mic. 6:1), the backbone of the land of Palestine, but more especially the seat of the 498h licentious and idolatrous cults, with the word of Yahweh: **I, even I, am bringing a sword against you.** The motif of the destroying sword is frequent in the prophecy; it is the most striking image of judgment by war and is even personified. The transition from mountains to people is natural, since it was upon the high-places (Heb. *bāmôth*) that Israel practised the 'abominations' of nature worship. Land and people were bound by strong psychic ties (cf. Isa. 24:5; Jer. 3:2; Rom. 8:20–2). Fertility worship exerted a strong fascination over its devotees. The reforms of 621 under Josiah were followed by sharp reaction after his death in 609 B.C. The *ḥammānîm* or incense altars (4, 6) are known from excavations, and the word appears on one of them from Palmyra in Syria (ARI (1942), 146, 215). The high-places will be ruined, the cult and its practices brought to an end, and the devotees lie slain about the altars. The word rendered *idols* is the Heb. *gillûlîm,* a contemptuous term which the prophet employs frequently. His frequent repetition of it accentuates his disdain and abhorrence.

8-10 Survivors of the Sword—The passage may well i have been inserted by Ezekiel in later years. In exile the survivors will remember Yahweh, i.e. they will call to mind his saving power and help. 'When I have broken their wanton heart': RSV represents a slight emendation of the Heb. 'I have been broken'. Through judgment Yahweh has overcome the inveterate fascination of the fertility cults. Israel will now experience utter revulsion to the lewd practices of the high-places and acknowledge that Yahweh alone is the true God, that he is true to his word, and that it was his judgment that brought her back to him.

11-14 The Exultancy of Scorn—Through dramatic gestures and triumphant shout, the prophet is to rejoice over God's judgment upon the abominations of the house of Israel. Pestilence, sword, and famine take their terrible toll (cf. 5:12, 12:16). **14. Riblah,** on the Orontes.

VII 1-27 A Day of Doom—The chapter contains 499a both prose and poetry. Unhappily, the text is often corrupt and the literary sequence confused. Yet the poetic sections are among the most stirring in the book; the short staccato lines (2*b*–3, 5*b*–7, 10–11) quiver with animation and the repetitions are charged with emotion. The prophetic theme of the Day of Yahweh dominates the whole (Isa. 2:12–22; Am. 5:18–20; Zeph. 1:7, 14–18; cf. also Jl 1:15; Mal. 3:19). The verb *to come* is repeated some thirteen times.

1-13 The End has Come—8–9 parallel 2–4 and b represent a later recension Ezekiel develops in his own way the words of Am. 8:2: 'the end has come upon my people Israel'. The opening exclamation, 'An End!' is elaborated with increasing concreteness and detail, each line making more explicit and more terrible the inevitability of the imminent event. Yahweh's decision is irrevocable; nothing can avert it. The time when injustice, arrogance, and violence flourished is over. All considerations of buying and selling are out of the question. It is a time of tumult, doom, and great wrath, the Lord's *dies irae.*

14-27 Disaster upon Disaster—Men go out to c battle, but there is no strength for waging it. Within the city, the sword will slay; outside, pestilence and famine will devour. The few survivors will wander over the mountains like moaning doves. **18.** Utterly undone, they observe the ancient rites of mourning. Their silver and gold are of no avail now. There is nothing to stay their hunger. **21.** The precious jewels out of which they fashioned images will become the plunder of the Babylonians, 'the worst of the nations'. Their houses will be occupied, their holy places profaned. So long as the Temple stood, Yahweh's presence was with them. To him they could repair for help and support. **22.** But now his presence will depart, his face be turned away, and 'brigands' will profane 'his treasured place'. **26.** In vain will they seek out the prophet for an oracle, or the priest for

499c Torah, or the elder for counsel (cf. Jer. 18:18). The king will mourn, the prince be in despair, the hands of the people of the land be palsied with terror. Disaster follows disaster until the end. Jeremiah could view quite otherwise the passing of the great institutions of Israel's religion ; for Ezekiel it is an event of unexampled judgment and doom. Yet Yahweh has his purpose through it all : *that they shall know that I am Yahweh,* Israel's sovereign and only God.

d **VIII-XI Visions of Idolatry and Doom**

VIII 1-18 The Alien Cult in the Temple—Some fourteen months after the vision of the glory of the Lord, in the middle of September 592 B.C., Ezekiel is sitting in his house with the elders of Judah before him. What their mission is we are not told, but it is probable that they have come to inquire for a word from Yahweh. The prophet falls into a trance and sees a form resembling a man clothed in the intense fire and light of theophanic appearances. It puts forth a hand (cf. 2:9) and transports him by the forelock to the inner gate of the Temple in Jerusalem (cf. the similar experience of Habakkuk in Bel). This does not suggest that the prophet actually journeyed to Palestine ; more likely, everything takes place in vision in his own house. He may well have retained memories of what he had seen in Jerusalem or been influenced by reports reaching Babylonia. **5.** At Yahweh's command he looks to the north, at the entrance of the altar gate, and there he sees the image (Heb. *semel*) which provokes Yahweh's jealousy, i.e. his zeal for his own exclusive deity and lordship. In all probability this image is the ' figured slab ', containing cultic and mythological scenes, familiar to us from excavations at Tell Ḥalâf and Zenjirli (ARI, 165–6, 221). Such worship is an intolerable offence to Yahweh's holiness and honour. **7.** Then Ezekiel is taken to the door of the court and is commanded to dig a hole in the wall. **10.** Through it he sees mural paintings containing pictures of ' creeping things ' and other mythological scenes, motifs which seem to point to syncretistic practices of Egyptian provenance (ibid., 166). Seventy elders are engaged in secret mysteries with censers in their hands (cf. Num. 7:14, 20 ; H. G. May, *Material Remains of the Megiddo Cult* (1935), 18–19, Plate xvii). Jaazaniah is probably the son of the Shaphan connected with the Reform of 621 (2 Kg. 22:3). Greater abominations follow. **14.** At the entrance of the north gate of the Temple Ezekiel sees women weeping for the return of Tammuz, Sumerian Dumuzi, beloved of Ishtar and god of shepherds and the subterranean ocean, whose departure into the underworld each year caused the death of all vegetation. Tammuz may be compared to Canaanite Baal and Syrian Adonis. Yet the prophet is to behold even greater apostasies. **16.** Within the inner court of the Temple twenty-five men, their backs to the sanctuary, are worshipping the sun (cf. Dt. 4:19 ; 2 Kg. 23:5–11 ; Jer. 44:17. See H. G. May, ' Some Aspects of Solar Worship in Jerusalem ', ZATW 55 (1937), 269–81). **14.** The strange allusion to ' putting the branch to the nose ' is some obscure rite, probably connected with practices of the Adonis cult (cf. Isa. 17:10). As in ch. 7 the situation becomes ever more intense and aggravated, the abominations are greater and greater, so that no alternative is left but doom and the departure of the glory (cf. 6).

e **IX The Carnage of Jerusalem**—The vision is followed by a loud call (cf. 1:4–3:15) for executioners to approach, and behold (cf. 8:2), six men, i.e. angels in human form, come from the north with weapons of destruction in their hands (cf. 2 Sam. 24 ; 2 Kg. 19:35) and after them a seventh, a heavenly scribe in white linen (cf. Dan. 10:5, 12:6 ; Rev. 15:6) with a writing-case in his girdle. The seven angels appear again in Tob. 12:15 ; Enoch 20:1–8, 87:2 ; Rev. 8:2, 6. They may be compared to the seven planetary gods referred to in an inscription of Adad-nirari III (810–783 B.C.) in which the god Nabu writes in the Book of Fate with a stylus in his hand. **3.** The Heb. for ' writing kit ' is cognate with the Egyptian *gsty,* present on many reliefs. The seven angels take their position beside the bronze altar, the old altar of the Temple of Solomon (1 Kg. 8:64), which King Ahaz replaced and moved to the north of the great stone altar (1 Kg. 16:14). **4.** The glory of God (cf. 8:4) then directs the angelic scribe to pass through the city and place a mark, the Heb. letter *tāw*, in proto-Hebrew the form of a cross, upon the foreheads of all the pious who lament and grieve over the abominations of the city (cf. Exod. 12:23 ; Rev. 7:3 ; cf. Isa. 44:5). Instructions are given to the six angels to destroy without pity all the people of the city, except those marked with the *tāw*. **6.** They must begin the awful carnage at the Temple, for there Yahweh was most present ; there his holiness had been most profaned, and his Torah most defied. The executioners begin with the company of seventy elders (cf. 8:11) and receive instructions to defile the sanctuary with the corpses of the slain. **8.** The prophet, who has been present all the while, now finds himself alone. Aghast and in despair he asks whether Yahweh will destroy all the Israelites who are left, whether there is no limit to the divine wrath. But his plea is rejected (cf. Gen. 18:23–32 ; Am. 7:1–6 ; Jer. 14:11–12, 15:1). Yahweh's decision is final ; Jerusalem must be completely destroyed. At that point the angelic scribe with his writing-case reports that he has done what God had commanded. 499e

X. Only a nucleus of the original account seems to be preserved (2, 7, 18–19, 11:22–5), but it has been supplemented by other traditions, drawn for the most part from the throne-chariot vision (1, 3–6, 8–17). f

2, 7, 18-19 Conflagration of the City and the Departure of the Glory—The angelic scribe in linen is commanded to enter the whirling wheels (Heb. *galgal* ; cf. the *'ôphannîm* of 1:15–21), to fill his hands with the burning coals among the cherubim (cf. 1:13), and to scatter them over Jerusalem (cf. Gen. 19:24–5). In 7 it is a cherub who gives the fire to the man in linen, but the LXX makes the latter the subject, which is probably right. The holiness of the fire is so great that only the angelic scribe in linen may perform so awesome a task (cf. 9:11). Nothing is said about its actual execution nor do we have any description of the burning city. We may have another instance here of the prophet's reticence before the supremely holy or the utter horror of the spectacle (cf. also ch. 9). Now that the terrible judgment upon the city is completed Ezekiel sees the glory of the Lord leave the threshold of the Temple, ascend the throne-chariot, and pause at the east gate (cf. Julian Morgenstern, ' The Gates of Righteousness ', HUCA 6 (1929), 1–37).

XI 22-25. Again the chariot takes off and comes to a stop on the Mount of Olives, in full view of the city. g
In the Midrash Rabba on Lam. 82 we read, ' Rabbi Jonathan said : For three and a half years the Shekinah tarried on the Mount of Olives in the hope that Israel would repent, but they did not.' Now that the long vision is over, the Spirit transports the prophet back to the exiles in Chaldaea. There he reports all the things that the Lord had given him to see.

X 3-6 The Cherubim—The cherubim, standing at h
the south side of the Temple, are waiting for the glory to mount the throne-chariot. The house is filled with a cloud (cf. Exod. 33:9f. ; 1 Kg. 8:10–11 ; Isa. 6:4 ; also Exod. 24:15–18), and the court is radiant with the presence of the glory. The whirr of the wings of the cherubim resound to the outer court, like the voice of El Shaddai (see 1:24). The man in linen, obeying the command to enter the whirling wheels (cf. 2) stands beside a wheel.

8-17. The passage parallels 1:1–28*a* closely. It is hardly a parallel recension to it, however, but may represent a later tradition. In **14,** which is awkward in its context (omitted by LXX[B]), the word ' cherub ' is an obvious error and should be read ' ox ' (cf. 1:10).

499h **21-22.** The chief purpose here is to identify the living creatures of ch. 1 with the cherubim.

500a **XI 1-21.** This section falls into two divisions: a denunciation of Jerusalem's false councillors (1–13) and a promise of future restoration to the exiles (14–21). The former is an independent piece, drawn here by its association with the vision in the Temple; the latter comes from a later period in Ezekiel's ministry, intended perhaps as an answer to the prophet's cry: 'Ah, Yahweh, wilt thou make a full end of the remnant of Israel?' (13*c*). The invective reflects a period of sore perplexity, the promise a time after the tragedy at Riblah (2 Kg. 25:18–21).

b **1-13 Prophesy, O Prophesy!**—Through an ecstatic experience Ezekiel is again brought to the east gate of the Temple (cf. 10:10, 44:1). The opening words indicate a new literary unit (cf. 8:3) and describe an event quite different from those in chs. 8–10. The city is still standing and the ungodly have not been annihilated. At the door of the gate, a place of assembly (cf. Jer. 26:2), Ezekiel sees a council of twenty-five men, not the sun-worshippers of 8:16. Among them are Jaazaniah, son of Azzur, not the person by the same name in 8:11 nor the Jaazaniah of 2 Kg. 25:23, and Pelatiah, 'princes of the people'. The former name appears on the famous seal discovered at Tell en-Naṣbeh (ZATW 51 (1933), 150ff.). They were doubtless men of influence and power. But what is the wicked counsel they are giving? Many see a reference to the machinations and intrigues of the pro-Egyptian party, urging revolt against Babylon; others see an allusion to the social abuses and corruption of domestic relations similar to those of Mic. 2:1ff. (Bewer, Cooke, Fohrer). The latter view is more probable. One of the Lachish letters (No. vi in ANET, 322), is similarly critical of the princes. In characteristic fashion and in the manner of the Lachish ostracon the words of the councillors are quoted (3), but their precise meaning is by no means clear. H. G. May (119) thinks they express their sense of insecurity (cf. 8), but there is little to suggest that the cauldron here was a symbol of destruction (cf. 7, 11). Rather, the cauldron represents the city, the flesh its leaders. They consider themselves favoured since they have not been taken into exile. They are the good flesh from which all the bones have been taken and cast away (cf. Jer. 24:3ff.). 'The time is not near to build houses,' they say. The meaning is obscure, but the implication is surely sinister. The councillors probably are seeking to take advantage of the unhappy social conditions after the first exile in 597 B.C. **4.** To this situation Ezekiel is urgently called to prophesy, and the Spirit grants him inspiration to hear the divine oracle (5*b*–12). Yahweh knows the plans they devise and the ends they seek. The city is filled with their victims. **7.** This *invective* is followed by the prophetic *threat*, introduced characteristically by 'therefore'. The meaning of the proverb of the cauldron and the flesh is quite other than they suppose. It is the slain who are the flesh; it is they who have been rescued by death. There is no irony here as many scholars suppose, but rather a ghastly portrayal of the actual situation. **8.** Once the leaders feared the sword, but the sword will destroy the city and they will be sent into exile (7:21, 28:10, 30:12, 31:12). **10-11** are either a later amplification by Ezekiel himself or a later tradition from Ezekiel's disciples. Their absence from LXX[B] is not decisive against their originality.

c **14-21 Promise of Felicity**—A new literary unit opens in the characteristic manner of the prophets. It is primarily an oracle of salvation (Joachim Begrich, 'Das priesterliche Heilsorakel im AT', ZATW 52 (1934), 81–92). While the passage is late, it may well belong to Ezekiel. It attaches well to 11:1–13. The answer to Ezekiel's poignant plaint in 13 is a decisive negative. **15.** The leaders in Jerusalem, dominated by the orthodoxy that land and God are inseparable, have interpreted the exile in two ways: (1) the exiles have gone far from Yahweh's presence, and (2) consequently the land has fallen to them for a possession. 500c
16, 17. To this radical misinterpretation of the divine activity, Ezekiel is granted two great oracular assurances, introduced by 'Therefore say, "Thus says Yahweh"'. It is true that God has removed his people and scattered them among the nations; *nevertheless* he himself has been a sanctuary to them, though 'in small measure', for in exile they could not observe the practices of the Temple cult. Here Ezekiel is again joining himself with Jeremiah (Jer. 24:7, 31:33, 32:39); yet he speaks more in the manner of a priest than his contemporary. The second assurance is full of promise: Yahweh will gather his scattered people, will assemble them and bring them home; he will restore the land to them again, and their worship will be cleansed of all its foreign accretions. **19.** But more than all this, through an act of pure grace he will give them one heart or mind (RSV*n* and Syr. read 'a new heart'; cf. 18:31, 36:26; Jer. 32:39), put a new spirit within them and their stony hearts he will make hearts of flesh. So, inwardly transformed and renewed, they will obey and serve him and thus become sons of the covenant again. In all such passages, it is important to observe that Yahweh speaks in the *first* person; it is not Ezekiel's own word about Yahweh's act nor an expression of his own hope and piety uttered in prayer. It is the voice of Yahweh himself which gives the assurance its meaning and power, and upon this the exiles must rely.

22-25. See §499*g*

XII 1-20 Symbols of Exile and Siege—As the 501a
inaugural vision of 1:1–3:15 was followed by a series of acted symbols, so the vision of the departure of the divine glory in ch. 10 is followed by two further symbols of exile (1–16) and siege (17–20).

1-16. Again Ezekiel becomes a sign to the house of Israel (6*d*, 11; cf. 4:4ff., 24:24, 27; Isa. 20). But the narrative of the exile as it stands is confused, due to the fact that a later interpretation has been assimilated to the original prophecy. The prophet's auditors have not responded to his words and acts (cf. 2:5ff., 3:26f.); their minds are dominated by optimistic convictions that Jerusalem will be spared further doom and that the exile will be short. To dispel such illusions the prophet is commanded to enact the role of an exile. During the day he is to gather together his few belongings, the absolute essentials for the long and trying trek from Jerusalem to Babylon, and to journey to another place. Bertholet takes this to mean a town near Jerusalem, but this is not the representation of the passage. In the coolness of evening he digs through the wall, the sun-dried brick of the Babylonian houses, and goes forth with his baggage on his shoulder. He is naturally asked what he is doing, and the next morning the answer is given him: 'I am a sign (*môphēth*) for you; as I have done, so it shall be done to them (the inhabitants of Jerusalem); they shall all go into exile'. But later events made the symbol susceptible of quite another meaning. The dramatic act is now interpreted as referring to the escape of Zedekiah by night (note 'in the dark', 5–12), his attempted disguise, his capture in the plains of Jericho ('cover his face', 7, 12), and his blinding at Riblah (2 Kg. 25:4–7; Jer. 52:7–11). **10** contains the parallel to 11: 'This oracle concerns the prince in Jerusalem' (RSV). **15.** The prophet concludes in his usual manner: 'and they shall know that I am the Lord . . .' The exile, far from being the defeat of Yahweh, is a demonstration that he is a God of righteousness and justice; through it his people will come to recognise and confess (lit. 'declare' or 'recount') their abominations (cf. ch. 8), and honour him as God alone.

17-20 Fear and Trembling—The symbol is por- b
trayed in the customary form of command (18) and interpretation (19–20). Bread is to be eaten in anxiety and water drunk in fear and trembling (cf. 4:10–11, 16–17). The prophet represents the people.

501b What he is doing they will do when the land lies desolate. Ezekiel is not giving merely a vivid illustration here. He mysteriously embodies the coming event within him, and he does so because he is acting at the behest of Yahweh, whose word is fulfilled in event. The ' people of the land ' (*'am hā-'āreṣ*) is the gathering of the men of a territory for political action (L. Rost in *Otto Procksch Festschrift* (1934), 146).

c **XII 21-XIV 11.** Five independent literary units (12:21–5, 26, 28, 13:1–16, 17–23, 14:1–11) are united by a common theme : true and false prophecy (cf. Jer. 27–9). The section is illuminating for its understanding of the nature of biblical revelation.

XII 21-28 The Word of God Fulfilled—The two prophetic oracles (21–5, 26–8) are so closely parallel in form and content that they have been considered to be variant recensions, but such parallels are not unusual in Ezek. and they are seldom exactly alike. Both contain a reflection of popular attitudes toward the prophet's message (22, 27). Ezekiel had long proclaimed the imminence of divine judgment. But the days passed on, each longer than the preceding, and nothing occurred (cf. Mt. 24:48ff., 25:5ff.). Here, as elsewhere, Yahweh cancels and reverses the facile proverbs of impatient majorities (23, 28) : ' The days are at hand, every vision will be fulfilled ' (23*c*). The word he speaks will be performed (25). It is a rebellious house which questions what he has spoken. Israel must live by faith in his word. The second oracle (26–8) also deals with fulfilment. The reality of the prophet's vision is not denied, but it is misunderstood and corrupted. Israel interprets it as referring to a time far off ; thus the urgency of the word, the actuality of its fulfilment, and its present relevance are dissipated. The prophet proclaims a ' now and here ' ; imminence and immediacy are the religious expressions of the power and validity of the divine imperative. ' It is peculiar to prophetism that it is unconditionally certain only in religious-ethical judgment, not in historical ' (Herrmann, 83).

502a **XIII.** The chapter is composed of two units, companions to each other. One is directed to the false prophets, the other to the false prophetesses. The literary type of both is invective with accompanying threat or oracle of judgment. It is likely that accretions have been made in the course of the history of the tradition. There is no reason for finding reflections of the fall of Jerusalem in 4–5, 9 ; the language of 4–5 is plainly figurative, and the reference to the ' register of the house of Israel ' (9) is by no means necessarily late. The date may be set at about 587 B.C.

b **1-16 Against the False Prophets**—The opening words are the same as in 12:1, 17, 21, 26. Ezekiel is commanded to prophesy *against* the prophets of Israel, probably the professional cult prophets. It is a bitter invective which he is to launch against them. Here again he is one with his prophetic forebears : Micaiah (1 Kg. 22), Isaiah (28:7–13), Micah (3:5ff.), and above all Jeremiah, many of whose words are similar to Ezekiel's (Jer. 2:8, 5:31, 6:13–15, 8:10–12, 14:14–16, 18:18, 23:9–32, 26:8–11, 27:9–18, 28:1–17, 29:21–32). That there were prophets prophesying in Babylon we know from Jeremiah (29:21ff.). Ezekiel offers us an exhaustive bill of particulars. The prophets prophesy out of their own minds ; they have not heard the word of God (2*a*, 7*b*). Indeed they think that they have mastery over his word, that it can be induced at will. They see nothing at all in vision (3*c*) but their own delusions (7*a*). They speak what the people wish to hear : prosperity, success, peace ; not God's word of judgment or his call to repentance. They have not stepped into the breaches when the city was stormed and pierced by the enemy (6–7). They have not built a wall for the protection of the people and have left them defenceless in time of battle in the day of the Lord (5). They solemnly repeat the prophetic words of inspiration, ' the oracle of Yahweh ', but it is mere formula, just as they invoke the Spirit, which is their own, not Yahweh's. They have not been sent, as the authentic prophet always 502b
was (cf. Jer. 23:21). They mislead the people that all is well (10), when they should have confronted them with the dire peril of their age, as did the prophets of former times. They speak falsehood, their divination is deception, their visions are fabricated. They daub the walls with whitewash so that the cracks may not be seen (10), so inveterate is their optimism (cf. Mt. 23:27). They recognise no transcendent judgment upon themselves and are blind to God's will and purpose in history. Yet they expect their words to be fulfilled. The consequence is inevitable : observe the repeated *because* and *therefore* in 8–16. Yahweh's word is succinct and direct : *I am against you* (8). They will be excluded from the council of the people, and their names will not appear in the book of the house of Israel (9), probably the book of life (Exod. 32:32f. ; Ps. 69:28, 87:6 ; Isa. 4:3 ; Lk. 10:20 ; Rev. 3:5, 13:8). The whitewashed walls will fall upon them (cf. Mt. 7:24–7). Yahweh will reveal himself in terrible judgment upon those whose mission it was to proclaim judgment and repentance.

17-23 Against the Prophetesses—Ancient Israel c
was not without women prophets : Miriam (Exod. 15:20) and Deborah (Jg. 4:4) are both given this title, and Josiah consulted Huldah the prophetess when the Book of the Covenant was found (2 Kg. 22). The accusation is the same as in the foregoing section : the prophetesses prophesy out of their own minds. They resort to all kinds of strange magical devices. The source of these may be seen in the Akkadian Maqlu and Shurpu texts (see Isaac Mendelsohn, *Religions of the Ancient Near East* (1955), 212–19 ; W. H. Brownlee, ' Exorcizing the Souls from Ezekiel 13:17–23', JBL 69 (1950), 367–73). The consummate and bitterest irony of both prophets and prophetesses is that they are the embodiment of all that prophecy is not ; thus the women hunt for the lives of men who belong to Yahweh ; they profane his holiness ; they bring death to those who should live and life to those who should not live ; they discourage the righteous and encourage the wicked. But the end of the day is with Yahweh : he will deliver his people from their hand. ' Then you will know that I am Yahweh.'

XIV 1-11 The Faithless Elders—1. A group of the d
elders of Israel are sitting before Ezekiel, presumably in his own house (8:1, 20:1 ; cf. 2 Kg. 6:32). Their mission is not stated, but it may be inferred that they are seeking an oracle from Yahweh. The oracle comes but is quite the contrary of what they expect. **3.** In pregnant style Yahweh informs Ezekiel that ' these men ' have become apostates. They have admitted the idols of their captors into their hearts ! Foreign worship doubtless had its insidious attractions for worshippers of the imageless Yahweh cult. The lure of the visual triumphed over the authority of the revealed word. But Yahweh demanded an exclusive worship (cf. Exod. 20:2–5 (E) ; Dt. 6:13ff. and *passim*). How can he be consulted by those who have syncretised with alien cults ? The reply is a decisive rejection of their request. **4-11.** Instead, Ezekiel gives them an oracle of judgment, but in the form and style of casuistic law. With piercing irony he says that the apostates who consult a prophet of Yahweh *shall* receive a direct answer from him. Thus he ' will lay hold ' of the hearts of all those estranged from him through idols. The implication appears sinister, although 11 suggests that through the divine judgment Israel will no more go astray from him but will again become his covenant people. So he calls Israel to repent (cf. Jer. 3:12, 14 ; Zech. 1:3, 4 ; Mt. 3:2). 7 is almost a word-for-word parallel to 4, but adds a reference to the strangers (*gērîm*), whom several scholars interpret as proselytes (cf. also the LXX). As for the apostates Yahweh is determined in his opposition to them (8*a*), their infidelity will be long remembered in Israel as a sign and proverb (RSV ' byword ' ; Heb. *māshāl*), and Yahweh will cut them off from the

502d midst of his people (cf. Lev. 20:3, 5, 6). Thus they will know that he is Yahweh. If the prophet answers them with an oracle, he has deceived himself and been recreant to his calling. Yahweh will deceive him, so the logic of the prophet runs, without recognising the presence of secondary forces (cf. 1 Kg. 22:18–23 and cf. Jer. 20:7). Throughout the passage Ezekiel is strongly influenced by the tradition of priestly Torah; especially by such formulations as appear in the Holiness Code (Lev. 17–26). There is no coercive reason for rejecting these as late. The language may have been current in his time, or the Holiness Code may be dependent upon Ezekiel. (See W. Zimmerli, 'Die Eigenart der prophetischen Rede des Ezechiel', ZATW 66 (1954), 1–26.)

e **12-23 Personal Responsibility**—The basis of all biblical morality is that Israel is accountable to God for its conduct (W. Eichrodt, *Man in the OT*, Studies in Biblical Theology, No. 4 (1951), 9ff.). This was the meaning of the covenant relation, and it was the task of both prophet and priest to remind Israel of her obligation as the people of Yahweh. In the present passage, as elsewhere, Ezekiel presses the demand to its extreme. He asserts the unconditional validity of the dogma: every man must personally give answer to God for his conduct. In the characteristically formal and stylised manner of priestly legalism (cf. chs. 18, 23), he develops his theme by citing four instances of divine judgment: famine, wild beasts, sword, and pestilence (cf. Gilgamesh Epic, XI, 177–85 for interesting parallel, in ANET, 95). Upon each judgment there follows the same inevitable conclusion (14, 16, 18, 20): even if Noah, Daniel, and Job were in the land, their exemplary righteousness would avail only for themselves (contrast Gen. 18:22–3). These heroes of faith go back to early times; Ezekiel, priest that he is, is fond of recalling the ideally pious men of venerable tradition. Jeremiah (15:1) in a similar context appeals to Moses and Samuel as intercessors. The name Noah appears in ancient Babylonian texts (J. Lewy, 'Nāḫ et Rušpān', *Mélanges Syriens offerts à M. René Dussaud* i (1939), 273–5); the figure of Daniel (cf. 28:3) may have its ultimate source in the Canaanite legend of Aqhat (ANET, 148–55) where he is known as the righteous judge of widow and orphan (cf. W. F. Albright, 'The Traditional Home of the Syrian Daniel', BASOR 130 (1953), 26f.); the reference to Job is derived from the ancient story which lies behind the prologue and epilogue of Job. They could save only themselves, not even their sons and daughters. (Cf. Noah and Job.) See M. Noth, 'Noah, Daniel, und Hiob in Ezechiel XIV', VT 1 (1951), 251–60. 21–3 might seem logically to contradict the foregoing because survivors remain after the destruction, but these are not righteous men. They survive only to demonstrate to the exiles the depth of their guilt and the absolute justice of Yahweh. Thus they will be comforted, for they will see that Yahweh has not acted without cause against Jerusalem, but in righteousness.

503a **XV 1-8**. Again Ezekiel avails himself of a traditional theme, one that is particularly rich in its historical and literary associations (e.g. Gen. 49:11; Num. 13:23–5; Jg. 9:8–13; Ps. 89:9ff.; Isa. 5:1–7; Jer. 2:21; Hos. 10:1). But as usual he transforms the imagery to conform to his own theology. Instead of the tame vine with its luscious fruit (cf. Jer. 2:21; Hos. 10:1), he selects the wild vine of the forest. It is useless and worthless, either for making a tool or as a peg. How much more worthless it is if it has been burnt at both ends, leaving the middle still filled with sap. So it is with Israel, the wild vine. Yahweh has consigned it to the flames, none shall escape, and the land will lie desolate (cf. Isa. 6:13).

b **XVI 1-43 An Allegory of Jerusalem's History**—This elaborate composition is probably derived from a folk-tale (cf. 44–58 and ch. 23) and composed before 587 B.C. Though allegorical, it has the force of invective (14, 19, 23, 30) and threat (35–43). Its theme is expressed succinctly in Isa. 1:21: 'How the faithful city has become a harlot!' The motif is familiar in other literatures (H. Gunkel, *Das Märchen im AT* (1921), 113ff.; H. Gressmann, *Mose und seine Zeit* (1913), 7–16). Here its source may be found in the Near Eastern fertility cults. The forces of vitality and procreation are understood as due to the sexual relationship of the god and his consort; worshippers engage in all kinds of licentious rites to participate in the mysteries of fecundity. Hosea is the first prophet to apply the myth to Yahweh and Israel (see H. G. May, 'The Fertility Cult in Hosea', AJSL 48 (1932), 89ff.). Although Amos (5:25), Hosea, and Jeremiah (2:2f.) all recognised a time of fidelity, Ezekiel, going beyond the Deuteronomic historians (G. von Rad, *Studies in Deuteronomy*, Studies in Biblical Theology, No. 9, 74–84), knows of no such period. To give force to this conviction the prophet tells his story.

503b

c **1-7.** The purpose is to portray the abominations of Jerusalem (1; cf. chs. 7–8). Its origins are pagan. The father is Amorite, a west Semitic people (Gen. 15:16, 48:22; Num. 21:13, 21, 31ff.; Jos. 7:7) referred to in the Tell el-Amarna letters as *Amurrū*. The mother is Hittite (Gen. 27:46, 28:1; Jos. 1:4 (D)), a non-Semitic people. As an outcast and exposed foundling about to perish from neglect (cf. Dt. 26:5), the child is rescued by a passer-by, and thanks to his care grows to be a stately young woman. The description is realistic; the Oriental observes no reticence in such matters.

d **8-14 The Bride of Yahweh**—The second episode opens with the marriage. The passer-by spreads his skirt over the maiden (Ru. 3:10), plights his troth (RSV, Heb. 'gave an oath'), and enters into the marriage contract (i.e. the covenant, Prov. 2:17; Mal. 2:14). He clothes her in elegant apparel, puts sandals of leather on her feet (Lk. 15:22–5), and adorns her lavishly with jewels (Gen. 24:22); moreover he places a regal crown on her head (see J. G. Wetzstein, *Zeitschrift für Ethnologie* 2 (1873), 287–94). She grows ever more beautiful, and her fame spreads far and wide. Many scholars see an allusion here to the splendours of Solomon's reign (1 Kg. 10; cf. Lam. 2:15).

e **15-22 Infidelity and Betrayal**—Forgetting the days of her youth (22), the bride offers herself to any passer-by (Gen. 38:14; Jer. 2:20, 33). Her garments are used for adorning pagan shrines (16; cf. 7:20) or for clothing images (Jer. 10:9), her jewels for male symbols, and her food for sacrifices to other gods. Her sons and daughters she offers as sacrifice (Dt. 12:31; 2 Kg. 16:3; Jer. 7:31, 19:5; Mic. 6:7).

f **23-29.** After an urgent invective (23), the indictment continues. She builds a vaulted chamber, probably the brick pedestal in Assyrian inscriptions portraying prostitution (see Fohrer, 88), and a lofty place in every square, the cult elevations symbolising the sacred marriage of the fertility goddess, as in Mesopotamian representations of the ziggurats (Fohrer, ibid.). From cultic transgressions the prophet turns to political intrigues and alliances (26–9). She plays the harlot with Egyptians, Assyrians, and Babylonians. The description may refer to foreign relations in the time of Hezekiah, for the details fit those of the Taylor prism from the time of Sennacherib and 2 Kg. surprisingly well (see Otto Eissfeldt, JPOS 16 (1936), 286–92).

g **30-34 The Limits of Depravity**—Here is the culmination of the indictment; it may, however, represent a later expansion. The woman is worse than the professional harlot since she gives gifts to her lovers (31–2; cf. Hos. 8:9; Mic. 1:7).

h **35-43 The Inevitable Consequences**—Such depravity cannot go unpunished. **35.** The prophetic note rings out clearly. Yahweh will gather her lovers to look upon her nakedness and shame. Her end will be as her beginning but more tragic. Her cultic symbols will be shattered; she will be deprived of her gifts and stoned. **43.** The inevitability of the prophet's **because . . . therefore** comes to a moving climax: *because* Jerusalem did not remember the days

503h of grace, *therefore* judgment will follow as the night the day.

i **44-58.** The invective and threat represent a later expansion of the tradition. Again Ezekiel quotes a popular proverb, 'Like mother, so daughter'. Jerusalem's two sisters (cf. ch. 23; also Jer. 3:6–11), have been visited with terrible judgment (Gen. 19; 2 Kg. 17), but by comparison to Jerusalem are relatively innocent (51–2; cf. Jer. 3:11). The city must bear the shame of her humiliation (cf. Jer. 3:25). Then surprisingly, another reversal! In his wrath Yahweh remembers mercy. Not only will Samaria and Sodom be restored to their former estate, but even Jerusalem so that Yahweh's grace will move her to a deeper sense of shame for her past.

j **59-63 An Everlasting Covenant**—Jerusalem has borne the divine judgment for breaking the covenant, but it is not within her power to abrogate it. Yahweh will remember the original event at Sinai (cf. 8) and establish with her an everlasting covenant. His grace of remembering evokes Jerusalem's response, and at long last she too will remember her ways (cf. 22, 43) and no longer be consumed in shame. If the words are not from Ezek., they represent the same tradition.

504a **XVII 1-21 Zedekiah's Breach of Treaty**—Ezekiel's preoccupation with contemporary history is vividly illustrated in this chapter (see R. H. Pfeiffer, *Introduction to the OT*, 531–2). Like Jeremiah (ch. 27) he views the events of his time in the light of an overruling divine sovereignty and urges subjection to Babylonia. It is probable that he is employing motifs derived from Babylonian art and literature. Under the guise of an allegory, or parable (Heb. *māshāl*; cf. 21:5, 24:3. See Eissfeldt, *Der Maschal im AT*, 14–16), in which one series of figurative events (1–10) is paralleled by another series of literal happenings (11–21), he portrays Zedekiah's breach of treaty with Nebuchadrezzar, king of Babylon, and his appeal to Pharaoh Neco, king of Egypt, for aid. Thus the nature symbolism of the Near East is transformed into the realities of contemporary international relations (cf. Artur Weiser, *Glaube und Geschichte im AT* (1931), 22–32). The date of the passage is 588 B.C. Nebuchadrezzar, 'a mighty eagle' (cf. Dt. 28:49; Jer. 48:40, 49:22; Lam. 4:19; Hab. 1:3), comes to 'Lebanon', i.e. the city of Jerusalem (cf. Isa. 10:34; Zech. 11:1–3), where he seizes Jehoiachin, 'the topmost twig', deports him to Babylonia, 'a land of trade' (Heb. *K^{e}na'an* or Phoenicia as in 16:19), and settles him in the capital, a city of merchants (cf. the Yaukin inscriptions). In his place he sets on the throne Zedekiah (2 Kg. 24:17; Jer. 37:1), 'beside abundant waters', and establishes him 'like a willow twig' (Heb. *ṣaphṣāphāh*, only here in OT. See G. R. Driver, *Biblica* 35 (1954), 152). Nebuchadrezzar's design was to make Judah a friendly vassal to strengthen his position against Egyptian intrigue. It became a humble tributary, 'a low spreading vine'; its policy was pro-Babylonian, 'its branches turned toward him'. But it survived under a benevolent policy, 'and became a vine and brought forth branches and foliage.' While Jehoiachin and Zedekiah were brothers, they had different mothers; therefore, the one is a cedar, greatly loved by his contemporaries, the other a lowly but flourishing vine. Ezekiel now adapts the original folk account which lies at the basis of the allegory and adds a second 'eagle' (7*a*, Heb. *one*; LXX *other*), Pharaoh Hophra (Jer. 44:30), to whom the Jewish king turns for support against his Babylonian overlord. Ezekiel upholds the sanctity of the treaty, pronounces this defection rebellion, castigates Zedekiah for his treason (20), and denounces the breach of treaty as a breach with Yahweh (16–21).

b **22-24 Yahweh's Intervention**—If the passage is not from Ezekiel's hand, then it must be attributed to the tradition stemming from him. Yahweh now takes the place of the king of Babylon in 4–6. From the topmost branch of the cedar (the Davidic dynasty) he will take a tender shoot (cf. Isa. 11:1) and plant it 504
upon Mt Zion, a 'lofty mountain' (cf. Isa. 2:2; Mic. 4:1; Zech. 14:10). It will grow into a majestic tree. In its shade all kinds of peoples will dwell. All the nations will know the wonder of Yahweh's work, how he has brought low the mighty and exalted the humble (cf. Lk. 1:52), how he dries up the green tree and gives new life to the dry.

XVIII Vindication of the Justice and Honour of God—Here we see Ezekiel in the fourfold role of pastor, theologian, priest, and prophet. He shows himself an heir to a long tradition of cultic and moral laws, of Temple ceremonies and teaching, of Deuteronomic reflection, and of prophetic proclamation. The chapter belongs to the later period of Ezekiel's prophetic career. c

1-4. The prophet quotes a current proverb (cf. Jer. 31:29) and rejects it emphatically with the divine oath, 'As I live, says the Lord Yahweh'. According to the view prevailing among the exiles, their plight was to be explained by the ancient doctrine of corporate guilt: the sins of the fathers were visited upon the children to the third and fourth generation (cf. Exod. 20:5, 34:7; Num. 14:18; Dt. 5:9; Lam. 5:7). Ezekiel forbids them to repeat the proverb. It is an attempt both to exculpate the guilty, and to impugn the righteousness of God. The lives of all men belong to him, the father as well as the son, and for all there is the same fundamental law: *the person who sins shall die.* The doctrine of individual responsibility (cf. 3:16–21, 14:12–20, 33:1–20) does not begin with Ezekiel (cf. Dt. 24:16; 2 Kg. 14:6), but it is carried to the greatest extreme by him. In this he is motivated by his concern not only to preserve the honour and righteousness of God, but also to give comfort to the discouraged and down-hearted. He speaks as a pastor, to be sure, but also as a theologian. Yet the statement that the sinner must die is more than a dogma; it is also an affirmation of faith. God does not act arbitrarily or capriciously. In the following verses (5–18) he elaborates his central theme by three illustrations drawn from successive generations. d

5-20. First, he takes the case of one who does righteousness and justice (*mishpāṭ* and *ṣ^{e}dhāḳāh*), and proceeds to clarify their meaning: the observance of cultic and moral laws. Here he is dependent upon past and current legal formulations, some of them doubtless from the Temple *tôrāh* (cf. 22:6–12, 23:37–9; Isa. 33:15f. See J. Begrich, 'Die priesterliche Tora' in *Werden und Wesen des ATs*, BZAW 66 (1936), 63ff.); others from legal codes (e.g. Exod. 20:1–17, 37:14ff.; Dt. 27:15–26; the Holiness Code). Such formulations were not unfamiliar to the pre-exilic prophets (cf. Jer. 7:9; Hos. 4:2). **9.** The man who heeds these injunctions is righteous; he shall surely live. **10-13.** But the son who does not follow in his father's footsteps shall not live. **14-18.** If in turn he begets a son who turns from the evil way of his father, that son too shall live. Ezekiel now draws the consequences from the three examples: every man is personally accountable to God. He is unwilling that his fellow-exiles should resign themselves to an evil fate. Nor does he seek to schematise existence into a hard and fast theological dogma; behind all he says is the urgency of the prophet and the compassion of the pastor. The alternatives of life and death (cf. Dt. 30:15ff.; Jer. 21:8) may refer to survival and destruction in the imminent judgment; yet there is more than an implication that the righteous experience life and the unrighteous experience death here and now. While illness, suffering, and adversities are weaker forms of death, happiness, prosperity, and well-being are the content of true life (see Aubrey Johnson, *The Vitality of the Individual in the Thought of Ancient Israel* (1949), 94–107). e

21-24. Ezekiel presses his great affirmation further. If the wicked man repents, his past will not be remembered against him; and if the righteous man turn to evil his past righteousness will not avail him. God f

504f does not desire that any man die, but only that he should turn from his evil way and live.

25-29. The problem is not of the divine righteousness but of the injustice of Israel. Precisely because of its injustice, it is blind to the ways of God.

30-32 Exhortation to Repentance—The old prophetic cry rings out again, **Repent and turn!** He who turns to Yahweh in obedience and trust will create for himself a new heart and a new spirit (11:19, 36:26; also Jer. 32:39). That these are in reality only gifts of divine grace the prophet would be the first to admit. The two statements do not contradict each other, as personal experience eloquently testifies.

g **XIX Lament over the Princes of Israel**—In the literary form of a lament, with its characteristic *ḳînāh* metre (3:2), Ezekiel addresses himself to the theme of the destruction of the three princes of Israel. His imagery is clearly derived from the royal ideology of the Davidic house: the *lion* (Gen. 49:9; Num. 23:24, 24:9; Mic. 5:8; cf. 1 Kg. 10:19–20. See the royal lion on the seal of Shema from Megiddo in ANEP, No. 276) and the *vine* (Gen. 49:11–12). The sceptre belongs to the same context (Gen. 49:10; Num. 24:17). The lament is superbly ordered, as the repetitions show. The mother (2*a*, 10*a*) is Judah; the first young lion is Jehoahaz (2 Kg. 23:31ff.; cf. Jer. 22:10–12), who reigned for three months and was carried off by Neco to Egypt (4*b*; 2 Kg. 23:33); the second young lion is Jehoiachin (5*b*–7; 2 Kg. 24:8ff.), who was deported to Babylon in 597 B.C. (9; cf. 2 Kg. 24:12–13; Jer. 22:24ff.). The description of the captives in 4, 9 is reminiscent of Assyrian lion-hunting; this probably explains the references to hooks (cf. Isa. 37:29). In **8** the reading of RSV*n*, 'from the provinces', is to be preferred.

505a **10-14 The Vine of Judah**—The symbol is a favourite with Ezekiel (cf. chs. 15, 17). **11.** Zedekiah is portrayed as the strongest stem of the vine, which became a royal sceptre. Then comes the tragic reversal. The vine transplanted by the water became fruitful because of many waters (cf. 17:5, 8; Jer. 17:5–8), thus producing a strong stem for the sceptre, but is uprooted and withered by the east wind and is transplanted in the wilderness where fire consumes it so that it ceases to be a sceptre (cf. Jg. 9:15).

b **XX 1-44 Prophetic Interpretation of Israel's Past and Future**—As in chs. 16 and 23, the prophet surveys Israel's past history (1–32) and future hope (33–44). Like the Deuteronomic authors of Jg. and Kg., Ezekiel schematises the past in conformity with his theological views: Yahweh's *oath for* and *against* Israel (5, 6, 15, 23); *promise* or *threat*; *saving* or *destroying activity*; *instruction* or *rebellion*; *wrath* or *grace* (9, 14, 21*b*–22). His one dominant concern is Israel's gross infidelity, its apostasy to other religions, and its profanation of his holy name. The single key by which he unlocks the past is Israel's disobedience. As in ch. 16, he traces her sin to the very beginning of her history. Some scholars deny that Ezekiel is the author of this passage (Hölscher, May); others credit him with practically the whole of it (Herrmann, Bertholet, Pfeiffer, Fohrer). The original prophecy has probably been somewhat expanded.

c **1-4 Occasion**—On 1 September 590 the elders come to Ezekiel for counsel (cf. 8:1, 14:1). The object of their inquiry is not given, but it may be inferred from 29–31*a*. It may be that they were concerned with the problem of worshipping Yahweh in a foreign land, where they were separated from the Temple, its sacrificial rites, and other cultic celebrations. It is probable that they sought to syncretise with the religious practices prevalent about them (cf. 32). The reply to the query is a decisive rejection (cf. 14:3). Ezekiel is instructed to remonstrate with them and reproach them for their abominations (4).

d **5-9 Israel in Egypt**—**5.** Israel's history begins with her election as the people of Yahweh (*bāḥar*, 'choose' is used only here in Ezek. but often in Dt., e.g. 4:37, 7:6f., 10:15, 14:2 and later in Second Isa., as in 41:8–9, 43:1, 44:1–2. With a solemn oath (RSV *swore*; Heb. 'lifted my hand'), Yahweh made him- 505d
self known to them in the covenant words 'I am Yahweh your God', and **6** promised he would spy out for them a land, the 'most beautiful of all lands' (cf. Jer. 3:19; Dan. 11:16, 41, 8:19). **7.** But he accompanies his solemn promise with demands. They must cast out the idols of Egypt (cf. Jos. 24:4; also Lev. 18:3). for *he* is their God. **8.** But they rebelled and would not obey; so he intended to vent his wrath upon them but instead acted 'for his name's sake' (Ps. 106:8; Isa. 43:25, 48:9; Jer. 14:7, 21), lest the nations would construe the judgment as a demonstration of his weakness and thus profane his name (cf. Num. 14:13ff.).

10-14 In the Wilderness—So he delivered them e
from Egypt and again guided them through his laws and statutes at Mt Sinai that they might live by obedience and service (cf. Exod. 20:12; Lev. 18:5; Dt. 4:10, 5:16). **12.** To the gift of the law he added the gift of the Sabbath (cf. Lev. 19:3, 30, 26:2). Its observance would be an eternal sign that the holy God had made them a holy people (cf. Exod. 31:12–17 (P)). **13.** Again Israel rebelled, rejected the ordinances, by whose observance they might live (cf. Ps. 19:7ff., 119:17, 25, 37, 92), and profaned his sabbaths. Again he considered pouring forth his wrath and destroying them but again acted for his name's sake, that his name might not be profaned.

15-32. This section develops the same thought as in the foregoing, though with slight variations. Ezekiel is saying that the story of Israel's waywardness and blasphemy has been the same from beginning to end. **25f.** Yahweh's judgment upon his people was ever more severe, so that he even gave them evil ordinances by which they might be perverted and child sacrifices instead of holy offerings that they might be corrupted and 'in order that he might horrify them'. The prophet knows that sin leads to greater sin, perversion to deeper perversion. **28.** For the worship which Yahweh had ordained for Israel they substituted the licentious nature cults of the high-places, engaged in 'detestable things', and thus defiled their great heritage. Such a people cannot receive an oracle from God, except one of prophetic judgment.

33-44 Yahweh's Sovereignty over the Future— f
In mighty power Yahweh will demonstrate his sovereignty: **I will be king over you!** His people will be gathered from the dispersion and will enter the wilderness again (Hos. 2:6, 12:10). As at Sinai, Yahweh will enter into judgment with them, and they will pass under his rod as sheep under the shepherd's staff (37; Lev. 27:32; Jer. 33:13). **38.** The rebellious and apostate will be purged and will not return to Palestine. Ezekiel is employing motifs of the new Exodus, the new wandering, the new return, which were to be developed by Second Isaiah. **39.** Let those who would have idols serve them, if they do not wish to live a life of obedience. But Yahweh's holy name will not be profaned. **40.** A refined and purged people, prepared to dedicate itself to Yahweh in complete devotion, will worship him on his holy mountain. There he will accept their sacrifices; like a shepherd he will lead his people to the land promised to their fathers and manifest his holiness before all nations—a magnificent contrast to the sordid picture of profanation and blasphemy and corruption (1–32). Here the air is at last serene and clear. Ezekiel is the mighty prophet of the holiness of God, for he has himself experienced its reality as a priest in the Temple's precincts. **43.** Superbly he has described the evil memories of the awful past and the radical reversal when Yahweh acts 'for his name's sake' and manifests his honour and sole deity in the world.

XX 45-XXI 32 Judgment by Sword—Four literary 506a
units (20:45–21:7, 21:8–17, 18–27, 28–32) are brought together because of the role played in them by the sword. In all except the third it is Yahweh's sword

506a which is the instrument of judgment. Here Ezekiel employs a favourite motif, one appearing some eighty times in his prophecy. Its origin is probably in the Holy War (H. Fredrikssen, *Yahwe als Krieger* (1945), 95–7 ; G. von Rad, *Der Heilige Krieg im alten Israel* (1951), 50–68) and Near Eastern mythology (H. Gressmann, *Der Ursprung der israelitisch-jüdischen Eschatologie* (1905), 75–82). For Israel the motif was legendary in associations (Gen. 3:24 (J), 4:23–6 (J) ; Jos. 5:13–15) and was employed by prophets (Jer. 47:26f., 50:35ff. ; Zeph. 2:12) and later apocalyptists (Isa. 27:1, 34:5f., 66:16) with telling effect (see Dt. 32:40–3). For Ezekiel it was a symbol of portentous and ominous import.

b **XX 45-XXI 7 Fire and Sword**—Yahweh's figurative instructions (20:45–9) are interpreted (21:1–7) in a manner similar to 17:1–10, 11–21. The fire is employed as symbol of the destroying sword. The prophet is commanded to look steadily towards the south (Heb. *têmānāh*, i.e. Jerusalem, 21:2*a*), to preach (lit. ' pour out ' or ' drip ' as in Am. 7:16 ; Mic. 2:6) against the south (Heb. *dārôm*, i.e. the sanctuary as in 4 MSS, LXX, Syr.), and to prophesy (cf. 14, 28) against the Negeb, the region *south* of Palestine, here the land of Israel (21:3). Yahweh is about to kindle a forest fire (Ps. 83:14 ; Isa. 9:18, 10:16–19 ; Jer. 21:14; cf. Gressmann, ibid, 53–4), which will devour both green tree and dry, i.e. both righteous and wicked from south or north (20:47, 21:4). **49.** Ezekiel demurs since he had been accused of always speaking in allegories or parables and riddles (cf. Mk 4:10–11), an accusation amply substantiated by the foregoing prophecies (cf. 33:32). **21:6, 7.** The word of doom is grievous to Ezekiel. This, too, is portent, for he represents the people in their approaching grief and embodies the revelation of the imminent judgment.

c **XXI 8-17 The Fateful Sword**—In their original form these verses were in poetry, but the text is so disturbed that it is difficult to restore it. **9.** The oracle opens with an apostrophe to the sword : read ' Sword, sword, sharpened and polished ! ' Yahweh makes ready the sword for slaughter, but who is to wield it we are not told—an ominous touch. The prophet will cry out and wail, for it is directed against his own people (cf. 6 ; Jer. 4:8, 19ff.). **14.** He must prophesy and clap his hands, so that the sword may magnify itself threefold and strike like lightning ; and cut right and left, so that the slaughter may be complete.

d **18-27 The Sword of the King of Babylon**—A symbolic act. The prophet is to re-enact Nebuchadrezzar's march (*c.* 588 B.C.). As he comes to the parting of the ways he resorts to divination to learn whether he is to go to Rabbath-Ammon (modern 'Ammân) or to Jerusalem. He shakes his arrows (1 Sam. 20:2–22 ; 2 Kg. 13:14–19), a common practice among Arabs (Cooke, 232) ; consults the teraphim, probably images in human form (1 Sam. 19:13, 16) ; and inspects the liver, a familiar ancient practice known as hepatoscopy (ANEP, Nos. 594–5). Jerusalem is indicated. **23.** To the people this will seem false divination, so incredible is it, but their guilt must be punished. **25.** Zedekiah, the desecrated and profane prince (Heb. *nāśî'*, thus often in Ezek. of the kings of Judah), will be dethroned. **26.** Again Ezekiel describes the great reversal : RSV **things shall not remain** (26 ; Heb. lit. *this not this ; exalt the debased, and debase the exalted* (cf. Lk. 1:52). In a word, *ruin, ruin, ruin*, nothing but *ruin* ! Then comes the surprising word, reminiscent of the oracle to Judah in Jacob's Blessing (Gen. 49:10*b* ; cf. ch. 19), ' until he comes to whom the right belongs ', i.e. to whom the crown will be given.

e **28-32 The Sword upon Ammon**—Originally Ammon had sided with Babylonia (2 Kg. 24:2) but later allied herself with Judah (Jer. 27:2ff.). After the fall of Jerusalem she exploited the tragic situation (cf. 25:1–7*a*). Ammon will be completely lost to memory.

507a **XXII 1-31 A Faithless and Perverse Generation** —The chapter is composed of three invectives (1–12, 507
17–18, 23–30) with corresponding threats (13–16, 19–22, 31). The original oracles have probably undergone substantial expansion ; 23–31 may not belong to Ezekiel ; in that event, it represents a tradition close to him. Again we see Ezekiel in the guise of both priest and prophet, as the many affinities to the Holiness Code (Lev. 17–26), on the one hand, and to the pre-exilic prophets, on the other, amply attest.

1-16 ' Woe to the bloody city ! '—**2.** Yahweh b
addresses the prophet with great urgency. **4f.** Because of her abominations Jerusalem is ' full of tumult ' and consciously brings near the day of reckoning. In 3*b* read for MT ' a city that sheds blood ' (RSV) : ' Woe to the bloody city ' (LXX). The keyword of the entire passage is ' blood ' (2, 3, 4, 6, 9, 12). Among the sins of blood-guiltiness are acts of violence (6), like Jezebel's murder of Naboth in 1 Kg. 21:5ff. and sexual offences (10–11), like those enumerated in the Holiness Code (Lev. 18:17ff., 20:11ff.). But social sins are also castigated : **7a** contempt of father and mother (cf. Exod. 20:12 (E)), **7b** oppression of the resident alien, the orphan, and the widow (cf. Exod. 22:22 ; Dt. 10:18, 24:19–21, 27:19 ; Isa. 1:17 ; Jer. 7:6), **9** slander (cf. Lev. 19:16 ; Ps. 15:3), **11** bribery and extortion (cf. Dt. 16:19 ; Ps. 62:10). Idolatry has made Jerusalem an unclean city (3–4). **12.** She profanes the sacred and has forgotten her God. **13.** In a gesture of scorn Yahweh strikes his hands together (cf. Job 34:37 ; Isa. 2:6) and scatters his people among the nations. For the catalogue of offences given in this oracle, cf. 18:15ff.

17-22 A Consuming Fire—Employing a notable c
figure of Isaiah (1:22, 25) and Jeremiah (6:27–9 ; cf. 9:7 ; Isa. 48:10 ; Zech. 13:9 ; Mal. 3:2f.), Ezekiel compares the house of Israel to the metals of the refining furnace and pronounces the whole of it dross. Yet they must all enter again into the furnace of affliction and divine fury. Then they will know that Yahweh has brought this terrible judgment upon them.

23-31 The Roll Call of the Guilty—The prophet d
reviews the past in retrospect. Judah is a land where no rain falls (cf. Isa. 5:6 ; Zech. 14:17). The princes are like roaring lions in their rapacity (cf. 19:3, 6 ; Jer. 2:15, 4:7) ; the priests, instructors in the Torah, violate and profane the holiness they were meant to preserve (Lev. 19:8, 26:34, 43 ; Jer. 2:8 ; Zeph. 3:4). **28.** The prophets whitewash the shaking walls (cf. 13:5ff.) and divine lies (Jer. 2:8*d* ; Zeph. 3:4). **29. the people of the land** (the fully qualified citizens) follow their princes in all kinds of social evils : extortion, robbery, oppression of the poor and needy. So degenerate was the land that Yahweh could find no-one to stand in the breach (cf. 13:5 ; also Gen. 18:22ff.; Isa. 59 ; Jer. 5:1ff.). Everyone is corrupt ; therefore doom is certain.

XXIII 1-49 The Faithless Sisters—In the literary e
guise of an allegory, containing invectives (5–8, 11–21, 36–45) and threats (9–10, 22–35, 46–9), the faithlessness of Samaria and Jerusalem is portrayed at length. Literary features resemble ch. 16, although in the latter passage the offences are primarily cultic. The language is even more revolting than in ch. 16, but it shows profound insight into the nature and depth of sin and apostasy. It is best understood as the speech of almost unbridled rage and disgust (cf. 18*b*, 28*b*). The prophet's sense of the utter holiness and purity of Yahweh is reflected in it. It is likely that oral folklore lies at the basis of the allegory. For the same tradition, see Jer. 3:6–11. In the Ugaritic pantheon El has two wives ; thus this tradition, as well as other elements, may have its source in the Ugaritic poems (cf. Fohrer, ad loc. ; C. H. Gordon, *Ugaritic Handbook* (1947), Text 52). The chapter is composite : 31–5, 36–49, and probably 28–30 represent an expansion of the text.

1-4 Oholah and Oholibah—The two sisters, with f

507f similar names, reflecting similar nature, were brides of Yahweh (cf. ch. 16, Jer., Hos.), but already became harlots in their early youth. The original folk-tale (1, 2, 4) is adapted to insert the dominant theme (3: 'from the beginning Israel was apostate' (cf. ch. 16)). Oholah means 'who has tents', Oholibah, 'my tent is in her' (cf. Esau's wife Oholibamah, 'tent of the high place', Gen. 16:15, and especially the tent of the gods among the Canaanites in C. H. Gordon, ibid., No. 128, iii, 1, 18. So H. G. May, loc. cit., 188).

g **5-10 Israel's Harlotry with Assyria**—The sins are political alliances. Ezekiel may have been thinking of Jehu's tribute (see Black Obelisk of Shalmaneser III in ANET, 281 ; ANEP, 351–5) and of Menahem's tribute (2 Kg. 15:19 ; Hos. 3:13, 7:11, 8:9, 12:2). Israel brings love gifts to Assyria (Hos. 8:9–10).

h **11-19 Judah's Harlotry with Assyria and Chaldaea**—Jerusalem did not profit from the fate of Samaria but surpasses her in obsession for other nations. She also made alliances with Assyria, notably under Ahab (2 Kg. 16:7, 9 ; Isa. 7:1–8:22). **18.** The pictures of images of the Babylonian cult so stirred her passions, she became so dissolute and defiled, that Yahweh turned from her in disgust. She repeats the scandalous years of her youth. There need be no allusion here to contemporary events (i.e. Zedekiah's alliance) as most scholars think (cf. May, ad loc.). The historical perspectives are more general.

i **22-35 Oholibah must be destroyed**—The passage contains four threats (22–7, 28–31, 32–4, 35). Judah, like Samaria, is to be destroyed by the very nation to which she had gone for salvation. Indeed, Babylonia, like Assyria, is the instrument of the divine judgment (cf. Isa. 10:5ff. ; Jer. 27:6ff.). The barbarous cruelty of the time is reflected in 25 (ANET, 215 ; ANEP, Nos. 362, 368, 373). The original threat (3) ends appropriately by an allusion to Egypt (27 ; cf. 3 and 19–21). In sharp contrast to the concrete detail, 28–31 are general, though the motif of harlotry is pronounced. In 32–4 Ezekiel employs the image of the cup of fate (cf. Ps. 11:6, 60:6, 75:9 ; Jer. 25:15ff., 49:12–13, 51:17–23 ; Lam. 4:21 ; Hab. 2:16), alters it to refer to Samaria's cup. May properly compares the 'cup of scorn' in the Ugaritic texts (192 ; cf. Gordon, op. cit., Texts 51, iii, 1, 16). For the mythology associated with this image, see H. Gressmann, *Der Ursprung der israelitisch-jüdischen Eschatologie*, 129–36.

j **36-49 The Common Fate of the Sisters**—The sisters are described together and share a common fate. Here the offences are both political and cultic. Worship of Molech and child sacrifice did not inhibit the guilty sisters from entering the sanctuary the very same day! The portrait of the harlot (40–2) is familiar (Prov. 7:16 ; Jer. 4:30). It is hard to believe that the righteous men of 45 refer to the nations ; as the executors of judgment (24) they were performing Yahweh's commission. The judgment is portrayed briefly but with utter finality: **49 your lewdness shall be requited of you.** Then, again, **you shall know that I am Yahweh.**

XXIV 1-27. The text of this chapter is both corrupt and disordered. It falls into two main divisions: the allegory of the cauldron (1–14) and the death of Ezekiel's wife, a symbol of Jerusalem's fall (15–27). Each of these in turn is composed of two parts. It is characteristic of Ezekiel's literary craft to divide units in this manner.

k **1-14 The Allegory of the Cauldron**—Some scholars see two separate allegories here (1–5, 6–11), but the thought is so closely interwoven that it is better to think of a single literary unit with two allied acts. Again the prophet employs a motif drawn from pre-exilic prophecy (Mic. 3:3), one which he has employed before (11:1–13). He is instructed to write down the precise day of the beginning of the siege of Jerusalem, 15 January 588 (cf. 2 Kg. 25:6=Jer. 52:4 ; Jer. 39:1). Knowing that the Babylonian army was on the march,
he may well have had a premonition that it was on 507k
that day that they would strike. Then he is told to perform a symbolic act. One may well imagine that he was engaged in preparing a stew (cf. 2 Kg. 4:38) in a copper cooking-pot (11 ; see J. L. Kelso, *The Ceramic Vocabulary of the OT*, American Schools of Oriental Research (1948), 27) when the deeper significance of his act was revealed to him (cf. Jer. 4:11f. ; 18:2ff.). The cauldron was Jerusalem, the contents its guilty inhabitants, who are to be taken from the cauldron (6*c* should precede 6*ab*). The second part of the symbol concerns the rusted cauldron. The rust is Judah's blood-guilt (6*a*, 7-9), her social and political enormities (13*a*). Like the blood of Abel it cries to heaven for vengeance, since it has not been covered or expiated (Gen. 4:10 ; Job 16:18). So the terrible fire is kindled again, the broth emptied out, the bones burned. Then it is set empty upon the coals until the copper is smelted and the rust completely consumed. **14** seals the verdict. Yahweh's decision is irrevocable.

15-27 The Death of Ezekiel's Wife—The prophet l
is not to bewail the death of his wife nor engage in any of the usual mourning customs (2 Sam. 15:20 ; Jer. 16:7 ; Mic. 1:8, 3:7). The command is especially grievous because his wife was 'the delight of his eyes'. The prophet places the event in the service of his prophetic office. **19.** When the exiles inquire of the prophet concerning his unusual behaviour, he is to proclaim Yahweh's word: the Temple is to be profaned, but the event will be so utterly disastrous that there will be no thought of lament and mourning. Impressively the interpretation reaches its climax toward the very close of the prophetic ministry of judgment: **24 Ezekiel** (named only here after the superscription!) *shall be to you a sign ; according to all that he has done you shall do.* **25-7.** These final verses present almost insuperable difficulties. Many solutions have been proposed, none of them entirely satisfactory. Originally 3:22–7, 33:21–2 may have appeared here ; if so, 26–7 were substituted for their removal.

XXV-XXXII Prophecies against the Foreign 508a
Peoples—From its beginning the history of Israel was involved with that of other nations. The earliest traditions already reflect a deep awareness of this relationship (cf. Gen. 12:1ff.). Since history is viewed as the primary area of the divine revealing, the prophets naturally have much to say about them (e.g. Isa. 13–23 ; Jer. 46–51 ; Am. 1:3–2:16 ; Obad. ; Nah. ; Zeph. 2:4–15). Like Jer. and Am., Ezek. contains oracles against *seven* nations: Ammon (25:1–7), Moab (8–11), Edom (12–14), Philistia (15–17), Tyre (26:1–28:19), Sidon (28:20–6), Egypt (29–32).

XXV Oracles against Ammon, Moab, Edom, b
and Philistia—The oracles are brief, and stereotyped and formal in construction (note the *because . . . therefore* of invective and threat) ; the imagery and diction relatively undistinguished ; and the thought and religious value limited. The writer confines himself to the behaviour of the nations after the fall of Jerusalem.

1-7 Oracle against Ammon—Cf. 21:28–32. c
Ammon's offence is its raucous jubilation over the profanation of Yahweh's sanctuary, the desolation of Judah's land, and the exile of its people. For her offence Ammon will be given over to the bedouins to the east (cf. Jg. 6:3, 33, 7:12, 8:10). The capital city, Rabbath-Ammon (21:20), will become pasture-land.

8-11 Oracle against Moab—Again Ezekiel recalls d
no early memories (e.g. the Balaam oracles, Num. 22–4 ; the conflict with Mesha, 2 Kg. 3 and the Mesha Inscription, ANET, No. 274). **8.** Moab denied the uniqueness of Israel: Judah is like all other nations. The green mountain slopes, the beauty of the land, with its cities, will therefore be exposed to the bedouins, and will cease to exist. Beth-jeshimoth is modern Tell el-'Azeimah, north-east of the Dead Sea ;

508d Baal-meon, Ma'în, nine miles east of Dead Sea, Kiriathaim, modern el-Qereiyât, ten miles below Baal-meon (May, 202. See Nelson Glueck, *The Other Side of the Jordan* (1940), 134–9 for details).

e **12-14 Oracle against Edom**—See also ch. 35. Esau was brother to Jacob, and the histories of the two peoples were closely related (for details, see Fohrer and May). Edom's transgression was the revenge it took on Judah after the conquest of the land. The judgment is therefore severe. Anti-Edomite polemic is frequent in OT (Ps. 137:7; Isa. 34:5ff.; Jer. 49:7–22; Jl 3:19; Am. 1:11–12).

f **15-17 Oracle against Philistia**—The Philistines entered Palestine *c.* 1170, and Israel's early history was especially involved with them (cf. Jg. 13–16; 1–2 Sam.). Her 'eternal hostility' toward Israel will bring about her destruction. The Cherethites (cf. 2 Sam. 8:18, 15:18, 20:7; 1 Kg. 1:38, 44) are usually associated with the inhabitants of Crete, whence the Philistines are supposed by many to have come. In a withering paronomasia their doom is sealed: *hikhrattî 'eth kᵉrēthîm, I will cut off the Cherethites.*

509a **XXVI 1-XXXVIII 19 Tyra delenda est**—The judgment against the ancient Phoenician city is developed at length in a variety of literary genres and in prevailing poetic form. The reasons for this elaboration are (*a*) the important role played by Tyre in contemporary international politics, (*b*) its pre-eminence as a mercantile city, for the writer a symbol of human self-sufficiency and *hybris*, and (*c*) its exploitation of Judah's fall to its own advantage. The Tell el-Amarna letters contain communications from Abimilki, king of Tyre (ANET, 147). During the period of the United Monarchy and again in the time of the Omri dynasty the economic and political interests of Israel and Tyre were closely related. The city is frequently mentioned in the Assyrian annals. It was the gateway to the Mediterranean Sea, being situated on an island about a half-mile from the mainland. Nebuchadrezzar laid siege to it for thirteen years (*c.* 585–572 B.C.; cf. Eissfeldt, 'Das Datum der Belagerung von Tyrus durch Nebuchadnezar', *Forschungen und Fortschritte* 10 (1934). During this period the oracles were composed.

XXVI 1-6 The Spoil of Nations—The prophet receives his oracle in the twelfth year (LXXᴬ; MT *eleventh*), i.e. 585 B.C. See §494*a*. The fall of Jerusalem had removed a commercial rival. The 'gate of the peoples' is destroyed, and Tyre can now gather the tolls imposed upon merchants passing through. But the last word is with Yahweh: **Behold, I am against you, O Tyre** (for style see §494*d*).

7-14 Nebuchadrezzar's Siege—The judgment becomes concrete. Yahweh sends the Babylonian monarch and his host against the city with all the implements of siege and attack. **8.** The **roof of shields** is literally the shield which covers the entire body (Heb. *ṣinnāh*; see Ges.-Buhl, ad loc.). **11.** The **mighty pillars** may refer to the sacred pillars in front of the temple of Melkarth (Herodotus, *History*, ii, 4), which perhaps had cosmic significance (cf. also the Temple of Solomon, 1 Kg. 7:15ff.; see ANEP, No. 739). **12.** The proud mistress of the sea will fall into the sea (cf. 3), and will never be rebuilt.

b **15-18 A Dirge on Tyre's Fall**—In the hey-day of Tyre's prosperity the coastlands and their princes were in terror of her might; now in the hour of her fall they are appalled by her fate. They had benefited from her commercial power and wealth; now that she has vanished they are stricken in grief by her passing (cf. Isa. 47:1–3, 52:1–2; Jer. 48:18; Lam. 2:10), and intone the dirge for the dead (17*b*–18). May felicitously compares the grief of El in the Ugaritic texts (see Gordon, *Ugaritic Literature* (1949), 42). This lament is paralleled by 27:28–36.

c **19-21 The Descent to Sheol**—The prophet characteristically heightens old motifs. The flood waters (3, 12*c*) now become the cosmic flood. The great abyss (Heb. *tᵉhôm*) with its many waters (*mayim rabbîm*) will engulf Tyre. The mythological context is deepened by the descent into the underworld (Heb. *bôr* is the same as Sheol, 31:14–18, 32:17–32), an allusion rich in literary associations in Israel (Job 17:13–16, 33:19ff.; Isa. 14, etc.), in the ancient Near East, and Greece and Rome. Tyre now joins 'the people of old' (*'am 'ôlām*) among the 'primeval ruins' of primeval time (cf. 32:27). 'Rather than conquer the chaotic waters like Yahweh or the Canaanite Baal, Tyre would be conquered by them and descend to the lower world' (May, ad loc.).

d **XXVII Tyre, Mistress of the Seas**—The compiler of the book has interwoven two originally separate literary units: a long allegorical lament on the great ship Tyre, in the usual *ḳînāh* metre (1–9*a*, 10–11, 25*b*–36), and a prose catalogue of Tyre's commercial market (9*b*, 12–25*a*). The former shows the prophet at the height of his literary powers; the poem is carefully composed (cf. 3*b* with 10*c* and 11*b* and 4*a* with 25*b*–26) and is singularly rich in imagery and illuminating detail. The latter is formal and stereotyped in style in the manner of the Priestly historian. Both passages have special interest for the historian of ancient culture.

e **1-11, 25b-36 Lamentation over Tyre**—The poem falls into two parts: a description of the ship (3*b*–9*a*, 10–11) and of its destruction (25*b*–36). The city is judged by its own pretentious words: 'I am perfect in beauty' (cf. 28:2, 29:3). **4.** For **your borders** many read 'you magnified yourself' (*giddᵉlûkh* for *gᵉbhûlāyikh*, Bertholet, Fohrer). Ashurbanipal describes Tyre as dwelling 'in the midst of the sea' (ANET, 296, 297). **5-7.** To the construction of the ship the Anti-Lebanons contributed cypress wood, the Lebanons cedar, Bashan in northern Transjordan oaks (Isa. 2:13; Zech. 11:2), Cyprus ivory-inlaid planks (see May, ad loc.), Egypt sails of embroidered linen (Heb. *shēsh bᵉriḳmāh.* See Ges.-Buhl, ad loc.), Elishah (?) blue and purple (i.e. blue purple and red purple. See Maisler, BASOR 102 (1946), 7–12; C. F. A. Schaeffer, 'Une Industrie d'Ugarit—La Pourpre', *Les Annales Archéologiques de Syrie* 1 (1951), 188–92). **8f.** The ship is manned by representatives of the Levantine cities. **10f.** Other peoples, too, have contributed to the splendour and beauty of the city. **25b.** Heavily laden it ventures boldly into the high seas and is wrecked **in the heart of the seas** where Tyre had deemed itself supreme (cf. 4*a*, 25*c*, 26*d*, 27*g*, 32*cd*, 34). The sea destroys the mistress of the sea; this is the irony of the whole lament. The sailors and pilots return to the mainland to intone a dirge (cf. 26:17–18). The arrogant and self-sufficient city has come to a tragic end. Tyre is gone forever (36; cf. 26:21).

f **9b, 12-25 Tyre's Commercial Hegemony**—Tyre is the centre of a world market. Fohrer has suggested that an original Egyptian version has been appropriated here (158). In conformity with the formal style, the cities are given in geographical order: from Tarshish (probably Sardinia, W. F. Albright, 'New Light on the Early History of Phoenician Colonization', BASOR 83 (1941), 17–22) in the west to Rhodes (Heb. *Dᵉdhān*; read *Rōdhānîm* with several MSS), from Edom in the south to Damascus in the north. For identification of the more than a score of place-names, see Fohrer or May, ad loc. The unity of the passage is seen in the relation of beginning and end (12, 25). **ships of Tarshish** probably mean 'refinery fleet', cf. Albright, loc. cit.

510a **XXVIII 1-26**. The chapter is composed of four literary units: an oracle in the characteristic *because ... therefore* structure (1–10; cf. ch. 25), an allegorical lament (11–19), a threat (20–3), and an oracle of salvation (*Heilsorakel*) (24–6). The proud pretensions of the king of Tyre are elaborated in the symbolism of ancient myths. These are probably derived from Phoenicia (Canaan). The theme of the myth is the exaltation and humiliation of the man who pretended to be God. Its affinities with the Paradise story (Gen. 2:4*b*–3:24) and the taunt against the king of Babylon

510a in Isa. 14:12–20 are apparent, but, as usual, the prophet employs traditional materials to suit his particular needs, and bodies forth his theology in the maximum imaginative forms at his disposal.

b **1-10 The Pride of Tyre**—The oracle is superbly constructed. It has two divisions: invective and threat (2*b*–5, 6–10). As often in OT literary compositions, the theme is succinctly stated in the first lines (2); this is then repeated at the most strategic points. The king of Tyre claims to be a god (2*cd*, 6*b*, 9*a*), but he is man and not God (2*b*, 9*c*; cf. Isa. 31:33). Above all, the king is a paragon of wisdom (2*g*, 3*a*, 4*a*, 5*a*, 6*b*, 7*d*), wiser than Daniel (Heb. *Dan'ēl*), probably related to the Dan'il of Ugarit in the Aqhat narrative (ANET, 149–55) and the much later book of Daniel (2:23, 4:8f., 5:11, 14. See Martin Noth, VT 1 (1951), 251–60). See also 14:14–20. Precisely because Tyre makes such claims it will suffer great calamity (6*b*–8). Its wisdom will be destroyed, and she will be cast into Sheol (31:15–17, 32:18–32). Tyre is not immortal, but will die the death of men (8*b*, 10*a*; cf. Ps. 82), for the sovereignty of the last word belongs to Yahweh (10*c*).

c **11-19 Dirge over the Tyrian King—11.** The king of Tyre was a **signet of perfection** (cf. Jer. 22:24; Hag. 2:23), perfect wisdom (cf. 2–7), perfect beauty (cf. 27:3). He is the primeval man (*Urmensch*) of the Paradise story. The myth in Ezek. has striking differences, however: **14** the dwelling is both the garden of Eden (cf. 31:8–9, 16) and **the holy mountain of God,** perhaps Mont Casius, the impressive mountain to the north-east of Ugarit (see Eissfeldt, *Baal Zaphon* (1932), 14ff.). The primeval king is adorned with many precious stones; he walked in the midst of stones of fire (i.e. precious stones?); a guardian cherub protects the primeval dwelling from outside invaders (contrast Gen. 3:24). The 'fire' (14*d*, 16*e*) which surrounds her becomes her destruction (cf. the sea in ch. 27).

d **20-23 Threat against Sidon**—The nature of Sidon's guilt is not mentioned. In the day of her judgment, Yahweh will manifest his glory and holiness.

e **24-26 The Future Security of Israel**—The 'thorns and briers' with which the neighbours of Israel persecuted her (cf. Num. 13:55; Jos. 23:13) will be removed. Yahweh will manifest his holiness among the nations by restoring his people to the land he gave Jacob. Their erstwhile foes (cf. ch. 25) will be judged, and Israel will live in security and peace.

XXIX-XXXII. The oracles against Tyre are followed by seven oracles against Egypt. These are arranged chronologically, except for the intrusion of 29:17–21. Egypt had long played an important role in the international affairs of Western Asia.

f **XXIX 1-6a The Great Dragon**—The oracle is dated January 587 (LXX[B] 586, accepted by Fohrer and others), and is directed against Hophra (Greek, Apries 588 to 570 B.C.). Yahweh is *against* the pharaoh (26:3, 28:22), the great dragon or crocodile who reclines securely in the canals and branches of the Nile, boasting that the Nile belongs to him, 'the self-begotten sun-god of Egypt' (May), for he made it (Heb. text is corrupt; RSV follows Syr.; cf. 9*c*). The motif of the great dragon is widely diffused, especially in the Near East. In Mesopotamian mythology it is the chaos monster (Gunkel, *Schöpfung und Chaos im Urzeit und Endzeit* (1895)); in the Canaanite Râs Shamra texts it is called Leviathan (Ps. 74:13–14; Isa. 27:1), which may be the source of the allusion here (see Eissfeldt, *Baal Zaphon*, 27ff.). The motif is common in the OT (cf. 32:2–4; Job 9:13, 26:11–13, 40:25; Ps. 68:22, 31, 89:11, 104:6–9; Hab. 3:6–15). Yahweh will punish the hybris of Pharaoh; the dragon will be captured with hooks together with the fish of the streams (4*af*, 5*d*), i.e. the mercenaries of Egypt.

g **6b-9a The Broken Reed**—Because Egypt is an unreliable support (cf. Isa. 20:5–6, 30:1–5, 31:1–3; Jer. 2:36, 42:7–43:13) Yahweh will bring the sword 510g
upon her and reduce her to a desolate waste. The figure of the reed (2 Kg. 18:21 = Isa. 36:3) was especially appropriate for a land of reeds (Exod. 2:3–5; Isa. 19:6).

9a-16 A Lowly Kingdom—The oracle seems to be h
a parallel recension of 29:3–9*a*. **10.** From Migdol (modern Tell el-Ḥeir) in the far north to Syene (modern Aswân) in the far south Egypt will be uninhabited. **11.** According to the redactor the desolation will last forty years (cf. Judah's punishment in 4:4–6); **14** then Yahweh will return Egypt to Pathros, Upper Egypt, the land of her origin (Herodotus ii, 4, 15), and there she will survive as a lowly kingdom. Never again will she be able to exalt herself, nor will Israel turn to her for aid.

17-20, 21 The Wages of Nebuchadrezzar—The i
oracle is dated on the spring New Year, 570, the latest of all the prophet's words. For thirteen years Nebuchadrezzar had laid siege to Tyre, but his rewards were not commensurate with his labours. The prophet's doctrine of rewards and punishments again finds expression here. Nebuchadrezzar had acted at the behest of Yahweh and will be rewarded for his services. Ezekiel is writing long after the oracles against Tyre. That his prophecies had not been fulfilled does not disturb him. Yahweh's sovereignty will yet be demonstrated. Interestingly, a single verse is added to this final oracle. The horn which is to sprout may be a reference to the restoration of the Davidic line (Ps. 132:17). All four oracles of the chapter end with the momentous words: **then they will know that I am Yahweh.**

XXX 1-9 The Day of Egypt—Against the general j
background of the Day of Yahweh (cf. ch. 7; Isa. 2:12–17; Am. 5:18–20; Zeph. 1:7, 14–18) the imminent fall of Egypt is predicted. There is nothing new in this oracle; indeed the passage is little more than a catena of previously employed lines. With the removal of 5 and 9, a general structure is discernible, however. After the announcement that the Day of the Lord is near, Egypt's destruction by sword is described, then the fall of her mercenaries and allies. In 3*d* and 9*d* RSV interprets the meaning by adding 'doom'.

10-12 Nebuchadrezzar and Yahweh—Yahweh uses Nebuchadrezzar, king of Babylon, to destroy the land of Egypt, but he himself will dry up the Nile. He has spoken, and his word will actualise itself in the event.

13-19 The Cities of Egypt—The ancient Hebrew k
was fond of such enumerations as we have here. The mention of one city after another impressively accentuated the completeness of the destruction of the land (cf. Num. 21:27–30 (E); Isa. 10:27*b*–34; Am. 1:3–8; Mic. 1:10–15; Zeph. 2:4; cf. also Isa. 16:7–9; Jer. 48:45f.). The order in which the cities are named is confusing. For modern identifications, see May, ad loc.

20-26 The Broken Arms of Egypt—The threat is l
dated April 586. **21.** The arm of Egypt has been broken, but it has not been bound up or bandaged. The allusion is the attempt of Pharaoh Hophra in 588 to relieve the beleaguered city of Jerusalem (Jer. 37:4–10). But the mission was ill-fated, so that the army was forced to return (Jer. 37:4–10). Now Yahweh will strengthen the arms of Nebuchadrezzar (24*a*, 25*a*), and will break both arms of Egypt (22*b*, 24*b*, 25*b*).

XXXI 1-18 The Great Cedar—The general unity 511a
and structure is clear: an allegorical poem describing the incomparable beauty and magnitude of the cedar (2*b*–9) and a prose section portraying its fall. The theme is succinctly stated in 3*a* (cf. 27:2*b*, 28:2*b*; this is elaborated at the close of the poem (8) together with a climax in 9. The second division has two parts (10–14, 15–18), similarly introduced; 18 gathers together the whole by repeating the opening theme and the summarising judgment of 17. The

511a prophet makes use of motifs and symbols elaborated before (e.g. ch. 17, 19:10–14, 26:19–21, 28:11–19) as well as a variety of mythological elements from Near Eastern epics and tales and the OT (e.g. Gen. 2:4*a*–

b 3:24 ; Isa. 14). The central symbol is the world tree, whose roots were watered by the primeval abyss with its streams (Heb. *t^{e}hôm*, 4, 15), and whose heights reached into the heavens (3*b*, 5*a*, 10, 14*a*). Compare Dan. 4:10–12, 19–27, which employs the same myth. The text of 3 is insecure. RSV emends the impossible *Assyria* of the Heb. *'aššûr* to *I will liken* (*'ashw^{e}khā*). The tree symbolism is illustrated by similar representations in Near Eastern mythology (see A. J. Wensinck, *Tree and Bird as Cosmological Symbols in Western Asia* (1921), 25–35 ; Gunkel, *Das Märchen im AT*, 22ff. ; Gressmann, *Der Messias*, 266f.). The other trees of the forest are watered by the same primeval deep (4–5, 15–16) but cannot rival it in height or beauty. The association with the Garden of Eden (9, 18) has been encountered before (28:13f.) ; it is here obviously located among the Lebanons. 'To the Israelite, all the glory of the earth was summed up in the thought of Yahweh's garden' (S. Mowinckel,

c *He that Cometh* (1957), 81). The allegory seeks to describe the greatness and prosperity of Egypt. But Egypt failed to realise that her greatness was not of her own making ; she apotheosised herself in the figure of the divine king (cf. 29:3) when in reality her greatness and beauty was the work of Yahweh (cf. 9: *I made it beautiful*). Therefore she must submit to a transcendent judgment. Nebuchadrezzar and his army will destroy it ; the nations will no longer find security under its branches (6*c*, 12–14). Like Adam and Eve it will be cast out from the garden (11*b*) ; like the king of Babylon in Isaiah's taunt it will enter the shades of Sheol (Isa. 14:9–11 ; cf. 14*b*–17). The descent into the underworld (cf. 26:19–21 ; Isa. 14:5–32) is evidently derived from a much more expanded mythology from Canaan or Mesopotamia, and the allusion to the garden-of-Eden story, while intelligible, does not harmonise well with the context. Yahweh causes all nature to participate in lamenting the terrible fall : the deep grieves and its many waters (*mayim rabbîm*) are stopped ; the Lebanons are shrouded in mourning-garments ; and the trees languish (15). In superb fashion, after the annihilating judgment the prophet inquires again about Egypt's incomparable glory and greatness 'among the trees of Eden'. It will be brought down to the underworld, with the uncircumcised and those slain by the sword, i.e. the murdered and executed (see Eissfeldt, 'Schwerterschlagene bei Hesekiel', *Studies in OT Prophecy*, ed. H. H. Rowley, 73–81).

d **XXXII 1-8 The Capture of the Dragon**—The poem, hardly a lamentation (2), either in metre or content, is companion to 29:1–6*a*, where the figure of the dragon (reading *tannîn* with RSV for MT *tannîm*. See K-B, ad loc.). The prophet is again dependent upon the Mesopotamian myth of the chaos-dragon, Tiamat, who was slain by Marduk (Enuma Elish iv, in ANET, 66–7). **2.** Pharaoh, king of Egypt, considers himself a lion (so MT and RSV, but many scholars emend the text : e.g. 'you must keep silent like a fish of the sea' (Fohrer) or 'Woe to thee, O Pharaoh, how thou art destroyed' (Bertholet). 'The royal sphinx was a lion-bodied creature' (May, ad loc. ; cf. 19:2–9). But he is in actuality the dragon monster of the chaotic deep which snorts and sprays with its nostrils (2*d*, RSV 'rivers', the emendation in the Heb. is very slight), muddies the waters with its feet, and disturbs the rivers of the deep. **3.** But it will be caught in a net (cf. 12:13, 17:20, 19:8), the beasts will devour its carcass (cf. Ps. 74:14), its flesh will cover the mountains and fill the valleys, and its blood will drench the earth. All these motifs are present in the Mesopotamian epic. The destruction of the dragon comes with the Day of Yahweh. **7-8** describe the universal disaster in which the light of the heavenly luminaries will be extinguished and the earth will lie in primeval darkness (cf. 7:2*b*–13, 30:2*b*–3 ; Isa. 13:9f., 51:6, 60:19 ; Jl 2:2, 10, 31, 3:15 ; Am. 5:18–20, 8:9). 511

9-16 The Sword of Terror—The text is corrupt and the composition disordered. The peoples which once feared Egypt's power will now be appalled at its terrible fate, and will tremble in dread for their lives. **11.** Nebuchadrezzar will come with his armies. This insertion of historical elements in the midst of mythological contexts has been encountered before. **13.** The beasts (note the plural here !) will be destroyed by Yahweh ; **14** the turbulent waters (cf. 2) will be stilled and will flow clear and smooth like oil through the desolated land. The foregoing words (perhaps *originally* 2*b*–15, though 9–15 have been edited and transformed) will be sung as a lamentation over Egypt. e

17-32 The Denizens of Sheol—The date is 27 April 585. The prophet is instructed to wail over the 'multitude of Egypt', and his word will have the colossal effect of sending it down to the underworld of Sheol. The passage is notable for its formal and repetitive style (cf. 14:12–20, 27:12–25), which in this instance is not without impressiveness. **19.** The prophet summarises in a succinct couplet the grandeur and collapse of Egypt (19, 31:2*b*–18). Most remarkable is the frequent repetition of the *uncircumcised, slain by the sword*, all of whom descend into Sheol (18*d*, 23*a*, 24*e*, 25*e*, 27*a*, 29*b*, 30*a*) the land of the dead. (See Eissfeldt, ibid. 81.) **21.** The mighty who lie buried in Sheol greet the coming of Egypt with scorn and mockery. Then, almost in the manner of Dante, the denizens of the Pit, the mighty conquerors of history, pass in review—Assyria, Elam, Meshech and Tubal, Edom, the princes of the north, and the Phoenicians. The list is strange ; one might have included other names, but the prophet has his own reasons for the ones he gives. Each seems to be assigned a special place. In **27** the negative should be deleted ; Meshech and Tubal lie with the fallen mighty men of primeval time (with emended text ; MT reads 'of uncircumcised'). f

XXXIII-XXXIX Prophecies of Restoration and Renewal—The fall of Jerusalem marks the turning-point in Ezekiel's ministry. His dire predictions have been fulfilled ; the city lies in ruins and its inhabitants have been carried into exile. In these chapters the prophet looks forward to a new age of national revival and moral renewal. Significantly, the section opens with Yahweh's demand for personal responsibility, both for Ezekiel himself and for every individual. 512a

XXXIII 1-9 The Call of the Watchman—This account is very similar to 3:16*b*–21, which properly belongs in this context. The prophet resorts to his favourite motif of the sword (cf. 21:9ff., 30:4, 21f., 38:21). The figure of the watchman is drawn from the daily experience of the people. On his watch-tower he guards the vineyards (Isa. 5:2) ; as shepherd he protects his flock (1 Sam. 17:34–6) ; in time of war he sounds the alarm of the approaching enemy (2 Kg. 9:17ff. ; Jer. 4:5f., 6:17 ; Hos. 5:8 ; Am. 3:6). See also Isa. 21:11f. ; Hab. 2:1. **1-9.** Ezekiel must warn the people of imminent danger ; he is to be constantly on the *qui vive* for Yahweh and the people. If anyone fails to give heed, he is himself solely responsible. But the watchman's very life depends upon fulfilling the task assigned to him. b

10-20 The Justice of God—Wasting away with guilt and despair, the people find themselves face to face with the issue of life and death : **How can we live ? 11.** Yahweh answers with an emphatic assurance that he takes no pleasure in the death of the wicked but only desires repentance : **Turn back, O turn back from your evil ways ; for why will you die, O house of Israel ?** (cf. Jer. 3:12, 4:1, 15:19 ; Hos. 7:10, 11:5 ; Am. 4:6–11). No man knows the day of accounting (cf. Mk 13:24–6 ; Lk. 12:35–8). The righteous man cannot count on his past righteousness ; neither will the past evil life c

512c of the wicked be held against him if in the day of Yahweh's judgment he has repented. (Cf. 18:21–32.) Life is more than physical vitality, and death more than a physical end. Rather men can choose life and death (Dt. 30:15–20) ; repentance is the open door to life, and obedience to the **statutes of life** is the way of life (33:15 ; cf. 20:11, 21 ; Lev. 18:5).

d **21-22 The City has Fallen**—These verses should follow 24:25. If the autumnal reckoning is followed (see May, ad loc.), the date would be 8 January 585, about six months after the fall of the city. This seems unduly long for the journey, but it need not be supposed that the fugitive left immediately after the event. The fugitive's words are tense in their brevity : **The city has fallen** (lit. 'smitten'). In an ecstatic experience the previous evening Ezekiel found himself able to speak again after the period of dumbness. Yahweh's silence was past. It was time for a new beginning.

e **23-29 Abraham our Father**—Those who were left in the city of Jerusalem interpreted their status as a sign of Yahweh's approval and sanctified it by an appeal to Abraham, to whom Yahweh had given the land and from whom they had sprung (Gen. 12:1ff. ; Isa. 51:1–2). Cf. Jn 8:33–9. Ezekiel answers their facile distortion of God's will and purpose by a bitter invective (25–6) and threat (27–8). In the time of terrible doom they will come to know that Yahweh is Lord, and that he is a God of righteousness.

f **30-33 The Prophet as Minstrel**—The occasion is uncertain. Perhaps Ezekiel's words of assurance had filled the exiles with expectations of a happy future. At any rate, he has now become a popular prophet. They listen to him as to a minstrel who sings pleasant ditties and plays his instrument well. But they do not grasp the purport of his message, for their minds are all fixed on gain. The prophet will not be misled. The time will surely come when they will be compelled to realise that they must be not only hearers but also doers of the word (cf. Isa. 29:13 ; also Mt. 7:21 ; Mk 3:35).

513a **XXXIV 1-16 The Shepherd and his Flock**—While the chapter shows signs of unevenness and possibly of composite authorship, it is governed by the common theme of the shepherd and his flock. In a biting invective (2–6) followed by a threat and a transformed oracle of salvation (8–10*a*, 10*b*–16), the prophet delivers a severe indictment of the past rulers of Israel. The designation of the rulers as shepherds appears not infrequently in the OT (1 Kg. 22:17 ; Isa. 44:28 ; Jer. 10:21, 23:1–6, 25:34–8 ; Mic. 5:5) and in the literature of the ancient Near East. The relation of this passage to Jer. 23:1ff. is so close as to suggest possible dependence. **2b-3.** Ezekiel condemns Israel's former kings for exploiting their subjects to their own advantage, **4** for neglecting their elemental obligations as rulers, and **5-6** for allowing them to be scattered throughout the earth. The responsibilities of the good king implied in the indictment reveal a lofty conception of the royal office. Yahweh will bring to an end the evil rule of the past, will rescue his people from the voracity of the kings, and will himself become their shepherd (cf. Ps. 23:1, 74:1, 95:7 ; Isa. 40:11, 49:9–10 ; Jer. 31:10, etc.). Refashioning the motif of the Day of the Lord, the prophet describes Yahweh gathering his flock on a day of clouds and darkness and becoming their faithful shepherd (cf. 3–6 with 14–16).

b **17-22 The Judgment of the Flock**—Yahweh will judge between sheep and sheep, between the strong and the weak, the fat and the lean. Cf. Mt. 25:32–3. The social abuses of the past are described in the characteristic imagery of the prophet.

c **23-24.** Yahweh will set over his people his servant David, who will be their prince (*nāśī'*). The days of the kingdom are over, but the prince will serve as Yahweh's representative in the new age. The word 'servant' may be drawn from the ideology of the sacral kingship (2 Sam. 3:18, 7:5 ; 2 Kg. 8:19 ; Ps. 89:4, 21). There is no thought here of the actual return of David, as some scholars have believed ; rather we must think of the perpetuation of the Davidic dynasty. Yahweh is the saviour and deliverer of Israel, not the prince. Yet the prince is the ruler, the shepherd who will feed them. The 'messianism' of this passage may be compared to 17:22–4, 37:24–5.

25-31 The Age of Peace—In the new age Yahweh will make a new covenant (Isa. 54:10) ; the wild beasts will be driven into the wilderness (Isa. 11:7–8, 65:25 ; Hos. 2:18), and showers of blessing will revive the thirsty land. Trees will yield abundant fruit and crops will flourish (27, 29). The reign of peace is reflected in freedom from bondage and foreign oppression, in the wonderful fertility of the land, and in the absence of all fear. The classical expressions of the covenant relation are finally expressed in the climactic words about the Davidic prince and the felicity of the new age. **31.** The final verse seems out of place here ; possibly the redactor considered it a suitable finale to the whole. Here the covenant promise is superbly worded in the language of the shepherd ; yet, significantly, the final words drop the imagery : **I am your God, says the Lord Yahweh.** d

XXXV 1-15 The Desolation of Edom—The fourfold invective and threat in the customary *because . . . therefore* style (1–4, 5–9, 10–12*a*, 12*b*–15) is a counterpart to the invective and threat of 36:2–7 (cf. 25:12–14). The first is addressed to Mt Seir, the mountains of Edom extending east of the Wâdī 'Arabah, from south of the Dead Sea to the Gulf of 'Aqaba ; the second to the mountains of Israel, the spine of the land (cf. 6:1ff.). The same terminology and motifs appear in both, and together they form the introduction to the words of promise in 36:8ff. Both sections open with a characteristically succinct statement : 'Behold, I am against you, O Mount Seir, and I will stretch out my hand against you' (35:3) and 'For, behold, I am for you and I will turn to you' (36:9). The keynote of the oracle is *desolation*, which reaches its climax in 14–16. Edom had taken advantage of Israel's plight during the siege of Jerusalem and in the time following. Israel's bitter resentment breathes through many OT passages (Ps. 137:7 ; Isa. 34 ; Lam. 4:21f. ; Ob. ; Mal. 1:2–5). The hostility between the two peoples was of long standing, reaching back to the contentions between Jacob and Esau (Gen. 25:22–3, 27:41 ; cf. also Mal. 1:2–5) and continuing through the centuries (2 Sam. 8:13 ; 1 Kg. 11:14–22 ; 2 Kg. 8:22–4, 14:7, 16:6 ; Am. 1:11–12). The invectives establish the case against Edom : (*a*) her perpetual enmity against Israel and particularly her exploitation of Israel's humiliation after 586 (5), (*b*) her ambition to possess both Judah and the land formerly occupied by the Northern Kingdom, possibly as a reward for her support of the Chaldaeans (10), and (*c*) her arrogance, blasphemy, and sinister exultation in the hour of Israel's desolation. Despite Israel's deserved punishment, she is still Yahweh's people ; her land is Yahweh's land, for Yahweh is there (10*b* ; cf. 48:35) and her future is in his keeping. Edom therefore must be destroyed. **11b.** Yahweh will make himself known in judgment, and then they will know that his sovereignty rules over the destinies of men and nations (4, 11–12, 15). e

XXXVI 1-15 The Transformation of the Land— f
The oracle falls into two parts : invective and threat (1–7) and transformed oracle of salvation (8–15). Addressed to the mountains of Israel (see 35:1–15), the whole section is an excellent illustration of the Hebrew understanding of nature as alive and sentient, possessing a psychical life of its own (cf. Isa. 1:2 ; Am. 4:6–11 ; Mic. 6:1–3). The land participates in the life of its inhabitants (8–15), hears the words addressed to it by Yahweh, its possessor (1, 4, 15), and is obedient to his bidding. **5.** In derision the enemy gloats over their desolation and their possession of it : **Edom gave my land to themselves as a**

513f **possession.** Such contempt arouses Yahweh's ' hot jealousy ' (lit. ' fire of my jealousy '); the offence to his honour and holiness must be avenged. **7.** The nations will suffer the same reproach they have heaped upon Israel. This characteristic reversal introduces the oracle of felicity (8–15). In joyous anticipation of Israel's return home the mountains break forth in fruitfulness : **8. you will yield your fruit to my people Israel, for they will soon return home. 9.** After Yahweh's solemn assurance of his favour, **Behold, I am for you, and will turn to you,** the blessings of the new age ensue. The mountains will no longer bereave the nation of her children (14). The last clause of 15 is corrupt; perhaps we should read ' no longer bereave your nation ', reading the verb *t^eshakk^elî* for *takhshilî*.

g **16-32 The Transformation of the People**—Israel had defiled and polluted the land by her conduct (17 ; cf. 18:6). Her occupation of it was conditional. Her failure to heed Yahweh's righteous demands had incurred his judgment (18–19 ; cf. 35:11*b*). Yet it was precisely the demonstration of his righteous judgment that had led to more grievous sin, for the nations interpreted the desolation as evidence of his inability to save it from conquest, exile, and exploitation. **20.** Thus Israel had caused his holy name to be profaned among the nations. Israel had made the holy land unholy ; yet her holy God must maintain his holiness in the earth. **21.** Therefore he spared them (RSV ' had concern for ') for the sake of his holy name. Yet, if the holiness of his great name was to be vindicated among the nations (cf. 20:9, 14, 22 ; Mal. 1:11), then his people must be radically transformed and become a new and holy people. **24.** First of all, of course, they are to return to their land. **25.** Yahweh will sprinkle clean water upon them to purify them from the stain and guilt of the past (Ps. 51:7). **26.** But the transformation goes deeper. He will give them a new heart, a disposition and will responsive to his purposes and requirements (cf. Ps. 51:10 ; Jer. 31:33). The induration of their stony heart will be transformed into the sensitiveness of a heart of flesh. He will do yet more : his gift of a new spirit will enable them to render him the obedience which is his due (cf. Ps. 51:11–13). **28.** In the transformed land they will renew the covenant bond. Blessings will abound. **29, 30.** Yahweh will summon the grain to abundance (cf. Hos. 2:21–2) and prosper the yield of field and tree so that they may never suffer again ' the disgrace of famine '. The holy land is a land of plenty, an idea congenial to the priestly mind. Then they will remember their evil past and loathe themselves for all they have done. The land is restored and the people renewed for the sake of Yahweh's holy name and honour. 33–8 represent a parallel tradition.

h **33-36.** The desolate land will become like Eden. Through all the mighty deeds of Yahweh the nations will come to know that it was he who brought about the great reversal. The words culminate in another great asseveration : **I, Yahweh, have spoken, and I will do it.**

37-38. As the flocks stream into Jerusalem to be offered for sacrifice at the sacred festivals, so the ruined cities will throng with Yahweh's flock, the sheep of his pasture. Cf. Isa. 54:1–3 ; Zech. 2:4.

514a **XXXVII 1-14 The Valley of Dry Bones**—The prophet feels himself in the grip of Yahweh and in a trance is brought to a plain, perhaps the same as that where the glory of Yahweh appeared to him (3:22–3). It is a vast battlefield (9) strewn everywhere with the bones of men long dead. **2.** He traverses the field all about and sees that they are very many and very dry, i.e. all vitality has long since gone from them. **3.** To Yahweh's question, **Can these bones live ?** he has no answer. It would seem to be utterly impossible. **4.** But then Yahweh commands him to prophesy, to address them, and to call upon them to hear. It is a wonderful reflection of the power of the prophetic word that even dead men's bones can be so quickened into response. **5.** Then follows the central line of the whole vision : **Behold, I will cause breath** (Heb. *rûaḥ*) **to enter you, and you shall live. 7.** Ezekiel heeds the divine commission and forthwith hears the strange sound of rattling. The bones are moving, everywhere assembling themselves about their original bodies. The gathering of sinews and flesh and skin is an admirable example of Hebrew ideas of anatomy, as the entire context is of biblical anthropology (cf. Gen. 2:7). **9.** But now, appropriately, Ezekiel must prophesy again, this time to the breath, and command it to come from the four winds (the plural of *rûaḥ*) and breathe upon the slain. **10.** The bodies become alive because it is the Spirit which gives life (Gen. 6:17, 7:15, 22) : they rise to their feet, **an exceedingly great host** (Heb. *ḥayil gādhôl m^e'ôdh*). **11.** The interpretation of the vision makes it clear that the bones represent Israel ; there is no suggestion of the resurrection of the individual here, but only of the nation (contrast Isa. 26:19 ; Dan. 12:2). The content of death is despair, hopelessness, the sense of being ' cut off '. To experience these is to experience death (see Aubrey R. Johnson, *The Vitality of the Individual in the Thought of Ancient Israel*, 88–107). **12-14.** Israel is to rise from the dead, to become the living community of the future, to live by those things that constitute true life (cf. 18:20–4, 33:10–16). All this is the work of the Spirit of God. When this transformation is wrought Israel will know that Yahweh has spoken and performed it.

15-28 The Restoration of the United Kingdom— b
The prophet is commanded to take two sticks or staffs, inscribe them with the names *Judah* and *Joseph* (cf. Isa. 44:5 ; Zech. 11:7–15), and join them into one, symbolic of the reunion of the two kingdoms. One king will rule over them. The restoration of the United Kingdom is not only national, however. Israel will not defile the land (36:16, 21). Yahweh will save her from all future apostasy (36:27), purify her from all uncleanness (36:25), and bring her into a new covenant relation (36:28). Under the rule of his servant David (34:23–4) she will live in obedience and faithfulness (36:27) and occupy the land of the fathers (36:24). The covenant of peace (34:25 ; cf. Num. 25:12 ; Isa. 54:10 ; Mal. 2:5), like all the blessings and benefits of the new age, will be everlasting. But above all else Yahweh will dwell in the midst of his people. The presence of his sanctuary in their midst is a pledge that the covenant has been renewed, and because of it the nations will see that Yahweh has sanctified his people and has set them apart. The vision of the new Temple in chs. 40–8 follows naturally upon this section.

XXXVIII-XXXIX The Invasion of Gog and c
Yahweh's Final Victory—The two chapters, inserted between the prophecies of national restoration (33–7) and the description of the Temple and its community (40–8), form an independent section ; yet they are so related in language, style, and point of view that they cannot in their original form be denied Ezekiel. They are parallel drafts of the same event : the invasion of Gog, the leader of the forces which launch a final assault upon the people of God. Historical considerations are by no means primary here. Legendary and mythological motifs intermingle : materials from the primeval *Urzeit*, prophetic representations of the Day of Yahweh, and floating oral traditions. These are employed to portray Yahweh's final triumph over the evil hosts which seek to threaten his sovereignty. The two chapters will be discussed together, according to their major themes.

XXXVIII 2 Gog the Invader—In characteristic d
fashion the divine oracle is given at once : **Behold, I am against you, O Gog** (38:2, 39:1 ; cf. 13:8, 30:22, 34:10. See §495*d*). But who is Gog ? He is said to be from Magog, probably a legendary assonance with Gog. In Gen. 10:2 ; 1 Chr. 1:5 ; and Rev. 20:8 Magog is a person. Many identifications have

514d been proposed for Gog, among them a god Gaga in Enuma Elish III, 11 ; Gyges, king of Lydia in Asia Minor (*c.* 690–657 B.C.), called Gugu in the Ashurbanipal Cylinder ; Ga-gai-a, mentioned in the el-Amarna letters as a land of barbarians ; Alexander the Great ; Antiochus Eupator. He comes from the extreme north and may possibly be the Northerner referred to by the prophet Joel and others (Jl 2:20 ; cf. Isa. 14:13 ; Jer. 1:14, 4:6, 6:1. See Arvid S. Kapelrud, *Joel Studies* (1948), 93–108). But above all he is the demonic and sinister leader of the peoples who are to make the final assault against the people of God (see H. H. Rowley, *The Relevance of Apocalyptic*, 33f., 40, 70).

e **5, 6. The Invading Peoples**—With Gog are associated many peoples : Meshech and Tubal, of whom he is prince (27:13, 32:26 ; cf. Assy. *Tabal* and *Musku* ; also the Μόσχοι and Τιβαρηνοί of Herodotus ; Gen. 10:2 ; 1 Chr. 1:5) ; Persia, Cush, and Put (27:10 ; Gen. 10:6) ; Gomer (Assy. *Gimirrai*, Greek Cimmerians ; cf. Herodotus i, 1–3f. ; Homer's *Odyssey* xi, 14ff. ; Gen. 10:2) ; Bethtogarmah (Assy. *Tilgarimmu* ; Gen. 10:2) ; Sheba, Dedan, Tarshish (27:12, 20, 22 ; cf. Gen. 10:7, 4). It is clear that the writer is availing himself in part at least of ancient traditions lying behind Gen. 10. The peoples come from widely separated parts of the earth, a mighty host, like a cloud (38:7–8, 15–16), to wage battle under the mighty Gog. **Israel's Time of Peace**—Israel lives at the centre of the earth (see 5:5) in peace and security, **a quiet people who dwell securely** in unwalled towns and villages without gates (38:8*d*, 11, 14 ; cf. Zech. 2:4). But the Day of the Lord is near (39:8*b* ; 38:7, 10, 14, 18, 19, 39:11). It is a day of judgment upon the enemies of Israel, of
f Yahweh's victory and vindication. **4-6. The Defeat of Gog**—The annihilation of Gog and his mighty hosts (38:4–6) is described in language characteristic of the eschatology of doom (Isa. 2:14–15 ; Zeph. 1:7, 8, 14ff.). The mythological colouring of the account is pronounced (38:19*b*–21). The earth will quake, and all nature will tremble—the fish of the sea, the birds of the air, the beasts of the field, all creeping things which creep on the face of the ground, and all men on the face of the earth (Isa. 2:14–15 ; Zeph. 1:3); the mountains will be cast down, the cliffs fall, and every wall tumble (cf. Gen. 1 ; Ps. 46 ; Jer. 4:23–6). Yahweh summons every kind of terror against Gog (Jer. 25:29, contrast 36:29), including sword, pestilence, and bloodshed, and will rain upon his hordes and peoples torrential rains, hail, fire, and brimstone (Gen. 19:24 ; Isa. 34:9).

g **XXXIX 9-15.** His vast armaments will serve as fuel for his people for seven years, and so great will be the number of the dead that it will take seven months to bury them in the Valley of Abarim east of the Dead Sea, which is now to be named ' The Valley of Gog's hordes '. The Day will be Yahweh's great sacrificial feast (39:17–20 ; cf. Isa. 34:6 ; Zeph. 1:7, 8). The prophet strains every nerve to describe the momentousness of the event, and in his characteristic Hebraic manner enters into vivid and concrete detail. **The Former Prophecies**—The prophecies of doom of former times are said to allude to the final victory of Yahweh over Gog (38:17). Which prophecies the writer has in mind is not clear ; surely many of them referred to historical enemies like Assyria or Babylonia. He may have Jeremiah's oracles on the ' foe from the north ' in mind or oral traditions, or this may be a characteristic coalescence of past prophecy to focus it upon the final time. **Yahweh's Holiness and**
h **Glory**—It is Yahweh who called the hosts from the uttermost parts of the earth to wage war against his people (38:4ff.), but only that he might establish his sovereignty over the nations and vindicate his holiness before their eyes (38:16*b*), and make himself known (38:23). Thus they may come to acknowledge that he is the Holy One of Israel and realise that his name may no longer be profaned (39:8). He will show
forth his glory among the nations (39:21 ; cf. Isa. 514h
40:5). He will reverse the fortunes of Israel (39:25) : the spoilers will be despoiled, the plunderers plundered (39:10*b*). The integrity of his holy name will be preserved (39:25). The nations will come to understand the meaning of the exile and the return : they will see that Yahweh was working out his purpose in the one as well as the other, that he is a God of justice and mercy and that in his wrath he remembers mercy (39:25, 28). No longer will he hide his face in wrath from Israel when he pours out his Spirit upon them (36:26–7).

The Gog Tradition—Just as these prophecies about i
Gog are deeply rooted in ancient traditions and prophecies, so they became the source of later prophetic oracles and visions in which God's final and decisive act in history was proclaimed, notably in the apocalypses (Enoch 56:5–8 ; 4 Ezr. 13:5, 8ff. ; Rev. 22:7–10 ; cf. also Isa. 66:15–19 ; Jl 2:23–32 ; Zech. 12:1–14:21).

XL-XLVIII Vision of the Temple and the Temple 515a
Community—Ezek. opens and closes with a vision of the glory of God. The elaborate detail of the opening vision culminates in the revelation of the divine glory (ch. 9) ; the architectural detail of the first section of the closing vision (40:1–43) reaches its climax similarly in the return of the glory to the new Temple (43:1–9). Because of Israel's gross profanation and desecration of Yahweh's dwelling (cf., e.g., ch. 8), the glory had departed from its ancient habitation (10:18–22, 11:22–5). But Yahweh will restore his people to their land, a new nation and a purified people (chs. 34–9), and will dwell in their midst (20:40–4, 37:26–7). In the description of the Temple complex the prophet is influenced by his memories of the Temple of Solomon, by the fortified sanctuaries of Babylonia, and by his own distinctive theological viewpoint. While chs. 34–9 are dominated by national interests and the role of the priesthood is completely absent, here the latter occupy a central position and the national features are wanting. It is noteworthy that the spatial dimensions and details are presented in the context of narrative, a characteristic feature of Hebraic mentality. The basis of the new theocracy is the presence of Yahweh in the midst of his people : these chapters are therefore the climax of the whole book, and gain their momentous significance by all that has preceded them. The Epistle to the Hebrews and other sections of the NT, in turn, are to be understood in contexts such as this.

XL-XLII The Temple and its Courts b
XL 1-5 Introduction—At the beginning of the year 573 B.C. (so LXX) Ezekiel is transported in vision to a high mountain (Isa. 2:2 ; Mic. 4:1 ; Zech. 14:10 ; Mt. 21:6 ; Rev. 21:10) and sees spread out before him a building-complex, with walls and gates, like a city. **6ff.** Finding himself at the east gate he meets a man like a figure of bronze, his architectural guide (cf. Zech. 1:9, 11, 13, 2:5 ; Rev. 21:15), with a measuring-reed in his hand. The reed is about ten feet four inches in length. Ezekiel is ordered to concentrate intently on all that he is to see, for he must report his vision to the exiles.

6-16 The East Gate—The East Gate, in direct line c
with the main approach to the Temple, especially in the celebration of the New Year, was of great cultic importance (see Julian Morgenstern, ' The Gates of Righteousness ', HUCA 6 (1929), 1–37). The Temple area is an elevated pavement and is designed to separate the holy from the profane (42:20). Ascending the seven steps (so LXX ; cf. 22, 26) they arrive at the threshold and then the passageway of the gate, where there are three guard-rooms facing each other on each side, all of them a perfect square and of the same dimensions. Beyond the passageway is a second threshold and the vestibule of the gate leading to the court. The architectural features have affinities with Syrian and Palestinian temples, such as those at Carchemish (Galling, *Biblisches Reallexikon*,

515c 523, No. 4) and Megiddo (ANEP, No. 721 ; cf.
Carl G. Howie, *Date and Composition of Ezekiel*, 43–6).
d **17-19 Pavement and Rooms**—Along the wall of
the outer court, to a depth of the length of the gates,
runs a large pavement with thirty chambers, probably
symmetrically arranged, although this detail is lacking.
The *lower* pavement is distinguished from the *higher*
pavement of the inner court. The degrees of holiness
are represented by the increasing elevation of the
various parts of the Temple complex. The distance
from the end of the east gate to that of the inner court
measured a hundred cubits.
e **20-27 The North and South Gates of the Court**—
These structures are exactly the same in architectural
design as the East Gate. The prophet's characteristic
repetitive style and love of detail is to be noted. His
priestly interests and mentality continually assert
themselves. **28-37 The Gates of the Inner Court**—
The gates are of the same construction as those of the
outer court, with the exception that there are eight
steps leading to them instead of seven, and that the
vestibule at the opposite end is a real vestibule to the
Temple. **38-43 Tables for Sacrifice**—The arrangements for the sacrifices at the inner gateway are here
described. While the exact location is omitted, the
reference may be to the east gate or possibly to all
f three gates. **44-47 The Priests' Rooms**—Ezekiel
is now led to the inner court where he sees two rooms
at the side of the north and south (LXX) gates, the
former for the priests who have charge of the Temple
precincts, the latter for those who have charge of the
altar. The court is a perfect square. **48-49 The
Vestibule of the Temple**—The elevation of the
vestibule is ten steps higher than the inner court.
The guide measured the vestibule ; its length was
twenty cubits, its breadth twelve (LXX). The
pillars probably stood in front of the vestibule, and
correspond to the Jachin and Boaz of Solomon's
temple (R. B. Y. Scott, ' The Pillars of Jachin and
Boaz ', JBL 58 (1939), 143–9 ; H. G. May, ' The Two
Pillars Before the Temple of Solomon ', BASOR 88
(1942), 19–27).
g **XLI 1-26**. The general structure of the Temple with
its vestibule (*'ûlām*), nave (*hêkhāl*), and most holy place
(*d^{e}bhîr*) corresponds in general with Near Eastern
sanctuaries, such as those at Tell Tainat (ANEP,
No. 739) and Khorsabad (Gordon Loud et al.,
Khorsabad (1936)). For details see G. Ernest Wright,
' Solomon's Temple Resurrected ', BA 7 (1944), 65–77.
1-4. The prophet is now led to the nave (Heb. *hêkhāl* ;
cf. Sumerian *egal*, Akkad. *ēkallu*), the large inner room
or holy place, but the guide enters the Most Holy
Place alone. This small room to the rear of the Temple
is called elsewhere the *d^{e}bhîr*, probably to be derived
from Arabic *dbr*, ' back ' or ' rear '. The entrances
to the vestibule, nave, and Most Holy Place are
increasingly narrow, symbolising the degree of their
sanctity. The Priestly writer of Lev. 16 records that
only the high priest is permitted to enter the *d^{e}bhîr*
and then only on the Day of Atonement. The descrip-
h tion of the room is characteristically reserved. **5-15a
The Side Chambers**—Along three sides of the
Temple the side chambers are ranged, thirty to each
story. What purpose they served we are not told, but
they may well have contained Temple furnishings or
objects connected with its service or gifts. The Temple
was elevated upon a platform or terrace about ten feet
above the level of the inner court. To the west of the
Temple was a large building, ninety by seventy cubits.
Here again we are not told its purpose ; it may have
been used for storage. The Temple building with the
surrounding yard was one hundred cubits square.
i **15b-26 The Interior of the Temple**—There is
much that is obscure here, but it is clear that the
interior was elaborately panelled ; from the ground
to the windows the walls are covered with carved
figures of cherubim and palm trees. Archaeological
parallels have been found in the ivory inlays from
Samaria (Wright, ibid., Figs. 5–6). Before the entrance

to the Most Holy Place stood an altar of wood, which 515i
the guide calls ' the table which is before the Lord '.
Archaeological illustration of such an altar has been
seen in temples at Bethshean and Ugarit (see May,
296). For the table of the Presence, cf. Exod. 25:23–30 ;
Lev. 24:5–9 ; 1 Kg. 20.
XLII 1-20 The Chambers of the Priests—1, 10. j
North and south of the Temple and facing the Temple
yard are three-storey buildings, each arranged in two
blocks. **13.** These contain the priests' rooms. They
are peculiarly holy, for there the most holy offerings
are stored and consumed, and there the priests keep
the holy garments which they wear when they minister
before the Lord. **14.** Once they have entered the holy
place, they are not to enter the outer court without
first leaving them in the rooms reserved for this
purpose. Only the building to the north is described
since the one to the south is exactly the same in
structure and dimensions, in accordance with the remarkable symmetry of the whole Temple complex.
The detailed description is often obscure. The whole
Temple area is a perfect square of 500 cubits, approximately 860 feet, on each side. The great wall is
designed to separate Yahweh's holy dwelling from
human habitations. To enter the Temple is to enter
the sphere of the holy ; there the distance between
God and man is overcome in acts of prayer and
contrition and sacrifice (cf. Heb. 9:1–14).
XLIII 1-12 Yahweh's Return to the New Temple k
—Now that the vision of the new Temple is over and
Ezekiel has been shown its gates, courts, walls, and
sacred precincts, all is in readiness for the event to
which the long description leads. **2.** Yahweh approaches the city from the east, not only because he
had gone to the east upon his departure (11-23), but
also because the east gate is associated with the cultic
rites of New Year's Day. **3, 4.** The auditory, visual,
and psychical manifestations are the same as those
we have encountered before : the sound of many
waters, the intense radiance of the glory (cf. 1 Kg.
8:11 ; Ps. 24 ; Isa. 6:1–3 ; also Exod. 40:34–8), the
prophet's prostration, and his transportation by the
Spirit. **6.** As usual, the vision is preliminary to the
audition (6–12 ; cf. 43:6 and 1:28*b*). Yahweh comes
to dwell as king among his people, one of the major
motifs of biblical faith (1 Kg. 8:27 ; cf. also Ps.,
Second Isaiah). The Temple is his throne (Jer. 14:21 ;
also 3:17, 17:21) and his footstool (Ps. 132:7, 99:5 ;
Lam. 2:1). Such representations are familiar in the
inscriptions and reliefs of other Near Eastern peoples
(see ANEP, Nos. 456–60, 493, 545). In the new age
of Yahweh's tabernacling among his people the Temple
will no more be unclean, either by the ' harlotry ' of
the apostate cults (cf. ch. 8), or by the proximity of the
royal tombs. Indeed, the holiness of the Temple is
such that there is no room for a royal palace or similar
structures, in contrast with the pre-exilic Temple of
Solomon (1 Kg. 7). **7, 9.** The return of the glory of
God to the restored Temple means two things :
**Yahweh will dwell in the midst of his people
for ever,** and **12 the ' law ' of the temple is
holiness.**
13-27 The Altar and its Ordinances—This section 516a
has probably been misplaced (after 40:47 ?). The
description of the altar may reflect Mesopotamian
cosmic associations, as is suggested, for example, by
the word *'^{a}rî'ēl* (RSV ' altar hearth ' ; cf. Akkad.
Arallu, either ' underworld ' or ' mountain of the
gods '), and may have been transmitted to Israel
through Phoenician influence (W. F. Albright, JBL 29
(1920), 132–47, ARI, 150–2). The definite article
appears before the word ; render in 15 ' the mountain
of God ', in 16 ' the Ariel '. The altar is impressive
in its dimensions ; its base eighteen cubits square,
its height twelve cubits including the horns. Erected
upon a base, it rose in three square blocks, each smaller
in size than the preceding. Its increase in height,
like that of the Temple, symbolises increasing sanctity ;
the dimensions, too, probably have symbolic signi-

16a ficance. Like the famous altars at Ba'albek and Petra, it is approached by steps. The ordinances which follow are designed to insure the sanctity of the altar. Elaborate sacrifices are to be offered for seven days to make atonement for the altar and to purify and consecrate it, and from the eighth day on the priests are to offer burnt and peace offerings. When all the ceremonies have been completed, Yahweh will accept his people.

b **XLIV 1-3 The Closed East Gate**—From the inner court (43:5) Ezekiel is led to the east gate of the outer court where he sees that the gate is shut. The guide explains that it is to remain closed since Yahweh had returned to his Temple through it (43:4) ; no human foot may therefore violate its holiness. A remnant of sacral kingship may be preserved in the single exception that the prince may enter the gate to 'eat bread'.

c **4-31 The Temple Personnel**—Yahweh had explained to the prophet 'the Torah of the temple' and had answered the cultic question, 'Who shall enter Yahweh's holy courts ?' Now he is given the Torah which is to govern the Temple personnel (44:5). The solemnity and importance of the event of the new Torah is indicated by the opening theophany (44:4), which introduces the long audition. The personnel of the Temple is to be reorganised, and the laws of holiness are to be observed strictly.

d **6-9 Exclusion of Foreigners**—In the Sinaitic covenant Israel had become a holy people dedicated to the service of Yahweh (Exod. 3:12, 5:3, 14:5). Yet in the pre-exilic sanctuary foreigners had performed some of the services (e.g. the Carites in 2 Kg. 11:4–8). Their presence is an offence to Yahweh, a profanation of his holiness, and a breaking of the covenant. So Yahweh gives a new Torah for the sanctuary. **10-14. The Levites** are to assume their duties, such as guarding the gates, slaughtering the sacrificial animals, and performing the services of the outer courts. Josiah's reformation of 621 B.C. had made just provision for the Levites (Dt. 18:1–7), but the Jerusalem priests had dealt more harshly with them (2 Kg. 23:9). Ezekiel makes a sharp distinction between the Levites and the priests of the Temple. The former are reduced to menial tasks, a punishment for their guilt in the worship at the high-places. It may be due to this situation that few Levites returned from Babylonia with Ezra (Ezr. 2:36–40, 58) ; later times sought to improve their lot (cf. G. von Rad, *Das Geschichtsbild des chronistischen Werkes* (1930), 98ff.). They came to occupy a place of distinction in the Second Temple,
e above all in the Temple choirs. **15-31 The Zadokite Priests**—The legitimate priests of the sanctuary are to be the sons of Zadok (15). They are to be in charge of the sanctuary, to 'come near' to Yahweh, to minister before him, and to offer sacrifices. Originally Zadok may have been a Jebusite priest (H. H. Rowley, 'Zadok and Nehushtan,' JBL 58 (1939), 112–41). When Abiathar was deposed because of his espousal of the cause of Adonijah, Zadok became the chief priest, and his line continued until the Maccabaean period. Among the covenanters of Qumrân he still holds a position of great importance. The holiness of the priests is expressed in the special linen garments they are to wear when they enter the inner court (cf. also Exod. 28:39ff. ; Lev. 6:36, 8:24f., 16:4), for which there are good Syrian and Phoenician parallels. Further regulations follow : **20** the priests may not shave their heads nor allow the hair to grow long ; **21** they must not drink wine before entering the inner court ; **22** they may marry a virgin of Israelite birth or the widow of a priest ; **23** they must teach the people the differences between clean and unclean ; **24a** they must settle disputes in their own court of law ; **24b** they are responsible for the proper observance of the festivals and the sanctification of the sabbaths (cf. 22:26) ; and **25-7** they must keep themselves from contact with the dead except in the case of near relatives. **28.** They shall have no inheritance in Israel, for Yahweh alone is their inheritance ; 516e
nor shall they have possessions, for Yahweh is their possession. One is reminded of the Qumrân covenanters, a pre-eminently priestly community. The revenues of the sanctuary are to be paid wholly in kind (cf. Dt. 18).

XLV 1-8 Allotment of the Land to the Holy f
Community—The passage is out of place here (cf. 44:28) and belongs with 47:13–48:36 ; it is parallel with 48:8–22, which is more complete, however. The radical reconstitution of life requires a new allotment of the territory. It may be compared to the list of Levitical towns in Jos. 21:1–42 (cf. Lev. 25:33–4 ; Num. 35:1–8 ; 1 Chr. 6:1–81). Yahweh instructs the people to set apart a sacred reserve of 25,000 by 20,000 cubits, which is to be divided into two rectangular strips of identical dimensions : the one to the north to be assigned to the Levites, the one to the south to the Zadokite priests. The Temple area lies within the latter region, but is surrounded by an open space of fifty cubits in width. South of the sacred area is another rectangle of 25,000 by 5,000 cubits, reserved for the city of Jerusalem. The whole forms a perfect square of 25,000 cubits to the side or about 8·3 miles. To the east, extending to the Jordan, and to the west, extending to the Mediterranean Sea, lies the domain of the prince. The land is assigned to him by Yahweh ; he therefore holds it in trust and has no cause for expropriating the property of his subjects (cf. 1 Kg. 19).

9-17 Rights and Duties of the Prince—The g
stirring exhortation of 9 with its solemn oracular opening (cf. 44:6) is in the manner of the pre-exilic prophets : **Execute justice and righteousness.** In contrast to his predecessors, like Jehoiakim, the prince may not resort to violence or oppression. A prophetic *tôrāh* follows : **You shall have just balances, a just ephah, and a just bath.** The demand for honesty in weights and measures is a constant motif in prophetic religion (Dt. 25:13–16 ; Am. 8:5 ; Mic. 6:10) and was perpetuated by the wisdom writers (Prov. 11:1, 16:11, 20:10, 23) and the Holiness Code (Lev. 19:35). The duties of the prince are then described. His function here is cultic. Since the people offer him revenues in kind, which were not at all excessive, it is his duty to provide the various offerings for the sacrifices at the festivals, the new moons, and sabbaths. Thus all the offerings go through his hand, and he offers them for the whole people (cf. the Athenian ἄρχων βασιλεύς and the Roman *rex sacrificulus*).

XLV 18-XLVI 15 Festivals and Offerings— 517a
Annually, at the beginning of the first and seventh months, marking the division of the religious calendar, sacrifices of atonement are to be offered for the sanctuary (cf. 43:18–27). These days of atonement are in preparation for the celebrations of the Passover and a second festival, not named, but probably intended to be the Feast of Weeks (see Julian Morgenstern, 'The Calendar of Ezekiel 45:18–25', HUCA 21 (1948), 493–6). Observe again how Ezekiel stresses temporal as well as spatial symmetry. In 20 read with LXX 'first day of the seventh month'. The duties and obligations of the prince are purely cultic in nature. No king ever sat on the throne of David after Ezekiel's time, but in the period of the Hasmonaean princes their constitutional status was largely defined by their high-priestly functions.

XLVI 1-15 From the celebrations of the two festivals b
the prophet turns to the offerings for the sabbaths and new moons. The opening verses parallel 44:1–3 ; there the east gate is shut and only the prince may enter the vestibule to 'eat bread' ; here the inner gate is also to remain closed on working-days, but it may be opened on sabbaths and new moons (the first day of the month). **2.** The prince may not proceed beyond the threshold of the east gate to enter into the inner court, but from his position he can see the priests offering his sacrifices on the great altar and

517b join in the worship. **3.** The people worship at the entrance of the east gate in the outer court. The prince's offerings on the sabbath are described in 4f., on the day of the new moon in 6f. The only difference is that on the latter day a young bull is added. **9.** The worshippers are to leave in orderly manner and must use the gate opposite to that from which they entered. **10.** Prince and people are one in their worship : when they enter, he must enter ; when they leave, he must leave. **12.** When the prince wishes to make a free-will offering (cf. §544*c*) the east gate is to be open as on the sabbath and new moon. **13-15.** For the daily burnt offerings the prince also makes provision.

c **16-18.** The property of the prince is inalienable and must remain within the family. He may bequeath it to his sons ; but if any of it is given to his officials, it must revert to him in the year of release, probably the sabbatical year (cf. Jer. 34:14 ; cf. also §516*f*).

d **19-24 The Kitchens**—At the west end of the row of rooms running parallel to the north and south of the Temple (42:1–13) are the kitchens reserved for the priests. Here they boil the guilt and sin offerings and bake the cereal offering. The food is especially holy and must in no event be brought into contact with the outer court lest its holiness produce evil effects upon the people (cf. 42:14, 44:9).

e **XLVII 1-12 The Sacred Stream from the Sanctuary**—The dominant motif of the prophecy, Yahweh's self-manifestation in glory, here reaches its climax. The glory dwells in the adytum of the sanctuary, in the centre of the land and of the holy community, yet it extends its power and beneficent gifts through the land (cf. Isa. 6:3). In the new age conditions will return to what they were at the beginning ; nature will be transformed by the presence of the divine glory in the midst of Israel (cf. Isa. 40:5, 41:17–20, etc.). Ezekiel employs the old mythological motif of the river of God with its life-giving waters, but employs it in his own way in the light of his conception of a Temple-centred land. From beneath the threshold of the east gate of the sanctuary, he sees a stream of water issue forth to the east, from the holy mount to the lifeless waters of the Dead Sea. The guide measures the depth of the river as it flows on its course, first only ankle-deep but finally so deep that one cannot pass through it. **6.** The significance of the transformation must not be lost upon the prophet. As the stream empties into the Dead Sea, its waters become fresh and healthy like the Mediterranean Sea and swarm with fish. **10.** From Engedi, modern Tell el-Jurn on the western shores of the Dead Sea, to En-eglaim, probably modern 'Ain Feshkhā, two miles to the south of Khirbet Qumrân, fishermen dry their nets. **11.** The prophet's realism is seen in his reference to the salt water of the swamps and marshes ; the region is still famous for its salt deposits. **12.** On both sides of the river the prophet sees many trees. They bear fruit every month (cf. Ps. 1:3), and their leaves are for healing (Exod. 15:22–6). The fruit is abundant and the leaves do not wither because the water flows from the sanctuary. The sources of this tradition of the miraculous river are less historical (e.g. Isa. 8:6) than mythological, as Ugaritic and OT parallels attest. In Ugarit Mt Ṣaphon, the dwelling of the gods, was called the 'sources of the rivers' ; in Ps. 46:5 ; Jl 3:18 ; Zech. 14:8 the river plays a similarly important role. See Rev. 22:1–2. While this passage has often been given allegorical interpretation, its true significance lies in the life-giving forces which stream from the sanctuary.

f **13-23 The Boundaries of the Land**—The land is to be divided equally among the twelve tribes of Israel, Ephraim and Manasseh to receive the portion of Joseph (cf. 37:15–22). All the tribes are to occupy western Palestine. The northern boundary extends from a point on the Mediterranean to the entrance of Hamath (2 Kg. 14:25 ; Am. 6:14), probably near Kadesh on the Orontes (see Map 6 at end of this volume), on to Hazar-enon, north of Damascus and

the Ḥaurân ; the eastern is formed by the Sea of 517
Galilee, the Jordan, and the Dead Sea ; the southern runs through Meribath-kadesh, i.e. Kadesh-barnea, probably 'Ain Qedeis, the Brook of Egypt, the Wâdi el-'Arîsh, to the Mediterranean, which also forms the western boundary. No distinction is to be made between the native-born Israelite and the resident alien. A similar representation is given in the Holiness (Lev. 17:15, 19:34, 24:16) and Priestly (Num. 15:29–30) codes (cf. §230*e*).

XLVIII 1-29 Tribal Allotments—The passage is g
set in the framework of the northern and southern boundaries of the land (1, 28 ; cf. 47:15–17, 19) and amplifies the instruction of 47:21. The tribal divisions are described in short, stereotyped, and identically constructed sentences (2–8*a*, (23), 24–9) ; 48:8*b*–22, an expansion of 45:1–8, is a description of the great square containing the sacred area and the allotment to the city of Jerusalem. The allotments are, of course, purely theoretical and schematic and show little correspondence with historico-geographic location or the relative size of the populations. Each tribe is assigned a strip of territory of the same width, running parallel east and west the breadth of the land. From north to south the first seven tribes are ordered as follows : Dan, Asher, Naphtali, Manasseh, Ephraim, Reuben, and Judah. To the south the order is Benjamin, Simeon, Issachar, Zebulun, and Gad. Jerusalem is the only fixed point in the description and occupies its historic position ; its centrality in Israel's sacred past, memories associated with the pre-exilic Temple, and Ezekiel's theology would require it. Judah lies to the immediate north, Benjamin to the south ; this, too, is an attempt to do justice to their historic relationship to the city. Dan and Asher are given their approximate historical position in the north, and Simeon is appropriately placed in the south. On the other hand, the northern tribes of Issachar and Zebulun are also assigned to the south, while the Transjordanian tribes of Reuben and Gad are located north and south respectively of the area containing the sacred districts. The concubine tribes are farthest from the Temple complex. In the description of the great square it is noteworthy that the city in the southern portion is surrounded by an open region to insure the sanctity of the Temple complex.

30-35 The Holy City—On each of the four sides h
of the city there are to be three gates, named after the twelve tribes of Israel, Interestingly, Levi is included among the northern exits, while Ephraim and Manasseh are represented by Joseph among the three exits on the east. Rev. 21:12–14 is dependent upon this passage ; there, however, reference is made to the twelve foundations of the wall, on which are inscribed the names of the twelve apostles. The circumference of the city is about six miles. **35.** As a climax the city receives a new name, corresponding to its new status : **Yahweh is there** (cf. Isa. 1:26, 60:14, 18, 62:2 ; Jer. 3:17 ; Zech. 8:3). In a word it summarises not only the closing and culminating chapters of the prophecy, but also the dominant consciousness and central concern of Ezekiel, the priest and prophet, from beginning to end.

Bibliography—Commentaries : A. Bertholet, HAT (2nd ed. 1936) ; J. A. Bewer, Harper's Annotated Bible (1954) ; G. A. Cooke, ICC (1951) ; A. B. Davidson and A. W. Streane, CB (1916) ; G. Fohrer, HAT (1955) ; J. Herrmann, KAT (1924) ; I. G. Matthews, *An American Commentary on the OT* (1939); H. G. May, IB vi (1956).

Other Literature : A. Bentzen, *Introduction to the OT* (1948) ; O. Eissfeldt, *Einleitung in das AT* (2nd ed. 1956); C. G. Howie, *The Date and Composition of Ezekiel* (1950); R. H. Pfeiffer, *Introduction to the OT* (1941) ; H. Wheeler Robinson, *Two Hebrew Prophets* (1948) ; H. H. Rowley, 'The Book of Ezekiel in Modern Study', BJRL 36 (1953), 146–90 ; J. Ziegler, *Ezechiel*, Septuaginta XVI, 1 (1952).

DANIEL

By J. BARR

8a **Divisions of the Book**—1. *By contents* the book divides into two sections: firstly the stories, comprising chs. 1–6, stories related about Daniel and his companions under the Babylonian and Median kings; and secondly the visions, comprising chs. 7–12, basically four in number, related by Daniel in the first person for the most part. In the first part Daniel appears as interpreter of heavenly secrets; in the second they are told to him and he has difficulty in understanding them. The atmosphere of the two sections is very different, the fairly straightforward narrative of the first contrasting strongly with the cryptic obscurity of the second. Yet a number of important connections between the language and matter in the two sections remains, e.g. between ch. 2 and ch. 7.

b 2. *By language*—The beginning of the book (1:1–2:4*a*) is in Heb., and so are chs. 8–12; the rest is in Aram. The division by language does not agree with that by contents given above, ch. 7 especially belonging by language to what precedes and by content to what follows. Different attempts have been made by scholars to explain the strange change of language within the book. The writer of this article would suggest that the procedure is in conscious imitation of Ezr., which drew on a source already written in Aram., introduces this source in quoting a letter of the Persian administration and continues thereafter in this language (Ezr. 4:7). The passage might well be of special interest in Daniel's time because it ends with the dedication of the new Temple (Ezr. 6:16–18). Our author, having certain traditions in Aram., introduces them with direct speech in the same way (2:4) and assumes that the language used by the Persian administrators in Ezr. would also be used by the 'Chaldeans' in Babylon; and takes it to be proper, in starting with the new language, to insert the tag 'in Aramaic' which he found in the received text of Ezr. (4:7). Coming to the end of his Aram. material, he naturally reverts to Heb., as Ezra did, without ceremony.

c **Origin of the Book**—It is almost universally held among scholars that the complete book as we now have it was written in the time of Antiochus IV Epiphanes (175–163 B.C.) and more particularly after the desecration of the Temple by him in 168 and before its reconsecration by the Maccabees in 165. Chs. 8–12 mention the 'abomination of desolation' which he built upon the altar but still look forward to the coming end of this time of trouble and sacrilege. It is probable however that the stories of chs. 1–6 originated in the Diaspora under the Persian or early Greek empires, for their original setting is not in a situation of persecution of Judaism by the state. Nevertheless, inasmuch as they dealt with the problem of the loyal Jew within a heathen empire, they remained relevant in Antiochus' time and would be reinterpreted for that situation. It is unlikely that the stories existed in written form separately before the present book was written. The writer has set down the oral tradition about Daniel and added to it the visions which are his own creation, intending the two to
d belong together. Within the book as a whole ch. 7 has a cardinal place, for it belongs to both sections and
unites them. It is perhaps probable that the basic 518d
elements of ch. 7 existed in oral tradition from about the time of Alexander and his first successors, but that in Antiochus' time they were moulded into the present form and, because of their special nature, received a much more thorough remoulding to fit the new situation than was given to anything in chs. 1–6. 8–12 then are a kind of commentary on ch. 7 after a further
development in the historical situation. The language e
of the book is of a late character, and in particular the occurrence of Gr. words is a decisive argument against the 'conservative' opinion that the book was written by Daniel himself.

The Figure of Daniel—Whether a Daniel in fact f
attained high position at the Babylonian or Persian courts is hardly possible for us to say. The name occurs in lists of exilic date, Ezr. 8:2; Neh. 10:6, but there of men of priestly family. More important is the appearance of the name along with Noah and Job in Ezek. 14:12–20, where Daniel seems to be regarded like Noah as an example of righteousness from remote antiquity (cf. the appearance of the Enoch figure in apocalyptic in the same way). Further, the Ugaritic texts of the 14th cent. B.C. know of a Daniel who is a righteous king and judge. It seems probable that Daniel was the name of a hero of legend, used in different ways at different times, and prominent especially in the story-telling of the Persian and Greek Diaspora, where he personified in story the practical and theological problems of the Jews in that environment. Our author gathers and writes down the Daniel tradition, and in the visions which he himself produces writes in the name of Daniel, clearly because he sees the older Daniel tradition and his own newer work as an integral whole.

Historical accuracy—The writer's knowledge of the g
Babylonian and Persian times in which the scene is set depends rather on popular tradition and on scattered biblical references than on exact historical information, and thus presents a mixture of true reminiscence and inaccurate surmise. The user of this commentary should make constant reference to the article on *History of Israel—II Post-Exilic*. In particular mention must be made of the position of the Medes and the king Darius the Mede in this book. At times it lumps Medes and Persians together—so 5:28, 6:8, 8:3, 20. Elsewhere it distinguishes the two, and this is specially significant in the important picture of the four kingdoms. The separate place given to Media was justified by the leadership of that people in events at the end of the 7th cent. B.C. and by references to them in biblical prophecy. The error of Dan. is to place the Median empire after the Babylonian and to make the Medes conquerors of Babylon, giving the Babylonian, Median, Persian and Greek empires as the succession of four. To this he was moved by a simple belief that Medes and Persians belonged together, so that it would not be natural to see the former as simultaneous with the Babylonian empire and no world-rulers, and yet that they were sufficiently distinct to require separate treatment as successive régimes. To this should be added the influence of passages like Isa. 13:17, 21:2; Jer. 51:11, 28, etc., which prophesy the destruction of Babylon by the

518g Medes more clearly and explicitly than any biblical passage describes Cyrus as the destroyer of the Babylonian régime. Darius the Mede is in all probability a figure constructed purely on the basis of the above theory of the Median empire. On Belshazzar and the circumstances of the fall of Babylon see commentary on ch. 5 (see §523).

h It is important to recognise how far the writer is determined in his historical and theological opinions by the earlier scriptures of Israel. For his view of history, a case in point would be his belief in the existence of four kings of Persia (7:6, 11:2). In the OT four *names* of Persian kings occur (Cyrus, Darius, Xerxes, Artaxerxes). Some of these names were in fact borne by more than one king, but our author, or rather the tradition behind him, concludes for four kings in all. His removal of the name Darius to serve for a Median and not a Persian king does not affect this list of four, for he knew from Neh. 12:22 of a 'Darius the Persian' who would certainly not be his (fictitious) Median Darius, but would, he would assume, be the same Darius whom he knew from Ezr., Hag., and Zech. For other examples cf. commentary on 1:1.

The historical accuracy of the book increases as we come down into the Greek period (especially ch. 11) where the history is however traced cryptically in visionary form. The writer's view of history is a theological one, for the rise and fall of historical powers is in the hand of God, and the secret times of his intervention are made known by him to the prophets and to such interpreters as Daniel.

i **Additional Daniel Tradition**—Certain traditions about Daniel and his friends are not to be found within the canonical Heb.-Aram. book, but exist in the Gr. texts of Dan., and appear in English versions of the Apoc. as Sus., Bel and S 3 Ch. These represent further living development of the Daniel tradition beyond what we have in the canonical book.

519a **I Daniel's Coming to Babylon and his Education in Wisdom**—This chapter may be seen under two aspects. Firstly it serves as an introduction to the whole book, describing Daniel's coming to Babylon and the beginnings of his skill in wisdom and interpretation. Examples of this skill will be unfolded in the succeeding chapters, and further we are introduced to the three companions who will be the centre of interest in ch. 3. It is reasonable therefore to suppose that the material of 2–6 lay complete before the author when he wrote the present form of ch. 1. This need not mean another author.

Secondly, however, the chapter contains the first of the Daniel stories proper, telling how he and his friends refused the rich food of the royal court and yet were better nourished on their simple fare. This story is not merely introduction but stands on an equal footing with the others of 2–6. There is no reason to believe that it was specially invented for its present place; it is more likely that it had its own existence in oral tradition before it was incorporated in the introduction. The use of Heb. suggests that it had a rather different history of transmission from the Aram. stories of 2–6.

b **1. In the third year:** this would be 606; but that date would be before Nebuchadnezzar's victory over Egypt and his accession to the Babylonian throne. The date is inexact. In all probability the writer intends the great deportation of 597, which followed soon after the death of Jehoiakim and in which his son Jehoiachin was taken to Babylon (2 Kg. 24:10–16). A rather vague mention of an attack by Nebuchadnezzar on Jehoiakim appears however in 2 Chr. 36:5–8, and under the influence of this tradition the writer has read the 'three years' of 2 Kg. 24:1 as if they meant the first three years of Jehoiakim's reign. The writer makes Daniel's career begin from the earlier deportation rather than from the greater disaster of 586 when Jerusalem was destroyed, because great interest was commonly attached to the first deportation. From it are reckoned the seventy years of Jer. 29:10; it has indeed been suggested that the giving of the date 606 is an attempt to make the period of 70 years work out more exactly—not a very probable suggestion. Among the exiles of the first deportation Ezekiel worked; to them Jeremiah sent promises of blessing if they would seek the welfare of their new home in Babylonia; and the king then deported, unlike the unhappy Zedekiah, lived to enjoy in the end a release from hardship. For Mt. 1:11 the first deportation was the end of an era. 519b

c **2. The land of Shinar:** Babylonia. An archaic phrase, suggesting the land where of old Nimrod dwelt and where the tower of Babel (Babylon) was built and destroyed (Gen. 10:8–10, 11:1–9). **The vessels:** recapitulating 2 Kg. 24:13 and preparing for the part taken by these vessels in ch. 5. Not only drinking-vessels are meant, but any kind of temple furniture; it is the vessels for liquid however which figure in ch. 5. The dedication in the temples of captured vessels was common practice; cf. Jos. 6:19. **His god:** Bel or Marduk, whose great sanctuary was in Babylon. **3. The royal family:** it would also be possible to translate as if three classes of people were involved, viz. Israelites, Babylonian princes, noble Babylonian children. We cannot deduce for certain whether Daniel and his friends are thought to belong to the royal family of Judah; unless the mention of a Daniel as a son of David in the (late) 1 Chr. 3:1 counts for anything; or we may regard the wisdom in which Daniel excels as a kingly attribute. The youths to be chosen are to be talented both physically and mentally; and these endowments are to be developed by a suitable diet and an advanced education. The purpose primarily is that the splendour of the palace should be embellished by the beauty and culture of the young attendants.

d **4. The letters and language of the Chaldeans:** the word 'Chaldean' may have two senses in Daniel: (1) The Kashdu or Kaldu, a people of lower Babylonia, who eventually expanded to dominate the country; the Neo-Babylonian kings and their empire are usually called 'Chaldean' in the OT. So Dan. 5:30, 9:1. (2) 'Wise men', 'astrologers'. So Dan. 2:2, etc. Astrology was highly developed in Mesopotamia, as were other methods of divining and influencing the future. This sense of the word, not native to Babylonia, was well known in the Graeco-Roman world. In this verse it is difficult to draw the exact boundary between the meanings. Probably the Akkadian tongue and its mysterious writing (cuneiform) are intended, but the culture thus revealed would largely consist of astrology, magic and the like. We cannot force the writer to be more precise than he is; he is only giving a general impression.

e **6f.** The Jewish youths bear names of familiar Heb. patterns; they are theophoric names, the ending *-el* meaning 'God', the ending *-iah* meaning Yahweh. The new names given by the chief eunuch are rather obscure, but clearly stand outside the Israelite religious world and indicate the changed lot of the youths, who must take their names from the world where their destiny now lies. The conception of the name as a living expression of the dominant force in one's life is common in the OT and in the ancient East generally. Belteshazzar clearly represents some Babylonian name, and in 4:8 it is regarded as containing the divine name Bel. In fact it is more probably a name in the form of a prayer—'Protect his life!' or 'Protect the life of the king!' Its similarity to the name of Belshazzar (5:1) is notable; in the Gr. translation they in fact were identical. In the name Abed-Nego the latter part may well be the divine name Nebo (Nabu) distorted, perhaps intentionally; and the other two names may also have been distorted in the tradition. A reasonable possibility however is that Shadrach stands for Marduk (like Nisroch, 2 Kg. 19:37) and that Meshach stands for Sheshach (cipher for Babylon, Jer. 25:26).

519e In the Gr. period it was common for Jews of Hellenistic sympathies to adopt Gr. names similar to their own Jewish name, e.g. Jason instead of Jesus. This may have given extra point to these verses; but it would be too much to say that the verses are polemic against the adoption of foreign names. No objection is raised by the heroes of the story, and the new names are used occasionally afterwards.

f **8f.** Concerning the king's rich diet, however, Daniel is adamant. The objection does not come from a puritanical opposition to delicacies as such, but from the likelihood that they would contain either meats forbidden by the Law (Dt. 14) or foods which had been offered to idols; to eat of such would be a ritual defilement. The chief eunuch is cordially sympathetic to Daniel, a result of divine action on his behalf. The type of literature represented in these stories and in other late books like Est. and Tob.—all stories of captivity and diaspora—does not describe Jewish life in exile as continual misery and torment; the Jew in exile is often successful, on good terms with authorities and even with kings, except when accident or the machinations of enemies temporarily shatter these good relationships. A good deal of the style in this respect goes back to the story of Joseph in Egypt.

g **10ff.** Nevertheless the official is responsible for the nourishment of the youths; to deviate from the royal diet would do them no good, and he would be punished. Daniel therefore turns to a subordinate official and obtains permission for a ten days' test on a vegetable diet. Such a diet was safe from the risk of defilement; Josephus (*Life*, ch. 3) tells of pious Jews who lived only on figs and nuts, and cf. Tob. 1:10–11; 2 Mac. 5:27. Ten days is a short time to expect to see results in; presumably the plan would have been detected if the test had been continued longer, and of course the shortness of the time emphasises the remarkable results. Contrary to all expectation the four youths appear better nourished at the end of the test than those who enjoyed the royal diet. Thus ends the first of the Daniel stories proper; what follows (vv. 17–21) is supplementary. The purpose of the story is not merely to encourage scrupulousness in diet; that good Jews will be scrupulous is taken for granted. The point is the contrast between the results that such scrupulousness would naturally be expected to produce (loss of good appearance and therefore of favour and success) and those which it in fact produces (better appearance, greater favour and success). Practising Jews can in fact win favour and high standing in the Diaspora, just as Joseph once did in Egypt. Nehemiah, highly placed at the Persian court, is an example in more recent times. Not only the colouring but the point itself of the story is of the Diaspora. It therefore had no original connection with Antiochus Epiphanes and his attack on Palestinian Judaism; the story is not of endurance under persecution from without but of gaining favour in a foreign environment.

h **17-20.** The growth in learning of Daniel and his friends is only loosely connected with the foregoing. It does not mean that the mental growth was a direct result of the vegetable diet, or that it was a reward given by God to the youths in return for their piety. The two processes are parallel. As the vegetable diet mysteriously leads to bodily beauty, so God adds wisdom in their mental training. **Visions and dreams:** traditionally a great means of revelation to the prophets (e.g. Num. 12:6, though with another word for 'vision'; Isa. 1:1, with words of the same root). In chs. 1–6 however Daniel, unlike the prophets, does not have visions of his own but interprets those of others; his vision in 2:19 contains an interpretation, not an original revelation. He is the wise man in the tradition of Joseph rather than the prophet. All the four youths excel in their education, but only Daniel has the interpretative gift. **20. Magicians:** divination and magic were highly developed in Babylonia. The greater excellence of the Jewish youths has been forgotten by the king in ch. 2; unevennesses of this kind in the narrative are of small moment to the writer, and arise from the loose connection which originally existed between the stories. 519h

21. The first year of King Cyrus: 539 B.C., when he became king of Babylon, and not the date when he became king of the Persians. In 10:1 we have however a passage dated in the third year of Cyrus. The point here is probably that Daniel remained throughout the period from the deportation down to the epoch-making rise to power of the Persian empire. i

II Nebuchadnezzar's Dream—We here enter the realm of Apocalyptic so characteristic of Dan. Apocalypse means unveiling or revealing. 520a

1-11. The Babylonian magicians are skilled in interpretation of dreams. But Nebuchadnezzar cannot even remember, or will not tell, what the dream was which he wants them to interpret. This is too much for the magicians. Nevertheless they will be put to death if they fail to interpret the dream.

1. The second year: this date appears not to fit with 1:5, 18, where a three years' training was fixed for Daniel. The difficulty may be overcome by suggesting that Daniel's training began in the *rēsh sharrūti* or accession year, which was not counted as one of the regnal years. Even so the three years would not be three full years. It is more probable that the writer simply did not bother about such things. He must nevertheless have had some reason for giving the second year as the date here. Most likely, having made Nebuchadnezzar active in the third year of Jehoiakim (1:1), he regards that as Nebuchadnezzar's first year; and from Jer. 46:2 he knows of Nebuchadnezzar's great victory at Carchemish in the fourth year of Jehoiakim. The year of the dream is therefore the year of Nebuchadnezzar's great triumph. In any case the writer is interested in giving a historical setting for his stories, and this fact is important even though we may know that his dates are frequently inaccurate. The divine revelation is linked to the actual movement of world history. **4.** With the words b
of the Chaldaeans (see on 1:4) the language changes to Aram., and remains so continuously until 7:28; the change is marked by the words 'in Aramaic'. For the reasons for the change, see §518*b*. A fragment from Qumrân shows the change at exactly the same point as in the traditional text. **Interpretation:** Aram. *pishrā'* = Heb. *pesher*, from a root meaning to unloose; the word used by the Qumrân sect of the meaning or interpretation of biblical passages. **8f. Time:** a cardinal concept of Daniel. Trying to gain time, lit. 'buying time', here means simply postponing the evil day; the phrase is taken up by Paul in Eph. 5:16; Col. 4:5. **Till the times change:** the noun is in fact singular. This may mean in the first place merely 'until something happens to distract me from my purpose', but cannot be entirely separated from v. 21, where it is God who changes times. The magicians have only a vague hope for a changed time; such a hope, says the king, will be disappointed. He thus prepares by contrast for what is to come. **11. The gods:** this also unconsciously prepares for the revelation to come. For the Chaldaeans there are the magic techniques, which will not work without certain information, and there are the gods, who know but are too far off to be induced to reveal their knowledge. **Flesh:** mankind, as frequently.

12-24 Daniel offers to interpret the Dream— c
Daniel apparently knows nothing of the matter until the guards set out to kill the wise men, including himself and his friends. He now approaches the king, obtains the grant of time to interpret the dream, and seeks divine assistance. **14. Arioch:** the name probably taken from Gen. 14:1, as having an archaic Mesopotamian flavour; so Jdt. 1:6. **Captain of the guard:** literally, 'chief of the slaughterers'—the same title as Potiphar had, Gen. 37:36, one of the many similarities between the Joseph story and this one. **18. The God of Heaven:** this title is prominent in the Persian period, e.g. Ezr. 1:2; Neh. 1:4.

520c **Mystery:** the word is *rāz*, borrowed from Persian, and later translated into Gr. as *mystērion*. In the Gr. Bible Dan. is the main source for this word, which had great importance in the NT and at Qumrân. Basically it means simply 'a secret', but it attains a deeper meaning in Apocalyptic. The mystery is the divine plan or purpose behind history. By Daniel's time the prophetic tradition has become long. The interpretation of history can no longer be made only at one or two points, but must extend over a longer process. But because the process is long and complicated its meaning becomes obscure and mysterious.

d **20-3. Daniel's hymn of praise:** he blesses God; to bless God is to recognise him as the source of strength and welfare. The Name is the manifestation of being. The hymn is in verse and is a free composition in liturgical style; it is distinctly a wisdom hymn, praising God as the source of wisdom and (v. 22) remembering those things which lie beyond human grasp but are known to God (cf. especially Job, e.g. 38:19–20). **21. Times and seasons:** not the regular periods like months and years, although 'time' is used for 'year' in Dan., but the periods of power allotted to states and empires. That God 'makes periods to alter' and removes and appoints kings is a central theme of Daniel, cf. chs. 4–5. There is no direct polemic against astral religion in these verses, although their point of view is of course one which must contradict the idea of a fate guided by the stars. The insertion of the hymn at this point adds to the dramatic tension as we wait to hear of the dream.

e **25-35 The Dream**—Daniel tells the king that in his dream he had seen a colossal human statue of brilliant and terrifying aspect. Its fabric was composite: the head of gold, the upper part of the body of silver, the lower part of bronze, the legs of iron, the feet of iron and ceramic combined. As he watched it, he saw a stone quarried 'by no human hand', which struck the statue on the feet and shattered it. The stone grew and became a mountain which filled the whole earth. **28. There is a God in heaven who reveals mysteries:** these words express the essence of apocalyptic. In the context the point is twofold; first to make a contrast with the magicians, who cannot reveal the true mystery, second to lead up to the revelation itself. **In the latter days:** the phrase is a characteristic one of the prophetic eschatology (cf. Isa. 2:2; Hos. 3:5). Time is real and not illusory; the divine life does not manifest itself in a timeless sphere; God's intervention is to be looked for in the latter days. **30.** The revelation is to be explained not from its source, e.g. in Daniel's wisdom, but from its purpose, i.e. that the king should understand. **31ff. The Image:** colossal figures were common in the art of the Near East. The combination of different materials, e.g. overlaying with gold and ivory, was well known; but the statue in the dream is of course no description of any real statue. As a figure it has both disunity and unity. The disunity appears in the different metals, which become less precious as we go lower, but on the other hand become stronger, until paradoxically we find fragile ceramics in the feet. On the other hand as being one statue the whole has a certain unity. The change of metals is no doubt a traditional motif; the best-known example is Hesiod's use for succeeding ages of mankind.

f **36-45 The Interpretation**—To Nebuchadnezzar it is a sketch of the future history of empires up to the time when God sets up his kingdom. To the author and his first readers, in the Greek period, it is rather a sketch of history from the Babylonian down to the Greek empires; they now therefore stand in the last period, awaiting the next stage of the appearance of God's kingdom. It is highly probable that the four kingdoms are the Babylonian, Median, Persian and Greek (see §518*g*). The idea of the division of the world's existence into periods is a common one. But, in conformity with the Israelite interest in history, the periods are not succeeding legendary conditions of humanity (Hesiod) or successive cosmological states of created things (Iranian religion); they are historical periods of imperial domination. Daniel does not have 'four world-periods'; he does not imagine that history begins with Nebuchadnezzar. The series begins from the exile of the Jews and leads to the kingdom of their God; it is not a scheme of universal history but an eschatological scheme with a particular starting-point. The scheme is not cyclic, for the divine kingdom does not pass away. **37-8. King of Kings:** mainly a Persian title, known from inscriptions; cf. Ezr. 7:12. The universality of Nebuchadnezzar's empire extends to birds and animals—perhaps a reminiscence of Adam in Gen. 1:28. Cf. 4:12. The splendour of this empire seems to be accepted; Nebuchadnezzar here is not the pattern of godlessness, nor a symbol of Antiochus Epiphanes.

g **40.** The fourth (Greek) kingdom is given more detail. Being stronger than the others, it is fittingly symbolised by iron. Strictly speaking the fourth kingdom succeeds only the third, but within the unity of the figure it may be regarded as succeeding and destroying the first three. The thought here naturally goes beyond the strict interpretation of the statue. **41. Divided:** in effect, 'composite'. Many hold that this refers to the Ptolemaic and Seleucid houses as heirs of parts of Alexander's empire. But more probably it refers only to the paradoxical mixture of the greatest strength and the greatest weakness. The difference of strength between the Seleucids and the Ptolemies hardly corresponded to that between iron and clay. **43. In marriage:** literally, by the seed of man. This could refer to dynastic alliances between Seleucids and Ptolemies, cf. 11:6ff.; perhaps more probably it represents the fusion of races in Hellenistic times, suggesting the circumstances of the Tower of Babel (Gen. 11)—a passage of which the present chapter seems to bear certain reminiscences. Note that there is no hint of persecution of God's people by the fourth kingdom; this could in any case hardly be fitted into the figure, but may indicate that this material is older than Maccabaean times. Israel is not mentioned in connection with the kingdom of God, but this can hardly be taken to mean that Israel had no part in the purpose envisaged. The mountain from which the stone was cut and the mountain which it becomes are hardly to be divorced from the mountain of the gods in ancient religion, and more specifically the 'mountain of the house of Yahweh' (Isa. 2:2–4); as the cultic centre of the Israelite community, it is to be also the centre of the world. The stone is the eschatological kingdom of God, and breaks the succession of foreign dominations which has lasted since the exile began. God alone 'without human hand' sets up this kingdom. For further developments of the thought of this chapter see ch. 7. **46.** A rigorist should no doubt have rejected the offering and incense. The writer includes them as a dramatic climax. In any case the king recognises that Daniel is only a servant of his God. As in most of the stories of this type, the end shows the king glorifying the one true God.

521a **III The three Confessors in the Fire**—Nebuchadnezzar builds a golden statue and commands all men to worship it. The three youths do not obey, and being denounced to the king by certain Chaldaeans are thrown into a furnace of extreme heat. Nevertheless they are not consumed but walk unharmed in the midst of the fire; and with them is a fourth whose aspect is like a 'son of the gods'. They are liberated, and the king declares the greatness of their God.

1-7 The Image—Whether of a god or of the king, true Jews would not worship it. **1. Dura:** not known, unless the name be taken from the great city of Dura Europos on the Euphrates. **2.** The style of Dan. delights in long lists; many of the words are Persian, and in the list of musical instruments below some are Gr. **8.** While the king is responsible for the initial idolatrous requirement, it is not he but the jealousy

521a of subordinates which brings the Jews into actual danger (cf. ch. 6; Est.). **15. Who is the God?** The question heightens the dramatic expectation. **16.** They need not answer; it is a time for action, not for words; God is able to save them, and in any case they will not obey the king. **19ff.** The furnace: of the kiln type, with the opening in the top through which the men were thrown, and also one at the side below, through which the king could see. **25. Son of the gods:** an angel, as frequently, e.g. Job 1:6. The appearance of the angel is the dramatic climax of the story.

b **23.** After this verse the Gr. version has the long insertion known as 'The Song of the Three Children'. The absence of Daniel from the story is noticeable, and it is to be explained by the separateness of the stories in tradition before the present book was composed. The chief point of this story is the miraculous intervention of God to save his faithful, and his presence with them in the fire in the person of the angel, cf. Isa. 43:2. It is essentially a miracle-tale and should not be over-moralised into an exhortation to martyrdom. The original setting is before the time of the Maccabees; it is not a general persecution of Judaism, but an occasional drive for conformity which is specially dangerous for those Jews who have positions of influence, because of the jealousy of others.

522a **IV Nebuchadnezzar's Chastisement**—Nebuchadnezzar dreams of a great tree overshadowing the whole world and its life. An angelic visitor commands that it should be cut down and only the stump left; 'he', i.e. the person represented by the tree, is to partake of the mind and life of the beasts, until he learns that the true God rules the kingdom of men. Daniel interprets this as meaning the king himself, and the events come to pass as foretold. At the end of the prescribed period the king recovers his reason and praises the Most High God.

Historically there is no evidence for a madness of Nebuchadnezzar, and it is unlikely that much historical truth is to be sought or found in the story. In any case the term 'madness' does not exactly fit the situation here. The story has a relation of form with strange popular tales about great persons, of which Herodotus for example has many, e.g. the story of King Pheros' blindness, Herod. II, 111. In any case our present story, being theologically interested, is quite transformed from the normal spirit and interest of such folklore.

b It has sometimes been held that the behaviour of the king in this story is characteristic less of Nebuchadnezzar than of Nabonidus, the last of the Neo-Babylonian kings. J. T. Milik has published (RB 63 (1956), 407–15) an Aram. text from Qumrân which appears to be part of a prayer of Nabonidus, who fell sick while at Têmã and was sent by God a Jew who reminded him of his past idolatries and recalled him to the worship of the true God. If this interpretation is correct, it shows at least that stories similar to ours were told of other monarchs by the Jews; and it makes it likely that our story did at an earlier stage tell of Nabonidus rather than of Nebuchadnezzar. And since Belshazzar was in fact the son of Nabonidus, the Belshazzar tradition in the following chapter was at this time historically accurate in representing him as the son of the central figure of the preceding story.

c The literary form is peculiar, in that Nebuchadnezzar speaks in the first person, as if writing a public edict. From v. 19 however the third person is used for Daniel's words and the following events until v. 34 when the king recovers. This change of person, if not logical, is quite natural. The idea of the king writing in the first person is in the first place probably inspired by documents like the Cyrus edict of Ezr. 1:2ff.; and the Cyrus edict has not only supplied something of the form but has done something to encourage the idea that great emperors may indeed confess the true God. The piety of the king suggests a pre-Maccabaean origin for the story; but in Maccabaean times it would carry the lesson that a proud Antiochus could suffer in 522c
the same way—and there were those who called him Epimanes (mad) in mockery of Epiphanes (God Manifest). The story has much in common with ch. 2 (theme of dream and interpretation), while its central emphasis, namely that God rules in the kingdom of men, leads on to ch. 5 and is in fact re-emphasised there.

1-18 The Dream—1-3. For the combination of d
epistolary style and metrical doxology cf. Darius in 6:25–7. **8. The name of my god:** see on 1:7. **The spirit:** as source of prophetic inspiration, especially in the later prophets, Num. 24:2–3; Ezek. 11:5, and of Joseph's interpretative powers, Gen. 41:38. 10–17. The closest parallel to the vision is Ezek. 31 where Pharaoh is likened to a cedar which is destroyed; behind this lies (Ezek. 31:8–9, 18) the tree of life in the garden of God (cf. Gen. 2:9), a common mythical figure and connected with the king as the source of life and fertility for society. Against the continuing mythological harmony expressed in the tree-of-life concept Daniel asserts the power of God in historical action to destroy the harmony; only when God restores life to the stump can the human kingdom continue. **13. A watcher:** a common term for angelic beings in apocalyptic. **15. The stump:** the leaving of the stump probably means leaving the possibility for a new growth in time to come; the metal band may both prevent further growth for the present and prevent the rotting and disintegration of the stump. There may be some influence from Isa. 6:13. **15-16.** The words pass by an easy transition from the stump to the person involved.

17. The Most High: an old divine name, which e
enjoys a certain revival in late Judaism, mainly because of its universality of sense. **Lowliest of men:** cf. 1 Sam. 2:6–8; the exaltation of the lowly is a common theme. **19-33. Interpretation and fulfilment.** Daniel's reluctance to explain the dream shows a real sympathy and respect for the king. He wishes it applied not to the king but to his enemies. **27. Break off:** i.e. perhaps 'commute, exchange, your sin for practice of righteousness'. The thought is like that of Ezek. 18:21–4, and neither supports nor denies the idea that good deeds have atoning power. Righteousness may have the later sense of 'almsgiving' (cf. Tob. 12:8–9). Even a foreordained judgment may be turned aside by repentance (cf. Ezek. 18:27–8), and in this case no action takes place for a year, v. 29. **30. I have built:** Nebuchadnezzar's great achievements in building are well known from inscriptions. It was from the palace roof that Nebuchadnezzar cursed the eventual conqueror of his empire in the curious tradition known to Abydenus and quoted by Eusebius (*Praeparatio Evangelica*, IX, xli, 6). He wishes that the eventual conqueror might 'be driven through the desert, where there is no city or track of man, where wild beasts have their pasture, and birds do roam, and that among rocks and ravines he might wander alone'—perhaps a related tradition to the one of our chapter.

33. In the story the king does not become insane; f
it is not a human heart imagining itself to be a beast, but the removal of the human and its replacement by the bestial (v. 16). The bestial heart produces bestial appearance and characteristics. In any case the difference between madness and transformation is too subtle for ancient times. **34-7. Restoration.** Reason is lacking to the beast's mind, but returns when the human mind is restored. **35. The host of heaven:** things celestial, as compared with things terrestrial. Either stars or angels might be meant, but most probably the totality of celestial beings. The basic message is of the precariousness of great human achievement, in the building of empires or of great cities, both of them the characteristics of high civilisation. This precariousness remains even when the civilisation (in the person of the king) is on fairly good terms with the representative of Israel's God. Only

522f the will of the Most High God holds humanity at its greatest above the level of the beast. The pride of the great civilisations is the negation of this truth. Earlier Israelite reflections on the Mesopotamian civilisation, so much more developed than their own, appear in Gen. 11:1–9; the newer picture of Dan. 4 arises from the Jewish Diaspora within the great civilised centres; Dan. 7 develops the theme farther, when the bestiality is turned against God himself.

523a **V Belshazzar's Feast**—Belshazzar is represented as the son of Nebuchadnezzar and the last king of the Babylonian empire. At a great feast in his palace he calls for the vessels of the Jerusalem Temple and drinks from them. A hand appears and writes a message on the wall. The wise men are unable to read it. Daniel is summoned and recapitulates to the king the story of Nebuchadnezzar's chastisement and shows how its lesson has not been learned. He reads and interprets the message. In the same night Belshazzar is slain and the kingdom passes to Darius the Mede.

b Historically it is certain that the last king of the Babylonian empire was Nabonidus (555–539 B.C., Bab. Nabu-na'id). Three kings and seven years separate his accession from the death of Nebuchadnezzar (562). Belshazzar was son of Nabonidus but was associated with him in the administration, and represented the monarch especially after his departure to Têmâ in North Arabia, where he stayed for many of the later years of his reign. It is a reasonable conjecture, but has no positive proof, that Nabonidus married a daughter of Nebuchadnezzar after he became king; but Belshazzar was already prominent early in his father's reign and could not have been a son of this marriage. Babylon fell to the Persian troops under a general Gobryas; Nabonidus was not in the city at the time; it is uncertain whether Belshazzar was, but Xenophon tells of the slaying of 'the King' during the entry. The 'Prayer of Nabonidus' from Qumrân shows that at least certain Jewish traditions knew of the last king of Babylon by name, and knew of his dwelling at Têmâ.

The fall of Babylon was an event which made a deep impression on the popular imagination, and traditions about it were probably widespread; in them good tradition was mingled with inaccuracies. Herodotus, Xenophon and our chapter are all examples. Our chapter does not know, or ignores, the fact that Nabonidus was the real king; it would seem to regard Belshazzar as son and immediate successor of Nebuchadnezzar, although a more subtle and more accurate interpretation is possible; and most serious of all, it names one Darius the Mede as conqueror of Babylon rather than Cyrus the Persian. The first Darius was of course a Persian and began his reign in 521.

c **1. A great feast:** that a feast was held on the night of the fall of Babylon is related also by Herodotus and Xenophon. The essential point as Daniel relates it is not the luxury of the feast but the use of the vessels of the Jerusalem Temple (cf. 1:2). Their profanation is an insult to the God of Jerusalem, a proclamation that as the God of a conquered people he no longer counts as an effective agent in history. The story intends to show that the God of the conquered people is still Lord not only in the hearts of the surviving faithful but in the affairs and policies of the conquerors. He can appoint and depose them at his will. The understanding that God had appointed foreign nations for the conquest of his people and would bring these conquerors also in due time under judgment exists in earlier prophecy (e.g. Isa. 10:5–19, 24–7; Jer. 25:8–14). The present story is thus a narrative confirmation of the truth of such prophecy.

d **5-9 The Writing on the Wall**—The king sees the writing clearly in the light of the candelabrum on the white plaster. Only the hand up to the wrist is visible. The question is now the double one of the reading and interpretation of the writing, just as in ch. 2 it is the relation and interpretation of the dream. **7. The third ruler:** this title is probably a true memory of an Akkadian title for a class of officials, and the original numerical sense of 'the third man' (i.e. the squire in the chariot along with the warrior and the driver) was lost. One need not try therefore to specify who were the two who had precedence over Daniel. On the other hand the story seems to have reminiscences of the Joseph story (Gen. 41:42–3), and in that passage Joseph clearly becomes chief minister of Pharaoh. 523

10-24 Daniel meets the King—The queen is probably the queen-mother, widow of Nebuchadnezzar, and doubtless witness of Daniel's abilities during his reign. **12. Solve problems:** literally, 'loosen knots'. Since the word 'knots' is used for magic spells, this has also been taken to mean Daniel's power to frustrate magic; but the solution of knotty problems is a better sense here. **17-23.** Daniel's speech presupposes the content of ch. 4. The lesson taught to Nebuchadnezzar was lost on his son. He had every opportunity to know and acknowledge the Most High God, but now had defied him.

24-28 The Writing and its Interpretation—These two elements are kept separate throughout. The interpretation assumes a certain latitude in dealing with the words as read, and depends upon the fact that in Aram. as in Heb. the consonants give the basic meaning of a root while a variation of vowels gives a change of grammar and sense within this general meaning. The reading, MENE MENE TEKEL and PARSIN, is most plausibly interpreted as a sum of money: 'Counted: a mina, a shekel, and divisions of a shekel.' It is unlikely that each of these monetary units is intended to refer to kings or empires. MENE: from the root to count or number; its interpretation is that God has numbered the kingdom of Belshazzar. The first MENE (= 'counted') does not figure in the interpretation. TEKEL: from the root 'to weigh'; the corresponding Heb. noun 'shekel' means a weight or a coin. A testing of Belshazzar's kingdom by weight finds it defective and therefore subject to rejection. PERES: from the root 'to divide'. PARSIN is the plural, or more probably the dual ('the two halves'). In this case the interpretation makes a double play on the word, for it signifies the division of the kingdom, but also the Persians (*pārās*) who with the Medes succeed to it. The Babylonian empire was not in fact divided, but was taken over by the Persians; but the idea is probably of the sharing out of profits or spoils, and beyond that of division as the fitting nemesis on an empire which gloried in its universality. e

29-31 Conclusion—29 relates Belshazzar's fulfilment of his promise; it will not support speculations about Belshazzar's spiritual state, such as that he was unconcerned about what he has just heard, or that his conversion came too late. The divine word is followed swiftly by its execution. On the Medes and Darius, see §518*h*. f

VI Daniel in the Lions' Den—A story with marked similarities to ch. 3. The leading administrators of the empire, jealous of Daniel, propose a decree which they know he will not obey. Advised of this disobedience, Darius unwillingly enforces the prescribed penalty; but by divine aid Daniel escapes from the lions, and the king decrees that all should fear Daniel's God. As in the other stories, the background is not of the persecution of the Jewish religion. The king favours Daniel and sympathises with his faith; the enemies who manoeuvre the king into sentencing Daniel are moved not by religious hatred but by jealousy of his fame and success. g

1. Satraps: Est. 1:1 gives the number of provinces as 127. The figure is probably a picturesque exaggeration; Herodotus gives the number for Darius I as 20, and this king's own inscriptions give numbers between 20 and 30. **6. Came by agreement:** the exact sense of the word here is uncertain, and the margin gives another suggestion, 'came thronging'; so also in vv. 11 and 15. **4. Error:** more exactly, h

523h slackness or remissness. **8. Law of the Medes and the Persians:** it is not likely that their laws were in historical fact any more irrevocable than those of other nations. The same view appears in Est. 1:19. **10.** Daniel's practice of prayer, probably indicative of the custom of the Diaspora in late Persian or Greek times; the kneeling posture, the time thrice daily, the direction towards Jerusalem. **16-17. The den:** pictured as an underground pit or cistern, with an opening and a lid on the top, not perhaps a realistic lions' den. Bentzen has pointed out that in the Psalms the underworld is sometimes pictured as a cistern (Heb. *bōr*), and traces the thought of the plunging of the hero into the realm of death as a background for our story (Aage Bentzen, 'Daniel 6. Ein Versuch zur Vorgeschichte der Märtyrerlegende', *Festschrift Alfred Bertholet* (1950), 58–64). **18. Diversions:** the exact meaning is uncertain. Darius can neither eat nor sleep for worry about Daniel. This story more than any other emphasises the king's friendship for the hero and his respect for his God. It is not a martyr legend in the usual sense, but in part at least an illustration of how a Jew may serve the heathen king faultlessly and be his friend, and how it is only through slander that he is made to suffer for his religion. Behind this may lie however hints of submersion in the underworld and escape from death. **24.** Daniel's enemies suffer the fate they planned for him, as Haman was hanged on the gallows he had prepared for Mordecai; cf. also Dt. 19:16–19. **25-7.** A decree of Darius, comparable in form and content to those of Nebuchadnezzar in ch. 4. **28.** This verse is the clearest evidence of the book's belief in a Median empire between the Babylonian and the Persian.

524a **VII-XII Four Visions seen by Daniel**—The style now changes. Daniel himself sees the visions rather than interprets them. The attractive story-telling of the first six chapters is left behind and the atmosphere becomes darker and more mysterious. The visions are dated in succession in the first year of Belshazzar, the third year of the same, the first year of Darius the Mede, and the third year of Cyrus. Though the style changes here, the language does not go back to Heb. until the beginning of ch. 8. The visions have in common the long history under foreign dominion, the final outburst of evil, and the approach of the end.

b **VII The Vision of the Four Beasts and its Meaning**—This has close connections with the great image of ch. 2. Four beasts come up from the sea; they are like a lion with eagle's wings, a bear, a leopard and a nameless and terrible monster with ten horns; another little horn comes up and destroys three of the previous horns. A great judgment follows and the fourth beast is slain. The 'son of man' appears and is given the kingdom. This is interpreted to mean a series of kings or kingdoms; the fourth beast is a destructive kingdom, its horns are its kings; the little horn will seek to intrude into the divine realm and will be given power for some time; but his overthrow will follow and the kingdom will pass permanently to the 'Holy Ones'. Certain roughnesses or discrepancies exist within the chapter, and it is possible that some parts of it are older than others. Unlike the other visions in the following chapters, it does not mention the 'abomination of desolation', the desecration of the Temple by Antiochus IV.

c **1. The first year:** no certain reason can be given why this year rather than another; perhaps the accession of the last king of a dynasty was a good time for a revelation about the fall of empires. **2. The great sea:** the chaotic sea of mythology. The beasts emerge from chaos. A good deal of the description of the beasts is suggested by traditional mythological art. **4. The first beast:** the four beasts are usually understood by modern scholars to represent the Babylonian, Median, Persian and Greek empires respectively, cf. ch. 2. It is not however easy to trace a special significance for every feature of each beast as an indication of the empire which it represents, and too much attention should probably not be given to such details. It is noticeable that in the interpretation following practically nothing more is said about the first three beasts. In v. 4 however we can see a very probable allusion to the chastisement of Nebuchadnezzar (ch. 4) when the proud eagle's wings are plucked off and the mind of a man is given to the lion. The voracious appetite of the second beast will be because the Medes were the conquerors of Babylon in the opinion of our writer. Why the beast was raised up on one side is quite obscure. The four heads of the third beast are probably the four kings of the Persians, cf. §518*h*. The fourth beast is not like any natural animal. Its great strength refers originally perhaps to the fabulous achievement of Alexander, about whose time an earlier form of the picture of the four beasts may have arisen. The ten horns are kings of the Macedonian-Seleucid empire, and to begin with the reference may have been indefinite, i.e. an actual prophecy from early Macedonian times. The new empire is to be longer-lasting than its predecessors. In Antiochus' time an attempt is made to fit the reference exactly to him as the last in the series. This procedure explains why it is rather difficult to fit the horns exactly and without doubt into the series of the kings. The little horn is Antiochus IV Epiphanes, and the three whom he displaced are most probably his elder brother Seleucus IV, the son and heir of the latter, Demetrius, later to be king, and his younger son, also Antiochus, the child co-regent of Antiochus IV in his earlier years. The first seven would then be: 1 Alexander; 2 Seleucus I; 3 Antiochus I; 4 Antiochus II; 5 Seleucus II; 6 Seleucus III; 7 Antiochus III. The eyes of the horn are human eyes, but its mouth speaks presumptuously. It is remarkable that no action beyond this is at this point ascribed to the horn.

d **9-12 The Judgment—Ancient of days:** at Ugarit the god El is called 'the king, father of years'. The point here is the venerability of the judge, cf. Job 29, a contrast with the impudent parvenu kings and empires. The scene of the court, the thrones, the fire, the myriads of ministers, are developed from other appearances of God in the OT, e.g. Dt. 33:2; Isa. 6; Ezek. 1. The passage is poetical. The horn continues its proud speaking in face of the court and the beast is slain. V. 12 is difficult; it is usually taken to mean that the other empires had not been so hostile to the true God, and would eventually be incorporated in the coming kingdom. Such places as Babylon, Media and Persia still existed, although without imperial dominion of their own. In 2:35 however all the kingdoms were destroyed simultaneously.

e **13-14 One like a Son of Man**—The word 'man' in Heb. and Aram. is generic in sense and means 'mankind'. 'Son of man' is therefore a normal expression for a single human being. The first point is therefore the contrast between this figure and the bestial figures preceding. It is commonly held that here he is a human figure representing Israel as the beasts represented the other empires. But the fact that he comes with the clouds of heaven, i.e. that he is a celestial being, unlike the other beings who arise from earth or sea, is also important. The appearance or likeness of a man is in fact a normal expression for an angelic manifestation in Dan. (8:15, 9:21, 10:5, 16, 18) and elsewhere in the OT, e.g. Jg. 13, and even for a divine manifestation (Ezek. 1). The 'son of man' or rather the One like a Man is then what we would call an angel, one of the holy ones or their representative. He has a relation to Israel, for he serves the God of Israel; but is more than a figure for Israel. In the interpretations following he merges back into the host of the holy ones. The further comprehension of his significance depends on the question why what we call 'angels' are so often described as 'man' and why on the other hand 'man' is sometimes brought so close to God, especially in his capacity as a ruler (Gen. 1–2; Ps. 8); and with this place of man

524e as ruler hangs together the question of the relation of the 'Man' here to the Messiah. There is no specific reference here to the Messiah as such, but there is a certain overlapping and community of expression; the Messiah is the king, and the king is also *ben 'ādhām*, 'man', in Ps. 80:17, cf. 146:3. Nor can we neglect the use of 'son of man' for Daniel himself (see on 8:17). But what we have here in essence is an eschatological appearance of an angelic being as man in heaven.

f **15-18 The First Interpretation**—The beasts are here interpreted as kings, not as kingdoms, but perhaps no real distinction is intended; this only gives a very general interpretation, perhaps to give vividness to the question and answer to follow, which concentrate on the fourth beast. **18. The saints:** Aram. *ḳaddîshîn*, lit. 'holy ones', and almost certainly not human saints but angelic holy beings, as the normal usage in the OT (see Martin Noth, 'Die Heiligen des Höchsten', in *Interpretationes ad Vetus Testamentum Pertinentes* (1955), 146–61). The kingdom is in the hands of the angels of God forever. The passage is strongly eschatological; what is now to be done is not followed by another periodical cycle but lasts for ever.

g **19-28 The Second Interpretation**—Not yet satisfied, Daniel seeks an understanding of the fourth beast and the details relating to it. Vv. 21–2 have sometimes been regarded as secondary, intruding as they do between the question and its answer a further narrative about the little horn and in particular the new statement that the horn made war with the holy ones. Most probably it is an afterthought, perhaps of the original author himself, put in to provide the basis for the words of the interpretation in v. 25 about wearing out the saints. Noth (op. cit.) thinks that these verses alone understand the 'holy ones' as the pious Israelites; but if the word usually means angels it may do so here too; the horn makes celestial warfare with some temporary success, cf. 8:10–12. **25. Shall wear out:** as of old clothes. Noth however (op. cit., 154–5) connects this word with Arabic *balā* meaning to test, to treat roughly, to harm, and translates 'will sorely hurt'. The parallelism here of 'the Most High' and the 'Holy Ones of the Most High' might support our view that the latter refers to celestial beings. **To change the times and the law:** the changing of the times is hardly a calendar reform of Antiochus, but an attempt to do what, as is expressly stated in 2:21, only God can do, namely to alter the allotment of time for imperial dominion; the law (*dāth*) may simply be the equivalent of Heb. *tôrāh* and refer to Antiochus' attack on the Jewish religion; but in the context it may mean as in 2:9, 13, 15 the royal sentence or judgment which condemns or terminates the little horn and which it vainly seeks to overturn. **For a time, two times, and half a time:** usually taken to be a cryptic expression for 'three and a half years'. 'Time' here is *'iddān*, while another word, *zᵉmān*, was used above of changing the times. The time of the power of the little horn will be half of the seven-year period, hallowed in the law of Israel as the period of the sabbatical year. Ch. 9 is another essay in the use of this period in the apocalyptic understanding of history. Cf. the time of Nebuchadnezzar's chastisement, ch. 4. The period is fairly general here; chs. 8–12 try to be more specific, and take the desecration of the Temple as a fixed point for the beginning of the time. In the event the desecration did in fact last just over three years.

h **27. People of the saints:** commonly taken as the pious of Israel; but if the saints are the holy angels, as affirmed above, then the sense is Israel as the people who belong to the Holy Ones, or more probably the people or host (*'am*) composed of the Holy Ones. The phrase 'The people (*'am*) of the army of the Holy Ones' occurs in a passage from the Dead Sea Hymns.

Ch. 7 is in many ways the centre of the book of Daniel, and the link between the stories of 1–6 and the succeeding visions. It shares the language of 2–6 but the atmosphere of 8–12. If the interpretation of ch. 7 given above is correct, its setting is largely the heavenly realm into which the last of the representatives of the bestial empires seeks to intrude. The actual act of presumption, the desecration of the Jerusalem Temple, is not mentioned, but appears in the following chapters which work out more closely the historical development of the assault on Judaism. The destruction of the beast and his works, however, is more clearly foretold here than in what follows. It would seem possible that the tradition about the succession of beasts began in the early times of the Greek empire and that the present form of the chapter was reached early in Antiochus' reign, and had in mind his interference with the high priesthood and his plundering of the Temple; the actual desecration had not yet taken place. 524

VIII. A vision of the history from the rise of Alexander the Great down to the time of Antiochus IV, with its climax in the desecration of the sanctuary at Jerusalem and the interruption of true sacrifice there; and a prophecy of the restoration thereof. The general lines of the vision and its interpretation are fairly straightforward, but there are some difficulties in detail. The language is now Heb. The chapter is a restatement of the theme of ch. 7, with the difference that the great desecration is now central. The central interest is less the destruction of the enemy than the restoration of the sanctuary. **1-2.** No special reason can be seen why it was the third year, unless it was thought that Belshazzar reigned only three. The vision may have been at Susa as the future capital where he might see the coming fate of Persia; cf. how Ezekiel's first vision is in Babylonia in the last years of Judaean independence (Ezek. 1). **The river Ulai:** Susa was near the river known to classical authors as Eulaeus. The LXX understood this as a gate, and this might be possible (*'ûbhāl* from Akkad. *abullu*, city-gate), but the river-bank as site for a vision accords well with Ezek. 1 and Dan. 10:4. 525

3-14 The Vision—**3. On the bank:** lit. in front of the river. As the interpretation will tell us, the ram is the Medo-Persian empire; the Persians rose to power later than the Medes, and exceeded them in it; hence the later horn was the higher. The Medes and Persians are here not separated into two distinct empires as commonly in the book, see §518*g*. The passage thinks of them as starting from the east (cf. Isa. 41:2, 46:11), and therefore does not mention the ram as charging eastward, although this empire did in fact extend into India. The he-goat is the Greek empire, and the great or conspicuous horn is Alexander. Because of the speed of his approach he does not touch the ground. The Persian empire is destroyed, but Alexander himself dies, and the four conspicuous horns are the four successor kingdoms in Macedonia, Asia Minor, Syria and Egypt. **9-12. Antiochus IV. Towards the south:** his campaigns against Egypt in 169–168. **Towards the east:** Antiochus planned an advance to reconquer lost territory in the north and east when the Romans prevented expansion in the Mediterranean area. The campaigns did not begin until 166–165, which seems too late for the writing of this passage; perhaps it was sufficient that the plans were made, unless there be a confusion with the eastern conquests of Antiochus the Great. **Toward the glorious land:** lit. towards the Beauty, a term used for the Holy Land in Ezek. 20:6, and in Dan. 11:16, 41 in the phrase 'land of the Beauty'; the phrase here may be a later addition to the text. The text of 11–13 is very obscure and precision cannot be reached in its interpretation. The little horn assaults the celestial world, v. 10, cf. 7:21, 25. The angels and the stars are alike powers of the celestial world, and are related one to another. **Prince of the host:** 'prince' (*śar*) in Dan. usually means the great angelic beings, cf. 12:1 etc., and should be so taken probably here and in v. 25, though the following mention of the sanctuary rather suggests God. b

We now reach the centre of the outbreak of evil c

525c under Antiochus, with its two aspects, the desecration of the Temple by the heathen altar and the interruption of true sacrifice, the continual offering morning and evening. **12. The host:** the meaning of this clause is very uncertain; the RSV translation probably takes it to mean a host, i.e. an army, of disloyal Jews, who sided with Antiochus. Another interpretation could take it of an armed garrison of Antiochus to support his religious innovations, translating: 'And a host was appointed against the continual offering.' Or the word 'host' may be excised and the passage translated 'And the transgression was set upon the continual offering'—so roughly LXX and Theod. **13-14** bring the climax of the vision. Daniel hears the holy ones discuss the time for which the vision will remain true; the answer is 2,300 evenings and mornings, i.e. 1,150 days with the two daily sacrifices. This is only roughly equal to the $3\frac{1}{2}$ years of 7:25. 1 Mac. 1:54 dates the desecration on 15 Kislev 168 B.C., and in 4:52 puts the resumption of true sacrifice on 25 Kislev in 165 B.C. The reason why precisely 1,150 days are mentioned is not clear; cf. the figures in 12:11–2. The transgression that makes desolate is doubtless identical with the 'abomination that makes desolate' of 11:31, 12:11, and usually taken to be a play on *baʿal-shᵉmîn*, the syncretised Hellenistic-Syrian deity, corresponding to Zeus Olympius, whose altar was set up in the Temple. 'Transgression' or 'abomination' takes the place of the name *Baʿal*, *shōmēm* or 'desolating' the second word (= 'heaven'). The form of the expression differs in detail in the various occurrences, and the article twice occurs in the first element but never in the second.

d **15-27 The Interpretation**—Daniel still does not understand, and Gabriel appears before him. This is the first case of an angel being given a proper name, and Michael, also in this book, is the only other case in the OT. These two also appear in the NT. Other apocalyptic works like Enoch had a luxuriant crop of angel names. If, as seems likely, Gabriel is the speaker in chs. 10–12, he seems to be chief of the angelic host of God, and at any rate is the messenger to Daniel. His first revelation to Daniel in v. 17 is that the vision applies to the end-time; the eschatological sense is heightened. **Son of man:** the phraseology of revelation to the prophet or seer, taken from Ezek. 2:1 etc.

e **18. Deep sleep:** commonly caused by supernatural influence, benumbing the human sense, as in Gen. 2:21; 1 Sam. 26:12. **On my feet:** cf. Ezek. 1:28–2:1. The gist of the angelic interpretation of the vision has been mentioned in the commentary above. **19. The indignation** seems to imply that the whole history of the present and intervening times is the outworking of the divine wrath; the importance of the vision is that it sees a term to this wrath. The last words of v. 19 suggest, perhaps deliberately, the famous passage Hab. 2:3 concerning the certainty that prophecy will be fulfilled however long the delay. **23. Their full measure:** introduces a fresh theological reason for delay in fulfilment, that of a measure for evil which must first be filled up—drawn from Gen. 15:16, which also explains why a promise is not at once fulfilled (cf. 2 Mac. 6:14; 1 Th. 2:16). **Riddles:** usually taken to mean Antiochus' skill in double-dealing, but more probably means that he can interpret heavenly secrets as Daniel could (5:12) but as the earlier kings Nebuchadnezzar and Belshazzar could not; this is part of his intrusion into the heavenly realm. Of the end of the oppressor it is said only that it will be by no human agency, cf. 2:34; but no vivid account is given of it, and the emphasis is on the time limit for the restoration of the sanctuary rather than on the fate of the enemy.

f **26.** The vision is to be sealed up; this element explains to the reader in the 2nd cent. why the vision seen in Belshazzar's time is unknown to him until now. The meaning is rather 'stop up' as of a well than 'seal up' as of a document; both of these are

525f involved in 12:4. That in the end Daniel still does not understand is in part a literary device leading on to the next chapters; but the vision and interpretation are clear enough in fact, and Daniel's failure to understand seems to be little more than a mere device, cf. 12:8.

526a **IX The Seventy Years**—Daniel seeks with prayer an understanding of the prophecy of Jeremiah which seems to mention the term of the desolations of Jerusalem as being seventy years (Jer. 25:11, 29:10). The difficulty is that if the vision of the last chapter is true and a desolation is to come at a time long after the Persian empire is fallen, then the word of Jeremiah would have shown itself unreliable. The answer of Gabriel is that the decree is for seventy weeks of years (i.e. 7×70 years), and he analyses this period into three sections of seven, sixty-two and one weeks respectively. **1-2.** The year is, by Daniel's chronology, that of the fall of Babylon (5:31) and therefore one in which the meaning of the Jeremianic words would be a relevant question.

b **3-19 The Prayer—Seeking him by prayer:** lit. 'to seek prayer', as if prayer did not come by itself. The prayer has many common phrases and some community of style with other prayers such as those in 1 Kg. 8; Ezr. 9; Neh. 9, and indeed much of its diction can be regarded as scriptural quotation. But this is natural in liturgical style, and this prayer has a certain unity and completeness in itself. It is then not merely a mosaic of quotations constructed *ad hoc*, but a real liturgical prayer probably going back to exilic times and perhaps revived in the time of Antiochus. It falls into three sections: (1) 4–10: confession of sin and acknowledgment of shame; (2) 11–14: recognition that the disaster was clearly foretold in the law and was therefore a true expression of the will of God; (3) 15–19: supplication for the restoration of Jerusalem for the sake of God's own name and glory. Like other Jewish prayers, it shows a certain oscillation between the second and third persons in addressing the Deity; it alone in Dan. uses the divine name Yahweh. From a certain repetitiousness in vv. 3–4 and 20–1 it has commonly been argued that this prayer is a later interpolation into the text, which could read straight from v. 3 to v. 21; but this need not be so. As a literary device the prayer fills out the chapter, concentrates attention on the desolation and restoration of the city and Temple, and takes up the time until Gabriel arrives.

c **Gabriel's Appearance and Words—21. In swift flight:** a probable translation of an obscure phrase; 'in great weariness' would also be possible. The time of the evening sacrifice is a regular time of prayer, cf. 6:10. **The seventy weeks:** Jeremiah's prophecy probably meant that the whole space of a man's life, about seventy years, must pass before Babylon fell. The interpretation here depends on the sabbatical year of Lev. 25; the sabbath of the land is in the seventh year; Lev. 25:8 provides the phrase 'weeks of years'; Lev. 26:34 (cf. 'sevenfold', v. 18 etc.) and 2 Chr. 36:21 see the desolation of the land in the exile as the keeping of its sabbaths. The new interpretation then is that 490 years will see the end of desolations of all kinds. The words 'of years' are not in the text of v. 24 but are clearly meant.

d The meaning of the time limit is to be the eradication of sin, the completion of atonement, the establishment of an everlasting right order and a holy sanctuary. We should perhaps read with the Kᵉthîbh 'to shut up transgression and to seal up sin'. To seal prophet and vision, however, seems to mean to confirm their truth by the event. The details of the time scheme are difficult to work out, for we do not know how many years the author believed to lie between the time of Darius and his own time. He would almost certainly have a good chronology back to Alexander, because the Seleucid era was the public reckoning; but his chronology for the Persian period was probably quite erratic, and he had very little biblical data to

526d help him here. It is difficult to interpret the last of the seventy weeks otherwise than of the time of Antiochus IV. It is usually held that the reckoning begins from the fall of Jerusalem; that the Prince Anointed is Zerubbabel or more probably Joshua the high priest known from Haggai and Zechariah; and that the second Anointed One who is cut off is Onias the high priest, who was ousted from his position by his brother Jason soon after 175 and was killed three years later at the instigation of Menelaus another pretender (2 Mac. 4:7–8, 23–35). The words of the beginning of the reckoning in v. 25 would seem in themselves rather to indicate the permission to rebuild Jerusalem given by Cyrus and known from Ezr. 1 and Isa. 44:28. In any case the total number of years, 490, does not fit in with the chronology now known to us; but this is not a reason for extending the period down into post-Maccabaean times; the ending of the period is the most certain thing about it. **26. And shall have nothing:** obscure. No true successor, perhaps. The verse goes on to announce Antiochus' assault on city and sanctuary, and the cataclysm and conflict of this last time. **A flood:**
e a reminiscence of Isa. 8:8, perhaps. **27. A strong covenant:** refers to the Jewish supporters of the Hellenisation programme. The centre of the time scheme as elsewhere is the cessation of true sacrifice and the appearance of the desolator, and the half of the week here fits with the 3½ times, or years of 7:25. **Upon the wing of abominations:** picturing the coming horror like an evil bird, if this is the right text and translation. Some have held it to refer to a wing or pinnacle of the Temple, translating ' and on the Wing an abomination that makes desolate ', cf. Mt. 4:5. Once again no clear picture is given of the destruction of the enemy, still less of the future restoration. The central point is that the desolation of the sanctuary and the interruption of sacrifice are the very last elements in the time of tribulation which Jeremiah foretold. With the end of the time comes the full restoration which was still awaited from Nebuchadnezzar's time right down to Antiochus; it is a restoration of the holy place and the holiness and righteousness which have their centre in it, and with this difference from the situation before 586 B.C., that an end is now made of the sin and iniquity which brought destruction on the holy city of old. As so often in Dan., the interest is in *interpretation*; but here it is the interpretation not of dreams and visions but of the scriptures, a growing emphasis in the Judaism of this time and one now known especially from the Dead Sea Scrolls.

527a **X-XII The Last Vision**—The three chapters belong together and provide much the longest single episode in the book. The natural division of the material is: (1) 10:1–11:1, the appearance of the angel to Daniel and their conversation; (2) 11:2–12:4, the revelation itself; (3) 12:5–13, the epilogue. The central section is a review of the coming events down to Antiochus' time and into the sequel; only as the review passes into the future (at the writer's time) does the angelic force of Michael intervene. Ch. 10 gives in advance a certain understanding of the position of the great angels, not only as revealers to Daniel, but as actors in the historical movement.

b **X The Meeting with the Angel—1.** A brief summary in the third person, cf. 7:1. No reason is readily apparent for the date in the third year of Cyrus, unless it is to indicate that the Persian empire is now fully established (1:21 might have been taken to mean that Daniel's life ended with Cyrus' accession) and that Daniel has not returned with the first of the liberated exiles to Jerusalem. **Conflict:** may mean the great conflict which is the content of the vision or the great effort which it involves for the seer. **Understood:** rather ' attended ', the same word as ' perceived ' in 9:2. That Daniel did not in fact understand is clear from 12:8, cf. 8:27.

c **2-9 The Angelic Appearance**—Daniel's mourning and fasting are a preparation for revelation, cf. 12. It 527c fits in with the *askēsis* (i.e. self-discipline) with which some of the early prophets practised the divine ecstasy, an experience which seems to have moulded this chapter. There is no obvious significance in the date in the first month; this is the month of the Passover, but the feast would be over before the twenty-fourth. **4. The Tigris:** there is no good reason for excising these words as a gloss, as many scholars do, simply because ' the great river ' usually means the Euphrates. The Tigris is one of the rivers of Eden (Gen. 2:14). **5. Uphaz:** occurs in Jer. 10:9, which may be the source of the reading here; but no such place is known, and one should perhaps read either ' Ophir ' or ' and fine gold '. The linen garments are priestly; for the girding with gold Bentzen also compares the man of Ezek. 9:2 with his writing-case. The description in general gives the impression of bright light as the medium in which the heavenly visitor lives. His name is not given, but it is reasonable to suppose he is Gabriel. The appearance has strong reminiscences of the divine epiphany of Ezek. 1, and like Ezekiel Daniel falls down and has to be raised up (Ezek. 1:28–2:2). Daniel's companions (otherwise unmentioned) do not see the vision, for which cf. Paul's conversion, Ac. 9:7, 22:9. The deep sleep as in 8:18.

10-21 Daniel thrice revived—First, he is uplifted d but trembles; hearing the words of the angel he is dumb (cf. Ezek. 24:15–27, 33:21–2). Secondly, his dumbness is removed, but he can speak only to show his lack of strength for speech. Thirdly, he is strengthened with words rather like those of Jos. 1:6–7, 9, and is able to listen with attention. The point is the shattering effect of epiphany and revelation, based perhaps on the traditional prophetic ecstatic experiences but more carefully delineated here; but the experiences are probably related also to the content of the revelations—it is when he hears that the content will be the future of his people that Daniel becomes dumb, and when he is strengthened he can hear of the angelic conflict and the long story of the next chapter.

10-14 tells why Daniel had to wait twenty-one days e for the revelation. **13.** The ' princes ' are celestial beings who contend for the place of the nation they protect. The angel of Persia seeks to withstand that secret guidance of his nation for the sake of Israel which is part of the apocalyptic theology; v. 20 indicates how the angel of Greece will do the same. Behind the brief statements here there is a great deal about the angels which is presupposed by the writer and which we have to guess at to some extent. **I left him there:** this is the reading of the Gr. texts; but the Heb. gives the perhaps better sense ' and I personally was superfluous there ', ' was not needed '. 10:20–11:2*a*. The text seems in some disorder here. There seem to be two groups of sayings, firstly those about the heavenly contest (20*b*, 21*b*, 1) and secondly those about the purpose of announcing truth (20*a*, 21*a*, 2*a*). It may be that the two series have become mixed up and should be read separately. The reference to Darius in 11:1 is difficult linguistically and takes us back to the beginning of the preceding empire; the Gr. versions read ' Cyrus '. But this is hardly reason to excise the reference, which must be to the co-operation of Michael and Gabriel at the transition from the Babylonian empire to the Median. ' The book of truth is God's record of the past and the determined future ' (Montgomery).

XI 2-XII 4. The history from Cyrus down to Antio- 528a chus' time and beyond seen as divinely planned. It is usually held that v. 39 brings us down to the writer's time, and from v. 40 on we have only prognostications of the future. It is not likely however that 2–39 are written merely to lend an air of probability to what follows by giving the impression that prophecy has been fulfilled so far at any rate. The purpose is rather to see the relevant history as divinely foreknown from the past through the present and on into the future.

528a The last of these should not be emphasised at the expense of the first two. The cryptic and allusive language emphasises the divine origin of the plan which Daniel himself does not comprehend.

b **2-4.** The third of the future Persian kings is, when Cyrus is included, the fourth of all. **He shall stir up:** this translation would seem to indicate Xerxes and his attack on Greece in 480; then the four would be Cyrus, Cambyses, Darius, Xerxes. But could they really suppose him to be the last of the Persian kings, especially when Artaxerxes is known from the OT itself? A better translation would be: 'It shall all stir up the kingdom of Greece', i.e. the riches of the last king will provoke the Greek aggression. In this case the four would probably be the four names of Persian kings occurring in the OT, see §518*h*. 3–4 give the story of Alexander, cf. 8:5–8. The successor states to his empire were not ruled by his own family, nor had they the strength of his own dominion.

c **5-9 Early Seleucid History**—The king of the south is Ptolemy I son of Lagos, who established himself in Egypt after Alexander's death. Another officer in the army, Seleucus, at first received no province, at Triparadisus in 321 received Babylonia, but in 316 had to take refuge with Ptolemy and served him in the war against Antigonus, 315–312; in 312 he recovered Babylonia, and this year was the beginning of the era by which events in the Seleucid empire were dated. The great territories in the east fell under him, so that he seemed stronger, as our text tells us, than his former master Ptolemy. **6.** Antiochus II about 252 married Berenice, daughter of Ptolemy II; this political marriage brought upon her and her child the vengeance of the divorced queen Laodice. **7.** The 'War of Laodice' followed, Ptolemy III brother of Berenice invading Syria in 246 and seizing Seleucia, later returning to Egypt with much booty. In 242–240 Seleucus II attempted reprisal operations against Egypt without success. **10-19. Antiochus III the Great (223-187):** v. 10 includes his brother and predecessor Seleucus III, unless the singular should be read. **His fortress:** the frontier town of Gaza; Antiochus operated against Egypt from 219, and was sorely defeated at Raphia in 217 (v. 11). **12.** But the Egyptian success was not permanent. **13.** Antiochus renewed the attack (204–197). **14.** Introduces subversive activity against the Ptolemaic régime, including action by violent elements among the Jews; these would likely be pro-Seleucid groups and the forerunners of those who were to incite Antiochus IV to his interference with traditional Jewish religion. This was done 'to fulfil the vision' but fails, for the time is not yet ripe, and to exchange one foreign rule for another does not bring in the final kingdom. Or it may mean that but for this action the fulfilment of the prophecy would never have come. **15.** Antiochus won a great victory at Panias in 198 and took Sidon by siege; Palestine now belongs to his empire. He now makes peace and marries his daughter Cleopatra to Ptolemy V; but if this is a move to secure influence in Egypt it does not succeed. **18-19.** After this Antiochus advances in Asia Minor towards the west (the Aegean coastlands) and is rebuffed by Roman power; the commander is the consul Scipio at Magnesia, 190 B.C. The peace terms impose a heavy indemnity in cash and the retreat of the Seleucid power east of the Taurus. The financial burden of the peace produces henceforth two important factors in Seleucid policy: the shortage of money, leading to Antiochus' own death while trying to spoil a temple treasury in Persia (187), and the interest in consolidating the empire in Syria and the east.

d **20-39 Antiochus Epiphanes (175-163)**—20 is a brief mention of Seleucus IV (187–175) and the attempt of his minister Heliodorus to seize the Jerusalem Temple treasure, an attempt foiled by a supernatural apparition (2 Mac. 3). **21.** Antiochus was brother of Seleucus, and displaced the latter's son in the succession. Cleopatra died in 174/3 and the advisers of the young Ptolemy favoured the recovery of Coele-Syria and Palestine from the Seleucids; in such a situation the Jewish area was a vital frontier province. **22.** Antiochus' operations were successful. **23.** Meanwhile appears the first desecration of the lawful priesthood when Onias was murdered (cf. 9:26) and the support for Antiochus from the Jewish Hellenisers, although his partisans are few. **24.** Plans for campaign are worked out, preparations are made by depredation and bribery. **23-8.** In 170/69 we have a full-scale campaign; nominally its aim is to protect the rights of the young Ptolemy, who falls into his hands and is left as puppet king, although the friendship is simulated (27). At this time Antiochus, hearing of disturbances at Jerusalem and interpreting them as revolt, marched there, committed a massacre, and entered the Temple to confiscate what he could of its treasure (28). In 168 another campaign is interrupted by the Roman envoys who, knowing now of their decisive victory over Perseus of Macedonia at Pydna, demand of Antiochus an immediate retreat. These are the ships of Kittim, a term originating from Kition in Cyprus, but coming to be used for an invader from overseas; it is now well known from the Dead Sea Scrolls; cf. Num. 24:24. It is after this that the desecration of Jerusalem takes place; according to 1 Mac. 1:54 on 15 Kislev, i.e. in the winter. Jewish reactions vary, some supporting the new measures, others opposing them and suffering for their opposition. **34. A little help:** usually taken to be the e

Maccabaean uprising; Daniel does not commit himself to full support of this, because (1) of the dubious motives of some who do support it; (2) it may have seemed too much an attempt to win victory by human hand and not by the hand of God (2:34, 8:25). **36-9.** The new cult in Jerusalem was not strictly a Greek cult, but rather a typical Syrian syncretism; Antiochus so magnifies himself as to neglect his own religious tradition. **Beloved by women:** perhaps Tammuz-Adonis, cf. Ezek. 8:14. **38. God of fortresses:** the God of the Akra, the fortified Hellenistic city at Jerusalem which is now in Antiochus' eyes the constitutional capital of the Jewish nation. **39.** A small textual change would give the sense: 'and he shall appoint for the strong fortresses the people of a foreign god.'

40-45. The writer foretells the end of the matter. f

An Egyptian attack will be answered by an overwhelming counter-offensive, in which Egypt and all her resources will fall into the hands of the northern king. The Glorious Land is again occupied but her neighbours are for the most part exempt, perhaps in reminiscence of the position of Edom during Nebuchadnezzar's attack on Jerusalem in 586. The tidings which cause the tyrant to retire northwards are perhaps suggested by 2 Kg. 19:7 (of Sennacherib). The writer seems now to neglect entirely the political realities of the situation; for any new attack on Egypt would have provoked Roman retaliation; and the Romans, who by now could be seen to be candidates for the fifth world empire, are quite neglected in the forecast here. Such things do not worry the writer, who sees events theologically and is interested above all in the dark hints which the scriptures give. **45** forecasts the pitching of the royal pavilion between Zion and the Mediterranean coast; this is usually held to be the sinister first step to an attack on the holy city, but this is not clearly stated. Antiochus in fact lost his life in Persia in another attempt to seize temple funds. But here once again there is only the barest mention of the end of the oppressor, and one can hardly say that the chapter concentrates on his catastrophe. The emphasis is not so much on it as on what follows (12:1–3), in which the writer has more positive things to say.

XII 1-4. A time of troubles is still to follow, such as g

has never been; but Michael now stands up to support his people; and they all escape, all who are written in the book. It is in principle the people of the Jews

528g who escape ; the qualification reminds us that some of them at least have not been faithful and are not written in the book. The resurrection of the dead is not seen as universal here ; the point is that where reward or punishment are deserved, the sleepers should awake to receive them. Israel was rather reserved in older times towards ideas of a life beyond death, except for the survival of one's 'name' in land and offspring, partly because of distrust for the dying and rising gods of mythology. This form of mythological threat is by the time of our writer largely overcome in Israel, and it is now possible to state in a new form the victory of life over death for the faithful. No clear concept of 'eternity' is involved, still less does it mean timelessness ; the contrast is between continuing life and continuing corruption and abhorrence (cf. Isa. 66:24). No picture is drawn of the conditions of this coming time ; Dan. does not enter into descriptions of the coming paradise. Stress is laid rather on the place of the wise and of those who turn others into the right way. **4.** The prophecy is to be sealed up for the present ; meanwhile men will go in all directions to seek guidance (cf. Am. 8:12) in order that knowledge should increase (perhaps so translate the end of the verse).

h **5-13 Conclusion**—Daniel again asks what shall be the term of the expectations. **6. The end of these wonders:** or perhaps, 'the time or term of the promises'. The angelic visitor declares again that 3½ years will be the time. Daniel still does not understand ; but here he must rest satisfied (v. 9), for the matters are closed and sealed until the end-time, when, it is implied, their sense will become clear. Until then evil will continue, and understanding will belong only to the wise. 11 and 12 give further figures for the time of waiting, and these do not quite agree with those already given (cf. 8:14). It is commonly held that the figures here (1,290 and 1,335) are additions to the book made when the 1,150 days of 8:14 had run out and the end had still not come. This is not a very satisfying interpretation but it is difficult to find a better. **13. Till the end:** omitted by the Gr. versions and perhaps not in the original text. **Allotted place:** lit. 'your lot', a word much used later in the Qumrân community, where it may mean a rank, an office, a group or a destiny. 528h

Bibliography—COMMENTARIES: A. Bentzen, HAT (2nd ed. 1952) ; A. A. Bevan, *A Short Commentary on the Book of Daniel* (1892) ; R. H. Charles, Cent.B and *A Critical and Exegetical Commentary on the Book of Daniel* (1929) ; S. R. Driver, CB (1900) ; K. Marti, KHC (1901) ; J. A. Montgomery, ICC (1927) ; F. Nötscher, Ech.B (1948).

OTHER LITERATURE: W. Baumgartner, 'Ein Vierteljahrhundert Danielforschung', ThRs (NF) 11 (1939), 59–83, 125–44, 201–28 ; H. L. Ginsberg, *Studies in Daniel* (1948) ; M. Noth, 'Das Geschichtsverständnis der alttestamentlichen Apokalyptik', in *Gesammelte Studien zum AT* (1957) ; H. H. Rowley, *Darius the Mede and the Four World Empires in the Book of Daniel* (1935), 'The Unity of the Book of Daniel', in *The Servant of the Lord and other Essays* (1952).

HOSEA

By P. R. Ackroyd

529a **The Prophet**—Information concerning the prophet himself is limited to the statement of his name and that of his father in 1:1, and the particulars of his marriage and children in chs. 1 and 3 (cf. below). From other parts of the book, little definite can be deduced. It is most natural to assume that he was from the Northern Kingdom of Israel, though his actual birthplace is not named. Deductions from the wide range of imagery which he uses are not very satisfactory. It is possible that 9:7 indicates that he was mocked by his contemporaries as a prophet, and this may mean that he was a professional *nābhî'* : the reality of his prophetic calling is everywhere apparent in both narratives and oracles.

b **Period of Activity**—1:1 also indicates the period to which later compilers attributed the work of Hosea. (On this, cf. below ad loc.) That there are many allusions to contemporary events and conditions, and particularly to the political situation in Israel during the last years of her existence as a kingdom, is abundantly clear (though Nyberg interprets the material wholly of religious conditions). The allusions are, however, often difficult to interpret, and it is not always clear whether Hosea is referring to some event in the immediate past or to more remote periods when he speaks, for example, of Gibeah or of Gilgal (cf. 9:9, 10:9 ; and 9:15). It has been very reasonably maintained that certain parts of the material (notably in 5:8–7:16) belong to the period of the Syro-Ephraimite war (cf. especially Alt, *Kleine Schriften* (1953), ii, 163–87). More doubtful is the suggestion that 11:9 indicates that the prophet's activity continued after the fall of Samaria.

c **Personal Life and Experience**—The most discussed aspect of Hosea's experience is his marriage, described in two sections in chs. 1 and 3. The varieties of interpretation are so many that they can only be very briefly indicated here. (A recent survey is in Rowley, 'The Marriage of Hosea', BJRL 39 (1956–7), 200–33.)

(*a*) The narratives may be interpreted as allegory, and not as descriptions of real events. Such a view does less than justice to the prophet's experience, and meets with the difficulty that some of the details (e.g. the name of the woman in 1:3) find no explanation. A modified allegorical view maintains that ch. 3 does not describe real events, but is an elaboration, perhaps during the Exile, of the earlier, genuine Hosea material. While this interpretation successfully by-passes the difficulties of ch. 3 in relation to ch. 1, it must be doubted whether such a later interpreter would have left so many uncertainties concerning the relationship between the two narratives.

d (*b*) The two narratives may—and this is most natural—be taken to refer to the same woman. Full justice is then done to the prophet's experience, but very great uncertainty inevitably exists as to the relationship between the two sections of the material. The most popular view—that ch. 3 is the sequel to ch. 1—demands some imaginative reconstruction of the intervening events. Did Hosea's wife leave him, and fall into slavery, so that he had to buy her back? Or did he divorce her (cf. 2:2) and so remarry her, in spite of Dt. 24:1–4 (cf. Jer. 3:1)? If the second narrative is the sequel, is it not reasonable to expect greater clarity of reference back from ch. 3 to ch. 1? 529d Alternatively, it may be felt that the two narratives are parallel, not in the sense that they record the same story—which they clearly do not—but in the sense that each relates an aspect of the marriage experience, in ch. 1 concerned with the children, and in ch. 3 concerned with the nature of the husband-wife relationship. This view, which appears to the present writer to arise more naturally out of the text than the alternatives, does full justice to the allusive nature of the material, and also to the divergent literary form—biographical and autobiographical—in which the two narratives are couched. It must, however, be acknowledged that the relationship between the two parts of the story is still by no means easy to determine.

(*c*) A third alternative, presented in a variety of ways, is to consider that the two narratives refer to two different women. While we may regard as very improbable a view such as that of Nyberg that the two marriages represent the relationship between Israel and the two deities Yahweh and El Elyon, there is something to be said for the more moderate view that ch. 1 describes the real marriage relationship, and that ch. 3 depicts the performance of a prophetic symbol, the purchase and holding in seclusion of a cult-prostitute, as a symbol of what God intends to do to his disobedient people. e

Two points may be added. Firstly, an interpretation which pictures the events as normal—a straightforward marriage according to the custom of the time—has probably more to commend it than a too far-fetched symbolism. We know of other prophets, e.g. Jeremiah and Ezekiel, for whom the normal events of their lives became pregnant with meaning, and who could quite properly say therefore, as Hosea said, that it was God who had thus ordained the course of their experience. Secondly—and here is the strength of the allegorical interpretation—for Hosea and his followers it was the *meaning* of the events rather than the events themselves which was significant and worthy of preservation. We cannot necessarily expect to get behind the allusiveness of the description. It may be doubted, therefore, whether it is proper to utilise the prophetic sayings of ch. 2 in order to fill out the picture of the marriage. Ch. 2 is best treated as 'a collection of detached sayings, not forming a coherent whole, but all turning upon the same subject, the relationship of Yahweh to Israel, pictured as his wife' (Eissfeldt).

The Message of Hosea—With all its variety, the message of the prophet may nevertheless be drawn together under two main aspects, the intimacy of the relationship between God and his people, and the inevitability and utterness of God's judgment. These are the two focal points, and the insistence upon the former makes the latter all the more vivid, while the relationship between the two aspects of the prophet's thought makes intelligible his words of hope. f

The husband-wife symbolism of the opening chapters is echoed elsewhere in the book, especially in allusion to Israel's apostasy. It is amplified by the use of a variety of other pictures which express something of the same intimacy of relationship : Israel as the child,

529f taught to walk (11:1ff.), or the not infrequent use of the symbol of Yahweh as healer (cf. 5:13, 6:1, 7:1, 11:3, 14:4). The same intimacy is expressed in characteristic terms such as righteousness, justice, loyalty, mercy, knowledge of God (cf., e.g., 2:19, 4:1), some of which carry overtones of the covenant relationship or of the close fellowship expressed most fully in terms of husband and wife. It is not surprising that the prophet's personal experience and his understanding in it of God's relationship with Israel, have led to some overstressing of the tenderness of Hosea. He has been pictured popularly as the prophet of mercy, which is only a part of the truth, and by itself presents a very inadequate picture of the prophet's understanding of the contemporary situation. Yet it is in this personal experience, particularly as it is set out in ch. 1, that the prophet proclaims most harshly the repudiation of his people by Yahweh, the covenant rejected because of Israel's unfaithfulness. The names of the three children are all words of utter judgment, and when they were subsequently reinterpreted, whether by the prophet himself, as seems quite possible, or by his followers, it was not because judgment is escaped, but because the activity of God towards man is two-sided.

g The repudiation of Israel, and the harshness of the judgment, arise out of her failure in both religious and political life. Not that these are really separable in the mind of the prophet, for both foreign alliances and religious apostasy arise ultimately from the same root, lack of trust in her own God. Israel's search for political security in a variety of foreign entanglements is on a par with her search for material well-being, the fruits of the earth, fertility and life, not from her God but from the gods of Canaan. The religious life of the time is unacceptable because it is offered by a people impure, and therefore cultically unfit (cf. 4:1–3), and because it represents a wrong understanding of the nature of God, who is largely conceived in terms of contemporary Canaanite religious standards. The repudiation of the sexual ritual (cf. 4:7ff.) follows properly upon the repudiation of wrong ideas about the nature of God (cf. 4:6).

h Hosea's polemic must be understood against the background of Canaanite religion, and the misconception of Yahweh in Israel which he traces to it. The assimilation of Yahweh with Baal, indicated in the prophet's repudiation of the title Baal for Israel's God (2:16f.), and at the same time the acceptance by some within Israel of Baal as the giver of life and fertility, call forth his most insistent protests. If there seems no adequate reason for going so far as Nyberg in interpreting everything in the book in terms of polemic against such religious tendencies, yet it is clear that the prophet's thought is dominated by the danger which threatens the religion of Israel. The book itself constitutes a very valuable source of information concerning Baal and the points of contact and contrast between the religion of Baal and that of Yahweh (cf. Östborn, *Yahweh and Baal* (1956)).

i Of even greater interest is the nature of the polemic, and the use which the prophet makes of terminology deriving from Canaanite religion. While evidence of this needs to be weighed very critically (cf. Östborn, op. cit. and H. G. May, 'The Fertility Cult in Hosea', AJSL 48 (1931–2), 73–98), there seems little doubt that Hosea did much for the reinterpretation of Yahwism within the terminology of the religion of Baal, and in particular took over the metaphor of the marriage bond, and stressed the reality of Yahweh's concern with the natural order, which many of his contemporaries associated much more nearly with Baal, or with a Yahweh who had become in effect equated with Baal. In this respect, it is perhaps not inappropriate to see in Hosea a presentation of the positive side of the repudiation of the religion of Canaan which is expressed in such negative terms in Dt., where the religion of the Canaanites is to be so completely destroyed (e.g. Dt. 12:2f.).

A similarly positive approach can be seen in Hosea's 529
view of the wilderness period as a time of discipline, to which Israel is to return (cf. 2:14f., 12:9). Unlike the Rechabites to whom Canaan was utterly evil and to whom a return to a wilderness type of life appeared desirable, Hosea—in common with other prophets—represents an appropriation of the life of Canaan, and an application of the principles of the religion of Yahweh to the new situations which the settled life and the development of its civilisation had brought to a formerly semi-nomadic people. Here too a comparison may be made with Dt., which pictures Israel as once more at the threshold of the promised land. For Hosea, as for Dt., Canaan is 'Yahweh's land' (9:3).

The Book of Hosea—There are many textual prob- j
lems in Hosea, especially in chs. 4–14; inevitably many points of obscurity remain, even though respect for the MT has grown in recent years (cf. Nyberg), and much that formerly appeared obscure has come to yield good sense. Yet it remains clear that there are many points of textual corruption.

The literary problems are also considerable (cf. Lindblom, *Hosea literarisch untersucht* (1927), especially ch. 2). The analysis of the material itself is difficult to determine. Commentators vary in their approach, and while some (e.g. Robinson) subdivide the material into the smallest units, others (e.g. Driver, LOT, 303f.) think in terms of larger addresses. A compromise appears more satisfactory than either (so Wolff, Frey, and cf. below), for while the units may often seem to be short, there appear to be linkages of thought ('kerygmatic unity', Wolff) between successive sections which suggest the growth of larger complexes. Whether these are the result of the prophet's own activity (cf., e.g., Wolff), or are to be understood as the product of the *traditio* of the prophet, is less easy to say with precision. It is not unnatural to suppose that the primary impetus towards the formation of the tradition and so towards the gathering of the words of the prophet into related complexes goes back to the prophet himself. But this is very far from saying that the book as we have it is due to the prophet. Many attempts have been made to arrange the material in a more satisfactory order (e.g. chs. 2 and 9). These do not appear to be convincing, for they suggest a logic of construction which does not belong to the prophetic material. There is in the prophetic books evidence enough of a tendency for like material to be placed together in the growth of the tradition, without it being necessary to believe that there ever was a form of the book in which all that the prophet said on one particular topic stood in a single context.

It must be observed, finally, that the book has come k
down to us through the tradition of Judah (cf. on 1:1), and in some passages (cf. on 4:15, 6:11, 10:11, 11:12, 12:2) it seems evident that 'Judah' has been substituted for 'Israel'. In this 'glossing' of the text, it is evident how the words of the prophet have been used and interpreted in later circumstances. Yet while this appears likely in a number of cases, it does not automatically follow that every reference to the south is later reinterpretation, for (especially in 5:8–7:16) it appears reasonable to suppose that the prophet himself was conscious of the relationship between the people to whom his message was especially directed and the related people of the south, among whom his words were to live on and be a continued source of inspiration and understanding of the divine word.

I 1 Superscription—The opening verse, similar to 530a
those which stand at the head of other prophetic books (cf. Zeph. 1:1 for an exact parallel), introduces both a historical note and one piece of personal information. The verse in its present form is likely to reflect the southern, Jewish, view, for (as in Am. 1:1) Jeroboam II is mentioned after the kings of Judah (but cf. below on 2*a*). It is clear from 1:4 that

530a Hosea prophesied during his reign. That he continued to prophesy later is probable, and it may well be that he did in fact continue as late as the reign of Hezekiah of Judah. The lack of reference to the kings of Israel after Jeroboam II may be due to the belief that they were no longer proper kings (cf. 8:4), or simply to the southern view that kingship in the north was disreputable (cf. 1 and 2 Kg.). The mention of the name of Hosea's father is presumably a piece of genuine tradition, and is not derived from the oracles. More significant than either of these points is the opening phrase, with its recognition of the unity of the divine message, transmitted through the activity of the prophet (cf. Zeph. 1:1, and contrast Jer. 1:1 ; Am. 1:1).

b **2-9 The Prophet and his Children**—The narrative relates in the third person Hosea's marriage and the birth of three children. Like the other narrative, in the first person, in ch. 3, it does not purport to be a full description of the prophet's life and experience, but alludes to events only because of the significance which they have within the delivery of the divine message. The wider problems have been discussed above (§§529*c*–*e*), and it is here appropriate simply to let the text speak for itself and assess its significance without prejudice.

2a provides in reality a new heading 'The beginning of Yahweh's speaking through Hosea'. This rendering avoids the impression (created by RSV) that the narrative which follows describes Hosea's call to prophecy ; it may simply mean 'this is the first section of the material', and it is possible that the 'again' of 3:1 is in reality a corresponding explanatory note. Since MT marks a division after these words, it is also possible to link **2a** with **1b** and render : 'In the days of Jeroboam . . . was the beginning . . .'

c The whole section contains a message of sheer judgment (with the exception of **7**, which is best understood as a gloss on **6**, perhaps with an allusion to the events of 701 B.C., as elaborated in the 'prophetic legend' of Isa. 36–9, or even, in view of the Chronicler's belief in Yahweh's saving Judah, belonging to a later reflection upon the meaning of the history. The text rather curiously contrasts 'saving by (the agency of) Yahweh' with 'saving by military power' ; less probably we may render 'I will deliver in my capacity as Yahweh'). **4.** The name of the first child—Jezreel—pronounces judgment upon the royal house of Jehu, of which Jeroboam II was the last great ruler. It is natural to see here an allusion to Jehu's *coup d'état* and the massacre of the royal family of the previous dynasty (2 Kg. 9–10) ; Hosea's view of the events differs from that of Elisha and his associates. Kingly rule in Israel is to come to an end (cf. Am. 7:7ff.) ; the judgment on the royal house, as in 1 and 2 Kg., means judgment upon the whole people. The word of judgment is elaborated with another, probably genuinely Hoseanic, saying in **5**, possibly referring to the Assyrian onslaught of 733, when the valley of Jezreel did fall into Assyrian hands. A broader concept may be present, for the opening phrase (cf. Isa. 7:18ff.) suggests the dark 'day of the Lord', and the historic battleground of Jezreel may have been interpreted as the scene of a more final conflict (cf. **11** and Isa. 9:4, 'day of Midian').

6. The second child's name reveals a further stage of judgment. The name may be interpreted as an impersonal passive : lit. 'it is not pitied', i.e. 'no pity is found'. There is a clear allusion to God's former mercies to his people, which now come to an end. The last phrase is very difficult to translate. RSV is possible, but grammatically not easy. Other renderings suggested are : 'I will forget them', 'I will strongly attack them', or, perhaps best, 'for I will remove it (i.e. my mercy) from them' (Wolff).

d The third child, whose conception is noted as taking place after the weaning of the second, i.e. probably two or three years later, brings the culminating word of judgment. Israel is no longer the people of God.
The point is emphasised by the direct address to the 530d
people in **9** ; and strikingly by what is to be understood as a change, a negation, in the divine name itself. RSV*n* indicates that MT has not been followed ; it really says 'I am Not-Yahweh to you' (actually 'Not-Ehyeh', for as in Exod. 3:14 God uses the first-person form *Ehyeh* when he refers to himself). LXX and RSV follow the covenant formula of Exod. 6:7, etc.

The whole stress lies upon the apostasy of Israel and e
the judgment which falls upon the people, eventually to be repudiated as God's people. This is made clear too in the introductory description of the entry upon the marriage in **2** ; the wife and the children are symbolic of the apostate state of Israel, expressed in terms of sexual unfaithfulness, for Israel has abandoned her God and worships other gods (so again in ch. 2 and elsewhere). The sexual terminology is particularly appropriate because of the emphasis on fertility in Canaanite religion, though it is more difficult to be sure how far Hosea refers to the actual worship of other gods and so to complete abandonment of Yahweh (this seems clear in 2:5), and how far he refers to the 'Canaanising' of Israel's religion, the worshipping of Yahweh as Baal, possibly with a female consort (cf. Jg. 6:25, and the association of female deities which appears to be indicated in the Elephantine papyri, cf. §102*e*). If the woman herself were one who had engaged in such sexual ritual, seeking fertility in a rite which equated Yahweh with Baal, then the description of her would be all the more pointed. The children too would be properly described as 'children of harlotry', both because they are symbolic of apostate Israel (cf. 2:4) and also because they owe their birth—as the cult would understand it—to the fertility granted by the god.

This last point is particularly illuminating for the f
naming of the first child. It seems not impossible that the name Jezreel—meaning 'El sows'—was chosen because the gift of the child was felt to be due to the fertility granted by means of the sexual rite. It may then be understood as being a 'normal' naming, in the sense that the name was chosen within a certain conception of religion ; it is interpreted by Hosea or his successors in 1:5, 1:11, 2:22f. If this is so, it may not be altogether improper to see the name of the third child also as having a double meaning : the symbolic sense is clear in the interpretation, but it might also mean 'not my kin' and so imply that Hosea did not recognise the child as his own. The fact that no such double interpretation is immediately observable for the second child's name is not necessarily an objection, since we can hardly expect to understand fully the circumstances in which such names were given (cf. Koehler, *Hebrew Man* (1956), 66f.). The name Gomer and the name of her father—unless the text should be emended to indicate her home-town (Diblaim, ? = Diblathaim, Num. 33:46)—appear to be simply elements in the prophetic tradition, and attempts at finding allegorical or other explanations have not been successful.

The tone of Hosea's message is set by this opening g
passage, and it is important to lay emphasis upon it, since it runs so directly counter to the popular notion that Hosea, in contrast to Amos, is the prophet of mercy and love. In so far as such a description may be applied to him, it must be applied in the context of a message of judgment which sees the apostasy of Israel as deserving nothing less than the complete repudiation of the covenant relationship.

I 10-II 1 (in the Heb., II 1-3) The Day of Jezreel 531a
—It is most convenient to treat this section of promise as consisting of loosely linked sayings, expressing different answers to the word of judgment in 1:2–9. Thus **10** provides a direct answer to **9** (for 'in the place where . . .' render 'instead of it being said to them'), and links with the promise of a renewal of the covenant, the fulfilment of the promise of the patriarchal sagas (cf. Gen. 32:12). Judgment in terms of depopulation appears elsewhere in Hos. (e.g. 9:12, 16f.). The

531a description of the people as 'Sons of the living God' stresses God as the giver of life, in contrast to Baal; the God of Israel is the living God, not bound in the cyclic pattern of dying and rising (cf. Hab. 1:12, reading 'Thou shalt not die'). The people owe their life to him, and are no longer therefore to be 'children of harlotry' (1:2). **11** deals with the reunion of Israel and Judah under one 'head'. Is the term 'king' avoided (cf. 8:4), or is there perhaps a thought of a return to the idyllic pre-monarchial days (cf. 2:14–15)? In 2 Chr. 13:12 God himself is the 'head' of Judah. The last part of **11** is difficult. Many commentators have sought an allusion to return from exile (reading 'lands' for 'the land'). But the phrase might mean 'go up' to appoint their ruler, to some centre of pilgrimage, presumably Jerusalem if this is a later southern comment; or Exod. 1:10 may be compared, where the same expression, rendered in RSV 'escape from the land', has been plausibly explained as meaning 'take control of the land'. There would then be an allusion to the recovery of land occupied by Assyria, and this might allow the passage to belong to the last years of Israel or, perhaps better, to the period of Josiah. Yet another suggestion sees the phrase as an interpretation of Jezreel, 'God sows', and meaning 'they shall sprout up again from the earth', which might allude to increase of population, or to the sowing again of the deported (cf. 2:23). The idea of the 'day of Jezreel' may be linked with 1:5, unless the suggestion be preferred that 'day of Yahweh' be read here, and Jezreel regarded as the first word of the next verse. **2:1** reinterprets the names of the second and third children (cf. 2:23); since these children are symbolic of the whole people, there is no need to follow RSV in reading singular for plural forms (cf. RSV*n*).

b **II 2-15 Israel's Unfaithfulness**—It is improbable that these verses form an oracular unit, but there is a clear interrelationship of ideas between the various sections. All are concerned with an indictment of the unfaithful wife Israel, in terms of judgment or of discipline. They are followed by 16–23, which in many respects corresponds to 1:10–2:1, producing a similar structure of judgment and promise to that observed in the opening chapter of the book. Yet here too judgment and promise are interdependent, and the link may be seen clearly in the use of the idea of discipline which is taken up and elaborated in the last part of the chapter.

c **2-5** forms the first unit, perhaps to be further subdivided into **2-3**, **4-5**. Here the children are first invoked to plead with Mother Israel, denounced as now divorced because of her unfaithfulness, that she should renounce her adultery, lest she become an unfruitful land. The stripping of the adulteress is in accordance with ancient custom (e.g. at Nuzu; cf. Gordon, ZATW 54 (1936), 277ff.), and no doubt represents both punishment and also repudiation of the husband's responsibility to provide clothing (cf. Exod. 21:10). The words used for harlotry and adultery in **2** may be intended to suggest actual visible marks, the prostitute's attire or perhaps even wounds incurred in fertility ritual (cf. Zech. 13:6). Israel—now as land—deprived of her husband becomes infertile; the blessing of rain (**3**) belongs to Yahweh. A slight shift of thought is observable in **4-5**, where the children—the people as sons of the land—are also condemned because of their mother's behaviour. They share in the faithlessness of the one who bore them, and who believes that it is her lovers (i.e. the Baals) who provide the produce of the land.

d **6-7** introduces a new idea, repentance, though this is not excluded from **2-3**. Here Israel is to be protected from her own wilfulness, being enclosed like a wild beast with thorn-hedge and loose stone wall. A slightly different image in **7** depicts her searching eagerly for her lovers but unable to find them. The allusion is possibly to cultic practice, the search for the god being a common element in cults which involve
a dying and rising deity (cf. 5:6). Israel's failure to 531d
find the Baals—by implication it is Yahweh who protects her from finding them—leads to a recognition that she was better off with her first husband, Yahweh. (For the thought, but in reverse, cf. Jer. 44:17.)

8-13—perhaps made up of smaller units—takes up the e
thought of **5**. Israel did not recognise that it was Yahweh who gave the produce of the earth. **9.** The unfaithful wife will lose her right to be supported by her husband, **10** and as in 3 she is left to shame and contempt (cf. Lam. 1:8; Nah. 3:5ff.), her lovers powerless to help, just as Baal was powerless to help his prophets in the Elijah narrative (1 Kg. 18). **11.** The removal of fertility from the land carries with it the end of 'her mirth'; **12** her religious festivals, the vines and figs, symbols of peace and well-being (1 Kg. 4:25 etc.) are made into a jungle (cf. 2 Sam. 18:8) and devastated by wild beasts (cf. Isa. 5:1–7). **13.** The reason is plainly set out, for here Israel is described as decking herself in finery—no doubt the proper garments for religious ritual, but here suggestive of the tawdry adornment of the prostitute. The lovers are named; they are the Baals. The title Baal is that given to the king of the gods, and god of fertility and weather in the Râs Shamra texts. The plural use here is probably a reference to the various local names under which this god was known in different parts of the land. Israel has forgotten God (cf. Dt. 6:12ff. etc.); the statement is underlined by a concluding 'oracle of Yahweh'.

14-15 returns to the thought of 6–7, but more force- f
fully. Yahweh is boldly depicted as a young lover, a seducer, leading the woman away from her lovers, and enticing her back into the wilderness, speaking to her as a lover speaks (cf. Jg. 19:3; Ru. 2:13; Isa. 40:2). **15** should begin: 'And from there . . .' for it is not in the wilderness that the new fertility is to come, but as Israel re-enters the promised land, through the valley of Achor, the scene of Achan's sin (Jos. 7:24ff.), now become the door of hope (cf. Isa. 65:10). Israel will respond, accepting anew the bond of marriage: 'From there she shall answer.'

The interplay of ideas is vivid in the whole section. g
God suffers from Israel's unfaithfulness, and though judgment is pronounced, yet he seeks to win her love afresh, by loving words, by warning and protective action. The whole passage presents more vividly than any other the utilisation of the Canaanite idea of sacred marriage. Hosea uses these ideas to combat Israel's wrong practices and to present a deeper notion of the relationship between Yahweh and his people. Unlike the Rechabites, Hosea does not wish a return to the desert and its conditions; but sees such a return as a preliminary to a new entry to the land which belongs to Yahweh (9:3).

16-23 The Day of the New Covenant—A loose h
collection of sayings, introduced more than once by 'in that day', elaborates the promises already indicated in **14f.** **16** envisages a new confession of faith by Israel; she is to acknowledge Yahweh as her husband in the new marriage bond, but to use for this a term which has none of the alien religious associations of the term Baal. This latter term means husband, or lord, or owner, but has undesirable overtones. Heb. proper names, both biblical and non-biblical, show that it was regularly used with reference to Yahweh (cf. the Samaria ostraca of this period, W. F. Albright, ARI (3rd ed. 1953), 160); even in 1 Chr. 12:5 a name Bealiah appears, 'Yahweh is Baal'. **17** forbids the ritual invocation of the Baals: to mention is to invoke formally. Later scribes took these words of Hosea literally and substituted *bōsheth*—shame—for Baal in proper names (e.g. 2 Sam. 2:8). **18** pictures Yahweh as mediator of a new covenant with the animal world, to the advantage of Israel; it is a restoration to the state of peace which existed before man's sin (Gen. 3:15, cf. Isa. 11:6–8). The land is to be freed too from the threat of war, and Israel is to enjoy peace and security (cf. Lev. 26:6). The picture

531h of judgment in terms of wild beasts may be seen in such a passage as 2 Kg. 17:25ff.

i In **19f.** the theme of **16** is again taken up. Israel is to be betrothed, the bride-price is to be paid and the legal formalities are concluded which make her wife. The bride-price is here not inappropriately expressed in terms of those qualities which guarantee an enduring bond, right action, right ordering of life, loyalty, love and faithfulness—though these translations only touch on the depth of meaning contained in the words, some of which reappear elsewhere in Hosea. **20.** Instead of being forgetful of God, Israel will know him.

j In **21f.**, Jezreel, here representing Israel, finds fertility and life; the sequence of terms—perhaps derived from some cultic form—traces the source of blessing from God himself, through heavens (rain) to the land, and hence to its products. **23** opens with what may well be a punning interpretation of Jezreel (though the feminine object 'her' (RSV*n*) makes the precise connection not certain), and leads into another reinterpretation of the other two names, the covenant formula being again freely used (in MT the response is simply 'My God', expanded by LXX, RSV).

The repudiation of Israel is followed by the establishing of a new covenant, a new marriage bond. This is achieved on the one hand by the removal of the Baals, and on the other by Israel's response to God's love and entreaty. The new covenant will endure, for it is God himself who establishes it firmly (19f.).

532a **III Hosea's Marriage**—If 1:2–9 is concerned with the marriage because of the children, 3:1–5 is concerned with another aspect, namely the position of the wife. In this respect there are clearly many links of thought between chs. 2 and 3. The allusive nature of the narrative again makes it difficult to be sure of the exact course of events. In 1 the 'again' is clearly intended in MT as part of the divine speech (cf. Exod. 3:15; Zech. 1:17, 11:15), but it is possible that it should be linked to 'the beginning' of 1:2 and regarded as merely resumptive. 'Beloved of a friend', i.e. a kept woman or (as LXX, Syr), with a slight emendation 'loving a friend', expressing the idea of Israel's active unfaithfulness. If 'adulteress' is taken literally, then it is natural to think that the woman in question was a previously married woman, and so, presumably, had formerly been Hosea's wife. Yet the use of the same Heb. root in parallel with the word for harlotry in 2:2 (cf. 4:13f.) suggests that too strict an interpretation is not necessary. In so far as the interpretation of the narrative dominates, it is not unnatural to think that the concept of the woman as symbolic of adulterous Israel, unfaithful to her first husband, has influenced the phrasing. **1a** makes the interpretation clear, referring to Israel's religious failure. **2,** like the mention of the name and parentage of the wife in 1:3, introduces a matter-of-fact element into the narrative. The price, partly in silver, partly in kind (LXX has 'jar of wine' for 'lethech of barley'), cannot be easily computed; it may be approximately the price of a slave (Exod. 21:32). But there is no means of determining whether the purchase is redemption from slavery or the payment of a normal bride-price (cf. 2:19f.). The unusual word for 'bought' perhaps indicates bargaining, but is used in Dt. 2:6 alongside another, more common, word; it may mean 'to recognise', i.e. to 'acknowledge as his property' (cf. Tushingham, JNES 12 (1950), 150ff.). **3.** For a long period, the wife is to be protected from going astray, and also deprived of normal marital rights; the possibility that this is seclusion because of the holiness which clings to one who has been associated with sacred fertility ritual may provide a clue to the meaning of 3:1 and 1:2. In **4f.** this marriage bond is explained. The crucial point in the narrative is the idea of discipline. If the symbol is interpreted exactly, the deprivation is of legitimate (ephod—probably a
cultic vestment) as well as illegitimate (pillar—symbol 532a
of deity; teraphim—household gods) cult-objects and other practices. That 2:9ff. depicts Israel deprived of God's gifts makes it reasonable to assume that to Hosea some, if not all, the possessions mentioned here are good. The deprivation is not permanent, and the time will come when, as in 2:14f., 16, 20, 23, Israel again seeks Yahweh, and approaches him in awe. The mention of 'David their king' appears to be a later addition, and possibly so too the phrase 'in the latter days' which is more characteristic of the south (cf. Isa. 2:2 etc.).

IV 1-3 Yahweh's Controversy with Israel—An b
introductory phrase ('word of the Lord', cf. 1:1 and Am. 3:1, 4:1, 5:1) stands at the head of a long, often rather loose, collection of prophetic sayings extending to the end of the book. The first oracle is in general terms, and may be regarded as setting the tone; it indicates the nature both of Israel's failure and of God's judgment. **1b** states the basic failure: lack of fidelity (cf. 2:20), lack of loyalty (RSV 'kindness' is too weak), lack of knowledge of God, which means lack of fellowship with God (cf. Mic. 6:8). The people's unfitness to appear before God and hence its rejection and judgment, are expressed in **2** with a list of crimes (all meriting the death sentence if 'stealing' is interpreted as in Exod. 21:16) strongly reminiscent of the decalogue of Exod. 20 and Dt. 6. The statement is fundamental to Hosea's thought, and it expresses the nature of his condemnation of the totality of the people's life, and especially its religious failure; for to appear before God in an unfit state for worship makes worship itself a disaster, and a source of danger rather than of blessing (cf. 6:6, 9:4, Am. 4:4f.; and cf. Ps. 15, 24; Isa. 33:13–16).

2b would be better rendered: 'they (i.e. the crimes c
listed) are spread abroad (in the land—so LXX; possibly the phrase belongs here rather than at the end of **1**): bloodshed meets bloodshed'. Alternatively the word rendered 'they break all bounds' may indicate another crime, i.e. violence. **3** contains the threat of judgment, and the tenses should therefore be rendered as futures: for 'mourns' translate 'shall dry up'; to 'languish' may mean 'to become barren' (cf. Jer. 15:9). The judgment reveals that intimacy between man's behaviour and the fruitfulness or barrenness of the earth which is a characteristic of ancient thought (cf. 2:18; Gen. 3:17f.; Hag. 1:9–11; Rom. 8:20f.).

**IV 4-V 7 Priest and People: the Religious 533a
Failure of Israel**—The section is built up of various oracles, mainly centred upon the failure of the priesthood and other leaders, to carry out their duties, with the result that the people is brought under judgment. **4:4-6** and **7-10** contain two judgments on the priesthood, the main object of God's contention (cf. RSV **4b**). The first condemns the priesthood for failure to inculcate knowledge of God in the people. They are condemned, not because they are priests, but because they are no longer priests (Wolff). **6.** They have forgotten the *tôrāh* which is the priest's privilege (cf. Jer. 18:18), and so God himself will forget them, and will cut off the priestly line. A similar judgment is passed upon the priesthood in **10**, though the point of the second oracle (7–10) is that the priests have flourished, greedy in their appetites (8), as religion has flourished. This reflects the prosperity of the period of Jeroboam II, a prosperity in which religion shared; in 10, sacrifices are multiplied, and the priests who take their share encourage this merely outward observance. Furthermore, they engage in sexual ritual, but it will not produce the desired effect of bringing fertility. So the line will come to an end.

The opening words of **4** are very obscure. Perhaps b
this is a pious marginal comment: 'When God judges, man dare not object'. MT might be emended slightly to give the sense 'it is not an ordinary man, not just anyone who is to be rebuked, but the priest'. MT in **4c** has 'thy people are as those who strive

583b with a priest'. RSV represents a fairly simple emendation of the text; or **4-5** may be emended to 'And with you, O idol priest, is my contention. For behold you stumble . . .' In **5** the reference to prophet has been considered a later addition; but although the prophet does not again appear in this passage, the parallelism makes the reference not out of place. It is not impossible that here we have a reference to the religious functionary (cf. A. R. Johnson, *The Cultic Prophet in Ancient Israel* (1944)) who appears to be active by night (cf. Zech. 1:8), while the priest ought to deliver his *tôrāh* by day. **5c** is probably corrupt, and may be simply a duplicate of the opening words of **6**. This verse provides a striking series of contrasts: you reject me, I reject you; you forget me, I forget your children, i.e. cut you off.

c Syr. and Targ. suggest that **7c** should be rendered: 'They exchange their glory (i.e. God) for shame'; MT may represent a scribal correction made for theological reasons. **9** opens with a proverbial saying: 'like people, like priest'—special privilege does not avail. **10** brings again, as in chs. 1–3, the emphasis on the sexual aspects of the worship; here it is indicated as being actual apostasy, though it may well be that the sexual rites were regarded as appropriate to a Yahweh pictured in terms of Baal. The last word of 10 belongs in MT to **11**. The transfer is not really necessary, as the text may be rendered: 'for they desist from worshipping the Lord'. **4:11-14** and **15-19** are concerned with the consequences for the people. **12**. Because of the failure of the priesthood, the people practise idolatry and forsake God. **13**. They engage in alien worship in cult-places—hilltops and trees; for 'poplar' read 'storax'; **13b, 14c** the young women engage in sexual ritual, clearly connected with bridal ceremony (cf. 1:2). It is possible that Dt. 22:14ff., with its insistence upon the virginity of the bride, is designed to counter such alien practices in Israel. The men, too, are involved in similar rites: the whole people is without understanding.

d **14a** may be taken as excusing the young women because they are not responsible for the sin into which they are forced (so RSV). It is better to render the line as a question; the interrogative particle—though not essential—could have been lost by haplography. In **15-19**, **15** is obscure. Its first two words may, with LXX, be joined to **14**, and rendered 'with its harlots' or 'harlotry'. It seems probable that 'Judah' is here a gloss, and with small emendation the verse might then be rendered 'Thou Israel, do not incur guilt: do not go to Gilgal, nor go up to Bethel' (Beth-aven—house of iniquity—is probably a derogatory name for Bethel). The people is here warned not to engage in religious practice, whether pilgrimage-feast or cultic formula 'as Yahweh lives'. Am. 5:5 may be compared. It is not so much an injunction against ritual involving a Canaanisation of Yahweh, as one against the worship of Yahweh at all; for the guilty people by approaching him calls down disaster upon itself. **17** and **18** are textually difficult. The word rendered 'joined' may be translated 'bewitched'; 'let him alone' is a strange expression, and perhaps the words are the corrupt opening of a phrase ending with 'in an assembly of beer-drinkers' (**18a**). In **18c**, MT has 'Her shields (? rulers) with shame love "Give ye" (? bribes)'. The last phrase might mean 'Her shield (i.e. her god, cf. Ps. 118:9ff.) is a shameful thing' (cf. 4:7). With a little emendation and a different interpretation of the word for shields (RSV has 'glory') we may render: 'Her shameless one loves shame', an appropriate parallel to the harlotry of **18b**. **19** pictures the people carried away by a storm-wind in the day of disaster, though the text is not without difficulty.

e **V 1-7** repeats the pattern of 4:4–19. The priests, and with them here the king and royal house (for 'house of Israel', read 'princes' or 'prophets of Israel'), are condemned; they have acted corruptly. 'For the judgment pertains to you' means either
'You are responsible for justice' or 'Judgment falls 583e
upon you'. The former is appropriate: though the latter is parallel to the last clause of **2**. Hence (**3-7**) guilt has come upon the whole people (cf. 1:4–5). Allusions are made (**1b, 2**) to various places, presumably at which cultic failure had notably occurred, though some political reference may be present. **2a** should probably be rendered: 'they have made deep the whoredom of Shittim' (cf. Num. 25:1), representing the consonants of MT, which is very obscure. In **4** the impossibility of recovery for Israel is indicated; such is the people's condition that they are not merely 'stubborn' (cf. 4:16), their actions have cut them off from God and made an approach to him impossible. **6**. Though the attempt is made to approach God with sacrificial offerings, he has withdrawn himself and become inaccessible. The deity is departed, ritual searchings are in vain (an allusion to common cultic practice); hence the fields are to meet with disaster. **7**. The deceit practised by Israel is the birth of children within an alien cult, possibly a further allusion to the narrative of Num. 25. **7c** is difficult; an attractive alternative rendering of the consonants of MT is: 'Now an invader shall devour their fields' (Eitan).

V 8-VII 16 Political Failure—The opening sum- f
mons to sound the alarm of war in **8** may be compared with the opening of a new section in similar terms in 8:1. Although there is no complete unity of material within the intervening section, yet there is no very sharp dividing line, and much of it is concerned with the political aspects of Israel's (and Judah's) failure. Very generally, all or part of this is assigned to the period of the Syro-Ephraimite war (cf. 2 Kg. 16:5–9; Isa. 7:1ff.), and, although the vagueness of the political allusions makes this not essential, it is true that many of the oracles would fit well into this situation (cf. especially Alt, *Kleine Schriften* (1953), ii, 163–87 (originally published 1919).

V 8-15 show God bringing judgment upon Israel and g
Judah. Whereas elsewhere in the book allusions to Judah may well be properly regarded as elaborations of the text, here the references to the Southern Kingdom are so integral to the text that it is difficult to excise them without creating undue disturbance. It may indeed be desirable to add a reference to Judah in the fourth line of **13**: 'and Judah sent to the great king'. Since the sounding of the alarm in **8** suggests invasion from the south, there is perhaps good reason for thinking in terms of an invasion by Ahaz into Israel at the moment when the Assyrian response to his invitation for aid was becoming effective. Similarly **10** might be regarded as an allusion to the removal of the boundary between the two kingdoms, as Judah presses north. During these years of Assyrian pressure on Israel, resulting in the cutting down of the Northern Kingdom to a comparatively small area around Samaria, Judah may well have been rewarded by being given some part of the border territory. Hosea—like Isaiah—recognises that this comes under the judgment of God, even though for the moment it may appear to be successful policy. The reason for the disaster is indicated in **11** and **13**. The last word of **11** is obscure, and RSV 'vanity' represents an emended text. The allusion might be religious, but more probably, in view of **13**, it is political. Disaster is associated with the political manoeuvres of the two kingdoms, for the people imagine that they can find new hope by appealing to Assyria for help. As far as Israel is concerned, this is most naturally to be understood in terms of Hoshea's submission, but it might be more generally interpreted in the light of the earlier experience of Menahem, whose establishment on the throne with Assyrian support had not brought lasting peace. **14**. Judgment comes from God, who tears like a lion (cf. 13:7f.). **15**. The withdrawal of God brings distress (cf. **7**). In **8**, MT has 'after you, O Benjamin', which, if correct, might be a battle-cry (cf. Jg. 5:14). 'among the tribes' in **9** might be

533g 'against the tribes'. **12.** For 'moth' the rendering 'mould' (Driver) is preferable. **13.** The 'great king' (cf. 10:6) is the Heb. equivalent of the Assyrian *šarru rabû* ; the form is slightly unusual, a more normal expression appearing in Ps. 48:2. In **14** 'and go away' is probably intrusive, repeated from the beginning of **15**. For 'acknowledge their guilt' perhaps read 'are made desolate' (Driver).

534a **VI 1-6 Israel and her God**—The division into sections is here problematic. The LXX (and so RSV) provide a linking-word to make 5:15 introductory to this passage. It is preferable to recognise that there are here two elements, a confessional liturgy in **1-3**, appropriately placed after the recognition of divine withdrawal in 5:15, and a statement of divine requirements in **4-6**, a sort of 'priestly oracle' in answer to the people's appeal. In **1-3** Israel is depicted as having come to her senses, making an act of penitence before God, and seeking him in the confidence that he alone is the one in whom her hope lies. This may be compared with 14:1–8, and it may be that these passages should be regarded as taken from contemporary usage, appropriate to some fast-day proclaimed in a time of distress and danger (cf. Jer. 36:9). **4-6**, with its critical appraisal of Israel's love, has often been thought to suggest that the penitence is here being represented by Hosea as shallow, a statement of overweening confidence that God will forgive—*c'est son métier*. But there does not seem to be any real necessity for distinguishing so sharply between true and false penitence. Elsewhere Hosea speaks of the impossibility of Israel finding her God because of the barrier of her sin ; yet he also shows that it is only when Israel does seek for God that she can find life, and the appeal to the past experience of the people and to God's redeeming and healing activity is pointless without the possibility of real penitence and restoration. In some ways **4-6** does present the other side of the approach indicated in 5:5–7. **4.** The shallowness of Israel's love and the judgment and warning given by the agency of the prophets (**5**) usher in the statement of the priority of God's requirements. **6b** indicates that **6a** is to be taken as a statement of what God requires as first essential, namely loyalty to the covenant, rather than as a negation of all sacrificial observance. As we have already seen, worship which is offered by those unfit to stand in the presence of God (cf. Ps. 15) courts disaster.

b In **2**, the expression 'two days, three' is a numerical device common in proverbial literature (cf. Prov. 30:15–31), and known from Râs Shamra to stand for an indefinite statement. There may well be an allusion here to contemporary religious ideas of the resurrection of fertility deities. In **3d** MT has 'early rain', rightly emended in RSV to 'water'. **5c** has 'and thy judgments are light which issues forth' but a simple redivision of the consonants gives the RSV rendering.

c **7-10** contains a catalogue of sins, associated with particular places. If the opening of **10** is read, more probably, as 'At Bethel' the series is well rounded off with a reference to apostasy at the great royal shrine (cf. Am. 7:13). The allusions are, however, obscure, and may well be to contemporary events unknown to us. **7.** It is best to take Adam as a place-name, and not, as MT, to read 'like Adam', since the parallel 'there' suggests a locality. **10b**, with only a small emendation, may be rendered : 'There Israel was defiled in virtue of the harlotry of Ephraim'. **11a** is a clear gloss, reminding the later reader that the judgment pronounced upon Israel was to fall equally upon the south.

d **VI 11b-VII 10** is mainly concerned with the corruptions of Israel's political life. The metaphors in **7:4, 6-8** from baking may provide a reason for this material having been grouped as it now stands. Again there is inevitable uncertainty as to the meaning of the various allusions, though it seems not improbable that the intrigues around the kingship during the twenty years before the fall of Samaria provide a fitting setting. **6:11b-7:2** provides a general introduction to these more specific statements. The revealing of God's redemptive purpose makes plain the deceitfulness of Israel ; the past is not just wiped out, but Israel's deeds stand before God (**2**, cf. Weiser). **3-7** have been understood as a general condemnation of the kingship of the north, or of kingship as such. Many commentators emend **3** to read 'In their wickedness they anoint kings', but MT reads perfectly satisfactorily, perhaps with an allusion to a coronation ceremony and suggesting in **5**, if the next verses are part of the same oracle, that even as one king is crowned, the courtiers are conspiring against him at a drunken orgy. **4-6.** There are several obscurities in MT, and RSV represents a reasonable reconstruction. The precise nature of the metaphors remains, however, like the allusions, somewhat obscure. **4b.** One picture seems to be that of an oven which is allowed to grow cold, so that, presumably, the food is never properly cooked. **6b.** Another picture is of the roaring up of the fire in the morning, after it has been damped down at night. **7** suggests that the attempt to save the people is made by continually setting up new rulers, but 'none of them calls upon me'. **8-10** takes up a similar picture, a cake placed on the ashes, which, if not turned, will be burnt on one side, though the first line seems to have a different idea, namely the mixing of Israel with alien life like the mixing of oil and meal. The result is that disaster comes upon the people without their being aware of it. Yet, for all this (cf. Isa. 9:12, 17, cf. also Am. 4:6–11), they do not return to God. **9c** may be better rendered 'hoar hairs are grey upon him' (Driver).

e **VII 11-13** describes political folly in terms of foreign alliances, perhaps with an allusion to the intrigues of Hoshea, the last king of Israel. **13.** The desire of God to redeem (an allusion to the Exodus) is frustrated by the duplicity of his people. One possible emendation of MT in **12c** is represented by RSV ; another possibility would be 'I will chastise them according to the abundance of their evils.'

f **14-16** turns back again to the religious aspect of the failure. Israel only pretends to return to God, but in fact engages in alien ritual. Because of this apostasy, Israel will find herself again in the bondage of Egypt, mocked by her overlords. In **14** 'gash themselves' is the most probable rendering, though the MT has an almost identical word meaning 'to assemble themselves' or 'to excite themselves' (cf. Syr.) ; 'they rebel' also represents an improvement on MT 'turn aside'. In **15**, it is possible that the word translated 'trained' really means 'strengthened', and that it has been glossed by the more common Heb. word. Only one of these is rendered in LXX. The opening of **16** is obscure, though the general meaning is plain from the context, and RSV represents a simple correction. An alternative reading is : 'They return to the High One (probably Baal) . . . through the insolence (or 'stammering') of their tongues, i.e. their stuttering (a gloss on the synonym) in the land of Egypt.'

535a **VIII 1-14 The Breaking of the Covenant**—The chapter does not form a unified oracle, but may not inconveniently be regarded as a series of sayings linked to the ideas of **1-3**, in which Israel's breaking of the covenant is indicated. Here, as in 5:8, the war alarm is sounded ; disaster threatens Israel, **1** like a bird of prey and **3** as an enemy. The disobedience of Israel is to the bond of loyalty established between God and the people, and expressed in the law which should govern her conduct (**1b**). 'For a vulture' (**1**) represents a slightly emended text ; the MT must presumably be rendered 'like a vulture it (i.e. disaster) is over the house of the Lord' (perhaps better 'house of Israel'. This meaning may be intended by MT, or the reference may be to a temple). **2a** is difficult : it seems to contain a cultic invocation to God (cf. Ps. 84:3), and its insincerity is commented upon in **3**.

535a But the order of words is peculiar. Wellhausen rendered 'To me they cry, My God: but (we) I know thee, O Israel.'

b **4-7** is mainly concerned with idolatry and its consequence in natural disaster. **4.** The opening lines on kings and princes may be an odd fragment, not really part of the oracle, but if rightly here, then there is a parallel drawn between kingship and idolatry which suggests hostility to the ideas of 'sacral' kingship familiar in Canaan and also in Israel. The suggestion of Nyberg that here and in **10** 'kings and princes' are divine titles does not seem appropriate. More satisfactory is the suggestion (Haupt, Driver) that the verse should be translated: 'They have taken counsel, but not of me; they have got advice, but I know not (of it)'. **5.** In particular the oracle is concerned with the 'calf of Samaria', which is commented on in more detail in **6**; a wooden image, possibly gold-covered, it is to be reduced to 'splinters' or 'will go up in flames' (RSV*n*). It is described appropriately as a 'not-God'. **5b** sounds like an interjected cry of distress at the recalcitrance of the people; the opening words of **6**, unintelligible as they stand, may be taken at the end of **5**, as RSV. Frey emends to: 'How long will they not cease from idolatry, for who has ever made a God?' which provides a clear link with **7**.

c **8-10** denounces Israel's policy of foreign alliances, another aspect of the breach of the covenant, for Israel no longer trusts in her God. The section is linked verbally to the previous one, for the last word of **7** and the first of **8** are from the same root. The same metaphor as is used in ch. 2, the desire for lovers, is here applied to foreign policy; **9c.** Ephraim has bargained for lovers, **10a** has gone a-bargaining among the nations. The remainder of **10** is difficult. A threat is expected, but the word 'gather' is most naturally used in a good sense (so LXX). The next phrases are reminiscent of 3:4; the rendering 'cease' may perhaps be obtained from the Heb. verb: 'and they shall have a little leisure from setting up kings and princes' (Driver); 'anointing' represents an emended text.

d **11-13** depicts the unavailing multiplying of sacrifices, which will not prevent the people from being sent back into Egypt as punishment (cf. 7:16). The LXX appropriately add 'and they shall eat unclean things among the Assyrians' at the end of **13**. A very small change of pointing would allow **11** to read:

> Though Ephraim has made many altars to atone,
> yet they have become to them altars of sinning.

13a might be rendered:

> They may sacrifice my sacrificial gifts
> and may eat flesh.

linking to **13b**.

e **14** is an isolated phrase, reminiscent of Am. 1 and perhaps out of context. Yet it reiterates the warning that there is no protection from disaster in the building of palaces and fortresses, when Israel has forgotten her maker.

f **IX 1-9 Disaster—Exile—at hand**—In **1-6** the theme of religious failure is again taken up, and the allusions in **1** and **5** have suggested that these verses may derive from words spoken at the autumnal festival. **1.** 'Exult not' represents a fairly simple emendation of MT; alternatively, render 'with exultation'. **2.** The crops fail because of Israel's apostasy, whether it be that they are worshipping Baal, or offering wrong worship to Yahweh. The imagery of **1** is that familiar from elsewhere in the book, suggestive of Canaanite fertility practice. **3** brings the threat; they are not to remain in the 'land of Yahweh' but go into exile in Egypt and Assyria (cf. 8:13). It is significant that the land is thus described, for it reiterates the idea that the return to the wilderness (2:14f.) is to be only temporary. **4-6** is best understood as repeating the same ideas. 535
Alien worship is disastrous, and produces defilement; it is not acceptable to God (**4b, 4f.**); exile is at hand, and their cult-objects (**6** probably this is the allusion of 'precious things') and shrines (so Sellin; lit. tents) will be overgrown. The alternative interpretation of **4-5** is that it refers to the cessation of worship in exile, but in that case the last clause of **4** is strange. In **4** 'please' might be rendered 'offer'; this meaning would support the second interpretation suggested above. MT in **6** speaks of 'going from ruin', i.e. from a desolated land. The parallel supports the conjecture 'to Assyria'.

7-9 is a further threat of disaster, with an allusion to g
some past failure at Gibeah (? cf. Jg. 19ff., or 1 Sam. 10:26), also alluded to in 10:9. The references here to the prophet are very difficult to interpret. They are often taken as an expression of the popular judgment on the prophet, who is prevented (**8b**) from carrying out his appointed task. Yet if the earlier reference to 'prophet' in 4:5 is not excised, it does not seem inappropriate to see here an allusion to contemporary prophecy and its failure. The prophet is the watchman, but, like the priest, he has failed in his task. The obscurity of the text makes a judgment impossible, though **8** stresses again that the greatest danger to Ephraim lies in her false religious life. In **7** 'Israel shall know it' should be rendered 'Israel shall be humiliated' (Winton Thomas).

IX 10-XIII 16 (Heb. XIV 1) Israel—then and now 536
—It seems not unreasonable to view this section as having in some measure a unified theme. The various smaller units which it comprises stress in one way or another the differences between the Israel that God called from Egypt, and the Israel which developed so soon into disobedience and apostasy. Not inappropriately the whole section is followed by an oracle of penitence in ch. 14.

IX 10-17 The deep-rooted Evil of Israel's Life— b
Here **10-14** may be separated from **15-17**, both passages having the same basic theme. In **10-14** the stress is laid at the outset on the unexpected delight of God's choosing of Israel—grapes in the wilderness (cf. Jer. 2:2f.), and the first-fruits of the fig-tree (cf. Isa. 28:4 for a different use of the idea). But immediately, even during the wilderness period, Israel went astray at Baal-peor (cf. Num. 25), and this apostasy brings now the judgment appropriate to the sin of joining in the alien fertility cult—no birth, cutting off the line, miscarriage. The nation is cut off from future life. In **10** the phrase 'in its first season' is omitted by Syr. and by many commentators; it is perhaps a gloss emphasising the idea of Israel as the first-fruits. 'Baal' or some other divine name is probably to be read for the MT 'shame'; similarly MT has 'detestable things' in the last line, probably replacing some other word, possibly 'cult prostitutes'. RSV represents the probable sense of the difficult last line. **12b** is obscure, Nyberg suggests 'when I take vengeance upon them' (cf. Syr.); another suggestion, based upon an emended text, is 'if they wean their children then they will be ashamed of them', providing a link to **13**. MT in **13** has 'Ephraim as I saw Tyre planted (feminine) in a meadow'. An alternative to RSV is 'Ephraim I see as a guilty man, his children are given for a prey'. The basic idea in both verses is disaster to the children who perpetuate the people's life.

15-17 is a similar oracle, tracing corruption to Gilgal c
(cf. 4:15, 12:11) with a possible allusion to the kingship (cf. 1 Sam. 11:15), but more probably a general reference to apostasy. The same disaster is indicated in **16f.** as in **10-14**. The recognition of this as a parallel oracle appears to be better than the commonly adopted suggestion of placing **16** after **13** because of the similarity of idea. More probably the two passages have been put together because of their related content. It is also to be noted that **14** and **17** have a certain parallelism of structure, representing a kind

536c of prophetic comment (cf. Zech. 3:5) on the appropriateness of the disaster (' My God ' in **17** is strange, but not impossible ; in **14** the prophet himself pronounces the final judgment).

d **X 1-8 Inescapable Disaster**—There is a verbal link in **1** to the previous section (cf. 9:10). In **1-2** the theme (cf. 4:7ff.) is taken up of the luxuries of Israel's religious life corresponding to her prosperity. **1.** For ' improved ', ' made more abundant ' may be preferred (Gordis). It does not seem to be implied that the cult objects are regarded as illegitimate, but that Israel's apostasy makes them the object of God's wrath. **2.** For ' false ' the alternative rendering ' divided ' (AV, RV) suggests a people whose allegiance wavers between Yahweh and Baal (cf. 1 Kg. 18). For ' bear their guilt ' perhaps render ' be made desolate ' (Driver). **3-8** indicates the desperate situation, with all help gone. The people do not fear God, nor can they see any hope in the royal house, whose policies are futile ; **4** the ' judgment ' which the king should uphold has become a poisonous weed. **5.** Equally impotent is Samaria's idol, an object for which men tremble instead of a power to protect (for Beth-aven cf. 4:15, though here a reference to Bethel is less appropriate and a more general reference to some religious building may be intended). **6.** The idol itself is carried captive (cf. 1 Sam. 4 ; Isa. 46:2) as tribute to the king of Assyria, and the people left in a state of shame, that is of recognising their powerlessness. The same motif reappears in **7-8,** where the reference to the king may in fact be to the idol and possibly **7a** should read : ' Samaria and her king (idol) . . .' **7b** is perhaps an allusion to Exod. 32:20. **8.** With the captivity of the idol and the destruction of the cult places, fertility is gone from the land, and the people in shame seek to be hidden from the disaster (cf. Isa. 2:19, 21). 'Aven' is probably the same as Beth-aven in 4:15 ; see §533*d*.

e **X 9-15 Sin from the Days of Gibeah**—The opening here alludes to an ancient act of disobedience (cf. 9:9) which makes Israel—still standing in the same sin—liable to disaster at the hands of the nations. **9b.** ' there they stand ' suggests a corrupted picture of battle, perhaps linked to the following phrase which might be read ' Shall not war overtake the wayward people at Gibeah ' (Reider). MT in **10a** has ' in my desire ' which perhaps means simply ' when I choose '. There is possibly a precise allusion in ' double iniquity ' which is now obscure to us. **11-12** is best understood as an interjected statement of Israel's obedience and God's requirements. For ' and I spared ' read ' and I put the yoke on ' and follow with ' and ' rather than ' but '. 'Judah ' is probably a gloss, and the text may then be rendered ' yoking Ephraim to plough, making Jacob to harrow '. Here is obedient Israel, submitting rightly to the yoke. **13** sharply contrasts the actual condition, and so (**13b-15**), because Israel has trusted in military power rather than in obedience to God, a great disaster comes upon the people and royal house. **14** alludes to a notable event, possibly an invasion of Gilead by Salamanu of Moab, probably in the not very distant past. LXX, followed by some commentators, find a reference to Shallum's destruction of the house of Jeroboam, but this appears to be an attempt to find a well-known event suitable to the occasion. In **15** MT ' Bethel ' is to be preferred to RSV ' house of Israel ' ; the reference to Beth-arbel in **14** suggests a reference to a particular city here. MT ' at dawn ' (RSV ' in the storm ') is also possible, perhaps meaning ' at the beginning of his reign ', but more probably suggesting a disaster like that which overtook the Assyrians in the reign of Hezekiah (cf. Isa. 37:36), dawn being an appropriate moment for a divine visitation.

f **XI 1-7 Out of Egypt I called my Son**—The same theme of the divine call and of Israel's disobedience is taken up again (**1f.**), with an even clearer allusion to the Exodus as the moment of divine choice. But this was followed by apostasy. **2.** The text is not quite in order, as RSV*n* indicates ; the opening ' they called ' of MT could refer to the Baals enticing Israel away from God ; Nyberg suggests that the plural forms refer to the messengers sent from God, but nothing in the context supports this. **3-4** elaborates the pictures of divine care, continuing the picture of God and Israel as parent and child. **3b** has ' he took them up in his arms ', an awkward change of person, but not so unusual in Hebrew as it appears in English. The reference to God as healer also recalls the Exodus (cf. Exod. 15:26). **4.** ' Cords of compassion ', lit. ' cords of a man ', may perhaps be an error for ' cords of love, or truth ', parallel with love in **4b.** Driver proposes ' bands of leather ' and ' bands of hide ' stressing the strength of divine attachment. The text of the second part of **4** is difficult, and a very attractive rendering, demanding little emendation and extending the picture is : 536f

> And I was to them as they who lift a babe upon their bosom,
> And I inclined to them and gave them food.

The tone changes in **5-7**, which contain the threat of judgment. Israel's spurning of God's care brings inevitable doom. MT has a negative at the beginning of **5**, which makes it better to render the verse as a question : ' Shall they not return . . . ? ' The reference to Egypt and Assyria may be paralleled in 7:16, 8:13, 9:6. The text of **6f.** is obscure in several respects. **6.** ' Rage ' would be better as ' whirl ', suggesting the swiftness of warfare, though in **6** emendation is not difficult to produce RSV. Another suggested rendering for ' fortresses ' (MT ' counsels ') is ' disobedient acts ' (Driver). **7a** might be ' My people is inclined to apostasy ' or (emended) ' sick in apostasy ' or ' has wearied me with its rebellion '. An alternative, which links well with **7b**, is ' My people is dependent upon my turning back ' ; **7b** is literally ' Though they call to 'Al (? ' him on high ', or read ' Baal ') none at all will exalt ' (perhaps ' he (Baal) could not lift them up ' or ' he does not arise '). The last phrase could be emended to : ' Can I desist from showing mercy ? ' which would link well with a positive interpretation of the next verses.

XI 8-11. The major problem here is to decide 537a
whether **8-11** is entirely hopeful, or whether it conceals words of judgment, elaborated with a message of compassion. **11:12-12:1** (Heb. 12:1f.) does not seem to go with the next section, and although it appears to be independent of 11:1-11 as it now stands, may perhaps represent another oracle of judgment appropriate to the main tenor of ch. 11. **11** is clearly a message of return from exile, and provides an answer to the oracle of 11:5. The same might be said of **10**, though here the picture of God as a lion is an unusual symbol for hope (cf. 5:14, 13:7) ; the original idea may rather be that of God as a lion with its young coming out eagerly after its prey, and in that case the final line may really belong to **11.** **9** is normally rendered as a series of questions. Much depends here on the weight given to ' I am God and not man '. Is it that God, unlike man, is willing to forgive ? Or is it that God is not a man to change his mind ? Man may overlook sin : God in his holiness cannot. In the latter case the sense of **8** may be appropriately linked as an interjection of God's great compassion for Israel, the child whom he has called and cared for, but whom he must judge. This sense corresponds well with the oracles of ch. 2. ' Even if God must punish, that does not imply that he has ceased to love ' (Mauchline). Attractive as it may be to find here an oracle of hope, the general context and much of the wording strongly suggests that original words announcing inevitable judgment have been elaborated, by the prophet or his successors, with a message relieving their darkness. The reference in **8** to Admah and Zeboiim (cf. Dt. 29:23) appears to be a variant of the Sodom and Gomorrah story (cf. Isa. 1:9). The last

537a clause of **9** is obscure, though RSV provides a reasonable reading, which may also be rendered : 'Shall I not come to destroy?' The last phrase of **10** might be emended to 'from Egypt'. **11a.** 'come eagerly' should be (like **10**) 'come trembling'.

b **XI 12-XII 1** resumes the theme of deceitfulness, and of the futility of the foreign policy of Israel. As the text stands **12b** indicates by contrast the faithfulness of Judah, though MT has a plural where RSV has 'Holy One'. The text is not altogether simple, and it would not be difficult to render :

Judah goes in and out with El (or possibly Baal)
and is intimate (confiding) with the gods

where 'holy ones' is taken to mean alien deities, though an alternative would be to read 'cult prostitutes'. If 'El' is used in a good sense, then the second clause is perhaps a contrast : at one and the same time Judah has dealings with El (her own God) and consorts with other deities. It is possible that 'Judah' here has been substituted for an original 'Israel'.

c **XII 2-11 (Heb. 3-12) God's Controversy with his People**—**2.** A general introductory word of warning ushers in **3-4** a series of allusions to the patriarch Jacob-Israel, with an ascription of praise and **6** an injunction to obedience. **7.** In the sequel another picture is given, of Ephraim the trader (literally Canaanite), priding himself in his wealth, interpreted as implying divine favour, which cannot avail to clear him of his guilt. **9.** He is to return to the desert (cf. 2:14f., 3:4). **10f.** A further oracle comments on the warning given by the agency of the prophets, and the disaster to the cult-places which is coming as a reckoning.

d The picture of Jacob here is most often taken to be a further indictment of the people : their corruption reaches right back to their forefather, the deceiver. Yet it must be recognised that this is not very clear in the text, and that Jacob is described rather as the one who prevailed with God (4). His craftiness (3 'taken by the heel', cf. Gen. 25:26, i.e. 'deceive, trick'), as in the Gen. narrative, is to be viewed rather as a virtue, and he is one who strove with God, and found blessing, 'wept' (using 'all the usual ways of imploring God for blessing' (Bentzen)) and found grace. This interpretation suggests a link of thought with the confession of faith in Dt. 26:5ff. ; the theme, as in 11:1, of divine protection on which Israel now (8) prides itself falsely.

e 'Judah' in **2** may well have been substituted for 'Israel' to provide an application to later needs. In **4** MT has 'with us', which is perhaps correct, for the people *now* is in a real sense identical with Jacob *then*, and the call for obedience applies equally to the patriarch and to his descendants. In **5b** 'his name' is literally 'his memorial', i.e. 'that by which he is invoked'. **7.** 'Oppress' could easily be read as 'defraud'. **8b** is obscure, but might be better rendered :

All his gains are not sufficient
for the sin (guilt) he has incurred.

9. 'Dwelling in tents' is likely to have a double allusion, to the 'day of meeting' at Sinai, and to the 'appointed feast' in the autumn (Tabernacles). **11a** may be readily emended to 'In Gilead there was iniquity, yea they became naught (or 'loved vanity')'. 'Bulls' should perhaps be read 'to bulls' or 'to demons'.

f **XII 12-XIII 3 (Heb. XII 13-XIII 3).** A similar passage depicts the past and the present. Admittedly the divisions of the material are far from clear, and it is possible to divide at the end of the chapter, or after **13:1.** Yet **13:1** appears closely linked to **12:14**, and an equally clear link appears with **13:2f.**, whereas **13:4** begins a new statement. Here too, in **12:12**, the patriarch Jacob is mentioned, and there is simply an indication of his wanderings (cf. Dt. 26:5). **13.** The Exodus is summed up in terms of prophetic guidance 537f and deliverance. The 'prophet' is a description of Moses, which is of great interest (cf. also Ps. 105:15 with reference to Abraham and Isaac). **13:1ff.** This initial favour has been followed by increasing apostasy. Such a description of the material makes it unnecessary to view **12:12** as a misplaced fragment of the Jacob material in 12:3f., as suggested by the brackets of RSV. **12:14** and **13:1** are obscure. Particularly difficult is **13:1a**, which might be rendered 'When Ephraim spoke stammeringly, or in trembling' or emended to 'When Ephraim spoke my law' (cf. LXX 'declarations of right'). This leaves the subject of 'he was exalted' open to question : is it God? or Moses? or an allusion to the primacy of Ephraim among the tribes (cf. the Joseph traditions and particularly Gen. 48:8–22)? Perhaps this last is the most probable, and the guilt and apostasy of **1b-3** stand out all the more sharply in contrast. RSV in **2b** represents a reasonable emendation of the text, which is clearly corrupt. **3.** A series of pictures describes the rapidity of the disaster which is coming.

XIII 4-11 God's Care and Israel's Forgetfulness g —The same theme recurs, **5** this time with a mention of the provision of nourishment in the wilderness period, **6** which was followed by disobedience and forgetfulness, with Israel ascribing her blessings to others (cf. ch. 2). **7f.** So now God is like the wild beasts of prey to his people, and Israel's trust in earthly rulers to deliver them from the coming judgment is vain. To **4** LXX appropriately add 'who established the heaven and created the earth, whose hands created all the host of heaven, and I did not show them to you in order that you might follow after them. And I brought you up (i.e. out of Egypt).' **5.** 'Knew' is better rendered as 'cared for', a proper sense of the Heb. verb (cf. Am. 3:2). **6a.** MT has 'according to their pasturing', i.e. 'as they were fed'. **7.** 'I will lurk' is uncertain : LXX suggest a rendering 'on the way to Assyria'. **8.** RSV paraphrases the last clause, which actually reads 'the wild beasts will rend them' ; an alternative is to read 'there dogs will devour them' for the previous clause. MT in **9** reads : 'He has destroyed you, O Israel : but in me is (as) your helper'. An alternative to RSV is 'If I destroy . . . who is as your helper?' **10a** is again obscure, but RSV gives the most probable sense, and it seems most appropriate to regard this verse and the next as providing not a general comment on the illegitimacy of kingship, but upon the powerlessness of kings to deliver, and upon the low ebb to which the monarchy has sunk in the last years of Israel's existence as a kingdom.

12-16 (Heb. 12-XIV 1) Oracle of Judgment— h Although it is possible that the section is made up of smaller units, it may be treated as one because of the unity of its theme. It offers in **15f.** a gruesome picture of the disaster which is imminent, the land deprived of water, the precious things (presumably of palace and temple) torn away, and the horrors of war as in Am. 1:13. **16.** For 'bear her guilt' render 'be made desolate' (Driver). The reason for the disaster is indicated in **12** where the iniquity of Ephraim is described as stored, preserved for the day of judgment ; nothing will escape its proper retribution. **13** offers a vivid picture of the failure of Ephraim ; like a child about to be born, Ephraim is summoned by the birth pangs, but he refuses to respond. A momentary glimpse of hope is thus again lost to sight. In this context of failure and disaster, it appears clear that the original meaning of **14** must have been gloomy. This is apparent in the last phrase of the verse, and in the light of this the opening questions expect a negative answer, and the address to Death and Sheol in effect means 'Bring your disaster now to Ephraim'. RSV, following LXX, Syr. and 1 C. 15:55, has 'where' ; the peculiar form in MT (cf. AV, RSV*n*), if correct, would emphasise the idea of the divine bringing of disaster. The interpretation of the verse in a hopeful

37h sense (cf. LXX, 1 C., Luther), while it is attractive, does not do justice to the context, and is only possible if the last clause of **14** is regarded as disconnected. If **14** is independent, then the opening can be rendered as a statement: 'I shall ransom', and the major part of the verse may be regarded as a gloss. The words in **14** rendered 'plagues' and 'destruction' may perhaps best be rendered 'sting', the former requiring only a transposition of two consonants (Reider). In **15** MT has 'among brothers', amended to 'like a reed' in RSV: the MT might contain an allusion to a political situation, or to the former place of Ephraim (cf. 13:1).

i **XIV 1-8 (Heb. 2-9) A Liturgy of Repentance**—Appropriately enough, the words of Hosea are rounded off with a word of hope, whose form (cf. 6:1–3) is that of a liturgy, in which the people respond to the exhortation to repent, and so find themselves brought to restored life and prosperity. The question has often been asked as to whether this passage is genuine, or represents a late addition to the book. The answer is best to be seen in the closeness of the relationship between the language and imagery used here and that found in the remainder of the book, not only in the hopeful passages (11:8f., 2:15–23), but also in the overtones of the messages of judgment and discipline, particularly in chs. 3 and 12. In any case, what is here presented is a picture of what can happen, rather than a description of an actual occurrence. The people is exhorted to acknowledge sin and to present itself before God 'with words', i.e. the proper liturgical forms of address. The divine forgiveness will find its response in the people's vows ('fruit of our lips' **2**, rather than MT 'calves, our lips'). **3.** The form of penitence is appropriate to the failure; alliances and idolatry are repudiated. The final clause emphasises justice, that other aspect of prophetic teaching, though here the phrase is somewhat loosely attached and may be a later addition. **4-7** pictures the divine response, healing, love and fertility for the land, the exact opposite of the disasters brought upon Israel by her sin. Vividly, in terms reminiscent of Ca., the abundant new life is described. **8.** The passage concludes with a further renunciation of idolatry, though the exact meaning of the verse is not clear. The suggestion that the four lines of the verse should be regarded as spoken alternately by Ephraim and God is ingenious, but lacks any real foundation. It is better to treat the words as part of the divine address—returning to the first-person form of **4-6** after **7** in the third person (so MT; RSV emends). Admittedly it is unusual to find God describing himself as an 'evergreen cypress', but such a phrase is not impossible. **8b** is the real crux. Emendations or alternative renderings suggested are 'I have afflicted and will restore him', which is appropriate; 'I have answered and I affirm it'; and 'I am his Anath and his Asherah' which is very bold, but not out of harmony with the general tenor of the book. It links 537l
well with **8cd**, and it is furthermore easy to understand that the text would be changed from a form which would certainly seem objectionable to later readers. It does not seem impossible that Hosea, who claims so firmly that it is from God and not from the Baals that Israel's life and the fertility of the land come, should also claim that Israel does not need any other deity, male or female, beside her own. When we recall the association with Yahweh of other deities (cf. 1:2–9), we may well believe that Yahweh was regarded in some circles in Hosea's time as having a female consort.

The phrase 'take away all iniquity' in **2** represents j
a free rendering of a rather unusual Heb. text. Perhaps MT should be emended to: 'All of you say to him: Take away iniquity' or 'Thou canst forgive all iniquity' or 'Indeed, forgive' (Gordis). In **5**, MT has Lebanon (perhaps accidentally from **6f.**); an easy emendation gives 'poplar' (better 'storax', cf. 4:13). For 'shall strike' we may emend to 'shall spread out (his roots)'. **6** compares the fragrance to that of the cedars of Lebanon. MT in **7** is literally: 'They that dwell in his shade return'; the third-person form may be kept, in spite of the context, for such changes are common in Heb. poetry. **7b.** 'As a garden' represents a straightforward emendation of MT; alternatively, we may read 'as corn', using the noun which is in MT. To 'wine of Lebanon', 'wine of Helbon' (cf. Ezek. 27:18) may be preferred, a place north-west of Damascus, noted for its wine.

9 (Heb. 10) Postscript—A wisdom saying, reflecting k
on the teaching of the book, brings it to a close. (For a similar note, cf. perhaps Zech. 8:9.) The reader is reminded that the words of the message, rightly understood, bring blessing; but to the wicked they bring disaster. Appropriately, the double-edged nature of the divine purpose is here emphasised, for the tension between the blessing which God intends and the disaster which Israel provokes is a marked feature of the prophet's thought.

Bibliography—COMMENTARIES: S. L. Brown, WC (1932); T. K. Cheyne, CB (1884); W. R. Harper, ICC (1905); A. van Hoonacker, EBib. (1908); R. F. Horton, Cent.B (1904); S. M. Lehrmann, Soncino Bible (1948); J. Mauchline, IB VI (1956); T. H. Robinson, HAT (2nd ed. 1954); E. Sellin, KAT (1929); A. Weiser, ATD (1949); H. W. Wolff, BK (1956–).

OTHER LITERATURE: H. Frey, *Das Buch des Werbens Gottes um seine Kirche. Der Prophet Hosea* (1957); H. S. Nyberg, *Studien zum Hoseabuche* (1935); H. Wheeler Robinson, *Two Hebrew Prophets* (1948), 11–61; G. Adam Smith, *The Book of the Twelve Prophets* (1928), i, 219–379; A. C. Welch, *Kings and Prophets of Israel* (1952), 130–84.

JOEL

By L. H. BROCKINGTON

538a The prophet Joel, of whom we know nothing beyond his own name, his father's name, and the message contained in the small book, bears a popular name found some twelve times elsewhere. If, as is possible, but not proved, the name means 'Yah is God' it may be associated with the name Elijah which bears a similar meaning with the two component parts in the reverse order. His father Pethuel bears a name which does not occur anywhere else. The occasion of the message of Joel was a locust plague of unprecedented severity and its content was a summons to fasting and contrition and a warning that the plague of locusts may be the herald of the day of Yahweh.

b The book cannot be dated with certainty, but in all probability is a product of the early part of the 4th cent. B.C. The facts upon which a date may be based are these. There was a devastating locust plague in the prophet's day so severe that the daily sacrifices had to be discontinued. The Israelites are scattered among the nations (3:2) which implies that the Exile had already taken place and that at least some Israelites are still not returned. The Phoenicians and Philistines are accused of trading Israelites with Greeks, selling them into slavery (3:4–6). These appear to be three definite historical facts for which a date ought to be readily determinable. But that does not prove to be so in actual fact. There is no other record of such a locust plague, and in any case locust plagues were doubtless of fairly common occurrence, although not by any means as severe as that described in Jl. They would be talked about for the next year or so, but it is unlikely that note would be taken of any locust plague to record its date. That some Israelites are scattered implies a date after the Exile. The selling of Israelites by Phoenicians to Greeks would be unlikely earlier than the 4th cent. B.C. when Greek contact with Palestine began. It is remotely possible that the enslaving may have been done by Ptolemy (Soter) son of Lagus in 320 B.C. when, according to Josephus (*Contra Apionem* I, 209, 210) he entered Jerusalem with his army. 3:17 refers to an invader who may be the same enemy. These facts therefore yield nothing definite. There are two other features of the book, however, which, while not helping to provide a definite date, do at least confirm the impression that the book is a late one. First there is a parody of Isa. 2:4 (Mic. 4:3) in 3:10. Now many scholars maintain that the oracle belongs to neither Isa. nor Mic. and that it is a later insertion in both books; moreover, a parody, to be effective, must be of something that is familiar to the hearers. Secondly, the descriptions of the day of Yahweh are couched in terms that are more in keeping with apocalyptic literature than prophetic, e.g. the universal outpouring of the spirit of prophecy (2:28, 29), the cataclysmic changes of sun, moon and earth (2:30–2), the assembling of the nations to the valley of Jehoshaphat for judgment (3:2, 12, cf. Zech. 14:1–5) and the flowing of a healing stream from the Temple in Jerusalem (3:18, cf. Ezek. 47:1ff.; Zech. 13:1). None of these features in themselves would stamp a work as apocalyptic, but taken together they make it very probable that the book, though not a full apocalypse, yet belongs to literature that is moving towards what finally blossomed out in Dan. and subsequent apocalypses. 538b The line between prophecy and apocalyptic cannot be drawn with any degree of certainty, or even the date at which apocalyptic may be said to begin be determined beyond doubt. H. H. Rowley is cautious of designating anything earlier than Dan. as apocalyptic, although he recognises that there was a transition period between prophecy and apocalyptic (*The Relevance of Apocalyptic* (2nd ed. 1947)). S. B. Frost, on the other hand, would draw in as much post-exilic material as possible (*Old Testament Apocalyptic* (1952)). In any case, apocalyptic was a late post-exilic product of Israel's literary genius. However, it did not spring up overnight, and although it took the crisis of the Maccabaean War to precipitate it as a separate type of literature, there had been several anticipations of it, as in Jl.

This book, then, is to be regarded as a product of c the transition period between prophecy and apocalyptic. It is essentially a prophetic book however and its message is a typical prophetic interpretation of a contemporary disaster. The prophet experienced the terrible plague and shared with the people in celebrating a national day of prayer and fasting, but he also interpreted the event for his fellow countrymen as might be expected of a true prophet. He saw in it a token and symbol of the day of Yahweh, or rather, of the kind of punitive disaster that would precede and herald the day. Once the prophet had embarked on this prophetic work the locust plague fell into the background and other figures for devastation and destruction came forward, i.e. an advancing army and a forest fire. To crown it all there is a picture of the upheaval of the normal course of events; the spirit of God will be poured out on everybody alike, old and young, slave and free, and there will also be catastrophic changes in natural phenomena (2:28–32). It is these things that bring the book very close to apocalyptic.

Uncertainty about the unity of the book has some- d times been felt. Here and there one finds sudden transitions in subject-matter, for instance at 2:28 there is a distinct change from the present situation caused by the locusts to a future time which can most naturally be described as eschatological. Further there are changes of person (cf. 2:19*b*–20, 21–4, 25–9) and of verse to prose (2:30). One theory put forward is that the book is a liturgy composed for two or more sets of voices and used on the occasion of a severe locust plague. This would account for the changes in style and in person, but there are no obvious marks of liturgical origin. Another suggestion is that the book has been subjected to successive editings in a gradual process of compilation. One recent study along these lines attempts to establish that Joel was a Temple-prophet, a younger contemporary of Jeremiah, whose prophecies were edited, expanded (especially 2:28–3:21) and written down by his successors among the Temple-prophets. It is argued that some of the language of the book is reminiscent of that used in the Canaanite ritual and that its full implication would be understood by the author's contemporaries (A. S. Kapelrud, *Joel Studies* (1948)). It is probably best however to regard the book as the work of one

38d author, a man called to prophetic activity by a contemporary disaster who responded to the urgency of the situation and who widened the horizon of his message to embrace all mankind in a visitation of God which the locust plague could betoken. The rapid changes of mood, subject-matter and person, within the book, reflect the urgency of the situation.

39a **I 1-12.** The ravages of a plague of locusts; the distress of the people. **1.** ' Aged men . . . all inhabitants '; cf. the similar linking of the two in v. 14. **4.** Four words are used for locusts. They probably represent local names, and perhaps also show different stages of growth. ' Cutting locust ' also in 2:25 and Am. 4:9 : ' swarming locust ' translates the commonest Heb. word for locust and may have reference either to their great numbers or to the fact that they are full grown : ' hopping locust ' also in 2:25; Ps. 105:34; Jer. 51:14; Nah. 3:16, the root of the word implies quick movement : ' destroying locust ', probably the locust at its most vigorous stage, the word implies the stage following the sloughing of the skin : it occurs also in 2:25, 1 Kg. 8:37; Ps. 78:46; Isa. 33:4. **5.** Drunkards : to pick out such a group as specially hard hit, a group that would normally be least affected by trouble, lends vividness to the utterance. It may even be possible that the grape harvest was just about to be made. ' Sweet wine ', the pressed-out juice of the grapes. **6. A nation** is used metaphorically for the locust swarm, cf. Prov. 30:25f. for a similar usage. ' Lion . . . lioness ' : Heb. parallelism lends itself to pairing or coupling of words of this sort to include a whole species or category. **8. Like a virgin:** a particularly poignant case of hardship is instanced. **9.** The picture of devastation and destruction is complete : food utterly fails, with not enough to maintain the daily offerings to God.

b **13-18.** The priests are called upon to mourn and lament for the loss of the daily offering, and also to proclaim a national day of fasting and prayer. **14.** ' Solemn assembly ', probably a specially proclaimed public holy-day; Isaiah has strong words to say about such days when they are not sincerely celebrated (Isa. 1:13). **15-18.** Then there follows a form of words to be used for the occasion. **15.** The devastation left by the locusts heralds what will happen when the day of Yahweh comes. The day of Yahweh was a familiar theme of the prophets, but they were concerned to show that it would not be the day of gladness and rejoicing which popular imagination expected but one of darkness and distress (Am. 5:18–20) because God would come to punish the wicked (Zeph. 1:14–16). In origin it may well have been an expectation of the day when Yahweh would gain victory over Israel's foes, giving great joy and satisfaction to the people. The prophets were convinced that it was not Israel's foes alone whom Yahweh would come to punish, there were many in Israel who would be visited for their sins.

c **19-20.** A cry of distress for the ravages of fire followed by drought. This appears to be a separate oracle, in the first person, that has nothing directly to do with the locusts and shows the author already looking beyond the plague to the conditions that would herald the day of the Lord.

d **II 1-11.** A call to be alert because the day of Yahweh is near. It gives a picture of the conditions that will prevail when the day of Yahweh approaches. It may well spring out of the experience of the locust plague, but develops the imagery beyond that naturally applicable to locusts. Three fresh ideas are introduced : that of sheer gloom (cf. Am. 5:18, 20; Zeph. 1:15*b*), that of an advancing army leaving ' scorched earth ' in its train, and that of the convulsions of earth and heaven. The first two lines of v. 2 are identical with Zeph. 1:15*b*, and reminiscent of Am. 5:20. There are touches in the description of the army in 3–9 that are similar to the advance of the hordes of Gog in Ezek. 38, 39. **11.** But whatever descriptions are used, we are reminded that it is the Lord's host, he is behind it, he utters his voice and thus gives expression 539d
to his power.

e **12-17.** The prophet returns to the actual situation caused by the locust plague and calls, in Yahweh's name, for heartfelt repentance. Vv. 12, 13 are a sincere plea for genuine contrition, not in outward show which was disliked by all the prophets, but by the true feelings of the heart that will match the gracious and merciful character of Yahweh. This is a familiar description of Yahweh's character and appears in practically the same words in Exod. 34:6; Ps. 86:15, 103:8; Jon. 4:2. The priests are invited to join in the general penitence after they have proclaimed a national day of fasting and prayer. The phrasing of 15f. echoes that of 1:14 and 2:1. **17.** It is not clear exactly what is meant by **Between the vestibule and the altar**; possibly it implies an act of intercession to God who is approached through the altar on behalf of the people gathered in the outer court. Or it may be the directive for a processional act of some kind. The danger that Israel should become a byword among the nations seems more natural to a time of defeat under enemy attack than to the devastation caused by locusts. ' Where is their God? ' i.e. to fight for and to protect them.

f **18-29.** The Lord's response to the nation's penitence. He will send them food in plenty, remove the ' northerner ' out of harm's way and finally renew the gift of prophecy and vision. **20.** What is meant by the **northerner**? In using the word the author almost certainly passes from description of event to anticipation of the future, a future that is eschatological. The locusts would not come from the north; the word must therefore be used in a somewhat sinister sense to represent the evil from the north that would come upon Israel before God's day of judgment (Jer. 1:14, 4:6, 6:1; Ezek. 38:6, 15, 39:2). (Facing eastward brings the north on the left hand —the sinister side.) Another possibility is that the Heb. word is a transliteration of the Gr. word *tuphōnicos* which could be rendered ' the typhonic (or tempestuous) destroyer '; cf. Ac. 27:14, ' a tempestuous wind called the northeaster '. **23.** For **early rain** another possible translation is ' rich food '. If this were to be accepted we should have to regard the last phrase ' the early and the latter rain, as before ' as a gloss consequent upon taking *môreh* in the sense of *yôreh*. **28f.** The gift of prophecy would be a mark of the age of fulfilment such as Moses heralded when he pleaded that ' all the Lord's people ' might be prophets, Num. 11:29. The gift was to be universal; young and old, master and servant alike, will all share in it and will all prophesy and receive revelation in dream and vision. Fulfilment was reached with the gift of the spirit at Pentecost following the Resurrection.

g There is sometimes felt to be a liturgical significance in the fact that 19*b*–20 are in the first person, 21–4 in the third person and 25–9 again first person, but the change of person is not necessarily to be so interpreted. The prophets often passed vividly from one mode of expression to another.

h **II 30-III 8.** Further oracles about the conditions that will prevail in the days that will herald the coming of Yahweh. This section is in prose and may have been uttered on a different occasion from the previous oracles. It is however readily linked to what precedes by the supernatural phenomena, in different realms, with which the one ends and the other begins. The day of Yahweh will be heralded by changes in the physical nature of sun, moon and earth. In ancient times events in the natural world were readily believed to be in sympathy with events in history. **30.** ' Portents ' are signs such as God alone, in his power, can produce; they are mostly supernatural.

540a **III 1-3.** Judgment on the nations in the valley of Jehoshaphat. The valley has nothing to do with the king of that name. It is not at all certain that the prophet had any particular valley in mind. What mattered to him was that God's judgment would

540a take place there, and this is symbolised by the name which means 'God has judged'. In v. 12 the play on the word is actually made. The name 'Valley of decision' in 14 may refer to the same valley in the prophet's imagination. Neither valley need be identified with any known valley but they will not be far from Jerusalem itself. In Zech. 14:4 the prophet envisages a valley actually being formed by Yahweh for his purpose.

b **4-8**. Tyre and Sidon and the coastland southward into Philistia are to be punished for selling Jews as slaves to the Greeks. This may be an expansion of 3:3: 'have given a boy for a harlot, and have sold a girl for wine'. Tyre, Sidon and Philistia will therefore be deemed to be included among the nations referred to in v. 2. The historical background of such slave traffic is not known to us. If we knew of the occasion it would be some help in fixing the date of the book. Some think that Ptolemy (Soter) son of Lagus took Jewish captives when he invaded the land in 320 (see §538*b*).

c **9-18**. A summons to the nations to military alertness ready for the challenge of the day of Yahweh when there will be a judgment in the valley of Jehoshaphat, also called the valley of decision (14). This will be followed by the purging of Jerusalem and renewal of prosperity. Who is included in the summons? Certainly the nations who are to face judgment, but possibly also the Israelites who are to fight on the Lord's side. Even Yahweh himself is included (11). **10** is a parody of lines from the oracle now found in Isa. 2:2-4 and Mic. 4:1-4. To have full effect it is essential that a parody shall be of something well known. Whatever its date of composition therefore we may assume that it was a well-loved oracle in Joel's day. There are several other passages in this section which have close parallels elsewhere: 15 with 2:10, 16*a* with Am. 1:2, 16*b* with Ps. 46:1, 17*ab* with Jl 2:27, and 17*c* with Isa. 52:1. The poem however is not just a string of quotations: it is not a patchwork but a poem in its own right showing acquaintance with previous literature. **18.** The conception of a fountain issuing from Jerusalem is probably a deliberate echo of Ezek. 47, but the valley of Shittim is unidentified. The name means acacias. It is probably another symbolic name used by the prophet to describe perhaps the same valley as that previously mentioned and now turned over to more peaceful purposes. 540c

19 returns to the theme of judgment and singles out Egypt and Edom as particularly deserving judgment. Egypt was an old enemy and Edom was especially hated after 586 when she took delight in Judah's downfall (Ob. 10-14). d

20, 21. Judah and Jerusalem will be rehabilitated. With the words 'The Lord dwells in Zion' the book ends on a similar note to Ezek., 'And the name of the city henceforth shall be, The Lord is there.'

Bibliography—COMMENTARIES: J. A. Bewer, ICC (1912); S. R. Driver and H. C. O. Lanchester, CB (1915); A. van Hoonacker, EBib. (1908); R. F. Horton, Cent.B; K. Marti, KHC (1904); T. H. Robinson, HAT (2nd ed. 1954); E. Sellin, KAT (2nd ed. 1929); G. W. Wade, WC (1925); A. Weiser, ATD (2nd ed. 1956).

A. S. Kapelrud, *Joel Studies* (1948).

AMOS

By J. P. HYATT

541a Amos is the earliest of those OT prophets whose utterances are preserved for us in the form of a book. The date which is given in the superscription (1:1) is substantially correct, being confirmed by the evidence of the book itself as to the general historical background. Allowing time for the prosperity of Jeroboam II's reign to develop into the state of luxury and licence such as Amos describes, the prophet may be assigned to about 750 B.C., or a little earlier.

b Amos was a shepherd and dresser of sycamore trees, who received a divine call to prophesy while following his flock (7:14f.). The call probably came to him in the form of visions, described in 7:1–8:3. The only public appearance of which we have record was at Bethel, in the Northern Kingdom. There he came into conflict with Amaziah, priest of the royal sanctuary, who expelled him because he thought Amos was stirring up sedition and rebellion. Most scholars believe that Amos prophesied only in the Northern Kingdom, perhaps also in towns other than Bethel which are mentioned in his book. It is not impossible, however, that he prophesied in Judah ; he mentions Zion in 6:1, and both Zion and Jerusalem are named in 1:2 (this verse may be editorial). To Amos the Hebrews were one, and 'Israel' included Judaeans as well as inhabitants of the Northern Kingdom (3:1).

c Amos prophesied at the end of a fairly long era of peace and prosperity. Jeroboam II and Uzziah had long and outwardly successful reigns ; they defeated their enemies and gave the people peace. Some of the Israelites lived in great wealth, in large fine houses, where they ate rich food and spent much of their leisure in banqueting. Many of the people were very 'religious', paying their tithes, attending religious festivals, making elaborate sacrifices, and so on.

Yet there was much corruption in commercial and civil life, with oppression of the poor by the wealthy, bribery in the law courts, and other forms of social injustice. There must have been a large number of landless poor and slaves who supported the small class of the wealthy. Licentious rites were performed in the name of religion.

d The message of Amos to the people living under such conditions may be summarised as follows : 'Because of your repeated transgressions against Yahweh, you must be punished. The Day of Yahweh is about to come, and it will be the opposite of what you expect it to be, bringing national defeat, destruction of the land, and the exile of many to a foreign country. There is only a small ray of hope for you : if you will seek the Lord and establish justice in your land, Yahweh may be merciful to a remnant.' While Amos never names the foe which, as an agent of Yahweh, he expected would come to exercise judgment upon Israel, he probably had in mind the Assyrians.

e The text of the book has, on the whole, been well preserved, and contains a surprisingly small amount of secondary material. It is not known whether the original collection of the utterances of Amos was made by the prophet or by one or more of his disciples, either during his lifetime or later. The visions in chs. 7–9, reported in the first person, have the best claim to have been written or dictated by Amos

541e himself. It is possible that the book preserves only a small portion of the prophet's words, and that his public career extended over a much longer period than is suggested by the biographical material in ch. 7.

Of the secondary passages in this book, the most significant are the appendix, added to express hope which would counteract the generally pessimistic message of Amos, 9:8*c*–15 ; the 'doxologies' which have a style different from Amos', and reflect a later theology, 4:13, 5:8f., 9:5f. ; and the message against Judah in 2:4f. The following verses may also be secondary (see below for details) : 3:7, 5:13, 6:9f.

542a **I 1f. Superscription and Motto**—These two verses have been prefixed to the oracles of Amos by an editor, in order to inform the reader of the prophet's place of origin and occupation, the date of his prophecy, and in 1:2 the key-note of his message. No information is given concerning Amos' father or other forebears ; this has been thought to indicate that he came from a very poor family with no social distinction. **1. among the shepherds of Tekoa:** the word for shepherd here is not the ordinary one, but *nôḳēdh*. In the OT it is found elsewhere only in 2 Kg. 3:4, where it is applied to Mesha, king of Moab, as a sheep-master or sheep-owner. The Arabic *naqad* is used of a breed of sheep valued highly for their wool. In Akkadian *nāqidu* was used for 'shepherd', sometimes connected with temples. Haldar believes that Amos was a 'keeper of the temple herd', and thus a cultic official (*Associations of Cult Prophets among the Ancient Semites*, 79, 112). He cites a Ugaritic text in which a certain individual is designated as both 'chief of the priests (*rb khnm*)' and 'chief of the *nqdm* (*rb nqdm*)'. This is very slender evidence indeed, and Amos's attitude toward the popular cult of his day makes it highly improbable that he was a temple official of any kind. Tekoa was 12 miles south of Jerusalem, about 3,000 ft. above sea-level. To the east, looking toward Moab and the Dead Sea, was a desolate and wild region, later known as 'the wilderness of Judaea'. **Uzziah** reigned 783–742 B.C. and **Jeroboam** reigned 786–746 B.C., **two years before the earthquake:** cf. Zech. 14:5 and Jos. Ant. IX, x, 4. The date of this earthquake cannot be precisely determined. As the margin of RSV indicates, the phrase may mean 'during two years', that is, duration rather than a fixed point of time.

b 2 is to be taken as a 'motto' of the book, summarising at the outset the message of Amos as one which emphasises Yahweh's judgment. This judgment affects nature as well as man. The verse is often considered to be editorial, but there is no decisive reason for denying it to Amos. It is an excellent example of Hebrew poetry ; it consists of two couplets with 3:3 metre and with synonymous parallelism.

c **I 3–II 5 The Sins of Israel's Neighbours**—The prophet begins by arraigning Israel's neighbours. For each of them Amos describes typical sins and pronounces doom. The separate oracles are arranged according to a pattern which is adhered to rather strictly. Amos apparently chose to make a denunciation of the sins of surrounding peoples lead up gradually to a sudden and more detailed denunciation of the sins of Israel. The oracles against Philistia, Tyre,

542c Edom and Judah have been questioned, and the present order may not be original. A more natural geographical order would be: Aram, Ammon, Moab, Israel. However, the reasons advanced for questioning the authenticity of some of the oracles are not valid, except that against Judah; there is no need to try to rearrange the oracles as we think the prophet should have spoken them.

These oracles reveal an important aspect of Amos' conception of God. Yahweh, the God of Israel, can and will punish foreign nations for their sins, which here are all examples of excessive cruelty in time of war. Thus Yahweh must be able to make moral demands upon those nations and to that extent be their God as well as Israel's.

d **I 3-5 Damascus**—This city was the capital of the kingdom of Aram or Syria, which until recently had been engaged in a severe struggle with Israel. Damascus stands here for the whole nation, which is condemned for unwonted cruelty in time of war.

3 For three transgressions of Damascus, and for four: for transgressions that have been repeated over and over, and are excessive, more than enough to bring punishment. Cf. a similar idiom in Prov. 30:15, 18, 21, 29. **I will not revoke the punishment:** Heb. is literally 'I will not cause it (*or* him) to (re)turn', but the significance is obscure, since it is difficult to determine the reference of 'it', and the exact meaning of the verb. RSV takes 'it' to mean the punishment of the nation; other suggestions are that it means 'my word', 'my anger', or 'the Assyrian king'. The most natural interpretation is to suppose that the antecedent of 'it' is the nation which has just been named, and that the meaning is 'I will not cause the nation to turn to me in repentance', or 'I will not restore it (to my favour)'. Cf. especially the use of the idiom in Jer. 15:19, 31:18. **threshed Gilead with threshing sledges of iron:** Gilead was a region of Israel in Trans-Jordan near Damascus; the Syrians are condemned for cruelly mistreating prisoners-of-war by running over them with threshing sledges having iron teeth.

e **4 Hazael** founded the reigning dynasty in Syria; see 2 Kg. 8:7–15. **Ben-hadad:** there were at least three kings of this name in Syria; see 1 Kg. 15:18, 20:1; 2 Kg. 13:24.

5 the bar of Damascus: the bar of the city-gate. **Valley of Aven,** or **On:** the broad fertile valley or plain lying between the Lebanon and Anti-Lebanon mountains. MT is pointed to read Aven which means 'vanity', and often stands for idolatry; an alternative vocalisation is *On* which was the name for the Egyptian Heliopolis (Gen. 41:45), and may have been used for the Syrian Heliopolis (Ba'albek). **Beth-eden:** a city in Syria, either modern *'Edēn*, 20 miles north-west of Ba'albek, or modern Jubb 'Adīn, 25 miles north-east of Damascus; or the equivalent of Bīt Adini of the Assyrian inscriptions, on the Euphrates River. The last identification is more probable, since we cannot be certain that the towns in Damascus existed in ancient times. **Kir:** the location is quite uncertain; perhaps identical with ancient Ur, in Mesopotamia, modern el-Muqayyar. According to Isa. 22:6, it seems to have been in or near Elam. Am. 9:7 says that the Syrians came from Kir, and 2 Kg. 16:9 that the king of Assyria took the people of Damascus captive to that place (732 B.C.).

f **6-8 Philistia**—An oracle against the Philistine cities, four of which are here named—Gaza, Ashdod, Ashkelon, and Ekron. These cities were all in the south-western part of Palestine; the fifth city of the Philistine confederation was Gath. This oracle is considered secondary by some scholars for several reasons: the omission of Gath is explained by the fact that this city had been destroyed at the time the oracle originated, and it is believed it was not destroyed until 711 B.C.; the sin of the Philistine cities in 6*b* is almost identical with that of Tyre in 9*b*; and the phrase, 'remnant of the Philistines', suggests a late date. These reasons are not conclusive, and we know too little about the 542
history of Philistia to press these arguments.

6 carried into exile a whole people to deliver them up to Edom: slave-trading on a large scale; cf. 9*b*. The reference may be to some raid in which the Philistines procured slaves for the Edomites to sell again. According to some scholars 'Edom' is a mistake for 'Aram', since the two words are easily confused in Heb.; if so, the reference may be to some episode in Hazael's campaigns (2 Kg. 12:18). Yet it is better to leave the text as it stands.

9-10 Tyre—This was the most important commercial g
city of Phoenicia, and here stands for the whole land. Tyre is charged with committing a sin similar to that of Gaza. This oracle has been questioned because of this similarity, and also because of the brevity of v. 10, the usual formula being incomplete. These reasons are hardly valid.

9 did not remember the covenant of brotherhood: if a covenant with Israel is meant, we may recall the covenant between Hiram and Solomon (1 Kg. 5:1) and the marriage of Ahab to Jezebel, daughter of Ethbaal (1 Kg. 16:31). Yet the reference may be to a covenant between Tyre and some non-Israelite nation.

11-12 Edom—The Edomites inhabited originally the h
mountainous region in the extreme southern part of the Trans-Jordan territory, extending down to the Gulf of 'Aqaba. At the time of the Babylonian capture of Jerusalem, 586 B.C., the Edomites took advantage of the situation to move over into southern Palestine and take possession of some Judaean territory. As a result of this, bitter enmity arose between Edom and the Judaeans (cf. Ps. 137:7). Some scholars believe that this oracle is late, originating after 586 B.C. Yet the Edomites and Israelites had frequently been at enmity; for example, in or near the time of Amos, King Uzziah is said to have restored Elath, an Edomite city, to Judah (2 Kg. 14:22). The sin of Edom, described in 11*b*, probably had to do with unusual and excessive cruelty in war, but the time and precise nature of it are not known.

12 Teman: a district in the north of Edom. **Bozrah:** apparently the capital of Edom at this time; modern Buṣeira.

13-15 The Ammonites—These people occupied the i
territory in Trans-Jordan between the Jabbok and the Arnon rivers. They were old enemies of the Hebrews. Jephthah defeated them (Jg. 11:32) and David completely conquered them (2 Sam. 12:26–31). They are reported in 2 Chr. 26:8 to have paid tribute to Uzziah. Like the other nations they are accused of great cruelty in warfare.

13 The sin with which the Ammonites are charged is mentioned elsewhere in OT, sometimes with reference to the Hebrews themselves (2 Kg. 8:12, 15:16; Hos. 13:16). **Gilead:** Israelite territory to the north of the Ammonites; the Ammonites may have taken over some of the Gileadite land at the time the Israelites were at warfare with the Syrians, when Gilead was often the battle-ground.

14 Rabbah: the capital city, sometimes called Rabbath Ammon; the site of the modern capital of the Hashemite Kingdom of Jordan, 'Ammân.

15 their king: possibly read 'Milcom', the national god of the Ammonites; this reading is supported by some MSS of LXX.

II 1-3 Moab—This nation occupied the high plateau j
east of the Dead Sea. It was subdued by David, and again by Omri; later it regained its independence. Amos gives here a typical instance of Moabite cruelty. The Moabites are accused of burning the bones of a king of Edom to lime. They reduced the body to ashes by burning it, possibly in order to use the ashes for plaster (as the Targum says). No other record of this has been preserved, and we cannot identify the king involved, but in any event a monstrous act of desecration is implied. For a body to fail to receive an honourable burial, or to be dese-

42j crated after burial, was considered a great crime by the Semites generally, as indeed by most peoples of the world. It is significant that the Moabites are condemned for an act of cruelty against a king of Edom; the implication is that Yahweh is concerned with the relationship between these two countries, not simply with the relationships between Israel and foreign nations.

2 Kerioth: a city of Moab, presumably the capital; cf. Jer. 48:24.

k **4f. Judah**—This oracle is to be considered as secondary, for the following reasons: (1) The language is similar to that of Deuteronomic writers; (2) the sin of Judah lacks the concreteness and vividness of detail found in most of the preceding oracles, and the punishment is not elaborated (cf. 1:10, 12); (3) it seems unlikely that Amos made a distinction between the two kingdoms of Judah and Israel, but in his message 'Israel' is the whole nation; see especially 3:1. Most modern critical commentators believe this oracle is not genuine, but a few defend its genuineness, including S. R. Driver.

4 their lies: their idols, inasmuch as they were false and misleading.

l **6-16 The Sin and Doom of Israel**—After condemning the surrounding nations in a manner with which his hearers no doubt agreed, Amos suddenly turns and confronts Israel, beginning with similar words. Israel is condemned now with great severity, and in much more detail than the other nations. Whereas the latter had been judged sinful for their excessive cruelty to other nations in time of war, Israel is condemned because Israelite has oppressed Israelite and the people have been faithless to their God. While it is possible that this section is composed of several originally separate oracles, it can readily be divided as it now stands into three parts: (1) Israel has transgressed by social injustice and false worship, 2:6–8; (2) these sins have been committed in spite of what Yahweh has done for the nation in the past, 2:9–12; (3) the coming doom of the nation, from which there is to be no escape, 2:13–16.

m **6 sell the righteous for silver, and the needy for a pair of shoes:** rapacious creditors sell their debtors into slavery for trifling debts. This may have been done within the law, but was wrong in Yahweh's eyes. **7. trample the head of the poor into the dust of the earth:** the rendering is uncertain; a more natural translation of MT is that of AV—'pant after the dust of the earth on the head of the poor'. The meaning of RSV is obvious; the meaning of the translation just suggested is that the wealthy are so greedy that they even long for the dust which the poor throw upon their head in time of mourning—an obvious exaggeration. **go in to the same maiden:** Heb. lacks any word for 'same'. It is lit. 'go in to a (*or* the) girl'. This is frequently taken to mean resorting to a sacred prostitute, for which the Heb. word is *ḳ^{e}dhēshāh*, a practice condemned in Dt. 23:17 and elsewhere. It may mean simply resorting to a common harlot; in either case Amos would say, **so that my holy name is profaned. 8.** The first half of the verse may have reference to the practice of 'incubation', sleeping in a temple or its precincts in the hope of having a vision of the deity worshipped there. The Covenant Code forbade the keeping of a poor man's garment after sundown if it were taken in pledge (Exod. 22:26–7). **the wine of those who have been fined:** an obscure phrase, possibly meaning wine which had been pledged to creditors who lost no time in foreclosing in order to drink the wine in temple feasts; or wine secured by priests as 'fines' from worshippers. The whole picture here is one of social injustice, practised in the name of law and religion, and of religious practices filled with revelry and immorality.

n **9.** Amos now begins to rehearse what Yahweh has done for the nation in the past; Israel should have responded to his deeds on their behalf with grateful obedience and worship instead of the rebellion they 542n
have manifested. The word 'I' is in emphatic position—'Yet it was I who . . .' **the Amorite:** a word generally used in north-Israelite tradition (E) for the pre-Israelite inhabitants of Canaan. **10.** The exodus from Egypt, the wilderness wandering, and the invasion of Canaan are here summarised. **11. Nazirites:** see Num. 6 for a description of the life of these people who took vows to refuse to partake of anything produced from the grape-vine, to let their hair grow long, and to avoid contact with the dead. They were primitivists who rebelled against Canaanite culture and sought to continue the type of life led in the desert (cf. the Rechabites, Jer. 35).

12. Here begins the description of Israel's doom. o
Yahweh will bring destruction, and those who are usually looked upon as defenders of the nation will not be able even to save themselves, much less the nation they should protect. **I will press you down in your place:** the rendering is quite uncertain; other possibilities are: 'I will make a groaning under you, as a cart groans . . .' or 'I will make you totter in your place, as a cart totters . . .' The latter, which involves an emendation of the verbs to forms of *pûḳ*, is probably to be preferred. The figure is that of a cart or wagon so completely loaded with sheaves that it collapses; it represents the complete destruction which is about to come upon Israel.

III 1-V 17 Oracles concerning Israel's Sin and 543a
Doom—This consists of three main divisions, each of which begins 'Hear this word . . .' (3:1, 4:1, 5:1). This arrangement seems to be editorial, and somewhat artificial, since oracles placed together frequently have little similarity in subject matter.

III 1-2 Israel's Election and Special Responsibility—Israel has been chosen by Yahweh; this choice gives to Israel, not special privilege, as the people apparently believed, but special responsibility. When Israel does not live up to this responsibility she will be punished severely. This oracle was perhaps intended to answer the popular objection made to the oracles in the preceding chapters, which implied that Israel would receive from Yahweh the same treatment as other nations. Amos believed in the divine election of Israel, but he did not follow the popular belief that this election gave to the nation special privilege and exemption from punishment.

1 against the whole family: some critics think this b
is an editorial addition, designed to include Judah in the oracle. This is by no means certain. There may be, however, some confusion in the verse, since it begins with the prophet speaking about Yahweh and ends with Yahweh speaking in the first person. Such confusion is not without parallel in the prophets, since the prophet identified his message so closely with the word of the Lord. **2. You only have I known of all the families of the earth:** the word 'known' here is virtually equivalent to 'chosen'. The verb is often used in Heb. of very intimate and personal knowledge; it is used sometimes of marital relations. In Gen. 18:19 RSV renders 'I have chosen him' where the Heb. is literally 'I have known him'. Cf. also especially Hos. 13:5 (where MT is not to be emended).

3-8 The Prophet's Authority to speak—This c
section is made up largely of a series of rhetorical questions, all implying a cause-effect relationship. There is a problem as to where the climax comes: is it at the end of v. 6, or at the end of v. 8? If the climax is at v. 6, the series of questions leads up to the assertion that it is Yahweh who brings about the misfortune of a city. If the climax is at v. 8, they lead up to the assertion that the prophet speaks because the Lord has spoken; he cannot avoid prophesying when the Lord speaks to him. The latter is preferable. If the climax is in v. 6, then vv. 7–8 are to be considered as a separate oracle, which is thus quite fragmentary. Also, v. 6 contains two rhetorical questions similar to the preceding verses, whereas v. 8 contains two decla-

543c rations : 'The lion has roared . . ., The Lord God has spoken'. The whole section is thus an *apologia* of the prophet in which he asserts that his authority is derived from Yahweh ; he is under divine compulsion to prophesy, and he cannot escape his task. Other prophets spoke similarly ; see especially Jer. 20:9.

d **3 unless they have made an appointment :** both text and translation are uncertain. The rendering of MT may be, 'unless they have agreed (to walk together)'. On the other hand, LXX implies that the Heb. was *nôdhā'û* rather than *nô'ādhû,* since it reads, 'unless they know each other'. As a general truth, all renderings seem somewhat uncertain, inasmuch as casual meetings might occur either in the desert or in town life. There is a slight preference for following the LXX. **7** is prose rather than poetry, and is almost certainly an editorial gloss. It interrupts the natural sequence of this series of questions, is not appropriate at this point, and the phrase 'his servants the prophets' is characteristic of the Deuteronomists. It probably originated as a comment by a reader, possibly at first in the margin. It embodies a very important Hebrew idea, which as such is not foreign to Amos. The Heb. *sôdh,* here rendered 'secret', may mean either counsel or council. For the idea of a council (or assembly) of Yahweh, see Jer. 23:18, 22 ; Ps. 82:1, 89:7. **8. The lion has roared :** the figure of a lion occurs somewhat frequently in Amos, who must have derived it from his experience as a shepherd ; see 1:2, 3:4, 12.

e **9-11 Foreign Nations summoned to witness the Fall of Samaria**—People who are in the strongholds of Assyria and Egypt are summoned to assemble on the mountain of Samaria to see the oppressions in that city and witness the downfall of the land. Samaria as the capital city of the Northern Kingdom stands for the kingdom as a whole, but Amos may have thought that deeds of oppression and violence were greater there than elsewhere. He implies that the sin of the nation is so deep and so obvious that even the pagan nations could recognise it.

f **9 Assyria :** Heb. is 'Ashdod' ; RSV here follows LXX in reading 'Assyria', on the assumption that the original text had *'ashshûr* rather than *'ashdôdh.* Since Ashdod was only a city in the Philistine confederation, and Assyria a large and powerful nation, the latter supplies a more natural balance to Egypt. The emendation cannot be considered certain ; Amos nowhere else names Assyria. **mountains of Samaria:** LXX has singular 'mountain' ; this may be correct, the reference being to the mountain on which the city of Samaria was erected.

11 An adversary shall surround the land : Amos apparently believed the coming punishment of Israel would be at the hands of a foreign nation which would bring destruction to the land and exile for many of the people ; however, he never names the nation, though he may have had Assyria in mind. Cf. 5:27, 6:14. If he prophesied before the rise to power of Tiglath-pileser III (745 B.C.), he may not have been as sure of the identity of the foreign nation as later prophets were.

g **12 Total Destruction of Samaria**—In a vivid figure derived from shepherd life, Amos here pictures the destruction of the people of Samaria. According to the law of Exod. 22:13, a man entrusted with the keeping of an animal would not have to make restitution if he could provide evidence that the animal had been torn by wild animals. This verse should not be used as evidence for the survival of a remnant (as in 5:15) ; the remnants of the sheep would have value only to prove that the animal had been slain. The picture is really one of total destruction.

with the corner of a couch and part of a bed : this rendering is approximately correct, but the precise meaning of the word translated 'part' is not known. The word is *d^{e}mesheḳ,* similar to the Heb. for 'Damascus'. The meaning may be 'silken cushions' (damask) or 'leg' (cf. Reider, JBL 67 (1948), 245–8).

13-15 Doom upon the Altars of Bethel and the Homes of the Wealthy—This oracle continues the prophecy of doom, with details which describe the destruction of the sacred altars, as well as the homes of the wealthy. When Yahweh brings punishment on Israel, even the altars will be destroyed ; these were supposed by the people to provide sanctuary in time of trouble, but Amos says they will not be spared in the general doom. 543

14 the horns of the altar : these provided refuge for a man who had committed accidental homicide ; see 1 Kg. 1:50. Altars found in excavations frequently have projections at the four corners ; these had the practical function of holding bowls of incense, and possibly animals, on the altar. **15. the winter house with the summer house :** probably not separate houses in different parts of the land, but different parts of one large house, the warmer part being used in the winter and the cooler in summer ; cf. Jer. 36:22. **houses of ivory :** either (1) houses made of white stone which turned to an ivory hue when weathered ; or (2) houses filled with furniture having ivory inlay and ivory-inlaid wood-panelling. Cf. 1 Kg. 22:39, and for examples of the ivories found in the excavation of Samaria, some of which may be from the time of Amos, see J. W. and Grace Crowfoot and E. L. Sukenik, *Early Ivories from Samaria* (1938). To Amos all of these are striking examples of the luxurious living of the wealthy who oppress the poor.

IV 1-3 Doom of the Women of Samaria—Amos denounces the wicked frivolity of the women of the upper classes, charging that they urge their husbands on in acts of injustice and oppression to provide them with the luxuries they demand, such as strong drink. When the punishment by war comes, the women will suffer dreadfully. 544

1 cows of Bashan : Bashan was a fertile district east of the Sea of Galilee, noted for its prize cows. Amos uses this figure to describe the lazy and unthinking lives of the women. **who oppress the poor, who crush the needy :** it is possible that some women engaged in business activities in which they directly oppressed the poor ; that women did sometimes engage in such activities in ancient Israel is shown by a passage such as Prov. 31:13–24. **3. you shall go out through the breaches :** when the enemy captures Samaria and breaks down the wall, the women will be carried out captive through the breaches in the wall. **you shall be cast forth into Harmon :** a place 'Harmon' cannot be identified ; emend *ha-harmônāh* to *hammadhmēnāh* and translate, 'you shall be cast on the dung-heap'. This is a vivid figure to describe the fate of the wealthy but wicked women of Samaria.

4-5 The Sanctuaries as Places of Transgression —With caustic irony Amos summons the people to come to Bethel, or to Gilgal, only to transgress against their God. The words may have been uttered at Bethel (cf. 7:10–17) at the time of some great religious festival when throngs came to the sanctuary to make their offerings and revel in feasting. Nowhere else does the prophet speak so bitterly against the prevailing cultus. Fosbroke has rightly said that Amos saw the offerings of the people 'as the means through which human beings gave expression to a total attitude toward God, which would to all intents and purposes treat him as one of themselves and draw him into comfortable fellowship so that what they called worship was but subordinating him to the satisfaction of their appetite for pleasure and the exhibition of their own importance' (IB vi, 805). b

4 Bethel was the site of a royal sanctuary of the Northern Kingdom (7:13). **Gilgal** likewise was the site of a sanctuary ; it was the town bearing that name in the Jordan Valley near Jericho. **bring your sacrifices every morning, your tithes every three days :** probably it is better to read, 'bring your sacrifices in the morning, your tithes on the third day'. The reference would then be to a festival on which c

44c sacrifices were offered on the first day, and tithes on the third day. If RSV (the usual rendering) is correct, Amos is ironically summoning them to be over-punctilious in their religious acts. The 'sacrifices' (Heb. *z^{e}bhāḥîm*) involved the offering up of animals, which were slaughtered by the priests and then in part eaten by the worshippers in a ritual feast. For the Deuteronomic law of tithing, see Dt. 14:22–9. Tithes were offered every year. In most years they were used for ritualistic feasts, but every third year they were set aside for the use of the Levites, sojourners, fatherless and widows. **5. Offer a sacrifice of thanksgiving of that which is leavened:** for the later (P) law of the thank-offering see Lev. 7:12–15. The law forbade the offering up of leaven with the sacrifices (Exod. 23:18; Lev. 2:11, 6:17), but we can hardly think that Amos was castigating the people for breaking a ritual law. **proclaim freewill-offerings, publish them:** make a great show of offering more than was required by the law, by bringing voluntary offerings. **for so you love to do:** the climax of Amos' indictment of the people for their sham religion. They make their elaborate and costly offerings to the Lord because it is what *they* love to do, not because they wish to give to God their moral obedience. In most cases the bringing of what we call 'sacrifices' did not actually involve sacrifice on the part of the people, for much of what they brought was used for merry festivals at the sanctuaries.

d **6-13 Repeated Chastisements have been Futile** —In five strophes, each of which ends with the same refrain, Amos describes the punishments that have been sent upon Israel by Yahweh in the past for the purpose of chastening them and inducing them to return to him; yet all of these have been futile, and Israel has continued in its ways. Now the nation must be prepared to meet God in judgment. For both form and content cf. Isa. 9:8–10:4, 5:25–30. The section is important as showing that the prophets sometimes composed their poetic oracles in a series of strophes; here the strophes vary in length but are marked off by a common refrain. It is important also as showing that Amos thought of Yahweh as controlling Nature; he thought of God as having direct and immediate control over the forces of nature. Yet the prophet was not interested simply in showing that Yahweh had such control, but rather that he used natural calamities as means of chastising and seeking to chasten Israel. Further, he implies that Yahweh is a God of love and mercy, who seeks through chastening to cause Israel to return to him; yet his love is not endless and the nation must meet a final punishment for its continued rebellion. The theology is similar to that of the visions in 7:1–9, and to the implication of 1:3, 6, 9, 11, 13, 2:1.

e **6 I gave you:** the word **'I'** is emphasised, as in 2:9. Heb. is literally 'and also I . . .' It is not certain whether this oracle, vv. 6–13, was originally composed to follow vv. 4–5. In any event it is appropriate to its present position; there is a contrast between the people's love for offering up elaborate sacrifice and Yahweh's repeated punishments of them. Their elaborate cult did not accompany moral uprightness; rather, the people continued in their sin and had to be chastened by God. **yet you did not return to me:** the word rendered 'return' (*shûbh*) often means 'repent'. That is essentially its meaning here; repentance meant turning to Yahweh and turning away from transgression.

f **7** It is significant that Amos believed Yahweh, God of Israel, could send or withhold rain; such control of nature was often ascribed by the Hebrew people to Baal, god of the Canaanites. Prophets such as Elijah, Amos and Hosea insisted that the Israelites did not need to worship Baal in order to secure fertility of their crops, but must serve Yahweh alone. **I would send rain:** RSV correctly translates the verbs here, which are imperfect, or perfect with *waw*-conversive, as indicating repeated action. Because this strophe is much longer than the others, some scholars believe 544f
that some of the lines, as in *7b–8a*, have been added. **10 after the manner of Egypt:** the meaning is probably 'like the pestilences of Egypt'. The Heb. might be rendered 'by way of Egypt'. Some scholars emend *b^{e}dherekh* to *k^{e}dhebher*, 'like the pestilence of Egypt'. **I carried away your horses:** the Heb. 'with the captivity of your horses' (see RSV*n*) is awkward, and may be a gloss; some emend *sh^{e}bhî* to *ṣ^{e}bhî* and render 'together with the best (lit. beauty) of your horses'.

11 as when God overthrew Sodom and Gomor- g
rah: see Gen. 19. Amos knows the tradition of the overthrow of these cities, but he did not necessarily know J in a written form. **you were as a brand plucked out of the burning:** you as a nation were just barely saved at the last moment. We do not know the event to which this refers, whether military invasion, earthquake, or some other calamity.

12 The conclusion of the oracle, warning Israel that she must now meet Yahweh in judgment because she has repeatedly refused to repent. The nature of the impending judgment is vague, perhaps purposely so. The thought is not that some individuals may prepare to meet God by now repenting, and thus be spared, though most of the nation will be destroyed. **13** is an addition to the words of Amos, like 5:8–9 and 9:5–6. These 'doxologies' are unlike the genuine words of Amos in both thought and form (a series of participial clauses in Heb.), but like later passages such as Second Isaiah, Job 38, and some of the Psalms. They may be fragments of a hymn which were inserted by an editor of the book at what he considered to be appropriate points. He wished to remind the reader of the vast power and transcendent majesty of Yahweh.

V 1-3 Lamentation over the Fall of Israel— h
Amos pronounces an elegy over the fall of Israel, which is considered complete and irreparable. He uses the Heb. perfect, translated as a past tense in English, but the reference is to the immediate future rather than to the past. The metre is of a type which is called *ḳînāh*, after the Heb. word which is here rendered 'lamentation'. It has three beats followed by two beats, thus giving a limping rhythm which is suitable for a dirge or elegy.

2 virgin Israel: Israel personified as a virgin woman; cf. the frequent use of 'daughter Zion' in other OT books. **3** is prosaic, and may actually be prose, in spite of the fact that it is printed as poetry by RSV. Some scholars consider it a gloss to explain v. 2. It lacks the vividness and sense of complete disaster which are characteristic of Amos.

4-15 Exhortation to seek Yahweh, mingled with i
Denunciation—This section may consist of several originally distinct oracles, but it is difficult to determine how they should be divided without having a number of small fragments; hence it is best to consider the section as a whole, and note how it consists of exhortations to seek Yahweh, or to seek the good, that alternate with denunciations of specific sins. Here are the most hopeful passages in Amos' message. He calls upon his hearers to seek Yahweh in order that they may live, or be saved in the coming destruction, and he suggests in some detail what the seeking of Yahweh means. It means to seek good rather than evil, to hate evil and love the good, to establish justice and fairness where injustice and dishonesty have existed, and to give up the useless sham religion which depends upon the piling up of sacrifices in the sanctuaries. Vv. 8–9 are a secondary doxology, like 4:13 and 9:5–6.

4 Seek me and live: to 'seek' a God had usually j
meant to go to a sanctuary and there seek from a priest or prophet an oracle or an answer in some manner to a specific question. Here it is beginning to have a deeper and more profound sense, as it has in Dt. 4:29; Jer. 29:13–14, and other writings of later date. The verb 'live' also has here a somewhat deeper meaning than physical survival through disaster (not survival in the hereafter), approaching

544j the idea of living in fellowship and right relationship with God. **do not seek Bethel:** Bethel was the place where the royal sanctuary was located (7:13); it was also the name of a deity (cf. Jer. 48:13; the deity is well known in Assyrian sources). There may thus be a *double-entendre* here. **Gilgal** and **Beer-sheba** were both sites of sanctuary; on the former see 4:4; the latter was in the extreme south of Judah, and was associated especially with the legends concerning Isaac. **Gilgal shall surely go into exile:** the Heb. has a play on words: *haggilgāl gālōh yighleh*. *An American Translation* (Powis-Smith–Goodspeed) seeks to reproduce this in English: 'Gilgal shall go into galling captivity'.

7 The transition from v. 6 to v. 7 is difficult in Heb., which does not contain the second person plural ('you who' of RSV). It is probable that we should emend *ha-hôph^{e}khîm* to *hôy hôph^{e}khîm*, and read 'Woe to those who turn . . .' Cf. 5:18, 6:1.

k **8-9** constitute the second interpolated doxology; see the note on 4:13. Here the interpolation is made in an awkward manner, interrupting the natural sequence between v. 7 and v. 10. **Pleiades and Orion:** these two star groups are named also in Job 9:9, 38:31. **9. who makes destruction flash forth . . .:** Yahweh controls the destinies of men in history, sometimes overthrowing the strong, as well as controlling the forces of nature. For attempts to emend and translate this verse so as to see in it the names of several other stars or constellations, see Cripps, *Commentary*, 297–9.

l **10** continues naturally after v. 7, with further description of those upon whom woe is pronounced. **reproves in the gate:** the gate, or the public square just inside a city gate, was a place of public meeting, where court was frequently held. **11. houses of hewn stone:** houses thus made were more durable than those made of loose stone picked up on the site, but in the coming judgment these would prove insecure. **13** differs in tone from the context, and in fact from the whole book of Amos; it sounds more like an aphorism, such as one might find in a wisdom writing, than a prophetic oracle. It is prose, and is most probably a gloss by a reader who, struck with the great evil of the time, believed that a prudent man could only keep silence, for anything he might do would be useless and endanger himself. Such an attitude of resignation is not characteristic of Amos. The only way in which the verse could be interpreted as by Amos is to consider it as deep irony and sarcasm; however, the literary form is not like that of Amos.

m **14 Seek good and not evil:** thus Amos explains, at least in part, what he means when he says, 'Seek the Lord and live' (v. 6). **15** expresses somewhat hesitantly the idea of a remnant. This verse is considered by many critics to be secondary, inasmuch as Amos does not elsewhere express clearly the hope of a remnant. However, the literary form, the hortatory tone, and the conditional nature of the hope speak in favour of his authorship.

16-17 A Day of Lamentation—When Yahweh passes through the midst of Israel in judgment, there will be wailing and mourning on every hand. The language suggests judgment by pestilence (cf. Exod. 12:12), but the prophet may have in mind military invasion, as is usually the case in this book.

16 those who are skilled in lamentation: professional mourners; cf. Jer. 9:17–22.

545a **V 18-VI 14 Woes upon Israel**—This section can be divided into three subdivisions, each of which begins with 'Woe to . . .' such-and-such a group in Israel, 5:18–27, 6:1–3, 6:4–14. The division is somewhat artificial, since the subject matter is not homogeneous; in general, the subject is the coming punishment in the Day of Yahweh. (Note that Heb. does not have 'Woe to . . .' in 6:4; see below.)

b **V 18-20 The Day of the Lord**—The prophet pronounces woe upon those who desire the coming of the Day of the Lord, as if it were to be a time that would 54
be desirable, a day of light, victory, and joy. Amos declares that it is to be the exact opposite of what the people expect it to be: darkness and gloom and defeat. It is clear from this passage that there was a popular expectation of a Day of Yahweh, which was not a creation of the prophet. Amos' contribution is to insist that it will be a day of darkness and punishment which will be a surprise to those who hold the popular view.

19 The vivid figures here emphasise both the unexpected nature of the Day of Yahweh, and the inescapability of judgment.

21-27 Yahweh's Rejection of the Cultus, and c
Israel's coming Exile—This section is probably to be taken as a single oracle, though there are difficulties in connecting 25–7 with 21–4. Speaking in the first person through the prophet, Yahweh declares that he rejects the costly and elaborate ceremonialism by which the people of Israel have sought to worship him. They must renounce it if they are to receive Yahweh's deliverance. The true demand of Yahweh in the wilderness period was not for sacrifices and offerings (v. 25); because the Israelites have depended so much upon these, they will go into exile along with the false gods they have worshipped. This is the strongest utterance in Amos against the popular cultus. In the light of it and of other passages such as 4:4–5, it is difficult to see how Amos could have believed that Yahweh demanded only the purification or simplification of the cultus (as many scholars think) rather than its renunciation.

21 your feasts: better, 'your pilgrim festivals'; d
Heb. *ḥagh* is related to the Arabic *'al-ḥaj*, 'the pilgrimage' (to Mecca). **your solemn assemblies:** better, 'your festal gatherings', which were often very joyous affairs. **22. burnt offerings:** usually, whole burnt offerings. **24. But let justice roll down like waters:** it is perhaps better to render, 'in order that justice may roll down like waters', etc. Amos calls upon the people to take away the noise of their songs and harps in order that God may send his salvation and deliverance upon them. 'Righteousness' here means God's deliverance, salvation, as in Isa. 46:13, 51:1, 5, 6, 8 and other passages; 'justice' has a similar meaning, as in Dt. 33:21; Isa. 42:1, 4. See Hyatt, 'The Translation and Meaning of Amos 5:23–4', ZATW 68 (1956), 17–24. The usual interpretation is that this is an exhortation to men to establish social justice and righteousness. Right conduct is contrasted with elaborate cult. Weiser interprets the verse so that the subject is God's destructive judgment, which flows upon the people like a continuous stream of water; he rearranges the order of verses so that 24 follows 25 (*Die Prophetie des Amos*, 223–5).

25 The answer to this question is No. Amos believed e
that sacrifices and offerings were not made in the wilderness period and thus were not a part of Yahweh's original demand upon Israel; cf. Jer. 7:22–3. **26. Sakkuth** and **Kaiwan:** names of Assyrian deities (or a single deity) associated with the planet Saturn. The Israelites are here represented as taking their idols with them into exile, in a procession with themselves as captives.

27 is denied to Amos by many scholars. Amos does not elsewhere speak so directly of exile into a foreign country, but there is no compelling reason to think that he could not have done so.

VI 1-7 Woe to the Self-satisfied, Luxury-loving f
Leaders—The prophet denounces those leaders who are comfortably at ease and smug in Zion and Samaria, putting far away the evil day, and indulging in revelry and luxury, with no thought of the ruin of their nation; they shall be the first to go into exile.

1. in Zion is considered by many to be a gloss, or a corruption for another word, on the theory that Amos did not address Judah or Jerusalem. Yet there is no valid reason for thinking that Amos may not on

545f occasion have spoken to or of Jerusalem. **the notable men etc.:** text and translation are uncertain; the lines are probably to be taken as ironical. **2. Calneh:** a city in northern Syria, near Aleppo. **Hamath the great:** a city of Syria on the Orontes River, modern Ḥamā. **Gath:** in south-western Palestine, one of the Philistine confederation of five cities. The usual interpretation of this verse is that these are cities which have been destroyed by the Assyrians. Thus, the last two lines should be emended to read: 'Are you better than these kingdoms? Or is your territory greater than their territory?' The implication is that Israel (or Samaria) cannot hope to escape the same fate which has befallen them. Yet it seems that these cities were destroyed by the Assyrians after the time of Amos—Calneh in 738, the other two in 711. Hence, many critics consider the verse an interpolation, interrupting the thought between 1 and 3. It is likely that the line on Gath is an interpolation, since it was not comparable in size or importance with the others. The rest may be genuine, and refer to the weakening of these cities a century before under Shalmaneser III (859–824 B.C.), according to T. H. Robinson. Another interpretation takes the MT as it stands, and supposes that the question is: Are these states better or greater in extent than Israel? Since the answer is No, the implication is then that Israel's failure to live up to her obligations is all the more serious. Maag puts the verse in quotation marks, as spoken in pride by the 'notable men' of v. 2.

g **4 Woe to** is not in the Heb., but is supplied in RSV, because 4–6 continue the denunciation begun in 1. This is valid, but the close connection of 4–7 with 1–3 must not be overlooked. **beds of ivory:** probably beds with ivory inlay (as Targum indicates); see comment on 3:15 for archaeological discoveries at Samaria. **5. like David:** possibly a marginal gloss; it is lacking in LXX, and makes the poetic line too long.

8 Yahweh will deliver up the City—A fragment of an oracle, placed here because of its similarity to the foregoing. Yahweh swears by himself—for he cannot swear by anyone higher—that, because of his hatred of Jacob's pride and dependence on material strongholds, he will deliver up the city and all its inhabitants. The reference may be to Samaria, but this is not certain; the Heb. does not actually have an article before 'city'. The deliverance may be to siege and captivity, or to pestilence.

h **9-10 Horrors of a Plague**—This is apparently also only a fragment, which RSV is correct in printing as prose. Many scholars doubt that it is from Amos; at any rate, it adds nothing to our understanding of his message, but only reflects popular beliefs and practices. The background is a time of plague, which may have attended a siege. The plague is so great that all die, or at least only one man survives in a house of ten. That one is so fearful that he will not mention the name of Yahweh, lest Yahweh break out in anger against him. There are several difficulties of translation and interpretation, but the general picture is clear.

9. he who burns him: Heb. is literally, 'his burner'. It means either (1) one who cremates the dead; cremation was rarely practised among the Hebrews (1 Sam. 31:12), but may have been used in time of plague; or (2) one who burns spices for the deceased; see 2 Chr. 16:14, 21:19; Jer. 34:5, which are all instances of royal burial.

i **11 Destruction of Houses at Yahweh's Command**—A third fragment, in which Yahweh commands that both great and small houses are to be smitten, either by earthquake, or by an enemy in war.

12-14—The Fate of a People of Unnatural Conduct and Foolish Pride—The Israelites have turned justice and righteousness into something bitter and poisonous; this is as unnatural and useless as for horses to run on rocks, or for a man to try to plough the sea with oxen. Further, they have shown a silly pride in minor conquests. Yahweh is therefore about 545i
to raise up against them a nation that will oppress their whole country.

12 Does one plow the sea with oxen: this render- j
ing, undoubtedly correct, rests upon a redivision of the Heb. word at the end of the line, reading b^{e}*bhākār yām* instead of *babb*^{e}*ḳārîm*. **13. Lo-debar:** name of a town in Trans-Jordan (2 Sam. 17:27), also meaning 'a thing of nought'. **Karnaim:** probably a town in the same region (1 Mac. 5:26, 43, 44; possibly the same as Ashteroth-Karnaim, Gen. 14:5), also meaning 'horns', a symbol of strength. The Hebrews had probably captured these two towns in their recent wars with the Syrians, and took a foolish pride in small victories. **14. a nation:** probably the Assyrians, but it is noteworthy that Amos never names them. **entrance of Hamath:** the northern limit of Israelite territory; either the pass between Mt Hermon and Lebanon, a little north of Dan, or the northern end of the broad valley between the Lebanon and Anti-Lebanon, where the district of Hamath began. **Brook of the Arabah:** a valley (wadi) in the region extending from the south end of the Dead Sea to the Gulf of 'Aqaba. Jeroboam II is reported to have restored to Israel these two northern and southern boundaries (2 Kg. 14:25).

VII 1-IX 8 Visions of Amos, with Oracles and k
a Historical Narrative—This long division closes the original book of Amos. The visions are narrated in the first person, and quite probably were written or dictated by the prophet himself. In spite of the fact that they now stand at the end of the book, it is a plausible theory that the first three (or four) visions constituted the call of Amos to a prophetic career. At the end of the first two visions he intercedes with Yahweh not to destroy Israel, and his petition is granted. At the end of the third Amos is made to feel that Israel's sin is so deep that further stay of judgment is not possible. The historical narrative in 7:10–17 is most valuable, and gives us our only direct insight into his activity. In chs. 8, 9 oracles are placed after the visions which may not have originally been connected with them.

The conception of God's nature implied in the visions is important. Twice the prophet has a vision in which he sees a great destructive force, and intercedes with Yahweh not to destroy Israel, but to forgive. Each time Yahweh repents, or relents from his intention to destroy, as a response to his prayer. Thus Yahweh is conceived to be a God of mercy, ready to forgive. Yet there is an end to his patience and his willingness to forgive, and the time comes when Israel must be punished for her deep and lasting sin. The God of Amos is not a stern, cold deity of strict justice; there is an important element of loving mercy in his nature.

VII 1-3 Vision of the Locusts—Amos has a vision, 546a
in the spring, in which he sees Yahweh forming locusts, which are on the point of causing great destruction. When he prays Yahweh to forgive Jacob, because he is so small, Yahweh repents, and stays the destruction. Palestine was subject to very destructive locust plagues. The vision probably grew out of his actually seeing a swarm, or many swarms, of locusts, and in his imagination he saw the possibility of their consuming all the herbage of the land.

1 latter growth after the king's mowings: presumably, the king had the right to the first mowing, before the owner made his own, but of this practice there is no other evidence. Some scholars refer to 1 Kg. 18:5, but it is doubtful that this is the same practice. **2. When they had finished . . .:** better, with slight emendation of the consonantal Heb. text, 'When they were about to finish eating the herbage of the land'.

4-6 Vision of Fire—The prophet, probably in the b
heat of midsummer, has a vision of a great supernatural fire which had already destroyed 'the great deep', a region believed to exist under the earth, and

546b was about to eat up the land. Again he intercedes, and a second time Yahweh repents.

7-9 Vision of the Wall—Amos in vision sees Yahweh standing beside a wall, with a plumb-line in his hand. Yahweh has apparently tested the wall and found it to be untrue. This is a symbol that Yahweh has tested Israel and, finding her most corrupt and untrue to her God, he is now going to destroy his people, and even the royal sanctuaries and the royal dynasty will be brought to an end. This time there is no prayer of intercession, but Amos becomes convinced that the judgment is inevitable.

c **10-17 Amos expelled from Bethel**—This is a most valuable historical narrative, telling how Amaziah, the priest of the royal sanctuary at Bethel, expelled Amos from northern Israel because he thought the prophet was preaching conspiracy. The narrative is placed here probably because Amos at Bethel narrated his third vision, with its threat of destruction both to the sanctuaries and to the royal house. **11** reports a similar oracle of the prophet in which he issues a threat against the king.

d **12 O seer, go, flee away . . .:** Amaziah speaks contemptuously to Amos, using the word ' seer ' as a term of contempt ; he tells Amos to leave the Northern Kingdom and go back to his native Judah and make a living by prophesying there. **14. I am no prophet, nor a prophet's son:** translation and meaning are uncertain. The Heb. has no copula corresponding to ' am ' of the English rendering. It is equally possible to translate as past tense : ' I was no prophet . . . but I was a herdsman ' etc. The RSV rendering implies that Amos did not want to be considered as a *nābhî'*, either because the prophets had become commercialised and in other ways corrupt, or because they were accustomed to engage in political activity. A strong case for reading as past tense has been made by H. H. Rowley (' Was Amos a Nabi ? ', *Otto Eissfeldt Festschrift* (1947), 191–8). It is so translated by LXX, Syriac, and many moderns ; it is strange that Amos should disclaim any connection with the ' prophets ' of his time, and then in the next breath say that Yahweh had sent him to ' prophesy ' to Israel. Elsewhere Amos speaks favourably of prophets (2:11, 3:7). He is here claiming above everything else that he is a prophet by divine constraint, and not by training or by his own choice. The second half of the phrase can mean literally ' nor a prophet's son ' or ' nor a member of a group of the sons of the prophets (a prophetic guild) '. **herdsman:** better, ' shepherd ', as in 1:1, emending *bôḳēr* to *nôḳēdh* ; the resemblance of the two words in Heb. is very close. **dresser of sycamore trees:** in order to practise this occupation, Amos had to travel, since the sycamore did not grow at so great a height as Tekoa. It was a seasonal occupation, followed by Amos in addition to his shepherding duties. The fact that he had these two occupations seems to indicate he was a poor man, and militates against the suggestion that he was a temple official. **16-17** are spoken directly to Amaziah and show the complete fearlessness of Amos, who had the last word (an oracle from Yahweh) in the exchange with the priest.

e **VIII 1-3 Vision of the Basket of Summer Fruit**—In this fourth vision Amos sees a basket of the fruits which ripen at the end of the summer (note the chronological sequence of the first, second and fourth visions). Meditating on the Heb. word for summer fruit, *ḳayiṣ*, the prophet hears Yahweh speak an oracle in which the first word is *haḳḳēṣ*, ' the end ', which Yahweh is about to bring upon his people. There is probably a *double-entendre* in this vision : there is a pun on the word for summer fruit, and the summer fruits themselves suggest the end of the summer season. **3** is a picture of devastation that will result at the invasion of the land.

3 The songs of the temple: as RSV*n* indicates, *hêkhāl* may be either ' temple ' or ' palace '. Some scholars emend *shîrôth* to *shārôth*, and thus read ' singing-women ', or to *śārôth*, ' princesses '. In either case **54** then the verb is to be rendered, ' shall wail (*or* howl) '.

f **4-8 Oppression of the Poor, and Greediness of Merchants**—This oracle is not directly connected with the fourth vision, but immediately after that vision an editor has placed several oracles of varied content, generally dealing with the oppression and the impending doom. Here Amos denounces those who oppress the poor, in language reminiscent of 2:6–7, and the dishonest and greedy merchants, who are anxious for the holidays to end so that they may sell their wares, and who use dishonest measures in their dealings. By the close connection of the two ideas in this passage, it is implied that the dishonest merchants are the ones who oppress the poor. The end of the oracle describes the punishment which is coming upon them through an earthquake.

g **5** The new moons and sabbaths were religious holidays, days both of religious observance and cessation from work (2 Kg. 4:23 ; Isa. 1:13 ; Hos. 2:11). **ephah:** a dry measure, probably used in selling grain, the standard being approximately 23 litres. **shekel:** a weight, the standard about 11½ grammes (not a coin at this time). **7. The Lord has sworn by the pride of Jacob:** elsewhere in Amos Yahweh swears by himself (6:8) or his holiness (4:2). Thus ' the pride of Jacob ' is probably a synonym of Yahweh himself, and we should render ' excellency of Jacob '. **8.** It is uncertain whether this verse is to be connected with the preceding or with the following verses. RSV takes it with the preceding ; it apparently describes an earthquake as the means of punishment of the dishonest and oppressing merchants. It seems that a verse such as this is needed to supplement v. 7, but punishment by earthquake is unusual in Amos. Some critics consider 8 secondary, like 9:5.

h **9-10 Darkness and Mourning on the Day of the Lord**—A description of the Day of the Lord, with the same elements found in 5:16–20, darkness and mourning. According to Assyrian records and the calculations of modern astronomers, there was an earthquake in June 763. This may have influenced Amos in the prediction here of the going down of the sun at noon, and darkening of the earth in broad daylight.

11-12 Famine for the Word of the Lord—Yahweh will send a famine upon the land, not a literal famine for bread, but a famine of hearing the word of the Lord. Though the people may wander all over the known earth seeking it, they will not find the word of the Lord. To both the prophet and the people at large this would be a great disaster, even though they conceived the nature and content of the word of the Lord to be different. To Amos it was a word of judgment, unwelcome to the people. Yet they were accustomed to seek Yahweh's word frequently at the sanctuaries on many occasions and in many crises. Failure of Yahweh to give them direction through his word—which might be considered by the prophet as a false word—would be indeed a great disaster in their eyes.

i **12 wander from sea to sea:** though the meaning could be, ' from the Dead Sea to the Mediterranean ', the context and the usual meaning suggest rather, ' from one end of the world to another ' (cf. Zech. 9:10 ; Ps. 72:8).

13-14 Punishment of Idolaters—This oracle has a close connection with vv. 11–12, and is taken by some to be part of a single oracle. But the phrase ' In that day ' suggests a new beginning, and ' thirst ' here is a literal thirst for water. Those who are denounced are the idolaters, even the young men and women who engage in idolatry.

j **14 Ashimah:** a deity worshipped in the Northern Kingdom by men of Hamath, according to 2 Kg. 17:30, and known also in the Elephantine papyri in the compound name Ashem-Bethel. **the way of Beer-sheba:** reference is often made to the fact that Moslems swear by the pilgrimage to Mecca, but it is doubtful that a similar practice is indicated here. Most likely we should emend the consonantal text *drk* to

46j *ddk*, *dôdh^ekhā*, and render ' as thy Dod (*or* thy patron deity) lives'. The word *dôd* occurs in the Mesha Inscription, line 12, as the name or epithet of a deity; if not a proper name, it seems to mean kinsman, friend, or the like. This emendation is in part supported by LXX, ' thy god '.

47a **IX 1-4 Vision of Yahweh standing beside the Altar**—Amos has a vision of Yahweh standing near an altar and saying that the sanctuary will be destroyed and with it all the worshippers, who will be quite unable to escape from the avenging wrath of God. This vision may have taken place at the sanctuary at Bethel, just before the prophet left there to return to Judah; cf. 7:10–17, 3:14. 2–4 depict vividly the pursuing wrath of Yahweh which cannot be escaped anywhere in the universe as known to the Hebrews.

b **1 beside the altar:** the Heb. may equally well be rendered ' upon ' or ' above '; either would be possible in a vision. **Smite the capitals:** the capitals on the pillars that support the temple. The verb is imperative, but it is difficult to determine to whom the Lord is speaking; it is hardly the prophet himself. Because of this difficulty, many scholars emend and slightly rearrange the text to read as follows: ' I saw the Lord standing beside the altar, and he smote the capitals and the thresholds shook, and he said: I will shatter them on the heads of (*or* with an earthquake) all the people.' Such a reading removes the difficulties involved. **2. Sheol:** the great subterranean region to which it was believed all the dead would go (not a place of punishment at this time). **3. Carmel:** the mountain at the western end of the Plain of Esdraelon. **serpent:** probably a mythical monster believed to live in the sea. **captivity:** even in a foreign land they cannot escape the power of Yahweh. **2-4** are often compared with Ps. 139. In that Psalm the emphasis is on the universal protecting care of Yahweh, whereas here it is on his avenging wrath which cannot be escaped.

c **5-6 Yahweh the God of the Universe**—This is the third of the three doxologies which have been added at appropriate places in the work of Amos; cf. 4:13, 5:8–9. Like the others this one stresses the work of Yahweh in creating and sustaining the universe. It is very appropriate following 2–4.

5 rises like the Nile . . . sinks again, like the Nile of Egypt: the annual overflow of the Nile which makes possible the fertility of Egypt; cf. 8:8.

7-8b Yahweh, the God of the Nations, will now destroy the sinful Kingdom of Israel—In two rhetorical questions Amos indicates that the Israelites are like the Ethiopians in Yahweh's view, and that Yahweh has not only governed the history of Israel but also that of the Philistines and Syrians. But the eyes of the Lord are upon sinful Israel, and he will destroy it from the face of the ground. This oracle ends the genuine words of Amos, and the hopeful appendix begins with the last line of v. 8.

d **7 Are you not like the Ethiopians to me, O people of Israel?:** The usual interpretation of this is that Yahweh has care and concern for the far-off Ethiopians, who lived south of Egypt, as well as for the Israelites. Perhaps Amos does not mean to say that the relationship of Yahweh to the Ethiopians is as close as to the Israelites (see 3:2), but he nevertheless implies that in some real sense Yahweh is their deity as well. Some scholars, thinking this view too exalted or universalistic for Amos, believe the verse is secondary, or adopt one of the following meanings: (1) ' Are you not in your conduct in my sight like the Ethiopians?' 547d
—that is, apostasy has become a second nature, and you can no more change than can the Ethiopians (cf. Jer. 13:23); (2) ' Now that you have broken your side of the covenant, you are not different in my sight from the Ethiopians, with whom I have not had a covenant.' **Caphtor:** Crete, and probably also southern part of Asia Minor. **Kir:** identification not certain; see 1:5.

8c-15 Appendix to the Words of Amos—Most e
modern critics take the view that the present ending of the Book of Amos is secondary, seeking to close the words of this prophet on a note of hope. Critics disagree as to just how much constitutes this appendix. It seems best to consider the last line of v. 8 and all that follows as secondary; there is a slight possibility that v. 10, or vv. 9–10 (which are very difficult of interpretation) may be from Amos. The appendix itself is probably not a unit, but consists of at least three separate additions (8*c*–10, 11–12, 13–15).

8 except that I will not utterly destroy the house f
of Jacob: the intention of this is apparently that Judah will be saved. The line directly contradicts the preceding line. **9** is very difficult to interpret; it is hard to tell whether it is a threat or promise. The reference is probably to the exile and dispersion of the Hebrews, particularly following the destruction of Jerusalem in 586 B.C. **all the nations:** the phrase is characteristic of later prophecies and additions to the prophets. **pebble:** the usual rendering is ' kernel (of grain) ', but in the only other occurrence, 2 Sam. 17:13, the meaning is pebble, and this is borne out by Targum, Aquila and Vulgate. If this meaning is correct here, the figure is apparently that of a sand-sieve, in the using of which the sand falls to the ground and the pebbles remain in the sieve. Here the pebbles represent the sinners that are to be punished, as v. 10 indicates. Some critics give an opposite interpretation, particularly if they adopt the meaning ' kernel ' for the Heb. *ṣ^erôr*. That which remains in the sieve is the good grain that is preserved. Thus the verse is a promise, to which v. 10 offers a contrast. If there is a clear-cut division here between the righteous and the sinners, the verses could be from the prophet. **11** presupposes the fall of Jerusalem. **the booth of David:** the dynasty of David which had come to an end with the fall of Jerusalem in 586 B.C. **12** reflects the fact that the Edomites had taken advantage of the situation at the time of the siege and capture of Jerusalem to take possession of Judaean territory; see Ob. 10–14; Ps. 137:7–9, etc. **13-15** predict unparalleled productivity of the soil, rebuilding of the cities, and restoration of the people to the land with a promise they will not be exiled again. These are frequent elements of exilic and post-exilic eschatological promises.

Bibliography—COMMENTARIES: R. S. Cripps (2nd ed. 1955); S. R. Driver, CB (1901); H. E. W. Fosbroke, IB vi (1956); W. R. Harper, ICC (1910); T. H. Robinson, HAT (2nd ed. 1954).

OTHER LITERATURE: A. S. Kapelrud, *Central Ideas in Amos* (1956); V. Maag, *Text, Wortschatz u. Begriffswelt des Buches Amos* (1951); J. Morgenstern, *Amos Studies*, i (1941); A. Neher, *Amos: contribution à l'étude du prophétisme* (1950); J. D. W. Watts, *Vision and Prophecy in Amos* (1958); A. Weiser, *Die Prophetie des Amos*, BZAW 53 (1929).

OBADIAH

BY L. H. BROCKINGTON

548a The prophecy falls into two parts: the first a threat of vengeance on Edom for her gloating over Jacob (Israel) at the time when Jerusalem fell in 586 B.C., and the second a prophecy that when the day of Yahweh dawns thus on Edom its horizon will be widened and punishment will fall on other nations too. The section which tells of the Edomite joy at Jacob's calamity (11–14) is so vivid that it was almost certainly written while the memory of it was still fresh, i.e. not very long after 586. If that is so, the rest of the material that refers to Edom must be regarded as prophetic prediction of a downfall that took place some time before 312 B.C. at which date we know that Nabataeans occupied Petra. The date should probably be brought much earlier still; inscriptions show that while at about 600 B.C. the governor of Ezion-geber was still an Edomite, by the 5th cent. Arab names are found there; moreover, Mal. 1:3, written about 460, may be taken to mean that the Arabs had already invaded Edom by 460. We may, then, date the book before 460 and as soon after 586 as may be reasonable.

b Doubts are raised as to the unity of the book, short though it is. The reason lies in the twofold division into which the book readily falls, the dividing line being at v. 15 where the day of Yahweh is introduced. The first part of the book is concerned solely with Edom and of this section 15*b* is clearly the closing sentence. The second part is eschatological in character and deals with the revelation of the day of Yahweh upon the nations. Some scholars think that the second part is entirely independent of the first, perhaps added very much later, and that the introductory sentence to this second part is 15*a*. There is no urgent reason, however, to dissociate the two parts in this way. What we have in this book we find also in Jl: a contemporary situation is seen by the prophet as a token and symbol of the day of Yahweh and from the point at which the day of Yahweh is introduced the prophet no longer speaks of the local event, but of the world-wide eschatological one. The closing section, vv. 19–21, is a prose appendix, possibly fragmentary, though not out of harmony with what precedes it, giving some details about the distribution of the land when 'the kingdom shall be the Lord's'.

c Literary interest is roused by the fact that much of 1–14 is found also with some small differences of text and order of sentences in Jer. 49:7–16 (22). It would be difficult to say which was written first; both may have come from a common source, but the section in Jeremiah is generally regarded as a later addition to the work of that prophet. Although there is no close similarity, a day of vengeance on Edom is also described in Isa. 34:1–17 and 63:1–6, and a similar vindictive attitude towards Edom is found in Ezek. 25:12–14, 35:1–15, 36:5; Jl 3:19; Am. 1:11–12; Mal. 1:2–5.

d The **title** (v. 1) is unique in consisting of two words only: Obadiah's vision. The nearest parallel to its form is Isa. 1:1 but there further details are added.

1-14 The Contents of the Vision—A threat against Edom for her behaviour when Jerusalem fell. **1.** The phrase 'We have heard' suggests that the vision was auditory and that the prophet hears the nations telling of the revelation made to them. The pronoun may
refer to any nation or nations except, of course, Edom. 548d
Yahweh's own words begin at v. 2. **3.** 'Of the rock' is probably an allusion to Sela ('rock') the capital city of Edom, in later times known as Petra. **5, 6** must be understood to mean that even if thieves come they do at least leave something behind them whereas when God visits the destruction is complete. This is clear from the parallel in Jer. 49:9 where, apart from a different order of clauses, the phrase 'if plunderers by night—how you have been destroyed!'—does not occur. If this phrase is original it seems to have been misplaced from the end of the verse. **7.** 'All your allies', probably adjacent Arab tribes. The last phrase seems to be an afterthought where it stands. In point of fact Edom does seem to have been noted for wisdom. Eliphaz, Job 2:11, was a Temanite (i.e. from a district in Edom). **9.** 'By slaughter' has every appearance of belonging to the next verse—the preposition is the same as that used with 'violence'.

In vv. 11–14 the prophet describes the day of e
Israel's distress and speaks vehemently of Edom's proud gloating. 'You stood aloof' (cf. Ps. 38:11 for the use of the phrase); here it seems to mean aloof but not uninterested. '**Foreigners**': the Babylonians. **12.** 'gloated'; this and other OT references to the behaviour of Edom show that the Edomites took advantage of the weakness of Judah after 586, raiding the country, harassing the people and annexing territory.

15-18. After the vivid description of Judah's humilia- f
tion the prophet threatens its return upon the head of Edom. If 15*a* is in its original position it indicates a bold contrast between Judah's day of humiliation—a day of pride to Edom—and Yahweh's day of visitation and punishment on Edom. Obadiah's picture of the day of Yahweh resembles that of other OT prophets, cf. Am. 5:18. In Isa. 34:8, 63:4 it is a day of vengeance on Edom. It is the day on which Yahweh will act (cf. Mal. 3:17) in vengeance and requital. The prophet may have thought at first only of Edom, but the very mention of the day of Yahweh brought with it an inevitable widening of the horizon. **16.** For the cup of disaster cf. Isa. 51:17; Jer. 25:15. **18** introduces another figure, that of a destructive fire coming out of Jacob and Joseph, cf. Jotham's fable, Jg. 9:15–20, and also Ps. 21:9. This verse closes the oracle about the day of Yahweh.

19-21, written in prose, unlike the rest of Obadiah, give g
details about the Israelite occupation of the land on their return from Exile. They lack an introduction, and it is not clear why Benjamin should possess Gilead. **20.** Halah is probably Halah of 2 Kg. 17:6. Sepharad occurs only here and is possibly Sardis, the capital of Lydia. **21.** 'Saviours': probably rulers, cf. Jg. 3:9, 15; but LXX implies a passive form, those who are saved, i.e. the Israelites delivered from Exile and recovered from the Diaspora.

Bibliography—J. A. Bewer, ICC (1912); S. Bullough, Westminster Version (1953); A. van Hoonacker, EBib. (1908); R. F. Horton, Cent.B; H. C. O. Lanchester, CB (1915); K. Marti, KHC (1904); T. H. Robinson, HAT (2nd ed. 1954); E. Sellin, KAT (2nd ed. 1929); G. W. Wade, WC (1925); A. Weiser, ATD (2nd ed. 1956).

JONAH

By L. H. BROCKINGTON

549a The story of Jonah has become one of the most familiar of stories, and only the barest outline is necessary here in order to indicate its purpose. A prophet, Jonah by name, is told to go and preach at Nineveh because of the wickedness of the people and bring them to repentance. He is unwilling to go and seeks means of avoiding the call. The plan he adopts and puts partly into action fails, and he finds himself forced to carry out his mission. The people of Nineveh repent at his preaching and in consequence God relents and forgoes his threat of punishment on them. At this Jonah is very angry and disconsolate, and, filled with self-pity, wishes to die and escape it all. In this mood his anger and indignation are roused for a plant which offered him temporary shelter from the scorching heat but then quickly withered. Through this incident he is brought to realise that God has pity on whom he will, no matter what nation they belong to, even if they be wicked Ninevites.

b The clear purpose of this story is to show that Jonah was in the wrong both in refusing to preach to the Ninevites and in being angry at their repentance and forgiveness. In other words, the message of the book is that in the providence of God even a non-Israelite people might turn to him in repentance and worship him.

c The book may be described as a written sermon in story form based on Jer. 18:8: 'If that nation, concerning which I have spoken, turns from its evil, I will repent of the evil that I thought to do to it.' This is clearly alluded to in 3:10. In the course of the sermon the author not only demonstrates the possibility of a heathen city repenting and turning to God, but draws attention also to the love, mercy and forgiveness of God, and, in the person of Jonah, strongly rebukes those who would be unwilling to see God's mercy extend beyond Israel. There are the foundations here of a strong missionary spirit. Such a missionary outlook was rarely made articulate in Israelite literature. Isa. 40–55 contains the clearest expressions of it.

d It has been mentioned that the author seems to have based his book on Jer. 18:8, but this is not the full extent of his indebtedness to already existing literature. First there is the name of the prophet whom the author uses as his victim to be held up to scorn and contempt; this comes from 2 Kg. 14:25 where some territorial expansion by Jeroboam is said to be according to the word of the Lord 'which he spoke by his servant Jonah the son of Amittai, the prophet, who was from Gath-hepher'. Jonah's wish that he might die seems to be modelled on that of Elijah, 1 Kg. 19:4–8, although the mood of the two men is vastly different. Then there are two motifs which seem to be drawn from folklore or legend, one that of the great fish which can swallow a man alive and vomit him out still alive and the other that of the rapidly growing plant which provides shelter for a day and then withers. That of the great fish is to be found in classical literature; that of the plant is not attested elsewhere. These motifs may have been drawn from oral tradition and need not be supposed to have been already in written form in Israel. They provide a colourful background to the author's story and enable him to develop it quickly, using the first to illustrate the futility of disobedience to God's commands and to provide the means to bring Jonah back where he started, and the second to elicit Jonah's anger and self-pity and thus to make him face the unreasonableness of his anger about God's grace towards Nineveh. In addition to these a psalm was incorporated in ch. 2. Though not found in Ps. it is probably one that was familiar to the first readers of the book. 549d

It may be assumed that all these things that the author drew from literature and tradition were familiar to practically everyone at the time the book was written; they would not have full force as illustrations if they were not. What was new was not the material but the use made of it. It was probably not a bit novel to tell the story of a man swallowed by a great fish, but it was novel and at the same time significant that the man afterwards preached to a heathen audience and brought them to repentance. e

The author's choice of Nineveh as the scene of Jonah's preaching may well have been dictated by popular tradition about the city as one of the most depraved of non-Israelite cities, a tradition which Nah. probably helped to foster. Tradition may well have painted the inhabitants blacker than they were, and if, as seems possible, the book was written after the Exile, there had been plenty of time since Nineveh's fall in 612 B.C. for such a tradition to have grown. f

Date—If it be accepted that the book is intended to show that God's mercy extends to non-Israelite nations, it is extremely probable that it was written some time after the Exile, after the writings now found in Isa. 40–55 in which the universalism of Yahweh is plainly expressed and reiterated. The occasion for a renewed presentation of the idea may have been such a time as that reflected by the age of Nehemiah and Ezra, a time at which Israelite particularism was rampant and the Jews had little or no thought for anything beyond their pride in the possession of the exclusive worship of Yahweh and in the purity of their race. g

If the prophet's name was taken from 2 Kg. 14:25, if 3:8–10 is dependent on Jer. 18:7–12, and if Jonah's mood in ch. 4 is comparable with, and perhaps dependent on, that of Elijah in 1 Kg. 19, and these are all highly probable, then we must think of a date later than Jeremiah and than the compilation of Kg. Moreover, Nineveh is mentioned in such a way as to preclude the possibility that it was written while the city still stood. It was written long enough after the fall of Nineveh in 612 B.C. for the city to have become a legendary place of great size and notoriously evil. This all points to a post-exilic date, but all certainty about date ends there. It could have been written at any time between the end of the Exile and 200 B.C. by which time it had apparently gained its place among the twelve minor prophets (Sir. 49:10). The language is also indicative of a late date, having several words and phrases that belong more to Aramaic than to Hebrew. h

Two references to Jonah are given in the record of the teaching of Jesus, Mt. 12:39–41 and Lk. 11:29–32. The significant point in both is that as Jonah was a i

549l sign to the men of Nineveh so would Jesus be to the men of his generation, but a more evil generation. Only the Matthean version speaks of the three days in the fish and the mention of it is generally felt to be out of keeping with the context. In the thought of Jesus the thing that most mattered about Jonah was that he preached to Nineveh.

550a **I 1-3.** Jonah is commissioned to preach to Nineveh but runs away from the task. The name Jonah, son of Amittai, is probably taken from 2 Kg. 14:25 where a prophet of that name from Gath-hepher prophesied in the time of Jeroboam II (781–740). The name Jonah means ' dove ' and Amittai ' truth '. It is not improbable that the meaning of the names may have led to the author's choice of name for his subject. Nineveh was the capital of Assyria until 612 B.C. when it fell before the combined forces of Babylonians and Medes after a two and a half months' siege. It had had a long history of nearly 2,000 years, but did not become a capital city until the time of Sennacherib (704–682). Excavations have shown that the city wall was about seven and a half miles long. Tarshish is commonly identified with Tartessus on the Guadalquivir in Spain. Jonah, like other prophets before him, although for different reasons, shrank from the call made to him and the task assigned him. His reason was not the difficulty of the task, but his own unwillingness to face the possibility that the Ninevites, a non-Israelite people with a bad reputation, should repent at his preaching and worship Yahweh.

b **4-6.** So strong a gale springs up that the sailors are forced to lighten ship, but Jonah sleeps on, much to the captain's chagrin. ' Each cried to his god ' (5) : we are to think of a cosmopolitan company on board owing allegiance to a number of gods among whom the captain seems to reckon Jonah's God as simply one other (6) but the story cleverly hints that only Yahweh had effective power (14).

c **7-10.** Believing the calamity to be due to some wrong done by one of the men on board the sailors discover who it is by lot and learn from Jonah why he is there. Mention of the name of Yahweh immediately produces an atmosphere of awe and alarm.

d **11-16.** At his own request Jonah is thrown into the sea and the storm subsides. The sailors, in their relief, sacrifice to Yahweh and make vows. How they handled the sacrifice on board ship was a detail outside the range of the author's interest. It is noteworthy that, almost incidentally, the author here introduces a delightful illustration of his main theme ; Jonah shows himself willing to give his life for the sake of the Gentile sailors.

e **17.** A great fish swallows up Jonah and he remains within it for three days. There is no need to speculate either upon the identification of the fish with any known species, or upon the probability of remaining alive within such a fish for three days. The tale is simply used rhetorically as a device for bringing Jonah back to where he began as quickly as possible.

f **II 1, 10.** Jonah prays to Yahweh from inside the fish and the fish then disgorges him on dry land. We are left to decide for ourselves where the land was, presumably not far from Joppa where his voyage began.

g **2-9.** A psalm is introduced here as though it were the prayer used by Jonah in the fish. In effect the psalm is the thanksgiving song of an individual who has been rescued from drowning. **2.** ' Out of the belly of Sheol ' is a unique phrase and probably a metaphor comparable with our ' at death's door '. Sheol is used in a similar way in Ps. 30:3. Cf. the phrase in v. 6 : ' Thou didst bring up my life from the Pit '. **4** indicates how deep-seated in Israel was the idea of the limited range of God's sovereignty. Not only was it limited to Israelite territory but in Sheol the dead could not worship or praise him (Ps. 6:5, 88:5, 10–12). Even in post-exilic times, when a universalistic note was sounded, as in this book, there were still many allusions to other gods. **6.** ' At the roots of the mountains ' : another possible translation 550 is ' in the crevices of the mountains '. According to ancient cosmogony the mountains were set in the waters of the sea. **9.** ' Vowed ', cf. 1:16 ; it was customary for the Hebrews to make vows when they were in dire distress and then to ' pay ' them in the presence of a congregation of worshippers (Ps. 116:14, 18).

The psalm is not applicable to Jonah's condition h although it could be claimed that it makes a fitting interlude in the story. Some ingenious commentators however have suggested that Jonah's relief at being rescued from drowning by the fish was so great that he felt compelled to recite this psalm inside the fish ! There may have been two reasons why this psalm was chosen for inclusion here. First because it speaks of the dangers of the sea, and second because the mention of sacrifice and vow in v. 9 are reminiscent of the sacrifice and vows made by the sailors in 1:16.

III 1-5. When the call comes a second time Jonah 551 responds to it without hesitation. He had learned his lesson that Yahweh must not be disobeyed. The account of Jonah's preaching at Nineveh may have been in George Fox's mind when he visited Lichfield and afterwards wrote : ' So I went up and down the streets crying with a loud voice, " Woe to the bloody city of Lichfield ! " ' Nineveh is described as so vast that it was a three days' journey across it. This detail, like that of the ' king of Nineveh ' in v. 6, is part of the storyteller's art and does not lend itself to critical examination. The city was, in fact, less than three miles across. ' Yet forty days ' (4) : LXX has ' Yet three days '. ' The people of Nineveh believed God ' (5) : this is just what Jonah had feared might happen and why he had run away from the task at the first call. In his belief, Yahweh was the God of the Jews only, and he, like the majority of his fellow-Jews, was very jealous of this privilege.

6-9. Proclamation by the king of Nineveh of a general b fast by man and beast in the hope that God would repent and turn away his anger. Nineveh, of course, had no king of its own ; its king would be the king of Assyria and would rightly be so called. The summons to both man and beast is characteristic of the Hebrew manner of making an exhaustive phrase ; the penitence is to embrace every single soul. With v. 9, cf. Jl 2:14*a*.

10. God, seeing this genuine penitence, changes his c plans about them. This is in fulfilment of such a promise as that of Jer. 18:8 of which it is also verbally reminiscent.

IV 1-5. Jonah is angry and perplexed at what has d happened. This is what he feared, and knowing God to be gracious he wonders what will become of the city. This is an important clue to the interpretation of the book. Jonah did not want the Ninevites to repent and be forgiven, because they were foreigners, who, in his view, as in that of so many of his fellow-Jews, had no claim on the love of God. God asks Jonah, ' Do you do well to be angry ? ' but at first Jonah, perplexed, has no answer. Some further revelation must follow. **2b** is identical with Jl 2:13*b* and both are based on Yahweh's own declaration of his nature in Exod. 34:6, 7. Jonah's longing for death is similar to that of Elijah in 1 Kg. 19:4, but Jonah's mood is very different from that of Elijah. In **5** Jonah is said to make a booth for shade from the hot sun, but if we press this detail the story of the plant in the following verses loses much of its point. On the other hand, there is clearly a break in the narrative at this point. Jonah obviously has much more to learn and in the interval provided by v. 5 he may be thought to be undergoing preparation in his own mind for the further revelation that is to come.

6-11. Jonah, thankful in his chagrin for the shade of e a plant, is brought to a more bitter mood when he finds the plant withered and shadeless next day. In this mood he is awakened to the pity that God feels for Nineveh, a city of 120,000 souls. God's words to Jonah might be thus paraphrased : ' You are terribly

551e upset about that plant, which cost you no pains at all, which you did not cultivate, which grew overnight, and faded overnight; but what of me? Should I not be distressed concerning this teeming great city, Nineveh?' (S. H. Blank, HUCA (1955), 29). The plant is usually identified with the castor-oil plant, known as *Ricinus* or Palma Christi and having hand-shaped leaves. Jonah's self-pity must be regarded as the connecting link between his anger, so strongly expressed in 9, and his pity for the plant (10). The book ends quietly, yet strikingly, with the concern of God for the bewildered souls in Nineveh, upwards of 120,000, and also for their cattle. It is an impressive finish and sets the seal on the whole book: God loves and cherishes all that he has made, even the poor ignorant folk with their cattle in that depraved city of Nineveh. 551e

Bibliography—J. A. Bewer, ICC (1912); A. van Hoonacker, EBib. (1908); R. F. Horton, Cent.B; G. A. F. Knight, Torch Commentary (1950); H. C. O. Lanchester, CB (1915); C. Lattey, *The Book of Jona*, Westminster Version (1938); K. Marti, KHC (1904); T. H. Robinson, HAT (2nd ed. 1954); E. Sellin, KAT (2nd ed. 1929); G. W. Wade, WC (1925); A. Weiser, ATD (2nd ed. 1956).

MICAH

By D. WINTON THOMAS

552a According to the editorial **superscription** (1:1), Micah's prophetic activity fell in the reigns of Jotham (739–734 B.C.), Ahaz (733–721 B.C.), and Hezekiah (720–693 B.C.). This statement, so far as the last named is concerned, receives confirmation from Jer. 26:18f., from which it is clear that Micah's prophecy concerning the fate of Judah (3:12) was remembered a century or so later. This Jeremianic passage has been thought to provide the approximate date of Micah's prophetic activity, the years shortly before 701 B.C., when Sennacherib, king of Assyria, invaded Judah, forming the most probable background of the prophecies. The passage need not, however, imply that all Micah's prophetic utterances were delivered in the reign of Hezekiah. An earlier dating may accordingly be allowed for some passages. For example, 1:2–9 could belong to a time prior to Sargon's capture of Samaria in 721 B.C. (Samaria still stands, 1:6), and 1:10–16 could as well be assigned to 711 B.C., when Sargon subdued Ashdod and Gath (1:10), as to 701 B.C. The book of Micah itself gives no decisive evidence as to the beginning of the prophet's activity. If, as is possible, his activity spanned the reigns of Ahaz and Hezekiah, the superscription would to this extent preserve a true tradition. No passage in the book appears to have the reign of Jotham as its historical background.

b If Micah did in fact prophesy in the reigns of Ahaz and Hezekiah, he will have known of military and political events of the greatest moment. He shows, however, little direct concern with them. The arch-foe, the Assyrians, are not even mentioned by name in the authentic parts of his book. In his disregard of the significant events of his day he differs markedly from his older contemporary and statesman, Isaiah of Jerusalem. His chief concern is with the sins of Judah and its capital, Jerusalem, with which Samaria, the capital of the north, is associated (1:5), and with the divine punishment which will inevitably result from them. This is the main topic of chapters 1–3, which, except for 1:1, and perhaps 1:7 and 2:12f., may be regarded as the genuine work of Micah. The remainder of the book is generally denied to him. Chapters 4 and 5, which form the second main part of the book, and which contain passages which look forward in hope beyond the approaching catastrophe, are in the main exilic or post-exilic in origin, but contain also pre-exilic material, viz. 4:9f., 5:5f., and possibly also 4:6–8 and 5:10–15. Pre-exilic material in the third main part of the book (chapters 6–7) is found in 6:9–16, and possibly also in 6:1–5, 6–8 and 7:1–4. Of all this pre-exilic material, 6:6–7:4 has the best claim to be considered as the genuine work of Micah.

c Only the first three chapters of the book may accordingly properly be used as a basis for a characterisation of the prophet Micah. In 1:1 he is described as being of Moresheth (Heb. 'the Morashtite', cf. Jer. 26:18), no doubt to distinguish him from the dozen or so other bearers of his name in the OT, and more particularly from Micaiah, the son of Imlah, who lived in the reign of Ahab (1 Kg. 22:8ff.). His home, Moresheth-gath (1:14), which may have been a dependency of the Philistine Gath, or near to it, is the modern Tell el-Judeideh, in the Shephelah, which 55
the prophet knew so well (1:10 ff.). Since, as in the case of Amos (1:1), the name of his father is not given, it has been inferred that he belonged to the peasant class. 2:11 has been taken to imply that he was a professional prophet, but in 3:8 he stands in opposition to the professionals. Like Amos (7:14f.), he is not of their company, but a simple man from the country, who recognised and earnestly condemned the evil consequences of the inhuman behaviour of the ruling classes in his day (3:1–4). In him the oppressed poor found their spokesman against the rich (2:1f., 8f., 3:3, 9f.). Micah attacked not only the social, but also the religious conditions of his time. The venality of prophet and priest especially evoked his strong condemnation (3:5, 11). Underlying the moral decline in his day he saw a perverse religiosity—the belief that Yahweh would in all circumstances protect Judah, the home of his people and the seat of his worship (2:6f., 3:11). The maintenance of outward ceremony in religion was all that the people cared about. Against this kind of thinking Micah set the ethical character of religion, and on it he based his call for social justice. God is above all else a god whose law it is that men treat each other justly, and, if his law is disobeyed, he will not hesitate to destroy his people, and Jerusalem and the Temple with them (3:12). In these first three chapters Micah is seen as a man with a profound and clear sense of the divine demand for morality and justice, and with a deep consciousness of the strength given to him by the living God to proclaim this demand passionately and unyieldingly (3:8). He made no great contribution to the development of Hebrew religion. Yet he has claims to be considered one of the great prophets. His significance lies in the fact that he, the last of the four great prophets of the 8th cent. B.C., found, as did the first, Amos, in the moral law of God the source, and centre, of true religion. Well has he been called 'an Amos *redivivus*' (E. Sellin, *Introduction to the OT* (1923), 175).

I 1 For the editorial superscription, see §552*a*. d
'Saw' is used in the transferred sense of 'heard' (Am. 1:1), unless 'saw' (Heb. *ḥazah*) has the double sense which 'observe' has in English. **in the days of . . . kings of Judah:** these words are probably a later addition which may derive from the same editor who was responsible for Hos. 1:1 and Isa. 1:1, or it may be modelled on these passages.

2–9 The Divine Judgment on Israel and Judah e
—All the nations of the world are warned that Yahweh will descend cataclysmically from 'his holy temple' (Ps. 11:4; Hab. 2:20), 'his place' (Hos. 5:15), that is, from heaven, and 'tread upon the high places of the earth' (Dt. 33:29; Am. 4:13), to the accompaniment of volcanic eruption and earthquake (Jg. 5:4; Ps. 18:7ff.; Hab. 3:6) (2–4). Yahweh's intervention is the result of the sins of the kingdoms of the north and south, the capital cities, Samaria and Jerusalem, being the focal points of the divine punishment at the hands of the Assyrians. Samaria will be razed to her foundations, her stones will roll down the hillside into the valley below, and she will become a ruin 'in the open country'. The fertile hillside, on which she was situated, will be given over to the cultivation of vines,

52e and her ' images ' will be destroyed (5–7). The coming judgment will reach the city gate, the very heart of Micah's own land, even ' to Jerusalem '. Micah knows that the punishment is deserved, but he cannot escape a certain sympathy with his people (8). In anticipation of the evils to come, he goes about in mourning for them. His lamentation and wailing resemble the yelling jackal and the mournful sounding ostrich (Job 30:29; Isa. 13:21f.). He walks ' stripped ', i.e. barefoot, and ' naked ', i.e. having discarded his outer garment (Isa. 20:2f.) (7–9). **7** may be a later addition. **the hires thereof:** read either ' her images ' or ' her Asherahs '. **the hire of a harlot** is the money or valuables paid to cult prostitutes which made possible the provision of costly temple furniture, such as idols plated with silver and gold (in Dt. 23:18 the bringing of the hire of a harlot into the temple is prohibited). The enemy will carry away the silver and gold plating, and will use it again in his own temples as a means of paying prostitutes. Another view is that the provision of idols was made possible by the material prosperity which the people imagined came to them through the favour of the Baalim (Hos. 2:5). **her wound is incurable.** cf. Jer. 15:18.

f **10-16 Lament over Judah's Ruin**—This section, which can only be made intelligible by extensive emendation of the MT, pictures the advance of a hostile army (Isa. 10:27ff.) from the south-west in the direction of Jerusalem, and the sufferings of places in the Shephelah which lay on the route of the invader. The places and the sufferings they endured are linked together in the original Hebrew by means of word plays and assonances. Gath may be identified with 'Arâq el-Menshîyeh or with Tell eṣ-Ṣâfî; Lachish with Tell ed-Duweir; Mareshah with Tell Sandaḥannah; and Adullam with Tell esh-Sheikh-Madhkûr. The location of the other places mentioned is less certain. Zaanan may be the same place as Zenan (Jos. 15:37) and represent an older pronunciation, and Maroth is perhaps a scribal error for Jarmuth (Jos. 15:35) or Maarath (Jos. 15:59).

The cities' sufferings are severally depicted—their inhabitants roll on the ground (10), are led away by the conqueror, barricade themselves (11), anxiously wait for good news (or ' are in very great anguish ' (12)), flee in chariots (13), resemble a wady whose waters fail (14; Jer. 15:18), fall into enemy hands, while ' the glory of Israel ', the fleeing nobles, seek refuge in the cave of Adullam (15; 1 Sam. 22:1). Jerusalem is bidden to shave her head, make herself bald, like the bareheaded ' griffon-vulture ' (rather than ' eagle '), in mourning (Isa. 22:12; Am. 8:10; in Dt. 14:1 the practice is forbidden) for her lost cities with their inhabitants, her delightful children (16). **10.** For **tell it not**, that is, ' do not declare (these sufferings) ' (2 Sam. 1:20), perhaps read ' rejoice not '. **weep not at all:** better ' weep not in Baca ' (a place otherwise unknown). **11.** Perhaps translate ' Blow ye the trumpet, thou inhabitant of Shaphir; from her city Zaanan came not forth; Beth-ezel is a place of mourning, withdrawing from you her support '. **12. the gate of Jerusalem.** Possibly read ' Shaaraim ' (Jos. 15:36). **13. the beginning of sin:** perhaps Lachish is regarded as a seat of licentious worship; or, since the city was in close contact with Egypt, it may be a symbol of political dependence on that country; or possibly it was thought to be a chariot city (1 Kg. 10:26; trust in horses was regarded as a major sin of Israel by Hosea, 14:3). **14. parting gifts,** i.e. a marriage dowry (1 Kg. 9:16). Zion is to say farewell to Moresheth-gath, as to a bride who is lost to her family.

553a **II 1-5 The Inhumanity of the Rich and its Punishment**—Micah here attacks the rich who make plans (by night, Ps. 36:4) to take possession, illegally and ruthlessly, of the fields and houses of the poor (Isa. 5:8ff.; Am. 4:1). Their plans will, however, be thwarted by Yahweh's counterplan, and punishment —the figure of the inescapable yoke betokens exile or slavery—will fall, not on individuals only, but on the whole people of Judah (1–3; Am. 3:1). The taunt song which shall be raised over Israel (4f.) envisages the occupation of the land by the Assyrians, who will take possession of the fields and allot them in turn to settlers. **3. haughtily:** better ' erect '. The text of verse **4** is particularly uncertain.

6-11 A Disputation between Micah and his Opponents—This section, though possibly of independent origin, stands in close connection with what precedes. The text is frequently uncertain. The section begins with a resentful protest by the rich against Micah's prophetic message which is not to their liking (6; Isa. 30:10; Am. 2:12, 5:10, 7:16). They believed that Yahweh would continue in his patience, and would not allow them to come to harm, so long as they walked ' uprightly ', which for them meant the correct observance of the demands of the cultus (7; **my words:** read ' his words ', with LXX). They reveal the same self-confident state of mind which Amos, Hosea and Isaiah had to combat. Micah replies that Yahweh will not be satisfied with their cruel behaviour, as if they were foreign enemies, towards those who live peaceably. They even tear the clothes off the people's backs (as security for debt, in violation of Exod. 22:26f.), drive out ' the women ' from their homes, and rob ' young children ' of their fathers (' my glory ' perhaps means the yeomen of Israel; Isa. 5:13f.). The poor man and his family are at the mercy of the rich landlords (8f.). But, because the rich by their conduct have infected the land with ' uncleanness ' (Lev. 18:25; Zech. 13:2), it is no longer a resting-place for them, and they will be driven out (10). Verse **11**, which should probably be read with verse 6, depicts the kind of professional prophet who offers a fair prospect to his patrons and so is acceptable to them. The rich have no use for a Micah, for whom to prophesy of ' wine and strong drink ' would be a lie. b

12f. Yahweh's Ingathering of the Scattered Exiles—These two verses, which interrupt 2:11 and 3:1, are of uncertain date. Most probably they are a post-exilic addition, being words of comfort which describe the way in which Yahweh will gather in the exiles of Judah and Israel, as a shepherd gathers his sheep, and bring them back to their home pasture in Palestine. Yahweh will break through the prison of their exile, whence they will emerge under his leadership (Isa. 40:10f., 52:12; Jer 31:10f.). **13. their king** is synonymous with ' the Lord '. If these verses should refer to Judah after 721 B.C., this verse would picture a breaking-out from Jerusalem, in which Judah was obliged, under heavy enemy pressure, to concentrate (Isa. 29:1ff.). The reference may, however, be to Sennacherib's invasion of Judah and the siege of Jerusalem (701 B.C.). Another possibility is that there is no reference here to real historical events, the verses being a piece of post-exilic apocalyptic writing, which treats of things which are to happen in the last days. c

III 1-4 A Condemnation of the Ruling Classes—Micah here condemns those who should, more than others, care about justice, the ' heads of Jacob ' and the ' rulers of the house of Israel ' (1). They have indeed deliberately chosen evil (Am. 5:14), and they go to uttermost lengths in their oppression of their fellow citizens. They who should have been guardians behave like wild beasts, tearing the flesh of the poor and crushing out their life (2f.; Isa. 3:15; Am. 2:7). Their evil deeds will, however, bring upon them fearful punishment, for they will be forsaken of God in their time of need (4; Isa. 1:15). d

5-8 A Condemnation of False Prophets—The prophets who prophesy for reward (2:11) readily prophesy prosperity to their clients if they are well fed by them; if they receive from them less than satisfies them, they ' declare war ' against them, i.e. they subject them to every kind of harm and injury (5). e

553e So the gift of prophecy will be taken from them; it will be 'night' without vision, 'darkness' and no 'divination', and 'seers' and 'diviners' will stand 'disgraced', for they are out of touch with God (6–7). Micah is not accusing these prophets of not having been sent by God. He does not deny to them divinely inspired communications. What he attacks is their corruption of these communications for their own ends. In opposition to these venal prophets, Micah, in full consciousness, claims to be a true prophet of the Lord. He is inspired, not by gifts, but by divine 'power' and a sense of what is right. From Yahweh too comes his moral courage to carry out his difficult mission of declaring to his people their sins (8). He is the agent of, and answerable to, Yahweh alone. **7. cover their lips.** A sign of shame (Lev. 13:45, of a leper) or of mourning (Ezek. 24:17).

f **9-12 The Punishment for the Injustice and False Confidence of the Rulers is the Destruction of Jerusalem**—Verses 9–11 contain a comprehensive denunciation of the unjust rulers of the people—of the rich, who build their houses by means of forced labour and confiscation of the goods of the poor (1 Kg. 21:1ff.; Isa. 5:8; Jer. 22:13; Am. 5:11); of the judges, whose verdict in the courts may be bought for money (Isa. 1:23, 5:23); and of the priests and prophets, who teach and prophesy for gain (Isa. 28:7; contrast Mal. 2:7). These leaders of the people are under the illusion that Yahweh cares nothing for social justice, and that the presence of the Temple in Jerusalem and the worship offered there guarantee them his continuing favour (2:6f.; Jer. 5:12, 7:4). This attitude is the antithesis of the religion of the true prophet, and Micah declares that only the total destruction of Jerusalem, the centre of Judah's sins (1:5), can expiate so heinous an offence (12; Jer. 26:18, see §552*b*).

g **IV 1-5 The New Jerusalem the Religious Centre of the World**—Verses 1–3 = Isa. 2:2–4, save that Mic. 4:4 is omitted in Isaiah. Perhaps these verses are not original either to Micah or Isaiah. Their main thoughts find their parallels in late passages. In this post-exilic section are reflected the hopes and ideals of a devout exile who directs his gaze to the new Jerusalem whither pilgrims from all nations will pour in (Isa. 66:23; Jer. 3:17; Zech. 8:20ff.). Conspicuously high (1; Zech. 14:10), it will be the religious capital of the world, whence Yahweh's teaching and instruction for the good life will flow (2; Isa. 30:20f.). Yahweh will be judge, settling the nations' quarrels, and implements of war will be put to peaceful use, for the threat of war will give place to a state of universal security, when men will no longer be called away from their quiet pursuits for military service (3f.). To **sit under** the **vine** and **fig tree** (4) was a proverbial expression for rural calm and prosperity (1 Kg. 4:25; Zech. 3:10). In verse 5, which is probably a later addition, the writer recognises the reality of other gods worshipped by the heathen. But Yahweh is his God.

h **6-8 The Restoration of Judah**—This section is probably of exilic or post-exilic origin, though a pre-exilic date has been claimed for it (the 'kingdom' is referred to in verse 8). In some respects it resembles 2:12f. (7:12; Ezek. 34:11ff.; Zeph. 3:10). Israel is scattered among the nations, but Yahweh, the shepherd of his flock, will gather them together, the limping with the straying and sickly (rather than 'cast off') sheep, and bring them home again, making them strong and acting as their leader (6f.). **8.** The **tower of the flock** is Jerusalem, the headquarters of Yahweh, Israel's shepherd, whose leadership will be widespread. Shepherds in Israel kept a look-out from wooden structures overlooking sheepfolds against attacks on their sheep by wild beasts (2 Chr. 26:10). **The former dominion** refers to the kingdom under David and Solomon, with Jerusalem as the capital of the whole nation.

i **9-10 Jerusalem's Exile and Deliverance**—Perhaps these verses should be transposed before verses 6ff. They belong to a time when threat of siege hung over Jerusalem, probably to 587 B.C. Jerusalem is all confusion, terror and noise, writhing in agony. There is indeed a king in Jerusalem, namely, Zedekiah, but so weak and helpless is he (Jer. 38:5) that the writer could well ask if there is no 'king' in the capital. Soon the inhabitants of Jerusalem must surrender and leave the city as prisoners and be taken 'to Babylon'. Yahweh, however, will deliver them thence. 553i

554a **IV 11-V 1** (Heb. 4:11–14) **The Destruction of the Nations—11-13** is of an apocalyptic character, and is in marked contrast to verses 9f. There is the familiar figure of the assembling of the nations against Jerusalem, eager to see it defiled and to feast their eyes upon its destruction (7:10). The nations do not, however, understand Yahweh's plan (Isa. 55:8f.), that it is their own destruction which is being divinely prepared (11f.). Jerusalem is ordered by Yahweh to destroy these nations. He will give her the strength—the iron horn and the bronze hoofs—necessary to carry out the order, and the spoil she takes from her enemies shall be consecrated to Yahweh (13). The passage is probably later than Ezekiel, since whose time the idea of enemies assembling against Jerusalem and their destruction was a firm element in Jewish apocalyptic (Ezek. 39:4ff.; Isa. 17:12ff., 41:11ff.; Zech. 12:1ff.). **13. thresh** is a figure for conquering and destroying enemies (Am. 1:3). **horn:** the figure is that of an angry ox goring the foe (Dt. 33:17). **devote.** The custom of consecrating the plunder taken from conquered foes to Yahweh was very old (Jos. 6:24). **Lord of the whole earth** is a post-exilic phrase (Zech. 4:14, 6:5). **5:1**, a fragment of a poem, which, like 9f., has the siege of Jerusalem as its subject, has been added to 4:11–13. Like 9f., it could refer to the siege of Jerusalem by Nebuchadrezzar. Perhaps it should be placed before verse 11. **strike upon the cheek:** a gross insult (Job 16:10).

b **V 2-4** (Heb. 5:1–3) **The Promised Messiah**—The exile and the return to Jerusalem are here presupposed. A Messiah, who will belong to one of the oldest families, that of David (Ezek. 34:23f.; Am. 9:11), will come out of 'Bethlehem Ephrathah', despite its insignificance (2; Mt. 2:5). Until his birth Israel will be given up by Yahweh (3). But the Messiah will later restore the fortunes of both Israel and Judah, for his greatness will extend to the ends of the world (Zech. 9:10), and peace and security will be enjoyed everywhere (4). **2. Bethlehem** is probably an explanatory gloss on Ephrathah, the latter being a name of Bethlehem. Or perhaps Ephrathah was the name of a district, to which Bethlehem belonged (Ru. 1:2, 4:11; 1 Sam. 17:12). **for me:** Yahweh is the speaker. **3. the rest of his brethren:** perhaps an allusion to Isa. 7:3.

c **5-6** (Heb. 4–5) **Overthrow of Assyria—And this shall be peace** (5) is an editorial introduction to the rest of the section, which may have belonged to a longer poem dating from the time of Sennacherib's invasion of Palestine (701 B.C.). This dating is preferable to a later date. The verses can hardly belong to the preceding section, for there is no mention of the Messiah. Here it is the people who speak. They are confident that they will not lack the leaders to defeat the Assyrian attack and to take the war into the enemy's camp and destroy him. **5. seven . . . eight** is a Hebrew mode of indicating an indefinite number (Prov. 30:15, 18, 21, 29; Ec. 11:2; Am. 1:3); whatever the demand for leaders may be, it will be met. **shepherds, princes** are terms for leaders (Ezek. 34; Zech. 11). **princes of men** are perhaps leaders chosen from the ranks of the populace, not from princely families. **6. land of Nimrod** is Assyria (Gen. 10:8f.).

d **7-9** (Heb. 6–8) **The Remnant of Yahweh's People will overcome all Nations**—These verses are post-exilic in origin. Israel, dispersed throughout

554d the world, is the subject of two similes which picture her victory over the nations. First, the remnant is likened to the 'dew' and the 'showers', which come from Yahweh and which make the 'grass' grow; the grass needs no human help. So, through Yahweh's, not man's, favour, the power of the remnant will increase, and her victory over the nations be made sure (7). Secondly, the remnant is likened to a destroying 'lion' among defenceless sheep; the nations are powerless before Israel's supreme might (8; Hos. 5:14). 9 is probably an editorial addition which may originally have followed 4:13.

e **10-15** (Heb. 9-14) **Israel's Punishment**—In this denunciation of Israel's sins, which may be pre-exilic in origin, though an exilic or post-exilic date has been assigned to it, Yahweh declares that he will remove from Israel means for waging war (10 f.), 'sorceries' and 'soothsayers' (12), and the furniture of idolatry (13f.). **10. horses, chariots,** for war purposes (Isa. 2:7, 31:1; Zech. 9:10). **11. cities** means fortified cities. **12. from your hand.** Perhaps a reference to manipulation on the part of the sorcerers. **13f. pillars.** Upright standing stone pillars (Gen. 28:18; Dt. 16:22), and sacred wooden posts ('Asherim') were a regular feature of Canaanite shrines (Exod. 34:13). **cities.** Better 'sacrificial stones' (T. H. Gaster, JTS 38 (1937), 163, without the usual recourse to emendation of the MT). **15** may be a later addition. It might more suitably follow 5:8. The heathen ought to recognise Yahweh as the true God of the world; if they will not hear, then destruction is their fate (Isa. 60:12). Yahweh desires a world-wide kingdom.

f **VI 1-5 Yahweh's Lawsuit against Israel**—This section is probably post-exilic, but a pre-exilic origin is possible. It is independent of 6–8, being probably a fragment of a longer address whose conclusion has not been preserved.

The law-court scene between Yahweh and Israel is frequent in prophetic literature (Isa. 3:13ff., 5:3ff., 43:26; Jer. 25:31; Hos. 4:1, 12:2. See B. Gemser, 'The *rîb*—or controversy—pattern in Hebrew mentality', in *Wisdom in Israel and in the Ancient Near East* (*Supplements to Vetus Testamentum III* (1955), 120–137)). Here Yahweh is both prosecutor and judge, and Israel the defendant. 1a is spoken by the prophet to the people, and 1bc and 2 by Yahweh to the prophet, who, as Yahweh's representative, argues his case before the 'mountains' who are the witnesses. The mountains are older than man, and have known all Israel's history, and are therefore good judges as to Yahweh's righteousness. 3–5 contain Yahweh's case against Israel. Has he, he challenges Israel, ever 'wearied' them, by making too hard demands upon them (Isa. 43:23; Jer. 7:22), or by not fulfilling his promises (Jer. 2:31)? Did he not deliver them from Egypt (Exod. 3ff.), send them leaders, 'Moses, Aaron and Miriam' (the two last named are mentioned only here in the whole of the prophetic literature; Exod. 15:20; Ps. 77:20), turn Balaam's curse into a blessing (Num. 22ff.), and make possible the crossing of the Jordan 'from Shittim to Gilgal' (Jos. 3:1–4:20)? By all these acts of salvation Israel should know her obligation to Yahweh (Dt. 8:2). It is not actually stated that this obligation has been unfulfilled by Israel It. has to be inferred. **2. you enduring foundations:** perhaps better 'hear, ye foundations'; the foundations of the earth are the mountains or their bases. **5. from Shittim to Gilgal** is probably a later gloss by someone who missed a reference to the crossing of the Jordan. Shittim, east of Jordan, was the last camping-station in Moab before the Jordan was crossed; Gilgal was the first station west of the river.

g **6-8 Yahweh's Demands**—These verses are an independent fragment. The reference to child sacrifice in verse 7 suggests a date in the reign of Manasseh (692–639 B.C.; 2 Kg. 21:6). It is doubtful, however, whether Micah lived on into his reign. The omission of Manasseh's name from the superscription (1:1) may be an argument against the probability that 554g he did. Possibly the reign of Ahaz (2 Kg. 16:3) is the background of these verses. The fragment could thus originate from the period in which Micah lived, and could indeed come from the prophet himself, though the style, vocabulary, and the note of tenderness which it displays hardly favour its ascription to him. By some it is regarded as post-exilic.

The people ask the prophet how it can atone for its sins. Shall it come before Yahweh with 'burnt offerings' and 'calves', 'thousands of rams', 'ten thousand rivers of oil', and, the crescendo heightening, the sacrifice of the 'first-born' (6f.)? The prophet's answer (8) is that Yahweh's demand is not for more and more offerings, but for the doing of justice, the pursuit of kindness, and the exercise of humble piety. Micah's reply is the very opposite of the popular view of religion, that all that Yahweh requires of men is a constant and unceasing supply of offerings. Yahweh, the lord of universal morality, demands first of all morality from men. In his reply the prophet provides a comprehensive summary of the teaching of Amos (5:24), Hosea (6:6, 11:1, 8) and Isaiah (6:5, 29:19), which is the finest guide to practical religion to be found in the OT. It has something of the sound of a catechetical lesson for the young; cp. Prov. 15:8, 21:3, 27. **6. calves a year old** are more valuable than younger ones (Lev. 9:3). **8. walk humbly.** The Heb. phrase means literally 'walk carefully, circumspectly, guardedly' (see JJS, i, 4 (1949), 182–6).

9-16 The Dishonest Traders of Jerusalem and their Punishment—These rather obscure verses, 555a which recall 2:1ff., consist of several fragments which have no connection with what precedes. Verse 12 should perhaps be placed before verse 10. The section is probably pre-exilic, and the ideas are Mican, but the language may be an argument against attributing it to the prophet.

The attack here is upon the traders of Jerusalem. They have amassed wealth by dishonesty in their commercial transactions, they have used false weights and measures (10f.; Dt. 25:13ff.; Prov. 20:10; Am. 8:5). But punishment will overtake them (13), and in the face of the advancing enemy the harvest will be interrupted, the 'olives' and 'grapes' trod but not enjoyed, and there will be near-starvation (14f.). The Hebrew text of verse **14** suggests that the reference may be to a decrease in the birth-rate and the destruction of even those who are born. **16** may be a later addition. The condemnation of the keeping of 'the statutes of Omri' and 'all the works of the house of Ahab' may refer to the cult of the Baal. In 1 Kg. 16:25f. Omri is roundly condemned. As the founder of a dynasty in northern Israel, he may be taken to represent all in the life of the Northern Kingdom which ultimately brought about its downfall. Ahab is likewise condemned in 1 Kg. 16:30 ff. Perhaps his ill-treatment of Naboth (1 Kg. 21) is in mind here. **hissing.** A sign of scorn (Jer. 25:9, 51:37). **9. city.** In the OT Jerusalem is only rarely referred to as 'the city' (Ezek. 7:23); it is similarly referred to in the Lachish letters. **tribe.** Judah is addressed. **assembly of the city** is the general meeting of Jerusalem's citizens for the deliberation of their affairs.

VII 1-4 Lament for Jerusalem's Injustice and its Punishment to Come—These verses, which have b no connection with chapter 6, may be pre-exilic in origin, and may be the work of Micah, though they recall later passages like Isa. 56:10 ff., 57:1f., 59:1f. The text is badly preserved, especially in verses 3f. The prophet thinks of himself as one who, 'when the summer fruit has been gathered' and the vintage gleaned, can find no grapes or early fig to eat (1; Isa. 28:4; for the comparison of Judah and Jerusalem with a vineyard, cp. Isa. 5:1ff., 27:2ff.). He can find no 'godly' or 'upright' man (Jer. 5:1ff.) in the land, only murder and self-seeking (2). The 'prince', in his capacity as judge (2 Sam. 15:2ff.; 1 Kg. 3:16ff.), and the 'judge' likewise, look for bribes, and the

555b leaders have only to express their desire, however evil, for it to be done (3). But the best of them are no better than briers and thorns (2 Sam. 23:6), which will take fire at once when the day of punishment foretold by the prophets arrives (4; for prophets as 'watchmen', cp. Isa. 21:6; Jer. 6:17; Ezek. 3:17; Hab. 2:1).

c **5-7 Universal Mistrust**—These verses, probably of post-exilic date, are a parallel to 7:1–4 rather than a continuation of it. There is mistrust everywhere—of neighbours, friends, even of one's own wife (5; the ascending scale is noteworthy). There is no honouring of parents (the great Semitic virtue, Exod. 20:12, 21:15, 17; Dt. 21:18ff.); 'son' and 'daughter' show no respect for 'father' or 'mother', and the 'daughter-in-law' defies her 'mother-in-law'. 'A man's enemies' include the servants of the house as well as his near relatives (6; Job 19:15). The dissolution of social and family ties is complete. **7** is probably an addition by a pious scribe who, in the midst of universal mistrust, expresses his own trust in Yahweh who may be relied upon to hear his prayer.

d **8-10 Israel's Deliverance from the Heathen**—These verses, which form an independent unity, probably of exilic or post-exilic origin, contain the first of three songs which tell of the superiority of Zion over the heathen. Zion is here represented as an individual taking up a lament. The enemy, possibly Edom, derides Zion, asking where her God is (10). Zion retorts that, though she fall, she will rise again; she will emerge from the 'darkness' of calamity to the 'light' of salvation (8; Isa. 42:16, 60:1ff.). She has had to bear this calamity, not because of any virtue on the part of the enemy, but because of her sins against God, which she now confesses. Yahweh is about to execute judgment on her behalf, and will deliver her from enemy oppression. Then the tables will be turned, and Zion will gloat over the discomfiture of her foes (9f.; Ps. 25:2, 30:2, 35:19, 24; Ob. 12f.).

e **11-13 Jerusalem Restored: Return of the Exiles**—This is the second of the three songs. Verses 11f. can hardly be later than the time of Nehemiah, in whose days the walls of Jerusalem were rebuilt (Ezr. 4:7ff.; Neh. 1ff.). The song may belong to the period of Nehemiah or it may be earlier, but it is hardly earlier than the exile. In verse 11 Jerusalem is addressed. Her 'walls' are to be rebuilt (Ps. 102:13ff., 147:2), and her border will be greatly extended, an idea often associated with the coming of the Messianic age (Isa. 26:15; Am. 9:12; Ob. 19f.; Zech. 2:4, 10:10). Peoples from all parts of the world will come to the restored capital, from 'Assyria to Egypt', i.e. from north to south, and from Tyre (so read for 'Egypt', with LXX) to the 'River' (the Euphrates), i.e. from west to east (12; Isa. 27:12f.; 555e Ezek. 34:13; Zech. 10:8ff.). **12. from sea to sea** probably refers to the Mediterranean and the Persian Gulf, but it may also be a general phrase indicating world-wide extent. Probably no definite 'mountains' are in mind. **13** may be a later addition. **The earth** refers, not to Palestine, but to the heathen lands outside it. The fate which was promised the heathen in verse 10 has overtaken them.

14-20 Israel's Prayer for Yahweh's Forgiveness—This, the third song, is a kind of psalm (Ps. f 95:7, 100:3, 106:7ff.), and may be assigned to the late post-exilic period. It begins with a prayer to Yahweh to 'shepherd' his people (Gen. 49:24; Ps. 23:4), who are the 'flock' of his 'inheritance' (Dt. 9:29; Ps. 28:9, 74:1). For the moment Israel dwells alone on the wooded hills (3:12), surrounded by 'garden land', to which access is denied her by her enemies. Israel's prayer is that Yahweh will again give her the fat pasture land of 'Bashan' and 'Gilead' which she once possessed (14; Jer. 50:19). The acts which Yahweh will perform will be as awe-inspiring as when he wrought the miracle of bringing Israel out of Egypt (6:4), and the nations who see them will be thrown into confusion, 'lay their hands on their mouths', i.e. be reduced to silence (Jg. 18:19; Job 21:5, 29:9), and suffer loss of hearing (15f.). They will prostrate themselves in the dust in terrified submission to Yahweh (17). The next three verses (18ff.) are praise to Yahweh as the only God who forgives sins. He has no equal (Ps. 86:8, 89:6; Isa. 43:11); there is a limit to his anger; he will annul Israel's sins, and he will manifest his 'faithfulness' and 'steadfast love' to the descendants of 'Jacob' and 'Abraham' in accordance with his earlier promises (Gen. 22:15ff.; Ps. 105:8ff.; Isa. 41:8ff.). **19. tread iniquities under foot** is a unique expression in the OT; sins are personified as enemies also in Gen. 4:7; Ps. 65:3.

Bibliography—Commentaries: J. A. Bewer, *Harper's Bible* (1949); K. Marti, KHC (1904); T. H. Robinson, HAT (1938, 2nd ed. 1953); E. Sellin, KAT (2nd ed. 1930); J. M. P. Smith, ICC (1912); G. W. Wade, WC (1925); A. Weiser, ATD (1949, 2nd ed. 1956).

Other Literature: G. R. Driver, 'Linguistic and Textual Problems: Minor Prophets II', JTS 39 (1938), 264–8; K. Elliger, 'Die Heimat des Propheten Micha', ZDPV 57 (1934), 81–152; J. Jeremias, 'Moreseth-Gath, die Heimat des Propheten Micha', PJB 29 (1933), 42–53; J. Lindblom, *Micha, literarisch untersucht* (Acta Acad. Aboensis, Humaniora vi, 2 (1929)); W. Robertson Smith and T. K. Cheyne, EB iii (1911).

NAHUM

By J. P. HYATT

556a The book of Nahum is unique among the books of the OT classified as prophets. Here the reader finds no condemnation of Israel and no call to repentance or reform, but a series of poems exulting over the fall of Nineveh, capital of the Assyrian Empire.

Nineveh fell to the Babylonians and Medes in the late summer (July-August) of 612 B.C. The capture of the city is recorded in the Babylonian Chronicle which says that the Babylonians and Medes turned the city into ruins and heaps of debris, and captured many prisoners, although the king of Assyria and his army escaped (see ANET, 304f.).

b According to a widely prevalent view, the work of Nahum of Elkosh consists of 1:11, 14, 2:1, 3–13, 3:1–19. He addresses Nineveh in the second person, and then proceeds to describe in vivid terms the sack of the city and exile of her citizens. Then, in ch. 3, he pronounces woe upon the bloody city, attributing her destruction to her 'harlotries'. He asserts it is Yahweh, the God of Israel, who causes Nineveh's punishment.

To the work of Nahum a later writer has prefixed a poem, 1:2–10, which is an alphabetic acrostic—at least in part. Approximately fifteen letters of the Heb. alphabet are used, but the order has been disturbed. Possibly the editor who found and used this poem did not understand its acrostic form; or perhaps it has been marred by copyists. The Heb. text of this section is very poorly preserved. According to the general view, 1:12, 13, 15 and 2:2 were interpolated within Nahum's long poem, largely to promise hope to Judah, probably by the editor who prefixed the acrostic poem.

c It is certain that Nahum lived near the time of the fall of Nineveh in 612 B.C., but did he prophesy before, during, or after that event? Did he actually predict Nineveh's fall, or only describe it after the event? Scholars have been divided on the answers to these questions. Those who believe he lived before the capture of Assyria's capital point to the verses which use the Heb. imperfect, most naturally translated by the English future tense—2:13, 3:5–7, 11, 15. Others who believe that the prophecy was composed *post eventum* point to the vivid and realistic details in sections such as 2:1, 3–10, 3:1–4, 12–13, 18–19. According to the principles of Heb. grammar, the imperfect verbs may be translated by the present tense in English. It is possible, therefore, that Nahum began to write—or proclaim his message orally—during the siege of Nineveh, and completed his work after the successful capture. At any event, the last two verses appear to look backward to Nineveh's fall rather than forward.

d The view which is generally prevalent concerning the composition of this book has been contested by some scholars. In 1907 Haupt offered the theory that the book is a liturgy of four poems composed for the celebration of Nicanor's Day in 161 B.C., incorporating two poems written by an eye-witness of Nineveh's fall. P. Humbert believes that the book was a prophetic liturgy composed *after* the fall of Nineveh, to be used at the Jewish New Year Festival in the autumn of 612.

Haldar has advanced the theory that the book originated in an association of cult prophets who made use of ancient mythical and ritualistic themes, for the purpose of propaganda against Assyria and holding 556d
out hope of national restoration of Judah. In his theory the poems were composed shortly before 612 and, though they made use of ritualistic themes, they were not intended for use in the Temple liturgy.

Superficially, Nah. appears to have little or no e
religious value. The author has even been classed among the nationalistic 'false prophets' who were condemned by such men as Micah and Jeremiah. However, this is too harsh a judgment. Nahum may have been a cult prophet associated with the Temple. He had a strong sense of the sovereignty of God, and of Yahweh's lordship of history. Yahweh controls the history of the mighty Assyria as well as of Judah. Also, the book is a great rebuke of militarism, illustrating the principle, 'All who take the sword will perish by the sword' (Mt. 26:52). The Assyrians were known as one of the most cruel and ruthless people of the ancient world.

This book contains some of the finest poetry in the OT, particularly the sections in chs. 2 and 3 usually attributed to Nahum. The poetry is vigorous, concrete, and concise. The staccato effect of lines such as those in 2:1, 3–9, 3:1–3 is well reproduced in RSV. As a martial poet the author ranks alongside, or only a little below, the one who composed the Song of Deborah in Jg. 5.

I 1 Title—Nahum means 'comforter'; it may 557a
not have been the prophet's birth name, but one given to him because of the nature of his message, which gave comfort to Judah. **Elkosh:** the location is not certainly known. Since at least the 16th cent. A.D., legend has placed the tomb of Nahum at Al-Qûsh, near Nineveh, and some scholars have thought the prophet lived in Mesopotamia. Jerome located the site in Galilee. Most likely it was in south-west Judah, near the site of ancient Eleutheropolis, modern Beit Jibrîn.

2-10 The Avenging Wrath of Yahweh—Yahweh is a jealous and vengeful God, who marches through whirlwind and storm to destroy the enemy, but is a stronghold to those who trust in him. This section contains the fragments of an alphabetic acrostic poem. Some fifteen letters of the Heb. alphabet are used to begin lines, but they are not all in correct order. Probably an editor used part of an old poem which is here imperfectly preserved.

2b is apparently the N stanza, and perhaps should follow 9*a*. **3b-5** reminds one of the Nature theophanies in the OT; cf. Dt. 33:2; Jg. 5:4–5; Isa. 50:2; Hab. 3:3–15; Zech. 9:14. **9. he will not take vengeance twice on his foes:** this translation is based on emendation of the Heb. text, which may be rendered: 'affliction will not arise twice'. Humbert interprets this line to mean that Nineveh has already been destroyed, and will not be destroyed twice.

I 12f., 15, II 2 Comfort for Judah—These verses b
have a common theme, comfort and hope for Judah, which will not suffer again at the hands of wicked Assyria. They are generally considered to be late interpolations of the poetry of the prophet Nahum, probably by the editor who prefixed the acrostic poem, or by others as a series of marginal notes. This view is somewhat strange, since in point of fact the oppres-

557b sion of Judah did not cease with the destruction of Nineveh ; the oppression by the Babylonians proved to be far worse than that of the Assyrians, culminating in the capture of Jerusalem and loss of independence. The verses could be original ; the poet addresses Assyria in 1:11, 14 and Judah in 1:12–13, 15. **15a** is very similar to Isa. 40:9, 52:7. The **good tidings** is news of the destruction of Nineveh. **Keep your feasts, O Judah:** if original, these words indicate the friendliness of Nahum to the temple ritual ; he may have been a temple prophet. **the wicked:** Heb. 'Belial', an evil spirit, eventually a synonym of Satan. **2:2** seems very much like a late interpolation, looking forward to the restoration of both Judah and Israel, the Southern and Northern Kingdoms.

c **I 11, 14 Nineveh's Crime and Punishment**—Nineveh is addressed in the second person in both of these verses. One came out from Nineveh plotting evil against Yahweh, but now Nineveh's name is to be uprooted and she is to be destroyed. According to the prevalent interpretation, these are the opening words of Nahum, so far as his words are now preserved. **11.** The reference is to an Assyrian king who plotted evil against Judah, probably Sennacherib, who invaded the land in 701 B.C. (cf. Isa. 10:5ff.). **14.** The second person pronouns are pointed as masculine, signifying the king of Assyria, or the people of Assyria personified ; some scholars would point as feminine, and make the reference be to Nineveh. The Assyrian idols will be powerless before Yahweh.

d **II 1, 3-5 The Attack on Nineveh**—In a passage of great effectiveness the poet describes the irresistible attack of the army on Nineveh.

1. The shatterer is the army of Babylonians and Medes under their kings Nabopolassar and Cyaxares. In the second half of the verse, the Heb. uses the so-called infinitive absolute, which expresses the force of the verbs with great emphasis. **4. The chariots** are those of the attackers rather than defenders. **5. the mantelet:** the meaning of the Heb. *sōkhēkh* is not certainly known. The literal meaning is 'a coverer' ; it probably refers to a siege engine, with battering-ram, of the type known from Assyrian wall sculptures ; see ANEP (1954), Nos. 367–9, 372–3.

e **6-9 Flight and Capture**—These verses depict vividly the capture and plundering of Nineveh, and the flight and exiling of her people. **7. its mistress:** the meaning of Heb. *huṣṣabh* is quite uncertain. Some take it to refer to the Assyrian queen, others to an Assyrian goddess, perhaps Ishtar. Haldar thinks it means the statue of a deity. In form it appears to be the hoph'al of a verb *nāṣabh* meaning 'set up, establish'. Many scholars emend the Heb. to read *hûṣ*[e]*'āh*, 'she was taken away'.

10-13 Nineveh's Desolation—This is a mocking lament over the desolation of Nineveh. Lions figure prominently in Assyrian sculptures and inscriptions. Here the Assyrian army is represented under the figure of a lion that returns after its depradations to its den—that is, Nineveh the capital. **12** represents the ferocity and ruthlessness of the Assyrian army. **13.** It is Yahweh, **the Lord of hosts,** who is really in control; he destroys the place of refuge to which the Assyrian plunderers were accustomed to return.

f **III 1-7 'Woe to the Bloody City'**—This is a new description of Nineveh's fall, with addition of the reason for it—the 'harlotries' she has practised. **2-3** are an unusually effective description of the tumult and confusion at the capture of Nineveh ; there is a staccato rhythm, and piling up of nouns with few verbs. **4.** Assyria is being punished **for the countless harlotries of the harlot,** who had seduced and bewitched other nations by her guiles and charms. The figure of the harlot is applied elsewhere to Israel (Hos. 2:5), Jerusalem (Ezek. 16:15), Babylon (i.e. Rome, Rev. 18:3) and others. **5-6** describe the punishment which Nineveh as a wicked harlot must receive. She is represented as being treated in the manner which was customary for a harlot or adulteress ; cf. Jer. 13:22–7 ; Ezek. 16:37–43 ; Hos. 2:3, 9. 557f

8-10 Nineveh is not better than Thebes—Thebes (Heb. *No-Amon*, 'City of Amun') was the Egyptian capital, situated on the Nile in southern Egypt ; it was captured by Ashurbanipal, the Assyrian king, in 663 B.C. It was long one of the world's leading cities. At the time of its capture Egypt was ruled by kings from **Ethiopia** ; she received help from **the Libyans** on the west. **Put** cannot be certainly located. In Gen. 10:6 Put is one of the sons of Ham, along with Ethiopia (Cush), Egypt, and Canaan. It may have been Somaliland on the Red Sea. For all her strength Thebes was carried away and captured ; Nineveh cannot expect a better fate. g

III 11-19 Nineveh must fall—11. You also will be drunken: drunkenness, caused by drinking from the cup of Yahweh's fury, was a figure of divine condemnation and punishment ; cf. Ps. 75:8 ; Isa. 51:17, 22 ; Jer. 25:15–29 ; Lam. 4:21 ; Ezek. 23:32–4 ; Hab. 2:16. **12-13** emphasise the weakness of Nineveh, and the ease with which it could be captured. The picture is exaggerated ; though Assyria had been declining in strength since the death of Ashurbanipal, Nineveh did make a fairly strong stand against her enemies. **14** seems to refer to preparations to withstand siege ; the arrangement of the various parts of the poetry is not chronological. **15a-17.** In spite of its great numbers of people, Nineveh will not prevail against the enemy. **16.** Probably the first line should be emended to read as imperative : 'Increase your merchants'. **18. O King of Assyria** is a gloss ; it is the nation that is being addressed. The king himself was considered to be a 'shepherd'. **18-19** appear to have been written after Nineveh's fall, and are considered by some scholars to be secondary. This view is hardly necessary ; the poet-prophet may well have written in part after the fall ; see §556*cd*. h

Bibliography—COMMENTARIES : A. B. Davidson, CB (1920) ; S. R. Driver, Cent.B ; K. Elliger, ATD (3rd ed. 1956) ; A. van Hoonacker, EBib. (1908) ; F. Horst, HAT (2nd ed. 1954) ; W. A. Maier (1959) ; K. Marti, KHC (1904) ; W. Nowack, HKAT (3rd ed. 1922) ; E. Sellin, KAT (3rd ed. 1930) ; J. M. P. Smith, ICC (1911) ; C. L. Taylor, IB (1956).

OTHER LITERATURE : A. Haldar, *Studies in the Book of Nahum* (1947); P. Haupt, 'The Book of Nahum', JBL 26 (1907), 1–53 ; P. Humbert, 'Le problème du livre de Nahoum', RHPR 12 (1932), 1–15.

HABAKKUK

By J. P. HYATT

558a Habakkuk is the sceptic among the prophets. He raises the question of theodicy: how can a just God allow the wicked to oppress the righteous? His answer, given in 2:4, has become one of the most frequently quoted verses of the Bible, but not quite in the meaning intended.

The book opens with a complaint regarding the oppressions of the wicked (1:2–4), and foretells the coming of the Chaldaeans as agents of divine justice (1:5–11); then abruptly the question is raised as to how a just and pure God can permit the wicked to oppress the righteous (1:12–17). In 2:1–5 the answer is given: judgment will come in time upon the wicked, and in the meantime the righteous man lives by his faithfulness. A series of five Woes are hurled at the wicked (2:6–20). The book closes with a splendid poetical description of Yahweh's march from Sinai to save his people (ch. 3).

b This book gives the impression of being well unified, and some scholars insist that the whole book was written by a single man for a specific historic occasion. Yet, when one studies carefully the separate parts, several questions arise: Is the oppressor of 1:2–4 a foreign nation, or some element in Judah? If the Chaldaeans are represented in 1:5–11 as a divine agent to deliver from oppression, how can they be represented in 1:12–17 as wicked conquerors? Against whom are the Woes of 2:6–20 directed? What is the relevance of the psalm of ch. 3 to the historic situation of chs. 1–2? Many different answers have been proposed to these questions.

c According to Karl Budde, the oppressors of Judah are the Assyrians, from whom the Chaldaeans will deliver the Jews. The date of the book, then, was about 615 B.C. According to other scholars, Hab. 1:5–10, and perhaps 1:14–17 in an earlier form, were anonymous prophecy used by the prophet Habakkuk, who lived shortly before the time of Cyrus the Great.

The prophecy is assigned to the Greek period, about 331 B.C., by Duhm and C. C. Torrey, who maintain that the word *Kittîm*, 'Greeks', originally stood in 1:6, where the Heb. text now has 'Chaldaeans'; and, according to Torrey, at 2:5 the original reading was *hay'wānî*, 'the Greek', where *hayyayin*, 'wine', now stands.

d P. Humbert, in a full-length study (1944), maintains that Habakkuk was a cultic prophet who received a revelation in the Temple and wrote his book (all three chapters, with only a few glosses) to be performed as a liturgy in 602–601 B.C. The oppressive tyrant from whom the Chaldaeans are expected to give deliverance is none other than King Jehoiakim of Judah, who is the wicked one of 1:2–4, 12–17, 2:6–19.

The older view, represented by S. R. Driver and others, is probably correct. The first complaint, 1:2–4, has to do with internal corruption rather than a foreign enemy. 1:5–11 was delivered sometime after the Battle of Carchemish in 605 B.C. Later the disillusioned prophet wrote 1:12–17 when the Chaldaeans proved to be oppressive. Still later are 2:1–5 and whatever is genuine in 2:6–20; the Woes may be later than 597 B.C. when the Chaldaeans first took Jerusalem. Thus Habakkuk's prophetic career spanned a long time, perhaps from early in Jehoiakim's reign to near the fall of Jerusalem. It hardly seems appropriate for a message such as his to have been used as a Temple liturgy, and only by a *tour de force* can Jehoiakim be made the wicked tyrant of the book, though it is not impossible that 2:9–11 may have been spoken against him. 558d

Ch. 3 is quite different in tone from the first two chapters, and has the kind of apparatus, including musical directions, that is found with many of the Psalms. It is probably secondary, but it does employ some very early mythological themes. Some recent critics, such as W. F. Albright and P. Humbert, believe Habakkuk was author of the psalm (see §559*f*). e

Among the scrolls found in the first cave at Wâdī Qumrân (the so-called 'Dead Sea Scrolls') was a *pēsher* (commentary) on Habakkuk 1–2. This work sought to explain how Habakkuk had prophesied events happening in or near the interpreter's own day. E.g. the Chaldaeans of 1:6 are explained as the *Kittî'îm*, the Seleucid Greeks or, possibly, the Romans, who invaded Palestine. The Qumrân scroll is valuable for correction of the MT at a few points which will be noted below. Complete absence of ch. 3 from this scroll does not necessarily prove that it was not recognised as part of the prophetic book when the *pēsher* was composed; it may be that the interpreter of chs. 1–2 could not use ch. 3 for his purpose.

I 1 Title—Habakkuk: the name appears in LXX as *Hambakoum*; it may be related to the Akkad. *ḫabbaququ* (or *ḫambaququ*), the name of a garden plant and a fruit tree. Nothing is known about the prophet outside this book, except in legends which arose at a later time. In Bel, one of the apocryphal additions to Dan., it is said that he was of the tribe of Levi, and that he was transported by an angel of the Lord, by the hair of his head, from Judah to Babylon in order to feed Daniel in the lions' den. The same legend appears in *The Lives of the Prophets*, preserved in Gr., where he is said to be from the tribe of Simeon (see ed. by C. C. Torrey (1946), 43–4). 559a

2-4 Complaint against Yahweh for tolerating Wrong—In bitter remonstrance with Yahweh, the prophet asks how long he must cry out for help and look on trouble, destruction, violence, and the failure of the law while Yahweh remains indifferent or powerless. While this is often interpreted as referring to conditions created by an external enemy, it is more likely to refer to internal strife and wrong-doing. This is made almost certain by **4** with its reference to **the law** and the failure of **justice**. Those who think this book is a liturgy interpret this as a collective complaint, uttered by the prophet in the first person as representative of the community.

5-11 The Chaldaeans as Ministers of Divine Justice—Yahweh addresses the evil-doers (in second person plural), warning them he is about to perform a work they would never have believed: he is raising against them the dread power of the Chaldaeans, who are already carrying destruction to the ends of the earth. Chaldaea was a province of southern Babylonia. By 626 B.C. the Chaldaean Nabopolassar established the independence of the kingdom of Babylonia from Assyria, and began to plan an attack on Assyria, whose capital, Nineveh, fell in 612 B.C. to the Babylonians b

559b and Medes. In 605 B.C. at the Battle of Carchemish, the Babylonians decisively defeated the Assyrians and Egyptians, and began to invade Syria and Palestine. The date of this oracle is probably soon after that time. From 605 to 597, the Chaldaeans invaded Syria-Palestine nearly every year, to keep the inhabitants reminded of Babylonian power.

5. Look among the nations: LXX reads 'Look, ye faithless ones'; this may be correct, for it seems to be supported by the comment on this verse in the Qumrân scroll, though the text of the verse is largely missing. **6.** The description here and in the following verses could actually fit either the Chaldaeans or the Greeks. **9. terror of them goes before them:** the translation is very uncertain. The third word in Heb. can mean 'eastward'. Duhm emends the first word *m^{e}ghammath* to *miggōmer*, translating 'from Gomer (Cappadocia) they march eastward', and interprets the sentence as describing the eastward march of Alexander's armies. **10. they heap up earth:** for a siege mound; those who date Habakkuk in the Greek period think this refers to Alexander's siege of Tyre. **11. Then they sweep by like the wind and go on:** translation is uncertain. Heb. is lit. 'Then wind (or spirit) moves past and goes by'. The reference could be to a change of purpose by the invader. **guilty men:** instead of MT *w^{e}'āshēm*, the Qumrân scroll has *wysm*, probably to be read *w^{e}yāśîm*. So translate 'and this one (i.e. the Chaldaean nation) makes his might his God'.

c **12-17 Remonstrance with Yahweh over the Inhumanity of the Wicked**—Abruptly the prophet asks the question: Why does the Holy One, whose eyes are too pure to look on evil, look on silently while the wicked swallows up one more righteous than himself? He describes the oppression of the nations with the figure of fish being caught by a fisherman. Almost universally interpreters have thought the wicked here are the Chaldaeans, when the prophet sees that they, although appointed as agents of the divine justice, are less righteous than the Judaeans. It is not likely that the wicked one here was King Jehoiakim, as Humbert believes. The date of this section must be several years after 1:5–11.

12. We shall not die: this is one of the ancient 'emendations of the Scribes' (*tiḳḳûnê sōph^{e}rîm*). The original reading was 'Thou diest not'. Yahweh was an ever-living deity, who did not die periodically as many of the ancient vegetation gods (such as Baal) were believed to do. **14.** The oppression of the Jews and other peoples by the Chaldaeans is vividly portrayed under the figure of the fisherman; it emphasises the helplessness of the victims and cruelty of the conquerors. **16. Therefore he sacrifices to his net:** this is figurative, and we need not search for a literal truth here. Yet, note that Herodotus says the Scythians made an annual sacrifice to a sword as an image of their war god (*History* IV, 62). **17.** In the Qumrân scroll this verse reads: 'Therefore he draws his sword (*ḥrbw*) continually, to slay nations without mercy.' This may have been the original reading, since it has an internal consistency that is lacking in MT (one slays with a sword, not with a net). The verse may be a gloss to explain the figure in 14–16; otherwise the section has two endings, each beginning with 'therefore'. The verse is nevertheless appropriate.

d **II 1-5 The Oracle from Yahweh**—The prophet stations himself on a watch-tower, to seek a revelation from God. The oracle soon comes, and he is asked to write it plainly on tablets, so that one may read it running: 'Behold, he whose soul is not upright in him shall fail, but the righteous shall live by his faithfulness (his loyalty to God and his promises).'

1. I will take my stand to watch etc.—the prophet was often thought of as a watchman; see Isa. 21:6–9, 56:10; Jer. 6:17; Ezek. 3:17; Mic. 7:4. Because of the use of the word *mishmereth* here (usually translated 'watch-tower'), Humbert conjectures that Habakkuk was a cultic prophet, since that word is used for a priestly station or office in 2 Chr. 7:6, 8:14, 35:2; 559d
Neh. 7:3, 13:30. While this is an attractive suggestion, it is not a necessary conclusion. **on the tower:** the Qumrân scroll reads 'my tower', a conjecture already made by some scholars. **I will answer:** Syr. has 'he will answer', probably correctly.

2. make it plain upon tablets: probably tablets e
of wood or stone in a public place, hardly clay tablets; cf. Isa. 8:1, 30:8. Humbert thinks they were tablets in diptych form in the Temple; Habakkuk as a cultic prophet received the oracle in a temple. However, the phrase **so he may run who reads it** suggests a public place in the open, with large characters.

3 is an admonition to have patience. The vision may seem slow in coming, but it is sure to come, since it is Yahweh who makes the revelation.

4 is quite difficult of translation; the meaning, however, is probably expressed in RSV with fair accuracy. The oracle is stated as a general truth, but the application to the question of 1:13, and the relationship between the Chaldaeans and Jews, is immediately apparent. **the righteous shall live by his faith:** the meaning here is not the same as in the NT passages which quote this verse (Rom. 1:17; Gal. 3:11; cf. Heb. 10:38). *'^{e}mûnāh* is faithfulness, moral steadfastness, trustworthiness, loyalty to Yahweh and his covenant, etc. The meaning is close to that of *ḥesedh*, with which this word is often joined. The transition to the NT meaning of trust in a person can be seen in the comment here in the Qumrân scroll: 'Its interpretation concerns all those who observe the *tôrāh* in the house of Judah, whom God will rescue from the house of judgment, because of their toil and their faith in the teacher of righteousness.'

5 is a most difficult verse. The translation of the f
first two lines is uncertain, and the relevance to the preceding or following section is unclear. RSV gives a possible rendering of MT. If correct the meaning is apparently that the oppressor, against whom the following Woes are to be hurled, boasts like a person filled with wine, but is unstable and never satisfied. Instead of the word *hayyayin*, 'wine', the Qumrân scroll has *hôn*, 'wealth'. Though this is usually taken to be a tendentious reading which reflects the Qumrân sect's doctrine of the communal ownership of property, it could be original; if so, the reference is perhaps to the wealth of the Chaldaeans, as compared with the relative simplicity and poverty of the Judaeans. Various emendations have been suggested, such as (1) *hayyôneh*, 'the oppressor'; (2) *hay^{e}wānî*, 'the Greek'; or (3) a reading which makes the first word *hôy*, 'woe', such as 'Woe to the treacherous dealer, the haughty man . . .' **His greed is as wide as Sheol:** Sheol, the place of the dead, is personified and pictured as being insatiable; cf. Prov. 27:20, 30:15–16; Isa. 5:14. The latter part of this seems to be descriptive of the Chaldaeans.

6-20 Woes on the Evil-doer—Five Woes are here g
hurled against an evil-doer (or evil-doers) described as rapacious, unjust, iniquitous, violent, and idolatrous. The literary form is similar to Isa. 5:8–24, where there was originally a series of seven Woes. It is customary to interpret these as directed toward the Chaldaeans, or specifically the Chaldaean king. Humbert thinks King Jehoiakim of Judah was the tyrant against whom they were hurled, but it is hard to believe that vv. 8, 10, with their references to many nations or peoples would fit the Judaean king. It is not necessary to suppose that all of these originated at the same time. 14 is an intrusion from Isa. 11:9, and 18–19 may be much later than the other parts of this section.

6-8 was probably directed against a Babylonian king, such as Nebuchadnezzar, who conquered or exacted tribute from lands that had been under Assyrian control. **9-10** reminds one of the malediction directed against King Jehoiakim in Jer. 22:13–17. This may have been influenced by that passage, but seems to have been directed against a foreign ruler who conquered many peoples. **12-14.** A malediction against

559g one who builds his cities on bloodshed, perhaps by forced labour ; cf. Jer. 22:13, 17 ; Mic. 3:10. **14** is apparently secondary, having little relevance to the context ; it is almost identical with Isa. 11:9.

h **15-17.** The figure here is that of drinking the wine of wrath ; the thought is illuminated by Jer. 25:15–29, by which it may have been influenced. Though generally interpreted as applying to the Chaldaeans, this Woe may have been directed originally against Judaeans, especially in the light of Jer. 25:18, 29. **15. his wrath:** this conjectured reading is supported by the Qumrân scroll. **17** may be out of place ; it is more appropriate after 12–13. **Lebanon** was often a source of cedar-wood for building purposes.

18-19. These verses should be reversed to give a more natural reading, with **Woe** at the beginning. It is somewhat strange that a Jewish prophet should condemn a Chaldaean for idolatry, though of course not impossible. Many interpreters consider these verses secondary, written under the influence of Second Isaiah ; cf. Isa. 41:6–7, 44:9–20, 46:6–7 ; Jer. 10:2–9, etc.

20. Yahweh is Lord of **all the earth** and commands respectful silence, in contrast to the helpless and useless idols. As the book now stands, the verse forms a good transition to the theophany of ch. 3.

i **III The Psalm of Habakkuk**—This is called 'a prayer of Habakkuk', but only v. 2 has the form of a prayer, addressing Yahweh in the second person. Succeeding verses describe in highly imaginative, mythological phrases the coming of Yahweh from the sacred mountain to save his people. The closing verses express the intense joy of the author in his fellowship with God.

A majority of critics deny this poem to the prophet Habakkuk, because of the presence of the liturgical directions in 1, 3, 9, 13, 19, such as many Psalms have ; the absence of indications of historical events, and thus the tenuous relationship to chs. 1–2 ; and the general difference in literary *genre* from the rest of the book. It appears to many critics that the poem originated in post-exilic times, found its way into a collection of poems, where it was provided with notations and attributed to Habakkuk (cf. the ascription of Ps. 146–8 to Haggai and Zechariah in LXX), and it finally became joined to the prophecy of Habakkuk.

j For recent studies see W. A. Irwin, 'The Psalm of Habakkuk', JNES I (1942), 10–40, who sees the influence of the old cosmological myth best known in the Babylonian *Enuma elish* (especially IV, 28–132), and thinks the poem may be of pre-exilic origin ; 559j
and W. F. Albright, 'The Psalm of Habakkuk', in *Studies in OT Prophecy Presented to Professor Theodore H. Robinson*, ed. H. H. Rowley (1950), 1–18, who sees the influence of Old Canaanite (Ugaritic) mythology of the triumph of Baal over the primordial Sea (chaos), especially in 8–15, and thinks it was composed by Habakkuk, a prophet-musician who lived in a strongly archaising period.

It seems possible—if not very probable—that the prophet Habakkuk made use of ancient poems, to which he added 3:16–19. In its present form and position the poem has a powerful message : Yahweh, the God who created the world by subduing Chaos and once delivered his people from the Red Sea, is ever available for the salvation of his people and for fellowship with those who serve him.

1. According to Shigionoth: Ps. 7:1 is called 'a k
Shiggaion of David'. **Shigionoth** is apparently a plural of that word, whose meaning is unknown. **3. Teman:** a synonym here for Edom ; properly a district in the north of Edom. **Mount Paran:** a mountain near, or possibly synonymous with, Sinai (cf. Dt. 33:2). **7. Cushan:** probably not Cush (Ethiopia), but a land near Edom and Midian. **8** reflects the myth of a primordial conflict between a deity and the Sea ; for the Ugaritic myth, see ANET, 129ff. **10.** Cf. Jg. 5:4–5. **11.** Cf. Jos. 10:12–13 ; Ps. 19:4–6. **13. thy anointed:** the people as a whole (as in the first line), or the anointed king. The closest parallels with the Babylonian creation epic are in 13*b*–14. In that epic Marduk splits the skull of Tiamat (IV, 130ff.). **16-19** express the quiet and full confidence of the author (or the community if the poem was used liturgically) in the power of Yahweh.

Bibliography—Commentaries: A. B. Davidson, CB (1920) ; S. R. Driver, Cent.B ; B. Duhm, *Das Buch Habakuk* (1906) ; K. Elliger, ATD (3rd ed. 1956) ; A. van Hoonacker, EBib. (1908) ; F. Horst, HAT (2nd ed. 1954) ; K. Marti, KHC (1904) ; W. Nowack, HKAT (3rd ed. 1922) ; E. Sellin, KAT (3rd ed. 1930) ; C. L. Taylor, IB vi (1956) ; W. H. Ward, ICC (1911).

Other Literature: K. Budde, EB *sub* Habakkuk, and *The Expositor*, Fifth Series, 1 (1895), 372–85 ; K. Elliger, *Studien zum Habukuk-Kommentar vom Toten Meer* (1953) ; P. Humbert, *Problèmes du livre d'Habacuc* (1944); C. C. Torrey, 'Alexander the Great in the OT Prophecies', *Marti Festschrift*, BZAW 41 (1925), 281–6.

ZEPHANIAH

By J. P. HYATT

560a The book of Zephaniah has three divisions that are well defined: ch. 1 describes the coming Day of Yahweh, which is to bring punishment upon Judah and cosmic desolation; ch. 2 extends the scope of the punishment specifically to certain foreign peoples—the Philistine cities, Moab and the Ammonites, the Ethiopians, and Assyria with its capital Nineveh; and ch. 3, after a second pronouncement of woe upon Jerusalem, describes the coming judgment upon the nations, the purification of the speech of the peoples so that all will call upon Yahweh, and the exaltation of Israel when she will be free of her enemies.

The prophet Zephaniah lived in the latter part of the 7th cent. B.C., probably as a contemporary of Jeremiah. It was a time when foreign influence was strong in religion and at the royal court, and hence there was much apostasy from Yahweh, practical scepticism, and social corruption. The first verse states that the word of Yahweh came to Zephaniah 'in the days of Josiah the son of Amon, king of Judah'. Most scholars therefore date this prophet under King Josiah before the Deuteronomic Reformation of 621, when such conditions must have prevailed. Many think that his prophecy was inspired by the invasion of Palestine by the Scythians a few years before that time. A few date the prophet under Josiah after 621 B.C.

b Yet there are difficulties in the generally accepted view, most of which can be resolved by supposing that Zephaniah prophesied under King Jehoiakim (609–598 B.C.), when most of the old pre-Deuteronomic practices were revived and Judah was threatened by the Chaldaeans. There is little reason to believe that Zephaniah's prophecy was inspired by the Scythians. Our information concerning those people is very meagre; in any event they did little damage in Palestine, and none in Egypt. Since they were allied with the Assyrians, we can hardly believe that the prophet predicted they would destroy Assyria (2:13–15). Dating Zephaniah under Jehoiakim enables one to consider as genuine all, or most, of the oracles against foreign nations in ch. 2; otherwise it is difficult to see their appropriateness to the conditions prevalent just before 621. Furthermore this view gives a natural explanation for 'the remnant of Baal' in 1:4, and makes it more likely that the prophet was a descendant of King Hezekiah, who ruled Judah 715–687. 1:1 places him in the fourth generation after Hezekiah. Such a view only requires that 1:1*b* be considered as a late editorial note that is slightly in error.

c Zephaniah the prophet was akin in spirit to Amos and Isaiah, whose influence pervades his work. He was of royal blood, and was intimately acquainted with court circles, concentrating his interest on Jerusalem. His prophecies are characterised by great moral earnestness and a strong sense of judgment, but show little literary distinction, apart from the classic description of the *dies irae* in 1:14–18, and a few vivid figures such as those of 1:12. In both style and thought he is characteristically a prophet of doom. It is generally agreed that 3:14–20 are later than Zephaniah; possibly all of 3:9–20 is late. Yet the prophet occasionally perceived a ray of hope, as in 2:3.

I 1 Title—This is the longest of the prophetic genealogies. **Hezekiah** probably was the king who ruled over Judah 715–687. The other individuals named here are otherwise unknown. **Cushi** is usually a Gentilic, meaning 'the Ethiopian'. 561a

I 2-6 Universal Doom—Yahweh is about to cause universal desolation, which will sweep away men and animals. His hand will be stretched out especially against Judah and Jerusalem for their idolatry and apostasy.

2-3 are denied by some scholars to Zephaniah because they believe he did not prophesy world-judgment, but only the desolation of Judah. This is arbitrary. **4. the remnant of Baal** is most naturally interpreted as referring to the remnants of Baal worship after Josiah's attempted extermination of the false cult in 621 (cf. §560*b*). Some interpret as 'Baal to the last vestige', comparing Isa. 14:22, 17:3; Am. 4:2. **5.** Worship of **the host of the heavens** was a prominent feature of Assyrian religion; it flourished especially under Manasseh (2 Kg. 21:3ff.). **Milcom**: the god of the Ammonites (1 Kg. 11:5, 33; 2 Kg. 23:13). This is the reading of most versions; Heb. has *malkām*, 'their king'.

7-9 The Day of Yahweh's Sacrifice—The day of the Lord is to be a time when he has a great sacrifice for his guests, and punishes various groups for yielding to foreign influences, and for injustice and oppression. **7.** Yahweh's judgment on Judah is represented under the figure of a sacrifice. This figure, first used by Zephaniah, is elaborated in Isa. 34:6; Jer. 46:10; Ezek. 39:17ff.; Rev. 19:17f.; cf. Isa. 25:6. Judah is the victim, but it is not clear who **his guests** are, perhaps the armies of an enemy, such as the Scythians or Babylonians. The details of the figure should not be pressed. On silence at a sacrifice, cf. Hab. 2:20; Zech. 2:13. **9. every one who leaps over the threshold:** the translation and meaning are quite uncertain. The reference may be to some form of social injustice, involving unlawful entry into the homes of the poor; or the reference may be to some cultic act. The threshold was widely held in ancient times to be the abode of spirits and demons; 'leaping over the threshold' may have been a superstitious act to avoid contact with them. The practice may be related to the story in 1 Sam. 5:1–5. Gerleman has suggested the rendering, 'everyone who mounts the pedestal (of an idol)', and thus considers it a form of idol worship. b

10-13 Wailing in Jerusalem—On the day of the Lord wailing is to be heard in various quarters of Jerusalem. **the Fish Gate:** mentioned in Neh. 12:39; apparently in the north wall. **the Second Quarter:** probably a section of the city on the north side; the prophetess Huldah lived there (2 Kg. 22:14). **the hills:** probably a section within the walls of Jerusalem. **11. the Mortar:** thought to have been the upper part of the Tyropoeon Valley within the walls of Jerusalem, a centre of trade and industry. **12. thickening upon their lees:** a figure drawn from wine-making; wine has to be stirred and poured from vat to vat; otherwise it becomes syrupy and sweet, and lacking in strength and proper taste; cf. Jer. 48:11. The figure is used for the slothful and c

561c indifferent people. **Who say in their hearts . . . do ill:** those who deny the power of Yahweh in the lives of men, the morally indifferent. **13. Though they build houses . . . drink wine from them:** derived from Am. 5:11, and placed here by an editor, where it is not appropriate; the day of the Lord is hastening too rapidly for such lines to be in place here.
14-18 The day of the Lord as a dies irae—The day of the Lord is now very near, a day of Yahweh's wrath, of great distress, devastation, defeat, and darkness. This classic description formed the basis of the medieval hymn, 'Dies irae', attributed to Thomas of Celano. Zephaniah has greatly expanded the description in Am. 5:18–20; cf. other descriptions in Isa. 13:6–13; Ezek. 7:5–9; Jl 1:15, 2:1–2. It is difficult to determine whether this was inspired by the danger of invasion by a known enemy such as the Scythians or Babylonians, or by general apocalyptic expectation. **16.** Mention of **trumpet blast and battle cry** suggests a human enemy. **18a** has been interpreted as referring to the time when Psammetichus, king of Egypt, bought off the Scythians, as reported by Herodotus (*History* I, 104–5). On the other hand the prophet clearly predicts universal destruction in 18*b*. Some scholars deny 18*b* to Zephaniah because of the universal scope of Yahweh's destruction which it implies.

d **II 1-3 Summons to seek the Lord in order to avert his Wrath**—The prophet addresses the **shameless nation** to come together and seek to escape the day of Yahweh's wrath, and then addresses specifically the **humble of the land,** admonishing them to seek righteousness and humility. The text of **1-2** is very difficult; some help can be secured from the LXX. It is likely that Judah is addressed, but some scholars believe the 'shameless nation' is the Philistines, referred to in 4–7. **1. Come together and hold assembly:** this translation is very uncertain, and the command is colourless; probably emend to read 'Be ashamed together and feel shame' (*hithbōshᵉshû wābhōshû*). **3** is frequently considered secondary, since 'the humble of the land' developed as a clear-cut group in post-exilic times, when righteousness and humility were greatly emphasised. But there is no valid reason to doubt that Zephaniah held out some hope of escape, particularly for the humble, the opposite of the proud whom he condemned; cf. the similar injunction in Am. 5:6, 14–15.

e **4-7 Oracles against the Philistines**—These people lived in south-western Palestine, originally in a confederation of five cities, of which the four named here were still standing; Gath had been destroyed earlier (2 Chr. 26:6). No bitterness is expressed here against the Philistines. **Ashkelon:** the Scythians are reported by Herodotus to have pillaged the temple of Venus at Ashkelon. Nebuchadnezzar captured and destroyed Ashkelon in 604 B.C. (Wiseman, *Chronicles of Chaldaean Kings* (1956), 69). It was probably from Ashkelon that a king named Adon wrote a letter in Aramaic to the Pharaoh of Egypt appealing for aid against the king of Babylon, found at Saqqârâ (Memphis) in 1942 (Dupont-Sommer, *Semitica* I (1948), 43–68). **5. Cherethites** (Cretans): the Philistines came from the Aegean region, including the island of Crete; cf. 1 Sam. 30:14; Ezek. 25:16. **O Canaan, land of the Philistines:** read 'I will humble you (*'akhnîʿēkh*), O land of the Philistines'. **7.** The first clause and the second sentence are probably post-exilic additions, glorifying the remnant of Judah, whose fortunes are to be restored.

f **8-11 Oracle against Moab and the Ammonites**—Great bitterness is expressed against the people of Moab and Ammon, who lived east of Jordan and the Dead Sea, for their taunts and boasts against the people of Judah; their lands are to be destroyed. This oracle is widely considered to be an addition to Zephaniah, reflecting the bitter feelings in Judah aroused by Moabite and Ammonite invasions of Judah at the time of the Babylonian capture of Jerusalem (Ezek. 25:1–11; cf. Jer. 48:1–49:6). Yet, if this were the occasion, it is strange that there is no oracle 561f
against Edom, which aroused particular hatred in Judah by its invasions at that time (Ps. 137:7–9; Ob.). A more likely occasion is the time of the invasions by bands of Moabites, Ammonites, and others in 602 B.C. (2 Kg. 24:2). If Zephaniah prophesied under Jehoiakim (see §560*b*) this oracle may be a genuine utterance of the prophet. The last sentence in **9** is probably a post-exilic addition, like part of 7 (see above). **11** is prose, and fits the context poorly. It is very probably a post-exilic addition by someone who was influenced by the universalism of Second Isaiah. He conceives the various heathen nations as worshipping Yahweh each in its own land. The word rendered **lands,** *'iyyê*, is a favourite word of Second Isaiah, usually translated 'coastlands' or 'isles' (Isa. 41:1, 5, 42:4, 10, 12, 49:1, 51:5).

12 An Oracle against the Ethiopians—This is a g
very brief and obscure oracle that seems to be only a fragment of a longer oracle directed against the Ethiopians; or it may have been originally written in the margin and subsequently found its way into the text. Ethiopia (Heb. *Kûsh*) was on the southern border of Egypt. It is difficult to determine if this verse refers to inhabitants of that country as such, or if the Egyptians are sarcastically referred to as Ethiopians because Egypt had been ruled by an Ethiopian dynasty 712–663 B.C. (XXV Dynasty). If the latter, the oracle may date from shortly after the Battle of Carchemish in 605 B.C., when the Egyptians and Assyrians were decisively defeated by the Babylonians.
13-15 Oracle against Assyria and Nineveh its Capital—The oracles against foreign nations end with this exultant cry over the destruction of Assyria. **13-14** are cast as prediction, but **15** has the tone of accomplished fact. Assyria was weak after the death of Ashurbanipal (*c.* 633 B.C.). Nineveh, its capital city, fell to a coalition of Babylonians and Medes in 612 B.C. The city which had long been the proud mistress of an empire is now to become desolate, the haunt only of animals. She is condemned for her pride in 15. On the whole this oracle seems to be prophecy after the event, and probably comes from shortly after 612 B.C. Cf. the description of Nineveh's fall in Nah.; cf. also the description of Edom's desolation in Isa. 34:11. Some scholars consider 2:13f. as genuine prediction, and 15 as an editorial addition after Nineveh's fall.

III 1-7 The Sin of Jerusalem contrasted with h
Yahweh's Righteousness—From these prophecies of destruction on foreign nations we are now led back to the sins of Jerusalem that drew down Yahweh's wrath. Jerusalem has proved to be **rebellious and defiled**, accepting no correction, her rulers rapacious as evening wolves, her prophets wanton and faithless. With such crimes she cannot escape Yahweh's judgment, for he is righteous and faithful. The nations he has already destroyed are witnesses to his righteousness. This section is fully within the tradition of pre-exilic Hebrew prophecy.
3. The **officials** (Heb. *śārîm*, often rendered 'princes') are members of the king's court and administration; they and the judges are described as being greedy and selfish, looking out for their own interests. **that leave nothing till the morning:** the translation is uncertain; lit. meaning seems to be 'that did not gnaw bones in the morning'. **4.** The **prophets** are faithless to their calling as Yahweh's spokesmen; the **priests** profane the sacred and do violence to *tôrāh*, the priestly 'instruction', not the law in the sense of a body of literature; cf. Hag. 2:11; Mal. 2:6–9. **5.** Yahweh, on the other hand, is righteous—that is, he is faithful, dependable, and just. **6-7.** Yahweh's destruction of foreign nations was intended to serve as an example to Judah, but she refused to accept correction and continued to be corrupt.

8 Destruction of the Nations by Yahweh's Wrath i
—Yahweh is now about to destroy the nations and consume the earth in the heat of his anger. **Therefore**

561i does not follow logically upon what precedes. One expects pronouncement of judgment upon Jerusalem for the sins just enumerated ; instead there is pronouncement of destruction upon the nations, and indeed all the earth. The assembling of the nations for judgment reminds one of Jl 3:2 ; Zech. 14:2 and other late passages. Yet this prophecy of universal destruction is like 1:2–3, 18 ; it is probably the end of Zephaniah's own words. **as a witness :** this follows LXX and Syr. in vocalising the word *l*^{e}*ʿēdh*, rather than *l*^{e}*ʿadh* as MT has it, ' to the prey ' or ' for ever '. For Yahweh as witness cf. Jer. 29:23 ; Mic. 1:2 ; Mal. 3:5. Here he is both witness and judge.

9-10 Conversion of the Nations to Yahweh Worship—A different spirit is found in these verses. The nations are to be converted to the worship of Yahweh by having their speech purified ; cf. Isa. 19:18. **my suppliants, the daughter of my dispersed ones :** the text is difficult ; probably emend to read ' to the uttermost parts of the north ' (*ʿadh-yark*^{e}*thê ṣāphôn*).

j **11-13 A Righteous Remnant shall remain secure**—Judah shall be purged of her pride, and a humble and righteous remnant remain. The idea is one familiar in post-exilic Judaism ; cf. the editorial 561
additions in 2:7, 9.

14-20 A Final Prediction of Joy and Restoration—The book closes with a vivid picture of the golden age : Judah is to rejoice over the defeat of her enemies, and the presence of Yahweh in her midst as warrior and king. The outcast and dispersed will be returned to Zion. The tone of these verses is very different from the authentic words of Zephaniah in earlier parts of the book ; they come from an editor (or editors) who, imbued with the spirit of Second Isaiah, thought the prophecy must end on a note of hope and joy. **14-15** is similar in form to the ' psalms of Yahweh's enthronement '—cf. Ps. 47, 48, 95–9.

Bibliography—COMMENTARIES : A. B. Davidson, CB (1920) ; S. R. Driver, Cent.B (1906) ; F. Horst, HAT (1938) ; J. M. P. Smith, ICC (1911) ; C. L. Taylor, jun., IB VI (1956).

OTHER LITERATURE : Gillis Gerleman, *Zephanja, Textkritisch u. literarisch untersucht* (1942) ; J. P. Hyatt, ' The Date and Background of Zephaniah ', JNES 7 (1948), 25–9.

HAGGAI

By P. R. ACKROYD

562a **The Prophet**—Concerning the personal life of the prophet Haggai, we have no information beyond that which is to be found in the book, together with the statements in Ezr. in which he and Zechariah appear, prophesying to the Jews (5:1) and encouraging the rebuilding of the Temple (6:14). There seems every probability that the Ezra narrative is dependent upon the same traditions as appear in the two books (Hag. and Zech. 1–8, q.v.), so that no independent testimony is available. The name of the prophet, connected with *ḥagh* = festival, most probably indicates that he was born on a festival day. Speculation concerning the prophet's age is not profitable ; one tradition describes him as a young man when he returned from Babylon (so Epiphanius) ; 2:3 has been thought to suggest that he was of great age. It has usually been assumed that he and Zechariah came from Babylon with Zerubbabel.

b **The Historical Situation**—The dates in the book (1:1, 15, 2:1, 10, 20) indicate the second year of Darius I of Persia (522–486 B.C.) as the period of the prophet's activity. The prophecies themselves also indicate the period before the completion of the building of the post-exilic Temple, completed, according to Ezr. 6:15, in the sixth year of Darius. The indications of troubles in the Persian empire which may be found in Zech. 1:11 and inferred as a background to the prophecies of Hag. 2:6ff., 21ff., make such a date in the early years of Darius I entirely probable (on the dating cf. Ackroyd, JNES 17 (1958), 13–22). Some Jews had returned from the exile in Babylonia, and the immediate concern of the prophecy is almost entirely with the urge to rebuild the Temple.

c **The Message**—The prophet addresses his message to the two leaders, Zerubbabel, described as ' governor ', and Joshua the high priest, and to the people—the ' people of the land ' (2:4). Those addressed are also described as ' the remnant of the people ', both in the command to the prophet (2:2) and in the descriptive passage 1:12–14. This usage suggests an important aspect of the post-exilic community's understanding of its nature and function : it consists not simply of the survivors of disaster, but of a remnant in an eschatological sense. The ' shaking of the earth ' (2:6) ushers in a new age, in which the nations will bring their tribute to the restored and glorified Temple. Zerubbabel will become the ' signet ', the executive officer of a new rule, and the people are the saved remnant who inherit the promises of the past. These and similar points are even more clearly brought out in Zech. In Hag., this new age is inextricably linked with the rebuilding of the Temple.

d **The Compilation of the Book**—It is reasonable to suppose that the book contains only a small part of the whole message of the prophet. The somewhat artificial nature of the introductory formulae to the various oracles, as well as the indications of some disorder in the material (1:15*a* is apparently out of place, and 2:15–19 has been annotated and may well not belong with the preceding oracular utterance), make it clear that the prophet himself was not responsible for the present form of the oracles. The occurrence of some rhythmic passages, e.g. 2:4–5 (omitting the gloss in 5*a*), 2:14, may point to an original poetic form, 562d
but this can hardly be recovered without doing violence to the present text (cf. Bloomhardt, ' Poems of Haggai ', HUCA 5 (1928), 155–95). Perhaps Haggai spoke in rhythmic prose rather than in the poetic form so common in the prophetic books.

That a selection has been made and provided with e
a historical framework, in which the precise dates belong, raises the question whether it is possible to discover the purpose for which the prophecies were issued in their final form. This may best be answered by considering Hag. together with Zech. 1–8, where so many of the same interests are revealed and the same style of arrangement and dating may be observed (cf. Ackroyd, ' The Book of Haggai and Zechariah 1–8 ', JJS 3 (1952), 151–6). If 2:10–14 has been subsequently reinterpreted to point to the Samaritan community, then a link with the period and purpose of the Chronicler (probably 4th cent. B.C.) might not be inappropriate. Subsequent reinterpretation is also to be seen in the glosses (2:5*a* and 17) and in further glosses which appear in the Gr. text at 2:9 and 14, showing how the prophetic message retains its vitality and continues to provide the word of God for later generations (cf. Ackroyd, ' Some interpretative glosses in the book of Haggai ', JJS 7 (1956), 163–7).

I 1-11 Prophecies concerning the Rebuilding of f
the Temple—The opening verses of the book contain a series of loosely connected prophetic sayings, concerned with the present economic distresses of the Jewish community in Palestine, and the relation between these distresses and the failure to rebuild the Temple. The passage contains a number of introductory expressions, in addition to the main dated preface in **1**—so **3** and **7**. A concluding phrase can also be seen in **8**. There are here in all probability five brief sayings, **2**, **4**, **5-6**, **7-8**, **9-11**, gathered together because of their related subject-matter.

2-4. The message to the leaders—though in reality g
to the whole community—concerns the dilatory behaviour of the people, who refuse to regard the moment as opportune for rebuilding. **4**, **9**. Yet they themselves are able to live in their own houses, and it is possible that the use of ' panelled ' in **4** indicates even some degree of luxury. The word may, however, merely signify ' roofed ', in which case a contrast is drawn between a ruined Temple and properly roofed houses. **10-11**. The failure to rebuild the Temple is to be regarded as directly related to the present drought and famine ; and (6) such is the economic situation that men's labour is futile (11) and their wages are worthless by the time they are brought home (cf. Zech. 8:10. On the purse with holes, cf. R. Loewe, ' The Earliest Biblical Allusion to Coined Money ', PEQ 87 (1955), 141–50).

The well-being for which the people long cannot h
be enjoyed until they set their life in order. They must therefore learn from these distresses, and realise that they cannot expect to find blessing while they neglect their God. **9** probably means that God despises (RSV ' I blew it away ') the offerings which they make at present (rendering ' into the Temple '—lit. ' the house '—instead of ' home '), because of the state in which the Temple has been left neglected. That only

562h wood is to be fetched for rebuilding suggests either that stone was plentifully available in the ruins, or that the stone structure was standing and needed only the panelling and roofing which would make the Temple a properly constructed place of worship. **8**. When this repair work has been carried out, God will take pleasure in it and appear in glory. The presence of the glory of God in the Temple is a mark of divine favour and blessing (cf. Ezek. 43:4).

i The appeal of Haggai is not, as has sometimes been thought, to the people's self-interest ; it is that they should recognise that life cannot be properly lived, cannot enjoy the well-being which is God's purpose, unless due honour is given to God by recognising his primary claims (cf. Mt. 6:33). ' The chief motive is that Yahweh will come to his own and receive due honour in the service which is proper to him ' (Horst).

In **2** the text ought possibly to be read as ' The time for the house of Yahweh to be built has not now come '. In **10** ' their dew ' is a better reading, parallel to ' its produce '.

563a **12-14 The People's Response**—A historical note records the response of leaders and people to the prophet's message. It is significant that the community is here referred to as ' the remnant '. In Ezr. 1–6 it is the returned exiles who are said to have rebuilt the Temple, and this appears to be a reinterpretation of the message of Haggai. The oracles were originally addressed to the community as a whole, with no reference to returned exiles or others.

The people are represented as being in awe at the message of God, spoken by the prophet who is here emphasised as coming ' in the commission of the Lord ' (so **13**, better than ' with the Lord's message '), and they are exhorted with the encouragement that God is with them (cf. 2:4–5).

b **15a**. This odd date may be intended as a note of the point at which the actual rebuilding began, and in this case a reading ' from the twenty-fourth day ' would provide a better link. Or it may be a fragment of an introductory formula, to which many commentators attach the loose vv. 2:15–19, though the reference there to the ninth month makes the position awkward. We have to recognise an indication of some disorder in the present arrangement of the prophecies, and the probability that no completely satisfactory rearrangement is now possible.

c **I 15b-II 9 Prophecies concerning the Glory of the Temple**—Two related prophetic oracles appear in this section, introduced by the dated formula of **1:15b, 2:1-2**. **3-5** is an encouraging message to those engaged in the rebuilding, exhorting the people to realise that though the Temple they are now seeing before them appears as nothing compared to memories of the former Temple, yet they must recognise the presence of God with them and the spirit of God in their midst. Whether any had survived the long period between the destruction of Jerusalem and the rebuilding seems improbable—it was nearly seventy years. Ezr. 3:12 which speaks of such aged men may well be based upon exegesis of the Haggai oracle.

A gloss in **5**, ' the promise that I made you when you came out of Egypt ', emphasises that the new age is like that of the Exodus. God is again in the midst of his people, and they need therefore have no fear.

d The second saying, **6-9**, is clearly connected in thought. Perhaps the uncertainties of the first years of Darius I's reign have given rise to the expression of the confidence that soon the earth will be shaken (cf. also 2:20–3), and the age of salvation will be ushered in, when blessing will be spread abroad from Zion. The picture in **7-8** is that of the nations paying tribute to the Lord, to whom indeed all treasures really belong. **7**. The word translated ' treasures ' is singular, but since the verb is plural, it is normally proposed to read it as a plural form. It is also possible that we might render it as ' that which is desired (by the Lord) ' out of all the nations ; in other words, that God will call to himself those out of all the nations
whom he desires (cf. Zech. 8:20–3). **9**. The phrase 563
' in this place ' may indicate Jerusalem, or the Temple itself, pictured as the centre where God dwells and from which prosperity and blessing are radiated abroad.

10-14 A Priestly Decision—The oracle of **14** is e
given on the occasion of a question directed to the priests concerning the contagious nature of holiness and uncleanness. **11**. Asking the priests for their *tôrāh* —' directive ' (literally)—may have been deliberately undertaken to provide the occasion for the oracle ; or it may be that the question appeared to be a divine command when the prophet realised the word which he had to speak on the occasion. The first part of the question concerns the possibility that the holiness of sacrificial flesh—perhaps killed and carried home—could spread its holiness to other objects. This is stated to be impossible. But the opposite, the contagion of uncleanness from contact with a dead body, may spread readily (cf. Lev. 21:11 ; Num. 9:6f., 19:11–13). **14**. In rhythmic form, the prophet then declares that this *tôrāh* applies to the people.

The immediate point of the oracle seems to be a f
condemnation of the people because of their neglect of God and his Temple, with a resultant failure in their life. ' There is a " dead thing " among them ' (Barnes) —that is, the Temple lying in ruins. It is possible that the prophet is recognising further that mere rebuilding will not of itself spread holiness throughout the land, and an early gloss (found in the Gr.) elaborates this with reference to social evils and injustice as the root causes of disaster (cf. Zech. 7:8ff.).

An alternative explanation, offered originally by Rothstein, has been accepted by a number of more recent commentators. As the passage now stands chronologically linked with 2:1–9, it may be wondered why so discouraging a message should have been given at this juncture to the Jewish community. To regard the message as applicable to the Samaritans—or perhaps more particularly to the rulers in Samaria, descended from the Assyrian settlers (cf. 2 Kg. 17:24ff., so Elliger)—would remove this difficulty. There would then be a link with Ezr. 4:1–5 which speaks of hostility occasioned by the refusal of the Jews to allow their co-operation in rebuilding.

But it is not clear why the phrase ' this people ' and its poetic parallel ' this nation ' should be used in a different sense here from that in 1:2. The possibility that the passage, originally applicable to the Jewish community, has been given a later, anti-Samaritan interpetation, may be suggested as a third alternative.

15-19 Past Distresses and Future Blessing— g
Many commentators place these verses with 1:15*a* at the end of ch. 1 (or after 1:11). They are only loosely attached to 2:10–14 by the linking phrase ' and now '.

15. The people are enjoined to consider their past situation—how they fared (so RSV 15–16*a*, Heb. ' since they were ') in the days before stone was placed upon stone in the Temple (15); **16f.** economic disasters, famine, natural disasters. But now there is to be a change of fortune, and blessing already appears in the vine and the fig-tree, the pomegranate and the olive.

The passage is complicated by the addition of a comment mainly from Am. 4:9 in **17**, appropriately comparing how the people of Amos' time did not learn from their past experience. The words ' yet you did not return to me ' in RSV are taken from Am. to replace the expression in the Haggai text, which is grammatically awkward. There is a further addition in **18**, identifying the date of the laying of the foundation-stone. It has thus become difficult to see in what situation the message was originally given, but there appears to be a fairly close connection of thought with the oracles of 1:2–8.

20-23 Message of Promise to Zerubbabel—As in h
2:6 there is to be a ' shaking of the earth ', in which God's intervention in the affairs of men will be known.

563h 2:6–9 suggested a time of blessing and recognition of God in his Temple ; here the picture is of Zerubbabel appointed as the signet-ring (cf. Jer. 22:24), the representative of God, the chosen one. The power of human rulers is to be overthrown (the second phrase 'of the kingdoms' in **22** should probably be omitted), and Zerubbabel occupies a place of authority in the new age.

i This oracle raises most acutely the question of Haggai's political outlook. Did he envisage the downfall of the Persian empire, and Zerubbabel as an independent ruler, a new David? Is the fact that Zerubbabel does not appear again after this period an indication that he was removed by the Persians because of his political aspirations? (cf. Waterman, 'The Camouflaged Purge of Three Messianic Conspirators', JNES 13 (1954), 73–8). Of this latter there is no evidence, and since OT personages often appear and disappear in the records without any explanation, not much weight need be given to it. Ezr. 6:14 implies that both Haggai and Zechariah were still active when the Temple was rededicated. The emphasis in Zechariah on 'by my spirit, rather than by might' (cf. Zech. 4:6) and the fact that such stress is laid here 563i upon divine intervention, suggest that the hope was really of a new divine age, and that, like earlier prophets, Haggai was more concerned with God's activity than with human aspirations after independence (cf. Bentzen, 'Quelques remarques sur le mouvement messianique . . . de l'an 520' RHPR 10 (1930), 493–503).

Bibliography—Commentaries : W. E. Barnes, CB (1917) ; S. Bullough, *Obadiah, Micah, Zephaniah, Haggai, Zechariah*, Westminster Version (1953) ; S. R. Driver, Cent.B (1906) ; K. Elliger, ATD (1951) ; A. van Hoonacker, EBib. (1908) ; F. Horst, HAT (2nd ed. 1954) ; H. G. Mitchell, ICC (1912) ; E. Sellin, KAT (1930) ; G. Adam Smith, Ex.B (1928) ; D. Winton Thomas, IB vi (1956).

Other Literature : P. R. Ackroyd, 'Studies in the Book of Haggai', JJS 2 (1951), 163–76, 3 (1952), 1–13, 'Two OT historical problems of the Early Persian period', JNES 17 (1958), 13–27 ; J. W. Rothstein, *Juden und Samaritaner* (1908) ; H. W. Wolff, *Haggai*, Biblische Studien 1 (1951).

ZECHARIAH

By P. R. ACKROYD

564a The generally accepted division of Zech. into two sections is here followed, since the marked differences of style between 1–8 and 9–14, as well as the disappearance of the prophet's name after 8, make it improbable that Zechariah had anything to do with the latter half of the book.

FIRST SECTION I-VIII

b **The Prophet**—As with Haggai, no independent information is available concerning his personal life. He is mentioned with Haggai in Ezr. 5:1 and 6:14. A Zechariah of the family of Iddo occurs in Neh. 12:16, and Iddo in Neh. 12:4, as one who came from exile with Zerubbabel and Joshua. Berechiah, father of Zechariah according to 1:1, is not mentioned in Neh., and the name may have been inserted by confusion with the Zechariah of Isa. 8:2. The punctuation of the Heb. text in 1:1 makes Iddo the prophet, suggesting an attempted link with Iddo in 2 Chr. 12:15, 13:22. The family clearly has priestly associations. The age of the prophet is unknown, unless he is to be identified with the ' young man ' of 2:4.

c **The Historical Situation** is the same as in Haggai. The dates in 1:1, 7 and 7:1 cover a longer period of time, from the second to the fourth years of Darius I of Persia. It seems not impossible that some of Zechariah's hostile utterances against Babylon might be of earlier origin. That Zechariah continued to prophesy after the rebuilding of the Temple has sometimes been denied ; yet some sayings (e.g. 6:14, 7:2–3) might presuppose its completion, and according to Ezr. 6:14 he was actively concerned in the final stages.

d **The Message**—As in Hag., there is considerable interest in the rebuilding of the Temple (1:16, 4:7–9, 6:12f., 15) ; the city of Zion is to be chosen again by God (1:17, 3:2, 8:1ff.), and this emphasis may be compared with passages such as Isa. 52, 60 and 62. The long period of distress occasioned by past failure is over, and now, though outward signs do not appear favourable (1:12), God is proclaimed as preparing judgment for the nations, and deliverance and prosperity for Jerusalem and Judah. The connection between the Temple and the new age is not explicitly stated, but implied, especially in 7–8.

e More elaborate prophecy appears in Zech. than in Hag. concerning the future age, and particularly the place to be occupied by Zerubbabel, the Branch (3:8–10, 6:12f.). The double leadership of the community is not always clearly described, perhaps because the text in 6:9–15 has later been adapted ; but the two leaders appear in 4 symbolised as olive trees beside the lamp-stand, and 6:13 speaks of ' peaceful understanding ' between them. To look for political motives in the prophecies (e.g. in 2:1–5), or to find evidence of friction between the leaders in 6:13 or in 3, does not do justice to the stress laid by Zechariah upon divine power and saving grace. The new age is the result of God's return to his people (8:3), bringing blessing for them and for ' many peoples ' (8:22).

f **The Prophet's Experience**—The prominence of visionary experiences in these chapters suggests that 564f
Zech. marks the transition from prophecy to apocalyptic. But while the images of the visions are often strange, they are not given the elaborate interpretations characteristic of apocalyptic, and they have that immediacy of experience which is characteristic of the earlier prophets (cf. Am. 7). They are experienced in a special state of mind, compared with ' waking from sleep ' (4:1). With this may be compared Lk. 9:32 and the description of an Akkadian oracular dream : ' When he (the seer) awoke, Ishtar showed him a night vision ' (cf. ANET, 451). The compelling character of the experience does not exclude the prophet's own self-consciousness, as may be seen from his questions and even his intervention in a visionary experience (3:5). Stress is laid upon the authority of the prophet's mission, recognisable in the events about which he prophesies (2:9, 4:9).

The Compilation of Zechariah I-VIII—The central section 1:7–6:15 contains a series of eight visions, elaborated and explained with prophetic material. There is here a deliberate structure, possibly undertaken by the prophet himself, in which the visions are forcefully combined, and their significance drawn out by comments derived from other prophetic sayings of Zechariah. There is a brief admonitory introduction (1:1–6), and a conclusion consisting of sayings concerned largely with the future age (7–8). Much of this material is homiletic in tone, which suggests that the original messages of the prophet have been elaborated and expounded, perhaps first by the prophet himself, and subsequently by disciples and followers. The ethical stress (cf. 1:1–6, 7:4–14, 8:14–17) is in large measure to be found in these homiletical passages, though it is not entirely absent elsewhere (e.g. 3:1–5, 5:1–4). g

As in Hag. it is possible that some reinterpretation may have had in view later events, and possibly the Samaritan schism (cf. 7:1–3) ; such a date for the final compilation might suggest why there was added the further collection of 9–14, though the dating and allusions of these chapters are extremely difficult to determine.

I 1-6. The opening verses of a prophetic book not infrequently set the tone for what follows (cf. Isa. 1 ; Jer. 1 ; Ezek. 1–3). Here a saying which bears some resemblance to other passages (e.g. 7:8–14, 8:14f.), provides an appropriate introduction, and by its hortatory tone suggests that the purpose of the collection of words of Zechariah is to encourage obedience and the learning of wisdom from the past experiences of the people. To the generation of Zechariah, the lesson had been learnt that, as their fathers had refused to hear the appeal of God to ' return to me . . . and I will return to you ', so they had brought disaster upon themselves. 565a

If in **6** ' overtake you ' is read for ' overtake your fathers ', the appeal is certainly more forceful, and the closing sentence can then be understood as a comment upon the situation, like that found in Hag. 1:12–14 ; when the people heard the message of Zechariah, they repented and acknowledged the justice of God's dealings with them and thus showed themselves to be unlike their fathers. Such an interpretation avoids b

565b the contradiction which otherwise appears between **4b** and **6b**. It may also help to explain the rather abrupt **2**, which intrudes into the conventional introductory formula. It may be regarded as in parenthesis, explaining the reason for the prophecy ('Now the Lord was very angry . . .') or explaining to its later readers the situation in which the prophecy was uttered and alluding to the hardships of the post-exilic group addressed originally by the prophet (cf. Hag. 1:6–10, 2:15–19).

c The day of the month is missing in **1**; Syr. adds 'on the first of the month'. The repetitive style, e.g. in **3**, may be in part due to textual error, but it is not without its effectiveness; so too are the rhetorical questions in **5**, which resemble the style of Mal. and of homiletical passages such as 2 Chr. 13:4–12. **4.** The use of the term 'former prophets' (cf. 7:7, 12)—later applied to the books Jos. to 2 Kg.—stresses the sense of continuity in the prophetic tradition, and the enduring vitality of the word of God (cf. **6**).

d **I 7-VI 15 The Visions and their Interpretation**

I 7-17 First Vision: the Horsemen—The introductory formula of **7** clearly does not belong with the description of the vision which follows. It is simply a conventional form, and the last phrase should be rendered 'saying' (so AV)—i.e. 'as follows'. What follows is not strictly a word to the prophet, but a description given by the prophet of his vision. The night vision was of a man on horseback among myrtle trees in a glen, with a group of horses—presumably with riders (cf. 11)—behind him. These are patrols, sent like the Persian mounted posts, to go to and fro in the earth. Their report is that peace is restored in this period of upheaval at the accession of Darius I.

e **12.** The meaning of the vision is brought out when the divine messenger asks, in words reminiscent of the psalms of lamentation (cf. 79:5), 'How long' Jerusalem and Judah are to remain unconsoled. **13.** God himself gives a direct and comforting reply. He is jealous for Jerusalem, and angry at the nations which have gone beyond his command in oppressing his people. Although outward events do not seem to indicate God's working, he is intervening on behalf of his people and Jerusalem. Some of Zechariah's contemporaries no doubt saw in the upheavals a sign of hope that national independence was at hand. Zechariah's answer, in accord with the teaching of earlier prophets, is that judgment and deliverance are the prerogative of God. The nations which are his instruments fall under judgment (cf. Isa. 10:12–19).

f **16** and **17** add two further sayings of the prophet, introduced by 'Therefore' and 'Cry again'. The first provides a promise of God's return to Jerusalem and of the rebuilding of Temple and city. The second speaks of the change of fortune which will accompany this return. Both sayings may be earlier utterances here used to comment upon the vision and its interpretation.

g **7.** The naming of the month is probably a later comment (cf. 7:1, also §37*l*). **8-10** are not easy to follow since the persons involved are introduced without explanation, and the sudden change from the angel of **9** to the speech of the horseman in **10** may be due to confusion in the text. The colours of the horses too are not clear, since the second word 'sorrel' may mean 'bright red'. There would then be two colours: 'red', i.e. light brown, and 'white'. That the colours have significance is unlikely, since no interpretation is offered in the context. The use of similar imagery in Rev. 6 has led some commentators to read back meanings into this passage; LXX render the passage with four colours, probably intended to be symbolical.

h **12.** For the expression 'seventy years' (cf. 7:5) cf. Whitley, VT 4 (1954), 60–72, Orr, VT 6 (1956), 304–6 and Ackroyd, JNES 17 (1958), 23–7. It would seem probable that the expression is in some way related to the length of the period between the fall of Jerusalem and the rebuilding of the Temple. Alternative renderings may be suggested for 'they furthered 565h
the disaster' (15) as 'they multiplied the disaster', and for 'overflow' (17), where the sense may be 'While my cities are yet deprived of wealth, the Lord consoles Zion anew . . .'

I 18-II 13 (in the Heb. 2:1–17) **Second and Third** i
Visions: the Horns and the Man with the Measuring Line—Two visions are placed together in this section, each briefly interpreted, and followed by a small group of sayings which link them together and comment upon their meaning. The first, **1:18-21,** is of four horns, representing the powers hostile to Judah. The use of the horn as a symbol of royal power is very ancient, cf. 1 Sam. 2:1 and 10 (RV). No attempt is made to indicate whether particular kingdoms are intended. **21.** These horns are to be cast down by divine agents of destruction (cf. Ezek. 21:31). The use of the expression 'terrify them' is perhaps best understood as expressing the effect of divine action on the nations (the object 'them' cannot refer to the 'horns', but only to the 'nations'). The construction rendered 'so that no man raised his head' might be linked to the following words (omitting 'and'), and rendered as 'in such manner that none may lift up his head'. The vision is linked with 1:15, and may belong to the period of turmoil at the outset of Darius I's reign, though it could come from an earlier period of Zechariah's activity.

II 1-5. The second of the two visions describes a man j
setting out to measure Jerusalem. Two angelic beings appear, coming out perhaps from the gateway of heaven imagined by the prophet as the scene of the vision. The interpreting angel is instructed to tell 'that young man' that Jerusalem will be like 'open villages' unwalled because of the size of its population. God's protection of it will be as a wall of fire, and the presence of God will be within the city (cf. Ezek. 43:1–5 and Hag. 1:8, 2:7). It is not clear whether the 'young man' of **4** is the same as the man of **1-2**. Jerome appropriately suggested that he was the prophet. The search for a political background—an attempt to rebuild the walls which Zechariah regarded as showing lack of faith—hardly seems necessary in view of this emphasis.

Four sayings follow. **6-7** exhorts escape from k
Babylon, the hostile 'land of the north'. Instead of 'I have spread you abroad' we may render 'I have caused you to fly (with wings)'. **8-9** links closely to 1:18–21, explaining the reversal of Judah's fortunes. The phrase 'after his glory sent me' is evidently corrupt: an alternative suggestion is 'whose glory has sent me', but the method of referring to God is abrupt and awkward. **10-12** links closely to 2:1–5 and enlarges the picture of the gathering of the exiles by including the gathering of the nations, who are to become 'my people' (cf. 8:20–3 and the covenant formula in Jer. 7:23, etc.). **8-9** and **10-12** lay emphasis on the authentication of the prophet's message which will be provided by the events foretold. **13** reads like a liturgical formula, an appropriate word invoking awe at the divine appearing (cf. Hab. 2:20).

III Fourth Vision: the High Priest in the 566a
Heavenly Court—1-5. Joshua is described as standing clothed in filthy garments before the angel of the Lord, accused by the Satan. The Lord rebukes the Satan, and at the angel's command Joshua is clothed in clean garments. At the same time the declaration is made that 'I have taken your iniquity away from you'. **6-7.** The vision is followed by a special pronouncement to Joshua and by **8-10** sayings concerning the Messianic figure described as the 'Branch' and the new age when all guilt will be removed from the land and peace will reign.

In the interpretation of this chapter, much depends b
upon the division of the material, since it is possible that **6-7** are part of the vision and express its real significance. If this is the correct view, then it is not unnatural to see in Joshua the actual high priest, whose office is in some way attacked. If he was a newly

566b returned exile (cf. Neh. 12:1), there might have been some in Jerusalem who regarded him as unfit for priestly office because he was polluted by exile. Or he may have been in Judah all the time, functioning as priest and regarded with hostility by the returning exiles. Either interpretation indicates a division within the community which the prophet wishes to heal. These interpretations do not do justice to the actual text of the vision itself in **1-5**, nor to the function of the high priest as representative of the people. It is significant that in **2** the emphatic statement is made that it is ' the Lord who has chosen Jerusalem ' who rebukes the Satan, and that Joshua (less probably Jerusalem) is a ' brand plucked from the fire '. (This expression may be proverbial, appearing in similar form in Am. 4:11.) God has delivered a remnant from disaster, and this is represented by Joshua. The replacing of Joshua's dirty clothing by clean garments, and in particular the placing of a clean turban upon his head, denotes the forgiveness and cleansing of the community he represents. The turban's connection with atonement is clearly indicated in Exod. 28:36ff. The function of Joshua is elaborated in **6-7.** Here he—and perhaps through him the priestly order (cf. **8**)—is given charge over the Temple (cf. Exod. 28:29f. ; Num. 27:18ff. ; Ezek. 44), and right of access among those who stand in the heavenly council.

c The relationship between this and **8-10** lies in the relationship between the Temple and the hopes of a new age (cf. Hag.). In **8** Joshua and his fellow-priests are ' men of a sign ' (cf. Isa. 8:18) who in some way symbolise or guarantee the coming of ' my servant the Branch ', i.e. Zerubbabel (cf. 6:12, and also Isa. 4:2 ; Jer. 23:5, 33:15). Emphasis in **9** is laid upon the removal of the land's guilt (cf. 5:1–11), the stone with its seven facets being best understood as a gem worn in the high-priestly diadem, again emphasising his atoning function (cf. Exod. 28:36). The passage ends with a typical description of the new age (cf. 1 Kg. 4:25 ; Mic. 4:4).

d The main action of the vision is performed by the angel of God, yet in **2** the text has ' the Lord '. Possibly, as in Jg. 6:11–24, this is a simple interchange. The figure of the Satan (with the article, not ' Satan ' as RSV ; cf. 1 Chr. 21:1) appears here, as in Job 1–2, as the accuser, the counterpart of the messenger of God. **4.** The word rendered ' rich apparel ' is to be explained as ' clean white garments '. The narrative of the vision is self-contained apart from the ' I said ' of **5.** This sudden change of person may be a device to lay emphasis upon the importance of the turban in the investiture.

e This vision has been compared with the Adapa myth (cf. ANET, 101–3) in which Adapa appears in mourning-garments before Anu, and his garments are changed. The resemblances are slight, but behind the vision there may lie a real ritual performed by the high priest on behalf of the people, not unlike that undertaken by the Babylonian king in penitential garments in the New Year ritual.

f **IV Fifth Vision : The Lamp and the Olive Trees**—The order—vision, interpretation, additional comment—found in other passages, is here disturbed by a group of sayings concerning Zerubbabel (*6b*–*10a*) placed in the middle. This is clear from the sequence in the text from **6a**, ' Then he said to me ', to **10b**, ' These seven are the eyes of the Lord '.

g **1-3.** The vision itself is introduced by an extended statement emphasising the nature of the prophet's experience. He sees a lamp-stand with its bowl upon it, and on this seven lamps each with seven lips (nozzles to contain the wicks, rather than ' pipes ' as RV which suggests the transmission of the oil from the olive trees, cf. 12). Beside the lamp are two olive trees. **10.** The interpretation points first to the seven eyes of God, ranging throughout the whole earth, expressive of the omniscience of God and the range of divine rule. **14.** A second stage of interpretation describes the olive trees as ' sons of oil ' (RSV ' anointed '), representing Zerubbabel and Joshua as the two agents of the divine purpose. A third interpretative element is found in 12, where the text is not altogether clear, and it appears to be suggested that the olive trees provide the oil directly to the bowl of the lamp (' Two branches of olive trees ' is a further detail not mentioned in the original vision). This represents an extension of the basic idea, pointing to the function of the two leaders in contributing to the well-being of the community. The last phrase of **12** might be emended to read ' emptying oil into the golden bowl '. **566g**

h The assumption that the lamp-stand is intended to be a ' seven-branched candlestick ' (so RV ; cf. Exod. 25:31ff.) meets with some difficulty in explaining the ' bowl ' at the top. More natural is the view that the lamp is an elaborate form of the ancient lamp with a nozzle to hold the wick : a large bowl upon a stand has seven lamps upon it, each with seven wicks. The whole picture is one of divine watchfulness (cf. 1:8–11), with a new note in the description of the place of the two leaders in the divine ordering of the world. The seven eyes ' ranging ' or ' wandering ' may be a metaphor derived from mythological ideas connected with the seven wandering planets. Emphasis and deliberation are given to the passage by the repetitions (e.g. 4–5).

i **6b-10a** consists of several short sayings concerning Zerubbabel and the Temple. **6b** stresses the divine power by which Zerubbabel's work is to be undertaken; political aspirations and the use of wrong methods are repudiated. **7** might reflect a time of depression (cf. Hag. 2:3) and gives the assurance that all difficulties will be overcome ; the headstone will be brought forward with shouts of ' How beautiful it is '. **8-9a** stresses the completion of the Temple by Zerubbabel, and in **9b** the note is added (cf. 2:9) that this will show the validity of the divine oracle declared by Zechariah. **10a** expresses a similar note of confidence in the divine power. The words rendered as ' plummet ' are difficult : a ' stone separated, set apart ', may be intended, since a plumb-line is hardly in place here.

j This group of prophetic sayings is evidently out of place. It would fit after 3:8–10, emphasising the function of Zerubbabel, who has just been described as the ' Branch ', or it could stand before or after 6:15. A better position would be after 4:14. It is simpler to recognise that an insertion has been made—awkward though it may appear—to bring out the deeper significance of the vision. The watchfulness of God and his appointment of Zerubbabel and Joshua are closely linked with the Temple-building ; as in Hag. this is intimately related to the promises of a new age.

567a **V 1-4 Sixth Vision : The Flying Scroll**—The prophet sees an immense flying scroll, representing the curse which goes out over the whole land. **3b-4** may be regarded as a fuller explanation of this visionary experience. Special reference is made to two classes of criminal : the thief, typical perhaps of deception, and the false-swearer (so **4**, the word ' falsely ' in **3** is not in the Heb. text, though obviously implied), typical perhaps of wrong dealings between men, rather than the religiously unfaithful. The main stress is upon the divine purification of the land by the destructive agency of this ' oath ' which brings disaster upon the houses of those who are committing social evils.

b The meaning of **3b** is not clear. The phrase rendered ' henceforth according to it ' might be interpreted as ' according to the wording on one side . . . on the other side '. The word translated ' cut off ' really means ' be purged out ' and also ' go unpunished '. A small emendation would give ' how long already has he remained unpunished '. But a rendering ' purged out ' is most appropriate. The opening words of **4** are in the past tense, and perhaps so to be rendered as indicating that the divine judgment is already in progress.

c **5-11 Seventh Vision : The Woman in the Ephah**—An ephah (cf. §34*l*) appears, and is defined as

567e 'their iniquity' in all the land. Upon the top is a cover of lead, and when this is lifted, a woman can be seen sitting inside. She is 'Wickedness' and after she has been thrust back into the ephah—as if she were trying to escape—the cover is replaced and two women with stork's (or heron's) wings carry it away to Babylon (Shinar ; cf. Gen. 11:2). There the ephah is set up in a house specially built for it.

d The text has a number of obscurities. **6.** 'Their iniquity' is the LXX reading, where the Heb. has 'their eye' : it is not quite clear, however, in what sense the ephah is 'iniquity', nor what is its relationship to the woman it contains. In **11** 'house' should be rendered 'temple' : the verbal forms are unusual, but the meaning is probably 'when it (the temple) has been prepared, then it (the ephah) will be placed there upon its pedestal' (RSV 'base'). The picture is of 'Wickedness'—best construed as godlessness or idolatry—carried away and worshipped, appropriately enough, in Babylon, the hated land of exile. Although it is the ephah which is set up, it is 'idolatry' itself which is worshipped. In the previous vision the land is purged of social evils ; here of apostasy.

e **VI 1-8 Eighth Vision: Four Chariots**—From between two bronze mountains come four chariots with various coloured horses ; they represent the messengers of God, going out from his heavenly council, travelling in different directions to patrol the earth. **8.** The phrase 'Then he cried to me' shows that special interest is concentrated upon the horses which go to the north, where they have 'set my spirit at rest'. The resemblances to the first vision are apparent and it is hardly surprising to find that there has been some mutual influence, especially in the ancient versions, where, for example, LXX read 'mountains' for 'myrtles' in 1:8, and discover four colours in the first vision like those of the eighth. In **2**, four colours are indicated, though the last is not clear : two words are used, one of which means 'speckled' (Gen. 31:10), and the other, used again at the beginning of **7**, may mean 'red', or more probably 'strong ones', i.e. 'steeds'. Possibly this word was original to **7** and has then been understood as a colour and added to **2** to explain the nature of the speckled horses.

f The difficulties are greater in **6** and **7**. No mention is made in the Heb. of the red horses, and it may be that we should add 'the red ones went out to the east country' at the beginning of **6**. Yet since the interest is only in the 'north', such completeness is unnecessary ; sufficient is said here and in **7** to indicate the function of the chariots. The white horses are described in the Heb. as going 'after them', that is the black horses which have gone northwards. An easy emendation gives RSV 'toward the west country', but whether this is accepted depends in part upon the interpretation of **8**. The opening of **7** looks rather like the beginning of another statement about one chariot and its horses, but this may be due to the interpretation of the word rendered 'steeds' as 'red ones' (cf. RV for a rendering in accordance with this).

g The real crux is the interpretation of 'spirit' in **8**. Are the chariots hostile—war-chariots—and is 'spirit' equivalent to 'anger'? If so, **8** means 'they have quietened, appeased my anger', i.e. shown my displeasure on Babylon (cf. 2:6–7). Alternatively, the chariots, coming from the heavenly council, may simply be messengers, and the sense may be 'they have set (an alternative interpretation of the Heb. verb) my spirit upon the north country', i.e. stirring up the spirit of the exiles, renewing their life (cf. Ezr. 1:5). This interpretation would provide a close link with the symbolic action which is described in 6:9–15, and would explain the linking together of these two passages. It is not impossible that the two aspects of the divine spirit are here combined, and if the Heb. text is followed in **6**, so that both black and white horses go northwards, symbolism might be looked for in the colours, expressing judgment and wrath upon Babylon, and promise and the stirring up of new life for the exiles. 567g

The two bronze mountains in **1** may be derived from some mythological idea, perhaps a reminiscence of a ritual with horses and chariots of the sun-god. If the two bronze pillars, Jachin and Boaz, in Solomon's Temple were known to represent mountains, the picture might be of God holding court in his temple and sending out his messengers thence. h

9-15 A Symbolic Action: the Crowning of Joshua—9-11. The prophet is commanded to make silver and gold into a crown (or crowns) to be placed on the head of Joshua the high priest. **12, 13.** The symbolic action is accompanied by an oracle concerning the 'Branch', a promise of the rebuilding of the Temple, and of peaceful rule by governor and priest. Various returned exiles share in this, and are witnesses of what has been done (**10, 14**). A promise of the gathering of distant Jews to rebuild the Temple is followed by an exhortation to obedience to God's word (**15**). i

The rendering of the passage is not easy. In **10-11** the sense appears to be 'Something is to be taken from the exiles, namely from Heldai, etc. . . ., i.e. take silver and gold . . .' **10b** is perhaps overweighted (RSV tacitly omits one phrase 'and come thou'), but might be emended slightly to read 'and come with them on the same day and enter the house . . .' RSV moves the phrase 'who have arrived from Babylon' from the end of **10** to a more logical position. The oracle in **12** is poetic in form and should read : j

> Behold the man, Branch is his name,
> Where he is, there is sprouting up,
> And he shall build the Temple of Yahweh.

The last phrase is omitted by some commentators as a duplicate of **13a**, but this is unnecessary if **13** is treated as a new prophetic utterance. It seems clear that the oracle in **12** has a direct allusion to Zerubbabel (cf. 3:8), whose name (*zerbabili*) means 'sprout of Babylon'. (The same Heb. root is used in **12** for Branch and 'sprouting up'.)

The interpretation of **13** depends closely upon that of **11**. Here the plural 'crowns' of the Heb. could easily be emended to a singular, more appropriate to the crowning of one individual, unless by 'crowns' is meant a double crown. It has often been thought that the reference should be to Zerubbabel, the Branch, rather than to Joshua ; or alternatively, in view of **13**, that both are to be symbolically crowned. The latter is attractive, in view also of the vision of the two olive trees in ch. 4. The poetic oracle of **13** could then be satisfactorily rendered : k

> And *he* (emphatic, i.e. Zerubbabel) shall build the Temple of Yahweh,
> And *he* (emphatic, i.e. Joshua) shall bear his glorious office (of priest),
> And he (Zerubbabel) shall sit and rule upon his throne,
> And he (Joshua) shall be as priest upon his throne (or LXX 'at his right hand')
> And peaceful counsel shall be between them both.

The absence of Zerubbabel's name has often been taken to indicate that he was removed by the Persians for Messianic pretensions (cf. §563*i*) ; of this there is no clue in the text. That prominence should later be given to the high priest is to be expected, in view of the political position occupied by him in the later post-exilic period. Yet in view of the saying to Joshua and his associates in 3:8, Joshua may here, privately or publicly, be crowned as a symbol of the crowning of the Branch.

14. The placing of the crown in the Temple as a memorial, witnessed by the returned exiles (10), appears to be an extension of the symbol, stressing the validity of the prophet's word, as does also the second l

567l clause of 15 (cf. 4:9). Helem appears in the Heb. for Heldai (14), and 'for grace' instead of Josiah. The latter may be a relic of a fuller expression. 15 relates the building of the Temple to the gathering of Jews from other lands (cf. 8:7f.). The stress laid here on the part played by the exiles in rebuilding points the way to the later idea that it was they alone who had actually rebuilt it (cf. Ezr. 6:16), though no such exclusive view is found in Hag. and Zech. The last part of **15** should be read as an incomplete conditional sentence: 'And it shall come about, if you will diligently obey . . .', possibly intended as an allusion to Dt. 28:1, indicating the blessing that will follow from obedience. The blessing upon the returning exiles provides a close link with 6:8. The promise that Zerubbabel should rebuild the Temple may belong to an earlier period, but provides a fitting conclusion to the vision series.

568a **VII-VIII A Collection of Prophetic Sayings**

VII 1-3 A Question about Fasting—A new and later date introduces an inquiry addressed to priests at the Temple and to prophets, concerning the observance of the fast in the fifth month. This fast celebrates the burning of the Temple (2 Kg. 25:8f.; Jer. 52:12ff.), and the rebuilding would suggest that its observance is now out of date. The most difficult problem here concerns the names in **2**, for the rendering 'the people of Bethel' represents an interpretation; the text contains only the place-name. Nor is it clear why messengers should be sent from Bethel, unless the passage is to be interpreted as connected with Samaritan hostility (so Rothstein, L. E. Browne). A better suggestion is to regard Bethel as the first part of the name Bethel-sharezer, since Sharezer is an incomplete form, and to render 'Now Bethelsharezer and Regemmelech and their men had been sent . . .' Or, if Regem is a corruption of Rab-mag, the chief officer (cf. Syr. and Jer. 39:3, 13), we might emend slightly to read 'Now Bethelsharezer, the chief officer of the king, had sent his men . . .' The names suggest Babylonian Jews, and this might account for the curious lapse of four months between the date of the fast and the date of the inquiry, unless the date in **1** is of independent origin, as may appear in the lack of connection between its wording and that of the story which follows. RSV omits 'separating myself' (RV) in **3** with the main LXX manuscripts. Some of the ancient versions translate as a further question 'Shall I separate myself?' The connection of consecration with fasting makes it reasonable to accept the Heb. text. The name of the month in **1** is probably a later explanatory addition as in 1:7. It is not easy to see where the answer to the inquiry is to be found. **4-7** are an address to the people as a whole, not to the messengers. More appropriately the answer may be seen in 8:18-19 which speaks of the turning of fasts into seasons of joy.

b **4-14 Prophetic Sayings forming a Sermon on Obedience**—Linked to the question about fasting is a prophetic saying, **5-7**, introduced by the formula **4**, condemning the wrong observance of fasts (cf. Isa. 58). The people of the land (cf. Hag. 2:4) and the priests are together warned that their celebrations are like their eating and drinking: they honour themselves not God. They should have considered the prosperity of Judah and Jerusalem in the past, and recalled what the former prophets (cf. 1:4) had said. **5.** It is possible that the rather terse 'Was it for me that you fasted' means 'Judah brought the disaster upon herself; her own failure, not God's, made fasting appropriate'. This is elaborated in the latter part of this chapter. The reference to seventy years (cf. 1:12) is more precise than the general term used in **3**, and may represent an explanatory note. The fast of the seventh month has been interpreted as celebrating the murder of Gedaliah (2 Kg. 25:25; Jer. 41:1-2), but the connection is not certain.

c **8-10**. A new prophetic saying interrupts the sequence of ideas, to elaborate what is meant by the teaching of the prophets. The phrases are reminiscent of earlier prophecy (cf. Hos. 6:6; Am. 5:14f., etc.) and are not unlike the language of Deuteronomic catalogues of obedience (e.g. Dt. 26:12ff.). Special concern is enjoined for those who are without protection—the widow, the orphan, the sojourner and the propertyless man. A similar passage appears in 8:14-17. 568c

11-14 resumes the warnings of 5-7. The refusal of the people of the past to hear the prophetic message resulted in the judgment of exile. In language again strongly reminiscent of the Deuteronomic homilies (e.g. Dt. 30), the people are warned by the experience of the past not to fail, lest by their disobedience they should hinder the coming of the age of salvation with which the sayings of the next chapter are concerned. **12** emphasises the unity of the prophetic message, because of its inspiration 'by his spirit'. **13** vividly changes in the middle into the first person (so RV correctly) and thereby the effect is heightened. The emendation to the first person at the beginning of the verse in RSV somewhat weakens the effect. d

VIII 1-23 A Collection of Ten Prophetic Sayings, marked by introductory formulae—A number of these sayings overlap other material in Zech. 1-8, and there are also allusions to other prophecy, notably Hag. They provide a picture of the age of salvation, when the promises of God will be fulfilled and blessing will come upon Jerusalem and her people, and through them upon the world. e

(1) **1-2**. The divine jealousy wears a double aspect; it burns with anger against evil, but it is also on fire to bring blessing to Zion (cf. 1:14f.). f

(2) **3**. God's return to Jerusalem will bring blessing, and the renamed city will express his holiness (cf. 1:16f., 2:10). The renaming of the city is reminiscent of Isa. 62:12 and Ezek. 48:35 and its faithfulness is stressed in Isa. 1:26. 'Holiness is the nature of the God who is enthroned in the Temple; faithfulness characterises the people living in the city' (Elliger).

(3) **4-5**. The city of the future is to be secure (cf. 2:4), and its inhabitants enjoy the divine blessing of long life (cf. Exod. 20:12; Isa. 65:20, etc.).

(4) **6**. Men's doubts are answered by the assurance of God's power. A saying possibly originally referring to the rebuilding of the Temple (cf. 4:7, 10; Hag. 2:3) is here applied appropriately to the age of salvation. The text would be clearer if rendered: g

If it seems too wonderful in the eyes of the remnant
of this people,
Is it then too wonderful in my eyes? says the Lord
of hosts

(omitting 'in those days' as wrongly copied from **10** or as added later to comment on the faith of the returned exiles).

(5) **7-8**. The scattered Jews will be restored to Jerusalem from all the earth—east and west being general terms rather than referring merely to Babylon and Egypt (cf. 2:6-13, 6:15). With them the covenant will be renewed (cf. Hos. 2:23, etc.) in mutual faithfulness and righteousness (cf. Hos. 2:19).

(6) **9-13**. A more elaborate promise of blessing and the renewal of former fortunes is here expressed in terms closely related to the language and thought of Hag. (cf. Hag. 1:6-11, 2:15-19). The verses have been thought to contain glosses from Hag. (e.g. in 9; cf. Hag. 1:2) or even to contain actual sayings of Hag. It seems more probable that here genuine sayings of one or both prophets have been elaborated into a little homily contrasting the distresses of the returned exiles (**10**; cf. Hag. 1:6)—or of the exilic period—with the blessings which are to be in the day of the remnant (**11**) and enjoining faith in those who now hear the prophetic message, that they should equally cast off their fear and be strong (**9, 13**; cf. Hag. 1:12, 2:5. Cf. Ackroyd, JJS 3 (1952), 151-6). h

In **9**, the reading 'since the day' follows LXX. The text actually means 'the prophets who were (active) in the day . . .' The allusions of **10** are rather more detailed than in Hag. 1:6 and 2:16f.; possibly there i

568i is some indication of the internal social problems raised for the returned exiles by the loss of their family property, and an allusion may be found to the hostility described in Ezr. 4–5, apparently on the part of the authorities, mainly in Samaria. In **12** the opening phrase is obscure : it may mean ' the seed shall be prosperous ', i.e. shall grow abundantly (cf. Hag. 2:19), or it could be rendered as ' its seed (i.e. that of the remnant) shall prosper '. LXX renders ' I will sow prosperity '. **13** may be compared with Gen. 12:2f., 22:18 ; men will mention Judah (and Israel, unless this is a gloss) to invoke a blessing upon themselves, and no longer to invoke a curse.

j (7) **14-17**. The devising of calamity on those who provoked God's wrath is here contrasted with his devising of good. But the word of assurance ' fear not ' (cf. 9, 13) is followed by a further emphasis on obedience (cf. 7:9–10). The saying closely resembles 1:1–6 and 7:4–14, and draws attention to the new age with its hopes and obligations. In **16**, the phrase ' that are true ' is probably due to the repetition of the word ' truth ' from the preceding phrase or influenced by a similar expression in 7:9. Read : ' Render in your gates judgments that make for well-being '—the reconciliation of contending parties and hence the well-being of the whole community. God's hatred (**17**) of the devising of evil by men (cf. 7:10) and of false swearing (cf. 5:3–4) is expressed by a technical term from marriage law (cf. Gen. 29:30f. ; Mal. 1:2f.) : God's ' insuperable disinclination ' against these things.

k (8) **18-19**. This is best regarded as the real answer to the inquiry in 7:2–3, though the list of fasts is fuller, including the fourth month (perhaps cf. 2 Kg. 25:3–11 ; Jer. 39:2), and the tenth month (perhaps cf. 2 Kg. 25:1). Fasts are to be converted into ' joyful festivals ' (19). Again the promise is followed by an injunction to faithfulness and reconciliation.

(9) **20-22**. The peoples—clearly non-Jews in **22**—are to come to entreat God's favour at Jerusalem (cf. 2:11 ; Isa. 2:2–4 = Mic. 4:1–3). The opening of **20** could be rendered : ' Again it shall be that . . .' where the ' again ' may be simply a resumptive word. In **21**, for ' at once ' render ' most certainly ' ; the closing phrase is very emphatic : ' Let me go, yes, me too '. Targum adds : ' said each to the other ', but the comment is better regarded as an emphatic interjection, either by a pious scribe or like the striking first-person form in 3:5.

(10) **23**. Universalistic ideas are welded to particularism. If all nations are here summoned to share in God's blessing, they must nevertheless recognise the special revelation of God through his people. To ' take hold of the robe ' probably means to ' accept the Jewish way of life ' and so, perhaps, to ' become a proselyte '. Where judgment foretells decimation (cf. Am. 5:3), the word of promise assures a tenfold increase. On ' God is with you ' cf. Isa. 7:14, 45:14.

SECOND SECTION IX-XIV

569a **Authorship and Structure**—The second part of the book consists of two groups of material introduced by the heading ' Oracle '. The same heading appears at Mal. 1:1, and since the book known as Malachi is also anonymous, it appears that three collections of prophetic material have been placed at the end of the ' Book of the Twelve '. Eventually the last was regarded as a separate book, while the first two came to be linked with Zech. 1–8.

b The very fact that this linking of 9–14 with 1–8 took place argues for some recognition of common ideas or interests. The disappearance of the personal names and clear allusions to the period of Darius I which mark 1–8 makes it clear that 9–14 are independent of Zechariah, and linguistic and stylistic considerations point the same way (cf., e.g., H. G. Mitchell, *Zechariah*, ICC (1912), 232–49) ; but certain points of contact may be noted. Thus, for example, the divine protection of 9:8 resembles that of 2:5 ; 569b
the wording of the commands to the prophet in 11:4, 13, 15 is not unlike that of the visions in 1–6, and perhaps more particularly of 6:9–14. More evidently, too, the whole emphasis on divine deliverance and the age of salvation provides close contacts, though the distinction must be observed between the immediacy of the promises of the new age in 1–8 (especially 7–8), linked to the rebuilding of the Temple, and the apocalyptic tone of 9–14.

The structure of 9–14, divided as it is into two c
collections, has been explained in various ways. On the analogy of Isa. 40–55 and 56–66, it has sometimes been thought proper to speak of a Deutero- and a Trito-Zechariah. Yet within 12–14 it is clear that 12:1–13:6 is hardly by the same author as 14, and it is more satisfactory to think of the building up of collections of material, belonging perhaps to various prophets and to various stages, than to think of one author or two for the whole. The problem of authorship is intimately linked with that of dating, and it may be doubted whether a completely orderly picture can be drawn of the process by which 9–14 has been formed. Some scholars think of early material (especially in 9–11), perhaps even of pre-exilic material (so e.g. Horst), to which later oracles have been added and the whole glossed and worked over in a third stage (so A. Jepsen, in ZATW, NF 16 (1939), 242–55 ; cf. also Elliger, Horst, Mitchell). It may be questioned whether an exact distinction can be made between the material of these varying stages.

Dating and Interpretation—The variety of datings d
to which sections of these chapters have been assigned does not inspire great confidence in any of those proposed. They have ranged from pre-exilic dating (as early as 740–730 B.C.), to the later Maccabaean period (so e.g. Kennett in Peake (1st ed.), and Oesterley and Robinson, *History of Israel* (1932), ii, 212ff., 242ff., 258ff., 304ff.). Most favoured is the assigning of some part at least of the material to the early Greek period (cf. the detailed historical discussion of 9:1–8 by K. Elliger in ZATW, NF 21 (1950), 63–115) ; though it must be admitted that assigning material to periods in which knowledge of Jewish history is very limited—as it is for the period from Alexander the Great to Antiochus III—is just as hazardous as the confident dating of it, on the basis of supposed allusions, in periods about which information is full—as, for example, the Maccabaean period.

It may be wondered whether the attempt to date e
is the most useful approach to the material. Kremer has listed thirty interpretations of the three shepherds of 11:8 (*Die Hirtenallegorie im Buche Zacharias* (1930), 17ff., 83ff.) of which some are too improbable to merit mention. That phrases which have been interpreted as historical allusions may have another origin will appear in the discussion of individual sections ; the same point has been made in the interpretation of psalmody in recent years. There are inevitably many points at which it must be confessed that we do not sufficiently know the events to be sure of a historical attachment for the oracles ; and it may be more useful to see in them messages which, however much originally conditioned by particular situations, have been preserved because they were discovered to be readily applicable to new needs.

The Message of IX-XIV—If chs. 1–8 show the place of f
the newly returned exiles in the coming age of salvation, chs. 9–14 are concerned in a manner much more nearly that of apocalyptic (cf. S. B. Frost, *OT Apocalyptic* (1952), 125–39), with the woes and distresses which usher in the final age, and with the establishment of the final divine rule. Jerusalem—which is in 8:20–3 a rallying-point for many peoples—is again described as the centre of a renewed land, in a new age (so especially ch. 14), and the nations, defeated by God in their attempts to frustrate his purpose, may be seen to have some hope of sharing in the worship of God.

569f The emphasis on the new age, and the fulfilment of men's hopes at a time which knew many distresses and uncertainties, is perhaps the reason for the not infrequent quotation from 9–14 in the NT (cf. Mt. 21:5 (cf. Jn 12:15), 26:15, 31 (Mk 14:27), 27:9 (quoted as Jer., perhaps because here Zech. 11:12–13 is combined with allusions to Jer. 32:6–15), Jn 19:37 (cf. Rev. 1:7)).

570a **IX 1-8 An Oracle of Judgment and Promise**—Judgment is proclaimed against some of the cities and states to the north of Israel, as well as against those of Philistia (1–6). The Philistines are to be incorporated into Judah (7) and God will protect his people (8).

The title 'Oracle' appears here as in 12:1, Mal. 1:1. The phrase which follows: 'the word of the Lord', is to be treated as part of the oracle and not as a further title. Vividly the divine word, representing the actual presence of God, is described as being 'in the land of Hadrach' (not 'against', RSV), and having Damascus as its resting-place. **1b** is difficult: RSV follows an emended text. The Heb. as it stands could mean 'For men look to the Lord (or, reading 'Aram' for 'man' (Adam), 'for Aram looks to the Lord'), and so do all the tribes of Israel'. This last phrase may simply be a gloss; or perhaps it should be emended to produce some place-name parallel to 'Aram'.

b **2-4** are clearer, depicting the vaunted wisdom—here, skill in diplomacy—of Phoenicia (cf. Ezek. 27, 28) and contrasting God's judgment. **3-4** may be rendered:

> Even though Tyre has built a citadel (cf. 2 Chr. 8:5 etc.; the word puns on 'Tyre') for herself...
> Behold, the Lord will impoverish her . . .'

5-6 depicts the judgment continued upon Philistia (cf. Jer. 25:20; Am. 1:6ff.; Zeph. 2:4), dismayed at the fate of Phoenicia. 'A mongrel people' suggests a half-Jewish population (cf. Dt. 23:2), but the term may be more general and refer to the settlement of foreign colonists. **7** describes the incorporation of Philistia, from which wrong practices are removed—the eating of blood and unclean flesh; **7b** calls Philistia a 'remnant', a clan of Judah (repointing the word translated 'governor' in AV. The Heb. word may, however, be rendered 'friend', cf. K-B), with an allusion to the incorporation of the Jebusites. This shows a remarkable breadth of vision (cf. 8:20–3). **8** depicts God's protection (cf. 2:5, 8:4f., 10f.); God in his temple (or his land—cf. Hos. 8:1 etc.) guards his people. The last phrase might be slightly emended to read 'Now I have looked upon his affliction.'

c Much in these verses suggests the time of the Assyrian conquests, and the reference to Israel in **1** would then be appropriate. The city of Hadrach ceased to exist in the 8th cent. B.C., and the apparent independence of the Philistine cities also fits that period. But a later date, particularly the period of Alexander the Great, is also possible. The name of Hadrach was used for an Assyrian province (Ḥatarikka), and possibly continued to be used under the Persians. The siege of Tyre by Alexander represented the most stubborn resistance with which he met, and the situation in Philistia corresponds well with the events of that period. Certainly **7-8** are more suitable to a later date with their universalistic outlook, and the relationship to Zech. 1–8 suggests that earlier ideas are here elaborated, and earlier prophecy has perhaps been used to explain the situation of Judah in a crucial age. The uncertainty of dating makes it advisable to deal gently with the text, rather than emending to produce readily intelligible allusions.

d **9-10 The Coming King**—The words of this saying, so appropriately providing a comment on the divine rule of 8, are reminiscent of psalmody, and in particular of passages which describe the functions of the king, the anointed. He is described as 'triumphant'—actually 'righteous' or better 'declared right, acquitted'—which is paralleled by 'victorious'—meaning 'given the victory'. The king is what he is by divine action, not by human power. He is also humble, riding upon an ass (cf. Gen. 49:10f.). Only one animal is meant: 'ass' and 'foal of an ass' are poetic parallels. The humiliation and vindication of the king may often be seen in the psalms (e.g. Ps. 89:38–45, cf. A. R. Johnson, *Sacral Kingship* (1955), 102ff.). Here the king (cf. Ps. 2:8, 72:8; Mic. 5:4) is given world-wide dominion, as in Akkadian royal psalmody; his kingdom stretches to the cosmic waters at the ends of the earth. His reign is one of peace and disarmament (cf. Ps. 46:9; Isa. 2:4= Mic. 4:3). The proposal to read a third-person verb —'he will cut off'—in **10a** lessens the vividness of the divine utterance. 570d

11-16 The Restoration—The theme of deliverance is continued with a summons to the prisoners to return and receive a double portion because of their sufferings (**11-12**). **11.** The description of the prison as a 'waterless pit' is perhaps due to a gloss from Gen. 37:24, but serves to suggest that the prisoners are exiles, in the barrenness of life far from home. They are to return to a 'stronghold'—but the word is of uncertain meaning, and should perhaps be emended to 'return in crowds' or 'to the daughter of Zion'. This deliverance is accompanied by divine warlike activity (**13-15**); God bends Judah as a bow, and fills the bow with Ephraim as an arrow. He uses his people as a sword to brandish. **13b** is overloaded, and 'over your sons, O Greece' is probably to be regarded as an explanatory gloss. It is, however, an indication of an early application of the prophecy, though precise historical reference cannot be given since either Ptolemies or Seleucids could be so described. e

In language reminiscent of Jg. 5:4 and Hab. 3:3, a theophany is described. God appears 'over his armies' (**14a**) and protects his own (**15a**). **15b** is obscure, and might be slightly emended to read 'and the slingstones (i.e. his people) shall devour flesh', The picture in this and the following phrases is then not unlike the great sacrificial battle-feast of Ezek. 39:17–20 (cf. Isa. 25:6); in this picture the LXX 'their blood' is preferable to the Heb. 'they are turbulent', and the last phrase of **15** pictures the drenching of the corners of the altar in the sacrificial ritual. **16.** The day of battle is a day of deliverance for God's people. **16a** might be better divided and emended to read: f

> The Lord their God will save them
> On that day he will feed them like a flock.

The sudden change of picture in **16b** is strange; the word rendered 'shine' means 'wave to and fro'.

IX 17-X 2 The Giver of Life—**17** is most often linked to 9:11–16 as a concluding picture of the day of salvation. Yet the rendering of **17a** as 'How good and fair he is' (Horst) suggests a link with **10:1-2** (cf. van Hoonacker, who, however, rearranges the text unnecessarily). A new stress is laid upon divine provision of the fruits of the earth (cf. 8:12), which are to be seen as divine blessings and not as provided by some mechanical religious device (**2**; cf. Hos. 2). **17b** may originally have read: 'He makes grain and new wine to flourish', the additional words being attempts to define the meaning more closely. The thought fits well with **10:1**, where God is described as giving rain and vegetation to man (cf. also 14:16f., Jer. 14:2–6). Small changes in text and punctuation would give in **1b**: g

> It is Yahweh who makes storm clouds
> who makes rain to fall.
> He gives bread to man
> the vegetation in the field.

In **2** various means of giving omens are said to be worthless and as a result the people are desperate for h

70h want of proper leadership. The relationship to the previous verses is not very close. The mention of teraphim has suggested an early date but we have no information as to when they ceased to be employed as a means of divination (cf. Ezek. 21:21). There is no good reason for believing that diviners and magicians were unknown in the post-exilic period. The oracle provides an explanation—wrong religious practices—for the delay in the coming of the new age. The reference to shepherds (**2**) provides a link of thought to the following passage, unless **3a** is to be interpreted as referring to the failure of Judah's leaders and regarded as the conclusion of this oracle.

i **X 3-12 The Battle for Deliverance and the Return of the Exiles**—God, through his people strengthened to battle on his behalf, brings a new hope and a day of return from exile. In many points, the wording of this passage is reminiscent of 9:11–16: God's people are again described as warriors, the agents of a victory which is divinely achieved; again the exiles are promised return. Whereas the earlier passage thinks of the covenant and Sinai theophany (9:11, 14), here the picture is of the passage of the sea (**11**), and a re-entry of the promised land (**10**).

j The passage consists partly of prophetic oracle (**3b-5**) in which God's care for Judah expresses itself by giving strength for battle. **4** is difficult, and it seems probable that the concluding clauses are explanatory: the corner-stone (cf. Jg. 20:2 etc.), the tent-peg (cf. Isa. 22:23) and the battle-bow, are symbols of charismatic leadership rather than weapons of war, and the Targum's discovery of a reference to the Messiah—from Judah (**3**)—is a not inappropriate reinterpretation of the idea. The future of the people will be in the hands of native rulers of (Davidic) line (cf. Mic. 5:2–5). In **5** 'together' is really the last word of **4**, but best read with the following clause. The word 'foe' does not appear in the text: 'trampling (them) like the mud' would be an alternative possibility.

k The remainder is in the form of a direct address by God, promising similar strengthening for ever—this time for Judah and Ephraim (**6-7**; cf. 9:13). In **6**, 'I will bring them back' represents a mixed form in the Heb.—two readings are preserved, 'I will cause them to dwell' and that of RSV; either is suitable. **7** is similar to 9:15, though rather less stark. **8-11** represents God 'whistling' for the exiles, as formerly he was described as summoning Assyria (cf. Isa. 5:26, 7:18). **8.** 'For I have redeemed them' may be a gloss, but a suitable comment, recalling the Exodus as does **11**. **10d** may be compared with Jos. 17:16f.; the reference to Gilead and Lebanon implies the outspreading of the returned exiles to refill the land occupied in the time of David. **11a** reads 'And he (one) shall pass through the sea, adversity': Egypt should be read for the last word. **11b** is also not clear and may be a gloss from 9:4, perhaps because the word for adversity, *ṣārāh*, was connected with Tyre—*ṣōr*. **12** reads 'they shall walk in his name', rendered 'glory in his name' by LXX; the former is perfectly satisfactory. 'Oracle of Yahweh' closes the section.

l Interpretation is difficult. **3a**, as we have seen, may simply be the conclusion of the preceding oracle. If it is the opening of this section, its reference to shepherds and he-goats—leaders of the flock—must be to foreign rulers. (For the metaphor cf. Isa. 14:9; Ezek. 34:17; cf. J. G. S. S. Thomson, SJTh. 8 (1955), 406–18.) No specific reference to foreign rulers appears in the remainder of the passage. The sentence is similar to material in 11:4–17, 13:7–9. The occurrence of Judah alone in **3b-5**, and of Judah and Ephraim in **6-7** suggests that the former is a separate oracle, here reinterpreted in a particular historical situation. But it is more doubtful to affirm that Egypt and Assyria (**11**) are the Ptolemies and Seleucids, or their predecessors in the period of struggle after the death of Alexander. Egypt and Assyria appear similarly, for example in Isa. 52:4, as representing the older disasters to the chosen people from which God brought deliverance. If precise definition is impossible, the general picture is of restoration through a new Exodus which ushers in the new age (cf. Isa. 51:9–11; Hos. 2:14f., etc.). 570l

XI 1-3 A Taunt Song—Vividly the Lebanon is invoked to open the doors like the gates of a besieged city to invaders, and fire devours the cedars, as so often cities were burnt after their capture (**1**). In **2** 'thick' forest would be better rendered as 'inaccessible'. The picture changes in **3**: the shepherds lament the despoiling of their 'glory'—Jer. 25:36 has 'pasture' in a similar expression. The lions roar because the jungle thickets (pride) of Jordan (cf. Jer. 12:5; GAB, Pl. 26) are devastated. The renderings 'ruined', 'despoiled' and 'laid waste' all represent the same Heb. word, and inevitably the sonority of its repetition is lost by using various English equivalents. 571a

Cedars are symbols of power in Isa. 10:33f. (Assyria) and Ezek. 31:1–18 (Egypt), and more generally in Isa 2:13. No precise reference can be indicated here, and the Ezekiel parallel shows that the localisation of the power is in no way connected with the northerly situation of Lebanon. The poem forms a triumphant conclusion to 10:3–12. b

4-17 Allegory of the Sheep and the Shepherds—A new style—much more closely akin to Zech. 1–8 and to Ezek.—is observable in the opening and again in **13** and **15**. Probably the opening phrase should be read: 'Thus Yahweh said to me' (cf. 15). The prophet is commanded to carry out a symbolic action, though its nature is such that it is impossible to be sure how far it could actually be performed; it is perhaps rather to be regarded as a literary device moulded upon prophetic symbolism (cf. Ezek. 37:16ff.). c

He is first (**4-7**) to act as shepherd to a 'doomed flock'—the chosen people are in the hands of those who kill them and go unpunished, caring only for their profit (**5**). The last phrase of **5** suggests that the shepherd is to be a good one, contrasted with those at present employed by the owners. If so, the gloomy note of **6** is intrusive. But **5** could also be interpreted as meaning 'Their shepherd (singular, i.e. the one they employ, whom the prophet represents) does not spare (singular verb) them': the singular verb, emended by most commentators, can then be preserved. **6** makes clear that the action of the prophet leads to rejection and doom; RSV 'his shepherd' is emended from 'his neighbour'—either is appropriate. The message of doom is not contradicted by **7**, which describes two staffs, named 'favour' and 'union', for the sequel shows that while the purposes of God are thus revealed as good, the disobedience of the people frustrates those purposes, and so God does not have pity. 'Those who trafficked'—lit. Canaanites—appears wrongly divided in the Heb. text into two words. Might these 'traffickers' be tax-gatherers? (cf. Mitchell). d

8a introduces 'the three shepherds', quite unconnected with what precedes and follows. It is clear that here is an interpretative comment arising out of some unknown situation. The variety of interpretations reveals the impossibility of recognising this situation. Only if the main section can be dated, is it possible to narrow the choice down to a later event. e

8b-11 resumes the symbol. **9.** The shepherd is seen to fail, and becomes indeed one who has no pity. **10.** The first staff is broken and the covenant brought to an end. It is described as with 'all the peoples', but in view of 14 it would be better to read 'all the people'. **11.** The merchants recognise the divine word. At this point there is but a thin line between actual symbolic action and allegory; it is not so difficult to visualise the prophet in the sheep-market, dressed as a shepherd, and breaking a staff to represent his repudiation of the sheep. The onlookers see the divine purpose clearly (cf. 2:9, 4:9 for similar stress on authority). f

571g A further element follows in **12-14**. The shepherd is paid his wages. Scornfully (' the magnificence of the price ', is the wage too small ?—was it a slave's price (cf. Exod. 21:32) ?) he casts it to the smelter in the Temple foundry (cf. Torrey, JBL 55 (1936), 247–60 ; Delcor, VT 3 (1953), 73–7—not ' treasury ' (RSV), which represents an emended text. The significance of the payment is lost, unless it reappears in 13:9. **14**. The second staff is broken, and the union of Judah and Israel is at an end. Dependence on Ezek. 37 seems evident, and we know of no later event other than the Samaritan schism as an appropriate occasion for this breach between north and south. The allusions are, however, so obscure as to make a dogmatic statement unjustifiable.

h **15-17** describes a further symbolic action or allegory. It appears to allude to a particularly evil ruler over the land—or the earth (**16**), and possibly marks a further elaboration of **4-14**. The passage puns on ' foolish ' and ' worthless '. **16** has some curious words : ' the sound ' should perhaps be ' the hungry ', ' tearing off their hoofs ' may be rendered ' tearing off pieces of them '. **17**. Doom is pronounced on the worthless shepherd in a poetic utterance.

The original gloomy note of the whole section is lightened with this divine act of judgment. It is possible that it has been elaborated to suggest universal judgment : ' all peoples ' (**10**), and ' this land ' (**6**) may be rendered ' the earth '.

i **XII 1-XIII 6 The Deliverance and Purification of Jerusalem and Judah**—The introductory phrase in **1**, like that at 9:1 and Mal. 1:1, appears as a heading to the whole section 12–14. It is expanded with a statement of the creative activity of God, reminiscent of Second Isaiah and of the creation narratives (especially Gen. 2:7). When Jerusalem is attacked by the nations (cf. Ezek. 38f. ; Mic. 4:11–13), God makes the city a ' cup of reeling ' (**2**, cf. Jer. 25:15ff. etc.). **2b** is obscure and is perhaps a gloss to include Judah with Jerusalem. The text might be emended to : ' there will be against Judah a siege like the siege against Jerusalem '. Pictures of disaster brought by God follow in **3** and **4a** ; a stone causes injury (actually the meaning is ' lacerate oneself ') or, emending the text, is allowed to fall ; panic strikes the enemy, elaborated in **4b** as blindness for the nations while the people of Judah are regarded with
j favour. In **5**, the clans of Judah are represented as acknowledging the divine protection of Jerusalem ; the Heb. reads : ' strength for me are the inhabitants of Jerusalem '. **6** pictures God spreading disaster among the nations like fire among trees, or among the corn-sheaves, while Jerusalem remains securely in its place. **7**—with a change to third-person forms descriptive of God—introduces a curious hostility to the house of David and the people of Jerusalem, but this is immediately countered by the picture of divine blessing in **8**. The phrase ' angel of the Lord ' is probably inserted to soften the bold description of the house of David as ' like God '. **9** should be read ' I purpose to destroy ' rather than ' seek ' which suggests uncertainty as to the outcome.

k Attempts to discover a historical situation in these verses are precarious ; the onslaught of the nations is an apocalyptic picture possibly connected with the royal liturgy as found, for example, in Ps. 2. The somewhat awkward alternation between Jerusalem and Judah may be due to different sayings being gathered into a unit, or to some elaboration of earlier material with an eye to a particular situation. Our knowledge of the post-exilic period is so patchy that such allusions as those of **7** ought not to be tied down.

l The same uncertainty attends the interpretation of **12:10-13:1**, in which a great lamentation is described, ending in a promise of a fountain of water to cleanse Jerusalem and the house of David (cf. Ezek. 47:1ff. ; Jl 4:18). The description is given in rhythmic form (**12-13**, using the 3:2 measure characteristic of the lament)—the families and their womenfolk mourn separately ; first two royal clans, David and Nathan 571l
(cf. 1 Chr. 3:5 ; Lk. 3:31), next two priestly clans, Levi and Shimei (cf. Num. 3:18), and finally the rest of the people (**14**). The mourning is such that it is compared with that for an only child, or a first-born son (**10b**), and compared also with the ritual weeping for Hadadrimmon in the plain of Megiddo, an allusion to the lament for the fertility deity, here identified with Hadad—the storm deity, and Rimmon, the chief god of Damascus (cf. 2 Kg. 5:18). The Râs Shamra tablets provide direct evidence of such practices in the Canaanite area (cf. ANET, 139), and ' weeping for Tammuz ' is mentioned in Ezek. 8:14. The mention of Megiddo suggests an allusion to the death of Josiah (cf. 2 Chr. 35:25) ; Syr. brings this out by speaking of ' the mourning for the son of Amon '.

10. This mourning is associated with the pouring m
out on the house of David and the people of Jerusalem of a ' spirit of compassion and supplication '. This spirit leads the people to ' look on me (so Heb. text : RSV ' him ') whom they have pierced '. Three main lines of interpretation are possible : (1) Adopting the reading ' him ' (cf. Jn 19:37), we may look for a historical character who was murdered and whose death is repented by those who inflicted it. Onias the High Priest of the 2nd cent. is a favourite candidate, but there can be no certainty. Nor is it certain that the subject of ' they have pierced ' is the same as that of ' they look ', so that it cannot be stated dogmatically that the character in question is now venerated by his murderers. (2) Or we may look, as is very often done, to the Suffering Servant figure of Isa. 53, and think perhaps in terms of some eschatological myth, connected with one who suffers and for whom lamentation is made ; the rituals alluded to in **11** would be not inappropriately applied to such a figure. (3) It cannot be denied that the more difficult reading ' they look on me ' gives a satisfactory sense if the following clause is interpreted as metaphor rather than as literal statement. The LXX render : ' they will turn towards me because they have insulted me ' (lit. ' danced in triumph '). Delcor has pointed to the similarity of this chapter to Ezek. 36:16–28, and notes that the term used there for ' profaning the name ' of God is one which can also have the meaning ' pierce ' (RB 58 (1951), 189–99). On this interpretation, the divine act of deliverance (**12:2-9**) is followed by a divine gift of repentance and cleansing (**12:10-13:1**).

This in its turn is followed by an elaboration of the n
idea of cleansing (**13:2-6**), where it appears that the evils of idolatry and false prophecy to be removed are just those which can be regarded as particularly wounding to God. There is concentration on false prophecy (cf. Neh. 6:12–14) ; older prophetic sayings are here reinterpreted to show how the external trappings of the prophet—the hairy garment, the ecstatic practice —are being misused (cf. Dt. 13:5, 18:20 ; Am. 7:14). **6** alludes to the lacerations of prophetic ecstasy (cf. 1 Kg. 18:28), which the false prophet excuses as resulting from a brawl. The meaning of this last phrase is however by no means clear, though this interpretation seems more likely than that the ' friends ' should be regarded as ' lovers ' with an allusion to fertility-cult practices.

XIII 7-9 Disaster and Purification—This poetic 572a
utterance is placed after the shepherd pictures of 11:4–17 by many commentators. But it is not possible to be sure that the shepherd of **7** is identical with any of the shepherds in ch. 11. It is better to treat this saying as separate, and as linked in thought with 12:1–13:6. God brings disaster ; leadership gone, the people are scattered (**7b**, cf. 1 Kg. 22:17 ; Mt. 26:31). This is an occasion for purification, but only of a remnant ; one-third is preserved and refined like gold or silver, so that a new people is formed for God, and acknowledges him (cf. Hos. 2:23 etc.). The picture of refining (cf. Ezek. 22:17ff.) perhaps provides a link with 11:13. The description of the shepherd as ' the man who stands next to me '—an associate of

572a God, a suitable term for a royal figure—perhaps suggests a disaster to some messianic personage (should we compare 12:10?), so that the picture is of messianic woes ushering in the final age (cf. Mk 13 etc.).

b **XIV The New Age**—The use of the introductory 'And it shall be on that day' (**6, 8, 13**) marks off sections of the material of this chapter; 'the day' or 'that day' gives, as in 12:1–13:6, a confident glimpse of the new age to come. The chapter consists of various elements, though it is uncertain whether an original coherent picture has been elaborated by annotators, or whether various separate sayings have been brought together because of their general similarity and common theme. The whole passage abounds in allusions to other OT material, and shows the fullest development of apocalyptic style in 9–14.

c **1-5** describes an onslaught on Jerusalem (cf. 12:2ff.) in which the city is taken with violence and its booty divided within the walls. **2.** Half the population goes into exile, but half is preserved in the city. Vividly the contrast is drawn between those who 'go forth' to exile (**2**) and God who 'goes forth' (**3**) as on a great day of battle. The allusion is probably to the cosmic battle (cf. Job 38:22f.) or possibly, as the Targum suggests, to the conflict at the crossing of the Sea (cf. Isa. 51:9ff.). **4.** At the theophany on the Mount of Olives, the mountain is split in two (cf. Nah. 1:5; Hab. 3:6, etc.); a great valley opens up from east to west. The note 'which lies before Jerusalem on the east' may be designed for readers (outside Palestine) unfamiliar with the topography of the city; or it may serve to draw attention to such a passage as Ezek. 43:2 (cf. Ezek. 11:23), where the glory of God comes from the east. The obscurity of **5** makes it uncertain whether the valley is opened up as a way of escape or as a channel for the waters to the Dead Sea (**8**). The difficulty in **5** is occasioned firstly by three occurrences of a word *nastēm*, from the root meaning 'to flee', and secondly by the geographical allusions. *Nastēm* could be punctuated as *nistām* and mean 'stopped up': RSV renders the first occurrence thus. The upheaval caused by God's appearance blocks a valley, and the terrified population escapes as at the time of the earthquake mentioned in Am. 1:1. It would, however, be better to render all the occurrences of the word in this way (cf. LXX) and read: 'and it shall be blocked as it was blocked in the days of Uzziah' (cf. Jos. Ant. IX, x, 4), since God's appearance and the statement of **2**, 'shall not be cut off from the city', make the idea of flight

d altogether inappropriate here. The 'valley of my mountains' is probably an error for 'the valley of the mountains' (which appears subsequently). This could be emended to 'valley of Hinnom'; but probably should be interpreted as a phrase for the Kidron valley between Jerusalem and the Mount of Olives. Instead of 'for . . . shall reach the side of it' Abel renders 'from Goa to Yasol' (cf. RV Azel. Cf. RB 45 (1936), 398f. and H. Vincent, *Jérusalem* I (1912), Pl. I). The whole phrase may, however, be another topographical note to explain that the obscure 'valley of the mountains' actually lies adjacent to the Mount of Olives. The last clause of **5** has some confusing possessive forms; as it stands it could be an interjection of confidence: 'The Lord *my* God will come, and all the holy ones—the heavenly host—will be with you (i.e. Jerusalem).'

e **6-11** describes the new age and the transformation of the land (cf. Ezek. 47–8). The text of **6** is obscure (cf. RV); as it stands it means 'there shall not be light, precious things shall be gathered together'. The latter phrase is probably to be emended to 'cold and freezing', and it seems better to omit the word for 'light' and gain a hopeful statement comparable to **7**. The new age will see the end of the present seasonal divisions (cf. Gen. 8:22), and of day and night; water will be abundant all the year round (**7f.**). The bracketed phrase in **7** may be a pious comment: 'God only knows when this new age will dawn'; or possibly it means '(continuous day) is known to God'—he dwells in eternal light (cf. Isa. 60:19f.). **8** is reminiscent of Ezek. 47:1ff. and Gen. 2:10ff. **10-11** pictures the whole land of Judah (Geba to the north, Rimmon to the south, marking the boundaries of the kingdom; cf. 2 Kg. 23:8 for a similar expression) brought to the level of the Jordan valley; Jerusalem alone remains on high (cf. Isa. 2:2 = Mic. 4:1), securely inhabited since the divine 'ban' is no more. The city is occupied to its boundaries; the east-west limits are the gate of Benjamin (possibly the Sheep-gate) and the 'former gate' or 'Corner gate'—these are alternatives, though it is not certain which is the original reading; the north-south limits are the Tower of Hananel and the king's wine-presses, probably to be sought in the extreme south of the city, near the king's garden (cf. Neh. 3). God is established as king over all the earth, his name confessed by all (**9**; cf. Dt. 6:4).

12-15 brings further pictures of disaster upon the f
nations. Men and beasts will rot away as they stand (**12, 15**). Panic brought by God will turn men against one another (**13**; cf. Jg. 7:22 etc.). **14a** (if it is not a gloss referring to some particular situation, cf. 12:2) should be rendered 'fight in Jerusalem', i.e. against the nations, and **14b** then indicates the spoiling of those who have oppressed the city. The section appears to be a collection of independent sayings.

16-19 holds out the hope that even the survivors of g
the nations will come yearly to worship at the Feast of Booths, when the kingship of God is acknowledged (**16**; cf. 9; cf. A. R. Johnson, *Sacral Kingship* (1955), 51f.). The connection of the water libations at this feast with the coming of the rains is indicated by the threat of **17**, elaborated in **18** to specify a separate punishment for Egypt since lack of rain does not affect that land. The awkward expression 'then upon them shall not [omitted by RSV] come' might be rendered as a question: 'shall there not come?' or it may be an error for such an expression as 'the Nile shall not rise' (cf. Targum). **18c.** 'that do not go up . . .' appears to be wrongly added from **19**.

20-21 emphasises the holiness of Jerusalem and Judah h
in the new age. Even the horses' bells—originally designed to avert evil spirits—will be inscribed like the high-priestly diadem (cf. Exod. 28:36); perhaps the meaning is that the secular power will be brought entirely within God's domain, since horses are symbols of military strength (cf. Isa. 31:1ff.). The ordinary vessels are perhaps to be made of gold like the bowls before the altar; or perhaps they are to be used for blood like these bowls because of the multitude of worshippers; every vessel will be sacred, so that all may sacrifice. The meaning of 'trader' in **21** is uncertain. Possibly it refers to the exclusion of commercial practices (cf. Mt. 21:12f.). Rendered as 'Canaanite' (cf. 11:7, 11) it might refer to the exclusion of aliens, but the universalism of the previous verses is against this. It might be an allusion to the excluding of the Samaritans (cf. the limits of the land in 10 which exclude the Samaritan territory).

Bibliography—COMMENTARIES: W. E. Barnes, CB (1917); S. Bullough, *Obadiah, Micah, Zephaniah, Haggai, Zechariah*, Westminster Version (1953); R. C. Dentan, on chs. ix–xiv, IB vi (1956); S. R. Driver, Cent.B (1906); K. Elliger, ATD (1951); A. van Hoonacker, EBib. (1908); F. Horst, HAT (1954); H. G. Mitchell, ICC (1912); E. Sellin, KAT (1930); G. Adam Smith, Ex.B (1928); D. Winton Thomas, on chs. i–viii, IB vi (1956).

OTHER LITERATURE: K. Galling, 'Die Exilswende in der Sicht des Sacharja', VT 2 (1952), 18–36; T. Jansma, 'Inquiry into the Hebrew Text and Ancient Versions of Zechariah 9–14', *Oudtestamentische Studiën* 7 (1950), 1–142; L. G. Rignell, *Die Nachtgesichte des Sacharja* (1950); J. W. Rothstein, *Die Nachtgesichte des Sacharja*, BWANT 2 (1910).

MALACHI

By L. H. BROCKINGTON

573a The literary structure of Mal. is unique among the books of the prophets. It comprises six sections, each opening with a statement to which a question, usually of deprecation, is put and the theme is then enlarged in brief argument. 2:17–3:4 offers a brief example: You have wearied me with your words. Yet you say, 'How have we wearied the Lord?' By saying, 'Everyone who does evil is good in the sight of the Lord, and he delights in them.' Or by asking, 'Where is the God of justice?' The section then goes on to say that God will indeed appear to judge and will be like a refiner's fire; no-one will be able to endure his coming.

b These are the six sections:

(1) **I 1-5.** Yahweh's love for Jacob is greater than his love for Esau. This is the only one of the six sections that does not contain a reproach on Israel.

(2) **I 6-II 9.** Honour is withheld from Yahweh by both priests and laymen.

(3) **II 10-12, 13-16.** The men of Judah have been faithless to God by marrying foreign women and adopting their heathen worship.

(4) **II 17-III 5.** The people have denied Yahweh's justice; he will therefore visit them in judgment.

(5) **III 6-12.** Tithes have been neglected, which is tantamount to robbing God.

(6) **III 13-IV 3.** Worship is despised and neglected, but true God-fearers will earn their reward.

c The book bears the same introductory title as does each of the additions to Zech. (9:1 and 12:1). The three collections of prophecies which bear these titles (Zech. 9–11, 12–14; Mal. 1–4) may have been added by the same editor who then affixed the same introductory formula to each. On the other hand, Mal. may have been added later and the formula copied from Zech. 9:1 or 12:1. If the Mal. chapters were added at the same time as the last chapters of Zech. we must assume that they were subsequently separated from the others in the interests of making a book of twelve prophets. But in that case, as a separate book, a name had to be found for it, and the editor seems to have turned to the beginning of ch. 3 and found it in the Heb. word *mal'ākhî* 'my messenger'.

d Whether or not the Mal. chapters were added at the same time as the last chapters of Zech., they seem to be somewhat earlier in their date of composition. The date is usually thought to be about 460 B.C. for the following reasons:

(*a*) The people have returned from Exile and are under the rule of a governor (1:8), and the Temple services have been resumed for long enough for the priests apparently to have become weary of the performance of them (1:13) and for irregularities and neglect to have crept in. (*b*) Such references as there are to the pentateuchal laws and institutions have affinity with Dt. rather than with the other codes. This suggests a time before Ezra to whom, it is thought, the promulgation of the priestly code is due. The following parallels may be noted between Mal. and Dt.:

Mal. 1:2	God's love for Jacob	Dt. 7:8	
Mal. 1:9	God does not show favour	Dt. 10:17	
Mal. 2:1, 4, 3:3	Priest and Levite are synonymous; Levites may offer sacrifice	Dt. 18:1	
Mal. 2:6	The law of truth in Levi's mouth	Dt. 33:10	573
Mal. 4:4	Revelation to Moses on Horeb	Dt 4:10	

(*c*) The fact that some of the community have married foreign wives, 2:10–12, seems to show no knowledge of the reforming work of Nehemiah and Ezra. Nehemiah returned in 444, so we must think of that date, or shortly before it, as the very latest at which the book could have been written. (*d*) Slackness in the payment of dues which is complained of in 3:8 was one of the things which Nehemiah had to reform.

On the other hand, there are several things that demand as late a date as possible, consistent with the facts already mentioned. First, the Edomites are threatened with disaster, indeed, it may already be beginning to overtake them, 1:3–5. This will refer to the Arab invasion of Edomite territory which finally resulted in the setting up of a Nabataean kingdom there. The exact date of this is not known; it took place before 312 (see on Ob.). Second, the abuses in worship imply a considerable lapse of time after the enthusiasm of the initial restoration in 516 after the Exile. Third, the high praise offered to the purity of heathen sacrifices, 1:11, is more in keeping with the temper that prevailed in some hearts after the Exile than anything in the pre-exilic period. If this evidence taken together is valid, and if we may, on the basis of it, assume a date at about 460 B.C. the book becomes a valuable contemporary witness to conditions shortly before the return of Nehemiah. e

(1) **I 1.** The editor's introduction to the book. 574
The first part of the verse 'The oracle of the word of the Lord' is identical with that in Zech. 9:1 and 12:1, although set out differently in RSV. It may be the work of the editor of the twelve minor prophets, or it may be that of the editor who added the last part of Zech. Malachi is a transliteration of the Heb. word for 'my messenger' found in 3:1 and its use here as a proper name is probably to be assigned to the editor who finally decided that there should be a Book of the Twelve Prophets, each bearing a prophet's name. In LXX the name Malachi is put at the head of the book and in the first verse it is translated thus 'by the hand of his messenger'.

2-5. Yahweh loves Jacob more than Esau. This is the first of the six sections into which the book may be divided. The statement 'I have loved you' is made and then the question asked which elicits the answer that God's love for Jacob is greater than for Esau, Jacob's own brother. This is the only section which does not contain a reproach. **3. I have hated:** this attitude of Yahweh to Edom reflects, of course, Israel's own attitude to Esau. Although it could be said that it was a true reflection on their mutual feeling at any time in their history, it was doubly true after 586, cf. Ps. 137:7; Lam. 4:21f.; Ob. 18–21. **I have laid waste:** if it is established that the book was written in the first half of the 5th cent. B.C. this will probably have to be understood as a 'prophetic perfect', for it is unlikely that by this time the Nabataean invasion would have progressed so far that the Edomites were already contemplating rebuilding the ruins. This disaster to Edom will, in effect, be a further revelation b

574b to Israel of Yahweh's power which the prophet seems to expect to take place within the lifetime of those to whom he spoke so that they would see it with their own eyes. **5. Beyond the border of Israel:** Yahweh's power, as great as his love for his people, extends beyond Israel's border in the exercise of his love for them. Here, as occasionally elsewhere in the post-exilic period, universalism makes itself heard in Israel.

c (2) **I 6-II 9.** The honour due to Yahweh is withheld from him by priests as well as by laymen. The priests are to suffer punishment for it. This section, like those to follow, begins with a reproach to which the priests' question implies that it is unjustified. The argument then maintains that improper sacrifices cannot honour Yahweh and that in this matter the laymen are no better than the priests. In the course of the development of the theme two statements are made of far-reaching implication, namely that God's name is great among the nations (11) and that it is feared among the nations (14). We may perhaps draw the inference that Israel's sin is great indeed in daring to offer inferior worship to God : even heathen nations, not chosen by God, offer acceptable worship to him.

d **8.** 'Blind animals', cf. Lev. 22:20, 22 ; Dt. 15:21, 17:1, where blemished animals are forbidden for sacrifice and blindness is mentioned as one of the blemishes. **9. Entreat the favour of God:** the phrase originally had a strong anthropomorphic sense implying that man by his worship could remove the signs of anger and displeasure from the face of God. By the time this was written it had come to be a metaphor for prayer. **10. Shut the doors:** because it would be far better not to sacrifice at all than to continue the present sham. The Gentiles offer a more acceptable worship without the specific Israelite ceremonial. This, at all events, is one possible meaning of v. 11 which can be read as affirming that even Gentile nations recognise the greatness of God's name and offer sacrifices that are pure in his sight. Another way of taking the verse is to imagine groups of Jewish worshippers offering sacrifice on foreign soil, i.e. among the nations and witnessed by them so that the Lord's name is great among them. Direct evidence in support of either view is lacking, but the plain sense of the words favours the former view. **12. when you say:** not in so many words but in their bearing and behaviour. **14. and vows it:** this will refer, not to the regular offering which would require no vow, but to the offering a man might vow to make in time of distress if his prayer should be granted. Lev. 22:18ff. specifies a male without blemish for the burnt-offering for vows.

e Uncertainty is sometimes expressed about the genuineness of vv. 11–14, for they appear to be concerned with laymen and their offerings whereas 6–10 and 2:1–9 are addressed solely to the priests. They may be a later insertion, but even if that be so, they are fully in keeping with the thought of the rest of the book.

f **II 1-9** is a continuation of 1:6–14 and threatens the priests, the house of Levi, with punishment for their failure in their duties. **2. give glory to my name:** by making sincere worship ; cf. 1:6 where the word is translated 'honour'. 'I will curse your blessings' : the priestly blessing was a most solemn part of the service (see Num. 6:22–7) and ultimately came to be the only occasion on which the divine name was actually pronounced in Israel. To threaten that the blessing be turned into a curse was to undermine and overthrow the whole fabric of institutional religion in Israel. For the ominous nature of curses see Dt. 27 and 28. **3.** The fouling of their persons which, by virtue of their priesthood, should be kept ritually clean at all times, is another reversal of the normal character of the priesthood. **4. my covenant with Levi:** cf. Num. 25:12, 13 where a covenant of a perpetual priesthood is mentioned but is promised to Phinehas son of Eleazar son of Aaron. Such a covenant is

indirectly implied in Dt. 33:9 and is there associated 574f
with Levi. The natural conclusion to draw from this reference by Malachi to Levi is that the prophet is in the same tradition as Dt. (18:1) according to which Levite and priest were virtual synonyms. The description of it as a covenant of peace comes from Num. 25:12. **7.** 'messenger' is the same Heb. word as that in 3:1 and is a unique description of the priest as the Lord's messenger. It is significant that Malachi should so speak of the priests and also use the same word for the herald of the Lord's coming. One is bound to wonder whether the herald would, in fact, be a Levite.

(3) **10-16.** A charge of faithlessness to Yahweh by 575a
marrying foreign women who worship other gods and of neglecting their own wives whom they married in a covenant relationship ratified by Yahweh. This section differs from the others in having no initial statement. It opens with a question which deprecates any suspicion of faithlessness amongst those who are descended from one father and are under the same covenant. This is answered by a charge of faithlessness and of profaning the covenant. **10.** 'One father' probably means God himself (cf. Dt. 32:18 ; Isa. 63:16), although it could be understood to mean either Abraham (as in Isa. 51:2, 63:16) or Jacob (cf. 2:12, 3:6 and Isa. 43:27). The covenant of our fathers is that made on Sinai in the records of which is embedded a prohibition of intermarriage with non-Israelites (Exod. 34:16 ; Dt. 7:3, 4). **11.** By 'married the daughter of a foreign god' the prophet implies that, like Solomon, they have not only taken foreign wives but have accepted the heathen worship to which they were accustomed in their own lands. Vv. 13, 16 imply that they then divorced their Israelite wives. This was not only an affront to the nation but to Yahweh himself who had witnessed the covenant which every marriage renewed. **12** seems to envisage the deprival of both civil rights and religious privileges : the offender will have no-one to witness or answer for him in a court of law or to make an offering for him in the Temple. This latter illustrates the absorbing interest which Malachi shows in the Temple services and their maintenance.

13-16 form an appendix to 10–12 and utter a con- b
demnation of divorce. This really brings forward yet another reason why God will not accept the sacrifices made by Israelites ; they make a show of penitence but their married life gives the lie to it all. **15.** This verse is difficult almost beyond solution, as will be seen by the two footnotes in RSV. Two words occur twice over in the verse and appear to be key words if only we had a clue to the way they are meant to be taken in the context. The words are 'one' in clauses *a* and *c* (rendered in *c* by the pronoun 'he') and 'spirit' in clauses *b* and *c* (rendered in *c* by 'yourselves'). There seems little doubt that the repeated 'one' echoes the 'one God' of v. 10. 'Spirit' may be the spirit of God invigorating the spirit of life in man, in which case clause *c* could be translated 'take heed to the spirit that you possess' ; or it could mean in *b* the life-giving spirit of God and in *c* the life-force in man. Godly offspring probably means children who are worthy of the one God who created both parents. We might paraphrase the verse in this way : 'Let us bear in mind that the One God has made us (or, with slight vowel change, her, i.e. the wife) and sustained his life-giving spirit in us. What, then, would this one God expect of us, if not an offspring worthy of him ? Guard, therefore, the life you owe to his spirit and do not be unfaithful to your true wife.'

(4) **II 17-III 5.** The people have denied justice : c
they have said that Yahweh is indifferent to what is right and that he is not a God of justice. They will learn the truth when he comes for judgment and appears like a refiner's fire. 'My messenger' (3:1), Heb. *mal'ākhî* ; it is from this that the name in the title of the book was probably taken. He is described as a messenger of the covenant and is thus indirectly

575c linked with the passage in 2:7ff. where the priest is a messenger of the Lord of hosts and enjoys a covenant of peace. There is some uncertainty as to whether vv. 2–4 describe the activity of the messenger or of Yahweh himself. God's judgment will be made from the Temple itself, his dwelling-place on earth, but its officers must first be purified. **5** tells of the actual judgment and the kind of people who will fall under judgment : sorcerers (cf. Exod. 22:18 ; Isa. 47:9, 12), adulterers (Exod. 20:14 ; Dt. 5:18), those who swear falsely (Lev. 19:12), those who oppress the hireling in his wages (Lev. 19:13 ; Dt. 24:14) and the widow and orphan (Exod. 22:22 ; Dt. 24:17), and those who thrust aside the sojourner (Exod. 22:21f. ; Dt. 24:17).

d (5) **III 6-12**. Tithes have been neglected. If the people remember their duty and give up robbing God by withholding their proper dues then he will richly bless the produce of their land. **6**. ' I the Lord do not change ' : this may be in answer to criticism made by the people about Yahweh, but many times in the OT the contrast between God in his moral purity and man in his weakness is drawn, e.g. Num. 23:19. **7**. The apostasy spoken of was worthy of death, but God, faithful to his people, has not destroyed (consumed) them. **9**. ' Cursed with a curse ' : cf. Dt. 27 and 28 for the threat of curses upon those who fail to keep the law. ' Windows of heaven ' : cf. Gen. 7:11 ; 2 Kg. 7:2. **11**. The ' devourer ' is doubtless one of the ways in which people spoke of locusts, cf. Jl 1 for the destruction that could be wrought by locusts and the several names given to them. **12**. ' Call you blessed ' : cf. the opening word of Ps. 1. ' Land of delight ' : cf. Isa. 62:4, ' You shall be called My delight is in her ' (Heb. *Hephzibah*).

e (6) **III 13-IV 3**. The worship of God is despised and neglected ; men deem it preferable to be arrogant and wicked for they seem to suffer no punishment for it. But there are some true God-fearers whose names will be recorded in the book of remembrance and who will be God's special possession when he comes to punish the wicked. When that day does come the plight of the wicked will be terrible indeed, while the righteous will be vindicated as they share in the trampling down of the wicked. **16**. ' Book of remembrance ' : cf. Exod. 32:32 ; Ps. 56:8, 69:28, 139:16 ; Isa. 4:3 ; Dan. 12:1. **17**. ' Special possession ' : cf.

Exod. 19:5 ; Dt. 7:6, etc. **4:2**. ' Sun of righteousness 575e
with healing in its wings ' is a figure of speech probably based on the conventionalised representation of the sun god as a winged disc in Egyptian, Babylonian, Assyrian and Persian religious art (see ANEP (1954)). ' Leaping like calves from the stall ' : cf. Ps. 29:6. **3**. ' You shall tread down the wicked ' : for the triumph of the pious over the wicked see Am. 9:12 ; Mic. 4:13, 7:17.

4. An exhortation to observe the law of Moses. Horeb f
is the name given to the mountain in Dt. In LXX this verse is placed to follow 5f. and thus to stand last in the book. Whether that was its original position or not, it is most likely editorial and intended to make a fitting end to the Book of the Twelve.

5, 6. The promise of the coming of Elijah to herald g
the day of the Lord. Malachi came to be regarded as the last of the prophets. It was very probable, therefore, that when men's thoughts turned to the expectation of a messenger to herald Yahweh's coming as expressed in 3:1 they would think not of a future unnamed and unknown prophet but of a former prophet. Elijah was a very natural choice for he had not died on earth but had been taken up into heaven, 2 Kg. 2:11. This, therefore, seems to be an editorial note offering an expansion of 3:1. It is the first reference to Elijah as the forerunner of the Messiah but it was an idea that came to stay and is found again in 1 Enoch 90:31 ; Mt. 11:14, etc. Elijah caught the imagination of the Jews who held him in special honour, cf. Sir. 48:1–12. In later times a place was laid for him at the Passover meal. They confidently expected that he would return to prepare the people for the crisis which would usher in the messianic age. Very fittingly, the OT, in the form in which we now have it, closes on this note of expectation that one of Israel's greater prophets would return to herald the coming of Jesus the Messiah.

Bibliography—W. E. Barnes, CB (1917) ; A. von Bulmerincq, *Kommentar zum Buche des Propheten Maleachi* (1932 ; *Einleitung* 1926) ; S. R. Driver, Cent.B ; K. Elliger, ATD (3rd ed. 1956) ; A. van Hoonacker, EBib. (1908) ; F. Horst, HAT (2nd ed. 1954) ; C. Lattey, *The Book of Malachy*, Westminster Version (1934) ; K. Marti, KHC (1904) ; E. Sellin, KAT (2nd ed. 1929) ; J. M. P. Smith, ICC (1912).

THE LANGUAGE OF THE NEW TESTAMENT

By N. TURNER

576a **(a) Hellenistic Greek**—Careful study of secular Greek literature of the last three centuries B.C., and what we know besides of the *spoken* Greek of this period, is still essential to the NT student who would examine the records at first hand.

The language in which these records were originally written is almost certainly Greek, though quite definitely their authors would almost all have spoken in Aramaic as well. In some cases it is possible that first drafts of their work were in Aramaic. The Greek in which the books are now extant belongs to that variety and period of the language known as Hellenistic. Anyone who has studied the Classical language of the great dramatists, the great prose authors, or the renowned orator Demosthenes, and whose studies have taken him no further will fail to understand the language of the NT. In vocabulary and style, but much more in thought-content, it is almost an entirely new language. Several influences brought this about, some gradual and some very sudden.

b First, the language itself is descended from the old dialect of Athens, called Attic (itself slightly Ionised in the Aegean 'Empire' of Athens), which tended to supplant all other dialects and was taken by Alexander the Great in his conquests and colonisations (334–320 B.C.) far and wide through the eastern Mediterranean, Syria, Palestine, and Egypt. After that, though the Romans conquered Greece, the Greek language conquered the Romans and followed them westwards. In the process, quite naturally, the old Attic was modified by the nations through which it spread, until it became a great universal language to which we have given the name of *Koine*, the cosmopolitan dialect in which many Greek dialects had some share but wherein Attic was the foundation of them all. Now scholars are in the main agreed that this language, especially in its more colloquial form, is that of the NT authors. This has come about in consequence of the discoveries and conclusions of Grenfell and Hunt, Deissmann, Thumb, and Moulton and Milligan. Deissmann claimed that the total of peculiarly 'biblical' words in the NT was only one per cent of its whole vocabulary. Before the work of these scholars our knowledge of Hellenistic Greek was dependent on its literary remains which were written in a 'literary Koine', sometimes, as in Polybius, with careful avoidance of hiatus. It was obvious that the NT differed from the language of the literature of its period, especially when the latter revived specifically Attic tendencies. There are very few atticisms in the NT, but many striking instances of the unfettered flexibility of the colloquial speech. Moreover, the NT language was thought to be very different from the stylistic aspirations of would-be *literati* such as Philo and Josephus. New papyrus discoveries in Egypt seemed to reveal a type of Greek which was almost exactly that of the NT.

c The characteristics of the language were a simplification of the verb system, a great display of the use of prepositions and compound verbs, simple syntax, and a tendency to disregard the rules of concord. This and the fact that so many new words 576c
had been coined makes a Classical grammar and lexicon virtually useless to the student of the NT. He will derive more profit from studying sensibly the indices to the published volumes of papyri of the Ptolemaic period and the illuminating works of Mayser on the grammar of these texts.

There has been somewhat of a reaction against the more extreme position of these pioneers, even among those who still maintain that the NT language is a form of Hellenistic Greek. Dr Milligan himself had said in his final preface to the renowned *Vocabulary of the Greek NT* that the NT language was half-way between literary and popular usage. There is certainly a case for arguing that it is often more akin to the literary *Koine* than to the vulgar papyrus texts. Mk and Rev. do indeed come very near the market-place at times, but Paul was usually, and Pet. and Jas always, decidedly literary in style. There is a certain affinity between the language of these writers and that of Polybius, Plutarch, and Lucian. It may be argued that Lk.-Ac. and Heb. are much nearer to the literary than to the colloquial *Koine*. While one may therefore appreciate the enthusiasm of those scholars who first investigated the papyrus texts from the rubbish heaps of Egypt and saw in their language a startlingly close affinity with that of the NT, there is a danger that they may have gone too far at times in claiming that the NT language was simply the vernacular *Koine* of the period adapted to the needs of Christian disciples. A great deal more than was ever realised may be involved in that word 'adapted'.

For a careful and attractively written statement of d
the argument just briefly stated the student should consult Mr E. K. Simpson's *Words Worth Weighing in the Greek NT* (1946), a lecture published by the Tyndale Press. He will find there a considerable number of important words on which the papyri throw no light at all, but which receive illumination from their usage in literary Hellenistic writers. The Pauline word *redemption* is a splendid example (Rom. 3:24, 8:23), and Mr Simpson gives citations from Menander and Strabo which the lexicons have neglected.

Dr Moulton was induced to modify his earlier views slightly, but he still maintained that in the vast majority of cases it is to the unliterary *Koine* we must turn for help. It seems to me that neither this position nor that of Mr Simpson will adequately explain the characteristics of the language of the NT. To an alternative suggestion we now turn.

(b) Biblical Greek—For the last three centuries B.C. 577a
the chief centre of the Hellenistic language which we have been discussing was not Greece, strange to say, but the empire of the Ptolemies with their capital at Alexandria. In the Egyptian city during these centuries lived thousands of Jews who had left their own land and settled here, as well as in many other centres, for various reasons. Gradually they lost all knowledge of their Aramaic mother-tongue and could understand only Greek. For this reason, it seems that in the middle

577a of the 3rd cent. B.C. the OT scriptures had to be translated from Heb. into Greek. So popular was this translation that even before it was completed it had gained almost as much reverence as its Heb. original—at least, outside of Palestine. In the NT many of the quotations from the OT are from this Greek version and not from the Heb., which is conclusive proof that the Greek version (or perhaps versions) had a vast influence on some at least of the early Christian writers. The kind of Greek they write is in vocabulary and style exactly that of the Bible (= LXX). One would expect the vocabulary to be similar, dealing with the same themes of God and redemption and religious history, but research into the syntax of the Greek OT has shown a remarkable similarity to that of the NT (cf. 'The Unique Character of Biblical Greek', by the present writer in VT 5 (1955), 208–13) ; it might have been written at almost exactly the same date, so little development is there from the Greek OT to NT.

b What does this mean ? The NT language was in many respects that of the literary and unliterary *Koine*, but in addition to this the NT writers had imported into it the style and (as almost everyone recognises now) the religious content of the Greek Bible. It is hoped that, one day soon, what Mayser has done for the papyri, someone may do for the **syntax** of biblical Greek (the OT and NT and pseudepigrapha and similar works) ; and another useful authority is the English translation (1962) of the useful Blass-Debrunner, *Grammatik des NT Griechisch*, which though brief is so excellent from the point of view of the student anxious to see both the papyri and biblical Greek parallels. And with regard to the thought-content, the lexicon of Bauer and theological lexicon of Kittel-Friedrich are much more valuable to the student than either Grimm-Thayer on the one hand or Moulton-Milligan

c on the other. What we require is a lexicon comparable with Liddell and Scott which gives the meanings not only as they were in earlier times but as they are found in the Greek Bible, the later versions of Aquila, Theodotion and Symmachus, in the pseudepigrapha and kindred 'biblical' works, and in the literary and spoken Greek of NT times. For it is likely that any important word in the NT will, since Classical times, have passed through the hands of Hellenistic writers of Alexandrian and Roman times (Dionysius of Halicarnassus, Polybius, Plutarch, etc.), and through the language of everyday life for many centuries. But it will also have come under religious influence, and have changed its meaning there, too. Granted that the Greek of the NT was the living language of the day, as it was both written and spoken, it should also be insisted that it was a language impregnated by the Bible, its Semitic idioms and thought-forms. Who has ever read Rom. without realising that Paul was steeped in the language of the Greek and Heb. OT, and yet he speaks the language of an educated man in spite of his copious use of biblical phraseology. Preachers are guilty of this sometimes in their sermons ; their source is the Bible and their language tends to be moulded on it too.

d Let us see how the biblical content has changed the whole meaning of the Greek. There is a solid group of very important words on which the usage of the *Koine* can shed little, if any, ray of light. Such words as *brother*, *parousia*, *fellowship*, *eternal*, *apostle*, *bishop*, *presbyter*, *saviour*, *to preach*, are now Christian technical terms charged with a new significance. No acquaintance with Classical authors will help in the exposition of these words to a Christian congregation. The whole content of meaning comes from the NT itself and the Bible that lies directly behind it—the OT. Hence the importance of knowing the biblical Greek authors of the inter-testamental period ; we must see how *they* used the words, because that is the best approach to the way in which their spiritual descendants, the Christian writers, would use them.

e Recently Professor H. S. Gehman has shown that the word for *holy* is incomprehensible in the Greek OT in a number of cases, unless one is conversant with the Heb. text (VT 4 (1954), 347). This is also true in the NT, where the writers apparently assume a knowledge of OT Greek terminology. It is part of Dr Gehman's thesis, which he developed with other words in the earlier volumes of VT, that there existed such a thing as a distinctively biblical Greek, not intelligible to non-Jews without a knowledge of the Bible. As to whether this sort of Semitic Greek was ever actually spoken, whether there was a vernacular Jews' Greek, that seems not at all unlikely ; at least for a certain period of time. Dr Gehman argues persuasively to this end (ibid. 1, 90) ; he says that in bilingual areas the masses do not keep both languages separate, and there would be a transitional period when Greek-speaking Jews spoke Greek with 'a pronounced Semitic cast'. He regards this as temporary (ibid. 3, 148), but I would think that many of Jesus' disciples, including Paul, were in this bilingual category and that they spoke as well as wrote in this Jewish Greek. It is noteworthy that a well-known specialist in the Greek OT, the Cambridge scholar Dr Peter Katz, has come to a similar conclusion. After discussing the syntactical features of the aorist optative in the LXX, he raises the question whether it stems from (or itself influenced) the living speech of the Alexandrian Jews without being simply a mechanical invention of the translators themselves ('Zur Übersetzungstechnik der Septuaginta', *Welt des Orients*, ii, 272f.). He is not denying that the basis of the language is Hellenistic Greek as far as sounds and spelling, accidence, and even syntax are concerned ; but he has moved a long way from Deissmann in concluding that it has become so idiomatic as to be in a certain sense different.

The history of the **optative mood** in the centuries just before and just after the apostolic age is complex. 578a
In both literary and colloquial Greek of the post-Classical period there was at first a gradual decay and subsequently a revival of the mood ; in the first place the revival was due to atticistic influence, a nostalgic pedantry seeking the forms of the past, but the revival spread. Now the period in which this mood was least in favour, the half-way house between the setting in of decay and the beginnings of revival, is the period when the NT and later books of the LXX appeared. This is remarkable, because the biblical books on the contrary display a comparative fondness for the optative mood. There are 539 instances in the LXX and 68 in the NT. (Thus, one for every four and a half pages of Swete, and one for every nine and a half pages of Nestle.) Having collated the results of the researches of Mayser and Horn,[1] I find the distribution of the optative of Wish in all the Ptolemaic and post-Ptolemaic papyri which they examined to be (centuries B.C. and A.D.) as follows : iv B.C. 2, iii B.C. 5, ii B.C. 23, i B.C. 1, i A.D. 1, ii A.D. 8, iii A.D. 6, iv A.D. 4 ; later centuries 8. Not a great number, and particularly few in the NT period ; yet there are as many as 40 instances of this kind of optative in the NT itself, the LXX maintaining the same average per page. The semi-cultured or atticistic revival of the mood in conditional and final clauses did not commence before ii A.D. in secular Greek, and only slightly then ; the majority of instances adduced by Horn are in the Byzantine period ; yet we find this revival anticipated as early as the LXX and NT. It is surprising also to find that Lk. employs the mood eight times in indirect questions, for this usage had almost disappeared in pre-Christian times. What is the reason for the b
abnormal lingering of the optative in biblical Greek alone ? Is it the conservatism of religion ? Is it after all only the atticising scribes of biblical MSS, confusing like-sounding endings ? Dr Katz justly explains the aorist optative by the influence of the Heb. jussive. That is probably true as to its origin, but may there

[1] R. C. Horn, *Use of Subj. and Opt. Moods in the non-literary Papyri* (1926)

8b not have been contributory factors to its preservation in biblical Greek? The Volitive (Wish) optative (*May such and such happen!*) is in fact admirably suited to pious aspiration and longing; it is, as it were, sacred syntax. This may have assisted its survival in religious circles. One cannot dismiss the possibility that Volitive optatives owe their preservation to their incidence in the solemn diction of Christian devotion and synagogue liturgy. They appear in the LXX, and that version became the Church's Book. It is a form of speech well fitted for the lips of pious folk. 'Let it be to me according to your word!' (Lk. 1:38). 'May you live in harmony with one another!' (Rom. 15:5). 'May the God of hope fill you with all joy!' (Rom. 15:13). 'May our God direct our way to you, and may you increase in love!' (1 Th. 3:11f.). 'May the God of peace sanctify you wholly!' (1 Th. 5:23). 'Now may the God of peace . . . equip you with everything good that you may do his will, working in you that which is pleasing in his sight, through Jesus Christ; to whom be glory for ever and ever. Amen' (Heb. 13:20 ff.). As Dr Katz points out, in some more elaborate instances from the LXX, it is particularly where God is the subject that the aorist optative and not the future indicative is used: 'while all sentences in which the people of Israel is the subject have the verb in the future, no matter whether what is stated about the people is the cause or the consequence of divine action' (op. cit., 272). This is true of Dt. 28, the chapter which contains the great liturgical passage, and of one secular papyrus of i A.D. which herein shows the influence of biblical Greek (cf. Dr Katz, 272f.).

c The distinction from secular, particularly colloquial, Greek is further shown by the **use of prepositions** with their cases. With most prepositions there is close agreement between the LXX and NT, and a difference from the use which has been observed in the Ptolemaic papyri. The biblical books display a more rapid tendency to drop one or more of the cases. Moreover, some prepositions, frequent enough in biblical Greek, occur hardly at all in the secular language whether written or spoken. It is not claimed that these new prepositions are due to direct Semitic influence, but that these prepositions are characteristic of biblical Greek.

d In many respects the development of the **Perfect tense** has reached a stage in the NT corresponding fairly closely with that reached in the vernacular, as Chantraine demonstrated (P. Chantraine, *Histoire du Parfait grec* (1927), ch. 9). However, there are some very important respects in which this is not so. The resultative Perfect, which flourished during the Classical Attic period, continued during the next period in both literary and vernacular texts; but the NT represents a new development. Here the number of resultative Perfects is few indeed, and the use of this form is limited to a small number of verbs, except in the rather emphatically solemn and strained style of the Fourth Gospel. Moreover, although one can cite a few examples in the Ptolemaic papyri of the periphrastic tense with Perfect participle, there is nothing in the secular texts which can compare with the fondness for this usage which is apparent in the LXX and NT. Mayser's examples are very few, and even Chantraine will not dismiss the probability of Aramaic influence. The Perfect tense in general is much rarer in the NT than in the popular language, and it preserves a good deal more of its old force. While the old intransitives have almost all disappeared in the *Koine*, in the NT we do still have a few, especially where they can be understood with a *present* meaning (e.g. *to be dead, to be at hand, to trust, to open, to be lost*). Moreover, in the NT some perfects are still true perfects, in spite of the prevailing tendency elsewhere at this time and the universal confusion in the Ptolemaic and Imperial papyri. It is remarkable that even in the more 'colloquial' Mk a significant distinction is sometimes made. The usual English versions apparently 578d do not think there is any special force in the Perfect in Mk 15:44, for they render Mk's Aorist and Perfect in exactly the same way. I see no reason why we should not give the evangelist credit for some subtlety there; he makes Pilate say: 'Is he *dead* already! When *did* he *die*?' This quaint old-fashioned exactitude of language is also observed by Paul, who avoids using the Perfect of the death of Christ and one suspects that is because in the old-fashioned usage of the Perfect that would mean that Christ was now dead. Which God forbid! In the language of the apostle, unlike that of his secular contemporaries, the old distinction between the tenses was still very much alive. It should further be observed that the oft-repeated *it is written* is correctly used in the NT, and that other Perfects retain their true present force.

e Now the reason for this is all-important because it introduces us once again to the question of **Semitic influence** upon the language of these writers. Dr Matthew Black has drawn attention (*An Aramaic Approach to the Gospels and Acts*[2] (1954), 93, 254) to the influence of Semitic usage on the Greek Aorist in the NT. Thus the Aorist in Mt. 23:2 'defies analysis on Greek lines', and has the force of a Semitic stative Perfect, as Wellhausen had observed. Dr Black instances also Mk 1:8 (most modern translators have corrected RV's erroneous alteration of AV), Mt. 14:31 ('Why dost thou doubt?'), 10:25, 13:24, 18:23, 22:2; Lk. 1:46, 7:47, 11:52, 14:18, 20; Jn 11:14. In all these the Aorist is 'used either of a general truth or an immediately completed act'. We suggest that the same Semitic influence contributes to the fact that so many perfects in the NT retain their true perfective force, in contrast with contemporary usage in secular Greek, and that the old intransitive perfects with their present meaning still persist in the NT, again in defiance of general usage in the *Koine*.

f Dr Moulton would not attribute the definite article, when used with a noun in the Vocative case (or Nominative case used vocatively, whichever nomenclature is preferred), to Hebraic influence. In Greek it is only used in addressing subordinates, especially slaves. Its use in addressing God would be particularly harsh to Greek ears. But it is so found, almost uniquely, in the LXX and NT. Not all the instances can be explained as exclamation or statement (i.e. Nominative case), rather than address.

g The position of the attributive adjective (and participle) in relation to the substantive and article is in the Ptolemaic papyri quite different from that in biblical Greek. The article before the substantive is very frequently omitted in Hellenistic Greek and particularly in the papyri; but this is extremely rare in biblical Greek. Moreover, the tendency in the papyri by the time of the NT is for the repetition of the article before an adjective after a substantive to be a very rare method indeed, and yet it occurs frequently in biblical Greek even where there is no emphasis. Similarly ἐκεῖνος and πᾶς in biblical Greek prefer the position they have in Heb.; cf. VT 5 (1955), 209, 211.

579a These instances by no means exhaust the peculiarities of biblical Greek syntax, but they indicate a fruitful line of research for those students who may not be satisfied with the Deissmann-Moulton position and on the other hand are not convinced that the language of the NT is any nearer to the literary Hellenistic writers of the time. The study of syntax from this point of view is one which has been largely neglected. There is no doubt that there are words and phrases on which a study of the secular papyri and inscriptions alone has been able to shed any light. But usually these words are not those which touch the heart of the Christian message, but words like *force* (Mt. 5:41), *pure milk* (1 Pet. 2:2), *he has a receipt* (Mk 14:41), *genuineness* (1 Pet. 1:7), *charge to my account* (Phm. 18), *set foot on* (Col. 2:18), *age* (Mt. 6:27), *collection* (1 C. 16:1), *metaphorical* (1 Pet. 2:2), *publicly portrayed* (Gal. 3:1). One is very grateful indeed to have new light

579a shed on these somewhat obscure words, although even here not everyone is convinced that the papyri have given us the correct meaning as far as the NT is concerned. Where the papyri leave us lamentably in the dark still is in the case of those all-important words by which the Christian faith stands or falls. One looks in vain in secular texts for any help on such vital words as *angel, truth, devil, covenant, church, gospel, propitiation,* and *idol* and cognate words. All these words gain far more in interpretation from a study of the OT and their context in the NT than from a knowledge of the non-Christian *Koine*. For instance, the word for *idol* which meant merely *phantom* or *likeness* in secular Greek was not applied outside the biblical language to the images of heathen deities, much less to the gods themselves. This was a Semitic creation, and so were the numerous compounds which sprang from this meaning of the word : *idol's temple, food sacrificed to idols, worship of idols, full of idols.*

b Other words still have the secular meaning alongside the new Christian one. Professor G. D. Kilpatrick has argued in *The Bible Translator,* 7 (1956) ('Some Notes on Marcan Usage') that *word* is used in two completely different senses in Mk, and that, strangely enough, one meaning occurs exclusively in the first four chapters and the other exclusively in the remaining chapters. In the first it means technically the Message of either Jesus or the Christian Church, whereas later it is used in the normal Greek sense of *utterance*. Thus RSV renders it 'what they said' (5:36), 'saying' (7:29), 'said this' (8:32). We have also *principalities* and *authorities* in both the secular sense and the biblical: rulers on earth and heavenly beings. The point is not simply that a specialised kind of writing has given a new shade of meaning to ordinary words, but more. The meaning of those words has been entirely changed. The words belong to a new language; only the letters remain. In many cases, when it is intended to express a certain meaning, the ordinary and obvious word for this in Hellenistic Greek seems to be deliberately set aside and a less obvious word is used in its place. Thus, several obvious words might have been used for Christian instruction, but the extremely rare *catechesis* word-group was adopted and made the basis of this idea. The same applies to the choice of the characteristic word for Christian love. It might often have seemed appropriate for the Christian author to have used the normal Greek word for *reverence, piety, holy, godless, deathless,* and *preacher*; but no Christian author actually ever did. Instead he preferred the rarer word and transformed it into a common word in the Christian vocabulary.

Dr Peter Katz has drawn attention to several notable cases of homonyms, where a word derives an entirely new meaning because of confusion on the part of a LXX translator between a Greek word and a Heb. root of the same letters. Thus, 'Be it far from thee' or 'God forbid' in the LXX and NT (Mt. 16:22) was fashioned after the Greek word for *merciful* merely because this consisted of roughly the same sounds as the Heb. word, without any link in meaning between the two homonyms (review of Blass-Debrunner's *Grammatik* in *Theologische Literaturzeitung* (1957), cols. 113f.). Again, through the confusion of Heb. roots by the LXX translators, even the author of Heb. (3:16) has given the new meaning *were rebellious* to a compound verb whose simplex in Greek had the different shade of meaning, *to embitter* (quoted by permission from 'Un-Greek Meanings from Confusion of Hebrew Homonyms', in P. Katz, *Text of the Septuagint*; cf. also, based on 5
Katz, W. Michaelis, *Theol. Wörterbuch z. NT,* vi, 125ff.).

It is by such study that we really come to grips with c
the NT language. We must appreciate its religious antecedents and expect to find in the Greek OT, pseudepigrapha, and apocalyptic literature the best illumination. Study of papyri and literary Hellenistic authors must not be despised, but the rich rewards will come from Semitic study. In this field a very important contribution has recently been made which must have far-reaching effects on all future assessments of the nature of biblical Greek. It is the brilliant discussion by Matthew Black already referred to, in which the extent of Aramaic influence on the language of the Gospel writers is examined (*An Aramaic Approach to the Gospels and Acts* (2nd ed. 1954)). He modifies the extreme position of Torrey and Burney, that their language is direct translation Greek, because he shows that the Aramaisms are strongest in the words of Jesus and this may point merely to an Aramaic sayings-source behind the Gospels. It seems to leave open still the question whether the evangelists themselves were writing a Semiticising Greek, or merely translating, or even just thinking in the syntax of their original Aramaic tongue while writing Greek.

Bibliography—The best list of books is that found in d
Blass-Debrunner, *Grammatik des NT Griechisch*[9] (1954). Among the books there mentioned the following should be specially noted : F. M. Abel, *Grammaire du grec biblique* (1927); W. Bauer, *Griechisch-Deutsches Wörterbuch zu den Schriften des NT und der übrigen urchristlichen Literatur* (5th ed. 1958; an Eng. tr. of 4th ed. has appeared); E. de W. Burton, *Syntax of Moods and Tenses in NT Greek* (1893); A. Deissmann, *Bibelstudien,* in English as *Bible Studies* (1901); R. Helbing, *Die Kasussyntax der Verba bei den Septuaginta* (1928); A. N. Jannaris, *An Historical Greek Grammar* (1897); M. Johannessohn, *Der Gebrauch der Kasus und der Präp. in der Septuaginta* I (Kasus) (1910), II (Präp.) (1925); Kittel-Friedrich, *Theologisches Wörterbuch zum NT* (1933 onwards, unfinished), some articles as English books; E. Mayser, *Grammatik der griech. Papyri aus der Ptolemäerzeit,* various dates for each part, indispensable; Moulton's *Grammar,* 2 vols.—the 3rd vol., Syntax, is now in preparation; Moulton and Milligan's *Vocabulary* (1914–29); T. Nägeli, *Der Wortschatz des Ap. Paul* (1905); H. Pernot, *Études sur la Langue des Évangiles* (1927), excellent; F. Preisigke, *Wörterbuch der griechischen Papyrusurkunden* (1914–27), indispensable; J. Psichari, *Essai sur le Grec de la Septante* (1908); H. Ljungvik, *Beiträge zur Syntax der spätgriech. Volkssprache* (1932), very useful for NT syntax; L. Radermacher, *Das Griechisch des NT im Zusammenhang mit der Volkssprache* (1925 ed.), very useful; H. St. J. Thackeray, *A Grammar of the OT in Greek* (1909), the syntax volume was never written.

To Debrunner's list might be added the following : Abbott-Smith's *Manual Lexicon* (1921), brief but usually reliable and up to date on the *Koine* meaning of words); Matthew Black, *An Aramaic Approach to the Gospels and Acts* (2nd ed. 1954); Peter Katz, *Gnomon,* 27 (1955), 87–91, an excellent review of Black; C. H. Dodd, *The Bible and the Greeks* (1935, now reprinted), shows the importance of LXX-study for determining the real meaning of important NT words, e.g. *sin, atonement*; M. Johannessohn, *Das biblische ΚΑΙ ΕΓΕΝΕΤΟ und seine Geschichte* (1926); C. F. D. Moule, *An Idiom Book of NT Greek* (1953).

THE TEXTUAL CRITICISM OF THE NEW TESTAMENT

By K. W. Clark

580a **Need and Objective**—It is well known that the primitive Christian gospel was initially transmitted by word of mouth and that this oral tradition resulted in variant reporting of the original word and deed. It is equally true that when the Christian record was later committed to writing it continued to be subject to verbal variation (involuntary and intentional) at the hands of scribes and editors. The earliest written Gospel, by Mark in Rome, was promptly copied for wider circulation and was soon known as far as Ephesus and Antioch. The correspondence of Paul was collected and copied and early circulated between Italy and Syria. Each hand-produced copy, however, contained its own deviations in the form of error or of editorial revision by the theologian-scribe. From the very beginning manuscript copies of NT books showed an increasing amount of variation in the text, and within a single century the original compositions were greatly altered.

All the autographs of NT books and of the earliest collections of books have disappeared—such as the Pauline Corpus (about A.D. 95) and the Four Gospels (about A.D. 130). Nothing remains from any scribal hand earlier than A.D. 200 (except a tiny fragment of the Gospel of John). The few copies that survive from the period 200–500 clearly attest the variety of textual forms which had developed from the original Gr. documents. It is this state of the text that has called forth 'textual criticism' as a means to the recovery of the original textual form.

It was realised even in early Christian centuries that the original Gr. documents had been altered in the process of transmission. Certain of the early Fathers, such as Origen (185–253), discussed at times the true form of the text. But the Gr. NT settled into a popular 'ecclesiastical' text throughout the Byzantine centuries, undisturbed by critical investigation. This Byzantine Gr. text continued in use in the Eastern Empire while the Latin Vulgate translation held the field in the West. When the printing-press was developed in the 15th cent. it became mechanically possible, for the first time in history, to produce two or more copies of a complete book in exact duplication. The Gr. NT was first so duplicated in 600 copies of the Complutensian Polyglot in Alcala in 1514, but the form printed was the Byzantine 'ecclesiastical' text which in its adulterated form had become popular. With very little change, and with no critical improvement, this popular text continued to pour from the presses in thousands of copies until the beginning of the 20th cent. Throughout these centuries it served as the Gr. base for exegesis and for translation into the numerous modern languages, including the Anglican versions from Tyndale in 1525 to the RV of 1881. The inadequacy of this popular Byzantine Gr. text came to be fully realised in the West only in the 19th cent. Consequently, 'textual criticism' has only lately been recognised as a discipline prerequisite to better exegesis and translation.

b **The task of the textual critic** is to bridge the centuries between his own age and the primitive Christian era by reconstructing for his contemporaries 580b
the original NT text as known to the early adherents of the faith. For many centuries of Christian history believers seemed unmindful of textual alterations and therefore felt no need and made no serious effort to recover a text truer than the one they possessed. In the absence of ancient manuscript witnesses, the numerous Byzantine copies of later date were generally accepted as the traditional text. This late form of the text was familiar to all and remained firmly established in use until the 18th cent. The first serious doubt arose in the 17th cent. when Christian scholarship in the West was confronted with a 5th-cent. witness of different textual character. This was an Alexandrian MS which was carried to London in 1627 (and still remains there in the British Museum, designated as **Codex Alexandrinus**). This was followed by the discovery of other manuscript witnesses of even earlier date, which clearly pointed to the fact that the prevailing Gr. text was substantially different from the original. The desire to reconstruct the lost original, along with the reappearance of ancient copies long lost from view, caused the development of the modern scientific discipline known as textual criticism. Its achievement to date has been to provide Christians with a Gr. text of the NT scriptures more trustworthy than any in use since the 6th cent. However, it is not to be thought that the 'original' text has now been fully recovered, for significant discoveries and important refinements of text and method continue to cast more light upon the problem.

Source Materials—The source materials with which the textual critic works are the surviving hand-written 581a
copies of NT text, which range from the 2nd cent. onwards. These manuscripts are of four types, according to their contents. Of primary value are the copies of NT books in a continuous text substantially as it appears in modern published editions. Second, there are the copies of church lectionaries, in which the canonical text is broken into daily readings (not all of the NT appears in this arrangement, whereas some parts are used more than once within the year's liturgical sequence). Third, there are the copies of NT books in a number of translations which reflect the Gr. original, the most important of which are the earliest versions such as Latin and Syriac and the Egyptian dialects. Fourth, there are the manuscripts of patristic works in Gr. and other languages ; commentaries and homilies by the church Fathers beginning with the 2nd cent., in which hundreds of quotations of NT passages give evidence of the text as each Father knew it in his own region.

The first type, preserving each book in continuous b
text, is highest in value for three reasons: it preserves the text in the original language (Gr.), it preserves the entire text as a unit, and it comprises the largest number of copies (about 3,000 manuscript witnesses). However, it is not to be supposed that all these manuscripts contain the entire Gr. NT, for prior to the beginning of printing it was seldom that a scribe wrote all the NT in one book. The contents most

581b common were the Four Gospels (a *tetraëvangelion*), surviving today in about 2,000 copies ranging from the 3rd cent. to the 18th. Much less often a scribe copied the Acts of the Apostles along with the Pauline and General Epistles (a *praxapostolos*), which we now possess in about 400 copies (plus about 300 copies of the Pauline Epistles alone). The book most seldom copied was the Apocalypse of John (or, the Revelation), for which we have only about 250 copies. It often circulated alone and only infrequently was joined to other books. When the complete NT was copied as one, the Apocalypse more often was excluded, so that a NT of twenty-seven books was rare and only about 50 such copies are preserved today.

c **The second type,** the church lectionary, has long been used for public reading during the liturgy. Of this form there are about 2,000 ancient copies known, divided into a major division of *evangelia* (with Gospel lections) and a minor division of *apostoloi* (with lections from the Acts and the Epistles).

d **The third type,** consisting of the early translations into various languages, provides testimony to the Gr. text for the place and time in which each was made. Since the Old Latin and Old Syriac translations (before A.D. 200) antedate the oldest surviving Gr. manuscripts, the critic finds such witnesses of great value. Still other translations made from the Gr. before A.D. 500 were the Coptic, Armenian, Georgian, and Ethiopic. Each language is represented by scores or even hundreds of manuscripts, but in distinguishable recensions which thus present the textual critic with the initial task of reconstructing the form of the original translation before he is able to use it in reconstructing its Gr. base.

e **The fourth type,** quotations by the Fathers, is a particularly valuable source because the writer is definitely known as to date and locale. Certain of the Fathers wrote so much and quoted so often that nearly a complete NT can now be excerpted from their works. A problem relating to this type, however, is the question whether there was intended an exact quotation, or a memory quotation, or a theological revision, or merely an allusion These patristic works too have been copied and preserved in so many manuscripts that the specialist must first derive from their differences a 'critical text' of each document before it is fully useful as an original witness to the Father's scripture. These Fathers witness to the text not only in Gr. (Justin, Irenaeus, Clement of Alexandria, Origen, Hippolytus, Eusebius, Chrysostom, etc.) but also in Latin (Tertullian and Cyprian in North Africa ; Novatian, Hilary, Ambrose, Jerome and Augustine in Europe) and in Syriac (Aphraates and Ephrem) and in other languages.

All of these types of source material for the textual critic of the NT form a great mass that must be examined, in a collaborative effort of hundreds of scholars through generations of research. These materials are scattered in libraries around the world, many of them difficult of access (in Sinai, Athos, Jerusalem, Damascus, Kiev) and yet increasingly available through photographic expeditions and publications. This host of witnesses to the original NT is by far the greatest among all literary works in history, a fact which offers both promise and problem to the critic. If all these multilingual witnesses were in agreement, or if only the most ancient copies agreed, the reconstruction of the lost original text would be simple and assured ; but these witnesses yield many thousands of textual variants and attest recensions differing from the earliest recording, with the result that the textual criticism of the Gr. NT is the most intricate and massive operation within the discipline of textual research.

f The search for the original text has been stimulated by a series of **significant discoveries,** in recent centuries, of Gr. copies of early date. In 1627 the 5th-cent. Gr. Bible, Codex Alexandrinus (now in the British Museum), was presented to King Charles I as a gift from the Patriarch of Constantinople. It was centuries 581g
older than the medieval sources thus far consulted for printed editions, and attested a text decidedly different from the common 'ecclesiastical' text. This discovery received more scholarly recognition than had the private acquisition by **Theodore Beza** in 1562 of a 5th-cent. Graeco-Latin copy of the Gospels and Acts, from the monastery of St Irenaeus in Lyons (now in Cambridge University). About the same time Beza acquired also another Graeco-Latin manuscript of the 6th cent., containing the Pauline Epistles, from the Clermont monastery near Beauvais (now in the Bibliothèque Nationale). In 1636 Archbishop Laud presented to the Bodleian Library in Oxford a Graeco-Latin copy of the Acts written about A.D. 600. It is probable that it was brought to Canterbury in A.D. 669 by Archbishop Theodore but it remained long neglected until its textual similarity with Codex Bezae was noted. About 1700 the young French scholar, Pierre Allix, discerned a 5th-cent. Gr. Bible text still partially visible underneath a 12th-cent. text of Ephrem's treatises. This copy had come from the East after 1500 into the Medici library and was taken by Catherine de Medici to Paris (now in the Bibliothèque Nationale). Thus during the 17th cent. notable discoveries were made of more ancient textual traditions dating from the 5th and 6th cent., which seriously challenged the 'ecclesiastical' text so long in use.

The most important discoveries have occurred within the last century. In 1859 the German scholar, **Tischendorf,** brought forth from hiding at St Catherine's monastery in Sinai (now in the British Museum, as Codex Sinaiticus) a Gr. Bible copied in the 4th cent.—the earliest witness until then accessible. Furthermore, its NT text of twenty-seven books was found to be complete, along with the Epistle of Barnabas and the Shepherd of Hermas (breaking off at Mandate IV, iii, 6). About the same time another Gr. Bible of about A.D. 350 (largely complete, without the Apocalypse) was made available through a publication of the Vatican where it may have reposed at least since 1481, although it first came to general notice when Napoleon carried it off to Paris for a period. These two last codices, **Sinaiticus** and **Vaticanus,** are now recognised as sister codices from Egypt of about the same date, attesting in common the most trustworthy Gr. NT yet available to us. In 1906 Charles Lang Freer secured another 4th-cent. Gr. manuscript at Giza (now in the Freer Gallery of Art in Washington), containing the Four Gospels in the 'Western' order: Mt., Jn, Lk., Mk (as in Codex Bezae). But about 1930 discovery drew another century closer to the original NT when A. Chester Beatty acquired three 3rd-cent. papyri from Egypt, of the Gospels and Acts, the Pauline Epistles (30 of its leaves acquired by the University of Michigan), and the Apocalypse of John. The most recent find (about 1955) is a manuscript of the earliest date, a papyrus in excellent condition acquired by Martin Bodmer of Geneva, containing the Gospel of John written about A.D. 200, or about a century after its original composition. Other manuscripts in the same group include texts of the Gospel of Luke and I Peter, of slightly later date. All our witnesses prior to 400, whether on papyrus or on parchment, come from Egyptian Christianity and therefore the primitive text in Egypt is the earliest form more immediately capable of being reconstructed.

Method—If the manuscript sources from which we 582a
must recover the text of the Gr. NT were but few, the method required to accomplish the task would be simple. It would then be possible for any single scholar to compare manuscript with manuscript and, keeping *all* the variants in mind, to make a judgment between an original and a derived reading. However, it must also be kept in mind that such simplicity would come only at the expense of confidence in the result ; for when the surviving copies of a text are numerous and offer the scholar more variations from which his

582a critical choice may be derived, it is much more likely that the original reading has somewhere survived among the manuscript witnesses. Consequently, it should be recognised as fortunate that so many manuscript copies have survived, although this circumstance has created the most intricate textual problem in seeking to recover the lost original text of the Gr. NT.

An intricate problem calls for a highly developed technique and such a technique has been applied in recent generations to the textual criticism of the NT, in part similar to the method employed to recover other lost autographs. The natural place to begin is with the earliest extant witnesses, and this requires a new approach and a fresh study at any time when a still earlier manuscript is discovered. For example, in the 17th cent. the best basis was the 5th-cent. Codex Alexandrinus whereas in the 19th cent. the best basis was the witness of the 4th-cent. MSS Vaticanus and Sinaiticus. In the 20th cent. the 3rd-cent. Beatty Papyri and Bodmer Papyri provide the best starting-point. It is essential for the textual critic to take up a new position whenever discovery carries him back in time.

b Since survivals before A.D. 500 are few the logical step is to compare such witnesses with one another (the **external method**) in order to discover any readings in which they differ. Such differences must then be resolved if possible on the basis of a set of principles, in order to judge which is the best reading (the **internal method**). The first step is merely fact-finding in order to bring to light the explicit problem, while the second step is one of great difficulty which calls for the most learned judgment possible. At this point the problem and its solution must be kept isolated from the critic's theology (although they demand the fullest understanding of the author's theology). Neither can the critic rely upon 'majority rule' among his manuscript witnesses, nor upon seniority.

c How then can we decide between variant readings as to which one should be accepted as original? Foremost is the principle of contextual (Hort: 'intrinsic') probability, which means that judgment is based not only on the sentence structure and its sense and on its place in the immediate argument but also upon the author's literary style and habit and upon his characteristic views and basic theology. This leads to the companion principle of deviational (Hort: 'transcriptional') probability, which means that one reading can be explained as a scribal derivative from the other (rather than the reverse). The clearest example of this principle is the scribal error so obvious that it is readily corrected, but more often the decision is more difficult between deliberate variants that make sense. For example, it may be recognised that the scribe (present or previous) exhibits a theological interest which might cause him to change the text of his exemplar (cf. Jn 1:18, referring to Jesus as 'only God' or as 'only son'). There are many additional factors which enter into the formulation of a judgment as to which is a primary and which a secondary reading. Another principle is a venerable one: 'the shorter reading is to be preferred' as original, on the ground that scribes tend to expand rather than to compress. Of course, what scribes in general (or even one specific scribe) tend to do cannot be relied upon to happen everywhere, and yet this rule has limited value. The principle that the older witness is to be preferred also has limited value, but cannot be automatically or always accepted. The example of Jn 1:18 (above) may illustrate and test this principle, since Bodmer Papyrus II (P^{66}) about A.D. 200 attests the reading 'only God' and this is supported by the 4th-cent. witnesses Vaticanus and Sinaiticus; whereas only later witnesses attest the form 'only son'. This same reading may illustrate again the principle: 'the more difficult reading is to be preferred' (propounded by Bengel in the early 18th cent.), based on the logic that scribes tend to simplify rather than to complicate the thought. In order, however, to use this rule properly it is necessary to be familiar with *their* thought rather than our own. 582c

As a result of applying such principles at thousands of points in the text, each manuscript thus studied reveals the character of its text—excellent or corrupt, integrated or agglomerated, consistent or erratic, conservative or 'sporty'. Once a manuscript has had its character fully and fairly evaluated, it provides still another principle: a reading in the better manuscripts is to be preferred. Although no single rule is all-sufficient, the full set of principles here listed can be applied to check one another and to provide a consistent criterion. Finally, the critic is forced to employ his last device in the case of textual corruption so primitive that all surviving manuscripts record only the deviation. The possibility of corruption is indicated only by an exegetical perplexity which seems to demand textual correction, but since there is no choice of explicit variants in any known manuscripts the critic must resort to 'conjectural emendation' (a shrewd deduction as to the original form). This device, which is rarely called forth, may be illustrated at 1 Pet. 3:19 where the traditional English version states that Jesus came to life in the spirit 'in which also he went and preached unto the spirits in prison'. The idea expressed here has long been a creedal problem, and the English Quaker Rendel Harris proposed an emendation to relieve the difficulty. The Greek for 'in which also' looks like the four letters for 'Enoch' who, it is recorded, made a proclamation in Sheol; hence, the original of 1 Pet. conjecturally read: 'Enoch preached . . .' Moffatt and Goodspeed accepted this conjectural emendation, yet there is always great caution felt toward this method. d

The science of textual criticism has certain more immediate objectives and tasks. Everyone understands the effort to recover the original NT text. This discipline is properly called **higher criticism**, by which is meant that it concerns itself with discovering the original (like seeking the upper source of a stream). To recover the NT writings in original form is the ultimate goal and will always be the main objective of textual criticism, as it unites with other disciplines to penetrate to Christian origins. But textual criticism has other tasks that belong to **lower criticism**, concerned with tracing the course of transmission (like exploring the lower course of a stream). It asks: How has the NT been transmitted to our time? What is the history of the text through the centuries? Through what hands has it passed, or what tributaries have affected it? What theological and social forces, what economic and political forces have affected its text? This sort of inquiry performs at least three services: it contributes to historical theology, it illumines church history, and it enables the textual critic to retrace the process of change which the text has undergone and thus to exscind accumulated error. e

For the lower criticism of the text the source materials are massive, and therefore the method must differ. Since there are thousands of medieval copies of the Gospel text it would be a fruitless and endless task to compare manuscript with manuscript, so the method described above for primitive manuscripts must be modified. Because a large proportion of the original NT text has never been corrupted it would be helpful to isolate the debatable passages from the universally attested text. Therefore the textual critic simply adopts some printed Gr. text as a control (necessarily one available to all, and preferably the same one to be adopted in all studies), and proceeds to compare (i.e. collate) individual manuscripts with *it*. Wherever he finds a difference in a manuscript it is recorded in its collation and the final list exhibits the textual contour of that manuscript, which is then ready for analysis and classification. The bulk of the NT text that is common to all can be set aside, and numerous manuscripts can now be compared with one another

582e by collating each one with the control base. In a typical Byzantine manuscript of the Four Gospels, collation of the text with a printed 'Received Text' will yield about 2,500 variants. Perhaps 300 readings will be unique in this manuscript, most of them of little consequence. Probably 1,500 other differences will be textually meaningless (spellings, itacisms, simple transpositions, etc.). There may then be left about 700 readings which are substantial enough to portray character, and thus the textual labour has been pared down to the significant core. If then additional manuscripts should be added to the study, each one would add only a few hundred significant readings not already in view. In this way hundreds of Byzantine copies can be handled for classification into sub-groups, as a physician might analyse for categories of blood types. Although 2,000 Gospel manuscripts have survived, surely many times that number have perished; and yet the numbers are still sufficient to show here and there the more intimate textual kinship of a 'family'. The more types and families it is possible to identify, the more is the maze of sources reduced to order, and the critic may deal more simply with a representative or an ancestor instead of the group.

It has come to be recognised that the NT text early took different forms in different geographical areas. For example, the region of Calabria in southern Italy used a text which is recognised in manuscript survivors today in a group known as 'Family 13'. Although it is not possible always to localise a 'family', several other such groupings have been assembled, such as 'Family 1' and 'Family 2412' and also the several categories in von Soden's classifications. Geographical characteristics in the text may be identified through quotations by some Father, or in the evidence of a regional version, or in some unusual reading in a local lectionary. But the broadest groupings less closely knit are recognised as 'recensions'. These are the major general classifications, such as 'Egyptian', 'Western', 'Caesarean', and 'Ecclesiastical'; and all manuscripts fall into one of these (or contain some mixture of them).

The manuscript materials and procedures for textual criticism may be described in the metaphor of a starry sky (much better than that of a family tree). Let each star represent a manuscript, varying in comparative age and size and everyone unique. They appear to be innumerable and at first in no pattern of relationship, and yet they are all related to one another by an elemental textual gravitation. There are far more than we normally see (though some have perished) and we have not yet discovered them all although a new one comes into view periodically and revises our textual astronomy. We begin to see consistent clusters or constellations, small and large, which hold together and as units are related to other clusters or stars. When visibility is best we perceive a broad milky way with a special density of units (like a textual 'recension'). Yet many are still unclassified and undescribed. The textual critic is the astronomer who explores and discovers, describes and classifies, then realigns and adjusts his chart of the textual heavens.

583a **History of Criticism**—Textual criticism as a modern science began about three hundred years ago with scholars like Brian Walton and John Fell. Of course, the earlier centuries too reflect a concern with textual variation, both in the original Gr. and in the translations. At some time (between A.D. 350 and 700) standard forms emerged in major languages: the Greek *koinē*, the Syrian Peshitta, and Vulgates in Latin, Ethiopic and Georgian. In the West the Latin Vulgate was continually subjected to textual emendation—a process punctuated by frequent remedial editions.

The Gr. NT has long remained little disturbed in the Eastern Orthodox Church, where it has always continued in liturgical use. In school and home a modern Gr. 'translation' is used. But the Gr. NT that was traditional in the East was revived in the Latin West during the Renaissance, and was soon being printed there and sold by the thousands. The Gr. text in the Complutensian Polyglot (1514) was traditional and had no critical consequences. The Graeco-Latin editions of Erasmus printed by Froben (1516–35) were also traditional and of no critical merit, but became the cornerstone of the NT text for three hundred years, both in the Gr. and modern-speech versions. This text was published with only slight revision and in increasing numbers by Stephanus in Paris (1546–1644), by Beza in Geneva (1565–1611), by the Elzevirs in Leiden (1624–78), and by many another. Yet none of these editions of the 'Received Text' was prepared with serious textual criticism.

b When Brian Walton published his great Polyglot edition in London (1657), he was the first to report the variants of Codex Alexandrinus recently brought to London. Although his traditional printed text was to prevail for almost two hundred years longer, Walton's recognition of the 4th-cent. MS was the beginning of a fundamental critical process. Walton also consulted about thirty other Greek manuscript witnesses, including the two given by Beza to Cambridge about 1582, the Codices Bezae and Claramontanus of the 5th and 6th cent. A younger contemporary, Bishop John Fell of Oxford, extended these researches and published his own text in 1675. In a marginal *apparatus criticus* he exhibited textual variations culled from over a hundred manuscript witnesses in Gr. and in various translations. The NT text of this edition was of the traditional 'ecclesiastical' form, and it was widely printed in England and on the Continent. John Fell had a protégé at Oxford, John Mill, who spent thirty years collecting additional manuscript evidence for his edition of 1707, in which he reported finding about 30,000 variants in his manuscript witnesses. The realisation of this fact shocked many in that day, and yet the state of knowledge today multiplies that figure many times. But a start had been made in demonstrating a weakness in the traditional text inherited from the Byzantines. As Fell had encouraged and supported Mill, so Mill in turn inspired Richard Bentley of Cambridge who proposed to revise the Gr. text more drastically. Although he failed to produce an edition before his death in 1742, he did publish his 'proposals' in 1720 as the basis for the projected text. He proposed: (1) that the text then in use must be revised according to the new evidence, (2) that the numerous variants would reduce to only about 200 debatable readings, (3) that the clue to an authentic reading lay in the agreement between the oldest Gr. copies and the OL, and (4) that secondary confirmation could be derived from the earliest translations and from quotations in the Fathers. This was the most enlightened effort in textual criticism up to that time, and even though it did not issue in a reconstructed text it had great influence upon successive critics.

c The Fell-Mill-Bentley texts and studies did not go unchallenged; indeed, there was a full round of sharp debate. The conservative view may be represented here by Dr Daniel Whitby who feared lest scriptural authority and personal faith be undermined. The supporters of the new textual discipline may be represented by Dr Francis Hare who argued that the sacred scriptures require the same critical (though reverent) treatment for emendation and interpretation as is applied to the classics. The debate reflected the strong attachment to the 'Received Text' which was not to be broken for still another century. But the period of textual research in England from Walton to Bentley caused the initial estrangement as it exhibited the hitherto unrealised variety of witness.

d The following era was constructive and was carried forward by a series of Continental scholars. The German Lutheran theologian, J. A. Bengel, pursued textual investigations from his youth which resulted

583d in a new Gr. edition in 1734, with an *apparatus criticus* of variant readings. He rarely ventured to change the text itself but did note in the margin new readings that had strong support. He applied Bentley's theory when he set up a classification of Codex Alexandrinus and the OL as the 'African natio', to be accepted as the earliest textual evidence. His 'Asiatic natio' was a catch-all for the later Byzantine manuscripts, which though numerous are outweighed by the other select class. With Bengel, we begin to see the lines of the fuller picture that later developed. The Swiss scholar, J. J. Wettstein, in youth collated manuscripts for Bentley, and later (1751–2) published a Gr. edition of little merit. His chief contribution was the initial check-listing of about 200 Gr. NT manuscripts known in the West, using the alphabet for symbols as Bentley had proposed. It was, however, another German who carried on from Bengel—the Lutheran theologian, J. S. Semler, 'the father of German rationalism'. He reaffirmed Bengel's principle of individual merit rather than majority rule. Although he did not publish a text, in 1767 he further refined the classifications of Bengel into Alexandrian and Occidental (thus dividing the 'African natio'), and Oriental (the 'Asiatic natio'). His student was J. J. Griesbach who published three editions of the Gr. NT beginning in 1774, with an *apparatus criticus*. His classification of witnesses as adapted from Semler distinguished the Alexandrian (the oldest and best), the Western, and the Byzantine (late and corrupt). His NT still retained the traditional text, although the final edition in 1805 showed the trend to be new and was influential in the editions of numerous minor editors. Two other scholars in Germany represent the earliest Roman Catholic interest in the Gr. text of the NT. J. L. Hug, Professor of Classical Philology at Freiburg, examined Codex Vaticanus in 1809 (while it was held in Paris by Napoleon) and established its date as about A.D. 350. His pupil was J. M. A. Scholz, Professor of Theology at Bonn, whose published text (1830–6) included the extension of Wettstein's check-list of known manuscripts to about one thousand. However, the main critical development circumvented these two scholars, as it passed from Griesbach to Lachmann.

Throughout the period of German textual scholarship from Bengel to Scholz, all the printings of the Gr. NT repeated the traditional 'ecclesiastical' text with but little alteration. Yet the insecurity of this text increased as the manuscript evidence mounted. Furthermore, its late origin came to be realised, in contrast with the antiquity of Alexandrian witnesses. An incipient history of transmission was reflected in the first efforts to classify the manuscript copies according to the various textual forms found, and this in turn provided a method by which an early prior form of the text might be identified. It was now fully understood that a few early witnesses might outweigh the mass of traditional copies. Critical principles had been formulated in readiness for a scientific procedure.

e The beginnings of the *critical* text of the NT in use today came with **Karl Lachmann**. He was a classical philologian who acted upon the principles advanced by his theological predecessors. He boldly set aside the Textus Receptus and created a text *de novo* (1831). This Gr. text was derived objectively from the most ancient manuscript witnesses, while setting aside the later Byzantine copies. Lachmann opened the door for which others had been preparing the key. His principles were similar to those enunciated by his predecessors. It was he, however, who acted upon these principles as he determined to derive his new Gr. text from his 'Oriental' or African class of witnesses which had come to be trusted. He too subscribed to the set of critical rules which had been developed. He too rested on the testimony of the OL and the early Fathers. What was new about Lachmann was that, instead of trying to mend the later 'ecclesiastical' text, he avowedly embraced a more ancient form. So about four hundred years after the Byzantine Gr. text was revived in the Latin 583e
West, western Christianity recovered the more primitive Greek base while the Eastern Church continued in the use of its traditional text.

Constantine Tischendorf was a youthful student f
when Lachmann's text first appeared in 1831, and was stimulated to devote his life to textual research. In persistent and wide travels he was highly successful in discovering additional and even older sources and in collating the text of the most important witnesses. Chief of his discoveries was the 4th-cent. Codex Sinaiticus at St Catherine's monastery, which contained a complete Gr. NT. Tischendorf's first published text came in 1841 (when he was but twenty-six) and he continued throughout his life to issue new and improved editions. He formulated some additional rules of procedure: (1) the Gr. witness is superior to any translation, (2) an ancient reading is not to be rejected even though all Byzantine copies differ, (3) a reading in hellenistic idiom or in the author's own style is to be preferred, and (4) where it seems obvious that a scribe has harmonised (with another Gospel or with the LXX), such a reading is to be rejected. By the time of Tischendorf, established canons of criticism had made the discipline highly objective and scientific. Accessibility to new resources of great age and high character had provided trustworthy witness direct from the 4th cent. Tischendorf's crowning achievement was his *editio maior* (1869–72) shortly before his death. It contained his most critical text (the first to be revised by reference to Codex Sinaiticus), and an *apparatus criticus* of high accuracy which is still the best available. The simple tools first forged by Fell and Mill almost two centuries earlier were here both justified and superseded.

The generation of Tischendorf was one of textual giants, for besides him there were such figures as the Englishmen Tregelles, Burgon, Scrivener, Hort, and Westcott. After a period of German leadership from Bengel to Tischendorf (1734–1872), the textual centre shifted again to England. **B. F. Westcott and F. J. A. Hort** collaborated for thirty years and produced the Gr. NT text still basic in western critical exegesis. This Westcott-Hort 'Neutral' text relies heavily upon the great 4th-cent. pair of Vaticanus and Sinaiticus. It does not carry an *apparatus criticus* but assumes the evidence published by Tischendorf. The chief contributions of Westcott and Hort are their superior critical text, the theory of the transmission of the text in the early centuries, and the definition of scientific method in textual criticism.

Since the Westcott-Hort text appeared, much g
important textual research has been accomplished although the new knowledge has not yet been fully assimilated. Such researches have exposed the limitations of the 'Neutral' text but have not yet provided a better one. Still older manuscript witnesses than Westcott and Hort had at hand have since been discovered and have been examined, but their witness has not yet been articulated into the textual schema. The new research has cast doubts upon the concept of textual transmission which underlies the technical procedure of Westcott and Hort in deriving their critical text, but as yet a more adequate explanation has not become apparent. For the time being, the Westcott-Hort 'Neutral' text (or another only slightly altered) continues to serve the interpreter, while we await the fruition of contemporary labours.

For example, an additional early recension unknown to Westcott and Hort has been discerned by Streeter and the Lakes and others, called the 'Caesarean'. Furthermore, the broad stream of the later traditional 'ecclesiastical' text is now recognised to consist of numerous distinctive tributaries, through the work of von Soden and K. and S. Lake and many another. Among the many Byzantine manuscripts groups of textual relatives have been recognised by the Lakes and Ferrar, as 'Family 1' and 'Family 13'. The investigation of the text as preserved in the liturgical

583g lectionaries offers a new approach to the primitive period, although this study is still in its infancy. New discoveries of important witnesses in the last seventy-five years have been numerous, some of them quite sensational. From St Catherine's monastery in 1892 came the first report of a 4th-cent. copy of the Gospels in the Old Syriac. From Giza in 1906 came the Freer MSS, including a copy of the Gospels in Gr. written about A.D. 400. From Tiflis the witness of Codex Koridethi written about A.D. 750 first emerged in 1913, displaying a text of the Gospels of 'Caesarean' character. From Egypt about 1930 came the Chester Beatty papyri of three NT MSS (Gospels and Acts, Paul, Revelation), which though fragmentary preserve substantial blocks of the Gr. text from the 3rd cent. A final example of such discovery are the Bodmer papyri (Luke, John, 1 Peter) which also attest the Gr. text in Egypt in the 3rd cent. The initial studies of most such early witnesses lend primary confirmation to the 'Neutral' text, and yet call for a bold reassessment of the critical text and of the primitive transmission.

h Textual criticism today has a strong ally in the camera. Photographic facsimiles of many key witnesses have become available to all. The microfilm camera has brought whole collections of manuscripts from inaccessible Eastern repositories into western libraries and private studies. Collations of texts have been made by the hundreds, vastly multiplying the early accumulations of Fell and Mill. World catalogues of extant manuscripts have grown larger with Scrivener, von Soden, and Gregory, and their successors. But, alas, the efforts made since Tischendorf (by von Soden and Legge) to organise the growing textual witness into a systematic and trustworthy *apparatus criticus* have fallen short. Such an effort has been renewed (since 1948) in the International Greek New Testament project, with plans to complete an eight-volume report of known variants as a basic reference work for the textual critic. Tischendorf based his *apparatus criticus* upon his own critical text; the projected one will exhibit all readings against the Textus Receptus (because the great majority of MSS cited are of this same type, and therefore the mass of variants will be greatly reduced). The projected *apparatus criticus* is to cite each MS completely, and report evidence on any reading fully (both for and against). Such a reference work is a prerequisite to the task of defining the process of textual transmission, and to any successful effort to reconstruct the original Gr. NT.

Yet there have been many new critical texts published since the Westcott-Hort of 1881. Some have been frankly synthetic, such as the Weymouth 'Resultant' text (1886) and the Nestle text (1898, etc.). All have been eclectic, achieving no more than minimum revision of the 'Neutral' textual form, in a number of itemised readings where choice involves a subjective balance. The British and Foreign Bible Society and the American Bible Society have sponsored separate plans to publish texts for use in missionary translation. But the *magnum opus* that may succeed the 'Neutral' text (as closer to the original) must await more fundamental and systematic researches.

584a **History of the Text**—The importance of knowing how the NT text was transmitted in the early centuries has gradually come to realisation. Indeed, it is now perceived that the critic must ascertain this history in order to evaluate and interpret the testimony of each manuscript. If one is to judge the authenticity of an attested variant it is necessary to know not only the date of the witnessing manuscript but also its place and relationship among all manuscripts. It is now obvious that *counting* manuscripts will not determine a true reading, for the majority often attest a late and popular variant. It is further recognised that *dating* manuscripts will not determine a true reading, for even the earliest manuscripts may preserve a provincial or recensional variant. The geographical *placement* of manuscripts will not determine an original reading, for this may yield evidence only of rival local texts from which choice must still be made. Besides all this, it is required to learn the textual *relationships* of manuscripts and the textual development they represent. Only the knowledge of this textual history will enable us to fix a proper value upon each manuscript witness to a variant, or to understand the general character of an individual manuscript. 584

When Bentley proposed in 1720 that the original Gr. NT could be recognised wherever the Gr. and Latin texts agreed, he implied a simple textual history. From his conclusion that Codex Alexandrinus and the pre-Vulgate Latin were in close accord he deduced that it was the primitive Gr. text that descended in both lines. This was the earliest hypothesis of textual 'history' but Bentley's own researches did not confirm it. The younger contemporary critic in Germany, J. A. Bengel, also reflected this textual theory in his 'African' class of witnesses. Bengel further postulated that textual corruption had infected and discredited the mass of later manuscripts (his 'Asiatic' class). He felt therefore that the best guides back to the original text were the Codices Alexandrinus and Bezae, especially when supported by the early Latin witness. His successor, J. S. Semler, believed that Bengel's African text was especially centred in Alexandria and had been used by Origen and other Egyptian Fathers and also underlay the Coptic and Ethiopic versions. But Semler was the first to make explicit the growth of a different ('Occidental') recension in the West, preserved in the Latin version and Fathers. He was the first to suggest the view that an Eastern ('Oriental') recension might have been made under Lucian the Martyr in his school at Antioch. This theory of the early development of three regional recensions was accepted by his student, J. J. Griesbach, who explicitly labelled the corresponding Gr. manuscripts and the translations attesting each recension. Thus a 'history of the text' was being evolved even while the latest and poorest textual form (the 'Textus Receptus') continued to be published and used. b

Karl Lachmann is justly noted as the innovator of the modern critical text of the NT. His achievement, however, rests upon the conception of the textual history which his predecessors had been developing. From them he learned to respect their African witnesses (his 'Oriental' Codices Alexandrinus, Vaticanus, and Ephrem Syrus; and Origen). From them he learned to distinguish a western, Italian recension (his 'Occidental' Codex Bezae *et al.*; the Latin version, and Irenaeus). From them he learned to trust the textual kinship between these two recensions. From them he learned to disregard the mass of later Gr. copies as untrustworthy descendants. The formulation of a textual history was a long collaborative development from Bentley to Lachmann, and was essential to the result achieved in the Lachmann text. Tischendorf's procedure in editing his critical text is evidence of his acceptance of essentially the same textual history. c

In the course of these researches there were certain critics who interpreted the phenomena differently and therefore arrived at a different textual history. Wettstein opposed the Bentley-Bengel 'history' with the argument that agreement between early Greek witnesses and the Latin showed that the former had been 'latinised', and he therefore concluded that the text had been better preserved in the later traditional Gr. copies. Scholz also took this position and further discredited the ancient Gr. manuscripts on the ground that their very survival was due to their disuse and rejection as false witnesses. The views of Hug were unique in his time and were not accepted by others although they now appear to have been prophetic insights. He insisted that the mass of manuscripts showed a degenerated text by about A.D. 250. He believed that the LXX and the NT together shared a threefold revision: by Origen in Palestine, by Hesychius in Egypt, and by Lucian in Antioch. He

584c held that the first of these was the best text, preserved in Codex Bezae and the OL along with Origen and Clement of Alexandria and the Sahidic and Syriac versions. All these views have been seriously held by one or another respected critic, at some time since then, and some are still in good standing.

d However, the main development in constructing the textual history descended from Bentley and Bengel, through Semler, Griesbach, Lachmann, and Tischendorf, to Westcott and Hort who brought it to its full fruition. They claimed for their critical text of 1881 that it was a 'Neutral' text of the early 2nd cent. known throughout the East (which Gregory later frankly called 'original'). This text was free from Western corruption and is attested chiefly in the surviving 4th-cent. Egyptian Codices Vaticanus and Sinaiticus upon which the editors relied. Immediately behind this 'Neutral' text lay the original apostolic text of the 1st cent. (for those books written at that early date). Directly descended from the 'Neutral' text was a polished revision of Alexandria in the 3rd cent. (recognised today in Codices Ephrem Syrus and Regius, as well as Egyptian Fathers and dialects). Another distinctive text derived from the original was called 'Western', for despite its origin in Syria in the 2nd cent. (cf. the Old Syriac) it is preserved in Latin or bilingual manuscripts (D, D_2, OL) and the western Fathers. Its distinctive character of fulsome paraphrase and interpolation was the result of editorial revison. Finally, there was the 'Syrian' revision (possibly by Lucian, or his Antiochian school) made about A.D. 300. It very soon became standard and was so generally accepted that the great mass of manuscripts still surviving belong in this category. The revision is marked by textual mixture and conflation and editorial 'improvement'. It was this text that was printed from the time of Ximenes and Erasmus, persisting even beyond the critical editions of Lachmann and Westcott-Hort, and that was translated and interpreted in many languages. It still had its 19th-cent. champions in Scrivener and Burgon, and the latter especially attacked the character of Vaticanus, Sinaiticus, and Bezae. But textual criticism had succeeded in outlining, however imperfectly, the course of textual transmission and thereby recovering a primitive and superior Gr. NT. Practically all the critical texts published since 1881 also rest upon this textual history refined by Westcott and Hort.

e The Westcott-Hort textual theory was the natural culmination of the dominant critical development since Bengel, and was probably the superior interpretation of the fact that distinctive texts existed in the earliest centuries. Although further discovery and research have raised many questions about this reconstruction of textual history, they have not yet yielded any clear pattern to displace it. Are the 'Neutral' and 'Alexandrian' forms really two distinct texts? Is the 'Neutral' text free from corruption? Is it the primitive text or rather an early derivation? Was it disseminated widely or only in Egypt where all its earliest extant witnesses were written? Did Egyptian Christians have also the 'Western' and 'Syrian' texts? Are any of the Westcott and Hort texts local or regional (Alexandrian, Eastern, Western, Antiochian, or Syrian)? Were the 'Western' and 'Syrian' texts deliberate revisions or natural growths? Can the 'Western' form be claimed as a distinct text? Is the 'Syrian' form one text or many? To ask these questions is to suggest necessary qualifications to the general theory, even where no clear response is possible. To qualify the theory at any or all points is not necessarily to refute or nullify it. The problem of the early history of the Gr. NT text still remains alive and fluid.

f **The major change since Westcott and Hort** has been the recognition of still another early text called the 'Caesarean' or 'Family Theta'. Its witnesses are found in all regions and as yet its relationships are obscure. The fuller realisation that the 'Western' text is universally attested from earliest times has led 584f some critics (Hilgenfeld and Zahn in Germany, A. C. Clark in England, and H. A. Sanders in America) to conclude that *it*, rather than the 'Neutral' text, is the primitive form. Among the mass of 'Syrian' manuscripts, groups with closely similar texts have been identified descending from older (but now lost) exemplars. Each group is designated after its dominant member, such as 'Family 1' and 'Family 13'. Each group, in turn, may belong to a larger and broader text, like the 'Theta text', and thus some order begins to emerge out of the mass and a pattern of transmission begins to form. Each group, small or large, points back to its master text which thus may be reconstructed to enable the critic to work with a few types rather than the multitude of individual variant members. The greatest advance in this effort was accomplished by Hermann von Soden (1902–13) who arranged hundreds of the Byzantine manuscripts in a few textual types. Thus the complex history of the text in the later Byzantine centuries has begun to yield to the science of textual criticism.

The need to improve upon the Westcott-Hort theory is clearly seen in the light of recent sensational discoveries. The Beatty and Bodmer papyri from the 3rd cent. have presented the critic with both problem and possible solution: problem, because they do not fit into our present theory; and possible solution, because they provide for the first time extensive portions throughout the NT of a more primitive text. The initial reaction has been to describe these new Egyptian texts as 'mixed': that is, a mixture of the forms already known in 'the great uncials' of the 4th and 5th cent. But this is standing on one's head to interpret the evidence, thus explaining the earlier text from our prior and partial understanding of the later. It is required of the textual critic now to dismiss such presuppositions and to assume an entirely new vantage-point. He must first analyse these 3rd-cent. texts as the earliest witnesses we possess, and only then look through them anew and with an open mind at the later copies. It is at least possible that such a new beginning may come to confirm the general theory of Westcott and Hort, but it is equally possible (and highly desirable) that it would instead result in a far more adequate history of the early text. In any case, textual criticism now stands at that point of need, to find the meaning of the Beatty and Bodmer texts for the transmission of the original Gr. NT. When that history is understood, the original text itself will come closer.

Theological Significance—The ultimate objective of 585a textual criticism is theological. It seeks to recover the true text of any Father as a means of understanding his theology, and particularly his interpretation of scripture. It reconstructs the text of 'Family 13', for example, in order to make available the theology of a Calabrian community in the medieval centuries. It would fix the various textual types which descended to Christians in the middle ages so that we may read aright their understanding of the faith. All such specific studies are essential parts of the dominant search for the original Gr. NT itself, which is the foundation of all Christian theology in any time and place. Far from being a literary study in an ivory tower, as is often supposed, textual criticism pursues its research at the very centre of Christian faith and life.

When Bentley announced in 1720 that he had found 30,000 textual variants in the later manuscripts he examined, he did not create these differences but merely recorded the fact of their existence. In the 20th cent. possibly 300,000 variants have accumulated. Although their discovery has revealed that some erroneous readings have crept into the Gr. text used by theologians, it is this very knowledge that has made possible a more trustworthy text as the basis of theological interpretation. Yet it must not be supposed that every variant discovered, even in an ancient manuscript,

585a involves correction of the original text, for the new variant itself may be a secondary reading. Nevertheless it should be recognised that as a result of textual criticism the Gr. text now in use is substantially different and far more accurate than the text of the early 19th cent. Consequently, theological interpretation also has yielded a more penetrating understanding of the Gospel as originally recorded.

b It has sometimes been declared that textual researches have no effect upon the doctrines of the church, although it has always been the very purpose of these researches to clarify our understanding of scriptural doctrine. It is quite true that many textual variants are trivial and that most have no doctrinal significance. Hort himself ventured the estimate (*Introduction*, p. 2) that significant variation 'can hardly form more than a thousandth part of the entire text'. This would be equivalent to only twenty lines of solid text in a Nestle edition, which is far too low an estimate. But the important insight is that we cannot by counting words measure the theological clarification afforded through textual improvement. The significant result lies not in the many thousands of orthographic or stylistic variants but in the *few* readings that open new theological vistas.

Illustration may be seen in two simple passages where the variant involves but a single word. The familiar verse in Rom. 8:28 reads in the AV: 'All things work together for good to them that love God'. This idea is based upon the late 'ecclesiastical' Greek text, but when the Codices Alexandrinus and Vaticanus came to light (later than the AV) they revealed a text with 'God' as the subject of the verb 'to work'. Lachmann's text in 1831 was the first to make this correction to the original, and a century later this reading was further confirmed by the new Beatty Papyrus from the 3rd cent. The English translation now reads (RSV): 'In everything God works for good with those who love him'. The textual correction of the single word, which had been lost for many centuries, adds depth to the theologian's interpretation. While it does not overturn a doctrine, it does affect our affirmation of belief in God. Again, another familiar passage is found in 1 Jn 4:19, which reads in the AV: 'We love him because he first loved us'. This translation is correctly made from the 'ecclesiastical' text as printed in the 16th cent. When Tischendorf found Codex Sinaiticus, he noted that the pronoun was made explicit: 'We love God . . .' But again the Codices Alexandrinus and Vaticanus were found to read without this object, and critics since Tischendorf have judged this to be the original form. Therefore, it is now translated (RSV): 'We love, because he first loved us'. So once again our theology is affected by the correction of a single word, and once again we are led to a greater depth of understanding in our relation to God. Instead of a *quid pro quo*, there is the description of the Christian quality of love created by God's initial love for us, whereby we become the agent of God's love for man. 585

A substantial body of such textual choices has been created by theological interests. It was a theological concern of the authors in the first place that determined the formulation of the original text. It was the theological interests of patristic editors and interpreters of successive generations that caused revisions in the original text. The critic is concerned to recognise such interests and the relevant textual variants in the history of Christian thought. He is also called upon to distinguish the secondary from the primary and, wherever in the text a secondary reading has come to stand in the place of the original, to discover the error and restore the true text. The Gr. NT text suffered increasing corruption through fifteen hundred years, but textual criticism through the last three hundred years has reversed this process by its constructive and reverent service. c

Bibliography—F. Buhl, 'Bible Text', *New Schaff-Herzog Encyclopedia* (1908); A. Fox, *John Mill and Richard Bentley* (1954); C. R. Gregory, *Canon and Text of the NT* (1907); F. G. Kenyon, *Handbook to the Textual Criticism of the NT* (1912²), *Recent Developments in the Textual Criticism of the Greek Bible* (1933), *Our Bible and the Ancient Manuscripts* (rev. ed. 1939), *The Text of the Greek Bible* (rev. ed. 1949); K. Lake, *The Text of the NT* (rev. ed. 1928); E. Nestle, 'Bible Versions', *New Schaff-Herzog Encyclopedia* (1908); I. M. Price, *The Ancestry of Our English Bible* (rev. ed. 1956); A. T. Robertson, *Studies in the Text of the NT* (1926), *An Introduction to the Textual Criticism of the NT* (1928²); S. P. Tregelles, *An Account of the Printed Text of the Greek NT* (1854); L. Vaganay, *An Introduction to the Textual Criticism of the NT* (1937); Westcott and Hort, *The NT in the Original Greek*, with Introduction and Appendix (1881–2).

THE EARLY VERSIONS OF THE NEW TESTAMENT

By B. M. METZGER

586a **Introduction**—From the point of view of origin, the early versions of the NT were products of the missionary activities of Christian evangelists and their converts in various lands to which the Gospel had been carried. Though many of the better educated persons of that day throughout the Mediterranean world knew enough Greek to read the NT in the language in which it was originally written, obviously for those whose mother tongue was another language, as well as for the many who knew no Greek, translations into the native vernaculars were of the utmost value. Thus it came about that during the 2nd and 3rd cent. renderings of one or more Gospels and other books of the NT were made into Latin, Syriac, and Coptic. During the following centuries other versions were made, some from the original Greek, others from one of the three earliest versions. These subsequent versions include (in the approximate order of their appearance) the Gothic, Armenian, Georgian, Ethiopic, Nubian, Sogdian, Old Arabic, and Old Slavic versions. Later versions (such as Frankish, Anglo-Saxon, Persian, and later Arabic versions) fall outside the scope of this article, as do the translations at the time of the Renaissance and the Reformation into the several vernaculars of Europe.

Our knowledge of the early versions depends upon a study of the manuscripts by which they have been transmitted, as well as upon an examination of the form of Scriptural quotations made by ecclesiastical authors in the several languages. In some cases these sources are extremely abundant (there are more than 8,000 manuscripts of the Latin Vulgate, and literally hundreds of thousands of Latin patristic quotations); in other cases they are quite limited in number and extent (for the Gothic version but six manuscripts containing portions of the NT are known today, and among these none preserves any part of Acts, Hebrews, the General Epistles, or Revelation).

If it be asked, What are the chief uses of the early versions to the NT scholar? the answer is twofold. They are extremely valuable to the textual critic confronted with variant readings, for in some cases (notably the Old Latin and Old Syriac) the version represents a stage in the transmission of the text which is earlier than the stages reflected in the overwhelming number of Greek manuscripts. The early versions are no less valuable to the exegete in tracing the history of Christian interpretation of a given passage of Scripture, for he finds embodied in the vernacular translations the current understanding of the meaning of the passage.

I THE LATIN VERSIONS

b **A The Latin Versions before Jerome**—Augustine tells us that, though it was possible to count the number of those who had translated the Hebrew OT into Greek (traditionally there were seventy translators), the Latin translators were innumerable, 'For in the early days of the faith, no sooner did anyone 586b
gain possession of a Greek manuscript, and imagine himself to have any facility in both languages (however slight that might be), than he made bold to translate it' (*de doctr. Christ.*, ii, 11). The advice which Augustine gives his readers is to prefer the *Italic* (or Itala) version, 'for it keeps closer to the words without prejudice to clearness of expression' (ib. 15).

Where it was that the very first attempts were made to translate the NT into Latin has been much disputed. Though some scholars have suggested Italy, and others have favoured Antioch of Syria, it is likely that Roman Africa was the birthplace of the Old Latin version. The wooden and literalistic style which characterises many of the Old Latin translations suggests that early copies were made in the form of interlinear renderings of the Greek.

Today scholars have traced the family relationships of the thirty or so surviving manuscripts of the Old Latin NT, and have classified them into sub-groups designated the African, European (or Italian), and Hispanic families. In general the type of NT text which is preserved in Old Latin witnesses belongs to the so-called 'Western' family (for this terminology, see §582e).

B Jerome's Latin Vulgate—It was the confusion c
among the Old Latin manuscripts that led Pope Damasus (A.D. 366–384) to request the chief scholar of Western Christendom at that time, Eusebius Hieronymus (Jerome), to make an authoritative version of the Latin NT. In 383 Jerome sent Damasus the first instalment of his work, the Four Gospels. These were followed by the rest of the NT (and later by the OT). His methodology was a sound one; he tells us that he made a careful comparison of the old Greek manuscripts of the NT and altered the current Latin rendering only when a real change of meaning was necessary, retaining in all other cases what had become the familiar Latin phraseology. Despite Jerome's scholarly qualifications for this kind of work, and despite the essentially conservative nature of his rendering, many of his contemporaries severely criticised him and refused to use his revision. During subsequent centuries, however, the intrinsic worth of Jerome's version came to be appreciated, and eventually it was accepted throughout Western Christendom, thus earning for itself the name Vulgate (*vulgata* [*versio*], 'the common version').

It was inevitable that, in the course of transmission by recopying, scribal carelessness corrupted Jerome's original work. In order to purify the text several medieval recensions were produced (notable among them were those of Alcuin, Theodulf, and Harding; related to these in purpose were the 'Correctoria' collected by scholars at the University of Paris and elsewhere).

The influence of the Latin Vulgate has been simply enormous. The Anglo-Saxon translations were made from it, as was Wyclif's English version, while other English versions from Coverdale's onward have been

586c much influenced by it. The religious terminology of the languages of western Europe has been in great part derived from or influenced by the Vulgate (e.g. words like justification, sanctification, salvation, regeneration, election, reconciliation, satisfaction, sacrament, communion, congregation, orders, penance, and priest). On 8 April 1546, the Council of Trent pronounced an anathema upon anyone who does not receive the ancient Vulgate edition as the authentic version of the Scriptures.

II THE SYRIAC VERSIONS

587a Syriac, a Semitic language, was the Aramaic dialect used at Edessa and in western Mesopotamia until, after the 13th cent., it was superseded by Arabic. It was similar to but not identical with the Aramaic dialect used in Palestine during the time of Christ and his Apostles. Though one might suppose that the contents of the Gospels, reflecting as they do Palestinian syntax and vocabulary, would have been transferred directly into Syriac, this does not appear to be the case. It was the Greek Gospels which were translated into Syriac, as is proved by the presence of occasional transliterations of Greek words into the Syriac (e.g. Mt. 26:28, the Greek *diathēkē* is used instead of the native Semitic word).

b **A The Old Syriac Version**—The earliest translation of any part of the NT into Syriac appears to have been made during the 2nd cent. Whether it was one or more Gospels as such, or a series of pericopes translated for liturgical purposes, or Tatian's Diatessaron (a harmony of the Four Gospels woven into one account), has been debated at length by scholars. Unfortunately we no longer possess Tatian's famous Diatessaron in its entirety, for he was later adjudged a heretic and copies of his Harmony were sought out and destroyed by ecclesiastical authorities. Except for a tiny fragment in Greek, all that we have today are secondary and tertiary witnesses to Tatian's remarkable work, the most important of which are an Armenian translation of Ephraem's commentary on the Diatessaron (*c.*365) and certain Arabic, Persian, Middle Dutch, and Old Italian Harmonies that are more or less closely related to Tatian's original work.

Related to the type of Scriptural text employed by Tatian is the Old Syriac version (but whether as ancestor or cousin is much disputed). Two manuscripts of the Gospels in this version (both somewhat fragmentary) are extant, one discovered by William Cureton at the middle of the last century and now in the British Museum, the other discovered by Mrs Agnes Smith Lewis at the Monastery of St Catherine on Mt Sinai in 1892. Both manuscripts date from about the 5th or 6th cent. and preserve a most interesting form of the text of the Gospels, one which goes back to the 2nd cent. and is characterised on the one hand by certain harmonistic readings and on the other by paraphrases which reflect knowledge of Palestinian topography and local custom.

c **B The Peshitta Syriac Version**—As Jerome's Latin Vulgate was prepared in order to provide a standard Latin version, supplanting the various Old Latin texts, so in the Syrian Church a revised translation was made in order to supply a standard version of the NT. Until the middle of the 19th cent. it was commonly supposed that the Peshitta NT dated from the 2nd cent.; the discovery of the Curetonian manuscript of the Old Syriac version, however, showed that this view was untenable, and subsequently the conjecture that the NT Peshitta was the work of the Syrian ecclesiastic, Bp. Rabbula of Edessa, in the first part of the 5th cent., came to be generally held. More recent investigation, however, has tended to suggest that the Peshitta is the product of several hands, different in methods and techniques, and that it may have been made toward the middle or end of the 4th cent. Whenever it was made, the translation endeared itself so thoroughly to all groups of Syrian Christians that it remained the standard version for both the Jacobites and the Nestorians when the Syrian Church was divided in A.D. 431. The original Peshitta version contains only twenty-two books of the NT (it lacks the so-called Antilegomena, viz. 2 Pet., 2 and 3 Jn, Jude, and Rev.).

The characteristics of the Peshitta text are a certain smoothness and grace which stand in contrast to the singularities of the Old Syriac. Apparently the form of the Greek text current in the patriarchate of Antioch was taken as the basis of the revision which produced the Peshitta. It is noteworthy that scribes have transmitted the Peshitta text with extreme fidelity; indeed, this version was handed down from generation to generation with fewer variant readings than is the case with any other ancient version.

C The Philoxenian and/or Harclean Versions— d
Much controversy has marked the investigation of these versions (or this version). The scanty and ambiguous evidence in certain colophons found in several Harclean Syriac manuscripts has been interpreted in opposite ways. (1) It has been held that the version, which was produced in A.D. 508 for Philoxenus by Polycarp, his chorepiscopus, was thoroughly revised in 616 by Thomas of Heraclea (Charkel) and issued as a new version with marginal readings from two or three Greek manuscripts. (2) On the other hand, it has been argued that Thomas merely reissued the Philoxenian version, essentially unchanged except for the addition of certain marginal notes. According to the former opinion there were two separate versions, the later one being provided with marginalia; according to the second opinion, there was but one version, which was republished with variant readings in the margin. Unfortunately no modern critical edition is available, and separate studies are far from satisfactory in presenting the whole body of evidence. Despite the lack of agreement among scholars as to who produced what, it is generally acknowledged that the type of text preserved in some of the Philoxenian and/or Harclean manuscripts is of great antiquity, and, for Acts at least, is the second most important witness to the 'Western' text.

D The Palestinian Syriac Version—Until two e
centuries ago the Aramaic literature of the early Christians of Palestine was unknown except for a few scattered words preserved in Greek. In 1758 two Maronite scholars, the brothers Assemani, published a lengthy description of a vellum manuscript in the Vatican Library which contains a Lectionary of the Gospels in the Aramaic dialect used by Christians in ancient Palestine. Strangely enough, this manuscript had to wait another century (1861–4) before it was edited in its entirety. Subsequently two other Gospel Lectionaries, as well as portions of other books of the Old and New Testaments, written in the same dialect, were discovered and edited. Though popularly called 'Syriac', the only claim which this version has to be regarded as Syriac is the form of the script in which it is written; the language is properly described as a western dialect of Aramaic (Syriac is an eastern dialect of Aramaic).

Although earlier scholars supposed that this version preserved the *ipsissima verba* of Christ, it is now recognised that the text of the Gospels was translated from a Greek original. When the rendering was made has been a moot question; some time during the late 4th or early 5th cent. appears to be as likely a date as any. The version is remarkable in that it is the only one used by any considerable body of Syrian Christians which contains the *pericope de adultera* (Jn 7:53–8:11).

III THE COPTIC VERSIONS

Coptic, the mother tongue of native Egyptians in 588a
the early Christian centuries, is the descendant of the ancient language of the Pharaohs. No longer written

588a in hieroglyphics or in the subsequent demotic script, the Coptic language used a modified Greek alphabet. There were many dialects of Coptic, spoken at different localities stretching from north to south along the Nile River.

A The Sahidic Version—It was in the south (that is, in Upper Egypt) that the need for translating the NT first arose. The dialect used here was Sahidic. Scholars think that the Gospels were translated into this dialect about the middle of the 3rd cent., and the rest of the NT shortly thereafter.

The manuscript remains of the Sahidic version are not so abundant as one could wish, nor have all of them been utilised in critical editions. It is not surprising, therefore, that different opinions exist as to the textual characteristics of this version. Most investigators find that the Sahidic discloses a tendency toward the Alexandrian text, but that it also preserves several noteworthy 'Western' readings.

b **B The Bohairic Version**—In the north, or Lower Egypt, the Bohairic dialect was predominant. This differs from Sahidic chiefly in orthography, but also in vocabulary and syntax. Textual materials in Bohairic are much more numerous than in any other Coptic dialect, yet, with few exceptions, most manuscripts are relatively recent in date (for example, no extensive manuscript of the Acts or Pauline Epistles is older than the 12th cent.). Scholars have proposed widely divergent dates for the origin of the Bohairic version, ranging from the 2nd to the 8th cent. Recent studies suggest that it was made about the 4th cent. The textual characteristics of the version reveal a close relationship to the Alexandrian family, with a limited number of readings peculiar to itself.

c **C Other Coptic Versions**—Other Coptic versions are represented in fragmentary manuscripts of the Achmimic, sub-Achmimic, Middle-Egyptian, and Fayyumic dialects. Except for a manuscript of the Gospel according to John in sub-Achmimic, dating from the 4th cent., most of the remains are too scanty to permit confidence in analyses. A study of the Johannine manuscript discloses that the sub-Achmimic version, like the Sahidic version to which it is related, has close affinities with the Alexandrian group of NT witnesses.

The study of the Coptic versions is still far from being advanced, and many problems remain to be solved. Particularly perplexing are questions of the nature and degree of interrelation of the several translations, as well as the possibility of stages of revision within a given version.

IV THE GOTHIC VERSION

589a The Gothic version of the Bible is noteworthy on several counts: its translator, Ulfilas, created an alphabet and reduced the Gothic language to writing; it is the earliest known literary monument in a Germanic dialect; and it is the only version of which all the known manuscript evidence has been utilised. Ulfilas (whose name, which is variously spelled, means 'Little Wolf') was born in the region of the lower Danube about A.D. 310, was made bishop of the Goths probably about 341 at Antioch, and died at Constantinople in 383. His translation of the NT is very faithful to the original, frequently to the point of wooden literalness, retaining the Greek order of words at the expense of what is believed to have been the true Gothic idiom. At the same time, in the renderings of individual words Ulfilas was an apt and forceful translator, comparable in certain respects to Luther.

The most complete of the half-dozen known Gothic manuscripts (all of them being fragmentary) is a *de luxe* copy dating from the 5th or 6th cent. It has portions of all four Gospels, which stand in the so-called 'Western' order (Matthew, John, Luke, and Mark). It is written on purple vellum in large letters of silver ink, whence the name commonly given to this manuscript, *Codex Argenteus*, i.e. the Silver Codex. 589a
The initial lines of the Gospels and the first line of every section of text are in gold letters. Today this celebrated manuscript is in the Library of the University of Uppsala. All the other manuscripts of the Gothic NT, with exception of a vellum leaf from a bilingual Gothic-Latin codex discovered earlier this century in Egypt, are palimpsests (i.e. manuscripts whose writing has been erased and which have been reused to receive other writing).

Opinion is divided as to the precise textual complexion of this version and its relation to the Old Latin. Whatever may be the ultimate verdict as to the time and circumstances when the Gothic underwent a certain latinisation, it is undeniable that the Old Latin manuscript Brixianus (*f*) agrees with the Gothic in a significant number of readings which differ from both the Old Latin and Vulgate forms of text.

V THE ARMENIAN VERSION

Christianity was introduced into Armenia sometime b
prior to A.D. 300. Though in the western areas of Armenia Greek influence from the Christian Churches of Asia Minor made itself felt, in Greater Armenia the chief influence came from Syrian Christianity. Toward the close of the 4th cent. Armenia was divided politically, and the western part was allotted to Constantinople, while the eastern, and larger, part went to the Persians. It was subsequent to the partitioning of Armenia that Mesrop (*d.* A.D. 439; also spelled Mesrob), a soldier who became a Christian missionary and teacher, saw the need of having a translation of the Scriptures in the vernacular. As Ulfilas did for the Goths, Mesrop created a new alphabet and, with Sahak, an able prelate, translated the NT into Armenian. Whether this translation was made from the original Greek or from an intermediary Syriac version has been debated by scholars. The inclusion of the apocryphal Third Epistle of Paul to the Corinthians in the early canon of both the Syrian and Armenian Churches, and the presence of traces of Syriac orthography of proper names and Semitic syntax in the Armenian text point to a strong influence from Syria. The earliest Armenian version appears to have undergone a subsequent revision sometime between the 5th and 8th cent. Most extant manuscripts embody this revision, which shows traces of a more hellenised form of text. Whether the Greek text which served as the basis of the revision was predominantly Caesarean or *Koine* in textual type is a problem which has not yet been satisfactorily clarified.

On the whole, the Armenian version is one of the most beautiful and accurate of all early translations of the Scriptures. Sometimes called 'the Queen of the versions', it is worthy of far more attention than scholars have been accustomed to give to its study.

VI THE GEORGIAN VERSION

Of all the early versions of the NT, probably the c
least well known is the Old Georgian, for here, if anywhere, the labourers are few! The people of Caucasian Georgia, that rough mountain-district between the Black Sea and the Caspian Sea, received the Gospel during the first half of the 4th cent. The time and circumstances of the translation of the Scriptures into Georgian, an agglutinative language not known to be related to any other, are hidden in the mists of legend. According to an Armenian tradition, Mesrop, the creator of the Armenian alphabet, also invented and introduced a new alphabet into Georgia. Probably the Gospels and certain other parts of the NT were translated during the first half of the 5th cent. The Book of Revelation was not translated until the end of the 10th or beginning of the 11th cent.; it was done

589c by Euthymius, one of the Georgian monks of the Iviron Monastery on Mt Athos who helped to inaugurate a new stage in Georgian ecclesiastical literature (the Athonite School).

Textual critics are not agreed as to the base from which the Georgian NT was translated. Although ecclesiastical tradition asserts that it was made directly from the Greek, only a few scholars today find evidence which supports this view. Most of those who have studied the problems at first hand believe that it was translated from a Syriac or (more probably) from an Armenian original. At a subsequent date the version appears to have been revised, and certain readings, based on Armenian influence, were supplanted by a stronger Byzantine influence in syntax and style.

VII THE ETHIOPIC VERSION

d According to tradition, the beginnings of Christianity in Ethiopia go back to very early times. Whether the Ethiopian eunuch whom Philip converted (Ac. 8:26–39) was successful in introducing the Gospel among his countrymen, we have no knowledge. The first evidence for any considerable amount of influence of Christianity in that country comes from Athanasius, who reports that he consecrated Frumentius, a Syrian, as bishop of Ethiopia just before the middle of the 4th cent. By about 340 ʽEzānā, king of Axum, who had become a Christian, decreed that his kingdom should become Christian. Whether Frumentius began the work of preparing a translation of the Scriptures into Ethiopic, or whether (according to Abyssinian traditions) this was done by a group of nine Syrian monks who as Monophysites fled after the Council of Chalcedon in 451 from Syria to Egypt, whence they made their way to Ethiopia, is not known. In any case, whoever the original translators were, at times they followed the Greek text slavishly, even as regards the order of words, but at other times, perhaps where the Greek proved to be too difficult for them, they paraphrased wildly, producing a Targumised rendering.

Unfortunately for the study of the earlier Ethiopic NT, no manuscript is known to antedate the 13th cent., and most date from the 16th and 17th cent. About the 14th cent. an extensive revision of the Ethiopic text was undertaken on the basis of the medieval Arabic text current at Alexandria. The characteristics of the text prior to this date can be ascertained only with difficulty, chiefly from quotations made by earlier Ethiopic ecclesiastical writers and from the relatively few Biblical manuscripts that antedate the process of Arabicising. The analyses which have been made of this earlier form of the text disclose a mixed type of text, predominantly Antiochian or Syrian in complexion, but with occasional agreements with certain early Greek witnesses (P^{46} and B) against all other witnesses. The little that is known of this version in the NT suggests that it deserves far more attention than it has received heretofore.

VIII THE NUBIAN VERSION

e The conversion of Nubia as a nation, located between Egypt and Ethiopia, probably took place about the middle of the 6th cent. Under the jurisdiction of the patriarchate of Alexandria, the Nubian Church increased and flourished until the 14th cent., when the growing power of the Arabs overwhelmed the country and the whole population embraced Islam.

Of the Scriptures, all that survives is a fragmentary manuscript, dating from the 10th or 11th cent., containing portions of an Old Nubian Lectionary for Christmastide. Pericopes from the Apostolos and the Gospel preserve short sections of Mt., Lk., Rom., Gal., Phil., and Heb. The textual character of this version has not yet been analysed.

IX THE SOGDIAN VERSION 589f

The Sogdian language, which belongs to the Indo-European family of languages, flourished in Central Asia from about A.D. 500 to 1000. In addition to extensive remains of Buddhist and Manichaean texts, certain Christian documents have also been discovered in this Iranian dialect. Besides several hagiographical treatises, portions of Mt., Lk., and Jn in the form of a lectionary, as well as small fragments of 1 C. and Gal., have been preserved. Preliminary studies indicate that the Gospel material was translated from the Syriac Peshitta.

X THE OLD ARABIC VERSIONS

Whether any part of the NT had been translated into Arabic prior to the rise of Islam is a mooted question. It is known that Christianity had penetrated the Arabian peninsula before the birth of Mohammed, but whether this would have demanded a translation of the Scriptures into the vernacular (the ecclesiastical language seems to have been Syriac), has been variously answered. Subsequently to the rise of Islam, renderings of the NT into Arabic were made from Greek, Syriac, Coptic (various dialects), Latin, and from combinations of these. As a consequence, the study of the Arabic versions is exceedingly complicated, and many problems remain to be solved. g

Among the earliest translations into Arabic is that prepared in A.D. 724 by John, bishop of Seville, with the intention of helping Christians and Moors. According to Padre Juan de Mariana (1537–1624), copies of this rendering were still to be seen in parts of Spain in his day. In 946 Isaak Velásquez of Córdoba translated the four Gospels into Arabic. The importance of this version is heightened by its preservation of many archaic readings from the Old Latin.

In Egypt during the 13th cent. two Alexandrian recensions were produced. Hibatallāh ibn al-ʽAssāl revised an Arabic text translated from Coptic, making use also of other Arabic translations from Greek and Syriac. This version was supplanted by the so-called Alexandrian Vulgate, a rendering which takes into account Coptic, Syriac, and Greek texts. The Alexandrian Vulgate enjoyed general acceptance in the Coptic Church, and is said to have formed the basis of all printed editions of the Arabic Gospels since 1591.

XI THE OLD SLAVIC VERSION

With exception of Jerome, more is known of the life and work of Cyril and Methodius, the apostles to the Slavs, than of any other translator of an ancient version of the Scriptures. Sons of a wealthy official in Salonika, they are credited with the creation of the Glagolitic alphabet, and perhaps also of the so-called Cyrillic alphabet. According to tradition, soon after the middle of the 9th cent. they began the translation of the Gospel (probably a Greek lectionary) into Old Bulgarian, which is also called Old Church Slavonic. On the basis of about a dozen manuscripts of the Gospels, dating from the 11th to the 14th cent., the Old Slavic text has recently been edited and its textual complexion analysed. The text belongs basically, as one would expect, to the later *Koine* or Byzantine family, but it also contains not a few earlier readings of a ' Western ' and Caesarean type. h

The rest of the NT has been studied chiefly from a grammatical and lexical point of view, and as yet no comprehensive analysis has been made of its textual affinities.

Bibliography—GENERAL: F. F. Bruce, *The Books and the Parchments* (1950) ; F. G. Kenyon, *Our Bible and the Ancient Manuscripts* (5th ed. 1958) ; B. M. Metzger, ' The Evidence of the Versions for the Text of the NT ', in M. M. Parvis and A. P. Wikgren (eds.), *NT Manuscript Studies* (1950), pp. 25–68 and 177–208; Metzger, *Annotated Bibliography of the Textual Criticism of the NT* (1955), pp. 27–65, and ' A Survey of Recent Research on the Ancient Versions of the NT ', NTS 2 (1955), 1–16; Ira M. Price, *The Ancestry of Our English Bible*, corrected ed. by W. A. Irwin and A. P. Wikgren (1951); H. Wheeler Robinson, *The Bible in its Ancient and English Versions*, enlarged ed. (1954); Arthur Vööbus, *Early Versions of the NT, Manuscript Studies* (*Papers of the Estonian Theological Society in Exile*, No. 6) (1954).

LATIN VERSIONS: Teófilo Ayuso Marazuela, *La Vetus Latina Hispana*; vol. i, *Prolegómenos, introducción general, estudio y análisis de las fuentes* (1953); Jan O. Smit, *De Vulgaat, Geschichte en harziening van de Latijnse Bijbelvertaling* (1948).

SYRIAC VERSIONS: Louis Leloir, ' Le Diatessaron de Tatien ', in *L'Orient syrien*, 1 (1956), 208–231 and 313–334; Arthur Vööbus, *Studies in the History of the Gospel Text in Syriac* (*Corpus Scriptorum Christianorum Orientalium*, vol. 128) (1951).

COPTIC VERSIONS: Paul E. Kahle, *Bala'izah, Coptic Texts from Deir el-Bala'izah in Upper Egypt* (London, 1954); Winifred Kammerer, *A Coptic Bibliography* (1950).

GOTHIC VERSION: G. W. S. Friedrichsen, *The Gothic Version of the Gospels, a Study of its Style and Textual History* (1926), *The Gothic Version of the Epistles, a Study of its Style and Textual History* (1939), *Gothic Studies* (1961); Fernand Mossé, ' Bibliographia Gotica, a Bibliography of Writings on the Gothic Language ', *Medieval Studies* 12 (1950), 237–324.

ARMENIAN VERSION: Stanislas Lyonnet, *Les origines de la version arménienne et le Diatessaron* (1950); Erroll F. Rhodes, *An Annotated List of Armenian New Testament Manuscripts* (1959).

GEORGIAN VERSION: D. M. Lang, ' Recent Work on the Georgian NT ', *Bulletin of the School of Oriental and African Studies*, 19 (1957), 82–93; Joseph Molitor, ' Georgien und seine Bibel ', *Trier Theologische Zeitschrift* 62 (1953), 91–98, ' Die georgische Bibelübersetzung, ihr Werdegang und ihre Bedeutung in heutiger Sicht ', *Oriens Christianus*, 4th Series, 1 (1953), 23–29.

ETHIOPIC VERSION: J. A. Montgomery, ' The Ethiopic Text of Acts of the Apostles ', HTR 27 (1934), 169–205; Arthur Vööbus, *Die Spuren eines älteren äthiopische Evangelientextes im Lichte der literarischen Monumente* (1951).

ARABIC VERSIONS: Georg Graf, *Geschichte der christlichen arabischen Literatur*, i (1944), 85–195; J. A. Thompson, *The Major Arabic Bibles*, reprinted from *The Bible Translator* 6 (1955).

OLD SLAVIC VERSION: B. M. Metzger, *Chapters in the History of New Testament Textual Criticism* (1963), ch. 3.

THE LITERATURE AND CANON OF THE NEW TESTAMENT

By J. N. SANDERS

I LITERATURE

590a The NT can hardly be considered as literature at all, except in the most general sense of the term. The aesthetic motive, and the desire to produce fine writing as something worth while in itself, are foreign to its authors, whose aims were urgent and practical. This is true even of such books as Heb. and 1 Pet., the style of which is rather more literary than the rest. Much of the NT is of course fine literature—even in the original Greek—but none of it was written simply as 'literature'. Paul writes with effectiveness and indeed eloquence, but the inspiration behind Rom. 8 or 1 C. 13 is religious, not aesthetic. The NT provides many illustrations of the truth of Longinus' dictum that 'Sublimity is the echo of greatness of soul'. But this was achieved, as was salvation by the Gentiles, by those who were not looking for it. The NT was brought into being to meet the needs of the Church by men who were apostles, evangelists, prophets, and teachers first, and writers by necessity. To understand their writings requires some insight into the needs they were designed to satisfy.

b The first Christians were probably many of them literate, though few can have had any literary training. This is the impression made by what is known of their social origins, and it is confirmed by their writings. The Christians by and for whom the NT was written were not men of leisure, and without leisure literary culture was impossible.

c The NT itself reveals little acquaintance with any literature other than the OT. The letters of Paul, and the speeches attributed to him in Ac., contain a quotation from Menander in 1 C. 15:33, one from 'Epimenides', followed by another from Aratus, in Ac. 17:28, and one again from 'Epimenides' in Tit. 1:12. His acquaintance with philosophy was superficial, and he can have understood its aims no better than the philosophers at Athens understood his. The author of Heb. probably had a profounder insight into philosophy, but the extent of his acquaintance with philosophical literature is a matter of dispute. Lk. 1:1–4 echoes the cadences, and repeats the conventional claims, of the Hellenistic historians, but there the resemblance ends, fortunately perhaps for our estimate of Luke's credibility. Their comparative indifference to pagan literature was on the whole an advantage to the writers of the NT. They gained thereby in freshness and freedom from stale conventions and artificial rhetoric.

d Their intimate knowledge of the OT on the other hand is too obvious to require proof. In striking contrast to their scanty allusions to pagan literature they continually quote and expound the OT. It, and the Jewish literature dependent upon it, nourished the piety of the early Gentile Christians no less than it had done that of Jesus himself. Many apparent examples of the influence of Greek philosophy in the NT are in fact indirect, mediated through the OT Wisdom Literature. It is not therefore surprising that the OT provided the first Christian writers with
literary models. What is surprising is that it did not 590
provide more.

The reason for this is not that the NT writers took e
their inspiration from the OT, and their literary models from contemporary Hellenistic literature, but rather that they were not conscious literary artists, obeying a convention, and imitating the correct models, like Hellenistic authors, but rather practical men falling into familiar forms when these happened to provide them with effective means of expression, in the case both of the oral and written literature.

Thus John the Baptist and Jesus resembled the f
OT prophets in the style of their teaching because it was similar to theirs in purpose. Jesus used parables, as the Rabbis did, and for the same reason. If they ever existed as documents, Q must have been something like Prov., and Proto-Luke something like Jer.—but not in either case because the author had set out to imitate them. There are of course examples also of the conscious following of OT models, particularly when they had proved popular in later literature. Rev. is a case in point. Mk 13, Jn 14–16 and Ac. 20:18–35 are examples of 'Farewell Discourses', popular in later Jewish literature, and again with OT precedents. With the recent growth of typological exegesis, examples have been found in the Gospels of imitation of OT models, but these are usually more obvious to their discoverers than to others. Lk. 1 and 2 clearly borrow a great deal from the OT, particularly in the Canticles, but it is hard to believe that Luke really meant them as an equivalent of Gen. (see M. D. Goulder and M. L. Sanderson, 'St Luke's Genesis', JTS 8 (1957), 12–30). Mt. has often been said to provide a Christian Pentateuch, or, according to A. M. Farrer (*St Matthew and St Mark* (1954)), a new Hexateuch. On the whole, the NT is remarkably independent of the OT so far as concerns literary form.

It is even more independent of Hellenistic literature. g
In this it is in striking contrast with the earliest Christian graphic art (admittedly of a later period) which follows slavishly the conventions of Hellenistic painting, utilising, for example, Orpheus charming the beasts as the pattern for Christ the Good Shepherd. In literature, the NT writers were Christians first, and writers by necessity; in painting, the artists were artists first, and Christians by accident.

In Greek literature the traditional forms for religious h
and philosophical subjects were the heroic hexameter poem (Hesiod, Parmenides, etc.) and the dialogue. Neither was by any means obsolete by NT times. The *Sibylline Oracles* are an example of Jewish adaptation of the hexameter poem. But the poetry of the NT derives entirely from that of the OT prophets and psalmists. The dialogue, devised by Plato and also used by Aristotle, had many imitators. The *Hermetica* use the dialogue form: so do, at a later date, the Christian philosopher Justin Martyr and the pagan satirist Lucian. From time to time Paul drops into dialogue (cf. Rom. 3:27–31; 1 C. 15:35), but this is simply due to his recollection of actual disputes, not

590h to compliance with a convention. In Jn there are passages of dialogue, like the conversation of Jesus and the Samaritan woman (Jn 4), where it is difficult to suppose that the author can rely on an eye-witness. The sceptic may suggest that here the author was drawing on his imagination, and following a familiar convention. But it is more likely that he was drawing on his own experience of conversations with unbelievers, if he is in fact writing such passages out of his own head.

591a In NT times the most familiar form for philosophical writing was the *diatribe*, virtually a sermon, designed not merely to instruct, but to convert, the listener or reader.[1] The *diatribe* was designedly informal, colloquial, vivid, and unsystematic. Jewish preachers in the synagogues of the *Diaspora* doubtless adopted the form, since their purpose was the same, and the Christians followed them. Jas reads very much like a *diatribe*, and Paul's Epistles, which no doubt often echo his sermons, have affinities with the form. Here is an example of real resemblance between the NT and Hellenistic literature, due to the close similarity in aim between the Apostle and the pagan philosopher.

b The same holds good in the case of the epistle, the literary form taken by the greater part of the NT. It has abundant parallels in pagan literature, but the letter is so natural a form to use that it is unnecessary to suppose that Paul wrote Epistles because Plato had. Nevertheless, the various forms taken by the letter in Classical literature all find parallels in the NT. But it is perhaps significant that the type least well represented is the essay in epistolary form. Most of the NT Epistles are genuine letters.

c The letters of Plato and Cicero range in form from purely personal communications to 'open letters', epistolary pamphlets in which the authors explain and defend their opinions and their conduct. So too do those in the NT. The Epistles of Epicurus had a purpose very like that of Paul's, for they were the means whereby he communicated his teaching and held together the 'societies of friends' who followed him (for a specimen cf. C. K. Barrett, *The New Testament Background* (1956), 73–75).

d In historiography and biography the parallels are less exact, since the difference of motive between Hellenistic historians and biographers and the evangelists was greater than that between pagan and Christian letter-writers. The Hellenistic writers were primarily rhetoricians and moralists.

e The unfortunate precedent set by Thucydides of putting speeches into the mouths of the principal personages at appropriate moments, in order to explain the motives for their actions, was followed with more enthusiasm than discretion by men who had neither his political insight nor his sense of the appropriate. Luke is often described as a Hellenistic historian, and the speeches in Ac. are interpreted accordingly as free compositions. There is undeniably some resemblance (more perhaps to Jewish works like 1 and 2 Mac. which were influenced by Hellenistic historiography than to the profane authors themselves), but Luke was probably more faithful to his sources than the average Hellenistic historian. The speeches in Ac. are probably only to a limited extent his own compositions. Their diversity of character suggests that he took over many of them from his sources. The variations in the three accounts of Paul's conversion, in his own narrative in Ac. 9, and in speeches attributed to Paul in Ac. 22 and 26 are most readily explained on this assumption.

f Justin Martyr describes the Gospels as 'memoirs' (ἀπομνημονεύματα), but he is writing for pagans, and uses the closest analogy he can find. Yet the Gospels are not really very much like Xenophon's *Memorabilia* or Plutarch's *Lives* (see below, §593*l*). Their closest parallel is perhaps Philostratus' *Life of Apollonius* (cf. C. K. Barrett, op. cit. 76–78), but that is later than the Gospels, and may have been influenced by them. 591f

g Thus, though the literature of the NT does present certain similarities with contemporary Jewish and Hellenistic literature, it is in the main something new, reflecting the fact that it came into being to serve the needs of a society which, for all the analogies it affords to contemporary religious societies, was also in itself essentially new. It reflects the richness, variety, and vigour of this new society, and of its faith, life, preaching, and worship.

h The Church showed a certain reluctance to commit its teaching to writing. The attitude expressed in 2 Jn 12 and 3 Jn 13 is not unique. Jesus himself had left no written records, and the tradition of his teaching was preserved orally for a considerable time. Papias shows a preference for oral tradition—'I did not think that I could get so much profit from the contents of books as from the utterances of a living and abiding voice' (Eus.HE iii, 39).

i This is partly due to the expectation of an early *Parousia*, but cannot be wholly accounted for by this, since it persisted after that expectation had begun to fade. It is partly due to the non-literary character of the early Christian society. It is also a characteristic of at least one section of the Jewish community, for all the Rabbinic teaching was preserved orally until a time later than the NT. There is a certain analogy also to Greek philosophy. Socrates wrote nothing, and the dialogues of Plato and Aristotle were popular works only; their advanced teaching was oral. The works of Aristotle which we now have were his own lecture-notes, unearthed and published long after his death. On the other hand, within Judaism the considerable apocalyptic literature and the writings of the Dead Sea community show that not all Jews were averse to written literature. These, however, may be special cases. The apocalypses were meant to have the authority of Scripture itself (which neither Rabbis nor apostles claimed). The Dead Sea community was different in character from the Christian, though not unlike what the latter might have become if it had remained wholly Jewish. Comparison of the two literatures reveals many parallels in thought and language, but not in literary form. For anything in Christian literature at all closely resembling the *Manual of Discipline* or the *Habakkuk Commentary* we have to wait until the post-apostolic period.

j So, however it is explained, we must recognise a certain reluctance on the part of Christians to begin a written literature. Some twenty years elapsed between the Crucifixion and the first book of the NT, most probably 1 Th. Nearly another twenty passed before the first extant Gospel was written, Mk (if indeed it is such); and this may have been the first written Gospel. What happened in the oral period was of immense importance, and has left clear traces in the written literature.

k Reluctance to write does not imply indifference to accurate preservation. It is not improbable that Jesus and his disciples were as careful as the Rabbis that their teaching should be remembered accurately. The teaching of Jesus is in a form well suited for memorising, and in the original Aramaic this would be even more obvious than it is in translation.

592a The first task of the Christian Church was to convert men to faith in Jesus Christ, the second to instruct converts in the Christian life. Thus the earliest literary forms were the sermon and the catechism. Both have left their traces in the NT.

b Thus in the sermons attributed to Peter in Ac. it is possible that we have outlines of the early apostolic preaching, reproduced on the whole faithfully, as the primitive character of their contents suggests. The Gospels themselves, in their narrative parts, consist largely of sermon-material, in the form of brief, self-contained *pericopai*, such as would have served for sermon-illustrations or texts for sermons. No actual primitive sermons have survived in full, though Jn

[1] In paganism the nearest thing to conversion was the decision to become a philosopher—cf. A. D. Nock, *Conversion* (1933).

592b may give a good idea of their character. Thus in Jn 6 the narrative forms the text of which the meaning is expounded in the discourse which follows. Though the discourse doubtless contains much material derived from the teaching of Jesus, it seems to owe its actual shape to a Christian preacher.

c Catechetical instruction was based on the teaching of Jesus. Jeremias has argued (*The Parables of Jesus* (1954)) that much of Jesus' teaching, particularly in the parables, originally had a polemical character, and underwent a certain amount of distortion in the course of adaptation to catechetical instruction. But the substantial faithfulness of the tradition is illustrated by such an example as Mk 2:18–20, in which 20 is a later comment, added to justify the practice of fasting, but nevertheless leaving the original saying unchanged. The large aggregations of teaching-material in the Gospels (e.g. Mt. 5–7) seem to derive from compilations made for catechetical purposes. The Epistles also contain passages of moral instruction which seem to follow a common pattern, and for the same reason.

d It is not easy to say how soon the preaching of the gospel and the instruction of converts necessitated a written literature. The four Gospels are the earliest documents we possess, but they may well incorporate earlier written compilations. At one time documentary analysis of the Gospels was carried to excess, and then, with the development of Form Criticism, there came a reaction towards emphasising the oral character of the tradition. Recently, however, the posthumously published work of W. L. Knox (*The Sources of the Synoptic Gospels*, i (1953), ii (1957)) has postulated the compilation of both narrative and teaching material in written form as an intermediate stage between the purely oral tradition and the Gospels.

e In principle, there was no absolute necessity for any written material, at least while the apostles were still alive, and written records may only have begun when the original 'eye-witnesses and ministers of the word' were no longer available. It is highly unlikely that any of the four Gospels antedates the deaths of the chief apostles. The Church may have been driven to putting its tradition into writing when it was in danger of being lost, as the Rabbis were. Nero's persecution and the Jewish War would provide the impetus.

f On the other hand actual eye-witnesses of Jesus' ministry were not the only preachers of the gospel: in the Gentile mission especially they must have been quite exceptional. But the fact of the existence of the Gospels shows that Gentile Christians were interested in Jesus' ministry, and from an early period preachers may have been equipped with tracts containing compilations of the deeds and sayings of Jesus, and of OT texts vindicating the Christian gospel. Whether this is capable of proof depends on detailed examination of the Gospels, a task beyond the scope of this article.

g The worship of the Church also made an important contribution to the literature of the NT. 1 C. 14:26 illustrates the richness and variety (as well as the danger of confusion) in early Christian worship. Confessions of faith, prayers, and hymns have all left their mark. But here written forms can hardly have developed in NT times. *Didache* ix and x provides a form of eucharistic thanksgiving, but assumes that it will not necessarily be followed, since it says that the prophets are to be allowed to offer thanksgiving as much as they wish. Yet before the stage of written forms, found in embryo here, there was a certain formalisation of liturgical language, and a production of fixed oral formulae, hymns, etc., which have left traces in the NT. There are words like *Amen*, *Maranatha*, and *Alleluia*, and passages like the hymn in Phil. 2:5ff.; the credal formula in 1 Tim. 3:16, and the 'faithful sayings' in the Pastoral Epistles. Rev. is rich in liturgical language. But none of these necessarily presuppose anything in writing earlier than the documents in which they are found. The earliest Christian liturgical document is 1 Pet., if F. L. Cross's suggestion is correct, that it represents a Paschal liturgy (*1 Peter, a Paschal Liturgy* (1954)). The need for a regular series of lections for Sunday worship has been suggested by Archbishop Carrington as a motive for the production of Mk (*The Primitive Christian Calendar* (1952)). If so, liturgical motives were indeed influential in moulding the literature of the NT. 592g

But of all the needs of the early Church which the NT was written to satisfy, that for the control, guidance, and edification of the newly founded congregations was the first to lead to the composition of works still extant. Of these, the genuine Pauline Epistles are the first. These are not treatises, written at leisure, but real letters, produced amid many distractions for urgent practical purposes. The collection which has been preserved is clearly incomplete, and also bears traces of editorial activity, most obvious in 2 C., which may be made up of substantial portions of two separate letters and a fragment of a third. The Pastoral Epistles (1 and 2 Tim. and Tit.) which as they stand are unlikely to be entirely Pauline, may nevertheless incorporate fragments of personal letters (see P. N. Harrison, *The Problem of the Pastorals* (1921)). h

All the genuine Epistles, even Phm., are letters to churches. The occasions for the letters are very diverse. 1 and 2 Th. were written to encourage a newly founded church to persevere in the faith and to clear up misunderstandings of Paul's teaching; 1 and 2 C. to answer questions that had been put to Paul, to regulate the discipline and worship of the Church, and to defend his teaching and authority; Gal. to define Paul's attitude to the Jewish Law and the authorities of the Jerusalem church, and again to vindicate his apostolic authority; Phil. to thank the church for a gift, to give news of their messenger, and to warn against subversive influences; Col. to combat erroneous teaching in a church which Paul had never actually visited; Phm. to restore the runaway slave Onesimus to his master, and to ensure that he would be treated in a Christian fashion. Rom., the letter most like a treatise, is still a genuine letter, and not just an essay in epistolary form, since it has a precise purpose, to prepare for Paul's projected visit to Rome by dispelling erroneous ideas about his teaching and explaining the purpose of his visit. i

Rom. 16 is a self-contained 'letter of recommendation' written for the deaconess Phoebe, interesting as an example of a kind of letter much used in the early Church, to assure a Christian traveller of a welcome in a strange church, and his hosts of his good faith. Paul alludes to such letters in 1 C. 16:3 and 2 C. 3:1. Cf. also 3 Jn 9f. j

Eph., if an authentic Pauline letter, is unique in as much as it appears to have no definite occasion or purpose in view; and it is this which, as much as anything else, makes it difficult to accept its authenticity. C. L. Mitton (*The Epistle to the Ephesians* (1951)) writes persuasively in support of the view that it is the work of a disciple, designed as a compendium of Paul's teaching to form a preface to the collected letters. For a contrary view, see the present writer's article in *Studies in Ephesians*, ed. F. L. Cross (1956). k

The authenticity of 1 and 2 Tim. and Tit. is also questioned, even more generally than that of Eph. As they stand, they seem to reflect a stage of development in Church organisation impossible in Paul's own lifetime. They thus raise the whole problem of pseudonymity in Holy Scripture. The later Church certainly tried to exclude pseudonymous works from the Canon, but the criteria which it employed laid too much stress on orthodoxy, and too little on the critical considerations which weigh with modern scholars, for its efforts to be entirely successful. This was not, however, because pseudonymity as such was regarded as improper, but because pseudonymous works were generally heretical. Ancient opinion on pseudepigraphy was very different from modern, for in ancient 593a

93a times there was no idea of copyright—nobody made money by literature, except copyists. The pseudonymous books in the NT represent sincere, if to our minds ill-advised, attempts to express what their real authors felt Paul or Peter would have wished to say in the circumstances in which the letters were written. The compiler of the Pastoral Epistles had the added motive of preserving some fragments of Paul's personal correspondence. They are in the Canon because the Church acknowledged the correctness of their teaching rather than the names under which they were published.

b The genuine Pauline Epistles all fall within a period of some twelve years, approximately A.D. 50–62, and are thus in all probability the earliest NT writings. Heb., which does not pretend to be Pauline, is probably a genuine letter, though it is not easy to reconstruct the circumstances in which it was sent. The fact that it has no address is not necessarily an argument against its epistolary character. The address may have been suppressed in furtherance of the attribution to Paul. It may have been written shortly after the fall of Jerusalem to Jewish Christians in Rome by a Hellenistic Jewish Christian of Alexandrian origin.

c The other Epistles are a very miscellaneous collection. Jas and Jude are letters only in name : they have no precise address, and are really tracts. They are probably not pseudonymous, though it is questionable if they are really works of the ' brethren of the Lord '.

d 1 Pet., if it is a genuine work of the Apostle, must belong to the early sixties, and be a circular letter to the churches of Asia Minor. If it is not Peter's, its date and provenance remain a mystery. 2 Pet. is a late pseudepigraph, based on Jude, and, like it, a tract denouncing heresy.

e Of the three Epistles of John, 1 Jn is a letter only in name, and in fact a meditation on a number of themes found also in the Fourth Gospel. 2 and 3 Jn are genuine letters, 2 to a church, quaintly personified as ' the elect lady ', and 3 to an individual, Gaius, presumably a person of some influence in the same church. They are anonymous, though in 2 and 3 Jn the author speaks of himself as ' the Elder '. He is clearly the author of 1 Jn ; whether or not he had any part in the production of the Gospel and Rev. is a question beyond the scope of this article.

f Rev., whether it is the work of John, as it claims to be, or a pseudepigraph, like the Jewish apocalypses on which it is modelled, included seven letters of exhortation and rebuke to the churches of Asia. Its purpose is to encourage its readers to face persecution, and, like most of the post-Pauline letters and tracts, to warn against moral laxity and doctrinal error.

g These works, with the exception of 2 Pet., all fall within the period A.D. ±65 to ±100. This is also the period of the Four Gospels and Acts. It was a time of consolidation, when the Church, now firmly rooted in Syria, Asia Minor, Macedonia, Achaea, Rome, and almost certainly also in Alexandria, finally separated from Judaism, and warned by the Neronian persecution of the hostility of the Empire, turned to the development of its inner life, its liturgy, and its organisation. The Gospels reflect this situation in various ways. Unlike much of the material which they incorporate, they were designed not so much as missionary literature as for the use and edification of the Church.

h This is more obviously the case with Mt. and Mk than with Lk., its sequel Ac., and Jn. Mk is the Roman Gospel, and, if it is the earliest of the four, it must be dated not long after the Neronian persecution. Mt. is of Syrian origin, and, while keeping the Marcan framework, incorporates a large amount of other, mainly catechetical, material, generally abbreviating Mk in the process. Both, however, may well have had a similar purpose, use in the worship of the Church, and have been so used from the time of their compilation. 593h

i Lk., Ac., and Jn reflect the new situation in a different way. They can be understood as having been written not exclusively for Christian readers, but also for pagans, and so as anticipating to some extent the apologetic literature of the 2nd cent., with which they have certain affinities. Lk. and Ac. resemble the works of those Apologists who tried to reassure the Roman authorities that Christianity was not a danger to the security of the Empire, Jn those which presented the Christian faith in such a way as to appeal to those who had hitherto looked for salvation in philosophy or the Mysteries. This is by no means their sole purpose, but it is a characteristic which must not be ignored.

j Lk. and Ac. may in fact have originated through Luke's desire to explain to a potentially sympathetic Roman, ' Theophilus ' (probably a pseudonym), the character of the Christian ' Way ' and Paul's part in it.

k Jn, published in Ephesus at the end of the 1st cent., embodies a highly individual and probably primitive tradition, Judaean in origin, derived ostensibly from the Beloved Disciple, and substantially, if not completely, independent of the other three. Its material seems to have been used in sermons, and so, though in its final form it may well have been designed for pagan as well as Christian readers, it is also very much a ' Church ' book.

l In the ' gospel ' the Church produced its most characteristic literary form, and our Four Gospels, different as they are, have, as Gospels, a fundamental similarity that quite outweighs their differences. We must not think of the Synoptic Gospels as ' historical ', and Jn as ' theological '. All four are both. The ' gospel ', basically a narrative of events, testifies to the fact that Christianity is a historical religion, based upon events that actually happened. But these events must be understood as the saving acts of God, and for this a mere record of events, however accurate, would be inadequate. So the Gospels do not set out merely to impart information, or even, in the manner of Plutarch, to present men with an edifying example, but to create and foster faith in Jesus as Christ and Lord. This does not mean that they are indifferent to truth, mere hagiographical romances. But it does mean that what they have to say can only be seen to be the truth by those who are willing to share their faith. Like the rest of the NT, they confront us with a person and a challenge.

II CANON

594a By the end of the period during which the twenty-seven books which eventually made up the NT were compiled, the literature of the Church included, in addition to these, a number of other works, *I Clement*, the Epistle attributed to Barnabas, the works of Hermas, the *Didache* or *Teaching of the Twelve Apostles*, and the Epistles of Ignatius and Polycarp. It was soon to have (if indeed it did not already possess, at least in part) a varied assortment of other books, Gospels, Epistles, Acts, and Apocalypses, many of them bearing the names of apostolic authors, and some written in the interests of various heresies. At first all these books circulated more or less widely and enjoyed varying degrees of popularity, those eventually accepted into the Canon as well as those eventually denied admittance to it. None had at first an authority equal to that of the OT, but it was only a matter of time before the Church began to select from the mass of writings which it possessed those to which it would attach a special authority.

b The idea of a ' Canon ' or list of authoritative books was inherited by the Church from Judaism, though the Canon of the OT itself was by no means fixed in the 1st cent. of our era. The word ' Canon ', κανών, *regula* in Latin, meant a ' level ' or ' ruler ', as used by

594b a carpenter or a scribe. From this literal sense various metaphorical ones were derived, the two most relevant to our purpose being (1) a *rule* of conduct, belief, etc., and (2) a *list* or *catalogue*. It is in the first sense that the word appears in Christian usage in the 2nd cent., e.g. in Irenaeus ; it is applied to the tradition of the Church, the 'rule of truth' or 'of faith', ὁ κανὼν τῆς ἀληθείας, τῆς πίστεως, which was of course *unwritten*. As applied to the written Scripture, the word is first used in the second half of the 4th cent. by Athanasius, and then is derived from the second sense already mentioned, that of a *list*. But this sense was inevitably coloured by the other usage already long familiar in the Church ; though the word itself comes into use at a relatively late period, the *idea* of an authoritative 'list' or canon of Scripture is much older.

c The formation of the Canon was a process of selection, whereby the books to be read publicly in the Church were distinguished both from those which were orthodox but not of sufficient authority to merit public reading, as for example *Hermas*, and from those which were to be rejected absolutely, as spurious and heretical. The ostensible criterion was that of authorship by an apostle or the immediate disciple of an apostle, whose authority it was deemed to possess : the effective criterion was that of conformity to orthodox teaching. For, since the teaching of an apostle must be by definition orthodox, and the Church of the 2nd cent. had no other means of distinguishing genuine from pseudonymous apostolic works, orthodoxy tended to become synonymous with apostolicity.

d Thus the pseudonymous *Gospel of Peter* was rightly excluded, but the no less pseudonymous 2 Pet. was included. Heb., though it did not claim to be by Paul, was eventually deemed to be his, and so admitted, in spite of scruples in certain quarters. And the doubts felt about the orthodoxy of Rev. were not outweighed, in the minds of those who wished to exclude it, by the early testimony to its apostolic authorship. But on the whole (if it does not sound patronising to say so) the Church performed the task of selection with remarkable discrimination. No apostolic work was excluded, and the only book which really got in by mistake is 2 Pet. A stricter definition of apostolicity might have excluded Heb., but that would have been a real loss.

e A variety of reasons led to the formation of the Canon.

A most powerful consideration was the great authority attached to 'words of the Lord'. These were of decisive authority for Paul, as is shown by 1 C. 7:10, 9:14, 11:23ff. ; 1 Th. 4:15. Jesus himself had claimed for his own words an authority even greater than that of the OT—'You have heard that it was said to the men of old . . . but I say to you' (Mt. 5:21f., cf. 27f., 31f., 33f., 38f., 43f.)—so that it is not surprising if his Church gave them an authority at least equal to that of the OT. This applied from the first not only to the words preserved in the oral tradition of Jesus' teaching, but also to those of Christian prophets speaking in his name. Of the passages referred to above from Paul's Epistles, some no doubt allude to such prophetic 'words of the Lord'. This being so, it was by a natural development that when books began to circulate which either recorded the tradition of the Lord's own teaching or were written by apostles, men believed to hold the Lord's commission, they acquired an authority as Scripture alongside the OT. Their quotation implies that they possess this authority.

f Moreover for the majority of Christians in the 2nd cent. the OT must have been very hard to understand. It could often be given an edifying interpretation only by the most ingenious allegorisation, which would contrast with the more immediately intelligible message of the Gospels and Epistles. Highly educated persons like Justin Martyr might enjoy the intellectual challenge of the OT, but the very real difficulty which ordinary Christians felt in appreciating it is shown by the popular appeal of Marcion, who boldly threw it overboard and substituted a new Scripture. 594

Christians of the 2nd cent. also felt acutely the contrast between the age of the apostles and their own day. They felt themselves called upon to conserve the truth then revealed, and though men like Papias might express a preference for the oral tradition, the written word inevitably increased in authority. g

The most powerful motive, however, which was in effect decisive, was the desire to preserve the Church from heresy. The Gnostics in particular claimed to derive their teachings from secret traditions entrusted by the Apostles to their favourite disciples, which were accordingly of superior authority to the public tradition to which the Catholics appealed. They also circulated pseudonymous Gospels and Acts in support of their doctrine. In reaction to these, Catholic writers like Irenaeus emphasised not only the apostolic tradition but also the apostolic writings which had been used in the Church from the earliest times. h

But important as were the Gnostics in this, the most influential figure was the great heresiarch Marcion. He denied that the God of the OT was the Father of Jesus Christ, and repudiated the OT entirely. In its place he put his *Euangelion* and *Apostolikon*, i.e. expurgated versions of Lk. and of ten Pauline Epistles, Gal., 1 and 2 C., Rom., 1 and 2 Th., *Laodiceans* (Eph.), Col., Phil., and Phm. The precise effect of Marcion's bold innovation has been the subject of much debate. According to Harnack and, more recently, J. Knox (*Marcion and the New Testament* (1942)), Marcion was responsible for the creation of the Catholic Canon of the NT. This is, however, probably an exaggeration. The other motives that have been noticed might well have produced eventually a NT Canon in the Church, but it is undeniable that Marcion provided a powerful stimulus in accelerating the process. For a careful study of this question see E. C. Blackman, *Marcion and his Influence* (1948), 23–41. i

Montanism was also influential. The movement began as a protest against the tendency of the Church in the 2nd cent. to regard the decisive epoch of revelation as lying in the past, and so to disallow the possibility of fresh truth being revealed through prophecy. This the Montanists claimed was being done by their prophets, to whose utterances they accorded an authority higher than that of the apostles. So here also the Church was compelled to face a challenge and to define more precisely the limits of revealed truth. j

Though the factors making for the formation of the Canon of the NT are clear enough, the actual stages of its accomplishment are, in the earliest period, very obscure. The collection of the four Gospels and of the Pauline Epistles, each into a single book (which the use of the *codex* facilitated), was no doubt an important stage in the process. 595a

When the Gospels were first collected into one is unknown. They were originally the Gospels of distinct churches, and local patriotism and conservatism may well have tended to limit their public use to the areas in which they originated. It is quite possible that the fourfold Gospel was a Catholic counterblast to Marcion's single Gospel. The first traces of acquaintance with the Gospels are of Mt. and Lk. in the *Didache*, of Mk in *Hermas*, and of Jn in Ignatius. But actual references to them as written works are not so early. Souter (*Text and Canon of the New Testament* (1954), 147) claims that the earliest of these are a passage from *Didache* viii 2 in which the Lord's Prayer is introduced by the words 'as the Lord commanded in his gospel, pray thus', and one from Ignatius (*Philad.* viii 2) which he punctuates ἤκουσά τινων λεγόντων ὅτι, "ἐὰν μὴ ἐν τοῖς ἀρχαίοις εὕρω, ἐν τῷ εὐαγγελίῳ, οὐ πιστεύω", so as to mean, 'I heard some saying, "If I do not find it in the archives b

595b (i.e. in the Gospel), I do not believe it ".' Though the *Didache* passage is not quite explicit, that from Ignatius, as Souter takes it, is unequivocal. But if the comma is omitted after εὐαγγελίῳ, it yields a different, and perhaps more natural, sense. ' If I do not find it in the archives (i.e. in the OT), I do not believe it in the gospel ', which is not necessarily a *written* one.

c Papias, contemporary with Marcion, testifies both to the existence of written Gospels, and to the preference for oral tradition. According to R. G. Heard (' Papias' Quotations from the NT ', NTS I 2 (1954), 130–134) Papias ' cannot be shown conclusively—so far—to have used any of our Synoptic Gospels ', though there is ' a strong probability ' that he used Jn.

d There is an indubitable reference to written Gospels, later than Marcion, in Justin Martyr (Ap. i, 66, 3), ' The Apostles in their Memoirs, which are called Gospels, handed down that it was commanded them thus ' (ἐν τοῖς . . . ἀπομνημονεύμασιν, ἃ καλεῖται εὐαγγέλια). Since in a later passage (67, 3) he speaks of them being read with the writings of the (OT) prophets and commented on in the homily during Sunday worship, it is clear that he regarded them as Scripture. Though his quotations are inexact and anonymous, it is nevertheless probable that he knew our four Gospels, which his pupil Tatian certainly did. (See R. G. Heard, ' The ἀπομνημονεύματα in Papias, Justin, and Irenaeus ', NTS I 2 (1954), 122–129).

e About A.D. 160 the Gnostic Heracleon wrote a commentary on Jn, which implies that he gave it the status of Scripture. Tatian, about A.D. 170, quotes Jn twice as Scripture (*Or. ad Gr.* xiii 1 and xix 4), as does Theophilus of Antioch also some ten years later. Tatian's *Diatessaron*, compiled from the four Gospels, is the first clear testimony to their supremacy in the estimation of the Church, while at the same time the combination of the four into a single narrative reflects the older preference for a single Gospel. By the time of Irenaeus, however, the fact that there are four Gospels, no more and no less, is quite taken for granted (see Souter, op. cit. 156ff.).

f The rise of the Pauline Epistles to a status equal to that of the OT is better documented than that of the Gospels in its earlier stages, since with Paul there is no question of a continuing oral tradition to complicate matters. Clement of Rome and Ignatius both seem to have known the Epistles as a collection, and evidence of a knowledge of all of them, with the understandable exception of Phm., but including both Heb. and the Pastorals, can be found in one or other of the Apostolic Fathers. (For details see *The New Testament in the Apostolic Fathers*, 1905.) ' Barnabas ' and Polycarp appear to regard the Epistles as Scripture, and 2 Pet. 3:16 certainly does. Marcion must have known the Epistles as a collection before he made his own edition of them. Justin knew the Epistles, but they do not appear to have possessed for him an authority as high as that of the Gospels. Athenagoras, before A.D. 180, and Theophilus of Antioch, however, quote Paul as an authority in doctrine. Irenaeus clearly accepts the Epistles as Scripture, with an authority comparable to that of the OT, but less than that of the Gospels,

g Before the time of Irenaeus little is known of the other NT books. Rev. has left the most traces of use—it was known to Clement of Rome, ' Barnabas ', Papias, and Theophilus, and valued highly by Justin and Irenaeus as the work of the apostle John. Next come the apostolic works 1 Pet. and 1 Jn. Polycarp knew both. Papias, according to Eusebius, quoted 1 Jn. Irenaeus knew 1 Pet. and 1 and 2 Jn. Ac., though known to Clement, was in an anomalous position as neither a Gospel nor the work of an apostle. It may, however, have come into favour as giving a picture of Paul that contradicted Marcion's, showing him as a collaborator with the other apostles instead of their opponent. For Irenaeus, it is on the fringe of

the Canon. Heb., on the other hand, though 595g
known to several of the Apostolic Fathers, was not accepted by Irenaeus ; but he quoted *Hermas* as Scripture.

By the end of the 2nd cent. much more information h
is available. Irenaeus' Canon consisted of the Four Gospels, the thirteen Epistles of Paul, 1 Pet., 1 and 2 Jn, Rev., *Hermas*, and Ac. Further evidence comes from the *Muratorian Canon*, Tertullian, and Clement of Alexandria.

The *Muratorian Canon*, an anonymous fragment, i
85 lines long, with a corrupt text and in barbarous Latin, is nevertheless of great interest. It appears to be the translation of an official Greek document emanating from Rome in the late 2nd cent., listing the books which are to be accepted as apostolic and to be read in Church. (Text and notes in Souter, op. cit. 191ff. ; translation in Bettenson, *Documents of the Christian Church* (1943), 40f.) Its beginning is lost, but its reference to Lk. and Jn as the third and fourth gospels implies acceptance of Mt. and Mk. It accepts Ac., the thirteen Epistles of Paul, 1 and 2 Jn, Jude, Rev., and the *Apocalypse of Peter*, ' which some do not wish to have read in Church '. *Hermas* is rejected with remarkable emphasis. An emendation has been suggested to make a mention of the Epistles instead of the *Apocalypse* of Peter, but this is unlikely.

Tertullian, a later contemporary of Irenaeus, j
furnishes evidence for N. Africa. Besides the four Gospels, thirteen Epistles of Paul, Ac., Rev., 1 Jn, 1 Pet., and Jude, which he accepts, he knows Heb., but assigns it to Barnabas, and does not regard it as part of the NT. *Hermas* he accepted until he became a Montanist.

Clement of Alexandria, another contemporary, has k
a larger and less clearly defined Canon than the Western authorities considered hitherto. Thus in addition to the four Gospels he accepts as lesser authorities the Gospels *According to the Hebrews* and *According to the Egyptians*. He accepts Heb. as Pauline in addition to the thirteen Epistles, 1 Pet., 1 and 2 Jn, Jude, ' Barnabas ', Ac., Rev. ; and also the *Apocalypse of Peter*, *I Clement*, *Didache*, and *Hermas* : he may also have known Jas, 3 Jn, and 2 Pet.

In the following century Origen (*d*.254), the l
greatest Biblical scholar of the early Church, distinguished ' acknowledged ' from ' disputed ' books. According to Eusebius (HE vi, 25) the ' acknowledged ' were the four Gospels, thirteen Pauline Epistles, 1 Pet., 1 Jn, Rev., the ' disputed ' 2 Pet., 2 and 3 Jn, and Heb. His observations on the authorship of Heb. (Eusebius, HE vi 25, quoted in Gwatkin, *Selections from Early Christian Writers* (1920), 142ff.) are a model of critical acumen. Elsewhere Origen himself shows that he regarded Ac. as ' acknowledged ', and Jas and Jude as ' disputed '. He was stricter than Clement of Alexandria in not allowing *Hermas*, ' Barnabas ', or the *Didache* to rank as Scripture. After Origen, Rev. was seriously challenged for a time in the Greek Church ; and when Eusebius of Caesarea in the 4th cent. came to draw up lists of ' acknowledged ' and ' disputed ' books, he was inclined to include it in the latter.

Eusebius' ' acknowledged ' books are (HE iii 25) m
the four Gospels, Ac., Paul's Epistles, 1 Jn, 1 Pet., and (somewhat hesitantly) Rev. Eusebius himself regarded Heb. as Pauline, but knew Rome did not (HE iii 3). ' Disputed, but known to the majority ' are Jas, Jude, 2 Pet., and 2 and 3 Jn. Amongst the books he rejects outright are *Hermas*, the *Apocalypse of Peter*, ' Barnabas ', the ' so-called *Teachings of the Apostles* ', and the *Gospel according to the Hebrews* : he would like to include Rev. among these, but tradition was too strong for him. Thus his Canon is virtually ours, for the Greek Church did not maintain his careful distinction of ' acknowledged ' and ' disputed but known to the majority '—

595m the latter soon became 'acknowledged'. The influence of the West overcame his scruples about Rev. And so Athanasius' *Festal Letter* of 367 (text and translation in Souter, op. cit. 196–200) gives our NT in the familiar order, except that the 'Catholic' Epistles follow Ac. Nevertheless certain books lingered on the fringe of the Eastern Canon as is shown by some early MSS: thus ℵ includes 'Barnabas' and *Hermas*, A *I* and *II Clement*, at the end of the NT.

n Evolution was slower in the West and in the Syriac-speaking Church. In the West, Heb., though often regarded as canonical, was generally quoted anonymously; Marius Victorinus (*c*.360) is the first to quote it as Paul's. Augustine in his earlier writings ascribed it to Paul, but in his latest quotes it anonymously. Its final acceptance was due to Jerome, as was that of Jas, 2 Pet., 2 and 3 Jn, and Jude, doubtless under Greek influence.

o In the Syriac-speaking Churches Tatian's *Diatessaron* was for long preferred to the four Gospels, though they were in fact translated about A.D. 200. The 'separated' Gospels did not come into general use until the turn of the 5th cent., in the Syriac *Peshitta* version. This included also the fourteen Epistles of Paul, Ac., 1 Pet., 1 Jn, and Jas. This remained the Nestorian Canon, but in the 6th cent. the Syrian Monophysites, under Egyptian influence, finally adopted the familiar Canon of twenty-seven books. 595

Thus the formation of the Canon was accomplished almost, we may say, unconsciously; Synods and Councils played a very minor role, merely ratifying what the common mind of the Church of their time had already accepted. p

Bibliography—M. Dibelius, *A Fresh Approach to the NT and Early Christian Literature* (1937); E. Fascher, *Vom Verstehen des NTs* (1930); A. Harnack, *Die Entstehung des NTs* (1914), Eng. trans., *The Origin of the NT* (1925); E. C. Hoskyns and F. N. Davey, *The Riddle of the NT* (1931); C. L. Mitton, *The Formation of the Pauline Corpus* (1955); A. Souter, *The Text and Canon of the NT* (1913, [2]1954); B. F. Westcott, *A General Survey of the History of the Canon of the NT* (1855, [7]1896); Th. Zahn, *Geschichte des ntlichen Kanons* (1888–92), *Grundriss der Geschichte des ntlichen Kanons* ([2]1904).

FORM CRITICISM OF THE NEW TESTAMENT

By E. DINKLER

596a **Definition of the Term**—Form Criticism of the NT has two aims—to explain the literary character of the Gospels and their place in the history of literature, and to analyse the material used by the evangelists and trace it back to the oral tradition and the sociological roots conditioning its forms. While the second concerns Form Criticism proper, the first is sometimes included in, and sometimes defined separately as, *Gattungsgeschichte* (history of types of literature). This article deals with both aspects.

Assumptions: (*a*) The literary-critical research into the Synoptic Gospels, which is concerned with their historical and literary interrelation, must be supplemented. Whether it be the classical two-sources theory, or B. H. Streeter's four-Gospel theory, or any other hypothesis—all, in general, open to question—about the interdependence of the Gospels (see §§653–8), the NT student has to go further in his investigation and to ask about the growth of an oral tradition behind the written documents. (*b*) The Gospels as a whole consist of many smaller units or pericopes, which have their own development and roots in the life of earliest Christianity, but use a common literary form to be found in Judaism or Hellenism. Because Form Criticism searches for the origin and history of the smaller units it finds its main subject-matter in the gospel tradition, where the evangelists collected given material, working it over as redactors. Later on it was applied to Ac., the Epistles and even the Book of Rev., since students recognised that here too traditional material is taken up as confessions, hymns, etc.

b **History of Form Criticism**—The term *Formgeschichte* was used first by F. Overbeck in 1882 and expressly taken up by M. Dibelius in 1919. As *Gattungsgeschichte* it was developed by H. Gunkel and H. Gressmann with reference to the OT. It was primarily from this quarter that a group of German NT scholars was influenced, and developed after World War I—independent of each other—the method of Form Criticism in order to overcome the deadlock of the *Religionsgeschichtliche* school. The latter had questioned the historicity of the Gospels as 'biographical' accounts and stressed the point that even the earliest evangelist, Mark, was dependent on a theological tradition to which he added a Christology of his own. Form Criticism tried, therefore, to disentangle the different layers of tradition, and to rediscover the historical growth of the 'forms'. The first step was done by K. L. Schmidt (1919), when he analysed the different pericopes by separating the traditional material as such from the additional framework. Schmidt showed clearly that all details referring to time and place were added later mostly by the evangelist himself, who grouped his material together and then gave it a historical situation or context. M. Dibelius, in his classical book on Form Criticism, was primarily interested in the reconstruction of the conditions under which the forms of the gospel material were created. His method tried to exclude as far as possible all subjective judgment and to stress the 'anti-individualistic and sociological' point of view. On the one hand, he concentrated on the earliest oral tradition, leaving aside the question of historical authenticity; on the other, he searched for the influences determining the forms. This leads to the question of the *Sitz im Leben*, which Dibelius recognises in the preaching of earliest Christianity. Preaching means missionary as well as edifying proclamation, catechetical as well as apologetical teaching. A more radical approach is made by R. Bultmann, who handles Form Criticism in combination with literary criticism and with *Sachkritik* (criticism of contents), and thus becomes the most influential leader of this approach. He consciously includes the question of historical authenticity and handles Form Criticism as only one—though decisive—tool for the reconstruction of the Synoptic tradition. He emphasises that the historical-philological method can be only one method among others, yet that it has various points of view and approaches which should be used together. 596b

In recent years three tendencies can be noticed: (1) Form Criticism was transformed more into a history of the evangelist or redactor, investigating his special motifs and theological perspective, so that the individual composer of the Gospel as a whole became better known. (2) Form Criticism was used for non-synoptic books of the NT in order to recognise, for instance, Pauline liturgical material, hymns, legal quotations or in 1 Pet. fragments of catechetical instruction. (3) W. L. Knox tried to correct the assumption of Form Criticism, that the earliest strata belong to an oral tradition, seeking to establish the existence of so-called 'tracts', smaller collections about sayings and doings of Jesus. He discovers a tract of conflict-stories, of a Twelve-source (previously assumed by Eduard Meyer, 1921), of miracles and of parables, etc., suggesting their literary fixation around the year A.D. 40, probably in the churches of Jerusalem and Antioch. The tendency is to postulate a higher historical reliability for the Synoptic accounts. Though critical with regard to Form Criticism, Knox follows its method of separating tradition and redaction. His own method may be described as a variation of Form Criticism.

Form Criticism of the Gospels—A comparison, c carried out by K. L. Schmidt, of the Synoptic Gospels with the general history of literature demonstrated that the Gospels are a literary phenomenon *sui generis*. They are neither biographical accounts nor strict historiography, because they write with the purpose 'that you may believe that Jesus is the Christ, the Son of God, and that believing, you may have life in His name' (Jn 20:31). The impulse of the evangelists in writing, whether Synoptics or Jn, was not concerned with factual knowledge but with Christological faith. Therefore we do not have descriptions of Jesus' character, his messianic development, his outward appearance or his social conditions—except perhaps in Lk. The leading standpoint is the foundation of faith. This interest determines the choice, the form of the material and its chronological setting. The smaller entities collected and connected have

596c literary parallels only in folklore—not literature as a piece of art—and should be understood according to the laws of such 'minor literature'.

d **(a) The Reconstruction of Forms**—Because all smaller units were first handed down orally, i.e. according to the memory of witnesses and hearers of the *kerygma*, the tradition concentrated upon characteristic points, either on some typical feature or short sayings, never on extensive 'sermons', but on 'logia' and 'parables'. No report really goes beyond the occurrences of a single day ; there is nowhere a complicated *symposion*, but only two or three interlocutors participating in discussion, or Jesus with a group of anonymous questioners or opponents. Even the opponents are not differentiated or individualised : they are 'Pharisees and Scribes' in general. Taking up critically the development, i.e. starting out with Mk, proceeding to Mt. and the more profanely educated writer Lk., and ending with the literary style of the apocryphal Gospels, one discovers tendencies in the developing tradition and even literary laws, which permit and encourage conclusions with regard to the earliest—presumably oral—strata of this process : e.g. Mk 9:17 tells of a father, who brought Jesus to his son 'for he has a dumb spirit'. Mt. 17:15 goes more into detail : 'for he is an epileptic and suffers terribly ; often he falls into the fire and often into the water'. Lk. reports further symptoms of the illness, adding that he was the father's only child (9:38f.). Or, according to Mk 14:47, one of the followers of Jesus 'drew his sword and struck the slave of the high priest and cut off his ear.' Lk. (22:50) knows that it is the right ear, and Jn (18:10) even gives us the names, Peter and the slave's name Malchus. There are more features of this kind which demonstrate that the earliest tradition reported the essentials only, names, places and times being added later as a frame mostly by the evangelist. The Passion and Easter stories represent an exception, where the literary laws are somehow broken down by the new content and a longer period in chronological order had to be reported. Here perhaps even eye-witnesses may be assumed, such as Peter or the anonymous young man with a linen cloth (Mk 14:51), or, for other parts, Simon of Cyrene (Mk 15:21). In the Passion stories narrative material is given and early compositions used by Mk, and all are further developed in Mt. and Lk. Yet even the Passion narrative taken up and worked over by Mk cannot be regarded in its details as an historical account although this part of the Gospel has undergone less changes than the shorter units. How did the Passion narrative come to be fixed so early ? Obviously because the salvation event *κατ' ἐξοχήν* here is given as it was needed for preaching purposes from the very beginning of the Christian Church. It opened the eyes and ears of hearer or reader to the eschatological action of God. And further, the Christian Church was forced by its Jewish environment to interpret the Crucifixion in the light of Jesus' Resurrection, and, last not least, to show that everything occurred *κατὰ τὰς γραφάς*. Here again Form Criticism demonstrates that even the Passion narratives have their *Sitz im Leben* and a Christological purpose.

Turning back to the form as such, we follow Bultmann's categories and distinguish two main groups of material : sayings and narratives.

597a **(b) Sayings of Jesus**—At first we have the *Apophthegmata* (Dibelius calls them *Paradigmata*), characterised by a short scene explaining the situation, yet actually merely framing a single saying of Jesus. The inner connection of scene and saying is important. The saying can be a response to the question of a disciple or of a Scribe (see, e.g., Mk 2:1–12, 2:23–8, 3:1–6, etc.) or sometimes to a sincerely searching individual (e.g. Mk 10:17–22, 12:28–34 ; Mt. 11:2–9). Another type is the biographical *apophthegmata*. They too point always to a significant saying (e.g. Mk 6:1–6, 10:13–16, etc.). The form as such has analogies in Judaism and in Hellenism, but at least in Mk the Jewish form proves to be more akin. The formulation of this tradi- 597
tion, therefore, can be assumed in Palestine and seems to be earlier than the *apophthegmata* in Lk., where a Hellenistic pattern is apparent (e.g. Lk. 17:20f.). The distinction between 'earlier' and 'later' must only be understood with regard to literary fixation, not as pointing *per se* to a higher degree of authenticity. Though there are times when historical reliability can be answered with a high degree of probability, e.g. when Mk 2:18f., 2:23–6 and 7:1–8 tell about the disciples—not about Jesus—that they transgressed the Sabbath law and that Jesus had to defend their doing so, at the same time such compositions may have had their origin in the early Church, reflecting a polemic, refuted by an authentic or sometimes invented word of Jesus.

Furthermore, we have the 'logia' of Jesus which lack the setting of any particular situation. One group has analogies in the Jewish Wisdom literature. It sometimes contains a general truth (e.g. Mt. 6:34*b*, 12:34*b*, 24:28), or a religious truth (e.g. Mt. 6:19–34), without any eschatological teaching ; nor is it related to the specific teaching of Jesus. The question of authenticity cannot be easily decided. A second group of prophetic and apocalyptic 'logia' is more closely related to Jesus' eschatological proclamation (see especially the Beatitudes, Mt. 5:3–9, but also Lk. 12:8–9 and perhaps Mk 13:3). But here again the decision about authenticity is difficult, e.g., when Mk 13:3–27, a whole apocalyptic sermon of Jesus, is composed of often unrelated sayings. Apparently Jewish apocalyptic fragments (13:7f., 12, 14–20, 24–7) are combined with Jesus' 'logia'.

Further there are the 'logia' concerning the law, some of which go back to Jesus (e.g. the antitheses, Mt. 5:21f., 27f., 33–7), while others have their origin in experiences or also in the apologetics of the earliest congregations (e.g. Mt. 12:5f. or 18:15–22). Here again we do not have any firm criteria as to their authenticity.

Finally with the 'parables' we are on safer ground. Their form shows they were not meant as allegories and that where allegorical traces or interpretations are found, they present *a posteriori* additions. In the parables we have perhaps the clearest criteria for tracing them back to the teaching of Jesus himself. The assumption of their authenticity is supported by the fact that their meaning does not point to general religious-ethical truth—as A. Jülicher stressed—but is bound up with the eschatological teaching of Jesus—so C. H. Dodd and J. Jeremias. The explanation in Mk 4:10–12 that parables should protect the secret of the kingdom of God against outsiders is obviously the dogmatic theory of the evangelist.

(c) Narratives—In the foreground are the 'miracle b
stories' (Dibelius's *Novellen*). Their form in Jewish and Hellenistic literature is well known, especially that of healing miracles. First the situation of the sick is given, perhaps also the futile efforts of physicians or magicians are emphasised. Secondly the action of healing follows. Thirdly the effectiveness of the healing and the awe of the witnesses is reported. It is characteristic for the Gospels that they do not describe a magical procedure in detail, but stress the healing word of Jesus and even preserve it in a foreign tongue : *Talitha kumi*, Mk 5:41 ; *Ephphatha*, Mk 7:34. Sometimes additional 'novelistic' features may be added (Mk 5:13 and 5:43). There are numerous legends, mostly concerning the person of Jesus. The term does not imply an historical evaluation. It is strictly meant as pointing to a literary form, *legenda*, i.e. something to be read. One connotation is to speak of a 'pious story'. (The modern use of the word legend is misleading, since it refers to something which is unverifiable and unhistorical.) A Gospel legend may go back to an historical event, but need not be particularly concerned with it. The intention is to edify the hearers or to glorify the central figure. An example of this form may be the infancy-narratives (Mt. 1, 2 and Lk. 1 and 2), the baptism of Jesus (Mk

97b 1:9–11), Jesus 12 years old in the temple (Lk. 2:41–52), the confession at Caesarea Philippi (Mk 8:27–33), the transfiguration (Mk 9:2–8) or Peter's miraculous catch of fishes (Lk. 5:1–11). Most parts of the Passion and Easter narratives belong to this form, which has its roots in the worship of the earliest Christianity.

c **(d) Results of Form Criticism**—The work, mostly analytical, may sometimes give the impression that the Gospels are unreliable historical sources. Such is not the case. The positive results may be summarised in three points :

(*a*) The different forms used by the Synoptic Gospels are recognised. In principle they are acknowledged today, though the terminology may differ.

(*b*) With regard to the history of the tradition of smaller units one must acknowledge that their *Sitz im Leben* lies in the preaching and worship of the earliest Christian congregations. The historical Jesus cannot be directly approached except through the medium of the post-Easter faith of his witness. Faith, worship or cult, and preaching set forth and shaped the 'forms'.

(*c*) Form Criticism has given positive answers to exaggerated scepticism because it lays bare the earliest layers of tradition. It has made obvious that the very earliest forms are characterised by simplicity and concentration upon the essentials, lack of magical traces or picturesque additions. Later times, especially in the apocryphal Gospels but also in Mt. and Lk. over against Mk, present an enlargement of 'novelistic' features.

Present-day Gospel research tends in two different directions : either it is more concerned with the Gospel as a whole and therefore with the specific work of the evangelist as redactor, or once more it is interested in the historical Jesus of the pre-Easter period. Both tendencies, however, presuppose and must indeed use the method of Form Criticism.

d **Form Criticism outside the Gospels**—The general principles were applied also to all NT books outside the Synoptic Gospels, although one has to recognise here different presuppositions, in so far as we do not have before us books resulting from a redacted work. An exception may be Ac., where the author, Luke, has made use of material previously formed, as we find it in the speeches, sermons, legends about persons or general historical narratives. Form Criticism has in Ac. analysed forms (see especially M. Dibelius), and thus not only reconstructed the early Christian preaching of the second half of the 1st cent., but also sharpened our eye for the recognition of Luke's own literary contribution.

Form Criticism is more complicated and controversial when applied to John's Gospel—as practised, e.g., by Bultmann, who reckons with a 'revelation' source of gnostic origin and one or two redactors, who misplaced units. On the other hand, we have scholars like C. H. Dodd and R. H. Lightfoot, who take the inner integrity of the present book as evident. Fruitful seems to be the cautious usage of Form Criticism in order to recognise confessional sentences, hymns, parenetical or catechetical material quoted in books, which are considered to represent integrities. Such passages are recognisable either by their introduction (e.g. οἴδαμεν ὅτι, οὐκ ἀγνοεῖτε, or by their style (e.g. relative clause, use of participial construction) or 597d
rhythm. The confessions seem to have had first a short formula pointing solely to Jesus as Christ or as *Kyrios* (1 C. 12:3 ; or Ac. 8:37, the Western Text). When enlarged they refer to the *kerygma*, the central Christ event : 'God raised him from the dead' (Rom. 10:9 ; see also Rom. 1:3f.), or explicitly 'received' and 'delivered to you as of first importance', the well-known *kerygma* of 1 C. 15:3ff. Yet often it is difficult to recognise smaller quotations of confessional sentences—as for instance 1 Pet. 1:20, 3:18f., 22—because the author apparently refers to formulae already known to the hearer. Closely connected with these confessions—according to content not to form—are the *hymns*. They concern Christ as redeemer. It is acknowledged that Paul in Phil. 2:6–11 quotes a hymn just as in Col. 1:15–20, which most likely originally had a larger text. Other examples are 1 Tim. 3:16 and 1 Pet. 2:21–4.

Parenetical and *catechetical* material can be found *passim*. Admonitions have shaped the catalogue of virtues (Gal. 5:22f. ; 1 Tim. 6:11 ; 2 Pet. 1:5–7) and vices (Rom. 1:29–31, 13:13 ; 1 C. 5:10f., etc.), whose forms go back to hellenistic origin. They are not particularly related to faith in Christ, but are giving typical examples. Such is the case also with regard to the *Haustafeln*, where the Christianisation of a formerly hellenistic pattern can be observed by comparing Col. 3:18ff. with Eph. 5:22f. and their later stage in the Pastoral Letters.

Other parenetical material obviously takes up Jewish and OT traditions. Especially the Holiness Code of Lev. seems to have played an important role in earliest Christianity. P. Carrington and E. G. Selwyn have proved how often Lev. 17–20 shows up in passages like 1 Th. 4:1–12 ; 1 C. 6:1–11 ; 1 Pet. 1:15ff., 2:12, etc. It is highly probable that this material—though different in forms—is catechetical and has its *Sitz im Leben* in pre-baptismal teaching of the Church.

As to the overall picture one must say that Form Criticism outside the Gospels and Ac. has still a formidable task before it and that more research is required in order to discriminate the small units or quotations out of fixed forms. Yet one result seems clear : all smaller or smallest units have their origin in the worship of the earliest Church, be it in sermons, liturgies or in baptismal rites and catechetical teaching. Perhaps one may go one step farther : most of these small units bring us back to the time before Paul's letters and thus to the decades after Christ's death and resurrection.

Bibliography—R. Bultmann, *Die Geschichte der Synoptischen Tradition* (3rd ed. 1957) ; O. Cullmann, *The Early Christian Confessions* (1953) ; M. Dibelius, *From Tradition to Gospel, Gospel Criticism and Christology* (1935), ThRs (NF1) (1929), 185–216, (NF3) (1931), 207–42 ; C. H. Dodd, *The Parables of the Kingdom* (1935) ; A. Fridrichsen, *Le problème du miracle* (1925) ; F. C. Grant, *The Growth of the Gospels* (1933) ; W. L. Knox, *The Sources of the Synoptic Gospels* I (1953), II (1957) ; K. L. Schmidt, *Der Rahmen der Geschichte Jesu* (1919) ; V. Taylor, *The Formation of the Gospel Tradition* (1933).

THE JEWISH STATE IN THE HELLENISTIC WORLD

By W. D. DAVIES

598a **The Dispersion**—Although the Jews have been especially connected with one land, that of Palestine, from the beginning of their history they have also been a wandering people. Abraham, who went forth not knowing whither he went (Gen. 12:10ff.), became not only their father but their prototype; and so too Jacob, Joseph, Moses were all journeying men (Gen. 28ff., 37ff. ; Exod. 2ff.) That already before the emergence of the prophets they were a dispersed people can be deduced from the hope, expressed by Isaiah and later prophets, for their unification and return to 'Israel' (Jer. 3:12f., 31:4–20; Ezek. 36:16–38, 37:24). Nevertheless, it was the deportation of the Northern Kingdom of Israel to Media by the Assyrians about 722 B.C., and more especially, since the northern tribes were apparently lost by assimilation or absorption, that of the Southern Kingdom of Judah by the Babylonians in 586 B.C., that first caused the growth of a large Jewish community outside Palestine. For a thousand years after Cyrus (538 B.C.) well-organised Jewish communities lived in Babylon. Remaining in living contact with the Jews of Palestine, they eventually gave to the world the Babylonian Talmud. But the Jews spread early to the West also. Through the discovery of the Elephantine papyri we now know that there was a colony of Jewish soldiers in the city of Yeb (Elephantine) in Egypt at the beginning of the 6th cent. B.C. They worshipped Yahweh but as one of a pantheon ; he had a consort Anath, the queen of heaven. The reference in Jer. 44:17 as well as others to Egypt in Jer. 24:8, 26:23, 42:14ff, 43:1ff, 44:11ff. have now become clear. (Probably the worship at Elephantine is typical of much in pre-Deuteronomic religion.)

b Thus before the advent of Alexander the Great (356–323 B.C.) Jews were already widely scattered, but his work stimulated further dispersion. Alexander founded the city of Alexandria (331 B.C.), and Ptolemy, who seized Egypt upon his death and soon after subdued Palestine, if he did not deport Jews thither, at least greatly encouraged their movement to Alexandria and other parts of Egypt ; and there from this time on Jews multiplied. Apart from the Babylonian and Alexandrian, we cannot know how most of the other Jewish communities outside Palestine, many of which were naturally very insignificant, came into being. But certain factors help to explain their remarkably frequent incidence. From the time of Ptolemy I (320 B.C.) political and military unrest often broke out in Palestine. Persecutions under Antiochus Epiphanes (175–163 B.C.) caused many Jews to flee to Egypt, Mesopotamia and Greece, and deportations took place possibly under Ptolemy I and certainly after Pompey's conquest of Palestine (63 B.C.). Such conditions made emigration attractive. Again, despite the continual bleeding of its population through war, and despite periods of comparative plenty, the land of Palestine was too poor to maintain its people. Emigration was a dire necessity. Jews did not share the widespread tendency in the Graeco-Roman world in this period to avoid having children, nor did they practise the exposure of children at birth. Hence, wherever they 598
settled, they tended to be more prolific than their neighbours. Moreover, mobility and intermingling characterised not only the period of Alexander the Great himself but that of his successors. Not only had the Exile familiarised Jews with movement but in the Hellenistic Age a man's fatherland tended to be where his fortune brought him. Thus trade carried people with it. The Jews had taken to commerce since the time of Solomon and conditions in the post-Alexandrian world opened doors for them everywhere. Finally, apart from the acquisition of converts to Judaism, and they were considerable, the Jews absorbed into their ranks other peoples of Semitic stock, especially Phoenicians, so that their numbers grew not only by natural increase but by the acquisition of outsiders.

For the above and other reasons, the Jews multiplied greatly in the Graeco-Roman world. A passage in 1 Mac. 15:16–23 makes this clear :

> 'Lucius, consul of the Romans, to king Ptolemy, greeting. The envoys of the Jews have come to us as our friends and allies to renew our ancient friendship and alliance. They had been sent by Simon the high priest and by the people of the Jews, and have brought a gold shield weighing a thousand minas. We therefore have decided to write to the kings and countries that they should not seek their harm or make war against them and their cities and their country, or make alliance with those who war against them. . . .
>
> 'The consul wrote the same thing to Demetrius the king and to Attalus and Ariarathes and Arsaces, and to all the countries, and to Sampsames, and to the Spartans, and to Delos, and to Myndos, and to Sicyon, and to Caria, and to Samos, and to Pamphylia, and to Lycia, and to Halicarnassus, and to Rhodes, and to Phaselis, and to Cos, and to Side, and to Aradus and Gortyna and Cnidus and Cyprus and Cyrene.'

How widespread Jews were is clear. Josephus quotes c
the geographer Strabo (64 B.C.–A.D. 24) that 'Now these Jews are already gotten into all cities, and it is hard to find a place in the habitable earth that hath not admitted this tribe of men, and is not possessed by them . . .' and that Josephus agrees with this appears from the BJ II, xvi, 4 (see Jos. Ant. XIV, vii, 2 and cf. Jos.BJ VII, iii, 3). But his apologetic interests make Josephus' work suspect. More important is a letter from Agrippa I to the Emperor Caligula (A.D. 37–41) cited by Philo in Legat. xxxvi, 281–2, which mentions Jews in Egypt, Phoenicia, Syria, Coelo-Syria, Pamphylia, Cilicia, Asia Minor as far as Bithynia, Pontus, Europe, Thessaly, Boeotia, Macedonia, Aetolia, Attica, Argos, Corinth, the Peloponnesus, and the islands Euboea, Cyprus, Crete, Euphrates, Babylon. No reference to Rome appears here, but Horace and Cicero mention Jews in Rome in their time, the 1st cent. B.C. And although this can be

98c exaggerated, probably large numbers of Jews were taken prisoners to Rome by Pompey after the destruction in Jerusalem in 63 B.C. The numbers of Jews in the Empire in the 1st cent. (1,000,000 in Egypt, 50–60,000 in Rome in the time of Tiberius (A.D. 14–37) and in all the Empire 6–7,000,000 (J. Juster, *Les Juifs dans l'Empire Romain* (1914), 1,210)) have been greatly exaggerated. The revolt against Rome in A.D. 66–70 lowered the numbers of Jews in Palestine but the Jews in the Dispersion were not much affected by it and remained numerically strong up to the time of Justinian (A.D. 527–65) Exact figures cannot be given for them.

d Can we discover the economic strength of Jewry? While the literary remains of Dispersion Jewry and the evidence of the Jewish catacombs indicate that most Jews were poor, nevertheless it can hardly be doubted that much economic power was in Jewish hands throughout the Empire. That Diaspora Jewry sat loosely to the revolt in A.D. 66–70 suggests that their condition, economically and otherwise, was not as desperate as was that of their Palestinian kinsmen. They were often traders, and so tended to concentrate in towns and commercial cities, such as Alexandria, Antioch and Rome where the intermingling of peoples was greatest. In some areas they had monopolies, e.g. in textiles in Babylon. They took over the dyeing industry from the Phoenicians and those of glass and jewellery were largely in their hands. Nor should the exports of Jews in Palestine be forgotten, e.g. in asphalt and wines. Such Palestinian export activity involved Jews of the Diaspora. Throughout the Empire there were rich Jews capable of giving large donations to synagogues and to charity, and considerable sums of money could be sent from the Diaspora to Jerusalem. Josephus refers to exceedingly wealthy Jews in Alexandria (Ant. XVIII, vi, 3), and they were not confined to that city. Nevertheless, in our period, Jews did not show any special predilection for commerce, and were not restricted to a few well-defined callings. There were among them common soldiers, army commanders, 'policemen', tax-collectors, peasants, farm-labourers, 'industrial' labourers, etc. Probably, however, the *proportion* of Jewish merchants to Jewish labourers was considerably higher in the Dispersion than in Palestine itself, and Jews were frequently found in the 'professions', as writers, artists, poets, historians, philosophers and doctors. Nevertheless, it must be emphasised that in the Diaspora as in Palestine the Jew in our period remained predominantly agrarian. 'The commercial Jew' was not yet (see Jos.c.Ap. i, 12).

99a **The official Roman Attitude towards the Dispersion**—From the above it will have emerged that apart from those in Palestine itself and those scattered all over the Empire, Rome had to come to terms also with two centres of Jewry, outside the Empire in Babylon in the East, and within the Empire in Alexandria and Rome in the West. Two factors made this imperative. First, the term Dispersion must not be allowed to suggest merely diffusion, because the numerous and powerful Jewish communities, although widespread, were also integrated. True their relation to Palestine was more like that of a Greek colony to its motherland, sentimental, rather than like that of a Roman colony, which was bound legally to Rome; and every Diaspora Jewish community had a real independence from Palestine and from every other Jewish community. Nevertheless, Diaspora Jewry did turn to Jerusalem and to its Temple as their spiritual centre. Moreover, Palestinian Judaism had contacts with all parts of the Hellenistic world. The annual half-shekel tax which every Jew paid to maintain the Temple cult bound him to Jerusalem wherever he was, and pilgrims from the Diaspora visited the city in large numbers annually (Jos. Ant. XIV, vii, 2; BJ, VI, xi, 3). By the 1st cent. every large city in the Empire had its synagogue or synagogues and these gave to Judaism everywhere an unmistakable unity and cohesion. Emissaries from the Palestine synagogues 599a
visited those in the Dispersion so that there was considerable reciprocal interchange of thought. Rome confronted, therefore, a Jewry not only ubiquitous but in a real sense unified: it had to tread warily. Secondly, Rome was compelled to give full weight to the existence on its Eastern boundaries in Babylon of a powerful Jewry which was in close touch with Jerusalem. There a Parthian empire came into existence in 58 B.C.—a force formidable even to Rome, and there came into being a Parthian party among Palestinian Jews which could exploit any anti-Roman situation (see Moore, *Judaism* (1927), i, 74). These two factors help us to understand the extreme sensitivity of Rome to the Palestinian scene and to Jewry, and the special treatment that the latter received from Rome. This last cannot be accounted for simply in terms of Rome's toleration of religious and 'national' peculiarities: it rests on political necessity also.

But what was this special treatment? In a milieu b
where gods many and lords many coexisted in mutual tolerance, there was One jealous God who demanded sole allegiance to Himself, the God of the Jews. But Rome also was jealous and from all its peoples it too demanded certain acts of obedience which were incompatible with absolute allegiance to Yahweh. It followed that Rome had either to persecute His worshippers or else grant them special privileges. For many reasons Rome chose the latter course. In many localities Jews had long enjoyed freedom to pursue their peculiar customs, and Rome, conservative by nature, was loath to introduce any innovation at this point or to allow communities under its sway to do so. But, more important, while a friendly Jewry could be a source of military strength (and Jewish soldiers were notoriously loyal to their leaders), a hostile Jewry could also constitute an enemy of formidable might, especially in alliance with Parthia. Moreover, in Palestine itself the international significance of the Jewish state enabled its rulers to further the cause of the Dispersion with Rome. Thus the relations between Rome and Dispersion Jewry came to be governed first by an agreement with Simon the Maccabee (141–135 B.C.). Rome thereby was to provide liberty of worship for Jews everywhere in its domains. These privileges were later guaranteed by Julius Caesar (about 48 B.C.) through a decree of the Senate (Jos. Ant. XIV, viii, 5, XIV, x, 1ff.). The decree was a perpetual one. That it was reviewed by Augustus and other later emperors proves the necessity for its renewal, as well as the good faith of the Romans. Moreover, except that after A.D. 70 they were made dependent upon the payment of a tax (see below), the revolt of A.D. 66–70 did not affect the privileges of the Jews of the Dispersion, because on the whole they had not participated in it. What these privileges amounted to in nature and scope we shall now briefly indicate.

First, as to their scope. In theory, they applied to c
all born Jews everywhere, except to Jews who were citizens of Greek or Roman cities and to proselytes (Jos. Ant. XIV, x, 20, XVI, vi, 3). In practice, they were accorded to all Jews who practised their religion, and proselytes are to be included in this category (Jos. Ant. XIV, x, 13, 16; G. F. Moore, *Judaism*, 1, 233f.).

Secondly, as to the nature of the privileges. They d
had to do only with the religious status of Jewry, not with their civic status. The chief privilege allowed the Jews was that they were not asked to worship the Roman gods. But in the matter of Emperor-worship their situation was more complex. They could not be excused participation in this, and fixed punishments were decreed against all who refused to conform to it. Nevertheless, certain aspects of the cult of the Emperor were modified so as to meet the scruples of Jews. Following the example of the Seleucids and Ptolemies (Philo, Legat. xxi, 33, Flac. vi; Jos.c.Ap. XI, vi, 73), Julius Caesar saw to it that Jewish convictions were respected in the Imperial cult: thus

599d Jews were allowed to avoid using names suggesting the divinity of the Emperor ; oaths to the Emperor asked of Jews were carefully screened so as not to offend their religious sensibilities. They were allowed to celebrate imperial festivals of all kinds in their own manner : up to the time of Caligula in A.D. 19 they were excused from participation in public games in honour of the Emperor : instead of rendering offerings to the Emperor and his family in pagan temples, Jews were allowed to pray for them in their synagogues and in the Temple in Jerusalem ; prayers could also be substituted for sacrifices to the Emperor (Philo, Flac. xxxvii ; Jos.BJ XI, x, 4). Jews were not compelled to construct synagogues to the Emperor's honour but could instead dedicate them to him. Furthermore it was forbidden to place imperial or other images in the synagogues ; this included images on Roman standards. Though Jews were expected to bow before the Emperor when speaking to him, they were not asked to worship the images of the Emperor or to prostrate themselves before them. In all these ways it was made possible for Jews to participate in Emperor worship without violation to their faith. Note, however, that such participation, though on their own terms, was compulsory.

600a But the privileges had also a positive content. Jews were given the right to unite in services for worship and sacrifice. Their observance of the Sabbath was carefully respected. On that day no Jew could be summoned to justice, no contribution could be required of him, no forced labour demanded. If the State distributed alms on a Sabbath, arrangements were made for the Jews to receive their share on another day. Military discipline recognised the Sabbath and no Jewish soldier could be made to march on that day. Rome honoured also the Sabbatic year during which the Jews were not taxed (this privilege was later ignored when the Empire became financially straitened). Jews could observe their own festivals and were not compelled to attend pagan ones ; they were allowed to make pilgrimages to Jerusalem, to the Temple, as long as it stood, and later to the city itself. Their dietary laws were given due consideration ; wherever they were numerous enough and so desired Jews were granted the right to establish their own markets. In the services of worship Jews were allowed to use Hebrew and to observe their own calendar for the religious year. The Hebrew scriptures were declared to be sacred and the violation of them a sacrilege (see, e.g., Jos. Ant. XX, v, 4). Finally, we come to the unusual privilege allowed to Jews to contribute money to the Temple at Jerusalem, even though the exportation of money for commercial purposes was illegal. Every Jew at the age of 20 was expected to pay half a shekel annually to the Temple. In addition both Jews and Greeks were allowed to send gifts in money, and sometimes in precious metals, there. Called ' sacred money ' ever since the 2nd cent. B.C. the transportation of it was protected by Rome and minutely regulated to ensure safety from brigands and dishonesty. The theft of the ' sacred money ' was declared to be sacrilege (Jos. Ant. XVI, vi, 4). The magnitude of this privilege was apparent : so much so that Titus can be made to declare that the Jewish revolt of A.D. 66–70 was waged with Roman money (Jos. Ant. VI, vi, 2). But not only could Jewry export money to Palestine, they could also maintain their own funds. They could unite into associations, for worship, with their own treasuries ; these associations were variously designated and this may suggest that they differed in organisation. But, however organised, they were not ordinary *collegia* but constituted a distinct category of associations, membership in which was by birth. Not only Jewish particularism but the Roman law was anxious to maintain this national character of the associations. Moreover the extent and complexity of their jurisdiction set them apart from mere *collegia*. They controlled the marital, financial and judiciary life of their members.

The result of all these privileges will be apparent. 600b Granted, partly at least, because Diaspora Jewry constituted a cohesive unity, which as friend or foe Rome could not ignore, these very privileges deepened this unity still further and this increased the significance of Jewry. And here it is essential to realise that the various Jewish communities were legally part of one Jewish nation. The right of association was not granted to each community in isolation but to the Jewish people *en bloc*. Although each Jewish community was free to enjoy peculiarly local privileges, each was also legally subordinate to central Jewish authority. The High Priest at Jerusalem was the chief of Jews everywhere and Rome dealt with him on behalf of all Jews. Thus Hyrcanus II was not only High Priest but ethnarch of the Jews (Jos. Ant. XIV, x, 2, XIII, xiii, 1) ; he had rights of jurisdiction and taxation over the Dispersion Jews. Moreover before A.D. 70 the Sanhedrin at Jerusalem had jurisdiction over all Jews in matters religious and political. The various communities, however, differed greatly in organisation. Usually each had a council of elders, chosen for sagacity, not age, to safeguard its financial and religious rites. The council had a president, a scribe, and ' rulers ' to execute its decisions ; it could levy taxes and collect money for synagogues, hospitals, schools, and it could also receive gifts. The community also had the right to defend its members at law, and, after permission from the procurator, to send delegates to the Emperor. Moreover, it could honour its benefactors in various ways. But, as in Palestine, so in the Diaspora, the Synagogue, with its trained Rabbi, was the centre of the community. Its books were to be respected by all ; asylum could be found within its walls. Its schools and libraries flourished and were usually honoured, as were the Jewish cemeteries.

The civil status of Jewry was more ambiguous than c their religious. The law of the land in which they dwelt was the law for the Jews. Nevertheless certain legal privileges were also theirs. In the granting of these, a sharp distinction was drawn between Jewish citizens and Jewish resident aliens :

Jewish resident aliens

(*a*) Could marry according to Jewish law
(*b*) Could practise polygamy
(*c*) Could follow Jewish laws of succession
(*d*) Could be tried by the Roman governor
(*e*) Could be flogged, expelled, imprisoned
(*f*) Did not have the right to the highest offices in the State
(*g*) Usually dressed like Romans

Jewish citizens

(*a*) Could marry according to Jewish law but only because this was not in conflict with Roman law
(*b*) Could not practise polygamy
(*c*) Could only follow Roman laws of succession
(*d*) Could also appeal to the Emperor
(*e*) Were free from flogging, expulsion and imprisonment
(*f*) Had the right to the highest offices (e.g. there were Jewish senators)
(*g*) Had to dress as Roman citizens

Among privileges granted to all Jews we have noticed d that they could not be summoned to law on the Sabbath or feast days. Although legally expected to use Roman forms in the drawing up of contracts, Jews did draw up such in Jewish forms adding the minimum of necessary Roman formulae. Litigation between Jews was allowed to follow Jewish practice. But the Jews had no jurisdiction in matters of penal

600d law in the Dispersion (compare Palestine where also the Great Sanhedrin, contrary to the previously held view, was *probably* not competent in capital cases; see J. Jeremias, ZNW 43 (1950–1), 145-50. The Diaspora Jews could only inflict flogging, scourging, imprisonment). An important point to notice is that the whole of a local community could be held responsible for a crime committed by one Jew. Thus in the case of a rebellion by a few the whole Jewish population could be massacred. Crimes of a political nature, e.g. in sedition or turbulence or rebellion, were not treated as simply murder.

e Two things remain to state. As to military service, Jews, under the Ptolemies and Seleucids, serving in various national units, e.g. the Macedonian, were disciplined and loyal. They were first exempt from military service in 49 B.C., but we do not know how long the exemption lasted: we do find Jewish soldiers in Syria at the end of the 1st cent. As to taxation, it seems that Vespasian was the first to level any special taxes on the Diaspora Jews, although Rome had continued the taxes placed on Jews in Egypt by the Ptolemies. After A.D. 70 Vespasian ordained that Jews should pay annually the two drachma which they had previously paid to the Temple at Jerusalem to Jupiter Capitolinus. Called the 'Jewish Tax' it was ostensibly levied for religious purposes but actually fell into the imperial coffers. Under Vespasian all *practising* Jews were so taxed, but under Domitian *all* Jews by birth were made subject to it. A special organisation was created at Rome to deal with it, though even in this matter the religious susceptibilities of Jewry were respected: the tax could not be collected on the Sabbath or festival days.

601a **Anti-Judaism**—Thus Jews in the Hellenistic Age were privileged. But they were not therefore safe. Privileges usually evoke protests; and attacks upon Jewry then, as so often since, were common. It is erroneous to refer to these attacks as anti-semitic, because that term presupposes the developed racial theories of the 19th cent. Best is it to use the word 'anti-Judaism'. At first contacts between Jews and Greeks were military and highly favourable. To the Greeks, Jews at first appeared as an admirable school of philosophers, and in the persecutions under Antiochus Epiphanes it was to Sparta that many Jews turned. Spartan discipline and Jewish legalism were congenial. We do not hear of a specific pogrom till Roman times, when Augustus deprived the Greek inhabitants of Alexandria of their Senate and allowed them only titular magistracies, and at the same time confirmed the Jews in all their rights. There were further outbreaks against Jews in the time of Caligula: the wealthy Jews of Alexandria were driven to the Delta and four hundred of their houses sacked. According to Jos.BJ XI, xviii, 7–8, iii, 1, 3, in the late sixties, 50,000 Jews were killed in Alexandria. Moreover while the exact nature of the expulsions of Jews from Rome under Tiberius (A.D. 19) and Claudius (probably A.D. 49–50) is uncertain, they do point to the insecurity of Jewry even in Rome itself. And anti-Judaism, although it only broke out into open violence in the Roman period, had old roots. First, the Hellenistic Age was syncretistic. While Aristotle had accepted the near-dogma in Greece that Greeks were essentially superior to other men, Alexander the Great, his pupil, rejected this: for him there was neither Jew nor Greek: he desired their fusion, and that of all men, in a common Hellenic culture. But the universalism of Alexander and of the Hellenistic Age demanded a religious pluralism which Jews could not countenance. However far they could go towards assimilation, the commandments under which they lived, 'Thou shalt have no other gods before Me', made final assimilation impossible. For the Gentile, freedom and universalism meant in the *sphere of religion* the right to worship any god as one pleased: for the Jew, it could only mean the worship of the living God before whom there was none other.

Thus the Jews were accused of being atheists, the point of which was not that they were what we should call speculative atheists, nor that they objected to images (the Jews were not always 'imageless' and not the only imageless worshippers). They were atheists because they actually opposed 'gods'—the gods of the State and of the Gentile world (cf. Jos.c.Ap. I, xxxiv). But this fundamental religious stumbling-block engendered also *social tensions.* The Jew was a creature apart. The fence of the Law which protected him became an offence. Thus the observance of the Sabbath struck Greeks as utterly irrational. For the refusal of the Hasidim to defend themselves rather than violate the Sabbath, the Greeks had only contempt. To them only fanatics could observe the dietary laws, which gave to Jews a reputation not only for blind credulity but for inhospitality; the refusal to participate in Gentile meals, private and public, gained for them the reputation of being unsociable monsters. They were accused of human sacrifice (which they had early condemned). According to Damocritus (1st cent. B.C.) Jews captured a stranger every seven years and sacrificed him to their God; and Apion asserted that a captured Greek was found put to death in the Temple by Antiochus Epiphanes. They were claimed to have no regard for any man. Moreover there were *philosophic attacks* on Jews. The philosophies usually emphasised universalism and rationalism. These were solvents of nationalism. To recognise distinctions between Jew and Greek and barbarian was objectionable, and the Stoics especially resented Jewish particularism. This comes out in 4 Mac. 5:8ff. where Antiochus Epiphanes argues philosophically with Eleazar concerning the partaking of swine's flesh: his reasoning was doubtless often followed: 'And Antiochus seeing him, said, I would counsel thee, old man, before thy tortures begin, to taste the swine's flesh and save your life; . . . For wherefore, since nature has conferred upon you the most excellent flesh of this animal, do you loathe it? It seems senseless not to enjoy what is pleasant, yet not disgraceful, and from notions of sinfulness to reject the boons of nature . . .' 601b

Again the *political aspect* of anti-Judaism is real. To the Roman government Judaism was merely one among many foreign cults being propagated in the Empire and invading Rome itself. And Rome was increasingly being filled with Eastern sects, mystery, magical, astrological, philosophic. Confined to foreigners these were tolerated, but when they began to undermine the ancestral forms of Roman religion measures were taken against them, but on the grounds not of religion but of morality. Nor was it difficult to justify these measures. Many of the sects were often immoral; thus the attacks on the Bacchanalia by Rome in 186 B.C. were probably necessary. Not only morally were the sects dangerous but also politically. They provided cells around which factions could grow. Thus Judaism shared in a widespread and real suspicion of Eastern groups. Moreover, the intransigence of the Jews in Palestine and especially their openness to Parthian influences, made Jews everywhere more politically suspect: the 'central government' had every reason to be wary of them. On the other hand, from the point of view of the local communities within which they dwelt, the Jews were especially privileged by the 'central government'. Many of their privileges were maintained forcibly by Rome so that they could easily be regarded as partisans of Rome against the local population. *Economic reasons* for anti-Judaism do not appear to have been especially operative. But there can be little doubt that Jews would be unpopular on account of the export of money for the Temple tax from areas which could well do with it themselves, and measures for its protection had to be carefully devised: the fact that Vespasian thought it worth while to perpetuate the tax after A.D. 70 indicates how considerable it must have been. c

601d The above factors, and others, combined to produce anti-Judaism. In Latin authors an item not hitherto mentioned by us is apparent : Horace, Strabo and Ovid found the *aggressive proselytism* of Jews offensive. Nor must this be underemphasised : conversion to Judaism, unlike conversion to less demanding religions, meant usually a complete break with nation, family, friends and the old life and it, therefore, appeared inhuman. How much Cicero knew about Jews is uncertain. He does not use the stock terms of abuse to which we shall shortly refer, and his reference to the Jews as ' a nation born to be slaves ' is merely rhetorical hyperbole. More important than stray references in Latin authors is the specific anti-Judaistic literature that developed. This was Alexandrian and expressed the Egyptian point of view. Since the beginning of the 6th cent. (Elephantine) Jews had represented in Egypt foreign overlords : those who came with the Ptolemies were likewise ' alien '. So it came about that with Egyptians, and also with Greeks, in Alexandria Jews were unpopular. A long tradition of anti-Judaism created a convention of anti-Jewish accusations. In the 3rd cent. B.C. Hecataeus of Abdera, a Greek living in Egypt, gave the Egyptian version of the Exodus. A pestilence caused by the anger of the gods at the presence of foreign elements in the population led to the expulsion of Jews. Most of these settled in Palestine. There Moses, famous for his wisdom and valour, ordained for them an inhospitable and inhuman way of life. Another Egyptian, a priest, called Manetho, in the same century, wrote a history of his people the thesis of which Josephus has preserved for us. The Exodus from Egypt was really the defeat and expulsion of certain rebellious Egyptians who had been isolated as lepers and criminals. In the 2nd cent. B.C. Mnaseas, a highly rhetorical historian in Alexandria, held Jews to ridicule because they worshipped God in the form of an ass, the ass, in Egypt, being a symbol of evil. This charge reappears in the 1st cent. B.C. in the work of Posidonius, Apollonius Molo, who taught Cicero and Caesar, and in that of Apion, a Greek grammarian of the 1st cent. A.D. who wrote a work against the Jews to which Josephus replied in *Against Apion*. Damocritus in the 1st cent. B.C. we referred to above. Thus even if we cannot strictly speak of anti-Semitism in the racial sense in our period (while the Greeks before Alexander had attached a certain theoretical importance to purity of descent and though Romans often made pretensions to this, feelings of racial purity did not play any significant role in the Hellenistic Age), there was a marked anti-Judaism.

602a **The Reaction of the Dispersion Jewry to the Gentile World**—How did Jewry react to the pressures in the situation we have just outlined ? Indistinguishable in dress and speech they were yet ' different '. We can assess their response to the Graeco-Roman world from the literature they produced and otherwise. First, since Greek became their language it became necessary to translate their sacred scriptures into that language and there came into being a translation of the OT into Greek which is now called the Septuagint (LXX). Two approaches to this translation are possible. First, that it is a translation of a particular Hebrew text of the OT which it can help us to recover. Since, until the recent discoveries in the Dead Sea area, the earliest extant complete manuscript of the Hebrew Bible dates from the 10th cent. A.D. and the earliest text of the LXX from the 4th and 5th cent., the LXX was regarded as very important as a tool for the recovery of the Hebrew text. But, secondly, there is the view that it is essentially a targum, not a translation ; that it grew up naturally in the synagogues as the OT was translated and interpreted, i.e. that there was no one original Greek version so that the manuscripts of the LXX do not go back to one archetype. The recent ' Dead Sea ' discoveries perhaps suggest that the former view is to be preferred. In any case the author of the Letter
of Aristeas tells us that seventy-two elders were sent 602
from Palestine to Alexandria in Egypt to translate the Law of Moses into Greek. In the course of time the title ' The Translation of the Seventy-Two ' became ' The Translation of the Seventy ', and came to include the translation of the prophetic and hagiographic portions of the Hebrew Bible. The aim of its authors was not to produce a good translation but one as faithful as possible to the original Hebrew. Because of this it is so inelegant that it could by no means have tempted its readers with the seductions of the Greek language. Nevertheless, though to cultured Greeks it must have seemed barbaric, its importance cannot be exaggerated. The process of harmonising (as far as this was indeed possible) the Jewish translation and, later, the Palestinian Christian tradition with Hellenism, which ultimately resulted in Christian Theology, was made possible because of the LXX, so that Christian thought owes an immeasurable debt to it. So too the rapid spread of Christianity into the Graeco-Roman world in the early centuries of the Christian era was largely helped by the fact that Christian missionaries had a Greek text of the scriptures of the OT.

The LXX was primarily intended for worship. b
There came into being also a considerable literature partly at least to satisfy the historical curiosity of Jews of the Diaspora. We note only the work of Demetrius (3rd cent. B.C.), who wrote a brief chronological history of Israel, of Eupolemus (*c.* 150 B.C.), who wrote a largely legendary history of the Jews, and of Artapanus (before the 1st cent. B.C.). More important are 2 and 3 Mac. : 2 Mac. is a Greek epitome of a Greek work in five books by Jason of Cyrene in N. Africa, who is otherwise unknown. It deals with 175–161 B.C., roughly from the persecution of Antiochus Epiphanes to the victory of Judas Maccabaeus over Nicanor. Legendary and picturesque, it provides classical examples of martyrdom and so had much influence ; it also throws light on the Pharisees and the doctrine of Resurrection. 3 Mac. has nothing to do with the Hasmonaeans : it relates Ptolemy's attempt to enter the Jerusalem Temple in 27 B.C. But still more important were the works of Josephus (born A.D. 37–8), namely (1) *The Jewish War*, written, soon after A.D. 70 probably, to discourage further revolt. This gives a survey of Jewish history in the Hellenistic-Roman period, skilfully and without embellishment. (2) *The Jewish Antiquities*, in twenty books, written during Domitian's reign (A.D. 81–96), seeks to show his people as worthy of Roman respect (Josephus himself was by then out of favour with Rome). It covers from the patriarchs to the Babylonian exile and up to the outbreak of the war against Rome. It is our chief if not our only source for Jewish history in the Hellenistic-Roman period. To the second edition of this Josephus added an appendix on his own life ; and later his work *Against Apion*, in two books, to refute calumnies against the Jews made not only by Apion. It is also a defence of Jewish culture and law.

The literary works so far mentioned, although with c
the exception of Jos.c.Ap. not designed to be apologetic, in fact tended to be such. But there also arose a literature deliberately designed to defend and propagate Judaism. Jews wrote under the names of real or imaginary Gentile authors to do this. Much of their work has been lost and only the briefest mention of what is extant is possible : the work of Pseudo-Hecataeus, a Jewish apologist whose real name and date are unknown, preserved in parts in Clement of Alexandria and Eusebius ; *The Letter of Aristeas*, by a Hellenistic Jew, describing the translation of the Law, with apologetic embellishments (after 200 B.C.) ; Pseudo-Phocylides, *The Wise Menander* (a Jewish pseudepigraph of the Hellenistic Age designed to convey Jewish ideas under the cloak of the famous Attic poet), *The Sibylline Oracles*. In most of the apologetic and missionary sources three emphases

602c appear, on monotheism and the evils of idolatry, on the spiritual nature of true revelation, and, oddly enough, on the election of Israel : it was its very awareness of being chosen which supplied the dynamic for Israel's missionary work.

d In addition to such works of apology, contact with Greek philosophy led the Jews of the Diaspora to a more logical or systematic or metaphysical presentation of Judaism to the Hellenistic world. Thus there appeared *The Wisdom of Solomon* (see §337*f*), which used Greek philosophical and ethical terms and notions. Another pre-Philonic work is that of Aristobulus, who probably lived in the 2nd cent. B.C. He attempted to harmonise the Law of Moses with the teachings of Greek philosophy in a work called *Interpretation of the Law of Moses* or *Interpretation of the Sacred Laws*, in which is given an allegorical interpretation of the anthropomorphisms of the Pentateuch : Homer and other poets are shown to quote scripture, and Pythagoras, Plato and other Greek thinkers to be dependent on Moses. 4 Mac. urges that the virtues desiderated by Stoics and Platonists are to be achieved by obeying the Law of Moses. But the greatest writer in this genre was Philo of Alexandria, who is now recognised to have been not merely an eclectic but an original philosophical thinker : it was he who gave the greatest impulse to the fusion of Greek and Oriental thought, which was to play so important a part later in Christianity. Born about 20 B.C. in Alexandria, of a wealthy family and influential, the one thing about which we can be certain is that in A.D. 40 Philo headed a Jewish legation to Rome to protest to Caligula against the pogrom instituted by Egyptians and Greeks, aided by Roman officials, in Alexandria. His writings were voluminous and can be classified as follows : (1) Writings of purely philosophical content, (2) interpretations of the Pentateuch : these included an allegorical commentary on Genesis ; questions and answers on Genesis and Exodus ; a historical-exegetical commentary on the Mosaic Law, (3) historical-apologetic writings. His work reveals the same duality as his life. Thus, while he observed the Law of Moses, he attended the Greek theatre, enjoyed athletic contests, and was well acquainted with Greek poetry and philosophy. So too in his writings, Jerusalem and Athens come to terms. We cannot enter into details here, we can merely indicate that two views of Philo have been suggested. One emphasises his ' poetic ' or ' mystical ' insight and sees him as a mystic who used Judaism as a peg on which to hang his understanding of life as a ' mystery ' : on this view he is more Hellenistic than Hebraic. The other view urges that Philo was essentially a Jew who used Hellenistic philosophy as a peg on which to expound Judaism. This second view is the more widely held. Like Aristobulus, Pseudo-Aristeas and others, Philo was concerned to show that life according to the Jewish Law was compatible with Greek culture and philosophy. Moses contained all that Greek philosophy had to teach : throughout his work Philo was concerned to make this last the handmaiden of Judaism.

This brings us next to another aspect of the interaction between Judaism and Hellenism, that of assimilation. This is attested in certain literary forms which appear among Diaspora Jews. The language and style of Greek epic and dramatic poetry were adapted to biblical themes. The work of three writers who attempted this, and three only, has come down to us : (1) Philo the Elder, an epic Jewish poet who wrote in the 2nd cent. B.C. According to Eusebius, he wrote an epic on Jerusalem ; (2) another writer Theodotus (2nd cent. B.C.) wrote an epic, *On the Jews* ; (3) Ezekiel (3rd–2nd cent. B.C.) composed tragedies on biblical themes. He wrote a Jewish drama on the Exodus, in a Greek manner, which has reminiscences of Herodotus. He was aiming probably at impressing Gentiles as well as encouraging Jews.

e But not only in the realm of literature was there assimilation. Recently archaeological studies in
particular have revealed the very great extent to 602e
which the Jews of the Diaspora, and even of Palestine, had come to share in the artistic impulses of their Gentile neighbours. Excavations of synagogues of the period and finds of objects of all kinds have uncovered mosaics of great beauty, painting of human, animal and floral figures on biblical and other themes. Thus in the most important monument of Jewish antiquity at Dura-Europos on the middle Euphrates in Syria, dated by inscription in A.D. 245, the entire walls of the synagogue have been found covered with biblical scenes. In addition the Hellenism which had penetrated Diaspora Judaism had also made inroads into Palestinian Judaism. Even Rabbinic methods of exegesis have been claimed to be Hellenistic in origin. Thus the gulf between the Judaism of the Diaspora and that of Palestine, which it has been customary to emphasise, was far less than had been supposed. Indeed some scholars have urged that while it is convenient to distinguish between Diaspora and Palestinian Judaism the distinction between them is in fact largely unreal ; but this is to go too far.

The Attraction of the Dispersion for the Gentile 603a
World—We can now ask about the results of the efforts which Judaism made to come to terms with the Hellenistic world and to present its faith to it. We noted previously that one of the factors explaining the remarkable extent of the Diaspora was the accession of converts. Among those attracted to Judaism two types are to be distinguished. First, there were the proselytes proper, i.e. Gentiles who were so drawn to the Jewish faith that they undertook all the steps necessary to become ' Jews ' in the full sense, i.e. circumcision, baptism, the presentation of an offering in the Temple (the offering of a sacrifice however was not one of the conditions of becoming a proselyte but only a condition precedent to the exercise of one of the rights of a proselyte, i.e. participation in a sacrificial meal). There was much discussion as to whether circumcision was absolutely necessary for proselytes. Since this last was one of the chief stumbling-blocks to Gentiles who would accept Judaism, especially for Greeks who resented all mutilation of the body, there were more female proselytes than male. But in addition to the proselytes proper there were other Gentiles who were attracted to Judaism, its worship, its tradition, its ethics, who did not however actually become proselytes (not only circumcision would keep them from this but also, as we saw, the complete severance of old ties that conversion to Judaism involved). These were called ' God-fearers ' or ' devout '. Often the son of a father who was a God-fearer would take the further step and become a proselyte. God-fearers were more numerous than proselytes, but the existence of both these types suggests at least a sympathetic understanding on the part of Jewry. Nevertheless, although a man such as the Gentle Hillel would welcome proselytes, there is evidence that there was much suspicion of them. They were prone to backslide into paganism and in times of persecution to become informers. The degree to which Judaism in the time of Jesus was missionary has been much disputed. Proselytism, moreover, was obnoxious to some and Judaism often attracted adherents not by its propaganda but by the silent witness of its life. Nevertheless the evidence suggests that Judaism in the 1st cent. was moved by a direct missionary passion which it has not known since and had not known before. Mt. 23:15 is not untrue to history in so far as it points to this. In any case whether as a result of the unobtrusive attraction of its life or of its missionary zeal, Judaism in our period drew proselytes and God-fearers. This it was, along with his desire to preach first to his own people, that led Paul, wherever he went, to the synagogues, where not only Jews but also proselytes and God-fearers congregated.

The Significance of the Dispersion—Our brief b
survey of the Jewish state in the Hellenistic world is completed. Finally, it remains to indicate the bearing

603b of what we have written on the early Christian movement. The existence of Diaspora Jewry ensured for it at least three elements of crucial significance for its growth—widespread synagogal organisations which it could use as bases in the Graeco-Roman world ; a large body of proselytes and near-proselytes ready to give heed to a Palestinian faith ; and a medium of interpretation, in the LXX and in the work of figures such as Philo, whereby such a faith could be made presentable to the Hellenistic world. On these grounds particularly the Diaspora was a preparation for the Gospel. Moreover, for many years up till the time of Nero, Christianity was able to shelter under the privileges given to Jewry and thus to gain strength in its very infancy In this sense, while Palestinian Judaism was the matrix within which Christianity was born, Hellenistic Judaism—to make a distinction which we have above seen to be dubious—turned out to be its fondling-nurse.

Bibliography—Sources : Of outstanding importance is *Corpus Papyrorum Judaicarum*, vol. i, edited by V. A. Tcherikover and A. Fuks (1957). The Prolegomena, pp 1–111, is the latest treatment of our theme. Masterly and comprehensive, unfortunately it could not be used in the above work. R. H. Charles, *The Apocrypha and Pseudepigrapha of the OT* (1913) ; T. Reinach, *Texts d'auteurs grecs et romains relatifs au Judaïsme* (1895) ; W. N. Stearns, *Fragments from Graeco-Jewish Writers* (1908) ; Works of Philo and Josephus in the Loeb Classical Library ; the Septuagint and its history, see under Canon and Text of the OT above ; very useful is C. K. Barrett, *The NT Background : Selected Documents* (1956).

Other Literature : N. Bentwich, *Hellenism* (1919) ; E. R. Bevan, *Hellenistic Judaism* in *The Legacy of Israel*, ed. by I. Abrahams, E. R. Bevan, C. Singer (1927), 29–68 ; A. Causse, *Les Dispersés d'Israël* (1929) ; E. R. Goodenough, *By Light, Light : the Mystic Gospel of Hellenistic Judaism* (1935), *Introduction to Philo Judaeus* (1940), *Jewish Symbols in the Greco-Roman Period* (1953, etc.) ; J. Juster, *Les Juifs dans l'Empire Romain*, i, ii (1914) ; W. L. Knox, *Pharisaism and Hellenism in Judaism and Christianity, Pharisaism and Other Cultures*, ii, 61–114 ; R. Marcus, *Hellenistic Jewish Literature* in *The Jews : their History, Culture and Religion*, ed. L. Finkelstein, ii (1949), 745ff. ; Oesterley & Robinson, *History of Israel* (1932), ii ; R. H. Pfeiffer, *History of NT Times with an Introduction to the Apocrypha* (1949) (the bibliographies on pp. 531ff. are invaluable); M. Radin, *The Jews among the Greeks and Romans* (1915) ; E. Schürer, *Geschichte des jüdischen Volkes im Zeitalter Jesu Christi*[4] (Eng. tr. also) ; H. A. Wolfson, *Philo*, i, ii (1947). On proselytism : B. J. Bamberger, *Proselytism in the Talmudic Period* (1939) ; W. G. Braude, *Jewish Proselytising in the first five centuries of the Common Era* (1940) ; P. Dalbert, *Die Theologie der Hellenistisch-jüdischen Missions-Literatur unter Ausschluss von Philo und Josephus* (1954).

THE DEVELOPMENT OF JUDAISM IN THE GREEK AND ROMAN PERIODS

(*c.* 196 B.C. – A.D. 135)

BY M. BLACK

4a What we know as Judaism, as distinct from the ancient religion of Israel, is a post-exilic phenomenon, emerging towards the close of the Persian period, at the time of the Restoration under Ezra and Nehemiah. In its earliest form its dominant characteristics were legalism and nationalism, and these it never lost through all the changes of the next five centuries (see further, §607*b* and §§614–19). But in addition, Judaism as a religion acquired in this period new and, to a large extent, foreign elements, which eventually came to be grafted on to the stock of the traditional religion. These religious developments ' between the Testaments ' are of special importance for the student of the NT.

HISTORICAL DEVELOPMENT

For a general introduction to this subject, see §§98–104 and §§42–4.

b The world-empire of Alexander the Great, which succeeded that of Persia, did not long survive Alexander's early decease (323 B.C.). Out of it emerged three great Levantine powers, two of which, next only to Rome itself, were to determine the course of Jewish history during the three centuries before the Christian era : they were Syria, under the Seleucids, and Egypt of the Ptolemies. (The third portion of Alexander's Empire, Macedonia, under the Antigonids, was too remote to affect Palestine.) It was chiefly the Seleucid empire, and, in particular, the oppressive policy of its most notorious ruler, Antiochus Epiphanes—made Emperor of Syria in 175 B.C.—which brought about the first of a series of crises within Judaism which profoundly affected its religious development.

Antiochus sought to mould the Jewish nation, with its ancient religion and customs, to the pattern of hellenistic life (and incidentally to provide himself, by their subjection, with an open highway into Egypt). He failed signally in both aims, but not till after a long and bloody struggle.

The key to Antiochus's policy was the Temple priesthood, in particular the office of High Priest ; and it was from this centre that he sought to carry out his hellenising reforms. The reigning High Priest Onias III was deposed and replaced by a Seleucid upstart by name Menelaus, who was a Benjamite and not even of high priestly birth. In 174 B.C. Onias III was assassinated by an agent of Antiochus.

c It is to this period we are to trace the rise of the 'Ασιδαῖοι or **Hasidaeans** (Heb. *ḥ*^{a}*sîdhîm*, the ' pious ones '), fanatical loyalists for the Law and the old religion and customs now threatened by the inroads of Seleucid hellenism. The Hasidaeans were not only to provide the religious backbone for the political resistance under the Maccabees, but represented, in an almost literal sense, the Remnant of the nation which was to carry forward the great religious tradition of Israel's past. They included a synagogue of scribes, probably lay-scribes (1 Mac. 7:11–17), 604c
and were also joined by loyal members of the priesthood (cf. E. Bevan, *Jerusalem under the High Priests*, 72). The later party of the Pharisees were the descendants of these lay scribes among the Hasidaeans (the Sadducees were descended from the corrupt hellenising priesthood and members of the Jewish aristocracy who were prepared to deal with Antiochus). The later priestly sect of the Essenes, including or along with the Qumrân sectarians (see below, §605*c*) goes back to the priestly ' seceders ' from the Temple led by Onias III. Many scholars identify the Teacher of Righteousness and founder of the Qumrân sect with the martyred Onias (this murder of a Jewish High Priest became a *cause célèbre* in the ancient world. It has left its mark at Dan. 9:11, 25 (the Anointed One who is ' cut off ') ; Zech. 12:10, 13:6 ; 1 Enoch 90:8 (see R. H. Charles, *1 Enoch*, in loc.) ; the story is told at 2 Mac. 4:30–8 and at 2 Mac. 15 Onias is represented, along with Jeremiah, as a kind of celestial champion of his people, a Jewish Stanislaus or Thomas à Becket).

Though resistance was at first passive (a group of d
Hasidaeans allowed themselves to be slaughtered on the Sabbath rather than infringe the commandments by defending themselves, 1 Mac. 2:36), the crisis produced fighters as well as martyrs. A family of priestly origin, the House of Hashmon, the aged Mattathias and his five sons, John, Simon, Judas, Eleazar and Jonathan, raised the standard of revolt. Mattathias was succeeded by the most famous of his sons, **Judas,** nicknamed **Maccabaeus,** the Hammer (of the Gentiles). A period of guerrilla fighting with the Seleucid forces of occupation and commanders sent by Antiochus ended in the capture by the Jews of the last stronghold of the Syrian resistance in Jerusalem, the Akra or Citadel defending the Temple. (Antiochus was heavily engaged elsewhere in his Empire, and this contributed not a little to the Maccabaean successes.) The liberation of the land was celebrated by the **rededication** of the Temple (165 B.C.), an occasion commemorated thereafter by the Feast of Hanukkah (the 'Εγκαινία of Jn 10:22). The Hasmonaean dynasty founded by the House of Hashmon was to last for another century, the two brothers of Judas, Jonathan and Simon, succeeding him, to be followed in turn by John, the son of Simon, known as Hyrcanus. (For a full account of the history of the period, see E. Bevan, op. cit., 69ff.)

Within this period the most important internal e
development within Judaism was the rise to power of laymen, particularly lay scribes, leading to the emergence in the reign of John Hyrcanus of a democratic party known as the **Pharisees,** challenging the traditional rule of the landed aristocracy backed by the priestly caste, the basis of the Sadducean party. There is little doubt that it was this progressive lay wing in Judaism known as Pharisaism which opened wide the door to new religious developments.

604e The derivation of the name Pharisee is obscure; they were the 'separate ones' (*perûshîm*), but 'separated' from what (or whom) is not certain. Lauterbach suggests 'from the priesthood', and Moore and Finkelstein 'from uncleanness' and 'people of the land'. Their main characteristics were their legalistic rigorism (cf. Jos. BJ, I, v, 2; II, viii, 14, *Vita* 38, Ant. XVII, ii, 4). Pharisaic legalism took a special form: it consisted of a tradition of *halākhôth*, legal interpretation of the Torah or Law of Moses which came in time to be more important than the Law itself, and was more often than not read into the text of scripture than exegetically derived from it. It was this adaptability of Pharisaism which gave it much of its strength: new legal rulings could be devised to meet the changing situation in Judaism, even if only lip-service was paid to the original meaning of scripture. The Sadducees, on the other hand, were the traditionalists in another sense; they abode by the original literal meaning of scripture, with the result that their system was inevitably static, rigid and conservative. Pharisaic legalism and respect for the 'tradition of the elders' are reflected in the Gospels (Mt. 15:2; cf. Mk 7:3, 5): since all life was regulated by Law and Tradition, Pharisaism produced a mass of legal rules covering all situations, with the inevitable consequence that they magnified trifles and in doing so trifled with magnitudes (Mt. 23:23). But, especially in the hey-day of their influence, the Pharisees were also the innovators in things religious; one other derivation of their name makes it equivalent to the name 'Persian', and many of the new ideas brought into Judaism by the Pharisees came from Persia. (See below, §607*a*) It goes without saying that they were intensely nationalistic and exclusive (they themselves constituted, in their own eyes, the true Israel).

f The **Sadducees** were the priestly and aristocratic bureaucracy of Judaism. They are not simply to be identified with the priesthood, though many of them belonged to the upper ranks of the hierarchy, but included also members of the landed aristocracy. Religiously they represented a purely conservative reaction to the progressive views of the Pharisees, rejecting whatever positive doctrine the Pharisees advanced. In adhering to a literalist view of scripture, they denied the validity of Pharisaic tradition: the Pharisees believed in a divine purpose in history; the Sadducees maintained the freedom of the individual to shape his own destiny and the course of history: the Pharisees taught a future life and belief in angels; the Sadducees held to the old belief in Sheol and rejected angelology (cf. Ac. 23:8), etc. Their positive characteristics belonged to the secular sphere; they were wealthy and people of high social standing (Jos. Ant. XIII, x, 6). Their manners were boorish to the point of rudeness even among themselves, and in the administration of justice they were harsh and severe. 'The Sadducees of history are a body of practical men running the affairs of their nation on what would nowadays be called common-sense lines making the best bargain they can for their people—and incidentally for themselves—in the existing circumstances. For ideals and programmes we must look elsewhere, to the men who wrote the Apocalypses, codified the Law and tradition, or founded the Community of the Essenes' (T. W. Manson, *The Servant Messiah*, 15).

It was due mainly to the intrigues and irreconcilable conflict of these two opposing parties within the Hasmonaean state that the Jews finally came to lose their political independence. Under Hyrcanus's successor, Alexander Jannaeus (104–78 B.C.), this domestic feud reached its climax; after the death of Alexander, the brief reigns of his successors, his wife Alexandra Salome (78–69 B.C.), Hyrcanus II and Aristobulus were terminated by both parties appealing for help to Rome. Pompey marched on Jerusalem (63 B.C.) and a new epoch in Jewish history was begun. After this Rome ruled by client kings, among whom Herod the Great took a worthy place, for, though responsible in the 60 last resort to Rome, he enjoyed sufficient independence, due largely to his own personal prestige, to make his own mark on history; some of the impressive ruins of his great buildings, such as those at Samaria, still stand. With the end of his reign and the outbreak of fresh internal dissension, Rome took over the direct administration of the country under her procurators.

The rule of Roman procurators, including Pontius 60 Pilatus (A.D. 26–36), continued till the outbreak of open rebellion in A.D. 66 (see G. W. Wade, *NT History*, 57ff.). The whole country was seething with rebellion, fomented by religious agitators (among whom Rome classed John the Baptist). The centres of trouble were in the numerous groups and sects, especially those opposed to the Pharisees and the Sadducaean hierarchy. It was extremist groups such as the Zealots which gave most trouble (see below, §605*d*) and which led to the final outbreak. But it is in this whole sectarian movement that we find the key to an understanding of this century, not only of its political development, but also of its religious apocalyptic fermentation. Moreover, it is in this area of the background of the NT documents that the Qumrân discoveries have most light to shed.

Next to the Pharisees and Sadducees Josephus places **b** the **Essenes** as the 'third philosophy' of the Jews. As J. B. Lightfoot remarked (*Colossians and Philemon*, 80), the Essenes constitute the 'great enigma of Hebrew history'. This is not to say that we do not possess a fair amount of information on the subject: both Josephus and Philo report on the sect (BJ II, viii, 2; *Quod omnis probus liber*, §12), and the location of a large settlement of Essenes by the elder Pliny (*Hist. Nat.*, v, 15) in the area where the new Hebrew Scrolls were discovered is a fact of importance for the identification of the Qumrân sect with the Essenes. What makes any reconstruction of the history and character of these sectarians difficult is our dependence, hitherto, on sources which are Greek, not Hebrew: we see the Essenes through the eyes of Greek writers who are not above idealising Essenism or accommodating it to more familiar hellenistic patterns of thought. This does not mean, however, that some general idea of the origins and essential features of what has come to be called Essenism is no longer possible. The most widely accepted view derives the name 'Essene', 'Εσσαῖοι, from Syriac *ḥsayâ*, 'pious (ones)' (Lightfoot, op. cit., 351). It seems fairly certain that this sectarian movement within Judaism had its origins some time before the 2nd cent. B.C. (the Essenes are first mentioned by Josephus in the reign of Jonathan), and it may even have a remoter background in the ancient tribal asceticism of Israel. In the form in which we meet it in the pages of Josephus and Philo it emerges as a priestly and monastic (or semi-monastic) order of Jewish ascetics, opposed both historically and on principle to the Temple and its sacrificial cultus, and cultivating a strict *Apartheid* from the world of men and cities which it sought to ensure by an elaborate performance of baptismal rites. A sacred meal occupied a no less central place in the religion of the sect, and some form of communism of possessions was practised. Such a brief characterisation of Essenism takes no account of other features mentioned by Josephus or Philo which may or may not have belonged to the essential structure of the order, such as the Essene practice of divination, their peculiar methods of studying scripture (their devotion to Moses and the Law goes without saying); their rites of initiation into the order by stages of baptismal purification belong to their central rites of lustration.

The relation of the **Qumrân sectarians** to the **c** Essenes is still a debated problem, but the majority of scholars hold that the two groups, if not identical, are closely related (cf. M. Burrows, *The Dead Sea Scrolls*, 273ff.). The non-Pharisaic Palestinian sects in the 1st cent. B.C. appear, for the most part, to have been

605c fragmentations of a widespread baptising movement, characterised mainly by its opposition to the Pharisaic-Sadducean theocratic bureaucracy in Jerusalem, and substituting baptismal rites and a sacred meal for Temple sacrifice (cf. J. Thomas, *Le Mouvement Baptiste en Palestine et Syrie*). These 'non-conformist' sectarian 'Baptists' were even more radical in their interpretation of the Law and their nationalism and exclusiveness than the Pharisees themselves. They also observed a different calendar from the official calendar of the festivals agreed each year between Pharisees and Sadducees in Jerusalem. The movement, split up into different sectarian groupings, appears to have extended from Samaria in the north (possibly including a sect of Nasarenes located in the region of Gilead) to the Judaean desert in the south, and comprising, in addition to the various Samaritan heresies (cf. J. A. Montgomery, *The Samaritans*, 252ff.), other baptising and generally also ascetic sects such as the Masbotheans, the Morning Bathers (or Hemerobaptists), and the Sabaeans (see W. Brandt, *Die jüdischen Baptismen*). The Qumrân sectarians belonged to this widespread *mouvement baptiste*. In addition to their legalism, the Qumrân sect, like the Essenes, practised a form of community of property and cultivated also a prophetic type of religion in which we find a number of interesting points of contact with the NT (see M. Burrows, *The Dead Sea Scrolls*, 333ff.). The sect was also, like Pharisaism, at any rate in its hey-day, open to the reception of new ideas from its hellenistic and Syrian environments. (See further below, §607*ac* and §§614–19.)

d In addition to this *mouvement baptiste* mention must also be made of several other sectarian movements of the period, most of them political in character. Beyond the name, little is known about the **Herodians** except what the NT reports. They appear to have been less a religious sect than simply a party of the friends and supporters of the Herod family, in particular of Herod Antipas ; the 4th-cent. Greek father Epiphanius tells us that they regarded Herod as the Messiah. The party figures in the primitive traditions of the Gospels, from which we may perhaps infer that they were an important factor in the historical situation of that time, though they disappeared early from the Palestinian scene. The **Galileans** (cf. Ac. 5:37) are identified by Josephus with a group of Pharisaic zealots ; he tells us (Ant., XVIII, 1, 6) that their love of liberty was unconquerable (they regarded God alone as their only Lord and Master). He considers them important enough to be classed as a 'fourth philosophy' (next to Pharisees, Sadducees and Essenes). Again this group must have been important politically in the first century ; they no doubt represented an extreme form of Pharisaism. Another important group of Jewish nationality were the **Zealots** ; the Ζηλωταί were 'activists', who regarded themselves as the zealous agents of the wrath of God and the instruments of His deliverance of His people. Phinehas (Num. 25:10–13) was their ideal, and they kept alive the spirit of Maccabaean resistance (they may have included in their numbers descendants of the Maccabaean family). Josephus (BJ, IV, iii, 9) makes them a separate sect, but in this he is probably mistaken ; Hippolytus treats them as a branch of the Essene movement (*Refutatio omnium haeresium* ix, 26), but there were probably 'zealots' in all parties willing to unite for common action.

606a Some account of Roman rule in the 1st cent., preceding the destruction of Jerusalem (A.D. 70), and of the sporadic outbreaks of revolt and persecution (in the Diaspora), will be found elsewhere (see J. P. V. D. Balsdon, *The Roman Empire in the First Century*, W. D. Davies, *The Jewish State in the Hellenistic World*). To complete the sketch of historical background something must be said about the main events leading up to, and the course and character of, the final Jewish attempt to assert its independence, the Revolt of Bar-Cochba (*c.* A.D. 135).

In spite of the almost total destruction of the Jewish nation in A.D. 70, the conflict between Roman and Jew especially in Palestine continued unabated, ready to break out again at any time with fresh fury. The persecution of Christians was, in fact, only in a sense incidental to the imperial anti-Jewish pogrom, since Christians were classed as Jews. The specific charge preferred against Jews and Christians alike was one of *atheismus*, rejection of the old gods. In the short reign of Nerva (96–98), Domitian's harsh measures against the Jews were relaxed ; profession of the Jewish religion was officially no longer *atheism*, taxes on Jews were reduced and the common charge brought against Jews of tax evasion was dropped. It was the next Emperor Trajan, who, in pursuit of imperial expansion in the East, again came into open conflict with Judaism and prepared the ground for the final tragic flare-up under his successor Hadrian. 606b

Trajan's successor, the Emperor Hadrian, began with a Jewish policy of promises and concessions, including the promise to restore the Temple in Jerusalem ; and it was Rome's failure to keep this promise which led to the Second Revolt. In A.D. 130 Hadrian visited Palestine in person and reported all quiet to the Senate on his return. The Temple was to be rebuilt —but it was to be a Roman temple dedicated to Capitoline Jupiter, and Jerusalem was to be renamed *Aelia Capitolina*, making it the Rome of the East. The site of Golgotha, already a place of pilgrimage for Christians, was obliterated and replaced by a temple of Aphrodite (the imposing ruins of which are still extant).

Jewish reaction could not be long delayed : the old hatreds welled up. Secret arsenals were laid down and preparations for war extended far beyond Judaea. The revolt was finally led by a figure of heroic legend, known as Bar-Cochba or Bar-Cosiba, but it was the great teacher and scholar **Rabbi Akiba** who gave brain and heart to the movement. c

Bar-Cochba was to prove the Hannibal or Brennus of the **Second Jewish Revolt**. Nothing at all is known of his family origins or early life. His real name was Bar-Cosiba, where Cosiba appears to be a place name ; Bar-Cochba was a messianic name given him by Akiba. The story is that so powerful was the immediate and first impression that his physical appearance and personality made on Akiba that he declared : 'That is the King Messiah !' and at once applied to him the messianic proof-text, 'There shall come a Star out of Jacob' (Num. 24:17). So great were the hopes set by Akiba on his Star from Jacob that he proclaimed the imminent realisation of the messianic kingdom.

So far as Jewish sources are concerned there does not appear to have been any attempt to attribute supernatural powers to the new Messiah ; it is from pagan accounts we learn that he blew burning tow from his mouth so that he might seem to be breathing fire.

Much of this is heroic myth, deserving as little credence as opposite attempts of anti-Jewish minds to belittle the Jewish hero. He seems, at any rate, to have been a man of some stature, an inspiring leader in the tradition of the Maccabees, but with far greater military forces under his command ; Jewish sources put them at 400,000 ; the Hellenistic historian Dio Cassius gives the number as 580,000.

At first Hadrian paid little attention to the news from the East, but, as one report of defeat after another reached him, he sent out powerful reinforcements, under some of his best commanders. These fared no better than their predecessors. The situation had developed into a challenge to Roman power, as well as a serious threat to her whole empire in the East ; the Palestinian landslide might soon precipitate an avalanche.

Their initial successes gave rise to a false sense of security among the Jews ; the victory of Jewish arms seemed secure. Jerusalem itself appears to have been

606c in Jewish hands, though the Holy City played no part in this war. No doubt plans were afoot for the reconstruction of the Temple, but there is no mention of this in any records ; the situation was, in reality, too unsettled for such long-term schemes of rebuilding. To celebrate their independence Bar-Cochba had special coins struck (' the coins of the Revolt '). Bar-Cochba's state had been in existence two years (A.D. 132–4) before Hadrian took effective measures to quell the revolt. He finally recalled Julius Severus, one of his most capable commanders, from Britain, where he had just successfully crushed another freedom-loving people ; Severus was given the task of reconquering Judaea for Rome.

Julius Severus avoided a major battle and continued to engage the Jews in a slow and bitter war of attrition. Judaea was virtually under blockade. Roman tactics consisted in isolating groups or small bands of insurgents, and the Romans made the most of their advantage in cavalry in which the Jews were virtually entirely lacking : they also made the fullest use of the weapon of terror ; no quarter was ever given, captives being put to death immediately. The end came with the fall of the central Jewish defensive position at Bethar where Bar-Cochba and the flower of his remaining forces with numerous refugees were destroyed.

DEVELOPMENT OF RELIGIOUS IDEAS

607a The religion of ancient Israel, in post-exilic as in pre-exilic times, was the product of its history. The most important events religiously as well as politically were the successive dominations of Palestine by the Seleucid and the Roman empires. The fanatical resistance of the Jewish people to their conquerors led not only to the rise of an independent state under the Hasmonaeans, and, for a brief period, of a second Jewish state under Bar-Cochba, but—and this was of fundamental importance for the history of Judaism as a religion—to the engrafting on the stock of the ancient Hebrew monotheistic culture of a new set of religious ideas and beliefs, with a new kind of literature, apocalyptic, as its chief vehicle of expression. The old biblical ideas continued to live on ; there were times, especially of renewed political hope, when the ancient Davidic expectation of political restoration flared up again. But these were short-lived, and the main orientation of the Jewish mind in this period was towards a supernatural and extra-mundane salvation. It is for this reason that these centuries are so important for the student of the NT, for it is within this category of religion and literature the NT itself falls.

The origins of this religious development are to be traced ultimately to Persian influence. No discoveries in recent years have altered the judgment of C. W. King and G. F. Moore on this question : ' Now it was from this very creed (of Zoroaster, *c.* 5th cent. B.C.) that the Jews derived all the angelology of their religion . . . the belief in a future state ; of rewards and punishments, the latter carried on in a fiery lake ; . . . the soul's immortality, and the Last Judgment—all of them essential parts of the Zoroastrian scheme, and recognised by Josephus as the fundamental doctrines of the Judaism of his own times ' (*The Gnostics and their Remains* (London 1887), 120). ' The eschatology of Judaism has an unmistakable affinity to that of the Zoroastrian religion in the separation of the souls of the righteous and wicked at death, etc. The resemblances are so striking that many scholars are convinced that this whole system of ideas was appropriated by the Jews from the Zoroastrians, as well as that Jewish angelology and demonology were developed under Babylonian and Persian influence ' (*Judaism II*, 394). It seems likely too that the new religious rites, especially that of baptism, had a similar origin (cf. J. Thomas, *Le Mouvement Baptiste en Palestine et Syrie* (Gembloux 1935), 417ff.).

This does mean that such ideas remained a foreign 60
element in Jewish religion, without becoming assimilated to the ancient Hebrew tradition. The idea of **life after death,** for example, is an apparent instance of a new departure, since it stands in complete contrast to the old ideas about Sheol. Yet the idea occurred, perhaps independently, to the prophets (cf. Isa. 26:19 ; Dan. 12:2, 3), and, when it did lay hold on the Hebrew mind, it was in response to the tragic loss of the flower of Jewish manhood in the Maccabaean persecutions and martyrdoms (cf. 2 Mac. 7:9). It is typical for Hebrew thought that in its earliest, crudest form, it should have meant nothing more than the revivification and reconstitution of the physical body (cf. also 2 Bar. 49:1–50:4). It was in the refinement and development of such ideas which occur independently to all peoples that Hebrew borrowing on Persian sources becomes evident. When the doctrine of the immortality of the soul is professed among Jews (cf. Jos. BJ II, viii, 11) we may be sure that we have a foreign importation. On the other hand, the Pharisaic doctrine of a glorious spiritual body after death (cf. 2 Bar. 51:2–10 ; 1 C. 15:44) bears the mark of Hebrew originality. The doctrine, on the other hand, that the individual becomes ' like the angels ', which appears to be that of the Qumrân scrolls (cf. Lk. 20:36), looks more foreign than native (see further, §§614–19). The whole eschatological scheme, however, of the Last Judgment, rewards and punishments, etc., within which immortality is achieved, is manifestly Zoroastrian in origin and inspiration.

Such new religious developments did not, of course, in any way affect the fundamentals of the traditional Hebrew religion, its monotheism and its emphasis on the Law. If anything, they intensified Jewish national feeling ; and they are found side by side with the rigorous observance of the Law that was reintroduced by Ezra and Nehemiah at the time of the restoration.

The channel by which these new ideas reached the c
popular mind ran through the sects or religious parties. There is no doubt that the Pharisees, in particular, played an important role in this respect. T. W. Manson writes : ' The living branch of Judaism was the Pharisaic . . . I am not concerned to decide the question whether their characteristic doctrines were derived from Persia or were the development—under Persian influence—of the ideas already implicit in Hebrew religion. The point is that the new ideas were developed, and developed by the Pharisees ' (*The Servant Messiah*, 20). But other equally important sectaries, especially in the 1st cent., were introducing new religious ideas into Judaism. The movement of baptising sectarians, e.g. from Samaria to the Dead Sea, brought not only their baptismal and other rites from the farther East. It seems entirely probable that the beginnings of Gnosticism are to be traced to this sectarian ferment within Judaism in the 1st cent. B.C. ; the ' gnosticism ' of Simon Magus about the year A.D. 35 (cf. Ac. 8:9ff.), according to which the Samaritans regarded Simon as ' the great power of God ', was not an isolated phenomenon of this sectarian nonconformity of the 1st cent. B.C. (see further below on 1 Enoch, §§608*d*, 609*a*). An incipient type of Gnosticism can also be traced in the DSS.

This new kind of religion was given literary expres- d
sion in a new type of ' prophecy ', called apocalyptic, the beginnings of which are to be found already in the later sections of Isa. 24–7, and in other late books such as Ezek., Jl, Zech. 12–14 and Dan. Its chief extra-canonical representatives are the various writings ascribed to Enoch and Baruch, *The Testaments of the Twelve Patriarchs*, 4 Ezra, and in some of the new Hebrew scrolls. As contrasted with the prophetic writings, the main features of this apocalyptic literature are : (*a*) it is pseudonymous, a book is attributed to a past worthy of Israel's history who is made to depict in visions the writer's conception of the eschata ; (*b*) it is marked by excessive employment of symbolism, in particular, animal figures, and makes free use of

7d mythology (the Book of Rev. is a typical example of this kind of literature); (*c*) it is almost exclusively concerned with eschatology, the Last Judgment, Heaven and Hell, the Life After Death, etc.; it develops a conception of a transcendent Messiah in striking contrast to the political or Davidic Messiah of the OT prophets. The latter continues to occupy a central place in Jewish thought, but even this figure comes in time to be transformed.

8a **The Messianic Hope**—The classic conception of the OT of the restoration of the glories of the Kingdom of David under a 'Son of David' (2 Sam. 7; Ps. 2; Isa. 6, 11:4, 56:18–20, etc.) remains central in the thought of Judaism. It is the main form of expectation in the Qumrân scrolls (see below). It is especially in Pharisaic Judaism, however, and in particular in the *Psalms of Solomon* (1st cent. B.C.) that we find the fullest expression given to this idea in our period. There is nothing superhuman or supernatural about this figure: the Anointed Lord (or the Anointed of the Lord) is to reign as an actual king of David's line in a restored Israel. Nevertheless, he is to be raised up by God Himself, to whom alone is known the time of his coming (17:23, 47, 18:6). His rule is to be spiritual, holy, wise and just. He is not to be an aggressive conqueror trusting in force of arms, but in Jehovah (cf. Isa. 9:6; Zech. 9:11; Mic. 4:1). At the same time, he is to overthrow the supremacy of the Gentile rule and to destroy them utterly from Jerusalem and the borders of Israel (17:25, 27, 31), driving out also the renegades of Israel itself who have obtained unlawful possession of the land. In general, the figure may be described as 'Solomonic', but it is the figure of one 'greater than Solomon', King David's 'greater son', who is to restore Israel and gather the dispersion into a new Jerusalem.

It is in its ethical features that this ideal of a personal Messiah of Pharisaism constitutes so remarkable a *praeparatio evangelica*: the ideal Messianic king's personal purity from sin, e.g., is to be the measure of his authority (17:41); and under him all his subjects shall become holy and 'sons of God' (17:30; cf. Rom. 8:15; Mt. 5:45, etc.).

b The new Hebrew scrolls know of three coming eschatological deliverers of the true Israel, of which two have been described as 'Messiahs', a priestly Messiah and a secular Messiah, the warrior Son of David of traditional Jewish belief; the third expected deliverer is the **prophet like Moses** promised at Dt. 18:15–18.

There is reason to believe that this last figure was one of the liveliest popular expectations in the NT period, among Samaritans as well as Jews and Christians, as we learn from the patristic writers as well as from the NT itself (Jn 1:31, 6:14; cf. 7:40; Ac. 3:22ff., 7:37). How prominent a place it occupied in the beliefs of Qumrân, it is difficult to judge: apart from a reference to the prophet in the document called *The Manual of Discipline* and the occurrence of Dt. 18:15, 18 as a proof-text in a small collection of *testimonia*, there is nothing else to guide us. It is possible that the sect at one time regarded their founder, the Teacher of Righteousness, as this promised Prophet.

The **Qumrân sect** believed not only in the Davidic Messiah, especially in his role as coming conqueror of the heathen, but also in an eschatological High Priest who (as one would expect in a priestly sect) takes precedence of the secular leader, e.g. at a banquet described in the so-called *Order of the Congregation* at which both are present. The two figures have been held to correspond to the Messianic High Priest of the *Testament of Levi* 18 and the Davidic king of the *Testament of Judah* 24, and to the Moses-Aaron, Joshua-Zerubbabel, and, in later times, Eleazar-Bar-Cochba partnership.

The Davidic figure known as 'the Prince' (as in Ezek.) is described in a collection of blessings, in the following terms:

For the Blessing of the Prince of the Congregation,... 608b
May the Lord exalt thee to an everlasting height, and
as a tower of strength on a lofty rampart.
Thou shalt smite the peoples with the power of Thy
word (*lit.* mouth);
With thy rod thou shalt lay waste . . . the earth,
And with the breath of thy lips thou shalt slay the
wicked,
With a spirit of counsel and eternal might;
A spirit of knowledge and of the fear of God;
Righteousness shall be the girdle of Thy loins,
And faithfulness the girdle of Thy reins;
And He will set thy horn with iron and thy hooves
with brass . . .
. . . Thou shalt tread down the nations as mud in
the streets,
For God has raised thee up [established thee] as the
sceptre of rulers.
They shall come before thee and worship thee,
And all the nations will serve thee,
And by His holy name He will make thee great
And thou shalt be as a lion
. . . tearing and there is none to restore; . . .

It is possible that it was this form of expectation of two Anointed leaders, a Davidic king and a priestly Messiah, which gave strength and inspiration to the Second Jewish Revolt, as it had very probably also done in the First. The Battle Scroll (a description of the impending Armageddon) has a figure, in addition to the High Priest, who closely resembles the Warrior Messiah.

A totally different form of messianic expectation is c that which derives from Dan. 7:13, the vision of one 'like a **son of man**', coming with the clouds of heaven to the ancient of days to receive an eternal kingdom. For Daniel the 'one like a son of man' is symbolic of a future glorified Israel, destined to triumph over the heathen empires. The figure of the Son of Man reappears in 1 Enoch (37–71), but there it is no longer a symbol but an individual, a supernatural being who is to appear at the end of time as the vicegerent of God to judge mankind. This supernatural Judge or Messiah is also called 'the Elect One' and 'the Righteous One'; both titles are applied to Christ in Lk.-Ac.; Lk. 9:35, 23:35; Ac. 3:14, 7:52, 22:14. He also reappears in 2 Esd. 13, the Man from the sea.

Until recently the section of Enoch called the *Similitudes* (37–71) in which the Son of Man appears has been d assumed to be both Jewish and pre-Christian. But, like 2 Enoch, now conclusively shown to be syncretistic work with Christian elements, the *Similitudes* have not been freed of all suspicion of Christian influence or tampering; no trace of these chapters of 1 Enoch has been found at Qumrân. It may be too (even granted a pre-Christian Jewish book) that earlier interpretation was wrong in assuming too hastily that the central figure was an individual, not, as in Dan., corporate and symbolic of Israel; perhaps the idea of the Son of Man in Enoch, like the idea of the Servant of the Lord in Second Isaiah, was both individual and corporate. An older tradition of Son of Man belief appears too to be embedded in chs. 70–1, where the Son of Man is unmistakably identified with the glorified patriarch Enoch himself. In that case we may require to assume a pre-Christian form of Jewish mystic 'gnosticism', where the figure of Enoch was the centre of belief as a divine-human mediator, and coming world Judge. But such a 'mysticism' may well all be post-Christian and derivative, as much in the mysticism of the Hebrew 3 Enoch appears to be.

The Eschata—The origins of the copious growth of 609a apocalyptic speculations about the Eschata, the Last Judgment, Kingdom of God, Heaven and Hell, etc. are to be traced to a reinterpretation of the Day of the Lord of the OT prophets. Originally the Day of the Lord was to be a day of Judgment on Israel (as in Am. and the pre-exilic prophets), but, after the Exile, the Day of the Lord came more and more to be

609a looked on as a day of triumph for Israel, and of doom for the heathen. This latter idea is perpetuated in apocalyptic writings, but with a new extra-mundane orientation. The Day of the Lord, when Israel is to be fully and finally vindicated before the Gentiles, will be the end of all history : Israel will be glorified and the heathen world destroyed. An important modification of this cruder eschatology in the direction of Am. and pre-exilic prophecy, is to be found in Dan. 7 where ' the saints of the Most High ' are not to be identified with the nation, but with the true spiritual Israel within the nation (even the righteous dead are to share in the triumph of the true Israel by rising from the dust of the earth, 12:2). The conception is further developed and transformed in 1 Enoch, where the universalist note of Second Isaiah is struck and the idea of judgment applied (as it had been in the OT) no less to the individual than to the nation or group : the Last Judgment is no longer a national vindication or the vindication of a purified remnant within the nation ; all men must finally submit to the divine judgment and their destiny will be decided solely on the basis of righteous or unrighteous conduct in their lifetime.

Out of this period of Judaism there thus emerges one of the classic conceptions of religion, the idea of a great and universal **Judgment**, both of the living and the dead, which the NT inherited and reinterpreted in relation to the Second Coming of Christ. It is central not only in post-exilic Judaism, but in the whole scheme and structure of the Christian religion. In this respect the place it occupies in Michael Angelo's famous murals in the Sistine Chapel is symbolic : behind everything, the creation of the world and the history of the chosen people, beyond the Altar and the drama of Christian worship, the Last Judgment looms, universal and inevitable.

b The precise expression **Kingdom of God** nowhere occurs in apocalyptic literature in its familiar NT sense, but the essential idea of the divine reign is no less prominent in these sources than in the OT itself, only it is again a divine rule or sovereignty to be established after the consummation of all things through the Last Judgment.

In an important passage in the *Assumption of Moses*, ch. 10, we are introduced to a further development, which is again taken up and reinterpreted in relation to Christ in NT scripture. The reign of God will not only be established by a judgment (and destruction) of men and nations. Evil is conceived as a cosmic force and the world as the Kingdom of Satan and his demonic powers (an idea found also in the new Hebrew scrolls) ; and the final triumph of the reign of God will bring the total destruction of the reign of Satan.

And then His Kingdom shall appear throughout all
His creation,
And then Satan shall be no more
And sorrow shall depart with him . . .
For the Heavenly One will arise from His royal
throne,
And He will go forth from His Holy habitation
With indignation and wrath on account of His
sons . . .
For the Most High will arise, the Eternal God alone,
And He will appear to punish the Gentiles,
And He will destroy all idols
And thou, Israel, shalt be happy, . . .
And God will exalt thee,
And He will cause thee to approach to the heaven
of the stars.

As has been noted, this same type of dualism is characteristic of the DSS. The Age is an evil one ; there is a conflict between the forces of light and of darkness, between the spirit of truth and the spirit of error (as in the Johannine writings but also in the *Testaments of the Twelve Patriarchs*). The Battle Scroll describes an eschatological warfare in which the ' children of light ' defeat the ' children of darkness '. 60

c Speculations about **heaven and hell** are particularly characteristic of the Enoch literature. 1 Enoch develops the idea of heavenly abodes for the righteous after death (and before the Last Judgment) and of places where the wicked are held until the Judgment and their punishment in Gehenna (e.g. 1 Enoch 27:61). The abode of the righteous is known as Paradise, a Persian word for a park or garden, and the picture of heaven is filled out by descriptions of a restored Eden. The opposite of Paradise is **Gehenna**, originally the ' vale of Hinnom ' south of Jerusalem, at one time a place for burning the city's rubbish and associated with the Moloch sacrifices of ancient times (2 Kg. 16:3, 2:6), but now become an apocalyptic symbol for the place of horror and torment for the wicked. It was the ill reputation assigned to this place by Jer. (7:32, 19:6 ; cf. Isa. 31:9, 66:24) which led to its adoption by the Apocalyptists as a symbol for the punishment of the wicked in the fires of torment after the Judgment (cf. Enoch 90:28f., 27:1f., 54:1f., 56:3f.). The graphic descriptions of this place in the apocalypses are notably absent from the NT, which uses the image mainly in a symbolic sense.

Whereas, however, Gehenna is used to symbolise the final end of the wicked, it should be noted that Paradise is an intermediary state or place only. Heaven itself is represented in Apocalyptic literature as ' the renewal of all things ' in heaven and earth, ' a new heaven and a new earth ' (as in the book of Rev.), the main OT source for which being Isa. 65 (where the return of the conditions of Eden is envisaged). So also in the DSS we meet with the idea of the restoration of ' the glory of Adam ' and the New Creation.

The Close of an Epoch—What may be termed apocalyptic Judaism came to a virtual end with the destruction of Jerusalem in A.D. 70. It was to be succeeded by the perpetuation in the Judaism of the rabbis (the descendants of the Pharisees), of the religion of the Book, the legalism and exclusive nationalism, which have gone to the making of what is called ' normative ' Judaism. The Judaism of the apocalypses, with its fanatical political hopes, revived again, for a brief period, side by side with the Judaism of the Law, in the Bar-Cochba period : but it ceased to exist, except in esoteric groups, in A.D. 135. Its religious successor was to be found in the religion of the NT, not of the Talmud and Mishnah.

Bibliography—E. Bevan, *Jerusalem under the High Priests* (1904) ; M. Black, ' The Eschatology of the Similitudes of Enoch ', JTS, N.S. 3 (1952) ; M. Burrows, *The Dead Sea Scrolls* (1955) ; H. Graetz, *Geschichte der Juden* (1888) ; T. W. Manson, *The Servant Messiah* (1953) ; J. A. Montgomery, *The Samaritans* (1907) ; W. O. E. Oesterley, *The Jews and Judaism during the Greek Period* (1941) ; H. H. Rowley, *The Zadokite Fragments and the Dead Sea Scrolls* (1952) ; J. Thomas, *Le Mouvement Baptiste en Palestine et Syrie* (1935).

See also Bibliography to *Contemporary Jewish Religion*.

THE ROMAN EMPIRE IN THE FIRST CENTURY

BY J. P. V. D. BALSDON

0a By Julius Caesar's will, made six months before he was murdered on 15 March 44 B.C., C. Octavius, grandson of his sister Julia, was left as chief heir to his estate and adopted into the Julian family. Octavius was 18 years old when Caesar was killed and on adoption he became C. Julius Caesar Octavianus (Octavian). Devotion to Caesar's memory was so strong among Caesar's troops and veterans that in the autumn of 44 two legions deserted the consul Antony and joined Octavian, together with a number of Caesar's discharged veterans. With the acquisition of this private army, Octavian adroitly outmanoeuvred first the Senate, then Antony and Lepidus, with whom he combined in a triumvirate at the end of 43. The tyrannicides Brutus and Cassius were defeated at Philippi in 42. Lepidus retired into private life, and survived. Antony, with Cleopatra, committed suicide after losing the battle of Actium in 31.

People might—and for centuries did—question the integrity of much that Octavian had done in the thirteen years in which he was making himself master of the Roman world, but nobody has ever questioned the immensity of his final achievement. After decades of civil war he restored peace—the *Pax Augusta*; for Augustus (Σεβαστός) was the name which he accepted when in 27 B.C. he 'restored the republic'. The 'restored republic' was, of course, the republic with a difference. Augustus was, and in each successive year, it seemed, would continue to be, one of the consuls. Augustus, too, was entrusted with those provinces in which the greater part of the Roman army was stationed, on the understanding that he could remain in Rome and govern them by deputies (*legati Augusti pro praetore*) appointed by himself.

The settlement lasted for four years. Then in 23 B.C. a serious conspiracy was detected, and Augustus appreciated that the reality of his power must be more adroitly concealed. So he ceased to hold the consulship and instead assumed the power (without the office) of tribune, the *tribunicia potestas*. This, with special grants such as a seat between the consuls in the Senate and the right to claim priority for business which he introduced in the Senate, restored to him the authority in Rome which, in resigning the consulship, he had abandoned. As for imperial administration, he was granted an overriding right to interfere in the affairs of the 'public provinces', whose governors were appointed by the Senate, if on any occasion he should think this necessary.

This was, to all intents and purposes, a final settlement. The 'principate' had now taken shape. Augustus was Princeps—First Man in the State—and men referred to him as such. His personal prestige, the familiar republican concept of *auctoritas*, was unrivalled, as he pointed out himself in the *Res Gestae*, the autobiographical record which he prepared for inscription on his mausoleum. In his deportment there was no sign of the autocrat, nothing to remind people of his great-uncle, the Dictator; on the contrary it was *civilitas* that he embodied.

b Inefficiency, no less than corruption, disfigured senatorial administration under the Republic and 610b
helped to bring about the Republic's collapse, and as Augustus set about the task of reconstruction, it was clear that, apart from closer supervision, far more talent was required for responsible posts in administration than the senatorial class could supply. So a second 'public service', the equestrian service, was established.

To engage in a senatorial career a man required to have property to the value of a million sesterces and to possess on his tunic the broad stripe (the *latus clavus*) for which, if his father was not a senator, he made application to the Princeps. To engage in an equestrian career, it was necessary to possess 400,000 sesterces. While the financial secretaries of public provinces were quaestors (senators), the financial secretaries of the imperial provinces were procurators (equestrian). Equestrians commanded infantry and cavalry units of the auxiliary troops and, on the Emperor's nomination, they governed the less important provinces. The most important posts for which they alone were eligible were those of Controller of Food (*Praefectus Annonae*), whose duties were of the first importance for morale in the city of Rome, 200,000 of whose citizen-residents were entitled to a free monthly corn ration; the Prefect of the Praetorian Guard (at first nine cohorts, mostly stationed outside Rome under Augustus, after that with barracks just outside the city wall); and the Prefect (Governor) of Egypt, a province which senators were not allowed even to visit without a permit from the Emperor.

The Emperor was responsible in the last resort for the administration of his own provinces, for all questions concerning the fighting-services (including supplies, posting, promotion, and gratuities), the food supply, in particular of the city of Rome and of the armies, frontier policy and general questions of imperial finance. This meant that in Rome he needed a large, dependable and, at the top, a highly skilled staff of what today would be called civil servants. That senators should occupy such dependent positions was out of keeping with Roman tradition, and equestrians were not employed regularly until the time of Hadrian. What Augustus did was to follow the tradition of rich private individuals, and to build up a great private service of freedmen and slaves, for whom vast office buildings were constructed, on the Forum side of the Palatine. These freedmen and slaves were organised departmentally, and at the heads of the various departments were freedmen of the highest ability—in particular the Emperor's financial secretary (*a rationibus*), his personal secretary (*ab epistulis*), and his legal secretary (*a libellis*). Here and in certain of the equestrian posts under the Emperor's direct supervision were the seeds, though they did not germinate for a century and a half, of ultimate bureaucracy.

Augustus' military and administrative command c
(his *imperium*) and his tribunician power were voted to him by the Senate at regular intervals, and it was a matter of the first importance to him to ensure that his new form of government should survive when he

610c himself was dead. It was unthinkable that Rome should return to the inefficient cut-throat amateurishness of republican government; on the other hand, it would have been in conflict with the whole spirit of his settlement for him to attempt to name a successor. The problem presented itself early, for he was seriously ill in 23 B.C.; he had no son, only a daughter, Julia. All that he could do was to associate others with himself in administration, by securing to them the grant of *imperium* and of *tribunicia potestas* like his own; and, wisely or unwisely, he chose to marry such men to Julia. There were, in succession, three of them: Marcellus, his nephew; M. Agrippa, his invaluable chief-of-staff, and finally his stepson, Tiberius Claudius Nero. When Augustus died in A.D. 14, Tiberius, a man with a distinguished military career behind him, was already a full associate in both *imperium* and *tribunicia potestas*, but he was a man whose private life Augustus had wrecked. His succession to Augustus was unpopular in Rome, both because it marked the continuance of the principate, whose inevitability some stubborn republicans still refused to accept, and because of the morose and unsympathetic character of Tiberius himself.

d Tiberius was 54 when he became Princeps, and he lived to the age of 77. He was conscientious and efficient and in general the provinces were well governed under him; but at Rome from 23 onwards, when his only son Drusus and his adopted son and nephew Germanicus were dead, public life was disfigured by the steadily increasing horror of trials for treason (*maiestas*), from few of which men escaped with their lives, such trials being held for the most part before the Senate. If Tiberius did nothing to encourage these trials, he did nothing to suppress them either; and in 26, perhaps through fear of assassination, with great irresponsibility, he retired to live on the island of Capri. Sejanus, sole Prefect of the Praetorian Guard, whom alone he trusted, took advantage of his opportunity, but his conspiracy was unmasked in 31. When Tiberius died in 37, Germanicus' son Gaius (Caligula), 25 years old and completely unprepared for his new responsibilities, succeeded; he was murdered after three and a half years of capricious despotism. His uncle, Claudius, brother of Germanicus, previously considered by his family to be no more than an eccentric, if gifted, pedant, was proclaimed Emperor, against the wish of the Senate, on the impulse of the Praetorian Guard; he was 49 years old, and ruled for nearly fourteen years, from 41 to 54. The conquest of Britain, planned by Gaius, was accomplished in 43; recognition was given to the important services of freedmen in the imperial administration by allowing greater prominence in public life to the most outstanding of them, particularly the *ab epistulis*, Narcissus and the *a rationibus*, Pallas—a move highly offensive to conservative prejudice—and a liberal policy was followed both in the extension of Roman *civitas* and in widening the field outside Italy from which the Senate was recruited. Literary sources represent Claudius as the tool of his scheming freedmen and successive wives; but the multitude of his enactments, preserved on stone or on papyrus, distinguished in every case by his markedly individual manner of thought and expression, prove him the author of the enlightened policy which marked the whole of his administration. His successor Nero (his great-nephew, stepson, and adopted son) ruled well as long as he enjoyed good advisers (Seneca and the Prefect of the Praetorian Guard, Burrus), but after Seneca had been forced into retirement and Burrus died in 62, he was the victim of bad advisers and of his own wilful and irresponsible aestheticism. At Rome the great fire of 64—the prelude to the first persecution of the Christians—was followed by the very serious conspiracy of Piso in 65. Three years later the largest of the Gallic provinces revolted under its governor Vindex, himself a Gaul by origin; the revolt was suppressed by the army stationed on the Upper 61
Rhine, but Sulpicius Galba, an austere man of good family with a creditable record of public service, who was legate of Hispania Tarraconensis and who had supported Vindex, was proclaimed Emperor by his troops. Except, naturally, among the armies on the Rhine, he received widespread support in the provinces and in Rome, and Nero, who had returned earlier in the year from a tour of Greece, committed suicide.

Galba was accepted as Emperor by the Senate; but in January 69 the armies on the Rhine proclaimed the governor of Lower Germany, A. Vitellius, son of a distinguished father, Emperor, but when they reached Italy, it was to fight not Galba but Otho, who had killed him. Victory over Otho made Vitellius Emperor, but he was defeated at the second battle of Bedriacum by the legions of the Danube and of the East, who had risen in favour of Vespasian, then commanding the armies in the siege of Jerusalem, who had been proclaimed Emperor at Alexandria on 1 July. The records of Galba, Otho, and Vitellius during their short principates gave nobody cause to shed tears over their failure to consolidate their rule.

From 70 to 96 Rome was governed by the Emperors e
of the Flavian house (by Vespasian till 79, his elder son Titus from 79 to 81, and Domitian, his younger son, from 81 to 96). While the Emperors down to Nero had sprung from the Julii and the Claudii, families distinguished in republican history, the Flavians were a middle-class Italian family. Vespasian's father had been a tax-collector. The former extravagance of social life at Rome was at an end, although the extravagance of public building continued. Nero's Golden House was destroyed, and on part of its site the Colosseum was built by Vespasian; and Domitian's palace was the start of the spectacular *domus Augustiana* which spread over the whole of the south-eastern half of the Palatine. As concerned the form of government, the events of 69 had demonstrated so clearly the power of the armies (men uninterested in constitutional niceties) to make and unmake emperors, that there was no longer any need to mask the reality of imperial power. The Flavian emperors, therefore, did not hesitate to hold the consulship frequently; Vespasian and Titus were censors (as no earlier emperors but Claudius had been) and Domitian assumed the title *Censor Perpetuus*. Vespasian even placed his son Titus and another senator in command of the Praetorian Guard.

Vespasian restored a stable administration to the empire; Titus' rule was short and ineffective; Domitian, a man of strong character and great efficiency, but disfigured by a streak of sadistic cruelty, was confronted, through no fault of his own, by more serious frontier troubles on Rhine and Danube than any previous emperor. He fought one war on the Rhine and two on the Danube, without any success to balance the heavy losses that were suffered; there was a military revolt on the Rhine in 88 and the threat of conspiracy in Rome in 93. His rule became more and more oppressive, and there was a return to the treason trials which Rome had suffered under Tiberius. In 96 Domitian was killed, having lost support everywhere except in the armies.

Nerva, whom the Senate proclaimed to succeed him, f
was an old man and would certainly have gone the way of Galba if he had not at once adopted a man who commanded the army's support. This was Trajan, a Roman born in Spain, then campaigning on the Rhine. Trajan succeeded in 98 at Nerva's death, and ruled until 117. He was completely successful in restoring Roman fortunes on the northern frontiers and after his second Dacian war (105–6) the kingdom of Dacia (modern Rumania) was annexed, and made a Roman province. We are assured by his contemporaries, Tacitus and the younger Pliny, that his government was considerate; and we have unique evidence of his care for the welfare and good govern-

10f ment of the provinces in the letters which he wrote to Pliny in the years 111 to 113 when, because of its unsatisfactory condition, Bithynia was taken from the control of the Senate and placed under the Emperor's supervision. Trajan died in the East in 117, after annexing Armenia and campaigning against the Parthians in Mesopotamia—a campaign whose ultimate purpose is anything but clear. Hadrian succeeded him, and Rome and the Empire both settled down to a century of good and wise administration.

1a More and more, important questions of domestic and imperial policy, instead of being discussed by the Senate, were settled by the Princeps, often after discussion with his counsellors (who were called 'amici principis', if their relation to him was a close one), but we have little first-hand evidence of such consultations. There was a corresponding change in the life of senators. For senators under the Republic political life in Rome, particularly the tenure of magistracies, was a primary, provincial administration a secondary, activity; under the Empire the position was reversed. The biography of Agricola by his son-in-law Tacitus illustrates the change. Agricola's career as a soldier and as a provincial administrator was a distinguished one; during his magistracies and as a senator, he did little of interest or importance.

There were no appeal courts in criminal cases at Rome. As courts of the first instance, the praetor's jury courts of the Republic (the *quaestiones*) continued, but the important criminal cases were heard either by the Emperor, sitting with a *consilium* of advisers, or by the Senate, whose function as a court of law was not republican, but started with Augustus. Impeachment of ex-governors of public provinces normally took place before the Senate; when a case was referred from the provinces to Rome either on the authority of a provincial governor or because the accused was a Roman citizen and, as such, entitled to claim trial in Rome, it normally went (like that of St Paul, Ac. 22:25–29, 25:10–12) to the Emperor, who also heard cases which had to do with members of the armed forces.

b Julius Caesar's Gallic wars had advanced the Roman Empire to the Rhine, and expensive military failures across the Rhine between 9 and 16 showed the conquest of Germany to be unfeasible; so that the Rhine and Danube were accepted as the northern boundaries of the Empire, garrisoned by standing armies in permanent legionary camps (*castra*) or auxiliary fortresses (*castella*). The large standing army on the Rhine was prepared for trouble from German tribes across the river and also to deal with insurrection at their back in Gaul, as happened in 21 and, more seriously, when Vindex revolted against Nero. The only time when there was serious danger was when in 69–70, because of the civil wars, the army on the Rhine was seriously depleted. In 69 the Danube was crossed by marauders from the North for the first time, and here the pressure became more and more dangerous, and was only arrested, for half a century or so, by Trajan. In the East lay Parthia, the sole surviving power comparable with Rome, but internal dissensions and frontier troubles in the north and east absorbed the whole of Parthian attention, and there was never any serious danger of her invading the Roman Empire. Recurrent trouble with Parthia, especially under Nero, had to do with the position of Armenia, across the Upper Euphrates, which, for the sake of prestige, both Rome and Parthia wished to control as a client kingdom. Trajan annexed it and made it a province, but Hadrian abandoned it.

c Rome administered her empire directly through provinces or, in the case of districts on the fringe which were not thought ready for direct administration, through client kings. The public provinces were, in general, the most civilised and in none of them except Africa were any legions stationed; their governors were proconsuls (ἀνθύπατοι: Ac. 13:7 (Cyprus); 18:12 (Achaea)), and were chosen by lot or appointed directly in the Senate. The imperial 611c
provinces, whose governors were appointed by the Emperor, were of four sorts: those in which more than one legion was stationed, whose governors were ex-consuls (e.g. P. Sulpicius Quirinius, legate of Syria in A.D. 6; Lk. 2:2), and whose legionary commanders were normally ex-praetors; those with a single legion (like Judaea after 70), or with no legion at all, whose governors were ex-praetors; Egypt, with an equestrian governor (called *Praefectus Aegypti*), and two equestrian legionary commanders under him; and provinces (like Judaea before 66) governed by equestrian procurators or *praefecti* in which only auxiliary troops were stationed (cf. Ac. 10:1).

The public provinces at the time of Augustus' d
death were Hispania Baetica, Gallia Narbonensis, Macedonia, Achaea, Asia, Bithynia, Cyprus, Crete, and Cyrene, Africa (with its one legion) and Sicily. Africa and Asia were the most distinguished of these appointments, and were usually held by ex-consuls about fifteen years after their consulship.

Imperial provinces with more than one legion stationed in them at the time of Augustus' death were Hispania Tarraconensis (3); Lower Germany (the northern section of the west bank of the Rhine) (4); Upper Germany (the southern section of the west bank of the Rhine) (4); Pannonia (3); Dalmatia (2); Moesia (2); Syria (4); Egypt (2). Imperial provinces without legions, governed usually by ex-praetors, were Lusitania, Gallia Lugdunensis, Aquitania, Belgica, Galatia; those governed by equestrian procurators or *praefecti* were Rhaetia, Noricum, Sardinia-Corsica (since 6 B.C.) and, since A.D. 6, Judaea.

Judaea, a client kingdom under Herod the Great, became a second-class imperial province in A.D. 6, two years after Herod's death; it was governed by an equestrian procurator and Caesarea Sebaste on the coast was wisely chosen instead of Jerusalem as the headquarters of the Roman administration (cf. Ac. 23:31–5; 25:4–6). This arrangement was interrupted from 41 to 44 when Claudius allowed Agrippa to rule Judaea as client king, and ended with the Jewish revolt of 66.

Under Tiberius Cappadocia passed from the status of client kingdom to being an imperial province governed by an equestrian procurator; Gaius separated Numidia (with the legion) from Africa, and so removed the anomaly of a legion stationed in a public province. Two fresh legions were raised for the invasion of Britain, which Claudius accomplished successfully in 43; also, under Claudius, a number of new second-class imperial provinces were established, administered by equestrian procurators: Thrace, Mauretania Caesariensis, Mauretania Tingitana (both freshly annexed) and, on the death of Agrippa in 44, once again, Judaea.

With the two legions raised by Gaius or Claudius e
for the invasion of Britain and a new legion raised by Nero himself, the army had risen from 25 to 28 legions at the end of Nero's reign, stationed 1 in Spain, 1 in Gallia Lugdunensis (a temporary posting), 4 in Britain, 4 in Lower Germany, 3 in Upper Germany, 2 in Pannonia, 1 in Dalmatia, 3 in Moesia, 3 in Syria, 3 in Judaea (for the war which had broken out in 66), 2 in Egypt, and 1 in Numidia.

Vespasian was responsible for two important changes in the eastern part of the Empire. A new first-class imperial military province with two legions was created on the Upper Euphrates, out of Galatia, Cappadocia, Pontus Polemoniacus and Armenia Minor and, once the Jewish war was over, Judaea was made an imperial province with a regular garrison of one legion.

In the East Trajan made a province of Arabia Petraea; in the West there had, since the accession of Domitian, been a great change in the military centre of gravity, as legions had been switched from the Rhine to the Danube to meet increasing pressure from

611e the North. After Trajan's second Dacian war and the constitution of Dacia as a first-class imperial province, there were thirteen legions on the Danube, while at the end of Nero's principate there had been six; seven legions on the Rhine and in Britain, while under Nero there had been eleven.

The total legionary strength of the Roman army at Augustus' death (25 legions) amounted to about 150,000 men; the total of the auxiliaries was about the same. Recruiting was generally from volunteers, sometimes by levy. Legions were recruited from Roman citizens, though if such men were in short supply a recruit might be given citizenship when he joined. Recruits for the western armies came chiefly from the western provinces (and, after 70, only a few from Italy); for the eastern armies, from the eastern provinces, especially from Asia Minor. Auxiliary units were cavalry (*alae*) or infantry (*cohortes*), and were often specialists. They served for twenty-five years (five years longer than the legionaries) and, in addition to their gratuity, they received citizenship on their discharge. On discharge, soldiers settled largely in districts where they had been stationed. While there were small coastguard and naval units at various places, there were only two large naval bases in Italy—at Misenum, north of the bay of Naples, and at Ravenna in the Adriatic—and two Roman fleets, manned by slaves and freedmen.

612a The law in any province was laid down in that province's charter, given at the time of its creation (the *lex provinciae*), supplemented and modified by later enactments from Rome of particular or universal application, decrees of the Senate and edicts and rescripts of the emperors. The particular privileges enjoyed by Jews in the eastern provinces (exemption from military service and from the obligation to obey a summons to court on the Sabbath) were set out in edicts which they succeeded in obtaining from Julius Caesar and Augustus, and which were binding on the governors of all eastern provinces. Except as covered by such privileges, all inhabitants of provinces except *civitates liberae* and *foederatae*, whose independence was usually the reward of service to Rome in days before the province was created, were subject to the law of the province and to the absolute authority (*imperium*) of the governor. Inhabitants of provinces were Roman citizens (*provinciales*) or non-Romans (*peregrini*); emancipated slaves were *liberti*. Inhabitants of *coloniae* and *municipia* were Roman citizens; Julius Caesar's proposal to give Latin rights, perhaps even Roman citizenship, to all cities in Sicily was not carried out, but in Spain from the time of Vespasian the towns had Latin rights—which meant that their ex-magistrates became full Roman citizens. The commonest path to Roman citizenship in the Empire was service in the auxiliary forces.

b The progressive development of the Roman Empire, so far from being in the (modern) direction towards secession and ultimate self-government of the various subject units, was towards attracting Roman citizens from the provinces in increasing numbers into the imperial administrative services, as senators and as *equites*. Some of these men came from families with native origins, some were descended from earlier Roman settlers. Enlightened Roman policy in this matter was admirably stated by Claudius in a speech which partly survives. It was from Narbonese Gaul and Spain that the best of the fresh blood came in the 1st cent. and a half of the Empire. The Spaniard Cornelius Balbus in 40 B.C. was the first 'provincial' to become consul. By Nero's time Seneca and many other prominent Romans came from Spain. Trajan, born in Spain, was the first 'provincial' to be Emperor. The influx of senators from the eastern provinces of the Empire came later, but there are interesting examples in the 1st cent. A.D. of men entering the Roman administration in the East. Philo's nephew, Ti. Julius Alexander (whose father, a Jewish customs officer in Alexandria, had received Roman citizenship) turned gentile, became a Roman *eques*, governed Judaea as procurator under Claudius, was made Prefect of Egypt by Nero and as such was responsible for the proclamation of Vespasian as Emperor. He was subsequently commander-in-chief of the Roman army under Titus in the last stages of the Jewish war, and was important enough to have a statue erected at Rome; the suggestion has even been hazarded (E. G. Turner, *Journal of Roman Studies* 44 (1954), 54–64) that he became Prefect of the Praetorian Guard. Many professional men, especially doctors, in Rome, were freedmen of eastern origin. An interesting pair of brothers, both freedmen, emancipated by the daughter of M. Antonius the triumvir, were (Antonius) Pallas, the talented financial secretary (*a rationibus*) of the Emperor Claudius, and his brother (Antonius) Felix, appointed Procurator of Judaea in 52, before whom St Paul appeared (Ac. 24). 612

Latin was the official language in the western provinces of the Empire, on the Danube and in Africa and Mauretania; Greek was the official language elsewhere; but, while the use of Latin was taught and encouraged as a part of romanisation in the West, nothing was done to suppress the everyday use of native languages anywhere (cf. Ac. 14:11); the tribune at Jerusalem was surprised that St Paul spoke Greek (Ac. 21:37).

The Roman Empire brought a general improvement everywhere in the material conditions of living. On land the fastest speed of travel was, as it was until the 19th cent., the speed of the fastest horse on the best of roads; and good road-making had from early republican times been an important part of the Roman genius. All over the Empire, it was the work on which the armies, when not campaigning, were employed. Based on the roads was a well organised, empire-wide, public posting service. Sailing was all but suspended during the winter months. In summer persistent winds made Mediterranean voyaging faster generally from west to east than from east to west, and in late July and August, when the Etesian winds blew, a voyage from the Straits of Messina to Alexandria in good conditions took from seven to ten days. On land and sea alike travel appears to have been reasonably safe. c

New towns, especially in the western provinces, followed the traditional Roman model and were based on a central piazza (the *forum*, with temple and town hall (*curia*)), with public baths, water and drainage systems, even theatre and amphitheatre. As the younger Pliny's letters from Bithynia show, over-ambitious enterprise in a world where town councillors (*decuriones*) were sometimes corrupt and contractors dishonest, might bring such building schemes to disaster; and this was a danger to which the good provincial governor's eyes were always open. Many public amenities, especially in the 1st cent., were the gifts to their home towns of rich individual benefactors. d

There were local taxes, collected by local officials, and public taxes which either were collected through Roman tax-farming companies (*publicani*) or native contractors, or else they were paid into the financial treasury of the province through the staff—many of them local employees—of the quaestor or procurator, as the case might be. There is no reason to think that taxation was oppressive.

The Emperor was the single bond of the whole Empire. His head was portrayed on most Roman coins (gold and silver coins were minted centrally under his direction at Lugdunum in Gaul); and the imperial cult was the means by which loyalty was everywhere expressed. Such cult had been accorded in the eastern Mediterranean world to Hellenistic kings and, as the Roman republic annexed their kingdoms, Rome, the Senate and, if they were not firm in their refusal, Roman proconsuls took the place of the Hellenistic kings as objects of a cult which later, 613a

13a under the Empire, displayed itself unofficially in all kinds of extravagances, but, at official level, was carefully controlled, though by sensible Emperors it was never rigidly enforced. In Rome and Italy the 'genius' of the living Emperor, but not the Emperor himself, might receive sacrifice; in the provinces 'Rome and Augustus'. More than this, certain Roman Emperors were officially consecrated and became 'divi' after their death, as Julius Caesar had done: Augustus, Claudius, Vespasian, Titus, and Trajan. There were temples of Rome and Augustus in eastern provinces, altars at first, then temples, in the West. The cult was organised, with priests, by a variety of units, in particular by cities and by provinces. In provinces there were councils of provincial representatives (who were sometimes consulted on administrative matters by governors) as well as priests; these were κοινά in eastern provinces and, copied from them, *concilia* in western provinces. In Italy and on the Danube and in western provinces freedmen took a prominent part in the cult. All over the Empire sacrifices and games took place on festivals, in particular on the Emperor's birthday.

b The absence on these festive occasions of Jews and, in due course, of Christians could not but be conspicuous. Jews were happy to pray for the Emperor in their synagogues, as they emphasised, but they were not able to take part in pagan sacrifice to his divinity. This attitude provided an irresistible temptation to their pagan enemies in cities of the eastern Mediterranean, particularly in Alexandria, whose inhabitants resented with equal intemperance the distant dominion of Rome and the presence in Alexandria, in their ghetto and outside it, of large numbers of Jews. (The earliest evidence of the Jew as a moneylender comes from Egypt in the time of Gaius.) Gaius had no personal responsibility for the pogrom which broke out in Alexandria in August 38 or for the consequent conflicts between Greeks and Jews in Judaea, though there was little discretion about his treatment of the Jewish delegates from Alexandria (graphically described by Philo, one of their number, in his *Legatio ad Gaium*) or in the instruction—which he subsequently revoked—that his statue should be placed in the Temple at Jerusalem. We have evidence both from Josephus and from a papyrus of the concern of Claudius at his accession in 41 to restore peace in Alexandria and in Judaea alike. An interesting inscription from Nazareth, known since 1878 but first published in France in 1930 (see F. de Zulueta, *Journal of Roman Studies* 22 (1932), 184–197), in which the Emperor threatens the death penalty for interference with, or the removal of bodies from, tombs, may belong to any date from Augustus to Claudius; it might be a consequence of Pilate's having reported to Rome on the disappearance of Christ's body from the tomb on the lines suggested by the priests (Mt. 28:12–15), but it is probably much earlier.

c In the province of Judaea, despite the concessions which Rome had made from the start to Jewish idiosyncrasy (the Emperor's head was not portrayed on the provincial currency, and there was no representation of him on military standards carried by the troops in the province), anti-Roman feeling was strong, fostered by the Sicarii, and open revolt broke out in 66, when Gessius Florus was procurator. There followed the Jewish war, of which Josephus' account survives, the Roman army of three legions being commanded by Vespasian and by his son Titus, who destroyed Jerusalem in 70. After this Judaea was governed by an imperial legate of senatorial rank and was garrisoned permanently by a single legion. Worship in the temple at Jerusalem was forbidden, and the annual gift of two drachmas a head which before this had been sent by Jews from all over the Empire to Jerusalem was made a compulsory tax for payment to Rome (the *fiscus Judaicus*). The exaction of this tax may have helped to make Roman officials conscious of the distinction betweeen Jews and 613c
Christians.

There was unrest again in Jerusalem under Trajan, and serious rebellion under Hadrian; and there were serious Jewish revolts also in Cyprus, Alexandria, and Cyrene.

Jews, together with Isis-worshippers, were expelled d
from Rome under Tiberius in 19 after the detection of particular scandals; and they were expelled again (Priscilla and Aquila among them: Ac. 18:2) by Claudius, probably in 49. Rightly or wrongly Suetonius, writing seventy years later, suggested that the rioting which led to this expulsion was not unconnected with the presence already of Christians in Rome.

As is shown by the edicts and rescripts of the wiser rulers (Julius Caesar, Augustus, and Claudius) and by what we know from, among other sources, the Acts, the Roman administration never sought to antagonise the Jews, but on the contrary made every possible concession to meet inconveniences arising out of Jewish observance of the Sabbath. The Jews did not proselytise actively, and trouble only arose when the mutual antipathy of Jews and gentiles (Greeks) provoked a Roman administrator to an indiscretion or the intransigence of either party prevented him from turning a blind eye to their disagreement, as (Ac. 18:17), left to himself, he wisely inclined to do. Christianity, on the other hand, confronted the Roman government with a difficult problem because it set out to win converts and because its cult was believed, however mistakenly, to include criminal practices (infanticide, cannibalism, and incest). For similar reasons Druidism was suppressed in Gaul because it involved ritual murder, and the worship of the Great Mother was carefully watched because it involved castration. The first certain mention of Christians outside holy writ relates to the year 64 (a few years after the probable date of St Paul's arrival in Rome), when they were arrested and, in circumstances of detestable cruelty, executed in Rome because of their supposed implication in the great fire, a charge which, though in fact baseless, acquired credibility from their supposed criminal habits (*flagitia*). There was possibly a further persecution at Rome at the end of Domitian's reign, but light is first thrown on Christianity from a Roman source in the letter written to Trajan by Pliny as governor of Bithynia in 113, and in Trajan's reply. Just as the effect of widespread conversions was feared on economic grounds by the temple silversmiths of Ephesus (Ac. 19:24ff.), so in Bithynia a heavy fall in the sale of sacrificial meat from the temples as a result of conversions to Christianity led to the laying of information against Christians, of which the governor was forced to take cognisance. Pliny's test of whether an accused person was a Christian was whether he was prepared to perform a formality of the imperial cult (which to the Christian was a matter of 'worshipping the beast': Rev. 20:4) and to curse Christ. Those who refused were executed. Though the ground of Roman persecution of Christianity lay in fact in the alleged criminal practices of Christians (cf. H. M. Last, 'The Study of the Persecutions', *Journal of Roman Studies* 27 (1937), 80–92), Pliny told Trajan that, despite examination and torture of suspects, he had no evidence at all to support this allegation, and Trajan gave instruction that no attention was to be paid to anonymous accusations.

Rome never lost its contempt for the East. The e
East spawned emotional and exotic cults (*superstitiones*), every one of them concerned, however crudely, with the spiritual life of the individual. These cults spread west, at their best challenging the cold formality of orthodox Roman religious belief (*religio*), at their worst challenging traditional standards of moral conduct—especially Isis worship, which spread from port to port with the sailors; Cybele worship; Mithraism, the religion for a soldier. And on the

613e heels of oriental cults, with its fatal attraction for individuals of all classes in Rome, came astrology. It was from the far East, by the trade routes which came overland through Syria and by the Red Sea through Egypt, that some of the most seductive enticements of material extravagance reached Italy and Rome—silks from as far as China, perfumes and spices from Arabia. The western Empire was a source of strength ; the eastern Empire, on the other hand, was the source of material and moral degeneration : so, from Augustus to Trajan, the moralists—and most Roman writers were moralists—preached : Horace, Seneca, Tacitus, Juvenal. Even the observance of the Sabbath by the Jews was stigmatised by both Juvenal and Tacitus as a sign of indolence. 613

Bibliography—*Cambridge Ancient History*, volumes x (1934) and xi (1936), with full bibliography, covering the period 44 B.C. to A.D. 192 ; C. N. Cochrane, *Christianity and Classical Culture* (1944) ; A. H. M. Jones, *The Herods of Judaea* (1938) ; *Oxford Classical Dictionary* (1949) ; M. Rostovtzeff, *The Social and Economic History of the Roman Empire*, (2nd ed. 1957) ; G. H. Stevenson, *Roman Provincial Administration* (1939) ; R. Syme, *The Roman Revolution* (1939) ; J. Wells and R. H. Barrow, *A Short History of the Roman Empire* (5th ed. 1950).

CONTEMPORARY JEWISH RELIGION

By W. D. DAVIES

614a The first century in the history of Judaism has long been recognised to have been a period of transition. Persian, Greek and Roman influences had, by that time, left their mark on Judaism to make it varied, complex and fluid. The Pharisaic forces, which triumphed at Jamnia, where Jewish scholars congregated after A.D. 70 to preserve, unify and revivify Judaism, were already powerfully active before that date. However they were not in sole control, but coexisted with others, which failed to survive the disaster of the Jewish war against Rome. Thus the solidified Rabbinic or Pharisaic Judaism which emerged after A.D. 70, and whose monument is the Mishnah, was more unified than that which had prevailed before, in the time of Jesus. Compiled at the end of the 2nd cent. A.D., *The Mishnah* is a systematised collection of regulations derived from the oral tradition. What was not included in the Mishnah was partly preserved in the *Tosephta*, a body of material similar to the Mishnah in form and content (see Strack, *Introduction to the Talmud and Midrash* (Eng. tr. 1931)). There can be little question that, however much Pharisaism gave to Judaism after A.D. 70 a continuity with that before A.D. 70, the religion of the Jewish people, when Jesus was born, was far more variegated than it subsequently became, and hence more difficult to describe (see G. F. Moore, *Judaism* iii, 17f.).

b This has been reinforced by two developments in recent scholarship. First, in the past, a rigid distinction was drawn between Judaism in Palestine, which was uncontaminated to any considerable degree by Gentile influences, and the Judaism which developed outside Palestine, which had assimilated much from the Graeco-Roman culture within which it grew. There has now, however, developed a more realistic appreciation of the extent to which Palestine had been for a long period, since the time of Alexander the Great, subject to Hellenistic influences. Archaeologists have revealed in the Synagogues of Palestine a considerable Greek influence ; Rabbis have been discovered to have tasted Greek culture and it has been claimed that even their exegetical methods are adaptations of Greek traditions. In the realm of ideas, on immortality, anthropology and, possibly, time, and in the sphere of institutional life, in the Synagogue, Greek influences and terminology are traceable. Nor must the regular intercourse between the Diaspora Jews and Palestine, and especially Jerusalem, be forgotten. This meant that Palestinian Judaism was not closed to Diaspora ideas and habits. On the other hand, despite the greater ease with which Graeco-Roman forces could impress the Judaism of the Diaspora, the real contact which the latter maintained with Judaism at its cultural and religious centre in Palestine, to which we have just referred, the maintenance of the annual half-shekel tax (see §600*e*), and the visits from the emissaries sent from Jerusalem to the Diaspora—all this meant that Judaism everywhere preserved an unmistakable unity which found expression in the ubiquitous Synagogue, which was both a sign and cause of this unity. Thus, Philo of Alexandria agreed in crucial matters with the Rabbis of Palestine, and it is a strikingly significant fact that the Jews of the Diaspora were prepared to substitute 614b
Aquila's rough Greek translation of the OT for the LXX, in order to retain a text more in accord with Rabbinic exegesis. Thus the division of 1st-cent. Judaism into distinct Palestinian and Hellenistic compartments has broken down.

But there is, secondly, another development not c
unconnected with this. Since 1947 we have been in possession of the manuscripts called the Dead Sea Scrolls. While there is no unanimity about their place and date of origin, so that we must use them very cautiously, most scholars have regarded them as pre-Christian and emanating from a sect possibly akin to Essenism which itself is an extreme form of Pharisaism. While the DSS are not revolutionary they have reinforced what we have just written, for there were Greek books discovered in the 'library' of the legalistic community that was centred at Qumrân, (though the presence of Greek books does not necessarily mean their acceptance). The DSS also support the recent tendency to emphasise that the Judaism of the time of Jesus was far less monolithic and more complex and changing than older scholars had supposed. Like the language of the time, which the Scrolls have revealed to be in process of development, so too the religion.

The variety of its sects and movements we cannot d
attempt to describe in detail. With one point only can we stay. Our customary understanding of the relative importance of the various groups we owe to Josephus, who gives the impression that the Pharisees were the dominant group in Judaism before the time of Jesus, and the central part they play in the Synoptics has served to confirm this impression. It is probable, however, that Josephus has exaggerated the role of the Pharisees. They were probably not as influential as he suggests. Rather they coexisted with other groups, which he mentions, surrounded by a vast majority of 'people of the land', who were largely unaffected by religion. It is possible also that the Zealots, for example, were more significant than previously recognised, through the early years of the 1st cent., the Maccabaean tradition of revolt having lived on to that time. Again if the DSS are Essene or quasi-Essene, as is held by many scholars, more attention must in future be given to the role of the Essenes in the 1st-cent. scene : but this is still not to be emphasised because of the uncertainty as to the origin of the Scrolls.

To sum up, then, studies since the first Peake e
commentary was published in 1919 have underlined the falsity of any sharp dichotomy between Palestinian and Diaspora Judaism, and the variety, complexity and transitional character of Jewish religion in the time of Jesus. The details of this variegated complexity we cannot here describe, but only what is largely common to all the groups of the period in different degrees. This common element we can with caution disentangle, but with the caveat that, as here formulated, it is an abstraction, a skeleton at best, which was clothed upon very variously by the several groups. Nevertheless, just as it is possible to speak of the characteristics of American Protestantism, even though it is divided into more than two hundred sects, so we can seek to

614e describe the Jewish religion of Jesus' day despite its fragmentation.

615a **I Assumptions (1) The One God: Monotheism**—We begin by noting certain assumptions which the religious Jew in the time of Jesus would make; and we use the word 'assumptions' advisedly, because the Jews belonged to the Semitic world. This differed from the Hellenistic, and especially at one point. The Greek mind sought to understand the world from within the world, by the rational observation of men and things: it sought to explain God from the world and its life, not the world and its life from God. But the Semitic mind was different: it discovered the 'Living God', a spirit, personal and transcendent, burning in his purpose, which gave meaning to life from outside life. The existence of this God was not a quandary for the Semitic intellect, but an assumption; not the conclusion of Semitic thought but its postulate. And, through the fires of exile and persecution, by the 1st cent., monotheism had become general in Judaism (Jdt. 8:18).

Sometimes reasons are given for God's existence by Josephus (Ant. I, vii, 1) but both he and Philo, as well as the Rabbis, would agree essentially that, except in the case of rare souls like Abraham, God was known not by reason but by revelation. And the One God was the constant theme of their thinking. Often conceived anthropomorphically, especially in popular utterances, nevertheless the majesty, spirituality, immutability, holiness and mysterious providence of God the Creator is so fully attested that anthropomorphism was not the only or the dominant category in the 'theology' of the time. For example, as the Bible was transmitted, awkward texts dealing with God were changed. Similarly in the LXX, the Targums, and the Rabbis, phrases unworthy of the transcendent God were changed. The same concern to preserve the 'otherness' of God prompted Jews to exclude the pronunciation of the name *Yahweh* from the public reading of scripture as early as the 3rd cent. B.C., the term *Adonai* being used in its stead. The incommunicable name was rendered in the LXX as *Kyrios* (Lord); the Targums most often substituted for *Yahweh* the term *Memra* (Word); and in the liturgy of the Day of the Atonement, the High Priest, who was to utter the name Yahweh, pronounced or mumbled it so that no-one could understand it (see Jerus. Talmud, Yoma III, vii, 40*d*). Probably this separation of the Divine Name arose through contact with Hellenistic thought in the 3rd cent. B.C. To give a proper name to God spelt idolatry: it was to suggest that He was a god among gods. To avoid using his Name was therefore to preserve His transcendence. At the same time it was to refuse to confuse the sacred and the profane. Hence the same influence lies behind the avoidance of the name, as lies behind the emphasis on things clean and unclean, mentioned later.

But did not this insistence on the 'otherness' of God banish him from his world? Was the warm nearness of God (Dt. 6:17; Ps. 73:25f., 139), lost in the experience of 1st-cent. Judaism, and was not that religion, therefore, dominated by fear and not by love? G. F. Moore (HTR (1921), xiv, 197ff.) has warned us against regarding the 'otherness' of God, in the Judaism of our period, as necessary transcendence. Judaism safeguarded the awareness of the nearness of God in several ways. While God was in heaven and man on earth, nevertheless, through his Shekinah (Heb. from the verb meaning 'to dwell') and His Glory (see TWNT under *doxa*; also Arndt-Gingrich-Bauer, *A Greek-English Lexicon* (1957), 202f.), the Jew could experience His very presence on earth. The Shekinah filled heaven and earth, but was especially located in the land of Palestine among His people. Again God was present among His own in His Holy Spirit. It has been customary to regard 1st-cent. Judaism as an arid desert unwatered by the Holy Spirit. The functions of the Holy Spirit had by then been relegated to the past, to prophecy, which no **615**
longer existed, to the composition of the sacred scriptures, which had been closed. But certain individuals were claimed to possess the Spirit, and there was a strong belief that God still spoke to his people through his own 'voice' or 'the daughter of a voice' such as was heard at Jesus' baptism. Nevertheless, until recently it could not be claimed that the awareness of the Spirit was a marked feature of 1st-cent. Judaism. But, in the light of the DSS, we can now say that there were certain people, in the 1st cent., who did have a vivid awareness of the Spirit. The sect from which the Scrolls came was a community in the Spirit. The exact significance of the Spirit in the Scrolls has to be carefully assessed, but the sect does seem to have combined the strictest adherence to the Law with a vivid pneumatology.

The angelology of the period is also noteworthy as **b**
a means whereby, in the popular mind, as well as in apocalyptic circles, the 'immanence' of God was preserved. The Sadducees rejected this; Philo seems to have assimilated the angels to Greek heroes; the Pharisees recognised angels but were chary of overemphasising their role from fear of polytheism; Josephus oscillates between the recognition and rationalisation of angelology. It was apparently among apocalyptic writers and the Essenes that angels enjoyed most popularity; the DSS are particularly rich in reference to angels. Two factors may account for the development of angelology; (1) the love of fables and stories expressed in *Haggadah* (Homiletic, often fanciful interpretation of scripture, as contrasted with *Halakah*, specific direction for life: this is authoritative (see Strack, op. cit.)), and (2) the need to recognise, while safeguarding His transcendence, that God did concretely intervene in the world. While the Rabbis were careful to insist on the distinction between God and the angels by forbidding their adoration, nevertheless the necessity for this interdiction itself proves how real was the belief in angels. What then were they? There are two types: the first, the good, constituted a vast company surrounding God in heaven, and whenever he appeared to men. They continually sang his praises, frequently intervened in the history of Israel, had a role in the promulgation of the Law on Sinai (Jubilees 1:27ff.; Gal. 3:19; Ac. 7:38), and assisted God in his judgments. Later, guardian angels were allotted to individuals. As to the character of the angels, they were elemental spirits connected sometimes with natural phenomena like the wind, clouds, fire, etc. (1 Enoch 60:11–21; 2 Enoch 29:1–3); they were immortal and dwelt in heaven; they did not marry (1 Enoch 15:4–7; Mt. 22:30). They were given personal names (Tob. 3:17; 1 Enoch 9:1) and divided according to rank (Tob. 12:15), the seven chief ones being Uriel, Raphael, Raguel, Michael, Saraqael, Gabriel, Remiel (1 Enoch 20:1–8). The other type of angels, the bad, the demons, lay in wait to injure the souls of men. They were variously regarded as born of the sons of angels and the daughters of men (Gen. 6:1–4), or as originally supernatural beings who revolted under the leadership of Satan against God. Whatever their origin they became incredibly numerous, Enemies of men, they infested them with diseases, corrupted them with bad teaching, and accused them before God. They often chose as their dwelling-places cemeteries and ruins. The chief of the demons was variously known as Satan, Beliar, Beelzebul, Azazel, Mastema, Sammael.

It cannot be argued that demons helped Judaism **c**
to preserve itself from an overemphasis on transcendence, although the good angels do serve this function. The same is also true of the concept of wisdom which developed. In Prov. 8, Sir. 24 and Wis. 7:22–8:1 wisdom appears in a personified form, even if it is not a person, a mediator between God and the world. Thus instead of following a tendency, which may perhaps be discerned in the OT, to recognise distinctions within the Godhead in order to

615c express the richness of His nature, Judaism developed a number of abstract terms which seem to be personifications of attributes of God, the Shekinah, the Spirit, the Wisdom, etc. These avoided anthropomorphism and transcendentalism. Nevertheless, the necessity for these personifications must not lead us into thinking that the predominant note in 1st-cent. Judaism was one of fear before the High God. While the passages defining the fear of God as the beginning of wisdom are familiar (Prov. 1:7), and although it can probably be claimed that the phrase 'the fear of the Lord' is the Rabbinic equivalent to our term 'religion' (see *Mishnah Aboth* 1:3, 3:9), the love of the Lord is as emphasised as His fear (e.g. *Yebamoth* 48*b*; *Mekilta* on Exod. 22:20; *Mishnah Sotah* 5:5). It agrees with this, that God is referred to in Israel not only as 'Our King' but as 'Our Father'. This usage goes back to the 1st cent. God the creator of all is, however, mainly addressed as 'Father' in a national not in an individual sense (*Mekilta* on Exod. 20:6, however, speaks of 'My Father'). (See J. Jeremias on 'Kennzeichen der ipsissima vox Jesu' in *Synoptische Studien* (München 1953), 86–8.)

There is, then, in Judaism a noble awareness of the One God. But the universalism implicit in this coexists with a belief in God's special relation to Israel.

616a **(2) His People: Nationalism**—We stated above that the belief in God, in Judaism, was not the outcome of reflection but of revelation. But this revelation was given in and through a particular event, the Exodus of Israel from Egypt. The very act in which the Creator of the whole universe was revealed was also the act which gave birth to the people of Israel as a nation. To put it technically, both universalism and particularism are conjoined in the revelation of God. The belief was natural that there was a relation of peculiar intimacy between God and His people Israel. This is clearly traceable in the OT, Apoc. and Pseudepigrapha. By the 1st cent. it was an axiom among religious Jews. The Rabbis avoided the use of phrases like 'the God of Israel', 'the people of God', because they disliked using the Divine Name, but the truth that Israel was in fact the people of God they cherished ardently. Israel, to them, was God's peculiar possession, His very own property. One Israelite was more to God than the whole world. The Song of Songs was interpreted in terms of Israel's bridal relation to God, although this metaphor was not otherwise used without reserve. Israel was also the first-born of God. According to some, it was only when they acted as such that Israelites truly were the sons of God, but others held that whether sinful or not they were sons, who enjoyed God's favour: the cause of Israel was the cause of God: in their affliction He was afflicted and He acts as their guardian and guide. Although he punishes Israel for her sin she can never be exterminated nor finally abandoned by God.

b But this peculiar relation between Israel and her God was not unconditioned. While God had chosen Israel to be his people, not because of any merit that she possessed, but out of sheer grace, nevertheless in choosing Israel God foresaw that she alone would be able to accept the Law. Although not chosen for merit, she had exhibited merit. And, in fact, the gift of the Law did give to Israel a superiority over the nations, and laid upon her the duty of manifesting God to them. She was to do this by fidelity to the commandments even unto death. The very reason for Israel's existence was that she should be able to accept, to study, to observe the Law and thereby glorify God's Name. Thus she was a holy, just and virtuous people assured of the Age to Come. From this it was not a big step to the belief that Israel was an eternal people; and her history was idealised from this point of view. Not only was excellence ascribed to the people of Israel herself, but also to the land she occupied. There it was that the Shekinah loved to dwell, because God had sanctified it: there also above all was the Holy Spirit to be experienced within the holy community in the holy land: according to 616b some, the inhabitants of Palestine were to be the first raised from the dead in the Messianic Age; thus there was advantage as well as merit in living in Palestine, and to quit it, in the eyes of many, was to sin. And at the centre of Palestine stood Jerusalem, the centre of the world. The idealisation of Jerusalem continued from OT times and it became not only the geographic centre of Jewry but a geographic expression of their faith.

Such being the relation between God and Israel and c her land, what was the attitude of Judaism towards the Gentiles? This was at least twofold. On the one hand Israel's superiority over the pagan world was emphasised. The Gentiles were enemies of God, guilty of idolatry and immorality; they had oppressed Israel, especially under Antiochus Epiphanes. In choosing Israel God could not but have acted exclusively: He had rejected the Gentiles, a natural name for whom was 'sinners'. There were declarations of hatred towards the Gentiles, although the terrible times and circumstances of these sometimes explain them. Before the time of Jesus it was customary to refer to the Gentiles under the figures of beasts (e.g. in Dan.). But on the other hand there is a kindlier attitude towards them. Some Rabbis are careful to explain that the Gentiles too had been offered the Law, and it was therefore their fault that they were not in the covenant. Attempts were made to excuse the Gentiles' failures and recognition given to their virtues: they were not so much deliberate transgressors of the Law as sinful because they were following their ancestral customs. Examples of filial piety and of justice were noted among them. Much in their manners and physical habits attracted leading Jews, e.g. Hillel, and we have previously noted the intercourse between Jews and Gentiles in the 1st cent. There were regular prayers for the Emperor and at the feast of Tabernacles bulls were slaughtered to expiate the sins of the Gentile world. In the Messianic Age many expected the Gentiles to be converted. It agrees with all this that despite its 'nationalism' or 'particularism' Judaism recognised and emphasised the unity of all mankind, as *Mishnah Sanhedrin* 4:5 shows.

There is evidence too that in the 1st cent. Judaism d had an uneasy conscience about the Gentiles. A symptom and result of this was a widespread missionary movement in which many proselytes were gained. We can use the term missionary of the proselytising done by Judaism as long as we remember that conversion to Judaism *ipso facto* meant naturalisation into the Jewish people.

Thus Judaism in our period, as later, was a blend e of a religion, a people, a country. Was this blend fortunate? To the nation, the religious connection gave not only its very existence but a strong bond of unity and continuity. Thus in a time of national danger Judas Maccabaeus appealed to the religion of the people as its strength. Proselytism moreover increased the nation's expansion numerically and geographically. The religious observances were also marks of nationality, and so religious loyalty always served national ends. And herein was the price that Judaism paid for its religio-national character. At times religious loyalty *subserved* national ends. The too close identification of the interests of Yahweh and his people meant that the universal religion could be degraded to be merely the religion of a people. This was particularly true in times of national stress, and especially after A.D. 70, when Jewish survival was at stake.

(3) His Law: Nomism—So far we have noted two 617a assumptions in Jewish religion, the reality of the living God, and the eternal relation between Him and Israel. The link between them was the Law, which was the condition upon which Israel had been chosen to be the people of God. Here we shall merely attempt a summary of what it stood for in 1st-cent Judaism.

617a The term ' law ' is here used to translate the Hebrew word *tôrāh*. And the objection has been raised that the English word ' law ' translates not so much this Hebrew term *tôrāh* as the Greek mistranslation of it given in the LXX, i.e. *nomos* (law). Torah is a wider term than the English ' law ', and stands for teaching of a religious kind, and, indeed, for what we should call ' revelation ' : it is not strictly or merely legal in its connotation. This objection is valid, but nevertheless the legal emphasis in torah is unmistakable, a major part of torah is in fact *nomos*, law. The singular term *tôrāh* came to be applied to the totality of the divine revelation given at Sinai, and this included the commandments of God. The torah was deemed to have existed before creation, but the category of pre-existence does not seem to have been a very significant one in Judaism, since pre-existence was ascribed to many items. What was more important was that, long before the 1st cent., the torah had been identified with Wisdom, which was both pre-existent and the agent of creation. Thus the torah came to be conceived as the ground plan of the universe, which God himself had studied and made the very instrument of creation itself. As we should put it, the universe was founded on ' the Law '.

Nevertheless, important as was its cosmic significance, Judaism was primarily concerned with the Law as it had been revealed in history at Sinai. And here it is essential to grasp that it was not by the exercise of any rational faculty that Israel had been led to the Law : she did not discover the Law for herself, far less invent it. Rather was the Law a gift given to a stiff-necked people, a gift which was not even understood in all its parts. This was one of the most favoured themes of Jewish discussion and study, the giving of the Law, not mediately (this was emphasised) but directly, not secretly to an esoteric group but to all the people. And it was this experience that Judaism was concerned to re-enact in every generation (see *The Passover Haggadah*).

b But what precisely was the content of ' the Law ', which had been given by Moses and handed on from generation to generation ? There were, first, the ten commandments, which are the essential part of the whole Law (so Philo) ; secondly, the Pentateuch, to which the term *torah* is most often applied ; thirdly, the whole of the OT. The writings of the OT were declared to ' defile the hands ', i.e. to be sacred, because they were the works of prophets speaking in the Holy Spirit, so that they can be regarded as the Word of God. According to the Rabbis and to Josephus we find the words of God himself in the Scriptures ; according to Philo the writers wrote their own words under the influence of the Holy Spirit, which was *par excellence* the spirit of prophecy. While, however, the whole of the OT was sacred, primacy among its documents was enjoyed by the Pentateuch. While the rest of the OT would eventually disappear the Pentateuch would persist into the Age to Come. But, in the fourth place, in addition to the written Law there was the ' oral Law '. Dt. 17:8–12 makes it clear how, from an early date, Israel recognised the necessity for accommodating or adapting the Law to changing circumstances. It was this that led to the growth of the oral Law or to what is referred to in the NT and by Josephus also as the ' traditions of the fathers ' ; it arose as a protective hedge around the Law. Let us look for instance on how oral laws governing the observance of the Sabbath grew. The written Law forbade work : but the question inevitably arose as to what constituted work. In their anxiety to avoid any infringement of the written Law the Rabbis eventually enumerated a large number of definitions (39 in all) of work to be avoided : thus was precept added to precept (*Mishnah Shabbath* 7:1f.).

c The impact of the oral Law was to make the Law livable and practicable. It became a maxim that no decree should be enacted which it was beyond the power of the majority in the community to perform. In the interests of this principle biblical prescriptions were modified and even annulled. A good example of this is the *Prozbol* of Hillel. According to Dt. 15:2 all loans were remitted in the seventh year. This could lead to fraud and oppression (Dt. 15:9), so Hillel enacted the rule of the Prozbol, which was a declaration made before witnesses, a court of law, by a creditor, to the effect that the loan in question would not be remitted under the terms of the seventh-year law (see *Mishnah Shebiith* 10:4). Not all groups in Palestine accepted the oral Law as binding. Thus the Sadducees, although they did not reject the tradition, nevertheless rejected its authority. Moreover, there were varieties of traditions which were accepted as binding by some and not by others. Thus Hillel and Shammai differed in so many points of interpretation that there was a danger that there should develop two laws in Israel : it was the necessity to counteract this danger that led the Rabbis at Jamnia to declare that it was the tradition according to the House of Hillel that was to be followed.

What was the relative importance of the oral Law ? In principle it enjoyed the same authority as the written Law, and some Rabbis even accorded to it a higher authority than to the latter. This was made possible by the claim that the oral Law, like the written Law, went back to Sinai. All the Law had been shown to Moses on Sinai ; all rabbinic decisions, all grammatical and other matters affecting the Law —all were traced back to Sinai. This can hardly be taken by us as a judgment of historical fact : it merely reveals the value attached to the oral Law. Historically the oral Law developed very gradually, and various theories have arisen to describe its growth. The evidence suggests that it was its authority as tradition that most weighed, not its relation to the scriptures. For a long time the oral tradition was not written down: it is possible and even probable, however, that little collections of ' laws ' were made by Rabbis in the 1st cent. : in any case by the end of the 2nd cent. the oral Law was codified, though not completely, in the Mishnah.

d We may finally note, in order to emphasise the centrality of Law in Judaism in our period, as always, that Moses as the mediator of the Law dominated the Jewish imagination like a colossus, and that the view was generally held that the Law, given through him, was eternally valid, although we are not to rule out the possibility that there was a considerable speculation on the advent of a ' New Law ' in the ideal future. And to the Law unquestioning obedience was to be rendered, both in the present and future. While the Rabbis did seek to give reasons for their obedience or for the laws which they had to obey, in the last resort the Law was obeyed not because it was understood but because it was commanded : for the religious Jew it was not primarily to reason why but to obey and, if necessary, to die in total commitment (see *Midrash Rabbah* on Num. 19:2).

618a **II Activities**—So far we have pointed out that 1st-cent. Judaism assumed a God who had called Israel to be his people and supplied her with his Law as guide and way. This meant that Judaism was a religion of gratitude for what God had done for, and given to, His people. But gratitude is a dynamic emotion : it necessarily resulted in attempts at responding to what God had done and given. These created certain activities which the Law itself demanded. It is with these that we are now concerned.

b First we note the significance of the Temple worship. The ease with which Judaism was able to survive the fall of Jerusalem and its Temple in A.D. 70 has led to the claim that already before that date the hold of the Temple on the people and leaders of Jewry must have been weak. Were the Rabbis slightly embarrassed by the sacrificial system ? Did the more intelligent and sophisticated among them sigh with silent relief when the Temple fell ? Already in the time of Jesus the Synagogue had replaced the Temple as the significant

618b religious institution in Israel: the Rabbi or the Scribe, not the priest, was the real shepherd of the people. But we should not too easily endorse this view. To judge from the NT Jesus regarded the Temple as of great significance. But, this apart, the centrality of the Temple in the mind of Ezra and Nehemiah continued into the Maccabaean period, while the frequently moving descriptions of its ritual which we find point to its vitality. Moreover, although the Rabbis after A.D. 70 found substitutes for the worship of the Temple in fasting, study and prayer, nevertheless their utterances show how deep was the attachment of Israel to the Temple also. The sheer actuality of the Temple and its ritual must not be discounted. In Jesus' day it had been restored by Herod and stood out strikingly in gold and white, so that its glory was praised afar: the stream of sacrifices offered could not but have made a deep impression. Thus it would be erroneous to overemphasise the extent to which already before A.D. 70 the Synagogue had replaced the Temple in the popular affection.

c Apart from the eminence it gained because of its place in the history of Israel and the impact of its traditional forms, the significance of Temple worship in Judaism was at least twofold. The Temple, firstly, was the place where the Shekinah loved to dwell. Its holiness and purity as the abode of the Lord was indicated in its very structure: the 'impure' were progressively excluded from the innermost shrine. Thus the Gentiles were only allowed into the section called the Court of the Gentiles, and into the Holy of Holies only the High Priest himself could enter, and that only after the most elaborate purifications. But, in the second place, the sacrificial system, controlled by the priests and centred in the Temple, was the means ordained by God for the expiation of sin and the reconciliation of his people to himself. Thus the High Priest on the Day of Atonement stood before God on behalf of all the people. To a 20th-cent. mind the gruesome accompaniments of the sacrificial system are revolting, but antiquity knew no such disgust. To 1st-cent. religious Jews, despite the condemnation of the abuse of the system in the prophets, and despite the corruption of its practice by the priests, it was a gift of God for their sake. Hence the act of sacrifice was performed with the minutest respect for details. Moreover, the intention of the priest and of him who offered sacrifice had to be pure and all had to be properly performed. Nevertheless the danger of mechanical observance was recognised. Sacrifice had to be accompanied by prayer, confession and restitution for the wrong done to the person injured. All this preserved sacrifice from being purely external.

d While the worship at the Temple signified the *perpetual* presence of Yahweh among His people, other activities of the religious life of the 1st-cent. Jew were connected with His *interventions* at different periods in the history of Israel. This is particularly true of certain Festivals which were observed, namely *Passover*, *Pentecost*, *Tabernacles* or *Booths*, the three pilgrimage festivals when many Jews went up to Jerusalem to worship with joy and thanksgiving. Originally these were connected with the agricultural year, but although the different prayers used show that they still retained something of their original character, they had come to have a national significance and their function to be largely that of strengthening national bonds through the forms of religion. Thus Passover recalled the deliverance of Israel from Egypt, Pentecost, the giving of the Law at Sinai, Tabernacles the sojourn of the people in the wilderness and the formation of the nation. The aim of such festivals was to make events in Israel's history, in which God had signally revealed himself, live again; they aimed at recreating in the experience of the Jew the experience of his people, and thus at incorporating him 'in Israel'. This comes out most clearly in the liturgy of the Passover, but it had become the real *raison d'être* of the other festivals mentioned, as also of the feast of *Dedication* (*Hanukkah* or the feast of lights), which celebrated the victory of Judas Maccabaeus and the recovery of Israel's independence under him (1 Mac. 4:36–61), and the feast of *Purim* which recalled the bloody triumph of Esther over Haman. Both these last fed the fires of communal awareness in a more directly 'nationalistic' sense. In addition, two other festivals aimed at the creation of a sense of sin, and the need for purity and forgiveness. *The New Year Festival* recalled the creation of the world: the New Year was the day on which God began to judge men and prayer was said that he might remember Israel in kindness. The other festival, *The Day of Atonement*, which Philo took to be the holiest of the Festivals, and which was for Jews 'the Day', was marked by fasting, long confession of sin, sacrifice. But, even on this day, joy was not excluded. 618d

So far we have noted the recognition of Yahweh's presence in the worship of the Temple, the commemoration and re-enactment of his past activity. We now turn to the guidance which God provided to his people in their daily lives, to the Law, the giving of which was commemorated at Pentecost, the demand of which was recognised by religious Jews all the days of their lives. How did the acceptance of the Law affect the life of a Jew? In the first place the centrality of the Law and the need for its study created an institution, the Synagogue. Already in the time of Jesus each village had its synagogue where the needs of prayer and study were met. (Note that along with the Synagogue went the school and by the 1st cent. A.D. the Jews had evolved a widespread system for elementary and advanced education.) There were Pharisees and teachers of the Law in every village of Galilee and Judaea and Jerusalem (cf. Lk. 5:17). Three main elements developed in the liturgy of the Synagogues, namely Prayer (including the use of psalms), the reading of scripture, the Homily. The meetings for worship took place regularly on the Sabbath, and on two other days of the week. No priests were necessary for their conduct, so that the Synagogue, as contrasted with the Temple, bore a lay character. While those who attended the Synagogue were not thereby in any way rejecting Temple worship, nevertheless the role of the Synagogue in the life of the people became such that many have claimed, as we saw, that it virtually overshadowed the Temple in importance before A.D. 70. And although this cannot be too much pressed, the significance of the Synagogue can hardly be overemphasised. It encouraged the growth of personal piety, it furthered the development of Pharisaic influence (Pharisaism was largely a lay movement), it helped to preserve the unity of Judaism everywhere. Above all the Synagogue made of the religious Jew a man of study and prayer (although the role of the Temple worship in the growth of the spirit of prayer should not be overlooked). The necessity for prayer and its importance is frequently the theme of the Rabbis. A day had to begin and end with prayer: there was an appropriate prayer for every significant act during the day. The posture for the saying of prayers and the direction in which they were to be uttered were closely defined. But this must not be taken to mean the mechanisation of prayer. While true prayers were believed to be answered, there was a full recognition of the vanity and futility of much prayer. Of the various forms of prayer we cannot here write; but, in view of the intensity of the prayer-life of Judaism, are we to think of a Jewish mysticism in the 1st cent.? The term 'mysticism' is a bog, because of its loose connotation. If by 'mysticism' is meant the absorption of the self in God, accompanied frequently by a rigid asceticism, then it is clear that there was much in Judaism which was not favourable to this. Suspicious of asceticism, because God had made all things good, Judaism also emphasised not individual absorption in God but membership in the people of God and obedience to his Law. Neverthe- e

618e less that Judaism knew the intensely personal relationship with God, which we sometimes refer to as 'mystic', cannot be doubted, except that the distinction between the creature and the Creator was always retained.

f But apart from the worship of the Synagogue, which its study had called forth, the Law pressed upon the Jew still more directly. Because it encompassed the whole of life it demanded tangible, visible signs of complete obedience to the will of God that it revealed. In this sense Judaism is full of symbolism. Thus there were certain external marks of the Jew. First, he was circumcised. Reasons given for the necessity for this were many. Circumcision denoted the consecration of the body to God; since it involved a certain shedding of blood, it could be regarded as a kind of sacrifice offered to God. But, however rationalised, circumcision became a mark of the people of the Covenant, who accordingly had something like a horror of the uncircumcised, and were prepared to give their life for circumcision. Secondly, the Jew was prohibited to wear garments made of mixed stuff; he wore *fringes* (see §222*f*) on the four corners of his cloak and *phylacteries* (Dt. 6:8) on his forehead or arm; he pinned a small object called the *m^ezûzāh* (literally 'doorpost'; see §234*g*) containing scriptural verses on his door. These things gave divine protection and, above all, reminded the Jews of the necessity to keep the commandments. But, thirdly, the consecration of all time to God was achieved by the Jews in the observance of the Sabbath, the seventh day of the week, which God had reserved for rest and sanctified. In keeping the Sabbath, Israel bore witness to its Creator, and actually participated in His holiness. All activity resembling work was prohibited on the Sabbath, but its mark was nevertheless joy. It was characterised by special food, clothes and a liturgy in the home. As a sign of the Covenant it was honoured unto death. As we have previously seen, every day was also marked by prayers—for rising and sleeping, for entering a house, for washing hands, for eating and other things. The birth of a child, his circumcision, his religious majority, betrothal, marriage, illness, death, funeral, mourning—all these events were consecrated by prayer. But not only were *events* thus marked for consecration, the Law also included *things* in its scope. Certain physiological functions were regarded as polluting. Contact with human corpses, lepers, impure animals enumerated in the Law—this physical contact was understood as a religious pollution, or rather there was no distinction drawn between the physical and the religious in this matter. And to recover 'purity' there were certain rites of purification to be recognised. Similarly there were certain dietary laws which had to be observed if the state of purity was to be maintained. Certain impure animals were 'forbidden'; blood could not be drunk and special precautions were taken in the slaughter of animals to avoid pollution.

g The results of these distinctions between things clean and unclean were far-reaching. It could and did lead to the serious consequence that sanctity was sometimes regarded merely as a material state, and that contact with Gentiles, who were in a condition of impurity, was not regarded as desirable. In this sense the observance of the Law could not but lead to segregation and particularism: the Law made it necessary for the Jew to avoid the pollution of the pagan world. For this reason, among others, it was better to live in Palestine than in the Diaspora. The ideal was *amixia* ('apartheid') and there are passages, mostly however later than the 1st cent., which suggest that there was an ethical standard for dealing with the Gentiles lower than that observed between the people of the Covenant. In fact, however, as we have previously insisted, there was much intercourse between even distinguished Rabbis, such as Gamaliel, and cultivated Greeks; the necessities of co-existence, the demands of sheer humanity, the duty of sanctifying the Name—all these modified the rigid separation demanded by the Law. 618g
Associated with the attitude to the Gentiles, however, is the 'intellectual snobbery', if we may so express it, which the religion of the Law would sometimes, at least, tend to foster. To be a good Jew one had to obey the Law; to obey the Law one had to know it; to know the Law one had to study it. Hence the ideal life was the studious life or, at least, study had to play an important part in it. The 'ignorant' could not be religious. Thus there arose sometimes within the circles of the pious, a contempt 'for lesser breeds without the Law', for 'people of the land', which is not an admirable feature of 1st-cent. Judaism. (On these, see Foakes Jackson and Lake, *The Beginnings of Christianity* (1920), 1439ff. H. Danby, *The Mishnah* (1933), 793, defines them as 'those Jews who were ignorant of the Law and who failed to observe the rules of cleanness and uncleanness and were not scrupulous in setting apart Tithes from the produce.') But this is not the last word. So far we have noted the centrality of religion for the Jew, his monotheism, his emphasis on the communal or national character of his religion, his nomism, and its consequent observances. And our last references to the Gentiles and to 'the people of the land' especially might create the impression that 1st-cent. Judaism was lacking in moral seriousness. Nothing could be farther from the truth. Alongside the Law and the Psalms the Jew also read the prophets. In the readings in the Synagogue all three had a place, though in what exact proportions we cannot say. (See Elbogen, *Der Jüdische Gottesdienst* (1931–); Jacob Mann, *The Bible as Read and Preached in the Old Synagogue* (1940).) Familiarity with the prophetic no less than the legal tradition we can assume. And with both prophets and law there naturally went an emphasis on morality, on justice, on family loyalties, on charity, on chastity and purity. That 1st-cent. Judaism was the heir of the prophets meant that it was set apart by its 'prophetic morality' from other religions of the time. Behind and in the intricate casuistry of its life, which, like all casuistry, could degenerate at times into pettifoggery and hypocrisy, we can discern the earnestness of the prophetic tradition and the 'exquisite sensitivity' of Pharisaism.

III Anticipations—But 1st-cent. Judaism was the heir also of apocalyptic literature and eschatological thinking in Israel. While the details of its *life* in the present were governed by the Law, its *thought* was largely controlled by the memory of the event in the past which gave the Law, the Exodus, and by an anticipation for the future which was largely determined by the character of the past. In Jewish eschatology, in the time of Jesus, as at other times, the end was to be as the beginning: the anticipation was grounded in memory. The hope of the end underwent many changes and emphases which are traced in §§604–9, to which the reader is referred. We merely note that it was very lively in the 1st cent. and led to much political unrest. 619a

Thus within the broad unity of thought and practice which have been indicated above there was a live fluidity. The mark of the Judaism of the time of Jesus was variety and change within a context of memory, anticipation, and present obedience to the Law. Perhaps in the intensity of its hope, its Messianic fervour, which led to so many outbreaks of short-lived Messianic claims, and in certain circles where the attempt at absolute obedience to the Law had led to something akin to the Pauline doctrine of sin and grace, as in the Dead Sea Sect, we see a Judaism at its 'boiling-point', if we may so put it (see W. D. Davies in *The Scrolls and the NT*, ed. K. Stendahl (1957), 281, *n*. 86).

Bibliography—SOURCES: OT, NT; *The Talmud* and *The Midrash* (Soncino trans.); *Josephus* and *Philo* in the Loeb Classical Library; C. K. Barrett, *The NT Background: Selected Documents* (1956); R. H. Charles (ed.), *The Apocrypha and Pseudepigrapha of the OT* (1913); A. Cohen, *Everyman's Talmud* (1932);

H. Danby (tr.), *The Mishnah* (1933) ; T. H. Gaster, *The Dead Sea Scriptures* (1956) ; J. Z. Lauterbach, *The Mekilta* ; C. G. Montefiore and H. Loewe, *A Rabbinic Anthology* (1938).

OTHER LITERATURE : S. W. Baron, *A Social and Religious History of the Jews* (1937, [12]1952) ; J. Bonsirven, *Le judaïsme palestinien au temps de Jésus Christ* (1935), i, ii ; W. Bousset-H. Gressmann, *Die Religion des Judentums im späthellenistischen Zeitalter* [3] (1926) ; A. Büchler, *Studies in Sin and Atonement in the Rabbinic Literature of the First Century* (1928), *Types of Jewish-Palestinian Piety from 70 B.C. to 70 C.E.* (1922) ; R. H. Charles, *Religious Development between the OT and NT* ; W. D. Davies, *Paul and Rabbinic Judaism* [2] (1956) ; J. Jeremias, *Jerusalem zur Zeit Jesu* i (1923), ii (1924), iii (1929) ; G. Kittel, *Die Probleme des palästinensischen Spätjudentums und das Urchistentum* (1926) ; J. Klausner, *Jesus of Nazareth* (Eng. tr. 1929) ; A. Marmorstein, *The Old Rabbinic Doctrine of God* i (1927), ii (1937) ; C. G. Montefiore, *Rabbinic Literature and Gospel Teachings* (1930) ; G. F. Moore, *Judaism*, 3 vols. (1927) ; R. H. Pfeiffer, *History of NT Times : with an Introduction to the Apocrypha* (1949) ; H. H. Rowley, *The Relevance of Apocalyptic* ([2]1947) ; S. Schechter, *Some Aspects of Rabbinic Theology* (1909) ; E. Schürer, *Geschichte des jüdischen Volkes im Zeitalter Jesu* (1901, [4]1907, 1909) ; S. Zeitlin, *The History of the Second Jewish Commonwealth* (1933). Illuminating on special points are L. Finkelstein, *The Pharisees* (1940) ; also W. R. Farmer, *Maccabees, Zealots, Josephus* (1956). The following articles in *A Companion to the Bible*, ed. T. W. Manson (1939), supplement in the most convenient and effective way what is written above : W. O. E. Oesterley, 'Angelology and Demonology' ; L. Rabinowitz, 'The Scribes and the Law', 'The Synagogue and its Worship' ; H. Wheeler Robinson, 'The Religion of Israel' ; N. H. Snaith, 'The Priesthood and the Temple'.

PAGAN RELIGION AT THE COMING OF CHRISTIANITY

By R. McL. WILSON

620a 'Remember that you were at that time separated from Christ, alienated from the commonwealth of Israel, and strangers to the covenants of promise, having no hope and without God in the world' (Eph. 2:12).

If there is perhaps a certain over-emphasis about these words, they are yet on the whole an accurate estimate of the religious situation of the pagan world at the coming of the Gospel, as seen through Christian eyes. It was not that the men of this period had no religion, since the Athenians, for example, could be described as 'very religious' (Ac. 17:22). Nor was it that the pagan world had no idea of God, for in fact there were in paganism 'many "gods" and many "lords"' (1 C. 8:5). Moreover there were in contemporary thought certain trends in the direction of monotheism. In the earlier part of the Hellenistic Age the dominant tendency was rationalistic and sceptical, but in the 1st cent. B.C. the tide had begun to turn. All such trends, however, all such evidences of a religious awakening, are still a very different thing from worship of the living God, and this is the essential point. The burden of Paul's indictment of the Gentile world (Rom. 1:19ff.) is that 'although they knew God they did not honour him as God', but 'exchanged the truth about God for a lie, and worshipped the creature rather than the Creator'. Jewish religious propaganda, again, had enjoyed a measure of success, but broadly speaking the world with which we are concerned is one which stood apart from Judaism, a world which with some few exceptions had no knowledge of the traditions of Israel, little or no acquaintance with the Jewish scriptures, and certainly no share in the heritage of the Jewish faith.

b The temper of the age from 323 B.C. down to the middle of the 1st cent. is admirably characterised in Gilbert Murray's phrase 'The Failure of Nerve'. The centuries immediately preceding the coming of Christianity were a time of upheaval, unrest and uncertainty, when men, perplexed and bewildered by the onrush of events, had lost their confidence and were yearning desperately for some assurance, some firmer ground of hope. They were beset by a sense of helplessness and insecurity, of being adrift in a fragile craft upon a waste of seas, at the mercy of wind and waves:

> Other life is a fountain sealed,
> And the deeps below us are unrevealed,
> And we drift on legends for ever.
>
> (Euripides, tr. Murray)

With the triumph of Augustus in 31 B.C., however, another note is heard. If the First Eclogue of Virgil gives poignant expression to the uncertainty of a time of reconstruction, the Fourth voices the hopes that were cherished of a new and better age.

c To understand the religious situation of the pagan world in the Hellenistic Age (*c.* 320 B.C. to A.D. 100) it is necessary to consider both the character of pagan religion and the history of its development. **The official religion of ancient Greece** centred in the 620
worship of the gods of Olympus, the gods of Homer and the Greek tragedians, but this was hardly a religion in our sense of the term. It had neither creed nor theology, nor did it require of the worshipper more than the fulfilment of certain purely external observances. These rites and ceremonies were held to be necessary to secure the favour of the gods, and failure to meet the obligations of the cult involved the risk of losing that favour, both for the culprit and for his community; but the religious content of these observances depended entirely upon the sincerity of the individual worshipper. In this connection we may note the persistence over several centuries of ideas concerning the obligation to observe the official cult. The accusation laid against Socrates and others was not so much of innovation or of the introduction of new gods, but rather of refusing to acknowledge the gods upon whose goodwill depended the welfare of the state. So also later, if one aspect of the charge against the Christians was that of *laesa maiestas,* their refusal to worship the emperor being construed as disloyalty, another was, as we see from Augustine, that the neglect of the ancient cults was detrimental to the interests of the empire. The disaster of A.D. 410 was interpreted by some as the consequence of the recent prohibition of the ancient Roman ritual. In the Hellenistic Age and under the empire it was possible for men to perform religious ceremonies in honour of gods in whom they no longer really believed.

It may be that the worship of the gods of Olympus d
was a genuine faith and inspired a genuine devotion down to the 4th cent. B.C.; it may be that this was so in individual cases even later; but it is worthy of note that one of Festugière's main examples of personal religion, and one in which Nock also finds an approximation to the idea of 'conversion', is drawn from Apuleius in the 2nd cent. A.D., and concerns the worship not of the Olympians but of Isis. It is significant that votive offerings in honour of Athene found on the Acropolis are numerous for the period before the Persian War (before 400 B.C.), but fell off later and in the Hellenistic Age (300 B.C. on) are scarce (Nilsson). As Nilsson puts it, Greek religion from the beginning was indissolubly linked with the community. It was 'that side of the communal life in which due respect was paid to the gods, and their goodwill and grace assured'. The worship of the Olympians was thus in the main civic and corporate, not personal, and the possibility of satisfying the deepest needs of the individual in and through this worship was severely limited. It could offer no real explanation of the mystery of life, no sense of purpose in human existence, no real comfort in adversity; nor did it provide an incentive for conduct, or an assurance of immortality.

To the decline and eventual collapse of this religion e
several factors contributed. For one thing, it was too closely associated with mythology, nor was the mythology capable of a real adaptation to meet the changing needs of the times. On the ethical side in

620e particular it did not keep pace with the developing moral conscience of the period. **Plato** in his *Republic* condemns the poets for teaching things unworthy of the gods, and in this he was not alone. **Euripides** openly censured the ethical shortcomings of the Olympians, while **Xenophanes** even earlier had declared that Homer and Hesiod ascribed to the gods all that among men was a shame and a reproach, and had ridiculed the representation of the gods in human form: the Ethiopians portray their gods as black and flat-nosed, the Thracians as red-haired and blue-eyed; if horses and cattle could paint, they also would doubtless depict the gods in their own likeness. From the sophists of the 5th cent. downwards, the philosophical tradition as a whole is strongly critical of the official religion. According to a theory commonly associated with **Euhemerus,** though not originated by him, the gods were simply human beings who had been deified for their achievements.

f The worship of the Olympians, again, was intimately connected with the city-state, many of these gods indeed being the patron deities of the several cities. In the Hellenistic period, however, the city-states were absorbed into larger units, the empires of **Alexander the Great** and his successors, and finally that of Rome. As Nock has noted, the conquests of Alexander had two main results of significance for religion: an increasing contact between East and West, which led to an influx of oriental religions into the Greek world, and a widening of men's horizons. Henceforth the Eastern Mediterranean, with most of the old Persian empire, was a single cultural unit, and under the Roman empire this was to be true also of the Mediterranean world as a whole. No merely local faith was adequate for these conditions. A faith for the times had to have a cosmic significance and a universal appeal, and this the Olympian gods did not possess. They were remote and apart, untouched by the feeling of men's infirmities. Moreover, the intellectual movements of the 5th cent. had asserted the rights of the individual, and the needs of the individual worshipper now assume a growing prominence. There is evidence of a real hunger of the heart which the worship of the Olympians could not satisfy. In the uncertainty of the times this worship was unable to provide the comfort of a living religious faith.

621a **Popular Religion**—Philosophical criticism and a developing morality, the decline of the city-state and the rise of great empires, increasing contact with men of other faiths and the growth of individualism, all these contributed in some degree to the undermining of the religion of ancient Greece. To some extent, however, it was only the educated who were affected. The lower classes continued to hold their belief in the old gods, although it was rather the minor deities who were thus revered. Less remote than the Olympians, they were nearer to the heart of the people. For the great gods of Olympus were not the only gods who claimed allegiance in the Hellenistic world, and on the level of popular belief we have to take account not only of religion proper but also of magic and superstition in many forms.

b If some of the Olympians were primarily the patron deities of particular cities, others had something of a pan-Hellenic character, like Zeus at Olympia or Apollo at Delphi. One cult which spread both widely and rapidly was that of **Asclepius,** the god of healing, introduced into Athens in 420 B.C., and into Rome in 293. 'Of all the Greek gods, he was surrounded with the warmest devotion and affection, and he kept his popularity until he had to give way to Christian saints who took over his activities' (Nilsson). Another worship, of special interest as foreshadowing things to come, is that of **Dionysus,** vividly portrayed in the *Bacchae* of Euripides. Thraco-Phrygian in origin, this cult produced an outbreak of religious frenzy when it first entered Greece. The adherents were mainly women, who wandered on the mountain-sides, dancing in ecstasy. As the frenzy reached its climax, they seized a beast, tore it in pieces, and devoured the flesh 621b raw. Dionysiac orgies have passed into proverb. This cult was tamed by the priests of the Delphic Apollo, who gave it a place in the state religion, and in time it became 'stereotyped and sterile' (Nock). It had, however, a real influence on the development of Greek literature, for dramatic performances were part of the worship of Dionysus, and from these stemmed the Attic tragedy and comedy.

Orphism, which was related to the Dionysiac c religion, never commanded the full assent of the Greek mind, and its influence at the coming of Christianity is difficult to estimate. But Orphic literature exercised a wide influence, e.g. on such men as Pythagoras, Pindar and Plato, and through the writings of Plato in particular certain Orphic ideas were assimilated into later Greek thought. Orphism 'maintained that all men have an inherited guilt which dooms them to a weary round of reincarnations unless by use of its means of salvation they win release' (Nock). It held that the body (*sōma*) is a tomb (*sēma*) in which the soul is condemned to suffer, but the initiate, freed by Orphic purification from earthly dross, can attain after death to immortality and blessedness. For the wicked, conversely, the future holds but punishment and retribution. This involved a transformation of the Homeric (and general Greek) idea of Hades as a realm of shadows, a transformation which was to have lasting effects. Orphism is important for its stress on sin and guilt, for its doctrine of salvation through purification and holy living, and for the influence which it exercised indirectly on later thought, but it was never a widely popular movement. In Nock's words, it produced 'an idea of conversion and a sacred literature but no church'.

Of greater (and increasing) importance were the d mystery religions, to which special attention must be given (see §623). The cults which flourished in the Hellenistic Age were mainly of oriental origin, but they had in classical Greece a precursor in **the worship of Demeter at Eleusis**. Originally the agrarian rites of a small community, this worship had developed into a 'mystery', initiation into which was open to members of any Greek state, male or female, bond or free. The candidate was required to pass through various grades of initiation, each with its appropriate rites, and on the completion of these requirements could look forward to a brighter future in the next world. The Athenians however attempted to exploit this cult for political purposes, and tried to persuade the other city-states to join together around these mysteries by sending tithes to Eleusis, an example of a not uncommon tendency towards the secularisation of religion.

Magic and Superstition—'The sharpest contrast e between the classical period and late antiquity', says Nilsson, 'is in the increasing spread of superstition and sorcery during the latter'. Here it should be noted that there was no clear line of distinction in antiquity between magic and religion. In some of the mystery rites the initiate passed through a symbolic anticipation of things to come—'a piece of sympathetic magic which ensured safety by a simulation here and now' (Nock). In the magical papyri prayers and hymns selected from the religion of the day are used. Ac. records the meeting of Christian missionaries with magical practitioners of various types, and on one occasion it is said: 'A number of those who practised magic arts brought their books together and burned them in the sight of all; and they counted the value of them and found it came to fifty thousand pieces of silver' (Ac. 19:19). It is an indication of the credulity of the times that such men as Simon Magus were able to command a following. Divination, again, was a part of religion, although the Roman Cato wondered how two *haruspices* (diviners) could pass each other in the street without laughing at the vanity of their profession, and Cicero was astonished that anyone

621e could believe in the office of *augur* (Angus). Disease was attributed to the activity of demons, and we read of spells and charms and amulets to ward off all kind of ills.

f **Fatalism**—' The best seed-ground for superstition is a society in which the fortunes of men seem to bear practically no relation to their merits and efforts' (Murray). And such was the society of the Hellenistic Age. One of the fundamental concepts of the religious thought of classical Greece was that of *hubris*, with its attendant *nemesis*. *Hubris* is presumption in any form, an overstepping of the bounds which is visited by the gods with requital. Thus Pindar warns his patrons against undue pride, for ' mortal things fit mortal men'. In the Hellenistic Age this idea disappears. No longer do the gods strike down those who climb too high. Yet men could not entirely avoid the thought of a higher power behind events, which exalted a man or cast him down ; and this power they found in *Tyche* (Chance or Fortune). The rapid rise and fall of kingdoms and of rulers, the changing fortunes of individual men, all the uncertainties of human existence, depended on the whim of a ' blind, fickle, capricious, unreliable ' Chance.

g A slightly different theory, upheld by the Stoics whereas that of *Tyche* was maintained by the Epicureans (cf. J. D. Duff on Juv. xiii, 86), was that of Fate (*Heimarmene*). It is sometimes difficult to determine whether Fate to the ancient world meant the will of the gods, or a power that is above even them. The decline of the old religion, combined with the rise of **astrology,** led to the belief that the world is governed by an unchangeable fate written in the stars or determined by them (cf. §624f.). This theory reached full development only through contact with Babylonian ideas, but the seed was already sown by Plato, who in his old age found in the heavenly bodies the true gods who followed immutable laws. For the Stoic, Fate is the Reason of the world, the law of God which is also the law of man's own nature. To live in accordance with one's true nature is to fulfil that law, to comply with the divine *Heimarmene*, whose service is perfect freedom. But in the later stages of the Hellenistic Age the heavenly bodies have become malignant powers and Fate a bondage from which men long to escape.

622a **Religion in Rome**—In religion as in other spheres

> Greece, captive Greece, her conqueror subdued,
> And Rome grew polished, who till then was rude.
>
> (Hor. Ep. II, i, 156f., tr. Conington)

The Greek influence on Roman religion goes back, however, well beyond the Roman conquest of Greece. From an early period the gods of Rome, Jupiter, Juno, Minerva, were identified with those of the Greeks, Zeus, Hera, Athene. In many respects indeed Rome may be considered as a Hellenistic city. Roman religion, like Greek, was polytheistic and largely concerned with the maintenance of right relations with the gods. The Roman *pietas* was formal and civic, and the primary function of religion was the promotion of the welfare of the state. At the same time there are differences to be observed. For one thing, the Senate exercised a measure of control over the introduction of new faiths, and although Rome was tolerant in admitting new gods prompt action was taken when a foreign religion seemed likely to infect society with a ritual contrary to the ancestral customs (*mos maiorum*). Thus after the introduction of Magna Mater from Phrygia in 204 B.C., the discovery that orgiastic rites were connected with her worship led to a decree that no Roman citizen should take part. In the same way, some twenty years later, the worship of Dionysus was suppressed. Nor are these examples isolated, for at various times we read of the expulsion from the city of philosophers and *rhetors* (itinerant preachers), or of Jews and astrologers.

b Again, the basis of Roman society was the family, and a prominent element in Roman religion was the worship of the Lares and Penates, the gods of hearth and home. This had its counterpart in the state festivals which served to maintain the sense of national solidarity. If the official religion of Rome was in some ways even more formal than that of Greece, it held out longer against the impact of philosophical criticism. Roman society after the Hannibalic War (202 B.C.) was still essentially a religious society. Some of the nobles, under the influence of Greek culture, might have begun to have their doubts, but the ordinary people still believed in the old gods and scepticism was not yet general. In this connection Smith refers to Polybius, who tries to explain away the attitude of the nobles towards religion in a way typical of a Greek rationalist, by suggesting that it was to keep the people in check, but really disproves his own explanation. The sceptical Carneades, at Cato's instance, was hustled from the city, whereas the Stoic Panaetius, with a finer feeling for Roman sentiment, could gain the confidence of the nobles. It is significant that it was Stoicism, always more in harmony with religion, which had the greatest appeal for the Romans.

After the fall of Carthage in 146 B.C., however, decay set in, and the history of the last century of the republic is one of a disintegrating society. While Rome remained a city-state, with a population mainly of the old Roman stock, the old ideals might be maintained ; but Rome was now fast becoming the capital of a world-empire, and the population ' an amalgam of all nations and creeds, a rootless proletariat, to most of whom the traditions of Rome and her *mos maiorum* were never known, by the rest of whom they were now forgotten ' (Smith). To this disintegration the acids of Greek scepticism contributed, as did the political history of the period. In Rome as in other great cities the growth of a cosmopolitan population led to the introduction of foreign cults, which promised to the individual worshipper happiness and eternal bliss, and gave to those who had neither privilege nor security at least the hope of deliverance from the bondage of remorseless Fate. These cults attracted chiefly the lower classes, who were also the most addicted to magic, astrology and superstition. The educated for the most part sought refuge in philosophy. The countryside, again, was more conservative than the city ; as Smith observes, ' if the countryside in later centuries could for so long withstand the onset of Christianity in its devotion to its own small gods, we should need some strong, compelling reason to explain its temporary eclipse at this time '. Once again, this living devotion is directed not to the great gods of official worship but to the minor deities, the gods of hearth and field. Augustus, when he became master of the world, attempted to restore the ancient order, with considerable success, but in the first century of the Christian era a change is noticeable. The old senatorial nobility was seriously weakened, and the composition of the ruling-class had changed from a predominantly Roman to a cosmopolitan ; there was in consequence a change in the whole tone of society. Juvenal can speak of Orontes flowing into Tiber (*Sat.* iii, 62) ; from this time on the oriental mystery religions assume an ever greater prominence. c

Rome, however, not only received, but also gave. The Romanisation of the Western provinces was much more thorough than the Hellenisation of the East. Latin was the language of the superior culture, and the native deities were Romanised and identified with the Roman gods. Rome herself had attained, even under the republic, to the status of a deity : ' the thrill of awe with which the provincials saw the advance of Roman power and Roman justice could only express itself in terms of an altar and incense ' (Murray). Closely associated with this reverence for the supreme city was **the cult of the emperor.** Augustus himself did not claim divine honours in d

622d Rome, but the *genius Augusti* was worshipped along with Dea Roma in the East, and some of his successors were not so scrupulous. At first the emperor was deified only after his death, and some who were felt to have been unworthy, like Nero and Caligula, were not deified at all ; but it was only a matter of time before the reigning emperor, like earlier rulers of Hellenistic empires, was regarded as a god in his lifetime. The idea goes back to primitive times and was to the native populations of Syria and Egypt almost a matter of course, although in Greece and Rome it was adopted only slowly. The one Hellenistic monarchy whose king was not regarded as a god was Macedon, and Alexander's claims were mocked, although they could not be resisted, in Athens. For Rome the beginning can be traced to the deification of Julius Caesar after his death. Augustus indeed had a better claim than many, for he had brought peace and security to the world after years of strife. In his case the inscriptions hailing him as Saviour were no conventional tributes, like so many tributes to a benefactor, but the recognition of a real service to mankind. Even so, as Epictetus was to observe, ' Caesar can give peace from war, but he cannot give peace from sorrow '. The cult of the emperor served as a bond of unity, linking the far-flung provinces in a common loyalty, but there were deeper longings which it could not satisfy.

e Tolerance in matters of religion was normal in the ancient world, except when some form of worship was felt to be undesirable. The Greeks, and the Romans after them, took it for granted that the gods of other peoples were simply their own gods under different names. The way was therefore open to any faith which did not offend against propriety. In the light of this the persecutions suffered by the Christian Church appear remarkable until it is remembered that they were due not to the fanaticism of the adherents of other faiths but rather to political factors. All that was required in the cult of the emperor was a prayer for the welfare of Rome, Caesar, and the empire as a whole, and the recognition of the divine destiny of Rome by means of a gift of incense ; but to Jew or Christian this was idolatry, apostasy from the true and living God. Judaism enjoyed something of a privileged position, but after the breach with the synagogue Christianity could no longer profit from being regarded as a Jewish sect. It was not that the faith became immediately illegal, but at least from the time of Nero it was certainly suspect. In the NT we can trace two widely differently attitudes to Rome : Paul insists on loyalty, and other writings, like the later apologists, reveal a desire to remove all suspicion of disloyalty ; but the author of Rev. looks on Rome with a ferocious hatred. By the end of the 1st cent. A.D. Christians had become ' a third race ', alongside Greeks and barbarians, and Tacitus can bring against them the charge of ' hatred of the human race '. The point of conflict was the refusal of the Christians to participate in the imperial cult. Pergamum, ' where Satan's seat is ' (Rev. 2:13), was one of the chief centres of the imperial cult in Asia Minor.

623a **The Mystery Cults**—Reference has already been made at several points to the oriental mystery religions, which attained to an ever increasing prominence in the Hellenistic Age, and particularly in the first centuries of the Christian era. This prominence is significant as an indication that rationalism and scepticism were not the only factors in the religious situation of the period. If in the earier part of the Hellenistic Age the tendency was in the direction of scepticism, the tide had turned by the 1st cent. B.C., and by the time that Christianity appeared on the scene it is possible to say that a real religious awakening was in progress. To this the prevalence of magic and superstition likewise point : men were becoming conscious of a need, and were in search of a faith to meet that need.

b In its origins Christianity itself must have appeared
to the men of the age as just another of these oriental 623b
cults. Like them, it came out of the East ; like them, it promised salvation. Like them also, it centred upon a Saviour who died and rose again, and like them it gave a special place to certain rites : baptism and a sacred meal. It is therefore only natural that questions should be raised as to the possible influence of these cults on the thought of the early Church, but here the greatest care is necessary. At a later stage indeed much was taken over and ' baptised ' into the service of the Christian faith : in Mithraism, 25 December had a special place as the birthday of the god ; the image-type representing the Madonna and Child has been traced back to statues of Isis and the infant Horus. It must be admitted that the Church in later ages absorbed into its belief and practice those elements which it could take over without doing violence to its own essential faith ; but this is a very different matter from the view that these cults exercised a formative influence upon Christianity in its earliest stages. And closer examination reveals certain decisive differences. For one thing, these religions are without exception mythological, associated in their origins with the renewal of vegetation in the spring ; in no case is the saviour an actual historical figure, who truly lived and truly died. Again, it is necessary to pay attention to chronology ; many of these cults were indeed widely current before the rise of Christianity, but we require to consider whether the suspected point of influence was already part of the cult, or whether, as the patristic writers allege, it was actually copied from Christianity itself. Finally, one of the distinctive features of NT Christianity is its capacity to adopt and transform the words and ideas of the world around, making them the vehicles for the expression of its own theology. We must therefore ask if such a man as Paul, in using language which recalls that of the mysteries, is employing it in ' mystery ' fashion, or giving to it a completely new and truly Christian connotation (cf. an article by B. M. Metzger, with full bibliography, in HTR (1955)).

The Propagation of these Cults was facilitated by c
the conditions of the time. The increased contacts between East and West after Alexander, the movements of population, whether voluntarily for purposes of trade or under compulsion, the spread of the Greek language as the common speech of the Eastern half of the Mediterranean world, and latterly, under the empire, the political unity and comparative peace which that world enjoyed, all contributed to the spread of these religions, and to that of Christianity itself. The roads built for the legions carried also the merchant and the evangelist. In 333–332 B.C. merchants from Citium in Cyprus resident in Athens were granted permission to build a temple, ' just as the Egyptians have built the temple of Isis ' (Nock). Such groups, like the synagogues of the Jewish dispersion, not only maintained the worship of their fathers in the lands of their adoption, but also served a missionary purpose.

At this point attention may be drawn to a notable d
feature of the period, the growth of small **societies** (*thiasoi*, *collegia*), associations of people who shared the same function, trade or profession, or the same religion. *Collegia* were known in Rome in the later days of the Republic, when they became so dangerously partisan that they were banned by Julius Caesar ; in the Hellenistic world similar private associations had had a long history (cf. Johnston, *Doctrine of the Church*, 5f.). These societies were not merely trade associations or guilds of craftsmen ; they had also a social function. They cared for the welfare of their members and arranged for their honourable burial, with due observance of the customary rites ; and they provided a fellowship to which the individual could resort, to which he *belonged*, and in which he could find some recognition and a measure of self-respect. Under the empire the number of such societies showed a remarkable increase. Some of them were no doubt originally

623d formed by resident aliens for the observance of their native worship, but these eventually lost their national character; some groups certainly at a later date served the purposes of the oriental cults.

e The strength of these religions is difficult to estimate, but two points must be noted: (i) 'For the subsequent expansion of cults from the Near East in Greece and in the West no worships are of great importance except those which were substantially translated into Greek and remade with Greek elements into cults which retained an Oriental flavour but were divorced from their original cultural and religious setting' (Nock); (ii) 'Apart from the one exception of Isis, who received a state temple under the reign of Caligula, no single example can be observed before the beginning of the 3rd cent. of the penetration of foreign cults into the circle of the traditional gods of Rome' (Altheim). The latter point is significant as indicating the popular character of these cults, over against the official religion of the state. Some measure of recognition might be granted to a particular cult, but we have also evidence, at any rate in Rome, of a certain resistance on the part of the authorities, especially where the worship was considered a potential danger to morality. Thus under the republic the shrines of Isis and Serapis were destroyed four times within ten years, while under Tiberius, as the result of a scandal, the temple was destroyed and the image thrown into the Tiber. Nevertheless the cult became official under Caligula.

f The first point requires fuller treatment, since it leads to consideration of the characteristic phenomenon of the age: **Syncretism.** From an early period the Greeks assumed that the gods of other nations were simply the familiar Greek gods under other names, an assumption which, it may be noted, explains the ethical shortcomings of the Olympians. When Zeus, for example, absorbed the chief god of some local cult, he was associated with a spouse who did not always correspond to Hera; as a result, he was finally credited with a host of consorts. Syncretism reached its climax in the Hellenistic Age, when the gods of oriental faiths were identified with those of Greece and Rome. Thus the Baal of Doliche appears in Rome under Vespasian as Jupiter Dolichenus, and is closely associated with Jupiter Heliopolitanus, the Baal of Heliopolis. Serapis again appears in Ptolemaic times as the god of a new cult which was to have a wide diffusion; he was to be 'an Egyptian to the Egyptians and a Greek to the Greeks' (Nock). The outstanding example, however, is that of Isis, who can be addressed as *una quae es omnia*, the goddess 'whose unique name in manifold forms, in various titles the whole world adores' (Apuleius, Met. xi, 5). Closely associated with this syncretism was the philosophical tendency to explain the gods as natural forces, or as so many manifestations of the one supreme God. These tendencies united to lead the Hellenistic mind towards monotheism. Here again the religious tolerance of the age may be noted; only Jews and Christians stood apart, and the Jews at least were subject to misconception, for the God of Israel was identified sometimes with Zeus, sometimes with Saturn, and also (by a misunderstanding of Sabaoth) with the Phrygian Sabazius.

g **The Ceremonies of the Mysteries** were, as the name implies, reserved for the initiate and our knowledge is therefore limited. Aristotle says that the candidate required not to learn anything but to receive an experience, and to be put into a certain frame of mind. By participation in these rites he became united with the god, even deified, and looked forward to eternal bliss. What initiation could mean is revealed in the pages of **Apuleius,** although of course he does not disclose the inner secrets. On the other hand, there is no idea in the mystery cults that initiation would make it easier to live a good life. Here a contrast is sometimes drawn between the mysteries and Christianity, but once more it is important to be exact: there is in the mysteries an ethical element, or at least an element capable of development in an ethical direction, but it was more a question of ritual purity than of genuine morality. Of a real spiritual dynamic and a demand for renunciation of the old ways and a renewal of life there is but little sign. The pagan **Celsus** contrasts the appeal of the mysteries with that of Christianity, the mysteries summoning the pure, Christianity the sinful; but the point is that Christianity claims a renewal of life. The convert could no longer continue in his sins. Again, it must be observed that initiation, like the *taurobolium* in the cults of Cybele and Mithras, must have been the privilege of the few; both were expensive, and open only to men of means. The average worshipper would take part only in the public ceremonies, in prayers and sacrifices.

The general character of the oriental cults has h already been outlined in describing the mysteries of Eleusis, which indeed exercised an influence on the development and Hellenisation of some at least among them. Originally fertility-cults, they became universalised by their transference to alien soil, and in the process also civilised. The more barbaric elements were as a rule removed or modified into something more in keeping with Graeco-Roman feeling; yet some such elements remained. Not until the time of Claudius could a Roman citizen become an *archigallus* in the rites of Cybele.

The individual cults varied in their range of dif- i fusion and in their power to attract adherents. The most widely popular, particularly in regions which had some connection with Egypt, was that of **Isis,** sometimes alone and sometimes in association with Serapis. This worship had a long history from its first appearance in the Greek world in Hellenistic Athens, and was the last of all to yield before a triumphant Christianity. The Syrian deities played a relatively unimportant role in Rome and flourished mainly in regions occupied by troops; their worshippers were either soldiers or of oriental origin. The worship of **Cybele,** on the other hand, was early Romanised, although it is not entirely certain whether Attis was already associated with the Great Mother in the earliest period. The spread of **Mithraism** again was largely due to the army; though in its origins it goes far back into Persian religion, and though under the empire it became widely popular, it did not attain to prominence until late in the 1st cent. A.D. This cult was unique in that its appeal was solely to men; moreover Mithras, before he reached Rome, had become a solar god and is identified in an inscription of the 1st cent. B.C. with Apollo, Helios and Hermes.

Finally, it should be noted that these religions made j a real appeal to the sentiments of the age. Their claims were cosmopolitan and universal, and they offered a genuine emotional satisfaction to people oppressed by the burden of life. They promised to their initiates escape from the bondage of Fate, deliverance from the power of the demons, and rebirth after death into life and immortality. They were popular because they ministered to a deeply felt need. The ultimate victory of Christianity was due to the fact that it could do all that its rivals promised, and do it better.

Philosophy and Religion—The criticism of the phil- 624a osophers was one of the factors which led to the collapse of the ancient Greek religion, but in the later Hellenistic period philosophy itself takes on something of the character of a religion. 'The attitude of Lucretius to Epicureanism', says Nock, 'is that of a man who has undergone the psychological experience which we call conversion'. The explanation lies in the character of Hellenistic philosophy itself, in the course of development of Graeco-Roman thought, and in the emphases which were dominant in the thinking of the period. Following the temper of the age, the Hellenistic schools departed from the metaphysics of Plato and Aristotle and stressed the problems of human

624a life, notably the conduct and happiness of the individual (Pfeiffer).

b At the beginning of the Hellenistic period we find five main schools, of which those of Plato and Aristotle soon lost ground, although the former in the Neo-Platonism of **Plotinus** was later to become once more prominent. Pythagoreanism also enjoyed something of a revival from the 1st cent. B.C., but the three schools which held the stage were the Cynic, Epicurean and Stoic. The characteristic aim of all three may be summed up as the self-sufficiency of the individual and his indifference to external circumstances, although they differed in the forms by which they gave expression to this ideal. The **Cynics** stressed the worthlessness of conventional standards and defined virtue as the capacity to reduce one's wants to a minimum. The typical Cynic is the famous Diogenes, and the stories told about him reflect the impression made by the movement. The later Cynics appeared as itinerant evangelists, and the influence of the Cynic diatribe has been detected in the NT.

c **Epicureanism** has unjustly suffered from a misunderstanding of its ethical ideal. Epicurus followed the Cyrenaic school of Aristippus in making pleasure the supreme goal of life, but in spite of Horace's *Epicuri de grege porcus* his emphasis was not (as with Aristippus) on the pleasures of the senses, but on *ataraxia*, serenity or impassiveness, even in the midst of adversity. In fact, to Epicurus 'pleasure' is not positive happiness, but rather lack of pain; as Murray puts it, this was a philosophy not of conquest but of escape. It did, however, inspire a real enthusiasm, as in Lucretius, whose great poem is the fullest extant exposition of the master's teaching. **Lucretius** wrote expressly to deliver men from the terrors of superstition. The gods exist indeed, but they dwell apart, in 'the lucid interspace of world and world', and have no concern with earthly things. Epicurus had been deeply impressed by the atomism of Democritus, and made it the foundation of his system. Since everything results by chance from a fortuitous combination of atoms, the soul is dissolved at death. There is no future for a man to fear. Religion, and ideas of immortality, are false. Epicureanism, however, did not become the dominant philosophy of the age.

d The most successful and influential school of all was the **Stoic,** which also offered the most acceptable solutions both to the metaphysical and to the practical problems of the time. According to Stoic doctrine, the cosmos emerges from fire and to fire returns in the final conflagration. The Stoic God, himself material, is the mind or soul of the universe, the immanent cosmic logos, a fiery spirit which reaches out to all parts of the universe through its 'seminal logoi' or powers. With this fiery spirit the human soul is essentially one, and to live in accordance with 'nature', with the highest dictates of one's own being, is to live in harmony with the divine purpose and so attain to virtue. There are of course variations in points of detail between the Stoic leaders, and particularly in regard to the final destiny of the soul. The system at its purest is represented by the early teachers, Zeno, Cleanthes and Chrysippus. Panaetius of Rhodes was more eclectic, accepting certain Platonic and Aristotelian teachings, and the process was carried still further by **Posidonius,** the last truly original Greek thinker, who built up a system combining Stoic and Platonic thought which was to become the dominant philosophy of the later Hellenistic Age. For Posidonius, 'the human soul is a portion of the fiery cosmic spirit, descending to earth to be imprisoned in the body and polluted by its passions. Here it yearns for communion with God and full knowledge, but they can be attained only through deliverance from the body and return to God' (Pfeiffer). In later Stoicism the original doctrine was modified in two directions: on the one hand a greater measure of transcendence was allowed to God, while on the other Posidonius admitted some hope of immortality 624d
at least for the great and good. Reincarnation, according to the Platonic tradition, is the punishment of the lowest class of earth-bound souls. The admission of even a partial immortality of course opened the way for a more general hope, such as was offered by the mystery religions. Stoicism indeed provided the vocabulary for the restatement of these religions (Reitzenstein), and **Philo of Alexandria** endeavoured to vindicate the intellectual respectability of Judaism by reading the philosophy of Posidonius into the OT.

Philo's method was that of allegorical interpretation: a deeper meaning was sought behind the plain surface of the sacred narrative. In this Philo was the precursor of a long tradition in the Christian Church, but he was also following a method which had earlier been applied in the attempt to make Greek religion rational. After the collapse of the official Greek religion men sought to salvage something from the wreckage, and one of the methods employed was that of reinterpreting the ancient gods as so many powers or manifestations of the supreme god, or as natural forces or elements controlled by him, and allegorising the myths into an edifying philosophy. As a result, the Stoics were able to combine the highest philosophy of the time with the most utter superstition. e

Science and Cosmology—The Hellenistic Age is marked by certain outstanding achievements in the realm of science, achievements which anticipated by centuries the discoveries of the modern world (see Pfeiffer, 110ff.). Aristarchus of Samos, for example, advanced the theory that the earth revolves around the sun, centuries before Copernicus. The accepted theory however was the geocentric, itself a novelty in this period: earth occupied the centre, and around it turned the spheres of the seven heavenly bodies; the eighth and highest of the heavens was the sphere of the fixed stars, in which the zodiac occupies the most important place. This 'new' cosmology involved profound consequences for religion and philosophy. Plato already had regarded the planets as divine and living bodies, but later thinkers were to develop the idea under the influence of Babylonian **astrology,** which 'fell upon the Hellenistic mind as a new disease falls upon some remote island people' (Murray). Once again the pioneer was Posidonius. In the developed systems of later antiquity, the soul belongs essentially to the Ogdoad, the realm of the supreme God above the seven heavens, but in this life it is subjected to the dominion of the planetary powers. The salvation for which men yearned was deliverance from the power of the stars. At its highest the astrological view of the universe could become an 'astral mysticism' (Cumont), in which the bliss of the elect consists in the contemplation of the movements of the celestial bodies; at the other extreme it could become a matter of equipping the soul with the passwords necessary to ensure its safe conduct through the heavenly spheres. f

The Dispersion—To complete the picture, some reference must be made to two further factors: the Jewish dispersion and the Gnostic strain. These may seem out of place in a discussion of pagan religion, yet both are relevant. The Judaism of the Hellenistic Age was not identical with the faith of the OT, nor yet with Rabbinic Judaism; nor was the Judaism of the dispersion exactly that of Palestine. In the wider environment of the Hellenistic world the Jew was brought into daily contact with men of other faiths. The Jews were indeed exclusive, and in such a city as Alexandria were exposed to the hostility of their Gentile neighbours; one of the commonest charges laid against them is that of 'hatred of strangers'. But there is evidence also of a considerable interaction of Jewish and pagan thought. If the Jews admittedly received, they also gave. The synagogue was not only a meeting-place and place of worship for the Jews; it was also a missionary centre. If many Gentiles were unable to become full proselytes because of the 625a

625a obligations imposed (such as circumcision), they could still remain as adherents on the fringe. It was among these that Christianity found its earliest Gentile converts. From the 3rd or 2nd cent. B.C., again, the Jewish scriptures were available in Greek translation, and the Jews moreover conducted a fairly extensive literary propaganda. Reference has already been made to Philo's allegorical interpretation of the OT ; Josephus, in addition to his historical works, also wrote against Apion an apology for Judaism. The influence of this propaganda is difficult to estimate, and it may have been confined to circles already attracted to Judaism, but Philo shows that it was certainly possible to present the Jewish faith in terms of the dominant philosophy of the time. If the Jews were unpopular, their religion exercised an attraction. Again, the Jews had a reputation in the world of magic, and the name of the God of Israel appears in the form JAO in the magical papyri. Of some syncretistic cults it is difficult to say whether we have to do with Hellenising Jews or Judaising Gentiles. The influence of Hellenism upon the Judaism of the last centuries before the Christian era was certainly very great, but as Dodd observes it would be a mistake to assume that the influence was always and entirely on the one side.

b **Gnosticism**—The Gnostic heresy reached its height in the second Christian century, when it constituted a real danger to the unity of the Church and the purity of its doctrine. Irenaeus then, and Hippolytus and others later, sought in their refutations to overthrow its teachings, and it is from their works that our main knowledge of the developed Gnostic systems is derived (but original Gnostic documents in Coptic are extant, most of them as yet unpublished). The origins of the movement, however, may be traced back with certainty into the 1st cent. A.D., and are possibly even earlier. The fact that the heresy combated in Col. seems to be a Gnosticism of a Judaising character, like the doctrines of the opponents attacked by Ignatius, suggests that there was a Jewish Gnosticism before there was a Christian. Here again, however, care is necessary. Irenaeus and especially Hippolytus regarded the Gnostic theories as the result of a dilution of Christianity by Greek philosophy, in Harnack's phrase ' the acute Hellenisation of Christianity ', but more recent research has tended to stress the oriental element. What is certain is that Gnosticism was strongly syncretistic ; almost the entire Near East has made its contribution (Quispel). But there is a real danger of reading back too much into an earlier period, and finding Gnosticism where none as yet truly existed. The mere occurrence of words like *gnosis* and similar terms is not decisive, since the sect of the Dead Sea Scrolls quite clearly claimed a special knowledge, which is however different from that of 2nd-cent. Gnosticism and also from that of Hellenistic syncretism.

c Closely associated with Gnosticism is the movement which produced **the Hermetic Literature.** Final proof of this association is afforded by the discovery in a Gnostic library in Egypt of a number of Hermetic texts. These also serve to show that the Gnostic movement in the widest sense was more than a Christian heresy ; yet Gnosticism and Hermetism are in many ways distinct. The Hermetic literature is more philosophical, more mystical, giving noble expression to what has been called ' the higher religion of Paganism '. Gnosticism on the whole is less philosophical, more mythological, and at times akin to magic. Both however at their best are capable of giving expression to a genuine religious feeling and a lofty aspiration.

626a The present article has aimed only at presenting a general picture of the religious situation of the pagan world at the coming of the Gospel, a situation which was the outcome of some three or four centuries of development from the greatest days of classical Greece, and of the penetration of Graeco-Roman thought and belief by ideas drawn from many sources, Greek and oriental, philosophical and religious. A general picture is inevitably distorted, above all in such a case as this. Not every Jew was a Philo, nor on the other hand was he like Philo's nephew, Tiberius Alexander, who to become a Roman procurator must have abandoned the faith of his fathers. Allowance must be made for the individual in all his manifold variety.

b One thing, however, is abundantly clear : that the religious development of the pagan world was in a real sense a preparation for the Gospel. The Christian faith emerged upon the stage of a wider world in a time of comparative peace, when its missionaries could travel in some security from the Euphrates to the English Channel ; when over a large part of the civilised world one common language was in general use, and when there were in most of the great cities communities of Jews, and synagogues in which to launch their mission. The breakdown of the ancient religion had left a vacuum in human life ; new ideas, new problems, new aspirations, all demanded fulfilment and satisfaction. In the fullest sense, the time was ripe for the launching of a world-religion. Christianity succeeded in ' the conflict of religions ' because it met and satisfied both the religious and the philosophical needs of the time.

Bibliography—C. K. Barrett, *The NT Background : Selected Documents* (1956) ; E. Bevan, etc., *The Hellenistic Age* (1923) ; R. Bultmann, *Primitive Christianity in its Contemporary Setting* (1956) ; G. H. C. Macgregor and A. C. Purdy, *Jew and Greek : Tutors unto Christ* (1936) ; A. D. Nock, *Conversion* (1933), ' Early Gentile Christianity and its Hellenistic Background ' (in *Essays on the Trinity and the Incarnation*, ed. A. E. J. Rawlinson) (1928) ; R. H. Pfeiffer, *History of NT Times* (detailed bibliographies) (1949) ; W. W. Tarn, *Hellenistic Civilisation*[2] (1930) ; P. Wendland, *Die hellenistisch-römische Kultur*[2] (1912).

GREEK RELIGION : A. J. Festugière, *Personal Religion among the Greeks* (1954) ; W. C. Greene, *Moira* (1944) ; W. K. C. Guthrie, *Orpheus and Greek Religion* (2nd ed. 1952) ; G. Murray, *Five Stages of Greek Religion* (1935) ; M. P. Nilsson, *Greek Piety* (1948), *History of Greek Religion* (1925).

ROMAN RELIGION : F. Altheim, *History of Roman Religion* (1938) ; R. E. Smith, *Failure of the Roman Republic* (1955).

MYSTERY RELIGIONS : S. Angus, *The Mystery Religions and Christianity* (1925) ; H. I. Bell, *Cults and Creeds in Egypt* (1953) ; F. Cumont, *Les religions orientales dans le paganisme Romain*[4] (1929, ET 1911) ; T. R. Glover, *Conflict of Religions in the Roman Empire* (11th ed. 1927) ; H. A. A. Kennedy, *St Paul and the Mystery Religions* (1913) ; R. Reitzenstein, *Die hellenistischen Mysterienreligionen*[3] (1927).

ASTROLOGY : F. H. Cramer, *Astrology in Roman Law and Politics* (1954) ; F. Cumont, *Astrology in Graeco-Roman Paganism* (1912).

HERMETISM : C. H. Dodd, *The Bible and the Greeks* (1935) ; A. J. Festugière, *Hermes Trismégiste* (1944–54) ; G. van Moorsel, *The Mysteries of Hermes Trismegistus* (1955). See also C. H. Dodd, *Interpretation of the Fourth Gospel* (1953).

GNOSTICISM : W. Bousset, *Hauptprobleme der Gnosis* (1907) ; F. C. Burkitt, *Church and Gnosis* (1932) ; H. Jonas, *Gnosis und Spätantiker Geist* (new ed. 1954) ; G. Quispel, *Gnosis als Weltreligion* (1951) ; R. McL. Wilson, *The Gnostic Problem* (1958). For the new Coptic texts see *The Jung Codex* (ed. F. L. Cross) (1955), and J. Doresse, *Les livres secrets des gnostiques d'Égypte* (1958).

THE DOCTRINE OF THE CHURCH IN THE NEW TESTAMENT

By G. JOHNSTON

627a When the Christian movement emerged within Judaism, nationalism was being fed on memories of the successful rebellion against the Syrians by the Maccabees (cf. Heb. 11:33–38) and various groups were seeking to maintain the character of Israel as a divinely chosen people. The easy-going Sadducees, the scholarly and devout Pharisees of Jerusalem and the towns, the monastic Zadokite Covenanters, and perhaps other baptist sects, were all actively expecting 'the era of favour', God's good time when he would rule the earth. The decisive mark of the Christians was not that they provided a rival school of biblical exegesis or a more efficient organisation for piety or an outlet for Zealots. It was rather their simple, audacious assertion that he who was to come (Lk. 7:19) had come; now they awaited his final victory (Ac. 2:36, 3:20, 13:23; 1 Jn 2:22, 5:20). Hence the doctrine of their 'Church' was tied indissolubly to their Christology.

b **Jesus and the Church**—In some sense, of course, this movement began when Jesus of Nazareth began his mission in Judaea and Galilee with the calling of disciples (Jn 1:35ff.; Mk 1:15ff.), although Simon Peter did not confess Jesus as the Messiah till the crisis of Caesarea Philippi (Mk 8:29 is preferable to Jn 1:41f., 49; cf. Jn 6:68f.; but an initial form of Messianic recognition is not improbable). In another sense there was no effective Christian society before the Resurrection, and all our NT documents come to us in the afterglow of Easter. A proper theology of the Church is, inevitably, post-resurrection. It is significant that of the Evangelists only Matthew uses the word 'church' (*ecclesia*, 16:18, 18:17), and that Luke introduces it without explanation after his account of Pentecost (Ac. 5:11). There is, however, not the slightest doubt that the Church is the outcome of Jesus' ministry and intention. When at the Last Supper he assembled his closest disciples for a unique rite, he expressed his desire that they should repeat it after his death (1 C. 11:25), in glad recollection that he had given his life a ransom for the commonalty of God's people (Mk 10:45, 14:24; cf. Isa. 53:11; 'the many' in *Zadokite Fragments*, CD 13:7, and *Manual of Discipline*, 1QS 5:22). The abiding question is whether Matthew correctly ascribes to Jesus the word 'church' in its Hebrew or Aramaic equivalent. Did Jesus organise his followers in such a way as this would imply? Fresh impetus to the study of this problem has been given by the evidence of the sectarian literature (constitutional and liturgical texts) from Qumrân, belonging probably to the period 160 to 31 B.C. Millar Burrows writes: 'More important than the form of organisation is what may be called the church idea, the concept of a spiritual group, the true people of God, distinct from the Jewish nation as such. In the Qumrân community's concept of itself can be seen an approach to this, doubtless without a full realisation of all its implications' (*The Dead Sea Scrolls* (1955), 332; cf. T. H. Gaster, *The Dead Sea Scriptures* (1956), 33).

It has long been known that *ecclesia* translates Heb. *ḳāhāl*, 'assembly', in Dt., 1–2 Chr., Ezr.-Neh., Mic., and elsewhere in the Septuagint, although in Exod., Num., and Lev. *ḳāhāl* is translated by *synagoge* ('synagogue'). In the Qumrân literature (QL) *ḳāhāl* appears so far (1957) about ten times: for a judicial assembly (1QSa 1:25) or an army (1QM 1:10). 'God's *ḳāhāl*' is the sign on a banner (1QM 4:10), and the same phrase is used in 1QSa for the holy convocation of God's people (cf. Dt. 23:1ff., in ref. to which Philo uses *ecclesia*). Far more important in QL are the words *sôdh*, *'ēṣāh*, *yaḥadh*, and *'ēdhāh*. 627b

Sôdh (counsel, foundation, assembly) appears in the *Manual* as the order into which postulants were advanced for a year before final admission into full membership (1QS 6:19). Prior to that they entered the **'ēṣāh** or council of the community, but did not share the board of the members (1QS 6:16). 'The council of the community' occurs frequently (e.g. 1QSa 1:26f.; 1Q14, 8–10, line 8). **Yaḥadh** may be used as an adverb, as in all examples in *The War of the Sons of Light against the Sons of Darkness* (1QM; cf. *Thanksgiving Hymns*, 1QH 3:22f.); or in the sense of 'in union with' (1QH 6:13, 11:11; 1QSb 4:26). One version in Greek of 1 Chr. 12:17 employs *henosis* ('union') for *yaḥadh* (alliance in battle is the context). But its technical use in the *Manual of Discipline* is for the Qumrân brotherhood or that Community to which the Qumrân 'camp' belonged. It is not distinct from Israel (1QS 8:5, 9:6), but embodies the true Israel and as such is God's holy *yaḥadh* (1QS 1:12, 9:2). It is the '*yaḥadh* of truth' (1QS 1:24), i.e. the Union of those Jews who have renewed the old Sinai covenant, believing that the Law is the Truth of God (1Q34b, 2:5–7 in Barthélemy-Milik, *Discoveries in the Judaean Desert I: Qumran Cave I* (1955), 154). This covenant was probably reaffirmed annually (1QS 2:19). They were pledged on oath to observe the Law of Moses and live together in brotherly love and mutual obedience (1QS 1:8–10, 6:22, 8:12–16; 1QM 10:9, 13:9f.; 1QH 6:9–11, 10:30, 11:11; CD 6:20, quoting Lev. 19:18 as does Mt. 19:19). The word *koinonia* (communion or fellowship, Ac. 2:42; 2 C. 13:14; 1 Jn 1:3) may perhaps represent *yaḥadh* in this technical usage.

'Edhāh is typical of 1QM, frequent in the two columns of 1QSa, but rare in 1QS. It is used of an army, whether God's angelic host or his human cohorts, or Belial's demonic hordes (1QM 1:10; cf. 1Q22, 4:1; 1QH 13:8; 1QM 2:1, 4:9; 1QH 2:22, 6:5; cf. CD 1:12, 3:9). It denotes a congregation of people, national or local (e.g. 1QSa 1:1, 20, 2:12; CD 10:4f.). The Covenanters were 'an *'ēdhāh* of truth resting on a firm foundation' (4Q pPs. 37:24). Israel in its corporate capacity is the Congregation over which the anointed High Priest and the anointed (lay) King are to rule (1QSa 2:12, 22; 1QSb 5:20; CD 7:17; 1QS 5:1).

Even for the Covenanters, then, 'Israel' is the proper title for the elect People of God (1QS 1:22f., 6:13, 9:3; 1QM 10:9–11), although 'Israel' sometimes means the laity in distinction from the priests and

627b levites (CD 10:6; 1QS 8:11). As in OT (Exod. 12:6; Num. 8:20; Ps. 74:2) the *ʿēdhāh* of God is Israel or the Jews in an organic unity, and the *ḳāhāl* (of God) is simply the assembled *ʿēdhāh*. Originally, therefore, '*Synagoge*' like '*Ecclesia*' could apply to all Israel, as the regular LXX translation of *ʿēdhāh*; but later it became the word for a local congregation or its place of meeting (like *k^{e}neseth* or *k^{e}nishta*). Note too that like *ḳāhāl Ecclesia* (Church) may refer to the whole People of God, his Israel, as well as to a particular assembly. Statistically, of course, most NT references are to local *ecclesiae* (e.g. 1 C. 16:19, the *e.* of Asia; 1 Th. 2:14, the *e.* of God in Christ Jesus which are in Judaea). No such phrase as 'The Church of Ephesus' or 'The Church of Galatia' appears (F. J. A. Hort, *The Christian Ecclesia* (1897), 115). 'Of God' is the proper qualification of *ecclesia*, and is always implied when the word is used technically of the Christian community. Some scholars have wrongly deduced from the statistics that universality was a federal outgrowth from a purely congregationalist beginning; but the 'catholic' concept was embedded within it through its heritage (cf. C. F. D. Moule, Colossians and Philemon, CGTC i (1957), 154f.).

c Within Judaism (a national religion) were diverse parties of Zealots, Sadducees, Pharisees, Essenes (including the *Therapeutae* of Egypt?), and the Zadokites of Qumrân (and Damascus? The meaning of CD 6:5 is disputed; see Rabin's edition, *The Zadokite Documents* (1954), 96). Whatever their origins and their relationship to Sadducees, Pharisees, or Essenes, the Zadokites were an esoteric brotherhood founded by a priest (the Teacher of Righteousness) and led by priests (CD 1:11, 14:6f., 20:32; 1Q pHab. 1:13, 2:2; 1QS 6:3, 14, 9:7, etc.). The structure was hierarchic, in three or four orders (priests; Levites; Israel; and proselytes: so CD; 1QS 5:6 may refer to proselytes). Each had to obey his superior, all must stay ritually pure through frequent ablutions (Qumrân is famous for its baths and cisterns), and be ready for the eschatological war and its tribulations (1QS 6:2, 1QM *passim*; CD 7:21; cf. *peirasmos* in the Lord's Prayer, Mt. 6:13). Repentance and trust in God were necessary (1QS 1:24–2:1; CD 15:7; 1QH 14:26), for they were the elect Remnant (1Q14, 10:7; 1Q31, 2:2; CD 4:4). In the desert this holy community prepared the way of the Lord (1QS 8:13f.; cf. Isa. 40:3; Mk 1:3). They were bound to contribute their possessions to the common chest (CD 14:13–17; 1QS 6:18–20), and they cared for each other (like the Essenes). Legalism is strangely mixed with grace in 1QH 12:4–9 and 7:17f. (cf. 1QS 10:1ff.). They were the 'Sons of Light' (1QM 1:1, etc.), and the 'Wise' to whom divine secrets had been revealed through prophetic teachers, inspired by the Spirit (1QS 3:13, 5:9, 9:12, 21; CD 12:21; 1Q pHab. 1:13; CD 1:11; 1QS 8:16 and CD 2:12; cf. Paul's teaching in 1 C. 1:20, 2:10–15). Whereas Christian 'mysteries' were revelations to be published abroad (1 C. 15:51; Col. 1:26f.; Eph. 1:9, 3:3), the truths of God are mysteries in QL requiring right expositors, and always to be hid from the profane (1QH 2:13, 4:27f., 18:11). Only once is the Isaian note sounded of a mission to all the nations (1QH 6:12). Moreover repentance is, illogically, tied to predestination (1QS 3:17–4:1, 15–26); and readiness to atone for the sins of Israel (1QS 8:4–9, 9:3–6) lies side by side with bitter enmity towards opponents, who would have claimed to be within Israel too (1QH 2:30f., 4:6ff.; 1QS 2:25, 3:1–5). Most significant is their insistence that initiates needed a cleansing by the Holy Spirit (1QS 4:21; 1QH 16:12; cf. Ps. 51:7, 10–12; Ezek. 35:25). This may be connected with baptism in water (1QS 5:13, 20), and if so baptism was probably repeated many times. Like the Pharisee, Saul of Tarsus (Phil. 3:3), some claimed perfect holiness in the sense of separation from the faithless and obedience to God's will; for the community was to have twelve or fifteen men 'who are perfect in all that has been revealed of the whole Law' (1QS 8:1–4, **62**
where possibly the three priests are to be included within the twelve). Then Israel would have a new, spiritual Temple, 'an eternal planting' (1QS 8:4–9, 9:3–6 seem to refer this to the entire community and not to the perfect alone). Did this remain an aspiration? Certainly their Messiahs, the High Priest and the Prince of the Congregation, did not arise; and by A.D. 70 they were disbanded.

d When we find that ideas of 'building', 'laying a foundation', 'the Rock' (i.e. God or his Truth), 'a tested stone' (Isa. 28:16) also occur (1QH 6:26, 7:8, 9:28, 11:15; 4Q pPs. 37:24), we are prepared to think that John the Baptist or even Jesus might have spoken like this (cf. CD 7:20*c*, 20:15; Lk. 1–2). For they too preached in the context of 'the end of the days', the *ḳēṣ* or *kairos* of God (i.e. time of destiny, the eschatological end, Mk 1:15; cf. 'hour' in Jn; CD 4:4, 9; 1Q pHab. 2:5). It is, nevertheless, improbable that Jesus had any direct link with Qumrân, and not certain that John the Baptist or his disciples (Jn 1:40ff.) could have provided one. Jesus was no ascetic, and not a Sabbatarian like the Zadokites (CD 10:14–11:18); so far as we know, he included no priests in his company, and assuredly he did not cast his Messianic hopes in terms of the High Priest as Head of the Congregation (1QSa 2:12, following Milik). The secret rules and doctrines were to be kept under a great oath of secrecy, so that the general public had only vague notions of them (e.g. Pliny, Philo, and Josephus, of the Essenes). How then are we to account for remarkable resemblances to apostolic Christianity? (*a*) Some of the priests mentioned at Ac. 6:7 may have been Zadokites or Essenes (Josephus says he had tried the Essene sect). (*b*) Paul, the Fourth Evangelist, the author of Heb. (note its Christology of the High Priest), and perhaps others may have had contacts with the Covenanters, if not membership in the community. (*c*) Many parallels have a common origin in OT and intertestamental literature. (*d*) Ideas spread in the general religious environment of the time.

e Did Jesus organise a *yaḥadh* within Israel or call into being a new structure quite distinct from Judaism? In a whirlwind ministry of thirty months, more or less, he taught in the Galilean synagogues for a while, proclaiming that the Kingdom of God had arrived in his own person (Mt. 11:25–27; Lk. 10:23f., 11:20, 17:21). As fellow-servants, heralds of the salvation, he sent out twelve selected men; and this means presumably that they shared the gift of the Spirit for the task (including the defeat of evil spirits; Mt. 10:6, 15:24; Mk 6:7; but contrast Jn 7:39, 20:22). Jesus may have intended by this that he and they, in T. W. Manson's words, should constitute the 'Son of Man', the regal saints of the Most High (Dan. 7:13, 22; cf. CD 20:8; 1QS 8:20, 23; 1QH 4:25, 6:5; 1QSb 4:27f.). Before his own generation passed men would see that the Kingdom had come with power (Mk 9:1). He invited them to perceive God active in his ministry and revelatory in his words, especially his riddles and parables (Mk 4:1–12). Those who did so and became obedient to his Father's will, he called his 'family' (Mk 3:35; cf. the emphasis in Jn and 1 Jn on the children of God). But there was a basic conflict between Jesus and important elements in the nation: whatever the merits of individual Pharisees, they rejected Jesus' teaching on the righteousness of love (Mk 3:6, 12:13); he showed no sympathy for the priestly Sadducean caste (Mk 12:18ff.), and his attitude to the cult, before the final crisis, is ambiguous (Mk 1:44, 11:15ff.). He acted with sovereign authority, but it was not acknowledged (Mk 1:27, 11:27ff.). He refused to be a new David, the leader of the War, and even challenged the popular concept of a Davidic Messiah (Jn 6:15; Mk 12:35–37). It seems unlikely that he wanted to be another Moses (despite the legislative power inherent in the office of the Messiah): yet he reinterpreted the Law (Mt. 5:22, 28). He was

7e a unique kind of Messiah, a layman who was the Son of the Father.

So the crowds deserted Jesus (though the Galileans may have hoped in him to the bitter end, in opposition to the Jerusalem hierarchy, Mk 14:2). Alternatively we must say that Jesus fled from the false enthusiasm of the multitudes, and he came to realise that he must suffer and die (Mk 8:31), for he satisfied neither the political nor the religious demands of his contemporaries and they misunderstood the way of the Father. In the last few months or weeks Jesus discovered that he would die alone, on a cross demanded by the Sanhedrin for a blasphemer, and erected for a rebel pretender by Pilate the governor. About this time he described the company of disciples as his 'little flock', because he was their God-sent shepherd (Lk. 12:32 ; cf. Jn 10:11), and he promised the Twelve seats at his royal table (Lk. 22:30). It is hard to see how one about to die could promise anything, unless he believed in a Kingdom beyond this earth or in a sudden divine intervention (as the apocalyptic dreamers expected). Perhaps he was satirically (or humorously) correcting his men, who aspired to a Kingdom like that of Rome. Cullmann would transfer the saying to Peter (Mt. 16:18) to the context of Lk. 22, but there is no evidence to support this. Despite the growing belief of modern Protestant scholars that it is genuine, Mt. 16:18 remains without parallel in the Gospels, especially the Petrine sections. It may be adapted to fit a Petrine primacy, and 1 C. 3:11 seems to contradict it (cf. Jn 21:15–19 ; and for building the Kingdom on a rock, *Odes of Sol.* 22:12). Better attested is the tradition that Jesus spoke of a new Temple (Mk 14:58 ; Jn 2:19), and his open attack on the Temple and the priesthood probably brought about his death (Mk 11:15–18). The conclusion must be that, while Jesus may have thought of his disciples as a *yaḥadh* or a *ḥ*^{a}*bhûrāh* (association), he did not organise a Community with a formal set of principles and a constitution, nor did he set out his teaching in writing. He was cut off in the midst of his work of recalling Israel to God as sovereign Father, and when he died he left behind him broken, disillusioned men and women (Lk. 24:21 ; Jn 20:19). Yet his legacy was his Spirit : in the darkness the light of God shone, and out of the ashes of defeat **the power of the Spirit brought victory and constituted a Church** (Jn 19:27, 30, 20:21–3).

f In the apostolic writings of the NT it is less a theological construct than an 'idea' of the Church that we find, for the marriage of Greek metaphysical thought to Hebrew prophetism had not yet taken place. The gospels, letters, homilies, and apocalypse of NT offer dynamic images and concepts ; and this is true without minimising the profound theological understanding of Paul, John, and the author of Hebrews. The Church is a house or a household (1 Tim. 3:15 ; Heb. 3:6) ; a flock (Jn 10:14–16 ; Ac. 20:28 ; 1 Pet. 5:3) ; a commonwealth (Eph. 2:12) ; a bride (2 C. 11:2 ; Eph. 5:23–32 ; Rev. 21:2, 9, 22:17) ; a temple (Jn 2:21 ; 1 C. 3:16f.). A congregation is a letter of testimonial to Christ and the Gospel, written 'with the Spirit of the living God' (2 C. 3:3). They are 'the company of believers' (Ac. 4:32 ; lit., the multitude, perhaps a translation of Heb. *rabbîm*, the many, used in QL ; cf. 1 C. 9:19 ; 2 C. 4:15 ; CD 13:7, with Rabin's note). They are 'Sons of Light' (1 Th. 5:5 ; cf. Mt. 5:14–16 ; Lk. 16:8 ; this is not a title for the Church, however). They are a brotherhood of love (Ac. 9:17 ; Phm. 16 ; Heb. 2:17, 4:14, 5:5–10 ; 1 Pet. 2:17, where *adelphotes* (brotherhood) occurs ; and Phil. 2:25, a brother, a colleague, and a comrade : see Lightfoot *in loc.*). Rom. 16:1–16 is important as a witness to the deep love that informed the churches. To meet the happy necessities of brotherliness Paul invented or reminted Greek words compounded with *syn*, 'with', the preposition of community.

8a **The New Israel**—The idea of the Church as the true Israel of God, the fulfilment of the promises, occupies 628a
a large place in the NT (Jn 4:22, 15, the True Vine ; Ac. 2:36, 3:19f., 10:32–40 ; Gal. 6:16 ; Phil. 3:3 ; Rom. 2:29 ; Jas 1:1 ; 1 Pet. 1:1, 2:4–10, classic for this conception ; Rev. 21:9–14, cf. 12:1–6). At 1 C. 10:18 'Israel' should be 'Israel according to the flesh' (cf. Rom. 1:3), and it implies as its opposite, 'Israel according to the Spirit'. But there is tension between this idea and that of a Church universal, a new creation, a people reborn by divine grace and power (Jn 1:12f., 3:3–6 ; Ac. 3:25, 4:27, 7:48ff., 10:47, 13:46f. ; 2 Th. 2:13 ; Gal. 3:23ff. ; Heb. 7:11, 8:8ff. ; 1 Pet. 1:20–25 ; 1 Jn 3:9). For an Israel after the Spirit could not be just a nation, and the Cross proved that the Jews had in fact rejected God and forfeited the right to the title of Israel. This fundamental conflict may easily be minimised if the New Israel idea is made primary. The NT writers did not do so, and it is but seldom that 'Israel' is applied to the Church (Gal. 6:16). Fulfilment of scripture is more commonly expressed (e.g. Mt. *passim* ; Lk. 24:26f. ; Jn 5:46 ; Rom. 9:25ff. ; 1 C. 15:3f. ; 2 C. 3:12ff.). Of course, some Christian Jews clung to the thought that they were merely the Israel of old reformed, and they observed Jewish rites and customs for two or three centuries ; but they were a dying cause. With Stephen and Paul a decisive change began, and before A.D. 60 Paul could speak of 'the Church of God' as a third alongside the Greeks and Jews (1 C. 10:32). Paul was well aware of continuity, as Rom. 9–11 suffice to prove. As the 'Seed of Abraham' the Church is at once the true Israel and the true Humanity (Gal. 3:6ff., 4:28 : Isaac born by miracle is the type of the Church ; cf. Jn 8:31–47 ; Heb. 2:16). Here belongs too the 'Adam' concept (Rom. 5:14 ; 1 C. 15:45–50 ; cf. Gal. 3:28). Christ and his people form a Unity ; hence the members are baptised into his risen life (Jn 15:5–10 ; Rom. 6:3–11, 13:14 ; Gal. 4:4–6, 5:24). To define the Church we should have to say that it is a resurrected Israel ; and that is more than a Reformation, for it is tied up with the Death and Resurrection of the Christ, the Son of God. The 'ecclesia' of God, the faithful who believe in the fact of the resurrection, the people empowered by the Holy Spirit in love and joy, the forgiven sinners who understand that Christ is their 'means of propitiation', is the form that the new Israel takes in history (Rom. 10:9 ; Gal. 3:2f. ; Heb. 2:4 ; 1 Pet. 1:12 ; 1 Jn 3:24, 4:13ff. ; Rom. 3:25 ; 1 Jn 2:2). Of course, the resurrection is not complete for the Church's life ; Christians are heirs of the Kingdom (Rom. 6:8 ; 1 Th. 5:9 ; Col. 1:12 with 1:13). Hence the Church remains an eschatological community, awaiting the end ; he who had come must also 'come again' (Jn 6:40 ; 1 Th. 1:10, 3:13 ; 2 C. 5:10 ; Phil. 1:6 ; Heb. 9:28, ; 1 Pet. 1:5, 7, 4:7, 5:4 ; Rev. 1:7, 22:12ff.). This note cannot be excised from the records ; but did the Church ever solve the problem posed by the reality that the Christ did not come again (cf. 2 Pet. 3:4) ? Out of this failure developed the institutions of the 2nd cent., Creed, Canon of the NT, and the Episcopacy in a monarchical form.

As we have seen, *ecclesia*, as denoting the whole b
People of God, had a 'catholic' significance from the beginning. When it became the normative title of the Christian community is not certain, but it was only a few decades after Easter at most. St Paul never calls a Christian congregation a *synagoge*, and he avoids Jewish titles except in OT quotations. The plural of *ecclesia* did not lessen its universality, but rather highlighted the meaning. For 1 Th. 1:1 and 1 C. 1:2 are typical : 'the *e.* of the Thessalonians in God the Father and the Lord Jesus Christ', and 'the *e.* of God which is at Corinth'. The Trade Union analogy is clear : each 'local' (as the Americans call it) is a part of the whole, like the synagogue in relation to the Jewish people. But each local congregation is in fact the Church in that place ; all were part of One Kingdom and sprang from one centre ; one Vine ; one

628b Flock. All were baptised into the One Christ (Ac. 2:38, 10:48 ; 1 C. 1:10) and were guests at One Table (1 C. 11:23–25). If as yet there was no credal formula there were definite apostolic traditions (1 Th. 3:6 ; 1 C. 15:3ff.) ; and to confess Jesus as 'Lord' bound all believers together (1 C. 12:3). Teaching this tradition and witnessing to this Lord was the essential work of the apostles and their colleagues. Hence the NT Church was truly a united, catholic society with a common faith (cf. Gal. 1:7–9) ; it is not credible that Paul was completely out of line with the original disciples in his statement of the gospel and his work of organising churches (see Gal. 1:19, 2:2). It is of such a Church that the author of Eph. speaks when he exhorts his contemporaries to maintain ' the unity of the Spirit in the bond of peace ' (4:3).

Just as theological orthodoxy had to be safeguarded, so unity also had to be achieved. Schisms, party-spirit, false ascetic practices, illicit behaviour at the love-feasts (the gatherings for worship and the Lord's Supper), and attacks on the sufficiency of Christ, all occurred during the NT age (cf. 1 C. 1:11ff. ; 2 Th. 2:2 ; Col. 2:18 ; Heb. 13:9 ; 1 Jn 2:22, 4:1 ; 1 Pet. 5:5 ; Jude 3 ; Rev. 1:4–3:22). It was out of such a situation that the doctrine was enunciated of the Church of God, the true Israel, the family of heaven.

629a **The Communion of the Holy Spirit**—Spiritual renewal was a distinctive feature of the Church, and no-one can miss the sense of excitement described by Acts and the Pauline letters. God in the last days had poured out his Spirit, the breath of life, source of wisdom and revelation (Jn 7:39, 20:22 ; Ac. 2:16ff. ; Heb. 2:4). In this respect the Church parallels the Qumrân community, but there is the difference that for the NT the holiness of the Spirit is defined in terms of Jesus. Again, the sharing of goods in the primitive Church was no legal condition of membership ; it was an expression of a new love (Ac. 2:44, 4:32–37 ; esp. 2 C. 8:1ff.). The Spirit did not stop to enquire if a convert was a Jew (Ac. 8:29, 10:44). Contrast the note of freedom and the fruit of the Spirit in Gal. 4:26–5:1, 22 with the predestined virtues and laborious discipline of 1QS 4:2–6, 8:20ff. Yet it was to ' holiness ' that God had called Christians and for this had bestowed on them his Holy Spirit (1 Th. 4:7f.). For Paul this gift of the Spirit was an ' earnest ' of the eternal life of the Kingdom (2 C. 1:22), and full redemption awaited the resurrection of the body (Rom. 8:11 ; 2 C. 5:1–5 ; 1 C. 15:42ff.). In his doctrine of the Spirit he provided a way to hold together the fact that the Kingdom had come and yet that Christ was still to come in glory. Thus the Church is a colony of heaven (cf. Phil. 3:20 ; Col. 3:1–4). The individual Christian is a shrine of the Spirit, for he and his Lord are united as in a marriage (1 C. 6:17–19), and a local *ecclesia* is a temple of the Spirit (1 C. 3:16). At Eph. 2:14–22 this concept is applied to the Church catholic (cf. Jn 2:21 ; 1QS 8:5f.).

b Once again, this is never presented in perfectionist terms : Ananias and Sapphira disgraced the fellowship ; John Mark hurt his colleagues Barnabas and Paul ; and many remained at the stage of spiritual infancy (Ac. 5:1–11, 13:13, 15:37f. ; Heb. 5:12–14 ; 1 C. 3:1–4 ; 1 Pet. 1:23–2:3). James warns teachers that they will be judged ' with greater strictness ' than others (3:1), and he makes the elementary point that profession of faith is sheer hypocrisy in the absence of the works of righteousness (1:22ff., 2:8 ; cf. Heb. 10:24; Rom. 12:9ff. ; Gal. 5:6, 14f. ; 6:9 ; 1 Jn 3:10). On the other hand, the emergence of Paul, Apollos, Peter, the writers of Eph., Jn, and Heb., demonstrates the intellectual power released in that creative age by the Spirit of Jesus. The Church of the Spirit is a divine-human phenomenon, unique among the societies on earth. ' The faithful Christians, filled with the power of the Spirit, are here and now being transformed so as to be like the Son of God, and the ecclesia is the concretion in a living organism of the grace of the Lord Jesus Christ, and the love of God, and the 6
fellowship of the Holy Spirit ' (E. C. Hoskyns in *Theology* (May 1927), 251).

The Body of Christ—Paul's supreme contribution to 63
the idea of the Church is that of the Body of Christ. We cannot delineate precisely its origins, though it must be related to the kind of teaching found in Mt. 10:40 and parallels ; 25:40, which in turn has roots in the Semitic sense of solidarity (the High Priest on the Day of Atonement represents all Israel before God ; and the sacral King too embodies his nation). Concepts of this sort, thought together with ideas of the world as a cosmic whole, of the Roman Empire as a body, and of the people of God as one in the last Adam, Jesus Christ, may have led the apostle to formulate his metaphor. Some scholars would seek its beginning in the word of Jesus over the bread at the Last Supper, ' This is my body ' (cf. 1 C. 10:16f.), and this is plausible. Others remind us of the identity between the risen Christ and his persecuted people expressed in the reply to Paul at his conversion (Ac. 9:4). At any rate, faith-union with the Lord Jesus gave the idea of the Body genuine power ; and faith-union meant love. For faith said, ' He loved me, and gave himself up for me ', and also, ' I have been crucified with Christ ; it is no longer I who live, but Christ who lives in me ' (Gal. 2:20 ; cf. Eph. 5:25, ' he loved the Church '). The sacrifice of Jesus laid infinite obligation on those who knew that he had expiated their sin and propitiated the Wrath of God (2 C. 5:21 ; Rom. 1:18, 2:8, 3:25, 5:1–11). It was divine love that had created, predestined, and justified the elect ; yet Paul does not speak as if only the predestined could accept the good news when they heard it (Rom. 8:29f., 10:8–10, 13 ; Gal. 3:9 ; cf. Eph. 1:4f. ; there is a similar note in Jn). Love in man answered love in God, and it is the greatest thing in the world (1 C. 13:13 ; cf. 1 Jn 4:7–12, 19). Converts were transferred from the dominance of one master, Sin, to that of the new Lord, Christ Jesus (Rom. 6:15ff. ; Col. 1:13f.). This new life was a re-creation of the Adam or Humanity of God, for Christ as the last Adam has become ' a life-giving Spirit ' (1 C. 15:45). Christians therefore share to some degree the exalted status of Christ : he is the Son, but the firstborn of a brotherhood which God has adopted as his family and given ' the Spirit of his Son ' (Rom. 8:14–25, 29 ; 1 Th. 4:8 ; Phil. 3:20f.).

What better concept than that of the body and b
its limbs ? In Rom. 12:3ff. it seems to be merely a social analogy, but 1 C. 12, taken in the light of the whole range of Pauline theology, proves that Paul has gone beyond mere metaphor. Christians were the limbs of the Messiah, and therefore his servants, expressing his mind and will (Col. 1:24). It is as if the risen Lord actually lived in the churches to direct, teach, and bless them. ' For just as the body is one and has many limbs, and all the limbs of the body, though many, constitute a single body, so is it with the Christ ' (1 C. 12:12). Of this Body the lifeblood is the Spirit, the power of God the Creator. From applying this idea to a local congregation Paul passes in Col. to refer it to the Church catholic, exactly as we should expect. The Church as the Body (in the Spirit) takes the place of the ' body of flesh ' which was crucified (Col. 1:18, 22). But now he also says that Christ is the Head of the Body, and it may be thought that this does violence to the original metaphor which identified Christ with his Body. Paul, however, elsewhere speaks of Christ as the Head, supreme over every man (1 C. 11:3), and the thought of supremacy was important in the Col. situation (cf. Moule, op. cit., 67f.). The Pauline disciple who wrote Eph. perceived the significance of this doctrine of the Body, and he displays profound understanding of its meaning. If we may say that the Creator is fulfilled by his creation, so may we say that Christ is completed by his Body, the Church (Eph. 1:22f.). This Body is not yet complete ; it is growing and expanding, and its ultimate goal is the very fullness of God himself (Eph. 3:17–19, 4:13 ;

630b what the fullness of God means is not, however, quite clear). As the Body the Church is an ordered society, with officers who perform their God-given or Christ-given functions (1 C. 12:28 ; Eph. 4:7–12 : 'for the equipment of the saints [i.e. the members] for the work of ministry, for building up the Body of Christ' ; ministry belongs to the whole Body as such). It must of course be one, else it could not be a Body at all (1 C. 1:13, 12:12 ; Eph. 4:1–6). In 1 C. 12 Paul is as much concerned to teach that people with their own gifts should realise that they belong to one another ; endowments are for the common good. Diversity in unity is the ideal, not uniformity. Nothing really mattered save a spirit of mutual forbearance and help (Gal. 5:25–6:5 ; Col. 3:12ff.) ; sex was not abolished, but there was a different tone to the sex-relationship ; racial characteristics remained, and slavery was allowed to continue, but what a change the brotherliness of the Body should make ! (see Phm. *passim*). As the author of Heb. put it, Christians were all of one (2:11) ; and so all were expected to live a life worthy of Christ and the Gospel (1 Th. 4:1ff. ; Phil. 1:27, 2:1–11, 4:2f. ; Eph. 4:20ff.). Such a life would not happen automatically, nor even from attendance at the baptismal bath or the Lord's Table (1 C. 10:1ff., 11:17ff.). Unity, peace, and purity could not be options in the Church ; they were obligatory, and the law of love, which fulfilled the Law, also exceeded the righteousness of the Scribes, the Pharisees, and the Essenes.

c Christ expressed his will through recorded words and the inspired utterances of apostles and prophets (1 C. 7:8, 10, 12, 25, 40, 14:5). Certain OT regulations remained valid (Rom. 13:9f. ; 2 C. 6:14–7:1 ; but the Jewish elements in the heresy at Colossae were rigorously denied, Col. 2:11–13, 16). Plenary meetings of a local church dealt with cases of discipline under local leaders (1 C. 16:16 ; Phil. 1:1), yet even in his absence the apostle-founder had rights and powers. He was their spiritual father or mother or nurse (1 Th. 2:7 ; Gal. 4:19 ; 1 C. 4:15, 5:3f. ; 2 C. 2:6–11, 13:10 ; cf. 1QH 7:20f.). Paul obviously expected his congregations to make the appropriate arrangements for meetings, worship, and the sacraments. They existed to praise and serve God, shining as lights in the dark world of sin and fear. For their well-being he himself constantly prayed, and he desired that Christians should never cease from prayer nor quench the power of the Spirit (1 Th. 5:12ff.).

Nowhere in NT is the Church a religious community 630c ruled by priests who can dispense sacramental blessings, though the whole Church may be called priestly (1 Pet. 2:5, 9 ; Rev. 1:6). Such language is rare and not typical, even after full allowance has been made for Rom. 15:16 and Phil. 2:17. Christians were to offer themselves 'as a living sacrifice' (Rom. 12:1), or to present 'a sacrifice of praise to God, that is, the fruit of lips that acknowledge his name' (Heb. 13:15). This meant doing good to all men, beginning with the household of faith (1 Tim. 6:18f. ; 3 Jn 5, etc.). The Church, as the communion in which the Spirit takes flesh, where Christ the living Saviour feeds his disciples with his flesh and blood, where God creates and re-creates, is a sacramental society ; it is 'of God', called, sustained, and to be glorified by God ; to whom therefore the Church and all its servants ascribe glory, majesty, and everlasting praise.

Bibliography—D. Barthélemy and J. T. Milik, *Discoveries in the Judaean Desert I: Qumrân Cave I* (1955) ; M. Burrows, 'The Manual of Discipline', *The Dead Sea Scrolls of St Mark's Monastery*, vol. ii, fasc. 2 (1951) ; C. Rabin, *The Zadokite Documents* (1954) ; E. L. Sukenik, *The Dead Sea Scrolls of the Hebrew University* (1955).

E. Best, *One Body in Christ* (1955) ; L. Cerfaux, *La Théologie de l'Église suivant saint Paul* (1942) ; O. Cullmann, *Christ and Time* (1951) ; N. A. Dahl, 'Christ : Creation and the Church', in *The Background of the NT and its Eschatology*, ed. W. D. Davies and D. Daube (1956) ; W. D. Davies, *Paul and Rabbinic Judaism* (rev. ed. 1955) ; C. H. Dodd, *According to the Scriptures* (1952) ; *The Apostolic Preaching and its Developments* (1936) ; R. N. Flew, *Jesus and His Church* (2nd ed. 1943) ; Stig Hanson, *The Unity of the Church in the NT—Colossians and Ephesians* (1946) ; F. J. A. Hort, *The Christian Ecclesia* (1897) ; George Johnston, *The Doctrine of the Church in the NT* (1943) ; J.-L. Leuba, *NT Pattern* (1953) ; E. Mersch, *The Whole Christ* (1949) ; E. Percy, *Der Leib Christi* (1942), *Die Probleme der Kolosser- und Epheserbriefe* (1946) ; J. A. T. Robinson, *The Body* (1952) ; A. Schlatter, *The Church in the NT Period* (1955) ; K. L. Schmidt, *The Church*, tr. J. R. Coates from TWNT (1949) ; H. J. Schoeps, *Theologie und Geschichte des Judenchristentums* (1949) ; L. S. Thornton, *The Common Life in the Body of Christ* (1942).

THE CONSTITUTION OF THE CHURCH IN THE NEW TESTAMENT

By G. JOHNSTON

631a **The Twelve and the Apostolate**—In an earlier essay it was suggested that Jesus, cut off in the midst of his life-work, did not organise a community with rules of membership, rites, and officials. He did, however, summon followers to his cause and sometimes to the sacrifice of home and livelihood. From these, we are told, he selected Twelve (Mk 3:14–19; Mt. 10:2–4; Lk. 6:14–16; cf. Jn 6:67, 71, 20:24; Ac. 1:13, 26; 1 C. 15:5), three of whom, Peter, James, and John were allowed to accompany him on special occasions (Mk 5:37, 9:2, 14:33). Peter and John were prominent in the primitive Church (Ac. 3:1, 4:13, 8:14, 12:2f.). James is mentioned at Ac. 1:13 and 12:2 (his death). These three may be the 'pillars' of Gal. 2:9, although most scholars would identify James there with the Lord's brother (Gal. 1:19). Gaster injudiciously says that the three pillars and the Twelve Apostles are recalled by 1QS 8:1, where the *Manual of Discipline* lays it down that in the council of the community there shall be twelve perfect, holy men and (or, including) three priests (*The Dead Sea Scriptures* (1956), 99). More properly the *Manual* passage reminds one of the clergy and laity in 1 Clement 40ff. and the famous reference to James the Lord's brother by Hegesippus (*ap.* Eus.HE II, xxiii, 4–6: he was called 'the Just', was a Nazirite, and interceded in the sanctuary (of the Temple?) for the people). A. Ehrhardt has founded on such references the theory that James of Jerusalem continued within the Church the High-Priestly succession from Israel; thus the Church was a better Qumrân Community! (*The Apostolic Succession in the First Two Centuries of the Church* (1953)). There is insufficient evidence to support the view that Jesus and James, like John the Baptist, belonged to a priestly family. It is no accident, of course, that a Jewish sect with Messianic hopes should have organised itself round a council of Twelve, the number of the tribes of Israel (cf. 1QM 2:2f.; Rev. 21:12–14). Hence Jesus might naturally symbolise his cause in the Twelve; but hardly in Seventy (or, Seventy-two), the mythical number of the nations (cf. Lk. 10:1ff.; Jn 21:11 for the number of the fish). Jesus required assistants if he was to reach all his fellow-Jews in the time available before the expected dénouement. They were to be his companions, the core of the holy Remnant within Israel; and he sent them out in his name to preach the Kingdom, and with authority (*exousia*) to expel demons (Mk 6:7, 12). No saying of Jesus is better attested than that which identifies him with those who were thus 'apostled' (Mt. 10:40; Lk. 10:16; Jn 13:20; cf. Mk 9:37; Mt. 18:5; Lk. 9:48; Jn 17:18, 20:21). The Church is an 'Apostolic' society, empowered with the Spirit of Jesus and sent out as his representative. (*Shālîaḥ* is the Hebrew for 'apostle', but the meaning of Christian Apostleship is not to be deduced from Hebrew models.) The Apostle is a herald (cf. Isa. 40:9; Rom. 10:14–16; 2 C. 5:20; but not all preachers were Apostles). Whether Jesus called the Twelve 'Apostles' is doubtful (Mk 6:30; Lk. 6:13; the title was appropriate in relation to their mission, but its use in the Synoptics may be coloured by later usage). 631

Who were these Twelve? We can be sure only of nine: Simon (Peter or Cephas; note the curious word order in 1 C. 9:5; cf. Gal. 2:8f.); Andrew, his brother (they were fishermen); James and John, the fisher sons of Zebedee; Philip (of Bethsaida, the original home of Andrew and Peter, Jn 1:44); Judas Iscariot (in Jn he is son of Simon Iscariot); Bartholomew; Thomas (the Twin); and another Simon (the Cananaean, Mk; the Zealot, Lk.; brother of Jesus? cf. Mk 6:3; 1 C. 9:5). Thaddaeus is not in Lk. or Jn. Matthew 'the tax collector' suggests an early identification with Levi, son of Alphaeus, but this is uncertain (Mt. 10:3; Mk 2:14). James of Alphaeus (Mk 3:18) may refer to a son or brother of Alphaeus and thus to Levi (called James in Bezan text of 2:14), or to his brother; on slender grounds a few identify him with James the Lord's brother. Judas of James, not Judas Iscariot (Lk. 6:16), may be a son or brother of James: but which James? He too might be Jesus' brother. Nathanael appears only in Jn, like the mysterious and probably fictional 'Beloved Disciple'. (Jn 7:5 and Mk 3:21, 31ff. make it most unlikely that Jesus' brothers were disciples before Easter.) Only the most ingenious juggling can reduce these names to twelve. To say the least, tradition was unclear about their names, and may have been equally confused about their function and status. In Ac. 1 they compose a sacred college, essential to the life and mission of the Church, yet NT evidence as a whole hardly bears this out.

The relation of the Twelve to the Apostles of the b
post-Easter Church corresponds to that of the Church to the nation Israel, at once one of continuity and discontinuity. Judas forfeited his place by apostasy, and the other eleven could not have had an inalienable title to theirs. If *exousia* in Mk 3:15 implies that they had received a gift of God's power (the Spirit) in order to exorcise the evil spirits, then they lost it by faithlessness and desertion (Mk 14:50). Jesus may have anticipated a new day when he would be vindicated and his disciples restored (Mk 13:11; Jn 14:18, 26; Lk. 22:31), but much water would have to flow under the bridges of history before that happened. Were the resurrection visions not necessary, in part at least, in order to restore the disciples? Thus Peter's threefold denial was balanced by a threefold pardon, according to Jn 21:15ff. (This is the truth of symbol and imagination, but it was no merely subjective hallucination: it was proved at Pentecost and in the struggles of the Church.) The complement of the Twelve was made up by the election (if one may describe a sacred lot in this way!) of Matthias rather than Joseph Barsabbas (Ac. 1:23–26; the latter is Barnabas in the Western text; cf. Ac. 4:36). Nothing else is known of these two men, who disappear immediately into the anonymity of 'the apostles' and thus belong to primitive Christian folklore. Some ten years later, about A.D. 42, James bar-Zebedee was killed by Herod Agrippa I, yet there was no election of a successor. There may have been no surviving

631b candidates, and at any rate the number was limited. As companions of Jesus the Twelve had no successors. It was Easter and Pentecost, then, that constituted the Apostolate as well as the *Ecclesia*.

c The word 'apostle' is probably non-technical in ref. to Titus, Epaphroditus, and others, including perhaps Apollos (2 C. 8:23 ; Phil. 2:25 ; 1 C. 4:6, 9, 9:5f.). The case of Barnabas is interesting : At Ac. 13:2f. he is sent out from Antioch on a mission, as at 11:22 he had been sent down from Jerusalem to Antioch, on an 'inspection' ; and so he might have been regarded as an apostle of these churches, in relation to specific commissions. But in Ac. 14:14 he and Paul are described simply as apostles, as though both were on the same level. Now, Paul was more than a congregational delegate, and it would seem that Barnabas was in the full sense an Apostle. There were opponents of Paul whom he dubs 'false apostles' (2 C. 11:5, 13 ; cf. Rev. 2:2, and the tests for false apostles in *Did.* 11). Andronicus and Junias are called apostles in Rom. 16:7 (where RSV 'among' is preferable to 'in the sight of').

In addition, there are James the Lord's brother and Paul. Gal. 1:19 implies James's right to the title of Apostle, but nowhere else is it used of him. (Ac. 12:17 cannot refer to the son of Zebedee, unless it is misplaced ; cf. 12:2.) 1 C. 15:7 mentions a special resurrection appearance to James, and that would put him in the same category as Paul. Paul's claim did not go unchallenged (2 C. 11:4f., 13, 22f.), and he insists on his true Jewish origin and the immediacy of his call, like Isaiah's or Jeremiah's (Phil. 3:5 ; Gal. 1:1, 7, 10, 12, 15f.). Thus we have the Twelve, a few others like Barnabas, Paul of the Gentiles, and James of Jerusalem (who was no missionary). Midway between James and Paul stands Peter, according to Acts. The conditions for the Apostolate on this evidence are three : (*a*) *companionship with Jesus and restoration by visions of the risen Lord* (Ac. 1:8, 21f., 10:41 ; cf. Jn 15:26f., 20:21f. ; 1 C. 15:5) ; (*b*) *a resurrection appearance, including a commission* (1 C. 15:7f. ; Rom. 1:1, 5) ; and (*c*) in Paul's defence in 2 C. 11:21–12:13 he relies on '*the signs of a true apostle*' (signs, wonders, and miracles) and *his own missionary sufferings*. In other words, the churches were the proof of the divine power and the apostolic claim (cf. Ac. 2:3f., 3:7f., 8:15ff., 12:6ff. ; 1 Th. 1:5 ; Rom. 15:19). So far as we know, James of Jerusalem could fulfil only the second condition ; some of the Twelve only the first (for it is a legend that they all went out into the four corners of the earth, like Thomas the putative founder of the Indian Mar Thoma Church).

d The duties of the Apostles in the first few years of eschatological excitement were *to guide the Church* (e.g. in the meetings for prayer and the breaking of bread in their homes ; the election of the Seven to assist in the distribution of goods to groups of Hellenistic Christian Jews) ; *and to exercise oversight of new churches* (e.g. in Samaria and Antioch ; presumably also in the churches of Judaea, Gal. 2:22). Ac. 10:44f. show that the gift of the Spirit was not tied to apostolic laying-on of hands (contrast 8:17, 19:6). No satisfactory theory of the relation of primitive baptism to the reception of the Spirit has been proposed ; cf. Gal. 3:2, 27 ; 1 C. 12:13. The picture was not uniform, and we do injustice to the evidence if we try to force it into a consistent pattern. It is possible, however, to infer that the Apostles had a function which must be called an *episcopacy* in the light of Ac. 1:20, 8:14ff., 11:22 ; and the relation of Paul to his churches. Greek *episcopein* translates the Hebrew root BKR, and a parallel may be found in the 'overseer' (*m^{e}bhakkēr*) or 'inspector' (*pāḳîdh*) of the Zadokite communities (CD 9:18, 13:7, 14:8 ; 1QS 6:12, 14, 20 ; he is administrator, teacher, and spiritual guide ; cf. the wise man, 1QS 3:13, 9:21 ; the parallel is not exact).

e Was Paul subject to the oversight of the Jerusalem Apostolate ? Gal. 1–2 indicate that he was not. Yet he and they belonged to one Body and he was scrupulous to maintain unity. His policy of admitting Gen- 631e
tiles without demanding circumcision (i.e. incorporation into Israel and the covenant of the Law) provoked a major crisis within twenty years of Easter, as a result of which Peter was recognised as leading one mission, Paul another (Gal. 2:8f.). Paul guided his churches, taught them the traditions, and shared in the disciplining of their members in his absence (1 C. 5:3ff., 7ff., 11:23, 15:3). But the 'circumcision party' challenged his authority constantly (Ac. 15:1ff. ; 1 C. 7:17ff. ; 2 C. 11:5–12:13 ; Gal. 2:3f. (Titus was not circumcised) ; 2:12, 5:11, 6:12–16 ; Phil. 3:2f. (from Rome at the end of Paul's life ; cf. 1 Clem. 5) ; Rom. 2:25–3:31). James is associated with this opposition group in Gal. 2:12, with no implication that they only pretended to come from him. When Paul was arrested, James and the church apparently did not lift a finger to help him. James belonged with a Judaising type of Christianity.

Such an interpretation has been too long discredited by the fantasies of the Tübingen School of F. C. Baur, although it explains the dualism of the NT documents. A persuasive mediating hypothesis has been put forward by J.-L. Leuba. The Twelve, including James the Lord's brother, were the institutional element in the Church. Appointed by Jesus, they stood in direct continuity with Israel and were commissioned to preach to the world (Mt. 28:19 ; Ac. 1:8). They received the Spirit by right, for they had a *character indelebilis*, effaced neither by incredulity nor by treachery (Thomas and Judas !). One cannot distinguish between the Twelve and the Spirit (Ac. 5:1–11). As the Twelve are to the Church, so is Peter to them. 'The Church is a hierarchical body in which the Twelve, with Peter at their head, hold a central position and wield powers of administration'. Thus the Twelve had a 'centrifugal tendency'. Contrast St Paul ! Suddenly, at his conversion he became the absolutely last (and thirteenth) Apostle, chosen in spite of being a Jew. Only after the Forty Days of Easter, and beyond Israel's borders, was he called : to demonstrate to Jewry that its salvation must come from the Gentiles (Rom. 11:13, 24). His name, appropriately, was Saul and he was descended from the charismatic northern kingdom of Israel. He received the Spirit (like King Saul) in the moment of his call, and only because he did so did he become an Apostle. As the Twelve are the 'institution' (lawful authority on the horizontal level), so he is the 'event' (direct intervention of the Holy Spirit on the vertical). Paul had to enter the Church ; the Twelve were the Church right from its origins (not simply after the scattering of Ac. 8:1). Hence Paul like everyone else had to profess their doctrine and accept their rule. Fortunately there was mutual recognition, and God bound them both in the unity of the one body. Paul submitted to the Twelve, who for their part saw in him God's charismatic instrument for the evangelisation of the world. To depreciate Paul is to be a Judaiser ; to depreciate the Twelve is to be a Marcionite (J.-L. Leuba, *NT Pattern* (1953), 51–92).

This remarkable thesis has the merit of showing that f
both institutional and 'spiritual' factors operated in the Church from the beginning, although it is hard to see a clear picture in the first days and one cannot agree that the Twelve could lay claim to the Spirit as of right. For that would destroy the personal relationship between God and his people. James could not have been one of the original Twelve, and there is no evidence that he was co-opted like Matthias. His standing depended on his vision of the Christ, his caliphate position as a brother of the Founder, and his personal qualities. Leuba relies too much on words of the Risen Lord as though they were *ipsissima verba* rather than the inspired utterances of prophets. Surely the Twelve required for their *diaconia* (service) an endowment of the Spirit similar to St Paul's ? Nor is Leuba quite fair to Paul's conviction (inherited from Stephen ?) that the Spirit in the Church had to

631f burst the skin of the old order (Mk 2:22). Flesh and Spirit; Letter and Spirit; Hagar and Sarah; the *paidagogos* and the free sons: all represent the deep cleavage between Israel after the flesh and the Church of the Spirit (Gal. *passim*; 2 C. 3:6; Rom. 7:6). Jesus did not, like the founder of the Zadokites, simply renew the Sinai covenant and re-enact the Mosaic Law; but some Judaising Christians would have limited Christianity to that. Leuba's scheme is too neat, everything is too beautifully balanced, and he makes the fatal mistake of assuming that Acts and the Pauline letters tell the whole story about the primitive Church and its constitution. Paul was simply one missionary to the Gentile lands; he did not limit himself to non-Jews, as Gal. 2:9 might suggest, for the Gospel was for the Jew first (Rom. 1:16; 1 C. 9:20; Ac. 13:14, etc.). Hence the Pauline churches were mixed communities of Jewish and Gentile converts.

632a **Jerusalem before A.D. 70**—The government of the Jerusalem Church, at first under the Twelve Apostles, soon passed to a presbytery of elders (*zᵉkēnîm*; Ac. 15:4, 6, 22, 21:18), on the model doubtless of the synagogues and the sects (cf. CD 9:4; 1QS 6:8; at Qumrân the High Priest was to be the head of the Congregation, and the local brotherhoods were ruled by priests). Peter was a leader and spokesman almost without peer, as the traditions of Mt. 16:18; Jn 21:15ff.; 1 Pet. 5:1 indicate. The status of the Seven is obscure: were they 'elders' or 'deacons' or merely an *ad hoc* group? If they were assistants to the Apostles, they might have been deacons, but they did little serving of tables. Philip and Stephen were evangelists (Ac. 6:1ff., 8:5, 26ff.). Jerusalem also had its prophets (e.g. Agabus, Ac. 11:27, 21:10; cf. 21:9, the prophetesses of Caesarea; 1 C. 12:28; Eph. 4:11). What role in government the prophets played is not stated; some Apostles and certain presbyters may well have been prophets too. 1 C. 12:28 must be seen in the context of 1 C. 12:4–10 which makes the prophet simply one among many who have received a *charisma* or a *diaconia* or an *energema* (working) from God for the common good. Corinth apparently was blessed with too many prophets, all competing for a hearing during the time of worship! Paul therefore gave directions about their duty (1 C. 14:29ff.). It would seem to follow that prophets did not as such have political power. Ehrhardt makes the curious deduction from 1 C. 14:29 and Rev. 10:11 'that the prophets were . . . allotted a general task of proclaiming the Christian message for all times' (op. cit., 86). Paul the Apostle was also Paul the Prophet, gifted with 'tongues' (1 C. 14:18f.; cf. 13:2, 7:40). The same conclusions follow from Rom. 12:4ff.

James's 'presidency' of Jerusalem is an inference from Ac. 12:17, 15:13, 21:18; and a precarious one, not 'plainly described' (Ehrhardt, op. cit., 13; cf. Easton, *The Pastoral Epistles* (1947), 174, 195, where he says that James and the elders formed 'a new Sanhedrin for the new Israel'). Ehrhardt independently has taken up and developed the theory that James headed the Christian Sanhedrin, but on flimsy NT grounds: the use of *presbyters* instead of *archontes* or *gerontes* (titles for elders in Diaspora synagogues); Jewish presbyters were the associates of the chief priests as members of the Sanhedrin; the Bezan text of Ac. 15:5 and 21:18ff. seems to portray James in this commanding position, which the evangelist Philip and the prophet Agabus resisted (op. cit., 25–30). Codex Bezae may indeed represent a 2nd or 3rd cent. idea, but that is not the view of Luke! Since NT provides comparatively little evidence for the idea of Apostolic succession, Ehrhardt turns to the succession lists of the 4th cent., 1 Clem., and Hegesippus. Unfortunately he begins by assuming that the Church is Apostolic 'with regard to its canon, its creed, and its ministry' (op. cit., 20). The student of the NT is not allowed to make such assumptions. Nor is it right, without very careful precautions, to work back from the Fathers of the late 2nd and early 3rd cent. to the canonical writers. No case for regarding James as the Christian High Priest has yet been made good. 632

The laying-on of hands (Ac. 6:6, 13:3; cf. 1 Tim. 4:14; 2 Tim. 1:6; but not Heb. 6:2, which may refer to baptism and reception into membership) included blessing, the conferring of authority, and commendation to God or the Spirit (Ac. 14:26). The Jewish elders were thus ordained, with reference to the case of Joshua (Num. 27:18, 23; Dt. 34:9).

Antioch and Paul's Churches—Syrian Antioch had teachers and prophets (Ac. 13:1–3) who sought the guidance of the Spirit. But the report of Barnabas and Paul on their mission was made to the entire congregation (14:27; cf. 6:2 for Jerusalem). We should therefore understand Ac. 14:23 (presbyters appointed in the new churches of Asia Minor) as referring to meetings of the congregations, with the missionaries presiding. These elders are known also as 'bishops' (Ac. 20:28; Phil. 1:1; cf. 1 Tim. 3:2, 5:17; Tit. 1:5, 7), and they are the *prohistamenoi* of 1 Th. 5:12 (cf. 1 C. 16:16 and the *hēgoumenoi* of Heb. 13:7). Some, if not all, of the members who had special gifts (*pneumatica* or *charismata*) were probably elders (Rom. 12:4ff.; 1 C. 12:4–11, 28f.). Paul as the founding missionary and an Apostle (in the narrow sense) had a special authority (*exousia*) for building up the Church (2 C. 13:10) and the right to maintenance (Gal. 6:6; 1 C. 9:3ff.). Thus each local church had a presbytery of bishops who arranged meetings, debated heresy and moral questions, and celebrated the Sacraments. Since committees need chairmen, and the Spirit came in diverse ways and degrees, there must have been presiding presbyters or bishops. Here we see the first delegation of the original Apostolic prerogative of episcopacy; and it is to a presbytery in a local church. Deacons are named; that is all (Phil. 1:1; cf. pos. Rom. 16:1, but Phoebe may not have been a minister). Women might be prophetesses (1 C. 11:4), but Paul did not allow them to share in the public worship and government of the congregation (on the pattern of the synagogue). Priestly service is alluded to in Rom. 15:16 and Phil. 2:17, but not in reference to local ministers. The church is a communion serving the Gospel (Rom. 1:12, 12:1; Phil. 1:5, 27), whose example is the Lord who came to be a servant (Phil. 2:1–13). It is an autonomous part of the one Body, with Christ as its Head. His words, if available, settle any issue (1 C. 7:10); otherwise his Apostle, who has the Spirit, may teach Christian duties (1 C. 7:12ff.). This did not mean that Paul always got his own way nor that he was exempt from making mistakes. 633

Admission to the Church was by faith, followed by Baptism (Rom. 10:8ff.; Gal. 2:16ff.; Col. 2:11f., 3:1ff.), and families belonged to the Christian community, as they had done to Israel, whether or no children were baptised as a sign and seal of their membership (cf. the 'circumcision made without hands' of Col. 2:11 and the contagious holiness idea of 1 C. 7:14).

Later NT Period—The preaching, teaching, and pastoral work of the ministry is prominent in the rest of NT (Jn 10:16, 17:20; Heb. 13:17: where Christian obedience to leaders is stressed; Jas 3:1, 5:14: where the elders pray for the sick and anoint them with oil; 1 Pet. 5:1–5: pastors have before them the example of the chief Shepherd, Christ, the meek and lowly one who died for his people. Christ is 'Bishop of your souls' also, 1 Pet. 2:25). It is very significant that Heb., despite its Christology of the true High Priest, has nothing of a Christian sacrificial system or a Christian priesthood; no such system is necessary, since Jesus has made the supreme sacrifice 'once for all'. Heb. 6:6 and 1 Jn 5:16 refer to the mortal sin of apostasy, which is unforgivable (the sin against the Holy Spirit? cf. Mk 3:30). Nothing can be drawn from the 'royal priesthood' of 1 Pet. 2:9 for the constitution of the Church (cf. Rev. 1:6). In Eph. 2:20, 4:11f. the Church is founded on the apostles and prophets (Christian, not OT), Christ Jesus being the 634

634a chief cornerstone (Isa. 28:16); and Christ (rather than God or the Spirit as in 1 C. 12) has given to the Church the ministry of apostles, prophets, evangelists (unPauline; why are they required in addition to the first two?), teaching pastors (the Greek indicates one office). Yet it is the whole Church of the saints to whom the work of ministering is committed, and the business of the officers is the equipping of the members of the Body to discharge it. This doctrine of the 'gift of ministry', derived from Paul, corresponds to Christ's choice of the Twelve and it is important in the total picture. Ministers, although elected by the congregation (Ac. 6:3), are marked out by the divine Spirit; cf. 1 Tim. 4:14; 1 Jn 4:1f. (the Spirit can be tested). The Elder of 1–3 Jn, like the 'Timothy' and 'Titus' of the Pastorals, may have been one of those eminent men (*ellogimoi andres*) to whom 1 Clem. 44:3 refers; but there is insufficient evidence for a precise estimate of his powers. Archbishops did not exist in the 1st cent. (It would be different if we could prove that Diotrephes, 3 Jn 9, was a monarchical bishop, as Harnack thought.) Easton thinks that Timothy and Titus in the Pastorals, which he dates about A.D. 95 before Ignatius of Antioch, are 'in everything but the title' the monarchical bishops of the Ignatian type (op. cit., 177). This is still more true if we date them about A.D. 125–35. The regulations of these epistles, however, tell us little about the constitution of the Church; presbyter-bishops must be wise and capable, teachable and temperate, once married, and so on. Deacons too must be of sound character and faith. (Easton's note on 1 Tim. 3:9 is strange; a bishop as one of a council was subject to correction; a deacon dealt individually with needy people, hence he must be of right faith and good conscience!) The women of 1 Tim. 3:11 are probably wives of deacons, but the widows of 5:9ff. do the work of the 2nd and 3rd cent. deaconesses (cf. Ign. *Smyrn.* 13:1; Hipp. *Apost. Trad.* 11). In Rev. 1:16, 20, etc., the angels of the churches are symbolic figures, stars in the right hand of the heavenly Son of Man, and not local bishops. This was the view of Lightfoot in his famous dissertation on the Christian Ministry. Ehrhardt sees in these angels the bishops who represented Christ in his sacerdotal ministry, like the Jewish High Priest who was the *mal'ākh* or angel of God (op. cit., 79, 107).

b The Constitution of the Church in the later NT period cannot be fully explored without reference to the Apostolic Fathers and the Apologists of the 2nd cent., but this is beyond the scope of this essay: the books listed below should be consulted. It is possible to discern in NT itself the growth of early 'catholicism', with a system of orthodox tradition, Scriptures of the NT as well as the OT (e.g. 2 Pet. 3:15; see A. E. Barnett, *Paul Becomes a Literary Influence* (1941)), and a developing Liturgy (A. B. MacDonald, *Christian Worship in the Primitive Church* (1934)). The Apostles have become historic personages, the preachers and founders of the first generation (Heb. 2:3; Eph. 3:5; 2 Tim. 3:10ff.; Rev. 21:14; Jude 17; 2 Pet. 1:16ff.). In one sense, as we have seen, they could have no successors (as companions of Jesus); in another, by the nature of the case, no others were allowed to succeed, namely, as eyewitnesses of the Resurrection. Only in the function of episcopacy could they have successors, hence the institution of the presbyter-bishops and the growing importance of the local ministry. 'Appoint therefore for yourselves bishops and deacons worthy of the Lord, . . . for they also minister to you the ministry of the prophets and teachers. Therefore do not despise them, for they are your honourable men together with the prophets and teachers' (*Did.* 15:1f.; the date of the *Didache* is very uncertain, and this may be archaising). Election by the local church did not disappear in the NT age, and there is an element of 'congregational democracy' that persisted into the 2nd cent. The debate regarding the development of the monarchical episcopacy out of the primitive Church Order still goes on; but the most natural view is that one of the presbytery of bishops became permanent president and drew to himself several originally separate functions. Even so, it was as yet a congregational and not a diocesan episcopacy. 634b

Bibliography: COMMENTARIES on NT books, esp. the Pastoral Epistles—M. Dibelius (1931); B. S. Easton (1947); J. Jeremias (1934); C. Spicq (1947). Acts—F. F. Bruce (1951); Foakes Jackson and K. Lake, *The Beginnings of Christianity*, Part I (1920–33); W. L. Knox, *The Acts of the Apostles* (1948). 1 Peter—F. W. Beare (1947); E. G. Selwyn (1946).

OTHER LITERATURE: S. G. F. Brandon, *The Fall of Jerusalem and the Christian Church* (1951); R. Bultmann, *Theology of the NT*, II (1955); G. B. Caird, *The Apostolic Age* (1955); H. von Campenhausen, *Der urchristliche Apostelbegriff* (1948); O. Cullmann, *Peter: Disciple, Apostle, Martyr* (1953); M. Dibelius, *Paul*, ed. W. G. Kümmel (1953); A. Friedrichsen, *The Apostle and his Message* (1947); M. Goguel, *L'Église primitive* (1947), *The Birth of Christianity* (1953); A. Harnack, *The Constitution and Law of the Church* (1910); K. Heussi, *War Petrus in Rom?* (1936); K. Holl, *Gesammelte Aufsätze zur Kirchengeschichte*, II (1927–8); T. G. Jalland, *The Origin and Evolution of the Christian Church*, n.d. (1948); K. E. Kirk (ed), *The Apostolic Ministry* (1946); G. Kittel and G. Friedrich (ed.), *Theologisches Wörterbuch zum NT* (1933–); J. Knox, *Chapters in a Life of Paul* (1950); W. L. Knox, *St Paul and the Church of Jerusalem* (1925), *St Paul and the Church of the Gentiles* (1939); W. G. Kümmel, *Der Kirchenbegriff und Geschichtsbewusstsein in der Urgemeinde und bei Jesus* (1943); J.-L. Leuba, *NT Pattern* (1953); H. Lietzmann, *Petrus und Paulus in Rom* (1927), *The Beginnings of the Christian Church* (rev. Eng. tr. 1949); J. B. Lightfoot, 'The Christian Ministry', in *Saint Paul's Epistle to the Philippians* (7th ed. 1883), 181–269; W. Lowrie, *The Church and its Organisation* (1904); T. W. Manson, *The Church's Ministry* (1948); P. H. Menoud, *L'Église et les ministères selon le NT* (1949); J. Munck, 'Paul, the Apostles and the Twelve', in *Studia Theologica*, III (1950); A. D. Nock, *St Paul* (1938); K. H. Rengstorf, *Apostleship* (Bible Key Words from TWNT, tr. J. R. Coates) (1952); H. J. Schoeps, *Theologie und Geschichte des Judenchristentums* (1949); E. Schweizer, *Das Leben des Herrn in der Gemeinde und ihren Diensten* (1946), *Gemeinde nach dem NT* (1949); R. Sohm, *Kirchenrecht*, I (1892); B. H. Streeter, *The Primitive Church* (1929); J. Weiss, *Primitive Christianity* (1937).

CHRONOLOGY OF THE NEW TESTAMENT

By G. OGG

635a A 17th cent. scholar described one of the many problems which this subject involves as a *magnis contendentium studiis agitata quaestio.* The same may be said of nearly all the rest of them. They are almost all so difficult that, in the present state of knowledge, solutions of them can be only more or less probable; and only a reasonable probability is claimed for those presented here. Except where otherwise indicated, the years mentioned are *anni Domini.*

CHRONOLOGY OF THE LIFE OF JESUS

b **His Nativity**—According to Mt. 2:1 and Lk. 1:5 the death of Herod the Great is a *terminus ad quem* for the Nativity. Particulars given by Josephus indicate that Herod died early in the year beginning 1 Nisan 4 B.C. It is commonly held that the first to effect the equation 754 A.U.C. = A.D. 1, and so to fix the Christian era, was Dionysius Exiguus (6th cent.). But some now claim that this era was introduced by Hippolytus and adopted in the East and that later Dionysius made it popular in the West. (See Hatch, *An Album of Dated Syriac Manuscripts* (1946), 19)

c Jesus was born at the time of an enrolment ordered by Augustus throughout 'all the world' (Lk. 2:1–7). This was not the census of 8 B.C. (*Res gestae*, 2, 8), for a rescript from Cyrene dated 7/6 B.C. indicates that by then no census of the non-Roman population there had been made. (See Anderson in *Journal of Roman Studies*, 17 (1927), 33ff.) That Dio (liv, 35, 1) points to an empire-wide census made in 11 B.C. is doubtful, and the passage itself seems untrustworthy. Ramsay's attempt (*Was Christ born at Bethlehem?* (1898)) to relate the enrolment of Lk. 2 to periodic enrolments in Egypt, has not outlived the criticism that Egypt was not Judaea. 'All the world' may be a 'pleasant hyperbole' which 'ought not to be pressed too far' (MMV s.v. οἰκουμένη). Herod being a *rex socius*, Augustus is hardly likely to have ordered an enrolment throughout his territory without a compelling reason. Learning, however, in 12 B.C. of an ominous state of affairs in Herod's house, he may have proceeded by means of an enrolment to prepare for possible disorders; and Herod, thinking of the future good of his family, may have been willing that this enrolment should be made.

d Lk. 2:2 dates the enrolment of 2:1 'when Quirinius was governor of Syria'. But Quirinius, who became governor of Syria in 6, is not known to have held that office at an earlier time. Various solutions of this difficulty have been suggested. That Quirinius governed Syria immediately before Titius is a narrow possibility. Ramsay held that Quirinius governed Syria jointly, first with Titius and then with Saturninus, when conducting the Homanadensian war. But competent classical scholars now maintain that Quirinius conducted this war when governing Galatia or Galatia-Pamphylia. Corbishley's conclusion (in *Journal of Roman Studies*, 24 (1934), 43ff.) that Quirinius governed Syria immediately after Titius rests on a rearrangement of paragraphs in Josephus for which the reasons given are unsound. Moreover all these theories are open to the objection that Quirinius is hardly likely
to have been twice appointed governor of so important 635
a province. The inference long made from the inscription of Tibur that he was so, is not now allowed; and indeed opinion is no longer unanimous that this inscription relates to him. The suggestion to substitute for Quirinius the name Saturninus on the authority of Tertullian, can satisfy no-one who knows how unscrupulous Tertullian was in chronological matters. Lazzarato's contention that Quirinius was *praepositus* not *Syriae* but *orienti* (*Chronologia Christi* (1952), 51ff.) goes beyond the plain meaning of Lk. 2:2. The assumption seems inevitable that Lk. 2:2 is an insertion made by a person who wrongly identified the enrolment of Lk. 2:1 with a well-known enrolment of Judaea made by Quirinius in A.D. 6/7.

It is possible that about the time of Jesus' birth e
interest in Jewish Messianic expectations was quickened in the East by a remarkable celestial phenomenon. The star (ἀστήρ), of the Magi, long considered supernatural, was identified by Ideler (*Handbuch der math. u. techn. Chronologie* (1825–6), ii, 408) with Jupiter and Saturn in conjunction in 7 B.C. But ἀστήρ means a single star, not an assemblage of stars. Moreover the belief that a conjunction of Jupiter and Saturn had Messianic significance cannot be traced farther back than the 11th cent., and it is difficult to see how a conjunction of planets can have suggested to astrologers the birth of an eminent person. Cardano's theory that the star of the Magi was a stella nova has found new adherents. More noteworthy is a growing tendency to identify it with Halley's comet seen in 12 B.C. So brilliant a spectacle may well have prompted the Magi to inquire whether Jewish hopes had been realised.

It is doubtful if Lk. 3:23 can serve any chronological f
purpose. Its correct rendering is disputed; the originality of the 'thirty' has been denied; and the activity which Jesus is said to have begun may have been a responsibility assumed by him in the 'silent' years and mentioned in the paragraph that preceded the genealogy in the document from which the genealogy was extracted.

The statement 'Thou art not yet fifty years old' g
(Jn 8:57) admits of several explanations. But had Jesus been in his thirties, the Jews, seeking to give their reply all possible point, would have said not 'fifty' but 'forty'; and the Asian elders quoted by Irenaeus (*Adversus haereses*, ii, 22) affirmed that Jesus was at least forty when he taught. Irenaeus was convinced of the trustworthiness of this testimony, and it ought not to be rejected because of the impossible conclusions he came to in combining loyalty to it with loyalty to the Gospels. Nor ought these conclusions to be fathered on the Asian elders. Unlike Irenaeus they may have rejected the 'thirty' of Lk. 3:23 and have carried Jesus' birth farther back than that verse taken with Lk. 3:1 admits.

As the year of the Nativity, 11 or 10 or 9 B.C. seems probable. Its month-date is unknown. (See Cullmann, *Weihnachten in der alten Kirche* (1947))

The Beginning of his Ministry—To date this two 636
passages are examined. (1) According to Jn 2:20, at the first Passover of Jesus' ministry, the Jews said to him, 'Forty and six years was this temple in building'.

636a They referred, it is usually assumed, to the Temple then standing. Josephus in Ant. xv, 380 records that Herod the Great undertook to build this Temple in the eighteenth year of his reign. Comparison with Dio liv, 7 shows that this date, and not another given in Jos.B. J. 1, 401, must be accepted; and since the said eighteenth year was 20–19 B.C., it is often inferred that the first Passover of the ministry fell in 27 or 28. But Herod made considerable preparations before building started, and the time they took may not be included in the 46-years' building period mentioned by the Jews. Since the most natural rendering of their words is 'In forty and six years was this temple built' (Westcott), the completion of the 46-years' period may not have coincided with Jesus' visit to Jerusalem. Moreover, that the Jews spoke of the Herodian Temple is uncertain. Neither Heracleon nor Origen assumed that they did so. For all these reasons Jn 2:20 cannot be used with any certainty to determine when Jesus' ministry began. (2) Lk. 3:1–2 dates the call of the Baptist in a considerable chronological notice, in which, however, the only precise time-indication is 'the fifteenth year of the reign of Tiberius'. Many have assumed that here the years of Tiberius are reckoned not from the death of Augustus (19 August 14) but from the time when he became co-regent, and consequently that his fifteenth year means 26, 27, or 28. But there being no trace of this reckoning in patristic or Jewish writings or on coins, that assumption must be rejected. Since the dating of events by the effective years of a king's reign becomes difficult after his death, it is likely that here the years of Tiberius' reign have been brought into coincidence either with the years of the Syrian calendar, in which case his second year began on 1 October 14 and his fifteenth year on 1 October 27, or with the years of the Jewish calendar, in which case his second year began on 1 Nisan 15 and his fifteenth year on 1 Nisan 28. According to reliable tradition Luke was an Antiochian Syrian. That suggests the use here of the first of these methods of computation. But as Girard has shown (*Le Cadre chronologique du Ministère de Jésus* (1953), 43–58), in all ancient writings which provide a reliable synchronism the fifteenth year of Tiberius includes part of 29. For that reason and particularly because it is the key to Josephus' chronology of the Herods and because Lk. 3:1–2 appears to come from a Baptist source, the second method is to be preferred and John's call dated within the year commencing 1 Nisan 28. He had already baptised many when he baptised Jesus (Lk. 3:21). But precisely how long this was after 1 Nisan 28 cannot be determined.

b **The Duration of his Ministry**—The Synoptics refer to only one Passover, that of the Passion, in the period of Jesus' ministry. This suggests that the ministry lasted only one year, and no Synoptic passage bears unquestionable evidence that it lasted any longer. Jn, on the other hand, mentions three Passovers in the same period (2:13, 6:4, 11:55), and that number cannot be reduced. Attempts to identify two of these Passovers have not succeeded nor has the attempt to show that the reference to a Passover in 6:4 was not read by certain patristic authorities and ought therefore to be deleted. According to Jn the ministry thus lasted at least two years. This divergence between the Synoptics and John is, however, not real, being due to the fact that the former concentrate, apart from their Passion and Resurrection narratives, on the Galilean ministry.

'There are yet four months, and then cometh harvest' (Jn 4:35*a*) cannot be a proverbial saying. Such a saying would have given the actual interval between seedtime and harvest, which was six months (*Jer. Ta'anith*, 64*a*). Some understand the words literally, but maintain that Jesus was looking on fields of summer grain. Biblical and Rabbinical writings refer, however, only to the harvest gathered at the Passover season, and the kinds of grain which are sown today in spring were unknown in Palestine in NT times (Holzmeister, *Chronologia Vitae Christi* (1933), 146f.). Jesus must then have passed through Samaria four months before the usual harvest, therefore in winter. 636b

The feast of Jn 5:1 has been identified with Purim, but that seems impossible. The time-note 'after this' (μετὰ ταῦτα, on which see Lohmeyer, *Galiläa und Jerusalem* (1936), 6) indicates a considerable interval between the events of chs. 4 and 5; but Purim, falling in Adar, was celebrated soon after Jesus' return to Galilee. Two attempts are made to identify the feast of Jn 5:1 with the Passover of Jn 6:4. (1) In Jn 6:4 'nigh' is said to mean 'recently past'. That, however, the μετὰ ταῦτα of Jn 6:1 makes impossible. (2) Jn 6 is read between Jn 4 and Jn 5. But the μετὰ ταῦτα of Jn 5:1 then dates the feast of that verse a considerable time after the Passover said to be nigh in Jn 6:4, and this rearrangement of chapters, while found in Tatian, *Diatessaron*, has no manuscript authority. Now there was no feast except Purim between the time of Jesus' return to Galilee and the following Passover. Consequently, since the feast of Jn 5:1 cannot have been Purim or the Passover of Jn 6:4, it must have been either the Passover of the year preceding that of the Passover of Jn 6:4 or some feast of the interval between these Passovers, and is perhaps best identified with Tabernacles. This necessitates a Passover between those of Jn 2:13 and Jn 6:4. Jesus' ministry thus lasted three years plus the time—two months at least (Mk 1:13; Jn 1:29, 35, 43, 2:1, 12)—from his baptism to the first Passover.

The End of his Ministry—All four Gospels put the Crucifixion on a Friday. According to John this Friday was 14 Nisan, the day in the evening of which the Passover was eaten, but according to the Synoptics it was 15 Nisan. c

There is no satisfactory resolution of this difference. 'The passover' in Jn 18:28 cannot mean the *Chagigah* made ordinarily on 15 Nisan, nor can the Passover of Mk 14:17ff. have been a Passover-*Kiddush* observed in the evening of 13 Nisan, for that *Kiddush* was observed at the beginning of the Passover meal. The thesis that there was an observance of Passover at different times by different parties is attractive but cannot be substantiated. According to Chwolson (*Das letzte Passamahl Christi* (1908), 37ff.), when 14 Nisan was a Friday, owing to the proximity of the Sabbath the passover lambs were slaughtered on 13 Nisan, and some ate the Passover in the evening of that day, others twenty-four hours later. But present-day Samaritan practice indicates that when 14 Nisan was a Friday, the killing began earlier than usual on that day. Billerbeck (in SB (1922–8), ii, 812ff.) maintains that, owing to a dispute in the year of the Crucifixion between the Pharisaic and Boethusean-Sadducaean parties regarding the commencement of Nisan, its fourteenth day was for the former a Thursday and for the latter the Friday following. But two killings were sanctioned, and each party ate the Passover on its own 14 Nisan. All this appears, however, to be conjecture. According to Jaubert (in RHR146 (1954), 140ff.), in the year of the Crucifixion 14 Nisan of the official year was a Friday, but Jesus observed Passover on 14 Nisan according to an old Jewish year, which 14 Nisan was Tuesday in Passion week. If, however, the meal of that Tuesday evening was a Passover, there must have been two killings, and of that at any time there is no evidence. Moreover, for the Jewish consciousness before 70 a Passover without a lamb that had been ritually slain would have been inconceivable. Of these chronologies the Johannine is the more likely for several reasons. (1) Notwithstanding recent denials, certain features of the Synoptic tradition contradict its chronology. The 15th Nisan was a holy convocation on which only the preparation of food was allowed (Exod. 12:16). On it, therefore, Jesus cannot have been arrested, Joseph cannot have purchased linen and the arresting

636c party cannot have carried arms. (2) 1 C. 5:7f. suggests that in the Pauline churches the Crucifixion was remembered on 14 Nisan. (3) Until the 3rd cent. the Johannine chronology was the prevalent one throughout the church. (4) Until the Middle Ages the whole church used leavened bread in the Eucharist.

The year of the Crucifixion is determined mainly in three ways. (1) The dating *consulibus Rubellio Gemino et Fufio Gemino*, i.e. 29, is chosen because given in many patristic writings and thought to embody a reliable tradition. But in early times the Crucifixion was by no means universally assigned to 29, and almost all the writings, of which the earliest is the *Adversus Judaeos* of Tertullian, which give the Gemini dating belong to the Latin West. Tertullian can have obtained it from a report of the Crucifixion which Pilate had sent to Tiberius only if a report was sent, and of that there is no evidence. In 29 the 25th March, a month-date for the Crucifixion found in many early writings, was a Friday, but in all likelihood 14 Nisan in that year was Monday 18 April. It is thus almost certain that 29 was not the year of the Crucifixion. (2) Help is sought in the history of Herod Antipas (Jos. Ant. xviii, 109ff.). When Aretas, king of Arabia Petrea and father of Herod's wife, learned that he was about to divorce her, he made this a commencement of enmity, and in the war that followed, apparently in 36, Herod was defeated. Now it is argued that since this defeat was considered a judgment upon him for killing John the Baptist, John must have died immediately before the war. Accordingly John's death is dated 34–35 and the Crucifixion 35 or 36. But retribution is not always immediate, and the reference to a *commencement* of enmity suggests that some time passed before the war started. Moreover these dates would create serious difficulties for the Pauline chronology. (3) Recourse is had to astronomy, the data being that the Crucifixion occurred on Friday 14 Nisan or, if the Synoptic chronology of Passion week be accepted, Friday 15 Nisan of one of the years of Pilate's procuratorship, 26–36. In NT times the Jewish year was lunisolar, comprising twelve months, to which another was added as required in particular by the state of the crops. The beginning of the month was determined by observation made in the evening of the 29th day of the month. If by a certain hour on the following day reliable witnesses reported that they had seen the new moon, that day was declared the first of the new month ; otherwise it was reckoned the thirtieth and last of the month. Astronomers have thus to determine when the moon became visible. Now Fotheringham, using observations made in Athens in 1859–80, and Schoch, using ancient Babylonian observations, have each arrived at a formula which gives in terms of its azimuth the minimum altitude which the moon must have for visibility. Fotheringham (in JTS 35 (1934), 158ff.), who prefers Schoch's formula when it differs from his own, concludes that in the period that has to be considered 14 Nisan was a Friday only in 30 and 33, and a Thursday only in 27. Abnormal conditions are of course possible, but it should be noted, in view of recent assertions that the Last Supper was a Paschal meal, that Gerhardt's conclusion (in *Astron. Nachrichten* 240 (1930), 156) that 14 Nisan was Thursday 6 April in 30 necessitates the assumption of ' an extremely early visibility of the crescent ' (Fotheringham). There are thus three possible dates of the Crucifixion —11 Apr. 27, 7 Apr. 30 and 3 Apr. 33, and conclusions already reached necessitate the choice of the last. The Passover of Jn 6:4 was thus that of 32, and the first Passover of Jesus' ministry (Jn 2:13) that of 30.

THE APOSTOLIC AGE: ITS ABSOLUTE CHRONOLOGY

637a **Paul's Flight from Damascus**—Of the Nabataean official whom he mentions in 2 C. 11:32 Paul says that he was the ethnarch of Aretas and also that he guarded the gates of Damascus to arrest him. The only conclusion consistent with *both* these statements is that Aretas then possessed Damascus and that this official governed there in his name. This use of ' ethnarch ' for ' governor ' is explained by Schürer (in *Studien und Kritiken*, 72 (1899), 95ff.). Coins show that Damascus was in Roman hands until 33–4. When in 37 Vitellius the legate of Syria marched against Aretas, he left Damascus in his rear. Apparently it was still in Roman hands. Accordingly the *terminus a quo* of Paul's flight is 37, and of his conversion 34 (Gal. 1:18).

b **The Death of Agrippa I**—Agrippa received the tetrarchies of Philip and Lysanias with the title king shortly after Caius' accession on 16 March 37. As 1 Nisan 37 was 5 March, the second year of Agrippa's reign began on 1 Nisan 38. When he had reigned three years, therefore in his fourth year, 40(1 Nisan)–41, he received the tetrarchy of Antipas. On 25 January 41, on Claudius' accession, he received Judaea and Samaria. He then reigned over all the territory that had belonged to his grandfather. Since he did so for three full years and died in the seventh year of his reign, his death occurred between 25 January and 1 Nisan 44. This conclusion, based on Jos. Ant. xix, 274, 343, 350f., suggests that a coin of Agrippa's eighth year discussed by Reifenberg in PEF 67 (1935), 80 was minted in anticipation. Agrippa's persecution of the church, which took place at Passover (Ac. 12:3), cannot be dated later than 43 ; and Ac. 12:19*b* refers perhaps to no more than the interval from Passover 43 to Agrippa's death.

The festival in progress in Caesarea when Agrippa died (Jos. Ant. xix, 343ff.) may have marked Claudius' triumphant return from Britain or have been a celebration of quinquennalia instituted in 9 B.C. by Herod the Great and commencing on 5 March, the foundation-day of Caesarea (Eusebius, *Mart. Pal.* xi, 30).

c **The Famine under Claudius** (Ac. 11:28) was apparently the famine of Jos. Ant. xx, 101 which oppressed Judaea in the procuratorship of Tiberius Alexander (46–48). Helena, Queen of Adiabene, coming to Jerusalem, found it at its height and, moved with compassion, fetched much corn from Egypt. Now papyri from Tebtunis indicate that there were famine conditions in Egypt in 45 (see Gapp in HTR 28 (1935), 258ff.). The high price of corn in August, September, and November of that year must be put down to a bad harvest in the preceding spring or to an anticipated bad harvest in spring 46. The fact that Helena's servants secured much corn quickly indicates that by the time they went to Egypt the situation there had improved. It is then to be concluded that in Judaea there was a bad harvest in 46 or 47, and that Helena showed her generosity about Passover (Jos. Ant. iii, 321) 47 or 48 shortly before the new harvest in Judaea and so when the situation there was at its worst. The Antiochian Christians doubtless sent relief immediately, but not before, they knew that it was needed. The Famine Relief Visit of Ac. 11:30 must accordingly be dated winter 45/46 or 46/47.

d **The Year of Sergius Paulus' Proconsulship of Cyprus** (Ac. 13:7)—The name L. Sergius Paullus occurs in an inscription (*Corpus Inscriptionum Latinarum*, vi, 31545) containing a list of curators of the Tiber in Claudius' reign. But the inscription cannot be dated more closely, nor is it known that this man was appointed to Cyprus. The concluding lines of an inscription from Soloi (Hogarth, *Devia Cypria* (1889), 114), dated 25 Demarchexousios and year 13, mention a reform when Paulus was proconsul. But the epoch of the year-reckoning is unknown ; and these lines being almost certainly a postscript, the date of the proconsulship of this Paulus may differ considerably from that of the inscription proper. At present the only certainty which inscriptions give regarding the Paulus of Acts is that he was not proconsul in 51 or 52 (*Corpus Inscriptionum Graecarum*, 2632).

e **Claudius' Expulsion of the Jews from Rome**

637e (Ac. 18:2)—This is mentioned but not dated in Suetonius, *Claud.* 25. Orosius in *Hist.* VII, vi, 15 puts it in Claudius' ninth year, 25 Jan. 49–24 Jan. 50. He errs apparently in saying that he found this date in Josephus. His actual source of it may have been trustworthy—Julius Africanus has been suggested, but it remains unknown.

f **The Year of Gallio's Proconsulship of Achaia**—An inscription from Delphi [1] enables this to be determined with considerable exactness. It is a rescript of Claudius regarding the boundaries of the sacred domain of Delphi. In it the number of his imperatorial acclamation, K⊏=26, is clearly legible. Now his 27th *acclamatio* is mentioned in an inscription (*Corpus Inscriptionum Latinarum*, vi, 1256) on an arch of the Aqua Claudia which was consecrated on 1 August 52,[2] and his 22nd *acclamatio* in an inscription (*Corpus Inscriptionum Latinarum*, iii, 476) side by side with the eleventh year of his tribunicial power (25 January 51–24 January 52). Claudius was thus acclaimed for the 23rd, 24th, 25th, 26th, and 27th times within the period 25 January 51–1 August 52; and it being unlikely that he was so all five times in 51, he was in all probability acclaimed for the 26th time in the first half of 52. Gallio had already investigated the boundary question and communicated his findings to Claudius before the rescript was issued. Accordingly it is almost certain that it belongs to the closing months of Gallio's year of office and that that year was 51 (summer)–52.

The Jews brought Paul before Gallio not when the latter *became* but when he *was* proconsul (Ac. 18:12). They waited apparently until they had such knowledge of him as seemed to warrant the hope that he would decide in their favour. But they doubtless also sought to avail themselves of his inexperience, and combined dispatch with caution. It may then be assumed that they acted within a couple of months of Gallio's arrival. Paul's coming to Corinth eighteen months earlier (Ac. 18:11) is accordingly to be dated early in 50.

g **The Year in which Festus succeeded Felix** is in Eusebius, *Chronicle*, Armenian Version, the last year of Claudius, and in Jerome's Version the second year of Nero. Josephus assigns the events of Felix's procuratorship to Nero's reign (Ant. xx, 160 ff.), but apparently adopts a story which, ignoring the fact that Nero early in his first year dismissed Pallas from court (Tacitus, *Ann.* xiii, 14f.), gave a false reason for the failure of the Jews to secure Felix's condemnation, namely the intervention of his brother Pallas 'who was at that time held in the greatest honour' by Nero. According to Jos. Ant. xx, 136ff. Felix succeeded Cumanus, apparently in 52. But according to Tacitus, *Ann.* xii, 54, for some time prior to 52 he governed a part of Judaea, while Cumanus governed the rest, and then in 52 became governor of the whole. This opens the possibility that much of what happened during his stay in Judaea occurred under Claudius and that he was recalled soon after Nero's accession. But here Tacitus probably follows a tradition which in hatred of Felix sought to involve him in responsibility for the enormities of his predecessor's administration. Certainly Josephus, presumably the better informed, knows nothing of a twofold procuratorship of Judaea.

The time-indications of these authorities thus provide an insecure basis for the so-called antedated chronology advocated by Petavius (*De doctrina temporum* (1627), 2, 176) and adopted by Harnack (*Chronologie der alt-christl. Lit.* (1897), i, 233ff.), Schwartz ('Zur Chronologie des Paulus', *Göttinger Nachrichten* (1907), 263ff.), Lake, etc. which assigns the change of office to 55 or 56. According to the more obvious interpretation of Ac. 24:27 Paul was arrested at Pentecost two years before Felix was recalled. If then his first visit to Corinth ended in autumn 51 and his arrest was in 53 or 54, the events of Ac. 18:18–21:16 occupied less than three years. But the Ephesian ministry alone was nearly three years in length (Ac. 20:31). 637g

Festus died in office. Thereafter lawlessness reigned for at least three months, and the new procurator was in Jerusalem at Tabernacles 62 (Jos.B.J. vi, 300 ff.). Festus thus succeeded Felix in one of the five years 57 to 61. Most scholars adopt 59 or 60, but some now prefer 61. According to Jos. Ant. xx, 195 an embassy which with Festus' permission carried a dispute about buildings to Rome received help from Poppaea, Nero's wife. Now she became his wife in May 62, also the buildings referred to may have been begun in Felix's procuratorship, and the few other events of Festus' period of office need have occupied no long time. It is thus probable that Festus was still alive in April 62 and that he succeeded Felix in 61. Those who favour an earlier year maintain that Poppaea is here called Nero's wife euphemistically or proleptically. The reasons based on Ac. 24:10 and Jos. *Vita*, 13ff. often given for putting the change of office not earlier than 60 are reasons for assigning it to 61.

THE APOSTOLIC AGE: ITS RELATIVE CHRONOLOGY

33-35. In its early pentecostal days the church grew rapidly and soon came into conflict with Jewish authorities. While it may be doubted if passages such as *Ascension of Isaiah*, ix, 16 and Irenaeus, *Adversus haereses*, i, 30, 14 embody trustworthy tradition regarding the period from the Resurrection to Paul's conversion, the events of Ac. 1–8 may have occupied but one and a half years and Paul's conversion have taken place in 34 or 35. 638a

35-46. From Damascus Paul returned to Jerusalem 'after three years' (Gal. 1:18). Leaving Jerusalem he sojourned in Syria and Cilicia until called to Antioch, a year before the Famine Relief Visit to Jerusalem. Of its possible dates only the earlier, winter 45/46, allows sufficient time for the events following up to Paul's first arrival in Corinth. b

Certain scholars consider, however, that in Ac. 11:27–12:25 this visit is put *before* the persecution by Agrippa. This raises the problem of Paul's Jerusalem visits recorded in Acts and of the identification with them of the visits mentioned in Galatians. The principal more recently suggested solutions of it are the following:

(1) Attempting a chronological order of events based mainly upon the time-indications contained in Paul's epistles, Knox [1] puts Paul's conversion in 37, his first visit to Jerusalem (Gal. 1:18; Ac. 9:26) in 40, his second visit (Gal. 2:1–10; Ac. 15:1–30, 18:22), after a missionary journey in Asia Minor and Greece, in 51, his third and last visit (Ac. 21:17ff.) in 53.

(2) Lake inserts Ac. 12:1–24 before 9:32 and regards the Famine Visit and the First Missionary Journey as doublets of the Council Visit (Ac. 15:1–30) and the Second Missionary Journey.

(3) Several scholars maintain that in Ac. 11:27–12:25 the Council Visit, which they identify with that of Gal. 2:1, is wrongly described as a Famine Relief Visit but correctly dated, and hence that the Council Visit was earlier than the persecution by Agrippa. Goguel in RHR 65 (1912), 285ff. puts the Council late in 43 or early in 44. But Paul's conversion, since it took place fourteen years earlier, must then be dated *c.*29/30, which is too early.

(4) Others maintain that following an Antioch source in Ac. 11:27–30 and a Jerusalem source in Ac. 15:1–30, Luke has made two visits of one, which one is given its correct chronological location in Ac. 15 and is described from his own standpoint by

[1] Text in Lake, 'The Chronology of Acts' *Beginnings of Christianity* (1920-33), I, v, 445ff.
[2] Frontinus, *De aquaeductu*, 13, ed. Grimal (1944), II.

[1] *Chapters in a Life of Paul* (1950). On his conclusions see Ogg in ET 64 (1953), 120 ff.

638b Paul in Gal. 2:1–10. But the Antioch source was presumably not just the cash book of the church there. Whilst recording the generosity of the Antiochian Christians, it cannot have been silent about discussions in Jerusalem which much concerned them.

(5) The position defended by Plooij (*De Chronologie van het Leven van Paulus* (1918), 10 ff.) seems the most satisfactory. Luke's phrase 'about that time' (Ac. 12:1) indicates only a general synchronism; and since in the paragraph Ac. 12:1–24 which lies between his references to the Famine Visit he brings up the history of events in Palestine to the time of it, it follows that according to him it took place *after* Agrippa's death. The Famine Visit was two years earlier than the visit of Gal. 2:1 (=Ac. 15), but Paul had no occasion to mention it and has not done so.

c **46-47.** Cyprus, to which Paul and Barnabas sailed on their First Journey, had a considerable Jewish population, and Ac. 13:5f. indicates that they visited most of its synagogues. Landing in spring 46, they may have stayed until autumn and then, crossing to Pamphylia, have reached Pisidian Antioch before winter. In Phrygia and Lycaonia they founded several churches and may have returned to Syria in autumn 47.

d **48-53.** After attending the Jerusalem Council early in 48, the fourteenth year after his conversion, Paul started on his Second Journey and first visited Lycaonia. He then entered a new field described as 'the region of Phrygia and Galatia' (Ac. 16:6). The part of it which he traversed first was Phrygian in population; the other part was Galatian and so was the territory in the heart of Asia Minor which, since the time of Attalus I, had been the home of certain Gallic tribes. The verb διῆλθον rendered 'they went through', may denote a journey in the progress of which missionary work was done (MMV s.v.), and here that meaning is made likely by the words 'having been forbidden *to speak the word* in Asia'. Paul, it appears, stayed in this new field sufficiently long to found churches there and did not proceed to Troas until spring 49. Crossing then to Europe, he reached Corinth early in 50. After the Gallio incident he remained in Corinth 'many days longer' (Ac. 18:18). But that expression cannot here denote more than one or two months (see Wieseler, *Chronologie des apostolischen Zeitalters* (1848), 46). Paul's return to Antioch is accordingly to be dated autumn 51. Its cause is unknown. It may have been sickness, and his stay in Antioch, given as 'some time' (Ac. 18:23), may have extended until spring 53.

e **53-59.** Starting then on his Third Journey, Paul passed through the Cilician Gates and proceeded to Galatia (in the ethnographical sense) by a road east of the one he took on his previous visit (contrast Ac. 16:6 and 18:23 and charts 2 and 3 in Metzger, *Les Routes de Saint Paul* (1954)). Traversing the country from east to west he may have made a considerable stay. From Galatia he proceeded to Phrygia and thence to Ephesus. A recapitulating reference to this journey in Galatia and Phrygia appears in the words 'Paul passed through the upper country' (Ac. 19:1), and there the verb suggests an extensive missionary labour which may have occupied eighteen months. The arrival in Ephesus may then be dated autumn 54.

The Ephesian ministry lasted for three years (Ac. 20:31), i.e. two years and several months. The riot of Ac. 19:23ff., of the occurrence of which during a celebration of the Artemisia there is no indication, probably obliged him to leave Ephesus somewhat sooner in 57 than he had purposed, and he spent the autumn in Troas and then crossed to Macedonia. Early in 58 he received heartening news about the church at Corinth and, relieved of anxiety, moved southwards evangelising as he went and going perhaps as far west as Illyricum (Rom. 15:19). He spent three months, those of winter (Ac. 20:6), in Greece and was back in Jerusalem by Pentecost 59.

f **59-64.** Arrested then, he remained a prisoner in Caesarea for two years (Ac. 24:27). On Festus' arrival in 61 he appealed to Caesar and, as Ac. 27:9 indicates, sailed for Rome in the autumn. Shipwrecked on Malta, he wintered there and, early in 62, reached Rome, where he continued in easy imprisonment for 'two whole years' (Ac. 28:30), therefore until 64. What followed is uncertain. But it seems probable that he suffered in the Neronian persecution or that he was tried, condemned and executed shortly before it so that in tradition his death was ascribed to it.

Cullmann in his study *Petrus* (1952) concludes that Peter came to Rome towards the end of his life, worked there for a short time and suffered under Nero. Katzenmayer in *Internationale kirchliche Zeitschrift* 31 (1941), 36ff. puts his arrival in Rome and martyrdom there very early in Nero's reign. But Heussi in TLZ 77 (1952), 67ff. denies that Peter ever went to Rome and, making a large use of the 'were' (ἦσαν) of Gal. 2:6, concludes that he died *c.*55 or 56 (on this conclusion see Aland in NTS 2 (1956), 267ff.). Robinson in JBL 64 (1945), 255ff. suggests that the other place to which in Ac. 12:17 Peter is said to have gone may have been the place of glory, and consequently that he may have died in Jerusalem in 44.

In Jos. Ant. xx, 200, in a passage which may be an interpolation, the martyrdom of James the Lord's brother is put in the period of anarchy that followed the death of Festus in 62. In a passage of Hegesippus, quoted by Eusebius (*Hist. eccl.* II, xxiii) and clearly legendary in character, it is apparently put nearer the Fall of Jerusalem. Debate continues as to whether the tradition of a long residence of the apostle John in Asia ought to be accepted or his death put with that of his brother in the persecution by Agrippa.

Bibliography—C. J. Cadoux, 'Chronology of the Apostolic Age', JBL 56 (1937), 177ff.; G. B. Caird, *The Apostolic Age* (1955), Appendix A; C. Cichorius, 'Chronologisches zum Leben Jesu', ZNTW 22 (1923), 16ff.; J. Dupont, *Les Problèmes du Livre des Actes* (1950), 51–70; O. Gerhardt, *Der Stern des Messias* (1922); F. K. Ginzel, *Handbuch der math. u. techn. Chronologie*, 3 vols. (1906–14); U. Holzmeister, *Historia Aetatis Novi Testamenti* (1938); J. Jeremias, *Die Abendmahlsworte Jesu* (1949); C. King, 'The Outline of the NT Chronology', CQR 139 (1945), 129ff.; E. Meyer, *Ursprung u. Anfänge des Christentums* (1923), iii; P. V. Neugebauer, *Astronomische Chronologie* (1929), i–ii; G. Ogg, *The Chronology of the Public Ministry of Jesus* (1940); E. F. Sutcliffe, *A Two Year Public Ministry* (1938); J. Wellhausen, 'Noten zur Apostelgeschichte', *Göttinger Nachrichten* (1907), 1ff.

THE LIFE AND TEACHING OF JESUS

By J. W. Bowman

9a **The Early Years**—It seems quite clear that at no time in its history has the Christian Church thought of its Founder's life as beginning with the manger in Bethlehem. Each of the four evangelists gives expression to this fact in his own way. The Fourth Evangelist, whose background appears to have been that of Hellenistic Judaism, employs the current *logos* doctrine to indicate the eternal character of him who became flesh as Jesus of Nazareth. Mark, less the theologian than John but sharing with him a certain flair for the dramatic, throughout his Gospel allows the facts to speak for themselves, until at the close they culminate in the amazing cry of the Roman centurion, 'Truly this man was God's Son' (15:39). The separate traditions of the virgin birth which are found in the Gospels of Mt. and Lk. represent a third endeavour to express the eternal Sonship which characterised Jesus of Nazareth (Mt. 1:18; Lk. 1:34f.).

b In addition to the accounts in the Gospels other NT writers in one way and another give expression to the Church's conviction on this point. In the Revelation to John, not only does the eternal Christ say for himself, 'I am the first and the last, and the living one' (1:17f.), but he is also acclaimed 'Word of God' (19:13) and 'Lord of Lords and King of Kings' (17:14). For the author of Hebrews, he is the eternal Son of God through whom the latter created the universe (1:1–14). For Paul, he was 'in the form of God' before he became man (Phil. 2:5–11). Contemporary Form Criticism, allying itself at this point with the school of Comparative Religions, commits itself to a belief in the legendary nature of the so-called 'birth narratives' of the Gospels. These it is said partake of the same nature as pagan accounts of apotheosis. The unique simplicity of these narratives, however, together with their undoubted wish to set the birth of Jesus in the framework of the Hebrew prophetic teaching, suggests rather that they represent the Church's attempt to dramatise for popular understanding its faith in the genuine eternity of the Son's nature. And that the evangelists believe these birth narratives to be founded upon historic fact there can be no question.

c A second characteristic of the Church's Gospels which impresses the reader is the lack of any endeavour on the part of their authors to present a comprehensive survey of the life of Jesus as a whole (see §641*c*). Both Mt. and Lk. place the birth narratives within the framework of the Idumaean dynasty of Herod the Great and Lk. gives them the larger reference of the reigning Roman emperor. Thereafter no dates are given nor are any events narrated until the appearance of John the Baptist in the Jordan valley when Jesus was approximately thirty years of age, with the single exception of his attending the Feast of the Passover as a youth (Lk. 2:41–51). Lk. alone among the evangelists is concerned to suggest that Jesus' development 'in wisdom and in stature' followed the normal pattern of the life of a Jewish lad. Long before Jesus' day the synagogue had become the teaching, as well as the worship, centre of the Jewish world. With the other boys at Nazareth, Jesus no doubt attended the *Bêth hassēpher* (house of the book) in which the local *ḥazzān* or custodian of the synagogue scriptures would serve as instructor, the OT in Hebrew 639c
being the principal textbook in the school. In sug- d
gesting that Jesus' questions and answers amazed the Rabbis as he talked with them in the Temple (Lk. 2:46), Lk. no doubt wishes to imply that Jesus' development was somewhat precocious. Jesus was at that time only twelve years of age and Rabbi Judah ben Tema (end of 2nd cent. A.D.) is authority for the statement that not until after the *miṣwah* ceremony (at thirteen) and the attainment of his fifteenth birthday was the Jewish boy ready to study the Talmud, that is, to indulge in the involved and often hair-splitting rabbinical discussions about the scriptures (M. Aboth 5:21). But whatever his precocity Jesus was not privileged to sit like Paul at the feet of one of the great contemporary Rabbis and his teachings never displayed the characteristics of their exegetical method.

The Contemporary Culture—At the same time it is e
possible that, in addition to learning to read the classical Hebrew of the OT scriptures, as T. W. Manson has pointed out (*The Teaching of Jesus* (2nd ed., 1935), 46ff.) Jesus may have known enough of the rabbinical Hebrew employed in the classroom and in learned discussion to meet the Rabbis on their own ground (Mk 7:1–23). It was perhaps for this reason that his pharisaic enemies, as well as his friends and disciples, at times addressed him as 'Rabbi'. Raised as he was in 'Galilee of the Gentiles' our Lord may also have possessed, in addition to his native Aramaic, an elementary knowledge of the *lingua franca* of the Roman empire, Hellenistic Greek, and even some small smatter-
ing of Latin. Jesus' native Galilee was the crossroads f
of the world and had been such for centuries past. One of the great highways connecting East with West in Jesus' day ran from Ptolemais on the Mediterranean seacoast, across the hills north of his native Nazareth and so down to the southern end of the Sea of Galilee, and then across the Jordan into the Greek Decapolis. A branch of this same road ran south to Nazareth itself and so across the hills southeast of Mt Carmel, down to the Plain of Sharon and on to Egypt. As a boy, therefore, Jesus must have seen the Roman legions passing along the road below his native town, as well as merchants from far-off Persia and India with their caravans of camels. The learning of the Greeks, too, had been introduced into Galilee centuries before his day and Greek was the language of commerce and trade, as of literature and art, even as Latin was that of the custom house and the Roman legionary.

As compared with the city of Jerusalem and Judaea g
generally Galilee in Jesus' day lacked sophistication. The Temple nobility, made up generally of Sadducees, were of course concentrated in the capital city of the Jewish world. The great Rabbis among the Pharisees also made the capital city their headquarters, although their disciples were scattered through the empire and were to be found wherever the synagogue went. The aristocracy of Galilee, aside from the Herodian house whose capital centre was at Sepphoris during Jesus' boyhood and at Tiberias in his later years, was composed of a relatively few large landowners, some of whom would no doubt belong to the more aristocratic among the Pharisees (the Shammaites). By and large, however, the small landowners and the artisans and

639g traders were either Ḥasidim (the truly religious and non-sectarian Jews of the day) or Zealots (members of the nationalistic party). Both of these groups would be looked upon with scorn by the Pharisees and their Rabbis as *'Ammē hā-'āreṣ* or common and religiously illiterate people of the land. Of such the great Hillel is reported to have said, ' An *'Am hā-'āreṣ* cannot be saintly' (M. Aboth 2:6). Our Lord's family and the majority of his disciples undoubtedly were drawn from this group (Ac. 4:13). One of Jesus' disciples, indeed, was known as Simon the Zealot and it is possible that Judas Iscariot received his sobriquet from his association with the *sicarii* or ' dagger men ', apparently an inner circle of the nationalist party (i.e. ' Iscariot' may stand for *sicarius* plus a prosthetic *aleph* represented by ' I ').

h It is possible also that Jesus as growing boy and young man came in contact with the Essenes, of whom Josephus remarks (Jos.B.J. II, viii, 4) that ' many of them dwell in every city ' (i.e. throughout Palestine). Possibly such groups are to be identified with the ' camps ' of which we read in the Dead Sea Scrolls (e.g. Dam. Doc. 7:6, 14:8f.). It may be that through the influence of this sect Jesus and his contemporaries came in contact with the esoteric literature known as Apocalyptic. For it does seem that this literature had a greater vogue among the less sophisticated Galileans than in Judaea. It is true that in the Gospels no mention is ever made of either Essenes or Qumrân community. None the less, it appears that teaching similar to that of this sect is reflected in the beliefs and practices of the later Hebraic and Hellenistic branches of the Christian Church and it would not be strange if such had had an impact upon the circle in which our Lord grew up as a boy and young man. The Qumrân community considered itself to represent the ' remnant ' of the later prophetic literature of the OT, ' the elect ', ' the righteous ', ' the saints of God '—in other words, the ' people of God ' of both Psalms and Prophets. In their judgment they were also an eschatological community living in the ' last times '. Like all others who treasured the Apocalyptic Literature, written approximately from 175 B.C. to A.D. 100, they believed in the kingdoms of God and Satan, respectively, which they peopled with angels and demons as well as with those men who were styled by them ' the sons of light ', on the one hand, and the ' sons of darkness ' on the other, cf. esp. *The War of the Sons of Light and the Sons of Darkness*.

i It is an undoubted fact that the Church to which we owe our Gospels was an apocalyptic Church, believing in the series of ideas about which we have just been speaking. It is not strange, therefore, that these Gospels should reflect such beliefs. It is a moot question, however, how far our Lord accepted or was influenced by them. The so-called school of ' consistent eschatology ' of Johannes Weiss and Albert Schweitzer held that all of Jesus' teaching was to be understood from the standpoint of such apocalyptic ideas. However, few if any would subscribe to this extreme position at the present day. It may be pointed out, for example, that Jesus' teaching reflects at least equally the ideas and teachings of contemporary Pharisaism, so much so that the ' Old Liberal ' school of criticism was able to declare him merely a somewhat heretical Rabbi, not too far removed from the Pharisaic Rabbis of his day ! The truth is that innumerable similarities may be pointed out between the teachings of Jesus and those of Pharisee, Essene or Qumrân sect, Apocalyptist, and even Sadducee. And yet with all these similarities, there is a distinctive note in Jesus' teaching which sets it apart from that of all his contemporaries. Like any wise teacher, he simply employed the thought-frames and idioms with which his hearers and disciples were familiar, and in them he presented the distinctive message which his Father had given to him to teach and preach.

640a **John the Baptist**—Jesus' ministry was immediately preceded by that of another, John the Baptist, conducted mainly in the Jordan valley. For at least one **64**
hundred and fifty years the voice of prophecy had been stilled. There is a traditional saying which reflects the accepted belief of the Pharisaism contemporary with Jesus, to the effect that—' When the last prophets, Haggai, Zechariah, and Malachi died, the Holy Spirit ceased out of Israel ; but nevertheless it was granted them to hear [communications from God] by means of a mysterious voice (the *bath qol*) ' (see George F. Moore, *Judaism* (1927), i, 421). This *bath qol* (lit. ' daughter of a voice ') was the rabbinic equivalent of our ' echo '. None of the great Rabbis of the period immediately preceding or succeeding the beginning of the Christian era claimed to hear more than an echo,
therefore, of God's voice speaking to them. John the **b**
Baptist, however, an ascetic in both dress and habit of life, spoke with a ring of authority like that of the old prophets of Israel. It seems clear that John had no developed theological or ethical message to present to his people. At best he was merely a ' voice crying in the wilderness ' who exemplified the spirit of Elijah, the prophet whose coming again was anticipated in popular belief ' before the great and terrible day of the Lord ' (Mal. 4:5 ; Mk 9:12). John was an apocalyptic figure announcing the near approach of God's judgment on men's sins and proclaiming a baptism of repentance unto remission of sins in preparation therefor. The baptism by John in running water was an apocalyptic sacrament that to his mind symbolised the genuine baptism in the stream of fire issuing from the throne of God, which the ' Coming One ' proclaimed by him would administer (see Carl H. Kraeling, *John the Baptist* (1951), 118–122). John never applied the term ' Messiah ' to the Coming One whom he announced. This Coming One was to act as judge of men, sorting out the chaff from the wheat on the threshing-floor of judgment in his time, and the figure who most nearly fits this description is that, not of the Messiah as popularly conceived, but rather of the ' Son of Man ' of 1 Enoch 37–71, who comes for judgment rather than for the salvation of the people of God.

In his home at ' Nazareth of Galilee ' Jesus heard of **c**
this new prophetic movement inaugurated by John and so, coming down from his native hills to the Jordan valley, Jesus purposed to ally himself with it. By way of explanation Mt. says that this was to ' fulfil all righteousness ', that is to identify himself wholly with mankind in the endeavour to fulfil all of God's righteous demand upon man. The repentance (cf. Heb. *shûbh*) which John preached, in the language of Hebrew prophecy stood for a complete about-face of the human personality, a turning away from selfish ambitions and desires to fulfil the will of God for one's life. Like all prophetic messages, accordingly, John's represented a call to decision to submit oneself to the Lordship of God. Jesus could no more resist the claims of such a call than could any of his contemporaries. In obedience, therefore, to the prophetic voice represented by John he came to seek baptism at the latter's hand. The Gospels in one way or another all record that as he came out of the waters he received definite signs of the divine approval of his action.

Jesus' Baptism and Temptations—The evangelists **d**
are united in their testimony that from this moment the Holy Spirit of prophecy came upon Jesus in a unique way and that that Spirit remained with him to direct and teach throughout his ministry. Moreover, the voice of his Father spoke to him saying, ' Thou art my Son, the Beloved One ; with Thee I am well pleased '. It is probable, as Mk implies, that none but Jesus heard the voice speaking to him out
of heaven. For it is characteristic of the voices of **e**
scripture that they are heard only by those prepared to receive them (cf. Jn 12:27–30 ; Ac. 22:7–9). And yet this voice, though spoken only to Jesus himself, is clearly indicated as being an objective one ; it is the voice of the eternal Father speaking to his eternal Son.

40e It quotes, moreover, from two passages of scripture—Ps. 2:7 and Isa. 42:1. The former of these is from a coronation psalm, wherein is narrated the coronation of the reigning messiah by the Lord God himself. In the psalm the words 'Thou art my Son' form the first part of the coronation formula which serves to constitute the reigning king of Israel or Judah as the Lord's current viceroy. Equally, in the latter quotation is to be found the ordination formula of the Suffering Servant of Yahweh pronounced by the Lord himself. As used of Jesus, accordingly, these combined formulae serve at once to declare him Messiah and Suffering Servant of the Lord.

f So far as our information goes, this is the first instance in all Jewish literature in which the concepts of Messiah and Suffering Servant are combined in referring to a single individual. If then, as we have suggested, Jesus was ready to hear this voice speaking to him it must have been because he was already prepared in mind and will to combine these two concepts with reference to himself. Some scholars call attention to the fact that neither in the formula here used nor in its immediate context is there a reference to the thought of suffering. (Thus Vincent Taylor, *The Gospel According to St Mark* (1952), 617; but cf. Oscar Cullmann, *Baptism in the NT* (1950), 16f.) This, however, can only be incidental. The Servant Psalms of Deutero-Isaiah were for the Jew as for us a unit and no thought of the Servant could at any time exclude that of his attendant suffering to save. Moreover, were no thought of suffering to be present here, there would be nothing new about Jesus' combining the concepts of Messiah and Servant of Yahweh in his thinking. The high priest, the reigning king, the prophet of God, indeed all Israelites, were servants of the true and living God according to the OT teaching. Again, the temptations of Jesus, which for the Synoptic Gospels form the second half of one event with the baptism of Jesus, remain inexplicable unless from the baptism onward two conceptions of Messiahship were battling for acceptance in his mind. These will be that of a national hero occupying the throne of David and concerned to muster an army with a view to overthrowing the foes of Israel, on the one hand, and on the other that of a great moral or spiritual figure whose deep concern for his people transcends (while including, to be sure) their mere political interest.

g The key to a right understanding of the meaning of the temptations for Jesus himself would seem to lie in the answers which he gives to the tempter. These are all taken from Dt. 6 and 8, and occur in contexts in which the 'chosen people' are themselves said to be passing through experiences like to those of Jesus on this occasion. If we follow the account in Mt., which appears to give us a sequence more psychologically probable than that in Lk.'s account, the first temptation will be one to employ powers which as Son of God Jesus knows himself to enjoy, but powers far transcending those of man. The temptation arises quite naturally out of the human experience of hunger and Jesus in rejecting it in terms of Dt. 8:3 manifests his decision to make the surrender to which all men are called and to follow at every point God's will for his life. The second temptation, following quite logically upon the first, will be, then, to test God and see whether he will measure up to the needs of one who has wholly dedicated himself to the doing of God's will. But, once again, our Lord (even as all men must do) refuses to try God at this point (Dt. 6:16). These first two temptations, as T. W. Manson has pointed out (*The Teaching of Jesus*, 196f.), are respectively to *disobedience* and *distrust*, and they rather clearly point to a tension within the mind of one who like Jesus has just committed himself to the new movement of the Spirit of God employing the prophet
h John. The third temptation—one to *disloyalty*—even more pointedly relates to our Lord's immediate situation. For there can be no mistaking that here the claims of two types of Messiahship are in question, 640h
one to be God's Messiah and the other Satan's. That such tension should exist in the mind of Jesus would seem to indicate that these two conceptions of Messiahship were very far apart indeed. Although without hesitation he brushes the third temptation aside in the words of Dt. 6:13f., there can be no doubt that Lk. is right in hinting that the tempter returned to him more than once through his ministry (4:13).

Jesus, who on the authority of the tradition followed i
by Lk. was about thirty years of age at this time (3:23), was according to Jewish standards now mature and 'ready for authority' (M. Aboth 5:21). He had already seen much of life and of men (Jn 2:25); above all he knew what his own people had done to men of prophetic insight before him (Mk 12:1–12). Accordingly, it should not surprise us that from the beginning of his ministry Jesus knew, with the assurance which moral insight gives, that his path would be a thorny one like to that of the Servant of Yahweh. None the less, he set his face resolutely to follow in the way of his Father's will.

Jesus and the Baptist—The Synoptic Gospels tell 641a
us nothing of Jesus' activity until the arrest and consequent close of the ministry of John the Baptist (Mk 1:14f.). The Fourth Evangelist alone suggests that there was a certain overlapping of the two ministries, during which both leaders and their disciples were engaged in preaching and baptising (Jn 3:22–4:3). That such overlapping should have occurred is, of course, to have been expected, and that there should have arisen a certain rivalry between the two bands of followers is also by no means unnatural. The Gospels indeed, and even the Book of Acts, bear witness to the continued loyalty of John's disciples to their master even after the ministry of Jesus had gotten well under way (Mk 2:18–22; Ac. 18:24–19:7). The Jews' religious leaders (Pharisees, Sadducees, and the representative elders of the people) had no love for John the Baptist, possibly for the same reason which Josephus, himself a Pharisee, attributes to Herod Antipas, viz. that of fear for the political repercussions of such a prophetic movement (Jos. Ant. XVIII, v, 2). Possibly we should think of these leaders as instigating trouble for John with Herod Antipas, even as they did later for Jesus before Pilate (Mk 6:14–29). This would explain the remark of the Fourth Evangelist that Jesus withdrew to Galilee from the neighbourhood of the Baptist's activities upon information that the Pharisees were concerning themselves with both the latter's and his own ministries (Jn 4:1–3), as well as Jesus' subtle question with reference to the Baptist's ministry during Passion Week (Mk 11:27ff.). At all events it was after John's arrest that Jesus felt called upon to enter actively upon his distinctive ministry (Mk 1:14f.). In Jesus' view John the Baptist incarnated the spirit of that Elijah who was to come to prepare the people of the eschatological period in which his own ministry was to be carried out (Mt. 11:2–15; Mal. 4:5). That Jesus had the highest esteem for John the Baptist as the final representative of the Hebrew prophetic movement there can be no doubt. But it is equally clear that to our Lord's mind, while John represented the close of an epoch, he himself inaugurated a new one (Lk. 16:16).

With the arrest of John, Jesus moved into Galilee b
and there embarked on his own distinctive ministry which was to end in the cross. John as we have seen had laid the groundwork for the new prophetic movement with a call to repentance; our Lord took up his ministry with a repetition of the same message, adding, however, 'The time is fulfilled, and the kingdom of God is at hand; repent, and believe in the Gospel' (Mk 1:15). To the mind of the Church responsible for the Gospels and to that of our Lord himself if the Church's witness be correct, the word 'fulfilment' which Jesus used from the beginning of his ministry onward, served to mark off that ministry, not alone

641b from that of John the Baptist, but also from that of all the prophets which had preceded him. Whereas the latter spoke always in terms of 'promise', Jesus was conscious of being one upon whom the 'ends of the ages' had come.

c **The 'Messianic Secret'**—As we endeavour to discover a consistent view of Jesus' ministry and teaching, two difficulties, first pointed out by Wilhelm Wrede and later taken with great seriousness by Albert Schweitzer (*The Quest of the Historical Jesus* (Eng. trans., 2nd ed., 1911), 331–335) confront us. These concern (1) the fact that the various pericopes, or several elements of the narrative, are united by means of ligatures of which there is at least a reasonable doubt whether they lay in the tradition as it came to the hands of the evangelist, or contrariwise were the product of his own fertile imagination; and (2) the presence in both narrative and teaching of 'a dogmatic element' which appears to be superimposed upon the ministry and to motivate it throughout. Form Criticism, as exemplified in the work of K. L. Schmidt, Martin Dibelius, Rudolf Bultmann, R. H. Lightfoot, Vincent Taylor, and others makes much of the former of these problems (see §§596ff.). Form critics indeed rather generally hold that it is no longer possible to give a connected account of the ministry of Jesus or to be certain of the order in which he presented his teachings. All that one may hope for is to rescue a series of disconnected nodules composed of both events and teachings as they group themselves into some sort of pattern at the hands of the Early Church's evangelists and teachers. As for the latter phenomenon (the so-called 'dogmatic element' of Wrede), Bultmann and his associates hold the view first elaborated by Wrede and the Old Liberal school that Jesus of Nazareth was a simple Rabbi of a somewhat heretical type. The Church on the other hand thought of him as Messiah, Son of God, Son of Man, and Suffering Servant. But finding no grounds in either the work or teaching of Jesus in support of these high views of his person, the Early Church invented the so-called 'Messianic Secret' to vindicate its views of its Lord. In this phrase reference is made to the fact that throughout the Gospels Jesus is said to have silenced his disciples, the demons, and any others who proclaimed his Messiahship, thereby giving the impression that it was a *secret* to be held during the days of his earthly ministry and revealed only by the Church after his withdrawal from the scene. Form critics and all others who accept the 'Messianic Secret' theory of Wrede, accordingly, look with suspicion upon those passages in the Gospels in which any awareness on Jesus' part relative to the nature of his person is indicated. For, say they, this 'dogmatic element', unhistorical in the extreme as it is, has been allowed to control the tradition and impair its value as history.

d In the present article, we shall take the position that the extreme scepticism above indicated is without justification. While by no means incognisant of the contribution made to our understanding of the ministry and teaching of Jesus by the form critics, particularly as regards the *Sitz im Leben* (or circumstances in which the Church found itself) which contributed, we believe, not so much to the creation as to the preservation of the tradition, we find conclusive evidence that the creative personality behind the Christian movement was none other than Jesus himself. It is our conviction that Jesus created the Church, and not the Church Jesus! Our reasons for so concluding are as follows: *first*, the *a priori* consideration that it is more likely that a spiritual and highly ethical movement such as the Christian Church should be established upon that Church's true witness to and understanding of its founder than the reverse; *secondly*, the undoubted fact that behind our four canonical Gospels there lie at least five distinct sources which by and large bear the same testimony to Jesus' consciousness of mission and purpose; *thirdly*, the fact that the reported *actions* of Jesus, perhaps even more 64
than his words, witness to a single motivation on his part from the beginning to the end of his ministry; and *fourthly*, that although it is true that all the evangelists believe in Jesus as Son of God and Redeemer of mankind, they none the less are concerned for the most part to allow the facts to speak for themselves and in some instances even appear to be unaware of the significance of the very events which they report.

When, in the light of the rather generally accepted solution of the Synoptic and Johannine problems and of the contribution made by the form critics, we read anew the canonical Gospels, a certain pattern of consistency appears to emerge in Jesus' ministry and teaching. This pattern of consistency is not one which we should expect of lesser men than Jesus of Nazareth. 'There is a type of consistency that is "the logic of fools", but there is also a type that because of its depth of insight gives us a picture of a mind possessed of vast, even universal, comprehensiveness. No merit attaches *per se* to the simple pattern of the liberal Rabbi Jesus of an older generation, nor to the equally naïve apocalyptic Jesus of the present. Jesus Christ by all accounts must have been an exceedingly complex person. The pattern of consistency which we seek for his speech and actions must prove equally so, and a kind of *a priori* taboo ought to attach to any endeavour to explain him that obviously ignores this fact' (cf. J. W. Bowman, *Prophetic Realism and the Gospel* (1955), 214f.). We agree with C. H. Dodd in remarking, 'I can see no reasonable ground for rejecting the statements of the Gospels that (for example) he [Jesus] pointed to Ps. 110 as a better guide to the truth about his mission and destiny than the popular beliefs about the Son of David, or that he made that connection of the "Lord" at God's right hand with the Son of Man in Daniel which proved so momentous for Christian thought; or that he associated with the Son of Man language that had been used of the Servant of the Lord, and employed it to hint at the meaning, and the issue, of his own approaching death. To account for the beginning of this most original and fruitful process of rethinking the OT we found need to postulate a creative mind. The Gospels offer us one. Are we compelled to reject the offer?' (cf. C. H. Dodd, *According to the Scriptures* (1953), 110). e

It is not contended that Jesus ever considered himself to be Messiah after the pattern entertained by the common man of his day, rather that the prophetic doctrine of the 'remnant' (composed of the morally mature in Israel who voluntarily chose God as their sovereign Lord) called for a Messiah qualified morally and spiritually to lead such a redemptive community. It is our contention that Jesus so interpreted the Hebrew prophets before him and that he saw himself chosen of God to be that moral and spiritual leader of his people. His activities during his ministry, even more than his teachings, point to the correctness of this conclusion. Further, it should be obvious that the establishment of this thesis does not depend upon the discovery of an exact sequence in which these activities occurred. It is enough for our purposes to establish that they did occur and that it is to their significance that the Church bears testimony in its early evangelistic preaching and teaching. f

Three of the sources (Mk, L, and Jn) lying behind our four Gospels testify to two facts which conjointly have significance; viz. (*a*) that Jesus sometime toward the beginning of his ministry chose twelve disciples to be with him and to see his mighty works and hear his teachings, and (*b*) that at the same time he was exciting both popular approval and bitter enmity, the latter finally resulting in his extirpation from the synagogue in 'his own country'. The number of the disciples is significant in view of the traditional number of the twelve tribes of Israel. As Jesus went about among the villages of Galilee at the head of this little band he would seem to be acting out a parable before all who could count, indicating (after g

41g the fashion of the prophetic 'memorial sign') the presence in Israel of the Messiah and the redemptive remnant. It seems evident that at his trial the endeavour was made to prove that Jesus had made claims to Messiahship but adequate testimony to his having made verbal claim to the office and title was not forthcoming. No doubt his enemies had seen the inner significance of his choosing exactly twelve disciples, even as they entertained grave suspicions that other of his actions were intended to 'speak louder than words'. Indeed, it is highly significant that Jesus chose disciples at all. The only Hebrew prophet on record as having chosen a follower was Elijah and this choice is stated to have been the result of an explicit command of God (1 Kg. 19:16, 19ff.). Nor is there any record that the great Rabbis of the day or John the Baptist chose disciples. Jesus' action in this respect was therefore unique, and that it had significance must have been obvious to friend and foe alike who were acquainted with the prophetic 'acted parable'.

42a **Jesus' 'Mighty Works'**—All the evidence which we possess points to Jesus' looking for much fruitage from his ministry in the towns and cities on the northern shore of the Sea of Galilee. It is Capernaum, Chorazin, and Bethsaida—all located in this vicinity, which come in for his bitterest invective because of their lack of response to his ministry of word and deed (Mt. 11:20–24; Lk. 10:13–15). After the Baptist's arrest he had apparently made Capernaum his home and the centre of his wider mission (Mk 1:14, 21; Mt. 4:12–17). And, indeed, during this early Galilean period, all signs point to Jesus' mounting popularity and to the flocking about him of great crowds to hear his message and to receive healing of their various diseases (Mt. 4:23–5:1; Mk 1:45).

b There can be no doubt that it was during this period that John the Baptist, hearing from prison of the nature of Jesus' activities, sent his disciples to seek of Jesus some sort of witness regarding his consciousness of mission. This is not surprising in view of the nature of John's testimony to the 'Coming One' as about to assume the role of Judge of mankind. Jesus' reply on this occasion to John's disciples is characteristic. For at no time would Jesus decide for another with reference to his own person and work. Even to the highest religious authorities of his day who had been unable to discern the divine power at work in the ministry of John, Jesus would not disclose the authority by which he carried on his own mission (Mk 11:27–33). As on all other occasions, so now Jesus merely pointed to the evidence and suggested that the Baptist make up his mind for himself. His rejoinder, however, on this occasion is deeply significant, as it appears to say in almost so many words—'Blessed is the man who on the basis of the evidence concludes rightly about me' (Mt. 11:6). Nor is it surprising that John should have been perplexed, as the evidence cited by Jesus all points toward redemptive activity rather than to the judgment which John had anticipated!

c The evidence was of two kinds, (*a*) evangelistic activity consisting in the preaching of the 'gospel to the poor', and (*b*) the carrying out of the implications of such preaching in the form of philanthropic work calculated to ameliorate man's distresses at every level of his life. All of the Gospels and the sources lying behind them bear joint witness to this two-fold nature of Jesus' ministry. Throughout that ministry word and work supplemented each other in a remarkable fashion. It is true that Jesus would perform no *sign* of an unmistakably supernatural kind such as his enemies constantly demanded of him (Mk 8:11f.). To have complied with such a request would have been quite out of character on the part of Jesus who by all accounts never set out merely to prove anything about his person or mission. It was characteristic of him rather that he looked for that spiritual insight in men with which they could very well pass their own judgments. 'He who has ears to hear', he remarked on more than one occasion, 'let him hear' 642c
(Mk 4:9).

Jesus' 'mighty works' were always done specifically d
in response to the temporal needs of men. He healed the sick because they needed healing and his compassion went out to them in their infirmities (Mk 3:1–6). He cleansed the lepers because he was 'moved with pity' toward them (Mk 1:41). Lk. tells us that he raised from the dead an only son of a widow because he felt 'compassion on her' (Lk. 7:13). Jesus' miracles commend themselves to us, not as works done with a view to exhibitionism, but rather as the normal expressions of the life and power of one such as he. The great miracle recorded in the Gospels is Jesus' own person. His 'mighty works' are merely the natural expression of that person. They are the product of the divine power which worked through him, that 'something greater' than Jonah, or Solomon, or even the Temple itself, which was present in him (Mt. 12:6, 41, 42). In a very real sense, therefore, Jesus' miracles were 'memorial signs' for those who possessed the spiritual insight to discern in them the sovereignty of God at work in the midst of his people; they were, so to speak, 'acted parables', demonstrating the presence of the kingdom of God as having arrived in and through Jesus. And thus, while they were done for purely humanitarian reasons, they formed a definitive part of Jesus' teaching ministry. Of the disciples who were privileged to observe his many mighty works Jesus might well ask, 'Do you not yet understand?' (Mk 8:21).

The so-called '*nature miracles*'—the stilling of the e
tempest and the waves, Jesus' walking upon the waters, the multiplication of the loaves and fishes, and the like—have not unnaturally disturbed many minds. By form critics they are classified as legends, not unlike those to be found in the lives of the saints and familiar to the student of comparative religions. It is to be observed, however, that not all of these nature miracles are upon the same level. As regards Jesus' 'walking on the sea' (Mk 6:49), it is suggested that the Greek idiom may mean merely 'on the seashore'. As regards the stilling of the waves, the best suggestion is perhaps that of Vincent Taylor, to the effect that 'the miracle was probably a miracle of divine providence. Jesus trusted in God and his trust was not deceived'. For he was 'sustained by the belief that "his hour was not yet come."'[1] Again, the two occasions on which Jesus is said to have fed the multitudes, like the Last Supper itself, are acted parables symbolic of the kingdom banquet at which Jesus as the viceroy of God is host and his disciples experience the joys of Kingdom salvation. Jn 6:25–65 furnishes us with the best commentary which we have on this nature miracle. Finally, it was characteristic of all Jesus' miracle working that the exercise of his powers came as response to faith on the part of the recipient (Mk 4:40, 5:34, 36). Where faith was not present, our Lord could not perform his mighty works (Mt. 13:58). In summary, it may be said then that the mighty works of Jesus had religious value in that they (*a*) drew forth faith on the part of the needy, (*b*) performed a salutary redemptive function, and (*c*) were active agents of the kingdom and power of God, which were present among men because of Jesus.

Jesus' Teaching: (a) Forms—Like all genuine 643a
teachers who have learned how to communicate to those who are being taught, Jesus adapted his teachings as to both method and content to the intellectual and spiritual stature of his hearers. First and last he observed the pedagogical principle—'to him who has will more be given; and from him who has not even what he has will be taken away' (Mk 4:25). Generally speaking, Jesus had three types of auditors—his disciples, his enemies, and the multitudes. Accordingly, in observing the principle just enunciated, he taught *the people* usually through the medium of parables, attractive stories adapted to drawing atten-

[1] cf. Vincent Taylor, *The Gospel According to St Mark*, 273

643a tion and readily remembered; *his enemies* with the reserve and caution which their attitude demanded (Mt. 7:6); and *his disciples* with an abandon and freedom that never ceased to amaze and intrigue them (Mk 4:33f.).

b In the Jewish literature Jesus is without doubt the master *par excellence* of the story parable. There is considerable overlapping in the tradition at this point and no doubt some doublets occur, but certainly between fifty and sixty distinct story parables are preserved for us in the sources of the Gospels. It is a chief characteristic of the story parable that but one major point is intended on the part of the narrator. Jesus' parables generally follow this pattern, although we incline to the belief that some scholars have overworked this principle in rigidly adhering to the 'one point theory' as a final criterion of genuineness. There is certainly no *a priori* reason why Jesus may not have allegorised his own parables, as in the case of the parable of the Sower (Mk 4:10–20). The Fourth Gospel contains a number of allegories attributed to Jesus, such as those of the Vine and the Branches, the Good Shepherd, and the like; while some of the Synoptic parables, such as those of the Wicked Husbandmen and the Prodigal Son, exhibit the characteristics of the allegory.

c The literary forms adopted by Jesus in teaching his disciples appear to have been particularly the sermon and the poem. The *sermon*, a literary product of the Hebrew prophet's artistry, received its name (Lat. *sermo*—word) from the fact that it contained an oracle of the Lord which the prophet believed he had received to deliver to the people. It is characterised by possessing a single theme which is developed and illustrated throughout by the preacher, who as he draws to a conclusion exhorts his audience to take to heart and live out the implications of the gospel message thus presented. Jesus' sermons include the 'Sermon on the Mount' (Mt. 5–7), the 'Sermon on a Level Place' (Lk. 6:17–49), the 'Charge to the Twelve' (Mt. 10), the 'Parables of the Kingdom' (Mt. 13), and the 'Discourse on the Last Things' (Mk 13). Probably other sermon fragments are to be found in the so-called 'Upbraiding of the Cities' (Lk. 10:13–15) and the 'Weeping over Jerusalem' (Lk. 13:34f.). These latter are also to be identified as *doom-* or *taunt-*songs such as are found in, for example, Mic. and Am. Jesus' sermons abound in *aphorisms* such as, 'You are the light of the world', 'Judge not, that you be not judged', 'The Sabbath was made for man, not man for the Sabbath; so the Son of Man is Lord even of the Sabbath', 'I am the door of the sheep', and 'I am the bread of life'.

d It is becoming increasingly clearer that Jesus was a poet of no mean ability, and that much of his sermonic material (as well as, indeed, that of his story parables) was cast in the form of Aramaic poetical structure. Aramaic *poetry* was characterised by rhyme, rhythm, parallelism of verse structure, and such rhetorical features as the pun, paronomasia, alliteration, word-play, and the like. The arduous and fruitful labour of a succession of scholars over a period of fifty years has made it appear as nearly certain as the case will permit that Christian Palestinian Syriac is substantially like the Galilean Aramaic spoken by our Lord and his disciples. Intensive study of this type of Syriac has made it clear both that 'an Aramaic sayings-source or tradition lies behind the Synoptic Gospels', that this tradition is found 'most frequently and sometimes exclusively, in the words of Jesus', and that generally speaking these words both in sermon and in story parable are cast in the form of Aramaic poetry. For on examination Jesus' teachings clearly exemplify the marks just noted (cf. M. Black, *An Aramaic Approach to the Gospels and Acts* (2nd edit. 1954), 206).

e The significance of this discovery that much of Jesus' teaching was cast in the moulds of Aramaic poetry and that to all intents the Christian Palestinian Syriac which we possess in the form of lectionaries **643**
approaches his mother tongue is manifold. To begin with, poetry is the form in which most primitive literatures are cast. Its rhythmical nature appeals even to the illiterate and renders it easy to remember. Then, too, the phenomenon of parallelism in Semitic poetry serves much the same purpose that the formal definition of words does in plain prose, the various members of the verse serving to define one another by means of antonyms, synonyms, or more complicated synthetic structure. All of the Beatitudes (Mt. 5:3–10) may be allowed to serve as examples of synthetic parallelism, wherein the second member of each verse completes the meaning of the first member. Synonymous parallelism is found at Mt. 7:7 in the saying 'Ask, and it will be given you; seek, and you will find; knock, and it will be opened to you'. An example of antonymous parallelism occurs at Lk. 13:30—'And behold, some are last who will be first, and some are first who will be last'. The new light cast upon the teachings of Jesus through our more perfect knowledge of the Christian Palestinian Syriac is of a quite varied character. Two examples must suffice for our purposes here. When the Greek of a passage like Mt. 11:28–30 is translated into Palestinian Syriac, it is seen to exhibit alliteration, rhythm, and even rhyme, thus:

> Come unto me, all ye that labour and are heavy laden
> ('^{e}tho l^{e}wathi kull^{e}khon d^{e}lahain ut^{e}'inin *or* t^{e}' ine mobh^{e}lin),
> And I will give you rest
> (wa'^{a}na 'aniḥ^{e}khon).
> Take my yoke upon you and learn of me
> (qabb^{e}lu niri ('oli ?) '^{a}lekhon ul^{e}madhu minni);
> For I am meek and lowly in heart
> (da'^{a}na n^{e}yaḥ w^{e}' enwan b^{e}libba(i)):
> And ye shall find rest for your souls
> (w^{e}tishk^{e}ḥun niḥa l^{e}naphsh^{e}khon).
> For my yoke is easy, and my burden is light.
> (d^{e}na'im niri ('oli ?) w^{e}qallil mobh^{e}li)! [1]

A contribution of an entirely different type is to be found at Mt. 7:6 where it is suggested that instead of reading, 'Give not that which is holy unto the dogs', we should read rather:

> Give not a ring unto dogs,
> Neither cast your pearls before swine.

The reason for the change from *holy* to *ring* is that in the Palestinian Syriac and in the Aramaic which Jesus spoke, the words for holy and ring are exactly alike so far as the consonants are concerned, thus holy is *qudhsha* and ring is *q^{e}dhasha*. In the text which originally contained no vowels the word would appear merely as *qdsh*, which could mean either holy or ring. Obviously, ring is better than holy at this point as it serves to balance 'pearls' which are referred to in connection with the swine.[1]

Jesus' Teaching: (b) Content—As regards the **644**
content of Jesus' teaching, our sources appear to be agreed that from the beginning he employed the prophetic word 'gospel' as definitive of his message. As we have already observed, Mk preserves the tradition that after John's arrest Jesus began to proclaim, 'The time is fulfilled and the kingdom of God is at hand; repent, and believe in the gospel' (1:15). Similarly, Mt. remarks that Jesus came 'teaching in their synagogues and preaching the gospel of the kingdom' (4:23), and Lk. says that on the occasion of Jesus' trial sermon in the synagogue in Nazareth he read from Isa. 61:1f., applying the saying to himself the while, 'The Spirit of the Lord is upon me, because he has anointed me to preach the gospel to the poor' (4:18*a*). In the Hebrew of the OT the verb employed at this and like passages is *bissēr* which (unlike its noun *b^{e}sôrāh*) refers to the distinctive message regarding the salvation with which

[1] cf. M. Black, ibid., 140f., 146f.

644a God would provide his people, that is, *to the gospel*. In the Christian Palestinian Syriac lectionaries the same noun and verb are always employed to refer to Jesus' distinctive message and his annunciation of it. Further, it is scarcely open to question that Jesus' linking the idea of the Kingdom of God with the term 'gospel' is derived from such a passage as Isa. 52:7, which may be translated thus :

How beautiful upon the mountains are the feet of him
who brings good tidings (*mᵉbhassēr*),
who publishes peace (*mashmîaʿ*),
who brings good tidings of good (*mᵉbhassēr*),
who publishes salvation (*mashmîaʿ*),
who says to Zion, 'Your God reigns'.

From the very beginning of his ministrv, therefore, Jesus assumes the role of the Gospel Herald who declares that the epoch referred to in the writing of the prophet has now arrived ; Jesus' contemporaries stand upon the very threshold of the Kingdom's inauguration. In the light of the context, both of John the Baptist's preaching and of the Deutero-Isaianic passages to which Jesus' use of the terms 'gospel' and 'to preach the gospel' distinctly refer, it is undoubtedly right in some sense to refer to Jesus' preaching as first and last eschatological.

b To conclude, however, as Albert Schweitzer and his followers have done that this eschatological gospel must be interpreted in terms of the contemporary apocalypticism is to go beyond the evidence supplied by our gospels. Schweitzer believed that Jesus was twice mistaken about the near approach of the Kingdom's consummation, which he believed Jesus to have prophesied both at the first sending forth of his disciples (Mt. 10:23), and again following the resurrection (Mt. 28:7). But to identify the so-called Galilean 'resurrection appearances' of the Risen Lord with the anticipated consummation of the Kingdom is a questionable procedure and open to grave doubt. As for the saying at Mt. 10:23, 'For truly, I say to you, you will not have gone through all the towns of Israel, before the Son of Man comes', it is to be noted that, as is generally recognised by scholarship, this chapter is a composite one, combining elements taken from more than one passage in Q with the actual instructions given to the disciples on this occasion as recorded by Mk (6:7–13) and even with some portion of the eschatological discourse (Mk 13:9–22). A careful study of the words and ideas involved in Mt. 10:9–15, 23, would seem to indicate that this portion of the passage was taken from the more original statement of Q as found in Lk. 10:4–15. The saying then about the coming of the Son of Man in Mt. 10:23 is to be understood as a rewording of Lk. 10:11*b*, which reads 'Nevertheless know this, that the kingdom of God has come near'. Mt. here has understood Lk.'s 'kingdom of God' to refer to the Church of Christ, and, as in other passages, he has employed the term 'Son of Man' in the corporate sense as referring to that Church (cf. for example, Mt. 16:18, 27f. ; Mk 8:38–9:1 ; Lk. 9:26f.). In any case, it is improbable that Jesus used the term 'Son of Man' with reference to himself before the confession of Peter at Caesarea Philippi (see below), and the Q passages employed here by Mt. are inserted by Lk., who usually has the better ordering of the Q materials, after that incident.

c For a right understanding of the nature of Jesus' eschatological teaching regarding the Kingdom, several facts are to be observed, (*a*) 'kingdom' in Hebrew, Aramaic, and Greek is in the first instance an abstract term meaning 'sovereignty' or 'lordship'. Accordingly, for the Kingdom of God to be near at hand will mean for Jesus that God's lordship is about to be realised in some sense in human experience. (*b*) T. W. Manson has demonstrated (conclusively in our judgment) that *before* Peter's confession at Caesarea Philippi, Jesus spoke of the Kingdom of God as *something that was about to come* and that *after* the confession his message was 'The Kingdom has now come. Come in' (cf. Mk 1:15 ; Lk. 10:9, 11 with Mk 10:15, 23:25 ; Lk. 11:20, 22:29f.). Accordingly, the Kingdom will have come, in Jesus' meaning of the term, with the confession of Peter. For to acknowledge God's Messiah (his viceroy) will be the same as to acknowledge God's lordship itself. When a man does this, then the Kingdom has come in his experience. It is instructive to note that in the language of contemporary Judaism, 'to receive the yoke of the Kingdom of God' (M. Berakoth 2:1) was an individual experience on the part of any Jew who daily recited the *Shemaʿ* (or Jewish creed beginning with Dt. 6:4ff.). Jesus uses the same terminology ('to receive the Kingdom of God') with regard to those children (and those like children) who come to himself, saying of such that 'to such belongs the Kingdom of God' (Mk 10:14f.). It seems quite clear from the above considerations and like passages which may be cited (Lk. 11:20, 16:16, 17:21) that Jesus taught the Kingdom of God to have come through him and more particularly through men accepting him as God's Messiah. The Kingdom was, therefore, in the teaching of Jesus, in the first instance an individual experience of God's lordship over the life of the disciple who acknowledged the same. But there can be no doubt that Jesus also had in view a group, the prophetic remnant composed of his little band of disciples, in whose corporate experience of fellowship with one another and with Jesus as their Lord and Master the Kingdom was realised (Mt. 8:11f. ; Lk. 12:32, 22:29f.). Finally, Jesus also no doubt looked forward to the final consummation of the Kingdom of God at the end of history and on more than one occasion expressed himself after this fashion (Mk 8:38, 13, 14:62).

This gospel of the Kingdom which Jesus elaborated d in parable and sermon, in aphorism and poem, was above all things a redemptive message. It was like a treasure which a man came upon in a field, like a pearl of infinite price for which one might seek all one's life, and in either case (whether discovered accidentally or after long search) it was of more value than all things that one possessed (Mt. 13:44–46). It was like a banquet to which God invited men from East and West, from North and South to come and sit down at his table, to enjoy his fellowship and the rich repast which he had to offer (Lk. 13:29). It was characterised by God's redemptive grace which called to partake of his banquet 'the poor and maimed and blind and lame' (Lk. 14:21). The God whom Jesus taught to be King in this Kingdom was also Father, a father who yearned over his son departed into a far country and spending his livelihood in riotous living (Lk. 15:11–32). He was like the owner of a hundred sheep who, when one of them goes astray, leaves the 'ninety-nine on the hills' and goes in search of the stray, and when he finds it rejoices 'over it more than over the ninety-nine who never went astray' (Mt. 18:10–14).

Mt. gives us an example intended certainly to be e typical of the way that Jesus taught and preached this gracious gospel of the Kingdom, particularly to the more intimate circle of his own disciples, in the so-called 'Sermon on the Mount' (Mt. 5–7). Whether or not Jesus preached the sermon exactly as it stands before us in the first Gospel is a moot question. Most scholars believe that the evangelist has combined two sermons from his Q and M sources, adding thereto perchance a verse here and there from some extraneous source in the tradition available to him. Be this as it may, the sermon as it now stands is a fairly unified whole developing first and last the single theme of *Kingdom-Righteousness and the manner of its attainment*. The sermon opens with the Beatitudes, a short poem in two stanzas of four verses each, in which Jesus in a few swift strokes paints a portrait of the 'son of the Kingdom' as he traverses the highway of life from spiritual poverty to riches. The first

644e word of each Beatitude (blessed) is a predicate adjective intended to give expression to the fact that the gospel of the Kingdom enunciates a series of gracious gifts which God has to give to his people, the second member of each verse accordingly indicating some one or other phase of this divine blessedness, thus, 'the poor in spirit are blessed, because the Kingdom of God is theirs'. Having drawn in bold lines the portrait of the son of the Kingdom, Jesus next proceeds to suggest how that son will act, first in relation to his fellowman (5:21–48), and secondly in relation to God (chap. 6). This portion of the sermon constitutes an exposition of the two great commandments which our Lord considered to sum up all the duty of man in the realms of religion and ethics (Mk 12:28–34). There can be no question that in this extended passage Jesus intends to set up a perfect standard for his disciples and that he will allow no deviation from that standard. 'Ye shall be perfect as your Father in heaven is perfect' (5:48). The question not unnaturally arises, then, has anyone ever been as good as this or can anyone be as good as this? Our Lord's answer to this question in Mt. 7:1–5 is in the negative. All men have either the mote or the beam in their eyes; all live in glass houses; all are in the same boat which, being full of holes, is sinking! And now the principle of God's grace which is at the heart of the gospel message emerges as one inquires, how then is the divine righteousness to be obtained? The answer is 'Ask, and it will be given to you; seek, and you will find; knock, and it will be opened to you' (7:7). Thereafter the sermon closes with a series of four doublets illustrative respectively of the two ways, the two types of teachers, the two kinds of disciples, and the two houses, all of which are intended to express the fact that to this gospel of the Kingdom man may make either a saving or a condemning response (7:13–27).

645a **Training of the 'Twelve'**—It is clear that as he taught and preached the gospel of the kingdom after the fashion above described and at the same time performed his mighty works of physical, emotional, and spiritual healing, thus bringing the gospel to bear on every phase of human life, Jesus' popularity grew by leaps and bounds. Crowds thronged him on every side, so much so that he and his disciples were not able to eat in quiet. When it was learned that he was at home in Capernaum, the house was thronged so that no-one could get in at the doors. To escape the multitudes, he pushed off across the lake at times or withdrew from Galilee into distant parts (Phoenicia, Decapolis, Mount Hermon, and the like). His very friends began to say that he was undoubtedly 'beside himself' that he should allow himself to be thronged in this unseemly fashion.

b But in all these labours and amid the apparent confusion, Jesus ever has his eye upon his disciples. At times he leads them aside to pray and rest or for special seasons of teaching in private. The suggestion on the part of some form critics that this privacy is suspect is lacking in imagination. Even if one were to grant the contention of the 'consistent eschatologist' that Jesus anticipated the consummation of the Kingdom of God before the close of that generation, yet it is clear that he expected his disciples to proclaim the coming of the kingdom throughout the cities and towns of Israel and certainly such proclamation required from Jesus a certain amount of training in their message and mission. Such training, as the evangelists suggest, could only be undertaken in seclusion from the vast multitudes which thronged about this little band.

c Having seen Jesus' mighty works, then, and listened both publicly and privately to his teaching and preaching of the gospel of the kingdom, the disciples were relatively prepared to go out on their own with a view to evangelising and carrying out the implications of the gospel message in healing the ills of men. No doubt during the Galilean ministry Jesus sent out his disciples on more than one occasion with a view to such evangelistic and philanthropic effort. Lk. alone among the evangelists suggests that our Lord also sent out seventy(-two) others as well (10:1–22). We incline to the belief that this is a doublet of the sending out of the twelve disciples, as the Greek characters for twelve (ιβ) and seventy-two (οβ) exhibit little difference and may easily be confused by a slip of the pen. As we have already seen also, Mt. appears to believe that Lk.'s material in this chapter refers to a mission of the twelve (cf. Mt. 10). Be this as it may, it is clear at all events that Jesus was training up his twelve disciples to be the nucleus of a redemptive society which should carry his gospel of the kingdom far and wide.

d The culmination of this period of activity comes as Jesus turns his feet toward Caesarea Philippi at the foot of Mount Hermon with a view to a quiet time of retreat with his disciples away from the multitudes. Having seen Jesus' mighty works and heard the nature of his message, these disciples should now be prepared for the examination which he expects to give them. The first question, 'Who do men say that I am?' is of no particular significance. It serves merely as an introduction to the question of prime importance which he has to ask. What the people think is never of great significance either to Jesus or to those like him of prophetic stature! The expected answer (and one verified by all of the evidence at our disposal), to the effect that the people consider Jesus 'one of the prophets', is provocative and serves as a stimulus to the imagination and insight of the disciples. The challenge is even greater if the Fourth Gospel be correct in suggesting that about this time a certain spirit of defection has set in, a spirit already infecting some of his fringe disciples so that they 'drew back and no longer went about with him' (Jn 6:66). Moreover, all the sources are agreed that up to this point Jesus' disciples have not adopted the popular appellative of 'prophet' to apply to Jesus. He is to them their Rabbi and it is as such that they constantly refer to him. Now, however, when Jesus asks the important question, 'But who do you say that I am?' Peter with a flash of real insight exclaims, 'You are the Messiah' (Mk 8:29). No doubt the title has quivered on Peter's lips before now, even as there is some small evidence that others may so have spoken of Jesus before this time (Jn 1:14). But Peter's declaration is unique on the present occasion. It is one thing to bandy about a title loosely and with only a passing thought of its significance. It is something else to utter the title of Jesus after so long an association with him. This is a declaration of faith on Peter's part charged with deep conviction and no doubt strong emotion. Little wonder that Jesus charges his disciples not to employ the title in speaking of him to others. For it is open to grave misconception and is to be employed of Jesus only as he is prepared to accept it of himself. And to understand how this is will require much training and real insight into the nature of his ministry and aims.

e How true this is will immediately appear. For having seen them pass this first examination, Jesus is now prepared to advance his disciples to a further understanding of the meaning of Messiahship for him. They are now prepared to call him Messiah. But if he is to accept this title, he must now interpret it for them as he has understood it at least from the time of his baptism at John's hands. Mk is our principal authority for the observation that immediately following the experience at Caesarea Philippi, Jesus brings two new notes into his teaching. In that directed to his disciples he begins to lay stress upon the suffering element involved in his own Messiahship. On three separate occasions according to Mk he makes this theme of suffering and death, as well as of his following resurrection, the distinctive characteristic of his teaching (Mk 8:31–33, 9:30–32, 10:32–34). At the same time, while redoubling his efforts with the

645e multitudes, he begins to sound the note of warning that discipleship will prove a costly experience for them. 'If any man would come after me', he begins now to say to the multitudes, 'let him deny himself and take up his cross and follow me' (Mk 8:34). Lk.'s special source also bears testimony to this new sombre element in Jesus' preaching to the crowds (Lk. 14:25–33). Indeed, Lk. has the strongest statement at this point of any of the evangelists. For he places Jesus' challenge in the form of a universal negative to which there can be no exception for any cause, 'Whoever does not bear his own cross and come after me, cannot be my disciple' (14:27).

f Bultmann among modern scholars has committed himself to the assertion that the three predictions of Jesus' passion and resurrection are *vaticinia ex eventu*, on the ground that the source common to Mt. and Lk. (Q) does not contain these predictions (cf. R. Bultmann, *Theology of the NT* (1951), i, 30). The argument, however, overlooks the fact that the source Q contains no reference whatever to Jesus' passion either as prediction or as historic event. Surely the author of this source knew of Jesus' passion as event! It seems obvious, therefore, that his lack of any reference to the passion is due to his interest for the moment lying in another direction. The account of Peter's 'rebuke' of Jesus' reference to his anticipated passion and of our Lord's answering rebuttal of Peter in the strongest terms is our best guarantee of the genuineness of these predictions. In the Fourth Gospel the role played by Peter on the occasion of the feet-washing in the Upper Room is the counterpart of his attitude on this occasion (Jn 13:6–10). It seems strange that Bultmann should be concerned to deny Jesus' insight at this point. For no-one has given stronger expression to the prophetic character of Jesus' teaching than he. Nor has anyone stated in clearer terms the essential unity of the eschatological and ethical elements in the teaching of Jesus. 'Both things,' he remarks, 'the eschatological proclamation and the ethical demand, direct man to the fact that he is thereby brought before God, that God stands before him; both direct him into his Now as the hour of decision for God' (ibid., 21). If these things be true for man generally, are they not also true for Jesus? And can it be that with all his prophetic insight, his understanding of human nature, his observation of the fickleness of the crowds as they begin to count the cost of discipleship, his certain knowledge of the hostility of the religious authorities, yet Jesus does not foresee for himself that this is his hour of decision and of reckoning? Indeed, had the gospels not recorded such insight on the part of our Lord, certainly we should have had to infer it!

646a **The 'Call' of the Church**—From this time onward, on the testimony of all of our sources, the term 'Son of Man' begins to have frequent mention on our Lord's lips. As Jesus uses this term it acquires the two motifs of *humiliation* and *exaltation* on one occasion and another. Thus, both motifs appear in the passage Mk 8:31–9:1. Moreover, it seems that at times the term has an individual reference to Jesus and at others a corporate reference to his body of disciples. The impression one gleans is that generally speaking the humiliation passages have the individual reference to Jesus most clearly intended, whereas the exaltation passages are those in which the corporate Son of Man is in mind.[1] Jesus may very well have derived the term in its corporate aspect from the well-known passage at Daniel 7:13, from which there can be little doubt the author of 1 Enoch 37–71 also took the exaltation motif. (It is still a moot question among scholars as to whether the figure of the Son of Man in the Similitudes of 1 Enoch is to be reckoned as a corporate or an individual figure, or perhaps as both together.) Jesus' application of the term to himself, and more particularly with the motif of humiliation, may have been derived from a passage like Ps. 8:4.

[1] cf. H. H. Rowley, *The Relevance of Apocalyptic* (1944), 115

But if, as we believe, he thought of himself in terms of the Suffering Servant of Yahweh, this would sufficiently account for the stress on the humiliation aspect when he used the term Son of Man with the individual reference. For as Rowley, who agrees that Jesus thought of himself in terms of Messiah, Suffering Servant and Son of Man, remarks, 'It was quite impossible to bring the Suffering Servant into association with these other terms without their transformation. For this meant that by suffering his mission was to be fulfilled, and by bitter humiliation at the hands of men.'[1] 646a

Mk significantly attaches the transfiguration temporally to the confession at Caesarea Philippi (9:2—'after six days'). This temporal reference is the more significant as it is the only one of an exact nature to be found in Mk's Gospel between the early events of chapters 1 and 2 and Passion week. This can only mean that these two events, like those of Jesus' baptism and temptation, formed for the tradition which Mk is following two sides of one experience. That this impression is accurate is further suggested by the fact that Jesus selected only three disciples, Peter, James, and John, to accompany him up the Mount of Transfiguration. Was this not because only James and John had come to share the insight suggested in Peter's confession? If so, then no doubt they were chosen as being alone worthy of experiencing the vision along with Peter. The opposing suggestion, that the evangelists are wrong at this point and that only Peter experienced the vision, finds support neither in the findings of modern psychology nor in the best accounts which we possess of genuine spiritual experience. Rather, it is in accord with both these authorities that all may experience the spiritual vision who are ready to see it. And our Lord's selection of these three would seem to suggest that to his mind they were all ready for it. Schweitzer (*The Quest of the Historical Jesus* (1911), 383f.) has suggested that the chronological order of the two incidents of confession and transfiguration should be reversed. He bases his suggestion on (*a*) Lk.'s 'great omission' of the material found in Mk 6:47–8:26 together with the possibility of some confusion in the ordering of Mk's series of events here, and (*b*) Jesus' attributing of Peter's insight at Caesarea Philippi, not to 'flesh and blood', but to a revelation from the 'Father who is in heaven' (Mt. 16:17). It is to be noted, however, that Lk. was characteristically selective in his attitude toward the Marcan material which at this point he may have considered involved a number of doublets (as indeed, many scholars also believe); and in any case there can be no question about the proper ordering of the two events with which we are here concerned. Lk. retains them both and in the same order as Mk! As for Schweitzer's suggestion relative to Jesus' comment in Mt.'s special source on the origin of Peter's insight, this appears to be peculiarly artificial and quite out of character on Jesus' part. Jesus characteristically looked for men to have eyes that could see and ears that could hear, quite irrespective of an overpowering event such as the transfiguration must have been. Moreover, it seems characteristic of such overpowering events in the scriptures that they come as climactic experiences at the end of a long period of preparation accompanied by progressive insights, and as confirmatory of the latter rather than as their cause. This was certainly true of Jesus' own baptismal vision and everything seems to point to its being true in the present instance. b c

It is possible, as has often been suggested, that in the present vision, Moses stands for the OT Law and Elijah as a representative of the prophets. The suggestion, however, does not appear to be very penetrating as it is not obvious what place the Law would have in a vision at this point. It seems more likely that Elijah stands as the exponent of the type of moral decision resulting in the creation of the prophetic d

[1] cf. *The Rediscovery of the OT* (1946), 297

646d 'remnant' (1 Kg. 19:18 ; Rom. 11:4), and that Moses' presence is justified as the exemplar of the great prophet who leads his people in exodus out of the land of bondage. Jesus, too, was about to lead a new people in 'exodus' (cf. the use of the word at Lk. 9:31) ; also like Elijah he was calling men to make the moral choice that constituted the new 'remnant' (Mt. 6:31). In line with this interpretation of the presence here of Moses and Elijah, it is to be noted that the transfiguration finds its chief significance as staging the 'call' of the Church, just as at the baptism the 'call' came to the Church's Leader. Consequently, as the voice from heaven at the baptism spoke only to Jesus, here it addresses rather his disciples with the words, 'This is my beloved Son ; listen to him'. Once again it is intelligible that such an overwhelming experience should be kept secret at Jesus' own request until after his resurrection. If it was of a character to require that a selection be made from among the original disciples for those ready to receive it, surely the narrating of it to others must await the gift of the Spirit to the Church, in accordance with the principle which our Lord had previously enunciated, viz. 'to him who has it shall be given'.

647a **Close of the Ministry**—The evangelists are agreed that no little time after these events Jesus left Galilee and went up toward Jerusalem (Mt. 19:1 ; Mk 10:1 ; Lk. 9:51 ; Jn 7:1). The Fourth Gospel, indeed, suggests that this final period of Jesus' ministry began about the time of the Feast of Tabernacles in the autumn (7:2), carried through the winter Feast of Dedication (10:22f.), and so to the Passover of the following spring (12:1ff.). Lk.'s long distinctive section extending from 9:51 through 18:14 and containing mention of Jesus' evangelistic efforts in Samaria (9:52), Galilee (17:11), and the Jordan valley (18:35), as well as Judaea itself (10:38–42), is inserted at this point. One gains the impression, however, both from the general character of the ligatures with which Lk. connects the various passages in this section, as well as from detailed overlapping between the material here with that of the other evangelists, that Lk. included in this long insertion many incidents and teachings regarding whose chronological sequence he had no information.

b We have no certain means of knowing how long Jesus' entire ministry lasted. But whether short or long, it was certainly characterised by two things which are exemplified in the two stories with which it closes, (*a*) Jesus' constant challenge to men to leave all and follow him, and (*b*) the spirit of compassion with which he responded to faith in himself and his mission. The first of these stories, that of the request of James and John to sit at his right and left hands, respectively, in his kingdom (Mk 10:35–45), also illustrates the moral obtuseness of Jesus' little band of followers. In spite of frequent warnings that the ordering of the kingdom is unlike that of this world (Mk 10:31), yet Jesus' most intimate disciples still long for position and prestige. Characteristically, the other ten are indignant when they hear of the request of James and John ! Jesus' saying on this occasion is further proof of his certain realisation that suffering and death is to be his final lot—'The cup that I drink you will drink ; and with the baptism with which I am baptised, you will be baptised'. The other story which we find at this point is that of the blind beggar, Bartimaeus. As is his wont, Jesus responds to his cry, 'Jesus, Son of David, have mercy on me !' with a display of that compassion which always responded to faith in himself (Mk 10:46–52).

648a **Passion Week :** (*a*) **Opening Events**—The relative importance of the events and teaching of Passion Week for an understanding of the significance of Jesus' life and ministry, as this was viewed at all events by the early Church, is readily seen in the fact that from one-fourth (Lk.) to one-third (the others) of their space is devoted to this last week by the four evangelists. Moreover, much of the Church's early preaching recounts the events of Passion Week 648a and indicates their redemptive significance in the light of the teachings of the prophets of old (Ac. 2:17–36, 7:1–53, 13:15–41 ; 1 C. 15). Form critics have made one of their major contributions at this point in suggesting that the relatively 'formless' and unified character of the Passion and Resurrection narratives is evidence of the early date of their production. For to acquire 'form' (in the sense of a well-rounded residue resulting from frequent repetition in the Church's teaching ministry) requires time. At a very early date the Church required an apologetic for the crucifixion of its Messiah which from the beginning formed a 'stumbling block to Jews and folly to Gentiles' (1 C. 1:23). It is intelligible, therefore, that the narrative of the resurrection appearances should early be written down in conjunction with the account of our Lord's passion with a view to forming just such an apologetic. This freezing of the tradition at an early date would explain the comparative absence of 'forms' in the accounts of passion week. It is even possible that, when on his first missionary journey Paul took along John Mark as the *chazzan* or custodian of the Christian scriptures for use in the Jewish synagogues, it was these already written Passion and Resurrection narratives to which reference is made (Ac. 13:5). Possibly we should think of the Passion and Resurrection narratives as existing in two separate forms for each. For the Passion narrative at all events Mk is our principal source and it is possible that Lk. had a separate account which he combined to some extent with Mk's. Jn also appears to have had distinctive materials of his own which he follows. As for the Resurrection narratives, that of Mk followed by Mt. refers to Galilean appearances of the risen Lord, while there also existed a Lk.-Ac. tradition recounting only Judaean appearances. In the Fourth Gospel, ch. 20 follows the Jerusalem tradition, while ch. 21 contains that of Galilee.

Two features of Jesus' activity during this last week b of his life are particularly noteworthy, (*a*) his self-assurance, and (*b*) the universal scope of his gracious redemptive purpose. A previous generation of scholars thought to see vacillation, hesitancy, even uncertainty with regard to the nature or scope of his mission in the account of his frequent journeys across the lake and his visits to the region of Tyre and the Decapolis, even timidity in his withdrawal from the region ruled over by Herod Antipas. However this may be (and we believe it to represent a misinterpretation of Jesus' actions), there can be no question that during Passion Week Jesus is entirely in command. His disciples had been amazed at his determined spirit as he approached Jerusalem for the last time (Mk 10:32). This spirit of assurance never leaves him to the end. Everything happens as he wills that it shall happen and at the time which he has determined for it. And yet, throughout all this confident activity, Jesus in act and word exhibits a gracious redemptive purpose. It is with this purpose that he successively challenges the nation and its ruling classes, the city of Jerusalem and its multitudes, to exhibit faith in himself as the moral and spiritual leader whom God has appointed for them. Amid this week's rapidly shifting scenes, one gains the impression that Jesus sees his ministry drawing to a focus. His 'hour' has at last arrived. And he will see it through in masterful fashion.

The week begins with three notable events—the c banquet at Bethany with the anointing of Jesus, the so-called 'triumphal entry', and the cleansing of the Temple. There is some uncertainty as to the timing of the first of these events. Mk (followed by Mt.) simply says that it was 'while he was at Bethany in the house of Simon the Leper' (14:3), but Jn dates it specifically and probably with accuracy as 'six days before the Passover' (12:1), which appears to mean the evening of the Sabbath previous to Jesus' crucifixion. Lk. has a third account of an anointing which he

48c places in the early days of the Galilean ministry (7:36–38). In this first of the week's incidents, the note of authority on Jesus' part which is characteristic of this week's happenings emerges. He insists that the woman is to be permitted to perform this service for him in spite of an apparent waste, and he interprets her action as an anointing of his body for burying (Mk 14:6–8). On the woman's part this act was doubtless intended as an expression of gratitude for some great thing that Jesus had done for her (cf. Lk. 7:47). In the Fourth Gospel it is Mary of Bethany who performs this deed of service and no doubt it is intended to reflect her thankfulness for the raising of her brother, Lazarus (Jn 11).

d The second incident of the week's activities, the so-called 'triumphal entry', occurring on the day following the Jewish Sabbath (i.e. on our Sunday), again exhibits a sureness of touch on Jesus' part that is unmistakable. This appears at once in the careful arrangements which he has made for the occasion. A colt is to be found tied and ready for his use. Moreover he has appointed the passwords for those involved, viz. 'Why are you doing this?' to be asked of the disciples whom he shall send to bring the colt, and 'The Lord has need of it', the reply to be given the questioner. Schweitzer has suggested, we believe correctly, that the Church has misunderstood the nature of the event which follows. This is no 'triumphal entry'; rather it exhibits tragic lack of spiritual insight on the part of Jesus' disciples, as well as on that of the multitudes. There is here a 'dogmatic element' superimposed upon the narrative, but the superimposition of this element is made by Jesus himself and not by the later Church. Jesus on this occasion is consciously fulfilling the prophecy of Zech. 9:9 with a view to challenging the capital city to see in him God's true Messiah. But neither the city nor Jesus' own disciples discern his purpose and they give him merely the reception accorded to the usual pilgrim band coming up to Jerusalem from the ends of the earth to worship at the feast. It was customary to sing the Hallel Psalms (Ps. 113–118) on the occasion of the three major feasts of the Jewish year—Tabernacles, Passover, and Weeks. These were sung by the pilgrim bands themselves as they marched along the road from Galilee through Peraea, and up from the Jordan valley at Jericho to the Holy City. They were also sung antiphonally by Levitical choirs, the priests, even the keeper of the Temple gates, and the multitudes themselves. Ps. 118 was sung as the multitude approached the Temple; v. 19 is clearly the cry of the pilgrim band for the opening of the Temple gates that they may enter in and v. 20 is similarly the reply of the keeper of the gates. By v. 25, accordingly, the band have arrived at the inner court of the Temple as they cry out, 'Hosanna (Save us), we beseech thee, O Lord!' And again, 'Blessed be he who enters in the name of the Lord!'

e The Mishnah is authority for the fact that relative to the feast of Tabernacles, at all events, the schools of Hillel and Shammai disputed regarding when the *Lulab* (i.e. the bundle of palm-, myrtle-, and willow-branches employed on the occasion) should be waved. The former traditionally waved the *Lulab* with the singing at the beginning and end of the psalm and at v. 25, while the latter performed this ceremony additionally at the second half of v. 25 (M. Sukkah 3:9). It seems likely, therefore, that the 'layers of leaves' which Mk says the people on this occasion had cut from the fields (11:8), and which Jn alone calls 'palm branches' (12:13), were being employed as expressions of the exuberant joy which went with the singing of the Hallel psalms. But that Jesus was being greeted by the crowds as Messiah there is no evidence in Mk's account. It is true that the other three evangelists contain phrases which may be interpreted as Messianic ascriptions on the part of either the multitudes or the disciples (Mt. 21:9; Lk. 19:38; Jn 12:13). But when the crowds in the city inquire who Jesus is, according to Mt. the answer is not that 648e
he is the Messiah, rather merely that he is the prophet from Nazareth (Mt. 21:11), and in the Fourth Gospel the statement is distinctly made that even the disciples did not understand until after the resurrection what they had done on this occasion (Jn 12:16). Accordingly, the incident appears to have been a piece of 'emblematic prophecy' on Jesus' part, in which he consciously threw out a challenge to the capital city to accept him as Messiah. But the challenge was not even understood, much less accepted!

The third incident of the week, the cleansing of the f
Temple, is placed by Mk on Monday. The Fourth Gospel has recorded the same incident much earlier in the ministry of Jesus. In spite of the efforts of some scholars to discount the evidence for misplacement of certain sections in this Gospel and particularly to justify an early date for this incident in the ministry of Jesus, it does not appear to us that the early date can be allowed. The evidence for misplacement in the Fourth Gospel appears rather clear (cf. 2:12, 3:22). Moreover, the challenge to the Temple authorities which is involved in this incident appears more fitting at the end than at the beginning of Jesus' ministry; while the reference to the destruction of the Temple and Jesus' raising it again recorded both in the Fourth Gospel (2:20) and in Mk at the trial before the Sanhedrin (14:58) is more likely to have been remembered by Jesus' enemies to be brought forward at his trial if it had only recently been made. The incident once again reflects that mastery of the situation characteristic of Jesus' attitude during Passion Week. The Temple markets, called in the Talmud 'the bazaars of the sons of Annas', were under the control of the high-priestly family who presumably let out stalls for the purpose of selling the animals required for sacrificial purposes. The trade was legitimate and afforded real assistance to worshippers in the Temple. Jesus' objections to it appear to have been two-fold, (*a*) that it offended against the principle of universalism at the heart of all true religion, and (*b*) that the type of control involved was debasing the practices of religion to a materialistic level. The first of these charges (represented in a quotation from Isa. 56:7 and found in Jesus' words, 'Is it not written "My house shall be called a house of prayer for all the nations"?') has reference to the fact that this market was carried on in the Court of the Gentiles, wherein alone non-Jews were permitted to worship within the Temple area. It was mere mockery to suppose that genuine worship could be conducted in the midst of the obvious confusion of a market-place. The second quotation involved in Jesus' statement ('But you have made it a den of robbers') is from Jer. 7:11 and has reference to the fact that following Josiah's reforms the pollutions of the high places had been simply transferred to the Temple at Jerusalem! Our Lord conceived the materialism exemplified by the high-priestly clan in making their privileged position a source of revenue to be of an equally gross nature.

The religious authorities sensed the challenge g
involved in Jesus' action with reference to the Temple markets. And, indeed, it seems quite evident that there was a 'memorial sign' involved in Jesus' action on this occasion just as clearly as at the so-called 'triumphal entry'. Here perhaps we should see a symbolic action intended to direct the Temple authorities' thoughts to Mal. 3:1, 'The Lord whom you seek will suddenly come to his temple'. In any case, as W. G. Kümmel has remarked, 'Jesus by this act indubitably claims to realise already . . . the eschatological hour as the eschatological saviour, and thus claims to perform a messianic action' (cf. his *Promise and Fulfilment* (1957), 118). But, as on former occasions, so now Jesus would not give a straightforward answer to a question relative to his person or work. His method had always been to present the evidence and expect the answering faith to respond to it with insight. In the present instance this method-

648g ology was clearly indicated in the reference which our Lord made to John the Baptist. And his refusal to state the authority for his actions in this context rather clearly suggested that those who had not the spiritual insight to discern the nature of the authority with which John the Baptist spoke, would also fail to discern the authority behind his own ministry (Mk 11:27–33).

649a The nature miracle of the 'cursing of the fig tree' recorded by Mk and Mt. at this point in the narrative has caused considerable difficulty, particularly because of its apparent pointlessness (Mk 11:12–14, 20–24). As it stands in the Gospels, it is a bit of emblematic prophecy intended to illustrate the power of prayer when accompanied by faith in God, the same motif in fact as that found in the source Q at Mt. 17:20 and Lk. 17:6. While Lk. has no reference to the miracle, he does have a parable of a Fig Tree at 13:6–9 whose point appears to concern the comparative failure of a people like the Jewish nation to respond to the graciousness of God's dealings with it. Some have suggested that Lk.'s parable has been converted by Mk into a miracle, but this seems doubtful in view of the great difference in detail between the two. The nature miracle, however, contributes little to the account of Passion Week save as further evidence of Jesus' thorough mastery of the situation.

b (*b*) **Pronouncement Stories**—The Tuesday of Passion Week has often been called 'the day of questions' or 'controversies', inasmuch as Mk has here grouped together a series of Apophthegmata or Pronouncement Stories in which as usual Jesus is said to have given a cryptic answer to his friends or enemies on one or another theme. The only reference to time, however, is to be found at Mk 11:20 and it is quite possible that, as in the case of the conflict-stories (2:1–3:6), this series actually represents a pre-Marcan complex. However, the note of authority and even finality in

c Jesus' pronouncements in these stories well accords with his general attitude during Passion Week. The appropriateness of the parable of the Wicked Husbandmen (12:1–11) which Mk interjects at this point is obvious. The parable approaches, if it does not quite measure up to, the sort of allegorising which is to be found in the Fourth Gospel. As Vincent Taylor remarks, 'The owner is God, the Son is Jesus, the vineyard is Israel, the husbandmen are the Jewish leaders or possibly the people as a whole, and the slaves are apparently the OT prophets' (*The Gospel According to St Mark* (1952), 472). The authenticity of this allegory has often been called in question but it can only be so on the part of those who do not accept the evangelists' picture of a Jesus who knew himself to be God's Son in a unique way and who was aware of the nature of his calling. That Jesus should have employed this parable with its final quotation from Ps. 118:22f. during Passion Week would seem more likely than at any other time during his ministry. It accords well with the tone of authority characterising this week's teaching and might well have led to the endeavour to arrest him which is noted by Mk (12:12).

d The questions put to Jesus in the following series of Apophthegmata (Mk 12:13–34) are quite typical of the interests of the groups concerned. The Pharisees with the Herodians question him regarding the poll tax; the Sadducees on the matter of resurrection; and a scribe with regard to the importance of the six hundred and thirteen commandments said by the Pharisees to constitute the Mosaic law. Jesus' answer in each case is typical and there is no reason to doubt the genuineness of either the incident or the answer. He suggests that the poll tax be paid to the Imperial government because this is the right of the ruler. The deduction is not to be made, however, that Jesus intended to equalise duty to God and duty to state. On the contrary, he makes it abundantly clear that duty to God comes above all other duties (Mk 12:29f.; Mt. 6:31). One of the major disputes between the Pharisees and the Sadducees concerned the matter of the resurrection of the dead, the latter contending that 649d the OT scriptures contained no such doctrine. Jesus' reply in the words of Ex. 3:6 constitutes an *argumentum ad hominem* which any Jew, including the Sadducee, was bound to respect. The type of argument involved probably approximates as nearly to that employed by the Rabbis as anything in the teaching of Jesus. It is significant that our Lord's doctrine of the resurrection exhibits a far less developed statement than that to be found in Paul (1 C. 15). It is typical also of Jesus' general attitude to the problems of religion and ethics that in his reply to the scribe regarding the chief commandment he should quote the well-known beginning of the Shema' (Dt. 6:4f.) as indicating one's primary duty to God, and that duty wholehearted love. Similarly, Jesus quotes Lev. 19:18 as embodying all one's duty to one's neighbour. Surely it is not amiss to conclude that for Jesus these two attitudes toward God and man constitute a summary of one's total obligations in the fields of religion and ethics.

The story of the so-called 'widow's mite' (Mk e
12:41–44) also illustrates the fact that in the field of social ethics as in that of religion Jesus was always concerned with spirit and not with amounts, with quality and not with quantity. In Jesus' pronouncement involving Ps. 110:1 it is probably a mistake to understand him as denying the Davidic Sonship of the Messiah. His point would seem to lie rather in the field of emphasis, for sons of David could then have been reckoned by thousands! As Walter Lowrie has remarked, 'It can be proved that in a closely knit nation which began with a few million people every man is related to every other and is descended from *every* individual . . . who lived a thousand years before' (*The Short Story of Jesus* (1943), 5). Jesus' meaning, then, will be that a right understanding of the Messiah's person is to be arrived at by stressing his lordship rather than his sonship to David. As C. H. Dodd has indicated (in *According to the Scriptures* (1953), 110) the large use of Ps. 110 by the Church in her later scriptures is best explained by the hypothesis that Jesus himself had employed this coronation psalm in some context such as the present one.

Both Mk in the present context and the source f
Q elsewhere (Lk. 11:42, 44) testify to Jesus' roundly criticising the scribes of his day for their religious exhibitionism, greed, excessive religiosity, and insincerity of motive. Mt.'s special source, from which his 23rd chapter is largely derived, if anything indulges in an overstress on Jesus' invective against the contemporary scribes on these and like counts. That the scribes, who were largely of the Pharisaic persuasion, laid themselves open to criticism there can be no doubt. There were, however, good men among them and rabbinical tradition itself is sufficiently self-critical to demonstrate as much. Much of that same criticism, however, justifies Jesus' invective: one passage, for example, suggests that there are seven types of Pharisees of whom only one is pleasing to God!

(*c*) **Jesus' Eschatological Teaching**—The problem 650a
of Jesus' eschatological teaching, and particularly that regarding the consummation of the Kingdom of God, emerges at this point because Mk has devoted his 13th chapter to a statement of it (cf. also Mt., chs. 24 and 25; Lk. 21:5–36). It is impossible, however, to take this chapter and its parallels as the criterion for our Lord's teaching on this topic. To begin with, probably most scholars would rate it a *sententia accepta* that this 'Little Apocalypse' is a product of the thinking of the Church and not Jesus' teaching at all. Even if one were to accept T. W. Manson's estimate (*The Teaching of Jesus* (2nd ed. 1935), 262) 'that Mk 13 is a compilation containing genuine utterances of Jesus, but that the way in which the sayings have been arranged is such as to give a wrong impression of his eschatological teaching', obviously it is not permissible to start with this chapter in attempting to reconstruct our Lord's eschatological message. We incline toward

650a Manson's thesis but with some modification. There is undoubtedly in the chapter a certain confusion relative to the two events of, on the one hand, the destruction of the Jewish state, and, on the other, the end of the age and the coming of the Son of Man. On the whole, however, it would seem that this teaching is intended to be taken rather *as a warning* than for any normative value—a warning against imagining that any event within history, such as wars, famines, earthquakes, and the appearance of false Messiahs, should be taken as harbingers of the end of the age and the Son of Man's appearance (cf. vv. 5–8, 21–23). In our judgment Jesus here as elsewhere is employing the terminology of the teachers of his day as any good teacher will do, but, on close examination, it appears that in that terminology he teaches his own distinctive message which is poles apart from theirs! (And *to this extent* only we would agree with Bultmann's thesis that Jesus' teaching requires to be *de-* or perhaps better, *re-mythologised* for modern consumption.) Accordingly, while parting company with W. G. Kümmel's view that this and the like passages, 'represent primitive Jewish-Christian traditional material' which does not 'belong to the oldest Jesus tradition', we would arrive at the like conclusion with him that 'it follows conclusively that this message stands in complete contrast to the *Weltanschauung* of apocalyptic; therefore the significance of his proclamation that the Kingdom of God is imminent cannot lie in the *fact* that the end of the world is near, but must be looked for elsewhere' (*Promise and Fulfilment*, 104).

b Jesus did believe in the consummation of the Kingdom at the end of the age, but he taught quite clearly that there would be no precursory signs of the end (Mk 13:32–37; Lk. 12:39f., 17:23–30, 21:34–36), and he also made it clear that he knew nothing whatever regarding the time element involved (Mk 13:32–37). Jesus taught, as we have already seen, that the Kingdom of God was present in him and in his saving activities. In a real sense, therefore, the eschatological time had already begun in and through him. And yet he also believed and taught that the consummation of the Kingdom awaited the end of the age. Again to quote Kümmel (op. cit., 151), 'Jesus' message concerning the future was not intended to be an apocalyptic revelation, but a prophetic message concerning the imminent Kingdom of God, so that the apocalyptic interest in the date and the premonitory signs is necessarily lacking in Jesus'. A passage like Mk 9:1, accordingly, cannot be taken as applying to the consummation of the Kingdom. Otherwise it is quite out of character in the context of Jesus' teaching as a whole. It must be understood rather in the larger context of Mk 8:34ff. as referring to the progressive coming of the Kingdom as men individually take up the cross and follow after the Master.

651a (*d*) **The Last Supper**—The Jewish leaders sought to arrest Jesus secretly lest there be an uprising among the people (Mk 14:1). That they found ready assistance in the person of a disciple, Judas Iscariot, is beyond question, as the later Church would never have invented such treason within the little band about Jesus (Mk 14:10f.). Schweitzer's suggestion that Judas betrayed, not only the place of rendezvous where Jesus might be discovered, but also the *Messianic secret* is probably correct. As we have seen, Jesus for reasons of his own had refused to have the secret told. Moreover, as we have been noting, during Passion Week it was Jesus (not his disciples nor the multitudes) who pressed forward his claims to Messiahship. In doing so our Lord's motivation was to call forth spiritual insight. Judas, on the contrary, whose motives are at best obscure, knew that for the Jewish leaders the term 'Messiah' could have no other meaning than the lower, nationalistic one. In their overweening desire to maintain the prestige they enjoyed under the Roman rule, then, the knowledge of Jesus' claims on their part could lead to but one end for him—crucifixion.

The historical problem as to whether Jesus died on Nisan 14 or 15 still awaits solution. If on the 14th, as the Fourth Gospel appears to suggest (Jn 18:28, 19:14), then the last supper which Jesus ate with his disciples may have been the *Ḳiddûsh* (sanctification meal in preparation for the Sabbath or a feast day), or in any case a *Ḥabhurah* or fellowship meal such as was commonly observed among friends. If on the 15th, then the last supper will of necessity be the Passover meal (Mk 14:12). Either solution is attended with considerable difficulty of a harmonising type. In any event it is clear that everything proceeds according to Jesus' own predetermined plan. As in the case of the entry into the city and Temple on the preceding Sunday, Jesus again has made all preparations for this event secure. His two disciples are to find the house in which arrangements are to be made as they follow a man 'carrying a jar of water', a sight seldom if ever seen in the East where it is the women who draw water and carry jars upon their heads. On this occasion the password is 'The Teacher says, "Where is my guest room, where I am to eat the passover with my disciples?"' (Mk 14:13f.). There can be little doubt that this secrecy is due to Jesus' firm determination to carry through his plans for this final week to the last detail. He is prepared 'to give his life as a ransom for many' (Mk 10:45), but he will die only after he has given every group in the contemporary Jewish society an opportunity to accept him and only after he has made his last preparations for the future of his band of disciples; only indeed, at the right time and for the cause that he claimed to be the Messiah. The various accounts of the *last supper* leave no doubt that the Church understood its Lord consciously to be presiding here at a memorial feast significant at once of the eternal banquet in the Kingdom of God and also of his own cruel death on the cross. At this banquet Jesus acts as host in his Father's name. Likewise, his breaking of the bread in conjunction with the words 'This is my body' and his pointing to 'my blood of the covenant, which is poured out for many' can have but one reference—the cross. 651b

Singing a hymn (no doubt Ps. 118), the little band moves out to the garden on the slope of the Mount of Olives. In spite of obvious difficulties in the narrative, there is verisimilitude in the prayer of our Lord on this occasion—'Abba, Father, all things are possible to thee; remove this cup from me; yet not what I will, but what thou wilt' (Mk 14:36). The sleepiness of the disciples, the kiss of the traitor, the artless and futile use of the sword, and the flight of the disciples are all of the same character. Mk's possibly autobiographical account of the young man who 'ran away naked', too, is a convincing touch (Mk 14:51f.). c

(*e*) **The Trials of Jesus**—The accounts of the two trials of Jesus, the religious trial before the Sanhedrin and the civil trial before the Roman governor, are found in all four Gospels. That Jesus was condemned on both occasions there is unanimous testimony. Beyond this basic fact, however, there is comparatively little agreement in detail. Mt. generally follows the tradition of Mk; Lk. employs on the whole his special source; while Jn again follows materials of his own. There is general agreement regarding the defection of Peter, a notable point as it proves that the incident took deep root in the mind of the early Church. Only the Fourth Evangelist, or at any rate the author of Jn, ch. 21, recounts the morally and psychologically probable story of the risen Christ's helping this repentant disciple to pull his life together after this event (21:15–19). The haste and confusion displayed at the hearings before the High Priest and Sanhedrin are intelligible in view of the occurrence of the feast and the Sanhedrin's understandable desire to avoid an uprising among the people. That Jesus openly pressed his claims to Messiahship before the Sanhedrin must remain in doubt, in view of the diverse statements in the Gospels. It is likely that he merely d

651d answered the High Priest, 'Am I?' or 'Is that what you say?' At the same time, it seems equally certain that he pointed at once to his usual teaching, 'you will see the Son of man seated at the right hand of power and coming on the clouds of heaven' (Mt. 26:64; Mk 14:62; Lk. 22:67–71). In other words, as on all other occasions, Jesus refused to determine the issue regarding his own person, merely presenting the evidence of his words and works in the hope that these would call forth faith in the heart of his interrogator. The evidence on this occasion was sufficient to convince the Sanhedrin that he without doubt made exalted claims for himself and it was on these grounds alone that he was condemned.

e The accusation before Pilate is cleverly put—Jesus claims, it is averred, to be 'the King of the Jews' (Mk 15:2). The phraseology employed here accords with the nationalistic interpretation of Messiahship and the Jewish leaders are well aware that an accusation clothed in such terms will gain ready hearing in the court of the Roman governor. Jesus' reply to Pilate regarding his claims is as enigmatic as that given before the Sanhedrin. All three of the synoptists record the answer as either, 'You have said so', or 'Do you say so?' It is more in character that Jesus should have put his answer in the second form, and the Fourth Gospel distinctly records it so, 'Do you say this of your own accord, or did others say it to you about me?' (Jn 18:34). Pilate's vacillation and suggestion that, as it was usual at a feast to release a criminal, he might absolve Jesus from the due process of law is in accord with what we know otherwise of Pilate's character. Time-server that he is, he finally delivers Jesus to be crucified. Thus is our Lord condemned before both religious and civil courts, and by Jews and Gentiles alike.

652a (*f*) **Crucifixion and Resurrection**—The crucifixion follows the usual Roman pattern but with modifications. Roman justice is tempered with Jewish mercy in that Simon of Cyrene is made to carry Jesus' cross and that the 'wine mingled with myrrh' prepared as a sedative by the women of Jerusalem to alleviate the pain of crucifixion, is offered to Jesus; this he refuses. The same note, or at any rate a deep sense of respect, is shown in the action of a member of the Sanhedrin, Joseph of Arimathea, in asking for the body of Jesus and laying it away in his own new 'rock-hewn tomb' (Mt. 27:57–61; Lk. 23:50–53). David Daube has suggested that this action of Joseph was intended to preclude that the body of Jesus should be buried in one of the two plots commonly maintained by the Jewish court for the corpses of criminals (*The New Testament and Rabbinic Judaism* (1956), 310ff.). This picture of the mingling of justice and mercy, however, is coupled with another—that of ridicule and callousness. Jesus is crucified between two common bandits; the chief priests and others pass by mocking him; the soldiers after cruelly scourging and treating him with contempt cast lots for his clothing. The picture of Jesus on the cross, while differing in great detail in the various Gospels, is one of dignity, forgiveness, compassion, and triumph. Lk. alone has recorded the notable words, 'Father, forgive them; for they know not what they do' (Lk. 23:34), and the Fourth Evangelist the note of triumph in the words, 'It is finished' (Jn 19:30). Jesus died on Friday (Jn 19:31), and if Jn's dating be correct, then at the approximate time when the paschal lamb was being slaughtered in the Temple (Mk 15:34–6) (M. Pesaḥim 5:1; Jos.BJ, VI, ix, 3).

b The accounts of the empty tomb and resurrection appearances are difficult if not impossible of harmonisation. The essential facts are clear, however—the tomb found to be empty on Sunday morning, the announcement that the Lord had risen, and the testimony that on one occasion and another he had appeared to many. As previously suggested, there appear to be two *loci* about which the resurrection appearances of the risen Lord cluster—Galilee and Judaea. Mk's 652
sixteenth chapter breaks off at verse eight in the middle of a sentence, but there is a suggestion that he knew of a series of appearances in Galilee (7). And it is highly probable that Mt. in his account has followed Mk's Galilean tradition. Lk.-Ac. knows only of the Judaean tradition, while the Fourth Gospel contains both (cf. chs. 20, 21). Paul, too, apparently is acquainted with both Galilean and Judaean traditions (cf. 1 Cor. 15:3–11). The suggestion that it is the primitive Church in these two localities which is responsible for preserving the tradition the more intimately known to each, as being locally of more interest and importance, is a good one. This is both psychologically sound and also helpful in establishing the authenticity of the separate traditions. Schweitzer's suggestion that Jesus contemplated leading his disciples into Galilee with a view to establishing there the Kingdom of God in its consummated form lacks verification. The traditional view that the resurrection appearances were meant to teach the Church of Christ that their Lord was always present in their midst by his Spirit has more to commend it. Only Lk. concludes the ministry with a clear account of the Ascension (Ac. 1:6–11). Thereafter the risen Lord returns to his new body, the Church, indwelling it by his Spirit from Pentecost onward (Ac. 2).

Bibliography—For the LANGUAGE of Jesus: Matthew Black, *An Aramaic Approach to the Gospels and Acts* (2nd ed. 1954); Friedrich Schultess, *Grammatik des Christlich-Palästinischen Aramäisch* (1924), *Lexicon Syro-palaestinum* (1903); C. C. Torrey, *The Four Gospels* (n.d.).

For the BACKGROUND (Jewish and Gentile): Gustaf Dalman, *Jesus-Jeshua, Studies in the Gospels* (1929); Herbert Danby, *The Mishnah* (1933); David Daube, *The NT and Rabbinic Judaism* (1956); C. H. Dodd, *According to the Scriptures* (1953), *The Bible and the Greeks* (1935); Louis Finkelstein, *The Pharisees* (1940); G. H. C. Macgregor and A. C. Purdy, *Jew and Gentile, Tutors unto Christ* (1936); C. G. Montefiore, *Rabbinic Literature and Gospel Teachings* (1930); G. F. Moore, *Judaism in the First Centuries of the Christian Era, The Age of the Tannaim* (3 vols. 1927–30); E. Schürer, *The Jewish People in the Time of Jesus Christ* (5 vols. 1885); H. L. Strack and P. Billerbeck, *Kommentar zum NT aus Talmud und Midrasch* (5 vols. 1922–8); also studies on the Dead Sea Scrolls.

For the LIFE of Jesus Christ (*a*) the problem of orientation and motive: G. K. A. Bell and A. Deissmann, *Mysterium Christi* (1930); J. W. Bowman, *The Intention of Jesus* (1943, Eng. ed. 1945); O. Cullmann, *Christ and Time* (1950, tr. from Ger. ed. of 1948); C. H. Dodd, *History and the Gospel* (1938); G. S. Duncan, *Jesus, Son of Man* (1949); F. C. Grant, *The Gospel of the Kingdom* (1940); E. Hoskyns and N. Davey, *The Riddle of the NT* (1931); John Knox, *Christ the Lord* (1945), *Criticism and Faith* (1952), *The Man Christ Jesus* (1941); T. W. Manson, *The Servant-Messiah* (1953); W. Manson, *Jesus the Messiah* (1943, Amer. ed. 1946); J. Marsh, *The Fullness of Time* (1952); V. G. Simkhovitch, *Toward the Understanding of Jesus* (1921–47); (*b*) history of the lives of Jesus and chronology: C. C. McCown, *The Search for the Real Jesus* (1940); G. Ogg, *The Chronology of the Public Ministry of Jesus* (1940); A. Schweitzer, *Vom Reimarus zu Wrede; eine Geschichte der Leben-Jesu-Forschung* (4th ed. 1926, Eng. tr. 1910); see also art. 'From Schweitzer to Bultmann', *Theology Today* (July 1954); (*c*) lives of Jesus: S. Cave, *A Plain Man's Life of Christ* (1941); M. Goguel, *Jesus* (2nd ed. 1950, Eng. tr. 1933); L. de Grandmaison, *Jesus Christ—His Person—His Message—His Credentials* (3 vols. 1930–4); C. Guignebert, *Jesus* (1935); J. Klausner, *Jesus of Nazareth* (1926); W. Lowrie, *The Short Story of Jesus* (1943); G. H. C. Macgregor, 'Recent Gospel Criticism and our Approach to the Life of Jesus', ET (Mar.

1934) ; T. W. Manson, 'Is it Possible to Write a Life of Christ ? ', ET (May 1942) ; V. Taylor, same title, ET (Nov. 1941).

For Jesus' TEACHING (*a*) general : John Bright, *The Kingdom of God* (1953) ; C. H. Dodd, *Gospel and Law* (1951) ; T. W. Manson, *The Teaching of Jesus* (2nd ed. 1935) ; (*b*) Sermon on the Mount : J. W. Bowman, *The Gospel from the Mount* (1957) ; Dom J. Dupont, *Les Béatitudes* (1954) ; A. M. Hunter, *A Pattern for Life* (1952) ; H. Windisch, *Der Sinn der Bergpredigt* (rev. ed. 1937, Eng. tr. 1951) ; (*c*) Parables : C. H. Dodd, *The Parables of the Kingdom* (3rd ed. 1936) ; J. Jeremias, *Die Gleichnisse Jesu* (1947) ; A. Jülicher, *Die Gleichnisreden Jesu* (2 vols., 2nd ed. 1899) ; (*d*) eschatology : C. J. Cadoux, *The Historic Mission of Jesus* (1941) ; H. A. Guy, *The NT Doctrine of the 'Last Things'* (1948) ; W. G. Kümmel, *Promise and Fulfilment* (1957, tr. from 3rd Ger. ed. of 1956) ; R. Otto, *Reich Gottes und Menschensohn* (1934, Eng. tr., 2nd ed. 1942) ; A. N. Wilder, *Eschatology and Ethics in the Teaching of Jesus* (rev. ed. 1950) ; (*e*) the problem of 'myth' : H. W. Bartsch, *Kerygma and Myth* (2 vols. 1953–5) ; Ian Henderson, *Myth in the NT* (1952) ; G. V. Jones, *Christology and Myth in the NT* (1956).

THE SYNOPTIC PROBLEM

By C. S. C. WILLIAMS

653a The Synoptic problem is that of determining the relationship of the first three Gospels. At one time it was thought that oral tradition in the Church led to similar presentation of the written Gospels, but this theory was abandoned when it was seen that oral tradition alone cannot account for the many close resemblances and even identical expressions in the Synoptic Gospels, however retentive the Eastern mind may have been. With the rise, however, of Form Criticism (see §§596–7), oral tradition has come back into play and despite the arbitrary and subjective opinions of many Form critics, it must be allowed that the phrasing of an account of an incident reported in the Gospels may be due, in part at least, to the influence of oral tradition upon members of the Christian community among whom the evangelists moved. Just as few judges would now appeal to Natural Law as an entity in itself but would apply what they imagine to be 'the principles of natural law' perhaps in any particular case, so NT critics have rejected the theory of oral tradition but apply it to particular sections of the narrative; e.g. Lk. 21 differs from Mk 13 in ways that suggest that Luke relied here more on oral tradition than upon his copy of the Marcan Gospel.

b **(1) The Priority of Mark**—The subject-matter of only 65 verses out of 661 in Mk is absent from Mt. Only one-third of Mk is not found in both Mt. and Lk. but almost all this one-third is found either in Lk. or in Mt., in fact all but 31 verses, apart from minor omissions which do not affect the sense (Mk 1:1, 2:27, 3:20–1, 4:26–9, 7:3–4, 7:32–7, 8:22–6, 9:29, 9:48–9, 13:33–7—though Mt. has much similar material elsewhere—and 14:51–2). The priority of Mk and its use by Mt. and Lk. follows from these facts. (Roman Catholic critics, however, being bound by the decision of their Biblical Commission of 26 June 1912, conclude that Mt. in some form was prior to Mk., a common form of this view being that a proto-Mt. written in Aramaic existed before Mk.)

The view of the priority of Mk is corroborated by the use, in the main, of the vocabulary of Mk by Matthew and Luke or by one of them where the other deserts Mk, e.g. Mk 11:1–10, cf. Mt. 21:1–9 and Lk. 19:28–38. It is corroborated also by the order of incidents related by Mk being kept by Mt. or Lk.; again, where either Mt. or Lk. deserts Mk, the other almost invariably keeps Mk's order, the exception being Mk 3:31–5. The preservation of Mk's order in the second half of Mt. is especially striking, though earlier (in Mt. 8–13), Mt. does not keep that order so strictly. On the ordinary supposition of the existence of Q (from Quelle, 'source'), a second source besides Mk common to Mt. and Lk., it is to be noted that after the Temptation story, which had to stand before the opening of the Ministry, the Q sayings of Jesus are not put by Mt. and Lk. into the same setting on any occasion. Matthew and Luke seem to have used Mk as their skeleton and to have inserted other material to form the flesh and blood of their Gospels. Matthew has done so by letting one saying or incident call to mind another from a non-Marcan source and he has conflated or welded them together; Luke has worked by adding strips or blocks of material together, some of which may have been already collected, probably by himself, before he 65
acquired his copy of Mk. Matthew, using Mk as his chronological basis, has expanded Mk by inserting material peculiar to himself into Marcan contexts, e.g. in Mt. 16:17–19, Matthew has an insertion of three verses peculiar to himself which may go back to three separate sayings of Jesus and which Matthew thought appropriate to the account of the Confession of Peter at Caesarea Philippi. Matthew's principle of adding like to like is seen in the accretion of parables appended to his version (Mt. 23–4) of Mk's apocalyptic ch. 13. Similarly, the whole of the Sermon on the Mount seems to have been built up by Matthew from non-Marcan material and inserted before Mt. 7:29 to illustrate Mk 1:22, 39. Luke's method is different. Between the Baptism and Temptation of the Lord on one side and the Last Supper on the other he almost invariably inserts non-Marcan blocks of material into Marcan, e.g. Lk. 6:20–8:3, 9:51–18:14 and 19:1–27, blocks partly of Q sayings and partly of material peculiar to Lk. (For the view that these blocks were already formed when Luke found his Marcan 'skeleton', see §655*a* on Proto-Lk.) But 55 per cent of the language of Lk. is that of Mk and this percentage rises to 69 in citations of the words of Jesus.

c A further corroboration of Mk's priority is seen in the refinements of his grammatical style and of his phraseology by Mt. and Lk., often of identical words or terms which would offend later writers or better stylists. For instance, in Mk 11:1–10 and its parallels noted above, Mk's historical present tenses are avoided by Mt. and Lk.; both the latter alter Mk 11:4f., which is repetitive, Mt. summing it up in six words and Lk. also abbreviating it. Mark may have used a codex or book-form for his work (C. H. Roberts) but, especially if they used the roll-form, Matthew and Luke needed to compress their material within the limits of 25–30 feet of a portable roll. Many of their refinements to Mk would occur to anyone writing better Greek or wishing to avoid giving offence to the religious scruples of later Christian readers.

d Dom B. C. Butler (*The Originality of St Matthew* (1951)) may be cited as typical of Roman Catholic scholars who question the priority of Mk. He suggests that instead of holding that Mk led to Mt. on one side and to Lk. on the other, it is equally possible that Mt. led to Mk and Mk to Lk.; he claims that there is one chance in two that Mk copied Mt., the alternative being universally ruled out that Lk. led to Mk and Mk to Mt. Like other Roman and some Anglo-Catholic writers he rejects the theory of Q (see §654*b*) and he accepts Augustine's view that Mark was 'a kind of lackey and abbreviator of Mt.' He fails to explain why Luke, if he knew Mt., followed Mt.'s order only when it had appeared in Mk's, or why there are so few agreements on order against Mk found in Mt. and Lk. Anyone working through a Synopsis in Greek, as Augustine was not able to do, studying the order of incidents as well as the language of the Greek original, not the Vulgate Latin, would be convinced of Mk's priority if he approached the subject without prejudices already formed (cf. H. G. Wood, ET 65 (1953), 19). Freed from the burden of the Biblical Commission, all scholars would recognise the truth

53d of Mk's priority even if it involved casting doubt on the validity of the Petrine commission of Mt. 16:16ff.

Another instance of giving priority to Mt. is L. Vaganay (*Le problème synoptique* (1952); cf. ETL (*Ephemerides Theologicae Lovanienses*) 28 (1952), 238–56). He postulates seven stages in the composition of the Synoptic Gospels: (1) oral tradition (O), (2) written evangelical essays (E) including certain catechetical elements put into writing, (3) an Aramaic Gospel of Mt. (M) and its Greek translation (Mg), M thus lying at the base of all the Synoptic tradition, (4) a second Synoptic source complementary to M, which is called S, or in its Greek dress, Sg, which is different from the Q of Protestant scholars, (5) Mk (Mc), (6) the Greek canonical Mt., and lastly (7) Lk. (Lc). However, J. Levie, ETL 31 (1955), 619–36, asks, 'Is Mk the source of the Greek Mt. or is an Aramaic Mt. the source of both?' Another writer seeking to preserve the dogmatic priority of Mt. is P. Parker (*The Gospel before Mark* (1953)), who postulates the existence of K, a kind of proto-Mt. consisting of Mk and the material peculiar to Mt. which he supposes Mk abridged at Rome giving it a pro-Gentile bias; Mt. combined K with Q and Lk. used Mk and Q; dependence of Mt. on Mk is thus avoided.

54a **(2) Ur-Markus**—At one time the question was asked whether Mt. and Lk. had before them an earlier form of Mk than the one that we can reconstruct mainly from the Alexandrian and Western texts. If so, it was felt that this would account not only for any positive agreements between Mt. and Lk. against Mk but also for the 'omissions' of parts of Mk by the other two evangelists. As for the common omissions, they are few, amounting, as has been said, to 31 verses. Because Mt. conflates his material, he sometimes appears to omit from Mk, but does not do so in fact. Lk.'s omissions, amounting to 155 verses, are more striking, especially that of Mk 6:45–8:26. The common agreements, if one rejects the view that Lk. used Mt., can be explained as refinements of Mk which would leap to the mind of any Greek writer, or as due to the scribal corruption of Mk's text which made it appear to differ from that of Mt. and Lk. or to similar corruption, frequently by a process of harmonisation, to the text of Mt. and of Lk., or as due to the influence on Mt. and Lk., when they are following Mk, of Q or some similar material.

To account for the omission by Lk. of Mk 6:45–8:26, Streeter suggested that a mutilated copy of Mk lay before Luke, this copy omitting 6:53–8:21; hence came Lk.'s mention of Jesus praying alone and his insertion of 'Bethsaida' into the first section of the story of the feeding of the multitude, Lk. 9:10 (cf. Mk 8:22; Lk. 9:18, cf. Mk 6:45). Streeter and others have urged also that as the original ending of Mk is lost after 16:8, it is unlikely that two recensions of Mk, Ur-Markus and Mk itself, were current in the primitive Church and known to the other two Synoptic evangelists and that neither contained the 'original ending', unless it is postulated with R. H. Lightfoot that Mk intended to end his Gospel at 16:8 on a note of numinous awe and not to record any appearances of the risen Lord.

However, G. A. Barton, JBL 48 (1929), 239ff., follows Goodspeed in thinking that Mt.'s ending was based on Mk's original ending which is lost and that it underlies Mt. 28:9f., 16–19*a*, 20; that Mark issued two editions of his Gospel, the first (a copy of which came into Luke's hands) lacking Mk. 6:48–8:26; 9:28, 29, 43 and 10:1–10, 35–41 and the ending; this edition was issued *c.* A.D. 46–7 while the later edition approximating to 'our' Mk appeared from Rome *c.* A.D. 65–70. Whereas Streeter maintained that if Ur-Markus ever existed, we have it and not the later recension, Barton suggested that Mt. and Lk. used different recensions of Mk.

b What was in effect another form of the Ur-Markus theory was suggested by Dr T. F. Glasson (ET 55 (1944), 180 ff.) who put forward a tentative hypothesis that Mt. and Lk. may have used a 'Western' text of Mk; this, however, does not seem to fit the facts, nor is it likely that the 'Western' recension goes back as far as the 1st cent., when Matthew and Luke wrote. 654b

(3) Q—The usual view among non-Roman and most Anglo-Catholic scholars is that Matthew and Luke used a common source or sources besides Mk. This source cannot be defined exactly as some of it may appear in Mt. or in Lk. where the other omits it, and as both Matthew and Luke may omit some parts of it, just as they omit some, though not much, of Mk in common. It is no argument against the existence of Q to say that different scholars have drawn up different lists of its contents. The list suggested by T. W. Manson (*The Sayings of Jesus* (1950), 15f.) may be a slight underestimate if the contexts surrounding the verses indicated are sometimes to be included too: Lk. 3:7–9; 4:1–13; 6:20–3, 27–33, 35–44, 46–9; 7:1–10, 18–20, 22–35; 9:57–60; 10:2–16, 21–4; 11:9–13, 29–35, 39, 41, 42, 44, 46–52; 12:2–10, 22–31, 33, 34, 39, 40, 42–6, 51, 53, 58, 59; 13:18–21, 24, 28, 29, 34, 35; 14:26, 27, 34, 35; 16:13, 16–18; 17:1, 3, 4, 6, 23, 24, 26, 27, 33–5, 37. Some scholars have treated such passages as coming from a single document (cf. B. S. Easton, *The Gospel according to St Luke* (1926), 98f., where he gives a list of passages having no parallel in Mk but where the agreement between Lk. and Mt. is so close as to render the use of common Greek originals indubitable). On this view to split Q into two or more documents would be to introduce needless complexity. Easton suggested that the Greek style of the passages in his list is remarkably uniform and that only the difference between the Aramaic original and a close Greek translation separates us here from the actual words of Christ; he maintains that the interests of the source point decisively towards a Palestinian origin and that the date of Q may not be later than *c.* A.D. 50. (The serious charge that Q never existed and that Luke used Mt. instead would remove all trace of this early source of Gospel material; see §654*g*.)

The view, however, has been maintained that c
Q consists of more than one document. There is a striking measure of agreement between Mt. and Lk. in some Q passages, not all; some passages seem full-bloodedly Q while others are anaemic. It was for this reason that Bussmann (*Synoptische Studien* (1925–31)) distinguished passages showing close agreement (T) from those where there is great variation (R); he thought that the language of T differed from that of R and suggested that T was derived from Greek, R from Aramaic common material, and that in R passages we find some 122 translation variants which help to account for the divergence between Mt. and Lk. (But 'translation variants' appear also in T passages and some of those in R may be due to editorial modification rather than divergent translation.)

C. K. Barrett (ET 54 (1943), 320 ff.) would go farther. He thinks that Q material came from a number of non-Marcan sources used by Mt. and Lk., just as Mk itself is in all probability the product of several sources. He considers the degree of agreement not only in words but also in traditional background between Mt. and Lk. when they were reporting sayings of the same purport and after examining Lk. 6:29, 11:44, 12:6, 16:16, 6:20–6, 13:22–30 and 12:54–6, he suggests that Matthew and Luke, in collecting their material, used traditions which were similar but not identical rather than that each had identical copies of one source. If, he argues, Matthew and Luke were both using the same continuous source, we should expect to find in them the same agreement in order which, generally speaking, they show in following Mk. Even if the larger blocks of Q material be separated from the shorter Q sayings which show no common order in arrangement, one finds that four blocks followed by a sixth and seventh correspond in order (Lk. 3:2–22, Mt. 3:17; Lk. 4:1–13, Mt. 4:1–11; Lk. 6:20–49, Mt. 5:1–7:27; Lk. 7:1–10, Mt. 8:5–13; Lk. 9:57–10:24, Mt. 8:19–22; Lk. 11:14–32,

654c Mt. 12:22–45) but the other seven blocks of Q show no such correspondence. Any similarity that exists, he maintains, can be accounted for by the common order corresponding to the outline in Mk. Therefore the theory must be discarded that the order of the Q sections in Mt. and Lk. indicates that they were taken from a source. Similarly W. L. Knox (*The Sources of the Synoptic Gospels*, ii, ed. by H. Chadwick (1957)) assumes that Q existed but he finds it necessary to insist that it is simply a hypothetical document and that the evidence for a single document Q as the source of all or most of the material common to Mt. and Lk. is by no means conclusive. He prefers to speak of 'Q tracts'.

d However, in two important articles, (*a*) ET 21 (1934), 71ff. and (*b*) JTS, N.S. 4 (1953), 27–31, Dr Vincent Taylor has reconsidered the evidence. In (*a*) he reviewed the reasons given for the differences in the Qness of Q material, viz. : (i) editorial modifications, as Harnack maintained, (ii) the existence of different recensions of Q, (iii) Streeter's theory (*The Four Gospels* (1924), 238ff.) of the overlapping of parallel versions of Q taken from different centres of church life, and (iv) Bussmann's theory (§654*c*). He finds some truth in all four theories ; except for (iii) and (iv) they are not mutually exclusive though these two provide alternative explanations of the same literary phenomenon. Streeter's theory has the merit of being simpler than Bussmann's and it can account for the existence of some of the 'translation-variants' by supposing that Mt. conflated Q material with M material (peculiar to himself), because these sources included similar sayings. Both may have been in part Aramaic sources resting on Aramaic tradition. In (*b*) he considers the order of the Q material, setting aside an (A) group of passages where the linguistic agreement between Mt. and Lk. is relatively small and where Mt. may be dependent on another source as well, besides Q, e.g. Lk. 10:25–8, Mt. 22:34–9 ; Lk. 12:54–6, Mt. 16:2f. ; Lk. 13:23f., Mt. 7:13f. ; Lk. 13:25–7, Mt. 7:22f., 25:10–12 ; Lk. 14:25–7, Mt. 22:1–10 ; Lk. 15:4–7, 10, Mt. 18:12–14 ; Lk. 19:12–27, Mt. 25:14–30. Another group (B) consists of short sayings which either Mt. or Lk., though generally Mt., to judge from his conflationary methods, has tended to insert in another context. He takes the five groups in Mt. of sayings and parables of Jesus, chs. 5–7, 10, 13, 18, 23–5 and sets out in one column the Lucan Q sayings, then in columns two to five those in each of the five blocks of Mt., and finally in a sixth column the sayings in the rest of Mt. Even including the B passages, though not the A, the sequences in this arrangement are striking and suggest that Matthew and Luke used a common documentary source. When one considers the strong Qness of many Q passages, the phenomenon of doublets where Mt. and Lk. seem to follow Mk in one place but reproduce from a second source almost identical teaching in another context, and the 122 translation-variants of Bussmann, 'the manifest signs of a common order in Mt. and Lk. raise the [Q] hypothesis to a remarkable degree of cogency, short only of demonstration.'

e The point that the amount of verbal agreement between Mt. and Lk. is so great as to exclude the possibility of our having two independent Greek versions of an original Aramaic Q, while we find verbal differences pointing to translation-variants comparable to those found in the two Greek versions of the Book of Dan., was developed by T. W. Manson, ET 47 (1935), 7ff., who maintained that as far as evidence of translation goes, the earlier form of the Greek is Lk.'s, while Mt.'s is a revised form. From the parallels Lk. 11:41, Mt. 23:26 ; Lk. 6:37, Mt. 7:1 ; Lk. 12:39, Mt. 24:43 he deduces that Lk.'s version is the more primitive, and he takes the differences between Mt. 7:12, Lk. 6:31; Mt. 6:28, Lk. 12:27 to be due to variant renderings of the Aramaic. He suggests that an Aramaic Q for Aramaic-speaking Christians consisted of teaching of Jesus and that it contained four sections, Jesus and John the Baptist, Jesus and His disciples, Jesus and His opponents, and Eschatology. In this article and elsewhere (*The Sayings of Jesus* (1949), 16f.) he has made the valuable suggestion that it was to Q that 'the oracles' refer in the disputed passage of Papias quoted by Eus.HE III, xxxix, 16 : 'Such then is Papias' account of Mark. But the following is the statement concerning Matthew : " So then, Matthew compiled the oracles in the Hebrew language ; but everyone interpreted them as he was able." ' Here 'Hebrew' means 'Aramaic' and it is possible that Papias or his source attributed to Mt. what should have been attributed to Q. 'The statement of Papias which cannot be made to fit the Gospel of Matthew except by a forced and unnatural interpretation, does, when taken in its simple and natural meaning, fit a document such as Q like a glove.'

f It is usually assumed that Q contained little, if any, narrative and consisted chiefly of sayings of Jesus and, despite F. C. Burkitt, did not include a Passion narrative, which the Form critics would say was fused into a single unit of oral tradition in the crucible of Christian preaching and teaching. Being formless, the Q sayings were no longer preserved after they were included in Mt. and in Lk.

The whole existence, however, of Q has been the subject of attack, not entirely by Roman Catholic scholars. To some the problem seems hardly worth discussing. 'The pressure of contemporary problems is too great for it to matter much whether Q was in one piece, or was a series of disconnected leaves . . . some of which Luke and Matthew had in common, while each had leaves unknown to the other ; or whether there ever was a Q at all or not. Perhaps one of my students was right when he said in an examination that Q was Lk.'s German source' (E. R. Goodenough, JBL 71 (1952), 2).

g To Dr A. M. Farrer it seems possible to dispense with Q by supposing that Luke read Mt. and Mk. (*Studies in the Gospels*, ed. D. E. Nineham (1955), 55–88). On this view Lk. was not a mere scissors-and-paste compiler inserting blocks of material into a Gospel strip by strip but a genuine author with a Pentateuchal arrangement in mind not so clear as Mt.'s had been, but still discernible. Against this the questions have been put: 'Could Luke really have left out so much of Mt. because it did not attract him? Could he really have broken up the well-arranged Matthaean discourses to put the fragments in settings that are usually inferior? It has been proved by Sir John Hawkins that there is not a single case after the story of the Temptation in which Lk. agrees with Mt. in inserting the same saying at the same point in the Marcan outline. Now could Lk. really have been so wilful as to alter all the contexts of these non-Marcan insertions in the Marcan settings found for them by Mt.?' (W. H. Blyth Martin, *Theology* 59, 431 (1956), 183). Other difficulties in the way of his hypothesis Dr Farrer deals with ingeniously and often convincingly, e.g. 'there are texts in Mt. which Lk. would not have omitted, had he been acquainted with them' or 'where Mt. and Lk. give the same saying of Christ, Lk.'s wording sometimes has the more primitive appearance', though on this latter point Dr Farrer has to prove that Mt.'s is invariably the more primitive, whereas most scholars agree that sometimes Mt. is giving the earlier version and sometimes Lk. Another difficulty that he recognises in the way of his hypothesis is that 'the order in which Lk. places the material common to himself and Mt. is mostly less appropriate and less coherent than the order it has in Mt.' But he finds purpose in Luke's method of taking apart Mt.'s sermons and rearranging them ; but his difficulty here is to prove that Luke was working, not on Q alone, but on Mt. Another difficulty is that the existence of 'doublets' and of 'translation-variants' has not been explained on this view. Therefore, though any theory which obviates mere hypothesis, and Q is such, is to be given serious

654g attention, especially if it avoids multiplying entities beyond necessity, this one raises considerable difficulties and is unlikely to win general acceptance.

655a **(4) Proto-Luke**—Instead of regarding Lk. as a late 1st-cent. Gospel presenting us with his own architectural plans, it is well to return to the older theory of B. H. Streeter (*The Four Gospels*; cf. his introduction to the 4th ed.) according to which about A.D. 70–80, Luke, having formed an early draft of gospel material and Q sayings plus L material (material peculiar to himself) already, came into possession of a copy of Mk which provided him with a chronological scheme not hitherto available and which he used, not as a primary source, but as a supplementary source to his Q+L or Proto-Lucan draft. It cannot be said too often that the theory of Proto-Lk. is sometimes attacked or abused as though the claim were made that this early draft were a complete Gospel in itself, with a Passion narrative at the end, as well as an introduction, 3:1–4:30, and a long middle section, 9:51–18:14. For example, S. M. Gilmour rejects the proposition that Q+L or Proto-Lk. was such a complete Gospel and goes on to reject the proposition that Q+L provided Luke with a framework for the final draft of his Gospel and that into this Gospel he inserted supplementary excerpts from Mk (*A critical re-examination of Proto-Luke*, JBL 67 (1948), 143–52). But as one of the severest critics of the theory, J. M. Creed, admitted (ET 46 (1946), 103), if this hypothesis were used simply to cover the very common theory that Q, as Lk. knew it, was already combined with some of the material peculiar to himself, he was not concerned to dispute it but he did take exception to any view which made out that Proto-Lk. equals Q + narrative extending from the beginning of the Ministry to the Passion and Resurrection and that this Q+L was the foundation document of Lk., Mk's material being secondary additions to our 3rd Gospel and the excision of the Marcan texts from Lk. leaving us with an independent non-Marcan source covering the whole range of the Gospel story. As Streeter and the other notable champion of the Proto-Lucan theory, Dr V. Taylor, described Proto-Lk. as a kind of 'half-way house' to a Gospel or as a 'first draft' rather than a complete work, many critical shafts leave them unscathed. Reduced to its essentials, the theory is that Luke had already formed Q+L material to be an early draft, and that it is seen now in Lk. 3:1–4:30, 6:12–8:3, 9:51–18:14, 19:1–27 and perhaps 22:14–24:53. To this the Infancy stories of 1:1–2:52 may have been added last. In Lk. as we have it, alternate strips of Marcan and non-Marcan material lie side by side and in the non-Marcan material we have Q filled out with L material. On this view it is easy to understand the omissions from Mk by Luke, as on no other view, because Mk was not Luke's primary source. 'Omissions' is therefore the wrong word. Also on this view one can understand why the careful sixfold date of Lk. 3:1f. stands where it does and the genealogy in 3:23–38, which one might have expected in Lk. 1.

b At the same time, if it could be proved that the Lucan Passion narrative was derived from a non-Marcan account and that excerpts from Mk have been inserted into this non-Marcan narrative, the theory of Proto-Lk. would be greatly strengthened. Here opinions are divided. On one side it is argued that Mk is the main source of Luke's Passion narrative and on the other that Luke's Passion narrative is based on a non-Marcan account into which extracts from Mk have been inserted. One critic may say that the 'insertions' summarise the contents of Lk. 22:14–24:12 and he may stress the fact that the Marcan phrases appear very nearly in the order in which they are found in Mk. Another critic will say that the 'insertions' are heterogeneous, including Lk. 22:19*a*, 22, 34, possibly 46*b*, 50*b*, 52–3*a*, 54*b*–61; 23:3, 26, 34*b* (possibly), 38, 44f., 50–4 and possibly 24:10, and the fact that they are inserted almost in the Marcan order is not unexpected. J. M. Creed (ET 46 (1934), 101ff. and his *Commentary on Luke* (1930)) maintains 655b Luke's indebtedness throughout to Mk. But A. M. Perry (ET 46 (1935), 256ff.) stresses (*a*) that whereas in Luke's account of the ministry of Jesus Lk's verbal correspondence with Mk is 53 per cent, this drops to 27 per cent in the Passion narrative; (*b*) that Luke indulges in liberty of transposition four times as freely as before when he comes to the Passion story; (*c*) that while the Passion story is only two-ninths as long as the narrative of the Ministry in Lk., it contains twice as much interwoven matter (three points made by Sir John Hawkins); and (*d*) that it is significant that Lk. omits many Marcan items, e.g. Mk 14:26–8, 41f., 51f., 56–61; 15:16–20, 29, 34f., 44*b*. Perry asks pertinently, 'Why did Luke change his editorial method of using Mk when he entered upon the Passion narrative?' He concluded that Creed seems to have made the mistake of assuming that no other *could* parallel Mark.

c Other attacks on the view that Luke was not indebted primarily to Mk for his Passion narrative have come from M. Goguel (HTR 36 (1933), 1–55) and from Dr G. D. Kilpatrick (JTS, N.S. 1 (1950), 56–60; cf. JTS 43 (1942), 34ff.); the latter has been answered effectively by Dr V. Taylor (ET 67 (1955), 15).

Apart from the Passion narrative in Lk., large blocks of material seem derived from Q+L and not from Mk to any great extent. Even this has been queried, e.g. by C. S. Petrie (ET 54 (1943), 172–7), who has examined Lk. 3:1–9:50 for dependence on Mk. His arguments met with a complete refutation by Dr V. Taylor (ibid. 219–22). Though suspicion and dislike of the theory of Proto-Lk. as a preliminary draft of gospel material have led to more abuse of it than argument against it (Dr Farrer has pronounced (*A Study in St Mark*, 210) that it is incapable of reasonable defence!), it is hard to resist the moderate conclusions of Dr V. Taylor that the existence of a document Q+L, consisting of a form of Q supplemented by material from Lk.'s special tradition, at a time earlier than the composition of the 3rd Gospel, is a reasonable and justifiable assumption and that 'it is a possible view that the 3rd Gospel consists of Q+L, a Lukan Passion narrative, the Birth Stories and Mk.' Like the theory of the existence of Q, the Proto-Lucan theory survives, and premature announcements of their demise are 'greatly exaggerated'. Both theories, however, are ignored rather than answered by critics who see in the Evangelists architects working on grand theological constructions of their own rather than compilers of the traditions, written and oral, handed on to them.

d Recently, however, two articles have examined in turn the contents of Lk. 9:51–18:14 (C. F. Evans, in *Studies in the Gospels*, ed. by D. Nineham (1955), 37–53) and of Lk. 1–2 (M. D. Goulder and M. L. Sanderson, JTS, N.S. 8 (1957), 12–30). The former set side by side sections from Lk.'s great central section and sections from Dt. Though sometimes the resemblances of subject-matter and phraseology may be accidental, it is striking that the sections parallel one with another follow the same order in the two very different works. The latter article, entitled 'Luke's Genesis' seeks to show that Lk.'s Infancy Stories were intended by the evangelist to correspond to the opening book of the Pentateuch. It may be suggested that with the exercise of only a little ingenuity a theory could be advanced that other portions of Proto-Lk. besides Lk. 9:51–18:14 now fit into a Lucan Pentateuch, consisting of sayings and deeds of Jesus about which Luke had heard before he read the Marcan Gospel and which he grouped, *faute de mieux*, into a Pentateuchal pattern until he found Mk's chronological scheme, for what it was worth, available. Such a theory might call for less ingenuity than one which treats the 3rd Gospel, as we have it now, as though it were arranged in such a pattern.

Whatever be the merits of a theory of a 'Proto-

655d Lucan Pentateuch', it has been suggested (ET 64 (1953), 283ff.) that Luke composed a primitive draft of gospel material and that this formed the 'first treatise' sent to Theophilus (Ac. 1:1); that at a later date Luke found a copy of Mk, which has influenced his Acts so that, later still, Luke, writing out the 3rd Gospel, has not repeated the parallels to Mk which he had used in Acts. (The possibility remains that the 'first treatise' was such a Proto-Lucan Pentateuch leading up to but not narrating the death of One greater than Moses.) This theory was accepted and elaborated by H. G. Russell (HTR 48 (1956), 167ff.). The ordinary assumption that the whole of the 3rd Gospel must have been written before Acts needs to be challenged.

It has been Dr V. Taylor himself who has pointed out one of the weakest spots in the Proto-Lucan theory (ET 67 (1955), 16), namely, the gap in Proto-Lk. before Lk. 22:14 which can be accounted for possibly on the supposition that the section preceding this verse, based upon Mk, was allowed to take the place of an originally Proto-Lucan section.

656a (5). Streeter drew attention to the **four-document hypothesis,** that besides Mk and Q we have L (material peculiar to Lk.) and M (material peculiar to Mt.) in our Synoptic Gospels, which has replaced the old two-document hypothesis of Mk and Q alone. Whether, however, L and M were documents rather than collections of oral tradition is incapable of proof.

b As B. S. Easton says in his commentary on Lk., a subjective element is bound to exist in any list of this sort; his list differs from that below. He argued in JBL 29 (1910), 139–80, and 30 (1911), 78–103 that the Greek material in his list of L passages has a peculiar vocabulary, different from Lk.'s. He notes as characteristics of L its strong LXX colouring and frequent Semitisms, its intensely Judaistic outlook, its hatred of the scribes, Pharisees and well-to-do classes and its Judaean or even Samaritan, not Galilean, interests. Even if L was not a document but a collection of oral material, there is nothing in Easton's arguments to forbid our following Harnack in thinking that such a person as Philip the Evangelist or one of his daughters supplied some of the L material; the author of the 'We-sections' of Acts, probably Luke, stayed with them at Caesarea for 'some days'. Though this is pure speculation, it is more probable than the Form-critical assumption of a 'common stock' of gospel stories (derived from whom?) told in the community by anyone but 'eye-witnesses' (*autoptai*, Lk. 1:2) or 'witnesses' (*martyres*, Lk. 11:48, 24:48; Ac. 1:8, 22, 2:32, 3:15, 5:32, 10:39, 41, 13:31, 22:15, 26:16), or than the idea of Luke and his fellow-Christians not asking about Jesus of those who had seen him during his ministry and who still survived. If the suggestion is accepted that Luke had in mind a first draft of gospel material corresponding to a new Dt., he would have selected suitable stories which he heard probably in Palestine to fill out the Q sayings at his disposal. This would have been about the time of Paul's last visit to Jerusalem, *c.* A.D. 55–8. Easton (*Commentary on Luke*, 29) and others have noted that a cycle of L material overlaps similar material in the 4th Gospel; some of the stories may have been drawn from Judaean sources, probably some at least from Christian women. It is characteristic of Lk. to select stories to show what the Faith has done for women and vice versa.

656c PASSAGES OF LUKE ASSIGNED TO L

Passage	Subject	Passage	Subject
1:5–2:52	Infancy narratives	13:31–3	Departure from Herod and Galilee
3:10–14	Teaching of John the Baptist	14:1–6	The man with dropsy healed
3:23–38	The genealogy of Christ	14:7–14	Teaching on humility
4:16–30	Christ's rejection at Nazareth	14:28–33	On counting the cost
5:1–11	Draught of fishes and Simon's call	15:1–32	Parables of the lost sheep, the lost coin and the lost (prodigal) son
5:39	Old and new wine (but cf. the variant reading of Mk 2:22)	16:1–13	The shrewd steward
7:11–17	Raising of the widow's son at Nain	16:14f., 19–31	Misuse of wealth and Dives and Lazarus
7:36–50	The woman who was a sinner	17:7–10	The servant's wages
8:1–3	The ministering women	17:11–19	Healing of ten lepers
9:51–6	Rejection in the Samaritan villages	17:20f.	Kingdom of God (but cf. Mk 13:21)
10:1	Mission of the seventy(-two)	18:1–8	The importunate widow and unjust judge
10:17–20	Their return	18:9–14	The Pharisee and the publican
10:25–8	The lawyer's question (but cf. Mk 12:28–31)	19:1–10	Zacchaeus
10:29–37	The good Samaritan	19:11–27	Parable of the pounds (but cf. Mt. 25:14–30, the parable of the talents)
10:38–42	Martha and Mary	19:37–40	Entry into Jerusalem (cf. Mk 11:9f.)
11:1–8	Teaching on prayer (but cf. Mt. 6:9–13)	19:41–4	Lamentation over the city
11:27f.	Blessedness of the Mother of Christ	20:18	The strength of the stone
11:37–41, 53–4, 12:1	Inward as against outward purity	21:5–36	The Apocalyptic discourse (cf. C. H. Dodd, *Journal of Roman Studies* 37 (1947), 47–54); cf. Mk 13
12:13–21	Parable of the rich fool		
12:35–8	On watchfulness (but cf. Mt. 25:1ff.)		
13:1–9	Call to repentance		
13:10–17	The woman with a spirit of infirmity healed		

7a MATTER PECULIAR TO MT., M

1:1–2:23	Infancy stories
3:14f.	Reason for the Baptism
4:13–6	Fulfilment of Isa. 9:1f.
5:1, 5, 7–10, 14, 16f., 19–24, 27f., 31, 33–7, 38–9*a*, 41, 43; 6:1–4, 5–8, 10*b*, 13*b*, 16–18, 34; 7:6, 12*b*, 15, 19f., 22	Passages in Mt.'s Sermon on the Mount, some of it editorial but much of it from reliable sources, if not from Q from which Lk. has omitted it
8:17	Fulfilment of Isa. 53:4
9:13*a*	Fulfilment of Hos. 6:6
9:27–31	The healing of two blind men (cf. Mk 10:46ff.)
9:32–6	The healing of the dumb demoniac, and preface to the Mission of the Twelve
10:5*b*	Command to go to the House of Israel
10:8*b*, 16*b*, 23, 25, 36, 41	Sayings chiefly of a missionary character
11:1	? editorial
11:14f.	(cf. Mk 9:13)
11:20	? editorial
11:28–30	The invitation to the heavy-laden (cf. Sir. 51:23–7)
12:5–7	Probably three sayings of Jesus spoken at different times, here expanding the story of the plucking of corn
12:17–21	Fulfilment of Isa. 42:1–4
12:36f.	Judgment on idle words
12:40	(cf. Lk. 11:30)
13:24ff., 44, 45f., 47ff., 51f.	Parables of the tares, hidden treasure, pearl of great price, draw-net, with an ending (to a parabolic source ?)
14:28–31	Peter on the water
14:33	(cf. Mk 6:51*b*)
15:12–14*a*	The Pharisees and the blind
15:23f.	Pro-Jewish-Christian expansion of the story of the Syro-Phoenician woman
16:12	Explanatory note about the 'leaven'
16:17–19	Probably three separate sayings attributed to Jesus, bearing on Peter and inserted here to expand the commission to him (cf. on 12:5–7)
17:6f.	Expansion of Mk's story of the Transfiguration
17:13	Explanatory note about 'Elijah'
17:24–7	The coin in the fish's mouth, which reads like Jewish-Christian Midrash
18:4	(but cf. Lk. 14:11, 18:14)
18:10	Introduction to the story of the lost sheep (cf. 18:14, a conclusion to it)
18:16–20	Expansion of the duties to fellow-Christians
18:23–35	Parable of the unforgiving servant, no doubt authentic
20:1–16	Parable of the labourers in the vineyard, also authentic
21:10*b*f.	Introduction to the story of Christ in the Temple
21:14–16	Healings in the Temple and the fulfilment of Ps. 8:3
21:28–32	Parable of the two sons, no doubt authentic
21:43	Explanatory note
22:6f.	A late addition to the parable of the wedding-feast, and 22:11–14, the parable of the wedding-garment, probably a different parable, the beginning of which is lost, that Mt. has conflated awkwardly
23:2f., 5; 23:7*b*–10; 23:15–22; 23:27*b*–28; 23:32f.	An expansion of the woes against scribes and Pharisees (but for 33 cf. Lk. 3:7)
24:10–12	Three sayings, probably originally separate, serving here to expand the beginnings of the Messianic woes
24:14*b*	A conclusion to a section or lection
24:20*b*	'Flight . . . on the sabbath', a Jewish-Christian addition
24:30*a*	An expansion based on Dan. 7:13
25:1–13	Parable of the ten virgins, probably authentic
25:31–46	The picture of the last assize, no doubt authentic also
26:1	Introductory to the Passion narrative
26:25	A secondary addition to show that Jesus knew the betrayer (cf. Lk. 22:23, which seems more primitive)
26:50	(cf. Lk. 22:48)
26:52*b*–54	(cf. Rev. 13:10)
27:3–10	Death of Judas and fulfilment of Zech. 11:12 (cf. Ac. 1:15ff.)
27:19, 24f., 62–6 and 28:11–15	A cycle of Christian Midrashic stories about Pilate, much of which may be secondary
27:43	A fulfilment of Ps. 22:9
27:51*b*–53	Portents at Jesus' death, also Midrashic in character
28:2–4	The earthquake and the angel at the tomb, possibly three originally separate phrases, the second of which may have at one time referred to Christ, brought together here by Mt. to expand the story of the Resurrection (cf. on 12:5–7, 16:17–19 above)
28:11–15	The bribing of the soldiers, which may be secondary material
28:16–20	The command to baptise

7b The summary of M material serves to show its lack of homogeneity. While some passages, especially the parables, are reliable, one cannot be so sure of all the OT fulfilments and Midrashic expansions, nor of the verses interpolated probably from separate sources into the Marcan context. Streeter thought that the Infancy stories, that of the coin in the fish's mouth and those inserted into the Passion story belonged to a cycle of oral tradition at Antioch.

Both the M material and Mt.'s way of handling Mk have raised the question why Mt.'s Gospel was needed in the Church. Some have found in it a work in the production of which contemporary liturgical custom was an important element, notably Dr G. D. Kilpatrick. Though a liturgical exposition provides many fresh insights, the view of K. Stendhal (*The School of St Matthew*) is more valuable; he rejects both the liturgical interpretation and the Form-critical view of Dibelius that 'in the beginning was the sermon'. A Matthean school is a more natural *Sitz im Leben* (setting in life) for 'a systematising work, an adaptation towards casuistry instead of broad statements of principles, the reflection on the position of church leaders and their duties, and many other similar 657b

657b features which all point to a milieu of study and instruction.' Against Dibelius he makes the good point that many elements in Mt. could not be preached! Not only does the idea of a 'school' agree with what is known of synagogue practice and of much that may be assumed of Jesus as a Rabbi with his disciples, but Stendhal can cite the evidence of the Qumrân scrolls, especially the Manual of Discipline with its outline of the doctrine and discipline of a Jewish sect and the Commentary on Habakkuk for its exposition of the OT. In this light Mt. seems the product of a school for teachers and church leaders, representing a manual for teaching and for administration in the church. Noting that the OT citations in M are freer than those where Mt. is based on Mk, he compares the *midrash pesher* of the Qumrân sect, in which the basis of the rules lay in the supposed fulfilment of the prophecy rather than in the OT texts themselves. It may be that the 'secondary' elements in M were derived from a school and that in such a school of Mt. or some other church leader that change of emphasis in Jesus' teaching was effected to which J. Jeremias has drawn attention in his work on the parables. In any case, Streeter's contention still stands that the Judaistic tendency of M is pronounced, and that the Judaistic sayings peculiar to Mt. did not occur originally in Q and were not there to be omitted by Lk. owing to his pro-Gentile tendencies.

658a (6). Synoptic criticism since the 1930s has tended in one of two directions, either (*a*) towards further analysis of the **possible sources** of the Gospels or (*b*) towards the treatment of each Gospel as a whole, the work of a theologian rather than a compiler, with perhaps a **pattern or cycle of patterns** to be discerned in his work by those with eyes to see.

(*a*) If Q existed, was Q one of the sources of Mk? Or were they independent overlapping traditions? Either view is more plausible than that Q depended on Mk (Wellhausen's view). An examination of the non-Marcan contacts between Mt. and Lk. with any typical section of Mk where all three overlap raises the problem why, if Mk knew Q, he did not use it more; the omission of the more missionary sayings of Q is especially surprising. It seems that Mk may have written for a church, probably that at Rome, which knew a version of Q, but that he assumed a knowledge of it and wrote almost independently; cf. T. E. F. Honey, JBL 62 (1943), 319–31, and B. H. Throckmorton, ibid. 67 (1948), 319–29.

The present writer suggested (McNeile, INT, 56ff.) that sources may be seen in Mk, including, as Dr Dodd suggested, a summary outline of Christ's life, traces of which are found in Mk 1:14f., 21f., 39; 2:13; 3:7*b*–19; 6:7, 12f. and 30 (ET 43 (1931), 396–400); this point has been challenged by Professor D. Nineham (op. cit. 223ff.) in a comment on the appeal to the 'outlines' of the ministry in Ac. 10 and 13. The dilemma is proposed: either the apostles themselves used a formal and traditional outline, which is unlikely, or the outlines in Ac. were invented by Lk., in which case the evidence for independent tradition disappears. But, as Professor Moule has urged, 'Who ever said that the apostles used a formal and traditional outline? The point is simply that if the Ac. outline was really apostolic (and such as therefore eventually became traditional) then it is probably authentic' (JTS, N.S. 7 (1956), 281f.).

Again, C. H. Turner's theory of a Petrine source is challenged only by those who maintain the improbable view that the apostles and other eye-witnesses had little or no influence on the evangelists. The Petrine source included probably Mk 1:16–39; 2:1–14; 3:13–19; 4:35–5:43; 6:7–13, 30–56; 8:14–9:48; 10:32–52; 11:1–33; 13:3–4, 32–7; 14:17–50, 53f., 66–72. In all these passages Peter's original 'we' has become 'they'. Peter and the other apostles are not spared by Mk and the vividness of the narratives points to an eye-witness as the source. There may be also a cycle of conflict-stories, 2:15–3:6 and 12:13–27 and a collection of parabolic material, 4:1–34. Again, a complete 65
cycle of stories in 6:31–7:37 is duplicated by another similar cycle in 8:1–26.

In *The Sources of the Synoptic Gospels*, i, St Mark, edited by H. Chadwick (1953), W. L. Knox studied the compilations of sources probably underlying Mk and other synoptic strata and he believed it possible to identify not only the conflict-stories, 1:40–3:6, as a source and a 'book of parables', 4:1–34, but also a 'Twelve-source' which was 'mainly a summary with one or two incidents showing Jesus' dealings with the Twelve and a Passion story'; the death of John the Baptist, 6:16–29; the Corban story, 7:1–23; a 'book' of localised miracles, 7:32–7, 8:22–6 and 10:46–52; a denunciation of the Pharisees preserved in Lk. 11:37–52 and Mt. 23:1–6, cf. Mk 12:37*b*–40 which with some genuine material was the basis of this source; the Marcan apocalypse, Mk 13, though this may have been compiled out of smaller units; and a Passion story independent of the Twelve-source. Though anyone but a Form critic would welcome such an attempt to cut down by about thirty years the supposed interval between the events of the Gospel and their first appearance in writing, confidence in the 'sources' suggested is shaken by the repetition of Meyer's 'Twelve-source' as against a 'Disciples-source', though C. H. Turner had proved such a distinction improbable, if not impossible (JTS 28 (1927), 22ff.). After a minute analysis of Marcan usage, Turner concluded that Mk represents a natural development in the ministry of Jesus by which he restricted his teaching gradually to a few chosen followers and that the disciples chosen to receive this later teaching are described indifferently as the Twelve or the disciples. Again, the modern tendency in regard to Mk 13 is to treat it as a whole and as an integral part of the entire Gospel (cf. G. R. Beasley Murray, *Jesus and the Future* (1954), 146).

(*b*) The other tendency to follow up and, in part, b
to revolt from Form criticism takes us beyond the limits of the Synoptic Problem.

For example, Dr P. Carrington (*The Primitive Christian Calendar* (1952) has discerned a 'proto-Mk' (and a 'proto-Mt.') in use as a lectionary for Sundays of the Jewish lunar year, Mark composing paragraphs for each Sunday and taking the Hebrew ritual and agricultural year as his basis. A mystical interpretation of the seed-parables and some (slight) evidence from chapter enumerations in ancient MSS are cited in support; this theory has met with severe criticism from Dr R. P. Casey, *Theology* 55 (1952), 362–70, and Dr A. M. Farrer (CQR 153 (1952), 501–8), though it is a better theory at least than the Form-critical one that Mk was composed for lectionary reading by prisoners-of-war, as it were, behind bars cut off from home (i.e. apostles and other eye-witnesses). Dr Farrer himself (*A Study in St Mark* (1951); 'Loaves and Thousands', JTS, N.S. 4 (1953), 1–14; *St Matthew and St Mark* (1954)) has taken the concept of 'pattern' from the anthropologists and Gestalt psychologists and has followed the trend apparent in modern studies in English literature to 'make sense of what you have' in place of speculating on an author's sources and to discern in a literary work, taken as a whole, images 'considered as symbols whose recurrent use creates patterns of meaning through which we apprehend the real content of the work and the prime and dominant concerns of the writer' (H. Gardner, *The Limits of Literary Criticism* (1956), 18). Arguments based on number-symbolism are also employed to elucidate the eisegesis. Attractive and stimulating as this method of approach is, confidence in it is undermined by a number of retractations of earlier statements made by Dr Farrer and by serious weaknesses in it (cf. H. Gardner, op. cit. 20–39; S. H. Hooke, CQR 154 (1953), 44–52, and R. P. Casey, op. cit. 369f.). There are limits to what typology can prove, as G. W. H. Lampe and K. J. Woollcombe have shown ('Essays on Typology', *Studies in Biblical Theology* 22 (1957)).

658b As Miss Gardner says, 'This method does nothing to illuminate, and indeed evaporates, St Mark's sense of what we mean by historical reality . . . I cannot feel satisfied with a literary criticism which substitutes for the conception of the writer as a "man speaking to men", the conception of the writer as an imagination weaving symbolic patterns to be teased out by the intellect.'

c Yet what if there was indeed one source at least beneath the second half of Mk? There may have been a pattern of exposition dependent on a pattern of events and their interpretation, summed up in the words, 'Jesus died to open the Kingdom of heaven to all believers'. M. Kiddle (JTS 35 (1934), 45ff.) went far to proving that by putting Jesus to death the Jews excluded themselves from God's plans and that by that death the Gentiles were given access to the Kingdom. If so, the pattern of exposition in Mk 11–end followed the pattern of events and their interpretation made almost certainly by Jesus himself, not by the evangelist nor by the 'community behind the evangelist' for neither of these would have had the originality or the temerity to rivet such a pattern on to the gospel story. The OT studies of J. F. H. Gunkel and the sociological works of E. Durkheim have led many in the last forty years to treat the primitive community as a closed system with inherent laws of its own being; we need to remind ourselves that even if the Gospels are primarily theological rather than biographical documents, it was the Gospel which created the Church, not vice versa, and that much of real historical value underlies the written or oral sources of the Synoptic Gospels because they are dependent on the Apostles and eye-witnesses of the ministry of Jesus. 658c

Bibliography—B. C. Butler, *The Originality of St Matthew* (1951); F. C. Grant, *The Growth of the Gospels* (1933); A. von Harnack, *The Sayings of Jesus*, tr. by J. R. Wilkinson (1908); Sir John Hawkins, *Horae Synopticae* (1899); W. L. Knox, *The Sources of the Synoptic Gospels*, ed. H. Chadwick, i (1953), ii (1957); D. E. Nineham (ed.), *Studies in the Gospels* (1955); A. M. Perry, *The Sources of Luke's Passion Narrative* (1920); V. H. Stanton, *The Gospels as Historical Documents* (1909); B. H. Streeter, *The Four Gospels* (4th ed. 1930).

THE THEOLOGY OF THE NEW TESTAMENT

By JOHN MARSH

659a **The Importance of the NT for Theology**—However much Christians differ among themselves as to the relative importance of scripture, the Church, and the testimony of the Holy Spirit for the task of formulating a Christian theology, they will at least agree in asserting that any work of theology inconsistent with or contradictory of the NT, however theological it be, cannot be reckoned as a work of Christian theology. This means that the NT is more than the common possession of the various Christian churches ; it is, in some way not easy to define, a common norm. It stands for all Christians as the diet of their devotions, the ideal of their conduct, and, most significantly for our present purposes, as the supreme fountain and test of Christian theology.

b Christian theology is distinguished from all other theologies by one unparalleled feature. From the metaphysical systems of Aquinas and the schoolmen on the one hand to the exclusively scriptural position of Calvin on the other there is a consensus of opinion that the distinctively Christian assertions made by Christian theology can be made only because certain things have happened, things to which the NT is the only adequate witness. The NT witness is to Jesus Christ, and it is in the NT alone that we gather fruitful data for a theology deriving from him. Secular writers mention his historical existence and refer to his death ; apocryphal authors relate marvels and wonders more magical than religious ; only in the NT are we given information about him which can generate the profound truths of Christian theology and sustain the faith of the simple believer alike in prosperity and adversity, in life and death.

c But it is only an approximation to the truth to say that the NT contains the story of Jesus Christ, and the Christian theologian reflects on the story and elaborates his metaphysics and his doctrine. For one thing, the NT contains much more than narrative (five only of its twenty-seven books can be reckoned as narrative, and even they not without important qualifications) ; and for another, even its admittedly narrative parts are not without some important theological formulations. Further, in the non-narrative parts of the NT we learn some facts about the earthly life of Jesus of Nazareth which are not recorded elsewhere. Yet it would be a most grave error to suppose that it is the earthly life of Jesus of Nazareth to which the NT as a whole, or in its several parts, bears witness. Rather must it be read in each and all its parts as witnessing to him who is the Word made flesh, Jesus Christ, the same yesterday, today and for ever, Son of God, son of Mary, God and man, Saviour of the world. We may rightly apply to the whole of the NT what the author of the Fourth Gospel wrote of his own work (knowing, as we suppose, the portrait of Jesus as given in at least Mk and Lk.), ' These are written that you may believe that Jesus is the Christ, the Son of God, and that believing you may have life in his name ' (Jn 20:31).

d When this is understood it can be asserted, with some approximation to the truth, that the NT ' tells a story ' and that the theologian draws out and 65
systematises the truths contained in, or implied by, the story. It relates the birth of Jesus, the Christ, his life, ministry, passion, death, resurrection and ascension ; it recounts the outpouring of the spirit on the Church, tells of Christ's dealing with the Church which is his body, and anticipates a final appearance of the saviour. It is only when this story has thus been fully told that the theologian can properly ask what truths it implies about God, about Jesus Christ, about the Holy Spirit ; about the Church, the Ministry and the Sacraments ; about man and the universe in which he lives ; about time and history and the eternity that lies beyond.

The NT ' tells a story ' ; the theologian expounds e
those truths about God, man and the universe which must be true if the story be told. The task of NT theology is thus exegetical rather than purely speculative or dogmatic ; and exegetical in a double sense : first, in that the doctrines about God, man and the world which it propounds must be such as follow from, and in turn explicate, the story that is told ; and second, in that it must take into full account the significance of the theological forms in which the NT story is itself cast. The NT writers made use of the rich and profound theology of the OT, and of the forms in which it was cast, in order to portray, in the very way their story was told, not only that certain events took place, but that in taking place they possessed a specific theological significance to which the OT forms and stories were, in their view, a divinely appointed anticipatory type.

In the article on the Theology of the OT (§§121*d–f*) f
the author has spoken of the dominant position occupied in the ' kerygma ' of the OT by that complex of historical events which are commonly referred to as ' The Exodus '. He has indicated how that event assimilated other historical traditions into itself, and how finally it became the point from which the doctrine of God as creator of heaven and earth was affirmed, and the basis also for the confident hope that beyond any fulfilment of itself in any historical occasion, it would be the clue to the meaning and the recognition of what God would finally do with his world (cf. §§121*d*, 126*h*, 128*g*). It is in this context of meaning that the NT must be read and understood, if we are to recapture for ourselves the theological assertions that its writers thought themselves to be making. For in the NT we must note two things : first, that, as in the OT, there is one central event, or rather complex of events, which assimilates other historical traditions to itself, which generates both a new doctrine of creation, and a new anticipation of the ' end of the world ' ; and second, that this is not merely placed alongside or offered instead of the Exodus story, but, on the contrary, is deliberately related to it as both fulfilling and transcending it.

But such indication of theological meaning by the g
application of OT persons and happenings to parts of the NT story is not confined to the use of the ' Exodus '. Many figures are taken (e.g. Moses,

659g Elijah, David, Jonah) to articulate meaning into the NT narrative, and many incidents are recorded which, though apparently superficial (e.g. the statement in Mk 1:6 that 'John was clothed with camel's hair, and had a leather girdle around his waist'—see below, §662*a*), are to a mind sensitive to OT allusions, rich in theological meaning. Moreover, just as in the OT the central event is used in the description of other historical situations (e.g. the crossing of the Jordan, Jos. 3:16), so the central event of the NT is used in the history of the early Church, thereby asserting it to have a certain theological significance. So one of the chief tasks of NT theology is to remain constantly alert to the OT 'overtones' of the NT text, to consider how much positive meaning is indicated by each OT allusion, and to what extent the OT reference must be understood as pointing to something that transcends it.

h This task needs to be done, though it must be done somewhat differently, for the non-narrative as well as for the narrative sections of the NT. But it must be done alongside other similar tasks, for it was not the OT alone which gave possibilities of understanding the NT to its first readers. Many NT terms (such as 'kyrios') had Hellenistic as well as OT overtones; and a number of NT stories (e.g. the Magi) have parallels in literature other than the OT. Nevertheless it remains true that the basic, and by far the most important, instrument for interpreting the NT is the OT. Other instruments may be helpful; this alone is indispensable. Jesus himself was a member of the OT 'Church' and first learnt, and then taught, about God in OT terms; the high probability is that OT words and thoughts lie behind every book of the NT; and the Christian Church considered itself to be the true successor, as the New Israel, or the Israel of God, to the people of God in the OT, or Israel after the flesh.

660a In §121*f* the author writes, 'Both Testaments then, have a *kerygma*, a proclamation of the acts of God. In the case of both we are faced with the ultimate question of the truth of the *kerygma* proclaimed. Two questions are in fact involved, the question of the accuracy of the events of history recorded and the question of the relation between these events and the alleged complicity of God in them.' It is important always to be clear which of these two questions is being asked, and in regard to which of them any arguments or evidence produced is advanced. For to establish one answer is by no means to establish the other; nor does failure to establish one itself imply failure to establish the other. We might, for example, find incontrovertible evidence that the events at the Red Sea as described in the J sections of Exod. took place as there stated; but that would not at the same time prove that God was complicit in them. We might, on the contrary, reach the point of having to confess that, so far as we could tell, we should never know 'what actually happened' on the night that Moses led some Hebrews out of Egypt, but that would not debar us from believing it to be true that on that night a great work of God was done, in actually bringing into existence a community of people that has had a continuous existence ever since as the 'People of God'.

b **We can distinguish four stages** in the development of the events that we refer to as the Exodus from Egypt. **The first stage** is the actual historical occasion, and while we rightly believe ourselves to have some data for recovering, to a certain extent, a true idea of 'what really happened', we have to confess that we cannot now, with present evidence, recover the event accurately in all details. **The second stage** is the literary report of the 'Exodus', which, by common consent, we can identify in what has become known as the J strand in the narrative of Exod. We need to remember, even here, that the story of the wonder at the Red Sea is preserved for us only because it had already, by the time of the production of the J record, established itself in the folk-memory of a people worshipping Yahweh, as the definitive story of their origin as his people. In this form of the story we are told (Exod. 14:21) that 'the Lord drove the sea back by a strong east wind all night, and made the sea dry land, and the waters were divided.' **The third stage** is the later modification of the story, found in the later literary strands of the Pentateuch, in this instance in P, where, in a context of misgiving on the part of the people, the Lord tells Moses: 'Lift up your rod, and stretch out your hand over the sea and divide it' (Exod. 14:16). Moses obeyed, and the report of his action immediately precedes the portion from J already quoted. This 'addition' in the later version of the story is not merely an illustration of the 'heightening of the miraculous element' so often traceable in the history of folk-tales; it is also, and much more characteristically, an attempt to make it unavoidably plain that it was Yahweh, and not the fortuitous blowing of the wind, that effected Israel's deliverance from Pharaoh and his army. Thus a common literary device is made to serve a profound and specific theological purpose. **The fourth stage** in the development of the Exodus motif in the OT is when it is used either as a means of interpreting other past events, as it is in recounting the crossing of the Jordan (Jos. 3:7–17), or as a means of discerning and foretelling the shape of future events, as when a later prophet used the Exodus imagery to embody his anticipation of a return to Palestine from Babylon (e.g. Isa. 43:14–21). In this use of the Exodus the significant thing, even for the original writer, is not the precise physical affinities that the use of the imagery may seem to assert (after all, a prophet of the Exile would know how physically different the route from Babylon to Jerusalem was from that going from Egypt to Palestine!), but the theological fact of the act of God to deliver, and in some sense thus to constitute or reconstitute his people.

c By the time that our earliest present literary references to the events of the Exodus were written down, that occasion had already become the focal point of the story of God's bringing his people into historical existence. But these earliest references are, as our present evidence suggests, separated by something like 300–500 years from the historical occasions they recount. The biblical story is ineradicably theological, it was meant to say not only that Israel escaped from Egypt, not only that God acted in a certain way on that night, but, even more, that what God did on that occasion can be properly understood only in the light of what had been done before, and of what was done afterwards, and was still to follow. The Exodus, that is to say, became part of the history of the people of God, and the *crux interpretationis* of that history. But while the story of the Exodus could thus serve to quicken and sustain the faith of Old and New Israel alike, it is by its very nature an embarrassment to the inquirer who wants to know 'what exactly took place'. It is of no avail to answer such an inquirer with the biblical answer that, whatever may appear now to be 'reporters' inaccuracies', the theological assertion made by the story as it stands is absolutely true—God did act, and by his action create, call and consecrate a people to himself. There is no simple way to avoid or overcome the inquirer's embarrassment. The story is in a form that was designed, not to tell us 'what exactly took place' in the inquirer's sense, but to bear witness that God was complicit in the event of the Exodus, which remains for all time a norm of divine saving action in history. In one sense of the words, then, we cannot now recover 'what exactly took place' and so satisfy man's historical curiosity; in another sense we may be said to know by the witness of the OT narrative, 'what exactly took place', i.e. that God called, constituted and consecrated his people in a miraculous deliverance on that night, and this can satisfy the man of faith.

d These considerations are not irrelevant when we

660d come to consider the narrative of the NT. For in spite of the fact that the latest of the NT writings is vastly nearer the events of the life of Jesus and that the earliest documents may go back to within a decade or two of his death, the fundamental problem of the relationship of historical to theological statement remains. The NT no more wants to tell us 'what exactly took place' in the historical inquirer's sense than the OT does ; that is plain from the use of the Exodus and other OT elements in providing the narrative form for many NT events. To use the necessary and fruitful distinction made by Luther, the NT does not seek to impart 'history-knowledge', but 'faith-knowledge' ; though we must be quick to add that the faith-knowledge is about God's actions in history. But even this distinction must not be overstated, for we must not separate the realms of faith and history, either as if the 'history' which is the object of Christian concern could be a different history from that which is the concern of the historian as such, or as if the alleged complicity of God could be known without the event in which he was complicit having taken place. Christianity must needs insist that the history which is the core of its gospel ('good news'), and in the end, all history, is not only a succession of occasions in a space-time continuum, but a whole which finds its abiding significance through the complicity in the events of the continuum of a God who transcends it ; and that the knowledge of the divine acts which give meaning to the Christian core and the whole of history alike cannot be known other than as ingredient in actual historical occasions.

e This can—and should—be illustrated by **what Christians have come to know as the Resurrection.** Those are equally wrong who think that the only point about which satisfaction is required is what we may call the sheer physical fact of the resumed life of Jesus after a well-attested death upon the cross. Neither the mere possession of accurate information about the resurrection as an event in human history, nor even the mere occurrence of that event itself, will save the soul of a single hearer. As Luke put it at the end of the story of Dives and Lazarus : 'If they do not hear Moses and the prophets, neither will they be convinced if some one should rise from the dead' (Lk. 16:31). A miracle of that kind, unrelated to anything else, can produce no real convictions. On the other hand Christian hope of immortality is vastly different from a belief in 'survival' or in the 'immortality of the soul'—beliefs which can be held on psychical, psychological and metaphysical grounds. The Christian anticipates more than that his soul will survive his body, or that it will prove to be 'immortal' ; his hope is that he will be 'with Christ in God', and the assurance of that hope is derived from the actual resurrection of Christ from the dead, not as one isolated individual, but as the 'first fruits' of those who have fallen asleep, as the representative, indeed, of a new humanity (cf. 1 C. 15:20–2). Thus, while Christians cannot say 'exactly what happened' when, 'on the third day' he rose from the dead, it is of the utmost importance for them that the historicity of the resurrection be established. There is perhaps no more reliable and remarkable evidence than the fact that the first witness to it whose testimony still survives is the apostle Paul. At the time of the crucifixion Paul was a most zealous Pharisee (Ac. 22:3, 26:4, 5 ; Gal. 1:14) who, within a few years of Christ's death, was known as a determined and enthusiastic persecutor of the infant Church (Ac. 8:3, 9:1, 22:4, 5, 26:9–11 ; 1 C. 15:9). It is clear from Festus' remark to King Agrippa that the recognised difference between Jews and Christians turned upon the truth or falsity of the Christian view that Jesus, who had died, was alive (Ac. 25:19). So Saul the Pharisee would have been aware of all the Jewish arguments for denying the Christian assertion ; yet, in spite of that knowledge, he is the first extant witness to the fact of the resurrection : 'he was raised on the third day in accordance with the scriptures'. That is to say, the whole story of Israel-after-the-flesh as we have it in the OT cannot be rightly understood save as leading up to, and being fulfilled in the resurrection of Jesus Christ, nor can that astounding event be understood as anything but meaningless marvel unless it be viewed as the crown and substance of the whole life of the people of God. 66

There is a sense in which it is wrong to speak of the theology of the NT. The NT does not stand on its own ; it did not fall from heaven ready written, as some other scriptures claim to have done. It belongs to the Church, and the theology it contains, implicit or explicit, is the theology of the Church. The NT took shape both as a canon of scripture, and as individual books because the Church wished to make plain, first to itself, and later to the world, what her life consisted in and how it was to be experienced and understood. This has enabled a number of theories to be advanced about **the origin of the Gospels and Epistles :** the Gospels have been seen as originating in the preaching of the Church, in its eucharistic worship, in its evangelism and its conflicts with Gentiles and Jews ; the Epistles have also been traced to a variety of origins. The truth is probably that in many ways, some realised at the time, and others not envisaged until afterwards, the various books were written and the canon of scripture formed so that the many-sided but unitary life of the Church should be seen in its true perspective and full depth. No part of the Church's life, the NT seems to say, may be properly experienced at a superficial level. The 'biography' of the founder was not simply a tale from human history and no more ; it was a story told to reveal the wonderful work of the incarnate Son of God as the saviour of the world. The preaching of the gospel was not simply a moralist's exhortation to virtue in this life ; it was the proclamation in faith of a divine fulfilment of all God's dealings with man and his world in the person of Jesus Christ. The worship of the Church was not simply the emergence of a new rite cleverly combining the Temple Passover and the local synagogue in a weekly service faintly tinctured with 'mystery' ; it was a real communion with a present saviour who had died and risen again, mediated by effective symbols and acts. Christian moral vigour was not an early sample of 'puritan' reaction against social decay ; it was, at its best, a conscious and humbling awareness that the reality of Christian virtue lay not in any personal triumph, but in a victory of grace where Christ was the believer's true life. The Church's community was not simply a strong bond between members of a reformist movement ; it was, the Church declared, a transcendent bond between all its members effected by God and for which no other language was adequate than the paradox of Christ being all and in all. He was the body ; all they were members. 66

It is possible, and in some sense necessary, to reduce all NT theology, and even to test all Christian theology, by one word—Christ. Each book of the NT bears witness to him, certainly in its own way, though to the same assertion of Lordship about him. It has been wrong, for example, to think that the Gospels (at any rate the Synoptics) testify to 'the Jesus of history' while other parts of the NT witness to 'the Christ of faith'. Each and all are concerned with a Jesus of history who is the Christ of faith, and with a Christ of faith who is the Jesus of history. Admittedly different theological languages are found within the NT, and the formulations, say, of Hebrews are very different from those of John or Peter or Paul. But in the books that seem most to deal with 'the Jesus of history', viz. the Gospels, the story has been so told as to leave it abundantly plain that the historical person is himself the divine object of faith : and in books like the Epistles and Rev., where there seems little interest in the narration of historical details of Christ's earthly life, it is equally clear that they would b

661b never have been written but for the conviction that the divine Lord to whom they testify had been incarnate in human history and had there effected the work of man's salvation. It is precisely in its testimony to the divine person and work of Christ that the NT writers make statements and narrate stories in such a way that the theologian studying their writings can discover and formulate what their witness to Jesus Christ involves for the whole range of theological inquiry.

c This article is written upon the widely accepted, but still honourably disputable, view that Mk was the first of the canonical gospels to have been written. To take another view would not of itself invalidate the theological comments that will be made, though it would, obviously, entail a somewhat different setting out of the material. We must now pass to an all too brief, but, I trust, not wholly inadequate **theological evaluation of Mark,** and then of the work of the three later evangelists.

662a Mark, or the editor of Mk, has given a sound clue to the purpose of the Gospel in the opening words **'The beginning of the gospel of Jesus Christ, the Son of God'.** The good news concerns a man Jesus, who fulfilled a specific role, Messiah or Christ, in the life of the people of God, and was himself related to God in a unique way as 'Son'. The story of the good news, however, goes back a long time before Christ was born; it can be seen as the fulfilment of hopes that the prophet Malachi had that a divine messenger would come and the Lord suddenly visit his Temple; and it can be seen as the fulfilment of the hopes that Isaiah had in the time of the Exile that a way back to a true life with God would be prepared. Now, says Mk, the 'messenger' and 'preparer' has really come in the person of John the baptiser. Seen in the light of the two OT passages quoted John's ministry is to prepare for the coming of God to his people. This is further borne out by the description of John in terms which once had been sufficient for Ahaziah to recognise as a description of the prophet Elijah (2 Kg. 1:8), and his food is described in terms (Mk 1:6) which make it plain that he is concerned to keep the law (Lev. 11:22) and yet knows himself possessed of special enlightenment to announce a great victory about to be won (1 Sam. 14:24–31). The act of baptising another person was itself quite new and unique. By John's baptism of repentance for the forgiveness of sins in the setting that Mk gives it by association with Malachi, Isaiah and Elijah, we are to understand that it was related in imagery to the crossing of the Red Sea under Moses (the baptism of the 'old Israel', cf. 1 C. 10:1, 2), and that John was calling his people to repent of their past, to confess their sins, to be baptised, i.e. enter a new Israel, because he was profoundly convinced that there was about to come among them one who would give the reality of which his (John's) baptism was still only a symbol.

b Jesus came from Nazareth and was **baptised by John,** thus indicating his self-identification with his own people (it is often forgotten by theologians that becoming a man means becoming a member of a particular race and nation!) and his repentance with and for them. When he came out of the water (in the imagery of the Mosaic Exodus, when he came to the place where a new relationship with and service of God could be initiated) he heard a voice from heaven, which said: 'Thou art my beloved son; with thee I am well pleased'. In the Exodus imagery context this means that in Jesus God sees the new beginning of the life of his people (cf. Hos. 11:1, 'When Israel was a child I loved him, and out of Egypt I called my son'). Jesus is, from the beginning of the Gospel, more than a *mere* individual; he is the new people of God, its life and its reality. The 'pleasure' of God is a figure derived from the first of the Servant Songs, and surely indicates that the Life of the new 'Son' or 'people' of God would, like that of the servant in Isaiah, attain its victorious felicity only through suffering and death. 662b

The Temptation is given an emphatic theological significance by its position. Like the old Israel after the Exodus, the new 'Son' is tested in the wilderness, the forty days being some equivalence in imagery for the former forty years. Mk underlines the fact that it was the Spirit which drove Jesus to his temptation, and we are meant to understand this as another sign of his divine difference from Israel after the flesh. But Mk gives a clear sign that what was going on in the baptism and temptation was more than the making of a new Israel; it was the creation of a new humanity. 'He was with the wild beasts' (Mk 1:13) is a contrasting reference to the first Adam, who with the wild beasts lost his proper manhood; but Jesus, the new and, in Luther's term, 'proper' man, did not lose, but kept his divine manhood, so that when in Mk 1:14, 15 we read of his proclamation of the kingdom of God, we are meant to understand that proclamation as deriving, at least in part, from knowledge gained by his victorious though mortally crucial struggle with *the* adversary of both God and man. c

Mk at this point gives what has been called a 'summary' of Christ's teaching. Certainly it is brief; but it is also adequate to the developing theme of the Gospel. After the careful attempt to indicate that in Christ the life of the new Israel had triumphantly begun, that good news is proclaimed as the beginning, not of a series of individual reactions, but of a realm or kingdom of God. What has begun, in Mk's view, is neither the merely individual life of a founder of a new religion, nor the mere beginning of a new society; it is both in one, and the Kingdom is proclaimed because the Christ is there, and the Christ is there since God has acted to re-create his people in his Son. d

Next Mk tells of the calling of four disciples to 'follow' Christ. Even so early in the Gospel this invitation has a more than spatial significance. From the manner of his call it is plain that from the start the disciples were to share in the saving mission of Christ: 'I will make you become fishers of men'. This is but a further development of Mk's theme that the coming of Jesus Christ as the Son of God is at one and the same time a fact about an individual and a fact about a society. The disciples are to share in his 'work'. e

It is only when the life of the new Israel has been thus in principle filled out that Mark records a miracle, or 'sign' of the kingdom's presence. But what took place in the synagogue at Capernaum, at any rate on Mk's showing, was not a detached marvel by an individual thaumaturgist, but a manifestation of the power of the life of the new Son or people of God as it had been established in the new community of Jesus Christ and his 'followers'. The same can be said, *mutatis mutandis*, of all the other events which Mk records as having taken place on the first Sabbath of the new community which has been happily called 'The Day of the Lord'. f

Before another day begins for the Lord himself, he seeks a desert place for early prayer, 'a great while before day' (Mk 1:35). His 'proper manhood', preserved in spite of the devil's temptation, was not something to be 'taken for granted', but like all true personality, human or divine, exists and persists only in communion. That fact receives its appropriate recognition when Jesus was asked to stay with those he had already helped; he proposed instead to expand the area of his work—to widen the area of the divine communion (Mk 1:38). g

The story of the healing of the leper (Mk 1:40–5) tells how an excluded member of the people of God was restored to its society (cf. v. 44). The Messiah came to gather together in one the scattered people of God (Jn 11:52). It serves also to show that from the beginning of the ministry Jesus realised the importance of establishing the communion of the new h

662h Israel in its proper divine reality. The injunction to silence is not simply the preservation of a secret, but rather an attempt to obviate any attempt being made to exploit his miraculous powers for less than their proper end. The leper did not keep silence, and the consequent publicity given to his thaumaturgical power was such as to restrict the journeyings of Jesus to uninhabited places for a while.

663a In ch. 2 of Mk we come to the beginning of the so-called 'conflict stories'; and such indeed they are, though there is room for debate as to what part of the conflict took place between the 'historical Jesus' and his Pharisee contemporaries, and what part, if any, must be understood as embodying a later conflict over his person between the Christian Church and the Jews. However that issue be decided, the theological centre of the story as Mk tells it lies in the perception by the Scribes that **Christ's announcement of forgiveness of sins** to the sick man was nothing other than a covert and presumptuous blasphemy. The miracle that Jesus wrought in reaction to their rejection of his implicit claim was certainly marvellous; a paralytic was made to walk. But that healing, miraculous though it was, was but the lesser and physical sign and counterpart of a much greater miracle. For a disabled body to be restored to such health that it could become a normal unit of society was indeed wonderful; but for a diseased spirit, in the grip of sin, to be restored to its proper place and relationships in God's Kingdom—that was something far more wonderful. Jesus knew, John the Baptiser knew, the whole of contemporary Judaism knew, that when the Messiah came to put relationships right between men and God, there would be an abundance of the lesser physical signs serving as evidence of Messiah's presence. This Marcan story of a miracle or sign is thus told on the understanding that the real burden of the opposition to Jesus lay in the Scribes' emphatic rejection of Jesus' implicit but real exercise of a divine authority and nature.

b The two other conflict stories in ch. 2 turn on the same issue of the divine nature of Jesus Christ. In the discussion about fasting Jesus refers to himself as the bridegroom, therewith saying two things: first that he is the 'husband' of the New Israel to whom he is betrothed, as Yahweh was the bridegroom of the Old Israel whom he had taken to wife, and second, that the New Israel was like a betrothed maiden, already established in the relationship of marriage (she could, for example, be divorced) though the actual marriage ceremony and the consummation thereof was still to come (Rev. takes up the theme with its proclamation that 'the marriage of the Lamb has come', Rev. 19:7). In the story of the dispute over plucking ears of grain, Jesus likens himself and his disciples to David and his companions when they were given showbread from the shrine at Nob. He thus likens himself to an anointed king who has not yet assumed his sovereignty, because the present ruler is still in office: he is the new David, the new 'Lord's anointed', who will supersede the present rulers of the nation, and has already been appointed thereto by God. His person, his mission, and the dedication of himself and his disciples to it, are the basis for his being able apparently to contravene a valid regulation.

c In ch. 3 we read (vv. 13–19) of **the appointment of the Twelve**. Two things must be noted as of theological significance: (i) there is little room for doubt that this act was intended to be a manifest sign of the formation and presence of a new Israel, where Jesus had the place of Yahweh and the Twelve took the place of the Patriarchs and/or their tribes. (ii) 'He appointed twelve, to be with him' states more than a spatial fact: they were to be with him by way of a union so close that they would lose themselves to find themselves; and because they were in this way to become part of his very nature, they were to be enabled to do his work: 'to be sent out to preach and have authority to cast out demons' (Mk 3:13).

In ch. 4 we have some illustrations of the teaching of the Messiah, the Son of God, who had come. This activity of the Messiah, like his miracles, forms another testimony to his person. If Dr Dodd is right, as he seems to be, the parable of the sower points 'to the facts of past and present history as showing that the time has come when the gains of the whole process may be realised'. But the parable points to this only because it is uttered by him in whom the realisation is fulfilled. And this is indicated by the comment on the parabolic method to be found in 4:11: 'To you has been given the secret of the Kingdom of God, but for those outside everything is (or rather 'happens': Greek—*γίνεται*; Luther—*widerfahrt*; French—*se passe*) in parables'. That is to say that the parabolic form—a story that can be understood on two planes, the direct, literal, and the metaphorical, cryptic—is itself a 'parable' of the actual life of Jesus Christ. To those who have been called to be with him and follow him the mystery of the Kingdom is revealed, for they know that in his person the king is himself present; but to the 'outsider' it is all a piece of historical happening with none of the revelatory content that the Christian affirms. The gospel story can be told as a piece of history; indeed it must be so told, for it is history. But the gospel story is more than history; it is revelation and saving act of God. Or to put it in other terms, to the Jewish opponent Jesus is a Galilean carpenter turned itinerant evangelist, while to the Christian *the same Jesus* is the incarnate Son of God at his saving work. 663d

In ch. 5 Mk tells the story of how Jesus raised the daughter of Jairus from death. As in other instances when he exercised his miraculous powers he charged those who saw the wonder 'that no one should know' about it (Mk 5:43). We have seen already in the Marcan narrative that the physical miracle is done for the sake of the spiritual, of which it is but a reflection. The strength and wholeness restored to the body of the paralytic is but the reflection of the strength and wholeness restored to the soul by the forgiveness conveyed in Christ's presence and person. So here, the calling back to life from physical death is not intended as the reality of the gift that Jesus brought to Jairus' daughter. His gift of wholeness, made available by his real miracles to some whose sicknesses he cured, is the same reality that is given to the dead maiden as the miraculous work of Christ's power. And it must be clear that one whose writ runs beyond the boundaries of physical, terrestrial existence must himself be a nature of a transcendent reality. e

In ch. 6 the progress of the Twelve in their growing into the nature, work and destiny of their master is carried a stage farther. They are sent out on a mission, equipped, by Christ's endowment, with 'authority over the unclean spirits' (Mk 6:7). When they had completed their tasks, they returned to Jesus (6:30). Their work evidently bore fruit, for thousands came out to follow Christ, even though he was seeking quiet retreat. What is clear, looking back to the past, is that in a lonely place the new leader or shepherd of the pilgrim people of God fed the newly pledged new Israel with miraculous food, as Moses had done before him. What is clear, looking forward to the future, is that the evangelist could not write of that meal (or of the meal with the four thousand) save in manifest eucharistic terms: 'Taking the . . . loaves . . . he looked up to heaven, and blessed, and broke . . . and gave . . .' (Mk 6:41; cf. 8:6). But again, in the eloquent reserve of the evangelist, the difference between the 'new Moses' and the old is significant, though not stridently accented: Moses was not himself the feeder of Israel in the desert, and even though the manna prefigured the eucharist, it was in essence food for the body; but Jesus was himself the feeder of the new Israel in the lonely place, and though the food was for physical satisfaction, its main significance was as the prefiguring of the eucharist 664a

64a where the physical is made so overwhelmingly the vehicle of the spiritual.

b After this 'Last Supper of the Galilean Ministry' and its restatement in a form which speaks of the provision of privilege and sacrament for the Gentile as well as for the Jew. Mk tells us that 'Jesus went on with his disciples to the villages of Caesarea Philippi'. Here he asked for some report on their experiences uring their mission: **'Who do men say that I am?'** (Mk 8:27). They told him of a number of speculations about his identity. He was thought of as 'John the Baptist returned to life', as 'Elijah' or, simply, as 'one of the prophets'. That is to say, the crowds they had addressed looked upon him as a forerunner of the Messiah; he was another, even if the last, figure to appear before the redeemer himself came. But when Jesus asked the disciples for their own answer to the same question, Peter declared: **'You are the Christ'**, thereby confessing that in the view of those within the circle of the disciples a decisive step forward had been taken in the ability to perceive the real character and person of Jesus. In effect Peter says that Jesus is not one of the figures heralding the Messiah, but Messiah himself. Surely Mk is making it quite plain that, however much they still had to learn (and it was much) about the destiny of Messiah, the disciples had not been witnessing the events of his life undiscerningly: to them had been given 'the secret of the kingdom of God' and they had perceived the meaning of the 'parable' which was his life. This granted, it is much less likely that the Lucan and Matthean versions of Peter's confession are theological intrusions, but rather quite sound exegesis of Mk's text, independent of any decision as to what form of words Peter used on the actual historical occasion.

c The confession is followed immediately by teaching about the human and divine destiny of the Messiah confessed and recognised. If Peter's confession may be thought to represent some perception of the first part of the utterance by the heavenly voice which Jesus heard at his baptism, Jesus' teaching may perhaps be taken as his leading the disciples on to the second part, where his own person and destiny is set out in terms of the Servant in the Servant Songs of II Isaiah. Be that as it may, this at least is clear, that after the rebuke to Peter for thinking 'humanly' about the destiny of Messiah, Jesus proceeds to teach disciples and multitudes alike (8:34) that to follow him is to be made a partaker of his destiny as well as of his nature. Messiah himself must be killed; the disciple too must take up his cross, and lose his life in order to find it. And however scholarly opinion may finally judge on the life of the early Church, the point for NT theology remains the same: the disciple shares both his master's nature and destiny.

After six days Jesus took Peter, James and John up a high mountain and was transfigured before them. The fact that some modern scholars have concluded that this incident is really a displaced account of a post-resurrection appearance of the risen Lord is itself a pointer to what was surely an underlying theological concern of the evangelist, viz. to make it quite clear that the person who walked the Galilean ways with his disciples was the same, unchanged person who appeared in his resurrection body after his death and burial. Whatever be the correct view of the origin of the story, its present place in the gospel narrative is tantamount to an assertion that **the Jesus of history was always the glorified Christ of faith,** and that the glorified Christ of faith is none other than the Jesus of history. In narrative form the evangelist is here making an important Christological statement, which can be paralleled by other formulations, in the Prologue to the Fourth Gospel, in the Epistle to the Hebrews, and in the ecumenical creeds of the Church.

The appearance of Moses and Elijah indicates again Mk's understanding of the Person and Work of Jesus as fulfilment. Law and prophecy find their fulfilment in Christ, as do the persons and the functions of Moses and Elijah. 664c

The presence of the three disciples marks a further stage in their growth not only in their understanding of Jesus, but also into his person and destiny. They were afraid, though they wanted to be there (9:5, 6; and the desire to 'be there' was clearly more than geographical!); they heard a voice, which took them to the point at which Jesus stood when he heard a voice at his baptism. The heavenly voice came out of the cloud, which, like the cloud that descended on the tabernacle in the wilderness, signified the presence of God, and on this occasion said: 'This is my beloved Son; listen to him' (9:7). The disciples now have their faith in Jesus as the Son of God confirmed by a voice from heaven; they do not hear any citation from the Servant Songs of II Isaiah. The reason for this is plain—they have already heard the consequence of such citation from the lips of Jesus himself—and they had protested against such a destiny for the Messiah. But now the heavenly voice confirms them in their perception of Jesus as a being on the other side of the line dividing forerunners from Messiah, sons of men from Son of God, and further exhorts them to 'listen to' Jesus, i.e. believe him when he speaks of his tragic destiny as Messiah and Saviour. It is significant that, even though they still do not fully understand (as their actions at the 'Triumphal Entry' show) they never again protest against his prediction of his passion and death. d

Later in the chapter we have a silent but eloquent testimony to the advance into conscious recognition of the solidarity between Jesus and the disciples. John reported that they had seen 'a man casting out demons in *your* name' and had forbidden him to do so (9:38) as he 'was not following *us*'. Jesus replied that he should not be stopped, because anyone working a mighty work 'in *my* name' could not go on to speak evil of him; and then he added: 'For he that is not against *us* is for *us*' (9:40). e

St Mark's narrative of the Passion opens in ch. 11 with the story of what has come to be called **the Triumphal Entry**. The story yields, as scholars observe, a number of historical conclusions (e.g. that Jesus must have been in or near Jerusalem more than Mk 1–10 relates, or he would not have been able to make arrangements for the use of the colt), though its main purpose is to give a theological background to the beginning of the Passion. Mk does not himself mention the passage in Zech. that the incident so quickly calls to mind, but to the ear of an OT student the story must suggest that the prophecy is meant to indicate the meaning of the Entry. Zechariah tells Jerusalem 'Your king comes to you; triumphant and victorious is he, humble and riding on an ass, on a colt the foal of an ass' (Zech. 9:9). This is a prophecy of a victorious messiah-king, but one who, by the sign of riding on an ass (as distinct from a horse, which was the animal of war) was to seek and gain his victory without the use of arms. This is further elaborated in Zech.; 'I will cut off the chariot from Ephraim and the war horse from Jerusalem: and the battle bow shall be cut off, and he shall command peace to the nations; his dominion shall be from sea to sea, and from the river to the ends of the earth.' Jesus is evidently saying by this dramatised claim to fulfilment of a prophecy that, contrary to the hopes of those who want to make him king and to restore a Davidic empire by force of arms, he proposes a peaceful way to his end, though his dominion shall be universal. The action of the disciples invites him to another road to his rule. They act in symbolic imitation of the followers of the fierce Yahwist rebel leader Jehu, who put their garments under Jehu when they proclaimed him king (2 Kg. 9:13). The crowd who spread leafy branches were repeating in hopeful symbol the greeting that Jerusalem gave to Simon Maccabaeus when he entered Jerusalem in triumph in 141 B.C. At the beginning of the last week of his life Jesus was still 665a

665a affirming a messiahship that sought conquest in peace and not by war, while the disciples and the crowds agreed in perceiving his messiahship, though neither group yet appreciated the significance of his own expectations. He sees himself as the anticipated king and Messiah of God's people, on his way to the establishment of his universal and imperishable kingdom.

b However the cursing of the fig tree be related to actual historical occasions it is hard to doubt that the fig tree stands for the old Israel, which had not borne fruit, and which Jesus would have to reject, because it had rejected him. This parable-miracle is therefore rightly interrupted by the story of **the Cleansing of the Temple.** For not only was the act of cleansing in itself an assumption of authority greater than that of its constitutional guardians—the High Priest and the Sanhedrin—but it was also a dramatic proclamation of an universalism upon which post-exilic Judaism had turned its back. The chief priests tried to secure an admission from Jesus that his action was tantamount to an assumption of divine authority (i.e. also nature), but Jesus does not submit to their trap (11:27–33). When he expelled from the Temple those who bought and sold, and overturned the money-changers' tables, he was doing something very different from a simple removal of 'commercialism' from the Temple precincts. Jesus knew as well as any that coin changes were necessary, given the situation as it was. It was precisely that situation which Jesus was radically opposing. Ever since the days of Ezra and Nehemiah post-exilic Judaism had, not without good reason, adopted a policy of estrangement between Jew and Gentile. Certainly pre-exilic Judaism had suffered because of intermarriage between Hebrews and Canaanites. Religion had become syncretistic, politics embarrassed, and national morale had evaporated. The restorers of the Jewish state sought to avoid these evils and forbade intermarriage, and adopted a general anti-Gentile policy. But, as books like Ru. and Jon. show, this was perceived by some as a radical failure in the inescapably universalist mission of the people of the 'God of the whole earth'. In cleansing the Temple Jesus shows himself to be wholeheartedly on the side of the universalists. 'Is it not written, "My house shall be called a house of prayer for all nations"? But you have made it a den of robbers' (11:17). Robbers have treasure. It is stored in their den, and kept there for themselves. Israel had treasure. It was her revealed religion, revealed to her 'for all the nations of the earth', but she had, as it were, stored it in her den, and kept it for herself. The wall that kept the Gentile from access to the inner place of the divinely revealed religion, the temple moneys in Jewish coinage necessary even to purchase a dove for sacrifice turned the house of what should have been a universal temple into the shrine of a nationalist deity. This was a contradiction of the religion God had revealed, and the precise opposite of the universal hope that Jesus had embodied on the previous day in acting to invest his mission with the universalism contained in Zech. No wonder that the authorities sought to kill Jesus after these two points had been made so crystal clear, the (to them) presumptuous claim to authority and a denial of the national policy for the Jewish religion.

c As Mk tells **the story of the last night** that Jesus was with his disciples, it is plain both that he regards the fact of its being the Feast of the Passover as important, and that he lays emphasis on the initiative of Jesus himself (cf. 14:13–16) in precipitating the climax in a context of the Passover and all its associations with the Exodus. This is not the place to engage in a full-scale discussion of the 'eucharistic sayings' of Jesus, but since Jesus would have shared the common beliefs of his people that the prescriptions for the observance of the Passover were given to Moses by God himself, for him to have presumed to make any sort of alteration in the rite was to claim, at least implicitly, a status other than human. Mk's narrative leaves it clear that the coming sacrifice of Jesus (body and blood being a pair of sacrificial terms) would be the occasion for the advent, in a new way, of the Kingdom of God (14:25). When Jesus was arrested and tried before the Sanhedrin the High Priest asked him: 'Are you the Christ, the Son of the Blessed?' (14:61). Jesus answered: 'I am; and you will see the Son of man sitting at the right hand of Power, and coming with the clouds of heaven' (14:62). This quotation from Dan. 7:13, 14 is Jesus' claim that his crucifixion must be understood not as death, but as his going to the Father to receive his universal and imperishable kingdom. 66

d Though the Twelve had been appointed to be with Jesus, the community falls apart during this night, which the Lord set in the terms of Zech. 13:7–9, where beyond the smiting of the Shepherd and the scattering of the flock, some are refined as silver in the fire. Judas betrayed Jesus; Peter denied him; they 'all forsook him, and fled'. They were not with him at the end. The end came in a darkness repeating that of the night of Exodus from Egypt, though by contrast here it is the Son or people of God, the true Israel who was 'smitten'. And even this true Israel was smitten to the point of the nemesis of the Old Israel, viz. in being 'forsaken of God'. This is the ultimate 'disintegration', and nothing short of miracle could possibly reintegrate.

e Here we see the consummate artistry of Mk's narrative of Easter Day, which ends with the words 'they were sore afraid' (16:8). What was the fear of the women, and doubtless of the disciples? It was the fear they had known when, on the way to Jerusalem, he had told them that he must suffer and rise again (10:32). It was the fear of Jairus when his daughter died (5:36). It is the fear they had when he stilled the storm (4:41). It is the fear felt in the presence of death, and of God's power to act even there. Now the women (and the disciples) realise the truth of the prophecies of death and resurrection, and gain a new sense of the demand to 'be with him'; they knew what it meant to take up the cross, that the road to his glory and his kingdom lay through death. His call was more than ever before a demand for total committal. As the gospel ending as the triumph of resurrection becomes known beyond the cross, it is understandable that human hearts should quail in awe at what had been done, and what was being asked of them thereby.

f How we may summarise, then, the basic theological themes of Mk? The Gospel tells the story of the beginning of a new Israel or Son of God in the divine human person of Jesus. It brings the story of the Exodus to provide categories of interpretation to the life and death of Christ. It tells of the proclamation of the Kingdom of God as a present reality, and reports the miracles which are signs of its presence. It recounts how the power of the new Son is adequate to withstand the Adversary, to work effectively beyond what sin and death can do to men; and how, finally, he can defeat the assault of death upon himself. It tells how the Son from the beginning was the centre and the life of a community, of how the community was disintegrated at Christ's death and awed by his resurrection. As a book which is intended to explain the Christian community to itself, it has the seeds of all later theology in it, as it sets the seal upon all that had been wrought hitherto. In the remainder of this article we shall be concerned to see how the basic themes of Mk are expounded in other NT writings.

666a Matthew takes the 'beginning of the gospel' back to Abraham, the great 'father' of all Jews (Mt. 3:9; Jn 8:39). As God once began the life of a people in Abraham, so now he began anew in Christ. A new Israel had come into being, and the divine act by which it began is conveyed in the passive voice of 1:16: 'Joseph the husband of Mary, of whom Jesus was born'. Mt. takes up Mk's Exodus material as

666a the means of expounding the story of the new Israel, and tells of a flight into Egypt (2:13–23) as a prelude to the Marcan 'passage through the Red Sea' and adds a fuller exposition of the 'New Law', in the 'Sermon on the Mount' (5:1–7:28). Mt. adds to the baptismal story a saying which makes it clear that Jesus is not confessing his own sins in seeking baptism by John, but was fulfilling the 'righteousness', the steadfast purpose, of God. Mt. enlarges Mk's temptation narrative by making it clear that the essence of the struggle with the Adversary was on his willingness to believe that he was the Son of God, and not to 'put it to the test' in action or passion or to deny it by worshipping the ruling power of evil. The presentation of the 'New Law' in 5:1–7:28 shows in its antithesis of 'You have heard . . . But I say to you' that **Jesus assumes the place of the divine lawgiver** to the Old Israel. For the failure of men to read the signs of the time he reserves a strong rebuke (16:1–4). Mt. has been charged with adding theology to a simple story in his account of Peter's confession, but he has but given voice to Mk's clear teaching that Jesus is a nature on the other side of the line which distinguishes men from God, as well as a figure on this. Mt. further cites Zechariah's prophecy to give meaning to the 'Triumphal Entry', even modifying the details (two animals instead of one) to ensure that its relevance will not be missed. We hear that Jesus knows that his 'time' had come as he began to prepare for the Passover (26:18 ; cf. Jn 7:6, 8:20, 13:1, etc.). At the time of the crucifixion we read of the appearance of many who had fallen asleep, a statement anticipating the Johannine treatment of Christ's power over death (27:52, 53 ; cf. Jn 5:25, 11:25). By repeating the words of the first temptation on the lips of scoffers at the crucifixion Mt., like Jn, means us to understand that the fundamental crisis of Jesus was the same throughout the ministry. In the account of Easter Mt. tells of an appearance to the disciples, and provides a narrative equivalent to what in Lk. we know as the Ascension ('All authority . . . has been given to me') and the gift of the Spirit ('I am with you alway'), together with a commissioning of the apostles ('Go therefore and make disciples of all nations').

b Lk. also expands and expounds Mk. He takes his genealogy through Abraham back to Adam. Not only a new Israel, but a new manhood has begun in Christ. Like Mt., Lk. makes it plain that the new manhood began by a new creative act of God (to which parthogenesis, however conceived, can only point). Lk. retains the Exodus formulation of the pattern of the ministry, though he gives his new law, as the Pentateuch had given the old, in two recensions. To the appointment of the twelve, symbolic of the new Israel, Lk. adds the appointment of the Seventy (Num. 11:16–25). Lk. can also link beginning and end of the ministry in an identity of meaning. The baptism in Jordan will be fulfilled in the cross (12:50), and it is envisaged, with Mk and Mt., that the disciples will share the tragic destiny that the baptism represents. Lk. in the body of his Gospel continues the basic themes of Mk and at the end is careful to underline the initiative of Jesus in arranging for his death to occur at Passover time (22:7–13). In the narrative of Easter Day Lk. is fuller than Mk or Mt., but emphasises that the eleven and all the rest (24:9) found belief in the resurrection hard. At the end of his Gospel (24:25–7, 44–5) Lk. repeats what he had said of his narrative at the start—that it was to set in order the things that 'had been fulfilled' among us. His last story is of an ascension on what, Ac. 1 apart, we should take for the evening of Easter Day.

c In the perspective of a theological examination of the four Gospels Jn does not appear as the perverse theologiser of an otherwise simple story, but as the one who most clearly and fully expounds what the Church already had in Mk, Mt. and Lk. Hence his selection of typical signs only, hence his concern by varying historiographical means, to show that the 666c essential crisis produced by the incarnation was not simply a matter of one week, but of the whole life and ministry. Jn begins his Gospel with the words from the beginning of Gen. in the Septuagint OT, 'In the beginning . . .', thus indicating not only that Israel and humanity was recreated in Christ, but the whole universe as well. **The 'prologue' summarises the story of the Word** as he sought embodiment in the life of a people of God, and Jn thus explicitly completes what had been implicit in the opening verses of Mk. To avoid any misinterpretation of Mk he makes it clear as soon as Jesus appears that he is the very Lamb of God—the beginning and end of the story are conjoined. Again, Jn displaces (surely deliberately !) the story of the Cleansing of the Temple, as if to say 'The story of the Passion and Crucifixion did not begin just a week before Christ died ; his whole life was passion and crucifixion.' Similarly the community of the Master and the disciples is unmistakably not a natural group flowering into something transcendent, but from the start emphatically an association of Messiah and his saints (1:35–51 ; cf. especially the reference to Mic. 4:4 in v. 48). The Fourth Gospel gives what seems to be a different treatment to miracles. What has happened is that Jn has taken stories from the Synoptics, or used similar ones, and placed each kind in its true synoptic perspective as but a 'sign' of the presence of the Son of God in his kingdom. The first sign of turning the water (of Jewish purification) into wine shows that he who is the true bridegroom of God's people or bride has rendered all other purification superfluous in his own self-giving. The unbelievable miracle is not the changing of the water, but the arrival of the God-man. A miracle in Jn is thus meant to portray not the physical event as itself the wonder, but the physical event as a sign of another more excellent miracle, that the Son of God has come in the flesh, and men, endowed with divine insight, can recognise him. This is as true of the healing of the paralytic (cf. 5:24) as of the giving of sight to the man born blind (cf. 9:35–8), or of the raising of Lazarus (cf. 11:24–6).

Jn handles the Exodus material as it is applied to d the gospel story somewhat differently from the Synoptists. He retains only part of the opening cycle, but introduces the imagery in a new form with the Baptist's confession that Jesus is the Lamb of God (1:29, 35). He also changes the application at the end of the ministry, for instead of the Last Supper being the point where, as an actual Passover, Exodus meanings are applied to the death of Christ, Jn tells us that Jesus died at the very hour that the Passover lambs were being slain in the Temple, and indicates that he was our 'Passover' by reporting that 'not a bone of him shall be broken' (19:36). In the Synoptics it might seem that the humiliation of the cross was the preliminary, and only the preliminary, to the glory. But in Jn **the cross is itself the point of glorification** (3:14, 8:28, 12:32, 17:1). Though in Jn the cross must not be separated from the previous ministry, it must not be separated on the other hand from the resurrection and ascension. And the resurrection narrative itself contains elements that are set out in temporal separation elsewhere. The ascension is clearly conceived as taking place on Easter Day. The gift of the Spirit and the Apostolic commission are related as taking place on the evening of Easter Day, and Jn ends his Gospel by repeating the simple but profound formula of a disciple's call : 'Follow me' (21:19). Thus Jn has told the Synoptic story so that neither docetism nor adoptionism can explain it, indeed so that only a Chalcedonian Christology is adequate ; and he has told it so that nothing less than a Trinitarian theology will bear the weight of the good news that the Gospels contain.

The teaching of the Gospels reinforces our con- 667a clusions. Mk summarised Jesus' teaching as 'The time is fulfilled, and the Kingdom of God is at hand ; repent,

667a and believe in the gospel.' The precise meaning of 'at hand' is still disputed, but there is a fair consensus of opinion that it indicates Christ's belief that in his own person the great reign or rule of God had begun. God's kingly rule had 'come upon' men in the works and person of Jesus (Lk. 11:20). Yet though the Kingdom is present in Christ, something is still awaited, and this finds expression in many parables—the small seed which will produce a hundredfold, the leaven that leavens the whole dough, the mustard seed that becomes a great tree. At present the rule of God demands its own quality of manhood, clearly set out in the Sermon on the Mount. The ethics of the Kingdom are not however external laws, but flow from inward springs of action. As still to come the rule of God involves its servants in darkness as well as light, tragedy as well as victory. Jesus identified the figure of the triumphant Son of man with that of the Suffering Servant, and proclaimed his own inevitable death as the road to his final reign; he also made it clear that those who were with him would have to share the same destiny (Mk 8:34f.). Thus the final embodiment of the Kingdom lies on the other side of tragedy, death and time. The question about when it will be finally accomplished cannot be answered: that is something hidden in the knowledge of the Father (Ac. 1:7). But we have clues about what the advent of the Kingdom will be like: (*a*) the 'end' will supervene on a history that appears quite normal (Lk. 17:26f.); (*b*) there will be an intensification of the conflict between good and evil as the end draws near (Mk 13:7f.); (*c*) the end will involve the breakdown of the physical universe (Mk 13:24–6); (*d*) the Son of Man will finally separate good and evil (Mt. 25:31–3); (*e*) the bliss of the final Kingdom will far outweigh the previous struggle and sacrifice (cf. Mk 10:29f.). The reality of the Kingdom is the open presence and undisputed authority of Jesus Christ.

b The titles used by and of Jesus further illustrate Mk's themes. **The Son of Man,** the one title which Jesus alone used to describe himself, is both the title of a supernatural, divine being and the name for the community of the saints of the Most High (Dan. 7:18). This title, individual and societary together, is joined by Jesus to the destiny of the Servant of II Isaiah: 'The Son of man must suffer' (Mk 8:31 etc.). (It is only after this is clear that Jesus speaks of the 'coming' of the Son of Man!) 'Christ' is used about Jesus, and not by him, probably to avoid embarrassing contemporary associations. The Messiah could be a divine figure; he was certainly to be the centre of a new Israel. 'Lord' is used, as a title, only after the resurrection (Lk. 24:34; Ac. 2:36). For the Jews the name implies worship, being the same word in the Greek OT as was used of Yahweh, and for the Greeks it had a religious usage too. Son of God, as we have seen, combines individual and societary meanings, and, in spite of much pleading to the contrary, seems to rest on the way Christ spoke of himself (cf. Lk. 10:22; Mt. 11:27; Mk 13:32). Yet, though the title claims a unique sonship, Jesus is the unique son not as an isolated individual, but as the reality of a new corpus—the corpus Christi, the body of Christ.

c The Gospels tell the story of the coming of the new Son or people of God in the person of Jesus Christ, and point their meaning by Exodus analogies. The book of Acts tells the story of the coming of the Son or people of God in the community of the Church, and points its meanings by Exodus and gospel analogies. The life of the new corporate son, like that of the new individual Son, bears the stamp of the Exodus pattern. If we may think of the cross and resurrection, which fulfilled the baptism for the individual son, as *the* baptism of the new corporate son (thus giving a basis for Paul's teaching on baptism as 'dying with Christ') then the forty days of the tabernacling and teaching of the Lord are the Exodus imprint of the preparation in the wilderness, and the gift of the Spirit at Pentecost, 66
with phenomena associated with the giving of the law on Sinai, is the enactment of the new law, not on tables of stone, but upon human hearts. The miracle of Pentecost was not the wind or the fire, or even the speaking with tongues, it was the fact that at last lips that had been dumb now for the first time proclaimed Jesus as both Lord and Christ. This was the basis for a plea for repentance and baptism (cf. Mk 1:15), and we read elsewhere that, like Jesus, the early Church preached the Kingdom (8:12, 14:22, 20:25, 28:23, 30).

Acts is a book of the Holy Spirit. His work is clear from Ac. 2. He re-creates the apostolic fellowship in the power and integrity it had when Christ was with them. 'The Lord is the Spirit' (2 C. 3:17). And with the Lord present, the signs are evident again. The blind receive their sight (9:18), the lame walk (3:8), the dead are raised up (9:31, 20:9–12), the poor have good tidings preached to them (4:32–5). In the life of the Church the Spirit occupies the place as counsellor that Jesus had taken in the days of his flesh (13:2, 15:28, 20:28). For the rest, though Ac. is primarily the story of the spread of Christianity from Jerusalem to Rome, it gives a clear-cut picture of the kerygma of the early Church, curiously like the theological structure of the Gospels: the time is one of fulfilment (2:16, 3:18, 10:43, 13:27, 32); Christ has done good and mighty works (2:22, 10:38); he was in God's purpose delivered up to death (2:23, 3:13–15, 4:10, 5:30, 10:39, 13:28, 9); he was raised from the dead (2:24, 32, 3:15, 4:10, 10:40, 13:30); he was exalted to the right hand of God (2:33, 3:21, 5:31); he will sum up or judge all things (3:20, 21, 10:42); men must therefore repent and know forgiveness (2:38, 3:19, 4:12, 5:31, 10:43, 13:38–9).

Acts is also the book of the Church. It began in d
the close corporate unity and common sharing that the new Israel had known during Christ's lifetime, and it was nourished by 'the apostles' teaching, the fellowship, the breaking of bread, and the prayers' (2:42). From the first, as Stephen's speech shows, it believed in its own universal mission. It used the sacrament of baptism 'into Christ', and the 'breaking of bread' which in essentials is our own Eucharist, commemorating the death of Christ, celebrating his presence with his people, and anticipating his final reign. In the Church it is Christ who must reign, not James, nor Peter, nor Paul; this is exemplified in the story of the Apostolic Council in Ac. 15 where after previous discord, Christ by his spirit brings his people to an obedient unity. The first creed of the Church seems to have been: Jesus is Lord; and Ac. shows on many occasions that the greatest content in that brief creed was the affirmation of the resurrection of Jesus Christ from the dead (see refs. above, and 17:3, 18, 31, 23:6, 24:21, 25:19, 26:23). As the risen Lord among his people he ruled in his Church, and the Kingdom was still a present reality awaiting its final consummation. It is significant that Paul should in many ways undergo experiences on the pattern of his Lord—three days sightless and without food, i.e. practically dead, before he receives his sight, is baptised and enters the new life of the Kingdom; he goes up to Jerusalem knowing that his end will meet him there. So is the identification of destiny and meaning of life set out in the approximation of Paul's story to that of his master.

How are the basic Marcan themes handled in Paul? 668a
They are all substantially developed. Paul affirms the humanity of Jesus 'who was descended from David according to the flesh' ((Rom. 1:3) and yet, as divine, is to be confessed as the one in whom 'all things were created' (Col. 1:16), and, as 'the image of the invisible God' (Col. 1:15), he is moreover the one through whom God will 'reconcile to himself all things' (Col. 1:20). Thus, as in the Gospels, **the Person and Work of Christ cannot be separated.** The recon-

668a ciliation of all things will be effected as God 'makes peace by the blood of his cross' (Col. 1:20), and the work of reconciliation has actually begun since God 'has delivered us from the dominion of darkness and transferred us to the kingdom of his beloved Son'. Paul nowhere relates the story of the crucifixion, but no writer puts the cross more in the centre; he expresses in a variety of theological statements and brilliant metaphors those meanings of the crucifixion which the evangelists conveyed in their allusions to the OT or by other interpretative historiographical devices.

b Mk's ecclesiological theme naturally receives much attention in Paul, since he is writing to the churches. If the evangelists' stories of Christ calling 'those whom he desired' (Mk 3:13) to be his disciples, and of his willing association with publicans and sinners may be read as their account of God's action to bring sinful men into right relationship with himself, then Paul's statement of 'justification by faith' can be seen as the theological counterpart of the gospel narrative. For Paul declares that God 'justifies the ungodly' (Rom. 4:5) not on any basis of work or merit, but simply by faith in Christ, in what God had done to put men right with himself. Justification is not, of course, the only metaphor Paul uses, though it is a dominant one, but the bases of the other images (adoption as sons, redemption from slavery, deliverance from evil, etc.) are to be seen in the gospel narratives, and they leave the same theological situation exposed as does the metaphor of justification. If Christ's fellowship with the disciples, particularly with the Twelve, unbroken by their dullness, unfaithfulness and sin, be the evangelists' story of how community between God and man was maintained in Christ, Paul's image of the Church as the 'body' of Christ is a more theological and compendious way of indicating the organic unity which Christ's presence with his own bestows. And it is important to remember that in 1 C. 12 where this imagery is most clearly developed, we are invited to think of the body of Christ in Eucharistic terms, for Paul recited at the end of ch. 11 the account of the Last Supper which he had received, where the Lord had said of the bread which was broken: 'This is my body'.

c But faith in what God has done in Christ to put men right with himself is not belief in a universal proposition on the basis of its one-time exemplification in history. The evangelists exhibited discipleship as man's being brought to share the very nature and destiny of Christ himself (cf. Jn 17:23), and Paul writes similarly of being a Christian. At our baptism we who are Christians 'die with him' (Rom. 6:8) and the life we now live is not ours *simpliciter*, for God 'has made us alive together with Christ . . . and raised us up with him, and made us sit with him in the heavenly places' (Eph. 2:5, 6). It is not surprising therefore that Paul could write: 'it is no longer I who live, but Christ who lives in me' (Gal. 2:20).

Yet Paul is far too sensitive to the realities of life, of his own life, to suppose that to say all this is to claim that the life of the Christian is from baptism onwards one of complete moral and spiritual perfection. The Christian knows, as other men know, the perpetual and fatal weakness of human nature—its sinfulness. If acceptance by God were to depend on the attainment of perfection, man's predicament would be utterly hopeless. 'Who will deliver me from this body of death?' is Paul's and every sinner's last cry of despair. But in the gospel, **in justification,** there is an answer to that despair: 'Thanks be to God (who will deliver me from this body of death) through Jesus Christ our Lord'. The paradox of the Christian life, as Luther saw so clearly, is that the Christian believer is at one and the same time a justified person and a sinner ('*simul iustus et peccator*'), in right relationship with God, although sinful.

d Justification is thus not an idea which Christians conceive, but an act wrought by God in Christ in
which they trust. Baptism is that point in the life 668d
of man when he first claims (or has it claimed for him) that the divine act is that which is to be his ultimate trust and hope. There, as Paul expounds the rite, the Christian dies and rises with Christ. The rest of the life of the Church, as Paul presents it, is concerned constantly to recall Christians to this justifying act of God, wherein all human hopes are centred. The great duty of preaching is to 'preach Christ crucified' (1 C. 1:23); the repeated celebration of the Lord's Supper is to 'proclaim the Lord's death until he come' (1 C. 11:26), as it is the means by which 'we who are many are one body, for we all partake of the same loaf'—i.e. the Eucharist is the means by which, humanly speaking, we are maintained in our paradoxical state of simultaneous sinfulness and justification.

But if the paradox were the last word, Paul's e
theology would be incomplete. For our union with Christ, our being 'in him', our 'membership' of his body, means that we are united with one who has 'sat down at the right hand of the Father'; and even now, joined to him, we share the heavenly session. But the time will come when what is now anticipated, though real, will become the fullness of reality. It cannot be too strongly stated that for Paul, as for the evangelists, the 'end' has come: Christians are already in 'the Kingdom of God's beloved Son' (Col. 1:13): but the very emphasis on such present triumph is the surety that all ambiguity will eventually be done away. The day when 'Christ will appear' (Col. 3:4) may not be discerned beforehand, and if Paul began by thinking of the Parousia as something temporally imminent, and in the imagery of contemporary Judaism (as he does, very largely in 1, 2 Th.), he later finds that what has to be said on the basis of Jesus Christ, incarnate, crucified, risen, ascended, regnant, means the supersession of such a time scheme and such symbols by a conception of a cosmic destiny centred in Christ, who will 'sum up' all things, when, beyond the bounds of history, he yields his universal and eternal kingdom to the Father.

Meanwhile, the certain hope and the universal f
answerability of man leads to a new formulation of the moral life. To continue the moral struggle is worth while not because we can attain perfection—or have been promised it—in this life, but because, while sinners, we are promised forgiveness and justification. In continuing it the Christian, knowing that no social, racial or economic differences make any difference at all to the common sinfulness in which all men stand, recognises that in every moral and social relationship there must be mutual rights and responsibilities. Christians, writes Paul, are to subject themselves to one another (Eph. 5:21) and gives a number of revolutionary concrete illustrations: man and wife, parent and child, master and slave—in each of these relationships both sides have rights, and both have responsibilities. In treating of individual moral character Paul sees the whole process of growth in virtue as a 'putting on of Christ' (*enduein*) and in some measure all that the whole society of Christians can do is, by grace, to become 'a perfect man' (*eis andra teleion*, Eph. 4:13). As in the Gospels, so in Paul, ethics are fundamentally eschatological just because they are Christological.

In the Epistle to the Hebrews we also find some 669a
interesting appearances of the Marcan themes. God has revealed himself in his Son (1:1) born of David's line (7:14). He is described in terms of the Suffering Servant as 'bearing the sins of many' (9:28). He 'endured the cross' (12:2), was raised from the dead (13:20) and is at the right hand of God (1:3). The ecclesiological theme finds some new development. There is a presentation of the life of the Christian Church in terms of a new Exodus (3:7–19), and **the great chapter on faith** speaks of the pilgrim people of God. The writer sees the community of those who are in Christ consisting not only of those still alive on earth, but of all the saints and patriarchs who are in

669a him. The Christian life is like the last laps of the great marathon races of the Olympic games which were run in the Stadium itself, in presence of the great crowd of spectators ; the Christian life is thus one lived 'in sight of the end' (the finisher of our faith) and before the great cloud of witnesses—the saints who have already gone into the heavenly realm.

b The images which the author uses to write of the creation and continuance of the community between God and man in Christ differ from Paul's, though manifesting the same theological concerns. He retains some reference to the second coming of Christ (9:28, 19:25, 37) but his chief means of articulating the difference between the imperfections of this age and what lies beyond is an almost Platonic distinction between the earthly and the heavenly (though this was not entirely unknown to Paul, cf. 1 C. 15:49). This distinction is significantly used of the work of Christ, considered both as a deed of atonement, and as a gathering of a new people of God. Christ's work is that of a great High Priest, and being done in the real, i.e. the heavenly, temple, needs but to be done once. So the Christ who was tempted like ourselves is also the one heavenly man and priest : in him we are joined with the heavenly world 'once and for all'. He has thus opened up a new way or an access to God himself. He has taken our own humanity up to God, and there continually—and, we cannot but suppose, effectually—intercedes for us.

The writer also formulates his ecclesiological theme in Exodus terms in a passage where he contrasts and yet compares the access of the Old Israel to Mount Sinai with that of the New Israel to Mount Zion, the true and heavenly Jerusalem. The New Israel continues, as it displaces, the Old.

c The First Epistle of Peter, as we might expect from a letter which has still some claim to have been at least 'dictated' by the apostle to Silvanus, has many characteristics in common with Mk, and some that develop Mk's themes. Like Mk, Pet. sees the story of Jesus as fulfilling the anticipations of the prophets of old times who 'spoke beforehand of the grace that was coming to us' (1:10). Of the person and work of Jesus he bears witness parallel to Mk, Paul and Heb. Jesus is 'our Lord Jesus Christ' who, in a phrase reminiscent of Paul and Jn, is said to have been 'predestined before the foundation of the world'. His work is, as in parts of Mk, identified with that of the Suffering Servant of Isaiah (2:22, 24) ; and Pet. reminds us of Heb. and of Paul when he writes that Christ died 'once for all' as the 'just for the unjust' (3:18). What Mt. embodied in his narrative of the dead saints rising at the time of the resurrection, Pet. incorporates in his reference to a preaching to the spirits in prison (3:9f.), i.e. those in Hades.

Pet., with the other apostolic writers, bears witness to the fact of the resurrection (1:3) and ascension (1:21), and to the gift of the Spirit (1:12). He also looks forward to an 'uncovering' or 'manifestation' of Christ at the end (1:7 and 5:4). All this may be expressed as the 'Word of God which (or better 'who') lives and abides for ever !'

d The ecclesiological theme is also pronounced. Before conversion we are like straying sheep, but as Christians we are sheep that have returned to the true shepherd of our souls (2:25). This shepherd, to use a Johannine phrase, 'gave his life for the sheep', and Pet. uses the Passover imagery when he says that, like a paschal lamb without spot or blemish, Christ ransomed us from futility. It is clear that with other NT writers Pet. sees the Church as a New Israel replacing the Old—'you are a chosen race, a royal priesthood, a holy nation, God's own people'. But he reminds the Church of the universal mission to which it is called : to 'declare the wonderful deeds of him who called you out of darkness into his marvellous light'. This the Church must do until Christ is revealed (1:7, 13, 4:13, 5:1, 4).

Much of what Peter has to say of the life of Christians is theological. **It is new birth, it is sanctified by** 669
the Spirit ; it must be upright and commendable by a good conscience (2:15, 20, 3:16, 4:2) ; then, even when persecution comes, Christians will know that Christ's spirit still rests upon them (4:12–16). Nor is the hope of a Christian confined to this world, for Pet., as other writers, tells of a glory to come (1:7, 4:13, 5:1, 4, 6, 10).

Theologically the Epistles of John are closely 670
related to the Fourth Gospel. There is no doubt of the writer's intention to articulate the same profound Christological concern as is voiced in the Gospel. He writes of what he has seen and heard and touched of the word of life ; and he is perfectly clear in his insistence that Jesus Christ has come in the flesh. No other NT writer has stated the Christological theme more emphatically or succinctly than the author of these letters (I, 1:2 ; I, 2:8, 12, 14 ; I, 3:23 ; I, 4:2, 9, 14, 15 ; I, 4:10 ; I, 5:1, 5, 10). The work of the Son has been to deal with our sin, **by expiation** (I, 1:7, 9 ; I, 2:2), **by taking away sins** (I, 3:5), and **by destroying the works of the devil** (I, 3:8). The author in his own way states the same paradox that Paul stated when he spoke of the sinner being justified. In this epistle it is stated that 'in him (Jesus Christ, who appeared to take away sins) there is no sin' (I, 3:5). Therefore it follows that 'No one who abides in him sins' (I, 5:6). Yet the author is far too aware of the frailties of human nature to give vent to a doctrine that believers are made perfect at once, here and now. Rather all through the epistle we must remember what was said at the beginning, that 'if we confess our sins, he is faithful and just, and will forgive our sins' (I, 1:9). So it is 'in this (that) love is perfected with us, that we may have confidence for the day of judgment' (I, 4:17).

The ecclesiological theme is also firmly embedded b
in the letter. The first-person plural in which the epistle is written is more than an editorial 'we' ; it represents the community of those who know that Jesus Christ has come in the flesh and inaugurated a new fellowship with the Father and the Son (I, 1:3), and binds them in a new bond of love with their fellow believers. 'We know that we have passed out of death into life, because we love the brethren' (I, 3:14). And all such knowledge is the gift of the Spirit which Christ has given (I, 3:24). So ethic and eschatology derive from the coming in the flesh of the Son of God, who abides with and in his people.

Admittedly the letters do not exhibit the funda- c
mental truths of the gospel in terms of OT history and theology ; but that lack, understandable in terms of the Hellenistic community addressed, only serves to emphasise the centrality of the Christological and ecclesiological themes, which, without the OT references, are recognisably dominant in these epistles.

For all its strange and puzzling imagery the book 671a
of Revelation also bears witness to the fundamental theological themes of the rest of the NT. Through the strange apocalyptic imagery in which the author conveyed his message to persecuted Christians there shines very clearly the light of NT theology and Christology. Some critics of the book have found some of its ideas sub-Christian, even its idea of God ; but it must be pointed out that the God of Rev. is the Father of Jesus Christ (1:6, 2:27, 3:5, 21, 14:1) the Saviour, and that the end of all the struggle and tragedy in the book is the final overthrow of evil and the perfect rule of God and the Lamb. Rev. has an exalted statement of the Christological theme : Christ is of David's line (5:5) and yet the essential Son of God, the Word of God (19:13), the first and the last (1:17, 2:8, 22:13) even as God himself is (6:10), and he is Alpha and Omega (22:13). His crucifixion is central to an understanding of his place in the universal purpose of God—he is the lamb slain from the foundation of the world (13:8 RV), and, using the lamb image in another way known to

671a Judaism, he is a leader of divine power and victory (cf. 17:14). Here, as elsewhere in the NT, the humiliated and the exalted Christ are one and inseparable. And here, as elsewhere, his work is to set his people free from sin, though here the liberation is envisaged in powerfully dramatic, historic and eschatological terms. And at the end of the whole drama of history and its climax comes the final peace and reign of God and the Lamb, shared by all Christ's people in the heavenly and new Jerusalem.

b Thus the ecclesiological theme is also firmly stated. The book begins with letters to the Asian churches about to undergo persecution. The whole drama of the book, cosmic in its reaches, is fundamentally the drama of the history of the people of God. They repeat the pattern of his life in theirs: 'He who conquers, I will grant him to sit with me on my throne, as I myself conquered and sat down with my Father on his throne' (3:21). But the conquest is not the unaided victory of men, as if man's place in heaven can be earned. For when the Lamb is at last married to his bride (the Church), and the bride has made herself ready for the great consummation of her betrothal, it is 'granted to her to be clothed with fine linen, bright and pure' (19:8), and when the author goes on to say that the fine linen is the righteousness of God's saints he is putting into other words a conviction basic to Paul—that our righteousness is not our own, but God's gift. We do not give him our goodness, but he gives it to us.

c But Rev., by its emphasis upon what is to happen at and before the end of history, brings into sharp relief one essential factor in the whole range of thinking that begins with the life of Jesus as reported in the Gospels. Jesus knew that his own life was a 'fulfilment' of the story of the ancient people of God; he knew that his own baptism was a fulfilment of the baptism of the old people of God in the Red Sea, of their baptism in the Jordan under Joshua; but he also knew that his baptism in Jordan was also something that had to be fulfilled, and it is plain that he saw the fulfilment in the cross and resurrection. It is equally plain that neither he nor the Church saw even the cross and resurrection as the end 'absolutely'; still the people of God must await a fulfilment; and Rev. underlines this. This thought was comfort to the Church undergoing or about to undergo persecution; it learnt to live with the uncomfortable present because it lived near the comfortable end. And the Church has continued to do that all down the ages. In our own century the churches that have been persecuted have found comfort and strength and courage in the contemplation of the end when Christ shall have put the last enemy under his feet. It will be so till the end comes. The possibility of living near something that may be far off is realised by the whole world in the mid-20th cent. Ever since 1945 the world, though nominally at peace, has been living perilously near to another world war; sometimes it is very near, sometimes farther off, but never far enough away to be forgotten. So it is with the end of which Christians dream—though their end is certain, while the third world war may never come. All the conditions for the coming of the end have been fulfilled; God has nothing more to do in the way of preparation; Christ has no more to do in the way of preparation. We live in a period when the end is always 'near' though it may be temporally far off still. This is the message of Rev., which through imagery that is alien to the 20th cent. was written to assure us that however much the evidence may suggest the contrary **God has not ceased to reign, nor Christ to be Lord**. Even so, come, Lord Jesus.

d The NT, as we said at the start, is not a treatise in theology. It is fundamentally the telling of a story, with material from the life of the Christian Church which provides a necessary and normative commentary on the story. The story is necessary because basic to Christian faith is the conviction that God has acted decisively in history; the commentary is 671d
necessary because the fullness of the good news that constitutes the gospel cannot be conveyed or apprehended in a one-dimensional telling of the gospel story. Even in the Gospels themselves theological depth is gained by the use of a number of historiographical devices enabling the writers to exhibit the two indispensable elements of the one gospel story—the heavenly and the earthly, the eternal and the temporal, the eschatological and the historical. Thus the evangelists not only 'tell us the stories of Jesus' but also make theological comment upon it as they tell it. The writers of Ac., of the Epistles and of Rev. do not add much (though they do add something) to our knowledge of the 'stories of Jesus'; yet, though they are predominantly 'commentary' on the story, are all greatly concerned that the whole commentary, as indeed the whole life of the Church, should be based firmly upon the one gospel story. The story was propagated by preaching; and so the apostle is anxious that he should preach 'Jesus Christ and him crucified' (not some Christ-figure of the theologian's brain, but the Christ of the story that spoke of death upon a cross in history): it was made the constant food of the believer's religious life in the worship of the Church, particularly in the Eucharist, where the Christian ate bread and drank wine and so fed on Christ; and so the apostle is anxious that what was done at the Eucharist should be unambiguously done 'in memory of him': it was set forth as the pattern of all Christian action and passion; and so the apostle is anxious to show how all the moral demands of the Church are really a request to 'put on Christ', i.e. not general ethical truths, but particular duties flowing from a committal of the self to Jesus Christ: it was summarised into certain affirmations of belief; and the apostle was anxious that every formula used and offered for use in the Church should not fail to miss either the heavenly or the earthly significances of the story. Thus, though the NT is not itself a treatise in theology, it is without doubt an exceedingly theological document.

The task of the theologian is very different from 672a
that of the NT writers in many ways, but fundamentally is continuous with it; in his own day he must seek to ensure that both 'heavenly' and 'earthly' parts of the story are given their due place in all the activities of the Church. His task may be looked at in two stages. There is the stage of what is called 'Biblical Theology' where the scholar traces a theme or themes of scripture and explores its theological significance. This theological task is in principle no different from that performed by the NT writers themselves whenever in their works they leave us clues to show that the story of Christ and his Church is but the fulfilment of the story of God and his people in the OT; it is in essence, indeed, an '*imitatio Christi*', for Jesus did precisely this for the two disciples who walked to Emmaus on the first Easter Day, as he did for the eleven who met later that evening in Jerusalem, as he did, according to his own claim in Lk. (24:44), during his earthly ministry. If this means that by examining the great themes of the Bible, such as covenant, word, shepherd, temple, righteousness, exodus, etc. we find ourselves again and again being pointed to Jesus Christ as the final point of reference and of fundamental meaning for all such themes and terms, we shall have understood both why the scriptures of the NT were collected into a canon, and why biblical theology itself must flower into something fundamentally systematic. Indeed, within the NT itself the process of systematisation has already, and of necessity, begun. The Church had to fashion a new language for itself in order to make use of its fundamental story both for the nurture of its own life in worship, catechetical instruction, discipline and confession of faith, and for its mission to the world, as it undertook the immense tasks of evangelism, and of wrestling with the rival religions and systems of

672a thought that were also claiming the loyalties of men, Stoicism, Gnosticism, the Mystery Religions, etc.

b The thing that marks Christianity out among all the great religions of the world is that, if it is to speak in its own distinctive way about God, it cannot dispense with the telling of a story, the story that goes 'from Genesis to Revelation'. But to tell a story which recites how the God who made the universe took pity on fallen and rebellious man, how he gathered and consecrated a people to himself by his own call to them in the events of history interpreted by the prophet Moses, how he persisted with and disciplined his people for centuries, how finally he came in the form of a man and in the person of his Son himself to inaugurate the historical and trans-historical reality of the final and indissoluble people of God, and how that led to all that is recorded in the Gospels—to tell such a story is inevitably to be involved in the making of a great number of theological presuppositions. If the Christian story as contained in both Testaments is to be told, then certain things have to be asserted about God, both about his own eternal nature and about his relationship to the creation and the creatures he has made ; about the character of the world in which men find themselves caught in an inextricable network of evil, both physical and moral ; about the extent and power of the evil in the world which required the redemptive act related in the NT and prefigured in the OT ; about the nature of the redeemer himself who works a redemption in history that is effective eternally ; about the nature and purpose of history itself, and about its 'end' ; about the nature of the secular societies of men, and about the 'supernatural' society of the Church. Indeed we might properly say that the whole purpose of Christian theology is to make articulate what it is precisely that the 'telling of the Christian story' requires us to believe. It is this conviction that has led the Church to formulate 'doctrinal standards' and to make a vital distinction between orthodoxy (what really flows from the Christian story) and heresy (what does not so follow, but really denies it). Sometimes, of course, the telling of the Christian story seems to require us to believe what seems wholly paradoxical, though something which we must assert since it is the only basis for the telling of the biblical story. Thus if we are to tell the story of a God who finally redeems the whole world to himself, as the Christian scriptures require us to do, we cannot but assert both God's omnipotence (or else we could not be assured of his ability to redeem the world in the end) and man's freedom (or else we would either have to attribute man's sin to God, or be found in doubt again as to the possibility of God achieving his full purpose).

c The great ecumenical creeds of Christendom wisely did not set out to be a full statement of Christian theology ; they are, in essence, the treasured affirmation of the necessary elements of the 'story' that the Christian has to tell. They are normative for doctrine, and witnesses to the truth, rather than statements of doctrine that follow from the acceptance of the basic Christian truth. But this leads us to the final point that must be made about the NT itself, about NT theology as men seek to articulate it, and about the whole enterprise of Christian theological statement. None of these is ultimate. One thing alone is ultimate —the life of God with man, which he has been pleased finally to establish in human history in and through Jesus Christ, mediated continually through the Holy Spirit. In collecting and authorising the books of the NT as a canon of scripture the early Church was not ultimately concerned that future generations should merely learn that certain events took place in an obscure part of the Roman Empire at the beginning of our era ; for, as Luther emphasised, 'history-knowledge does not save a man ; indeed it is possible to know *that* Christ lived and died and even that he rose from the dead, and still be without his salvation'. The early Church transmitted its scriptures in an ultimate concern that future generations should meet and trust the same Lord Jesus Christ whom the apostles had known and to whom they had witnessed, the same Lord whom the early Church had known and believed, and through whom it had fellowship with the Father. The NT is not an end in itself ; it is a handmaid to the living reality of the Church, a witness to the life that it lives with God, or rather that God is pleased to live with and in and through the Church. Theology is also a handmaid and witness. Biblical theology points to the centrality of the person of Jesus Christ for the story that Christians have to tell, as well as for the ideas that are involved in the telling. The great ecumenical creeds of the Church likewise witness to God's gracious life with his people, demanding not belief in their formulae as such, but rather in their formulae as guardians of that area of human thought and language within which the Church may hopefully and truthfully bear witness to the innermost reality of its life. It is important in this connection to notice that the creeds use terms in their formulae which do not derive from scripture; which points eloquently to the fact that neither scripture nor creeds are ultimate as words, but as witness to the God who is the life of his people as Father, Son and Holy Spirit, creator, redeemer and sanctifier. Likewise the task of systematic theology is to build a rounded structure of Christian thinking upon the basis of biblical theology and creedal definition, and by this means to bear witness to each succeeding generation in the language familiar and useful to it, what is the area of human thought and language within which effective testimony can be borne to the great and gracious reality of the Church's life—God with us, Immanuel, the heart of biblical theology, the essence of creed and system, and the one hope of every Christian man.

Bibliography—R. Bultmann, *Theology of the NT* (1955) ; C. H. Dodd, *The Meaning of Paul for to-day* (1920), *Parables of the Kingdom* (1935), *History and the Gospel* (1938), *According to the Scriptures* (1952) ; A. M. Hunter, *Introducing NT Theology* (1947), *The Unity of the NT* (1952) ; A. Richardson, *An Introduction to NT Theology* (1958) ; E. Stauffer, *NT Theology* (1955).

In addition, particular studies by : Bultmann, Cullmann, Dodd, Jeremias, Stauffer, etc.

MATTHEW

By K. STENDAHL

73a **Introduction**—Studies of the relation between the synoptic Gospels during the last century and a half have—rightly—led to an almost universal acceptance of Mk as the oldest Gospel and upon that basis the origin of Christianity in the ministry of Jesus is now commonly described. It is worth remembering, however, that at least from the time of Irenaeus and early canonical witnesses, Mt. was for seventeen centuries 'the first Gospel' in a most real sense. It supplied both the frame and the basic shape and colour to the church's image of Jesus Christ. It outweighed not only Mk, but also the other Gospels in the readings assigned for the Sundays and Holy Days of the church year, and other Gospels filled in where the Matthean picture was felt to be incomplete. This fact may well have had deeper significance for the history and the theology of Christianity than will ever be properly assessed.

b There must have been many reasons, internal as well as external, for this great success of Mt., but it could hardly have happened without enthusiastic support from one of the more important centres of early Christianity as, for example, Antioch, even if the place of its origin may have been rather in the Syrian inland where Christianity was strong and of diversified nature with a rich amount of Jesus traditions available, in some quarters with distinctive Jewish features. One could also seek for its origin somewhat closer to Palestine, such as one of the Phoenician cities, but none of those places assumed any greater role in early Christianity. For example, Caesarea (by the Mediterranean) could well have hailed Peter as its apostolic founder (see Ac. 10), a fact which tallies with Mt.'s conspicuous emphasis on Peter's leadership ; but Caesarea as a Roman centre was perhaps not that haven for Jews, either before or after the Jewish war (A.D. 66–70), which much of the material in Mt. would require as a matrix.

c While the image of the Gospel writers as 'authors' —with or without specific channels of inspiration— has faded away under the impact of comparative synoptic studies and under the impact of Form Criticism, it would be wrong to picture Matthew as a mere redactor who brings together material from different and sometimes conflicting sources as best he can. This would be misleading in at least two ways : (*a*) At almost every point where Mt. makes use of material found in Mk or Lk.—i.e. where we can study his method and procedure—he gives it a special emphasis (e.g. 27:57–61), a different application (e.g. 18:10–14), or a new context, especially by bringing together sayings of Jesus into virtual discourses (see §673*h*). Thus we are able to discern the rather clear traits of a 'Matthew' in the details as well as in the total arrangement of his Gospel, and there is no reason to believe that he has not played the same formative role when handling material to which we happen to have no parallels in the Gospel tradition. (*b*) In carrying out his work by such an interpretative use of earlier material, written as well as oral, Matthew does not work in a vacuum, but within the life of a church for whose needs he is catering ; his Gospel more than the others is a product of a community and for a community. G. D. Kilpatrick has argued for such an understanding of Mt. in terms of the 673c
liturgical and homiletic needs, and over against the catechetical elements. We have elsewhere (in *The School of St Matthew*, 1954) suggested a somewhat broader and yet more specific interpretation of the nature of Mt. by calling it a handbook for teaching and administration within the church, and we have compared its form with the Manual of Discipline from Qumrân. This is not to deny that Mt. basically is and remains a Gospel, but that which gives to Mt. its specific features could well be understood from the interest in having the Gospel material in such a form that it answered the needs for which such manuals existed.

With such confidence in the creative forces of the d
Matthean church and in the possibilities of analysing and grasping in what manner and for what reasons Matthew presents his material as he does, the following commentary tries to present Mt. without any specific theory about his sources. While his dependence upon Mk is considered the basic fact for Matthean interpretation, and while the material common to Mt. and Lk. could be called Q, no distinction has been made between other sources, e.g. Bacon's N source (certain haggadic traditions among Aramaic-speaking Christians of north-eastern Syria) and the commonly accepted M source over against the work of Mt. proper ; cf. the article on 'The Synoptic Problem' (§§653–8).

Already the dependence of Mt. on Mk makes it e
hard to uphold the old tradition that Mt. should be a translation from an Aramaic Gospel. This view has its root in Papias' statement (*c.* 135), quoted by Eusebius (HE III, xxxix, 16) : 'Matthew collected the oracles in Hebrew language, but everyone interpreted [or translated] them as he was able' ; and it is not even clear whether this statement originally refers to Mt.'s Gospel, although Eusebius understood it to do so. C. C. Torrey, (*The Four Gospels*, 1933, 279), as well as modern Roman Catholic scholars like Benoît and Vaganay who assume an Aramaic original to Mt., all admit that 'our' Mt. has been worked out in Gr., dependent upon a Gr. Mk, and thereby the Aramaic original is at least twice removed, back into what must appear to many of us the mist of unwarranted hypotheses.

Mt. is readily described as **the Gospel which has the** f
strongest Jewish flavour. Its birth narratives are centred around the Davidic descent of Jesus, the Kingdom is usually called 'The Kingdom of Heaven' (lit. 'of the Heavens' with the Semitic plural *shāmayim* retained, as it is rarely in the LXX). The Sermon on the Mount and ch. 23 are spelled out with the Pharisees in focus. When the message of Jesus takes the form of antitheses over against the teaching of the Jews, this form urges a more radical obedience to the Law (5:17–48) and the Christian is he who has a higher degree of 'righteousness' (5:20), a key-word to Mt. (3:15, 5:6,10, 6:33, 21:32 ; see A. Descamps, 'Le christianisme comme justice dans le premier évangile', *Ephem. Theol. Lov.* 22 (1946), 5–33). Mt. retains the command to the disciples 'not to go to the Gentiles' (10:5, cf. 7:6, 15:26) and the Son of Man is to come before the cities of Israel have been visited by the

673f disciples (10:23). On the other hand, Mt. ends on a strong universalistic note, 'make all the nations my disciples' (28:18–20; cf. 24:14), and sees the Jews as having forfeited their right to the Kingdom (8:11, 22:8). The Kingdom is now given to 'a nation which brings forth its fruit' (21:43, cf. 3:8f.), and that 'nation' is the church. One can even speak about 'The Gentile bias in Matthew'; see K. W. Clark, JBL 66 (1947), 165–72.

g The Gospel is related to Judaism in two ways. It understands the Christian faith and life not as a new religion but as a new constituency of Israel, where the last have become the first: a messianic community which is the true heir to the OT and which, after the exaltation of Jesus, contains also Gentiles, the very 'last'. It argues for the right to understand itself as such over against the Synagogue with which it still is in constant discussion. Secondly this rootage in Judaism may well be epitomised in the suggestion that the Gospel grew out of a 'school' led by a converted rabbi (see 13:52), where Jewish methods of teaching and studying were applied to the new cause. From this 'school' originate also the eleven 'formula quotations' (...this happened in order to fulfil what was said by the prophet: 1:23, 2:6, 15, 18, 23, 4:15f., 8:17, 12:18–21, 13:35, 21:5, 27:9f.). In these quotations Mt. applies rules for interpretation similar to those used at Qumrân and arrives at a substantiation of the claim that the church is right in hailing Jesus of Nazareth as the Christ, and his believers as the true heirs to the prophecies and their promises (see K. Stendahl, op. cit.).

h This is part and parcel of **the ecclesiastical nature** of the Gospel. Mt. does not think in ideas or doctrines. To him the question is: Who will inherit the Kingdom? The answer is clear: the church, i.e. those who recognise Jesus as the Messiah. In this church the Gospel serves as a manual with the teaching of Jesus assembled under appropriate **headings in five discourses** each of which ends with the same formula (7:28–9, 11:1, 13:53, 19:1 and 26:1) and all of them preceded by narrative material which usually follows Mk's order but sometimes (especially chs. 8–9) is enlarged to give fuller examples to what is to be treated in the discourse. There is nothing to suggest that this five-fold structure in Mt. was meant as a 'New Pentateuch' (see 5:21–48), and it is preceded by the Nativity and followed by the Passion and Resurrection:

i Chs. 1–2 The birth of Jesus, the Son of David, called the Nazarene.

Section I

(*a*) 3–4 Narratives: The Kingdom announced by John and Jesus. Short glimpses from the ministry in Galilee.

(*b*) 5–7 The Sermon on the Mount: Ethics for the Kingdom; the higher righteousness.

Section II

(*a*) 8–9 Narratives: The ministry described as one in which the disciples are to share.

(*b*) 10 Discourse on the Mission and the Martyrdom of the disciples.

Section III

(*a*) 11–12 Narratives and debates, both indicating the difficulties of outsiders to understand that the Kingdom is at work in Jesus.

(*b*) 13 Discourse on the nature of the coming of the Kingdom (parables).

Section IV

(*a*) 14–17 Narratives and debates with the disciples, rather than the outsiders, in focus.

(*b*) 18 Discourse on fraternal relations among the disciples and on church discipline.

Section V 67

(*a*) 19–(22)23 Narratives and debates in Jerusalem, sharpening the issue with the Pharisees and the authorities.

(*b*) (23; see §691*a*) 24, 25 Discourse on the eschaton, the Parousia and the proper way to wait for its coming.

26–28 The Passion, the Resurrection and the charge to the eleven disciples.

It remains an unsolved problem how and why the j
Gospel came to circulate under the name of Matthew, who only in this Gospel is identified with a tax-collector called by Jesus (see 9:9, 10:3). But it is highly unlikely that the man responsible for this Gospel had lived on the despised outskirts of Jewish religious life, nor does the Gospel itself (the title was certainly added later) intimate that Matthew was its author. All information to that effect in the Church Fathers seems to depend on Papias's statement quoted above. (For an ingenious explanation, see B. W. Bacon, *Studies in Matthew* (1930), 37–49.) Could it have received its title since the church in which it originated hailed Matthew as its patron apostle? The date is usually set after k
A.D. 70 due to: dependence on Mk; the way in which Mt. refers to the fall of Jerusalem, e.g. 22:7 (but this verse could have suffered change at a later date), and 24:9–15 as compared with Mk 13. Mt. is known and quoted in the early 2nd cent. (Ignatius?, Didache, Papias). Many of the arguments for a relatively late date of Mt. are based on the conviction that so 'formal' and ecclesiastical a Gospel presupposes a relatively long period of development away from the 'informal' beginnings of the church, but the nature of the Qumrân community indicate that this is not necessary. On the contrary, Mt.'s understanding of Jesus as the founder of a community within a Jewish matrix but with a new constituency has a more original ring than much of the Marcan, Lucan and Pauline interpretation of Jesus Christ (cf. §§639–52).

I 1-17. (The) book of (the) genealogy (*biblos* 674
geneseōs) refers either to the whole Gospel or only to 1-17. While the term can introduce narrative material, e.g. in Gen. 5:1, it is probable that it here has the limited meaning of 'genealogy'. In 18 the narrative starts with a somewhat different use of the term 'genesis'. 'Jesus Christ': a formula where Christ (the Anointed One, the Messiah) has become almost a second name. In Mt. it is found only here and in 18 (see also 16:21). In Mk it is found only in 1:1 (not in Lk.), and it is the term by which Jesus is referred to in the introductory phrases of all the Epistles and in Rev., and should not be over-interpreted as a conscious statement about the Messianic character of Jesus; cf. 16. The genealogy in Mt. differs considerably from that in Lk. 3:23–8. In Lk. the line goes back to Adam, the 'Son of God', and it goes via David's son Nathan. In Mt. the line goes from Abraham via David and Solomon. Mt. follows information found in 1 Chr. 2 and 3 and Ru. 4, and that in their Gr. form (LXX). From Zerubbabel on, we have no biblical records, but Jewish genealogies were available and highly treasured
(Jos. Vita i, 6; cf. Phil. 3:5). **17** makes clear what b
is Mt.'s intention with the genealogy. Abraham and David are the significant ancestors. There is no interest in anything beyond Abraham, the father of the Israelites. And Jesus is of royal descent. He is a son of David. Among the three Messianic figures of the Qumrân community, the Prophet, the Messiah of Aaron and the Messiah of Israel (1QS 9:10–11), the genealogy identifies him with the last, the royal and Davidic, the non-priestly Messiah. This impression is strengthened by the line via Solomon, cf. 22:41ff.
While Mt. reports 3 times 14 generations, it is striking c
that the third group contains only 13. It is as hard to believe that one link should have been completely lost in the transmission of the text, as it is to think

674c that Mt. just couldn't count. Is it totally excluded that Mt. counts the Messiah (16) as the 14th, while Jesus is the 13th? 'Christ' should then refer to Jesus in his risen state and/or at his Coming (parousia) at the end of time. We should then have here the strong futuristic eschatology of the primitive church, which is clearly expressed in Ac. 3:20–1. This would give special weight to the Matthean expression 'called Christ', cf. 'Simon called Peter' in 4:18 and 10:2
d as compared with 16:18. **16.** The Gr. text behind RSV and AV is supported by our best MSS. The textual tradition displays considerable variety in this verse, a sign rather of dogmatic concern than of original confusion in the tradition. Among the variants especially the reading of Syr. Sin. deserves attention: '. . . Jacob begat Joseph; Joseph, to whom was betrothed Mary the virgin, begat Jesus who is called the Messiah'. This reading could be used to substantiate the view that the genealogy of Jesus in its original form did not presuppose the virgin birth. The two main reasons against such an interpretation are: (*a*) that 'begat' does not necessarily refer to physical paternity. If a man acknowledged his son's paternity, there were no further questions (Baba Bathra 8:6), and the whole of Mt.'s birth story—with its reference to the virgin birth (18-25)—is centred around Joseph. (*b*) The reader is prepared for this 'holy irregularity' by the reference to four women in the genealogy (3, 5, 6), a most unusual feature in Jewish genealogies; consequently the genealogy itself is leading up to the 'virgin birth'. Tamar (Gen. 38), Rahab (Jos. 2), Ruth (Ru. 4:13–22) and Bathsheba ('the wife of Uriah', 2 Sam. 11). Different suggestions have been given for a 'common denominator' for these four women. The concern of Mt. for the Gentiles or for sinners hardly suffices, and neither Tamar nor Ruth were considered sinful, but both were hailed as ancestors of the future Messiah (Tamar through Perez as in 3). Both Tamar and Bathsheba were good Israelites, and Jewish tradition went far in whitewashing Bathsheba. But all four were 'misunderstood' in their own time, but redeemed in the
e light of God's history. Thus the genealogy is geared towards the 'irregularity' in the birth of Jesus and the reading of the Syr. text is not out of the context of the 'virgin birth'. It may even be a more original reading, and thereby a key to understanding how and why Mt. reports the 'virgin birth'; see 18–25.

f **I 18-II 23. The Matthean Birth Stories** have few points in common with the Lucan accounts. The striking differences are: in Mt. (*a*) Joseph is the central figure; (*b*) apparently he and Mary *live* in Bethlehem; (*c*) only by special revelation are they later on led to Nazareth; (*d*) the story develops by guidance received in dreams; (*e*) each detail happens in order to fulfil prophecy; (*f*) none of the events
g mentioned in Lk. are referred to in Mt. Points (*a*), (*d*) and (*e*) suggest that Mt., in giving this story its form, has drawn upon traditions available to him. Point (*e*) may suggest that he confined himself to material for which he found scriptural basis. The five 'formula quotations' in this section are followed by six more spread over the whole Gospel. A study of these suggests that they are the product of Matthean study of Scripture applied to Marcan or other material available to Mt. (see K. Stendahl, *The School of St Matthew*, 1954) and consequently are neither *testimonia*, nor quotations chosen by Mt. around which a story was built up. Their aim is rather an apologetic one: to make acceptable as divine will what otherwise would seem strange or insignificant. The guidance of God is guarded from two sides: (*a*) the action is intimated by dreams, and (*b*) obedience to these dreams leads to fulfilment of prophecy. The abundance of these quotations in chs. 1, 2 (5 of the 11 found in the whole Gospel) suggests that Mt. here is free to let his own way of writing dominate his presentation.

h **I 18-25.** Mt. knew of a tradition which spoke of a **virgin birth**. It may be, however, that this term is 674h
misleading for Mt.'s account. **20.** If we try to free ourselves from all that Lk. tells us and from later christological discussions, we find that the emphasis is on overcoming Joseph's hesitancy to marry Mary and to accept her child as a son of David (20: 'Joseph, Son of David'). What is told here is a heightening of the miraculous way in which, according to the OT (Sarah: Gen. 18:11–14; Rebekah: 25:21; Hannah: 1 Sam. 1:4–20), the birth of significant persons takes place through divine intervention. The holy spirit is not personalised as in Lk. 1:35. Isa. 7:14 is quoted in the LXX form with the word 'virgin'. While MT has the broader sense 'young woman', the LXX chose the word 'virgin'. This choice does not witness to a Jewish expectation of a messianic virgin birth, in any other sense than: Messiah will be the first-born. While the formula quotation must be a contribution by Mt., it here is meant to be within the message of the angel. **23.** The main emphasis seems strangely enough to be on Emmanuel, and this is heightened by the added translation: 'God with us'. **21.** This use of Emmanuel strengthens the point made about the name 'Jesus', i.e. he who is going to save his people from their sins. These were two synonymous ways of speaking about the Messianic age. The meaning of 'Jesus' (Heb. *Yēshūa'*) is supposed to be understood, i.e. was known to the addressees of Mt. The original intention of Mt. is even more obvious if we follow Syr. Sin. in reading 'She will bear *you* a son . . . (21) and he took his wife and she bore a son and he called his name Jesus', i.e. without the conscious stress on the virginity in the phrase 'but knew her not until . . .' (24–5).
Thus we face an account which knows of a 'virgin i
birth', but the supernatural element is neither stressed nor glorified. It rather has the form of a divine overcoming of a stumbling-block and counteracting of misunderstanding and slander. Such slander is well known in this connection in later Jewish tradition.
19. Joseph was a righteous Jew, and as such he *had* j
to divorce his fiancée in this case, but on the other hand he did not want to scandalise her. Thus he wanted to do it 'quietly', without lawsuit. Talmudic evidence points to a Galilean origin of the tradition, since here—but not in Judaea—those engaged did not come together prior to the marriage, see SB I, 45ff.

II 1-12. The royal, Davidic line from ch. 1 is con- 675a
tinued in 2. The newborn king receives homage, his birth as a Davidide in Bethlehem (cf. Jn 7:41) is attested according to scripture and the threat to the ruler (cf. 27:11–31) is recognised. The legend of the magi and the plans of Herod are woven together so that it is difficult to see any independent function of the story of the magi or the significance of the star. Many parallels have been suggested: the coming of Parthian magi to Nero in A.D. 66 and the stars which accompanied the birth of important men, Suetonius' report on the oracle about the birth of Augustus which led the Senate to the decision that no-one born that year should be allowed to live. It is striking that Mt. does not relate the star to Num. 24:17; the Messianic star became significant in the Qumrân community and in the early church (Justin, *Dial.* 32) and is reflected in Rev. 22:16 together with the
'root', cf. Mt. 2:23. The 'magi' were originally b
a class of priests among the Medes, but in Hellenistic time the word stands for men from the East (or Egypt) who possess astrologic/astronomic wisdom. It can be used in a good sense as in our passage, as well as in a bad sense (as in Ac. 8 and 13). The occurrence of the star or the constellation has been used as a means to date the birth of Jesus, usually with reference to the combination of Jupiter and Saturn in 7 B.C. Ignatius combines the star and the term 'magi' (*in malam partem*) so as to show that Christ has 'dissolved all magic' (Eph. 19). But in Mt. the magi give glory to the birth of the Son of David. Their character of

675b Gentiles is not consciously stressed in the story. The point seems to be homage and celestial corroboration in general. 'The whole of Jerusalem' is identified with Herod, and there is no note of joy among the Jews as in the homage paid by the Lucan shepherds (2:8–20). **II 9.** The motif of the star showing the way is an additional feature, not decisive for the main line of the story. In later tradition the magi became kings under the influence of passages like Ps. 72:10 ; Isa. 49:7, 60:10 (so Tertullian) ; they were supposed to be three since there were three kinds of gifts (5th cent.) ; they got names (Kaspar, Balthasar and Melchior; 8th cent.) ; and in the 14th cent. Kaspar became a Moor. **6.** The quotation is from Mic. 5:2 and follows neither MT nor LXX. It is an example of Mt.'s way of adapting prophetic texts in the light of their fulfilment. MT : 'Bethlehem Ephrathah [cf. 18 below], who is little to be among the *clans* of Judah' is changed, partly on the basis of the Heb. consonants, to 'Bethlehem, in the land of Judah, by no means are you smallest of the *rulers* of Judah', a form which brings out more strongly the positive Messianic note.

c **13-23.** If 1-12 had a legendary character of a more general Hellenistic type, this can partly be said also about this section. While not unique in antiquity, the cruelty of Herod had become proverbial even in Rome. But the massacre of the children is not mentioned by Josephus, who tells about many of the ferocities of Herod. The miraculous rescue of a royal child is well known from folklore and history (Heracles, Romulus and Remus, Sargon, Cyrus) and from the OT (cf. Moses, Exod. 2). In addition to the general character of this legendary material, the impact of Jewish haggadah may have had influence, perhaps especially the passover haggadah, where Laban (i.e. the half-Jew Herod) is more wicked than Pharaoh, and Jacob is sent to Egypt by the divine word (see D. Daube, *The NT and Rabbinic Judaism* (1956), 189–92). The style is haggadic, but is used with economy ; there is just enough to trace the main line of the flight, its justification and its end, all supported by scripture and guided by dreams. Egypt was a natural asylum for
d Jews. It is also worth noting that the Qumrân community did not return to its centre, which had been destroyed by earthquake in 31 B.C., until just after the death of Herod in 4 B.C. The reign of Herod lived in memory as one in which Messianic tendencies were not welcome in Judaea. The quotation in **15** from Hos. 11:1 is based on the Heb. text and presupposes a tradition about a flight to Egypt. Apart from such a
e tradition, there is nothing Messianic about it. **16-18.** The two years indicates that the magi are thought of as having seen the star long before, or it is just an inconsistency in the tradition. Again the quotation is based on the Heb. text, but no intentional changes are made. It is one of the more far-fetched formula quotations in Mt. ; but Jewish tradition connected Ephrath (cf. MT above to 6) with Bethlehem (MT and LXX to Gen. 35:19). Thus the quotation stresses the significance of Bethlehem as the place of revealed history and thereby all the quotations in ch. 2 find their common denominator in their geographical significance. Bethlehem—Egypt—Bethlehem—and
f . . . Nazareth. **19-23.** Herod died in 4 B.C. and his realm was divided among his three sons : Archelaus became ethnarch of Judaea, Samaria and Idumaea ; Herod Antipas became tetrarch of Galilee and Peraea ; and Philip tetrarch of the land east and north of Galilee. Archelaus was more to be feared than his brothers, and partly on the request of the leading Jews he was summoned to Rome in A.D. 6 and exiled to a place called Vienna, on the Rhône south of Lyons. **20.** 'The Land of Israel', a term used only here in the NT, carries the connotations of the Moses story as compared with the more geographical Judaea, Galilee, etc. The same is true about the plural '*those* who sought the child's life' (e.g. Exod. 4:19).
g So they find their way to Nazareth. Here Mt. catches up with what is taken for granted in Mk (1:9) ;
Lk. (1:26) ; Jn (1:45f., 7:41) ; Ac. (10:38). The 67
adjective *nazōraios* (cf. Mt. 26:71) has given rise to considerable discussion. Since the town Nazareth is unknown prior to the Gospels, and *nazōraios*, especially in Ac., is used by outsiders as the name for the Christian sect or party (24:5), and since Epiphanius speaks of a pre-Christian group called *nasaraioi* and the Mandaean literature uses the *natzoraje* about themselves, the suggestion was made (by Lidzbarski and others) that this adjective originally designated a pre-Christian sect out of which Jesus and the church emerged (the term having the meaning 'observant'). Nazareth would then be just invented as a false historisation. It has, however, been shown (by G. F. Moore, in *Beginnings of Christianity* i, 426–32 ; H. H. Schaeder, TWNT iv, 878–84; and W. F. Albright, JBL 65 (1946), 397–401) that *nazōraios* is a natural form of a Gentilic adjective to the Galilean-Aramaic Nāṣ^{e}rath, and the Mandaean term should be understood as derived from the Syriac term for Christians, cf. M. Black, *An Aramaic Approach . . .* (1954^{2}), 143–6. The Marcan form *nazarēnos* may be another of the Latinisms of the second Gospel ; cf. *essaioi* (Philo)—*essēnoi* (Josephus, mostly)—*esseni* (Pliny). The reference to 'the prophets' (plural) is somewhat vague. It is not impossible that this vagueness is intentional and allows the double reference to *nēṣer* (sprout) in Isa. 11:1 and *nāzîr* in Jg. 13:5, the former with explicit reference to Messiah in the Targum. The point of the quotation is nevertheless not to prove the messiahship of Jesus, but to account for and defend his Galilean background, cf. Jn 7:41–3.

III 1-5. All the four Gospels begin with **John the Baptist**, and Ac. 1:22, 10:37 suggest that the work 67
of the Baptiser even belonged to the kerygma. The problem of the relation between John's work and that of Jesus looms larger in the Fourth Gospel (1:19–51, 3:22–4:3), but among the Synoptics Mt. is the one most concerned to give to the Baptist his proper place in the plan of God (3:13–15, 11:7–19, 14:1–2, 17:9–13, etc.). That the relations between the early church and the followers of John remained a problem is seen in Ac. 19:1–8. The activities of John the Baptist are known also from Jos. Ant. XVIII, v, 2) and the short account there given agrees on the whole with the picture of the Gospels : He was called 'the Baptist', he taught baptism and demanded an ethical life ; he was killed by Herod Antipas, who feared that John's activity could lead to a revolt, presumably of a messianic nature. In Lk. the traditions about John's origin, his miraculous birth, his entering upon the great line of the *nazirs* of God (Lk. 1:15), and his dwelling in the wilderness 'till the day of his manifestation before Israel' (1:80) are described in strict OT terms (3:2). Mt. 3 changes to present tense, an historic present which could well be retained in the translation : 'In those [well-known and crucial] days John the Baptist appears . . .' To the general reference 'wilderness' (Mk), Mt. adds 'of Judaea'. The place
for John's activity is unknown (cf. Jn 1:28 : Bethany on the other side of Jordan ; 3:23 : Aenon, near Salim). Jordan as the river used is well attested (Mk 1:5, 9), and is hardly only a theological addition, although it had great typological significance in later Christian interpretation (see J. Daniélou, *Sacramentum Futuri* (1950), 233ff.). In Lk., John's stay in the wilderness is actually prior to his Baptist activity. **2.** The content of John's preaching is summarised in exactly the same words as the initial message of Jesus (not so Mk and Lk.), see 4:17. **3-4.** 'For this man b
is the one spoken of . . .' While Lk. (and Mk with a conflated quotation) refer the quotation from Isa. to the whole activity of John, Mt. refers it to the person John. The quotation is not new with Mt., and it requires its LXX form. This form made it easier to use it as the Gospels saw it. The Heb. text must be read with a colon after 'crying' : 'A voice crying : In the wilderness . . .' and in that form it was used by the Qumrân community (1QS 8:14) with reference to c

676c the study of the Law at the community centre in the wilderness of Judaea (cf. K. Stendahl, *The School of St Matthew*, 48, 217). Even with the LXX it took some adaptation in the light of messianic fulfilment to fit it into the Gospel meaning : ' the Lord ' (Yahweh) was read as referring to Christ, and thus ' of our God ' in Isa. 40:4*b* was rendered by a simple ' his '.

d **4-5.** The description of John's clothes points to the picture of a prophet (Elijah, 2 Kg. 1:8) and the life of the wilderness, the *nāzîr* ideal rather than asceticism of a dualistic sort. The Ebionite Gospel found a reference to the manna behind the reference to the honey but the Synoptics have not seen any allusion to the Exodus at this point. There is no similarity to what we know about dress and food at Qumrân. John's activity is seen as Judaean and as felt in Jerusalem.

e **6-10.** The baptism is performed by John or under his supervision and it is accompanied by confession of sins. Here the Qumrân material has bearing on John's baptism. The yearly rites of lustration in 1QS 2:19–3:12 are described in a language which suggests its origin in the priestly lustrations at the Temple (see N. A. Dahl, ' The Origin of Baptism ', in *Festschrift S. Mowinckel* (1955), 36–51) ; yet the eschatological claims of the community make them significant for true belonging to the chosen ones of God. But the water does not help if one falls short of the moral and communal standards of the community—then he is not even allowed to undergo the baptism. While Mk 1:4 speaks about a baptism of repentance to the remission of sins, Mt. gives a picture of John which puts him closer to the Qumrân contention where repentance is the condition for baptism and where remission of sins is not mentioned. This becomes even more clear in **7-10** where the emphasis is on the fruits of repentance. Mt. and Lk. draw from the same source, but Mt. has narrowed the address of these words to the Pharisees and the Sadducees, while Lk. has ' the multitudes ' (cf. Mt. 16:1–12 with par. in Lk.). The objective in being baptised is to escape the wrath of God's ultimate judgment. AV and RSV : ' who warned you . . .' ; but perhaps rather : ' who gave you the idea that you could escape . . .' In the imminent judgment it is the fruits, the deeds in accordance with repentance, which count ; the trust in belonging to the people of Israel is of no avail, a theme most fully elaborated in Jn 8, cf. Jn 15:6, and Mt. 21:33–46, in close relation to the Baptist's ministry (32).

f **11-12.** At this point Lk. (3:15, like Jn 1:20 ; cf. Ac. 13:25) is anxious to sharpen the line between Jesus and John the Baptist by mentioning that some people entertained the idea that John was the Messiah. Mt. and Mk give only the statement by the Baptist, and Mt. ties it to the reference to the impending judgment. John's baptism is one of preparation and repentance ; but there will follow a messianic baptism and this is not only a preparation, not even preparation for the Spirit, but it will give the Spirit. This expectation was also that of Qumrân : ' In the season of the decreed judgment, the Holy Spirit will come over man, [either man in general ; or to One Man, i.e. the Messiah, and through him to those chosen for an eternal covenant] as a baptism ; but there will be a fiery visitation over the sons of perversion ' (1QS 4:9–26) ; cf. Test. Levi 18. See also J. A. T. Robinson, HTR 50 (1957), 175–92. ' He who comes after me ', especially in the form the phrase has in Mt., may have an intentional double meaning : (*a*) the one to come later ; (*b*) my disciple (as in 16:24, cf. 4:19 ; see also Jn 1:15). A disciple should serve his master as a slave. The difference between ' carry the sandals ' (Mt.), ' loose the laces of the sandals ' (Mk, Lk.) could go back to one Aram. expression (so McNeile, ad loc.).

g **13-17.** At this point Lk. brings his account about John's activities to an end : John is put into prison and the **baptism of Jesus** is described as an epiphany while all the people were baptised, but John is not mentioned as the agent. In Mk John is the agent and Jesus' baptism is treated as a matter of course, 676g
but in Mt. Jesus ' comes ' (the present tense, retained in the AV, alerts the reader to something important) from Galilee to John and his intention is stressed : in order to be baptised by him in the river Jordan. **14.** John tries to prevent this (*diekōlyen* : imperfect of attempted action) and Jesus urges him to let it be so now in order to fulfil the plan of God, which in Mt. has ' righteousness ' as its ultimate goal (see 21:32, cf. Lk. 7:29 and Mt. 6:33 ; this seems to be the understanding also in Ignatius, Ep. to Smyrna 1:1); cf. Mt. 17:24–7. John's objection is a general statement of inferiority to Jesus, but may in Mt. show concern for later church problems as those in Ac. 19:1–8. The problem is that of inferiority-superiority, not that of the sinless Son of God accepting a baptism of repentance, as it is expressed in the *Nazarene Gospel* : ' In what have I sinned, that I should go and be baptised by him ? ' Mt. (differing from Mk 1:4 and Lk. 3:3) does not speak of sins or forgiveness of sins in relation to John's baptism, see 26:28. **16-17.** Now h
the heavens open up (cf. Jn 1:51) and the Spirit of God descends upon Jesus as a dove (seen only by Jesus ; so also Mk ; Lk. : ' in the form of a dove ' ; in Jewish literature the dove is the symbol of Israel ; cf. Philo, *Qu. rer. div.* 25, 48 : dove symbol for Wisdom, *Nous* and *Logos*). The voice from heaven is the *bath-ḳôl* (the ' daughter of the voice ', i.e. the ' echo ' of the Spirit which spoke to the prophets), in the period when the Spirit was not available to the people as it should be again in the time of consummation. The saying of the voice differs in the three Gospels and the MSS show considerable confusion and mutual influence of the parallels on each other (cf. also 17:5). Basically the allusion is to Isa. 42:1 but the striking *'ebhedh/pais* (servant or child) has been changed to *huios* (son), perhaps under influence of Ps. 2:7 (cod. D in Lk. has Ps. 2:7 in a straight quotation). Mt. has directed the words to the bystanders. The actual source for the quotation is significant for the understanding of the baptism of Jesus. If the text be a conscious reference to Isa. 42, it can form the basis for understanding Jesus as the *'Ebhedh Yahweh*, the Servant (so O. Cullmann, *Die Christologie des NTs* (1957), 65), and the baptism takes on the connotations given to that term e.g. in Mk 10:38 : the baptism of suffering and death, cf. Mt. 20:22–8. If the relation to Ps. 2:7 is carried out, the point is ' messianic enthronement ', see Mt. 17:1–8. In both cases, however, the primary significance is the announcement of Jesus as the chosen one of God (to ' in whom I am well pleased ', cf. Lk. 2:14 and for the Qumrân material, E. Vogt in K. Stendahl, *The Scrolls and the NT* (1957), 114–16). There is little or no indication that Mt. is aware of Jesus' baptism as a prototype for the baptism practised by the church. The accent is on Jesus' manifestation as the one endowed with the Spirit.

IV 1-11. Mt. and Lk. draw their material about **the** 677a
temptation from the same source. The strict LXX nature of the OT quotations, which form the substance of the pericope, indicate that it had been cast in its form in a Greek-speaking milieu. The difference in order may be due to Lk.'s use of the reference to angels in Mk 1:13 within the dialogue (4:10), omitting it in the final section since it is Satan who suggests angelic assistance, and thus contrary to Jesus' answer in 4:10 ; cf. also Mt. 26:53 (see, however, Lk. 22:43, if genuine). To Lk. the Gethsemane temptation is the b
continuation of the temptation (4:13) ; not so Mt., where the victory over Satan is definite, and in the light of which Peter is rebuked (16:23). Mk's short reference, 1:12 (especially the enigmatic ' among the wild beasts '), may suggest that Mk presupposes his readers to be familiar with a fuller account. What he says about the angels suggests, however, less of a real struggle and gives the note of a sham fight to the incident. All the synoptic Gospels relate the Tempta- c
tion to the baptismal epiphany of Jesus and it is the Spirit (which Jesus has just received) which leads him

677c into the wilderness (cf. perhaps 1 Tim. 3:16). The forty days (Mt.: 'and nights'; cf. Exod. 34:28) remind us of Moses and all the answers of Jesus have the Exodus as their setting (Dt. 8:3, 6:16, 6:13). The point intended in Mt. is clear: Jesus rejects the false understanding of his power. The conversation has the form of rabbinic controversy with biblical proof-texts, and a later apologetic interest in the church's clarification of its understanding of the Messiah may have given the form to this well-structured tradition.

d **10.** Mt. (and Lk.) retain the name Satan in what appears to be *ipsissima verba* of Jesus (cf. 12:26, 16:23) while *diabolos* ('devil'; **1, 5, 8, 11**) occurs in passages where the activity of the church can be surmised (e.g. 13:39, 25:41). Mt.'s 'the Holy City' (Lk.: Jerusalem) has distinctly Jewish flavour.

e The three temptations are: (1) Either to use spectacular 'magic' or to use his power for selfish means. In either case the incidents of Peter and Simon Magus (Ac. 8), Paul and Elymas (Ac. 13) illustrate the issue in the early church; cf. however the feeding of the multitudes in the desert (14:13–21, 15:32–9). (2) The spectacular signs which the Jews requested will not be given (12:38–42, 16:1–4); cf. however ch. 24 and 26:64. (3) The earthly glory of the Messiah is a satanic temptation (16:23, 26:53); cf. however 28:16–20. The mythical element is not strong, cf. the *Gospel of the Hebrews*: 'My mother the Holy Spirit [feminine in Heb.] took me by one of my hairs and brought me to . . . Mount Tabor.' It is, however, significant that the christological title around which the pericope centres is 'Son of God'. Satan knows who he is, and so do the evil spirits (e.g. 8:29) but nobody else in Jesus' surroundings in the early stages of his ministry. The form of the question '. . . if you are the Son of God . . .' always has a note of temptation in the Gospel: 16:15–23, 26:63, 27:40;

f cf. Wis. 2:18. The term *peirasmos* means not only 'temptation' but also 'trial' or even 'tribulation', cf. 6:13 and 26:41. In this pericope, however, 'temptation' covers the meaning well although it should be remembered that by overcoming Satan Jesus has withstood the assault of him who puts Jesus' followers through trials and tribulations, trying to make them apostates, see 24:12, 22, etc.

g **12-25.** Mk and Mt. state that Jesus' teaching starts after the imprisonment of John the Baptist. Mt. is moving rapidly and with great economy to his first discourse (chs. 5–7) and is only interested in setting the stage for it. He does so by summarising Mk's so-called 'Day in Capernaum' (1:18–38). This makes it possible to see what Mt. considered essential in the ministry of Jesus: (1) He taught in Galilee of the Gentiles; (2) He announced the Kingdom of Heaven; (3) He called disciples; (4) He worked miracles of healing; (5) The impact of his ministry was widely recognised from Syria in the north to Jerusalem in the south and Decapolis in the east.

h **12-16.** Apparently Mt. is—perhaps rightly—under the impression that Nazareth is not in the territories of Zebulun and Naphtali, but Capernaum is. Thus Jesus' moving to the latter is significant for the fulfilment of the prophecy (Isa. 9:1–2), and Mt. understands its reference to the sea as referring to Capernaum's location by the Sea of Galilee (in Isa.: the Mediterranean). The quotation is adapted on the basis of Heb. text to make this meaning clear. The point is again (cf. 2:23) to give valid reasons for a Messianic ministry in Galilee, and this is made even more stable than in Mk (1:21) by saying that

i Jesus 'settled down' in Capernaum, cf. 9:1. **17.** Some MSS (Syr. Sin. Cur.; k) and Fathers have only: 'The Kingdom of Heaven is at hand', but it is easier to understand the addition of 'repent' as an indication of what Mt. felt was required of his hearers. Mt. concentrates on what he must have considered the nucleus of the message and does not retain Mk's references to the fulfilment of time and acceptance of the good news. The Gr. word translated 'repent' (*metanoeite*, lit. 'change your mind') is in NT times and especially in eschatological literature equivalent not to 'grieve for one's sins' (*niḥam*) but to 'turn around, return' (*shûbh*). This 'conversion' is the radical conversion to God of an apostate nation and in the OT it finds its strongest expression in Jer. It is the appropriate attitude in the time when the Kingdom is at hand. The Kingdom j 677

of Heaven is Mt.'s term for the Kingdom of God (see above, §673*f*; cf. however 'Kingdom of God', 12:28, 19:24, 21:31, 43), and it has a Jewish flavour in avoiding the mentioning of 'God', but Mt. does not generally subscribe to this attitude of awe (see e.g. Mk 14:61 and Mt. 26:63). The Kingdom is the paramount subject in Jesus' teaching in the synoptic Gospels, while the term occupies a humble place in Jn and the other NT writings. The term as used in the NT suggests more than a reference to God's 'sovereignty' or 'reign' in an abstract or moral sense. It is a synonym for 'the age to come' (see 12:32), and Jesus does not claim to bring in a new concept about this coming age, but draws upon common Jewish expectations (cf. the parables about the Kingdom in ch. 13). The age of all-embracing bliss and righteous- k

ness is now at hand: *engiken*, 'it has come near and is near now'. C. H. Dodd (*The Parables of the Kingdom* (1936), 43ff.) insisted that this meant the Kingdom had actually arrived, identifying *engizein* with *phthanein* ('come upon' in 12:28) and suggesting the same Aram. expression behind the two. There are, however, good reasons against such an identification (see, e.g., W. G. Kümmel, *Promise and Fulfilment* (1957), 23ff., 105ff.), and it would be misleading to move beyond the meaning that its powers are in operation in, with, and around Jesus; but since the Kingdom is not an abstract expression for God's sovereignty but stands for a new and different age, it is yet to come; cf. also *engiken* in Jas 5:8. **18-23.** Next (following Mk) l

comes **the calling of four disciples**, three of whom, Simon Peter, James (Gr. *Jakobos*), and John, form the group of closest associates to Jesus (see 17:1–8; cf. 26:37). Mt. gives both the name Simon and Peter (see 16:18) at this point, indicating that Peter was a name given to Simon later (*legomenos*: 'called'; cf. 1:16). All four men were fishermen and in Mk they are thought of as living in Capernaum (Jn 1:44: Bethsaida as Peter's home-town). 'Follow after . . .' m

is a technical term for discipleship. It was by following his master also in a quite physical sense that a Jewish student was trained and his life under the 'yoke' (11:29, 23:4) was shaped. Also the phrase 'and he called them' has a precise and formal ring, but this is based on Christian tradition and the revival of prophetic calling, e.g. Elijah's call of Elisha in 1 Kg. 19:19–21, where Elisha is taken from his work and leaves it and his father. 'Fishers of men' in the meaning used here has become a powerful image in the Christian tradition. Used in a good sense it has no known precedent, and witnesses to the social matrix of Christianity. **23-5.** Before his first discourse, Mt. n

gives a summary of Jesus' activity: he travels widely in Galilee. Every Jew had the right to teach in the synagogue, and one who came visiting was often invited to do so. The term 'teaching' commends itself to Mt. (cf. Mk 1:39—and 1:21) when he mentions the synagogues. But his message was the good news that the Kingdom was at hand. This was accompanied by healing. These healings are what here brings his fame to spread widely. Syria was the name of the Roman province to which also Palestine belonged, but it could also refer to the land north of Galilee. The term 'all Syria' may indicate that Mt. uses the name in the inclusive Roman sense (cf. above, §673*b*). The crowds that follow Jesus are from all over Palestine. Apart from Judaea, the population was highly mixed—in Decapolis the Jews must have been in the minority. Yet there is no awareness of this 'problem' here. Jesus' contacts with Gentiles are treated as rare exceptions later on in the Gospel (8:5–13, 15:21–8),

677n and Mt. apparently thinks of those who followed him as Jews.

678a **V 1-VII 29 The Sermon on the Mount**—The first of the five discourses which constitute the most striking feature of Mt.'s treatment (see §§673*hi*). Its location as well as its composition is clearly Matthean. While some of the material is found in Lk., especially in Lk. 6:20–49 (starting with beatitudes and ending with the parable of the builders), but also scattered in the Lucan Travel Narrative (9:51–18:14), Mt. has created a discourse on the challenge and reward of the life of the disciples. Apart from the dependence on material common to Lk. and Mt., this discourse shows a growth of catechetical material. 'He reflects but does not directly record early oral tradition' (F. V. Filson, 'Broken Patterns in the Gospel of Matthew', JBL 75 (1956), 231). In the cases where we have parallels in Lk., the Matthean forms of the material display more of structure and ecclesiastical codification, but this should not lead to the conclusion that Lk. is always closer to the original. The Lucan form has been written to correspond closely with Lk.'s point of view, and the Lucan discourse in ch. 6 has *its* features of composition, centred around
b the concept of humility as such—Mt. has given enough of a background for the first discourse: Jesus' teaching and healing activity is well under way. He has called his first disciples and many people are following him. 4:24-5 shows some dependence on Mk 3:7–12, and the mountain where Mk (and Lk.) see Jesus calling his disciples (3:13) is made the appropriate scene for the discourse. The traditional division of chapters obscures how closely 4:24-5 is related to the discourse, as is the similar section in Lk. 6:18–19, both sections being immediately preceded by the calling of disciples.

c **V 1-2.** Mt. sees Jesus go away from the people to teach his disciples. The mountain is hardly a hill serving as pulpit before the multitudes but, as it is in Mk 3:13 and often in Lk., a place of privacy (so 14:23; cf. also 17:1 and 28:16). It has often been understood as a reference to Jesus as 'the prophet like unto Moses' (Dt. 18:15; cf. 1 Mac. 14:41; 2 Mac. 8:1–8), the mount being a 'new Sinai'. Such a typology is, however, far from compelling. This is the first time the word 'disciples' is used. The comprehensiveness of the term cannot be understood in the light of what Mt. has told so far (Simon Peter, Andrew, James and John; 4:18–22) but is based on the distinction between the people (even those who followed him) and the 'disciples'. **He sat down,** i.e. the practice of synagogue (Lk. 4:20) and of the schools.

d **3-12.** Both in Lk. and Mt. the **Beatitudes** have the marks of Semitic poetry. When Mt. gives a longer series of beatitudes without the woes, he uses his material as his first presentation of Jesus' teaching. Mt.'s beatitudes have somewhat the same function within the Gospel as Lk.'s 'programmatic' sermon in Nazareth (4:16–30), with its quotation from Isa. 61:1–2 and its prophecy about the messianic bliss of the poor and oppressed (cf. G. D. Kilpatrick, *The Origins . . .*, 82, about this sermon in Q, but not used by Mt.). The form **blessed are . . .** is well known from the OT, especially the Psalms and the Wisdom literature. The ethical note is stronger in Mt. than in Lk. (**3** 'in spirit', **7-9**) and consequently the Wisdom tradition is more clearly retained: this accounts for the third person instead of Lk.'s second-person address, but the accent is rather eschatological. The beatitudes are not primarily a description of the true virtues or an exhortation to the right life, but a reinforcement of the promises of the Kingdom with its approaching
e bliss and directed to the disciples. **3. Poor in spirit** (Lk. 'poor') is a correct interpretation of the Heb. *'ānî* as used in Jewish piety in the time of Jesus, the so-called *'anāwîm* piety; *'ānî*, *'ānāw*, and *'ebhyôn* are synonyms for this attitude and the meanings 'poor' (*ptōchos*), 'meek' (*praÿs*) should not be too neatly distinguished. Goodspeed's translation 'feel their spiritual need' is a modern over-interpretation. 678e
The Pharisees identified themselves with this attitude of 'poverty' and humility over against the fellow travellers of Hellenism and Roman politics. So did the Qumrân sect (4QpPs 37, 1QS 4:2–6). **4. Those who mourn** points in the same direction: the
oppressed, those 'who look for the consolation' of a f
humiliated Israel (Lk. 2:25). **5.** An allusion to Ps. 37:11, a psalm which is very close to the whole series of beatitudes and which was given an *ad hoc* interpretation in the Qumrân sect as a prophecy in process of fulfilment through the establishment of their messianic community (4QpPs 37). The Western texts have 4 and 5 in reversed order, whereby 3 and 5 form a *parallelismus membrorum.* **inherit the earth** (or 'the land') as a parallel to 'receive the Kingdom' makes clear how the Kingdom is understood as the
realisation of Israel's hope. **6.** While Lk. speaks about g
hunger and thirst as such, not necessarily in a plain material sense, Mt. understands it clearly as metaphorical (see F. M. Cross, *The Ancient Library of Qumrân* (1958), 67, on Lk. 6:21 as a reference to the messianic banquet, a reference which is woven together with the words about the poor in 4QpPs 37). **The righteousness** (with article, cf. **10**) is a crucial term for Mt. (see further §673*f*). Were it not so, it could mean simply 'those oppressed', 'the underdogs'. But in Mt. it has the further meaning of the vindication of God's people as the goal of history. This justification is a gift of God to the suppressed, cf. 1QS 11:12–15.
7. Here we meet the 'principle of reciprocity' as used h
in the Gospels (see 6:14f.; cf. 7:1). 'Show mercy and mercy will be shown to you' (i.e. by God) circulated as a logion of Jesus outside the Gospels (an *agraphon*, unwritten saying; 1 Clem. 13:2). Polyc. 2:3
combines a series of such sayings. **8.** In Ps. 24:4 the i
access to the Temple on Zion is for him who has clean hands and a pure heart. In Jas 4:8 the 'pure heart' is the opposite of the 'double mind', cf. Mt. 6:22. **To see God** (only here in the synoptics) is a synonym for the final bliss of the Kingdom, cf. Rev. 22:4 (Ps. 17:15, 42:3) and 2 Esd. 7:98: '. . . for they hasten to behold the face of him whom they served in life and from whom they are to receive their
reward when glorified.' **9.** In the term **peacemakers,** j
'peace' does not carry the full meaning of the Heb. *shālôm* (neither as a greeting (Lk. 10:5, cf. Mt. 10:13) nor as the comprehensive term for ultimate well-being), but refers to the non-militant character of the true disciples of the Kingdom (so in Jas 3:18, cf. 1 Enoch 52:11). It is not impossible that Mt. here has a mistranslation or interpretation of an Aram. word of the same stem as 'peace', meaning 'perfect' or 'honest'. According to Hos. 1:10, the Israel restored shall be called 'sons of the living God'. This terminology is well alive in Jewish expectations, Ps. Sol. 17:30; cf. 44-5 and 11:25. The beatitudes in **8** and **9** are not to be understood as consciously ethical statements. The future tense ('shall see'—'shall be called') refers primarily to the contrast of
reward in the age to come. **10-12** lend further support k
to such an understanding. As in 3 the Kingdom is what matters and all the words which have served as synonyms for the coming of the Kingdom give way for a final reference to it. While Lk. refers to the Son of Man, Mt. has 'me' (see 8:20). The true spirit of humility is heightened to that of martyrdom. The cause is once more summed up in Mt.'s term 'righteousness' (cf. 6). The reward is stressed and is not identified with the share in the Kingdom as such but seems to imply a more specific reward for those who have suffered persecution and derision. The question of reward was handled with sophisticated care by the rabbis but Jesus is less concerned about the dangers involved in such exhortations, see also 19 and 46; cf. 19:29. Lk. is aware of the fact that no persecution or ridicule has taken place so far ('when that day comes'); Mt. speaks right into a situation of such pressure. For the idea of the prophets as martyrs—

678k which is not based on the OT accounts—see 23:34. In the light of the Qumrân texts and *Mart. Isa.* Jesus may here refer to his disciples as 'prophets' as the Essenes considered themselves and were considered by Josephus (see K. Schubert in K. Stendahl, *The Scrolls and the NT*, 122f.).

l **13-16.** On the basis of separate logia where the metaphors **salt** and **light** were used (Mk 9:50, 4:21; Lk. 14:34f., 8:16, 11:33), Mt. has construed a double parable (cf. 13:44–6). All the editions of the sayings about salt refer to discipleship. The connotation of 'salt' in rabbinic metaphorical language is mainly 'wisdom' and this is indicated by the fact that the basic meaning of the verb *mōranthē* (RSV: 'has lost its taste') is also 'to be foolish'. The strong emphasis on 'you' may give the clue to the logion in Mt.: *You* (and not the official representatives of Jewish wisdom and tradition) are the truly wise, while they have fallen hopelessly behind (see also W. Nauck, 'Salt as a Metaphor in Instructions for Discipleship', *Studia Theologica* (1952), 165–78). Other possibilities: It is a warning, or the point is—as it may be in **14**—that just as salt cannot lose its taste, so the disciples will serve as the salt of the world by inner necessity. The first of the above-mentioned interpretations is possible also for **14-16**, as Mt. has understood the sayings and especially for the purely Matthean form of **16**. Jesus' disciples are the true light and their example will arouse the admiration which belongs to the true Israel when God's name is honoured
m by the Gentiles, cf. Rom. 2:24 and 9:8, 15:31. **17-20.** Apart from a short logion, related to the discussion of divorce in Lk. 16:17, and Mk 13:31 (24:35), this pericope is peculiar to Mt. H. Ljungman, *Das Gesetz erfüllen* (1954), has given good reasons for taking it as a unit. The *Sitz im Leben* is the different attitudes toward the Law in early Christianity. Some attempts were made to revise the Law for Gentile as well as for Jewish Christianity, as did the Ebionites, cf. Ac. 15 (see H. J. Schoeps, *Theol. und Gesch. des Judenchristentums*, 1949). **19.** Those who take such an approach in practice and teaching are here called 'smallest in the Kingdom'. For such an approach to 'wrong teaching', cf. 1 C. 3, where the dissenters are saved, but with a narrow margin. For Paul the Law is also undivided (no distinction between cultic and moral commandments) and for 'Mt.', who also had a somewhat academic background (see above, §673*g*), the same is true. While Paul sees the Law as obsolete in a certain sense (Gal. 3:24), Mt. follows a less drastic line, prefigured in the type of Jewish expectation where the coming of the Messiah would imply a sharpening of the Law to its ultimate implications of holiness (cf. W. D. Davies, *Torah in the Messianic Age . . .* (1952)). To him the Pharisees are—as they were to the men at Qumrân—'the seekers of smooth things', i.e. those who made the Law practicable and thereby broke its ultimate demand by their casuistry. This understanding of our pericope calls for a drastic revision of our picture of what according to Mt. was the issue in the encounter between Jesus and the Pharisees.

679a **21-48.** In this light the **antitheses** which now follow appear to be examples of the sharpening of the Law, its restoration in its ultimate radicality. Here is not a New Law and not a New Moses, but a Messianic intensification, producing the true righteousness which belongs to the Kingdom. This is done with great emphasis on such attitudes and virtues which were high-lighted in the Beatitudes, a fact which has led to a romantic modernisation of the Sermon on the Mount. The point is not inner motivation compared with pharisaic casuistry, or warm concern for human values as opposed to hair-splitting legalism. We are faced with Mt.'s collection of statements concerning the superior righteousness and its root in Jesus' messianic restoration of the Law

b **21-26** The contrast **you have heard . . . but I say** is somewhat similar to the formula in rabbinic texts ('I hear . . . but you must say . . .') used to distinguish
between the literal meaning of scripture and its valid 679
(halachic) interpretation (see D. Daube, *The NT and Rabbinic Judaism* (1956), 55–62) but it differs from such usage strikingly when Jesus turns it around and claims his own authority: 'but *I* say unto you . . .' Such a form presupposes an authority far beyond that of the scribes (see 7:28). 'The men of old' refers both to the Law itself (Exod. 20:13; Dt. 5:17) and to prevailing interpretation of these commandments in Judaism, i.e. both written and oral Law. **22.** 'without
cause' (AV) is wanting in the best texts. The word c
'brother' looms large in this pericope as well as in the Sermon on the Mount as a whole. In the light of the disciplinary rules from Qumrân with their high ideals of brotherhood within the community we must raise the question with new seriousness whether the ethical concern here is intramural (relations between the disciples as members of a community) rather than rules for human behaviour in general. The Jews understood 'brother' to be 'Israelite' but it is often said that Jesus broke through such a particularism. That is certainly true, but in this context the focus can well be that of the disciples in their mutual relations. Such an interpretation has much to commend it, especially since the relation between cultic action and the mutual forgiveness of the brethren is a strong motif in Mt. (see 6:14, 18:15–20), and it is in such a context that the logion about sacrifice and forgiveness (23–4) is
most understandable. The references to 'the council' d
and 'Gehenna' are an obvious device for crescendo, especially if—as is quite possible—the obscure term 'raka' was a stronger invective than 'fool', cf. 23:16–22. The Gehenna (Heb. *Gê-Hinnōm*) of fire belongs to the apocalyptic topography. The actual valley of Hinnom (Jos. 15:8), south of Jerusalem, was here transformed into the hell of fire (1 Enoch 54:1–2; 2 Baruch 85:13). **23** and **24** deal with the case where somebody has a (just) claim against you, not where you feel hostility towards your brother. (Thus we are close to the problem of attitude towards enemies, 43–7.) In both cases the emphasis is on the urgency for reconciliation. The Mishnah says that the Day of Atonement does not atone for offences against one's neighbour, unless one reconciles him (Yoma 8:9; cf. Mt. 3:7–10). **25-6** is found in the context of eschatological urgency in Lk. (12:57–9) and this seems more congenial to the logion, and Mt. presents it here where the eschatological note adds urgency to the plea, an urgency which is implied in the Sermon on the Mount already by its prologue, the Beatitudes.
27-32. A similar intensification is given to the com- e
mandment about adultery (Exod. 20:13; Dt. 5:17). In the Decalogue as well as in Jewish interpretation, this commandment referred only to the breaking into another man's marriage (a qualified theft). It is hard to trace how and when it came to affect premarital behaviour and the extramarital relations of the husband. Jesus identifies lust and action, disregarding the well-developed distinctions of the scribes between
intention and action. **29-30** is one of the Matthean f
doublets and has its parallel in 18:8–9 and in Mk 9:43–8 (see J. C. Hawkins, *Horae Synopticae* (1909[2]), 64–87). There is no need to suggest two sources (Mk in ch. 18 and M (see §653*d*) in ch. 5) since such doublets occur in Mt. also where there is no indication of different sources (e.g. 16:19/18:18, 9:27–31/20:29–34) and are the consequences of Mt.'s method. He found good reason to make use of the passage in this context, and found it natural to give the passage also in its Marcan context. **30.** *Skandalizō* (AV: 'offend'; RSV: 'cause to sin') has the root meaning of 'stumbling-block', see 11:6. **31-2.** A 'doublet' g
(cf. 19:9) although the wording is somewhat different; sometimes explained by two sources (Mk and M). It is more plausible that Mt. lifted the material from Mk 10:11–12 (Mt. 19:9) and wrote it up in a more full and formal style in the framework of his antitheses. It belonged there since the point was the restoration of the true Law and Mk knew of a case where Jesus

9g even went beyond what Moses had given men for their lack of ability to live according to God's will (see Mt. 19:7–8). The clause ' except in the case of unchastity ' (or : ' fornication ', but *porneia* may also include ' adultery ') is usually considered a later concession to compromise in church discipline. This is not necessary : (1) Divorce was not ' allowed ' but *required* by Jewish law in the case where the woman had committed adultery (cf. 1:19) and this fact may have been in the picture from the beginning, but not spelled out in the other Gospels. (2) There is a difference in form and function between the general principle and the actual practice. In Mt. with its formal features of a manual, a clause like this could be expected. See further, note to 19:9.

h **33-37.** The words about swearing take the place of the commandment in the Decalogue concerning false witness, following those concerning murder and adultery. There is a close affinity to Jas 5:12, where they have a possibly more original form. In Jas there is no reference to them as a logion of the Lord, and it is quite possible that both Jas and Mt. draw upon Jewish material, cf. *Pseudo-Phocylides* 16 and Did. 2:3 where ' thou shalt not commit perjury ' is linked to ' thou shalt not bear false witness ' and ' thou shalt not be double-tongued '. It is in such a context of Jewish moral codes rather than in the OT or in rabbinic discussions about oaths (cf. 23:16–22) that this collection has its proper background, and Mt. has cast such material in the form of an antithesis. Gr. *epiorkeō* means both ' commit perjury ' and ' break an oath ' ; the latter translation fits perhaps better the following ' but you shall redeem to the Lord your oaths '. Josephus mentions the Essene aversion to oaths (Jos. BJ (II, viii, 6) ; they ' regard it as worse than perjury '; an antithetical form, as in Mt.) and he gives their attitude the same significance as in Mt. : a word of truth does not need such support. The Qumrân Manual of Discipline as well as Josephus (II, viii, 7) show that the oath had a significant role in their rites
i of initiation. **36.** cf. 6:27. **37.** Since the masculine and the neuter form of ' evil ' coincide here, it is hard to decide whether ' evil ' or ' the Evil One ' is meant. If the *Stichwort* principle for the arrangement of material is at work here, ' evil ' would be a meaning which **37** and **39** could have in common, but this meaning is less likely in 39 and less natural in 37 ; ' Evil One ' is Satan in 37 and ' evil one ', enemy in 39, is also a strange combination, but a *Stichwort* does not need to imply similar meaning even if it is conscious, see 16:23 and 24 (*opisō mou*). This antithesis is rather an occasion for ethical instruction than a genuine antithesis in the main line of Mt.'s argument, but it was part of the ethos of radical obedience.

j **38-42.** The second part in Mt. refers to ' insult ' (**39 :** Gr. *rapizō*), while Lk. (6:29–30) thinks of violence and robbery. The insult may also be indicated by ' the right cheek ', i.e. slapping with the back of the right hand, but ' right ' could be an over-concrete expression, cf. ' right eye ' in 29. ' One who is evil ' (RSV) gives the best sense in the context, cf 37. **38.** The famous principle of retaliation (Exod. 21:24 et al.) which is found already in the Laws of Hammurabi forms the first part of the antithesis. In keeping with the piety displayed in the Beatitudes, the attitude of not insisting on one's right is spelled out. The issue is not the principle of love over against that of justice, but as in Rom. 12:18–21 ' live peaceably with all . . . never avenge yourselves ' is motivated by ' leave it to the wrath of God ', so the behaviour here described presupposes vindication by God in the near future. Now is the time when one can and shall live so. The note sounded in Rom. 12:21, ' overcome evil with good ' (indicating that love is more effective), is not to be found in Mt. But the words about reward (46) point in the same direction. **40** seems to refer to the OT : If you have to give up your coat (the long robe), give also the cloak which according to Exod.
22:26 you have the right to keep. **41** refers to the 679j
right of the government or the army to request services. The ' mile ' is a Roman measurement (*mille passuum*= 1 mile) ; the Roman soldier had the right to require non-Roman subjects to carry his equipment one mile, cf. 27:32. Hence the anti-zealotic note in the Sermon on the Mount is apparent. For **42**, cf. Exod. 22:25.

43-48. Most of the sayings in this antithetical section k
are found without antithesis in Lk. 6:27–8, 32–6 (for Lk. 6:29–31, see above, Mt. 5:38–41 and 7:12). **You shall love your neighbour** is found in Lev. 19:18, and belongs to the core of Jewish catechism together with the second table of the Decalogue (see K. Stendahl, *The School of St Matthew*, 136–8) ; the negative counterpart about hating one's enemies has puzzled Jewish and Christian scholars alike. It cannot be found as a quotation, nor can it be considered as a fair interpretation of Jewish ethics of the time, even if it is allowed for that the Semitic ' to hate ' may mean ' love less ', ' let come second in value ' (cf. Lk. 14:26, ' not to hate ', meaning ' to love more ' in Mt. 10:37). The terminology ' to love—to hate ' does, however, belong to that of Jewish ethics and especially when the eschatological tension divides mankind into two camps—*tertium non datur*. The Qumrân material is revealing. Within one homogeneous document (1QS, the Manual) we find statements like these : ' I will repay no man with evil's due—with good will I pursue a man ' (10:18) ; ' . . . But my anger I will not turn back from wicked men ' (20) ; ' . . . Now these are the rules of the way for the wise man in these times, with regard to his love as well as his hate : Let there be eternal hatred toward the men of the Pit . . .' (9:21 ; cf. 1:3–4, 9–10). While the statements in Mt. 5:38–41 could be understood in line with the piety of humble non-resistance, waiting for the judgment of the Lord (1QS 10:19 and even more Test. Benj. 4:1–5:5), the antithesis in **43ff.** goes beyond the eschatological pattern of such piety with its sharp language of hate, a hate which is grounded in God's own hatred of evil. The attitude called for by Jesus is grounded in God's concern for both good and evil, and that even without any reference to a possible repentance on the side of the unrighteous (this is hardly implied in ' pray for
your persecutors '). The overall principle from 5:20 l
(' the righteousness which exceeds that of the Pharisees ') comes to the fore : **47** Jesus requires something more (Gr. *ti perisson*) and finds the behaviour of his Jewish opponents equal to that of tax-collectors and Gentiles (Lk. : ' sinners ', cf. Mt. 6:7 and especially 18:17 where tax-collectors and Gentiles retain their bad connotation even in a Christian setting in spite of passages like 9:9–13 and 15:21–8). When Justin refers to this passage he displays good insight by changing to : ' what *new* do you do ' (1 Apol. 15:10 ; cf. Jn 13:34). **46.** Here, as elsewhere, Jesus speaks about ' reward ' (5:12, 6:1f., 5, 16, 10:41f., 20:8) ; on this in relation to rabbinic teaching, see note to 5:12 and M. Smith, *Tannaitic Parallels to the*
Gospels (1951), 54–77. **48** could be a concluding state- m
ment to the whole series of antitheses as well as to 43–7 proper. It is based on Lev. 19:2 (' be holy as I am holy ') rather than Dt. 18:1 where the word ' perfect ' (*teleios* in Gr., *tāmīm* in Heb.) is used. The emphasis is on the parallel between God's attitude and man's (' sons ' = ' children of God ', 45–7) and while it is true that the Heb. word does not imply ' perfection ' in a pedantic sense (' absolutely flawless '), this should not be an excuse for the interpreter to force the saying within the boundaries of that which is ' humanly possible ', cf. 19:26. The question of possibility is not in focus. The Lucan ' merciful ' is more suitable to the context of the pericope as well as to Lk.'s presentation of Jesus at large ; Mt.'s *teleios* may be due to his interest in having a term which fits the whole of 17–47 ; cf. also 19:21. **48.** ' You ' is strongly emphasised, again in keeping with the antithetical intention of Mt.

680a **VI 1-18.** Some reliable MSS start ch. 6 with a connecting ' but ' (*de*), thereby balancing the demand for more intensive piety with the warnings which now follow when the superior righteousness, mentioned in 5:20, is spelled out in traditional terms : **Almsgiving —Fasting—Prayer.** In the terminology of the synagogue ' righteousness ' could have the specific meaning of ' alms ' (which accounts for such a reading in TR and consequently in AV), but this makes ' alms ' in 2 almost redundant. The main argument in **1-18** is against hypocritical behaviour. The teaching of the Pharisees contained similar warnings, cf. 23:1–36.

b **2-4.** The reference to sounding the trumpets may be metaphorical ; it could also refer to official drives for alms in connection with public fasts. ' Hypocrite ' in Gr. actually means ' an actor ' but in the LXX it is used in the sense ' impious ' (Job 34:30, 36:13) and its Heb. equivalent takes on the connotation of hypocrisy. In Ps. Sol. 4:7, 25 the Pharisees use it about the Sadducees ; cf. below 16-18. ' . . . they have received (the term is that of a commercial transaction : ' signed the receipt ') their reward '. Here the reward is recognition and repute, and the antithesis between those who had had their reward on earth and those who had to wait for it till the coming age was a commonplace in Judaism, cf. Mk 10:30. It has found its strongest expression in Dives and Lazarus (Lk. 16:19–31). AV, based on TR, has ' reward thee openly ' here and in 6, apparently a gloss.

c **5-8.** The offerings at the Temple were accompanied by public prayer (Ac. 3:1) ; the synagogues functioned as temple extensions for this purpose but when the hour came, the prayer could also be performed in the streets (cf. Moslem practice). It goes without saying that neither Mt. nor Jesus criticised public worship as such, but he was aware of its temptations —as were the Pharisees themselves. **7-8** and the Lord's Prayer are brought in here and break the strict pattern of 1–18 : not the hypocrites, but the Gentiles are in focus—there is no indication that these are identified in Mt.'s mind. **8.** The foreknowledge of the Father is stressed without any recognition of ' the answer to prayer ' as a theoretical problem. A similar saying is found in 6:32, where again the attitude of the Gentiles is identified with ' will to have ' while the Christian attitude is to seek the Kingdom. The Lord's Prayer follows exactly the same line : it is the Prayer for the coming of the Kingdom.

d **9-15 The Lord's Prayer**—Both in Mt. and Lk. (11:1–4) the Lord's Prayer is given as *the* Christian prayer : In Lk. by the preceding contrast and parallel to John the Baptist's prayer(s), in Mt. by an emphatic ' Thus you shall pray *in this way*'. The prayer is available in three forms : Mt., Lk. and the Didache (8:2). Mt. and the Didache are virtually identical. In the majority of MSS the Matthean form has influenced the Lucan text, so the differences are few (so in AV, cf. RSV), but in the best MSS the difference is substantial. It is usually held that Lk.'s shorter and less formal prayer is the more original one. Already the Lucan ' Father ! ' over against the typically Matthean ' Our Father who is in heaven ' points in that direction. But difference between the two forms cannot be understood only in terms of ' Mt.'s liturgical accretion over against Lk.'s greater simplicity '. As especially E. Lohmeyer has shown (*Das Vater Unser*, 1952[3]), the difference is one between two different ' theologies ' : In Mt. the setting is thoroughly eschatological ; in Lk. there is more concern for the daily life, the End is not in the process of breaking in, the eschatological tension is relatively low. Furthermore, retranslations into Aram. may suggest a Galilean form in Mt. and a Jerusalem form in Lk. The choice between the two forms is consequently related to the total understanding of the historical Jesus. If Mt. translates the Gospel into the terms of Jewish eschatology (so recently E. Stauffer, *Jesus and His Story*, 1960), then Lk.'s form is preferable ; but if Mt. (and Mk) is basically right in his understanding 68
of Jesus, then the Lucan form is suspect of being a form of the Lord's Prayer found in a tradition where the prayer had become a prayer for daily use and with the more general concerns of Christians in this world.

e In Jewish prayers from the 1st cent. and on, many phrases have a ring similar to those found in the Lord's Prayer : Thy name is holy—Forgive us, our Father, for we have sinned—Magnified and hallowed be His great Name ; may His Kingdom reign—Our God who art in heaven . . . establish Thy Kingdom continually—cause us not to come . . . into the hands of temptation. In the ' Eighteen-Prayer ' (*Shemoneh-esreh*) the middle prayer (the ninth) reads ' Bless this year unto us . . . together with every kind of produce thereof . . .' It is preceded by the prayer for forgiveness and other manward gifts, while the prayers for the restoration of Israel follow. Thus the structure is that of the Lord's Prayer (Kingdom—Bread—Forgiveness and Protection) in reverse. While the imagery is similar, the eschatological intensity is the great difference as, e.g., ' Thy kingdom come '(not : ' reign ' or ' continually '). **9b.** ' . . . who is in heaven '.

f The Jewish parallels above (cf. also, e.g., Wis. 2:16) indicate that it was not unique to call God Father, but it became a prominent and distinct Christian usage, and plays a significant theological role already in Paul's epistles, even by retaining the Aram. ' Abba ' (Rom. 8:15 ; Gal. 4:6 ; cf. Jesus' prayer, Mk 14:36, see Mt. 26:39). **9c-10.** The first three prayers

g express one and the same thought. The verbs in passive form as well as ' the Name ' are in keeping with the laws of reverence in Jewish prayers. God is asked to let that time come when he will be the Holy One in the eyes of the nations, i.e. the coming of the Kingdom when his will is made manifest on earth (*r^{e}'ûthā'* = Heb. *rāṣôn*, translated ' will ' (*thelēma*) in Ps. 40:9 (Heb. 10:7), but usually = *eudokia*, ' good will ' in the sense of ' election ', see 11:26). With such an interpretation the thought has striking similarity with the song of the angels (Lk. 2:14 : ' Glory to God in the highest and on earth peace among men of God's good pleasure ') and the Qumrân parallels strengthen such an exegesis (cf. E. Vogt in K. Stendahl, *The Scrolls and the NT*, 114–17). Then the translation should be ' manifest thy will ', which is the more natural translation (so Burney ; Aram. *tith'^{a}bhēdh* (Dalman, Kuhn [Lohmeyer] is based on understanding ' will ' in a more ethical sense). Thus the ethical note is—to say the least—not at the fore in this part of the prayer. It asks for the establishment of the Kingdom of God, by God for us, not by us for God.

h **11.** The prayer for bread continues to puzzle the interpreter. The Gr. word *epiousios* has not been found (reports to the contrary notwithstanding). Mistranslations from the Aram. have been suggested (see M. Black, *An Aramaic Approach*, 150–3 : Give us our bread today and tomorrow = day by day). From the Gr., the meaning ' necessary ' (*epi tēn ousian*) is as hard to accept as Jerome's *supersubstantialis* (*ousia* = *substans*). The meaning is based rather on *ep-iousa*, ' that which is coming soon '. This agrees with the *Gospel of the Hebrews* : ' that of tomorrow ' (*māḥār*, the word used by Black in his idiomatic interpretation). Thus the bread is related to future and this is what the word in the Lord's Prayer wants to convey, well in keeping with the future element in the prayer so far. It is worth considering whether this term refers to the messianic banquet (cf. notes to 5:6). In 1QSa the meal as actually practised in the community is described in the terms of its messianic consummation and the Matthean form of the prayer may refer to the same high tension between today and tomorrow. This has then taken the place of the prayer for the annual produce of the earth in the Jewish prayer—well in line with 6:32–3 : It is the Kingdom that matters! **12.**

i The ' debts ' (Did. : singular ; Lk. : ' sins ' ; for the translation ' trespasses ' in different English Bibles, see IB, i, 102–3). The word is used only here and in

680i Rom. 4:4 ; and ' debtors ' is a common Jewish term for ' sinners ' and for ' guilty ' in a general sense (e.g. Lk. 13:4), i.e. those on whom we have a just claim (the opposite in 5:23). The terminology may have a more precise meaning within the community (see note on 14). The best texts use the aorist, which does not necessarily require a translation into past tense (' have forgiven ' ; so RSV), but sees the act of forgiveness as fact rather than as repeated action. In what sense this is a condition, see note to 14.
j **13.** The word ' temptation ' (*peirasmos*) can also mean ' trial ' or ' test '. Especially in parallel with 13*b*, this might be the meaning : Do not put us to that ultimate test where no-one can stand (cf. 24:22 : ' If those days were not shortened, no flesh would be saved ')—but save us from the Evil One (or : from evil ; Did. : from all evil ; cf. 5:39). Behind ' lead us not ' stands a Semitic causative, but the question whether God sends temptation is hardly involved. The accent is on the trial of the chosen ones, and it is far from the more ' athletic ' attitude towards temptations as muscle-builders for the faithful as in Jas 1:2 ; cf. Jas 1:12–14. In Mt. the concept is closer to 1 C. 10:13, see also the Gethsemane scene, 26:36–46, and K. G. Kuhn, ' New Light on Temptation . . .', in K. Stendahl, *The Scrolls and the NT.*
k **13c.** A doxology (see RSV*n*), found in later MSS and (a shorter one) in Did. Its source may be 1 Chr. 29:11. It was a Jewish practice to end public prayers with such doxologies, although they were not in the text (J. Jeremias, *Unknown Sayings of Jesus* (1957), 28). In the light of the above interpretation, it was well
l chosen with its reference to the Kingdom. **14-15.** Thus the prayer in its Matthean form is a prayer for the Kingdom, an expanded *Maranatha* (1 C. 16:22) and appropriately related to the messianic meal since all the accounts of the institution of the Lord's Supper contain the eager look towards the coming of the Kingdom (see 26:29). Why does Mt. then centre attention on the prayer about forgiveness when he sums up the prayer ? The clue may be found in 18:15–20, where the ' omnipotence of prayer in the name of Jesus ' is vested in a community where mutual forgiveness is urged to the extent that he who does not co-operate in this venture of full and open brotherhood has to be excommunicated. Thus the prayer of the messianic community presupposes a mutually forgiven community. Only on this condition can the church pray with power. The group discipline of the Qumrân community is centred around the question of the access to its inner sanctum, the meal, and the immediate connection in the Lord's Prayer between the prayer for the eschatological meal and the mutual forgiveness (11–12) points in the same direction. It is only in the light of later theological distinctions that this ' condition ' for God's forgiveness raises theological problems. In the context of the messianic self-consciousness of the early church the condition of living according to the nature of one's calling was not jeopardising the grace of God (see 22:14) ; see also notes on 18:15-20.
m **16-18.** The saying about fasting follows the main pattern of 1–18, and that in its shortest form. Mt. has not seen fit to bring in any further teaching of Jesus at this point, as e.g. that given in 9:14–17. Anointing was a symbol of joy, forbidden for days of fasting. Thus the saying (*a*) can mean ' do behave as usual ' ; or (*b*) it may be a command which grew out of the answer of Jesus in 9:14–17, combining the practice of fasting with Jesus' reference to nuptial joy. In Did. 8:1 we read : ' Let not your fasts be with the hypocrites, for they fast on Mondays and Thursdays, but you fast on Wednesdays and Fridays.' Here ' hypocrites ' has totally lost its meaning and is just ' the Jews '.
681a **VI 19-VII 29** offers material which has been brought into the Sermon on the Mount by Mt. in such a manner that we find no clue as to his arrangement. Most of it is found in different places in Lk., although ch. 7
follows more closely what is found in Lk. 6 and leads 681a
up to the parable which concludes the ' sermon ' both in Lk. and Mt. While the material is of a general ethical nature, Mt. occasionally brings to it the urgent concern for the Kingdom as the decisive feature (e.g. 6:33).
VI 19-24. The repeated antithesis in 1–18, **reward** b
from men/ reward from God, leads to this saying. In Lk. 12:33f. it refers to alms and so do references to treasures in heaven like Test. Levi 13:5, Tob. 4:9 ; cf. also Lk. 16:9. **19.** Gr. *brōsis* describes any act of ' eating ' or corrosion : ' rust ' (AV, RSV) suggests metal while ' worm ' (RSV*n*) suggests cloth. The word for ' corrupt ' or ' consume ' (*aphanizō*) is the same used for ' disfigure ' in 16. It may be the *Stichwort*,
which brought these passages together. **22-3.** While c
Lk. (11:34–6) treats this saying under the heading ' light ', Mt. has given it what seems to be the better context, i.e. that of generous giving. In a Jewish setting this should be the right one since the ' evil eye ' is a term for ' niggardliness ' as in 20:15, while the characteristic Hellenistic Greek words for generousness in giving are the adverb *haplōs*, and the noun *haplotēs* (see e.g. Jas 1:5). But *haplous* (meaning ' single ') translates the OT *tām*, in terms of undivided commitment and obedience to God. Such an interpretation is reasonable in the general context of Mt. but strained within this parabolic saying, unless it is considered a conscious play on the Aram. word *shᵉlîm* (Heb. *tām*), which has the possible double meaning of ' health ' and ' undivided commitment '. If the saying is understood as a genuine parable with ' picture ' plus ' application ', the meaning ' sound ' is the only one needed. Heart (21) and eye (22) are both centres of the person according to OT and
Jewish anthropology. **24.** It may be that the word d
haplous (' single ') suggested this saying at this point (Lk. 16:13). Mammon is used in Rabbinic texts without any bad connotation (' property '), e.g. in legal texts like Mishnah Sanhedrin, a fact which adds sharpness to this antithesis of Jesus (cf. Lk. 12:13).
25-34. A good example of similarities between Mt. and e
Lk. : While there are differences in wording (e.g. ' the birds '—' the ravens ') there is striking similarity in details which appear rather casual (e.g. 30, ' O men of little faith '). There must be a common source to which Mt. in this case has given his accent of ' righteousness ' (33). **25.** The word *psychē* may mean both ' life ' and ' soul ' (cf. 16:26). While the translation ' life ' is more natural to our ears, the parallelism ' soul-body ' suggests such an understanding, provided that it is understood in its Semitic framework : soul and body make up the whole man as God's creation.
The argument is that of rabbinic interpretation, called f
' light and heavy ', i.e. ' if so—how much more ', cf. 7:11. ' Take thought ' (AV) or ' be anxious ' (RSV) ; perhaps ' worry ' catches the meaning better (31 and 34). **27.** Both ' stature ' (AV and RSV*n*, so in Lk. 19:3) and ' span of life ' (RSV) is possible ; the latter is the more usual meaning in Gr. The whole passage is mainly within the traditional thought pattern of Jewish wisdom and stresses the dependence on God with the appeal to the Jew over against the Gentiles (32). This was also the emphasis when the argument was one from nature in 5:43–8. **30.** ' Little-believing ' refers here to lack of trust in *God*, cf. however the references to *Jesus*' power in 8:26, 14:31, 16:8. There may be a similar connotation in 30,
referring to the situation of the Kingdom. **33.** Mt. g
brings the ' righteousness of God ' into parallelism with the Kingdom. Both are the object for man's undivided concern, and both are about to be given. This adds intensity to the insights of Jewish wisdom (the two sentences in 34 have Rabbinic parallels and should be considered as ironic proverbs) and makes it more imperative to leave the worries for the terrestrial tomorrow. The Gr. has two words for ' evil ' ; earlier the word *poneros* has been used and it describes what is objectively evil (in the eyes of God) ; *kakos* is often

681g that which is subjectively evil (from a human point of view), hence RSV's translation ' trouble '.

h **VII 1-5. 1.** The conjunction of finality ' that ' (Gr. *hina*) is a stronger rendering of an Aramaic *de* than the form in Lk. 6:37 ; the passive constructions ' be judged ', ' be measured to . . .' are especially in Mt. clearly referring to God's judgment of man, not to other men's judgment as such, although those may be the vehicles of God's judgment. Consequently the reference is not necessarily eschatological. **2.** The idea of measure for measure is well known in Jewish material (Sotah, 1:7). In contrast to the renunciation of the principle of an eye for an eye (5:38) as valid for human retaliation, this very principle is upheld here as valid for God's dealing with man, and it is used as a warning against hypocrisy. **3.** The saying about the splinter and the log is consciously ridiculous in good oriental
i fashion, cf. 19:24. The whole saying on judging has apparently been a popular one in the early tradition, as can be seen from the way in which it was expanded on the pattern of mutuality (Lk. 6:38 ; 1 Clem. 13:2 ; Polyc. 2:3, etc.). In Mk 4:24 the saying about the ' measures ' is applied to the willingness to receive the Gospel. **2b** may also imply a reference to the two ' measures ' by which God judges the world according to rabbinic views : Mercy and Justice. If so the meaning is : If you want to be judged in mercy, apply such a measure here and now.

j **6.** A recognised *crux interpretum.* In Did. 9:5 it refers to the closed table of the Eucharist, and the Ebionite Jewish Christians find here explanation for the resistance to their doctrines (*Clementine Homilies* 3:5 and *Recognitions* 3:1). No satisfactory explanation of why Mt. brings in the saying at this point can be given. McNeile's suggestion (*Commentary on Matthew*) is not impossible : a counter-weight to the preceding stress on ' not to discriminate ', cf. 18:15–20 and 23–35. An original meaning in line with 15:26 (and 10:5), i.e. against mission to the Gentiles, is not impossible. Dogs and swine were both ' unclean '. For the combination, cf. 2 Pet. 2:22.

k **7-11. Ask, seek, knock** are used as general expressions for man's confident attitude towards the heavenly Father. Jewish texts speak about ' knocking at the doors of mercy '. In Mt. it has no specific relation to the door in v. 14 ; rather to the situation in Lk. 11:5–8. **11.** ' you who are evil ' is here a comparative statement (cf. Mk 10:18) rather than a statement of what human nature is. In Lk. the saying is in the more natural context of teaching about prayer, and it is made specific by referring to the prayer for the Holy Spirit (Mt. : ' good things ').

l **12.** In Mt. the **Golden Rule** stands alone as a logion in its own right and in the form of a general rule (*panta* : ' whatever ') ; in Lk. it is integrated among other sayings on love for enemies (6:31). It is well attested from Judaism as well as in other religions and cultures. Much attention has been given to the fact that all of the Jewish examples of this rule are in the negative form (e.g. Hillel : ' What you do not like yourself, you shall not do to your neighbour '), while Jesus uses the formula in a positive form. The positive note in Jesus' ethics may be rightly stressed on other grounds, but it remains a puzzling fact that if this were to be the point, the Early Church apparently did not see it. When the Golden Rule is referred to in Did. 2:1 (combined with the double commandment in Mt. 22:37f.) and in the Western Text to Ac. 15:28, it is in the negative form. Mt. has the concluding remark :
m ' For this is the Law and the Prophets ', i.e. it is a conscious summation of God's revelation just as Hillel's rule was explicitly so. It must therefore appear quite odd when the Golden Rule is used as an epitome of what was new with Jesus. It is quite the contrary, (1) because it was *not* new, and (2) because the accent falls on its identity with the old revelation, cf. 1 Jn 2:7.

n **13-23.** While the preceding sayings in ch. 7 have been of a rather general ethical nature, the remainder of the chapter has a clear reference to the eschatological **68**
crisis at the same time as they show distinctive marks of the catechetical function of the material in the Matthean church. **13-14.** What appears in Lk. 13:23f. as a direct question to Jesus, is in Mt. cast in the familiar pattern of the Two Ways (Did. 1:1, Barn. 18:1 with OT and Jewish antecedents ; see Dt. 30:15 ; A. Seeberg, *Der Katechismus der Urchristenheit* (1903) ; Ph. Carrington, *The Primitive Christian Catechism* (1940). The antithesis between the Many and the Few (cf. 22:14) is stressed. The striking—and unexpected—feature within this pattern in Mt. is, however, that the narrow door and road is hard to *find.* No stress is laid on the fact that the road would be hard to walk : *tethlimmenē* means ' pressed together ', and *eurychōros* ' roomy ' ; the RSV's ' hard ' and ' easy ' are somewhat misleading. **15-23** are addressed against false teachers ; the shorter parallels in Lk. speak of man in general. It is a warning for the church situation (' false prophets ' : Mt. 24:11, 24; Mk 13:22, with reference to the future). The saying about tree and fruit was deeply rooted and widely applied in the tradition, cf. 3:10, 12:33–5, 15:13 (Jn 15:1ff. ; Jas 3:12). **19.** The Matthean emphasis on being ' thrown into the fire ' is not in Lk., cf. however Lk. 3:9. **21-3** pictures the judgment day (' that day ' = ' the day of the Lord ') and the saying sharpens the warning given in 15:20. Jesus is here speaking as the Judge of that day (cf. Mk 8:38) while in Lk. 13:22–30 the same function is referred to a ' householder '.

24-27. In 15–23 the emphasis has been on ' doing the **o**
will of the Father ' or : ' producing fruit '. In both cases the Gr. word is the same : *poiein.* This is also the central word in 24–7. **24.** The parable of the house-builders is usually understood as a concluding statement for the whole Sermon on the Mount. Its place in Lk. 6 and the generalising ' Everyone then who . . .' in contrast to what has been addressed to the false ministry, strengthens such an interpretation. It is in view of an impending *catastrophe* that there is wisdom in following the teaching of Jesus in deed. This element in the parable seems to be more than incidental. For the distinction, hear/do, see also 13:18–23, 21:28–32, 22:1–14, 23:1–3, 25:31–46, *et passim* in Mt.

28-29 is the first of the five basically identical con- **p**
cluding statements by which Mt. brings a discourse section to a close (see above, §673*h*). It is apparently taken from Mk 1:21–2 ; cf. 27. ' As one having authority—and not as the scribes ' has a quite specific meaning in Mt. While the scribes argued from scripture and tradition, giving evidence of the chain of interpreters, Jesus had spoken in his own name : ' but I say unto you '. To Mt. this places Jesus within the Messianic realm of fulfilment and power ; cf. 28:18–20. See however D. Daube's suggestion that Jesus behaved as an ordained Rabbi with the power to promulgate new decisions, not like just any scribe (*The NT and Rabbinic Judaism* (1956), 205–16).

VIII 1-XI 1 constitutes the *Second Section* in Mt. **68**
(see above, §673*i*). The narrative part is obviously arranged by Mt., using Mk 1:40–2:22 as the basic frame into which earlier Marcan material (8:14–17) as well as later (8:23–4, 9:18–31) has been brought to give a fuller picture of the ministry as a background to the charge given to the Twelve in ch. 10.

VIII 1-4. The story of healing of a leper, as all the **b**
other accounts taken over from Mk, is shortened in Mt. (not so in Lk.), reduced to its essentials, and stripped both of the plasticity of story-telling and of the terms which describe Jesus' emotions in strong language (see e.g. Mk 1:43). **2.** ' . . . and worshipped him ' (AV) ; ' . . . knelt before him ' (RSV) : as one does before gods and kings, 2:2, 4:9 ; Jn 4:20–4. Only in Mt. is this behaviour mentioned as one of human recognition of Jesus ; in Mk (and Lk. ; cf. Ac. 10:25–6) only the demons (Mk 5:6) do so and the soldiers do it to ridicule (Mk 15:19) but for Mt. see also 9:18, 14:33, 15:25 (18:26), 20:20 and 28:9, 17. **4.** The command not to broadcast the healing and to perform

2b the sacrifice prescribed (Lev. 14:4–7) 'as a testimony to them' is retained; the contrast between 'the priest' (sing.) and 'them' (pl.) has led RSV to translate 'the people', but the technical use of 'the priest' (as representative of the priesthood) makes such a change unnecessary.

c **5-13.** The account is again more concentrated; the Jews pleading for the centurion as for a benevolent friend is typically Lucan. **6.** The Gr. word for slave or servant (*pais*) may also mean 'son' as it does in 17:18; the traditional rendering 'servant' is enforced by Lk.'s *doulos* (7:2). Parallels like 15:21–8 (and 10:5) and the syntax of **7** with its strong accent (in Gr.) on 'I' suggest that this verse should rather be read as a question: 'Should *I* come and heal him?' Then (cf. 15:21–8) the humility of this Roman officer is described and his simple confidence in Jesus' power over demons and sickness is displayed, and the healing performed at that very moment and from a distance. **11-12.** But the pericope functions as a saying statement of doom over the reluctant Jews, a saying which Lk. has in a more systematic context (Lk. 13:28–30). On the messianic banquet as the symbol of the Kingdom, see 26:29.

d **14-17.** The healing of Peter's mother-in-law (14–15; Mk 1:29–31) is given in short sentences. Note the change from 'and she served *them*' (Mk, Lk.) to the more Christocentric 'she served *him*' in Mt. **16-17.** Again the Marcan account (1:32–4) is slightly shortened, the reference to the demons' knowledge of Jesus' identity is omitted (while it is developed in Lk.: 'Christ'), but Mt. gives here the first of his formula quotations within the account of the ministry of Jesus
e (see above, §673*g*). **17.** This formula quotation is Mt.'s way of giving a clue to a messianic understanding of Jesus: not by demons but by Scripture! The quotation is from Isa. 53:4 and based on the Heb. text. It by-passes all known Jewish interpretations (where these words had been spiritualised as referring to 'sins and hardships') in applying the text to a healing ministry. The use of Isa. 53 shows no understanding of that text in the redemptive sense in which it came to be used in the main tradition of Christian
f interpretation; cf. however 20:28. When the exorcism is described in **16** as performed 'by word', cf. 8, this is in line with Mt.'s consistent suppression of the details about healing procedure; cf. Mk 7:31–7 (Mt. 15:29–31) and Mk 8:22–6; Jn 9:1–7. The point is one of heightening the unique power of Jesus rather than one of 'religion' contra 'magic'. There is no conscious reference to God's creation by word (Gen. 1); cf. however 27.

g **18-22. 18.** The stage is being set for the stilling of the storm (Mk 4:35), but two sayings on discipleship precede the actual account. The 'scribes' (i.e. those who teach in the synagogues on the basis of some formal training), are not automatically enemies to Jesus, but potential and actual disciples ('another of the disciples', **21**; and 13:52). 'Disciples' is used either in the broader sense of those who listened to Jesus with appreciation, or it indicates how these logia were used for the instruction of Christians in the Matthean church. 'Teacher' and 'Lord' are titles of courtesy without any specific theological overtones, cf. 23:8–10. The two sayings point to the urgency and the hardship of true discipleship. The reference to the non-disciples as dead should not be over-interpreted in a Johannine sense (e.g. Jn 5:24); it
h is just a strong metaphor. **20.** This is the first time the **Son of Man** is mentioned in Mt., where it (as also in Mk and Lk.) occurs only on the lips of Jesus. It is often held that in this and other passages (11:19, 12:32) Son of Man is an over-translation in the Gr. Gospel tradition of an Aram. idiom which meant only 'I'. See Mt.'s 'I' in 10:32 and 5:11 for Son of Man in Lk.; and Mt.'s Son of Man for Mk's 'I' in 16:13. On three different usages of the title Son of Man: (*a*) as coming in glory; (*b*) as suffering; (*c*) as Jesus' self-designation during his earthly ministry,
see R. Bultmann, *New Testament Theology*, i (1951), 682h
26–32; cf. J. A. T. Robinson, *Jesus and His Coming* (1957), with the distinction of visitation and vindication in relation to the Son of Man. Since there are obviously genuine statements of Jesus (not to be credited to the later church) in the first category, it would be a strange coincidence of language if these were technical and not referring to Jesus but to a celestial figure, while the same Aram. term would also have been used conspicuously often by Jesus in an innocent meaning of 'I' without any reference to the Son of Man. It was rather the only term which Jesus wanted to use during his earthly ministry—and the traditions retain it as such; after the Resurrection it is not used; Lk. also refrains from using it in Ac.; cf. Mt. 26:64.

23-27. The Marcan account—in another context i
(4:35–41)—is more detailed. **26.** The harsh rebuke to the disciples is toned down to 'little-believing'. The word 'save' is used in the NT both for help in this world and for salvation.

28-34. What is retained of the account in Mk 5:1–20 j
is what mattered to Mt. For the location of 'Gadara', see §701*c*, where the original in Mk is correctly 'Gergesenes'. In Mt.'s tradition there were two demoniacs (as he has two blind men, 9:27–31, and two asses, 20:29–34). The territory was mainly Gentile and this may account for the swine (unclean and not kept by Jews) in the story. The demoniacs seem to be thought of as Gentiles and prototypes for the mission to the Gentiles. While the blind see him to be Son of David, 9:27, the demons recognise him as Son of God (cf. Mk 3:11, 5:7, 15:39). The idea of k
an anticipation of the church's ministry to the Gentiles accounts for the way in which Mt. has changed Mk's (and Lk.'s) plea of the demons not to be tormented into the statement: 'Have you come here to torment us *before the set time*?' This is in accordance with Mt.'s view of Jesus' *earthly* ministry as one to the Jews only (10:5; cf. 28:16–20). Were this saying not only in Mt., it would be enough to refer to Test. Levi 18:12, 1 Enoch 16:1, Jubilees 10:8–9, where the destruction of the demons is one of the features of the Last Judgment. The plea of the citizens that Jesus leave them and their swineherds in peace is either just a storytelling device, or perhaps is intended to anticipate refusal of the church in those parts of Palestine.

IX 1-8. 1. Capernaum is to Mt. Jesus' home town l
(cf. 4:13). The story is, as usual, told in a stricter and more economic form. **3.** This is the **first clash between Jesus and Jewish authorities** ('some of the scribes'; so also Mk). The point at issue is the forgiveness of sins which here is held to be identical with healing. Jesus shares such a view (for a more sophisticated approach to the problem of sin and sickness or calamities, see Lk. 13:1–9; Jn 9:2–5), and the accent is—especially in Mt.—not on the healing as such, but on the power of forgiveness. **8.** All the Synoptics use strong language to express the reaction of the people, and Mt. uses the term 'they were afraid', which occurs in relation to divine manifestations like the Transfiguration, 17:6, and the Resurrection, 28:5, 10. The interplay between 'Son of man' (6) and 'men' (8), the latter only in Mt., could support the view that the former meant just 'man', but the context of **6** suggests rather: The Son of Man, whom you expect as the celestial being of the end, has already power to forgive sins now 'here on earth'. And the plural 'men' in **8** is influenced by the fact that the church has the authority to practise such forgiveness (see 18:15-20).

9-13. On the name Matthew in **9**, see above, §673*j*. m
The call of this customs official only sets the stage for the next encounter between Jesus and his opponents. There are few differences between Mk and Mt. It is not clear in Mk or Mt. whether the meal was held in Jesus' house or in that of the tax-collector (so Lk.), but Jesus is pictured as the host (*sunanekeinto tō Jēsou*). **10.** They 'sat at table', literally reclined, which was

682m the Graeco-Roman custom followed also at Jewish banquets, and referred to in the references to the messianic banquet, 8:11. The conversation which is the nucleus of this incident suggests that the issue seen by the evangelists is more than that of Jewish regulations concerning meal fellowship : Jesus has come to call (i.e. invite) sinners to the Kingdom. This would not be an answer to the objection, were not the idea of the messianic banquet in the picture. **13.** The quotation from Hos. 6:6 which Mt. brings in here and in 12:7 does not fit organically, but was apparently a handy and useful slogan in discussions with the Jews ; ' go and learn ' is a well-known Jewish formula for such references. Are ' healthy ' and ' righteous ' (12, 13) used with irony, or does Jesus recognise his opponents as in some sense acceptable to God, only pleading for a place also for the despised ? The latter possibility should not be excluded too quickly under the pressure of later developments of the Christian message.

n **14-17.** The relation between Jesus (and his disciples) and the disciples of John is in focus at several points in Mt. ; apart from 3:13–17, the main passages are in 11:2–19, 14:1–12, 21:32. At this point the interest is centred not on their positive or negative interrelation but on the radical ' newness ' of Jesus' message and mission. **16, 17.** The parables (Lk. calls them so : 5:36) of the patch and the wineskins point to this non-compromising newness, and fit better to **15a** than to **15b** ; reference is to the place of fasting in the ' post-ascension ' rather than ' post-crucifixion ' (*aparthē* —' is taken away ') situation. The imagery about the bridegroom is not incidental ; it is of the same cloth as that of the banquet and belongs to Messianic eschatology. **15b** is often understood as a later adjustment to the continued practice of fasting in the church, see Did. 8:1, quoted above in note to 6:16–18.

o **18-34.** Before introducing the second discourse (ch. 10), Mt. brings in three more healing incidents in order to have examples of the three objects for Messianic deeds as mentioned in 11:5 : the blind, the deaf and the dead. This also makes the background to 10:1 more complete. In the case of the blind, this arrangement causes one of the doublets typical for Mt. (9:27–31 and 20:29–34). The Marcan material is slimmed down to bare necessities. **25.** For parallels, see Elijah (1 Kg. 17:17–24), Elisha (2 Kg. 4:17–37) and Peter (Ac. 9:36–42) ; in all cases they are alone. Jesus' garment has a fringe or rather ' tassel ' (Num. 15:38–41 ; Dt. 22:12) of the sort the Pharisees made broad (23:5) to display their piety. Broad or not, this liturgical element in the garment of the pious Jew is mentioned as worn by Jesus, cf. 14:36. In all three instances Mt. gives or retains a reference to the great impression Jesus made, and on its spread over the country, and this also points to the passage where the narrative is taken up again : ' the deeds of the Christ ' in 11:2. **34.** To complete the background to the discourse in ch. 10, the reaction of the Pharisees is brought in here with terms which receive their full significance in a later context (12:22ff.). The verse is missing in some MSS apparently since it was felt to be superfluous, but Mt. thought it to be necessary for a reference in the following speech (10:25).

683a **35-38.** Just as the first of the discourses (the Sermon on the Mount) was preceded by a statement about Jesus' general activities in the synagogues (4:23), so also here : **The commission to the Twelve** is preceded by a saying, lifted from another context in Mk (6:34, cf. Mt. 14:14) and enlarged in some general similarity to Jn 4:35. In Lk. this logion is related to the commission of the 72 (10:1ff.), as is a good deal of the following discourse. **36.** The allusion is closest to Num. 27:17, but could well be a general figure of speech within the framework of OT language (1 Kg. 22:17 ; Isa. 53:6 ; Ezek. 34:5, etc.). **37.** The imagery of harvest—not sowing—suggests that Jesus' ministry and that of the Matthean church is one of the end rather than a new beginning, cf. Jas 5:7–8.

X 1-4. 1. . . . his twelve disciples are introduced here as well known to the reader, although they have not been mentioned before. There is only reference to their power of performing the miracles which Jesus has just completed, and no mention of a message, see, however, 7 ; they are to extend Jesus' active compassion for the people (9:36). Only in **2** does Mt. call them ' apostles ', a term used more consistently by Lk., perhaps in the perspective of his second volume, the book of Acts. For Mt. the basic picture is that of a teacher with his disciples. Their number is unanimously understood in the Gospel tradition in relation to the 12 tribes of Israel (19:28), cf. the ' twelve ' in the Qumrân community (1QS 8:1–10 and Rev. 21:14). The names of the Twelve are c listed also in Mk 3:16–19 ; Lk. 6:13–16 and Ac. 1:13–16. The special features in Mt. are : the position of ' Simon called Peter ' as the first is emphasised ; Matthew is referred to as ' the customs officer ', cf. 9:9 ; some MSS have Lebbaeus instead of Thaddaeus. This broken tradition was reconciled in the TR into ' Lebbaeus, called Thaddaeus '. ' Simon the Cananaean ' is hardly a geographic adjective, but was presumably correctly translated into Gr. by Lk. : ' Simon called the Zealot ' (6:15). C. C. Torrey's suggestion that the same applies to Iscariot, the Aram. for ' of falsehood, of betrayal ' (HTR 36 (1943), 51–62), has been well enforced by B. Gärtner, *Horae Soederblomianae* 4 (1957) ; verse 4 could then be read : ' . . . Judas the Iscariot, who also (as his name rightly says) was the one who betrayed him.' RSV leaves the *kai* (here = ' also ') untranslated. Very little is known d about most of these Twelve, and their role may have been so confined to the church of Jerusalem (cf. Ac. 8:1) and the Jewish Christianity which was cut off from the main stream of the Christian expansion after A.D. 68, that not even their names were known with precision in the Gentile centres where the Gospels took form. The legends and the patron-claims in diverse corners of primitive Christendom are of a considerably later date, and are based on the biblical record as are, e.g., the traditions about Alphaeus as identical with Clopas etc., see R. Harris, *The Twelve Apostles* (1927), and J. Munck, ' Paul, the Apostles and the Twelve ', *Studia Theologica* 3 (1949), 96–110.

5-42 forms a typical Matthean *discourse*. Mt. has e brought together diverse material on (*a*) **5-15** the missionary task of disciples in a leading position (cf. Mk 6 and Lk. 9 and 10) ; (*b*) **16-25** the plight of disciples when opposed by the authorities (cf. Mk 13 and Lk. 21, i.e. from the so-called ' apocalypse of Mk ' with its Lucan parallel ; cf. also the farewell speeches in Jn) ; (*c*) **26-42** the conditions of discipleship in more general terms (cf. Mk 8 ; Lk. 12, et al.). This Matthean arrangement leads to some duplication in Mt., see 15:24, 16:24-5, 18:5, 24:9, 13. The discourse contains almost no material peculiar to Mt. (5–6, 8, 16*b*), and Mt.'s role is that of an arranger and shows these words of Jesus to be highly relevant for the situation of the church in which he lives. Thus the speech has become a ' manual ' for the activities of the teachers and leaders of the early church.

5-15. Mt.'s picture of Jesus' earthly ' ministry ' as well f as that of the disciples is here one confined to the Jews, and especially to ' the lost ' among the Jews, presumably the ones despised by the Pharisees, i.e. the *'am hā-'āreṣ*, the people who did not take upon themselves the precise obedience to the Law as expounded by the Pharisees. It is quite clear from 28:16–20 that this particularism of Jesus and his disciples was not practised in the Matthean church when the Gospel was written. Why, then, was it so carefully and forcefully retained in this discourse (cf. 23), which—more than the logia in Mk and Lk.—is adapted to a valid manual for the church ? Mt.'s creative way of using sources makes it insufficient to assign these sayings to Jewish-Christian sources. The reason is rather seen in Mt.'s understanding of this particularism as the actual behaviour of Jesus during

3f his earthly ministry. The great commission with
reference to the whole world is preceded and conditioned by the resurrection and enthronement of
Jesus, see note to 28:16–20. Before that date only
Jews are addressed, and the exceptions are real
exceptions which do foreshadow—but only foreshadow
—what is to come (8:11–12, 15:21–8 and perhaps
8:28–34) ; see J. Jeremias, *Jesus' Promise to the Nations*
g (1958). **8.** The *gratis* saying was a common *bon mot*
in missionary circles, cf. 2 C. 11:7, which Paul also
balances over against the right for the apostle to
receive free room and board, a rule which rests on a
'Word from the Lord', 1 C. 9:14 ; in 1 Tim. 5:18
it is quoted from 'Scripture'. How significant and
controversial this question of support to travelling
teachers and apostles was in the early church is clear
from the lengthy discussion in 1 C. 9 and Did. 13, and
from the conspicuous emphasis on *hospitality* among the
virtues in the epistles (Rom. 12:13 ; 1 Tim. 3:2 ; Tit.
1:8 ; Heb. 13:2 ; 1 Pet. 4:9). **23.** The reference to
light travel may be rightly understood by Lk. as a
sign of haste (Lk. 10:4). 'Worthy' is a keyword
in this chapter : **10** (AV) ; in a more technical sense :
11, 13 bis, **37, 38.** It refers to those who accept the
invitation (see 22:8). **12.** The greeting *shālôm*,
'peace', is conceived of as far more than a greeting :
the disciples carry with them and offer the peace of the
Kingdom, see also 40. **14.** To turn them down is to
place oneself under God's wrath and judgment and
this is manifested by prophetic action. The pattern is
one of houses and cities, not individuals. **15.** This is the
visitation of the people on a grand scale, just as Paul
thinks in cities and countries, and as Yahweh dealt
with Sodom and Gomorrah in olden times.
h **16-25. 16.** The proverbial saying (only in Mt.) about
the wise serpents alludes to Gen. 3:1 where the
same Gr. word is used ; it is a matter of 'prudence'
rather than 'wisdom'. Mt. accentuates : 'Behold
I send you'. This verse opens also the section on
the hardships of the disciples and the sayings are for
the church rather than for a mission of the disciples
during Jesus' earthly ministry ; **17-25** is a slightly
revised edition of Mk 13:9–13, cf. Mt. 24:9, 13.
18. The word 'testimony' is derived from the Gr.
stem 'martyr', which later acquired the meaning
'one who *dies* for his faith', but here has the meaning
of a 'witness' who gives testimony for God. When
before Gentile authorities, this testimony is also for
those represented by their leaders ('and the Gentiles',
18). Since they witness for God, the martyrs can count
on the Holy Spirit (1 Pet. 4:14, cf. Mart. Isa. 5:14,
and the term *Paraclete* in Jn 14:16, 26). On **21-2**
and its relation to Mic. 7:6 used as a messianic
prophecy, see **34-6. 23** is one of the focal points for
i A. Schweitzer's thorough-going eschatology (*The
Quest of the Historical Jesus*, 358–63) : Jesus 'does
not expect to see them back in the present age'
(358) and 'the non-fulfilment of Mt. 10:23 is the
first postponement of the Parousia' (360) ; see,
however, W. G. Kümmel's balanced criticism in
Promise and Fulfilment (1957), 61–4. **22.** Mt. sees
this saying as referring to the mission of the church,
and lets the coming of the Son of Man refer to the
victory beyond the grim and painful end, where the
reference to Israel's cities gives an authentic ring in
keeping with the framework of the Matthean discourse.
24-5. The reference to the similar fate of the teacher
and master is found in a similar context and meaning
in Jn 13:16, 15:20, while Lk. gives the saying a more
enigmatic setting and form (6:40).
j **26-33.** A block of sayings parallel in Mt. and Lk.
(12:2–9). But in Mt. the first two of them are applied
to the duty of the apostles and teachers to pronounce
openly also what they have been told privately (cf. 28:20).
28. They have nothing to fear from men who can only
kill the body, but they should be afraid of him who has
power to destroy both soul and body in Gehenna, i.e.
the fiery hell of Jewish eschatology. Is this God,
or the Son of Man as judge (25:31–46), or Satan ?
Most commentators argue for the former as did the 683j
Church Fathers, this—it seems—for partly theological
reasons, in order to keep the dualism down as much
as possible. But in the time of ultimate trial and
temptation the power of Satan is great (6:13, 24:22).
For the distinction soul-body in Mt., see 6:25, 26:38.
The only thing worth fearing is not to be on Jesus'
side by failure to confess him before men. The
distinction between Jesus and the Son of Man on the
Day of Judgment—if it is a distinction in Mk 8:38—
does not occur in Mt. where the Gr. uses straight
first-person singular.
34-39. Different from its original meaning, Mic. 7:1 k
had been already used by the Jews as a picture of the
divisive impact of the Messiah. So also here and in **21.**
This is contrary to the expected role of Elijah, according
to Mal. 4:5–6. What follows is the same principle in
reverse : The disciple has to sever the relations with
his family (cf. 4 QTest. 16f., where Dt. 33:8–11 is
quoted in a series of testimonia). **38.** The saying
about the cross may refer rather to the shame of being
an outcast than to the pains of death. This saying is
a doublet in Mt., cf. 16:24–5.
X 40-XI 1. The end of the discourse comes back to l
the task of the disciples as travelling missionaries ;
they are not only equipped with Jesus' power to heal.
They are true emissaries for 'a man's emissary is like
the man himself' (Berakoth 5:5) ; in this sense Jesus
(and the Father) are identified with the disciples,
a principle expanded in 25:31–46. In **40-2** it gives
weight to their mission and a promise of reward to
those who receive the emissary well. Thus the second m
discourse ends on the note of church ethics and
promise of reward for those who recognise Jesus Christ
in the activities and the agents of the church. **XI 1.**
Jesus is described as continuing his mission on his
own but there is no conscious attempt to describe a
return of the Twelve (cf. Lk. 10:17–20). In ch. 12
they seem to be around again (see note to 12:1), and
it may well be that ch. 11 is thought of as covering
a period when they are absent and Jesus receives the
emissaries of John and speaks to the people.
XI 2-XIII 54. The *Third Section* of Mt. with its 684a
discourse on the Teaching of Jesus about the Kingdom
(ch. 13) is, as all the others, dependent on the material
found in Mk (2:23–4:34) but this Marcan material
is prefaced by a major section on John the Baptist
(11:2–19 ; cf. Lk. 7:18–35), the Woes on the cities
of Galilee, the Thanksgiving to the Father and the
Invitation to the heavy-laden (20–30 ; cf. Lk. 10:13–15,
21:2). While chs. 8–10 have given the picture of the
Ministry of Jesus, chs. 11–13 form basically a section on
the response or the lack of response and it is also in
such a context that the parables on the Kingdom are
to be seen.
XI 2-19. 'the deeds of Christ' is used by Mt. b
here in the language of the church ; it hardly refers
to 'messianic deeds'. The coming one (*ho erchomenos*,
cf. 3:11) is obviously a technical term for a messianic
figure, Prophet or Messiah, but it is not known as a
title in Jewish texts, although the idea of his coming
is a commonplace, see 21:9 (Ps. 118:25). The quotation is basically from Isa. 61:1, but substitutes 'sight
for the blind' for 'freedom for the captives' (cf.
LXX and Lk. 4:18). All deeds thus mentioned
have been fully exemplified in chs. 8–10, hence
the descriptive introduction in Lk. is not called for in
Mt. **6** gives the basic theme for the whole Third c
Section in Mt. (see above, §673*i* ; cf. 13:21, 57) :
skandalizesthai (RSV 'take offence') actually means
'be caused to fall (into sin or apostasy)', cf. 16:23
and, for an even more concrete expression, Rom. 9:33 ;
1 Pet. 2:8. This is perhaps not with special reference
to John, but rather to his disciples and others who
do not recognise Jesus' messianic claim and who
thereby stumble and fall off the way of righteousness
which John had paved (21:32). **7-19.** The reed refers d
to the cane grass on the banks of Jordan. **8.** The royal
attire may refer to Davidic-messianic expectations.

684d John was recognised as a prophet (**11** : 'has risen' is only used in this sense about prophets) and his relation to Jesus and the Kingdom is now assessed by Mt. To him (as to Mk 9:13, but not to Lk.) John is identified with Elijah as a forerunner of the Kingdom. **14.** The phrase 'if you are willing to accept it' indicates the esoteric and 'difficult' character of such an identification, see further 17:9–13. This special role is given to John on the basis of a revised form of Mal. 3:1 where the forerunner was *God's* forerunner, not that of a Messiah. Nevertheless the point is not to exalt the role of John but to sharpen the contrast between the period of the Law and the Prophets which reaches its climax in John and the
e period of the Kingdom of Heaven. **12.** Mt. pictures the transitional situation—'from the days of John the Baptist until now'—with a phrase which remains a veritable *crux* of interpretation : **12b** reads either : 'the Kingdom of Heaven suffers violence (passive) and men of violence grab it' or 'the Kingdom of Heaven manifests itself violently (or: powerfully ; reflexive) and keen and daring men take hold of it'. The latter meaning fits better into Mt.'s context, but the former—taken as a reference to Zealots and others who entertain military dreams of Israel's deliverance—is more natural from a linguistic point of view ; cf. W. G. Kümmel, *Promise and Fulfilment* (1957), 121ff. In whatever way the intermediate situation be described, the prophetic ministry of John was the last phase and predicted climax before the
f coming of the Kingdom. **16-19.** A saying akin to the issue in 9:14–17 is used to round off the assessment of John's relation to Jesus ; **19** the final logion remains obscure, as it seems to have been almost from the very beginning, since the manuscripts both in Lk. and Mt. vary : 'deeds'/'children'. It is unlikely that Wisdom here is identified with Jesus (cf. below to 23:34), and yet there is a striking affinity to what follows in **25-30**, where Jesus assumes the function of Wisdom as described in Sir. 51:23–7 ; **19c** the preposition (*apo*: AV 'of' ; RSV 'by') may have the force of 'over against', but that would require 'children' : The Wisdom of God (moving towards its goal) cannot be hampered by those who claim to be the sons of Wisdom, i.e. the Pharisees and others who take offence. With 'by his deeds' the thought comes close to 21:28–32 and that seems to be Mt.'s understanding ; cf. also Jn 5:36.
g **20-24.** Lack of response is once more (8:11f., 10:15, 21:28–32) pointed out by an unfavourable comparison between the Jews and those whom they despised. **23** is an allusion to Isa. 14:13, 15 (in its Heb. form). The future tense used in **22** and **24** presupposes a resurrection of both good and evil at the Day of Judgment.
h **25-30.** The hymnic character of these verses is recognised with precision since Eduard Norden (*Agnostos Theos*, 1913) drew attention to a pattern of such 'self-revelations' : (*a*) Thanksgiving to the Father for received revelation ; (*b*) statement of its content ; (*c*) invitation and appeal. This structure gives Mt.'s form as the complete one priority over the Lucan form (only *a* and *b*), cf. also the close link with **19.** The language has a strong Semitic ring (see e.g. **26** ; cf. W. L. Knox, *Some Hellenistic Elements in Primitive Christianity* (1944), 6ff.) and its Near Eastern background was established by T. Arvedson, *Das Mysterium Christi* (1937). At this point the Synoptic tradition comes very close to the Johannine, both in style and content (Jn 3:35, 17:2, 7:29, 10:14, 15). Consequently we are inclined to consider the passage as having originated from an interplay between actual words of Jesus and the formative activity of a church similar
i to that behind the Fourth Gospel. **25-6** continues the basic theme of chs. 11–13, the resistance to revelation on the part of the scribes and Pharisees. This is hailed as according to God's gracious plan (*eudokia*), see note to 6:10. In **27** recognition of Jesus' true identity is a mystery which only the Father can disclose, and this
is truly Matthean as we find it in 16:16f.; the parallel 68
turn of the argument is less natural in Mt. but the crucial function of Jesus as the only true revealer is not far from his messianic function in the Sermon on the Mount, 7:29. The idea of sonship has no clear implications of pre-existence or specific christological
speculation, cf. 3:17. **28-30.** The invitation is cast j
in words similar to those spoken by 'Wisdom' in Sir. 51:23–7. The Rabbis spoke of the 'yoke of the Law' as the glorious obedience to God which freed man from obligations to the world, and gave 'rest' and 'peace of mind'. But Jesus criticised this 'yoke' as heavy and wrong (e.g. 23:4), and presents his own teaching as an alternative *halachah* (i.e. legally binding statements). This *halachah* is characterised by his humility, his concern for the despised who did not dare to think that the yoke of the Law was for them. The yoke stands for the burden, not for the means by which loads are carried. For a later use of this saying see Did. 6.
XII 1-13. Two incidents centred around the question k
of the Sabbath. In Mk and Mt. these are the *only* places where **Jesus' attitude to the Sabbath** is dealt with explicitly (cf. 24:20), while Lk. makes more of it (13:15f. and 14:3 in addition to 6:1–11). At this point Mt. comes back to Mk's outline (2:23) and this gives the impression of the disciples being back from their missionary tour, but this is neither stressed nor even consciously meant in Mt., and according to the Marcan outline they are neither commissioned yet (3:13–19) nor sent out (6:7–11). Both these incidents are given in the form of the typical 'pronouncement story' or 'paradigm' : the narrative itself, told with great restraint and economy, functions solely as a 'candlestick' for a pronouncement of considerable
weight and importance. **1-8.** For the scriptural and l
Mishnaic basis for this controversial action of the disciples, see Dt. 23:25 and Mishnah Shabbath 7. On the showbread, see Exod. 25:30 et al. Mt. gives a double illustration and the terminology of the second is in keeping with Jewish tradition. Mt.'s understanding of the incident is clear from 6 and 8 : By the rabbinic principle 'if the lesser, then the greater' it is obvious that Jesus as the Son of Man has even more right than David and the priests to overrule the Sabbath laws ; and when he does so, it opens up possibilities for mercy. On 'man/Son of Man' in this passage,
see Mk 2:27–8. **9-13.** The argument is once more based m
on 'if the lesser, then the greater', and the incident of healing is not told as a miracle as such—this was more significant in Mt., chs. 8–9. The behaviour taken for granted in **11** is apparently correct to the Pharisees—but not to the Essenes who denied even such help on the Sabbath (CD 11:13–14).
14-21. Following Mk (3:6–12) Mt. has here a refer- n
ence to the decision of Jesus' enemies (for Herodians, see Mk 3:6) to get rid of him and Mt. introduces the following phrase so that the incidents more closely related to this decision (15 : 'aware of this') and by giving one of his formula quotations, 18–21. This quotation gives a deeper significance to the now necessary emphasis on secrecy. The quotation from Isa. 42:1–4 shows obvious marks of Mt.'s own exegetical reflection on the Heb. text (see K. Stendahl, *The School of St Matthew* (1954), 107ff.).
22-37. The miraculous powers of Jesus are discussed o
(but not in Mk). These powers raise the messianic hope in the minds of people, and are given in the Matthean form : 'Son of David' ; but the Pharisees ascribe them to 'black magic'. **25.** This sets the stage for a full-length apologia by Jesus, who is introduced with a supernatural touch ('knowing their thoughts'). The structure is that of Mk 3:23–30 and most of the sayings are found also in diverse places in Lk., but Mt. has given it his own accent and understanding. **25-9** makes the somewhat humorous point p
that whatever way you look at it, Satan's power is apparently broken—either because he has come in opposition to himself (26) or because somebody who

684p is stronger has come. **27-9.** This line of argument has
been woven together with a direct attack on the
Pharisees, originally on the Jews in general, according
to Bultmann (1957[3]), and Mt. also uses the logion in
30 in this argument. **27** is one of the crucial passages
in the Gospels for our knowledge of Jesus' understanding of his person and his ministry (see W. G. Kümmel,
Promise and Fulfilment (1957), 105–9) : The kingdom is
at work in Jesus' activity. **28.** For the use of ' Spirit '
here (Lk. ' the finger of God ') cf. the quotation from
Isa. 42 in 18 with its accent on the hiddenness. In
q **31-2** the double aspect of the veiled and yet real
manifestation of the Spirit in Jesus' activities is stated
by Mt. (cf. Mk 3:28–30). There is the distinction
between the blasphemy against the Son of Man,
which can be forgiven, and the blasphemy against the
Holy Spirit, which cannot ; i.e. during the ministry
of Jesus it was ' permissible ' and understandable not
to recognise Jesus as the Messiah, but after Pentecost
r there was no excuse, cf. 21:32. **33-7** (not found in
Mk) take off from this point where it is made clear
that the confession to Jesus is what counts, and this
confession, although it consists of such insignificant
things as words (*argos*, 36, not ' careless ' or ' idle ' but
' insignificant '), is all-decisive and reveals the true
nature of him who utters the words, cf. Rom. 10:10.
s **38-42.** The argument continues logically (*apekrithēsan*,
here rather ' answered ' (AV) than ' said ' (RSV)) :
If you say this then you are under obligation to give
us a ' sign '. None of the synoptic Gospels refers to the
healing-miracles of Jesus as ' signs ' (as does Jn).
The sign required must be a spectacular and celestial
one, ' a sign from heaven ', 16:1 ; cf. the Joel prophecy
in Ac. 2:17–21. The Marcan tradition (8:11–12, cf.
Mt. 16:1–4) says ' no sign ' (using a Semitic ' if ' as a
negation, which could have been the starting-point
for the tradition found in Mt. and Lk. : ' if not '
t = except that of Jonah). But is it Jonah as a prophet
who experienced the response of repentance as it
appears in **41** and to which **42** is a natural parallel in
good Semitic style ? Or is the sign of Jonah the
three days in the grave, as in **40** ? Strangely enough,
when Justin (*Dial.* 107:2) gives the latter interpretation, which he expands, he quotes Mt., leaving out
40. It is therefore reasonable to suppose that 40 is
not original in Mt. and that the interpretation which
it gives to the Jonah sign, though of early Christian
origin, does not represent Mt.'s understanding. To
him the sign of Jonah is the preaching ministry, a
ministry which was successful among despised Gentiles;
cf. 8:11, 10:15, 11:20–4. On the queen of Sheba
coming to Solomon, see 1 Kg. 10.
u **43-45.** This logion seems to have a more correct
context in Lk. (11:24–6). The language is that of
common Jewish folklore. The desert—in the OT as
well as in the NT—is a place of the demonic (cf.
4:1–11). It is a warning against backsliding, which
Mt. tries to fit into the context of the preceding
criticism of Jesus' own generation of Jews.
v **46-50.** Mt. had little interest in the descriptive and
47, not found in some of the best MSS, was added
under the influence of Mk-Lk. to give more life to the
background of Jesus' saying. In Mk (3:31–5) the
mentioning of Jesus' relatives may be thought of as
the climactic conclusion of what is mentioned in
3:20–2, viz. their attempt to take care of their strange
son and brother. In Mt. there is no interest in their
coming as such, but a contrast is given to the new
family of messianic fellowship. **50.** To do the will of the
Father may, in this context, refer to accepting Jesus
rather than general obedience in the realm of ethics.
685a **XIII The Third Matthean Discourse** follows
and expands the material in Mk 4, and consists of
parables, which are presented as spoken in public
and interpretations of a private nature ; cf. however
44-50. Much is made of the contrast between the
public and the private or even secret aspects of Jesus'
teaching, and the parables here assembled are of a
special kind : those about the Kingdom and the way
in which it comes ; how or why it is received or not 685a
received, see 10-17. See *The Life and Teaching of
Jesus* (§§643*ab*), and for a more detailed study of
the parables, see especially J. Jeremias, *The Parables
of Jesus* (1954). **1-9.** What is the ' point ' of this b
famous **parable of the sower** ? Like many of the
parables on the Kingdom, and different from many of
the other parables, it ends on a positive and happy note :
in spite of much apparent loss, there will be a glorious
and sure crop ! Thus the emphasis falls on encouragement for the disciples or for those concerned about
the Kingdom. Their work and hopes as well as Jesus'
own work will not be in vain. For the interpretation,
see 18–23 below.
10-17. The discussion about whether Jesus used c
parables (*a*) as a conscious method of a veiled witness
(Gr. *parabolē*, Heb. *māshāl*, also means ' enigma ') or
(*b*) in order to make his point plain and simple, is
usually based on **13** or rather Mk 4:10–12 (see also
Jeremias, op. cit., 11ff.). On the basis of the underlying Aram. saying, both possibilities were open to
those who had to render this saying into Gr. Mk
with *hina* (' in order that ') in 4:12 seems to follow (*a*)
while Mt.'s *hoti* (' because '), 13, would rather fit (*b*).
Mt.'s total understanding of Jesus' use of parables
comes nevertheless closer to the first alternative, and
this not only due to his dependence on Mk 4:10–11,
but also by his using the saying in Mk 4:25 (cf. 25:29)
at this point (12) with reference to ' the mysteries of
the Kingdom ' : these were not to be given to outsiders
(11*c*). This stern attitude has to be understood not
about parables in general (as for example those in
Lk. 15), but specifically about the **parables which deal
with the Kingdom,** and which in its veiled form
announce its coming. Such an understanding is also
strengthened by Mt.'s use of the logion in **16-17** at this
point, cf. Lk. 10:23–4. **14-15.** The full quotation from
Isa. 6:9–10 may be a later expansion prefaced by the
formula of fulfilment (see K. Stendahl, *The School of
St Matthew* (1954), 129–33). If original in Mt., we
see again that the use of parables is not taken as a
pedagogical device in a modern sense, but is according
to the plan of God (cf. 35).
18-23. The interpretation of the parable about the d
sower moves towards allegorisation—but Jesus is not
actually made ' the Sower '—and Mt. ties up the
interpretation with what has gone before (10–17)
by stressing the ' understanding ' of the word (19
and 23). The different types of soil become illustrations for different types of men.
24-30 and **36-43.** The **parable of the tares** and its e
interpretation are found only in Mt. While being
quite different from the Marcan parable of the seed
growing secretly (Mk 4:26–9), it could be a parallel
tradition with its reference to what happens while the
farmer sleeps and with its urging of patience. Two of the
three parables in ch. 13 peculiar to Mt. (the tares and
the drag-net) focus upon the ' end of (this) age ' (**39f.**
and **49**). The parable itself seems to have its point in
the command not to weed out the tares, but wait for
the harvest. In its context in Mt. this could be
understood as an argument against premature judgment in matters of church discipline (cf. 18:15–22),
but is perhaps rather meant as a further reference to
the situation which applies to Jesus' earthly ministry,
where the ultimate dividing line is not yet drawn
(cf. 12:31–2). **36-43.** In the interpretation, the f
eschatological accent is stronger and makes the
parable all-inclusive (**38 :** ' the field is the world ')
and the accent is not on waiting, but upon the consummation. **41.** The Kingdom of the Son of Man,
from which ' those who cause evil and those who do
evil ' are weeded out, could be either the whole world
or the church or—and that is most probable—Israel
as the centre of the world, cf. 8:11f. **43.** The climax
is, in style, an allusion to Dan. 12:3, where we find
a pointed reference both to ' the righteous ' and to
' those who *understand* ', a term prominent in ch. 13
(13, 14, 15, 19, 23, 51).

21

685g **31-33**. Two short parables, the first also in both Mk and Lk., the latter in Lk. only and almost identical. The description of the tree may allude to Dan. 4:21 where it refers to Nebuchadnezzar (a Gentile). The leaven in Jewish imagery refers to what is unclean (cf. 16:6–12, 1 C. 5:6–8), but this may be incidental. The parables are hardly meant to describe the way in which the Kingdom grows or how the Gospel slowly permeates the world. The point is one of encouragement and awareness of the Kingdom's hidden beginnings in Jesus' ministry.

h **34-35**. Mt. renders Mk's concluding remark about Jesus' use of parables by a chiastic parallelism with biblical ring and adds to it one of his formula quotations. Ps. 78:2 is here used as prophecy (some MSS refer it even to Isaiah), as is Ps. 110 in 20:43f. The quotation is reinterpreted on the basis of the Heb. text so that it now refers to the revelation of that which was hidden up to this time. This, again, strengthens the view that, to Mt., the use of parables was a way to reveal and yet to do so in a veiled manner according to the rules of Jewish apocalypticism. But to the disciples the inside story can and should be given; cf. the similar role of the Teacher of Righteousness, 1QpHab. 7:1–5. **36-43**. See above, with **24-30**.

i **44-50**. It appears from the arrangement of ch. 13 that Mt. may have consciously meant the three parables about the Treasure, the Pearl and the Drag-net for the disciples only: they continue on the note given in **36-43**. The first two have their point in the joyous determination of him who finds—it is not clear whether the behaviour in **44** was felt to be as unethical as it may strike us. If it was, this only intensifies the parable (cf. Lk. 16:1–8, 18:1–6). The hiddenness as well as the emphasis on 'finding' is not accidental (cf. 7:14), and goes well with the address to the disciples, as does the joy. **47**. The parable of the Drag-net turns the attention once more to the conclusion.

j The perspective is universal ('every kind of fish'; cf. Jn 21:11 with reference to the 153 fishes, see §758*i*). The accent falls not on the waiting period, but on the separation of the elect from the evil ones. As told to the disciples, the parable seems to have a glorious rather than a threatening function, although the phrase 'out of the midst of the righteous' can also have been read as a cleansing of the church from its false members.

k **51-52**. Mt.'s concluding remark on the parables about the Kingdom stresses once more the 'understanding': a disciple is he who 'understands', who sees through the veil of the parabolic revelation. The words about the scribe who has 'become a disciple' (*mathēteutheis*, cf. 27:57 and 28:19) with this kind of understanding of the Kingdom is often taken as a self-portrait of the author of the First Gospel (so e.g. von Dobschütz and Bacon). The order 'new and old', not old and new, may be significant in that connection since Mt. is anxious to relate the new (Jesus' messianic manifestation and teaching) to the old (the promises of the OT), cf. 7:12.

686a **53-58**. The usual formula by which Mt. concludes the five sections with their discourses forms here a more integral part of what follows as the beginning of the *Fourth Section* (13:54–19:2), a section where there is little deviation from Mk 6–9 until Mt. comes to the point where he elaborates Mk 9:33–43 into a discourse on church discipline, 17:24–18:35.

54. Since Mt. goes directly from the discourse on parables—and the passages dealing with Wisdom (11:19ff.)—having used the material in Mk 5 in earlier contexts, it appears that the words about 'wisdom' and the 'miraculous power' are a summary of what has been dealt with in Sections II and III of

b the Gospel, but this may be incidental. Unlike the account of Jesus' rejection in Nazareth given in Mk (Mk 6:1–6), (*a*) **55** Jesus is not called 'carpenter', but 'the carpenter's son', and (*b*) **58** the statement about his inability to perform any miracle is toned down to 'and he did not perform many miracles'. The MSS are somewhat at variance about the names of Jesus' brothers (Mt.: Joseph or Joses or Johannes; Mk: Josetus or Joseph or Joses). 686b

XIV 1-12. Herod Antipas, correctly called tetrarch by Mt. and Lk. (Mk: king) was the son of Herod the Great and inherited Galilee and Perea from his father. Josephus tells of a marriage of his which was against the Law (Lev. 20:21), and about his putting John the Baptist to death (Jos. Ant. XVIII, v) but he does not connect these two incidents. Josephus sees John as apprehended for fear that his influence over the people may lead to a revolt. **1-2** gives a revealing insight into religious expectations in Israel at the time: Jesus is considered 'John risen from the dead'. Mt. gives this 'parallel' to Jesus' resurrection as a matter of course; it should be noted as significant for early interpretations of Jesus' resurrection and the miracles performed in his name (Ac. 2–3). The details of John's death are reduced to a minimum in Mt., and the point seems rather to be to introduce the material where Jesus is revealed in his messianic manifestations. It also serves as a reason for Jesus to withdraw from the public scene into remote and partly Gentile territory. c d

13-21. There he performs a miracle which has both OT and messianic connotations (Elisha in 2 Kg. 4:42; Elijah in 1 Kg. 17:9–16; cf. on Moses, Jn 6:32). The terminology in **19** may show some influence from the account of the Last Supper (26:26) and consequently from the meal practice of the church. The twelve baskets seem to be related to the twelve disciples, see 15:32–9; in the feeding, as well as in this whole Fourth Section, the disciples play a strikingly significant role. The whole event is perhaps even originally understood as a 'messianic banquet'. e

22-36. As Jesus in a veiled way has manifested himself as the Messiah by the feeding of the multitudes, so he now manifests himself openly to the disciples in the storm, and they hail him as the Son of God (33); **27** the *egō eimi* may have a numinous and divine ring (not: 'It is I', but: 'I AM'). In the Matthean form we find here material on discipleship with Peter as *the* disciple (28-31 only in Mt.). The walking on the water is told as a study in discipleship and faith (cf. G. Bornkamm, *Überlieferung . . .* (1960), 48–53). **34-36**. In shortened form Mt. retains a connecting account about healing. On the 'fringe of the garment' see §682*o*. f

XV 1-20. The notice about a stay in the area (the plain) of Gennesaret, south-west of Capernaum, 14:34, supplies a more natural scene for an encounter with officials from Jerusalem. Mt. makes **1-20** into a closed unit by returning in **20** to the question raised in **2**. The requirement of hand-washing was a typical Pharisaic tradition, where the requirement for the priests (Lev. 22:1–16) were applied to the rank-and-file Jew—a principle of the priesthood of all believers which was at the very root of Pharisaic concern for the Law. The antitheses in the Sermon on the Mount had the form of sharpening the Law to its ultimate intensity, and the casuistry of the scribes was criticised for its evasive and slackening tendencies (cf. also 19:4–12). The material in ch. 15 is not so different, though the form is more precisely that of controversy, perhaps under the influence of the debate going on between synagogue and church. **3**. The principle of the (oral) Pharisaic tradition is challenged and called hypocritical as conflicting with the basic commandments of God. **7-9**. This is done by an *ad hoc* rendering of Isa. 29:13 based on the LXX, and consequently coined in a Greek-speaking community. **4-6**. The criticism has been substantiated by reference to how somebody can make a votive gift (to the Temple?) instead of taking care of his parents. **10-11**. After such demonstration of how their tradition overrules the Law, the question of hand-washing is criticised on internal grounds and (**13**) a logion which could well have referred to persons—the elect compared with the unbelievers—is applied to the regulations of g h

6h the Pharisees as 'not planted by God', and linked with the saying about blind leaders (Lk. 6:39, cf.
i Rom. 2:19). In **10** the verbs technically applied to parables in ch. 13 ('hear and understand') have been used, and in **15** Peter now refers to 11 as a 'parable'; this may well remind us of how bold Jesus' interpretation was felt to be, since we would hardly find 11 to be a parable or an enigma. **19**. Mt.'s list of vices is considerably shorter than Mk's, but he adds 'false witness'. This as well as blasphemy (RSV 'slander') may well have the more precise religious sense to Mt., and not a merely ethical one.

j **21-31**. The issue about clean and unclean is closely related to the attitude towards the Gentiles, and Paul's epistles make it quite clear that it was in matters of food laws that the tensions between Jews and Gentiles, both in and outside the churches, came to the fore. Mt. has either rewritten what he found in Mk at this point (7:24–30) or had a source with quite distinctive features. His use of 'Tyre and Sidon', 'Canaanite', 'Son of David' (cf. 9:27; and 'the God of Israel') gives an archaic tone to the pericope, compared with Mk's more geographical and 'contemporary' terminology. The interplay between Jesus and his disciples gives the impression that the text was used as a guide to the proper handling of similar matters in the church. In keeping with 10:5, Jesus insists on his call to the children of Israel, but the point of the story is apparently the significance of the exception or the extension granted on the basis of
k the woman's strong and humble faith. The healing is quite incidental; what counts is the attitude to the Canaanites, the chief enemies in the time of the Judges, as the epitome of the heathen. There was nothing offensive to Mt., who lived and worked in a church which happily accepted Gentile Christians, in the harsh words to the woman. On the contrary, hereby the faith of the Gentiles was glorified and Jesus' words just witnessed to the great fact that Gentiles could *now* share in the riches at the table of
l God's children, cf. 8:5–13. **29-31**. It may well be that Mt. thinks of this summary as a generalisation of what has just happened, a ministry under the eyes of the Gentiles and even to their benefit. Thus they praise 'the God of Israel'. On all sides of the lake of Galilee, but especially on its eastern shore (Mk: Decapolis), were many non-Jewish settlements.

m **32-39**. Mt. shares with Mk the double tradition of a feeding of the multitudes, while Lk. has only the one in Mt. 14:13–21, and Jn 6 shows signs of both combined. In all six accounts a voyage across the lake follows. Thus they all may stem from one and the same tradition. Many reasons have been suggested to account for this duplication in Mk and its retention in Mt. (See e.g. Ph. Carrington's suggestion of a lectionary where the calendar required such a pattern, *The Primitive Christian Calendar* (1952), 16.) One real possibility is that the feeding of the 4,000 refers to the Gentiles and E. Lohmeyer (*Komm. Mt.* ad loc.) strengthens this view by reference to the seven baskets = the seven deacons (Ac. 6:1ff.) over against the twelve baskets in 14:20 = the twelve disciples (as representatives of the twelve tribes of Israel; see also Lohmeyer in JBL 56 (1937), 235f.). **30**. Neither Magadan nor Dalmanutha (Mk) can be identified. Some MSS read Magdala, i.e. on the eastern side of the lake.

37a **XVI 1-4**. Mt. follows Mk in letting the second feeding prompt a request for a sign from heaven (so also Jn 6:30), although he has dealt with this matter in 12:38–9. **2b-3** is missing in some of the best MSS; these verses may have come into Mt. under the influence of Lk., where the argument is more clear. The text in Mt. would imply that even when the signs are very similar, they are made quite distinct.

b **5-12**. This short discourse on leaven is of interest as an example of how a saying of Jesus could be used on the basis of association (leaven-bread) in relation to the accounts of the feeding of the multitudes and how it thereby was given additional implications in the preaching and interpretation of the church. Thereby 687b
two thoughts were woven together: (*a*) I have taken care of your physical needs; (*b*) don't be deceived by the teaching of the Pharisees and the Sadducees. The interpretation of teaching being equivalent to bread is brought out with more force and clarity in Jn 6.

13-23. One of the most debated pericopes in Mt. c
In Mk we find the account of how the disciples for the first time recognise Jesus as the Messiah; Peter speaks for them (cf. the confession of Peter in the similar context after the feeding and the sea voyage in Jn 6:68–9). While this is of great significance to Mk, the main point for him is the first prediction of the Passion; the climax of the pericope is the rebuke of Peter—with an eye to the disciples (Mk 8:33). Mt. retains the Marcan account with few changes: (*a*) **13**. 'Son of Man' instead of 'me', the most striking example of the interchangeability of these, see note to 8:20. (*b*) **14**. Jeremiah mentioned by name, presumably since he was often listed first among the so-called 'latter prophets' in Jewish canon. (*c*) **16**. 'Son of the living God' added to 'Christ'. **21a**. 'Jesus Christ': in some of the best MSS (ℵ and B), but only here in context in the Synoptics and out of line with Gospel usage, cf. 1:1 and 1:18; hence hardly a genuine reading. **21b**. Jerusalem mentioned but not the Son of Man, and Mk's reference to Jesus' open language is omitted. **22**. Peter quoted and the reference to the other disciples omitted. **23**. *skandalon*, 'stumbling-block' or something that causes to fall and sin. The pericope thus still has the point of rebuke at its end, but the balance has been shifted to the majestic statement about Peter which Mt. has brought into this Marcan structure (17–20). In Mt. this is not the first time the disciples recognise Jesus as the Son of God (14:33) but the title Christ-Messiah has not been used before on the lips of the disciples. 17–20 seems d
to be a Matthean (for another view, see Oepke, in *Studia Theologica* 2 (1948)) tradition about why Simon was called Peter (see Mt.'s omission of 'and he added the name Peter to Simon' in Mt. 10:2; Mk 3:16). The Aram. *Cepha(s)*, which is not used in the Synoptics, but usually by Paul, cf. Jn 1:42, is identical in form as a name and as meaning 'rock'. This name has nothing to do with stability of character; **17** indicates that Peter's personal qualifications matter little. But Peter is made the leader of the church, cf. especially Lk. 22:31–4; Jn 21:15f. This church is spoken of in mythological and apocalyptic terms as an edifice (cf. 1QS 8:7, about the leaders at Qumrân and its parallel in Rev. 21:12) in close proximity to the gates of hell (Hades or Sheol). An Aram. fragment to Test. e
Levi 2:3–5 found at Qumrân may give an astonishing complex of parallels to this passage and even to its connection with the country around Caesarea Philippi (13), on the slopes of Mt Hermon and at the sources of the river Jordan, since this area played a role in Jewish apocalypticism as a place of revelation and as a meeting-place for the upper and the lower world, **18-19**, see J. M. Allegro, *The Dead Sea Scrolls* (1956), 143ff. **19**. The keys of the Kingdom are a symbol f
of Peter's power as the leader of the church. 'To bind and to loose' can either refer to the authority to promulgate binding rules (*halachah*) or to the practice of church discipline, ℵB, ad loc. Although these two functions were closely related in the life of the synagogue, it is probable that Mt. intentionally uses the saying in the former sense here (i.e. Peter the 'chief-rabbi') and in the second sense in 18:18, where the saying is not tied to Peter in person. In the Gospels g
the word *ekklēsia* (church) occurs only here and in 18:17. The question usually raised is then: Did Jesus use the word *ekklēsia* or did he even think in terms of a church or a community as the consequence of his ministry? The material from Qumrân with its community structure adds considerably to the probability for such thoughts and terminology. On the h
history of exegesis of **17-20**, see O. Cullmann, *Peter* (1953), 158–69, where also the different attempts to

687h interpret the ' Rock ' as something else than ' Peter in person ' are in most cases shown to be expressions of Protestant bias. The distinction between the person Peter and the faith which he has presupposes a sophistication of a sort not to be expected in our text. On the other hand, the role of Peter is here understood as unique at a specific juncture of God's history, and its repetition in the bishops of Rome is quite another matter. On the historicity of the pericope, see Cullmann, op. cit., 170–212 ; A. Oepke and W. G. Kümmel in *Studia Theologica* 2 (1948), 110–65
i and 7 (1953), 1–27. **21-3** plays with force on the motif which was of utmost significance to the early church, both in its apologetic and its missionary task : a crucified Messiah renounced by the Jewish leaders in Jerusalem. Even if there was a place in Jewish eschatology for an expected ' suffering Messiah ' (see W. Zimmerli, J. Jeremias, *The Servant of God*, 1957), the Gospels all indicate that the disciples did not have such expectations regarding Jesus : pericopes like this one could hardly serve as a mere literary device to give more effect to Jesus' statements. Jesus may well have spoken about his death and resurrection (or : exaltation, cf. 26:64) ; he can hardly have done so with as much precision (Mt. : ' on the third day ' ; Mk : ' after three days ') as here. The accent falls rather on his suffering than on his death, this in contrast to Pauline Christology.

j **24-28.** As expected in this section of Mt., only disciples are addressed (Mk : ' the crowd together with the disciples '). Mt. has used these sayings once before, in the discourse to the messengers of the Gospel, 10:33, 38f. It is striking that Mt. has not retained the pointed words about how the Son of Man will be ashamed of those who have not been willing to take upon themselves the shame of the discipleship of Jesus (Mk 8:38, see Mt. 10:33). The whole tone of 24–8 does not seem to recognise that there are such among the disciples (and yet the *Stichwort* is *opisō mou* which is used in quite opposite directions : 23—' get behind me (Satan)'; 24—' follow me (ye disciples)'), and **27** refers to the good recompense on the other side of trial and tribulation : the allusion to Ps. 62:13 (' he shall repay every man according to his deed ') is used as in the Psalter referring only to God's steadfast love towards the righteous. This good connotation is intensified in **28** where the coming of the Kingdom is expected within a generation. But coming in what sense ? The variation in the different synoptics at this point (Mk 9:1 ; Lk. 9:27) and in the MSS witness to the problem which they faced in this matter, cf. 24:34–6, and Jn 21:21–3.

k **XVII 1-13.** Modern studies (especially H. Riesenfeld, *Jésus Transfiguré*, 1947 ; cf. G. H. Boobyer, *St Mark and the Transfiguration Story*, 1942) have stressed the amount of cultic and mythological motifs from the OT and Jewish eschatology which underlie the account of the transfiguration. The prevailing interpretations of the story as a post-resurrection appearance projected back into the ministry of Jesus hardly account for many of its precise details. The group of the Three (Peter and the sons of Zebedee) form an inner circle among the Twelve in the Gospels (26:37, 20:20) and in Gal. 2:9 we find three ' pillars ', but there James is the Lord's brother with that name. Thus the group of Three, just as that of the Twelve, seems to have a significance in itself apart from who they may have been, as both have at Qumrân (1QS 8:1–8, see F. M. Cross, *The Ancient Library of Qumrân* (1948), 174f.), and it is worth noting that they are singled out as having received special revelation. The basic pattern of the transfiguration is that of the Feast of Tabernacles (e.g. the three booths) as the inauguration of the New Age with Jesus enthroned as a high-priestly Messiah.

l **9-13.** In the light of this epiphany with its strong manifestation of the Age to Come with its ' rest ' (**4** : ' it is well for us to be here ', cf. RSV's somewhat more pedestrian : ' it is well that we are here '), the Kingdom has drawn more close than expected and
Jesus is more than a forerunner of that Kingdom. 68
Yet the restoration of all things has not taken place, as it was expected to be carried out by Elijah (Mal. 4:5). Now John is identified with Elijah, but since he was not accepted, he could not do what he was expected to ; yet God's time-table cannot be upset thereby, and it will force itself through by suffering, as will also the ministry of Jesus. The identification of John as Elijah was not as self-evident as Christian exegesis makes us believe, see J. A. T. Robinson in NTS 4 (1957–8), 263–81.

14-21. In the larger context of instruction to the m
disciples Mk 9:14–29 has been reduced to a minimum as far as the healing is concerned, and by adding the Logion found in Mk 11:22–3 Mt. gives teaching about the power of faith. **17.** It is significant that he retains the words ' how long am I to be with you ', i.e. the note of the image of Jesus as ' visiting ' the world to get his church started (cf. Jn 14:9). **21** is missing in the best MSS and seems to be due to influence from Mk 9:29 in a later stage of its textual tradition. On the relation between prayer and the power of miracle, see however 6:14 and 18:15–20.

22-23. Following Mk 9:30–2 (minus the reference to n
the lack of understanding on the part of the disciples and their fear for asking further), Mt. gives the second —or third (see 9–13)—prediction of the death and the resurrection, now causing no questions but only sorrow.

24-27. The half-shekel tax is the one paid yearly by o
every adult Jewish man to the Temple. The story is found only in Mt., where it is naturally connected with Peter as the chief apostle. Its point of departure is the fact that Jesus did recognise the Temple and did pay such tax : **25** Peter's answer is a plain yes. This must have raised certain questions at a later date and those receive an answer here, in keeping with, for example, 3:15, i.e. Jesus does certain things which, strictly speaking, he did not have to do as the Son of God. The miraculous element serves this dialectic by letting the Father supply the coin. The tendency of the story seems to be that Jesus' action could not be made a basis for making Christians continue to pay the Temple tax.

XVIII 1-XIX 1. The incident in 17:24–7 sets the 68
stage for, or could even be considered the introductory part of, the *Fourth Discourse* in Mt., which deals with the relation between ' the sons ' (17:26) and gives admonitions, warnings and ordinances for the life together and for church discipline.

XVIII 1-9. Mt. reduces the narrative element in Mk b
and forms a statement which does not deal with a concrete rivalry of the Twelve, but with the ranks in the Kingdom. The Qumrân literature has shown the importance of rank in the structure of that sectarian Judaism, both in the visions of the heavenly future (1QSa) and in the actual life of the community (1QS 2:19–25, 6:8–13). **4.** In both respects Jesus hails the child as the ideal, not on the basis of innocence, but of humility, and the child becomes the symbol for the rank-and-file disciple in constant danger of deception from proud and clever people (cf. 25:31–46). This picture of the disciples is consistent in all the Gospels, cf. Lk. 12:32, Jn 10, and may well say something about the nature of the early Christian community as well as of those who gathered around Jesus as relatively uneducated and helpless in the more or less academic climate of synagogue Judaism ; cf.
Paul's concern for the weak brethren. **6-9** is a string c
of sayings held together by the term *skandalon*, ' stumbling block ', i.e. that which causes man to stumble, to fall, to become an apostate, to take such offence (hence our ' scandal ') in Jesus, as to deny him (cf. especially 11:6, 15:12, 24:10, 26:31ff.). Only 6 deals with ' the little ones ', to which Mt. returns in 10. Mt. may have understood the *skandalon* sayings as urging the expulsion of false teachers (for a quite different use of the metaphor (8) in an ethical context, see 5:29–30). **7** (cf. Lk. 17:1) sees the role of these

8c *skandala* as the device for testing the true believers (cf. 24:10ff.) and the statement is identical in its theology to that of Paul in 1 C. 11:19, cf. also Mt. 26:24.

d **10-14**. From here on to the end of the chapter Mt. goes off on his own, and becomes more specific in his material about the life together, perhaps with the general statement on 'peace with one another' (Mk 9:50*b*) as a guide for his thought. In **10** the parable about the Lost Sheep (Lk. 15:3–7) is introduced by a reference to how the guardian angels of the rank-and-file disciples are of the highest rank, close to the throne of God. The Qumrân texts witness to their view of worship together with the angels as a sign of the community as consisting of the true Israel, close to its consummation (e.g. 1QSa 2:10; explicitly as guardians of the meek and needy, the orphans and the despised, see 1QH 5:20–2). (**11** has weak support in the MSS and seems to have come from Lk. 19:10.)

e In Lk. the parable about the Lost Sheep—together with the Lost Coin and the Prodigal Son, both only in Lk.—exemplifies Jesus' attitude towards the sinners among the Jews and is directed explicitly against the criticism of the Pharisees and the scribes (Lk. 15:1). In Mt. the use of the parable is totally different. This is clear already by the context, which deals with the 'little ones' as the rank-and-file believers. The lost sheep is now described three times as 'having gone astray' (12 bis and 13), a significant term for Mt. in his description of apostasy (24:4, 5, 11, 24). Mt. also avoids the term *metanoia*, 'repentance' (Lk. 15:7, 17:3, 4), which for him is confined to initial conversion. Thus it deals with the brother who has lapsed, or is in danger of doing so, and the parable introduces the following pericope with its more specific regulations about handling matters of church discipline.

f **15-20** The three-step procedure suggested here in matters of correction of a brother (private—before witnesses (cf. Dt. 19:15)—before the full assembly) is found in the Qumrân Manual of Discipline (5:25–6.1, cf. CD 9:3). In Qumrân the disciplinary action is necessary since membership there is proleptic membership in the New Covenant, about to be made manifest. It is not an educational device for producing good and serious members. This seems to be even more so in the Matthean church since there is no gradation of the punishments, no short-term expulsions (as at Qumrân). **18, 19**. He who does not conform and is not 'gained back', is excommunicated: 'considered a Gentile and a tax-collector'. Such a description appears strange in a Gospel where these were the very persons who put Jews to shame by their faith (8:1–11, 9:9–13, 15:21–8). But apart from their faith in Jesus they are still the chief examples of those
g who are not to inherit the Kingdom. The word *ekklēsia* (church) as well as the saying about binding and loosing occur here as they did in 16:18–19. The latter saying (now in plural and not confined to Peter) refers to forgiveness and its grim counterpart, the
h definite curse (cf. Jn 20:23) The omnipotent prayer is not mentioned in general (as in 21·22) but with special reference to the authority of the witnesses (or the leaders) to act according to **18**, and the famous saying 'Where two or three are gathered together . . .' is here clearly meant as a promise that Christ himself is acting with the church in matters of this sort ('two or three' both in **16** and **20**). A close parallel to this understanding and this procedure is given in 1 C. 5:4, see C. H. Dodd, *New Testament Studies* (1953), 58ff; cf. also 6:14–15, and K. Stendahl, 'Prayer and Forgiveness', *Svensk Exegetisk Årsbok* 22–3 (1957–8),
i 75–86. **21-35.** But Mt is anxious to end on the note of forgiveness to the utmost, and this he achieves by the words to Peter (in Lk. 17:4 not to Peter and with the generalising 'daily' which is typical for Lk.; cf. Lk. 9:23, 11:3), and the full-length parable of the Unmerciful Servant, where the accent falls not on behaviour in general but on the inter-fraternal relations and their debts or obligations to one another (cf.
§673*i*). But just as the merciful king and the 688i
heavenly Father are severe in their judgment, so the church, though ready to forgive, is forced to judge those who jeopardise the brotherhood. The plot as well as the *dramatis personae* have some affinities to the Unjust Steward (Lk. 16:1–8; cf. also the talents, Mt. 25.14–30) but they can hardly be considered as having their root in common.

XIX 1-2. The usual concluding sentence, marking j
the end of Mt.'s Fourth Section and the beginning of the Fifth. Mt. says explicitly that Jesus leaves Galilee. He is on his way to Jerusalem (20·17).

XIX 3-XXVI 2. *The Fifth Section* is even more than 689a
the preceding one shaped by the Marcan outline since Mk already has a real discourse within this section (Mk 13) Mt has few changes (see 21:10–17) but some substantial additions (20:1–16, 21:28–32, 22:1–14, the expansion of Mk 13:37–40 into a full-length speech against the Pharisees, and five additional 'parables' at the end of Mk's eschatological discourse).

XIX 3-12 The question of divorce, touched upon in b
the Sermon on the Mount (5:32) comes now in the context of debate. The schools of Hillel and Shammai discussed this matter on the basis of the phrase 'some indecency' in Dt. 24:1, the very quotation to which Jesus' opponents refer (7), and which may account for the reference to unchastity in 9 (even more so in 5:32, see T. W. Manson, *The Teaching of Jesus* (1935[2]), 292). The form of the argument is of a type recognised in Jewish exegesis: the more original, the weightier. A reference to the intention in the creation (Gen. 1:27 and 2:24) outweighs the ordinances of Moses (cf Gal. 3:17; and the Ebionites who used the principle of 'Laws given after the "Golden Calf" are invalid'). The tendency here as in the Sermon on the Mount is one of sharpening the Law towards the heavenly fullness (Gen. 1 27 and 2:24 are 'pre-fall' sayings; cf. Mt 22:30) On 'except for unchastity', see 5:32; the MSS are rich in variants at this point, mostly due to attempts of harmonisation with 5:32.
10 is a good indication of how stern this teaching was c
in Jewish ears, especially since marriage was a duty to a Jew. **11-12** 1 C. 7 indicates that marriage or re-marriage was a problem in the early church and Mt.'s saying may well serve as a guide in the same general manner. While celibacy is allowed (as it was not to the Pharisees), not only where imposed by nature, but also for the Kingdom's sake—and then even commendable—it is not required for everybody. This attitude has its parallel among the Essenes where some were celibates and others lived a married life 10–12 resembles in form what all the synoptics have after the words to the Rich Youth (see 25ff): a further clarification in the form of a dialogue.

13-15. The association in Mk (and Mt-Lk.) seems d
to be the simple one of Marriage-Children In Mt. 18:3 the children were used as examples of humility; here the question of their place in the Kingdom is treated for its own sake. There is no basis for thinking that the disciples display a common Jewish attitude and that Jesus enunciates a new and more gracious one. O. Cullmann (*Baptism in the NT* (1950), 71–80) has drawn attention to the term 'hinder not' (**14**: *mē kōlyete*) as a technical term in connection with baptism (see e.g. Mt. 3:14; Ac. 8 36, 10:47); hence this logion could be intended as relative to the order of infant baptism. Blessings of the sort mentioned here were common in Judaism.

16-30. Mt. has small but most significant differences e
from Mk (and Lk) **16-17**. He has softened Mk's 'Why do you call me good?' (due to 20:15 as referring to Jesus?) and he has brought the theme of 10–12 into this pericope by his 'if you want to be perfect' (21), thereby indicating that poverty (rather than altruistic giving) is the highest stage of obedience, a note missing in Mk. **19**. The quotations from the latter part of the Decalogue were combined with Lev. 19:18 in Jewish catechism as they are here. Jesus does not criticise the man's confident confession of

689e obedience to the Law by a deeper interpretation of the
commandments (as does, e.g., the apocryphal *Nazarene
Gospel* at this point) **22.** It is intimated that the price
was too high for the young man and this prompts the
words about the dangers of wealth. It is especially
Lk. who labours this theme, but it runs through all
the Gospels and is a commonplace in Jewish piety
as well, where from the prophets and on, 'rich' and
'transgressor' are often synonyms (see e.g. Isa 53:9).
27, 29 But the disciples are hailed as having become
f truly poor for Jesus' name's sake. **28.** They are
promised reward and Mt. here brings in the 'great
promise' (Lk 22:28–30, in connection with the Last
Supper and the messianic banquet) to the Twelve:
they shall become the 'rulers' ('judge' in the sense
of 'rule' as in, e g, Ps 2·10; 1 Mac. 9:73; Ps. Sol.
17:26) of the New Israel in the time of the 'rebirth'
(*palingenesia*), a word used only here and in Tit. 3:5,
there with reference to baptism. Josephus uses it
about the restoration of the Land of Israel, and it
has a good deal of that concrete connotation in Mt.
29, on the other hand, speaks with the timeless and
general 'everyone who . . .' but Mk's clear distinction
between 'already in this age' and 'in the age to
come' has been lessened or deleted. **30** refers to
'the reversal of the conditions' This logion is also
the concluding climax of the following parable, which
Mt. consequently considers as an illustration.
g **XX 1-16.** The vineyard is a much loved image from
the OT and in Jewish teaching. It usually has the
connotation of 'Israel' (Isa 5) and it may have that
here, but the interpretation does not hinge upon such
an allusion. There are three main possibilities of
interpreting the parable · (*a*) It is basically an apologia
for Jesus' ministry to the despised and has its point
in 15; it is, then, a Matthean parallel to the parables
in Lk. 15. (*b*) It is concerned with the nature of reward
and has its point in the fact that everyone gets the
same pay (10–12). (*c*) It is less concerned with Jesus
and more with the reversal of order and has its point,
and perhaps its root, in the logion in 16 (and 19:30).
The second alternative seems to be the weakest, since
the equal pay is a natural device to make the story a
vivid one. Actually Mt. uses different degrees of
reward (see e.g. 5:19). While alternative (*a*) could be
the original meaning, still the first-last motif is so well
woven into the story that (*c*) is as possible, and 19:30
and 20:16 are not identical as we would expect if that
verse were just tagged on by Mt **15.** RSV's alternatives 'Do you begrudge my generosity' or 'Is your
eye evil because I am good' are based on the idiomatic
use in biblical Greek of 'evil eye' = non-generous,
see 6:22–3. **16b.** 'Many called and few chosen'
is not found in the best MSS; cf 22:14.
h **17-19.** Mt. follows Mk in this third general prediction
of the death and the resurrection. The last journey
to Jerusalem, the reference to the Gentiles as executioners and tormentors, and the mentioning of the
cross are here for the first time. Mt. does not retain
Mk's vivid description of the disciples following behind
Jesus in fear and trembling.
i **20-28.** The issue which was raised in 18:1–5 is now
specifically connected with the sons of Zebedee,
although the pericope here too turns into a statement
on the ethics of discipleship Mt. brings the mother
into the picture, perhaps not in order to protect the
prestige of the two brothers but to protect Peter from
having been so disregarded by them **22** ('*you* do not
know . . . are *you* able .') shows that the mother is a
later addition: only the sons are in the picture.
Their vision of the Kingdom is confirmed as valid
but in that Kingdom everything is planned and
predestined by the Father. **22.** The cup of suffering
also is in 26:39; cf Isa. 51:17 The parallel sentence
about baptism is not well attested in Mt., but came
j from Mk 10:38 into later MSS. **24-8.** The indignation
of the ten others leads over to the logion about 'to
serve rather than to be served'. **28.** Mt. follows Mk
almost verbatim all through the famous saying about
'a ransom for many'. To this saying we may 689
observe that it actually occurs in an ethical setting and
not as a theological or kerygmatic statement in its
own right. Already this should warn us against
pressing it for Christological significance. Jewish
martyrological texts (e.g. 2 Mac. 7:37; 4 Mac. 6:28
and 17:21f.) describe the death of the faithful as
producing ransom for Israel ('many' is a semitism
for 'all', the whole people or the whole church, cf.
26:26; see J. Jeremias, 'Das Lösegeld für Viele',
Judaica 3 (1948), 249–64). Many commentators find
here an allusion to Isa. 53:11f.
29-34. *Two* blind men, as Mt had two demoniacs k
(8:28; Mk in both cases only one). Mt. gave the
same incident in 9:27–31 in order to have all types of
miracles exemplified. In ch. 9 they were admonished
not to tell the miracle; now there is no place for such
admonition, but instead they follow Jesus, i.e. as
disciples.
XXI 1-9. Jesus enters Jerusalem from the East, 690
having come down through Perea and thus avoided
Samaria, as the good Jew was supposed to; Samaria
is never mentioned in Mt. (except in the prohibitive
command, 10:5), or in Mk. This takes him over
the Mount of Olives on the slopes of which the messianic manifestation at the entry takes place. This
Mount is important in Jewish eschatology both as the
place where Messiah will appear, and as the place
of universal resurrection (cf. 27:52f.). The entry is
arranged by Jesus himself and all concern for secrecy
is gone. Jesus comes out into the open and the tone of
chs. 21–3 is quite provocative. In the account of the b
entry, Mt. follows Mk, but he finds it unnecessary to
tell how Jesus' predictions of what would happen
when they went to get the ass came true (Mk 11:4–5);
Jesus' command is enough. **3.** 'The Lord' could be c
Jesus or God. **5.** The formula quotation is from
Zech. 9:9 with the introductory words from Isa.
62:11. The quotation is based on the Heb. text, and
its parallelism is understood as referring to both the
young ass and its mother. **7**. On the reason for this
and the following puzzling plural 'and he sat upon
them' (RSV: 'thereon', since it could also refer to
the garments), see K. Stendahl, *The School of St
Matthew* (1954), 119. The palms are not mentioned
(cf. Jn 12:13); the scene is one belonging either to
the Feast of Tabernacles with its processions and its
Hosanna or to the Hanukkah (Rededication of the
Temple, cf. 1 Mac 13:51). The latter would lead
naturally to the cleansing of the Temple; the former
fits well into the connection between Tabernacles and
Messianic expectations (see §687*k*). **9.** In Mt.
Hosanna has become a liturgical shout of joy and
has lost its original Heb. meaning: 'Save now!'
It is taken from Ps. 118:25f., a psalm in the so-called
Hallel (Ps. 113–18), which was sung at Tabernacles
and Hanukkah as well as at Passover (26:30).
10-17. Mt. is less interested in the day-by-day events d
of Jesus' last days in Jerusalem than is Mk and arrives
at a more simplified picture. **11.** Jesus is followed by
an enthusiastic crowd, mostly from Galilee; they
hail him as the prophet Jesus from Nazareth, and he
goes to the Temple and performs the cleansing right
away. Some of the Marcan details are omitted,
especially 11:16 and the reference to the Gentiles in the
quotation from Isa. 56:7, which may point to a restoration of the Court of the Gentiles as a true part of the
Temple, in view of the consummation where also the
Gentiles shall worship in the Temple But to Mt. the
cleansing is just a majestic epiphany (cf. Mal. 3:1ff.)
and Jesus is still surrounded by the crowd who hailed
him at his entry. **14.** The reference to healing
strengthens the messianic note. **16.** The quotation
is based on the LXX: 'praise'; MT: 'strength'.
17. During the Passover festival most pilgrims had to
lodge outside the crowded city.
18-22. The way in which Mk and Mt. place the e
story about the fig-tree in connection with the visit
to the Temple suggests that it is meant as a prophetic

690e action (see e.g. on Agabus, Ac. 21:11f.), prefiguring the fall of the Temple and the judgment over the Jewish nation as such, cf. also Lk. 13:6–9. Jesus did not find fruit, i.e. the faith in him which he had the right to expect. Like many words and works of Jesus, this one also had a more general implication in the teaching and preaching of the church. **20-2** is an example of such didactic usage in the early tradition; cf. 17:20. On omnipotent prayer, cf. also 6:14f. and 18:19.

f **23-27** The first of five controversies (21:23–22:46) in the form of questions and answers are similar to such material in the Talmud. Mt. follows Mk and the clash between the officials of Judaism and Jesus is
g told with force and precision. **23.** Jesus teaches in the Temple, i.e. in one of the porticos around the Court of the Gentiles (see Jn 10:23); the question about his authority could refer to the fact that Jesus was not an ordained teacher (a 'scribe'; cf. 7:28). No teaching is mentioned in Mk and 'these things' (**23, 24, 27**) refer rather to the cleansing of the Temple, the arrangement of the entry (and, to the evangelists,
h also to the prophetic cursing of the fig-tree). To answer by asking another question is typical of rabbinic debate, and is not necessarily evasive, but may rather lead to the right answer or trap the opponent in a concession which implies the answer to the original question, see e.g. 41. **25, 26.** John's significance is here centred in his baptism rather than his preaching. The argument is perhaps of the type 'if (not) the lesser, then (not) the greater', i.e. if they could not discern who John was, they will not be able to discern who Jesus is. **27.** They are forced to admit their incompetence as teachers ('we do not know')

i **28-32.** The parable (only in Mt.) may have the same root as the Lucan one about the two sons (15:11–32). The different MSS vary considerably but give basically two alternatives: (*a*) the text used in the English translations, where the one who said 'no' but repented is hailed as the obedient (so in most MSS); (*b*) the one who said 'yes' but did not go is said to have done the Father's will (cod. D et al.). This must mean that the opponents are pictured as stubborn, insisting that the 'yes' which Israel gave (as the only one) when the Law was offered to the nations at Sinai is what really counts. Cod. D and Syr. Sin. combine this reading with one without the negation in **32b**: 'but when you saw it, you *did* repent afterwards', a word to those Jews who did become disciples
j of Jesus. **32** ties the parable to John the Baptist in accordance with the preceding pericope (especially 25*b*). The 'way of righteousness' may well be the way leading to the true 'righteousness', which to Mt. is a synonym to the Kingdom; cf. 3:15, 5:20, 6:33.

k **33-46.** An allegory rather than a parable, i.e. the details and not only the total thrust of it have significance for the understanding: the owner of the vineyard is God, the vineyard is Israel (allusions are made to Isa. 5:1–7), the workers are the leaders of the nation. **38-43.** The hope of the workers to inherit the vineyard if they kill the heir is a literary rather than realistic feature in the story. The notion of Jesus as the Son does not go beyond what Mk and Mt. have intimated earlier—it has no overtones of divine nature. or power as such. But the outcome of the story is one degree sharper than what has been found in Mt. so far: the Jewish nation has forfeited its elect status as a nation and the Kingdom will be given over to a new 'nation', i.e. the church (only Mt.). The 'stone-prophecy' (Ps. 118:22–3) strengthens this emphasis on the new 'edifice'. **44,** found in the majority of MSS, is missing in the Western text and comes from Lk. 20:18; cf. 1 Pet. 2:6ff. **41** is a device by which the opponents are made to write their own condemnation. While **43** speaks about the whole nation, **45-6** returns (following Mk) to the distinction between the apostate leaders and the multitudes who hail Jesus as a prophet (as they had done with John, see 26).

XXII 1-14. Mt. has a royal marriage feast, which 690l gives a more eschatological tone to the story (Lk. 14:16–24: a *man* gives a *dinner*; cf. 25:14 where Mt. has 'a man' and Lk. 'a king'). In Lk. the same is achieved by the introductory words about the messianic banquet (Lk. 14:15). **3.** In Mt. already the first invitation is turned down, and the second leads to such behaviour as the one mentioned in 21:35–6. **7.** Here it is usual to see a reference to the Jewish War and the destruction of Jerusalem in A.D. 70 as a punishment on those who turned down the invitation of Jesus and the church. This is plausible since the details are out of line and harmony with the story itself. **9.** The usual reversal takes place and the unexpected guests come in (cf. 20:1–16). **10.** 'Both good and bad' may be used in a neutral sense meaning 'everybody', but is rather setting the stage for what follows in 11–14: awareness of the need for church discipline.
11. The wedding garment symbolises the ethical quality m
expected in the church (cf. Rev 19:8), see also 7:21–3. The rational problem of how they could have such garments, being ushered in from the highways and by-ways, is irrelevant to Mt. **14.** The epigrammatic logion 'many are called but few chosen' refers either to the surprise of those Jews who knew they were duly called, but proved to belong to those not chosen; or it refers more specifically to 11–13, as a warning to the Christians not to trust their calling in such a way that they are proven not to belong to the elect. In both cases the idea of election is not set over against man's deed as in later Christian theology, but man's behaviour indicates whether he is elect or not: 'chosen' in **14** and 'worthy' in **8** are synonymous. See K. Stendahl, 'The Called and the Chosen', in A. Fridrichsen et al., *The Root of the Vine* (1953).

15-22. In this and the following three controversial n discussions (15–46) Jesus is pictured as disappointing his opponents by giving answers which were fully acceptable, at least to the Pharisees, a fact of which Mt. is quite conscious (23:3). **16.** The Herodians, mentioned only here by Mt. (cf. Mk 3:6 and 8:15) were presumably pro-Roman and their presence accentuates the political trap which the question is supposed to be. **16b** is meant as flattery; 'God's Way' is a Jewish catechetical term which was taken up in what became the trade-mark for the early church: 'The Way' (Ac. 18:25f., 9:2, et al.). **19-21.** Jesus asks for the kind of Roman coin used for taxes (*dēnarion*; in contrast to 17:24–7 with the Syrian coins used for Temple tax). The Imperial tax was the more offensive to the Jews since it was paid in coins with the glorified head of the Emperor (RSV: 'likeness') and inscriptions which spelled out the religious and cultic nature of the Caesar (e.g. *divus* and *pontifex maximus* on Tiberius' coins). Jesus turns this evidence in the opposite direction: 'Give then *back* (*apo-dote*) to Caesar . . .' Stated with ingenious simplicity, this coincided with the view of the Pharisees, who, while resenting the Romans, considered insurrection a lack of faith in God's own power to set Israel free. Thus Jesus could apparently not be labelled a political rebel, in spite of the mass demonstration at his entry into Jerusalem.

23-33. Resurrection (of the righteous or of all men) o was taught by the Pharisees, who appeared as modernists to the Sadducees in this respect, cf. Ac. 23:6–8. The latter upheld the basic OT view that there is no resurrection (see art. 'Hell' in A. Richardson, *A Theological Word Book of the Bible*, 1950). The concept of resurrection has its root in the transformation of cultic and royal ideology into apocalyptic expectations (Isa. 26:19; Dan. 12:2), but the Sadducees based their teaching on the Torah only. **32.** Hence Jesus bases his answer on Exod. (3:6), which they did recognise as a valid basis. **33.** It is not reported whether they accepted his interpretation, although it did impress 'the multitudes'. The argument is one of high-handed Jewish exegesis: Isaac became 'patriarch'

690o after the death of Abraham, and Jacob after the death of Isaac; yet the Lord speaks to Moses as if they were simultaneous with one another or with Moses. Hence they are alive to God and a prototype for the resurrection '*of* the dead' (**31** and only there; otherwise in the NT: '*from* the dead'). **24-7.** The levirate marriage (Dt. 25:5–6, cf. Gen. 38:8 and Ru. 3:9–4:12), an extreme case of which is chosen by the Sadducees as ridiculous, was actually the only answer to the question of 'eternal life' in early Israelite faith: life through the offspring (24: 'raise up offspring', *anastēsei*, 'resurrect'). Jesus cuts through the question as irrelevant. 'The resurrection' (30) is spoken of not as an event but as an enduring state in the life of the Kingdom. Angelology was actually as objectionable to the Sadducees as was resurrection, see Ac. 23:8.

p **34-40.** The Pharisees were satisfied with this answer but Mt. sees them still trying Jesus (not so Mk), and now on his understanding of the Law. **35.** 'Lawyer' (*nomikos*, only here in Mt.) is a man learned in the Law of Moses, i.e. a 'scribe'. Yet this is not a genuine controversy tradition and Lk. uses it in a different context (10:25–8). In Mt. and Mk *Jesus* brings together the love of God (Dt. 6:5) and the love of the neighbour (Lev. 19:18). Actually this combination was known in Jewish catechism (Test. Issachar. 5:2) and in Lk. it is so presented, cf. also Mt. 19:19. For the interest in such an epitome of the 613 commandments of the Law, see §674*l*.

41-46. Mt. makes use of the context by having the question about the Davidic Messiah directed to the Pharisees and achieves thereby a continued discussion where Jesus now takes the initiative (cf. Mk 12:35) and thus Mt. achieves a climax in the series of controversies, where Jesus emerges as the champion (46).
q 'Christ' is here 'Messiah' and not a name for Jesus. The Psalms were prophetic ('in the spirit'); cf. Mt. 13:35. Ps. 110 is composed for a king ('my lord') but the Davidic authorship taken for granted here leads into an enigmatic argument. Is this originally a refutation of a Davidic requirement for Jesus as the Messiah in a tradition (Mk, for example) which did not know of any Davidic descent of Jesus? It could not have such a meaning to Mt., whose whole Gospel stresses the Davidic element, see chs. 1–2. Mt. may have understood this as an indication that 'Son of David' is not a sufficient title for Jesus, since David himself called this son of his 'lord'. D. Daube (*The NT and Rabbinic Judaism* (1956), 158–69) has given good reasons for this as the original meaning since the question is one of Haggadah, where two conflicting texts often were shown to be true (here e.g. Isa. 11:1, 10 and Jer. 23, as well as Ps. 110:1).

691a **XXIII 1-36.** This section could be considered the first part of the *fifth discourse* in Mt., a public part followed by a second part for the disciples only (chs. 24, 25). We may prefer to see ch. 23 as a climax to the controversies, and to the public ministry of Jesus as a renunciation of the Judaism upheld by its leaders, which in Mt. 23:2 are the Pharisees and scribes, the Sadducees being of no consequence in the Diaspora, especially after A.D. 70. The scene is still the Temple. The material here assembled expands the remarks in Mk 12:37–40 and much of it is found
b in Lk. 11:37–52. Is the criticism in this discourse aimed at actual hypocrites among the Pharisees or against 'Pharisaism' as a system which is wrong in its basic principle? In Did. 8:1 'hypocrites' had become identical with 'Jews' (see Mt. 6:16), and in this discourse we find the church on its way to such a clear-cut identification, where Judaism, and especially Pharisaism, has become somewhat of a man of straw for self-reassuring attacks. But there is enough of genuine material, which can well be identified with the actual teaching of Jesus. He did not enunciate principles, nor did he aim at a new approach to religion, but he taught with prophetic consciousness in a nation where he found the strongest resistance among those who were its spiritual leaders. This must have sharpened his eyes for their shortcomings— 69
most of which they would admit themselves, at least when they were among themselves, as the Talmud shows quite clearly. See e.g. I. Abrahams, *Studies*
in Pharisaism and the Gospels (1924), 29–32. **2.** The c
Seat of Moses was an actual seat in the front of the synagogue where the authorised teacher sat (E. L. Sukenik, *Ancient Synagogues in Palestine and Greece* (1934), 57–61). Is **2-3a** meant to be a recognition of the authority of Jewish *Halachah*, both in principle and in its actual pronouncements? That would be hard to understand in the light of e.g. 15ff. It is tempting to say that the point is only to give the maximum force to the denunciation of the behaviour of the scribes (3*b*). **4** refers to the 'yoke' (see 11:28) which they imposed on people in trades and walks of life where it was much more difficult to fulfil the requirements than for the scribes who had ordered their lives to suit their own arrangements. The social tension between the scribes and the people at large is already behind this saying and comes to the fore in **5-13.** 'Phylacteries' are small cases containing a piece of vellum inscribed with short passages from Exod. 13 and Dt. 6 and 11, which were tied to hand and forehead in obedience to Exod. 13:16; Dt. 6:8, 11:18. Such phylacteries have been found at Qumrân (with slightly different texts; see K. G Kuhn, *Phylakterien aus Höhle 4 von Qumran* (1957). On the 'fringes' or 'tassels', see §682*o*. On the motif
of ostentation, cf 6:1–18. **8.** 'Rabbi' was not yet an d
official title for the scribes, but was about to become such in NT times, and Mt. translates it 'teacher'. **9.** The same seems to have been true about 'father'. **10** may sound as an anticlimax and has been considered as a variant of **8** (so Wellhausen, Dalman, et al.), but if 'master' (*kathēgētēs*) is the equivalent of Heb. *môreh*, the technical term for the Teacher of Righteousness at Qumrân, then it is the proper climax, making Jesus Christ *the* 'Teacher'. **11, 12.** To this is added one old (20:26–7), and one new saying about humility. **13-14.** In Lk. (11:52) this logion gives the climax to the criticism of the Pharisees, and that on good grounds. In Mt. it is the first of seven 'woes'. For the keys, cf. 16:19, where Peter is given the keys when *he* is made the promulgator of *Halachah*. **14** is missing in the best MSS and comes from Mk 12:40. **15.** Judaism was a missionary religion in the time of Jesus, but only in areas where there was already a Jewish synagogue. A proselyte has taken a step beyond the so-called 'men who feared God' (e.g. Ac. 10:2, 13:16) and become circumcised. The verse may have the same problem in mind which Paul encounters among the 'Judaisers' (e.g. Gal. 5:2ff.).
16-22. The intention behind the rulings of the e
scribes here under criticism was a good one: they were against insincere oaths and this led them to discourage oaths by the most holy things, allowing such by what appeared more removed from the centre of holiness. Such rulings are ridiculed here by the hermeneutic rule 'if the lesser then also the greater'. **17.** The word for 'fool' (*mōros*) used here is the same
which in 5:22 is tantamount to murder. **23-4.** The f
tithing of vegetables and spices was over and above what the Law required (Dt. 14:22–3), but is mentioned in the Mishnah as practised and required by the Pharisees. 'Justice' (so RSV; AV: 'judgment' means 'right judgment'; Gr.: *krisis*; Heb.: *mishpāṭ*), 'mercy' and 'faith' (i.e. 'fidelity', not belief) are all three social virtues; cf. the famous Mic. 6:8; Prov. 14:22; Jer. 5:1. No special case is in view but the implication is the same as when Hos. 6:6 is quoted in 9:13 and 12:7. The dialectic: 'the former you ought to do' (RSV's 'to have done' is not a necessary translation of *poiēsai*)—'the latter you should not neglect' expresses well the attitude of Jesus towards the Pharisees: they do too little, not too much; cf. 3 and 5:20. **24** gives the same criticism in colourful language. The Talmud's 'he that kills a flea on the Sabbath is as guilty as if he killed a camel' (Shab. 12*a*)

91f gives the background to this saying, which is more natural
in Aram. where 'camel' and 'gnat' are similar in
g pronunciation. **25-8.** The theme from ch. 15 comes
here in more apodictic form, but both examples are
highly rhetorical since certainly the cleansing of the
inside of the vessels was more important to the opponents
and since the point in chalking the tombs was to mark
them so that nobody contracted defilement unwittingly
by walking over them (cf. Lk. 11:44). **28.** The
criticism of the scribes and Pharisees comes out here
h in the sharpest form ever in Mt. **29-36.** Apparently
the word 'tomb' (27 and 29) ties this saying together
with the preceding one (*Stichwort*). The picture of
the prophets as martyrs is not based on the OT record
but on Jewish tradition (cf. 5:12), and with special
reference to Jerusalem (37), Lk. 13:33; this martyrological aspect is most clearly expressed in Heb. 11:32–8.
29. 'The prophets and the righteous', cf. 13:17;
'righteous' is an important term for the true martyrs,
cf. 35. The 'hind-sight' recognition of these martyrs
is used to prove the continuity in Israel's apostasy, not
the change of attitude. Lk.'s 'but you are building'
(11:48) and Mt.'s 'you are sons' (31) may well
translate the same ambiguous phrase in Aram. (see
M. Black, *An Aramaic Approach* . . . (1954²), 11f.).
i **32.** With this verse the style changes to that of an apocalyptic oracle which concludes the discourse against
the Pharisees at the same time as it leads over to (37–9)
the prediction of Jerusalem's destruction and the apocalypse proper (ch. 24). The apocalyptic style
accounts for the imperative 'fill up the measure . . . !'
and the 'behold' in **34** (*idou*, not translated in RSV)
as well as the first-person (speaking on God's behalf?)
'I send you', without the reference to a quotation
(cf. Lk. 11:48, 'the Wisdom of God'; Mt. 11:19,
25–30). The fate of the emissaries of God and/or
Christ resembles that of the disciples in 10:17, 23 and
Lk. (11:49) even couples 'prophets' with 'apostles';
thus the language is coloured by the experiences of
the early church. The death of Jesus and the martyrdom of the church is seen all through the history
of God's people (cf. 1 Tim. 2:16). **35.** Zechariah
the son of Berachiah is the OT prophet Zechariah, but
the Jewish tradition, as well as the LXX texts about
the different Zechariahs, show some confusion and the
saying could also refer to Zechariah the son of Jehoiada,
mentioned as a martyr towards the end of the last
book of the Jewish canon (2 Chr. 24:20–2; cf. also
Isa. 8:2), or to a Zechariah son of Baris, who was
martyred in the Temple shortly before the fall of Jerusalem in A.D. 70 (Jos. BJ iv, 5:4). The precise description in **35b** may speak for the third alternative.
j **37-9.** Here Jesus speaks in the great style of a prophetic
oracle. He speaks on behalf of God in first-person
singular with the long history of an apostate Israel in
view (for such a derogatory survey of Jewish history,
cf. Stephen's speech in Ac. 7) and at the same time
as the Messiah who is to come in glory, cf. 24:30–1.
The term 'from now on' (**39**: *ap'arti*; AV: 'henceforth', RSV: 'again'?), peculiar and important for
Mt.'s eschatology, is now introduced and is repeated
in 26:29, 64. Not so in Lk. where this saying with its
allusion to Ps. 118:26 (cf. Mt. 21:9) is placed in an
earlier context (13:34–5) and given as history so as to
refer to the entry into Jerusalem.
92a **XXIV-XXV.** By making the oracle about Jerusalem
the climax of the denunciation of the Scribes and the
Pharisees, Mt. has already set the stage for what
follows, *The Fifth Discourse*, and he has no use for
'The Widow's Mites', which in Mk 12:41–4 and
Lk. 21:1–4 gives concretion to *their* criticism of the
Pharisees (especially Mk 12:40; Lk. 20:47: 'widows'
houses'). In **XXIV** Mt. follows Mk 13 closely and
with few additions or changes. Consequently we may
here satisfy ourselves by giving attention to what is
peculiar to Mt., referring to the commentary on Mk
13 for the bulk of the exegesis. Mk's ending of the
discourse (13:33–7) with its call for watchfulness, is
enlarged into a series of sayings, semi-allegorical
parables, some of which are found in Lk., but there 692a
without special reference to the parousia or the end.
XXIV 1-3. Following Mk 13:1–4, the prophecy about b
the destruction of the Temple leads to the discourse
(cf. 23:1), which is wholly directed to the disciples in
private. **3.** Both '(your) coming' (*parousia*: 3, 27,
37, 39) and 'the close of the age' (RSV) or 'end of
the world' (AV), cf. 13:39, 49, 18:20, are terms
peculiar to Mt. in the Gospels, and these two terms
make the question in 3 much more precise in Mt.
than in Mk. Mt. uses 'parousia' as a technical term
for what came to be called the Second Coming of
Christ, but which originally was *the* Coming (see e.g.
Ac. 3:20, cf. Mt. 1:16*c* and Heb. 9:28).
4-8 (Mk 13:5–8). In the general warning for the c
false messiahs (cf. 23-6) Mt. has 'I am the Messiah
[Christ]' whereas Mk has 'I am', which could be
read as the formula of divine self-presentation, see
14:27. **7.** The war may to Mt. be the Jewish War,
A.D. 66–70, and famine had heightened the expectations also among the Christians (see Agabus' prophecy
in Ac. 11:28). **8.** *Ōdinai* (RSV 'sufferings') are
actually 'birth-pangs', an imagery not accidental in
eschatological language, where the New Age or even
the Messiah is born out of the tribulations of the Old,
or out of the sufferings of the community of the elect;
cf. Jn 16:21, for Qumrân: 1QH 3:9f.
9-14. Mt. has used most of the material in Mk 13:9–13 d
in 10:17–30. What he gives here is rather a summary,
stressing the hatred between men for Jesus' sake, and
in **12** he gives a logion which sharpens this fact drastically. The important saying in Mk 13:10 is expanded
and stressed as a climax: the Gospel shall be preached
in the whole world, before the end comes. There is no
limitation to the Jews at this point, for Mt. understands
this to refer to the post-resurrection situation and the
task of the church, cf. 28:18–20.
15-22. 'The abomination of desolation' is mentioned e
in Dan. 9:27, 11:31, 12:11 and there it refers to the
statue of Zeus which Antiochus Epiphanes set up in the
Jerusalem Temple, see 1 Mac. 1:54ff. Mk may have
Caligula's (A.D. 37–40) threat of similar desecration
in mind; in Lk. the 'desolation' refers to the fall of
Jerusalem (21:20). **15.** Mt. refers to the Temple
explicitly (the Holy Place; the lack of article does
not make it indefinite), but he does not have any more
explicit references than Mk to the Jewish War or the
withdrawing of the Christians from Jerusalem in
A.D. 68. The language is apocalyptic; 'he who reads
[or recites] let him understand' adds to this flavour.
20. Mt. adds 'or on a Sabbath'. Apparently the
Matthean church kept the Sabbath, cf. 12:1–8.
22. The shortening of the tribulations for the sake of
the elect is a motif in Jewish eschatology (2 Bar.
20:1–2); it shows how the Christian knew that he had
no chances against the adversary or the temptations
to give up, if they came over him with full and unlimited
forces; cf. the Lord's Prayer, 6:13, and 26:41.
23-33. Mt. retains Mk 13:21–3 and adds a saying f
which Lk. gives in a more general form in a different
context (Lk. 17:23–4, 37). There is no point in
looking for the Messiah in the wilderness (as John the
Baptist or the Qumrân community) nor in hidden
places, as e.g. the Jews later could think of Messiah
as hidden in the slums of Rome (see E. Sjöberg, *Der
verborgene Menschensohn in den Evangelien* (1955), 72–80,
cf. Justin, *Dial.* 49:1); now it is time for the Parousia
of the Son of Man (here clearly identified with the
Messiah: 23–26–27) and that will be a spectacular
and cosmic event. While Jesus' ministry was a hidden
manifestation of the Son of Man, his Parousia will be
seen by all. **28** seems to be a proverb which Mt.
and Lk. associate with this type of prediction.
RSV has felt the same need as did Lk. to use the nobler
word 'body' instead of 'corpse' or 'carcass'. Gr.
aetoi are actually 'eagles' but e.g. Aristotle and Pliny
counted the vultures to be 'eagles'. The point may
be: there will certainly be signs as visible as the
vultures in the sky, once there is reason for their being

692g there. **29-31.** Immediately after those hard days are over the cosmic manifestation of the Son of Man will take place. This is the Parousia and Mt. adds two motifs to those in Mk 13:24–7: (*a*) **30.** When seeing the Sign of the Son of Man, i.e. his manifestation on the clouds, 'the tribes shall mourn', an allusion to Zech. 12:10–12 which is worked out more fully in Rev. 1:7 and Jn 19:37. Zech. refers to a mourning of repentance granted by God to Jerusalem and 'they shall mourn for him whom they have pierced'. But to Mt. it is rather a mourning of the lost who see the elect being gathered. (*b*) **31.** The trumpet is mentioned only in Mt., cf. Isa. 27:13 with reference to the return from the Dispersion; there is no reference to the resurrection as in 1 Th. 4:16. All is within one generation (cf. 34) and the 'gathering' of the elect removes them from a world about to be destroyed, cf. also 40–1. **32-3** is, almost verbatim, Mk 13:28–9.

h **34-41.** In 16:28 Mt. made it clear that some of the first disciples would live to see the Parousia. He reinforces it here, following Mk 13:30–2. **36.** RSV has good textual basis for retaining 'nor the Son'. Its disappearance in some MSS may have been due to theological reflection upon such a limitation of the Son's knowledge; this is more likely than attributing its insertion in some MSS as due to the need for an 'excuse' for Jesus' miscalculation. **35** is here with specific reference to this prophecy, while it formed part of a logion with more far-reaching implications in 5:17.

i **37-41** (also Lk. 17:26f., 34f.). Mt. stresses the 'nobody knows' by the explicit interpretation of the Noah example: **39** 'and they did not know until the flood came...' There is no typological use of the Noah story, as e.g. in 1 Pet. 3:20f. In Lk. the Noah saying
j is coupled with one about Lot. **40-1** stresses not so much the surprise as the sharp cleavage. The language suggests once more (see 31) a gathering of the elect. The word translated 'taken' (*paralambanetai*) has the connotation of 'receive' or 'take to oneself'; cf. e.g. Jn 14:3.

k **42-51.** The short sayings in Mk 13:33–6 are of the same sort as the more expanded traditions which Mt. and Lk. (12:39–46) have. Lk. treats the parable of the Two Servants as an interpretation of the one about the Householder (see especially Lk. 12:37, cf. Mk. 13:37). He has the latter addressed to Peter and the apostles as those who are expected to be wise stewards and servants, watchful and caring for the master's household. **49.** Mt. makes this point even more clear by '*fellow*servants'. But still the accent falls on watchfulness in view of the surprise arrival of the Son of Man (as 'a thief', **43**; cf. 1 Th. 5:2, Rev. 16:15). It is possible that **45-51** originally applied to the Jewish leaders.

l **XXV 1-13.** While the parables about the Kingdom in ch. 13 were introduced by the formula 'The Kingdom of Heaven is like...' we read here 'Then the Kingdom of Heaven *shall be* like...' The wedding motif as well as the basic point of this parable is also in Lk. (12:35–6), but the point in Mt. is made by stressing the wisdom of five of the maidens, the careful planning (2: *phronimos*; cf. 25:45), rather than the staying awake, and **13** is repeated as the refrain from the preceding chapter, but does not fit too well for the details of the Matthean parable since all ten fell asleep (5). Some good MSS read 'the bridegroom *and the bride*' in 1 and this may well be the original reading. By omitting 'the bride' the parable becomes an allegory, the groom being the Messiah (cf. 9:15 and 22:1–14). The delay of the bridegroom (5) has often been understood as Mt.'s awareness of the fact that the Parousia had been expected longer than one first thought, but it can just as well be an integral part of the story. Sayings about the closed door and the sharp judgment over foolish late-comers were also circulating in another context, as found in Lk. 13:25 (cf. Mt. 7:22–3). It is the second time Mt. gives a marriage scene with this kind of 'unhappy end' (see 22:11–14).

14-30. Lk. gives his form of this parable so as to 692 correct the expectation that the Kingdom was to appear immediately (19:11–27, cf. Ac. 1:6, 7) and his version of the parable has its own problems. In Mt. the point about the proper behaviour while the master is away—and that for a long time (19)—is made more clear. It gives instruction for the Christian life, as does the following **31-46.** For the value of the talent see §36*d*. The use in English of 'talent' for 'gift' stems from this parable.

31-46. The traditional designation of the parable as n
concerning **The Last Judgment** may be somewhat misleading since it promises an answer, or even *the* answer, to the question: How and on what grounds is man to be judged on the Day of Reckoning? This then leads to an impasse when the question is raised (*a*) whether this is the judgment on the whole world or on the Christians only; or (*b*) whether faith as an acceptance of Jesus Christ (see e.g. 12:36–7) suddenly counts for nothing. But the function of this parable is totally within the framework of what has preceded it, viz. instruction to the disciples about the demands on them while waiting with the church for the Parousia. The scene is that of contemporary Judaism, and the Son of Man in his glory is the King and the Judge (cf. Ac. 17:31; see also Th. Preiss, 'The Mystery of the Son of Man', in *Life in Christ* (1954), 43–60). The point made is partly the same as in 7:21–3 (where there is also the note of surprise), 16:27 and 10:33.
Yet there is something new here: the parable should o
be understood as Jesus' farewell speech, his testament to his disciples. The accent falls not so much on the surprise, or the *unconscious* goodness or badness; that is only a rhetorical device which gives further weight to the repeated sentence: 'Truly I say to you, as you did it—or did it not—to one of the least of these my brethren, you did it—or did it not—to me'. Thereby Jesus, at his departure, makes the rank-and-file brother in need his representative, he identifies himself with him. This is the testament which goes well with Mt.'s great concern for the least of the brethren, cf. 18:6–35. The absence of the Lord has become a creative motif in the life together of the church, and 26:11 seems to strengthen this interpretation; it may even indicate the heart of the whole parable (also with its 'what she could, she did', Mk 14:8).

XXVI 1-5 gives the familiar concluding phrase to 693
the Fifth Section of the Gospel and leads over into the *Passion Narrative*. One of the striking features of Mt.'s Passion narrative as compared with Mk's (which he follows closely) is the transformation of the reports given in Mk into direct speech by Jesus (26:7, 36, 38–40, 42; see N. A. Dahl in NTS 2 (1955–6), 30). We find it already in **2** and it is not a merely stylistic feature. Jesus is in command: he gives the orders; here is the Messiah who knows what is going to happen and 'speaks it into effect'. **3.** Thus Mt. treats the meeting of the chief priests and the elders as if it were the effect of Jesus' words in **2**: 'Then...' On the dates of Passover, see notes on 17–19. Caiaphas was High Priest *c.* A.D. 18–36; the deliberations are described as informal. **5.** 'Not during the feast' is a strange saying in view of what follows, but with John's chronology it could be upheld. J. Jeremias suggests that 'not in *tē heortē* (feast)' could mean 'not in the festal crowd' (*The Eucharistic Words of Jesus* (1955), 48). The 'two days' in 2 suggests that this is on Wednesday, cf. 17–19. **6-13.** The Marcan b
account is compressed to its essentials. The fact that Jesus visits a leper, i.e. presumably one whom he has healed, attracts no attention in this context where even in Mk the preparation for the Passion dominates. **10.** Jesus' reading of thoughts is an added feature in Mt. Mt. and Mk have understood **13** as referring to the fact that the woman is mentioned in the Gospel, cf. however commentary to Mk 1:1; but J. Jeremias (*Jesus' Promise to the Nations*, 1958), has an alternative view of the original meaning of the saying when he takes 'gospel' as in Rev. 14:6f.: 'When God's angel

693b announces the eternal Gospel to the world [i.e. on the day of Judgment] then this deed of hers shall be mentioned before God, to a gracious remembrance [i.e. saving judgment] ', cf. also notes to 25:31–46.

c **14-16.** The weight of the dramatic progress is heightened by Mt.'s ' then ' (*tote*) in **14** (Mk : ' and '). There is no explicit reference to a Satanic inducement as in Lk. 22:3 and Jn 13:27 or to Judas being a thief (Jn 12:6). On Judas, cf. 10:4 and 20–5, 27:3–10. The last of these passages is prepared for by the reference to the thirty pieces of silver (Zech. 11:12).

d **17-19.** As was the case in the entry pericope, 21:1–9, so also here : Jesus gives orders and Mt. does not even find it necessary to describe that it was as he had told them. How could it be otherwise ? **18b.** The majestic note is especially strong : ' My time is nigh ; at your house *do I* celebrate [straight present tense] the

e Passover '. The chronology of the Passion narrative is one of the most puzzling problems of NT studies. The discussion can be best surveyed in J. Jeremias, *The Eucharistic Words of Jesus* (1955). All the Synoptics have thought of **the Last Supper** as a Passover meal and have dated it according to the official Jewish calendar. Jn (18:28, 19:14, 31) on the other hand dates the crucifixion as coinciding with the slaughtering of the lambs; hence he places the Last Supper twenty-four hours earlier than the Synoptics. A meal (without a lamb) which was not a Passover or : a ' Diaspora Passover ', held on the eve of the 14th of Nisan, instead of the regular date of the 15th etc., has been suggested (see B. Gärtner, *John 6 and the Jewish Passover*, 1959), as well as differences in calendar in various parts or sects of Judaism. The solar calendar used at Qumrân may shed new light on the whole problem by showing that the Sect always celebrated Passover on Tuesdays, see A. Jaubert, *La date de la Cène*, EBib. (1957). If Jesus followed such a calendar, many problems would be solved, by allowing enough time both for the Sanhedrin's and for Pilate's activities. But it creates some new problems : e.g. how could such a tradition be forgotten so completely that the Synoptic Gospels all conform to the official Jewish calendar ?

f **20-25.** Mt. has omitted the suggestive allusion to Ps. 41:9 in Mk 14:18. Otherwise he follows Mk and adds a direct question from and answer to Judas. ' You have said it ' is a literal translation of the Greek. rendering an Aram. expression which usually means ' yes ', but could also mean ' you say so, not I ', cf.

g 64 and 27:11. **24. The role of Judas** is necessary in order to fulfil the scriptures, but woe to that man who is the instrument for this purpose (cf. 18:7 on *skandalon*). This saying allows us some insight into the complex relation between determinism and free will in Judaism as well as in the early church. What has to happen will happen, but this does not make an excuse, nor is Judas considered a helpless victim for a superimposed fate. It is an interplay of determinism and free will, taught also by the rabbis; and at Qumrân those who joined ' by free will ' became thereby ' the elect ', cf. 22:14.

h **26-30.** The Matthean words of institution follow closely those in Mk 14:22–4, but are somewhat more symmetrical and transform the descriptive phrase in Mk 14:23*b* into a command, i.e. has a more developed liturgical formula, with the addition ' for the remission of sins ', an element which was conspicuously missing in 3:2 where Mk and Lk. mention it in relation to John's baptism. To Mt. the forgiveness of sins was apparently tied to the ' new covenant ' through Jesus Christ, cf. 20:28 and 6:11f. On the relation of the Marcan-Matthean words of institution to those in Lk. and in 1 C. 11:23–5, see Jeremias, op. cit., and K. G. Kuhn in K. Stendahl, *The Scrolls and the NT*

i (1957), 65–93. **29** sheds important light on the nature of the Last Supper and its repeated use in the Matthean church. This meal is an anticipation of the messianic banquet which Jesus will celebrate in his Kingdom and—Mt. adds—' together with you ' ; see also

5:6, 8:11 and Lk. 22:29–30 where the banquet is 693i
combined with the thrones for the apostles, see Mt. 19:28. The Matthean ' from now on ' stresses the marked interval between now and the Parousia, cf. 39. **30.** The Passover was followed by singing the second half of the so-called Hallel, Ps. 115–118.

31-35. Once more the Matthean ' then ' marks the j
dramatic progress. The prediction of the scattering of the disciples is enforced by a slightly adapted quotation from Zech. 13:7 (see K. Stendahl, *The School of St Matthew*, 80–3). **32** appears strange since it seems to break the context between **31-33** and it is missing in the Fayyum fragment. It may be that Mt. has understood the saying as if Jesus meant Peter to be the shepherd and the other disciples as the flock, pointing beyond their defeat to a gathering in Galilee, cf. 28:7 ; Jn 21:15ff.

36-46. The group of the three (Peter and the sons of k
Zebedee, cf. 17:1–8) is closer to Jesus also in his anguish and Peter is their leader (40 ; cf. 17:4). Mt. follows Mk closely, and lessens the strong language of Mk slightly : **37** : ' be sorrowful ' ; Mk 14:33 : ' be scared ' ; **39** : ' fell on his face ' (Gr. aorist) ; Mk 14:35 : ' threw himself on the ground ' (Gr imperfect for repeated action). The Matthean form of the story shows some signs of having been used for instruction in prayer since it, in addition to the ' My Father ', has two verbatim allusions to the Lord's Prayer : **41** and **42.** ' Temptation ' is here rather ' trial ', ' assault by the enemy ' (6:13), and this is made clear by the saying about the willing spirit and the weak flesh, which cannot withstand the assaults. The basic narrative is one about Jesus as left alone by even his closest disciples. Still, God is with him, cf. 27:46. Gethsemane is described as a victory over the temptation, rather than as a gathering of strength through prayer (so Lk.). The majestic note is recaptured as Jesus goes to meet his executioners.

47-56. Judas comes with a group from the Temple l
guard and there is no indication in Mt. that Roman soldiers were involved at this stage. Mt. deletes Mk's ' scribes ' as incorrect in this official context. The ' sign of the kiss ' had made itself a well-remembered place in the tradition, but it is hard to see why it was necessary, although one should not picture Gethsemane as a desolate place in meditative moonlight on this evening when there were pilgrims all over the place. **50.** The translation of Jesus' words to Judas remains uncertain, see RSV. The total image of Jesus in Mt.'s Passion narrative suggests a majestic ' My friend, do what you came for ', cf. Jn 13:27. **52.** There is no reference to a healing of the servant (as in Lk. and Jn), but in **53** Mt. adds the logion about the sword and his right to call on angelic legions ; in the War Scroll from Qumrân, the angels are joining forces with the righteous, 1QM 7:6. But Jesus is clear regarding his mission, and the fulfilment of the prophecy in 26:31 requires this kind of band to take the man who has been within reach of the authorities in the Temple daily. The reference to the scriptures is mentioned by Mt. as if *it* created the flight of the disciples (' then ', **56b**).

57-75. In the Fourth Gospel the interplay between m
the Roman authorities and the Jewish leaders in the execution of Jesus is close from the very beginning (18:3, 12, etc.) and the leaders are pictured as being anxious to keep good relations with Pilate (11:48) for which reason Jesus is crucified as a political threat and a liability to the Jews. There is also explicit reference to the fact that the Jews at this time had not the authority to inflict capital punishment (18:31). The Synoptics picture a more formal **procedure of the Sanhedrin**, but the account does not agree with the Mishnaic requirements for legal procedure in matters of capital charges, which should be carried out in daytime and on two consecutive days and with private interrogation of the witnesses, etc. (Mishnah Sanhedrin). Even if all of the regulations now in the Mishnah were not in force *c.* A.D. 30, the account in the Gospels gives the impression of extraordinarily

693n great haste in the procedure. This has led to the suspicion that the proceedings in **57-75** are an adjustment, the outcome of a quite obvious theological interest to make the Jews responsible for the execution of their own Messiah. It was to the interest of the early church in the Roman Empire to minimise the fact that its founder had been crucified by the Roman authorities; this may also have been a contributing factor. For a full discussion, see G. D. Kilpatrick, *The Trial of Jesus* (1953); S. Zeitlin, *Who Crucified Jesus?* (1942); J. Blinzler, *Der Prozess Jesu* (2nd ed. 1955) and E. Stauffer, *Jerusalem und Rom* (1957). The basis for every interpretation must be that Jesus was crucified by Roman authorities and consequently as a messianic rebel. The diversified Gospel traditions can hardly be wrong when they all agree in giving some role to the Jewish leaders in this procedure, and the question whether there was an official act of the full Sanhedrin is of somewhat less significance. The Gospel writers did not have access to more than general reports about what had happened and on the basis of these they described the proceedings as best they could.
o Mt. shows more knowledge of procedure than does Mk. He mentions a full meeting of the Sanhedrin first on the following morning (27:1 : 'all') but Mk has it that night, 14:53; **60-1** seems to imply that the witnesses were not giving false testimony but reported a prophecy which Mt. proudly recognises as true. The direct question about Jesus' eschatological identity is required not because of inconclusive witnesses but because of Jesus' majestic silence—a strong motif in all the Passion narratives, cf. Isa. 53:7.
p **63.** 'The Christ, the Son of God' is the language of the Church rather than of the Jewish leaders, cf. Mk 14:61, 'Son of the Blessed One'. **64.** Both Mt. and Lk. avoid Mk's straight 'I am' in the answer to the question. While the phrase used (*su eipas*) must mean 'Yes' in 25 (cf. 27:11), it is probable that here it is intentionally evasive and even more so through the following 'but' (*plēn* could be translated 'furthermore', but retains its adversative character). Thus, even in this situation, Mt. thinks of Jesus as avoiding identifying himself with the Messiah before the Jewish leaders, and as placing the emphasis on the enthronement (Ps. 110:1) of the Son of Man. Mt.'s 'from now on' refers to the situation of the church with the Son of Man as the Lord and King and makes the second part of the quotation (Dan. 7:13) into a different sentence predicting his Parousia in due time. See however J. A. T. Robinson, *Jesus and His Coming* (1957), 43ff., with reference to the coming on the clouds as a vindication, the Son of Man being lifted *up* towards God as is the case in Dan. This may be
q the original meaning of the saying. **67-8** (cf. 27:27-31) presupposes that they veiled his face as Mk says. Mt. adds 'Christ' and this is not inconsistent with the evasive answer given by Jesus. Naturally Jesus was the Messiah and was judged as a false Messiah. It is only *Jesus* who cannot say so due to the hiddenness of his office.
r **69-75. The denial of Peter** is told with more balance and dramatic progress by Mt. than by Mk. **73.** The reference to his Galilean accent is made more explicit, and Mt. retains—as he does rarely—Mk's 'immediately' for dramatic reasons (74).
694a **XXVII 1-2.** The wording is strikingly unaware of what has happened the night before. The expressions are those used already in 12:14, 22:15.
b **3-10.** By placing the account of the death of Judas at this point (and it is an obvious insertion, cf. Mk 15:1 and 2), Mt. indicates that he understands the decision of the Sanhedrin as the crucial one (**3**: 'that he was condemned') The reflection on what seems to be a pre-Matthean tradition about Judas (i.e. that he was paid, Mk 14:11, cf. 26:15; that his deed was necessary for the fulfilment of scripture, Mk 14:21, cf. 26:24 and Ac. 1:16; and that his violent death was connected with a graveyard called the Field of Blood, Ac. 1:15-20) has in **9** materialised into one of Mt.'s most pointed

formula quotations. The Matthean use of the quotation 69
from Zech. 11:12-13 (cf. 26:15) with certain allusions to Jer. 18:2-3 and 32:6-15 (allusions which must have strengthened Mt.'s interpretation, hence the reference to 'Jeremiah') hinges upon the Heb. words *yōṣēr* and/or *'ôṣār* since they can mean both 'potter' and 'treasurer/treasury'. Hence the priests, who recognise that this money cannot be put into the treasury, bring this prophecy to its fulfilment without knowing it when they purchase the potter's field. See further K. Stendahl, *The School of St Matthew*, 120-7, cf. B. Gärtner in *Studia Theologica* 8 (1954), 16-20. The Matthean understanding of the priests' action is similar to that of the Fourth Gospel in 11:49-52, and the Matthean 'then' (*tote*) in 9 accentuates the unconscious but glorious way in which the fulfilment comes about.
11-26. Differing from the account in Jn 18:33-7, c
Jesus is never alone with Pilate. **11.** The title under discussion is now 'King of the Jews', which was the only terms on which Jesus could be presented as objectionable to Pilate, i.e. as a messianic revolutionary. The answer once more (cf. 26:25, 64) leaves the situation in doubt, and in **12-14** there is complete silence; cf. especially Jn 18:34: 'Do you say this (that I am the King of the Jews) of your own accord, or did others say it to you about me?' where the silence is only
before the Jews; cf. also 19:20. **16.** The political d
aspect becomes even more pronounced in the **choice between Jesus and Barabbas.** Mk 15:7 presents Barabbas as one who has committed murder during an outbreak of insurrection, i.e. a man under similar accusation as the one now brought against Jesus. Barabbas was not a 'criminal', but a Jewish fanatic. In Mt. this is less obvious, but in **17** Mt. stresses the alternative between the two; it may even be that Mt. knew them both as having the name 'Jesus' (so in Syr. Sin. and Caesarean texts). In Mt. Jesus is presented to the people as Jesus 'called Messiah' (18, 22; Mk: 'King of the Jews'). **18.** Mt. places less stress than Mk on the fact that it was the chief priests who were jealous, but the reference to jealousy
gives sense only if it is so understood. The incident e
before Pilate has two distinctive features found only in Mt.: (*a*) **19** The dream of Pilate's wife. This has a particularly Matthean flavour since chs. 1-2 were held together by dreams; '... this righteous man' may mean only 'innocent' in the technical sense; cf. variant readings in 4 and 24. The verse may be an anticipation of: (*b*) **24** Pilate, led by the guidance received by his wife's dream, demonstrates how he has no guilt in Jesus' execution, and the Jews accept willingly the responsibility. This is as hard to accept as an actual procedure on the part of the procurator, as it is illuminating for our understanding of the tendency in all the Gospels: it was the Jews who crucified their own Messiah, cf. Ac. 3:13-15.
27-31. The mocking by the Roman soldiers—which f
had a parallel with more Jewish ('prophesy!') flavour in 26:67-8—has few distinctive Matthean details: the royal motif is strengthened by the reed used also as sceptre. Similar mocking scenes are known (Philo, in *Flaccum* 5-6) and may be late disintegrated forms of the Near Eastern New Year's rites (see R. Delbrueck in ZNTW 41 (1942), 124ff.). The 'crown of thorns' is not necessarily thought of as painful, but long thorns could have been used as 'rays' as in the radiant crowns pictured on Tiberian and other coins, see H. St J. Hart, JTS 3 (1952), 66-75. According to tradition they let Jesus keep the crown, but that is not expressly stated in any of the Gospels.
32-57. Simon from Cyrene is only a name to Mt., g
and thus Mk's reference to his sons is omitted (Mk 15:21). The Roman soldiers acted within their right, see above, 5:41. 'The cross' may refer to the beam to which the hands were to be fastened and which was fixed to a pole already raised on Golgotha. On the location of Golgotha and the Tomb, see A. Parrot,

94g *Golgotha and the Church of the Holy Sepulchre* (1957).
h **34.** The 'wine with gall', if compared with Mk's
'myrrhed wine', appears to be a conscious allusion
to Ps. 69:21 (LXX: 'gall'; MT: 'poison'), one
of the Psalms which was used from earliest time in the
Church in its teaching and liturgy, cf. Jn 2:17;
Rom. 15:3; Jn 15:25; Mk 15:36; Jn 19:28;
Ac. 1:20; cf. C. H. Dodd, *According to the Scriptures*
(1952), 57–9. **34b.** This is alluded to in 48, but in
34 the reference is more rational, i.e. to the offering of
such a drink as a sedative. Jesus refuses it, apparently
a 'heroic' note; cf. the perhaps docetic development
in the Gospel of Peter (4:10): 'as one feeling no
i pain'. Ps. 22 even more than Ps. 69 has had a
formative role in the Passion narrative and, as
M.Dibelius suggests (*From Tradition to Gospel* (1935), 184),
they were used in connection with the telling of the
Passion story long before there was a fixed account.
35. Some MSS (see AV) give an explicit formula
quotation, but such must be an accretion, using the
exact wording of the LXX (cf. 13:14–15). Originally
there was only the allusion to Ps. 22:18. **36.** The
watching is mentioned only in Mt., perhaps in anti-
j cipation of 62–6 (cf. 61). **37-44** follows Mk closely
with its further allusions to Ps. 22:7 (**43**, Mt. also
alludes to Ps. 22:8). This allusion is strengthened in
Mt. by the explicit reference to 'the Son of God'
which brings the whole incident very close to what is
described in Wis. 2:6–20, with its allusions both to
Isa. 53 and Ps. 22. The result of the 'test' in **40** is
k given in 54 on one level by the centurion. **44.** The
reference to the 'robbers' is expanded in Lk. and in
the Gospel of Peter, where they are understood as
criminals, but in Mk and Mt. it is not necessarily so;
they may well have been Zealots of Barabbas' kind,
l see 15–18. **45-50.** All the Gospels report the darkness
from noon to three p.m. and the Gospel of Peter
elaborates the theme, as does Mt. in 51–4. Again
Ps. 22 (now v. 1) breaks into the Passion narrative,
in Mt. now in a form which is meant to be Heb. (Mk
rather Aram.). **46.** The cry of utter desolation raised
grave problems in the later development of Christology,
solutions to which are intimated in the variants of
some MSS and in the Gospel of Peter, see K Stendahl,
The School of St Matthew (1954), 88–7. The mishearing
of Elijah for Eli is somewhat easier to account for in
Gr. than in Aram. and even more difficult in Heb.
But it seems to have belonged to the role of Elijah to
m rescue in time of need (SB iv:2, 769–71) **48.** The
drink offered to Jesus is now vinegar (cf. 34), according
to Ps. 69:21, perhaps a doublet of the same original
notice. Mt. may have understood it as sedative or
only as fulfilment of prophecy, but in the Gospel of
Peter (5:16) this drink is understood as causing
premature death; see above to 34: Ps. 69:21 in
n MT reads 'poison'. **51-7.** The curtain of the Temple
was between the Holy and the Holy of Holies (Exod.
26:31–7). No interpretation of its rending is given in
the Gospels; cf. however Heb. 6:19, 9:12, 24, 10:19–22.
It may have been to Mt. a sign of how the Temple is
to be destroyed by Jesus (26:61f.), or even of the new
era when Gentiles are full members of God's people.
It may also be just an additional element in the
cosmic upheaval at the death of the Messiah as a
o righteous martyr. In **52-3** Mt.—and he alone—
offers what must have been a piece of a primitive
Christology. The resurrection of the righteous
('saints') was expected as one of the great events of
the End, and it was expected to take place at Jerusalem when the Mount of Olives split in two; out of
that split the dead were to appear. Here the earthquake at Jesus' death (cf. also 28:2) performs the first
part of this event while a second (their appearance)
comes first after Jesus' resurrection. It is easy to see
how such a witness to the significance of Christ's death
and resurrection did not survive in the main stream
of the tradition, since it did not fit into what came to
be the basic Christology with Jesus as the 'first fruit
of those who had fallen asleep' (1 C. 15:20), all the

rest awaiting the general resurrection (1 Th. 4:16). 694o
But the point made in **51-2** is clear: with Christ the
general resurrection has begun; cf. also Ign. Mag. 9:2.
54-56. In Mt. the Roman centurion (Mk uses the p
Latin form of his title, but Mt. and Lk. have the
Greek equivalent) is a witness to the cosmic events
(Mk: only the actual death) and these prompt what
Mt. must have understood as a confession, which a
Gentile, not a Jew, made. The women give continuity q
to the story, cf. 61 and 28:1ff. Here as in the lists of
the Twelve (10:2–4) and of the brothers of Jesus
(13:55) there are some differences between the names
of the men, presumably disciples, and these women
who were their mothers, differences which the latter
MSS harmonised, cf. Lk. 8:3; Jn 19:25. Mt. either
identifies the mother of the Zebedees with Mk's
Salome, or substitutes the 'mother of the Zebedees'
as better known to him.
57-61. Mt. has no interest in presenting Joseph of 695a
Arimathea as do Mk, Lk., and Jn (19:38–42), i.e.
as an honoured member of the Sanhedrin who had
been positively inclined towards Jesus. **57.** In Mt.
he is pictured as a disciple, who is rich enough to own
a tomb in the vicinity; 'who was a disciple' translates Mt.'s specific term *mathēteuesthai*, 'be taught',
or 'become a disciple', see 13:52, 28:19; cf. Ac.
14:21. Thus, just as John the Baptist's body was buried
by his disciples (14:12), so also with Jesus. Mt. also
leaves out the reference to the 'day of preparation'
(Mk 15:42), and the amazement of Pilate (15:44),
both elaborated in Jn 19:31ff., cf. Gospel of Peter
5:15, where the eclipse is combined with the commandment in Dt. 21:22–3 (cf. Ac. 5:30, 10:39; Gal. 3:13)
that 'the sun should not set upon one put to death'.
60. On the other hand Mt. adds that the tomb was not
used before and this may imply the faith of this Joseph,
for if he considered Jesus a criminal the Law forbade
him to use the grave again; it may also be just a note
of honour. **61.** It is a consistent trait in Mt. that b
there is constant watch over what happens: 36 (the
soldiers), 55 and 61 (the women; Mk 15:47 says only
that they saw where he was buried, thus asserting that
they went to the right tomb on Sunday Morning),
66 (the guard); and 28:1–15.
62-66 is setting the stage for 28:11–15, both peculiar c
to Mt., as is seen already from the references to the
stealing of the body in **64** and in 28:13. **65** Pilate's
answer has an irony which shows knowledge of the
final outcome. **62.** It is hard to imagine the chief priests
and the Pharisees as going to Pilate on the Sabbath,
but Mt. avoids mentioning the Sabbath and speaks
of 'the day after the day of preparation', i.e. the first
day of the feast of the unleavened bread. This
whole tradition is clearly apologetic and is meant to
refute the criticism which is mentioned as current
among the Jews in 28:15.
XXVIII. Mt.'s account of the **resurrection** follows d
basically that of Mk (similar in Gospel of Peter) over
against that of Lk. and Jn 20 (cf. 21). **7.** The women
receive an angelic message, while the appearance is
promised to occur in Galilee (cf. 26:32) as it also does
in 16; on the end of Mk, see commentary on Mk
16:8. In Lk. (and Jn 20) both the angelic message
and the appearances occur in or around Jerusalem.
But Mt. has not only the angelic message, but in **9,**
10 the same message is given to the women also by
Jesus himself, and they worship him, but this is told as
something preparatory rather than as a decisive
manifestation. On the problem of Galilee-Jerusalem,
see R. H. Lightfoot, *Locality and Doctrine* (1937) and
L. E. Elliott-Binns, *Galilean Christianity* (1956)
1. Mt.'s accent again falls on what is watched and e
by whom, and consequently Mk's reference to the spices
for anointing is omitted when the women are re-
appearing on the scene 'to see the tomb'. **2-4** is f
a 'description' of the actual resurrection event.
There is no such in Mk, Lk. or Jn, but in the Gospel
of Peter (9:35–11:44) the account is more elaborate
and describes how Jesus walks out of the grave, 'his

695f head reaching above the heavens'. The Matthean account in 2–4 is strikingly free from any mentioning of Jesus. It is apparently an early stage in the growth of the precious answer to a question which the earliest records did not answer, viz. the 'how' of the resurrection. Due to the insertion of 2–4 in the Marcan context, the women are pictured as watching the earthquake (cf. 27:51–3) and the descent of the mighty angel
g which paralysed the guard with terror. **5-8.** The 'young man' in a white robe (Mk 16:5) is in Mt. the mighty angel from 2–4 (angels had no wings in the 1st cent.). It is somewhat surprising that Mt., who has often stressed Peter's role, does not retain Mk's special reference to him (Mk 16:7); nor does he stress that Jesus had predicted the appearance in Galilee, perhaps because he is concerned about the Jewish accusation that the disciples staged what they were expecting to happen. **8.** Mk's much discussed reference to the total silence of the women (16:8) is changed into its opposite in Mt.: With fear and great *joy* do they run to tell the disciples. **9-10.** Here Jesus calls the disciples 'my brethren', cf. 12:49 and 25:40.
h **11-15.** While the Gospel of Peter quite naturally has the guard reporting to Pilate (11:46–9), Mt. gives the astonishing picture of these Roman soldiers going to the Jewish authorities. But this whole incident is prompted by the need to answer a concrete accusation, known to be current in the days of the evangelist.
i In either case the empty tomb is recognised as a fact. The argument centres around how it became empty. It is therefore reasonable to suggest that the resurrection tradition in the Gospels has its nucleus not in visions and revelations but in an experience of an empty tomb. But around this basic tradition Mt. has accumulated what by contrast is even more obviously accretion both of legendary (2–4) and apologetic (27:62–6 and 28:11–15) material. This type of reflection on the empty tomb does not weaken the validity of the nucleus of the tradition.
j **16-20.** Mt. is the only one of the Gospels that we can be sure has a genuine ending (Lk. leads over to Ac.; see §§714*b*, 758*f* on Mk 16:8 and Jn 20–1), and it has the form of a glorious epiphany on a mountain in Galilee, appointed by Jesus (not, as has been suggested, 'where Jesus had proclaimed (his Law)', i.e. the one mentioned in 5:1). The mountain here is of mythological rather than geographical significance, cf. 4:8. **17.** 'Some doubted', but this point is not expanded (cf. Thomas in Jn 20:24–9), nor are those who doubted less recipients of the command that follows. This note must rest on early tradition and serves perhaps only to stress the greatness of the revelation. There is no description of Jesus (as e.g. in 17:2), the accent falls on his words.
k **18.** The word '. . . therefore . . .' is significant. His charge to the Eleven rests upon the fact that he is now the enthroned Messiah, the King, with power both in heaven and on earth, cf. 6.10*c*. *Therefore* the time has come for them to do what he never did except in reluctant anticipation: to go to the Gentiles.
l **19.** This mission is described in the language of the church and most commentators doubt that the trinitarian formula was original at this point in Mt.'s Gospel, since the NT elsewhere does not know of such a formula and describes baptism as being performed in the name of the Lord Jesus (e.g. Ac. 2:38, 8:16, etc.). Neither Mt. nor any of the other Synoptics describes Jesus as practising baptism; the disciples only in Jn 4:1–2. On the other hand, a reference to the practice of the church (with or without a trinitarian formula) is well in keeping with this epiphany, which pictures the situation of the church in all its other details. On 'make disciples' as a technical term in
m Mt., see 13:52 and 27:57. The teaching of Jesus is here described as 'commandments' to be 'observed' or 'kept' (**20**), following the terms used for the Law of Moses (e.g. 15:4, 19:7, 17). Here rather than in the Sermon on the Mount (see notes to 5:21–48) could we speak about Jesus as a New Moses. At the same time we find that category greatly transcended and the 695m 'commandments' may well include such things as the keeping of the meal (26:26–8; cf. Justin, 1 *Apol.* 66:3), and the orders of church discipline, 18:15–22. By n
20 the words of Jesus fall definitely into the pattern of a Testament, a farewell speech (see J. Munck, in *Aux sources de la tradition chrétienne*, Mélanges Goguel (1950), 165). Jesus' guidance of his church when it carries out his ordinances was seen in 18:20 and here the same presence—for their actions rather than for their contemplative awareness—is promised 'to the close of the age' (the temporal reference peculiar to Mt. 13:39f., 49, 24:3; cf. Heb. 9:26), gives a clear picture of what to Mt. is the period of the church: From the resurrection of Jesus from the dead and his enthronement as the exalted King to the time of consummation which is yet to come, cf. chs. 24–5. In this interim there is the activity of the church in mission and teaching, an activity which has prompted the composition of this Gospel and left its distinct marks on its outline as well as in its details.

Bibliography—The Synoptic Gospels are best studied with a 'Harmony'; *Gospel Parallels* (New York 1949), based on RSV and on A. Huck's Synopsis (9th ed. 1936), contains also translations of Huck's alternatives from the MSS and non-canonical parallels. See also J. C. Hawkins, *Horae Synopticae* (1909²)

COMMENTARIES: W. C. Allen, ICC (1907); P. Benoît, *La Bible de Jérusalem* (1950); Sh. E. Johnson, IB vii (1951); E. Klostermann, HNT iv (1927²); M. J. Lagrange, EBib. (1948⁸); E. Lohmeyer, *Des Evangelium des Matthäus*, ed. W. Schmauch (Mey., Sonderband) (1956); A. H. McNeile, *The Gospel According to St Matthew* (1915); A. Merx, *Die vier kanonischen Evangelien* (1897–1911); C. G. Montefiore, *The Synoptic Gospels*, 2 vols. (1927²); T. H. Robinson, The Moffatt NT Commentary (1928); A. Schlatter, *Der Evangelist Matthäus* (1929), SB i and iv, 1–2 (1922–8); J. Wellhausen, *Das Evangelium Matthaei* (1904).

OTHER LITERATURE: B. W. Bacon, *Studies in Matthew* (1930); M. Black, *An Aramaic Approach to the Gospels and Acts* (1954²); G. Bornkamm, 'Enderwartung und Kirche im Matthäusevangelium', in *The Background of the NT and its Eschatology*, ed. W. D. Davies and D. Daube (1956); G. Bornkamm et al., *Überlieferung und Auslegung im Matthäusevangelium* (1960); B. C. Butler, *The Originality of St Matthew* (1951); K. W. Clark, 'The Gentile Bias in Matthew', JBL 66 (1947), 165–72; D. Daube, *The NT and Rabbinic Judaism* (1956); A. Descamps, *Les justes et la justice* (1950); A. Farrer, *St Matthew and St Mark* (1954); F. V. Filson, 'Broken Patterns in the Gospel of Matthew', JBL 75 (1956), 227–31; B. Gärtner, *Horae Soederblomianae* 4 (1957); E. J. Goodspeed, *Matthew, Apostle and Evangelist* (1959); J. Jeremias, *The Parables of Jesus* (1954), *Unknown Sayings of Jesus* (1957), *Jesus' Promise to the Nations* (1958); G. D. Kilpatrick, *The Origins of the Gospel According to St Matthew* (1946); W. G. Kümmel, *Promise and Fulfilment* (1957); K. Kundsin, 'The Matthean Tradition', in *Contemporary Thinking about Jesus*, ed. Th. Kepler (1944); T. W. Manson, 'The Life of Jesus: . . . (4) The Gospel according to St Matthew', BJRL 29 (1945/6), 392–428; E. Massaux, *Influence de l'Évangile de saint Matthieu sur la littérature chrétienne avant saint Irénée* (1950); P. Nepper-Christensen, *Das Matthäusevangelium—Ein judenchristliches Evangelium?* (1958); P. Parker, *The Gospel before Mark* (1953); M. H. Shepherd, 'The Epistle of James and the Gospel of Matthew', JBL 75 (1956), 40–51; K. Stendahl, *The School of St Matthew and its Use of the OT* (1954), (ed.), *The Scrolls and the NT* (1957), and 'Quis et unde? [Mt. 1–2]', ZNTW 72 (1960); B. H. Streeter, *The Four Gospels* (1924); V. Taylor *The Names of Jesus* (1953); C. S. C. Williams, *Alterations to the Text of the Synoptic Gospels and Acts* (1951); H. Windisch, *The Meaning of the Sermon on the Mount* (1951).

MARK

By R. McL. Wilson

696a **Introduction**—Long regarded as no more than an abbreviation of Mt., and hence comparatively neglected, Mk is now commonly recognised not only as the earliest canonical Gospel but also as one of the sources used by Mt. and Lk. in the composition of their works. It is therefore a primary authority for our knowledge of the life and teaching of Jesus. The earliest reference to Mk by name appears to be that of **Papias** (*c.* A.D. 140), who quotes a still older authority: 'Mark, who had been the interpreter of Peter, wrote down accurately everything that he remembered, without however recording in order what was either said or done by the Lord. For neither did he hear the Lord, nor did he follow him, but later as I said (attended) Peter, who adapted his teachings to the needs (of his hearers) but had no intention of giving a connected account of the Lord's oracles. So then Mark made no mistake in writing down some things as he remembered them; for he made it his one care not to omit anything of what he had heard or to set down any false statement therein.'

b There are several problems connected with this tradition, and it is probably not to be taken entirely at its face value. In particular the association of Mk with Peter should not be understood to mean that the Gospel records the testimony of an eye-witness throughout. It has been more accurately described as an expansion of the primitive kerygma (cf. Dodd, *The Apostolic Preaching* (1944), 46ff.), or as the recollections of an eye-witness noted down by his disciple and supplemented by material from other sources (Taylor). This is however the unanimous tradition of the earliest authorities, and is repeated with slight variations by later writers. Moreover, we can trace in these later versions of the tradition a growing tendency to make Peter more and more responsible for the work, and correspondingly to diminish the contribution made by Mk. Since it is difficult to see why the association should ever have been made without good reason, the ascription of the Gospel to the comparatively unknown Mk, rather than to some more prominent figure, must be considered a strong argument for the authenticity of the tradition. The later forms of the tradition can indeed be explained from the known concern of the Church to emphasise the apostolic character of its authoritative books, over against the many apocryphal and heretical documents which were in circulation. The earliest form of the tradition again suggests a date after the death of Peter (so Irenaeus and the anti-Marcionite Prologue), while on internal grounds the book would seem to have been written before the Fall of Jerusalem in A.D. 70. A **date** between A.D. 65 and 70 would most nearly fit the facts. The **author** is generally identified with the Mark who figures in the NT (Ac. 12–15; Col. 4:10; Phm. 24; 2 Tim. 4:11; 1 Pet. 5:13). As to the place of writing, the tradition is unanimous, with one late exception, that the Gospel was written **in Rome,** and with this the internal evidence is entirely consistent. If it is dangerous to lay emphasis on the Latin words which Mk transliterates (which may have belonged to the common Greek of the period), there is also the fact that he is at pains to explain Jewish customs to his readers, and that when he preserves the actual Aramaic words of Jesus he is careful to add a translation. He is therefore writing at any rate for a predominantly Gentile public. Moreover, as Branscomb notes, a Roman origin would go far to explain the ready acceptance and rapid dissemination of the Gospel. It would also explain the inclusion and preservation of Mk among the Gospels finally admitted to the Canon. 696b

c According to Papias, Mk wrote accurately but not in order. Evidently the Gospel had suffered by comparison with some other work (probably Jn, possibly Mt.), but there has been some debate as to whether Papias meant literary or chronological order. In point of fact, Mk does present a clear sequence of development in the ministry of Jesus, and it is therefore probable that Papias' comment is to be understood as meaning that the Gospel does not have the orderly arrangement of a finished literary composition. With the rise of **Form Criticism,** however, the question has been raised again in another form: working on the theory that the material was originally current in isolated units or pericopes, K. L. Schmidt endeavoured to show that the framework was an artificial construction, the work of the evangelist, so that even in Mk we have no sure basis for the chronology of the life of Jesus. It is probable that many of Mk's stories were used in the early propaganda of the Church, for example in preaching, and some of the material may already have been collected into larger complexes before he made use of it, but C. H. Dodd has shown reasons for believing that Mk also had at his disposal a general outline of the whole ministry (see his *NT Studies* (1953), 1ff.). As Dodd puts it, 'It is hazardous to argue from the precise sequence of the narrative in detail; yet there is good reason to believe that in broad lines the Marcan order does represent a genuine succession of events, within which movement and development can be traced'. A particular narrative (e.g. the plot of the Pharisees and the Herodians, 3:6) may occur too early because it was already associated in the tradition with material appropriate to a particular point in the story, but we have no ground for thinking of 'a heap of unstrung pearls'. It is difficult to believe that early Christians would be satisfied with isolated narratives, without some general knowledge of the story as a whole.

d **Characteristics**—The outstanding characteristic of this Gospel is the **realism and vividness** of the narrative. Shorter as a whole than either Mt. or Lk., Mk is frequently fuller and more elaborate in its descriptions, and abounds in graphic detail as to the manner, look and gestures of Jesus: he looks round with anger (3:5), or takes a child and sets him in the midst (9:36), or takes an invalid by the hand (1:31, 5:41, cf. 1:41). As Hunter notes, it is Mk who gives us 'four unforgettable pictures of Jesus': asleep on a pillow in a storm (4:38), taking the children 'in the crook of his arm' (10:16), looking with affection on the rich young man (10:21), and finally, striding ahead of the disciples, a lonely figure, on the road towards Jerusalem (10:32). So also it is Mk (6:39f.) who lets us see the five thousand squatting down upon the grass 'like so many garden plots' (see 'Torch' Commentary (1948), 21).

696e Allied to this is the **candour** of the narrative. Mk does not spare the disciples, or gloss over their faults. Comparison with Mt. and especially with Lk. is instructive (e.g. at 10:35 James and John themselves ask special favour ; in Mt. the plea is made by their mother). This candour extends even to the description of Jesus : 'No other evangelist is so "familiar" in his references to Jesus. No other evangelist dwells so often on his human emotions' (Hunter). He is moved with pity (6:34), marvels at the unbelief of his fellow-countrymen (6:6), or grows indignant at the conduct of his disciples (10:14). At some points indeed Mk's treatment seems to have shocked his successors (e.g. Mk says that in Nazareth Jesus was *unable* to do any mighty work, Mt. simply that he did not many). This is the more striking in that for Mk himself Jesus is beyond question the Son of God. This note is struck in the opening verse, and resounds again and again in the Gospel. It is strong evidence for Mk's reliability that he shows so little tendency to recast his materials to match the theology of a later day.

f Another feature of the Gospel is its strongly **Semitic colouring**. Not only does Mk record on occasion the original Aramaic words of Jesus, but his own Greek bears clear marks of Aramaic tradition. There are grounds for suspecting Aramaic sources behind the Gospel, though whether written or oral it is impossible to say (cf. Black, *An Aramaic Approach to the Gospels and Acts* (2nd ed. 1954). The importance of this is that a work so deeply coloured by Semitic usages must, in the main, bear a high historical value (Taylor). It has sometimes been alleged that the Gospels derive much of their colouring from the theology of the Hellenistic Church, but in Mk at least we are very close to the original source in oral (Aramaic) tradition. The Gospel is therefore a historical document of supreme importance.

697a **I 1-13 The Beginning of the Gospel**—Where Mt. and Lk. begin with nativity stories, Jn with a 'philosophical' prologue, Mk opens with the ministry of John the Baptist. The book is a Gospel, not a biography. Originally the reward given to the bringer of good tidings, 'gospel' came to mean the good news itself. Its application to the document containing the news is even later. The Gospel of Jesus Christ is not only the message he proclaimed (1:14), but also that of which he is himself the central figure. **1** is probably intended as a title, either for the account of John's ministry or (better) for the Gospel as a whole. Turner would link with 4, taking 2f. as a parenthesis (the beginning of the Gospel was John the Baptist's preaching), but though parentheses are a feature of Mk's style this usage should not be unduly pressed. The words 'the Son of God' are probably original (*a*) because of the weight of MS evidence, and (*b*) because this is a fundamental part of Mk's Christology.

b **2-8 The Ministry of John**—The first quotation is from Mal. (3:1 ; cf. Exod. 23:20), hence some MSS emend to read 'in the prophets' ; whether Mk was in error or 2 is a later insertion (it is missing here from Mt. and Lk.), 'in Isaiah the prophet' is probably original. The Jews expected Elijah to return to prepare the way for the Messiah (cf. Moore, *Judaism* (1927–30), ii, 357ff.), and the early Church saw the fulfilment of this hope in the ministry of John. He is described in terms which recall Elijah (2 Kg. 1:8 ; cf. the prophet's hairy mantle, Zech. 13:4), but he is more than a prophet ; the characteristic of his ministry from which he derived his name is that he baptised. His mission was to recall the people to obedience, 'repentance' signifying not merely sorrow after sin but a return in loyalty to God. Of this return baptism was the outward symbol. John's preaching is more fully recorded in Mt. and Lk. ; Mk is concerned only with his prophecy of one greater than himself, for whom he was not fit to perform the duties of a slave. **6.** Certain locusts were reckoned clean (Lev. 11:22), but some ancient commentators held that locust-beans are meant. **8.** It has been suggested that the original contrast was between John's baptism by water and the Messiah's baptism by fire (in judgment —cf. Mt. 3:11), and that Mk introduced the reference to the Spirit under the influence of Christian practice ; or that the original phrase was 'with wind and fire' and that πνεύματι was taken to refer to the Holy Spirit. Cf. Ac. 1:5, 11:16, where the saying is ascribed to Jesus. 697b

c **9-11 The Baptism of Jesus**—That Jesus, who was without sin (Heb. 4:15), submitted to a baptism 'for forgiveness of sins' had begun to cause some perplexity by the time of Mt. (3:14 ; cf. 'The Gospel according to the Hebrews', James, *Apoc. NT* (1924), 6), but Mk does not feel the difficulties. It may be that Mk regarded the Baptism as the moment at which Jesus received the endowment of supernatural power (note the association of the gift of the Spirit with Baptism, e.g. Ac. 19:5–6), but whether the earliest Christology was 'adoptionist' is an open question. Certainly the problems raised by later theological reflection are not yet even on the horizon. For Jesus this was (*a*) an act of self-dedication to his mission, and (*b*) an act of self-identification with the sinners he had come to save. Moreover this submission to baptism at the hands of John is the real foundation of the Christian sacrament (cf. Cranfield in SJTh. 8 (1955), 55). Mt. and Lk. imply that others also heard and saw (cf. Jn 1:32), but in Mk the vision and the voice come to Jesus alone ; they convey to him the divine attestation of his Messianic destiny. The words of the voice recall Ps. 2:7 ; Isa. 42:1, but neither is quoted exactly ; the echoes however are significant : Ps. 2:7 is 'the coronation formula of the Messianic king of Israel', Isa. 42:1 'the ordination formula of Isaiah's Servant of the Lord' (Hunter). It is probable that this association is to be traced not merely to the evangelist, nor to the early Church, but to Jesus himself (cf. W. Manson, *Jesus the Messiah* (1943)). The term 'beloved' is used in LXX of Abraham's only son and Jephthah's only daughter, and is practically equivalent to 'only begotten' (see Turner in JTS 27 (1926), 113ff.). The comparison of the Spirit to a dove probably goes back to Gen. 1:2.

d **12-13 The Temptation**—Mk merely records the fact ; for fuller details we must turn to Q (Mt. 4:1–11 =Lk. 4:1–13). The forty days recall Moses and Elijah (Exod. 34:28 ; 1 Kg. 19:8 ; cf. also the forty years in the wilderness). The narrative is intelligible only in the light of the baptism : 'A time of dedication . . . is inevitably followed by a time of testing' (Luccock). It should be noted that the Temptation was not an isolated fact, met and overcome at the very outset of the ministry ; the pressure lasted to the end, at every Pharisaic demand for a sign, when Peter rebelled against the thought of his Master suffering (8:32f.), and even in the last hours upon the Cross (15:29ff.).

e **14 The Opening of the Galilean Ministry**—Mk fixes upon the arrest of John as the decisive moment for the beginning of the ministry of Jesus. There is room between vv. 13 and 14 for a period of activity side by side with that of the Baptist, recorded by the Fourth Evangelist from his own special tradition (Schmidt).

14-15 A summary of the message of Jesus. The note of fulfilment is one that resounds throughout the entire NT—it was a fundamental part of the primitive kerygma that in Jesus the ancient prophecies and promises had been fulfilled (cf. Dodd, *The Apostolic Preaching* (1944)). Here 'the time fixed in the counsel of God has fully come'. The way had been prepared by John, and indeed in the entire history of Israel, as also in the history of the world at large ; now the hour has struck. The kingdom of God is fundamentally his sovereignty, his rule in the hearts of men, not a Utopia of material well-being (cf. Bright, *The Kingdom of God in Bible and Church* (1955)). Jesus here

7e takes up the age-old Jewish hope, but gives to it a new intensity and a new depth of meaning. The word rendered 'is at hand' has given rise to some debate: C. H. Dodd argues for the translation 'has come' (*The Parables of the Kingdom* (1936)), but others have found this difficult. It is dangerous to distinguish rigidly between 'realised' and 'futuristic' eschatology: the kingdom is present in Jesus and his ministry (cf. Lk. 11:20) but it awaits a consummation that is yet to come. This sense of the imminence of the kingdom gives a note of urgency to the message: there is still time for 'repentance', but that time is short. But unlike John Jesus proclaimed not merely judgment but a gospel, 'good tidings'. In **14** some scholars prefer the AV reading 'the gospel of the kingdom of God'; the phrase 'the gospel of God' is Pauline (Rom. 1:1, 15:16; 2 C. 11:7; 1 Th. 2:2, 8f.).

f **16-20 The Call of the First Disciples**—Taylor (against Bultmann and others) thinks there is good reason to believe this story rests ultimately on the reminiscences of Peter. Many scholars have felt that the response of the disciples is more intelligible if they had previously had some contact with Jesus (cf. Jn 1:35–42). The 'sea' of Galilee is really a lake (so Lk.); Mk's use of 'sea' is 'thoroughly Semitic' (Black). Note the prominence in Mk of the idea of following Jesus. According to Bishop (*Jesus of Palestine* (1955), 63), 'Peter and Andrew were standing knee-deep in the water, when they cast their nets, which is the usual practice still for fishermen by the Lake'. Mk does not necessarily suggest any special sacrifice on the part of the disciples—they could return to their fishing (cf. Jn 21:3); Levi later (2:14) much more literally burned his boats.

g **21-39 A Day in the Life of Jesus**—This section contains four narratives covering a period of twenty-four hours and based on the earliest personal testimony. It is probably intended to give a typical picture of the early ministry. Like Paul later, Jesus at first used the opportunities afforded by the synagogue. The note of assurance and authority in his teaching, by contrast with the traditionalism of the scribes, created a sensation. The scribes were the professional teachers of the Law, and appear often in a bad light; but cf. 12:34. No details of the teaching are given, but only that it was interrupted by the demoniac. 'The Holy One of God' was not a Messianic title but Mk evidently saw in it a recognition of the supernatural character of Jesus (cf. 1 Kg. 17:18). Belief in demon-possession was one of the characteristics of the age, and one which seems remote from modern views; yet must it be confessed that there is a demonic element in the world and in the life of man. The rebuke uttered by Jesus was enough to effect the cure, and at once his fame spread (**28**: Mk is vague; Mt. understands 'all Syria', Lk. merely 'the country round Capernaum'). The astonishment of those present arose partly from the authority of the command, partly from the fact that Jesus cast out the demon with a word, without the use of 'psychic' phenomena to prove the reality of the cure. Cf. on 5:1–20 below. **29**. Turner observed that if the third person plurals (in the AV) are changed to first person we have something that looks like a first-hand eye-witness account. That the invalid could serve (at the evening meal) demonstrates the completeness of her recovery. **32**. Mt. here has one phrase, Lk. the other, but Mk's double phrase is not so redundant as at first appears. It was a Sabbath, and only after sunset was it lawful for the crowds to bring their sick. Mk presents a vivid picture of the eager throng, the whole town pressing round the door. **34**. Many MSS add 'to be the Christ' (an assimilation to Lk. 4:41). This passage, with the many injunctions to silence in Mk, formed the basis of Wrede's theory of the Messianic Secret, on which it must suffice to say that the secret is not an invention of Mk: in such cases Jesus enjoined silence because he did not seek the reputation of a wonder-worker; his own conception of Messiahship was vastly different from that current among his contemporaries. **35-9**. Such withdrawals 697g
are characteristic of Jesus; in the solitude he sought renewal of strength in communion with the Father. Here however there may be also another motive: those who 'tracked him down' evidently thought he was missing a great opportunity (37), but Jesus may have seen his popularity as a temptation to depart from the true purpose of his ministry. **38** would then mean that he left Capernaum to avoid entanglement in a ministry merely of healing and of wonder-working. Some scholars however think Lk. has correctly interpreted Mk (4:43; cf. also Jn 18:37): 'for this purpose was I sent' (from the Father).

40-45. The leprosy here is probably not the leprosy of h
today but a skin disease; cf. Lev. 13:1–59 (Taylor). It involved, as did no other disease, exclusion from the community on the grounds of uncleanness. The story appears in another form in the fragments of an unknown Gospel (see Dodd, *NT Studies* (1953), 33ff.). In **41** the variant 'being angry' is probably original; the anger could be explained as indignation (*a*) at the breach of the law involved in the leper's approach, (*b*) at the doubt expressed in the words 'if you will', or (*c*) at the interruption of his ministry, but is most probably to be taken as the reaction of Jesus to the disease. The charge in 44 shows that on certain points Jesus explicitly recognised the validity of the Mosaic law. Once more, Jesus enjoins silence, but in vain. 'People came to him from every quarter', not so much for the sake of his message but in hopes of seeing wonders.

II 1-III 6 The Conflict Stories—This section illus- 698a
trates the growing opposition to Jesus on the part of the scribes and Pharisees, which finally reached such a pitch that they were prepared to enter into alliance with the adherents of Herod Antipas in order to encompass his destruction. The whole section may already have been brought together before it was finally incorporated in the Gospel (see Taylor, 91ff.), so that chronologically 3:6 may come too early, the plot against Jesus' life belonging to a later stage in the narrative. The section is however dramatically appropriate here as revealing the contrast between popular enthusiasm and official censure and preparing the way for what is yet to come; and 3:6 marks the climax.

II 1-12 The Healing of the Paralytic—Many b
scholars consider this passage composite, a miracle story into which a controversial section (5*b*–10) has been inserted. Certainly the story runs more smoothly without this section, and the repetition of 'he saith to the paralytic' in 5*a* and 10*b* is clumsy. On the other hand there is difference of opinion over the precise limits of the story of the healing (1–5*a*, 11f., or 1–5, 12?), and the difficulty sometimes found in the association of healing and forgiveness belongs to modern thought; in the ancient world sin and suffering were related as cause and effect. Moreover modern medicine is discovering a deeper relationship in the health of mind and body.

Mk thinks of a flat roof, covered with earth, Lk. (5:19) of a tiled roof. The men gained access to the roof by the outside stair, and literally dug their way through. The 'pallet' was the poor man's bed—Mk uses a colloquial word for which Mt. and Lk. substitute a politer but less appropriate term. 'Their faith' most naturally refers to the faith of the hearers, but most modern commentators include the faith of the paralytic himself; certainly Jesus normally looked for a personal trust in the sufferer who sought his help. 'Thy sins are forgiven' is an authoritative declaration, and it is this that arouses the anger of the scribes. Not even the Messiah was expected to forgive sins, which in the OT is the prerogative of God alone; hence the charge of blasphemy (as yet unspoken). On the surface, it is easier to declare forgiveness, which cannot be verified, than to restore a bed-ridden man to manifest health, but Jesus submits to the test. The implication is that he who can do the one can do the other. It should be noted that 12

698b refers only to the miracle, not to the forgiveness; again, the story as it stands appears in contrast with Jesus' persistent refusal to accede to the Pharisees' demand for a sign to vindicate his authority. This seems a further reason for considering the controversial section an insertion. A special problem concerns the use of the term 'Son of Man', which is almost entirely confined to the Gospels and there to sayings of Jesus. In Ps. 8:4 and in Ezek. the phrase means simply 'man', but this is inappropriate both here and in 28; the words seem clearly to refer in some sense to Jesus himself. In Dan. 7:13 there is a vision of 'one like unto a son of man', and in 1 Enoch the Son of Man is a supernatural figure; but it is not clear that this was a current Messianic term in the time of Jesus (cf. Jn 12:34 and Bernard in ICC *ad loc.*). In Dan. the phrase is interpreted of 'the people of the saints of the Most High', and this has led some commentators to understand it here as a reference to the Elect Community; in this case Jesus speaks here as representative and head of that community. Another possibility is that Jesus deliberately chose the title to provoke reflection: to claim Messiahship was to court misunderstanding, the popular conception being so far removed from his own; to claim to be Son of Man might make men think. The most striking feature is however his reinterpretation of the phrase, after Caesarea Philippi, in terms of the Suffering Servant of Isaiah. The splendid figure of apocalyptic thought ascends his throne through suffering.

c **13-14. The call of Levi** serves as introduction to the next conflict, over Jesus' association with the tax-collectors and sinners. Some MSS call him James, while Mt calls him Matthew (Levi does not appear in the list of the Twelve, 3:16–19); he was probably an official in the service of Herod Antipas.

15-17. The question of **table-fellowship** between Jews and Gentiles was a live issue in the early Church (cf. Ac. 11:3; Gal. 2:12), and it was probably this that led to the preservation of this story (Bultmann). The host was probably Levi, although if 13f. and 15–17 were originally independent 'he' and 'his' might refer to Jesus himself. Mk adds that Jesus now had many disciples, although he has so far mentioned only five. The tax-collectors here are not the *publicani* or magnates to whom the taxation of large areas was farmed out, but the local agents. The sinners are those who failed to observe the law by Pharisaic standards, the 'people of the land' (cf. Jn 7:49). That Jesus associated with such people was an offence to the strict Jews, as later to the pagan Celsus (cf. Orig., *c. Cels.*, iii, 59); but if Jesus did not condemn, neither did he condone—he came, as Lk. interprets (5:32), to call them to repentance, as a physician to heal the sick (17).

The **Pharisees** were the religious leaders of the time, although the Sadducees held the high priesthood. The descendants of the Hasidim who had supported the Maccabees, the Pharisees were devoted to the Law and endeavoured to apply it to every department of life. For this purpose they developed a tradition of interpretation by which action in every sphere of conduct was minutely regulated. In the Gospels they appear as the implacable opponents of Jesus, and the objects of his most searching criticism, but justice must be done to their ideals. If they were often guilty of complacency and even of hypocrisy, they set at their best a high standard and a noble ideal. In contrast to the Sadducees, they believed in a future life and recognised as authoritative not only the Pentateuch but also the 'prophets' and the 'writings'. The reply of Jesus to their criticism is probably to be taken as ironic: they believed they had no need of a doctor, and a doctor must go among his patients.

d **18-20 On Fasting**—The only fast required by the Law was that on the Day of Atonement (Lev. 16:29), but the Pharisees were accustomed to fast twice weekly, on Mondays and Thursdays. It has been suggested that John's disciples were fasting as a sign of mourning for their leader, which would place the incident after his execution. Some commentators hold 19*b* and 20 to be a later addition, intended to justify fasting by the Christian community, and claim that the prophecy of the Passion comes too early in the Gospel, but (as Taylor notes) criticism itself has weakened the force of this objection, since the incident may have happened later. As with the preceding narrative, interest in a question which was a living issue for the early Church may have contributed to the preservation of the story.

According to Taylor, the idea of **the Bridegroom** had, under OT influence, attained Messianic significance (cf. also 2 C. 11:2; Eph. 5:23ff., but cf. Jeremias, *The Parables of Jesus* (1954), 41 and *n.* 81 there), but Jesus does not here put forward a public claim to be the Messiah. 'The point of comparison is not the persons but the time: the kingdom of God is at hand' (Grant); it is therefore no time for mourning or for fasting. That time will come. The *Didache* (ch. 8) curiously misses the point: Christians are enjoined not to fast like 'the hypocrites', but to fast on Wednesdays and Fridays.

21-22. These two short sayings were probably originally independent, and it is impossible now to guess their context, but the general sense is clear: the new movement canot be confined within the limits of the old religion. The last clause is omitted in some MSS, and may be an assimilation to Mt. and Lk.

23-28. The law of Dt. 23:25, sometimes cited here, is e really irrelevant: it permits gleaning with the hand in a neighbour's field, as against reaping with a sickle, but says nothing at all about the Sabbath. Exod. 34:21 enjoins rest on the seventh day 'in plowing time and in harvest'. Reaping, grinding, and sifting are included among the 39 kinds of work forbidden on the Sabbath in the Mishnah (quoted in Barrett, *The NT Background: Selected Documents* (1956), 154). Jesus replies to the Pharisaic criticism with a characteristic counter-question (cf. 12:10, 26, etc.), appealing to the example of David (1 Sam. 21:1–6). The high priest was not Abiathar but his father Ahimelech, but in association with David Abiathar was much the better known. For the shew-bread, or 'bread of the Presence', see Lev. 24:5–9. **27f.** forms the climax to the story, but 'recent discussion tends to regard these sayings as isolated logia appended to the narrative for topical reasons' (Taylor, 218). The principle stated in 27 appears in Rabbinic teaching in the form 'The Sabbath is given over to you, not you to the Sabbath' (Barrett, 153), but the real problem lies in **28** (cf. 2:10 above). No Jew could admit that man is lord of the Sabbath. The alternatives are (*a*) that Jesus here makes a veiled claim, as man's Lord and Representative, to possess authority over the Sabbath, or (*b*) that 28 is a Christian comment expressing the conviction that Jesus is Lord of all that belongs to man (Taylor).

III 1-6. Like the preceding story, this probably owes f its preservation to the interest of the early Church in the question of **Sabbath observance**. According to Taylor, 'the story is not a Miracle-story because the healing is subordinate in interest to the religious question at issue' (but cf. Richardson, *The Miracle Stories of the Gospels* (1941), 77). In the Gospel of the Hebrews, according to Jerome, the man was a mason (see James, *Apoc. NT* (1924), 4f.). This section is particularly rich in touches of vivid realism.

The Rabbinic rule forbade healing on the Sabbath except when life was in danger. Jesus here meets the unspoken challenge with a counter-question which has a pointed and particular reference: 'Was it unlawful on the Sabbath to rescue a life from incipient death, and yet lawful to watch for the life of another, as they were doing?' (Swete). To this they had no answer. The anger of Jesus here (which Mt. and Lk. omit) is explained by the following words: a natural indignation at the obtuseness of men who are blind to the real moral values. The upshot of the growing hostility displayed in these stories was a plot between

698f the Pharisees and the Herodians against the life of Jesus, which may however belong to a later stage of the ministry. Other clashes are recorded later (3:19*b*–35, 7:1–23, 11:27–12:40).

699a **7-12.** A brief but vivid account of the interest aroused by the ministry of Jesus, people coming from far and near as the rumours of his healings spread. The section prepares the way for later narratives (cf. 10 with 5:27ff., 6:56, etc.). Once again we are told that Jesus enjoined silence upon the unclean spirits; he did not welcome their testimony, which might have involved misconceptions about his mission.

b **13-19 The Appointment of the Twelve**—The previous section records a withdrawal from the towns to the open air beside the lake; now Jesus seeks a greater solitude in the hills (Black suggests that the Aramaic word behind 'the hills' may mean either 'mountain' or 'open country' as opposed to inhabited places). The purpose of this withdrawal is the setting apart of the twelve (the number symbolises the twelve tribes of Israel, cf. Mt. 19:28; Lk. 22:30), whom Jesus appointed for the double purpose which is still the essential function of the Church: fellowship with himself, and the proclamation of the Gospel. Mk however probably has in mind not the later apostolic mission but that of 6:7–13. Despite its strong MS support, the clause 'whom also he named apostles' is probably an assimilation to Lk. 6:13.

Some of the disciples are no more than names to us, but others are specially singled out: Peter and James and John formed an inner circle (cf. 5:37, 9:2, and (with Andrew) 13:3); Simon the Cananaean was not a Canaanite, nor a man of Cana, but a Zealot (cf. Lk. 6:15), a member of the extreme nationalist group. **16** suggests that Peter received his surname here, whereas Mt. (16:18) puts it at Caesarea Philippi; but only later was Simon truly Peter. Boanerges is a transliteration of a Hebrew or Aramaic name for which various suggestions have been made; Mk's interpretation fits 9:38; Lk. 9:54. Levi is not mentioned, but has been identified with James the son of Alphaeus. The meaning of Iscariot is doubtful: the common interpretation 'man of Kerioth' would make him the one Judaean among the twelve. The name Judas itself was common (Jn 14:22 mentions another Judas, not Iscariot, among the disciples).

c **19b-35.** A series of sayings and stories illustrating further the conflict of Jesus with the authorities, and the charges brought against him. In 21 'they said' may be impersonal (Turner), but even so the friends of Jesus (his family?) are not absolved from blame; people were saying he was mad, and they believed and acted upon the rumour. It is however more natural to take 'his friends' as the subject throughout the sentence (so Taylor and others). If, as many scholars hold, the reference is to the family of Jesus, 21 anticipates 31ff.

d **22-26. The Beelzebub Controversy**—In the Q version (Mt. 12:22–6; Lk. 11:14–18), the controversy results from the exorcism of a dumb spirit. Some scholars find here two charges: (*a*) 'he hath Beelzebul', (*b*) 'by the prince of demons he casts out demons'; but others identify Beelzebul with the prince of the demons, i.e. with Satan (cf. 23). Baalzebub (2 Kg. 1:2) was the god of Ekron, but this form occurs here in no Greek MS; for the form Beelzebul many attempts at explanation have been made, e.g. that the Jews changed the name to give it a derisive sense. The point of the story lies however in the reply of Jesus, in which he turns the charge against his accusers: if Satan is casting out Satan he is hastening his own destruction. **27** (cf. Isa. 49:24f.) may have been originally independent, but is appropriate here: the exorcisms prove that the Strong Man's house has been entered; the Stronger (Lk. 11:22; cf. Mk 1:7), has come. In **23** 'parables' are mentioned for the first time. This word is much wider than 'illustration' or 'analogy', and goes back to the Hebrew *māshāl* (proverb, aphorism, illustrative story). See further on 4:1–11. Comparison of 3:23, 4:30, and 13:28 (RSV 'lesson') is instructive: in each case the Greek is literally 'parable'. 699d

e **28-30.** A solemn warning uttered with great emphasis. The Q version (Lk. 12:10; Mt. 12:32) occurs in a different context and contrasts a word spoken against the Son of Man (or a son of man, i.e. any man?) with speaking against the Holy Spirit. The sin against the Spirit is the wilful blindness of those who refuse to see, who persist in putting the worst construction on the acts of others, who as here ascribe a work of healing manifestly wrought by the Spirit of God to the agency of Beelzebub. Cf. Milton's Satan: 'Evil, be thou my good'.

f **31-35.** The point of this story lies in the saying in 34f., that the ties of common obedience to God take precedence over those of kinship. As on the mission field today, this must have had a very real relevance for members of the early Church. It is difficult to reconcile this narrative with the doctrine of the Virgin Birth, of which indeed Mk does not seem to know (cf. 6:3). The absence of any reference to Joseph may indicate that he was already dead.

700a **IV 1-34 A Chapter of Parables**—This section consists almost entirely of teaching, and illustrates the parabolic method characteristic of Jesus. From a comparison of 1 and 35 it would seem that Jesus spends the whole day in the boat and crosses the lake in the evening; but in 10 he is alone with the twelve, while 26ff. again appear to be spoken to the crowd (note 'he said to them', 11, 13, 21, 24, but simply 'he said' in 26 and 30). This suggests that Mk has inserted into a group of parables (*a*) some general comments, and (*b*) the interpretation of the Parable of the Sower.

The crux of the passage is **11f.**, which as it stands implies that Jesus deliberately made use of parables in order to conceal his message. This contradicts 33 ('as they were able to hear it'), and is moreover contrary to the evidence of the parables themselves: often the point is clear without any explanation, and indeed on one occasion the opponents of Jesus recognised that he had spoken a parable against them (12:12). Whatever else may be said, the teaching of Jesus was not an elaborate series of riddles designed to conceal the truth. Attempts have been made accordingly to explain **12** (which is based on Isa. 6:9f.) either as a case of the Semitic use of a final clause to express the result which actually followed or as due to mistranslation of the original Aramaic. It is however more probable that the present position of the saying is due to Mk, who has been misled by the occurrence of the word 'parable'. It may mean (*a*) an illustrative story or (*b*) a riddle, like the Hebrew *māshāl* (proverb, aphorism, etc.). The former sense applies as a rule to the 'parables' of Jesus, the latter is the meaning in this verse. Jesus may have reflected on the results of his ministry and his failure to convert the people and drawn his conclusion in the language of Isa. 6. By employing this saying as an 'explanation' of the use of parables Mk has produced an interpretation long felt to be intolerable; there can be little doubt however that it represents Mk's own view, the result of reflection on the failure of the ministry of Jesus and on the experience of the Christian mission: if the people would not hear, there must be some explanation. So Paul also speaks of the hardening of Israel (Rom. 9–11). Cf. further Jn 12:37–43.

b For centuries the accepted interpretation of the parables was allegorical (cf. for example Trench, *Notes on the Parables*): they were 'earthly stories with a heavenly meaning', and an attempt was made to find a spiritual significance for every detail. There was indeed much of value in such interpretation, and Mk interprets the Sower on just such principles, but modern research has questioned whether this is in fact the real meaning of the parables (cf. Dodd, *The Parables of the Kingdom* (1936); Jeremias, *The Parables of Jesus* (1954)). In point of fact the parable was a common method of illustration among Jewish teachers and the parables

700b of Jesus are similar in form to those of the Rabbis. According to the modern view, the typical parable presents one single point of comparison, whereas in allegory every detail is significant (cf. Bunyan's *Pilgrim's Progress*). This distinction must not however be pressed too far, since details may be added in the building up of the story (e.g. in the Parable of the Wicked Husbandmen, 12:1–9) which are suggested by their special appropriateness. Two questions here should be kept distinct: (*a*) what was the meaning Mk saw in the parables he included? (*b*) what was the original meaning of the parables in the mind of Jesus?

In Mk the parable of the Sower is interpreted as a parable of four kinds of soil, and is thereby made to stress the responsibility of the hearers. Modern interpretations take various forms: it is a reflection on the experience of Jesus as a teacher, or is intended to give encouragement to the disciples (though much of a preacher's effort may be wasted, yet he will see fruit of his labours); or again it refers to the preaching of the Kingdom of God. Dodd and others find the significance in the immediate situation of Jesus: despite unresponsive hearers, the field is white to the harvest (cf. Jn 4:35). The crop is ripe, and it is time to reap.

c **9.** A characteristic saying, impressing on the hearers the necessity of paying heed to his words; cf. 23, 7:16, etc.

11. 'The secret' (in the Gospels only here and in the parallels, but often in Paul) is the purpose of God concerning His Kingdom, now made known to the disciples. The word is common in contemporary Greek, especially in relation to the 'mystery' religions, but in NT 'there is no case in which it connotes secret rites or esoteric knowledge communicated to 'initiates"' (Taylor).

13. Mk records a number of rebukes to the disciples (4:40, 7:18, 8:18, 21, etc.), which Mt. and Lk. commonly tone down. Comparison is instructive.

d **14-20.** As already indicated, many scholars feel that this interpretation derives from the early Church, perhaps from Mk himself. The conditions reflected seem to be those of a later period. The interpretation may however be based on genuine reflections of Jesus about his mission.

21 reads strangely after 11f. Mk seems to understand the saying to mean that the 'secret' entrusted to the disciples is in time to be made known to all (T. W. Manson thinks he means it to refer to the coming manifestation of the Kingdom in power). Dodd suggests that the saying originally applied to the conduct of the religious leaders of the time, who hid from men the light of God's revelation (cf. Mt. 23:13; Lk. 11:52). The sayings in this group (21–5) appear in different contexts and with different applications in Mt. and Lk., and it has been held that Mk derived them from Q; but he may have taken them from another sayings-source, or from oral tradition. **24f.** emphasise again the responsibility of the hearer.

e **26-29.** The parable of **the Seed growing secretly** is peculiar to Mk. The traditional interpretation identifies the man either with Jesus or with the preacher, but Trench notes the difficulties which this involves. Dodd lists three lines of modern interpretation which compare the Kingdom (*a*) to the seed, (*b*) to the process of growth, or (*c*) to the harvest, and himself adds a fourth: the parable implies that the Kingdom is already present. 'The parable in effect says, Can you not see that the long history of God's dealings with His people has reached its climax? After the work of the Baptist only one thing remains: "Put ye in the sickle, for the harvest is ripe".' Cf. Lk. 10:2=Mt. 9:37f. But Mk may have seen here the assurance that the delay in the coming of the Kingdom was only apparent; the final result is certain (Grant).

f **30-32. A Grain of Mustard Seed** was proverbial for smallness among the Jews (cf. Mt. 17:20=Lk. 17:6), and Mk evidently saw here a comparison between small beginnings and great results. Dodd however, referring to Dan. 4:12; Ezek. 31:6, 17:23, thinks the 70
prevailing idea is that of growth to a point at which the tree can shelter the birds: 'in this parable Jesus is asserting that the time has come when the blessings of the Reign of God are available for all men'. As already noted, **33** conflicts with 11f. **34** may have been added by Mk in the interests of his theory, but may mean only that to the disciples further teaching was given (Taylor). The use of the imperfect tense in the Greek indicates that Mk is here recording Jesus' usual practice.

IV 35-V 43 Four Miracle Stories—These narratives 70
are different in style from those already related, and show an interest in detail for its own sake: e.g. in the reference to 'other boats' (35: 'probably a genuine reminiscence' (Taylor)), or to the rower's cushion (38). A boat is mentioned in 3:9 and 4:1, and this has suggested to some commentators that these three references were originally together, but were separated by the introduction of fresh material. Mk however seems to intend 4:1 and 35 to refer to the same day, and 3:9 to a different occasion. All four stories tell of events which took place on one side or other of the lake, which is subject to sudden storms (cf. SHG, 441f.).

35-41 The Storm on the Lake—When Jesus had b
finished his teaching the disciples simply put out with him in the boat. The story is remarkable for its graphic description of the storm, the waves breaking into the boat so that it began to fill, and for the contrast between the calm serenity of Jesus and the terror of the disciples. Their panic-stricken question (Wood's 'suggestion of complaint' is an understatement) is toned down by Mt. and Lk. One lesson of the story is the example of absolute faith and confidence set by Jesus, who here fulfils his own admonitions to trust in God; but it is not the whole point. In response to the disciples' appeal, Jesus rebukes the wind, as if it were a demon (the word 'be still' is addressed to the demoniac in 1:25), and in the ensuing calm the disciples ask each other the question which the story is meant to raise in the mind of the reader: 'Who then is this?'

It has been suggested that the command of **39** was addressed not to the wind but to the disciples, but this has no support in the narrative; on the contrary they are rebuked for lack of faith after the calm. The suggestion is an attempt to rationalise the miracle so as to match modern ideas and minimise the supernatural element; but if we eliminate the supernatural what we have left is certainly not the Christ of the Gospels (J. S. Stewart). The miracles are today a problem, where once they were regarded as the proofs of the divinity of Jesus; but if we once grant 'the Grand Miracle' of the Incarnation, the main objection to the other miracles falls to the ground (Hunter). They were not however wrought for their evidential value (Jesus consistently refused to provide the Pharisees with the sign they demanded); they are on the one hand works of the divine compassion, and on the other the signs of a new age already breaking in (cf. Bright, *The Kingdom of God in Bible and Church* (1955), 221). The simplest explanation here is that Jesus trusted in God and His trust was not deceived (Taylor). Mk may have inferred that he who could calm the storm was present still with his own amid the storms and stress of life (Grant) (cf. 6:45ff.). On the whole subject see Richardson, *The Miracle Stories of the Gospels* (1941).

V 1-20 The Gerasene Demoniac—Several elements c
in this story (e.g. the description of the demoniac, his association with the tombs, and the demand of Jesus to know the demon's name, which would convey power over it, cf. Gen. 32:29) reflect popular ideas, and some scholars have thought a story about some unknown Jewish exorcist has been transferred to Jesus; on the other hand 'the many artless details . . . are details taken from life' (Taylor). The story is 'a folk tale current in a pagan neighborhood, but a folk tale about Jesus' (Grant). The description of the scene

1c is vague, probably because Mk knew no more ; the variant readings are due to the fact that both Gerasa (Mk) and Gadara (Mt.) are some miles from the lake. Origen preferred 'the country of the Gergesenes', but Mk refers only to the country in general terms, i.e. the district of which Gerasa is the chief town, not to the town itself. What is clear is that we are here on pagan soil (Decapolis, 20), which explains the presence of the swine. As in 1:23 and 3:11, the demon recognises Jesus, and begs not to be tortured (cf. 1:24 and Philostratus, *Apollonius of Tyana*, iv, 25). 'The Most High God' was a common title for Yahweh in Diaspora Judaism, and is also the name of the deity worshipped by certain syncretistic groups, probably under Jewish influence (cf. HTR (1936), 39ff.). The name Legion given by the demon is variously explained as an attempt at evasion (giving a number instead of the name), as due to some experience involving a legion which lies behind the man's madness, or as indicating a divided personality (cf. 9, 'we are many'). The real problem lies in the destruction of the swine, although it may well be that neither Jews nor Jewish Christians would have been unduly perturbed by the loss of a herd of unclean beasts. Usually it is suggested that in a final paroxysm the man hurled himself upon the swine, and drove them over the cliff. The onlookers (and the man himself) then inferred that the demons had taken up a fresh abode. It may be noted that the miracles and exorcisms are not as a rule accompanied by 'proofs' of their reality (cf. on 1:28 and compare the story of Apollonius quoted by Barrett, *The NT Background* (1956), 77). Turner suggests that the loss of the herd weighed as nothing in comparison
d with the rescue of one single human being. **14ff.** relates the sequel : the herdsmen spread the news and brought a crowd to see what had happened. At the sight of the demoniac sitting 'clothed and in his right mind' they are overcome with awe, but 'the cure of a mere maniac was of less importance than the security of their property' (Turner), and they besought Jesus to depart. **19.** The charge given to the man is strikingly at variance with the injunctions to silence in other cases, but may be due to the fact that he was apparently a Gentile. Elsewhere Jesus seems to have regarded his mission as limited to 'the lost sheep of the house of Israel' (Mt. 15:24), and it is doubtful if this verse should be understood as implying a Gentile mission. 'The Lord' here as elsewhere refers to God, but the man tells what *Jesus* had done. Decapolis was a group of ten Greek cities mostly east of the lake of Galilee ; the names vary in different lists.
e **21-43** contains the story of the **raising of Jairus' daughter,** interrupted, **24b-34,** by another miracle. Lk. the physician tones down Mk's disparaging reference to the doctors in 26. Mt. specifies that it was 'the fringe' of Jesus' garment that the woman touched, one of the four tassels which the Law required. For Mk the story of Jairus' daughter is clearly a raising from the dead, but the words of Jesus in 39 ('she is not dead but sleeping') have suggested to some scholars that the child was not actually dead but in a trance (cf. Turner and Taylor *ad loc.*). Taylor observes that Mk has related the story with great objectivity in that another interpretation is possible. Mt. and Lk. both took him to mean that the girl was dead. **43.** The charge of secrecy here could not be obeyed, since the news was bound to spread ; but it may be that Jesus merely sought time to escape an embarrassing publicity. The significance of all four stories is well summed up by Wood : 'The memorable acts and utterances of Jesus which make these stories unique are all concerned with the maintenance of simple trust in God—a trust that triumphs over natural dangers, demonic powers, disease, and even death.'

02a **VI 1-6 The Rejection at Nazareth**—Lk. places this story at the beginning of the ministry (4:16–30), although his account indicates that Jesus had already become famous (cf. Lk. 4:14, 23). Wood suggests that Mk puts it here as the first sign of waning public interest : 'The disciples, in the next section, are warned to expect similar indifference and antagonism.' 702a
'His own country' is most naturally Nazareth (cf. 1:9 and Lk. 4:16) ; Mk, like Jn, makes no reference to the story of the birth at Bethlehem. Here in his own village, where all knew him, Jesus could make no impression ; their very familiarity with him obscured his real greatness. This was no prophet, but the boy who had grown up in their midst, whose family indeed were still among them. The phrase 'the son of Mary' might indicate only that Joseph was now dead (Turner), but it is contrary to Jewish custom to call a man by the name of his mother. For 'the carpenter' Mt. reads 'the son of the carpenter' (13:55), and many important MSS (including the Chester Beatty Papyrus P45) support a similar reading here ; the other reading may be due to revision under the influence of the doctrine of the Virgin Birth. Origen (*c. Cels.*, vi, 36) declares that no canonical Gospel describes Jesus as a carpenter. (For details see Taylor, 300)

The reference to the 'brothers' and 'sisters' of Jesus has also given rise to much discussion. The three main views are (*a*) that they were full brothers of Jesus (Helvidius) ; (*b*) that they were sons of Joseph by a former wife (Epiphanius) ; or (*c*) that they were cousins of Jesus (Jerome). Of these the last is open to conclusive objections, but the other two can both claim a considerable antiquity. The Helvidian is the simplest and most natural, but is difficult to reconcile with the doctrine of the Virgin Birth, especially in its elaboration into the doctrine of the perpetual virginity of Mary (see Taylor, 247ff. and literature referred to there). Turner remarks that if Jesus were younger than his brothers we can more easily understand their early attitude towards him (cf. Jn 7:3–5). **4.** Cf. the Oxyrhynchus logion (James, *Apoc. NT* (1924), 27) : A prophet is not accepted in his own country, nor does a physician work cures upon them who know him. **5-6.** Mk is unique in the boldness with which he records Jesus' inability to do any mighty work in Nazareth, and his amazement at their lack of faith. As Wood notes, this amazement is significant as showing how natural trust in God seemed to Jesus.

7-13 The Mission of the Twelve—This is a new departure, but is prepared for in 3:14. The instructions vary slightly in the different accounts (Mt. and Lk. forbid the staff, Mt. even the wearing of sandals (cf. Lk. 10:4) while both change the wearing of two tunics to the owning of them), but all show the same note of urgency that is revealed in Mk. The missionaries 'are to be like an invading army and live on the country' (T. W. Manson) ; their business brooks no delay (cf. Lk. 10:4 ; Mt. 10:23). Of the message with which they were entrusted nothing is said, but it must have related to the imminence of the kingdom (cf. 12 with 1:14). It was the reading of the Mission Charge that inspired Francis of Assisi to embrace 'the lady Poverty'. Deissmann (*Light from the Ancient East* (1927), 108ff.) thinks the 'bag' in **8** was the collecting-bag of the itinerant priest in some pagan faiths, in which he gathered alms. The directions of **11** 'reflect the actual practice of the earliest Christian missionaries' (Wood, comparing Ac. 13:51, 18:6). The action is symbolic, indicating that the place is to be regarded as heathen, but is not to be taken as an acted curse ; it is 'a testimony intended to provoke thought and to lead men to repentance' (Taylor). **13.** Anointing with oil is not mentioned in the Gospels except here and Lk. 10:34, and may reflect later practice (cf. Jas 5:14). b

14-29 Herod's Misgivings and the Death of John the Baptist—A dramatic interlude filling in the gap between the sending of the disciples and their return (30 ff.). Many commentators mark here the beginning of a new division of the narrative, in which Jesus moves for the most part outside Galilee, and hence beyond Herod's jurisdiction. Bethsaida (6:45, 8:22), Tyre and Sidon (7:24), Decapolis (8:31), and Caesarea c

702c Philippi (8:27) are all beyond the borders of Herod's territory. The fate of John may have counselled prudence, but Mk does not represent the movements of Jesus as a flight (Taylor compares Lk. 13:31f.). According to Josephus, Herod put John to death lest his influence over the people should lead to a rebellion ; the influence of Jesus must have appeared at least as dangerous. Herod (Antipas) became tetrarch of Galilee and Peraea (Mk's ' king ' reflects popular usage) on the death of his father Herod the Great. His brother Philip (tetrarch of Ituraea, Lk. 3:1) was the husband not of Herodias but of Salome, the husband of Herodias being yet another Herod (the name ' Philip ' is omitted here in P45, and is wanting in Lk. 3:19 and in some MSS of Mt. 14:3). Herod's rejection of his first wife in favour of Herodias led to a disastrous war with her father Aretas, king of Arabia, which some interpreted as a divine retribution for the death of John. Herodias appears here in the part of Jezebel to John's Elijah, and the story of Salome's dance has also been influenced by the book of Esther (cf. 22 with Est. 2:9, 23 with Est. 5:3). Much has been written both about the problems of chronology and about the discrepancies between Mk and Josephus, but these difficulties are not insuperable. Rawlinson suggests that Josephus writes some sixty years later as a historian concerned to trace the political causes of a war, whereas Mk recounts the rumours current in the bazaars at the time. There may however be a solid core of historical fact in John's rebuke of Herod and Herodias' consequent hostility, and Mk is certainly faithful to the character of Herod. To the credit of Herodias it should be added that when Antipas was banished to Gaul after an unsuccessful appeal to Caligula she shared his exile. **14f.** The various rumours about Jesus anticipate the reply of the disciples in 8:28. For the expectation of the return of Elijah cf. Mal. 3:1, 4:5 ; the fulfilment of this expectation is seen by Mk in John (cf. Mk 1:6, 9:11–13).

20 shows very clearly the mingled feelings with which Herod regarded John. **21.** Mk seems to suggest a celebration in Herod's palace at Tiberias, but Josephus says John was executed in Machaerus. It is not however impossible that the banquet was held in the fortress.

d **30-44 The Feeding of the Five Thousand**—Mt. (14:13) links this withdrawal to the news of John's death, but in Mk the motive is the need of the disciples for rest after their mission. In Mk they are called ' apostles ' only here and in 3:14 (where the phrase is probably due to assimilation). Another motive is the pressure of the crowd (cf. 3:20) which Mk alone records (31). The plan is frustrated by the people, who recognise the party and by going on foot round the head of the lake reach the ' lonely place ' first ; presumably the boat was delayed by an adverse wind. The words which describe the reaction of Jesus recall the OT (esp. Ezek. 34:5–6) : ' Though he has withdrawn to avoid them, he goes forth to welcome them. To him they seem like the shepherdless flock described in Ezek. 34 ' (Wood). Here the compassion is inspired by their lack of leadership ; in 8:2 it is the hunger of the people that is stressed.

For Mk the story of the feeding is quite certainly miraculous, and so it was interpreted down to comparatively recent times. Modern criticism has questioned it on various grounds, not all of equal force. Sanday is recorded to have said that he was inclined to regard the account as fact, save in one particular, that they were all filled. Some interpretations are simply attempts to rationalise the story into conformity with modern ideas (e.g. that Jesus and his disciples set an example of sharing which those who had food followed) ; others however contain a core of truth. Thus the present form of the story may have been influenced by 2 Kg. 4:42ff.—' It was inevitable that such a story as this, in the earliest Christian circles, should be told in OT language ' (Grant)—but this need not mean that it is only a myth created on the basis of the OT story. Again, there are definite associa- 70
tions with the Last Supper (cf. 41 with 14:22), which show that at any rate ' Mark has conformed the vocabulary of the passage to that of the Supper in the belief that in some sense the fellowship meal in the wilderness was an anticipation of the Eucharist ' (Taylor), but this again need not mean that the story is purely imaginative. As Taylor puts it, ' it is probable that the concrete facts are seen in the light of history to have a richer meaning '. For the early Church any such story must have taken on Eucharistic associations. The Fourth Gospel already ' makes Jesus himself draw the line from the miracle of feeding with material bread to the miracle of the Sacrament ' (Cullmann, *Early Christian Worship* (1953), 93). Since the Last Supper itself points forward to the Messianic Feast (cf. 14:25), the best hypothesis is probably that of Schweitzer, that this also is an anticipation of the Messianic banquet. The miraculous element should probably not however be excluded ; it is a miracle of divine compassion and a sign of the presence of the Kingdom. If it be objected that the story conflicts with that of the Temptation, it may be noted (*a*) that Jesus might have been prepared to meet the needs of others but not to satisfy his own, (*b*) that he immediately withdraws. The Temptation was to use his power as a means of securing men's allegiance, and this he still refuses to do.

37. The 200 pennyworth of bread and the green grass (39) are also mentioned in Jn 6:7, 10, which raises the question of the relation between the two accounts. The denarius was a labourer's daily wage. The vividness of Mk's narrative deserves attention.

45-52. In Jn (6:15) Jesus perceives that the people are e
on the point of making him king by force, and therefore withdraws to the hills. It is only afterwards, in the evening, that the disciples set out across the lake without him. Mk may preserve the true order of the events, Jn the explanation : the old temptation (cf. Mt. 4:2–4) is present again, in a particularly pressing form. Jesus constrains his disciples to go, lest they too catch the ' messianic ' fever. Not yet do they fully understand his mission (cf. 8:31–3). Then he sends the people away, at the cost of his popularity (cf. Jn 6:66). The miracle is difficult : ' One is tempted to believe that allegory has been materialised here ' (Wood). Some scholars have seen in it a misplaced Resurrection appearance, others attempt to rationalise it, but Taylor would seem to be right in urging that the story has a factual basis. Richardson (90 ff.) links with 4:35–41, and finds the main teaching of these two stories to be that ' Jesus shares the power of God as the Lord of the mysteries of creation ' ; a subsidiary theme (p. 92) is the assurance of the presence of the Lord with his own, even in the darkest hour (' the fourth watch ' (48, which implies the Roman not the Jewish reckoning) would be about 3 a.m.). **52** is Mk's comment (cf. 8:17–21), in which Taylor sees Pauline influence (cf. 2 C. 3:14, etc.). They ought to have seen the significance of the feeding of the crowd, but their minds were dull.

53-56. Mk's geography is distinctly vague : after f
setting out for Bethsaida (45) on the NE. shore of the lake, the disciples arrive at Gennesaret on the NW. side. The usual view is that the wind (48) caused a change of plan (but cf. 51) ; other alternatives are to read Capernaum for Bethsaida with Jn (6:17), or to assume that 53–6 is the true continuation of 30–2 (Wood). On 56 (' the fringe of his garment ') Wood comments : ' The example of the woman with the issue of blood had clearly been influential '.

VII 1-23 Further Clashes with the Pharisees— 703
The passage falls into three sections, and reveals the gulf which separates Jesus from the Pharisaic legalism. As Taylor notes, the validity for Christians of the scribal tradition (' the tradition of the elders ') was a living issue between Church and Synagogue in the early period : ' The question had far more than an academic interest, for the answer given to it decided

3a the issue whether Christianity was capable of becoming a world religion' (Taylor, 96). Cf. Ac. 11:1–18 and the Council of Ac. 15; also Gal. The explanatory comments (3–4, 11, 19) are probably due to Mk himself, as is the explanation in 2 that 'defiled' means 'unwashed'.

The Jewish practice of ceremonial washing of the hands before meals was a ritual act, intended to remove the defilement incurred by contact with the Gentiles, such as was inevitable in a district like Galilee. Mk's comment illustrates the meticulous care with which the rule was carried out, but shows also that like other good customs this practice had degenerated into formalism: concern for the minute details of ceremonial had supplanted genuine religious faith and devotion (cf. Mt. 23:23). The attitude of Jesus is not that such observances are wrong, but that they are receiving a disproportionate attention, to the neglect of the things which really matter.

3. One Greek word in this verse is not translated in RSV because no satisfactory explanation has yet been offered. The AV 'oft' is based on a variant reading. Literally 'with the fist', it has been variously rendered 'up to the elbow', or 'diligently'. Allen suggests that it refers to some particular method of washing, the precise nature of which we do not know. The reference to 'all the Jews' is an exaggeration.

4. 'when they come from the market place' is literally 'from the market place'. Black suggests 'anything from the market place'. 'Purify (literally 'sprinkle') is the reading of SB, but some other MSS read 'baptise', which Turner prefers: 'Nothing illustrates better the primitive atmosphere of Mk's Gospel than this use of the Greek word which became consecrated to the sacrament of initiation . . . in a profane or non-technical sense'. Taylor however suggests that the less familiar word ('purify') is probably original.

5. 'live' (Greek 'walk'): as Taylor notes, the Palestinian origin of the story is revealed by the use of this word (here only in the Synoptic Gospels) in the Pharisaic sense of Halakah or observance.

b The reply of Jesus takes the form of a counter-charge, pressed home in **8** and then illustrated by a concrete example (9–13); the whole section is then rounded off by an explanation of the true nature of defilement (14–23). The quotation from Isa. 29:13 is close to LXX, and some scholars think it may be due to the evangelist. Other sayings in this section may have been originally independent and brought together here by Mk for topical reasons (Grant notes that the need of the disciples for further instruction is 'a regular device of Mark for the introduction of additional teaching on a subject'), but while 18–19 and 20–3 may reflect early Christian interpretation, there can be no reasonable doubt that 9–13 were spoken by Jesus and illustrate his attitude to the oral law (Taylor). So also Taylor considers 15 'unquestionably genuine'.

The Rabbinic law as codified in the Mishnah here agrees with the attitude of Jesus, but this may be the result of later relaxation. Rawlinson suggests that Jesus may be referring to an actual case. It should be noted that while Jesus rejects the oral tradition (11–13) he explicitly accepts the Decalogue as binding (10; cf. 10:3). The law (Dt. 5:16; Exod. 20:12, 21:17; cf. Lev. 20:9) lays down the duty of honouring and caring for parents, but according to the scribal tradition a vow dedicating to the Temple what they might have gained for their support took precedence. This Jesus denounces as a tradition of men which conflicts with the will of God. The example moreover is only one of many.

c **14-23.** The important point here is the statement of principle, that nothing outward can defile; uncleanness comes from within. Ultimately, this implies the abrogation of the distinction between clean and unclean meats, although it is doubtful if Jesus would have countenanced a rejection by his disciples of the laws of Lev. 11. Certainly the disciples did not understand (17f.), nor did Peter, as Turner observes, 703c as late as the conversion of Cornelius. In view of the controversy in the early Church on these questions (e.g. Gal. 2:11ff.; Rom. 14; 1 C. 8, etc.), it may be doubted whether Jesus explicitly drew out the implications of his saying; in this case the applications (18*b*–19, 20–3) are the result of later reflection. The list of vices can be paralleled from Gal. 5:19–21 and similar passages; such lists were commonplace in Hellenistic popular philosophy, and were adapted by the Jews for their own purposes. Most commentators take 'envy' (22, lit. 'an evil eye') as referring to a jealous or grudging disposition, but Turner holds that it refers to 'the wide-spread superstition of the evil eye'; if there is no trace in Judaism of this superstition (Grant), Mk's Roman readers would have found no difficulty.

VII 24-X 52 Beyond the Bounds of Galilee— d Apart from the account in 9:30–50 of a journey through Galilee, this whole section is concerned with events which take place beyond Herod's jurisdiction, and it has been thought that Jesus went into retirement because the suspicion of the tetrarch had now been aroused against him. On the other hand Mk does not suggest that this was a flight, but only that Jesus was seeking privacy (24). (T. W. Manson, *The Servant Messiah* (1956), 71, suggests that it was a flight, not from the menace of Herod or the Pharisees but from the misguided enthusiasm of his friends.) As the disciples are not mentioned until 8:1, when Jesus is apparently back in the Decapolis, it would seem that the retiral was not intended for the training of the twelve (in Mt. 15:21ff. they are present). See further Taylor, 632ff.

24-30. The purpose of Jesus is however frustrated: a e woman (described as a Greek, i.e. a Gentile (cf. Gal. 2:3) by religion, and a Syro-Phoenician by race) hears of him and comes to seek healing for her child. The reply of Jesus seems harsh, but the Greek word refers to household dogs or puppies. The word 'first' in 27 has suggested Pauline influence to some scholars, but Taylor is probably right in suggesting a tension in the mind of Jesus concerning the scope of his ministry (cf. Mt. 15:24); the woman's prompt response, catching up his words, and her persistence win from Jesus his approval and the assurance that her desire is fulfilled. In Mt. (15:28) her request is granted because of her faith (cf. Mt. 8:13, in the only other story of a healing at a distance). Since cures in Mk are normally wrought by contact or by a commanding word, Taylor suggests the alternative explanation of supernatural knowledge. Richardson finds here 'the Pauline conception of the divine economy of salvation in story-form' (cf. Rom. 1:16, 10:12 and see *The Miracle Stories of the Gospels* (1941), 78f.).

31-37. The route described is circuitous and uncertain f (Taylor); Blunt declares the geography impossible. It may be that Jesus was still avoiding the territory of Antipas (Burkitt, Turner). Wellhausen conjectured 'Bethsaida' for 'Sidon', but while Taylor is inclined to accept this others reject it as unproved or unnecessary. The miracle which follows is peculiar to Mk. Wood suggests that Mt. omits it because the method (cf. 8:23) savours of magic, but Mt. 15:29–31 shows knowledge of it (Taylor). Grant (IB, vii, 757) gives extensive references to parallels in Jewish and pagan sources; cf. the cures attributed to Vespasian (Tacitus, Hist., iv, 81), also Jn 9:1–7.

As in 8:23, Jesus takes the man aside and seeks to avoid publicity; Turner notes that 'as the Ministry draws to its close, miracles become less and less an outstanding feature . . . Their significance belongs rather to the earliest stage'. **32.** The rare word *mogilalos* occurs in Isa. 35:6 LXX, where it means 'dumb'; this meaning would suit 37 and is favoured by Turner, but 35 suggests that the man was not dumb but stammered.

VIII 1-10 The Feeding of the Four Thousand— 704a The striking parallelism between 8:1–26 and 6:30–7:37

704a has often been observed, but it is not enough to say that this whole section is simply a doublet of the other: there are differences as well as similarities. Both the narratives of feeding are followed by a crossing of the lake, a controversy with the Pharisees, and a healing miracle, but the subject of controversy is different in each case, and the healings are also different, while 7:24–30 and 8:14–21 have nothing in common except the reference to bread. On the other hand, the perplexity of the disciples in 4 is strange if the previous feeding had taken place, and many scholars therefore feel that the two accounts of feeding at any rate are doublets. W. L. Knox argued from the language that 6:30 ff. is the Semitic, 8:1–9 the hellenised, version. For detailed discussion see Taylor, 628ff., where it is noted (after Weiss) that the same sequence of events lies behind Jn 6. Turner observes (*a*) that while all four Gospels record the first feeding, the second appears only in Mk and Mt. (the whole section is however part of one of Lk.'s major omissions); (*b*) the two accounts are suspiciously similar; (*c*) while the first is full of dramatic touches, the second is bare by comparison; (*d*) the introductory phrase in 8:1 'almost suggests the advent of intrusive material'.

Here, perhaps more than anywhere else in the Gospels, it is essential to distinguish between the scholar's question of the historical basis of the narrative and the evangelist's purpose in recording the incident. 'Mk, knowing a second version of this story, seems to have regarded it as a distinct event, and inserted it at this point, perhaps to show that Jesus did for the Gentiles what He had previously done for the Jews. If so, this is symbolically suggestive, and historically inaccurate' (Wood). Richardson (*Miracle Stories*, 88) finds the explanation of the whole section, 6:30–8:30, in the theological symbolism of the stories: the Blind Man of Bethsaida (8:22–6) is symbolic of the gradual opening of the eyes of the disciples. While this explains the evangelist's purpose, it does not mean that the stories have no historical foundation; rather should we say (with Taylor, 96) that the basis is historical but the narratives have been adapted for catechetical purposes. Both the stories of feeding then describe the same event, but Mk has used the second as a sign to the Gentiles, the first as a sign to the Jews. **8.** The word used for 'baskets' is different from that in 6:43 (they are distinguished again in 19–20); in Ac. 9:25 this word is used for a basket large enough to hold a man. **10.** The identity of Dalmanutha is unknown; the variants may be assimilations to Mt. 15:39.

b **11-13 The Demand for a Sign**—What the Pharisees sought was some token to attest the authority of Jesus (cf. 11:28), a miracle that would convince them. The word here rendered 'test' is translated 'tempt' in 1:13: the old temptation once more rears its head (cf. Mt. 4:5–7). 'The story reflects sound tradition in that it records the refusal of Jesus to accept the test of signs as a proof of his commission' (Taylor). Lk. adds 'except the sign of Jonah' (11:29; cf. Mt. 12:39). Only Mk refers to the emotion of Jesus.

14-21 The Leaven of the Pharisees—This paragraph is difficult, and many scholars think it composed by Mk. Certainly if 1–9 is a doublet of 6:30 ff. then 19–20 must be due to the evangelist; but **15** is undoubtedly genuine. Lk. (12:1) has it in a different context and interprets 'the leaven' as referring to the hypocrisy of the Pharisees, while Mt. (16:12) understands it of their teaching; Mk gives no interpretation, but 'leaven' is used by the Rabbis of an evil disposition (Taylor), and this would fit here. The saying is ignored in the rest of the narrative. The fault of the disciples is twofold: anxiety about bread (cf. Mt. 6:25ff.), and failure to perceive the significance of the feeding-miracles. It may be that 15 should be interpreted in the light of 11–13, as a warning against the wilful blindness that refuses to see the truth. Grant, following P45, etc., prefers the reading 'the Herodians'
but Taylor thinks it a correction influenced by 3:6 70
and 12:13.

22-26 The Blind Man of Bethsaida—The story is c
strikingly parallel to 7:32–7, and has been thought a doublet; but there are also differences. Mt. and Lk. both omit, perhaps because the gradual character of the healing seemed to detract from the power of Jesus. Some commentators refer to a Greek parallel, in which a blind man saw a vision: the god Asclepius forced open his eyes with his fingers, and the first thing he saw was the trees in the temple precinct. As before, Jesus takes the man aside, the method is the same, and again he forbids the man to tell the tale. RSV here follows the WH 'Neutral' text, but the 'Western' reading ('Tell no-one in the village') is strongly supported and Turner claims the case for its originality is unanswerable.

27-30 Caesarea Philippi: Peter's Confession— d
This passage is the climax of the first half of the Gospel; from this point the teaching of Jesus is addressed more exclusively to the disciples, and prophecies of the Passion figure prominently. Some scholars treat the story as a turning-point, and suggest that in Galilee Jesus hoped to convert the people to his own way of thinking; the knowledge that he must suffer came only later, when he found that conventional Messianic ideas were too firmly embedded to be changed. Certainly there is a contrast between the 'Galilean summer' and the more sombre tone of the later chapters (Daniel-Rops contrasts the smiling pastoral land of Galilee with the grim and barren uplands of Judaea), but this interpretation may owe too much to modern psychology. If the story of the Baptism does contain an allusion to Isa. 42:1 (cf. on 1:11), then Jesus may have envisaged the possibility of his rejection by his people from the first. If the injunctions to silence are rightly interpreted as due to a desire to avoid misunderstanding about his Messiahship, he may well have understood his mission in terms of the Suffering Servant from the outset; nor is this necessarily inconsistent with a hope of the conversion of Israel. At any rate, Caesarea Philippi marks a crisis: if the Twelve had penetrated no more deeply into his secret than the mass of the people, then he must have stayed his advance. Caesarea Philippi, the ancient Paneas, on the slopes of Hermon, was rebuilt by Herod Philip, whose name it bears to distinguish it from Caesarea on the coast, the seat of the Roman government. The answer given by the disciples to the first question recalls 6:14ff. Taylor notes the remarkable fact that despite the cries of the demoniacs (1:24, etc.) popular opinion does not hold Jesus to be the Messiah. **29** puts the decisive question, already prepared for in the first. Peter's reply is 'a profound act of faith' (Grant), although as the sequel shows he still shared the popular conception of the Messiah. The title 'Christ' occurs here for the first time in the Gospel (in 1:1 it is a proper name). The story should not be understood as if the disciples had never thought of this before. They had been with Jesus for some months, nor would they have followed him at first without some sense of his greatness; but 'what had been inchoate and provisional now became definite and irreversible' (Taylor). The charge to tell no-one is due once more to the danger of misunderstanding, all the greater now.

31-33. Blunt notes that from 27 on a change comes e
over Mk's narrative: hitherto the story has been apparently aimless, but now purpose and tragedy enter into it. The Son of Man in Dan. and 1 Enoch is a glorious and triumphant figure, but the teaching here combines this concept with that of the Suffering Servant. At one time it was thought that much in the prophecies of the Passion was *vaticinium ex eventu*, due to reflection by the early Church upon the Crucifixion, but scholars are now much more inclined to trace this combination of ideas to the mind of Jesus himself (cf. Hoskyns and Davey, *Riddle of the NT* (1936); Manson, *Jesus the Messiah* (1943)). It is certainly

4e probable that Jesus made several attempts to convey this completely new idea to the disciples, although it may have been in less explicit terms ; but Turner aptly observes that if the prophecy had been put into the mouth of Jesus by the disciples later we should have inevitably found the word 'crucified'. For Peter the very idea was intolerable : not yet did he fully understand. The associations with the temptation narrative in Q should be noted—hence the severity of the rebuke.

f **34-38.** A group of sayings stressing **the obligations of discipleship :** self-denial, obedience even to death, and loyalty (34). **35-7** are eschatological, and lay before the reader the ultimate issues : what is the supreme aim in life ? In **38** some scholars feel that Jesus distinguishes the Son of Man from himself, and suggest that he speaks of the Elect Community of Dan. 7, of which he is the head ; in this case the saying belongs to an earlier period (Taylor). A similar saying, perhaps in more primitive form, occurs in Q (Lk. 12:8–9 = Mt. 10:32–3). Commentators often note the direct relevance of these sayings for a Church in the fires of persecution. The reference to cross-bearing need not have alluded originally to the Crucifixion, although Mk no doubt so understood it ; nor is it merely a stoic endurance of the ills to which the flesh is heir.

IX 1 may be the introduction to the Transfiguration story, or the conclusion of the present section. Certainly Mk seems to have seen 'at least a partial fulfilment' in the Transfiguration (Taylor). Dodd argues for the translation 'has come with power', but this (realised eschatology) has not found general acceptance. The early Church expected the Second Advent within their own lifetime.

5a **2-8 The Transfiguration**—The mountain is traditionally identified with Tabor (1,000 ft. above the plain), but modern commentators prefer to think of Hermon (9,200 ft.). Both suggestions are however conjectural. Moses and Elijah represent the Law and the Prophets : their very presence is a sign that Jesus is Messiah, and this is probably the primary significance of the Marcan narrative (Taylor). Lk. adds that they spoke of his *exodus*, which he was about to accomplish at Jerusalem. Elijah is associated with the coming of the Messiah from the time of Mal. 4:5f., but evidence for a belief in the return of Moses is late, although Boobyer (*St Mark and the Transfiguration Story* (1942), 70) points out that it was current among the Samaritans. Moreover Dt. 18:15 appears to have been an important text for the sect of the Dead Sea Scrolls.

The precise form of the experience is difficult to determine, but the important thing is the revelation ; the details must remain matters of speculation. Modern scholars have interpreted the story as (*a*) a piece of symbolic writing to affirm the Messiahship of Jesus ; (*b*) a historical experience of a visionary character ; or (*c*) originally a resurrection-story which has been misplaced (see Boobyer, op. cit. ; Taylor, 386ff. for details). (*c*) is open to serious objections, and Dodd (*Studies in the Gospels*, ed. Nineham (1955), 25) declares on the basis of form-critical study that the Transfiguration story 'contrasts with the general type of post-resurrection narrative in almost every particular'. The weakness of (*a*) again is its failure to recognise any historical basis for the story (Taylor). There is most to be said for (*b*) and indeed Mt. already speaks of a vision (17:9), but allowance must be made for elaboration of detail as a result of later Christian reflection.

Mk certainly saw here a divine confirmation of the Messiahship of Jesus (Boobyer, 17f.), although opinions vary as to whether any further significance was found by him in the story. **5.** Peter's proposal is probably best understood as a desire to prolong the experience (Wood suggests that the excuse (6) is a genuine reminiscence from Peter himself). Turner (JTS 27 (1926), 121) notes that where Peter puts Jesus still on the same level as Moses and Elijah, the Voice marks the uniqueness of the Son. The cloud occurs 705a
as the symbol of the divine presence in the theophanies of the Exodus and at the dedication of the first Temple ; it was expected to reappear in Messianic times (2 Mac. 2:8). In NT it is connected with the Transfiguration, the Ascension and the Parousia (Swete). Mk appears to think of it as the vehicle of God's presence, the abode of his glory, from which he speaks (Taylor). The voice from the cloud echoes the words spoken at the Baptism (1:11), with the addition of 'listen to him' from Dt. 18:15 : the Prophet like unto Moses is identified with the Christ the beloved Son (Swete).

9-13 Elijah—The difficulty here lies in the question, b
12b, 'How is it written of the Son of Man . . . ?' which seems at variance with the context. Attempts have been made to rearrange the verses, but none are entirely satisfactory, and Taylor and others think them unnecessary (see *Jesus and His Sacrifice* (1937), 91ff.). Jesus as often replies to a question with a counter-question to bring out the really important issue : the suffering of the Son of Man. Another possibility is that Mk has momentarily reverted to indirect speech, and that 12*b* should be read as a statement, not a question ('he told them how it is written . . .'). In any case the reference is to Isa. 53 and similar passages (cf. Lk. 24:26–7). The question about Elijah is perfectly natural ; if Jesus is the Christ (8:29, 9:2–7), what of the expected forerunner ? (It is of interest here that the people held *Jesus* to be Elijah, 8:28.) Jesus first reaffirms the expectation (12*a*) and then (13) identifies Elijah with John the Baptist. **13.** The last clause is obscure, but may refer to 1 Kg. 19:2, 10 or to the traditions underlying Rev. 11.

14-29 The Epileptic Boy—Wood and Grant refer to c
Raphael's painting which reproduces Mk's contrast between Jesus seen in glory on the mountain and the disciples in the valley below. Mk and Lk. abbreviate drastically, and thereby lose 'genuine and valuable material (esp. 23f.)' (Wood). Some commentators explain the amazement of the crowd by suggesting that something of the glory of the Transfiguration was still to be seen on the face of Jesus, but Taylor observes that the objections of Swete are strong and that the situation in Exod. 34:29f., is different. The alternative is to explain the amazement as due simply to the sudden and unexpected appearance of Jesus. Wood thinks Weiss justified in citing 10:32 as the best parallel : 'Throughout this section, the very presence of Jesus evokes awe and wonder. Men are conscious of his dedication unto death.'

16. The question of Jesus is answered by one of the crowd, who explains that he has brought his epileptic son to the disciples in hope of a cure. Grant notes the 'tragic brevity' of the final words 'and they could not' (18, AV). Something still was lacking, and Jesus in his reply lays his finger on the weakness. The words impressively suggest his loneliness and isolation, his sense of the thanklessness of his task in the face of a world of unbelief. Wood cites Lk. 12:50, while Taylor refers to Mk 6:6, 8:12 and notes that in view of Jesus' expectation of death the saying is relevant to the situation. Mt. and Lk. omit the conversation with the father (21–4), perhaps simply for the sake of brevity, but possibly to avoid representing Jesus as seeking information (21) or because of the suggestion of doubt (22) ; in their accounts the cure immediately follows, but the vividness of Mk is wanting. The reply of Jesus seizes upon the doubt : 'If thou canst !' (RV is here 'more correct and more vivid' than AV (Wood) ; so too RSV). As so often in Mk, he once more emphasises the power of faith (cf. 5:34, 36, 11:23f. and see Cranfield in SJTh 3 (1950), 64). The father's response is on the surface inconsistent, yet is it realistic, at once a confession and an appeal ; but small though it be, his faith is enough (cf. Lk. 17:6). The close of the story recalls the healing of Jairus' daughter, but is not necessarily suggested by it (Wood). The question of the disciples is natural after their failure to effect the cure, but the reply is at first sight

706c surprising, since prayer is not mentioned in the story. Grant however sees here ' an authentic record of Jesus' own view ' : ' by prayer ' means ' a life of intimacy with God through personal communion '. The words ' and fasting ' are wanting in the best MSS, although some scholars favour their retention.

d **30-32 The Second Prediction of the Passion**—Some scholars think Jesus is still avoiding the attentions of Herod, and Turner suggests that the visits to Jerusalem of Jn 7:14 and 10:22 should perhaps be fitted into this period. In Mk however the desire for privacy is explained by Jesus' purpose to give further instruction to the disciples. The prophecy is briefer than 8:31, and slightly different ; in particular it refers to the ' delivering up ' of the Son of Man for the first time. This has been taken as an allusion to the treachery of Judas, but more probably refers to this ' delivering up ' as part of the counsel of God (cf. Ac. 2:23 ; Rom. 8:32). The failure of the disciples to understand is due to the revolutionary character of the prophecy ; they are still thinking in terms of the conventional Messianic expectation (cf. 34).

e **33-50**. Mk evidently intended this section as an illustration of the teaching given in private to the Twelve (Grant notes that 9:33–10:45 ' contains a whole series of discipleship sayings '), but it is not a connected discourse. Either Mk has drawn upon a sayings-source (Taylor) or he has himself ' strung together utterances and incidents belonging to different occasions ' (Wood) ; in either case the links are provided by catchwords (e.g. ' stumble ' (42ff.), ' fire ' (48f.), ' salt ' (50)). A special problem arises from the variety of forms in which some of these sayings are found in the four Gospels (cf. Dodd in NTS 2 (1956), 75ff.).

33-35 The Dispute among the Disciples shows how far they were from understanding the mind of Jesus, who seeks to correct their ambition by explaining the nature of true greatness, a theme further elaborated in 10:42ff. The connection of **36-7** with the preceding verses is obscure, since they do not continue the lesson. The Aramaic *ṭalyā'* however means ' child ' or ' servant ' (Black), and it may be that this key-word is the link. Turner observes that 9:37 would be more appropriate at 10:15, and 10:15 here ; the occurrence of the unusual word rendered ' taking them in his arms ' in both places suggests that there may have been some confusion. This vivid word occurs in Mk alone.

38-40. The story is linked to the previous verse and to 41 by the phrase ' in my name '. This is ' the only occasion in Mk where John is named alone, and significant of his surname as " a son of thunder " ' (Turner, cf. 3:17). The historicity of the story has been questioned on the ground that such exorcisms are unlikely in the lifetime of Jesus, but if he exercised the authority over demons described by Mk it is probable that some did try to use his name (cf. Ac. 19:13 ; a magical text contains an adjuration by ' Jesus, god of the Hebrews ').

42-50. In Mt. 10:40–2 the sayings found here in 37 and 41 are more closely related, but it is also possible to link 37 and 42 (cf. Mt. 18:5f.) ; in this case 38–41 may have been inserted because of the catchphrase ' in my name ' (this does not however affect the authenticity of these sayings). In the passage as it stands the connection runs from receiving a child (37) to the humblest service rendered to a disciple (41), and then in contrast to a warning against offending the humblest believer (42) ; this in turn leads to a warning against offences affecting oneself. No sacrifice is too great if entry to the Kingdom is assured. ' Hell ' is literally Gehenna, the valley south-west of Jerusalem which had been defiled by Moloch-worship (cf. 2 Kg. 23:10 ; Jer. 7:31, etc.), and was now symbolic of the place of future punishment (1 Enoch 27:2). The description is taken from Isa. 66:24 (RSV omits 44 and 46, rightly, with the best MSS). Later ideas of eternal punishment should not be read into these words, but neither should their sternness be watered down. The sayings in **49f.** are difficult, but the combination of salt and fire suggests purification (Wood, Taylor) ; ' salt ' in 50 takes up ' salted ' in 49, and 50*b* refers back to 34. ' The contribution of the disciples to the health of the world depends on their own wholesomeness ' (Wood). The saying occurs in different contexts in Mt. and Lk. 706f

X 1-12 The Question of Divorce—Mark seems to indicate a journey through Peraea, not through Samaria, to Jerusalem ; he also notes a resumption of the public ministry. The question regarding the legality of divorce is an attempt either to bring Jesus into conflict with the Law or to compromise him in the eyes of Herod (cf. 6:17f.), and hence is described as putting him to the test (cf. 8:11, 12:13ff.). The Law allowed divorce for ' unseemliness ' (Dt. 24:1), but there was a debate between the school of Shammai, which limited ' unseemliness ' to adultery, and that of Hillel, which allowed divorce even upon quite trivial grounds (e.g. if the wife burnt the dinner, or the man found some other woman more attractive). Some scholars refer the issue to this debate (as in Mt.), but in Mk it seems to concern divorce itself ; certainly Jesus proceeds to raise the whole question to a higher level. The law of Dt. 24:1 was a concession to ' the hardness of your heart ', but he cites Gen. 1:27, 2:24 as revealing the purpose of God from the beginning, and draws the inference ' What God has joined together let not man put asunder '. Wood thinks the exception in Mt. 19:9 ' probably interprets the teaching of Jesus aright ', in which case he agreed with Shammai ; but on this two opinions are possible. Paul follows Mk (1 C. 7:10 ; cf. Rom. 7:2–3 ; but see also 1 C. 7:15). What is vital here is the ideal of marriage advanced by Jesus. His words should probably not be treated legalistically, as affirming the absolute indissolubility of marriage (the hardness of heart is still a fact), but they do set the standard for the Christian ; ' in particular cases they need to be interpreted under the guidance of the Spirit ' (Taylor). The further reply to the disciples (11–12) puts both sexes on the same level, in contrast to the Jewish law, which allowed divorce only to the man. **12** has been explained as due to conditions in the Gentile world, but Burkitt suggests that Jesus is referring to the case of Herodias (6:17f.). The interpretation of the passage is complicated by textual problems, on which see Taylor, 416ff. 707a

13-16 The Blessing of the Children—This story is justly celebrated for its simple beauty and vivid realism. As always, the children are brought to see the great man ; ' that he might touch them ' suggests the hope that they might receive his blessing (Taylor compares Gen. 48:14). The disciples endeavour to save Jesus from embarrassing attentions, but the Master is greater than his followers. ' Here only in the gospels is indignation ascribed to Jesus ' (Taylor)—another vivid detail peculiar to Mk. ' Apart from the gospels ' says Burkitt, ' I cannot find that early Christian literature exhibits the slightest sympathy towards the young ' ; nor is there any parallel in ancient literature as a whole. **15** would suit the context better at 9:33ff. (Turner), but there is no warrant for the change. b

17-31 Riches and Rewards—Wood refers to Shakespeare (*Richard II*, V. v. 10 ff.) as having caught the contrast between this section and the last. The man is ' a young man ' only in Mt., a ' ruler ' in Lk. ; Mk here is indefinite. On the other hand, Mt. and Lk. both compress, omitting vivid details (the man ' ran up ' and ' knelt ', Jesus ' looking upon him loved him ', the man's face fell—all are in Mk alone). Mt. indeed appears to have been shocked by 18, which he recasts. The verse has long been a problem (Taylor lists six explanations), but is probably best taken as ' the expression of that humility which was part of the moral perfection of Jesus ' (Wood). As Grant says, ' Jesus has the natural attitude toward God of every pious and devout Jew '. The reference to the law (19) is notable as indicating Jesus' respect for the Law as a guide to conduct, although the c

706c sequel shows its ultimate inadequacy. 'Defraud not' (Mk only) is omitted by some important MSS, but is 'quite certainly genuine' (Turner; Grant compares Jas 5:4; Lev. 19:13; Dt. 24:14). The 'counsel of perfection' (21) should not be generalised; this was the crucial test in this particular case, but the barrier in other cases may be different. For the influence of this saying cf. Sabatier, *Life of St Francis*, 75, and Kirk, *The Vision of God*, 180 (Taylor). In the following verses Jesus drives home the lesson of the incident. The Western text reverses 24 and 25, enhancing the vividness of the detail and producing an argument in two stages, applied first to the rich, then to all. This would explain the increasing astonishment of the disciples, but some scholars think it too logical and due to the effort to smooth away difficulties. The saying about the eye of a needle should not be weakened by taking the 'camel' as a cable or the 'needle's eye' as a postern gate; the saying is a vivid hyperbole to express what is humanly impossible (cf. 26–7). The whole passage contains in germ Paul's doctrine concerning the law. Notable also is the identification of 'eternal life' (17), 'salvation' (26), and 'the kingdom of God' (23); cf. the Fourth Gospel. Peter's remark is probably not due to complacency, but is half a question: What shall we have? (explicitly so in Mt.). In reply Jesus gives a firm assurance, but it is not a 'purely rose-coloured prospect' that he holds out: 'besides the common love there will also be common sufferings' (Turner).

d **32-45 The Third Prediction of the Passion**—This passage introduces the final stage of the journey to Jerusalem: 'The goal of the journey is now disclosed, and there is to be no more delay' (Wood). This prediction (33f.) is the most detailed of the three, and corresponds most closely with the Passion story (cf. Taylor: 'In its precision the third is a *vaticinium ex eventu*'); but even yet there is no reference to crucifixion. It is still probable that Jesus often spoke of his approaching death, although the details may be coloured by knowledge of the events. The awe and amazement of the disciples probably reflect their sense of something imminent, but not yet understood. Their failure to comprehend is illustrated in **35-41,** where James and John attempt to forestall the others by claiming the places of honour. **39** has been thought to indicate that the disciples expected a brief period of trial, but is more probably the confident reply of men who had no real understanding of what lay ahead (cf. 14:29). A tradition ascribed to Papias says John, like James (Ac. 12:2), was martyred early in the history of the Church, but on this question scholars are divided (see Taylor, 442); it is doubtful how far this saying can be taken to confirm the tradition. Notable is the use of the cup (cf. 14:24, 36) and of baptism (cf. Lk. 12:50) as symbolic of Messianic suffering. Mt. (20:20 ff.) spares the two disciples; Lk. omits the whole story. The reaction of the other disciples is inevitably indignation (41), and this leads to a discussion of true greatness, culminating in the 'ransom' saying, 'one of the most important in the Gospels' (Taylor). This saying has been questioned as due to Pauline influence but, as Taylor justly says, Paulinism is rooted in primitive Christianity. 'Paul was not the earliest Paulinist' (Wood). In fact, the terminology is not Pauline, and the saying is best interpreted by Isa. 53:11f. The example of the Son of Man sets the true pattern for his followers: greatness is measured by service. For 'ransom' see Morris, *The Apostolic Preaching of the Cross* (1955).

e **46-52 Bartimaeus**—The story is notable for the persistence of the blind man, despite the rebuke of the passers-by, and for the use of the title 'Son of David' (here only in Mk as a form of address, although mentioned by Jesus himself in 12:35). Wood notes that from this point Jesus no longer enjoins silence: 'The appeal of the beggar is not rebuked like the confession of the demoniacs.' The name Bartimaeus, like the detail in 50 ('throwing off his mantle', etc.), 706e
is peculiar to Mk.

XI 1-10 The Triumphal Entry—Here begins a new 707a
section of the Gospel, narrating the work of Jesus in Jerusalem. Mk gives no indication that Jesus had been in Jerusalem before, but (*a*) the Fourth Gospel mentions a number of previous visits; (*b*) certain sayings in the Synoptic tradition imply a longer or more frequent ministry in the city than these Gospels now record (e.g. Mt. 23:37; Lk. 13:34); (*c*) Jesus had friends in the city (cf. Branscomb, 193ff.). Burkitt conjectured that the Entry took place at the Feast of Dedication (December), but T. W. Manson objects that this would be the most unlikely time of the year for the fig-tree to offer any promise of fruit. Many scholars however feel that Mk has compressed into a single week the events of a longer period.

The significance of the Entry has been variously estimated (e.g. the suggestion that a spontaneous outburst of acclamation was later reinterpreted in a Messianic sense; for the theories see Taylor, 451f.), but certain facts are clear: Jesus acted in deliberate fulfilment of Zech. 9:9, thereby not only laying claim to the homage of the people but also revealing the character of his own conception of Messiahship. It was this disappointment of their hopes which turned the crowd against him; there is no need for the suggestion that this was a crowd of Galilean pilgrims, and that the crowd which demanded the crucifixion was Judaean. Whether **9f.** (Ps. 118:26 with an added comment) was a Messianic greeting is more doubtful; Mt. 21:10f. seems to suggest that the people did not regard Jesus as Messiah. In its original context the verse invokes a blessing upon the pilgrim approaching the holy city for a festival, but as Turner notes it is specially appropriate here. If there *has* been reinterpretation here it has only revealed the true significance of the event; of the historical worth of the narrative there can be no question. 'The Lord' (3) could mean merely 'the owner', although Mk probably read more into it; the word is used of Jesus only here in Mk. The fact that the colt is unbroken characterises it as 'in some sense sacred' (Taylor cites Num. 19:2; Dt. 21:3; Turner adds Lk. 23:53). On 7f. Turner compares 2 Kg. 9:13; 1 Mac. 13:51. Blunt observes that it must have been a grievous disappointment to the crowd that Jesus ended such an entry with an anticlimax (11); in Mt. and Lk. the Cleansing follows immediately, but in Mk it is a day later.

12-14 The Cursing of the Barren Fig-tree—The b
story is difficult, but the objections raised against it are not all equally cogent (Taylor); the strongest is that the action is not worthy of Jesus. Some scholars take it as symbolic of the rejection of Israel, or as an acted parable, but the simplest explanation is that the parable of Lk. 13:6–9 has been transformed into a miracle story. Swete emphasises that it is not mere fruitlessness that is condemned, but fruitlessness in the midst of a display that promises fruit. Manson (BJRL 33 (1951), 278) notes that only the last clause of 13 fixes the incident at a time which makes nonsense of the story, and suggests that it occurred at the Feast of Tabernacles. Cf. also Richardson, *The Miracle Stories of the Gospels*, 55ff. Bishop (*Jesus of Palestine* (1955), 217) tells of a fig-tree bearing fruit on Good Friday.

15-19 The Cleansing of the Temple—To Hunter, c
this is the second of three great acts of Messianic symbolism, the first being the Triumphal Entry, the third the Breaking of the Loaf at the Last Supper. Lightfoot also (*The Gospel Message of St Mark* (1952), 60 ff.) finds a vital connection between the Entry, the Cleansing and the Passion. The story is told by Jn at the beginning of the Ministry, but is more appropriate in the context of the last days; Cullmann (*Early Christian Worship* (1953), 71ff.) suggests that Jn brought it forward for dramatic effect. There are however objections to the Marcan dating (cf. Taylor,

707c 461ff.). T. W. Manson (BJRL 33 (1951), 271 ff.; *The Servant Messiah* (1956), 78f.) thinks a good case can be made out for placing the Cleansing at the Feast of Tabernacles.

The market existed for the convenience of pilgrims, who had to buy victims for the sacrifice and also change their Greek or Roman money into the Jewish coinage in which alone the Temple dues could be paid. There was probably scope for extensive corruption, but the cleansing is not merely the indignant act of a reformer; it is a fulfilment of Mal. 3:1ff. The traffic took place in the court of the Gentiles, to which alone the Gentiles had access (only Mk completes the quotation in 17); moreover the protest is not only against priestly abuse, but also against popular irreverence (16—also peculiar to Mk). The use of the Temple court as a short-cut is forbidden in the Mishnah (Danby, 10). Taylor is doubtful how far Jesus intended to make a Messianic claim, except for those with eyes to see, but Lightfoot sees here 'the great act of the Lord as the Messianic king on his arrival at his Father's house', and 'a sign that the kingdom of God is already at the doors'. There is a real significance in the association of this event with the story of the Barren Fig-tree, whether the latter be taken as a parable or a miracle. The sequel is a plot against the life of Jesus (18), for the moment frustrated because he was still too popular.

d **20-25.** The sequel to the story of the fig-tree leads to a group of sayings about faith, prayer, and forgiveness which may have been originally independent (cf. Mt. 17:20; Lk. 17:6), since the lesson does not seem to follow from the incident. This does not of course affect the historical character of the sayings, which are undoubtedly genuine. **25** seems to show knowledge of the Lord's Prayer (cf. Mt. 6:14f., 18:35); here only in Mk does the phrase 'your Father who is in heaven' occur. **26** is rightly omitted as an addition from Mt. 6:15. The reference to removing mountains is metaphorical, emphasising the power of faith.

708a **27-33 The Question of Authority**—This is the first clash with the authorities in Jerusalem, who in the Passion Story are the chief opponents of Jesus (14:43, 53, 15:1; cf. 8:31); here probably a deputation is meant. The question put to Jesus concerns his authority, and probably arises from the Cleansing of the Temple. As often (e.g. 10:3, 12:16), Jesus answers with a counter-question, not to evade the issue but raising the fundamental point: 'If John's mission was from God, he had pointed to Jesus as the greater than himself for whom his work was but a preparation' (Turner). The question leaves the deputation in a dilemma (31f.), but carries a veiled claim that in fact he is the Messiah; like that of John, his authority is 'from heaven'.

b **XII 1-12 The Parable of the Wicked Husbandmen**—The Vineyard is a familiar OT metaphor for Israel (cf. especially Isa. 5:1f. LXX), and the story 'implies that Jesus felt himself to be God's last appeal to His people, and also thought their rejection of him would issue in his becoming the foundation of a new community which should inherit God's kingdom' (Wood). The authenticity of the parable has been questioned, on the ground that it is really an allegory and quite unlike the parables of ch. 4 (so for example Grant), but even among those who hold this view many see in it a nucleus of authentic words of Jesus. On the other hand the narrative is not pure allegory (Taylor), and the murder of the son (suspect as reflecting the theology of the early Church) 'betrays no reminiscences of the manner of the death of Jesus' (Dodd, *Parables of the Kingdom* (1936), 130). It may be that there has been some expansion (e.g. in the addition of the quotation of Ps. 118:22-3, also cited in Ac. 4:11; 1 Pet. 2:7; but cf. Taylor, 477), but it seems better to take the story as a whole as an authentic utterance of Jesus, reflecting the troubled conditions of the period. The parable 'stands on its own feet as a dramatic story, inviting a judgment from the hearers, and the application of the judgment is clear enough without any allegorizing of the details' (Dodd). Such elaboration as has taken place only serves to draw out the meaning more explicitly. **9.** Dodd quotes from Cicero the case of Marcus Brutus, who collected a debt from the corporation of Salamis by employing troops to besiege the town-council until five members died of starvation. **7** recalls Gen. 37:20. 708b

c **13-17 The Question of the Tribute Money**—As in 3:6, the Pharisees are associated with the Herodians. Wood suggests that perhaps they represent the two horns of the dilemma by which they try to catch Jesus. The question raised was a burning issue throughout the period up to the Jewish war, not so much because of the burden of the tax as because of its significance. It was paid directly into the emperor's treasury, and the coinage used was stamped with the name and image of the emperor, so that on both accounts it symbolised subjection. A significant point, which Lk. omits, is that the coin had to be fetched; either both Jesus and his opponents possessed no silver money (6:8 refers to copper) or they refused to use the pagan coinage (cf. Exod. 20:4). The delegation begins with flattery, but the trap is almost immediately sprung: 'Is it lawful to pay tribute to Caesar or not?' For Jesus to answer in the negative would embroil him with the Romans, while approval would incur the hostility of every patriotic Jew. The final answer (17) is not an evasion, nor is it a complete solution of the problems of Church and State, but it does lay down a fundamental principle: 'Jesus held that the claims of God are all-embracing (cf. Mk 12:29f.), but he does recognise that obligations due to the State are within the divine order' (Taylor). Loyalty to the emperor need not be inconsistent with loyalty to God although, as can be seen from 'the virulent hatred of Rome that runs through the Revelation of John' (Dodd (Moffatt Commentary), *Romans*, 201), there was to be a time when the two came into conflict.

d **18-27 The Question of the Resurrection**—The next attack comes from a different quarter. The Sadducees (here only in Mk) were the priestly aristocracy, and theologically conservative; they rejected such new developments as the doctrine of immortality, belief in angels and spirits (cf. Ac. 23:8), and predestination, all of which were held by the Pharisees. The problem propounded is an attempt to reduce to absurdity the doctrine of the resurrection by the use of a purely hypothetical example, possibly a stock argument against the Pharisees. The Levirate law (Dt. 25:5ff.; Ru. 1:11ff.; Boaz in Ru. 4 acted not as *Levir* (brother-in-law) but as *Gō'ēl* (kinsman)) was intended to ensure the continuance of the family; if literally fulfilled, it seemed to raise difficulties for belief in resurrection. Jesus in reply declares that the Sadducees are completely mistaken in assuming that the future life is merely a continuation of the present; it is in fact a different order of existence (cf. 1 C. 15:35ff.). In **26f.** Rabbinic methods of exegesis are applied to Exod. 3:6 to produce a positive argument; though strange to modern ways of thinking, it nevertheless lays hold of 'probably the strongest of all arguments for immortality, not the nature of man but the character of God' (Grant). The Jewish (and Christian) belief in the resurrection of the body (not of the flesh) is quite distinct from Greek ideas of the immortality of the soul (cf. also 2 C. 5:1-4).

e **28-34 The Supreme Commandment**—In the parallels (Mt. 22:35; Lk. 10:25) the attitude of the lawyer is hostile, but of this there is no sign in Mk; on the contrary, Jesus commends the scribe (34). This is important as a reminder that not all the Pharisees were antagonistic. The question is one which was often discussed, but 'there was no real doubt as to the greater commandment. The *Shema'* (Dt. 6:4f.) was repeated daily by the Jews', and was the foundation text of their monotheism (Wood). The distinctive feature of the reply given by Jesus is that he added to it Lev. 19:18. Hillel is recorded to have summed up the Law in the negative form of

8e the 'Golden Rule', and Akiba later called Lev. 19:18 the greatest principle in the Torah, but there appears to be no evidence for the combination of the two texts by any teacher before the time of Jesus. 'Love to God finds its only adequate fulfilment in love to one's neighbour . . . Love to one's neighbour must be rooted in love of God' (Wood). The implications have been much discussed—according to Lk. the lawyer himself sought further explanation, and received in reply the parable of the Good Samaritan. For the impression made by this teaching on the mind of the early Church, Taylor compares Gal. 5:14; Rom. 13:9; Jas 2:8; cf. also 1 Jn *passim*. **34** seems to imply a kingdom already present (Wood), or at least within reach (Dodd); 'he is near the kingdom in the sense that he recognises the sovereignty of God and has the right moral and spiritual disposition as it is described in the Sermon on the Mount' (Taylor). Taylor notes as of outstanding importance the authority with which the statement is made: 'The speaker is the Lord, and not only the Teacher.'

f **35-37 Messiah and Son of David**—Against the view that these verses come from the early Christian community Taylor argues that the one speaker to whom they can be credibly assigned is Jesus himself. Here he takes the initiative, himself posing a problem: current opinion, with strong support in OT, held that the Messiah would be of the house of David, but the 'Messianic' Psalm 110 speaks of him as David's Lord, which seems to be inconsistent. The exact significance of the question is difficult to determine: it has been thought that Jesus is contesting the Davidic descent of the Messiah, with the implication that he himself was not of David's line, but such a rejection of the OT testimony would not have passed unnoticed and the implication itself is decisively refuted by the universal witness of the early Church (for references cf. Taylor, 491). More probably the question should be linked with Jesus' reinterpretation of Messiahship. His purpose here is to provoke reflection and 'expose the futility of Messianic hopes which do not rise above the earthly and human plane' (Taylor), or to substitute the 'transcendental' concept of the Messiah for the political (Grant). The Messiah is 'more than the heir of David's glory' (Wood). A special problem arises from the acceptance by Jesus of the traditional ascription of the Psalm to David (see Turner's discussion). Wood remarks that Jesus starts from the scholarship current at the time, and that his use of that scholarship does not bind his followers to acceptance of it today. Turner aptly observes that Docetic tendencies have always been the most serious danger to Christian thought. The verses in fact epitomise the mystery of the Incarnation: here is one who is more than a Son of David, yet subject to the limitations of his time. 37*b* introduces the next section.

g **38-40 A Warning against the Scribes**—The previous section criticised the teaching of the scribes as inadequate (35); now Jesus proceeds to condemn their practice. The sayings have been thought a summary of or an extract from the longer discourse in Q (Wood, Taylor), but Grant is doubtful. The first charge is one of vanity and ostentation, the last of hypocrisy; between comes that of devouring widows' houses (presumably by abuse of their hospitality, but Wood suggests the taking of rich fees for pious services, or the harsh pressing of the rights of creditors). Care for the widow and the fatherless is frequently enjoined in OT, as their oppression is condemned (cf. Exod. 22:22; Isa. 10:2). The scribes are charged with violation of the law they profess to expound, but cf. 28–34 above. Turner would take 40 as a separate sentence ('those among them who devour . . . they shall receive severer judgment'), saying it is the only way to make the Greek grammatical.

h **41-44 The Widow's Mites**—The reference to widows in 40 and the fact that the scene is laid in the Temple may have prompted Mk to place this story here; its authenticity has been questioned, but without sufficient reason. 'The treasury' seems to refer to 708h
the chests ranged against the wall in the Court of the Women for the offerings of the people. Turner remarks that if only copper coins were allowed in the Temple a large contribution would necessarily make a good deal of noise. By contrast, the poor widow contributed 'two copper coins', the proverbial 'widow's mites' which make a farthing (AV; 'a penny', RSV; Mk a quadrans, the quarter of an as, of which sixteen made a denarius). No offering could be more humble, but 'subscription lists are dangerous things at best' (Turner). What Jesus saw was not the money but its value in terms of devotion and of sacrifice: it was all she had (Luccock: her next meal). Hence she has put in 'more than all' (Turner suggests 'more than all of them together').

XIII The Apocalyptic Discourse—The first two 709a
verses contain a prophecy of the destruction of the Temple, uttered in response to the admiring exclamation of a disciple: not one stone will be left upon another. In this Jesus stands in line with the prophets (Mic. 3:12; Jer. 26:6, 18; cf. 9:11), nor can there be any doubt of the authenticity of the saying. It appears in one form or another in all four Gospels; it was the subject of a charge brought against him before Caiaphas (14:58); it was flung in his face at the Crucifixion (15:29); and it appears to underlie the story of Stephen (Ac. 6:14); (so Turner). Moreover Jos. (BJ, VI, iv, 5ff.) says the Temple was destroyed by fire, of which there is here no hint (Taylor).

The remainder of the chapter is more difficult to b
account for. Since 1864 it has been generally agreed that the discourse, the longest attributed to Jesus in this Gospel, is composite, and the theory that it is based on a 'little apocalypse' has been widely accepted (see Beasley-Murray, *Jesus and the Future* (1954); also Taylor, 498f., Grant, IB, vii, 853ff.); but Turner justly remarks 'It is quite impossible to believe that the anticipation of the triumphant return of Christ could have had such firm hold on the first Christian generation, if it had not had deep roots in our Lord's own teaching'. More recently Taylor (636ff.) has urged on the basis of a detailed analysis that 'the Evangelist has combined several groups of sayings, some of which contained apocalyptic elements, and has not simply edited a Jewish-Christian apocalypse' (but cf. Beasley-Murray, 106ff.).

3-4. The scene changes from the Temple court to the c
Mount of Olives, associated by Zech. (14:4) with the coming of the 'day of the Lord' and by popular expectation with the appearance of the Messiah. In later writings it is the scene of the post-resurrection discourses of Jesus. See James, *Apoc. NT* (1924); also the *Apocryphon Johannis* 20:5 (ed. Till, TU 60 (1955), 81). The question of the disciples relates first to the destruction of the Temple, but the 'sign' concerning which they ask is that which precedes the end of all things, as in apocalyptic literature. Jesus replies with a warning against false pretenders (5f., cf. 21f.), and then prophesies 'wars and rumours of wars', to be followed by earthquake and famine. These are common apocalyptic expectations, as the references quoted by Taylor show (cf. also the 'apocalypse' of 2 Th. 2:1–10); but the important point is the injunction against alarm in 7: these things must take place, but the end is not yet. This is but the beginning (8).

9-13 contain a warning of the persecution in store for d
the disciples, which again includes an injunction against anxiety: even when they are brought to trial for the faith it is to bear testimony, and they are assured of the presence of the Spirit (11). This section would of course have a special relevance for a Church beset by actual persecution, and it may be that the recollection of the words of Jesus has to some extent been coloured by Christian experience. A special problem concerns the reference to the preaching of the Gospel 'to all nations' in **10**, which seems to show that Jesus envisaged the Gentile mission; on the other

709d hand it is difficult to believe that the early Church would have been so reluctant to undertake such a mission had so definite a statement been current in the tradition. It may be, as Taylor suggests, that Mk 'truly represents the mind of Jesus but does not give his *ipsissima verba*'. The whole section is a call to steadfast endurance, for 'he who endures to the end will be saved'.

e **14-20**. The phrase 'desolating sacrilege' comes from Dan. (9:27, 11:31, 12:11), where it refers to the pagan altar erected in the Temple in 168 B.C. by Antiochus Epiphanes. Some commentators take the prophecy here to mean the attempt of Caligula in A.D. 40 to set up his own statue in the Temple, but this threat was averted by the emperor's assassination; others see here a reference to Anti-Christ. Jerome says Pilate placed in the Temple an image of the emperor, a statement which Eisler explains as a misunderstanding of Pilate's action in bringing the standards of the legions (which bore medallions of the emperor) into the Temple (A.D. 19). The simplest explanation seems to be that the phrase is an echo of Dan. in a prophecy of trials comparable to those of that former age. The parenthesis to the reader has suggested to some that a written document (the 'little apocalypse') underlies this section, but it may be an allusion to Dan. ('a clue to Christian eyes, but an enigma to others' (Taylor)). Turner thinks it 'simply asks the reader of the gospel to look beneath the surface, for what is said is less than what is meant' (cf. Rev. 13:18). The rest of the section is a vivid presentation of the crisis: immediate flight is the only resource, and the least delay may mean disaster. The reference to winter (18) has in view not cold but the heavy rains, which 'turn the wadis into impassable torrents and make flight from danger difficult, if not impossible' (Beasley-Murray, 60). 21–3 repeat the warning of 5f., and have been thought a doublet of the previous passage.

f **24-27**. The prophecy reaches its climax in a forecast of heavenly portents, to be followed by the parousia of the Son of Man and the gathering of the elect. The whole discourse is then rounded off by a parable (28f.) and a series of sayings on the general theme of watchfulness. As the budding fig-tree is a sure sign of summer, so the tribulations mentioned are signs of the impending end; but of the precise day and hour no man knows. The one thing vital is that the Christian should be ready; the discourse ends on the note with which it began.

g **30** and **32** in particular have caused difficulty, the latter because of its limitation of the knowledge of the Son, the former because the prediction so emphatically made was not fulfilled. The problem of 30, which may be reflected already in 2 Pet. 3:3, was among the issues raised by D. F. Strauss and hence, as Beasley-Murray shows, was a factor in the growth of the 'little apocalypse' theory; that of 32 became acute with the rise of Arianism, which 'deduced an essential difference between an all-knowing Father and a not all-knowing Son' (Turner). The further problem of reconciling the two verses, as Wood notes, is removed by the 'little apocalypse' theory, but there is an alternative solution: 'It is of the glory of the Incarnation' says Taylor, 'that Christ accepted those limitations of knowledge which are inseparable from a true humanity.' Space does not permit of detailed discussion of the critical problems, which would in any case be out of place here; reference must be made to the literature cited above. At the same time some conclusion appears to be called for. The arguments in favour of the 'little apocalypse' theory are not all equally cogent, and in particular the attempt to remove the eschatological element from the teaching of Jesus is without justification. On the other hand, the occurrence of certain sayings in a different context in other Gospels seems to suggest that the discourse, like the Sermon on the Mount, is composite, and indeed it is difficult to imagine the disciples remembering the whole discussion in every detail. Many of the sayings are however unquestionably genuine (32 for example is one of Schmiedel's 'pillar passages'), although they may have undergone a certain modification in the light of later events. That Jesus at this point delivered an apocalyptic discourse is entirely credible; that this discourse is identical with Mk 13 is another question entirely. The simplest solution would appear to lie along the lines laid down by Taylor. According to Lightfoot (*The Gospel Message of St Mark* (1952)), the discourse was 'designed by the evangelist as the immediate introduction to the passion narrative', but it should perhaps be noted, with Beasley-Murray, that composition of the discourse as a whole by Mk does not preclude the authenticity of the sayings of which it is composed. The value of the discourse 'is independent of the question as to when it was spoken and whether or not it is a fusion of separate sayings.'

XIV 1-XV 47 The Passion Narrative—By common consent the story of the Passion and Resurrection of Jesus, 'the most closely articulated section in the gospel' (Taylor), was the first part of the tradition to be written down, or even to be told as a continuous narrative. As Dodd (*The Apostolic Preaching* (1944)) has noted, these events form part of the primitive kerygma; they were indeed so fundamental as to force upon the Church a comprehensive study and reinterpretation of the OT prophecies (cf. Dodd, *According to the Scriptures* (1952)). Their very interest and importance however made them the subjects of reflection, and hence of development. As Grant observes, comparison of Mk with the parallel narratives indicates that the Passion Story continued to grow even after the writing of this Gospel, although this does not mean that the additional material is fictitious. In Lk. in particular many scholars think there is reason to believe that an early and independent account has been combined with that of Mk. 710a

b **1-2**. The precise notes of time are a feature of the narrative, but they raise problems of chronology since the Marcan dating of the Last Supper and the Crucifixion conflicts with that of Jn (see below). In Mk again, the whole sequence of events from the Triumphal Entry to the Resurrection takes place in the course of a single week, but it has been suggested that in fact they extended over a longer period. On Mk's dating the Anointing in Bethany falls upon the Wednesday.

The Passover was the great Jewish festival which commemorated the Exodus from Egypt (cf. Exod. 12:24–7). The lamb was slain on the afternoon of Nisan 14 and the Passover meal took place that evening; the Jewish day began at sunset, so that by the Jewish calendar the meal was eaten on Nisan 15. According to Blunt the seven-day Feast of Unleavened Bread which followed was originally distinct, but Josephus speaks as if the two were equivalent (cf. Lk. 22:1 and see Exod. 12–13). **2** is difficult, since on Mk's account Jesus was crucified during the festival. The chief priests and scribes apparently wanted to act after the feast (but some scholars think *before* it); the treachery of Judas gave them their opportunity to act 'by stealth' and at once.

c **3-9 The Anointing**—Jn places the incident six days before the Passover (12:1), while Lk. has a similar story in another context (7:36–50). Later tradition, by combining all three narratives, identifies the woman (unnamed in Mk) with Mary Magdalene, but for this there is no warrant. The story with its graphic detail rests on good authority, while the variations in the later Gospels illustrate the development of the tradition (Taylor). Special interest attaches to the occurrence in both Mk and Jn of the rare word *pistikos* (here rendered 'pure', but cf. Black) and of the reference to three hundred denarii; but Jn says it was Judas who grumbled (12:4f., cf. Mk 14:4). The reply of Jesus is not a comment on the permanence of poverty, but contrasts the narrow con-

0c ventional attitude of the objectors with the lavish offering of an inspired devotion. Hunter suggests that the woman had penetrated into the secret of the Suffering Messiah, but Taylor thinks that anointing for burial was the interpretation Jesus himself put upon her action (so too Blunt). At this point there was but little that anyone could do for him : she had done what she could, 'rendered the only service within her power' (Taylor). 9 has been widely regarded as a later addition, but the absence of the woman's name favours the authenticity of the saying (Taylor).

d **10-11.** The story of **the treachery of Judas** affords 'a striking example of the growth of the tradition from one gospel to another' (Menzies). In Mk he does not ask for money ; in Mt. he does, and the sum agreed is named (cf. Zech. 11:12). Lk. explains that Satan entered into Judas, a point mentioned at a later stage by Jn (13:27 ; note also Jn 12:6). As Taylor observes, Mk's sober account is clearly primary ; the other evangelists are already embarrassed, and attempt to explain the treachery by avarice and Satanic inspiration. Various motives have been suggested to account for the treachery of Judas, mostly in an attempt to exonerate the traitor, but the most probable explanation is that he was moved by frustration and disappointment at Jesus' failure to seize his opportunities. Hunter suggests that realising the danger he tried to save himself by turning 'king's evidence'. What he betrayed was probably when and where Jesus might be conveniently arrested (Hunter ; cf. Jn 18:2). Mk simply states the facts, without entering into details.

e **12-16.** The narrative of **the preparation for the Passover** shows certain parallels to that of the Triumphal Entry, but these are not such as to suggest that the stories are doublets ; moreover the differences exclude this hypothesis (Taylor). The sign and the message given to the disciples (13f.), like some features in the earlier story, suggest previous arrangement, and hence either a longer ministry in Jerusalem or more frequent visits than Mk would lead us to believe. Lagrange explains that men carry leather bottles, women only pitchers, which would make the guide a distinctive figure.

The date in **12** is ambiguous, since the first day of Unleavened Bread was Nisan 15, while the following words show that Nisan 14 is meant. It may be that the phrase is used loosely for the whole festival, including the Passover, but Black (*An Aramaic Approach* (1954), 100 *n*3) suggests that it is a misunderstanding of the Aramaic for 'the day before the feast', i.e. the Day of Preparation. The furnishing of the 'upper room' may well have been less elaborate than we are apt to think (Grant observes that the setting in most paintings of the scene represents 'later European custom', and was probably derived from the illustrations in mediaeval Jewish Passover Haggadahs). It should be noted that no reference is made to the details of the preparation. How far sacrificial ideas were associated with the Passover at this time it is difficult to say : 'the later tendency was to subordinate the sacrificial element in the meal' says Taylor, but 'this tendency does not mean that sacrificial ideas were absent from the mind of Jesus . . . ; the words of institution suggest the contrary.'

f **17-21.** Before telling the story of the Last Supper Mk includes **the prophecy of the betrayal,** which Lk. places after the 'words of institution'. Once again Mk's account shows sober restraint in comparison with the other Gospels, and of its historical value there can be no doubt. In Jn the traitor is indicated (13:26), although it is said that no-one knew why Jesus spoke to him (13:28) ; in Mt. Judas asks with the others 'Is it I ?' and receives an affirmative reply (26:25). In Mk the reference to the dish (20) is not a sign but stresses the enormity of the act. That Jesus was aware of Judas' treachery is not improbable, but he could hardly have identified the traitor openly without provoking some action on the
part of the others. Mk thinks the Supper was a Pass- **710f**
over meal, hence commentators identify the 'dish' as that which contained the sauce which was eaten with the Passover lamb. As Grant observes, there is a divine necessity in the death of the Son of Man, but he himself accepted it ; there was a necessity in the betrayal, but the traitor also had the option of refusal. 'He is not the blind instrument of fate' (Taylor), but must bear the responsibility for his action. On **21** Taylor says it is intelligible only in the mind of one who has identified the Son of man with the Suffering Servant, and that it is more intelligible if it is original than if it is secondary.

22-25 The Last Supper—In Mk the Supper is a **711a**
Passover meal ; in Jn Jesus was crucified on the day when the Passover lamb was slain (cf. 1 C. 5:7). The alternatives are (*a*) that Jn advanced the date to secure the symbolism of Christ as the Passover lamb, or (*b*) that Mk put the Supper a day later in order to represent the Eucharist as the Christian Passover. On this point scholars are still divided : Taylor, 664ff., with most British scholars, favours the Johannine dating, but Jeremias (*The Eucharistic Words of Jesus* (1955)) and Higgins (*The Lord's Supper in the NT* (1952)) argue for the Marcan. Turner makes the ingenious suggestion that on the Passover evening, after the Crucifixion, the disciples were too grief-stricken to celebrate the festival, and that the following year they observed the Jewish Passover on the night of the Last Supper and on Nisan 15 kept the fast which ended in the Easter feast. This would explain the growth of the tradition, but must be regarded as conjectural. More recently Jaubert (RHR (1954), 140ff.) has attempted to resolve the difficulties by arguing that the Synoptists follow the old Jewish sacerdotal calendar (followed also by the sect of Qumrân), by which the Passover always fell on a Tuesday, Jn the Jewish legal calendar, by which the festivals fell on different days of the week each year. This however appears to be exposed to the objections raised by Jeremias against the similar view of Billerbeck. Since there are indications in the Synoptic tradition (cf. Taylor, *Behind the Third Gospel* (1926), 37, etc.) that the Supper was not a Passover meal, the balance seems to incline towards the Johannine date. The day of the Crucifixion was certainly Friday, but whether the Friday was Nisan 14 or 15 is not absolutely clear. More important is the significance of the Supper, which has been observed ever since as the central act of Christian worship. Here, in Taylor's words, 'the Marcan narrative commends itself as one of the oldest, if not the most ancient, of the accounts which reveal the singularly original manner in which Jesus conceived the nature of his redemptive death and related the Eucharist thereto'. The 'words of institution' are given in their simplest form, but are eloquent in their very simplicity. The Supper is at once an anticipation of the Messianic feast (cf. 25) and a bond of union (cf. 'covenant' in 24, recalling Exod. 24:8) ; the note of sacrifice is present in the Passover associations of the meal, and is explicitly brought out in 24 ('poured out for many'). 'This last time that he would touch wine before his death he consecrated it to a special relationship to the blood he was about to shed' (Turner). The new covenant of Jeremiah's prophecy is about to be inaugurated 'by the blood of a better sacrifice' (cf. Heb. 8–10). The Blessing (22) is an act of thanksgiving to God, and would probably take the normal Jewish form. The words 'for many' (24) imply not 'many' in contrast to 'all', but 'many' in contrast to 'one' ; cf. 10:45 ; Rom. 5:15–19 ; Isa. 53:11–12.

26-31. The story of **Peter's denial** 'must undoubtedly **b**
rest on Peter's own record' (Blunt). As Taylor observes, Christian tradition would not have preserved it except on the highest authority. Here the denial is prophesied, first in general terms with a quotation from Zech. (13:7, where LXX and Heb. are slightly different from Mk), then more directly in response to

711b Peter's reply. 28 seems to foreshadow appearances in Galilee (cf. 16:7), but Grant thinks both verses may be later additions. The 'hymn' (26), if the Supper was the Passover, would be the Hallel (Ps. 115–18). Only Mk mentions a double cock-crow.

c **32-42 Gethsemane**—Branscomb thinks this tradition of a period of anguish 'can scarcely be due to anything other than a recollection by certain of the disciples.' For comment Blunt refers to Heb. 5:7–10. Once again Peter and James and John are singled out : 'the three who had witnessed the anticipation of glory at the Transfiguration were now to witness something of the Agony' (Turner). As elsewhere, Mk gives prominence to the human emotions of Jesus. Here is no mere divine being, but one who was in every respect tempted as we are (Heb. 4:15), who in the fulness of his humanity shrank from the prospect that lay before him ; yet one also who bowed in perfect obedience to the Father's will. The Greek words rendered 'distressed' and 'troubled' (33) express the very deepest emotion. Here in the garden the old temptation once more rears its head, but even yet not for the last time (cf. 15:29ff.). In striking contrast, the disciples are found asleep (37) ; 'he who was ready to die with Jesus lacked the will to watch for an hour' (Taylor). The reference to 'temptation' is difficult. Dodd (*Parables of the Kingdom* (1936), 166) thinks of the impending attack, but Taylor argues that more is meant ; 'a definite peril' appears to be in mind. Hunter suggests the danger of apostasy, Menzies that of loss of faith in Jesus and his cause. If we recall 13:35 it may be questioned if the reference is intended to be specific ; for all their protestations (31), they are but human. Swete refers to Westcott on Jn 3:6 and Sanday and Headlam on Rom. 8:9 for the contrast of 'spirit' and 'flesh', but as Taylor notes it is not necessary to characterise the words as Pauline ; this is the common OT distinction. Another difficulty is the word rendered 'it is enough', which perhaps should read as another question, following the reading of D and other MSS : 'the end is far away?' On the contrary, the hour is at hand, 'the hour when the Messianic ministry of Jesus reaches its climax' (see Taylor, 556f. for details). It should be added that the scene in Gethsemane is fundamental for a right understanding of prayer, and especially of 'unanswered' prayer. The cup was not removed, but Jesus accepts his destiny in a complete self-consecration : 'not what I will, but what thou wilt'.

d **43-50. The arrest** is apparently made by a hired rabble, armed with 'such weapons as could be hastily collected by an irregular body of men called out to deal with a brigand' (Swete). There is no reference to the Temple police (Lk.) or to Roman soldiers (Jn). So in 48 Jesus condemns not the arrest itself but the manner of it. The kiss was a customary greeting for a Rabbi from a disciple (cf. Lk. 7:45), and would serve to identify Jesus among the group in the darkness. In Jn the bystander who drew his sword is said to have been Peter, and the high priest's slave is named as Malchus. Lk.'s note that Jesus healed the wound is 'thoroughly hagiographical' (Grant).

e **51-52**. Some commentators refer to Am. 2:16, but this is perhaps far-fetched ; others have seen here the author's signature, the young man being Mk himself, but this again is no more than conjecture. If the house of Ac. 12:12 was that in which the Last Supper was celebrated, it might have been Mk, but this is as much as can be said. 'Naked' does not mean 'unclad', but clothed only in a tunic (cf. Jn 21:7 and 13:4, which together make the meaning clear). As Bengel noted, the fine 'linen cloth' suggests that the young man belonged to a wealthy family.

712a **XIV 53-XV 15 The Trial and Condemnation of Jesus**—At this point there is some divergence among the Gospel narratives : in Mt. and Mk the 'Jewish trial' takes place at night and 'the whole council' holds a further consultation in the morning, after which Jesus is led away to Pilate ; in Lk. the trial is in the morning (22:66) ; in Jn the only note of time is 71
that it was early when Jesus was taken to the praetorium (18:28). Moreover in Jn Jesus is brought first before Annas, who is not mentioned in Mk, and only thereafter before Caiaphas, the ruling High Priest. Again, there is some doubt as to whether the session before the High Priest was a trial in the full sense. The Rabbinic regulations regarding trials (see Barrett, *The New Testament Background* (1956), 169ff.) are designed to give every opportunity for the presentation of evidence in favour of the defence, but it is still in debate how far these rules were in force at this period ; nor is it certain whether the Sanhedrin had the power to exact the penalty of death. The fact that Jesus was brought before Pilate, and not summarily dealt with, suggests that the trial of capital charges was one of the prerogatives reserved by the Romans to the provincial governor (cf. Jn 18:31). The responsibility for the condemnation of Jesus rests with Pilate, although there is a tendency in the Gospel narratives to try to transfer the burden from his shoulders to those of the Jewish people. Mk certainly regarded the examination before the High Priest as a trial, but the objections are so weighty that many commentators feel that what took place was 'probably a private examination *in camera*, conducted secretly by the powerful enemies who had Jesus in their hands' (Grant). By Jewish law the trial ought to have taken place by day, and the verdict should not have been reached until the day after. It is however only the *character* of the incident, not its historicity, that is in question.

55-56 The Jewish Trial—The attitude of the Council b
is hostile from the start. There is no reference to witnesses for the defence. According to Dt. 19:15 the testimony of at least two witnesses was necessary to sustain the charge. Some scholars suggest here OT influence (e.g. Ps. 27:12), but although no disciples were present Mk might have obtained his information from members of the Sanhedrin (Taylor suggests Joseph of Arimathea or Nicodemus).

57-59. Of the authenticity of the saying alleged c
against Jesus in 58 there can be no question, especially if with some scholars it is felt that Mk's suggestion that it was false (57) reflects the uneasiness of the early Church, which continued to frequent the Temple (cf. Ac. 2:46). Cf. 13:2 (probably the basis of the charge), 15:29 ; Ac. 6:14 ; in Jn 2:19ff. it is interpreted as a reference to the Resurrection. It may be, however, that the *form* of the saying has been altered, and that originally Jesus spoke in symbolic terms of the end of the old order and the beginning of a new. Taylor thinks he made the Messianic claim that he would establish the new Temple. The discrepancies in the evidence (59) suggest that the original saying was less explicit than 58 as it stands.

60-65. The High Priest presses the question, perhaps d
in the hope of provoking an incriminating answer, but Jesus remains silent. Only in response to the further question (61) does he make any reply. Turner suggests that as he avoided arrest before the advent of the feast so he 'would not be condemned on any less issue than his claim to be Messiah and Son of God' ; but it may be that both question and answer are seen through Christian eyes : 'both here and in 15:39 Mk reads a much deeper meaning into the title' (Taylor). 'The Blessed' is a reverential periphrasis to avoid pronouncing the name of God, but it is a disputed question whether the Messiah was in this period regarded as Son of God. In reply Jesus quotes Ps. 110:1 and Dan. 7:13. The historical character of this saying and its significance have been much discussed (cf. Taylor, 568f. ; Robinson in ET 67 (1956), 336ff.). Some good MSS read 'Thou hast said that I am', on which Taylor says that the reply is affirmative, but registers a difference of interpretation ; Jesus has his own ideas about Messiahship, which are not those of contemporary Judaism. Since it would account for Mt. 26:64 and Lk. 22:70 more

712d readily than the normal text, this reading may well be original. Whether the saying refers to the Second Coming is disputed : according to Taylor 'What Jesus claims is that the glorious destiny which belongs to the Messiah, described in different ways by the Psalmist and the prophet, will be seen to be his. The emphasis lies on enthronement, and on enthronement as the symbol of triumph,' cf. 8:38, 13:26–7, and see further Kümmel, *Promise and Fulfilment* (1957) ; Robinson, *Jesus and His Coming* (1957).

e To rend one's garments was originally a sign of grief (cf. Gen. 37:29), but in the case of the High Priest had become 'a formal judicial act minutely regulated in the Talmud' (Taylor). Turner says the clothes were those which could most easily be mended, but this is contradicted by Sanh. 7:5 (Danby, *The Mishnah* (1933), 392) : 'The judges stand up on their feet and rend their garments, and they may not mend them again.' It has been urged that nothing in the words of Jesus constitutes blasphemy in terms of Lev. 24: 10–23, but Taylor argues (*a*) that there is reason to think the concept of blasphemy was broadened ; (*b*) Jesus not only claims to be Messiah but that he will fulfil the prophecy of Dan. ; (*c*) the High Priest may have been disposed to put a damaging construction upon the words of Jesus. Mk evidently took the examination as a formal trial and the verdict as unanimous, but the wording of 64 suggests a judicial opinion rather than a sentence (Taylor contrasts 10:33 'condemn him to death' ; here 'deserving of death'). Turner however thinks it a definite sentence, although one which they had no legal power to execute.

f The story of the mockery is complicated by textual problems : Grant thinks the words added after 'Prophesy !' in Mt. and Lk. ('Who is it that struck you ?') originally stood in Mk (they are found in some MSS), but Taylor and others think they are an assimilation to Lk. In the latter case we should have two independent versions, of which Taylor thinks that of Lk. is nearer to the facts. In Mk the mockers appear to be members of the Council ; in Lk. they are 'the men who were holding Jesus'. The silence of Jesus (61) and the 'blows' (65) recall Isa. 53:7, 50:6 LXX (cf. Dodd, *According to the Scriptures* (1952)).

g **66-72.** The way has been prepared in 54 for **Peter's denial**. Greatly daring, he had followed into the courtyard and was warming himself at the fire when he was challenged by a maid. Embarrassed and aware of his danger, he gave an evasive answer and moved away ; the maid however persisted (the other Gospels vary here), and finally the bystanders explicitly charge him with being 'one of them', observing that he is a Galilean (Grant thinks the clause 'thy speech agreeth thereto' (AV) a gloss based on Mt., but Taylor raises the question whether it may not be original in Mk). From evasion Peter passes to denial, and finally accompanies the denial with an oath. The whole narrative is vivid and realistic, and it has been well said that if anywhere we have a reminiscence of Peter himself it is here. The denial was not due merely to cowardice ; it was the instinctive reaction of a man who knew he had gone too far. Some MSS omit the reference to the cock in **68,** but the evidence is variable and the omission is probably due to the desire to bring Mk into line with the other Gospels. For details see Taylor on 14:30, 68, 72.

713a **XV 1-5 The Roman Trial**—After the verdict in 14:64 the consultation in 15:1 is strange, and many commentators accordingly feel that 14:55–65 is an insertion by Mk into his original source, which would then agree with Lk. (22:66). Pilate was procurator of Judaea from A.D. 25/6 to 36. Taylor notes that the absence of any description either of the governor or of the place of trial shows that Mk wrote for readers who knew the facts. Pilate's question indicates that the authorities had resolved to proceed on the basis of the political aspect of Jesus' Messianic claims, an aspect hitherto not mentioned and of course quite out of keeping with Jesus' own conception. If the text of Mk be taken as it stands, it may perhaps be suggested that the evangelist thought the Council decided at the session during the night to bring Jesus before the governor on a capital charge, and then held a further consultation in the morning to determine the precise form of the charge to be preferred. The political implication alleged in Jesus' claim to Messiahship would of course bring him before Pilate as a rebel. It is however clear from 9f. that Pilate did not believe the accusation to be true. As in some MSS of 14:62, the reply of Jesus is affirmative, but implies that he would have put it differently (cf. Jn 18:33–7). As Grant notes, Lk. 23:2, 5 and Jn 18:33–19:16 help to explain the 'many things' of which Jesus was accused.

6-15 Barabbas—There appears to be no evidence for b
the custom of releasing a prisoner at the Passover, apart from the Gospels, although Taylor notes certain analogies in Livy and elsewhere. Grant thinks it scarcely necessary to brand the incident as fictitious, but Turner takes it as referring to an act of grace to mark a great occasion. Only in Mk does the crowd take the initiative (8). Some MSS here read 'cried out', but Swete thinks this misses a point of some importance : their advance 'was no less menacing than their shouts'. In Mt. 27:16f. some MSS give the name as *Jesus* Barabbas, which Origen says he found in very old MSS. Taylor and others think there is good reason to believe it original in Mt., and to conjecture that it was read in Mk. The omission is readily explained as due to the piety of a later age. As Luccock observes, there was much in Barabbas, the nationalist and man of violence, to win him the vote over Jesus in the courtyard of Pilate ; his way was in line with the popular expectation, the way which Jesus might have followed had he yielded to the Temptation which constantly beset him (cf. on 1:12–13). Much has been made of the fickleness of the people but it is not necessary to suggest that the crowd of the Triumphal Entry was composed of Galilean pilgrims while this was the mob of Jerusalem. Jesus' refusal to fulfil the popular hope is enough to explain the change in their attitude. Moreover the 'chief priests' and their agents were among them inciting them to choose Barabbas (11). The character of Pilate is vividly revealed in a few words : responsible as he was for keeping order, he was too weak to resist in the face of a threatened riot. His defence of the prisoner, says Grant, was only half-hearted. Taylor notes the consistent use of the word 'delivered' (the same word is used of the betrayal by Judas), and explains it by the belief that 'as the Suffering Servant, Jesus is "delivered up by the determinate counsel and foreknowledge of God" (Ac. 2:23)'. A significant contrast to these trial scenes is afforded by the *Bacchae* of Euripides (note also the dénouement of that tragedy).

16-47. Taylor drily comments that the industry with c
which parallels to **the Mocking** are gathered is not commensurate with the results obtained (646ff.). Many commentators refer to Philo's story of the insult offered to Agrippa I by the Alexandrians when he visited the city (*In Flacc.*, vi, 36–9). The soldiers would be provincials, from various parts of the empire, but not Jews (Swete), the Jews being exempt from conscription. 'Battalion' is misleading ; Turner suggests a company or platoon. Taking up the claim of kingship, they render to Jesus in mockery the honour which belonged to the emperor, On the whole section from 15 cf. Isa. 50:6 and see Dodd, *According to the Scriptures* (1952), 91.

21-32. Crucifixion was a Roman punishment reserved d
for slaves, although eastern in origin. The victim was fastened to the cross-bar and driven through the streets to the place of execution (cf. Plautus, *Mostellaria*, 56, with Sonnenschein's note). Death came through exposure and exhaustion, but the suffering might be prolonged. Cicero calls it *crudelissimum taeterrimumque supplicium.* Jesus apparently set out bearing the 'cross' (Jn 19:17), and Simon was pressed into service when he fell exhausted. Cyrene had a large Jewish

713d population, and Simon had probably come to Jerusalem for the Passover ; he is mentioned in a way which suggests that he was known to Mk and his readers (a Rufus is mentioned in Rom. 16:13). The wine drugged with myrrh was intended to deaden the pain, but Jesus refused it, 'willing to die with an unclouded mind' (Taylor) ; Turner recalls 14:25. The clothes of the victims were the perquisites of the executioners (Mk's language shows that he has Ps. 22:18 in mind, but this need not have suggested the detail). The third hour would be 9 a.m. (Jn 19:14 says 'about the sixth hour', probably following a different tradition) ; as Taylor notes, precise statements of time are a feature of the Crucifixion narrative. The reference to the superscription is in accordance with Roman custom (Taylor), and proves that Jesus was executed (*a*) by the Romans, (*b*) on a charge of claiming kingship (Grant). After 27 many MSS add a quotation from Isa. 53:12, probably derived from Lk. 22:37 (Swete, Taylor).

29-32. This section is full of OT echoes, which have influenced the form of expression (cf. Ps. 22:7, 109:25 ; Lam. 2:15). As often, 'facts are related in appropriate Biblical language' (Taylor). Notable are the allusion to the 'false testimony' of 14:58 and the recurrence yet again of the old Temptation (esp. 32).

e **33-39.** 'The whole land' probably refers to Judaea only, although the phrase could mean 'the whole world'. Taylor quotes 13:24 ; Am. 8:9 ; Jer. 15:9 ; Grant adds Isa. 60:2. The cry in **34** (the only word from the Cross in Mk) is from Ps. 22:1, and was probably uttered in Hebrew ; the Aramaic form could not have suggested 'Elijah' (Turner). The Gospel of Peter gives the rendering 'My power, my power' (Swete, 385). As Taylor notes, 'The depths of the saying are too deep to be plumbed, but the least inadequate interpretations are those which find in it a sense of desolation in which Jesus felt the horror of sin so deeply that for a time the closeness of his communion with the Father was obscured.' The view advanced by McLeod Campbell and others (*The Nature of the Atonement* (1906), 240f.) seems to deserve notice ; if Dodd is correct (see *According to the Scriptures* (1952)), such quotations are intended to recall not merely the actual text which is cited but the whole context, and the final note of the Psalm is not despair but one of confident faith. Even so, the sense of 'that alienation from God which sin brings with it' (Hunter) was undoubtedly real. No doctrine of the Atonement is adequate which fails to do justice to the cost involved to the Redeemer.

Elijah in Jewish legend is the guardian of the interests of Israel (Edersheim). Taylor refers to Billerbeck for the belief that he would come to the rescue of the godly in time of need. The incident of 35–6 is however more complex than appears (see Taylor, 594ff. for details ; he suggests combination of two traditions). The bystanders were probably Jews, and may have spoken in mockery, but the offer of the vinegar may have been meant in kindness. Cf. Mt. 27:47–9 ; Jn 19:28–9. **36** recalls Ps. 69:21, which may have influenced the wording although it need not have suggested the incident.

The 'loud cry' was not a cry of despair but the shout of a victor (Grant) ; cf. Lk. 23:46, where Lk. 'certainly intends to identify the "loud utterance" of Mk with his own "Father, into thy hands I commend my spirit"' (Turner). It was the manner of Jesus' death that impressed the centurion (39), not any external portents as in Mt. and Lk. (the textual evidence suggests that the original text of 39 contained a reference to the cry). Probably as a pagan he meant only that Jesus was more than human, a 'hero' or demi-god, but Mk very naturally takes his words as a full confession of the deity of Jesus. Lohmeyer observes that the confession surpasses that of Peter and asserts what to the High Priest amounts to blasphemy ; it is therefore of the highest significance from the point of view of Mk's Christology : he who was announced at the beginning as Son of God is now explicitly recognised as such. The reference to the rending of the veil of the Temple (38) may be 'a legendary addition doctrinal in origin' (Taylor ; Grant says the narrative is smoother if 38 is bracketed). The veil is the curtain between the Holy of Holies and the Holy Place, and its rending symbolises the opening of the way to God (cf. Heb. 6:19–20, 10:19–20). In the Gospel according to the Hebrews it is said that the *lintel* of the Temple fell down in fragments, but this is a further development. 713e

40-41. Mk completes his story of the Crucifixion by noting the presence of the women, whose loyalty 'surpassed that of the disciples' (Wood). Mary of Magdala is frequently mentioned, but only in Lk. 8:2 before the Passion Story ; she is not to be identified with the woman of Lk. 7:37 (cf. on 14:3ff. above). Salome is identified in Mt. 27:56 as the mother of the sons of Zebedee. The reference prepares the way for the story of the Empty Tomb. f

42-47. Crucifixion normally involved a lingering death (both Pilate and the centurion were surprised that Jesus died so soon), and the bodies were left hanging ; but Dt. 21:22f. enjoins the burial of dead criminals before nightfall. Apparently the Romans respected Jewish scruples in this as in other matters. Here there was an additional reason for haste, in that it was the day before the Sabbath. **43** emphasises the boldness of Joseph's action : 'The circumstances of the Passion, which wrecked the brave resolutions of the Apostles, made this secret disciple bold' (Swete). The fact that Joseph was able to buy the shroud (46) seems to indicate that the Passover day had not yet begun, and so to confirm the Johannine chronology. In Mk there is no anointing (cf. 14:8) ; in Jn 19:39f. the proper offices are duly performed. The rock-cut tomb is typical of the time and place. In Mt. it is Joseph's own new-made tomb ; in Lk. it had never been used (cf. Jn 19:41). The stone against the door was a protection against wild beasts and thieves (Menzies).

XVI 1-8 The Empty Tomb—'There can be little doubt that, when in the earliest preaching it was affirmed that God raised up Jesus from the dead (Ac. 2:24, 31f., 3:15, etc.), an empty tomb was implied, and further, that the same implication underlies the words of St Paul in 1 C. 15:3–5' (Taylor). There are however numerous critical problems about the story (see Taylor, 602ff.), especially when it is compared in details with the accounts in the other Gospels. In Mk and Lk. the women go to anoint the body (a day and two nights after death), in Mt. and apparently in Jn they go to see the tomb. The simplest explanation is that Mk is describing what he believed to have happened (so Taylor). On the other hand 'the theory that the whole evidence for the resurrection of Jesus goes back to the "wrought-up imaginations of a group of hysterical women" is quite impossible' (Grant). We have to account for (*a*) the transformation in the Apostles, (*b*) the conversion of Paul, (*c*) the subsequent history of the Church, and we must also reckon with the person of Jesus himself. As Hunter notes, there are three great witnesses to the reality of the Resurrection : the existence of the Christian Church, the existence of the New Testament, the existence of the Lord's Day. The evidence of Mk may not be conclusive for the modern mind, but as Wood rightly observes the issue 'cannot satisfactorily be discussed on the interpretation of the story in isolation.' 714a

The reference to Peter in **7** is emphatic, and there can be no doubt that the Denial is in mind (Taylor). The message takes up the prophecy of 14:28. In contrast with Lk. and Jn, Mk and Mt. seem to know only of appearances in Galilee.

It is now generally agreed that **9-20** are not an original part of Mk. They are not found in the oldest MSS, and indeed were apparently not in the copies used by Mt. and Lk. A 10th-cent. Armenian MS ascribes the passage to Aristion, the presbyter b

4b mentioned by Papias (ap.Eus.HE III, xxxix, 15). Some MSS give a shorter ending, but neither is in Mk's style ; the longer is indeed compiled from the other Gospels and from Ac. For details see Taylor, 610ff. ; Turner, 83ff. ; Grant, 915ff. Cf. also Moule in NTS ii, 58f.

Some scholars argue that Mk intended to end his work at 16:8, but most find it incredible that the Gospel could end in this way. Three explanations have been offered : (*a*) the mutilation of the original papyrus MS, (*b*) Mk's premature death, and (*c*) the deliberate suppression of the remainder of the book. The one thing certain is that if the conclusion has been lost it was at a very early date. Grant however rightly observes that if Mk closes without an account of any appearance of the risen Jesus it everywhere presupposes the Resurrection of our Lord.

Bibliography—Commentaries : The latest and most comprehensive critical commentary is that of V. Taylor, which contains an extensive select bibliography (xiii–xix). Other commentaries : A. W. F. Blunt (Clarendon Bible), B. H. Branscomb (Moffatt Commentary), A. B. Bruce (EGT), C. E. B. Cranfield (CGT), A. M. Hunter (Torch Bible Commentaries), Sherman E. Johnson (Black's NT Commentaries), E. Lohmeyer, A. Menzies, H. B. Swete, C. H. Turner (reprinted from *A New Commentary on Holy Scripture*, ed. Gore, etc.), H. G. Wood (Peake). See also F. C. Grant, IB vii (introd. and exegesis, with exposition by H. E. Luccock).

Other Literature : H. Baltensweiler, *Die Verklärung Jesu* (1959) ; G. R. Beasley-Murray, *Jesus and the Future* (1954) ; M. Black, *An Aramaic Approach to the Gospels and Acts* (2nd ed. 1954) ; G. H. Boobyer, *St Mark and the Transfiguration Story* (1942) ; C. H. Dodd, *The Apostolic Preaching and its Developments* (1944), *The Parables of the Kingdom* (1936), and *According to the Scriptures* (1952) ; H. A. Guy, *The Origin of Mark's Gospel* (1954) ; A. J. B. Higgins, *The Lord's Supper in the NT* (1952) ; J. Jeremias, *The Parables of Jesus* (1954), and *The Eucharistic Words of Jesus* (1955) ; W. G. Kümmel, *Promise and Fulfilment* (1957) ; R. H. Lightfoot, *The Gospel Message of St Mark* (1952) ; W. Marxsen, *Der Evangelist Markus* (1956) ; A. Richardson, *The Miracle-Stories of the Gospels* (1941) ; J. A. T. Robinson, *Jesus and His Coming* (1957).

LUKE

By G. W. H. LAMPE

715a **Authorship and date**—From the 2nd cent. (Irenaeus, *Adv. Haer.* III, i, 2 ; ' Muratorian Canon ' ; cf. the ancient ' Anti-Marcionite Prologue ' to Lk.) this Gospel and Ac. have been attributed to Luke, the companion of Paul (Col. 4:11 ; 2 Tim. 4:10). He is said by the above-mentioned prologue to have been a native of Antioch in Syria, a tradition found also, possibly independently, in Eusebius (HE III, iv, 6), and, by many early writers (following Col. 4:11), a doctor. How far these traditions are inferred from the ' we passages ' of Ac., including the short ' we passage ' in Ac. 11:27 in the ' Western ' text, the setting of which is Antioch, taken in conjunction with the Pauline references mentioned above, and how far they rest on genuinely independent records or reminiscences is quite uncertain. Probably some independent tradition about the authorship had come down to the 2nd-cent. writers, Lk. being otherwise an unlikely person (because of his obscurity in the NT) to have been selected on internal grounds alone as the author. The ascription to Lk. raises many difficulties, chiefly in connection with his account of Paul's life in Ac., but these are not insuperable. The place of writing is said by the same prologue (followed by Jer.) to have been ' Achaea '. It was certainly written in and for the Gentile Church.

b Its **date** is very uncertain. Some would place Lk.-Ac. before A.D. 64 on the ground that if it were written later it must have described the fate of Paul ; but this argument probably rests on a misunderstanding of the purpose and plan of the work. It is often suggested that Lk. 21:20ff., compared with the Marcan parallel, indicates a date subsequent to the fall of Jerusalem, but this need not be the case (see commentary). If Lk. 3:1 (Lysanias' tetrarchy) and Ac. 5:36–7 (Theudas and Judas) compel one to infer that Lk. had read (and misunderstood) Josephus, the date must be later than A.D. 93 ; but it is by no means certain that the apparent chronological inaccuracies contained in these passages are to be explained in that way. Lk.'s use of Mk will place his work later than *c.* 64 ; his ignorance of the Pauline Epistles will forbid a late date. It is very probable that Lk. was known to the Fourth Evangelist. A date *c.* A.D. 80–5 is usually assigned to the Gospel (see Jackson and Lake, *The Beginnings of Christianity* ii (1922), 355–8 ; Burkitt, *The Gospel History and its Transmission* (1911), 107).

c **Sources**—Lk. uses Mk, omitting, probably for reasons connected with his theological plan, Mk 6:45–8:26. In addition he uses much Q material, some practically identical with Mt. in language as well as content, some parallel in content but with considerable differences in wording (for the view that Lk. used Mt., see B. C. Butler, *The Originality of St Matthew* (1951) ; A. M. Farrer in Nineham, *Studies in the Gospels* (1955), 55–86). Much material in the Gospel is peculiar to Lk., and was believed by Streeter to consist of traditions gathered by Lk. at Caesarea from Palestinian sources. Streeter's designation (L) for this part of the Gospel can represent only a varied assortment of different material, some probably composed by Lk. on the basis of oral reminiscence, some derived from more firmly fixed tradition, written or oral. The theory of a ' Proto-Luke ' was advocated by Streeter and by Vincent Taylor (*Behind the Third Gospel* (1926)), who maintained that the first stage of the work was a combination of the Q and L material, subsequently combined with Mk after Lk.'s arrival at Rome with Paul. Whether the theory be accepted depends largely on how far it may be believed that Lk. has rewritten and modified his Marcan material, or how far it seems likely that whenever Lk. departs strikingly from Mk in reproducing episodes or sayings found in that Gospel he has in fact deserted Mk for a parallel non-Marcan source. On the whole it seems probable that Lk. handles Mk freely, modifying and supplementing as it suits his purpose. In any case, the structural framework of Lk. is Marcan, and it is hard to see how the supposed ' Proto-Luke ' could ever have stood on its own feet as an independent Gospel. The question whether Lk. used a Passion narrative independent of Mk is still open, though on the whole it seems probable that Lk.'s Passion story is taken from Mk, with modifications and additions from other sources. It has been suggested that the final welding together of ' Proto-Luke ' (Q and L) with Mk came later than the addition of Ac. to the original Gospel (' Proto-Luke ') ; see C. S. C. Williams, JTS 49 (1948), 204 ; but this theory has found little favour.

The Nature and Purpose of Lk.—The author's object was clearly to tell the story of the whole course of God's mighty acts in Christ, from the birth of the Forerunner to the proclamation of the gospel of salvation in the capital city of the Gentile world. The divine promises to Israel have now been extended to the Gentiles, their meaning having been revealed through the rejection and vindication of Jesus the Messiah. His rejection by his own people, his death and exaltation, and his acceptance by the Gentiles were determined by the counsel of God, and it is as the consequence of the glorification and vindication to which his death was the ordained and necessary prelude that repentance and forgiveness of sins are extended to the whole world. d

The Ascension of Jesus thus forms the turning-point in the Lucan narrative, linking the work of Jesus himself to the mission carried out in his name by his disciples to the ends of the earth ; or, rather, linking the operation of the Spirit of God in and through Jesus to the same Spirit's working in the Church. e

The scene of the beginnings of the fulfilment of God's promises is the heart of the old Israel, Jerusalem and the Temple. This is the setting for the opening chapters both of the Gospel and Ac. In the former, the rejection of Jesus and his acceptance after his resurrection by the Gentiles are hinted at in the episode of the Nazareth synagogue and the speech of Jesus on that occasion, which together form an introduction to Lk.'s entire story ; and, especially in the central section of the Gospel between the first prediction by Jesus of his coming death and resurrection (9:22) and the Passion itself, the constantly repeated theme is the contrast between the repentance and salvation of the outcasts (foreshadowing the Gentiles), together with the character and purpose of the mission of Jesus and his followers, and, on the other hand, the failure of Judaism to comprehend that mission, and its obstruction of the salvation of the outcasts and sinners. In f

715f Ac. the repeated theme is the offer of repentance and forgiveness to Israel, its rejection of the gospel, and the consequent opportunity afforded to the Gentiles to embrace the promises of God. Lk.'s narrative accordingly comes to a dramatic climax at its conclusion, when Paul, having, like Jesus himself, travelled up to Jerusalem in the revealed knowledge that suffering awaits him there, is brought by God's guidance, through his violent rejection by the Jews and the further 'passion' of the shipwreck, to Rome and preaches the gospel in the Gentile capital 'openly and unhindered', in the sure conviction that 'this salvation of God has been sent to the Gentiles: they will listen' (Ac. 28:28–31).

716a **The Theme of Lk.'s Work** is thus the progress of the gospel from its first beginnings to its arrival in the centre of the Gentile world, the nature of this gospel being summarily expounded in the speeches in Ac. and more fully set out in the author's first volume. A subsidiary motive is probably to explain to Gentile readers that, although Jesus was greeted as a king at Jerusalem and was put to death as an insurrectionary, and although his followers were imprisoned by Roman authorities, yet the kingdom of Jesus was not a political project and the Christian mission, like its author, was always recognised as harmless by the secular rulers except when Jewish hostility succeeded in so misrepresenting the position as to pervert their judgment. The strength of this motive, however, should not be exaggerated. Lk. is not writing an apology addressed to high Roman officials, whether or not his patron, Theophilus, may have been such a person. He is writing for those who have a wide sympathy with Samaritans and Gentiles, and who, like himself, see Christianity as a world religion; but this public consists of people who, again like himself, are steeped in the Septuagint Bible, probably as Gentile adherents of the Synagogue, and are concerned to hear, as it were, the risen Lord interpreting 'in all the scriptures the things concerning himself' (24:27).

b It is obvious that Lk. intends his work to be read as a single book in two volumes. The Church's mission to the world is an integral part of the gospel as Lk. understands it, and Ascension-Pentecost is not the end of one story and the beginning of another, but the climax of a single series of events and the hinge or bridge linking the death and resurrection of Jesus, the climax of his ministry, to the fulfilment which that preliminary climax had inaugurated. Lk.'s Gospel was not, therefore, intended to be read as a separate work in isolation from its sequel, and it is not possible to make sense of Lk.'s thought if it is detached from Ac. and read as though it were complete in itself. As a separate Gospel it is an unsatisfactory production, and it has undoubtedly suffered greatly from being isolated from its companion volume and included in the corpus of the four Gospels. Hence the profound religious meaning of Lk. has often been distorted and misinterpreted in terms of sentimental humanism or a 'social gospel'. When, however, it is read in conjunction with its author's second volume its deeper significance becomes apparent and we can more fully appreciate the wonderful beauty of the portrait of Christ which is here presented to us, and also the skill, the subtlety and the warm-hearted devotion of the great literary artist who has painted it. A fuller understanding of Lk.'s religious purpose can only lead us to acknowledge, in a new sense, the truth of Renan's description of this Gospel as the most beautiful book ever written.

c **The Theology of Lk.** is not easy to distinguish and evaluate. His ideas are not clear-cut, and in place of a few fully worked-out ideas he prefers to hold together a number of different theological motives, no single one of which is fully and clearly developed. He is also bound to a large extent by his sources, so that in the Gospel his distinctive thought is to be discerned mainly in the minor and sometimes subtle modifications which he makes in his material, in his rearrangement of its order, and in his placing it into new contexts. Nevertheless his writings show evidence of a distinctive outlook. It differs widely from that of Paul, lacking the Pauline interpretation of Christ's death, except in so far as it holds that Christ's rejection and death were part of the divine plan and that, by reversing the action of sinful men and vindicating his Messiah, God has opened the way to repentance and forgiveness to those who become Christ's people. It also lacks the Pauline preoccupation with the Law and justification, except in so far as it constantly sets the self-righteousness of Pharisaic Judaism over against the spontaneous love and forgiveness offered by Christ to outcasts and sinners. The point of contact between the thought of Lk. and Pauline Christianity is the common conviction of the supreme importance of the opening of the way of salvation to the Gentile world. The thought of the breaking down of the 'middle wall of partition' underlies the whole of the Lucan theology. Its similarity to the thought of the Epistle to the Hebrews is striking (see the full discussion by C. P. M. Jones in Nineham, *Studies in the Gospels* (1955), 113–43). It is possible that both authors owe much to the theology of Stephen and his followers (cf. W. Manson, *The Epistle to the Hebrews* (1949), 25ff.), but it is impossible to determine how far the ideas attributed to Stephen are authentic and how far they represent only the thought of Lk. It also has much in common with 1 Clement, notably in its emphasis upon Christ as the Servant of Isa. 53, the prominence of the idea of repentance, its idealised picture of the life of the primitive Church, the importance which it attaches to the apostles and the apostolic ministry, and its use of the concept of the Name of Christ. There are also points of contact between Lucan thought and that of the Pastoral Epistles, as for example in their common application to Jesus of the title 'Saviour', which is rare elsewhere in the NT.

It is possible that Lk. represents a common and widespread understanding of the Christian faith in the early Church, where this was not directly influenced by the advanced and peculiarly profound insights of St Paul and St John. Some of the characteristic elements in his theology may be summarised as follows. d

Christ and his Work—The theme of Lk.'s narrative is summed up in the speeches in Ac., the burden of which is that God sent his word to Israel in Jesus, who was anointed with Holy Spirit and power. His ministry of healing, with signs and wonders, began after John's teaching and baptism had prepared the way for him. He was rejected by his own people, the Jews; but his death, brought about by the ignorance and stubbornness of their leaders, was, in the counsel of God, ordained as the means of his exaltation to God's right hand and the reception of the Spirit to transmit to his followers. The apostles could, and were specially commissioned to, testify to his resurrection, and in his name they were sent to the whole world to proclaim in his name, and as the consequence of his exaltation to glory, repentance and forgiveness of sins. Of the climax of the gospel story (Ascension-Pentecost) his death is both a prelude and a part, for the time of his 'receiving up' (9:51) begins immediately after his anticipatory glorification upon the mountain, in the context of his repeated announcement of his approaching death and the beginning of his journey to the Cross. It is as one who was hanged on a tree that he was lifted up by God to glory. He enters into his glory through death at his resurrection, and fulfils his own prediction: 'the third day I finish my course' (13:32). This exaltation is consummated at the Ascension, when the prophecy of Ps. 110:1 is fulfilled and Jesus is seated at the right hand of God, as he had himself foretold in his reply to the high priest's court (22:69). e

Thus the picture of Christ's work painted for us by Lk. may be summed up in the sentence, 'Through death to the heavenly throne'. The theme is to some extent the ancient one of disaster and restoration, f

716f familiar in the OT ; but the hero of the story is now identified with the Servant of the Lord, whose mission was to be a light to the Gentiles, and he suffers and ascends as the one who goes before his people as their leader (*archēgos*, Ac. 3:15).

g Jesus is the Davidic Messiah (1:31–3 ; cf. 2 Sam. 7:12–16), and in Lk. his Davidic royalty is emphasised (Ac. 2:29–31, 13:23 ; cf. the greeting as king, Lk. 19:38, the charge before Pilate (23:2) and that brought against the preaching of Paul and Silas, Ac. 17:7). The birth of the Saviour, Lord Messiah, was in the city of David (2:11), and he was revealed in the Temple as the Lord's Messiah (2:26).

h As Messiah he stands in a unique relationship to God. He is 'Lord' from before his birth (1:43). Yet all this is proleptic. The infancy stories announce what Jesus is, and yet at the same time what he is to become when through death he enters into his glory and is made (Ac. 2:36) the Lord and Christ which he was proclaimed to be in the beginning, and which he already was in the predetermining counsel of God (Ac. 3:20–1). He is Son of God. This is a term denoting the relationship of the Messiah to God (cf. 4:41 : 'You are the *Son of God* . . . they knew that he was the *Christ*' ; Ac. 9:20 : 'He proclaimed Jesus, saying, "He is the *Son of God*" . . . proving that Jesus was the *Christ*'), and possibly the word *pais* (Ac. 3:13, 3:26, 4:27), if it means 'child' (RSV*n*) rather than 'Servant', may indicate that Jesus stands in the same relation to God as David (Lk. 1:69). The term also, however, indicates a special and deeper personal relationship to God (2:49), which is revealed most strikingly in the Q passage of Christ's thanksgiving to the Father (10:22). Lk. acknowledges the intimate union of the Son with the Father ; if, however, we inquire into its nature, the answer must be that it is a union brought about by the Son's possession in the fullest degree of the Spirit of God, and, on the human side, by his communion with the Father in prayer. Yet this is a complete union ; the word of Jesus is God's word ; his authority and power are divine ; he is the agent of God's judgment and God's forgiveness ; and the Spirit which motivates his ministry is the Spirit of God. His followers can identify the divine Spirit with the Spirit of Jesus (Ac. 16:6–7). His exaltation, furthermore, implies divinity ; he is 'Lord of all' (Ac. 10:36), identified with the 'Lord' of Joel's prophecy (Ac. 2:21, 38), and even, perhaps, identified in function with 'God' (Lk. 8:39).

717a Jesus is the bearer of the Spirit, and the agent through whom, as one 'anointed' with the Spirit, the Father is to bestow the same Spirit upon his people. As the Spirit-possessed Messiah, Jesus is the prophet like Moses (Dt. 18:15ff.), and the fulfilment of this expectation is central in Lk.'s thought (24:19, cf. Ac. 7:22 ; Ac. 3:22ff., 7:37). It is as the anointed prophet of Isa. 61:1ff. that Jesus announces his mission in the Nazareth synagogue, and this prophet is in all probability intended to be identified in the mind of his hearers with the Spirit-possessed 'Servant of the Lord' of the earlier chapters of Isaiah. By implication Jesus claims the title of prophet in his speech on the same occasion (4:24), and again in connection with his death (13:33). At Nain he is described as acting in a manner reminiscent of Elijah at Zarephath, and is greeted by the people as a great prophet whose appearance means that God has visited his people (cf. 1:68, 78). In 7:39 Jesus is evidently looked upon by many of the people as a prophet, or, according to a variant reading, *the* prophet (of Dt. 18:15). The voice from heaven at the Transfiguration, in its Lucan form, directly echoes the language of the Deuteronomic injunction to hearken to the prophet like Moses.

b As a prophet, Jesus is the bearer of God's word to Israel. In Lk.'s version of the story of his appearance in the Capernaum synagogue at the beginning of his healing ministry (4:32, 36; cf. Mk 1:22, 27), there is a singular emphasis upon his *word* which is authoritative and potent against the demons. Lk. calls attention to his spoken word as the means by which Simon's wife's mother was healed (4:39). After the healing of the leper, the crowds come to *hear* and be cured, that is, to benefit from a prophetic ministry which is like that of the prophet of Isa. 61 and is ascribed to Jesus in 4:18ff., in the Beatitudes, and in the answer to the messengers of John. 71

c As the prophet like Moses, Jesus naturally reproduces some of the characteristic features of Moses himself. This typology is most strongly brought out in the speech of Stephen, but it is indicated in the Gospel in the appointment of the Seventy in addition to the Twelve, in the bestowal by Jesus of the Spirit on those who are to succeed him in his mission, and perhaps in the allusion to the 'exodus' (RSV 'departure') which he was to accomplish at Jerusalem (9:31). If the suggestion be accepted that the central section of the Gospel was intended to form a new Deuteronomy, following the pattern of the teaching of Moses (see C. F. Evans in D. E. Nineham's *Studies in the Gospels* (1955), 37–53), the parallel with Moses will be greatly strengthened. The prophet like Moses also resembles Elijah, who received God's word in the wilderness, was persecuted, and ascended into heaven. Jesus is likened to Elijah in the episode at Nain, and especially in the narrative of the Ascension ; the task of restoring the tribes of Israel (Sir. 48:10) is probably transferred by Lk. from John the Baptist (whom, unlike Mk, he does not identify with Elijah) to Jesus, and from the preparation for the Gospel to the final judgment (Ac. 3:26).

d Like the prophet of Isa. 61:1ff., Jesus is sent by God (4:43, with a significant alteration of Mk), and, as the fulfilment of that prophecy, Jesus is identified with the Servant of the Lord. If the Alexandrian text is to be followed at 3:22, Lk. takes from Mk the words of the heavenly voice, saluting Jesus in terms which point to him as both Messiah and Servant. Like the Servant, Jesus is named from the womb ; he is the Servant who was 'reckoned with transgressors' (22:37) ; his 'setting of the face' to go to Jerusalem (9:51) may recall Isa. 50:7 ; and the terms *pais* (see above) and 'Righteous One' (Ac. 3:15, 7:52) may denote the Servant. It is as the Servant that Jesus is preached to the Ethiopian (Ac. 8:32ff.), but here the particular part of the Servant prophecy concerned with the Servant's redemptive and vicarious death is not quoted (this aspect of the Servant prophecies is in any case much less marked in the LXX than in the Hebrew text). For Lk. the chief significance of the Servant probably lies much less in the atoning character of his death than in the fact that the Servant was sent as a 'light to the Gentiles' and that he achieved his mission through suffering and death. Jesus was to be the light of the Gentiles (2:32), and in this respect the mission of the Servant is transmitted to the apostles (Ac. 26:17–18, 23 ; cf. 13:47). As the Servant, Jesus passes through death to accomplish the Gentile mission through the Spirit in his followers (2:32, 3:6 ; Ac. 26:23).

e Like the Servant, Jesus brings salvation to the ends of the earth. Great prominence is given by Lk. to the thought of Jesus as Saviour and of the effect of his mission in terms of salvation, from the infancy narratives (e.g. 1:77) to the declaration that this salvation had been sent to the Gentiles (Ac. 28:28).

f **Christ's Death** is foreshadowed in his rejection and attempted murder by his own people at Nazareth after the proclamation to them of his mission, and from 5:21 onwards the reader is prepared for the final conflict by a series of clashes between Jesus and the Jewish authorities, in which the narrow legalism of the old order is ranged against the mission of Jesus and his disciples in the power of the Spirit. The theme of the contrast between the mission of Jesus (and that which will be undertaken by his disciples) and the hostility of the Jewish leaders and their blind legalism, is continued throughout the Gospel ;

17f a climax is reached in 9 with the mission of the Twelve, the feeding of the multitude, Peter's confession, the teaching about the death of the Son of man and the suffering of his followers, and the start of the journey to Jerusalem which begins his 'receiving up'. Lk. emphasises the participation of Christ's disciples in his suffering and victory (9:23), and the connection of his death with his glorification. This is brought out in several peculiar details in the Transfiguration narrative, and in the linking of the Transfiguration with the Resurrection and the Ascension by the two witnesses who are present on each occasion, and, in the case of the Ascension, by the cloud (denoting the divine glory) into which Jesus enters permanently at the Ascension but which is also temporarily manifested at the Transfiguration. His approaching death, of which the reader is reminded by the repeated stress upon the journey to Jerusalem, is totally uncomprehended by the disciples, including those claimants to discipleship who offer to follow him wherever he goes (9:57ff.). It is a prelude, a 'baptism' to be accomplished, which will lead to his 'perfection' (13:32, RV). The way to the Cross is the setting of the teaching about renunciation and counting the cost (14:26ff.); that is, the way of death is to be followed by every disciple. Yet the ultimate note for the disciple is one of hopefulness and confidence (21:16ff., cf. Heb. 10:36). At the Last Supper Jesus speaks of his death as the prelude to his entry into the Kingdom of God; the disciples misunderstand him and dispute about greatness in the Kingdom, but the penitent robber realises that Jesus is to enter his Kingdom through death (23:42). In his death Jesus enacts the part of the Servant (22:37), and, although the moment of his deliverance into the hand of his enemies is the time of the 'power of darkness' (22:53), his death is the fulfilment of the prophecies (24:7, 26, 46), and the necessary and ordained prelude to glory (24:25). Because Jesus has been vindicated in his exaltation, repentance and forgiveness are open to all his people (24:47).

g The idea of the imitation of Christ in the martyr's witness and suffering is very prominent in Lk., e.g. in 12:8–12, 21:12–19; Ac. 14:22; and the parallel drawn between the death of Stephen and that of Jesus.

8a **The Relation between Jesus and his Followers** is in the writer's mind in very many parts of the Gospel. He accordingly devotes much attention to the choice by Jesus of those to whom the task of witnessing to Him will be entrusted, and through whom repentance and forgiveness will be preached to all the nations, to their preparation and training for their mission, and to the contrast between himself and his disciples on the one hand, and the leaders of Israel on the other. The latter had forfeited their place as God's chosen instruments both by their attitude to the outcasts and their rejection of the Christ. The theme of the future mission is interwoven with the narrative of Christ's attestation by mighty works, wonders and signs, from the call of the chief disciples onwards. It is especially prominent in the central section of the Gospel, where the thought of the advent of the Kingdom of God, in the mission of Jesus and in its future proclamation by the apostles is set alongside the judgment of God which that mission and proclamation are bringing, and will bring, upon the old order of Judaism. The climax of the disciples' preparation comes at the Last Supper, when Jesus covenants his kingdom to them and they are instructed in the true meaning of Christian authority as contrasted with worldly leadership. Like the man in the Parable of the Pounds, Jesus goes to receive his kingdom in heaven, leaving his disciples to administer his possessions; this means their exercise of the world-wide mission in his name and in the power of the Spirit received from him in his ascended glory. When he has ascended, the Church is left to follow him and to imitate him. He is enthroned in heaven, and is no
longer with them in person (24:44, 'While I was 718a
still with you'; contrast the Matthaean, 'Lo, I am with you always'). He is seen in special manifestations by Stephen and Saul of Tarsus, but the heavens must receive him (Ac. 3:21) and his return, in like manner to his ascension (Ac. 1:11), may be long delayed. In Lk. the perspective is drawn out; Christians must not believe that the Parousia is imminent; the conversion of the Gentile world lies ahead and must come first. The union between the glorified Christ and his people is an external one, in some respects like that between Christ and the Father. The Pauline sense of the indwelling of Christ in the believer and the believer in Christ is absent. Yet the bond between them is the Spirit which Jesus has sent, which is the 'Spirit of Jesus' and which is the possession of all those who repent and are baptised in his name. The concepts of Spirit and Name, rather than any idea of identity or indwelling, express the link between Christ and his Church. At the same time, this link is so close that the experience and mission of Jesus are repeated in the Church's early mission to Israel under the leadership of Peter, and again in the ministry of Paul to the wider world and ultimately to Rome.

Repentance and Forgiveness—These concepts are b
of cardinal importance in Lk., being the subject of the apostles' preaching and virtually identified with the content, or effect, of the Kingdom of God. John's mission was to make Israel repent, like Elijah in Malachi's prophecy, and so to make ready a people prepared for the Lord (1:17). His task was to bring about forgiveness, a role directly connected with his office as Christ's forerunner (1:77). His baptism was of repentance with a view to forgiveness, and he exhorted the people to bring forth fruits worthy of repentance (3:3, 8; cf. Paul's mission as described in Ac. 26:20). Sinners are called by Jesus to repentance (5:32; cf. the Marcan story of the forgiveness of the paralytic, 5:20ff.). The Lord's Prayer in Lk. includes a petition for forgiveness of sins; and through the vindication of the crucified Messiah repentance and forgiveness are to be universally proclaimed (24:47), and are available to those who are baptised as the people of 'Jesus Messiah' (Ac. 2:38). The acceptance of this gift will bring nearer the day of final fulfilment (Ac. 3:19ff.). It has been made possible by the Resurrection (Ac. 5:31; cf. Ac. 13:38), and is received by faith in Jesus as the Christ (Ac. 10:43). 'Repentance leading to life' is the effect of the extension of the gospel to the Gentiles (Ac. 11:18), and repentance and faith are the content of Paul's preaching to Jews and Gentiles (Ac. 20:21). What Lk. understands by repentance is explained in Ac. 26:18: the opening of the eyes so that there may be a turning from darkness to light and from the power of Satan to God. It is significant that repentance as well as forgiveness are subjects of the gospel-preaching. Both are gifts of God extended to men through Christ. Opposed to repentance and forgiveness is the divine judgment which is coming upon the old Israel (12:6–9, 13:1ff., 13:22–30, 34–5, 19:11ff., 19:44).

The Spirit—One of the most striking features of c
Lk.-Ac. is the prominence accorded to the Holy Spirit. As in the OT, the Spirit is the power of God, manifested particularly in prophesying and in ecstatic phenomena. The Gospel begins in the setting of a fresh upsurge of the Spirit's inspiration, and the narratives of John and of the infancy are full of allusions to prophetic inspiration, John himself being in the highest degree a Spirit-possessed prophet. This new revival of the prophetic inspiration is intended to point to, and witness to, Christ, and he himself is born through the operation of the Spirit and at his Baptism becomes the recipient of the Spirit in a unique manner and degree. The Spirit resting upon him is the power of his mighty works; in the Spirit he holds the closest converse with the Father, and as one anointed with the Spirit he is sent as the great prophet

718c like Moses. The pouring out of the Spirit by the ascended Christ is both the token of his Messiahship and the sign that the last days have dawned. From Pentecost onwards the Spirit is the guide and motive force of the Church's mission, and this is foreshadowed in the Gospel where Jesus promises the Spirit's inspiration to the faithful witness under stress of persecution, whereas the apostate commits the unforgivable blasphemy against the Spirit.

719a **I 1-4 Lk.'s Preface to his Work**—In the customary manner of a classical writer, the author addresses his patron, announcing the purpose of his work. This is probably intended to introduce both parts of Lk.'s work, the secondary preface to his second volume (Ac. 1:1) being intended to mark the continuity of the whole book and to recall to the reader what the author has said here (cf. the opening of the two books of Jos.c.Ap.). This preface is composed in the conventional style of classical rhetoric, in marked contrast with the extremely 'biblical' and Semitic language of the succeeding infancy narratives. 'Accomplished' may have the further sense of 'fulfilled' and refer to the fulfilment of the OT in the gospel events, but the verb does not necessarily imply this. 'Delivered' denotes an authoritative transmission, as from teachers to pupils, and covers both oral and written records. By 'eyewitnesses and ministers of the word' Lk. probably intends us to understand the original apostles, as the source of the authoritative tradition. Thus in Ac. 26:16 Paul declares that he was divinely commissioned as a *minister and witness* of the things in which Christ was revealed to him. The function of the apostles as witnesses is emphasised especially in Ac. 1:22 and 4:20. 'The word' is not Christ as the Word of God, but the Christian revelation or gospel.

b Lk. claims to have kept in touch with, or investigated, the course of events 'for some time past', that is, probably, from the beginning of the ministry of Jesus or John's baptism (cf. Ac. 1:22). This does not necessarily imply that he had participated in them, and it seems rather that he is distinguishing himself both from those who have already compiled narratives and from the authoritative witnesses. His account is 'orderly' as being arranged in a chronological order, corresponding to the movement of the Gospel events from Jerusalem to Rome. His literary patron, Theophilus, whom we cannot identify, may be a Roman official, but this is uncertain. 'Most excellent' is applied to the procurator of Judaea (e.g. Ac. 23:26), and is most commonly used in address to members of the equestrian order (representing the Latin style of address, *egregius*), though it is also used of senatorial officials. In dedications such as this, however, it is sometimes used as a complimentary address to non-officials, as in Jos.c.Ap. i, 1. It is uncertain whether Theophilus had merely been 'informed' or had been 'instructed' as a Christian. The verb may mean either (cf. Ac. 18:25 and 21:21); but the latter is perhaps more likely.

c **The Stories of the Birth and Infancy of John the Baptist and the Annunciation to Mary**—The remainder of chs. 1 and 2 form a theological prologue, explaining the rise of the Baptist as a great prophet and drawing out the parallels and connections between God's action towards the Forerunner and towards the Christ. Thus the reader knows, when the Gospel proper opens at 3:1, something of the nature of the person and mission of Jesus, and is ready to appreciate the importance of the witness to him borne by John, the last and greatest of the prophets of Israel. Lk. also explains in these narratives how the events which he is to record began in the context of a new revival of the prophetic Spirit in Israel. It has often been argued that a Semitic (probably Hebrew) source underlies this section. On the whole, however, it is more probable that Lk. is consciously writing 'biblical' language, and that he is greatly influenced in language and thought by the LXX, particularly the stories of Gideon, Samson and Samuel, and the Psalms.

5ff. Herod the Great reigned from 40 B.C. to 4 B.C. 719 It is typical of Lk. to give the word 'Judaea' the wide sense of 'the land of the Jews', and not to confine it to the actual province of Judaea. The division of Abijah is the eighth of the divisions of priests (1 Chr. 24:10) responsible in turn for performing the regular daily duty of the Temple. The name Elizabeth recalls that of Aaron's wife (Exod. 6:23). The details given here by Lk. serve to heighten the Jewish and OT colouring of the setting in which the gospel events begin. As in Ac., the story starts from Jerusalem and the Temple, moving out into a wider sphere. The whole work leads us from the Jerusalem Temple to Rome, the Gentile capital and the future main centre of Gentile Christianity. Here the narrative is moving wholly within the sphere of the piety of the Old Covenant, and the language is correspondingly Septuagintal. Zechariah and his wife are typical saints of the OT. Their story is evidently meant to recall that of Abraham and Sarah, and God's ancient promises.

9. The morning and evening offerings of incense. e Ps. 141(140):2–3 may be in the writer's mind, possibly to the extent of suggesting an allusion to dumbness. The narrative follows the usual pattern of OT stories of theophanies; cf. also the appearance to Cornelius (Ac. 10:3–4). **14.** 'Joy and gladness' are strongly emphasised in the Lucan writings, especially in connection with the activity of the Spirit. **15.** 'He shall drink no wine', etc., recalling Samson (Jg. 13:7), but probably not implying that John was to be a Nazirite; Lk. is presenting John as a Spirit-possessed person and a great prophet even from (or before, cf. 44) birth, like Jeremiah (Jer. 1:5) or the Servant of the Lord (Isa. 49:1, 5). John's mission is like that of Elijah, according to the proof-text of Mal. 3:22–3 and the account of Elijah in Sir. 48. He is to prepare a penitent and faithful Israel as God's people. **18.** There is a close parallel between the annunciations to Zechariah and to Mary of miraculous births. Gabriel's words in **19** recall those of the angel in Tob. 12:15. Gabriel is the bearer of revelations in Dan. 8, 9, 10, where Daniel also is stricken with dumbness (10:15). The sign of dumbness is more closely paralleled in Ezek. 3:26.

24-25. Elizabeth's withdrawal enables the news of her f conception to be first given to Mary by the angel. Her response to God's action is expressed in similar terms to that of Rachel (Gen. 30:23).

26. The Annunciation to Mary is so described g as to bring out the parallel between the conception of the Forerunner and that of Jesus. Joseph belonged to the house of David; Mary is related (36) to Elizabeth who was of Aaronic descent (5), so that the royal and priestly character of Jesus as Messiah is adumbrated (cf. *Test. Levi* 18, 1QS 9:10). **28.** The angel's greeting 'Hail' is Greek rather than Hebraic; it involves a play on 'favoured one' which can only be effected in Greek. Mary is a recipient of God's grace in a supreme degree. The addition to this salutation in some MSS is interpolated from 42. The supernatural naming of the child recalls Gen. 16:11 and Isa. 7:14, the latter being cited in **31**. The reader is told in 32–3 that Jesus is to be the Messiah of Israel, God's Son (cf. Ps. 2:7, and, for the expression 'Most High', Ps. 82:6), fulfilling the expectation of Isa. 9:6ff. **34.** Mary's question to the angel directly implies that her conception is to be virginal and even more miraculous than Elizabeth's. It is omitted by the Old Latin MS *b* (see §586*b*), which inserts 38*a* at this point, probably owing to scribal confusion between the two verses which begin, 'And Mary said'. **35.** The birth of Jesus is brought about by the coming of the Holy Spirit, or power of God, as the beginning of the Church's mission was to be effected by the bestowal of power on the disciples through the coming of Holy Spirit upon them (Ac. 1:8). This equation of the divine Spirit with the power of God is typical of Lk. The 'overshadowing' of the Spirit resembles the 'over-

19g shadowing' of the cloud, as the sign of the divine presence, at the Transfiguration (9:34); cf. Exod. 40:38. **37.** An echo of the word of the Lord to Sarah (Gen. 18:14). **38.** Mary's obedience, contrasted with the disobedience of Eve, has received much emphasis from Irenaeus onwards, and has been stressed to the point of making her a partner in the economy of redemption. Lk., however, does not dwell on this thought. Mary has received a promise of supreme grace and blessing, and, like Abraham, accepts it in faith, assenting to God's word with her 'Amen'.

h **39ff. The Story of the Meeting of Mary and Elizabeth** shows John as a prophet from before his birth, and as a witness already pointing to Jesus. The passage may owe something to Gen. 25:22ff. It is evidently intended to bring out the fact that the gospel events began in the context of a great revival of the prophetic inspiration. **42.** Elizabeth, as an inspired prophetess, greets Mary as the mother of her Lord and as blessed for her acceptancc in faith of God's promise. **46.** The hymn of praise is assigned to Mary in most MSS, but to Elizabeth by some of the Old Latin MSS, texts known to Origen, and Irenaeus (*Adv. Haer.* IV, vii, 1, some MSS; but at III, x, 1 this verse is cited in all MSS with the reading 'Mary'). The hymn (*Magnificat*) as a whole looks back to the song of Hannah (1 Sam. 2:1–10) and is a catena of OT reminiscences. **48a.** 'Low estate' might refer to Elizabeth's reproach of childlessness if the hymn were hers. **48b** recalls Gen. 30:13, and **50** Psalm 10:4 of the Psalms of Solomon. **55**, like much in this narrative, links the fulfilment of the Messianic hope of Israel with the original covenant promise to Abraham. The repetition in **56** of the name 'Mary' (cf. 46) has seemed to some to support the reading 'Elizabeth' in 46.

i **59-64. The Naming of John**—The name is given by inspiration; Elizabeth can know it only supernaturally, and the story implies that Zechariah is deaf as well as dumb. **67.** Zechariah, like so many other characters in this narrative, is inspired by the Spirit as a prophet. His song (*Benedictus*) is parallel to *Magnificat*, and is also made up of OT quotations. **70** is echoed, according to most MSS, in the speech assigned to Peter in Ac. 3:21. **76** asserts John's eminence as a prophet, Unlike Mk, this Gospel does not directly identify him with Elijah, but he is inspired in a similar way and carries out the expected work of Elijah. **77.** Salvation is a favourite Lucan concept; its interpretation in terms of remission of sins is typical of the thought of Lk.-Ac., and suggests that Lk. is the author rather than the transcriber of this poem. **78.** The word rendered 'day or 'dayspring' is the same as the word for the (Davidic) *branch* in Jer. 23:5; Zech. 3:8, 6:12. It may possibly have been misunderstood in the sense of *dawn* here, but the thought of this verse is paralleled in Isa. 60:1 and Mal. 4:2. The concluding words of the song interpret John's mission in terms of the messianic passage (Isa. 9:2) and the first 'Servant song' (Isa. 42:7). **80.** The picture of John's growth resembles what is said about Samson and Samuel in Jg. 13:24 and 1 Sam. 2:26.

720a **II 1ff. The Birth of Jesus**—Lk.'s narrative so far has moved in a purely Jewish atmosphere, and has been concerned with the fulfilment of the divine promises to Israel. The marvellous birth of John, the great prophetic Forerunner, has led on to the birth of the Messiah, announced in terms (1:28–35) which indicate a fresh creative intervention of God in history. Now, when he comes to tell the story of Christ's birth itself, Lk. begins to associate the gospel with the wider background of the Gentile world. The advent of Christ is linked with the enrolment of the whole world by Augustus, and although Lk. does not anticipate post-Constantinian writers in connecting the empire of Christ directly with the *pax Romana*, he is clearly anxious that the reader should be reminded of the relevance of the birth of Christ to the whole of Caesar's world, since he is to be 'a light for revelation to the Gentiles' as well as 'for glory to Israel'. 720a
Lk.'s eyes are already looking ahead from the Jerusalem of the beginning of his Gospel to the Rome of the last chapter of Ac.

In making his point Lk. seems to have made use of historical data with which he was imperfectly acquainted. A census was held about A.D. 6, when Quirinius was legate of Syria and Coponius procurator of Judaea (Jos. Ant. XVII, xiii, 5; XVIII, i, 1). This is referred to in Ac. 5:37, and Lk. was probably uncertain of its date and ignored the inconsistency involved here in associating it with the reign of Herod. A census ordered by Augustus could scarcely have taken place in Herod's dominions without provoking disturbances, and would be unlikely to be unnoticed by Josephus. Lk.'s allusion to this as the 'first enrolment' suggests that he is thinking of the census which, as the first to be held under the Roman administration of Judaea, caused the revolt of Judas of Galilee. There is evidence for the taking of a census every fourteen years in Egypt, the series possibly going back to A.D. 6; but there is no sure evidence for the extension of this system to other parts of the Empire at so early a date, and no mention is made by Josephus of regular enrolments. On the evidence of Strabo, combined with two inscriptions, the *lapis Venetus* and the very fragmentary *lapis Tiburtinus*, it has been argued that Quirinius was in Syria with an extraordinary legatine commission for military operations in Cilicia between 10 and 7 B.C., or possibly as holding a first governorship of the province from 3 to 2 B.C. If the former possibility were established, the historical problem would still not be completely solved; if the latter, the inconsistency with a dating in Herod's reign still stands. Tertullian (*adv. Marc.* iv, 19) dates the birth of Jesus in the governorship over Syria of Saturninus (9 to 6 B.C.), which may well be correct. b

An edict of C. Vibius Maximus, Prefect of Egypt, in A.D. 104 requires those away from home to return to their domicile for registration (*P. Lond.* cmiv, 20f.). This is often held to support Lk.'s statement about the census procedure (3–4); but Lk. envisages a return *from* the normal place of residence to the ancestral seat of a family, which is by no means the same thing. On all this very difficult historical problem see W. M. Ramsay, *Was Christ born at Bethlehem?* (3rd ed. 1905), and *The Bearing of Recent Discovery on the Trustworthiness of the NT* (1915); E. Schürer, *A History of the Jewish People in the Time of Jesus Christ* (2nd ed., tr. Macpherson, 1908), I, ii, 105–43; J. M. Creed, *The Gospel according to St Luke* (1930, reprinted 1942), 28–30; F. J. Foakes Jackson & K. Lake, *The Beginnings of Christianity* (1933), iv, 61–2; T. Corbishley in *Klio* 29 (1936), 81ff. c

Like Mt., but in a different way, Lk. combines the tradition that Jesus had his home at Nazareth with that which claimed that he fulfilled the Davidic promises by his birth at Bethlehem. In addition to setting the birth of Christ in the context of the Roman world, Lk. emphasises the Davidic Messiahship of Jesus through Joseph's lineage. It is characteristic of Lk. to lay stress on the fact that Jesus was a Davidic king, and at the same time to show that his kingship is of a new kind and politically harmless. **5.** Some of the ancient versions read 'wife' for 'betrothed', presumably to account for Mary and Joseph travelling together; hence the harmonising reading 'betrothed wife'. d

8ff. The Annunciation to the Shepherds—The declaration to shepherds of the birth of the Messiah suggests the favourite Lucan theme of the acceptance by humble, and often by outcast, people of revelation which the leaders of Israel are not given to perceive. The shepherds also recall David, and their association with Bethlehem is possibly linked with a connection of the 'tower of the flock' to which 'the kingdom' shall come (Mic. 4:8) with the 'tower of Eder (= 'flock')' in the region of Bethlehem (Gen. 35:19–21). The angel's words are parallel to the annunciations to Mary and Zechariah. His announcement is a 'gospel' e

720e of good news and joy (so often associated by Lk. with divine activity) to all the people of Israel. Jesus is proclaimed as 'saviour', a relatively infrequent NT title perhaps because of its associations with the imperial cult; Lk. may lay stress upon it here in the context of the allusion to the imperial power of Augustus, but cf. Ac. 5:31, 13:23. The title 'Lord Christ' (cf. Lam. 4:20 (LXX); Psalms of Solomon 17:36) belongs to Jesus from birth, but in a sense proleptically; he becomes Lord and Christ when he enters into his glory and takes possession of the fullness of these titles (Ac. 2:36). **14**. The angels' proclamation of the divine blessing of peace (a concept closely akin to that of divine grace; cf. Isa. 52:7 and 57:19, also Ac. 10:36) is made to those to whom God's favour is granted, that is, his covenant people. The alternative reading 'goodwill among men' is less probable. The meaning, however, is not dissimilar; the 'goodwill' is God's.

f **The Circumcision, and Presentation in the Temple**—The narrative in **21** continues the parallel with the story of John (1:59ff.). The presentation in the Temple recalls the dedication of Samuel, who typifies Jesus in his character as the great prophet (24:19; cf. Ac. 3:22). **24**. Hence the episode is seen as a presentation of the child (cf. Exod. 13:1) rather than a purification of the mother (Lev. 12), and speaks of 'their', and not 'her', purification, which some MSS have sought to correct. The offering is that prescribed for a poor person (Lev. 12:8). **25**. Simeon, like Joseph of Arimathaea (23:50–1), is not only typical of pious Jews, but also belongs to the number of those who had faith and patience to await in peace the fulfilment of the hope of Israel. Like most of the principal characters in the infancy narratives, he is inspired by the Spirit. 29ff. His song (*Nunc dimittis*) contains many echoes of the Second Isaiah, and emphasises the double mission of Christ to Jew and Gentile. **29**. 'Thy word', referring to the promise mentioned in **26**. 'Lord' is more properly translated 'master', used of God also in Ac. 4:24; Rev. 6:10 and frequently in 1 Clement. **30**. The prophecy of Isa. 40:5 is fulfilled; the implication is that all flesh will see the salvation of God; cf. Isa. 52:10 which is echoed in **31**. Like the Servant of Isa. 49:6, Jesus (and his apostles afterwards, cf. Ac. 13:47, also 26:18, 23) is to convert the Gentiles, along with Israel. The double approach to Jew and Gentile, adumbrated here, is worked out in Ac. The 'glory' is the revelation of God's glory to Israel (Isa. 40:5). The mission of Jesus will involve judgment on Israel, or be the sign of God's judgment through his rejection. **35**. The crisis of his advent reveals men's minds. Simeon's allusion to a 'sword' is a parenthetical foreshadowing of suffering—the first hint in the Gospel of the association of Christ's mission with suffering—or possibly a prediction that the crisis of judgment will affect Mary herself as well as Israel as a whole (cf. the similar thought in Heb. 4:12). Anna, whose name is that of Samuel's mother, is a prophetess. She is described in terms which recall Christian widows in the early Church. 'Redemption': i.e. deliverance; cf. 1:68, 24:21; Ac. 7:35; Heb. 9:12.

721a **39. The Return to Nazareth**—Lk.'s general reference to Christ's boyhood is parallel to the description of John the Baptist (1:80). **Jesus at Jerusalem**—The parents' visit recalls the story of Samuel (1 Sam. 1:7, etc.). Lk.'s purpose is mainly to contrast the relation of Jesus to God with his human parentage, to emphasise that this unique relationship existed before the experience of Jesus at his Baptism, and to set his obedience to Mary and Joseph in this context. Mary appears again only in 8:20 and Ac. 1:14. **52**. Lk.'s second summary of Christ's boyhood, with its emphasis on the reality of his humanity, is based on the account of Samuel in 1 Sam. 2:26; cf. the description of Moses, as a type of Christ, in Ac. 7:22.

b **III 1-2 The Mission of John** introduces the Gospel narrative proper after the prologue of the infancy stories. This is the beginning of the age of fulfilment, the epoch of the gospel, the mission of John forming 721b the hinge between the Old Covenant and the New, though he himself belongs to the former (Ac. 1:22, 10:37, 13:24). Lk.'s elaborate dating conforms to secular patterns, such as Thucydides ii, 2 (the closest classical parallel to this passage), and serves to set the Gospel event in the framework of world history. The fifteenth year of Tiberius: A.D. 28–9. Pilate was procurator from 26 to 36. Lysanias may be introduced to make four divisions (tetrarchies) out of Herod the Great's former kingdom; 'tetrarch', however, does not preserve its etymological meaning, and signifies only a minor prince. The only Lysanias known certainly is the king of Chalcis killed in 36 B.C. Jos. Ant. XIX, v, 1 mentions 'Abila of Lysanias', and xx, 7 tells of the former tetrarchy of Lysanias being given to Agrippa II in A.D. 53. Two inscriptions have suggested that a second Lysanias may have ruled at Abila. It seems probable, however, that, without necessarily having read and been misled by Josephus, Lk. may have had confused and unreliable information about the history of this district. Annas ceased to be high priest in A.D. 15. As father-in-law of Caiaphas he continued to exert much influence (cf. Ac. 4:6), but Lk. appears to think that the high priesthood was jointly exercised, which was not the case.

3-6. Lk.'s account of John's mission appears to be c based on Mk, but Lk. typically draws attention to the prophetic call of the great prophet, echoing Jer. 1:1 in his allusion to the coming upon him of the 'word of God'. This takes place in the desert, with which John is always associated (cf. 1:80) in harmony with the application to him of the prophecy of Isa. 40:3. Mk's description of John preaching 'a baptism of repentance with a view to forgiveness of sin' becomes of central importance in Lk. What was proleptically announced in John's mission is realised through the work of Christ and made effective in the Church (cf. Ac. 2:38), especially in the missionary labours of Paul (Ac. 26:20). John's baptism was a prophetic sign denoting the preparation for a coming divine judgment of a penitent and faithful people of God. **4b**. Lk. follows Mk in applying to John the text of Isa. 40:3, repunctuated in order to suit its fulfilment and with the substitution of 'his paths' for 'the paths of our God' (LXX). Thus by implication 'the Lord' is identified with Jesus. In Lk. the citation is continued so as to bring in the prophecy of universal salvation (foreshadowing the Gentile mission) already alluded to in 2:30. Like Mt., Lk. omits Mk's quotation of Mal. 3:1, probably because the text occurs in Q material which is used by Mt. and Lk. later (Mt. 11:10; Lk. 7:27).

John's Preaching—**7b-9** is Q material almost exactly d paralleled in Mt. In Lk. it is addressed to the crowds as a whole; in Mt. to the Jewish leaders. The coming judgment demands sincere repentance, not simply a confidence in physical membership of the covenant people, or participation in the merits of Abraham (cf. *Test. Levi* 15:4). The strongly eschatological character of John's prophetic preaching is striking. It is worked out in terms of day-to-day conduct in **10-14**, a passage peculiar to Lk. and in harmony with the picture in Ac. 1–5 of a society where 'repentance' has become effective. This teaching recalls the moral exhortations of the OT prophets. The injunction in **11** recalls the system of sharing property in the primitive Jerusalem Church. John's instruction to tax-collectors may be compared with the repentance of Zacchaeus (19:8) as a true son of Abraham (19:9; cf. 8 above). Lagrange's suggestion that the soldiers are armed attendants or agents of the tax collectors is unnecessary; the Greek denotes simply 'soldiers', who are evidently pictured as Jews rather than pagans. They may well be troops in the service of Herod Antipas. Their appearance here is in harmony with the interest shown by Lk. in devout soldiers such as Cornelius. **15** is peculiar to Lk. The Marcan prophecy of John that a 'mightier one' is

721d to come has been expanded by Lk. into a formal disclaimer by John that he is more than a forerunner or preparer of the way ; he is not himself the Messiah. That John's ministry took place in the setting of much varied messianic expectation is no doubt historically true ; but the Lucan picture of a general inquiry among the people of Israel whether John might be the fulfilment of their hopes is probably due to apologetic motives. Like the Fourth Gospel, Lk. presents John as a prophetic herald whose role is strictly subordinate to that of the Messiah. This is in sharp contrast with the account of John given by Josephus. Whether there is an implied polemic against a sect of followers of the Baptist remains uncertain. **16b** resumes Mk's narrative : John is unworthy to act as a slave to the coming agent of divine judgment, who will baptise with Holy Spirit and fire in a baptism for which John's water baptism is only a preparation. A bestowal of God's Spirit was expected in the age of future redemption and renewal (cf. Isa. 32:15 ; Ezek. 39:29 ; Jl 2:28–9), and this is associated with a Messianic hope in Psalms of Solomon 17:42 and *Test. Levi* 18. The allusion to the fire of judgment (cf. Isa. 4:4 ; Mal. 3:2–3) is added by Mt. and Lk. to the saying as given in Mk. This Q material extends through **17**, where the ideas of judgment and the salvation of a faithful remnant are prominent. Lk.'s conclusion (**18-20**) to his account of John emphasises that the people (i.e. Israel) received a *gospel* from him. John thus belongs in a sense to the age of fulfilment to which he pointed ; at the same time, by inserting a notice of his imprisonment at this point (cf. Mt. 14:3–4 ; Mk 6:17–18), Lk. makes it clear that John's mission had ended when the preaching of Jesus began, so that his work is primarily the closing stage of the OT prophetic dispensation. **19.** The husband of Herodias was Herod, a son of Herod the Great who lived privately and held no tetrarchy.

e **21-23 The Baptism of Jesus**—Mk is probably the source for this narrative. Certain minor agreements in wording between Mt. and Lk. against Mk are probably due either to coincidental improvements made by them in the language of Mk, or to the influence of OT language on both of them ; their common use of a different Greek word from that employed by Mk to describe the ' opening ' of heaven is probably due to the influence of Isa. 24:18, 64:1, and Ezek. 1:1.

f Jesus, according to Lk., participates in the baptism of all the people of Israel, identifying himself with those who were preparing for the coming judgment. Lk. alone refers to Jesus praying. In his view, the decisive turning-points in the gospel story take place in a setting of prayer. Prayer and the Spirit constitute the human and divine aspects of the relationship of Jesus to God. The actual baptism, perhaps to be interpreted as a prefiguring of Christ's descent to death, is mentioned only incidentally, the emphasis being laid upon the divine revelation which designates him Son of God. This is the anointing of the Messiah (Ac. 4:27, 10:38) with the Spirit of God (cf. Isa. 11:2 ; Enoch 62:2). Lk. characteristically heightens the concreteness of the appearance of the Spirit, ' in bodily form '. It is symbolical of the permanent and full endowment of the Messiah with the Spirit, unlike a partial and temporary prophetic inspiration. The imagery of the dove may possibly link the inauguration of a new covenant between God and man with the beginning of the first covenant with Noah. Spirit-possession is identical with Sonship. **22.** The reading of most MSS, reproducing Mk, combines the beginning of the Messianic (royal and Davidic) salutation in Ps. 2:7 with language which echoes Isa. 42:1, 44:2, alluding to the ' Servant of the Lord ', who is called ' beloved ' in Isa. 42:1 as cited in Mt. 12:18 (cf. Isa. 44:2). The ' Western ' text continues the quotation of Ps. 2:7 : ' today I have begotten thee '. The latter proof-text (cf. Heb. 1:5) is applied in Ac. 13:33 to the Resurrection ; it is perhaps unlikely that Lk. would have used it here of Christ's baptism. It is improbable that the ' Western ' reading was corrected in the interests of orthodoxy ; Ps. 2:7 is a constantly used proof-text in the later Church and there is no evidence that it was thought to express an adoptionist Christology. More probably the ' Western ' reading is due to assimilation to the familiar words of the Psalm. The text has not been assimilated to Mt., whose wording differs in minor respects. 721f

23-38 The Genealogy—This indicates the Davidic ancestry of Jesus, through Nathan, and his descent from the universal father of mankind. It is inserted here to present Christ's human ancestry in juxtaposition to his relation of sonship to God. **36.** Cainan occurs in Gen. 11:24 (LXX), but not in the Hebrew. The list is based on the Greek Bible. 722a

IV 1-13 The Temptations—This account is non-Marcan, except possibly for *1b–2a*, and is substantially, but not verbally, paralleled in Mt. The temptations are consequent upon the baptism of Jesus and the voice from heaven. The assurance of Sonship involves the temptation to fulfil ordinary messianic expectations and to put aside the vocation of Servant-Messiah which was expressed in the heavenly voice. This temptation was repeated, in part, at Gethsemane, and, according to Mk, at Caesarea Philippi. Jesus leaves the scene of John's mission, under the impulsion of the Spirit. Lk. heightens the impression given by Mk and Mt. that Jesus went into the desert in a state of Spirit-possession. The forty days, recorded by Mk, recall the experiences of Israel in the desert, Moses on Sinai and Elijah at Horeb. The first temptation is to interpret the assurance of divine sonship in a selfish and materialistic way. Its form is interesting in view of the feeding of the multitude later on; that miracle is not a selfish or arbitrary exercise of power, but a prophetic sign of Christ's gift to men of the true spiritual bread. It is countered by a quotation of Dt. 8:3. The second temptation also assumes the fact of divine sonship, and interprets it in terms of worldly or political power. These two temptations in Lk. lead on to the third in which the devil challenges the conviction of divine sonship itself in a temptation to put God to the test in a miracle of sheer wonder-working. It is in this last temptation that the devil quotes scripture (Ps. 91:11–12). **5-8.** This temptation may be related to the promise of world-wide dominion given to the Davidic king in Ps. 2:8, which continues the first part of the declaration of the voice from heaven (3:22). Lk. inserts ' in a moment of time ', as usual heightening the dramatic effect of the story. In this Gospel the kingdoms of the world belong now to the devil (cf. Jn 12:31, 14:30, 16:11). Authority and glory belong to Jesus as the overthrower of the devil (cf. 11:20) ; here he is promised the authority and glory of a kingdom conferred by the devil. The answer of Jesus is quoted from Dt. 6:13. In the last temptation the devil speaks in the words of Ps. 91, and is answered by Dt. 6:16. **12.** In Lk. there is no reference to the ministry of angels, mentioned in Mk and Mt. It is made clear that the temptations will be resumed, as in Gethsemane. b

14-15 The Beginning of the Galilaean Ministry— c
The short summary by Lk. is required by Lk.'s coming alteration in the Marcan order of events. Typically, Lk. brings Jesus into Galilee as a great prophet possessing the power of the Spirit. That a report went out about him does not imply that he had already carried on a ministry in Judaea ; it is rather an anticipation of the results of his teaching in the synagogues.

16-30 Jesus in the Synagogue at Nazareth—This d
narrative is probably based on Mk 6:1ff., to which Lk. has prefixed an introduction explaining more fully the circumstances implied in Mk, an expansion of the Marcan story, centred upon the proof-text of Isa. 61:1–2, and a speech (25–7) developed out of Mk 6:4 as applied to the wider sphere of Christ's rejection by the Jewish nation. The passage concludes with a furious attack upon Jesus (28–30) in which the rejection

722d of him which Mk implies is written up in the light of subsequent events, and placed in close parallelism with the murder of Stephen (Ac. 7:57–8). The expansion of Mk's story of the preaching in the synagogue may be based on the use of the same proof-text, together with other Isaianic prophecy, in Q material employed by Lk. at 7:22.

e As rewritten and expanded, this story announces the nature of the mission of Jesus, the words of Isa. 61 revealing the character of his messianic anointing by the Spirit (at his baptism), prepares the reader for his rejection by his own people, and hints at his acceptance by Gentiles. It thus unfolds the pattern of the subsequent history of Jesus himself and of his gospel as proclaimed by the apostles. It is thus an introduction to the whole of Lk.'s two-volume work. Its theme is taken up and echoed in the speech of Paul at Antioch (Ac. 13) with its setting in a synagogue and its sequel of a turning to the Gentiles.

f **16**. In Lk., Mk's undefined 'his own country' is explained as Nazareth. In the Fourth Gospel (Jn 4:44) the Lucan extension of this story to symbolise the Jewish rejection of the gospel is carried further and the 'country' of Jesus is thought of as the 'land of the Jews', 'Judaea'.

g **17**. The prophetic lesson would follow the reading of the Law. This passage is also introduced in the answer to John (7:22) and echoed in the Beatitudes. Jesus is presented here as a great prophet, and perhaps by implication as the 'Servant' in view of the close relation between Isa. 61:1 and 42:1. The anointing with the Spirit is recalled in Ac. 10:38. **18**. The 'sending' of Jesus introduces a theme on which Lk. lays some stress (cf. the alteration of Mk's wording at 4:43) and which is strongly developed by the Fourth Gospel. Lk. conflates Isa. 61:1–2 with Isa. 58:6 in order to introduce his favourite theme of 'release', a word generally used in the sense of 'forgiveness' (of sins), which is for him of the essence of the gospel. **19**. The 'year' is the age of fulfilment or Messianic era. **20**. The preacher or teacher sat (cf. 5:3; Ac. 16:3). 'Attendant' denotes the *ḥazzān* or beadle. In telling us that the eyes of the congregation were 'fixed' upon him, Lk. draws a parallel with Stephen at the opening of his speech of defence (Ac. 6:15); both speeches imply the end of the peculiar privileges of the old Israel, and both, in consequence of this, end with an attack on the speaker by his infuriated hearers.

h **22**. The saying of the people implies both a natural surprise and a complete misunderstanding of the mission of Jesus. 'Joseph's son' may be a softening of Mk's 'the carpenter, the son of Mary', but more probably a further indication of the people's ignorance. Lk.'s readers know, in the light of the infancy stories, that the people were wrong even in this assertion. **23**. A proverbial saying introduces the wider significance of the misunderstanding and rejection of Jesus by his own people. 'Capernaum' may be mentioned by inference from 14–15, but is more probably due to the author's failure to remember that the context of this episode in Mk (after many incidents at Capernaum) is no longer appropriate in its new setting before Jesus has worked at Capernaum. **25-7**. Like his great prophetic predecessors, Jesus will turn to the Gentiles. This hint is fulfilled, according to Lk., only after his exaltation, when the pattern of the Church's mission is one of rejection by the synagogue and acceptance by Gentiles (cf. Ac. 28:25–8). **25**. The mention of 3½ years agrees with Jas 5:17 against 1 Kg. 18:1; some influence may have been exerted on this reckoning by Dan. 7:25.

i **28-29**. The fate of Jesus at the hands of his own people is foreshadowed thus early in Lk. **30** suggests that the Resurrection and the ultimate triumph of the gospel are also foreshadowed. **31** resumes the narrative of Mk 1:21ff.

723a **31-38a Healings at Capernaum**—Jesus descends (a favourite expression of Lk., usually denoting—except in 9:37; Ac. 13:4, 21:3, 27:5—travel from Jerusalem or Judaea to Capernaum. This 'descent' may possibly symbolise Christ's going down, through the Church's mission, from Jerusalem, his own country, to the Gentile world. 'Galilee of the Gentiles' seems at times in the NT to convey this overtone; and, unlike Mk, Lk. emphasises that Capernaum is a city of *Galilee*, despite the fact that Nazareth was also such a city. **32**. Authority characterises the mission of Jesus. It is expressed in 'power' and exercised in works of power. **35**. In Lk. the impression given by Mk that the demon did much harm to the possessed is softened. In **36** there is great insistence on the power of the word of Jesus, who has been acknowledged by the demon as the Messiah, consecrated to God, the Holy One of God (cf. Jn 6:69).

38b, 39 Simon's Mother-in-law healed—Simon is introduced abruptly, Lk. having omitted the call of Simon and other disciples as given in Mk 1:16ff. 'They besought him for her' replaces Mk's 'they told him of her', possibly because it is thought that Jesus would not need to be informed. In Mk and Mt. the woman is touched by Jesus; here the fever is treated as demonic, and only the word of rebuke is needed. Thus the authority and power of Jesus are again illustrated, as in the cure of the demoniac in the synagogue. The insertion of 'immediately' in **39** (not found in Mk) heightens the miracle. In Lk., however, a laying-on of hands is inserted in the story of general healings which follows. b

A General Healing of the Sick—This takes place at sunset, i.e. as soon as the sabbath is ended. The imposition of hands is a sign of personal identification with another person, and so, in the case of the laying of hands on the sick, of healing. **41**. The confession of the demons is taken from Mk 3:11. Though the identity of Jesus is for the most part unrecognised, the demons know him, and acknowledge him as Messiah (Son of God). Lk. explains in this sense Mk's bald statement that they 'knew him', and makes their recognition take a quasi-credal form (cf. Ac. 8:37—some MSS—and Jn 6:69). c

Jesus leaves Capernaum and sets out on a Preaching Mission—**42**. Following Mk, Lk. describes Jesus setting out on a wider mission from which the crowds seek to deter him. The wording suggests that Lk. sees in this a hint of the wider mission of the Church to the world outside Palestine. **43**. 'I must' (cf. 2:49, 9:22, etc.); the mission of Jesus is ordained in the counsel of God. 'I was sent' emphasises the character of Jesus as the accredited agent of God, sent by him; Mk's 'I came out' is ambiguous and might denote only the departure from the city of Capernaum. In Lk. the purpose of this mission is to preach good news, and its content is said to be the Kingdom of God. **44**. Judaea probably means the land of the Jews; an explanatory variant reading gives 'synagogues of the Jews'; an inferior reading is 'Galilee', following Mk. The reference to Judaea is no evidence for a ministry in the actual province of Judaea. d

V 1-11 The Call of Peter, with James and John—The setting of this episode seems to be derived from Mk 4:1f. which Lk. omits at 8:4. The calling of these disciples is narrated by Mk (1:16–20), where the point of the story is the same: Simon (and Andrew in Mk) are designated as missionaries (catchers of men). Here the story is much fuller, and closely resembles Jn 21:1–14. It is intended to show Peter as one who was designated from the moment of his call to be the leader of the universal mission (cf. Ac. 2–5, 10, 15). The Fourth Gospel has transferred this commission to the post-Resurrection period and associated it with Peter's restoration after his denial of Jesus. It has also developed the symbolism. The Greek of this passage is full of typically Lucan words and idioms, including the use of 'lake' rather than 'sea' for the sea of Galilee. **4** is addressed to more than one person: Simon is the captain of the boat. **5**. Jesus is called 'Master' only in Lk. (cf. 8:24, 45, 9:33, 49, 17:13). e

723e 6. Contrast the unbroken net of Jn 21:11. **8.** The double name 'Simon Peter' (see Mt. 16:18) occurs only here in Lk., and some MSS omit 'Peter'. 'Lord' appears to have a full religious meaning here; contrast the title 'Master' above. Peter's sense of sinfulness is related to this; it is an expression of awe, and need not suggest that Lk. has antedated a post-Resurrection episode in which Peter was alluding to his denial of Jesus. James and John are subordinate in this story to Peter; the promise concerning the mission is here addressed to Peter alone. 'Fear not' is a phrase usually associated with a theophany. The disciples leave everything, as in the case of Levi (28).

f **12-15 The Healing of a Leper**—The call of Peter is followed by a series of stories from Mk. Lk. has first set out the nature of Christ's mission and the call of Peter to evangelise; now he relates a group of healings and other episodes which illustrate the attitude to Jesus of the Jewish leaders. Despite the adherence of Jesus to the provision of the Law when he heals an outcast leper, their hostility develops as he appears to blaspheme, to associate with outcasts from Israel, to set aside Jewish religious practice, and to claim authority for himself over against the Sabbath law. The section reaches its climax in their furious plotting against him (6:11). The early chapters of Ac. exhibit a similar pattern, leading up to persecution by the Jews.

g **12.** The episode, having lost its Marcan context, through the insertion of the story of Peter's call, is provided with an introduction, giving a very vague indication of place and time. 'Full of leprosy': 'full' in this sense is a common Lucan expression (cf. 4:1; Ac. 6:8, 9:36, 13:10). It heightens the dramatic force of the narrative. **14.** The law of Lev. 14:1ff. is fulfilled, as a proof of the attitude of Jesus to the Law. **15.** Healing is associated by Lk. with the hearing of Christ's word. **16.** A characteristic Lucan reference to the centrality of prayer in the ministry of Jesus.

h **17-26 The Healing of a Paralytic**—The authority of Jesus is demonstrated in respect of both forgiveness and healing. After another vague indication of the context, the narrative follows Mk. Lk., however, places the episode in a setting of teaching, and heightens the sense that this dramatic sign is given in a formal context of the assembled leaders of Judaism from all parts of Palestine. The mention of the 'power of the Lord' (i.e. the operation of the Spirit) is typically Lucan. **19.** Lk. alters the Marcan 'pallet' to 'bed' and adds detail to the letting of the man through the roof. **21ff.** The Jewish leaders accuse Jesus of usurping the divine prerogative; the sign of healing demonstrates that he is the Son of man who, in Daniel's vision, received authority to exercise the divine judgment. **25.** Lk. alone mentions the glorifying of God by the paralytic, and the fear of the bystanders.

724a **27-32 The Call of Levi and Christ's Attitude to the Outcasts**—The spiritual restoration of the sinner is linked to the forgiveness and physical restoration of the paralytic, as in Mk; cf. the saying about the mission of Jesus in 31, with the simile of the work of a physician. **27.** In Lk. stress is laid on the fact that Levi was a tax collector, and as such was an outcast. The Marcan description of him as 'son of Alphaeus' is omitted, probably because of the appearance of 'James the son of Alphaeus' in the list of the Twelve (6:15); for the same reason some MSS read 'James' for Levi in Mk 2:14. Only in Lk. is it said that Levi left everything (cf. 11). **29.** Mk's rather ambiguous language is clarified; the feast is in Levi's house. **32.** Christ has come to call sinners, not those who claim righteousness for themselves, like the Pharisees. Lk. adds 'to repentance', in accordance with the emphasis which he lays on repentance as the content of the preaching of Christ and the Church. Repentance follows Christ's calling, as its consequence, and is not a prior condition of hearing his call. **33.** This teaching leads to the objection by the Jewish leaders that the disciples of Jesus disregard ordinary piety as expressed in fasting. In Mk and Mt. this objection is a separate occurrence distinct from the dispute in connection with Levi. Lk. inserts 'often' and refers to prayers as well as fasting. The answer of Jesus foreshadows his death, already implied in the echo of the 'Servant' prophecies at his baptism. The parable may imply that Jesus is the bridegroom, as God was the bridegroom of Israel in the OT.

36-38. The old observances are now unnecessary hindrances. Mk speaks of patching an old garment with uncarded cloth. Lk. thinks of cutting a piece of a new garment to patch an old one, so as both to harm the new and to fail to achieve harmony with the old. The old system must be wholly replaced, new wine into fresh skins. **39.** Those who condemn Christ's attitude to Jewish observances and his treatment of the outcasts prefer the old to the new. The 'Western' text omits this verse, probably owing to Marcion, who must have misunderstood it as a commendation of Jewish conservatism. It may have had some influence upon the narrative of Cana in the Fourth Gospel. b

VI 1-5 Jesus and the Sabbath: the Cornfields— c
Following Mk, Lk. illustrates the new dispensation which replaces the observances of Pharisaic Judaism. In the first instance Jesus and the disciples commit a technical infringement of the Sabbath law, and arouse the opposition of the leaders of contemporary Judaism. **1.** Some MSS read as RSV*n*, 'on the second sabbath after the first'; this obscure expression probably means 'the second of a series' and, if a scribal gloss, may be due to a consideration of this passage alongside 4:31 and 6:3–4. David abrogated the Law in a case of need (1 Sam. 21:2–7; cf. Lev. 24:7–9). **4.** Lk.'s insertion of 'took' in addition to 'ate' and 'gave' might conceivably suggest that he sees a eucharistic analogy in this episode, Christ exercising his authority in order to give food to his followers. The language of Mk and Mt. would exclude this possibility. **5.** As Son of man, and by implication son of David, Jesus establishes his right to abrogate the Pharisaic interpretations of the Sabbath law.

6-12 The Man with a Withered Hand healed on d
the Sabbath—The preoccupation of the Pharisees with their legal institutions blinds them to the character of the saving mission of Jesus—a theme often repeated in this Gospel. Lk.'s introduction mentions Jesus teaching in the synagogue; otherwise the story follows Mk, with some heightening of dramatic interest in 8. **9.** Healing was allowed on the Sabbath in case of danger to life. 'Destroy' may allude to the conspiracy of the Pharisees against himself; their question was malicious. **10.** Jesus looks around on them, as he does on the Temple in Mk 11:11, with a scrutiny which sums up and judges. The opposition of the Jewish leaders reaches a climax.

The Call of the Twelve—In Lk. this follows im- e
mediately upon the plot of Christ's enemies. It is thus connected by anticipation with his death, and, by associating the Twelve with him in the demonstration of power before the great mixed multitude (17–18), it may foreshadow their universal mission after his resurrection.

12. The mountain (a better rendering than 'hills') f
is a scene of great and decisive events in the Gospels, especially where Jesus acts in the character of a new Moses. In Mk also the appointment of the Twelve is made there. In Mt. it is the scene of the delivery of a new Law. In Lk. this important point in the gospel is characteristically set in the context of prayer. In Lk., but not necessarily in Mk, the Twelve are commissioned out of a larger group of disciples. Lk. always thinks of them as 'apostles', a term very rarely used in the other Gospels; they are the designated missionaries and leaders of the Church from the time of their call. Their number suggests a disposition of the tribes of Israel under twelve judges, under the sovereignty of Christ as the new Moses (cf. 22:29–30).

724f 14. From this point onwards Simon is always referred to as Peter. As in Mt., but not in Mk, Andrew is grouped with his brother Peter. Judas the son of James replaces Thaddaeus (cf. Jn 14:22); the alternative translation 'brother of James' is due to an attempted identification of this Judas with the brother of Jesus and James (Mk 6:3). Only some of the Twelve were clearly remembered as individuals; their number was known more accurately than the names of some of them.

g **The Descent of Jesus with the Apostles into the Plain**—Here Jesus is joined by many disciples, in a wider sense of the term than the Twelve. **17.** He meets a great multitude of 'the people' (rather than 'people'), a phrase usually denoting Israel, but here comprising a mixed crowd including some from Phoenicia, representing the Gentiles. Judaea again denotes the whole land of the Jews. Lk. is following Mk closely, but to him this crowd may suggest a parallel with the scene at Pentecost. In Lk. Jesus here combines teaching with his healing. **19.** Lk. emphasises the divine power radiating from Jesus.

h **The Sermon**—Mainly Q material, with some sections peculiar to Lk. It is difficult to determine whether the Q passages in Lk.'s sermon represent a sermon recorded in Q in this form, to which Mt. has added much material, preserved by Lk. in its original Q contexts, or whether Lk. has broken up material already existing in a form approaching that of Mt.'s 'Sermon on the Mount'. The latter is more probable; Lk. seems to have required a different context for much of the 'Sermon on the Mount', within the part of this Gospel concerned with the journey of Jesus to Jerusalem.

i **The Beatitudes**—These are not to be understood as 'giving the qualifications necessary for admission to the Kingdom' (Plummer, *St Luke* (ICC), 178). They indicate the blessings which the Kingdom in the person of Jesus brings to disciples, to whom the sayings are addressed (20), and the reversal of the existing order which the Kingdom involves (cf. the theme of *Magnificat*). They comprise a reaffirmation, after the call of the apostles, of the proclamation of Jesus in the Nazareth synagogue; they re-echo Isa. 61:1ff., but less fully and clearly than Mt.'s longer version of them. If the Beatitudes were before Lk., in his Q material, in their Matthaean form, he may possibly have used them as the basis of his addition to the Marcan story of the preaching at Nazareth (4:17–21). It may be for this reason that he reduced the number of blessings from eight to four, having covered similar ground in his expansion of the Nazareth episode. **20.** The lifting up of the eyes indicates a peculiarly solemn action (cf. 16:32, 18:13; Mt. 17:8; Jn 6:5, 11:41). 'You poor' echoes Isa. 61:1 (LXX), and denotes the typical saints of Judaism, the poor, humble and pious. Whether Lk.'s version or Mt.'s is original, Mt.'s 'poor in spirit' well expresses the meaning of 'poor' here. **21.** 'You that hunger', an allusion to Ps. 106:9 (LXX; (107:9)) which refers to those whom the Lord has redeemed; cf. 1:53. **22.** Mt.'s simpler version of this saying has probably been expanded under the influence of the Church's experience of persecution by the Jews. Hence what seems to be an allusion to excommunication from the synagogue ('cast out your name as evil'); cf. Jn 16:2. 'Son of man' for Mt.'s 'for my sake': a reference to the *suffering* Son of man, in whose character his people participate. **23.** 'Leap for joy' for Mt.'s 'be glad', perhaps influenced by Mal. 4:2, which may also account for the addition of 'in that day' (cf. Mal. 4:3). Persecution has the character of the woes of the last days. '*Their* fathers': the Jews are beginning to be regarded as a distinct people, opposed to Christians.

725a **The Woes** are peculiar to Lk., and form a parenthesis, not addressed to disciples, indicating the condition of those who reject the Kingdom; cf. 1 Sam. 2:7ff.; Isa. 65:13–15, and cf. also the contrasting 'blessings' and 'woes' in *Magnificat.*

27-33, Q Sermon to Disciples resumed—The character of those who accept the Kingdom. **27** is more fully expanded than Mt.'s parallel, and is similar to Rom. 12:14. **29.** In Lk. the order of coat and cloak is reversed in comparison with Mt., Lk. possibly not understanding that in Palestine the cloak, used for sleeping out of doors, is likely to be the more important garment. **31.** The 'Golden Rule' summarises the preceding injunctions. **32-3.** Where Mt. speaks of tax-collectors and Gentiles, Lk. significantly has 'sinners', reflecting a less Jewish outlook. In view of 34 the RSV text of **35** must stand as against RSV*n*. 33–35*a* are peculiar to Lk.; 35*b*–49 is again paralleled in Mt. **35.** 'sons of the Most High': cf. Ps. 82:6. 36ff. These sayings may perhaps be related in Lk.'s thought to the exercise of pastoral discipline in the Church; hence his expansion in 37–8 of the saying as given in Mt. **38c** is also paralleled in Mk. The parable in **39** appears in Mt. 15:14 where it clearly refers to the Pharisees. **40** occurs in Mt. 10:24 and Jn 13:16, 15:20. It is applied here in a more general sense. In Lk. it means that to avoid becoming a blind guide one must exercise self-criticism. Lk. seems in these sayings to have in mind the disciple considered as an apostle; they are concerned with missionary and pastoral functions. This marks a difference from Mt.'s sermon, which applies to all Christians as such. **43-4.** Only a good disciple can (not be a blind guide but) produce good converts. A missionary who is a 'thorn' cannot bear fruit. **45-6** warns against false disciples. **47-9.** A more general precept for disciples. Lk. thinks of foundations securely built, Mt. of the choice of a stable site. There may perhaps be an allusion to Christ as the rock. 725b

VII 1-10 The Centurion's Servant—Like Mt.'s conclusion to the Sermon. Lk. points out that it was delivered in the hearing of the people (Israel), as a formal proclamation. The message of the centurion follows in Lk. immediately (contrast Mt.), perhaps in order that the proclamation addressed to the disciples may lead on to an incident foreshadowing the Gentile mission. Jesus does not actually meet the Gentile; Christ's ministry to Gentiles is to follow the Ascension, according to the plan of Lk. in Ac. (cf. Jn 12:20). The centurion is a pious sympathiser with the Jews, like Cornelius, but apparently not a proselyte; hence entry into his house would involve defilement for a Jew. **7.** 'Therefore . . . you' is omitted in the 'Western' text, probably by assimilation to Mt. The words are important for Lk.'s picture of the event; the centurion's trust in the authority of Jesus makes the latter's personal presence unnecessary. **9.** More clearly than in Mt., the point is made here that the faith of a Gentile is greater than Israel's; the reader is thus prepared for the later acceptance of the Gospel by Gentiles. c

11-17 The Raising of a Widow's Son at Nain—A passage peculiar to Lk. After healing a man at the point of death, Jesus raises one about to be buried; cf. the raising of the entombed Lazarus (Jn 11:1–44). He acts in a manner reminiscent of the great prophets, Elijah and Elisha. **13.** 'The Lord' is a title very often used in narrative in Lk. Mention of the compassion of Jesus in connection with miracles is very rare in the Gospels. **14-15.** The language here is echoed in the raising of Tabitha (Ac. 9:40). **15b** introduces a citation of 1 Kg. 17:23; cf. also 2 Kg. 4:36. **16.** Jesus is greeted as a great prophet (cf. 7:39, 24:19), in harmony with the Lucan presentation of him as the fulfilment of Dt. 18:15ff.; 'God has visited his people' in sending the prophet like Moses. **17.** 'Judaea' again denotes Palestine. d

18-23 John's Question—A passage of Q material expanded by Lk. After the climax of the miracles, John is told that Jesus is the great prophet; is he therefore the 'coming one' of whom he had prophesied (3:16)? The two disciples may represent the two witnesses prescribed by the Law for the establishment of the truth (Dt. 19:15). The testimony in **22** e

725e is based on Isa. 61:1ff. (and has thus possibly contributed as a source to the speech in 4:17f.) and Isa. 35:5–6 (cf. Ac. 3:8). No raising of the dead is mentioned in these OT passages; the allusion is to the raising at Nain.

f **24-35 Jesus describes the Work of John**—Q material. John was the great prophet of the old dispensation, and more than a prophet, being the messenger of Mal. 3:1. The latter text is cited, as in Mk 1:2, shaped by Christian usage. **27.** 'Before *thy* face', 'before *thee*'. The use of the text by Jesus implies a Messianic claim. **28.** John belongs to the old order, not to the Kingdom. **29.** The people (Israel) is contrasted with its official leaders, and is associated with the outcast tax-collectors in acknowledging God's righteousness. This foreshadows the rejection of Jesus by official Judaism. **31ff.** The comparison does not exactly fit the case. John and Jesus correspond to children who invite others to dance or to mourn. The reference is to games of weddings and funerals. **35.** God's wisdom is vindicated or acknowledged by those who respond to John and Jesus. This section is a climax in the Gospel. After the supreme miracle, and the declaration to John, Jesus explains how the leaders of Israel rejected John and the tax-collectors and sinners accepted him. So, by implication, will it be with Jesus.

g **Jesus is anointed by the Woman who was a Sinner**—A typical example of the outcast who accepts Jesus is contrasted with a Pharisee. The story has affinities with Mk 14:3–9 and Mt. 26:6–13. Lk. has probably taken the Marcan story and recast it so as to illustrate the same theme as that of the Parable of the Prodigal Son. Jn 12:1–8 combines elements of the Marcan and Lucan stories. **39.** The Pharisee is prepared to see in Jesus a prophet, or, as in some MSS, *the* prophet (i.e. the prophet like Moses (Dt. 18:15ff.). **40.** The host of Jesus in Mk 14:3 is Simon the leper. **41.** The parable does not exactly fit the case. The woman does not love because she has been forgiven, but vice versa. The Pharisee was negligent because he felt no need for forgiveness. The woman expressed her devotion, and is forgiven. **48** does not necessarily imply that she was not forgiven until this point. **49-50.** Objections are raised to the exercise by Jesus of his authority, as in 5:21. Faith is the response to forgiveness. 'Go in peace' recalls Eli's words to Hannah (1 Sam. 1:17). Faith apprehends salvation from both sin and disease (cf. 8:48).

h **VIII 1-3 Preaching Ministry**—Jesus travels with his disciples, preaching the good news of the Kingdom of God. Women accompanied Jesus in Galilee (cf. Mk 15:40–1). Mary Magdalene had been in an extreme state of demonic possession (cf. Mk 5:9). Joanna and Susanna are mentioned only in Lk. The entourage of Herod Antipas provided some converts (cf. Ac. 13:1). Jesus and the apostles were financed from the resources of sympathisers; cf. the system by which the primitive Church in Jerusalem was maintained, as described in Ac.

726a **4-15 The Parable of the Sower**—Marcan material with a revised introduction omitting the preaching from a boat, which has been used in the setting of the call of Peter. Lk. abbreviates Mk's parable, but makes few alterations. **5.** The treading under foot may indicate a rejection of the word before the devil takes it away. **6.** In Mk some seed fell on rocky ground, germinated quickly but was short-lived. In Lk. it falls on rock and withers before it is grown. Lk. emphasises the perfection of the harvest, omitting the Marcan thirtyfold and sixtyfold. **9-10.** In Lk. this discussion is applied to this particular parable only, and the idea of esoteric revelation is less prominent than in Mk; cf. 'others' for Mk's 'those without'. **10.** The parables have the effect of judging the hearers; to those without discernment they are obscure. The Marcan allegorical interpretation (11ff.) may not be original. **12.** 'Believe and be saved', i.e. 'be converted'; cf. Ac. 16:31. 'To believe' is virtually a technical term in the early Church for 'to be a Christian'. In Lk. the parable seems to be interpreted in terms appropriate to the Church's preaching after Pentecost. **13.** The joyful reception of the word suggests the quick germination of the seed on rocky ground as described in Mk. 'Temptation' means the same as Mk's 'tribulation or persecution'. 'Fall away' denotes actual apostasy, as against Mk's 'be scandalised'. **14.** In Lk. alone is there a reference to pleasures. In the conclusion, Mk says merely that they hear and receive the word and bring forth much fruit; **15** Lk. adds that they keep the word and produce fruit 'with patience'; that is, the opposite of apostasy. The word is to be kept in an honest and good heart (lit. 'beautiful and good'), according to the typical Hellenic moral ideal. 726a

Sayings on hearing the Word—Originally referring to the hearing of the parables of Jesus, these Marcan sayings are probably also related in Lk. to the apostles' mission (cf. 12:2) and the proclamation of the Gospel. **16** is paralleled both in Mk 4:21 and in Mt. 5:15. Lk.'s allusion to 'those who enter' may mean that he is thinking of the lamp in the porch of a Roman house, and possibly also of those who enter the Church (from without, like Gentiles; contrast Mt.'s reference to 'all in the house'). **18.** Lk.'s 'what he thinks that he has' brings out the meaning implicit in Mk. These sayings apparently stood both in Mk and Q and reappear in different contexts in Mt. and Lk. b

The Mother and Brethren of Jesus—This Marcan episode is used in Lk. to close the section on parables, Mk 3:35 being rephrased so as to refer, like the Parable of the Sower, to those who hear the word of God and do it. Through obedience to God's word, men enter into a close personal relationship to Jesus. The family's visit is the occasion for this declaration; it does not necessarily imply, in Lk., that they were disbelievers. Mk suggests this, but it would be inconsistent with Lk. 2:51. c

22-25 The Stilling of the Storm—The Marcan story, with a vague Lucan introductory note of time, demonstrates Christ's authority over the deep, i.e. chaos, regarded as a demonic force. d

26-39 The Gerasene Demoniac—The situation of his country 'opposite Galilee', and his heathenish language (28) suggest that the demoniac may be a Gentile. 'Son of God most high' is a title which might well be used by a pagan. **31.** Lk. clarifies Mk; the allusion is to Hades. Lk. also explains more exactly the meaning of 'Legion', a name which Jesus desired to know, either for exorcism or in order to recall to the madman his own personality. **32.** The presence of the swine suggests Gentile territory. **35.** In Mk the maniac is simply 'sitting', i.e. calm, and not wandering. Lk. adds 'at the feet of Jesus', i.e. as a convert or disciple. **37.** Lk. adds the reason for the request to Jesus to depart. **39.** The command to proclaim is in contrast with the usual injunction of secrecy; this may be related to the Gentile setting, and the absence of any likelihood there of a misunderstanding of the mission of Jesus in terms of popular Jewish messianism. The correspondence of 'God' and 'Jesus' is remarkable. If it is intentional, Jesus is seen as doing the work of God. e

The Daughter of Jairus—This miracle, by contrast, is in a strongly Jewish setting. It is taken from Mk. The number 'twelve' is prominent (**42**, where Lk. has transferred it from the end of the story in Mk to the beginning, and **43**) and may possibly be connected with symbolism denoting the people of Israel. Mt. emphasises the fact that the girl was actually dead before Jesus was informed about her. **43.** In Lk. the uncomplimentary reference to doctors is mitigated, and in some MSS omitted altogether, as in Mt. **44.** In mentioning the fringe of the garment, Lk. and Mt. agree against Mk, but there is some MS evidence for its omission here. If it is authentic, it may have been inserted by Lk. from Mk 6:56, which is a part of Mk that he omits to reproduce. **47.** The healing of f

726f the woman is witnessed by the whole people of Israel. This woman's disease rendered her ceremonially unclean. **48.** Faith is the necessary response to the outgoing of divine power ; cf. 50. **51.** In Lk. the order of disciples is changed. John precedes James ; Peter and John were the great leaders of the early Jerusalem Church. Lk. adds a reference to the parents. **54** is echoed in Ac. 9:40–1. **56.** This great miracle is followed by a command to secrecy, in contrast with the story of the Gerasene.

g **IX 1-6 The Mission of the Twelve**—Lk. sets the mission of the Twelve in the context of the triumphant progress of the mission of Jesus himself, after the great miracle of a raising from the dead. Thus it corresponds to the proclamation of the nature of the mission of Jesus to John's disciples after the earlier raising from the dead at Nain. It also foreshadows the world-wide mission of the Twelve after the resurrection of Jesus. **1.** The Twelve receive the power and authority which belong to Jesus. **2.** Lk. adds a commission to heal, inferred from Mk 6:13. Their journey is to be made without preparation. Lk. and Mt. agree against Mk in including a prohibition of staves, probably introduced from Q material (cf. 10:4), distributed by Lk. between his account of the Seventy and his mainly Marcan account of the Twelve. **4-5.** The early missionaries adopted these methods, establishing settled headquarters in urban centres, and adopting the gesture described in 5, as in Ac. 13:51.

h **7-9 The Reaction of Herod to the Ministry of Jesus**—In Mk Herod thinks Jesus to be John risen from the dead. The continuity of the work of John and Jesus is thus emphasised, and the death of John prepares the way for the death of Jesus. In Lk. Herod knows that Jesus cannot be John, and the rumours that he is a prophet lead him to ask who Jesus is and to desire to see him. The implication is still that Herod will prove hostile (cf. 13:31ff.) ; but Lk. makes little allusion to the death of John, and it plays a much smaller part in his story than in Mk's. **8.** The appearance of Elijah, Mal. 4:5 ; 'old' is inserted by Lk., perhaps because he does regard Jesus as a prophet, but a new and greater prophet.

i **10-17 The Twelve return; the Feeding of the Multitude**—Jesus withdraws to Bethsaida with the Twelve, but Lk. does not suggest, like Mk, that this was for rest. **12.** Lk. has retained the Marcan setting of the feeding in a *desert*. Jesus welcomes the crowds, speaking to them of the Kingdom of God as to the disciples after the Resurrection (Ac. 1:3 ; another great turning-point in the gospel story). Here the feeding, in which all are more than satisfied with the bread given by Jesus, is the immediate prelude to his teaching of the Twelve about the meaning of his suffering and death (cf. the explicitly worked-out theme of Jn 6). **14.** Lk. interprets Mk as indicating 100 groups of 50 each, possibly seeing a similarity with the disposition of Israel in Exod. 18:21. **16.** The language is liturgical, suggesting a direct connection with the Christian Eucharist, including the distribution of the elements by deacons. **17.** Jesus provides a superabundance. Basketfuls, corresponding in number to all Israel, and to the number of the apostles by whom the spiritual food of Christ is later on to be distributed, are left over after all are fed.

j After 17, Lk. omits Mk 6:45–8:26. This consists mainly of a crossing of the lake, miracles in Gentile country (in Lk. the Gentile mission of the post-resurrection period has only some slight adumbrations in Christ's ministry), the second feeding (probably representing a feeding of Gentiles), a miracle at Bethsaida (omitted also in Mt., perhaps because of the apparent difficulty involved in it), and an attack on Pharisaic traditions (perhaps inappropriate to Lk.'s readers).

727a **18-27 Jesus teaches the Twelve about his coming Death**—The first direct instruction about his destiny of suffering is set in a context of prayer. Lk. does not suggest that this takes place at Caesarea Philippi, as in Mk, or in a different locality from the feeding. 727 **19** repeats the rumours recorded in 8. **20.** Peter confesses Jesus as God's anointed (Messiah). This is not to be divulged, and Lk.'s direct connection of **21** and **22** makes it clear that this is because Messiahship is to be given a new meaning in terms of the Son of man who is to suffer in accordance with the purpose of God ('*must* suffer') indicated in the scriptures, and rise from the dead. **23.** The mission of Jesus as the suffering Son of man involves the participation in his self-sacrifice by 'all' who follow him. Lk. alters Mk's direct call to death by inserting 'daily' ; the disciple's participation in Christ's death is continual, as he enters into it by denying his self-centred life for the sake of Christ. **26.** Lk. alone refers here to the glory of the Son of man. The thought here is of the Christian who acknowledges the Gospel under persecution, and the implication is that he will share Christ's glory. This first reference to the glory and the Parousia of Christ is directly linked with the thought of his death. **27.** The Kingdom comes through the glorification of Christ through death and resurrection ; the Transfiguration is a foretaste of this.

28-36 The Transfiguration—The meaning of b Christ's glorification through death is demonstrated. **28.** Lk. substitutes eight days for Mk's six, perhaps to indicate the first day of the week and to underline the relation of the Transfiguration to the Resurrection. Prayer is again the setting of a momentous event, which, like the choice of the Twelve, takes place on the mountain which recalls the ascent of Moses. **30.** The appearance of the two men forms another link between this foreshadowing of Christ's glorification and both the Resurrection and the Ascension. **31.** 'Departure' (lit. 'exodus') may simply mean 'death' (cf. 2 Pet. 1:15) or may be meant to set the work of Christ in his death and resurrection in relation to the exodus of Moses and Israel. As the 'prophet like Moses', Jesus is attested by Moses and Elijah, the Lawgiver and the great Prophet, both of whom ascended to heaven. **32.** Cf. the narrative of Gethsemane (22:45–46). **33** suggests an allusion to the Feast of Tabernacles. **34.** The overshadowing of the cloud recalls Exod. 40:29. **35.** The salutation reaffirms the declaration at the baptism of Jesus ; 'my Chosen' is echoed in the scoffing of the rulers at the Cross (23:35) ; 'listen to him' is an application to Jesus of what is said of the 'prophet like Moses' in Dt. 18:15ff. **36.** The witnesses of the OT disappear. The disciples could not proclaim the meaning of this vision at the time (i.e. before the post-resurrection period) because they could not then understand it.

37-43 The Epileptic Boy—Lk., like Mt., greatly c shortens Mk. The failure of the disciples is connected with their lack of faith, i.e. their failure to understand the nature of Christ's mission in relation to his death. The rebuke in **41** appears to be addressed to them, and to refer to his imminent departure in death. This begins a section of the Gospel concerned largely with the preparation of the disciples for his departure and their refusal to comprehend.

43b-48 The Second Prediction of Death—Lk. lays d stress on the fact that this emphatic teaching was delivered in the context of the Galilaean mission at the height of its success, and also on the total failure of the disciples to understand. **46.** This is illustrated by their dispute about greatness, in the setting of the prophecy of the death of Jesus (cf. the dispute at the Last Supper). The disciple who acts as the least, or as a servant, in receiving a child in Christ's name, is the greatest. The child symbolises the humble. Jesus is the Father's representative.

49-50 The Strange Exorcist—Q material, probably e reflecting difficulties experienced in the early Church (cf. Ac. 19:3). This does not really conflict with 11:23.

The Journey to Jérusalem—The Galilaean ministry f is followed, according to the Synoptic (Marcan) outline, by the decision of Jesus to confront the leaders of Israel in Jerusalem, where he will be rejected and put

727f to death. The teaching given to the disciples, and the Transfiguration, have prepared the way for this. Into the Marcan framework of the journey Lk. inserts a great deal of non-Marcan material. It is unlikely that this was done merely because Mark's outline provided no place for it in either the Galilaean or the Judaean ministries ; it has been placed here as the most appropriate context, in the setting of the imminent death of Jesus, the preparation of his apostles, and the nature of his kingdom, of which they are to be the agents, contrasted with the narrowness and blindness of official Judaism.

g **51-56 The Samaritans**—The journey begins when the time of God's purpose is fulfilled. **51.** 'Received up', that is, exalted through death (cf. Jn 13:31). **53.** The Samaritans refuse to receive one who is apparently going on pilgrimage to Jerusalem. **54.** James and John expect Jesus to act like Elijah (2 Kg. 1:10–12). Some MSS supplement the citation of the latter passage with an explicit comparison with Elijah's action. Jesus rebukes the false ideas of Messiahship implied in the attitude of these disciples. His words are expanded in some MSS by what may conceivably be a Marcionite addition (cf. RSV*n*). This passage is peculiar to Lk.

h **57-62 Would-be Disciples**—The total self-commitment required of a disciple who intends to follow Jesus (to Jerusalem). Mainly Q material, but Lk. adds a third claimant (61–2), in a passage strongly reminiscent of the call of Elisha by Elijah (1 Kg. 19:19–20). Lk.'s account of the second claimant differs from Mt.'s in making him be called by Jesus and adding the command to proclaim the Kingdom of God.

i **X The Seventy**—Jesus appoints seventy (or seventy-two) other disciples, corresponding to the elders chosen by Moses (Exod. 24:1 ; Num. 11:16) and perhaps to the number of the nations (seventy-two in LXX ; Gen. 10). They are to precede Jesus on his way, the setting of their appointment being Samaria. Probably their mission foreshadows the universal mission of the disciples which is to be extended to every place where Jesus was about to come in the wider world beyond the borders of Judaism. Samaria is regarded as an intermediate point between the land of the Jews and the actual Gentile world (Ac. 1:8). Their dispatch 'two by two' (10:1) resembles the journeys by Paul and Barnabas (Ac. 13ff.). Paul and Silas (Ac. 15:40) and Peter and John (Ac. 8:14).

j **2-12.** The charge to the Seventy is composed of Q material, found in Mt. 9:37–8 and 10:7–16 as part of the charge to the Twelve. In Mt. only the Twelve are commissioned, and their work does not comprise any wider scope than the people of Israel. **2.** This saying is echoed in Jn 4:35, in the context of the expected and partly anticipated conversion of Samaria. **4** is referred to in 22:35 as though it were addressed to the Twelve, Lk.'s transference of it into this context being apparently forgotten. In Lk. the saying seems to refer to the urgency of the mission ; in Mt. to the maintenance of the missionary by his converts (as in 7 below). Cf. 2 Kg. 4:29. **7.** Lk. alludes to the eating of Gentile (in the context, Samaritan) food ; cf. 1 C. 10:27. On the maintenance of the apostles, cf. the Pauline echo of Christ's teaching, 1 C. 9:7, 14. **9, 11.** To the first proclamation of the near approach of the Kingdom, Lk. adds 'to you' ; it is to be accepted personally. This is absent from the second proclamation (peculiar to Lk.), where the Kingdom's advent is for judgment.

k **13-15.** Q. In Mt. this is a detached saying (11:21–3). The parallel in Mt. and Lk. is very exact. **15** cites Isa. 14:13–15, referring to the downfall of Babylon. The coming of the Kingdom involves judgment on those places where Jesus is rejected.

l **16** is paralleled in Mt. and Mk, probably occurring in Q and Mk. Lk. enlarges the saying in its negative aspect, and speaks of 'hearing' rather than 'receiving' (as Mt. 10:40 ; Mk 9:37), because he applies the saying to the apostolic preachers. Jesus is the Father's 727l
representative agent.

17-20 The Return of the Seventy—Peculiar to Lk. m
They triumph in the name of Jesus (cf. Ac. 3:16, 4:10, 4:30). The fall of Satan expresses the significance of the mission of Jesus, in the flesh and through the apostolic missionaries (cf. Jn 12:31), whose authority brings a fulfilment of Ps. 91:13, being superior to the power of Satan. For the thought of the heavenly book, cf. Exod. 32:33 ; Dan. 12:1.

21 The Thanksgiving of Jesus—Lk.'s introduction n
reminds us of the Spirit-possession of Jesus, and again connects joy with the Spirit's activity. The thanksgiving itself is Q material, prefaced in Mt. with the invitation to the heavy-laden, inappropriate in Lk.'s context of the apostles' mission. The 'wise' are the leaders of Israel, contrasted with the humble believers. **22-3.** In language reminiscent of Jn, Jesus declares himself the sole source of God's revelation, and asserts the intimate mutual knowledge of the Father and the Son ; 'delivered' may refer particularly to Christ's teaching, his words being given him by God.

23-24. A Q passage, referring in Mt. to the general o
use of parables, is applied to the disciples and their mission.

25-37 The Good Samaritan (cf. curious verbal p
echoes of 2 Chr. 28:15)—The introductory narrative seems to be based on Mk 12:28–31 (omitted by Lk. at 20:40). In Lk. the question concerns the gaining of eternal life, not the principal commandment of the Law (cf. 28). In Lk. the question is thrown back to the lawyer, who himself enunciates the summary of the Law, uniting Dt. 6:5 with Lev. 19:18 (cf. *Testament of Issachar* 5:2, 7:5 ; *Testament of Dan* 5:3, if these are pre-Christian). The parable is a highly finished story in an artificial setting. The real point seems to be the contrast between the care for the needy and oppressed shown by the outcast Samaritan, and the negligence of the leaders of Israel, which is due to their preoccupation with the ceremonial Law. The implied contrast may be between the attitude of Jesus and his missionaries to sinners etc., and the narrowness of Judaism. To approach a corpse would involve ritual contamination. The Lucan parable is followed by a Lucan narrative which suggests a relationship between Lk. and Jn.

38-42 Martha and Mary—Mary is the ideal disciple, q
who has chosen the good portion—i.e. of spiritual food. Textual confusion is probably due to an early misinterpretation of 'one thing' in a material sense, as 'one dish'. Conceivably the two women are also typical of the difference between Christ's true disciples and the Jewish leaders, preoccupied with trifling minutiae.

XI 1-4 The Lord's Prayer—Lk. places this in the 728a
setting of Christ's prayer and the disciples' desire to be taught to pray as John's followers were (cf. 5:33). The actual prayer may consist of Q material, the first, second and last petitions corresponding to Mt. exactly, the third being very similar (and including the unique word *epiousios* in each case) and the fourth fairly close.
2. 'Father' may be the original opening of the b
prayer (cf. Mk 14:36 ; Rom. 8:15 ; Gal. 4:6). 'Hallowed be thy name' is typical of Jewish ascriptions of blessing to God. A variant found in two MSS and in Gregory of Nyssa's exposition of the prayer, and known to Maximus Confessor, reads 'May thy Holy Spirit come upon us and cleanse us', in place of 'Thy kingdom come'. Marcion appears to have read this in place of 'Hallowed be thy name' (Tertullian, *adv. Marc.* iv, 26). The reading has affected Codex Bezae : 'May thy kingdom come upon us'. Despite Burkitt (JTS 26, p. 290), this is unlikely to be due to an alteration by Marcion. It may have entered the prayer as a variant for use at baptisms, the convert being enabled to say 'Abba, Father' and receiving the Spirit ; or it may quite conceivably be authentic. It is in harmony with Lk.'s view that the supreme object of prayer is the gift of the Spirit

728b (cf. 13). **3.** 'Daily' renders *epiousios*, a word believed by Origen to have been an original coinage in this prayer (*orat.* xxvii, 15). By Jer. it was translated *daily* here and *supersubstantial* in Mt. Contrary to some modern suppositions, it seems that there is no evidence for the word outside the Gospels. The probable meaning is 'of the coming day'. (See R. F. Wright, CQR clvii (1956), 340–5; M. N. Tod, ibid., clviii, 49–51.) Lk. emphasises the *continuous* feeding of the faithful by his use of the present tense. **4.** Lk. introduces his general emphasis on forgiveness of sins; contrast Mt.'s 'debts'. 'Temptation' denotes particularly the trial of persecution.

c **5-8 The Parable of the Friend at Midnight**—Peculiar to Lk. The sense is: 'you (cf. 'you who are evil' in 13) will give to a friend because of his importunity; how much more will God give freely?'

9-13. Q material, linked by Lk. to the preceding
d parable. It is thus used by Lk. to explain the point of the parable and to show how God, as Father, will always answer prayer. For Lk. the grand object of prayer is the gift of 'holy Spirit'; Mt. has simply 'good things'.

e **14-26 The Beelzebub Controversy**—Jesus casts out a dumb demon. In the Mt. parallel (Mt. 12:22) a blind and dumb demoniac is healed. Possibly there is an implied contrast here with the believer who receives the Spirit (13) and testifies (12:8ff.). He is accused of exorcising through the power of evil. This Q story also has a parallel in Mk 3:22ff. **16.** Lk. here inserts the demand for a sign from heaven, which Mt. places at Mt. 12:38, corresponding to Lk. 11:29. Lk. does this to emphasise that the miracles of Jesus *were* a sign, to refuse to recognise which is as bad as to ascribe them to Beelzebub. The demand for a sign is to 'try' Jesus. Possibly Lk. thinks of the third temptation (4:9) being renewed by this demand. **19.** Jewish exorcists are met with in Ac. 19:13ff.; Jos. Ant. VIII, ii, 5. **20.** The expulsion of demons is the sign which shows how the future Kingdom is operative now by anticipation in the works of Jesus. Lk.'s 'finger of God' (Mt. has 'Spirit') echoes Exod. 8:19 and may be meant to show Jesus as an antitype of Moses. The coming of the Kingdom means the defeat of the devil as ruler of this world. The parable of the strong man is paralleled both in Mt. and in Mk. Lk. has greatly developed its detail. Lk.'s addition
f of **22b** introduces an echo of Isa. 53:12, part of the Servant prophecies. **23** is a Q saying, in the same context in Mt. The advent of the Kingdom and the assault on the Devil by Jesus compel men to take sides in the conflict. **24-6.** Neutrality is impossible. One either receives the Kingdom or is repossessed by the evil spirit, returning to its house from which the 'stronger' (22) had expelled it, and introducing seven other spirits (cf. 8:2).

g **27-28 The Blessedness of Disciples**—Cf. Mk 3:31–5, in the same context in relation to the Beelzebub controversy. Some ascribe the work of Jesus to the Devil, some ask for a sign, some are ready to honour him on the purely human level, without accepting the Kingdom as it comes in his person—i.e. hearing God's word and keeping it (cf. Parable of Sower). The disciple is more blessed than one who is involved only in a physical relationship to Jesus.

h **29-32 Seeking for Signs**—Q material, with a Lucan introduction. The search for a sign is wicked. The only sign to be given is that of Jonah, who was a sign to heathen Nineveh, as Jesus is to Israel. **31.** Israel will be condemned by the eager response of a Gentile queen and the repentance of the Gentile Ninevites. The future tenses, 'shall be given', 'so will the Son of Man be', may indicate that the great sign will be the Resurrection, the thought of which may be implicit in the typology of Jonah (and made explicit in Mt.). This thought is, however, combined with that of the present confrontation of Israel by the mission of Jesus. It is, nevertheless, probably in Lk.'s mind that as the 'resurrection' of Jonah was the necessary prelude to
his mission to the Gentiles, so it will be with Jesus. 72
J. H. Michael (JTS 21 (1920), 146f.) argues for an early corruption, and an original reference to John (the Baptist) and not Jonah; but this is improbable. Codex Bezae omits 32.

33. The significance of Jesus is really plainly mani- i
fested. Cf. the use of this saying (in Mk and Q) at 8:16. **34.** To see the light of Jesus, however, demands undistorted vision, unlike that of those who will not see the significance of his signs. The light (vision) that one possesses may be itself darkness, blinding one to the meaning of Jesus, as in the case of those who still seek for signs, or attribute the genuine signs of the Kingdom to Beelzebub (34*b*–35). Those who have sound spiritual vision receive complete illumination, and the 'lamp' (cf. 33), which is the light of Jesus, will give them light (**36**, a verse omitted in the 'Western' text as confused or tautologous).

37-53 The Pharisees denounced—The reasons are j
here given for the blindness of the Pharisees to the meaning of Jesus and the Kingdom. Mainly Q material, with an introduction (**37-8**) probably derived from Mk 7:2, part of the long section of Mk omitted by Lk. Their lack of insight is due to preoccupation with legal minutiae. **41.** Wellhausen accounted for the curious form of this saying by postulating a confusion in an Aramaic original between *dakkî, purify*, and *zakkî, give alms*, or a mistranslation into Greek depending upon the similarity of these words; but the Greek is not impossible, and Lk. may well have recast the saying in order to emphasise the thought that the Pharisees give precedence to legal observance over care for their fellow men. True cleansing is effected by giving the contents of the dish as alms to the poor. **42.** Justice and the love of God have been subordinated to legalism. Mic. 6:8 is in mind here. Lk. has 'love of God' for Mt.'s 'mercy and faith'. **42b** is omitted by the 'Western' text, probably as a result of Marcion's editing. The rejection of the prophets foreshadows the Pharisees' rejection of Jesus. **49.** 'Wisdom of God' probably means 'God in his Wisdom', and does not allude to a 'Wisdom' book. The 'Western' text omits the phrase. Lk. has 'apostles' for Mt.'s 'wise men and scribes'. He is linking the mission of the prophets to that of the Church. **51.** Zechariah: see 2 Chr. 24:22. **52.** 'knowledge' signifies knowledge of God. Mt. has 'the Kingdom of Heaven'.

XII 1ff. The Witness and Character of Christ's 72
Disciples, contrasted with the Pharisees—The teaching to disciples consists mainly of Q material. Lk.'s introduction brings in the multitude, which is not apparently friendly.

1. Disciples are to avoid the hypocrisy of the Pharisees b
which is a pervasive evil influence. In the similar saying in Mk 8:15 (included in Lk.'s 'Great Omission' from Mk) their 'leaven' is contrasted with the bread given by Jesus. Mt. 16:12 refers the 'leaven' to the Pharisaic and Sadducean teaching. **2-3.** Lk. uses the Q material to show that the Pharisees' hypocrisy is to be unmasked by the proclamation of the Gospel, which will ultimately be announced publicly and unmistakably. Disciples are friends of Jesus (cf. Jn 15:14–15). They are to proclaim the Gospel fearlessly, fearing only the Devil, who might cast them into hell if they apostatised. God will exert his protective care over the faithful disciples, even in persecution (cf. 21:18). This does not necessarily mean physical safety, but the assurance that he who witnesses to Jesus, in time of persecution, will be acknowledged by him in his capacity as the glorified Son of man when he comes as judge, in the presence of the heavenly court. **10** (cf. Mt. 12:32; Mk 3:28–9). Lk. sets the saying about blasphemy against the Holy Spirit in the context of the witness of disciples under persecution (cf. Ac. 7). **11.** Since the confessor is to be directly inspired in making his speech of defence, apostasy involves a deliberate and total rejection of the Spirit. Whereas the martyr is pre-eminently Spirit-possessed, the apostate is an

9b unforgivable blasphemer, who, because he rejects the Spirit's inspiration, is a worse offender than one who, on a merely human plane, speaks against the Son of man. **12**. For the inspiration of the confessor see 21:14–15 ; Mk 13:11 ; Jn 14:26.

c **The Rich Fool**—Peculiar to Lk., who, as often, provides a dramatic setting to the teaching. The preceding teaching on God's providential care implies detachment from worldly concerns and covetousness ; **15ff**. addressed to the whole crowd. **14**. Cf. Exod. 2:14. If Jesus is a new Moses, he is a greater and different Moses. **22ff**. Q material, addressed to disciples ; the parable's meaning is drawn out in teaching about God's care for them. **25**. ' Span of life ' is probably the right rendering ; cf. Ps. 39:5. **30**. ' nations of the world ' replaces the ' Gentiles ' of Mt.'s parallel verse. The necessary condition of the assurance of God's providential care is that one should be seeking the Kingdom, which God will give to disciples. **33**. Almsgiving means treasure in heaven (cf. 11:41) ; the beginnings may perhaps be discerned here of the idea of almsgiving as a means of acquiring merit, but the principal thought is that the Kingdom, to which almsgiving is closely related, is the primary object of endeavour. Lk. may regard this saying as the basis of the sharing of property in the early Church.

d **35-48 Disciples as Servants of Christ :** Watchfulness and Stewardship—Peculiar to Lk., but perhaps containing a tradition used by Mt. 25:1–13. The disciples are left to administer Christ's household until he returns from the marriage feast (i.e. the heavenly banquet). They must be vigilant for him. **37**. Christ will minister to his faithful servants ; cf. Mk 10:45 ; Jn 13:4–5 (a dramatic representation of this theme). **40**. Jesus will come as the glorified Son of man. **41**. The characteristically Lucan dramatic interruption of the discourse leads to the point of the saying about vigilant servants, with a hint of Peter's leadership in the administration of Christ's household. **45**. Delay in Christ's expected coming must not lead to corruption in the apostles' stewardship. There may also be an implied contrast between them and the leaders of Judaism. **47-8**. Peculiar to Lk. The responsibility of the Jewish leaders is heavier than that of those, such as Gentiles, who did not share their privileges ; a similar responsibility falls on the apostles.

e **49-53 The Mission of Jesus effects a Judgment**—**49**. The ' fire ' probably signifies the fire of judgment, to be kindled as a result of the completion of his mission through death. **50**. For his death as a ' baptism ' cf. Mk 10:38. Jesus awaits the fulfilment of his work (cf. Jn 12:27), with perhaps an allusion to its foreshadowing in his baptism by John. The crisis of the gospel will produce strife and division, as in time of persecution. **51**. Lk. has ' division ' where Mt. has ' a sword ', possibly in order to avoid misrepresentation in political terms. **52f**. Based on Mic. 7:6.

f **XII 54-XIII 9 The Crisis of the Kingdom** should be discerned even by the general multitude ; its signs are already present. **57**. This is Lk.'s link between the discernment of signs and the other Q material on agreement with one's adversary, **58-9**, which in Mt. is a general precept whose context has probably been changed by Lk., as the retention of the singular ' you ', ' your ' indicates. In Lk. the saying refers to the urgent need for Israel to take action to avoid the imminent judgment, by repentance ; perhaps also the further thought that failure to repent will mean political destruction. The urgency of the crisis that confronts Israel is illustrated by incidents in which some individuals have already perished spectacularly. **XIII 1**. The news arrives of some Galilaeans being slain in a Temple incident. The episode is unknown, but historically plausible. It anticipated the slaughter of many worshippers in the Jewish War during the fighting between the rival factions in the Temple (Jos.BJ V, i, 3). **4**. Another group had previously been killed at Siloam, possibly Zealots who had 729f
attacked Pilate's aqueduct, which was constructed out of Temple funds. Much revolutionary activity was evidently going on, unrecorded by Josephus, as the episode of Barabbas shows. The incident foreshadowed the destruction of the city. Jesus says that all Israel, not merely individual sinners, is liable to perish if it does not repent, i.e. change its attitude to his mission. There may be an implicit condemnation of nationalist political ambitions. Israel will perish, as happened in A.D. 70. **6-9**. Israel is offered a last chance. This parable corresponds to the acted sign of the fig tree, omitted by Lk. from Mk 11:12ff. The tree is Israel. ' Three years ' indicates a complete period, in which every chance has been allowed, probably not a three-year mission by Jesus (cf. ' three measures ' in 21).

10-17. The Woman with a Spirit of Infirmity— g
Israel's repentance in face of the crisis of the Kingdom will be shown chiefly in respect of the treatment of those in bondage and the outcasts. The woman in the synagogue is bound (cf. **12 :** ' freed ' ; **15 :** ' untie ' ; **16 :** ' bound ', ' loosed '), and the implication of 16 is that a daughter of Abraham is being treated as an outcast (cf. 19:9). The rulers of Israel are blind to such needs because of their narrow legalism which prevents them from seeing the significance of the works of Jesus. **17**. The crowd, however, rejoices over them.

18-21 Parables of the Mustard Seed and Leaven h
—The former occurs in Mk 4:30ff. Lk.'s version on the whole resembles Mt. 13:31f. more closely than Mk, except in 18. Possibly Lk. is using a Q version, and Mt. a conflation of Mk and Q ; but in any case Lk. is rewriting fairly freely. The Lucan context is original. It is placed in contrast with the condemnation of Israel's narrowness, and Lk. is probably thinking of the world-wide extension of the Church, giving protection to the peoples of the world, like an empire. This is also the meaning of the Parable of the Leaven, similarly linked with the former parable in Mt. 13:33. Leaven is usually a figure for an evil influence ; here it denotes the all-pervasive extension of the Kingdom.

22-30 The Condemnation of Israel—**22**. Jesus i
extends his teaching over a wide area on his way to confront the leaders of Israel in Jerusalem. **24**. Paralleled in content, but not in wording, in Mt. 7:13–14 ; in Lk. this refers to the difficulty of repentance for Israel. **25-9**. Paralleled in Mt. in various contexts, but in Lk. related to the condemnation of Israel and the calling of outcasts into the Kingdom of God, a theme which begins with the question in 23, probably asking whether Israel as a whole or only a ' remnant ', is in the way of salvation (cf. Ac. 2:47). **26-7**. Similarly pointed by Lk. as a saying directed against the leaders of Israel ; note the Lucan phrase ' in our streets '. **27**. Citation of Ps. 6:9, Mt.'s parallel being closer to LXX. **28-9**. Paralleled in Mt.'s story of the Centurion (8:11f.). Lk. alone refers to prophets in this context, in harmony with his emphasis on the succession and the testimony of the prophets (Ac. 10:37, 13:27). Israel's leaders are cast out from the Messianic feast and replaced by a gathering in of God's people from all parts of the world, Lk. adding ' north and south ' where Mt. has only ' east and west '. **30**. From both the Marcan and Q traditions. In Lk. it signifies that the Gentiles will take precedence over the Jews.

31-35 Judgment on Jerusalem—Jesus must be 730a
rejected by the leaders of Israel in Jerusalem, like the prophets of old. Herod is hostile, as he had been to John ; these Pharisees appear to be friendly. Jesus cannot allow himself to perish obscurely in Galilee. **32**. Cf. the answer to John's disciples. Jesus will perform his great works for a definite, and short, time, and is then to go on his way for a definite, and short, time in order to challenge the Jewish authorities at Jerusalem. ' Finish my course ' : not merely referring to the Galilaean ministry, but also to his glorification (cf. 9:31, 51). **33**. Jesus is a prophet (cf. 24:19), for whose death the Jews, including the Pharisees) are

730a to be responsible. This means the condemnation of Jerusalem ; hence the lament of Jesus. This is Q material, in a context in Mt. (23:37, 39) which removes the ambiguity of Lk.'s v. 35, and makes it allude to the return of Jesus as Messiah, not to his entry (19:38). This is probably the intended meaning in Lk. also. **34** echoes Dt. 32:11. **35.** ' house ' : Jerusalem, rather than the Temple. A prophecy of destruction, after which Christ will return as Messiah (cf. 21:24, 27), to be greeted with the royal salutation of Ps. 118:26.

b **XIV 1-6 The Man with Dropsy**—The condemnation of the unrepentant leaders of Israel is renewed as they repeat their obstruction, on the grounds of legalism, of the mighty works of Jesus for men's deliverance. **5.** The difficult reading ' a son ' for ' an ass ' is textually preferable. It has been accounted for on the supposition of confusion between ' sheep ' and ' son ' (*ois, huios*), ' pig ' and ' son ' (*hus, huios*), or, in an Aramaic tradition, between ' animal ' and ' son ' (*beʿîr, bar*). The odd collocation may, however, be original, and depend on Dt. 5:14.

c **7-14 The Outcasts**—Israel is condemned for its narrow legalistic complacency, contrasted with the calling of the outcasts by Jesus. The arrogance of the Pharisees is illustrated by their conduct when invited to a feast ; cf. the Parable of the Pharisee and the Publican. **7-11** is also a parable, whose point is the Pharisee expectation of receiving the best places in the Kingdom of God as a matter of right. **11** recurs at 18:14 (Mt. 23:12). **12-14.** General advice, set in the context of the duty of inviting the outcasts, who have nothing to contribute to Israel, into the Kingdom of God, and applied in that sense (cf. the echo of **13** at 21. **14.** There will be recompense at the Messianic feast in the Kingdom of God (it is not implied that none but the righteous will rise) ; hence the exclamation in **15.**

d **15-24 The Parable of the Great Supper**—The theme is the position of Israel in relation to the outcasts, the point being made more strongly in Mt. 22:1–10, perhaps derived from a different source. **17.** For Lk. Jesus is the servant sent to announce the appointed time ; Mt. thinks of the prophets as servants (plural). **20.** Cf. Dt. 24:5. **21.** Cf. 13 ; the outcasts from Israel, such as tax-collectors and sinners, are to be brought in to the banquet in the Kingdom of God, in place of those who were originally chosen. In Lk., but not in Mt., a further extension of the servant's mission is indicated : into the more distant countryside, to compel, by urgent persuasion, those from far afield to enter the Kingdom in place of the leaders of Israel. The Gentile mission is foreshadowed. The main point of the parable is in **24.**

e **25-35 The Cost of Discipleship**—Christ's invitation nevertheless involves following him through suffering. The Messianic feast lies beyond the death of the Messiah. Jesus addresses the crowds who were accompanying him on the road to the Cross, and explains that discipleship involves the sacrifice of earthly ties and life itself. **26-7.** Paralleled in Mt. 10:37–8, but much more strongly worded in Lk. who adds a reference to ' wife ' (cf. 20). 27 is also paralleled in Mk 8:34, reproduced in Lk. 9:23 (Mt. 16:24). The suffering of the Messiah is implied, and the disciple must subsequently share in it. The parables of counting the cost lead to the demand for renunciation of all possessions, a thought which is prominent in Lk. **34-5.** Saying paralleled in Mt. 5:13. Lk.'s version seems to be influenced also by the Marcan form of it (Mk 9:50), and in this context refers to the zeal necessary for the disciple who is to face the cost of his calling.

f **XV 3-7 The Parable of the Lost Sheep**—Lk. sets three parables in the context of objections raised by the leaders of Israel to Christ's treatment of the outcasts. The Parable of the Lost Sheep occurs also in Mt. 18:12–14, but Lk. applies it to the contrast between Israel as the chosen people and the outcasts who foreshadow the Gentiles. **7.** Lk. also lays stress 73
on the repentance of the sinner, which is contrasted with the ' righteous ' who are really self-righteous. Neither the sheep, nor the coin can repent ; this may suggest that the sinner's repentance may be a gift of God, consequent on his being found, not the condition of his being found.

8-10 The Lost Coin, peculiar to Lk., presents the g
same truth, with less emphasis on the righteous who feel no need of repentance.

11-32 The Prodigal Son—Another Lucan parable h
declaring God's welcome to the outcasts (and, by implication, the Gentiles) and the recalcitrant attitude of the Jews. The point is the same as that of the preceding parables, more fully worked out in respect of God's love, the repentance of the outcast, and the blindness of the Jews to their obligations towards their ' unrighteous ' brethren. **13.** ' Gathered ' should perhaps be better rendered ' Realised '. **15.** The son's degradation suggests the application of the parable to Gentiles. **20.** The father's welcome precedes the son's confession, and begins while the son is still far off. **22.** The ring signifies authority in the household. **29.** The elder brother, in whose position the Jews stand, is wholly unperceiving. The basis of his relationship to his father is servitude, and keeping commandments in a Pharisaic manner. By calling his brother ' this son of yours ' he fails to recognise his brotherhood with outcast sinners. **31.** The privileged status of Israel and the Pharisees is recognised by implication. Lk. always sees the Christian mission as directed in the first instance to the Jews as the chosen people. **32.** ' Your brother ' corrects the unbrotherly attitude of the Pharisee.

XVI The Parable of the Unjust Steward—This is i
the most difficult of all parables, and no interpretation is wholly satisfactory. **1** suggests that the theme of the preceding parables is continued. If so, the leaders of Israel, who have behaved harshly to outcasts and aliens, are still in mind, this time as the stewards of God's people. A wise steward, seeing that he was to be dismissed, would conciliate his master's debtors out of his ill-gotten gains. Even if brotherhood does not induce the Jewish leaders to adopt a more liberal outlook, prudence ought to persuade them ; by their dispensation of their riches to those whom they have oppressed, they would gain eternal friends.

Difficulties in the way of this interpretation arise j
from the fact that the parable is addressed to disciples (1 ; cf. 9). Possibly 1 may be interpreted to mean that Jesus spoke to his disciples about the failure of the Pharisees ; but in this case 9 must also be addressed to the Pharisees, otherwise it must mean that, in contrast with them, the disciples are to make eternal friends by their dispensation of worldly things. This leaves it difficult to explain why mammon in 9 is ' unrighteous '. It is often said that the point of the parable lies solely in the steward's swiftness, resourcefulness and prudence ; disciples must act similarly in the crisis of the advent of the Kingdom ; but this breaks the connection with ch. 15, indicated by 1, and makes 9 very difficult. To make 8, 9 read as questions is to deprive the parable of much of its point. If the parable is meant solely to inculcate the need for decisive action in face of the crisis of the Kingdom, 10–13 can have had no original connection with it, their point being entirely different. That the lesson of the parable would in that case be based on the action of a wicked man is in itself no objection ; cf. 11:5–8, 18:1–8. On the whole, however, it is more likely that the parable is directed against the leaders of Israel as stewards of God's property. They should be making friends of those whom they have oppressed, so as to find security when their present position of worldly privilege collapses with the end of the old order. **10ff.** If they have not discharged their stewardship faithfully, including the use of their usurped privileges for the benefit of those whom they now treat as outcasts, they will not be entrusted with the

730j riches of the Kingdom, which are 'true' as opposed to 'spurious', and which belong to Christ and his followers ('our own' is a better reading than 'your own' in 12). Hence they cannot serve God and mammon (13: a Q saying, used as a general statement in Mt. and fitted to this context in Lk.). On this interpretation 1–13 is really addressed to the Pharisees, despite the introduction in 1; this accords with **14ff.**, where the Pharisees, as the real audience, understand the application to themselves, and Jesus attacks their justification of themselves on the score of their position of privilege, and, probably, the wealth which they often possessed. **15.** 'Abomination' implies that their self-justification is idolatry.

k **16-18 The Law and the Kingdom—16** is Q material (Mt. 11:12–13, undoubtedly the more original version). The dispensation of the Old Covenant ended with John as the forerunner. Now the Kingdom is proclaimed by Jesus as a gospel, and is open to all who force their way into it, unlike the old order represented by the Pharisees from which many are excluded. The Law itself, however, is not repudiated by the preaching of the Kingdom. It is not part of the Pharisaic 'abomination', but is fulfilled and so stands in its entirety. To repudiate it would be for Jesus to break the covenant, or marriage-bond, between God and Israel (**18**; a saying with a general application in Mt. 5:32, which is applied to the covenant relationship in this context, and possibly also in Mk 10:11–12).

731a **19-31 The Rich Man and Lazarus**—This parable resumes the attack on the leaders of Judaism for their attitude to outcasts, and by implication the Gentiles. Probably a folk-story has been employed for this purpose. **22.** The outcast reclines at table with Abraham, being by implication a son of Abraham (cf. 13:28–9, 13:16, 19:9). **24.** The representative of Pharisaism seeks comfort at the hands of an outcast. **29.** The scriptures, rightly understood, would suggest a different attitude on the part of Pharisaic Judaism. Repentance in this context means primarily the adoption of such an attitude. If the witness of scripture will not persuade, even resurrection will be insufficient; a hint of the consequences of the resurrection of Jesus himself.

b **XVII Teaching to the Disciples on Offences, Forgiveness, Faith and Service**—In contrast to the Pharisaic failure to exercise stewardship, the disciples are now taught about the nature of their stewardship in the Kingdom. **1-2.** Temptations to sin are inevitable, but those who cause ordinary believers to go astray will be punished; cf. 12:45ff. 'Little ones': i.e. humble believers (cf. Mt. 18:6; Mk 9:42). Lk. appears to preserve the Q version here of a saying found both in that tradition and in Mk. **3-4.** Q material (Mt. 18:15, 21–2). Lk. is typically emphatic in his mention of forgiveness and repentance, and probably applies the saying to the apostles' exercise of Church discipline. **5-6.** Another Q saying with a Lucan introduction (paralleled in Mt. 17:20). The 'sycamine' appears in LXX as equivalent to 'fig'. This may refer to the 'fig tree' of Judaism (13:6), to be removed by the disciples' faith. A similar saying in Mk 11:22–3 speaks of the removal of 'this mountain' (perhaps Jerusalem) in the context of the episode of the withered fig tree which certainly signifies Judaism. **7-10.** Peculiar to Lk. The disciples, unlike the Pharisees, must behave as God's servants, with no claim to merit.

c **11-19 The Ten Lepers**—The healing work of Jesus is bestowed on all the lepers alike; only the Samaritan responds. Thus the outcast is praised for his attitude, whereas the Jews are condemned. Jesus, on the way to Jerusalem, passes along the border of territory inhabited by the outcast Samaritans and the mixed population of 'Galilee of the Gentiles'. The story is peculiar to Lk., but may be founded on Mk 1:40ff. **18.** 'foreigner' is the usual LXX term for a heathen. This Samaritan may foreshadow both the Samaritans (Ac. 8) and the Gentiles who will respond to the act of God in Christ, in contrast to the Jews. **19.** 'Has made you well' is the same phrase as 'has saved you' (7:50); the same terms are used of healing and forgiveness. 731c

The Kingdom of God—While the Kingdom is manifested before their eyes, the Pharisees are still asking when it will come. Their attitude is contrasted with the faith of the 'foreigner'. **20.** 'signs to be observed': better, 'with watching for it'. **21.** When the Kingdom comes, it will have been already known and familiar to those who have accepted it as inaugurated by Jesus. 'In the midst of you' is improbable as a translation of *entos hymōn*. Three instances in Symmachus' version of the OT are the only real parallel for this meaning of the Greek phrase. The natural sense of 'within' is impossible in the context. More probably it means 'within your grasp', 'within your power to reach out and take', a sense which is attested in two papyri and apparently understood here by some patristic commentators, especially Tertullian (*adv. Marc.* iv, 35). See C. H. Roberts, HTR xli, 1 (1948). d

The Manifestation of the Son of Man—The Parousia is delayed, and the disciples will long to see one of the days of the Son of man. The latter might mean one of the days of Christ's self-revelation, such as the Transfiguration or the Resurrection; but more probably it means a day of the coming age of his full manifestation in power. There will be vain expectations, consequent upon the delay, but the appearance of the Son of man will be unmistakably brilliant. **25.** The necessary prelude to his manifestation in glory is his suffering and rejection. **26-7.** Noah typifies believers who are prepared for the revelation of the Son of man. Lk. adds to this Q passage the type of Lot, linked with Noah as an example of preparedness in disaster in 2 Pet. 2:5–8. **30.** The 'days of the Son of man' (26) are here explained as the 'day' when the Son of man is revealed. **31.** Paralleled in Mk 13:15–16 (Mt. 24:17–18) where it refers to the destruction of Jerusalem. Here it alludes to the urgency of preparation for the manifestation of the Son of man in his Kingdom. **33.** Q material (Mt. 10:39), also in Mk 8:35 (Mt. 16:25; Lk. 9:24), here signifying that the crisis and the urgent action necessitated by it involve a following of Christ in death, a taking up of the cross daily. **36.** The Western text inserts a saying similar to 35, found in Mt. 24:40. One will be taken into the Kingdom and another left, for the manifestation of the Son of man involves judgment. **37.** The disciples are still looking for the place of the Kingdom's arrival. It will come when the judgment that it brings is appropriate and the time is ripe; when, according to a proverbial saying, the corpse is present to attract the vultures. e

XVIII 1-8 The Unjust Judge—This parable indicates that the Kingdom will come in response to the prayer of God's elect for vindication. Even an unrighteous judge attends to a persistent complainer; how much more will God intervene to vindicate his people? Cf. the parable at 11:5ff. The question is whether the Son of man as the agent of divine judgment will find God's people faithful and steadfast when he appears. The delay in the Parousia must not cause any relaxation in the faithful vigilance of God's people. **1.** If this general introduction is not due to Lk.'s misunderstanding of the point of the parable, it means that prayer is regarded as being primarily directed towards the consummation of the Kingdom; cf. the second petition of the Lord's Prayer. **3-4.** Probably based on Sir. 35:15. **5.** 'Wear me out': lit. 'hit in the face' (cf. 1 C. 9:27), the probable meaning being 'treat roughly', whether physically or otherwise. f

9 The Pharisee and the Tax-collector—Like the last parable, this is peculiar to Lk. It reverts to the theme of the Pharisees in relation to the outcasts. Their self-justifying despisal of the outcast tax-collectors is opposed to true faithfulness, such as the g

731g Son of man ought to find at his coming. Righteousness earned by works is contrasted with faithful perseverance. The parable illustrates a doctrine of justification like that of Paul. **12.** The two fasts (cf. *Didache* 8:1) and the tithes on all his income are works of supererogation, not specifically commanded. **14.** The outcast who repents is accepted with God. 'justified' : cf. 7:29, 10:29, 16:15 ; Ac. 13:38.

h **15-17 The Children brought to Jesus**—Lk. here resumes Mk. The children are contrasted with the self-righteous Pharisee, for the Kingdom must be received as a totally unmerited gift, not earned by works. Having made this point, Lk. omits Mk's ending to the story. **15.** 'touch' in blessing.

i **18-30 The Rich Ruler**—From Mk. Reception of the Kingdom means total self-surrender, and in the case of the privileged rulers of Israel a change of heart towards the poor and outcast. The point of the parable is similar to that of the rich man and Lazarus. That this man was a 'ruler' might be inferred from Mk's detail about his wealth. Lk. is probably still thinking of the rulers of Israel and their ungenerous attitude to others. **19.** Lk. does not tone down the force of this saying, as Mt. does. **20.** The ruler is referred to the ordinary law which a Pharisee would observe. For the order of the commandments here, cf. Rom. 13:9 ; Jas 2:11. **21.** Lk. inserts 'all', thus strengthening the force of the command. The saying concerning the needle's eye is apparently not addressed to the disciples, as it is in Mk. For those who are in the position of the rich ruler entry into the Kingdom can be effected only by a divine miracle. **28.** Peter seeks an assurance that this has taken place in the case of the disciples. **29.** Lk. adds 'wife', as in 14:26. In the present age the disciples can receive more, perhaps especially in the form of the Christian fellowship.

j **The Third Prediction of the Passion**—All this depends on the fulfilment of Christ's mission of suffering and resurrection, for which they are going up to Jerusalem. Lk. alone refers here to the fulfilment of scripture (cf. 24:27, 45). **34.** He lays extreme stress on the disciples' failure to understand ; his omission of the Marcan story of the sons of Zebedee (and the transference of the sayings which it introduces to the context of the Last Supper) enables him to set the narrative of the blind man in dramatic juxtaposition to the blindness of the disciples.

k **35-43 The Blind Man at Jericho**—Jesus is attended by a pilgrimage crowd. Even before the entry to Jerusalem, he is a focus of messianic expectation, as the Davidic salutation indicates. As in Mk, the man's recovery of sight is linked with his following Jesus in the way to Jerusalem. Lk. alone mentions the people's praise to God.

l **XIX 1-10 Zacchaeus**—Peculiar to Lk. The outcast tax-collector is saved by Jesus, as being a son of Abraham. Zacchaeus is an important official at what was probably an important customs post. **7.** Even the crowd appear to join in the protest against Jesus entering his house, since he is a sinner. **8-9.** Zacchaeus' repentance is the consequence, not the cause, of the approach of Jesus to him, and salvation is equated with the gift of repentance. **10** echoes the theme of the parables in ch. 15.

m **11-27 The Parable of the Pounds**—Probably a version, from another source, of Mt.'s parable of the Talents (Mt. 25:14–30). The chief points are : (1) Christ's kingdom is not to appear now, as some expected ; he must depart in order to receive it. (2) This will involve his rejection by Israel and the consequent destruction of the nation. (3) The Kingdom will be administered by his disciples. (4) This will involve its continual expansion, in contrast to the narrow and self-complacent attitude of the Jewish leaders. **11.** The crowd evidently supposed that the kingdom was to appear as soon as Jesus entered Jerusalem ; but he is to ascend to heaven to receive the kingdom which is already his by anticipation. **23.** The task of the disciples is to extend the possessions of Jesus which have been entrusted to them, that is, to promote the coming world-wide mission. 731
26. A narrow adhesion to present privileges and possessions, in the spirit of Judaism, means their forfeiture. **27.** The coming judgment on the Jews. The parable may possibly be based on the journey of Archelaus to Rome to receive his kingdom, and the petition against him organised by the Jews (Jos. Ant. XVII, xi, 1).

28-44 The Entry into Jerusalem—Lk. follows the Marcan narrative with some variations and additions. 73
The entry is prearranged as a prophetic symbol through which Jerusalem is confronted with a king 'righteous and saving, meek and mounted on an ass' (Zech. 9:9ff.). **29.** Bethphage : a tract of the Mount of Olives and the outermost part of Jerusalem bordering on it. **30.** The colt is fit for a royal progress. **36.** A reminiscence of the accession of Jehu (2 Kg. 9:13). **37.** The descent of the Mount of Olives by which Jesus goes down to Jerusalem may stand in contrast to the return to the Mount before the arrest and for the Ascension. The crowd consists of disciples, and Jesus is openly greeted as king, on the ground of his mighty works. Lk. has rephrased the salutation as given in Mk, assimilating it to the cry of the angels (2:14). **39-44.** Lucan : the stones would cry out because the Messiah has come to the capital of Israel. **42.** In rejecting Jesus, Jerusalem has chosen the way of political nationalism, which will lead to war with Rome. The siege is exactly predicted (cf. Jos.BJ V, vi, 2, V, xii, 2) but although this may well be written after the event, it is not necessarily so. The siege imagery may be based on the OT, especially Isa. 29:3 (LXX) ; **44** echoes Ps. 137:9. In the coming of Jesus to Jerusalem God's decisive visitation in judgment has occurred.

45-48 The Cleansing of the Temple—**46.** Lk. has greatly abbreviated the Marcan account, and, surprisingly, omitted 'for all the nations' from the citation of Isa. 56:7. Lk. has postponed the subject of the relation of Christ to the Temple for treatment in the trial and speech of Stephen (Ac. 7) ; he also realises that the Temple is not in fact to be the house of prayer for Gentiles, since he is probably writing after its destruction. **47-8.** Jesus is listened to by the people of Israel in the Temple, while their leaders seek to kill him. b

XX 1-8 The Question about Authority—Jesus is teaching the people and proclaiming the gospel to them when the rulers of Israel come upon him to question his authority. **2.** Cf. the demand of the rulers for a sign in Jn 2:18. The question concerns the drastic action of the cleansing of the Temple, and also his teaching, for which he had not the authority of Rabbinic tradition. **4ff.** John was the prophet who pointed to Jesus, and his baptism prepared the way for the mission of Jesus. Through John's baptism Jesus was marked out as the Messianic Son of God. He now requires the leaders of Israel to declare their position concerning this, and they dare not deny that John was a prophet, for John's movement was popular and formidable. **8.** If they do not understand the meaning of John's mission, they will not accept a direct statement from Jesus himself about his own authority. c

9-18 The Parable of the Wicked Tenants—In Lk. this Marcan parable is addressed to the people as a whole. It explains the nature of the mission, and so also of the authority, of Jesus. The idea of Israel as God's vineyard is based on Isa. 5:1ff. ; the tenants are the leaders of Israel, the servants the prophets. Lk. emphasises the murder of the *son* by altering Mk so that the third servant is only wounded and not killed. **13.** 'Beloved', or perhaps 'only', recalls 3:22. Lk., like Mt., reverses Mk's order of events in **15**, so as to correspond with the actual death of Jesus outside Jerusalem ; cf. Heb. 13:12. **16** predicts the destruction of Jerusalem but, whereas Mt. 21:43 d

732d envisages the Gentile mission, Lk., like Mk, seems to allude to the coming Gentile domination over the land of Israel. **17.** Those who exclaim in horror at this prophecy are probably for the most part the Jewish leaders. Ps. 118:22 is cited, signifying the rejection of the Messiah. **18** indicates that this proof-text is already associated in Christian usage with Isa. 8:14 (cf. 1 Pet. 2:4ff.) and Dan. 2:44. **19.** The parable was directed against the rulers, who fear the people as a whole who presumably have been impressed by the teaching of Jesus.

e **19-26 Tribute to Caesar**—The rulers, having decided to attack Jesus, conspire to bring a political charge against him. Lk. omits Mk's mention of Pharisees and Herodians, and makes suborned agents of the priesthood responsible. Jesus decisively rejects the extreme patriotic position, and asserts that Caesar has a right to obedience, within the scope of man's all-embracing obligation to God. Ancient commentators find an allusion to man as the bearer of God's image. This would mean that the rulers of Israel, like the wicked shepherds of Ezek. 34, have neglected to render to God the human beings with whom he has entrusted them; this being more important than any question about secular allegiance. This is a possible, but perhaps unlikely, interpretation.

f **27-40 The Sadducee Question**—The Sadducees apparently wished simply to discredit Jesus by posing a trick question on the law of levirate marriage (Dt. 25:5–6) in relation to crude ideas about future life. **34-5.** In this age men marry, but in the age to come they are immortal, and do not marry, living for ever like the angels (cf. Enoch 15:6ff.). **35.** Lk. corrects Mk's apparent implication that all the sons of this age will attain the resurrection life. It is very unlikely that Lk.'s change in Mk's wording implies a view that men are fitted by celibacy in this life to attain the age to come; marriage is considered in this passage solely from the point of view of legal relationship and the procreation of children. No conclusions can be drawn from it concerning the character of Christian marriage. **36.** Attainment to the resurrection life is identified with sonship towards God. Belief in future life is grounded in God's calling of his servants and his unchanging purpose.

g **41-44 David's Son**—Lk. accepts the tradition that Jesus really was of Davidic descent. This Marcan passage means that Jesus is not *merely* the Davidic Messiah, but the Son of man who is to be enthroned at the right hand of God. Ps. 110:1 is a commonly used Christian proof-text; cf. Ac. 2:34; 1 C. 15:25; Heb. 1:13; 1 Pet. 3:22. It was probably interpreted messianically in 1st-cent. Judaism; otherwise this passage makes little sense.

h **XX 45-XXI 4 Denunciation of the Scribes**—From Mk; but in Mk addressed to disciples, like the parable of the Unjust Steward which also seems to be really directed against the Jewish leaders. The disciples are to guard against such conduct. The scribes are typical of the complacency and worldliness of the Jewish leaders and in contrast with them is set the Marcan episode of the poor widow's coins, the smallest permissible offering, yet more acceptable than the contributions of the rich. This story is in line with the repeated theme of this Gospel that the poor and outcast are vindicated over against the self-justifying rulers of Judaism.

i **XXI 5-36 The Apocalyptic Discourse**—**5-7** introduces the discourse; from Mk, omitting his reference to the Mount of Olives and the names of the disciples who question Jesus. The destruction of the Temple is certain and will be complete. **8ff.** The discourse proper; a modified form of Mk 13. It opens with a warning against false eschatological expectations. Those who 'come in my name' are probably persons claiming to be the Christ rather than Christian teachers announcing that the Lord has come. Lk. adds 'The time is at hand'; such a declaration is false, because the Parousia is delayed. Lk. substitutes 'tumults' (i.e. civil strife) for Mk's 'rumours of wars'. 732i
Such disturbances, on the lines of those of the Maccabaean age, are probably only part of the general apocalyptic imagery, and not to be identified with the events of A.D. 68. 'Not . . . at once': a stronger expression than Mk's 'not yet', emphasising the delay of the Parousia. **10** introduces the prophetic discourse. 'Nation will rise . . .': an echo of the judgment on Egypt in Isa. 19:2. Lk. adds pestilences to the famines and earthquakes, probably owing to literary convention (cf. Thucydides ii, 43) and assonance in Greek. All three are part of the apocalyptic imagery, and not to be identified with particular 1st-cent. events. Lk. anticipates 25 in his reference to prodigies. **12ff.** The whole discourse concerns the lot of the disciples, contrasted with the fate of Jerusalem. Lk. emphasises what is to happen *before* the end. Persecution by the Jews, with a repetition of what befell Jesus in being brought before kings and governors. Confession under persecution will be the supreme testimony to the Gospel. **14.** Lk. lays much stress on the inspiration of the confessors (cf. 12:11). Here he thinks of them as Christ's representatives, hence as being given 'a mouth and wisdom' by him (cf. Exod. 4:12; Jer. 1:9), rather than as inspired by the Spirit (as Mk and Mt.); cf. 12:12. This prophecy was fulfilled in the case of Stephen, and Lk. has adjusted Mk's wording here to draw out the parallel (see Ac. 6:10). **16.** Lk.'s rewriting of Mk 13:12 obscures the allusion to Mic. 7:6, but his addition of 'friends' may be derived from Mic. 7:5. **18.** Lk.'s apparent optimism is explained by **19**: the martyr wins life through his endurance, and God will preserve him even in death; cf. 10:19. **20ff.** In contrast, Jerusalem is to be destroyed. Whether or not Lk. is influenced by knowledge of the actual siege, he interprets Mk's 'desolating sacrilege', probably correctly, as destruction by enemy forces. **21.** This invasion means the evacuation of the city; cf. 17:31 (Mk 13:15–16). This need not refer to the flight of the Jerusalem Christians to Pella before the siege. **22.** 'Vengeance'; cf. Dt. 32:35, describing God's punishment of Israel. To emphasise the fact that the destruction is due to divine wrath Lk. rewrites Mk's (13:19) citation of Dan. 12:1. **23.** 'Earth': better, 'land' of Israel ('this people'). Lk. alters Mk in **24**, removing his statement about a shortening of the days and introducing the thought of the Gentile destruction and domination of Jerusalem, his language being derived from Zech. 12:2–3, part of which is quoted. The 'times of the Gentiles' are the period of Gentile domination, corresponding to that of the Jewish rejection of the gospel (cf. Rev. 11:2). **25** takes up the theme of 11, the apocalyptic imagery being based on Isa. 13:10. Lk. adds a citation from Ps. 65:8, on the disturbance of the sea and the nations. Ps. 65:9 may have influenced Lk.'s language about 'signs' here. **26** also reflects Ps. 65:8–9, in its references to troubles coming upon the world as a whole, and not Judaea only. The 'powers of heaven' (stars) echo Isa. 34:4 (LXX). **27.** Dan. 7:13–14 will be fulfilled in the coming of the Son of man for the redemption of his disciples. Lk. omits Mk's allusion to this prophecy in his narrative of the trial of Jesus, perhaps because, unlike Mk, he interprets it of Christ's *coming*, for which this context is appropriate, and not of his glorification in the Ascension. Lk. has 'cloud' for Mk's 'clouds', probably in order to bring the Parousia into the series of the Transfiguration and Ascension, where the 'cloud' also occurs. Lk. stresses the positive and joyful hope of redemption, i.e. the deliverance of the saints at the coming of the Son of man. **29ff.** Lk. marks off the parable of the fig tree by means of an introductory sentence. He adds 'and all the trees' perhaps to show that the fig tree does not have its special application to Judaism here (as in 13:6ff.). **31.** The Kingdom is here future, and means the full completion of God's rule through Christ. **32.** The fall of Jerusalem is temporally linked

732i with the redemption of the elect and the coming of the Kingdom. The words of Jesus are to stand though heaven and earth are destroyed. **34-6.** Lk. reproduces the substance of Mk's teaching on watchfulness, omitting his parable of a man going on a journey (Mk 13:34), since he has inserted a somewhat similar saying in 12:35ff. This passage owes much to Isa. 24:17ff., with a probable allusion in **35** to Jer. 25:29. The parallel with 1 Th. 5:3, 6, 7 is notable. Vigilance is associated with prayer. The redeemed will stand before the Son of man in glory; cf. the vision of Stephen (Ac. 7:56).

j **37-38 Summary of the Proclamation made by Jesus** to the whole people of Israel in the Temple. The lodging on Olivet corresponds to Mk's account of journeys to and from Bethany. The attitude of the people is contrasted with the plotting of the rulers (22:2).

733a **XXII The Betrayal—1-2.** Lk. abbreviates Mk, omitting 'not during the feast' as inconsistent with the subsequent event; Lk. is anxious to emphasise the Passover theme in the narrative of the Last Supper. He expresses the point of that Marcan clause, however, in 6 ('in the absence of the multitude'). **3.** Satan was directly responsible for Christ's death; cf. Jn 13:2, 27; 1 C. 2:8. **4.** 'Captains', i.e. commanders of the Temple police.

b **The Last Supper—8.** According to Lk., Peter and John as the chief disciples are sent formally to prepare the Passover. Lk. follows Mk very closely. The arrangements made in advance prepare the reader for an event of specially profound significance, as in the case of the entry to Jerusalem. **14.** 'The hour' of the Passover meal, perhaps also with a hint of the decisive hour of Christ's mission, so often spoken of in Jn. Mk has merely 'when it was evening'. Lk. typically speaks of the 'apostles' for Mk's 'the Twelve'.

c **The Institution**—RSV reads the 'shorter text', found in Codex Bezae and most of the Old Latin MSS. Two of the latter read 15, 16, 19*a*, 17, 18, and this order occurs with minor variations in the Old Syriac. Most of the MSS read the 'longer text' (15–20) as RSV*n*. This presents an extremely difficult problem. It should first be observed: (1) Lk.'s special concern is to show the Last Supper as a final anticipation, before Christ's death, of the Messianic feast in the Kingdom of God. Jesus is about to enter into possession of the Kingdom through death and glorification. This is to be brought about by the betrayal, for as Son of man he is predestined to die (cf. Ac. 2:23). Christ's followers, like their Lord, partake of the character of the Servant, and in that role they receive the covenant promise of the Kingdom. This is connected with Peter's fall, and his restoration to leadership. (2) Lk.'s possible sources. 17–18 appear to be derived from Mk 14:25, as the common use of the odd phrase 'fruit of the vine' indicates. 15–16 enlarges Mk's narrative by adding a parallel saying concerning the fulfilment in the Kingdom of the Passover meal, a saying about eating exactly balancing the Marcan saying about drinking. This may reflect the influence of Christian liturgical practice. 15–18 may, however, conceivably be non-Marcan. Then 24–30 may have followed 15–18 in a non-Marcan source. 21–3 (probably derived from Mk, 22 being certainly Marcan) may be thought to break the continuity, as does 19*a* (Marcan) and 19*b*–20 (perhaps partly Marcan), if authentic. (3) If the longer text is original, Lk. has either awkwardly conflated sources, inserting Marcan and Pauline material (or material from a source parallel to both Mk and 1 C. 11:24–5) into a basically non-Marcan narrative (15–18, 24ff.), or, more probably, taken some Marcan material and built it up in a prominent and emphatic position (15–18), intending to proceed to the next most important section of the narrative (24ff.), but has felt obliged to incorporate the substance of Mk 14:22–4 (with additions) and also Mk 14:18–21, both of which he inserts rather clumsily. (4) The longer 73
text is preferred (e.g. by Jeremias, *The Eucharistic Words of Jesus*, ET (1955), and Schürmann, *Biblica* 32 (1951), 364–92, 522–41) because the numerous small differences between the longer text and 1 C. 11:24 and Mk 14:24 suggest that it is unlikely that this text is an artificial correction of the shorter text. It is also difficult to account for Lk. writing the shorter text. (5) On this view, however, it is hard to account for the origin of the shorter text. It is sometimes ascribed to a desire not to reveal the central Christian mystery to the uninitiated, but any excision from the text for this reason would certainly have included 19*a*. Alternatively, it is thought that the shorter text was concerned to promote the separation of the eucharist from the *agape*; but the excision of 20 would be a strange way to effect this. The excision of 19*b* is not explained by this theory. (6) The difficulty of accounting for the appearance of the shorter text, if the longer be authentic, is a strong argument for the originality of the former, which may be preferred as being the harder. (7) If Lk. wrote the shorter text he has put Mk's saying about the fulfilment of the cup, with a similar saying about the fulfilment of the Passover meal, first. To him this conveys the primary meaning of the Last Supper. Then he has added Mk 14:22 in 19*a*, although it breaks into the sequence of his story. He has omitted Mk 14:23–4, having already mentioned the cup in 17–18. Lk. seems indifferent to the order of the bread and cup, perhaps because in his view the normal eucharist is merely the 'breaking of bread'; or because liturgical practice varied. (8) On this view, the longer text is an early attempt to bring Lk. into harmony with the Pauline and Marcan tradition. **15.** 'Again' (RSV*n*) may have been d
inserted to make it unambiguously clear that Jesus *did* eat the Passover. **16.** The Passover is fulfilled in the eschatological feast, which the cup also prefigures. **21-3.** Probably based on Mk. Lk.'s rewording of Mk in 21 may be influenced by Ps. 41:3, and is intended to clarify Mk, who might be taken (as by Mt.) to mean that a particular disciple was going to dip into the dish, whereas they all did so. 22 follows Mk closely; 23 corresponds to Mk 14:19, but the inquiry is among the disciples, not addressed to Jesus, thus avoiding obvious difficulties in the story. **24-7.** Probably Marcan with a Lucan introduction. The quarrel and the saying of Jesus have been transferred from the story of the sons of Zebedee to this setting, where the nature of Christ's Kingdom, now covenanted to the disciples with the pledge of the Messianic banquet, can be most effectively contrasted with the character of worldly sovereignty; hence Lk. omits the episode of the sons of Zebedee at 18:34. **24** follows naturally upon 15–18, and may possibly resume a non-Marcan source after the Marcan verses preceding it. **25.** 'Benefactors': a typical title of Hellenistic monarchs. **26.** It is assumed that the apostles are rulers of Christ's people or kingdom. 'Youngest' possibly denotes a junior member of the Church (cf. Ac. 5:6, 10); 'leader' is used of Judas and Silas (Ac. 15:22) and of Church leaders in general (Heb. 13:7, 17, 24); 'serves', cf. Ac. 6:2. **27.** Cf. 12:37 and the feet-washing in Jn 13:4ff. Jesus is the servant. **28** expands a version of a saying paralleled in Mt. 19:28. The Kingdom covenanted to Jesus by the Father is in turn covenanted to the apostles. As its administrators they are to share in it; hence they are to join with Jesus in the eschatological feast when he has come into his Kingdom (cf. 23:42), eating and drinking as the Last Supper foreshadowed. The covenanting of the Kingdom and this promise are the most significant events at the Supper, according to Lk. If 20 is authentic, its mention of the covenant is probably to be interpreted in this sense. The nature of the Kingdom and of the thrones of the apostles is to be explained in Ac. 1:6–8. **31-4.** The prophecy of Peter's denial looks forward, as Mk's version does not, to his restoration and leadership of

733d the apostles. Lk. sets this in the context of the Supper and the teaching about the Kingdom ; Mk on the way to Gethsemane. Satan has gained power over all the disciples (like Job), to 'sift' them. Jesus prays for Peter as the apostolic leader, that his steadfastness may not permanently fail. He is to be converted and strengthen the others. Peter prefers to trust in himself and asserts his devotion in words recalling Ittai's devotion to David (2 Sam. 15:20–1), a passage recalled also in Jn 18:1). 'Three times': his denial will be complete.

e **35-38.** Lucan. If Satan is to gain the disciples, their whole manner of life must alter. Their previous instructions are cancelled, and they are told to safeguard their lives by worldly means in view of the crisis of the arrest of Jesus. It is not probable that Jesus wanted swords to be carried to prevent a private assassination, or to identify himself and his followers with revolutionary 'transgressors'; the allusions to 'purse' and 'bag' would then be otiose and confusing. **35** quotes instructions actually given to the Seventy (10:1ff.). **37.** Isa. 53:12 is quoted, identifying Jesus directly with the Servant. The disciples' unperceptive literalism evokes an ironical dismissal of the subject.

f **39-46 The Prayer of Jesus**—Either non-Marcan, or a drastic abbreviation of Mk, the latter being more probable. Lk. does not name the place. **40.** 'Temptation': the trial of crisis ; cf. 11:4. **41.** 'knelt' in earnest prayer ; cf. Ac. 7:60, 9:40, 20:36. 'Father': cf. 11:2. **42b** echoes the Matthaean, not the Lucan, Lord's Prayer. **43-4.** Omitted in many MSS ; perhaps omitted by Marcion for docetic reasons, and by Alexandrians as doctrinally difficult. Cf. Heb. 5:7.

g **47-53 The Arrest**—Lk. suggests that Judas did not actually kiss Jesus, and omits Mk's story that this was a prearranged signal ; he may think of it as the regular sign of brotherhood within the Church ; hence the emphasis on 'with a kiss'. It is not clear whether this episode has any connection with the omission of the kiss of peace in the liturgy on Good Friday (cf. Tertullian, *orat.* 18). **49.** Lk. only. The question arises from the disciples' misunderstanding of the saying about taking a sword in 36-8. **50.** Closely paralleled in Mk ; Lk. adds the detail that the *right* ear was cut off (so also Jn 18:10), probably an imaginary graphic detail (like the right hand in 6:6) which does not necessarily indicate that the servant was fleeing with his back turned to the striker. Lk. adds the healing of the ear. **52.** Lk. pictures the Jewish authorities as coming out in person, as with Peter and John in Ac. 4:1. **52b** is closely paralleled in Mk, as is **53a**. **53b** introduces the idea of the hour appointed by divine providence, which is that of the apparent triumph of the devil (cf. Jn 13:30).

h **The Trial before the Sanhedrin**—In Lk. the Sanhedrin meets only in the morning, and the events at the high priest's house take place before any trial begins. The story of Peter's denial follows Mk, with minor modifications. Lk. omits Peter's cursing (**60**) and leads up to 'I do not know what you are saying', instead of giving this as Peter's first answer, as in Mk. **61a** is Lucan, probably inferred from Mk, since it explains how Peter connected the cock-crow with the prophecy of Jesus. If 62 is not authentic (there is some MS authority for its omission, and it may be interpolated from Mt.), 61*a* is Lk.'s dramatic climax to the story. **63.** Lk. corrects Mk's impression that the mocking was done by members of the Sanhedrin. **64.** Mt. and Lk. agree against Mk in adding 'Who is it that struck you?' unless Mk originally read this too ; but the weight of textual evidence is against this sentence in Mk. Streeter believed that Lk. has a better and independent account, to which both Mk and Mt. have become partly assimilated ; but Lk. may, like Mt., have inferred the above question from Mk's narrative, for it is implied in the blindfolding. **67.** The point at issue in the trial, according to Lk., is Messiahship, not Christ's attitude to the Temple, a subject which is going to be treated by implication 733h
in the story of the trial of Stephen. **69.** Christ's glorification is to begin from his condemnation and death. The Son of man is to be exalted, in fulfilment of Ps. 110:1. Lk. assumes that Jesus spoke only of his exaltation here, not of the Parousia ; hence he omits Dan. 7:13 (Mk 14:62), which he evidently understands as alluding to the latter event. **70.** Son of God : i.e. the Messianic son, the Davidic king of Ps. 110. Jesus does not deny this title, but accepts it in a protesting manner.

XXIII The Trial before Pilate—**2.** Lk. alone, i
either by inference from the Marcan narrative as a whole, or from a non-Marcan source, records the actual charge. It is centred on a claim to kingship, supported by a story that he forbade the payment of taxes. **3** is Marcan. **4.** Lk. makes clear Pilate's verdict of acquittal ; he is anxious to show in what sense Jesus was a king, and that his claim was non-political. **5.** Lucan : cf. Ac. 10:37.

The Sending to Herod—6-16. Peculiar to Lk. The j
episode may be based on Ps. 2:1–2 ; cf. Ac. 4:25–8. Herod may well have been at Jerusalem. Lk. may see in the incident a further opportunity of exculpating Pilate. **8.** Cf. 9:9. **11.** Lk. transfers the soldiers' mockery from the Romans to Herod's men. The gorgeous robe corresponds to the purple of Mk 15:17, and signifies burlesque kingship.

13-25 Pilate's Sentence—**14.** The acquittal is re- k
peated and Herod is also stated to have found Jesus innocent. **17** (RSV*n*) is added in some MSS to clarify Lk.'s narrative which is otherwise obscure, perhaps because he is linking together different sources. **19.** 'An insurrection' replaces Mk's 'the insurrection'. A tumult may have involved some of the followers of Jesus among the Galilaean pilgrims. Lk. may be toning down Mk's mention of the incident, for political reasons. **22.** Marcan passage, followed by the third acquittal. **24.** Lk. expands this passage, bringing out the full guilt of the Jewish leaders, not Pilate or Herod.

The Crucifixion—**26.** The Marcan episode of Simon 734a
of Cyrene. Lk. adds 'to carry it behind Jesus', recalling 9:23, 14:27. **27-31.** Lucan, probably based on the mourning of Jerusalem in Zech. 12:10–14. The woes are prophesied that will fall on Jerusalem in consequence of the rejection of Christ. Hos. 10:8 is cited in 30. **31.** If the Roman power deals thus with the politically innocent, what will become of the guilty, i.e. the zealots and revolutionaries? **32-3.** The fulfilment of Isa. 53:12, brought forward to clarify Mk's narrative. **34.** The prayer of Jesus, to which that of Stephen (Ac. 7:60) is probably a deliberately intended parallel. This makes the authenticity of the verse probable, although the MS evidence for including it and excluding it is very evenly balanced. **34b.** Marcan, alluding to Ps. 22:19. Verse 8 of the same Psalm underlies the Lucan v. **35**, which contrasts the looking on by the people with the scoffing of the rulers. **35b** echoes the thought of 9:35 and Isa. 42:1. **36-8.** Marcan. The offering of vinegar recalls Ps. 69:22. Lk. makes the title on the cross a climax to the mocking, altering its position in the story, and adding the sarcastic 'This'. **39-43.** Lucan, reasserting Lk.'s favourite contrast of the penitent sinner with the hard-hearted. **42.** Jesus is to enter the Kingdom through death, according to the more probable reading (RSV*n*). The reading 'in your kingly power' would suggest an allusion to the Parousia, which is unlikely. **43.** The criminal is to enter the abode of the righteous, with Jesus. **45.** Lk. adds a reference to an eclipse (RSV*n*), the variant readings being attempts to correct the apparent statement that an eclipse had taken place at the full moon, which would be an impossibility. **45b.** Marcan. The Temple is superseded, access to God having been opened by Christ. **46.** Lk., having omitted Mk's cry of dereliction, adds Ps. 31:6, with 'Father', expressing trustful commitment and voluntary acceptance of death. **47.** The centurion acknowledges, as a Gentile, that

734a Jesus was vindicated. Lk. adds the repentance of the crowds, which shows that only the leaders of the nation are wholly responsible and entirely impenitent. **49.** Mk mentions the women looking on from afar ; Lk. brings this directly into line with Ps. 38:11 and 88:8, 18, perhaps supposing the apostles to be present also.

b **50-56 The Burial**—Lk. explicates Mk's narrative, explaining that Joseph, though a member of the Sanhedrin, was good and righteous, in the class of people represented also by Simeon, who expected the Kingdom of God. Mt. and Jn make him a disciple. **54.** ' Preparation ' : Friday. **55.** The women could therefore become powerful witnesses for the Resurrection.

c **XXIV The Resurrection—1ff.** Lk. abbreviates the Marcan narrative, and alters it. **3.** Lk. alone records explicitly that they did not find the body ; it is implied in Mk 16:6. Lk. refers back to this at 23. Most MSS add ' of the Lord Jesus ', which is absent from the ' Western ' text and in part from the Old Syriac. This is likely to be a ' Western non-interpolation ', since it is difficult to account for the omission of the words, if genuine. Possibly, however, the omission might be due to confusion with v. 23 ; the expression ' the Lord Jesus ' is used of the risen Lord in Ac. 1:21, 4:33, 8:16. **4.** Lk. rewrites the story in his typical manner. The two men link the event with the Transfiguration and the Ascension. The former is also recalled by the ' dazzling ' apparel. **5.** In Lk. it is implied that the women ought not to be seeking Jesus among the dead for they should have remembered his words ; cf. Isa. 8:19. ' He is not here . . .' etc. (RSV*n*) is probably a ' Western non-interpolation ', perhaps an assimilation of the story to Mt., slightly reworded to fit the context ; it is not, however, an exact assimilation to either Mt. or Mk. **6b.** Lk. recasts the Marcan narrative ; he takes from Mk the reference to Galilee, but all the events of the post-Resurrection period are set in Jerusalem ; hence the angels remind the women of the previous words of Jesus instead of sending a message to the disciples about going to Galilee. Those words had been addressed to the disciples (9:22, 18:33) ; this does not imply that the women were with them then, for Lk. has rewritten his source rather roughly, in order to concentrate the beginning of the Church's commissioning by the risen Lord, and its preparation for the universal mission, in Jerusalem, like the beginnings of the preparation for the mission of Jesus himself. **9.** Like Mt., Lk. makes the women bring the news to the disciples, who here include others besides the apostles. **10.** A confused verse, with variant readings designed to improve its continuity with 9 and 11. The verse may be an explanatory note by Lk. or an early interpolator. The two Maries appear in the Marcan tradition, Joanna only in Lk. (cf. 8:3). **12** (RSV*n*). Usually reckoned as a ' Western non-interpolation ', 13 following more naturally on 9 without this verse. It has much in common with Jn 20:3–10, including verbal similarity ; but there are also striking differences between it and the Johannine tradition, where the point is the belief of the ' other disciple ', not the incredulity of Peter, and where there is no equivalent to ' wondering at what had happened '. An interpolation from Jn might have been expected to follow that tradition more closely. In Jn the episode precedes that of the angels at the tomb. 24 seems to refer back to this verse, but it speaks of ' some ', not of Peter only. 24 may be the source of the Johannine story, and of this verse if it is an interpolation. Possibly, however, the ' Western ' text may have omitted the verse, a parenthetical comment to explain that Peter did not absolutely disbelieve the women, because it did not seem to be in harmony with either 24 or the Johannine tradition.

d **13-35 The Emmaus Appearance**—Peculiar to Lk. A dramatically composed story, alluding to earlier Lucan material. **18.** Cleopas : cf. Jn 19:25. **19.** Jesus as a great prophet : the language used here is reproduced in Ac. 7:22 in the description of Moses 734
as a type of Christ. Jesus thus fulfils the expectation of the prophet like Moses (Dt. 18:15ff.). In Ac. 7:35 Moses is also described as a ' deliverer ', just as Jesus was looked upon as the one to redeem (deliver) Israel ; cf. Lk. 1:68, 2:38. **21.** It is implied that the disciples, or some of them, had in fact retained some memory of Christ's prediction of his resurrection ; cf. 7. **23** refers back to 3 ; **24** to 12 (if authentic) and to the tradition underlying Jn 20:3–10. **25** and **27** refer back to 18:31. Scripture as reinterpreted by Christians points to the suffering of the Messiah. This is the great turning-point in the interpretation of the OT, and it is reasonable to think that in essence it originated in the mind of Jesus himself. **26.** Christ, having suffered according to the prophecies, enters into the glory which is already his by anticipation. **30.** The breaking of bread is the means by which the risen Christ makes his presence known to the disciples. Fellowship with him after the Resurrection in the breaking of bread links the Eucharist of the post-Ascension Church (Ac. 2:42, 46) with the pledge given by Jesus at the Last Supper (22:19) and the feeding of the multitude (9:16). The language here used recalls especially 9:16. The passage reflects the experience of the early Church, and the historical details should not be pressed to the point of making them imply that Cleopas and his companion were at the Last Supper. **31.** Christ's disappearance implies that his physical presence is to be withdrawn from his disciples in the post-Resurrection age. **32** links the manifestation of Christ's presence through the breaking of bread with his self-revelation in scripture.

Appearances to Peter and the assembled e
Disciples—34. Lk. inserts, somewhat awkwardly, a mention of the appearance to Peter (cf. 1 C. 15:4). **36-43.** Perhaps the source of Jn 20:19–29. **36b** (RSV*n*) is probably a ' Western non-interpolation ', introduced from Jn 20:19, but it may conceivably be original, the ' Western ' text having omitted it because of a supposed discrepancy between the Lord's salutation and the subsequent terror of the disciples. **39** argues for the physical character of the Resurrection against the idea that the appearances were comparable to phantoms or the figures in a vision. **40** (RSV*n*) is probably another ' Western non-interpolation ' from Jn 20:20, but with ' feet ' (from 39) instead of ' side '. If, however, it is authentic, it may have been omitted as redundant after 39. **41-2** has probably influenced Jn 21:5. For the eating of fish at such a meal of fellowship with the Lord cf. Jn 21:13 and the feeding of the multitude. Some MSS interpolate ' and of a honeycomb ', perhaps influenced by the giving of milk and honey to the newly baptised at their first Communion. **43.** This meal, and that at Emmaus, are referred to in Ac. 10:41.

44-49 Christ's Charge to the Apostles—The f
gospel begins with his prophecies of his death, based on the OT. **44.** ' Still with you ' : contrast Mt. 28:20. Here Jesus is thought of as having been removed from the world by his exaltation. **45.** The basis of the gospel is the reinterpretation of the OT taught by the risen Christ to the apostles. The summary of the gospel is that Christ was destined to suffer and rise again, and that, in consequence of this, repentance and forgiveness of sins are to be proclaimed universally. The content of the world-wide preaching is repentance and forgiveness, and it is to be made to all nations (cf. Mk 13:10). **48.** The apostles are commissioned as witnesses. **49.** The promise was expressed in Jl. The Spirit is equated with divine power. As in the case of the gospel itself, the starting-point for the Church's mission in the power of the Spirit to is be Jerusalem.

50-53 Christ's Blessing and Departure—51. The g
direct reference to the Ascension (RSV*n*) might be a ' Western non-interpolation ', but more probably it has been omitted as apparently inconsistent with the beginning of Ac. Lk. has probably felt it necessary

84g to anticipate the narrative of Ac. in this way by concluding his first volume with a summary statement of the event which forms its climax and is the turning-point of the whole work. **52-3.** The first part of the gospel story has ended. The apostles look forward with joy to the fulfilment of the promise, and, as they serve God in the Temple, are in the same position as that of Zechariah when he had received the promise from the angel.

Bibliography—H. Balmforth, *The Gospel according to St Luke* (1930) ; Henry J. Cadbury, *The Making of Luke-Acts* (1927) ; H. Conzelmann, *Die Mitte der Zeit* (1954) ; J. M. Creed, *The Gospel according to St Luke* (1930) ; B. S. Easton, *The Gospel according to St Luke* (1926) ; N. Geldenhuys, *Commentary on the Gospel of Luke* (1950) ; A. Harnack, *Luke the Physician* (1907) ; E. Klostermann, *Das Lukas Evangelium* (2nd ed. 1929) ; M. J. Lagrange, *Évangile selon Saint Luc* (1921) ; A. Loisy, *L'évangile selon Luc* (1924) ; W. Manson, *The Gospel of Luke*, Moffatt Commentary (1930) ; A. Plummer, *St Luke*, ICC (5th ed. 1922) ; W. M. Ramsay, *Luke the Physician* (1908) ; B. H. Streeter, *The Four Gospels* (1924) ; Vincent Taylor, *Behind the Third Gospel* (1926) ; J. Wellhausen, *Das Evangelium Lucae* (1904).

C. F. Evans, 'The Central Section of St Luke's Gospel' ; C. P. M. Jones, 'The Epistle to the Hebrews and the Lucan Writings' ; G. W. H. Lampe, 'The Holy Spirit in the Writings of St Luke' : all in D. E. Nineham, *Studies in the Gospels* (1955).

JOHN

By C. K. BARRETT

735a **Introduction**—The origin of this Gospel is veiled in obscurity. Towards the end of the 2nd cent. a tradition became strongly established that it had been written by John the son of Zebedee (who was understood to be referred to in the Gospel itself as 'the disciple whom Jesus loved') not far from A.D. 100 (John was believed to have survived till the principate of Trajan). This tradition cannot however be traced early in the 2nd cent. It finds confirmation in some features of the Gospel itself, but is contradicted by others, and the position is complicated by both the similarities and the differences between Jn and the Synoptic Gospels. These points must be taken up one by one.

b **The Tradition**—Irenaeus (writing at Lyons, *c.* A.D. 180) wrote, 'Afterwards (sc. after the writing of the other Gospels) John, the disciple of the Lord, who also reclined on his bosom, published his Gospel, while staying at Ephesus in Asia' (*Adv. Haer.* III, i, 1 ; Eus.HE V, viii, 4). He supports this statement by an appeal to Polycarp (bishop of Smyrna ; died *c.* A.D. 155). He himself, he says, had as a boy heard Polycarp recount his 'intercourse with John and with the others who had seen the Lord' (*apud* Eus.HE V, xx, 4–8). Similar testimony is given by other writers of approximately the same date, and the connection between John and the Gospel seems at first sight secure. The earlier evidence is however much less satisfactory. Polycarp himself in his extant epistle makes no claim to personal contact with the apostle, and does not refer to the Gospel (though he does quote 1 Jn). Irenaeus's statement about Papias, which is similar to that about Polycarp, is almost certainly incorrect. Ignatius of Antioch, writing *c.* A.D. 112 to the church at Ephesus, makes no allusion to John, though he emphasises Paul's contacts with Ephesus. In fact, there is no *early* evidence to connect John with Ephesus, or with the writing of a Gospel. Accordingly, even if certain pieces of evidence which have been held to suggest an early martyrdom for John the son of Zebedee are discounted (and their validity is disputed), the Irenaeus tradition remains at least open to question.

c **Internal Evidence**—The Greek style of the Gospel has been variously assessed. Some have regarded it as translation Greek, behind which an original Aramaic Gospel can be traced. This view probably exaggerates, and it is doubtful whether any of the supposed mistranslations which have been alleged can be maintained ; but the Semitic element is sufficient to give weight to the belief that the evangelist was a Jew. This conclusion is supported (though not as strongly as is sometimes supposed) by the acquaintance which the Gospel suggests with Jewish customs and rites (see e.g. 5:10, 7:22f., 51, 8:17). It is very probable that the evangelist was a Jew, but by no means certain (as far as this kind of evidence goes) that he was a Palestinian Jew. Was he an eye-witness of the events he narrates, or of some of them ? In answering this question we can only appeal to the impression made by the Gospel upon the reader, and different readers have received widely differing impressions. The question is further complicated by the possibility that the evangelist may have used sources (see below), for it is possible that features that suggest the hand of an eye-witness may be due not 73
to the evangelist himself but to another whose work he used.

It is necessary at this point to raise the question of the 'disciple whom Jesus loved' (see 13:23, 19:26, 20:2, 21:7, 20). It has been maintained that this term describes (*a*) an 'ideal' disciple (possibly Paul) ; (*b*) John the son of Zebedee ; (*c*) another disciple, probably not one of the Twelve. On the whole it seems probable that the son of Zebedee was intended. Of this 'Beloved Disciple' it is said in 21:24 that he 'witnessed these things and wrote these things'—that is (probably), that he was the author of the Gospel as a whole. In 19:35 a disciple standing by the Cross (probably the Beloved Disciple is meant) is named as a witness. It seems that the Gospel itself claims at the least a connection (more than that if 21:24 is accepted as it stands) with John the son of Zebedee. This John, however, is a figure well known to us from the Synoptic Gospels.

Relation with the Synoptics—The first impression d
received by a reader who turns from the Synoptic Gospels to the Fourth is of difference : there is difference in style (easily noticeable even in translation), difference in chronology (the ministry lasts not one year but three ; the crucifixion takes place before, not after, the Passover meal), difference in locality (in the Synoptic Gospels Jerusalem is not visited till the last week ; in Jn, Jerusalem is frequently mentioned from ch. 2 onwards), difference in subject-matter (the Synoptic Gospels contain few long discourses, the Fourth contains no exorcisms), and to some extent difference in the presentation of Jesus himself. Along with these differences, however, there is an underlying similarity, which includes not only the basic outline (activity of John the Baptist ; a decisive journey from Galilee to Judaea ; crucifixion in Jerusalem and resurrection appearances) but also a good many details. The following list of events is by no means exhaustive.

	Mk	Jn
Work of the Baptist	1:4–8	1:19–36
Feeding of 5,000	6:34–44	6:1–13
Walking on the Lake	6:45–52	6:16–21
Peter's Confession	8:29	6:68f.
Entry into Jerusalem	11:1–10	12:12–15
Anointing	14:3–9	12:1–8
Last Supper	14:17–26	13:1–17:26
Arrest	14:43–52	18:1–11

To these we may add the recurrence of synoptic sayings in Jn (e.g. 4:44, 12:25, 13:20). On account of these parallels it is today very generally agreed that John was familiar with the synoptic tradition—that is, the traditional material out of which the Synoptic Gospels were composed. Whether he knew any of the Gospels themselves is disputed. A strong case can be made for his having known Mk, a fairly strong case for his knowledge of Lk. On any view of this question, however, one is bound to ask whether an apostle, equipped with such unrivalled first-hand knowledge as John the son of Zebedee must have possessed, would have (*a*) found it necessary to consult and use other authorities, and (*b*) come into conflict with the good

735d and early tradition of Mk on such an issue as the date of the crucifixion.

e No simple answer to the question of authorship is possible. As will appear below, the Gospel is early enough to have been the work of John the Apostle provided that the tradition that he lived to a great age is true. The reference made by Papias (*apud* Eus. HE III, xxxix, 3f.) to an 'Elder (presbyter) John' is itself too obscure to afford useful help. The traditional connection of the Gospel with the apostle John, supported as it is by the Jewish features of the Gospel, is not to be disregarded; but there are also in the Gospel Hellenistic features which probably represent the interests of the editor who gave it to the world. It is very probable that it rests upon not only the synoptic but also other independent traditions; and there is at least nothing to disprove the view that some of these may in some way go back to the apostle.

736a **Date and Place of Writing**—If it be correct (see above) that Jn used Mk we are provided at once with a *terminus post quem* of *c.* A.D. 70, or rather of 80 or 90, since we must allow time for the circulation of the earlier Gospel. It is probable (see the notes) that 9:22, 16:2 refer to a Jewish decision which was taken between A.D. 85 and 90; again, a date after A.D. 90 is suggested for the Gospel. A *terminus ante quem* is not easy to fix. Two papyri, one containing a few verses of the Gospel itself (P. Ryl. 457) and the other an apocryphal Gospel apparently dependent on Jn (P. Eg. 2), are to be dated probably not later than A.D. 150; these prove the circulation of the Gospel in the first half of the 2nd cent., and suggest that it was written not later than A.D. 140. Allusions to Jn in the newly discovered gnostic 'Gospel of Truth' do not take us much farther back. If it could be proved decisively that Ignatius (who died *c.* A.D. 112) quoted Jn the *terminus* could be taken much farther back; but this question is disputed. The traditional connection with John the Apostle makes A.D. 100 a more probable date than, say, A.D. 130; but greater precision is hardly to be obtained. The fact that the Gospel attained publicity so slowly, and was first used (so far as we know) by Gnostics, does not support apostolic authorship.

Tradition places the writing of the Gospel in Ephesus, and there is no decisive reason for rejecting it, though recently the claims of Alexandria have been urged.

b **Sources**—It has already been pointed out that Jn drew on traditions akin to or perhaps identical with those contained in the Synoptic Gospels. It is very doubtful whether it is possible to go farther with the source-criticism of the Gospel, which is marked by such a consistent unity of style that we should certainly not be able to pick out the 'Marcan' episodes if we had not Mk to guide us. Three main possibilities may however be mentioned, though serious examination of them would lead beyond the limits of this commentary.

c (*a*) It is easy to split up the Gospel into narratives and discourses, and it has been suggested that these were derived respectively from a 'Signs-source' and a source which has been called the 'Revelatory Discourses' (*Offenbarungsreden*). The primary objection to this hypothesis (in addition to the general uniformity of style which has already been noted) is that the narratives and discourses fit each other too well for it to be probable that they were originally distinct and were simply brought together and adapted to each other by the evangelist. This is not to say that the stories were not originally independent units of tradition or that Jn did not take over earlier discourse material (possibly even of gnostic origin); it does however seem probable that what he took over he digested so completely that it is no longer possible to distinguish sources in it.

d (*b*) It has been held that certain passages in the Gospel (e.g. 3:27–36) stand out as bearing marks of Aramaic origin. It is not impossible that these were drawn from an Aramaic source, whether this was 736d
translated by the evangelist or by some earlier writer. It is however equally possible that the passages in question were drawn from the main body of traditional material available to the evangelist.

(*c*) It has been held that in the Passion Narrative e
Jn draws upon a special body of material distinct from that used in the Synoptic Gospels. Here the real question is how the Johannine Passion Narrative is to be understood. Is it an independent historical narrative capable of standing on its own feet, or is it a Johannine rewriting of the Marcan Passion Narrative, embellished here and there with additional but subordinate details and rewritten in order to make more clearly the theological points Jn wished to emphasise? This is a disputed question, and an answer can be reached only by means of detailed examination and comparison of the two narratives.

Original Order—It has often been suggested that f
the Gospel as we have it is not in the form in which it left its author's hand. It has been subjected (so it is held) to redactional glosses and to disarrangements of its original order.

There is much to be said for the theory of redactional g
glosses. It is certain that 7:53–8:11 (the story of the adulteress) is an addition to the original text of the Gospel (see §759*d*), and very probable that 5:3*b*, 4 is an explanatory addition, to be rejected on textual grounds. The same may be true of 4:9*b*. Again, there is good reason to doubt whether ch. 21, though contained in all the MSS, formed part of the Gospel as originally planned (see §758*f*). It is however probable that the redactional glosses are few in number and small in extent. The evangelist was capable of making his own explanations, and it is unlikely that many additions have been made.

There is perhaps less to be said for the theory of h
textual dislocations, though it has often been supported on the ground that the passages alleged to have been displaced are all multiples of the same unit length, and might therefore correspond to sheets of the original MS. The suggestions that have found most favour are the following:

(*a*) 3:22–30 should be placed between 2:12 and 2:13, thus restoring the connection between 3:21 and 3:31, and improving the itinerary in ch. 2.

(*b*) Ch. 6 should stand between chs. 4 and 5. This again improves the itinerary.

(*c*) 7:15–24 should stand after 5:47. It continues the argument of ch. 5, and interrupts the connection between 7:14 and 7:25.

(*d*) 10:19–29 should stand after 9:41. This restores the connection between 10:18 and 10:30, and gives 10:21 a closer and more natural relation with the miracle of ch. 9.

(*e*) Chs. 15 and 16 should stand before 14:31, which is evidently the close of the Last Discourses.

The fundamental test by which all such proposed rearrangements must be judged is that of exegesis. If the Gospel makes sense as it stands there is no need to alter its order. In fact it is often found that though the changes proposed improve some connections they worsen others, and it is hard to accept any of them as proved.

Purpose; Historical Value; Interpretation—It 737a
has already been pointed out that the Gospel is related to at least three worlds of thought: to the primitive Christian tradition—at once historical and theological—about Jesus; to Judaism; and to Hellenistic thought. This triple background may be best illustrated by reference to Jn's use in the Prologue of the term 'Word' (see on 1:1–18). This is an ancient Christian term for the Gospel, the message of salvation of which Jesus himself was both the bearer and the subject; it occurs in the OT both for the command by which God created the world and for the prophetic message; and it was a technical term in philosophical use. To suggest however that Jn was concerned simply to make an amalgam of the

737a various kinds of religious thought known to him is to give an inadequate account of his purpose. For him, Judaism and Hellenism could never stand on the same level as the Christian faith. It was the Christian tradition he was concerned to expound in order ' that you may believe that Jesus is the Christ, the Son of God, and that believing you may have life in his name ' (20:31), and it is the Christian tradition that cements together the Jewish and Hellenistic terminology he employs in his exposition. The two strands of thought, which in the work of the Hellenistic Jew Philo lie in somewhat uneasy juxtaposition, are made one in common witness to Christ.

b Jn's theological purpose may be rather more narrowly defined in terms of two problems which beset those who professed the Christian faith at the end of the 1st cent. From within the faith itself arose the problem of eschatology : the expected time had long gone by, and Jesus had not yet manifested himself, as had been expected, ' to the world ' (14:22). From without, Christian thinkers were faced with the increasing pressure of Gnosticism (see §§625*b*, 864*b*). It is perhaps the supreme achievement of Jn that he saw his way through these problems, insisting that the answer to each was in the historic person of Jesus, whose life, death, and resurrection constituted already an eschatological event, perpetuated in the work of the Spirit, and formed thereby the means to the only true and saving knowledge of God (17:3).

c **Historical Value**—That Jn was concerned to emphasise the importance of the historical figure of Jesus does not mean that every detail of his Gospel is to be accepted as historically accurate. The deeds and words ascribed here to Jesus are open to historical investigation as are those contained in the other Gospels, and the many differences between Jn and the Synoptic Gospels raise special problems at this point. It is true that these differences have been exaggerated ; Jn was more of a historian than an imaginative mystic, and the synoptic writers too were concerned with the theological significance of what they described. But it remains true that they (on the whole) take one incident or saying at a time, allowing it to be interpreted in its own light, whereas Jn sets each unit of tradition in the light of his understanding of the total significance of Jesus. It was this total significance that he desired his readers to see, and the narrative details were made to bear witness to it. A probable example of this process (though some would dispute it) is to be found in the fact that Jn, who sees in Jesus the Lamb of God (1:29), alters the synoptic date of the crucifixion in order to represent Jesus as dying on the Cross at the moment when the Passover lambs were sacrificed in the Temple. It is no doubt true that, here and there, with greater or less probability, pieces of good early tradition, earlier and better perhaps than the synoptic tradition, can be detected within the Fourth Gospel, but it was not in order to preserve these that Jn wrote. He wrote in order to bear witness to the Saviour of the world and to the divine love which sent him to his incarnate ministry and death, and bald historicism was as alien to his purpose as unhistorical mysticism.

d **Interpretation**—The Gospel must be interpreted in the light of its author's purpose. To dissect it in the hope of finding pieces of verifiable historical tradition is as mistaken a process as to allegorise all its details as though the whole Gospel were a cryptogram. The Gospel is a work of history in which the author has handled the details with complete freedom, not arbitrarily but with the intention of bringing out the meaning of the whole story. It follows that it is particularly important to study this Gospel *as a whole* ; and also to be prepared to see the whole, or at least some aspect of it, in each unit of material. The Prologue (1:1–18) tells the story of the book as a whole, both historically and theologically : He who is light and life came to his due and proper place, was rejected by those who should have accepted him, but gave new birth and divine life to those who did receive him. **73**
The full story of his final rejection and victory is told in the Passion and Resurrection Narratives (chs. 18–20), and receives more detailed interpretation in the Last Discourses (chs. 13–17, where it is also preceded by a symbolic act—the feet-washing—which foreshadows the Cross itself). Between these points the significance of Jesus and his work is brought out in a series of ' signs ' (see on 2:11) and discourses ; in each, under a particular symbol, the *whole* truth is stated. Thus in ch. 6 Jesus feeds the multitude and declares that he is the bread of life ; but the discourse closes with the assertion that Jesus himself is eternal life for those who receive him. In chs. 8 and 9 Jesus heals a blind man and declares that he is the light of the world ; but the discourse ends with a penetrating summary of the ministry as a whole : ' I came into this world that those who do not see might see, and that those who see might become blind ' (9:39). And Jn affirms that all that Jesus was to men in the days of his earthly ministry, he is forever, through the Spirit (16:7–15).

I 1-18 The Prologue—Whereas Mk begins his account of Jesus with his baptism, and Mt. and Lk. **73**
with his conception and birth, Jn goes back to creation, and indeed beyond it. The historical activity of Jesus is put in an absolute theological setting in order that the reader of the Gospel may be placed at the point of view from which the story may be understood. It seems probable that the Prologue was written for the purpose of introducing the Gospel, though it has often been maintained that in constructing it the evangelist used an earlier document (possibly Semitic, possibly in verse form, possibly not Christian). For example, C. F. Burney regarded 6–10*a*, 12, 13, 15, 16*b*, 18 as prose insertions into an original Prologue written in Aramaic couplets. We may, however, feel confident that we read the Prologue now in the form in which Jn intended it to stand as the key to his Gospel. It falls into four parts.

1-5. Jn sets his story in a cosmological framework. ' In **b**
the beginning ' recalls Mk 1:1 ; also Gen. 1:1 and Prov. 8:22. ' Word ' is a term of wide background. In itself it suggests the issuing of thought in audible and intelligible form, and is therefore an appropriate title for the Revealer. In the OT it is used both of the creative command of God (Gen. 1:3, etc. ; Ps. 33:6), and of the divine message given to the prophets (e.g. Jer. 1:4). It suggests further the figure of Wisdom (cf. Wis. 7:22, 27), which, in Hellenistic Judaism (see §625*a*), came to be in varying degrees assimilated to the use of ' Word ' found in Hellenistic thought. By selecting this term Jn was able to evoke several themes useful for his purpose in describing the pre-existence of Christ ; but that which binds all together is the specifically Christian use of ' Word ' for the gospel message of salvation (e.g. Ac. 13:5). For Jn, the Gospel *was* Christ. Unlike the Baptist (6), the Word did not come into being, but ' was ' ; and was with God, and had the nature of God. He was the agent of creation (as was said of Wisdom, and of the Law, which sometimes was spoken of in personal terms). The division of words between 3 and 4 is in doubt, as RSV*n* shows. The marginal rendering is often preferred because it can claim the support of a number of early interpreters ; but the repetitiveness of the text (' was not anything made that was made ') is Johannine, and it is difficult to find any clear and satisfactory sense in the marginal rendering. ' Life ' and ' Light ' are both very characteristic words in this Gospel, which claims that Jesus is and gives life, and is and gives light. He is at the same time Saviour and Revealer ; and the act of salvation is revelation. The light shines—the present tense suggests that Jn is not referring to the particular event of the Incarnation. **5**. ' Darkness ' is not to be so rigidly defined as to suggest metaphysical dualism. ' Overcome ' represents a word which in Greek is ambiguous ; it means both ' overcome ' and ' understand '.

6-8. The coming of the light into the world is intro- **c**

738c duced by the testimony of the Baptist. He was not eternally pre-existent with God, but was God's envoy; he was not himself the light, but did bear witness to it. This was the purpose of his mission; see 1:29–34.

d **9-13.** Jesus himself was the true light—that to which partial and imperfect lights, such as the Baptist, bear witness. 'True' implies something like the Platonic relation of type and antitype, but also the more Biblical notion of that which God himself has promised and now brings to pass. It is probably correct to take 9 as in RSV text, and to see in it the first reference to the Incarnation: the pre-existent light now shines upon men, so as to expose them to judgment (cf. 3:19; 1 C. 4:5). Alternatively, 'coming' may be taken with 'man': '. . . the true light that enlightens every man who comes into the world'; i.e. every man. If this punctuation is accepted, it is natural to think that Jn refers to a universal reason (*logos*, to the Stoics) which is partially present in all men but was fully revealed in Christ. This, however, is scarcely consistent with Jn's thought in general. The next verses are most simply taken as an historical summary of the effects of the incarnation. The world (perhaps to be distinguished from 'all things' in 3 as the world of *men*) did not recognise him through whom it was made. The Jewish Messiah came to the place where he belonged, and the Jews ('his own home' and 'his own people' represent the same Greek word in the neuter and the masculine respectively) rejected him. The rejection however was not complete: those who received Christ were supernaturally born again as the children of God. In 13 there is some early MS support for the singular verb ('who *was* born'). This would be a direct reference to the miraculous birth of Jesus. It is probable that this variant is incorrect, but that Jn did intend to represent the new birth (cf. 3:3, 5) of Christians as parallel to the supernatural birth of Christ.

e **14-18** restate in more general terms, and with further reference to the Baptist (cf. 1:26f.), the effect of the incarnation. The eternal Word (1) came on the human scene not disguised as a man but actually as flesh—the raw material, as it were, of humanity. As the glory of God dwelt in the Tabernacle (Exod. 40:34), so the Word dwelt among us. Some think that Jn here refers to himself as an eye-witness; more probably 'us' means not the apostles alone but the apostolic Church built on their testimony and sharing their communion with Christ. 'Grace and truth' is an OT phrase; cf. e.g. Exod. 34:6. The revelation is given not in metaphysical but in moral terms. 'As of the only Son from the Father' might possibly, though less probably, be rendered, 'as of an only son from a father'. 16 is sometimes taken as a continuation of the Baptist's testimony; but probably again 'we' means the Church. Jn has in the Prologue used language which recalls that of the Greek philosophers; but the last contrast he uses to bring out the significance of Jesus the incarnate Word is with Moses, who was not suffered to look on God's face (Exod. 33:20). Moses might see God's back; but the Son rests ever in his bosom, and has revealed him to men.

f **19-34 The Testimony of John**—In the Prologue (1:7f., 15) John the Baptist appears as a witness. A historical account of his testimony, akin to that in the synoptics, is now given. John is not the Christ (it may be that, when the Gospel was written, there still were some who thought he was, and that the evangelist was correcting them); he is not Elijah (cf. Mal. 4:5 and contrast Mt. 11:14 etc.); he is not 'the prophet' (cf. 7:40; this is presumably not the 'prophet-messiah' of 6:14, since the Baptist has already denied that he is the Christ). He is no more than a 'voice', but a voice which becomes articulate in the words of the OT (Isa. 40:3). John is almost a personification of the witness of the OT. The question of 25 leads to John's positive witness. His baptism, no less than his words, points away from him and to Christ. Baptism with water suggests baptism with Spirit (33); the Baptist himself suggests the Unknown, with whom John is not worthy to be compared. 738f

Jesus is described as the Lamb of God (29), as he who will baptise with Spirit (33), and as the Son of God (34; a well-attested variant has 'the Elect One of God'). The origin of the term 'Lamb of God' is disputed. There may be reference to (*a*) the Passover lamb (Exod. 12) sacrificed at the annual festival, but not regarded as expiatory; (*b*) the lambs sacrificed daily in the Temple (Exod. 29:38–46); (*c*) the goats used on the Day of Atonement (Lev. 16:21f.), one of which carried away the sins of the people into the wilderness; (*d*) the lamb mentioned in the description of the Servant of the Lord in Isa. 53:7; or (*e*) to the lamb which plays a part in apocalyptic imagery (e.g. Rev. 14:1), and represents the Messiah, who purifies his people. In view of Jn's interest in Jesus as the true Passover (see §750*f*) it is probably best to suppose that the Passover lamb forms the background of the metaphor (cf. 1 C. 5:7), though it may also have been affected by Isa. 53. There is no need however to suppose that 'lamb' mistranslates an Aramaic word that should have been rendered 'servant'. **29.** 'Sin' is probably to be understood in the sense of guilt. The other terms used in describing Jesus portray him as the Messiah (this is true whether 'Son' or 'Elect One' is read), and insist that his person and work are to be understood in terms of the Spirit. g

28 Bethany—Confusion with 10:40, 11:1ff. may have helped to produce the variant *Bethabara*. Bethany is to be accepted; Jn refers to two places of this name.

35-51 The first Disciples—The paragraph opens with the repetition (from 1:29) of John's witness to Jesus as the Lamb of God. This testimony leads two of John's disciples to transfer their allegiance to Jesus. **38f.** Their contact with Jesus is described in some circumstantial detail, which is sometimes taken to point to the presence of an eye-witness: one of the two was Andrew; it is possible (but beyond proof) that the other was John the son of Zebedee. **41.** Simon, Andrew's brother, is next brought to Jesus, who confers on him the name Cephas (Peter; i.e. Rock). The new name may suggest a change in character, or that Peter will be the foundation of the Church (cf. Mt. 16:18), but Jn does not bring out either interpretation. 739a

The events so far described have taken place in Judaea (and presumably precede Mk 1:16–20). **43.** The small party now moves towards Galilee (Bethsaida is at the northern end of the lake). Philip is impressed by Jesus (45) as the one in whom the OT is fulfilled. **46.** Nathanael's objection presupposes a disparagement of Nazareth which is not easy to parallel. He is convinced by Jesus' supernatural knowledge—the fig-tree is probably mentioned only to identify the place where Nathanael was; allegorical significance should not be sought in it. Jesus however has not only seen Nathanael; he knows that he is a true and guileless Israelite. It may be that a contrast with Jacob (cf. Gen. 27:35) is intended. Nathanael's confession of faith is couched in the nationalist terms of Jewish Messianism; 'Son of God' need not here suggest more than 'king of Israel' (cf. Ps. 2:7). **51.** He is immediately taken further by Jesus' reply. He will henceforth see much greater things than a display of supernatural knowledge or second-sight. Jesus is the Son of man (see §641*e*), the representative or heavenly Man, who, as the figure of the ascending and descending angels shows, forms the place of mediation between heaven and earth. This representation of the unique mediatorship of Jesus seems to depend upon (*a*) an interpretation of Gen. 28:12, which may in turn owe something to a piece of Rabbinic exegesis in which 'on it' (sc. the ladder) was given the meaning (possible in Hebrew) of 'on him' (sc. Jacob), and (*b*) the traditional picture of the Son of man coming in glory with the angels (e.g. Mk 8:38). b

739b Not at the last day only, but always (to the eye of faith) Jesus unites God and man. The rest of the Gospel, with its 'signs' (of which the first follows immediately), is intended to confirm this belief.

c **II 1-12 The Sign at Cana**—The narrative itself is simply told. Cana was in Galilee (not, therefore, the Cana of Jos. 19:28), and it was there, not in Judaea, that Jesus' miraculous activity began. Three modern villages all bear names similar to Cana, and it is impossible to be certain which represents the ancient site. **1.** The mother of Jesus is never named in Jn; see 2:12, 6:42, 19:25ff. All the miracles take their origin in some kind of human distress (hunger, disease, death, etc.), nowhere more trivial than here. **3.** The simple remark, 'They have no wine', probably implies a request. The reply, 'O woman', is not harsh (cf. 19:26); but 'What have you to do with me?' emphasises the complete independence of Jesus; as in other miracle stories (e.g. 6:5, 11:6) he acts so as to bring out the fact that neither family, friends, nor circumstances can dictate to him. He acts only when the *hour* comes; this word refers primarily to the moment of death and exaltation (12:23, 27, 17:1), but also to anticipations of this moment in which the glory of Jesus is manifested (11). The six stone jars hold an immense volume; the Jewish rites of purification are not further specified—Jn was probably content to connect them in general terms with the old covenant which was about to be superseded. **7, 8** probably mean that the water put into the jars was turned into wine; but it is not impossible that Jn intends that, the jars having been filled, the water subsequently drawn became wine. **9, 10** give circumstantial details which demonstrate the truth of the miracle. **11.** The event is described as a *sign*. This is Jn's characteristic word for Jesus' miracles. In the synoptics it occurs principally in passages where Jesus is asked for a sign and refuses to comply with the request. The word has an important OT background (e.g. Exod. 4:8; Isa. 8:18; Ezek. 4:3), and also occurs in Greek philosophical and religious thought. In Jn it describes an act of Jesus which is a partial showing forth of the whole meaning of his ministry, death, and resurrection. Jewish legalism (represented by the water of ritual purification) becomes the gospel, the wine which brings gladness to the marriage feast (cf. Mt. 22:1–14, 25:1–13; Mk 2:19f.) of the kingdom of God. The miracles are not in themselves the gospel, but, as it were, miniatures in which it is represented; and by such signs (which Jn undoubtedly regards as historical and not merely allegorical) men may be brought to faith in the full significance of Jesus and his work.

d **13-25 The Cleansing of the Temple**—According to Jn, this is the opening event in Jesus' Jerusalem ministry; the synoptic parallel is in Mk 11:15–18, that is, at the beginning of Holy Week. It does not seem likely that so striking an event should have happened twice, and the Marcan dating should probably be accepted, though it has been urged that Mk, who knows of only one visit to Jerusalem, was bound to fit into it everything that happened in Jerusalem, and that his chronology is therefore mistaken. Jn and Mk agree that the event took place at or near Passover. **14ff.** The expulsion of the animals and traders is described in vivid terms. The trading carried on in the Temple was in principle convenient rather than blameworthy; but the practice was no doubt open to abuse. Jesus' action is explained in terms of the passage recalled by the disciples, Zeal for thy house will consume me (Ps. 69:9; in the Ps. the past tense, 'has consumed', is used); this is used as a simple proof-text. The fact that Jesus' work of purifying was accomplished at the cost of his life may also be in mind. Just as in Mk 11:28 the cleansing of the Temple is followed by the question, 'By what authority are you doing these things?' so here the Jews ask for a sign to give authority to Jesus' act (18; cf. Mk 8:11). The reply is worked out in **19-22**; it is first stated, then misunderstood, and then 73 explained in the light of later Christian reflection. Jesus does not directly predict destruction (19); his words are in effect a conditional sentence, but they are taken by the Jews as a claim that he could construct in three days that upon which armies of men had been labouring for forty-six years. The false accusation of Mk 14:58 comes to mind: 'We heard him say, "I will destroy this temple that is made with hands, and in three days I will build another, not made with hands."' It is possible that this charge was a perversion of some such words as those of 19. Jn explains that Jesus 'spoke of the temple of his body', thereby making a reference to the resurrection 'on the third day'. Behind the confident assertion of rebuilding probably lies the conviction, found in several apocalyptic sources, that, after the time of troubles, a new, or restored, temple would be granted to the people of God. But here what is promised is not merely a renewal of, or an improvement upon, Herod's Temple, or even Solomon's. The body of Jesus himself is the place where God and man are united; the reference is primarily to the incarnate Person as the centre of dealings between God and man, but so far as the Church is the Body of Christ it is also the new Temple.

20. Herod's Temple was begun in 20/19 B.C., but not completed until *c.* A.D. 63. The Jews' misunderstanding of Jesus' words is characteristic of this Gospel; cf. 3:4.

23-25. The request for signs (18) was not left un- e gratified, though Jn gives no particulars. But a faith based merely upon miracles is an inadequate (though real) faith (4:48, 14:11). Jesus could not confide himself to men who were merely impressed by miracles (cf. 6:15). He did not need to be told but knew the stuff of human nature (cf. 1:47).

III 1-21 Jesus and Nicodemus—Of Nicodemus we 74 know only what Jn tells us (7:50, 19:39). Evidently he is a representative and leading Jew (1, 10); and his conversation with Jesus readily passes into a conversation between Judaism and the Church (note the plurals in 7, 11). It may be significant that he comes to Jesus 'by night' (cf. 9:4, 11:10, 13:30). Like the men mentioned in 2:23 he has been impressed by the works of Jesus, and is prepared to accept the view that he comes from God; but evidently he is not one to whom Jesus can 'trust himself'. As a good Jew, Nicodemus is awaiting the kingdom of God (it is in this conversation only that the phrase 'kingdom of God' is used in Jn); Jesus asserts that before a man can see the kingdom he must be born 'anew'. This word could equally well be translated 'from above', and the ambiguity is intentional. **4.** Nicodemus understands the word to mean 'a second time', and takes it in the crudest and most literal sense. But though Jesus had indeed spoken of a second birth (or *begetting*), this was not to be, like the first, from a human source or origin, but from *above*, that is, from God himself (cf. 1:12f., an important comment on this passage). Mere waiting for the kingdom does not suffice; already, through Jesus, the Spirit is available as a re-creating agency, and men must accept by faith that which is offered to them now. The new order of existence stands beside the old, and the visible world of matter and the wind form an appropriate analogy of them. Note RSV*n*: 'wind' and 'Spirit' both translate the Greek word *pneuma*. In **5**, the contrasting pair is 'water and Spirit'. There is no ground for omitting 'water and' as a redactional note intended arbitrarily to bring in a reference to the sacrament of baptism; the allusion may be to Christian baptism, or to John's baptism, or perhaps to ordinary human birth. *Spirit*, at all events, refers to that which is not under man's control, whether in natural processes or religious rites; begetting from the Spirit implies a new existence whose origin is in God—theocentric, not anthropocentric, existence.

9. By all this Nicodemus is frankly puzzled; yet he b

40b of all men, as a professional exponent of the OT, should have understood that human existence is meaningless apart from God. **11f.** It is not easy to give a precise meaning to 'earthly things' and 'heavenly things'. The contrast is probably to be interpreted in terms of the earlier reference to the kingdom of God, which can be spoken of not directly but in terms of 'earthly things', such as birth, and the audible but invisible motion of the wind (cf. Mk 4:11f.). Among men, only one, the Son of man, has direct experience of the heavenly world (cf. 1:18). He it is who descends thence, and returns. But in what way? The question is answered in **14**; 'as Moses lifted up the serpent in the wilderness' (Num. 21:9). For 'lifted up' cf. 8:28, 12:32. Like 'anew', this is a word of double meaning, and points both to exaltation in glory, and to lifting up on the Cross. For Jn, these are two aspects of the same thing; the crucifixion of Jesus *is* his glory. The Son of man is lifted up *in this way* in order that (as those who had been bitten by serpents were cured when they looked at the brazen serpent) those who believe in him may be saved. How this is effected is explained more fully in 16–21.

c In the first place, the Incarnation and Crucifixion, that is, the descent of the Son of man, are a demonstration in action of the love of God, which is their cause and motive. **16.** It was God's intention that the world (cf. 1:10; the 'world' is mankind apart from, yet loved by, God) should be saved, and for that reason he sent his Son to act as revealer (1:18), and, by the knowledge of himself thus revealed, to give eternal life (17:3). **17.** Jesus did not come to judge (8:15), and the man who 'believes in him', accepts him as what he is, is not judged (condemned). **18.** Yet it is also true that he did come to judge (9:39), for the unbeliever, who has rejected the Son of God, has thereby condemned himself by refusing the salvation offered him.

d The theme of judgment and salvation is next worked out in the symbolism of light and darkness. For Jn (unlike some of his contemporaries) these are not components of an absolute dualism, but serve to express the decision for or against God which the mission of Jesus requires from men (cf. 8:12). His presence divides men into two groups; if in these verses the two groups are described in somewhat moralistic terms, this is determined by the use of the metaphor of light and darkness. **21.** That which makes deeds good, or rather 'true', is their being wrought '*in God*'.

e **22-36 Further Testimony of the Baptist**—In this paragraph Jn represents Jesus and the Baptist as pursuing their work at the same time; John had not yet been put in prison (24; cf. Mk 1:14). Where Jesus baptised (cf. 4:2) is not stated; Salim is probably (so Albright) the town SE. of Nâblus and Shechem; nearby is the modern 'Ainûn. **25.** The discussion with a Jew 'over purifying' serves only to introduce John's testimony.

That Jesus should have greater success than John is as it should be; it comes to him from God (heaven; 27). John was not the Christ, but his forerunner (1:20, 23, 26f.). Now that the Greater One has come, John must recede into insignificance. **29** may be merely a metaphorical way of saying this: in a wedding, the best man has a part to play, but cannot compare in importance with the bridegroom. There may, however, be an allusion to the OT figure of Israel as the bride of God (Isa. 62:4f.; Jer. 2:2, 3:20; Hos. 2:20, etc.); it is John's mission to present the bride to the Bridegroom (cf. Lk. 1:17).

f **31-36** may have been misplaced; some would put it between 2:12 and 2:13, others between 3:21 and 3:22. But **31** seems to develop naturally out of 30. The difference between John and Jesus is that the former is a man—commissioned, indeed, by God, but no more than a man; whereas the latter is the Son of God (1:6; 1:1, 18). **32** reflects 11; it no more contradicts **26** than 2:23. The many superficial
believers are not men to whom Jesus can 'trust 740f
himself'. To the 'no one' of 32 there are exceptions; and these, who accept Jesus' testimony, are not merely accepting the word of a man but asserting the truth, or faithfulness, of God himself, since Jesus does not speak his own words, but God's (34), and that in virtue of the Spirit, who remains upon him (1:32). The fullness of the Spirit ('not by measure') qualifies Jesus for his work. **35.** Father and Son are one through the Father's love, and the Son shares the Father's authority (cf. 5:19–23). **36.** It follows that the decision between belief and unbelief ('does not obey') *in the Son* is of ultimate significance, and leads either to eternal life or to the wrath of God. The evangelist does not tire of bringing out this decision as the main point in the earthly ministry of Jesus, and thereby pressing it upon his readers also.

For an important attempt to demonstrate that some verses in this paragraph go back to an Aramaic original, see M. Black, *An Aramaic Approach to the Gospels and Acts* (2nd ed. 1954), 108–11.

IV 1-42 Jesus in Samaria—Returning from Judaea g
to Samaria, Jesus 'had to' take (4) the usual route, which (as Josephus tells us) was that to the west of the Jordan. Jn has shown that Jesus is the fulfilment of the hopes of cultic (2:19) and of apocalyptic (3:3, 5) Judaism. He now shows that Jesus stands in the same relation to the hopes of the heretical Judaism of the Samaritans.

1-9 sets the scene upon which the conversation between h
Jesus and the Samaritan woman takes place. **1f.** The baptising activity described here is without parallel in the other Gospels; it has been pointed out that it makes more intelligible the practice of Christian baptism after the resurrection. **5.** Sychar is probably the modern 'Askar, which lies near to a site identified by ancient tradition with Jacob's well. **7.** The incident is opened by the request of Jesus for water. Here as elsewhere Jn emphasises that in his dealings with men the initiative always lies with Jesus; Jn also displays characteristic irony in representing the giver of living water as himself thirsty and in need of drink. **9.** The woman is surprised by the request, partly because conversation with a woman was regarded as undesirable in a Rabbi (cf. 27), and also on account of the tension between Jews and Samaritans. This is further described in 9*b* (omitted by some MSS but probably to be retained), which should be rendered, 'Jews do not use (vessels) with Samaritans'—because the ceremonial purity of Samaritans could not be relied on. The situation calls for clarification; this is supplied in the ensuing conversation.

10-15 develops the theme of water (see also 3:5, 7:37f., i
19:34). If the woman had been able to perceive the truth, she would have made the request for water. **10.** 'Living water' is ambiguous (cf. 'anew', 3:3). Jesus means 'water that gives eternal life'; the woman thinks that he means 'running water'. Even on this interpretation of his words, however, he would be representing himself as greater than Jacob—surely an absurd conclusion! Jn emphasises the irony of the situation. **13f.** In reply Jesus states the issue plainly. The water he speaks of is not that which (for the moment) satisfies physical thirst, but represents an unfailing spiritual supply which issues in eternal life. **15.** The woman still fails to understand.

16-26. Again Jesus takes the initiative. His words in 741a
18 may be a purely factual statement about the woman's past and illicit present (he has supernatural knowledge of such matters—1:47f.); or may be an allegorical comment on the imperfect religion of the Samaritans, based on their past adherence to various false gods (cf. 2 Kg. 17:30f.), and present improper worship of the God of Israel. **19f.** In any case the woman is impressed by his insight, and raises the standing question between Jews and Samaritans. **21f.** The first part of the reply does not mean that the question is irrelevant; it is the Jews, not the Samaritans, who stand within the main stream of biblical

741a revelation, and it is among them that salvation will (not for their exclusive benefit) emerge. **23.** Yet this future tense is an inadequate expression of the truth: 'will emerge', but better, 'is emerging' (cf. 5:25, 16:32). The place where God and man are united is neither Zion nor Gerizim, but the person of Jesus (cf. 2:21). **24.** 'God is spirit' recalls the anti-anthropomorphic propaganda of both Jews and philosophers, but can be understood here only in terms of the use of 'Spirit' in the Gospel as a whole. Cf. 6:63—God is the source of life, and himself inspires the true worship which he seeks (cf. 10, 14). 'Truth' (23, 24) points not simply to an alternative preferable to Gerizim and Jerusalem but to God's faithfulness in fulfilling in Christ that to which Jerusalem and Gerizim pointed. After this, there is only one thing more to say. The woman guesses it, and Jesus avows it: he is the Messiah, in whom the purposes of God are brought to fulfilment.

b **27-30.** The disciples return (for their surprise cf. 9), and the woman departs, with the same half-faith as that of 2:23. Cf. 39; meanwhile Jesus speaks with his disciples.

c **31-38.** Jesus has no need of the food which his disciples have brought. **32.** His food (which corresponds to the unfailing water-supply of 14) is obedience to God's will. This is the means of access to eternal life. The rest of his reply raises many questions. The sayings about sowing and reaping recall several synoptic sayings and parables; e.g. Mk 4:1–9, 26–9, but especially Mt. 9:37f. (= Lk. 10:2). The synoptic material brings out the double fact that the kingdom of God is both present and future; the same double fact lies behind the Johannine sayings also, but the emphasis is different. **35.** The common experience of men ('Do you not say?') is that between seed-time and harvest four months intervene (this corresponds closely enough with Palestinian agricultural practice); but Jesus declares that the fields are already waiting for the reaper. The interval between sowing and harvest disappears. **36.** The reaper is not merely doing his work, he is drawing his pay for work done. The fruit which he is gathering for the purpose of eternal life is represented in the first instance by the Samaritan converts (41f.), who prefigure the whole body of believers gathered (10:16, 11:52, 17:20, 20:29) into the Church. Thus the reaper has overtaken the sower; the time of fulfilment has come. **37.** The saying is a popular Greek proverb, which ordinarily expresses the sad reflection that men see the fruit of their labours falling to other hands. This human bitterness no longer obtains in the new circumstances (35f.); yet there is a limited sense ('here') in which the saying is true. This is stated in 38, where those who are addressed are told that as reapers they will enter into the work of others. This may be interpreted in three ways, and it would probably be wrong to exclude any of them. (*a*) The disciples are to take part in the work of 'harvesting' the believing Samaritans. (*b*) The apostles in their missionary work will enter into the labours of the prophets, of John the Baptist, and of Jesus himself. (*c*) When the Gospel was written the Church at large had entered into the labours of the apostles. Christian men work for God, but they have nothing which they have not received.

d **39-42.** The story is brought to a close with an account of the Samaritan response to the woman's testimony. Jesus stays with the Samaritans, but for two days only; it is not the incarnate Son but the Spirit who abides with men for ever (14:16). Jesus finally is described as 'the Saviour of the world' (cf. 3:16)—not of Jews only. The word 'Saviour' recalls many parallels in Hellenistic and oriental religions; but the God of the OT is a 'righteous God and a Saviour' (Isa. 45:21), and the OT sense of the word is determinative here.

e **43-54 The Officer's Son**—Cf. Mt. 8:5–13=Lk. 7:1–10 (the healing of the centurion's servant). **44** also recalls the synoptic saying about Jesus' 'own country', 74
but here (contrast Mk 6:1, 4 and parallels) the word refers not to Nazareth (or Galilee) but to Judaea; this was his 'own home' where his 'own people' did not receive him (1:11). The Galileans on the other hand believed in him. In this paragraph, however, Jesus moves out not merely into Galilee but into the heathen world, where he meets with the most favourable reception of all, for without signs and wonders (48) the officer (who may be thought of as a non-Jewish officer in the service of Herod Antipas) believes at the bare word of Jesus (50), prefiguring thereby the conversion of the Gentile world at large. The details of the story (49–53) are intended to show the exact correspondence of events with the authoritative statement of Jesus. **54.** Like the miracle at the wedding-feast at Cana (2:11), to which reference is made in 46, this is described as a sign. The cure of a dying boy, the proclamation of this cure, and the acceptance of the proclamation in faith, form a clear and effective picture of the work of Jesus as a whole.

V 1-18 Miracle by the Pool—Again (cf. 2:13) Jesus f
went up to Jerusalem to attend a feast (RVm, *the* feast, referring perhaps to Tabernacles; but the indefinite article is correct). The text of 2–4 is in some confusion. 3*b*–4 should be omitted (though there is somewhat better evidence for 3*b* than for 4); the reference to the angel is probably an attempt to account for 7. In 2 the reading that should probably be adopted is, 'There is in Jerusalem, by the Sheep Pool, that which in Hebrew (Aramaic) is called . . .' Reference to the 'Sheep Gate' (cf. Neh. 3:1, 12:39) is not required. The name of the structure having 'five porticoes' (which may probably be identified with the buildings of which ruins remain at the double pool of St Anna) is variously given in the MSS: Be(th)zatha is perhaps to be preferred, but Bethesda and Bethsaida are alternative possibilities. The scene is described and the healing simply narrated in **3-9**; some features of the story (e.g. the word for 'pallet', and the command, in 8) recall the story of the paralytic in Mk 2:1–12. **6f.** Whereas however in Mk Jesus is confronted not only with a man let down through a roof but also with the great faith of his four companions, in Jn Jesus as usual takes the initiative, approaching the sick man and eliciting a desire for healing.

9b. The second part of the narrative, which in turn g
leads to the discourse of 19–47, is introduced by the observation that the cure has taken place on the Sabbath. The complaint of **10** is justified within Jewish law, but the man, who does nothing but excuse himself (contrast the blind man of ch. 9), makes the obvious reply. Again in **14**, Jesus, who presumably could have avoided trouble had he wished to do so, takes the initiative. His words do not imply that the illness had been due to sin; in the manner of Lk. 13:1–5 they point beyond human calamity to final judgment. **16.** The Jews are now in a position to persecute Jesus for Sabbath-breaking. **17.** His answer recalls a Jewish controversy: In what sense could God himself, who ceaselessly sustains the universe, be said to keep the Sabbath? Various expedients were found to show that Gen. 2:2f. did not mean that God had ceased altogether from his activities. These arguments are presupposed: God is always at work—and so is Jesus. That is, when (for example) he cures a sick man, he is not to be ranked with a human doctor treating disease (which after thirty-eight years could well have waited till the next day), but with God, who is ever active in maintaining and restoring his creation. **18.** The Jews are not slow to see the point of this reply. They are right in noting that Jesus regards God as his 'own' Father, and claims to be equal with God; wrong in thinking that he is a man aspiring to equality with God; he is the Word of God (who is God, 1:1, 14) made flesh. The way is now prepared for a discourse of central Christological significance.

19-47 Jesus and the Father—The Prologue opens 742

742a with the assertion that 'the Word was God' (1:1). To this point Jn has now returned in his narrative (5:18, 'equal with God'). In view of what he has said, and in view of what he is going to say (especially the great 'I am' sayings, and the material in chs. 14–17), it becomes urgently necessary for him to clarify the relation between Jesus of Nazareth and God. The twin themes, of the divine status of the Son, and of his obedient dependence on the Father, are worked out in the ensuing discourse and debate. Theologically, the material in this chapter comes at the right point. This fact must be set against the narrative considerations which lead some to reverse the order of chs. 5 and 6 (see on 6:1).

b **19-30.** The main theme of this paragraph is stated in 19f. On the one hand, the Son has no activity independent of the Father. He is not a divine rebel (like Prometheus), but an obedient agent. His acts, including his actions on earth, reflect the acts of God which to mankind at large are invisible (1:18), but to him are visible. This involves on the other hand no limitation in the Godhead of the Son, for between Father and Son exists the mutual moral relation of love, and the Father shows the Son *all* that he does; it follows that the Son will perform more marvellous works than the cure of a sick man. Of the 'greater works' two examples follow.

c **23.** In order that the Son may be honoured equally with the Father, he is endowed with the two divine prerogatives of giving life (raising the dead) and judging (21f.). These are developed side by side in 24–9. For the pair of statements (which provides a key to what is said here), 'the hour is coming' (28) and 'the hour is coming, and now is' (25), cf. 4:23. The two themes (resurrection and judgment) may be understood in a straightforward apocalyptic fashion. A time will come when the dead will be raised and come out of their graves for judgment. For some this resurrection will result in life, for others in judgment (i.e. condemnation) (28f.). This is the hope of Judaism. But the same truth can be observed in the present as well as the future: 'the hour is coming, *and now is*'. **27.** It is the voice of the Son of God (who is also Son of man—truly man) that will quicken the dead at the last day; but already the voice of the Son of God is audible in his incarnate ministry, and already there are, not men physically dead in their tombs (but cf. Lazarus, 11:39, 43f.), but men who are spiritually dead to hear him and be quickened. Those who hear and believe have already eternal life, and for them the experience of death and judgment is already over (24f.). Jn's meaning is close to the Pauline doctrine of justification by faith. For those who hear and believe there is no condemnation (cf. Rom. 8:1), and the life proper to the Age to Come has already begun.

30. Reiteration of the main theme effects a transition to the next paragraph: the judgment of Jesus is righteous because he seeks the Father's will, not his own.

d **31-40.** The contradiction between 31 and 8:14 is superficial and apparent only. Jesus means that he does not act, or bear witness, independently of the Father, who is the 'other' of **32.** (In 32 'you know' is well attested instead of 'I know'; but the reading of the text is more suitable to the argument.) The witness to Jesus borne by the Father is expressed in various forms. (*a*) **33-5.** John the Baptist bore witness (cf. 1:7f., 15, 19, 32, 34)—witness of which Jesus himself had no need, though he was prepared to use it for the good of others (34). John was not the Light (1:8), but a derived ('kindled' is better than 'burning' in 35) light; and the Jews in their folly preferred the secondary to the primary, the witness to that to which he witnessed (cf. 39f.). (*b*) **36.** Greater than the witness of John is that of the works of Jesus (cf. 2:11); and their testimony is not that Jesus is an independent authority, but that 'the Father has sent' him. (*c*) **37f.** There is also a direct witness of the Father. The language here is complicated and
obscure; the key is in 1 Jn 5:9f. The testimony is 742d
not one that can be assessed by an impartial observer; it is apprehended only in the act and attitude of believing in Jesus. The unbelieving Jews accordingly fail to hear the Father's voice, and their failure corresponds to their unbelief. Because they do not believe they do not hear; because they do not hear they do not believe. (*d*) **39f.** The OT, of which John the Baptist is the final representative, also bears witness, and here the tragic error of the Jews is most clearly seen. They diligently examine the scriptures, believing that the process itself confers eternal life (Jewish literature is full of evidence both for the process and for the belief); yet they fail to see that the scriptures themselves point to Christ as the life-giver. Cf. (*a*) above.

41-47. From the exposure of Israel as foolishly mis- e
using the testimony God has richly supplied, Jesus moves to the attack. He and they represent two fundamentally opposite points of view. They do not love God or seek his good opinion; their aims are essentially human, their world man-centred. **43.** It follows that they will accept one who comes to them in his own name (there is no need to see here a reference to Bar Cochba, the messianic claimant of A.D. 132, and to date the Gospel accordingly); such a man they will be able to understand on their own terms. But the aims and motives of Jesus are God-centred; him therefore they reject. **45.** There is no need for Jesus to bring an accusation against them; Moses will do that (cf. 39f.). Moses, like other biblical writers, bore witness to the Christ; those who reject his testimony will not accept Christ.

Some think that 7:15–24 should follow at this point; see on that paragraph.

VI 1-15 Feeding of the Five Thousand—Cf. Mk f
6:35–44; also 8:1–9 (the four thousand). The incident has strong historical attestation, and there is no doubt that all the evangelists understood it as miraculous. No non-miraculous 'explanation' of it carries much conviction. Whether such a miraculous multiplication as the evangelists describe *could* take place is a question too wide to be handled here. The narrative as such calls for little explanation.

Jesus crosses the Sea of Galilee (also called 'of Tiberias' after a—mainly Gentile—town founded by Herod Antipas in honour of Tiberius; 1). This follows oddly upon ch. 5, located in Jerusalem, and for this reason some would take ch. 6 immediately after ch. 4 and before ch. 5. This rearrangement does to some extent smooth the itinerary; but we have seen reason to think that *theologically* ch. 5 is in the right place. **4.** The feast of Passover is mentioned not simply as a chronological note (according to Jn this is the second Passover of the ministry; cf. 2:13, 11:55), but also with a view to the interpretation (22–59), which recalls the Last Supper. **5.** As usual in Jn, Jesus takes the initiative. (The AV gives the Synoptic version of the distribution.) **9.** The 'lad' is not mentioned in the other Gospels; some see here the mark of an eye-witness, others an expansion of Mk 6:38 ('Go and see'). Cf. also 2 Kg. 4:42ff. The words of **11** recall the acts of the Last Supper ('took', 'gave thanks', 'distributed'); yet they were also natural acts at a Jewish meal. **12, 13.** The gathering up of the left-over fragments, again, may reflect only a characteristically Jewish respect for food; but the word used, and also the word for 'be lost', are Johannine words used for the gathering and perishing of *men* (see e.g. 11:52, 17:12), and it is possible that Jn means to represent this gathering symbolically.

The onlookers draw from the miracle the conclusion g
that Jesus is the Messiah. This belief is plainly visible in the attempt to make him a king (15), and is probably expressed also in the words, 'This is indeed the prophet' (14), 'prophet' being understood as a designation of the Messiah (cf. Dt. 18:15; and contrast 1:21, where 'the prophet' is not the Messiah). But Jesus' kingdom is not 'of this world' (18:36),

742g and he cannot submit to be made a king by men. He withdraws to the hills (15); yet the thought of Messiahship lies in the background of the great discourse of 22–59.

743a **16-21 On the Lake**—As in Mk (6:45–52), the feeding-miracle is followed by a crossing of the lake (from east to west—Capernaum, 17—in Jn), in the course of which Jesus, not originally in the boat, joins his disciples by walking on the water. According to Jn (19), the disciples had rowed 25–30 stadia (3–4 miles); according to Mk 6:47 they were in the 'middle of the sea'. The lake is about 7 miles broad at its widest point, so that the two statements correspond. It is accordingly impossible to believe that 'on the sea' (19) really means 'by the sea', though this is a possible translation of Jn's words: undoubtedly he means to record a miraculous event.

b The last two verses of this paragraph give rise to several questions. (*a*) The words of 20 agree with those of Mk 6:50. A literal translation would run 'I am: be not afraid', but comparison with 9:9 shows that the phrase means only 'It is I'; it is unnecessary to compare the other great 'I am' passages in this Gospel (see on 6:35, 8:24). (*b*) The statement in the RV that 'they were willing to receive him into the boat' (21) is at first surprising. Mistranslation of an original Aramaic ('they were glad') was adopted in RSV, but seems unnecessary, since the connection of thought is, 'they wished to take him into the boat but found they had already reached land'. (*c*) That the boat, 3½ miles out, should immediately reach land is a second miracle. 'He bringeth them unto the haven where they would be' (Ps. 107:30). It is unlikely that Jn means more than that the presence of Christ puts an immediate end to danger and conflict, though some have seen here the suggestion that through him the hoped-for future is already realised. Jn however makes no attempt to interpret this paragraph and it is probably to be regarded as a traditional pendant to the feeding-miracle.

c **22-59 Bread from Heaven**—In conversation and discourse, Jesus brings out the full meaning of what was pictorially represented in 1–15: his power to give men the bread of life. There is no parallel to this discourse in the Synoptic Gospels, but it is important to have in mind the synoptic accounts of the acts and words of Jesus with reference to the bread and wine at the Last Supper (to which there are no parallels in Jn). That the present chapter contains allusions to the eucharist seems beyond question (see especially 51–8); yet Jn is not simply introducing eucharistic theology but emphasising by all possible means that Jesus in his death for men gives them true life. The paragraph falls into four parts.

d **22-27.** These verses prepare for the discourse, both topographically and thematically. They are somewhat obscure in both respects. **22** must refer to an observation made the previous evening ('they *had* seen'); there was only one boat; Jesus had not entered it with his disciples; yet both Jesus and the disciples were missing. **23.** The other 'boats' may have been blown out of port in the storm (18). The crowd took advantage of them and came to Capernaum (24; cf. 59). **26f.** introduce the thought of the ensuing discourse. 26 cannot mean that the crowds were unaware that a miracle had been performed; awareness is shown by 14f.; but they were unaware of the *significance* of what they had seen. They see nothing more than the prospect of getting cheap meals without working (cf. 4:15). To this desire, **27** is a reply, which contains the whole discourse in germ. Men must work for their food, and for food which is not of temporal use only but produces eternal life. This food is given by the Son of man (see further §§641*c–g*), who comes into the world with the seal of God's approval. From this point the discourse advances by means of objections, questions, and misunderstandings on the part of the hearers.

e **28-40.** The crowds have heard the word 'work', and since their own religion consists in doing 'works' 74 which it is hoped will be pleasing to God they understand what Jesus has said in their own way. **28.** Read not 'the work' but 'the works'. **29.** But he speaks not of 'works' but of 'a work'; and this work is—to believe, not in Jesus for his own sake, but in Jesus as God's messenger. Before men will so believe, however, they must be convinced, and therefore ask for a sign. With the recent meal in mind it is natural to recall the OT miracle (Exod. 16:4, 13ff.; cf. Ps. 78:24); can Jesus show any parallel to that?

The answer (32) loses in clearness because two points are pressed into one sentence. These are: (*a*) It was not Moses who gave you the bread from heaven (but God); (*b*) It was not bread from heaven that Moses gave you (but merely bread 'that perishes'). It is the Father who gives the true (cf. 1:9, 15:1) bread from heaven—that of which all earthly bread, and even the manna, is but a parable. In **33** we could translate 'that which comes down' or 'he that comes down'. The Jews take the former interpretation (34); **35** Jesus corrects them in the first of the great 'I am' sayings (cf. 41, 48, 8:12, 10:7, 9, 11, 14, 11:25, 14:6, 15:1, 5): **I am the bread of life.** Like many other characteristic elements in the Johannine vocabulary, 'I am' has a complicated background. (*a*) It recalls passages in ancient literature where the goddess Isis declares her virtues and attributes. (*b*) It is an OT phrase, representing the majesty and person of the one true God (e.g. Exod. 3:14, 20:2; Isa. 51:12), and also connected with Wisdom. (*c*) It recalls the synoptic pronouncements of Jesus (e.g. 'I came', 'I say', and 'The kingdom of God is . . .'). In fact, all these Johannine sayings (see the notes) reflect synoptic material, applied to the person of Jesus himself by means of what must, to Jews and Greeks alike, have been a solemn and impressive phrase. Here the synoptic material recalled is Mk 14:22, the context of which shines through from time to time. The two parallel phrases in 35 say the same thing, but the reference to thirst recalls 4:14, and points forward to 53–6, and the allusion to the eucharistic cup. But in 35 Jn is not referring to the eucharist: the 'coming' is evidently a once-for-all coming in faith. For **36** cf. 26. In **37-40** the theme of coming to Jesus is developed. This is not an act which lies simply within the will of men who may or may not choose to 'work the works of God'. Before men can come, God must will their coming. Jesus has come down from heaven to do the Father's will; all whom the Father gives will come to him. Of the rest we hear nothing at this point. Those who come will receive eternal life, and be raised up at the last day. The last clause in 40 is somewhat awkwardly attached to the sentence, but there is no reason for regarding it as an insertion into Jn's text; *both* the realisation of eschatology in eternal life here and now, *and* the reaffirmation of futurist eschatology are intended, and no account of Johannine theology which fails to do justice to both can be regarded as satisfactory.

41-51. The discourse advances by means of an objection. f
The speaker is well known as Jesus the son of Joseph; it is absurd for him to claim that he has come down from heaven. This complaint however only serves to enforce the point made at the close of the preceding paragraph. The claim that the son of Joseph (Jn is probably aware of the Virgin Birth; see on 1:13) should be the heavenly Man is necessarily so offensive that none would believe it were he not appointed to do so by God. Those who are drawn and taught by God (Isa. 54:13) come to Jesus; otherwise this is impossible (cf. Mk 10:27). This however does not mean that men have an immediate knowledge of God in virtue of which they pass judgment upon the claims of Jesus. He alone has such knowledge (cf. 1:18). Men show by their response to him whether God has knowledge of them, and wills to give them to his Son. **47-51** make points which have already

743f been noted, and add two more. (*a*) Jesus is now the living bread which *came* down from heaven ; the allusion to the incarnation already implicit in 33 here becomes explicit. (*b*) In 51*b* Jesus says that the bread which he will supply is ' my flesh (which is given) for the life of the world ' (this, rather than that of RSV, is probably the original word-order). There is here a pointer to the fact that the self-giving of Jesus will be complete only in his death, which accordingly is necessary if men are to have life, and probably also to the eucharist. See below.

g **52-59.** Once more the Jews debate the words of Jesus : can he be proposing cannibalism ? For the misunderstanding cf. 2:20. The explanation which follows (53–8) uses eucharistic language and imagery, as the introduction of blood (53–6) shows. It is however significant that Jesus speaks not of ' body and blood ' (cf. Mk 14:22, 24) but of ' flesh and blood '. This common biblical phrase points to the complete humanity of the Son of man, which is indeed (55) that which supplies life to mankind. The discourse as a whole is summarised in 57. The Father sent the Son (as Son of man), and the Son lives not on his own account but by doing the Father's will (cf. 4:34). Through his complete sacrifice of himself arises the possibility that men may feed upon him, that is, may enter into a relation with the Son analogous to the Son's relation with the Father ; thus they will in turn have life (cf. 5:21). This is heavenly bread indeed ; those who ate the manna (though this was miraculous bread) died ; so will those who ate the five loaves (11f.). But to be united with Christ is to ' live for ever ' (note this interpretation of ' eternal life '—duration as well as quality is in mind).

744a **60-71.** This paragraph forms the close, in the Johannine story, of the Galilean ministry of Jesus. Like the ministry in Jerusalem (12:36f.) it ends in almost complete failure, relieved only by a confession of faith made by Peter on behalf of the Twelve (68f.) ; with this cf. the confession made near Caesarea Philippi (Mk 8:29 and parallels). Yet the terms ' failure ' and ' success ' are quite misleading in an account of the work of Jesus, for all that happens does so in accordance with the will of God.

The sentence in **62** is incomplete, and its interpretation remains in some doubt. It may mean ' If you see . . . then the offence will be greater than it is now ' : or ' If you see . . . then all will be well '. It is probable that Jn writes with studied ambiguity. The Son of man will ascend where he was before by way of the Cross ; it is where the offence is greatest that the resolution of the difficulty is to be found—by those who believe, or, to put the same thing more accurately, by those to whom the Father has granted the power to come to Christ (65). Faith and unbelief lie ultimately in the hands not of men but of God.

b The discourse on the bread of life is put in proper perspective by the reference to the Ascension, and to the Holy Spirit (63). Flesh as flesh belongs to the realm of the ' food which perishes '. ' The Spirit is that which gives life ' summarises the biblical doctrine of the Spirit. Jesus is he upon whom the Spirit abides (1:32), he who baptises with the Spirit (1:33) ; his words convey the Spirit and thereby life (cf. Dt. 8:3). It is in fact Jesus who gives life (cf. 1 C. 15:45) ; his flesh and his words are manifestations of himself.

Many defections (66) lead to a direct challenge to the Twelve (67). **69.** ' The Holy One of God ' (cf. Mk 1:24) is to be understood as a more general way of saying ' The Christ '. Jesus is sanctified as the emissary of God (10:36, 17:19). But even the orthodox phrases of the Twelve are no guarantee of faith. Jesus himself has chosen them (15:16), yet Judas the son of Simon Iscariot (there is much textual variation here ; Iscariot probably means ' Man of Kerioth ') is a devil (cf. 13:2). Jesus was not deceived in Judas (64, 71) ; it was as master of circumstances that he went to his death.

c **VII 1-13 Departure for Jerusalem**—This paragraph with its secret journey to Jerusalem (10) recalls 744c
Mk 9:30, and the Marcan theme of the ' messianic secret ' (see §641*c*). On the Feast of Tabernacles, which provides occasion for the decisive break with Galilee, see §§117*a–c*, and on 37f., 8:12. It is sometimes suggested that 7:1 would better follow ch. 5 than ch. 6 ; but we have seen that to reverse chs. 5 and 6 is to upset the theological development of the Gospel, and there is difficulty in 7:1 only if ' after this ' is taken to mean ' *immediately* after ' ; in fact, the note of time is quite vague. For the unbelieving brothers cf. Mk 3:21, 31–5, 6:3. **3f.** Their unbelief appears in their suggestion, which is based on purely worldly considerations. They believe that Jesus can work mircles, but this is at best an inadequate faith (2:23f.). He does not seek popularity ; his mission is bound to lead to hatred, because he tells men the truth about themselves. Moreover, he does not make plans for his own advancement, but obediently fulfils his Father's will. Hence he can move only on the divine monition. His independence of human constraint is again vindicated (9). His delayed arrival at the feast gives rise to discussion. That Jesus was a deceiver who ' led astray ' the people was a Jewish accusation (Sanhedrin 43*a* ; and Trypho in Justin's *Dialogue*).

8. The direct negative (I am not going up) was found d
difficult and altered by many copyists into ' I am not yet going up ' But the contradiction with 10 is superficial only ; Jesus means ' I am not going now, merely because you tell me to do so '.

14-52 Jesus at the Feast of Tabernacles—Not at e
the beginning of the feast, but in the middle of it, not therefore because his brothers urged him to do so, but when the ' hour ' (6) appointed by God had struck, Jesus went up to Jerusalem. His object was not to dazzle beholders with a display of power (3) but to proclaim the divine gift in obedience to the Father's will.

14-24. The question of **15** is sometimes thought to f
arise out of 5:47 ; but it is sufficiently explained by the fact that Jesus teaches in the Temple (14). But the onlookers have misunderstood him (as his brothers had) : he is not a prodigy of self-taught learning trying to make a name as a teacher. His teaching is not his own but God's—as can be recognised by anyone who seriously intends to be obedient to God. The very fact that Jesus does not seek notoriety for himself but the glory of God is his authentication. At **19** he carries the war into the enemy camp. The reference to Moses *may* arise out of 5:47 ; but it could equally arise out of 17, for to the Jews the will of God is expressed in the Law of Moses. This the Jews do not keep, for they are seeking to kill the innocent Jesus. **20.** They indignantly repudiate this charge, which however is clarified in the argument of 21–4. Jesus had performed the marvellous cure of 5:1–9—on the Sabbath. This had provoked opposition. Yet it was recognised rule and practice that boys born on the Sabbath should be circumcised on the following Sabbath (the eighth day). This was regarded not as transgressing but as upholding the Law. But what Jesus had done was to put right not one member only but a whole man. To condemn this as sabbath-breaking was a superficial and therefore false judgment.

25-36. The public activity of Jesus suggests that he g
may after all have been recognised as the Messiah ; this however (the Jerusalemites think) is impossible because the Messiah was to be of hidden origin (this belief can easily be paralleled), and the origin of Jesus was well known (cf. 41 and note). **28f.** The reply is that the information current in Jerusalem is true enough as far as it goes, but that it is irrelevant. Jesus did not present himself as the distinguished representative of a famous city ; he came from God, and he represented him who sent him. In this sense his origin is hidden, for his hearers do not know God. Within Judaism this was a very provocative assertion, but his angry adversaries were unable to arrest Jesus :

744g the moment appointed by God for the death of his Son had not yet come.

31, 32. Once more (cf. 2:23) many are moved to faith by the signs (of which Jn records but few), and the attempt to arrest Jesus now becomes official. **33.** Jesus replies in an enigmatic utterance. He has come from the Father, and he will go to the Father; he will then be out of his adversaries' reach. Their mistaken interpretation of his words is nevertheless in a sense correct (cf. 8:22). After his departure to the Father, the gospel will indeed be taken to the Greeks, and they, unlike the Jews, will accept it. The irony is characteristically Johannine; cf. the next paragraph.

h **37-44.** The Feast of Tabernacles lasted seven days, but the eighth day was marked by a closing festival; it cannot be determined whether Jn refers to the seventh day or the eighth. The punctuation of **37f.** is in doubt. It is possible to read *either* (i) If any one thirst, let him come to me and drink. He who believes in me, as the Scripture has said, 'Out of his belly shall flow rivers of living water'; *or* (ii) If any one thirst, let him come to me; he who believes in me, let him drink; as the Scripture has said, 'Out of . . .' Note that, if (i) is accepted, the living water flows out of the believer; if (ii) is accepted it may be said (as far as the construction goes) to flow out of the believer or out of Christ. The problems raised by this ambiguous sentence are not alleviated by the fact that the words quoted from 'scripture' do not point clearly to any passage in the OT. Cf. however Zech. 14:8 (particularly important because Zech. 14 is the prophetic lesson for the Feast of Tabernacles); also Isa. 12:3; Ezek. 47:1–12. It is also to be remembered that a notable feature of this feast was the drawing and libation of water (cf. on 8:12). On the whole it seems likely that, though the passage is rooted in OT thought and imagery, and in Johannine thought about 'living water' (cf. 4:10), its immediate starting-point is the rite practised at Tabernacles. Punctuation (i) may be accepted. Jesus first gives the invitation to drink *living* water; then promises, in the terms of Zech. 14, that supplies of water shall be located within the believer (cf. 4:14); though they will of course be in him only because Christ is in him.

i **40.** For 'the prophet' cf. 1:21. **41f.** is a good example of Johannine irony; the crowd dismiss the claims of Jesus for the wrong reason—he was in fact born not in Galilee but in Bethlehem (cf. on 1:13). But even if they had known this fact they would not have believed (28). **43.** Division results as in 9:16, 10:19; cf. 3:19ff. Jesus is again miraculously preserved; he is still awaiting his 'hour'.

45-52. The chapter ends inconclusively; indeed, it continues immediately in 8:12. Even the officers sent to arrest Jesus could not but be impressed by him. Not so the Pharisees, who have no time for the opinions of the *'am hā-'āreṣ* ('the people of the land', see §618*g*). Nicodemus (cf. 3:1) makes some sort of defence of Jesus, appealing to the law as it was carried out in Judaism at its best, but still, it appears, prepared to judge Jesus 'according to the flesh'. His views are ignored; it is impossible that a Galilean should be taken seriously. This does not appear to have been an opinion current in Palestinian Judaism.

j **VII 53-VIII 11 The Woman taken in Adultery**—See §759*d*

745a **VIII 12-59 Further Controversy in Jerusalem**—This passage should be taken as following immediately upon the debates at the Feast of Tabernacles (7:14–52).

b **12-20.** A new turn is given to the discussion by the pronouncement, **I am the light of the world**. This is certainly connected with the miracle of the next chapter (see especially 9:4f., 39ff.), and receives no explanation here, but serves to raise the question of witness-bearing. Like most of Jn's great Christological terms it has a complicated background. Not only in the OT but in most religions 'light' is used metaphorically to describe the forces of good, darkness serving as a complementary description of evil. In
some religions, light and darkness form the elements 74
of an absolute dualism, each being a necessary part of the nature of things. In biblical thought, however, both light and darkness are God's creatures, and light accordingly represents not so much the essence of God as his activity in doing good to men. Thus 'light' was naturally used as a description of the Law (cf. Ps. 119:105; Prov. 6:23), and also in a messianic sense (cf. in the Synoptic Gospels Mt. 4:16, 5:14; Mk 4:21; Lk. 2:32). A prominent feature of Tabernacles was the erection of a great lampstand in the Temple. Cf. 7:37f. In Jn also 'light' is not so much essence as act. In 12 it is used to describe the result of Christ's work (He who follows me . . . the light of life), and this becomes even clearer in the verses already referred to in ch. 9. That Jn was aware of the use made of 'light' in Hellenistic religious thought is probable, but he gives the term a primarily biblical sense, and builds his Christological thought upon the work of redemption.

13. But surely, when Jesus makes such pronounce- c
ments about himself he is not to be taken seriously. A man's testimony about himself naturally evokes suspicion. **14.** Jesus' reply is in formal contradiction with 5:31; the difficulty is not serious, since in each passage the argument is *ad hominem*. In general it is true that a man's testimony about himself is not to be relied on, for men are ignorant about themselves and speak not out of knowledge but out of self-interest. Jesus knows that he comes from God and goes to God (cf. 13:3); this qualifies him to bear witness, and to judge. **15ff.** His adversaries judge by outward appearance (cf. 7:24); if he judges at all (cf. 3:17) his judgment is in effect the judgment of two consentient judges—the Father and himself. For this reason his testimony must be accepted. But the Pharisees are still judging 'according to the flesh', and require Jesus, as it were, to produce his Father; they simply expose their own ignorance and unteachability. **20.** The 'treasury' cannot refer to the Temple strong-rooms; possibly to the place in the Court of the Women where the thirteen 'Shofar-chests' for the reception of offerings were situated.

21-30. Jesus has already declared (14) that his hearers d
do not know whence he comes and whither he goes. He now takes up the theme of his departure. They will die in their sins (cf. 9:41); they cannot follow him; as in 7:35, the Jews make a mistake which is nevertheless in a sense true. Jesus will not commit suicide, but he will of his own accord lay down his life (10:18). But this is not the present point. He and his hearers belong to two orders of existence, 'from below' and 'from above', 'of this world' and 'not of this world'. In these words the Jewish conceptions of 'this age' and 'the age to come' are reformulated, perhaps with some reference to Greek thought.

24. The radical sin which leads to death is the rejection e
of Jesus, failure to believe that 'I am'. For this expression cf. 6:35; here however it is without noun or adjective complement (so also at 28, 58, 13:19). The Greek words are found several times in the LXX (e.g. at Dt. 32:39; Isa. 41:4, 43:13, 46:4, 48:12; cf. also Exod. 3:14ff.). Isa. 43:10 is particularly suggestive ('that you may know and believe and understand that *I am*'). 'Am' is to be understood as, in the strictest sense, a continuous tense, implying neither beginning nor end of existence (see especially 58); it indicates the eternal being of Christ, and thereby places him on a level with God. This is the probable meaning of the words; yet they were not clear to the hearers, who ask, Who art thou? and receive an answer which has given much difficulty to expositors. **25.** The main possibilities (unless we reconstruct the text on the basis of a hypothetical Aramaic original) are: (1) Why do I talk to you at all? (2*a*) I am from the beginning what I tell you; (2*b*) I am what I tell you from the beginning. None of these can be excluded; (2*a*) may perhaps be preferred.

The remaining verses emphasise the unity (which f

745f includes a moral unity—29*b*) between the Son and the Father who sent him, and the complete failure of his Jewish hearers to understand what Jesus means. They will know, when they lift up the Son of man. For this *lifting up* see on 3:14. The glorification of Jesus through and beyond the Cross is meant. Upon these words many believed, but the inadequacy of their belief is immediately exposed.

g **31-59.** The first question raised is that of freedom. The ' believers ' assert that, as Jews, they have never been slaves ; they cannot therefore be made free. **34.** But they have misunderstood both slavery and freedom. Men enjoying complete political freedom may be, and indeed are, the slaves of sin ; and the only true freedom comes by abiding obediently in the word of Jesus. It is the truth (about God) which the Son declares, and *is*, that makes men free, for freedom is a relation with God which only God himself can create.

The Jews have described themselves as ' descendants of Abraham ' ; this leads to a second point. **40.** If they were truly Abraham's children they would resemble their father ; but in seeking to kill an innocent man, whose only crime is to speak the truth, they are as unlike Abraham as could be. Jesus is the Son of God, and declares the truth he receives from God ; but who can their father be ? **41.** The charge is repelled with a sneer ; *they* are the children of God ; Jesus (it is implied) was born of fornication. This slander was certainly current later ; probably it was used in anti-Christian propaganda in Jn's time, and perhaps earlier. But they are not God's children ; if they were, they would love his Son. The Son claims no independent rights, but emphasises once more that he has been *sent*. If men will not listen to what he says it is because the message which has been entrusted to him is quite foreign to them. No : their father is the devil ; that is why they seek to kill, and prefer falsehood to truth. **47** sums up the argument so far : he that is of God hears Jesus, others do not.

h **48.** All this can however be dismissed as madness. The context (49) suggests that 'to be a Samaritan' means ' to have a demon ', i.e. to be mad ; but it cannot be proved that this is the meaning of the phrase. Of course, Jesus is not mad, but he is certainly unusual in that he seeks not his own glory but God's. In turn, the Father seeks his glory, and judges those who abuse him. **51.** Suddenly the offer of eternal life is made ; and this, to the unbeliever, is conclusive proof of madness. Anyone would think that Jesus was greater than Abraham ! The reply to this comes in **56** ; it is very carefully prepared for in 54f. Jesus is no braggart ; yet it is true that he, alone in the whole company, knows God. Therefore it can be said that Abraham, who, according to Rabbinic exegesis, had seen the day of the Messiah, had seen the day of Jesus, and greeted it with joy. **57.** Such a statement, on the lips of a comparatively young man, was manifestly absurd. But it is such calculations as this that are absurd. Abraham was a man who, like all men, came into being at a particular time and lived for a limited period. The continuing and eternal existence of Christ (' I am '—see on 24) precedes, as it also follows, all such transient phenomena.

Once more (7:30, 8:20), Jesus escapes his attackers unharmed.

746a **IX 1-41 The Man born Blind**—This chapter develops the saying of 8:12 in the light of a simple miracle story, which has no synoptic parallel (but cf. Mk 8:22–6, 10:46–52). The story itself is recounted in the plainest historical terms ; interpretative material occurs mainly in 3ff., 39ff.

b **1-7,** the miracle. Jesus is presumably still in Jerusalem. The blind man does not approach him, but is singled out by Jesus' own will (cf. 5:6). **2.** A theological problem (to the terms of which parallels exist in Jewish literature) is raised by the disciples. Jesus' reply does not deny the possibility of a general relation between sin and suffering, but does deny a specific and personal relation. In any case, all events that contribute to the activity (' works ') of Jesus have a special place within the purpose of God, and it is in the light of this purpose that they must be evaluated. The abounding of sin forms a suitable context for the super-abounding of grace (Rom. 5:20). In Christ the human scene becomes a stage for God's self-manifestation. **4.** This will not always be so. The ministry of Jesus will before long end in his death. This, however, though true, is not the whole meaning of the verse, which is deliberately cast in the plural (' *We* must . . .'). A time-limit is imposed upon the Church's activity also, just as death brings to an end each man's work. **5** makes clear the sense in which 8:12 is to be taken. Jn is not using the term ' light ' to denote a metaphysical concept but the means by which God brings salvation to men. Jesus *in the world* is its light because he offers life and light to the world, as the ensuing narrative will illustrate.

c **6.** The narrative now proceeds in straightforward fashion. For the use of spittle in cures cf. Mk 7:33, 8:23 (there are non-biblical parallels too). **7.** For the Pool of Siloam cf. (in the LXX) Neh. 3:15 ; Isa. 8:6. See also Gen. 49:10*n*, where the similar name Shiloh was interpreted messianically. The water used in the libations at the Feast of Tabernacles (7:37f.) was drawn from Siloam. Jn treats the name as if it were derived from the Hebrew verb *shālah*, to send. Jesus himself is the ' sent one' (e.g. 10:36), and he gives to men light, and the water of life. Moreover, the man himself is sent by Jesus to the pool, so that his cure is made by Jesus to depend upon his obedience to his mission. The notion of sending plays so important a part in Jn's thought (e.g. 20:21) that it is probably right to see here some such thoughts as these. When the man obeys, his cure is immediate.

d **8-34.** The cure is investigated. The blind man is interrogated by the Jews, and their examination of him becomes as it were a trial of Jesus. (It is worth noting that Jn has no parallel to the synoptic account of a Jewish trial of Jesus in the Passion Narrative.) The Jews in the end pass their verdict on Jesus (24), but in doing so they condemn themselves (41 ; see below). **14.** That which sets the examination in progress is the fact that the cure has taken place on the Sabbath (cf. 5:9). **16.** Since Jesus has undoubtedly performed acts of work on the Sabbath it is impossible to believe that he is ' from God '. But this conclusion provides one horn of a dilemma : for who can believe that a sinner should perform such a mighty work ? Hence there arises division among the Pharisees. **17.** The blind man himself is questioned, and gives the opinion that the miracle-worker is a prophet. This is probably to be understood as a stage on the way from ignorance and unbelief to belief (38). **18.** The man's parents are called in, but refuse to give more than evidence of identification, because they fear the Jewish decision to excommunicate anyone who confesses Jesus to be Christ. **22.** The form in which Jn expresses this decision probably reflects the drawing up (in A.D. 85–90) of a Synagogue Benediction designed to exclude Jewish Christians. **24.** There is thus nothing to do but recall the formerly blind man, and exercise authority. ' Give God the praise ' probably means ' Admit the truth '. It is now settled that Jesus is a sinner, and therefore cannot be responsible for the cure. But the man will not be browbeaten. He maintains the one thing he knows : I was blind but now I see. He has still not reached the full faith of 38, but will not retreat from what he has attained. **27.** The Jews, taunted by the healed man, become angrier. **28f.** They are confident that they represent the authentic religion of the OT and Judaism, which goes back through Moses to God himself. In comparison with a connection of this kind, Jesus, being of unknown origin (cf. 7:27f.) has no authority whatever. (The ' whence ' of Jesus is a matter of importance in Jn's thought ; cf. e.g. 8:23). **30.** A strange piece

746d of ignorance on the Jews' part! Only one who came from God could achieve a unique miracle. The argument of **31** does not imply that God does not hear the prayer of a *penitent* sinner. **34.** The Jews are reduced to abuse, and *cast out* the man who has ventured to disagree with them (cf. the work of the Good Shepherd in the next chapter).

e In **35-41** the meaning of the event is laid bare. First, Jesus inquires into the meaning of the man's expulsion from Judaism. Is it due to genuine belief (in the Son of man—though many later MSS have 'of God')? No, for the man is not yet fully informed. Jesus discloses his identity; the man believes and worships. There can be little doubt that Jn intends us to see here the spiritual counterpart of the physical cure which has already been performed. The man has believed in the light and become a son of light (12:36). **39.** Secondly, Jesus declares the purpose of his mission: he has come into the world 'for judgment' (cf. 5:22, 8:15f.). This judgment takes place in two ways. One has already been indicated in the illumination of the blind man. Those who are aware of their blindness and ignorance (cf. 25, 36) may be made to see, because they will be prepared to believe in the light when it shines upon them. The other way in which judgment takes place is condemnation. Those who are confident of their own power to see become blind, because they refuse to look at the light (cf. 5:40). **40f.** Thirdly, this aspect of the judgment is applied to the Pharisees. It is precisely because they are confident of their own ability to see apart from the light which shines in the world in the person of Jesus that they are under sentence of blindness. There is no verbal parallel to this saying in the Synoptic Gospels, but Mk 3:29 is a close substantial parallel. For the language, cf. also Ps. 146:8; Isa. 6:10, 29:18, 35:5, 42:7, 18f.; Mk 4:11f.; Jn 12:40.

747a **X 1-21 The Good Shepherd**—1-5 of this chapter are described in 6 as a 'figure' (RV 'parable'; Gr. *paroimia*, not *parabolē*), but neither these verses nor the section as a whole is much like the synoptic parables. There is no story or description of a particular shepherd, but a series of observations upon the general subject of sheep and shepherds, combined with interpretative material, with direct intrusions of interpretation into the symbolism (e.g. *I am* the good shepherd, 11). There are of course synoptic parallels to the imagery, especially Mt. 18:12ff.; Mk 6:34.

Jn makes no break between ch. 9 and ch. 10, but the latter is not a direct continuation, though it refers to the neglectful behaviour of the appointed shepherds (cf. 9:34), and to the care of Jesus for his own (cf. 9:35, et al.).

Authentic shepherds use the door of the fold; others (who may be distinguished by their failure to acknowledge Jesus Christ; cf. 1 Jn 4:2f.) are not merely unauthorised shepherds but thieves and robbers (cf. Ezek. 34, an important part of the background of Jn 10). It is not so much false messiahs as the many 'saviours' of the Hellenistic world who are in mind. The true shepherd proceeds by the appointed way, and is recognised by the porter and by the sheep themselves. He leads his sheep out (to pasture), and they follow him because they know his voice. On the importance of hearing the words of Jesus see 5:24, 18:37. Evidently his hearers on this occasion did not 'belong to his sheep' (26), for they failed to understand his symbolic language. He continues, casting the symbolism in the form of two 'I am' sayings: I am the door (7, 9), and I am the shepherd (11, 14).

b The term 'door' appears to be used in different senses in the two verses in which it occurs. In 7f. the theme is *approach to* the sheep: the elect of God can be reached only through Christ. (In 8, 'before me' gave difficulty to copyists and interpreters. It is certain that Jn cannot have meant that the patriarchs and prophets of the OT were 'thieves and robbers'; the reference is, as in 1, to those who teach a way of salvation apart from Christ.) In 9, the theme is the *movement* of the sheep themselves; it is through Jesus only that men have access to eternal life. The word 'door' had many religious connections in antiquity; Jn reflects some of these, but is not simply dependent on any of them. What he means to convey is the centrality and all-sufficiency of Jesus in salvation. 747b

The term 'shepherd' also was widely used; its OT background (Ps. 23:1, 80:1; Isa. 40:11; Jer. 31:10; Ezek. 34; Zech. 11:4-9, et al.) is particularly important, as well as the synoptic tradition (above). The main point is given in **10.** The purpose of the shepherd is to give life to the sheep. The theme of mutual knowledge and recognition is again brought out (8, 14f.), and emphasises the contrast between the hireling and the shepherd. It points to the fact that the shepherd (of his own accord) *lays down* his life for the sheep. For this reason the shepherd is described as *good* (cf. the use of 'true', 1:9, et al.). **16.** The shepherd's mission extends to sheep which are not 'of this fold'. The world-wide mission of Christianity will include Gentiles as well as Jews within the people of God. c

In **17f.** stress is once more laid upon (*a*) the freedom of Jesus from all human constraint, and (*b*) his complete obedience to the Father.

19. Jesus' words divide his hearers; cf. 7:43, 9:16, and especially 9:39. For the charge that he 'has a demon, and is mad' (one charge only—madness is caused by demon-possession), cf. 8:48. But the problem of 9:16, 33 recurs: neither Jesus' words nor his actions suggest demonic activity. d

22-42 Debate at the Feast of Dedication—This section continues the debate on the person of Jesus which has proceeded in Jerusalem since ch. 7; but the time mentioned (Dedication—December) is some two and a half months after Tabernacles (7:2, 14, 37). Jn probably intends the present stage of the debate to be regarded as a climax (see 40ff.); it is not resumed until the public ministry as a whole is summed up in 12:36-50. On the Feast of Dedication see §§37*i*, 604*d*; there seems to be no symbolical purpose in the reference. For 'Solomon's Portico' cf. Ac. 3:11, 5:12. It was probably on the eastern side of the Temple, but complete certainty cannot be attained. **24.** For 'How long will you keep us in suspense?' we should probably translate, 'How long do you mean to annoy, distract, us?'; that is, the question arises from enemies, not from honest seekers after truth. It is implied that no plain and unambiguous statement about messiahship has been made; yet Jesus answers, **25,** 'I told you, and you do not believe'. In fact both the Jews and Jesus are right. Only to the Samaritan woman (4:26) has Jesus unequivocally declared his messiahship, but his works bear witness concerning him, and many of his symbolic utterances could only be interpreted messianically. It is **26f.** which provide the clue. No matter how openly Jesus speaks, those who are not his sheep will not believe; no matter how obscurely he speaks, those who are his sheep will understand. The cause of misunderstanding lies not in him but in the listener. **28.** Out of the mutual recognition between Jesus and his own comes the gift of eternal life, and the ultimate security of believers, that is, of those who stand under the authority of Jesus (in his hand). **29.** This authority, and this security, are moreover the authority and security of God himself; **30** say 'Jesus' and you have said 'God'. This unity between Father and Son is not merely cosmological or metaphysical; the moral relationships of love and obedience are primary (17). **31.** But essential relationship (cf. 1:1f., 5:18) is also implied, and it is this that enrages the Jewish audience. **33.** To blur the distinction between God and man is blasphemy because it infringes God's majesty; man can never make himself God. It is important to grasp this—a true biblical thought—for it is the key to the difficult paragraph that follows. It is not incorrect to speak of the argument based on Ps. 82:6 (quoted in 34) as *ad hominem*—here is a point in their own law e f

47f which the Jews will have to explain away. But the argument is more than this, for the Psalm speaks not of men 'making themselves' gods, but of the movement of God to men through his word; and that which is seen in the ministry of Jesus is the supreme movement of God to men in his personal Word (1:1). **36.** He whom God thus sanctified and commissioned cannot be accused of blasphemy when he asserts a relationship with God for which God himself is responsible. **37f.** bring back the stress to the activity rather than the person of Jesus. The questions men must consider are whether he acts in obedience to the Father, and whether his work brings eternal life to men. **39f.** After an unsuccessful attempt to arrest him (cf. 7:30, 8:20, 59), Jesus withdraws across the Jordan (cf. 1:28), and returns to the scene of the Baptist's work, having now completed (in all respects save the Passion) what the Baptist, representing the OT itself, had foretold. The believers of **42**, of whom no more is heard, represent the fruit of this ministry of fulfilment.

48a **XI 1-44 Lazarus**—Jesus' stay on the far side of Jordan is terminated (though not instantly—6) by the sickness and death of Lazarus, who in 1f. is somewhat clumsily introduced by reference to his sisters, Mary and Martha. The sisters have not previously been mentioned in Jn, but are both mentioned in Lk. 10:38f. (Jn's reference would certainly be more intelligible if he could assume knowledge of Lk.; see §735*d*), and **2** points forward to the anointing story of 12:1–8. The appeal of **3** is presumably sent before Lazarus's death (of which Jesus therefore must learn supernaturally—11, 14) in the hope that Jesus will come and cure the sick man. **4** also presupposes supernatural knowledge of the ensuing course of events. The end of the story will not be death but the glory of God (cf. 40), revealed in the actions of his Son, who accordingly shares in the glory given to the Father. **5.** The explicit statement that Jesus loved the family at Bethany is probably intended to emphasise the paradox of 6; instead of hastening to the relief of his friends, Jesus stayed where he was. The motive for the delay is hardly the hope of performing a more wonderful miracle—this would be entirely foreign to Jn's mode of thought—but to emphasise that the acts of Jesus are determined neither by his foes nor even by his friends (cf. e.g. 2:3f.) but wholly by the command of God. At the moment ordained by God, Jesus proposes to return to Judaea (7); but the disciples are not slow to see the dangers of such a plan. They are answered in **9f.** While opportunity lasts, the will and work of God must be done; the night comes soon enough. The metaphor is simple, but especially appropriate on the lips of Jesus (for 'hour' cf. 2:4, 8:20; for 'light' cf. 1:9, 8:12, 9:5, 12:46).

b In **11** Jesus declares his knowledge of Lazarus's death, and his intention to raise him up, but in veiled language, which is misunderstood. The misunderstanding is significant, however; for Christians, death is a sleep, and after death they will be saved (in 12, 'recover' translates a Greek word which in other contexts would be rendered, 'be saved'). From one point of view the end of the sign is the glory of God (4); from another it is the faith of the beholders (15). For Thomas the Twin cf. 14:5, 20:24–8, 21:2. He is without hope, and without understanding, but loyal. **17.** Lazarus has been four days dead when the party reaches Bethany (not the Bethany 'beyond the Jordan' of 1:28, but another village, a bare two miles from Jerusalem). **19.** The duty of consoling the bereaved has always been emphasised in Judaism, and there is nothing to suggest that the Jewish mourners were
c insincere. **22.** Martha, meeting Jesus, expresses the thought implied in 3: even now, she is not without hope. **23** is so phrased as to set in motion the ensuing conversation, which brings out the point of the story. 'Your brother will rise': the words are deliberately ambiguous. They forecast the events about to take place; **24** but Martha, notwithstanding the belief
tentatively expressed in 22, does not take them in this 748c
sense, but in terms of the belief of Pharisaic Judaism that the dead, or at least the righteous dead, will rise again at the last day. This belief is perfectly correct, but Martha states it incompletely: The dead do not rise up in virtue of some inward quality of their own, but because they are raised up; and they are raised up by Christ (5:25, 6:39). **25.** In other words, '*I am* the resurrection and the life'. (It is possible that 'and the life' should be omitted, with some old versions and the Chester Beatty Papyrus; little difference is made to the sense.) For the 'I am' formula see on 6:35. It is the Son of God who has life *in himself*, and gives life to the world (e.g. 6:33). This will be manifest at the last day, but it is also manifest wherever the Son of God is present. This does not mean that miraculous anticipations of the last day take place wherever he appears, but that appropriate revelations of his life-giving power may always be expected. This truth is now stated more precisely. First, the believer who dies (as Lazarus has done) will come to life (not necessarily as Lazarus will do, but certainly at the last day). Secondly, he who believes, and thereby is truly alive (cf. 20:31), will never die (that is, physical death will not mean the end of his life, which is eternal). **27.** Martha's reply, which may possibly echo early Christian formularies, is properly directed to the person of Christ, who himself is the truth about man's future. The three phrases are perhaps best taken as separate parallel statements of the truth: Jesus is the Christ; the Son of God; he who comes into the world (i.e. as its Saviour; cf. 3:16, 31, 6:14). The conversation breaks off here (though **28** implies that Jesus has summoned Mary); there is no more to say.

29. For a few verses the narrative moves smoothly d
on. Mary shares Martha's real but not perfect faith (32). **33** expresses the emotion of Jesus in vivid language; RSV fails to express the sense of anger which the Greek implies, and which can be removed only by adopting an inferior reading or emending the text in terms of a hypothetical Semitic original. But why should Jesus be angry? There is nothing to suggest that the tears of 33 are hypocritical, nor can we say that Jesus is angry at the unbelief of the Jews (37 does not necessarily express scepticism—and Jesus himself wept; 35). Perhaps the explanation is that Jesus perceived that a miracle, and a public miracle with all its power not only to evoke and confirm faith but also to provoke and stimulate unbelief (46ff.), was being forced upon him (cf. Mt. 9:30; Mk 1:43, where the same Greek word for anger is used). **38.** Again the story moves on. Lazarus was laid in a tomb constructed and sealed in what was a common Jewish manner. He had been dead four days; in Jewish belief, the soul after the third day ceased to hover over the body; death was complete and dissolution in full course. Martha, notwithstanding 21–7, still does not expect, in these circumstances, to see a miracle. **40.** For the 'glory of God' see 4.

In view of **42** it has been said that Jesus prays aloud only in order to impress the crowd. This is in a sense true; but what he impresses upon the crowd is not his own personal greatness but, on the contrary, the fact that he is in all things dependent upon the Father who sent him. He draws men's attention from himself to God. **44.** Lazarus comes out of the tomb still wrapped in the linen strips that had been bound about his body. But beneath them he is alive, and needs only to be released.

It is inevitable that the problems raised by the e
miracle-stories should come to a head at this point, though it is in fact doubtful whether, if the concept of the miraculous be granted at all, it is possible to distinguish degrees within it. All that can be said here is that the historian as such cannot pronounce for or against the historicity of miracles without going beyond his own field, either as sceptic or believer. In dealing with this miracle, he may assert, on the one

748e hand, that there is no indication that Jn has simply created a story out of nothing—it is much more probable that he is using traditional material, even if he has introduced into it theological utterances intended to make its point clearer ; and, on the other, that it is difficult to account for the absence of this story from the synoptic tradition, and to find a place where it could fit into the synoptic story. He will moreover draw attention to the curious parallel in Lk. 16:19–31—a parable. The plain fact, however, unwelcome as it may be to those who like clear-cut pronouncements, is that we have no means of investigating the peculiarly Johannine traditions before they were written down in the Gospel.

749a **45-54 The Plot against Jesus**—The raising of Lazarus had the effect which all manifestations of divine power have ; some it moved to faith (45), others to unbelief (46). The report brought before the Pharisees leads to the decisive plot against Jesus' life (53).

So striking and public an act evidently brought about a crisis for the officials of Judaism, and a meeting of the Sanhedrin (see §777*i*) was convoked. Its proceedings are reported with biting irony. The Jews propose to restrain Jesus to prevent men from believing in him, and the Romans from doing away with the (holy) place (i.e. the Temple), and the Jewish nation. By crucifying Jesus they brought about exactly what they sought to avoid—the world-wide Christian mission, and the capture of Jerusalem (in A.D. 70). Caiaphas (see further 18:13), who happened to be high priest at that momentous time, went further. Better, he suggested, that one man should die for the people than that the whole nation should perish. This was unconscious prophecy. Jesus did die *for the people* ; politically, the nation perished, but those who accepted the Crucified did not perish but received eternal life (3:16).

b Further, Jesus did not die for the (Jewish) people only ; through his passion God drew together (10:16, 12:32, 17:20) all those whom he had chosen as his children. Behind the language used in this verse (52) lie the Jewish thought of the Dispersion, and the Stoic-Gnostic conception of men in whom seed-like fragments of divinity give them a natural kinship with God ; but Jn reproduces neither of these. For him, men become children of God by receiving *the* Son of God (1:12) ; Christ both makes and unites the children of God.

The situation had now become so dangerous (53) that Jesus, in order not to precipitate the Passion before the appointed moment, drew his public ministry to a close and withdrew with his disciples to Ephraim—probably the modern Eṭ-Ṭaiyibeh, four miles NE. of Bethel.

c **XI 55-XII 11 The Anointing**—The final Passover (cf. 2:13, 6:4) was now near. The Jews themselves made the customary preparations, and there was, in view of the official plots against him, doubt whether Jesus would present himself in the city for the feast.

Six days before Passover Jesus came to Bethany (within two miles of the city—11:1, 18). Notwithstanding the official opposition, large crowds assembled, attracted partly by the prospect of seeing Lazarus (12:9), and many believed in Jesus (11). The sign had had the customary effect (cf. 2:23). Meanwhile, at a feast attended by Lazarus and his sisters, the anointing of Jesus took place (12:2, 3). The relation between this narrative and the parallels in the Synoptic Gospels is complicated. In Lk. 10:38–42 Jesus is entertained in the house of Mary and Martha (there is no mention of Lazarus). An anointing story is given by Mk (14:3–9 ; Mt. 26:6–13), and another by Lk. (7:36–50), in a different context and differing in some material particulars. In Mk, the anointing takes place in Bethany, in the home of Simon the leper. It is performed by an unnamed woman, who pours ointment over Jesus' feet. The act is related to the burial of Jesus. In Lk., the event takes place in the house of a Pharisee. The woman who anoints Jesus is unnamed, 749 but described as a sinner. She wets his feet with her tears, wipes them with her hair, kisses them, and anoints them. There is no reference to the burial. The details of the Johannine story, which has points of resemblance to both the Marcan and Lucan stories, will be noted in what follows.

3. The ointment used is described in the same terms d as in Mk ; it is particularly striking that Jn uses the very rare word *pistikos*, which is probably derived from an Aramaic word for the oil produced from the pistachio nut but indicates here Jn's use of Mk rather than knowledge of Aramaic. Mary anoints Jesus' feet and wipes them, after anointing, with her hair. It is possible, especially in the light of Jewish parallels which speak of the diffusion of Abraham's good works, that the last sentence in 3 is a symbolic equivalent of Mk 14:9. **4f.** The complaint is here ascribed to Judas only (cf. Mk 14:4f.). The agreement between Jn and Mk in the estimate of the value of the ointment is striking, and not easily explained as due to coincidence. Care for the poor and care for the dead (both good works on which Judaism laid much stress) are here contrasted as in Mk 14:7.

7. ' Let her keep it for the day of my burial ' is obscure. e In Mk a similar saying is differently worded, and it is clear that the woman has actually done by anticipation something which later there was no opportunity to do—Mk 16:1, 6 show the women prevented by the resurrection ; the body of Jesus was never anointed, *except by anticipation.* In Jn, however, anointing is carried out on a lavish scale (19:39), so that there is no need to say explicitly that Mary was anointing the body of Jesus for burial, though tradition demanded some allusion to the last rites. It is sometimes supposed that Jn means, ' Let her keep that part of the ointment which has not been used . . .' ; but this is to miss the spirit of the narrative. ' Let her keep this in her memory . . .' makes good sense but is a doubtful rendering of the Greek. It is possible that ' keep ' should be taken in the sense of ' observe ' (as e.g. at 9:16) : ' Let her observe the rite now with reference to the day of my burial '. But none of these suggestions is entirely convincing. Jn himself may have viewed the incident as symbolic of the anointing of Jesus for his office as king of Israel. It is significant that, in comparison with Mk, he reverses the order of the Anointing and the Entry ; Jesus enters his capital as its anointed king.

XII 12-19 Jesus enters Jerusalem—As in the f preceding narrative, Jn seems to be dependent on Mk (11:1–10), but lays special emphasis on two points : (*a*) It is as king that Jesus enters the city (see above). In **13** the quotation from Ps. 118:25f. is supplemented by the words, ' Even the King of Israel '. It is possible that the words of the Psalm were originally used with out messianic intention (they originally meant, ' Blessed in the name of the Lord be he who comes '), but the messianic interpretation appears already in Mk. (*b*) The disciples did not understand the event until after Jesus had been glorified. Only in the light of his completed work of crucifixion and resurrection, and through the work of the Spirit (16:13), could they understand the mingled contemptibility and glory of the triumphal entry of the meek and lowly king who rode upon an ass, and the testimony to this of scripture (Zech. 9:9).

It is doubtful whether any special significance can g be found in the use of palm-branches, though they suggest the rites of Tabernacles, and perhaps of Dedication, rather than of Passover. **15.** The opening words (Fear not) of the quotation from Zech. 9:9 differ from all other forms of that verse (Rejoice greatly) ; possibly Isa. 40:9 was subconsciously combined with it. **17.** The importance of Lazarus in the unfolding of the Johannine story is underlined. **19** is written in Jn's ironical style ; the Pharisees themselves mean only to draw attention to Jesus' popularity, but they are made to express themselves

49g in a way that suggests Jesus' mission to and salvation of the world (cf. e.g. 3:16).

50a **20-36 The Greeks at the Feast**—' Greeks ' means non-Jews ; the fact that they had come ' to worship ' does not prove that they were proselytes ; cf. Ac. 8:27. They represent the Gentile world from which, when Jn wrote, the majority of Christians were drawn. It is not through accident or careless writing that, after they have been mentioned in 20, they are lost sight of, and never in fact appear in the presence of Jesus. The paragraph as a whole is designed to show that the world-wide Christian mission presupposes the death and glorification of Jesus : **24** the grain of wheat must first fall into the ground and die in order that it may bear fruit. It is characteristic of Jn that this piece of symbolism, which is used in the Synoptic Gospels (Mt. 13:24–30 ; Mk 4:3–9, 26–9, 31f.) with reference to the kingdom of God, should be applied to the person of Jesus himself, who concentrates in himself the meaning of the kingdom. Cf. also 1 C. 15:36ff., which is very close to Jn's usage, and may have been known to him. This earlier NT application of seeds and sowing is sufficient to account for Jn's words ; there is no need to think of the mythical use in some ancient religions of the natural cycle of growth and decay. As in the Synoptic Gospels the kingdom is thought of as passing through a period of obscurity before it comes in power, so is this true also of Jesus himself. And now the moment is come for the Son of man to be glorified—in death (23). Like the seed symbol, **25f.** recall synoptic material (Mt. 10:39 ; Mk 8:34f. ; Lk. 17:33, 14:26). What is true of Jesus is true also, *mutatis mutandis*, of his disciples. For them too the way to life lies through the renunciation of life.

b **27-30.** There is one synoptic narrative which makes this theme particularly clear—the story of Gethsemane. Jn does not use the story as a whole, but takes from it the account of Jesus' prayer and resignation to the will of God. It makes little difference whether (with RSV) we place a question-mark after ' Father [cf. Mk 14:36], save me from this hour ', or a full-stop. If the prayer is offered, it is instantly reconsidered. Jesus has not come so far only to turn back before completing the mission on which he has embarked. **28.** What he seeks is expressed in the prayer, ' Father, glorify thy name '. Not because Jesus himself needed confirmation for his faith, but for the benefit of the bystanders, a divine voice answers. God's name has already been glorified (e.g. in the signs—11:40), and will be glorified (in the death and exaltation of Jesus). Presumably it was not those who ascribed the sound to thunder, but those who thought an angel had spoken, who derived advantage from the heavenly voice. **31.** It is perhaps this distinction, between hearing and deaf listeners, that suggests the next verse. This is the judgment—that some hear and others do not. The present moment is also the time for the expulsion and defeat of the power of evil, the ruler who has usurped this world and alienated it from God ; positively put, Jesus, lifted up on the Cross (33) and thereby exalted (Jn chooses deliberately an ambiguous word), will draw all men away from Satan and to himself.

c But here is a problem. If ' lifting up ' is taken to refer only to death, it is implied that the Messiah (for which Son of man seems here to be taken as a synonym) will die ; but this is contrary to the belief, grounded (as was believed) in scripture, that the Messiah should be eternal. Jesus does not reply directly, but uses once more the imagery of light and darkness. ' Lifting up ' implies at least this, that a time-limit is imposed upon the opportunity granted to men to accept the light and themselves acquire its nature (36).

The opportunity is in fact immediately concluded. **36b.** The light of the world went into voluntary concealment. The final summing-up of the ministry follows ; thereafter, the converse of Jesus with his disciples, and the Passion.

37-50 The Conclusion of the public Ministry— 750d
The scene from which Jesus withdrew was, notwithstanding his many signs, a scene of failure. **37.** ' They '—the Jews in general—did not believe in him. This was not unforeseen ; indeed it took place that scripture (Isa. 53:1) might be fulfilled. They could not believe because God himself had blinded their eyes and hardened their hearts, as Isaiah, because he saw the glory of Christ himself, declared (Isa. 6:9f.). This OT passage is quoted in Mk 4:12, and Paul also sees (Rom. 9ff.) in the unbelief of Israel part of the divine plan. **42.** No crudely mechanical determinism is involved, for Jn immediately notes exceptions to his general statement—' Nevertheless many believed '. The root of the trouble is revealed in **43** : those who are primarily interested in the praise (glory) of men cannot hope to see the glory of God. Man-centred existence can only be hardened by God's word.

44-50. Yet only in a secondary sense is this God's e
intention. Jesus speaks what may be described as an epilogue to the main action of the Gospel. He has come into the world as its light not in order that men may be blinded but that they may not remain in darkness ; not to judge the world but to save it (46f.). His coming has the significance of the coming of God himself. He does not speak from himself, but says only what the Father commands him to say. It follows that to accept Jesus is to have the life which Jesus himself enjoys as the result of obedience to the command of God (50). But those who prefer the darkness of egocentricity will inevitably be judged, and will be responsible for their own judgment. The word of Jesus, which is the word of God, the word which they have rejected, will be their judge. They have loved their own lives (25), and at the last day they will lose them. The shining of the light, though intended to bring salvation, splits men into two groups according to their reaction to it.

XIII 1-30 The Last Supper—The public ministry f
over, Jesus takes supper with his disciples on Passover eve. In the Synoptic Gospels also a supper is recorded for the night ' in which he was betrayed ', but according to them (Mk 14:12, 16, 17, etc.) the meal was the Passover itself ; that is, they place the supper, and accordingly the crucifixion also, a day later than does Jn (all evangelists agree in placing the supper on a Thursday, the crucifixion on a Friday). There seems to be no satisfactory way of reconciling the two dates, and in face of this conflict some maintain the Johannine, others the synoptic, chronology, while others think it impossible to date the crucifixion precisely. The following arguments have been used : (*a*) In favour of the Johannine date : The synoptic story is inconsistent—some passages (e.g. Mk 14:2 ; Lk. 22:15) point to the Johannine date ; a trial would not have been held on Passover night ; the disciples would not have borne arms on that night, nor would Simon of Cyrene have been ' coming in from the country ' (Mk 15:21) the following morning ; the synoptic dating arose because Jesus was identified with the Passover lamb (1 C. 5:7), and the supper in which he explained the significance of his body and blood was therefore naturally, but erroneously, supposed to have been a Passover meal. (*b*) In favour of the synoptic date : All the above arguments are held to be illusory—the synoptic passages alleged to be inconsistent with the synoptic date are in fact consistent with it, and Passover time, while the pilgrims were still in the city, was precisely the time when a ' false prophet ' should be executed in order that ' all Israel ' might ' hear and fear ' (Dt. 17:13) ; several features in the meal—its time, the fact that the participants reclined, the use of wine, the explanation of foods used—suggest that it was a Passover meal ; the Johannine date, which represents Jesus as dying at the hour when the Passover lambs were sacrificed, might well be due to identification of Jesus with the lamb of God (1:29). If the supper was not the Passover

750f (and it seems probable that it was), it can only be described as an *ad hoc* religious meal ; a ' Passover *Ḳiddûsh* ' it certainly was not.

751a Jesus took part in the meal knowing fully his relation to God and to his own. **1.** He loved them ' to the end ' ; this means ' up to the last moment ', but also (and the ambiguity is characteristic) ' utterly ', ' completely '. All that follows is to be understood as an act of love. **2.** Over against Jesus stands Judas Iscariot, now fully in the hands of Satan. **3ff.** In full awareness of the total situation, Jesus proceeds to perform the menial task of washing his disciples' feet. To this process, Peter, guided by a false scale of moral values, objects ; having part of the truth explained to him he next seeks to have not his feet only but also his hands and his head washed, failing this time to see the theological point. The symbolic act of feet-washing, which foreshadows the crucifixion itself, has three meanings : (*a*) It reveals the love of Jesus for his own ; he will perform on their behalf the humblest act of service. (*b*) As an act of love, it serves as an example (14f.). (*c*) As an act of love, it is an act of cleansing, which is essential to fellowship with Christ (8). The feet-washing itself is a parable of this cleansing ; so, in another way, is baptism, but Jn is not simply illustrating the importance of baptism. Here (as in ch. 6) he is primarily concerned with the historic and universal act of redemption which underlies and gives significance to the sacramental act. This suggests that in 10 the marginal reading is to be followed rather than the text of RSV. He who has once participated in the redemptive work of Christ (which the feet-washing foreshadows) *is* clean —Peter's desire for more washing is pointless. On the other hand, no quantity of water will cleanse Judas, the tool of Satan (11 ; cf. 18).

b The example of humble love is one that Jesus may well expect to be followed. **16.** His servants are not greater than he ; yet conversely as his envoys they truly represent him. **20.** That is, in the Christian mission it is God himself that men encounter.

c In **21-30**, the traitor, Judas Iscariot, is dealt with. In Mk (14:18, 20) there is a general prediction that one of the Twelve will betray Jesus ; in Mt. (26:25) the traitor is named. Mt's version of the story raises the difficult question why none of the Twelve took any steps to hinder Judas's plan. Jn reduces, but does not eliminate, the difficulty by representing the disclosure as made to one disciple only. This disciple reclines (on the left side) with his head ' close to the breast of Jesus ', occupying the place of second-highest honour (the disciple on the other side of the Master would have the highest place). He thus has an opportunity of seeking confidential information. He is described as one ' whom Jesus loved ' (23). Cf. 19:26, 20:2, 21:7, 20 ; and see §735*c*. The association of this disciple with Peter lends weight to his traditional identification with John Zebedee. There is nothing in the present context to suggest that he represents an ' ideal ' disciple.

In ambiguous words (27, 29) Jesus bids Judas go about his work ; Satan takes full possession of him, and he goes out into the night (30). The meal was no doubt taking place at night (though this is more natural for a Passover than for an ordinary supper) ; but Jn thinks of darkness in another sense (cf. 1:5 etc.).

d **31-38.** In these verses we pass from the narrative of the supper to the discourses of chs. 14ff., and the prayer of ch. 17 ; themes which will be developed in detail in these later chapters—the departure and glory of Jesus, the command of love, and the approaching failure of the Twelve—are adumbrated here.

31. The past tense ' glorified ' can be used because the Passion has been anticipated in the feet-washing, and is viewed as already in a sense complete. The Passion *is* the glory of the Son of man ; themes which are often chronologically distinguished in the synoptic Son of man sayings are here combined. **32.** God will glorify the Son of man ' at once ' : there will be no 751
need to wait till the *parousia*. **33.** But in the compound of suffering and glory to which he will shortly go, Jesus will be alone. Not even the Twelve can follow him (yet ; cf. 36). Peter himself must learn the self-despair which will result from his denial before he can truly follow (cf. 21:19).

Jesus leaves his followers one command : **34f.** it e
is by their mutual love that they will be recognised as his disciples. It is only superficially that this appears to be a narrower command than that of Mt. 5:44 ; the mutual love which exists within the Christian society is of a special kind, which reflects the mutual love existing between the Father and the Son (see on 15:12–15). The existence of such love is the distinguishing mark of the Christian society. The commandment is described as ' new ' (34) not because nothing like it had ever been uttered before (cf. Lev. 19:18), but because it reflects the relations within the Godhead, and, still more, because it belongs to the new age which the work of Jesus introduced (cf. 1 Jn 2:8).

XIV 1-31. It is possible to regard this chapter as f
containing all that Jn intended to put into the Last Discourses ; see on 31. Certainly the main themes are raised here : the departure and return of Jesus ; the revelation of the Father ; the union of the Son, and of believers in him, with the Father ; prayer ; the Paraclete ; the obedience of believers to Christ in love. In their position and in their contents these discourses afford a partial parallel to the eschatological discourse of Mk 13 (and parallels), which otherwise does not appear in Jn.

1 follows closely upon 13:33, 38 : notwithstanding g
Jesus' imminent departure, and Peter's denial, there is no reason for fear. Rather, the disciples must trust the Father and the Son (it is better, with RSV, to take ' believe ' as imperative each time it occurs, though ' Ye believe in God, believe also in me ' is not impossible). **2.** There is room for them in heaven ; that is, they will always be able to *abide* with God (the word ' rooms ' is cognate with the common and important Johannine verb ' to abide '). The construction and punctuation of the next sentence are doubtful. The translation in RSV is possible ; perhaps better is to take ' if it had not been so I would have told you ' as a parenthesis and to link the clauses on either side : ' . . . there are many abiding-places, for I go to prepare a place '. **3.** In any case, the departure of Jesus on this mission implies his return. The primitive Christian tradition spoke of a return of Christ : he would come as the Son of man with power and glory, and he would come soon. The latter part of this hope had already when Jn wrote been disappointed, and reconsideration of Christian eschatology was demanded (see §737*b*). In the present chapter can be seen what Jn made of the theme of the Coming of Christ. Four points may be distinguished : (*a*) Jesus will return to his friends after his crucifixion : 19. (*b*) Jesus and the Father will come to abide with those who love Jesus and keep his word : 21, 23. This is not a public manifestation (like the *parousia* in popular expectation), but a manifestation to faith. (*c*) This abiding presence of Christ is effected by the Paraclete (see below) : 16f., 26. (*d*) Though Jesus thus *comes* in the present, it remains true that he *will come*, though no attempt is made to say when this future coming will take place : 3.

In **4** the awkward wording of the text is more h
probably original than the smoother sentence of the margin. The stress on the ' way ' is important ; all Jn's religious contemporaries would have agreed with him that it was essential that the soul should find its way out of its evil environment into heaven and to God. Many shared Thomas's bewilderment. **6.** The answer of this Gospel is clear. Jesus himself is the way, the truth, and the life (for the ' I am ' formula see on 6:35). He is the truth and the life because he is the way to God, who is truth and life.

51h To know him is to achieve the goal of all those religious seekers whom Philip (8) represents. Jesus reveals the Father because he never acts or speaks from himself but is always obedient. For this reason, the works which he does are a valid witness to his person and mission (cf. 5:36), which may form the foundation, or at least the occasion, of faith.

i **12.** A new situation is introduced, however, by the impending departure of Jesus. This is not to be regretted. He will answer his disciples' prayers, and they will do 'greater works' than his. This does not mean 'more astounding miracles', but works even more plainly revealing the purpose of God—that is, the gathering of many believers into the Church. On men's side, it is required that they keep Christ's commandments (15; also 21, 23).

52a **16.** The presence of Christ will be supplied by 'another Counsellor'. The word thus translated is *paraklētos*; it is uncertain how it should be translated, and there is therefore much to be said for transliterating it as Paraclete. The same word is used in 1 Jn 2:1 of Christ. See also 14:26, 15:26, 16:7–15. Etymologically the word signifies one 'called to one's side', that is, as helper, often as legal advocate (perhaps, therefore, Counsellor). This fact however must not be allowed to outweigh three other important considerations: (*a*) In the passages where the word occurs, the Paraclete-Spirit instructs believers in the truth communicated by Jesus, and convicts the world—i.e. acts as teacher, and as counsel for the prosecution (not defence). (*b*) Cognate words are very commonly used in the NT for Christian preaching. (*c*) Cognate words are used to represent not consolation in general but the consolation to be expected in the messianic age. Accordingly, the Paraclete seems to be primarily the Spirit who operates in the Christian proclamation of the redemption effected in Jesus the Messiah, and thus confirms and instructs the Church, and pricks the conscience of the world.

b The Paraclete-sayings are sometimes regarded as insertions into discourses already complete without them, but it is probably better to regard them as an integral element in an attempt to re-express the doctrine of Christ's 'coming'. To this Jn turns again explicitly in **18f.** The language suggests the return of Jesus in the 'resurrection appearances', but these do not exhaust the meaning of 19f. **19** should perhaps be translated, '. . . because I live and you shall live', thus explaining the difference between the disciples, who will see and have fellowship with Jesus because they have received the gift of (eternal) life, and the world, which has excluded itself from this gift. This theme is developed in **21-4.** Jesus manifests himself not to the world but to his own, because he and they, together with the Father, form a circle of love and obedience, within which mutual knowledge is possible. (For the Paraclete in **26,** see above; his function here is that of teaching and reminding; he brings no new truth, but applies what Jesus has already said.)

c The chapter closes with a return to the theme of the opening verses. The departure of Jesus should mean not fear but peace and joy, for he is going from the humiliation of his earthly ministry to the glory of the Father. The departure will take place in the faith-shaking events of the crucifixion; but the disciples will be forewarned. The crucifixion is engineered by the devil (working e.g. through Judas), and he will seem to win a victory; but what appears to be his victory is in fact his defeat (12:31). So far from condemning Jesus, he is himself judged (16:11). **30.** Better than 'has no power over me' is perhaps 'has no claim on me' (reflecting a Hebrew expression). **31** can be punctuated, 'But that the world may know that I love the Father, and do as the Father has commanded me, rise, let us go hence'. However it is punctuated, the last five words (cf. Mk 14:42) give rise to a difficult problem. They suggest that at this point the party left the upper room, and that chs. 15, 16, 17 were spoken between it and the garden
beyond Kidron (18:1). This is almost inconceivable, 752c
though some believe it. Alternative views are as follows: (*a*) The difficult words must be otherwise understood; perhaps 'Let us rise and go *to the Father*'; or 'Let us go out to face and attack the ruler of this world'. (*b*) The discourses must be rearranged. The simplest form of this hypothesis is that the material should run: 13:1–31*a*; chs. 15, 16; 13:31*b*–38; chs. 14, 17. (*c*) 13:31–14:31 and chs. 15–17 should be regarded as alternative drafts of the last discourses, both of which were eventually incorporated in the Gospel. On this view, 14:31 was originally intended to precede immediately 18:1. There can be no doubt that 13:31–14:31 and chs. 15ff. have much in common.

XV 1-17 The true Vine—If either of the views d
(*b*) and (*c*) mentioned in the last note is correct, it will follow that this paragraph stands in immediate contact with the narratives of the supper. This recalls the synoptic words ascribed to Jesus in explanation of the cup: This is my blood of the covenant, which is poured out for many. Truly, I say to you, I shall not drink again of the fruit of the vine . . . (Mk 14:24f. and parallels). Other passages in the Synoptic Gospels contain symbolic language based on vines and vineyards; see Mt. 20:1–16, 21:28–32; Mk 12:1–9 and parallels; Lk. 13:6–9. All these parables recall the OT description of Israel as a vine (e.g. Ps. 80:8–15; Jer. 2:21; Ezek. 15:1–8, 19:10–14).

The Johannine discourse begins not in the character- e
istically synoptic form of a parable, but with the pronouncement 'I am'; see on 6:35. The true (cf. 1:9) vine is to be found not in Israel, but in the Messiah, the Son of God. It is he who, by the shedding of his blood (cf. Mk 14:25, the fruit of the vine), makes possible the existence of the *true* people of God, whose members are what they are in virtue not of their physical descent but of their abiding in him. As often in Jn, the Christological term draws attention rather to the work than to the essential status of Christ. The Father as 'vine-dresser' stands over the whole process, directing its outcome; Christ the vine is the means by which men are related to God. **2.** The unfruitful branches may be thought of as unbelieving Israelites, who will be cut away from God's plant (cf. Mt. 15:13; Rom. 11:17); more probably as unfaithful Christians. Fruitful branches are pruned (the word is a technical term). **3.** The disciples however have already undergone the process of purgation (cf. 13:10), of which the instrument has been the total message of divine truth (not a particular 'word') spoken by Jesus. It remains for them now to *abide* in him; apart from such abiding there is no prospect of fruitful life. **7.** Fruitful life is further defined as communion with God in which prayer is always answered. The alternative is simply excision from Christ and consequent destruction (6).

With **8** the discourse moves out of symbolism into f
direct speech. 'To bear much fruit' is to live the life of true discipleship and thereby to glorify God. The thought moves between God's initiative in love and man's loving obedience. Glorify God by fruitful discipleship: **9** but this is possible only within the mutuality of love which exists between Father and Son; **10** yet again, disciples must abide in this love by keeping God's commands.

The substance of God's command is itself love. This is the theme of **11-17.** The disciples are to love—one another (12, 13, 17); not because Jn thinks it unnecessary that Christians should love their enemies (Mt. 5:44), but because the mutual love of Christians is in a peculiar way related to the mutual love between the divine Persons (above, 9; cf. 13:34). **13.** Their love will be expressed most clearly in self-sacrifice. But the somewhat unusual expression used here recalls its use elsewhere in the Gospel (e.g. 10:11); before any of the disciples could lay down his life for another, Christ had laid down his life for them all. **16.** The initiative is therefore exclusively his; they have not

752f chosen him, but he has chosen and appointed them. They are not his slaves, but his friends, standing within the circle of mutual knowledge and love, of which Father and Son are the coincident foci. The metaphor of fruit-bearing returns once more, again in connection with prayer (16 ; cf. 7) ; and the paragraph ends with an emphatic reiteration of the command to love.

753a **18-27 The Hatred of the World**—The previous paragraph has dealt with Jesus and his friends (13ff.), the small group united to him by their love, their obedience, and their prayers. This group however lives in the *world* (cf. 1:10 etc.), and it is as characteristic of the world to hate as it is of the Christians to love. **19.** The world can only love its own, but the Christians are Christ's, so that the world's hatred of them is simply a continuation, or further expression, of its hatred of Christ (18), whom it hates precisely because he is not ' its own ' but stands over against it, bearing witness to its sin, and demonstrating a kind of life, and in particular a kind of love, which is diametrically opposed to its own. **20.** The disciples need expect no better fate than that which befalls Jesus (cf. 13:16) ; at the same time they may expect no worse success. They have kept the word of Jesus, and they will find others who will keep theirs.

The reaction of the world however is even more significant than this, for a reaction to Jesus is a reaction to God. **21, 23.** It is God whom men fail to recognise, and indeed hate. **25.** Their hatred, though real, is, as scripture attests, baseless (cf. Ps. 35:19, 69:4). Note that in 25 ' law ' means not the Pentateuch but the OT as a whole ; cf. 10:34. This uncaused hatred has been released through the ministry of Jesus, which has therefore had the effect of unveiling the sin of the Jewish people and leaving them without excuse (22, 24 ; cf. 3:19ff.).

The hatred of the world for the Church is thus traced back through Christ to God. The same path may be pursued in the opposite direction under the word witness. It is God himself who has testified to mankind through the ministry of Jesus ; **26f.** he continues to bear witness through the mission of the ' other Paraclete ', who in turn operates continuously with the ministry of the disciples. He bears witness, and they bear witness, on the basis of their long relation with Christ. The Paraclete is here said to proceed from the Father (who is thus the ultimate agent in witness-bearing).

b **XVI 1-15 The Judgment of the World**—We have learnt in the preceding paragraph that the separation of the Church from the world is a matter not of social but of ultimate theological significance. The world's attitude to the Church arises out of and reflects its attitude to God ; its condemnation of the Church means its own judgment by God. The theme of judgment is now developed, not (as in the synoptic apocalypses) in an account of what will take place at the end of world-history, but in a description of the work of the Paraclete in the life and experience of the Church.

Jesus warns his disciples of the fate they may expect ; undoubtedly there were Christians who, surprised by persecution, ' fell away ' and gave up their faith (cf. 6:61). For the threat of excommunication see on 9:22, where the same word occurs. Worse than this is in store ; in the folly of perverted loyalty and enthusiasm men will put Christians to death. Behind their enmity will lie not merely political suspicion and social friction (though of course it is easy to see these in the history of the persecutions) but failure to recognise God the Father, and Christ. This point has already been emphasised in ch. 15. To know these things in advance will be a source of strength and comfort to those who suffer ; they will know that their Master has not been surprised by opposition, and that their sufferings have a place in the fulfilment of his purpose. There was no need to tell them earlier ; Jesus himself was with them and could care for them and preserve them from despair. Now, the moment of departure to the Father, is the time for such communications. 75

There is a superficial difficulty in **5** (None of you asks me . . .) ; cf. the questions of 13:36, 14:5. But Jesus does not say, None of you *has* asked me. He is dealing with the disciples' *immediate* reaction to his announcement of his impending departure. **6.** He declares that he is going away, and immediately their hearts are full of grief ; **7** but if they had for a moment considered where Jesus was going they would have perceived that his departure was for their advantage. He was going to the Father, and only so could he send them the Paraclete (see on 14:16). We now have a fresh account of the Paraclete's work. c

8. The Paraclete will convince the world of sin, and of righteousness, and of judgment. The word ' convince ' is one which is regularly used of the operations of the conscience, and it is no doubt correct here to see a work of the Spirit upon the conscience of the world. Jn has however already pointed out that the world itself cannot receive the Paraclete (14:17), and accordingly we should think of the effect upon the world of the Spirit-inspired preaching of the Church. The sense in which the Paraclete convinces ' of ' sin, righteousness, and judgment is brought out in the following verses. ' Of ' must be understood in the light of 8:46 : the Spirit will convict the world of sin —as a fact in itself ; of righteousness—as a fact in Christ ; of judgment—as a fact in the Ruler of this world. This interpretation is the most probable, though an attractive alternative can be expressed thus : The Paraclete will convince the world of its erroneous notions in respect of sin, righteousness, and judgment. d

The Paraclete will convince the world of sin because the sin of the world has been completely manifested in its failure to believe in Jesus ; here its egocentricity became perfectly manifest in its rejection of God and assertion of itself. He will convince the world of righteousness—' because I go to the Father, and you will see me no more '. The departure of Jesus to the Father means his crucifixion and resurrection, and this twofold event means at once the offering of a perfectly obedient life and the ratification of that life by God's acceptance of the offering. He will convince the world of judgment because in the crucifixion and resurrection the Ruler of this world has been judged and thrown down ; see 12:31, 14:30. That which appeared to be the condemnation of Jesus was, by God's act in the resurrection, turned into the condemnation of his accusers, and of the great Accuser. Thus the Paraclete brings to bear upon the conscience of the world the acts of God completed in the death and resurrection of Jesus. e

12. So far Jesus may instruct the disciples ; more they cannot receive, nor is it necessary that they should. **13.** The Spirit, who will communicate divine truth (' what he hears '), will guide them into all the truth. He will announce the ' things that are to come '. It is true that, from the viewpoint of the supper, these might refer to the Passion, and that, as we have seen, the Spirit will apply the events of the death and vindication of Jesus to men's consciences. But this is not the viewpoint from which Jn writes, and ' things that are to come ' points rather to the last (eschatological) events. One would expect sin, righteousness, and judgment to be manifested at the Last Day—as indeed they will be ; but this manifestation is anticipated by the Spirit's work in the conscience. f

One would also expect the glory of Christ to be manifested at the Last Day ; but the Paraclete will anticipate this glory too, by bringing home to men the truth of what Jesus had said (not bringing out some new and independent revelation), and revealing his unity with the Father.

16-33 Victory over the World—In this last paragraph of the Upper Room discourses the characteristic dialectic language of the Gospel reappears—the going and coming of Jesus, grief and joy, tribulation 754

4a and peace, asking and receiving, seeing and not seeing, parable and open speech, faith and unbelief, the world and God.

The preceding paragraph, 1–15, deals mainly with the work of the Paraclete, who realises in the present world the effect of the Last Judgment. It would however be incorrect to draw from this observation the conclusion that Jn has lost interest in eschatology in the ordinary sense. That this is not so is shown by the opening verse of the new paragraph, **16.** As it stands, this verse is, and was no doubt intended to be, ambiguous. It might, and at first sight appears to, refer to the events immediately in prospect : Jesus will after his crucifixion disappear into the tomb, and reappear on Easter Day. But it could equally be interpreted, and in the sequel many points suggest that it should be interpreted, of the removal of Jesus from bodily sight at the Ascension and his return at the Last Day. **20.** This too is a period in which the world will rejoice in its successful attacks upon a powerless and apparently undefended Church (e.g. 15:18, 16:2), a period in which the Church will experience a sorrow which the return of Christ will turn to joy. **21.** The figure of the woman whose travail pains are turned into joy by the birth of her child recalls Isa. 26:16–19, 66:7–14, where the messianic salvation which relieves the affliction of God's people is compared to the relief and joy of childbirth. The point of this imagery is that the death and resurrection of Jesus are described as eschatological events, and his withdrawal to heaven and return in glory are set forth as prefigured and anticipated in the death and
b resurrection. **22.** 'I will see you, and your hearts will rejoice' recalls Isa. 66:14, 'You shall see, and your heart shall rejoice' ; the change from 'You shall see' to 'I will see' emphasises the initiative of Christ in the process. It is because the disciples' joy depends not on themselves but on him that no-one can take it away from them. It rests upon the reconciliation between God and man which is effected in the person of Jesus, and the visible expression of this reconciliation and communion is prayer ; it follows that the Christian life will be marked by trustful, and answered, prayer, and it is in this prayer that Christian joy is perfected. **23a.** 'To ask questions' translates a different Greek verb from 'to ask' (23*b*, 24). It is right to distinguish the two words. In the time to which these verses refer the disciples will ask (i.e. make requests), but they will not need to ask questions (such as those of 17f.), because the Spirit will lead them into all the truth.

c **25-33.** A new paragraph takes up two themes from 16–24 : (*a*) The disciples will not in the future need to ask questions (23), because Jesus will henceforth speak not in figures (cf. 10:6) but plainly (25) ; (*b*) they will be able to pray with assurance that their prayers will be answered. **27** does not mean that the Father's love is contingent upon men's love for and belief in Christ. Jn is reverting to the terms of 15:13ff., where Jesus and the disciples are seen to stand in a complete circle of love ; here it is stated that the Father himself stands within the circle. **26.** The mediatorship of Jesus does not mean any disharmony within the Godhead. **28.** Jesus comes from and departs to the Father.

d **30.** But the disciples anticipate the future, confident that they have now completely understood the truth, which is in fact still veiled in 'figures'. They 'know' and 'believe'. Their misplaced confidence must be broken before they can learn the truth. **32.** So far from having reached satisfactory knowledge and faith, they are about to desert their Master and leave him to his fate. True, he will not be alone ; but it is the Father, not they, who will accompany him.

33. This devastating disclosure is not however made with the purpose of destroying but establishing their peace. 'This' (better, 'these things') might refer simply to the preceding prediction ; they will be reassured when they recall that Jesus himself foretold their desertion. More probably it refers to the contents of the discourses as a whole, which interpret both the sufferings of Christ and the sufferings of the Church in such a way as to make peace possible. The ultimate ground of peace in the midst of tribulation is the fact that Christ has overcome the world (cf. 1:10). It is overcome (*a*) through being redeemed, and (*b*) through the overthrow of the Ruler of this world (11), who is responsible for the transformation of God's creature into his enemy. 754d

XVII The Prayer of Jesus—It was pointed out above (on 16:23f.) that communion with God reaches visible expression in the practice of prayer. This is no less true of the Son of God, whose unity with the Father is, in his incarnate life, expressed in prayer—and supremely, as far as the Fourth Gospel is concerned, in this prayer. It is for this reason that the prayer sums up what has been delivered about the work of Christ in other forms in other parts of the Gospel. It emphasises his obedience to the Father ; the fact that his obedient death reveals the glory of God ; the choice of the disciples out of the world ; the revelation made to them ; their unity in love ; and their eternal dwelling in Christ and in God. The prayer falls into four parts. e

1-5. Jesus prays that his approaching death ('the hour') may prove to be the means by which Father and Son are mutually glorified (in the completion of the work of redemption). It is by the Passion that the Son will exercise the authority he possesses over all mankind, and the purpose of his authority is the giving of eternal life to all (in Greek the neuter of the word 'all' is used to express more strongly the unity of Christ's inheritance among men) which the Father has committed to him. **3.** 'Eternal life' is here defined as arising out of and consisting in the knowledge of God. In this definition Jn reflects both the convictions of the OT (e.g. Prov. 11:9 ; Hos. 4:6 ; Hab. 2:14), continued in post-biblical Judaism, and those of Hellenistic, and particularly of Gnostic, thought (e.g. *Corpus Hermeticum*, x, 15, This alone means salvation for man, the knowledge of God). But for Jn, knowledge of the 'only true God' is incomplete without reference to 'Jesus Christ whom thou hast sent'—that is, it is only possible to speak satisfactorily of the knowledge of God in the context of the historic mission of Jesus. **4.** In this mission Jesus has glorified God by completing the task entrusted to him. **5.** It remains for the Son to return to the glory he enjoyed before his incarnate life. f

6-19. Jesus prays for his disciples. To them he has revealed the name (i.e. the nature and character) of God. What they have learnt is that the mission of Jesus is from God ; that is, that God is to be known in Jesus Christ, and that the work of Jesus is to be understood as the work of God. It is for them Jesus prays, not for the world ; not because God does not love the world (3:16), but because the only hope for the world is that it should cease to be the world (creation existing in and for itself) and become, like the disciples, the property of God and Christ (10). **11** describes the situation that will obtain between the Ascension and the *parousia*. The Son will be no longer in the world but with the Father ; the disciples will be left in the world. **12.** Henceforth therefore they will lack the direct protection that Jesus has given them (only Judas has perished, and that in fulfilment of Scripture—Ps. 41:9 ; cf. 13:18), and he prays the Father to guard them, and preserve their unity (11 ; see further below). **13.** For the joy of the disciples cf. 16:22 ; **14** for the hatred of the world cf. 15:18–27. **15.** They are in the world but not of it ; in the world they must remain, but by divine aid they will be preserved from the Evil One (rather than 'from evil' ; cf. 1 Jn 2:13f., 3:12, 5:18f.). **17ff.** In the concluding verses of this paragraph Jesus speaks of his dedication of himself to his mission, which is the ground of the dedication of the disciples to theirs. **19.** 'I consecrate myself' does not necessarily contain a reference to sacrifice and death, though this may be g

754g implied by ' for their sake '. It is the truth, the truth which consists in the word of God, in and by which the disciples are to be consecrated. It must be remembered that for Jn Jesus himself is both the Word (1:1, 14) and the Truth (14:6).

h **20-24.** The scope of the prayer is extended to later generations of believers, whose Christian life is dependent upon the apostolic proclamation of the eye-witnesses. The purpose of the mission referred to in 18 is that men who belong to the world (9) may transfer their allegiance to Christ. The content of Jesus' prayer is that all believers may be one (21; cf. 22f., 11). The way in which this prayer for unity is to be understood is made clear in the words ' As thou, Father, art in me, and I in thee '. The Father is active in the Son (14:10), and the Son abides in the Father, and has no meaning independently of him. They are one (10:30) not in identity, but in mutual love and consentient activity. The unity of the Church is correspondingly to be a unity in God; as such, it will be the supreme human testimony to the truth of the claim that Jesus is God's authorised emissary. Cf. what was said on 15:12–17; the disciples form a circle of love which includes also both the Father and the Son. The existence of any part of this circle bears witness to the whole. **22.** The glory given by the Father to the Son and by him to the Church is the glory which is completely manifested in the crucifixion and resurrection; the lot of the Church in this world is therefore most fully realised in affliction and in sacrificial witness to the truth.

In 21, 23 the goal is that the *world* may believe and know. Contrast 16:33; but in fact the two passages are not inconsistent, for when the world recognises the truth about Jesus it ceases to be the world, and thus, *as world*, is overcome. Finally, **24,** believers are not to be left in the world (11); they are to be with Christ (cf. 14:3), sharing the eternal love and glory of the Godhead.

i **25f.** Jesus reviews the results of his mission. He came into a world ignorant of God with the knowledge the world lacked. His disciples do not, for they cannot, share his immediate knowledge of the Father, but they recognise that Jesus has been sent from God, and that he therefore is the Revealer. They have accepted the revelation that he gives; but the intended result of this disclosure is not the production of a circle of gnostics, but of a group of men who love God and love one another. Love, not gnosticism, is the goal of God's act of revelation and redemption in Christ.

755a **XVIII 1-11 The Arrest**—This narrative is closely, though not precisely, linked with what goes before (' when Jesus had spoken these words '), and leads immediately into the Passion narrative. There are fairly close parallels in the Synoptic Gospels (e.g. Mk 14:43–50), but the Johannine story differs from the synoptic in the following important points: (*a*) Topographical and other details are introduced. The names Kidron (cf. 2 Sam. 15:23 etc.), Peter, and Malchus (10) were probably drawn by Jn from tradition, since it is hard to see that they serve any theological purpose. Whether they are further to be regarded as legendary additions to the tradition is a question scarcely capable of certain answer. (*b*) The Romans are introduced at the beginning of the Passion narrative (3, ' band '; 12, ' captain '; these are technical terms denoting a cohort—nominally 600 men—and a tribune of the Roman army); in the Synoptic Gospels they do not appear till a much later stage, when Jesus is brought by the Jews before Pilate. It is plausibly argued that Roman authorities, if they had once laid their hands on Jesus, would not have handed him over to a native court; this Johannine variant therefore seems secondary. (*c*) The synoptic narrative of the agony in Gethsemane is entirely omitted, though 11 (cf. Mk 14:36) suggests that Jn knew it. It may be right here to compare Jn's omission of the Transfiguration. Jn desired to suggest not that there was in the ministry of Jesus *one* moment of glory, and *another* of costly and sacrificial obedience, but that glory and obedience together marked every step he took. (*d*) Throughout Jn emphasises the authority of Jesus. It is he, not Judas or the tribune, who takes the initiative. He goes out voluntarily to his arrest; he questions his captors, **6** and fells them to the ground with a word; he rebukes and also preserves his disciples. (*e*) He thus fulfils (9) his own promise (17:12) that he will keep his own from destruction, or rather foreshadows by this act of self-sacrifice which saves the disciples from arrest and punishment the full meaning of his mission.

3. The ' officers ' who join the Roman cohort would be the Temple guard, a sort of military police. b

5. On ' I am ' see on 6:35, 8:24. Here it need not mean more than ' I am Jesus of Nazareth, the man whom you seek '. Cf. 9:9.

12-27 Jesus, Caiaphas, and Peter—In this paragraph, at least two narratives are woven together. c One tells a straightforward story: at the time of the arrest two disciples followed Jesus; one was known at the high priest's palace and was thus able to secure admission for himself and for his companion Peter; what becomes of the disciple ' known to the high priest ' we do not hear, but Peter abuses his privilege by vehemently denying his connection with Jesus. It is true that his three denials are divided, one (17) taking place before the high priest's interrogation of Jesus, and two (25ff.) after it, but there is nothing unnatural or difficult in this. The other narrative recounts what happened to Jesus himself, and is by no means so easy to put together. **13.** Jesus is first taken to Annas, described as father-in-law of Caiaphas the high priest (cf. 11:49). **19.** After Peter's first denial we read that the high priest (who according to Jn's own account was Caiaphas) questions Jesus. **22** shows that a dispute with the high priest is still in mind. But in **24** ' Annas sent him bound to Caiaphas the high priest '. These statements clearly do not make a consecutive narrative; it is no doubt for this reason that a few textual authorities alter the order of the verses; e.g. the Sinaitic Syriac has the order 13, 24, 14, 15, 19–23, 16–18. A similar reconstruction was suggested by Luther, and many modern scholars have in various ways attempted to improve upon the traditional text. There is no doubt that the text is difficult, but the difficulty may go back to Jn himself. It may ultimately be due to the fact that the Marcan Passion narrative (on which Jn was probably dependent, though some would deny this) suggests that there were two Jewish trials (see Mk 14:53, 15:1). Jn may have developed this hint without noting that he had not been entirely consistent in detail.

The hearing before the Jewish authorities is not d dealt with as fully as in Mk 14:53–64, possibly because Jn has already (chs. 7–10) brought out the issues between Jesus and the Jews, and accordingly wishes to develop a different point by expanding the conversation between Jesus and Pilate (see below). The relation between Annas and Caiaphas is not mentioned elsewhere, but is by no means improbable. In **14** Jn recalls the fundamental interpretation of Jesus' death (11:50ff.).

15. The ' other disciple ' is sometimes identified with e the beloved disciple (13:23). This is possible but by no means certain. It is in fact not probable that John the son of Zebedee would be ' known to ' the high priest, for the word used suggests a closer acquaintance than is probable between a provincial fisherman and the head of Church and State. **16.** It is uncertain whether the last words should be translated ' he brought in ' or ' she admitted ' Peter.

It may be implied by 19ff. that the hearing was informal; if formal, the high priest should not have addressed to Jesus direct questions which might have led him to convict himself. The verses are perhaps intended by Jn to bear witness to the impasse which existed between Jesus and the authorities of his own race: it remained for him only to deal with Pilate.

55f **XVIII 28–XIX 16 Jesus and Pilate**—In this long paragraph, which begins with the transference of Jesus from Caiaphas's court to Pilate's, and ends with the final decision to crucify him, Jesus holds long conversations with Pilate, and Pilate speaks with the Jewish leaders; but Jesus himself has no more dealings with his own people. The fundamental points in the story are shared by Jn with Mk: the examination of Jesus before Pilate, Pilate's unwillingness to condemn Jesus, the reference to Barabbas and to the custom of releasing one prisoner at Passover, the scourging, the mockery, the clamour for the death of Jesus, and the handing over for crucifixion. Another common point of great importance is the theme of the discussion between Jesus and Pilate—kingship. It is probable that Mk is Jn's source, and that, though Jn has (as will appear) brought out a number of theological points more clearly, he has not improved upon Mk from the historical point of view. This is shown e.g. by 19:1–3, where the scourging and mockery (which are intelligible enough in Mk) appear unmotivated, since at this point Pilate has decided to release Jesus. Jn retains the narratives, partly because they were in his source, and partly because they helped to prepare for the theological hints which follow (see below).

g **28.** The Jews who brought Jesus from Caiaphas to Pilate would not themselves enter the Praetorium, because they intended later in the same (solar) day to eat the Passover. This verse brings out clearly Jn's dating of the Passion, which differs from Mk's (see on 13:1). The point however is by no means clear, since there seems to be no reason why even if the men had entered heathen precincts they should not have taken the required bath and been 'clean' in time to take part in the Paschal meal.

h **29ff.** Pilate's attitude to the Jews is surprising, especially as **31** (in the Johannine context) shows that Pilate does not know that a capital charge is involved. He simply wishes a Jewish case—probably of no great importance—to be tried in a Jewish court. **30** shows a hardly credible insolence, and throws doubt upon Jn's editing of his Marcan material. The question whether Jn is right in putting into Jewish mouths the statement (31) that 'it is not lawful for us to put any man to death' has been much disputed, and agreement has not been reached. If the Jews had themselves put Jesus to death the method employed would have been not crucifixion but stoning; hence 32 (cf. 12:32f.).

56a **33.** Pilate re-enters the Praetorium and his first conversation with Jesus ensues (33–8). It deals with kingship. Pilate begins with a direct question; but the issue is not so simple as that suggests. **34.** What prompted it? It was a Jewish, not a Roman charge; a Roman can only inquire what Jesus has done to incur hatred and justify the accusation. **36.** The reply is not direct. A kingdom may be 'of this world', or not. If Jesus' kingdom were of this world he and his followers would take appropriate action against the Jews; but this they have not done. It follows that his kingdom has a different origin. **37.** It also follows that he is a king, as Pilate concludes, with astonished emphasis on 'you'—'So *you* are a king'. Jesus does not deny this definition of his person, but it is not his own ('*You* say . . .'). His own account of his mission is different. He has come to bear witness to the truth; not to assert his own sovereignty, but to reveal God, whose kingdom is the truth faintly adumbrated by every earthly kingdom (cf. 19:11). Only those who are from the beginning directed by the truth can recognise it; it follows that Pilate need not stay for an answer to his question (38), What is truth?

b He is nevertheless convinced of Jesus' political innocence, and sees a means of releasing him in the custom (Mk 15:6 and parallels; otherwise unattested) of freeing a prisoner at Passover. Surely to release the 'King of the Jews' would be a popular step! But Jesus is not the kind of king the Jews desire. They prefer Barabbas the robber, that is, probably, the armed rebel (cf. Mk 15:7). **19:1.** Surprisingly (see above), however, Pilate has Jesus scourged, and the mockery follows. The crown of thorns should be thought of not as an instrument of torture but, like the purple robe, as a mocking mark of kingship. The mockery makes it very probable that the charge brought to Pilate by the Sanhedrin was, as Mk but not Jn states, that Jesus claimed to be Messiah, i.e. king of the Jews. 756b

5. Jn has already developed the theme of kingship theologically (18:33–8); he now develops it dramatically. The divine king is introduced as the man. But there is truth in this, though Pilate is unaware of it (cf. 11:51), for Jesus is the Man, the Son of man; that is, the heavenly and representative Man, who is also the Redeemer. c

But he is not a man whom the people want. They are set upon crucifixion, and Pilate, still convinced of Jesus' innocence, wishes (in Jn metaphorically) to wash his hands of the matter. **6** might well have been the end of the proceedings, but a further theological theme is raised in **7**: Jesus has not only claimed to be the messianic king, he has made himself out to be Son of God. This claim frightens Pilate, and leads to his second conversation with Jesus (8–11). His question, 'Where are you from?' recalls Lk. 23:6, but must here be understood in the light of the claim to be Son of God, and of passages such as 3:8, 8:14, 9:29. It is for this reason that Jesus does not answer. There is an answer to the question, but it is not one that Pilate can understand. **10.** Jesus' silence however is surprising on ordinary terms; a prisoner should not treat in this cavalier fashion one who has absolute authority over life and death. **11.** But that is just the point: Pilate has at most a secondary, derivative authority; Jesus has the authority of one who is from God, the source of all authority. **11b.** 'He who delivered me to you' is probably Judas (cf. 6:64, 71, etc., where the same word is used); possibly the Jews (or Caiaphas; cf. 18:30, 35).

Pilate is still anxious to release Jesus; but the argument of **12b** determines his action. If he releases Jesus he will be delated as tolerating *maiestas*, or treason. **13.** He brings Jesus out to the Pavement, Gabbatha (for suggestions with regard to this locality see most recently W. F. Albright in *The Background of the NT and its Eschatology* (ed. by D. Daube and W. D. Davies (1956), 158f.)), and sits on the judgment-seat. It would be possible to translate, 'made him (i.e. Jesus) sit on the judgment-seat'. This would accentuate the irony of 'Here is your King!' (14, cf. 5). Pilate's hand has been forced; but he in turn provokes the Jews to blasphemy and apostasy (cf. Jg. 8:23; 1 Sam. 8:7: there is danger lest even a Jewish king should obscure the divine sovereignty under which Israel lives). d

Note the careful statement of date and hour in **14.**

XIX 17–30 The Crucifixion and Death of Jesus—Once more, the Johannine narrative is substantially the same as the Marcan, but certain differences stand out. **17.** In Jn, Simon of Cyrene (Mk 15:21) disappears, and Jesus carries his own cross; **22** Pilate refuses to alter the wording of the *titulus* on the cross; **24** the soldiers' gaming for the clothes of Jesus is given explicit scriptural attestation; **26f.** Jesus commits to each other as mother and son his own mother and the beloved disciple; **28** his thirst and the draught of vinegar are also given specific reference to the OT; there is no mocking by the onlookers, and **30** instead of a cry of dereliction (Mk 15:34) Jesus utters at the moment of death an affirmation that his work is complete. e

It is in general easy to understand the motivation of these changes. The addition of OT references causes no difficulty. In the matter of the *titulus* Jn emphasises once more the theme of kingship, which has already been underlined in conversation between Jesus and Pilate (18:33–8). There must have been f

756f many trilingual notices in Jerusalem (cf. those that warned Gentiles not to transgress the appointed limits in the Temple); the effect of 20 is to proclaim the kingship of Jesus to the whole world. The objection made by the Jews is readily intelligible; not only was Pilate suggesting that a dead man on a cross was the only kind of king they were likely to get, he was implying an act of sedition on the part of the nation as a whole. It is again perhaps an aspect of kingship when Jesus appears, much more clearly than in Mk, to be in control of the events in which he takes part. Perhaps for this reason Jn notes that Jesus carried his own cross, though here the Fathers may have been right in comparing Jesus with Isaac, who also (Gen. 22:6) carried the means for his own sacrifice. Jesus also, even when on the cross, makes arrangements for his mother's future. It is possible that Jn saw in this event a further theological point—the incorporation of the ancient church of Israel into the new apostolic community—but unlikely that he simply created the story in order to make this point. Above all, it is to be noted that, in this narrative, Jesus dies, one might almost say, at his own volition, and ends his life with a word which means probably not 'Life is ended' but 'The work is done'.

g A few points of detail call for attention. 'Skull-place', Golgotha (17), is not certainly identified. The name probably refers to the shape of the hill. Jn shows no interest in the two robbers (contrast Lk. 23:39–43); he mentions them in view of 31–7. The publication of a *titulus*, or public notice, at an execution (19) was common, and the clothes of the victim seem to have been a perquisite of the soldiers who carried out an execution. In 25 it is probable that Jn refers to four women, though the names can be arranged to refer to three, or even two. In 29, 'hyssop' should be read, with the MSS; 'javelin' is a conjecture, superficially attractive because hyssop is an impossible material for proffering a sponge, but to be rejected in view of the Paschal associations (cf. Exod. 12:22) of the narrative as a whole.

h **31-42 The Burial**—Jn records the deposition and burial of the body of Jesus more elaborately than any other evangelist, though the main outline of his narrative is similar to Mk's.

31. The day of the crucifixion was the 'Preparation'—that is, the day before the Sabbath (not as in 19:14 the day before Passover). It cannot however have been simply for this reason that the Jews wished the bodies to be taken down, since the law of Dt. 21:22f. applies to any day. Nevertheless, what would have been undesirable on any day would be doubly so on the Sabbath, especially as this was a great Sabbath—either because (on the Johannine dating) it was the first day of Passover, or (on the synoptic dating) because it was the Sabbath on which the Omer sheaf was presented (Lev. 23:11). The *crurifragium*, or breaking of the limbs, was sometimes an independent punishment, and was sometimes combined with crucifixion.

757a It was unnecessary to break Jesus' legs; he had died much earlier than many victims of crucifixion. Instead a soldier pierced his side with his lance. In both these events Jn finds theological significance. **36.** The fact that no bone of Jesus was broken was the fulfilment of prophecy. It is possible that the reference here is to Ps. 34:20, which speaks of God's care for the righteous; more probable that Jn is thinking of Exod. 12:46; Num. 9:12, that is, of the Passover regulations. Jesus died as the true Passover. **37.** The lance-thrust also fulfils prophecy: Zech. 12:10, which Jn quotes in agreement with the Hebrew against the LXX. But he notes also that it resulted in the effusion of blood and water (34). The next verse (35) shows that Jn regarded this as a fact of great importance, and as a fact rather than a mere symbol. The event Jn describes is physiologically possible, and it is probable that his first intention was to demonstrate (perhaps against docetic heretics) that Jesus really died; his death was not a matter of appearance only. It is, however, further probable that Jn saw in what he narrated primarily as a historical fact a second meaning. Water and blood are in this Gospel significant words; see especially 3:5, 4:14, 6:53ff., 7:37f., 13:5; cf. 1 Jn 5:6, 8. Christ is the dispenser of the water and blood by which men are regenerated and live, and these issue precisely from his death, which is the means by which salvation and eternal life are achieved. It is, further, true that water and blood suggest baptism and the eucharist respectively; these sacraments find their meaning only in the death of Jesus which is the life of men.

b The historical facts just discussed are vouched for by a witness (35; cf. 21:24). It is a reasonable guess that he was the beloved disciple (19:26), but this cannot be taken as certain. Whoever he was, he *saw* and *testified*; and 'he' knows that what he says is true. It is not clear who 'he' is in this sentence. The most natural suggestion is that it refers back to the witness; some have taken it to refer to the writer, others even to God or to Christ. It is not claimed here that the witness was the writer of the book, but that he supplied this piece of information. The aim of his witness is not simply 'that you too may believe that blood and water issued from Jesus' side', but 'that you too may become believers', i.e. Christians (cf. 20:31). For the bearing of this verse on the question of authorship see §735*c*.

c **38ff.** Jn proceeds to the burial. Joseph of Arimathaea (Mk 15:43), who asks Pilate for the body of Jesus, is joined by Nicodemus (3:1), and together they lay Jesus in a tomb situated in a garden near the place of crucifixion. The burial, done in the Jewish style, is carried out in the most sumptuous manner. **41.** The tomb was new, as befitted the body of Jesus.

Jn adds to Mk's account of Joseph that he was a secret disciple. It is possible that he intends that this should be understood of Nicodemus also, though neither 3:1–15 nor 7:50f. implies his conversion.

d **XX 1-18 The empty Tomb and first Resurrection Appearance**—In this narrative, which shows occasional contacts with the Marcan fragment (Mk 16:1–8), Jn skilfully combines the tradition of the empty tomb with that of resurrection appearances.

e Mary Magdalene arrives at the tomb very early on Sunday morning. Seeing the stone removed, she reports this suspicious circumstance (she evidently—2, 13—suspects tomb-breaking, a not uncommon crime) to two leading disciples, Peter and the disciple whom Jesus loved. **4-6.** Of these, the beloved disciple proves the swifter runner but Peter the more impetuous investigator. There is little to see in the tomb: the linen cloths (19:40), and, by itself, the napkin which had been wrapped round Jesus' head (cf. 11:44). Comparison with the resurrection of Lazarus might suggest (though it is well to draw such conclusions with great caution) that the body of Jesus had in some way passed through the cloths in which it had been wrapped, leaving them empty. **8.** It is implied that Peter observed what was to be seen but did not grasp its significance; not so the beloved disciple, who 'saw and believed'—that is, believed that Jesus had risen from the dead. When Jn wrote, it was common Christian conviction that the resurrection had been foretold in the OT (e.g. 1 C. 15:4); the disciple, however, the first Christian believer, was dependent solely upon what he saw (see below on 20:29). It is neither said nor implied that the witness of his eyes was or should have been unnecessary. 'Saw' does not empty 'believed' of its meaning; nothing he saw or could have seen could have proved that Jesus had been raised up, and an empty tomb does not prove Christianity to be true. Yet faith rests upon the historical testimony of those who saw and bore witness.

f **11-16.** The men withdraw, but Mary remains at the tomb. When she looks in, it is no longer empty. To the angels who appear, she repeats the story about the violation of the tomb. The angels however are

57f forgotten and disappear from the story as she turns and sees one whom she takes to be the gardener (cf. 19:41). She fails to recognise the appearance of Jesus, but not his voice as he calls her by name. The good shepherd calls his own sheep by name, and they hear his voice (10:3 ; contrast 18:37f.). **17.** Jesus' reply to her exclamation calls for some explanation. 'Do not hold me' represents a Greek sentence which means literally either 'Stop touching me' (implying that Mary was touching him) or 'Do not attempt to touch me' (implying that she was about to touch). The prohibition itself contrasts with 20:27, and the reason given for it is obscure : 'I have not yet ascended to the Father'. It seems to imply that there will be a later moment, after the Ascension, when touching will be permissible. This seems hardly intelligible, though some have held that Jn believed the Ascension to have taken place between 20:17 and 20:27. This view finds support in the fact that in 20:22 the Spirit is bestowed on the disciples ; cf. 16:7, where it is pointed out that the coming of the Spirit is dependent on the departure of Jesus. The return of Jesus to the Father is indeed an essential element in Jn's thought ; see 3:13, 6:62, 7:33, 39, 13:1, 3, 14:4, 28, 16:5, 17, 28, 17:13. Only in this return are the ministry and the passion complete. In general, Jn does not draw a clear distinction between resurrection and ascension, but in the resurrection narratives he is compelled by circumstances to do so, though not to the extent of providing, as Lk. does, a separate Ascension narrative. Perhaps the best way of interpreting 17 is to suppose that the reference to 'my brethren' is parenthetical, so that the verse may be paraphrased : 'Stop touching me ; it is true that I have not yet ascended, but I am about to do so ; this is what you must tell my brothers'.

In the last words of 17 Jesus distinguishes between himself and his relation to God, and his disciples and their relation to God. To each, God is 'God and Father' ; he calls them his brothers. Yet he is God's Son eternally ; they are God's children only through him (1:12).

g **19-31 Second and third Appearances of Jesus**—After Mary's report (20:18) the day passes ; the disciples, afraid of the Jews who have slain their Lord and cannot be well disposed towards them, meet behind locked doors ; and Jesus (it is implied that he has passed through the doors miraculously) joins them. Jn does not define the meaning of the term disciples. He uses the word frequently, and it certainly does not always refer to the Twelve (whom, as in 24, he sometimes mentions explicitly). The only synoptic parallel to this incident (Lk. 24:36ff.) implies a larger group than the Eleven alone (Lk. 24:33, the Eleven and those who were with them). The description however of Thomas as 'one of the Twelve' (24) might suggest that those to whom the appearance of 19–23 was granted were the Ten. But uncertainty must remain, and it is impossible to assert that the words of 21ff. were spoken to the apostles alone. See below.

Jesus greets his disciples with the common Semitic salutation, but probably a fuller Christian sense is to be found in the word 'peace' (cf. 14:27, 16:33). **20.** He shows his wounded members, no doubt for identification, and to show that his body is 'real' and not a phantom. **20b** contains a verbal allusion to 16:22.

58a **21.** Jesus repeats his greeting ; and transfers to his disciples—to the Church—his own mission ; cf. 4:38, 13:(16), 20, 17:18. It is because he has been sent from the Father that the work of Jesus has its significance ; it is because they have been sent by Jesus that the subsequent work of the disciples has meaning and effect. As in the mission of Jesus men were confronted by the living God (e.g. 1:18, 14:9), so in the apostolic mission of the Church they will be confronted by Jesus the Son of God. This fact may be illustrated by the Rabbinic use of the Hebrew verb *shālaḥ* (to send) and the derived noun which means 'accredited envoy', but it is in no way dependent on 758a
this use—it arises simply out of the words of 21.

22. The Church then inherits a mission from Christ ; b
but it is not a mission which it can perform unaided. The moment has now been reached when the promise of the gift of the Spirit, dependent upon the exaltation and departure of Jesus (7:39, 16:7) can be fulfilled. 'He breathed into them' recalls verbally the Greek of Gen. 2:7 : this is the moment of the new creation, when a new humanity comes into being through the work of the second Adam. It is further (see on 16:8–11) the Holy Spirit who produces the effect of the apostolic preaching in convicting the world of sin, righteousness, and judgment. This operation is treated more explicitly in **23.** This verse can be taken most simply to refer to baptism, in which sins are remitted ; if it is withheld, sins are retained. But the verse ought not to be restricted to this one interpretation. The ministry of Jesus himself had the twofold effect of remitting and retaining sins (see 3:19ff., 9:40f.). It is this ministry that is perpetuated in the work of the Church, and in the Church's mission the same twofold effect is observed (e.g. 1 C. 1:23f. ; 2 C. 2:15f.). This verse teaches that this twofold effect is not arbitrary or fortuitous, but of absolute, divine significance.

24-29. On the first Easter Sunday one of the Twelve, c
Thomas (11:16, 14:5, 21:2), was missing. He felt forcibly the points noted above on 20 ; it was absolutely necessary to establish, by physical tests, the identity of the risen Jesus with the incarnate and crucified Jesus, and the reality of the risen body. On the next Sunday (the placing of the resurrection appearances on Sundays may reflect the Church's habit of worship on that day) Jesus again came, in the same way, to his disciples. He offers Thomas the test he requires ; but Thomas, without availing himself of the opportunity, makes the supreme confession of faith. This is Jn's final Christological pronouncement. 'Lord' recalls the early confession of faith, Jesus is Lord ; 'God' is the ultimate deduction that must be drawn when 'Lord' is taken seriously (as in the OT) ; cf. 1:1, 5:18, etc.

Johannine Christology has reached its climax ; d
but this does not mean that Thomas has reached the climax of Christian blessedness. His faith rests upon sight (the question in RSV—'Have you believed?'—could equally well and perhaps better be taken as a statement) ; future generations of Christians, who do not see the risen Christ, as Thomas did, will believe on the basis of the apostolic testimony alone. They are not for this reason to be pitied ; they are blessed. Their faith is not of the kind that rests upon signs and wonders (4:48), but clings to the word of Christ alone (cf. 1 Pet. 1:8).

It can scarcely be doubted that 30f. form the end e
of the Gospel as originally planned. On the origin of ch. 21 see below. For the meaning of 'signs' see on 2:11. John's purpose in writing has been to evoke and foster (this verse does not enable us to answer the question whether he wrote for believers or unbelievers) faith in Jesus as Christ and Son of God. This faith is the way to life.

XXI The Appendix—The Gospel comes to a close f
with the statement of its purpose in 20:30f. Who added ch. 21, and why? It is evident that the Gospel was never published without its last chapter, and this fact, together with its stylistic resemblance to the rest of the Gospel, suggests that it was a supplement added by the evangelist himself. Again this view have been urged (*a*) certain stylistic differences, more perceptible in Greek than in English, between chs. 1–20 and ch. 21 ; (*b*) the fact that the author would probably have felt free to remove the concluding verses 20:30f. and place them after the supplement, whereas a second writer would not ; and (*c*) certain differences between the eschatological outlook of 21:20–3 and that of the rest of the Gospel (see below). Students of the Gospel are by no means agreed on this issue.

758g **1-14 The Appearance by the Lake**—A group of seven disciples (of whom the beloved disciple—7—was one; he may but need not have been one of the sons of Zebedee), led by Peter, make for the Sea of Tiberias (6:1) to fish. Their action is difficult to understand after the events of 20:19–29; what follows would be more intelligible as a first appearance than a third (14). Hitherto the Johannine appearances have been in Jerusalem (like the Lucan; Mt., and apparently Mk, place them in Galilee).

h **3**. The fishing has been unsuccessful. **6**. Acting on Jesus' instructions, however, the disciples make a huge catch. This miracle closely resembles that of Lk. 5:4–7, which does not take place in a resurrection appearance. It prompts the beloved disciple to recognise the Lord. As at 20:8, he is the quicker in perception, but, as at 20:6, Peter is the more impulsive in action. With natural Jewish respectfulness he seizes his outer garment and swims to shore. The rest follow, dragging the net which they had been unable to draw.

9. Arrived on land they find preparations for a meal afoot. There is already fish on the fire, but they are invited to add from their own stock of 153 large fish, and to join Jesus (there is now no doubt who he is) at breakfast.

i How is this story to be interpreted? It may of course be a straightforward historical narrative. The disciples may have despaired of their mission, returned to Galilee, gone fishing, seen Jesus, caught 153 fish (which, in accordance with custom, they would count and perhaps remember), and eaten breakfast. It seems however probable that the author intended at least some features to be taken allegorically. (*a*) A meal of bread and fish recalls 6:11, and both meals have probably eucharistic associations. (*b*) The catch of fish seems to represent the result of the apostolic mission. The number 153 may suggest the sum total of believers (either because it was believed that there were 153 species of fish, or because 153 = 17 + 16 + 15 + . . . + 3 + 2 + 1, and 17 = 10 + 7, the mark of perfection and completeness). **11**. Notwithstanding the number and variety of the fish, the net did not break: the Church contains all sorts and conditions of men.

759a **15-25 Jesus, Peter, and the beloved Disciple**—The first paragraph (15–19) deals with the reinstatement of Peter, who, after his threefold denial, three times declares his love for Jesus. In the first two questions 'love' represents the Greek word *agapan*; in the last question, and in all the answers, it represents *philein*. It is sometimes supposed that a difference is intended, but this seems unlikely; cf. e.g. 14:23 (*agapan*) and 16:27 (*philein*). 'More than these' probably means 'more than these other disciples do' rather than 'more than you love this fishing-gear, which represents your secular life'; both meanings, however, are possible. Peter, on the ground of his love, is installed as shepherd. For Jesus and his sheep, see 10:1–16, 26f.; for Christian ministers as shepherds, see Ac. 20:28f.; Eph. 4:11; 1 Pet. 5:2ff. **19**. Peter moreover will not only be a pastor, he will be a martyr; that is, he can now *follow* Jesus (as in 13:36ff. he had been told he could not). He will glorify God by the obedience and faith shown in his death. Whether **18** implies death by crucifixion is not quite certain, but probable. When this chapter was written Peter had in all probability already suffered, and this passage may be taken as early and good evidence for his martyrdom.

b **20**. The predictions about Peter break off, and interest is turned to the beloved disciple. He appears, and the word is surely significant, already *following*. Martyrdom is perhaps the clearest and simplest way of following Christ and bearing witness to him, but it is not the only way. The beloved disciple also follows, and bears witness. **22**. Peter's inquiry is met with rebuff. Whatever be God's will for the beloved disciple is no business of Peter's; it is his to follow, and not to concern himself with the destiny of others. 759 But in the form in which the rebuke was cast was a reference to the coming of Christ, and this, the writer tells us, was misunderstood. Men expected the *parousia* to take place before this disciple's death; it seems probable that his death had already happened when this chapter was written and had caused disappointment and distress. The writer (who deals with the eschatological hope and its postponement in what seems a more material way than that in which these are handled in the rest of the Gospel) explains that no prediction had been made at all; Jesus had said only, 'What if . . . ?'.

Peter, then, is to follow, to be a shepherd, and to c bear witness by his death. The beloved disciple also follows, and bears witness, though in a different way. His witness consists in attesting the truth of the gospel story, and indeed in writing it (**24**). 'These things' may refer to the last paragraph (15–23), to the whole of ch. 21, or, more probably, to the whole Gospel. This verse was presumably added to the Gospel by those who published it, in the belief that the book had been written by the beloved disciple. It recalls 19:35, where however it is not said that the witness *wrote*. It is possible that here 'has written' means 'has caused to be written' (cf. 19:19), but in the absence of further evidence this cannot be regarded as a likely solution of the problem. Who 'we' are, is another problem that cannot be solved. We may think of the church in Ephesus, if that is where the Gospel was written, and recall the statements in Clement of Alexandria and the Muratorian Canon that others encouraged Jn to write and assisted him. Cf. also 1:14; the Gospel as a whole conveys the witness of the apostles which is now the witness of the Church, which can still use the first-person plural: We beheld.

For **25** cf. 20:30.

VII 53-VIII 11 The Woman taken in Adultery— d
It is certain that this narrative is not an original part of the Gospel. It is omitted by most of the earliest and best Greek MSS, by the oldest versions (Syriac, Coptic, and some of the Old Latin), and by the earliest Fathers. The MSS which do contain the paragraph do not all place it at this point; some even place it after Lk. 21:38. Yet the story is probably ancient; there is evidence that Papias recorded a story 'about a woman accused in the Lord's presence of many sins'.

VII 53, VIII 1 suggest a setting in the synoptic record of the last week in Jerusalem (cf. Mk 11:11f., 19f.; Lk. 21:37). It is significant that the woman was 'caught in the act' (4) of adultery; eye-witnesses were necessary if punishment was to be inflicted for adultery. 'In the law' (5): cf. Lev. 20:10; Dt. 22:22ff. According to the Mishnah, stoning is the punishment when the woman is betrothed, strangling when she is married.

It is fruitless to ask what Jesus wrote on the ground (6); he simply refuses to pass judgment. His answer (7) is designed to have the effect described in 9. He does not condemn (11); he came not to condemn but to save (3:17, 8:15). Yet his very presence has the effect of judging the self-righteous accusers (8:16; cf. 9:39ff.). For his last words to the woman cf. 5:14.

Bibliography—Commentaries: C. K. Barrett (1955); W. Bauer, HNT (1933); J. H. Bernard, ICC (1928); R. Bultmann, Mey. (1957); E. C. Hoskyns (1947); M. J. Lagrange, EBib. (1947); R. H. Lightfoot (1956); A. Loisy, ed. 1 (1903), ed. 2 (much altered) (1921); G. H. C. MacGregor, Moffatt NT Commentary (1928); H. Odeberg (1929); A. Schlatter (1948); R. H. Strachan (1941); H. Strathmann, NTD (1951); W. Temple (1945); J. Wellhausen (1908); B. F. Westcott (1880, 1908).

Other Literature: B. W. Bacon, *Fourth Gospel in Research and Debate* (1918), *The Gospel of the Hellenists,* ed. C. H. Kraeling (1933) ; C. F. Burney, *Aramaic Origin of the Fourth Gospel* (1922) ; C. H. Dodd, *Interpretation of the Fourth Gospel* (1953) ; J. Drummond, *Character and Authorship of the Fourth Gospel* (1903) ; P. Gardner-Smith, *St John and the Synoptic Gospels* (1938) ; J. R. Harris, *Origin of the Prologue to St John's Gospel* (1917) ; W. F. Howard, *Christianity according to St John* (1943), *Fourth Gospel in recent Criticism and Interpretation* (rev. ed. 1955) ; E. K. Lee, *Religious Thought of St John* (1950) ; C. Maurer, *Ignatius von Antiochien und das Johannesevangelium* (1949) ; P. H. Menoud, *L'Évangile de Jean d'après les Recherches récentes* (1947) ; E. Percy, *Untersuchungen über den Ursprung der johanneischen Theologie* (1939) ; W. Sanday, *Criticism of the Fourth Gospel* (1905) ; J. N. Sanders, *The Fourth Gospel in the early Church* (1943) ; E. Schweizer, *EGO EIMI* (1939) ; E. F. Scott, *The Fourth Gospel : its Purpose and Theology* (1906).

THE APOSTOLIC AGE AND THE LIFE OF PAUL

By W. D. DAVIES

760a By the Apostolic Age we mean roughly the period in the history of the Christian Church from A.D. 30–100. (The historicity of Ac. is here treated with respect. For a radical criticism of this position, see John Knox, *Chapters in a Life of Paul* (1950) ; for a defence, G. H. C. Macgregor, IB ix (1954).) Behind it, as its background, stands the life, death and resurrection of Jesus of Nazareth ; and particularly the last, because it was the encounter with the Risen Lord which impelled his scattered followers to reassemble at Jerusalem. Ac. makes the disciples remain in Jerusalem after the Resurrection. In Mt., Mk, Jn they are in Galilee whence, we presume, they returned to Jerusalem. That there developed a Galilean Christianity as urged by E. Lohmeyer, *Galiläa und Jerusalem* (1936), remains conjectural. (See G. B. Caird, *The Apostolic Age*, 88f. On the Resurrection as such, see R. Niebuhr, *The Resurrection and History* (1957).) But to reassemble was not enough. Although it is possible to over-emphasise the despair following the death of Jesus, the Apostolic Age, strictly speaking, began when the disciples ceased to be merely an expectant enclave, and became a witnessing community. According to Ac. 2, this happened with the coming of the Spirit on the day of Pentecost. And the community that emerged from the experiences of that day, marked by baptism, teaching, fellowship, breaking of bread, prayers, and above all by the presence of the Spirit and communal sharing of goods, was well-knit and self-conscious, under the leadership chiefly of Peter.

b These main forms are noted in summaries of the life of the primitive Church which the author of Ac., who may have inherited them, gives in Ac. 2:42–7, 4:32–5, 5:12–16 and other shorter ones (see on these P. Benoît in *Aux Sources de la Tradition Chrétienne* (1950)), but it would be erroneous to think of it chiefly as an organisation : it was more an organism. The rudiments of order were there, but far more characteristic was the ardour of life under the guidance of the Spirit. Nevertheless, this did not signify the mild anarchy of a horde of undisciplined enthusiasts. The first believers were not neophytes in religion. Belonging, many of them, to the ' pious of the land ', they were not only acquainted with synagogal forms, but had precedents for the organisation of their life in various groups of dedicated people within Judaism, who had drawn up rules for their life together. Members of the dissident sect centred at Qumrân *may* have joined the community bringing influences, forms and possibly an exegetical tradition (K. Stendahl, *The School of Matthew* (1954)) from their former life (J. Daniélou, *Les Manuscrits de la Mer Morte et les origines du Christianisme* (1957)). In any case, when the necessity arose, the community, despite its marked spontaneity and enthusiasm, showed itself prepared to ensure that all things should be done decently and in order. That necessity arose early. Two groups soon emerged in the community ; they are termed in Ac., Hebrews and Hellenists. The former represented Aramaic-speaking Christians, the latter probably Greek-speaking Jews who had become Christians and who may have had connections with the Diaspora and were **76** likely to be more open to Hellenistic influences than were the Hebrews. According to Ac. 6:1ff. the Hellenists complained that the Hellenist widows were being neglected in the distribution of alms, which seem to have taken the form of free meals. Other factors besides this may have caused friction. Differences in language can be irksome (even though Ac. assumes that the leading Hellenists at least were bilingual (Ac. 21:40)). The native-born Aramaic-speaking Palestinians may have revealed an irritatingly superior attitude towards the Greek-speaking and possibly Diaspora Jews. To meet the challenge to its unity, the community, at the instigation of the Twelve, chose seven men, all bearing Greek names, who were to deal with the distribution of alms. Thus the Hellenists were accorded proper recognition.

c But the significance of the appointment of the seven was not exhausted in the serving of tables. According to Ac. 6:7 there followed an increase of the community. Priests were attracted to it (was it by the signs of its ordered life ?), and, of the seven, those whose activity is recorded became preachers, and it was the preaching of the chief of the Hellenists, Stephen, that precipitated the first persecution in the history of the community. This probably reveals the underlying source of the tension caused by the Hellenists, namely, their radical approach to Judaism. Hitherto the primitive community had not felt it necessary to emphasise any distinction between itself and Judaism. The first believers had been Jews or proselytes to Judaism (Ac. 2:11), they attended the Temple, celebrated the Jewish festivals, kept the Law. They attracted priests and Pharisees (Ac. 2:47, 4:4, 5:14, 6:7, 15:5), who apparently continued in their former way of life. Gamaliel was able to secure an easy toleration for them, despite the fears of the Temple authorities, the Sadducees, that they might provoke disturbances and rouse the wrath of Rome against Jewry. All this suggests that the attitude of the earliest believers to Judaism was positive as well as negative. They were aware of the continuity between the New Israel and the Old even while they condemned the latter for her rejection of Jesus. Their condemnation of Israel was not total, but sorrowful and designed to call forth her repentance (Ac. 2:36ff., 3:19f.). That the earliest community was loath to mark itself off decisively from the Old Israel appears also from the tardiness with which it came to call itself the people or Israel of God. The term *ecclesia* occurs first in Ac. 5:11, but at the beginning more common were terms such as ' the disciples ' (Ac. 1:15), ' brethren ' (1:16), ' those that believed ' (2:44), ' the saved ' (2:47). Similarly, although the first day of the week, Sunday, soon came to be celebrated as the Lord's Day, this was not, at first, in any opposition to the Sabbath, which continued to be observed along with it. It was later, and at Antioch, not in Jerusalem, that the name ' Christians ' came to be used and that outsiders came to recognise Christianity as an independent religion (Ac. 11:26).

0d But with Stephen the case was different. The aim of his speech (Ac. 7) has been variously understood, either as a call to the Jewish-Christian community to forsake the old securities offered to it by Judaism, Palestine, the Temple, the Law, or as an indictment of the Old Israel as apostate. Whichever be the immediate purpose of the speech, its implication is clear. To Stephen Israel has been apostate throughout her history : her rejection of Jesus is merely the culmination of a series of misdeeds. Christianity must break with Judaism because the two are incompatible. The origin of Stephen's radicalism has been variously sought, in the teaching of Jesus, in an anti-cultic tradition within Judaism, in the criticism of the Temple and of the ' orthodox ' understanding of the Law revealed in the Dead Sea Scrolls, it being claimed that sectarian influences of the Qumrân variety were already at work in the Church. Similarly the ultimate impact of Stephen on early Christianity has been differently assessed. Stephen's teaching, it has been urged, greatly influenced the debate within the primitive community on the significance of the Jewish cultus, and it is the matrix from which such a document as the Epistle to the Hebrews ultimately emerged. But it is more likely that Stephen's attitude was too radical for the Church at large. His total dismissal of the Jewish tradition was not permanently influential in the Church, which preferred to regard its faith as the fulfilment of Judaism not its annulment.

e Of the immediate impact of Stephen's teaching, however, Ac. leaves us in no doubt. He had brought into prominence the revolutionary character of the new faith and advocated its independence from Judaism. The reaction of Jewry was swift and violent. The persecution that broke out probably touched the Hellenists only. Ac. merely states that the apostles remained in the city, and they are unlikely to have remained there unless there were other Christians around them. And had the persecution been general they themselves would hardly have escaped it. The Hellenists, however, were compelled to flee and their flight was to have momentous consequences. (Not all, however, even of the Hellenists, fled Jerusalem : some at least returned, Ac. 9:27.) Hitherto the Church had confined its activity to Jews. But with the scattering of the Hellenists the new faith inevitably began to confront the Gentile world. One of the seven, Philip, evangelised Samaria. True, the people of Samaria were circumcised, but the Jews had no dealings with them. Moreover, Philip's work brought him into contact with Simon Magus, who is a familiar figure in the history of ' Gnosticism '. The details of the story of Philip's meeting with Simon may be legendary, but in the rejection of Simon we see a premonition of the attitude which the Church was later to take towards Gnosticism and of the dangers which awaited the Gospel as it spread outside strict Judaism. In addition, Philip went to the villages of Samaria (Ac. 8:25), he appears on the road from Jerusalem to Gaza (8:26), at Azotus (8:40) and Caesarea (8:40). We read of Hellenists going to Jews in Phoenicia, Cyprus and Antioch, ' speaking the word to none except Jews ' (Ac. 11:19) (there may have been missions to Alexandria and Rome also). Some Hellenists from Cyprus and Cyrene, however, preached at Antioch to the Gentiles, and that with remarkable success. Thus there emerged a novel phenomenon, Gentile Christianity, and it was in Antioch, as we previously noted, that the disciples were for the first time called Christians (Ac. 11:26).

61a The emergence of this ' new ' Christianity raised the question, inevitably, of its relation to the mother community in Jerusalem. The latter sent emissaries to inspect the new brethren, and it is clear that, despite the development of new groups of Christians, the Church was still conceived as a single entity centred at Jerusalem. Communities outside were not autonomous, but extensions of the Church in that city and subject to the authority of the leaders there. It is probable that this situation tended to consolidate 761a
the primacy of Peter (but see Loisy, *The Birth of the Christian Religion* (Eng. tr. 1948), 103), because it was he who travelled most to visit the new communities. He thus became more and more known so that in certain sections of the Church he came to be regarded as the rock on which the Church was built, although this view of him may well go back to the time of Jesus himself (Mt. 16:18). And the role of the Church at Jerusalem, and indeed of the city itself, in the Apostolic Age is noteworthy. Some have claimed that the relation between the Church at Jerusalem and communities elsewhere came to resemble that between the Temple at Jerusalem and the rest of Jewry. Just as a Temple tax was laid on the latter, so Christians outside Jerusalem contributed money to the Church there. Moreover, because, in accordance with traditional eschatological thinking within Judaism, the expectation was strong that the final act of history would take place in Jerusalem, the missionaries of the Church, wherever they were, centred their eyes on that city : all roads for them led to Jerusalem because of the eschatological dogma that we have mentioned (Munck, *Paulus und die Heilsgeschichte* (1954) ; Davies, NTS 2 (1955), 60–73). However, it is best to regard the ties binding Christians to the Jerusalem Church as those of Christian brotherhood and gratitude (Dodd, *Romans* (1932)). For Paul at least the Jerusalem above had early replaced the Jerusalem below as the centre hope (Gal. 4:23ff.), and it was only in the first stages of the Apostolic Age that Jerusalem had anything like an effective hegemony. The flood of Gentile Christianity was soon to carry the ark of the faith its own way, free from the control of Jerusalem, honoured as she continued to be. When the Gentile Church emerged at Antioch the fateful ' leap ' from the Palestinian to the Hellenistic world had been taken ; and it was away from Jerusalem.

But, within the city itself, the departure of the b
Hellenists opened the way for the increasing Jewishness of the Church, which, in turn, made the way into it attractive to more Jews. Through losses and through its gains the entrenchment of the Church in Jerusalem within Judaism deepened. Thus for an undefined period it lived at peace. Nevertheless, just before Passover in A.D. 44, in order to appease the Jews, Herod Agrippa put to death James, the son of Zebedee, and imprisoned Peter. Why? This sudden attack is a reminder that the history of the Church in this period can only be understood over against the mounting tension between Jew and Gentile in 1st-cent. Palestine, a tension which created among Jews an irritated sensitivity against any blurring of the distinctions between Jew and Gentile. Thus Herod Agrippa himself, while he was capable of playing the Hellenistic sovereign outside Jewish circles, was careful to play the part of an observant Jew within them and thus gained the favour even of the Pharisees. So, as long as Jewish leaders could be sure that Jewish Christians were not departing radically from Judaism, all was well. But before A.D. 44 Peter received a Gentile, Cornelius (Ac. 11), along with other Gentiles, into the Church at Caesarea. The occasion was marked by great enthusiasm, and the alarm among Jews was natural. This was shared by Jewish Christians themselves, and Herod Agrippa was not slow to exploit it in the way we have indicated. Whether Peter's action had created a gulf between him and Jewish Christians is not stated. Ac. merely notes that after his escape from prison Peter left Jerusalem for another place never to return (Ac. 12:17). The leadership of the Church at Jerusalem fell to the ' safe ' James, the brother of the Lord. Some claim that in A.D. 44 dynastic supplanted apostolic Christianity at Jerusalem. Probably, not only his dynastic connection with Jesus, but also his intense personal piety accounted for the emergence of James, the brother of the Lord, as leader. Everything that has come down to us about him points to an observing Jew, who had become a

761b Christian without making a radical break with Judaism. His prominence after A.D. 44 was not wholly a new thing. Probably from the earliest days of the Church he had become one of the 'pillars'. As brother of the Lord he would be regarded as one who had special knowledge of him, and, in addition, although we know nothing of his conversion (for presumably during the ministry of Jesus he had been sceptical) his witness to the Resurrection gave him much weight.

c Of the history of the Church at Jerusalem between A.D. 44 and the fall of Jerusalem in A.D. 70 we know very little. This may be due to the uneventful nature of its life or to the fact that the author of Ac. had no traditions or, at any rate, none which he considered reliable about this period. Tradition asserts that James was the first bishop of Jerusalem. Apparently he had such personal power that he was virtually, even though not in name, the first monarchial bishop, possibly the *desposunoi* (the family of Jesus) were gathered around him also in positions of authority. There can be little doubt that, under James, the Church became increasingly Judaistic and critical of Gentile elements in the community. Numerically, therefore, it prospered, conversion from Judaism being comparatively simple, although economically the Jerusalem Church never recovered, apparently, from the early ill-fated 'communistic' experiment: it was in such straits that the Gentile churches had to help it. Attempts at toning down the 'Judaism' of Jerusalem Christianity, however, and at minimising the gulf between Gentile and Jerusalem Christianity break down on the opposition which the Pauline mission so often encountered from Jewish Christians, who, whether they were direct emissaries of the Jerusalem Church or not, probably did represent the predominant point of view of that Church, even if not of James himself. It is illuminating that, when Paul visited Jerusalem in A.D. 58, James had to take precautionary measures before he was allowed among the faithful (see Munck, op. cit.).

d Nevertheless, while fully recognising the sympathy with which James, the brother of the Lord, regarded and was regarded by Judaism, his devotion to the Lord must not be minimised. His faith led him in A.D. 62 to pay the price of martyrdom. The cause of his death at the hand of Annas, the High Priest, is difficult to assess. The traditions about it diverge (Jos. Ant. XX, ix, 1; Eus.HE ii, 23. See M. Goguel, *The Birth of Christianity* (1953), 124–32). The weight of evidence suggests perhaps that the cause lay in the personal jealousy which Annas felt towards James: this would explain the peculiarity that it was James alone of the Christians who was struck, though to remove the leaders in order to scatter the flock is a familiar strategy among persecutors. And, on the other hand, even the modicum of openness to the Gentiles the Jewish Christians may have had was distasteful to the authorities. In any case, as the shadows of the revolt against Rome gathered, the Christians in Jerusalem, now deprived of James, found themselves out of sympathy with the Zealots, and, in obedience to a revelation, they left the city for refuge in Pella probably in A.D. 68. The number of the Christians who left was probably small, otherwise they would not have been allowed to go. There is nothing to suggest that it was detachment from the national aspirations of their people after the flesh nor indifference to the fate of Jerusalem that induced them to depart, naturally as their conduct was so construed by Jewry. What is clear is that they rejected the extreme militarism of the Zealots and obeyed what they regarded as the will of God. It has been customary to claim that, at Pella, Jewish Christianity, isolated from Judaism and from the main stream of Christianity, gradually petrified, and died without significance. On the basis of sources claimed to underlie the pseudo-Clementine literature and the translations of Symmachus, the attempt has recently been made to prove that Jewish Christianity continued to play a leading **76** role—well organised and missionary—in the life of the Church, that Jewish Christians proved to be the most determined opponents of Gnosticism and especially of Marcion (H. J. Schoeps, *Theologie und Geschichte des Judenchristentums* (1949)). The disputed validity of this rehabilitation of Jewish Christianity cannot be discussed here. In the same way, the significance of the fall of Jerusalem in A.D. 70 has been reopened in recent scholarship. Was that the decisive event in Christian history which relegated Jewish Christianity to insignificance and opened the way for the triumph of Gentile Christianity? We shall deal in detail with this below: here suffice it merely to assert that it is still more probable that 'the leap' of Christianity to the Gentile world had been safely accomplished long before A.D. 70.

The leap to which we have referred we owe in part **76** to the pressure of persecution. After the martyrdom of Stephen, the Hellenists left Jerusalem; and after the persecution under Herod Agrippa, Peter and possibly other Jewish Christians left Jerusalem also and became missionaries at large. Their activities we noted above, and particularly that at Antioch some preached to the Gentiles. Here it was that the Gospel took a 'leap' into a new world. The term 'leap', however, suggests too deliberate a movement. The first preaching to the Gentiles was not a conscious policy, but the inevitable concomitant of any preaching in such a cosmopolitan centre as Antioch. Gentiles, already attracted to Judaism, heard the Gospel preached in synagogues and possibly elsewhere. They believed and were not turned away by the Church. And as at Antioch so in other cities. The activity of most of the Hellenists is unknown to us, but, from scattered references in the NT, we must conclude that the Gospel took root in many cities through their labours and those of others. Although these references do not always make it clear that the groups of Christians called into being in various places were always composed of Gentiles, it is probable that some Gentiles at least were included among them, especially in view of the frequent presence of Gentiles in synagogues, which were the usual points of departure for Christian missionaries. Barnabas and Mark worked in Cyprus (Ac. 15:39); the brothers of the Lord and the other apostles were active in missionary work: that they were accompanied by their wives suggests that their periods of labour were protracted (1 C. 9:5). By A.D. 49 Christianity had reached Rome: that the Church there survived the expulsion of the Jews under Claudius, the Emperor, in A.D. 49, probably means that it must have been composed of some Gentiles. In A.D. 42–3 there were disturbances in Alexandria, possibly caused by opposition to Jewish-Christian missionaries who had come from Syria. Apollos, a Christian from Alexandria, is found in Ephesus before Paul arrived there (Ac. 18:24f.). According to 1 Pet. there were churches in an area including Pontus, Galatia, Cappadocia, Asia and Bithynia, the date of whose foundation, and its manner, we do not know. The ascription of the epistle to Peter *may* point to the fact that the apostle himself perhaps did labour in these parts: there is evidence that he visited Rome. But very many others who spread the Gospel have left no memorial. That Paul drew a sharp distinction between churches that he himself had founded, and those that he had not, points to a wide growth of churches other than the Pauline (Rom. 15:20). Paul's activity took place within the context of a vast missionary expansion. Because at first not many wise and noble were converted (1 C. 1:26ff.) (a fact which, however, must not be exaggerated in view of figures like Barnabas, Paul, Erastus the city treasurer, Gaius, who entertained Paul and allowed the Church to meet in his house (Ac. 18:8, 19:3; Rom. 16:23; 1 C. 1:14)), the exact steps in the spread of Christianity could pass unnoticed, not only by secular historians, but also by those who came to positions of authority

2a in the Church itself. Moreover, Ac. has so elevated Paul that others who laboured have been dwarfed, and any assessment of the rise of Gentile Christianity must allow for the possible distortion introduced by this concentration of Ac. on Paul. For example, we must somewhere find in a non-Pauline milieu a piety profound enough to produce the Epistle to the Hebrews.

b Nevertheless, it is not without much justification that Ac. has so presented Paul. He himself tells us that he had laboured more abundantly than any of the other apostles (1 C. 15:10; 2 C. 11:23), and doubtless the transition of Christianity from the Palestinian to the Hellenistic world is best mirrored for us in his life. That transition could not but be difficult. The language of Palestinian Christianity had to be reinterpreted; the ethical tradition of Judaism, which Jewish Christianity had been able largely to assume, could no longer be taken for granted, and the need for catechetical instruction on a new scale and on a different plane arose; theological and moral problems, beyond the limits of this article to describe, emerged in Paul's churches and in those of others, and lay behind the ceaseless activity of the apostle. And, because he stimulates and at the same time confronts these problems, as well as because of his unique role as the apostle to the Gentiles, Paul demands extensive consideration.

3a Since the apocryphal writing *The Acts of Paul* (see M. R. James, *The Apocryphal NT* (1924), 270ff.) must be dismissed as legendary, we have two sources for Paul's life, Ac. and his own epistles. Where these disagree priority must be given to what Paul himself wrote, but the historicity of Ac. must be treated respectfully. Paul-Saul (he had both names from birth because the Jews were accustomed to having Jewish names among their own different from those they used in the outside world) was a 'Hebrew born of Hebrews', an Aramaic-speaking Jew (Phil. 3:4ff.). But he was born outside Palestine in Tarsus in Cilicia where his father had achieved Roman citizenship, of which Paul, who had inherited the same citizenship, was proud. This presupposed a comparatively high social status, and probably gave to Paul from the first a certain imperial awareness. Much has been made of Paul's Tarsus background, namely, that since he was familiar with a type of Hellenistic Judaism or Diaspora Judaism, which was less sure of itself than the more authentic and integrated Rabbinic Judaism of Palestine, the transition to Christianity was easier for him than had he been a Palestinian Pharisee. Moreover, as a Dispersion Jew, of warm human sympathies, particularly in a city with pretensions to philosophy as well as to commerce, Paul would early be aware of the larger world outside Judaism, and, therefore, long preconditioned for his future work as a Christian missionary to Gentiles. But caution is necessary in all this. By the time of Paul the distinction between the Judaism of the Dispersion and of Palestine had become very fluid. In addition, although born in Tarsus, we cannot be sure that Paul was brought up there: he may have left for Jerusalem at an early age and spent the years of his youth entirely in that city. The pertinent part of Ac. 23:3 suggests this (W. C. van Unnik, *Tarsus of Jerusalem* (1952), see G. Ogg, SJTh. 8 (1955), 94–7). But, even if we reject this view (Gal. 1:21 is against it) and think of his upbringing as at Tarsus, Paul's home there would almost certainly have been a bit of Palestine across the sea. This would be doubly the case if we accept a tradition preserved by Jerome that Paul's parents had come from Gischala in Galilee, so that he would be the child of first-generation emigrants, as likely to be repelled or at least frightened by his Gentile environment as attracted to it. And in Jerusalem, where he probably studied under Gamaliel, possibly for the Rabbinate, his training would be thoroughly Jewish and, indeed, Pharisaic. His eagerness in religion and in his studies, as in all he undertook, enabled him to outstrip his contemporaries in zeal for, and knowledge of, the Law (Gal. 1:13f.; Phil. 3:5ff.). That the 763a
Dispersion was a broadening and disturbing influence on him it would be idle to deny, but by far the most formative factor in Paul's background was Judaism. This accounts both for the violence of his initial reaction against the Gospel, and the cogency with which later he could expose the weakness of life under the Law, and puncture the pretensions of many who gloried in it, even while he honoured the Law (Rom. 7:12). Judaism he could defend and attack from within; the treatment of his opponents in Gal. is especially instructive here.

A student of Gamaliel's could not but be aware of b
the Christian movement. That Paul saw Jesus in the flesh we cannot say. To judge from the twofold, pointed mention of his name in Ac. 7:58f., for the author of Ac. it was Paul's connection with the martyrdom of Stephen that was especially significant. Possibly he had been among the Cilician Jews with whom Stephen had argued (Ac. 6:9). In any case it is in connection with the radicalism of the Hellenists that we first encounter Paul. Untouched by the mild tolerance of Gamaliel, with which indeed he may have been impatient. Paul recognised the incompatibility between 'Christianity' and Judaism and responded promptly. After ravaging Christians in Jerusalem and Judaea, although his victims did not always know who struck them (Gal. 1:22f.), he asked permission from the High Priest to persecute Christians in Damascus (Ac. 9:1). Why Paul selected Damascus Christians for his attack we cannot be certain. They may have been Hellenists who had fled thither, although to judge from the figure of Ananias, a Jewish Christian, there were other Christians in the city. That the Christians were sufficiently numerous to warrant the special attention of the persecutor indicates how rapidly Christianity had spread. Possibly a centre such as Damascus, which was often 'a haven for heretics', had attracted the earliest Christians. That the High Priest had the right to authorise Paul on his 'mission' we know from 1 Mac. 15:15.

Four accounts of what happened to Paul on the way c
to Damascus appear, in Ac. 9:1–19*a*, 22:3–16, 26:4–18; Gal. 1:11ff. In form these recall descriptions of the call of major OT figures, Isaiah, Jeremiah, Enoch, The Servant of the Lord (cf. especially Jg. 16:17; Ps. 21:10–11, 70; Isa. 6, 49:1–6; Jer. 1:4–10; Ezek. 1–2:8; 1 Enoch 14:8–16:4. See Munck, *Paulus und die Heilsgeschichte* (1954), 15–25). But this formal similarity is deceptive and must not be allowed to dictate our understanding of the 'conversion' as the call of another prophet, even though the prophet of the New Age. Nor must the term 'conversion' itself mislead us. Paul was not rescued from a life of aimless dissipation to a life of Christian virtue, but from one kind of devotion, that to Judaism, to another, that to Christ. Three motifs emerge implicitly, if not explicitly, in all the accounts. First, Paul became convinced of the Reality of the Risen Christ. His 'vision' on the road to Damascus was deemed by him to be qualitatively different from all other visions he had himself experienced (for his evaluation of these see 2 C. 12:1ff.) and comparable to that vouchsafed to Peter, James, the Twelve and the five hundred brethren (1 C. 15:3–10), on which the preaching and faith of the Church was based (1 C. 15:14). Secondly, Paul realised that, when Christians were persecuted, the Lord himself suffered: this he later expressed by asserting that the Church was the Body of Christ. (When Paul is persecuting Christians the voice of the Risen Lord asks him, 'Saul, Saul, why do you persecute *me*?' Ac. 9:4. J. A. T. Robinson, *The Body* (1952).) Thirdly, Paul knew that necessity was laid upon him to preach the Gospel to the Gentiles (Ac. 9:15, 22:15, 26:17f.; Gal. 1:15). The above motifs are intimately connected. Paul understood his experience of the Risen Lord as an act of the sheer grace of God (1 C. 15:9ff.); Jesus had appeared to *him*, the arch-persecutor. But not only did this justify the preaching

763c of Christians, that the crucified Jesus of Nazareth was Messiah and Lord, a claim which in the eyes of Paul was an accursed one (Gal. 3:13). The Risen Lord had identified himself with his own, that is, with 'the second-rate Jews' (for that is how Christians must have appeared to Pharisees) who constituted the Church. Thus he had also validated their claim to be the Messianic community, the people of God. But it was this last that had infuriated Paul, the Pharisee. That *'am hā'āreṣ* ('people of the land') should presume to be the people of God was to him intolerable. At his conversion the Lord himself revealed his error to him. But, if Paul had been wrong about the *'am hā'āreṣ*, was it not possible that he was also wrong about the Gentiles? Would not the Risen Lord identify himself also with them? Conversion thus came to spell mission: the barriers were down. The intensity of Paul's devotion to the Risen Lord became commensurate with his erstwhile opposition to him and his.

764a The accounts of the conversion suggest that all this matured quickly in Paul's mind. But that he became immediately aware of the significance of Christ for the Gentiles is open to doubt. His life for thirteen or fourteen years after his conversion must be a matter of conjecture. After his conversion he went off alone to Arabia (the Nabataean kingdom). That he preached to Gentiles there we cannot know. When he returned to Damascus, according to Ac., he preached in the synagogues of the city: no mention is made of any direct appeal to the Gentiles. Although the extreme steps taken by the local Jews to destroy him might be taken to point to this, nevertheless the mere fact of his conversion might sufficiently account for these. According to Ac. 22:17ff., Paul received the specific call to preach to the Gentiles in a special vision given to him in the Temple at Jerusalem three years after his conversion (Gal. 1:18), the implication being that before this Paul had confined his preaching to Jews. The passage does not suggest a second conversion (cf. Phil. 3:7–11, which seems to refer to a single event when Paul had counted all things lost for Christ), but it may indicate that the apostle's full realisation of the meaning of his conversion came, not at once, but after some time. Unfortunately Paul's own account in Gal. 1:1ff. is given in a context of controversy over the nature of his apostleship: in this he emphasises the independence of his call from all human authorities, even the leaders of the Church at Jerusalem; he ignores the role of Ananias. But the essential truth of his version cannot be doubted. Not till three years after his conversion did he go up to Jerusalem to see Cephas, and even then it required the sponsorship of Barnabas to allay suspicion of him among the Jewish Christians of the city (Ac. 9:26ff.). It agrees with this, that Gal. 1:18f. makes the visit brief and private.

b All this indicates not a well-known disciple already engaged in missions to the Gentiles but one still indistinguishable from Jews (Ac. 9:26). Ac. 9:29, taken at its face value, would exclude any Gentile mission by Paul before this time: the difficulties of this verse and the differences between Ac. 9:26–9 and Gal. 1:18f. cannot be discussed here. After this first visit Paul retired to Tarsus, and for fourteen years worked in Cilicia and Syria, on his native heath as it were (Ac. 9:30; Gal. 1:21, 2:1). Of these years we know nothing. But we do know that at some period in his life Paul must have wrestled with the OT in the light of Christ: possibly it was during these silent years that he became mighty in the scriptures from the Christian point of view, and worked out the implications of his acceptance of Christ. We also know that when Barnabas had visited Antioch to inquire into the results of the preaching to the Gentiles there, and approved of it (Ac. 11:22–6), he turned for help in such work to Paul who was at Tarsus. Possibly therefore the latter had already gained some kind of reputation in work connected with the Gentiles. Equally possible is it that Barnabas knew of the vision which Paul had received in the Temple (Ac. 22:17ff.) and his 76
preoccupation with this problem, and that it was his invitation to work at Antioch that brought Paul's resolution to go to the Gentiles to the boil. At any rate the epistles and Ac. reveal that Paul came to regard himself, whether immediately at his conversion or gradually through meditation upon its significance, as *the* Apostle to the Gentiles and was so regarded by others. For a person of Paul's strong natural quality and deep loyalties the transition from 'particularism' to 'universalism' we can assume to have been painful and gradual. Whatever the anticipations of this in the silent years at Tarsus, significant or merely sporadic, it was when he joined Barnabas at Antioch that Paul's full stature as missionary to the Gentiles began to appear. He then emerged from a long obscurity to occupy the stage and, according to Ac., to dominate it. For the sake of clarity we shall now state concisely his missionary activity and then seek to understand what lies behind it all—the purposes, problems, prizes and the person of Paul.

According to Ac. 11:26ff. Barnabas and Paul c
laboured for a year at Antioch. Their success was such that the Church emerged in the eyes of Gentiles as an entity distinct from Judaism. During this period a prophet from Jerusalem called Agabus came to Antioch, and predicted a famine which took place in the reign of Claudius. The Antiochene Church decided to send Barnabas and Paul to Jerusalem with relief for Christians there (Ac. 11:27ff.). According to Ac., this was Paul's second visit to Jerusalem since his conversion. Presumably, therefore, it coincides with that described in Gal. 2:1–10. But the difficulties in the way of their identification have led many to reject it. Unless we adopt an extreme scepticism as to the historicity of Ac., as does John Knox in *Chapters in a Life of Paul* (1950), two live alternatives emerge, to identify the visit described in Ac. 11:29–30 or that in Ac. 15:1–29 with that in Gal. 2:1–10. The former position, much favoured by British scholars and most recently by Gregory Dix (*Jew and Greek* (1953), 22ff.) enables us to reconstruct events as follows.

Apparently Jewish and Gentile Christians at Antioch d
had been worshipping together on the basis of equality. Doubtless Jewish Christians had continued to observe the Law as much as was possible. Nevertheless, they had broken bread with uncircumcised Gentiles. From the point of view of Judaism they themselves had *ipso facto* become unclean, and so cut off from the community of Israel. Gentile-Jewish 'intercommunion' at Antioch, then, if we may so express it, was no creation of Paul's but of the Jewish Christians who preceded him there. Barnabas, who had come down from Jerusalem to inspect the situation, had not condemned it. At this juncture occurred Paul's second visit to Jerusalem. Note especially that the political situation at that time was particularly delicate on the question of Jewish-Gentile relationships. Direct Roman rule had been restored in A.D. 44; in A.D. 45 Theudas rebelled, so that the temper of the time was not conducive to such 'reconciliatory' experiments as Paul and Barnabas were conducting at Antioch. For the visit itself, we have to go to Gal. 2:1–10. In the charged atmosphere of the city it was held discreetly in private. Paul laid before the Jerusalem leaders, James, Cephas and John, the Gospel which he proclaimed among the Gentiles lest he should have laboured in vain (Gal. 2:2). In this Gospel the leaders saw nothing lacking. They did not insist on circumcision or on the observance of the Law for Gentile converts but gave to Paul and Barnabas the right hand of fellowship, recognising that they should go to the Gentiles, just as Peter had been entrusted with the mission to the Jews. Paul and Barnabas granted the only request made by the Jerusalem leaders, namely, that in their work they should remember the poor of the mother-Church.

One difficulty arose owing to the presence of certain e
spying false brethren, possibly Jewish Christians

764e of the extreme Pharisaic persuasion or Jews. They demanded the circumcision of Titus, a Greek who had accompanied the apostles to Jerusalem, probably on the assumption that he would be accepted without difficulty as were his like at Antioch. Whether their demand was accepted is not certain. Paul perhaps did circumcise Titus to avoid giving offence : his manner of referring to the matter suggests that he found it embarrassing. The crucial point, however, is that the Jerusalem leaders accepted the Gentile mission without conditions. Thus the subsequent missionary activity of Paul and Barnabas went under way with the full consent of the Jewish-Christian leaders at Jerusalem. Paul's practice of admitting Gentiles into the Church, without insistence on circumcision or observance of the Law, was under no cloud of disapproval from the 'pillars' of the Church. Indeed it could not be, because it was merely the continuation of that already blessed before his day by the Jerusalem Church in the person of Barnabas. When therefore Paul and Barnabas, accompanied by John Mark (Ac. 12:25) returned to Antioch, the Church there continued on its way without interruption, Jewish and Gentile Christians ate together on an equal basis. Peter, who visited them a little later (is Antioch 'the other place' referred to in Ac. 12:17?), fell in naturally with this practice, until 'certain men from James' (emissaries or passers-by from Jerusalem?) objected, at which Peter withdrew from table fellowship with Gentile Christians. Paul accused Peter of hypocrisy. Probably the charge derives its force from the political situation. To avoid offence to Jewry was imperative. Those 'from James' may have so persuaded Peter, who as a matter of political expediency desisted from intercommunion. But such expediency appeared to Paul as hypocrisy. So he withstood Peter to his face. He raised the question not of expediency but principle.

f Nevertheless, despite these disturbances, the Antiochene Church prospered. Manaen, a member of the very court of Herod, was converted. Pulsating with life the Church later sent forth the two apostles Barnabas and Paul, together with John Mark as an assistant, to what was regarded as their God-given task of evangelising the Gentiles. Before we trace Paul's missionary labours, however, a caution is necessary. The travels are usually treated after a threefold pattern, as if Paul undertook three journeys of a distinct character from Antioch as his base. As far as it goes this convention is acceptable, but it blurs two things : first, that, although Antioch was the immediate base for the journeys, the ultimate one was Jerusalem ; and, secondly, by exaggerating the distinctness of these journeys, especially the second and third, it loses the unified character of all Paul's missionary work. This is best thought of as one activity turning round Antioch, but beginning and ending in Jerusalem. With this caveat we trace the journeys ; for the correspondence of Paul, the reader is referred to the introductions to the various epistles.

765a Taking their way from Antioch through Seleucia to Cyprus, Paul and Barnabas preached at Salamis and Paphos, thence they went to Perga in Pamphylia (here for an unknown reason, not creditable in the judgment of Paul, Mark left them for Jerusalem) and missionary work followed in Antioch in Pisidia, Iconium, Lystra, Derbe. From there—possibly because Tarsus, to which they would come next if they advanced, had already been evangelised by Paul—they returned to Pisidian Antioch, and via Perga and Attalia to Antioch in Syria again (Ac. 13, 14). An almost tangible tentativeness hangs over this first journey, even though 'Barnabas and Paul' soon changes to 'Paul and Barnabas'. Was it because he sensed this tentativeness that Mark left? Cyprus was chosen perhaps simply because it would be familiar to Barnabas. Paul and Barnabas possibly left the Pamphylian plain, not from policy, but because of an illness referred to perhaps by Paul elsewhere as a 'thorn in the flesh', so that the evangelisation of the cities from Pisidian Antioch to Derbe, in the Roman province of Galatia, was not 765a
a long-deliberated plan : the arrangements seem to have been extremely fluid. All this, however, is conjectural. What is certain is that the work was effective : converts probably came from the lower classes ; the conversion of a proconsul Sergius Paulus is an event of note. And, as were the converts, so were the places visited 'insignificant'. There was no concentration on important cities. The towns visited were remote: their inhabitants, not so much Greek as mixed. Did Paul, the Cilician, feel more at home amid mixed, Oriental Greeks than among purer types? He frequented their towns more often. Or was it that the culturally backward places were more easy to approach? Healings and exorcisms particularly impressed the people visited (Ac. 13:4ff., 8ff.), and while the Jews and proselytes were converted the mission was most successful among the Gentiles, to whom because of violent Jewish opposition (Ac. 13:45, 50, 14:2, 19ff.) Paul and Barnabas deliberately turned (Ac. 13:47, 14:21) (for Gentile opposition see Ac. 14:5).

On their return to Antioch Paul and Barnabas b
reported that 'a door of faith had been opened to the Gentiles'. Such was indeed the real significance of their 'first journey'. Tentatively, but deliberately and effectively, the Gospel had been presented to Gentiles outside Palestine. Previously this had happened sporadically and usually as an unavoidable concomitant of preaching in synagogues. There was now a Gentile mission. But this could not spell peace. A short time after their foundation the Galatian churches (Pisidian-Antioch, Iconium, Lystra, Derbe) were troubled by Christians (whether Jewish Christians sent from Jerusalem or Gentile Christians is debated) who claimed that circumcision and the observance of the Law were obligatory on all Christians, that Paul was not a true apostle and had wrongly taught the Galatian churches to indulge in freedom. To meet the situation it is probable that Paul wrote Gal. in which he raised the issue of circumcision as a principle : to insist on this was to annul the Gospel, however advantageous it might be to do so in the immediate circumstances. This could not go unnoticed. Pharisaic Jewish Christians appeared in Antioch from Jerusalem. Discussion and dissension followed until the Antiochene Church decided to send Paul and Barnabas with others to discuss the issue of circumcision. There followed what is usually referred to as the Apostolic Council. Peter took the position we may loosely call 'open communion'. James substantially agreed, but suggested a compromise : Gentiles were not to be troubled with circumcision and the Law, but were nevertheless to abstain from the pollutions of idols, unchastity, what is strangled, and blood. The Church adopted a decree to this effect which it sent to the churches of Antioch, Syria, and Cilicia. Highly diplomatic, the decree is a compromise : it neither condemns their opponents nor praises Paul and Barnabas. Its significance is momentous. It did *not* insist on circumcision and the Law for Gentile Christians. Virtually, if not explicitly, the Pauline position was endorsed by the Jewish-Christian Church at Jerusalem. (Perhaps the decree is a version, not too clearly understood by Ac., of the Noachian commandments, the minimum of demands laid by Judaism on all men.) Henceforth the acceptance of Gentiles could proceed unhindered. Paul had proceeded without the authority of the decree : others less venturesome had hesitated. Now they need hesitate no longer : the way was open for the widespread development of Gentile Christianity. (The reconciliation of Ac. and Gal. cannot be examined here : the above reconstruction stands or falls with the identification of Ac. 11:27–30 with Gal. 2:1–10, which enables us to place Gal. before the Council of Jerusalem, Ac. 15. If Ac. 15 = Gal. 2 then Gal. must be later than the Council. See commentaries on Ac. and Gal., and Caird, op. cit., 198ff.)

After the Council Paul and Barnabas continued to c
preach at Antioch. They shortly, however, decided

765c to revisit the recently founded churches. Barnabas wanted to take John Mark with them, but Paul, who may have been fractious because the Council had not more unreservedly endorsed his position, refused to do so because of Mark's previous defection. So they went separate ways. Barnabas and Mark to Cyprus: Paul and Silas (Silvanus) through Syria and Cilicia, Derbe, Lystra and Iconium. A missionary tour through Phrygia and Galatia followed, but they avoided Asia where lay Ephesus, Miletus, Smyrna, Pergamum (the proconsular province of western Asia is meant here by 'Asia'). In Mysia they were constrained from going into Bithynia but proceeded to Troas, where, in a vision, Paul was bidden to go over to Macedonia. They crossed to Samothrace, thence to Neapolis, Philippi, Amphipolis, Apollonia, Thessalonica, Beroea, Athens, Corinth, and it is to this period that the Thessalonian correspondence belongs. At the last place Paul stayed for a year and six months (Ac. 18:11) but finally left for Syria accompanied by Priscilla and Aquila, a Jew and his wife from Italy, with whom Paul stayed at Corinth. After calling at Cenchreae and preaching in the synagogue at Ephesus, despite requests that he should remain, Paul left Priscilla and Aquila there and returned via Caesarea to Antioch. The second missionary journey reveals how careful Paul still was to avoid offending Jews. His vow at Cenchreae and his circumcision of Timothy (symbol of the effectiveness of the first journey) point to his practice of observing the Law and expecting other Jews even as Christians to do so (a sign not only of his national awareness but of his grace). Nevertheless, although prominent ones were converted (Ac. 18:18, 17), the opposition of the Jews was marked (17:5, 13, 18:6ff.). They enlisted Roman support by representing the missionaries as revolutionaries bent on another 'kingdom'. And even though the authorities failed to distinguish Judaism and Christianity, Paul was led not only to avoid presenting the Gospel in terms of the Kingdom of God, on political grounds, but also, for self-protection, to insist on his rights as a Roman citizen. Does his imperial awareness reveal itself otherwise? Perhaps it does; but we are not certain. Certainly he did not concentrate on the great imperial cities: the rich Asian centres he left aside, as we saw, and only touched at Ephesus on his return journey. Nevertheless the crossing to Europe was a very self-conscious one: the geographic, if not imperial, awareness is unmistakable in Ac. and the epistles. But, on the other hand, although he could not but have been quickened by the change from the somewhat backward areas where he had hitherto laboured to the more civilised world of Philippi, it is odd how Paul tarried at Neapolis, a place more akin to the wild area he had left, as if again the areas resistant to pure Hellenism, for Macedonia was such, attracted him.

766a The third journey undertaken by Paul followed almost immediately (Ac. 18:23). Travelling through the region of Galatia and Phrygia (Ac. 19:1) he came to Ephesus, by what route we do not know. There Christians who knew only the baptism of John the Baptist (an interesting sidelight on the way in which Christianity had spread in various forms) demanded some attention, but Paul concentrated on the synagogue. But, after three months, Jewish opposition compelled him to make his headquarters, like some travelling philosopher, in a hall belonging to a certain Tyrannus, where for two years the apostle evangelised both Jews and Greeks. Healing and exorcism accompanied his work which was so effective that the trade in pagan religious shrines was threatened not only locally but throughout all Asia (Ac. 19:26). Persecution broke out against Paul now in the name of Gentile religion: the Jews' role therein is obscure (Ac. 19:33f.). It became wise to leave, and, as he had previously resolved, Paul went through Macedonia to Greece with the intention, after returning once more to Jerusalem, to go to Rome (19:21). After three months in Greece, a plot against him by Jews made 76
him return by land to Macedonia, and, accompanied by a delegation of considerable size, he sailed from Troas past many small places (he omitted Ephesus to save time to be at Jerusalem for Pentecost) to Caesarea in Syria and there stayed with Philip the Evangelist, before leaving for Jerusalem to lodge with Mnason of Cyprus, an early disciple. (During this journey the Corinthian correspondence came into being, probably written from Macedonia and Ephesus, and the Epistle to the Romans.)

This last journey reveals at once that all tentativeness is gone. b
The first journey, in the light of the last, appears almost preparatory, as if Paul had then kept to out-of-the-way places, whereas in the last he has reached out confidently to Ephesus with his powers at full stretch. Deliberateness has replaced tentativeness: this deliberateness expresses itself not only in the direct descent on Ephesus, in the effectiveness of the labour, but also in the fixity of purpose with which at its close he set his face to go to Jerusalem. The impressive entourage which accompanied him as if to give him support, as he took his collection—which had long occupied his attention—to the poor of the city, and the repeated warnings he received not to go to that city, lend to this visit to Jerusalem, his last, a kind of tragic triumph. So much is this so that the magnitude of the other resolve Paul made during his Ephesian ministry, to go to Rome, can be overlooked. What Paul expected in Jerusalem is disputed. What transpired, according to Ac., was somewhat as follows. His report of the work among the Gentiles was well received (21:20) and Paul showed himself anxious to conciliate his kinsmen. At the suggestion of James he performed the necessary rites of purification for himself and paid the dues necessary for the release of four other men from their vows. But the Jews were not to be placated. Paul was accused in general terms of 'teaching men everywhere against the people and the law and this place' (21:28), and specifically of having introduced a Greek into the Temple. A mob dragged him from the Temple, and the Roman authorities had to intervene to save his life. These last would have scourged him had not Paul revealed his Roman citizenship (22:26ff.), when the Roman tribune concerned allowed Paul to address his fellow countrymen—the Chief Priest and the Sanhedrin. But this created further dissension.

Forty Jews vowed to taste no food till they had killed c
Paul. The plot was foiled by Paul's nephew who had received information which he passed on. The tribune arranged for Paul to be taken to Caesarea under strong escort to face the governor Felix (23:16ff.), Five days later Ananias the High Priest with some elders and a spokesman, Tertullus, laid the case of Paul before Felix. The latter, hoping that Paul would bribe him (a hope quite in character with what Roman historians write about Felix), kept Paul in custody, only with liberty and access to his friends. When Felix was succeeded by Porcius Festus, Paul was left in prison out of consideration for the Jews. A Jewish request for a trial in Jerusalem was refused by Festus who insisted that the trial should be in Caesarea. When Paul was asked if he should be tried in Jerusalem he rejected the suggestion, quite naturally, and appealed to the Emperor. Festus and Herod Agrippa, before whom Paul also appeared, as before Bernice, Agrippa's sister, both felt him to be innocent. But to Caesar he had appealed and therefore to Caesar he had to go. There followed, how soon or late we do not know, Paul's journey to Rome where he was greeted by the brethren. He was allowed to stay by himself with the soldier who guarded him. There he lived for two years at his own expense: disputes with the Jews continued (28:17–28) but Ac. leaves him preaching and teaching openly and unhindered (28:30–1). For the remainder of Paul's life we are dependent on the Pastoral Epistles and on tradition. According to Clement of Rome (1:5) he went to the

766c 'limits of the west': this would agree with Paul's own assertion (Rom. 15:24, 28) that he proposed to go on to Spain after visiting Rome. Several Fathers of the Church accept the tradition of a visit to Spain. If we accept the authenticity of the Pastorals, they are to be placed after this visit to Spain. To judge from them, Paul went again to Ephesus, Macedonia, Greece. Perhaps he was arrested a second time at Troas (2 Tim. 4:13), and slain in Rome in the Neronian persecution (according to Eusebius in A.D. 67). Tertullian thinks he was beheaded. Of all this, however, we cannot be certain. A tradition first found in the *Acts of St Paul* places his martyrdom on the left bank of the Tiber, about three miles from Rome. There is no reason to doubt the tradition of Paul's martyrdom, and it is probable that Eph., Phil., Col., Phm. were written during his time in Rome (but see G. S. Duncan, *St Paul's Ephesian Ministry* (1929)).

767a Can we discern behind the above bare bones of Paul's career the dominating aims which governed him. Two interpretations have been urged, one old, the other recent. To begin with the new approach, Munck (*Paulus und die Heilsgeschichte* (1954)) has claimed that the whole life of the Apostle was lived in the conviction that he was *the* apostle to the Gentiles, that on his evangelism depended the incidence of the return of the Lord and the advent of the End of all things. Paul was dominated by an eschatological dogma about his peculiar role in world history (according to Schweitzer the same was true of Jesus). Since the tradition of eschatology to which Paul belonged expected the final scene of history to be enacted in Jerusalem, then for him all roads led, not to Rome, but to the city of David, the centre of his universe present and future. Hence his anxiety to keep in touch with Jerusalem: hence the collection for the saints there, which was designed to provide tangible evidence of the success of his mission and which therefore had eschatological significance. This alone accounts for the widely representative character of the people who accompanied him on his last visit to Jerusalem, when the collection was handed over. They came from Paul's major missionary fields (Ac. 20:4–5) at a considerable cost, and had Paul been concerned merely with relief he would hardly have squandered money so lavishly. His aim was otherwise, namely, to confront the city of Jerusalem with an impressive representation of believing Gentiles. Their gifts were to fulfil OT prophecies that the Gentiles should come to Jerusalem bringing their tributes with them: their presence was to stimulate the conversion of the Jews and hasten the End. We thus understand better Paul's readiness to face suffering and even death in visiting Jerusalem, his view of his own witness before the authorities of this world as 'a sign of the End'.

b Much in this approach is salutary. Paul did labour under the cherished conviction that he was *the* apostle to the Gentiles; he was under *necessity* to preach to Gentiles: he did see the centre of his world in Jerusalem rather than Rome. But difficulties arise. By the time when Gal. was written Paul was thinking of a Jerusalem above, and, more important, while he continued in his latest epistles to await the Parousia, nevertheless his emphasis seems to have changed from the expectation of the End to the present reality of the redemption wrought by his Lord. Certainly in his later years he was not *dominated* by the expectation of the immediate advent of the End. Had the collection for the saints had the decisive eschatological significance alleged, Ac. would hardly have ignored it. Moreover, a geographic awareness does seem to enter into Paul's activity especially when he crossed to Europe. This leads to the older approach to Paul, the traveller.

c It is particularly associated with Sir W. M. Ramsay. To him Paul thought as a Roman citizen. His missionary strategy was to concentrate on centres of imperial significance, so that the Roman imperial policy finds its counterpart in Pauline missionary policy. And clearly Paul did centre his work in certain cities—Tarsus, Damascus, Antioch, Corinth, Ephesus, Rome, not to speak of Jerusalem. But, on the other hand, we saw, first, that he also visited, apparently for personal reasons in the case of Cyprus, less significant places. It is not clear that Antioch in Pisidia, Lystra, Iconium, Derbe were 'significant' centres of Roman penetration: authorities differ on this and these cities were regarded by some as out of the way. And, secondly, that Paul should have gone to the chief cities was natural if not inevitable, but this must not be taken to mean that he was necessarily thinking of a 'divine commonwealth' set over against or parallel to the Roman. The only thing certain is that Paul first approached the Jews: he therefore sought out synagogues. After his experience on the first journey, the tentativeness of which we noted, he became more deliberate and geographically conscious. Thus the second journey up to Troas was largely a prelude to the descent upon Europe. As his deliberateness grew, his work followed more and more the pattern laid down by the imperial government, but not because he had become the Christian counterpart of an imperial strategist. This was due merely to the fact that his work could thus be most efficiently executed. Thus Spain, not Rome, was his goal in the West. Paul was thinking not of capturing the Empire but the whole known world. Ac. has perhaps made him more 'Roman' than he was. To think of him as a calculating strategist either bent on Jerusalem or Rome is erroneous. He was rather bent, whenever and wherever he could, on building the body of Christ. Sometimes this demanded speedy passage from city to city: sometimes as at Corinth and Ephesus a prolonged stay in one place; sometimes retracing his steps. But shortened as he thought the time to be before the End, Paul's speed was unhurried, dictated by no eschatological dogma or imperial policy. To build the body of Christ in places mean and not mean, among Jews first and, when they rejected his message, among the Greeks—this was his aim, to create a body wherein was neither Jew nor Greek, bond nor free, male nor female 'in Christ'.

d And from this grew the antagonisms that he aroused. First, there was Jewish opposition. As we saw, the violence with which Jewry reacted to the emergence of Gentile Christianity is to be understood against the very inflammable situation which existed between Jews and Gentiles in 1st-cent. Palestine. The fires which broke out in A.D. 66–70 had long been smouldering. To blur in any way the distinction between Jew and Gentile was to become an enemy of 'the people'. And the Gentile mission did precisely this: it endangered the solidarity of Jewry against the Gentile world. And a still more tangible political factor was involved. Judaism was a *religio licita* with a privileged status, the price of which was eternal vigilance. When the Church claimed to be the true Israel it could also claim the same privileges as did Jewry, and for a long time doubtless did. And the Church's insistence on this claim had not only a theological but also a political perspective: it took place against a legal background. Especially when Gentiles entered the Church, legal and political differences might easily arise with Rome. To avoid this it was to the advantage of Jewry to oppose the new Israel on political grounds by emphasising its seditious character and thus making clear to Rome the distinction between Jews and Christians. Equally advantageous politically was it for Christians to deny this distinction.

e But Paul had also to face the opposition of Jewish Christians. The earliest Christians clung to the forms of Judaism. When members of the Church introduced Gentiles there was opposition when they departed from these forms. Not all the Jerusalem Church was in opposition. James and the leaders never insisted on the necessity for circumcision for Gentile Christians and Peter had more in common with Paul than even with

767e James. Nevertheless a group of Jewish Christians in Jerusalem insisted on circumcision : they were Paul's chief opponents—at Galatia, Corinth, Antioch these appeared or their emissaries. Attempts made to deny this by minimising the differences between the Jerusalem Church and Paul and claiming that the 'Judaisers' were not Jewish Christians connected with Jerusalem but Gentile Christians who had been overzealous for the Law, are not convincing (see Munck, op. cit.). The Judaisers were probably Pharisaic Christians, and it is essential to understand why Paul opposed them. His conversion had revealed to Paul that the grace of God was towards the 'outsiders'. It was his very understanding of his conversion and of the Church that was at stake, therefore, in his conflict with his Jewish-Christian opponents. To insist on circumcision and the Law was a denial of the nature of the Church as a community founded in the grace of God towards the ungodly. Paul was prepared to allow Jewish Christians to live *as Jews*, himself to be a Jew in order to win Jews ; he probably observed the Law as much as possible all his days ; his agony over his people never abated. But on the issue that the Law was *necessary* to salvation he could not compromise. No considerations of policy or expediency could justify this. The struggle over the Law is, therefore, a struggle over Paul's understanding of God's act in Christ and of the Church as his Body.

f And it was the same struggle over the nature of the Church that lies behind the attacks on his apostleship. This was a convenient means of attacking all he stood for. Paul's insistence on the validity of his apostleship arises in controversy with Judaisers. And his defence of his apostleship as independent of the Twelve, true as it is, nevertheless hides from us his oneness with the Twelve also, a oneness he was prepared to do much to maintain. Paul was not so much an apostle of liberty from the Twelve as the Apostle of the universal Church : it was over the unity of the Church that he defended his apostolate and opposed Judaisers. Nor was he the apostle of liberty from all law. In the Gentile churches he found opponents of a more Hellenistic or pagan origin. We see them in 1 C. claiming that entrance into the Church conferred a kind of supernatural status beyond good and evil to which ethical conduct was irrelevant (1 C. 4:8, 6:12–20, 10:6–13). They were the objects of Paul's discipline. And his concern for them was increased when Jewish-Christian opponents of his invaded the Church : antinomianism and legalism could make strange bedfellows. Both 1 and 2 C., Rom. and Col. show how Jewish legalism and asceticism recur, how sin was always ready to enter in under cloaks of grace or of law. And the expectation of the End could also create moral problems (see 1, 2 Th.). From many sides Paul was faced with the need for moral discipline. He, who seemed to Jewish Christians to annul the Law, must have seemed to the Gentile churches a moralist. Paul, apostle of freedom, was a catechist.

g Thus he was a complex figure : but this very complexity helps to explain the greatness of his achievement. Although he did not labour alone, he more than any other was responsible for the rapid spread of Christianity in the mid-1st cent. ; albeit unwittingly he can be claimed to have laid the foundations for later Christian theology ; he gave the Gentile churches order in worship and in organisation. He understood the Graeco-Roman world, and was yet rooted in Judaism, so that he was able to plant a Palestinian Gospel in an alien world and yet keep it true to its root ; while his imperial awareness kept Christianity from conflict on any large scale with Rome. Paul's prizes were great. As a person he gained friendship and hatred : sensitive and courageous, passionate and sagacious, uncompromising and yet capable of being all things to all men, he is a vivid figure. Who touches him, touches a man who remained true to the kindred points of heaven and earth.

h Ac. ends with the imprisonment of Paul in Rome. Thereafter we have no narrative of events which we 767
can follow. We have to rely instead on indirect indications in the literature of the Church and in the history of the Roman Empire. The period between the death of Paul and the end of the 1st cent. has rightly been referred to as a tunnel or a twilight. But the attempt to understand it must be made. To begin with, it is essential to re-emphasise that Paul had not laboured alone : Paul was doubtless the best-known 1st-cent. missionary but not the only one. Thus, besides him other missionaries, great and small, 'authorised' and 'unauthorised', had carried Christianity to Asia Minor, Macedonia, Greece, Italy and Egypt. During the 1st cent. churches came to be firmly planted in all these areas. Geographically two things are noteworthy. First, the development of the Church seems to have been associated particularly with certain 'metropolitan' centres : in the period up to A.D. 70 Jerusalem, Caesarea and Antioch played the leading role, in that from A.D. 70–200, Antioch, Ephesus and Rome. This markedly metropolitan characteristic of the Christian movement persisted into the 2nd and subsequent centuries when great city churches became centres for the literary, textual, ecclesiastical and theological life of the Church. And secondly, the Church outside Palestine necessarily became far stronger than that inside Palestine, until finally the centre of gravity of the Church moved from Jewish to Hellenistic Christianity. This shift produced problems.

I The Church and Judaism—In this connection 768
the significance of the fall of Jerusalem in A.D. 70 has recently been re-emphasised. 'After the Resurrection experiences', writes Brandon, 'the next most crucial event in the life of the Christian Church was the overthrow of the Jewish nation in A.D. 70' (*The Fall of Jerusalem* (1951), 251). And it is with this event that Gentile Christianity really supersedes Jewish. The death of the great Paul left the narrowly nationalistic Jerusalem Church in a dominant position, but fortunately for the future of Christianity Jerusalem fell to Rome in A.D. 70. Paul, as a result, was rehabilitated and the Gospel freed for the world. The link between the Church and the Synagogue was effectively severed. The weaknesses in this theory are evident : (*a*) the antithesis drawn between Pauline and Jewish Christianity cannot be substantiated ; (*b*) there is no evidence that the fall of Jerusalem rehabilitated Paul. What Brandon calls 'the rehabilitation of Paul' is better described as a revival of interest in Paul which came much later, probably with the publication of Ac. ; (*c*) The Church as a whole did not become Paulinist after A.D. 70.

But more important than all such points of detail b
is the fact that the 'leap' from Palestinian to Gentile Christianity had occurred long before A.D. 70. The fall of the city at that date could, at best, only place the seal on what was already achieved, namely, the predominance of Gentile Christianity. Any undue emphasis on the fall of Jerusalem is, therefore, to be avoided. And with this it agrees that apart from Mk 13 and its parallels the references to the fall of Jerusalem in the NT are few. Christianity reacted to that event much as did Judaism itself. Already before A.D. 70 Judaism had really found an effective centre for its life in the Law and the Synagogue : already the significance of the Temple had possibly become secondary, so that its fall, despite the despairing sorrow which it caused to many at first, was soon surmounted : it was for a school not for a temple that Rabbi Johanan b. Zakkai prayed when Jerusalem was falling. So too was it with Christians. The role of Jerusalem and its Church in the early days of Christianity was an important one, but already the centre of Christian life had found elsewhere its root. Sorrowful as it must have been to many Christians no less than to Jews, the fall of the city did not, as far as we can judge from our sources, deeply influence the development of the Church. For them the fall of the

8b city was a vindication of their faith and a sign of the end, but it seems that this did not breed vindictiveness : the interpretation of the results of A.D. 70 as a punishment for the incredulity of Jewry came later.

c We have stated that there was no vindictiveness on the part of Christians towards Jews. This is true both before and after A.D. 70. The NT reveals both criticism of Jewry as in Mt. 23 ; Jn ; Rom. 2:1ff., and a yearning for their repentance and conversion, as in the early chapters of Ac. ; Rom. 9–11, and even in the Fourth Gospel, which is often taken to be particularly opposed to 'the Jews', the desire of the author is for their salvation (Jn 5:34). There is much evidence that there was considerable interchange of thought between Jews and Christians up to the end of the 1st cent., and Jewish scholars have contrasted the 1st and the 2nd cent. in this regard. In the latter opposition to Christianity among Jews became bitter, because of the failure of Jewish Christians to join the forces of the revolt under *Bar Cochba*. But the bitterness already existed in the first century after A.D. 70 both because of the failure of Christians to fight against Rome and because of the danger which Judaism recognised in the growing Christian movement. The Rabbis who gathered at Jamnia after A.D. 70, and who assumed the leadership of Jewry, took active steps to prevent the inroads of Christianity. The fixation of the Jewish canon of scripture about this time may have been provoked by the need to define what constituted 'scripture' in view of the use of the OT and Apocrypha and Pseudepigrapha by Christians. Regulations were drawn up to ensure that Jews should not fast on the same days as Christians. A prayer referred to as *Birkath ham-Mînîm* was introduced to make it impossible for Christians to participate in synagogue worship: miracles and the *bath ḳôl* (literally, 'a daughter of a voice') were discredited as media of revelation as a counterblast to the emphasis placed upon them by Christians. There can be little question that after A.D. 70 Judaism was increasingly shutting itself in against Christianity ; the forces which led to their later rigid separation were already working despite the agony in many a Christian of Jewish origin on behalf of his people. It should be noted that by A.D. 70 any advantage that Christianity may once have gained from association with Judaism was gone : in any case since the persecution under Nero in A.D. 64 Christians and Jews were distinct in Roman eyes. Most of the literature which expressly deals with the relation between Judaism and Christianity belongs to the 2nd cent., but we can read Paul's understanding of this in Rom. 9–11, and it is probably legitimate to regard the Gospel according to St Matthew (A.D. 75–100) as a presentation of Christianity as, in part at least, the reformation of Judaism—a plea to the people of the Old Covenant.

9a **II The Church and the Caesars**—The friction between Jews and Christians was accompanied by that between the latter and the Roman Empire. What we may call the pre-conditions for Imperial suspicion of Christianity were exceedingly rich. There was, first, the simple fact that Christianity was associated in the Roman mind with Judaism. That Christianity arose within Judaism worked at first as an advantage to it. Judaism was ascribed privileges which, as long as the distinction between the two religions could be overlooked, Christianity could share. This circumstance probably helped the initial spread of Christianity and partly explains why Christians laid such emphasis on being the true Israel : the acceptance of their claim to this title brought tangible benefits : they could thus pass under the protective umbrella of Judaism. But the opposite was also true. Their connection with Judaism gained for Christians the ill odour which fell upon Jews. We need merely add that the constant unrest in Palestine would also react very unfavourably against a Palestinian faith. 'Palestine' to Rome was synonymous almost with revolution. After the death of Herod the Great in 4 B.C. it saw a series of revolutionary movements of a fanatical kind. There were riots in that year ; ten years later in 769a
A.D. 6 Judas of Galilee rebelled—there was to be no king but God and therefore no taxes to be paid to Rome ; and there followed the birth of that revolutionary party which was to plunge Jewry into revolt in A.D. 66–70, the Zealots. There is little doubt that the attitude of Roman officials towards Christianity would from the first be prejudiced by their knowledge of its Palestinian origin. But, secondly, Christianity was from 'the Orient'—which again is relevant to the understanding of the Roman attitude towards it. As Rome grew to be a cosmopolitan centre, it attracted cults from the Orient, from Italy, Greece, and later from Galatia and Egypt. Many of these were gradually adopted by Rome as its own and control could be exercised over them. However there also crept into the city other cults which were not recognised. Towards all these Rome showed a watchful tolerance. As long as they were not a menace to the morality and safety of the State they were unmolested. But occasions arose from time to time when Oriental cults did cause moral and political concern. Thus by 186 B.C. Bacchic associations had developed in Rome which became hotbeds of moral corruption, forgery, murder and political conspiracy. The authorities were compelled to take appropriate measures against them. The cult of Isis spread to Rome, and in its name particularly revolting incidents occurred in the 1st cent. B.C and later. Not without reason therefore would another movement from the Orient be scrutinised by Rome, and especially one from Palestine (see Tacitus, *Annals*, xv, 44).

Christianity from the first would suffer from a kind b
of guilt by association. And there were aspects of the Christian movement itself which could not but incite suspicion and ultimately opposition : (*a*) Fundamental was the nature of the Christian message as often popularly preached and understood. Christianity did not only participate in Jewish monotheism and was thus jealous and 'intolerant' of any other gods, one of the major causes of anti-Judaism, it also proclaimed the imminent advent of God's vicegerent to establish His Kingdom, when there would be an end to the existing order, and the kingdoms of this world, including Rome, would become the Kingdom of God and of His Christ. Nor was this proclamation made tepidly but by fervent enthusiasts. Christian preaching could not but disturb a necessarily watchful empire (Ac. 17:6f.). (*b*) Romans would also be alarmed by the 'hatred of the human race' which Christianity seemed to inculcate. The Christian faith was not only intolerant of Roman gods but of social practices which to the Romans seemed enjoyable or harmless. The stern morality of Christians precluded participation in festivals, feasts, games and even in weddings and funerals with their pagan friends. Thus their conduct would appear as inhuman as it was blasphemous and atheistic. Moreover, often Christians would be uneasily yoked in marriage with unbelievers and the strained relations which could arise between husbands and wives, parents and children are reflected in the ethical exhortation given in the NT (see Eph. 4:22ff. ; Col. 3:18–22). (*c*) Again, as Ac. 19:24ff. makes abundantly clear, there were economic motives for opposition which Christianity called into play. Providing for the religious needs of the various cults in the Graeco-Roman world was a considerable industry and a religion that threatened this last could not but bring wrath upon its head. Nor was this wrath insincere. The 'gods many and lords many' of that world might seem non-existent to Christians but to their worshippers they were real. So too the frequent indifference of Christians in public and civic affairs, which were inevitably compromised by their pagan associations and which, in any case, belonged to a world which they deemed to be passing, would also make for unpopularity. Despite the evidence that occasionally Christianity invaded the more privileged sections of Roman society, neverthe-

769b less most Christians were of low degree and much of Christian preaching and worship had an uncomfortable economic relevance (1 C. 7:21f. ; Phm.), as we should expect from point (*a*) above. The political and economic relevance of the Gospel must not be too much sacrificed to ' the spiritual ' (see A. N. Wilder, *Studies in Honour of C. H. Dodd* (1956), 509–36).

c The preconditions for persecution will now be clear. On the Roman side, cosmopolitanism bred both tolerance and, in times of crisis, insecurity and consequently intolerance ; on the Christian side, intransigent claims, the ' scandal ' of the Gospel, created its own ' intolerance '. Moreover, there were theological considerations preconditioning Christians to an expectation of suffering and persecution. Their Lord had suffered and so must His followers also : this was to be their normal lot. Nevertheless to picture the lives of 1st-cent. Christians as one continuous stretch of harrowing persecutions would be unjustified, although there can be little doubt that in that century persecution was a constant and real possibility. Actual persecution began with the Jews. Ac. reveals a rough pattern. Christian preaching called forth the envy of the Synagogue. This in turn instigated mob violence and led to Roman intervention. And despite the difficulty of distinguishing Christians from Jews at first, their presence as a disturbing factor among Jews could not long have escaped Roman vigilance. Gentile persecution broke out first perhaps at Philippi, a Roman colony, and the matter led to a Roman court (Ac. 16:12ff.). To judge from Ac. Christianity in itself was not regarded as illegal *from the beginning*, and despite its tendency to present the relations between Christianity and the Empire in a favourable light, this is probably to be accepted. Did a change come with the first great persecution ? This occurred in A.D. 64 under Nero. Not only does this persecution show that Christians were known under that name in Rome in A.D. 64, as a sect distinct from Jews which was unpopular ' on account of the abominations which they perpetrated ', it also ensured that henceforth the hatefulness of Christianity was established. Did this lead to a change in the Roman policy towards Christians ? There is no evidence that the persecution under Nero spread outside Rome, so that there does not seem to have been an immediate change of policy, at any rate. The fall of Jerusalem in A.D. 70 helped further to distinguish Christians from Jews and it has been claimed that in the Flavian period there was a change. Whereas previously, as under Nero, for example, Christians were punished when they were charged with definite offences, e.g. hostility to society, they began now to be punished ' for the name ' ; i.e. the mere acknowledgment of Christianity in itself involved immediate condemnation. But the weight of the evidence is against this. The letter of Pliny to Trajan asking for advice on policy implies that previously there had been no official policy. Moreover Trajan, in his reply, makes it clear that Christians as yet were too insignificant to require such a policy. Persecution ' for the name ', i.e. for the mere profession of Christianity, would go back at least to Nero's time : it merely meant that Christians as such were regarded as ' enemies of the race ', and therefore could at the discretion of the magistrates be persecuted. There is not one passage in the NT where the phrases ' for the name ', ' in the name ', ' on account of the name ' denote any particular kind of persecution which is more official than any other kind.

d We find, then, that in the 1st cent. Christians were sometimes persecuted although there was no statutory enactment to this effect. The response of Christians to this state of affairs is illustrated in the NT itself. The preservation of Jesus' words in Lk. 22:25–6, in criticism of Gentile authorities, suggests what may have been a prevailing attitude among Christians. Yet the preservation of those in Mk 12:17 is also significant : Christians were to obey the civil authorities in matters where this did not compromise the demands of God. Paul's advice in Rom. 13:1ff., as that in 1 Pet. 2:13ff., **76**
falls in line with this. The State is valued as a dyke against the evil forces in society but there is nothing of the Hellenic conception of the State as existing for the good life or as being the chief or only educative influence upon human nature. We could hardly expect this when as in the reign of Domitian (A.D. 81–96) persecution raged, nor indeed during most of the period. Persecution created its own response. The author of Rev. came to regard the State as essentially opposed to God. This extreme attitude did not become typical (1 Tim. 2:2), but in our period while there was no enmity to the State as in Rev. there was always a nervous watchfulness ; it is not for nothing that the Fourth Gospel was careful to insist that Christ's Kingdom was not of this world.

III The Church Consolidates—Neither the defen- **77**
siveness of Judaism nor the persecution of Rome availed to stem the growth of Christianity. The Church was too well launched in the Gentile world to be seriously affected by any Jewish policies ; and persecution was intermittent. While its disruptive effects are not to be minimised (1 Pet. 4:12 *et passim*), it was the problems of success that mainly faced the Church in the last decades of the 1st cent. But before we examine these we note that the passage of time alone brought major problems with it. Under Nero Peter and Paul lost their lives, and the tradition that the Apostle John lived to old age to the end of the century is highly dubious. The history of the other Apostles is hid from us. What is certain is that by the period with which we are concerned those who had first led the Church had mostly passed away. Those upon whom the Church depended as witnesses to the life, death and resurrection of Jesus were no longer available. This fact was doubly serious when the Church was becoming increasingly Gentile and thus inevitably alien to the forms in which the Palestinian Gospel was couched and to the Judaic root from which the Gospel had sprung and which to some extent determined its genius. There was a danger that the historical ground of Christianity should be lost in the mists of the past. The Church had expanded into the Graeco-Roman world, into a rich world of many religions and philosophic cross-currents. Above all was it a syncretistic world. Particularly potent among the circles in which the Gospel spread were those usually referred to as ' Mystery ' and/or Gnostic. Oriental, Hellenistic and Jewish currents had combined among certain groups to produce the belief that salvation was by participation in a ' Mystery ' or by ' Knowledge ' (*gnosis*), not so much intellectual knowledge, as that derived through a tradition about man's origin and destiny and which culminated in a vision of the divine. Such ' knowledge ' usually implied the recognition that man's life in the flesh was due to his fall from another sphere, so that there often accompanied it either an extreme disparagement of the flesh leading to asceticism or an extreme indifference to the flesh leading to licentiousness. The Gospel could easily have become domesticated in the Graeco-Roman world by becoming a ' Mystery ' without living roots in the Jesus of history and in the morality of the Hebraic tradition. To prevent this was the ' agonic struggle ' of the Church. (This is the error in the claim that the Christian faith adopted the sacramental and ideological framework of the Mysteries and itself became a Mystery : this was precisely what the Church resisted. (See Loisy, *The Birth of the Christian Religion* (1948) for this now generally rejected thesis.) The nature of the problem emerges in the NT itself (Col. 2:8ff. ; 1 Tim. 1:3ff., 4:1ff. ; 2 Tim. 3:1ff. ; Tit. 1:10, 3:9 ; 2 Pet. 2:1ff.).

These dangers the Church met in a threefold way. **b**
First, the Synoptic Gospels emerged to preserve the story of Jesus ; and this is part of the Church's answer. The Gospel according to St John carries the battle farther and uses the weapons of the Hellenistic world to present the Gospel to it. All the Gospels are

770b designed to preserve the historical and ethical root of the Faith against those who would substitute for it a 'mystery' or 'gnosis' that was frequently amoral if not immoral. The emergence of the Gospels is part of that impulse which later led to the formation of the Canon. But, secondly, the NT itself also reveals the second weapon forged by the Church. The essential content of Christian preaching and teaching which we can discern in certain passages of the NT shows that, even though we cannot think of any single fixed form, the main elements of the Faith were presented in a loosely schematic form. But we can go farther than this. The earliest NT documents also reveal unmistakable traces or outcrops of confessional formulae, incipient credal forms which the Church seems to have used at baptism and otherwise from the first (see J. N. Kelly, *Early Christian Creeds* (1950); O. Cullmann, *The Earliest Christian Confessions* (Eng. tr. 1949)). In these documents, moreover, the forms are evidently alive; they participate in a spontaneity which is unmistakable, they appear as the inevitable expression of the pulsating faith of the Church. But in later documents of the NT there is a change. The credal formulae have become the *necessary* expression of faith (see, e.g., 1 Tim. 4:16). The change is significant. The 'credal' elements come to have a defensive and polemic intent. Their aim is to protect the faith against misinterpretation. Thirdly, there is one further development in the later decades of the 1st cent. designed to close the breaches caused by Judaistic, Hellenistic and imperial forces. Persecution in weakening the Church revealed the necessity for organisation: 'heretical' movements in splitting the Church revealed the necessity for control. Two broad classic views of the early Church have emerged in the past. According to the one the Church was a unity from the first—a creed, an apostolate, an organised body, integrated and disciplined. According to the other the Church at first lived in a 'mild anarchy' of the Spirit as a band of spirit-filled enthusiasts. As we saw, both these extreme positions are distortions. Ordered the early Church was, but, even more, guided by the Spirit 'which bloweth where it listeth'. There was a great diversity of organisation, presbyterial, congregational, episcopal (see B. H. Streeter, *The Primitive Church* (1929)). The NT reveals the process whereby this diversity of organisation begins to give place to a unity—the episcopal, and, by the beginning of the 2nd cent., Ignatius, bishop of Antioch, seems to make union with God and with Christ dependent on membership in the Church and loyalty to the bishop. The stages leading to this cannot be traced here.

c The emphasis on the ministry which emerges later in Catholicism was already being called into being by those pressures to which we have referred above: to these there may possibly be added another influence which can only be mentioned. The recently discovered Dead Sea Scrolls *may* provide another clue to the increasing organisation of the Church. After A.D. 68, when Qumrân, probably their headquarters, was destroyed by the tenth Roman legion, it is possible that numbers of the Dead Sea Sect joined the growing Church and brought to it their rigid traditions of discipline and order. Their presence 770c in some strength in the Church might have lent added force to that impetus to organisation to which we have referred. But this possibility must be treated with caution until the evidence is better sifted (see J. Daniélou, op. cit.).

For whatever causes, the Apostolic Age however does end set towards the later Great Church. Romanising forces (these if we follow one school, as we saw above, were already present in Paul's activity), Hellenising forces, Judaising forces—all these were at work in the world which the Gospel entered and we have seen how the Church reacted to them. Whether in meeting these forces as it did the Church 'fell' from its pristine purity or merely developed what was always implicit in its life lies outside the scope of this article to discuss.

Bibliography—S. G. F. Brandon, *The Fall of Jerusalem and the Christian Church* (1951); F. C. Burkitt, *Christian Beginnings* (1924); G. B. Caird, *The Apostolic Age* (1955); P. Carrington, *The Primitive Christian Catechism* (1940), *The Early Christian Church: 1 The First Christian Century* (1957); O. Cullmann, *The Earliest Christian Confessions* (Eng. tr. 1949), *Peter* (Eng. tr. 1953); Gregory Dix, *Jew and Greek* (1953); C. H. Dodd, *The Apostolic Preaching and its Developments* (1936); M. Goguel, *L'Église Primitive* (1947), *The Birth of Christianity* (Eng. tr. 1953); A. E. G. Hardy, *Christianity and the Roman Government* (1925); A. Harnack, *The Mission and Expansion of Christianity* (1908); F. J. A. Hort, *Judaistic Christianity* (1894), *The Christian Ecclesia* (1897); K. Lake & H. J. Cadbury, *The Beginnings of Christianity*, v, (1933); K. Latourette, *The History of the Expansion of Christianity*, i (1937); J. Lebreton & J. Zeiller, *The History of the Primitive Church* (1942–6); H. Lietzmann, *The Beginnings of the Christian Church* (1953); E. Meyer, *Ursprung und Anfänge des Christentums*, iii (1923); A. Momigliano, CAH, x; J. W. Parkes, *The Conflict of the Church and Synagogue* (1934); H. J. Schoeps, *Theologie und Geschichte des Judenchristentums* (1949); B. H. Streeter, *The Primitive Church* (1929); J. Weiss, *The History of Primitive Christianity* (Eng. tr. 1937); K. H. Weizsäcker, *The Apostolic Age of the Christian Church* (Eng. tr. 1894–5); H. B. Workman, *Persecution in the Early Church* (1906).

On the life of Paul: W. D. Davies, *Paul and Rabbinic Judaism*[2] (1956), chs. 1, 4, 5, 6; G. A. Deissmann, *Paul: A Study in Social and Religious History* (1926); Dibelius & Kümmel, *Paul* (1953); G. S. Duncan, *St Paul's Ephesian Ministry* (1929); A. M. Hunter, *Paul and his Predecessors* (1942); J. Klausner, *From Jesus to Paul* (1944); W. L. Knox, *St Paul and the Church of Jerusalem* (1925), *St Paul and the Church of the Gentiles* (1939); J. Munck, *Paulus und die Heilsgeschichte* (1954); A. D. Nock, *St Paul* (1938); W. M. Ramsay, *St Paul the Traveller and Roman Citizen* (1897); A. Schweitzer, *Paul and his Interpreters* (Eng. tr. 1912).

For archaeological details, see G. E. Wright, *Biblical Archaeology* (1957), 245ff. For the NT and the Dead Sea Scrolls, see *The Scrolls and the NT*, ed. K. Stendahl (1957); M. Burrows, *The Dead Sea Scrolls* (1955), *More Light on the Dead Sea Scrolls* (1958).

ACTS

BY G. W. H. LAMPE

771a **Authorship**—Acts is, as the preface (1:1) shows, a continuation of a single work addressed to Theophilus (cf. Lk. 1:3) of which the Third Gospel is the first volume. See the introduction to the commentary on Lk. (§715*a* above). The continuity of theme, the frequent implied allusions in Ac. to the contents and words of the Gospel, and the very close similarity of style and vocabulary bear out the obvious meaning of the preface. A case against the single authorship of Lk. and Ac. was built up by A. C. Clark (*The Acts of the Apostles* (1933), 395ff.) on the basis of statistics of vocabulary, particularly in respect of particles and conjunctions, but W. L. Knox (*The Acts of the Apostles* (1948)), after re-examining Clark's contentions, concludes that 'Clark's linguistic researches . . . tend to prove that the same hand is responsible for the final compilation both of the Acts and of the Gospel.' It is only reasonable to suppose that it is the same hand that has added the two prefaces and the incidental pieces of 'scholarship prose' and that it is the hand of the writer of the 'we-sections'. There seems no reason to doubt that it is the hand of Luke 'the beloved physician'. The work is called *The Acts of the Apostles* and ascribed to Luke by the Latin version of Irenaeus (*Adv. Haer.* III, xiii, 3, III, xiv, 1). The Muratorian Canon, of approximately the same date as Irenaeus (*c.* 180–90), also assigns the book, which it calls *The Acts of all the Apostles*, to Luke. The so-called 'Anti-Marcionite Prologue' to Lk., after stating that Luke, a Syrian doctor from Antioch who had been a companion of Paul and finally died in Boeotia at the age of eighty-four, was the author of the third Gospel, adds that afterwards he wrote the Acts of the Apostles. The date of this prologue, which was assigned by D. de Bruyne (RB 40 (1928), 193ff.) to the 2nd cent., is, however, uncertain and may be considerably later (see R. G. Heard, JTS, N.S. 6 (1955), 1ff.). From the time of Irenaeus onwards this book is regularly
b attributed to Luke (see §715*a* above). The internal evidence of both volumes would accord well with the external tradition that they are the work of Luke, the companion of Paul, but for certain features of the narrative of Ac. which present a difficulty to this view. They consist chiefly of: (*a*) supposed historical discrepancies. These are to be found in connection with the story of the conversion of Paul, where the part played by Ananias is not mentioned in Paul's letters (see 9:10ff.), the situation at the time of his escape from Damascus (9:23–5) does not seem to be precisely the same as that described in 2 C. 11:32–3, and the visit to Jerusalem (9:26–9) appears to be much longer and more full of preaching activity than the fortnight's semi-private visit recorded in Gal. 1:18–19; and in connection with the 'Jerusalem Council' of ch. 15, where the narrative in Ac. is very hard, and probably impossible, to harmonise with Gal. 2:1–10. These discrepancies are discussed at length in the commentary. A less important conflict seems to exist between the account of the journeys of Silas and Timothy in 17:15 and 18:5 and that implied by Paul in 1 Th. 3:1–6. Other difficulties arise from (*b*) the episodes known to us from the Pauline letters which Lk. omits to mention, such as the troubles in the Corinthian church which form so large a part of the subject-matter of 1 and 2 C., the sufferings undergone 771b
by Paul at Ephesus (1 C. 15:32; 2 C. 1:8), and the great collection for the Jerusalem church (Rom. 15:25ff.; 1 C. 16:1ff.; 2 C. 9), which is, at most, only obliquely mentioned in 24:17, though it was of immense importance to Paul and the omission of any reference to it leaves the presence of Paul's companions on his final journey from Corinth (20:4) unexplained. To these omissions might be added Paul's sojourn in Arabia (Gal. 1:17), and some of the sufferings enumerated by Paul in 2 C. 11:23ff. It may be also objected (*c*) that the author of Ac. shows little acquaintance with Pauline theology; some of the most fundamental and distinctive doctrines of Paul are absent from the thought of this writer, such as the sacrificial character of Christ's death and its atoning efficacy, and the contrast between grace and law, faith and works, in relation to justification (13:39 is often thought to be un-Pauline in its brief treatment of justification, and the implied allusion to Christ's blood as a covenant-sacrifice in 20:28 may be thought to stand out as an exception to the general theology of this author, and perhaps as a direct reproduction of Paul's actual words). These objections are cumulatively weighty, but do not preclude the possibility that Ac. was written by a friend and companion of Paul. Those under the heading (*b*) are relatively unimportant. They are largely derived from a misunderstanding of the nature and scope of Ac. The book does not set out to write a history of the apostolic Church, still less a biography of Paul (see §§715*a*, 716*a*). The author's treatment of events is highly selective, and nothing is included, except the details contained in the 'we' passages, which does not directly contribute to his stylised picture of the progress of the gospel. The omission of much that Paul mentions concerning his experiences is only to be expected. The discrepancies under (*a*) above show that the author did not have the Pauline letters as a source for his work. They also show that he depended rather on Church traditions for his information (especially, in all probability, those of Jerusalem and Antioch for the narratives relating to Paul's conversion and the 'Jerusalem Council') than on Paul's own reminiscences, heard at first hand. This need not imply that the writer never travelled with Paul, though it does mean that Paul probably spoke rarely of the past (which we should infer from his letters) and also that the author was not a really intimate friend with an insight into Paul's deeper thought. Ac. gives the impression of being written, from a developed theological standpoint, a very considerable time after the events which it records. The events are set in a distant perspective, and the author's own acquaintance with Paul has itself taken its place in this distant view along with the traditions which he has heard in the churches. It has, in fact, become 'stylised' in the process by which the writer paints his own distinctive picture of the movement of the gospel to Rome. Like his contemporaries, the author would probably find the more profound insights of Paul's teaching difficult to assimilate, even if he had read the letters. Without them, and since there is no need to suppose that Paul's everyday conversation on board ship was devoted to wrestling with the meaning

771b of the Atonement and Justification, there is no need for surprise that the distinctively Pauline insights are not reproduced in Lk.-Ac. On balance, there is no reason to reject the ancient ascription of the work to the Luke of Col. 4:11. It is likely, however, that we must accept the probability that he is not entirely accurate in his narrative of the 'Jerusalem Council' despite the many attempts which have been made to harmonise Ac. 15 with Gal. 1–2. See §791*b–e*.

c **The 'we' passages** present a subsidiary problem. It is usually held that they are the work of Luke himself, the compiler of the whole work, and that they are inserted without a change of pronoun in order to show that the author was himself present in those parts of the history. This is very probable. The style of these passages is characteristically Lucan; they are more closely related to the rest of Luke's writing, in vocabulary and style, than is, for example, Luke's Marcan material after he has worked it over. The detailed narrative which these passages contain, mainly accounts of voyages, is out of keeping with the author's general practice elsewhere of moving rapidly from one major episode to another without describing the intervening journeys, and it seems most probable that the author has so strong a personal interest in this material as to be willing to sacrifice his usual speed of movement, and a good deal of space, in order to bring it in. These passages may well be part of a diary actually kept at the time of the events, on which Luke draws long afterwards. It is less probable that they are the work of someone other than the final author. Not only does the similarity of language and style tell against this view, but it is difficult to account for the retention of the first person in the final incorporation of the passages into this book. The appearance of the first-person 'diaries' of Nehemiah and Ezra in the work of the Chronicler could, indeed, furnish a precedent, but Luke's work seems to be more artistically conceived than that of the Chronicler. On the other hand it must be admitted that Ac. is roughly finished and has not been carefully revised (see e.g. 3:16, 4:25 and §796*b*). On balance, it is likely that these passages are from Luke's own notes. It is much less probable that the intervening passages between 16:19 and the end are worked up from the same notes, cast into the third person. The treatment of Paul's stay in such places as Corinth and Ephesus (see §§795*h*, 797*b*) strongly suggests that the author of the book was not an eye-witness of the events there. It remains hard to discover why the first-person notes cover only the narrative of sea voyages and the events which occur soon after Paul and his companions have come ashore, and why the diarist always slipped out of the picture as soon as his friends had established themselves at their destination.

d **Date**—See introductory commentary on Lk. (§715*b* above). Assuming that Ac. was written after Lk. (for the contrary view, that Ac. preceded the Gospel in its early form, see C. S. C. Williams, JTS 49 (1948), 204ff., *The Acts of the Apostles* (1957), 14), it must have been composed between the publication of Mk (*c.* 64) and the latest date at which it would still be possible for the author to write on this subject in ignorance of the Pauline letters. It is not necessary to suppose, though it is likely, that the Gospel was written after the fall of Jerusalem (70); it is on the whole unlikely that 5:36–7, 21:38; Lk. 3:1 (see §721*b*) imply that Luke had seen, and misread, Josephus, which would involve a date for Lk.-Ac. later than 93. The points which Lk. is at pains to make, that Christianity is the true religion of Israel and that it is no threat to the peace and security of the Empire, would be important at any time in the 1st cent., but especially when the Church was being actively repudiated by the synagogue, and the Roman world had become aware of the Church as an independent body, distinct from Judaism. The presentation of the story of the gospel's rejection by the Jews and its acceptance by Gentiles, its progress from Jerusalem to Rome, in the highly selective and stylised manner of this book, could hardly be carried out until after a relatively long interval of time had elapsed. A date in the eighties would seem most probable. 771d

Canonicity—Ac. seems to have taken some time to establish itself as a widely read book in the Church. The chief reason for this is that, with the incorporation of Luke's first volume in a corpus of four Gospels, his second volume tended to be read as an independent work and therefore lost much of its meaning. In comparison with the Gospels and the Epistles it would seem to have relatively little value for the immediate needs of the Church and it would tend to be regarded simply as an early work of Church history, of comparatively little doctrinal or devotional importance. The following passages in 1 Clement have been thought to contain allusions to Ac.: 5:4, 7 (Ac. 1:25), 18:1 (a combination of OT texts partly similar to 13:22), 2:1 (a different form of the saying attributed to Christ at 20:35), 59:2 (an OT reminiscence echoed also at 26:18). In Ignatius possible echoes of Ac. have been traced in *Magnesios* 5:1 (Ac. 1:25) and *Smyrnaeos* 3:3 (10:41). Parallels have also been seen in *Barnabas* 5:9 (1:2), 7:2 (10:42), 19:8 (4:32); the last-mentioned occurs also in the *Didache* 4:8. This work affords possible echoes in its use of *pais* ('son' or 'servant') for Christ (9:2, 10:2; Ac. 3:13, 26, 4:27, 30), though it is very improbable that it does in fact borrow from Ac. Other possible allusions have been seen in 2 Clement 1:1 (10:42), 4:4 (4:19, but more probably alluding to Mt. 10:28), 20:5 (3:15, 5:31). It is possible that there may be actual echoes of Ac. among these suggested parallels, but in no single case is it absolutely necessary to suppose such dependence. There is a better case for the view that the Epistle of Polycarp shows direct acquaintance with Ac.: 1:2 (2:24), 6:3 (7:52), 12:2 (20:32). Justin alludes to Ac. (cf. esp. *1 Apol.* 50:12), along with the Gospels and Epistles. Irenaeus discusses the contents of much of the book at length (*Adv. Haer*, III, xii, 1ff.); see above, §764*a*. From his time onwards it is often cited, and from the Muratorian Canon included in the undisputed books of the Canon. It has been suggested that there is an allusion to Ac. 3:26 in the Valentinian *Gospel of Truth*, 22:20; but the parallel is not close enough to indicate dependence. 772a

Purpose and Scope—Ac. is not an entire work, to be read by itself, but the second part of Luke's *ad Theophilum*. It cannot, therefore, be properly understood unless it is read as the continuation of the Third Gospel. It is, indeed, intended to be a part of the Gospel, and not merely a sequel to it; still less is it meant to be an early essay in Church history. The gospel events extend from the annunciation of the birth of the Messiah's forerunner to the proclamation of the Kingdom of God and the teaching of 'the things concerning Jesus as Lord and Messiah' in the capital of the Gentile world. The gospel is not only the proclamation that the messianic promises of God are fulfilled in Jesus, but also the declaration that through his saving work Israel has been reconstituted; though the leaders of the covenant people rejected first Jesus and then his apostles, Israel has been given a new structure by the operation of the Spirit through the apostolic mission. It is continuous with the Israel of old, but the present leaders of Judaism fail to recognise this. It is, however, no longer confined to those who accept the Mosaic Law, but extends to all, including uncircumcised Gentiles, who have faith in Jesus. This re-creation of Israel is made possible because God has vindicated and exalted his Messiah, showing that his death was not the contradiction and scandal that it seemed, but that it was purposed by God as the road to his glory. The glorification of Jesus in the Ascension is thus the decisive turning-point of Luke's work, but it is by no means the end of his story; it demonstrates that Jesus is Lord and Messiah, but it remains for Luke to tell how the people of the Messiah was brought into being out of the faithful among the Jews and out of Samaritans and Gentiles. b

772b The first volume had told how Jesus, as the Davidic Messiah and the prophet like Moses (see Ac. 3:22 ; Lk. 4:18ff.), had proclaimed the Kingdom of God (whose ' content ' is later defined in terms of repentance and forgiveness of sins) to Israel. This ' salvation ' was attested and effected by ' signs and wonders '. Jesus was rejected by the leaders of Israel, mainly on account of his attitude to those who were outcasts from the people of God and the narrow legalism of the Jewish authorities, and was put to death. This was in accordance with the divine will revealed in Scripture. God vindicated him in the Resurrection, of which the apostles, already appointed to become his envoys to the world, were eye-witnesses, and he was exalted to heaven as Lord. In the second volume Luke describes the making-up of the number of the apostolic witnesses, the coming on them, through the exalted Lord, of the Spirit that was upon him in his ministry, and their proclamation of salvation (repentance and forgiveness), through faith in him, to a mixed multitude at Jerusalem, symbolical of the nations of the world, and then to the people of Israel, in the inspiration and power of the Spirit. The preaching is accompanied by signs and wonders, performed through the power of the name of Jesus, which are parallel to those wrought by him in his earthly ministry. Converts are baptised in his name and the community of the reconstituted people of God is established, possessing a unity and harmony that finds expression in the common sharing of property. The gospel is accepted by the crowds, but rejected by the priestly leaders. It is under the divine guidance and by the divine power that this mission is carried on ; hence no human authority can interfere. Even when the apostles are imprisoned they are miraculously set free. The final clash between the Christian missionaries and the Dispersion Jews at Jerusalem leads to the martyrdom of Stephen in which the death and glorification of Jesus is reproduced in his disciple.

As a consequence of this martyrdom and the ensuing persecution, the mission moves out to Samaria and then to the Gentiles, always under divine guidance. It is by this divine guidance that Peter baptises the Gentile household of Cornelius, and the extension of the Church is again accompanied by signs and wonders. Meanwhile the leader of the Gentile mission has already been converted by a direct appearance of the glorified Lord, and changed from the Church's chief persecutor to its principal missionary to the Gentile world. The divine power is also demonstrated in Peter's release from Herod's prison and the spectacular end of Herod. The mission, under Paul's leadership, then proceeds through Asia Minor, and later into Europe, directed first to the Jews in every city and then to the Gentiles when the Jews reject the gospel. Two secondary, but important, themes receive special emphasis in the later chapters, that Christianity is a fulfilment of Judaism, a development in full harmony with all that was best in the tradition of Israel ; and that Christianity was always befriended by Gentile local authorities and Roman governors and officers (the governor of the first province visited by Paul becoming a convert), except when misunderstanding was caused by the malicious hatred of the Jews. Finally, through Paul's ' passion ', his trials and imprisonments, there comes the triumphal entry of the gospel into the capital of the Gentile world. Even the storm and shipwreck cannot hinder it, and signs and wonders continue to accompany and attest it. Paul makes his last missionary appeal to the Jews at Rome, and, when they reject his gospel, turns to the Gentiles, confident that they will accept it. Thus the work is brought to a triumphant conclusion.

c The author's method of presenting this part of the gospel is by means of a series of dramatic scenes or pictures. There is little continuous narrative, but rather an impressionistic treatment of the events so that the meaning of the story can be concentrated in a few vivid episodes. Thus the call and empowering of the apostles to proclaim the gospel to the world is 772c focused pictorially in the fiery tongues of Pentecost and the preaching of Peter to a crowd drawn from all the ends of the earth ; the great step forward by which Gentiles were brought directly into the people of God is dramatically portrayed in Peter's vision at Joppa and the coming of the Spirit upon Cornelius ; the relations between Christianity and the imperial authorities are not analysed but vividly presented in such tableaux as the conversion of the proconsul of Cyprus (in face of the machinations of a Jewish false prophet) and Gallio driving Paul's malicious accusers from his tribunal. The claim that the gospel is the fulfilment of the best in Judaism is embodied in the scene of Paul dividing the Sanhedrin on the Pharisaic doctrine of resurrection. The unity of the Spirit in the primitive Church is shown in the picture of a community possessing all things in common and in the dramatic fate of those who tried to deceive the Spirit for selfish advantage. Certain episodes of central importance in the progress of the gospel have their significance brought home to the reader by being repeated, always with such minor variations as may serve to avoid tedium : this is notably the case with the conversion of Paul and the vision of Peter.

Speeches are inserted at frequent intervals, in order to d interpret for the reader the content of the gospel, whose progress is presented in Luke's series of stylised episodes. In these speeches the gospel is set forth in its relation to particular situations : Peter's speech at Pentecost declares the fulfilment of the messianic promises in the resurrection of Jesus and the outpouring of the Spirit. His speech at the Temple (3:12–26) shows that in Jesus the prophecies are fulfilled, that Jesus, despite his death at the hands of the Jews, has been glorified by God, that through him there is salvation, and that therefore Israel is called to repent. The speech of Stephen shows that Jesus, as the prophet like Moses, stands in the succession of those deliverers whom the leaders of Israel have always persecuted, that the rejection of him by the Sanhedrin is part of the whole pattern of their resistance to the Spirit by their idolatry, their failure to understand and keep the Law and their devotion to the man-made Temple. Peter (10:34–43) and Paul (13:17–41) declare the outlines of the gospel as preached to Jews, showing, in particular, how the scriptural prophecies and promises are fulfilled in it. At Athens and Lystra there are examples of the preaching of the gospel to pagan audiences, where the appeal to scripture would be useless. The speeches of Paul, from 22:3–21 onwards, show how Christianity fulfils the hopes and aspirations of Pharisaic Judaism. In all of them the meaning of the Church's mission is set out, as the meaning of the mission of Jesus was declared in the speech at Nazareth (Lk. 4:23–7).

The question remains open whether these speeches e are Luke's free composition or, if not, to what extent they may be based on actual records or memories of what was said by those to whom they are attributed. The method of such OT writers as the author and compilers of Deuteronomy and the historical books, as well as of Greek and Roman historians, is to compose speeches, suitable to the characters concerned, representing what they would have said in the particular circumstances and enabling the reader to grasp the inner significance of the events. Luke seems to follow the same practice. In his case the object is to make explicit the nature of the apostolic preaching. In so far as he follows existing models, these would seem to be contained in the OT. Thus the speech of Stephen is closely modelled on the ' Deuteronomic ' psalms. The style of the speeches is Lucan. Those which embody the missionary preaching to Jews, especially 10:34–43, are composed in a highly ' biblical ' style, using many words and phrases from the LXX, and at times the mosaic of scriptural expressions becomes so complicated as to confuse the grammar and obscure the sense. This is not out of keeping with Luke's

772e manner, as seen particularly in Lk. 1–2. They contain echoes of Luke's Gospel (e.g. 7:22, Lk. 24:19 ; 3:21, Lk. 1:70), and occasionally matters which Luke might have been expected to treat more fully in the Gospel seem to have been postponed to these speeches : e.g. the question of the Temple, passed over very lightly in Lk. 19:45–6 and omitted from the trial of Jesus, is taken up in the speech of Stephen. The speeches sometimes echo one another, e.g. 3:22, 7:37 ; their frequent allusions to the OT are to the text of the LXX, even in the speech assigned to James at Jerusalem (15:16–18). The speeches at Lystra and Athens seem to be typical of Jewish and Christian preaching to the heathen world, owing much to OT thought, with probably some admixture of those ideas which could be shared by Stoics. On the whole, it is likely that the speeches are Luke's composition. Comparison with the NT Epistles tends to show that Luke was able to reproduce in general outline what was in fact the substance of the early Church's preaching. In a few places he seems to have taken pains to insert certain touches for the sake of verisimilitude : e.g. the reference to justification in the speech of Paul (13:39), though whether this represents Paul's own teaching on the matter is doubtful. One speech appears to stand out as an exception : that of Paul at Miletus (20:18–35). This is comparatively full of Pauline echoes and ' rings true ' as a speech of Paul in a way which differentiates it from the other speeches. It may well be that notes of this speech were included in the ' travel diary ' of Luke and that he wrote it up from a solid basis of personal reminiscence. On the difficult problem of the speeches see M. Dibelius, *Studies in the Acts of the Apostles* (1956) ; C. H. Dodd, *The Apostolic Preaching and its Development* (1936) ; B. Gärtner, *The Areopagus Speech and Natural Revelation* (1955) ; C. F. Evans, JTS, N.S. 7 (1956), 25ff. ; C. S. C. Williams, *The Acts of the Apostles* (1957).

773a **The Theology of Acts**, for the most part expressed in the speeches, but implicit in the structure and movement of the whole narrative, is discussed in the commentary on Lk., §716*c* ff. above.

b **Sources**—No solution of the problem of Luke's sources for Ac. can be more than guesswork. In the Gospel Luke was dealing with fairly closely defined and established traditions, and his principal source (Mk) lies before us. In Ac. we have no similar check on any part of his material, and there is no reason to suppose that traditions about the early life and mission of the Church were remembered and handed on in the way in which traditions of the deeds and words of Jesus were transmitted in preaching, teaching, liturgy and credal summaries. Luke himself might well think it possible to *preach* the good news of the Gentile mission or of Christianity as the ' true Judaism ', but there is no reason to suppose that others before him had thought this, still less that they had acted on that idea. It is therefore unlikely that he possessed extensive written sources. E. Haenchen (*Die Apostelgeschichte* (1957), 78) believes that the insertion of an apparent afterthought in 18:19 (see §796*b*) implies that Luke added a sentence to a document lying before him ; but the difficulty here is more probably due to Luke's hastiness in writing and his failure (observable in several places) to revise his draft thoroughly. The ' travel diary ' probably existed in the form of notes made long ago by the author himself (see above, §764*c*). It is likely that the episodic character of the narrative, especially from 16 to the end, if it is not due entirely to Luke's own method, may indicate that he used the traditions of individual churches (Philippi, Corinth, Ephesus, etc.) rather than a connected story of the missionary journeys, such as might be preserved at Antioch. The conventional division of 13:4–21:27 into three ' missionary journeys ' does not, in any case, correspond to actual divisions in Luke's narrative. 1–5 is probably based on traditions derived from the Jerusalem church. 6, 8:1–3, perhaps 9, 11:19–30 and 12:24–5 may represent a cycle of traditions about the
' Hellenists ' and their missionary activity, of which 773b
the story of Paul's conversion may have formed part, or the latter may have been an independent story inserted in this cycle by Luke (as the Epistles show, it was not derived from Paul himself). The fact that this material leads on without a break into 13–14 perhaps indicates that the whole of this cycle originated in the church at Antioch. Possibly 15 also belongs to it rather than to the Jerusalem church. 8:4–40 is presumably derived from stories about Philip, perhaps circulating at Caesarea. A tradition about Peter's mission underlies 9:31–11:18 (though after the beginning of the story of the vision at Joppa it is hard to say how much remembered tradition lies behind Luke's elaborate ' writing-up ' of the story). 12 may be a part (possibly displaced) of the same cycle of Petrine tradition, emanating either from Caesarea or Jerusalem, or it may be an independent story circulating in Jerusalem. A switch from one of such cycles to another is probably to be discerned at 6:1, 8:4, 9:31, 11:19 and 12:1. C. C. Torrey (*The Composition and Date of Acts* (1916)), held that 1–15 was translated from an Aramaic document. W. L. Knox (*The Acts of the Apostles* (1948)), supported this theory in respect of 1–5:16. There has been more general support for the theory that some, at least, of the speeches in the first half of Ac. are translated from Aramaic. This hypothesis rests on the existence of supposed Aramaisms in Luke's Greek and on difficulties in the Greek that are explicable as the result of mistranslation from Aramaic. In very many cases, however, the alleged ' Aramaisms ' are either actual citations from the LXX or imitations of the style and vocabulary of the LXX. Other supposed Aramaisms have been shown to be good *koinē* Greek. That Luke was probably ignorant of Aramaic is suggested by his attempt to translate ' Barnabas ' and his confusion over Bar-Jesus and Elymas. Any theory of a document underlying the whole of chs. 1–15 has to postulate a pre-Lucan author of this part of Ac. whose thought and methods were indistinguishable from Luke's. In fact, it is most improbable that any part of Ac. is translated. See H. F. D. Sparks, JTS, N.S. 1 (1950), 16ff.

Text—The text of Ac. presents a very difficult problem. c
The two main groups of MSS are the ' Alexandrian ' (Vaticanus, Sinaiticus, Chester Beatty papyrus, etc.) and the ' Western ' (Bezae, Floriacensis, marginal readings in the Harklean Syriac, etc.). The Western text differs from the former to so great an extent that it has been supposed to represent a different recension. A. C. Clark (*The Acts of the Apostles* (1933)) believed that it was the better text, representing more nearly what Luke wrote. This is very unlikely. Its readings have to be treated on their merits, and some are interesting, but for the most part the Western text is an expanded version. Luke's narrative is not thoroughly revised. It is often abrupt and too concise. The Western text smooths over the rough joints, adding explanatory details. It also tries to improve awkwardness of style. See, e.g., 2:47, 3:11, 8:39, 10:25, 16:35. In few cases, however, does this text add anything which could not be inferred from the Alexandrian text or plausibly guessed. Certain common tendencies in the Western readings suggest that behind this text there is an editor with views of his own. These tendencies include a certain magnifying of the apostles and their authority, especially Peter (e.g. 5:39, 11:1, 15:2, 5), a pious insistence on giving the full titles of Christ (28:31 is the most notable of many examples), extra emphasis on the guidance of the Spirit (e.g. 19:1–2), and, oddly, a depreciation of the importance of women in the story (e.g. 17:4, 12). Some of the notable Western readings include : (*a*) 8:37 (the insertion of a credal affirmation, which was felt to be implicit and fitting to be expressed), (*b*) 11:28 (the insertion of a ' we ' passage at Antioch), (*c*) 12:10 (the reference to ' the seven steps '), (*d*) 19:9 (Paul occupied Tyrannus's hall from the fifth to the tenth hour), (*e*) 20:4 (Gaius of Doberus,

773c in Macedonia, instead of Derbe, a Gaius having apparently been mentioned as a Macedonian in 19:29). See the commentary on these readings. In fact, all these readings seem to be the work of a careful reader, intent on smoothing out difficulties and adding explanations of questions that might occur to other diligent readers. Some are over-clever. It is improbable that any are to be preferred to the Alexandrian text.

d **Chronology**—The chronology of Ac. is discussed in the larger commentaries. The principal data are the death of Herod Agrippa I in 44 (probably 10 March), the famine of 11:28 which may be identical with that which, according to Josephus, was severe in Palestine between 46 and 48, and the dating of Gallio's proconsulship by the Delphi inscription (see commentary on 18:12).

774a **I 1-2 Preface recapitulating the Theme of Luke's Gospel**—' First ' meaning the former of two is common in Hellenistic Greek (cf. 12:10) and does not imply that a third volume was projected. This second volume of Luke's work opens with a renewal of the first volume's dedication to Theophilus (see §719*a*), and a glance at its subject-matter which leads directly into the narrative which continues it. ' Began ' is not emphatic, and is little more than an extended form of the past tense, ' did and taught '. The allusion is to the mighty works of Jesus and to his teaching (cf. Lk. 24:19). ' Taken up ' : the point at which the first volume ended. Even if the direct allusion to the Ascension in Lk. 24:51 should be omitted with the Western text (which is by no means certain), this passage indicates that the words ' he parted from them ' in that verse denote a final departure, the moment of Jesus' exaltation. Old Latin readings (Augustine, *De Consensu Evangelistarum* 4:8) try to harmonise this passage with the ending of the Gospel by omitting ' he was taken up, after '. ' Commandment ' probably refers to Lk. 24:45–9, not to v. 4 below, though the text is difficult ; the Western text tries to improve it by adding ' and commanded them to preach the gospel '. ' Through the Holy Spirit ' may refer to the choice of the apostles, made under the inspiration of the Spirit (cf. Lk. 6:12–13, which sets their appointment in the context of sustained prayer). Alternatively, it refers to the instruction given by Jesus to the apostles (i.e. the eleven)as his chosen missionaries.

b **3-11 The Promise to the Apostles and their Commissioning**—' To them . . .' : this sentence marks the transition from Luke's first volume to his second. ' Appearing ' translates a participle which means ' being visible ' ; it does not imply that Jesus appeared in a vision. Tob. 12:19 may be in mind here. ' Forty days ' : cf. 13:31, which indicates a similar tradition of an interval between the Resurrection and the Ascension, apparently conflicting with Lk. 24:51. The deliberate parallels with, and echoes of, Lk. 24:46–53 in this passage, however, suggest that Luke saw no inconsistency between Ac. and the Gospel and did not intend to correct the narrative contained in the latter. The explanation of his introduction of the forty days may be found in typology, the story in Ac. being modelled on 1 Kg. 19:8, the forty days of Moses on Sinai before the giving of the Law (itself corresponding to, and typical of, the events of Pentecost), and perhaps also the forty days of the Temptations. Forty is a ' sacred ' rather than an exact number. (See J. G. Davies, *He ascended into Heaven*, 47–56.) ' The kingdom of God ', to come in fullness at the Parousia, will begin to become effective among men when the apostles enter upon their missionary task ; cf. 6–8. **4.** ' Staying with ' : RSV*n* is probably correct. The verb probably means ' eating salt with ', the allusion being to the fellowship meals (like that of Emmaus) in which the disciples encountered the risen Christ (cf. 10:41). Alternatively, the verb is a variant spelling for *synaulizomai* (instead of *synalizomai*), meaning ' lodge with ', which itself has a little support in the MS tradition. Just as the gospel began in Jerusalem (Lk. 1:5ff.), so the apostolic mission begins there. Luke is insistent that the events in which the Church's mission began happened either in or very near Jerusalem, from which the story moves gradually into the Gentile world and Rome itself. ' The promise ' : see Lk. 24:49.

5. John's baptism was preparatory for the ' baptism ' c with the Spirit, promised for the last times (cf. Lk. 3:16) and now to be fulfilled when Jesus has been exalted at the right hand of God (2:33). **6.** ' So when ' introduces the main narrative, beginning with the commissioning of the apostles. Their question does not necessarily indicate a merely worldly or materialistic conception of the kingdom. They would naturally suppose that the Resurrection and the imminent fulfilment of the eschatological promise of the Spirit's coming (cf. ' in the last days ', 2:17) meant the immediate consummation of the Kingdom of God and the fulfilment to themselves of the promise that they exercise its authority over the tribes of Israel (Lk. 22:30). Jesus tells them (i) that speculation about the imminence of the end is to be discouraged (cf. Lk. 21:8–9), in accordance with the general teaching of the Lucan writings that the Parousia is to be long delayed ; (ii) that the world is first to be evangelised (cf. Mk 13:10) ; (iii) that the kingdom is to be opened to those who stood outside the old covenant ; (iv) that the kingdom is to be exercised, until the Parousia, in and through the preaching of the gospel ; (v) that the apostles are to be the judges of the renewed Israel (cf. Lk. 22:30) by virtue of being the chosen witnesses who will bring the gospel of salvation and judgment to all the nations. **8.** The apostles will perform their task as witnesses in the power of the Spirit. The Spirit, whose work is to testify to Jesus (cf. Lk. 12:12) will bear witness in the apostolic mission which he inspires and directs. The stages in their mission, indicated here, correspond with the plan of Ac. : chs. 1–7 deal with Jerusalem, 8–9 with Judaea and Samaria, and the rest mainly with the Gentile mission, culminating at Rome. The advance from Jerusalem to Rome, from the Israel of old to a predominantly Gentile Church, is reflected in the ' missionary strategy ' of the apostles : to the Jews first, as the people of God's covenant ; then, when the Jewish leaders reject the gospel, to the Gentiles. In the background of Luke's thought here there may be the mission of the ' Servant ' (Isa. 49:6) to be a light to the Gentiles and to bring salvation to the ends (so LXX) of the earth.

9-12 The Ascension—The commissioning of the d apostles and the promise to them of the power of the Spirit is the last utterance of Jesus on earth. Luke pictures his exaltation (cf. Lk. 22:69 ; Jn 17:11 ; Eph. 4:8–10 ; Phil. 2:9 ; Heb. 1:3) as a physical event, comparable with the ascension of Elijah. Elijah's disciple, Elisha, was promised a double share of his master's spirit if he saw him being taken from him (2 Kg. 2:9). The disciples of Jesus similarly ' look on ' as he is taken, and they receive the Spirit from him at Pentecost. They are witnesses of his glorification as well as of his earthly life and his resurrection. The cloud is the sign of the divine presence ; cf. the translation of Moses (Jos. Ant. IV, viii, 48) and of Enoch (Enoch 39:3), and especially Luke's own account of the Transfiguration (Lk. 9:34–5) where, as at the Resurrection (Lk. 24:4), there are two heavenly witnesses, as here. cf. also Rev. 11:12. **10.** White robes are the symbol of a heavenly being (cf. Lk. 9:29, 24:4). The angelic messengers explain the meaning of the departure of Jesus. He is now exalted in glory and will not again be seen in his own person, except in extraordinary revelations (cf. 7:55–6) until the Parousia. Meanwhile the apostles are to move on to their task of administering his kingdom on earth by proclaiming the gospel of which they are the commissioned witnesses, united to the ascended Jesus by the promised Spirit. **11.** ' Men of Galilee ' : a typically Greek rhetorical opening to a speech, characteristic of Luke's style in the speeches in Ac. The earthly life of Jesus is now at an end and he

4d is to be known in a new mode until the Parousia when he will come as Son of man ' in a cloud with power and great glory ' (Lk. 21:27). This will not be soon; hence the apostles must not ' stand looking into heaven '. **12.** Olivet is to be the scene of the coming of the Lord in the last days, to do battle for Jerusalem (Zech. 14:4). ' Sabbath's journey ' : 2,000 cubits (Exod. 16:29; Num. 35:5). The short distance indicates that Jerusalem or the immediate surroundings is the focal point of the Church's mission, where it begins and from which it spreads.

e **13-26 The Replacement of Judas**—The ' upper room ' may be the scene of the Last Supper, and was possibly located in the house of Mary the mother of John Mark (12:12). The beginning of the active mission of the Church is prefaced by a list of the eleven apostles as its nucleus and, by virtue of their commission as witnesses, its leaders. In contrast with Lk. 6:14–16, John comes before James, as befits Peter's associate as a leader and spokesman of the primitive Church (3:1ff., 4:13ff., 8:14ff.). Thomas appears before Bartholomew and Matthew. **14.** Prayer is the setting for the major events of the gospel in Lk. This is the prayer of expectation of the coming of the Spirit, parallel to the prayer of Jesus at his baptism (Lk. 3:21). ' With one accord ' is a favourite expression of Luke's, serving to emphasise the unity of the Christian community. The Western text, interpreting ' women ' to mean ' their wives ' (probably rightly), adds ' and children '. Mary is mentioned separately to distinguish her from the apostles' wives, to link the beginning of Ac. with the opening of Luke's first volume, and, with the mention of the brothers, to indicate that the family of Jesus were among the original nucleus of the Church, though they had not always been favourably disposed to him in his earthly life: cf. Mk 3:21, 31; Jn 7:5, a tradition reinforced by the fact that James the Lord's brother was not put forward as a candidate for the place of Judas; he was presumably not qualified as a witness of the ministry of Jesus, although he did see the risen Lord (1 C. 15:7) and may have been converted on that occasion with the other brothers. **15.** Peter appears from the first as the leader. ' Brethren ' is a semi-technical term for ' Christians '. To prevent confusion with the ' brothers ' of Jesus, the Western text has substituted ' disciples '. ' Persons ' : literally ' names ' (cf. Num. 1:18, 20, 26:53, 55, LXX). 120 : i.e. ten times the number of the Twelve, who were about to be brought up to their original strength. Perhaps cf. Zech. 8:23. Luke almost always prefaces numbers with ' about ' ; see note on 27:37.

775a **Peter's speech** is less likely than any other in Ac. to represent what was actually said on the occasion to which it is assigned. It looks back on the events of the Passion from a considerable distance in time, reminds the audience of what had in fact just happened, and refers them to the Greek Bible for an explanation of the events. ' Brethren ' again represents a Greek rhetorical opening. ' Scripture ' : what Judas did was in accordance with the divine purpose as disclosed in the scriptures when these are rightly understood. It was part of the providentially necessitated Passion of the Messiah. ' David ' : i.e. Ps. 69:25, 109:8 (see 20 below). **17.** ' Numbered ' : cf. Lk. 22:3. ' Ministry ' : i.e. apostleship. The word can refer to any service to the community undertaken for God. **18.** The account of the death of Judas, inserted for the benefit of the reader rather than Peter's audience, differs from that in Mt. Another tradition, of Judas swelling to a monstrous size, is cited by Apollinarius from Papias. There was a natural tendency to imagine a horrible end for the traitor and this story may be influenced by Num. 5:21–2, with Ps. 109:18 and 69:24. ' Field ' is properly ' small estate '. The Greek translated ' falling headlong ' means properly ' becoming prone '. The strange expression may be due to the influence of 2 Mac. 9:8, where Antiochus Epiphanes, the persecutor, ' was brought down to earth ' by falling from his chariot, and possibly Wis. 4:19 : ' he will dash them (i.e. the persecutors of the righteous) . . . to the ground ' ; but Luke may simply mean that Judas fell so heavily (? from the roof of his farmhouse) as to burst his body. Despite F. H. Chase (JTS 13 (1912), 278ff.), it seems improbable that the Greek could mean ' swelling up ' rather than ' becoming prone ' or ' falling flat '. **19.** Akeldama can represent the Aramaic for ' field of blood '. An ingenious suggestion that it can be a transliteration of ' field of sleep ' and that such a term might have been used to designate a cemetery, would bring the original basis of this story into line with Mt. 27:7–8 ; but there is no evidence for this phrase meaning a cemetery in Aramaic. This is obviously Luke's information for his readers, not Peter's for an Aramaic-speaking audience in Jerusalem. **20.** Ps. 69:25 and 109:8 are loosely quoted, the former being altered to suit its application to a single individual ; it presumably refers to Judas's farm rather than his office as an apostle, since otherwise it would be contradicted by the appointment of Matthias. ' Office ', on the other hand (literally ' overseership '), refers to his place as an apostle.

21-22. The qualification for apostleship in the full b
sense (as opposed to the office of a missionary envoy of a local church, cf. 14:14) is to have been an eyewitness of the gospel events (cf. Lk. 1:2) from their beginning (John's baptism) to the Ascension, although the function of an apostle is primarily to witness to the Resurrection. This implies that other disciples besides the eleven were present during the ' Resurrection appearances '. ' They put forward ' : i.e. probably the whole community. Popular choice is also implied in 6:4. The Western text has the singular verb, supposing that Peter chose the two candidates. Nothing is said about the criterion by which these two were selected from those qualified. For ' Barsabbas ' the Western text has ' Barnabas '. There is confusion over this name (meaning either ' son of the sabbath ' or ' son of the aged '), the Western text reading ' Barabbas ' for another ' Barsabbas ' at 15:22. Greek and Latin names were frequently adopted by Jews, and these often resembled the Jewish name as closely as possible : thus Joseph Justus and Jesus Justus (Col. 4:11). Papias told a story of this disciple drinking serpent's poison unharmed (Eus.HE III, xxxix, 9). Nothing further is known of Matthias, though Clement of Alexandria (*Stromateis* IV, vi, 35) identified him with Zacchaeus, which is obviously impossible. He was remembered, not for himself but as the person by whom the twelve patriarchs of the true Israel were brought again to their appointed number. **24.** No-one could be ordained a member of the Twelve. Hence this appointment is unique, for an apostle could be commissioned only by the Lord himself, either in the flesh or, as here, in answer to prayer by the medium of the casting of lots, as by the Urim and Thummim (cf. 1 Sam. 14:41, LXX), through which God's will was directly revealed. The prayer was probably addressed to Jesus as Lord, since he is the chooser of apostles (cf. 1:2). ' Knower-of-the-hearts ' occurs frequently in liturgical passages from Hermas to the Apostolic Constitutions, where it is used of Jesus. The title ' Lord ' (*Māran*) was applied to Jesus by the primitive Aramaic-speaking Church and is very frequent in Lucan usage. Once again Luke lays stress on prayer as the setting of a turning-point in the gospel story.

25. ' Ministry and apostleship ' denote two aspects of the function of an apostle : he is a servant of the community and a commissioned representative envoy of Christ. ' His own place ' is paralleled in Ignatius, *Magnesians* 5:1 : ' each man shall go to his own place ' (i.e. life or death), but we need not suppose a borrowing.

II 1-13 The Coming of the Holy Spirit at Pentecost—The harvest Feast of Weeks (Lev. 23:15–21 etc.) 776a
had by the time of Luke come to have historical significance as the commemoration of the giving of the

776a Law. This fact has considerably influenced Luke's description of the event. 'All' would naturally refer to the 120 of 1:15, though 14 (below) suggests rather that it means the Twelve. 33, however, may imply that the ecstatic excitement is spreading among a wider group while Peter and the eleven are confronting the people. 'Together' emphasises, once again, the unity of the brethren. **2.** The sound recalls Sinai, as also does the appearance of fire. 'Wind' and 'Spirit' are closely related in Hebrew and Greek speech and thought, and wind and fire appear in the story of the Lord 'passing by' when Elijah visited the mountain of the Law (2 Kg. 19:11ff.). The Spirit and the fire of judgment belong to John the Baptist's expectation of the future coming of the 'stronger one' (Lk. 3:16). There may perhaps be a reminiscence of Isaiah's vision (Isa. 6:4) in the 'filling' of the 'house'.

b **3.** Luke thinks of the Spirit as the witness to Christ (cf. the Johannine *Paraclete*) in the mission of the Church and the proclamation of repentance and forgiveness to the world. The Spirit inspires and directs the Church's preaching and its inner life, and is manifested chiefly in the prophetic gifts required for the mission; hence the coming of the Spirit takes the form of the gift of tongues. The effect of Spirit-possession is to enable the apostles to proclaim the gospel to all nations. Luke sees in the crowd of Pentecost pilgrims, drawn from all over the Dispersion, a foreshadowing of the world-wide mission which was about to begin from Jerusalem. Luke is accustomed to present great themes in terms of single dramatic events; hence the details of this scene should not be pressed. It is a picture of all the nations hearing the gospel, each in its own tongue, as the Law was believed to have been proclaimed by angels at Sinai to all the nations in their own languages. **5.** Sinaiticus omits 'Jews'. If this were correct it would mean that the mission to Gentiles began at the very outset, at any rate according to Luke's view. This is very unlikely. If it were so, the subsequent story would be unintelligible. The crowd was probably made up of devout Jews whose dispersion over the whole world made them symbolical of the future world-wide Church. **6.** Luke supposes that the apostles were inspired to speak foreign languages; it is only on this supposition that the story makes sense. It need not follow that he has in fact misunderstood the nature of the 'speaking with tongues' that was practised at, for example, Corinth (1 C. 14). That phenomenon may have included both unintelligible utterances and speaking in foreign tongues (cf. J. G. Davies, JTS, N.S. 3 (1952), 229ff.). The whole scene is a proleptic summing-up in a symbolical picture of what is to be the theme of Ac.: the Spirit-inspired proclamation to the whole world. It would be to miss the point if we were to object that Diaspora Jews, mainly city-dwellers, would be more likely to understand Greek and Aramaic than the local languages of the countryside of the various lands in which they lived, or that it is surprising that they knew the apostles to be Galileans.

c **9. The list of the nations** may be based on an astrological catalogue in which each country was allocated to one of the signs of the Zodiac. Such a catalogue was drawn up by Paul of Alexandria in A.D. 378, using much older material; this strikingly resembles Luke's list in order and content (F. Cumont, *Klio* (1909), 263ff.; S. Weinstock, JRS 28 (1948), 43ff.). Luke's list proceeds from east to west, beginning with Rome's great rival empire, Parthia, the biblical Medes and Elamites representing the eastern 'ends of the earth', and going through Asia Minor as far as the province of Asia, back along the southern part of Asia Minor to Egypt, omitting Syria and Palestine, where a Galilean could not need a special gift of tongues to make himself understood, and thence to Cyrenaica, and to those Jewish visitors to Jerusalem who were, like Paul, Roman citizens and might be Greek-speaking or Latin-speaking. Judaea seems altogether out of place between Mesopotamia and 77
Cappadocia. Tertullian (*Adversus Judaeos* 7), and Augustine (*Contra Epistulam Fundamenti* 8), read 'Armenia' for 'Judaea'. Another variant is 'Jews'. Burkitt conjectured 'Gordaia' or 'Gorduaia' (Kurdistan). A better conjecture might be 'Galatia'. Armenia appears next to Cappadocia in the table of Paul of Alexandria and may be right; or 'Judaea' might be an early interpolation by a scribe who failed to understand how Judaea could be omitted from the list. **10.** 'Jews and proselytes' sums up the religious condition of this great crowd. Although it symbolises all the nations, the crowd did not actually consist of Gentiles, and the Gentile mission, adumbrated in this scene at Pentecost, does not begin until Peter goes to the house of Cornelius. **11.** Cretans and Arabians: Crete appears with Cilicia in the astrological table, and Arabia might correspond with the 'Red Sea and Indian country' which is the last item in it. These two places, however, seem to have been added as an afterthought, for the list goes from east to west. The theory may be right that a very early scribe added 'Arabians' in the light of Gal. 1:17, and 'Cretans' because of the traditional association of Crete with Titus (Tit. 1:5); see Knox, *The Acts of the Apostles*, 82. The addition could scarcely be Lucan, for Luke ignores Paul's visit to Arabia and probably did not know the tradition of a connection of Titus with Crete. Without Judaea, Crete and Arabia the number of regions is twelve, corresponding to the apostles, but without any implication that each apostle concerned himself with one particular country. **13.** 'New wine', i.e. unfermented. The accusation on the part of some of the crowd that the apostles are drunk serves both to illustrate the nature of their enthusiasm and to lead into the speech of Peter.

14ff. Peter's Speech—The style of this speech is 77
typically Lucan, and combines certain conventions of Greek rhetoric, such as the opening address, with a generally biblical style and vocabulary. Peter begins by refuting the accusation of drunkenness: at so early an hour as 9 a.m. this would be inconceivable. The apostles' apparent madness has a very different cause: the promise of the last days has been fulfilled, and the Spirit, whose outpouring on all Israel was expected at the final consummation, has actually come upon 'all flesh'. **16.** 'Joel' is omitted from the Western text. Other prophetic citations appear in Ac. without a mention of the particular prophet by name (cf. 7:42, 13:40, 15:16). Jl 2:18–32 is cited to show that the 'last days' have come, the ancient expectation has been fulfilled and the Spirit is outpoured, no longer upon special individuals such as prophets and rulers, and it is through Jesus as the exalted Lord, risen from the dead and ascended into heaven, that the Spirit has been given. The quotation follows the LXX with minor modifications in the Alexandrian text and considerable variations in the Western. The textual problem is difficult (see *The Beginnings of Christianity*, iv, 21ff.). 'In the last days' is read by the Western text, with the support of Sinaiticus and other MSS. The LXX, reproduced by Vaticanus and others, has 'after these things'. The former reading explains that Luke interpreted the LXX phrase as meaning 'in the age of fulfilment' which has begun, although the final consummation is not yet (cf. 1:7–8), so that the Church lives in the intermediate age between its inauguration and its completion. 'All flesh' in the prophecy meant all Israel. Luke may intend the phrase to suggest the universality of the Church, though he is clear that this implication of Joel's words was not realised until a later stage in the mission. The Western text may be seeking to emphasise this implication with its curious change of 'all flesh' into the plural. 'Those days': i.e. the times of the end. **18.** Prophecy is regarded as the principal manifestation of the Spirit. The Pentecostal tongues are a form of prophecy, for they testify to Christ, and this is the chief work of the Spirit in the Church and to the world. It is to em-

777a phasise this aspect of the Spirit's advent that the reference to prophecy, found in LXX only in 17, has been repeated here in the Alexandrian text. **19-20.** The natural portents signify the last times. ' blood and fire and vapour of smoke ' is omitted in the Western text, which probably sees the prophecy as fulfilled in the signs and wonders performed by Jesus and subsequently by the apostles. All MSS agree in inserting ' signs ' into the LXX text, as a first step in the adaptation of the prophecy to the situation of the Church's mission. **21.** ' the Lord ' : 38 shows that Joel's allusion to God is reinterpreted as a reference to Jesus. Indeed, the promise of salvation to those who call on the Lord's name introduces the second part of the speech : the claim that Jesus who was crucified has been exalted as Lord and Messiah. **22.** ' Of Nazareth ' : see *The Beginnings of Christianity*, v, 357 ; M. Black, *An Aramaic Approach to the Gospels and Acts*, 143ff. The adjective *Nazōraios* used here cannot properly be derived from *Nazareth*. There is much confused etymology in the primitive tradition between *Nazareth* (and *Nazarene*) and perhaps *nēṣer* (branch) and *nāzîr* (Nazirite), possibly also with *nāṣôrayyā'* (observants), a name which may have been given to the Baptist's disciples. Jesus was attested as the messianic bringer of the promised reign of God by the mighty works, signs and wonders (cf. 19) which God wrought through him (cf. Jn 14:10). As God's Spirit worked in him, so, now that he has been vindicated and exalted, the same Spirit will work through his followers (43). **23.** The scandal of a crucified Messiah does not invalidate God's attestation of him. His death was part of the divine plan revealed in scripture, when rightly understood. The human responsibility is laid directly on the Jews, whose rejection of the Messiah is underlined by the fact that they employed heathen (' Lawless ' men) to crucify him. **24.** The action of the Jews was reversed by God's deed in raising him from the dead. His vindication, like his death, was purposed by God and declared in scripture. ' Pangs of death ' is a LXX expression (Ps. 18:5, 116:3) based on a mistranslation of the Hebrew for ' bonds '. Luke uses it as a conventional piece of biblical language, capable, without absurdity, of being the object of ' loosed '.

b **25.** Ps. 16:8–11 (LXX), referring originally to a righteous sufferer whom God has rescued from an untimely death, is reinterpreted in the primitive Christian tradition as David's prophecy of a Messiah who would never be deserted by God (contrast Mk 15:34, omitted by Luke), but would be preserved by God's presence even through death itself. **29.** The tomb of David, mentioned by Jos. Ant. VII, xv, 3 etc., is evidence that David did not speak of himself in this psalm. He must have been prophesying the resurrection of his descendant, the Messiah Jesus. **30.** ' Sworn ' : an allusion to Ps. 132:11. The direct speech of the LXX has been reproduced indirectly, with consequent awkwardness. Hence the Western text has expanded the passage : ' that of the fruit of his heart ' (probably a corruption of the LXX ' belly ' ; Luke has altered the LXX because this word means for him ' womb ') ' according to the flesh ' (cf. Rom. 1:3) ' he would raise up the Messiah and set him . . .'
32. The speech passes from scriptural prophecies to the testimony of the apostolic eye-witnesses to the fulfilment of the OT. The apostles authenticate the gospel by their witness. **33.** Resurrection and exaltation are here brought together as one event. Jesus is exalted at God's right hand as the Messiah who is ' Lord ' (Ps. 110:1). He has received the promised Spirit (cf. Lk. 24:49) to pour out on his people. That this has actually occurred is manifest to the crowd. **34.** David himself was not exalted. In Ps. 110:1, therefore, he is again referring to the Messiah who was to come. **36.** The conclusion of the speech : Jesus is revealed to Israel as Lord (Ps. 110:1) and Messiah, even though Israel's leaders have crucified him. He was Lord and Messiah from his birth
(Lk. 2:11, cf. 1:43), but through death and exaltation 777b
he has taken possession of his throne at the right hand of God and has been ' made ' what he had already been designated as being ; cf. Rom. 1:4.

The Response to Peter's Speech—37. The people c
are ' cut to the heart ' (Ps. 109:16, LXX) in penitence for the death of the Messiah. Peter acts throughout as the spokesman of the apostles as a body. **38.** Repentance is expressed in baptism, as in the mission of the Baptist. Now, however, the sign employed by him has acquired a new meaning in consequence of the death and exaltation of Jesus as Messiah. It is now baptism in his name, i.e. into his ownership and authority, so that the baptised become his people. Forgiveness of sins and possession by the Holy Spirit are gained through membership of the Messianic community. The Spirit, imparted in baptism, is evidently thought of here as the basic inward principle of the life of the Christian community and its individual members. There is no indication that all the converts became ecstatic prophets or spoke with tongues. Luke, however, conceiving the Spirit to be pre-eminently the Spirit of the Church's proclamation of the gospel, tends to confuse two aspects of the Spirit : as the Spirit who was in Christ and who now dwells in his people, linking them with the ascended Lord, and as the source of the special inspiration manifested in prophecy and tongues.
39. Jl 2:32 appears to be conflated with a reminiscence d
of Isa. 57:19, suggesting that ' far off ' denotes distance in space rather than time, and that a hint of the coming mission to distant parts of the world may be intended. **40.** ' Crooked generation ' : cf. Dt. 32:5 and Ps. 78:8. **41.** ' Received ' : the Western text has ' believed ', so making it clear to the reader that ' received ' indicates the necessary response of faith made by candidates for baptism to the preaching of the gospel. ' Souls ' : a LXX expression for ' persons '. ' Three thousand ' is perhaps intended as a contrast with the three thousand who fell after the idolatry of the golden calf (Exod. 32:28).

A Summary of the Characteristics of the Life of e
the Primitive Community—42. The apostles' teaching would include public teaching in the Temple (3:12ff., 4:2) and teaching within the Christian body. ' The fellowship ' refers primarily to the sharing of property (45), but it also has a wider application. The sharing was an expression of the unity and harmony of the believers, manifesting their possession by the Spirit. The ' breaking of bread ' (cf. Lk. 24:35) is probably already a quasi-technical name for the common meal which was the setting of the primitive Eucharist (cf. 6:1). It does not necessarily imply that no cup was drunk. Possibly the use of wine may have been confined to the solemn commemoration of the Resurrection on the first day of the week, but even the Sunday Eucharist is described simply as a gathering for the breaking of bread (20:7). The prayers are the Jewish prayers in which the first Christians participated (3:1) and, no doubt, specifically Christian prayers both within and outside the context of the eucharistic meal.
43. ' Fear ' : i.e. awe at the wonders and signs, the f
visible evidence that the new age had dawned. **44.** ' Together ' emphasises the unity of the Christian society, which was expressed in the sharing of resources. **45.** The Western text adds ' daily ' to ' distributed ', suggesting a regular ' dole ' from the common fund. The Alexandrian text is probably right in attaching ' daily ' to 46. **46.** The Christians did not cut themselves off from the Temple. On the contrary, they, as the part of Israel which accepted Israel's Messiah, frequented the centre of Israel's religion, and exercised all their religious rights as Jews until their proclamation of Jesus to the leaders of Israel met with rejection. On the other hand, the peculiarly Christian observance of the eucharistic meal took place in private houses. The Greek can mean either ' in their homes ' or ' from house to house ' ; cf. 6:1. The joyful character of the Christian common meal is emphasised. **47.** The

777f Christians found favour with the people, i.e. Israel, as a whole, despite the attitude of the rulers. The Western text goes further and reads ' the whole world ' instead of ' all the people '.
48. The Greek is awkward. ' The Lord added those who were being saved daily together '. Instead of writing ' added to their number ' or ' added to the Church ', Luke has made use of a favourite expression from the LXX, where the phrase ' together ' occurs in the Psalms some fifteen times, sometimes with the full meaning of ' coming (or ' acting ') together ', sometimes as little more than an emphatic phrase signifying something like the English ' altogether ' or ' wholly '. ' Those who were being saved ' : i.e. by ' calling on the name of the Lord ' (21). These are the true Israel, who were being chosen out of the ancient people of God.

778a **III 1ff. The First Sign of Healing**—This story illustrates the signs and wonders, parallel to those of Jesus, performed in his name by his followers. Like the miracles of Jesus, they are effective signs that the ' age to come ' has already dawned and is now operative. The story begins abruptly, and although Luke has carefully set it in its present context, he seems to have retained its original form as an independent unit of the oral tradition. The Western text, on the other hand, provides it with a connecting link with the preceding sentences. **1.** Peter and John are the leaders of the community. ' The ninth hour ' (3 p.m.) was one of the regular times of prayer, corresponding to the hour of the evening sacrifice in the Temple. **2.** The healing is parallel to that effected by Paul at Lystra (14:8–10). ' Beautiful ' : the position of this gate has not been established. Much later tradition identified it with the Shushan Gate, on the east side of the Temple, in the outer wall. The Nicanor Gate, on the east side of the Court of the Women, has also been suggested. **4.** ' Gaze ' is a favourite expression of Luke. **6.** The ' name ' signifies the authority of Jesus the Messiah, exercised by his followers and made effective in acts of power. Solemnity is added to the formula by the use of the full title, including ' of Nazareth '. **7.** Peter raises up the lame man. The healing foreshadows, in a measure, the raising of the helpless to new life in the power of the name of Jesus. The physical contact expresses the link established between the patient and Jesus in the person of his apostle. In the mention of ' feet and ankles ' there is, contrary to the opinion of some commentators, no technical medical terminology. **8.** The completeness of the healing is emphasised, with an allusion to Isa. 35:6, a prophecy of the blessings of the age to come. **9.** All the people, i.e. Israel, witness this healing, which is the great sign attesting the gospel to the old Israel in Jerusalem. **11.** The ' portico called Solomon's ' was probably on the east side of the Temple, the Beautiful Gate either leading into it from the eastern outer wall (if it was the Shushan Gate) or out of it to the west into the Court of the Women (if it was the Nicanor Gate).

b **12ff. Peter's Speech in the Temple**—This takes its starting-point in the amazement of the people. It is designed to show that it is the power of the name of Jesus alone which has made the lame man strong. This is because Jesus, though rejected and killed, has been vindicated and glorified by God. His suffering was really in accordance with God's plan, made known by the prophets. Israel must now repent, so that the Messiah may return and fulfil all God's purposes for his people. He is the promised ' prophet like Moses ' (Dt. 18:15), whom to disobey means destruction. The ancient promises of God to his covenant people are fulfilled in Jesus, and to that people the blessing of repentance is now first offered. This is the principal summary given us by Luke of the verbal proclamation of the gospel to Israel, accompanying and interpreting the acted sign of healing. The people of Israel are challenged in the very heart of their religion, the Temple itself.

12. ' This ' : perhaps better ' him '. ' Piety ' : this 778c
presumably means that the apostles have not acquired, through personal piety, special merit with God so as to persuade him to do a miracle. Some MSS find the expression difficult and read ' authority '. **13.** The speech appeals to the God of the old Covenant (cf. Exod. 3:15). ' Glorified ' might refer either to the manifestation of his glory in this miracle or to his exaltation, but the latter is more probable. The miracle is evidence of his authority and power as the Lord enthroned at God's right hand. ' Delivered up ' : i.e. to the Roman authority. The blame is firmly laid by Luke on the shoulders of the Jewish leaders. They rejected Jesus and their ' denial ' of him in Pilate's court is like the denial of him by apostates (cf. Lk. 12:9). Pilate, on the other hand, as Luke so strongly emphasises in his Gospel, acquitted him. **14.** cf. Lk. 23:18ff. ' Holy ' : cf. Ps. 16:10 ; Lk. 4:34 ; Ac. 4:27. ' Righteous ' : cf. 7:52, 22:14 ; Jas 5:6 ; 1 Pet. 3:18. This is a messianic title in Enoch 38:2, 53:6. It is unlikely to be connected with the ' Teacher of Righteousness ' of the Qumrân community. **15.** ' Author ' : cf. 5:31 ; Heb. 2:10, 12:2. The word conveys the idea of ' originator ' and also of ' leader ' or ' pioneer ', i.e. one who goes ahead to bring his followers after him. If it has the latter sense here the phrase must mean ' leader into life '. ' Author ' is more probably right. Jesus is the author of life as being raised from the dead ; but the word is used as a description of the eponymous heroes of ancient cities, and C. S. C. Williams remarks that it ' could be used of quasi-divine founders of colonies '. He asks whether it may therefore imply ' a comparison between Joshua and Jesus, both of whom led God's people into a holy land '. ' Witnesses ' : the apostles guarantee the truth of the gospel by their witness to the Resurrection.

16. The healing has been wrought by the authority of d
the name of Jesus, to which there corresponds the faith of the patient (which itself comes from Jesus), as in the miracle-stories of the Gospels. There it was faith in Jesus in person ; now it is faith in his name, i.e. his continuing and present power. A desire to lay stress on the appeal to faith and the response of faith, together with an awkward allusion to the fact that the lame man was well known to the witnesses of the healing, and with a rather curious reference to the ' strengthening ' of the patient (echoing 7 above), has produced a harsh and difficult sentence. C. F. D. Moule has suggested that Luke left three alternative forms of this sentence in his unrevised MS, and that these have been combined by an editor. But the sentence, though awkward, is not impossible.
17. The direct appeal to the audience begins here. The Jews are partially excused even though they killed the Messiah, for they and their rulers acted in ignorance (cf. Lk. 23:34), and unlike Judas they may repent and be forgiven. **18.** The suffering of the Messiah was foretold by all the prophets collectively. **19.** Repentance consists in a returning to God. ' Refreshing ' : i.e. the time of the Parousia or the completion of the age of fulfilment.

20. Jesus will be sent again from heaven, where he is e
enthroned until the time of the end. He is the Messiah, previously ordained by God. There is no need to suppose that this speech implies that Jesus was not Messiah, but only Messiah-designate, before the Ascension—a view which would directly contradict 18 above. For a contrary interpretation (that this passage expresses a primitive ' Elijah Christology ') see J. A. T. Robinson, ' The Most Primitive Christology of all ? ' JTS, N.S. 7 (1956), 177ff., ' Elijah, John and Jesus : An Essay in Detection ', NTS 4 (1958), 263ff.

21. ' Establishing ' : i.e. the time of the end, when f
God's declared purpose will be finally brought to its accomplishment. This will be the age of new life, the ' times of refreshing '. ' Prophets from of old ' is a direct echo (unless the Western text should be right in omitting ' from of old ') of Lk. 1:70. **22.** Jesus is

78f the 'prophet like Moses' (Dt. 18:15), a thought which plays a prominent part in Luke's Christology. As the prophet he must be obeyed, and the Jews who reject him will be destroyed out of God's people. The implication is that Christians are the true Israel. Two texts, Lev. 23:29 and Dt. 18:15, have been combined in **22-3**, having perhaps already been drawn together in Christian tradition as a proof-text.

24. The Greek is very awkward. The verse does not mean that proof-texts were found in every individual prophet, but that the prophets as a body spoke of Christ. Samuel is singled out as the first prophet, Moses having been already mentioned separately, and as the one who pointed to, and anointed, David (cf. 13:20). **25.** Israel, Peter's audience, are the heirs of the blessing of the covenant and the promises declared by the prophets. **26.** 'Raised up', not in the Resurrection, but in the sense that God sent him (cf. Jg. 2:16, 18, 3:9, 15, etc.). The blessing promised to Abraham's seed is given to Israel through Jesus and through the message of repentance and forgiveness.

g **IV 1ff. The Appeal to Israel is rejected by the Nation's Leaders**—Although it meets with a ready response from the people (4), it is rejected by the leaders, and the warnings of Jesus concerning the persecution of his disciples (Lk. 12:8ff., 21:12ff.) are fulfilled. The 'priests' are those responsible for the regular duty in the Temple. The 'captain of the Temple' may be the 'sagan', a high official ranking next to the high priest, or perhaps more probably one of his subordinate officers who assisted in his task of maintaining order in the Temple. The 'Sadducees' were not an official body like the priests, but the party, priestly and aristocratic, to which the high-priestly families belonged and which, rejecting the oral tradition, adhered to the written Law alone, denying the Pharisaic beliefs in future life, angels and demons. They 'came upon' the apostles in the manner of the chief priests and others when Jesus himself taught in the Temple (Lk. 20:1).

h **2.** 'In Jesus': perhaps better 'proclaiming the resurrection that had taken place in Jesus'. The Sadducees object to this as a frontal attack on their beliefs. Luke is anxious to show that the opposition to the gospel within the old Israel came from the Sadducee party, whose influence ceased with the fall of Jerusalem. He represents Pharisaic Judaism as much more friendly to the Christians, and the gospel as the culmination and fulfilment of the religion of the OT as rightly interpreted. This theme is developed in the speeches made by Paul in his defence.

i **4.** The speech of Peter had had impressive results. Luke's figure is not an accurate estimate. It is a round number, perhaps suggested by the feeding of the multitude (Lk. 9:14). **5.** The Sanhedrin, which could not lawfully meet at night, assembled in the morning. This is a solemn assembly of the leaders of Israel, the 'rulers' being the priests, assisted by the elders (originally the heads of the leading families), and the scribes who for the most part belonged to the Pharisaic party. 'In Jerusalem' might seem otiose, were it not that Luke mentions this fact in order to make his readers understand that in this scene the apostles of the Messiah confront the rulers of Israel in the sacred city itself. **6.** Luke seems to think that Annas was the reigning high priest, whereas he held office from A.D. 6–15 and remained very influential during the reign of his son-in-law Caiaphas. John may perhaps be identified with Jonathan (so the Western text) who succeeded Caiaphas in 36. Alexander is unknown. **7.** The inquiry is not directly concerned with resurrection, but with the power and authority of the name of Jesus.

j **8. Peter's Speech to the Sanhedrin**—In Peter's case the promise of Jesus is fulfilled that 'when they bring you before . . . the rulers . . . the Holy Spirit will teach you in that very hour what you ought to say' (Lk. 12:11–12). **9.** Peter's ironical opening, to the effect that the apostles are being examined by a

criminal court concerning a 'good deed' of healing, 778j
leads into a proclamation of the gospel to the rulers of Israel. The regular pattern of Christian 'confession' of Christ under persecution is already established; a trial is an opportunity to make a missionary speech under the direct inspiration of the Spirit. **10.** The lame man has been healed in the power of the name of Jesus. Peter goes on to preach the resurrection of Jesus as Messiah, after the same Sanhedrin had crucified him. **11.** The proof-text from Ps. 118:22 was important to the primitive Church (cf. Lk. 20:17; 1 Pet. 2:7), since it was taken to refer to the rejection and vindication of Jesus. It is cited elsewhere from the LXX, but here it has apparently been derived from an independent version, perhaps contained in a collection of scriptural proofs like those peculiar to Mt. **12.** 'salvation' and 'saved' have a double meaning, alluding to 'healing' and also to 'salvation' in the full Christian sense.

13ff. The Decision of the Sanhedrin—'Boldness' k
is the characteristic disposition of the free man, as opposed to that of the slave in relation to a master or the subject to a despot. It is peculiarly characteristic of the freedom of speech enjoyed by Christians under the inspiration of the Spirit (cf. Lk. 21:15). 'Uneducated and common': properly 'illiterate and amateurish', as opposed to 'educated and professional'. 'With Jesus': i.e. as disciples during his earthly life. **14:** cf. Lk. 21:15. **16.** The Sanhedrin has to confess that a notable sign has been manifested to all Jerusalem. **19-20.** The authorities' attempt to silence the gospel is frustrated; see note on 5:29. **21.** The people as a whole, in sharp contrast with the rulers, enthusiastically accept the sign and the preaching. **22** emphasises the wonder and greatness of the sign.

23ff. The Prayer of the Persecuted Church— l
'Friends': literally 'their own people'. The Christian community, or at least its inner nucleus, is here thought of as a small group, despite the 8,000 converts, able to meet together in one place, perhaps the house of Mary (cf. 12:12). 'Together' indicates the unity of Christians in the Spirit as a worshipping body. **24-30** probably represents a typical early Christian liturgical prayer. It is constructed on the model of OT prayers, especially that of Hezekiah in 2 Kg. 19:15–19; Isa. 37:15–20, the language of which (LXX) has been directly imitated here. **24.** 'Sovereign Lord': cf. Lk. 2:29; the address to God, recalling his almighty power in Creation, echoes Isa. 37:16. **25.** The order of the Greek words is impossible, though RSV gives the sense correctly. There is probably very early textual corruption, all the easier MS readings being attempts to correct the difficulty. 'By the Holy Spirit' may be an early interpolation. Torrey suggested a mistranslation of an Aramaic original: 'that which our father, thy servant David, said by command (literally 'by the mouth') of the Holy Spirit'; but the relationship between David and the Spirit would then be extraordinary, for the Spirit would surely speak by David's mouth, not vice versa, and the solution implies that Luke was content to let an impossible sentence stand in his text. C. F. D. Moule (ET 65 (1954), 220f.) thinks that here, as at 3:16, phrases in Luke's draft, intended as possible alternatives, were allowed by an editor to stand together. In this passage this is an attractive explanation. 'Servant': or possibly 'son', as in 27. **26.** The citation is from Ps. 2:1ff., which the primitive Church read as a most important Messianic text. To the Christians the psalm spoke of a persecuted Christ, and it was directly applicable to the story of the Passion.

27. 'For truly': an echo of Isa. 37:18. 'servant': Jesus, like David, is the messianic son or servant of God (cf. 25 above). He was anointed as Messiah at his baptism. 'Herod etc.', corresponding to the kings, rulers, Gentiles (Romans) and peoples (of Israel) of the psalm. The hostility of Pilate and Herod

778l to Jesus, which is here implied, is scarcely in accordance with Luke's own Passion narrative, and suggests that this typological interpretation of Ps. 2 was taken over by Luke from early tradition without adjustment. **28.** The sufferings of the Messiah, nevertheless, were in the purpose of God. **29.** 'And now, . . . look': cf. Isa. 37:20, 17. 'Servants': literally 'slaves', answering to 'Sovereign Lord' (or 'master') of 24. 'Speak thy word': i.e. to pursue the Church's mission of preaching the gospel. **30.** The gospel is proclaimed, in the power of the Spirit, by word and signs, the mighty works of Jesus being achieved through his name. 'Hand': the language here is solemn and biblical. The 'stretching out of the hand' of God is the exercise of his power for salvation.

31. 'Shaken': the sign of God's presence; cf. Exod. 19:18; Isa. 6:4. 'Filled with the Holy Spirit': the Pentecostal advent of the Spirit is here confirmed in face of the opposition of the Jewish authorities. The Spirit, as always, inspires and empowers the missionary enterprise, so that the Christians preach the gospel with the 'boldness' which is the characteristic effect of the Spirit's operation. This is not, as has sometimes been supposed, an alternative version of the Pentecost story itself. The Pentecostal coming of the Spirit, conceived of by Luke as the Spirit of the mission finding expression in prophecy and preaching, is fully consistent with the renewal and enhanced experience of his presence among Christians according to particular circumstances.

779a **32ff. The Progress of the Church and its Fellowship**—There is no break in the narrative here. The presence of the Spirit is expressed in two ways: externally in the mission to Israel, and internally in the unity of the brotherhood itself, where perfect harmony is given practical expression in the sharing of property. **33.** 'Power': i.e. the power of God manifested in the signs and wonders prayed for in 30. These signs accompany the unique work of the apostles, to attest the Resurrection. 'Grace': the favour of God, which blessed the life of the community. **34.** cf. Dt. 15:4.

b **36.** Barnabas is singled out as an example of how the members of the community sold their property for the common good. We are not told whether Mary's house (12:12) had been left in her private possession because it served as a meeting-place. The name Barnabas cannot be translated 'Son of Encouragement' (or 'Exhortation' or 'Consolation'). The suggestion that Luke has confused the name Barnabas with Manaen (Menahem) in 13:1 is possible; the latter could be so translated. The similar difficulty over Elymas (13:8) indicates that Luke did not know Aramaic. 'Barnabas' might conceivably mean 'son of a prophet', or 'son of (the god) Nebo', but neither is likely (and certainly not the latter) to have been given as a surname by the apostles.

c **V 1ff. Ananias and Sapphira**—Deliberate offence against the unity of the brotherhood for private advantage is a sin against the Spirit. The destruction of Ananias and Sapphira is a 'mighty work' of God, corresponding to the grace (4:33) which brought unity and harmony to the Church. **2.** 'Kept back' is an echo of Jos. 7:1. Luke draws a parallel with the story of Achan who, like Ananias, kept back part of what had been dedicated to God, and so, in effect, stole it. **3.** Ananias is inspired, not by the Spirit but by Satan, the adversary, whose part he has taken in deceiving the Spirit in the Church. **4.** The sale of property was apparently voluntary. The offence consisted in pretending to give the full value and in fact holding part of it back. **5.** 'Died': the Greek word is used also of the divine punishment of death inflicted on Herod Agrippa (12:23). 'Fear': awe at the manifestation of God's avenging justice. **6.** 'Young men' (cf. 1 Pet. 5:5): literally 'younger men'; probably not an 'order' analogous to 'elders', nor parallel to the 'novices' in the Qumrân community. In 10 the word means simply 'youths'. **9.** 'Tempt': literally 'test', i.e. by provoking the Spirit (cf. Exod. 17:2). **11.** 'Fear': see note on 5 above. 'Church' is here used for the first time in Ac. to denote the Christian community, the 'congregation' of God's people. 779

12ff. Signs and Wonders—A summary of the Church's situation, largely repetitive of 2:43–7. The prayer of 4:30 continues to be answered. 'All': presumably the apostles, using Solomon's Portico as their meeting-place for teaching the people. **13.** A difficult sentence. 'The rest' are probably their non-Christian opponents who dared not join with them (in questions and disputation), but the expression is very strange, and 'the rest' may be an early corruption of the text; 'rulers' has been suggested as a possible emendation. The people (of Israel) honour the apostles. **14.** 'Added to the Lord' is an expression for conversion and membership of the Church which is used again in 11:24. **15-16** is apparently based on Mk 6:55–6 (Mark's word 'pallet' in the vulgar tongue is reproduced here), which Luke omitted in his Gospel, but uses here. Peter's position as leader of the apostles is strongly emphasised. It is parallel to the position of Paul in the days of the Gentile mission (19:12). **15.** 'Overshadow': cf. Lk. 1:35, 9:34; always used of the divine presence and power. d

17ff. The Renewed Hostility of the Authorities—This large-scale mission of healing revives the hostility of the Sadducees. There is no necessity to suppose this episode to be a doublet of 4:1ff. 'Rose up' (Gr. *anastas*): a variant in some Old Latin MSS reads 'Annas'. 'Jealousy': i.e. at the success of the apostles' mission. cf. 13:45 and 1 Clement 5:4, 5, referring to the tribulations of Peter and Paul. e

19ff. Deliverance from prison by miraculous means is a prominent theme in Ac. (cf. 12:6–11, 16:26ff.). The progress of the gospel cannot be hindered by the imprisonment of the missionaries, who are released so that they may, at least, have the opportunity of making their defence in open court and so continuing their testimony in a manner which brought a special blessing and inspiration of the Spirit. **20.** 'This life': the life inaugurated by Christ's saving work; cf. 13:26. **21.** 'Council and . . . senate': Luke is laying great stress on the formality of this occasion. The apostles are to give their testimony before the supreme council of the Covenant People. Luke uses OT phraseology (cf. Exod. 12:21, LXX), and a solemn repetitive biblical style. 'Senate' thus repeats 'council', and the translation should be 'even (rather than 'and') all the senate'. There is no reason to think that Luke supposes that two assemblies were involved here. **22.** 'Officers': members of the Temple police. **24.** 'Captain': see note on 4:1. **24.** 'What this would come to': not a 'biblical' but a literary Greek phrase, peculiar to Luke in the NT. **26.** The goodwill of the people as distinct from the rulers is again stressed. f

27. The Appearance of the Apostles before the Sanhedrin—**28.** 'strictly charged': literally 'commanded with commandment', a piece of biblical language from the LXX. 'Blood': the high priest fears that the Christians intend to avenge the death of Jesus. **29.** 'obey God . . .': cf. 4:19 and Plato, *Apology* 29D, possibly known to Luke. g

30-32 Peter's Defence—The testimony delivered by Peter as spokesman for the apostles is that God vindicated and exalted Jesus, despite his violent rejection by the leaders of Israel. Through him repentance and forgiveness are given to Israel, and the apostles are witnesses to this gospel through their possession by the Spirit. It is an echo of the speech in 3:13ff. The gospel is continuous with the revelation of God to Israel, for the God who raised Jesus is the God of the patriarchs and the old Covenant. The gospel fulfils the scriptures. 'You'; the guilt falls squarely on the Jewish authorities. 'Tree': Dt. 21:22; cf. 10:39, 13:29; Gal. 3:13; 1 Pet. 2:24. **31.** 'Leader h

779h and Saviour' : cf. 3:15, 7:35 (of Moses as a type of Christ). Jesus is the leader and captain of his people, like Moses (cf. Heb. 2:10, 12:2) and a saviour or liberator. 'Saviour' is a title rarely given to Jesus in the NT, but relatively common in Lk.-Ac. 'Repentance and forgiveness of sins' : the primary content of the Lucan Gospel. Repentance is not merely a human preparation and qualification for forgiveness ; it is itself a divine gift. **32.** The apostles guarantee this gospel as eye-witnesses. The Spirit testifies in them. Codex Vaticanus omits 'whom', reading 'and God has given the Holy Spirit'. This is almost certainly an accidental error.

i **The Decision of the Sanhedrin—33.** 'enraged' : literally 'sawn asunder' or 'cut to the quick' with fury, as were the Sanhedrin at Stephen's trial (7:54). The apostles are nearly put to death. **34.** Gamaliel was a descendant of Hillel and was himself a famous rabbi ; according to 22:3 he was the teacher of Paul. As a Pharisee he is inclined to favour the Christian movement, in contrast with the complete hostility of the Sadducees. Luke lays stress on this favourable attitude on the part of an honoured doctor of the Law. Christianity is the fulfilment of the scriptures, and a wise Pharisee would be unwilling to condemn it. He would at least wait to see whether the movement were blessed by God.

j **35 Gamaliel advises Caution**—False messianic movements tend, as always, to come to nothing, but if the Christian cause is blessed by God it is bound to prosper and cannot be suppressed. **36.** Theudas was a *soi-disant* prophet who proposed to emulate Joshua and lead an army of his followers dry-shod across Jordan. The procurator Fadus suppressed this rising, between A.D. 44 and 46. Unless there was an earlier, unknown, Theudas, also a revolutionary leader, Luke, in writing a speech suitable to Gamaliel (and very probably representing his attitude correctly), has inserted a chronologically impossible allusion. See Jos. Ant. XX, v, 1. **37.** Judas the Galilean raised a revolt in A.D. 6, when the first census was held by the Romans, on Judaea becoming a province of the Empire. Quirinius was then the governor of Syria. Luke appears to have mistaken both the date of Theudas in relation to Judas, and also the date of the census (Lk. 2:2). It is more questionable whether the source of the former mistake can be a misreading of Jos. Ant. XX, v, 2. Josephus there mentions the death of the *sons* of Judas 'who caused the people to revolt from the Romans when Quirinius was conducting a census of the Jews'. This passage occurs almost immediately after Josephus's narrative of Theudas. The meaning of Josephus, however, is perfectly clear and does not lend itself to such a misunderstanding. Moreover, Luke includes particulars of Theudas, such as the number of his followers, which are not given by Josephus, and he presumably, therefore, used some other source of information. We need not necessarily suppose that Luke wrote after the publication of Josephus's work (A.D. 93). On the other hand, it does not seem possible to defend the accuracy of Luke in respect either of the census or of Judas, despite the efforts of Sir William Ramsay to establish a previous governorship of Syria by Quirinius and a fourteen-year census cycle going back before A.D. 6 and including the territory of Herod the Great.

'Scattered'. Luke's second example is not very apt. The movement led by Judas did not collapse with his death, but grew into the formidable Zealot faction.

k **38.** 'So in the present case' : a form of expression derived from the LXX, used in the prayer at 4:29. 'Of men . . . of God' : cf. Lk. 20:4.

l **40ff. The Apostles triumph through Suffering**—'Beat' : according to the penal practice of the synagogue ; cf. 22:19 ; Mk 13:9 ; 2 C. 11:24. **41.** From the Christian point of view, all persecution is 'for the name'. **42.** The apostles have triumphed as 'confessors' under persecution, and the preaching of Jesus as the Messiah goes on unhindered. Their release was apparently followed by no further action against them on the part of the authorities, at least 779l
until the persecution following the death of Stephen, and even then the apostles themselves were not involved.

VI 1ff. The Appointment of the Seven—The story 780a
moves on from the apostles' encounters with the leaders of Israel to the appointment of the Seven. Here hints of a wider mission to the Jewish Dispersion, represented by Greek-speaking Jews, begin to appear. This leads to the final challenge to the Jerusalem authorities by Stephen, whose martyrdom and the persecution which ensues lead to the spread of the Church into Judaea, Samaria and the Gentile lands. 'These days' : a connecting link between the sections of Luke's work, and perhaps also between different sources used by him. 'Disciples' occurs here for the first time in Ac. In the rest of the book it occurs frequently as a synonym for 'brethren' or 'Christians'. See note on 19:1.

'Hellenists'. This word is so rare as to present a b
puzzle to later copyists who show, by their frequent confusion of it with the common word 'Hellenes' ('Greeks' or 'Gentiles') that they probably treated both words as though they were identical in meaning. That the primitive community included Gentiles in considerable numbers is, however, incompatible with the subsequent narrative in Ac. It is true that the verb from which 'Hellenists' is derived means primarily 'to Graecise' and might certainly signify 'to follow Greek customs or habits' ; but Chrysostom (*Hom. 14 in Ac.*) recognises that the noun means 'Greek-speakers', and this is fairly certainly correct. The theory has been advanced (see Cullmann, JBL 74 (1955), 213ff. and *The Scrolls and the NT* (ed. Stendahl), 18ff.) that the 'Hellenists' were 'Hellenising syncretists' among the Jews, whose hostile attitude to the Temple was similar to, and connected with, that of the Qumrân sect. But the group contrasted with the 'Hellenists' is not a party of 'Hebraisers', but 'Hebrews', and to interpret 'Hellenists' as meaning 'syncretistic Jews with leanings towards Hellenism' is very difficult. Further, although the attitude of Stephen towards the Temple partly resembles that of the Qumrân sect, he was also accused of subverting the Law, whereas the Qumrân sect was 'puritanical' in its devotion to the Law. The Hellenists were in all probability Christian converts from among the Dispersion Jews resident in Jerusalem, who, as Christians, may have differed from the 'Hebrew' Christians, not only in language (the 'Hebrews' being Aramaic-speaking) but also in their attitude to the Law and the Temple. The apostles themselves, and presumably also the 'Hebrews', continued to frequent the Temple : Stephen regards the foundation of the Temple as a cardinal error. Paul himself was originally a 'Hebrew of Hebrews' (Phil. 3:5), and this probably indicates an attitude of devotion to Law and Temple, since he was himself a Jew of the Dispersion from Tarsus, who spoke Greek ; but Paul does not contrast himself as a 'Hebrew' with Jews who were syncretistic Hellenisers, but with Christians ; so that it is unlikely that his use of the term in Phil. 3:5 throws light on the meaning of 'Hebrew' as a designation
of a particular class of Christians. Too much should c
not be made of possible differences between Stephen's party and the 'Hebrews' over the question of the Temple. Luke always implies that the Temple had its due place in a Judaism which was intended, and ought, to find its proper fulfilment in Christianity ; but that, as the symbol of a Judaism which denied its rightful inheritance by rejecting the Messiah, the Temple was no more than a monument of apostasy. 'Distribution'. The sharing of resources by the Christians apparently included a daily 'ministration' of relief, either in the form of a common meal or by way of doles distributed by the apostles. Widows would have been prominent among the necessitous people for whom provision was made. It is difficult to reconstruct the precise historical situation. The

780c whole passage is influenced by Num. 11:1–24, where Moses appoints seventy elders to assist him in satisfying the needs of the 'murmuring' multitude. **2.** The Twelve (cf. 1:26, 2:14; 1 C. 15:3–5), as the nucleus and leaders of the community, summon a general meeting of the 'disciples'. They think it right to devote themselves to the preaching of the gospel, and not to administer poor-relief. The Seven were to take over this task, but in fact Stephen and Philip are presented to us as evangelists. **3.** 'Pick out': cf. Num. 27:16ff.

d 'Seven men'. They are not described as 'deacons', though the function for which they are appointed—the administration of poor-relief—is work which deacons performed in later times. As antitypes of the elders of Moses, they might rather seem to be forerunners of the Christian elders. Their task of ministering to the 'Hellenist' widows may be connected in the mind of Luke with the mission of the 'seventy' (Lk. 10:1) and perhaps with the seven basketfuls associated with the feeding of the four thousand with seven loaves, recorded by Mark (8:1–9) as occurring in the course of a visit by Jesus to Gentile lands, and omitted by Luke in the Gospel. 'Of good repute'. The congregation as a whole selects these ministers, who have to be well attested by public opinion. 'Full of the Spirit': cf Num. 27:18, which is probably imitated here (hence the absence of 'Holy'). They do not receive the Spirit from the apostles at their ordination, but are already possessed by the Spirit, here regarded primarily as the Spirit of wisdom. 'Appoint'. The people as a whole select, and the apostles appoint. 'Duty' is more nearly represented by 'office'. **4.** 'Prayer': cf. 1:14. The ministry of the word is the evangelistic task, in which, in fact, Stephen and Philip were to play a prominent part. **5.** 'Pleased'. The language is solemnly biblical. The chosen men all have Greek names. Stephen is an inspired man, full of faith, by which may be meant the peculiar gift (cf. 1 C. 12:9) needed for the performance of signs and wonders (see 8 below). Nicolaus is a proselyte, the others being presumably Jews by birth. Antioch is mentioned as his home, probably because Luke was specially interested in the origins of the Church there. He was early identified with the founder of the Nicolaitan heresy (Rev. 2:6, 15), cf. Irenaeus (*Haereses*, I, xxvi, 3), Clement (*Stromateis*, II, xx, 118). **6.** They prayed: i.e. the apostles. The symbolism of the laying-on of hands is primarily concerned with 'solidarity' between persons, or the self-identification of one person, in respect of his status, office, quality, etc., with another. Thus it denotes the taking of a person into association with the holder of an office or the possessor of a spiritual gift, so as to become his *alter ego*, as in the case of Joshua and Moses (Num. 27:18, 23). The inspiration of, and possession by, the Spirit is thus thought of as transferred. In ordination it denotes the imparting to the candidate of the status and office possessed by the ordainer, and the transference to him of a share in the divine gifts and blessings accompanying that status and office (cf. 13:3; 1 Tim. 4:14, 5:22; 2 Tim. 1–6). In healing it denotes the self-identification of the healer with the healed and the imparting to the latter of the blessings enjoyed by the former (cf. 9.17, 28:8). Hence this sign was used in the appointment of the Seven to indicate that they became the associates of the apostles in their ministry and deputies for them in their supervision of the community.

e **7 A Summary of the Church's Progress**—The mention of priests is the only indication that the mission was making such important headway among the religious leaders of Judaism. Such a fact as this explains why there was so much opposition to the Pauline attitude to Gentiles, which could destroy a real possibility of the conversion of Israel. There is no evidence to suggest a link between these priests and those of Qumrân.

781a **8 The Arrest of Stephen**—'Grace and power': the favour of God, responded to by Stephen's faith (5), confers on him the power to work signs and wonders. The Western text adds 'through the name of Jesus Christ'. **9.** The Dispersion Jews evidently had their own synagogues in Jerusalem. It is not clear whether Luke refers to one, two, or five synagogues. 'Freedmen': probably Jewish freedmen, perhaps descended from Pompey's captives, but the juxtaposition of this social group with two regional synagogues is odd, and the Armenian and Syriac versions suggest the possible variant 'Libyans'. Paul himself may possibly have belonged to the 'Cilician' group. 'Disputed'. The Dispersion Jews attack Stephen, who evidently conducted a preaching mission among them. **10.** 'Could not withstand': cf. Lk. 21:15. 'Wisdom and Spirit': cf. 3 above. **11.** There is a close parallel, strongly emphasised by Luke, between the 'passion' of the first martyr and that of Jesus. 'Instigated' recalls Mk 14:56, omitted by Luke in his Gospel but echoed here. Stephen is accused of blasphemous attacks against the Law and the Temple. The charge of blasphemy repeats that brought against Jesus. **12.** Here the people, as well as the rulers, are hostile, but they are stirred up by the leaders as in the Passion of Jesus. The trial is before the Sanhedrin, which had condemned Jesus on a similar charge. **13.** 'False witnesses': cf. Mk 14:56–7. **14.** The charge brought against Jesus is transferred to Stephen, who is alleged to have said that Jesus will destroy the Temple and subvert the Law; cf Mk 14:58; Jn 2:19ff. The reference to the 'customs' of the Jews alludes in the main to the attitude of Jesus to the Temple and to the laws of ritual purity. **15.** 'The face of an angel'. Stephen, in fulfilment of the promise of Jesus (Lk. 12:12), is inspired by the Spirit to testify to the court. The inspired confessor is like an angel (cf. Est. 15:13, LXX) and reflects God's glory like Moses (Exod. 34:29ff.).

VII Stephen's speech has presented much difficulty b to commentators. It is not a defence against the charges on which he was tried, and it does not make its point explicitly until the last sentences. It must be remembered that even an actual speech made on this occasion by Stephen would not take the form of a denial or a disproof of the charges. It would naturally be a missionary speech, a 'confession' of Christian faith under persecution, inspired by the Spirit To make such a speech was a principal object of the Christian martyr. But this speech is exceptionally long, and occupies a very substantial proportion of Luke's work. He must therefore attach great importance to it, and a comparison of it with the other speeches shows that it is addressed to the reader rather than the supposed audience. Luke intends to mark an important stage in the narrative. Hitherto the gospel has been presented to Israel, and the leaders of the nation, represented by the Sadducee party, have rejected it and persecuted Christ's witnesses. Now, when the Diaspora Jews find the gospel, as preached by the Hellenist Stephen, incompatible with their devotion to the Temple and the Law, the whole system of Israel's religion is brought to the point of decisive challenge. The speech of Stephen tells the reader that in rejecting that challenge Israel was denying its own history and inheritance. It was rejecting that to which its own history pointed, when rightly understood; and yet in another sense it was fulfilling its own tradition, the tradition of those who betrayed Joseph, rejected Moses, turned to idols, broke the Law and sterilised their religion in an almost idolatrous devotion to the man-made Temple. The rejection of the Messiah was in keeping with the long history of Israel's resistance to the Holy Spirit, for Jesus is the true redeemer of whom Moses was the type; he is the promised prophet like Moses; in him as the 'righteous one' the Law is fulfilled; and he has superseded the Temple as the focal point on earth where God encounters man.

The speech is a review in the Deuteronomic manner c

781e of God's dealings with Israel, similar to Ps. 105 or Ps. 78. It is full of citations and echoes of the LXX. Its point is conveyed by means of subtle selection and emphasis in this handling of a familiar theme.

d **2ff. The Patriarchal History and the Rejection of Joseph**—The speech opens, as usual, with a typical Greek rhetorical address, after which it is largely a catena of carefully selected OT texts. 'God of glory', a phrase from Ps. 29:3, meaning 'glorious God', here perhaps conveys an allusion to the divine glory bestowed on Christ.

The impression that Abraham was called by God before he left Ur, and that it was after his father's death that he migrated from Haran, is easily obtained from Gen. 11:32 and 15:7, though in both cases it is at variance with the narrative.

5. 'No inheritance'. Great stress is laid in 2–7 on the fact that the original promises were given to Israel's ancestor when he was a wanderer, constantly moving on from his settled abode, outside the promised land. When he did enter Canaan, he received no permanent possession there, but only a promise, which the Christian reader would understand as fulfilled in his seed, Jesus.

6-7. 'Four hundred': cf. Gen. 15:13 (LXX). 'This place': Exod. 3:12 has been altered, 'place' (i.e. Canaan) being substituted for 'mountain'. **8.** The original covenant, sealed by circumcision, was concerned with the promises of God, especially of redemption, and not immediately with the holy land, the Law and the Temple.

9. The story of Joseph foreshadows that of Jesus. The original founders of Israel, the patriarchs, were jealous of Joseph, as the chief priests were of Jesus' disciples (5:17), rejected him and sold him into Gentile hands. God was with him, delivered him from all his afflictions and gave him favour with Pharaoh, so that he was made governor of all his house, as Jesus was delivered from death and exalted as Lord over God's people. 'Wisdom': cf. 22, where Moses resembles Joseph as a type of Christ. **13.** 'Second visit'. Possibly the two visits of the brethren, like the two 'visits' of Moses to the Israelites, correspond to the two advents of Christ, but this is unlikely. In the former case it is the brothers who visit Joseph, not vice versa. **15.** Jacob, Israel's eponymous ancestor, also went as a stranger to a Gentile country, and there he and the patriarchs died, having no inheritance in the promised land except for the tomb, bought from heathen Canaanites (in the locality of Samaria and Mt Gerizim, the antithesis of the holy city of the Jews) in which their bodies were later buried. The speech confuses, or conflates, the burials of Jacob at Hebron and Joseph at Shechem (Gen. 33:19, 49:31).

e **Moses and his Rejection by Israel—17.** 'Time of the promise drew near'. The language is reminiscent of the fulfilment of God's promises in Christ. Moses is portrayed throughout this speech as a type of Christ. **19.** 'Dealt craftily': cf. Exod. 1:10 (LXX). **21.** Moses was brought up in a Gentile palace, not among the people of God, still less in the holy land. **22.** He resembled Jesus in his growth in wisdom (Lk. 2:52), his 'favour with God' (20; cf. Lk. 2:52), and in being 'mighty in his words and deeds' as Jesus was (Lk. 24:19), who is the 'prophet like Moses' (37). For the Egyptian learning of Moses cf. Jos. Ant. II, ix, 7ff; Philo, *De Vita Moysis* 1:5. **23.** 'Visit his brethren', like Christ who was sent to Israel, bringing God's vindication of his people. **25.** God was giving 'deliverance' (literally 'salvation') by the hand of Moses, but Israel did not understand. Like Joseph before him and Jesus afterwards, Moses is rejected. He is driven out as an exile in an alien land. **26.** 'Brethren'. The teaching of Jesus and his work of reconciling men to one another as sons of God is adumbrated here. **27.** 'Thrust him aside' (cf. 39), as the Jews 'thrust aside' the gospel (13:46). **29.** 'Fled'. Exod. 2:15 makes Pharaoh responsible for his flight. Here for typological reasons his brethren bear the responsibility for his exile. Moses himself 781e
was a stranger in a foreign land, like Abraham and the patriarchs and like Israel in the desert. **32.** The mission of Moses is continuous with God's original election of Israel and his promises to the patriarchs. The episode of the bush corresponds to the heavenly voice at the baptism of Jesus. **33.** Moses is both likened to Jesus and also contrasted with him as the lesser to the greater: cf. Lk. 3:16. The holy ground of God's self-revelation is in a foreign land. **34.** Moses is sent to his brethren, like Jesus (Lk. 4:18, 43). **35.** He was 'denied' (RSV 'refused'), as was Jesus by Israel's leaders (3:13–14); but he was sent by God to be a ruler and redeemer (RSV 'deliverer'), as also was Jesus (5:31, cf. Lk. 24:31). 'Hand of the Angel': i.e. hand of God, by whose power Moses wrought signs and wonders. The 'hand' of God is a concept parallel in the OT to the 'Spirit' of God (that rested on Jesus). The parallel between Moses and Jesus is again emphasised, in respect of the performance of mighty works. **37.** Dt. 18:15, a most important text in Luke's Christology: cf. 3:22; Lk. 24:19. **38.** 'Congregation': cf. Dt. 4:10, 9:10. Moses was with the assembly of Israel at Sinai, but he was the unique mediator to whom the angel of God spoke and to whom was given the 'living oracles' of the Law. The 'angel' is equivalent to the divine presence, but later Judaism also believed that angels were the subordinate ministers through whom the Law was mediated (Gal. 3:19; Heb. 2:22). **39.** Israel disobeyed even Moses, to whom the angel spoke, and they rejected him. They 'turned to Egypt' (Num. 14:3) in their hearts, by thrusting their leader and redeemer aside and reverting to pagan idolatry.

The Idolatry of Israel—41. The idol-sacrifice at f
Sinai and the rejoicing 'in the works of their hands' are the first open expression of Israel's constant tendency to rebel against the Spirit of God. God 'gave them over' to the idolatry which they had deliberately embraced: cf. Rom. 1:24ff. **42-3.** Am. 5:25–7 (LXX), with the variant 'Babylon' for 'Damascus'. The text's original meaning is doubtful. It is interpreted here to mean that from the wilderness days Israel has sacrificed, not to God but to idols. 'Moloch': cf. 2 Kg. 23:10; Jer. 32:35 (LXX). The LXX 'tent of Moloch' appears to be a mistranslation of 'Sikkuth your king' (an Assyrian deity). 'Rephan' (Western text 'Rempham'; other variants: Remphan, Rompha, etc.) was read by the LXX for Hebrew 'Chiun' (an Assyrian god identified with Saturn). This name may be an error for 'Kaiphan' ('Kaiwan'), or may represent the substitution of an Egyptian equivalent for Saturn ('Repa') for the Assyrian. This prophecy is freely cited by the 'Zadokite Fragment' (a document emanating from the Qumrân sect), 9:4–9. 'Babylon' is probably substituted for 'Damascus' in order to make the prophecy refer directly to the *Jews*, and to lay stress on the fact that their punishment actually did take place. It is conceivable, but unlikely, that Luke is thinking of the events of A.D. 70 and equating Rome with Babylon as in 1 Pet. 5:13; Rev. 18:2. The Western text corrects to 'into the parts of Babylon'.

The Tabernacle and the Temple—44. The 'tent g
of witness' was made according to the divine pattern. It was a movable tabernacle, signifying that God's presence among his people in this mode was transitory and impermanent, destined to be replaced, like the Law, when the promises were fulfilled in Christ. **45.** 'Joshua': Gr. 'Jesus', the leader of Israel into the promised inheritance. **46.** David sought to find a habitation (more correctly 'tabernacle'): Ps. 132:5. The best MS tradition reads 'house of Jacob', but this may represent an early corruption caused by the occurrence of 'house' in the next sentence, combined with the familiarity of the phrase 'house of Jacob'. **47.** Solomon replaced the divinely planned movable tent with a permanent house. In this context it is implied that the foundation of the Temple was a

781g misguided act. God does not dwell in ' things made with hands '. This expression conveys a suggestion of heathen temples and idols (cf. 17:24) and is a reflection on the Jerusalem Temple : cf. the allegation of the false witnesses at the trial of Jesus (Mk 14:58). The phrase ' the Most High ' is most often used of God in connection with the recognition of the true God by pagans, and in opposition to heathen deities. Here it heightens the contrast between God and man-made temples. **48.** ' Prophet ' : Isa. 66:1–2 (LXX). **49.** ' What is the place ? ' : LXX, ' What sort ? ' The reading of Ac. agrees with that of the citation of the same verse in the *Epistle of Barnabas* 16:5, raising the question whether Luke and ' Barnabas ' used a book (or perhaps an oral collection) of ' testimonies '.

h **51-53 The Attack on Israel's Leaders**—Having rehearsed the history of Israel's stubborn refusal to fulfil their true calling and their continual failure to understand God's dealings with them, the speech breaks out into a direct attack upon the contemporary leaders of the nation. ' Stiff-necked ' : like Israel at the time of the apostasy over the golden calf (Exod. 32:9, 33:3). ' Uncircumcised ' : cf. Jer. 9:26. ' Resist the Holy Spirit ' : i.e. in rejecting the Spirit-inspired leaders and especially Moses, the prophets and now the ' prophet like Moses ' ; cf. Isa. 63:10. **52.** In later Jewish legend the prophets were for the most part believed to have been martyrs. This is connected here with their prophetic testimony to Christ. ' Coming ' : a term specially associated with the Messiah. See Kilpatrick, JTS 46 (1945), 136ff. ' Righteous One ' : cf. 3:14. Jesus is perhaps identified here with the righteous ' Servant ' and possibly also with the persecuted and vindicated ' righteous man ' of Wis. 2–3. The leaders of Israel are the betrayers and murderers of the Messiah. **53.** They received the Law from the mediating angels themselves (i e. they were uniquely privileged in being brought into contact with the divine Lawgiver), yet they did not keep it. This does not mean merely that they committed transgressions, but that they apostatised from it and so failed to see that it pointed to Christ and that by him it is superseded, like the Temple.

i **The Martyrdom of Stephen—54.** The speech had reached its climax. It is not really interrupted by the fury of the audience. For the reaction of the Sanhedrin there was plenty of excuse ; their national history had been recounted as a story of constant opposition to God's covenant purpose and of rejection of his agents. Israel had been portrayed as a race of idolaters ; the building of the Temple had been represented as a major error in religion. They themselves had been likened to the slayers of the prophets and denounced as murderers of the Messiah. They had apostatised from the Law, and they were an idolatrous and (spiritually) uncircumcised people. ' Enraged ' : as at 5:33. **55.** Stephen has an inspired vision : in the Spirit he sees the divine glory and Jesus exalted at God's right hand (Lk. 22:69 ; cf. Mk 14:62). ' Standing '. Ps. 110:1 speaks of ' sitting ' at God's right hand. The picture of Jesus ' standing ' at God's right hand is probably derived from the vision of the Son of man in Dan. 7:13, where the glorified Son of man is, by implication, standing before God. **56.** ' The heavens opened ' : as in a theophany (cf. Lk. 3:21), so that the martyr is granted a vision of the exalted Christ in heaven. ' Son of man ' is used as a designation of Jesus only here, outside the Gospels. The vision of the suffering and glorified Son of man, promised by Jesus at his trial (Mk 14:62 and parallels) is granted to the martyr who shares in his death. **57.** The claim to see Jesus sharing in the glory of God and exalted as the Son of man is, of course, blasphemous in the ears of the Sanhedrin, since Jesus had been himself condemned as a blasphemer. Their violent reaction suggests a lynching rather than a judicial verdict, sentence and execution. Luke pictures the Sanhedrin as a body liable to violent outbursts of emotion (cf. 5:33, 23:10). **58.** ' Cast him out of the city ' in accordance with the prescribed practice 781 (cf. Num. 15:35) ; but the further implication is that the inspired witness to Jesus is ejected from the midst of Israel. It was the duty of witnesses to execute the sentence. Saul was apparently present as a prominent onlooker ; cf. 22:20. **59.** The prayer of Jesus at his death (Lk. 23:46, echoing Ps. 31:5) is repeated by the martyr and is now addressed to Jesus as Lord. **60.** Stephen kneels in prayer and echoes the prayer of Jesus for the forgiveness of his murderers (Lk. 23:34). This gives support to the authenticity of the textually doubtful passage in Lk. (see note on Lk. 23:34). A close parallel is drawn between the death of Jesus and that of the martyr who is peculiarly inspired by the Spirit of Jesus and, sharing in his death, is enabled to reproduce its quality.

VIII 1-4 Persecution and Dispersion of the Church—1. Saul is brought into the centre of the story after being casually mentioned above. ' Judaea and Samaria ' represent the next stage after Jerusalem in the expansion of the mission and in the plan of Ac. The gospel has been offered to Jerusalem and rejected ; its violent rejection is the point of departure for its presentation to the wider world. It is difficult to judge the extent of this persecution. In 3 a general and intense persecution is indicated, but 14 suggests a different state of affairs. The persecution seems in fact to have been confined to the Hellenist part of the Church and to have affected chiefly Stephen's associates. The part played by Saul has probably been exaggerated by the tradition ; the great apostle must have been also the great persecutor. The apostles, at any rate, were left in Jerusalem to continue the general direction of the mission, whether in hiding or in peace. 782

2. ' Devout men ' : possibly pious Jews, if 3 is to be b taken as an indication that a Christian funeral would have been impracticable because of the persecution. If this is so, the burial of Stephen at the hands of pious sympathisers among the Jews resembles that of Jesus carried out by Joseph of Arimathaea (Lk. 23:50–1). But the story of the funeral may rather be a conventional ending to a narrative of martyrdom. It indicates the beginning, by the time of Luke's writing if not of Stephen's death, of the Christian practice of attaching high importance, and paying great honour, to the burial, remains and burial-place of a martyr (cf. the *Martyrdom of Polycarp*, 18). **3.** ' Laid waste ' is a verb often used of ' mangling ' or ' mauling ' by wild animals. The role of Saul is difficult to determine ; whether he was acting as the agent of the Sanhedrin or of one or more of the synagogues of the Dispersion in Jerusalem, for Luke he is virtually the sole, and autocratic, persecutor. **4.** ' Now ' introduces a new narrative, and probably a change to another source. ' Went about ' is a common expression in Ac. for making a missionary journey.

5-8 Philip's Preaching in Samaria—Philip's name c appeared next to that of Stephen in the list of the Seven (6:5). ' A city '. The principal Alexandrian MSS read ' the city ', which would mean Sebaste, the ancient Samaria ; but elsewhere in the NT Samaria always denotes the country, not the city, and ' a city ' is probably right. It has been suggested that this city might be Gitta, the home of Simon Magus according to Justin (*1 Apology*, 26). In preaching to Samaritans Philip was taking a momentous step. They were the ancient enemy of the Jews, detested by them as a mongrel race of semi-heathen heretics. **6-7.** Philip's preaching, like that of Jesus and of the apostles and Stephen, was accompanied by the ' acted preaching ' of signs. Demons were cast out, as by Jesus in Galilee, and the signs foretold in Isa. 35:6 attest the working of the Spirit and the advent of the age of fulfilment. **8.** ' Joy '. The Lucan writings often call attention to ' joy ' and ' gladness ' as the expression and consequence of the Spirit's active presence.

9-13 The Conversion of Simon Magus—Simon has d played a most important role in Church history as the first of the great leaders of Gnosticism and the rival and

782d foe of Peter. The mass of legend about him goes back to Justin (*1 Apology*, 26, 56; *Dialogue*, 120). Irenaeus, and especially Hippolytus, describe the Simonian Gnostic system of belief and the antinomian practice of the sect. Simon is the villain of much early Christian fiction, notably the *Clementine Recognitions* and *Homilies*, and the *Acts of Peter with Simon*. It is by no means certain that the founder of the Gnostic sect was really this Simon of Samaria. Justin himself, who tells us that Simon came from Gitta, was a native of Samaria and might be expected to have authentic information about him; but he does not allude to Ac. His account of Simon's career in Rome includes some obviously erroneous matter, at least in so far as he apparently believed a statue to the god Semo Sancus to have been erected in honour of Simon as 'Deus sanctus'. See R. P. Casey, *The Beginnings of Christianity*, v, 151ff.; E. Haenchen, *Zeitschrift für Theologie u. Kirche*, 49 (1952), 316ff.; E. Amann, *Dictionnaire de Théologie Catholique*, xiv, cols. 2130 ff.

e 'Somebody great': cf. 5:33. **10.** Simon seems to have claimed to be the manifestation on earth of the Great Power, i.e. the Deity. According to Justin and later writers, his consort Helena was supposed to be an embodiment of the 'primal thought' proceeding from the supreme Deity. 'Of God' may be a mistaken explanation of an unfamiliar term which Luke cites (cf. the insertion of 'called') without fully understanding its meaning. **11.** Simon has nothing in common with the normal religion of the Samaritans, but according to Luke he had gained immense prestige among them by his acts of magic, extending over a long period. **12.** Philip's preaching announces the approach of the Kingdom of God and its effective exercise in the present order through the power of the name of Jesus the Messiah. The Samaritans looked for the coming of a 'messianic' figure, the *Taheb*, identified with the prophet of Dt. 18:15. 'Baptised': cf. 2:38. **13.** The power of the name of Jesus Christ was demonstrated in Philip's signs and mighty works. Even Simon the magician was amazed.

f **14-25 The Visit of Peter and John, and the Rebuke of Simon**—The Jerusalem church is regarded by Luke as the headquarters of the Church's mission, and the apostles as its directors and controllers. They now send the two leaders of the original mission in Jerusalem, Peter, the chief and spokesman of the apostles, and his associate John (cf. 3:1, 11, 4:13). The suggestion that this John might be John Mark and not the son of Zebedee (*The Beginnings of Christianity*, iv, 92; E. R. Annand, SJTh. 9 (1956), 46ff.) does not fit the facts of the situation. Their object is evidently to set the seal of apostolic approval on Philip's revolutionary step of extending the mission to Samaria.

g **15.** The apostles' ratification of Philip's mission takes the form of prayer that the new converts may receive the Holy Spirit. Though they had been baptised in the name of the Lord Jesus, in accordance with Peter's command to the crowd at Pentecost (2:38), the Spirit had not yet come upon them. The implication is that the Spirit here means the Pentecostal manifestation of the Spirit in 'tongues' and perhaps prophesying; for it is clear that a striking and obvious external manifestation was expected, and that when it occurred Simon was immensely impressed, to the extent of wanting to buy the authority to give the Spirit himself (18–19). It is also clear that the coming of the Spirit in this mode was expected usually to accompany baptism (cf. 2:38) and that the absence of Pentecostal manifestations in Samaria was abnormal and unexpected. It cannot be supposed that the Spirit as the principle of the unity, love and joy of the Christian community was absent from the Samaritan converts who had been baptised in response to the preaching of the Kingdom and the Name of Jesus as Lord, in a setting of mighty works and signs. Nor is it easy to believe that the coming of the Spirit, as the inner principle of Christian life, was normally dissociated from baptism in the name of Jesus Christ, or that it 782g
was mediated only through the Twelve. From
Tertullian (*De Baptismo*, 8) onwards there was a h
tendency to regard the bishop's imposition of hands upon, or 'consignation' of, the newly baptised as the particular sacramental sign of the coming of the Spirit, but of this, as a regular practice, there is no evidence in the NT, apart from Heb. 6:2, a passage whose meaning is itself in doubt. Here the circumstances are evidently extraordinary. The apostles were not visiting Samaria to 'confirm' the baptised, like a modern bishop. They were confirming the extension of the mission to Samaria and ratifying Philip's preaching and baptisms. 19:5–6 describes another extraordinary initiation of disciples, as, in a different way, does 10:44. According to the late Dom Gregory Dix, what was happening at Samaria was an 'ordination of prophets'. This is not quite correct, for prophets were not ordained as such; but it is true that the apostles' prayer and imposition of hands were the means by which the Spirit of prophecy and tongues (the 'missionary' Spirit of Pentecost) came upon Samaritan believers, marking a new stage in the mission and a total change in the relation of Jews to Samaritans, within the Church. This is a Samaritan Pentecost, as 10:44 is a Gentile Pentecost. The Spirit who guides and inspires the mission is manifested in this new centre of the Church's work, in phenomena like those at the Jerusalem Pentecost. The Samaritans are given a participation in the Spirit that possessed the original apostles. When the two chief apostles visit Samaria from the hated rival sanctuary at Jerusalem, pray for the converts and give them the ancient sign of 'solidarity' and self-identification, the laying-on of hands, the Spirit received by the apostles at Pentecost and manifested in 'tongues' is imparted to the Samaritans, now joined with their former enemies, the Jews, in the community of the Church.

19. 'Power': more correctly 'authority'. **20.** i
'Perish': literally 'be for destruction' (cf. Dan. 2:5; Theodotion). Simon wanted to buy the gift, not of the Spirit but of authority to confer the Spirit. **21.** 'Neither part nor lot' is an OT phrase (cf. Dt. 12:12), here denoting excommunication from the Church. The language of this passage is especially solemn and 'biblical', full of echoes of the LXX. **22-3.** Simon's grievous sin does not preclude hope of repentance and forgiveness. 'Gall': cf. Dt. 29:18; Isa. 58:6. **25.** The apostles return to Jerusalem and another story about Philip is introduced.

Philip and the Ethiopian Eunuch—26. Curious j
verbal similarities have often been pointed out between this passage and Zeph. 2:4, 11–13, 3:4, 10, LXX. These may be due to sheer coincidence, or to Luke's having for some reason had the language of that passage of the Bible in his mind as he wrote. 'Angel of the Lord': Philip was divinely guided to meet the Ethiopian. This expression, where we might have expected a reference to the Spirit of the Lord (cf. 39 below), is common in the OT (cf. especially 2 Kg. 1:15). 'South'. The alternative translation 'at noon' seems less probable, but, since travellers would not normally be on the road at noon, it might, together with the curious note that it was a desert road, imply that for Philip to meet anyone at such a time and place was humanly improbable. 'Desert', however, might allude to Gaza rather than the road. Old Gaza was destroyed by Alexander, and New Gaza in A.D. 66. Gaza is the last town before the desert road to Egypt begins.

27. 'Ethiopian' means, not Abyssinian but belonging k
to Meroe, the modern Sudan. Ps. 68:31 may be in mind here, but although this man comes from the ends of the earth he is clearly not a heathen. His conversion may foreshadow the extension of the mission to the farthest parts of the world, but his significance lies less in the fact that he was an Ethiopian than in his being a eunuch. Eunuchs were outside the community of Israel (Dt. 23:1). The gospel, having

782k been preached to the outcast Samaritans, now comes to a representative of another class of those excluded previously from the covenant people. ' Candace ' is a title of the ' Ethiopian ' queen-mothers, who, being regarded as consorts of the sun, maintained the real power in their hands, although their sons reigned as the nominal sovereigns. ' Worship '. The eunuch was probably of the class of ' God-fearers ', Gentile adherents of Judaism who did not, or could not, become actual proselytes. **30.** In the Greek there is a play on the words ' understand ' and ' reading '. The eunuch was reading aloud, as was apparently the

l usual practice in antiquity. **32.** Isa. 53:7f., part of the last ' Servant ' poem. This is one of the relatively few direct citations of the ' Servant ' poems as prophecies of Jesus. It refers to the death of the Messiah, but is otherwise hard to interpret. ' Justice was denied him ' : literally ' was removed ', either meaning ' was denied him ' or possibly referring to the removal of his judgment (i.e. his condemnation) by the Resurrection. It is significant that Luke does not quote any part of the poem dealing with vicarious atonement for sin, which is in any case a less prominent theme in the LXX than in the Hebrew text of the poem. For Luke the death of the Messiah is the necessary road to his glory, but the idea that by it sin was expiated plays little part in his thought.

m **34.** The eunuch's question leads to Philip's preaching, which was not confined to this scriptural text but made it the starting-point. **36.** ' Prevent ' : cf. 10:47. This was possibly a conventional formula at the admission of a candidate for baptism. As in 16:33, baptism is administered without preparation or probation apart from the initial preaching and the candidate's assent to it. An addition (37) in the later MSS, with much support from Western patristic citations, from Irenaeus onwards, adds the eunuch's confession of an early creed : ' I believe that Jesus Christ is the Son of God '. **38.** Unlike Jewish proselyte baptism, Christian baptism was evidently not self-administered. **39.** The Spirit caught up Philip like an OT prophet (cf. 2 Kg. 2:16). The Western text says that ' Holy Spirit fell upon the eunuch, and an angel of the Lord caught up Philip '. This is probably an attempt to show that the eunuch received the Spirit, like Jesus on emerging from the Jordan, and so to tidy up an apparent difficulty in the narrative. ' Rejoicing '. The frequent association of joy with the Spirit may imply in any case that the eunuch departed possessed by the Spirit ; cf. 13:52, 16:34. **40.** Azotus is the ancient Philistine city Ashdod, whence Philip conducted a mission up the coastal district of Palestine to Caesarea (cf. 21:8).

783a **IX 1-9 The Appearance of Jesus to Saul—1.** Saul is consistently represented as a violent enemy of the Christians, and as the instigator and conductor of the persecution. ' Disciples ' : cf. 6:1. This chapter contains many different words descriptive of the Christians. **2.** The letters were presumably from the Jerusalem Sanhedrin to the synagogues of the Jewish community in Damascus. The question of the rights of the Jerusalem authorities over members of synagogues in the Dispersion is much disputed. Damascus was the home of a large Jewish colony. It probably included the ' covenanting ' sect which produced the ' Zadokite Fragment ' and is to be identified with the Qumrân community. Saul's mission may have been to arrest Christian Jewish fugitives from Jerusalem. A right of extradition was granted by Rome to Simon Maccabaeus as high priest in respect of fugitives to Egypt (1 Mac. 15:21). ' The Way ' : cf. 24:14. A designation applied by Christians to themselves ; cf. the OT expressions ' way of the Lord ', ' way of righteousness ', etc. Christianity was *the* way of life.

b **3.** The manifestation of Jesus, classed by Paul as one of the ' Resurrection appearances ' (cf. 1 C. 15:8), is described in terms appropriate to a theophany. The light signifies the glory of the exalted Lord. The details of this event vary slightly in the repeated accounts

of it given in Ac. ; thus in 26:13 the light shone round 783
Saul's companions as well as himself. **4.** ' Fell to the ground ', like the profaner of the Temple, Heliodorus, on whom there came ' great darkness ' (cf. 8 below) ; see 2 Mac. 3:27–8. ' Saul, Saul '. The name is given here, and in the parallel passages, 22:7, 26:14, in its Semitic form, though usually it appears in the Greek form. This harmonises with 26:14, where Jesus is said to have spoken in Hebrew (i.e. Aramaic). ' Persecute me '. As the persecutor of the Church, Saul was persecuting Christ himself in the person of his people ; cf. Lk. 10:16. **5.** Saul acknowledges Jesus as Lord. **7.** ' Hearing ' : cf. Dt. 4:12, which suggests that Saul's companions heard the Lord's voice, not simply the voice of Saul. **8.** Saul's overthrow is complete. In his blindness he is reduced to the state
of his opponent in 13:11. **9.** Saul's fast is probably c
due to his state of shock, of which his blindness is another symptom. It might also suggest to Luke the fast undertaken by converts before baptism ; cf. *Didache* 7:4. The three days might well bring home to Saul himself the reality of the baptismal symbolism of death, burial and resurrection with Christ, which plays so prominent a part in his own theology.

10-19 The Vision of Ananias and the Baptism of Saul—Ananias (see also 22:12) was a pious Jewish 784
Christian, well known in Damascus. He may have been a refugee from Jerusalem or possibly even a Galilaean disciple from the pre-Resurrection period. Paul never mentions him in the autobiographical parts of his letters. The language in which his vision is described is strongly biblical. With **10** cf. 1 Sam. 3:4. **11.** ' Called Straight ' : i.e. ' Straight ' is a name and not merely a description. The details given in the vision serve to heighten the effect of this providential dispensation for Saul's conversion. ' Praying '. As usual in Luke's writings, events of special importance, especially those involving divine revelation, occur in the setting of prayer. **12.** Many MSS add ' in a vision ' after ' seen '. The omission of these words is probably accidental, or possibly intended to improve the word-order. In any case it must have been in a vision that Saul saw Ananias. The vision within a vision is remarkable. **13.** ' Saints ' is a common Pauline description of Christians as the people consecrated to God, used also in this chapter and in
26:10. **14-15.** The great contrast here is between b
Saul as he himself intended to be (14) and Saul as he was chosen to be according to the divine purpose. He is a ' vessel of (God's) choice ' to carry the name of Christ (i.e. the content of the gospel) to Gentiles and kings and the sons of Israel. This foreshadows his leadership of the Gentile mission, his witness before Agrippa II and Caesar, and his mission, at the same time, to Israel. **16.** The gospel of the name involves the suffering foretold by Jesus for his disciples. **17.** Ananias calls Saul a ' brother ', i.e. a Christian. Jesus is the Lord whose ' apostle ' (the verb *apostellō* is used) Ananias now is, commissioned by him to give Saul healing and to enable him to receive the Spirit. This seems to have taken place when Ananias gave Saul the sign of self-identification and ' solidarity ' in the laying-on of hands and thus associated him with the community of believers represented by this disciple. **18.** ' Scales ' is not a medical term, except in relation to diseases of the skin. Tob. 11:13 may be in mind here. ' Baptised '. Here the coming of the Spirit may have preceded baptism and been connected rather with the recovery of sight and the laying-on of hands, the sign of unity with the Christian society. On the analogy of 8:18 and 19:6, it is likely that ' Holy Spirit ' here denotes the Pentecostal manifestation of the Spirit, empowering Saul as an apostolic missionary. The ' illumination ' of baptism (cf. Heb. 6:4) was associated in Saul's case with a physical recovery of sight, and his baptismal ' resurrection ' corresponded with recovery from a death-like condition. **19.** ' Took food ', referring to the completeness of Saul's recovery,

784b and perhaps also the breaking of the baptismal fast; the language is entirely unliturgical.

c **20-22 Saul's Preaching at Damascus**—Paul himself (Gal. 1:17) indicates that he went to Arabia directly after his conversion. He might indeed, nevertheless, have stayed 'several days' with the Damascus Christians, preaching there, but 23 suggests that Luke did not know of the visit to Arabia and thought that Saul remained in Damascus until he went to Jerusalem. **20.** Luke's whole emphasis in this story is upon the wonder of the persecutor's transformation into a missionary. Saul's preaching concerns the messiahship of Jesus (**22**), and hence his messianic sonship in accordance with Ps. 2:7 (cf. 13:33). The phrase 'Son of God', however, occurs only here in Ac., and may possibly be introduced to indicate what was to become the central theme of Pauline teaching. **21.** 'Amazed'; cf. Lk. 4:22. 'Made havoc': the word means *sack* a city, or *ravage*; cf. Gal. 1:13, 23. 'Proving': i.e. by reference to the OT.

d **23-25 Saul's Escape**—**23.** 'Jews'. According to 2 C. 11:32 it was the ethnarch of Aretas, the king of Nabataea (Arabia) who tried to capture him (probably lying in wait for him outside the gates), presumably as a consequence of trouble caused by his missionary activity in Arabia. **25.** As Luke pictures this incident, the Jews are watching the gates to prevent Saul going out. The disciples ('his disciples' may be an early corruption for 'the disciples', i.e. the Christians) lower him from the wall between the gates.

e **26-30 Saul's Visit to Jerusalem and Departure to Tarsus**—**26.** Luke lays stress on the close association of Saul with the apostles at Jerusalem, and their authorisation of his ministry. Paul's own account in Gal. 1–2 gives a very different impression. Luke probably bases his account on the tradition handed down from the Jerusalem Christians. **27.** 'The apostles' are evidently the Twelve, still apparently resident in Jerusalem as the governing body of the Church. **28.** A close association is implied between Saul and the apostles. His conversion and mission are thereby attested and recognised. **29.** According to Luke, Saul actually followed in the footsteps of Stephen, preaching and disputing with the Jews of the Dispersion (Codex Alexandrinus has the variant *Hellēnes*, Greeks, for *Hellēnistai*, Greek-speaking Jews). The effect is the same as in Stephen's case; they try to murder him. According to Gal. 1:18–19 Saul's visit to Jerusalem lasted only a fortnight and he met only James, the Lord's brother, in addition to Peter. **30.** In 22:17–21 Saul's departure is prompted by a vision in which he is divinely commissioned to go to the Gentiles. The two accounts are not incompatible. The violent rejection of his preaching at Jerusalem leads to his departure, which was probably decided upon both by himself and the 'brethren', and thus to missionary work in the region of Tarsus (Syria and Cilicia, Gal. 1:21). The story of Saul thus reproduces the history of the Church's entire mission in its pattern of rejection by Jews and acceptance by Gentiles.

f **31 A summary of the state of the Church** at the critical moment when Peter's missionary journey begins, which was to lead to the extension of the mission to Gentiles. 'So' introduces a new section of the book. Hitherto it has dealt with Judaea (Galilee, as a part of the land of the Jews, is mentioned here, but nothing is said about the mission there) and Samaria. Now the turning-point is reached when the final stage begins which is to take the story to the ends of the earth'. There is slight MS evidence for 'churches' instead of 'church', but it is likely that Luke used the singular here, in the sense of the universal Church. 'Comfort': Gr. *paraclēsis*, the peculiar work of the Spirit as *Paraclete*. It probably means 'exhortation', referring to the inspired preaching and teaching by which the inner life of the Church was enriched and its numbers increased.

g **32-35 Peter heals Aeneas**—'Among them all': literally 'through all', an odd expression, perhaps meaning 'through all the areas mentioned' (i.e. in 784g 31). Peter may be pictured as touring all the lands in which the Church had by now been established, in a kind of pastoral visitation. **33.** The Church is already established at Lydda, north-west of Jerusalem. The cure of this paralytic recalls Lk. 5:18–26, as the raising of Dorcas recalls that of Jairus's daughter. The signs of Jesus are reproduced in the Church's mission through the power of his name. **34.** 'Heals', or perhaps 'has healed'. This is a favourite word of Luke's, perhaps with a play on the name Jesus (*iatai se Iēsous*). 'Make your bed': literally 'spread your couch', either to lie on, or for a meal. **35.** It is not stated whether or not Aeneas was a Christian. These people who 'turned to the Lord' are presumably Jews. 'Sharon' is the coastal plain of Palestine.

36-43 Peter at Joppa: the Raising of Dorcas— h **36.** 'Disciple' in the feminine form of the Greek occurs only here. 'Tabitha' (Aram.) and 'Dorcas' (Gr.) mean 'Gazelle'. **37.** 'Upper room': cf. 1 Kg. 17:19. The stories in 1 Kg. 17 and 2 Kg. 4 have influenced this narrative, together with the story of Jairus's daughter. **38.** 'Two men': cf. 10:7, 11:30, etc., perhaps connected with the idea of two witnesses authenticating a message. **39.** 'Widows': cf. 6:1. Although not yet, in all probability, a defined 'order' in the Church, the widows in each Christian community would receive relief and support from its resources. Here they point to their clothes, which Tabitha had made for them. **40.** cf. 2 Kg. 4:33. Jesus acted similarly in the house of Jairus (Mk 5:40, the wording here being closer to Mk than to Lk. 8:51). 'Prayed'. This miracle, like so many other important events in Luke's writings, is set in the context of prayer. 'Tabitha rise': an echo of the Aramaic preserved in Mk 5:41, where, by assimilation to this passage, 'Tabitha' is read in some MSS for 'Talitha' (maiden). Luke rendered the Marcan phrase somewhat differently (Lk. 8:54). 'Opened her eyes': cf. 2 Kg. 4:35. 'Sat up': cf. Lk. 7:15. **41.** 'Hand': as at the raising of Jairus's daughter (Lk. 8:54). **42.** This sign results in many conversions (from Judaism) at Joppa. **43.** Simon's trade as a tanner may be mentioned to avoid confusion with Simon Peter (10:5–6). According to the oral Law a tanner's trade was unclean; but there is no indication that Luke intends his readers to have this in mind, and it is not clear how strictly such provisions of the Law were generally observed at this period in non-Pharisaic Judaism.

X 1-8 The Vision of Cornelius and his Embassy 785a **to Peter**—**1.** Caesarea, a seaport, was the old 'Strato's Tower', renamed by Herod the Great. It was the seat of the Roman administration of Judaea. 'Italian Cohort': probably *Cohors II Miliaria Italica Civium Romanorum Voluntariorum* (i.e. of freedmen), an auxiliary unit of archers. Its presence in Syria before A.D. 69 is attested by an inscription (Dessau, *Inscriptiones Latinae Selectae*, 9168), but there is no evidence to show whether it was at Caesarea as early as this. Cornelius strongly resembles the centurion of Lk. 7:2–10. He is 'devout', i.e. a 'God-fearer', a Gentile adherent of the synagogue, interested in the Jewish faith and performing typical works of Jewish piety reminiscent of Tob. 12:8. **2.** 'The people': i.e. Israel. **3.** The ninth hour (3 p.m.) was the hour of prayer (3:1) and a time of day at which a vision such as this must be objectively real; Cornelius was not asleep in bed and dreaming. 'Angel of God'. The great event of a Gentile conversion is brought about by a theophany like those in Luke's infancy narratives. This story has some close resemblances to the beginning of the Gospel, the appearance of the angel to Zechariah in the Temple (Lk. 1:11ff.). **4.** 'Memorial'. Cornelius's prayers and alms are like a burnt sacrifice (Lev. 2:11); cf. Tob. 12:12. **5-6.** The approach of Cornelius to Peter, as well as Peter's response, is due to a direct divine command. **7.** Cornelius sends two household servants and a batman who was also 'devout'. A centurion, although

785a comparable in some respects with a modern warrant officer, in others resembled more nearly a major, being a kind of company commander.

b **9-23 Peter's Vision and the Arrival of Cornelius's Messengers**—**9.** Again, a major event in the story begins in the setting of prayer. The sixth hour (noon) was not a regular hour of prayer (but cf. Ps. 55:17). **11.** 'Saw the heaven opened': a phrase denoting a theophany or, as here, a special revelation from God (cf. Lk. 3:21; Ac. 7:56). Peter's vision has often been described in psychological terms, its chief constituent elements being his hunger, his perplexity about the possibility of extending the mission to Gentiles, and the sight of a sail being lowered in the nearby harbour (or possibly of an awning on the roof, which would be needed in the heat of noon). **12.** cf. Gen. 1:24 and 6:20. **13.** Peter is told to 'kill', the word being commonly used of sacrificial slaying. This is perhaps intended to point the paradoxical contrast between the divine command and the uncleanness of the animals; but the verb can have an entirely 'secular' sense.

c **14.** Peter's reply is an echo of Ezek. 4:14. **15.** God has cleansed these creatures by his command to eat of them. It is unlikely that there is a direct echo here of Mk 7:19. **16.** The threefold occurrence emphasises the importance of the divine command. **17.** 'Mean'. The sequel shows that it meant the abolition, for the Church, of the distinction between Jew and Gentile. Hence the vision might suggest an allegorising interpretation of the Mosaic food laws, such as is found in a developed form in the *Epistle of Barnabas*, where the laws are made to relate only to ethical conduct. It must be remembered, however, that the question of food laws was very closely bound up with that of the admission of Gentiles to the Church. The extension of the mission raised the problem of table fellowship and this in turn brought up the whole question of the validity of the Mosaic food laws. **19.** Peter is prompted by the Spirit to go with the messengers and not to hesitate. The whole episode is worked out under direct divine guidance. Some MSS omit 'three'; Codex Vaticanus reads 'two', perhaps supposing the soldier (7) to be an escort for the two messengers. **22.** cf. the description of the centurion in Lk. 7:4-5. 'Jewish nation' is a Gentile way of describing the 'people', as Israel is generally termed in Luke's writings. 'Directed': cf. Lk. 2:26.

d **23-34 Peter's Arrival at the House of Cornelius**—**23.** The brethren from Joppa (six in number) act later as witnesses to the divine action towards Cornelius (11:12). **24.** Cornelius assembles friends and relatives to meet Peter. The 'Gentile Pentecost' accordingly happens to a group, not an individual or even a single family, and a nucleus of the Caesarean church is formed. **25.** The Western text adds a verbose account of Peter's approach, the announcement of it by a slave and Cornelius meeting him. **25-6.** Cornelius seeks to worship Peter as though he were an angel. **27.** Peter finds the 'congregation' assembled indoors. It was 'unlawful' for him to go in to them, but his vision had shown that the Law was no longer valid in this respect. 'Another nation' is a common LXX word with a contemptuous implication: it suggests a heathen outsider. 'Any man'. The personal language (contrast 14) makes explicit the meaning of the vision. **30.** 'Four days ago'. The Greek is obscure, but RSV gives the probable sense. 'Bright apparel' indicates a heavenly being. The repetition of Cornelius's story serves to heighten its importance and solemnity as a narrative of God's direct intervention. **33.** 'In the sight of God'. Biblical language is thought by Luke to be appropriate for so 'devout' a Gentile.

e **34-43 Peter's Speech**—This speech uses a stilted biblical vocabulary and style, which at times produces very awkward Greek. It begins with a reference to the actual situation. God shows no partiality; he has no favourites, not even a favoured nation. **35.** God accepts from every nation those whose manner of life is like that of the 'devout' Cornelius. Those who live 785e
like Jews are accepted by God even though they are outside the boundaries of Israel. This is a different doctrine from the Pauline teaching on justification, though it has points of contact with the thought of Rom. 2:14-15. **36.** 'Word': i.e. the gospel. Some MSS make this a plain statement: 'He sent the word . . .' (cf. Ps. 107:20). The content of the word is the coming of peace (cf. Isa. 52:7) between God and man (probably also between Jew and Gentile) through Jesus Christ, who is Lord of all men, not of Israel alone.
37. The gospel began with the ministry of Jesus in f
Galilee after John's baptism. 'Beginning': the participle in Greek is here used, as elsewhere in Luke's writings, indeclinably and adverbially. The gospel narrative here is a compressed summary of Luke's Gospel without the prologue (the infancy narratives). **38.** 'Anointed' as Messiah with the Spirit and power, at the Baptism. The passage with which Jesus announced his ministry (Isa. 61:1-2; Lk. 4:18) is echoed here. This description of Jesus as the Spirit-possessed agent of God is typical of Luke's Christology. 'Doing good'. The earthly ministry does not usually receive so much emphasis in the missionary preaching, but cf. 2:22. **39.** The gospel is guaranteed by the apostles' testimony. 'Country of the Jews': i.e. Galilee and the road up to Jerusalem. Luke uses 'Judaea' in a wide sense to mean 'the land of the Jews' including Galilee (cf. Lk. 4:44). 'Hanging him on a tree': cf. 5:30. **40.** The Resurrection is attested by the specially chosen witnesses to whom alone God made Jesus manifest. Their testimony rests on their experience of the risen Christ in the post-Resurrection meals (1:4, cf. Lk. 24:30, 43). **42.** 'Commanded': cf. 1:8; Lk. 24:47-8. 'The people': i.e. Israel. 'Ordained'. Jesus is the appointed judge of the living and the dead; that is, he is the Son of man (cf. 17:31). **43.** The content of the gospel is forgiveness of sins through faith in Jesus. The OT prophets testify to this, their witness confirming the apostolic preaching. This forgiveness is open to all men, not only to Jews.
44-48 The Coming of the Spirit upon the Gentiles, g
and their Baptism—**44.** The Spirit comes upon Peter's Gentile hearers, as at Pentecost. This second Pentecost is a major turning-point in the mission. **45.** 'Circumcised'. The Jewish Christians who accompanied Peter from Joppa. 'Gift of the Holy Spirit'. The Pentecostal endowment of the missionary Spirit, manifested in 'tongues'. The Western text has 'other tongues', pointing the parallel with Pentecost. **47.** 'Forbid': cf. 8:36. Possibly a quasi-technical term in connection with candidates for baptism. 'Received'. On this extraordinary occasion, unique except for the parallel of Pentecost, the coming of the Spirit is unmediated. This does not make baptism superfluous but indicates that those whom God has chosen must forthwith be received into the Christian community by baptism. On this marvellous occasion, however, baptism is not the effective sign of the coming of the Spirit, but follows it. 'Just as we have': i.e. like the original disciples at Jerusalem. **48.** 'In the name': i.e. as Christ's people, belonging to him and owing allegiance to him. This phrase does not necessarily indicate the wording of the baptismal profession of faith, but it was probably an assertion of belief in Jesus Christ as Lord or as Son of God (cf. 8:37, Western text). 'Some days'. Peter does not merely visit the Gentile household and go away again, but stays in the legally unclean place for some time.
XI 1-18 The Jerusalem Church approves Peter's 786a
Admission of Gentiles—**1.** The story of the extension of the Church's mission to Gentiles continues to a climax in the recognition by the Jerusalem church of God's acceptance of the converts at Caesarea and its implications for the future. 'Heard' implies that the authorities of the Church in Jerusalem (the whole community is associated with the apostles) took official cognisance of the great step taken by Peter

86a and, when he came and reported to them, required him to give an account of what he had done. In similar language we are told of the Jerusalem church taking cognisance of the extension of the mission to Samaria (8:14) when they sent Peter and John to investigate and approve the revolutionary action of Philip. Similarly at 11:22 they take cognisance of the formation of a mixed Jewish-Gentile church at Antioch and send Barnabas to look into the situation there. The Western text adds a verbose introduction to this narrative, which implies that Peter did not go to Jerusalem until a considerable time after the events at Caesarea and that he finally went there in the course of a preaching tour in which he fulfilled a long-standing desire to go to Jerusalem. In this version Peter's subordination to the Jerusalem church is much less apparent.

b **2.** ' The circumcision party '. Those who opposed any relaxation of the Law in respect of intercourse with Gentiles ; cf. 15:1ff. **3.** The dispute refers to table fellowship with Gentiles. The question of table fellowship naturally arises in connection with the baptism of Gentiles, but, according to Luke (who may to some extent have confused two issues here) it was the former which was now in dispute. **4.** ' In order ' : cf. the phrase used in Lk. 1:3. Peter's defence consists in a narrative of the divine guidance which had led him to Cornelius, and the manifestation of the Spirit which came upon Cornelius and his household and made it imperative to baptise them. The repetition of this story serves also to impress it upon the minds of Luke's readers as an event of the greatest significance. **5-16.** In retelling the story Luke avoids repeating himself exactly. Several minor points are mentioned here for the first time, and certain features of the previous version are now omitted. **11.** ' We were ' : i.e. Peter and the six brethren (12). It was not previously stated that any other Christians were lodging with Peter when the messengers arrived from Cornelius. The Chester Beatty papyrus and other MSS avoid any discrepancy by reading ' I was '. **12.** ' Without hesitation ', or possibly ' without making any distinction ' between Jews and Gentiles. ' These six brethren ' are the Christians who accompanied Peter to Caesarea and are now present as witnesses. Their number was not mentioned in the previous narrative. It may possibly be connected with the idea that seven witnesses (the six and Peter) guaranteed the truth of the story (cf. the seven seals of Rev. 5:1).

c **14.** The angel's message to Cornelius is expanded in the light of the event. **15.** Peter's speech in Cornelius's house, intended primarily for Luke's readers, is omitted here. The Spirit is said to have come as he began to speak (contrast 10:44). ' On us at the beginning ' : i.e. the apostles at Pentecost. **16.** Peter's defence is clinched by a quotation of the words of Jesus (cf. 20:35). The reference is to 1:5 ; the promise of the Pentecostal gift has been fulfilled for these Gentiles. **17.** God gave the same gift of the Pentecostal manifestation (in ' tongues ') to the Gentiles at Caesarea as to the Jerusalem Christians when they acknowledged Jesus Christ as Lord. Peter could not hinder God (cf. 10:47) by refusing to baptise them. **18.** Peter's opponents acknowledge the act of God and recognise that repentance leading to life (the content of the apostles' gospel) has been granted to Gentiles without the necessity for them first to become Jews. The Gentile mission is thus officially authorised and the later protests of the Judaising party are regarded by Luke as unrepresentative of the Jerusalem authorities.

d **19-26 The Church at Antioch : Preaching to Gentiles : Barnabas's Visit—19.** ' Now ' begins a new section of the book, and probably indicates a transition to a different source. The mention of Stephen links this story with 8:4. The rejection of the gospel by the Jerusalem Sanhedrin leads to a double extension of the mission to Samaria and to the Gentiles. ' Phoenicia ' : cf. 21:4, 7, 27:3. ' Cyprus '. Despite
the impression given by 13:5-12, Paul and Barnabas 786d
were apparently not the first missionaries there. ' Antioch '. The capital of the province of Syria and the third city of the Empire, with a large Jewish colony and many proselytes (cf. 6:5 and Jos.BJ VII,
iii, 3). **20.** ' Men of Cyprus and Cyrene ' : like e
Barnabas (4:36) and Lucius (13:1). ' Greeks ' : Codex Vaticanus and other MSS read *Hellēnistai* for *Hellēnes*, reflecting the inability of scribes to distinguish between the two words. The story makes no sense if these are not Gentiles, admitted into the Church without first being circumcised as Jews. The content of the preaching of these Greek-speaking Jewish missionaries is that Jesus is Lord. The title was not a Gentile innovation, but was used by Palestinian Christians from the outset. The missionaries are unknown Christians, not appointed as ministers of the Church, who probably evangelised in the ordinary course of their business. Thus the founders of the church at Antioch, like that at Rome, were anonymous laymen. **21.** ' Hand of the Lord ' : i.e. God, not Jesus. This is an OT expression ; 2 Sam. 3:12. God acknowledged their mission and blessed it, and it met with great success. **22.** ' To the ears ' : cf. Isa. 5:9 (LXX). The new development was reported to Jerusalem and Barnabas was sent to investigate the situation. **23.** ' Grace ' : the divine favour (cf. 21) manifested in the progress of the mission. In the Greek there is a play on the words ' grace ' and ' was glad '. ' Exhorted '. Barnabas was a ' son of exhortation ' (or ' encouragement ') ; cf. 4:36. ' Stead-fast purpose ' : a biblical expression found in Ps. 10:17 (Symmachus). **24.** ' A good man ' : cf. Lk. 23:50. Barnabas was ' full of the Holy Spirit and of faith ' like Stephen (6:5). Hence the approval of the mission, conveyed by Barnabas, is prompted by the Spirit, the guide, inspirer and counsellor of the Church's mission
to the world. ' Added ' : cf. 2:41, 47. **25.** Barnabas f
brings Saul back from Tarsus (cf. 9:30). According to Gal. 2:1, Saul had been there for something like fourteen years, either from his conversion or from his departure from Jerusalem (9:30). No such interval is suggested by Luke. Barnabas recognises him as the most suitable person to take a leading part in a mixed Jewish-Gentile community. **26.** Saul and Barnabas joined in the regular life of the Antiochene church, the latter remaining there to assist in the work of this new community. ' Met with ' might specially refer to the meetings for worship. The alternative translation, ' were guests of ', is unlikely to be right. ' Christians ', i.e. Christ's people, the people of the Messiah. There is no necessary reason to suppose that this was a nickname given by the non-Christian population ; ' called ' might refer to the community's designation of itself by this name. It is, however, likely that the name was given by the heathen population when the Christian body began to be distinguished from the Jewish community.

27-30 The Prophecy of Agabus and the Mission 787a
of Relief—27. Christian prophets were prominent in the early years of the Church. Luke thinks of them as men peculiarly inspired to act as the mouthpiece of the Spirit in promoting and guiding the missionary enterprise. Here they seem to be associates of the Jerusalem apostles. **28.** ' Agabus ' : see 21:10. ' Claudius '. This note is meant to impress on the reader the fact that the prophecy was fulfilled. The suggestion is that at the time of the prophecy Claudius had not yet become emperor (A.D. 41). There was a serious famine in Palestine and the East between 46 and 48. The Western text reads ' And there was much rejoicing ; and when we were gathered together one of them named Agabus spoke, foretelling . . .' This reading gives the first of the famous ' we ' passages ; but it probably arises either from a confusion of Luke with Lucius (13:1) or from the tradition that Luke was an Antiochene. In the Western text's typically verbose expansion a scribe might thus have thought fit to indicate Luke's presence at Antioch. The new

787a community in the Gentile city gives expression, by the collection it takes, to the solidarity of the churches outside Palestine with the mother church of Jerusalem. The contribution of relief as a sign of loyalty, to which Paul attached so much importance (cf. 2 C. 9 etc.) is introduced here by Luke, at the outset of the Gentile mission ; he omits the great Pauline collection for the Jerusalem church, apart from an obscure allusion at
b 24:17. **30.** ' elders '. The presiding body of the Jerusalem church, presided over (15:13) by James, the Lord's brother. James and the elders formed the governing body of the Jerusalem church after the apostles had left the city. They may be a body set up on the model of the elders of a Jewish synagogue or even of the national Sanhedrin (with James as a Christian counterpart of the high priest). There has been speculation whether this body replaced the Seven, and whether its members were then increased to seventy. If the latter were the case, the further question arises whether Luke's account of the choice and sending out of the seventy disciples represents a reading back into the gospel history of the origins of an institution that was later well known ; but this seems improbable.

Barnabas and Saul now become envoys of the Antiochene church.

c **XII 1-4 The Martyrdom of James and Arrest of Peter—1.** ' About that time ' : i.e. while Barnabas and Saul were in Jerusalem. The vague note of time introduces a new story. Luke's knowledge of the order of events in this part of the book may have been uncertain. Peter's escape from prison may possibly have antedated his journey to Lydda and Joppa, in which case this attack on the Church's leaders may have arisen out of the persecution of the Hellenists. Herod Agrippa I, grandson of Herod the Great, had originally been given the former tetrarchies of Lysanias and Philip by the emperor Gaius. In 39 he received Galilee, previously governed by Herod Antipas. Claudius added Judaea and Samaria, making him a ' client ' king of a considerable Jewish state. ' Laid violent hands '. The translation should be : ' took it in hand (or ' set his hand ') to maltreat . . .' The Greek expression is perhaps taken from 1 Esd. 9:20. Herod's motive, as an ambitious and self-seeking ruler in high favour with the emperor, may have been to
d conciliate Jewish religious opinion. **2.** The execution of James raises the question whether the prophecy of Mk 10:39 was also fulfilled in the case of John. Luke's failure to mention the death of so important a leader is a strong argument against its having taken place now. (See *The Beginnings of Christianity*, iv, 133f. ; R. H. Charles, *Revelation* (ICC), 1, xlv ff.) **3.** If ' Jews ' means the people as a whole, it stands in striking contrast with Luke's usual picture of the attitude of the people as opposed to the rulers. Possibly the term has come to be used here, as in the Fourth Gospel, in the vague sense of ' Jewish opponents of Christianity ' ; but cf. 11 below. The language of this story, and especially this verse, is strongly biblical. ' Unleavened bread ' : i.e. the days following the Passover ; but Luke uses this phrase as synonym for ' Passover ' (cf. Lk. 22:1). **4.** There is a parallel here with the Passion narrative. Herod intends to avoid disturbance, or perhaps to respect Jewish religious feeling, by delaying a public execution until after the festival (cf. Mk 14:2). ' Four squads ' : possibly so divided as each to be responsible for one of the four night watches ; but Luke may suppose that all four were on duty simultaneously to preclude an escape such as that of the apostles (5:19). This deliverance is regarded by Luke as wholly miraculous.

e **5-19 Peter's Deliverance from Prison—5.** This great act of God takes place in a setting of prayer. **6.** All the details emphasise the miracle : Peter is asleep, rather than considering the possibility of escape ; he is between two soldiers, bound with two chains ; sentries before the door preclude the possibility of access on the part of anyone from outside. **7.** ' Appeared ' : cf. Lk. 2:9. The light is the divine 787
glory accompanying a heavenly being. In every detail of the story it is the angel who acts and gives orders and Peter's part is merely to obey. He is in fact unconscious that what he supposes to be a dream is actually happening. **10.** ' They went out '. The f
Western text adds ' they descended the seven steps '. Some commentators believe that this is an authentic detail recorded either by Luke or by an editor who had correct information about Jerusalem as it was before A.D. 70. C. S. C. Williams may well be right, however, in his suggestion that the Western editor has, as often, added a piece of otiose imaginary detail (' they descended the steps ') and that a marginal query (ζ in Greek, an abbreviation for ζήτει, meaning ' query ') was taken by the scribe of Codex Bezae or its ancestor for the figure (ζ′) denoting ' seven '. The query would probably refer to a doubt whether or not the gloss about the steps was part of the text. Another quite probable solution is that the Western editor has imported a detail from Ezekiel's description of the Temple gates (Ezek. 40:22, 26). This would be quite in his manner. We do not know where Herod's prison was, but it may well have been in the fortress of Antonia next to the Temple. **11.** The impression given here is certainly that the whole people was now hostile. ' Sent his angel and rescued ' : an echo of Dan. 3:95 (Theodotion). **12.** ' House '. g
The place of meeting of the Jerusalem congregation. Possibly this was the scene of the meeting of the disciples before Pentecost and of the Last Supper. It was not, however, apparently the place where James and the leaders were to be found (cf. 17). John Mark was the kinsman of Barnabas (Col. 4:10), who took part in the first missionary journey of Paul and Barnabas (13:5) and left them at Perga (13:13), afterwards accompanying Barnabas to Cyprus (15:37). cf. 2 Tim. 4:11 ; Phm. 24 ; 1 Pet. 5:13. It is uncertain whether this John Mark is identical with the Mark who was, according to Papias, the ' interpreter ' of Peter and the writer of the second Gospel. There is a possibility that he was the ' disciple whom Jesus loved ' and who took the mother of Jesus to his home (Jn 19:26). ' Praying ' : see note on 5 above. **13.** ' Door of the gateway '. A fairly large house is h
implied ; there is a gateway leading into a courtyard, into which the rooms of the house open. Rhoda comes from the house to answer the door. **14.** ' Joy ' : cf. Lk. 24:41. **15.** The miracle of Peter's release is so astonishing that the Christians think Rhoda must be mad. ' Angel ' : cf. Mt. 18:10. It was believed in Pharisaic Judaism that men had spiritual counterparts in their guardian angels. **17.** ' Motioning '. A gesture used by a speaker about to begin an oration (13:16, 21:40). James seems to be recognised here by Peter (the original leader of the Jerusalem church) as his successor. James was not an apostle in the sense of being a member of the Twelve, for, once the number of the ' patriarchs ' of the new Israel had been made up by the divine appointment of Matthias, there could be no addition to it. Nor could there be successors to the Twelve, since as ' patriarchs ', the original witnesses and the foundation members of the Church, they could not be succeeded. Hence James the son of Zebedee was not replaced as Judas had been. The Lord's brother, however, played a leading part in the Jerusalem church (cf. Gal. 1:19, where Paul reckons him among the ' apostles ', in a rather wider sense of the term, and 2:9). After Peter's departure, he, together with the ' elders ', administers the government of the Mother Church. ' Another place '. Peter now seems to have become a travelling apostle (1 C. 9:5 ; Gal. 2:11). This phrase probably means ' elsewhere ', i
without any indication of a particular place ; otherwise Antioch would be intended (cf. Gal. 2:11), or, if Luke's order is incorrect, Lydda and Joppa. That it denotes Rome is highly improbable, and virtually impossible unless ch. 15 is misplaced or unhistorical. **18-19.** The reaction of Herod is like that of the

87i Temple authorities in 5:22ff., but now the guards are 'led away' (to execution (cf. Lk. 23:26), as the Western text's 'killed' makes clear). **19.** 'Judaea' here means Jerusalem and its immediate surroundings.

j **20-23 The Divine Vengeance on Herod**—Herod's death is the typically frightful, divinely inflicted, death of a persecutor ; see note on 23. Jos. Ant. XIX, viii, 2 gives a different account. There the king's death is a penalty for accepting the plaudits of the people of Caesarea when, dazzled by his silver robes reflecting the morning sunlight as he entered the theatre, they cried out that he was a god. Unlike Luke, however, Josephus tells us that Herod looked up and saw an owl sitting on a rope. Years before, when Herod was a prisoner of Tiberius, a German fellow-prisoner had pointed to an owl perched in a tree over Herod's head, declared that it was an omen of his speedy release, but warned him that when next he saw an owl he would have but five days to live (Ant. XVIII, vi, 7). He was immediately seized with violent pain and died five days later. The wide differences in detail between these stories are strong evidence that Luke had not read Josephus. **20.** Perhaps this was a personal quarrel ; more probably it was an economic dispute connected with trade from northern Palestine through Tyre and Sidon. The coast towns depended for food on the hinterland, ruled by Herod, who was perhaps trying to divert trade through Caesarea. **22.** 'God'. Why they so shouted is not explained. Something like the story of the splendour of Herod's royal robe seems to be implied. **23.** The Western text adds 'while still alive'. cf. the deaths of the persecutors, 2 Mac. 9:5–9 (Antiochus), Jos. Ant. XVII, vi, 5 (Herod the Great), Eus.HE viii, 16 (Galerius).

8a **24 The Progress of the Mission**—Another brief summary of progress.

25 The Return of Saul and Barnabas—Codices Sinaiticus and Vaticanus, and other MSS, read 'to Jerusalem'. This, as the apparently harder reading, is probably right. It may well be intended to be read with 'mission' : i.e. they returned, having fulfilled their mission to Jerusalem. An alternative possibility, though less likely, is that Luke, or a very early copyist, carelessly wrote 'Jerusalem' for 'Antioch'.

b **XIII 1-3 The Sending-out of Barnabas and Saul by the Church at Antioch**—Barnabas and Saul are classed with the prophets and teachers. Prophets and teachers appear together in Paul's list of *charismata* ('gifts of God') in 1 C. 12:28. The function of both was, at least in part, to interpret the OT prophecies and to demonstrate their fulfilment in the gospel ; this required the inspiration of the Spirit who spoke through the OT prophets, and prophets and teachers were thus alike Spirit-possessed men. Luke, however, also emphasises the prophetic gift of declaring the purposes of God for the future, as in the case of Agabus. Barnabas was Spirit-possessed (11:24), as was also Saul (9:17). According to Luke's understanding of the Pentecostal gift, this would probably mean that they were to be reckoned among the prophets or the
c inspired teachers. Nothing is known of Symeon (see note on 15:14). The fact that his colleague Lucius came from Cyrene is no adequate reason for his identification with Simon of Cyrene (Lk. 23:26). Lucius was often identified by ancient authors with Luke himself, doubtless wrongly. Manaen was a member of the court of Herod Antipas (literally, he was his 'foster-brother'). This title was applied to boys brought up with a royal prince, who became his companions at court. Luke knows of another member of Herod's court circle (Lk. 8:3). On Manaen's name see note on 4:36.

d **2.** 'Worshipping the Lord' : an expression common in the LXX for 'doing service', especially by prayer. Prayer is again the setting for an important turning-point in the story, and its solemnity is emphasised by the association with fasting, which, itself, is often the preparation for receiving divine revelation. The Holy Spirit presumably spoke through one or more of the prophets. The Spirit is the guiding inspiration of the 788d
mission, and it is directly due to his revelation of God's will that this journey is undertaken by the commissioned representatives of the Antiochene church. 'Set apart' : a term used in the LXX of the consecration of the Levites (Num. 16:9 etc.) and Aaron (1 Chr. 23:13), and also by Paul of his call to be an apostle (Rom. 1:1 ; Gal. 1:15). Here it denotes the consecration of Barnabas and Saul to the work to which God had already called them, i.e. the mission sponsored by the church at Antioch. **3.** Fasting and prayer are emphasised by this repetition. The imposition of hands, which always denotes solidarity and self-identification, here signifies particularly the formal commissioning of the missionaries to act as representatives of the Antiochene church and with the solemn blessing of their colleagues. After this Barnabas and Saul are called 'apostles' by Luke. This is a secondary use of the term : they are envoys of the church at Antioch. Paul certainly did not ascribe his status as an apostle of Jesus Christ to this commissioning (Gal. 1:1). It is not, however, an 'ordination' to a definite office in the Ministry. Barnabas and Saul already possessed the same status as 'apostles and teachers' as those who laid their hands on them.

4-12 The Mission in Cyprus—'So' introduces a e
new stage in the narrative. It is the Holy Spirit (not the human agents) who directs the mission and sends out the missionaries. Seleucia is the port of Antioch. Luke, with his keen interest in sea travel, often mentions the ports at which the missionaries embarked and landed. Cyprus was the home country of Barnabas and a suitable field for his work, as it had a large Jewish population. Herod the Great had been granted by Augustus a half-share in its rich copper mines. **5.** Salamis is the port facing Syria, on the east coast. The mission is, as usual, directed to the Jews and the preaching takes place in the synagogues. The task of John, i.e. John Mark, as their 'assistant' or 'minister', may have been simply to look after food and lodging and do the 'odd jobs', but possibly it was to act like the *ḥazzān* in the synagogues, attending to books and documents, perhaps also teaching converts. The 'ministers of the word' of Lk. 1:2 are different ; they are the preachers of the gospel, like Paul (26:16) and, if they are not identical with the apostles, they certainly include the latter. John is a minister, not directly 'of the word', but of the
two missionaries. **6.** Paphos, at the opposite (SW.) f
end of Cyprus, was the administrative capital. Magicians were numerous in the more heterodox fringes of Judaism (cf. 15:13ff. ; Jos. Ant. VIII, ii, 5, XX, vii, 2). 'False prophet' : i.e. he was apparently an inspired man, who opposed the preaching of the gospel which a true prophet would be bound to assist. **7.** Sergius Paulus, the propraetor of the senatorial province, is called by courtesy 'proconsul'. An inscription (CIL 31545) mentions him as one of the *curatores riparum et alvei Tiberis* ('guardians of the banks and channel of the Tiber') during the reign of Claudius, probably not long before he was made governor of Cyprus. Luke's picture of a Roman governor having a Jewish *magus*, probably an astrologer and prognosticator, among his companions is by no means improbable. This first mention of a Roman official outside Judaea shows him to be friendly to the missionaries and anxious to hear the word of God. If he was interested in Jewish religion, this too is not unlikely. The point of this story is that a Jew who was, as a false prophet, an agent of the devil (10), tries to prevent the friendly Gentile, the representative of the Roman state, who is ready and anxious to hear the apostles, from embracing the gospel. By the power of the Spirit (9) he is defeated, Saul vanquishing him as Peter had overcome the enemy who interfered with the mission to Samaria. Thus the pattern of Luke's two-volume book, rejection of the gospel by Jews and acceptance of it by Gentiles despite Jewish hostility, is

788g repeated here. **8.** ' Elymas ' is not a translation of Bar-Jesus, nor an equivalent of it. The problem is complicated by the reading of the Western text, ' Hetoimas ' (' *paratus* '). Some attempts at a solution are desperate, such as the idea that Elymas may be a corruption of *ho loimos* (' the pest '). Another view is that ' Bar-Jeshuah ' (Bar-Jesus) should be read as ' Bar-Yishvah ' (cf. Ishvah, Gen. 46:17 ; 1 Chr. 7:30) and that this name comes from a verb which can mean ' make ready ' so that it could be represented in Greek by ' *Hetoimos* ' (' Ready '). This would be plausible, but it is doubtful if the Hebrew verb can have this meaning. It might, however, derive some support from the reference in Jos. Ant. XX, vii, 2 to a magician from Cyprus, only a few years after this time, called ' Atomos ', which might represent ' Hetoimos '. Possibly, on the other hand, ' Hetoimos ' may represent Josephus's ' Atomos ', the Western editor having identified that character with this magician. If so, there remains a theory that ' Elymas ' is derived from the Arabic *'alîm*, meaning ' wise ' and that it was really *magus* which was represented by ' Elymas ', and not ' Bar-Jesus '. Luke is unreliable in the interpretation of names (cf. 4:36). ' Faith ' is here used in
h the sense of ' the Faith ', the Christian gospel. **9.** Not only would Saul in any case have probably adopted a second, Greek or Roman, name, like so many other Jews, and, like them, have chosen one which resembled his Jewish name, but, as a Roman citizen, he would have had *praenomen*, *nomen* and *cognomen*. His *cognomen* was Paulus. There is no reason to suppose that he adopted this name now for the first time, or that he took it from Sergius Paulus like a general taking a title from a defeated enemy (e.g. Scipio Africanus). Origen, who discusses this possibility, points out that Luke implies that he had always been ' also called Paul '. Moreover, his Gentile name is brought into the story before the proconsul has been converted. Most probably Luke thinks it appropriate to begin to use this name (invariably used in the Pauline letters) when the scene has moved to Gentile territory and the story begins to be concerned with the Empire as a whole, and not merely with the neighbourhood of Palestine, and with imperial rulers. In Gentile lands the apostle would have been called, by himself and others, Paul. ' Holy Spirit '. It is as one inspired by the Spirit that Paul defeats the false prophet. **10.** This denunciation is a mosaic of LXX phrases and words. ' Straight paths ' : the direct progress of the mission. **11.** ' Hand of the Lord : usually mighty in healing and saving, here in judgment. ' Blind ' ; cf. Dt. 28:28f. ' For a time ' : cf. Lk. 4:13. This is not an irrevocable penalty. The punishment of Bar-Jesus may be likened to a conversion (such as Paul's) in reverse. **12.** Luke clearly supposes that the Roman governor was actually converted. The mission begins with a spectacular triumph, foreshadowing a conversion of the powers of the Gentile world to Christ, which the hostility of a ' son of the devil ' could not prevent.

789a **13-15 The Arrival at Pisidian Antioch**—**13.** Paul is now represented as the leader, rather than Barnabas, his senior in the Church. Perga : a city, whose seaport was Attalia (14:25), in Pamphylia, a district on the south coast of Asia Minor, west of Cilicia and east of Lycia. No reason is given for the return of John, which was not merely to Antioch but to his home in Jerusalem. Various explanations have been suggested : that the visit to Asia Minor involved a change of plan, John having, as it were, ' signed on ' for a journey in Cyprus only—he later returned there with Barnabas (15:39)—but it would seem more natural then for him to turn back before the voyage to Perga ; that the original plan included Perga, but not the districts of Pisidia and Lycaonia in the interior (Sir W. Ramsay supposed that the visit to these upland areas was undertaken because Paul, as a sufferer from malaria (cf. Gal. 4:13), was unable to stay in the unhealthy coastal plain), and that John was unwilling to go so far from their base ; or that John disapproved of the mission to Gentiles as exemplified in the conversion of Sergius Paulus. The fact that he went back to Jerusalem, where he would find sympathy with this view, lends some support to this last theory, but like all others, it is a guess. John's reasons may have been purely private. **14.** This Antioch, founded by b
Seleucus Nicator, was now in the Roman province of Galatia, in a district which had a considerable Jewish population. In accordance with their normal practice the missionaries appeal first to the Israel of old, represented by the local synagogue. **15.** The service comprised the recitation of the *Shema'* (Dt. 6:4–5), the ' Eighteen Benedictions ' and a blessing, the readings from the Law and the Prophets, and a sermon which might be delivered by any suitable person at the invitation of the ' rulers ' (cf. Lk. 4:16). The president of the meeting, who arranged the service, was called ' ruler of the synagogue '. Apparently other leading members of the congregation might also have this honorary title. The invitation was probably given to Paul as a Pharisee and so to his companion, who was a Levite and a notable person at Jerusalem. At this stage the missionaries are not yet notorious as troublemakers in the synagogues.

16-41 Paul's Speech in the Synagogue—**16.** The c
usual practice of the preacher was to sit (the posture of a teacher) ; cf. Lk. 4:20. Paul is here depicted as an orator, making a typical rhetorician's gesture as he begins, and using the Greek rhetorical address ' men of Israel '. ' Fear God ' : referring to the Gentile ' God-fearers ' (cf. 10:2). **17.** The speech is similar in pattern to those in chs. 2 and 3. It follows the method used in Stephen's apology, of tracing the history of Israel to show the working-out of God's purposes for Israel. The promises lead to Jesus who is Israel's saviour, the messianic descendant of David. The mission of the Baptist was a preparation for his coming. His death, for which the inhabitants and rulers of Jerusalem were responsible, was in accordance with the prophecies. God vindicated him in the Resurrection, of which the apostles are witnesses. The Resurrection fulfils the scriptures according to their proper interpretation. Forgiveness of sins is now offered through him ; the prophets afford warnings of the consequences of rejecting this gospel. Beginning with the choice of Israel's ancestors, Paul goes directly to the redemption from Egypt. The language is full of
echoes of the LXX. **18.** ' Bore with '. A better- d
attested variant in the LXX (Dt. 1:31) reads ' cared for '. The Hebrew ' carried ' could be translated ' nursed ', ' cared for ', or ' tolerated '. In this passage the better MS tradition reads ' bore with ', but the corruption is very easy and the sense of ' cared for ' is better. **19.** ' Four hundred and fifty '. The Western text takes this to be the period of the Judges, perhaps by calculating the years assigned to the Judges according to the Hebrew text. The text of the majority of MSS understands this as the period from the entry into Egypt to the completion of the conquest
of Canaan. **20.** Samuel (cf. 3:24) is important as the e
first of the prophets. **21.** Saul is mentioned with some emphasis, to make the point that God's original choice of a king did not fall on David. Saul was given to Israel and reigned 40 years (cf. Jos. Ant. VI, xiv, 9), but God removed him and raised up David. Similarly, God has now raised up the son of David to replace the régime of those who have opposed the divine purpose for Israel. Saul is the type of those who, having been appointed by God over his people, resist him and are rejected. It is very unlikely that he is singled out for mention because he belonged to Paul's own tribe of Benjamin (Phil. 3:5) and bore the same name. The contents of the speech, in any case, suggest that it is
Luke rather than Paul who is speaking. **22.** The f
citation combines 1 Sam. 13:14 ; Ps. 89:21 ; and Isa. 44:28. The same combination (of the first two texts) occurs in 1 Clement 18:1, raising the question whether Clement knew Ac. or used a traditional proof-text which was also employed by Luke, perhaps

789f from a collection of testimonies in which the two texts already appeared in combination. **23.** The messianic promise is fulfilled in Jesus, who is a saviour for Israel (cf. 5:31 ; Lk. 2:11). **24.** 'Before his coming', literally 'before the face of his coming', an expression based on Mal. 3:1–2, a standard proof-text concerning John the Baptist (cf. Lk. 7:27). John's baptism was the prelude to the gospel (10:37, cf. 1:22). His mission was addressed to all Israel. **25.** cf. Lk. 3:15–16. John denies that he is the promised Messiah. 'Worthy' is used also in Jn 1:27, but not in the Synoptic Gospels in this connection. Luke may have followed his normal practice of varying the wording of passages which he repeats, and, since there are many points of contact between the Fourth Gospel and the Third, we may suppose that the author of the former, knowing Luke's Gospel, may also have read
g his second volume. **26.** A formal repetition of the opening address, embracing Jews and Gentile God-fearers, serves to emphasise the vitally important theme of the death and resurrection of the Messiah. The hearers of the speech and their contemporaries are the generation for whom the promise of salvation has been fulfilled. 'salvation': the deliverance of God's people (cf. 4:12, 7:25, 16:17 ; Lk. 1:77). **27.** The Jews of Jerusalem were ignorant of Jesus and of the meaning of the prophets whom they heard read each sabbath (cf. 3:17). Yet in condemning Jesus they unwittingly fulfilled God's plan declared by the prophets (cf. 3:18). Luke here suggests that the Jews, and not only Pilate, recognised Jesus to be innocent. He means that they could not find a genuine charge on which to accuse him. **29.** His narrative here is extremely compressed in order to avoid lengthy repetition of what the reader has been told earlier in the book and in the Gospel. This has affected the narrative of the burial, which is ascribed to the Jews,
h Joseph of Arimathaea not being mentioned. **30.** The Resurrection reversed the action of the Jews and vindicated Jesus as Messiah. **31.** This is attested by his witnesses to Israel, the apostles who accompanied him from Galilee to Jerusalem (cf. 1:21–2). Paul and Barnabas are not among these witnesses. Luke does not recognise the appearance on the Damascus road, as Paul himself did (1 C. 15:8), as part of the evidence for the Resurrection, and the qualifications of the Twelve included, besides the ability to testify to the Resurrection, knowledge of Jesus in his earthly ministry, which neither Paul nor Barnabas possessed. 'Many days': cf. 1:3. **32.** On the basis of the apostles' testimony the missionaries proclaim the good news of the fulfilment in this generation of God's
i promises to Israel. **33.** The best textual tradition has 'our children', probably as a result of a very early corruption. Probably Luke wrote 'to us and our children' (cf. 2:39) ; it would be easy for 'to us and' to drop out. Alternatively, 'our' is a mistake for 'us': the promise made to the fathers has been fulfilled 'to us, the children'. The Messiahship of Jesus is demonstrated from Ps. 2:7 (cf. Lk. 3:22). 'Second Psalm'. The Western text reads 'first'. Origen and 3rd-cent. rabbinic sources tell us that in Hebrew MSS the first two psalms were combined. Tertullian and Cyprian quote passages from Ps. 2 (Latin) as from the first psalm. The Western editor is probably familiar with the Latin psalter and possibly also knows of the Hebrew arrangement. The Chester Beatty papyrus reads 'the psalms', which may possibly be original, both numbers having been inserted later according to different traditions of enumeration.
j **34.** Isa. 55:3 (LXX) is cited to prove the fulfilment of the messianic promise in the Resurrection ; verbal similarity in Greek ('the holy things', 'thy Holy One') leads on to the familiar proof-text for the Resurrection (Ps. 16:10) cited already at 2:27. Here it interprets the 'holy things of David' (Isa. 55:3) as meaning Jesus as the 'Holy One'. **36-7.** The argument repeats that of the Pentecost speech. David died and saw corruption : so the promise of Ps. 16:10
refers not to him but to his descendant. **38.** The 789k
climax of the speech : forgiveness of sins is available through Christ, and is offered for acceptance now ; cf. 2:38, 5:31, 10:43. **39.** 'Freed': literally 'justified', i.e. 'put in the right' with God in respect of all those things (i.e. sins) from which the Law could not give liberation. The terminology is Pauline : everyone who believes is justified in Christ, or by Christ. But it is questionable whether the theology is Pauline. This depends on whether 38–9 is taken to imply that the observance of the Law can justify men up to a point, faith in Christ coming in to give justification beyond that point, or whether it is taken to mean that the Law could not justify at all, but that Christ, through faith, can. Luke seems to be deliberately using terminology which he knows to be Pauline, without having read the Epistles or fully understanding what Paul meant. Luke, however, sufficiently indicates that the speech adopted an attitude to the Law which shocked the orthodox. **40.** The speech ends with a warning from Hab. 1:5 ; cf. 3:23.

42-49 The Reaction of the Jews: the Missionaries 790a
turn to the Gentiles—42-3. Luke's compressed narrative is somewhat difficult to follow, but the meaning is that as the congregation goes out of the synagogue some ask the missionaries to speak on the next sabbath. When the meeting had finally dispersed, many followed Paul and Barnabas, who continued preaching elsewhere. 'Grace' is here practically equivalent to 'the gospel'. **44.** The preaching appears to have attracted a mixed multitude, not all of whom were Jews or 'God-fearers'. **45.** 'The Jews' are presumably the authorities of the synagogue and its more orthodox members. They are filled with jealousy from their desire to safeguard the sanctity of the Law and their fear of a gospel which might break down the distinction between Jew and Gentile. Such a gospel would, as one of its first effects, sweep away the 'God-fearing' adherents of the synagogue. **46.** The principle of the mission is explicitly stated. The gospel must go first to the Jews, according to the divine purpose. Since they reject it, the missionaries turn to the Gentiles. This pattern is constantly repeated up to and including Paul's preaching in Rome. 'Eternal life': the life of the age to come, made available
through Christ. **47.** Like Jesus (Lk. 2:32), the b
missionaries fulfil the role of the Servant who was a light to the Gentiles (Isa. 49:6). In Luke's view the importance of the Servant as a type of Christ and his apostles lies primarily in the fact that he was commissioned by God to 'restore the preserved of Israel' and to 'bring salvation to the uttermost parts of the earth'. **48.** The response of the Gentiles at Antioch is typical, and symbolical of the joyful acceptance of the gospel by the Gentile world as a whole after it has been rejected by the Jews (cf. 28:28). 'Ordained to eternal life', or 'appointed to the life of the age to come', i.e. the resurrection life gained through faith in Christ. The converts are those whose 'names are written in heaven' (Lk. 10:20). In God's eternal purpose they are predestined to life in Christ ; but this predestining purpose is effected in and through their response to the preaching of the gospel, not apart from it. **49.** The gospel spreads through a wide area, evidently through the agency of converts in addition to the apostles.

50-52 Persecution and Departure of the Mis- c
sionaries—50. The Jews incite the socially important women among their Gentile adherents. Women tended to be numerous among those who were attracted to Judaism, and women in Asia Minor enjoyed a higher status and more freedom than in most parts of the ancient East. It may have been largely through their wives that the leading citizens were induced to take a hostile attitude to the missionaries. **51.** This gesture was commanded by Jesus (Lk. 9:5, 10:11). It probably indicates a breach of all fellowship with the inhabitants and an abandonment of the city to God's judgment. Iconium lay some 80 miles SE. of Antioch

790c along the Via Sebaste, on the borders of Phrygia and Lycaonia. Paul and his companions evangelised the main urban centres, from which the gospel spread to the surrounding country (cf. 49 above). Luke is therefore not concerned with what happened between their departure from one city and their arrival at another, except when he was himself present and the journey was a sea voyage, in which he takes a detailed interest. **52.** 'Disciples': i.e. the new church at Antioch which flourished despite persecution. 'Joy' is as always associated with the presence of the Spirit.

d **XIV 1-7 Preaching at Iconium. Persecution, and Departure to Lystra and Derbe—1.** The preaching is again directed in the first place to the Jews in the synagogue. Many Jews and Greeks are converted, the latter probably being 'God-fearers' attached to the synagogue. **2.** The hostility of the Gentiles is due to the Jews who incite them against Paul and Barnabas. **3.** Unless 3 and 2 were written in the reverse order, for which there is no evidence, no active persecution broke out for some time. The Western text smooths out an awkward narrative with several additions, such as 'the Lord soon gave peace', after 2. 'Boldly': the characteristic attitude of the Spirit-inspired preacher (cf. 9:27, 18:26, 19:8, 26:26). The declaration of God's grace towards men is attested by signs and wonders, which accompany the work of Paul and Barnabas as they did that of the Twelve in Jerusalem (cf. 5:12, almost exactly reproduced here).

e **4.** The effect of the Jewish hostility, and at the same time the witness of God in signs and wonders, is to divide public opinion. Paul and Barnabas are here described as 'apostles'; cf. 14 below, and see note on 13:3. **5.** 'attempt': more correctly, 'movement' or 'intention'. The 'rulers' are possibly the leaders of the synagogue, but more probably the local civil authorities. **6.** Lystra was a Roman colony 23 miles SW. of Iconium, also in Lycaonia but on the border of Phrygia and probably a Phrygian rather than a genuinely Lycaonian town. Derbe, the modern Kerti Hüyük, is about 56 miles SE. of Lystra (see M. Ballance, *Anatolian Studies*, vii (1957), 147ff.). **7.** Preaching went on in these towns and neighbourhood for an unspecified time.

f **8-14 The Healing of a Lame Man at Lystra: Paul and Barnabas are taken for Gods**—The story of the cripple is closely parallel to that of the cripple at the Temple. The works of Jesus (cf. the healing of the paralytic at Capernaum) are reproduced, first in the proclamation of the gospel to Jerusalem under Peter's leadership, then in the mission to the Gentile world led by Paul. There are echoes of words and phrases used in 3:2–10 which emphasise the parallel. The greatness of the sign is stressed by the threefold insistence on the man's helpless state. **9.** 'Faith': cf. Lk. 5:20 and many other instances in the Gospel, Ac. 3:16. **10.** 'Stand upright': cf. Ezek. 2:1. 'Sprang up and walked': cf. 3:8; Isa. 35:6.

g **11.** The crowds take the apostles for gods walking the earth in the likeness of men. The nature of the Lycaonian language is obscure. Most, if not all, of the people would probably have understood Greek; but the apostles naturally would not have understood Lycaonian. The scene of the legend told by Ovid (*Metamorphoses* viii, 626ff.), of the visit of Zeus and Hermes to Philemon and Baucis, was Phrygia. Inscriptions relating to Zeus and Hermes have been found near Lystra, but they date from the 3rd cent. (W. M. Calder, Exp. 7th ser. x (1910), 1ff, 148ff.; cf. ET 37 (1926), 528). **12.** Barnabas was taken for Zeus (and his name is before Paul's, contrary to Luke's practice since 13:13; so also at 14 below, but cf. 15:12) probably because he was silent, suggesting the silence and impassibility of the supreme deity. Hermes was represented by Paul the orator. Hermes, according to Iamblichus (*De mysteriis Aegypt.*, i) was the 'leader of words' and the communicator of divine revelation. **13.** The 'garlands' were of wool, adorning the sacrificial victims. 'Gates': apparently the city gates, where possibly the cripple had been lying 79
begging. **14.** 'Apostles': see note on 4 above. 'Tore their garments': cf. Jdt. 14:16–19, which has influenced Luke's language here. This is probably, as in Jdt., a sign of grief and distress, not a formal token of hearing a blasphemy (as in Mk 14:63).

15-18 Paul's Speech at Lystra and its Effect— h
Unlike all the other speeches in Ac. except 17:22–31, this is directed to pagans. It is a short polemic against idolatry, speaking of the revelation of the one true God. It is on the usual lines of Jewish and Christian propaganda towards polytheists. **15.** 'Of like nature': cf. Jas 5:17. The speakers share the same feelings as their audience and, perhaps by implication, are quite unlike the impassible deity. 'Good news': the 'gospel' is that now there is no longer any excuse for idolatry, since the true God has revealed himself; but this point, clearly made in 17:30–1, is here left obscure. 'Turn to a (better 'the') living God': cf. 1 Th. 1:9. 'Vain things': i.e. idols; cf. Jer. 2:5 (LXX). 'the heaven' etc.: cf. Exod. 20:11. **16-17.** God has allowed the heathen to go their own way, excusing their ignorance, although in fact he made himself known in the blessings of nature. The implication, made explicit in 17:30–1, is that God has overlooked the idolatry of past generations, but has now so revealed himself that there is no longer any excuse for it. 'Food and gladness': cf. Ps. 145:15–16 (LXX).

19-20 Paul is stoned. Visit to Derbe—The abrupt i
change from divine honours to stoning led the Western text to add a passage about the apostles staying and teaching in Lystra and how the Jews from Antioch and Iconium incited the people against them. Lystra seems to have had no Jewish residents. 'Stoned': cf. 2 C. 11:25. **20.** The Western text suggests that the disciples surrounded him, presumably in his defence, until the evening when the crowd dispersed and he rose up.

21-28 Mission in Derbe. Return to Syrian j
Antioch—The mission to Derbe is, by contrast, highly successful. Paul and Barnabas return, instead of going on to Syria overland, in order to visit and consolidate their churches, despite the extreme danger involved in this. **22.** 'Continue in the faith'. Possibly this means 'continue to be faithful', but more probably 'faith' here means 'the Faith' as at 13:8. 'Enter the kingdom of God': it is through tribulations that Christians enter into the life of the age to come (cf. Lk. 21:19) and, like Jesus, into the resurrection glory (cf. Lk. 24:26). This truth makes a special appeal to Luke, who emphasises its universal application by using the first person. **23.** The apostles organise k
a local ministry for the new churches, on the lines of that of the synagogue. The elders (at Ephesus, 20:17, 28, they are also called 'overseers' or 'bishops') form a governing body, presiding over the worship and administration and discipline of the congregation. In the first instance, they would have been literally 'elders', senior men among the converts. Like the commissioning of the missionaries, their appointment is accompanied by prayer and fasting. 'Believed': literally 'had believed', i.e. 'to whom they had been converted'. **24-5.** On the return journey Perga was evangelised for the first time. They then sailed from Attalia direct to Antioch. **26.** Luke carefully reminds the reader that Paul and Barnabas had been commissioned by the church at Antioch for the work they had now carried out. This may be intended to show why they did not go up to Jerusalem to report to the authorities there. **27.** They reported to the whole church, not merely to its leaders. 'Gentiles' refers to the events at Pisidian Antioch and afterwards, and prepares for the dispute in ch. 15. **28.** There is a long interval after the return to Antioch. According to one theory Paul wrote *Galatians* during this period, having heard that Judaisers were perverting his converts in the province of Galatia in which his journey had lain.

XV Historical problems are raised by this chapter, 791

791a and many theories have been advanced for their solution. Space does not allow a full discussion of these. Luke's story tells how Judaisers came from Jerusalem (24 indicates that they purported, at any rate, to be an official delegation from the Jerusalem church) to Antioch, insisting that Gentile converts should be circumcised according to the Law. After considerable debate, Paul and Barnabas were sent to discuss the matter with the apostles and elders. On their arrival, Christian Pharisees demanded that Gentile converts be subjected to circumcision. A meeting took place and Peter reminded it of the conversion of Cornelius, objected to putting an intolerable burden on the Gentile converts, and claimed that Jew and Gentile alike would be saved by grace. Paul and Barnabas narrated the signs and wonders done through them among the Gentiles. James declared that the scriptures revealed that God's purpose was to create a covenant people out of the Gentiles, and gave judgment that Gentile converts should be required only to observe four precepts required by God to be observed by all men. This decision was embodied in a letter and conveyed by Paul and Barnabas to Antioch.

b **Among the difficulties** presented by this account are the following :

(1) It is not clear who the Judaisers were, or whom they represented.

(2) Unless the Cornelius episode were regarded as merely an isolated and extraordinary case in which God approved the baptism of a Gentile, the question at issue in 15:1, 5 had been settled in 11:18 ; and Luke certainly does not suggest that that episode was anything but extremely significant for the Gentile mission as a whole or that it was without relevance for general expansion of the Church. If it was a significant episode then it involved the admission of the uncircumcised into the Church. No Jew would ever have objected to the reception of Gentiles if they were prepared to be circumcised and observe the Law.

(3) The 'decree' of the council relates apparently to the minimum requirements for table fellowship between Jewish and Gentile Christians. The question of the conditions on which Jewish Christians could eat with Gentile believers at the agape-Eucharist and at ordinary meals, and therefore of what rules must be observed by Gentile Christians if the unity of the Church were to be maintained, would inevitably arise once Gentiles were dispensed from circumcision and the full obligation of the Law. Here, however, this seems to be the main point at issue, and nothing is directly or explicitly said about the question of circumcision itself, over which the dispute had arisen and which was the matter referred to the council for decision.

(4) Paul never alludes to this decision in his letters. The problem of the Christian attitude to food offered to idols was important to the churches in Gentile lands, and Paul was called upon to give directions about it, especially in Rom. 14 and 1 C. 10. This matter was the subject of a formal and solemn resolution of the leaders of the Jerusalem church ; yet Paul never alludes to this or invokes its authority, even though he began his second journey carrying copies of the 'decree' to give to the churches in Asia Minor.

(5) In Gal. 2 Paul states that, on the second of the two visits he had paid to Jerusalem up to the time of writing the letter, the question of circumcision arose, particularly with reference to the case of Titus, and that agreement about Paul's mission to the Gentiles was reached between himself and James, Peter and John. Later, at some time unspecified, 'certain men came from James', and as a consequence of their attitude, Peter, who had joined in table fellowship with Gentiles, now withdrew, 'fearing the circumcision party'. Barnabas, too, was 'carried away'. Paul then publicly rebuked Peter and asserted the gospel of justification by faith as opposed to legalistic works. James had, apparently, changed his attitude (unless, indeed, the James whom Paul mentions in company with Peter and John was the son of Zebedee and not the Lord's brother). This is hard to square with Ac. 15, and Paul says nothing in his letter to the Galatians about this decision of the Jerusalem church. 791b

(6) The narrative of Ac. is notoriously difficult to harmonise with Paul's own account of his visits to Jerusalem in Gal. 1–2. In Ac. there are his visit after his conversion, the 'famine visit' with Barnabas (11:30), and the visit (again with Barnabas) to this council. In Galatians there are two visits, one after his conversion, the other with Barnabas and Titus when he 'went up by revelation', the question of circumcision arose and his Gentile mission was recognised by James, Peter and John. These are only some of the difficulties raised by this chapter. It must also be c
observed that the speeches of Peter and James are more likely to represent Luke's presentation of the matter to his readers than to reflect accurately what the speakers actually said. The speech of Peter presupposes a knowledge on the hearer's (or rather the reader's) part of the events of ch. 10, which not all his audience could be expected to share (or, if they could, then the dispute about circumcision ought never to have arisen), and it takes up an attitude to the Law, as a burdensome yoke, which can scarcely reflect the opinion of the Jerusalem Christians. That of James is based upon the exegesis of texts of the LXX, unlikely in a speech by a 'Hebrew' Christian to fellow 'Hebrews'. A further problem arises over the textual phenomenon in 20.

Many theories have been proposed for the resolution d
of these difficulties. The view that *Galatians*, a letter sent to the converts made on the first journey, was written between the arrival of the Judaisers at Antioch (cf. Gal. 2:12) and the journey of Paul and Barnabas to Jerusalem is attractive. It solves the problem of Paul's visits to Jerusalem by identifying the second in Gal. with the second in Ac. and supposing that 'by revelation' alludes to the prophecy of Agabus. It involves difficulties in the dating of Gal. and does not explain why the 'apostolic decree' is still left without mention in Rom. 14 and 1 C. 10 ; nor is it easy to explain why the two accounts of the 'famine visit' should be so dissimilar.

It is possible to hold that the 'council visit' and the 'famine visit' were really identical and that the decision of the council represents the pact described in Gal. 2:9. In that case Luke has mistaken the order of events and put the council too late : it should come at the end of ch. 11 and precede the first missionary journey. The controversy which gave rise to it would then be concerned with Gentile converts made at Antioch or during Paul's activities in Syria and Cilicia (Gal. 1:21). This, however, makes the attitude of James and his emissaries (Gal. 2:12) inexplicable. There are the further difficulties that if this were the case Paul would surely have mentioned the 'decree' in Gal., and also that circumcision was the question at issue on the second visit to Jerusalem whereas the decree dealt with table fellowship.

It is perhaps more probable that Luke has fused e
together two stories. One concerned a dispute about circumcision which led to Paul and Barnabas going to Jerusalem, the question of circumcising Titus, and a pact with the leaders of the Jerusalem church. This is described by Paul in Gal. 2:1–10 and by Luke in the opening verses of Ac. 15 and the notice of the 'famine visit'. This, then, was Paul's second visit, and possibly it may have synchronised with Peter's visit at which he defended his action in the house of Cornelius (11:2ff.). The second story concerned a later dispute about food laws in connection with table fellowship in mixed churches. It may have been preceded by a dispute stirred up, once again, by Judaisers from Jerusalem at Antioch (Gal. 2:12), confused by Luke (15:1ff.) with the previous dispute about circumcision. A meeting was held to settle this matter and a letter embodying the decisions about

791e table fellowship was sent to the churches in Syria and Cilicia. Luke has a tradition about this meeting but has fused it with the story about the dispute concerning circumcision. He is mistaken in supposing that Paul and Barnabas were present at this council, and he really knows only what was decided ; the speeches of Peter and James are his own free composition. Paul did not know of the meeting and its decisions, and hence did not refer to them in his letters. It has been often observed that in 21:25 James seems to be informing Paul about the ' decree ' as though he were ignorant of it (though in fact this is more probably Luke reminding his readers of it). On this view the date of Gal. is not restricted to the (very early) period before the council met, and several of the other main
f difficulties disappear. The question remains why Luke arranged his material in an historically mistaken order. The chief reason, apart from misinformation, is probably that Luke wishes to reaffirm the fact that the Jerusalem church both approved the Gentile mission (11:18) and also endorsed the admission of Gentiles without circumcision (but with elementary rules for table fellowship) once again after the first missionary journey. He probably wishes to show (*a*) that James and the ' apostles and elders ' disapproved of the Judaising party, who claimed to speak in their name ; (*b*) that they recognised the divine approval of Paul's Gentile mission, both in the signs and wonders done in Asia Minor and also in the prophetic scriptures rightly interpreted ; (*c*) that Paul was scrupulously loyal to the authorities at Jerusalem in carrying out his Gentile mission. The speeches put into the mouth of Peter and James are designed to explain this to the reader, who is given an emphatic reaffirmation of the legitimacy of Paul's ' turning to the Gentiles ' directly after the wonders of the first missionary journey have been related.

g **1-5 Controversy concerning the Admission of Gentiles—1.** cf. Gal. 2:12. From 24 it appears that Judaea means Jerusalem and that these Judaisers claimed the authority of James and the elders. **2.** The dispute was sharp ; the word rendered ' dissension ' suggests a state of strife and disunity. ' Appointed ': the Western text, which has a verbose opening to this story, states that the men from Jerusalem ordered Paul and Barnabas to go up, but its editor tends to magnify the authority of Jerusalem. Probably it was the church at Antioch which appointed Paul and Barnabas as its envoys. ' Some of the others '. If there is a fusion of the story of two visits, this group could include Titus (Gal. 2:1ff.), but there is no evidence that Luke knew of him. **3.** The reception given, evidently by Jewish Christians, in Phoenicia and Samaria to the news of the conversion of Gentiles indicates the general support on which Paul and Barnabas could count. Judaisers were few and confined to ' Judaea '. **4.** Similarly, the leaders at Jerusalem welcomed them in a way which would not be possible if they stood on the other side in the great ' dissension '.
h ' Apostles and elders ' : 12:17 gave the impression that the leadership of the Jerusalem church had passed to James and a body of elders (cf. 11:30) and that certainly Peter and probably also the other apostles had left Jerusalem after the persecution of Herod had caused the death of James and nearly brought about the death of Peter. In this narrative James seems to be the president. Yet the apostles are present as well as the elders, and Peter appears as one of the former. Nothing is said about how he came to return to Jerusalem. This seeming confusion may support the view that Luke is working with two stories which originally dealt with separate events, and that Peter and the apostles belong to one of these (perhaps identical with the ' famine visit ' and conceivably also with 11:2ff.) and James to the other. ' Declared ' : as in the case of Cornelius, the divine approval of the Gentile mission is attested by the acts of God done
i through the missionaries. **5.** Whoever the Judaisers who came to Antioch may have been, the legalist party at Jerusalem consists of converted Pharisees 79
(the Western text identifies the former with the latter). The conversion of a large enough number of Pharisees to be influential in the Church represents a remarkable advance since the time of Gamaliel's benevolent neutrality and shows how promising the mission to the Jews must have seemed and correspondingly how much might be lost by supporting the Pauline mission.

6-21 The Debate and Decision—6. From 12 it 79
appears that this was a general meeting of the congregation and not merely a council of its leaders. **7.** The speech of Peter is couched in strongly biblical language. ' Early days ' : the meaning is obscure. ' Early ' probably means ' of the beginning ', and this presumably refers to the beginning of the Gentile mission. The conversion of Cornelius was not long ago (the speech, of course, represents Luke's review of the situation rather than Peter's words at the time). Yet, in Luke's picture of the events, the conversion of Cornelius was a beginning, the origin of the mission to the Gentiles. ' Choice '. Peter's reception of Cornelius into the Church was directly due to the will of God. He was a chosen instrument. ' Gospel ' occurs only here and at 20:24, though the corresponding verb is common in Luke's writings. **8.** ' Who knows the heart ' : cf. 1:24. The coming of the Spirit upon these Gentiles was the sure proof of their acceptance by God, equally with the original disciples. **9.** ' Made no distinction ' : cf. the possible translation of 10:20. ' Cleansing ' : cf. 10:15, 11:9. The cleansing of Gentiles from heathen defilement which, in the Judaisers' view, would be effected by circumcision and obedience to the Law is performed by God in granting them the gift of faith. This implied antithesis of faith to law is one of the closest approximations of Lucan to Pauline thought. **10.** If faith takes the b
place of law in this respect, then the Law is an unnecessary yoke. The ' yoke of the Law ' was a familiar Jewish phrase, but in the sense of an obligation that was at the same time a blessing and a privilege. For Luke it is a burden too heavy for the Jews and intolerable to Gentiles who are ' cleansed by faith ' and ' saved by grace '. This, again, represents an approach to Pauline theology, but without Paul's deeper understanding of the Law as an instrument of human self-righteousness, or of the Law as ' established ' through faith in Christ. ' Make trial of God ' : cf. Dt. 6:16 (Lk. 4:12) ; Ps. 78:18. To impose the Law on Gentile converts would be to challenge God's acceptance of them on equal terms with the original disciples, demonstrated in the gift of the Spirit and the cleansing of their hearts by faith. ' Disciples ' : i.e. Gentile Christians. **11.** Since the Jews have been unable to bear the yoke of the Law, salvation, for them as for the Gentiles, will be by faith. This is a different attitude from that of Paul with his confidence in his own righteousness attained by perfect observance of the Law (Phil. 3:6). Luke maintains, rather, that the Law had been an intolerable burden to everyone. On the main issue, however, he reproduces the Pauline doctrine that salvation is by grace and faith and not through the Law. He represents the Jerusalem apostles, in the person of Peter, as endorsing this doctrine and so being in complete agreement with the Pauline gospel as preached to the Gentiles. **12.** Peter's c
speech ends the dispute. The ' signs and wonders ' attest God's guidance of the Gentile mission. There seems no particular reason why Barnabas should here be mentioned before Paul. See note on 14:12. Luke does not record what they said. His readers certainly know the story already, but Luke might have been expected to repeat it briefly, so far as the signs and wonders were concerned, for the sake of emphasis, as in the case of Cornelius and the conversion of Paul. Is it possible that Luke's source for the narrative of a meeting concerning table fellowship included no reference to Paul and Barnabas, but that, having conflated this story with one dealing with circumcision and placed it after the mission of Paul and Barnabas,

792c he mistakenly supposed that they were present, and
d inserted this brief summary? **13.** James presides and gives the decision. As the head of the Jerusalem church he exercised great authority, even Peter being afraid of his emissaries at Antioch (Gal. 2:12). If the James of Gal. 2:9 is the Lord's brother, he is there mentioned before the leading apostles, presumably because he had already taken over the leadership (a pointer to the story of Peter's imprisonment being misplaced from before 11:30 and perhaps from before 9:32ff.). **14.** 'Simeon'. James is made to use a Semitic form of Simon Peter's name (cf. 2 Pet. 1:1), perhaps to indicate that he is supposed to be speaking in Aramaic, despite the fact that his OT citations are from the LXX. Since the reference to God's choice of the Gentiles 'at the first' clearly alludes to 7 above, the suggested identification of Symeon with the Simeon of Lk. 2:25 (with an allusion to Lk.2:32)—so Chrysostom—or with Symeon surnamed Niger (13:1) misses the point. 'Visited': cf. Lk. 1:68, 78, 7:16. 'People for his name': i.e. a covenant people, a renewed Israel. **15.** 'The prophets' (cited, as usual, from the collected book of the Twelve Prophets) afford proof to reinforce what Peter had said. In most of Luke's speeches scriptural proofs clinch the argument after the acts of God have been narrated and before the speech reaches its conclusion. Here the act of God is narrated, and a general argument stated, in Peter's speech; the scriptural proofs and practical conclusion are assigned
e to James. **16.** Am. 9:11, the points where the LXX, cited here, differs from the Hebrew being vital to the application of the text. 'The dwelling (literally 'tent' or 'tabernacle') of David' is probably understood as a prophecy of the restoration of David's kingdom, not to the nation of Israel (cf. 1:8) but as the new universal people of God. If, however, 'tent' or 'tabernacle' ought to be more strictly interpreted, the allusion is to the resurrection of the body of the crucified son of David, making it possible for all men, including Gentiles, to seek the Lord. **17.** The Hebrew reads 'that they may inherit what remains of Edom and of the other nations over which my name is named'. This speech depends upon the Greek text. **18.** 'Known from of old' is an addition from Isa. 45:21. **19.** James concurs with Peter's view that Gentiles should not be subjected to the Law. Luke makes the great Jewish-Christian leader actually describe this as 'troubling'
f or 'annoying' them. **20.** The requirements for table fellowship are reduced to four essentials: abstention from 'pollutions of idols', i.e. eating meat which had been offered in an idol temple before being sold in the market, and *a fortiori* participation in pagan cultic meals; abstention 'from unchastity', i.e. probably marriage within prohibited degrees (Lev. 18:6–18) or possibly mixed marriages with pagans (cf. 2 C. 6:14); abstention from 'what is strangled' and from 'blood': i.e. from meat that had not been killed in the prescribed fashion (kosher). These conditions are probably derived from Lev. 17:8–9 (sacrifices not offered to the Lord); Lev. 17:10–12 (eating blood); Lev. 17:13 (ritual slaughter of animals taken for food); Lev. 18:6–18 (prohibited degrees). All these commandments are prescribed for the 'strangers' among the Israelites as well as for the original covenant people. They appear also among the seven precepts believed by the later rabbis to have been enjoined upon Noah's sons, the ancestors of the entire human race. The Alexandrian text, which gives all four conditions, is therefore probably correct. The Chester Beatty papyrus, with some support, omits 'and from unchastity', probably because this seemed, superficially, to be out of place in what appeared to be simply a food law. The Western text omits 'and from what is strangled', and in most MSS adds 'and whatever you do not wish to be done to yourselves, do not do to others', thus turning the prohibitions into moral injunctions, 'blood' being interpreted as 'bloodshed' or 'murder'. This would bring them into line with the penitential discipline of the early Church which
treated apostasy, murder and fornication as the three 792f
major sins. This reading cannot be authentic. A simple moral law would not have been transformed into a food law; the tendency would be in the opposite direction, though the prohibition against eating blood lingered on (cf. Minucius Felix, *Octavius* 36:6; *Epistle of Lyons and Vienne* in Eus.HE V, i, 26; Tertullian, *Apology* 9:13). This version would also imply that a special warning had to be given to Gentile converts against such sins as murder, and that this was expressed in the form of asking them to 'abstain' from it. The only possible alternative to the adoption of the Alexandrian text is to suppose that the original text read 'from the pollutions of idols and from blood', that some scribes, represented by the Chester Beatty papyrus etc., took this to be a food law and added, for explanation, 'and from what is strangled', while others, represented by the Western text, understood it as a moral law and added the prohibition against the third major sin, 'and from
unchastity'. But this is much less likely. **21.** A very g
obscure verse. It may possibly mean that a literal interpretation of the prophecy in 16 is impossible because Israel now extends over far wider regions than the kingdom of David (cf. Ropes, JBL 15 (1896), 75ff.). But this is most improbable. Alternatively it may mean that from the beginning of the Dispersion the Law has been proclaimed in the synagogues throughout the world; therefore the Gentiles ought to know what the Law specially prescribes for them (i.e. Lev. 17, 18, mentioned above) and understand why these requirements are accordingly demanded of them. The suggestion that it means that all those converts who want more of the Law than is here demanded can easily get it by attending the synagogues, seems implausible.

22–29 The 'apostolic letter'—**22.** The whole as- h
sembly makes the decision to send its own envoys back to Antioch with Paul and Barnabas. This decision emphasises the authority of the Jerusalem church. 'Barsabbas': cf. note on 1:23. 'Silas' is almost certainly identical with the Silvanus of 2 C. 1:19; 1 Th. 1:1: 2 Th. 1:1, and probably also 1 Pet. 5:12. 'Leading men' is not an official title. They were in fact prophets (32). **23.** The letter repeats what has been already told in the narrative; repetition once more serves to emphasise an important event. The letter is addressed to the Gentile Christians at Antioch and the neighbourhood, including Syria and Cilicia, but not to the converts in Galatia, the scene of Paul's missionary journey—possibly another pointer to the decree having no direct connection with Paul or his activities. The decree cannot, in any case, have been meant to apply only in the regions near Antioch, and this does not explain the absence of any reference to it in Rom. or 1 C. **24.** The Jerusalem church disowns the Judaisers who went to Antioch (1 above); but Gal. 2:12, if it refers to the same events, states that they were emissaries of James. **25.** 'In assembly' translates Luke's favourite expression 'with one accord'. **26.** 'Risked': better 'devoted'. **28.** The inspiration of the Spirit who directs the entire mission is unhesitatingly claimed for the Church's decision. **29.** The textual phenomena are as in 20. The Western text also adds to the words 'do well', 'being borne by the Holy Spirit'.

30–35 The Return to Antioch—**31.** 'Exhortation': 793a
i.e. the *paraclēsis* by which they were assured of their unity with the Jewish Christians, or possibly the edification which they received from the prophets' preaching. **32.** The Christian prophets largely concerned themselves with exhorting the faithful and edifying the Church (cf. 1 C. 14:3). Hence their function is often closely associated with that of teachers (13:1). **33.** Judas and Silas return to the Jerusalem church. A number of MSS add **34**, explaining that Silas stayed at Antioch (so making 40 easier).

36–39 Preparation for the Second Journey; the b
Quarrel between Paul and Barnabas—**36.** 'After

798b some days' is not so much a note of time as of a transition to a new episode. Paul proposes to return and inspect (oversee) the converts in Asia Minor. At this stage he did not plan a new missionary campaign. **38.** Again no reason is given for John Mark's withdrawal or Paul's disapproval of it. **39.** The Greek indicates that this was a very bitter quarrel. It is quite uncertain whether it was made worse by Barnabas being won over by Judaising emissaries of James (Gal. 2:13) and the implication that he was not wholly devoted to the principle of the Gentile mission; it seems improbable that this was the case. By the time of writing 1 C. 9:6 Paul was prepared to think of Barnabas as a colleague in the apostolic mission. 'Cyprus': cf. 4:36.

c **40-41 The Departure of Paul and Silas—41.** Luke has not mentioned a mission in Syria and Cilicia, though the address of the council's letter has informed the reader that there were Gentile churches there. Gal. 1:21 indicates a long period of activity there by Paul before he went to Antioch. 16:4 indicates that Luke believes that Paul and Silas were carrying the council's letter on this journey.

d **XVI 1-5 Visit to Derbe and Lystra. Circumcision of Timothy**—Paul alone is mentioned; the mission is wholly in his charge. He revisits his churches, approaching overland from the east. 'Timothy': cf. 2 Tim. 1:5. Such a mixed marriage was contrary to the Law. From the Jewish point of view Timothy was a Jew, being the son of a Jewish woman; but his status was irregular and anomalous, since although he was legally a Jew he was uncircumcised and presumably lived like a Gentile until his conversion, or the conversion of his mother (and grandmother, 2 Tim. 1:5; but the picture of his upbringing given there and in 2 Tim. 3:15 can scarcely be reconciled with what we are told here). **2.** Timothy has so high a reputation among the Christians of Lystra and Iconium (indicating that he may have been already a travelling preacher) that Paul is anxious to take him, perhaps to do the work undertaken by Mark on the
e first journey. **3.** The circumcision of Timothy seems astonishing in the light of Gal. 5:2ff. and of Luke's own account of the decision taken at Jerusalem. Luke, however, represents Paul as acting on this journey in full harmony with the Jerusalem church. This would have been broken if he had taken as a colleague, in a mission approved by the Jerusalem authorities, one who, though a convert of good repute, had a most unacceptable history in Judaism (which was known to the Jews in Asia Minor), being a technically illegitimate child brought up, from the legal standpoint, as a heathen. Timothy was not in the same category as Gentile converts, and the Jerusalem decisions could not be applied to him. It would give great offence to Jewish Christians if he were treated like a Gentile convert, since he was not now being admitted to baptism but commissioned as an accredited missionary in an expedition sent out by Antioch with the full approval of Jerusalem. Paul could not afford to prejudice his mission by disregarding the scandal which would ensue; and Ac. 21:26 and 1 C. 9:20 indicate that Paul would go to any lengths to avoid this, short of denying salvation by faith in Christ.

f **4.** Paul acts as the representative of Jerusalem in delivering the council's decisions, which are now made known beyond the area to which they were formally addressed (15:23). **5.** A typical summary of the progress of the Church.

6-9 Journey to Troas. Call to Macedonia—Luke tells us practically nothing of the journey, save that the guidance of the Spirit brought the missionaries, contrary to their own plans, to Troas and thence to Macedonia. The mission is always under the direct guidance of the Spirit; consequently the reader is not told where, if at all, Paul preached or by what route he travelled from the 'cities' (4), i.e. Lystra, Iconium and probably Antioch, to Troas. It is not certain whether 'Phrygia and Galatia' in the Greek means 'Phrygia and the Galatian country' or 'the 79
Phrygian-Galatian country'. The phrase in 18:23, if meant to be an exact parallel, points to the former. It is doubtful whether Luke means the borderlands of Phrygia and Galatia, i.e. country which, although Phrygian, was in the province of Galatia, or whether he means Phrygia and the country inhabited by people of Galatian race, perhaps the district of Pessinus. If the former, Luke is referring to the district of Pisidian Antioch. If the latter, it is possible to fit a mission to 'north Galatia' into the itinerary at this point and to suppose that the people there were later the recipients of *Galatians*. But the impression is that the journey to Troas was pursued as directly and quickly as possible. Paul's intention had been to travel westwards from Pisidian Antioch to the big cities of the province of Asia, such as Ephesus. This the Spirit forbids, probably through dreams or visions. While they were travelling north-westwards, probably in the region of Nacoleia and Dorylaeum, they planned to turn north into Bithynia, probably making for the other group of large towns on the coast, Nicaea, Nicomedia, etc. This was also forbidden. **7.** It is h
most significant that the Holy Spirit (6) is recognised by Luke as the Spirit of Jesus. This is implied in what we are told by him about the operation of the Spirit in the earthly ministry of Jesus and, through the exalted Lord who sends the Spirit, in the ministry of the Church. The phrase may mean that Silas as a prophet spoke in the name of Jesus ('Thus says the Lord', i.e. Jesus). **8.** Troas: a seaport at the north- i
west corner of Asia Minor. Having been brought to the sea against their own inclinations, they must have been uncertain where to go. They were guided by a vision which convinced them of God's call to go to Macedonia. **9.** The nature of the divine guidance is here described in detail. It is useless to inquire how, in a vision, the man of Macedonia was recognised as such. The words 'vision' and 'appear' make it clear that the man was a dream figure.

10-15 Journey to Philippi. Conversion of Lydia j
—**10.** The beginning of the first 'we' passage. If, as is probable, Luke is indicating that he was present, it does not necessarily follow that he joined the party only at Troas. Nor is the structure of the narrative intended to make the reader necessarily infer that the writer in the first person must be either Silas or Timothy. **11.** The 'we' passages in describing voyages give much detail about the course and the time, in contrast to Luke's stylised narratives of the land journeys. 'Samothrace': a mountainous island rising to a great height, half-way between Troas and Neapolis. They would anchor there for the night. 'Neapolis': the terminus of the Via Egnatia, leading across northern Greece to the Adriatic and so to Rome; the port of Philippi, which was a Roman colony with a large population of veterans settled by Augustus. 'Leading city': literally 'first city of the district'. It was not the capital of the province or of any district of it. Important towns that were not capital cities might, according to 2nd- and 3rd-cent. evidence, have the title 'first' conferred upon them. If this were the case of Philippi, for which there is no other evidence, 'leading' would probably represent this title. There is slight MS evidence for the reading 'city of the first district'. This would refer to one of the four divisions of Macedonia created by Aemilius Paulus in 167 B.C. These were apparently maintained after the country became a province. Livy xlv, 29 indicates that Philippi was in fact in the first district. The corruption is easy and this reading may well be right. **13.** 'Outside the k
gate'. Philippi apparently had no synagogue and Jews met for worship outside the town. 'We supposed'. The missionaries had evidently had no contact as yet with the Jewish inhabitants. A Western variant reads 'it was customary for prayer to be made'; but this is probably secondary. 'Place of prayer'. This term can mean 'synagogue', but Luke does not use it elsewhere in this sense. It probably

3k denotes a place out of doors where a few Jews, mainly women, came together on the sabbath. 'Sat down': not necessarily as formal teachers, but for normal conversation. **14.** 'Lydia'. Thyatira, a centre of the purple-dye industry, was in Lydia. Possibly 'named' is an interpolation, and we should read 'a Lydian woman' (so in 40); but 'named' may stand and 'Lydia' still be a personal nickname. 'Worshipper of God': i.e. a 'God-fearer'. 'Opened her heart': cf. Lk. 24:45. **15.** 'Baptized'. As in the case of the Ethiopian (8:36) and the gaoler (33 below), baptism is administered immediately upon profession of faith. 'Household'. The family and its domestic household are regarded as a unit from the point of view of Church membership. 'Faithful to the Lord': i.e. one who has genuine faith. Lydia's house became the 'base' for the work in Philippi (cf. 40).

l **16-18 The Cure of a Possessed Girl—16.** The beginning of this story took place before the meeting with Lydia. 'Spirit of divination: literally 'Python', a name derived from the serpent slain by Apollo at Delphi. Since the Delphic priestess was inspired to give oracles, a 'python spirit' meant a spirit of soothsaying. **17.** 'Most High God'. A title often used of the God of Israel by Gentiles (cf. Lk. 8:28 where, as here, it occurs in the utterance of a demoniac). It was also employed in syncretistic cults in which a supreme deity whose title was derived from Judaism was worshipped along with pagan gods. A similar syncretism produced the cult of Sabazios-Sabaoth. But there is no reason to suppose that this soothsayer or her owners were devotees of such a cult. This address to Jesus is in fact made by the spirit speaking through the girl and is directly parallel to Lk. 8:28 where the demoniac is probably also a heathen. 'The way of salvation': cf. Lk. 1:77, 79; Ac. 4:12, 13:36. **18.** The exorcism is in the name of Jesus Messiah, as in the case of the 'signs' of healing. There may be a deliberate play on 'gone' (literally 'gone out'); the spirit had 'gone out' and with it the owners' hope of gain had 'gone out'. The Western text finds this odd and alters the wording. The first 'we' passage ends here. Nothing is said to indicate what became of Luke (assuming he is the author of the diary in the first person), until he appears again on the journey to Troas (20:5). He may have remained in Macedonia, possibly at Philippi. The distribution of the 'we' passages indicates that he was generally present on voyages, but never stayed very long in Paul's company once they had gone ashore.

4a **19-25 Arrest, Beating and Imprisonment of the Apostles—19.** 'Market place'. The forum of Philippi where, as archaeology has shown, the court and prison were situated. 'Rulers': a general term for the local magistrates. **20.** 'Magistrates': properly 'Praetors', here, as in inscriptions from other places, used of the *duoviri*, as the chief magistrates of a colony were usually styled. 'Disturbing our city'. The charge is designed to appeal to anti-Jewish prejudice. The missionaries are accused of disturbing public order, and in particular of introducing illegal customs. This may mean proselytising which, especially among Roman citizens, was illegal and not covered by the toleration accorded to the actual practice of Judaism by Jews. Luke is careful to show that the hostile action of Roman authorities was based on a complete misunderstanding of the situation. **22.** The crowd is hostile, being anti-Jewish. 'Garments'. RSV translates correctly. The idea that the magistrates followed the practice of the Jewish high priest on hearing blasphemy and tore their own garments is quite impossible. 'Rods': cf. 2 C. 11:25. **24.** As in the parallel case of Peter in ch. 12, the security of the imprisonment is strongly emphasised. Paul and Silas are put in the 'inner prison', probably an underground dungeon, with their feet fastened in wooden stocks.

b **25-34 The Miraculous Deliverance of Paul and Silas**—This is wrought in answer to prayer. The singing of hymns recalls the account of Joseph in the 794b
Testament of Joseph 8:5, but it is not impossible that the latter is dependent on Ac. **26.** In answer to prayer there comes an earthquake, the shaking of the foundations (cf. 4:31) and the opening of the doors. A further miracle unfastens the fetters. **27.** The gaoler wakes up and is going to commit suicide immediately (cf. 12:19). The details of the dramatic story cannot be pressed so as to include an answer to the question how Paul knew that the gaoler was drawing his sword, when the latter could not see whether the prisoners were still there. **29.** The gaoler apparently knows that the prayers of Paul and Silas are the cause of the earthquake, though he was asleep at the time. Probably he knew that they were preachers of a new God, and now sees that this God has been shown to be powerful to rescue his servants. **30.** The Western text adds that the gaoler was careful to secure the other prisoners before bringing out Paul and Silas. 'To be saved': the typical question of the intending convert. **31.** The 'way of salvation' (17) is through faith in Jesus as Lord. **31-2.** The conversion is not of the gaoler individually, but of his whole household. See note on 15 above. **32-3.** The baptism takes place immediately after they have received the word of the gospel. **34.** The meal might possibly include a post-baptismal Eucharist, but nothing is said to indicate that it was not merely an ordinary meal. Rejoicing, however, is usually a token of Spirit-possession consequent upon believing in God, i.e. upon conversion and baptism.

35-40 The Magistrates apologise. Departure c
from Philippi—The praetors' lictors are sent to release the missionaries. Paul refuses to leave without a personal apology from the magistrates themselves, who have violated the law by beating Roman citizens. Both Paul and Silas evidently possessed the citizenship. The magistrates accordingly come in person and apologise. The missionaries, however, have to leave Philippi after visiting Lydia and the Christians whose headquarters are now apparently at her house, and 'exhorting' the brethren (see note on 15:32). In telling this story Luke has shown how the guiding hand of God brought the mission across the sea (it may be significant that the voyage was performed in something like record time (cf. 16:11, 20:6) and, after an apparently disastrous reverse in a Gentile city, effected a mighty act of deliverance. This resulted in Paul and Silas receiving the homage of the gaoler (29), converting him, receiving an abject apology from the rulers in person, and practically going out of Philippi in triumph. The Gentile mission, at its entry into Europe, is blessed with the same great acts of God as the mission in Jerusalem, and Paul and Silas stand in the same relation to the former as Peter and John to the latter. From Luke's point of view the triumph is all the greater in that it involved deliverance through, and in spite of, suffering. The pattern of Christ's triumph through death is thus reproduced in his apostles. It would spoil the story, as Luke sees it, if Paul and Silas had claimed their citizen rights in the first place, when they were sentenced; and it is reasonable to suppose that Paul saw the matter in a similar light. The situation at 22:25 is quite different. There it is most important for Paul to secure a fair hearing and for his mission to be vindicated. The sufferings at Philippi are alluded to in 1 Th. 2:2, but without reference to the miraculous deliverance.

XVII 1-10 Tumult at Thessalonica—1. Philippi, d
Amphipolis, Apollonia and Thessalonica lie between 30 and 37 miles apart from each other. This fact has suggested the possibility that Paul may have made the journey in three stages, each of one day. This would imply that he rode. It is very doubtful, however, if Luke's narrative should be pressed to yield detailed information of this sort. Luke telescopes some journeys, omits others, and when he describes a stay in a particular place he is inclined to proceed directly from the start of the work there (often accompanied by some 'sign'

794d or other striking incident) to its close (generally brought about by some kind of persecution). His picture of the mission is stylised, and designed to show how the Holy Spirit brought the gospel to Jews and Gentiles. He does not set out to give a precise record of journeys except in the diary of sea voyages given in the first person. Luke is writing the second volume of a Gospel, not the detailed history of Paul's missions. Thessalonica was the seat of the proconsul of the province and was the capital of the second district of Macedonia. Here Paul was once again in a city with a considerable Jewish population and there was an opportunity to open his mission in the synagogue.

e **2.** RSV*n* reads 'three sabbaths'. The preaching is concentrated on the theme that Jesus is the Messiah, and that the apparent scandal of his death, and his resurrection, are proved from scripture to have been divinely ordained. **3.** 'Explaining': literally 'opening' (cf. Lk. 24:32); i.e. revealing their relevance to Christ and his death. 'To suffer and to rise': cf. Lk. 24:26, 46; Ac. 3:18, 26:23. The vivid touch given by direct speech is found also at 1:4, 23:22, 25:5. **4.** Paul's preaching converts many of the Gentile adherents of the synagogue, and some influential women. The Western text takes the latter to be 'wives of influential men', and, through a misunderstanding, speaks of Gentiles (heathens) as well as God-fearers. **5.** The persecution at Thessalonica, according to Luke, was initiated by Jews, jealous because of the conversion of the numerous 'fringe' of 'God-fearing' adherents of their synagogue. 1 Th. 2:14, on the other hand, suggests that the Thessalonian Christians suffered at the hands of their own countrymen. The Jews here collect a mob of hooligans (the 'rabble' of the market-place). 'Jason' is a name not infrequently adopted by Jews, especially those whose Jewish name was Joshua (Jesus). Presumably Jason was a convert whose house, like Lydia's, had become the centre of the mission. 'People' does not denote a democratic tribunal, but the riotous mob. **6.** 'City authorities' (*politarchs*): the magistrates of the municipality. This title occurs frequently in inscriptions from the Macedonian cities, and is virtually confined to that region. 'Turned the world upside down': more literally 'disturbed the (civilised) world'. The same word occurs in 21:38 where the participle, used absolutely, means 'who raised a revolt', and in Gal. 5:12

f of those who disturb or upset Paul's converts. **7.** Jason was the missionaries' host. It has been suggested that he procured for Paul the work by which he maintained himself in Thessalonica (cf. 1 Th. 2:9). 'Another king'. This charge resembles that brought before Pilate (Lk. 23:2). Luke never hesitates to admit that Jesus was called a king (e.g. Lk. 19:38) and that this was liable to be misinterpreted in a political sense; but he insists that the charge that Jesus or his followers preached sedition was brought maliciously by Jews and that the Roman authorities perceived it to be false. On this occasion the local authorities were alarmed, probably because Paul's preaching had been concerned with Christ's kingdom and the phrase had been misinterpreted. **9.** 'Security': i.e. probably a legal undertaking not to harbour the Christians. Hence Paul could not return to Thessalonica (cf. 1 Th .2:18).

g **10-13 The Mission at Beroea**—Beroea was in the third district of Macedonia, lying south of the main Via Egnatia. It also possessed a flourishing Jewish community. **11.** 'Noble': properly 'high-minded', i.e. willing to pay serious attention. 'Examining the scriptures' to see whether the scriptural proofs adduced by Paul were well founded. **12.** Many Jews were converted and a number of Gentiles, prominent men and women. The Western text reads 'many men and women of the Greeks and prominent people'; cf. note on 4 above. **13.** The Thessalonian Jews repeat their tactics of stirring up a mob.

h **14-15 Departure from Beroea and Arrival at Athens**—**15.** The Western text, not realising that Luke means that Paul went by sea to Athens, adds that he passed through Thessaly but was prevented 79
from preaching there. Silas and Timothy stay to establish the Thessalonian church, and rejoin Paul at Corinth (18:5). Luke has probably omitted some complicated movements (cf. 1 Th. 3:1).

16-21 Paul disputes at Athens—Athens, at this i
time small and politically insignificant, here represents the Greek philosophical world. 'Provoked': literally 'stirred to fury'. **17.** The reference to preaching in the synagogue appears rather oddly between the reference to the pagan idolatry of Athens (16) and the speech to pagan philosophers. It is probably meant only to indicate in a conventional way that the approach to Gentiles was duly preceded, according to the plan of the mission, by preaching to Jews, and so to lead on to Paul's general conversation with all comers in the market-place. Here alone does Luke tell of Paul actually addressing Gentiles directly, apart from the short episode at Lystra; for Luke, at any rate, it is as the scene of a speech to Gentiles that Athens is important. If the arguments in the synagogue are historical they produced singularly little effect, for no Christian community is mentioned as having emerged out of the synagogue and its God-fearers. The approach to Gentiles begins in an unusual way with disputations in the market-place, somewhat in the manner of Socrates. **18.** Paul encounters Epi- j
curean and Stoic philosophers. The former, with their materialistic outlook based on the atomic theory of Democritus, denied divine providence (all things coming into being and passing away through purely fortuitous combinations of atoms) and immortality. It was their 'atheistic' view of reality (they did not deny the existence of gods, but held that they were unconcerned with the world) which chiefly differentiated them from the Stoics. Ethically there was little practical difference between the Epicurean quest of pleasure and the Stoic aim of living in accordance with nature. Both objects were to be achieved by a severe self-sufficiency and detachment from ordinary passions. It would probably be the Epicurean part of Paul's audience who mocked at his teaching about the resurrection of the dead (32 below), and perhaps also who contemptuously called him a 'babbler'. Paul's speech is designed to appeal more powerfully to the Stoics with their belief in an immanent divine reason pervading the cosmos, maintaining the order of nature and the moral law which is made known to the conscience. The object of the wise man, according to their system, is to live in accordance with the divine law expressed in the universal order of nature.
'Babbler' (literally 'seed-picker'), a word descriptive k
of a bird picking up grain, then applied to a scavenger, and so to one who picks up and retails second-hand scraps of knowledge. 'Foreign divinities'. This is almost identical with the charge brought against Socrates (Xenophon, *Memorabilia*, I, i, 1). From Chrysostom onwards commentators have generally supposed that 'Resurrection' (*Anastasis*) was understood to be a goddess, and this is more likely than that the idea of 'gods' was suggested by allusions by Paul to Jesus, the Father and the Spirit. **19.** Areopagus. l
Luke gives a dramatic picture of Paul expounding his teaching to this ancient and venerable court, which had acquired such great prestige under the Empire that Cicero ascribed to it the government of the Athenian state (*De natura deorum*, II, xxix, 74). In view of 18 it would seem that those who 'brought him' were unfriendly and that Luke thinks of this as a trial for disturbing the peace with subversive religious teaching. On the other hand, 20–1 suggests a more friendly inquiry by people with a craze for new-fangled ideas. Probably the two aspects are combined in Luke's mind: Paul is brought for trial before the court which embodies the most ancient and revered traditions of Athenian religion and culture; and the Athenian philosophers, with their craving for novelty, ask Paul to lecture. Luke is giving an impressionistic picture of Paul at Athens, and it is probably useless

941 to press him for accuracy in detail. Little is known of the precise powers and function of the Areopagus at this time. It probably exercised control over matters of religion and morals. Whether there was, as B. Gärtner holds (*The Areopagus Speech and Natural Revelation*, 59), an 'education commission' of the Areopagus is doubtful, and depends mainly on the interpretation given to Plutarch, *Cicero* 24:5, which does not readily suggest a formal jurisdiction over the 'university of Athens'. If, however, there was such a commission, it would presumably maintain order among the wandering scholars who gave lectures, and keep out seditious and subversive speakers. Luke, at any rate, seems to depict a mixture of a judicial inquiry and a public lecture, or perhaps university sermon. If it was mainly an inquiry it would probably take place in the *Stoa Basileios* in the market-place, rather than on 'Mars' Hill', the original meeting-place of the Areopagus. The hill would certainly seem an inconvenient place for any kind of meeting, unless the object were to find a quiet spot away from the city. 'Know'. The repeated mention of the Athenians' anxiety to know leads up to Paul's text, the 'unknown God'. **20.** 'You bring'. The same word is used of Socrates introducing strange gods (Xenophon, *Memorabilia*, I, i, 1). **21.** This was a proverbial characteristic of the Athenians.

95a **22-31 The Speech before the Areopagus**—**22.** 'In the midst' as an orator before an impressive audience. The phrase does not help to indicate whether or not the scene was 'Mars' Hill'. 'Men of Athens': the classical opening address. 'Very religious'. The same word is used by Festus at 25:19. As he is there writing to a Jew it is unlikely to be meant contemptuously, and here, in the orator's preamble, it cannot be intended as an insult. It describes a religious devotion which may be genuine and praiseworthy, but which the speaker does not share: cf. the modern use of 'religion', 'religious', in 'Of course, I'm not a religious person' and 'So and so seems very interested in religion'. Though Paul indicates that he stands outside the Athenians' religion, his words could

b be taken as a compliment. **23.** No evidence has yet been found for the existence of any such dedication. When authors refer to altars of 'unknown gods' they appear to mean altars without a dedication to a named deity. Such passages as Pausanias, V, xiv, 8 (Olympia), I, i, 4 (Athens), Diogenes Laertius 1:110 (Athens), Philostratus, *Vita Apollonii*, VI, iii, 5 ('... at Athens where altars even of unknown gods are set up'), probably do not imply more than this, and do not refer to actual dedicatory inscriptions 'to unknown gods'. Even if they did, there would still be no evidence for the use of the singular. A fragmentary inscription from Pergamos (2nd cent. A.D.) has been implausibly restored as reading 'to the unknown gods', but this should probably read 'to the most holy gods'. Luke had perhaps read about the existence at Athens of altars to unknown (i.e. unnamed) deities, and built this speech round the idea of a dedication to the unknown God, whom Greek paganism worshipped in ignorance and who is revealed to Christians. 'You worship as unknown'. The inscription is a witness to the Athenians that they are ignorant of God. They ought to have known him, since all men are dependent upon him for life and health. Yet they seek to worship him, even though they are ignorant of who he is. The emphasis, if not the basic thought, of Rom. 1:22–5 is different. There the Gentiles have preferred to worship the creature rather than the Creator, and have been punished by being allowed to continue in

c idolatry. **24.** A paraphrase of Isa. 42:5. God is Creator and he governs the universe as its Lord. He therefore cannot live in 'shrines made with hands' (cf. also 1 Kg. 8:27ff.). The same term is used here of heathen temples which was applied to the Jerusalem Temple in 7:48, and the argument there employed against the Temple at Jerusalem is here used against heathen sanctuaries (cf. 7:49–50). **25.** That God is self-sufficient and has no need of man's service is a 795c thought common to Hebrew tradition (cf. Ps. 50:12), especially in the Greek period (2 Mac. 14:35; 3 Mac. 2:9), and to philosophical Greek and Roman thinkers, especially of the Stoic school. In a different sense the idea that God wants nothing from men would appeal to Epicureanism with its aloof deities. 'Life and breath'. Isa. 43:5 reads '... and gives breath to the people upon it and spirit to those who walk in it'. Luke has substituted 'life' for 'spirit', perhaps because the latter might be confused with the peculiarly Christian gift of the Holy Spirit; he may also be influenced by 2 Mac. 7:23, 'the creator of the world, who fashioned the generation of men ... in mercy giveth back to you again both your spirit and your life'. On the side of Greek thought there is the association of Zeus with *zōē* (life). **26.** 'From one'. d

The Western text with some other support adds 'blood', probably failing to realise that the reference is to Adam, the concept of the primal man being, as syncretistic Gnostic systems indicate, not unknown to Hellenism. The common humanity of all men, sharing the same nature, was a prominent idea in Stoicism, which finds a point of agreement here with the Hebraic concept of Adam as man's common ancestor, though scarcely with the use of the Adam idea in Rom. 5. **26.** 'Periods' of history and the disposition of the nations ought to be seen as vehicles of God's self-revelation. **27.** The purpose of this revelation is that men should seek God (through the recognition of him in his works, cf. Wis. 13:1–9 and especially 6, a passage echoed in Rom. 1). 'Feel after' suggests the groping of a blind man (cf. Isa. 59:10). 'Not far'. This would be understood in Hebraic thought in terms of God's dealings with his people: cf. Ps. 145:8; Jer. 23:23. It would also be familiar to Stoics, who believed that God is with man and within him (cf. Dio Chrysostom, 12:28; Seneca, *ep.* 41:1), and would understand this pantheistically.

28. It is very doubtful whether 'In him we live ...' e is really a quotation. The commentary of Isho'dad of Merv (*c.* 850) ascribes both this saying and also 'For we are indeed his offspring' to 'heathen poets'. It then states that the latter is cited from Aratus, and the former from 'Minos'. The passage which Isho'dad quotes from 'Minos' includes also the line about the Cretans which is cited in Tit. 1:12 and is attributed by Clement of Alexandria to Epimenides (it certainly occurs in Callimachus's *Hymn to Zeus*). It has therefore been concluded that the whole passage quoted by Isho'dad comes from the epic on Minos and Rhadamanthus by Epimenides. It is more probable, however, that Isho'dad is referring to an apocryphal 'Minos' poem, and not to the epic of Epimenides. Theodore of Mopsuestia, on whom Isho'dad mainly relies, does not mention 'Minos'. It is certainly improbable that Paul would cite with approval a poem whose object is to assert the eternal existence of Zeus. See M. Pohlenz (ZNTW 42 (1949), 69ff. 'Poets' (**28**) need not in fact refer to more than one poet. The idea of God's omnipresence is present in the poem of Aratus from which 'For we are indeed his offspring' is quoted. It is also familiar in Judaism (cf. Ps. 139). 'For we are indeed ...' is quoted from Aratus of Soli, *Phaenomena*, 5. The fact that the preceding lines of the speech echo the theme of the whole of the opening part of this poem suggests that Luke, or the writer of this speech, knew the original and is not merely reproducing a hackneyed quotation. A similar line occurs in Cleanthes, *Hymn to Zeus*, 4. This thought, too, is fully biblical; cf. Lk. 3:38: Adam as God's creature is God's son. **29.** If men f are God's offspring, they ought not to suppose that God can be truly represented by works of art created by their own hands. Here is a standard Jewish and Christian argument against popular polytheism, but hardly effective against the philosophers; cf. Wis. 13:10. **30.** God has not punished men for their ignorance (cf. 23 above). Contrast the thought of

795f Rom. 1 that God has punished men's idolatry by letting them continue in it. 'Repent'. The general theme of the gospel preaching is here applied particularly to repentance from idolatry by recognition of the true God. **31.** God 'will judge the world' in righteousness (cf. Ps. 9:8 etc.) by a man (suggesting to a Christian reader, but not to the supposed audience, the Son of man exercising the divine judgment) whom he has appointed, giving assurance of this in the Resurrection. 'Assurance' is a unique use in the NT of the ordinary word for 'faith'.

g **32-34 The Effect of the Speech**—**32.** Epicureans would be especially contemptuous of the idea of resurrection. It is hard to say whether those who did not mock were serious in saying 'We will hear you again', or whether this is a polite but final dismissal. No Greek philosophers would take kindly to a doctrine, not of immortality as some of them could understand it, but of a 'resuscitation of corpses'. Any idea of a trial seems to have disappeared at this stage. **33.** For the most part the audience had rejected Paul's teaching. This does not imply that Paul went out disheartened, determined never again to adopt the technique of a cultured sermon, but to stick to the 'simple gospel'. If this speech does at all represent Paul's own methods, there is no evidence that he ever thought them ineffective or abandoned them. In fact, however, the speech is probably a composition by Luke, using much standard material from Jewish and Christian apologetic against polytheism. **34.** On the contrary, Paul was distinctly successful at Athens, where his discourse converted a member of the Areopagus among other people. Dionysius is said by Dionysius of Corinth (Eus. HE III, iv, 10, IV, xxiii, 3) to have become bishop of Athens.

h **XVIII 1-11 Paul's Mission at Corinth**—Corinth was an important commercial centre linked by busy trade routes with the eastern Mediterranean and with Italy and the West. It now had something of a Roman as well as a Greek character, having been refounded by Julius Caesar (Old Corinth was destroyed by Mummius in 146 B.C.), and planted with settlers. Its population was always largely cosmopolitan. It was a place where many cults found a home and it was notorious for immorality. **2.** There seems no good reason for Ramsay's suggestion that Aquila may have been a freedman of the *gens Pontia* at Rome rather than a native of Pontus. Priscilla: the Prisca of Rom. 16:3; 1 C. 16:19; 2 Tim. 4:19. 'Claudius had commanded'. Suetonius (*Claudius*, 25) states that Claudius had expelled from Rome the Jews who were 'incessantly causing tumults with Chrestus as the instigator', probably a garbled version of disturbances in the Jewish community at Rome consequent upon the arrival of Christianity there. Orosius gives the date of this order as A.D. 49–50 (the ninth year of Claudius). It is uncertain whether Aquila and Priscilla were

i already Christians before they met Paul. **3.** 'Tentmakers'. Apart from resources supplied by his converts at times, the Epistles show that Paul prided himself on being self-supporting, and not exercising his right to be maintained by his churches. The word is better rendered 'leather-workers', and probably refers to the felted goat-hair cloth called *cilicium* because it was a special product of Cilicia (the neighbourhood of Tarsus). This was used for many purposes besides tents. Codex Floriacensis, the Syriac Peshitta and patristic commentaries indicate that the word was understood as 'leather workers'. **4.** Paul begins his Corinthian mission with an appeal to the Jews. There was apparently but one synagogue, possibly that of which an inscribed lintel has been found. Paul's work probably occupied him throughout the week, confining his preaching to the sabbath. 'Greeks': i.e. God-fearers. **5.** Silas and Timothy: see 17:14–15. 'Occupied'. If his friends brought funds (possibly from Philippi (cf. Phil. 4:15ff.)), Paul could devote more time to the mission. His message is the Messiahship of Jesus. **6.** Here the pattern of the mission seen at Pisidian Antioch, and on a larger scale in the missions to Jerusalem, Samaria and the Gentiles, and indeed in the whole structure of the Lucan writings, is again reproduced. The Jews reject the gospel and Paul turns to the Gentiles. 'Shook out his garments': cf. Nah. 5:13; a gesture of repudiation and separation. 'Blood be upon your heads': cf. 2 Sam. 1:16; Mt. 27:25. The Jews bear the responsibility of rejecting the gospel. **7.** Paul leaves the synagogue and

j takes up his quarters with one of the God-fearers whose conversion had presumably infuriated the authorities of the synagogue next door. The establishment of the Christian mission next door to the synagogue, with a converted ruler of the synagogue as a member, must have aggravated the situation considerably. 'Titius'. Codex Sinaiticus and other MSS read 'Titus'. Others omit the name. 'Titus' is probably due to the tendency of ancient commentators to identify this man with the Titus of Gal. 2:1. Either the omission of the name, or its insertion into the text, might be due to an easy corruption, but probably 'Titius' should be read. **8.** 'Crispus': cf. 1 C. 1:14. This conversion was obviously of much importance for the mission in Corinth and made a great impression. 'Ruler of the synagogue': see note on 13:15. 'Household': see notes on 16:15, 33–4. The baptism of Crispus, and presumably of his whole household, was carried out by Paul himself (1 C. 1:14). **9.** A special vision of the Lord encourages Paul to make an unusually long stay in Corinth. **10.** cf. Isa. 43:5. 'Many people': i.e. those who will receive the gospel. **11.** As usual, Luke says little about the progress of the local mission between its spectacular opening and the events with which it ended.

12-17 Paul is accused before Gallio—Gallio was k

the brother of Seneca and uncle of Lucan, the poet. An inscription from Delphi, recording the emperor's decision on a dispute referred to him by Gallio, includes in the imperial title the 26th salutation of Claudius as *imperator*. The figure 26 is actually legible in the inscription, which is pieced together from four fragments, and the reference to salutation as *imperator* seems to be a secure reconstruction. Other inscriptions show that the 22nd, 23rd and 24th salutations occurred in Claudius's eleventh year as emperor (25 January 51 to 24 January 52). The inscription on the Claudian aqueduct at Rome gives his salutations as 27; Frontinus (*aqueduct.* 13:14) states that the dedication of the aqueduct, when this inscription was set up, took place on 1 August 52. The strong probability is that the 26th salutation took place in the twelfth year of Claudius's reign, between 25 January and 1 August 52. Gallio was in office then. The normal practice under Claudius was for provincial governors of the less distant provinces to leave for their provinces at mid-April (Dio Cassius, LX, xvii, 3). It is unlikely, from the circumstances recorded in the Delphi inscription, that Gallio assumed office only at the beginning of May 52. The previous year is more probable, though we do not in fact know for how long Gallio held office. It is probable, though not certain, that v. 12 implies that Gallio had only recently come to the province. If he took over his duties in early May 51, Paul would have arrived in Corinth in the winter of 49–50, which accords well with Orosius's dating of the edict which caused Aquila and Priscilla to come to Corinth shortly before Paul. 'A united attack'. l

Probably they were trying the mettle of the new governor. Luke's picture of Paul's stay in Corinth is 'stylised'. It is focused round one central theme: that when the gospel was rejected by the synagogue Paul turned to the Gentiles and conducted a most successful mission. The Jews did their utmost to enlist the Roman power on their side, but failed totally to achieve their malicious purpose. It is, again, the theme of the whole of Lk.-Ac. **13.** Luke does not make it m

clear what the charge was. From 15 it seems that the 'law' means the Jewish Law, and, indeed, it would not appear that any Roman law made Paul's activity

5m illegal, since he could not be accused of making Jewish proselytes of Roman citizens (unless Titius Justus were one). On the other hand, the Jews were surely optimistic, even if they were dealing with an inexperienced governor, if they supposed that a Roman tribunal would protect the orthodoxy of the synagogue against heretics. Gallio, however, makes it reasonably plain that this was their hope, since he not only refuses to call on the defendant to speak but pithily and concisely explains that the Jews have alleged no crime of any description against him ; his opinion of them is then forcibly expressed when he has them driven from the tribunal. Thus, as at Philippi, the triumph of Paul and the gospel is complete ; here it is by the civil authority vindicating him to the fullest conceivable extent ; there, when the civil authorities had been so misguided as to condemn him they were compelled to offer him abject apologies. Luke probably intends the reader to see here a pointer to what was to happen
n to Paul when he appealed to Rome. **15.** The dispute is about empty theological phrases and terms (presumably including ' Messiah ' ; cf. 5 above), and questions of the Jewish Law. **17.** The context indicates plainly that an anti-Jewish mob (no doubt correctly interpreted by the Western text as ' all the Greeks ') seized and beat the ruler of the synagogue, Sosthenes, who had presumably brought the prosecution against Paul. Only an attempted identification with the Christian Sosthenes of 1 C. 1:1, which is most improbable, has confused the interpretation of this sentence. Gallio paid no attention to this final and crushing humiliation of Paul's adversaries.

96a **18-22 Departure from Corinth, Journey and Arrival at Antioch**—This passage presents historical difficulties. Some commentators suggest that it is a fictitious account by Luke of a supposed visit to Jerusalem, modelled largely on the final visit. There is no good reason, however, for doubting that Luke's narrative of the journey to Ephesus is historically correct, and also the story that Paul went to Antioch, possibly by way of Caesarea. The visit to Jerusalem which Luke intends to indicate in 22 is less plausible, though not impossible ; the preaching in Ephesus (19*b*–21) is difficult to reconcile with 19*a* and with the
b general impression of haste in this journey. **18.** ' Syria '. Antioch, his starting-point, is probably meant. ' Priscilla ' is mentioned before Aquila, perhaps as being the more important of the two in the work of the Church. ' Cenchreae : the eastern seaport of Corinth. ' Cut his hair '. This indicates that Luke, who is always anxious to lay stress on Paul's Jewish piety, thinks that Paul had taken a temporary Nazirite vow. It may mean that he was discharging a vow made at Corinth ; the end of the successful mission, signalised by his departure, may have been the occasion for this. But it is possible that the head was shaved before the hair was left to grow during the period of a vow. In that case Paul was taking a vow at Cenchreae, intending to discharge it at Jerusalem. **19.** The Western text smooths out difficulties by inserting at 21 the statement that Priscilla and Aquila were left at Ephesus. 19*a* makes good sense, but 19*b*–21 may be an afterthought intending to show that the beginnings of the Ephesian church were really due to Paul and not to Apollos and Aquila and Priscilla. The general impression given by the narrative is that the journey was being carried out in haste (the Western text adds to 21 a statement that Paul was hurrying to get to Jerusalem to keep ' the approaching festival ' ; cf. 20:16), and it seems odd that Paul should take the time to start a mission in the Ephesian synagogue. It may have been the case, however, that Paul was delayed at Ephesus, perhaps waiting for another ship to Syria, and had time on his hands, Luke may have left his narrative in a rather rough or unrevised state, having noted that Priscilla and Aquila were left at Ephesus, and then added a summary of what Paul did at Ephesus himself while waiting there. This section of the book reads like a series of hastily compiled notes. **21** prepares the reader for the story in ch. 19. **22.** Paul disembarks 796c
at Caesarea and, according to Luke, goes up to Jerusalem and greets the church there. There can be no doubt that Jerusalem is indicated : ' go up ' and ' go down ' are almost technical terms for travelling to and from Jerusalem, and could not be used in this way of going from the harbour at Caesarea to the meeting-place of the local church and back again. Luke presents Paul in this second missionary journey as an envoy of the Jerusalem church, following the council in ch. 15. He naturally supposes that on the completion of the journey Paul would report to those whom he represented, so that the Jerusalem church would be fully apprised of, and would approve, the mission in Europe. Whether Luke is correctly informed is another matter. It seems improbable that Paul visited Jerusalem on this occasion. The visit in ch. 21 is prepared for with great care, and the Epistles show that the collection from the Gentile churches was intended as an impressive gesture of solidarity between the new communities and Jerusalem. That visit, with the offerings of the Gentile churches, seems to be the first official contact between the new churches, through their apostle, with the Christians of Jerusalem. In view of the events at his final visit, it seems strange that Paul could visit Jerusalem, even for a very short time, without running into personal danger, though the taking of a vow may have been intended to demonstrate his loyalty to Jewish traditions and avert the wrath of those who believed him to be a subverter of the Law among the Jews of the Dispersion (cf. 21:21). If Gal. ought to be dated during the ' third ' missionary journey, near the time of the writing of Rom., this visit would again raise the problem of reconciling Gal. and Ac. There is no place in the former for this visit, yet, if it had taken place, Paul would almost certainly have felt bound to mention it. ' Antioch ' : the real base for the second journey, and the place to which, rather than Jerusalem, Paul would naturally return.

23 Journey into Asia Minor—' Departed '. The d
start of the ' third missionary journey ' ; but in fact the labours of Paul from the departure from Antioch soon after the Jerusalem council to the final visit to Jerusalem are presented by Luke as a continuous whole, scarcely broken by the brief return to Jerusalem in 22. ' The region of Galatia and Phrygia ' : see note on 16:6. This might denote the region of Pisidian Antioch, Iconium, etc., or the more northerly regions of Galatia, followed by Phrygia. In either case, however, Paul is ' strengthening ' the disciples, i.e. revisiting his converts and not breaking new ground.

24-28 Apollos—The Western text has the longer e
form ' Apollonius '. Codex Sinaiticus and others read ' Apelles ', seeking to identify him with the Apelles of Rom. 16:10. This Alexandrian Jew was an eloquent interpreter of the scriptures : i.e. able to interpret the OT in a Christian sense and trace the prophecies and types and their fulfilment. He seems to have been a prototype of the later Alexandrian exegetes. The guess of Luther, taken up by T. W. Manson, that he wrote the Epistle to the Hebrews is attractive. **25.** He had been instructed in the Christian ' way ' and was an inspired preacher and an accurate teacher of the Christian belief about Jesus. He was ' boiling with the Spirit ', meaning the inspiration of the Holy Spirit. Yet in his case the prophetic gift was not associated with baptism, for he knew no other baptism than that of John, which Christ's disciples probably continued to administer until it was transformed into baptism in the name of Jesus in consequence of his death and resurrection. The spiritual status of Apollos is very obscure; but in some degree he was evidently out of touch, especially as regards baptism, with the post-Pentecostal Church. **26.** Apollos conducts a mission among the Ephesian Jews. He is then given fuller instruction in the ' way of God ' (not ' the things concerning Jesus ' which he knew well) by Priscilla and Aquila (the order of whose names is reversed in the Western text). **27.** ' Brethren '.

796e Probably as a result, mainly, of Apollos's preaching, a church now existed at Ephesus ; cf. Luke's picture of Paul's earlier work there (19 above). 'Wrote'. Letters of commendation for Christians travelling to strange towns were a feature of the Church's organisation (cf. 2 C. 3:1). 'Achaia'. Apollos became a very prominent leader at Corinth, ranking in the minds of his Corinthian partisans with Peter and Paul (1 C. 1:12, 3:6, 4:9). **28.** The work of Apollos is concerned with refuting the Jews by preaching the Christian interpretation of the OT, which drew scriptural proofs from the prophecies to show that Jesus is the Messiah.

f **XIX 1-7 Paul at Ephesus: Baptism of Disciples previously baptised into John's Baptism—1.** Apollos is mentioned here to link what follows with the narrative just completed. 'Upper country': i.e. the hill country inland from Ephesus. 'Disciples'. In Luke's writings this word, used absolutely, always means 'Christians'. In all probability these were converts made by Apollos during his mission at Ephesus. Like him, they knew only John's baptism (cf. 18:25). They may have been Christians of a 'pre-Pentecostal' kind, comparable in their religious state with the Twelve before Pentecost. Their number (twelve) may therefore be significant. They are the original nucleus of the Ephesian church, the future headquarters and focal point of Paul's Gentile mission and the place where he spent a longer time than in any other centre, as the Twelve had been the nucleus of the church in Jerusalem. Through Paul they receive baptism in the full Christian sense, and by the sign of identification with Paul, the laying-on of his hands, they are associated in the apostolic mission and receive the Pentecostal Spirit of the missionary enterprise, manifested in 'tongues' and prophesying. Like the establishment of a new centre of the mission in Samaria, this is a major turning-point in the history of the gospel, and a new focus of the Pentecostal Spirit comes into being through the presence of Paul, who, although not one of the Twelve, was a Spirit-possessed missionary. The imposition of hands on the Ephesian disciples and on the Samaritan converts is the closest approximation which Ac. offers to an ordination of apostles : not that the apostolate of the Twelve could be imparted to others, nor in the sense that there was a formal ordination to the office or status of apostle in a broader meaning of the term, but in so far as a nucleus of believers in a new centre of the mission received the same gifts of the Spirit as were bestowed on the Twelve, in order that they might carry the mission a stage further. There is certainly a possibility that Luke misunderstood the story, and that these men were members of a sect of John the Baptist's followers. This interpretation is attractive, in that it enables Jn 1:19–27, 3:28–30 to be interpreted as a polemic directed against a Johannine sect at Ephesus ; but it is very improbable. 'Disciple' means 'Christian' ; 'believed' (2) means 'were converted and baptised as Christians', and Paul would not have expressed the surprise implicit in his question (2) if these men had been non-Christian followers of John. **2.** 'That there is a Holy Spirit': cf. Jn 7:39. The meaning is, as the Western text expands it, 'that any people are receiving the Holy Spirit', i.e. that the baptism with the Spirit foretold by John has become a reality to those who are baptised in the name of Jesus as Lord (cf. 5). **3.** 'Into what?' Paul asks what baptism they had received ; he does not imply that they had been baptised into another name. **4.** They had received the baptism of repentance, which, according to John's preaching, was preparatory for the coming of Christ (cf. Lk. 3:16 ; Ac. 1:5, 11:16) and the baptism of the Spirit which he was to inaugurate. Luke here interprets John's preaching in the light of Christian reflection upon it ; John did indeed point to a 'coming one', but he spoke of him as the future judge rather than as the object of faith. **6.** Paul had not received the Pentecostal Spirit himself through one of the Twelve, but the disciple Ananias had laid his hands upon him, having been sent to do this in order that Paul might both recover his sight and be filled with the Holy Spirit (9:17). There is no evidence at all for the view that in every case where the Spirit of tongues and prophecy was imparted through the laying-on of hands, this was done through the agency of the Twelve. The case of Samaria was special, and the presence of apostles from Jerusalem was essential there. Paul associates these twelve disciples with his own mission and his own spiritual gifts. **7.** 'About'. This does not imply that there were not in fact exactly twelve. Luke's curious habit is to qualify all numbers in this way : cf. 2:41, 4:4, 5:7, 36, 10:3, 13:18, 20, 19:34.

g **8-20 Preaching at Ephesus: Signs and Wonders —8.** 'Synagogue'. Had the 'disciples' not been Christians, Paul would presumably have approached the Jews in the synagogue before anyone else, according to his usual practice. 'Boldly'. Paul spoke in the characteristic fashion of one inspired by the Spirit. 'Kingdom of God': cf. 1:3. Paul's preaching probably concerned the fulfilment by Christ, now realised proleptically, of the promises of God's kingdom. **9.** Following its usual course, the gospel is rejected by the majority of the synagogue, and continues to be proclaimed to a minority of Jews and to Gentiles. 'The Way': see note on 9:2. 'Withdrew'. The mission causes a schism from the synagogue. 'Hall of Tyrannus'. A lecture-hall either used or owned by Tyrannus, possibly a philosopher. The Western text adds 'from the fifth to the tenth hour'. The editor has naturally asked himself, 'What happened to the lectures of Tyrannus?' and given the likely answer that Paul and his congregation occupied it during the hot hours (11 a.m. to 4 p.m.) when the lecturer was taking his siesta. **10.** 'Two years' to which should perhaps be added the three months of 8 and the 'for a while' of 22. Much missionary activity was based on Ephesus ; hence the great importance of the renewal of the Pentecostal gift at the foundation of the Church there. The gospel was taken to Colossae, Laodicea and other places ; so that it was heard throughout the province of Asia. Luke says nothing of Paul's serious anxieties concerning the Corinthian church during this time. **11.** Paul's Gentile mission is accompanied by the same 'signs' as those performed in Palestine by Peter (cf. 5:15). 'Hands' may be meant literally: he laid hands on the sick. **12.** 'Handkerchiefs'. The miraculous power which authenticates the mission of Paul is conveyed, according to Luke, by all forms of contact with his person, including cloths which had touched his body. cf. Lk. 8:44. **13.** Jewish exorcism (cf. Lk. 11:19) was well known in antiquity, and its methods were often believed to have been derived from Solomon. Here they begin to use the name of Jesus as a potent charm (cf. Lk. 9:49). **14.** 'High priest'. Sceva was never a high priest in Jerusalem. Possibly he held a pagan high priesthood, perhaps of the imperial cult ; more probable than this view that he was a renegade Jew in an important pagan office is F. C. Burkitt's suggestion that the exorcists claimed (entirely fictitiously) to be the sons of a high priest at Jerusalem, so as to let it be thought that they knew the sacred and ineffable name of the Most High, and were therefore powerful exorcists. The Western text reads 'priest' only. 'Seven'. In 16 'all of them' translates a Greek word usually meaning 'both'. Probably this is an early example of later Greek usage in which it may refer to more than two. It has, however, been suggested that 'seven' may have been interpolated here from a marginal sign for 'query' being mistaken for the figure 7 (cf. note on 12:10), or that 'Sceva' was confused with the Hebrew 'Sheva' (seven) ; but these theories are unnecessary. **15.** The h
demon knows Jesus and the apostle who preaches him (cf. 13), but will not recognise any authority in the name as pronounced by non-Christians. **16.** The false exorcists are at the mercy of the demonic power. The episode serves to magnify Paul's mission. **18.**

796h Many who were already converts confessed to the practice of magic and disclosed it although they had apparently not done so at their baptism. **19.** ' Ephesian writings ', i.e. books of spells, were famous. ' Pieces of silver ' : i.e. drachmas. **20.** The mission at Ephesus makes great progress ; the Word of the Lord cannot be obstructed by Jewish hostility, the practisers of magic, or, as the story goes on to show, the fury of a mob incited by malicious opponents.

797a **21-22 Paul's Plans for the Future**—Paul's resolve to revisit Greece, and so to go to Jerusalem to mark the completion of this mission based on Ephesus, was inspired by the Spirit who directed the progress of the gospel. To translate ' in the Spirit ' by ' in his spirit ' (cf. ' in the heart ', 5:4) is probably wrong. Paul believes it to be the divine purpose (' I must ') that he should take the gospel to Rome, the capital of the Gentile world, completing the final stage of the mission ' to the ends of the earth '. Thus the last scenes in Luke's story are foreshadowed. **22.** ' Timothy ': cf. 1 C. 4:17, 16:10, which may allude to this visit. ' Erastus ' : cf. Rom. 16:23 ; 2 Tim. 4:20, but not necessarily the same person.

b **23-41 The Riot of the Silversmiths**—After describing the great success which attended the preaching at Ephesus, Luke goes on to the events which preceded Paul's departure, in which, again, his cause triumphed over opposition. Luke says nothing about troubles at Ephesus mentioned in 1 C. 15:32 ; 2 C. 1:8, nor about his dealings, from there, with the Corinthian church. ' The Way ' : cf. note on 9:2. ' Demetrius ' has been identified with a *neopoios* mentioned in an inscription (*Ancient Greek Inscriptions in the British Museum*, 3:578), but this is by no means certain. *Neopoios* was the title of the members of the body responsible for the maintenance of the temple. Literally it means ' shrine-maker ', and Luke may have misunderstood the term. Silver shrines, presumably miniature, designed as votive offerings, such as Luke indicates here, have not been discovered, nor are they mentioned by ancient writers. Demetrius may have been a maker of silver statues and a temple warden. ' Artemis ' was the famous Ephesian goddess of fertility, identified by the Greeks with Artemis. She was a form of the ancient Asian Great Mother, depicted in her statue as ' many-breasted ' (but the numerous ' breasts ' have been supposed by some to represent a bunch of dates and by others a swarm of bees !). **25.** Demetrius organises the skilled craftsmen and ordinary workmen in defence of their trade, which is now endangered by Paul's success in converting very many pagans, directly and indirectly, throughout the province of Asia. **26.** Paul had been preaching to Gentiles against polytheistic idolatry (cf. 17:29). **27.** The temple was one of the ' seven wonders ' of the world. The cult of Ephesian Artemis was in fact widespread. **28.** ' Great is Artemis ' : a ritual acclamation of the goddess ; cf. Bel 18. **29.** The theatre at Ephesus is very large and evidently served as a public meeting-place. ' Macedonians '. Aristarchus was from Thessalonica, Gaius from Derbe (20:4) ; but if the Western text's reading should be right (' Douberios ', from Doberus, a Macedonian town, instead of ' Derbaios '), both men were Macedonians. If the Western reading at 20:4 is, however, a scholarly conjecture designed to reconcile that passage with ' Macedonians ' here, the plural ' Macedonians ' may be a corruption of the singular (an easy corruption), and the adjective would then apply only to Aristarchus. **30.** Paul wished to confront the mob
c himself ; cf. 21:40. **31.** The cities of Asia formed a religious league for the promotion and administration of the cult of Rome and the emperor in the province. Their elected representatives, the Asiarchs, formed the council of the league, which maintained the cult and also acted as a political link between the provincials and the emperor. Luke as usual emphasises the good relations between Greek and Roman officials and Paul. **32.** Apparently this meeting was in theory a constitutional democratic assembly of the citizens (cf. 40).

33. The situation is very obscure. Luke appears to 797c
mean that Jews in the crowd put up Alexander to make it clear that the Christians were not Jews and so to save themselves from being involved in a pagan attack on the former. ' Prompted '. The Greek word may mean ' instructed ', but it has caused difficulty to copyists who have substituted several variants. Alexander might be referred to in 1 Tim. 1:19, and/or 2 Tim. 4:14, but this is highly improbable. ' Motioned with his hand ' in the regular manner of an orator opening his speech. **34.** The mob does not in fact differentiate between the Christians and the Jews who are evidently already highly unpopular. **35.** ' Town clerk ' : the secretary or executive officer of the municipality, presiding over the assembly. ' Temple keeper ' : a title sometimes given to a city, especially one which maintained a temple of the imperial cult. An inscription attests its application to Ephesus as the guardian of the temple of Artemis (CIG 2972). ' From the sky '. The image, like many others, was believed to have fallen from heaven (possibly a meteorite). The clerk reassures the crowd that nothing can damage the fame and prestige of the goddess of Ephesus. **37.** Paul's companions, and, by implication, himself, are obviously innocent of any of the offences committed from time to time by Jews (cf. Rom. 2:22). **38.** ' Proconsuls ' does not mean that there was more than one provincial governor, but that the proconsular courts were available. **39.** ' Assembly ' : i.e. in the regular course of the assembly's formal meetings. **40.** The clerk is afraid that the Roman authority will punish such disturbances, perhaps by abolishing the limited autonomy enjoyed by the city of Ephesus. **41.** The assembly is formally dismissed as though it had been a regular meeting. Paul has again been vindicated by the authorities after riots had been stirred up by his enemies in a Gentile city.

XX 1-6 Paul's Visit to Greece and the Beginning d
of the Journey to Jerusalem—**1.** Luke makes it clear that Paul's departure was in fulfilment of plans made under divine guidance before the riot (19:21) and not as a result of it. The narrative is extremely abbreviated. ' Exhorted ' : i.e. Paul preached to the brethren so as to strengthen and encourage them ; cf. 15:32 etc.). **2.** Paul is concerned to strengthen and build up his churches in Macedonia. ' Greece ' occurs only here in the NT. In fact Paul travelled to Corinth, having met Titus in Macedonia (2 C. 2:12, 7:6ff.). **3.** During the ' three months ' Paul probably wrote the Epistle to the Romans (cf. Rom. 15:23–33) and may have conducted or organised, either from Corinth or, on his way thither, from Macedonia, a mission as far as Illyricum (Rom. 15:19). ' Plot '. Paul's Jewish enemies planned to kill him on the voyage, or perhaps at Cenchreae when he embarked. The suggestion that he had planned to sail on a ship conveying Jews from Corinth to the Passover at Jerusalem seems probable ; possibly they intended also to steal the collection for the Christians at Jerusalem which, as we know from the Epistles (cf. 24:17) he was carrying on this journey. He therefore returned by land. The Western text misunderstands the situation, not connecting the plot with the decision to abandon the direct voyage, and ascribing this decision
to a revelation by the Spirit. **4.** The text is confused, e
Luke not having made it clear who went with Paul ; scribes have accordingly tried to clarify the matter, without success. The Western text, with other support, reads ' accompanied him as far as Asia ', probably supposing that Paul's seven companions went with him only as far as Troas. ' Sopater ' is perhaps identical with the Sosipater of Rom. 16:21. These companions are evidently (to judge from the Epistles) representatives of the churches bringing their contribution to the collection for the Jerusalem Christians. ' Aristarchus ', already mentioned as a Macedonian (19:29), has an unknown fellow delegate, Secundus. Timothy and Gaius belong to Lystra and Derbe respectively (but see note on 19:29). Tychicus and

797e Trophimus are really Ephesians, as the Western text here describes them (cf. 21:28–9). No mention is made of Corinth or Philippi. It has been conjectured that Paul himself represented the former and Luke the latter ; but this is improbable (contrast 1 C. 16:3ff.). Luke may have reduced the number to seven, seeing a parallel between the financial assistants of Paul, chosen by the Gentile churches, and the Seven of 6:1ff., chosen by the Jerusalem church as financial assistants to the Twelve. Against this is the fact that Luke says virtually nothing about the collection except by inference in 24:17, and we should not know the reason for the presence of these seven men with Paul

f if we had not the evidence of the Epistles. **5.** The first-person diary is resumed here (see 16:17). It is not clear how many of the party went on in advance. If all the seven with Paul, then ' we ' must refer to the diarist and others, but not Paul. Yet elsewhere the diarist always means by ' we ', ' Paul and I (and others)'. It would be strange, too, if Paul did not visit Philippi. ' Accompanied him ' (4) indicates that the whole party of seven did not go on, leaving Paul and the diarist behind. Probably the two Asian representatives went on to make travel arrangements. **6.** Paul presumably kept the Passover at Philippi. ' Five days ': contrast 16:11.

g **7-12 The Raising of Eutychus**—' First day '. Sunday is already observed (cf. 1 C. 16:2 ; Rev. 1:10). In Luke's ' telescoped ' narrative the foundation of a church at Troas has not been mentioned. ' Break bread '. It is not clear whether this was the Eucharist alone (with a discourse), or whether a common meal (agape) preceded it. Like the Last Supper it is held in an upper room. **8.** Possibly the lights are mentioned in order to refute, in passing, malicious rumours that Christians held orgies in the dark ; but such rumours had probably scarcely arisen so early as the time of Luke. More probably Luke wants simply to explain that the smoky and hot atmosphere sent Eutychus to sleep. The Western text reads ' small windows ' for ' lights ', but this does not harmonise with the ' window ' of 9, and does not explain either why Eutychus went to sleep or how he came to fall out. **10.** ' Bent over him ': literally ' fell upon him '. This great miracle of raising from the dead, corresponding to the raising of Dorcas by Peter, is closely parallel to the raisings performed by Elijah and Elisha (1 Kg. 17:21 ; 2 Kg. 4:34–6). ' Be alarmed ': literally ' make a disturbance ' ; cf. Mk 5:39, which Luke reproduces here rather than in Lk. 8:52. ' His life is in him ' does not, of course, mean that Eutychus had not died, but echoes 1 Kg. 17:23. **11.** ' Broken bread ', referring not to Paul alone, but to the congregation's Eucharist which had been preceded by the sermon. It is not clear whether ' daybreak ' means Sunday or Monday morning. Luke seems generally to use Greco-Roman reckoning, and to think of the day as extending from dawn to dusk rather than sunset to sunset. Hence he probably means that the meeting began on Sunday evening.

h **13-17 Journey from Troas to Miletus**—**13.** Paul went directly across country to Assos, avoiding what could be a tedious voyage if the wind were contrary rounding the cape between Troas and Assos. The subsequent voyage is described baldly and concisely in the manner of a ship's log. This is a very different kind of narrative from Luke's usual highly selective story, but there is no reason why, when he wrote up the history of the mission from a theological and apologetic standpoint, he should not have used notes made by himself long before for quite different purposes. ' Samos '. The Western text adds ' and having stopped at Trogyllium ' (see RSV*n*), probably because the editor realised that from Samos to Miletus was too long for a single day's journey and supposed that they must have spent the night at the only convenient harbour, Trogyllium, north of Miletus. Ships put in for the night whenever possible. **16.** Ephesus would have been off the course. Paul was anxious to reach Jerusalem quickly, both to present his collection and also to arrive in time for Pentecost, another demonstration to the Jewish Christians of his respecta- 797

bility as a pious Jew. **17.** ' Sent to Ephesus ' implies i

a considerable wait at Miletus. ' Elders ' : cf. 14:23. The *presbyteroi*, who are the senior and leading members of the Ephesian church, are addressed (28 below) as *episcopoi* (' overseers '). The two terms are clearly synonymous here. Possibly the former was more generally used in Jewish-Christian circles, being derived from the synagogue (cf. James's elders at Jerusalem, 11:30 etc.), and the latter among Gentiles (cf. Phil. 1:1). More probably, the term ' elder ' denotes the status in the community (as a senior and responsible person, a convert of relatively long standing) of a man appointed as a minister in a local church, and the term ' overseer ' or ' bishop ' denotes the function which such a person is appointed to perform : the direction and oversight of the worship, teaching, discipline, finance and social work (care of the sick and poor, etc.) in the local church. It is not certain that all ' elders ' invariably exercised the active function of ' oversight ' : 1 Tim. 5:17 may suggest that they did not ; but there can be no doubt that until the rise of ' monarchical episcopacy ' all ' overseers ' were ' elders ', and in this passage the Ephesian ' elders ' are all ' overseers '.

18-35 Speech to the Ephesian Elders—This is the j

only speech in Ac. in which Paul addresses Christians. It is a sample of the strengthening and encouraging exhortation (*paraclēsis*) so often mentioned (see note on 1 above), though here there is the special theme of farewell. This is the last message of Paul, on his way to probable martyrdom, to his principal Gentile church. It is a strongly defensive speech, suggesting that, even if opposition to him had not in fact developed at Ephesus, making it necessary for Paul to make an *apologia* to the elders, Luke, at least, is concerned to give his readers a defence of his hero against all possible detractors of his memory, perhaps some who misused his name to promote antinomian heresy. It is to some extent based on 1 Sam. 12:3ff. The speech refers, first, to Paul's first arrival at Ephesus. **19.** ' Serving the Lord ' : a Pauline phrase, common in the Epistles ; cf. also Lk. 16:13. The noun ' servant (of God) ' occurs in Lk. 2:29, 17:10 ; Ac. 4:29, 16:17. ' Plots ' probably refers to the general character of Paul's life rather than to particular events at Ephesus. **20.** This probably means only that Paul openly declared everything that was essential to the gospel, not that he was believed, either in his own day or at the time when Luke wrote, to have kept some teaching secret. **21.** His gospel was a message of repentance, and faith in Jesus as Lord and Messiah. This was

what was chiefly signified in baptism. **22.** ' I am k

going to Jerusalem ' : cf. Mk 10:33, perhaps reproduced here after being omitted at Lk. 13:22ff. ' Bound in the Spirit '. The journey is performed under the direct compulsion of the Spirit's guidance. **23.** The Spirit, presumably testifying through prophets, warned Paul to expect imprisonment. Luke may already have Agabus (21:11) in mind ; but Agabus's prophecy may only be typical of warnings such as had already been given to Paul. **24.** The Greek is difficult ; it seems to mean, ' I do not take any account of my life as precious to myself '. ' Accomplish my course ' : cf. 2 Tim. 4:7, which is probably derived from this speech. ' Grace of God '. Paul's mission is to testify to the gospel, here described in thoroughly Pauline terms. **25.** This gospel is equivalent to the preaching of the Kingdom, i.e. the future reign of God made present in Christ. ' No more '. Luke evidently knew of no return of Paul to Asia. If Paul did revisit Ephesus after being released from Rome, as the Pastoral Epistles would suggest, Luke must have written Ac. before that happened. It is much more probable that this was really Paul's last visit to these people. **26.** Paul has preached the whole gospel of judgment and salvation, and so he escapes the con-

797k demnation of the ineffective prophet (Ezek. 3:18, 20).
l **28.** Now that the apostle will no longer be able to guide his churches, the local ministers must bear the responsibility for maintaining the faith against the false teachers whom Paul foresees. They have the pastoral oversight of the community, like the 'shepherds' of Israel (Ezek. 34; Zech. 10:2–3, 11:4–17); cf. Jn 21:15ff.; 1 Pet. 5:2. 'Guardians' ('overseers' or 'bishops'): see note on 17 above. The Holy Spirit guides and inspires the Church in the appointment of ministers, as in all other aspects of the mission. 'Church of the Lord'. The Alexandrian MSS for the most part read 'of God'. This is probably right. 'His own blood' should probably be translated (as RSV*n*) 'the blood of his Own'. The misrendering of this as 'his own blood' probably led the Western text and a number of other MSS to alter 'God' to 'the Lord'. 'Obtained'. The corresponding noun is used of God's 'acquisition' of Israel as his own people (cf. Eph. 1:14; 1 Pet. 2:9). Through the death of Christ the Christian Church has been made the covenant people, the community which is the peculiar possession of God. The word does not mean that God 'purchased' the Church at the price of Christ's blood (as a ransom paid to the devil, or to God's own justice). The Greek means '*through* the blood', and there is an allusion here to the covenant sacrifice of Sinai (Exod. 24:8). The thought that Christ's death corresponds to the sacrifice with which the old covenant was inaugurated is much more Pauline than Lucan. Luke does not use sacrificial language about Christ's blood except in the longer text of the narrative of the Last Supper, which is probably not authentic (see note on
798a Lk. 22:20). **29.** 'Departure'. The Greek more commonly means 'arrival', but there is some classical and Hellenistic evidence for the opposite sense. Here it refers to Paul's death. 'Fierce wolves'. False teachers (cf. Mt. 7:15) are often so called in 2nd-cent. literature. Luke depicts Paul as prophesying the advent of false teachers and heretical Christians. The rise of Gnostic or quasi-Gnostic beliefs, such as were prevalent at Colossae, is probably indicated. **31.** 'Be alert': cf. Mk 13:35, 37; Lk. 12:37; 1 Pet. 5:8, which may allude to catechetical instruction under this heading, given to candidates for baptism. 'Three years': cf. 19:8, 10, 22. **32.** Paul commends his hearers to God (Codex Vaticanus and other MSS read 'the Lord') and to the gospel of God's unmerited favour to man. 'Build up': i.e. build up the Church now and give its members the future inheritance which belongs to those who have been made God's holy people (cf. Eph. 1:14, 18; Col. 3:24; 1 Pet. 1:4). Apart from 26:18 (in a speech also assigned to Paul) there is no parallel to this language in Lk.; but it is certainly, though not exclusively, Pauline. **33.** Paul's insistence on working to maintain himself and to avoid being a burden to his converts is dramatically introduced in language reminiscent of 1 Sam. 12:3–4. **34.** There is a typically rhetorical touch in 'these hands'. **35.** Just as the other speeches in Ac. end with an appeal to an OT text, so Paul's farewell ends with a saying of Jesus. It may well be authentic, but it is not recorded in the Gospels. Luke may have known it through oral tradition but decided not to use it in his Gospel, or he may have found it in material which he used for this speech (possibly an actual summary of what Paul said). There is a parallel in 1 Clement 2:1.
b **36-38 The Elders' Farewell to Paul**—**36.** Prayer follows Paul's address. **37.** cf. Gen. 33:4.
XXI 1-6 Journey to Tyre—**1.** The diarist continues his 'log'. Cos, Rhodes and Patara (in SW. Lycia) may be the daily stages of the voyage. The Western text, with the Vienna papyrus P[41], adds 'and Myra', probably because it was supposed that a change of ships must have been made there as it was on the voyage to Rome (27:5). Myra was a better-known port. There is no reason to suppose that this reading is more than one of the many over-clever conjectures of the Western editor. To go on to Myra in one day's 798b
sailing from Rhodes would not be possible. **2.** By changing ships they were able to get a direct passage across the open sea to Tyre, passing south of Cyprus. This voyage would require a large and fast vessel. The ship was due to terminate the voyage at Tyre and unload. **4.** 'Disciples'. The foundation of a church at Tyre has not been mentioned, but cf. 11:19. 'Through the Spirit'. These disciples seem to have prophesied collectively. Their warning is an example of what Paul had mentioned at Miletus (20:23), but Luke can hardly mean that the Spirit was actually telling Paul not to go to Jerusalem; he believed that he was 'bound in the Spirit' to go there (20:22). Rather, the prophets give warning that in going there he will find trouble awaiting him. **5.** cf. 20:36–7.
7-14 Journey to Caesarea. Prophecy of Agabus c
—**7.** 'Finished': literally 'continued'. Ptolemais (Acre) is about 27 miles south of Tyre. Here, too, there was a church. **8.** They probably came to Caesarea by sea. Philip was last mentioned at Caesarea (8:40). 'Evangelist' seems to denote any preacher of the gospel. Here it distinguishes this Philip from his namesake, one of the Twelve, with whom Eusebius (HE III, xxxi, 3, V, vii, 3) confuses him. **9.** 'Prophesied': i.e. had the gift of prophecy; perhaps cf. 2:17 (Jl 2:28f.). Though no mention is made of them prophesying on this occasion, Luke reminds the reader that Paul's journey to Jerusalem was accompanied throughout by prophesyings. **10.** Luke reproduces the 'diary' here without troubling to link its reference to Agabus with what he has already recorded about him in 11:28. So also with Philip. 'Judaea': always for Luke the 'land of the Jews', not simply the province. Hence Gentile Caesarea is not included in it, although it was the seat of the administration of the province. **11.** Christian prophets seem usually to have been concerned with pointing to the fulfilment of OT prophecy in Christ and so preaching Christ from the scriptures; also with exhorting and encouraging the believers. Agabus stands much nearer the ancient Hebrew prophetic tradition. He employs prophetic symbolism, in the manner of Isaiah (20:2), Jeremiah (13:1ff.) and Ezekiel (4:1ff.), to declare the purpose of God for the future. The sign is integrally related to the fulfilment. The future act of God is made present, and the prophet's action is an efficacious sign of God's revealed will, accompanied as it is by God's word spoken through the prophet. 'Thus says the Holy Spirit' corresponds to the Hebrew prophets' 'Thus says the Lord'. Paul's fate is to resemble that of Jesus; the Jews are to bind him and hand him over to the Gentiles (cf. 28:17). **13.** Jerusalem is likely to prove the place of death as for Jesus. There is a close parallel with the journey of Jesus to Jerusalem. 'To die . . . for the name': cf. 5:41; 1 Pet. 4:14. This has almost become a technical term for martyrdom. **14.** 'Will of the Lord': cf. Lk. 22:42. God's will is to triumph through suffering.
16-25 Arrival at Jerusalem. Interview and d
Agreement with James—**16.** Mnason was apparently Paul's host in Jerusalem. The wording of this verse does not mean that he entertained the party somewhere between Caesarea and Jerusalem. 'Early': i.e. original. Mnason was presumably a member of the Jerusalem church from its early days, like his fellow Cypriot Barnabas. **17.** 'Brethren'. Probably the Christians in general, possibly the Hellenist group in particular, such as Mnason and his friends. **18.** James and the elders are now the governing body of the Jerusalem church. The 'we' passage ends here. **19.** Paul reports on his ministry among the Gentiles. **20.** 'Glorified God'. Luke pictures the Jewish Christians as willing to accept the Gentile mission with thankfulness, but at the same time urging Paul to remember the strength and zeal of the Jewish-Christian community. Paul's work must not be allowed to upset them; hence the need for some spectacular demonstra-

798d tion that the reports about him are false and that he is a pious devotee of the Law. 'Thousands'. The figure is not meant literally, but it indicates the great success of the mission in Judaea. It was by no means clear that the future of the Church lay in the Gentile lands. **21.** 'Told'. The word probably means '(officially) informed', presumably by Diaspora Jews visiting Jerusalem. Paul is certainly not represented by Luke as acting in the manner alleged of him, as the circumcision of Timothy shows. **22.** Despite the 'glorifying of God', James and the elders are not prepared to risk any trouble with their Jewish-Christian disciples. In fact, when the disturbance arose it was caused by Diaspora Jews, not Jewish Christians (27). **23.** There are four Christians in Jerusalem under a temporary Nazirite vow. This was discharged, at the end of the period for which it was taken, by the shaving of the head and the offering of prescribed sacrifices. Paul is asked to pay the expenses of the sacrifices, and to 'purify himself' with them. This probably meant that he should undertake a ritual purification from the uncleanness contracted by his sojourning among Gentiles, a process which involved a cleansing on the seventh day (cf. Num. 19:12). This would prove to the 'zealots for the Law' (20) both that he was ready to do a good work, commended to pious Jews, in assisting the Nazirites, and also that he recognised the impurity of the Gentile world and was ready to conform to the ritual practices of Jewish piety in order to avoid offence to strict legalists. It is an extraordinary action for the Paul of the Epistles to perform; but it is not wholly incredible (cf. 1 C. 9:19f.), if his reception by James, and probably the acceptance of the offerings of the Gentile churches, depended on it. **25.** James recites the provisions of the decree of the council (15:20), possibly as though Paul had not heard of them, more probably in order to remind Luke's readers that, although Paul was pressed to conciliate Jewish-Christian opinion on this occasion, James had himself agreed that Gentile converts should not be subjected to the Law.

e **26-31 The Attempted Lynching of Paul in the Temple. His Rescue by the Tribune**—**26.** Paul arranges for the sacrifices to be offered when his seven days of purification have ended. **27.** 'Jews from Asia': see note on 22. The Jews of the Dispersion were especially sensitive to any betrayal or weakening of the Mosaic system by which they were distinguished from their pagan neighbours. They were therefore the great opponents of Stephen and of Paul (6:10–11, 9:29). These Jews would recognise Paul from having seen him at Ephesus. **28.** Paul is accused of teaching against the Covenant people of Israel (the 'people', as so often in Luke's writings), the Law and the Temple, a similar charge to that brought against Stephen (see 6:13 and note). 'Greeks'. For Gentiles to go beyond the barrier fencing off the Court of the Gentiles from the inner parts of the Temple was a capital offence. Notices were displayed to this effect: Jos.BJ V, v, 2 etc., cf. Eph. 2:14. Their presence would make the Temple itself unclean. **30.** The mob drags Paul out of the Temple itself and presumably the Temple police or the Levites close the entrances to it from the Court of the Gentiles. It would be in that court, visible to the guards on the fortress of Antonia, that the Jews set about lynching him. **31.** The military tribune commanded the auxiliary cohort which, with a cavalry squadron, garrisoned Jerusalem. The barracks were in the fortress of Antonia, overlooking the Temple area and linked with the outer court by steps (35). **32.** To intervene in case of riots in the Temple would be part of the cohort's regular duty and could probably be put into effect rapidly. **33.** 'Two chains': probably fastened to an escort on either side as a particularly secure form of custody, but possibly binding hands and feet in fulfilment of the prophecy of Agabus (11). The tribune inquires of the crowd. **35.** Although the 'diary' has ceased, this is a vivid piece of descriptive writing. Either Luke has seen what happened or he is able to imagine and depict the riot in a most realistic fashion. The steps led from the Temple to the barracks. **36.** 'Away with him': i.e. to death, a direct echo of the cry of the Jerusalem mob at the trial of Jesus (Lk. 23:18). **37.** 'Know Greek': better, 'speak Greek'; 'know' means 'know how to speak', not 'understand'. If Paul's question were expressed in anything like the words used by Luke, the tribune might well be surprised at being addressed in idiomatic and polite Greek by a supposed bandit chief. 'Egyptian'. An Egyptian false prophet is mentioned in Jos. Ant. XX, viii, 6, BJ II, xiii, 4. He led a large crowd (Josephus says 30,000, probably an error for 4,000—Δ = 4, Λ = 30) of terrorists to the mount of Olives, claiming that the walls of Jerusalem would collapse before them. This revolt was smashed by the procurator, Felix. Jos.BJ II, xiii, 5 says that the Egyptian led his men *out of* the desert; but in the same context Josephus mentions 'deceivers' who led their followers *into* the desert. This is another passage (cf. 5:36–7; Lk. 3:1) which might suggest that Luke depended on, and had misread, Josephus; but it does not necessarily do so, for rebel leaders usually made for the desert and it is likely that the Egyptian led his forces out and assembled them in the desert before marching on Jerusalem. 'Assassins': i.e. *Sicarii* ('dagger men'), armed terrorists. **39.** 'Jew': i.e. not an Egyptian, and one who had good reason to be in the Temple. 'Citizen of no mean city'. There is a play on the Greek words in which Paul expresses his pride in his Hellenistic inheritance, using distinguished literary Greek. The reference is to citizenship of Tarsus, not of Rome. **40.** 'Motioned': the orator's gesture (cf. 13:16, 26:1). 'Hebrew': i.e. probably Aramaic.

XXII 1-21 Paul's Speech to the Jerusalem Mob f
—**1.** The opening address is identical with that of Stephen's speech (7:2). 'Fathers' is more appropriate to a defence before the Sanhedrin; but perhaps Luke thinks of this as an apologia to Israel as such rather than actual words addressed to the mob. **2.** The address is in the people's own tongue. The whole purpose of the speech is to show that Paul was a zealous Jew who was converted by the Lord himself and supernaturally commissioned by him to go to the Gentiles. **3.** 'I am a Jew' is the key-note of the speech. It was as a loyal Jew, not an apostate, that he had entered upon the Gentile mission. 'In this city'. Although Paul came from Tarsus, great stress is laid upon his intimate connection with Jerusalem from his childhood. A similar biography in outline—'born', 'brought up', 'educated'—is given for Moses in 7:20–1. 'Gamaliel': see 5:34. 'At the feet': of a pupil 'sitting under' a teacher: cf. Lk. 10:39. 'Strict manner': i.e. as a Pharisee. 'Zealous for God', as a persecutor of Christians; cf. Gal. 1:14. The Vulgate reads 'zealous for the Law'. **4.** 'This Way': see note on 9:2. 'To the death'. Luke enlarges on his previous narrative in 8:2. **5.** 'Council': i.e. the Sanhedrin. **6ff.** The story of Paul's conversion is repeated in order to emphasise its crucial importance, as was also the story of Peter's vision and his visit to Cornelius. Minor variations lessen the tedium of this method. One of these is the mention of 'noon'. This implies that the appearance of the risen Lord was not an ordinary vision in the night. There may possibly be an allusion to Dt. 28:28–9. **7.** 'Of Nazareth' is added in this account. **9.** Another minor variant: in 9:7 Paul's companions hear a voice but see no-one. **12.** It is part of the argument to represent Ananias (in 9:10 merely a 'disciple') as a devout Jew in very good repute with the Damascus Jews. Paul, the zealous Pharisee, was given the assurance of God's new commission by an irreproachable devotee of the Law. **14.** It was the God of the patriarchs who ordained Paul's conversion, which was entirely in accordance with the true traditions of Israel and God's purposes for his people. 'Just One':

798f see 3:14 and 7:52. **15.** cf. 1:8. Paul's commission is like that of the original apostles. He will be a witness of the risen Lord. **16.** cf. 2:38. Baptism is in the name of Jesus in the sense that the baptised person acknowledges him as Lord (cf. 2:21) and is for remission of sins. **17.** This vision was not recorded in ch. 9. Paul's departure from Jerusalem is expressly commanded by the Lord in person because the Jews will reject his message and he consequently has a mission to perform to the Gentiles. The Lord reveals this commission to Paul in the Temple itself. Since it was at the heart of Israel's religion that Paul was ordered to undertake the Gentile mission, there could be no question of it involving apostasy. 'Trance': as when Peter was divinely instructed to go to Gentiles (10:10, 11:5). **18.** As always, the Gentile mission follows on the rejection of the gospel by the Jews. **19.** Paul's record as a persecuting zealot ought to have commended him to the Jews. **20.** 'Witness'. The word *martys* is beginning to acquire the particular meaning of a witness unto death. **21.** The Gentile mission is directly and explicitly ordered by the Lord.

g **22-29 Fury of the Mob. The Tribune is about to have Paul tortured, but learns that he is a Roman Citizen**—**22.** The mob's fury breaks out at the idea of a religious equality between Jews and Gentiles. 'Away with': cf. 21:36. **23.** 'Waved . . . and threw dust'. See Additional Note, 'Dust and Garments' (*Beginnings of Christianity*, v, 269ff.). Probably this is a spontaneous gesture of loathing and abomination, with no kind of formal or 'ritual' significance. **24.** The tribune, not fully convinced by his conversation with Paul (21:37–9), is evidently frightened by the fury of the mob and proceeds to put him to the torture by flogging in order to extort the truth from him. **25.** 'With the thongs'. Probably better rendered 'for the lash'. Here Paul claims the privileges of a Roman citizen under the *Lex Porcia* and the *Lex Julia* which prohibited the flogging of a citizen, at least as a mode of 'interrogation' or without formal sentence (cf. 'uncondemned', 25, 16:37). Little is known of the exact extent of a citizen's privileges in the provinces, or of how a claim to possess citizenship was verified. **28.** The tribune's citizenship, purchased at a high price, serves by contrast to emphasise Paul's status. The Western text reads 'I know for how large a sum I bought . . .' This is probably an attempt to tidy up Luke's rather elliptical Greek, and it is unlikely that it means 'I know *I* paid a great deal . . . (and you do not look the sort of person who could pay much)'.

h **30 Paul is released and brought before the Sanhedrin**—The tribune's object is to discover why Paul had provoked a riot among the Jews. It is impossible to say whether a relatively junior officer, acting for an absent procurator, could in fact order the Sanhedrin to meet in this way; but it need not be assumed that Luke's picture of the events is incorrect.

799a **XXIII 1-10 Paul's Appearance before the Sanhedrin**—The meeting dissolves in disorder. The purpose of Paul's address to the Sanhedrin is to demonstrate that Christianity is continuous with the best traditions of Judaism. In his Christian faith Paul is not a traitor to Pharisaism; on the contrary, that faith is the fulfilment of the messianic hope and of the beliefs of his native Pharisaism about the resurrection of the dead. **1.** 'Lived': literally 'conducted myself'. 'Good conscience': cf. 24:16; 1 Tim. 1:5, 19; 1 Pet. 3:16, 21, etc. Paul has no consciousness that his conversion has meant a breach of his religious duty as a Pharisee. Contrast Phil. 3:7–9. **2.** On Ananias see Jos. Ant. XX, ix, 1–2, BJ II, xvii, 6, 9. He was murdered by terrorists at the beginning of the Jewish War. The high priest represents Sadducee Judaism, with which Christianity has nothing in common. Paul's faith is a fulfilment of Pharisaism; but the Sadducee priesthood has had its day, and has no further place in God's purposes for his people. Ananias is represented as a caricature of a true high 799a
priest: a thug on the judge's bench. cf. Jn 18:22, which is clearly related to this passage; possibly the Fourth Evangelist had read Lk.-Ac. Paul's answer is not impossible in the light of 1 C. 4:12: indeed, it is in character; cf. Paul's outbursts of fury in Gal. 5:12; Phil. 3:2, etc. 'Smite'. This is not a mere imprecation, but a prophecy, which Luke probably regarded as fulfilled by the murder of Ananias (see above). 'Whitewashed wall'. Perhaps a common term of abuse: cf. Mt. 23:27. The point is the high priest's hypocrisy; his true character is masked by an outward show of sanctity. 'Contrary to the law'. Perhaps a reference to Lev. 19:15. **5.** Paul is deeply ironical; he will not recognise a high priest in Ananias. If the latter were in any real sense a high priest, Paul, as a devout observer of the Law, would never have dreamed of insulting him. Paul quotes Exod. 22:28. An odd interpretation of Paul's words, taking them excessively literally, has made them the basis of a theory that he suffered from bad eyesight. **6.** The attempt to play off Pharisees against Sadducees is by no means historically impossible; it serves, for Luke, to remind the reader that the best kind of Judaism was by no means wholly opposed to the fundamental Christian beliefs. Paul's claim to have been a Pharisee is borne out by Phil. 3:5, but here the point of his argument is that as a Christian he claims *still* to be a Pharisee. 'Hope': probably not the hope of resurrection, but the messianic hope. In claiming that Jesus was Messiah and that he rose from the dead, Paul is fulfilling the Pharisaic expectation of a messiah and belief in resurrection. **8.** The Sadducees denied resurrection (cf. Lk. 20:27) and hence (although this point is not mentioned elsewhere) a man's 'spirit' or 'angel' (cf. 12:15). 'Angel' cannot here mean 'angel of the Lord', nor, of course, does 'spirit' mean the Spirit of God, for both are prominent in the written Law, which the Sadducees accepted. 'All'; literally 'both', which is correct, assuming that 'spirit' and 'angel' are synonymous. **9.** cf. Pilate's acquittal of Jesus. The Pharisaic scribes admit the possibility that a 'departed spirit' (of Jesus) may have spoken to Paul. **10.** This violent uproar explains why Paul would not, for the future, submit to Jewish jurisdiction. The court nearly became the scene of a lynching. The rescue of Paul by Romans from the fury of the Sanhedrin is to be the prelude to his journey to Rome.

11 Paul's Vision of the Lord—This fury of the Jews b
and Paul's rescue by the Romans is, as the vision tells him, to be the means by which he will be led to the more promising task of witnessing to the gospel at Rome, now that Jerusalem has finally rejected it. The proceedings in the procurator's court are to be overruled by divine providence.

12-22 The Jewish Plot—**12.** The Jews' plot to kill c
Paul is a dramatic indication that he can hope for no justice at their hands. **14.** The vow is a most strict one: they will taste nothing until Paul is dead. A bogus reassembly of the Sanhedrin is the pretext for getting Paul out of the fortress of Antonia. **16.** Paul's nephew may have been a young member of the Sanhedrin, and so have known of the plot. The fact that he could talk privately with Paul indicates that the tribune was keeping him only in a kind of open arrest, and Paul's peremptory order to a centurion suggests that he was in high favour with the tribune. **20.** 'They were going to inquire'. Codex Vaticanus reads 'you were going', which is scarcely possible in the context. **21.** 'Promise': perhaps better 'consent'.

23-35 Paul is escorted to Caesarea and handed d
over to the Procurator—**23.** 'Third hour': 9 p.m. 'Spearmen': a word that does not recur until several centuries later, apparently meaning 'light-armed troops'. Codex Alexandrinus reads 'slingers', perhaps rightly. The enormous size of this escort is not necessarily incorrect. The disturbed state of the country might well necessitate the use of overwhelming force

799d if Paul was to be conveyed safely out of Jerusalem by night and down to Caesarea. **24.** Felix, the brother of Claudius's freedman and minister Pallas, was procurator from 52 probably to 59. **25.** 'To this effect'. Neither Luke nor Paul would have been likely to see the letter. Luke gives the gist of what must have been said, putting it in proper epistolary form. Its purpose is again to show that, from the point of view of the Roman authorities, Paul is perfectly innocent. **26.** 'Excellency': see note on Lk. 1:3. **27.** The blame for Paul's plight is put squarely on the Jews. **29.** 'Their law'. The tribune's view of Paul is identical with that of Gallio. **30.** A piece of new information is given to the reader: that the Jewish accusers had been enjoined to apply to the governor. **31.** 'Antipatris'. From here the route lay through mainly Gentile territory. The main escort was therefore no longer needed. **34.** Felix's question may imply that he had thoughts of remitting Paul to the jurisdiction of the governor of his home province; cf. Lk. 23:6. **35.** Herod's *praetorium* was the palace of Herod the Great, now the governor's headquarters.

e **XXIV 1-9 The Accusation of Paul before Felix**—**1.** The Jewish delegation, led by the high priest in person, comes to present the case against Paul through a professional pleader. Tertullus's speech begins in the customary way with a *captatio benevolentiae.* Its language is conventional, and has been influenced by 2 Mac. 4:6; but Felix did in fact take strong measures to suppress terrorism and establish peaceful conditions. 'Most Excellent': see 23:26; Lk. 1:3. **4.** 'Detain'. The cognate adjective means 'weary' (Job 19:2; Isa. 43:23, LXX), and the verb here probably means 'tire'. The language is a good reproduction of the stilted formal style of the professional rhetorician. **5.** The charge is that Paul is a general disturber of the peace, stirring up trouble among the Jewish population throughout the world, and a leader of the Nazarene sect. This is the general accusation, making Paul out to be a danger to the public peace. The particular charge of trying to profane the Temple is a concrete instance of his 'pestilential' conduct. The word used for 'profane' is the normal Greek term, immediately intelligible to a Gentile hearer, not the more technical word for Jewish ritual defilement. The Western text adds a passage (RSV*n*) which, as usual, explains the situation at greater length without adding anything which the reader either has not been explicitly told or cannot infer. To insert it would mean making 'him' (8) refer to Lysias, whereas it clearly denotes Paul, and would make Tertullus complain of the conduct of the tribune ('with great violence') before his superior, the governor, whose goodwill he has been trying so hard to win—a most improbable proceeding.

f **10-21 Paul's Defence before Felix**—The speech opens with another *captatio benevolentiae.* It does not imply that either Paul or Luke really dissented from Tacitus's opinion of Felix that he exercised the power of a king with the mind of a slave. Paul's object in visiting Jerusalem was that of a pious Jew: to worship (cf. 8:27). He had stirred up no disturbances; had not, in fact, spoken in public. He cannot, therefore, be proved to be a disturber of the peace. As for his religion, he is a loyal Jew, worshipping the God of his fathers according to the Way. **14.** This is represented as a sect, but Paul implies, by using the term 'Way', that it is a 'walking in the way' of righteousness within Judaism as rightly understood and interpreted. His Christian faith is in full accordance with the Law and the Prophets (cf. Lk. 24:44); **15** and its eschatological hope is shared by Pharisaic Judaism. His endeavour is, by following the Christian 'Way', to have a clear conscience as a faithful Jew. **17-18.** So far from profaning the Temple (Paul comes to the detailed accusation), he had come to bring alms and offerings to the Jewish nation, and was in the Temple in order to discharge a Nazirite vow. The 'alms and offerings' are presumably the collection undertaken in the Gentile churches (cf. Rom. 15:25ff.; 2 C. 9) as a great gesture of solidarity with the church of Jerusalem, impoverished by the early practice of sharing property and by famine. Luke's readers have not been told about this: the purpose of the journey of the various delegates (20:4) was not mentioned. Perhaps this is because, whereas to Paul this collection was of immense importance as a means of disarming the hostility of the Jerusalem church to his mission to the Gentiles, Luke has so taken the edge off the controversy as to suppose, both that the Jerusalem Christians would be satisfied by Paul's piety in undertaking the sacrifices for the Nazirites, and that Paul would be content without question to accede to their request to do this. Here the impression is given to the reader (perhaps resting on Luke's own misunderstanding of whatever he may have known about the collection) that the offerings were meant for the Temple, not for the Christian elders. **18.** 'Purified'. Paul himself had completed a ritual purification, so as not to defile the Temple. It was in this holy state, with no sign of public disturbance, that the Jews of Asia found him, and, by implication, it was they who created the tumult. If they had any charge against him it is they who should appear as his accusers; as for the high priest and his delegation, they found him guilty of no crime when he appeared before the Sanhedrin, and the only issue was the purely Jewish and religious question of belief in resurrection, on which Judaism itself was divided, and which was no concern of the Roman authority.

22-27 Felix postpones Paul's Case, and is later succeeded by Festus—**22.** 'Rather accurate knowledge'. The meaning of this phrase is doubtful, but it more probably means 'Knowing about the Way more accurately (as a result of Paul's speech)'. Felix decides to postpone judgment, but he is clearly disinclined to treat Paul as a criminal. He allows him a large measure of liberty, and the right to be visited by Christians. The result of the hearing is undoubtedly another vindication of Paul's essential innocence. **24.** Drusilla was the daughter of Herod Agrippa I and sister of Herod Agrippa II and Bernice. She had married Aziz, king of Emesa, but was enticed from him by Felix through the mediation of the Cypriot magician Atomos. Their son, another Agrippa, perished with his wife in the eruption of Vesuvius in 79 (Jos. Ant. XX, vii, 1-2). She was apparently interested in Paul and wanted to hear him. **25.** 'Justice': better 'righteousness', which, with self-control and the coming judgment, seems to have been the subject of Paul's discourse. Paul is again being presented as a pious Jew. Felix is frightened, as Herod Antipas had been of John's preaching (Mk 6:20). Felix again postpones action. **26.** He hopes for a bribe from Paul, or perhaps his relatives. Luke is careful to show that although Paul was kept in custody for two years (perhaps reckoned from his arrest), he was on good terms with the procurator. Festus succeeded Felix, but Paul remained a prisoner because Felix had not wished to offend the Jews by releasing him. g

XXV 1-5 Festus is informed about Paul—Festus goes to Jerusalem almost immediately after taking over the province. The Jewish leaders follow their previous plan, and plot to kill Paul on the way to Jerusalem. Festus insists that the trial shall take place at Caesarea, and asks leading Jews to come and prosecute Paul there. h

6-12 Trial before Festus. Paul appeals to Caesar—**6.** Festus hurries on the arrangements, and a trial is held without delay. **8.** Paul's summary of his defence is that he was innocent of any offence either against Judaism (the Law and the Temple; cf. 21:28) or against the Roman government. This is the double truth which Luke seeks to emphasise in every possible way. **9.** Festus offers the Jews a favour, and asks if Paul will stand trial at Jerusalem, but in the procurator's court, not in the Sanhedrin. Paul, however, will not go there. The Jewish charges have been proved groundless, and Paul will not submit to a trial i

799i in Jerusalem, even in the procurator's court. He appeals, as a Roman citizen, to the emperor's court. For the complex problems concerning the appeal to Caesar see H. J. Cadbury, 'Roman Law and the Trial of Paul', *Beginnings of Christianity* (Additional Note XXVI), v, 312ff. **12.** Festus consults his legal assessors and sanctions the appeal.

j **13-22 Festus consults Agrippa II**—Agrippa II was brought up at the court of Claudius, made king of Chalcis in the Lebanon region about A.D. 50, and later of the tetrarchies of Philip and Lysanias (cf. Lk. 3:1) with certain cities in Galilee and Peraea. His sister Bernice was betrothed to Marcus, the nephew of the philosopher Philo. Later she married Polemo, king of Cilicia, but left him and after A.D. 70 became the mistress of the emperor Titus. Festus seems to be genuinely puzzled by Paul's case. He seeks to interest Agrippa in it, as a Jew who had, moreover, been given the right of appointing the high priests. **15ff.** What had been only briefly indicated in 3 is now explained to the reader: the Jewish authorities had asked Festus, on his first arrival in the province, to condemn Paul. Festus had replied that to condemn a defendant in absence or without an open trial would be contrary to Roman law. He had accordingly arranged the trial at Caesarea, but the Jewish prosecutors had failed to make out a criminal case against Paul. The dispute was about their religion. **19.** The word translated 'superstition' is cognate with that which Paul used to describe the religious character of the Athenians (see 17:22 and note). The question at issue was whether Jesus was alive or dead. **20.** This is beyond the range either of the procurator's jurisdiction or his understanding. He had therefore asked Paul whether he would be tried at Jerusalem, where the Jewish authorities could be more fully represented and some light be thrown on this puzzling dispute; **21** but Paul had appealed to the emperor and was waiting in custody to be sent to Rome. Agrippa wishes to hear Paul, as Herod Antipas had wished to see Jesus (cf. Lk. 9:9, 23:8), and thus, like Jesus, Paul comes 'before governors and kings' (cf. 9:15).

800a **23-27 Paul comes before Agrippa**—**23.** Luke sets the stage for Paul's great speech of defence. Agrippa and Bernice come with royal pomp, attended by leading Gentiles of Caesarea, and the tribunes commanding the cohorts there. **24.** The picture of the 'people' shouting for Paul's death is more suggestive of the crowd at the castle steps than of the Jewish leaders with whom Festus had had to do. **25.** 'I found' repeats, for the benefit of Luke's readers, the procurator's conclusion that Paul was entirely innocent of any crime. This recalls Pilate's repeated acquittal of Jesus (cf. Lk. 23:22). **26.** Festus does not know how to frame his report to the emperor. 'Lord' is here an early instance (if it does not belong to Luke's time, rather than that of Festus) of the absolute use of *kyrios* to denote the emperor. Festus hopes to receive advice from Agrippa about this strange case, though it seems unlikely that there could, in fact, be any question of sending a prisoner without an accompanying dossier.

b **XXVI 1-23 Paul's Defence before Agrippa**—Agrippa now presides. Paul uses the normal gesture of the orator. An expansion of the text in the Harklean Syriac margin, probably representing the Western text, says that Paul spoke with boldness and with the 'advocacy' or 'encouragement' (*paraclēsis*) of the Holy Spirit. **2.** The speech opens with a conventional *captatio benevolentiae.* It begins in a good rhetorical style, but the syntax of the sentence breaks down. **3.** Paul intends to deal with the question of his attitude to Judaism, not with those criminal charges of which Festus had decided that he was innocent. Agrippa is expert in Jewish customs and controversies, and will understand. **4.** Paul's way of life, as a Jew and at Jerusalem ('nation' means the Jews, not the province of Cilicia), is generally known. **5.** The Jews have known 'for a long time past' (the Greek word occurs also at Lk. 1:3) that he belongs to the strictest school of Judaism, the Pharisee party (cf. 22:3). **6.** He is on trial, not because he has apostatised, but precisely because, as a loyal Pharisee, he rests his hope in the promise of God to Israel, i.e. the messianic hope and the hope of resurrection (which are brought together into one by their fulfilment in Christ). **7.** The idea of the deep piety of the whole Jewish nation, awaiting the fulfilment of God's promise, is well conveyed by the 'solemn' language of the 'twelve tribes' earnestly worshipping by night and day. It is therefore patently absurd that Paul should be accused by Jews. **8.** The Jews deny the resurrection of Jesus, but without good reason, since they believe in a general resurrection. **9.** Even Paul himself had done this (though he does not explain why), and had opposed the name of Jesus of Nazareth. **10.** He had persecuted the saints in Jerusalem, i.e. the holy people of God, the true Israelites. Paul's own part in the persecution, passed over very briefly in 8:3, is now described in more detail. **11.** Paul had tried to make Christians blaspheme Christ, as was done by later persecutors (cf. Pliny, *ep.* 10:96, *Mart. Polycarp.* 9:3), and perhaps by 'unofficial' enemies of Paul's own converts at Corinth (cf. 1 C. 12:3). His fury (cf. 8:3) urged him to extend the persecution to cities outside Judaea. **13.** This repetition of the story of Paul's conversion includes a more vivid account of the brilliance of the light from heaven, and a heightening of the effect: **14** all the party, not only Paul as in 9:4, fall to the ground. It is explicitly stated that Paul heard the voice in Aramaic, as was hinted in the use of the Aramaic form of 'Saul' in 9:4 and 22:7. 'It hurts you to kick . . .' is a Greek proverb, meaning that resistance is useless: 'you have met your master'. This thought is similarly expressed in classical literature, notably in Euripides, *Bacchae,* 794–5. It is more likely that Luke knew it as a widely quoted proverb than as a literary citation. There is no evidence for such a saying in Aramaic. Ananias is not mentioned here. The events are telescoped in order to make the essential point: that Paul, the devout Pharisee, was directly commissioned in a theophany, to which he could not be disobedient, to go to the Gentiles in the character of the 'Servant', and convert them, in accordance with Israel's hope, to the God of Israel. **16.** 'Stand upon your feet' echoes the commissioning of Ezekiel for his mission to Israel (Ezek. 2:3). The glorified Jesus has appeared in order to appoint Paul as a 'minister' and 'witness' to himself, i.e. to be an apostle (though Luke keeps this title, in its full sense, for the Twelve) or an 'eyewitness and minister of the word' (Lk. 1:2). **17-18.** Paul's mission is to the c
people of Israel and the Gentiles, like that of the Servant who was sent 'as a covenant to the people, a light to the nations, to open the eyes that are blind' and through whom God promised to 'turn them from darkness into light' (Isa. 42:7, 16). The conversion of the Gentiles is, first, from Satan's power to God. This is the conversion of the Gentiles prophesied in the OT, especially by the Second Isaiah. Secondly, it brings to them the forgiveness of sins which is the content, or effect, of the kingdom inaugurated by Christ (cf. Lk. 24:47; Ac. 1:6–8), and a 'lot' (like that of the covenant people) among those who are made God's holy people through faith in Jesus. **19.** Paul's response was to preach in Jerusalem, Judaea and the Gentile lands the repentance, accompanied by 'works worthy of repentance', from which no pious Jew could withhold approval (cf. Lk. 3:8). **21.** Yet it was for this that the Jews had actually tried to kill him within the Temple itself. So, with God's help, Paul continues to testify to what is no more than the fulfilment promised by the OT, that the Messiah must suffer (cf. 2:23; Lk. 24:25–6; nothing is said of the inner significance of Christ's death, but only that the apparent scandal of a crucified Messiah was willed by God), and that he, through being the first-fruits of the resurrection, would bring light, as being himself the

800c Servant, to Israel and the Gentiles (cf. Lk. 2:32). It has been suggested that the 'headings' of the preaching: 'That the Messiah must suffer', 'That, by being the first to rise, . . .' represent the heads under which an early collection of scriptural testimonies may have been drawn up. This is quite possible, though not necessarily the case.

801a **24-29 The Reaction of Festus; Paul's Personal Address to Agrippa—24.** Festus thinks that Paul is out of his mind. He cannot treat the idea of resurrection seriously; accordingly, he interrupts the discourse, which, like so many Lucan speeches, is dramatically broken off by an outburst from the audience as soon as it has reached its climax. Festus probably thinks, quite genuinely, that Paul's great learning in the Jewish scriptures has turned his head. **26.** Paul appeals to Agrippa, who understands these things (i.e. the resurrection of Jesus and the ensuing mission), since they have not happened in secret. 'Done in a corner' is another Greek proverbial phrase. Agrippa cannot deny their significance if he really believes the prophets. **28.** Agrippa's only reply to this appeal is a rather embarrassed half-jest. The Greek means: 'You make very little business in persuading (or, 'you take a very short time to persuade') me to turn Christian' (literally 'to make a Christian'). This last phrase has many parallels in the later patristic writers: e.g. 'to make a monk', i.e. 'to turn monk'. In 1 Kg. 20:7 (LXX) Jezebel asks Ahab, 'Is this how you now make (i.e. act the part of) a king?' Some MSS, unfamiliar with the idiom, have altered the text to the more usual 'become a Christian'. **29.** Paul's reply is that whether it were quickly or slowly accomplished, he could wish all his hearers to become Christians like himself, only without his chains.

b **30-32 The Verdict of Paul's Hearers**—The distinguished audience agrees unanimously that Paul is entirely innocent, and Agrippa's advice to Festus is that if Paul had not made his appeal to Rome (which must stand) he could have been released.

c **XXVII 1-13 The Voyage from Caesarea to Crete —1.** The Western text seeks to make it clear that the author of the 'we' passage, which begins here, was not himself subject to the procurator's decision. The 'Augustan Cohort' (*Cohors Augusta I*) was in Syria in the 1st cent. A.D., and apparently in Batanea in the time of Agrippa II. See *Beginnings of Christianity*, v, 443. It has been suggested that the name means rather 'cohort of the emperor's troops' and refers to the *frumentarii* who, at least as early as Trajan's reign, formed a corps of imperial 'special agents', all of the rank of centurion, concerned, among many other things, with secret-police duties. But this is unlikely; Luke generally takes trouble to give such details correctly. **2.** The first ship belongs to Adramyttium, SE. of Troas, and is visiting the ports of the Asian coast. 'Aristarchus': cf. 19:29, 20:4; Col. 4:10; Phm. 24. **3.** 'Sidon' is a port of call. 'Friends' may have been a term for 'Christians', like 'brethren'. Luke is concerned to emphasise the friendship of the centurion for Paul. **4.** The prevailing winds in summer are westerly; hence they sail to the east of Cyprus and then follow the coast of Cilicia and Pamphylia, aided by land breezes which offset the westerly wind. **5.** 'Sailed across' does not preclude a straight course parallel with the coast after they had sailed across from eastern Cyprus to the south coast of Asia Minor. The Western text adds 'for fifteen days'. **6.** At Myra, for which a number of MSS oddly read 'Lystra', perhaps by some confusion with the first letters of 'Lycia', they change to an Alexandrian corn ship, which would have sailed so far north in order to secure a favourable northerly wind from Myra towards Sicily. **7.** They are able to proceed slowly and with difficulty towards Cnidus, whence they sail south to the eastern side of Crete and along its south coast. **8.** 'Fair Havens' is an open bay, unsuitable

d for a prolonged stay. **9.** 'The fast' is the Day of Atonement (10 Tishri), usually falling in early October.

The sailing season ended on 11 November, according 801e
to Vegetius (*De Re Militari* 4:39), who also says that navigation was considered risky after mid-September. **10-12.** Luke does not explain clearly the dispute between Paul and the captain and the owner, nor what the minority implied in 12 wanted to do. If these were the captain and the crew, as opposed to Paul and perhaps his companions, they wanted to move westwards to Phoenix and winter there. Paul presumably advised them to stay at Fair Havens, but we are explicitly told that this was not a suitable harbour (12). Paul at this stage is apparently giving an ordinary judgment on the dangers of trying to go on. He is already in a position where, although a prisoner, he is given a hearing on such matters as navigation. Phoenix looked 'southwest and northwest' according to what is probably the best translation (RSV*n*). **13.** With a south wind blowing, they were able to coast along the southern shore of Crete towards Phoenix, about thirty miles from the western end of the island.

14-26 The Storm—14. A north-east wind off the 802a
Cretan mountains caught them and blew them out to sea. They were unable to head the ship into the wind, perhaps because of the violence of the waves, and consequently they ran before it. **16.** 'Cauda' and 'Clauda' are both textually well supported. See *Beginnings of Christianity*, iv, 332 for the view that the former is the Latin and the latter the Alexandrian form. Under shelter of the island, they were able to hoist the dinghy aboard. What tackle was used for this operation is uncertain. **17.** It was then necessary to 'undergird' the ship, which probably means that the hull was strengthened against the violence of the waves by being bound together. This might be done by means of a cable stretched from bow to stern above the deck, perhaps connected at each end with ropes passed under the keel. H. J. Cadbury (*Beginnings of Christianity*, v, 345ff.) describes this method, with an illustration of an early Egyptian ship braced in this manner. But the Greek word itself suggests something fastened *under* rather than *over* the ship. Or, the bracing cables might have been stretched laterally from rib to rib across the inside of the hull below the deck. A more likely explanation may be that cables were placed lengthwise round the hull and tautened. 'Measures' is probably the right rendering of a noun which might be abstract ('assistance'), or concrete ('tackle'). They were afraid of being cast up on the Greater Syrtis, a sand-bank west of Cyrene. 'Lowered the gear'. This operation also is obscure. It might mean 'unfurling the sails' (as some MSS understood it) in order to try to sail close into the wind and avoid being driven south-westwards. This would seem to be beyond the capacity of an ancient cargo ship. More probably it means 'lowering a sea-anchor' to act as a brake and give some stability. **18.** 'Throw the cargo'. If the cargo was jettisoned now, it is hard to understand why there was another lightening of the ship and jettisoning of the grain in 38, unless the wheat was in a hold and there was some kind of deck cargo as well. The phrase is taken from Jon. 1:5, which may have influenced Luke's narrative. **19.** On the third day they threw out all spare sails and tackle, possibly also the mainmast and sail. **20.** It was impossible to check their position owing to the cloudy weather. **21ff.** Paul's speech is in the rhetorical manner. He reminds them of his previous warning (10), but encourages them with the prophecy that only the ship, and no lives, will be lost. An angel of God has appeared, telling Paul that it is God's will to bring him before Caesar, so that he cannot perish on the journey. His fellow voyagers will be saved together with him. In this speech, which in content and style is very typically Lucan, even to the 'Septuagintal' language of the angel, Paul's journey to Rome is again shown to be directly purposed and guided by God. Paul and the whole company are saved from death simply in order that he shall reach Rome. **24** implies that in fact he did come before Caesar's court. **26.**

02a Paul knows that it is within God's purpose that they will run on an island.

b **27-44 The Shipwreck**—**27.** ' Adria ' included the sea between Sicily and Crete, according to Ptolemy. **29.** Fearing that they were going to run on to rocks, they put anchors from the stern to hold the ship off. **30.** The action of the sailors is puzzling. Some commentators find it so difficult to suppose that they believed it safer to try to get to land in the dinghy in darkness than to stay on board, that they think that Luke, and perhaps Paul, misunderstood the situation ; they were really going to put out anchors from the bow. But it is by no means impossible that they lost their heads. If this was so, Paul's orders to the centurion saved the situation ; if not, Paul was responsible for the wreck. It is not clear, however, whether the cutting adrift of the dinghy was Paul's idea. It was this which made it necessary to run the ship aground. **33-4.** Paul encourages the company to take food. There is an echo of Lk. 21:18 in 34.

c **35.** The language is eucharistic, speaking of the fourfold action of taking, giving thanks, breaking and eating ; but it is probably to be understood as the regular act of ' saying grace ', common to Christians and Jews. Since they all partake, it evidently cannot be the Eucharist itself. **37.** According to most MSS the numbers present are 276, but according to Codex Vaticanus and others, ' about 76 '. The former is quite possible, but Luke has the curious habit of qualifying the figure that he quotes with the word ' about ', and this suggests that the smaller number may be right. The corruption is very easy in either case. **38.** The grain is jettisoned and it is planned to bring the ship ashore in the bay now known as St Paul's Bay. **40.** The anchors are cast off, together with the ropes with which the steering oars were fastened to them. A small foresail is hoisted on the foremast. They drive ashore and strike a shoal with deep water on either side of it, but the stern begins to break up. **43.** The centurion again shows his friendship for Paul, in saving his life. **44.** ' Planks ' may have been used as cargo hatches, or to keep the cargo from shifting. ' Pieces of the ship ' might possibly be translated ' people from the ship ', implying that some were brought ashore on the backs of swimmers ; but this would hardly be expressed so baldly, and it would be a perilous and difficult affair.

03a **XXVIII 1-6 Reception in Malta. Paul's Miraculous Escape from a Snake-bite**—**1.** ' Malta ' renders ' Melite ' in most MSS, ' Melitene ' in some (an adjectival form agreeing with ' island '), and, by confusion, ' Mytilene ' in some of the Old Latin MSS. In view of Luke's data about the voyage, there can be no doubt that this was Malta and not Meleda, an island in the (modern) Adriatic, with which it has sometimes been identified. **2.** ' Natives ' : literally ' foreigners ' or ' barbarians ', i.e. non-Greek-speaking people. The Maltese spoke a dialect of Punic. **3ff.** The divine purpose in the rescue of the ship's company is shown by signs and wonders. Paul was ' twisting together ' a faggot of wood, when a snake bit his hand. Luke makes the Maltese, although not Greek-speaking, say that Justice (Gr. *Dikē*) will evidently not allow Paul, though saved from the sea, to live ; he must be a murderer. **6.** When no harm befalls him, they take him to be a god. The incident fulfils, for Luke and his readers, the promise of Lk. 10:19.

b **7-10 Healings in Malta**—**7.** This was not the only sign. Cures follow, beginning with the father of the ' chief man of the island '. This was the official title (cf. *Corpus Inscriptionum Latinorum* 10:7495). **8.** Paul heals the father of Publius by the laying-on of hands with prayer (cf. 9:17 ; Lk. 4:40). Healing is mediated with the same sign as ordination and the bestowal of the Pentecostal Spirit of prophecy and tongues. In all cases its primary significance is the Spirit-possessed person's identification of himself with the other party, and it is accompanied by prayer on behalf of the latter. **8-9** echo the story of the healing of Peter's
mother-in-law and the cures which followed it (Lk. 803b
4:38-41). **10,** RSV*n.* ' Honours ' is probably right. Though the word may mean ' fee ' (of a doctor), this meaning would be singularly inappropriate here.

11-16 Journey from Malta to Rome—**11.** At the c
end of winter they embark in an Alexandrian ship which had wintered at Malta. Its figurehead was Castor and Pollux, favourite deities of sailors, with a widespread cult in Egypt. **12-13.** The voyage is by way of Syracuse and Rhegium (Reggio) to Puteoli (Pozzuoli), near Naples, a terminal port for the Alexandrian corn ships. **14.** A church has already been established at Puteoli, and they stay a week with the ' brethren '. For the sake of descriptive emphasis Luke mentions the arrival in Rome, and then (**15**) goes back to tell how the Roman Christians came far out of the city to meet Paul. This is a sort of triumphal entry. ' Appii Forum ' is 40 miles from Rome on the Appian Way, and ' Tres Tabernae ' 30 miles. **16.** Paul is allowed to remain in ' open arrest ', living privately with a guard. The Western text prefaces this with the statement that the centurion handed over the prisoners to the *stratopedarch*, meaning by this probably the Praetorian Prefect or possibly the *princeps peregrinorum*, the head of the *frumentarii* (see note on 27:1).

17-28 Paul's Final Appeal to the Jews and d
Turning to the Gentiles—**17.** Paul invites the leaders of the Jewish community, and makes his last speech of defence. He has done nothing against the people of Israel or the Law, but was delivered over into the hands of the Romans by the leaders at Jerusalem : like Jesus (cf. 3:13, 2:23). **18.** The Roman authorities exculpated him. **19.** Yet he was compelled to appeal to Caesar against his own compatriots, although he was a perfectly loyal Jew. **20.** As he said in his previous speeches of defence, he is a prisoner for the sake of the messianic hope of Israel. **21-2.** Since the Jews at Rome have received no reports about Paul from Jerusalem, there is some chance for him to appeal to an unprejudiced Jewish audience, even though they have heard that ' the sect ' is ' everywhere spoken against '. It is strange that they are represented as being so ignorant of the Christian movement, seeing that there was a church in Rome, probably with many Jewish converts among its members, as the Epistle to the Romans indicates, and that disturbances caused by Christian missionaries may perhaps have led to the expulsion of the Jews by Claudius (see 18:2 and note). **23.** Paul's preaching to them consists of testimony to the Kingdom of God, that is, the gospel of God's reign established through his mighty acts in Christ ; that is synonymous with ' convincing them about Jesus '. As always, Paul's appeal, in preaching to Jews, is to the OT scriptures. **24-5.** The Jewish reaction is unfavourable. Some are convinced, but they leave him in a state of disagreement among themselves. **25-7.** Their rejection of the gospel was foretold by the Spirit through Isaiah in the words of Isa. 6:9-10, a standard proof-text for Israel's failure to receive the gospel (cf. Lk. 8:10 and, in full, Mt. 13:14-15). Isaiah thus prophesied Israel's rejection of the gospel ; but Ps. 67:2 is a promise that salvation will be given to the Gentiles and (**28**) Paul declares that this promise is fulfilled. The Gentiles will listen. Thus at Rome the pattern of the whole of Lk.-Ac. (set out in the speech at Nazareth, Lk. 4:23-8), and the pattern of the mission at Pisidian Antioch and Corinth, is repeated for the last time. The gospel, preached first to the covenant people, is rejected by them and given to the Gentiles, who will accept it. **29,** a repetition of 25, is added by the Western text.

30-31 The Gospel in Rome—Paul lives at his own e
expense, or perhaps ' in his own hired house ', and preaches to all who come to him. The gospel of the Kingdom of God, which is the teaching about Jesus as Lord and Messiah (**31**), is proclaimed in the capital of the Gentile world ' openly and unhindered '.

803e These concluding words are the triumphant ending of the gospel story which began in the Jerusalem Temple (Lk. 1:5ff.) and has brought salvation to the ends of the earth.

Bibliography—Commentaries and Works include: H. W. Beyer, NTD (1947); A. W. F. Blunt, Clarendon Bible (1923); F. F. Bruce (1951); H. J. Cadbury, *The Making of Luke-Acts* (1927; rev. ed. 1958); E. Haenchen (1957); E. Jacquier, *Les Actes des Apôtres* (*Études Bibliques*, 1926); W. L. Knox, *The Acts of the Apostles* (1948); K. Lake and F. J. Foakes-Jackson, *The Beginnings of Christianity* (5 vols.; vol. 4, Translation and Commentary (1920–33)); R. B. Rackham, Westminster Commentaries (1902); William Ramsey, *St Paul the Traveller and Roman Citizen* (1903); H. H. Wendt (in Meyer, 1913); C. S. C. Williams, Black's Commentaries (1957).

THE EPISTLES OF PAUL

By F. F. BRUCE

804a **Introduction**—On 17 July, A.D. 180, half a dozen humble people from the North African town of Scilli appeared before Saturninus, the Roman governor of the province, charged with belonging to a seditious organisation, the Christian Church. There was brought into court a box, containing the library of their small community. 'What have you in your box?' asked the governor. 'Our books,' they answered, 'and the letters of Paul, a righteous man.'

What strange potency was there in those letters of 'Paul, a righteous man', written over a hundred years earlier, which gave them such high value in the eyes of the unlearned Scillitan martyrs, so that they played a part in the evidence supporting the capital charge on which the martyrs were arraigned?

b Some two hundred years later, another North African, no plebeian but a professor of rhetoric, sat weeping in the garden of his friend Alypius at Milan and heard a child singing in a neighbouring house: 'Take up and read! take up and read!' Taking up the scroll which lay at his friend's side, he let his eyes rest on the words which we identify as Rom. 13:13*b*–14, 'not in revelling and drunkenness, not in debauchery and licentiousness, not in quarrelling and jealousy. But put on the Lord Jesus Christ, and make no provision for the flesh, to gratify its desires.' 'No further would I read,' he tells us, 'nor had I any need: instantly, at the end of this sentence, a clear light flooded my heart and all the darkness of doubt vanished away' (*Confessions* viii, 29). And what the church and the world owe to this influx of light which illuminated Augustine's mind as he read these words of Paul is something beyond our power to compute.

c In November 1515 a professor of sacred theology in the University of Wittenberg began to expound Paul's Epistle to the Romans to his students, and continued this course until the following September. As he prepared his lectures, he came more and more to appreciate the centrality of the Pauline doctrine of justification by faith. 'I greatly longed to understand Paul's Epistle to the Romans,' he wrote, 'and nothing stood in the way but that one expression, "the righteousness of God", because I took it to mean that righteousness whereby God is righteous and deals righteously in punishing the unrighteous. . . . Night and day I pondered until . . . I grasped the truth that the righteousness of God is that righteousness whereby, through grace and sheer mercy, he justifies us by faith. Thereupon I felt myself to be reborn and to have gone through open doors into paradise. The whole of Scripture took on a new meaning, and whereas before "the righteousness of God" had filled me with hate, now it became to me inexpressibly sweet in greater love. This passage of Paul became to me a gateway to heaven' (*Weimarer Ausgabe* liv, 179–87). And the consequences of this new insight which Martin Luther gained from the study of Paul are writ large in history.

d In the evening of 24 May 1738 John Wesley 'went very unwillingly to a society in Aldersgate Street, where one was reading Luther's Preface to the Epistle to the Romans. About a quarter before nine,' he wrote in his journal, 'while he was describing the change which God works in the heart through faith in Christ, I felt my heart strangely warmed. I felt I did trust in Christ, Christ alone, for my salvation; 804d
and an assurance was given me that he had taken my sins away, even mine, and saved me from the law of sin and death.' And Wesley's transition from 'the faith of a servant' to 'the faith of a son' was the event above all others which launched the evangelical revival of the 18th cent.

In more recent times the first edition of Karl e
Barth's commentary on Romans, written, as he said, 'with a joyful sense of discovery', fell 'like a bombshell on the theologians' playground' (to quote Karl Adam), and started something of which the end is not yet in sight.

But in all these personal experiences and historical movements it is Paul himself, with his many-sided and abiding vitality, who has stimulated thought and brought new light and power into human life—all because of those few letters of his which were preserved and collected by early Christians and have survived to the present day.

Significance of Paul's Epistles—Thirteen of the f
twenty-seven documents which make up the NT take the form of letters bearing the name of Paul as their writer. So far as the actual bulk of the NT is concerned, these letters occupy between one-quarter and one-third of the whole volume. The majority of them were written before any other NT document (some would except the Epistle of James); the earliest of them may go back to A.D. 48. This means that when the earlier Pauline Epistles mention a saying or action of Jesus, that mention is the oldest written account that we have, antedating the earliest Gospel record by several years. An outstanding instance of this is Paul's account of the institution of the Eucharist in 1 C. 11:23ff.; it is not always easy to remember that this is the oldest record of that event that has come down to us. Since our Gospels stand at the beginning of the NT, and deal with a period of time some years earlier than Paul's conversion and apostolic activity, we tend to forget that even the earliest of the four was not composed until Paul's career was wellnigh finished.

Nor do such considerations as these exhaust the significance of Paul's writings for the NT. Some decades after Paul's death, the collection and circulation of his letters played an important part in the emergence of the NT as an acknowledged collection of sacred scriptures.

Although the anonymous Epistle to the Hebrews has been traditionally ascribed to Paul (cf. the title in AV and RV), and was indeed bound up with the Pauline Epistles from the beginning of the 3rd cent. A.D. (as in the Chester Beatty papyrus codex known as P^{46}), it can in no sense be regarded as a Pauline document, and therefore finds no further mention in this article (see introduction to the commentary on Heb., §§880*b*–*e*).

Paul as a Letter Writer—The circumstances of 805a
letter-writing in antiquity may have some bearing on our interpretation of Paul's style and language, and on the textual criticism of his epistles.

Even where a form of shorthand was used (such as the *notae Tironianae* of Cicero's secretary), writing was a slow business compared with writing today—

805a although not so slow as O. Roller has argued in *Das Formular der paulinischen Briefe* (1933). (E. Percy has an acute criticism of Roller in *Probleme der Kolosser- und Epheserbriefe* (1946), 10*n*; see also S. Lyonnet, 'De arte litteras exarandi apud antiquos', *Verbum Domini* 34 (1956), 3ff.) We can hardly take seriously such a statement as J. Jeremias makes (following Roller), that 'the composition of a letter of the length of 2 Timothy demanded of the ancient art of writing not hours but days of laborious work' (*Das NT Deutsch: Die Pastoralbriefe* (1953), 5).

According to Roller, the roughness of the writing-material (especially papyrus), the inadequacy of the reed-pens and of the ink all contributed to the difficulty of the procedure. Where a letter or even a longer document was dictated, a common proceeding was for the scribe to take down the gist of it on wax tablets and then compose the fair copy at leisure in his own handwriting and style. The sender might check it to make sure that it conveyed the sense of what he wished to say, and add a few words of greeting in his own hand to certify the authenticity of the document (cf. 1 C. 16:21; Gal. 6:11; Col. 4:18; 2 Th. 3:17).

b Paul, it appears, made regular use of amanuenses in his letter-writing. Yet it seems plain that, for the most part, he did not give them merely the general sense of his communication and leave them to write it up in the conventional epistolary style of the day. The individual style which characterises most of his epistles tells its own tale. Paul dictated—and the scribe copied his words verbatim as best he could. Sometimes the work of copying would not be so difficult, where Paul develops a careful argument in a relatively calm mood; at other times the impetuous torrent of his thought carries him swiftly on, and we can only try to imagine how the amanuensis fared. Paul's mind ran ahead of his utterance, and the words as we have them seem sometimes to have overleapt a gap in order to catch up with his thought. Usually, we may suppose, it was one of Paul's friends and not a professional letter-writer who acted as his amanuensis. The only amanuensis whose name is given is Tertius, who sends his greetings in Rom. 16:22. Whether he did this at Paul's prompting or on his own initiative, Paul would have approved of the added salutation. Tertius may have been a professional amanuensis, since Romans is rather more formal than most of Paul's other letters; even so, he was evidently a Christian, since he sends his greetings 'in the Lord'. From the frequency with which Timothy's name is joined with Paul's in the superscription of letters (2 C.; Phil.; Col.; 1 and 2 Th.; Phm.), it has been conjectured that he commonly acted as the apostle's amanuensis.

c Of course, an author writing letters with a view to publication would be more careful to control their style than one whose letters were simply intended to convey information or instruction or greetings to the recipients. Paul's letters were intended in the first instance for the people to whom they were addressed, although there is evidence that some of them were intended to be read by others as well. In either case, they do not come into the literary category of the Epistles of Cicero or Pliny, and yet they have this in common with these literary collections, that in most of them the style is as recognisably Paul's own as the style of the Epistles of Cicero or Pliny is theirs. Here is a man with something to say, and what he has to say is so much part of the man himself that there can be nothing artificial or merely conventional about the way he says it. 'At last, at last, once again someone speaks in Greek out of a fresh inward experience of life. That experience is his faith. He is sure of the hope within him, and his glowing love embraces all mankind, to bring healing to whom he will gladly throw away his own life. It is as a substitute for his personal activity that he writes his letters. This epistolary style is Paul himself and no other' (U. von Wilamowitz-Möllendorff).

Where, however, a letter bearing Paul's name does 805c not present the same features of style as the majority do, the possibility that the amanuensis was occasionally given a greater measure of freedom in this regard should dictate caution in using the stylistic criterion alone in coming to a decision about the genuineness of such a letter.

Criteria for Dating the Epistles—Paul's letters d have not come down to us in chronological order. The order with which we are familiar—beginning with Rom. and ending with Phm.—is based on a twofold principle. Firstly, his letters to churches precede his letters to individuals; secondly, within these two groups, the letters are arranged roughly in descending order of length, from Rom. to 2 Th. in the first group and from 1 Tim. to Phm. in the second. (The main exception to this rule is that Gal. precedes Eph., although Eph. is slightly the longer of the two.)

When we try to arrange the letters in chronological order, we have two kinds of criteria to guide us. One is the presence of personal references in some of the letters which indicate quite clearly to which point in Paul's career they belong. Thus, 1 Th. was evidently written soon after his departure from Thessalonica, either during his stay in Athens or (more probably) shortly after he had settled in Corinth (cf. 1 Th. 3:1–6 with Ac. 17:1–18:5). It appears that 1 C. was written during Paul's Ephesian ministry (1 C. 16:8), while 2 C. was written shortly after the close of that ministry (2 C. 1:8ff., 2:12f.). Rom. was written when Paul was about to set out for his last visit to Jerusalem (Rom. 15:25), probably during the three months which he spent in Greece (Ac. 20:2f.).

But we are not always in the happy position of having such definite time-indications as these. Sometimes, as in Gal. 1:18–2:14, Paul's autobiographical references relate to the past, and we cannot be sure whether the past to which they relate is the immediate or the more remote past. At other times his personal notes relate to the present, but are not explicit enough to be set unambiguously in the context of our available outline of his life. Thus, when writing Phil., Col., Phm. and Eph. (the 'Captivity Epistles'), he was evidently deprived of his freedom, but it is not easy to determine to which of his frequent imprisonments (2 C. 11:23) these letters may belong.

Where the time-indication is an insufficient criterion, e we have to fall back on the more uncertain one of the development of Paul's thought. Here we must be on our guard, lest we find ourselves arguing in circles, determining the development of his thought from the order of his epistles and determining the order of his epistles from the development of his thought. But if we can establish some definite progression of thought on the basis of those epistles which can be dated on the strength of our former criterion, we may sometimes be able to suggest where, along the line of progression thus determined, the other epistles should most probably be placed. Even so, we must beware of assuming anything in the nature of 'linear progression' when we are trying to trace the advancing thought of such a man as Paul.

With this and every other proper proviso, we may consider the history of Paul's thought in relation to two quite different subjects: (i) his eschatological expectation; (ii) his conception of the church as the body of Christ.

(i) **Eschatological Expectation**—The Thessa- 806a lonian correspondence, which can be dated fairly accurately in A.D. 50, must be viewed against a background of eschatological excitement. Paul's converts at Thessalonica had clearly received some instruction from him about the Last Things (cf. 1 Th. 1:9f.; 2 Th. 2:5). This instruction reflected the eschatological discourse of Mk 13, or at least an earlier edition of that discourse, which may have circulated as a separate pamphlet during the scare of A.D. 40, when the Emperor Gaius ordered the erection of his statue in the Jerusalem Temple. It must have

806a seemed to many in that year that the abomination of desolation was about to be set up 'where he ought not' (Mk 13:14, RV); and although the threat came to nothing, the memory of it seems to colour Paul's description, ten years later, of 'the man of lawlessness' who 'takes his seat in the temple of God, proclaiming himself to be God' (2 Th. 2:3f.).

Paul had to leave Thessalonica hurriedly (Ac. 17:10), without completing the instruction which he was giving to his converts there; hence their bewilderment, first when some of their number died before the expected *parousia*, or second coming, of Christ (a problem with which Paul deals in 1 Th. 4:13ff.), and then when certain people tried to persuade them that the day of the Lord had already set in (2 Th. 2:1ff.).

b Along with the other elements in the primitive *kerygma* Paul had 'received' the belief that Jesus, whose messianic office had been confirmed by his resurrection, would return in due course as divinely appointed judge of the living and the dead (cf. Ac. 10:42, 17:31). The way to obtain a favourable verdict in that judgment, he held, was to be justified here and now by faith in Jesus. At Thessalonica he taught his converts to wait for the return of Jesus from heaven in terms which some of them misunderstood to mean that this event would take place while they were all still alive. Perhaps because of his hasty departure they did not realise that the resurrection of the just (which was to coincide with the parousia) would include not only the faithful of OT times but also believers in Jesus like themselves, if they died before he returned. When Paul wrote to reassure them about the lot of those of their number who had died already, he appeared to associate himself with those who would survive until the parousia: 'we who are alive, who are left until the coming of the Lord, shall not precede those who have fallen asleep' (1 Th. 4:15).

The language which he uses in this connection is markedly apocalyptic: the Lord Jesus is to be attended at his parousia by all his holy ones (1 Th. 3:13); he 'will descend from heaven with a cry of command, with the archangel's call, and with the sound of the trumpet of God' (1 Th. 4:16); 'the dead in Christ will rise first' and living believers will then 'be caught up together with them in the clouds to meet the Lord in the air' (1 Th. 4:17). The apocalyptic note is even more pronounced in the second epistle: not only have we the apocalyptic pericope in 2 Th. 2:3ff., where the Lord Jesus destroys the man of lawlessness 'by his appearing and his coming'; but in 1:7 he 'is revealed from heaven with his mighty angels in flaming fire', to execute vengeance on the ungodly and 'to be glorified in his saints' (v. 10).

But in spite of the eschatological interest of these two epistles (which is due to the nature of the problems which were exercising the minds of the Thessalonian Christians), their dominant note is ethical. Even if the parousia be near at hand, that must not be used as an excuse for slacking and failing to earn an honest living; still less must it be used for failing to maintain the strictest moral standard. Paul presents the parousia pre-eminently as a grand incentive to holiness and sobriety of life.

c In 1 C., written about four years later than the Thessalonian correspondence, we find substantially the same eschatological teaching as in 1 Th., but the apocalyptic note is not so prominent. More attention is paid to the resurrection of the dead as the harvest of which Christ's resurrection was the first-fruits, Paul's treatment of this topic arising out of an actual situation in the Corinthian church. On the day of resurrection, he says, it is a 'spiritual body' that will be raised, and simultaneously 'we shall be changed'—i.e. 'we' who have not passed through death shall receive immortal bodies 'in a moment, in the twinkling of an eye, at the last trumpet' (1 C. 15:52). Here the conception of a 'spiritual body' marks a notable advance on current Jewish ideas. But if in this passage Paul still seems to associate himself with those who will be alive on earth at the parousia, elsewhere in the 806c
same epistle he associates himself with those who will be raised from the dead (1 C. 6:14). Yet the time will not be long delayed, and this has its implications for present family relationships and the like (1 C. 7:29ff.). When the time comes, Christ will exercise his judicial authority and apportion praise and blame (1 C. 4:4f., 5:5), and his people will share his judicial and royal dignity (1 C. 6:2f.).

Similarly in Phil. Paul can say that 'the Lord is at hand' (4:5); or, in greater detail, from heaven 'we d
await a Saviour, the Lord Jesus Christ, who will change our lowly body to be like his glorious body, by the power which enables him even to subject all things to himself' (3:20f.). Here certainly too much emphasis should not be placed on his use of 'we', for it is plain from other parts of this epistle that he viewed with equanimity either prospect—continued life or speedy death. It was better, he said, for his friends and converts that his life should be prolonged a while; but so far as he was concerned personally, death was gain: in fact his own preference would be 'to depart and be with Christ, for that is far better' (Phil. 1:23). Clearly he does not think of the interval between death and resurrection as a hiatus in his fellowship with Christ.

When we come to 2 C. 1–9, however, we are con- e
scious of a further advance. Here, as in 1 C. 6:14, Paul associates himself with those who will be raised from the dead (2 C. 4:14). But the resurrection principle is already at work in the servants of God; the spiritual body is even now being formed, as the inner man undergoes daily renewal (2 C. 4:16), and death will mean the immediate receiving of 'our heavenly dwelling, so that by putting it on we may not be found naked' (2 C. 5:2f.). (Cf. R. F. Hettlinger, '2 Corinthians 5:1–10', SJTh. 10 (1957), 174–94.) It may be that the deadly peril in which Paul found himself shortly before the writing of these words (2 C. 1:8ff.) had led him to consider more urgently than before what the believer's prospects at death would be. To be 'away from the body' would mean being 'at home with the Lord' (2 C. 5:8). But if not at a fixed point at the end of the age, then certainly after the completion of this earthly life, it remains true that 'we must all appear before the judgment seat of Christ, so that each one may receive good or evil, according to what he has done in the body' (2 C. 5:10).

In Rom. Paul lays stress not so much on the resur- f
rection from the dead at the end-time as on the inward participation in Christ's risen life which his people experience here and now, having been baptised into his death and raised with him to 'walk in newness of life' (Rom. 6:3f.). This experience is communicated through the Spirit, whose indwelling presence is the earnest of full and final resurrection (8:11, 23). The parousia is still seen as the day of judgment and review (2:16, 14:10ff.), and the day of salvation and glory (8:17, 13:11). But it is seen also as the day for which all creation eagerly waits—the day when the universe will be liberated from its bondage to frustration and futility to share 'the glorious liberty of the children of God' (8:19ff.).

This cosmic vision prepares us for the teaching of Col. and Eph., where Christ is presented as the one in whom God proposes to reconcile the universe to himself (Col. 1:20) and bring it to its consummating unity (Eph. 1:9f.). Yet at the end of his great period of letter-writing, as at its beginning, his prime purpose in presenting the parousia is to let it have its sanctifying effect on the present lives of Christians on earth: since they will be manifested in glory with Christ, their true life, when he appears (Col. 3:4), they must here and now reject what is unworthy of that prospect, and pursue what befits it (cf. Eph. 4:1).

Along with this progression in Paul's thought about g
the Last Things, some have recognised a growing appreciation of the positive worth of family relation-

806g ships. This is specially obvious with regard to marriage. When all due allowances have been made for varying conditions of context and life-setting, there is an unmistakable difference in tone between 1 C. 7:1–8, 26–38, and Col. 3:18f., not to mention Eph. 5:22ff., where the married state is treated as a divinely intended analogy of the relation subsisting between Christ and the church.

In terms of eschatological development, then, there seems to be some reason for dating Phil. along with the Corinthian correspondence, but Col. and Eph. definitely later.

807a (ii) **The Body of Christ**—An even stronger argument for dating Col. and Eph. some time after the Corinthian and Roman epistles is the apparent progress in Paul's thought of the church as the body of Christ.

The common life of Christians is first described in terms of the interdependent functioning of the various parts of a body in 1 C. 12:12ff. There the figure of the body is used as a simile: the head is one member among others, and an individual member of the church may be compared to the head or to a part of the head—an ear or an eye. So in Rom. 12:4f. the mutual and co-operative responsibilities of church members are compared to the diversity of functions performed by the different parts of the body as they work together for the health and efficiency of the whole. But in Eph. 1:23, 4:12ff.; Col. 1:18, 2:19, etc., Paul thinks rather of the relation which the church, as the body of Christ, bears to Christ as the head. Here there is no possibility of an ordinary member of the church being compared to the head or to part of the head; here, too, the body ceases to be used as a mere simile and becomes rather the most effective term which the apostle can find to express the vital bond which unites the life of the people of Christ with his own risen life. Whether this represents a spontaneous and inevitable advance in Paul's thinking about the relation between Christ and his people, or was due in part to some special stimulus, cannot be known for certain. It could well be that the form which his teaching on the subject takes in Col. reflects his vigorous reaction to the Colossian heresy. But it is very difficult to think of Paul writing in these terms to Colossae at the same time as he was writing his successive letters to the Corinthians (or very shortly after), and before he wrote to the Romans.

b It has, indeed, been suggested that Rom. in substance is earlier than the date implied by its personal references, and that its composition may have been spread out over a considerable time. G. S. Duncan, for example, believes it to be in essence earlier than 1 C., and to be the fruit of prolonged study and reflection on Paul's part when he first saw the road to Rome opening out before him (ET 67 (1955–6), 164). No doubt the main argument of Rom. is the product of long experience and reflection, but the form which the letter actually takes belongs to the beginning of A.D. 57, and it may safely be regarded as reflecting the mind of Paul at that time.

c The cosmic significance of Christ and the church, so fully brought out in Col. and Eph., is not absent from other epistles (cf., e.g., Rom. 8:19ff.; 1 C. 8:6); but Col. and Eph. present a more developed exposition of it. Once again it could be that Paul's thinking in this realm was further stimulated by the necessity of giving the Christian answer to the cosmic speculations of the Colossian heresy. In any case, it is difficult to suppose that Paul's fuller statement of the cosmic implications of the Gospel in these two epistles belongs to the same period as their more inchoate adumbrations in 1 C. and Rom.

d **Four Groups of Epistles**—While these two aspects of Paul's thought are limited in their value as criteria for dating his epistles, they do point to the same conclusions as far as they go. There are a number of chronological questions, however, which they leave unanswered. But we may now adopt the following tentative grouping of the epistles as a working arrangement. 807d

Group I

Galatians	Written from Syrian Antioch, A.D. 48
1 Thessalonians	Written from Corinth, A.D. 50
2 Thessalonians	Written from Corinth, A.D. 50

Group II

1 Corinthians	Written from Ephesus, A.D. 54
Philippians	Written from Ephesus, A.D. 54 (?)
2 Corinthians 10–13	Written from Ephesus, A.D. 55
2 Corinthians 1–9	Written from Macedonia, A.D. 55/6
Romans	Written from Corinth, A.D. 57

Group III

Colossians	Written from Rome, A.D. 60/1 (?)
Philemon	Written from Rome, A.D. 60/1 (?)
Ephesians	Written from Rome, A.D. 60/1 (?)

Group IV

Titus	Written from Ephesus, after A.D. 62 (?)
1 Timothy	Written from Macedonia, after A.D. 62 (?)
2 Timothy	Written from Rome, A.D. 64 (?)

This grouping raises a number of questions hitherto untouched, such as the position of Gal. among the letters of Paul, the arrangement of the Corinthian correspondence, and the authenticity of Eph. and of the 'Pastoral Epistles' (1 and 2 Tim. and Tit.). Another question, already ventilated but calling for further consideration, is the date and provenance of the 'Captivity Epistles' (Phil., Eph., Col., Phm.).

Group I Galatians—To place Gal. in Group I, e making it the earliest of Paul's extant letters, has the obvious disadvantage that Gal. is thus detached from its proximity to that other Pauline letter with which it has the closest affinity—Rom. Yet the main outline of Paul's understanding of the Gospel, as it finds expression in both these epistles, may well have taken definite shape within a short time of his conversion. Even on the earlier dating of Gal., it did not precede Rom. by more than nine years.

Paul's conversion must certainly have compelled him to think out, from the foundation upwards, the relation of the Gospel to the law and the true way of righteousness; and he probably arrived at his characteristic position on these matters in the earliest period of his Christian life. A revolutionary experience such as his tends to shake apart the component elements of one's former pattern of thought, when once their unifying principle (in his case, the observance of the law as the way to acceptance with God) is disturbed or removed; these elements then come together again to form a fresh pattern, around a new unifying principle (in his case, faith in Christ as the way to acceptance with God). What had formerly been to Paul the final proof of the impossibility of Jesus' Messiahship—the fact that he died the death on which a divine curse was pronounced—now became the centre of his Gospel: 'For all who rely on works of the law are under a curse; for it is written, "Cursed be every one who does not abide by all things written in the book of the law, and do them." . . . Christ redeemed us from the curse of the law, having become a curse for us—for it is written, "Cursed be every one who hangs on a tree"—that in Christ Jesus the blessing of Abraham might come upon the Gentiles, that we

807e might receive the promise of the Spirit through faith' (Gal. 3:10, 13f.). The problem presented to a mind like Paul's by the manner of Jesus' death (once he was convinced that Jesus had risen from the dead and was indeed the Messiah) cannot have waited long before finding a solution along these lines. On this score, then, the early dating of Gal. need not be objected to. However early Paul was confronted by the situation which is reflected in this epistle, he could not have dealt with it otherwise than he does here.

f But the early dating of Gal.—to a time shortly after his return to Syrian Antioch (Ac. 14:27)—is bound up with the following theses: (i) the churches addressed in Gal. 1:2 are those of Pisidian Antioch, Iconium, Lystra and Derbe, planted by Paul and Barnabas on their first missionary journey in Asia Minor; (ii) Paul's reference in Gal. 4:13 to his having preached the Gospel to them 'at first' (i.e. the first time or the former time) alludes to his journey from Pisidian Antioch to Derbe via Iconium and Lystra (Ac. 13:14–14:21*a*), the implied second visit being that which immediately followed when he and Barnabas, having reached the frontier between Roman Galatia and the kingdom of Antiochus, retraced their steps and revisited the churches which they had so lately founded (Ac. 14:21*b*–23); (iii) the Council of Jerusalem (Ac. 15) had not yet met (otherwise Paul could scarcely have failed to mention its decision in confirmation of his argument in Gal.); (iv) Paul's Jerusalem visits of Gal. 1:18 and 2:1 correspond respectively to those of Ac. 9:26 and 11:30.

g That the Jerusalem visits of Gal. 1:18 and Ac. 9:26 are identical is generally agreed, but the identification of the visit of Gal. 2:1 is disputed. Most expositors take Gal. 2:1–10 to be Paul's account of the Council of Jerusalem, and many of them, in view of the great difficulties in the way of reconciling this account with that of Ac. 15, are prepared to allow little historical value to the latter. A more moderate view is expressed by O. Cullmann: he identifies the two occasions, and supposes the record of Ac. to be right in its chronological placing of the meeting, but wrong in attaching the apostolic decree to it; the decree was drawn up later, without Paul's knowledge (*Peter* (1953), 42ff.). Another suggestion—that Gal. 2:1–10 records a private meeting between Barnabas and Paul and the 'pillar' apostles about the same time as the Council—has been criticised on the ground that 'we have no reason for supposing that the Church had by this date reached that stage of democracy in which the public meeting registers its assent to a decision reached in advance by its leading members' (W. L. Knox, *The Acts of the Apostles* (1948), 42). We may also mention the view (held by J. Wellhausen, E. Schwartz and K. Lake) that Ac. 11:30 and 15:2 refer to one and the same visit (that of Gal. 2:1), recorded variously in two of Luke's sources and wrongly applied by him to two separate occasions; the view (expressed by J. Knox) that Ac. 15:2 and 18:22 refer to one and the same visit (that of Gal. 2:1), which belongs chronologically to the position of Ac. 18:22; and the suggestion of T. W. Manson that the visit of Gal. 2:1 finds no mention in Ac., but was paid on the eve of Barnabas and Paul's departure for Cyprus (Ac. 13:2ff.).

The identification of the visit of Gal. 2:1 with that of Ac. 11:30 seems most satisfactory, not least in view of the Jerusalem leaders' closing appeal (Gal. 2:10) to Barnabas and Paul ('Only,' they said, 'please continue to remember "the poor"'), with Paul's added comment ('and in fact I myself had made a special point of doing that very thing')—specially apposite language in connection with a famine-relief visit.

h **Thessalonians**—It is unnecessary to add anything here about the two epistles to Thessalonica (which, with the possible exception of Gal., are Paul's earliest surviving letters), after what has been said above about their eschatological teaching (see §806*b*).

808a **Group II Corinthians**—The problems presented by Paul's Corinthian correspondence illustrate the difficulties under which the collection of his letters was first undertaken. 808a

The first epistle appears to be intact. But it was not the first letter that Paul sent to the Corinthian church; it was apparently preceded by another which is mentioned in 1 C. 5:9. It is unlikely that Paul is using the 'epistolary aorist' in this verse, as though he meant 'I am writing to you in this letter of mine not to associate with immoral men'; it is much more probable that he is referring to an earlier letter dealing particularly with that subject. This earlier letter may be designated 'A'; it must be regarded as lost, unless indeed a fragment of it is embedded in 2 C., where 6:14–7:1, warning Christians not to be 'mismated with unbelievers', seems to break abruptly into the context, which reads more smoothly when these verses are removed. This, however, would be a slender argument in itself, were there not other grounds for thinking that 2 C., as we have it now, is a composite document.

If the previous letter mentioned in 1 C. 5:9 be designated 'A', then our 1 C. may be designated 'B'. It was sent to Corinth from Ephesus (1 C. 16:8), possibly by the hand of Timothy (1 C. 4:17; read 'I am sending', with RSV*n*, rather than 'I sent' of RSV text; cf. 1 C. 16:10f.).

When we turn to 2 C. we again find reference made to a previous letter—a severe letter sent by Paul to the Corinthian Christians, which cost him much pain as he wrote it, and which, once it had left his hands, he regretted having sent, lest his readers should suffer too much pain when they received it. In it he presented them with something in the nature of an ultimatum, testing their obedience by a demand for disciplinary action against a certain member of their church. Its effect, however, was so unexpectedly good that it brought about a complete reconciliation between Paul and the whole Corinthian church, in which a strong opposition to his leadership had been growing (cf. 2 C. 2:3–11, 7:8ff.). b

It seems clear that this severe letter cannot be identified with 1 C., which does not exhibit the features ascribed to the severe letter. The person against whom the severe letter demanded disciplinary action can scarcely be the same as the incestuous man whose excommunication is enjoined in 1 C. 5:13. The severe letter was more probably a distinct document, written between 1 C. and 2 C., and we may designate it as 'C', in which case 2 C. may be designated 'D'. But 'C' may not be totally lost. It has often been noted that there is a strange break in argument and temperament between 2 C. 9 and 10; the note of gladness and reconciliation which is apparent up to the end of ch. 9 suddenly gives way to one of sharp remonstrance and almost violent defence of Paul's apostleship. Several features of the last four chapters of 2 C. correspond to what can be gathered about the severe letter from references to it in 2 C. 1–9; and it is not surprising that many commentators have concluded that 2 C. 10–13 represents the end of 'C', while 2 C. 1–9 (with the possible exception of 6:14–7:1, sometimes identified with 'A') contains the bulk of 'D' (whose ending has somehow been lost). The best statement of this view is found in J. H. Kennedy, *The Second and Third Epistles to the Corinthians* (1900); the unity of 2 C. is defended in the commentaries by J. Denney (1894) and A. Menzies (1912). But even if 2 C. 10–13 represents 'C', it can represent only part of it, for there is nothing in these four chapters about the demand for strong disciplinary action which the severe letter demanded (2 C. 2:5ff., 7:12). On the other hand, we may compare such pairs of passages as the following: (i) 2 C. 10:6 ('being ready to punish every disobedience, when your obedience is complete') with 2 C. 2:9 ('this is why I wrote, that I might test you and know whether you are obedient in everything'); (ii) 2 C. 13:2 ('I warned those who sinned before and c

808c all the others, and I warn them now while absent, . . . that if I come again I will not spare them ') with 2 C. 1:23 (' it was to spare you that I refrained from coming to Corinth'; cf. 2 C. 2:1); (iii) 2 C. 13:10 (' I write this while I am away from you, in order that when I come I may not have to be severe ') with 2 C. 2:3 (' I wrote as I did, so that when I came I might not be pained by those who should have made me rejoice'); (iv) 2 C. 11:1ff. (where, speaking ' as a fool ', he boasts of his qualifications) with 2 C. 3:1 (' Are we beginning to commend ourselves again?'). In each pair the quotation from 2 C. 1–9 could well echo or refer back to the accompanying passage from 2 C. 10–13. It has also been pointed out that 2 C. 7:16 (' I have perfect confidence in you ') might echo, with a prepositional change, 2 C. 10:1 (literally, ' I have confidence against you ').

d One difficulty remains: in 2 C. 8:6–24 Paul proposes to send Titus back to Corinth to complete the collection for Jerusalem, along with another Christian brother; in 2 C. 12:18 he says: ' I urged Titus to go, and sent the brother with him.' If 2 C. 12:18 refers to the same mission as 2 C. 8:6ff., then 2 C. 10:13 will certainly be a separate letter from 2 C. 1–9 (for the mission is future in 2 C. 8, past in 2 C. 12), but it will be a later, not an earlier letter, to be designated ' E ', not ' C ' (and ' C ' would have to be regarded as lost altogether). But 2 C. 12:18 more probably refers back to an earlier mission than that of 2 C. 8:6ff.—possibly to the time when Paul first conceived the plan of organising a collection for the Jerusalem church. It is evident from 1 C. 16:1ff. that the Corinthian Christians had already been informed about the collection, and they may have received their information from Titus and his colleague. In that case, we must distinguish three occasions on which Titus visited Corinth as Paul's envoy: (i) to announce the plan for the collection (2 C. 12:18); (ii) either as bearer of the severe letter or to ascertain how the Corinthian Christians had reacted to it (2 C. 2:12, 7:6f., 13ff.); (iii) to complete the business of the collection (2 C. 8:6ff.).

e However that may be, why should 2 C. have come down to us in this disorganised state? One suggestion is that the church of Corinth, about A.D. 95, was stimulated to a revival of interest in the letters which Paul had written to it forty years before, by the reception of a letter from Clement of Rome. Seeing how a leader in the church of Rome valued one of Paul's letters to Corinth (Clement invokes the authority of 1 C. in his expostulation with the Corinthians), the leaders of the church of Corinth may have set themselves to retrieve all they could of the remains of Paul's correspondence with their predecessors. These remains were by this time in a mutilated condition, but they pieced the fragments together to the best of their ability, putting what was obviously the opening salutation of a letter at the beginning and what was obviously the concluding greeting at the end—thus producing our 2 C., which is actually a combination of ' D ' and ' C ', with possibly a small fragment of ' A ' inserted half-way through.

Of course this is mere speculation, but it may not appear so totally unrelated to the probabilities of the case when we consider (i) that Clement does not appear to have known 2 C., and (ii) that 2 C., on internal evidence, does seem to incorporate parts of two distinct Pauline letters to Corinth.

809a **Philippians**—Phil. is here placed in Group II along with 1 and 2 C., on the ground that it is most probably to be assigned to the period of Paul's Ephesian ministry. While some scholars (e.g. G. S. Duncan) assign all the ' Captivity Epistles ' to the Ephesian period, and some (e.g. C. H. Dodd) assign them all to Paul's Roman captivity—not to mention those (e.g., most recently, L. Johnson in ET 68 (1956–7), 24ff.) who assign them to his two years' custody in Caesarea—there are others who separate Phil. in date and place from Eph., Col. and Phm. Of these some (e.g.
P. N. Harrison) prefer a Roman dating for Phil., while **809**
admitting an Ephesian setting for the others; some (e.g. C. J. Cadoux) date Phil. in the Ephesian period, but Eph., Col. and Phm. in the Roman period. This last position is the one represented in the present article, but the disagreement among scholars reflects the uncertainty of the evidence.

That Phil. is a ' prison epistle ' is clear: ' it has become known ', says Paul, ' throughout the whole praetorium that my imprisonment is for Christ ' (Phil. 1:13). It seems certain that the imprisonment is one which he is undergoing in the place from which he is writing. If (with RV and RSV) we take ' praetorium ' to mean the ' praetorian guard ', we must think of Rome (cf. AV ' in all the palace'); but elsewhere in NT the word denotes a Roman governor's headquarters, and the reference here could be to the administrative headquarters of the province of Asia. (Although it is urged that no instance can be adduced of the use of ' praetorium ' for the headquarters of a senatorial—as opposed to an imperial—province, there is no good reason why it should not have this meaning. Advocates of a Caesarea provenance can, of course, point to Ac. 23:35, where Paul is expressly said to have been kept under guard ' in Herod's praetorium ' at Caesarea, the capital of the imperial province of Judaea.) The Christians ' of Caesar's household ' (Phil. 4:22) were not necessarily attached to the imperial palace in Rome; the civil service of the empire was staffed by freedmen of the emperor, and such *Caesariani* were to be found in many provinces. The visit to be paid to Philippi by Timothy (Phil. 2:19) could be associated with Paul's sending Timothy and Erastus from Ephesus to Macedonia (Ac. 19:22); the ' true yokefellow ' of Phil. 4:3 could be Luke, who appears to have been in Philippi during Paul's Corinthian and Ephesian ministries—if this is a sound inference from the fact that the first ' we ' section of Ac. closes in Philippi (Ac. 16:17), while the second one begins there (Ac. 20:5f.).

But all this means that Ephesus cannot be excluded **b**
as the place where Phil. was written; it does not prove that Phil. was in fact written there. In favour of a Roman provenance certain similarities in language between Phil. and 2 Tim. are adduced, as though the possibility of Paul's life being poured out as a libation (Phil. 2:17) had become a certainty by 2 Tim. 4:6*a*, and his desire to be ' released ' (Phil. 1:23) was on the point of being fulfilled by 2 Tim. 4:6*b*. Against the argument that this section of 2 Tim. might itself be of Ephesian provenance, it has been urged that in Ephesus there must have remained for Paul the possibility of appealing to Caesar, but no such loophole of hope is suggested here. But we know from 2 C. 1:8ff. that Paul went through a period of distress in the province of Asia, if not in the city of Ephesus, which made him despair of life. The terms in which he describes this trouble indicate something other than a very serious illness. (And 1 C. 15:30–2 implies an experience of great peril at an earlier stage in his Ephesian ministry.) If G. S. Duncan is right in supposing that Paul was somehow involved in the situation attendant upon the assassination of Junius Silanus, proconsul of Asia, at the beginning of Nero's principate (A.D. 54), then an appeal to Caesar in those circumstances would have increased his danger rather than otherwise.

While there is no explicit evidence for Paul's imprisonment in Ephesus, his claim, at the end of his Ephesian ministry, to have endured ' far more imprisonments ' than his traducers (2 C. 11:23) shows that he must have been imprisoned on many more occasions up to that time than the one recorded in Ac. 16:23ff.

The terms in which he acknowledges the gift from **c**
Philippi (Phil. 4:10ff.) suggest that the interval between his departure from Philippi and the arrival of the gift was not so great as it must have been if he was writing from Rome; in fact, the whole passage is more intelligible if he had not yet paid a second

9c visit to Macedonia (Ac. 20:1–5). On the Roman dating the words 'now at length you have revived your concern for me' (Phil. 4:10*a*) have an almost ironical flavour. To reply that the following words, 'you had no opportunity' (10*b*), mean that all their gifts had been channelled into the collection for the Jerusalem church is inadequate; the collection did not occupy so many years as all that.

On the other hand, it may seem strange that in a letter written about the same time as 1 C. there should be no mention of the Jerusalem collection. If, however, the Philippians had just sent Paul a gift, it would have been a delicate matter to broach the question of a contribution for Jerusalem in the letter which conveyed his thanks for that gift. It would be better to entrust Timothy with instructions about the Jerusalem collection, which he could deliver by word of mouth.

The eschatological criterion, which has been considered above (§§806*dg*), points to an interval of time between Phil. and the other 'captivity epistles', with Phil. standing at the beginning of the interval and the others at the end.

d The greater part of the letter is devoted to friendly encouragement. There was little in the Philippian church that required to be set right, apart from some personal friction within its membership; hence the general exhortation to likemindedness in ch. 2, which is reinforced by the example of Christ's self-denial (vv. 6–11 may be an early Christian hymn, based on Isa. 52:13–53:12), and the specific exhortation to Euodia and Syntyche in 4:2 to 'agree in the Lord'. But in 3:2–21 a new note is introduced, so unlike the rest of the epistle that these verses have sometimes been regarded as part of a separate letter. This hypothesis is unnecessary; Paul's epistolary style does not always conform to those standards of neat and orderly arrangement which appeal to us.

The people against whom he puts his readers on their guard in 3:2ff. were not necessarily present at Philippi at that time, but other churches of his had been visited by them and found themselves involved in trouble and controversy in consequence; the church of Philippi must therefore be warned against them lest they should try to find an entrance there. They evidently included Judaisers of the class dealt with in Gal. The vigour of Paul's language in Phil. 3:2 (cf. Gal. 5:12) might suggest that, if we accept C. H. Dodd's theory of a psychological watershed in Paul's Christian life (dated in the latter part of his Ephesian ministry), Phil. should be placed on the earlier and not on the later side of it. Certainly this is not the tone which he employs in 1:15ff. towards those who 'preach Christ from envy and rivalry', but it is not necessary to identify the rival preachers of 1:15ff. with the 'dogs', 'evil-workers' and 'mutilators of the flesh' of 3:2. The former may be compared to the people who fostered party spirit at Corinth (1 C. 1:12), but Paul would probably not have admitted that what the people of 3:2 were preaching was the Gospel at all. That 'those who mutilate the flesh' (3:2) were not his straightforward Jewish opponents, but judaising Christians who tried to undermine his apostolic authority, seems plain (i) from the consideration that the Philippian Christians would have required little warning against Jewish opponents of Christianity, and (ii) from the following words about Paul's grounds for 'confidence in the flesh', had he been inclined that way. The parallel with his self-vindication in the 'severe letter' to Corinth (2 C. 11:16ff.) is obvious, and the language of Phil. 3:2ff. may very well reflect the apostle's state of mind at that particular time.

e **Romans**—Rom. can be dated rather easily; it was sent to Rome in anticipation of Paul's projected visit there (cf. Ac. 19:21), on the eve of his setting out for Judaea with the Gentile churches' contributions for the Jerusalem church. It is thus to this extent an 'occasional' letter, in that it was written to prepare the Christians of Rome for his visit; on the other 809e
hand, it is less of an occasional letter than most of his other epistles, for its main argument—an exposition of the Gospel as Paul understood and preached it—is not directed to a particular situation in the church addressed.

Since the outline of the argument of Rom. was not worked out in Paul's mind under the stimulus of a situation with which he suddenly found himself confronted, it is arguable that he had already drafted it. Some have gone farther than this; e.g. K. Lake, who suggested that Rom. 'was originally a general Epistle written by St Paul, at the same time as Galatians, to the mixed Churches which had sprung up round Antioch and further on in Asia Minor' (*Earlier Epistles of St Paul* (1914), 363).

There is some textual evidence that Rom. circulated f
in two shorter recensions than that which we know. Some texts omitted the destination 'Rome' in 1:7, 15; some brought the epistle to an end with the doxology (16:25–7) immediately following 14:23; while P^{46} bears witness to a recension which brought it to an end with the doxology immediately following 15:33. The recension which cut the epistle short at the end of ch. 14 was probably Marcion's; the following passage, with its statement of the value for Christian instruction of 'whatever was written in former days' (15:4) and its catena of OT quotations (15:9–12), would have been quite uncongenial to him. But the recension which omitted the reference to Rome in ch. 1 was probably not an earlier draft of the epistle but a draft which was sent as a general letter to other Pauline churches about the same time as the main copy was sent to Rome. The existence of a recension which omitted ch. 16 points in the same direction. Whether the greetings of ch. 16 were sent to Rome or Ephesus, they would have been sent originally to one church only. In either case the words 'All the churches of Christ greet you' (16:16) would be specially appropriate at the time when Paul was about to sail for Judaea, and had been joined by the delegates who were to carry their churches' gifts to Jerusalem.

While the main outlines of the argument of Rom. g
were worked out in Paul's mind long before he sent his letter to the Roman Christians, there are features in the course of his letter which reflect his actual dictation. His rhetorical questions (especially those put into the mouth of a supposed objector) and his sudden apostrophes are not simply to be explained as commonplaces of his discursive style. This is especially so in Rom. 9–11, where Paul wrestles with the problem of Jewish unbelief. In these chapters we can almost hear him thinking aloud, exploring one argument after another as he endeavours to reach the heart of the problem, until at last he concludes that 'God has consigned all men to disobedience, that he may have mercy upon all' (11:32). He must often have grappled with the problem before, but there is a spontaneity about these chapters which suggests that they proceeded from the actual situation. In Rom. 1–8 Paul has traced the course of God's saving purpose from universal sin to final glory, and inevitably there bursts forth the question which lay continually near his heart: Why have my own people not grasped this salvation with both hands—they in whose midst the preparation for it all was worked out?

Group III—This group comprises the later 'Captivity 810a
Epistles'—Phm., Col. and Eph. It has been suggested already (§807*a*) that the development of the conception of the church as the body of Christ in Col. and Eph. accords better with their later (Roman) dating than with an earlier dating.

Philemon—Phm., of course, is not an exposition of b
doctrine, but it manifestly belongs to the same date as Col. (cf. Col. 4:9). The argument that Onesimus, running away from his master in the Lycus valley, would be more likely to hide in the nearest big city, Ephesus, than in distant Rome, can be countered by the argument that he may well have thought distant

810b Rome a safer hiding-place than Ephesus. The balance of probability one way or the other is inconclusive. Paul's request to Philemon to get a guest-room ready for him (Phm. 22), because he hoped to be released and to pay him a visit, can also be accounted for either way. If he wrote from Rome, then the unforeseen situation which had developed since the writing of Rom. in A.D. 57 may have led to a modification of his plans, in that he now intended to revisit Asia instead of going on to Spain—or at least before going on to Spain.

How Onesimus got in touch with Paul we cannot say. But Paul's delicately insinuated hope in writing Phm. is that Philemon would send Onesimus back to him, to continue the personal service which Paul valued so highly. And the very survival of the letter is strong evidence that Paul had his way. Moreover, its inclusion in the Pauline corpus has been taken (especially by John Knox) as evidence that Onesimus himself had a hand in the compilation of the corpus.

c **Colossians and Ephesians**—Col. was written by Paul in consequence of a report, received from Epaphras, that the church of Colossae was in danger of accepting a Jewish-Hellenistic syncretistic teaching which was willing to accommodate some Christian elements in its scheme. In his reaction to this 'specious make-believe' (as he calls it) Paul developed his presentation of the cosmic role of Christ and the Gospel beyond the point which it had hitherto reached. The planetary powers, which played a decisive part in the 'Colossian heresy', were inferior to Christ (i) because they owed their existence to him, as the agent in creation, and (ii) because they were vanquished by him when they tried to overwhelm him on the cross.

The doctrine of the cosmic Christ was not a new thing with Paul: to him and his fellow-Christians there was 'one Lord Jesus Christ, through whom are all things and through whom we exist' (1 C. 8:6); this Christ was 'the power of God and the wisdom of God' (1 C. 1:24); and God through the Spirit had imparted to his people that hidden wisdom, 'decreed before the ages for our glorification', through ignorance of which the superhuman world-rulers had 'crucified the Lord of glory' and thus compassed their own doom (1 C. 2:6–10). And the liberation which Christ procured by his death was not restricted to mankind, but would ultimately be displayed in its cosmic outreaching (Rom. 8:19–22). But what was hinted at here and there in some of his other epistles is expounded more fully and systematically in Col. and Eph.

Justification by faith, fundamental as it is to Paul's thinking, does not exhaust his message. It was inevitable in the age of the Reformation that special attention should be concentrated on the principle by which the individual soul is accepted as righteous in God's sight. But it is regrettable that in consequence there has been a tendency among Protestant theologians to equate Paulinism so absolutely with the emphasis of Gal. and Rom. that the corporate and cosmic insights of Col. and Eph. have been felt to be non-Pauline. There is room in true Paulinism—and in true Christianity—for both these emphases.

d The difference in vocabulary which has been detected between these two epistles and their predecessors may be due in part to Paul's employment of the technical terms of a controverted system of thought in what has been called a 'disinfected' sense. As an apologist to the Gentiles, Paul was a pioneer in meeting opponents on their own ground and adapting their language to Christian usage, in order to show that the problems to which an answer was vainly sought elsewhere found their satisfying solution in the Gospel.

It may also have been the working out of his reply to the Colossian heresy that led Paul to develop his earlier picture of Christian fellowship in terms of the interdependent parts of a body to the point reached in Col. and Eph., where the church is viewed as the body of which Christ is the head. In this way he brings 81 out not only the living communion between the members but also the dependence of all the members on Christ for their common life and power; and he vindicates the supremacy of Christ against a theosophy which bade fair to set him on a lower plane than other celestial powers. In consequence these two epistles use 'body' in correlation with 'head' rather than (as in the earlier epistles) in correlation with 'spirit'; but this is no argument against common authorship.

While Col. and Eph. stand together over against the e earlier epistles, significant differences appear when they are compared the one with the other. Yet the significance of these differences should not be overrated. The fact that the technical terms used in Col. reappear in Eph. in new senses does not prove diversity of authorship; we have only to think of the variety of senses in which Paul uses Gr. *nomos* ('law') in Rom., and in any case it is a well-attested feature of less formal literature that 'a single word or phrase persists in the writer's mind by its own force, independently of any sense-recurrence' (E. Laughton, *Classical Philology* 45 (1950), 75).

From the theme of the cosmic Christ Paul went on to consider the cosmic role of the church as the body of Christ. From the thought of Christ as the reconciler of men to God he went on to consider Christ's role as the reconciler of men to one another, and especially of Jews to Gentiles. In Col. he unfolds the 'mystery' that Christ indwells Gentile (as well as Jewish) Christians as their hope of glory; in Eph. he goes on to unfold the 'mystery' of the uniting in one body of those who are thus indwelt by Christ—Jews and Gentiles alike. To one with Paul's Jewish antecedents, this could never cease to be the crowning wonder of God's grace.

If the author of Eph. was not Paul, he was the f greatest Paulinist of all time. That such a genius left no further trace in early Christian history is scarcely credible. For Eph. is a distinctive work with its own unity of theme. An atomistic study of it may make it look like a cento compiled from Paul's other letters, but when it is viewed as a whole, it has a unity which no mere cento could attain. It may justifiably be described as an exposition of the quintessence of Paul's teaching, but it is more than that: it carries on the teaching of his earlier epistles to a further stage of revelation and application, saying those things which Paul himself would have said had he advanced from his portrayal of the cosmic Christ in Col. to treat the cosmic role of the church. Some of its stylistic features would be accounted for if Paul employed as his amanuensis on this occasion one with a rather more classical style than the transcriber of Col.

The significant differences between Col. and Eph. are not inconsistent with the view that Paul, having completed his reply to the Colossian heresy, allowed his thoughts to run on in a less controversial vein until he was gripped by the vision which finds expression in Eph., and began to dictate its contents in an exalted mood of inspired meditation, thanksgiving and prayer. The resultant document was then sent as a general epistle—one might even say as Paul's testament—to the churches of Asia, by the hand of the messengers who were entrusted with the epistle to Colossae.

Group IV The Pastoral Epistles—The problem 811 of the Pastoral Epistles (1 and 2 Tim., Tit.) has not been solved to universal satisfaction. While the balance of opinion is preponderantly in favour of the position that they are not, as they stand, epistles of Paul, the case for their authenticity has been ably restated in recent years.

The main points urged against their Pauline authorship are: (i) their polemic against heresies which have a 2nd-cent. Gnostic (and even Marcionite) hue; (ii) their more stereotyped theological outlook, presuming a fixed body of orthodox doctrine called 'the faith'; (iii) the developed state of church organisation which they reflect; (iv) the difficulty of finding a

1a suitable setting for them in Paul's lifetime ; (v) the fact that early external evidence is not so strong for them as it is for the other Pauline epistles ; (vi) indications of borrowing from the other Pauline epistles ; (vii) their divergence in style and vocabulary from the other Pauline epistles and their affinity in this regard with 2nd-cent. Christian writings.

b The heresies envisaged in these epistles, however, do not have the fully developed character found in the 2nd cent. The reference, e.g., in 1 Tim. 6:20 to the 'contradictions (*antitheses*) of what is falsely called knowledge (*gnōsis*)' does not appear to have any special relation to Marcion's *Antitheses*. The emergence of a recognised body of belief by the 60s of the 1st cent. is not surprising ; we have traces of credal and catechetic summaries in generally undisputed epistles of Paul. The church organisation in the Pastoral Epistles has not reached the stage of development represented in the Ignatian epistles (*c*. A.D. 115). The threefold ministry has not yet been established ; church government by bishops (or elders) and deacons, such as we find in the Pastorals, is attested as early as Phil. 1:1. A 2nd-cent. date for these epistles (whether in more general terms or more specific, such as their recent ascription to Polycarp of Smyrna) is too late.

The difficulty of finding a setting for them in Paul's lifetime, as known to us from Ac. and Paul's other epistles, is admitted ; but since the Pastorals are in any case later than the other Pauline epistles, they must (if Pauline) belong to the closing years of Paul's life, about which we are poorly informed. To place them in Paul's closing years may involve a 'flight into *terra incognita*' (M. Dibelius), but that does not constitute a prima facie argument against this dating.

c The strongest argument against their Pauline date and authorship is that from style and vocabulary, presented in its most cogent form by P. N. Harrison in *The Problem of the Pastoral Epistles* (1921). Harrison's thesis has contributed more than anything else towards the widespread abandonment of belief in their authenticity. Yet the statistical presentation of the linguistic evidence from such a restricted field as the Pauline corpus is of limited validity ; and there are other conclusions than Harrison's which may account not only for the linguistic peculiarities of the Pastorals but for some of their other distinctive features too (cf. B. M. Metzger, 'A Reconsideration of Certain Arguments against the Pauline Authorship of the Pastoral Epistles', ET 70 (1958–9), 91ff.).

If it is difficult to accept all three in their present form as letters written or dictated directly by Paul, they may be held to represent the posthumous recension of a number of *disiecta membra* of Paul's correspondence (especially with Timothy and Titus) and other fragments, together possibly with some notes of his oral instruction on church order. Such a situation will best be appreciated by those who have had actual experience of the collecting, editing and publication of someone else's literary remains. If we envisage Timothy as specially active in this regard, possibly with some assistance from Luke, we may not be far wrong. Timothy is associated with Paul in the writing of other epistles (cf. 2 C., Phil. Col., 1 and 2 Th, Phm.); and Luke, who was Paul's only companion when 2 Tim. 4:11 was written, was evidently his amanuensis on that occasion. (But the style of the Pastorals is not Luke's.)

d The contents of the Pastorals may not be chronologically homogeneous (e.g. some advocates of an Ephesian provenance for the 'Captivity Epistles' bring 2 Tim. 4:6ff. into line with these). But if the Pastorals are dated in the interval between the termination of Paul's two years' imprisonment in Rome (say early in A.D. 62) and his death (probably an episode in the anti-Christian measures of A.D. 64), then one would have to suppose that he revisited the eastern Mediterranean lands. A further visit to Ephesus is not necessarily implied in 1 Tim. 1:3, taken by itself, as Paul's departure from Ephesus for Macedonia there mentioned could be the occasion 811d
referred to in Ac. 20:1. But 2 Tim. 4:19 ('Trophimus I left ill at Miletus') cannot refer to the Milesian visit of Ac. 20:15ff., for on that earlier occasion Trophimus continued to travel to Jerusalem with Paul. Tit. 1:5 certainly implies a visit by Paul to Crete more extended than anything that can be fitted into the coasting along the south shore of that island on the way to Rome, with a brief stay at Fair Havens, described in Ac. 27:7ff. Titus's mission to Dalmatia (2 Tim. 4:10) is probably later than his activity as apostolic delegate in Crete.

If Phm. was written from Rome, it contains evidence of Paul's intention to revisit Asia Minor before going elsewhere. And the combined evidence of the Pastoral Epistles implies a visit to Crete, Asia Minor, Macedonia and Epirus (Tit. 3:12). Whether after this he went to Spain or not is uncertain. But two or three years after the end of his first Roman imprisonment he was probably arrested again, tried and convicted on a capital charge at Rome, and executed. And the opinion which finds in this last phase of his life the setting for the valedictory words of 2 Tim. may well be right.

The Pauline Corpus—The earliest collection of 812a
Paul's epistles of which we have explicit information is that drawn up by Marcion at Rome about A.D. 144 as the second part of his canon. Part I was 'The Gospel' (a specially edited form of Lk.), and Part II, 'The Apostle', consisted of ten Pauline epistles (all except the three Pastorals), edited in accordance with Marcion's special theories. The implication of Tertullian's critique of Marcion (confirmed in the main by the express testimony of Epiphanius) is that in Marcion's canon the epistles appeared in the order : Gal., 1 and 2 C., Rom., 1 and 2 Th., Eph. (called by Marcion 'the Epistle to the Laodiceans'), Col., Phil., Phm. If the Corinthian correspondence was reckoned as one composite letter, and the Thessalonian correspondence similarly, then (apart from Gal.) the epistles are arranged in descending order of length. (It is interesting to observe how largely this principle has continued to control the traditional order of the Pauline epistles.) Harnack supposed that Gal. was placed first because its argument was so particularly congenial to Marcion's interpretation of the Gospel. More recently J. Knox has suggested that Marcion found the Pauline corpus of ten letters already arranged with Eph. at the head and Gal. immediately before Col., and that he made Gal. and Eph. change places. This suggestion has to be appreciated in the light of the view of E. J. Goodspeed and his school, that Eph. was composed as a prefatory statement of Paulinism to stand as an introduction to the Pauline corpus when first it was collected and published.

However that may be, the catholic leaders reacted to Marcion's teaching by defining their own acceptation of the canon, in which the NT did not supersede but stood alongside the OT, in which there was a fourfold Gospel and not Lk. only, in which there were not only Pauline epistles but epistles of other apostolic men, and not merely ten but thirteen epistles of Paul. And since the end of the 2nd cent. the thirteen epistles bearing Paul's name have invariably formed part of the NT canon.

But when we try to get behind Marcion to envisage b
the formation and history of the Pauline corpus before his time we are on uncertain ground. It is probable that the corpus of ten epistles was something which he inherited ; towards the end of the 2nd cent. the Chester Beatty codex P^{46} has apparently the same ten epistles, together with Heb., but without the three Pastorals.

It seems clear that a beginning had been made with the collection of Paul's epistles by A.D. 95, when the Epistle of Clement of Rome to the Corinthians was written. For Clement can quote 1 C. as readily as Rom., and he appears to know Eph. and Phil. as well.

812b There is some reason to think that he did not have access to 2 C., because it contains some passages which chime in with his argument so well that he would almost certainly have quoted them had he known them. Whether it was his evident knowledge and appreciation of 1 C. that stimulated the Christians of Corinth to gather the surviving fragments of Paul's correspondence in their church archives is a purely speculative question. But it certainly looks as if there were earlier stages in the interchange and circulation of some of Paul's letters, before the publication of the ten-letter corpus. On the other hand, we have to reckon with the practical certainty that his letters were not used as a source by the author of Ac. It may indeed be, as Goodspeed has suggested, that the publication of Ac. about A.D. 90 led to a revival of interest in Paul, in consequence of which his literary relics were collected. Whether, in addition, the task of collecting them was carried through at Ephesus (so Goodspeed); whether the prime mover in the work of collection was Onesimus, Philemon's former slave (so J. Knox, who further identifies him with the Onesimus who was bishop of Ephesus in the year of Ignatius's martyrdom, A.D. 115); whether the publication of the first Pauline corpus led to the formation of other Christian epistolary corpora (so A. E. Barnett)—these are hypotheses which cannot be verified in the present state of our knowledge.

c Possibly for a considerable time the second and enlarged edition of the Pauline corpus (comprising thirteen letters) circulated alongside the shorter ten-letter corpus; it may even have been published before the time of Marcion. Ignatius, for instance, appears to have some acquaintance with the Pastoral Epistles. And Tertullian's statement (*Prescription*, 38) that the Gnostic Valentinus (roughly contemporary with Marcion) 'appears to have used the entire canon' (unlike Marcion)—a statement confirmed in a general way by the recent publication of the Valentinian *Gospel of Truth*—possibly implies a certain recognition of the 2nd-cent. catholic canon of the NT, including thirteen Pauline epistles, even before the publication of Marcion's canon.

At any rate, the letters of Paul were in circulation throughout the Christian world early in the 2nd cent., and the publication of the Pauline corpus, together with the fourfold Gospel, and Ac. as the 'pivot' book, formed an initial and essential stage in the shaping of the completed NT canon.

d Even before the last decade of the 1st cent., some exchange of Paul's letters had probably already begun to be made between the churches to which they had been written. Indeed, he himself had encouraged such an interchange. However we identify the 'letter from Laodicea' of Col. 4:16, it is evident that the Colossian and Laodicean churches were called upon to exchange with each other the letters which they had received from Paul. It is probable, too, that Eph. from the start, and Rom. in one of its recensions, had the character of general epistles, not confined to one community only. Gal. was addressed to 'the churches of Galatia', not to one single church. We cannot be sure whether one copy only was sent, to be passed on from one church to another, or whether each church received its own copy (the latter possibility would have interesting implications for the early textual history of the epistle).

e Again, we must interrogate our various witnesses for the text of the Pauline epistles, in an attempt to discover whether they all represent a textual tradition which stems from the publication of the first Pauline corpus, or whether some evidence may not survive of the text of some at least of the epistles from a time antedating their publication in this form. The conclusion cannot be certain; but F. G. Kenyon's figures showing the measure of agreement and disagreement between P^{46} and other principal manuscripts reveal significant variations in this respect from one epistle to another; Rom., in particular, stands apart from the others (*The Chester Beatty Biblical Papyri*, Fasc. III Suppl. (1936), xv ff.). This state of affairs can best be explained if the textual tradition goes back to a time when the individual epistles circulated separately.

f **The Pauline Epistles and Early Christian Preaching and Teaching**—The epistles of Paul are our earliest written source of information about the apostolic preaching in the first days of Christianity. Since they were written for people who had already heard and believed this preaching, it is only occasionally that they make reference to it, when Paul wished to recall to his readers' mind something that they already knew; even so, we could reconstruct the main outline of the preaching, if it were necessary, from these epistles alone.

In his early preaching Paul laid emphasis on Christ's crucifixion (1 C. 2:2; Gal. 3:1), his resurrection, and his role at the parousia (1 Th. 1:9f.). The most notable kerygmatic passage in his epistles is 1 C. 15:3ff., where (by way of introducing an argument for the truth of resurrection) he reminds his readers of three essential elements in the message which they had received from him (as he himself had received it earlier)—Christ's death for their sins, his burial, and his resurrection on the third day. His death and resurrection are said to have taken place 'in accordance with the scriptures'; several eye-witnesses of his resurrection are listed, among whom Peter and James are mentioned by name. Paul's added reference to his own belated vision of the risen Christ is probably his personal contribution to the message which was proclaimed by all the apostles. He insists that on the basic facts there was no difference between his preaching and that of the other apostles (1 C. 15:11).

Further references in this and other epistles help to fill out the summary of the preaching. In 1 C. 11:23ff. he gives his account of the institution of the Eucharist—something again which he had 'received' himself before he 'delivered' it to his converts. (This is the oldest account of the institution, earlier by several years than that of Mk 14:22–5.) For the rest, we may summarise Paul's message thus: God, in the fullness of time and in accordance with prophetic scripture, has sent his Son Jesus as the Christ, who was born of the seed of David, lived under the law, taught the truth of God, was betrayed and crucified, dying the death which incurred the divine curse in order to redeem others from the curse incurred by sin; he was buried, was raised again the third day, appeared to many witnesses, was exalted to God's right hand, where he is now engaged in intercession for his people; he will reappear to judge the world, to raise the faithful departed, to consummate for his people the salvation which he has won for them, and to bring enduring bliss to all creation.

In general (as has been demonstrated outstandingly by C. H. Dodd), the outline of the early preaching which can be reconstructed from Paul's epistles is the same as that which can be traced in other NT epistles (notably Heb. and 1 Pet.), in the apostolic speeches reported in the first half of Ac., and in the Gospels (notably in the framework of Mk).

g If Paul's epistles show that he was at one with the other apostles on the basic facts of the Gospel, even if he interpreted and applied them in a way distinctively his own, they also show that his Christology was essentially the same as theirs. Such a significant feature as the application to Jesus of OT passages which speak of Yahweh (e.g. Isa. 45:23 in Phil. 2:10f.) is not peculiar to Paul; cf. the application of Isa. 8:12f. in 1 Pet. 3:14*b*–15*a*, and of Ps. 102:25–7 in Heb. 1:10–12. The 'wisdom' Christology of Col. 1:15ff. is paralleled in the prologue of Jn and in Heb. 1:2f.; Paul introduces it in a confessional context (Col. 1:13ff.; cf. Eph. 1:7f.) which appears to represent a wider Christian usage than his own (e.g. here we find mention of the 'remission (Gr. *aphesis*) of sins', whereas Paul's own preference is for more positive g terms which speak of God's justifying grace). The 'wisdom' Christology may reasonably be taken as one more of those things which Paul 'received' before he handed them on to others.

The portrayal of Christ's humiliation and exaltation in Phil. 2:5–11 reflects a 'Servant of the Lord' Christology (cf. §809*d*). E. Lohmeyer detected in this Christological passage a pre-Pauline hymn, while he emphasised its appropriateness to its context here. What is important is that in his Christology (as in his soteriology) Paul was not the complete innovator that some have imagined; he held in common with other Christians fundamental beliefs which he and they ultimately 'received from the Lord'.

h Furthermore, Paul's epistles are our earliest written source (see §804*f*) for primitive Christian ethical teaching. That this teaching goes back to the teaching of Jesus seems clear: we note the confidence with which Paul appeals to actual pronouncements of Jesus where they were available—on such a controversial question as marriage and divorce (1 C. 7:10f.), or even on the material support of those who preach the Gospel (1 C. 9:14). But even more than the teaching of Jesus, his life and character are presented as the supreme example and principle of Christian behaviour: when Paul wishes to commend to his readers the Christian graces (the very graces which characterise Jesus in the Gospels), he can sum up his teaching in the words: 'Put on the Lord Jesus Christ' (Rom. 13:14).

We may observe also the close logical connection brought out by Paul between the ethical teaching and the facts of the preaching. It is because his converts have accepted the truth of the Gospel story that it is incumbent on them to live in conformity with the mind of Christ. This is implied by the Pauline 'therefore' in such places as Rom. 12:1; Eph. 4:1; Phil. 2:12; Col. 3:5.

But these epistles bear witness, too, to the fact that at an early date Christian ethical teaching was classified in catechetical form for the more effective instruction of converts—the 'form of teaching' of Rom. 6:17 (RV). Cf., e.g., the catechetical teaching of Col. 3:5–4:6, falling into four paragraphs which may be collected under the respective captions 'put off' (3:5–11), 'put on' (3:12–17), 'be subject' (3:18–4:1), 'watch and pray' (4:2–6). That is to say, converts to Christianity must 'put off' old vices and 'put on' new virtues, they must display a spirit of yieldingness and mutual consideration in their relations with one another (and not least within the domestic circle), and their general behaviour must be characterised by vigilance and prayerfulness. The recurrence of such 'forms', under these or similar catchwords, in non-Pauline as well as in Pauline epistles, is best accounted for in terms of a common body of catechetical instruction rather than literary dependence of certain epistles on others. Even so, Paul reveals his distinctive lines of thought in his treatment of such common Christian property—e.g. in his use of the terms 'put to death' or 'reckon as dead' as alternatives to 'put off' (cf. Rom. 6:11, 8:13; Col. 3:5).

813a **The Pauline Epistles and Apostolic History**—The epistles of Paul provide valuable source-material both for Paul's own career and for early church history. They do not, of course, supply a continuous narrative such as we find in Ac., but they do give independent information on some crucial issues.

Here and there Paul in his epistles makes an autobiographical digression which illuminates what is left obscure in Ac. Thus we learn from the epistles more clearly than from Ac. that the central element in his conversion experience was the actual appearance to him of the risen Christ (1 C. 15:8, 9:1). The account of his persecuting zeal in Gal. 1:13ff. tallies well with the narrative in Ac. In the epistles and Ac. alike his conversion and earliest Christian activity are associated with Damascus, although Gal. includes reference to a stay in Arabia (1:17). In 2 C. 11:32f. his escape from Damascus in a basket is told as in Ac. 9:24f., but while 813a Ac. makes the Damascene Jews watch the city gates to catch him, Paul says it was the ethnarch of the Nabataean king Aretas who did so (this illuminates the reference to Arabia in Gal. 1:17). Where Ac. says that his first post-conversion visit to Jerusalem took place 'when many days had passed' (9:23), Paul tells us more precisely that it was 'after three years' (Gal. 1:18); where Ac. says that Barnabas 'brought him to the apostles' (9:27), Paul tells us (ibid.) that the only apostles whom he met on that occasion were Peter and James the brother of Jesus, and he adds that his visit lasted fifteen days, and that he spent those days with Peter. His statement that he 'was still not known by sight to the churches of Christ in Judaea' (Gal. 1:21) is not easy to square with Ac. 9:28f.; perhaps 'at Jerusalem' should be omitted from Ac. 9:28, and vv. 28f. should be taken as part of Barnabas's account of Paul's activity in Damascus. Paul's statement that he went from Jerusalem 'into the regions of Syria and Cilicia' (Gal. 1:21) agrees with the statement of Ac. 9:30 that he was shipped home to Tarsus. It is to Ac. that we owe the information that he was a native of Tarsus; the further information of Ac. that his name was Saul presents an 'undesigned coincidence' with the information of the epistles that he belonged to the tribe of Benjamin (cf. Rom. 11:1; Phil. 3:5). The autobiographical narrative of Gal. suggests further that he engaged in missionary activity (possibly among Gentiles as well as Jews) even before he joined Barnabas at Antioch. The latter episode is recorded only in Ac., but is supported by the appearance in the epistles of Paul and Barnabas as colleagues (cf. 1 C. 9:6; Gal. 2:1). It was evidently during those years in Syria-Cilicia (*c*. A.D. 42) that Paul had the strange experience described in 2 C. 12:2ff. During those years, too, may be dated his 'loss of all things' (Phil. 3:8)—a reference to disinheritance?—and some at least of the five beatings inflicted on him by Jewish authorities (2 C. 11:24).

The next incident to which Paul makes autobiographical reference is his Jerusalem visit of Gal. b 2:1ff. However this visit should be identified (see §807*g*), we are here given valuable information about a conference not recorded in Ac., at which the Jerusalem 'pillars' agreed that Paul and Barnabas should continue their Gentile ministry while they themselves would concentrate on apostolic witness to the Jews.

The account of the controversy during Peter's visit to Antioch (Gal. 2:11ff.) has no parallel in Ac., although we may link it with the arrival of Judaisers from Judaea mentioned in Ac. 15:1. The best attested text of Gal. 2:12 probably indicates one messenger from James whose representations to Peter persuaded him to withdraw from table fellowship with Gentile Christians at Antioch. Even so, the suggestion of a judaising Peter is as foreign to the epistles as it is to Ac. The point of Paul's rebuke to Peter in Gal. 2:14ff. is that Peter knew better; he did not by this time object on principle to table fellowship with Gentiles, but was 'acting a part' (as Paul put it) out of deference to the circumcision party. There is no good reason for linking the behaviour of Barnabas on this occasion (Gal. 2:13) with the contention which arose between him and Paul, according to Ac. 15:39, when they were on the point of revisiting the young churches of Cyprus and South Galatia.

From Ac., moreover, we should never have gathered that Paul had such a situation to face as that which he deals with in Gal. The silence of Ac. on such matters is no doubt bound up with the author's purpose and plan; but, for all our indebtedness to this author for our knowledge of the rise and progress of early Christianity, there would be more serious gaps than there are in our knowledge of the field covered by Ac. were it not for the first-hand information contained in Paul's epistles.

The same is true with regard to the tensions to c

813c which the Corinthian correspondence bears witness. We might well wish that this correspondence had been preserved to us entire—not only all Paul's letters to the Corinthians, but their letter to him (1 C. 7:1). As it is, the surviving correspondence gives us a vivid impression of the war on two fronts which Paul had to conduct—on the one hand, against those Gentile Christians who interpreted Christian liberty as licence and regarded ethical requirements as so many restrictions on the freedom of the truly spiritual man ; on the other hand, against those who followed him around and tried to impose a judaising legalism on the churches which he had founded. His apostolic claims were belittled by both sides—the ' spiritual ' party thought he was too influenced by old Jewish taboos and prejudices ; the Judaisers emphasised the apparent weakness of his commission, since he had not been one of Jesus' companions and delegates during his Palestinian ministry, but claimed to have been called to the apostleship later, in a vision. Some of these latter belittlers of Paul's apostleship compared his apostolic claims unfavourably with Peter's. Whether Peter himself ever visited Corinth, or even knew that some members of the church there formed a party which claimed his leadership, cannot be inferred with certainty from Paul's references to those Corinthian Christians who said : ' I belong to Peter ' (1 C. 1:12). But if Peter did know or approve of it in any measure, Paul could regard it as a breach of the agreement which he and Barnabas had reached with Peter and the other ' pillars' at Jerusalem. Those who claimed to act in Peter's name at Corinth represented themselves as building on the foundation which Paul laid (1 C. 3:10ff.). There was a way of doing this which Paul did not resent ; he seems to have been quite happy about Apollos's activity at Corinth after his own departure, although he deprecated the tendency to make Apollos a party-leader, just as he refused to be regarded as a party-leader himself. But the Petrine party, in claiming to build on Paul's foundation, did so in a manner which disparaged Paul's work. While they did not follow the cruder methods used by the Judaisers earlier in the churches of Galatia, immediately pressing the necessity of circumcision and so forth upon their hearers, their activity was perhaps regarded by Paul as all the more dangerous for that. How careful Paul himself was not to ' build on another man's foundation ' (Rom. 15:20) may be seen from the delicacy of his approach in Rom., where he writes to a Christian community which he had no part in forming.

d Paul's Ephesian ministry of nearly three years is sketched briefly in Ac. 19, only a few outstanding incidents being treated in detail (principally the riot in the theatre). The epistles written in that period throw further light on Paul's words to the elders of Ephesus in Ac. 20:19, where he reminds them of his tears and the trials which befell him ' through the plots of the Jews ' ; they also ease our sense of surprise at his forecast in vv. 29f. of the same speech, that after his departure his converts will be exposed to invasion by ' fierce wolves ' from outside, and to seduction by false teachers from within. The problem of the special perils which Paul had to undergo during his Ephesian ministry (cf. 1 C. 15:30–2 ; 2 C. 1:8–11, 11:23–9), with its bearing on the date of the ' Captivity Epistles ', has already been discussed (§809*b*).

e It is evident, too, from the epistles that Paul was greatly concerned at this time about the collection which he was organising in his Gentile churches as a gift and token of fellowship for the Jerusalem church. It is mentioned first in 1 C. 16:1ff., in terms which suggest that the Corinthians had already been informed about it (probably through Titus ; cf. 2 C. 12:18). Paul had also given instructions about it to the churches of Galatia (1 C. 16:1), probably when he passed that way on his return from his flying visit to Palestine in A.D. 52 (Ac. 18:23). He reverts to the subject in 2 C. 8:1ff., where (writing in Macedonia) he stimulates his Corinthian readers by telling them of his boast to his Macedonian friends that ' Achaia has been ready 81
since last year ' (2 C. 9:2), and by describing the zeal with which the Macedonian Christians, despite their poverty, actually begged for the favour of sharing in this good work. By the time he writes Rom., the collection of the money is almost complete, and he reveals something of the importance which he attaches to it (Rom. 15:25ff.). He is not sure if it will achieve its purpose and be ' acceptable to the saints ' in Jerusalem ; he asks the Roman Christians to pray that this may be so, and also that he may be ' delivered from the unbelievers in Judaea ' (Rom. 15:31). How necessary this last prayer was is clear from the narrative of Ac. 21–6.

But we should have gathered hardly anything about the collection from Ac., although the references to it in the epistles explain a few points in Luke's narrative. (i) Why did Paul resolve, after passing through Macedonia and Achaia, to visit Jerusalem before carrying out his plan to see Rome (Ac. 19:21) ? Because he wished to see to the safe delivery of the collection. (ii) Why was Paul accompanied by so many Gentile Christians when he set out on his last journey to Jerusalem (Ac. 20:4) ? They were delegates from the contributing churches (cf. 1 C. 16:3f.). (iii) What were the ' alms and offerings ' which Paul told Felix he had brought to his nation (Ac. 24:17) ? They were the contributions made by the Gentile churches.

The language of Ac. 24:17 may reflect the Jerusalem Christians' attitude to the collection. From Paul's point of view it was a voluntary gift which he had organised in accordance with his earlier promise to go on remembering ' the poor ' of Jerusalem (Gal. 2:10), and he hoped it would bind the Jewish and Gentile Christians more closely together. From the viewpoint of James and the other leaders of the Jerusalem church, however, it may have been regarded more as a tribute which Christians in other lands owed to Jerusalem, much as Jews throughout the world made a regular contribution to the Temple treasury. We may wonder why Luke is so reticent in the matter ; was the collection itself an item in Paul's indictment, being represented by his prosecutors as a diversion of money which ought to have formed part of the Temple fund (which was safeguarded by Roman law)?

While the narrative of Ac. has Paul's arrival and f
unhindered preaching in Rome as its goal, it is to the epistles (especially to Rom. 15:22ff.) that we turn for Paul's conception of his life-mission. For him Rome was to be a temporary halting-point on his way to Spain ; his aim was to cover as much as possible of the Mediterranean world with the Gospel. In the east he had evangelised ' from Jerusalem and as far round as Illyricum ' (Rom. 15:19) ; now he proposed to repeat his programme in the west. Egypt and Cyrenaica, like Rome itself, had already heard the Gospel, and it was no part of his policy to ' build on another man's foundation '. But in Spain there was virgin soil for sowing the good seed.

According to Rom. 11:13ff., Paul believed that Israel as a whole would one day accept the Gospel, despite its present unbelief (ascribed to a temporary ' hardening ') ; but Israel's turning to the Lord, with which the history of salvation would reach its climax, must be preceded by the ingathering of the full complement of Gentiles. And Paul was very conscious of his personal role as the chief instrument in God's hand for this Gentile ingathering. His apostleship to the Gentiles thus takes on an eschatological significance. Everything else is subservient to the fulfilment of his commission ; even his last defence when on trial for his life is remembered with special satisfaction because of the strength he then received ' to proclaim the word fully, that all the Gentiles might hear it ' (2 Tim. 4:17).

Bibliography—H. N. Bate, *A Guide to the Epistles of* 81
St Paul (1926) ; W. D. Davies, *Paul and Rabbinic Judaism* (1948) ; A. Deissmann, *Paul* (2nd ed. 1926) ;

814a M. Dibelius, *Paul* (1953); C. H. Dodd, *The Meaning of Paul for To-day* (1920), *NT Studies* (1953), 67–128, 'The Mind of Paul' (first published 1933–4); G. S. Duncan, *St Paul's Ephesian Ministry* (1929); E. J. Goodspeed, *The Meaning of Ephesians* (1933), *The Key to Ephesians* (1956); A. M. Hunter, *Paul and his Predecessors* (1940), *Interpreting Paul's Gospel* (1954); H. A. A. Kennedy, *St Paul's Conception of the Last Things* (1904), *St Paul and the Mystery-Religions* (1913), *The Theology of the Epistles* (1919); J. H. Kennedy, *The Second and Third Epistles to the Corinthians* (1900); J. Klausner, *From Jesus to Paul* (1944); J. Knox, *Philemon among the Letters of Paul* (1935), *Marcion and the NT* (1942), *Chapters in a Life of Paul* (1950); W. L. Knox, *St Paul and the Church of Jerusalem* (1925), *St Paul and the Church of the Gentiles* (1939); K. Lake, *The Earlier Epistles of St Paul* (1911); J. G. Machen, *The Origin of Paul's Religion* (1921); A. H. McNeile, *Introduction to the NT* (2nd ed. 1953), 124–99; T. W. Manson, *St Paul in Ephesus* (4 BJRL reprints, 1939–42), *St Paul's Letter to the Romans—and Others* (BJRL reprint, 1948), *St Paul in Greece* (BJRL reprint, 1953); C. L. Mitton, *The Formation of the Pauline Corpus of Letters* (1955); J. Munck, *Paulus und die Heilsgeschichte* (1954); A. D. Nock, *St Paul* (1938); W. M. Ramsay, *St Paul the Traveller and the Roman Citizen* (14th ed. 1920); A. Schweitzer, *Paul and his Interpreters* (1912), *The Mysticism of Paul the Apostle* (1931); C. A. A. Scott, *Christianity according to St Paul* (1927), *St Paul: the Man and the Teacher* (1936); G. Vos, *The Pauline Eschatology* (1952); G. Zuntz, *The Text of the Epistles* (1953). 814a

ROMANS

By T. W. MANSON

815a **Authorship, Occasion, and Date**—The Pauline authorship of Rom. is generally accepted by NT scholars : attempts to question it may be reckoned among the eccentricities of criticism. There is wide agreement that Paul composed it during his stay in Greece, probably at Corinth, mentioned in Ac. 20:2f. The date of this visit cannot be fixed with certainty ; but it took place in winter some time between late 54 and early 59. The Apostle's reasons for producing the work may be inferred from the contents of the letter itself and from its place in the larger context of his missionary work as revealed by the other letters and by Ac. The author looks back on a period of fierce controversy in which the adequacy of his Gospel had been questioned and his status as an apostle challenged. He had succeeded in re-establishing his authority at Corinth (2 C. 7:5–16), and it appears from Ac. 20 that he could count on the loyalty of the churches in Macedonia and western Asia Minor ; but we do not know how matters stood in Galatia, and we do know that, after earlier hesitations (1 C. 16:3f.), he had finally decided to pay a visit to Jerusalem, though with serious misgivings about the reception he would have there (Rom. 15:30–2). It seems as if he considered it essential to come to a fresh understanding with the authorities in Jerusalem before embarking on the new missionary enterprises which he had in mind. His future plans are stated in Rom. 15:23f. After his visit to Jerusalem he hopes to go to Rome, spend some time there, and then, with the support of the Roman community, begin missionary work in Spain.

b **Contents**—The contents of the letter answer to this situation. After the introductory verses (A), the major part of it (1:18–11:36) (B) is a calm vindication of the adequacy of Paul's Gospel, showing that it is the divine response to a universal human predicament ; that the Apostle is deeply conscious that both Jews and Gentiles are equally in need of it and deeply concerned that both Jews and Gentiles should accept it. He refuses to be thought of as a renegade Jew whose sympathies are wholly pro-Gentile. On the contrary he sees the epoch-making events which constitute the Good News as the culmination of Israel's history, the fulfilment of the Law and the Prophets. For the Jewish people to accept Jesus as Messiah and Lord and proclaim him to the world is to achieve this historic destiny. For Jews and Gentiles alike the acceptance of Jesus as Lord is the way to reconciliation with God, to sonship in his family, and citizenship in his kingdom.

The second major section (C) of the letter (12:1–15:13) draws out the ethical implications of this new status. Ch. 12 lays down the rules that govern the common life in the Body of Christ. Ch. 13 reaffirms the teaching of Jesus about the proper relations between the State and its subjects and indicates how a Christian minority should behave in a predominantly pagan society. In 14:1–15:12 Paul deals with the tensions that had arisen, and could easily arise again, between Christians of Jewish origin whose way of life in great matters and small had been formed by the Jewish Law and tradition, and Gentile converts to Christianity, for whom much of this code of behaviour
was pointless or positively repugnant. It is clear to 81
him, and he tries to make it clear to his readers, that the Christian life cannot be codified into a detailed system of rules and regulations, and that Christian liberty can flourish only if Christians learn two lessons : (*a*) to forgo the pleasure of imposing all their manners and customs on their fellow-Christians, and (*b*) to respect the conscientious scruples of other Christians even if they cannot share them. The essentials of Christian ethics are few and simple, though not easy ; on these Christians must be uncompromising ; on more peripheral matters they must learn to be tolerant.

The remainder of ch. 15 (vv. 14–33) (D) gives the Roman Christians an outline of Paul's plans for the future and asks them to pray for the success of his coming visit to Jerusalem. Ch. 16 (E) contains a commendation of the deaconess Phoebe to the recipients of the letter (1f.), numerous greetings from Paul to named individuals and groups (3–16), some brief warnings and exhortations (17–20), greetings from named individuals (21–3), and a doxology (25–7). At this point we are confronted by the most serious critical problem touching the epistle.

The problem of the last two chapters may be c
shortly stated thus : There is evidence that in the 2nd cent. Rom. was extant in three forms of varying length. The shortest ended at 14:23 in the middle of an argument which continues in the longer texts to 15:13. In other words this is a mutilated text and we have early testimony that the cut was deliberate and that it was made by the heretic Marcion.* The longest form is that which we have in our English Bibles, ending at 16:27. Now one of the main pieces of evidence for the existence of the short text is the fact that in many MSS the closing doxology (16:25–7) is placed after 14:23 and this placing can be traced back to a very early date. As the doxology is clearly meant to be the last word, it would be put at the end of the text. In 1935 the publication of the Michigan University's leaves of the Chester Beatty codex of the Pauline epistles (P^{46}) revealed that in this, the oldest known MS of Paul, the doxology was placed at the end of ch. 15. From this fact it was a natural inference that P^{46} is descended from an ancestor that ended at 15:33. This conclusion would hold whether the doxology (16:25ff.) is genuine Paul or a Marcionite interpolation, a question to be discussed in its proper place. In the meantime it may be noted that Paul clearly indicates the major pauses in his exposition by doxologies or benedictions which occur at 11:33–6, where the doctrinal section (1:18–11:32) ends ; at 15:13, the end of the ethical section ; at 15:33 at the end of the plans for future work ; and at three different points in ch. 16, vv. 20, 24 and 27, on which see the commentary. These are natural stopping-places in a way that 14:23 is not ; and it is a plausible suggestion that the doxology, 16:25–7, was first produced in Marcionite circles to soften the abruptness resulting from Marcion's cut at 14:23. In that case the appear-

* Marcion (*fl. c.* 150+) was an encratite (Christian ascetic), with strong prejudices against the Jews ; he rejected the OT altogether as scripture, and produced a bowdlerised version of the NT, with all passages removed which seemed to him most Jewish in character.—Ed.

5c ance of the doxology at the end of chs. 15 and 16 would indicate that it had been taken from the short form and added to the two longer forms.

d A century before P^{46} turned up it had been argued on internal evidence that the original letter to the Romans ended at 15:33 and that ch. 16 was a letter or part of a letter to some other church where Paul was already well known, had many friends, and could speak with authority. Considering the long list of names in 16:3–15, it appears that Prisca and Aquila were in Ephesus a few months before Rom. was written and that their house there was a meeting-place for the church (1 C. 16:19). We have no reason to suppose that they moved to Rome and gathered a fresh congregation in their house there between the writing of 1 C. and Rom. Further, greetings are sent to Epaenetus the first convert in Asia: he is more likely to be in, say, Ephesus than Rome. A number of persons are described as hard workers in the church in question or as fellow-workers with Paul: it is more likely that he knew such people in a place like Ephesus, where he had himself worked for a long time, than in Rome, where he was a stranger. The commendation of Phoebe (16:1f.) would carry more weight, and the warning (16:17–20) be more heeded if it came from the Apostle to a church in which he was already well known and greatly respected. In a word, ch. 16 reads very oddly if we think of it as addressed to a church to which Paul has just written the previous fifteen chapters in order to show, amongst other things, that he is the kind of Christian missionary that they can safely welcome to their fellowship and support in his enterprises.

e The best defence of the view that the whole letter of sixteen chapters was sent by Paul to Rome is C. H. Dodd's in his commentary on Rom. in the Moffatt series. This, however, was written before the discovery of P^{46}; and the evidence of this ancient MS may be thought to tip the balance in favour of the view that the Roman copy of Rom. did not have ch. 16. If so, we may conjecture that the letter originated as an attempt to set down Paul's mature and considered convictions about a number of theological and moral issues that had been burning questions for a considerable time before it was written. Some of these issues had perhaps been discussed at Corinth; and we may be sure that other Pauline churches would be eager to know the results of the debate, among them the churches of Asia, particularly Ephesus. As it was not Paul's intention to visit Ephesus on his way to Jerusalem, it would be natural for him to send a copy of the document there with the personal matters of ch. 16 added. Any further information would be supplied by Phoebe. Another copy comprising chs. 1–15 would be sent to Rome. These two forms of the text will thus go back to Paul himself. The shortest form, ending with ch. 14, was the result of deliberate mutilation by Marcion. For a fuller discussion of the problem reference may be made to the writer's article 'The Epistle to the Romans—and others' in BJRL 31 (1948), 224–40.

f It is evident from Ac. and Rom. that the Christian community in Rome was not founded by Paul. There is in fact no contemporary evidence of its having had a founder at all in the strict sense of the word. It is certain that Paul was in contact with it when he was awaiting trial in Rome, and probable that Peter was also associated with it towards the end of his life; but it was already there when they came to Rome, and the most likely hypothesis is that it came into existence through the migration of Christians from other places to the capital city of the Empire.

16a **(A) The Introductory Verses**

I 1-17 Greetings and Introduction of the main Theme of the Letter—The section is in three parts: (*a*) the opening salutation, rather more elaborate than in most of Paul's letters (1–7); (*b*) a thanksgiving to God for graces received by the readers of the letter, leading to personal relations between them and the Apostle (in the case of the Roman church these are 816a
plans for the future rather than memories of the past) (8–15); (*c*) a bridge passage leading from Paul's entire preoccupation with preaching the Gospel to the exposition of the Gospel he preaches (16f.).

Vv. 1–7 expand what in ordinary letters was said in a line or two. The essentials were the names of sender and addressee and the word of greeting: 'A to B his father greetings' or the like. Paul uses six verses to say who and what the sender is and comes to the addressees and greetings in v. 7. He is 'a servant of Jesus Christ' (cf. Phil. 1:1). 'Slave' gives the wrong emphasis: in religious usage in both OT and NT the stress is not on one person's rights of property but on the total loyalty and unstinted service given of right to God by his prophets or to Christ by his apostles. To Paul 'servant of Jesus Christ' is a title of honour not to be used indiscriminately: he has other designations for ordinary Christians—'saints', 'God's beloved' and so on. He was 'called to be an apostle' by God (1 C. 1:1; 2 C. 1:1) through Christ (Ac. 9:5, 26:15ff.; Gal. 1:1); and he is thus the authorised representative and agent of his master. The work to which he is allocated is the 'Gospel of God', i.e. that self-revelation of God in Christ which is good news for a lost and despairing world. What is now news was formerly promise. The Heb. scriptures, the OT, held the prophetic announcement of the good purpose of God lately realised in the fact of Christ.

For Jesus Christ is the content of the Gospel (3–6). The Gospel is about him, the Son of God, who stands in a unique relation to the Father (cf. 8:3; 1 C. 8:6; 2 C. 8:4; Gal. 4:4; Phil. 2:5–11; Col. 1:9–20) and plays a unique part in the deliverance of mankind from the domination of evil. His life-work brings together two orders of being. 'According to the flesh', i.e. in the natural order, he is a descendant of David and so may claim the title of Messiah or Anointed, the rightful king of Israel. **4.** 'According to the Spirit of holiness', i.e. in the divine spiritual order, he is 'designated Son of God in power' (cf. Lk. 1:35). The royal birth and the divine incarnation go together. In that case we should probably make a pause after 'holiness' and understand the next clause to mean that the title of 'Lord' belongs to Jesus Christ as a corollary to his being raised from the dead (cf. 1 C. 15:23–7; Phil. 2:9–11). **5f.** Through the Risen Lord Paul has obtained the privilege of being an apostle to all non-Jewish nations including the Roman people. His task is to claim men and women for Christ and to bring them in trusting submission to him. **7.** So we come to the addressees, the Christians in Rome (the absence of the place name here and at v. 15 in a few MSS is perhaps due to Marcion, who had been ejected from the Roman community). They are described as dear to God, having responded to his call and dedicated themselves to him. To them Paul wishes 'grace and peace'. Grace is the kindness shown by the powerful to the weak, the divine generosity coming to meet human need. Peace is the total well-being that results from this kindness. The source of these blessings is 'God our Father and the Lord Jesus Christ'. For Paul the essence of the Christian faith is to know God as Father (8:15; Gal. 4:6) and to acknowledge Jesus as Lord (1 C. 12:3; Phil. 2:11).

8. Here as often Paul finds something to thank God b
for in the Church to which he is writing, in this case the remarkable and widely known progress of Christianity in Rome. He declares how much he wishes to have part in this activity, and how earnestly he prays that he may after many delays succeed in fulfilling this long-cherished and often frustrated desire (9f., 13*a*). The first purpose of his visit would be to 'impart some spiritual gift to strengthen' them. The strength will not come from Paul but through him from God, as the Gr. clearly implies (11); but to exclude all misunderstanding it is made clear in **12** that the benefit will be mutual. Paul's second aim is active missionary work in the area served by the Roman community

816b (13*b*–15), because his duty as an apostle is one which recognises no barriers of race or culture.

c In **16f.** we have the transition from Paul's obligations as preacher of the Gospel to the Gospel which he has to preach. It is an understatement to say that he is ' not ashamed ' of it : he is proud to tell of this mighty act, *the* intervention of God in history. Here God has showed his hand, and it is a helping hand— ' for salvation '. One thing, and one thing only, is required on man's side : he must ' have faith ', the simple trust that will accept what God offers to all, in the first instance to Israel and then to the rest of mankind (here represented by ' the Greek '). In the gospel, i.e. in the fact of Christ, ' the righteousness of God is revealed ', it is invading our experience here and now. The ' righteousness of God ' is no abstract quality of ultimate Reality : it is the creative goodness of the living God in action. It can be argued that it is the Pauline counterpart to the ' kingdom of God ' in the teaching of Jesus (see W. Sanday, ' St. Paul's equivalent for the " kingdom of Heaven " ', JTS 1 (1900), 481–91). In both cases we have a divine intervention, which reveals God at work to deliver man from the powers of evil and to create that right relation between God and man which is man's true life. This revelation is ' through faith for faith ', more literally ' from faith to faith ', which may mean that it is a matter of faith from start to finish, but more probably that it is a revelation that springs from God's faithfulness and appeals to man's faith. The proof-text which Paul quotes (Hab. 2:4) could, as quoted, refer to either; and the ambiguity is older than Rom. The Heb. text of Hab. says that ' the righteous shall live by his (own) faith (or faithfulness) ' : the LXX that ' the righteous shall live by my (i.e. God's) faithfulness '. By omitting the possessive pronoun Paul leaves both possibilities open, and perhaps that is what he meant to do (cf. 3:1–4). Life is the portion of him whose rightness with God springs from God's faithfulness and his own faith.

817a **(B) The Christian Faith: God's Life for Man (I 18-XI 36)**

I 18-III 20 tells of the human predicament that calls for the Gospel. Men everywhere are estranged from the one true God. Either they do not acknowledge him at all or, if they do, their acknowledgment is formal and superficial and does not issue in full obedience to his will. All are subject to evil powers hostile to God ; and this means degradation and destruction for the race, since all are exposed to the corrupting influences of evil and to the wrath of God.
I 18-32. This is demonstrated first in the case of the non-Jews. The two counts in the indictment are idolatry and immorality, idolatry being the tap-root of evil. **18.** These things bring down the ' wrath of God from heaven '. The ' wrath ' is the obverse of the ' righteousness of God ' : his creative goodness is matched by his inflexible opposition to evil. The Bible knows nothing of a remote and impassive Absolute : it knows only the living God who will not condone evil, though he will do everything to turn the evildoer from his ways. The godless and wicked ' suppress the truth ' : they distort the knowledge of the one true God. **19f.** This knowledge God himself has made available to anyone who will consider the wonders of the created Universe (cf. Job 40:1–42:6 ; Ps. 19 ; Isa. 40:12–31). There his ' eternal power and deity ' are clearly reflected. In **21ff., 25** Paul argues that the indefensible thing is that, confronted by facts which pointed to the Creator of the world, men gave their reverence and gratitude, not to him, but to things created. The forces and mechanisms built into Nature became for them the final truth about Nature. The sun with its light and heat, the seasonal growth and decay, the mysterious reproductive power of living creatures, these and many other elements of creation were deified and allowed to usurp the place of the Creator.

b In a divinely ordered universe this could only be disastrous. Idolatry is the big lie that ' darkens the 81
mind ' ; it is the big sin that corrupts the will. Sexual excesses (24), homosexual perversions (26f.) and general moral degradation (28–31) follow on idolatry. Three times in these verses Paul declares that God allows these appalling things to happen. They could have been avoided if he had made robots instead of men. But he made men and they could be men only if they had the capacity for good or evil. At the same time he set them in an environment of natural and spiritual laws in which evil must be calamitous. Since the laws are his laws, their operation is properly said to be his doing : the wrath is ' the wrath of God revealed from heaven '. But divine retribution is not the last word. That rests with the Gospel.

In the catalogue of wrongs (29ff.) ' covetousness ' c
is hardly strong enough : ' rapacity ' is nearer the Gr. ' Gossips ' and ' slanderers ' both injure the reputation of others, the former by private whispering, the latter by open denunciation. ' Haters of God ' may be right ; but the usual meaning of the Gr. word is ' hateful to God '. The Gr. word translated by ' insolent ' means one who inflicts wanton injury or humiliation on another merely to gratify his own sense of power. ' Foolish ' implies lack of conscience even more than of common sense. The last word (32) is that the evildoers are not content to be what they are ; they must encourage others to go the same way to perdition.

II 1-III 20 The Indictment of Israel—2:1-10. 81
Paul argues (*a*) that the special position of the Jews gives them no right to sit in judgment on the rest of mankind or (**11-16**) to claim preferential treatment for themselves ; (*b*) **17-24** that knowing the Law is useless without obedience ; and (*c*) **25-8** that circumcision is a meaningless sign unless it signifies a cleansed heart. In that case it may be retorted (*d*) **3:1-9** that the status of Chosen People is illusory ; and Paul has to admit in the main this is the case. Jews and Gentiles *are* in the same boat, a fact which can be proved (*e*) **10-20** from the Jewish scriptures themselves.
II 1-10. The accusing finger turns from the Gentiles to Israel (cf. Am. 2:6ff.). In 1:32 the last word was of Gentiles who encourage evildoing. The Jew could say : ' We condemn it '. **2:1-3.** The answer is : ' In that case you condemn yourselves, for your own hands are not clean.' **4f.** God may be very patient with his Chosen People, but they abuse his patience at their peril. **6.** In the final reckoning nothing will be taken into account except what each person has done with the opportunities granted to him (cf. Job 34:11 ; Ps. 62:12 ; Prov. 24:12). Persistent effort to achieve a life of the highest quality will be rewarded with life of the highest quality. **7f.** Selfish disregard of truth and justice will bring the sternest retribution. **9f.** In either case the treatment will be the same for Jews and Gentiles.

11-16. The reason why no preferential treatment can b
be given to Israel is now stated. In these matters God has no favourites (11). Either you are subject to the Law of Moses or you are not. If you are, you will be judged by it ; and the test will not be knowledge of its provisions but obedience to them (12*b*–13). In 13 we have the first appearance of the verb ' to justify '. The verb and the cognate noun ' justification ' both have to do with right relations between God and man and the ways in which they can be established. Men are right with God when they are devoted heart and hand to him and are approved by him. In theory, at any rate, they can put themselves right with God by complete conformity to his will : ' the doers of the law will be justified '. They will be acceptable to God on their merits. Or they would be, if they existed. But in practice no-one gives this total obedience ; no-one is acceptable on his merits. They can become acceptable only if they are accepted by God. In order to become righteous they must first be put right with God. And only God can do what is needed. His doing of it is the Gospel.

818b In **14-16** the Gentiles who do not possess the Mosaic Law are considered. They too will be judged on their merits. They are not without moral insight. The debate between good and evil goes on in their minds and they can frame rules of conduct for themselves. If they are loyal to the good they know, they will be acceptable to God; but it is a very big 'if'.

c **17-20.** We return to the Jew with his immense spiritual heritage of which he is justly proud. With his pure religion and his lofty moral code he is uniquely fitted, he claims, to assume the spiritual leadership of mankind. The 'foolish' who need correction are the morally backward; and 'children' is used figuratively for 'immature' people of any age. The attitude portrayed was specially characteristic of Jewish communities outside of Palestine.

21-23. But mere possession of creed and code does not create leaders. Creed and code must be lived out before men. The spiritual education must begin at home. Paul is not asserting that all Jews commit all the sins he mentions: he does claim that too many of them fall too far short of the standards they set up. The particular charges are clear enough except that of 'robbing temples'. No really convincing explanation of this has so far been offered. **24.** The indictment is clinched by an OT text, Isa. 52:5.

d **25-29.** Circumcision, by no means an exclusively Heb. rite, had a special significance in the Jewish community as a token of membership of the Covenant People. Already in the OT it was emphasised that the vital matter was not the surgical operation but the dedication of the personality to God (Dt. 10:16, 30:6; Jer. 4:4). Paul insists on this in 25 and 28f. He also argues (26f.) that the uncircumcised Gentile who does what is right in God's eyes has a better title to membership of the Covenant People than the circumcised Jew who does not. 'Condemn' in 27 does not mean that the judgment will be carried out by the good Gentiles but that at God's judgment they will show up the errant Jews (cf. Mt. 12:41f.). Recognition as a true Jew depends not on external things but on inward dispositions; and it comes from God alone (29).

e **III 1-9.** If Paul is right so far, it may well be asked what is the use of being a circumcised Jew. He answers by naming the chief advantage, that 'the Jews are entrusted with the oracles of God' (1f.). The oracles are the commands and promises of God, the terms of his covenant with Israel. But (3) does not the failure of Israel to obey the commands release God from the obligation to keep his promises? No, says Paul, God stands by his covenant even if Israel defaults (4); and there is a text to prove it in Ps. 51:4. In that case, it is objected, God ought to be handing rewards to Israel, and not punishments. Our human instinct for fair play suggests that there is something wrong here (5). Paul denies this on the ground God has not only the covenant to keep: he has also to maintain order and justice in the world (6). In 7f. the same argument is used as in 5, but a new conclusion is drawn. The charge of being sinners should be dropped and we should go to all lengths in wickedness, that our extremity may be God's opportunity. Paul sternly rejects this view, the more sternly as he is falsely charged with holding it himself. This false charge may well have arisen out of the fact that he refused to subject his converts to the entire Mosaic Law. We come back to the original question in v. 9. Several translations of the Greek are possible. The most likely seems to be: 'What then? Are we Jews (in fact) worse off (than the Gentiles)? No, not entirely.' The Jews still have the covenant, even if they and the Gentiles are all 'under the power of sin'. But they no less than the Gentiles are in that state.

f This is shown by a catena of OT texts. **10-12** seem to be quoted inexactly from Ps. 14:1-3 or 53:1-3. **13** looks back to Ps. 5:9 and 140:3; **14** to Ps. 10:7; **15-17** to Isa. 59:7f.; and **18** to Ps. 36:1. These OT texts ('law' in v. 19 = OT) can refer only to Israel. It follows that no-one can defend himself; all are exposed to God's judgment. Why? **20.** Because no man can make himself acceptable to God by obedience to law, natural or revealed. For the law which demands righteousness cannot create it. What it does create is a sense of guilt. 818f

III 21-XI 36. We now come to the universal remedy for this universal sickness. Paul will describe the intervention by which all men are offered a new and right relation to God himself.

III 21-30. We begin with a summary statement. 'But now' (21) in Paul often marks the transition from theoretical discussion to realities. We have seen how men *might* become acceptable to God on their merits; but in fact they do not, and in fact God has provided another way in which they may be accepted by him (22). The Jewish Law is not it, though the OT tells of it; and the real advantage of the Jew over the Gentile is that the scriptures which contain his condemnation contain also the promise of better things—the creative goodness of God now offered to all who put their trust in Jesus Christ, all without distinction. **23** reasserts the universal need. It was a Jewish belief that Adam's sin lost him the supernatural glory that was his before the fall. His descendants inherit his loss just as they re-enact his fall. **24.** The remedy for this is that in the sheer generosity of God the unacceptable are accepted: their emancipation and restoration to their true Owner is Christ's doing. **25.** God put Christ forward as a *hilastērion.* The question is what Paul had in mind in using this Gr. word. (1) It has nothing to do with propitiation in the sense of placating an angry God. (2) C. H. Dodd has shown (JTS 32 (1931), 352–60) that in biblical Gr. the root meaning is twofold: (*a*) the mercy and forgiveness of God; (*b*) expiation, i.e. the removal of the defilements that unfit man for communion with God. (3) Grammatically the word may be an adjective (masc. or neut.) or a neuter noun. In the former case Christ is an expiatory agent or object; in the latter he is the locus of God's mercy and forgiveness. (4) Both meanings will yield a satisfactory sense; but in view of the usage of the Gr. OT we should perhaps prefer the latter. Christ crucified then takes the place of the mercy-seat in the Holy of Holies. 'God was in Christ reconciling the world to himself' (2 C. 5:19). Two things make the *hilastērion* what it is: the self-sacrifice of Christ ('in his blood'), and the faith of those who are to benefit by it. And all is done to make God's creative goodness visible and convincing. Before Christ there could be no radical dealing with the state of mankind. God could only be patient and forbearing with men, overlooking but not condoning their sins. With Christ comes the demonstration that God is not only righteous himself but also that he will accept men who have faith in Jesus. By faith those who are on their merits unacceptable can now be accepted (25*b*–26). 819a

It follows (27) that there is no room for 'boasting', the self-confidence that says: 'I have done my duty and I am not afraid to face my Maker.' For the rule of merit and reward has had to give way to the rule of faith. In the kingdom of God there are no self-made men, but only (28) men who have been accepted on their faith without reference to any merits they may claim. b

This is the only view consistent with real monotheism. Human sin is one and indivisible; and there is one radical way of dealing with it, which is the same for Jews and Gentiles. To bring in a second way is in effect to posit a second God (29f.), and the Jewish Law cannot tolerate that. To insist on the principle of one God and one way of salvation is to maintain the basic truth of the OT (31). c

IV 1-25. What has been said in 3·27–31 is illustrated and established by **the OT story of Abraham. 1.** The opening question should probably read, 'What then shall we say was found by Abraham . . . ?', to which the answer should be 'grace', i.e. God's favour (Gen. 18:3; cf. J. Jeremias in *Studia Paulina in honorem* d

819d *J. de Zwaan*, 147, *n*. 2). **2.** But it might be argued that he did not 'find' it but earned it. He could rely on his merits. To which the answer is 'Not before God' (cf. 15:17; Lk. 17:10). **3.** And the fact is that it was his faith in God that 'was reckoned to him as righteousness' (Gen. 15:6). Abraham did nothing but believe God's promise to him of a son and heir. **4.** This is different from dealings between men with their debits and credits. God was never in Abraham's debt. He gave him credit for his faith; **5** and he will give credit to anyone who believes in his readiness to accept men with no merits of their own. **6ff.** This 'reckoning', this giving of credit can be paralleled from Ps. 32:1f., where God refrains from reckoning a man's sins against him. Such a man is called 'blessed', which can only mean that God accepts him and gives him credit in spite of his lack of merit. This is not to say that Abraham had no merits: he was an excellent man. But the two texts together show that a man can be accepted by God, whether he has merit or not, simply on the basis of faith in God.

e **9-12.** Equally a man can be accepted whether he is a Jew or a Gentile—circumcision being regarded as the hall-mark of Judaism. Abraham was accepted by God (Gen. 15:6) before circumcision has even been mentioned. It is first commanded and practised at a later time (Gen. 17:9–14, 23–7); and it became the symbol of a status which Abraham had already acquired through faith. Abraham is thus the spiritual father of all who, through trusting God, receive the inward and spiritual grace of acceptance by him, whether or not they also have the outward and visible sign of circumcision. He cannot be claimed by those who think that circumcision is enough and refuse to follow his example of faith.

f **13-22.** Again the promise of a glorious future for 'Abraham and his offspring' cannot be tied up to the Mosaic Law. Vv. 13–16 must be read in the light of Gal. 3:16–29 and the whole passage (13–22) must be compared with Gen. 17f. It is likely that Paul took 'offspring' to refer in the first instance to Christ and then to the Church including both Jewish and Gentile Christians. The 'promise' seems to be that in Gen. 17:5, 18:18 and 22:17f. The essence of God's promises is that they are kept; and faith is the confidence that they are kept. But all this goes for nothing if enjoyment of the promises is confined to those who keep the Law (14). For (15) the 613 commandments of the Law can be broken as well as obeyed; and, as the Law has its sanctions, disobedience necessarily brings retribution (cf. 3:20).

g Therefore the basis must be faith on man's part and sheer generosity on God's. The latter guarantees the promise; the former ensures that all Abraham's offspring, the '*many* nations' (Gen. 17:5), whose father he is because they have faith like this, share in it, and not just those who adhere to the Law (16, 17*a*). The mention of Abraham's faith leads to a fuller account of it (17*b*–22). It consisted in taking God at his word when he promised to make him 'the father of many nations', and believing in the creative power of God to bring about the seemingly impossible (17*b*, 18). Abraham was, apparently, no longer capable of parenthood, and Sarah never had been; but God had promised them offspring and that was enough. Vv. 19–21 consist of six clauses of which the first three are contrasted with the last three, thus: (*a*) with no weakening of faith, (*b*) he faced the fact of his and Sarah's impotence, and (*c*) never doubted God's promise: on the contrary (a^1) he was strong in faith, (b^1) acknowledging the wonderful power of God (cf. Jn 9:24), and (c^1) certain that he could fulfil his promise. **19.** 'Barrenness', lit. 'deadness', a Heb. usage. **22.** It was faith of this quality that made Abraham accepted by God.

h In **23ff.** Paul argues that what is said about Abraham is universally applicable. Abraham believed that God would bring life out of death (= barrenness) in the birth of Isaac; we must believe that he has done so in raising our Lord Jesus from the dead. 81
Christ was delivered to death because of our misdeeds (cf. Isa. 53:4, 5, 12), and raised from death because of our justification (**25**). The preposition is the same in both clauses. He died because death is the inevitable result of man's disobedience: he rose again because God's purpose meant new life for a renewed humanity.

V 1-21. In this chapter the thought of 4:25 is developed 82
further. **1-5.** We begin with the immediate results of Christ's work, which are ours by faith. **1.** Our right relation to God is one of peace in place of our former hostility (5:10, 8:7; Col. 1:21). The authorities are divided between 'we are at peace' and 'let us continue at peace': the former gives the better sense. **2.** The peace has been made by God through Christ and Christians have their good standing now in God's kingdom by Christ's introduction, together with the assured hope of greater things to come. **3.** They can keep their confident assurance even though they must suffer for their faith. This way comes fortitude; and (4) so a sterling character is formed that expects great things from God. **5.** This expectation, far from being disappointed, is already being realised in an overwhelming experience of God's love, which comes through the Spirit's enabling us to say 'Abba, Father'.

6-11. Behind the peace we enjoy lies the reconciling b
work of Christ. **6.** 'Helpless' and 'ungodly', i.e. unfit for the moral and the religious life: the two hang together. 'The right time' is the time of man's extreme need. The death of Christ is the measure of the need. **7.** We are none too ready to sacrifice ourselves even for the just and the good; **8** but God proves his love by giving everything for us when we are worth nothing. **9.** Christ's sacrificial death has put us right with God; and that is the guarantee that we shall be delivered from the final retribution. **10.** Through it God has changed us from enemies to friends. For Paul it is always God who reconciles, and men who are reconciled to him. The reconciled share the life of Christ, and to share this divine life is to be saved indeed. **11.** In a word Christians are 'on top of the world' and they owe it all to God's reconciling work in Christ.

In the light of all this we can read the story of c
mankind, as told in the OT, with new understanding. The salient points are dealt with in verses **12-21**, which might be entitled 'Paradise Lost and Paradise Regained'. There are three periods: (*a*) Adam to Moses, (*b*) Moses to Christ, and (*c*) the new age begun in Christ. (*a*) **12-14.** The 'one man' is Adam. He let Sin loose in the world. 'Sin' in Paul has two main senses: (i) behaviour which runs counter to God's will and man's welfare, whether specifically forbidden or not; (ii) the evil power that promotes such behaviour. Only the context can tell us if it is 'Sin' or 'sin(s)' that is meant. Sin brought death; and universal sin brought universal death. This is Gen. 3 in a nutshell (cf. Wis. 2:23f.). **13f.** Sin is distinguished from 'transgression', which is the breach of a definite commandment. Adam had one commandment (Gen. 2:16f.) and he broke it. No further commandments were given until the Mosaic Law; and so there were no more acts of disobedience 'from Adam to Moses', though there was much evil-doing with consequent disaster. Meanwhile the world must await one who would succeed where Adam failed and stop the chain-reaction which he began.

The contrast between Adam and Christ is worked d
out in vv. **15-19.** Adam's trespass consisted in taking that to which he had no right: God's free gift is also something to which man has no right; and it is in every way a greater thing. 'Many' here means mankind in general. Adam brought them death: the generous gift of God in Christ is an antidote as far-reaching in its effects. **16f.** Another difference: Adam's disobedience set God's judicial activity (what the Rabbis called *middath haddîn*) into action and condemnation followed; but the wretched condition

20d of man in his sins aroused the divine compassion (*middath hăraḥ^{a}mîm*) to put things right again. Adam inaugurated Death's reign of terror over men : now men are given their true autonomy in life. It is God's free gift to us through Jesus Christ who inaugurates the new reign in life. **18f.** The sum of the matter is this : Adam's misdeed put everybody in the wrong, but Christ's good deed (i.e. his complete fulfilment of God's purpose for him) put them right again with God and restored them to life. Adam's disobedience made men unacceptable to God, but Christ's obedience will make them accepted by him. They will be new men living in a new world.

e **20f.** It is all very well jumping from Adam or Abraham to Christ, but where does Judaism come in ? What about the divine revelation on Mt Sinai ? Paul says that the more commandments you have, the more opportunities there are for disobedience and so for getting deeper into the mire. That is the bad side. The good side is that the Law, which so mercilessly measures man's degradation, shows the immeasurable goodness of God in Christ, delivering men from the tyranny of Sin and Death and naturalising them in his kingdom of righteousness and eternal life.

21a **VI-VIII** The next two chapters go more deeply into **the Christian's relation to the Law** ; and ch. 8 gives Paul's positive conclusions. Brunner justly says that these three chapters contain ' the key to the ethics of the NT ' (*The Divine Imperative*, 586). On the issue of Law and Gospel Paul is very sensitive because his teaching was misunderstood both by his critics in Palestine and by his supporters among the Gentile Christians (cf. 3:5–8). In these chapters he will show that the Christian attitude is neither defiance of the Law nor slavery to it, but insight into what its cumbrous and complicated machinery is meant to achieve and the awareness of spiritual resources more than sufficient for the achievement. These resources are possessed by those who are ' in Christ ' as parts of his Body, members of his Church, the new race of men which originates in him.

b **VI 1-11. 1** is antinomianism in its most repulsive form. Paul violently rejects it. Christians should be long past the idea of balancing sin against grace. **2ff.** Their life is now a matter of whose they are and whom they serve. Once they were enslaved to Sin, the evil power (6), but that is so completely over and done with that we can say that the old self is dead. **3f.** This death of the old self is symbolised and experienced in baptism, where the convert is united to Christ and shares in his death, burial, and resurrection. This union with Christ is also an assimilation : a death and resurrection like his (5) and a new way of living (4*b*) like his. ' Walk ' is a Heb. way of saying ' behave ' : Christians start out on the way of Christlikeness. **6.** More literally : ' we know that . . . in order that the body of Sin might be put out of action so that we should no longer be in servitude to Sin.' It is a question whether in ' body of Sin ' ' of sin ' is a possessive genitive or a genitive of quality. RSV takes the latter view which does not yield a very good sense. It is perhaps better to regard ' the body of Sin ' as the opposite of the ' body of Christ '. It is the mass of unredeemed humanity in bondage to the evil power. Every conversion means that the body of Sin loses a member and the body of Christ gains one. This takes place when the believer ' is crucified with Christ '. He ' dies to Sin ' (10 f.) as Christ did ; i.e. so far as the evil power is concerned he ceases to exist and is ' freed from Sin '. But as the old life is ended, a new life in Christ (11), in fellowship with him (8), begins. This life, like Christ's, is dedicated to God (10 f.). Christ was the first to break the dreadful solidarity of the body of Sin by his death. He there did something that he need not do a second time : it was a decisive victory (9f.). From that point the body of Sin must diminish in power as the body of Christ grows (6).

c **12-14** draws the practical conclusions. Since Christians are no longer part of the body of Sin, they must refuse 821c
all obedience to their former master. As members of the body of Christ they must devote themselves to serving God's purposes (12f.). Sin will not have the mastery any more ; because they are no longer under law, which can only demand good conduct, but under grace which inspires and creates it.

15-23. Antinomianism seizes on the supposed opposi- d
tion between law and grace : ' If we are under grace we can disregard the law.' ' At your peril,' says Paul. Even Christians have only two ways open to them, called ' sin ' and ' obedience ' and leading respectively to death and righteousness. Obedience is the link between law and gospel : it is what law demands and what Christ gave to God (cf. Phil. 2:8). All who are united to Christ, the obedient one, are committed to this obedience (16), to a bondage which is the only real freedom, freedom from what they hate and despise, freedom to live a good and holy life (18f.). How this came about is described in v. 17: it was by a willing acceptance of the ' standard of teaching ' or ethical pattern ' to which they had been committed ' when they were united to Christ who is himself the ' standard of teaching '. Vv. **20-3** emphasise the incompatibility of the two ways. No man can serve two masters. Slaves of Sin have nothing to do with righteousness : they can only do Sin's shameful work and draw Sin's pay, which is death ; a progressive deterioration of the whole man ending in complete destruction. Those who are set free from Sin and brought into God's service gain ' sanctification ', a progressive assimilation to the character of God revealed in Christ ; and this brings with it God's ' free gift of eternal life ', life of divine quality enjoyed in fellowship with Christ Jesus our Lord.

VII 1-6 is difficult because Paul is using two arguments 822a
at the same time. His contention is that Christians are not in servitude to the law. The first point is that the law has no power over the dead : this is stated in **1** and applied in **4a**, where the nerve of the argument is that Christ's bodily death broke the tyranny of the law and that those, who become members of (or cells in) his body (6:3–5), are set free as he is free. The second point is that the death of a Jewish husband releases his wife from the very strict laws governing her status. (In Jewish law ' adultery ' was *always* an offence of the wife and some other man against her husband. See T. W. Manson, *The Sayings of Jesus*, 136ff.) She can now remarry. The analogy in **2f.**, **4b** requires that the first husband = the law, the wife = the convert, the second husband = Christ. It breaks down because in the application it is the convert, not the law, that dies. This analogy cannot be pressed. All we can say is that conversion is the end of the old relation to the law and the beginning of a new life in Christ. The offspring (' fruit ') of the old marriage of unregenerate humanity to law was perverse conduct leading to death (**5**) : that of the new union with the risen Christ is conduct worthy to be offered to God (4*b*), the result, not of slavery to a ' written code ', but of indwelling divine power.

7-11. The close association posited in 1–6 between the b
law and man's sinful condition before conversion prompts the question whether law and sin are not identical. Paul says No, and explains how they are related. He constantly uses the first person in the account that follows. We may call it autobiography if we like, but here Paul's autobiography is the biography of Everyman. The law stamps some of my activities as sinful and makes me aware of them as my sins. Man in a state of nature has endless wants : he only begins to ' covet ' when some of his wants are barred by the law. **8.** But the law that forbids them cannot prevent them : indeed they seem to thrive on prohibition. We may say that without the law sin could not exist. In **9-11** we see how Everyman repeats in his own life the story of Adam : to begin with simply living at the natural level ; then the first awareness of a moral imperative ; sin becomes a living reality,

822b and man is destroyed. **10.** The law was meant to bring life through obedience (Lev. 18:5) ; but in fact it brought death, because (11) Sin engineered the fatal disobedience (cf. Gen. 2:17, 3:13).

c **12f.** It follows that ' the law is holy ', i.e. it is God's law ; and what it commands is God's decree, which is just and good. How then could it cause my death ? It did not. Sin did that, using the law for its evil ends, and so intensifying its own evilness.

d In **14-20** man's predicament is more closely analysed. He is no free agent to say Yes or No to the law's demands. The law belongs to the divine order : unredeemed man is ' carnal ', human, all too human. He is already Sin's slave, bought and paid for. **15.** ' I do not understand '—better ' I do not decide '. Man is not his own master : his best intentions are frustrated. **16.** He sees a moral ideal, which he must admire even though he cannot obey. **17f.** So it becomes clear that his real trouble is within himself, a conflict between his ' better self ' with its good intentions and his ' flesh ' with its instinctive reactions controlled by some evil influence ; and that evil influence dominates his life. **19f.** restate the symptoms and name the cause of man's moral sickness. The description is coloured by OT views of man's nature as a spirit-filled body (cf. L. Koehler, *OT Theology*, 135–47). The spirit that ought to be in control is constantly overpowered by another evil spirit, called Sin, which also occupies man's body and is the effective agent in his wrong-doing.

e Paul's findings about the natural man are finally stated in **21-5.** Frustration is built into his nature. **22.** He is constantly aware of the pull of moral ideals embodied in the ' law of God ' *and* (**23**) of the opposing pressure of forces within himself that make him the prisoner of sin. **24.** Helpless and miserable he cries for deliverance. From what ? Literally translated the Gr. can mean ' out of this body of death ' or ' out of the body of this death '. ' Of death ' may be a genitive of quality—' mortal body ' or ' body doomed to death ' —or a possessive genitive—' body of Death ', another name for the ' body of Sin ' (6:6). In the former case the body is that of the individual man ; in the latter it is the mass of unredeemed mankind. Paul's statements in Rom. 8:11, 23 ; 1 C. 6:15, 15:44 ; Phil. 3:21 ; 1 Th. 5:23 and above all 1 C. 15:51–7 (which is the best commentary on Rom. 7:24) seem to tip the balance in favour of ' this body of Death's '—unredeemed mankind under the rule of Death. Deliverance from it comes through Christ by incorporation into his body. This deliverance will be completed at the last not by man's becoming a disembodied spirit but by the transformation of his body, its adaptation to a new mode of existence.

823a **VIII** describes the life of those who are members of Christ's body, a life of freedom under the guidance of the Spirit. It means, first, ' no condemnation ' (1) for them : the verdict has been given against the real culprit—Sin (3*b*). In **2ff.** three laws are mentioned : (*a*) that of the Spirit, (*b*) that of Sin and Death, (*c*) the moral law, especially in its Mosaic form. The first two are more like our ' natural laws ', one bringing life and the other disaster. The moral law formulates ' just requirements ' (4) but cannot enforce them because of conditions in the ' flesh ' where the law of Sin and Death is at work (3*a*). It takes an act of God to bring about man's proper response to the claims of morality (3f.) The matter can be put thus : Moses' law has right but not might ; Sin's law has might but not right ; the law of the Spirit has both right and might. God's intervention (3) involved ' sending his own Son ' into the human situation dominated by Sin, not to be contaminated by it but to decontaminate it, in a word to expose and overthrow the power of evil in its occupied territory.

b **5-11.** The great divide in human life is now apparent : it is between living at the physical level, for physical satisfactions, with the certainty that it will all end when the physical resources are exhausted ; and living at the
spiritual level, for spiritual ends with the assurance 82
of life and peace (5f.). Those who remain at the physical level are inevitably at odds with God : their way of life compels them to reject God's way and makes it impossible for them to win his approval (7f.). But (9) Christians live at the spiritual level, if, as is the case, they are permeated by the spirit of Christ. Otherwise there is no sense in calling them Christians. **10f.** The indwelling of Christ does not exempt Christians from physical death which is the common lot because of sin ; but it brings life of a new quality, a life which comes from God because we are now right with him. In the end this spiritual life will prove stronger than physical death, and Christians will share in the resurrection of Christ.

The practical consequences follow at once. **12f.** c
The primary obligation of Christians is to embrace the spiritual way of life and reject its fatal opposite. To ' put to death the deeds of the body ' means simply to put an end to certain courses of action. The Heb. mind tends to measure ' life and death ' in terms of activity and inactivity. **14f.** ' Spirit-led ' and ' God-adopted ' are names for the same group of people whose lives are spent in the service, not of an owner whom they fear, but of a father whom they love. ' Sonship ', lit. ' adoption '. In Roman law adoption meant primarily coming under the authority of the new father, elsewhere in the Near East it meant becoming his heir. The latter idea is dominant here (17). **15.** ' Abba ' (cf. Gal. 4:6f.) is the Aram. word for ' father ', used by our Lord in his prayers (Mk 14:36) : it expresses the deepest trust and affection. For Paul the hall-mark of Christianity is to call God ' Father ' and Jesus ' Lord ' (1 C. 12:3), and mean it. In both cases the holy Spirit is at work in the believer ; and this is the essential ' speaking with tongues '. The RSV rendering of 15*b*–16*a* is possible : so is the more usual ' spirit of sonship whereby we cry ' Abba ! Father '. The spirit himself bears witness . . .' **16.** ' Provided we suffer '—better, ' if, as is the case, we suffer . . .' It is clear from 8:18, 36f. that the sufferings are not hypothetical but actual ; and the glorious inheritance is as sure as the present affliction.

In **18-25** Paul looks towards this glorious future so d
eagerly awaited by ' the creation '. ' Creation ' may mean either the cosmos or mankind (SB ii, 53f. ; iii, 245f.). If the former, Paul may have in mind Gen. 3:17f. and God's curse on the earth because of Adam's sin. The ' hope ' will be that which is expressed, for example, in Isa. 55:12f. The total picture will then be that of a redeemed humanity shown to be God's children and living in a transformed universe. The difficulty of this interpretation lies in **21** : it is not clear how the material world can ' obtain the glorious liberty of the children of God '. If, as seems more likely, ' creation ' = ' mankind ', the main contrast of the passage is between those who already ' have the first fruits of the Spirit ' (23) and the rest of mankind still ' subjected to futility ' and ' decay ' (20 f.) and suffering like a woman in childbirth (22), while they long for release from their bondage into the freedom of God's children (21). Christians are not exempt from this travail ; for what has been begun in them has yet to be completed when their bodies are set free at the resurrection and their full sonship is achieved (23). Meanwhile (24f.) they live in hope. Their salvation began and continues in hope. They would cease to hope only if all they look for were already at hand ; but this is not the case : they have much, but there is more to wait for. In this interpretation the total picture is one of a progressive salvation of which some already have some experience and in which all are destined to share.

26-30 returns to the working of the Spirit in the e
community as a ground of hope. In 26f we are shown believers experiencing emotions which they cannot put into words. Inarticulate sounds are all they can utter. These wordless utterances are the language of the Spirit, and God, who can read men's minds

3e (cf. Jer. 17:10 ; Jn 2:23f.), understands ; for what the Spirit begs for God's people is what he himself wills for them. **28.** The text and translation are uncertain : the possibilities are : (*a*) ' With those who love God, God co-operates in all things for good ' ; (*b*) ' With those who love God he co-operates in all things for good ' ; (*c*) ' With those who love God all things co-operate for good '. The difference between (*a*) and (*b*) is textual : in both cases the subject of the verb is God, explicit in (*a*), understood in (*b*). The difference between (*b*) and (*c*) is one of translation : the question is whether or not ' all things ' is the subject of the verb. Geographically (*a*) and (*b*) are at home in the Eastern communities, (*c*) in the West. A firm choice is difficult ; and, in the last resort, it does not greatly matter. For, whatever the grammatical subject may be, in Paul's world it is God who is in control ; and if ' all things work together for good ', it is he who makes them do so (cf. Phil. 1:12f.). **29f.** God's overruling is seen most clearly in the life-story of his chosen, who are ' called according to his purpose ', i.e. appointed to serve his ends (28). God's purpose, like himself, is from everlasting to everlasting. ' Foreknew ' means ' chose in advance '—a Hebraic use of ' know ' (Jer. 1:5 ; Am. 3:2 ; cf. H. H. Rowley, *The Biblical Doctrine of Election*, 18). ' Predestined ' means that God determined in advance the form their lives should take : they were to be Christlike. The pattern to which they are to be ' conformed ' is described in Phil. 2:7f. It is the form of an obedient servant. Christ's task is to bring men into the sonship —and service—of God, to be the senior member of a new human family in which all are brothers and sisters. The formation of these men and women begins with God's call to them. As they respond they come into their right relation to God ; and that means that something of the divine glory becomes theirs (2 C. 3:17f., 4:6). Note the tenses : all these things are already within Christian experience.

f **31-39.** This experience of God's goodness is the ground of unshakeable confidence. This confidence is not new (cf. 2 Kg. 6:15ff.) ; but it is vastly strengthened by what God has done, and will do, in Christ. ' Spare ' in **32** can mean either ' begrudge ' or ' spare ' : the former is preferable, for the emphasis is on God's generosity (cf. 5:8 ; Jn 3:16). In **33f.** we have two rhetorical questions (cf. Isa. 50:8f.). To both the unexpressed answer is ' Nobody ' and the reason why is given in the following statement : ' Who shall bring . . . ? (Nobody, when) it is God who justifies. Who is to condemn ? (Nobody, when) it is Christ . . . who is actually pleading our cause.' **35** continues the pattern with ' Who shall . . . ? ' though the possible separators are things rather than persons. Perhaps he is thinking of them as means used by personal adversaries ; certainly this first list is of things familiar to martyrs and confessors. **36**, borrowed from Ps. 44:22, was applied by the Rabbis to Jewish martyrs. Hostility to the true faith is fierce and ruthless ; **37** *but* we are winning a rousing victory ' through him who loved us ', i.e. through Christ who loved us and gave himself for us (cf. Gal. 2:20 ; Eph. 5:2, 25). The decisive battle of this campaign was fought at Calvary and the foundations of victory laid there. **38f.** If the hostility of men cannot break the bond between God and his people, neither can natural or supernatural forces. ' Angels ' may come from Satan as well as from God. ' Principalities ' and ' powers ' are probably personified, or personal evil forces. ' Height ' and ' depth ' are astrological factors. ' Things present ' and ' things to come ' stand for the march of events, which, apart from belief in God, tends to look like the ' trampling march of unconscious power '. Paul is not concerned to deny the existence in the world of forces which we can neither understand nor control : what he does deny emphatically is that any or all of them can touch the one thing that really matters, God's loving care for the younger brothers and sisters of his Son.

824a In chs. **9-11** Paul deals with the tragic fact that the Chosen People, whose whole history was a preparation for Christ (Gal. 3), to whom the Gospel was first offered by Christ and his Apostles, whose need of it has already been shown (Rom. 2:1–3:20), for the most part rejected Christ and persist in the rejection. He must show that this rejection, which on the surface looks like a frustration of God's declared purpose in the OT, is neither unforeseen nor unprovided for in the divine plan.

b **IX 1-3.** He begins with his own grief at what has happened and his willingness to lose his own place in Christ's kingdom, if that would enable his people to enter it. He belongs to them (11:1) and his attachment to them is closer than we can easily understand : in 11:14 he speaks of them as his flesh, i.e. he and they are one body by virtue of their common descent from Abraham. In **4f.** he speaks of their special privileges as Israelites. The ' sonship ' means that God is their father, the ' glory ' that he is visibly present among them. The ' covenants ' or charters are the old one given at Sinai and the new one announced by Jeremiah (31:31–4) and inaugurated by Christ (1 C. 11:25). The ' law ' and the ' worship ' are the appointed ways of serving and worshipping God. The ' promises ' express God's good purposes for Israel. They spring from great men ; and from them is sprung one who is greater than all men, God's Anointed. **5.** It is a much debated question whether the words ' God over all blessed for ever ' are to be taken as a further description of the Christ or as a separate doxology referring to the Almighty. The structure of the sentence favours the former view, though it gives a more advanced Christology than we find elsewhere in Paul. The most recent discussions by O. Cullmann (*Die Christologie des NT* (1957), 320f.) and V. Taylor (*The Person of Christ in NT Teaching* (1958), 55–61), show how difficult the problem is. Any solution must accord with the fact that there are two fundamental articles of Pauline faith—confession of God the Father (8:15) and of the Lord Jesus (10:9). These two must not be confused. Yet they are intimately related : ' God was in Christ reconciling the world to himself ' (2 C. 5:18f.) ; Christ is the likeness of God (2 C. 4:4 ; cf. Phil. 2:6) and the Son of God (Rom. 1:4). So we have two questions : (*a*) Did Paul assert here that Christ is God ? (*b*) if he had done so, what would he have meant by it ? We can make shift to answer the second question so far as it concerns the relations between God and Christ ; but on the first, complete certainty is not attainable.

c There is no doubt about Israel's place in God's purpose and it is unthinkable that God's declared intention should become a dead letter (6). We must therefore look more closely at the supposed rejection of God's plan by Israel and of Israel by God. Paul's first point is that ' Israel ' is not just an ethnological label. The true Israel does not include all who have the right pedigrees. The true children of Abraham are in some sense children of God (7f.) sprung from the fulfilment of God's promise to Abraham (9). This means that from the beginning there is a dichotomy : the line is traced through Isaac and not Ishmael. In the next generation it runs through Jacob and not Esau (10–13). Still later the nation is divided into the faithful Remnant spoken of by Isaiah (Isa. 10:22f., 1:9) and the others (27–9). Again in the days of Elijah there are loyal and disloyal elements among the people (11:2–4). And now in the time of fulfilment there are those in Israel who hear and accept the Gospel and those who do not (9:24, 11:17, 25). The nucleus of the true Israel is still Jewish, as Jewish as Paul himself, and Gentile converts are incorporated into the true Israel. Sweeping statements about failure and rejection are not true of Israel as a whole.

d Secondly, in so far as they are true of a part of Israel they reflect a temporary state of affairs. Certainly these people have been offered the Gospel and have rejected it (10:14–21) ; but the possibility of a change

824d is not excluded. Paul thinks of his own Gentile mission as a means to show his fellow-countrymen what they are missing (11:13f.); and he looks forward to a day when they will all be brought in (11:25–32).

e Thirdly, Paul maintains, God is in full control of the course of events from beginning to end. It is he who establishes Abraham's line in the first instance (9:7), he who prefers Jacob to Esau (9:13), he who determines who shall be 'my people' or 'not my people' (9:25f.), he who breaks off branches here and grafts on others there (11:17–24). The foundation principles of Paul's interpretation of the history of Israel are (*a*) that 'the gifts and call of God are irrevocable' (11:29), and (*b*) that 'God has consigned all men (including Israel) to disobedience, that he may have mercy upon all (including Israel)' (11:32).

f God's full control raises the age-old questions of man's freedom and responsibility. Paul denies that God's power is used unjustly (9:14), though his description of its exercise makes it seem arbitrary (9:15–18). To the objection that unlimited power in God means no responsibility in man (9:19) he can only reply by indignantly denying the right of the objector to make any objections: there is no argument with God. It must be allowed that Paul here (9:20–9) makes no attempt to anticipate Milton in justifying God's ways to man; and anyone who has really been gripped by Job 38:1–42:9 will understand his difficulty. In his eagerness to silence anything that looks like a criticism of the Almighty he bluntly insists that God is not accountable to anyone. But behind what looks very like bluster lies the deep conviction that in God's hands—and only there—absolute power cannot corrupt at all; and that only by absolute trust in God can a man discover for himself that this is so. This way of trust is indicated in 10:5–13: God has spoken and acted in Christ. He has shown his hand and his heart; and 'no one who believes in him will be put to shame' (10:11 quoting Isa. 28:16).

g The Jews who remain in unbelief do so because, instead of trusting God completely and putting themselves in his hands, they go on trying to provide God with valid grounds for accepting them on their merits (9:30–10:13). But this is not the whole truth. That the Gospel has been accepted only by a minority in Israel, while the rest struggle on at an impossible task (11:1–10), has merely served to further the wider purpose of God for mankind as a whole (11:11f.); and the success of the Gentile mission will in the end be the means of bringing over the recalcitrant Jews (11:13–32). Once the scope of God's purposes has been seen, however dimly, there is no room left for questionings or criticisms, but only for ever increasing wonder and gratitude (11:33–6). These are the main points in chs. 9–11. It remains to deal with some matters of detail not already discussed.

h **7ff.** Cf. Gen. 18:10, 14, 21:12; Gal. 4:21–31. **10f.** 'By one man' underlines the fact that Jacob and Esau had the same parents, whereas Isaac and Ishmael had only one parent in common. This and the fact that they were still unborn shows that their differing destinies depended entirely on the divine will. **12f.** Cf. Gen. 25:23; Mal. 1:2f. 'Esau I hated' is a Heb. idiom = 'I loved less', i.e. 'I preferred Jacob to Esau'. **15** quotes Exod. 33:19. Another Heb. idiom meaning 'I will have mercy on whom I please' correctly explained in v. **18**. **17.** 'I have raised you up' means in effect 'I have brought you on to the stage of history'. The quotation is from Exod. 9:16 and the point is the absolute power of God in history (see Rowley, *Bibl. Doct. of Election*, 132ff.). The entire material power of the Egyptian empire served as the *background* to the exodus; and the exodus is an essential link in the chain of God's gracious purpose. **19ff.** Cf. Isa. 45:9ff.; Wis. 15:7. **22ff.** The question posed in these verses is given no explicit answer. Perhaps the simplest one we can supply is that if God acts thus, he is consistent, since this is how he says he will act in the texts already quoted. The quotations from Hos. 2:25 and 2:1 in **25f.** originally 82[illegible] referred to the resoration of Israel to God's favour: they are given a far wider application by Paul—to Jews *and* Gentiles. **27f.** From Isa. 10:22f. In the Targum on Isa. 10:22 the 'remnant' is defined as those 'that have not sinned, or that have repented of (lit. 'turned away from') sin'; Paul would define it otherwise, in terms of faith. **29.** 'Children', lit. 'seed': how Paul would interpret it, may be gathered from Gal. 3. The text is Isa. 1:9. **33** gives a combination of two texts, Isa. 8:14 and 28:16. In the phrase 'believes in him' the words 'in him' are not found in the Heb. of Isa. 28:16 but only in MSS of the LXX. The effect of the additional words, which appear again in 1 Pet. 2:6, is to identify the stone with Christ. Perhaps it is a bit of pre-Pauline Christian exegesis (cf. A. M. Hunter, *Paul and his Predecessors*, 73ff.).

X 2. 'not enlightened', lit. 'not according to knowledge', particularly the knowledge that recognises things for what they are. **3.** When the way of acceptance was opened to them in Christ they ignored it and went their own way; **4** not perceiving that their way of law-keeping was superseded by Christ. **5** quotes from Lev. 18:5 (cf. Gal. 3:12): life is the sure reward for obedience to the law—if only men could obey. In **6-10** Paul reinterprets Dt. 30:11–14 so that Christ takes the place of the 'commandment' or 'word' of God. The justification, if any be needed, for this step is in the word of Jesus in Lk. 17:20f. (see T. W. Manson, *The Sayings of Jesus*, 303ff.). **9.** What Christ brings is appropriated by those who accept and acknowledge him as Lord (cf. 1 C. 12:3; Phil. 2:11). Inward faith puts a man right with God; **10** confessing of that faith joins him to the company of those who are in the way of salvation. **12.** Cf. 3:22f. As there is 'no distinction' between Jew and Gentile in their undeserving, so there is none in God's generosity towards them. **13.** In Heb. to 'call upon the name of the Lord' is to acknowledge him. This text from Jl 2:32 is to be understood in the light of what Paul has said in v. 9. In **14f.** he draws the missionary conclusions, fortifying them with the text Isa. 52:7. **16.** But preaching does not always get a response: Isa. 53:1 tells us as much. **17.** 'What is heard' means in Rabbinic usage the traditional Jewish doctrine, and Billerbeck suggests that in a Christian context it stands for the Gospel doctrine of salvation, a meaning which fits quite well in Gal. 3:2, 5; 1 Th. 2:13; Heb. 4:2 (SB iii, 283f.). **18** quotes Ps. 19:5 the message was not inaudible. **19.** Neither was it unintelligible. Moses (Dt. 32:21) and Isaiah (65:1) give proof to the contrary. The Gentiles were not very bright theologically—'a foolish nation'. They did not know how or where to seek. Yet *they* have found. Therefore mere ignorance is no obstacle. **21.** The real obstacle is obstinate disobedience; and that is Israel's trouble, as scripture shows (Isa 65:2). i

XI 1 asks a question which is already answered in the negative in Ps. 94:14. Paul himself and other Christian Jews are a living proof that God has not rejected his people (2, 7). However hopeless the case of Israel may appear to human eyes, e.g. Elijah's (1 Kg. 19:10), there is always a Remnant (1 Kg. 19:18). There was one in Elijah's day and there is one in Paul's (3ff.). **6.** And the existence of this Remnant is a demonstration of divine grace rather than of human merit. **7.** The rest of Israel 'were hardened', i.e. they were overtaken by a dullness of apprehension so that they could not receive the Gospel. **8ff.** This state is described in terms borrowed from Isa. 29:10 and Dt. 29:4 followed by a quotation from Ps. 69:22f. 'Feast', lit. 'table', in Rabbinic exegesis understood to mean the altar. This can be taken as a type of the whole ritual-legal system which fills its votaries with unjustified confidence while setting them to perform impossible tasks. **11.** Does this mean that there is no hope for any but the Remnant? Paul says No. The Gentiles have profited by their failure; and they will learn from the j

824j Gentile achievement. **12.** When that happens, it will mean incalculable blessing for the world. 'Failure' here probably means something like 'the fact that only a minority of them have accepted the Gospel'. This 'minority' stands in contrast with 'their full inclusion', i.e. the conversion of them all.

k **13a** means that what follows, down to the end of the chapter, is a warning to Gentile Christians not to presume on the favours they have been granted. **14.** 'My fellow Jews': lit. 'my flesh', an expression showing how strong the feeling of corporate solidarity was among Israelites. The apostle to the Gentiles is eager to have a share in the conversion of Israel. **15.** The reconciliation of the world (i.e. the human race) to God is the first stage of redemption; 'life from the dead' its consummation. **16.** 'The dough offered as first fruits' (Heb. *ḥallāh*) is the portion of dough ($\frac{1}{24}$) given to the priests as an offering to God. The rules about it in *The Mishnah* (trans. H. Danby, 83–8) are based on Num. 15:18–21. The due offering of the *ḥallāh* sanctifies the entire baking, says Paul (see further SB iv, 665–8). The quality of the root determines the quality of the tree. By 'first fruits' and 'root' Paul presumably means Abraham. Then the 'lump' and the 'branches' will stand for Israel, as Paul understands 'Israel', i.e. the faithful Remnant whose latest manifestation is the Church. This is the real Israel, which in **17** is now compared to an olive tree. The broken-off branches are the Jews who have refused to be part of the true Israel; the ingrafted shoots of wild olive are Gentile converts to Christianity, who by conversion become part of the true Israel. The 'richness', lit. 'fatness'. Dalman assures us (*Arbeit u. Sitte*, i, 680) that the wild olive produces no oil. This gives point to the caustic reminder in **18.** The new scions contribute nothing to the parent stock. **19.** The Gentile Christian flatters himself if he thinks this. **20.** The adverb *kalōs* is probably ironical and should be translated, 'Well, well!' rather than, 'That is true'. The true reason is now given: they lost their status through unbelief; you got yours by faith, and faith alone. Don't presume. **22.** The 'kindness' and 'severity' may well correspond, as Billerbeck suggests, to the divine attributes of mercy and judgment. See on 5:16f., §820*d*. To 'continue in his kindness' is to have it as God's gift and as the dominating influence on one's own conduct. **23f.** The gardening operations described in these verses are, as Paul admits, 'contrary to nature'; and it would be unwise to look to this passage for hints on how to manage an ordinary olive orchard. All that can be said is that the miraculous olive tree is intended to illustrate the miracle of grace.

l **25-32** state the conclusion of the whole matter. 'Wise in your own conceits' means relying on your own interpretation of history. It is opposed to the 'mystery', i.e. God's secret, his governing purpose in history made known in part to the prophets, and fully in the Gospel. The 'hardening' is spiritual obtuseness: they just cannot see the divine truth. It affects only part of Israel and only for a limited time, the time needed to bring in 'the full number of the Gentiles'. Does 'the full number' mean all the Gentiles there are or all that have been chosen for salvation? **26.** The fact that Paul expects 'all Israel' to be saved may suggest that he hopes for as much for the Gentiles. The proof-text in 26f. is a combination of Isa. 59:20f. and 27:9 (cf. Jer. 31:33). **28.** In the matter of the Gospel the recalcitrant Jews have turned against God's purpose; and this has been to the immediate advantage of the Gentiles. **29.** But on the long view God's purpose must and will prevail; and within that purpose they are God's Chosen People and he stands by his promises to the Patriarchs. **30-2.** 'Disobedience' is the basic meaning of the Gr. word used in these verses. In the NT it can be construed somewhat widely so as to include disbelief. The Jews could argue that they were doing their very best to obey God's law. To that Paul might answer that even so they were resisting
God's will by rejecting the Gospel. Perhaps 'resistance' 824l
expresses the thought of the Apostle a little better than 'disobedience'. Resistance at home sent the good news abroad: its success abroad will break down resistance at home. In the long run the scope of God's mercy becomes as wide as the world, which is precisely what God intended all the time. He has penned all mankind in the enemy's camp—this is the meaning of 'consigned all men to disobedience' (cf. Gal. 3:22)—in order to show mercy to them all. In **32** we have Paul's deepest eschatological conviction; and it is this conviction that prompts the outburst of adoration that follows.

33-36. The doxology closes the first part of the letter. m
The universal provision to meet a universal need shows the infinite resources of wisdom and power in God (33). He has no need of consultants or commissions of inquiry (34). He can finance his own undertakings (35). The proof-texts are from Isa. 40:13 and Job 41:11. Throughout the history of the world from its creation to the final consummation, in all the vicissitudes of history, it is he who brings men and things into existence, guides and controls them, and finally brings them to their predestined goal. There is no room on man's part for anything but awe and wonder, nothing that he can contribute but his adoration and thanksgiving.

(C) The Christian Way: Man's Life for God 825a

XII 1-XV 13. So we come to the second main section of the letter, in which Paul draws out the ethical implications of the foregoing theological teachings. He has shown how God has given new life to men in Christ: he will now show how men are to live that new life in Christ. It seems probable that just as there was an early formulation of the main points of the good news, which we call the *kērygma* (see C. H. Dodd, *The Apostolic Preaching and its Developments*), so there was an early description of the good life (on this see P. Carrington, *The Primitive Christian Catechism* and E. G. Selwyn's commentary on 1 Peter, 363–466). The new life from God and the new life for God make up the entire teaching of the epistle; and it is significant that they are presented in that order. In Paul's ethical teaching *noblesse oblige*; and he is here concerned to show what kind of conduct befits those who have been ennobled as sons of God and brothers of Jesus Christ.

XII 1f. Paul lays the foundation of Christian ethics: it is complete self-surrender to God. In this he follows the teaching of Jesus (Mk 12:28–34) who makes love to God the first obligation, followed by love of neighbour. **1** sheds a bright light on what is meant by the 'priesthood of believers'. **2.** Christians are not mechanically to 'do in Rome as Rome does': their nature is to be transformed by a revolution in their thinking, bringing with it a new sensitiveness on all moral issues. Conduct in accord with God's will means what is good in itself, acceptable to God, and the best that one can do here and now.

3-21. The new life is to be lived out in a new context, b
in a new human community called the body of Christ. It is significant that it is called the body of Christ and not the body of Christians: it depends for its existence and its unity on the steadfast purpose of Christ rather than on the variable enthusiasms of Christians. The body of Christ has a life of its own in which each Christian has a part to play. In **3** 'the grace given to me' means the part assigned to Paul, the job of an apostle. This entitles him to give the good advice which follows.

3-8 begins (3) with an admonition to the individual c
member to take a modest and realistic view of his own capacities. The equality in Christ of all Christians (Gal. 3:27f.) does not involve the spiritual omnicompetence of every Christian. The several parts of a human body have their several functions (4) and so have the members of the body of Christ (5). The thought is worked out more fully in 1 C. 12:6. 'The grace given to us' (6) has the same sense as in **3.**

825c Each member receives from God the gifts needed to do the task allotted to him by God, and each is to do his best with what gifts he receives. Examples follow. 'Prophecy', i.e. inspired declarations of God's purposes, must clearly be in accord with the Faith (cf. Dt. 13:1–5). **7f.** If the task is 'service'—especially care of those in need of help—get on with it. Similarly with 'teaching' the Christian way or 'exhorting', i.e. encouraging others to walk in it. He who shares his possessions with others must have his heart in the business (cf. 1 C. 13:3). 'He who gives aid': the Greek may equally well, and more probably, mean 'he who is a leader'; and this is how it is understood in the earliest versions. **8.** 'Cheerfulness': we are not only to be helpful but also glad to help.

d **9-21.** From functions in the fellowship we turn to Christian character and its manifestations, beginning with love that is sincere. 'Hate what is evil' is hardly strong enough: the Gr. word means to show hatred as well as feel it, to 'recoil with loathing from evil', the exact opposite of embracing what is good. **10.** The individual Christian must love the whole brotherhood; and out of this will grow a family affection between members. He must be more ready to show respect than to stand on his dignity. In **11** all is clear except that there is a variant reading 'time' for 'Lord'. If it is right, Christians are called upon to meet the demands of their own day and generation in accordance with God's will (see O. Cullmann, *Christ and Time*, 42). As the more difficult reading it has some claim to consideration. **12f.** present no difficulties. **14.** Some important MSS omit 'you', which may have crept in from Mt. 5:44. If this is right the Christian is to ask God's mercy on all persecutors, and not just on his own tormentors. **15** calls for true and wide sympathy. In **16** the RSV text 'associated with the lowly' is to be preferred to the margin. Christianity and self-esteem do not go together. 'Never be conceited': rather 'Don't overestimate your own wisdom' (cf. Prov. 3:7). **17-21** deals with the Christian's relations with other men when there is tension or strife. We must not think that one bad turn deserves another. 'But take thought . . . all' comes from the LXX of Prov. 3:4. Paul uses the text again in 2 C. 8:21. The sense is: 'Let your aims be such that men will see their nobility'. **18.** 'If possible' implies that there may be cases where it is not possible, where open opposition to other people becomes a Christian duty. 'So far as it depends on you' means that the Christian must do all he can do, without betrayal of what he sees to be right, in order to secure agreement. If he has done his best with no result, and the matter requires it, he must resist. **19.** But the duty of resisting evil does not mean the right to take vengeance for injuries to ourselves. Taking vengeance means being judge, jury, and executioner in your own case. The wrath of God is his inflexible opposition to evil whether exercised directly or through his appointed agent, the civil government (13:4). This is your best shield. The proof-text is from Dt. 32:35: it is quoted in the same form in Heb. 10:30. This form is nearer to the Targum of Onkelos than to MT or LXX. **20.** The right way to treat personal enemies is that laid down in Prov. 25:21f. The meaning of 'Heap burning coals on his head' has long been obscure. The best suggestion is that it is a reference to an Egyptian ritual in which a penitent showed his repentance by carrying on his head a dish containing burning charcoal on a layer of ashes (see S. Morenz in TLZ 78 (1953), 187–92). In that case the English equivalent would be 'you will make him wear a white sheet'; and the meaning 'by showing kindness to your enemy, you will make him ashamed of himself before God.' All is summed up in **21.**

e The injunctions in 12:17–21 pave the way for the definition of the rights and duties of the civil government in **13:1-7.** Paul writes to the Roman Christians as a subject of the kingdom of God, an Israelite of the tribe of Benjamin, and a citizen of the Roman Empire, 825e
and proud to be all three. What he says in this passage must be compared with 1 C. 6:1–11 in order to see what limits he sets to Christian appeals for State intervention or State interference with the life of the Christian community. And always it must be remembered that 'at the time when St Paul wrote Romans 13, the only alternative to the Imperial Roman Government was anarchy' (E. Bevan, *The Kingdom of God and History*, 66; on Paul's teaching about the State and the questions it raises, see O. Cullmann, *The State in the NT*, ch. iii; G. B. Caird, *Principalities and Powers*, ch. i; H. V. Campenhausen in *Biblical Authority for Today*, 299–303; H. H. Schrey, H. H. Walz, and W. A. Whitehouse, *The Biblical Doctrine of Justice and Law* (1955)).

XIII 1f. It is a debated question whether 'the governing authorities' refers to the State alone or 'to the State and to the angel powers which stand behind it' (Cullmann, op. cit., 114). That the Jews believed such powers to exist and influence the affairs of nations is hardly open to doubt; and it is likely enough that Paul shared the belief. In counselling obedience to the Imperial Government he may be held to imply obedience to the spiritual powers behind it; but—and this is the vital point—such obedience can be given by Christians to these authorities, of whatever kind they may be, only in so far as their commands are consistent with the rule of Christ. God is the supreme Power. He can be called simply 'The Power' (Mk 14:62; cf. Dalman, *Words of Jesus*, 200 ff.). All other power or authority is derivative, either authorised or permitted by him. Hence resistance to legitimate authority legitimately exercised is wrong. **3f.** It is assumed in these verses that the State is doing its appointed task of maintaining order and administering justice; and when Rom. was written a case could be made that the Roman Empire was doing its duty by its subjects. It is to be noted that Paul regards the State in its punishment of evildoers as the agent of God's wrath. **5.** The motive for obedience must be something more and better than fear of punishment: there must be awareness of a personal responsibility which may not be evaded. **6f.** The obligations of a Christian to the State include payment of taxes, direct and indirect, since the civil rulers are in God's service (whether they know it or not) and busy with their proper task, the encouragement of good and the repression of evil. They have a right both to your material and your moral support (cf. Mk 12:13–17) f

8. The sum-total of Christian ethics is 'to love one another'. There is no duty that is not included in 'love', and nobody that is not included in 'one another'. It is wrong to construe 'one another' as meaning fellow-Christians only. **9.** All the specific rules of conduct are particular applications of the general principle laid down in Lev. 19:18 and confirmed by Jesus himself (Mk 12:28–34). How Christians are to apply this great principle is indicated in Jn 13:34. **10.** The first half of this verse may be taken as a warning: some of the worst mischief in the world can be caused by people who set out to do good to their neighbours but do not love them. Love is the complete performance of what the law of God prescribes: it brings benefits to others, and does them no ill. g

11-14 contain the reminder that Christians are already living in the overlap of two ages (1 C. 10:11). The old order is moving to its close, and the new order to its consummation. Christians must be up and doing. 'Salvation' in **11** is the completion of what is already begun in the experience of believers; and it is already nearer than when they became believers. **12** Christians must be up and dressed not for night-life but for battle, what in the Dead Sea Scrolls is called 'the War of the Sons of Light with the Sons of Darkness'. This war and its equipment are described in Eph. 6:10–20. **13.** We are to behave decently as befits those who belong to the new order. This h

825h excludes drunken carousals, wanton debauchery, quarrelling and jealousy. In **14** the metaphor of Christian clothing is given a new turn. We are to 'put on the Lord Jesus Christ'. Paul uses the same figure in Gal. 3:27; and it is not impossible that it is a variant on the theme of incorporation into the body of Christ. Cf. Eph. 4:24; Col. 3:9–11. This would fit with the injunction not to make any further provision for gratifying the desires of the flesh. For they have taken off the old nature with its practices (Col. 3:9).

826a **XIV 1-XV 12** might be headed 'Traditions and Taboos', the small change of religion and morality, the scene of constant and often embittered conflict between the 'scrupulous' and the 'emancipated', the 'traditionalists' and the 'progressives', the 'old-fashioned' and the 'enlightened'.

Paul himself is quite clear that the basic principles of conduct, which he has expounded in chs. 12 and 13, will sweep away much of the dead weight with which the traditionalist encumbers himself. He is equally clear that the same principles will be a necessary brake on the headlong career of some progressives. He had learned a great deal in the disputes that arose out of Jewish-Christian devotion to ancestral Jewish customs; but he does not here raise that issue. He gives himself the widest terms of reference in discussing the problem. With the whole passage cf. 1 C. 8–10.

b **1-6.** He begins by asserting the right of both kinds of Church members to exist and to obey the dictates of their consciences. 'The man who is weak in faith' is the man whose Christian conviction is not strong enough to get himself free from the scruples or superstitions he may have brought in from his former religious belief and practice. 'Disputes about opinions' in contrast to the substance of the Faith, which is acknowledgment of God as Father and Jesus Christ as Lord. **2.** The first example of such disputes is that about food taboos. The robust faith of one Christian allows him to eat all kinds of food: another feels that he must restrict himself to vegetables. The distinction here can hardly be between Gentile and Jewish Christians; for vegetarianism was not a Jewish practice. But Jewish scruples may have been at work at three points: (*a*) the commonest meat available to Gentile Christians was pork, which was absolutely taboo to Jews; (*b*) Jewish food laws were specially exacting about butchering and cooking of meat; (*c*) Jewish hatred of idolatry put all the contents of the meat market under suspicion, since much of it came from animals sacrificed in heathen temples. Converts from heathenism to Christianity may well have been strongly influenced by the third of these scruples (see 1 C. 8–10). **3.** Paul deprecates not merely terms like 'libertine' and 'killjoy' but the whole attitude of mind that lies behind them. **4.** Christians are not called to be censors of one another's behaviour in these peripheral matters. They are answerable to their Master, Christ; and Christ has room for both. The weaker brother has his welcome and the stronger his standing, both as gifts from Heaven.

5 Judaism had its holy days. Pagan religion had its festivals. Pagan superstition had its lucky and unlucky days—as it still has. As we are concerned here with religious scruples, it is most likely that the scrupulous regard certain days as specially holy (cf. Col. 2:16). Others do not. Paul maintains that both alike should know what they are doing, and why. We may compare the story told in Codex Bezae (D) at Lk. 6:4: 'On the same day, seeing one working on the Sabbath, he (Jesus) said to him: "Man, if indeed thou knowest what thou doest, thou art blessed: but if thou knowest not, thou art cursed, and a transgressor of the law."'

c **6** explains what is the right motive behind the different practices; and **7f.** gives the theological principle lying behind the motive. Whatever we do and whatever may happen to us, the basic fact is that we belong to and acknowledge one Lord. This is the fact that must control both inward motive and outward act. 826c **9.** It was to win this lordship that Christ fought the decisive battle of Calvary. Note that the Gr. verb translated here 'be Lord of' is used in 6:14 where it is said that 'Sin will have no dominion over you'. Christ's victory removed the dominion over mankind from Sin to himself. **10.** This supremacy of Christ makes nonsense of the censoriousness of the scrupulous and the superiority of the enlightened; since both alike must answer to a higher authority. **11.** For proof Paul appeals to Isa. 45:23, a text which he uses again in Phil. 2:11. There he uses the text to prove that all must confess Christ as Lord: here he uses the Gr. verb in its other sense of confessing one's deeds to God. (RSV footnote is preferable to the text 'give praise'.) His interpretation is stated explicitly in v. 12. Each of us has to answer *for himself*; and that should keep us all fully occupied in minding our own business. The words 'to God' may well be a (correct) gloss. Many early authorities omit them.

Some positive advice is now offered in the light of d the principles just laid down: it extends from **14:13** to **15:6.** First of all (**13**) censoriousness must go, and its place be taken by a resolve to keep our fellow-Christians on their feet. **14.** Secondly, following the teaching of Jesus himself (Mk 7:14–19), Paul declares that there is nothing wrong with, let us say, a piece of pork or meat from a pagan sacrifice. On the other hand, if a Christian's conscience revolts against such food, he must obey his conscience; and (**15**) it is no kindness to him for the emancipated to ignore his scruples, and, by their example, lead him on to doubt or defy his own conscience. Christian liberty does not carry the right to destroy the moral integrity of a man for whom Christ died; and (**16**) insistence on this good thing, Christian liberty, must not be carried so far as to bring it into disrepute. **17.** Freedom from food taboos is a by-product, not the essence, of the kingdom of God; and Christian liberty is not primarily freedom to eat and drink what you like but freedom to live a new life dominated by the spirit of God. **18.** Such a life lived in the service of Christ has the approval of God and wins the confidence of men.

In **14:19-15:6** the application of basic principles is e continued. **19.** The aim of all Christians should be the peace, i.e. the total well-being of the Christian community, and the building up of its common life. The Gr. word translated here by 'upbuilding' and in 15:2 by 'edify' usually, if not always, in Paul lays the emphasis on the building up of the community and its life rather than spiritual improvement of individual members, though this is involved. **20.** 'The work of God' is the Church (cf. 1 C. 3:9ff.), and it is not to be knocked to pieces because some members will not control their appetite. Of course the food is harmless; but eating it is far from harmless if it causes the downfall of a fellow-Christian. **21.** It is better to waive all your rights if claiming them will mar his Christian life **22.** This does not mean giving up 'the faith that you have', i.e. your strong Christian convictions, including those concerning Christian liberty: it does mean concentrating on your duties in God's sight rather than your rights. The man who can make a decision here that will not bring discredit on himself is a man to be envied. He knows his rights but does not enforce them. **23.** On the other hand the man who indulges his appetite, when he is uncertain about the rightness of what he is doing, is already discredited. Where there is no Christian conviction there cannot well be Christian action, but only reaction to physical stimuli, which in effect means sin. At this point Marcion made the epistle end; but Paul had not finished and his argument continues in **15:1-6.** In these verses the main point is an appeal to the example of Christ. **1.** The strong characters in the Church must see the hesitations and inhibitions of the weaker members as an opportunity to give a helping hand. They are not to look after their own interests; but (**2**) each is to look after the interests of his neighbour

826e (fellow-Christian), for his good and for the building up of the common life (see on 14:19 above). **3.** For Christ did not look after his own interests. On the contrary he fulfilled the scripture (Ps. 69:9) by bearing the brunt of man's hostility to God ; and (**4**) the scriptures which are prophecy of Christ are precept for us. They call for all our endurance and they offer us every encouragement to cherish our highest hopes. **5f.** And it is Paul's prayer that God, who is the source of endurance and encouragement, will enable the readers to achieve within the fellowship a true common interest, with its standards set by Christ Jesus, and its results such that all can unite in praising God for them.

f **7-13.** The sum of the whole matter is stated ; and it is a call to let Christ set the pattern of Christian behaviour. 'Welcome' in **7** means all that it says and more—'take to your heart'. This is a corollary to the great maxim, the 'new commandment' of Jn 13:34, 15:12, 'Love one another as I have loved you'. **8.** Christ's ministry was to the Jews. He had to show God's truthfulness by confirming God's promises, that is, by making them come true. As Paul understands these promises and their fulfilment (see above, §§812*fg*), both Jews and Gentiles are to share in the blessings ; and that the Gentiles will do so and praise God for his mercy (**9**) is foretold in scripture. The relevant OT texts are given in **9-12.** They are : Ps. 18: 49 (= 2 Sam. 22:50) ; Dt. 32:43 (LXX) ; Ps. 117:1 ; Isa. 11:10 (LXX). **13.** The benediction which follows this catena of texts and picks up from them the ideas of joy and hope, suggests that the readers of the letter are mainly Gentile Christians. 'The God of hope' means the God on whom we may rest our hopes. Trust in him brings joy and peace ; and the Holy Spirit at work in the Christian's heart intensifies his Christian hope. So this section ends on the note that the Christian life is a joyful adventure on which we may embark knowing that the issues are in the hand of God.

827a **(D) Missionary Plans: Rome and the West**

XV 14-33. This section falls into three parts : (*a*) a general statement of Paul's missionary practice (14–21) ; (*b*) an outline of his plans for the immediate future (22–9) ; and (*c*) a request for his readers' prayers (30–2) ; rounded off by the blessing (33).

14-16. One gets the impression from these verses that the Roman community was something quite considerable, and its members not unaware of the fact. Paul is willing to admit every claim that can be made for them (14) ; but (15) he has his own God-given status (cf. Gal. 1:15f.), in virtue of which he makes bold to write them his little memorandum about essential Christianity (a deliberate understatement, if ever there was one). 'Very boldly'—better 'somewhat boldly'. **16.** His work is described in liturgical language. In his priestly work he serves under Christ in the preaching of the gospel of God. His object is to bring a consecrated offering that God can accept, namely, his Gentile converts.

b In **17-21** he speaks with justifiable pride about what he has already accomplished in the service and fellowship of Christ (17) ; but (18) in the last resort everything worth mentioning in his achievement is the work of Christ, who uses him and provides all the resources needed to secure the submission of the Gentiles to himself. The list includes 'natural' things like speaking and physical exertion, and (19) 'supernatural' things like 'signs and wonders'. Evidently Paul believed that he could perform miracles. The 'power of the spirit' is what finally effects a conversion, enabling the convert to call upon God as his Father and Jesus as his Lord. At the time of writing he has completed missionary journeys which have taken him round the north side of the Mediterranean as far as, but probably not including, Illyricum (the western part of modern Yugoslavia). He has concentrated on pioneer work (20) taking as his motto Isa. 52:15 (21). In 1 C. 3:10 he calls himself a layer of foundations on which others may build.

c **22-29.** Now that he has covered the ground from Jerusalem to the Balkans he can plan further work 827
in Spain (23f., 28). Note 'Jerusalem'—not Antioch. The Gospel begins from Jerusalem (Lk. 24:47), the place where Christ died and rose again. Italy is left out, presumably because Rome the strategic centre is already occupied by Christian forces. Only a brief visit to the city is contemplated ; and he hopes to enlist Roman support for his Spanish project. As we know from Ac. 21–8 these plans were completely upset ; and when Paul did come to Rome some three years later it was as a prisoner awaiting trial before the Imperial Court. Whether the journey to Spain ever took place we do not know. On the whole it is unlikely that it did. **25f.** The immediate task is to take to Jerusalem the money raised by the Gentile churches for the relief of poverty among the Christians there. On the collection see 1 C. 16:1–4 ; 2 C. 8–9 ; Gal. 2:10. On Paul's journey to Jerusalem with it see Ac. 20:3–21:19, 24:17. **26f.** 'They have been pleased' means that it is a voluntary contribution ; but Paul emphasises that there is a moral obligation (a 'debt'). What they send to Jerusalem can only be a small return for what has come to them from Jerusalem. In **28** 'delivered' represents a formal business term : he will hand the proceeds over under seal. **29** gives the ground of all his hope and confidence in planning for the future. 'The blessing of Christ' (this is the true text) is the secret.

30-33. His confidence will be all the stronger if he can d
rely on the prayers of the Roman community. The chief danger will be from the Jews of Judaea, in whose eyes Paul is a renegade. He is also concerned about the kind of welcome he will receive from the Jerusalem Christians (31). The account in Ac. does not suggest that they were very cordial on his arrival or very zealous in his interests when he was arrested. Some of the hopes expressed in **32** were realised (Ac. 28:14ff.) ; but any expectations he had of the Jerusalem Christians seem to have been disappointed.

If our answer to the problem of the last two chapters is correct, the copy sent to Rome ended here with the blessing in **33.**

(E) The Note to Ephesus 828a

XVI 1-23, (24), (25-27). Reasons have been given above (§808*d*) for thinking that this chapter was added by Paul to a copy of Rom. which he sent to Ephesus. **1f.** The note begins by commending 'our sister', i.e. fellow-Christian, Phoebe, 'a deaconess of the church at Cenchreae'. 'Deaconess' should perhaps be avoided here, as the word has modern connotations which may lead to misunderstanding. The Greek word used in *diakonos*, a noun of common gender denoting the holder of some office in the local church (Phil. 1:1). It would seem that this office could be held and its tasks, whatever they were, performed by men or women. (See further, W. Lock on 1 Tim. 3:11 (ICC) ; Hort, *The Christian Ecclesia*, 198–211 ; C. H. Turner in *The Ministry of Women*, 93ff.) We should translate 'deacon' or, perhaps better, paraphrase by 'who also holds office'. Cenchreae was the seaport of Corinth. **2** suggests that Phoebe has some business of her own to do in Ephesus, either church or secular. The word 'helper' may have a technical flavour. Phoebe may have championed the cause of Christians, including Paul, before secular authorities.

In **3-15** we have a long list of people to whom b
greetings are sent, beginning with Prisca (in Ac. Priscilla) and Aquila, whom we know from Ac. 18:2f., 18f., 24–6 ; 1 C. 16:19 ; 2 Tim. 4:19. They had come from Rome to Corinth and thence to Ephesus, where they still were when 1 C. was written. There is no evidence that they ever left Ephesus. Nothing more is known about the matter referred to in v. 4 ; but evidently Paul owed a deep debt of gratitude to them. Their house was a meeting-place for Christian worship (5) : no doubt they were fairly prosperous. The reference to Epaenetus as the first convert in the Roman province of Asia favours Ephesus rather than Rome as the destination of this note. Mary (6) is not

828b mentioned elsewhere: she and her work *for the addressees* are already well known to Paul. Where? Not in Rome. Andronicus and Junias, named only here, are called 'kinsmen', meaning probably no more than fellow-countrymen, i.e. Jewish Christians (cf. vv. 11, 21, 9:3). We do not know when or where they shared captivity with Paul. Evidently they are Christians of long standing and high reputation 'among the apostles'. The meaning of this last phrase is in dispute: were these two themselves eminent apostles (= missionaries), or were they highly esteemed by the Apostles? The latter is perhaps more likely in view of K. Holl's arguments (*Gesammelte Aufsätze*, ii, 47ff.). The names in verses **8-10** are only names to us, with the possible exception of Aristobulus, who *might* be the grandson of Herod the Great. The persons greeted would then be members of his household, and this would favour Rome as the destination of this chapter. But the identification is purely conjectural. In **11** Herodion is not otherwise known. Narcissus might be the Roman freedman put to death early in Nero's reign (Tacitus, *Ann.*, xiii, 1): this would favour Rome. **12.** The three women are known to us only as hard workers for the church, presumably some church known to Paul. **13.** The name Rufus appears in Mk 15:21, for a son of Simon of Cyrene. The name is a very common one; and there is no special reason for identifying this Rufus with that. His mother has treated Paul as a son. Where? The names in **14f.** are no more than names to us. They would seem to belong to the outstanding members of two distinct groups in the community; and knowledge of the kind involved here could surely come only from close personal acquaintance with the church concerned. It is to be noted that many of the names in 3–15 are slave-names, a fact which sheds light on the social standing of the first Christians. The 'holy kiss' (16) became a regular feature of the Communion service (see G. Dix, *The Shape of the Liturgy*, 105–10). The greetings probably cover all the churches with which Paul had been in touch since he left Ephesus.

c **17-20** are most readily understood as written to a church in which Paul was very well known and highly regarded. The warning against trouble-makers has affinities with Paul's words to the Ephesian elders (Ac. 20:28–32) and to the Philippian church (Phil. 3:17–19). Further, his complaint is usually that the trouble-makers intrude into churches which he has founded, and there challenge his authority and propagate a reactionary Jewish version of Christianity. They are against Paul the Apostle and the Pauline statement of the Gospel; and they are more likely to be at work in Pauline foundations than elsewhere. **17.** 'The doctrine which you have been taught' invites the supplement 'by me'. **18.** The trouble-makers are not in Christ's service, that is, they do not follow in the way marked out by him: rather they serve 'their own appetites', lit. 'their own belly'. This could mean merely that they are grossly self-indulgent; but a comparison with Phil. 3:17ff. suggests that here, as there, the persons in view are those who see the ultimate triumph of Christ in terms of material things and earthly pomp and power. They try to hold the Messianic hope without the Cross. Their weapons are fair words (cloaking ill deeds) and canting religiosity (without real religion); and innocent people are readily taken in by them. **19.** The 'obedience' is the trusting submission to God in Christ, mentioned in 1:5. When Paul says 'I rejoice over you', he surely means more than 'I am glad to hear about your obedience': rather he is like a proud parent exulting over the progress of his children. Paul knows these people and has followed their growth in the Gospel with eager and affectionate eyes. He wants them to be experts in goodness and inexperienced in evil. They will soon see (20) how God, the guardian of their true welfare, will reduce their worst enemy to complete impotence. At this point in RSV comes a blessing, which some MSS and versions place, with slight verbal variations, after **23** or **27**. We cannot 828c
be certain which is the right place; but the best MS authority puts it at **20**.

In verses **21-3** we have a list of people who send greetings. It is to be compared with the list of Paul's companions in Ac. 20:4. Timothy his faithful lieutenant appears in both lists. Sosipater here may be identified with Sopater there. Deissmann (*Licht vom Osten*[4], 372–7) made a case for equating Lucius here with Luke the author of the 'We-document' which comes in at Ac. 20:5. Arguments against the identification are given by H. J. Cadbury (*Beginnings of Christianity*, v, 489–95). It is possible that Deissmann was right. Jason does not appear in the list in Ac. Others are mentioned there who do not appear here.

22. Tertius who acts here as Paul's amanuensis is not d
mentioned elsewhere in the NT. **23.** Gaius is probably the Gaius of 1 C. 1:14, presumably one of Paul's first converts in Corinth. His house was big enough to be used for meetings of the church there. Erastus the city treasurer may be the Erastus mentioned in Ac. 19:22 and 2 Tim. 4:20; but the identification is far from certain. Still more doubtful is the identification of Erastus here with the Erastus of an inscription at Corinth, (see H. J. Cadbury in JBL 50 (1931), 122–38).
24. Quartus is unknown apart from this reference.
25-27. The question of the genuineness of this doxology has already been touched on above (§808*c*). There are two main grounds for doubting Paul's authorship: (*a*) The doxology was absent altogether from some very early forms of the text: in others its position varies, (i) after 14:23, (ii) after 16:23, (iii) in both places, (iv) after 15:33. Uncertainty of position is often a symptom of interpolation. (*b*) It is likely enough that the doxology was added by one of Marcion's followers to ease the abruptness of Marcion's ending. Later, with some adaptation, it was adopted by the orthodox and found its way into the great mass of MSS. According to Harnack there are two orthodox additions: (*a*) 'and the preaching of Jesus Christ' (25), (*b*) 'and through the prophetic writings is made known' (26).

In **25** 'my gospel' means the Gospel which I preach; and the 'preaching of Jesus Christ' is the preaching of which Christ is the subject-matter. The 'mystery' spoken of in **25f.** has close affinities with that spoken of in Eph. 3:3–6. The mystery will be the fact that the Gentiles are fellow-heirs with the Chosen People and the disclosure of it by God's command is to result in 'obedience to the faith', i.e. the conversion of the Gentiles. If the doxology is Marcionite, its composer may well have been influenced by the Eph. passage; and the similarity of the two pieces may have made it easier for the doxology to win acceptance. In **27** RSV follows the text of a few MSS headed by B. The majority have 'to the only wise God through Jesus Christ, to whom be glory for ever, Amen.' This is certainly the more difficult reading. If it is correct, it involves an anacoluthon, which could be an argument in favour of Pauline authorship.

Bibliography—Commentaries in English: C. K. Barrett (1957); Karl Barth, tr. from the German by Sir E. Hoskyns (1933); C. H. Dodd, in the *Moffatt Comm.* (1932); K. E. Kirk, *Clarendon Bible* (1937;) R. A. Knox, *A New Testament Commentary*, ii (1954), 68–125; A. Nygren (Eng. tr. 1952); W. Sanday and A. C. Headlam (ICC, 5th ed. 1902), gives (pp. xcviii–cix) a useful account of earlier expositions down to the end of the 19th cent. Their own commentary is a first-rate piece of work; E. F. Scott (1947). Careful study of Barrett, Dodd, and Sanday and Headlam will provide the English reader with practically all the information he needs in order to reach his own understanding of the Apostle's meaning.

Commentaries in other Languages: M. J. Lagrange, EBib. (6th ed.); H. Lietzmann, HNT (4th ed. 1933); SB iii (1926), 1–320; A. Schlatter, *Gottes Gerechtigkeit* (2nd ed. 1952).

I AND II CORINTHIANS

By C. S. C. WILLIAMS

829a Paul had stayed for eighteen months in Corinth during his second missionary journey, the date being *c.* A.D. 50–1, as the Gallio inscription shows (cf. A. H. McNeile, *St Paul, his life, letters and Christian doctrine*, Introduction), cf. Ac. 18:12, before he returned to Jerusalem and Antioch at the end of the 'second missionary journey'. Later he returned to Ephesus, Ac. 19:22, where he had been for about two years, Ac. 19:10, cf. 1 C. 16:8–9. Now Timothy has been sent to Corinth and salutations are given from the churches in Asia, especially from Aquila and Priscilla (or Prisca), cf. Ac. 18:2, 18, 26 ; Rom. 16:3 ; 2 Tim. 4:19, who had sailed with Paul to Ephesus where they remained to set up a house-church, Ac. 18:26. If time is allowed for his journeys since he left Corinth, Paul's letter may be dated *c.* A.D. 55-6, its place of origin being Ephesus.

b Corinth, the 'Vanity Fair' (T. W. Manson) of the ancient world, had been destroyed by Rome in 146 B.C. and rebuilt as a colony by Julius Caesar and Augustus. It lay on the trade route between east and west, Cenchreae, its eastern port and Lechaeum, its western, receiving a mixed population of Romans, Greeks and Jews. The moral standards of the city were low ; a verb formed from 'Corinth' meant to lead a dissolute life. Even if the thousand sacred prostitutes of Aphrodite no longer existed in Paul's day (cf Knox, *St Paul and the Church of Jerusalem*, 276), yet the temple of that goddess of 'love' dominated the city from the summit of Acrocorinth.

c Clement of Rome, *c.* A.D. 96, attests the Pauline authorship of 1 C. in his 1 Corinthians 47, as also does Marcion's acceptance of it *c.* A.D 140. Few modern critics contest this. The unity, however, of the letter has been questioned, especially by J. Weiss, M. Goguel and J. Héring. Héring finds a contrast between Paul's reference to his coming visit in 4 and that in 16, and another contrast between 10:1–22 with its rigorist view of pagan sacrifices and 10:23–11:1 which treats the problem in terms of tolerance towards a weaker, more scrupulous Christian. He finds also that 9 is misplaced. Accordingly he divides the letter into two parts (*a*) 1–8, 10:23–11:1, 16:1–4, 10–14, and (*b*) 9, 10:1–22, 11–15, the rest of 16, while 13 is a sort of 'hors-d'œuvre' ! However, as the notes below indicate, the letter is treated as a unity for the purpose of this commentary.

I CORINTHIANS

830a **I-IV Party Strife at Corinth**

I 1-9. Sosthenes is probably the ruler of the synagogue of Ac 18.17 An apostle denotes one who is specially sent ; Paul applies the term to more than the Twelve but he does not do so indiscriminately, e.g. to Timothy or Titus ; cf. *Apostleship* by K. H. Rengstorf, tr. by J. R. Coates (1952) For the Church, see Coates' translation of K. L. Schmidt's *The Church* (1950). Like the Post Office, the Church is one organisation with local branches and not formed out of local branches into one. A thanksgiving section normally followed a salutation in a letter of the period. Paul makes his thanksgivings theocentric.

b **10-17 Party Spirit among the Converts**—In Paul's absence Apollos had arrived at Ephesus and Aquila and Prisca had completed the conversion of this learned and eloquent biblical student from Alexandria from his being a disciple of John the Baptist into becoming a Christian. Apollos was then recommended to cross to Corinth to convert Jews. His work there met with success and a party calling itself by his name grew up in opposition to other parties, 1:12, cf. 3:6, no doubt without Apollos' approval. His eloquence and Alexandrian methods of interpreting the OT, probably allegorically, captivated many who contrasted the poor presence and feeble diction of Paul, 2 C. 10:10. Some of the converts however remained loyal to Paul, forming a Pauline party. Others claimed to belong to Cephas or Peter, which does not imply necessarily that Peter had visited Corinth but that some Jewish-Christians had arrived there claiming to represent the mother-church of Jerusalem which had had Peter as its first leader. There may have been even a Christ-party claiming to go back behind all parties to Jesus. More probably, unless the words 'And I of Christ' are a gloss, they represent Paul's own counterclaim. (The emendation by Perdelwitz of *Crispus* for *Christus* does not recommend itself. Still less is to be said either for the outmoded Tübingen theory that Judaistic Christianity was opposed to Pauline as thesis to antithesis, the thesis being Peter's and Christ's parties and the antithesis being Paul's and Apollos' or for the theory of Schenkel and others that a party distinguished between Jesus and Christ, Christ being a kind of Gnostic aeon or intermediary who descended upon the man Jesus and indwelt him before the crucifixion, deserting him then.) In rejecting all party labels in the Church Paul uses words about Baptism which, ripped from their context, seem to disparage that sacrament ; but he means that he was sent to preach ; no doubt he left it to his companions to baptise converts, as Jesus may have done, Jn 4:1f. The great store that Paul set by Baptism is seen in Rom. 6 Now Paul is glad that he has not baptised anyone, thereby giving him occasion to claim to belong to Paul's party, though he adds as an afterthought the names of those whom he had indeed baptised, including the household of Stephanas which probably, though not certainly, included children. The brilliant eloquence of Apollos and his allegorical or philosophical presentation of the Gospel might appeal to converts ; worldy wisdom does, blinding men's eyes to the truth. But the Cross contradicts this human wisdom.

c **13.** The voice heard at his conversion on the Damascus road convinced Paul that in attacking the Church he was attacking Christ. It is unthinkable to him that Christ's body should be split into sections. **14** Crispus, cf. Ac. 18:8. **16.** Stephanas, a companion of Paul now, cf. 1 C. 16:15, 17, may have jogged Paul's elbow or his memory ; he is not mentioned in Ac.

d **I 18-II 5 The Cross, foolishness to the world, is God's power and wisdom**—Human rhetoric, like that of Apollos presumably (cf. 2:1–3, 13, 3:1–4, 18, 21), and human wisdom are nothing compared with divine wisdom, cf. 2:7, 9, 3:18–20, 4:10, 19, 5:12–13, 8:1–3. Isa. 29:14 starts with a Greek word (*apolō*) like the name Apollos, 'I will destroy'. Men need saving far more than they need teaching. The paradox of the Gospel is that men must concentrate less on striving to reach God by their own unaided effort ; they must rely on faith instead. God

830d chose the 'foolishness' of the Gospel through which to reveal himself to men, while the Jews sought for signs from heaven, cf. Isa. 7:11; Jn 4:48, and the Greeks for human wisdom; the Cross is a stumbling-block to the Jews, cf. Dt. 21:23; Gal. 3:13, and mere silliness to the Greek. But the Christian knows the Cross to be God's power and wisdom; even the Corinthian converts knew it, far as they were according to worldly standards from being wise or powerful. Paradoxically God chose the foolish, weak, base and contemptible things to throw their opposites into confusion and by the incarnation Christ became the source of their strength, the divine Wisdom showing himself as righteousness, sanctification and redemption. This divine Wisdom, semi-personified in the Jewish Wisdom literature, became embodied in Christ, the foolishness of God being wiser than man's wisdom. Paul had not preached with eloquence at Corinth but after his visit to Athens he had determined to preach the doctrine of the Cross alone; the world has had enough teachers, it needs a Redeemer.

e **18.** Those in process of being saved, not those already saved, are in mind. **19.** Isa. 29:14 is cited loosely, cf. Ps. 32:10. **20.** The Greek wise man, the Jewish scribe and the ancient philosopher are set aside. **23.** Some Jews, as at Qumrân, may have held in pre-Christian times the doctrine of a suffering Messiah (cf. W. H Brownlee, BASOR (Dec. 1953), 8ff., contrast M. Burrows, *The Dead Sea Scrolls* (1955), 313f.) but none would have held that he would suffer crucifixion, cf Dt. 21:23. **30.** By his death Christ justifies us, i.e. sets us right with God, cf. Rom. 3:25; he sanctifies us by uniting us with himself, cf. Rom. 6; he ransoms us, cf Mk 10:45, by setting us free from all hostile powers, cf Col. 1:13, 2:14. **2:1.** Mystery (the reading attested by P[46], Chester Beatty) means God's divine plan, hitherto kept secret but now revealed openly, summed up in Christ for the Gentile world. Cerfaux may be right in his suggestion that the OT citations in this section came from a Florilegium of texts about human wisdom and its rejection.

831a **II 6-16 God's Spirit shows what Christian wisdom is**—Divine wisdom, which the spiritually adult receive, is opposed to human. Before Christ came and outside his present sphere of influence, angelic 'spiritual' beings held sway, among the Jews through the Law which they mediated to men according to late Jewish tradition, and among pagans through their kings and rulers, such as Pilate, cf. the 'elements of the world', Gal. 4:3, 9; Col. 2:8, i.e. the spiritual beings whose powers were exercised through the planets and stars of the physical world; such powers were now passing away, Col. 1:16 (cf. G. H. C. Macgregor, NTS 1 (1954), 1, 17–28). The Jewish rulers would never have put Christ to death if they had known the true wisdom, which would have delivered them from astral fatalism and from that 'failure of nerve' which was a weakness of both Jews and Greeks The 'hidden' wisdom enables the mature Christian to know that Christ's victory has been won over all hostile forces. How? By special revelation, as when Paul was carried up to the third heaven, 2 C 12:2–4? Or by listening to Christian prophets, cf. Rev 1:10, 4·2? Rather, by growing up 'in Christ' as a member of his Body, the Church. The Corinthian converts who boasted of their 'knowledge' were being puerile. For only the Spirit of God could reveal his mind. The mature Christian receives this Spirit while the 'natural' (*psychikos*) man—one who simply shares the principle of life with other animals—cannot perceive spiritual truths. The spiritual man perceives, searches and examines them. Isa. 40:13 had warned the Jews that none of them had grasped the mind of the Lord so as to instruct him. But the full-grown Christian is united with God through Christ; to that extent he knows God's mind and is subject to no human judgment.

b **9.** Isa. 64:3–4, combined with 65:17, may be echoed vaguely, though 'it is written' suggests an actual citation: Origen thought that the quotation was from the now lost Apocalypse of Elijah and if this work was earlier than Paul's, this is possible. The Jews of the Dispersion, like Paul, had more respect for non-canonical works than the Palestinian Jews. **11.** 'Of men' may be an interpolation, as the omission in some MSS suggests. **13.** 'Words' also may be an interpolation (Blass) but the sense is clear; 'we speak thus not to those with human wisdom but to those knowing spiritual truths, collating spiritual truths with spiritual.' 831b

III 1-17 Further Denunciation of party Spirit— c
Paul had insisted already on the unity of Christians all of whom were baptised into Christ; now he insists on that unity finding expression in daily work for God in the Church; he addresses his converts as babes in Christ, not ready yet for the spiritual nourishment of the grown up.

1-9. A new-born infant is fleshy (*sarkinos*), a piece of d
animated flesh; the Corinthians are fleshly too (*sarkikos*) in a more ethical sense; yet the former word carries some ethical opprobrium also, implying that the converts should have grown up spiritually; it is to be noted that envy and strife are spiritual sins, involving fleshly sinfulness; the word 'flesh' meant to Paul that element in man which sin has attacked, making it its bridgehead against man's spirit, so that the opposite to spirit is not flesh but sin. So long as the converts indulged in party strife, they showed themselves to be fleshly, not the spiritually gifted beings that they claimed to be, cf. chs. 14–16. **4.** Apollos and his party are still chiefly in mind. The absence of reference to Peter may be due to the latter's never having visited Corinth personally. **7.** The God who gives increase is something; the last two words are to be supplied. **9.** Apollos and Paul were both fellow-workers under and with God and the Church is part of his field or his building; Jesus had been a carpenter or builder and the metaphor of building up or edification recurs throughout the NT.

10-17. A sterner note is struck; if the reference in e
5–9 was to Apollos, here it is to a member of the Apollos party probably, who is warned of his responsibility before God. Paul had laid the foundation like a master-builder with God-given ability; others added on to the foundation but nobody could lay again the foundation which is Jesus Christ. The day of judgment would test their work whether it was costly or cheap, enduring or combustible; according to Mazdean beliefs the fire of judgment would be a molten fire indeed to sinners but like warm milk to the righteous; such beliefs may have penetrated into Judaism during the Persian period of domination, cf. Mt. 3:12. Paul is not speaking of purgatorial fires. Even the sinners would be saved, but they would lose their reward, as a builder whose work is destroyed by fire loses his materials and labour. The metaphor of building suggests to Paul God's shrine or temple, his Church, cf. 6:19. There is no contradiction between this title for the community and their inclusion of sinners who are offered the opportunity of being incorporated into Christ and his temple of the Messianic community of the End-time, proleptically present, cf. Eth. Enoch 91:13; Jub. 1:17. Probably Paul thinks of men such as the incestuous man of ch. 5, not of builders on his foundation, when he speaks of them destroying the temple.

III 18-23 The leaders of the Church belong to it, f
not the converts to them—The Stoic-Cynic term for the anti-philosopher was the 'fool' (*mōros*); the 'wise' man, as the world reckons wisdom, can become truly wise if he rejects human philosophy first and if he is prepared to be regarded as a 'fool'. Paul cites Job 5:13 and Ps. 94:11 loosely; he may have substituted 'the wise' for 'men' in the Psalm but Marcion and the Armenian with some Greek minuscules have 'men'; 'wise' may have come into the text from 18f. Everything belongs to the Christian on earth and in heaven and the Christian belongs to

831f Christ and Christ to God. Paul may have known from his early days at Tarsus Stoic phrases similar to his poetical, concluding sentences, such as 'All things belong to those who are wise' (Zeno) and Paul may thus be echoing such sentiments to show that the converts must not think of their belonging to any party leader but only to Christ alone, No apostle, still less any later church leader, is to come between the Lord and the Christian, cf. Rom. 8:32.

g **IV 1-13 Paul is judged by Christ, not by the converts**—The converts' fanciful bliss is contrasted with Paul's Apostolic condition. Christ has chosen some to be his ministers and stewards ; in a steward we expect reliability, not originality. If the converts judge Paul, that is irrelevant, because the Lord judges him, none else, not even Paul himself, though he knows himself. At the judgment-day God will reveal everything, even the heart's secrets. There was no real ground for the converts' self-esteem. Any gifts that they had were received through Paul from God. Their hypothetical spiritual wealth and royal status in the kingdom are contrasted with the actual lot of an apostle, a doomed gladiator, persecuted for all to see. How ridiculous to suppose that the converts were at ease in Zion already while an apostle is fighting for his life in the arena!

h **6b.** Probably an early marginal gloss has crept in, 'the *not* is written above the *-a*' (of *hina* in the last clause) and the attempted translation 'not to go beyond that which is written' should be abandoned (Baljon). **9.** Here as so often Paul maintains his own apostolic status. **13.** The words for refuse and offscouring may bear the special sense of the human victims chosen for pagan sacrifice in times of pestilence or calamity to avert the gods' anger.

i **14-21 A paternal Appeal**—Paul's mood changes, as so often, from severity to affection ; yet it is out of love that he will spare them, not out of weakness. Their relation is that of father and children while other 'apostles' were to them mere 'pedagogues', slaves conducting children to school, cf. Gal. 3:24 where the Law is called a pedagogue to bring men to Christ. Paul has written a letter which has probably gone by sea ; Timothy is to follow it overland, cf. Ac. 19:22, and he will call to mind Paul's ways in the Christian faith. Not that anyone, however bold, should imagine that Paul is afraid to come in person. He will come soon, if God wills, but the converts' response will decide if he is to come with a rod or in love.

j **17.** It seems here that Timothy may have been Paul's convert ; he was Paul's companion on the 'second missionary journey' especially at Corinth, cf. Ac. 16ff. ; 2 C. 1:19. The aorist tense means 'I am sending'. **18.** Paul probably thinks that any 'puffed up' converts, cf. 4:6, will say that he is afraid to appear personally. **20.** For the contrast between word and power, cf. 1 Th. 1:5.

832a **V The incestuous Man**—A different matter is now discussed. The Corinthian church had tolerated one of its members living with his stepmother. Such an offence was not found even among pagans for the Roman law forbade it ; and the Jewish law of Lev. 18:7f. was equally explicit. Paul says that the offender must be removed and, being really spiritually present with the church in Corinth, though physically absent, Paul has already passed judgment on the man ; he is to be cast out of the Church, the circle of light and life, into the outer pagan darkness and death where Satan reigns. The converts' complacency was misplaced. They claimed spiritual gifts but they forgot that a little infection can make the whole body corrupt, a little leaven permeating the whole life of the Church. A strict Jew made a careful search before every Passover for the least particle of leaven in his dwelling and with relief he cast it out before the Paschal rites began. Christ is our Paschal lamb, cf. Dt. 16:6. 'Become what you are', true sincere Christians without any trace of corruption in the body. Paul had already written on this grave matter, warning them not to mix with self-lovers and other sinners. Part of this warning note 832a may well be preserved in 2 C. 6:14-7:1. But the converts had misinterpreted the note to mean that all contact with sinners was to be avoided, which was impracticable. Paul explains that he was concerned with sinners within the Church, not those outside who are to be left to God's judgment. The Church must eliminate sin from within. The Jewish custom of excommunicating offenders was continued presumably in the Church, the apostles having the right to 'bind and to loose' or declare what was forbidden or not and to remit or retain sins, cf. Mt. 16:19, 18:18 ; Jn 20:23. In 2 C. 2:5ff. Paul assumes that he has power to remit a sentence (where he is dealing probably with a different offender from this one).

4. The solemn language including the sacred name b suggests that Paul is quoting from the rite of excommunication. **5.** Physical death as well as spiritual is envisaged, the two being linked together in early Christian thought ; by 'flesh' Paul means here the entire man, seen from one aspect, just as man's spirit is the entire man seen from another. He constantly stresses that 'flesh' is transient and mortal, as opposed to God's power to save or make alive, cf. 15:53 ; 2 C. 10:2f. **7.** This is the only passage in Paul's letters that can be taken to mean that Christ died at the time of the slaughter of the Paschal lambs before the Passover meal, cf. Jn 19:14 and contrast the synoptic chronology. A. Jaubert has suggested that in Jesus' day two calendars were in use, the legal one, cf. the synoptic tradition, and a sacerdotal calendar attested by the book of Jubilees and the Qumrân sectaries, cf. the Johannine account (RHR 146 (1954), 140-73).

VI 1-11 The Scandal of Christians using pagan Courts—A link with the preceding chapter may be 833a supplied by supposing that a relative of the incestuous man was threatening to sue him before a pagan court and that Paul was aware that at Corinth Christians were habitually using the courts for suits against one another. If such a link existed, it might explain why in the next section, 12-20, questions of chastity and robbery are still in mind. 5:12 had implied that the Church judges its own members ; now Paul insists that Christians must settle their own disputes. In the Messianic age the saints would judge the world, under God, Dan. 7:22 ; Wis. 3:8 ; Sir. 4:15 ; Enoch 1:38 ; Rev. 20:4 ; now Jesus as Messiah and Son of Man had come. 'Son of Man' perhaps still had a corporate meaning running back to Daniel's 'one like unto the son of man' who represented the saints of the most High ; so those 'in Christ' would take part in the final trial when even angels would be judged, i.e. when the evil spiritual forces behind the world would be subject to Messianic judgment. If Christians were to judge the highest known form of created beings, much more should they judge one another in secular matters. Why set up as judges the heathen who are counted as nothing in the Church? A wise Christian to act as judge would be far better. Better also to accept a wrong inflicted or to let oneself be defrauded. There must be no mistake ; sexually indulgent, greedy and unscrupulous persons will not inherit God's kingdom Once the converts had been in that category ; now they were baptised Christians, sanctified and set right with God, in Christ's name, as his property and as belonging to God's spirit.

1. According to the Manual of Discipline judicial b decisions among the Qumrân sectaries were made by the general assembly, but according to the Damascus Document by four judges from Levi and Aaron and six from Israel. But to turn a member over to a pagan court for capital punishment was in itself a capital offence (M. Burrows, *The Dead Sea Scrolls* (1955), 235). **4.** It is best not to read a question- but an exclamation-mark at the end of this verse and to take 'those set at nought' to mean heathen (judges) ; yet Paul did not condemn pagan law any more than he condemned the 'natural order' *in toto* ; he could appeal later from Jewish injustice to the highest pagan court, the

833b Emperor's, and he recognised that the pagans are a 'law unto themselves', Rom. 2:14, having a 'natural law' in their hearts. **9f.** Did Paul know that such sinners had been brought before the courts at Corinth? Or that sexual offences and stealing often have a common root? Or was he condemning self-love in every form? **11.** As the converts' (Gnostic) intellectualism has been pricked, so is their moral pride. It was by Christ's saving acts and by baptism into his Church that they had been rescued from the slime of self-love.

c **12-20 Liberty is not licence; licence destroys unity with Christ**—If the Christian was free from the Jewish Law as Paul had taught his converts, perhaps in the very words 'All things are lawful', that did not mean that they could be licentious. To such a misquotation of his preaching he replies both that not everything is expedient, i.e. if it involves spiritual ruin, and that he will not become a slave to anything. Licence is enslavement to lust. The converts could say that the lower appetites need satisfaction. Paul replies that the physical organs like the stomach are perishable. Viewed as a whole, the body is not something evil and should not be dedicated to evil, such as to fornication, but to the Lord just as the Lord gives himself to the body (in the Eucharist). The body is something which God can raise up, as he raised his Son. The tendency of early Gnostics was to disparage the body as material and so, on their view, an evil thing with the consequence either that men were encouraged to sow wild oats in the fancy that the soul would not thereby be endangered or that a too rigorous asceticism was pursued, the spiritual element being used to crush the material. The Christian doctrines of the Incarnation and Resurrection stood opposed to such teaching of an antithesis between spiritual and material, and in chs. 10–11 Paul will refer to the Eucharist, the chief material vehicle and instrument of Christ's spiritual power for men. Christ became man, Spirit became matter and in man's risen life his spiritual body will be raised up as part of the whole man which has been nourished spiritually on Christ in the Eucharist. No Christian could commit fornication with a 'sacred' or any other prostitute and remain in union with Christ because Christians share in Christ's body; 'they are not *like* but *really* Christ himself in his own body and life' (A. M. Ramsey, *The Gospel and the Catholic Church* (1936), 35). A Christian is not his own and cannot do what he likes with his body; he is bought with a price, ransomed and redeemed, cf. Mk 10:45. The pagan world was all too familiar with the slave-market and pagan inscriptions at Delphi show that a slave could be manumitted on payment to the gods; equally the Jew was familiar with the idea of deliverance from bondage in Egypt and with the thought of 'ransom' associated with that saving act of God. A Christian's body is God's shrine; Philo could have said the same of man's soul, not of his body, just as Philo could have uttered most of the prologue to the Fourth Gospel except the all-important words, 'The Word was made flesh'.

d **13b.** Héring notes that Christ's body is for Paul a metaphysical reality, which, thanks to the Eucharist, already extends its sway to the physical sphere where the future body of the resurrection is prepared. While 'flesh' shows how far man corporately has moved away from God, 'body' can show how close man corporately can come near again to God, cf. 15:50; yet both terms stand for an entire man, not for distinct elements in him. With his 'body' a convert is a member of Christ, the body thus being an instrument of the Spirit; but if he becomes a victim of sin's attack on the 'flesh' and commits fornication, then the union of his 'body' with Christ is destroyed. **18.** Here 'body' represents man's personality; having sexual relations outside marriage affects one at the root of his personality. Paul is not to be taken to mean that other sins, e.g. pride or sloth, do not have such lasting consequences.

Paul turns now to a letter from the converts asking 834a
for guidance on certain problems. Paul's reply to each point in turn is prefaced usually with 'now concerning', 7:1, 25, 8:1, 12:1 (16:12?), cf. 1 Th. 4:9, 13, 5:1 and the letter of the Emperor Claudius to the citizens of Alexandria, A.D. 41 (H. I. Bell, *Jews and Christians in Egypt* (1942), 1–37).

VII Problems about Marriage, Celibacy and Divorce—It is probable that some incipient 'Gnostics' at Corinth despised marriage, thinking perhaps that all Christians should live 'spiritually' without cohabiting even if they were married.

1-9 On Marriage in general—Celibacy was not a b
Jewish ideal, though some Rabbis remained unmarried; Paul, who had no doubt trained formerly to be a Rabbi, was unmarried and preferred Christians to be as he was in view of the impending Messianic woes which on the Jewish theory would inaugurate the Kingdom and in view of the distractions from God's service involved in the married state. (K. E. Kirk, *The Vision of God* (1920), 75ff. stresses the second of these two points, saying that Paul advances other reasons for preferring celibacy to marriage which do not depend for their validity on the imminence of the Lord's Parousia.) Yet Paul allows marriage, stipulating that it must be monogamous and that within marriage conjugal rights must be conferred. Each partner belongs to the other and such rights are not to be withdrawn unless temporarily to give scope for prayer, permanent withdrawal being morally dangerous. Paul had no command to this effect from the Lord or the Church but he makes this concession to the 'spiritually' minded. Personally he would prefer all to remain as he was, unmarried, but different men have different gifts, i.e. all have not the gift of continence. The unmarried and widows (or should we read 'widowers'?) are advised to stay unmarried but, if they cannot, to marry, which is better than to be consumed with illicit passion.

5. cf. Testament of Naphtali, For there is a season for a man to embrace his wife, and a season to abstain therefrom for his prayer, cf. Ec. 3:5. (But were the Testaments post-Pauline?) **8.** The change of a single letter would give the reading 'widowers'.

10-16 On Divorce and mixed Marriages—Paul c
distinguishes carefully between Christ's teaching and his own judgment, cf. 12. He must have known some of the *ipsissima verba* of the Lord on this point, though probably not in the form of Mt. 5:32, 19:9; Mk 10:9; Lk. 16:18. He assumes that divorce is forbidden to Christians by the Lord but he allows the wife to separate if she remains single. Marriages with non-Christians, for which Jesus had not legislated, are presumably those where one partner has been converted since marriage rather than where a Christian marries a pagan. These partnerships are not to be broken for the Christian sanctifies the bond As Schweitzer says, the corporal effects of being in Christ are so real that marriage with an unbeliever extends the relationship to him or her and to the fruit of such marriage (*The Mysticism of Paul the Apostle* (1931), 128). For the partner's and the children's sake the marriage should continue, but if the partner withdraw, the Christian husband or wife is not enslaved, which means presumably that he or she may remarry and that there is no necessity to maintain a relationship where strife and not peace will be found: such a partner could hardly tell for certain that the pagan would be converted.

17-24 Vocation and the Status Quo—In view of the d
approaching End and of the Christian heritage, each should stay as he is whatever the lot be that has fallen to him; such was Paul's advice in the churches that he founded. A circumcised Jew should not undergo an operation to remove the traces when he is converted nor should a pagan become a circumcised Jew before becoming a Christian; neither circumcision nor uncircumcision matters, but only keeping God's laws. The slave should remain as he is,

834d contentedly ; even if he can become free, he had better use his servile state as a Christian. For the Christian slave is God's freedman and the Christian free man is Christ's slave. Christians were bought with a price, cf. 6:20, and they cannot be enslaved to any man. Let everyone stay as he was when converted. These words were based on Paul's judgment not on Christ's precepts, but it remains true that a Christian's duty is to serve God faithfully in that state of life to which it shall please (not 'has pleased') God to call him.

17. Paul does not distinguish between a job which is a vocation in itself and a job into which the vocation to serve as a Christian has to be taken. This is unfortunate ; it is not invariably true that 'to work is to pray'. **21.** 'Use it rather' may mean 'use the chance to become free' but the context suggests rather the alternative, 'use your present state to show that you are a Christian' ; if so, Paul was hinting at the distinction required in the note on 17. **22.** Cf. Augustine, 'Deus quem nosse vivere est ; cui servire regnare est' and Cranmer's translation of this second phrase, 'Whose service is perfect freedom'.

e **25-38 Advice on Virgins**—Three views have been maintained on this point : (*a*) The virgins are daughters of men whose right it was to give them in marriage. The RV adds the word 'daughter' consistently in these verses. (*b*) This is the earliest evidence for the custom which grew up of men and women vowed to celibacy living under the same roof. (*c*) The virgins are maidens engaged to young Corinthians who, like the girls' fathers, were anxious in view of the Parousia whether they should marry or not. (*a*) is the traditional view. A father would not want his daughter to start a family at the time of the Parousia, cf. Mk 13:17 ; but if his prohibition against their marriage proved unseemly, the girl being of full age and temperamentally suitable for marriage, he should let them marry and no sin would be involved. Against this interpretation it is urged that Paul does not use the word 'daughter' at all and the wording of 36–8 is against this meaning, for the charge of unseemly behaviour would be difficult to define and the context would call for the word 'daughter' in the Greek, especially in the phrase 'let them marry'. (*b*) The custom of *virgines subintroductae* may have arisen early and this would explain the reference to virgins here, cf. Hermas, *Sim.* ix, 11 ; Eus.HE VII, xxx, 12 and the third Canon of the Council of Nicaea. Before monasteries and nunneries were built, the custom was common ; bishops fulminated and councils legislated against it as it was open to scandal, cf. S. Jean Chrysostom, *Les cohabitations suspectes*, ed. J. Dumortier (1955). Against this interpretation it is argued, chiefly by Roman Catholic scholars, that Paul would never have countenanced such a dangerous practice. Yet in the first fine careless rapture of the Christian Church, the dangers would not have been obvious and Paul, naturally inclined to asceticism, may have overlooked them. (*c*) The maidens are already engaged and Paul is dealing in 25–35 with the problem whether their fiancés should marry them as much as in 36–8. (On views (*a*) and (*b*) 36–8 stand in a separate category from the preceding verses.) Paul advises that the marriage should take place if the man cannot exercise self-control or if his refusal would not be proper, but that it would be better still to remain unmarried. On this view Paul is not considering *virgines subintroductae* but his advice may have helped that custom to arise later, cf. H. Chadwick, NTS 1 (1955), 4, 267f.

f **25-35.** Paul declares that the *ipsissima verba* of Jesus do not cover the case(s) under consideration and that he has to rely on his own judgment as that of one to whom God has shown mercy. The imminent distress meant the Messianic woes before the End, the time before which is shortened, cf. Mk 13:30. 'Detachment' should be the Christian's motto with regard to marrying, mourning, merrymaking or purchasing goods ; otherwise distractions will follow. An unmarried person can concentrate on the Lord's service but the married person has to think of and give pleasure to the partner. 834f

38. In late Greek *gamizō*, despite its classical meaning 'to give in marriage', may have come to mean 'to marry' like *gameō*.

39-40 Second Marriages—These are allowed explicitly for a widow, and presumably for a widower, g provided that the marriage is to a Christian ; yet Paul speaking not with Christ's authority but with that of the Spirit would prefer widows to remain as they were. It may be that a class of widows was growing up in the Church already, cf. Ac. 6:1ff. ; 1 Tim. 5:3ff. Throughout the whole chapter Paul shows himself in favour of asceticism, cf. Rev. 14:4. He was not in a position to recognise the value of the humanist spirit in Christian ethics nor the dignity of Christian marriage nor its capacity for bringing out Christian virtues. Yet unlike the Marcionites and Manichaeans later, he does not maintain that marriage is evil. But the day was to come when virginity was to be exalted above the married state as though it were superior, cf. Novatian, *De bono pudicitiae*, vii. It is superior—only for those specially called to it.

VIII-XI 1 Meats offered to Idols—The problem 835a put to Paul would easily arise when meat left over from sacrifices to an idol in a temple would be offered for sale in the market-place, slaughterhouses in Greece being usually attached to a temple. A host might hold a meal even inside a pagan shrine where again the meat might seem polluted in the eyes of a scrupulous or 'weak' Christian, cf. MMV, 138, citing a 2nd-cent.-A.D. papyrus, 'Chaeremon requests your company at dinner at the table of the Lord Serapis in the Serapeum tomorrow, the 15th, at 9 o'clock.' The majority at Corinth apparently repudiated the idea that an idol was real or the god that it represented was real and disregarded the scruples of the 'weak' brethren, maintaining that as an idol is nothing, the meats in question were clean. Paul answers that knowledge is not enough. Love must be allowed to settle the problem, not superior knowledge ; the latter makes men conceited, the former strengthens the Church ; if any man loves God, he is known by God (he does not say 'he knows God', cf. 1 C. 13:12 ; Gal. 4:9) ; that constitutes true knowledge. In a different sense the Christian knew that there is but one God ; so an idol is nothing and the Gentile gods, the lords many and gods many, are unreal compared with God the Father, the source of all things and the goal of each of us or with the Lord Jesus, the agent of all creation to whom we owe our being. Not every Christian knew that an idol is nothing ; some had been accustomed to idolatry and in their recent past took idols to be real. We who are 'strong' must remember that our meat or abstinence from it will not be in question on the day of judgment. We are not to cause the 'weak' to stumble or to destroy the brother for whom Christ died by letting us be seen to disregard his scruples. Rather than do that, Paul would prefer to become a vegetarian all his days.

J. Weiss, followed by F. B. Clogg and J. Héring, b thinks that 8 and 10:23–11:1 come from a different letter from 10:1–22 as in the former passages Paul is tolerant towards the 'weak' while in the latter he is rigoristic, arguing that a Christian cannot approach the table of demons and the table of Christ. Paul believed, however, in the power of demonic influence at work before Christianity appeared and still at work outside Christianity especially through pagan rulers, cf. 2:6. Could not Paul have said 'Inside the Church idols of course are nothing, but outside they are powerful'? In any case, Paul could be brilliantly inconsistent ; he does not furnish a systematic theology but throws out flashes of insight. The Hebrew mind could hold opposites together and state each side of the truth without seeing any inconsistency. It may seem strange that he does not quote the Apostolic Decree

835b of Ac. 15:20, 29, 21:25. Perhaps as he moved westwards he preferred to argue the question *de novo* without reference to the authority of the Jerusalem church. Or perhaps the text of the Decree is misplaced in Ac. and should be dated later, so that Paul did not yet know its exact terms (cf. T. W. Manson, BJRL 24 (1940), 59–80).

c **VIII 2.** ' So Socrates recognised that he was wiser than others, in that while all alike knew nothing, he alone was aware of his ignorance ' (Peake). **5.** The Corinthians would think of the gods of their city, Aphrodite or Aphrodite-Tyche, Apollo (seven columns of whose temple still stand there), Athena the Horse-tamer who bridled Pegasus, Poseidon the god of sea and earthquake, Hera (Juno), Serapis, Bacchus and Aesculapius the god of healing, not to mention the cult of the emperor (cf. O. Broneer, *The Biblical Archaeologist*, 14 (1951), 4). **6.** The poetical, Christological statement may be compared with the ' hymn ' in Col. 1:15ff. which makes explicit what is implicit here. Paul answers in advance the Gnostic and Marcionite heresies. Father and Son are one in creation and redemption. **7** The Alexandrian reading is probably correct, *sunētheia*, by custom, not *suneidēsei*, by conscience. **11b.** The atoning value of Christ's death is assumed here, cf. Rom. 3:22. Paul's assumptions are as valuable as his statements.

836a Two different views are taken of ch. **9.** It can be argued, as by Héring, that there is no connection between it and 8 ; that it is a vindication of Paul's apostolic status and in line with 1–4, though it does not discuss whether Paul should be followed rather than any other apostle but rather whether Paul was truly an apostle, and that this question should come logically before any problems of marriage or meats ; and that it belongs to 10:1–22, 11–15, 16:5–9 and 15–end. On the other hand it can be argued, as by Moffatt, that this chapter is not primarily a vindication of Paul's apostolic status and rights nor is it a digression. Just as Paul refused to insist on his rights as an apostle, so the majority of the converts should not insist on their rights to despise and repudiate the scruples of the ' weaker ' brethren. When Paul began to argue about certain subjects, like the Law or his own status in relation to the Twelve, he was apt to digress.

b **IX 1-18.** In a series of short rhetorical questions, like those of an ancient Diatribe writer, Paul asserts his freedom and apostolic rank, which may have been thought to have been conferred by seeing the (risen) Lord. In any case the Corinthian church was the seal upon his apostleship. If he had wished, Paul could have lived off his converts ; again, he could have gone on his apostolic journeys accompanied by a wife like the other apostles and the Lord's brethren, including Peter. Barnabas and Paul had waived their apostolic rights ; it is possible that they were therefore ranked with the ' apostles of the churches ', 2 C. 8:23, presumably on a lower grade than that of the Twelve. If so, the spirit of Mt. 10:7–14 was being forsaken. The allegorical meaning of Dt. 25:4 still stood ; a soldier has a right to his pay, a farmer to his harvest, a shepherd to his flock. Paul had not insisted on his rights as he did not wish any charge of self-interest to hinder the spread of the Gospel. But the implications of Mt. 10:10 and Lk. 10:7 still remained just as the ministers of temple and altar still lived by those objects. He still refused payment and valued this refusal as a ground for boasting. Not that he could boast of being a preacher ; the message of the Gospel was imposed on him and woe to him if he failed ! Being under commission to preach, he did so free of charge.

c **1.** Having seen the Lord (cf. Ac. 1:2f.) and having won converts and having suffered for Christ, Paul could claim to be as good an Apostle as any of the Twelve. **5.** Cephas (Peter) is not excepted from the Apostles but singled out for special mention as one whose wife accompanied him on his missionary
journeys undertaken after he relinquished to James the 836c
headship of the church at Jerusalem. The reference to Barnabas suggests that the ' irritation ' of Ac. 15:39 was temporary and that he, Mark and Paul were reconciled, cf. Col. 4:10 ; 2 Tim. 4:11.

19-27. In his deep desire to make converts, though d
free, Paul had made himself an absolute slave to men to win them, becoming a Jew to Jews and a Gentile to Gentiles. He would be anything to anybody to convert him. Why ? For the sake of the Gospel, that he might share with them in it. The effort required was like that of a competitor in an athletic contest. In a race only one man wins ; the Christian must win his race. A competitor undergoes severe self-discipline in training to win a corruptible crown. Paul runs without faltering ; his blows, as of a boxer, hit their mark, his opponent being his own body which he pummels into subjection, so as not to be rejected himself after preaching to others.

19. Paul could go so far in his efforts to win men to Christ that the charge of hypocrisy has been brought against him, e.g. for his action when he went to Jerusalem for the last time and appeared in the Temple as a Jewish-Christian, Ac. 21:24 (some have doubted the historicity of that scene). Yet Paul was a Pharisee converted to Christ and he may have dressed as a Pharisee, though he did not force Judaism, still less Pharisaism, on Gentile converts and though he knew that Christianity is far more than a baptised Pharisaism. **25.** Paul is thinking probably of the Isthmian games near Corinth at which he may have been present ; he may even have seen the mosaic floor of the office of the director of the Isthmian games depicting a victor at the games, palm in hand, offering thanks to the goddess of Good Fortune (Tyche), and wearing a crown of withered celery (*sic*), cf. Broneer, op. cit., 93. For the metaphor of the ' unfading ' crown of the Christian, cf. 1 Pet. 5:4 ; Rev. 2:10 ; Tertullian, *De Corona*.

X 1-13 Paul has hinted that the crown may be lost ; 837a
now he returns to the subject of idol meats, linking the two themes by a solemn, Rabbinic-sounding warning, based on OT types against various forms of sin. He assumes that the Church is the heir of the OT scriptures, being the true Israel of God, and he works out his exegesis on lines which would have been familiar to the Rabbis or to Philo. At the back of his mind is the fact that even the sacraments of Baptism and the Eucharist do not guarantee victory to the Christian. In speaking of Baptism he refers to the Rabbinic traditions of the Exodus story based on Ps. 105:39 as well as on Exod. 13:21, cf. Wis. 10:17, 19:7, the early days of the Israelites being the type of those of the Church. The ' cloud ' could be taken to be a type of Baptism, of which the sea is also introduced as a type, though Exod. 14 suggests that the Israelites walked through the Red Sea on dry ground. (It is possible that in this passage we have the earliest evidence for the existence of proselyte baptism among the Jews, cf. J. Jeremias, ZNTW 28 (1929), 312ff. Paul's references to the cloud and the sea follow not the OT but the lines of Tannaitic Midrash because it provides a theological basis for the already established custom of such baptism, cf. T. F. Torrance, NTS 1 (1954[a]), 150f.)

Just as baptism into Moses was for all, so all in the b
desert shared in the type of the Eucharist, the manna and the water from the rock, the spiritual or supernatural rock. That rock was Christ, the pre-existent Christ. For the manna, cf. Exod. 16:4, 35 ; Ps. 78:24 ; Wis. 16:20, and for the rock, cf. Exod. 17:6 ; Num. 20:2–13 ; as there are two different accounts of the rock being in two places, Rabbinic exegesis could explain the rock as moving with the Israelites from one place to another. Philo could also identify that rock with the Wisdom of God. W. L. Knox maintained that since Paul's comparative failure at Athens he revised his eschatological message of the Gospel to show that Christ is not only the End but

837b also the Beginning and the Wisdom of God, the agent of God in creation, cf. Gen. 1:1 ; Prov. 8:22 ; Col 1:15ff. (*St Paul and the Church of the Gentiles*, 8–9, 123f.)

c In the light of the Song of the Well, Num. 21:16–18, with its supernatural power, Paul could pass from the thought of angelic force behind the water to that of Christ as the source of the water, water and Spirit being closely connected in Hellenistic Judaism with the divine Wisdom The types in 6ff. are not parallels so much as warnings ; even if Christians have access to Christ, the power of God and the wisdom of God, 1:24, they may still fall and be destroyed. Failure may come through giving way to evil desires, cf. Num. 11:4, 33f., as the Israelites had lusted after the flesh-pots of Egypt and had been destroyed · or to idolatry, as the Israelites had indulged in idolatrous dancing and revelry, Exod. 32:6, 19 : or to impurity, 'fornication' being connected with idolatry in the OT, cf. Num. 25:9 (where 24,000 not 23,000 is given as the number of the dead Israelites) : or to presuming on God's mercy, thereby testing him, as did those whom serpents destroyed, Num. 21:4–6 ; or to murmuring and grumbling, as did those struck by the destroying angel, Num. 16:41–50. These were warnings written for us on whom the ends of the ages have come ; this is probably an eschatological phrase ; the present age and the coming age may be visualised as two separate 'lengths' overlapping now for Christians. The future Kingdom (which is always a present reality outside this age) has been brought within our experience by Christ (W. D. Davies, *Paul and Rabbinic Judaism*, 314ff.). But M. M. Bogle (ET 67, 8 (1956), 246f.) connects the word for 'ends' with perfection and suggests that the language is not eschatological but sacramental ; 'we to whom the eternal mysteries have come down'. Though this would have point in a context about Baptism and Eucharist, it is the less probable interpretation. Paul continues : let no convert be too confident that he can stand, though only the temptations within man's capacity to endure have befallen them and God will not allow superhuman temptation to attack them without providing also a way of escape, that they may bear it.

d **14-22 Idol Sacrifice**—The converts are to flee from idolatry. The Lord's cup of blessing, which in turn is blessed by men, effects fellowship with Christ's blood and the bread which we break with his body. Partaking of the one bread, the many communicants become one. Take as an example the historic Israel. Those who ate Jewish sacrifices were partakers of the Jewish altar. An imaginary objector may then ask 'Then is the sacrificial meat anything?' We know that pagan gods are nothing, yet demons exist, cf. Dt. 32:17, and to offer them sacrifices is to enter partnership with them. A Christian cannot partake of the Lord's cup and of that of demons. We claim to be 'strong' ; are we stronger than God? Are we able to provoke him to jealousy by siding with such a rival as a demon? (Dt. 32:21). As Héring observes, Paul speaks here, as in ch. 5, of a metaphysical and not merely moral union with Christ.

e **16.** The stress here is on the unity of communicants one with another, cf. *Didache* 9 ; Cyprian, *Ep.* 63, 13. **17.** Whatever may have been the origin of Paul's doctrine of the Body of Christ, whether Stoic, Gnostic, OT or Rabbinic, here at least the influence of the Eucharist on his thinking is clear (Rawlinson, *Mysterium Christi*, ed. G. A. Bell (1930), 228).

f **X 23-XI 1.** The threads of the argument in 6:12 are picked up but Paul is concerned now not with the strong Christian so much as with the effect of his action. He must consider his brother's interest. Any meat put up for sale in the market could be freely bought without asking its origin, because it belonged to God ; and if one accepted an invitation from a heathen, one should eat things set on the table without question. Yet if attention is called, presumably by the host, to the meat having come from a pagan 837f temple, the Christian should abstain, so as not to warp the conscience of others who may consider a Christian eating such meat to be without a conscience. However, another man's conscience is not the yardstick for one's own and if thanks to God have been given over the meat, a Christian may eat of it. Everything, including eating and drinking, is to be done to God's glory, without causing offence to Jews, Gentiles or the Christian Church. Paul sought the good of others always and had earned the right to say 'Imitate me, as I imitate Christ'.

26. cf. Ps. 24:1. **32.** The 'third race' of Christians is already here !

XI 2-13 The Scandal of unveiled Women—Some 838a Christian women at Corinth were praying and prophesying in public worship with heads uncovered. This offended Paul's tastes and though he may have heard of it privately (for he does not begin 'Now concerning' as if in answer to a question), he gives his opinion. His repugnance to the growing custom was no doubt due to the conventions of the ancient world, according to which ladies appeared in public with a veil covering their hair, ears and forehead, or else they were no ladies. The advice is given about women engaged in public praying and prophesying, i.e. preaching, but it would apply doubtless also to all Christian women meeting in a house-church for worship. If they appeared to be ladies of easy virtue, the good name of the church would suffer. Paul adduces certain arguments, physical and theological, for observing the conventions, though one should not dismiss his arguments as mere rationalisations or bad excuses for a good reason. They are, however, weak, as he himself seems to recognise in 13f. when he falls back on an appeal to the custom of the churches and to what is fitting. An objector could have replied that b in Christ Jesus there is neither male nor female, Gal. 3:28, and that only by a bad Christian could Paul's estimate of relative importance be maintained: (*a*) God, (*b*) Christ as agent in creation, (*c*) man and (*d*) woman in that descending order ; and that if a Christian woman is 'covered' by her long hair, that is a sufficient veil for her ; and that to argue that if she is uncovered, she might as well be shaven, is absurd ; or that Paul would have been on surer ground if he had argued that unveiled women in church are liable to distract men (not angels) from prayer and worship or that the function of women is different from men's and that this fact cannot be overlooked.

Paul puts forward the physical arguments for c woman's inferiority, using the word 'head' loosely of the relation of God to Christ and of Christ to man as well as of man to woman. Men in the new age, as opposed to Jews, prayed with heads uncovered, following no doubt the example of Jesus ; the women who had accompanied him must have been veiled and the custom continued in the church outside Corinth. Paul held that a man covering his head to pray dishonoured it, while a woman unveiled dishonoured hers, the former by wearing a badge as it were of inferiority though he is supreme over created things, the latter because she would not seem better than a harlot punishable as such by having her head shaven. The word 'glory' is difficult and probably the word *dogma* for *doxa*, 'copy' for 'glory', should be read (Ginsburger). **7b** may be an interpolation ; otherwise the same emendation should be made there too. Paul's theological argument is based on the Jewish belief derived from Gen. 6:1–4 that *'elōhîm* or angelic beings lusted after women ; if a woman is unveiled in prayer she has no protection against evil angelic forces, the spiritual plane which she has entered being dangerous ; her veil would be her 'authority' against them, cf. Tertullian, *De virginibus velandis*, vii, *De Oratione*, xx-xxiii, *De cultu feminarum*, ii, vii.

3. Here is the first-known expression of the doctrine d of Christ's headship later elaborated in Col. and Eph.

838d **10.** The variant *velamen* for authority is probably an easier reading. If Paul had preached at Corinth on the fall of the angels according to Gen. 6, his allusion would have been clear, cf. Eth. Enoch 6–7, 67–8, 106:13f; Slavonic Enoch 7:18; Jubilees 5:1; Bar. 56:8–13 **11.** It is only 'in the Lord' that men and women have any sort of equality, being as Christians complementary the one to the other. **14** argues that if nature covers woman with long hair, grace demands that we veil her head as well. Paul's arguments, weak as they are, were sufficiently weighty for the custom of women being 'covered' in church being maintained in Britain until the Second World War.

e **17-34 The Misuse of the Lord's Supper**—Again there is no 'Now concerning' to serve as an introduction to an important topic of which Paul had had news. He was in no position to confer praise and he gave at least partial credit to the rumour that the converts had forgotten the original meaning of the Supper and concentrated attention solely upon the social side of the ceremony. Not only did they neglect the religious significance of the rite but they also made the social aspect of it an occasion for the wealthy alone to meet convivially without waiting for their poorer brethren to join them. The 'parties' so formed may not have been those of 1:12 but may have been based rather on rank or wealth; worse still, the convivial gatherings of the wealthy were in danger of becoming orgies of gluttony and drunkenness. It would be better for the converts to eat their meals at home, if they wanted no more than that, rather than that they should disgrace the Church of God.

f Paul then reminds them of the original solemnity of the Lord's Supper, the tradition of which he had received ultimately from the Lord but immediately through the church at Antioch, and corroborated no doubt by what he knew of similar teaching at Jerusalem. The words of 'institution' are recorded for the first time in any extant Christian writing. The lack of 'balance' between the two halves of the 'words' points to their primitive character, the liturgical tendency being to harmonise one 'word' with the other. To Paul not only is the Church the Body of Christ but on a deep level the Christians share together spiritually in his body through partaking of his body and drinking his blood spiritually re-presented before God each time that they perform this rite, so making a memorial of him. The cup is the new covenant to which Jer. 31:31 had pointed forward, a 'better covenant' than any sacrificial covenant of ancient Israel, Exod. 24:8, or any covenant of the Qumrân or Damascus covenanters or sectaries. Thus the Church proclaims the Lord's death till he returns. To eat the bread or drink the cup of the Lord unworthily is to be guilty with regard to Christ's body and blood. Hence the vital necessity of self-examination before participation; else, judgment is brought on oneself through failure to discern the Lord's body. For this reason many Christians have fallen sick or even died for outside the circle of light and life sickness and death prevail. Yet if the converts examine themselves, they escape judgment; being judged by the Lord, we are trained like children so as not to fall under the judgment coming onto the world. The Christians are to wait for one another before they partake or else to eat at home. Paul will make other regulations when he comes.

g **19.** It may be an unrecorded saying of Christ, 'There needs must be divisions among you', cf. Mt. 18:7; the reason for including this saying here would be that such divisions are a test for Christian faith; if he fails, a Christian is rejected (*adokimos*). **20.** At Corinth Paul had taught the converts apparently to combine the Eucharist with an Agape or social meal: later when Mark and other evangelists wrote their accounts of the institution of the Eucharist, the social element had already disappeared. Was Paul's stern warning given here responsible for separating the Agape from the Eucharist? This is more probable 838g than that we should agree with Dr Wand that the Agape was a late importation into Christianity and that the Last Supper or Eucharist was never celebrated in New Testament times as part of or in conjunction with a full meal. **23.** The preposition 'from' denotes that the tradition came through the Church, not by Christ's direct revelation to Paul; O. Cullmann holds that the word 'Lord' is a designation for the oral tradition about Jesus (SJTh 3, 2 (1950), 180 ff.). **24.** Only Lk. 22:19*b*–20 of the Synoptic Gospels contains the command to repeat the rite; though this part of Luke's text is omitted in some Western MSS, it is probably part of his authentic text, not due to insertion from the present Pauline passage; any similarity of language used by Paul and by Luke may be due to familiarity with liturgical usage. 'Remembrance' is best taken in the sense of 'memorial', cf. Exod. 13:9, not, following J. Jeremias, as a prayer of Jesus to be remembered by God (*The Eucharistic Words of Jesus*, tr. A. Ehrhardt (1955), 161–5). **29.** The body is the Church, according to A J. B. Higgins, *The Lord's Supper in the NT* (1952), 73.

XII-XIV Spiritual Gifts—Paul had been asked to 839a
pronounce on the gift of speaking with tongues, glossolalia, to which he reverts in ch. 14. It is a common critical fallacy to differentiate between speaking in foreign tongues and making ecstatic, unintelligible noises, and to proceed to interpet Luke's account in Ac. in terms of the former and Paul's references to glossolalia in terms of the latter, and in the light of this supposed contrast to maintain that the author of Ac. could not have been Paul's companion. Paul is alluding to a gift latent in many people of all times to utter noises, intelligible or not, under stress of deep emotion or when the 'censor' of the psyche is removed by hypnosis, narcotics or drugs, cf G. B. Cutten, *Speaking with Tongues* (1927) For the later history of the phenomenon, e.g. among the Montanists, the Little Prophets of the Cevennes, Irvingites and other revivalists and similar phenomena attested by spiritualists, cf. E. Lombard, *De la glossolalia chez les premiers chrétiens et les phénomènes similaires* (1910) and N. Whymant, *Psychic Adventures in New York* (1931).

It seems that there are four 'levels' at least of glosso- b
lalia: (*a*) inarticulate sounds, (*b*) articulate sounds resembling words, (*c*) coined words and phrases, (*d*) the utterance of some words or phrases in a foreign tongue (Cutten). A possessed person, usually but not invariably a woman, may pass from one to another level in succession. Paul rates this psychological gift below the other, moral gifts of the Spirit. The history of glossolalia confirms the correctness of his estimate that the psychological gift was apt to lead to pride for its possessor and not to the edification of the Church.

XII 1-3. Those speaking in the Spirit should be tested, c
cf. 29; 1 Jn 4:1. If the possessed person curses Jesus by saying that 'Jesus (is) anathema', he is not possessed by God's Spirit as is one who says that Jesus is Lord. The acknowledgment of Jesus as our Lord (*Māran*) goes back to the primitive Aramaic-speaking Jewish Christians of the early days and it was not, as Bousset thought, due to Greek-speaking Christians familiar with the 'gods many and lords many' of the pagan world.

2. The text is probably corrupt (though *-ate hoti hote* is well attested, *hoti* should probably be omitted). Paul could remind his converts that some of them not long before were liable to be inspired by idols and pagan deities like the Pythian goddess.

4-11. As glossolalia is only one of many gifts of the d
Spirit, Paul considers the value of some of the others, which appear as functions, not distinct offices, of members of the Church. The Spirit is the donor in each instance and each gift contributes to the corporate life of the body of Christ, the Church. The one Spirit, Lord or God, is at work in the body; the embryonic Trinitarian formula is to be noted, cf.

839d Rom. 12:6–8 ; 2 C. 13:14. The Spirit enables each independent member to function, whether his gift be a word of wisdom (moral teaching?) or a word of knowledge (of God), or a deep faith in God, or a gift of healing or of the ability to work miracles or to preach or to discern spirits or (last in the list) to talk in tongues or to interpret them. All gifts are given in proportion to the Spirit's will and are all grace-gifts, freely conferred.

e **12-31 The metaphor of the body is elaborated**—The body is a perfect unity, made up of many parts, each interdependent, the function of each, however humble, being necessary to the well-being of the whole. So too with the members of Christ's body. The analogy, which calls for little comment, was a widespread one for the body politic, cf. the speech of Menenius Agrippa to the Roman plebs, Livy ii, 32, 8 ; Epictetus, *Dis.* ii, 10, 3 ; Dion. Hal., *Ant. Rom.* iii, 11, 5. But Paul starts from the one body and explains why it must have more than one member or else not be a body ; he does not start from the many to reach the one. Nor is his metaphor used to insist on the rights of the many but on their duties.

13b. Were made to drink ; the reference is probably not to the cup of the Lord's Supper but to Baptism as in 13*a*. **28**. cf. the list of functions in Rom. 12:6–8 ; Eph. 4:11.

840a **XIII The Hymn of Love or Self-giving**—This chapter is not a Pauline interpolation as Héring takes it but a dithyrambic outburst typical of Paul's inspired utterance linked to ch. 12 by 13:1 and 8, and to 14:1 by its theme of self-giving Love or Agape, as opposed to Eros, desire to gain, cf. A. Nygren, *Agape and Eros*, tr. A. G. Hebert (1936) ; H. Riesenfeld, *Coniectanea Neotestamentica* 5 (1941) ; J. Moffatt, *Love in the NT* (1929). Christian Agape should be compared with the nearest Hindu 'parallel' in the Ramayana of Tulsi Das, *bhakti*, which falls far below the supreme Christian virtue. Without the gift of God's essence, self-giving Love, Paul maintains that any Christian sacrifice is valueless, like the resonant gongs and tinkling cymbals of pagan worship ; the former phrase was used proverbially of empty wind-bags. Even the gift of preaching and of understanding all divine secret plans or having all sacred knowledge, and even the gift of faith that could move mountains (Mk 11:23), without Agape, is valueless. Even giving away all possessions piece by piece, including the body itself, is profitless without Agape. The characteristics of Agape are to be long-suffering, kindly disposed, not given to envy or to self-display, to conceit or misbehaviour, to self-seeking, rage or bitterness. Agape does not brood over wrongs, is pleased not with injustice but with truth and is always forgiving, trusting, hopeful and patient. Agape is indestructible. Prophecies, tongues, knowledge all perish but not Agape. They belong not to the mature but childhood stage. A metal mirror gives but a dim reflection ; in this life we see God's truth like that ; but then we shall see clearly and know for certain as God knows us. Faith, hope and Agape remain in that new age which has already begun.

b **2**. Again Paul reveals that he knew a collection of the *ipsissima verba* of Jesus. **3**. The variant 'that I may boast' is better attested textually, especially by Alexandrian MSS, than 'that I may be burnt', though the latter suits the context well and if it is original may show that Paul was thinking of Indian gymnosophists who burned themselves alive, like the Indian who accompanied Porus' embassy to Athens, where Paul may have seen his grave. **7**. For *stegei*, bears, *stergei*, cherishes, was a variant known to Cyprian. **8**. Again Paul pricks the bubble of gnosis or knowledge. **12**. Paul may have thought of the sorcerer's magic mirror which revealed a destined bride, cf. 2 C. 3:18. **13**. Faith, hope and love are the three theological virtues displacing the four cardinal, pagan virtues, soberness, understanding, righteousness and courage, Wis. 8:7. It is beside the
point to inquire how faith and hope 'remain' in the 84
New Age as well as Agape, since Paul is thinking of the overlapping period of the two ages, the present and the coming, which the Christians enjoy, cf. on 10:11.

XIV Prophecy and Speaking with Tongues—Paul c
reverts to the subject raised in 12. (Those who take 13 to be an interpolation from another Pauline work maintain that 12:31 should be followed by 14:1*b*, 1*a* being redactional.) In the early Church glossolalia and prophecy were both considered signs of God's Spirit being present and of his kingdom having arrived. Paul enjoyed the exercise of glossalia himself more than his converts but he wanted to limit its use in public assembly, maintaining that prophecy was a more important gift. The Christian prophets were inspired preachers, proclaiming God's will and foretelling the results of failure to obey it. Apparently they had, at times at least, clairvoyant faculties, enabling them to read the minds of those present, v. 25. Even if they spoke in an ecstatic condition, they had their gift under control and they presented it with and to the intelligence ; they could cease if another was due to speak in turn, for the prophets' spirits were subject to them as the spirits of those speaking with tongues were not.

1-19. Above all Agape is to be sought, and, among d
spiritual gifts, prophecy or preaching is to be desired most. Anyone speaking with tongues is at one with God and is not understood by his audience since he discourses about secret divine plans ; but anyone who prophesies builds up the Church by his preaching and comforts and consoles the hearers, so that the one gift edifies the speaker, the other the Church. Paul wishes that all could speak with tongues but he would have preferred all to prophesy, as prophecy is the greater gift (cf. Num. 11:29), unless the glossolalia is interpreted that the Church may be built up or edified. If Paul arrived exercising his glossolalia, what profit would it bring unless he made it into revelation, knowledge, prophecy or teaching? A lifeless instrument of music, wind or stringed, cannot play a recognisable tune unless it plays different notes, and unless a trumpet sounds clearly, how can it summon to battle? So a Christian, to be understood, must speak intelligibly or else talk to the wind. There is an infinite number of sounds in the world, none of them meaningless. But any 'Greek', not knowing a 'barbarous' tongue, would find that a barbarous word estranges him from the speaker and vice versa. If the converts were anxious for spiritual things, let them ask for such gifts as would be more than abundant for the edification of the Church. A glossolalist should pray for the gift to interpret ; the spirit of a glossolalist, not his understanding, prays fruitlessly. Both understanding and spirit have their place in singing and in praying. Else, when a blessing is given in the spirit, how will an uninitiated member present be able to say 'Amen', if he is ignorant of what is said? The thanksgiving may be excellent but the other man is not edified. Paul can be thankful that he can outstrip all his converts in glossolalia but he would prefer to speak a few words with his understanding than a myriad of words in glossolalia.

10. 'Sounds' may mean 'words' here. **11**. To a e
Greek anyone without a knowledge of Greek was a barbarian. **13ff**. These verses do not necessarily mean that the usual content of glossolalia was a prayer though often it may have included an ejaculation of praise to God. **16**. In many an early house-church there must have been members of a family present, not yet fully converted. They were uninitiated (*idiōtēs*) and almost on a par with the unbeliever. **16f**. The reference may be to the Eucharistic form of prayer or to any prayer of thanksgiving in a wider sense. (The former had no fixed liturgical form for many years, cf. *Didache* 10 ; Justin, *Apol.* 65.)

20-25. For all his disparagement of human wisdom f
Paul insists that Christians must use their brains in adult fashion, not being intellectually childish like the

840f incipient Gnostics, but remaining infants so far as vice goes. As Isa. 28:11 had foretold, the Lord would speak to Israel by men with other tongues and yet they would refuse to hear them. Instead of believers being impressed by glossolalia, Paul maintains that this phenomenon should impress unbelievers, while prophecy is a sign rather for the believer than the unbeliever. Any uninitiated person coming into the assembled church and hearing them speaking with tongues will call them mad, while if all prophesy (in turn) that person will find that the prophets can read his very thoughts, speaking to his condition, and the stranger will become a worshipper, recognising that God is with his new Israel indeed.

21. As J. G. Davies says, 'it is reasonable to assume that St Paul understood glossolalia to be talking in foreign languages' (JTS, N.S. 3 (1952), 28–31). **23.** Clairvoyancy and thought-reading were characteristics of OT seers, cf. 1 Sam. 9:15ff. ; 2 Kg. 5:20ff., and presumably of NT prophets also ; or did Paul mean no more than that by preaching they convicted the uninitiated in his conscience ?

g **26-40 Rules for Worship**—At the moment all are anxious to show off their gifts in public worship, whether it be psalm, teaching, revelation, a 'tongue' or its interpretation. But all should be done to build up the Church. Only two or at the most three are to speak with tongues, taking it in turn, and one is to interpret, but if no interpreter is there he should keep silence and speak to himself or to God. But two or three prophets are to preach while the others exercise discernment on what is said. The preacher must fall silent if anyone else in the congregation has a revelation to give. All can take it in turn to preach, for mutual enlightenment and strength. For the prophetic gift is under control of the prophet and God wills not confusion but peace. Such was the custom in all God's churches (but should v. 33*b* be taken with 34–6 as in RSV ?). Some scholars think that **34-6** are interpolated verses, apparently contradicting 11:5, 13, which seem to allow a woman to prophesy or pray in church so long as she is veiled. Some Western texts, including D, G put 34–5 after 40 ; yet this may not be so much a sign of interpolation as of the bewilderment of the Western scribe(s) at the apparent contradiction. Other scholars (e.g. Héring) take the passage to prohibit women joining in a discussion of the prophecy or sermon ; should they wish to do that, let them do so at home with their husbands, cf. W. J. Sparrow Simpson, *St Paul and the Ministry of Women* (1920), according to whom Paul thought that women should in their subservience to men remain in a public service both covered and silent. Paul did not forbid private instruction by women, e.g. by Priscilla who instructed Apollos, but Paul never contemplated women becoming priests or overseers, or even public preachers. After all, says Paul, he could speak from wide experience. The faith had neither started nor ended at Corinth.

To conclude, any claimant to a prophetic or spiritual gift must allow that Paul's message is on a par with God's command, cf. 2:16*b*, presumably because Paul speaks with the Spirit ; else, the claim cannot be recognised. While glossolalia is not to be forbidden, prophecy is a more desirable gift to seek.

841a **XV The Resurrection of the Dead**—Christian doctrines rest on the belief that Christ rose from the dead. The subject is raised here because Paul had heard apparently that questions were asked at Corinth not so much about the resurrection as about the nature of the risen body. The absence of the phrase 'Now concerning' suggests that this was not one of the specific questions put to Paul for him to answer. Pharisaic Jews would think of the risen body reanimated, the human being, body and soul, forming one whole. God had seen at creation that his work, including man, was good. Despite man's fall, his risen state would be in a new heaven and earth. On the other hand the Greeks at Corinth who held any belief in an after life would think in terms of the immortality 841a of the soul apart from the body ; to them the body was the tomb of the soul, the *sōma* was a *sēma*. Death would liberate the soul. To the Pharisaic Jew, with whom naturally Paul had most sympathy, Paul would have said that the risen body is not crudely material, though in some sense continuous with the earthly body ; he does not define the nature of that continuity. To the Greeks Paul would have replied that there is to be a body, but a spiritual one which will be the clothing (cf. 2 C. 5:3) of the personality of the risen Christian ; the body is the organ of the spirit's expression and in the coming age there will be the appropriate organ for man to use, in a way which will preserve his continuity and identity. The whole basis of this belief is the resurrection of Christ and the knowledge that Christ appeared with a risen body after death to his disciples. Without that resurrection Christian faith is futile and Christian standards of life pointless. But Christians rest assured ; the life-giving power of the Spirit is a present possession, a guarantee of future bliss, and Christ's resurrection is the surety for the resurrection of those 'in Christ'.

The importance of this, the earliest discussion of b Christian belief in the resurrection, cannot be exaggerated. It assumes that Paul has already given his *kērygma*, or form of the Apostolic preaching, including the doctrine of the resurrection of Christ and also some of his *didachē* or teaching based on it, which he now supplements ; in doing this he appeals to history and to the evidence of historical eye-witnesses of appearances of the risen Lord, many of whom were still alive. He gives a list of them, which, it is well to remember, is probably incomplete.

1-11. Paul gives the 'knowledge' that the converts c needed, the reminder of the Gospel preaching which he had proclaimed already and which they had received. It was the basis of their salvation if they held it fast, not having made their act of faith with rash impetuosity. For he had handed on to them among the most important facts which he had received from the Church (in Antioch ?) that Christ died for our sins as the OT scriptures foretold, and that he was buried and that he rose on the third day according to the same scriptures. So far probably Paul is recording his kerygma. Now he adds a reference to the appearances of the risen Lord to Peter (cf. Lk. 24:34), then to the rest of the Twelve, then to more than five hundred brethren, probably in Galilee, most of whom were still alive ; then to James, the Lord's brother, who had not believed before the resurrection in Jesus (Jn 7:5) but who became head of the primitive Jerusalem church, then to all the Apostles ; then to Paul himself who felt that he had entered on the 'new creation', being born again, in an untimely way (or was it that some converts called him 'the abortion' ?). He felt unworthy to be called an apostle, as he had persecuted the Church. Yet he is what God has made him. Not being one of the original Twelve, Paul has to stress his labours for Christ to show that he was as good an Apostle as any. His pattern of the apostolic kerygma did not differ from the Apostles'.

2. The Greek text is difficult but the sense is clear. d **3f.** The empty tomb of Christ is assumed, cf. Ac. 2:25–8 ; the scriptures may mean especially lists of Testimonies or OT proof-texts pointing to Christ (cf. Ac. 26:23) together with their contexts, cf. C. H. Dodd, *According to the Scriptures*, who shows how deeply the consciousness that Jesus was the Suffering Servant of Deutero-Isaiah entered into the mind of the primitive Church, cf. V. Taylor, *The Names of Jesus*. **4.** Included in the primitive kerygma is a mention of the 'third day', cf. Mk 8:31, 9:31, 10:34, 'after three days'. When Christians searched the scriptures daily to see if the things said of Christ were so (Ac. 17:11), they found that Hos. 6:2 supported this belief, 'on the third day he will raise us up'. It is highly improbable that this citation was the sole source of the belief about Christ. **5.** The 'Twelve' is already

841d a technical term ; the variant, the Eleven, found mainly in Western MSS, is due to scribal reflection that Judas had hanged himself.

e **12-19.** By repeating the vitally important evidence for the historical facts of Christ's saving work, Paul forestalls any possible argument that all belief in any kind of resurrection, Christ's or Christians', may be rejected. Because Christ has risen, resurrection is possible, and if it were impossible Christ could not have risen. Paul assumes by implication the reality of Christ's manhood at this point. If Christ had not risen, Christian preaching would be futile, and the Apostles would be false witnesses, faith would be vain and converts would be back in their former sinfulness and the faithful departed would have been destroyed by death. If in this life Christians had nothing but hope in Christ, they would be the most pitiable people on earth. Paul had probably met men who had known Christ in his Galilean days but who were without knowledge of a faith in his saving acts of death and resurrection ; to them Christ had given hope of a great prophet and no more.

f **20-28.** In fact we are in no doubt about the resurrection ; we know the eye-witnesses to it and its power in us. Christ was the *aparchē*, the first-fruits, rising from the dead at about the time when the sheaf of first-fruits was offered in the Temple on Nisan 16th. Christ was the *rêshîth*, cf. Col. 1:15ff., which guaranteed the rest. *Rêshîth* in the opening word of Gen. 1 (when God created Adam) is an operative word to Paul ; all men unredeemed are in Adam, as all men redeemed are in Christ, Rom. 5:12ff. Christ is everything for redeemed man that *rêshîth* and (*ap*)*archē* can possibly mean ; in him all things are created, by him and into him ; he is the beginning, sum total and head as well as first-fruits (C. F. Burney, JTS 27 (1926), 160ff.), cf. Col. 1:15–20.

g The resurrection is to take place in 'stages', first, Christ's, then those belonging to him at his second coming, then comes the end when Christ will hand over the kingdom to the God and Father, when he has annihilated all spiritual enemies, till when his kingdom must continue ; the last enemy to be destroyed will be death. Ps. 8:6 pointed to Christ, the 'man' of the Psalmist being equal to the 'Son of Man' ; the Son of Man Christology probably continued in the early Church, cf. Ac 7:56, though, to be intelligible to Gentiles, Paul preferred to speak of the second Adam instead

h **23.** Paul may be using the imagery of some Jewish apocalypses and of the later Rabbis, who distinguished between the days of the Messiah and the coming age, as he does too in Col. 1:13 apparently. Though the resurrection of Christ meant the defeat of hostile spiritual powers, their total destruction would not be completed till the Second Coming when the Messianic reign would begin, those 'in Christ' sharing this rule with him ; death which had had no right to attack man's body, though it has a hold on man's flesh, will be destroyed before the end of all things or final act in the divine drama. (Paul does not say here whether he envisages a general resurrection of all the non-faithful at the end. But if *telos* does not mean 'end' or 'finally', it may mean 'the rest' or 'remainder' (so in Aristotle and Arrian), and the thought of a second, general resurrection may be read into the passage, as by J. Weiss and Lietzmann.) **25.** Cf. Ps. 110:1. **27** cf. Ps. 8:6. The Psalmist's words in Paul's mind have given a subordinationist bias to the words which follow Later, the Church had to safeguard the faith against the heresy of Marcellus of Ancyra by inserting the words 'Whose kingdom shall have no end' into most of the Eastern conciliar creeds, cf. Lk 1:30 At the end Christ would render back to the Father the Messianic dignity but his Sonship which had been pre-existent would be his. **28.** Paul does not mean that all things, good or bad, will be equally divine (he was no pantheistic Hindu) but that God's sovereign sway will be exercised universally.

29-34 If there were no resurrection, Christian action 841
would be futile. Why are Christians baptised for the dead ? Why did apostles like Paul run the risks that they did ? By his justifiable pride in his converts he can swear that he dies daily. Supposing our existence were only on the natural plane, what would have been the object of his struggle with beasts at Ephesus ? If there is no resurrection, the hedonistic outlook summed up in Isa. 22:13 would be appropriate. But the converts must not be duped ; as Menander of Athens, the 4th-cent.-B.C. dramatist, had said, 'Evil communications corrupt good manners'. Let them come to their righteous senses and cease sinning.

29. B M. Foschini has catalogued over sixty different j
interpretations of this verse ; 'dead' can be taken to mean 'dead in sin', or 'on behalf of the dead' can be taken separately with a question-mark, as Foschini suggests ; or a reference to martyrdom which was treated as the equivalent of baptism for the unbaptised has been found ; or else deep-seated textual corruption is postulated, for which Héring finds evidence in the future tense ('what shall they do ?') instead of the present. But it is best to take the verse literally to refer to vicarious baptism undertaken by Christians on behalf of dead friends and relatives ; this custom would arise naturally out of a misunderstanding of the necessity for being 'in Christ' (Schweitzer). St Paul does not commend the practice but it lingered on among the followers of Montanus and Cerinthus and it was found as late as the 5th cent. among the Marcionites to whom the Armenian father Eznik refers. It probably dates back to a time before the schismatics hived off from the great Church. **32,** however, is best taken metaphorically. Ac. does not relate a literal exposure of Paul to wild beasts at Ephesus, where some at least of the Asiarchs are said to have been his friends. As a Roman citizen he would have been able to claim exemption from such a fate.

35-49 The Nature of the risen Body—Paul may k
have in mind his imaginary objector rather than a real one who supposed that there was only one kind of flesh on earth and one of body in heaven. Even the senseless man of Ps 14:1 who denied God's existence would have to admit that a seed must die after it is sown, that it may be given life. The seed is not exactly the same as the body that is to be, for God gives it a body appropriate to it. There is difference as well as continuity between the earthly and the heavenly body. Paul, like Galen, thought that there were different kinds of flesh of men or beasts, of birds or fish ; so there are earthly and heavenly bodies, the former sown in corruption but raised in incorruption, the latter radiating light and glory, according to the nature of each. Other antitheses connected with the two bodies are dishonour and glory, weakness and power, natural (sharing the principle of life common to all creatures) and spiritual. Gen. 2:7 proved that both bodies exist and the citation can be taken to point to the first as opposed to the second Adam, cf. Rom. 5:12–21 ; 2 C 4:6, 5:17 ; Gal. 6:15 ; Col. 3:10 for this Adam-Christ typology. Paul treats the question of resurrection as a corporate not individual one, cf. W. D. Davies, *Paul and Rabbinic Judaism*, ch. 3 As Adam had stood in the OT generically for all mankind, now Christ stands for the whole of redeemed humanity.

42. The dead : the gist of the argument is that the l
actual physical particles of the earthly body are not raised up but that a spiritual body or expression of the man's whole self, continuous with his earthly body but different from it, will be provided for him on the heavenly plane. A. Feuillet points out that the contrast in 2 C. 5:1–3 between the earthly and the heavenly tabernacle awaiting the Christian is paralleled here by the contrast between the first and the second Adam ; the heavenly tabernacle he takes to be Christ's glorified body, cf. J. A. T. Robinson, *The Body* (1953) (RSR 44, 2 (1956), 161–92 and 3, 360–402). Without losing his personal identity, the risen Christian will be 'in Christ', as in a sense he is on earth already, and

l will be part of the glorified body of Christ. **49.** Some MSS have the future tense 'we shall bear'; but in view of the present participation of the Christian in Christ, the subjunctive 'let us bear', attested by the Chester Beatty papyrus and others, is better.

m **50-58 The Transformation into the risen Life**—The argument of 42 is picked up. Paul and his converts expected the Parousia to occur before their death. How would those still alive fare at the second coming? (cf 1 Th. 4:13–17, where the lot of those Christians who had died already is discussed). Not all would die but when the trumpet sounded for the last events (cf. Zech. 9:14; Mt. 24:31; 1 Th. 4:16; Rev. 11:15), those on earth would be transformed. They would partake of the heavenly body, as if they had died, while the dead would be raised incorruptible. The Jewish-Christian apocalyptic imagery of the trumpet is still in Paul's mind but he uses terms like incorruption and immortality for the benefit of his Greek readers. These describe the garment of the corruptible and mortal body, Resurrection and transformation (change) are treated as synonymous terms. Isa. 25:8 is not quoted but echoed and the triumphant citation of Hos. 13:14 follows, for the grave has lost its victory and death its sting. To Paul the Mosaic Law was like a 'hot fomentation to bring to the surface the poison of sin in the body' (N. P. Williams). Rom. 7 describes the power of the Law over man and his consequent guilt, ending in a similar outburst of praise to God for deliverance from the 'body of this death'. Paul closes here with an appeal for steadfastness and perseverance; Christian effort is not in vain, cf. 32.

50. cf. J. Jeremias, NTS 2 (1951), 3, 151–9. **51.** The variant readings 'We all shall sleep but we shall not all be changed' and 'we all shall arise but we shall not all be changed' are inferior and probably due to scribal reflection that Paul and his readers had all died before the Parousia. **55.** 'The Christian died with Christ to the sin brought out by the Law; hence sin lost that which conferred on it its strength, while with the paralysis of sin, death lost its power to sting. And the powerlessness of death came to light especially in its reversal in the resurrection' (Peake).

a **XVI Items of Business and Personal Affairs and Salutations—1-4.** Instructions are given about the collection for the saints, the poor Christians of Jerusalem, whose economy seems to have suffered from the voluntary communism of the early days of the Church there (Ac. 4:32) and from the famine (Ac. 11:28). Paul was anxious to cement the Gentile-Christians with the Jewish-Christians by encouraging the former to send contributions to the latter, cf. Ac. 12:25; Rom. 15:27; 2 C. 8:4ff. This payment would correspond to the half-shekel sent by every male Jew of the Dispersion to the Temple. Nothing is known of the details of the collection from the Galatian churches but Gal. 2:10 speaks of Paul's promise to arrange one. It seems that the first day of the week, the day of Christ's resurrection, was already the special day for Christians to meet together, cf. Ac. 20:7; Rev. 1:10. Paul suggests tactfully that the collection be made once a week so that the money should not be contributed hurriedly on his arrival or pass through his own hands but be entrusted to delegates who would accompany him with it to Jerusalem. So he forestalled any accusation that he or his companions profited by the collections, cf. 2 C. 12:16. A reference, **5-9,** follows naturally to his own plans; the present tense 'I am going through Macedonia' is probably to be given a future meaning; Paul is still at Ephesus (8f.), intending to travel not by the fast sea route but overland via Macedonia to Corinth. He was detained at Ephesus by great opportunities for effective work and by the pressure of many enemies. He hoped to spend the winter in Corinth or at least some time there with the converts, if the Lord willed it (cf. Jas 4:15), before being sent on his way by them.

b **10-11** give a reference to Timothy's mission, cf. 4:17; Ac. 19:22. There seems to have been a certain diffidence in Timothy's character, cf. 2 Tim. 1:7 (probably a genuine fragment). Paul uses a conditional clause here, not a temporal one, perhaps because he feared that Timothy would hesitate to go to Corinth after all. Paul makes a special appeal for a good reception for him and for his respectful treatment since he works, like Paul, for the Lord. Paul was eagerly awaiting his return 'with the brethren'; were the latter Corinthian delegates perhaps already in Ephesus or Ephesian Christians? (Héring connects these two verses with his 'earlier' letter, and he connects 5–9, which contradict 4:19, he thinks, with the 'later' letter.) If the 'brethren' of **12** are the same as those of 11, they were probably Corinthian delegates in Ephesus. **13f.** give a brief exhortation to be watchful, cf. Mt. 25:13, in view of the End, to be steadfast in faith, manly and strong. 842b

15-17. Stephanas and his household are commended; he had been the 'first-fruits of Achaia' (contrast Ac. 17:34) and he had done outstanding service to the 'saints'; to such labourers for Christ submission is due. Fortunatus is unknown; the name was common and it is rash to identify him with the Fortunatus of Clem. Rom., *1 Cor.*, 65, 1 written nearly fifty years later. Achaichus is also unknown; this may mean the Achaian (slave). All three made up to Paul for his separation from the converts. c

19-24 Salutations and possibly a liturgical Fragment—Asia, approximately the western third of our Asia Minor, included Mysia, Lydia, western Phrygia and Caria and was one of the wealthiest of the Roman provinces. Aquila and Prisca (or Priscilla), cf. Ac. 18:2, 18, 26; Rom. 16:3; 2 Tim. 4:19, were originally Jews from Pontus; they had reached Rome and had been expelled under Claudius' decree (Suetonius, *Claudius*, 25, 4), probably *c.* A.D. 49. At Corinth they met and worked with Paul, presumably already having become Christians; they left with Paul and set up a church-house in Ephesus; Rom. 16:3 may be part of a letter sent to Ephesus or of a chapter added to the original Rom. 1–15, which had been sent to the West by Paul. In line with the current tendency to discern traces of liturgical language embedded in the NT, J. A. T. Robinson found such traces of a liturgical sequence in 20–4, by comparing this passage with the language of the *Didache* 10:6, cf. Rev. 22:20; Justin, *Apol.*, 1, 65. The supposed 'sequence' may have run as follows, as Robinson suggests: d

℣. Let grace come and the world pass away
℟: Hosanna to the God of David
Deacon?: If any man is holy let him come, If any man is not let him depart
℣: *Maranatha*
℟: Amen.

This 'sequence' may have come after the 'Agape' or social meal and before the Eucharist began. Mutual greetings and the kiss of peace would be exchanged (JTS, N.S. 4 (1953), 38ff.). E. C. Ratcliff (ib.) compares Rom. 15:30–3 which points to a request for prayer, a kiss from all and a doxology according to P^{46} (at the end of ch. 15). On such a view we have evidence a century older than Justin's for part of the 'Eucharistic sequence' in the worship of the church and for the view that the pattern of such worship was fixed at Corinth less than a quarter of a century after the resurrection. *Maranatha*, 'Come, O Lord', is probably a liturgical cry, transliterated into Greek from Aramaic. In itself it is enough to disprove Bousset's theory that the worship of Jesus as Lord was an importation into primitive Christianity by Greek converts perhaps at Antioch; it goes back to Aramaic-speaking Jewish-Christians probably of the mother-church at Jerusalem, where Jesus was worshipped as Lord from the first.

842e 23. Grace in Pauline language means the unmerited love and power of God through Christ at work in men's souls. 24. Finally, the great theme of Agape or self-giving Love, ch. 13, is picked up before the letter closes.

Bibliography is given at the end of 2 C.

II CORINTHIANS

(For an explanation of the departure from the traditional order of chapters see §§844a–d.)

843a This letter probably consists of at least four fragments of Paul's correspondence with Corinthian Christians. These four fragments are:

(A) VI 14–VII 1
(B) X 1–XIII 10
(C) I–VI 13; VII 2–IX
(D) XIII 11–14

b (A) **VI 14–VII 1 A Warning against Contamination**—This section has been interpolated into its present context and if it is excised it leaves a continuous argument in 6:13 and 7:2. This section is different in tone from its environment, teaching a baptised Pharisaism, a complete separation for Christians from pagan ways of life. The Christian is to keep away from all unsuitable ties, sexual and other, because righteousness and iniquity have nothing in common any more than light and darkness or Christ and the prince of demons, Belial. A believer has nothing to do with an unbeliever, any more than God's temple with idolatry, for it is the Christians who are a temple of the living God. Loose quotations follow, given in the Pharisaic manner, from Lev. 26:12; Ezek. 37:27; Isa. 52:11; Ezek. 20:34, 41; Jer. 31:1; Isa. 52:11, 43:6. A Christian possessing these promises cleanses himself from any contamination of flesh or spirit, cf. 1 Jn 3:3.

c 1 C. 5:9f. shows that Paul had written a letter in this vein which the converts had misunderstood, taking it to mean that they must go out of the world. The interpolated fragment may well be the letter to which 1 C. 5:9f. refers. The language of the Qumrân sectaries, especially their use of 'Belial', which occurs as 'Beliar' in the better-attested text here and which does not occur elsewhere in the NT as a personal name for Satan, is extremely close to the wording of this fragment, cf. M. Burrows, *The Dead Sea Scrolls* (1956), 334.

844a (B) **X 1–XIII 10.** This is an extremely caustic and severe passage which is not likely to have followed originally upon 2 C. 1–9 in which allusions to such a severe letter are found. A probable suggestion is that 10:1–13:10 forms part of Paul's severe letter, the original opening and ending of which have been lost when an editor compiled the Pauline letters to Corinth.

b Allusions in 1–9 to a severe letter are found in 2:4, 7:8; cf. 3:1, where the implication is that in a previous letter Paul has had to resort to self-commendation. Further, 2:3 seems to presuppose 13:10, 1:23 to presuppose 13:2 and 2:9 to presuppose 10:6. If on this view 2 C. 10:1–13:10 is read in what was probably the original order, before 1–9 and 13:11–13, we see Paul's moods changing from bitterness to joy and from despair to exultation and we are spared the necessity of explaining why his moods changed in the reverse direction if the chapters are read in the order printed in our Bibles, just as we are spared the difficulty of making out that 1 C. was in whole or part the 'severe letter' which had been sent.

c Admittedly there is no textual evidence for this dislocation. All MSS, including the 3rd-cent. Chester Beatty papyrus codex, P[46], as well as the Alexandrian uncials Bℵ and the Western D, give the traditional order, which has been challenged since Semler's day during the last two centuries simply on the grounds of internal evidence. Yet the papyrus sheets of the original roll or codex could easily have become loose and the Pauline editor could have been faced with the problem of fitting the fragments together as best he could. As 2 C. was apparently less popular and less copied than 1 C. in the early Church, the editor may not have begun his work of compiling 2 C. till the end of the 1st cent. or the beginning of the 2nd. While Clement of Rome, *c.* A.D. 96, quoted 1 C. frequently, he does not use 2 C., though the theme of 'rebellion' would have been much to his purpose! In the 2nd cent., Polycarp (A.D. 120–35) and Irenaeus and the Muratorian canonist (both *c.* 180) seem to have known 2 C. but it is doubtful whether earlier writers, e.g. Ignatius (*c.* 115), did.

d On the other hand, it must be admitted that scholars like A. H. McNeile, J. H. Bernard and R. V. G. Tasker maintain that the traditional order is correct.

e On the usual, modern view, after writing 1 C. Paul paid a second visit to Corinth in keeping with his plan announced in 1 C. 4:19ff., 11:34, 16:3, 8. It was a flying visit, unrecorded in Ac. because Luke was concerned with the spread of the Gospel from Jerusalem to Rome, not with all the minor movements of Paul. This visit was a failure, 2 C. 2:1, 12:14, 13:2. Paul returned to Ephesus feeling crushed and humiliated; he wrote the severe letter pouring into it all his anger and sorrow, thereby revealing his character as in no other epistle. For he had been deeply offended by someone (unknown) at Corinth, who had launched a personal attack upon him. The offender was probably not the incestuous Corinthian of 1 C. 5:1ff., despite J. H. Bernard's arguments (*Studia Sacra* (1917), 232ff.). for Paul would never have considered the sin of incest a personal matter, as this was. His own apostolic status was denied; he was said to be arrogant and self-seeking, a weighty letter-writer but an ineffectual and contemptible speaker; and the majority at Corinth had countenanced the attack. Paul sent his indignant reply by the hand of Titus, 2:4, demanding the punishment of the offender. On our view this letter included 10:1–13:10. It was a crisis in Paul's life. He had been led by the Spirit into what is now called Europe; he had had to be smuggled out of Thessalonica. In the university city of Athens, the 'educational committee' of the court of the Areopagus had smiled politely but incredulously at his Gospel of Jesus and the resurrection. Now it seemed that even at Corinth his mission had failed. Paul left Ephesus for Corinth via Troas. Titus was not there to meet him and to tell him about the effect of the severe letter. In his anxiety he went along the road to Macedonia along which Titus had to travel, 2:12f., and at last they met. To Paul's unbounded relief and joy the news was good. The Corinthian community had come round to Paul's side against the offender and his apostolic authority was no longer flouted. Out of a full heart he could now write his paean of thanksgiving, 1–9. He was as glad as Titus was for the latter to return to Corinth, taking an almost incoherent outburst of joy ahead of Paul, who would strengthen the Macedonian church and then follow Titus to Corinth himself.

f **X 1–6 A Warning of impending Discipline**—Paul, who knew Christ's characteristic meekness and consideration for others, makes them the basis of an appeal which answers the taunt of his opponents that he is humble in their presence but a bully when he is absent. He begs that on his arrival he may not have to show them personally the source of his courage and audacity as if he walked according to the standards of the flesh, that bridgehead in men's make-up which sin had made its own. He may be in the flesh but his weapons are not fleshly ones but divinely powerful enough to demolish strong-points or the ramparts of speculation built up to withstand the knowledge of God and sufficient to capture every theory in order to subject it to Christ and alert enough to pass sentence on any act of insubordination, as soon as the majority

4f of the Corinthian community should capitulate. Paul loves to contrast the weakness of the flesh with the power of God, cf. 1:17 ; Rom. 6:19, 8:3 ; 1 C. 15:43 ; Gal. 4:13.

g **7-18 Justifiable Boasting**—To face plain facts, Paul belongs to Christ as much as anyone making such a boast. He feels free to boast about his authority which God had given him to build up and not to destroy the church in Corinth. But he does not intend to browbeat the converts by letter. Had not his opponent said that Paul's letters are powerful and imposing but his personality feeble and his speech contemptible? He will not compare himself with those who blow their own trumpets. He boasts, but only within limits, setting his own standard against himself. The standard for him is marked out by God and its limit is on the far side of the Corinthian church. He is not transgressing his limits in exercising authority there ; he had been the first evangelist at Corinth. He would never encroach on other's territories, cf. Rom. 14:12 ; 1 C. 4:3–5. Rather, he hoped that the church there would increase and expand so as to enlarge his proper limits beyond Corinth. In any case, Jer. 9:23f. taught that if anyone boasted, he should boast about the Lord. Self-praise is not acceptable compared with the praise conferred by the Lord, who had given Paul his apostolic ministry.

h **XI The 'Foolishness' of Paul**—The withering sarcasm of this chapter shows how deeply Paul was hurt by the insult that he had received. Behind his biting phrases lie a deep affection and concern for his converts. Paul has been called a 'fool'. Very well, let them bear with a little 'folly' from him. As the Lord is 'jealous' for his people, so is Paul for the Corinthians. He had arranged a wedding-contract between the church of Corinth, the 'chaste' maiden, and Christ himself ; but as Eve had been duped by the serpent, it seemed as though the church was being won away from Christ. They could tolerate some intruder giving them a different version of the Gospel of Jesus from that which Paul preached or a different message of the Spirit from his. Why not tolerate Paul too? Paul is one of the genuine apostles, on a par with the Twelve, not with these apostolic delegates, these 'super-apostles' who claimed probably (despite F. V. Filson) to represent the mother-church. Paul gave his message clearly for all to understand, though he did not claim eloquence but knowledge, the real knowledge of God seen in Christ, not any knowledge of the incipient Gnostic. As in 1 C. the 'foolishness' of God was seen to be wiser than men's, like that of Apollos, so now Paul's 'foolishness' should be seen to be wiser than that of any eloquent Jewish-Christian emissary.

i **7-15.** Paul was a 'fool' to take nothing from the converts ; they merely turned round and said that he thereby showed that he ranked himself below the Twelve, who were paid for their ministrations according to the precept that 'the labourer is worthy of his hire', Lk. 10:7. He is glad to boast of financial independence of the church at Corinth. He had refused his pay and he would continue to do so in order not to be a burden on the community. (We know that the Macedonian converts gave him financial assistance, Phil. 4:19, and that his own work as a tentmaker contributed to his necessities and to those of his companions, Ac. 20:34. The Jew saw no shame in a teacher making a living with his hands. But the Greek thought manual occupations to be menial.) Apart from the apostles who had seen the Lord during his ministry or after his resurrection or both, many could call themselves 'apostles' even if they were merely sent on some *ad hoc* errand from a church such as that at Jerusalem. Paul had not only seen Jesus on the road to Damascus, he had also suffered in his service. Meanwhile, no wonder that these false apostles dress up as Christ's apostles ; Rabbinic legend told of Satan's ability to dress as an angel of light. Their fate would accord with their deserts.

16-32. Speaking as a 'fool', not as an inspired 844j
apostle, Paul is compelled to boast to prove his apostleship genuine. The converts in their 'wisdom' endured fools readily enough ; they endured a man who claimed control of their souls or spent their money or deceived them or strutted about arrogantly or even buffeted them. Paul could not compete with that. They were emissaries of the Jewish-Christians? Paul was a Jew through and through, a real minister of Christ as his suffering proved. So he recalls his toils, the beatings, the imprisonments for the sake of the Gospel. He had been at death's door ; five times the Jewish authorities had had him lashed with forty stripes, except one. Three times he had been flogged by the Roman lictors. He had been stoned once, three times shipwrecked and for twenty-four hours adrift in the ocean ; continually travelling, facing dangers from rivers and robbers, from Jews and Gentiles, in cities, deserts and at sea ; in danger from false Christians ; suffering toil and hardship, often sleepless, hungry and thirsty ; lacking food, warmth and clothing and all the rest, not to mention the pressure of anxiety every day, his concern for all his converts. Which of them was weak without him being the same? Which had his faith upset without Paul burning with indignation? Paul's boasting consists of his weakness in suffering for Christ and the Gospel. The first, most bitter taste of humiliation for Paul the apostle was when he had been lowered in a basket from a hole in the wall at Damascus to escape the clutches of the ethnarch of king Aretas, cf. Ac. 9:25. (The ethnarch may well have been a sheikh outside the city waiting for Paul to come out of the city gates ; this is easier than to suppose that Aretas was master of the city or that the vast number of Arabs there necessitated his appointment to be governor.)

24ff. We see that Luke in Ac. has underemphasised k
Paul's sufferings, and has not made too much of them. The shipwrecks may have occurred off Cilicia early in Paul's Christian ministry unrecorded in Ac.

XII 1-10 A Vision recalled—Boasting about visions 845a
is out of place but Paul is compelled to recall one which he, 'a man in Christ', had had fourteen years previously. God and not he himself knew how the trance came ; he was snatched up to the third heaven, which according to late Jewish belief was the highest heaven of all. He heard ineffable words on entry into Paradise. Paul would not boast of himself, except of his weaknesses, but he would mention that vision, though if he wanted to do so he could boast of much else without being a 'fool' ; but he wanted to be accepted for nothing less than what his words and deeds were worth. He had had many visions but to prevent him from being too superior about them, he was given a 'thorn in the flesh' to buffet him. Three times he had begged the Lord to remove his trouble but the answer to his prayer was a negative ; 'My grace is enough for you ; for power is made perfect in weakness'. Boasting of his weakness, he knows that Christ's power rests on his life, as God's cloud of glory of old had rested in the Temple or even on two pious Jews studying the Law together. Being strong when he is weak, he is content for Christ's sake with weakness, insults, persecutions and calamities. Said to be 'beside himself', he could tell of such an incident. Recalling it, he could come to terms with life. This experience, according to Dr C. H. Dodd, had a profound influence on Paul's development (BJRL 17–18 (1933–4)). It helped to effect a radical change in his attitude to the Gentile world and in his message to it. 'He withdrew his claim on life for power, predominance and conspicuous success. He was reconciled to
experience.' His eschatology changed from being a b
futurist, Jewish-Christian eschatology as that of 2 Th. 2, into being a sublimated or realised eschatology. Though even in the last group of letters he was to cry still, 'The Lord is at hand', yet now it is Christ, as the Wisdom of God and with God in the beginning,

845b who confronts him. 'Christ is the end for Christ is the beginning, Christ the beginning for the end is Christ.' Hitherto Christ had been to Paul the End; now he is to be the Beginning, cf. Col. 1:15ff. Set right with God or justified, the Christian is made a part of the new creation corresponding to but better than the creation of Genesis. Paul could become world-affirming and not world-denying; even the 'household codes', baptised from their Stoic forms, were to form part of his message since he perceives now the worth of the natural order (cf. W. L. Knox on Christ as Wisdom in *St Paul and the Church of the Gentiles*, 125ff., and contrast J. Lowe, JTS 42 (1941), 129ff. and W. D. Davies, *Paul and Rabbinic Judaism* (1948), 285–320).

c 7. The nature of the 'thorn in the flesh' is unknown; epilepsy, malaria, stammering and blindness have all been suggested. C. G. Jung has suggested that the blindness was psychogenetic; that long before conversion Paul had been a Christian, resisting the faith fanatically; at last on the way to Damascus the 'unconscious complex of Christianity broke through into consciousness. Because he could not see himself as a Christian, having resisted Christ, he became literally blind; that resistance was as usual apt to recur and with it the psychogenetic fit' (*Contributions to analytical Psychology*, tr. by H. G. and C. F. Baynes (1945), 257). But why does Jung assert that Paul from time to time resisted Christ later? Jung's desire to eliminate the supernatural has probably a simple psychological explanation.

d **11-21. The 'Fool' and 'Nonentity' speaks**—The converts, having failed to vouch for Paul, forced him to boast and he has written indeed like the 'fool' that he has been called. Though a 'nonentity' he is on a par with the super-apostolic legates from Jerusalem. The works which reveal an apostle, miracles, wonders and acts of power, were all performed patiently at Corinth. In every way Corinthian Christians were treated like other Christian communities, with one exception; the former were not burdened with Paul's upkeep; they are asked sarcastically to forgive him for that. Paul is ready for the third time to visit them and still he will be no burden. For he wants them, not their money. Children do not store up for parents but parents for children; Paul would gladly spend and be spent for his converts; is he to be given less affection by them because he has lavished more on them? Very well, he had not been a burden, but he had been 'deceitful', they said, using his messengers to get money after all from Corinth. Titus and his brother (Luke?), he replies, had been asked to go as messengers and they had made nothing out of the converts. Paul too had acted in precisely the same way. If Paul's argument for his defence has been lengthy in their view, he has spoken before God in Christ so as to build up the Church. He fears that on his arrival they will find each other far from pleasant; the converts may be guilty still of moral lapses and he may be humiliated by God in front of them, mourning for those who have committed for some time various sins including sins of the flesh, without repenting.

e **XIII 1-10 Paul the Mouthpiece of Christ's Power**—Paul is about to pay them the third visit; he cites Dt. 19:15 with a twinkle in his eye, not because he intends to call witnesses literally against the offender, whose offence was well known, but because Paul hopes to be 'third time lucky'. If he comes, sinners past and present will suffer and the Church will be given a proof that Christ speaks through Paul. Paul does not tell them that in rejecting the Gospel of Christ, they had rejected themselves from God's saving plan, but that Christ is powerful and no weakling. Crucified in his weakness, Christ lives by God's power; the weak in Christ shall live by God's power with him. They are not to test Paul but themselves. Christ is in them unless they have been put to the test and have failed, as Paul hopes that they will find that he has not failed. He prays that no harm befall them, not to

prove that he has passed any test but that they may 84
act rightly even if he seems to have failed. He cannot work against but for the truth. He is glad when the converts are strong, though he is weak; and he can pray for their restoration. Away from them he writes thus, so as in their presence not to deal abruptly with them as he could do in view of the divinely given authority conferred on him to build up and not to destroy them.

So this letter closes, revealing as no other does, the depth of his bitterness when he thought that the converts whom he loved had forsaken him.

(C) **I-IX The Letter written in Macedonia** 84
I 1-11 Salutation and Introduction—Paul is careful to say that his apostolic status was conferred by the will of God. Though Timothy (cf. 1 C. 16:10) had not succeeded in bringing the Corinthian church to order, he is selected again to appear in the salutation as Paul's companion. The blessing or thanksgiving which normally followed a salutation in a letter of the period is God-centred in Paul's letters; the tone of it, with its constant, throbbing word 'comfort' (which recurs ten times in five verses) is suitable if it is taken to follow reconciliation after the severe letter had had effect. Tactfully Paul avoids being too explicit about the need for this comfort. The wound must not be reopened. The comfort that he has received will be held as a stewardship, to enable him to comfort others in need of comfort; somehow Christ's sufferings are abundant in Paul's case, cf. Col. 1:24. Though Paul would have been the first to maintain that only Christ's sufferings have redemptive value, cf. 1 C. 1:13, and that the Cross was a completed act of God, yet so closely is he in union with Christ that any birth-pangs of the Messianic age still to be undergone by Christians are to be joyfully received and shared as part of Christ's sufferings, cf. Mk 10:39; Phil. 3:10, and Paul can gladly draw the converts' share upon himself.

In Asia Paul had suffered a crushing experience; b
so overwhelming was it that he expected to die, as though God's verdict of death was already passed on him. That experience drove him back to God who raises the dead. (Is this an allusion to the events behind 1 C. 15:32 or to a situation the gravity of which Luke has minimised in Ac. 19–20?) God rescues still and Paul asks for the prayers of the converts that he may still rely on his deliverance, cf. Ps. 9:10, and he asks that many may be made thankful for the answer to this prayer.

12-22 The divine, affirmative Answer 'Yes'— c
Paul can boast that he has been actuated especially in regard to Corinth by holiness and sincerity. His letters were written straightforwardly for all to understand; they have shown, like his life, that the converts have him as their basis for any boasting, as he has them, on the Day of the Lord. Confident of this, he had intended to visit them on the way both to and from Macedonia before leaving for Judaea. But had he proved fickle in altering his plans? Not 'fickle' in a worldly sense, which means answering 'Yes' and 'No' in the same breath. In an inspired 'aside' Paul comments on the nature of the Son of God proclaimed by all three companions at Corinth. Christ is the affirmative answer to all God's promises; all the hopes and aspirations of Israel were fulfilled in him. Believing in a God who carries out his promises, could Paul be anything but sincere? When the Church utters 'Amen', 'So be it', it endorses the truth of that preaching. Paul and his converts were together made over to God through Christ, consecrated, marked with his seal in baptism and given his Spirit as a pledge of the blessing to come, the Spirit being 'the anticipation of the end in the present' (Cullmann).

I 23-II 11 The Cause of Paul's Grief and its d
Outcome—He calls solemnly on God to punish him if he lies in saying that he wanted to spare the converts and so did not visit them (it was not that he favoured the Macedonians). Not that he lorded it over their faith for they had taken their stand firmly in the faith.

6d A second painful visit should not be made ; one was more than enough ! For if he grieved them, he cut off his own source of joy. He had written the severe letter out of bitter distress and anguish of heart, not to grieve his converts but to show them his affection. If anyone had pained Paul, the pain had been inflicted on all, or at least on a majority of them. But now all is well because the majority had come round to censure the offender so severely that there was danger of the man being overcome with remorse. Paul has even to plead for him that the converts may forgive and comfort him, letting him take the old place that he had had in their love. If they forgive the offender, Paul does the same for their sake in the presence of Christ. But if they fail to forgive him, Satan, whose wiles Paul knew all too well, would find a way of gaining advantage.

e **4.** There can be little doubt that this painful letter is not 1 C. but one couched in such terms as 2 C. 10:1–13:10. Although 1:23 is ambiguous, as are 12:14 and 13:2, the probable meaning is that Paul had paid two visits to Corinth and was intending to pay a third. **5.** The offence was personal but public ; it is extremely unlikely that the offender was the same as the incestuous man of 1 C. 5 ; Paul's reference to him having been punished enough distinguishes him from the incestuous man who had been ' handed over to Satan '. Probably this offender had flouted Paul's apostolic authority and the majority at Corinth had done nothing to support Paul.

f **II 12-17 The triumphal Procession of Christ**—When Paul reached Troas he was too restless and anxious to take advantage of the door of opportunity wide open to him. He yearned for Titus to bring news. But instead of relating what that news was (cf. 7:6) Paul bursts out in a great paean of praise for the triumph of Christ which carried Paul with it as victor over the Jewish Law. Paul's journey to Corinth became a triumphal procession ' in Christ ', giving off a fragrance of the knowledge of Christ in every place that he reached. This fragrance was the incense used in a triumphal procession (cf. Knox, *St Paul and the Church of the Gentiles*, 129*n*) and marked the triumph of Christ, Paul being the victim sacrificially offered as well as sharing in the victory. The fragrance was also the knowledge of God shown in the Gospel, a fragrant spice which brought life to the righteous and death to the unrighteous far better than the Law did, for which this claim was made. (In the exuberance of his delight Paul's language becomes involved and Rabbinic allusions flood into his mind.) The power of life and death in one's hands being terrible, he asks who is qualified for this ministry. No man. Yet he can claim not to have ' watered down ' the word of God like a dishonest wine-vendor with his wares, but to have preached sincerely, conscious of having been commissioned by God and of being in God's sight.

g **III 1-3 The Corinthian Church is his Commendation**—Afraid of appearing again to be praising himself, cf. 12:11, he says that he needed no recommendation from or to the converts such as Jewish-Christian emissaries needed and paraded, no doubt. The community at Corinth was his commendation, an open letter for all to see, written not on tables of stone but on the tables of the heart. The reference is not only to the giving of the Law, Exod. 24:12, 31:18, 32:15f., but also to the new covenant of Jer. 31:33 according to which the day would come when a new covenant would be written on men's hearts so that all should know God from the greatest to the least. (For the thought of the ' new covenant ' cf. 1 C. 11:25.) That day had come.

h **4-11 The new Ministry as opposed to the old**—Paul could write with complete assurance, not because his ' sufficiency ' was based on himself but on God. Perhaps Paul was thinking here of the popular, false etymology of ' Shaddai ' in the sense of ' sufficient '. God's sufficiency made Paul a minister of the new law or covenant, one of the Spirit and not of the letter, one leading to life and not to death. Paul is making 846h
no reference here to an ' underlying spirit ' of a set of rules. The ' law ' is indeed the Jewish Law but the Spirit is the Holy Spirit, cf. Augustine's *De Spiritu et Littera*. A legal religion imposes rules from without, a religion inspired by the Spirit imposes rules within. The legal one passes a verdict of guilty on the despondent sinner, the spiritual one infuses life and hope into him. Moses' face had shone with God's glory after talking with him, Exod. 34:29ff., and the old covenant had had a measure of divine, shining radiance, but it was transitory ; the new covenant is far more glorious, and is permanent. To administer the new covenant, as Paul did, is far more glorious than to have administered the old, as Moses had done ; Paul's implied contrast of himself with Moses would have shocked a Jew. Since glory means the radiant light of God's self-revelation, the Christian ministry dispenses a glory that reduces that of the OT to nothing ; the former remains, the latter has vanished.

9 The Ministry of Righteousness—God has taken i
action to set men right with himself, to make a new order, a new creation ; ' to justify ' is inadequately translated by ' to acquit ' ; men are reprieved from death and given life in a new creation, in which they share by belonging to the body of Christ (cf. O. C. Quick, *The Gospel of the New World* (1944), 54).

12-18 Paul can use great boldness and frankness j
of speech—He reads into the Exodus narrative the idea that Moses knew the transitoriness of his reflected glory and veiled his face to prevent the Hebrews seeing that glory fade. Even up to Paul's day the Jews could not do without a veil ; for in the synagogue a veil had to be placed on the ark of the Law. That was symbolic. The knowledge that Christ has outdated the Law is veiled from the Jews. Yet they have only to turn to Christ for the veil to be removed, cf. Exod. 34:33. The Lord is the Spirit and where he is, there is liberty from the Law. The Christian can boldly unveil his face and reflect and behold as in a mirror the Lord's glory, being ' magically ' changed into what he sees there through the power of the Spirit.

17f. Two phrases occur in two verses which seem to identify the risen Lord with the Holy Spirit and some scholars have accepted the view that Paul identified them ; others prefer to speak of ' equivalence of function ', the work of the Lord being undifferentiated from that of the Spirit, or they suggest that the ' Lord ' means ' God ', Exod. 34:34 being in mind ; or they maintain that in Christian experience Christ and his Spirit are one and that Paul meant no more than that (cf. D. R. Griffiths, ET 56 (1943), 81–3, cf. H. J. Carpenter, JTS 40 (1939), 31ff.). Griffiths points out how many different renderings of 18*b* have been made : (1) even as by the Spirit of the Lord, AV, (2) even as from the Lord the Spirit, RV, (3) even as from the Spirit which is the Lord, RVm, (4) even as from the Lord of the Spirit, (5) even as from the Lord who is spirit, cf. RSV, (6) even as from a sovereign Spirit, taking Kyriou as an adjective with Hort.

IV 1-6 The Light of the new Age and the Dark- k
ness of blinded Souls—Here Paul picks up the themes of 2:16 and 3:12. Such a glorious ministry as Paul had been given meant that he could never be a traitor to the word or indulge in shameful deeds or deceitfully falsify the Gospel, the truth of which, being sincerely preached, could be judged by every human conscience. If the Gospel is obscure and ' veiled ', it is so only for those who are perishing. God has allowed for a season the prince of darkness to dominate the present age, so that men are blinded, unable to see the light shed by the Gospel of Christ who is the image of God, as ' Wisdom ' in the Wisdom literature had been that image, a semi-personified being alongside God in creation. Christ, not the Law, is the light (cf. Heb. 1:3) and he is the master whose slave Paul is and whom Paul preaches. Had the converts said that the light that shone on Paul on the road to Damascus was an illusion ? It was as real as the light

846k which came from God at Creation. Being born into the new age is to partake of the new creation and God who gave light at the first creation gives light at the second. Knox brings out the connection assumed here between light and the pre-cosmic Wisdom of God in Jewish Hellenistic thought (*St Paul and the Church of the Gentiles*, 133). To Paul, Jesus is all that late Jewish thought took 'Wisdom' and God's Spirit to be, and more.

l **7-12 Christ lives in a dying Man**—Moffatt's translation of the first-person plural by the first-person singular is justified especially here. It is Paul who is conscious of the great paradox that a Christian minister presents. The treasure of the Gospel is entrusted to a weak vessel to show that divine not human power works thereby. Paul is 'down' but not 'out' physically and spiritually, continually re-enacting in himself the dying of the Lord that the life of Jesus might be brought out through his own body; that life is active for the converts while death is at work for Paul who refers here to his own sufferings.

m **13-18 Faith in the Unseen**—Paul speaks in language which a Greek as well as a Jew could understand. He appeals to the underlying faith of both his converts and himself, quoting a phrase from Ps. 116:10 (the reader being left, in accordance with Rabbinic custom, to complete the poem for himself), their faith being that God who raised Jesus from the dead will raise them too and place them together in his presence. Now it seems that having faced death, or at least the most dire threat of it, Paul has reached the conclusion that he may die before the Parousia, contrast 2 Th. 2. In the light of the coming of the resurrection, temporary affliction to man's outward nature counts nothing in comparison with his inward nature and the prospect of its eternal glory. The contrast between the outward and the inward man or between the seen or temporal and the unseen or eternal would appeal to the Greek mind, cf. Plato, *Republic* 588B. If the life of Jesus is made effective in the Apostle's mortal body, then a spiritual life is being built up in it, which will triumph soon. The glory far beyond all comparison outweighs the light affliction of the passing hour before the end. Paul plays on the Hebrew word for 'glory' which is cognate with that for 'to be heavy'; a Jewish audience would appreciate the point. In 15 Paul shows that his feet are planted firmly on this earth despite the lyrical outburst of his previous theological meditation: all that he does is done for the converts so that the more that God's gracious unmerited love is poured out, the more may thanksgivings arise and redound to God's glory.

16. cf. Rom. 12:1f. As 'flesh', man is decaying, but as 'body', which is man under another aspect, a man in Christ is being made into the body of Christ which is in the unseen world (cf. J. A. T. Robinson, *The Body* (1953), 76) The resurrection of the body begins at Baptism.

n **V 1-10 The Spirit as a First Instalment of the risen Life**—As a Hellenistic Jewish-Christian of the Dispersion, Paul is using language intended to appeal to Jew and to Greek, filling terms familiar to them with a new content, Christ and the risen life. (*a*) It is possible to take this passage to refer to the resurrection of the individual Christian. It may be that in 1 C. 15 Paul had written as if the Christian waits till the Parousia for his new body, while in writing 2 C. 5 the pressure of events has led him to hope for the heavenly body at death, or it may be that 'what looks like inconsistency is really due to the fact that he had not carried out an analysis of the stages of post-mortem experience' (Anderson Scott). From the image of the body as a dwelling or tent, Paul's mind passes to that of raiment. The spiritual body is eternal, in the heavens; a Greek familiar with Platonic 'ideas' would assent. This 'certain hope' makes Paul yearn to be covered with the new body, 'nakedness' being abhorrent to the Jew. He admits that, like every man, by nature he finds the thought of death repellent but he welcomes the thought of being 'covered' with **84** a heavenly body so that what is mortal may be swallowed up by life. He insists that it is God who effects this change by his Spirit; man cannot achieve it by his own efforts, however good. The Spirit is the guarantee or 'pledge and instalment' (Moffatt) of all that is to be given hereafter. The Church astounded Jew and Greek not by its doctrine of the Spirit so much as by its assurance that it had that Spirit already. Paul is supremely confident, come what may, life or death, for he knows that while he is in the earthly body he is away from the Lord, having to lead his life by faith without seeing Christ, but that if he dies—which he would prefer—he would reside with the Lord. His whole desire, either way, was to please the Lord, for every man has one day to stand before Christ's tribunal to receive his due reward or punishment for all that he has done on the natural plane. Accused of turning liberty into licence, Paul insists on moral responsibility for acts done in this life, every man's conscience before God being judged by Christ. (See the discussion in W. D. Davies, *Paul and Rabbinic Judaism* (1948), 308ff.)

(*b*) J. A. T. Robinson, op. cit., 77ff., maintains **o** that it is impossible to take 2 C. 5:1-10 to refer to individual resurrection for it carries on the thought of 4:16ff. The heavenly house is the body of Christ, the word for 'building' in Paul meaning the Church or the body of the Lord, cf. A. Feuillet under 1 C. 15:42. He may still think that not all the converts will die before the Parousia. The hope of the new body is expressed in terms of clothing-upon the present one but the disquieting thought exists in Paul's mind, cf. 5:3, that this frail body of flesh may not endure till the Parousia. On this view the language here does not contradict that of 1 C. 15 according to which the existing body will be transfigured and the new body given to the Christian at the Parousia itself. Whatever view is taken, it is most unlikely that Paul was here expressing himself simply as a Hellenist would have done in terms of immortality and not of the resurrection of the body (cf. R. H. Charles, *Eschatology* (1899), 395).

11-19 The compelling Love of Christ and God's Reconciliation—His opponents had apparently **84** charged Paul with a capacity for 'getting round' men as well as being 'beside himself'. Paul picks up these accusations and refutes them by raising his eyes to God; if he 'got round' men, it was with the fear of the Lord in his heart; God could see his utter sincerity, as the converts should have done. This was no self-commendation but a reason for the converts to take pride in him, not in those Jewish-Christians who boasted about the possession of mere externals, such as Jewish ancestry, cf. 11:22, or a commission from the Jewish-Christian leaders who had seen Jesus in the flesh, cf. 3:1. If he was 'beside himself' in ecstasy he kept that private between himself and God, but if sanity were claimed for him, he showed it in furthering the spiritual interests of his converts. For his life was subjected to a compelling influence, the self-giving love of Christ. He was sure that as Christ had died, all 'in Christ' had shared that death, and that he died on behalf of all so that they should live for him who died and rose again, not for their own selfish interests. All the usual standards of human **b** qualifications have gone. Christians do not judge others by externals. Even to have known the Lord during his ministry as the Twelve had done or even the ability to repeat his *ipsissima verba* counted for nothing compared with being 'in Christ' as part of the new age or creation, which is entirely God's act. God was in Christ reconciling the world to himself, the Father taking the initiative towards men and Christ never doing God's work more fully than he did on the Cross. The message of the reconciling work of God through Christ was entrusted to Paul and the Church; like other leaders of it, Paul was Christ's envoy through whom God made his appeal to men hostile to him.

c **14.** C. Spicq says that 'of Christ' after 'love' is both a subjective and an objective genitive and that the choice of the word for 'compels' suggests the overwhelming love of Christ on the Cross (*Studia Theologica*, 8, 2 (1955), 123ff.). **16.** It is not likely that 'to know Christ after the flesh' implies that Paul had set eyes on Jesus during the last week of the ministry, perhaps, in Jerusalem or that it means 'to have a Judaistic view of the Messiah'. The meaning given above is more probable; 'after the flesh' goes with the word 'regard'; hence RSV 'even though we once regarded Christ from a human point of view'.

d **V 20-VI 10 Christ's Envoy bears his Marks of Suffering**—Paul begs again as Christ's envoy that the converts will be reconciled to God. The appeal is made on behalf of Christ who made himself man unreservedly, except that he remained 'sinless', a negative word that fails to convey his positive purity; but Love made him to be sin on our behalf, cf. Rom. 8:3. Paul avoids saying 'God made him a sinner'; all things being in God's hands, God is subject of the sentence; but Paul means that in this evil world Love was bound to suffer as though it were as sinful as men, so as to set them right with God. A fellow-worker with God, he begs them to make the reception of the Gospel a success; he quotes Isa. 49:8 (LXX) from a Deutero-Isaianic Servant Song to prove that the time for God's favour, long promised to men, had arrived. With Jesus (the true Servant) the power and love of God in reconciling men to himself are at work here and now. But if the reception of the Gospel at Corinth should turn out to be a failure, Paul's ministry
e would be discredited. Yet the genuineness of his apostolic ministry had been proved by his sufferings for Christ. Again, under the stress of deep emotion both in recalling his bitter experiences and in being compelled to do so, Paul's phrases strike a poetical note, cf. 11:23–8; the sufferings are set out in phrases with a 'triple beat' and are followed in 6f. by mention of the underlying strength from God enabling him to endure, the Holy Spirit, sincere love, truth in word and God's power. Paul has used no weapons in the struggle except those of integrity, the only weapons that a Christian can use in attack or defence. An outburst follows telling of the paradoxes of the apostle's life, in which the taunts of his opponents are quoted again. Presumably they had called him a 'nonentity' and an 'impostor'. 'Paul gives noble expression to the thought that the nobler and more devoted the servant of God, the wider is his experience of men at their best and at their worst' (Strachan, MNTC, 123f.). The servant is not above his Master, the Servant fo the Lord. To Paul, Jesus was one who had been rich but at the incarnation became poor that we might become rich (8:9); a disciple also is poor to enrich many.

f **11-13.** Paul's affectionate longing for some response from the converts is revealed. The open nature of his speech is the measure of the large-hearted nature of the apostle. Did they talk about 'restraint' as if he restrained them in any way? No, any 'restraint' was imposed on their own affections by themselves. 'Play fair', as one says to children, 'and be large-hearted in turn to me', he pleads. (When André Gide says in *The Coiners* that such an appeal comes from the frustrated and self-consciously inferior, he is thinking of human and not divine love.)

g **VI 14-VII 1** is part of a separate letter discussed above.

VII 2-12 The divine Comfort brought through Pain—Perhaps Paul is again answering charges that he had 'wronged and corrupted' some converts or taken advantage of them. By 'corruption' we may understand a Jewish(-Christian) accusation that by forsaking the Law, Paul had undermined morality. Yet this answer by Paul was no condemnation, for how could Paul condemn those whom he held in his heart until death? He had complete confidence and great pride in them; after all his troubles they were the source of his comfort and delight. He recalls the 847g
deep anxiety that he had felt until he reached Macedonia because he had not known the outcome of the 'severe letter'; pressure from all sides came upon him, external conflicts and internal fears. The God, however, who comforts the downcast gave comfort to Paul by Titus' arrival and by the news from Corinth that the converts had been a comfort to Titus who could repeat to Paul that at last they yearned for the apostle, they were deeply penitent, they were entirely on his side. Looking back now on the 'severe h
letter' Paul might regret its tone but in fact he did not, at least not any longer, because he is glad that they accepted the pain as coming from God's hand. Every priest knows the difference between penitence and remorse. Paul distinguishes between 'godly grief' or the 'pain that God is allowed to guide' (Moffatt) and 'worldly grief' or remorse. The former leads to repentance and no regrets, the latter to spiritual death. The 'godly grief' has induced in the converts greater seriousness, anxiety to clear themselves, indignation, alarm, eagerness for Paul and a spirit of determination and relentlessness against the offender, cf. 2:6. They have proved themselves sincere. The severe letter has brought out not so much the offender's fault as the converts' attachment to Paul.

14-16 Titus' Share in Paul's Joy—Paul's tact is i
seen in including Titus' joy over the converts' change of heart. Titus had seen not only that Paul's pride in them was justified but also that the converts obeyed him with deference and trembling when they received him as Paul's messenger. As Paul had gone among them once in trepidation, 1 C. 2:3, so now they showed the same spirit to Titus Paul's joy and trust in them are complete.

VIII, IX. The collection for the poor saints of Jeru- j
salem. Paul valued highly the contributions made by Gentile-Christians to the Jewish-Christians of the mother-church, cf. Ac. 24:17; Rom. 15:26; 1 C. 15, which suggests that the Corinthian collection was complete and that Paul and his converts at Corinth were on good terms. Male Jews paid half a shekel as temple dues, thus binding Jews of the Dispersion with the Temple; so Paul cemented his Gentile converts and Jewish-Christians together, relieving the distress of the latter caused perhaps by the early 'communism' of the church in Jerusalem and by the famine, Ac. 2:44, 4:32f. and 11:27ff. Paul puts his appeal for money upon the highest plane, as for a 'grace', an act of loving help from God to men and a means of fellowship between Christians in the common life of the body of Christ.

**VIII 1-15 Paul holds up for imitation the church k
in Macedonia** at Thessalonica, Philippi and Beroea, which in spite of their difficulties poured out joyfully a spate of liberality from 'rock-bottom' poverty. This contribution had been made voluntarily when they had first given themselves to the Lord. Titus had been encouraged to make Corinth contribute in the same way and now Titus could complete his plan. This must have come after, not before, the 'severe letter' and the reconciliation which followed. Now the Corinthian church, being outstanding in every way, in faith, speech, knowledge, zeal and in love for Paul, must be foremost too in this act of graciousness. Paul is not issuing commands but adducing the zeal of Macedonian Christians for those at Corinth to emulate it.

In another great theological 'aside' (cf. §846*c*) l
Paul maintains in 8:9 that Christ was pre-existent with God with all the wealth of heaven's splendour but for our sakes he became poor that by his poverty we might become rich. The self-abasement of the incarnation is made here the basis of an appeal for charity in the same way as in Phil. 2:6ff. it is for humility. Paul's ethical teaching is rooted in doctrine. The pre-existence of Jesus with God is not the 'latent pre-existence' (Strachan) of the Law or the Tabernacle

847l according to Jewish thought within the mind of God but part of his eternal existence as divine. To Paul, Jesus was God who became man, not man who became God. Having taken the initiative in planning their charity, the converts should continue the good work so far as possible, each contributing according to his ability. This would not lead to distress at Corinth and superfluity at Jerusalem but would be a matter of 'give and take' (Moffatt). The present Gentile-Christian surplus could make good the Jewish-Christian deficiency; and the spiritual life of the mother-church would be the wealth in which the gift would be repaid. Exod. 16:18 is cited with its slight verbal connection with **14** in the words 'much' and 'little'; but the aptness of the quotation is not marked apart from the obvious moral of the original story that selfishness is not the best policy.

m **VIII 16-IX 5 A Commendation of the Collectors and a Note on the Christian Attitude to Almsgiving**—Once again Titus is tactfully mentioned; his enthusiasm for the generosity being displayed equals Paul's. Two other envoys are going with him, both unnamed in the present text (but were their names erased at some early stage?). The brother whose services to the Gospel are praised by all the churches (Moffatt) may have been Luke; according to Ac. 16:10, 17:1, the first 'we-section' reveals Luke with Paul at Philippi where Luke probably stayed on. He would have taken a leading part in building up the church in Macedonia and he would be an appropriate envoy to carry contributions to Jerusalem. Paul is most anxious to avoid the least breath of suspicion falling on the administration of this undertaking or on himself. It is probable that an envoy from Corinth was the other unnamed companion (Apollos? or Timothy?). They were 'apostles of the churches', 8:23, a rank presumably lower than that of Paul and the Twelve whose apostleship had been conferred by Christ. Paul goes on tactfully to show how he has held up the Corinthian converts before those of Macedonia as a model for generosity. The latter were told that the former were ready to make their contribution 'last year'. Paul is sending the brethren to ensure that the readiness is actual but he is most anxious not to extract the money under any kind of compulsion but to receive it as a voluntary offering. There is no need to suppose that 9 was written on a different occasion from 8. Paul has to labour the point that he wants a collection for the saints at Jerusalem, since the recent trouble had caused the subject to lapse.

848a **IX 6-15 The true Spirit of Giving**—A miserly farmer reaps little, a generous one much; but there should be no grudging or compulsion about giving. God loves a cheerful giver and can bless men with more than enough both to meet their needs and to allow for kind acts towards others. The charity (or righteousness which meant the same often in late Judaism) of God endures as Ps. 112:9 says and his gifts are scattered broadcast. God will supply the donors and to God will arise thanks for the donations. Contributions of this kind give rise to praise for the effect of the Gospel as well as for themselves. Christians 8
at Jerusalem will be attracted to the converts and will pray for them. Thanks be to God for his gift past all expression, for Jesus Christ, the embodiment of the self-giving of God, the source of all Christian giving.

(D) **Postscript XIII 11-14.** This section may be the 8
conclusion of 1–9 rather than of 10:1–13:10. It picks up the theme of unity, cf. 1 C. 1:10, 13; for the kiss of peace cf. Rom. 16:16; 1 C. 16:20; 1 Th. 5:26. In place of the pagan 'farewell', the Christian 'charis' (not dissimilar in sound) normally closes a Pauline letter. The familiar words of 13:14 may have become already a liturgical formula (Lietzmann), though there is no evidence for this and we may equally suppose that Paul was writing out of a full heart, meditating on the Christian experience of God through Christ; so the grace of the Lord is mentioned first. Communion of the Holy Spirit probably meant the participation by Christians in the Holy Spirit (cf. J. Y. Campbell, JBL 51 (1932), 353). Out of such experience of God the Trinitarian doctrine was to evolve, cf. Rom. 8:7ff. and 16ff. As Dr L. Hodgson says, 'We have found the doctrine of the Trinity to be the doctrine of God implied by the earthly life of Christ when that life was reflected on by Christians in the light of their experience of being adopted to share his sonship . . . It did not begin as a theological doctrine but as a religious outlook, the outlook of One who thought of himself as finding and doing his heavenly Father's will through the indwelling Spirit by whom he was one with the Father' (*The Doctrine of the Trinity* (1943), 83).

Bibliography—Commentaries: E. B. Allo (1 C., 1934, 2 C., 1937); C. T. Craig, IB x (1 C., 1953); F. V. Filson, IB x (2 C., 1953); H. L. Goudge, WC (1 C., 1903, 2 C., 1927); J. Héring (1 C., 1949, 2 C., 1958); H. Lietzmann, HNT (1949); A. Menzies (2 C., 1912); J. Moffatt, MNTC (1 C., 1938); A. Plummer and A. Robertson, ICC (1 C., 1911, 2 C., 1915); R. H. Strachan, MNTC (2 C., 1935); H. Windisch (2 C., 1924).

Other Literature: W. F. Arndt and F. W. Gingrich (Preuschen-Bauer), *A Greek-English Lexicon of the NT* (1957); G. C. Campbell, *The Corinthian Letters of Paul* (1947); O. Cullmann, *The Early Church* (1956); W. D. Davies, *Paul and Rabbinic Judaism* (1948); C. H. Dodd, BJRL 17 (1933), 91–105 and 18 (1934), 69–110, *The Apostolic Preaching and its Developments* (1936), *According to the Scriptures* (1952); J. R. Harris and V. Burch, *Testimonies* (1916); J Héring, RHPR 12 (1932), 300ff.; J. H. Kennedy, *The Second and Third Epistles of St Paul* (1900); W. L. Knox, *St Paul and the Church of Jerusalem* (1925), *St Paul and the Church of the Gentiles* (1939), *Some Hellenistic Elements in Primitive Christianity* (1944); T. W. Manson, BJRL 26 (1941), 101ff; O. C. Quick, *The Gospel of the New World* (1944); H. W. Robinson, *The Christian Experience of the Holy Spirit* (1928); J. A. T. Robinson, *The Body* (1953); B. Schneider, *Dominus autem Spiritus est* (1951); C. A. A. Scott, *Christianity according to St Paul* (1928); H. St John Thackeray, *The Relation of St Paul to contemporary Jewish thought* (1900).

GALATIANS

By J. N. SANDERS

850a **Authenticity and Integrity**—The authenticity of Gal. was unhesitatingly accepted in ancient times, and is not seriously questioned today. There are no grounds for suspecting that it may represent a conflation of letters sent at different times (as in the case of 2 C.), or that it circulated originally in different recensions (as in the case of Rom.). Indeed, Gal. has sometimes appeared to be so obviously the very type and norm of a Pauline letter that it has tended to bring into question the authenticity of other letters.

Its genuineness has however been questioned, first by Bruno Bauer (*Kritik der paulinischen Briefe* (1850)). But it may safely be said that if we have any genuine letter of Paul's, Gal. is one. Marcion accepted it as his, and placed it first in his expurgated edition of the Epistles. And this did not produce any orthodox reaction to deny its authenticity (contrast the attempt of the conservative Alogi to discredit the Johannine writings). Before the time of Marcion, there are clear traces of its use, the earliest being in 1 Clement.

b **The Destination, Date and Place of Writing** of Gal. present a problem, or rather a series of interrelated problems, to which there is not as yet any generally accepted solution. These are moreover involved in the equally vexed problem of the relationship between the accounts in Gal. and Ac. of Paul's relations with the church of Jerusalem.

c **Destination**. The alternatives are either that it is to the *Galatai* proper, i.e. to the descendants of the Gallic invaders who had established a kingdom in central Asia Minor during the 3rd cent. B.C.; or that it is to the inhabitants of the Roman province of Galatia, which included in the south many who were not of Gallic descent, and in particular to the churches of Pisidian Antioch, Iconium, Derbe, and Lystra, which Paul had first visited in company with Barnabas (Ac. 13:14–14:23), and at least twice since (Ac. 16:1–6, 18:23).

d **The Date and Place of Writing** are, if to the *Galatai* proper, not before Ac. 16:6, Paul's first opportunity to have gone through the old Galatian kingdom, and probably during Paul's stay at Ephesus (Ac. 19); or, if to the southern part of the province of Galatia, either (*a*) from Syrian Antioch just before Paul left for the Council of Jerusalem (Ac. 15:2f.) or actually during his journey thither (if it is held that that Council happened as described in Ac. 15, and that Gal. 2:1–10 refers to the same occasion as Ac. 11:30, 12:25); or (*b*) at the time and place which best accord with the internal evidence of the Epistle—probably Ephesus, as above, if it is held either that Ac. 11:30, 12:25 and 15:2ff. are variant accounts of the same visit, which Paul also describes in Gal. 2:1–10, or that Paul was not in fact present at the meeting which drew up the 'Decree' of Ac. 15:29 (see below, §852).

The opinion of the present writer is that the later date for Gal. is highly probable, and that its destination is rather more likely to have been South Galatia, or at least to have included South Galatia.

e In reaching a decision internal evidence is of great importance. This tells strongly in favour of a date close to those of 1 and 2 C. and Rom., with which Gal. has many similarities in mood and tone, and also in phraseology. If one discounts resemblances to Rom. on the ground of the similarity of subject-matter between Rom. and Gal., there are still sufficient parallels in phraseology with the letters to Corinth (and particularly with 2 C.) to suggest a similar date. The following may be noted: 850e

Gal. 1:6 *ἕτερον εὐαγγέλιον*, 2 C. 11:4 *εὐαγγέλιον ἕτερον*.

Gal. 1:9 *ὡς προειρήκαμεν καὶ ἄρτι πάλιν λέγω*, 2 C. 13:2 *προείρηκα καὶ προλέγω*.

Gal. 1:10 *ἀνθρώπους πείθω; ἢ τὸν Θεόν;* 2 C. 5:11 *ἀνθρώπους πείθομεν, Θεῷ δὲ πεφανερώμεθα*.

Gal. 2:4 and 2 C. 11:26 have the only examples in the NT of the word *ψευδάδελφοι*.

Gal. 3:3 *ἐναρξάμενοι πνεύματι, νῦν σαρκὶ ἐπιτελεῖσθε;* 2 C. 8:6 *ἵνα καθὼς προενήρξατο, οὕτω καὶ ἐπιτελέσῃ* (cf. Phil. 1:6 *ὁ ἐναρξάμενος . . . ἐπιτελέσει*, these being the only examples of *ἐνάρχομαι* and *προενάρχομαι* in the NT).

Gal. 6:15 and 2 C. 5:17 *καινὴ κτίσις*.

ζηλόω is used transitively twice in Gal. 4:17 (and passively in 4:18), and four times in 1 and 2 C. (1 C. 12:31, 14:1, 39; 2 C. 11:2—to which 1 C. 13:4 should possibly be added, though no object is expressed), and elsewhere in the NT only intransitively (Ac. 7:9, 17:5; Jas 4:2).

Also in favour of a late date is the most natural interpretation of Gal. 4:13, according to which Paul had visited Galatia at least twice when he wrote.

f The acceptance of the earlier date, on the other hand, has little or no support from internal evidence, and must be regarded as a consequence of the belief not only that Ac. gives a trustworthy account of Paul's visits to Jerusalem, but also that Paul has not omitted one of these visits from his narrative in Gal. 1. But it runs into the difficulty of accounting for disturbances arising in Galatia *before* the Apostolic Decree (which is addressed to Antioch, Syria and Cilicia only—Ac. 15:23), a difficulty which a later date avoids.

Gal. may even have been written from Rome. It is true Paul makes no reference to imprisonment, but if he was a free agent at the time of writing, it may seem surprising that, in view of the seriousness of the situation in Galatia, he did not hint at the possibility of personal intervention.

g The destination of Gal. is more difficult to decide. The *Galatai*, in the natural sense of the term, are the inhabitants of Galatia proper. If a late date for Gal. is accepted, visits to Galatia proper can be fitted into the narrative of Ac., at 16:6, and 18:23. The argument that Paul habitually used geographical terms in their official Roman sense only proves that he *could have* called the inhabitants of Pisidian Antioch, etc. 'Galatians'. It does not compel us to suppose that he *did* do so.

On the other hand, these *Galatai*, who remained for long relatively impervious to Hellenistic culture, seem unpromising subjects for Paul's missionary efforts. And the internal evidence of Gal. seems on the whole to favour South Galatia. Barnabas was with Paul when he visited South Galatia, but not when he could have visited Galatia proper, and the allusions to Barnabas in Gal. may suggest that he was known personally to Paul's readers. And the references to Paul's first visit in Gal. 4:13–15 fit in with the account in Ac. of Paul's visit to South Galatia. So perhaps South Galatia should have it. But the question of

850g destination is of less moment than that of date for the understanding of the Epistle.

h **Purpose**—Paul wrote in order to vindicate his authority as an apostle and the truth of the Gospel which he preached. His adversaries were trying to persuade the Galatians to accept circumcision, and attacking Paul's authority in order to urge their own opinions more effectively. They were presumably not natives of Galatia, who had thought of these ideas for themselves, but members of a kind of anti-Pauline mission to the Gentiles. Paul's main concern is with this judaising movement, but it is possible that there was also an opposite tendency towards antinomianism (more probably of native origin in Galatia) which gave him grounds for anxiety (see on 5:13ff.).

It is impossible to say whether Paul achieved his purpose. If the late date for Gal. is correct, he cannot have visited Galatia again in any case. It is by no means unlikely that the Galatian churches were unmoved by his appeal.

i The **contents** of this epistle fall into five groups:

I 1-5. Address

I 6-II 21. The vindication of Paul's Gospel and apostleship as given him by Christ himself, and acknowledged by the leading members of the Church of Jerusalem

III 1-V 12. Exposition of the place of the law in the scheme of salvation, and proof of the errors of Paul's opponents

V 13-VI 10. The moral consequences of Paul's doctrine

VI 11-18. Autograph postscript.

851a **I 1-5 Address**—**1.** Paul emphasises at once his independence and divine authority as an apostle, which his opponents in Galatia were denying, and which it was one of his main objectives to vindicate. **2.** 'The brethren who are with me' is an expression unparalleled in the addresses of other Epistles, though not in concluding greetings (cf. 1 C. 16:20; 2 C. 13:13; Phil. 4:21f.). Paul writes in his own name alone (so Rom., Eph.) or associates with himself persons whom he names—presumably as known to his readers (cf. 1 C., Sosthenes; 2 C., Phil., Col., Timothy; 1 and 2 Th., Silvanus and Timothy). Paul's purpose here is probably to let his readers know that his views have the support of the Christians with him at the time of writing, though their names would not mean anything to the Galatians. In view of the similar phrases at the end of other Epistles, there is no need to suppose that Paul was not in fact settled in one of his churches when he wrote—that, e.g., he was in prison or on the journey to Jerusalem for the council of Ac. 15 —though such a possibility is not excluded. For the meaning of 'Galatia' see above. **3.** Paul's customary and characteristic greeting. **4.** Paul asserts at once the basic message of the Gospel, which it is his concern to vindicate, no less than, and together with, his own status as apostle. An attack on one necessarily involves the other.

b **6-10.** In all his other Epistles, Paul begins with thanksgiving to God. But here the coldness and abruptness of his words show clearly his anxiety and grief. There is only one genuine Gospel, that which he had preached. That to which the Galatians are so quickly turning is a spurious substitute, however high the authority of those who preach it. **6.** 'So quickly' describes the speed with which their apostasy is being achieved. It may, but does not necessarily, mean that this was soon after their conversion by Paul. **10.** Paul throws back at his opponents their taunts that he is a mere time-server. Had he been such, he would not be writing as he does. But 1 C. 10:33 suggests that his opponents were echoing Paul's own words; his annoyance may be heightened by his awareness of an indiscretion.

c **11-17 The Origin of Paul's Gospel**—His Gospel, like his commission to preach it, is from Christ himself. Paul does not mean that his conversion involved the miraculous imparting of factual information. He must have known already what the Christians claimed, but their ideas seemed to him blasphemous nonsense. His conversion meant that he now knew that they were saving truth. So he had no need (16f.) to ask anyone for instruction. **13.** Paul does not say where or under what auspices he persecuted. Many scholars hold that it was in Damascus, and cite 22 in their support. **14.** Cf. Phil. 3:5f. and Ac. 22:3. The word ζηλωτής here and in Ac. need not mean that Paul had actually been a Zealot. **15.** Paul's vocation was ordained by God before his birth, as was Jeremiah's (Jer. 1:5). **16.** 'To reveal his Son' hints at Paul's claim to be an apostle in virtue of having 'seen the Lord' (1 C. 9:1). How soon after his conversion Paul felt the call to the Gentile mission is not clear—while still a Pharisee, he may already have been interested in converting Gentiles (cf. Mt. 23:15). For 'flesh and blood' cf. 1 C. 15:50. **17.** 'Go up' is almost a technical term for visiting Jerusalem, cf. Ac. 15:2, 18:22 (?). 'Arabia' is probably the kingdom of Aretas. Ac. does not mention this episode, but represents Paul as going to Jerusalem from Damascus, 9:23ff. Paul does not say why he went to Arabia. Various suggestions are made—to meditate in the desert, to visit Sinai, to preach. Possibly a brief period 'in retreat' was followed by some preaching, whereby Paul attracted the hostile attention of Aretas (cf. 2 C. 11:32). Damascus may have been under Aretas' jurisdiction at this period. If so, this may help to explain the silence of Ac. on Paul's Arabian visit.

18-24 Paul's First Visit to the Church of Jerusalem—This was not until three years after his conversion. Its date depends on that assigned to his conversion (for this see 'The Chronology of the NT', §638*a*). This visit was in private, and brief. Paul's purpose was simply 'to become acquainted with' (ἱστορῆσαι, translated 'visit' in RSV) Cephas, not to be taught or commissioned by him, or anyone else. **19.** Apart from Cephas, he only saw James the Lord's brother. It is not clear if Paul regarded him as an apostle. RSV appears to imply that he did, but the verse may mean, 'I saw no other apostle, but I did see James'. **20.** Paul's emphatic assertion of his truthfulness comes at this point because, if he had received his commission as an apostle 'from men', it must have been on this occasion, or never. He had acted as an apostle in Cilicia and Syria before his second visit. Ac. 9:26ff. puts this first visit in a different light, and adds some details. Of these, the part played by Barnabas in introducing Paul to 'the Apostles' is quite probable, But that Paul actually preached in Jerusalem (Ac. 9:29) is not very likely. **21.** According to Ac. 9:30, Paul went, via Caesarea, to Tarsus, the capital of the province of Cilicia, and, according to Ac., Paul's home (Paul himself never mentions this). If 'fourteen years' in 2:1 is correct, there is a considerable period of Paul's life of which we know nothing, except that at the end of it he spent a 'whole year' in Antioch with Barnabas (Ac. 11:26). It may well be that some of the missionary work placed later in Ac. was in fact done in this period (see J. Knox, *Chapters in a Life of Paul* (1954), 51ff.). **22.** If Paul had in fact been active as a persecutor in Jerusalem, this verse is hard to explain, unless 'Judea' can be understood as meant to exclude Jerusalem itself—which indeed must be the case if 22 is to be strictly consistent with 18—and unless further we are to suppose that the churches of Judaea were founded only after Paul's persecution had ended. d e

II 1-10 Paul's Second Visit to Jerusalem—The reconciliation of Paul's own account here with the narrative of Ac. is one of the most complicated problems in NT criticism, and one to which there is no generally accepted solution. All attempts at a solution involve difficulties of some kind. The reader must judge for himself. One thing however is certain. Paul is convinced that the highest human authorities in the Church approved of the Gospel which he was 852a

2a preaching to the Gentiles, and recognised that he and Barnabas had a special call to the Gentile mission. Those therefore who were disturbing the Galatians were unauthorised intruders.

b The traditional view of the occasion on which this understanding was reached between Paul and Barnabas and the 'pillars' is that it was on the visit recorded in Ac. 15. The persons concerned and the agenda at their meeting are, it is said, the same. Not quite the same, however, if the evidence of Gal. 2 is interpreted strictly, for Gal. has no mention of any other issue than Paul's Gospel and circumcision. Nothing is said about food laws. That topic apparently only arose later, out of the dispute at Antioch (Gal. 2:11ff.). A serious objection to this view is that Paul has passed over in silence the visit of Ac. 11. It is argued that Paul had no need to mention this visit, since on it he met no apostles. But, even so, his opponents might have made something out of his silence, and Paul could easily have avoided any misunderstanding by mentioning the visit.

c The majority of critics who do not accept the traditional view take one or other of the following lines:

(1) That the meeting of Gal. 2 took place on the visit of Ac. 11, when Paul and Barnabas took famine relief to Jerusalem. Since the discussions were in private (Gal. 2:2), the tradition followed by Ac. knew nothing of them, and only recorded the public purpose of the visit. On this view the 'revelation' of Gal. 2:2 is the prophecy of Agabus (Ac. 11:28) and Gal. 2:10 is an allusion to the relief taken on that occasion (then ἐσπούδασα ('I was eager', RSV) must be taken in a pluperfect sense, 'I had been eager'). It is a corollary of this view that Gal. was written after the dispute at Antioch (Ac. 15:2; Gal. 2:11), while Paul was on his way to the Council. It was addressed to the churches of South Galatia, which Paul and Barnabas had recently visited, and is thus the earliest
d of the Pauline Epistles. This is itself a difficulty (see §850*e*). It is also surprising to find trouble developing so early in the Galatian Churches. Furthermore, if this visit occurred fourteen years after Paul's conversion, it can hardly have been where Ac. places it, during the reign of Herod Agrippa (A.D. 41–4); if it was seventeen years after (as it must be if the fourteen years of Gal. 2:1 are counted from the first visit), it is quite impossible. In any case, the reign of Agrippa is rather too early for a relief mission, since the famine did not develop until after his death, reaching its greatest severity before the harvest of 48. A date in Agrippa's reign is however possible if 'fourteen' in Gal. 2:1 is a mistake for 'four', made by a very early copyist who perhaps had the 'fourteen' of 2 C. 12:2 still in his head. Though there is no MS authority for 'four', the change is easily explained: in Greek uncial letters, it only involves writing ΔΙΑΙΔ ('after fourteen') for ΔΙΑΔ ('after four'). Then a visit as early as the Passover of 42 would involve 36 (seven years before, counting inclusively) as the date of Paul's conversion, which is quite feasible. If this conjecture is not accepted, then the likeliest date for this visit on this view is 48 or 49 (fourteen years, again counting inclusively, from 35 or 36).

e (2) That Ac. 11 and 15 give two alternative and complementary versions of the same visit. This has the merit of making it unnecessary to postulate the early date for Gal., or the early development of trouble in Galatia. A further suggestion along this line is that the meeting need not necessarily be placed either in Ac. 11 or Ac. 15. If it is placed at Ac. 18:22, it has the advantage of filling the otherwise blank period of nearly fourteen years in Paul's life with the work described in Ac. 13–18, but the disadvantage of involving a drastic reassessment of the credibility of Ac. On this view also Gal. 2:10 is a reference to Paul's collection for the poor saints at Jerusalem which was a major preoccupation of his just before his last visit to Jerusalem. It is an advantage to have his agreement to organise this as close as possible to the actual 852e
collection.

Both these views assume that Paul accepted the f
prohibitions in the Apostolic Decree of Ac. 15:20. But it may be questioned whether this is the case: Paul never alludes to them in his Epistles, even when discussing 'food offered to idols' (1 C. 8:1ff.) and his discussion of that topic makes it difficult to believe that he accepted them. A third alternative is therefore conceivable, that Paul and Barnabas came to a private understanding with the 'pillars' about circumcision, either as early as 42 or as late as 48 or 49, and that after the dispute at Antioch Peter, James and Barnabas drew up the Apostolic Decree at a meeting at which Paul was not present. The author of Ac. knew that there had been a conference at which Paul *was* present, and wrongly supposed that it was the one which produced the Decree.

Two further problems arise: (1) Was Titus in fact g
circumcised, or not? (2) Who are the 'pillars'?

(1) Paul's embarrassment in 2:3–5 is obvious. If Titus was circumcised, Paul's opponents could make much of his inconsistency, and his willingness to 'please men'. Are we to understand **3** as 'Titus was not compelled to be circumcised (and was *not* circumcised)' or 'Titus was not *compelled* (but agreed) to be circumcised (in order to placate Christians of Pharisaic origin)'? In **5** the original reading of D, with some Latin support, omits the negative, reading 'to them we yielded submission': i.e. Paul agreed, no doubt reluctantly, to a concession in this one case, in order to secure approval of the general principle 'No circumcision of Gentile converts'. The textual authority is not strong, but it remains a possibility that Titus *was* in fact circumcised.

(2) In **9** Papyrus 46, D, G, the OL and Gothic h
versions, Marcion, Tertullian, 'Ambrosiaster', Jerome and Augustine read 'Peter, James and John'. This may be only a promotion of Peter (and 'Peter' instead of 'Cephas' is suspicious) but there is an outside chance that it is the true reading, and that the 'pillars' are Peter and the two sons of Zebedee, the three leading members of the Twelve. In that case the meeting of Gal. 2:1–10 could only have taken place before the death of James, say in 42. The reading 'James, Cephas and John' would be due to the identification of the meeting of Gal. 2 with that of Ac. 15.

11-21 Paul's Opposition to Peter at Antioch— i
Why or when Peter came to Antioch Paul does not say. Presumably the occasion is that described in Ac. 15:1f., though Ac. does not mention Peter, or any dissension between Paul and Barnabas on this issue. If the 'men from Judea' of Ac. 15:1 are the same as the 'men from James' of Gal. 2:12, then either they were not authorised to act as they did, or James had changed his policy since the agreement of Gal. 2:9. In the former case, why did Peter give way to them? If however the 'James' of Gal. 2:9 is the son of Zebedee, then James the Lord's brother was free to take this line, having been no party to the agreement, which may be a point in favour of the interpretation of 9 suggested above. But whatever their status or authority, they induced both Peter and Barnabas to give up eating with Gentiles, which presumably involved the abandonment of a common Eucharist.
14. Paul therefore accused Peter in public of incon- j
sistency. His report of his words to Peter merges into an exposition of the Gospel, and by the end of the chapter he has lost sight of Peter and Antioch. **15.** 'Gentile sinners' echoes, not without irony, the views of Paul's Jewish opponents: to Jews, Gentiles were 'sinners', as it were *ex officio* (cf. Mt. 18:17). **16.** To Paul, on the other hand, all men are sinners, and cannot expect acquittal before God's judgment seat on the basis of their own achievement of obedience to the Law. Christians are 'justified', i.e. 'pronounced not guilty', because they put their trust in Christ, and abandon the Law as a means of justification.

852j **17.** But (say the Jews) to abandon the Law is sinful. This, says Paul, leads to the absurd conclusion that Christ, who has induced us to abandon the Law, is 'an agent of sin'. **18.** The sinner is he who, by having recourse again to the Law, abandons Christ.

k **19.** The Law itself points to its own supersession, as Paul goes on to show, and so it is consistent with the Law to abandon it, for this 'death' brings a new life in God. **20.** The Christian in fact dies and rises to life again with Christ, so that Christ lives in him, in virtue of the Christian's faith in his atoning death (cf. Rom. 6:3–11). **21.** But if the Law is the means of justification, Christ's death was pointless. It is however God's means of grace, and accepting God's grace involves abandoning the Law.

853a **III 1-V 12. Proof of the truth of Paul's Gospel,** argued mainly from the OT itself.

III 1-5 Appeal to Experience—At their conversion the Galatians received the gift of the Spirit, because they believed Paul's preaching of Christ crucified. And they still enjoy that gift, as is proved by the miracles which God works among them. In all this it is faith, not the Law, that was decisive. And it is absurd for them now to submit to the Law in order to achieve a higher status than that already conferred by the Spirit, since the Law belongs wholly to the natural order (the 'flesh'), and so is intrinsically inferior to the Spirit.

b **6-14 The Superiority of Faith** is attested by the Law itself. **6.** To prove this, Paul quotes the case of Abraham (Gen. 15:6), and argues, **7,** that the true sons of Abraham are not his physical descendants, the Jews, but men of faith. **8.** That these would in fact be Gentiles is shown by the blessing of 'the nations' in Gen. 12:3. **10.** To rely on the Law, however, makes one liable to the curse of Dt. 27:26, instead of blessing, while, **11,** Hab. 2:4 (as Paul understands it) proves that to rely on the Law is vain, since it is faith that ensures God's gracious verdict of acquittal. **12.** Lev. 18:5 moreover shows that the Law has nothing to do with faith, but only with the performance of its commands. **13.** So, if men were left to the Law, they would (being sinners) fall under its curse. But Christ intervened on our behalf, and by his death on the Cross took upon himself the curse pronounced in Dt. 21:23, in order that, **14,** the Gentiles might inherit the blessing of Abraham, which Paul identifies with the promise of the Spirit, to the fulfilment of which he has already appealed (1–5). No doubt Paul, in his pre-Christian phase, made a great deal of Dt. 21:23. He now sees that its truth is on a profounder level than he then realised.

c **15-22 The Law and the Promise**—In order to illustrate his claim that the validity of the promise was not impaired by the giving of the Law, Paul uses an analogy, likening the promise to a man's will, which, once it has been properly made, cannot be altered or cancelled by anyone—not even, in some systems of ancient law, by the testator himself. **16.** According to Gen. 12:7 the promise was made to Abraham and his offspring (literally, 'seed'). Paul seizes on the fact that 'seed' is singular to argue that it means 'Christ'. This is apparently a mere quibble, but it conceals the real strength of Paul's argument, which rests on the (unexpressed) conviction that Christ is a 'corporate personality', who unites in himself the 'men of faith' who are Abraham's true
d descendants (as shown in 3:7). **17.** The Law therefore does not annul the promise. Paul uses here the word *διαθήκη* (translated 'will' in 15) which means both 'testament' and 'covenant'. The precise interval between the promise and the Law does not affect Paul's argument. He in fact follows the LXX rendering of Exod. 12:40. Here again Paul's argument is stronger than its verbal form suggests. The legalism which he is concerned to repudiate was in fact a much less ancient feature of Judaism than he realised, being post-exilic rather than Mosaic. But he does not consider the obvious rejoinder that the Law can be regarded (on his own analogy) as a valid 85
codicil to God's original 'will', and that observance of its provisions is a necessary condition of obtaining the promise. **19.** Instead, he explains that the Law e
was given 'because of transgressions'. The sense of 'because of', *χάριν*, is almost 'for the sake of'. By stating explicitly God's commands it makes men aware that they are in fact transgressors—cf. Rom. 3:20, 7:7. And in so doing, it actually stimulates sin (Rom. 5:20, 7:13). It is inferior to the promise both because it is temporary, lasting only 'until the offspring should come', and in the manner of its promulgation—and this latter in two respects. It was ordained (1) by angels (cf. Dt. 33:2 ; Ac. 7:53), whereas the promise was given by God himself, (2) through an intermediary, i.e. Moses (cf. Dt. 5:5 ; Heb. 8:6), while the promise was made direct to Abraham. **20.** The meaning of this verse is much disputed. If it is intended to elucidate 'intermediary', as it appears to be, then Paul has not expressed himself very clearly. His point seems to be that the Law is a *διαθήκη* not in the sense of a 'will', but of a 'covenant', or compact, which is made between two parties, and has to be negotiated by a third party, the 'intermediary', and depends for its effectiveness on both parties carrying out their obligations, whereas a 'will' depends only on the testator. **21.** But though inferior to the promise, the Law is not inconsistent with it. It cannot give life, because it cannot put men right with God. **22.** But by emphasising their sinfulness (and consequent need of salvation by some other means, i.e. by the grace of God) it prepares for the fulfilment of the promise.

III 23-IV 11 The Law and Faith—Further implica- f
tions of Paul's analogy of God's promise to a will.

III 23. Under the Law men are 'kept under restraint' (*συγκλειόμενοι*, the verb translated 'confined' in 22), but only for a time. The Law is in the position of a custodian (*παιδαγωγός*, the slave who took care of a child, particularly on his way to and from school), whose responsibility ends when Christ comes. **26.** All, Jews and Gentiles, are sons of God through faith, **27,** in virtue of their union with Christ ratified by baptism. **28.** This union makes irrelevant not only the difference between Jew and Gentile, but also those between slave and freeman, and male and female. **29.** The Galatians then, being Christ's (which they do not deny), are Abraham's offspring, and heirs of his promise. So the Law can do nothing for them.

IV 1-2. While an heir is a minor he has no more g
freedom than a slave, until he reaches the time laid down in his father's will for his coming of age.

3-9. Paul has argued hitherto that Jews have been in bondage under the Law, in order to dissuade Gentiles from putting themselves under it, and he now proceeds to show that Gentiles also have been in bondage. But his train of thought is made obscure by the fact that while in 3 and 8–9 he is thinking primarily of Gentiles, what he says in 4–7 really only applies to Jews. **3.** Christians were once 'slaves to the elemental spirits of the universe'. These *στοιχεῖα τοῦ κόσμου* are the demonic powers which control the stars, and through them the destinies of men. These astral demons haunted the minds of men in the 1st cent. A.D., and the conviction that Christ had conquered them is an important element in Paul's theology (cf. Eph. 6:12 ; Col. 2:20, and perhaps
also 'the rulers of this age' in 1 C. 2:6). Some critics h
prefer to take *στοιχεῖα* in its other accepted sense of 'elementary principles', the ABC, as it were, of religion and morals, since they find it hard to believe that Paul regarded the Jews as under the dominion of astral demons. Paul's thought is admittedly surprising, but 'elemental spirits' fits better with what he says in 8 and 9. His substantial point is that both Jews and Gentiles were in fact in bondage and fear, and moreover that the instruments by which this bondage was exercised, the Law and the elemental spirits, were both under the providence of God, and destined

853h to have their power taken away by Christ. **4.** Then, at the time which God had appointed, we attained to our inheritance. God 'sent forth his Son', a man born like other men, and, being a Jew, subject to the Law (cf. Phil. 2:6, 7).

i **5.** This was in order to free those who were likewise subject to it (cf. 3:13). Strictly, this applies only to Jews, but Paul's argument can readily be adapted to the case of the Gentiles, for Christ frees them from bondage as well as Jews. At this point Paul introduces two fresh analogies, 'redemption' and 'adoption', to describe the process by which men are put right with God. 'Redemption' is naturally suggested by his previous description of men as 'slaves', for it means emancipation by purchase. Paul may have at the back of his mind a familiar legal fiction by which this was accomplished: the slave, having acquired the money for his purchase, deposited it in a temple, the god of which then bought him from his master 'for freedom' (see C. K. Barrett, *The NT Background*
j (1956), 52f.). Paul speaks of Christians as 'adopted' because, unlike the 'heir' in his 'will' analogy, they are not in fact sons of the father, until the Father makes them so by incorporating them in the Son. **6.** Paul brings his argument back to its starting-point in Christian experience (cf. 3:2ff.), to the prayer, 'Abba, Father', inspired by the Spirit of the Son of God. According to Mk 14:36 this very phrase was used by Jesus himself in Gethsemane. But this bilingual invocation most probably occurs here because it represents the usage of the Hellenistic Church, which preserved the Aramaic 'Abba' characteristic of Jesus' own prayers, and added to it the translation 'Father'. **7.** Thus they are heirs indeed.

k **8-11.** Formerly however Christians were slaves of the elemental spirits to which they gave worship to which they were not entitled. **9.** But now they know God (not by any human wisdom), because God has known them—acknowledged them as his. How then can they relapse into slavery? **10.** Their observance of Jewish sacred days and seasons shows that they are in danger of this (cf. Col. 2:16). Sabbaths, new moons, etc. were of course regulated by the sun and moon (cf. Gen. 1:14) and this presumably supplies the connection. It is unlikely that Paul would regard a Jew who kept the Sabbath, etc. as worshipping the elemental spirits, but the logic of his argument leads to that conclusion. But for a Gentile Christian to start keeping them is another matter.

854a **12-20.** The thought in 11 of his labours among the Galatians leads Paul to digress from his argument into a direct appeal to his readers to resume their old relationship with him. **12.** His opening words are—no doubt intentionally—vague, meaning something like 'Imitate me (cf. 1 C. 4:16) by becoming free from legalism, for I showed myself free from Jewish prejudice by preaching to you'. There is no verb in the second clause in the Greek, and this interpretation involves understanding an aorist rather than a perfect, as in RSV. The thought recalls 1 C. 9:22. 'You did me no wrong' is best taken as a reference to the warm welcome Paul received among the Galatians.

b **13-15.** His first visit to them was due to an illness which had apparently caused him to change his plans. That Paul was subject to recurrent illness is the most natural explanation of the 'thorn in the flesh' of 2 C. 12:7. On the view that Galatia means the Roman province, this first visit was after Paul and Barnabas had crossed from Cyprus to Asia Minor (RSV's reference to Ac. 16:6 implies a different view). Paul may have caught malaria on that occasion, and gone inland to higher and healthier ground to recuperate. **14.** Instead of recoiling from Paul—thinking his illness a sign of divine displeasure (?)—the Galatians welcomed him. 'As an angel of God' may be a wry allusion to the Lystrans calling him Hermes, the messenger of the gods (Ac. 14:12). **15.** This may, but need not necessarily, suggest that his eyes were affected by his illness.

16-20. But now their former friendliness has changed 854c
to hostility, though all Paul has done is to be honest with them, **17,** unlike their present friends (his opponents) whose motives are selfish. They want to estrange them from Paul, and make them their own partisans. **18.** But to be the object of partisan enthusiasm is good if its cause is good. Such was the case when Paul was in Galatia and the object of their enthusiasm. The fact that he is now absent is no reason for a change in their allegiance. **19.** They are his 'little children' (Paul does not use the diminutive form *τεκνία* elsewhere), for whom he has suffered, and is suffering, pain like that of childbirth. Elsewhere Paul likens himself to a father (cf. 1 C. 4:15), here only to a mother of his converts. 'Until Christ be formed in you', i.e. until their conversion is complete. Paul usually speaks of Christians as being 'in Christ'; here, as in Rom. 8:10; 2 C. 13:5, it is Christ who is in the Christian. Both forms of expression are consonant with Paul's conception of the Church as the body of Christ. 'Formed' suggests (as do 'conformed' in Rom. 8:29 and 'changed into his likeness' in 2 C. 3:18) that Christians are destined to share the very nature of Christ.

20. Paul's wish to be present with the Galatians is d
natural enough: his wish to 'change his tone' is less obvious. Most probably he means adapting his speech to circumstances which while absent he cannot fully appreciate, or, less probably, changing from the written to the more effectual spoken word.

IV 21-V 12. Paul returns to, and concludes his e
doctrinal argument by (1) an allegorical exposition of the meaning of Abraham's two wives and their sons (4:21–5:1), and (2) a summary appeal to his readers (5:2–12).

IV 21-V 1. Paul argues *ad hominem* against those who 'desire to be under law', using the Law itself to demonstrate that Christianity is a new dispensation which supersedes the old, and so to meet the most powerful argument of his adversaries, that the Law is permanently binding. A subordinate purpose is to stress again the point which he has already established (4:7), that Christians are not slaves, but free, and must not submit again to slavery (4:31, 5:1). He calls his argument an 'allegory', by which he means an analogical or typological argument rather than an allegory in Philo's sense.

IV 22. As Abraham is the type of faith, so his son by f
the free-woman is the type of the Christian, and his son by the slave is the type of the Jew. **23.** This is borne out by the fact that the latter was born in the ordinary process of nature, while the former's birth was the result of God's promise and intervention. The Jews pride themselves on their physical descent from Abraham, but this is not, in God's purposes, decisive (cf. Lk. 3:8; Rom. 9:6–9). **24.** Their mothers likewise represent the two dispensations. Hagar represents that given on Mt Sinai, and, **25,** Paul notes in passing the appropriateness of the fact that Mt Sinai is in Arabia, the land to which Hagar took her son. (The text here is uncertain. RSV follows ABD, etc. while an equally strong group of MSS, headed by ℵCG, omit 'Hagar'. As 'Hagar' (in Gr. uncials ΑΓΑΡ) contains the same letters as the preceding word 'for' (ΓΑΡ), it is not easy to decide whether the longer ΓΑΡΑΓΑΡ or the shorter ΑΓΑΡ is original. But the general sense favours the longer reading.) Hagar corresponds to the actual Jerusalem, whose citizens are in fact slaves. **26.** But Sarah is the type of the spiritual Jerusalem, and the mother of the Christians, **27,** long barren, but, as Isaiah foretold (54:1), destined at last to have a greater progeny than the slave. **28.** Christians, therefore, like Isaac, are 'children of promise', and, **29,** further resemble him both in the persecution they suffer, and, **30,** in the guarantee that the sole inheritance is to be theirs (cf. 3:29). Paul here quotes what are in fact the words of Sarah (Gen. 21:10) as if they were God's. Then, **4:31, 5:1,** he draws his con-

854f clusion—to adhere to the old covenant is to choose slavery and to forfeit the inheritance of the Christian.

g **V 2-12.** Paul now appeals to his readers as man to man—' I, Paul '—putting the issue, circumcision or Christ, Law or faith, as simply as possible, and largely recapitulating points he has previously made. **3.** Cf. 3:10. **4.** Cf. 2:21. **6.** Cf. 3:28. The essential thing is faith expressing itself in love (cf. 1 Th. 1:3, ' work of faith and labour of love ')—here Paul looks forward to the next section of his letter, the development of the moral implications of his doctrine. **7.** Paul reassures the Galatians, using a favourite metaphor (cf. 1 C. 9:24, 26 ; Phil. 2:16), that hitherto they were making good progress. The implication is that they will soon resume their old course. **9.** He realises that his adversaries, who have so unsettled the Galatians, would, if left unrebuked, corrupt the whole community, working like yeast in dough, a metaphor which Paul also uses of the unrepentant sinner at Corinth (1 C. 5:6). **10.** But Paul is confident that the Galatians will heed his warnings, and that his opponents, whoever they are, will incur divine con-

h demnation. **11.** A slander which some (perhaps of antinomian tendencies) had used to discredit Paul was, apparently, that he himself preached circumcision. Absurd as this was, if one knew Paul's views, a certain plausibility might well have been given to it by his circumcision of Timothy (Ac. 16:3), who may be reckoned as himself a Galatian, on one possible interpretation of the term, and by the case of Titus (see on 2:3ff.), which had obviously embarrassed Paul. In answer Paul points to the attacks of which he is the victim. These are due to the offence which his preaching of the Cross has caused to those who regard observance of the law and not faith in Christ crucified as the means of salvation. Paul cannot, in reason, be maintaining both. **12.** In a final burst of sarcasm, Paul suggests that those who are so fond of surgical operations for religious motives should imitate the eunuch priests of Cybele, who were no doubt familiar in Galatia (cf. Phil. 3:2).

855a **V 13-VI 10 Teaching on the Christian Life—13.** Paul first takes up the theme of ' freedom ', so prominent in the earlier part of the Epistle (cf. particularly 5:1). His teaching on freedom from the Law was very liable to be misunderstood as antinomianism, especially by Gentiles, for whom the connection between religious faith and moral behaviour was by no means as self-evident as it was for Jews. That this was a very real danger is shown by the situation at Corinth, where one of the factions in the church apparently took this line. The antinomians claimed to be the truly ' spiritual ', in the manner of some later Gnostic sects. That a similar tendency existed among the Galatians is by no means unlikely. In any case (particularly if Gal. is from the same period as the correspondence with Corinth) Paul was well aware of the danger, and laid down a new principle of morality—love (ἀγάπη) at which he had already hinted in 5:6.

b He warns the Galatians not to let liberty turn into licence, by giving an opportunity to the ' flesh '. This does not mean that Paul was a dualist, regarding ' flesh ' as inherently evil. ' Flesh ' means simply man as creature, capable both of sin and of salvation. It was through man's wilful disobedience, and not through any inherent defect, that ' flesh ' has become the sphere within which evil has established itself, and reduced man to slavery (cf. Rom. 6:12ff, 8:4ff.). To be a Christian does however involve becoming a slave—by self-denying love—to one's neighbour.

c **14.** Paul turns to the advocates of the Law to point out that the only way of fulfilling the Law is by love (cf. Rom. 13:8ff.), citing Lev. 19:18 as a single precept summing up the whole Law. Jesus himself had used this text in the same way, according to Mk 12:31, but Paul gives no indication that he is consciously following him in this. The fact that Paul does not add Dt. 6:4f. (as Jesus does) rather suggests that he is

not. In Lev. ' neighbour ' means ' fellow-Israelite ', 85
but Gal. 3:28 shows that Paul imposes no restriction on its application. Here again Paul is in unconscious harmony with Jesus. **15.** Faction is not only obviously incompatible with love, but also a failing to which the Galatians were particularly prone (as Paul's repeated warning in 5:26 suggests).

V 16-26 The Opposition between Flesh and d
Spirit, cf. Rom. 8:2–13—**16.** Christians possess the Spirit of God (cf. 3:2) ; they must therefore let it control their actions, and produce its fruit in their lives. They must not at the same time think that they can give rein to the desires of their (fallen) human nature. **17.** If they try to do this, they are doomed to frustration, and find themselves in the state so vividly described in Rom. 7:15ff. **18.** (This frustration is the lot of those who are in fact under the Law, for they are trying to please God, but without the help of the Spirit.) But those who have the Spirit are not under the Law (cf. Rom 8:2) and so are not doomed
to frustration. **19-21.** For examples of other lists of e
vices cf. Mk 7:21f. ; Rom. 1:28–31 ; 1 C. 6:9f. Such lists were a favourite rhetorical device of the time. This one shows that for Paul ' flesh ' comprises the whole range of human nature, will and intellect, as well as passions. **21.** Though ' heirs ' (3:29, 4:7) Christians will not receive their inheritance unless their behaviour fits them for it (cf. Mt. 21:43 ; 1 C. 6:10). **22, 23.** Of the fruits of the Spirit love is the first to be mentioned, as the *sine qua non* of all the others. The prominent place given to joy is noteworthy : emphasis on it is characteristic of Paul (cf. Rom. 14:17, etc.). **23.** Law does not exist to deal with such things (note the emphatic οὐκ ἔστι), for ' it was added because of transgressions ' (3:19). **24.** The Christian can produce the fruits of the Spirit because he has died to the flesh, having shared in Christ's crucifixion (cf. 2:20) and entered a new, risen, life (cf. Rom. 6:3–6), that in the Spirit (cf. Rom. 8:11). **25.** So, if we live by the Spirit (as we do), we must behave accordingly.

VI 1-10 Practical Illustrations of Christian Love f
—1-5. The first is the help given by Christians to their brethren who have fallen into sin. One might suppose from what Paul has just been saying that, for him, sin by a Christian is theoretically impossible. But Paul has too firm a grasp of reality for such doctrinaire notions. Sin has indeed been dethroned, but is not immediately made powerless, and the Christian may still fall from time to time. His fellows must not despise him for this, but restore him (cf. the attitude he recommends towards the penitent Corinthian, 2 C. 2:7), and rather look at their own danger than the other's fault (cf. 1 C. 10:12). Restoration of the penitent involves the sharing of the burden of his grief and shame. The AV produces obscurity in 2 and 5 by reading ' burden ' in each case. In 2 the word is βάρος (literally ' weight ')—an extraordinary burden—in 5 φορτίον, a ' load ' (so RSV) that each must carry for himself, as a soldier his pack.
6. The second example is the practical expression of g
gratitude for spiritual benefits by supplying physical necessities (cf. Rom. 15:27 ; 1 C. 9:11 ; Phil. 4:15). **7-10.** This passage may be taken simply as containing general reflections conducive to the generosity recommended in 6. Coming where it does, however, it may have a more specific purpose, even though it is not explicitly formulated. If Gal. is to be dated (as seems most probable) at about the same time as the correspondence with Corinth, this passage may betray Paul's anxiety lest the disturbances which had so suddenly arisen in the Galatian churches should upset his plans for the collection for the poor saints at Jerusalem (cf. Rom. 15:25–7 ; 1 C. 16:1ff.). Paul had presumably given the instructions to which he refers in 1 C. when he was last in Galatia, on his way to Ephesus (Ac. 18:23). Gal. 2:10 may allude to them. The fact that he does not mention Galatia along with Macedonia and Achaia in Rom. 15:26 may indicate that his anxiety was justified in the event. The

855g collection was an opportunity to do good to the household of faith (10). Christians are all God's 'house-slaves' (οἰκεῖοι). Those who have opportunities of service to them are 'stewards' (οἰκονόμοι), servants entrusted with the management of their master's property, and particularly with the feeding of his household (cf. Lk. 12:42 ; 1 C. 4:1f.).

h **11-18 Postscript**—It was Paul's practice to add a postscript in his own handwriting to the letters which, following the usual ancient custom, he dictated to a scribe : cf. 1 C. 16:21 ; Col. 4:18 ; 2 Th. 3:17. That in Gal. is far the longest. **11.** The 'large letters' were due most probably not to Paul's clumsiness as a writer or to the weakness of his eyesight, but to a deliberate desire for emphasis. The letter could be held up in the church meetings for all to see. **12-13.** Paul delivers a last attack on his opponents. Their motives are a desire to avoid persecution as Christians (cf. 5:11) and an un-Christian pride in outward show. **14.** The only thing a Christian can be proud of is the Cross of Christ (which is the prime cause of offence to those whom his opponents would have the Galatians imitate). For by the Cross (or possibly 'through Christ' —the Greek is ambiguous) the power of the world has been broken (cf. 2:20 and Rom. 6:6), and Christians set free. **15.** For them the only thing that matters is the new life open to them in Christ (cf. 5:6 ; Rom. 6:4ff. and 2 C. 5:17). **16.** The true Israel is this new creation, upon which are poured the blessings which 'Israel according to the flesh' has forfeited (cf. Rom. 9:6ff.). 855h

17. Here Paul probably means to give a solemn warning that to attack him is sacrilege. He alludes to the scars left by his sufferings for Christ as the brand-marks of his master's ownership. Devotees were tattooed or branded (as well as slaves), and to attack them was to attack the god who owned them (cf. Herodotus II, 113, 'If any man receives holy στίγματα, giving himself to a god, it is not lawful to touch him'). i

18. For this form of final greeting cf. 2 Tim. 4:22 ; Phm. 25. 'Brethren' has a special emphasis in this place. Paul's last word to the Galatians is in effect a plea for reconciliation.

Bibliography—Commentaries : E. D. Burton, ICC (1920) ; G. S. Duncan (1934) ; M. J. Lagrange (1918) ; H. Lietzmann, HNT ([2]1923) ; J. B. Lightfoot (1865) ; W. Ramsay ([2]1900) ; H. Schlier, Mey. (1951).

J. Dupont, *Pierre et Paul dans les Actes*, RB 64 (1957), 35–47 (includes a full list of recent articles on the problem of Ac. and Gal.) ; J. Knox, *Chapters in a Life of Paul* (1954) ; W. L. Knox, *St Paul and the Church of Jerusalem* (1930) ; K. Lake, *The Earlier Epistles of St Paul* (1911) ; A. D. Nock, *St Paul* (1938).

EPHESIANS

BY H. CHADWICK

856a **Doctrine of the Epistle**—Ephesians is ' the crown of Paulinism ' (C. H. Dodd). The theme is the Church, one, holy, catholic, and apostolic, divinely planned and founded for the redemption of humanity in Christ in virtue of his reconciling work. It is of the *esse* of the Church that it be a unity, because it is the means of bringing unity to mankind. Its door is the baptismal font, the remission of sins, the gift of the Spirit, and the consequent assurance of election to the faithful, who must ever be reminded of that high vocation to which they are thereby called. The coherence of the Church depends on the realisation of the ideal of reconciling love between man and his fellow and upon the ordered life of the Church in dependence upon the apostolic ministry. Both this moral ideal and this ordered unity are on the one hand given, and on the other hand are objectives of striving. Within the Church there is one existing point of tension which is particularly important, namely that between Jew and Gentile. It is a *raison d'être* of the Church that it must transcend this division ; the reconciliation wrought by Christ's atoning death does not only make a way to God for the individual ; it has created the one divine society in which both Jew and Gentile are united.

b Into this society the Gentiles had no expectation of being admitted. The Jews were the exclusive inheritors of the promises of God under the covenant of which circumcision was the sign ; the Gentiles were ' alienated from the commonwealth of Israel and strangers to the covenants of promise '. Nevertheless, Christ's reconciling death has created the possibility of access to God even for those who had previously been ' without God '. This divine plan was unknown to previous generations, but now God has willed to disclose his eternal purpose, and by special revelation has chosen St Paul to be the apostle uniquely entrusted with the mission to the Gentiles, which therefore stands or falls with the recognition of his apostolic status.

But what is this Church in which Jew and Gentile are made one ? It is not that by baptism Gentiles are incorporated into Judaism, like synagogue proselytes. Nor does it mean that Christian Jews abandon the promises of God given to their fathers. The Church is God's new creation, and Christians are a ' third race ' (to use the language of some 2nd-cent. Christian writers), though not in such a sense as to be discontinuous with the old covenant. Gentile Christendom is universalised Judaism. Both Jew and Gentile, united in Christ through his reconciling death, have access by one Spirit to the Father.

c This high ecclesiology and the revolutionary interpretation of history which it implies differentiate Eph. more deeply from Col. (with which its kinship is otherwise obvious) than any other single factor. In Col. the fundamental question at issue is the dignity of the person of Christ and his lordship in the cosmic hierarchy. In Eph. the question is the catholicity and divine origin of the Church. The glory of the Head is now transferred to his Body. In this doctrine of the Church and its role in history, the affinities of Eph. are less with Col. than with the crucial statement of the unfolding divine plan set forth in Rom. 9–11, where St Paul sees Gentile Christianity as a parenthetic protestant movement to recall catholic Judaism to 856d
its true vocation ; as an independent movement its status is temporary and provisional. God's ultimate purpose is to reconcile in one Church both ' all Israel ' and ' the fullness of the Gentiles '. The position of the Gentiles within the people of God is compared to that of a branch grafted into a vine which may be cut off if it proves unfruitful. The line drawn in Rom. is extended in Eph. by its architectonic conception of the Church as a great building of which a permanent and integral part are the stones constituted by Gentile believers. The limited vision of Rom. 9–11 (with its half-apologetic attitude on behalf of the Gentile mission) has become replaced by an altogether wider and more confident idea of a permanent world-wide Church, universal in its range.

Implicit in all this is the need to answer certain questions. If the Church is that society by which God has appointed that his redemption in Christ shall be proclaimed to the entire human race, why has it arrived on the scene of history at so late a stage? And why is it subject to obvious and glaring limitations of time and space ? Eph. answers that the Church is not merely local and particular, nor is it merely of recent invention. Its message is to all generations (3:21). Its advent was in the mind of the Creator from eternity (3:9, 11), and he called it into existence in ' the fullness of time ' (1:10).

Authorship—In whose mind did these remarkable 857a
ideas originate ? It is one of the least important questions about the epistle, and at the same time one of the most fascinating and baffling. Eph. formed a part of the Pauline corpus of letters from the start, and no suspicion concerning its authenticity was entertained in the ancient Church. But in modern times its origin and purpose have been keenly debated, and the question remains open. On any showing Eph. is *sui generis*. The grandeur of its conception and its affinities with other Pauline letters, especially Col., make it hard to ascribe the document to anyone but St Paul. Yet if Pauline it is unique in respect of its style, theology, and atmosphere. Are these differentia such as to compel the conclusion that the epistle cannot be from the apostle's own hand ?

(1) Eph. differs from all other Pauline letters in b
that there is no specific public addressed and no concrete situation envisaged. It is a theological manifesto addressed to everybody in general and to nobody in particular. It lacks the strictly occasional character that marks all other letters in the corpus except perhaps Rom. which in this regard lies betwixt and between.

(2) The language and style are strangely unlike c
Paul's earlier letters. Col. presents some analogies ; even so Eph. makes surprising reading. It has elaborate and untranslatable genitival constructions, especially joining virtually synonymous nouns (cf. 1:5, 11, 19, 2:2, 14, 3:7, 6:10) ; and the style seems artificially complex and self-conscious. The first three chapters are reminiscent of nothing so much as the exalted language of early Greek liturgies, with which they share the characteristic that their effect is largely obscured in translation—notably in RSV where the vast sentence-paragraphs are broken up into short

857c units ; the AV, with all its portentous obscurity, conveys something of the right total effect.

d (3) The theology of the epistle, when examined in detail, shows some differences in emphasis from other Pauline letters. (*a*) The death of Christ, though basic to the author's theme in 2:13ff. as the ground of the reconciliation and unity of mankind, is less prominent than the exaltation of Christ. The author offers a *theologia gloriae* rather than a *theologia crucis*. The doctrine of redemption expounded in Rom. 3 (still for many readers naturally identified with 'Paulinism') is pushed into the background. (*b*) Eph. 1:23, 2:16, and 4:11 ascribe to Christ that which is ascribed to God in 1 C. 15:28 (all in all), Col. 1:20 (author of reconciliation), and 1 C. 12:28 (giver of ministry). (*c*) The Second Coming is conspicuously absent. It seems to have become replaced by the notion of the universal mission of the Church. The author thinks of a gradual growth towards the final consummation (2:21, 4:13) rather than of a catastrophic imminent return of Christ. The Church, like a building, will take time to construct and to attain to the 'measure of the stature of the fullness of Christ'. History continues ; the Church is involved in tomorrow and tomorrow and tomorrow. Christian children need to be trained (6:1ff., cf. Col. 3:20) so that the torch may be handed on. (*d*) If 4:9 is a reference to the Descent to Hades (which is unlikely), then it is unique in St Paul. (*e*) The exalted conception of human marriage in 5:21–33 is spectacularly different from the low and grudging doctrine of 1 C. 7 that it is allowable as a remedy against incontinence—as if marriage under the new covenant has a status comparable to that of divorce under the old. If 1 C. 7 may be taken at its face value (which is admittedly wildly improbable), this divergence must be fatal to Pauline authorship of Eph.

e (4) The atmosphere is that of a high catholicism. The Church is 'built upon the foundation of the apostles and prophets' (2:20), and is an established society which can look back on its divinely inspired founders. Does this imply the retrospective look of the subapostolic generation, strongly aware of its dependence on those who had actually heard the Lord (cf. Lk. 1:2 ; Heb. 2:3), rather than the contemporary look of St Paul himself? At 3:5 the epithet 'holy' is applied to the apostles and prophets ; does this reflect an idealisation of 'the saints' hardly possible in Paul's lifetime? (Surprising as it may seem, the answer to this last question is, Not necessarily at all. See the classic discussion of the early usage of the term 'saint' by H. Delehaye, *Sanctus* (1927), who shows that the later idealised usage may not be read back into the NT.) The emphasis on the divine gift of the apostolic ministry, and on the monolithic character of the Church over against the divisive and centrifugal doctrines of the heresies and sects (4:4ff.) again brings us near to the self-consciousness of the subapostolic Church. There is no great gulf fixed between 4:1f. and the doctrine of Apostolic Succession found in the first epistle of Clement or the strident emphasis on the ministry as a symbol and indispensable instrument of Church unity found in Ignatius of Antioch. If it is but a short step in idea, it may be urged that it must also be short in time—that Eph. belongs to the generation which naturally thought in this way rather than being an apostolic blueprint for a situation unlikely (it is thought) to have arisen already within the lifetime of the apostle.

f (5) Further evidence of maturity is seen in the attitude towards circumcision in Eph. It is certainly more tranquil than that in Gal. Eph. 2:11–3:21 presupposes that the Gentile mission is now accepted, and that the hard controversy over the terms of the admission of Gentile converts is a thing of the past. (As an argument against Pauline authorship, however, this last point cuts no ice. 1 C. 7:19 is equally tranquil about circumcision ; and if on the other hand it is urged that the genuine Paul could never have spoken of circumcision with the implied scorn of Eph. 2:11, 857f it may be countered that by the standards of Gal. 5:11 and Phil. 3:2, Eph. 2:11 is respectful to a degree.)

(6) The relation of Eph. to Col. has been appealed g to equally by both defenders and opponents of Pauline authorship. It is a relation far closer than that of Rom. and Gal. (though this is in some respects a relevant analogy). About a third of the words in Col. reappear in Eph., and the mind of the author of Eph. is obviously soaked in the language of Col. The 'borrowing', however, is no wooden or mechanical dependence. Eph. is not an ingenious stringing together of bits and pieces from Col. and other epistles, composed with the artistry of a Ravenna mosaic, but a masterful variation on the same general themes in language often verbally identical (Eph. 1:4 = Col. 1:22, Eph. 1:7 = Col. 1:14, cf. 20, Eph. 2:5 = Col. 2:13, Eph. 3:2 = Col. 1:25, Eph. 4:2 = Col. 3:12, Eph. 4:16 = Col. 2:19 ; Eph. 4:22–4 = Col. 3:8–10, Eph. 4:32 = Col. 3:12, Eph. 5:19–20 = Col. 3:16–17).

Nevertheless there are important differences in the way in which these identical words are used, in particular some instances where the same words express divergent ideas, a phenomenon requiring some explanation if it is supposed that Eph. and Col. come from the same mind and, though not so problematic, less than self-explanatory even if they do not. The example regarded by some opponents of Pauline authorship as decisive (!) is Eph. 4:15–16, where Christ is head of the body which is the Church, whereas in Col. 2:10 and 19 Christ is head of the body which is the cosmic hierarchy of being (angelic powers etc.). But the usage of Eph. is paralleled in Col. 1:18. And the other instances of this phenomenon are much less impressive. 'Mystery' in Eph. 1:9 and 3:3ff. means the secret divine plan to include the Gentiles within the scope of redemption ; this is a scarcely perceptible extension of the usage of Col. 1:26f. though standing in more marked contrast to Col. 4:3. 'Reconciliation' in Eph. 2:16 is of Jews to Gentiles (it is claimed), but of humanity to God in Col. 1:22 and of the cosmic hierarchy to God in Col. 1:20. (This last place, however, suggests that St Paul was prepared to be adventurous in his application of the doctrine of reconciliation ; and in Eph. 2:16 the notion of reconciling all humanity to God is clearly present.) *Oikonomia*, translated by RSV 'stewardship' in Eph. 3:2 (= 'the divine office' in the parallel, Col. 1:25), slides over into meaning the unfolding of the divine plan in Eph. 1:9 and 3:9 and it is possible that this may also be the meaning in 3:2. 'Fullness' (*plērōma*) is also said to be used quite differently in Eph. and Col. ; but the truth is that it is hard to be perfectly confident of its precise force in any passage of either epistle.

(7) Finally there remain more subjective con- h siderations, chief of which are the personal references to St Paul himself in 3:1–13, above all 3:8, 'I am the very least of all the saints', which to opponents of Pauline authorship seems an extravagantly ostentatious declaration of humility even by comparison with 1 C. 15:9. On the other hand it is not laid on with a trowel more thickly than the advanced claims to apostolic status in 3:1ff. At least the one is balanced by the other ; and to defenders of Pauline authorship (to be distinguished from defenders of St Paul) the entire passage may appear thoroughly in character.

Address—If Pauline, the letter can hardly have been 858a written to Ephesus, where St Paul had worked for about 3 years (Ac. 19:8–10, 20:31), or indeed to any Church with which the apostle was personally acquainted ; Eph. 1:15, 3:2 and the absence of any specific public are decisive evidence. It is very possible that this lack of particularity is connected with the omission of the words 'at Ephesus' in 1:1 by the high authorities followed by RSV, Sinaiticus, Vaticanus, Orig., 'ancient copies' known to Basil, and the Chester Beatty papyrus. Is Eph. an encyclical, as Ussher proposed (1654)? Was the place-name

858a originally left blank? Gal. 1:1 is admittedly different; but Gal., though an encyclical, is addressed to a concrete situation in a specific and geographically limited number of churches. No exactly parallel instance of a general letter with a blank address to be filled in by the messenger actually survives from the ancient world; but it would be hasty to dogmatise about the 'impossibility' of such a proceeding (see the excellent note of G. Zuntz, *The Text of the Epistles* (1953), 228). A papyrus find might be embarrassing any day. In any event the text with no place-name is awkward. RSV irons out its harshness; but to Origen it seemed so odd that St Paul should write to 'the saints who are' that he had to explain the strange phrase from Exod. 3:11 (they participate in him who is). It is therefore probable on linguistic grounds that originally there was either a blank or a name subsequently deleted.

b Marcion held that Eph. was the lost letter from Laodicea mentioned in Col. 4:16 (Tert., *adv. Marc.* 5:11, 17). Of this various interpretations are possible: (*a*) Eph. 1:1 came to Marcion, as it did to Orig., without a place-name, and on the basis of Col. 4:16 Marcion himself conjectured the identification with the Laodicean letter. (*b*) Eph. 1:1 came to Marcion with 'at Laodicea' already in the text. (*c*) Eph. 1:1 came to Marcion with 'at Ephesus' there; he deliberately deleted Ephesus and substituted Laodicea. Or did he only delete Ephesus without substituting Laodicea in the text (as opposed to the heading)? The textual problem of Eph. 1:1 is bound up with that of Rom. 1:7 and 15 where the words 'in Rome' are omitted by G and Orig. The authority for the omission of 'at Ephesus' is stronger than that for the omission of 'in Rome' and, whereas the former omission is certainly right if Eph. is Pauline, Rom. was certainly addressed, primarily if not exclusively, to Rome (cf. John Knox, NTS 2 (1956), 191–3). Nevertheless these two omissions of the place-name are probably to be ascribed to a single cause. T. W. Manson ('St Paul's Letter to the Romans—and Others', BJRL 31 (1948), 229) conjectures that Marcion is responsible for both: 'It is at Rome and Ephesus that Marcion received two great and humiliating rebuffs. It is conceivable that Marcion may have considered that the two churches that had contemptuously rejected the one man who really understood St Paul had thereby forfeited their status as recipients of a letter from the Apostle.' The only apparent alternative to this guess is to suppose that both Rom. and Eph. were originally encyclicals, Rom. being addressed primarily to the capital with some copies going elsewhere in which a blank would be needed in 1:7 and 15, and Eph. not being sent to any particular congregation or single province but to many churches throughout the Mediterranean world. The title 'to the Ephesians' may have been subsequently introduced either from a combination of Eph. 6:21 with 2 Tim. 4:12 ('Tychicus I have sent to Ephesus'), or because an archetypal copy originated in the archives of the Ephesian church. (It is noteworthy that the Chester Beatty papyrus, Orig., and probably also Tert. all attest the traditional title of the letter, though they have no mention of Ephesus in 1:1.)

c If Pauline, Eph. must have been produced in proximity to Col. Col. is a highly self-conscious essay in outclassing a potent gnostic movement, partly by flat denial of the heretical teaching, but partly (and significantly) by a positive incorporation of ideas and language drawn from the opposition within an orthodox framework. Eph. manifests the same tendency to use the gnostic vocabulary in a disinfected sense. The objection to Pauline authorship (mentioned above), based upon the observation that Eph. uses some of the same words as Col. to express different ideas, assumes that for St Paul ideas were always more important than words. This is risky. It is pertinent that without exception the words in question lend themselves to ambiguity, and that such transferences of meaning can be convenient, especially in irony or submerged 858
polemic (an art in which St Paul must be reckoned no mean master). They are all terms which may, with respect, be termed 'balloon-words', capable of inflation to a varied degree in accordance with the necessities of the moment. Confronted by the formidable movement in the Lycus valley, the apostle may well have felt it needful to issue a general counterblast against all such tendencies throughout the Gentile congregations. But in Eph. this is not the sole motive. Equally important for the writer is the assertion of Pauline authority over all these congregations, even including those which he had not founded (3:1ff.). What should be the relation of a Gentile but non-Pauline congregation to the apostle of the Gentiles? This explosive question determines a great deal of Eph.

If not Pauline, Eph. is the work of an intelligent d
and devoted admirer of the apostle (Onesimus and Tychicus are favoured candidates) who have may been personally acquainted with him and so formulated a summary of Pauline essentials for the generation after the apostle's death. Even during his lifetime his churches exchanged letters (Col. 4:16); but the impelling motive for issuing an authoritative corpus would not come until his death and it has therefore been urged (Goodspeed, Mitton) that it was the author of Eph. who first collected and launched the Pauline corpus. The conjecture has attractions. But there is no evidence that Eph. ever stood either first or even last in any form of the Pauline corpus attested during the 2nd cent. (for an attractive series of conjectures as to how it was displaced from its primacy see John Knox, *Marcion and the NT* (1942), 60ff.). And in so far as the theory presupposes widespread ignorance of St Paul's writings from his death to A.D. 90–5 (the presumed date of Eph.), it is open to *a priori* objections that cannot be countered by empirical facts (cf. T. W. Manson, JTS, N.S. 7 (1956), 286–9). Unhappily, therefore, there is no means of elevating the theory above the status of an interesting guess.

The conclusion must be that the arguments for and e
against Pauline authorship are delicately balanced. Neither side can appeal to any single decisive point; both depend upon the cumulative effect of all the evidence taken together. Ultimately the discussion turns on the bottomless problem: What manner of man was the apostle? If we begin from the conventional portrait, it is not easy to suppose Eph. to be Pauline. But the Procrustean picture may be mistaken. We have no sufficient ground for regarding him as a man incapable of producing Eph., and in any event the argument against the tradition, strong as it may be, falls some distance short of the demonstration claimed for it by the over-enthusiastic. The exegesis of the document is affected at few points, and in the ensuing commentary the author is called Paul without either apology or question-begging.

I 1-14 Salutation and Hymn of Blessing—After a 859
greeting like Col. 1:2 (for the text in 1:1 see above), Paul launches himself into an elaborate eulogy (cf. 2 C. 1:3ff.; 1 Pet. 1:3ff.) extolling the heavenly status of those who are in Christ. It reads like a baptismal hymn, with its stress on the high calling of God's adoptive sons, on the gift of the remission of sins, and on the seal of the Spirit, which impose on the believer the demand that he shall realise in this life that of the world to come. The exalted vocabulary is comparable to that of Col. 1:9ff., and is determined partly by the polemical undercurrent against gnostic claims to supply heavenly riches by a theosophical account of the angelic hierarchy, regarded as superior to Christ, and partly by the need to answer the question why the Church, as a divinely created society, has nevertheless appeared only recently. Hence the particular stress on grace and predestination. **9.** The Church was from the beginning in God's mind, and has appeared in the fullness of time. Though incarnate

859a as Man, as God's creative wisdom Christ is head of all angelic powers, and so in him all things find their apex or head, their coherence, and their principle of unity. He is the linchpin of the great chain of being, transcendent over it and at the same time immanent within the whole (cf. 2:20 ; 1 C. 15:24–8). By this language Paul imports a specifically Christian content into the contemporary cosmology for which there was no more pressing question than the source of harmony in a world of diversity and freedom. That immanent power of God which providentially guides the universe is identified with Christ.

12 speaks of **we who first hoped in Christ, 13** of **you**. Is the contrast between 'we Jewish Christians' and 'you Gentiles' (cf. Rom. 1:16, 'to the Jew first')? This fits 2:11ff., and for Paul's sense of the importance of such priority cf. Rom. 16:7. But it tells against this interpretation that hitherto in Eph. 'we' has apparently meant all Christian people ; the alternative is then to suppose it to mean 'we who put our hope in Christ before its final realisation' (cf. Rom. 8:24–5), and to take the contrast of 'we' and 'you' to be that between the universal Church and the readers of Eph. **13-14** mark the bridge between the introductory hymn (3–14) and the prayer (15–23). In the hymn the stress lies on that wealth of inheritance which is the present possession of the baptised believer. The prayer asks that this ideal may be realised in the future consummation. The link between this life and the salvation to come is the seal of the Spirit given as a 'guarantee' (2 C. 1:22), the first instalment which promises future payment in full. Tomorrow, though it remain tomorrow, is already here.

b **15-23. The intercession** prays for the grace of insight to discern the wonder of the body of Christ, for the awareness of what it means for the Church, in union with her Lord, that he has been raised not only from the dead but also far above all cosmic powers. He is thus supreme in the universe, and at the same time indwells his body, the Church, like the world-soul. The terminology here is technical and allusive which makes its drift hard for the modern reader to grasp. **23.** 'the fulness of him who fills all in all'. RSV is improbable though not impossible ; the verb is more naturally taken as passive, i.e. 'who is being filled', or 'that which is in process of being filled' or 'that which is in a state of being full'. Of the various interpretations may be mentioned : (A) Christ is attaining his full development and perfection in the Church (cf. Eph. 4:13 ; Col. 1:24) ; (B) The Church is that which is being filled by Christ who is himself being filled by the Father (cf. Col. 2:9–10)—this gives a forced sense to *plērōma* which means 'that which fills', not 'that which is being filled'. (C) Christ is head of the Church, his body (= the cosmic hierarchy), and is immanent within it so that he is that which fills the cosmic hierarchy as it attains to the maximum of its perfect plenitude. This last interpretation is the most likely ; it takes *plērōma* to be in apposition to the whole idea of the preceding phrase, i.e. as Christ transcendent over and immanent within the Church.

c **II 1-10.** The Church of which this exalted language has just been used in the first chapter is the creation of divine grace, by the word of truth (1:13). **1ff.** draws the sharp contrast between the high calling of the baptised and the sinful state of their unredeemed past. (In Eph. the lights and shades are extreme, the one setting off the other.) God's power is chiefly shown in mercy and pity to those whose existence, apart from his saving intervention, is death, a mere following of 'the course of this world', the evil condition of which is personified as the domination of demonic power in the sublunary sphere (almost universal contemporary belief). To regard the allusion to grace in 2:5 and 8–10 as an irrelevance, dragged in by a Pauline imitator who had to pack it in somewhere, is to miss the point. The interest, however, of **1-10** is that it forms the introduction to what follows.

11-22. The immeasurable grace of God has reached down so far that it extends to the Gentiles, who in 859c
Christ are made inheritors of God's promises to his people, thus fulfilling Isa. 57:19. It is this incorporation of the Gentiles which makes the Church something 'new' on the stage of history ; they are incorporated in 'one new man', i.e. Christ. The Mosaic law is abolished because it is limited to Judaism and is an instrument of racial exclusiveness (cf. Rom. 3:29–30), constituting a 'dividing wall of hostility'. cf. *Letter of Aristeas* 139, 'Our Lawgiver . . . fenced us round with impregnable ramparts and walls of iron that we might not mingle at all with any of the other nations, but remain pure in body and soul' (tr. Andrews). The unity is derived wholly from Christ of whose indivisible body both Jews and Gentiles are members. **20-1.** The metaphor of a body is fused with that of a building (with the minor inconsequence that the building is said to grow), that is God's temple, the foundations of which are the inspired apostles and (Christian) prophets (cf. 4:11 ; 1 C. 12:28). The contrast with 1 C. 3:11 is explained by the divergent interests and tendencies of the two passages ; both are in some degree polemical.

III. Why has this Church uniting Jew and Gentile d
only appeared so recently? It was an eternal part of the divine plan but hitherto has been kept secret. (For the Christian revelation as God's secret see the non-Pauline Rom. 16:25–6, Ignatius, *Ephes.* 19 etc. ; the theme is prominent in early Christian apologetic, and there is no need to suppose that the question failed to cross anybody's mind before A.D. 95.) The instrument of the disclosure is the apostle himself. **2** shows that Eph. is primarily addressed to Gentile communities owing nothing to Paul. Elsewhere (Rom. 15:20 and 2 C. 10:13–16) Paul displays some embarrassment about his relations with such churches ; Eph. offers a firm assertion of the apostles' authority as *doctor gentium* even over congregations whose existence was due to missionaries quite outside the Pauline circle. He has never visited them ; but they may learn to recognise him as indeed apostle of the Gentiles by what they read here. (The motivation of the passage is wholly intelligible if Eph. is Pauline ; if it is not, the passage must be ascribed to the enthusiasm of the disciple carrying him into panegyric.)

3 may refer either to 1:9–10 or less probably to Col. Goodspeed understands it to refer forward to the corpus of epistles to which on his hypothesis Eph. is the covering letter. **4. When you read:** for the exercise of apostolic authority by letter cf. 2 C. 10:9–10. **5.** Contrast Col. 1:25–6 where the secret is revealed to the entire Christian society, not merely to the ministry. Is this subapostolic clericalism? Or is it so formulated because in this context Paul is interested in affirming that his own jurisdiction is conjoined with that of the other universally recognised authorities? On 'holy' see §857*e* ; the epithet was naturally attached to prophets already (cf. Lk. 1:70 etc.), and could easily be transferred to other inspired authorities. **6.** Cf. Col. 1:27. **8.** Cf. 1 C. 15:9. **10** has a gnostic ring, but is paralleled in 1 C. 2:6ff.

13. The latent thought is perhaps that Paul's imprisonment and suffering are not to be understood as evidence of divine displeasure or refusal to authenticate his apostolic authority by success. For his suffering as being on behalf of all the Gentile churches (which implies that he is their unique representative and that all alike stand in a necessary relation to him) cf. 3:1, 6:19–20. **15. Every family:** a play on words, *patria* = family, *patēr* = father. The main notion is that the Church as God's family is a society that must ultimately be coterminous with humanity, because creation is the ground of redemption. But in detail the sense is less than clear. It might mean 'the whole family', i.e. either the Church or the family of mankind. But RSV is more likely right, in which case it may either mean 'every family, no matter where, is a family because it is derived from God's paternity', or refer allusively and polemically to gnostic theories of

859d the propagation of heavenly powers, as the aeons in the system of the 2nd-cent. Valentinians, a famous gnostic sect among whom this text was very popular (cf. note on 5:31–3); this explains the reference to families in heaven, an exegetical crux that has exercised commentators since Origen.

e **IV 1-16.** The shift to the moral implications of the high doctrine so far set forth is made only slowly. The stress lies on humility (because pride is the prime source of Christian disunity), on the unity in community created by the Spirit, and on the divine gift of the apostolic ministry. Although this unity is declared to be given, it is none the less the final objective of a gradual growth to maturity. The one Church already exists; at the same time it is an eschatological end to be realised in the future.
8-10. Ps. 68:18 means that the apostolic ministry is a gift of the ascended, triumphant Christ; its authority is therefore his. The parenthesis, a distracting digression, is intended to justify the forced exegesis of the Psalm-text by the Rabbinic (and typically Pauline) argument that an ascent implies a previous descent. **The lower parts of the earth:** i.e. in the incarnation, almost certainly not the Descent to Hades.

f **IV 17-V 20 The New Man**—The theological statement now passes over into an account of Christian conduct, expounded in a series of contrasts with the decadence of paganism. **18-19.** cf. Col. 1:21, especially Rom. 1:21ff. **24ff.** cf. Rom. 12–13; Col. 3:5ff. The moral demand of the Gospel is related to the response of the believer to the love of God in Christ. **26.** cf. Ps. 4:4. Resentment is a toxic emotion; do not brood on grievances. The sentiment is paralleled in Greek morality. **V 5.** cf. 1 C. 6:9–10. **11-14** are obscure because of the allusive references to 'light' in varying senses; the end of **13** is odd, and seems to mean that, being illuminated by Christ's light, believers are made light themselves, and stand out against the shame and darkness of pagan immorality. **14** quotes a lost baptismal hymn. **15.** cf. Col. 4:5. **19-20.** cf. Col. 3:16.

g **V 21-VI 19 Domestic Morality**—The primacy of humility means that Christian marriage is a relation of mutual giving and subordination. The submission of wife to husband is an earthly enactment of the heavenly relation between the Church and Christ. The author here picks up the 'cosmological' ecclesiology of 1:22–3. Contemporary religious philosophy and cosmology spoke of the union of the divine spirit with matter as a sacred marriage. Eph. transfers this terminology to the relation of Christ to his Church.
22. The end-phrase, seemingly more absolute than Col. 3:18, is explained by **23**, the thesis of which it already introduces. **26. with the word:** i.e. the baptismal liturgy, or the interchange of question and answer between the baptizer and the baptizand. 859
28ff. Various strands of thought intertwine (in a typically Pauline manner, cf. Rom. 7:1ff.). Just as the love of a husband for his wife is identified with the love of Christ for his Church, so also the care that an individual has for his own body is identified with the care Christ has for his Church. **31-3.** The natural interpretation is that Paul regards Gen. 2:24 as a symbolic reference to Christ's union with the Church, while granting that the literal reference to human marriage may well be a legitimate exegesis. It is a natural extension of the idea of Christ as second Adam (cf. Rom. 5; 1 C. 15), and implies that Eve is a type of the Church. The transition to 'gnostic' speculation is easy, and possibly there is also some veiled polemic against a rival, heretical interpretation of Genesis, offering speculation of the Valentinian type about heavenly aeons in male and female pairs (cf. also note on 3:15). cf. 2 Clement 14. **VI 1-9.** See on Col. 3:18–4:1.

10-20. The description of **the Christian warfare** is h
virtually the sole significant remnant of Jewish apocalyptic within the theological framework of Eph. The language of the divine war is drawn from Isa. 59:17f.; Wis. 5:17–20; cf. the description of Armageddon in Rev., and the Qumrân 'War of the sons of light with the sons of darkness'. The conflict between good and bad angelic powers is the only piece of apocalyptic which can readily fit into a hellenised, 'gnostic' doctrine of redemption. **19-20.** cf. 3:1–13. **21-24.** For the final greeting cf. Col. 4:7. The virtual identity of the two greetings is one of the weaker points in the case against Pauline authorship. Would not an imitator have varied it more drastically?

Bibliography—COMMENTARIES: T. K. Abbott, ICC (1897); F. W. Beare, IB (1953); M. Dibelius, HNT (1953); C. H. Dodd, Abingdon (1929); C. Masson (1950); J. A. Robinson (1903); H. Schlier (1957); E. F. Scott, Moffatt Commentary (1930).

OTHER LITERATURE: F. L. Cross (ed.), *Studies in Ephesians* (1956); E. J. Goodspeed, *The Meaning of Ephesians* (1933), *The Key to Ephesians* (1956); H. J. Holtzmann, *Kritik der Epheser- und Kolosserbriefe* (1872); F. J. A. Hort, *Prolegomena to Romans and Ephesians* (1895); W. L. Knox, *St Paul and the Church of the Gentiles* (1939); C. L. Mitton, *The Epistle to the Ephesians* (1951), *The Formation of the Pauline Corpus of Letters* (1955); J. Moffatt, *Introduction to the Literature of the NT*[3] (1918); E. Percy, *Die Probleme der Kolosser- und Epheserbriefe* (1946); J. A. T. Robinson, *The Body* (1952); H. Schlier, *Christus und die Kirche im Eph.* (1930); P. Vielhauer, *Oikodome* (1939).

PHILIPPIANS

By G. R. Beasley-Murray

860a I **The Occasion of the Letter**—The church at Philippi had sent Paul a gift by the hand of their messenger Epaphroditus, who was charged to assist the apostle in any way required. This letter is Paul's acknowledgment of their affectionate concern for him (Paul's 'receipt', Feine-Behm). Information concerning his own affairs is provided, yielding more encouragement than could well be expected. Account is further given of the ministry of Epaphroditus: the Philippians had heard of his illness; possibly they had not taken it seriously and had expressed disappointment at his inadequate service on their behalf; Paul reveals the gravity of their compatriot's earlier condition and commends him to them as worthy of honour. Paul's writings always advance beyond the merely mundane, and this, too, becomes an opportunity for 'imparting some spiritual gift' (Rom. 1:11). Lohmeyer urged that this last aspect is the only significant factor in the writing of the letter. The Philippians were in dire straits through persecution; bereft of their leaders, they had appealed to Paul for aid; the response is virtually a tractate on martyrdom, written by a martyr to a church of martyrs; this context accounts both for the joy of the letter and the divisions within the church (martyrdom brings pride as well as peace!). While Lohmeyer has exaggerated this feature, the element of truth in it may be gathered from 1:29–30. The Philippians had been refined in the crucible of suffering, hence apostle and community were closely drawn to each other (contrast the Corinthian correspondence, written to a church that knew no suffering for the gospel's sake, but which almost broke Paul's heart). The divisiveness of the Philippians should not be exaggerated; there is no such shadow over this fellowship as existed in some other Pauline communities (cf. 1 and 2 C.).

b 2 **Place of Origin**—(*a*) Rome is still favoured by most, since we know that Paul was imprisoned there, and the 'Praetorians' (1:13) and 'saints of Caesar's household' (4:22) are most naturally associated with that city. But there are serious difficulties involved in this identification. The opposition of the Judaists suits the earlier period of Paul's ministry better than the later; no reference is made to Paul's intention of journeying to Spain; the frequency of communication between the apostle and his friends is surprising in view of the length of the journey (it took anything up to eight weeks, yet no less than four journeys are presupposed prior to the letter's composition, and four after it, Paul's being the last, but spoken of as taking place 'soon'!); the inability of the Philippians to assist Paul (4:10*b*) is hardly comprehensible if Paul had ministered three years in nearby Ephesus and had been imprisoned two years in Caesarea without hearing from them. (*b*) Lohmeyer's revival of Caesarea as the place of writing, on the ground that Paul there first faced trial for life at the hands of the Romans and bore witness to governors and kings, has too many difficulties to be acceptable (there is no indication that Paul was in danger of death at Caesarea, and after his appeal to Caesar no plans for mission journeys immediately ahead were possible). (*c*) Ephesus is currently favoured by many as the most likely place of origin. The thought, style and vocabulary of Phil. are closer to the Corinthian letters than to Eph.-Col. (see Feine-Behm, *Einleitung*, ad loc.); an earlier date suits the time of Paul's struggle with the Judaists; the communications between Paul and the Philippians are more comprehensible if he was at Ephesus; his plans for journeys dovetail into those implied in 1 C. and Ac. (T. W. Manson's suggestion that Paul wrote the letter from Ephesus *in freedom*, immediately after the Jewish attempt in Corinth to get rid of him, is attractive but difficult to accept; Paul was not placed under arrest by Gallio, so far as we know, and Phil. 1:16f. would seem to imply that his prison experience was not past but present at the time of writing). 860b

3 **Date**—If Phil. was not written in the Roman imprisonment, the *terminus ad quem* is Easter 55, when 1 C. was written. On the assumption that Paul's plans for travel (2:19ff.) are identical with those mentioned in 1 C. 4:17, 16:10f., the two letters will not have been far apart; but since the Corinthians probably knew of Paul's sufferings in Ephesus (1 C. 15:32), they will not have been written together. Some time in the winter preceding A.D. 55 would suit this hypothesis best. c

I 1-2 Greeting—The contents of the letter (see 2:19ff.) show that Timothy is mentioned out of courtesy: the writer is Paul alone. The Philippians are addressed as 'saints', an OT term denoting Israel as holy in virtue of their divine consecration; Christians are holy in that they are God's property, called to a life of sainthood. 'Bishops and deacons' (better 'overseers and attendants') were names widely applied in ancient society; the former ranged in meaning from gods to building financiers, the latter from community officials to table servants; both terms were used in religious communities, particularly for those charged with administrative and practical responsibilities. Unlike apostles, prophets and teachers, the terms imply technical rather than charismatic offices (though men with 'spiritual' gifts would often have been chosen for them, and the dividing line between charismatic and practical was thin). It may be noted that in Wis. 1:6 God is *episkopos*, as Christ is in 1 Pet. 2:25, while Mk 10:43–5 represents Christ as the *diakonos par excellence*, a pattern for every servant of God. d

The officers are here mentioned because of their part in gathering and forwarding the monetary gift for Paul.

3-8. Thanksgiving—Every thought of Paul on the Philippians led him to thanksgiving on their behalf, and every prayer of his included joyful intercession for them (3–4). **5.** Their partnership (*koinonia*) in the work of the gospel was a prime cause of gladness; its continuance had lately been demonstrated in their contribution to Paul (*koinōnia* signifies partnership both by contributory service and by contributory gift, cf. Rom. 15:26). Paul at this point thanks not the Philippians for this partnership but God, the source of all Christian *koinōnia*. God had begun in their hearts the work of grace of which this was one of the fruits, and he would carry it through to completion right up to the day of Christ (6). The mention of grace till the parousia implies the negative thought, 'Therefore you will be acquitted in the judgment', and also the e

860e positive, 'Thereby you will experience the glory of the Kingdom' (cf. Mt. 25:31–46). Paul's confidence of this happy issue was born of a twofold consideration : 7 on the one hand he carried his friends in his heart, 8-9 with a 'Christ-Jesus yearning' over them (Dibelius) that expressed itself in earnest prayer ; on the other hand they were participators in the same grace that Paul knew in his defence and vindication of the gospel against its opponents (7) ; the Philippians, suffering in like manner as Paul (29–30), knew a like grace as he did.

f **9-11 Intercession**—An example of 'prayer with joy' (4). Its keynote is growth—that their love may 'grow and grow' (Lightfoot). Paul would have his pilgrims *progress*. And their progress should be in a love which, exercised in knowledge and perception, enabled them to approve things that excel (not merely to 'test things that differ', but to choose what is seen after testing to be superior). This concept of love is notable. Christian love is not blind, but discriminating ; it is the lodestone to guide through casuistry to appreciation of moral worth, the supreme ethical principle in matters of doubt. For Saul the Pharisee, as to his Rabbinic teachers, this had been the function of the Law ; but to Paul the Christian, after learning of Jesus, love was the purport of the law (Mk 12:29ff. ; Rom. 13:8ff.). The prayer closes with an outlook on the future, that the Philippians might be prepared in view of the day of Christ, **10** negatively as pure and blameless, **11** positively as embodiments of righteousness to the greater glory of God. To magnify that glory is the *raison d'être* of the Church and the purpose of redemption (2:11).

861a **12-18 Irrepressible Testimony**—Paul turns to his circumstances, for the Philippians were concerned about them. They may have imagined that he had been silenced ; in reality the testimony had been multiplied. **13.** On the one hand, his chains were seen in relation to Christ and had become a witness to all the 'Praetorians' (whether soldiers of the Praetorian Guard, members of the court at Paul's trial, or officials of a Government House) and to all others he encountered. **14.** On the other hand, the local church, following Paul's example, found courage to increase its endeavours to proclaim the gospel. The net result was an intensification of the mission, beyond what Paul had achieved in freedom. **15.** Not that all was done from the highest motives. Some were actuated by envy, others by delight in the cause. **16.** The 'men of love' saw the hand of God in Paul's imprisonment and supported his vindication of the gospel. **17.** The 'men of party-spirit' were rather concerned for their group and hoped by their success to add to Paul's burdens. The sectarianism of these men makes it likely that they were of the Judaising party, not Gentile Christians jealous of Paul. Far from being vexed, the apostle rejoiced. His sympathisers were doing well, while the Judaists had to toil strenuously to make any impression alongside Paul. **18.** The name of Christ was being spread abroad, and Christ was Paul's gospel! The Good News would make its impact despite its preachers. What happened to an apostle mattered little so long as the Name was confessed by men (2:11).

b **19-26 Unquenchable Hope**—By the prayers of his friends and the help of the Spirit Paul looked, as Job of old (Job 13:16), for 'salvation'—preservation through all trials unto the kingdom of glory. **20.** If released, he will serve Christ in the gospel ; if condemned, he will serve him by martyrdom. Christ is the beginning, end and inspiration of his life ; **21** to die will mean increased apprehension of Christ, therefore death is gain. Yet he cannot turn from life and ask for death, though the latter be preferable. **24.** The Philippians need his help. For their sakes and the further glory of Christ, Paul chooses duty and life and is confident that God will send him to them again (24–6).

The passage is noteworthy as an expression of the Christian view of life and death. Death is not only not feared ; it is willingly embraced, for it has been conquered. To the Christian *death* is Christ. But this does not involve, as with many, a despair of life, for life is of worth : *life* also is Christ. Paul turns from desire for more of Christ to duty to serve Christ, knowing that his destiny is in his Lord's hands. Life and death alike are under the sovereignty of Christ and have thereby won new significance. 861b

I 27-II 4 True Fellowship—A life worthy of the gospel, such as Paul appeals for, includes a unity over against the world without (1:27ff.) and one fruitful in the inner relations of the fellowship (2:1ff.). The former is expressed in a united front against the opponents of the gospel : the Christians' fearless bearing will provide a sign that the opponents fight God, not men ; and that opposition must lead to defeat, as surely as the perseverance of the Christians will issue in their salvation. Unity in the church will show itself in likemindedness, expressed in humility and concern for others (vv. 2ff.). In **2:1** the emphatic appeal to mutual oneness may be interpreted either from the human viewpoint ('If your life in Christ yields you any encouragement, if love has persuasive power, if fellowship in the Spirit means anything, if you have love and sympathy, fulfil my joy . . .'), or from the divine viewpoint ('If Christ gives any encouragement, Love any incentive, the Spirit real fellowship—in short, if God has shown love and pity towards us, fulfil my joy . . .'). On the latter interpretation it is a short step to regard 'love' in the second clause as that of the Father, as in 2 C. 13:13 (so Lohmeyer). Paul's adducing of the divine mercy as a basis of ethical appeal in Rom. 12:1 favours this second view. c

II 5-11 The Example of Christ—The occurrence in v. 5 of Paul's favourite expression 'in Christ Jesus' supports the RSV translation : the readers are to let that attitude prevail in their mutual fellowship which is characteristic of their communion in and with Christ. Since the latter is determined by the Lord, and not by the believer, a description of *his* 'attitude' fittingly follows. The Greek Fathers saw in this example the quality of humility, the Latin Fathers a self-denying concern for others : both are discernible in the preceding context (3–4) as well as in that which follows (7–8), and both find their perfect expression in obedience unto death (9). d

We have here an early hymn on the humiliation and exaltation of Christ (Lohmeyer divides it into six strophes containing three lines each). While it may have been composed by Paul himself, the unusual use of some of the terms, the employment of ideas not characteristic of Paul and the absence of concepts central to his thinking suggest that this is a pre-Pauline formulation, cited for its pertinence in this context. If so it may be necessary to distinguish between the intention of the hymn and the meaning it would have had for the apostle. Moreover it should not go unnoticed how far Christological thinking had gone at so early a date, and that independently of Paul.

Christ existed in the 'form' of God : whether this represents an inner quality ('specific character', Lightfoot) or external ('divine glory', Behm) or even 'status' (E. Schweizer), it is hard to determine ; the English term 'stamp' is not far from the idea. Existence on equality with God was not for him a 'treasure to be grasped'. It is not said whether this represents a treasure to be gained (*res rapienda*) or one to be retained (*res rapta*). On the former assumption a contrast could be in mind with one who did so view 'life on equality with God', whether it be the devil (as in Lutheran tradition) or Adam (it is possible to read every line in the light of Gen. 3, see F. C. Synge). Since however, 'life on equality with God' seems to be the correlate of 'existence in the form of God', but neither is equated with the messianic sovereignty bestowed upon humble obedience, it is better to

861d interpret the language as relating to the pre-existent Christ in the glory of God, possessing equality with God but not viewing it as a privilege that could not be forsaken (in Paul's mind the contrast could well be with the doubtful attitude of some of the Philippians, vv. 3–4, so Barth).
7. Christ emptied himself *by* taking the form of a servant. The nature of this ' kenosis ' (emptying) is explained by the clauses that follow. While theologians may legitimately consider its implications, the term has no metaphysical intention but indicates the abyss of humiliation to which renunciation led the Christ. If, as is possible, the language echoes Isa. 53:12, the view is strengthened that ' servant ' here connotes the Servant of the Lord rather than an ordinary slave. Whether or not we should go further with Lohmeyer and regard ' as a man ' as a literal rendering of ' one like a son of man ' (Dan. 7:13), so combining in this passage the Servant and Son of Man concepts, is more doubtful ; it presumes an Aramaic original for the hymn. **8.** The humiliation of the Christ reaches its limit in death—Paul characteristically adds, ' and that on a cross '.
9. In consequence of this renunciation, God exalted His Servant to unparalleled heights, with a view to the whole created orders yielding him at the last reverence as sovereign Lord (cf. Rev. 5:13 ; the exaltation is presumed as achieved in the resurrection, the acknowledgment at the parousia). The passage is modelled on Isa. 45:23, which proclaims the purpose of Yahweh to bring all nations to obedience to Himself. Lohmeyer insists that such is the meaning of the hymn : the three kingdoms of creation shall become the kingdom of God and of his Christ. For Paul's intention, however, it must be noted that he cites the same passage in Rom. 14:10f. in respect of the acknowledgment of human accountability to God in the judgment. The triumph described is the manifestation of messianic Lordship, attained as a result of the incarnation, not the assertion of the inherent glory of the divine Christ. The Servant-Son of Man is confessed as Lord, a perfected humanity is combined with the majesty of Yahweh. The universe gives glory to God and thereby attains the goal of its creation and redemption.

862a **12-18 Following in Christ's Steps**—The example of Christ and its divine vindication controls the appeal in 12f. ' In view of God's exaltation of the Christ (' Therefore '), achieve your salvation—pursue your Christian vocation to its victorious conclusion—with a like obedience (cf. 8) and with the humility of the servant (cf. 7). So surely as God gave glory to His Son, so will He give grace for the performance of His will to the end of the process.' **14, 15.** In contrast to this noble example, his readers are not to be like the Israelites, grumblers and a perverted generation (a ' triumphant parody of Dt. 32:5 ', Barth), but should be lightbearers, sending forth the rays of the word of life. Their faith in its manifold expression is an acceptable sacrifice to God : if Paul is called on to make his life's blood an accompanying libation, he is glad and congratulates his friends ; they are bidden likewise to congratulate him (17f.).

b **19-30 Apostolic Ministers**—Timothy is to be sent shortly to the Philippians, partly for Paul's own relief of mind when he learns of their presumed progress, partly that Timothy may exercise a similar pastoral function towards the Philippians as Paul would do if he were present (19–20). It is necessary that this church of his affection receive adequate care, should he be called to lay down his life. **21, 22.** Paul has no other colleague who can so take his place as this ' son ' of his, who served in the gospel along with him in a truly filial spirit. **23.** First he must see whether the magistrate's decision will be for liberty or for death. Thus the tension between hope and resignation unto death, observable in the apparently contradictory sentiments of vv. 17 and 24, is present in the paragraph as a whole. Paul is ready for either event and makes his plans accordingly.

25. If Timothy is to wait, Epaphroditus must come at once, for his own and for their sakes. The stress on his dignity and worth, the command to hold him and all like him in esteem (29), and the account of his dangerous illness (26ff.) suggest that an explanation was needed of the manner in which he had discharged his ministry. It may have been thought in Philippi that Epaphroditus had not adequately fulfilled his charge. Paul assures the church that such had not been the case. **30.** Epaphroditus had ' gambled with his life ' to perform service on their behalf and should accordingly be honoured. 862b

III 1-11 Righteousness human and divine—Through rendering the opening phrase of v. 1 as ' finally ', it is often thought that what follows either constitutes a digression or originally belonged to a different letter (cf. Polycarp's reference to Paul's *epistolas*—epistles ?—to the Philippians). But the phrase in later Greek often represents ' therefore ', and since Paul has not yet acknowledged the gift received from the Philippians it is better to interpret it so here. His readiness to ' write the same things ' most plausibly relates to the repeated exhortation ' Rejoice ' (cf. 3:1 with 2:18, which was the last exhortation given). **2.** The term ' dogs ' indicates that the warnings here are directed against non-Christian Jews, not Jewish Christians (the epithet may be a returning on their own heads of their customary estimate of the Gentiles, but cf. Rev. 22:15). Circumcision in the flesh, now that the Christ has come, is but an ' incision '—a mutilation that excludes from the people of God (see Dt. 23:1) : **3** true circumcision is a spiritual phenomenon (the three clauses provide Paul's reinterpretation of circumcision in Christian faith). Not that Paul can be charged with despising what he never possessed : he was born a Jew, not a proselyte ; he traced his ancestry to Benjamin, whom Rabbinism deemed as most highly favoured of the tribes (the Shekinah dwelt in Benjamin because he was the only patriarch born in the promised land) ; and he was Palestinian born, sprung from Palestinian Jews (a Hebrew born of Hebrews—so interprets Gutbrod, TWNT). As to his accomplishments, he had attached himself to the party in Judaism most devoted to the Law ; his loyalty as a Jew was seen in his enmity to the Christians who apparently opposed the religion of the Fathers ; his righteousness in the sight of the Law (viewed as a national standard of life—contrast Rom. 7) was flawless. c
7. All these advantages Paul at his conversion (' *I counted* ') viewed not simply as insignificant, but as loss, for they had hindered him from the fellowship of Christ. **8.** As a mature Christian Paul still maintains that attitude (' *I count* '), even describing his former advantages as filth. A more complete revulsion from his former attitude as an orthodox Jew could hardly be expressed ; it is not intended to be a characterisation of Judaism as such (cf. Rom. 7:12) but of the abuse of the ancient faith as a means of self-justification.
9-11. This renunciation Paul continues in order to gain Christ ; that he may be found in Christ (an expression including justification in Christ and fellowship with Christ) ; that he may know Christ, alike in the power revealed in his resurrection and in the fellowship created by his sufferings and maintained in sufferings ; and that he may be raised at the last day to be with Christ. These are continuing ideals of Paul : they are neither past strivings nor purely elements of eschatological hope, but indicate an ever deepening appropriation of Christ till it reaches its consummation in the final kingdom.

12-16 Conditions of Progress—Paul disclaims having reached the goal of his striving ; it is ever before him (the tenses of 12 are noteworthy : I did not attain it when I was converted ; I have not reached it in the present ; I press on to make it mine in the future). The attainment of this end is Paul's dominant concern, and to illustrate it he draws a picture of an d

862d athlete in the closing stages of a race. **13, 14**. As the runner does not look back, but at that point keeps his eye on the winning-post and makes a supreme bid for success, so he frees himself from the chains of the past and makes the fulfilment of God's call to him his sole aim. The intense language gives place to a quieter picture in 16: 'Let us *walk* in the light of our experience gained'. Persistence, as well as effort, are required for the completion of the heavenward vocation.

e **III 17-IV 1 Citizenship in Heaven**—The Philippians have in the apostle, his colleagues and those of their number who walk in their ways, concrete examples of Christian living. With them are contrasted professing Christians (Paul *weeps* for them) whose life denies the spirit of sacrifice and the judgment upon sin manifest in the cross; such men are dominated by greed, lust and the things of this world (18f.—the language is inapplicable to the Judaisers). Christians, on the contrary, are citizens of the Kingdom in heaven; set in this world as a colony of that realm, their interests cannot be confined to earth and their life is lived in obedience to the divine sovereignty. **20-1**. The Emperor-Redeemer is to manifest himself (the cult language of the Hellenistic rulers seems to be echoed here) and, by virtue of his cosmic authority and power, will transform the body which fetters us to our condition of humiliating impotence that it may become like his, sharing his glorious attributes and so enabling us to experience the power and freedom of the divine life (20f.). In face of such a prospect one thing above all matters: 'Stand firm in the Lord!' (4:1). Neither temptations of the flesh nor opposition of this world must rob us of such a reward.

863a **IV 2-9 Peace in the Church**—Euodia and Syntyche, who could not agree, are urged to do so 'in the Lord', i.e. in virtue of their common relation to Him. **3**. One designated as 'true yokefellow' is asked to help them, in view of their services to the church at Philippi; they had laboured along with Paul in the gospel and were regarded by him as fellow workers. Evidently Lydia and her friends (Ac. 16:13ff.) played no small part in the founding of the church at Philippi. 'Yokefellow' could be a proper name, 'Syzygos'; if so, 'True Yokefellow' implies 'Syzygos, rightly so named' (Vincent—cf. Phm. 11). Unfortunately no occurrence of the name in ancient writings has been found. The inscription cited by Dibelius concerning two gladiators, 'Each died as he conquered and slew his yokefellow', favours the usual interpretation; in which case the person referred to must have been an overseer (1:1), sufficiently prominent to be known without further definition. His endeavours to make peace between the two women would further the peace of the church.

4. 'Rejoice in the Lord' savours of a benediction, as well as being an exhortation (cf. Mt. 28:9, where 'Rejoice!' is rendered 'Hail!'). It is spoken in face of trials endured, for which forbearance is needful, and in prospect of the parousia, which introduces the time of supreme joy ('The Lord is at hand' is probably eschatological, despite Ps. 145:18; cf. *Barnabas* 21, 'The Lord is near, and his reward'). The eschatological tone may well occasion the call for abandonment of anxiety (cf. Mk 13:11), but the care of God for His children is a constant factor for every season (Mt. 6:25ff. may be in Paul's mind). **7**. When such confidence issues in grateful prayer, the peace of God, like a soldier, stands sentinel over the heart (cf. Ps. 125:1f.), more effective in its working than any device ('understanding') of man.

8. 'Whatever is true . . . think about': despite the endeavour of Lohmeyer to divorce these ideals from non-Jewish religious and philosophical thought and to keep them wholly within the OT horizon, on the ground that every term occurs in the LXX, it would seem that Paul here maintains a positive attitude to the world and exhorts that all that is noble in it be pondered. In the last analysis, the differentia of 863 Christian ethics is not its unique content but its motive and power—it is the ethics of gratitude and of grace. The distinctiveness of the Christian way is not forgotten: 'What you have learned and received' indicates the passing on of a Christian tradition; 'What you have heard and seen in me' indicates an exemplification characteristic of apostolic but not of pagan pedagogy.

10-20 A Gift to God—Paul's sensitiveness in respect b of receiving money is nowhere more apparent than in this expression of gratitude for the gift sent by the Philippians. He deeply appreciates their thought for him, but strives to make it plain that it is their consideration for and fellowship with him, implied in the gift, that gives him joy (10, 14). **11ff**. He does not write as one dependent on the gifts of others, **17** nor is he soliciting further donations. **18**. Their present to him was inspired by the love of God and so it is viewed as a sacrifice to God, as well pleasing as any offering given in the Temple ritual. **17**. Paul's chief concern is that his friends lay up treasure in heaven, not for a continuous supply of food for himself. **19**. He gives God glory for grace bestowed and for mercy assured for the future. If Lohmeyer's characterisation of the passage as 'thankless thanks' is an exaggeration, it yet points to the apostle's desire to deflect attention from money to the spiritual significance of this act of Christian charity.

11. 'I have learned to be *content*'. This key term of Stoic ethics (*autarkēs*) had been emptied of its technical significance in popular usage (*autarkeia* = the ability to be independent of all that is external), yet the present context presents a significant contrast to the Stoic ideal. **12**. Far from regarding external circumstances as irrelevant, Paul has been initiated into the secret of making both extremes of plenty and want minister to his good. This is not due to his own native ability; **13** his 'self-sufficiency' is a Christ-sufficiency. The Christian ideal has nothing in common with an ascetic denial of creation and society; rather, recognising the creation as proceeding from God, it seeks to use it without abusing it, to attain to maturity through a dependence on Christ in the fellowship of his people, and by honest labour to supply not alone one's own needs but also to contribute to those who cannot meet theirs (2 C. 9:8).

15. After Paul's founding the Philippian church and departure from them, they alone shared fellowship with him by sending financial aid and so freeing him for preaching. It is hardly to be deduced that Paul thereby conferred an honour on the Philippians not accorded to others (Schlatter, Lohmeyer); on the contrary, their generosity is implicitly contrasted with its lack in others and they are thanked for it (15–16: the apostle's refusal to receive money from the Corinthians was exceptional, due to a desire to dissociate himself from the covetous false teachers there, 2 C. 11:7–13). Paul maintained a policy not to accept support from a church he was founding, in order to provide an example for converts and to avoid the criticism of being a charlatan (1 C. 9:1–12; 2 Th. 3:7–10). The Philippians evidently helped him to uphold this policy in Corinth itself (2 C. 11:8f.).

15. It was as though they had opened a credit account with him ('giving and receiving' are the usual terms for debit and credit in book-keeping; **18** 'I have received full payment' cites the common formula for making out a receipt). The debt of love is paid, and the creditor is overwhelmed at the amount! The God who prompted the Philippians to meet his need will as surely supply every need of theirs (19)—not as a reward, but in virtue of the same grace.

21-23 Conclusion—The greeting is sent through the c overseers and deacons, to whom the letter was addressed (1:1). For the 'saints of Caesar's household', see the Introduction. If they were in Rome, a greeting from them to the hard-pressed Christians of Philippi would be particularly appropriate; if, as is more

863c likely, they were in Ephesus, the greeting may be sent as from members of the guild of 'Caesar's household' in that area (Duncan).

Bibliography—COMMENTARIES : K. Barth (4th ed. 1953) ; P. Bonnard, CNT (1950) ; M. Dibelius, HNT (3rd ed. 1937) ; G. Heinzelmann, NTD (5th ed. 1949) ; E. Lohmeyer, Mey. (9th ed. 1953); J. H. Michael, MNTC (5th ed. 1948) ; W. Michaelis, Theol. Hand-Komm. (1935) ; F. C. Synge, Torch Bible Comm. (1951).

OTHER LITERATURE : G. S. Duncan, *St Paul's Ephesian Ministry* (1929) ; T. W. Manson, 'The Date of the Epistle to the Philippians', BJRL, vol. 23, no. 2 (April 1939) ; W. Michaelis, *Die Datierung des Philipperbriefes* (1933) ; J. Schmid, *Zeit und Ort der paulinischen Gefangenschaftsbriefe* (1931).

COLOSSIANS AND PHILEMON

By C. F. D. MOULE

864a **Authorship**—The Pauline authorship of Col. has often been questioned. But its obviously close connection with Phm. (see below), whose genuineness there is no cause to question, makes it difficult to believe that it is not at least substantially Pauline. The theory that, though mainly Pauline, Col. has suffered interpolation, depends largely upon the fact that the description of Christ (especially in 1:15ff.) is in part unparalleled in the acknowledged Paulines. But there is nothing there, either in vocabulary or in ideas, which it seems impossible to attribute to the Paul who is known from other epistles, or even unlikely for him to have written, given the circumstances implied by the epistle. The relation of Col. to Eph. is indeed problematic ; but if suspicion is cast by the comparison, it falls more naturally on Eph. than on Col. (but see works by Synge and Coutts in Bibliography).

Place of Origin—The subscriptions which appear appended to the epistles in MSS assume that Paul was writing from Rome. But these are not demonstrably early or reliable, and other suggestions have been made. The so-called monarchian prologues (short introductions to the NT writings, believed to be connected with the heretic Marcion, *c.* A.D. 140) describe Col. as written from Ephesus (though they assign Phm. to Rome) ; and modern criticism has suggested Ephesus and Caesarea as alternatives to Rome. Ac. (23:35ff., 28:16ff.) is explicit about imprisonments of Paul at Caesarea and Rome, but is silent as to Ephesus (19:1–20:1). In favour of an imprisonment at Ephesus, however, it is urged that Ac. is demonstrably only selective (cf. 2 C. 11:23ff.) ; that the expectation of release and the request for accommodation at Colossae (Phm. 22) are highly improbable from the Roman imprisonment but natural enough from Ephesus ; and that the thought and style of our epistles are compatible with the earlier date. Similar arguments may be used for Caesarea. (Note, in passing, that critics vary as to whether or not to include Phil. and Eph. in the same chronological scheme.) Caesarea, however, is unlikely, since (to judge from Ac. 23:12ff., 25:2f., 28:18f.) Paul must have known that release there meant almost certain death by violence ; and Ephesus, though in itself a plausible suggestion, is not substantiated by any direct evidence (the building pointed out by guides as Paul's prison scarcely constitutes evidence of a reliable tradition). Rome therefore (unless the distance renders the request for accommodation, Phm. 22, absurd) remains a not unlikely claimant, though certainty is not attainable. The date of writing (see §798*d*) will be either between 54 and 57 or 61 and 63, according to one's choice of locality.

b **Circumstances**—The letters to Colossae and to Philemon undoubtedly belong together. In both alike the writer refers to his imprisonment (Col. 4:3, 18 ; Phm. 9, 13), Onesimus and Archippus figure, and greetings are sent from the same group of friends. Most of the recipients had apparently never met Paul himself (Col. 2:1), but had received the gospel through his friend, and perhaps convert, Epaphras (1:7, reading 'our behalf', cf. 4:12). Colossae, Laodicea, and Hierapolis formed a group of towns in a triangle of

about 6, 12, and 13 miles, in or near the Lycus valley 864
some 100 miles inland from Ephesus, and the Christians in them were evidently in close touch with each other (4:13–16). **The Colossian Error.** The chief purpose of Col. was evidently to combat serious error (see especially Col. 2:16–23) reported, presumably, by Epaphras, who, for some reason, was staying on with Paul. Reading between the lines, it looks as though the error in question had come from professing Christians, who affected a cult of angels and certain dietary rules and ascetic practices—though apparently without any noticeable improvement in morals (2:23)—and who were impugning the supreme and all-inclusive position of Christ in God's plan of salvation. This is the situation which called out a magnificent counter-claim in Col. About the precise nature of the error there has been much speculation. Very soon after the NT period there is evidence of attempts to combine the Christian gospel with systems of thought which were 'dualistic' in the sense that they drew a sharp distinction between matter, which they deemed essentially evil, and a divine and immortal and essentially good spirit. On this basis, sin was interpreted not so much in terms of the abuse of the will—disobedience—as in terms of the entanglement of spirit with matter—imprisonment. 'The fall', on this showing, would not be a fall of the whole man into disobedience, but of his spirit into the realm of matter ; and the glorious liberty of the children of God would be not release into obedient sonship (Rom. 8:21) but the release of the ethereal spirit from imprisonment in the flesh. Hand in hand with this system of thought there sometimes went an elaborate mythology of the stages of ascent through which a redeemed soul might rise on its way to freedom ; and speculation was rife about the angelic (or demonic) powers controlling the planets or the concentric zones of the universe, which had to be passed in the soul's ascent. To such systems of thought the term 'gnostic' is usually attached in modern descriptions, although this was not at the time a technical term for them. Indeed, in early days 'gnosis' could be used to designate orthodox Christianity, as *the* 'knowledge' *par excellence* (and see, e.g. 2 C. 11:6). In 1945, in Upper Egypt, documents were discovered giving earlier and more authentic information of Christian 'gnosticism' than had before been available ; and it is becoming clear that even in pre-Christian times this dualistic type of thought (or at least some aspects of it) had already penetrated areas of Judaism. The writings successively discovered near the Dead Sea from 1947 onwards have yielded impressive evidence of this ; and there seems to be no reason to doubt that this way of looking at man's predicament was widespread, and may well be represented in the errors attacked by Paul among the Lycus valley Christians. Col. 2:8–3:4 seems to point to an amalgam of Jewish, 'gnostic', and Christian ideas, and to certain evil consequences or attendant circumstances. Corresponding to Paul's denial of the value of this outlook and these practices, there is, on the positive side, his insistence that in Christ we have all : in Him dwells the 'fullness' (*plērōma*—later a technical term, at least in the 'gnostic' system of Valentinus, denoting the totality of the denizens of the

864b divine sphere, as contrasted with the world of gross matter) ; that He is God's secret truth (*mysterion*, see §866*b*) ; that He is supreme in and over creation ; that He is God's means of reconciliation and redemption. Thus, it is a plausible suggestion (if not demonstrably correct) that the Colossian error claimed, perhaps actually in the name of Christianity, that Christ was only one among the supernatural powers, and that salvation required, over and above baptism and faith in Christ, elaborate secret knowledge (' mysteries '), and the rigid observance of ritual laws. Paul himself probably believed in the existence of personal ' powers ', angelic or demonic, in the universe ; but, unlike these false teachers, he did not for one moment countenance the idea that Christ was but one among them.

COLOSSIANS

865a **I 1f. Greetings—1. an apostle** (see §631*a*) : Paul presents his credentials, as one personally commissioned by divine appointment. **Timothy :** for his life and character, see Ac. 16:1ff. ; Phil. 2:19–22 ; 1 Tim., 2 Tim. *passim*. **2. the saints** (*hagioi*) means ' the dedicated ones '. The word is closely linked with the OT word *ḳādhôsh* (Heb. *ḳ d š*) used both of God (as ' holy ', ' separate ') and of his own people (as ' consecrated ', ' separated '). Applied to God's people, it denotes not, in itself, ' holiness ' of character, but rather ' commitment ', ' consecration '.

3-14 Thanksgiving and Prayer—7. Epaphras : see §864*b*. The name is probably short for Epaphroditus, but circumstances do not suggest that this Epaphras is the same as the Epaphroditus of Phil. 2:25, 4:18. **9. spiritual wisdom and understanding** describes, for Paul, the quality of those who are receiving and responding to a full measure of knowledge of God's will ; i.e. all these words, ' knowledge ', ' wisdom ', ' understanding ', are related to a movement of the will. They mean more than mere perception and acceptance of some proposition with the mind. The whole Christian vocabulary of knowledge is very closely connected with obedience. This is where it differs from ' what is falsely called knowledge ' (1 Tim. 6:20). See §876*h*. **11. endurance** is the opposite of cowardice, **patience** the opposite of hasty temper or revenge ; **joy** is constantly linked, in the NT, with circumstances demanding these qualities (Mt. 5:12 ; Ac. 5:41 ; Jas 1:2f. ; 1 Pet. 4:13). **12. the inheritance of the saints in light** is the spiritual counterpart of the promised land which was the material goal of the exodus of the people of God (' the saints ') in the OT story. **13, 14 :** it is the kingdom of God's beloved Son (cf. the voice at the baptism and the transfiguration) ; it means, essentially, release from sin. There is no trace of any nationalistic or materialistic messianism here (cf. Rom. 14:17). Very seldom in the NT is reference made to the kingdom of *Christ* (it is usually ' of *God* ' or ' of heaven ') ; but see 1 C. 15:24–8, and Mt. 25:31 ; Rev. 11:15. A striking parallel to 13 is to be found in the words attributed to Paul in Ac. 26:18.

b **15-23 The Great ' Christology '**—Nowhere in the Pauline epistles is there a richer and more exalted estimate of the position of Christ than here. His work is related not only to the rescue of mankind from sin, but also (perhaps with special reference to current false teaching, see §864*b*) to the creation of the universe. He is associated both with the creation of the world and with God's ' new creation ', the church : He is both ' the first-born of all creation ' (15) and ' the first-born from the dead ' (18). He is the goal of creation (16, ' all things were created . . . for him ' ; contrast 1 C. 8:6 where only God Himself is the goal) and ' the head of the body, the church ' (18). In Him ' all the fullness (*plērōma*) of God was pleased to dwell ' (19, cf. 2:9). He is God's revealed secret (27, cf. 2:2f.). Thus, Jesus of Nazareth, who had been done to death as an insurrectionary some 30 years **865b**
(or less) before, occupies a position uniquely close to God in His creative and redemptive work. And this is inseparably associated precisely with that death on the cross. It was there that ' all things, whether on earth or in heaven ' were reconciled to God (20) ; there that estranged humanity was brought back to God (22) ; there that Christ faced the entail of men's sin, discharged their debt, and established their freedom (2:14f.). For the origin of these convictions, see §812*g*. It is (in all but the actual term) a ' Logos ' christology, like Jn 1:1ff. ; cf. Heb. 1:1ff. But whereas the Jewish conception of God's Wisdom or Word treats it as among created things, it would be a mistake to interpret 15 the first-born of all creation in this sense. In itself, the phrase could mean this, just as, in Rev. 3:14, ' the beginning of God's creation ' could mean ' the first thing created '. But this sense is neither borne out by 16 (where Christ is the agent of creation, not part of it), nor by the consensus of Christian experience and belief. Christ as Saviour is clearly more than a creature : as the later creeds put it, He is begotten, not created. Accordingly, the phrase here must mean either ' He who was born (later creeds would say ' begotten ') *before* all creation ' (cf. 17, ' He is before all things '), or ' the one who holds authority over all creation ', as the first-born is supreme over the rest of the family. **16. thrones,** etc. : there is ample evidence from the Jewish and Christian apocryphal literature (e.g. Enoch 41:9, 61:10) that these terms refer to the non-human, angelic or demonic ' powers ' thought of as peopling the universe and controlling the planets. If Paul shared with the false teachers this type of astrological superstition, he did not share one grain of their fear of, or attempts to propitiate, these sinister forces. He knew Christ to be Head over all ; and in Christ he knew that he and all Christians had the freedom of the universe. The modern equivalent of this is the freedom which Christ can bring to those who are hag-ridden by a no less real fear of fate or destiny, or who feel themselves caught up in the inexorable forces of materialism or of the social and economic order. **18. the head of** c
the body, the church : to us, ' the head ' suggests ' the brains ' of an organism. But here it may rather mean the ' Chief ' (cf. 1 C. 11:3 ; Eph. 5:23), the ' Leader ', the one who is supreme over the body (possibly even the ' origin ' of the body—see Eph. 4:16—however strange this may seem to us) ; cf. Eph. 1:22f. ; Col. 2:19. Only in Eph. and Col. is Christ the head of the Church ; in the earlier epistles He is (by implication) the body itself : 1 C. 10:16f., 12:12, 27 (cf. Rom. 12:5). In either case, this ' organic ' conception is distinctively Christian (some maintain, distinctively Pauline). Occasionally earlier non-Christian writers had already compared the universe or a state or a group of people to a body ; but the distinctive thing is that the Church is not ' the body of Christians '—a mere growing aggregate of persons—but ' the body of Christ '—part of an already existing personality. The most probable explanation of this striking usage is to be found in the discovery, common to all Christians, that Jesus, vivid historical individual though He was, was also in some mysterious way more than individual : He was, and is, an inclusive personality ; He *is* His people. To persecute Christians is to persecute Christ (Ac. 9:4f., etc.) ; to do something for the least of His brethren is to do it for Him (Mt. 25:40, etc.) ; and to be baptised into Christ is to become a limb of His body. It is in Eph. and Col., too, that the word ' church ' (*ecclesia*) is used not merely for the local gathering of Christians in a town or in a house (though it is also so used in Col. 4:16 ; Phm. 2), but also for the church universal. The word is emerging into its broadest and most theological sense. **19. fullness :** see §864*b*. Paul may be deliberately borrowing a technical term from the teaching which he is attacking, as much as to say, Christ includes within Himself all those supernatural

865c beings to whom you show such superstitious reverence; you treat Christ Himself as merely one of them ; but He transcends them all. On the other hand, ' fullness ' (a common word, both in OT and NT and elsewhere) need not bear a technical sense, either here or in the fuller expression in 2:9, where it seems to mean that God's full presence dwells in Christ: He is, in a uniquely complete sense, divine. Moreover, if we take it here, as in 2:9, to mean ' the whole fullness of deity ', this provides an intelligible subject for the verbs which follow : it means, virtually, ' God Himself ' ; and He it is who, in Christ, does the work of reconciliation (cf. 2 C. 5:19).
21, 22. And you . . . he has now reconciled in his body of flesh by his death : great stress is laid in the Christian gospel on the real incarnation and the real death. It is a real, physical body surrendered actually to death, by which God reconciles estranged men and women to Himself. There were plenty of thinkers who tried to by-pass this materiality : God, they said, can only have *appeared* to be in Christ; before the death the divine power must have been withdrawn ; there can have been no real union, they maintained, between God and man. It is this error that Paul guards against in his ruthlessly explicit phrase. **23. stable and steadfast,** like the well-founded house in the parable (Mt. 7:24-7). **which has been preached to every creature . . . :** it was a very important part of Christian expectation that the whole creation must hear the Good News before God's design was complete (Mt. 28:19 ; Mk 13:10, etc.). In what sense could this already be declared to have happened? Apparently, in the sense that *representatives* from every section of the known world had been evangelised. Even so, it is an exaggeration, and in Rom. 15:19-23 Paul more exactly limits it to the east, in anticipation of going on to Rome and Spain. Thereafter, with the keen expectation and ' foreshortening ' of a prophet's vision, he expected the ' End ', the final act of God's plan of salvation. It has been for countless generations since to learn a new perspective without losing the essentials of this hope.

866a **I 24-II 5 The apostle's share in the reconciling work of God in Christ, and prayer for Christian maturity in his friends**—In this section Paul expounds his place, as he understands it, in God's design of evangelism, and goes on (2:4ff.) to appeal for a corresponding steadfastness in the Lycus valley Christians. **24. I rejoice in my sufferings . . . I complete what remains of Christ's afflictions . . . :** this very startling phrase seems to mean (*a*) that the apostle's sufferings can be spoken of as Christ's afflictions because of the communion which a Christian, incorporated in Christ, holds with the Lord ; and (*b*) that it is the destiny of the ' corporate Christ '—the Church—to fulfil a certain tale of afflictions ; and that thus the apostle's hardships and privations, incurred in his calling, are a contribution made for the sake of the whole body, towards the discharge of this quota. It is clear that the faith of the NT is that Christ suffered once and for all, and that His self-surrender was complete and unique—the fountain-head of reconciliation, a free gift that cannot be earned ; yet, also, that those who are in Christ are caught up into this activity, and, though never able on their own merit to win their own salvation (still less that of others), are, by their very acceptance of this free gift, brought into the same stream of creative suffering. See especially Phil. 1:29f., 3:10 ; 1 Pet. 4:13 ; Rev. 1:9. Paul says that his sufferings are ' for your sake . . . for the sake of (Christ's) body, that is, the church ', because the obedience of any one limb of that ' body ' is necessarily for the benefit of the whole organism. But in his case it is further true that he, a Jew, is offering this devotion for the sake of the Gentile mission : in that sense, his sufferings in Christ are
b vicarious. **26. the mystery :** this very famous word stands, in the religion of the Bible, for ' God's secret purpose as divulged to his people ', ' God's open secret '.
In the pagan world, *mysterion* could mean a secret 866b
religious rite, or an object or teaching connected with such a rite ; and it was accordingly adopted by Greek-speaking Judaism for a divine secret, hitherto concealed but now divulged, or concealed from others but revealed to God's chosen (Dan. 2:28f., 47 ; cf. Tob. 12:7 (א)). More than ever, therefore, when Christians had recognised in Jesus God's unique act of salvation—the very focal point of all the beams of His light, the very hinge of His plan—it was natural to speak of the incarnation as the long-concealed and at last revealed *mysterion* (' hidden for ages and generations ' is a more natural interpretation of the Greek than RSV*n*). The word aptly conveyed the paradox of revelation—that it is offered to all and yet it is only the few who prove capable of receiving it ; that it is a secret, and yet an open secret. In the NT it is generally found, as here, in company with words denoting unveiling, revealing, divulging, making known (cf. Ignatius, *Ephesians* 19) : Mk 4:11 ; Eph. 3:3 are other important instances. In our passage, the ' mystery ' is first identified with ' the word of God ' preached by the apostle (cf. 4:3 below), and then, **27,** with **Christ in you, the hope of glory** (below, at 2:2, it is simply ' Christ '). This may mean that God's ' secret ' is the indwelling Christ—the character of Jesus reproduced in the believer's life through the Holy Spirit ; but ' in you ' may, perhaps more probably, be taken collectively, so that the mystery is Christ as found among the Gentiles—the Messiah in an unheard-of position ! In either case, it is an aspect of the gospel of the incarnation ; and it carries in it the ' hope ', or guarantee, of the revealing of God's presence—for that is what the Bible generally means by ' glory '. The Greek word (*doxa*), which in secular literature means ' opinion ' or ' reputation ', came more and more to bear the connotation of God's splendour seen among men (cf. Rom. 9:4). **28. in all wisdom** describes either the contents or the mode of the teaching : unlike false teachers (it may be), who perhaps reserved special wisdom for an inner circle of privileged initiates, Paul stresses that he keeps nothing back from anyone : all wisdom (the whole gospel) is offered to all—not some of it to only some of them. (' All wisdom ' is a not impossible translation here, despite the fact that in more precise Greek the words should mean ' every (sort of) wisdom '.) Or, alternatively, the teaching is performed ' with every sort of wisdom ', i.e. with all the equipment of understanding which God gives to a Christian teacher. **29 :** cf. Eph. 3:20 ; Phil. 2:13. A Christian's force of character and effectiveness in prayer (represented as a great athletic contest : striving, *agōnizomenos*) is God's own power at work within him. **II 1ff.** Paul's energetic and divinely empowered prayer for his friends is that they may be given confidence and unity, and may grasp the fact that having Christ (God's ' open secret ') they have all : there need be no question of worshipping or conciliating other ' powers ', or going in search of abstruse ' gnosis ' ; for Christ is the entire storehouse of God's wisdom and knowledge. **2. mystery :** see 1:26, above. **3 :** see 1:15-23, §865*b*, for the relation between Christ and wisdom.

II 6-III 4 Since, having Christ, we have all, do not let anybody sit in judgment on you for not adhering to arbitrary requirements—It is in this c
section that we learn most about the error at Colossae. See §864*b*. But its permanent value lies in the description of what Christ's death has achieved, and how it may be appropriated. **6. As therefore you received Christ Jesus the Lord . . . :** ' received ' (*parelabete*) is the regular word for accepting something handed on by tradition ; but the tradition here is not a mere statement or piece of instruction : it is Christ Himself ; He is identified with the gospel. Cf. Eph. 4:20, ' You did not so learn Christ ! ' ' Christ Jesus the Lord ' is a very rare phrase (only here and in Eph. 3:11) ; literally, ' the Christ Jesus the Lord '.

866c Without the definite articles it would probably mean 'Christ Jesus *as* Lord'; and with them it may possibly mean 'Jesus the Christ as the Lord'. If we knew more about the Colossians' error, it might be easier to divine the force of the phrase. **8. according to the elemental spirits of the universe:** so most modern commentators interpret *ta stoicheia tou kosmou*. Similarly some ancient interpreters had taken it to mean the astral spirits controlling the calendar and thus the ritual. But the evidence for *stoicheia*='elemental spirits' is (apart from other NT occurrences) all later than the NT; and it is possible that here it still means simply rudimentary notions belonging to a 'worldly' outlook. Besides 20 below, it occurs in Gal. 4:3, 9 (apparently of Judaism, and therefore, perhaps, in reference to the angels who, according to legend, mediated the Law); Heb. 5:12 (of elementary teaching); 2 Pet. 3:10 (perhaps of the physical elements). **9. For in him dwells the whole fullness of deity bodily:** see on 1:19, §865*c*. The chief problem here is 'dwells . . . bodily'. If it had been 'dwelt bodily', it would almost certainly have been a reference to the incarnation. But the present tense is less natural with such a connotation; and it may mean that in Christ the whole fullness of deity dwells *as in a body*—i.e. organised into a unity, as opposed to dispersed throughout the universe in the various 'principalities and powers': Christ represents 'integrated', not dissipated, divine power. Some ancient commentators took 'bodily' to mean 'in actual fact', as opposed to 'in mere seeming'; and this again would apply to a real (not 'docetic') incarnation. Perhaps it is best to accept a reference to the incarnation, taking the present tense as a terse way of saying 'dwelt and still dwells' (although the Greek perfect tense would be more natural for that).

867a **10. and you have come to fullness of life in him:** presumably the immediate reference is to false teaching which claimed that mere baptism into Christ was not the way to completeness: further degrees of initiation were required. **who is the head . . .:** see 1:18, §865*c*. **11-15.** In Rom. and Gal. faith-union with Christ is a very prominent feature of the meaning and means of salvation. Here in Col. the way of salvation is seen rather in terms of sacramental union. (The two are not discrepant: they are only different aspects of one reality.) Christians are spoken of as the body of which Christ is the head (1:18), and as 'circumcised', 'buried', and raised to life again with Christ (2:11–13, 3:1). It appears that Paul is viewing Christ's death as the deliberate surrender of His body in obedience to the will of God—a huge, all-inclusive act of obedience, to which Jewish circumcision might be viewed as a tiny analogy; an act of obedience which was the climax and implementation of Christ's own baptism of dedication, and which led, through the cross and the grave, to life. Each Christian, in baptism, is brought into this all-inclusive act of obedience—made one with Christ in death and burial and life. It is an organic conception, so vivid and realistic that in 1:24 the apostle can speak of his own sufferings as a share in the total sufferings of Christ which are yet awaiting completion in His body, the church (see notes there). But this conception of the relation of believers to Christ does not imply something mechanical, external, achieved merely by the enactment of the ritual of baptism. For the statements (in the indicative) of what Christians *are* by virtue of their incorporation are followed by injunctions (in the imperative) about what they are to *do* and to *become*: 'Set your minds on things that are above, not on things that are on earth. For you have died, and your life is hid with Christ in God' (3:2f.); 'Put to death therefore what is earthly in you' (3:5); 'Put on . . . compassion, kindness . . .' (3:12). It is the constant paradoxical refrain of the NT: Become what by God's grace you already are! **11.** This very difficult verse is best understood to mean that the death of Jesus on the cross is (in Paul's interpretation) real circumcision: it is the total surrender 867a
of the body to the will of God, of which the Jewish rite might be taken as a token or symbol. Now Christian baptism is incorporation into Christ and into that death of His (cf. Rom. 6:3ff.); in this sense it is the Christian version of circumcision—it is an identification with Christ in that circumcision-death of His. If so, **by putting off the body of flesh** either refers to the Christian divesting himself of his sensual unredeemed nature (for 'of flesh' in this sense, cf. 18 below)—losing his selfish character by 'burial with Christ'; or, less likely, it might be translated as parallel to **in the circumcision of Christ,** and made to refer to the death of Christ Himself: 'when Christ put off His physical body at His "circumcision"'; i.e. 'body of flesh' may either be a *moral* term for one's personality as sensually and materialistically disposed, or (less probably) a purely neutral term for (Christ's) physical body. **12.** The best comment, again, is Rom. 6:3ff. **13. the uncircumcision of your flesh:** i.e. a state of literal uncircumcision. As Gentiles, these persons had been outside the Israelite covenant. It is only in Christ that, despite still being Gentiles in external conditions, they had become part of real Israel; and that, only by the drastic total 'circumcision' which is baptism. **14. the bond:** the metaphor is that of an IOU, a written statement of indebtedness signed by the debtor himself (see Phm. 19 for the form). Instead of 'the bond . . . with its legal demands', translate, perhaps (with J. A. T. Robinson, *The Body*, 43, *n.* 1) 'the bond to the Law's demands'—i.e. the undertaking to discharge the requirements of God's Law which, in fact, man's conscience does 'sign' by its assent. (Eph. 2:15 has a different expression.) **nailing it to the cross:** a dramatic way of saying that when Jesus let Himself be nailed to the cross, He was thereby destroying the incriminating 'document' which stood against man. **15. He disarmed the principalities and powers . . .:** if we translate 'in him' (i.e. Christ), the subject of the sentence must be God; but it is possible (RSV*n*) to translate 'in it' (i.e. on the cross). Then the daring metaphor represents Christ as a victorious conqueror riding His cross like a chariot and leading the hostile powers (see 1:16, §865*b*) in triumphal procession at its tail (cf. 2 C. 2:14). 'disarmed': literally 'stripped', it may mean not that Christ stripped the hostile powers of their weapons, but that He stripped the powers themselves off Himself: putting off His body in death, He put off with it the last handhold that the hostile powers had. Or again, it may be reflexive, 'stripped Himself'; then the sentence will continue: 'and made a public example of the principalities and powers, triumphing . . .' In any case, the crucifixion is seen as the decisive contest in which the hostile powers, who held mankind in their grip, believed that they had conquered their enemy, but found instead that, having done their worst, they had only gained a Pyrrhic victory (see J. A. T. Robinson, *The Body*, 41). **16-23.** Here some b
of the practices and beliefs of the false teachers come to light: see §864*b*. **17. shadow . . . substance:** a contrast even more at home in Heb., e.g. Heb. 10:1. **18.** 'disqualify you', i.e. deny your claim to be genuine Christians. 'taking his stand on visions': literally, 'entering upon what he has seen'. The meaning is uncertain, but at any rate it suggests an unduly high estimation of alleged visions; contrast Jn 3:11, 32, 8:38; Rev. 1:2. **19. Head . . . body:** see 1:18, §865*c*. For the physiological metaphor, cf. Eph. 4:16. It looks as though the joints and ligaments are conceived as ducts for nourishment. But in any case the general sense of the metaphor is clear and telling. **20. elemental spirits:** see 2:8, §866*c*. **23. rigour of devotion:** better, 'voluntary devotion'—a single Greek word, perhaps coined by Paul, apparently with reference to the arbitrary nature of this asceticism. **are of no value in checking,** etc.: the sense is obscure; but this translation seems more

867b plausible than RSV*n*. **III 1-4.** Having attacked a false type of religion, Paul puts the positive side : Christians are dead and buried ; in baptism they have said goodbye to the old nature—the whole of fallen nature ; they are united with Christ in His death to all that, hence also in His resurrection. This is their actual condition (cf. 3:9, 10) ; now it is for them to realise and implement it. The paragraph illustrates the paradox, Become what you already are ! (see on 2:11–15). **1. . . . you have been raised :** only Col. and Eph. (2:6) use the past tense of the resurrection of Christians (contrast, e.g., Rom. 6:5)—a vivid description of sharing, here and now, the risen life of Christ (though not in the sense repudiated in 2 Tim. 2:18). **2.** ' things that are above ' : i.e. all that belongs to the will and purposes of God, the opposite of all that is trivial or selfish ; cf. Jn 8:23. **4.** ' When Christ who is our life appears . . .' : the hope to which Paul and other Christians look forward includes the manifesting of the Lordship of Christ in company with all his people ; cf. 2 Th. 1:10.

868a **III 5-IV 6 A practical application of Christian conviction — 5-17. General admonitions.** The ' Become what you are ! ' (see 2:11–15, §867*a* ; 3:1–4, §867*b*) is here made specific. **9.** ' put off ' : the baptismal divestiture (cf. 2:11), perhaps symbolised by the baptisand's undressing for descent into the water. **10. the new nature, which is being renewed in knowledge after the image of its creator :** ' the new nature ', ' put on ' by Christians, is Christ Himself (Rom. 13:14 ; Gal. 3:27). He is the ' image ' (or reflection) of God (1:15, etc.), the perfect, the last ' Adam ' (Gen. 1:26f. ; 1 C. 15:45) ; and consequently, once incorporated in the body of Christ, believers are progressively ' renewed ' so as to become like the ' image '. The difficulty is in the phrase **in** (literally ' to ') **knowledge :** perhaps the sense is that renewal brings us to a knowledge of God's will ; or that it brings both us and others to a recognition of the wonderful thing that has happened : what we ' are ' will only be fully known when we have fully ' become ' it. **12.** ' Put on ': see 9 above. **13.** ' as the Lord has forgiven you ' : cf. Mt. 18:33. Christianity with its gospel of new moral power—the clothing with the new nature—is a great deal more than the mere effort to imitate a perfect exemplar. But the appeal to Christ's example is nevertheless a part of it, cf. Rom. 15:3, 5 ; 2 C. 8:9 ; Phil. 2:5ff. **14.** ' love, which binds everything together in perfect harmony ' : *agapē* is that without which any attempt after virtue goes to pieces ; see 1 C. 13. **16.** ' Let the word of Christ dwell in you . . .' : i.e. the gospel, the ' Word ' uttered by Christ in His life and ministry and through His person, is to make its home in (or among?) them ; they are to be constantly with it, and it with them. ' hymns ' : see, perhaps, Eph. 5:14 ; 1 Tim. 3:16 for examples. **III 18-IV 1.** Such instructions about the relations between members of a household are found in both pagan and Jewish writers. The christianised form is notable chiefly for its stress on the reciprocal nature of the duties : parents and masters have duties as well as children and slaves. But there is no question of identity of position : the principle of subordination is assumed (cf. 1 C. 11:3, 14:34f. ; 1 Tim. 2:11–14 ; 1 Pet. 3:7). **22.** ' eye-service ' : i.e. probably, only such service as can actually be seen. The ideal is conscientious thoroughness, even where the work does not show ; the motive is undivided loyalty to God (cf. Mt. 6:24). **24. the inheritance :** i.e. the ' property ' which, paradoxically, this Master—the Lord God—will give to His ' slaves ' ; or else the ' promised land '—the inheritance destined by God for His people. Whatever the metaphor, it stands for that fellowship with God which is His gift to all Christians. **IV 2-6. Further general admonitions. 3.** ' a door for the word ' : perhaps what we might call ' an opening for evangelism '—a door through which the evangelist may pass with his message. ' the mystery of Christ ' : see 1:26, §866*b*. **5. making the most of the time** (so Eph. 5:16) : literally buying 868
up ' (or ' out ') ' the time ' (or ' opportunity '), i.e. either, buying up the whole stock of opportunity, like an eager purchaser ; or, emancipating, buying out, the opportunity which is like a slave in the hands of an evil master. **6.** ' seasoned with salt ' : Christians have no excuse for being dull and insipid in their conversation.

7-18. Messages, injunctions, and farewell—7. b
Tychicus : see Ac. 20:4 ; Eph. 6:21 ; 2 Tim. 4:12 ; Tit. 3:12. **9. Onesimus :** see §868*c*. **10. Aristarchus :** see Ac. 19:29, 20:4, 27:2. ' fellow prisoner ' is probably a metaphor meaning that, like Paul, A. had been ' taken prisoner ' by Jesus Christ (cf. 2 C. 2:14, and ' fellow servant ' in Col. 1:7). It is true that, as a companion on the voyage to Rome, A. *may* have literally shared Paul's imprisonment ; but the word here means ' prisoner of war ', which is inapplicable in that sense ; and it is applied to others in Rom. 16:7 ; Phm. 23. **Mark :** see Phm. 24 ; 2 Tim. 4:11. He is generally presumed to be the same as the John Mark of Ac. 12:12, 25, 13:13, 15:37–9, and the writer of the Gospel ; but this is not demonstrable. **11.** Of **Jesus Justus** the NT tells us nothing more. **These are the only men of the circumcision . . . :** this implies that the rest whose greetings are sent, including Luke, were Gentile Christians. **12. Epaphras :** see §864*b* and 1:7, 865*a*. **14. Luke :** only in Phm. 24 and 2 Tim. 4:11 is he again named in the NT ; but there is no need to doubt that he is the author of the Gospel and the Acts (qq.v.). **Demas :** see 2 Tim. 4:10. **15. Nympha and the church in her house :** ' house-churches ', i.e. assemblies in private houses, were the normal mode of meeting for worship and instruction before there were any special buildings for the purpose ; cf. Rom. 16:5 ; Phm. 2. Nympha (or possibly masculine, Nymphas, with the reading ' his ' or ' their house ') is otherwise unknown ; nor is it clear whether the house was at Laodicea or elsewhere. **16. the letter from Laodicea** (i.e., probably, Paul's letter *to* L., which was to be brought *from* L. to Colossae, in exchange for our present epistle) is lost, unless, with Goodspeed, we are to identify it with Phm. Marcion knew Eph. as ' Laodiceans ' (Tert. *adversus Marcionem*). The Latin epistle under that name in certain MSS is a patent forgery. **17. Archippus** may, as Phm. 2 suggests, have been son to Philemon and Apphia ; what his ' ministry ' (*diakonia*) was can only be guessed at ; but ' which you have received in the Lord ' seems to suggest something official. Was he a church officer, such as a deacon or an elder ? **18.** For Paul's autograph, see also 1 C. 16:21 ; Gal. 6:11 ; 2 Th. 3:17 (cf. 2 Th. 2:2) ; Phm. 19. It is very moving to picture this brief greeting in the prisoner's own handwriting.

PHILEMON

Philemon was, it seems, a Colossian Christian owing c
his conversion to Paul (Phm. 19). His slave Onesimus had run away, perhaps with stolen goods (18), and had somehow reached Paul in prison (10). Paul's letter to Philemon was written to support Onesimus as he bravely returned to his master. It may be that Paul had brought him for the first time to the Christian faith (10, if the syntax is strictly pressed, might be translated, ' my child whom I have begotten *as Onesimus* . . .') ; at any rate, the apostle sends him back as a changed character (formerly useless, now truly Onesimus, i.e. ' profitable ' !), as one for whom he had conceived a deep affection (12), and as a Christian brother to his master (16). And it is clear that Paul hopes that he will be released by Philemon for service with the apostle (13, 21). But he is determined that everything shall be above board, and that Philemon shall be free to do as he thinks best (14). If the Onesimus alluded to in Ignatius, *Ephesians* 1:3 as ' bishop ' of Ephesus is the same person, the possi-

868c bilities were indeed richly fulfilled. (For suggestions about the role of Onesimus in the collecting of the Pauline letters, see §810*b* and Goodspeed (bibliog.); and for a distinctly different interpretation of Phm. see Knox's *Philemon among the Letters of Paul*, who thinks that Onesimus' owner was Archippus, who was also the chief recipient of Phm., while Philemon had succeeded Epaphras as superintendent of the Lycus valley churches, and was appealed to to support Paul's

d request.) **The Problem of Slavery**. It outrages many readers of the NT that so evil an institution is not condemned but tolerated. It must be remembered, however, that in the circumstances, there was nothing—short of using violence, which seemed contrary to the spirit of Christ—that Christians (even those who were not themselves slaves) could do in the realm of external things, since they mostly had no vote and no political voice. What they could do, however, was to let the gospel through them create such relations between master and slave that the principle of one man owning and disposing of another became more and more unthinkable and obsolete. And Phm. is the clearest possible instance of this great force at work. That it has taken (is taking?) so lamentably long to turn this into universal practice and legislation is a reflection not on the weakness of the principle but on the failure of Christians to implement it when the power is placed in their hands. In the same way, other relationships are seen being transformed by the gospel in the NT: man and wife, parent and child, one member and another of the Christian fellowship, are placed in new positions of responsibility towards each other and in new attitudes of mutual concern. See especially Col. 3:18–4:1, §868*a*.

e **1-3 Greeting**—See Col. 1:1f., §865*a*; 4:15, 17, §868*b*.

4-7 Thanksgiving—6 is notoriously obscure. The most problematic phrase is **all the good that is ours in Christ**. Literally, it runs: '. . . that is in us to Christ', which is not very naturally turned as in RSV. Further, who is to enjoy 'the knowledge' of this, and to what purpose? Finally, what is **the sharing of your faith**? Various attempts at rendering or paraphrasing this include: (*a*) 'the faith you hold in common with us all'; (*b*) 'the participation of others in your faith'; (*c*) 'the communion' (with God and between Christians) 'arising from your faith'; (*d*) 'the communication' (to others) 'of your faith'; (*e*) 'the kindly deeds of charity' (cf. Heb. 13:16) 868e 'which spring from your faith'. The rest of the sentence will vary accordingly. C. H. Dodd continues (from (*a*)), '. . . may work out in a clear intuition of every good thing that brings us into union with Christ.' **7.** 'saints': see Col. 1:2, §865*a*.

8-20 The Request about Onesimus—9. 'ambassador': more probable here than RSV*n*, 'old man'; cf. Eph. 6:20. **10. Onesimus:** meaning 'profitable'; the same root is actually used in 20, 'I want some *benefit*' (see RSV*n*). **11. useless . . . useful** is thus probably a playful allusion to the name. **15.** 'forever': not necessarily a more profound phrase than 'for good' (cf. Exod. 21:6, in an exactly similar context), though it *could* mean 'for eternity', referring to the quality of friendships 'in Christ'. **16.** 'in the flesh and in the Lord': i.e. 'as a man and as a Christian'. **19:** see §867*a* on Col. 2:14. **your own self:** Philemon seems to have owed his Christianity to Paul. **20:** see 11 above.

21-25 Personal Details and Farewell—22. prepare a guest room for me: is such a request conceivable from Rome? See §864*a*. **23f.:** see Col. 1:7, §865*a*; 4:10, 14, §868*b*.

Bibliography—Commentaries: (*a*) C. H. Dodd (*The Abingdon Commentary*, L. B. Radford (WC), F. C. Synge, (S.C.M. 'Torch' Commentary); (*b*) T. K. Abbott (ICC—for Col.), J. B. Lightfoot, C. F. D. Moule (CGT), A. S. Peake (EGT), M. R. Vincent (ICC—for Phm.), A. L. Williams (CGT); (*c*) W. Bieder (Zürich—for Col.), M. Dibelius (HNT), E. Haupt (Mey.), E. Lohmeyer (Mey.), C. Masson (CNT), H. Rendtorff (NTD).

Other Literature: J. Coutts, 'The Relationship of Ephesians and Colossians', NTS iv (April 1958); G. S. Duncan, *St Paul's Ephesian Ministry*, and ET lxvii (March 1958); J. Dupont, *Gnosis* (Louvain, 1949); E. R. Goodenough, 'Paul and Onesimus', HTR xxii (1929); E. J. Goodspeed, *New Solutions to NT Problems* (Chicago, 1927), and *The Key to Ephesians* (1956); P. N. Harrison, 'Onesimus and Philemon', *Anglican Theol. Review* (October 1950); J. Knox, *Philemon among the Letters of Paul*, and *Marcion and the NT* (Chicago, 1942); E. Percy, *Die Probleme der Kolosser- und Epheserbriefe* (Lund, 1946); T. Preiss, 'Life in Christ', *Studies in Biblical Theology*, xiii (1954); J. A. T. Robinson, *The Body: a Study in Pauline Theology* (1952).

I AND II THESSALONIANS

BY W. NEIL

869a **Thessalonica,** now Saloniki, was one of the three centres which Paul, accompanied by Silvanus and Timothy, chose for his mission to Macedonia on his second campaign, which took the gospel through Asia Minor into Europe. It was a large and flourishing seaport situated on the great imperial highway, the Via Egnatia, which carried traffic from Asia across Greece to the Adriatic. Not only as the capital of Macedonia, but as a free city of the Empire, it enjoyed considerable importance and prosperity. There was a Jewish colony and a synagogue, with its usual fringe of Gentile adherents.

b **The Thessalonian Mission**—As described in Ac. 17:1–10 Paul had come to Thessalonica smarting from his ill treatment at Philippi, but, although his general reception by the Thessalonians was little better, it is notable that in these cities he was able to lay the foundations of what became two of the most outstanding Christian communities. After a short spell in which Paul addressed himself to the Jews, apparently with some success both among Jews and Gentile adherents, the narrative of Ac. suggests that the Jews, inflamed by resentment, organised a riot as a result of which Paul and Silvanus hurriedly left the city. It would seem from the evidence of 1 Th., however, that the mission lasted longer than the few weeks mentioned in Ac. 17:2, and in all probability there was a second phase in which the missionaries directed their appeal to the pagan population. This activity may have terminated in trouble with the civic authorities, as described in Ac., which made it advisable for Paul to bring his campaign to an abrupt end and to move on to Beroea.

c **The first Letter to Thessalonica**—From Beroea Paul had proceeded alone to Athens where his failure to make any impression on the critical inhabitants had so depressed him that on his arrival at Corinth, his next port of call, he had little heart for further missionary activity (1 C. 2:3). It appears that at this point he was not only physically ill but in complete ignorance of what permanent results had attended his Macedonian campaign.

Timothy and Silvanus had been left behind at Beroea, presumably to consolidate the work there. It is a mark, however, of the apostle's anxiety about Thessalonica that Timothy, who had been summoned from Beroea to Athens (Ac. 17:15), was immediately despatched to Thessalonica (1 Th. 3:1f.) to find out how the young community there was faring in face of official opposition and Jewish machinations, and to encourage it to stand fast in the faith.

It was perhaps not until Timothy and Silvanus arrived at Corinth with the news that the Thessalonian campaign had succeeded beyond all expectation, that the young Christian community was standing up to all opposition, and that its enthusiasm was attracting attention beyond Thessalonica itself, that Paul felt himself sufficiently reassured to launch into his normal missionary work (Ac. 18:5).

Before doing so, however, he dictated a letter to the church at Thessalonica, in which he congratulates it on its vigour and resistance in face of persecution, and deals also with one or two other matters which
required his attention. The Jews at Thessalonica had 869
apparently not been idle and were stirring up trouble within the Christian community by alleging that Paul was nothing more than a money-making charlatan. It would seem also that a particular problem had arisen among the Thessalonian Christians as to the fate of those who died before the Parousia, which, in accordance with the general tenor of the earliest missionary preaching, was regarded as close at hand. Would Christians who died before the Second Advent share in Christ's Triumph? Some of the members were also concerned to know when the Parousia would take place. Besides these main topics the apostle has something to say on the question of the Christian attitude to work, sex and Church order.

Date and Authenticity—It is impossible to say d
precisely when this letter was written. The date is controlled by the interpretation of an inscription at Delphi which suggests that the term of office of Gallio as pro-consul at Achaia began in A.D. 51. It was during his administration that Paul was haled before him by the Jews (Ac. 18:12). At that point the apostle had been for some time in Corinth, where he stayed in all eighteen months (Ac. 18:11, 18). If he reached Corinth a few weeks after leaving Thessalonica on his first visit, that would give us a probable date for the Thessalonian mission towards the end of A.D. 49, and for the first letter, which followed soon after, a date somewhere in the early part of A.D. 50.

Apart from the attack by Baur in the middle of the last century on the authenticity of the epistle, an attack which has since gained little or no support, there has never been any serious question as to the Pauline authorship of the first letter. It was included in Marcion's canon (*c.* A.D. 140).

The second Letter—Shortly after the dispatch of e
the first letter it would seem that Paul found it necessary to write to Thessalonica again. His first letter had apparently not been clearly understood. What he had said about the Parousia was being interpreted as a warning of its imminent approach. As a result of this, some of the Thessalonian congregation had downed tools and were excitedly preparing for the End. Paul has now to calm these people down and has in addition to remind the community generally of the recognised signs that must precede the End and to point out that none of them has as yet happened.

Authenticity—Within the past century the authenticity of this second letter has been much more widely challenged than that of the first. The doubts in the minds of the critics have arisen on account of such features as the large place given to apocalyptic imagery, the alleged difference between the affectionate warmth of the first letter and the chilly formality of the second, and the repetition of the same ideas and phrases in both epistles.

It has therefore been held that the second letter is a forgery, or that it was written by one of the other members of the missionary team. Some critics have held that if Paul is the author he must have intended the second letter to be read by a different circle, or, if by the same circle, then on a more formal occasion. None of these objections is now generally felt to be

69e strong enough to upset the traditional view, and while it cannot be said that the second letter does not give rise to certain critical difficulties, it can be said that none of them is sufficient to shake the unanimous testimony of the early Church that the letter is genuinely Pauline. Here the evidence is even stronger than in the case of 1 Th. since the letter is quoted as Pauline as early as Polycarp (*c.* A.D. 120).

I THESSALONIANS

70a **I 1-10 Greetings to the Church and Thanksgiving to God**—Paul gives thanks for the wonderful example of Christian faith and practice shown by the Thessalonian church. **1. Silvanus** (or Silas) (Ac. 15:22) and **Timothy** (Ac. 16:3) were Paul's companions on the second missionary journey and had probably shared with Paul in the foundation of the Thessalonian church, although Timothy is not specifically mentioned in Ac. 17:1–10. He had however had more recent contact with the Thessalonians than either of the other two missionaries (3:2). **3. Faith, love, hope:** the characteristic Christian graces, probably a pre-Pauline combination (cf. 1 C. 13). *Work of faith* is possibly faith in action in everyday life, whereas *labour of love* may be more particularly missionary activity. It is their *hope* in the coming Triumph of Christ that has produced their *steadfastness.*

b **4, 5, God . . . has chosen you:** the astonishing success of the Thessalonian mission could only be accounted for by the hand of God. He had singled out this tiny group to be his witnesses in the great pagan city. Paul felt that not only had he been guided to Macedonia (Ac. 16:6–10) but that also in the mission itself the evangelists had been unusually conscious that the power of the Holy Spirit was behind their preaching. **What kind of men:** he will describe this more fully in 2:1–12. **6. imitators of us:** as always the best Christian instruction is the example of the Christian instructor. **and of the Lord:** because the missionaries were men in Christ (cf. 1 C. 15:10). **affliction:** Ac. 17:6; 1 Th. 2:14, 3:3; 2 Th. 1:4. **with joy:** the Christian paradox (cf. 2 C. 6:9–10, 8:1–2; Col. 1:24; Heb. 12:2). **7. Macedonia and Achaia:** the Roman provinces, now constituting Greece, where missions had been started at Philippi, Beroea, Athens and Corinth as well as Thessalonica. **8. sounded forth:** the good news has reverberated from Thessalonica throughout Greece and the Christian witness of the Thessalonians is talked of even beyond it (cf. Ps. 19:4). **9.** Strangers talk about the success of the mission before the missionaries have a chance to tell them. **idols:** this suggests that the Thessalonians had been converted to Christianity from paganism and not from Judaism. The 'living and true God' is contrasted with the wood and stone of lifeless images.

c **10. To wait for his Son from Heaven:** this eschatological emphasis, unexpected here and prominent throughout these epistles, does not imply that the gospel as presented to the Thessalonians was in any way different from that proclaimed to Corinthians or Philippians. The first years of the Church were years of heightened tension when men were more than usually conscious of living in a new dimension. The miracles of Jesus had culminated in the supreme miracle of the Resurrection. This was followed by the dramatic events of Pentecost and the apostolic ministry, with its harvest of healed bodies and changed lives. Clearly God was in their midst and heaven was no longer remote from earth. Every Christian had become a citizen of both. It was this intense conviction of the historical triumph of Christ over sin, evil and death that produced the certainty on the part of the missionaries that the world at large must soon see for itself that this conviction was true. Christ would return to earth and after Judgment the righteous would receive their reward of everlasting 870c bliss while the wicked who opposed him would be correspondingly doomed.

It is impossible for us now to say how far this was d regarded as a programme to be fulfilled to the letter and how far it was recognised that the picture was symbolic. It is likewise impossible to say to what extent it was regarded by the missionaries as an event in the normal series of historical happenings. The limitations of language, and indeed of the human mind, make it inevitable that supra-historical events, like God himself, are spoken of to some extent in human terms. Myth and symbol are often the only means of expressing religious truth. Such word-pictures and poetic images cannot be translated into matter-of-fact scientific statements. The language in which the missionaries expressed their conviction of the ultimate Triumph of Christ and the moral order of the universe was borrowed from the terminology and symbolism of OT prophecy and Jewish apocalyptic.

10 is the traditional Jewish picture of the appearance e of God's Messiah in Judgment, combined with the claim of the apostles in the earliest preaching that Jesus had been proved to be the Messiah by the Resurrection, and that the only hope for Jew and Gentile was repentance and incorporation into the society which he had founded, before he returned to judge the world. This was the only way of escaping the *wrath to come.* It would be surprising if both missionaries and converts in these early days had not thought of this as on the point of happening. The OT prophets had always declared that the victory of God and the downfall of evil were just round the corner. The NT apostles had much more reason for sharing this belief. The form in which this conviction is expressed by Paul here and elsewhere in these letters (e.g. 4:16f.; 2 Th. 1:7ff.) reflects and repeats the normal terminology of early Jewish-Christian missionary preaching. What we generally think of as characteristically Pauline thought, as in Rom. and C., is his own individual interpretation of the apostolic gospel (e.g. 1 C. 15).

II 1-16 An apostolic Apologia—Paul refutes slander- f ous talk by his Jewish opponents and denounces them as enemies of God and man. **1. visit:** Ac. 17:1–10. **2. Philippi:** Ac. 16:11–40. **3.** Although the Jews are not mentioned specifically until v. 14 Paul is almost certainly replying to scandalous rumours which were being spread by them in Thessalonica about the missionaries and about Paul in particular. This was doubtless part of Timothy's news. In an age when itinerant philosophers and charlatans were rife it was an easy matter to suggest that the Christian missionaries were no better than the rest. **error:** this is probably in reply to the suggestion that a gospel of a crucified Messiah or a risen carpenter was arrant nonsense. **uncleanness:** the Jews prided themselves on their high standards of sexual morality. Many pagan temples on the other hand were little more than brothels. The insinuation here is that there was not much to choose between paganism and Christianity in this respect. **guile:** smooth-tongued oratory to wheedle money out of a credulous audience was part of the stock-in-trade of the wandering sophists. **4.** The missionaries' message was not their own invention. Its origin was the word of God, therefore their sole aim was to carry out his commands and not to seek popular acclaim.

5-8. Paul rebuts the innuendo that the apostles had g been interested in furthering their own private ambitions, financial or otherwise, pointing out however that they might have stood on their dignity as commissioned apostles of Christ. Instead of that they had cared for their flock as tenderly as a nurse for her children and had devoted themselves body and soul to their service. **7.** The word translated 'gentle' is replaced in many MSS by the word for 'babes'. The RSV translation seems preferable. **9-11.** The

870g best proof that the missionaries were no money-making sophists was the fact that they had made themselves self-supporting by the sweat of their brows and, here Paul varies the metaphor of v. 7, had treated the Christian converts with the affection of a father. Paul mentions elsewhere his practice of making himself independent by plying his trade during mission campaigns (Ac. 18:3; 1 C. 4:12). **12. kingdom and glory:** God is constantly calling us to live in the proper relationship to himself. By acknowledging him as Lord and King we become citizens of his kingdom, but its full glory awaits us in the age to come, provided we 'lead a life worthy of God'. **13.** If the message of the missionaries had merely been a man-made philosophy the young Church would not have been able to withstand opposition as it had done. **14.** Like their fellow-members in Jerusalem who had been scattered throughout Palestine by Jewish opposition (Ac. 8:1), the Christians of Thessalonica had had to face misunderstanding, ostracism, abuse and attack from their pagan neighbours.

h **15-16.** But behind pagan opposition lurked Jewish venom. Paul's denunciation is severe, and difficult to reconcile with his normal view that the Jews, despite their refusal to heed the prophets, or to recognise Jesus as the Messiah, and despite their crime of crucifying him, are still vital to God's plan of salvation and have been given a final opportunity to repent by having the gospel preached to them (cf. Rom. 9:1–5, 11:1ff.). The passage has therefore been thought to be an interpolation. v. 16*c* may indeed perhaps be a marginal comment by some pious scribe which has become part of the text, but Paul's strong words are perfectly explicable as an outburst of exasperation. It seems that just about the time when this letter was written from Corinth the Jews there too were beginning to show their teeth (Ac. 18:5ff.). **15. drove us out:** either Ac. 9:23ff. or Ac. 17:5ff. **16. fill up the measure:** the OT metaphor of drinking a cup, which could be filled either with punishment (Ps. 11:6) or blessing (Ps. 23:5). Paul's thought is that the Jews by preventing the spread of the gospel had added the last drop to the cup of their evil deeds which they must now drink themselves. **wrath:** the phrase may be proverbial. Paul uses it of the impending Judgment (cf. 1:10) rather than of the impending Fall of Jerusalem which must have seemed more than likely even twenty years before A.D. 70. But in biblical thought, historical events reflect theological patterns. God's final Judgment was foreshadowed by his imminent Judgment on Jerusalem (cf. Mk 13).

871a **II 17-III 13 Why Timothy was sent to Thessalonica**—Despite his intense concern to know how the young church was faring in face of local opposition, Paul was for some reason unable to return to Thessalonica. He therefore sent Timothy in his place and Timothy had now returned with the best possible news. Paul pours out his thanks to God for this and prays that he may yet be permitted to revisit the Thessalonian church and that God's blessing may rest upon them. **18.** Possibly one of the insinuations made by the local Jews at Thessalonica was that Paul had left his converts in the lurch to fight their battles alone. This would be particularly insidious if Paul had definitely promised to return soon. It is difficult to account for the vehemence of his assurances unless some such situation is envisaged.

b **Satan hindered us:** we cannot tell from this what it was that prevented Paul from returning to Thessalonica. If it had anything to do with the attitude of the authorities at Thessalonica or other local conditions, presumably the members of the church there would have known about it. Obviously some hostile influence—most likely Jewish (cf. 2:15–16)—was at the root of it, and had made it impossible for Paul to return. Illness (cf. 2 C. 12:7) would seem to be ruled out by the use of the plural 'us'. Contrast the phrase with Ac. 16:6–7 where the circumstances, equally obscure, were clearly regarded by Paul in retrospect as the providential guidance of God. **19-20:** an assurance that otherwise nothing would have prevented him from revisiting a church which stood foremost in his affections. Characteristically in this letter the thought is couched in eschatological terms as the presentation to Christ at his Coming of the souls who had committed themselves to him (cf. 1:10). 871b

The word translated 'coming', Parousia, was the normal Greek word used for the visit of a dignitary or royal personage, or the manifestation of a god. It is mainly in this sense that it is used in these letters and in the NT generally of the Second Advent of Christ. It should be remembered however that the original meaning of the word is 'presence'. It was the conviction of the Church that from the Resurrection onwards Christ was 'present' with his people (cf. Mt. 28:20; Jn 14:18–23). His Parousia in the technical sense would therefore be the full revelation of a Presence they had already known, and, conversely, the more strongly they felt his Presence the more intense became their hope of his immediate Parousia. c

III 1. Despite the indications that he was apparently far from fit at Athens (Ac. 17:14–15) Paul was so concerned about the Thessalonian church that he deprived himself of the help of Timothy in order to set his mind at rest. Timothy must have gone from Beroea to Athens in response to Paul's urgent need (Ac. 17:15) and from there was sent back almost immediately to Thessalonica. Luke does not mention this detail in his narrative. **2-3.** Timothy's importance and status are stressed to make it plain that he was no mere casual messenger but a fully accredited ambassador. He was the youngest of the missionary team and seems moreover to have been rather diffident (1 C. 16:10–11). His mission was twofold, to consolidate the mission work and to strengthen the church's resistance to the local opposition. **4.** Paul had warned them that persecution for Christ's sake was part of the cost of Christian discipleship (cf. Mt. 5:11). It was inevitable for both Jewish and pagan converts. **5. the tempter:** = Satan (2:18) in the person of the Jews who were trying to undo all the achievements of the campaign (cf. 2:1–12). d

6. Paul writes this letter just after Timothy has rejoined him at Corinth, to which the apostle had gone on leaving Athens. His report was so favourable that in spite of Paul's own difficulties there (cf. 1 C. 2:3) he took fresh heart for his own work. **8.** This striking sentence is the measure of Paul's pastoral concern. The success of the gospel was indeed all that he lived for. **9-10.** With a full heart the apostle reiterates his consuming desire to return to Thessalonica, the more so since he has heard from Timothy of some special problems that have arisen. Since he cannot deal with these in person he proceeds to discuss them in this letter (4:1–5:22). **11-13.** Before that, Paul utters a prayer that he may yet be allowed to revisit the young church, which he was in fact able to do some years later (Ac. 20:1) and that meantime God would grant them grace to grow in Christian love and service. As before (cf. 1:10, 2:19) Paul focuses this prayer on the impending Parousia and Judgment. **saints:** or 'holy ones'. Most likely the phrase is pictorial rather than doctrinal and is an echo of Zech. 14:5 (LXX). There it is used to enhance the impressiveness of the triumphal advent of Yahweh on the Day of the Lord, here of the Messiah on the Day of Christ. e

IV 1-12 Problems of Conduct—Paul turns to specific topics which have either been commented on by Timothy or have been raised by the Thessalonians themselves (4:1–5:22). Firstly, apparently, come matters to which Timothy has drawn attention f

71f (4:1–12). **1. Finally:** i.e. furthermore. **2. instructions:** the content of the missionary teaching during the campaign. **3.** There is no reason to suppose that relations between the sexes presented any greater problems in the Thessalonian church than elsewhere. Paul mentions this topic first because in any Christian community consisting largely of ex-pagans, acceptance of the Christian attitude to sex and marriage was probably the most difficult aspect of the gospel ethic. The pagan view in general was that sex behaviour on the instinctive level was natural and right. Sacramental fornication and phallic symbolism formed an integral part of many cults. Paul's description in Rom. 1:24ff. is not overdrawn. To step out of this atmosphere in a pagan city into an austere acceptance of monogamy or continence was no easy matter. Paul therefore states unequivocally the Christian obligation—self-control as opposed to self-indulgence, fidelity within marriage and chastity outside it. **4.** An alternative and perhaps better translation would be ' that each one of you know how to possess his body in consecration and honour '. This is a more profound insight in line with 1 C. 6:19 and Rom. 12:1. **6.** The sex instinct cannot be abused without all sorts of repercussions. ' Brother ' means ' any person '. Retribution is certain here or hereafter. **9.** Paul commends and encourages hospitality and help to those in need in Thessalonica and to Christian travellers from farther afield. **11.** A mild caution against irresponsible behaviour on the part of some members who appear to have suffered from Second Adventist hysteria. The matter is dealt with more fully in 2 Th. 3:6–13.

g **IV 13-V 11 Problems of Faith**—The apostle deals now with two aspects of the expectation of the imminent return of Christ, to which allusion has already been made in 1:10, 2:19, 3:13. (1) Apparently some members of the Thessalonian church had died since the missionaries left Thessalonica. The question that was exercising the community was whether these faithful departed, by dying before the Parousia, had forfeited their chance of taking their place in the company of the redeemed and sharing in the Lord's Triumph. This is dealt with in 4:13–18. **13.** Sleep was commonly used as a euphemism for death by Jews and pagans alike. Paganism was not quite without hope, since Platonists believed in the immortality of the soul and devotees of the Mystery Religions expected to survive death. But presumably Paul refers here to the great mass of pagans whose fatalism is reflected on their tombstones. **14.** The historical fact of the Resurrection of Christ is the basis of Christian hope in life beyond death. This translation implies that at the Parousia God will by the power of Jesus bring the dead back to life (cf. 1 C. 6:14). AV and RV prefer to take the words ' through Jesus ' after ' asleep ', thus implying that God will bring back to life the dead who have died ' through ', i.e., ' in ', Christ (cf. 1 C. 15:18).

h **15. the word of the Lord:** this does not necessarily point either to a saying of Jesus or to a special revelation given to Paul. The substance of the tradition, based on the words and works of Jesus, illuminated by the OT and handed on by the missionaries in their campaigns, was regarded as having divine authority (cf. 4:2). **we who are alive:** Paul at this time expected to live to see the Parousia. But while his views on the imminence of the Parousia did not change, he seems, probably as a result of his severe illness (2 C. 1:8–9), to have ceased to expect that he would still be alive when it took place (Phil. 1:20ff.). **precede:** i.e. shall not have an unfair advantage over those who have died previously. **16-17.** Paul's intention is to comfort the Thessalonians, not to supply a literal description of the end of the world. The last few words of vv. 16 and 17 provide the assurance for which the Thessalonians had asked. They also contain what is probably the only original Pauline teaching in this passage: viz. that those who die ' in 871h
Christ ' before his final Triumph remain ' in Christ ' until they are welcomed into his Presence to be with him for ever. The framework is presumably the traditional picture of the end-event as taught by the missionaries and which was largely familiar to the readers. It is made up mostly of OT allusions and images derived from descriptions of the descent to earth of Yahweh in Judgment as depicted by the prophets (cf. Mic. 1:3; Jl 2:1; Exod. 19:16ff.; Zech. 14:5). The dead will rise as in Dan. 12:2; Isa. 26:19*a*, and the living will be gathered up as in Isa. 27:12*b*, 13*a*.

(2) The second matter which was causing anxiety i
in the Thessalonian church was apparently speculation about the probable date of the Parousia and some apprehension about its effect. Missionaries schooled in the prophets might be able to reconcile their proclamation of the imminence of the Parousia with their lack of concern as to when it might take place but the simpler minds of their converts found this difficult. Paul teaches them here to distinguish between the imminence of the Parousia and its immediacy. The obligation of the Christian is to live his life in such responsible obedience to God that it is a matter of indifference to him at what point he might be called on to give a final account of his actions (5:1–11). **V 1-2.** Paul reminds his readers that as they know very well the Parousia will be sudden and unexpected (Mk 13:32). The day of the Lord = the day of the Son of Man (Lk. 17:30) = the day of Christ (Phil. 2:16). In the OT the day of the Lord was the prophetic conviction, expressed in dramatic form, that God would one day bring the present corrupt world order to an end, establish his sovereign rule, vindicate his servants and eliminate his enemies. Paul uses the phrase here of the Parousia which, in the thought of the early Church, would shortly fulfil the hopes of the prophets. **3.** Those who have cause to be alarmed are those who trust in some false security.
4-5. Christian men however have nothing to fear. j
They live in the light of the gospel, not in the darkness of unbelief. **6.** But they must not be complacent. Vigilance and sober responsibility are needful if the world, the flesh and the devil are to be resisted. The only sure defence is to don the Christian armour of faith, hope and love (cf. Eph. 6:11ff.). **9-10.** It is not the will of God that his people should perish. Christ died that we might live in the right relationship to God (' salvation '). This life in him, begun here and now, is something that physical death (' sleep ') cannot interrupt, and which will be fully realised in the age to come (Rom. 2:5–11).

12-22. Problems of Church Discipline—Paul k
rounds off his letter with some words on the respect owed to the leaders of the congregation, on the responsibilities of members towards one another, and on the place of emotional fervour in the services of the Church. **12-13.** It would seem from this that there was some resentment against the leadership of the community. There is no suggestion of any organised ministry. The leaders, probably elders (cf. Ac. 14:23) drawn from the more gifted members, are to be treated with deference in view of their important contribution to the life of the congregation. **14. the idle:** cf. 2 Th. 3:6–13. **16-18. rejoice . . . pray . . . give thanks:** ' the standing orders of the Christian church ' (Denney). This was written to people who had little cause either for joy or thanksgiving (cf. 3:3, 4:13). **19-22.** This probably refers to two manifestations of the Spirit which were common in the early Church—' speaking with tongues ' and prophesying (cf. 1 C. 14). Apparently the Thessalonians were not impressed by either. Paul urges them to recognise the value of these evidences of the presence of supernatural power but insists that utterances of this type must be subject to critical examination (cf. 1 C. 12:10).

871l **23-28 Final Message**—The letter ends with a prayer that God would draw the members of the young church closer to himself. The prayer is similar to that in 3:13. **23. spirit and soul and body:** not to be taken as psychological differentiation. Paul means the whole man. **27.** This is a strong command that every member of the community, including the members whose various problems have given rise to this letter, should hear its contents.

II THESSALONIANS

872a **I 1-12 The Judgment of God**—After the usual greeting and thanksgiving Paul assures the Thessalonians that the persecution which they are suffering is God's way of testing their faith. But God's justice is unswerving and the enemies of the truth will in the end meet the fate they deserve. **1-2.** cf. 1 Th. 1:1. **3-4.** Perhaps the Thessalonians had modestly deprecated the apostle's enthusiastic commendation of them in his previous letter. **5-7a.** Their knowledge of the help that God had given them to stand fast against all opposition should convince them that ultimately evil will be destroyed and that the gospel will triumph since this is God's world. They are being purified through suffering to take their place ('rest') among God's people in the age to come. **7b-10.** The theological conviction just expressed in 5–7*a* is now dramatically presented as the final scene of God's acts in history, the Last Judgment following the Parousia. Those who have flouted the will of God on earth, and rejected his word, will reap the consequences of their misdeeds in eternal separation from God ('destruction'). Those who have chosen to be his servants ('saints') on earth will share the glory of his presence for ever. The form in which the picture of Christ as Judge is expressed echoes the imagery of the OT conception of the Day of Yahweh (Isa. 2:10, 19, 21, 66:15). **11-12.** A prayer that God may sustain them in their present troubles and prepare them for the life of the age to come.

b **II 1-12 Antichrist**—It appears that some members of the Thessalonian church had either misunderstood Paul's references in his last letter to the suddenness of the Parousia (5:1ff.), or had been misinformed in some way that in the apostle's view the Parousia was on the point of happening. There was in consequence considerable excitement which Paul now wishes to allay. He reminds them of the recognised signs which would precede the Parousia, including widespread apostasy and the appearance of the Man of Sin. Since these things have not taken place there is no reason to expect the Parousia immediately. **1-2.** Paul refers here to what he has said in 1 Th. 4:16–17. Some of the congregation had apparently anticipated the Parousia by assembling to wait for it in a state of agitation as a result of a rumour that Paul had said or written that it might be expected at any moment. Paul does not seem to know how the misapprehension had arisen. **3.** He reminds them that certain things must first happen and rather impatiently refers to his instruction on this subject during the mission (5). The two preludes to the Parousia which are not yet in evidence are (*a*) the Rebellion and (*b*) the revelation of the Man of Lawlessness.

c (*a*) *The Rebellion* was a common feature in Jewish teaching about the end of the world. It was believed that before the end there would be a widespread apostasy from God. This was to be one of the many unnatural portents that would herald the Judgment (cf. 2 Esd. 5:1ff.). The belief was taken over into Christian apocalyptic (Mt. 24:10ff.).

d (*b*) *The Man of Lawlessness* or the Man of Sin, also called the Son of Perdition (i.e. one doomed to perish) and the Lawless One (8) presents an insoluble problem of interpretation. He is described as the emissary of Satan (9) opposing all forms of religion and claiming divine status (4). He is credited with supernatural gifts (9) and with power to attract many followers and lead them to destruction (10). He is even now active in the world (7) and would be fully revealed if it were not for some restraint which at present holds him in check (6). This restraining power will be exercised until its agent is removed (7). When this happens the Parousia of the Man of Sin will take place, but he and all his dupes will thereupon be destroyed by Christ at *his* Parousia (8, 9, 12).

e Attempts have been made to find a solution with reference to historical events, e.g. the Man of Sin has been identified with the Jewish people, the Roman Empire, Nero, the Pope, Napoleon, Hitler or Stalin according to the commentator's predilections. Similarly the 'restraining power' has been thought to be the Roman Empire or the preaching of the gospel, while the 'restrainer' has been equated with the Emperor Claudius or Paul himself. In view of such conflicting theories—for most of which a good case can be made out—it is difficult not to feel that the solution is to be found in theology if it is to be found anywhere. In the events of past and contemporary history, to which Paul makes such baffling allusion in this passage, the Church merely saw foreshadowed the ultimate issue of the divine economy. When scholars from Augustine downwards agree that only Paul and his readers held the clue to the full interpretation of this mysterious utterance, something may be said for trying to salvage what seems to be relevant for our own day.

f The end event, according to Christian hope, will be the Triumph of Christ and the vindication of his followers, a supernatural happening which can only be described in symbolism and imagery. Christ's victory is over sin and lawlessness, incarnated in human beings. Is not the Man of Sin a symbol of mankind's revolt against God, of the accumulated evil of this present age which has acquired a demonic power, and of the pride of man which seeks to usurp the authority of God? It is as impossible to say whether Paul literally expected the Advent of a supernatural Man of Sin as to say whether he literally expected him to be destroyed by the Advent of Christ as he describes it in v. 8. Thus while historical personages such as Antiochus Epiphanes and Caligula are doubtless embodied in the conception of the Man of Sin, this obscure passage finds most relevance as the symbolic expression of the cosmic battle between Christ and Antichrist, God and Mammon, which rages now and which will continue and intensify until the final Judgment falls on the world and the power of evil is vanquished by the power of God.

g **13-16.** Paul contrasts the gloomy picture of the followers of Antichrist with the happy position of the Christians, urges them to be staunch in the faith and invokes God's blessing. **13. from the beginning:** i.e. God's eternal purpose. **15. traditions:** instruction in the Christian life. **letter:** i.e. 1 Th.

h **III 1-18.** This final chapter is mainly concerned (6–15) with the problem of absenteeism already referred to in I, 4:11, 5:14. This had apparently become more serious. Some members had given up their normal employment in the mistaken belief that the end of the world was at hand. They were also upsetting others and preventing them from working. They were quite content that the community should support them in their idleness. Paul reminded them of his own example of hard work while at Thessalonica, and urged that slackers should be left to starve and be ostracised from the community. But his last word is that these offenders are still brothers in Christ.

Bibliography—COMMENTARIES: W. F. Adeney, Cent.B; E. J. Bicknell, WC; J. Denney, Ex.B; M. Dibelius, HNT; G. G. Findlay, CB; J. E. Frame, ICC; G. Milligan; J. Moffatt, EGT; W. Neil, J. Moffatt and Torch; A. Oepke, NTD; B. Rigaux, EBib.

THE PASTORAL EPISTLES—

I, II TIMOTHY AND TITUS

By A. J. B. HIGGINS

873a The question of authenticity is more difficult to decide in the case of the Pastorals than of any other NT document because of the close interconnection of several equally important factors. Among supporters of Pauline authorship may be mentioned Parry, Lock, Meinertz, Spicq, Jeremias, and Simpson, and among its opponents Harrison, Scott, Easton, Dibelius, and Gealy, although, with the exception of Dibelius, all the latter (along with Falconer, who proposes a somewhat complicated literary analysis) allow possible Pauline fragments. For the reasons given below the second view is adopted in this commentary.

b **1. External evidence.** The Pastorals all claim to be by Paul, and ancient orthodox church tradition, which always demands careful consideration, consistently accepts the claim. Yet, while the Muratorian Canon (*c.* 200) includes them, the incomplete Chester Beatty Papyrus of the Pauline epistles, of slightly later date, probably never included them. More controversial is their absence from Marcion's list (*c.* 150). Tertullian (*adv. Marc.* V, 21) says Marcion 'rejected' them. Another view, that they were written after Marcion, cannot stand if, as many scholars believe, they were used by Ignatius and Polycarp considerably earlier in the 2nd cent., and perhaps, though less certainly, by Clement of Rome (*c.* 96). It is much more likely that Marcion simply made use of a list familiar to him which did not include the Pastorals. Their absence from certain lists, together with the fact that they show knowledge of all the ten Pauline letters (P. N. Harrison, *The Problem of the Pastoral Epistles* (1921), 87ff., 167ff.) suggests that they are not of Pauline authorship (cf. C. L. Mitton, *The Formation of the Pauline Corpus of Letters* (1955), 38ff.).

c **2. Internal evidence**

(*a*) *Style and vocabulary.* Even in English the difference in style between the Pastorals and the ten Pauline epistles is discernible. The Pastorals lack the impetuous force and vigour of Paul's style, and are written in language which is slow, monotonous, and colourless. Even more important is the vocabulary. No fewer than 306 (305) words in the Pastorals are not in the Paulines. Of these 175 occur nowhere else in the NT, while 131 (130), although found in other NT writings, are not used in the Paulines. These are some of the results of P. N. Harrison's elaborate study (op. cit.), which concludes that the composition of the Pastorals belongs to the first part of the 2nd cent. because their language, apart from the borrowing of Pauline phrases, has far more in common with Christian and other writings of that period than with the rest of the NT. These results, while widely accepted, have not gone unchallenged. The inadequacy of statistics has been recognised, and it has been suggested that part at least of the vocabulary may be due to the special topics treated in the Pastorals, or to an amanuensis (Jeremias 5; cf. O. Roller, *Das Formular der Paulinischen Briefe* (1933)). E. K. Simpson (*The Pastoral Epistles* (1954), 13ff.) vigorously champions the cause of authenticity, but Harrison has subsequently produced fresh linguistic evidence in support of his case ('Important Hypotheses Reconsidered: III The Authorship of the Pastoral Epistles', ET 67 (1955–6), 77–81; see B. M. Metzger's critique in ET 70 (1958–9), 91–4.). The linguistic argument against authenticity is in itself strong (but cf. D. Guthrie, *The Pastoral Epistles and the Mind of Paul* (1956)), and becomes overwhelming when reinforced by other considerations. 873c

(*b*) *Doctrine.* Part of the purpose of the Pastorals is to denounce heresy and to stress the utter necessity of 'the faith' and 'sound doctrine'. The heresy has been variously explained as Jewish Christian, as gnostic, or as Marcionite. Most probably it is a later form of that Judaising gnosticism combated by Paul in Col. Here, however, in place of Pauline argument we have quite un-Pauline contradiction and denunciation, and the provision of orthodoxy as the antidote to false teaching. Pauline Christianity as the norm, demanding conformity, is the twin bulwark against heresy along with a firmly established church organisation. Behind the writer, then, lies the church as an established institution with its organised ministry, its clear-cut set of doctrines, and its system of worship, glimpses of which he supplies in liturgical quotations. It is little wonder that the Pastorals are 'ecclesiastical' in a way which is incompatible with Pauline authorship.

(*c*) *Church organisation.* Whether the stage of church organisation implied in the Pastorals is compatible with Pauline authorship is still in dispute. While it must be admitted that there is some ambiguity in the references to bishop and elders (deliberately so, according to B. H. Streeter, *The Primitive Church* (1930), 109f.), they, and other passages relating to church order are most satisfactorily regarded as further evidence of a post-Pauline date. Although 'bishop' and 'elder' seem to be synonyms in Tit. 1:5, 7, as in Ac. 20:17, 28 (RSV 'guardians'; cf. Phil. 1:1 'bishops' as a college of elders), and the same qualities are required of both, the latter point is cancelled out when it is remembered that substantially the same qualities are required also of deacons, while the use of 'the bishop' in the singular (1 Tim. 3:2; Tit. 1:7) seems to point to some differentiation from the elders. If this is regarded as inconclusive, there is the overriding authority possessed by 'Timothy' and 'Titus', in whom we may see 'the Ignatian [monarchical] bishops . . . in everything but the title' (B. S. Easton, *The Pastoral Epistles* (1948), 177). Equally compelling evidence of a date far later than Paul is the very fact that regulations for the various types of ministry are thought necessary, and this is especially true of the widows who formed a recognised group within the churches of Asia Minor in the early 2nd cent. 1 Tim. and Tit. utilise rudimentary church orders, which were the precursors of the later more detailed systems; but the difficulty of interpreting the relevant passages is due to the author's primary interest not in the offices themselves, which he takes for granted, but in the worthiness of office-bearers.

(*d*) *Pauline notes.* Even if these considerations were

873c invalid, there would remain the virtual impossibility of fitting the events presupposed in the Pastorals into the framework of Paul's life as known from his letters and from Ac. (but see J. V. Bartlet in Exp., Series VIII, v (1913), 28–36, 161–7, 256–63, 325–47). Hence the baseless hypothesis of a release from the Roman imprisonment with which Ac. ends and further journeys in the East, followed by a second imprisonment. Support for the theory of Paul's release is sometimes adduced from the statement in 1 Clem. 5 that he came 'to the limit of the West' as well, understood doubtfully (but cf. Simpson, 4) to mean Spain, and from the more explicit language of the Muratorian Canon which, however, is a mere inference from Rom. 15:24, 28. There is therefore no justification for assigning supposedly genuine Pauline fragments embedded in 2 Tim. and Tit. to a later period in Paul's career, as Harrison (op. cit.) has shown, though his subsequent reduction of the five notes originally suggested to three (in the article already mentioned ; see also 'The Pastoral Epistles and Duncan's Ephesian Theory', NTS 2 (1955–6), 250–61) betrays the subjectivity inevitably involved in such theories. Yet it is quite possible that there are some Pauline fragments, the most likely passages being 2 Tim. 1:15–18, 4:9–22 (in whole or in part) and Tit. 3:12–15.

d The commentary takes the epistles as their author-compiler intended them to be taken, as if written by Paul to Timothy and Titus. That is why the commentary does not speak of 'Timothy' and 'Titus', despite the view that the Pastorals are pseudonymous, nor take the epistles in the order 2 Tim., Tit., 1 Tim. frequently and perhaps rightly assigned to them on critical grounds. The date of composition suggested is A.D. 100–120, preferably towards the end of this period.

I TIMOTHY

874a Timothy at Ephesus is confronted with grave difficulties. False teachers have arisen who, in attacking the true faith, as had been foretold, threaten the religious and moral life of Christians. Paul sends him instructions for his guidance in this situation until he can come himself. These instructions are partly personal advice as to conduct which will set an example to others, and partly detailed directions for the organisation of the church, in which considerable importance is attached to careful scrutiny of the characters of office-bearers. The defence against heresy is 'the faith' itself and a well-organised church as 'the pillar and bulwark of the truth'.

b **I 1f. Salutation**—The greeting is somewhat formal and official, even having regard to Timothy's being *in statu pupillari* to Paul.
1. an apostle of Christ Jesus occurs also in the greetings of 2 Tim., 1 C., 2 C., Eph., Col., and is therefore Pauline, as is also the order 'Christ Jesus'. But 'Jesus Christ' is of about the same frequency in the 10 Paulines, whereas it occurs only 4 times in 1 and 2 Tim. as against 'Christ Jesus' 23 times. **God our Saviour** is an OT title applied to God 6 times in the Pastorals, but un-Pauline ; it is found elsewhere in NT only in Lk. 1:47 ; Jude 25. **Christ Jesus our hope :** cf. Col. 1:27, the probable source of a somewhat formal phrase which balances 'God our Saviour'. God and Christ are intimately associated in the command that Paul should be an apostle. **2. my true child in the faith :** Titus is addressed in closely similar terms (Tit. 1:4) ; **in the faith :** there is no article in the Greek (cf. RV), but this does not preclude here the objective sense, frequent in the Pastorals, of 'Christianity'. The addition of 'mercy' produces an un-Pauline form of greeting which is repeated in precisely identical language in 2 Tim. 1:2.

c **3-7 False Teaching**—Paul reminds Timothy of his earlier verbal charge. **3.** The occasion cannot be verified. Ac. 20:1 is ruled out by 19:22, unless Timothy had meanwhile returned to Ephesus. Otherwise the visit is an unknown one from Ephesus, or a 87
fictitious one after the 'first' Roman imprisonment. In **4-7** the **different doctrine** (3) is described in terms which make difficult exact definition of the nature of the heresy. Some explain the 'myths' and 'genealogies' as legends elaborated out of OT narratives and pedigrees similar to those in Rabbinic haggadah, the book of Jubilees, and Philo, but more probably we have to do with a kind of Judaising gnosticism (cf. Col.). In gnostic dualistic thought God is separated from the material world, and there is need of an 'endless' series of emanations or aeons to bridge the gap. **7.** Part of the undoubted Jewish element in the false teaching, whose exponents seek to be 'teachers of the law', consists of fanciful gnostic interpretations of the OT (cf. Easton, 113). Such doctrine must be opposed : not only is it inherently false, but it diverts the attention from the discipline of Christian living to useless 'speculations' (4) and 'vain discussion' (6), and its exponents flounder in ignorance both of their own premisses and of their statements about them.

8-11 The Place of the Law—Though the false d
teachers abuse the Jewish law, it has its own proper purpose. But the writer, in attempting to echo Paul's antithesis of law and gospel, misunderstands his attitude by asserting that the law was only for the grossly wicked, and therefore not for Christians, who did not commit these sins. According to Paul the law was a failure because not even the most righteous man could live up to it. The list of sins follows the second part of the Decalogue, but paraphrased into the grossest examples. **10. Sound doctrine**, meaning a system of belief, is confined to the Pastorals in the NT.

12-17 Persecutor turned Preacher—This digres- e
sion is suggested by 11, and is perhaps intended to revolve round and to illustrate the extract from some formulation of belief quoted in 15. **15. The saying is sure** (also in 3:1 ; 2 Tim. 2:11 ; Tit. 3:8) and the present fuller form (also in 4:9) precedes or follows the statement to which it refers. **And I am the foremost of sinners** (cf. 1 C. 15:9) seems too formalised for Paul (cf. Gealy), and **16** almost amounts to boasting. **17.** In this doxology the words **King of ages** and **only** are Jewish, **immortal** and **invisible** are Greek attributes of God.

18-20 Recapitulation of the Charge—The charge f
to Timothy is repeated, but the rest of the letter shows that it is not confined to opposing the false teaching (3f.). **18. The prophetic utterances** are the testimony of Christian prophets which accompanied Timothy's ordination (4:14). Ac. 13:1–3 provides an analogy. The metaphor of warfare (cf. 6:12 ; 2 Tim. 2:3f. ; 2 C. 10:3f. ; Eph. 6:10ff.) was familiar in philosophy and the pagan mysteries, and may have influenced Christianity ; but cf. also the 'War Scroll' of the Dead Sea sect. **20.** Hymenaeus (see on 2 Tim. 2:17f.) and Alexander, perhaps the coppersmith of 2 Tim. 4:14, in being **delivered to Satan** (the phrase is taken from 1 C. 5:5) were excommunicated, and perhaps also punished with some unspecified calamity, cf. Ananias and Sapphira, Ac. 5:1ff.

II 1-7 Christianity is for all Men—The thought g
flows from the necessity of all-embracing prayer to the universality of the Christian faith, and on to Paul as apostle of the Gentiles. The different names for prayers in **1** are 'liturgical pleonasm' (Easton, 120) and are not to be rigorously distinguished. **2** may repeat an actual Christian prayer (cf. Easton, 121). By **kings** successive Roman emperors are meant. Intercession for the Roman authorities will prove the loyalty of Christians (cf. Rom. 13:1–7 ; 1 Pet. 2:13f., 17*d* ; Tit. 3:1), enabling them to lead an undisturbed life 'in all godliness (= *pietas*) and gravity (= *gravitas*)' (RV), and is in accord with the universal scope of the gospel (4). **5f.** may be a citation or reminiscence of a primitive creed introduced here

74g because, as against gnostic notions, the mediator is a *man*. Note the striking juxtaposition of ' men ' and ' the man ' (*anarthrous* in the Greek). **7.** The words **For this I was appointed a preacher and apostle . . . a teacher** are repeated exactly in 2 Tim. 1:11. Note the telling position of the words in parenthesis after ' apostle ' ; but it is incredible that Paul should have written thus to his trusted lieutenant.

h **II 8-III 1a Conduct at public Worship**—The whole of this section directly concerns women, apart from **8**, which nevertheless, by laying it down that *males* alone should recite public prayers, is an integral part of it. **10-12.** The role of women is to perform good deeds, but in church they are to learn *in silence*—a sentiment entirely parallel with 1 C. 14:34f. That passage, however, is textually uncertain and may be a marginal gloss, and it also conflicts with 1 C. 11:2–16, which permits women to pray or prophesy in church ; if, however, it refers only to speaking with tongues, Paul is misunderstood in **11f. 13f.** The inferiority of women, disqualifying them from teaching or rule in the church, is inferred from Eve's creation after Adam and her deception by the serpent. In **15** the emphasis on child-bearing is directed against gnostic depreciation of marriage (4:3). The Greek plural (' they continue ') could refer to the children (Jeremias), but is more probably due to careless transition in thought from singular to plural. **III 1a.** Since the other instances of **the saying is sure** concern salvation the phrase goes with the preceding words ' Yet woman will be saved through bearing children ' (Parry, Lock, Falconer) rather than with 1*b* (AV, RV, RSV, Scott, Spicq, Jeremias). The poorly attested variant rendered by Easton, ' There is a popular saying ' (cf. Moffatt), referring to 1*b*, is due to the feeling that the solemn phrase was unsuitable.

75a **1b-13 Bishops and Deacons**—On **bishop** see introduction, 2*c*. The qualities required of a bishop (2–7) and of deacons (8–13) are partly identical. Some of the qualities of a bishop are repeated in Tit. 1:7f. (blameless, no drunkard, not greedy for gain, hospitable), and elders, like the bishop, must be blameless and married only once (Tit. 1:6*a* ; cf. also 6*b* with 1 Tim. 3:4). These qualities, which are not specially appropriate to office-bearers nor specifically Christian, are comparable with Hellenistic lists of virtues, e.g. of a king or a general (cf. Easton, 197–202). **2. married only once** (also 12 ; Tit. 1:6 ; cf. 1 Tim. 5:9 (of women)) implies either prohibition of digamy or refusal of office to those who, converted after marriage to an unbeliever, remarried (cf. 1 C. 7:15) rather than prohibition of the non-Christian practices of polygamy or concubinage or of remarriage after the divorce of a *Christian* partner, since a higher standard is required of office-bearers. **8.** Apart from Phil. 1:1, where the term (Greek ' servants ') may have a more general meaning, **deacons** are only named in the NT here and in 12, though the supposed origin of the diaconate is described in Ac. 6:1–6. In **11 the women** are more probably deacons' wives (in which case the ' deaconess ' Phoebe in Rom. 16:1 may be a ' servant ' of the church) than deaconesses, because the female counterparts of deacons in 1 Tim. 5:3–16 are the widows.

b **14-16 The Purpose of the Instructions**—They are to serve until Paul comes in person. In **15** the church **is the household of God** (cf. 1 Pet. 4:17), and **the pillar and bulwark of the truth,** a phrase only found here (but cf. 2 Tim. 2:19), ' the truth ' meaning objectively the Christian faith. **16.** This liturgical language leads on to a quotation from a hymn which crystallises **the mystery of our religion** (cf. 9, ' the mystery of the faith '), the essence of the revelation of divine truth in Christ. The incarnation is an epiphany ; **vindicated in the Spirit** is best explained of the resurrection (cf. Rom. 1:4, 8:11) ; **seen by angels** is difficult, but is best understood as referring to Christ's victory over spiritual forces (cf. e.g. 1 C. 2:8 ; Col. 1:20, 2:15).

875c **IV 1-5 Apostasy foretold**—That the expectation of apostasy and erroneous doctrines inspired by false spirits formed part of Christian apocalyptic is abundantly illustrated by the NT, e.g. Mk 13:22 ; 2 Th. 2:3–12 ; 1 Jn 2:18, 4:1ff. The writer regards himself as living in the ' later times ' foretold by the Spirit **expressly** (in scripture ?). In **3** depreciation of marriage and abstinence from certain foods are the characteristic features of the dualistic heresy, while the distinction between clean and unclean foods is also one of its Jewish elements. But the Essenes also (though not all, e.g. the Dead Sea sect) rejected marriage, and the Dead Sea scrolls point to some connection between gnosticism and certain kinds of unorthodox Judaism (cf. Bo Reicke in NTS 1 (1954–5), 137–41). **4** echoes the Christian view of food (cf. Mk 7:19*b* ; Ac. 10:15), but marriage is by implication included. **Thanksgiving** is essential for it is due to God and consecrates whatever food is received. In **5 the word of God** may refer to Gen. 1:31 ; more probably the verse means grace before food couched in biblical language.

d **IV 6-VI 2a Instructions in church Government**—This is a tolerably coherent though not very systematic section, in which the combination of more strictly personal advice to Timothy with instructions on church order is due to the author's endeavour to present his ecclesiastical aims in the guise of advice to Paul's ' true child in the faith '.

IV 6-16 The good Minister—These more personal injunctions form an apt introduction to what follows. In **6 these instructions** does not refer to 1–5 only, but to all which precedes, and resumes 1:3, 18, 3:14. **The faith** and **the good doctrine**, presupposing definite formulations of belief, are strongly contrasted with **godless and silly myths** (7) (cf. the RV rendering), for which see on 1:4. In **9 the saying** (cf. 1:15, 3:1) is the quotation in 8, which confirms the necessity of training in godliness (7*b*) by declaring its overwhelming superiority to athletic exercises. **10.** That the Christian life is a hard struggle is expressed in ' gymnastic imagery ' (Simpson) ; the motive power is the living God, and the prize his salvation. He is the potential Saviour of all men—that is his will (2:4)—but only believers will be saved. **11** continues personal advice to Timothy as to his conduct in commanding and teaching ' these things ' which have been laid upon him. In **12 let no one despise your youth** is perhaps inspired by 1 C. 16:11 ; for the flexibility of the meaning of ' youth ' see references in Gealy, 431. His youthfulness must be counteracted by his example even to people older than himself. **13. the public reading of scripture:** since the Greek has only ' reading ' (AV, RV), in addition to the OT, other writings also can be meant, such as letters (Eph. 3:4 ; Col. 4:16 ; 1 Th. 5:27) and ' memoirs of the apostles ' (Justin Martyr, *Apol.* I, 67). **Preaching** is literally ' exhortation ' (AV, RV) ; **teaching** includes instruction of catechumens. **14.** The **gift** is a special endowment received by Timothy through the laying-on of the hands of ' the elders ' (Greek ' presbytery ' (AV, RV)) to the accompaniment of **prophetic utterance** (cf. 1:18) whereby God's choice of him was made known. There can be no question here of Paul's initial choice of Timothy (Ac. 16:1–3), since the background of 1 Tim. and Tit. is most satisfactorily understood to be some system of church orders reflecting practice in the author's own day. Ordination by the laying-on of hands was adopted from Judaism (cf. E. Lohse, *Die Ordination im Spätjudentum und im NT* (1951)). The gist of **15** is ' practise what you preach ', and of **16** ' do not forget that your own soul also needs saving '.

e **V 1f. Old and Young**—Older members, both men and women, must be treated with the respect due to age, while younger members must be treated like (younger) brothers and sisters.

876 **3-16 Widows**—The care of widows enjoined in the

876a OT was continued by the church (Jas 1:27), but early presented a problem (Ac. 6:1). It is probable that the widows of Ac. 9:36ff. already formed not merely a group within the church but an embryonic order of church workers (cf. 36, 39) which is much more developed in 1 Tim. Roughly contemporary references to widows as a recognised body within the churches of Asia Minor occur in Ignatius (died *c.* 117), *Smyrn.* 13 and *Ep. to Polycarp* 4 ; cf. *Ep. of Polycarp* 4. Widows feature in the later church orders such as Hippolytus' *Apostolic Tradition*, and notably in the 3rd-cent. *Didascalia Apostolorum*, where there are both widows, who were pensioners and given to a life of prayer, and deaconesses who were church workers in the ministry of women corresponding to the deacons. In 1 Tim. the widows who both pray (5) and work (10) are virtually ' deaconesses in every regard but their name ' (Easton, 185). The whole section forms a unity whose purpose, however, is twofold : (i) to define who are **real widows** (3, 5, 16) and therefore deserving of respect and maintenance by the church ; (ii) to draw up rules for admission of certain of these to the list of widows who, in return for maintenance, do service to the church. The word ' widow ' has here three different meanings : (*a*) a woman whose husband has died, (*b*) a widow with no relatives to support her (' a real widow '), and (*c*) more technically, a member of the roll of widows. It cannot, of course, be supposed that only widows of sixty or over (9) qualified for *support*, for this would have ignored genuine cases of destitution among young widows.

(i) Two conditions concerning church support of widows are laid down. The first, in a positive form (4 ; cf. 16, which seems to concern a similar service possible for a younger widow ; cf. Scott 63) and a negative form (8), is that a widow with descendants must be supported by them ; the second (5f.) is that only widows who are devout and reject dissipation qualify for maintenance by the church.

(ii) Those to be enrolled must not only be ' real widows ' and devout, but also at least sixty years of age, not ' married more than once ' (see on 3:2), and with a reputation for good works (9f.). **11-13.** The objection to the enrolment of younger widows is due to bitter experience, for some have ' violated their first pledge ' (to Christ) by remarrying and by unseemly conduct. But older widows are not liable to the same temptations. **14.** It is therefore better for the younger ones to remarry and live a normal family life, an attitude which is un-Pauline (cf. 1 C. 7:25–31) in that the continuance of the world is taken for granted, but fully in line with the writer's anti-asceticism (4:3).

b **17-22 Elders**—It is the chief business of the elders to rule, and those who do it well and also engage in voluntary preaching and teaching deserve more pay than others. That **honour** does mean payment is clear from 18, where **the scripture** refers not only to the first quotation from Dt. 25:4, but also to the second which is exactly Lk. 10:7. The former passage is quoted in 1 C. 9:9, and a little later (1 C. 9:14) Paul alludes to a saying of ' the Lord ' similar to the second. But our writer goes further, and in **18b** equates the traditional word of Jesus with scripture. It is even possible that he knew Luke's Gospel, in which case he regards it as scripture equally with the OT. **19** refers to Dt. 19:15 (cf. Mt. 18:16 ; 2 C. 13:1). Nothing illustrates more unambiguously than 19f. the eminence of the position attributed to Timothy : he rebukes even elders. **21. These rules** are what has just been said. In **22 the laying on of hands** probably does not allude to the restoration of penitents, for which the rite was first used in the 3rd cent. (see Spicq, Jeremias), but to ordination of elders, despite the difficulty that in 4:14 it is *elders* who ordain ; perhaps this is implied here, with Timothy in charge.

c **23-25 Sundry Remarks**—**23** is another tilt at gnostic asceticism suggested by the end of 22. **24,** with its moralising on **sins**, also follows on 22, and is 87
balanced by **25** on **good deeds.**

VI 1-2a Slaves and Masters—Christian slaves must d
regard respect for their (heathen) masters as a means of upholding the honour of God and the gospel, while slaves with Christian masters must not take advantage of the fact, for although they are their brethren in Christ, they are still their masters in the world, and deserve all the more respect just because they *are* brethren.

2b-10 False Teaching and Money—After a re- e
minder to Timothy in 2*b* of all the instructions he has been given (literally ' these things '), we have another warning against the false teachers (3–5) whose wrong attitude to money leads to a contrast between false and true riches (6–10).

The language of 3–5 resembles that of 1:3–7. In **3 the sound words of our Lord Jesus Christ** are church tradition through which Christ speaks (see O. Cullmann, *The Early Church* (1956), 55ff.) and so are the same as **the teaching** etc. **5.** One of the effects of the false teaching is the erroneous notion that **godliness** (or religion) **is a means of gain** ; and so it is (6 ; RSV obscures the substantial repetition of the phrase : ' and godliness is a great means of gain ', cf. RV), though the gain is not money but **contentment** (the word is the Stoic ' self-sufficiency '). **7f.** The religious man is not concerned with material goods, which are only worldly appendages, except for the necessities of food and clothing. **9.** The disasters which overtake the covetous prove the truth of the proverb quoted in **10a** (for parallels in Greek (and Latin) writers see Lock, 69f., Dibelius, 66, Simpson, 86) ; **10b** love of money may lead to the worst of disasters, apostasy.

11-16 Challenge to Timothy—This section which, f
with its noble doxology, would have formed a splendid conclusion to the letter, appears to break the connection between the preceding section and 17–19, but this is typical of the indifferent arrangement of the document. **11.** The **man of God** (an OT expression, e.g. Dt. 33:1 ; 1 Sam. 2:27 ; 1 Kg. 12:22) is intended to be Timothy as representing responsible church leaders (cf. 2 Tim. 3:17). The language of **12a** is athletic (cf. 2 Tim. 4:7). **The good confession** is acknowledgment of the Lordship of Jesus (Rom. 10:9; 1 C. 12:3 ; Phil. 2:11). When was it made? Surely, as customarily, at baptism ; but some supporters of Pauline authorship (Jeremias, Simpson) suggest Timothy's ordination (Ac. 16:3 ?). But the reference to being called to eternal life is unsuitable for this. On the other hand 2 Tim. 3:15 may imply that Timothy was baptised in infancy, and so could not have made a confession. **13.** The mention of Christ **before Pontius Pilate** is a clear echo of a credal statement, adapted to the context by the employment, in **the good confession**, of the phrase used to denote Timothy's confession—like master like servant. In **14 the commandment** has a wide reference, being the same as ' the faith ' in 12. **The appearing** (' epiphany ') is here a substitute (cf. 2 Th. 2:8 ; 2 Tim. 1:10, 4:1, 8 ; Tit. 2:13) for *parousia* which elsewhere in the NT is the word for the apocalyptic coming of Christ. **15f.** The doxology, which adds to that in 1:17 the Greek epithet **blessed** (cf. 1:11) and the Jewish titles at the end of 15 (cf. 2 Mac. 12:15, 13:4 ; Rev. 17:14, 19:16), is couched in the language of Hellenistic Judaism and at least reflects a liturgical formula.

17-19 True Riches—Logically this follows 6–10, to g
which it is akin in dealing with ' the rich ', but the rich are an already existing group in the church, who are here advised of the Christian use of wealth. They are not attacked, but reminded of the true riches in the world to come which will be their reward for being **rich in good deeds** in this.

20f. Final Charge—Timothy is reminded of the h
essence of his instructions : to preserve the true faith when assailed by false teaching. **Contradictions of**

876h **what is falsely called knowledge** means the various points at which the false teaching opposes the Christian faith. This is the only occurrence in the Pastorals of the term *gnōsis* (knowledge), which aptly characterises the heresy. The attempt to see in the ' contradictions ' (Greek ' antitheses ') the book of *Antitheses* between law and gospel written by the heretic Marcion is untenable, because Marcion wrote later (*c.* A.D. 150) than the Pastorals, and his teaching was anti-Jewish, whereas the false teaching attacked in the Pastorals has a Jewish element **21b. Grace be with you:** this short benediction (cf. 2 Tim. 4:22) is certainly Pauline (Col. 4:18), but since ' you ' is plural it hardly fits a letter purporting to be addressed to Timothy alone ; it does, however, fit the contents, which are of wider application, and has been adopted for this reason.

II TIMOTHY

877a Paul, now imprisoned (1:16, 2:9) in Rome and expecting death by execution very soon, renews his exhortations to Timothy at Ephesus (1:18) · let him take courage from his own sufferings for the gospel in his struggle to maintain the truth in the face of heresy and moral corruption, and be sure to hand it on in turn to trustworthy ministers Despite the note of farewell, Timothy is finally bidden to hasten to him with Mark.

b **I 1f. Salutation—1 Paul, an apostle of Christ Jesus by the will of God,** is identical with 2 C. 1:1 and Col. 1:1, in which Timothy is joint author with Paul, and is chosen here for that reason (Easton). The verse repeats in different words the sense of 1 Tim. 1:1, and 2*b* repeats 1 Tim. 1:2*b*

3-5 Thanksgiving for Timothy's Faith—Paul, remembering Timothy's distress at their last parting, and longing to be reunited with his ' beloved child ' (2), is comforted by the conviction that he possesses the same faith which his grandmother and mother had before him. His mother is mentioned in Ac. 16:1 as a convert from Judaism.

c **I 6-II 13 The Call to Suffer**—Despite his undoubted faith Timothy needs to bestir himself to face his difficulties as a Christian leader without timidity and hesitation, and may take courage from the heavy trials his own teacher has to face.

I 6-14 Exhortation to Timothy—6. rekindle: better ' stir up ' (AV, RV). **The laying on of my hands** has been explained as confirmation (F. H. Chase, *Confirmation in the Apostolic Age* (1913), 35ff.), but the usual reference to ordination is preferable despite the apparent disagreement with 1 Tim. 4:14. **8.** The exhortation to Timothy to take his **share of suffering for the gospel** leads in **9f.** to a quotation or possibly adaptation of a Christian hymn. **10. Appearing,** a term current in Hellenistic religion and emperor worship and borrowed by Christianity in an apocalyptic sense (see on 1 Tim. 6:14) only here denotes the Incarnation. **12. I am not ashamed** despite my sufferings, so why should you be? **What has been entrusted to me** (lit. ' my deposit ') is the Pauline interpretation of the gospel which Timothy in his turn is to guard as ' the good deposit ' (so Greek in 14).

d **15-18 Disloyal and loyal Friends**—Possibly these verses form part of a genuine Pauline note (cf. Harrison, Falconer), or else record authentic tradition. The men in **15** are unknown (Hermogenes appears in *Acts of Paul* (M. R. James, *The Apocryphal NT* (1945), 272f.) ; also Onesiphorus (16), ibid., as Paul's host at Iconium) ; for **the household of Onesiphorus** cf. 4:19. That Onesiphorus is only mentioned in connection with his household in both places may, but need not, mean that he was now dead.

e **II 1-7 Renewed Encouragement to endure—2,** a very clear statement of the principle of transmission of tradition from one generation to another, skilfully combines two ideas : (*a*) the recipient has received the (Pauline) tradition indirectly by succession ' through ' (Greek *dia*) **many witnesses** between Paul's time and his own, and (*b*) Timothy received it directly from Paul **before** (Greek *dia*) **many witnesses** (at his ordination). In **3-6** the admonition to perseverance in Christian leadership is driven home by the examples of the good soldier, athlete, and farmer which the Lord will enable him to understand (7). 877e

8-13 Fellowship with Christ's Sufferings—Moreover, there is the promise of reward with Christ for suffering for the gospel (12*a*). In **8 Jesus Christ, risen from the dead, descended from David** is perhaps from an early creed (cf. Rom. 1:3f.) with the clauses in logical instead of chronological order. **9f.** Paul repeats the example of his own sufferings, and then quotes, with the usual formula **the saying is sure,** an extract (11–13*a*, or perhaps only 11–12*a*) from a baptismal hymn (cf. Rom. 6:8).

II 14-IV 5 False Teachers—The danger from false and corrupting doctrine is dealt with under various aspects in this long section which is the core of the letter. What precedes prepares for it (see on 2:14), and its warnings and advice are vitally urgent because the apostle is about to leave the scene (4:6ff.). f

II 14-19 Advice for Ministers—14. them (not in the Greek) means other ministers who are to receive from Timothy the same encouragement as he has received from Paul, in particular the substance of 8–13 (' these things ', AV, RV is better than **this**). **Disputing about words** (cf. 1 Tim. 6:4), **godless chatter** (16; 1 Tim. 6:20), and **their talk** (17) are all descriptions of the gnostic heresy (1 Tim. 6:20) also attacked in 1 Tim., with special emphasis on the fruitless and pernicious disputes both about its own terminology and terms like ' knowledge ' (cf. 1 Tim. 6:20) and ' resurrection ' (18 ; see below). The remedy is not to embroil oneself in discussions with the offenders, but to present the positive **word of truth** (15). **17f.** Hymenaeus (1 Tim. 1:20) and Philetus are examples of those who retained the term **resurrection** only as an accommodation, rejecting its fundamental Christian content and applying it to post-baptismal life in the Spirit (cf. Rom. 6:3ff.). **19.** Yet **God's firm foundation,** the church, is immovable and bears his **seal** or inscription (cf. Rev. 21:14) ; the first quotation is from Num. 16:5 ; for the second cf. Num. 16:26.

20-26 Personal Advice—The **great house** in **20** forms a link with 19 and continues the metaphor of the church as a building. The ignoble utensils (**vessels** gives too restricted a meaning) from which Timothy must purify himself are the false teachers, who must be expelled. But the metaphor is confused. **22a.** The **youthful** (cf. 1 Tim. 4:12) **passions** are the **controversies** (1 Tim. 6:4) of **23,** in which the heretics indulge. The advice in the preceding paragraph is thus repeated : the remedy is the practice of the Christian virtues (22*b*), and **24-6** the adoption of a patient and gentle attitude to the opponents who may thereby be led to repentance and so **escape** (lit. ' come to their senses ', after their intoxication with error) from captivity to the devil. g

III 1-9 Prophecy of the last Days—The last days will produce a final upsurge of evil before the Parousia. ' The conditions of this coming time are described by way of prediction, but the writer is plainly dealing with the situation of his own day ' (Scott, 117). The vices mentioned in 2–4 are typical of Hellenistic lists (for similar lists of virtues see on 1 Tim. 3:1*b*–13), are applied to the heretics, and constitute a much fuller variant of the same theme as in 1 Tim. 4:1f. **2. lovers of money:** cf. 1 Tim. 6:10 ; Tit. 1:11. **At 5** the writer abandons conventionalities and brings genuine charges against the false teachers. They hypocritically masquerade as orthodox Christians, but in actual fact they have long given up (**denying** is a perfect tense in the Greek) any claim that Christianity is a motive power in their lives (Falconer, less 878a

878a probably, explains ' power ' as Christ's resurrection ; cf. Gealy). **6f.** To some of them **weak women** (' silly women ' (AV, RV) is a more expressive rendering of the Greek diminutive of contempt) fall victims, corrupted by a life of dissipation and incapable of distinguishing fraud from genuine Christianity, **the truth. 8f.** These opponents, however, will ultimately be no more successful than Pharaoh's magicians in trying to imitate Moses (Exod. 7:11ff.) : truth will out. The names occur in late Jewish sources.

b **10-13 Paul's Example**—The true servants of God are bound to suffer, but let Timothy be encouraged by the example of others, especially that of Paul (cf. 1:12). The mention of the first three scenes of Paul's persecutions in **11** appears to be a purely literary allusion to Ac. (13:50, 14:5f., 19), although **what persecutions I endured** could have a wider reference (cf. 2 C. 11:23ff.). In **13** the word for **impostors** means ' magicians '—a reminder of the comparison of the false teachers with the Egyptian sorcerers in 8.

14-17 Encouragement of the Scriptures—15. A further source of strength is **the sacred writings** themselves, the Jewish scriptures on which Timothy was nurtured from infancy, and which if interpreted aright, i.e. from the Christian standpoint, provide instruction which will lead to salvation. ' Sacred writings ' is sometimes extended to include Christian literature (Scott, Gealy), but improbably, because it is the regular name for the OT in Greek-speaking Judaism. In **14 from whom** (plural) is intended to include others besides Paul, especially Lois and Eunice (1:5), among Timothy's instructors. In **16**, note and RV are preferable, the meaning being that every OT book also possesses its own practical value for the minister and his work as ' the man of God ' (17 ; 1 Tim. 6:11).

c **IV 1-5 Final Exhortation**—There is little time left for Paul to say more and the imminent crisis demands of Timothy utmost loyalty and perseverance in his calling. In **1 to judge the living and the dead** reflects a liturgical formula, cf. Ac. 10:42 ; 1 Pet. 4:5. The whole verse constitutes a very strong adjuration. **2.** First and foremost comes the preaching of the word, all the more pressing as the time is coming (and by implication is already present) when people will refuse to listen to it, because they have ' itching ears ' and have recourse to teachers who will tell them something new (cf. 3:7, and the Athenians in Ac. 17:21) and regale them with myths (1 Tim. 1:4, 4:7 ; Tit. 1:14). **5** sums up the only attitude possible for Timothy, a final reminder all the more urgent in view of 6f.

d **6-8 Paul's Departure and Reward**—The rest of this chapter provides most of the material for attempts to distinguish Pauline fragments in the letter. **6.** Paul's **departure** is imminent ; his blood is already on the point of being poured out as a libation to God (the same kind of sacrifice as in Phil. 2:17). The athletic metaphors of *7a* (cf. 1 Tim. 6:12) are continued in 8 in the thought of the victor's wreath.

9-18 Paul and his Friends—9 If Timothy is to come to Paul as soon as possible, what is the point of the detailed instructions he has been given in this letter ? **10. Demas** is in very different character from Col. 4:14 ; Phm. 24. **11** shows a different (and later) state of affairs from Col. 4:10–14 ; Phm. 23f., where Luke is one of several companions of Paul, among them Mark. **12 Tychicus** is to be succeeded by Mark as Paul's companion (Eph 6:21 ; Col. 4:7). **13.** The travelling-cloak, needed by Paul because of the approach of winter (21), may have been left at Troas on his departure for Assos (Ac. 20:13 ; Dibelius) **The books** are papyrus rolls, of unknown content ; **the parchments** are either vellum rolls included among ' the books ', or pieces containing legal documents (Scott, Easton). **Alexander the coppersmith** in **14f.** could be the same person as in 1 Tim. 1:20.

e **16-18** are problematic, and may be taken in either of two ways : (1) The **first defence** is the trial which ended a first Roman imprisonment with acquittal and made possible further missionary work before a second arrest. (2) Preferably, it is the preliminary investigation (*prima actio*) which went favourably. But it remains uncertain whether Paul's outlook is optimistic or pessimistic. If the former, the reference to preaching to the Gentiles in 17 could be prospective, but would be inconsistent with 6ff. Probably the intention in the context is rather to show that deliverance from death (*17b*) was only temporary : ' the time of my departure has come ' (6) ; what Paul looks forward to is *final* deliverance into Christ's kingdom (18, cf. 8). If so, the ' Gentiles ' must be the court which examined the case. 878e

19-22 Personal Greetings—19. For **the household of Onesiphorus** see on 1:16. In **20** both **Erastus** (Ac. 19:22 ; Rom. 16:23) and **Trophimus** (Ac. 20:4, 21:29) are known, but not the incidents mentioned. The Roman Christians in **21** are all unknown, unless Linus, as Irenaeus (*c.* 190) states, became the first bishop of Rome after Peter's death. In **22a your** is singular, referring to Timothy alone, in *22b* **you** is plural, including the persons named in 19 (see on 1 Tim. 6:21*b*) f

TITUS

Titus, left in Crete to build up the defective life of the churches there, is instructed in the qualifications necessary for ministers who will have to teach sound doctrine and confute the many false teachers who threaten the stability of believers. He is told what advice to give Christians for life both within the church and in the world outside, and is encouraged in his task by the reminder of the manifestation of God's goodness and grace in Jesus Christ. 879a

I 1-4 Salutation—This greeting is more formal even than those in 1 and 2 Tim., and strangely elaborate as a personal salutation ; but it is intended as an introductory definition of Pauline Christianity as the divinely ordained means to lead men by faith to the salvation promised ' ages ago ' (2) by God, because he has now revealed his word (3, **in** is not in the Greek) through it. **1. servant of God** is un-Pauline (cf. Jas 1:1). **3. God our Saviour :** see on 1 Tim. 1:1. **4. my true child in a common faith :** cf. 1 Tim. 1:2. b

5-9 The Appointment of Elders—In **5f.** Titus is reminded that he was left in Crete for the express purpose of appointing elders in the local churches which, by being properly organised, should be better able to deal with false doctrine (10ff.). The three qualities desired in elders (6) are included in the longer list required of the bishop in 1 Tim. 3:2ff. (see notes). The abrupt transition to **the** (so Greek) **bishop in 7** raises the question of the relation between him and the elders. The marked similarities between 7–9 and 1 Tim. 3:2–7 may be due to both having been taken from, or at least based on, some church order(s) dealing with bishops (so Falconer ; to Moffatt the verses here are merely an awkward intrusion) ; and **insubordinate** in 10 forms an excellent connection with 6, which ends with the same word. The writer himself seems to equate ' bishop ' and ' elder ' (see introduction, 2*c*). c

10-16 False Teaching—The heretics whom Titus must ' rebuke sharply ' (13) are described in much the same language as in 1 Tim. 1:3–7, 4:1–3, 7, 6:3–5, 20 ; 2 Tim. 2:14–18, 3:2–9, 13, 4:3f., so that the same sort of heresy seems to have flourished both in Asia Minor and in Crete. That this epistle alone (14) calls the myths (1 Tim 1:4, 4:7 ; 2 Tim. 4:4) **Jewish**, and alone (10) distinguishes **the circumcision party** among the false teachers, does not affect this impression, for the heresy in 1 and 2 Tim. was a form of Judaising gnosticism, and ' the circumcision party ' would be an appropriate name for d

879d unorthodox Jewish Christians who would especially favour the Jewish elements of the heresy. The quotation in **12** is a Greek hexameter line probably attributed here to the Cretan Epimenides (6th cent. B.C.). The reputation of the Cretans was such that 'to Cretise' became a synonym for lying. The proverbial saying is made to fit the false teachers fairly aptly because they lie in propagating false doctrine 'for base gain' (11). **14.** The **commands of men** are such things as prohibition of marriage and dietary laws (1 Tim. 4:3), to which is opposed in **15** the probably proverbial saying **to the pure all things are pure** (cf. Lk. 11:41 ; Rom. 14:14, 20). **16.** In the heretics' claim **to know God** we have allusion to 'the gnostic watchcry' (Easton ; cf. 1 Tim. 6:20 ; 1 Jn 2:4).

e **II 1-10 Christian Conduct in the Church**—Titus is bidden to inculcate conduct which **befits** (conforms to) **sound doctrine** (1:9 ; 1 Tim. 1:10 ; 2 Tim. 4:3) in five groups within the church : old men, old women, young women, younger men, slaves. The passage follows the pattern of Eph. 5:22–6:9 and Col. 3:18–4:1 (cf. 1 Tim. 5:1–6:2 ; 1 Pet. 2:18–3:7), but also contains marked resemblances to the ethical lists in 1:6–8 and 1 Tim. 3:1–13. **4f.** It is the business of the older women to train the younger ones ; **7f.** Titus as a young man himself is to be an example to his contemporaries.

11-15 The Ground of this Conduct—11f. Christians, whatever their station in life, must aim at the highest moral conduct because of the revelation, in the Incarnation, of God's grace which itself trains us **to renounce irreligion** etc. ; **13** moreover, we are inspired by the advent hope and **14** by the conviction of final redemption from all impurity.

11 gives the substance of **the doctrine of God our Saviour** (10), i.e. the Christian faith. In **13 our great God and Saviour Jesus Christ** is almost certainly correct (as against AV, RSV*n*) from the point of view both of Greek grammar and pagan religious usage, here imitated, in which the combination 'God and Saviour' was a commonplace (see Lock, Easton, Simpson, Gealy). **14. a people of his own :** the church has replaced Israel as God's chosen people (Exod. 19:5 ; Dt. 14:2 ; 1 Pet. 2:9). In **15** Titus, in discharging his commission **with all authority,** must let no-one **disregard** him (because of his youth, cf. 1 Tim. 4:12).

f **III 1f. Christian Conduct in the World—1.** The writer summarises the Christian attitude to the state ; cf. the longer treatments of the theme in Rom. 13:1–7 ; 1 Pet. 2:13–17), and **2** to non-Christians in general.

3-8a The old and the new Life—In **3** recollection of the vices of their own pre-Christian days is given as a reason for the display of gentleness and courtesy to their still-pagan neighbours by those who have been saved. The formula **the saying is sure** in 8*a* 879f (see on 1 Tim. 1:15) refers to a liturgical quotation which constitutes part of 4–7. The title **God our Saviour** in **4**, being characteristic of the Pastorals (1 Tim. 1:1, 2:3, 4:10 ; Tit. 1:3, 2:10), rules out this verse as part of the quotation. If 5–7 are taken as quoted from a baptismal liturgy, the quasi-Paulinism here does not come from the author himself, as it does elsewhere, but is an indication of the background of theological thought presupposed by the Pastorals. **5a** preserves the Pauline antithesis of works and grace, but in **5b** the view of baptism is un-Pauline if the meaning is that it is baptism in itself which effects **regeneration and renewal** by the Holy Spirit. That this is the meaning is borne out by the total absence in **7** of *faith* as that whereby we are justified (Rom. 5:1), despite the superficial resemblance to Rom. 3:24 of **so that we might be justified by his grace.** In our passage justification is obtained through the operation in baptism of the Spirit as the agent of Christ (6, cf. Jn 15:26 ; Ac. 2:33) ; to Paul justification is through the redemptive death of Christ (Rom. 3:24f.), and baptism is the symbolic authentication of the new life of faith in Christ (Rom. 6:3–11 ; Col. 2:12).

8b-11 Final Advice—8b. Titus must press home g **these things** (referring to 1–7), so that Christians will live out their profession in good deeds. **9.** Cf. 1 Tim. 1:4, 7, 6:4 ; 2 Tim. 2:23, and for **the law** cf. 1:10, 14. In **10 factious** (Greek *hairetikos*) is almost, if not quite, 'heretical', referring back to 9.

12-15 A personal Note and Greetings—The verses h may either come from a Pauline note (though the identity of **do your best to come** in **12** with 2 Tim. 4:9, cf. 21, arouses suspicion), or be written up from traditions otherwise unknown. While Tychicus and Apollos are well known, Artemas and Zenas appear nowhere else in the NT. **15.** With **grace be with you all** cf. 1 Tim. 6:21 ; 2 Tim. 4:22.

Bibliography—COMMENTARIES : M. Dibelius, HNT (1955[3]) ; B. S. Easton (1948) ; R. Falconer (1937) ; F. D. Gealy, IB xi (1955) ; D. Guthrie (1957) ; J. Jeremias, NTD (1953[6]) ; W. Lock, ICC (1924) ; M. Meinertz (1931[4]) ; J. Parry (1920) ; E. F. Scott, Moffatt Comm. (1936) ; E. K. Simpson (1954) ; C. Spicq, EBib. (1947).

OTHER LITERATURE : Articles in Dictionaries (especially *diaconos* in TWNT II, 88ff., *episcopos*, ibid., 604ff.) ; Discussions in Introductions to NT ; H. von Campenhausen, *Kirchliches Amt und geistliche Vollmacht in den ersten drei Jahrhunderten* (1953) ; P. N. Harrison, *The Problem of the Pastoral Epistles* (1921) ; F. J. A. Hort, *The Christian Ecclesia* (1914) ; B. H. Streeter, *The Primitive Church* (1930).

HEBREWS

BY F. F. BRUCE

880a The Epistle to the Hebrews differs from the other NT epistles in that, while it ends like a letter, it does not begin like one, and lacks the customary opening salutation with the names of the writer and addressees.

Its traditional title 'To the Hebrews' (Gr. *pros Hebraious*) goes back at least to the last quarter of the 2nd cent. A.D. Whether 'Hebrews' was intended as synonym for 'Jews', or to denote a particular class of Jews (cf. Ac. 6:1; Phil. 3:5), the title was probably an inference from the contents, which were regarded as being specially appropriate to Jewish Christians who were in danger of abandoning their Christianity and reverting to Judaism.

b **Authorship**—The epistle is quoted by Clement of Rome (*c.* A.D. 95), who, if he had any inkling of its authorship, gives no hint of it. But he does not quote it as Paul's, whereas he is glad to invoke Paul's authority when he cites admittedly Pauline epistles. In the 2nd cent. traces of our epistle appear in the *Epistle of Barnabas*, in '2 Clement', and possibly in Justin Martyr. Tertullian ascribes it to Barnabas, apparently in accordance with a tradition which he had received; this ascription may be due to an idea that the 'word of exhortation' (Heb. 13:22) would have come fittingly from the 'son of exhortation' (Ac. 4:36, RV). Since the author appears to have been a second-generation Christian (Heb. 2:3), the Barnabas ascription seems unlikely; but at least it was not handicapped by having a Pauline ascription to contend with. As late as the 4th cent. the Pauline ascription was resisted in the west; thus 'Ambrosiaster' (*c.* 375) did not include Heb. in the Pauline epistles on which he wrote commentaries, and to him it is always an anonymous work (A. Souter, *A Study of Ambrosiaster* (1905), 171f.). Pelagius regarded it as Pauline, though perhaps not on the same canonical plane as the thirteen epistles bearing Paul's name, on which he wrote commentaries. Jerome and Augustine treated it as Pauline, and the Pauline ascription persisted thereafter in the west until the 16th cent.

c But if the west was slow in making up its mind about the Pauline authorship, it was otherwise in the east, where the epistle was attributed to Paul from about the middle of the 2nd cent. Clement of Alexandria and Origen had sufficient sense of style, it is true, to feel uneasy about the Pauline ascription. Clement (*c.* 180) reports a belief that Luke translated it into Greek from the original language in which Paul wrote it (meaning Hebrew or Aramaic); but Heb. is patently no translation, but an original Greek composition. It is noteworthy, however, that the style of the epistle is closer to Luke's than to any other NT writer's. Origen (*c.* 230) ordinarily acquiesces in the Pauline ascription which he had received at Alexandria, but he knows that it is not at all certain: 'God only knows who really wrote it', he admits in a more critical moment.

d None of the suggestions about the author's identity which have been made in more recent times can claim to be more than guesses. Luther's suggestion of Apollos still enjoys considerable support, largely because of affinities which are detected between some phases of the argument and the Platonising tendencies of Alexandrian Judaism.

880d The author appears to have been a second-generation Christian (2:3), well versed in the study and interpretation of the LXX, master of a fine rhetorical style (quite different from Paul's)—we might say 'a learned man, . . . mighty in the scriptures' (cf. Ac. 18:24, RV). He was probably a Hellenist, inheriting the outlook of the Jerusalem Hellenists of Ac. 6–8, 11:19ff., the associates of Stephen and Philip, pioneers in the Gentile mission.

e The recipients of the letter certainly knew who the writer was (cf. 13:18f., 22ff.). Their own identity must be deduced from the contents of the work as much as his. They were Christians in danger of abandoning their pristine faith because of persecution and disappointment and perhaps also under the influence of strange teaching not unlike that refuted by Paul in Col. From the author's confidence that, even in their wavering, they will admit the authority of the OT, we may judge that they were converts from Judaism. Had they been Gentile Christians who were inclined to lapse, their only response to such an argument as 'Now if perfection had been attainable through the Levitical priesthood . . .' (7:11) would have been: 'We never thought it was!' We may think of them as converts from Diaspora Judaism, perhaps resident in Rome or its neighbourhood (a probable, but not certain, inference from 13:24*b*), who were strongly tempted to discontinue their Christian fellowship with its forward-looking challenge and slip back into the Judaism they had left. The author impresses upon them the finality of the Christian revelation, which is as substance to shadow when compared with the Judaism it has superseded; the imminent disappearance of the old sacrificial order; the horror of the irretrievable sin of apostasy; the blessedness of Christian hope. The general line of interpretation adopted in the following commentary owes much to that so persuasively expounded in W. Manson, *The Epistle to the Hebrews* (1951).

f We may describe the treatise as a written sermon (cf. 13:22) with an epistolary ending. From Dr Aileen Guilding comes the interesting suggestion that it may have been a sermon with special reference to Pentecost, since some of the most prominent OT passages used in it (especially Gen. 14 and Ps. 110) were prescribed for the season of Pentecost in the triennial lectionary of Palestinian and western synagogues (JTS, N.S. 3 (1952), 53). In any case, our author's use of the OT reflects a creative exegetical system. Noteworthy too is the way in which he repeatedly begins with a passage in the Psalms, treats it with a new Christian insight, then interprets in the light of that a relevant passage from the OT narrative books, and applies the resultant lesson to his readers' situation. His concentration on the OT description of the wilderness tabernacle and its ritual, rather than on the contemporary Temple cult at Jerusalem, when he undertakes to demonstrate the obsolete character of the Jewish ceremonial, may remind us of Stephen's sharp contrast between the tabernacle and the Temple (Ac. 7:44ff.); it also suggests strongly that the situation to which he was addressing himself was not a Palestinian one.

g If the situation envisaged in this epistle—that in which a group of Jewish Christians found themselves

880g in the seventh decade of the 1st cent.—is not likely to recur exactly at this later date, the epistle retains its abiding value for Christian faith. Its warnings are salutary whenever Christians are tempted by 'an evil heart of unbelief, in falling away from the living God' (3:12, RV); and among its positive contributions to the strengthening of Christian faith we may include its insistence on the finality of Christianity, the immutable trustworthiness of Christ, the perfection of his self-offering, and our consequent free access to God; the necessity of constantly pressing on in the steps of 'the pioneer and perfecter of our faith' till we reach our goal in the eternal city where he is exalted as priest-king for ever; together with its encouragement to have our hopes and purposes bound up with him and to preserve a proper detachment from mere tradition, from the external accidents of religion, and from all transitory institutions which sooner or later will be shaken into nothingness. Its lesson might almost be summed up in Herbert Butterfield's words: 'Hold to Christ, and for the rest be totally uncommitted.'

881a **I 1-II 18 The Finality of Christianity**

I 1-4 God's Final Revelation in his Son—In 1f. the progressive character of the biblical revelation is clearly set forth: the earlier stages by which **God spoke of old to our fathers by the prophets** were partial and piecemeal; the latter stage, in which he **has spoken to us by a Son,** is that of fulfilment. **2. in these last days:** an OT phrase indicating the time of fulfilment (cf. e.g. Isa. 2:2). The Son's pre-eminence is described partly in terms of the OT personification of divine Wisdom (2–4); cf. Prov. 8:22ff., where Wisdom is God's assessor at creation, and Wis. 7:26, where Wisdom is an 'effulgence (Gr. *apaugasma*, used here in 3) of everlasting light'. Similar language is used of Christ in Jn 1:1ff.; Col. 1:15ff. **3b** introduces the main themes of the epistle. **When he had made purification for sins** expresses the work of Christ in priestly language; **he sat down at the right hand of the Majesty on high** emphasises the finality of his work. The enthronement of Christ at God's right hand—an echo of the words addressed to the Davidic king in Ps. 110:1—is a regular feature of the apostolic preaching (cf. Ac. 2:33ff.; Rom. 8:34; 1 Pet. 3:22; Rev. 3:21*b*); but in Heb. it is viewed especially as evidence of the perfect and unrepeatable nature of his sacrifice on his people's behalf, and so of the finality of Christianity. Moreover, *sitting* in the presence of God was a royal prerogative of Davidic kings (2 Sam. 7:18; Ezek. 44:3). **4.** The significance of his superiority to angels, both by his title 'Son' and by his exaltation to the throne of God, appears in 2:3f., where the law, mediated through angels, is declared to be manifestly inferior to the gospel, inaugurated by the Son. **superior:** Gr. *kreittōn*, used 13 times in Heb. of Christ and his new order in comparison with what went before.

b **5-14 A Greater than Angels**—The Son's superiority to angels is established by a catena of OT quotations. Some of these had already become current as messianic 'testimonies'; others are probably used thus for the first time by our author. **5a** is a quotation from Ps. 2:7 (an oracle addressed to a Davidic king at his enthronement). **Thou art my Son** formed part of the heavenly allocution at Jesus' baptism (Mk 1:11). Ps. 2 is applied to the expected Davidic Messiah in Ps. Sol. 17:26; for its Christian use cf. Ac. 4:25f., 13:33; Rev. 12:5. **5b** is a quotation from 2 Sam. 7:14, where God gives promises to David regarding his son who is to build a temple; the words are applied to the Davidic Messiah in a fragmentary messianic anthology from Qumrân Cave 4; cf. J. M. Allegro, 'Further Messianic References in Qumrân Literature', JBL 75 (1956), 174ff. For the Christian belief that the 'holy and sure blessings of David' were fulfilled in Jesus cf. Ac. 13:34. **6** is a quotation from Dt. 32:43, LXX, which has a longer text—now attested in a Qumrân fragment—than MT; cf. Ps. 97:7. In Dt. it is God who is to be worshipped at the completion of his work; here **when he brings the first-born into the world** is our author's interpretation, perhaps reflecting a 'Son of man' Christology (cf. 2:5ff.), in which the heavenly Man, by divine decree, receives the homage of the angels at his appearing. **7** is a quotation from Ps. 104:4, LXX (MT means that winds speed on God's errands and fire renders him service). **8.** But the Son is granted a higher dignity, as the citation of Ps. 45:6 shows; he is addressed as 'God', his throne is everlasting, and his righteous government has won him supremacy over all other rulers. RSV*n* 'God is thy throne', as though the Son were upheld by God, is an improbable rendering; whatever be the merits of the RSV rendering of Ps. 45:6 ('Your divine throne endures for ever and ever'), our author certainly understood 'God' as a vocative, expressing a title of the Son (cf. Isa. 9:6, 'Mighty God'). **9. God . . . has anointed thee with the oil of gladness:** probably a reference to Jesus' endowment with the messianic dignity, which confers on him a rank above all other rulers. **thy comrades:** probably angel-rulers (but see note on 3:14, §882*b*). In 10–12 the language of Ps. 102:25–7, celebrating God's creative power and contrasting his eternity with the transience of earth and heaven, is applied to the Son, as the one 'through whom also he created the world' (2). **10. Lord** comes from LXX; it is absent from MT. The angels were but spectators of the creation (Job 38:7); the Son was the agent in the work.

13. Sit at my right hand: this invitation, already alluded to in 3, could never have been extended to angels; **14** they are servants, **ministering spirits,** but these words are spoken to the Son. These angels, whose service benefits **those who are to obtain salvation** (through the Son), are plainly different from Paul's 'elemental spirits of the universe' (Col. 2:20), with whom Christians should have no more to do. This chapter reveals a carefully co-ordinated system of OT exegesis.

II 1-4 The Gospel greater than the Law—The c emphasis on the angels' inferiority to the Son may partly be designed to counteract a tendency to angel-worship, as at Colossae. But the main purpose is to enhance the dignity of the gospel, brought by one who is so far superior to angels, and to warn the readers that the penalty for disregarding the gospel must be even more severe than for breaking the law. **1. lest we drift away from it:** Gr. *pararrheō* suggests drifting downstream past the landing-stage or a fixed object on the bank; apostasy may spring from neglect as well as from a wilful renunciation of the faith. **2. the message declared by angels:** for the angelic mediation of the law at Sinai cf. Ac. 7:53; Gal. 3:19. Other references occur in *Jubilees*, *Testaments of Twelve Patriarchs*, Philo and Josephus. In Heb. the law is not a principle set in opposition to the grace displayed in Christ's redemptive work, but an anticipatory sketch of that redemption. This author is more concerned with the sacrificial cultus than with the 'tradition of the elders', with the ritual law as a way of access to God rather than with the moral law as a means of life. **3. It was declared at first by the Lord:** cf. Mk 1:14f.; Lk. 4:18ff. **attested to us by those who heard him:** our author seems to include himself and his readers among the second-generation Christians who were converted through the apostles' testimony; he does not, like Paul, assert his independence of the apostles. **4. God also bore witness by signs and wonders and various miracles and by gifts of the Holy Spirit:** for these external manifestations and spiritual gifts which confirmed the gospel cf. Ac. 2:3f., 43, 8:7ff., 10:44ff., 19:6; 1 C. 12:1ff., 14:1ff.; Gal. 3:5; 1 Pet. 1:12. The testimony of the NT writers to these phenomena is impressively unanimous.

5-9 Men, not Angels, the Crown of Creation—It d

881d was commonly held that the various departments of the present world-order were placed under angelic administration (cf. Dt. 32:8, RSV; Dan. 10:13ff.); but in the world to come, the new age ushered in by the gospel, the Creator's original purpose will be achieved, whereby man is appointed king of creation. This purpose is stated in Ps. 8:4–6 (which in turn echoes Gen. 1:26–8), quoted here in 6–8. **6. It has been testified somewhere:** note how unconcerned our author is about the particular authors of OT documents. In the psalmist's original intention, 'man' or 'the son of man' is Adam, made but little lower than God and appointed to rule all creation. But here the words, instead of emphasising the dignity of Adam, are interpreted of the humiliation of Jesus (cf. Paul's conception of Jesus as the second Adam, e.g. in Rom. 5:12ff.; 1 C. 15:45ff.). In Jesus the sovereignty promised to man is realised; but because of man's sin it must be realised by way of humiliation, suffering and death. As the representative of men and **pioneer of their salvation** (10), Jesus must share in all the conditions of humanity, becoming **for a little while . . . lower than the angels** (9, following Ps. 8:5, LXX)—although he is essentially 'superior to angels' (1:4)—and enduring **death for every one.** And while the dominion of man, or rather of this Man, over creation is not yet universally apparent, Jesus' enthronement at God's right hand marks him out as the one **crowned with glory and honour** and therefore destined to exercise universal supremacy. **9. by the grace of God:** this appears to be a scribal emendation (Gr. *chariti theou*) for the earlier but difficult 'apart from God' (Gr. *chōris theou*), which in origin was almost certainly a marginal note intended to limit the scope of 'everything' (8) or 'every one' (9)—i.e. 'everything (or every one) apart from God'.

e **10-13 The Son of God one with his People—10. For it was fitting:** what is fitting for God to do can only be known by considering what in fact he has done. He has given Christ to be the 'pioneer' (Gr. *archēgos*, as in 12:2) who opens up the way by which his people find salvation and follow him into heaven (cf. 10:20). But the way to heavenly glory is the way of suffering, and in order to be his people's perfect representative Christ must suffer (cf. 5:8f.). He would not be exempt from their afflictions; his solidarity with them must be complete. He who makes his people holy is the Son of God; those whom he makes holy are through him the sons of God, acknowledged by him as his brothers. **11. have all one origin:** i.e. in God. The three quotations in 12f. show how our author finds Christ variously prefigured in OT. In Ps. 22:22 (quoted in 12) a man of God who has endured great affliction vows, in gratitude for his deliverance, that he will proclaim God's name (i.e. his character and reputation as vindicated by that deliverance) to his fellow-Israelites and sing God's praise when they are gathered together. The quotation of Ps. 22:1 by Jesus on the cross (Mk 15:34) made it easy for Christians to apply the rest of the psalm to him. In 13 two passages from Isa. 8:17f. are quoted; Isaiah, both by his patient and confident hope in God and by his identification of his sign-children with himself and his message, is recognised as a 'type' of Christ. Isaiah's sons and disciples embodied the nucleus of the saving remnant which was a dominant theme of his prophecy, and here they foreshadow the solidarity of Christ's people with himself and his work.

f **14-18 The Reality of Christ's High Priesthood—** But Christ's 'children' are human beings, sharers in flesh and blood; therefore, if there was to be true solidarity between him and them, he also must be truly incarnate (14*a*). **14b, 15.** But those who 'share in flesh and blood' die; Christ became incarnate in order that he might die—but in order further that by dying he might deal the death-stroke to the devil, the former lord of the realm of death, and liberate **all those who through fear of death were subject to lifelong bondage.** Only by becoming man could Christ conquer death, which man without Christ could never have done; until his conquest of death the devil seemed to have the last word. **16. he is concerned:** this RSV rendering weakens the sense of Gr. *epilambanomai*; cf. its use in 8:9 meaning 'to take (by the hand)'. The point here is that Christ laid hold, in order to help and save them, not of angels but of men—and since no-one can become a man without becoming a man of a particular family, Christ took hold of **the descendants of Abraham.** This may suggest not only his physical descent from Abraham but also 'the descendants of Abraham' in the Pauline sense (Gal. 3:29), i.e. those who believe. **17.** And now comes the first mention of the central theme of Heb., the high priesthood of Christ. A high priest must be truly one with his people, if he is to represent them adequately in the presence of God and **make expiation for the sins of the people,** i.e. remove their sins from God's sight (Gr. *hilaskesthai*). Our author, despite his frequent citation of Ps. 110:4 as the OT basis of this doctrine, prefers to call Christ '*high* priest' (and not simply 'priest'), probably because he wishes to set forth his priestly service in terms of the ritual of the Day of Atonement, when the high priest alone could perform the central act. **17. a merciful and faithful high priest:** cf. the Gnostic *Gospel of Truth* (Jung Codex, 19f., perhaps echoing Heb.), 'For this reason *the merciful, the faithful* Jesus was patient, bearing the suffering until he had taken this book' (*The Jung Codex*, ed. F. L. Cross (1955), 108). He can plead his people's cause before God and procure them effective help because he knows from personal experience the trials and temptations that beset human life. So his sufferings have not only perfected his obedience but also qualified him to be a sympathetic high priest (cf. 4:15, 5:7ff.).

III 1-IV 13 The Danger of missing the Heavenly Rest 882a

III 1-6 Jesus greater than Moses—1. Jesus, the apostle and high priest of our confession: as apostle, Jesus is God's messenger to men; as high priest, he is man's representative before God. If Moses (who in his day combined 'apostolic' and priestly functions) was faithful in the care of God's house entrusted to him (Num. 12:7), Christ's faithfulness was no less. **3-6a.** While Moses was but chief servant in God's house, Christ is set over the house, as Son of the divine Builder, and so bears greater responsibility and honour. If the context of Num. 12:7 contains a solemn warning against despising Moses, it must be more serious to despise one who is head of the house. Christ's superiority to Moses is emphasised partly in order to show again the superiority of Christianity to Judaism, but also because in some Jewish-Christian circles Jesus was viewed as a second Moses; here he is presented as being more than that. **5. to testify to the things that were to be spoken later:** this is amplified later with reference to Moses' role in relation to the tabernacle and the new covenant (8:5, 9:19f.). **6b. we are his house if we hold fast our confidence and pride in our hope:** better, 'the glorying of our hope' (RV); Christian hope is nothing to be ashamed of. The phrase 'firm to the end' (RSV*n*) is probably an insertion from 14; it is absent from P^{46}B and other early witnesses. The emphasis on the maintenance of hope was necessary at a time when the first expectant enthusiasm was growing dim. Note that, whether under Moses or under Christ, there is one continuous household of God (cf. 11:40).

7-19 Rejection of Christ worse than Rejection of Moses—In accordance with a primitive Christian catechesis reflected in 1 C. 5:7, 10:1ff., a parallel is drawn between Moses' days and those of Christ. If there were rebels in Moses' days who missed the promised blessing of entry into Canaan, so 'in these last days' there were signs of disobedience and b

882b unbelief which would forfeit the blessings of the new age. The quotation of Ps. 95:7–11 sums up the loss which the rebellious Israelites incurred in the wilderness; our author applies the psalm as a warning to his readers (7–11). **9. forty years:** particularly apt, if forty years had nearly expired from the new Exodus, the redemptive death of Christ (cf. Lk. 9:31). 'Today' (7) is still present (13); it is the day of opportunity; while it lasts, says our author, **do not harden your hearts** (8) but **exhort one another** (13). **12. an evil, unbelieving heart, leading you to fall away from the living God:** cf. the 'evil inclination' of the rabbis. This warning suggests something more serious than a relapse into Judaism; it implies outright apostasy. But a relapse from the gospel into Judaism would not be a mere return to a position formerly occupied, but a complete break with God. For those who had never received the final revelation in Christ, Judaism provided a means of access to God (albeit shadowy, inadequate and now superseded); but for those who had received that revelation to renounce it was the irretrievable sin against light (cf. 6:4–6). **14. we share in Christ:** lit. 'we have become comrades of Christ', for the word is the same as at the end of 1:9 (Gr. *metochos*). **if only we hold our first confidence firm to the end:** the conditional note is struck again, as in 6; continuance is the test of reality. All those Israelites who hardened their hearts and tempted God (tried to see how far his patience would abide their disobedience) had enjoyed his delivering mercy when they escaped from Egypt with Moses (16) and heard him speak when he gave the law at Sinai; but those initial experiences did not keep them from dying in the wilderness when they rebelled against God, or guarantee their entrance into the promised land at the end of the forty years (17–19).

c **IV 1-10 The Eternal Rest of God may be lost**— **1.** Therefore, let the readers not fail to attain the 'rest' which God has set before them as their goal, as the Israelites failed to reach Canaan. **2.** The good news which came to them did them no good because they did not accept it by faith. **because it did not meet with faith in the hearers:** our textual witnesses here exhibit 'a variety of ancient conjectures vainly striving to heal a primitive corruption' (G. Zuntz, *The Text of the Epistles* (1953), 16); but the general sense is plain enough. **3.** God's true rest is for men of faith. But what does God mean by **my rest**? It must be his resting after creation described in Gen. 2:2 (quoted in 4); the rest which may be forfeited is a share in God's unending sabbath rest. (In LXX the verb 'rest' in Gen. 2:2 is *katapauō*, cognate with the noun *katapausis* in Ps. 95:11; in MT two quite different Hebrew words are used.) But, our author proceeds, according to Ps. 95 the Israelites in the wilderness were not the only ones who might fail to enter the promised rest, for centuries later, 'in David' (i.e. in the Psalter) certain other people are warned to listen to God's voice 'today', lest they too harden their hearts and miss his promised rest. Therefore the 'rest' which the disobedient Israelites missed in Moses' day was not merely the land of Canaan, for the people addressed in Ps. 95 were already settled there. **8. if Joshua had given them rest:** 'Joshua' and 'Jesus' are two forms of the same name (cf. AV 'Jesus' here); it is significant in our author's eyes that the leader into the earthly Canaan bore the same name as the pioneer of our salvation, but the 'rest' into which Jesus brings his people is better than anything that Joshua's followers attained. **9. there remains a sabbath rest for the people of God:** Gr. *sabbatismos*, emphasising the connection with Gen. 2:2. There is no true rest on earth; the real sabbath rest is eternal, and into this rest (identical with the well-founded city and the heavenly country of 11:10, 16) God's faithful people will enter when their labour is done, as God himself rested when his work of creation was finished.

11-13 Exhortation to attain God's Rest—God is 882d
not to be trifled with. **12. For the word of God is living and active:** God's word, as occasionally in OT, is viewed as his messenger or agent. **sharper than any two-edged sword:** cf. Is. 49:2; Prov. 5:4; Jer. 23:29. There is a reference in *The Gospel of Truth* (Jung Codex, 26:2) to 'the judgment "which is as a drawn two-edged sword" which cuts in all directions' (*The Jung Codex*, ed. F. L. Cross, 119). So here God's word is the supreme judge, **discerning the thoughts and intentions of the heart.** Outward behaviour may be exemplary; a curb may be put upon unruly lips; but it is possible even so to cherish within a spirit of rebellion against God. But nothing is concealed from his sight. **13. laid bare:** lit. 'with neck bent back', ready for the death-stroke (Gr. *trachēlizō*); the inner self is exposed to the scrutiny of the supreme Judge, stripped of all disguise and protection.

So ends this extended 'warning passage' (3:7–4:13), and the writer resumes his main theme.

IV 14-VI 20 The High Priesthood of Christ 883a

IV 14-16 Christ's High Priesthood an Encouragement to his People—Reverting now to the subject introduced in 2:17f., our author presents the high-priestly office of Jesus as an incentive to perseverance. He endured every trial that his people are likely to undergo, and yet he remained steadfast throughout, and has now **passed through the heavens** to the very throne of God. **14. Jesus, the Son of God** is not disqualified by his divine origin from sharing in his people's troubles and sympathising with their weaknesses. **15. yet without sinning:** lit. 'apart from sin'; this does not mean that he experienced every sort of human temptation except temptation to sin, but rather that he sustained every form of testing that man could endure, without losing his faith in God or relaxing his obedience to him. Such endurance implies more than ordinary suffering, not less: 'sympathy with the sinner in his trial does not depend on the experience of sin but on the experience of the strength of the temptation to sin which only the sinless can know in its full intensity. He who falls yields before the last strain' (B. F. Westcott, *ad loc.*). **16.** He who won through victoriously is best able to help others; the throne of God where he is installed is a mercy-seat to which his people have free access to receive all the grace and strength they need to help them in the hour of trial and crisis.

V 1-4 A High Priest's Qualifications—But any b
high priest must fulfil certain conditions, and this is so with Jesus. **1.** The Aaronic high priests were appointed to represent men before God, principally in the presenting of gifts and sin-offerings; **2** they were required to have a sympathetic understanding of human weakness, being weak men themselves; **3** they had to present sin-offerings for themselves as well as for others; **4** they must be duly appointed in accordance with the divine ordinance. **2. deal gently:** a term of peripatetic philosophy (Gr. *metriopatheō*), contrasted with the Stoic's cultivated lack of feeling; it denotes 'the golden mean between indifference and mawkish sentimentality' (E. K. Simpson).

5-6 Christ designated High Priest by God—How c
do Christ's claims to be his people's high priest appear in this regard? That he had no need to present sin-offerings for himself has been implied already (4:16) and is emphasised later (7:27), but his capacity for sympathy is not diminished thereby. As regards his being 'called by God' (4), there is no question. **6.** For God, who in Ps. 2:7 hails the Messiah as his Son (5; cf. 1:5*a*), addresses him in Ps. 110:4 as a priest for ever, after the order of Melchizedek. Ps. 110:1 has already been cited with a messianic application (1:13), as elsewhere in the apostolic preaching. But our author is the only NT writer to quote Ps. 110:4. There is historical justification for applying these words to the Davidic Messiah, for David and his

883c successors, after the capture of Jerusalem from the Jebusites, appear to have acted as heirs to the dynasty of priest-kings of which Melchizedek was the best-known representative. Our author may not have been greatly interested in this historical argument, but he knew that Jesus, born into the tribe of Judah, could not be an Aaronic priest of the tribe of Levi (cf. 7:14); here, however, in a psalm which Christians recognised as messianic and as fulfilled in Jesus, was a direct word of God which declared Messiah's perpetual priesthood after another order, and this forms the text for the following exposition of Christ's high priesthood.

d **7-10 Christ's Experience of Suffering**—A high priest must be able to sympathise with others in their suffering; Christ's own sufferings qualify him in this regard. **7. In the days of his flesh:** i.e., while he was incarnate on earth; the phrase should not be pressed to imply that the writer thought Jesus was no longer incarnate after his death and exaltation. **Jesus offered up prayers and supplications, with loud cries and tears, to him who was able to save him from death:** usually understood as an allusion to the agony in Gethsemane (cf. especially Lk. 22:41–4). This may be so, but if it were not for the gospel narrative of the agony we might think the reference was to occasions on which Jesus prayed to God when his life was in imminent danger and was delivered from death. These moving words certainly make us wish that we knew the form in which the gospel story had reached our author. In any case, we can recognise clearly the motif of humiliation and suffering followed by exaltation and glory which so pervaded the primitive *kerygma*. **8. Although he was a Son:** 'Son though he was', the one who 'reflects the glory of God and bears the very stamp of his nature' (1:3), yet like his brethren he must tread the path which attains wisdom through suffering, a path which Greek thinkers also had recognised as divinely appointed for men. **he learned obedience through what he suffered:** not that he learned to be obedient through suffering for disobedience, as we do, but that he learned by his experience of suffering what obedience to God involved in man's life on earth. **9.** But this first-hand acquaintance with the cost of obedience was necessary in order to make him 'perfect', i.e. fully qualified from his present position of universal supremacy to procure **eternal salvation to all who obey him,** and to be their effective high priest in accordance with the divine designation (10).

e **11-14 The Immaturity of the Readers**—**11.** Before going on to elaborate further the theme of Jesus' high priesthood, our author expresses a doubt whether his readers are sufficiently mature to appreciate such teaching. This doubt leads him to warn them solemnly against the danger of staying where they are (and so inevitably slipping back) instead of pressing on. Although they have been Christians long enough to be teachers themselves, they need to learn the ABC of Christianity all over again. **12a. first principles:** Gr. *stoicheia*, here used in its primary sense of 'letters of the alphabet' (not 'elemental powers' as in Gal. 4:9; Col. 2:8). **12b. You need milk, not solid food:** for a similar contrast cf. 1 C. 3:2. (In 1 Pet. 2:2 milk is commended where 'newborn babes'—perhaps baptismal candidates—are addressed.) Indeed, the whole conception of spiritual maturity as requisite for a deeper understanding of the doctrine of salvation may have been influenced by Paul's argument in 1 C. 2:6, 3:1ff.—a specially interesting possibility if our author could be identified with Apollos, who is mentioned by Paul in that context. **14. mature:** 'perfect', 'full-grown' (Gr. *teleios*, also capable of meaning 'initiated'; but this idea is scarcely in view here). The man who is 'mature' in this sense is he who has truly appropriated the essence of the gospel in his heart and learned to regulate his way of life by it.

f **VI 1-8 No Second Beginning possible**—In spite of

883f the readers' immaturity, there is nothing to be gained by starting at the point where they were when they first heard the gospel. **1.** It has been argued (cf. A. Nairne, *The Epistle of Priesthood* (1913), 15) that all the features mentioned in connection with **a foundation of repentance of dead works and of faith toward God** are consistent with the creed of a Pharisaic Jew. **2. instruction about ablutions:** hardly a reference to Christian baptism; we are reminded rather of Jewish ceremonial purifications. At one time these things had served as a foundation on which they had been taught **the elementary doctrines of Christ** (1); but if they slipped back to their former ways no fresh building of that kind could be erected on the same foundation again. **4. those who have once been enlightened:** possibly meaning 'baptised' as it did in later Christian terminology (cf. also 10:32 and the baptismal hymn quoted in Eph. 5:14). **6. if they then commit apostasy:** this does not mean that our author 'will allow no forgiveness for Christian sinners' (F. C. Burkitt, quoted by Nairne, op. cit., 130), although Tertullian and others have understood him thus; he has in view the deliberate repudiation of a faith once embraced, the shutting of one's eyes to the light, the 'falling away from the living God' of 3:12. Those who act thus are guilty of an insulting renunciation of Christ and his cross, which must bring both into contempt. **7f.** The metaphor of the fruitless land is to much the same effect as Isaiah's song of the vineyard (Isa. 5:1ff.; cf. Lk. 13:6–9; Jn 15:6).

9-12 Further Encouragement to Perseverance— g
In spite of his solemn warning, our author does not believe that his readers have fallen from grace yet. He does not intend to frighten them, but to encourage them. So he reassures them of his confidence that the evidences of true salvation are apparent in their lives. He remembers their loving energy in serving their fellow-Christians, and assures them that God remembers it too and will reward them. What he really desires is that they should go on as they have begun, without flagging in their pursuit of the Christian hope, and thus at last inherit the promises which God holds out to his people. Once again, continuance is emphasised as the proof of reality. And in pressing on to receive the promises, they have as an incentive the exemple of men of God in earlier days.

13-20 The Certainty of God's Promises—**13. For** h
when God made a promise to Abraham, . . . he swore by himself: 'By myself I have sworn' (Gen. 22:16). The bare word of God is guarantee enough in all conscience—for **it is impossible that God should prove false** (18)—but when God swears by himself, having **no one greater by whom to swear** (13), he makes 'assurance double sure'. **18. two unchangeable things:** God's promise and the oath by which he confirms it. What was true of God's promise to Abraham is equally true of his promise to Christians; our author might almost have quoted Rom. 4:23f., 'But the words . . . were not written for his sake alone, but for ours also' (for 11:8–19 shows that Abraham was promised the same heavenly blessings to which Christians look forward). **19.** The sure hope that God will perform his promise to those who believe in him, and bring them right through to the end, is a great encouragement to persevere in faith, a veritable **anchor of the soul,** binding Christians firmly to their heavenly home, that Holy of Holies above where Christ has already entered as his people's precursor and representative, to fulfil the high priesthood of Melchizedek's order to which God has called him (20). These words not only bring our author back to the point from which he digressed in 5:10, but also anticipate the further teaching which he proposes to give on the heavenly sanctuary (cf. 8:1ff.). **19. behind the curtain:** i.e. the curtain that separated the inner sanctuary or Holy of Holies from the outer sanctuary in the wilderness tabernacle (cf. Exod. 26:31–5).

884a **VII 1-28 The Order of Melchizedek**
VII 1-3 Melchizedek the Priest-King—Our author now comes to grips with his central and positive theme. If we are to understand why Jesus should be called a priest ' after the order of Melchizedek ' (5:10, 6:20), we must refresh our memories about Melchizedek. And so, as his manner is, he goes back from Ps. 110:4 to Gen. 14. **1. Melchizedek, king of Salem, priest of the most high God,** according to Gen. 14:17ff., went out to meet Abraham on his return from the rout of Chedorlaomer and his allies, bestowed his blessing upon him and accepted a tenth part of the booty which Abraham had retrieved. In Christ the priesthood and kingship (not to mention the prophetic office too) coincide (cf. Zech. 6:12f.; Rev. 1:5f.). **2. king of righteousness:** etymology of the name Malki-ṣedeḳ. The ideal of righteousness (*ṣdḳ*) was strikingly associated with the city of Jerusalem from early times; cf. A. R. Johnson, *Sacral Kingship in Ancient Israel* (1955), 31ff. **king of peace:** ' Salem ' is treated as a variant of Heb. *shālôm* (cf. Arab. *salaam*), ' peace '. The collocation of righteousness and peace is naturally found suggestive (cf. Isa. 32:17). **3.** But not only are the statements about Melchizedek regarded as significant; significance is also found in the fact that nothing is said about his parentage or ancestry, birth or death (whereas in the Aaronic priesthood pedigree and age were of prime moment). This silence about the beginning and end of Melchizedek's life and office is linked with the designation ' a priest for ever ', a designation uniquely applicable to the Son of God, whose priesthood is not passed on to successors. A modern preacher might express the thought by saying that the facts revealed about Melchizedek and the facts concealed were alike divinely overruled in order that he might the more tellingly foreshadow the high priesthood of Christ.

b **4-10 The Greatness of Melchizedek—4. See how great he is!** The more clearly Melchizedek's greatness is attested by the narrative of Gen. 14, the more clearly will the superiority of Christ's priesthood (' after the order of Melchizedek ') appear. For one thing, Abraham paid tithes to Melchizedek (4) and received his blessing (6), in both ways necessarily acknowledging Melchizedek as his superior (7). But Abraham is the ancestor of the tribe of Levi, to which other Israelites are commanded to pay tithes (cf. Num. 18:21, 24ff.); thus Levi might be said to have paid tithes to Melchizedek in the person of his forefather Abraham (9f.). But in that case the Levitical priesthood is manifestly inferior to Melchizedek's, and therefore to Christ's. **6. him who had the promises:** cf. 6:13–15, 11:8–19. **8. it is testified that he lives:** i.e. in every OT reference to Melchizedek he is alive; there is no mention of his death; whereas there are frequent references to the Aaronic priests as dying and transmitting their dignity to others (cf. 23f.).

c **11-14 Imperfection of the Levitical Priesthood**—A further mark of the inferiority of the Levitical priesthood is the fact that Messiah is designated a priest of a different order. **11. if perfection had been attainable through the Levitical priesthood,** there would have been no need to introduce this new order. Its introduction implies not only the supersession of the Levitical priesthood, but also the alteration of the law which confined the priesthood to Levi's tribe and Aaron's family (12). For Messiah, as all knew, was to come (as Jesus did) of David's family and therefore of Judah's tribe (14), and so could never have been a priest under the old order. Our author does not mention the possibility that the earlier Davidic kings exercised a royal priesthood ' after the order of Melchizedek ' in Jerusalem, alongside the Levitical priesthood which tended the ark and its shrine. Nor does he entertain the idea of a Levitical Messiah, such as appears in the *Testaments of the Twelve Patriarchs* and the Qumrân texts: had he done so, he might have drawn inferences from the fact

that the mother of Jesus was related to Elizabeth, 884c
who was ' of the daughters of Aaron ' (Lk. 1:5). Such speculations were at best irrelevant to one who was concerned to expound the Melchizedek priesthood ascribed to the Davidic Messiah in Ps. 110:4. **12. a change in the law:** i.e. in the whole body of sacerdotal and sacrificial ordinances. The supersession of the law in Paul's epistles refers rather to the law interpreted by the ' tradition of the elders ' and viewed as the means of acquiring a righteous status before God (Rom. 10:4).

15-19 The Levitical Priesthood superseded by a Better—Not only the introduction of a new priesthood, but the terms in which it is introduced, proclaim the inferiority of the Aaronic order. For the priest ' after the order of Melchizedek ' is hailed as a priest ' for ever ' (17). **16.** Here our author sees a reference to the **indestructible life** which our Lord possesses in resurrection. The Aaronic priests were appointed by virtue of heredity, but none of them could enjoy the sacerdotal dignity in perpetuity. **a legal commandment concerning bodily descent:** RV, ' the law of a carnal commandment ', embracing possibly other features of the old order which laid stress on externalities (e.g. animal sacrifice) as well as the family qualification for priesthood. That priesthood, like everything else in the Levitical régime, was characterised by imperfection and transience; the new order which has replaced it is permanent and effective, **19** being bound up with the **better hope** of the gospel, which enables men, not merely in symbol but in spiritual reality, to **draw near to God.** d

20-22 The Divine Oath—The superiority of the Melchizedek priesthood is also shown by the fact that designation to this priesthood is confirmed by the oath of God; **21** again Ps. 110:4 is quoted: **The Lord has sworn and will not change his mind, ' Thou art a priest for ever ':** here the phrase ' after the order of Melchizedek ' is a later addition in the Western and Byzantine texts. But there is no mention of a divine oath in the Levitical law which appoints Aaron and his sons to be priests; **22** this betokens the inferiority of their priesthood to Christ's and the superiority of the new covenant which he guarantees to the old one under which they held office. e

23-25 A Priest who cannot die—The impermanence of the Aaronic priesthood was due in part to the mortality of the men who filled it. No individual among them could ensure permanent acceptance by God to those whom he represented. **24.** But Jesus, having died once for all (cf. 27), lives for ever and maintains his priestly office **permanently:** Gr. *aparabatos*, ' untransferable ', ' indefectible '. His priesthood ' is in its very nature unsupersedable, and . . . finality inheres in it ' (E. K. Simpson). **25.** Therefore those who approach God through him can count on his unceasing availability; he can guarantee their total and final salvation (as those earlier priests could not), **since he always lives to make intercession for them.** The picture of Jesus interceding for his people at God's right hand belongs to the kerygmatic foundation of 1st-cent. Christianity (cf. Rom. 8:34). The nature of his intercession may be indicated by Lk. 22:32; Jesus (that is to say) is doing for his people now what he did for Peter in the hour of temptation, procuring for them the necessary spiritual strength to keep their faith from failing (cf. 4:16). f

26-28 The Personal Character of the Priest—Above all, the priest's own character makes the chief difference to the priesthood. **26.** Our high priest is **holy, blameless, unstained,** and therefore has no need (as every Aaronic priest had) to offer a sacrifice for his own sins before presenting the people's sin-offering (cf. 5:3; Lev. 16:6, 11ff.). **separated from sinners:** ' in a different class from sinful men ' (W. Manson). **exalted above the heavens:** he has passed through them (4:14) to the throne of supreme majesty (cf. Eph. 1:20ff., 4:10). **holy,** g

884g **blameless, unstained/separated from sinners/ exalted above the heavens:** we should perhaps recognise here a tristich from an early Christian hymn in praise of Christ (cf. O. Michel, *ad loc.*). **28.** This is the kind of high priest that suits our case, one who has no sins of his own to expiate, like the priests appointed by the law; for he who has received his priestly appointment by the sworn word of God is the **Son who has been made perfect for ever.**

885a **VIII 1-IX 22 The Two Covenants**

VIII 1-7 Christ's Priesthood exercised in the Heavenly Sanctuary—1. the point in what we are saying is this: 'to crown the argument' (W. Manson). Christ, enthroned as high priest at God's right hand, ministers not in any earthly shrine but in the heavenly sanctuary above, a tabernacle not made with human hands. **2. which is set up . . . by the Lord:** the Greek clause echoes Num. 24:6, LXX ('like tabernacles which the Lord pitched'). Of this heavenly sanctuary the Mosaic tabernacle was a material copy. This idea of an archetypal sanctuary in heaven has usually been regarded as a sample of our author's Platonising tendency, after the manner of Alexandrian Judaism as seen in Philo. But biblical authority for the idea is produced from Exod. 25:40, where Moses is commanded to build the tabernacle in conformity with the pattern shown to him on Mt Sinai (5). **3. It is necessary for this priest also to have something to offer:** viz. (as stated in 7:27), the perfect and unrepeatable oblation of himself (cf. 9:14, 25, 28, 10:12). **4.** But it is an oblation which can be presented only in the heavenly sanctuary, for **if he were on earth, he would not be a priest at all**, because he did not belong to the tribe of Levi, from which the priests who served **according to the law** were exclusively drawn. **6.** And the fact that his ministry is discharged in heaven is a further token of its superiority, and of the superiority of the covenant mediated by him to the covenant enacted at Sinai. **7.** Moreover, the imperfect and transitory nature of that earlier covenant is declared by the necessity for a new one.

b **8-13 The Old Covenant obsolete**—What our author meant by saying that the new covenant was 'enacted on better promises' (6) now appears by his lengthy quotation from Jer. 31:31-4 (8-12). The promises are stated in the latter part of the quotation, from **10b I will put my laws into their minds** to **12b I will remember their sins no more**. No such promises were made at the inauguration of the Sinaitic covenant (Exod. 24:3ff.). Nor did Jeremiah leave the inferiority of the old covenant to be inferred from these promises; he explicitly contrasts it (to its disadvantage) with the coming new covenant. The new covenant, involving the spontaneous assent to the will of God planted in the heart, represents the attainment of the 'perfection' of 7:11 (cf. 9:14f., where fellowship with God is of the essence of the covenant). For a Pauline parallel cf. Rom. 8:4, where God's 'just requirements', which cannot be met in terms of law-keeping, are fulfilled in Christians 'who walk not according to the flesh but according to the Spirit'. Jeremiah's disillusionment after the reaffirmation of the covenant which formed part of Josiah's reformation (2 Kg. 23:3) may have impressed him with the need for a covenant which would be new in character as well as in point of time, new in a sense which would make the old one **obsolete** (13*a*). Now that Jesus had come and inaugurated this new covenant (our author may have had in mind the word of institution known to us from Mk 14:24/1 C. 11:25), the ceremonial which continued to be performed in terms of the old order was an empty husk, soon to disappear. **13b. ready to vanish away:** these words inhere in the logic of the situation, and do not necessarily mean that the Temple in Jerusalem was still standing, but they would be all the more effective if in fact the Aaronic priesthood was still carrying out its sacrificial duties.

IX 1-5 The Old Sanctuary—1. the first covenant had regulations for worship and an earthly sanctuary: our author has in mind the wilderness tabernacle (described in Exod. 25-31, 35-40) and not the Jerusalem Temple (with which indeed he may have had no first-hand acquaintance). Possibly, like Stephen (Ac. 7:44-50), he considered the portable tent-shrine more appropriate for a pilgrim people than a static building of stone. He gives a brief account of the two compartments of the tabernacle, with their furniture. **3. the second curtain:** i.e. the veil shutting off the Holy of Holies from the Holy Place; the first curtain or screen led from the court into the Holy Place (Exod. 26:36f., 36:37f.). **4. having the golden altar of incense:** this altar appears to have stood in the Holy Place, 'before the veil that is by the ark of the testimony' (Exod. 30:6). P. E. Kahle suggests that our author followed a Greek text exhibiting the same order as Sam., where Exod. 26:35 is immediately followed by Exod. 30:1-10 (*The Cairo Geniza* (1947), 146f.). But Exod. 30:6 (MT) places the incense-altar not only 'before the veil' but also 'before the mercy seat that is over the testimony' (this latter phrase is absent from LXX and Sam.); cf. 1 Kg. 6:22, where the incense-altar in Solomon's temple is the 'altar that belonged to the inner sanctuary', and 2 Bar. 6:7, where before the Chaldaean invasion an angel removes from the Holy of Holies various sacred objects, including 'the altar of incense' AV and RV text render 'golden censer' here; Gr. *thymiatērion* (which means 'censer' in LXX in 2 Chr. 26:19; Ezek. 8:11; 4 Mac. 7:11) denotes something into which incense is put, but 'altar of incense' is its more probable sense in this passage. **4. the ark of the covenant:** cf. Exod. 25:10ff., 37:1ff. **a golden urn holding the manna** (golden in LXX, not in MT), **and Aaron's rod that budded** were placed 'before the testimony' (Exod. 16:34; Num. 17:10f.). **the tables of the covenant:** i.e. the 'testimony' itself, which was to be placed in the Ark (Exod. 25:16, 21). In Solomon's Temple 'there was nothing in the ark except the two tables of stone' (1 Kg. 8:9). **5b. Of these things we cannot now speak in detail:** he implies, however, that he could enlarge on the symbolism of all these objects if he chose. 885c

6-10 A Temporary Ritual—The very furnishings and ritual of the tabernacle proclaimed the transitory nature of the covenant with which it was associated. **5.** The dwelling-place of God was in the inner shrine, over the 'cherubim of glory' which formed the visible pedestal for his invisible presence. But while the priests discharged their sacred duties daily in the outer shrine (particularly the burning of incense on the small altar), the inner shrine was entered only once a year, on the Day of Atonement, when the high priest passed through the curtain which normally barred access to the divine presence, to present the sacrificial blood as a propitiation for his own sins and those of his people (Lev. 16:2ff.). **9. symbolic for the present age:** not only 'a parable of the time then present' (AV), but 'a parable bearing on the present crisis' (W. Manson), emphasising the contrast between the free access to God guaranteed through Christ and the limited access allowed by the structure and ceremonial of the earthly sanctuary. **10.** So also the various offerings, food-laws and ritual ablutions prescribed in the Levitical law were external and material and temporary in intention, **regulations for the body imposed until the time of reformation.** d

11-14 Christ's Perfect Redemption—But now the 'time of reformation' is here, for the Messiah has appeared, **a high priest of the good things that have come** (reading *genomenōn* with P^{46}, B and other early authorities instead of *mellontōn*, 'things to come'), and he has entered the heavenly Holy of Holies on the basis of his own self-sacrifice (11, 12*a*). **11. not made with hands:** the idea of a sanctuary not made with hands goes back to the earliest forms of e

885e Christian teaching (cf. Mk 14:58 ; Jn 2:19ff.) ; it is specially associated with Stephen (Ac. 7:48). But while in some of those forms of teaching the reference is to the Church (cf. 1 Pet. 2:5), here it is to the celestial abode of God. **12. taking not the blood of goats and calves but his own blood :** RSV introduces a crudity of expression which our author is careful to avoid,; he does not say that Christ *carried* his blood into the presence of God. The Aaronic high priest did carry sacrificial blood into the Holy of Holies (7, 25), for the presentation as well as the shedding of the blood was required to complete the sacrifice ; but it was ' through his own blood ' (RV)—i.e. by virtue of his self-oblation—that Christ, having procured eternal redemption for his people, entered into the presence of God. Again, while the high priest of Israel had to repeat his propitiatory service in the Holy of Holies year by year (thus acknowledging the inadequacy of what he did), Christ's entrance **once for all into the Holy Place** (12*a*) bespeaks the permanent efficacy of his offering. **13f.** If external and ceremonial pollution might be removed under the old order by sprinkling with blood as on the Day of Atonement, or by such a rite as that of the Red Heifer (Num. 19), the self-oblation of Christ, a sacrifice offered on the moral and not on the ritual plane, will be even more effective in removing the real and inward pollution of guilt from men's conscience, and emancipate them from the **unavailing ceremonial** of Judaism to worship God in spirit and in truth. **14. through the eternal Spirit :** this suggests that Christ's sacrifice was the act of his own free will (cf. 10:7–10 ; Isa. 53:10 ; Mk 14:36)—which made it a true and efficacious sacrifice by contrast with all the shadow-sacrifices of the old order. In his application of the ritual for the Day of Atonement our author makes no reference to the ' goat for Azazel ' (AV ' scapegoat ') which carried away to an uninhabited spot the people's sins which had been confessed over it (Lev. 16:20–2) ; he concentrates only on the animals whose blood was presented in the Holy of Holies.

f **15-22 The Mediator of the New Covenant**—To follow the argument of this paragraph, we must remember that Gr. *diathēkē,* generally rendered ' covenant ', has the wider sense of ' settlement ' and sometimes means ' bequest ' or ' testament '. It is in this last sense that it is used in **16** and **17** (RSV ' will '), for this is the only kind of settlement that is invalid during the lifetime of the person who makes it. Westcott insists on the meaning ' covenant ' throughout, and appeals to the practice of sacrificing a covenant-victim (cf. Gen. 15:9ff. ; Exod. 24:5ff.) to confirm the irrevocability of a covenant. This idea is not excluded here, but the covenant-victim is not normally the person who makes the *diathēkē,* and it is that person's death that is required in 17. Our author uses *diathēkē* in the sense of ' will ' in 16f., because he has in mind the death of Christ as the event by which his new covenant becomes effective. **15. he is the mediator of a new covenant :** not merely as an intermediary between two contracting parties, but as God's representative in bestowing this ' settlement ' on men, and as the one who validates it by his own death. He is testator and executor in one. He is, to be sure, the covenant-victim, even as the old covenant was ratified by a covenant-victim's blood (18–20, quoting Exod. 24:6–8) ; but the covenant-victim by whose sacrifice the new covenant is ratified is also the mediator and guarantor of the covenant. **19. calves and goats :** ' and goats ' should probably be omitted with P^{46} and a number of other authorities (the words may have been added under the influence of 12). **with water and scarlet wool and hyssop :** these are not mentioned in Exod. 24 ; they may have been imported from the Red Heifer ritual (cf. 13). (It has been suggested. that in the old triennial synagogue lectionary Gen. 14 ; Exod. 24 and Num. 19 formed part of the Pentateuchal readings in three successive years prescribed about the season of Pentecost.) In Exod. 24:6 it is the altar, not the book of the covenant, that is sprinkled with 885f
half of the sacrificial blood to represent the Godward side of the covenant. For the other instances of blood-sprinkling mentioned in 21, cf. Exod. 29:12, 36 ; Lev. 8:15, 19, 16:14ff. **22. almost everything :** for exceptions to the general law that blood was necessary for cleansing from pollution and removal of sin cf. Lev. 5:11–13 ; Num. 16:46, 31:50.

IX 23-X 18 The Sacrifice of Christ 886a

IX 23-28 A Perfect and Unrepeatable Sacrifice—Material sacrifices might suffice for the ceremonial cleansing of an earthly sanctuary, but if sinful men are to approach God in a heavenly sanctuary, a sacrifice different in kind as well as better in degree is called for. Such a sacrifice has been provided in the voluntary self-oblation of Christ, which has entitled him to enter the true sanctuary above and represent his people before God. By his death he has consecrated the new covenant together with the heavenly sanctuary itself and everything associated with it (cf. 10:19ff.). No repetition of his sacrifice or of his entry into God's presence is necessary ; he has effected the removal of his people's sin from the sight of God once for all. **26. at the end of the age :** i.e. in the time of fulfilment (cf. 1:2 ; 1 C. 10:11 ; Gal. 4:4 ; 1 Pet. 1:20). Christ's appearing marks the end of the old age and heralds the age to come. Our author has turned back from his temporary contrast of the upper and lower worlds to the characteristically Jewish contrast between the two ages. **28. to bear the sins of many :** an echo of Isa. 53:12, not only identifying Jesus with the Servant, but showing that the distinctiveness of his sacrifice lay in his willing acceptance of suffering and death as an expiation for the sins of others. **will appear a second time :** as the Israelites on the Day of Atonement eagerly waited for the reappearance of their high priest after he had entered into the Holy of Holies, so the people of Christ wait for his *parousia,* knowing that he will not have to repeat the work of sacrifice (as the Aaronic high priest had to do) but that he will now make good to his people the final and eternal benefits of his one sacrifice.

X 1-4 The Old Order a Shadow—1. the law : b
i.e. the Levitical ceremonial, now superseded by the work of Christ. **a shadow of the good things to come :** cf. Col. 2:17 (where, however, it is food-laws and sacred seasons rather than the sacrificial ritual that Paul has in view). **the true form :** Gr. *eikōn,* here used of the reality itself ; under the old covenant a shadow or reflection of the heavenly reality was manifested on earth, but the new covenant imparts the heavenly reality itself. P^{46} apparently takes *eikōn* in the sense of a mere copy ; it reads : ' the law having a shadow of the good things to come and the copy (*eikōn*) of the realities . . .' Only the heavenly reality can bring perfection ; the inadequacy of the old shadow-order was seen in the constant repetition of sacrifices which were in any case ineffective. **4. For it is impossible that the blood of bulls and goats should take away sins :** this is in complete agreement with the argument of the great OT prophets, who maintained that the sacrificial ritual had value, at best, only if it expressed the spontaneous devotion of merciful, righteous and humble hearts.

5-10 The New Order the Reality—If the shadow c
belongs to the sphere of ritual, the reality belongs to the moral sphere. This is shown by the application to Jesus of Ps. 40:6–8, where the psalmist dedicates himself to do the will of God, knowing that this is a more acceptable offering than all material sacrifices. **5. a body hast thou prepared for me :** thus LXX replaces the MT of Ps. 40:6, ' thou hast given me an open ear ' (so RSV ; lit. ' ears hast thou dug for me '), by a paraphrase which puts the whole for the part ; he who listens obediently to God with the ear which God himself has made goes on to do the will of God with the rest of the body which God has created for him. **7. as it is written of me in the roll of the book** (Ps. 40:7) ; i.e., as it is prescribed

886c for me in the written law. To our author the book may have meant the whole OT, which bore witness to Christ. **8. Thou hast neither desired nor taken pleasure in sacrifices and offerings and burnt offerings and sin offerings:** these are the four main classes of Levitical sacrifices; the 'sacrifices' are the peace offerings, the 'offerings' are the cereal offerings. The whole passage strikes the authentic prophetic note, and is understood here as announcing the abrogation of the old order and the introduction of the new, based on Jesus' wholehearted devotion to his Father's will. **10. we have been sanctified through the offering of the body of Jesus Christ once for all:** i.e. we have been cleansed from *moral* defilement, as we could never have been by ritual ordinances. The use of 'body' rather than 'blood' here may be understood by the recent quotation of Ps. 40:6, LXX, 'a body hast thou prepared for me', which is interpreted not only of Jesus' incarnation but of his lifelong dedication to the will of God, culminating in his acceptance of the cross. 'Body' (here) and 'blood' (19, 29) represent, each in its own way, the total self-offering of Christ.

d **11-18 A Seated High Priest**—The Aaronic priests never sat down in the performance of their priestly duties, whether in the daily service or on special occasions like the Day of Atonement. Rightly so, says our author, for their work was never done. But Ps. 110 acclaims Messiah as a seated priest. (The 'enemies' of Ps. 110:1 are only mentioned in 13; their identity is not explored, as in 1 C. 15:24ff.) Christ's enthronement means that his sacrificial work is finished, that his self-oblation has accomplished once for all what generations of Levitical sacrifices had never done. **14. by a single offering he has perfected for all time those who are sanctified:** while the Levitical sacrifices, after hundreds of years, were no nearer the attainment of their aim than they had been at the beginning, the sacrifice of Christ has purified his people from sin (cf. 2:11) and assured them of permanent maintenance in a right relation with God. This complete removal and forgiveness of sin, we are reminded, was promised in Jeremiah's prophecy of the new covenant, already quoted in 8:8–12. **17. I will remember their sins and misdeeds no more** (Jer. 31:34): this promise in itself implies that no further sin offering will be necessary (18).

887a **19-39 Call to True Worship and Faithful Endurance**

19-25 God to be worshipped through Christ—**19. since we have confidence:** Gr. *parrhēsia*, primarily 'freedom of speech' but here 'freedom of access'. An enthroned high priest and the perfect sacrifice to which his presence at God's right hand bears witness give us every encouragement to 'draw near' (cf. Eph. 2:13, 18). **to enter the sanctuary by the blood of Jesus:** all danger of thinking in merely symbolical terms is removed by our author's insistence on the historical reality of Jesus and his self-oblation. The barrier which the veil presented in the old sanctuary is no longer there; in the heavenly sanctuary there is no analogy to the distinction between 'Holy Place' and 'Holy of Holies' (9:2ff.). **20. through the curtain, that is, through his flesh:** here we may detect an allusion to the rending of the veil which coincided with Jesus' death on the cross (Mk 15:38). The curtain is taken as a symbol of his incarnation; but because it is a torn curtain, it symbolises his crucifixion too. Both were necessary to open up our way to God. Westcott's interpretation, 'that is, the way of his flesh', which breaks the connection between the curtain and our Lord's humanity, is probably wrong. 'Blood' (19) and 'flesh' (20) alike denote his humanity, offered up in death to bring his people to God. **21. a great priest:** a variant rendering of Heb. *kōhēn gādhôl*, 'high priest' or 'chief priest' (e.g. Lev. 21:10). **over the house of God:** cf. 3:2–6. **22. let us draw near:** i.e. to worship God. **having our hearts sprinkled clean . . . and our bodies washed:** reflecting OT ceremonies for the removing of pollution; for sprinkling cf. Num. 8:7, 19:13ff. (alluded to in 9:13 above); for washing cf. Lev. 16:4ff., 22:6; Num. 19:7f. But here the sprinkling is inward and spiritual, the cleansing of the conscience, and while the washing of the body would certainly recall to the readers their baptism as Christians, it is not the outward bathing alone but its moral significance that is intended (cf. 1 Pet. 3:21). With this call to approach God through Christ comes a fresh call to go on confessing their hope steadfastly (cf. 3:6) in view of God's faithful promises, to help and encourage one another in Christian living, and not to grow slack in gathering together for mutual edification, especially as the day of review and decision was drawing near. **25. not neglecting to meet together:** the reference may be to a house-church or house-synagogue (Gr. *episynagōgē*) where this group had been in the habit of meeting; they were in danger of slipping back into the general life of the Jewish community to which they formerly belonged (cf. W. Manson, *The Epistle to the Hebrews* (1951), 69).

b **26-31 Warning against Apostasy**—A fresh warning is sounded against apostasy, for this seems to be the 'deliberate sin' (26) which our author has in mind. Repeating in different terms the argument of 6:1ff., he points out that those who renounce the sacrifice of Christ as the basis of their acceptance by God have no other sacrifice to help them. Failing the salvation which they have treated with contempt, their only prospect is the unmitigated severity of divine judgment. For the argument of 28f. cf. 2:2f. **29. profaned the blood of the covenant by which he was sanctified:** i.e. cleansed from sin (cf. 14); the apostate tacitly declares that the sacrifice of Christ has no such virtue after all. **outraged the Spirit of grace:** of whom they had become partakers (cf. 6:4). This passage was later used (e.g. by Tertullian) to support the argument that there was no forgiveness for post-baptismal sin. But the kind of sin that these theologians often had in mind was quite different from the unpardonable sin described here—the rejection of the only means by which pardon may be secured. **31. It is a fearful thing to fall into the hands of the living God:** these words, reinforced (30) by the quotation of Dt. 32:35f., afford a clear insight into our author's deep conviction of the awesome holiness of the divine majesty (cf. 3:12, 4:13, 12:28f.).

c **32-39 Fresh Encouragement to Faith**—After the warning of 26–31 (as after that of 6:1–8) he assures his readers that he has better hopes of them. **32. But recall the former days:** the remembrance of their earlier steadfastness in face of persecution should be an incentive to perseverance now. If a Roman group is addressed the circumstances referred to may be the riots associated with the name of 'Chrestus' (so Suetonius) which led to Claudius' decree of expulsion (Ac. 18:2). **after you were enlightened:** cf. 6:4. **33. publicly exposed:** Gr. *theatrizomenoi*, which has made some (e.g. Th. Zahn) detect a reference to Nero's persecution of A.D. 64), in which Christians were maltreated for public entertainment in the imperial gardens; but this identification seems to be excluded by 12:4. Perseverance is necessary in order to attain the fulfilment of God's promises, the expectation of which had enabled them to endure their earlier sufferings joyfully. **37. For yet a little while:** these words are taken from Isa. 26:20, but they serve here to introduce a free quotation of Hab. 2:3f., LXX, interpreted as a prophecy of the *parousia* of Christ. Verses 3 and 4 of Hab. 2 are reversed (37f.), with the effect of identifying 'my righteous one' with the man who perseveres in hope of the *parousia*; cf. T. W. Manson, 'The Argument from Prophecy', JTS 46 (1945), 129ff.; C. H. Dodd, *According to the Scriptures* (1952), 49ff. No middle way is allowed between pressing on in faith and shrinking back (39). To stand still is to slip back.

888a **XI 1-40 The Faith of the Elders**

1-3 The Nature of Faith—It is plain that in 'faith', as our author conceives it, hope plays a prominent part; faith is the 'firm assurance' (Gr. *hypostasis*, 'basis') of the fulfilment of our hope; it persuades us of the reality of what is not seen as yet, and enables us to act upon it. So Philo links 'faith towards God' with 'apprehension of the unseen' (*On Dreams*, i, 68). **2**. The commendation which men of old received from God for their faith is an example to their descendants. **3**. The creation of the material world by the divine decree (cf. Gen. 1:3; Ps. 33:6, 9; 2 Mac. 7:28) is something of which we can have no visible proof; it is to be apprehended by faith.

b **4-7 The Faith of the Antediluvians**—From the antediluvian world Abel, Enoch and Noah are selected as examples of faith: Abel (4) because of his acceptable sacrifice (Gen. 4:4*b*); Enoch (5) because he 'pleased God' (so Gen. 5:22, LXX, for MT 'walked with God') and God 'translated' him (so Gen. 5:24, LXX, for MT 'took him'); and Noah (7) because he believed God's warning of a coming deluge and took appropriate action in the absence of any visible signs (Gen. 6:13ff.). For Enoch and Noah cf. Sir. 44:16–18. **4. he received approval as righteous:** cf. Mt. 23:35; 1 Jn 3:12; these passages may go back to a common literary source, but if so, it is not extant. **he is still speaking:** a reference perhaps to Gen. 4:10; cf. 12:24 below. No reference is made to Enoch's apocalyptic visions. Enoch's faith is deduced from the statement that he 'pleased God' (**6** draws out the underlying principle, for the special benefit of the readers). **7**. Similarly the OT statement that 'Noah was a righteous man' (Gen. 6:9) is interpreted here in the affirmation that he **became an heir of the righteousness which comes by faith.**

c **8-12 The Faith of Abraham and Sarah**—Abraham's going forth at the call of God is a signal example of faith; he had nothing but the bare promise of God to rest upon, but he acted upon it as if it were already fulfilled and Canaan were his acknowledged possession. **9**. In fact it remained a foreign country to him all his days, and he lived there as a nomad alien, like Isaac and Jacob, who, as his descendants, were included in the divine promise. **10**. But, says our author, the heritage to which Abraham's faith really looked forward was no earthly Canaan but the eternal city of God, the 'sabbath rest' which remains for the people of God (4:9). **11. By faith Sarah herself received power to conceive:** it has been argued vigorously that 'Sarah herself' is a gloss which has entered from the margin, and that the original reference was to Abraham's receiving power to become a father at an advanced age, on the ground that the Gr. *eis katabolēn spermatos* (lit. 'for the deposition of seed'), denotes the paternal act of begetting and not the maternal one of conception, and also because Sarah's incredulous laughter (Gen. 18:12) was no sign of faith But 'even Sarah's acceptance of a promise which at first she seemed to hear with indifference is to the mind of the *auctor ad Hebraeos* a venture into the unseen world which faith makes real' (R. V. G. Tasker, NTS 1 (1954–5), 182f.). P^{46} and a few other witnesses read 'Sarah herself, who was barren . . .' **12. as good as dead:** Gr. *nenekrōmenos*, similarly used in Rom. 4:19. The figures of the stars and sand are taken from Gen. 15:5 and 22:17; it is in the context of the former passage that God is said to have counted Abraham's faith to him for righteousness.

d **13-16 The City of God the Home of the Faithful**—The thought of 10 is expanded in this paragraph. These patriarchs never saw the fulfilment of God's promise; yet they lived as if the promise was sure, and **died in faith. 13. strangers and exiles on the earth:** cf. Gen. 23:4. From the fact that they lived in Canaan as resident aliens, our author infers that the homeland which they really sought was the heavenly city prepared for them by God. Apart from this faith, they might have seized the opportunity to 888d
return to Mesopotamia; the fact that they did nothing of the kind proved the quality of their forward-looking faith. **16. God is not ashamed to be called their God:** because they were men of faith, God makes himself known as 'the God of Abraham, the God of Isaac and the God of Jacob' (Exod. 3:6).

17-22 The Faith of the Patriarchs—We have not e
yet finished with Abraham, Isaac and Jacob; further examples of their faith are Abraham's readiness to offer up Isaac (Gen. 22:1ff.), Isaac's blessing of Jacob and Esau (Gen. 27:27ff., 39f.), and Jacob's blessing of Joseph's two sons, Ephraim and Manasseh (Gen. 48:1ff.). As Abraham's obedience in the sacrifice of Isaac depended on his confidence that God, whose promises were bound up with Isaac's survival and posterity, would raise Isaac from the dead to ensure the fulfilment of those promises (cf. Gen. 22:5, 'we will come again to you'), so the blessings bestowed by Isaac and Jacob showed a similar belief that God would fulfil his promises. So too Joseph's charge concerning his bones (22) reflected his faith that God would bring Jacob's family back from Egypt to the land promised as their heritage (Gen. 50:25; Exod. 13:19; Jos. 24:32). **21. the head of his staff:** so Gen. 47:31, LXX, presupposing Heb. *maṭṭeh* for MT *miṭṭāh*, 'bed'.

23-28 The Faith of Moses—**23**. In the story of f
Moses, faith is shown first by his parents; had they, as Josephus says (Ant. II, ix, 3), some inkling of their child's destiny? **24f.** Moses' own faith appears in his great refusal. (After 23 there is a Western addition: 'By faith Moses when he grew up killed the Egyptian when he perceived the ill-treatment of his brothers.') He renounced the prospects which beckoned to 'the son of Pharaoh's daughter', to share the lot of a group of nomad-slaves, through faith in God's promises, which were bound up with the future of Israel. **26. abuse suffered for the Christ:** by prolepsis the experiences of the messianic people are viewed as those of the Messiah, in whose advent their destiny would be achieved. **he looked to the reward:** one which, like the city of God, lay beyond this earthly life. **27. not being afraid of the anger of the king:** this disagrees at first sight with Exod. 2:14f., but refers probably to Moses' abandonment of Egypt at the Exodus, after his vision of the Invisible King. The Exodus itself was attended by acts of faith, chief among which was the institution of the Passover, with the sprinkling of the blood, in obedience to God's commandment (Exod. 12)

29-31 Faith from Egypt to Canaan—**29**. It was g
faith in God's promise, spoken through Moses (Exod. 14:13ff.), that brought the Israelites safely through the Red Sea; the Egyptians, imitating their action without their faith, were drowned. **30**. It was in answer to faith in God's promise made to Joshua (Jos 6:2ff.) that the walls of Jericho collapsed. **31**. And Rahab's **friendly welcome to the spies,** the fruit of her faith in the power of Israel's God (Jos. 2:9ff.), secured the preservation of herself and her family (Jos. 6:22f.). Rahab's faith seems to have been a commonplace in early Christian preaching; it is adduced in Jas 2:25 alongside the 'binding of Isaac' to prove that faith without works is dead (these two incidents, common to Heb. and Jas, are not explicitly mentioned by Paul).

32-38 The Faith of other OT Saints—Later heroes h
of faith are mentioned more concisely. **33. conquered kingdoms, enforced justice, received promises:** a reference to various judges, kings and prophets. **stopped the mouths of lions:** a reference to Daniel (Dan. 6:22). **34. quenched raging fire:** the three Hebrew youths (Dan. 3:25ff.). **won strength out of weakness, became mighty in war, put foreign armies to flight:** a recurrent theme in Israel's history, from the judges to the Maccabees. **35. women received their dead by resurrection:** e.g. the widow of Zarephath (1 Kg. 17:17ff.) and the Shunam-

888h mite woman (2 Kg. 4:32ff.). **some were tortured:** more particularly the martyrs under Antiochus Epiphanes. **refusing to accept release:** their lives would have been spared had they consented to forswear their faith. **that they might rise again to a better life:** i.e. to the life of the age to come, by a 'better resurrection' than the resurrection to a further lease of earthly life referred to in 35*a*; cf. 2 Mac. 7:9, 11, 14 **37. They were stoned:** like Zechariah (2 Chr. 24:21). **they were sawn in two:** possibly a reference to Isaiah.

f **39-40 Their Faith vindicated when Christ came**—The faith of these OT believers is the more noteworthy because the promise which they embraced was never realised in their lifetime. **40.** If none the less their faithful endurance has won such glowing testimony, how much more (our author argues) should we who live in the age of fulfilment persevere in faith; for we have received **something better** than they experienced in their day. Their hope required for its perfection the realisation which we have witnessed: 'God in his good providence reserved the messianic *teleiōsis* of Jesus Christ until we could share it' (J. Moffatt, ICC, *ad loc.*).

889a **XII 1-29 Divine Discipline**

1-2 The Race of Faith—1 a cloud of witnesses: the men and women of ch. 11; they are witnesses not only to the power of faith but also to Christ before his incarnation, by which they have now, with us, been 'made perfect' (11:26, 40). The word 'witness' is here well on the way towards its special Christian sense of 'martyr' (cf. Ac. 22:20; Rev. 2:13, 17:6). **which clings so closely:** Gr. *euperistatos*, as of a long robe hampering the runner's feet; P^{46} reads *euperispastos*, 'distracting'. **2. looking:** Gr. *aphorōntes*, lit. 'looking away to', i.e. 'keeping our eyes fixed on'. **Jesus, the pioneer and perfecter of our faith:** he is the chief witness and exemplar, who completed the race of faith and reached the throne of God. **pioneer:** Gr. *archēgos*, as in 2:10. **for the joy that was set before him:** 'for' represents Gr. *anti*, denoting exchange or compensation, as in 16 ('for a single meal'). The joy comprises the completion of his work, his exaltation at the Father's right hand, and the consequent blessing of his people.

b **3-11 Christ's Example prevents Slackening—3. who endured from sinners such hostility against himself:** the more difficult reading 'against themselves' is better attested (by P^{46} ℵ D* etc.), but is probably either a primitive corruption or an intrusive gloss. **4. you have not yet resisted to the point of shedding your blood:** an argument against a date after A.D. 64, if a Roman destination be accepted for the epistle. **5f.** The quotation is from Prov. 3:11f. Suffering is a proof that we are true-born sons of God; though painful to the flesh, it is spiritually profitable. For the argument of 7–11 cf. Elihu's in Job 32–7. **9 Father of spirits:** i.e. our spiritual Father, as opposed to our earthly fathers (lit. 'the fathers of our flesh'); cf. 'God of the spirits of all flesh' (Num. 16:22, 27:16) and 'Lord of spirits' in 1 Enoch, *passim*.

c **12-17 Let nothing hinder**—He calls his readers to revive their own—or one another's—flagging spirits (12 is an echo of Isa. 35:3, and 13*a* of Prov. 4:26, LXX: 'make level paths for your feet, and make your ways straight'). Rough, untended roads would aggravate lameness. **14 Strive for peace with all men:** cf. Mt. 5:9; Rom. 12:18, 14:19. **the holiness without which no one will see the Lord:** cf. Mt. 5:8; 1 Th. 4:7. **15. that no 'root of bitterness' spring up and cause trouble:** an allusion to Dt. 29:18, LXX, 'let there be no root among you springing up in gall and bitterness'; but 'in gall' (Gr. *en cholē*) has by an interchange of two letters become 'cause trouble' (Gr. *enochlē*). **the many become defiled:** one such individual might infect the whole community with his poison. **16 that no one be immoral or irreligious like Esau:** 'like 889c
Esau' refers only to 'irreligious', not to 'immoral' (lit. 'fornicator'). Esau showed no appreciation of his spiritual inheritance (Gen. 25:29ff.); his case would be applicable to anyone who thought of renouncing Christian faith and hope for the sake of temporary ease or a respite from persecution. Esau's forfeiture of the first-born's blessing was irrevocable (Gen. 27:34ff.); this underlines the warnings previously given in this epistle.

18-24 Zion, not Sinai—The Israelites who met God d
at Sinai found that experience dreadful enough (for the details of 18–20 cf. Exod. 19:12ff.). **21. Moses said, 'I tremble with fear':** cf. Dt. 9:19, where Moses speaks of his second ascent of Sinai after the episode of the golden calf. But Christians have come to an even more awe-inspiring, though intangible, mountain—the heavenly Zion, the city of God. **22. innumerable angels in festal gathering:** attendants on God as at Sinai (Dt. 33:2), but not mediators of the gospel as they were of the law (2:2). The faithful on earth join in worship with the heavenly host (cf. Rev. 5:8ff.). **23. the assembly of the first-born who are enrolled in heaven:** Christians who, unlike Esau, value their birthright. **the spirits of just men made perfect:** the men of faith of ch. 11, who through Christ have now attained perfection in the well-founded city to which they looked forward (11:10, 14, 16). **24. the sprinkled blood that speaks more graciously than the blood of Abel:** Abel's blood demanded Cain's banishment from God's presence (Gen. 4:10ff.); the blood of Jesus brings us into God's presence (10:19).

25-29 Pay Heed to the Voice of God!—If it was e
death to disregard the voice of God that spoke from Sinai, it is more perilous still to disregard his voice when he speaks from heaven in the gospel (cf. 2:2ff.). **26.** At Sinai he shook the earth, but on a coming day, according to Hag. 2:21, he will shake heaven as well. **27.** That is to say, at the end of time God will so shake the universe that only the unshakeable things will survive. **28.** But the kingdom which Christians have received is one of the unshakeable things; its ruler is the royal priest on God's immovable throne. Let Christians therefore give thanks to God, and pay him acceptable and reverent worship, remembering that today, as at Sinai, **our God is a consuming fire** (echoing Dt. 4:24; cf. Isa. 33:14).

XIII 1-25 Final Exhortation, Benediction and 890a
Greeting

1-6 Ethical Admonitions—There was apparently a well-established ethical catechesis in the Church from early apostolic days, which lays down the main lines followed by the practical teaching in the NT epistles. So here **1** brotherly love, **2** hospitality, and **3** kindness to those suffering imprisonment and injustice are enjoined; **4f.** marriage and contentment are commended; sexual immorality and greed are condemned. A spirit of trust in God promotes contentment; since he has promised never to forsake his people (Jos. 1:5), they need have no fear (Ps 118:6).

7-16 The True Christian Sacrifices—7f The b
example of their leaders and teachers, from whom they first heard the gospel, should be a further incentive to faith, but the greatest incentive of all is the unchanging Christ (cf. 12:2f.). **9. strange teachings:** the context suggests that these had to do with external matters like food, which could bring no spiritual benefit to their adherents (cf. Col. 2:16ff.). Spiritual strength is fed by divine grace. **10.** If these teachings were bound up with the charge that Christians had no longer any altar (a charge levelled by pagans and Jews alike), let it be known that Christians *have* an altar, and a better one than was available to the priests of Israel in the tabernacle service. **11.** No part of the animals sacrificed for a sin offering on the Day of Atonement might be eaten; their bodies were burnt to ashes **outside the camp** (cf. Lev. 16:27). **12.** This analogy is followed in so

890b far as Jesus **suffered outside the gate** of Jerusalem as a perfect sacrifice for the purifying of his people; but his people who follow him outside the closed circle of Judaism know him as alive from the dead, one to whom they may go and from whom they may by faith derive abiding sustenance. **13f.** If 'going forth' to him involves abuse for his sake, such as Moses endured in his day (11:26), if it means leaving the shelter of a *religio licita*, that is a small price to pay for the privilege of inheriting the eternal city which Jesus ensures to his followers—a contrast to the earthly Jerusalem which was even then under imminent sentence of destruction. Therefore let them henceforth worship God through Jesus; this is the true spiritual worship of which the old sacrificial ritual was but a shadow. **15. the fruit of lips that acknowledge his name:** an echo of Hos. 14:2, where such praise is a more acceptable substitute for the sacrifice of calves. **16.** But praise should be accompanied by deeds of kindness and charity; these also are sacrifices that bring pleasure to God. The whole round of Christian life, in fact, is sacrificial in character.

c **17 Submission to Leaders**—Part of the trouble in the community addressed may have been a tendency to disregard their true leaders in favour of unsettling teachers. But these leaders ought to be respected and obeyed, for it is they, and not the purveyors of strange teaching, who have a real concern for their well-being and know that they will have to render God an account of their pastoral service. They should be helped to render this account with joy and not with sorrow.

d **18-19 Request for Prayer**—These verses imply that the writer is under some form of restraint, possibly in prison, but his conscience is clear, and he hopes that his friends' prayers will soon be answered in his restoration to them.

e **20-21 Benediction**—These two verses have the general structure of a collect in the third person: we have the invocation (**the God of peace**) followed by an adjective clause (**who brought again . . . covenant**), then the main petition (**equip you . . .**) and a secondary petition (**working in you . . .**), a pleading of the merits of Christ (**through Jesus Christ**), an ascription of glory to him, and the **Amen. 20. who brought again from the dead:** the only reference to Christ's resurrection in the epistle; its general argument makes it more appropriate to dwell on his direct passage from the place of sacrifice to the throne of God in the heavenly sanctuary (cf. Jn, where his 'lifting up' embraces both crucifixion and exaltation). **the great shepherd of the sheep:** an echo of Isa. 63:11. **the blood of the eternal covenant:** an echo of Zech. 9:11. 890e

22-25 Personal Notes and Final Greeting—22. f
my word of exhortation: this expression denotes a synagogue sermon in Ac. 13:15, and may here be used of an epistolary sermon which the preacher was prevented from delivering orally. **23. our brother Timothy:** we can only guess at the circumstances of Timothy's imprisonment and release; had he shared the writer's imprisonment (cf. 18f.)? **24. Those who come from Italy:** but the words might mean 'Those of Italy'; much will depend on whether we judge the epistle to have been sent to Italy or written in Italy.

Bibliography—Commentaries: J. Bonsirven (rev. 1956); A. B. Bruce (1899); A. B. Davidson (1882); M. Dods, EGT (1910); J. Héring, CNT (1955); G. H. Lang (1951); O. Michel, Mey. (1949); J. Moffatt, ICC (1924); A. Nairne, CGT (1917); F. D. V. Narborough, Clarendon NT (1930); W. Neil, Torch Commentaries (1955); A. S. Peake, Cent.B (1914); E. Riggenbach, ZK (1922); T. H. Robinson, Moffatt Commentary (1933); E. F. Scott (1922); C. Spicq, EBib. (1952–3); B. F. Westcott[3] (1903); E. C. Wickham[2], WC (1922); H. Windisch, HNT (1931).

Other Literature: K. Bornhäuser, *Empfänger und Verfasser des Hebräerbriefs* (1932); V. Burch, *The Epistle to the Hebrews* (1936); F. C. N. Hicks, *The Fulness of Sacrifice* (1930); T. W. Manson, *The Problem of the Epistle to the Hebrews* (Rylands Bulletin reprint, 1949); W. Manson, *The Epistle to the Hebrews* (1951); G. Milligan, *The Theology of the Epistle to the Hebrews* (1899); A. Nairne, *The Epistle of Priesthood* (1913).

A very full bibliography is given by C. Spicq, *L'Épître aux Hébreux*, i, 379ff.

THE CATHOLIC EPISTLES

By C. E. B. CRANFIELD

891a The Gr. adjective *katholikos* (derived from the adverb *katholou* or *kath' holou* meaning 'on the whole', 'in general') is found as early as Hippocrates (5th cent. B.C.) and is used by early Stoics, by Polybius (2nd cent. B.C.), by Dionysius of Halicarnassus (1st cent. B.C.), by Philo (1st cent. A.D.), and others, and means 'general' as opposed to 'particular'. The first person known to have used it with reference to the Church is Ignatius (martyred before 117), who uses it, in accordance with its ordinary meaning, of the universal Church in contrast with particular local churches. But the word soon acquired a further special significance in Christian usage as a result of the Church's struggle against heresy. The general consensus of the faithful was set over against the views of particular individuals and groups. So the word 'catholic' came to have the sense of 'orthodox' in addition to its primary sense of 'universal'.

b The first known occurrence of the adjective *katholikos* in connection with any of the Catholic Epistles is in the statement (Eus.HE, v, 18) of an anti-Montanist writer Apollonius (*c.* 197) that a certain Montanist called Themison wrote a 'catholic' epistle in imitation of that of the apostle (presumably John). A little later Clement of Alexandria refers to the letter given in Ac. 15:23–9 and also to Jude as 'catholic'. Origen (*c.* 230) uses *katholikos* with reference to 1 Jn, 1 Pet., and Jude, and also with reference to the Epistle of Barnabas. Dionysius of Alexandria (*c.* 260) uses it of 1 Jn in contrast with 2 and 3 Jn (Eus.HE, vii, 25). The first extant mention of 'catholic epistles' in the plural as the name of a group is by Eusebius himself (*c.* 310); but, as he speaks of 'the so-called catholic epistles' (HE, ii, 23), it would seem that the usage goes back beyond him. He includes in this group all the seven epistles which we know as 'Catholic'—i.e. **James, 1, 2 Peter, 1, 2, 3 John and Jude.**

c There has been a certain amount of controversy about the sense in which the term *katholikos* was originally applied to these Epistles; but there is no real doubt that it was used to differentiate them **as addressed to Christians in general** from the Pauline epistles which for the most part were addressed to individual churches. As far as 1 Jn was concerned (apparently the first to be so described) the appropriateness of the adjective is perfectly clear. 1 Pet., though addressed to the churches of a definite area, was general at least in comparison with most of the Pauline letters. In the case of 2 and 3 Jn the name was inappropriate; but it was not unnatural that, being attributed to the same author as 1 Jn, they should be included in the group for the sake of convenience. In the Eastern Church the name 'Catholic Epistles' has consistently been understood in this sense; but in the West the adjective 'catholic' was taken in its special doctrinal sense as meaning **recognised by the Catholic Church,** so 'authoritative', 'canonical', as opposed to other epistles which were not so recognised—hence the Lat. name *Epistolae Canonicae,* which was preferred in the West to *Epistolae Catholicae*.

892a It seems clear that by about the end of the 2nd cent. 1 Jn and 1 Pet. were recognised as canonical throughout the Catholic Church. About the other Catholic **892a**
Epistles doubts remained, though 2 and 3 Jn and Jude were probably generally accepted. Origen (185–255) whose chances of getting to know accurately which books were accepted as canonical in the different churches were particularly good, distinguished between those books that were universally recognised (*biblia homologoumena*) and those whose authority was disputed in some churches. 1 Jn and 1 Pet. he placed in the former category, the other five Catholic Epistles in the latter. About the genuineness of 2 and 3 Jn he himself expressed doubts; but 2 Pet., Jude and Jas he apparently himself regarded as scripture (he is actually the earliest writer to quote from Jas). Eusebius of Caesarea (*c.* 265–339) at the beginning of the 4th cent. similarly classifies 1 Jn and 1 Pet, as universally recognised, and the remaining five Epistles as 'disputed, but familiar to the majority'. But the **Festal Letter xxxix of Athanasius (367)**, which is the first document to declare that all the twenty-seven books of our NT, and only they, are canonical, betrays no consciousness of any doubts about Jas and the four shorter Catholic Epistles. The 4th-cent. canons of Antioch and Constantinople, on the other hand, excluded 2 Pet., 2 and 3 Jn and Jude, and in consequence the Syriac Peshitta version made under the authority of Rabbula, bishop of Edessa (411–35), also omitted them. The Philoxenian Syriac version (*c.* 508), however, included them, and it seems that about the beginning of the 6th cent. the whole of the Greek-speaking Church was agreed in accepting the canon as listed by Athanasius. Meanwhile in the West the disputed Catholic Epistles had established themselves as canonical, the speed with which this came about being to a large extent due to the influence of Jerome and Augustine (there is no known citation of Jas or 2 Pet. by a Western author until after the middle of the 4th cent.); and the Councils of Hippo (393) and Carthage (397) published lists of canonical books identical with that of Athanasius.

In the Gr. MSS, the ancient versions and the **b**
different lists of canonical books the position of the Catholic Epistles varies. But generally the Eastern Church tended to place them (as representing the Twelve Apostles) immediately after Ac. and before the Pauline corpus, while the Western Church tended to put the Pauline corpus (as being the older collection) in front of them.

The contrast between the Catholic and the Pauline **c**
Epistles is apparent at once. Paul's Epistles are for the most part addressed to individual churches; they are real letters, called forth by particular circumstances, concerned with the concrete and the individual, and full of evidences of the personal relationship between author and recipients. The Catholic Epistles (with the exception of 2 and 3 Jn and also 1 Pet.) are not really letters at all; rather they are tracts concerned with the dangers and problems confronting the Church as a whole at the times at which they were written and setting forth messages of general relevance. In view of this contrast it is hardly surprising that these books make a less immediate appeal than Paul's letters. Nor is it surprising that the fact that their canonicity was so long disputed makes the Catholic

892c Epistles (other than 1 Jn and 1 Pet.) seem to many to be of but doubtful authority. Add to this the pressing problem of pseudonymity attaching to 2 Pet., the fact that in the five chapters of Jas Jesus Christ is only twice mentioned, and the slightness of 2 and 3 Jn, and it is not difficult to understand why the Catholic Epistles (apart from 1 Jn and 1 Pet.) tend to be neglected.

d But before giving way to the temptation to relegate any or all of these five epistles to a kind of NT appendix, we shall be well advised to make a very special effort to approach them sympathetically. The fact that one 892d of them, Jas—the one which has been most severely belaboured with disapproval (e.g. by Luther)—has in our day begun to make itself heard as having a message of particularly urgent relevance for the Church of the West in the mid-20th cent., summoning it to test the reality of its faith and the sincerity of its professions (see, e.g., E. Thurneysen's *Der Brief des Jakobus* (1941)), should encourage us to maintain a patient expectancy with regard to the others.

For bibliography see under the separate epistles.

JAMES

By L. E. ELLIOTT-BINNS

893a Apart from 1:1 this writing has none of the characteristics of a letter, and is best regarded as a **homily**, delivered, in whole or in part, to a congregation. Some critics look upon it as a diatribe or a parenetic tract; but such terms are too technical. Jas as it stands, apart from a few insertions, seems to be a unity addressed to the same hearers, who were probably a Palestinian church. There is nothing in their circumstances to connect them with an 'ecclesiastical' environment such as Jerusalem. My own opinion is that they were Galileans, original followers of Jesus; the background is very similar to that of the synoptists. The attribution to James can hardly be original. Had it been by him it would not have remained so long in obscurity. Though it was probably known to Hermas at the turn of the 1st cent., it was not assigned to James before Origen and actually remained among the disputed books until the latest stages of the canon. This suggests that it came from some unimportant church and from a writer of no special prominence. He was, however, of mark among his flock, for he speaks with authority and occasionally indulges in chiding. He is utterly opposed to any kind of sham (belief must show itself in conduct) and is eminently practical. He was a teacher of ripe experience and a keen observer of human nature; his personal qualities, moreover, seem to have been enriched by inherited wisdom.

b The **style** is vivid and energetic, and the Greek is that of one who was skilled in the language and well acquainted with LXX. Though there are affinities with the 'wisdom' books the outlook is very different and the epistle can hardly be called a 'typical product of Hellenistic Judaism'; the methods, however, are not unlike those of the rabbis. Jas contains many likenesses to the sayings of Jesus, though in a vague form, and there are parallels with 1 Pet. and some of the Pauline writings, but the extent to which use is made of 'catechetical' material is doubtful, it is hardly in a form known to other writers.

c The **contents** suggest that the epistle came from a very early period in the life of the Church, before theological ideas had been worked out—there is no reference to the atonement or the resurrection. Jesus is named only in 1:1 and 2:1 and in neither case in such a way as to give convincing evidence that the mention is part of the original. The writer never refers to the earthly life of the Lord and for examples of conduct turns to the OT prophets and to Job (5:10f.). His mind was evidently soaked in OT, and for him and his readers it had the highest significance (he may have had a pharisaic upbringing). It has, indeed, been suggested that the writing was originally Jewish and that Christian interpolations are late. Such interpolations are not unknown (e.g. in *The Testament of the Twelve Patriarchs*), but the theory has not found much favour.

d The writing was almost certainly directed to **Christian Jews**; possibly with an eye to those Jews who had not yet made up their minds whether Jesus was the Messiah or not, hence perhaps its defective Christology. It should be noted that the Gentiles are completely ignored, and that there is no discussion about the conditions upon which they are to be 893
admitted to the Church.

I 1. This **ascription** is much too elaborate for what 894
follows and would suit better an utterance of an ecumenical nature. It was probably prefixed about the middle of the 2nd cent. when fresh interest was being aroused in James, and attempts made to exalt him (cf. the Clementine Romances and the literature behind them). 'A servant' is a sufficiently humble description, but it was widely applied to the servants of God; the conjunction of 'God and the Lord Jesus Christ' imply that the service is one and the same. The 'twelve tribes' represent Israel in its completeness, the ideal people of God (cf. Mt. 19:28; Ac. 26:7; Rev. 7:4ff., 21:12). The 'dispersion' suggests for some scholars Christians in exile from their heavenly home; others take it literally of scattered Christians.

The **name James** represents Heb. Jacob and was b
in very common use. It would not in itself denote any special individual, but here it is applied to James, 'the brother of Jesus'. This phrase has been taken in various ways: (*a*) literally (cf. Mk 6:3; Gal. 1:19), which is the most natural sense, and regards him as the son of Joseph and Mary by a birth later than that of Jesus (the so-called Helvidian view); (*b*) the son of Joseph by a previous marriage (the Epiphanian view); (*c*) the suggestion of Jerome that James was the *cousin* of Jesus. Jerome confessed that this view was his own invention and that it was far from convincing; nevertheless it was for long the official view of the Western Church; but historical criticism has made it difficult to hold, though both Lightfoot and Hort accepted it. It was the view of Palestinian Christians, so Hegesippus in the middle of the 2nd cent. (see Eus.HE, II, xxiii, iii, 20; see also 'Brethren of the Lord', HDB).

Greeting is typical of Gentiles rather than Christians (cf. Ac. 23:26. The only other occurrence is Ac. 15:23 in the letter from the council in which James of Jerusalem took a leading part).

2-8. Trials (not necessarily 'persecutions' of which c
there is no real evidence) are to be encountered with joy as coming from God. They are a 'testing' (better than 'proof') which discloses what is genuine in their faith or belief. Such testing produces 'steadfastness' ('patience' of EVV is too passive), a favourite word with James. But steadfastness is not an end in itself, it must have its 'full effect' and go on to something higher—perfection and the absence of any defect or lack. In characteristic style 'lacking' leads on to the next thought, for among the things which a man may lack is 'wisdom', the ability to guide his ways aright. This is a gift from the bounteous liberality of God in response to earnest and believing prayer. Faith is necessary; for the man who doubts, 'the double-minded man' is like a storm-tossed wave or a heaving sea. Such a man must not expect any gift from God and his vacillation and irresolution in prayer is typical of his whole character and conduct, for he has no firm footing in any of his paths.

9-11. The worldly status of a Christian is of small d
concern. The poor man can exult in the spiritual elevation which may accompany poverty; whilst the

894d rich man, if he suddenly loses his wealth—and wealth is a very precarious possession—should rejoice in the opportunity for spiritual and moral progress which such a deprivation may provide. In **11** there is a reference to Isa. 40:6 ; 'scorching heat' is better than 'hot wind' (RV). 'In the midst of his pursuits' is taken by many as when on a journey (cf. 4:13), but the use may be figurative.

e **12-18.** Blessed is the man who continues to be steadfast when exposed to trials, for he shall receive the crown of life (or living crown) which has been promised to those who love God (cf. 2:5). The standpoint of **12** differs from that of **2-4** where testing shows the genuineness of the belief, and the outcome is steadfastness ; here the successful endurance of trials is rewarded (as in Rom. 5:4). **Crown** has many meanings, but here seems to be the garland of victory of the athlete ; it is, however, an unfading crown and may go back to a saying of Jesus. It is also mentioned in Rev. 2:10 which Charles (ICC) thought later than the present passage. It is to be noticed that the idea of reward is not alien to biblical teaching ; virtue is *not* its own reward.

f **12ff.** 'Trials' become **temptations** (the same root in Gr.) when they link up with man's own nature. 'Desire' (**14**) is better than 'lust' of AV, being a more colourless word.

No man when he is tempted must try to evade responsibility by throwing the blame on his Maker. The nature of God demonstrates that he cannot be the source of temptation. Each man is led astray by his own desires ; these conceive sin, and sin, becoming mature, gives birth to death ('spiritual' rather than 'physical'). Thus we are given a kind of genealogy of sin, ending up with 'death' (cf. Rom. 6:23). By contrast the things which come down from God are all alike good, and he is not subject to change. For 'father of lights' cf. Job 38:7. The terms used in 17 are obscure, but the meaning is plain ; God does not alter like the heavenly bodies, which are in continual motion, or the shadows which they cast. Our very existence is due to the divine fiat and so we are his offspring, the first fruits, as it were, of his creatures. I find the reference here to the original creation, not as most scholars to the rebirth through the gospel (see NTS iii, 148ff.). First fruits may be used of the best in quality, as well as of the first in time.

g **19-27.** If we are to receive **the divine word**, or any other of God's gifts, we must have a right disposition (cf. Sir. 5:11), having ready ears, and self-control to check any impulse to hasty speech or exhibitions of anger, even to such as might seem to be excused as righteous indignation. Everything that defiles or is malicious must be rigorously avoided, and a spirit of meekness cultivated. **20.** 'Anger' comes in a little oddly. The 'righteousness of God' is that which God would approve, and it cannot be promoted by violent measures. 'Overflowing of wickedness' (RV) is not a happy phrase, and 'rank and excessive growth' as suggested by Hort is better. He and others render 'implanted' word as 'inborn'. It cannot be the same as 'the outward message of the Gospel'. Whatever the exact meaning of the 'implanted word' it brings salvation. **23.** But it is of no avail merely to listen to God's voice, there must also be willing obedience—the creed must become a code for action ; **24** otherwise the believer is like one who looks at himself in a mirror and speedily forgets what he is like. There may here be a contrast between contemplating the natural face as seen in a mirror, and the unchanging ideal which demands deep meditation and constant study. To merit the divine approval and blessing a man must accept a law which is liberty (cf. **12**), a law which because it is in full accord with the will of God is 'perfect', and is no longer a burden but a rule which is freely and gladly obeyed.

h It is all too easy for a man to imagine that he is 'religious', and to deceive himself by failing to control 894h
his tongue (cf. 3:2, 8 ; Mt. 12:36f.). Punctiliousness in outward observance is not the sum total of religion. Genuine religion is characterised by acts of benevolence to those in need and by the avoidance of such blemishes as come from too close a clinging to the world. 'God is Father, and he only receives the worship of love towards his needy children, and of purity from the world's selfishness (see 1 Jn 4:20)' (Moulton).

II 1-13. The text of **1** is difficult to interpret as it 895a
stands ; 'Jesus Christ' or perhaps 'the Lord of Glory' may have been a marginal gloss. The passage begins by the writer laying his finger on a serious defect in the assembly to which he and the readers belong ; a tendency to **servility** to rich and influential visitors. Such a practice was inconsistent with their profession, for as Christ humbled himself (Phil. 2:5ff.) there is no place for class distinctions among his followers, and such an attitude shows that they are divided in their minds and like judges who give corrupt decisions. In the eyes of the world those who lacked material resources were despised, but by heavenly standards they might rank very high (cf. 1:9 ; Lk. 12:21 ; 2 C. 6:10 ; 1 Tim. 6:18 and contrast Rev. 3:17), for God has chosen the rich in faith to be heirs of his kingdom. The rich on the other hand (and this made the conduct of the readers especially blameworthy) were often oppressors, bringing men into court by vexatious lawsuits and the perversion of justice ; they also blaspheme the 'name'. These rich men were not necessarily Christians or Jews or even partakers in such conduct ; but they were members of the same class.

2. assembly (Gr. 'synagogue') : either the assembling together, or the place where they met. The latter is probable here. **5.** 'chosen', cf. 'elect' of Rom. 8:33 ; Eph. 1:4, etc., but not implying any doctrine of 'election'. 'God's Kingdom [is] a reality of the spiritual order, entry into which depends upon spiritual conditions' (Quick, *Doctrines of the Creed*, 168). **7.** 'the name', i.e. of Christian or perhaps of Christ. It is often taken as a reference to baptism. If the offenders were Christians they may have brought discredit on the 'name' by their unworthy conduct ; but though this idea is found among the Jews, especially in later times, it is hardly in place here.

8-13. This may be a reply to those who pleaded that b
by honouring the rich they were fulfilling the **royal law**. But to love one's neighbour was hardly the same as exalting men simply for their worldly position. The law of liberty (1:12) applies to both words and deeds, but it penetrates to the motive behind them, and such servility was really a violation of the law quite as much as more flagrant breaches. The law is a unity and to break one commandment is in effect to break all. You cannot excuse yourselves for murder on the ground that you are innocent of adultery. Stern justice will be inflicted on those merciless to others ; for mercy triumphs over justice.

14-26. The writer deals with a 'superior' person, c
proud of his **orthodoxy**, and affirms that *real* orthodoxy, a right relation to God, is proved only by conduct. A profession of faith is of no avail for salvation, just as the expression of mere pious good wishes, unless accompanied by practical relief, is of no help to those in need. To repeat a creed and not to live up to it is as grotesquely futile as to feed the starving with unctuous good wishes. Faith if it is genuine must be demonstrated by works ; the demons believe, but their faith brings not comfort, but only terror.

The history of the Jewish people provides ready d
examples of the need for works to demonstrate faith. It was what Abraham *did* that declared him to be righteous ; Gen. 15:2, 8 showed that his belief was not fully effective before the offering up of Isaac (Heb. 11:17-19 connects the sacrifice with the resurrection. A ram is substituted for Isaac, but the object of the sacrifice is not propitiation, but a proof of

895d obedience. The sacrifice of Isaac is never connected with the atonement in NT). By that act the reality of his belief was both tested and deepened (Heb. 11:19) and he became worthy to be the 'friend of God' (cf. Jn 15:14f.). Another instance was the heathen Rahab. In these examples faith and works co-operate to their mutual advantage. A faith which remains inoperative, though it may have the semblance of life, is really a corpse.

e The relation of **Faith and Works** as held by James and Paul has been the subject of innumerable discussions, and various suggestions have been put forth: (*a*) They knew the teaching of one another and were opposed. The question as to which was the earlier comes into consideration in this connection but James seems to be prior in time. (*b*) James may have heard a distorted version of Pauline teaching. (*c*) There is, however, no fundamental contradiction between them, for here 'creed' stands in contrast with 'personal trust'. A formula to which they might both have subscribed could easily be found, such as 'Faith alone justifies, but not faith which is alone'.

896a **III 1-12.** This may be a separate document incorporated in the writing from which it differs in a number of ways (though possessing similarities) and uses semi-philosophical terms, perhaps in a popular manner, for since they are not explained they were presumably familiar to the readers.

Do not be over-eager **to instruct others**, for those who do so will be judged by a higher standard of attainment. Everyone slips occasionally, and it is only the mature Christian who can satisfactorily control his tongue; in fact he who can control his tongue can also control his whole conduct. So the bridle in the horse's mouth controls its whole body, and the rudder of a ship (though ships are so vast and exposed to fierce gales) directs its movements as the steersman exerts his will (or moves the rudder). The tongue like these is an insignificant part of the body, yet it is capable of exercising great influence. **5, 6.** Just as a small spark may set ablaze a large mass (of woodland), so the **tongue** (that evil world in our members, which contaminates the whole man) may kindle 'the wheel of nature' (or birth) It is itself set alight by the flames of hell (James transliterates Heb. Gehenna). Every species of the natural creation is brought into subjection by the human race, but no man seems able to restrain the tongue which remains an ever restless evil whose effects are like those of a lethal poison. **9.** By a monstrous inconsistency we use our tongues to bless God and to curse man who is made in his likeness—thus both blessing and cursing proceed from one source. Nature shows that this ought not to be, for the same fountain does not send forth both sweet water and salt, and trees produce only their characteristic fruits (two *good* fruits are unexpectedly given as examples: cf. Mt. 7:16).

b **13-18.** The truly **wise man** (especially one who would teach others) will exhibit his wisdom by appropriate conduct. Where there is bitterness and rivalry the boastful pretence to wisdom is a mere sham, and is not derived from God (cf. 1:5), but has its origin in the world, the flesh and the devil; and its fruits can so easily be disorder and worthlessness. The wisdom which comes down from heaven, on the other hand, has its own characteristic fruits which produce peace and steadfastness. The harvest of righteousness is the product of the seed of peace, and the reward of those who cultivate it.

Wis. 7:22ff. contains a description of true wisdom, but few of its twenty-one epithets occur in the present passage though some similar aspects of wisdom have a different adjective. The two lists should be compared. Meekness (**13**) in present-day popular use has lost much of its original nobility. For the Greeks it denoted a strong man's self-discipline and a wise man's humility. One who is strong, and knows it, will not be jealous of rivals or become fanatical. The partisan spirit is really a scorning of truth and a heaping up of lies.

896b **16.** Note the unproductive character of sin. Jealous partisans can never achieve any really good object and this is more damaging than actual mischief. **17.** 'without uncertainty' (cf. 1:6, 2:4), here probably best rendered 'impartial'.

c **IV 1-10.** The **things that make peace** are contrasted with the state of the community which is affected by continual 'warfare'. Such wrangling and bickering is the outcome of unbridled passions, of unbounded and uncontrolled desires, which find no enduring gratification. **2** is a very difficult verse to translate (cf. footnote). Hort rendered it 'Ye covet and have not: ye commit murder. And ye envy, and cannot attain: ye fight and war', which is perhaps the best that can be made of it. Real satisfaction can only be obtained in response to prayer; but your prayers are not answered because they rise from hearts given up to selfish and worldly concerns. **4.** 'Unfaithful creatures' is literally 'adulteresses', but must not be limited to one sex or to one sin; it applies to every Christian soul which is guilty of apostasy from God. It is impossible to be on terms of intimacy with the world and with God. God is a jealous God and will not accept a divided allegiance. **5.** 'Do you imagine that Scripture is meaningless when it tells you that "He yearns jealously over the spirit which he has made to dwell in us" (or "the spirit which he has made to dwell in us yearns for our love")?' God's yearning is no vague sentiment for he offers 'more grace' (Prov. 3:34). Grace here, as in the original, hardly means divine help, but rather divine approval. Acceptance by God is of greater value than the fleeting patronage of the world, and he looks with favour on the humble. Make your submission to God and stand up to the temptations of the devil for he will flee from you. God never turns his back on those who draw near to him (a phrase used of priests approaching the altar). But your contrition must be sincere, and manifest its sincerity by amendment in both thought and act, and even by a spirit of mourning and gloom. No definite passage can be cited for scripture in **5**. **8.** 'hands and hearts': this seems to refer to acts and thoughts, but in the ancient world sin could be regarded as a 'stain'. Note the parallelism between 'sinners' and 'men of double mind'.

d **11f.** This passage reverts to 1:26, 2:12, 3:2–12 (offences of speech). Moulton suggested that the **censoriousness** which the Jews habitually applied to Gentiles was now being applied to one another. They are too prone to criticise and condemn others. This is the outcome of a haughty spirit, for it sets aside the royal law (2:8) and him who gave it. God is the sole rightful judge and lawgiver, and his power of condemnation and acquittal is absolute; to seek to displace it is sheer folly.

e **13-17.** This and the following section denounce, in the spirit of the OT prophets, **the sins of the wealthy**. The warning here, although there is no mention of brethren, is addressed to those who know the law (**17**). The teaching is very similar to that of Lk. 12:18 and emphasises the foolishness of making plans as to time and place in view of the precariousness of life itself ('year' is contrasted with 'tomorrow'). There is no warning of the dangers which come from the possession of riches (cf. Lk. 6:24, 18:24, etc.). Such boastful self-confidence is sinful and shows a profane and worldly spirit, for all things depend on God and he cannot be left out of account. The sin is made worse when it is committed by those who claim to know what is good. The teaching is positive, sin is not only a commission of what is evil, but also the failure to do what is good. **15.** 'If the Lord wills' is not in form a Jewish expression.

f **V 1-6.** The writer now turns from those who are godless because they leave him out of account to those who are guilty of actual oppression; it seems to be more appropriate than the previous section to non-Christians or to nominal Christians (for similar passages cf. Isa. 5:8–10; Jer. 22:13f.; Am. 5:11;

896f Mic. 2:8f.). Woe to the rich, for grievous misfortunes are coming upon them. The things in which they delight are exposed to decay and destruction (cf. Mt. 6:19) and they themselves will be involved in a similar overthrow. **4.** They must not suppose that the complaints of the unpaid workers (here unlike Dt. 24:15 it is the wages which cry out) are unheard in heaven. Their luxury and extravagance are but the fattening of animals for the butcher (with a possible reference to the Day of Judgment or to the disorders which preceded the Fall of Jerusalem) and will be evidence against them (cf. RVm.), as will 'the righteous one' whom they have murdered. **6.** Many from early times took the reference to be to Jesus (cf. Lk. 23:47; Ac. 3:14, 7:52, 22:14) as did Moulton and others. But it seems better to take 'righteous' in a generic sense (cf. Wis. 2:2), though 'does not resist you' (if this is the right rendering and not 'set himself against you') recalls Isa. 53:7 (cf. Mt. 23:35).

g **7-11.** Be **patient** (not the usual word for 'endure' as in 1:3 and Heb. 12:1f.) but used in **11.** It means the opposite of impatience or short-temperedness, and is to be cultivated since it will not be for long (cf. Rom. 13:11; 1 C. 7:29; Rev. 1:3). The writing evidently belongs to a time when the coming (*parousia*) was still thought of as imminent, and not had yet become a 'technical term' (St Paul in addition to references to Christ (1 C. 15:23 etc.) uses it of his own coming (Phil. 1:26) or that of others (1 C. 16:17; 2 C. 7:6f.)). Let them learn a lesson from nature (as in Mt. 13:28ff.) for the cultivator of the soil must wait upon the operations of God. Meanwhile they must not complain, nor judge one another, for the judge himself will quickly come. Jewish history also furnishes a lesson (Moulton thought that the choice of examples shows that James was addressing Jewish hearers), for the prophets of old were patient under affliction, above all let them ponder on the classic example of Job who trusted in God (13:15) and remember God's mercy to him at the last (cf. 42:12).

h **12ff.** There follow a number of short **sharp admonitions** similar to those of 1 Pet. 2:17. **12** is a disconnected warning (unless 'swearing' is a sign of impatience) against a prevailing evil which is also found in Mt. 5:37 (many scholars regard the form here as earlier). What is condemned is the vain use of the name of God or a too ready resort to it. This may result in irreverence or in a debased sense of truth as something which need not be observed unless 896h supported by an oath.

13-18. In times of adversity **prayer** is a ready resort i (just as when things go well the feelings should find expression in praise) for prayer can meet all needs. Sickness should be dealt with by sending for the elders of the church (not for physicians, cf. Sir. 38:1ff.), that by their prayers and the use of anointing-oil (for the use of oil cf. Isa. 1:6; Lk. 10:34 and for 'means' Mk 1:41, 7:33, etc.) the sufferer may be restored to health. The **unction** of the sick man is to promote recovery; there is no suggestion of preparing him for his last journey. If sin is a cause of his trouble that too shall be forgiven (cf. Mk 2:1ff.). It is well to acknowledge faults to one another and not 'to one superior person' (Moulton). Prayer, if it comes j from one who is in right relations with God, has enormous power. In OT there is the well-known story of Elijah, no 'superman', but one like ourselves, in response to whose earnest prayers the heavens withheld rain for three and a half years, and then, again in response to his intercessions, were opened, the earth was refreshed and enabled to yield its beneficent produce (the account here disagrees in some minor details with that in 1 Kg. 17:1, 18:1, 42; cf. Lk. 4:25 and see commentaries). **19f.** is a return to the thought of **16.** Understand that he who has brought a sinner back when he has lost his way will save a life from death and cover a multitude of sins (Prov. 10:12). Critics are not agreed as to whose sins are 'covered', those of the rescuer, or of the sinner himself. Moulton thought it was very unlike NT to assert that successful preaching could atone for the sins of the preacher (cf. 1 C. 9:27; but cf. Ezek. 33:7f.).

Bibliography—COMMENTARIES by R. J. Knowling, WC; F. J. A. Hort (to 4:7 only), J. B. Mayor and J. H. Ropes, ICC.

M. Dibelius, Mey.; J. Marty, *L'Épître de Jacques* (1935); A. Plummer, Ex.B; H. von Soden, HC; B. Weiss and F. Hauck, ZK; H. Windisch, HNT.

OTHER LITERATURE: L. E. Elliott-Binns, *Galilean Christianity* (1956); F. J. A. Hort, *Judaistic Christianity*; Rendall Parry, *The Epistle of St James and Judaic Christianity*.

Spitta in *Gesch. u. Litt. des Urchristentums.*

I PETER

By C. E. B. CRANFIELD

897a This epistle needs no commendation. Its attractiveness is often acclaimed; its spiritual authority and relevance to the Christian's life in every age are undoubted. It is not, however, free from critical problems. The two main ones concern its authorship (and date) and its unity

b **Authorship**—A number of features have been alleged to be incompatible with Petrine authorship: (i) the good Gr style and literary vocabulary; (ii) the use of the LXX; (iii) the apparent echoes of Paul; (iv) the reference to suffering 'as a Christian'; (v) the lateness of evidence of its use (the first writer to show unmistakable evidence of acquaintance with it is Polycarp (*c.* 135)—though see 2 Pet. 3:1; it is not mentioned in the Muratorian Canon). It is further alleged (vi) that there are not the personal reminiscences of Jesus one would expect in a letter from Peter; (vii) that the references to the Holy Spirit are too meagre for a document of the apostolic age, and (viii) that it contains references to the ideas and practices of the Hellenistic mystery-cults so numerous as to suggest that the author was a Gentile, whose religious background was formed by the mysteries.

c Of these (i) and (ii) may perhaps be explained on the assumption that Silvanus (5:12) played the part of a responsible secretary rather than of a mere scribe writing to dictation. (It is natural to identify him with the Silvanus of 2 C. 1:19; 1 Th. 1:1; 2 Th. 1:1 and also, since Silvanus is the Lat., and Silas the Gr., form of the same Aram. name, with the Silas of Ac. 15–18, who according to Ac. 16:37 was a Roman citizen.) Since Silvanus is associated with the writing of 1 and 2 Th., it seems plausible to regard him as helping to account for (iii) also, though this is probably mainly to be explained by the existence of a widespread common stock of catechetical material in the early Church. As to (iv), it is surely pressing the language of 4:15f. too much to argue that at the time this was written the profession of Christianity must in itself have been a crime, and so to conclude that the epistle cannot be earlier than the time of Trajan's correspondence with Pliny (111–12). In fact, the persecution here envisaged may well be privately instigated rather than official. It is possible that (v) is due to chance; the absence of mention in the Muratorian Canon is perhaps due to that document's fragmentary nature. Eusebius, it is to be noted, classes 1 Pet. among the writings whose authority was never in dispute. Not much weight need be put on (vi) and (vii): the former is too subjective, and the weakness of the latter becomes clear, when it is remembered that in several Pauline epistles references to the Spirit are rare With regard to (viii) the alleged traces of mystery terminology are problematic, and it is doubtful whether any terms occur which cannot equally well be derived from other sources.

d There is a considerable body of critical opinion which regards the epistle as pseudonymous; an equally reputable body of critical opinion supports the Petrine authorship. The statement of F. W Beare that 'there can be no possible doubt that "Peter" is a pseudonym' is far more dogmatic than the present state of scholarly discussion justifies. The question is not yet settled. 897d

e **Date**—If the author is Peter, the date will be A.D. 63 or 64, the place of writing Rome. It is possible that 'Galatia' in 1:1 means only Galatia proper and that in referring to Asia the writer had only the NE part of the province of Asia in mind. In that case the areas mentioned in 1:1 would be areas that had not been evangelised by Paul. This would account for the otherwise surprising absence of any reference to him. If, however, the author is not Peter, a date in the reign of Trajan might seem most likely

f The other main critical problem is posed by the obvious break between 4:11 and 4:12 (marked by the doxology and 'amen' at the end of 4:11), by the fact that in the earlier part persecution is referred to as a remote possibility, while in 4:12ff. it is referred to as already beginning, and by some curious changes of tense within the first and larger division.

g **Various solutions** to this problem have been suggested. One that has attracted much attention recently is the **liturgical solution.** This is propounded by Preisker in the 3rd edition of Windisch's commentary on the Catholic Epistles, pp. 156ff. He finds in 1:3–5:11 a Roman baptismal liturgy in two parts The first part is for those who are being baptised and consists of a prayer-hymn (1:3–12); instruction (1:13–21), in which the aorist imperative (' be ') in 15 looks forward to the act of submission to baptism; a baptismal dedication (1:22–5), the perfect tenses of which indicate that the actual baptism has taken place between 1:21 and 1:22; a festal song in three strophes (2:1–10), which Preisker thinks was contributed by an inspired member of the church; exhortation (2:11–3:12) with a song about Christ (2:21–4) inserted; a revelation (3:13–4:7*a*); and finally a closing prayer (4:7*b*–11), which has been changed into exhortation because the whole is being sent as a letter. The second part, consisting of a revelation (4:12–19), exhortation (5:1–9), a blessing (5:10) and a doxology (5:11), is for the whole congregation. Thus, according to Preisker, it is only when the whole congregation is addressed that persecution is referred to as actually happening; for those about to be baptised or only just baptised persecution is still only potential. F. L. Cross has gone a step further and identified this liturgy with the celebrant's part of the baptismal eucharist of the Paschal vigil For a trenchant criticism of this liturgical solution reference should be made to C F. D Moule (see bibliography).

h Moule's own solution is that the whole of 1 Pet. was written specifically for the churches indicated in the greeting, but since some of these churches were actually being persecuted but others not, the writer sent two alternative forms, the messengers being instructed to read in each church the form appropriate to the particular situation.

i Perhaps the most likely suggestion is that in the composition of a letter to the churches indicated in 1:1, the author (or authors) decided to incorporate some material that was already in existence (1:3–4:11—probably a sermon to the newly baptised), because it

897l seemed eminently suitable for the purpose, along with fresh material composed with the present situation of these particular churches in mind.

98a **I 1-2 Salutation**—' The dispersion ' was used as a technical term to denote those Jews who resided outside Palestine, but its use here does not mean that the people addressed are Jewish Christians (several things in the letter suggest that they are mostly Gentiles—see 1:14, 18, 2:10, 18ff., 4:3)—it is rather an example of the Church's application to itself of terms which had been used with reference to the old Israel. Christians are a new dispersion, being resident aliens in this world (cf. 2:11). For ' chosen ' cf. 2:4, 6, 9, 5:13 : the word has a rich OT background (e.g. Dt. 4:37, 7:6f.). The Gr. represented by ' and destined . . . blood ' is perhaps better understood as three mutually independent phrases (cf. AV, RV) explaining ' chosen '. Their chosenness or election is grounded in the eternal purpose of the Father (cf. Eph. 1:4 ; 2 Tim. 1:9), is made effective through the sanctifying activity of the Spirit, and has for its goal their sharing in the benefits and obligations of the New Covenant established by the death of Christ. The last of the three phrases is reminiscent of Exod. 24:6–8. (Attempts to connect these three phrases with ' apostle ' (Selwyn) or with ' apostle ' and ' grace and peace ' (Beare) as well as with ' chosen ' seem strained.) For ' grace and peace ' cf. Rom. 1:7 ; 1 C. 1:3, etc. ; for ' be multiplied ' cf. 2 Pet. 1:2 ; Jude 2 and Dan. 4:1, 6:25.

b **3-12 A living Hope**—The letter begins with an ascription of praise to God (its form is characteristic of Jewish prayer) for what he has done for us in Christ. By the resurrection of Christ ' we have been born anew (better ' he has begotten us anew ', for God is the subject of the verb in the Gr.) to a living hope '. The metaphor (cf. 23, 2:2 ; Jn 1:13, 3:1–15 ; Jas 1:18 ; 1 Jn 2:29, etc.) witnesses to the tremendousness of what has been accomplished and—since a child does not assist in its own begetting—to the fact that it is altogether God's doing. The author probably has his own and his readers' baptism in mind (cf. the association of baptism and the resurrection of Christ in 3:21 ; see also Rom. 6:3–11). ' Hope ' is a theme-word of the epistle (cf. 1:13, 21, 3:5, 15). The idea, though not the word, is specially prominent in this section. **4**. The ' inheritance ' God has in store for them, unlike Canaan (the inheritance of Israel—e.g. Dt. 15:4, 19:10), cannot be ravaged by hostile armies (this is perhaps the significance of the word rendered ' imperishable ') or defiled by sin ; for it is ' kept [safe] in heaven for you ' (cf. Mt. 6:19f. ; Col. 3:1–3). **5**. ' Salvation ' is here clearly eschatological. cf. Phil. 3:20f. ; Col. 3:4, etc. In **6-9** a new theme-word occurs : ' rejoice ' (' joy '). In the light of the future salvation and the present hope and joy the ' various trials ' are seen in true proportion : they are but ' for a little while ', and serve to prove the genuineness of their faith. In **8** ' now ' implies a contrast with an unexpressed ' then ', when they will see him face to face. In **9** ' of your souls ' is equivalent to ' your ' (cf. 1:22, 2:11, 25, 4:19) : the whole, not merely a part, of them will be saved. **10-12** adduce two proofs of the surpassing worth of this salvation : the OT prophets looked forward to it ; it has not yet been revealed even to the angels. (A different explanation of the former of these has been suggested by Selwyn. He thinks that the prophets referred to are not OT but NT prophets ; that the Gr. behind ' the grace that was to be yours ' refers to the admission of Gentiles to the Church and the reconciliation of Jews and Gentiles in Christ ; that the Gr. which means literally ' the sufferings unto Christ ' means not the sufferings destined for Christ, but the sufferings that come to Christians as they seek to follow Christ (' the sufferings of the Christward way ') ; and that ' themselves ' in 12 means ' men of their own race '. But this seems forced.)

c **13-25 You shall be holy, for I am holy**—For the initial ' therefore ' cf. Rom. 12:1. The obligations follow from the possession of the living hope. Some prefer to take ' fully ' in 13 with ' be sober ', but it is probably better to connect it with ' set your hope '. Not only must they be sure to hope for the right object ; they must also hope for it wholeheartedly. In 14–23 the Christian life is characterised as obedience (14), holiness (15f.), fear of God (17), love of the brethren (22) ; and its motives are indicated : God is holy and you belong to him (15f.), you call the impartial Judge ' Father ' (17), you have been redeemed by Christ's blood (18–21), you have been begotten again of the Word of God (23). 898c

14. ' obedient children ' : the Gr. is perhaps better understood as a Semitic idiom meaning simply ' obedient people '. With the rest of the verse cf. Rom. 12:2. **15f**. The word ' holy ' has a long OT history. Used of God, it denotes the absolute authority with which he confronts men ; the holiness of Israel derives from God's choice (Israel is holy in that it specially belongs to him) and involves the obligation to act in accordance with his character. For the quotation see Lev. 11:44f., 19:2, 20:7, 26. **17**. cf. Mt. 6:9 ; Lk. 11:2 ; Rom. 8:15 ; Gal. 4:6. ' Fear ' is another theme-word : see 2:17f., 3:2, 15 (contrast 3:6, 14). **18f**. ' Were ransomed ' carries various associations. The Gr. verb is used in the LXX of the next of kin redeeming a relative who has been enslaved ; of the redemption of the first-born or of a life that is forfeit ; and, metaphorically, of deliverance from danger or distress, especially of God delivering Israel from Egyptian slavery and from the Exile. Outside the Bible it is used of the ransoming of prisoners of war, the manumission of slaves and the redemption of pledges. A slave might save up to purchase his freedom ; but their redemption from their former ' futile ways ' had cost more than ' silver or gold '. The latter part of **19** suggests the sacrificial significance of the death of Christ, probably with particular reference to the Paschal lamb. With **20a** cf. Ac. 2:23 ; Rev. 13:8. With **20b** cf. Ac. 2:17 ; Heb. 1:2, 9:26, etc. The final stage of history began with the Incarnation. **22**. ' Earnestly ' : the adjective from which the adverb here used is derived occurs in 4:8, and is translated ' unfailing ' : ' unfailingly ' or ' persistently ' would perhaps be a better rendering here. **24f**. To illustrate and confirm the phrase ' the living and abiding word of God ' in 23 the author quotes from Isa. 40:6–8. d

II 1-10 The People of God—**1-3** gathers up the preceding exhortation. In view of the proximity of the reference to birth in 1:23 it seems improbable that ' Like newborn babes ' is merely a strengthening of ' long for ' (the order of the words also tells against this) ; rather it refers to the fact that those addressed are still babes in the faith (newly baptised ?)—the fact which suggested the metaphor ' milk '. The word translated ' spiritual ' (*logikos*) perhaps means ' spiritual ' as opposed to ' material ' (cf. *pneumatikos* in 5, which is also translated ' spiritual ') or ' supernatural ' ; but it seems more natural to connect it, as AV (' of the word ') does, with ' word ' (*logos*) in 1:23. e

The core of 4–10 consists of 4, 5, 9. To come to Christ involves incorporation into that community which belongs to him, shares his election, and is the living temple of which he is the living foundation-stone : this community is the new Israel (9), whose twofold function is to offer up to God through Jesus Christ the sacrifice of its obedience (5) and to show forth God's mighty works (9). **4**. ' Come ' : better ' Coming ' (as in the Gr.). **5**. The verb translated ' be built ' is more probably to be taken as an indicative. **6-8** is a parenthesis explaining ' stone ' in 4. The first quotation is from Isa. 28:16. ' Cornerstone ' : here a foundation-stone seems to be intended : in Eph. 2:20 it is rather the keystone (see TWNT i, 792f., iv, 277–9). **7** explains that ' precious ' in the quotation describes what the ' stone ' (i.e. Christ) is for believers : the significance of the ' stone ' for f

898f unbelievers is then indicated by two other texts (Ps. 118:22 ; Isa. 8:14), the latter of which is commented on in 8*b*. With 'as they were destined to do' cf. Rom. 9. In **9a** four OT titles of Israel are applied to the Church (cf. Exod. 19:5f. ; Isa. 43:20f.). With **9b** cf. Isa. 43:10, 12, 21, 44:8. **10**, which recalls Hos. 1:6, 9f., 2:1, 23, is added in explanation of the phrase 'of him who called you out of darkness into his marvellous light' (9).

899a **II 11-III 12 Exhortation drawing out the moral Implications of the Gospel—11f.** forms an introduction to this division of the epistle. Since they are resident aliens in this world (cf. Gen. 23:4 ; Phil. 3:20 ; Heb. 11:8–10, 13, 13:14), they must 'abstain from the passions of the flesh'. 'Flesh' here means not merely one part of man's nature, but the whole in its alienation from God. For 'soul' see on 1:9. While 'flesh' describes man in his alienation from God, 'soul' describes him simply as an individual person, a self. **12.** The word 'visitation' can hardly refer to the trial in a human court of those addressed, for in the Bible the subject of 'visit' is usually God. The reference may be to God's visiting the Christians or their slanderers. If the former, it will be his visiting them in mercy and delivering them from their persecutors ; if the latter, it might be his visiting them in judgment and punishing them or his visiting them in mercy and opening their eyes to the truth. Or the reference may be in a general way to the final day of judgment.

b **13a** is usually understood as in RSV ; but the Gr. verb *ktizo* and its derivatives, of which the word here translated 'institution' (*ktisis*) is one, are elsewhere in the NT used only of God's creating. In view of this and also of the LXX evidence it seems difficult to take *ktisis* to mean an institution made by man. On the other hand, Hort's rendering 'divine institution among men' and the RSV note 'institution ordained for men' involve a strained interpretation of the adjective *anthrōpinos* ('human'). It seems better with W. Foerster (TWNT iii, 1034) to translate 'Be subject to every human creature for the Lord's sake' and to take this as introductory not only to 13*b*–17, but to the whole of the passage 2:13–3:12, the theme of which is the subordination of self to the welfare of others.

c In **13b** we then pass to the first example of this general rule. The Christian's obligation to his neighbour includes the obligation to fulfil his responsibilities as a citizen. **14** sums up the purpose of the state in God's intention. It is to restrain the worst excesses of fallen man's self-assertion by providing his selfishness with selfish reasons for doing right ('praise') and for not doing evil ('punish'). Christians, however, will fulfil their obligations as citizens not just for these reasons but 'for the Lord's sake' (13), 'as servants of God' (16). **17.** 'Honour all men' is the equivalent of what we suggested was the meaning of 13*a* : cf. 2:13, 3:1 ('be subject' and 'be submissive' represent the same Gr. verb) with 2:17 ('honour the emperor') and 3:7 ('bestowing honour'). 'Love the brotherhood' : within the wider area of obligation there is an inner circle, the Christian community, in which the uniting bond is more intimate. The third and fourth commands of this verse derive from Prov. 24:21 ; but there is a difference due to the fact that the writer does not like to use the same word of what is owed to God and what is owed to the emperor. In the context of a modern democracy 'honour the emperor' must include a whole-hearted acceptance of one's political responsibilities. On the state see also Mk 12:13–17 ; Rom. 13:1–7 ; 1 Tim. 2:1–7 ; K. Barth, *Church and State* (1939) ; O. Cullmann, *The State in the NT* (1957).

d **18-25** is addressed to slaves. The author does not discuss the institution of slavery, but simply addresses himself to the immediate personal problems of Christian slaves. It was the only practicable course for the tiny Church of the 1st cent. By accepting willingly and without resentment as a following in Christ's steps the unavoidable humiliations and sufferings they could transform what in itself was sordid and degrading into something dignified and noble, and attain an inner freedom. **18.** The word translated 'respect' here is elsewhere translated 'fear'. Fear of God rather than of their masters is probably meant (cf. 1:17, 2:17). With **19f.** cf. Lk. 6:32–4—though the RSV by translating *charis* differently in the two passages ('credit' in Lk. ; 'approved', 'approval' in 1 Pet. ('credit' in 1 Pet. 2:20 represents another word)) has obscured their similarity. **21.** The word translated 'example' means a copy-alphabet used by children learning to write or an outline or sketch requiring to be filled in or coloured. A cognate noun is used in Aeschylus of the 'print' of a foot. **22.** cf. Isa. 53:9. **24.** The fact that 'the tree' is accusative in the Gr. has encouraged some scholars to think the author has in mind a priest lifting a victim on to the altar or the scapegoat bearing Israel's sins into the desert ; but in NT times the accusative was often used where classical usage would have required the dative, and in 4:14 we have a fairly clear example of the same preposition (*epi*) with the accusative denoting *place where*. It is therefore unnecessary to try to give to *epi* here the sense of *motion towards*. 'On the tree' indicates the place where Christ fulfilled the Servant's ministry of vicarious suffering. 'He himself bore our sins' echoes Isa. 53:12. With **24b** cf. Rom. 6:1–11. 899d

III 1-6 is addressed to wives. This is much fuller than the following exhortation to husbands (7), probably because the writer recognised that the wives were in greater need of pastoral help than the husbands, since the lot of the Christian wife of a pagan husband was much more liable to be difficult and dangerous than that of the Christian husband of a pagan wife. **1.** Note that 'word' is here used in two different senses, first of the Word of God, then simply of 'speaking'. In **2** 'reverent and' represents an original 'with fear'. The fear is the fear of God, which expresses itself in an unassuming and yet dignified bearing towards other people : contrast the fear which is to be avoided (6). **6.** For 'calling him lord' see Gen. 18:12 in the RV : the RSV has 'husband' instead of 'lord'. e

7. The Gr. translated 'considerately' means 'according to knowledge' ; and the reference may be to understanding of the other person (so 'considerately') or it may be to knowledge of God. The latter is perhaps more likely : the point will then be that the husbands' treatment of their wives is to be governed by what they know of God's character and will. For the meaning of 'bestowing honour on' see on 2:17. The recognition that husband and wife are 'joint heirs of the grace of life' was incompatible with domestic tyranny. The last clause of the verse is both an indication that selfishness in the marriage relationship is a hindrance to the partners' fellowship with God and also a reminder that marriage should serve an end beyond itself, namely that fellowship with God. f

8-12 forms the conclusion of the section (or group of sections) which began at 2:11. **9.** The fact that God has called them in Christ in order that they may inherit the blessing he has in store for them is both the reason why they should answer evil with good and also the source of their strength to do so. **10.** The quotation from Ps 34:12 here takes a different interpretation from the meaning in the original Hebrew, as 'life' now comes to mean 'eternal life'. The man indicated by 1 Pet. 3:10*a* is the man who in this present life desires to set his heart upon the life that is life indeed, and hereafter to enjoy the good days of the age to come. g

III 13-IV 6 But even if you do suffer—13. The rhetorical question, which amounts to the statement that those who seek God's kingdom with their whole heart, though not beyond the reach of suffering, are beyond the reach of harm, takes up the last phrase h

99h of 12 (the word translated 'evil' in 12 is *kaka*, the verb translated 'harm' in 13 is *kakoō*). **14a.** 'Do suffer' here and 'should be' in 17 (both optatives in Gr.) suggest a remote possibility (see §897*f*). **14b-15a** is based on Isa. 8:12f. (LXX). In Isa. the Gr. which is literally 'fear not the fear of them' means 'do not fear what they fear'; but it is here used in the sense 'do not fear them'. Christians are to let the fear of Christ banish other fears from their hearts. The RV rendering 'sanctify' is to be preferred to 'reverence': the same Gr. word is used in Isa. 8:13. **15c.** For 'reverence' see on 2.

i From 18 to the end of 4:6 is the most difficult part of the epistle. The core of the first half (18–22) of this passage is 'For Christ . . . to God' (18), which brings forward a reason in support of what has been said in 17. The author appeals to Christ's passion, which he regards as an example ('also') but also as vicarious and atoning. But, since Christ's death cannot be rightly understood except in the light of its sequel, that sequel is indicated in the rest of 18–22, and at the same time a reference to baptism is introduced. **19** is best taken to mean that in the interval between his death and resurrection Christ preached to the dead (the men who died in the Flood being specially mentioned as outstanding sinners—if Christ actually went to *them*, then none could have been left out). (The textual emendation accepted by Moffatt, which introduces Enoch, is unconvincing, since Enoch comes in here very awkwardly. Equally unlikely is the suggestion that the reference is to a preaching by the pre-existent Christ through the mouth of Noah to those who, though now 'in prison', were at the time of this preaching still alive. The view accepted by Selwyn that the 'spirits' referred to are fallen angels and that the verb translated 'preached' refers, not to a preaching of the gospel, but to a proclamation of the approaching end of their power, though more probable than these other two suggestions, seems less natural than the interpretation indicated above.) **20b-21a** ('in which . . . saves you') makes a comparison between the water of the Flood and the water of baptism, between the eight people in the ark and the Christians who are being addressed, and between the deliverance of those in the ark and the salvation of the Christians. The OT event is regarded as a type or foreshadowing of Christian baptism. **21b.** The parenthesis ('not as a removal . . . conscience') guards against a possible misunderstanding. Baptism is not merely an external washing; it is the pledge of God's forgiveness. (The meaning of the Gr. translated 'an appeal to God for a clear conscience' is uncertain. The word *eperōtēma* should mean 'question'. It might possibly mean 'prayer', 'appeal'—in which case we might either translate as the RSV does, or else 'an appeal to God proceeding from a good conscience'. But there is some evidence that it was used of the formal question and consent that sealed a contract, so that 'pledge' is a conceivable meaning. Of the possibilities, 'a pledge to maintain a good conscience', 'a pledge proceeding from a good conscience', 'a pledge of a good conscience', the last is perhaps most satisfactory—baptism is a pledge of God's forgiveness.) **21c** indicates that the efficacy of baptism derives from Christ's resurrection. **22.** cf. Eph. 1:20–2; Col. 2:15

j **IV 1f.** picks up the argument of 3:18 (but with the additional meaning contributed by the reference to baptism) and repeats the moral exhortation in more general terms. The words 'arm yourselves with the same thought' are often taken as an exhortation to put on as armour the spirit of patience which Christ displayed, but the last part of the verse seems an extravagant way of saying that suffering thus patiently borne has a cleansing effect. It seems more likely that these words mean 'reckon that you yourselves have died with Christ' (cf. Rom. 6:1–14) and that the last part of the verse means that he who has by faith shared in Christ's death is in God's sight dead
to sin (cf. Rom. 6:7). **6.** Some take 'the dead' to 899j
mean Christians who have died (cf. 1 Th. 4:13ff.); others take the reference to be to the spiritually dead; but the most natural explanation is surely to connect with 3:19 ('the spirits in prison'). In the opinion of men they have had their judgment, but the gospel has been preached to them, in order that by God's power they may live. The Gr. *kata* in this verse twice rendered 'like' in the RSV is better translated 'according to': 'like' gives a definiteness of meaning that is by no means certain.

7-11 The Imminence of the End—With the first 900a
part of 7 cf. Mk 13:29; Rom. 13:12; 1 C. 7:29; Phil. 4:5; Heb. 10:25; Jas 5:8f.; 1 Jn 2:18; Rev. 22:20. According to many this insistence on the nearness of the Parousia is something that history has proved mistaken. For the view that it is, on the contrary, an essential insight of the gospel see C. E. B. Cranfield, 'St Mark 13', SJTh. 7 (1954), 284–303. **8.** For the connection of the demand for love with the nearness of the End cf. Rom. 13:8–14; Heb. 10:24f. The saying contained in **8b** was apparently proverbial in the early Church. Its derivation from Prov. 10:12 (cf. 17:9) is not certain, the LXX here differing widely from the Heb. Several interpretations of the words as they occur in 1 Pet. are possible: if your love for the brethren is real, you will be ready to forgive them again and again; if you love the brethren, God will overlook the multitude of your sins; you must love the brethren unfailingly since God's love has forgiven you so much. Of these perhaps the first is most probable. **9-11** consists of further exhortation in the light of the nearness of the End.

12-19 The fiery Ordeal—12-13. For the change of b
atmosphere perceptible at this point see §897*f*. These two verses say four things (either directly or indirectly) about persecution: it is characteristic of the life of Christians in this world; it tests the reality of their faith; it is a sharing in Christ's sufferings; it is a reason for joy. **14b.** For the suggestion that there is here a reference to the Shekinah see Selwyn *in loc.* But the difficult Gr. (literally 'the of (the) glory and the Spirit of God') is probably rightly translated by the RSV (except that 'spirit' should surely here be 'Spirit' as in 1:2). God's Spirit, who is glorious and the source of glory, and whose presence is the pledge of future glory, rests on the persecuted Church. The language is in part suggested by Isa. 11:2 (LXX). **16.** 'as a Christian': i.e. simply because one is a Christian, and not for any other reason. The name 'Christian' occurs in the NT only in Ac. 11:26, 26:28 and here. **17.** The idea that God's judgment begins at the Church is derived from the OT (e.g. Jer. 25:29; Ezek. 9:6). The thought is that the judgment will get more severe as it goes on. So, terrible though the ordeal of persecuted Christians is, it is less severe than that which unbelievers will have to endure. To try to escape persecution by apostasy would therefore be but to jump out of the frying-pan into the fire. Prov. 11:31 (LXX) is then quoted (18) in confirmation of what has just been said. **19.** The word 'creator' is probably chosen in order to suggest the almighty power which is able to save; the proof of God's faithfulness is the life, death and resurrection of Jesus Christ.

V 1-4 To the Shepherds of God's Flock—1. c
'Elders', though it clearly has an official sense here (contrast 5), probably includes all who have some sort of authorised pastoral function. If the author is Peter, the phrase 'a witness of the sufferings of Christ' will naturally refer to his having been an eye-witness of the Passion; but *martys* need not necessarily mean an *eye*-witness—it could mean simply 'one who testifies to'. (For another explanation see TWNT iv, 498f.) The last phrase of the verse may possibly refer to the author's having experienced at the Transfiguration a foretaste of that glory that would finally be revealed at the Parousia, or it may simply refer to his being (like any other Christian) an heir of the

27a

900c glory which will then be revealed. **2.** ' not by con-
d straint ' : e.g. they must not be reluctant to be pastors for fear of being more liable to persecution. With ' domineering over ' in **3** cf. Mk 10:41–5 (the same Gr. word is used in Mk 10:42—RSV : ' lord it over '). **5-11 Final Exhortations—5.** After a word specially addressed to the younger people (suggested perhaps by his use of ' elders ' in the technical sense in the previous section) the author bids all alike serve one another humbly. The word translated ' clothe yourselves with ' perhaps contains a reference to the apron which slaves wore. The last part of the verse is a quotation from Prov. 3:34. **6.** They are to recognise God's hand in the troubles that humble as well as in their joys. (For God's ' mighty hand ' see Exod. 13:9 ; Dt. 3:24, 9:26, etc.) Their troubles will not last for ever : those who now share Christ's humiliation will at his Parousia share his glory. **7.** cf. Ps. 55:22 ; Mt. 6:25–34. **8.** For Peter the command to watch must have had poignant associations—see Mk 13:37, 14:34, 38. **9.** They will be helped by remembering that they will not be suffering alone. In **10** ' himself ' is emphatic : their salvation is God's doing ; their hope is in his strength and faithfulness, not in their own ; cf. Phil. 1:6 ; 1 Th. 5:24.

e **12-14 Final Greetings**—Probably added in the author's own hand (cf. 1 C. 16:21 ; Gal. 6:11 ; Col. 4:18 ; 2 Th. 3:17 ; Phm. 19). **12.** For Silvanus see §897*c*. **13.** ' She ' is not likely to be Peter's wife : there is little doubt that it is the church that is meant (*ekklēsia* is feminine : in some MSS the word *ekklēsia* is actually inserted). ' Babylon ' probably stands for Rome : cf. Rev. 17 and 18. The RV ' elect together with you ' brings out the meaning of the Gr. better than ' likewise chosen '. ' Mark ' is presumably the evangelist, whom early tradition associates with Peter in Rome. For the ' kiss ' in **14** cf. Rom. 16:16 ; 1 C. 16:20 ; 2 C. 13:12 ; 1 Th. 5:26.

Bibliography—COMMENTARIES : (*a*) *in English, on the English text :* J. Calvin (1551 ; Eng. tr. reprinted 1948) ; C. E. B. Cranfield, Torch (1960) ; R. Leighton (posthumously published 1748) ; J. Moffatt, Moffatt NT Comm. (1928) ; A. M. Stibbs, Tyndale NT Comm. (1959) ; J. W. C. Wand, WC (1934) ; (*b*) *in English, on the Gr. text :* F. W. Beare (2nd ed. 1958) ; C. Bigg, ICC (1901) ; G. W. Blenkin, CGT (1914) ; F. J. A. Hort, on 1:1–2:17 only (1898) ; E. G. Selwyn (1946) ; (*c*) *in German :* F. Hauck, NTD (5th ed. 1949) ; H. Rendtorff, *Getrostes Wandern* (7th ed. 1951) ; E. Schweizer, Prophezei (1942) ; H. Windisch-H. Preisker, HNT (1951).

OTHER LITERATURE : W. Bieder, *Die Vorstellung von der Höllenfahrt Jesu Christi* (1949) ; W. Bornemann, ' Der 1 Pet. eine Taufrede des Silvanus ? ', ZNTW 19 (1919), 143ff. ; W. Brandt, ' Wandel als Zeugnis nach dem 1 Pet. ' in *Verbum Dei manet in aeternum : eine Festschrift für Prof. D. Otto Schmitz* (1953) ; R. Bultmann, ' Bekenntnis- und Liedfragmente im 1 Pet. ', *Coniectanea Neotestamentica* 11 (1947), 1ff. ; J. Coutts, ' Eph. 1:3–14 and 1 Pet. 1:3–12 ', NTS 3 (1957), 115ff. ; C. E. B. Cranfield, ' The Interpretation of 1 Pet. 3:19 and 4:6 ', ET 69 (1958), 369ff. ; F. L. Cross, *1 Pet., a Paschal Liturgy* (1954) ; O. Cullmann, *Peter : Disciple—Apostle—Martyr* (Eng. tr. 1953) ; G. Friedrich, TWNT iii, 705f. (on 3:19) ; J. Jeremias, ' Zwischen Karfreitag und Ostern ', ZNTW 42 (1949), 194ff. ; E. Lohse, ' Paränese und Kerygma im 1 Pet.', ZNTW 45 (1954), 68ff. ; C. L. Mitton, ' The Relationship between 1 Pet. and Eph.', JTS, N.S. 1 (1950), 67ff. ; C. F. D. Moule, ' The Nature and Purpose of 1 Pet.', NTS 3 (1956), 1ff. ; R. Perdelwitz, *Die Mysterienreligionen und das Problem des 1 Pet.* (1911) ; B. Reicke, *The Disobedient Spirits and Christian Baptism* (*Acta Sem. Neot. Upsal.* 13 (1946)) ; E. G. Selwyn, ' The Persecutions in 1 Pet.', *SNTS Bulletin* 1 (1950), 39ff., ' Eschatology in 1 Pet.' in *The Background of the NT and its Eschatology*, ed. W. D. Davies and D. Daube (1956) ; T. Spörri, *Der Gemeindegedanke des 1 Pet.* (1925) ; W. C. van Unnik, ' The Teaching of Good Works in 1 Pet.', NTS 1 (1954), 92ff.

II PETER

By G. H. BOOBYER

901a **Authorship and Date**—The writer claims to be Simon Peter (1:1); and by the end of the 4th cent. the epistle gained a place in the Church's canon of scripture (except in Syria) as the apostle's work. But for some three hundred years after its appearance, the Petrine authorship was frequently denied. Amongst modern Protestant scholars, it is usually regarded as one of the clearest examples in the NT of a pseudonymous writing. **(i) External Evidence**. (*a*) *To the end of the 2nd cent.*, there is no sure sign of its use by orthodox Christian writers, though the author of the Apocalypse of Peter may have known it. The Old Syriac and Old Latin versions omitted it. (*b*) *In the 3rd cent.*, there was both acceptance and rejection of the epistle. The Muratorian Canon (Rome, *c.* A.D. 200) seems not to have mentioned it. It is possible, though not provable, that Clement of Alexandria commented on it in his *Hypotypōseis*. Origen supplies the first certain reference to it (HE vi, 25:8), and indicates that some accepted it, whilst others did not. There is evidence of its approval in Egypt (the Sahidic and Bohairic versions), Asia Minor (Firmilian, Methodius) and Rome (possibly Hippolytus). (*c*) *The 4th and 5th cents.* Eusebius of Caesarea (died *c.* A.D. 340) evidently knew 2 Pet. as one of the 'catholic epistles' (HE ii, 23:25), but denied that Peter was the author, and classed it amongst the 'disputed' books (HE iii, 3:4, 25:3). Its absence from early editions of the Peshitta and the writings of Syrian Fathers like Chrysostom signifies its rejection by the Syrian Church. However, in the west, Jerome, though aware of doubters, accepted it as by Peter, and so did Augustine. **(ii) Internal Evidence**. Most Protestant NT scholars regard the internal evidence as weighing heavily against the Petrine authorship. The chief points are: (*a*) Differences from 1 Pet. in vocabulary, style and tone, too pronounced to be attributable to Silvanus's share in 1 Pet. (1 Pet. 5:12). Jerome records that this difficulty was felt in the early Church. (*b*) A stage of church life had arrived when a collection of Paul's letters existed, and could be set alongside the OT as in some sense 'scripture' (3:15f.). (*c*) The use of Jude implies a date later than Jude; and would a leading apostle like Peter have borrowed from the epistle of one who was not an apostle? (*d*) Doubt of the Parousia had become widespread and radical (3:3–13 and much more in the letter). (*e*) The Hellenistic colouring of some of the vocabulary and thought, e.g. the emphasis on knowledge (1:2 etc.) and the ideas of 1:3f. etc. (*f*) The underlying conception of the Church, the apostles, the scriptures and the faith discernible in several passages. The Church is the custodian of a traditional faith, embodied in the scriptures (including Paul's letters), and handed down from the Lord through the apostles, especially Peter and Paul. This faith is to be defended against heretics and interpreted to the faithful by accredited teachers. The individual prophet is in decline; the ecclesiastically authorised teacher of apostolic orthodoxy is taking charge. cf. 1:1, 12, 15, 16, 19f., 2:1, 10, 21, 3:2, 15f.

From the external and internal evidence, it is commonly concluded that 2 Pet. is a pseudonymous epistle and the latest document in the NT. Around A.D. 140 is frequently suggested as its date. Mayor thought that it could not be earlier than A.D. 125. M. R. James put it between A.D. 100 and 125. Spitta, Zahn and Bigg defended the authorship of Peter, and placed it A.D. 60–5.

b **Purpose**—The author's aim is clear enough. Being passionately concerned that his readers should not lose their promised entry into the eternal kingdom of Jesus Christ (1:11) in the coming Day of the Lord, he wrote to save them now from (i) antinomians and (ii) deriders of the hope of the Parousia. The attack on antinomianism is mostly concentrated in ch. 2; that on the scoffing of the Parousia expectation occupies chs. 1 and 3. But the polemic against both dangers is sufficiently intertwined to suggest that they arose from one and the same group of reprobates; cf. 3:3 etc.

Who were these perverters of the faith? Evidently erstwhile orthodox Christians (2:15, 20f.) who were misusing the OT (1:19ff.), the gospel tradition (1:15f.) and Paul's letters (3:15f.), expounding all of them falsely in the light of their own individually received revelations (1:20f., 3:16), whilst they set aside the guidance of the Church's acknowledged teachers. The fruits of their heterodoxy appeared in lives of greed, intemperance, insubordination and licentiousness, though they themselves claimed to have attained a form of spiritual freedom here and now (2:19) which could turn its back on the idea of fuller salvation at the Parousia. Indeed, they denied that there was substance in this hope (3:3f.).

The antinomianism assailed resembles that attacked in Jude (cf. §911*a*); but it had apparently gone to further extremes. Yet again there is no sure reason to suppose that the heretics of 2 Pet. were adherents of one or more of the Gnostic systems of the 2nd cent., especially when the necessary allowance is made for the hyperbole characteristic of diatribe of this nature in both Judaism and the early Christian Church. None the less, the situation was serious. Grievous errors ensnared the feet of Christian believers; and our author roundly denounced their seducers in his effort to strengthen the faithful 'in lives of holiness and godliness'.

c **Destination and Place of Writing**—To whom was the letter addressed? Few have followed the view of Spitta and Zahn that it was sent to Jewish Christians. Most scholars think that the readers were Gentiles or mostly Gentiles; and the later the epistle is dated, the greater is this probability. But where were they located? Zahn placed the readers in Palestine; Bigg and others in Asia Minor (3:1; cf. 1 Pet. 1:1); Mayor in Rome (see §904*c* on 3:15); whilst some like Moffatt see 2 Pet. as a homily in epistolary guise sent out to the whole of Christendom. The most relevant considerations seem to be: (1) The letter is almost entirely devoted to the rescue of its readers from antinomians and deriders of the Parousia. Is this somewhat restricted concern likely to have constituted nearly the total subject-matter of a short homily directed to the whole of Christendom? (ii) There are hints of personal relationships between the writer and the recipients (1:12–18, 3:1). (iii) As in Jude, the description of the dangers with which the readers are

901c beset is sufficiently particularised to suggest a specific emergency in a circumscribed locality or region (1:20, 2:10, 13, 19, 3:4, 16). (iv) If 3:1 alludes to 1 Pet., were not the readers of 2 Pet. in the areas mentioned in 1 Pet. 1:1? (v) Passages like 1:1 (cf. Ac. 11:13–18, 15, 6–11), 2:18, 20, 3:15f. suggest Gentile addressees.

On the whole, the conjecture that 2 Pet. was written to Gentile Christians in Asia Minor appears to have as much justification as any. The epistle gives no sign, however, of its place of origin. Egypt has been frequently proposed, largely on the ground of 2 Pet.'s relationship with the Apocalypse of Peter.

d **2 Peter and Jude**—cf. §911*c*. There are correspondences, some of them particularly close, between 2 Pet. 2:1–18 and Jude 4–13, 16; 2 Pet. 3:1–3 and Jude 17f. §901*a* has shown that 2 Pet is almost certainly later than Jude. If, then, the parallel passages arise from the dependence of one writer on the other (as most scholars maintain), it will be a case of 2 Pet.'s indebtedness to Jude; and this is the most widely accepted theory. It is thought to be the best explanation of such divergences of wording as occur in substantially parallel verses. These differences are said to be more intelligible on the hypothesis that 2 Pet.'s rendering is a later variation of Jude than on the view that Jude used 2 Pet. Furthermore, it is easier to understand why 2 Pet. should borrow heavily from Jude's single chapter than why Jude should extract some thirteen verses from 2 Pet. to republish them separately as the major portion of so short an epistle. Dependence of 2 Pet. on Jude is therefore a well-grounded theory; but whether the relationship is one of direct literary dependence is perhaps more questionable than is often supposed. 2 Pet. also appears to have had some connection with the rest of the pseudo-Petrine literature (especially with the Apocalypse of Peter) which began to appear in the 2nd cent.

902a **I 1-2 Greeting**—On the destination, see §901*c*. **1. a faith of equal standing:** i.e. 'a religion' or 'a saving gospel' of like privileges and benefits to 'ours' and otherwise described in 2 Pet. as 'truth that you have' (1:12), 'the way of truth' (2:2), 'the way of righteousness' (2:21), 'the holy commandment' (2:21), 'the commandment of the Lord' (3:2). For the writer, it was a body of truth to be taught, believed and lived; it had been delivered by the Lord through the apostles (2:21, 3:2, 15f.), and was conserved in the Church (1:12) and in the scriptures (3:2, 15f.). See §912*b* on Jude 3. **with ours:** probably 'with that of us Christians of Jewish descent', if 2 Pet. was addressed to Gentile Christians. But it could mean 'with that of us apostles' as distinct from the rank and file of Christians whether of Gentile or Jewish birth; cf. 1:1*a*, 16–18, 3:2*b*, 15f. **2.** The epistle emphasises **knowledge** of God and Christ as a means of salvation (1:3, 5f., 8, 2:20, 3:18). This emphasis supplies a corrective to the 'false words' of the 'false teachers' (2:1, 3. etc.).

b **3-15 Reminder of Christ's Divine Power and Coming Kingdom**—His power enables him to give life, participation in the divine nature and the promised entrance into his eternal kingdom to those who confirm their election with godly living. **3f.** The Hellenistic phraseology and thought are noteworthy, e.g. 'divine power', 'partakers of the divine nature'. **9. cleansed** includes an allusion to baptism. cf. Tit. 3:5; 1 Pet. 3:21, etc. **12.** cf. Jude 5. **truth that you have**—see on 1:1; cf. Col. 1:5f. **14.** cf. Jn 13:36, 21:18f.; Rev. 11:3–13 (*vide* Munck, *Petrus u. Paulus in der Offenbarung Joh.* (1950)); 1 Clem. 5:1–6:1; Ignat. ad Rom. 4:3. These passages show (cf. Cullman, *Petrus*, 73–169) that before the middle of the 2nd cent. there existed (i) a widely accepted tradition that Peter suffered martyrdom, and (ii) a tradition that Christ had predicted that this was to be Peter's lot in the apostle's old age. The writer of 2 Pet. will have been acquainted with both these traditions, and therefore intended 2 Pet. 1:14*a* as a reference to the apostle's martyrdom. **14b** is mostly 902
held to be a direct allusion to Jn 21:18f., or to some other version of the same incident. This is likely. It is not impossible, however, that 'soon, as our Lord Jesus Christ showed me' has also 1 Pet. 4:16–5:1 in mind (cf. 1 Pet. 4:7 etc.), especially if our author read 'witness' (Gr. *martys*) in 5:1 in the sense of 'martyr'—a meaning which Christians sometimes gave to *martys* by the beginning of the 2nd cent.; cf. 2 Pet. 3:1–2. **15** has been interpreted as a reference to (i) 2 Pet. itself; (ii) some pseudo-Petrine work (Apocalypse of Peter etc.); (iii) Mark's Gospel. Papias recorded a tradition that Mark derived his material from Peter (HE iii, 39:15, v, 8:2f.).

16-21 The Writer had received Divine Con- e
firmation of Christ's Prophesied Power and Coming—He had been an eye-witness of them at the Transfiguration (17f.; cf. Mk 9:2–8 etc.). The power and coming of the Lord as made known to the readers by the writer and other apostles were therefore no myths. **16. the power and coming:** in the exposition of the section, much turns on the sense of 'coming'. Chase and others have taken it to mean Christ's first coming, his life on earth before the resurrection. On this hypothesis, the Transfiguration (17f.) is cited as proof of the power of Christ on earth at that first coming. But amongst those whom the writer is addressing the 'power and coming' in question were evidently being represented as 'myths' (16*a*). If, then, the reference is to the first coming, what cogency was there in arguing from an event like the Transfiguration, taken from the first coming? Even the 'coming' itself was queried! This line of interpretation thus seems ill-fitting. It is, in fact, out of keeping both with the immediate context and with the content of the epistle as a whole. The rest of the letter makes it perfectly clear that what the false teachers did strongly dispute was the nature of the present divine power of Christ as Saviour and Lord and the hope of his Second Coming. Further, (i) 'coming' in 16 is the Gr. word *parousia*. This word the author uses again in 3:4, 12 of Christ's Second Coming, and elsewhere in the NT the Parousia of Christ is always his Second Coming; (ii) in the immediately preceding section (1:3–15), the readers are said to require constant reminder both of the divine power of Jesus Christ now as Saviour and Lord and of the promised entrance into his coming kingdom. cf. 2:1, 10. (iii) 1:19 represents what the apostles saw at the Transfiguration (17f.) as a confirmation of OT prophecies of Christ's Second Coming. (iv) The whole letter is anxiously concerned to justify belief in the Second Coming, since this belief had become a special target of the scoffers (3:1–13). The 'power and coming' of 16 are therefore the present power of the risen and exalted Christ as living Lord and his expected Second Coming. cf. also the following comments on 19ff. **19. prophetic word . . . sure:** i.e. the Transfiguration experience (17f.) confirmed OT prophecy. **a lamp . . . day dawns:** 'the day' is the day of the Second Coming (the Parousia). OT prophecy is to the Parousia as a lamp in darkness to the dawn. The 'prophetic word' in question will therefore be such OT predictions as the early Church interpreted as giving assurance of Christ's Second Coming. cf. Ac. 2:14–21, 3:20f.; 1 Pet. 1:10–12. Thus in 2 Pet. 1:16–19, the Transfiguration is used as a proleptic representation of the Parousia, as it is in the Apocalypse of Peter and possibly in St Mark's Gospel. **morning star . . . hearts:** for Christians, the Parousia will be the dawn of full and undying day, both outwardly and inwardly. cf. Rom. 13:12; 2 C. 4:6. **20f.** In the light of their context, the sense and implication of these much-debated verses seem to be: all scripture is God-given, through the Holy Spirit. Likewise, God alone unfolds its true meaning. He has revealed this to the apostles. In the case of scriptures relating to Christ's Parousia, he did so on the Mount of Transfiguration. The apostolic inter-

902e pretation of these and other passages is therefore to be heeded as authoritative, as against the private interpretations offered by the false teachers. cf. 1 Pet. 1:10–12 ; 2 Pet. 3:16.

903a **II 1-22 Denunciation of false, ungodly Teachers whom God will punish**—The chapter has close correspondences with Jude 4–16. Both sections condemn erroneous teachers in similar language, and refer to waywardness in Israel, the fall of the angels, Sodom and Gomorrah, Michael and the devil and Balaam's transgression.

1-3 False Teachers to be expected—cf. Jude 4–5. **1. people :** i.e. Israel. The reminder here of false prophets in Israel (cf. Dt. 13:1–6 ; Jer. 5:31, etc.) parallels the mention of unbelief in Israel in Jude 5. **will be . . . among you :** the appearance of false and impious teachers was one of the predicted signs of the End of the Age. cf. 3:3 ; Mt. 24:4–25 ; 2 Tim. 3:1–9, etc. **denying . . . bought them :** cf. 1 Pet. 1:18f. ; Jude 4. 'Master' seems to mean Christ, not God. They denied Christ in that their heresies and reprobate lives were a repudiation of his lordship. cf. 2:10, 1:16-19. **3. their condemnation . . . destruction . . . asleep :** compare the way in which Paul could personalise sin or death as men's destroyers, Rom. 7:11 etc.

4-10a Examples of how God rescues the godly and punishes the unrighteous—cf. Jude 6–8. Like Jude (and other NT writers) the author uses OT examples in the embellished or interpreted forms found in contemporary Judaism. **4.** An account of the punishment of the angels of Gen. 6:1–4 resembling that in Enoch etc. See §912*c* on Jude 6. cf. 1Pet. 3:19f. **5.** cf. 3:6 ; 1 Pet. 3:20. That Noah was 'a herald of righteousness' derives from Jewish tradition. cf. Jos. Ant. I, iii, 1 ; Jubil. 7:20–39 ; 1 Clem. 7:6, 9:4, etc. See SB iii, 769. Jude omits the instance of Noah. Did its presence in 1 Pet. 3:19f. (also after a reference probably to the fallen angels) induce 2 Pet to include it? **6-8.** See §912*c* on Jude 7. **9-10a.** Like the fallen angels of 4, the wicked dead are thought to be already undergoing punishment in hell until the Last Judgment. cf. 2:17 ; also Lk. 16:19–31 ; Enoch 22, etc. **despise authority** or 'lordship' : possibly with special reference to that of the angels and Jesus Christ.

b **10b-22 Further Description and Condemnation of the activity of the False Teachers**—cf. Jude 8–16. **10b-11.** The 'glorious ones' of 10*b* appear to be the angels who have sinned, including Satan The argument of 10*b*–11 will then be : even the faithful angels, greater as they are than the false teachers, do not revile the fallen angels. This is a generalisation about angels apparently based on Jude 9 (see §912*d*) and, possibly, a passage like Enoch 9. Bo Reicke holds that 'the glorious ones' included the angels believed to direct pagan states, and that therefore political disorder was one of the aberrations denounced (*Diakonie, Festfreude u. Zelos*, 355–67). **13.** There are uncertainties of text and translation. **suffering . . . wrongdoing :** Mayor, Knopf and others take the phrase to mean that by meeting self-destruction they will be defrauded of the anticipated gains of their wickedness. Their fate would thus resemble Balaam's (cf. 15). He perished without receiving his hire (Num. 24:11, 31:8). Some, however, would render as Windisch : 'being punished with the due reward of unrighteousness'. cf. Rom. 6:23. **dissipation :** whether this word (Gr. *apatais*, literally 'deceits'), or 'love-feasts' (*agapais*) correctly represents the original reading, disorderly love-feasts may have been one form of the revelry. cf. 1 C. 11:17–34 ; Jude 12. E. Käsemann, accepting *apatais*, sees a word-play in it : theirs were 'mock love-feasts' (*Apologie d. urchristl. Eschatologie*, 292ff.). **15f. Balaam :** see §912*d* on Jude 11. **20-2** relate to the libertine false teachers rather than to recent Christian converts whom they have corrupted. Hence these false teachers were formerly orthodox Christians (cf. 15,
20). Apparently the writer held doctrine similar to 903b
that in Heb. 6:4–8, 10:26–31, etc. **22. The dog . . . vomit :** cf. Prov. 26:11 ; SB iii, 773. **the sow . . . mire :** cf. Story of Ahikar, Syr. 8:18 (CAP ii, 772) ; SB iii, 773.

III 1-13 In spite of Scoffers, the Day of the 904a
Lord will come as predicted—The writer returns to his main aim which previously appeared in ch. 1—the vindication of the Church's hope of the Parousia. Scoffers of the Parousia are themselves a sign of the last days (2–4*a* ; cf. 2:1). Being wilfully indifferent to the ending of the antediluvian world by flood (4*b*–6), these scoffers obtusely ridicule the idea of the coming destruction of the present world, which will be by fire (7). The Lord's delay has its reasons (8f.) ; but the final conflagration is certain (10). The imminent day of God necessitates holy living and is hastened thereby (11f.) ; new heavens and a new earth follow (13). **1. This . . . second letter :** widely agreed to be a reference to our 1 Pet. **2.** With 2f., compare Jude 17f. **prophets :** i.e. the OT scriptures with special reference to prophecies thought to relate to Christ's Second Advent. cf. 1:19ff. **commandment :** see on 'faith' in 1:1. The scriptures and the account of the life and teaching of Jesus Christ, conserved in the Church and interpreted by apostles, are the ultimate authorities for Christian belief and practice. cf. 3:15f. ; Eph. 2:20. **3f.** The **scoffers,** like the 'false teachers' in 2:1, are a sign of the last days (3*b*) and are antinomian (3*c*). They thus appear to be the same perverters of the faithful as those castigated in ch. 2 ; but their ridicule of the Parousia requires special attention and refutation. Deriders of God's delay in bringing in the new age had appeared in Judaism (cf. Ezek. 12:27f. ; Mal. 2:17, 3:1, etc.), as well as in the early Christian Church (cf. 1 Clem. 23 ; 2 Clem. 11, etc.).

5f. The Gr. text contains obscurities. The writer's b
thought was probably either : (i) At God's word, heaven and earth were created out of the primeval water (Gen. 1:1–10) ; at God's word, both were destroyed by water at the Flood (Gen. 7, but interpreted as leading to the end of both heaven and earth, as in some Jewish belief, e.g. Enoch 83:3–5. cf. 1 Clem. 9:4) ; or (ii) At God's word, heaven and earth were created ; the earth, made out of the primeval water, lay between the waters beneath it and those above the firmament (Gen. 1:7 ; Ps. 24:2, 148:4, etc.); these waters beneath and above deluged it at the Flood (Gen. 7:11, 8:2) and destroyed it. The former interpretation looks preferable.

7. stored up for fire : vv. 7–13 are the only NT passage which speaks of the eventual annihilation of heaven and earth by fire. The OT does not explicitly attest the belief, though passages like Zeph. 1:18 ; Mal. 4:1, etc. associate fire with the coming Day of the Lord. In the ancient world, however, the idea of a coming world conflagration was widely diffused, and appeared in Jewish writings by the beginning of the Christian era. cf. 1QH 3:19–36 ; *Sibylline Oracles* 3:80–92, etc. ; SB iii, 773. **8-10.** The Day of the Lord tarries because God's measure of time differs from ours, his day being as a thousand years (8). cf. Ps. 90:4. He also desires to allow the utmost time for repentance (9). cf. Rom. 2:4 ; 1 Tim. 2:4 ; *Shepherd of Hermas—Similitudes* viii, 11:1. 1QpHab vii, 1–14 also offers an explanation of the delay of 'the end of time'.

12. hastening : 'As sins (cf. v. 9) delay the coming, so righteousness will accelerate it' (M. R. James, CGT, 32). cf. Ac. 3:19f. The Qumrân Covenanters regarded the study and strict practice of the Law as clearing the way for the Lord (1QS viii, 10–16, ix, 19f.). **13. new heavens . . . earth :** cf. Isa. 65:17, 66:22 ; Rev. 21:1.

III 14-18 Closing Exhortation to Purity and c
Stability—**15. So also . . . Paul . . . to you :** Mayor restricts the reference of 'so also' to the preceding injunction in 15, and sees in the phrase a sufficiently

904c specific allusion to Romans (especially to Rom. 2:4, 3:25f., etc.) to justify the conclusion that 2 Pet. was addressed to Christians in Rome (as some earlier expositors). But there is no apparent reason why 'so also' should not refer to 14, as well as to 15*a*.

16. of this (Gr., literally, 'of these') may then be an inclusive, repetitive phrase gathering up the reference to the events of the last days denoted by 'for these' in 14*a* and the exhortations in 14*b* and 15*a*. If so, the appeal throughout 14ff. is to the teaching of Paul 'in all his letters' (16). **all his letters:** these words taken with 'the other scriptures' (16*c*) suggest that the writer refers to a collection of Pauline letters acknowledged as authoritative. The apostates whom he is attacking evidently twisted the teaching of Paul, the OT and other writings revered by the Church to justify their own views. Paul's gospel of freedom from the Law to live in and by the Spirit was open to such abuse. cf. Jas 2:14–26. Was not Paul himself denounced as a libertine? The author of 2 Pet. evidently protests that unregulated private interpretations are as inadmissible for the Pauline epistles as for OT prophecy (1:20f.). The Church's accredited teachers are the true expositors.

d **the other scriptures:** what writings are here designated 'scriptures'? Certainly the OT (which from the first had been accepted scripture in the early Church) and the Pauline epistles; possibly other books as well, now in our NT or now treated as apocryphal. But the mention of Paul's letters followed by an allusion to 'the other scriptures' does not necessarily place the Pauline epistles fully on a par with the OT in scriptural authority. 'Scriptures' could have meant both the OT and other writings venerated and used in the Church's teaching or worship, these being thus at least on their way to equal recognition with the OT as canonical scripture.

A leading place in this second group of authoritative writings was here accorded to the letters of Paul. Where so high an assessment of the apostle's teaching appears, it is difficult to see the justification for E. Käsemann's contention that 15f. put Paul's apostleship in a 'peculiar twilight' (*Eine Apologie d. urchristl. Eschatologie*, 278f.). vv. 15 and 16 in an epistle purporting to come from Peter seem to reflect the view that in the guardianship and exposition of the Church's gospel the principal apostolic witnesses were Peter and Paul. cf. Ac. (the prominence given to both); Rev. 11:3–13 (?); 1 Clem. 5; Ignat. ad Rom. 4:3, etc. 904

Bibliography—COMMENTARIES: (i) *Commentaries in English*: W. H. Bennett, Cent.B; C. Bigg, ICC; M. R. James CGT; J. B. Mayor, Macmillan; J. Moffatt, Moffatt NT Commentary; R. H. Strachan, EGT; J. W. C. Wand, WC; (ii) *Other Commentaries*: J. Chaine; F. Hauck, NTD; G. Hollmann-Bousset, Schriften des NT ed. by J. Weiss; R. Knopf, Mey.; A. Schlatter; F. Spitta; G. Staffelbach; H. Windisch, [3] HNT; G. Wohlenberg, [3] ZK; W. Wrede; J. de Zwaan.

OTHER LITERATURE: G. H. Boobyer, 'The Indebtedness of 2 Pet. to 1 Pet.', *NT Essays* (1959), 34–53; F. H. Chase, HDB iii, 796–818; M. Goguel, *La Naissance du Christianisme* (1946) 455–69; H. Grosch, *Echtheit des Zweiten Briefes Petri* (1914); E. Käsemann, 'Apologie der Urchristlichen Eschatologie', *Zeitschrift für Theologie u. Kirche* (1952), Heft 3, 272–96; B. Reicke, *Diakonie, Festfreude u. Zelos* (1951), 352–67; H. Werdermann, *D. Irrlehrer d. Judas u. 2 Petrusbriefes* (1913). Introductions to the NT, especially A. H. McNeile (2nd ed.), J. Moffatt; histories etc. of the Apostolic Age.

I, II, III JOHN

By G. JOHNSTON

THE FIRST LETTER OF JOHN

905a **Introduction**—Although directed to a particular group (1:4f., 2:1, 5:13), 1 Jn is not an ordinary letter; it is a homily or tract, written at a time of schism (2:19), due to heresy. Some have dismissed it as 'the innocent prattle of a good old man', but Denney warmly commended it as 'the most passionate book in the New Testament . . . the most profound, the most searching, and the most impassioned of all' (*The Way Everlasting* (1911), 216). Its greatness consists in the penetration with which it expounds a single thought, that God is love; and Denney's judgment exaggerates its importance. The heresy was taught probably by several teachers (2:18), who claimed that their religious experience was immediate and perfect: (i) they were in communion with God; (ii) they had 'knowledge' of God, not mere faith; (iii) they enjoyed the vision of God; (iv) they truly loved God; and (v) they were themselves sinless (1:6, 8, 10, 2:3f., 9, 4:12, 20). John estimated their pretensions by the tests of moral obedience, brotherly love, and possession of the Spirit of truth; and none could truly have the Spirit who denied that Jesus Christ had come in the flesh (cf. 5:20 for a summary). For all his insistence that God's children cannot sin (3:9), the writer requires the orthodox to confess actual sins, in the assurance that Jesus died to save them and lives to be their Advocate (1:7–2:2). The heresy was some form of Docetism, i.e. the view that the man Jesus was not essential to the divine revelation. It was widespread in Syria and Asia Minor early in the 2nd cent. (Ignatius, *Trall.* 9f., *Eph.* 7), and was combated by the virginal conception stories of Mt. and Lk. as well as the fiery rhetoric of Ignatius. John avoids such a defence and simply asserts that the *Logos* or Word had become incarnate (cf. Jn 1:1–14, 6:51ff.; 1 Jn 1:1–3, 2:22, 4:2). Yet John's reaction was wholehearted, for the heresy threatened the very existence of Christianity and would have transformed it into an idealist metaphysic of absolute power as absolute love, with no real basis in history. Perfectionist claims might follow from saying that Christians had 'passed from death to life' (3:14), but they deny the proleptic character of justification (3:2; cf. Paul in Col. 3:3f. The early chapters of George Fox's *Journal* show the influence of certain elements in 1 Jn). John's purpose was to cut the wings of this gnostic mysticism and bring it down to earth (Théo Preiss, *Life in Christ* (1954), 27). Did he unduly narrow love to brotherly love? There is no exhortation to love the heretic, a biblical example too often followed by later Christianity.

b **Authorship**—Vocabulary, style, and similar ideas relate 1 Jn to the Fourth Gospel (cf. 1:1–5 with Jn 1:1–14). Each has its own stamp, of course, and the Gospel is four times as long. Common authorship might easily be assumed, and the onus of proof is on those who deny it. C. H. Dodd, however, challenges identity of authorship: 30 Gospel words are absent from the homily (*salvation, glory, judge,* etc.); 40 words in 1 Jn do not appear in Jn. Aramaisms are obvious in the Gospel, but 1 Jn has none, and it makes no use of the OT (apart from a reference to Cain at 3:12).
Highly significant is the quite different usage of 905b
compound verbs, prepositions, and particles (e.g. *oun,* 'therefore', 190 times in Jn, never in 1 Jn). The Gospel is very dramatic in style, the tract is monotonous. The teaching of 1 Jn about the second advent and the Spirit seems more primitive; 'Paraclete' refers to Jesus in 1 Jn, but to the Spirit in Jn. Again, the atonement doctrine of 1 Jn 2:2, it is said, has no parallel in the Gospel. For these reasons C. K. Barrett thinks that 1 Jn was written by 'a man of less profound mind than the evangelist' (*The Gospel according to St John* (1955), 51). Dodd ascribes 2 and 3 Jn to the same author as 1 Jn, despite their closer relationship to the Gospel in terms of vocabulary. Hence the Elder of 2 Jn 1 wrote the letters; someone else wrote the Gospel (*The Johannine Epistles* (1946), xlvii ff.; BJRL, vol. 21, no. 1 (April 1937)).

In reply, it may be said that divergences are c
accounted for by different occasions and purposes; that John had Aramaic sources, oral or written, available for the Gospel story; that primitive doctrine in 1 Jn merely shows it was composed prior to Jn, but dependent on the same basic teaching; that Jn 14:16 implies the use of 'Paraclete' for Jesus by the Evangelist, and that 'Lamb of God' (Jn 1:29) is an image containing some sacrificial elements, perhaps of a propitiatory nature. (For a minute scrutiny of the linguistic evidence, see the articles by W. F. Howard and W. G. Wilson in JTS, vols. 48 (1947) and 49 (1948).) The question of common authorship should perhaps be left open, because the Greek usage must not be underestimated; but certainly all four documents must emanate from a close circle. (There is, however, no good reason to link 1–3 Jn with Revelation.)

If the author was the Evangelist, he might be the d
Apostle John, in the judgment of many (see the commentary on Jn); but it is much more likely that he is the Elder of 2 and 3 Jn. Papias, in a famous reference, speaks about an elder John, a disciple of the Lord (Eus.HE III, xxxix, 4ff.). Irenaeus, who accepted 1 and 2 Jn as canonical, attributed them to John the disciple of the Lord, with the implication that this meant the son of Zebedee (*Adv. Haer.* III, xvi, 5, 8). Either Irenaeus was confused, or he deliberately gave the impression that John of Asia, the teacher of Polycarp, was the Apostle. An Asiatic provenance for the Elder is suggested by the quotation of 1 Jn by Polycarp (*Phil.* 7) and the Johannine influence on Ignatius; but it is not certain. The Elder must have been an influential figure, who had perhaps had immediate contacts with the Apostles (1:1–4; if he is also the Evangelist, he may have been a Palestinian Jew and a disciple of Jesus).

Date—The upward limit of dating is A.D. 155/6, the e
martyrdom of Polycarp, or the date of Polyc. *Phil.* P. N. Harrison divides Polyc. *Phil.* into two letters and places ch. 7 in the second. He dates it about A.D. 135, but it may in fact be twenty years earlier. The lower limit depends on the relationship to the Gospel; if prior, 1 Jn might be close to A.D. 70; otherwise, the evidence would be satisfied by a date near A.D. 100. This would agree with the prevalence of Docetism and the state of Church organisation

905e implied in the Johannine literature. In view of the remarkable parallels to the *Dead Sea Scrolls* from Qumrân, where the monastery was broken up about A.D. 68, it may be necessary to place 1 Jn earlier; but the present state of our knowledge does not permit us to say whether John had first-hand contact with the Essenes or Zadokites of Qumrân.

f Analysis of 1 Jn is difficult, for the thoughts are curiously convoluted; but there are natural breaks at 1:4, 2:17, and 5:12:

I 1–4	The Theme
I 5–II 17	Light and Darkness
II 18–IV 21	Truth and Falsehood
V 1–12	The Victory of Faith
V 13–21	Concluding admonitions

906a **I 1-4 The Theme**—Communion with God, which is life eternal, depends on the incarnation of Jesus Christ, the Son of the Father; and on genuine brotherly love within the apostolic community of his disciples.

What is Christianity? The paragraph emphasises (*a*) that eternal life has been made known in the historical Jesus (cf. Jn 17:3, 20:31) and (*b*) that the Church as an apostolic company actually handled, saw, and heard the divine logos who is the creative mediator of life (cf. Jn 1:3f.; Lk. 10:23f.; and the Valentinian gnostic claim, 'For when they saw and heard Him, He granted them to taste and to smell and to touch Him, the Beloved Son', *The Jung Codex*, ed. F. L. Cross (1955), 120). **1:1. from the beginning:** i.e. of Christianity, with perhaps a glance at the pre-existence of the logos. **Concerning the word of life** may mean 'concerning the gospel'; or, taking the genitive as explanatory, 'concerning the Word (logos) that is life'. John boldly calls the logos life because as the Father's Son he creates it. NT teaching as a whole affirms the revelation of life, writes John Baillie: 'that Christ is this life; and that He is this life because in Him God was revealed' (*The Idea of Revelation in Recent Thought* (1956), 55). Hence true life is communion with the Father and the Son, and it demands of men knowledge, pardon of sins, and moral obedience. John wishes to unite his readers with the apostolic Church, not simply in an orthodox confession, but rather in common love for the God revealed in Christ. Then will his joy and theirs be complete (cf. Jn 15:11; 2 Jn 4). Like a good teacher John rejoices when his scholars do well, yet his deepest concern is as bishop and father in God (2:1, 7). Note the place given by John to the Spirit of truth (4:1–6) and the Sacraments (5:8) in preserving the genuine, apostolic faith.

b **I 5-II 17 Light and Darkness**

I 5-10 Walk in the Light!—Here John refutes the heretical claims to have fellowship with God and to have no need for redemption from sin. The whole world, being subject to evil (5:19), needs Christ as Saviour; and the plain facts of life are that Christians who should not sin (3:9) are guilty of transgressions.

c **5.** 'God is light' means that God is knowable although invisible (4:20), for he reveals himself as love (4:7–12); and also that he is holy and morally perfect, for the darkness of sin does not exist at all in his Being. Contrast with this the dualism of the Persian religion of Ahura-mazda and Angra-mainyu, which may have influenced the Zadokites of Qumrân (*Manual of Discipline*, 1QS 3:18). John could have found the imagery in the OT (Gen. 1:3f.; Ps. 27:1; Isa. 50:10) or in the Christian tradition (Mt. 6:22f.; 2 C. 6:14; 1 Th. 5:4–8). He rejected a metaphysical dualism that would make Evil coeval with God, and drew the proper correlative for ethics: walk in the light! Heretical religiosity stressed 'experience', but John exposed its shallow pretence. In **7** we expect 'fellowship with him', but for this writer it was more important to remind Christians that to profess love for the Father whilst neglecting the Father's children, their own brethren, is sheer hypocrisy.

d **9.** Every sin must be confessed, in the awareness that God knows all (3:20) and that he is just. God will forgive in loyalty to his covenant and as the Father of the Son, who gave his life-blood as an atoning sacrifice (1:7, 9, 2:2). Sin is defilement, as well as lawlessness (2:12, 3:4), and must be expiated (cf. note on 2:2). To claim perfection is to make God a liar, for his revelation in Christ exhibits what sin is and how far short men fall. It is, however, God's gracious purpose that disciples should become sinless as his Christlike children (3:1–5). (See also D. M. Baillie, *To Whom Shall We Go?* (1955), 117–36, 178.) 906

II 1-6 The Test of Obedience—Now the writer speaks more directly in his own person, urging his friends to realise that the one sure way to prove fellowship with God is to do the will of God. (cf. CD 2:14 for this use of 'children': 'And now, children, hearken unto me, that I may uncover your eyes to see and to consider the works of God', tr. C. Rabin.) e

1. John writes, 'that you may not sin'. But he has already admitted that believers do sin: what then? Sometimes the sin may be so serious that nothing can be done about it (5:16). Otherwise, we have an Advocate with the Father, a Paraclete who will be heard (cf. Mk 8:38; Lk. 12:8f.; Jn 17:9ff.; Rom. 8:34; Philo, *vit. Moys.* II, 134). The Paraclete is the defence counsel or the intercessor (cf. Abraham's prayer in Gen. 18:23ff.). John, like the author of Hebrews, links the heavenly intercession of Christ to his atoning death (Heb. 2:17; cf. 4:14, 9:24). **2.** 'He is the expiation (*hilasmos*) for our sins' (cf. Rom. 3:25). 'Expiation' agrees with the notion of cleansing in 1:7, but Leon Morris (ET 62 (1951), 227ff.) has revived the case for 'propitiation' as better expressing the meaning. For it keeps the personal nature of the breach with God caused by sin, and the necessity of averting the 'Wrath' (which is no merely impersonal principle, as Dodd has argued). Neither word is quite adequate for the paradox that God who is light and love, holy and eternal, sent Christ as Saviour (4:10); the means of atonement is thus a personal life freely laid down (3:16). Forgiveness is always tragic, as Denney says, because it springs 'out of an agony' (op. cit., 300, 303f.). Note that the sacrifice was offered for the whole world (cf. 4:14; Jn 3:16). Dodd thinks that this implies an extension of Christian charity by John to all men, not simply to the brotherhood. The love which is commanded is caring unselfishly for others, rather than an emotional liking. f

7-11. 'Beloved, it is not a new commandment I am writing to you . . . Yet it is a new commandment I am writing to you—what is true . . .'. In this monotonous style John presses home his point. There is an echo of Jn 13:34f., for the 'eleventh commandment' is peculiar to Jn. As planets of the Sun of righteousness the enlightened are to shine; the fresh element in their loving is that it should be 'as he loved them'. ('He' and 'him' are often ambiguous in 1 Jn, referring either to Christ or the Father.) John's condemnation is directed against any who forget the elementary duty of the faith. The true light of God is shining on the road of life, so that there can be no 'scandal', no cause of stumbling (cf. Mt. 16:23, 18:7ff.; 1QS 3:20f., 'All who practice righteousness are under the domination of the Prince of Lights, and walk in ways of light; whereas all who practice perversity are under the domination of the Angel of Darkness and walk in ways of darkness', tr. Gaster). g

12-17. Children, fathers, young men: St Augustine thought these refer to the faithful generally (so Dodd); Origen took them to differentiate on the score of spiritual age. The verbal tenses ('I am writing . . . I write', lit. 'I wrote') are equally hard to understand. Probably some distinctions are in view in 'fathers' and 'young men' (cf. 1 Pet. 5:1, 5; Schnackenburg compares 1 Tim. 5:1f.; Tit. 2:1–8; there is a similar concern in 1 Clement). The faithful are 'children' in relation to John and to God. **12.** 'For his sake' should be 'through his Name' (there h

906h may be an allusion to Baptism). The elders ('fathers') know him who is from the beginning, i.e. the Word of Life (1:1) or God himself; and this is the warrant for their function in the community. The young men are victors in the spiritual warfare, for they have kept the Word of God (but this allusion is baffling). The solemn, rhetorical style recalls Jn 14–17.

i The first main section is concluded here with a stern warning against worldliness (cf. Mt. 6:24; 1QS 1:6). John sums it up as **lust of the flesh:** sensuality and sensuousness; **lust of the eyes:** covetousness and illicit sexuality; and **pride of life:** pretentious materialism or a reckless contempt for God like the rich man's in Tolstoy's *What Men Live By*. It is folly to prefer the things of this dying world to the eternal realities of life with God (cf. 2 C. 4:18; Heb. 11:27). **17.** 'Abides' should perhaps be 'will abide'. We expect here, 'but God is eternal', and some Latin texts supply, 'even as he himself abides for ever' (cf. Isa. 40:8; 1 Pet. 1:23f.). Prefer the shorter reading.

Man's love for God is mentioned twice, at **2:5, 15**; this is rare in NT, despite the great commandment (see Quell and Stauffer, 'Love', *Bible Key Words* from Kittel's TWNT, tr. J. R. Coates (1949), 45ff.).

907a **II 18-IV 21 Truth and Falsehood**

II 18-29 The Crisis has arrived!—'Hour' is a destiny-laden turning-point (cf. 'end' in Lam. 4:18, 'time' in Mk 1:15, and 'hour' in Jn 2:4, 13:1). With prophetic insight into the menace to the Church's life represented by his opponents John warns that the final judgment is at hand when Christ will appear (cf. 3:2, 4:17). He was proved wrong, and no man knows the hour (Mk 13:32f.). Yet this expectation was deeply embedded in the apostolic tradition and was sometimes coupled with the advent of a diabolical rival to Christ (Mk 13:6, 22; 2 Th. 2:3f.; Rev. 16:13). 'Antichrist', however, is found only here and at 4:3 and 2 Jn 7 in NT; the spirit of Antichrist means a false prophet speaking in ecstasy (cf. 1 C. 12:3). John was right to detect a supreme danger in the heresy. His statement, 'Jesus is the Christ' (22), has no merely Messianic significance, for its point is that 'Jesus' who was a **true** man is the Saviour of the world and Son of the Father (4:2, 14, 5:5f.). This coheres with Jesus' own teaching (Mt. 11:25–7) and the earliest creeds that call him *Maran*, our Lord (Rom. 10:9; 2 C. 4:5; Heb. 7:14).

b Traditionally John's chief opponent in Ephesus was Cerinthus (Iren., *Adv. Haer.* I, xxvi, 1; Eus.HE IV, xiv, 6). But **18** has several teachers in mind. It is not clear if they were excommunicated; at any rate for the Elder their departure was, in God's providence, to demonstrate that 'not one of them belonged to us' (**19**; RSV is too literal). **20.** In theory the faithful require no teacher, for they know the Truth (ultimate reality disclosed in a human life and given expression in doctrine) and have an 'anointing' from the Holy One. So they 'know everything' (RSV*n*; cf. 27). *Chrism* (anointing) is associated with doctrine in Ign. *Eph.* 17, hence Dodd refers this passage to initiation; but not to Baptism or the gift of the Spirit. The *chrism* is the apostolic gospel. This is far-fetched. More probably there is a reference to baptismal 'sealing' with the Spirit, as in 2 C. 1:22 (note too Jn 14:26, 16:13). John indeed exaggerates wildly, because the *raison d'être* of this homily is that Christians very badly need his instructions! Who will test the Elder? Like others he is subject to the tradition that stems from Jesus, and his own tests of obedience and love.

c **29** marks a transition, and may go with 3:1 'He' and 'him' should refer to Christ, who is about to come (28); but rebirth belongs with the Spirit (Jn 3:6–9) or the Father. 'Righteous' is used of God in 1:9 also (RSV 'just')

d **III 1-10 The Children of God confront the Children of the Devil—1** sounds flat in RSV. Translate, 'Behold what amazing love!' **2** links
vision with spiritual likeness in causal relation (cf. 907d
Mt. 5:8f.; Jn 14:9, 21, 17:24). Some take its last clause with 'we know', and a possible translation is: 'And what we shall be has not yet been revealed: we know that, and we know that we shall see him as he is.' In that event John may be refuting an heretical claim that vision, which they had (6), inevitably involves likeness, so that they cannot sin. But this may not have been a distinctively heretical idea: prefer the RSV.

1-3 say (*a*) our hope of being like Christ is grounded on our being God's children now (cf. Jn 1:12); (*b*) this demands purification, for Christ is pure, i.e. sinless (cf. 1:9, 3:5); and (*c*) for this reason the world no more recognises the disciples than it did Christ (Jn 1:10), indeed it hates them (3:13; Jn 16:33, 17:14).

4-10 centre on the proposition that 'he who does e
right is righteous'. This quite elementary principle was being subverted by a deceiving teacher, whose comfortable doctrine was that sin is an occasion for grace (cf. Rom. 6:1f., and Heine's famous aphorism that it is God's business to forgive), or that a true gnostic can never sin. But Christ came to destroy the Devil's works (cf. Heb. 2:14f.), for the Devil is the 'old sinner'. **8.** 'From the beginning' is difficult: 'from all eternity' would be Zoroastrian (the Devil is the dark side of God, says the Zen Buddhist-Christian syncretism of Alan Watts in our own day); 'from the start of history' is not satisfactory, if the Devil be a fallen angel; perhaps John means vaguely, 'from the start of sin'. At any rate, the sinner is a child of the Devil (a Semitic idiom), whereas the godly is a child of God (cf. Jn 8:37ff.). Godly is as godly does. Hence the children of God do not sin (theoretically?) seeing that they dwell in Christ (**6**) and God's seed dwells in them (**9**; RSV 'nature' is obscure). The seed may be the family of God collectively (Bengel, Moffatt); or the divine Word as in Mk 4:14; Lk. 8:11; Jas 1:18 (Augustine, Luther, Dodd). It is best with Law to take it as a new principle of life implanted at spiritual rebirth. John is emphatic that genuine fellowship with Jesus Christ prevents sinning, and this is an important thought; but John is no perfectionist (1:9). **10b** leads to the next application of the central concept, right action means brotherly love.

11-24a. Cain and Abel are types of the world and f
the Church. John seems to be dependent on Jesus' teaching as in Mt. 5:21f. He does not raise the questions, could Cain have done otherwise? was the Devil really responsible? but merely sets the orthodox over against their enemies. **19.** The former 'are of the truth', keep the divine law, and believe on Jesus Christ as Son of God (22f.). If they love one another, they hold fast to eternal life, which is theirs through faith and God's gift of the Spirit (14, 24). The opponents are the worldly in general, but presumably include the heretics. It may be that the latter had exhibited bitter antagonism to the orthodox (the *odium theologicum*). **17f.** show that John is aware how much his own followers have to be reminded to put their faith into deeds. Jesus Christ as always is the pattern, for love means sacrificial ministry and therefore may involve martyrdom (16; cf. Jn 15:13); and the hope of his people is in God, who knows everything and answers the prayers of those who do his will (20, 22). 'God's love' (17) is ambiguous but probably means love for God. **19f.** are difficult in Greek, but RSV offers a reasonable text. On **20** cf. a Qumrân hymn (1QH 11:7f.): 'in Thy counsel (is) all knowledge'. The note of mutual love in **23** points back to 3:11 and forward to 4:7 Meantime a new section is inserted at 24*b*.

III 24b-IV 6 Testing the Spirits—The proof of g
communion is in the Spirit God has given (Jn 14:16f.). Christians are anointed, because they are Messiah's people (Isa. 61:1–3), and God has breathed into them a new life characterised by the virtues of Christ, on

907g whom the Spirit rested. Yet, in spite of calling the Spirit 'the witness' (5:7, cf. Jn 15:26; Ac. 5:32), 1 Jn does not describe him as the Paraclete. 'Spirit of truth' is, however, common with the Fourth Gospel. One must admit that the pneumatology of the homily is simpler than Jn's. God inspires the orthodox, the Devil inspires the heretics (was it really as clear-cut as that?). The source of inspiration is to be detected in what the ecstatic says about the Incarnation: either concerning its reality or its method. For **4:2** may be either, confesses Jesus 'as Christ come in the flesh', or, confesses 'Jesus Christ, come in the flesh'. Victory is assured for the orthodox, since God is on their side and none is greater than he; and this must be a comfort when all the world goes after the heretic (**4:5**). It is obvious that the world will accept only an easy morality, and such success simply exposes the hollowness of the false teaching. In **6** we should perhaps omit the clause, 'and he who is not of God does not listen to us', as a gloss.

h **IV 7-21 Love is of God**—Here is concentrated the theology of John, who assumes the reality of God the invisible, and all that the prophetic faith of the OT had taught about his nature and will. Alongside the 'God is light' of 1:5 we must now set the 'God is love' of **8**. John does not mean that light is God, nor that love is God (the nouns are anarthrous; contrast the statement that 'sin is lawlessness'). In Corinth then, and in the western world today, it might be popular to equate love with God. John rather means that loving is the most characteristic activity of the Godhead, such love as was manifested at the Cross. God cares. This doctrine is 'our author's outstanding contribution to Christian theology' (Dodd). Of course, John's primary desire is to urge Christians to treat one another as God treats them, with gracious concern.

i **13.** Assurance and inward resource are bestowed on the faithful by God's Spirit (RSV 'his own' is somewhat strong). **16.** Abiding in love means to continue in loving actions and thus in fellowship with God, our final Judge. Such love takes terror from the expectation of the Judgment, for the loving life here and now is already a part of the eternal order. But there is a fear of the Lord that is wisdom: 'In all love there is an element of fear . . . Fear spiritualised is in all adoration' (Baron von Hügel, *Letters to a Niece* (1929), xx, xliii). **20** repeats the now familiar condemnation of one who claims to be loving God when clearly he 'hates' (i.e. dislikes, neglects, or hurts) his fellow-Christian (cf. Mt. 5:24; Mk 12:29–31); John has fully grasped his Master's teaching. Some Christians love too easily their distant, unknown brethren to the neglect of those on their doorstep; others refuse to help the far-off on the ground that charity begins at home! John might have added an injunction to love the enemy and the heretic; but his statement in **19** sublimely and simply defines the obligation of love, and makes it absolute: 'We love, because he first loved us.'

908a **V 1-12 The Victory of Faith**

1-5 recall 2:13, 3:1f., 10, 4:4. Belief in the Incarnation has at once two effects: (*a*) it brings the believer into the Family of God; and (*b*) enables him to conquer the evil influences of the world. There are also these corollaries: (i) that the believer should love God and the children of God; and (ii) that he should observe the divine commandments, which will not weigh him down because they flow from love (cf. Mt. 11:30). Nothing here is new, but the convolution of thought is typically Johannine.

b **6-12** deal with the historical life of God's Son, and the divine witness to it. RSV follows B (codex Vaticanus) in **6**; a few MSS substitute 'Spirit' for 'blood'; ℵ (codex Sinaiticus) and some important authorities read 'through water and blood and Spirit' (cf. **8**), which Moffatt and Dodd accept. **6b** is against the addition, and **7** seems to make a quite new point. Water and blood refer primarily to the baptism and death of Jesus, demonstrating that 908b
it was no phantom that went down into the Jordan and ascended the Cross. They may also allude to the sacraments of Baptism and the Lord's Supper; only, it is most unusual for 'blood' to represent the Eucharist (but cf. Jn 6:54). God witnessed to his Son at the baptism and the Transfiguration, according to the Synoptics (Mk 1:11, 9:2ff.; cf. 2 Pet. 1:16–21).

Primitive tradition showed Jesus as one who had c
been endowed with the Spirit, and Jn agrees (1:32–4, 3:34, 7:39; and the Paraclete promises). Similarly, the apostolic preaching was done in the power of the Spirit (Ac. 2:14ff., 5:32; 2 C. 12:12; Heb. 2:4), who spoke also through the Christian prophets (1 C. 12:10, 14:1ff.). Hence the witness of the Spirit was effectively displayed to those who had ears and eyes (cf. 1 C. 2:12–14). **7** contains in germ the great doctrine of the *testimonium internum Spiritus sancti*, without which it is not possible to express fully the meaning of the final revelation in the historical, but now ascended, Jesus. The Spirit is the Spirit of truth, because proceeding from the true God. (Note that the frequent reference to the Holy Spirit by this title in the Qumrân literature makes it now more probable that Jesus taught his disciples about the Spirit, as John above all suggests.)

8. The famous interpolation after 'three witnesses' is d
not printed even in RSV*n*, and rightly. It cites the heavenly testimony of the Father, the logos, and the Holy Spirit, but is never used in the early trinitarian controversies. No respectable Greek MS contains it. Appearing first in a late 4th-cent. Latin text, it entered the Vulgate and finally the NT of Erasmus.

The paragraph ends with the affirmation that e
eternal life is in the Son, to be enjoyed only by those who possess the Son (cf. 1:2, 2:23, 4:9). John is ruling out all who repudiate the Lord's humanity, rather than setting up anything like a Chalcedonian orthodoxy.

13-21 The Concluding Admonitions have at their f
heart a wonderful battle-cry: we know! With this reiterated indicative is asserted the completely superior position of John and his followers (even when an indicative is an atrocity in Greek, as in **15**). One may pray for an erring brother, knowing that God hears the petitions of the faithful; but intercession for one who is guilty of mortal sin is futile. In the context, this sin is either the denial of the Incarnation or the act of apostasy (cf. Mk 3:29; Heb. 10:26–31). **18** stresses the cleavage between Christ with his people and the Devil with his; no compromise is permitted; cf. the eternal enmity between those predestined to follow the spirit of truth and those who must follow the spirit of perversity in 1QS 4:17. **20f.** Christ has revealed the one true God, the source of eternal life (cf. 5:12; Jn 17:3, 20:31). 'This is the true God' does not refer to Jesus, as Stauffer thinks (*Theology of the NT* (Eng. tr. 1955), 114). Nevertheless to know the Son is to know the Father.

The end of the tract is abrupt. John's last word g
recalls the first Mosaic commandment: no other gods before me! For an idol is any substitute for the real God who is man's ultimate concern.

THE SECOND LETTER OF JOHN

Irenaeus (*Adv. Haer.* III, xvi, 8) and Clement of 909a
Alexandria (*Strom.* II, xv, 66, and the *Adumbrationes* where it is summarised) knew 2 Jn. The Muratorian (Roman) Canon, *c.* A.D. 190, accepted two letters of John, but doubts remained in the West, as Jerome tells us, until the 4th cent.; the Syriac East did not canonise the letters till the 6th cent. Both 2 and 3 Jn are footnotes to Jn and 1 Jn, and preserved presumably by being associated with one or other of them. No good reason can be given for supposing that 2 or 3 Jn is a forgery, or how in that case either could have survived. The date must be close to that of 1 Jn,

909a and the value of the notes is that they shed some light (tantalisingly dim) on the figure of the Elder and the situation of the Church.

b The address of 2 Jn is puzzling, but from **8** onward it is clear that a local church (Pergamum or the like?) is being warned by the writer against the same kind of heresy that is in question in the first epistle. 'The elect sister' of **13**, therefore, is the Elder's own church, perhaps Ephesus. Verse **4** implies either that the Elder had visited the church, or that some members had come to him. Intercommunication by letter and visit promoted the unity and catholicity of the Church, and hospitality had become a typical Christian virtue (Mk 6; Heb. 13:2; *Didache* 11–13, although the *Didache* may be archaising). So serious a view of the heresy is taken by the writer that he advises his readers not even to admit its exponents into their homes (cf. 2 Tim. 3:6f.). Bonsirven regards this as a sentence of excommunication from the apostle John.

c **1-3 The Salutation**—Unusual features are 'mercy' (not a Johannine word), 'the Father's Son', 'in truth and love', the repeated 'will be with us', and, of course, 'the elect lady'. We may compare 1 Tim. 1:1f. and 2 Tim. 1:1f., but contrast the openings of 1 Pet., Jude, and the genuine Paulines. The phrase 'will be with us' in **3** might be omitted as an example of dittography, only there is no MS authority for the conjecture. The entire opening of **1** is unnatural, perhaps due to the political situation in Asia Minor in the reign of Domitian (cf. 1 Pet. 5:13) or more probably to some domestic problems with which the Elder is concerned. RSV 'in the truth' may be correct, though the words can mean 'genuinely' (cf. 3 Jn 1). 'All who know the truth', the true gnostics, are the orthodox who acknowledge the Elder (cf. 1 Jn 2:21; Jn 8:32). Truth means more than doctrine set forth in propositions; it is final reality revealed in Jesus Christ and so belonging with grace and love (Jn 1:14; 1 Jn 4:8). 'Love is truth in human action; and truth is love in regard to the order of things' (Westcott). The second 'from' in **3** is deliberate, for it safeguards the dignity of the Son.

d **4-11 The Crisis**—Deceiving antichrist (see on 1 Jn 2:22) is abroad, and the price of surrender would be the loss of God himself because men are isolated from the Father unless they truly confess and serve the Son. Thus it is 'wicked work' (11) to seduce God's children from their proper allegiance. On the other hand, the gospel is good news that God loves, that in Christ there is salvation (8, a full reward), namely, eternal life (cf. 1 Jn 5:20). This is the secret of joy (4) Joy and love belong with light. What indeed is love without joy? Light reveals the truth concerning God's nature and his purpose for man. What then is love except obedience? **5.** 'That we love one another' sums up the Elder's teaching; on the 'new commandment' see notes on 1 Jn 2:7.

e **7-11.** The coming of Jesus Christ in the flesh is being denied (cf. 1 Jn 2:18). Dodd thinks the heretical teachers 'have set on foot a general appeal to the public', but it is more likely that the 'world' (7) is the realm of darkness, and the meaning is quite simply, 'many deceivers are abroad'. Westcott takes the present participle 'coming' (7) as futuristic, referring to the Parousia; and this would mark a material difference in the heresy being attacked. More consonant with the situation would be a reference to the Incarnation, the participle being aoristic (cf. 1 Jn 4:2). **8.** 'what you have worked for' is an easier reading, and the footnote is preferable. We teachers (says the Elder), who are the rightful interpreters of the faith (1 Jn 1:1–4), have laboured to establish our spiritual children in love and faith; their reward, and ours, is to be like Christ at his coming (1 Jn 3:1; cf. Jn 4:36 for the idea of reward, which is absent from 1 Jn). **9.** 'Any one who goes ahead' should refer in the context to theological issues, and so Westcott: 'entering on new regions of truth and leaving the old' This involves heretical boasting about superior knowledge. But that is contained in the next phrase, hence some prefer to translate, 'any one who takes the lead' (cf. 3 Jn 9). 'The doctrine of Christ' must refer to the point in dispute at 7 and in 1 Jn; so the genitive is objective. To abide in the doctrine (cf. Jn 8:31) is to abide in the Son, to be a friend of Jesus, a loyal member in the Church (1 Jn 2:22f.). Here the Elder asserts that the profession of orthodoxy involves fellowship with the Father and the Son (there are no references to the Spirit in 2 or 3 Jn). On his own showing, however, this does not follow at all. There may be an orthodox confession without true love, and that is a form of disobedience. Love is defined, e.g. in Jn 15:12; 1 Jn 3:16f., 5:16 (caring for each other as Jesus cared; if need be, martyrdom; intercession before God). We must assume that such teaching is embedded in the meaning the writer gives to 'having the Father and the Son'. 909e

12-13 Conclusion—'Come to see' is a paraphrase. f
Some texts read 'come'; the best ones have 'I hope to be with you', where 'with' means 'to enjoy personal relations with' (cf. Jn 1:2, 'with God'). 'Face to face' is literally 'mouth to mouth' (cf. 2 C. 6:11). There is no adequate substitute for personal meeting (see J. H Oldham, *All Life is Meeting*). In **12** there is strong textual support for 'your joy'. We may compare Jn 15:11, 16.24; 1 Jn 1:4. With 'I have much to write to you' Bonsirven compares the words of Jesus in Jn 8:26, 16:12, and 17:13.

THE THIRD LETTER OF JOHN

This note might be called 'To Gaius' (cf. Philemon), 910a
but its *dramatis personae* are four men—the Elder, Gaius, Demetrius, and Diotrephes. Demetrius, a travelling preacher perhaps or an Ephesian Christian, probably carried the letter to Gaius (**12**). It is by no means certain that Diotrephes and Gaius belonged to the same local church, for surely in that case Gaius would have known what had happened (**10**). Diotrephes likes to be 'at their head' (RSV omits 'their'). The 'us' of **9f.** may be a real plural, including Gaius and other supporters of the Elder (RSV 'my authority' and 'me'). Gaius knows to which church his friend refers Our estimate of the functions exercised by these three men depends partly on the same evidence. Gaius and Diotrephes may each be either member, leader, or bishop; and, if they are bishops in a monarchical sense, then the Elder holds or claims an almost archiepiscopal position. Against such an interpretation is the weak phrasing of **10**, where we should expect a strong statement of his authority. (The same argument tells against his being an apostle.) Also, the verbs in **10b** may be only conative, 'tries to stop . . . tries to expel'. If Gaius and Diotrephes belong to the same congregation, we may see a conflict within the eldership (cf. Tit. 1:5ff.; 1 Pet. 5:1ff.) On the whole, it is reasonable to deduce that all three men were leaders of consequence. The Elder's high standing would be enhanced if he were also the Evangelist and the author of 1 Jn, possibly a personal disciple of Jesus. 1 Clement refers to successors of the apostles who were the predecessors of the local presbyter-bishops in Greek and Asiatic churches towards the end of the 1st cent (e.g. Ignatius of Antioch), and to this group perhaps Timothy, Titus, and the Elder belonged. Yet it is more significant that the author of 3 Jn relies less on his official prestige than on personal influence. The charges against Diotrephes were ambition, and rejection of the Elder's friends. Was he, in addition, guilty of heresy regarding the Incarnation? There may be an implicit contrast with Gaius who professed and served the Truth; nevertheless, there is no explicit accusation of heresy, and we must conclude that that was not the real ground of their antagonism. We do not know

910a Diotrephes' side of the story; and, since there are usually two sides, he may have felt, not without cause, that the Elder was usurping more authority than he could properly claim.

b Analysis is simple: **1-8** deal with Gaius and his kindness to travelling missionaries; **9-11** advise him about the conduct of Diotrephes; **12** commends the bearer, Demetrius; and **13-15** conclude, in similar manner to 2 Jn 12f.

c **2.** Read (following Piscator), 'I pray above all that you do well and keep well, as it does go well with your soul.' **3.** Omit 'For' at the beginning. 'The truth of your life'—better, 'the truth you profess'. **3f.** 'follow the truth' does not quite catch the meaning of the original, 'walk in the truth' (i.e. in daily behaviour). **4.** 'joy' may be correct, although B (Vaticanus) and some editors prefer 'thanks' (*charis*; this word is rare in John, hence it is the more difficult reading here).

d **1-2 The Greeting**—Nothing else is known of Gaius. 'I love': the 'I' seems to be emphatic. Whatever others say, I assure you of my affection. 'In the truth' may mean 'sincerely', but **3** justifies 'the truth'.

e **3-8.** Christians visiting the Elder and his church have commended Gaius for the truth of his life, that is, for sound doctrine and conduct befitting his profession. (The word 'church' occurs in John only here and at 9f.). **4.** Such news gladdens the heart of the Elder as father in God to Gaius, and he gracefully encourages his 'child' to persevere in good works (6). 'As befits God's service', lit. 'worthily of God' (cf. Phil. 1:27; 1 Th. 2:12). **7.** 'Heathen' is lit. 'Gentile people', for by now a Gentile is a non-Christian (cf. Eph. 2:11, where 'in the flesh' defines 'Gentiles' in its more usual sense). Accepting food, money or shelter from the pagans would not have been treachery on the part of missionaries; the reference must be therefore to some further compromise or unchristian practices. Those who have gone forth 'for his Name's sake' (cf. Ac. 5:41; Rom. 1:5; 1 Pet. 4:14; Ign. *Eph.* 7) are the duly commissioned teachers who offer Christ the Lord as Saviour of the world; **8** Gaius may support such men as fellow-workers 'for the truth'. He should test the spirits (cf. 1 Jn 4:1). 910e

f **9-11.** Condemnation of Diotrephes answers the commendation of Gaius. 'I have written' could refer to 1 or 2 Jn (preferably the former, on the ground of content) or to some letter not preserved. **10.** 'Prating' is archaic in modern English: 'putting out gossip or slander about us' (cf. 1 Tim. 5:13). **11** reminds us of 1 Jn *passim*. God's children do good; the evildoer has not really seen God, whatever he may claim (see notes on 1 Jn 3:1–10).

g **12,** a testimonial for Demetrius, who adorns the Truth, is praised by the Elder and all who know him (cf. Jn 19:35, 21:24).

h **13-15 The Conclusion—14.** 'We shall talk' (a simple future). When the Christian says, 'Peace be to you', he means, 'The God of peace be with you, to bless and sustain you' (Jn 20:19; Rom. 5:1; Phil. 4:7). **15.** 'The friends' is uncommon, and lovely (cf. Jn 15:15). 'Greet the friends (or, my friends), each by name' (RSV misses the point entirely). The great Shepherd calls his own by name, and the true pastor of a church follows this example (Jn 10:3; Ign. *to Polyc.* 4:2; cf. Isa. 43:1; and *The Jung Codex*, ed. F. L. Cross (1955), 52). The absence of a 'grace' at the beginning and end of 3 Jn is noteworthy; perhaps it demonstrates the intimacy and authenticity of this letter to Gaius.

Bibliography—COMMENTARIES: J. Bonsirven, Verbum Salutis IX (1935; rev. ed. 1954); A. E. Brooke (1912); C. H. Dodd (1946); R. Law, *The Tests of Life* (1909); R. Rothe (1878); R. Schnackenburg (1953); B. F. Westcott (3rd ed. 1892); A. N. Wilder, IB, xii (1957); H. Windisch (1911; 3rd ed. rev. by H. Preisker, 1951).

OTHER LITERATURE: D. Barthélemy and J. T. Milik, *Discoveries in the Judaean Desert I: Qumrân Cave I* (1955); M. Burrows, *The Dead Sea Scrolls* (1955); M. S. Enslin, *Christian Beginnings* (1938); T. H. Gaster, *The Dead Sea Scriptures* (1956); T. W. Manson, 'Entry into Membership of the Early Church', JTS 48 (1947), 25–33; O. Roller, *Das Formular der paulinischen Briefe* (1933).

JUDE

BY G. H. BOOBYER

911a **Authorship and Date**—*External Evidence.* (*a*) To *c.* 200. Possibly known to Polycarp and the writer of the Didache; used by 2 Pet.; accepted in the Muratorian Canon; Tertullian attributed it to 'Jude the apostle'; Clement of Alexandria (*Hypotyposes*) expounded it. By *c.* 200, Jude was in fact widely esteemed as scripture and certainly at Alexandria, Carthage and Rome. (*b*) After 200. Origen attributed it to Jude, the Lord's brother, but indicates the doubts of some people; Eusebius classed it as 'disputed' though widely acknowledged; Jerome accepted it, but reports that many rejected it; Athanasius, Augustine and Cyril of Jerusalem approved of it; Cyprian, the Mommsen MS and Syrian church leaders neglected it and the Peshitta excluded it; the Council of Carthage A.D. 397 declared it canonical. In spite, therefore, of objections, arising chiefly, it seems, from its use of apocryphal writings (so Jerome), Jude established its place in the canon of scripture before the end of the 4th cent. *Internal Evidence.* The corrupt teaching and behaviour described were a somewhat gnostic type of antinomianism; but Jude's remarks do not necessarily stamp the 'ungodly persons' (v. 4) as members of any of the Gnostic sects of the 2nd cent. A.D. (Carpocratians, Cainites, Valentinians, etc.). 1 C., Col., the Pastorals, Rev. 1–3, etc. reveal serious evils in the Church from the Apostolic Age onwards, and those condemned by Jude could have arisen as early as, say, the eighth decade of the 1st cent. *Conclusions.* Jude (Gr. *Judas*) has been attributed to: (i) the Jude named with James (cf. Jude 1:1) in Mk 6:3 and Mt. 13:55 as a brother of Jesus (cf. 1 C. 9:5). Eusebius, relying on Hegesippus, reports grandsons of this Jude brought before Domitian and surviving until the time of Trajan (HE III, xixf., xxxii, 5). Did, however, a brother of the Lord write Jude 1*a* ('servant'), 3, 17f., 20? See §§912*be*. (ii) The apostle Jude: Lk. 6:16; Ac. 1:13 (cf. Jn 14:22). But this Jude was, correctly translated, 'son of James'; and note Jude 17f. (iii) Judas Barsabbas: Ac. 15:22, 27, 32 (HE V, xvii, 3). But there is no evidence that he could describe himself as 'brother of James'. (iv) Jude, a bishop of Jerusalem after the death of James, the Lord's brother (cf. Apost. Const. vii, 46; HE IV, v, 3, etc.). Is, then, 'brother of James' (Jude 1) a mistaken interpolation? (v) Some other unknown Jude, in which case his brother James is equally unknown. (vi) An unidentifiable person writing under the name of 'Jude'.

There is no conclusive case against Jude, the Lord's brother, being the author. If he wrote the epistle, it should probably be dated between 65 and 75. But possibly (vi) is the best theory, and passages like 3, 17f., 20 suggest a date 80–90. Some prefer 90–110.

b **Provenance and Destination**—There is no clear indication of either. The main proposals have been (i) that it was written from Palestine (especially Jerusalem), Syria, or Egypt (perhaps Alexandria); (ii) that it was sent to a church, or churches, in Palestine, Syria (especially Antioch), Egypt, Asia Minor or Corinth, or that it was a catholic manifesto to the whole of Christendom.

Jude addressed himself 'to those who are called', but this need not mean 'all who are called', the Church universal. The occasion of the letter as 911b
described in 3f., the contents, perhaps its briefness, point rather to recipients in a single church, or small association of churches, for whom the writer had some kind of immediate, pastoral responsibility. He writes as one dealing with a quite specific, local emergency. It is also to be noted that (*a*) the epistle was written in Greek; (*b*) the writer probably represented himself as one of the brethren of the Lord (1); (*c*) he assumes that James who became head of the Jerusalem church was held in esteem by the readers; (*d*) 'our common salvation' (3) could mean that the author, a Jew by birth, is addressing Christians of Gentile origin; (*e*) the epistle reflects a Jewish-Christian type of faith; (*f*) may be, apostles had worked amongst the addressees (17f.).

The evidence suggests that Jude was written to Greek-speaking Christians of Gentile birth. Since, however, James of Jerusalem and Jude his brother were leaders of special authority for them, they were probably adherents of the Jewish-Christian wing of the Church. They may therefore have been proselytes in Jewish synagogues, before they became Christians. Palestine or Syria (Antioch?) is a plausible conjecture for their location, and the writer may have been a Church leader in the same region. Chase's view that he wrote from Jerusalem seems unlikely, if the epistle is to be dated after the fall of Jerusalem in A.D. 70.

Jude and Other Writings—Jude drew on the c
OT (LXX), Enoch and the Assumption of Moses; and points of contact have been seen between Jude and James, Matthew, the Pastorals and the Didache. The most important question, however, concerns the parallel passages to much of Jude found in 2 Pet. See §§901*d*, 912. Spitta, Zahn and Bigg held that Jude borrowed from 2 Pet.; Chase, Mayor and most scholars today think that 2 Pet. used Jude. The hypothesis of a common source has had few exponents.

1-2 Greeting—1. brother of James: best taken 912a
as a reference to James, brother of Jesus, who became a leader of the Church at Jerusalem. Mention of him strengthens Jude's own authority. **2.** 'to those who are called'. See §911*b*.

3-4 Occasion of the Letter (cf. 2 Pet. 2:1–3)— b
Ungodly perverters of the faith had appeared amongst the Christians addressed. **3.** The author, already possessed of an eager desire to write about the salvation which he and the readers enjoyed in common, was constrained by the new danger to appeal to them to contend for the traditional faith. cf. Phil. 1:27; 1 Tim. 6:12; 2 Pet. 2:21. **the faith** here and in 20 has become the once-given compound of 'most holy' Christian belief to be guarded and used as the foundation of Christian thought and life. The phraseology suggests a date after 70 (cf. 'faith' in the Pastoral Epistles), though from the earliest years of the Church converts received truths to be believed. 'The faith' in this objective sense, or aspects of it, was also called the word, truth, teaching, commandment, preached message (kerygma), gospel, etc. It included brief creeds (cf. Rom. 10:9, 'Jesus is Lord'; Phil. 2:6–11, etc.); moral precepts in part derived from the teaching of Jesus; and accounts of his life, death and resurrection. Much of 'the faith' was in

912b fact material which was being put into the Gospels when Jude wrote. cf. Ep. Diog. 11:6, ' the faith of the Gospels '. **4. designated:** predicted in books regarded as scripture (the OT, Enoch, etc. cf. Jude 14f.), rather than primevally inscribed in books in heaven (Ps. 56:8, 139:16 ; Rev. 20:12 etc ; SB iii, 780 ; TWNT i, 772). **this condemnation:** their evil action and its punishment at the last judgment. cf. Gal. 5:10.

c **5-7 OT Instances of Sin and its Punishment** (cf. 2 Pet. 2:4–9)—The readers have full knowledge of all that is necessary for salvation, including the scriptures. But let them recall God's ways with evil-doers as illustrated in the unfaithfulness of Israel in the wilderness (cf. 1 C. 10:1–11 ; Heb. 3:7–4:11) ; the rebellious angels of Gen. 6 ; and Sodom, Gomorrah and the neighbouring cities (Gen. 19:1–28 ; Dt. 29:23). **6.** Jude describes the angels of Gen. 6:1–4 as bound and thrown into the dark depths of the earth to lie there until the Last Judgment. This version of the story resembles that in Enoch *passim* ; Jubil. 5:1–6 ; 2 Bar. 56:12–13, etc. cf. 2 Pet. 2:4; 1 Pet. 3:19f. ; 1 C. 6:3. **7. likewise:** the angels of **6** cohabited with women and the men of Sodom attempted sexual relationships with angels (Gen. 19:5–8). Both examples relate to copulation between divine and human orders of flesh and therefore exemplify ' unnatural lust '. For sins attributed to Sodom and Gomorrah, see SB iii, 571–4, 785f. cf. 2 Pet. 2:6 ; Rev. 11:8, etc. **of eternal fire** alludes either to the opinion that the area was still suffering from the effects of the fire and would continue to do so (Wis. 10:6f. ; Philo, *De Abr.* 140f., *Vit. Mos.* ii, 56 ; Jos.BJ iv, 483–5 ; Tert., *Apol.* xl) ; or to a belief that as the eternal fires of hell were partly located underneath that region they were used to consume the cities (JE v, 582f. ; Enoch 27, 67, etc.).

d **8-16 Conduct of the ' Ungodly Persons ' described and denounced** (cf. 2 Pet. 2:10–22)—They were licentious, insubordinate towards angels and men, covetous, intemperate, greedy, grumblers, boasters and flatterers. The interpretation of Jude's language should allow for some rhetorical exaggeration. **8. in their dreamings** is probably to be connected with ' reject ' and ' revile ' as well as with ' defile '. It may therefore mean that they claimed special revelations in dreams as the sanction of their infamous behaviour. **glorious ones:** angels. cf. 2 Pet. 2:10f. **9.** The archangel Michael himself did not presume to revile even a fallen angel like the devil, leaving the rebuke to God (Zech. 3:2). The altercation between Michael and the devil belongs to a legend from the Assumption of Moses. Whilst Michael was digging a grave to bury Moses, Satan appeared and unsuccessfully claimed the body. **11. way of Cain:** scarcely his fratricide, but cf. Jas 4:2 etc. ; perhaps it means 912d
some of the further sins imputed to Cain in Jewish and Christian tradition, e.g. selfishness, unbelief, opposition to God (Philo, *de Poster. Caini* 38f., 42, etc., Targ. Jer. Gen. 4:7 ; Heb. 11:4 ; 1 Jn 3:12 ; 1 Clem. 4:7) ; or, Cain seen as one whose transgression brought self-destruction, as in Wis. 10:3, 11:16 ; Jubil. 4:31f. ; Philo, *Quod det. pot.* 47f.). **Balaam's error:** Balaam of Num. 22–4 as depicted in Num. 31:8, 16 (cf. Num. 25) ; Jos. 13:22 and much subsequent Jewish and Christian tradition. cf. 2 Pet. 2:15f. ; Rev. 2:14. **Korah's rebellion:** Num. 16. **12. love feasts:** cult meals. Whether here associated with the ' Lord's Supper ' like the meal of 1 C. 11:17–34 is not indicated. cf. Ac. 2:42, 46, etc. ; 2 Pet. 2:13. The relation of Love Feast (Gr. *agapē*) to Eucharist in the early Church is a much disputed question. **13. wandering stars . . . ever:** cf. Enoch 18:12–16, 21:1–6. **14f.** Quotation from Enoch 1:9. **seventh:** Gen. 5:4–20 ; 1 Chr. 1:1–3 ; Enoch 60:8, etc.

17-23 Attitude required of the Faithful (cf. 2 Pet. e
3:1–13)—Heed apostolic warnings and remain established in the faith. **17f.** imply that the writer is not an apostle and suggest that he was living later than the apostles. Windisch : ' now is " the last time " ; then was the time of prophecy ' (HNT, 45). **they said to you . . . passions:** if a quotation, the source is unknown ; but it could be Jude's summary of the warnings of apostles as given, perhaps partly in person, to the readers. cf. Ac. 20:29f. ; 2 Th. 2:3–12 ; 1 Tim. 4:1–3, etc. **19. set up divisions:** their conduct resulted in factions in the Church ; or, they presumed to classify men as ' spiritual ', ' carnal ', etc. **22f.** cf. Didache 2:7.

24-25 Doxology—cf. Rom. 16:25–7. f

Bibliography—(i) COMMENTARIES IN ENGLISH : W. H. Bennett, Cent.B ; C. Bigg, ICC ; M. R. James, CGT ; J. B. Mayor, Macmillan and EGT ; J. Moffatt, Moffatt NT Commentary ; J. W. C. Wand, WC. (ii) OTHER COMMENTARIES : J. Chaine ; F. Hauck, NTD ; G. Hollmann—W. Bousset, *Schriften des NT* ; R. Knopf, Mey. ; A. Schlatter ; F. Spitta ; G. Staffelbach ; H. Windisch, HNT [3] ; G. Wohlenberg, ZK [3]; W. Wrede ; J. de Zwaan.

OTHER LITERATURE : F. H. Chase, HDB ii, 799–806 ; M. Goguel, *La Naissance du Christianisme* (1946), 455–69; J. B. Mayor, JTS 6 (1904–5), 569–77 ; B. Reicke, *Diakonie, Festfreude u. Zelos* (1951), 352–67 ; B. H. Streeter, *The Primitive Church* (1929), 178–80 ; H. Werdermann, *D. Irrlehrer d. Judas u. 2 Petrusbriefes* (1913). Introductions to the NT, especially A. H. McNeile (2nd ed.), J. Moffatt ; histories etc. of the Apostolic Age.

REVELATION

By N. TURNER

913a **Type of Literature**—There is one book in each Testament to which the Greek name *apocalypse* (unveiling) is given. Dan., which is the oldest of extant apocalypses, became a model for *Enoch* and subsequent specimens, of which Rev. is the supreme Christian example. Jews and Jewish Christians were fond of this type of book and produced many, especially in the period 100 B.C to A.D. 100. Rev. therefore is almost unique in the NT, although there are apocalyptic elements in the Gospels (Mt. 24, 25 ; Mk 13). When it was felt that they might throw some light on the Christian book, the Jewish apocalypses began to be studied rather exhaustively in modern times, and it is found that they were written in periods of stress to encourage readers to persevere in faith and good works. They often warn that further tribulation is yet to come, after which the patience of the saints will be rewarded by their receiving the Kingdom of God. Early Christians found comfort in these books during days of persecution. They themselves wrote but few, and they eagerly read and adapted Jewish ones : the *Ascension of Isaiah* and *4 Ezra* are well-known examples. Because Christians used them, in time the Jews looked askance at them and neglected them. Eventually the Church also lost interest. A few still retained their popularity, but these were a special type of apocalypse containing legends of paradise and hell (based on Jewish tradition) which circulated in many parts of the world during the Middle Ages. Of these, we have the *Apocalypse of Peter* and the *Testament of Abraham.* Our apocalypse is much more concerned with the course of world-history than with the fate of souls after death.

b There may have been a body of ' prophets ' for a time in the very earliest days of the Church, one of whose functions was to receive and propound visions of things to come. Our author does indeed class himself as such. There were prophets who foretold famines, and others who revealed God's will concerning Barnabas and Saul ; Paul mentions ' prophecy ' among gifts of the Spirit ; as a class they probably disappeared at about the time that apocalyptic ceased to be in vogue, thus following historically in the tradition of the Jewish apocalyptists. Their message was that the Kingdom of God, in its literal and material form, was shortly to come, with the signs already appearing. It was the message of the Little Apocalypse in Mk and of Paul's earlier epistles (2 Th. 2).

c **Scheme**—With great artistry, the theme is built up like a symphony in three movements : (1) Christ's message to the churches (1–3). (2) The Visions of judgment on the enemies of God and victory for the faithful (4–20). (3) God's Kingdom on earth (21–2). It weakens the effect if we analyse any farther. Every commentary has its detailed analysis ; and they are all different because the book was not constructed so meticulously. In all three movements Satan plays his part and is finally overthrown. With him falls that most devilish kingdom of Rome, and the way is opened to everlasting bliss. All the visions blend into one powerful (if crude) expression of faith, one vision. The consistency of tone is remarkable, especially as the author used most of his material at second hand ; and the language, so apparently eccentric and uncouth 913c to readers of classical Greek, is as naïvely beautiful as the theme itself.

Unity of the Book—That is why so few modern d writers have endorsed Harnack's approval of Eberhard Vischer's theory of seventy years ago, to the effect that movements 2 and 3 (cf. previous paragraph) are simply a Hebrew apocalypse (of date before A.D. 70), which was made Christian by the addition of an introduction and insertions (6, 7, parts of) and an epilogue (22). Others, who held that at least two Jewish sources were used in its composition, find slightly more favour (e.g. Spitta). The views of Weyland, Schmidt, and Weizsäcker were along the same lines and need not detain us ; no modern scholar takes much account of them, except to agree that the author of Rev. had a wealth of apocalyptic material to draw upon, especially in chs. 11 and 12. Some have been puzzled by this, marvelling that there should be such spiritual unity and power and at the same time a lack of sufficient in-weaving of the borrowed material. It is pointed out that many of the details of the narrative, e.g. in 12, are irrelevant. The difficulty is acute enough to have caused Dr Charles to suggest that a not over-intelligent disciple may have acted as editor after the author's death, and have finished the work of revision rather clumsily.

More recently the attempt has been made to revive earlier theories by suggesting that the seer wrote a Jewish apocalypse originally, that he was then converted to Christ and made his book Christian by means of a few additions (J. H. Michael, in ET (May 1948) ; cf. Torch Bible, 24*n*.). It can, however, be shown that the Christian implications are too closely woven into the fabric of the book, the OT quotations are always too carefully subordinated to a Christian context, to make such a suggestion very feasible (Preston and Hanson in the *Torch Bible Commentary*, 34–40). It is, however, often a matter of personal opinion, and the reader will have to judge for himself. This much can be said : there has been little agreement among scholars as to where the precise division between the sources is to be sought. The present tendency among writers on Rev. is to leave source-criticism alone and to seek for the author's meaning by taking the book as we have it. This is a pity, because to know where the author drew his material might help us to know the man.

The Value of the Book today—We need not go to e the other extreme of saying that the visionary John was ' a creative genius ' (Moffatt Commentary, xxv–xxvii). There is too much unassimilated second-hand material, and often it is employed pointlessly—obscure to us, to many early Christians, and to vast numbers of readers who decline to make it support their peculiar notions. The series of Visions (Seals, Trumpets, Bowls), can hardly be intended to be consecutive chronologically, since each describes the End ; and they must be parallel and alternative accounts of the End. In that case, they might either be derived from disparate sources and insufficiently assimilated ; or be intentionally parallel, with the design of rousing the faithful by one means after another to a sense of the reality of the End. Some

913e commentators prefer the latter alternative, unwilling to believe that John was anything but an inspired prophet and creative artist.

On the other hand, his prophecies did not come true, and that must affect our judgment of the book and the author. 'The best that can be said of it,' writes Loisy of the book, 'is that for centuries men have taxed their wits to find in it a meaning which is *not* there, for the simple reason that the meaning which *is* there was immediately contradicted by the course of events' (*The Origins of the NT* (Eng. tr. 1950), 11). Of course, the book may still have a value undreamed of by the author. Moreover, he was clearly well aware of the principles involved in remaining a faithful Christian, with the inevitable conflict between the Church's spiritual power and a force which trusts only in physical might. The need for that vision is always topical. Whether the visionary in this case had quite that clarity of vision which the modern commentator often likes to find in his work, is another matter. Evidently he believed in the ultimate victory of the Church, and this, unless crudely and violently interpreted, will be of permanent value to Christian faith. Nevertheless the solution which he adopts for the age-old problem of evil is not that favoured by all devout men. It is not dualistic, for it envisages the utter destruction of evil ; but it is not the universalistic solution either. Satan fails to be converted ; Babylon falls unrepentant. One will value such a solution according to the variety of Christian experience one has.

f Preston and Hanson have done their best to answer this kind of criticism, and especially that proffered by C. H. Dodd. 'The work of Christ is not so much a background, as Professor Dodd asserts, but is the centre. Nowhere in the New Testament is Jesus given higher honour than he is in Revelation' (*Torch*, 32). He receives the same worship as the Father, and OT concepts of Yahweh are extended to him. Nevertheless, they have to agree with Dodd's estimate of the seer, that 'his failure is in his attitude to the sinful' (p. 32), and although the seer is alleged to picture the Lamb as sprinkled with his *own* blood and as made worthy only by *self*-sacrifice to be Judge, many Christians will yet sympathise with Dodd, who writes : 'the God of the Apocalypse can hardly be recognised as the Father of our Lord Jesus Christ' (*The Apostolic Preaching and Its Developments* (1936), 86ff.). To excuse the absence of universalism the Torch Bible commentators invoke the phrase of F. D. Maurice : 'The impossible mercy of giving us the blessing of the light which we hate.' The point which they appear to miss is the force of a more fundamental question : How can the creatures of God permanently and finally hate a light which they were created to enjoy ?

Yet modern interpreters do agree that there exists a struggle between good and evil powers, and if John's prophecies failed of literal fulfilment there is a sense in which all ecclesiastical history has supported them, and individual experience agrees that Christian discipleship is hard and unpopular, though the end justifies the struggle. Apart from this, the relevance of Rev. today can hardly be as great as it was in the 1st cent. The seer had indeed a pastoral love for his readers. He saw them faced with an urgent situation ; he shared their persecution, for he was exiled in Patmos ; he knew that many of them would be martyred, and that some had only saved their lives by compromise. The last thing he wished was to make his message obscure, except where it was wise to be cryptic in such matters as the number of the Beast, and he is often at pains to explain his meaning. Besides, his readers were accustomed to apocalyptic modes of thought ; this was perhaps the best way to gain their ear. It has been doubted whether John himself really understood all that he wrote. Psychological study helps us to realise that ecstatic visions can be vividly remembered and at the same time cannot be so clearly put into words. Even so far as 913f his first readers were concerned, John may have failed in this respect. It is certainly very difficult to interpret the book in detail to the modern Christian. Assuming that the first readers knew the meaning of the details, the secret perished with them and cannot be recovered. In principle we understand, but John does not really live and move in our intellectual sphere. We sometimes experience what we think may be symbolically described in his word-pictures, but that does not tell us what his symbols mean. Did he really know himself? The number three means heaven, four means the earth, and the number seven is the blending of these two, or God dwelling with man ; but most of the rest is as obscure as the Jewish literature on which it is based.

It may, however, be read as poetry and in that way g
as an aid to devotion. It has inspired countless hymns. In a way, it is refreshing to turn from the gospel record of historical events and from the practical pastoralia of the epistles, to enter the holy realm where one may rest in the numinous thrill of a world wholly subjected to God and Christ.

Why did Revelation survive ?—As we shall see, 914a
it was not because its apostolic authorship was never in doubt, nor because of its own explicit claims to divine inspiration, nor even because of the popularity of the apocalyptic form of writing. The best suggestion is probably that of F. C. Porter : the reason why this strange book held its own in the Christian Church is 'the consciousness that, on the whole, the religious faith and feeling of the book predominate over its apocalyptic form, and give to apocalyptic language, which the majority cannot understand or accept in its literal sense, practically the value of figure for the emotional expression of Christian faith and hope. It is really as Christian poetry, rather than as the disclosure of mysteries of the unseen world and of the future, that the book has been valued, and, because valued, preserved and canonized by the Christian Church' (HDB iv, 241).

Who was the Author ?—It was the conviction of b
Dr Charles, who carefully examined the language, that this author could not have written Jn or the Johannine Epistles ; he was a Jew of Palestine, one John the Prophet, who migrated to Asia Minor (ICC on Rev., vol. i, p. xxxviii). Galilee was probably his original home, for the writers of apocalypses generally lived here, and not in Judaea, and this type of literature was usually read where the Law had least power. Though he was a devout Jew, and intimately acquainted with the Hebrew text of the OT, he had wide sympathies, and Dr Charles considered him to have been a spiritual genius (p. xliv). To the scholar, the most interesting feature is his tendency to invent his own grammatical rules at times, perhaps because his mind moved in terms of Semitic phraseology. It is not unlikely that John the Elder (author of the Gospel and Epistles) and John the Prophet belonged to the 'same religious circle', and the Prophet may have been the Elder's teacher (p. xxii). There are indeed some similarities of thought and language, particularly the vivid conflict of good and evil.

Evidently the author wielded great moral authority among the churches of Asia ; he writes almost like an apostle.

Even more controversial is the suggestion of Dr c
Charles that the author did not live to revise his work or put the material in the correct order, and that this was done by 'a very unintelligent disciple' (p. xxii), who yet knew more Greek, but not as much Hebrew, and 'was profoundly ignorant of his master's thought'. Take away the additions (about twenty-two verses) of this disciple, suggested Dr Charles, and the whole book progresses logically ; most of the visions can then be taken strictly in chronological order and are not recapitulatory (p. xxiii).

But there are still some (e.g. Lohmeyer) who support Harnack's view that Rev. and Jn have a

914c common authorship, not necessarily apostolic. One has to consider the possibility that Jn was originally written by the author of Rev. in Aramaic and subsequently translated into its present form ; that might account for the different kind of Greek in Rev.

We may be certain that the author's real name was John. If he were using a pseudonym he would hardly have chosen this common name, but rather some great name. He does not claim to be the apostle John, but the 'brother' of the recipients and a sharer of their troubles. Nevertheless, apostolic authorship is not an untenable supposition ; the author is indeed a son of thunder, indignant with the Church's foes, eager to destroy (as in Lk. 9:54) and ambitious to sit at Messiah's right hand in glory. It is hard to believe that anyone but an apostle would venture to write scathing letters to the churches of Asia, especially if the Apostle himself were living there, as tradition states. Moreover, although its reception into the Canon was slow, the very earliest traditions of the Church are strongly in favour of
d apostolic authorship. As early as about A.D. 136 Justin Martyr is the first to state that 'John, one of the apostles of Christ', is the author (*Dial.* lxxxi, 15). The Muratorian Canon (Rome, *c.* A.D. 170) supports this. The Lucan prologue of the Anti-Marcionite Gospel Prologues (A.D. 160–80) definitely mentions the apostle John as the author. Tertullian (*c.* A.D. 200) quotes 'the apostle John in the Apocalypse', and refers to the Holy City 'seen by the apostle John'. Irenaeus (*c.* A.D. 180) defends the apostolic authorship. It is clear that by 'John a disciple of the Lord' he means none other than the Apostle, for elsewhere he describes him as 'he who leaned upon his breast' (*Adv. Haer.* ii, 22, 5, iii, 11,1, iv, 20, 11, v, 35, 2). Moreover, Rev. is widely quoted as scripture without mention of authorship. The first traces of doubt appear in the 3rd cent. Heretics known as the Alogi disliked the book and ascribed it to another heretic, Cerinthus. This provided a reason for rejecting it. More orthodox churchmen disliked it because of its hard sayings in general, and particularly because Montanist heresies about the millennium claimed support from it. Marcion, of course, rejected it for its strongly Jewish complexion. There were doubts at Rome, where Gaius (*c.* 210) rejected it and ascribed it to Cerinthus, but they were short-lived, for Hippolytus of Rome in 205 wrote a book against the Alogi and another against Gaius, defending the authority and apostolicity of Rev. Apart from the hesitancy of Jerome, there were no serious doubts expressed after this in the West, and the position is ratified in the Canons of
e Cyprian of Carthage (*c.* 250). In the Eastern Churches Dionysius of Alexandria, *c.* 250, rejected apostolic authorship, partly because of doctrinal presuppositions of his own, but he was a scholarly pupil of Origen and rightly felt the linguistic difficulty of ascribing Jn and Rev. to the same author. He supposed that there must be another John, but all that he has to say is subjective evidence and is not based on any sound tradition. Eusebius of Caesarea (270–340) later took up the difficulties and suggestions of Dionysius and added his own guess that the other John was the Presbyter mentioned by bishop Papias of Hierapolis, whom he quotes (HE III, xxxix, 6). The suggestion has been revived of late, but even the 3rd cent. in the East saw the unquestioning acceptance of Rev. as apostolic by Clement of Alexandria and Origen. The main difficulties experienced at that time were those of the language and doctrinal presuppositions. Apart from this, there would probably never have been any doubt ; but it persisted into the 4th cent. until the acceptance of Rev. by Athanasius settled the question for Egypt and much of the East. Doubt persisted in the Syrian church in the 5th cent. and even after that. Dislike of Rev. was strongly expressed by half the Reformation scholars, including Luther and Erasmus, but it was never excluded from the Bible.

Dr Charles, who decisively favoured the view that John the Presbyter wrote Jn and the Epistles, argued 914f at length that John the Apostle was martyred very early (ICC i, xlvi–xlix). Nevertheless the evidence in support of this martyrdom is very slight and rests only on Jesus' prophecy (Mk 10:39), a Papias tradition supported no earlier than the 7th to the 9th cent., the doubtful 'statements' of some early writers and a 5th-cent. Syriac martyrology which simply states that James and John were killed in Jerusalem. Against this must be set another tradition which asserts that the Apostle lived to a very old age in Asia, and the definite evidence of such early writers as Justin, Irenaeus and Tertullian as to the apostolic authorship of Rev., and the fact that John the Presbyter is an elusive figure who depends entirely on second-hand evidence derived ultimately from Papias alone. Nor have we any real evidence that Papias' Presbyter had any connection with Asia Minor ; to suppose that Dionysius' remark, that there were the tombs of two Johns in Ephesus, proves anything at all is quite fantastic.

Date—(1) The earliest possible date would be the g
reign of Nero. The reference to the Temple in 11:1, 2 implies that it is still in existence, unless a spiritual temple or a reference to Ezek. 40 is intended. It is doubtful whether Nero's persecution was sufficiently sustained to provoke such a book as this, and the edict concerning emperor-worship which appears to be envisaged in 13:15 hardly belongs to this reign. The church of Ephesus, moreover, would scarcely have had time to forsake its first love (2:4).

(2) Some passages, such as that of the seven kings h
in 17:10, suggest the reign of Vespasian or Titus. The seer appears to live under the sixth of these emperors. If we omit the short reigns of Galba, Otho and Vitellius, and begin with Augustus, this gives us Vespasian as the sixth. But the same difficulty about emperor-worship meets us here. Vespasian did not insist on it.

(3) The most reasonable suggestion is the reign of Domitian (81–96) and this accords with the very early Church tradition of Irenaeus and also with the demand for emperor-worship in this reign and the fierce persecution of Christians (*c.* A.D. 92, according to Pliny). This is not to exclude the possibility that earlier material from the reigns of Nero and Vespasian has been incorporated into the finished work.

I Address and Preface—This introduces the 915a
Letters to the seven churches.

1-3 Title and Introduction—The oldest title was probably Apocalypse of John ; then, in the Latin Church, Revelation of John. 'Divine' appears no earlier than 4th cent. and simply means 'theologian'. **1. what must . . . take place:** the phrase follows Theodotion's, not the LXX, text of Dan. 2:28, 29, 46. Our author appears to use a version of Dan. like Theodotion's. But it might be taken from Mt. 24:6 ; Lk. 21:9. **soon:** conservative scholars try to see in this word the meaning 'quickly' (i.e. catastrophically) as well as soon, for the simple truth is that the events did not have an immediate fulfilment. But the meaning really is 'soon'. **made it known:** the Gr. is rather 'gave a sign'. **sending his angel:** a free translation for 'through his angel', which is preferable. The background idea is that in Jewish apocalyptic the revelation about the future was made through an angel, rather than given directly from the transcendent God. **2. bore witness to:** first of many important parallels with Jn, too numerous always to be noted, which do not prove identity of authorship but some clear connection between the thought of both : Jn 3:11. 'Bears witness' would be a better translation : it is the epistolary aorist. **even to all that:** the Gr. is limiting and means : 'as much as he saw of them'. **the word of God:** R. H. Charles did not take this personally of Christ, as in the Prologue of Jn, but as 'the revelation given by God'. But one does not *see* a spoken word. Some

915a therefore take it of the OT and take the next phrase, **testimony of Jesus Christ,** as meaning the NT. However, it must be part of his vision, because he saw it. An interesting alternative for **testimony of Jesus Christ** would be 'demonstrations held in honour of Jesus Christ' (cf. MMV, s.v. for papyrus support; but it is late: 3rd to 4th cent.). That would well describe the drama depicted in Rev. **3. read aloud:** the true meaning. **the prophecy:** presumably this very book. Note that the words rendered **witness, testimony,** and **keep** are key-words throughout the Johannine writings. But the wording is also very close to Lk. 11:28. The author seems to have known Mt. and Lk. **the time is near:** cf. Mt. 26:18.

b **4-8 Address and Greeting**—For the address, cf. Paul's epistles, which our author must have known. This form of address does not seem to be earlier than the NT. **4.** cf. Gr. of Exod. 3:14. 'The Seer has deliberately violated the rules of grammar in order to preserve the divine name inviolate from the change which it would necessarily have undergone if declined' (Charles, ICC i, 10). **and from the seven spirits who are before his throne:** though present in the MSS the words may possibly not be the author's but an early interpolation into Rev. (ICC i, 11–13). The seven spirits may be Babylonian or Persian symbols of the deity but are more likely to be the archangels of Judaism (cf. 8:2 note). It seems incredible that any author should place them here between the first and second Persons of the Trinity. On the other hand, scribes usually try to make things easier rather than more difficult, if they interpolate. It is just possible that the Holy Spirit is meant, symbolised as sevenfold. **5.** There is another grammatical howler in the Gr.: a nominative case in apposition with a genitive. The author several times indulges in solecisms of this kind. He may have been Semitic-speaking, with a very uncertain grasp of Greek; or he may have been feeling his way towards a kind of diction more suitable than the normal kind to the impressive nature of his subject. **first-born of the dead:** similar phrases occur in Paul (1 C. 15:20; Col. 1:18), here and elsewhere in Rev.; cf. Ps. 88:28 (RSV 89:27). 'First' may not be chronological so much as procedural; the whole phrase will then mean: 'Lord of the dead and king of the living'. **loves us . . . has freed us:** the correct treatment of the Gr. tenses is notable, first the present and then the aorist. An important theological point is nicely presented by the grammatical construction and (at least in 1–3) this author is not simply a barbarian in language. He means that God's love is continuous (present tense); but that the act of atonement was once only (aorist). The point is missed in AV, which was based on TR, a different text from that of RV and RSV. **freed:** AV 'washed' was based on an inferior text. **faithful witness:** Jn 18:37, Gr. of Ps. 88:38 (RSV 89:37). **6a** follows not the LXX, but Theodotion, in Exod. 19:16. **7a** again follows Theodotion, not LXX, of Dan. 7:13. Also at Jn 19:37. cf. 1:1 note. On the whole verse, cf. Mt. 24:30. **7b.** cf. Zech. 12:10; Jn 19:37. **even so. Amen:** the two words are really, 'Yes, yes!' first in Gr., then in Heb. But there is no clear reason for the repetition, and it should be noted that in 3:14 The Amen is a proper name for Christ. However, something similar occurs in 2 C. 1:20. **8.** There is no textual authority for omitting this verse, and Charles's argument from the context is weak. The linguistic argument, that this author never separates 'God' from 'almighty', is based on the assumption that the style of chs. 1–4 is consistent with that of 5–21. The phrase is indeed a translation of Heb. 'God of hosts', but the author often proves himself able to do strange things with his Greek and could easily split up the phrase.

c **9-20 Preface**—**9.** A humble self-description, extraordinary if the author was an apostle. It is a characteristic device of this author to avoid a genitive of quality and to substitute a co-ordinate noun in the same case; thus: 'made us a kingdom *of* priests'
(6), and here: 'the tribulation *of* the Kingdom', 915c
i.e. the Messianic woes which are already being endured. **share with you in Jesus:** RSV may not be justified in taking 'in Jesus' so closely with the verb. More probably it refers to the patient endurance, with which it is closely connected in the Gr., and should be '*of* Jesus' (cf. 2 Th. 3:5). That John was in Patmos as a punishment seems suggested by the similar phrase in 20:4, and Patmos appears to have been a penal settlement of the Romans. **10.** cf. Ezek. 3:12. The meaning is: 'I was in spiritual rapture', i.e. a trance. One cannot claim that the verb means 'fell into'; it is used as the simple verb *to be* in v. 9 and elsewhere in Rev. **the Lord's Day:** not quite the same phrase as 'the Day of the Lord' in the OT, with its Messianic associations, but probably Sunday. The adjective is the same as that used of the Lord's Supper which came to be associated with that day of the week. For the argument, cf. Charles (ICC i, 23) and his references. On the other hand 17:3 and 21:10 support the attempt to connect this trance with eschatology. In that case, the seer is experiencing a foretaste of things to come at the End, the demonstrations to be held in honour of Jesus Christ
(cf. 1:2 note). **11.** Seven is a symbolic number, but d
these particular churches may have been chosen as convenient centres, for they all lay on a circular road (unlike Colossae and Troas, which are omitted), and are mentioned in the correct order. **12. lampstands:** they burnt oil, but had the appearance of large candlesticks. Here they symbolise the revelation of God on earth. Besides their Jewish associations, they also figured in Bab. astrology. **like a son of man:** i.e. like a human being; this is not a reference to the title in the Gospels, but to Dan. 7. It should not be rendered: 'like the Son of Man' (RVm), because it *is* the Son of Man. But this author so often closely resembles *1 Enoch* elsewhere that here he probably had 46:1 in mind. **13.** cf. Dan. 7:13, 10:5. The description suggests a priest. **14.** cf. Dan. 7:9, 10:6. What is said of the Ancient of Days (God) in Dan. and *Enoch* is here applied to the Son of Man. **white as snow,** though retained in the MSS, may be a very early gloss (Charles). **15. burnished bronze:** no more than a possible translation. It may be an alloy of gold and silver (Suidas). The derivation of the Gr. word is uncertain; it appears to be compounded of two words: 'white brass' or 'brass of Lebanon' or 'gum of the colour of brass' or 'brass as clear as gum'. It can hardly be a gum, as that would be consumed in the furnace. R. Knox's 'orichalc' transliterates the Latin Bible. It seems to have been metal made from a yellow copper-ore, possibly an alloy. Latin is probably due to the derivation 'white brass' (understanding white as brilliance, not colour). **his voice was like the sound of many waters:** based literally on Heb. of Ezek. 43:2, on which Dan. 10:6 is also less closely
based. **16a.** cf. Isa. 49:2. **he held:** strictly: 'he e
had'; the same verb that RSV renders 'has' in 3:1, not the same as 'holds' in 2:1. **seven stars:** symbolism explained in v. 20. There are parallels in Mithraism; they may be accidental, but we do not otherwise knoww hence the seer drew the idea of holding stars. **16c.** Very close to Mt. 17:2. **17.** Closely based on Heb., not Gr., of Dan. 10:9, 10, 12. **I am the first and the last:** cf. Gr. of Isa. 48:12 (Theod., not LXX). **18.** Close to 2 C. 6:9. On the supposition that these verses form stanzas (Charles), the arrangement will not be as RSV, but: 'Fear not, I am the first and the last!—I live, I died!—And, behold, etc.' **I am alive for evermore:** cf. Dan. 4:31, 12:7, *1 Enoch* 5:1. **Death and Hades:** written as proper names on the ground that in Rev. they are personified (cf. 6:8, 20:13, 14); but death is not always personified, and it does not suit this context, for they are places to which access is sought, rather than persons who own a key. Through death Christ visits Hades and preaches. **19. is to:** translate:

915e 'must'. Usually in Rev. the verb has little more force than futurity, but here and in 3:10, 6:11 destiny is strongly implied. Lat. *oportet*. The phrase is from Dan. 2:29 (Theod.). cf. 4:1. **20. As for the mystery:** RSV, following Charles (ICC i, 34), differs from RV in taking this as a new sentence, not as an additional object of **write**. The grammar of the verse is highly irregular; there is much to be said for the supposition that the author had intended to revise his work grammatically. The **mystery** (as generally in NT) is the hitherto secret meaning which God would now reveal; the emphasis is on the secrecy of it, not on the difficulty of understanding it. **the angels of the seven churches:** there has been much speculation about their identity. They could hardly be the mere messengers who carried the letters. They may be the overseers (bishops) or presbyters set over the churches; if so, Rev. reflects a period when there had come to be one of these officers for each church of Asia. It is probably better to understand them as spiritual guardians and representatives (as Mt. 18:10; Lk. 1:19; Ac. 12:15), a view widely held in contemporary Judaism (*Jubilees* 35:17) and in Zoroastrianism (ERE vi, 118), although it is difficult to see how John could be commissioned to write to guardian angels. Each explanation is open to criticism, and perhaps it only means the church itself.

916a **II, III Letters to the Churches**—The opinion of Dr Charles, reached on linguistic grounds, was that the Letters are by our author but are an earlier composition, before the reign of Domitian, which he later incorporated in a larger work (ICC, i, 43); Charles was of opinion that these Letters were actually sent to the respective churches (i, 47).

II 1-7 Ephesus—1. The words of: In the NT the phrase is almost confined to these letters, but it is characteristic of the Gr. OT (some 330 times), with which our author must have been very familiar. **2. you cannot bear:** verbally as Jn 16:2. **who call themselves apostles:** probably a wider circle than the Twelve were known as apostles in the early Church. They were a class of official teachers. The Nicolaitans may have tried unsuccessfully to assume this role at Ephesus. **4. the love you had at first:** Paul had found the elders of this church very affectionate (Ac. 20:37). Strife and divisions had changed all this. This may however refer to their love to God. **5. Remember . . . repent . . . do the works:** Swete notes that this answers 'to three stages in the history of conversion'. Not conversion, however, but restoration after apostasy is envisaged here. **remove your lampstand:** the total destruction of the
b Ephesian church appears to be threatened. **6. Nicolaitans:** also mentioned in the Pergamum letter. It seems they were immoral and that they ate food which had been sacrificed to idols. They were Gnostics or some other heretical teachers, probably of the extreme antinomian type, who abused the liberty whereby Christians are free of the Law of Moses. **7** suggests that Rev. was intended to be read in public services. But the phrase is extremely common in the Gospels, which our author may have known. **him who conquers:** almost a synonym for the martyr in Rev., as a glance at 3:21 will show. His reward is immortality (**the tree of life**) in the holy city (**paradise,** cf. 22:2). cf. *Testament of Levi* 18:11.

c **8-11 Smyrna**—The origin of this church is quite unknown. Polycarp was bishop and suffered martyrdom here, A.D. 155. **8. came to life:** an accurate rendering of the Gr. aorist tense. RV wrongly emphasises the new life rather than the act of resurrection, making the same mistake in Rom. 14:9. For the same reason RSV is correct in rendering **who died** (not 'which was dead', RV), because the verb is that which the author regularly uses as the aorist of the verb *to be*. The expression is very strong; it is almost: 'who plunged into death and sprang to life'. Paul merely uses the aorist of the verb *to die* (Rom. 14:9); our author uses an equivalent of the aorist of the verb *to be* in conjunction with the adjective 916c
dead. It is effective language. **9. rich:** presumably in faith (Jas 2:5). **slander:** correct translation in this context; 'blasphemy' (RV) is the same crime directed against God. There were many Jews in Smyrna and their hostility to Christians is well attested (e.g. Polycarp). They **say that they are Jews and are not,** because the Christian Church is now the true Israel. Jn uses 'Israelite' in this sense: 1:47. **10. ten days:** probably suggested by Dan. 1:9f. The length of time appears to have no special significance. **crown of life:** reminiscent either of the Greek games (the victor's wreath) or of Jewish apocalyptic. But cf. Jas 1:12. **11. the second death:** a thoroughly Jewish rabbinic idea, referring to the awful possibility of perishing in the next world (20:14, 21:8), besides dying naturally.

12-17 Pergamum—It was particularly associated d
with emperor-worship (**Satan's throne**). **13. did not deny:** correct; aorist tense signifies a definite point of time, a particular persecution. **my faith:** a mistranslation. It is 'your faith *in me*'. Objective genitive (e.g. 14:12) is a favourite construction of this author. **witness:** the obvious meaning here is martyr, and the word later came to have this technical meaning. **14. a few things:** rather 'a little'. Besides the adverbial use of the plural word in this sense in Thucydides (3:73), we have the plural often enough in LXX for 'a little' (e.g. LXX 4 Kingdoms (=2 Kg.) 10:18; Sir. 31(34):10; Zech. 1:15), where the meaning 'few' is quite impossible. In this context Christ has only one thing, not a few things, against the Church. For OT source, cf. Num. 25:1f. Some have seen in this a veiled attack on Paul (cf. 1 C. 8:9f.), who ate this food but realised that it might offend the brethren. **15. So** rather obscures the meaning: 'in this way and in like manner', i.e. like the Ephesian church. **Also** must be taken closely with **you,** or the impression will be given that the sheltering of the Nicolaitans is a further point against the Church, whereas it is the only one. **17. hidden manna:** in line with Jewish apocalyptic tradition, our author thinks of this as now existing in heaven and as destined to appear on earth with the Messiah (cf. Jn 6). **a white stone:** there is some reference to pagan superstition here, although the secret name on this lucky charm will be a divine one. *Test. Levi* 8:14.

18-29 Thyatira—Of no importance. Dyeing was an e
industry (Ac. 16:14f.). **18. eyes:** 1:14*b*. **20. Jezebel:** some real person at Thyatira was encouraging broad-minded Christians to attend the dinners of the trade guilds in this city, since there was no harm (so Paul) in eating food offered to idols. She is condemned and given the name of Elijah's enemy. Compare v. 14, where the offences are mentioned in reverse order; perhaps at Thyatira it was necessary to emphasise that these trade dinners were licentious. cf. 1 Kg. 21:25. **22. I will throw her on a sickbed:** the future tense is justified (present with future meaning). So also is the rendering **sickbed,** for the parallelism with the next line makes some kind of affliction necessary in this line. However, the reference to a bed is not without its irony. **23. strike her children dead:** it seems unreasonable that her lovers are let off more lightly than her innocent children, unless (with Charles) we suppose that the interpretation is spiritual: the lovers, who can repent, being those at Thyatira who compromise with Gnosticism for business purposes, but the children being those who are heart and soul involved in it. **23b.** Two ideas are combined here which are also combined in Jer. 17:10. **mind and heart:** strictly in the reverse order in Gr. **24. what** f
some call the deep things of Satan: a compressed phrase meaning that the Gnostics call their knowledge 'the deep things of God' (cf. 1 C. 2:10), but they belong really to Satan. Some of the Gnostics, however, may have gloried in knowing the secrets of Satan. Another suggestion is: 'as they say' introduces the quotation from the apostolic decrees, 'I lay upon you no

916f other burden' (Ac. 15:28). **27. rule:** the verb has this meaning, but in LXX it often has another meaning, *destroy*, and the parallelism requires it here. **as when:** according to Charles (ICC, I, 77), this is not the meaning. As in the model (Ps. 2:9), there is a new sentence after **iron,** thus: 'Like earthen pots shall they be broken'; some Latin Fathers support this, and have the verb in the plural. cf. *Psalms of Solomon* 17:26. **27f. even as:** again RSV and others have probably misunderstood the parallelism. It is: 'As I myself received from my Father, so will I give to him the morning star.' Probably it is a reminiscence of Job 38:12 (compare vv. 31, 32); what was denied to the patriarch in his weakness will be granted to the overcoming Christian—all the power of God and knowledge of the deep things of God. Thus the parallelism is preserved: 'I receive power and knowledge from God, and I pass them on to you.' Venus is the morning star, but probably no connection of thought between this and the paramours of Jezebel is intended. There is no end to the fanciful interpretations of preachers: some have suggested that as the morning star is the last of the stars to set, so the Christian should be the last person to give in.

917a **III 1-6 Sardis**—A place of luxury and licence; which things affected the church. **2. awake:** with Goodspeed and Moffatt, but the Gr. is: 'Be watchful', or perhaps: 'Be alive' (as 1 Th. 5:10). So also v. 3: 'if you are not watchful'. **what remains:** Sardis was destroyed by earthquake in A.D. 17 and had been rebuilt, but this is a reference to spiritual wreckage. **3.** The Second Coming is meant; cf. Mt. 24:42. **4. names . . . people:** 'names' can legitimately be rendered 'persons' at this period and in this type of Gr. Omit 'people'. There is no suggestion of a church register. **for they are worthy:** the meaning must be exactly the same as in 16:6 where RSV renders: 'It is their due!' **5. white garments:** symbol of the heavenly bodies after

b resurrection. **book of life:** referred to in Exod. 32:32f., as containing the names of all living Israelites. To be blotted out of this book meant death: cf. Ps. 69:28. Here the conception is spiritual, the life being immortality. Dan. 12:1. This passage and 20:12, 13 throw some light on an interesting problem: the elucidation of the idea of books of judgment in contemporary Judaism. In the Ethiopic *Enoch* the seer saw the Head of Days upon his throne and 'the books of the living' were opened before him (47:3); assurance is given to the righteous that their names are written before the glory of the Great One (104:1), and transgressors' names shall be blotted out of the Book of Life and the holy books (108:3). The latter may be the 'heavenly tables' of *Jubilees* 19:9, 30:19. It seems that there were by this time (*a*) the heavenly tables in which the character of men was recorded, (*b*) the Book of Life, from which the ungodly will be blotted out, and (*c*) 'the book of those who will be destroyed' or *liber perditionum.* Two of these books are mentioned in *Jubilees* 36:10. Among the rabbis, Johanan bar Nappaha (died *c.* A.D. 290) taught that there were three kinds of record tablets, one having the names of the righteous, one the wicked, and one the middle class (Talmud tractate *Rosh Ha-shanah* 16*b*; Jerusalem Gemara 57*a*). Now in Rev. we are introduced to both kinds of record books at the Great Judgment, which is very illuminating: 20:12, 'books and another book'. These must be: first the Book of Life, and then the books in which all men's *deeds* are recorded. These latter books, to be used against men in the future judgment, may be alluded to in Isa. 65:6; Ezek. 2:10; Mal. 3:16, and they are plainly indicated in the pseudepigraphical and rabbinic literature. A heavenly voice tells Baruch, 'The Book will be opened in which are written the sins of all that have sinned, and likewise the treasuries in which the righteousness of those who have conducted themselves righteously . . . is collected' (Syriac *Apoc. Bar.* 24:1, cf. 30:2). Enoch is told to observe the 'heavenly tablets'; these he reads and also 'the Book of all the deeds of mankind' (*1 Enoch* 81:1, 2, 90:20). *2 (4) Esdras,* which may be influenced by Rev., states the time when these books will be opened (6:20). In the Talmud and Midrashim is the same idea: 'All your deeds are written in a Book' (*Pirkê Aboth* 2:1). Even needless words which pass between husband and wife are recorded against them in the hour of death (Talmud tractate *Hagigah* 5*b*). The same thought lies behind the judgment scene in the *Testament of Abraham.* Rev. therefore takes its place in the line of development which culminated in the more clearly defined doctrine, among the rabbis, of the Book of human deeds. It is true that there are other parallels to record books, as well as Jewish; but the parallels in Hindu, Buddhist and Muhammadan eschatology are not so close as those in the Jewish. **I will confess his name:** quite clearly the author knows and is borrowing from Mt. 10:32. 917b

7-13 Philadelphia—7. the key of David probably involves the admission to David's city, new Jerusalem. Much of the verse is from Theodotion's version of Isa. 22:22. **8. open door:** it may refer to missionary opportunities (as in 1 C. 16:9; 2 C. 2:12), but more clearly it refers to the previous verse. **9.** cf. Isa. 60:14 (Heb.). They are **Jews** in name only, as Paul also teaches in Rom. 9. **I have loved you:** a Hebraism meaning: 'I love you'. The model of the author was probably LXX of Isa. 43:4. **10.** If **my** is taken rather with **patient endurance,** as is lawful in Gr., the phrase will mean the gospel of the cross and passion. Otherwise, it is difficult. **11. crown:** 2:10 note. **12. never shall he go out of it:** 'Fixity of character is at last achieved' (Charles); but the idea is rather that of Jn 17:12, 18:9, eternal union with him. **which comes:** or 'will come', 2:22 note. c

14-22 Laodicea—14. Dr Charles thought this author knew Col. (ICC i, 94f.). cf. Col. 1:15, 18, but also Prologue to Jn: 'By him were all things made'. **17.** cf. Hos. 12:9: **you are wretched, pitiable:** there are definite articles before these two adjectives: 'You are the wretched one, the pitiable one'. **18. refined:** it may mean 'glowing' from the fire. **19.** It is strange that, of the two Gr. words for 'love', the one used here is not that in the Gr. version of Prov. 3:11f., from which this verse is taken, and in the NT (including Rev. 1:5, 3:9) when the love of Christ for man is meant. Dr Charles suggested that 'the exceptional use of the emotional word' is here deliberate (ICC i, 99). Although the Laodiceans do not deserve it, Christ feels for them the more unreasoning and passionate kind of love. **be zealous and repent:** the Gr. tenses are instructive: first present (i.e. 'be constantly zealous', a general command about a Christian virtue), secondly aorist or point-of-time (i.e. 'repent now', as a deliberate act, for the present state of affairs). The linguistic accuracy of this author is remarkable, considering his apparent carelessness in some ways. Is it really carelessness? cf. notes on 1:4, 5, 5, 20, 2:8. **20.** The hint of passionate love in v. 18 is repeated in this verse which appears to borrow, from Ca. 5:2, LXX, the thought of the lover seeking admission at night. The love is also individualised in this verse: **if anyone hears**. The next verse and the echo of Mk 13:29 imply that this knocking refers to the Second Advent, but it is not quite certain (cf. Jn 14:23). The tense of **stand** is against it; it is that of Mt. 20:6; Mk 13:14; Lk. 8:20; Jn 6:22, etc., and implies a semi-permanent or persistent stance. **21.** cf. Eph. 2:6; Col. 3:1 d

IV-V The Vision of Heaven—We turn from earth to heaven. He had been told to write what he saw, present and future things. He has already described the present condition of churches; now he turns his eyes above. Probably it is in ch. 6 that he begins to see 'what is to take place hereafter' (1:19). This is not to say that his material is in any sense original, being borrowed liberally from Isa., Ezek. and Dan., and probably extra-biblical books too. 918a

918b **IV God the Father and Creator—1. After this I looked, and lo:** a combination of LXX and Theodotion, Dan. 7:6. **open door:** or, 'a door was opened'; cf. *1 Enoch* 14:15; *Test. Levi* 5:1. **2.** In this vision of God, he is not described but simply compared with dazzling stones, and a rainbow hides him. cf. Ezek. 1:26, 28. **seated on the throne:** cf. the Gr. of Isa. 6:1; 3 Kingdoms (1 Kg.) 22:19. **4. twenty-four elders:** various interpretations have been given: glorified men or angels of some kind. In any case, they seem to represent God's People or servants. Through Judaism the idea may have come from Bab. astrology, not from the Jewish priestly courses. **5a.** cf. Exod. 19:16; *Jubilees* 2:2. **voices:** the Gr. is referring merely to the claps of thunder; there were no other voices. **6. a sea:** a sea in heaven in *2 Enoch* 3:3; *Test. Levi* 2:7. **living creatures:** cherubim (Charles, ICC i, 119–23). This is another case, as with Book of Life, where knowledge of the Jewish pseudepigraphical literature is essential to an understanding of Rev. Basically the ideas come from the OT, but the finished picture is that of *1 Enoch* 71:7, 39:12, 61:11f.; *2 Enoch* 19:16 (cf. Ezek. 1:5, 18). From the time of Irenaeus each of the creatures has been held to symbolise one of the four evangelists, with very little point. **8a.** cf. Isa. 6:2. **8c.** cf. Isa. 6:3. **9.** The tense has been correctly changed from the future of RV, back to that of AV. The Gr. future is an attempt to render the Heb. imperfect. **11. by their will** (RV, RSV) is correct. The lovely rendering of AV ('for thy pleasure') is not what the Gr. means. So the chapter ends with the emphasis on God the Creator. We turn now to God the Redeemer.

c **V God the Son and Redeemer**—Again there is the faithful harnessing of Jewish sources to a Christian purpose. Very little indeed need have been added, and it is this which gives us the strong impression that our author already had a Jewish work in front of him, or several fragments, and adapted them with the least possible effort. **1.** cf. Isa. 29:11; Ezek. 2:9, 10; Dan. 8:26. **in the right hand:** Gr. has '*on* the right hand', i.e. lying flat on the palm. **a scroll:** it is impossible from the word itself or the context to decide whether it was really a scroll and not a codex (book). It is possible, in the latter case, to punctuate differently: 'a book written within, sealed on the back with seven seals'. The LXX of Ezek. 2:10 makes this less likely, however. **2.** cf. Isa. 6:8. **3f. look into it:** Gr. has 'look *at* it'. **5. Lion:** cf. Gen. 49:9. **conquered:** 2:7 note. **Root of David:** cf. Isa. 11:1. It appears to imply that the rest of the tree has died; Christ represents a new
d beginning. **6. a Lamb:** cf. Isa. 53:7. Not the Gr. word used elsewhere for Lamb in the NT, except Jn 21:15. Moreover, the sudden transformation from a lion to a lamb is arresting. Some scholars have suggested that in the author's source another figure stood instead of the Lamb as though it had been slain. This might have been Metatron, who appears in rabbinic literature as a sort of mediator between God and the world; on one supposition as to the origin of the name Metatron, it would exactly fit the figure described here, who is before or in the midst of the throne. The Metatron conception may be as early as Philo (M. Black in VT I (1951), 217–19; for a summary of the Metatron conception, cf. H. Odeberg, *3 Enoch* (1928), 95–125), and it was unlikely to have been influenced at all by Christian thought. If these chapters were originally Jewish, much as they stand, it would be easy for a Christian to adapt them. In that case, in the source which he used, *aria* (lion) might easily have suggested to our Christian author *mria* (lamb or fatling, in a sacrificial sense; cf. Isa. and Am.). Others have suggested that the **horns** of the Lamb imply that in the original astrological sources of Rev. this was the Ram, a sign of the Zodiac. **horns and . . . eyes:** symbols of power and omniscience respectively. **sent out:** cf. Zech. 4:10.
e **8. which are the prayers of the saints:** this hardly accords with what is said of the function of 918e
incense in 8:3. The phrase, though in the MSS, may be a very early gloss. But cf. the Gr. of Ps. 140 (RSV 141):2. **9a. they sang a new song:** cf. Gr. of Ps. 143 (RSV 144):9; Isa. 42:10. **9d. tribe and tongue and people and nation:** Charles showed that this was taken from an older Aram. text of Dan. than the canonical (ICC i, 147f.). **11.** For the numeral, cf. Dan. 7:10. **13. To him who sits upon the throne and to the Lamb:** an advanced Christology. The magnificent description may be intended as an antidote to emperor-worship in the time of Domitian. This is part of what a modern writer has aptly termed the 'surrealistic artistry' of Rev. Sometimes, later on in the book, the surrealism reaches depths where it gives vent to feelings so vindictive and cruel as to be offensive to many Christian readers (e.g. 14:19, 20, 18:6ff., 19:2, 15). Had the author simply caricatured Roman heathenism, all would have been well, but he is in danger of grotesquely caricaturing Christian zeal and faith.

VI-VIII 5 The Vision of the Seven Seals—The 919a
seals may refer to contemporary events in history exclusively, but this is unlikely in view of the author's method, which was to use ancient sources. They may refer to great empires that are past. More likely is the view of Dr Charles (ICC i, 158) that the seals follow the pattern of events in Mt. 24; Mk 13; Lk. 21: war, strife among nations, famine, pestilence, persecutions, phenomena (earthquakes, eclipses, etc.). These are the six seals. In that case the seer may have known the Gospels or the Christian apocalypse which lies behind them. But Charles believed that he rearranged the order of the woes, in order the better to fit contemporary events (ICC, i, 160): possibly the Parthian empire, Rome, Domitian's edict, the martyrdoms under Nero. Nothing that Charles has to say discounts the possibility that both Gospels and Rev. are deriving their material from an older Jewish source. In any case, at this point in the book the depicting of the Church's struggles really begins.

VI The First Six Seals—1. one of: on both b
occasions the Gr. should be translated: 'the first of'. **2-8.** Some commentators have tried to see in these four seals the signs of the Zodiac; but the parallel is remote in the extreme. **2.** War is symbolised. The colours of the horses are suggested by Zech. 6:1–8, but not the functions. The white horse may be Parthia, Rome's dread enemy at this time. In 2–8, the wording is based on the Zech. passage, and it is notable that the Heb. text is followed here and the Gr. versions ignored. This is not the invariable practice of the author and argues for the use of various sources. **conquering and to conquer:** the first word refers to past achievements, and the rest to future threats, of the Parthians. **3f.** The opening of the c
second seal symbolises national instability ('rumours of wars'). This and the previous symbol are difficult to distinguish, but so are the first two woes in Christian apocalyptic (Mk 13 etc.). **5** symbolises famine: the third apocalyptic woe. **6. quart** is the amount a man would consume in a day, and the **denarius** was the whole of a day's wages. **harm not oil and wine:** there was a shortage of bread and superfluity of wine in Domitian's reign. This would accord with Irenaeus' date. **8** symbolises pestilence, the fourth woe. The context demands this as a translation, rather than Death. Charles rejects, as a scribal insertion: **and Hades followed him,** and also the last seventeen words of the verse (ICC i, 169–71). They are a summary of all the woes so far and not applicable solely to the fourth. cf. Ezek. 14:21. **9.** The fifth woe is Christian martyrdom. **under the altar:** the souls of the martyrs, having been offered in heaven as a sacrifice to God, are now safely preserved beneath his altar-throne. It is a favourite rabbinical belief, probably pre-Christian. **the word of God:** cf. 1:2 note. **the witness they had borne:** another way of taking this is at least as probable: it is Christ's

919c witness which they had received and faithfully kept, as suggested by Jn 3:32 ('no one receives his testimony'). Yet another interpretation is that suggested in the note on 1:2 : 'for the honour in which they held him'. **10. Sovereign Lord:** after Moffatt and Knox. They and RSV might have used this also in Lk. 2:29 (opening of Nunc Dimittis) ; 2 Pet. 2:1 ; Jude 4 (of Jesus), and (as indeed Moffatt and RSV do) in Ac. 4:24. But, in fact, a master of slaves is all that is meant. Almost, 'Sir!' (cf. modern Gr., 'reverend sir' ; MMV, s.v.). In the OT it translates *Adonai* (my Lord). **avenge our blood:** cf. 5:13 note, 2 Kg. 9:7. The vindictiveness of this prayer of departed saints, quite unlike anything in the Gospels and Pauline epistles, cannot be excused on any grounds. Lk. 18:7, 8 is a dubious parallel and is merely part of a parable. No divine rebuke is forthcoming. Our author's sympathies are fully with them. In the fall of Rome he hopes to see this prayer answered (19:2). The thought is very near to the notorious passage, *4 Ezra* 7:85ff., 93, 95, wherein the righteous delight
d to see the sufferings of the wicked. **11. a white robe** probably symbolises the glorified resurrection body, as in Judaism (*1 Enoch* 62, 108 ; *2 Enoch* 22) and on the Mount of Transfiguration. **were to be killed:** perhaps a reference to the imminent martyrdoms expected under Domitian, the previous martyrs being those under Nero. The idea that the End will come when the roll of the martyrs is complete is also found in *1 Enoch* 47 ; and there too the martyrs are an
e offering to God, as here. **12.** cf. *Assumption of Moses* 10:5, probably based on OT material. Phenomena preceding the End are described, as in Mk 13 and in traditional Jewish eschatology. The only reference which cannot be traced beyond doubt is that concerning every mountain and island (14). That of the fig-tree is from Isa. 34:4, not necessarily the Gospels. **13.** The stars falling is also from Isa. **14a.** cf. Isa. 34:4. **15b.** cf. Isa. 2:10, 19 ; Lk. 23:30. **16a.** cf. Isa. 2:10 ; Hos. 10:8. Rev. is based on the Heb., but Lk. 23:30 on LXX. **and from the wrath of the Lamb:** many scholars have regarded these words as an addition ; but they may not be a scribal addition so much as the Christian editor's attempt to render previous Jewish material suitable to his purposes. Not many such additions appear to have been made in these chapters (4–20) ; the Christian traces can be detached fairly easily, there are not too many of them, and the result is a consistently Jewish work. **17.** cf. Jl 2:11, 31*b* ; Nah. 1:6.
f **VII The Saints sealed**—This chapter comes in to interrupt the sequence between the sixth seal (VI) and the seventh seal (VIII), just as there is an interruption later between the sixth and seventh trumpets. Within the chapter, too, there is a marked dichotomy between the very exclusive Jewish verses (1–8), and the more universalistic Christian ones (9–17). Wherever the earlier views may have been derived, the language throughout is a unity.
g **1.** In Talmudic Jewish thought certain angels each have control over one of the elements. Thus, Gabriel was prince of fire. The same idea comes again in Rev. 16. **corners:** in Jewish thought a wind blowing from between the four quarters, i.e. from an angle, was a dangerous wind. cf. 20:8, also Ezek. 2:7 ; *1 Enoch* 34:3, 76. **3. sealed:** the idea is that God's servants are shown to be his against the time that Satan's host makes its final onslaught (9:4). **foreheads:** taken from Ezek. 9:4. cf. Rev. 9:4, 14:1, 22:4. **4. a hundred and forty-four thousand:** the square of twelve a thousandfold, a symbol of the completeness of God's People. Early Christians believed themselves to be the new and spiritual Israel. **every tribe:** not quite, for in the ensuing list Dan is omitted and Manasseh should be included in Joseph. Irenaeus suggested that it was because Anti-Christ
h was to descend from Dan. **5. Judah:** placed first, because of Christ's descent from him. **9-17.** This vision seems to be anticipatory and to have been
inserted here for the purpose of giving encouragement 919h
to the seer's own generation before the final struggle with Satan. **9. palm branches:** symbol of victory after war. **Lamb:** the simple insertion of this name in vv. 9, 10, 14, and its substitute for 'God' or 'Lion' in v. 17 are all that is required to make this thoroughly Jewish chapter Christian. In 14, if 'Lamb' were omitted, 'in the blood' could mean 'by martyrdom'. **10. Salvation belongs to our God:** cf. Ps. 3:8. **14. the great tribulation:** a reference to a definite event in the apocalyptic future facing the seer's generation (Mk 13:19). **washed their robes:** a familiar idea in the OT for putting on righteousness (Isa. 1:18f., cf. also Gen. 49:11). **15. shelter them with his presence:** this translation retains the idea of the Shekinah glory (Lev. 16:2 etc.), but RSV should have dealt in the same way with Jn 1:14. **16f.** cf. Isa. 49:10. **strike them:** this is not in any of the MSS (which read as AV), but is a very acceptable emendation of the text by Gwynn and Swete. **thirst:** the same meaning as in Jn 4:14 (unfulfilled desire). **17. shepherd** has obvious parallels with Jer. 10:11, and **springs** recalls Jn 4:14, 7:38. **17c.** cf. 21:4, Isa. 25:8.
VIII 1-5 The Seventh Seal—After the interruption i
we return to complete the seven seals. The last is opened in silence. **1. half an hour:** no satisfactory explanation of the length is possible. **2. seven angels:** the seven archangels of Jewish tradition are Michael, Gabriel, Raphael, Uriel, Raguel, Sariel, Remiel. They are known as 'the Angels of the Presence', closely connected with the person of God, as *-el* at the end of every one of their names implies (cf. 1:14 note). cf. Lk. 1:19 ; Tob. 12:15. **trumpets:** used eschatologically in the OT to announce God's judgment. cf. Isa. 27:13. **3. stood at the altar:** cf. Am. 9:1. **3.** The suggestion that the seer used more than one Jewish source is supported by the difficulty of this verse. Two altars are apparently envisaged here : those of burnt-offering and of incense, as in Herod's Temple. But there is one altar-throne in ch. 4, where the scene is based on the first Temple, as in Isa. 6. **4a.** cf. Ezek. 8:11.
VIII 6-XI The Vision of the Seven Trumpets— 920a
It is not at all certain whether this new series of judgments is intended to lead us forward chronologically or whether it recapitulates what has gone before from a different point of view. In any case, there is nothing very logical about the sequence.
VIII 6-IX The First Six Trumpets—**7. Fire** and b
blood, in an eschatological context, appear in Jl 2:30, quoted in Ac. 2:19. **8.** The background appears to be a mingling of the plagues of Exod. 7 with eschatology from *1 Enoch* 18:13. Throughout these verses most of the allusions have parallels in the OT. There is no need to assume Zoroastrian influence, except indirectly by way of the OT or Judaism. The four elements of earth, water, fire and air may form the basis of this vision and that of the Bowls, but the number has been increased to seven. Some would say that in order to do this, the author has repeated water and then added two Zodiac signs (Scorpio and Sagittarius), because a *scorpion* is mentioned in 9:5 and the horses with human faces (9:7), presumably centaurs who have bows and arrows and long hair, suggest Sagittarius, who in Zodiacs of Babylon and Egypt is depicted in precisely that manner. The ultimate origin of the material used by the author of Rev. is often very ancient, but we think that it always
comes to him through Jewish media. **IX 1. star:** c
cf. *1 Enoch* 86:1. Evidently an angel. **bottomless pit:** the provisional place of punishment for Satan and fallen angels, the final place being the Lake of Fire (ch. 22) ; but in common with Gehenna and the Lake it is a place of fire. **2.** cf. Gr. of Exod. 19:18 and Jl 2:10. **3a.** cf. Exod. 10:12. **5.** cf. 8:8 note. **6.** cf. Job 3:21. **7.** This and other verses here are reminiscent of Jl 2:4, 5, but cf. also 8:8 note. **11. in Hebrew . . . in Greek:** cf. Jn 5:2, 19:13, 17, 20,

920c 20:16. **14. Euphrates:** here was the border between Rome and her dreaded enemy, the Parthians. From here perhaps the seer expected the fulfilment of this prophecy of punitive invasion. cf. Gen. 15:18. **15.** Note that the four angels have some connection with days, months and years. Greek astrological gods and goddesses also controlled times and seasons, and the reference may have been to them, Judaised into angels. cf. 12:1 note. **20.** cf. Theodotion's version of Dan. 5:23. Also Ps. 113:13–15. But the combination of the worship of demons with that of idols is first found in *1 Enoch* 99:7, which passage therefore (rather than the OT passages) is the true parallel to this passage. **21.** As Dr Charles observed: 'Immorality of every description was the natural sequel of demonic worship and idolatry' (ICC i, 255). cf. Exod. 20:13; 2 Kg. 9:22.

d **X-XI 13 The Little Scroll, the Temple, the Witness**—Here there begins a parenthesis between the sixth and seventh Trumpets. The seer appears to have changed his position; hitherto he has been a witness but is now on earth (4). We expect to read of the seventh angel and Trumpet, but that is delayed until 11:14. The source of the author's material may change at this point, as some have suggested, but the Gr. language is still characteristic of our author.

e **X. 1. another mighty angel:** it may be Gabriel (Charles, ICC i, 259). **legs like pillars of fire:** cf. Dan. 10:6. **2. a little scroll open in his hand:** cf. Ezek. 2:9. The message of the tiny book concerns the whole earth, land and sea (cf. 6). **3. like a lion roaring:** cf. 11:10. **sounded:** RSV is weak; the point in the Gr. is that there was an articulate message in each of the seven thunders. **4.** cf. Jn 12:28. **5-6a.** cf. Dan. 12:7 (Theod.). **6b.** cf. Exod. 20:11. The correct translation is **delay**, although 'time' (RV) is linguistically possible. The idea is that the Day of the Lord is delayed until Antichrist is revealed. **7. mystery:** cf. 1:20 note. **his servants the prophets:** an OT phrase (cf. Am. 3:7), but Christian prophets are probably meant by our author. **9.** Reminiscent of Ezek. 3:1, 3. Probably the allusion is to the mixture of blessing and curse in the scroll. **11. I was told:** a neat way of avoiding the plural verb in the Gr. ('they say'), but it does not solve the difficulty. Who is speaking? cf. Jer. 1:10.

f **XI 1-13.** The parenthesis between the sixth and seventh Trumpets continues. It would all seem to involve preparation for the appearing of Antichrist in Jerusalem, whereas the author's main point appears to be his identification of Antichrist with Rome, rather than with anything Jewish. The identification with Rome is not absolutely certain, however, and the early Christian Antichrist was in some respects a Jewish one: cf. 2 Th. 2:4, 7. The language of these verses is slightly different from that usually found in Rev., and it may indicate the use of a different source here. **1.** cf. Ezek. 40:3, 41:13. **2. measure:** this action must be equivalent to that of the sealing, i.e. spiritual preservation, and to our author (as distinct from his source) the Temple will be the New Israel, the Christian Church. We must not press the meaning of the details (e.g. the altar) in this new Christian context. **trample:** cf. Zech. 12:3. **forty-two months:** the three and a half years have no apparent explanation or origin, as the duration of the final apocalyptic woe. cf. Dan. 7:25, 12:7. **3. my two witnesses:** in Jewish apocalyptic Enoch and Elijah were said to return before the Judgment but 5 and 6 of this chapter rather point to Moses and Elijah. **4.** cf. Zech. 4:2, 3, 14. **5. would:** a more satisfactory translation than RV. The word is often merely an auxiliary at this period of Gr. **fire pours . . .:** cf. 2 Sam. 22:9; Jer. 5:14. **6.** cf. Gr. of 1 Kingdoms (1 Sam.) 4:8. **7. the beast that ascends:** cf. Dan. 7:3; Rev. 13:1, 17:8. **7b.** cf. 13:7, Dan. 7:21. **8. the great city:** its reference here to Jerusalem raises the question whether it should be interpreted of Rome in the rest of the book. If so, we must accept the expedient that this section is from a different source, 920f one which equated the great city with Jerusalem (as Dr Charles). However, there is something to be said for the identification with Jerusalem throughout Rev.; one must not too easily assume that the book is directed against Rome rather than the Jews. We know all too little about the true interpretation of it. **Sodom:** this was the prophet's name for Israel: Isa. 1:10. **where their Lord was crucified:** one of the very few traces in chs. 4–20 of Christian influence, and, like the others, it would be an easy addition to make to a Jewish source. **10. exchange presents:** reminiscent of Est. 9:19. **11.** cf. LXX of Ezek. 37:10.

14-19 The Seventh Trumpet—14. Woes and Trumpets are now resumed. **15b.** cf. Ps. 2:2, 9:37. Slightly reminiscent of Mt. 4:8. **17d, 18a.** cf. Gr. of Ps. 98 (RSV 99):1. **18d-g.** a combination of the Gr. of Am. 3:7 and Ps. 113:21 (RSV 115:13). **19. the ark:** a reference to the Jewish tradition that the ark, which disappeared at the destruction of the first Temple, will reappear at Messiah's coming. g

XII The Portent of the Woman and Child—This chapter is more Jewish than Christian in conception and language; nothing is said of Jesus Christ's earthly life and work; and Michael, not Jesus, is the conqueror. But it has many mythological features which in themselves are neither Jewish nor Christian. They may be Persian, Egyptian or Greek (e.g. the sun-goddess and the Signs of the Zodiac). In any case, although the whole has been somewhat Christianised by the author, we must not press for the Christian meaning of details. The connection with what has gone before is very slight. Evidently the time has come in the drama when the struggle with Antichrist must begin. This is a kind of introduction to that. 921a

1. a woman: cf. Isa. 7:14. In the present Christian context it may be the Virgin Mary, or the Old or the New Israel. Some suggest that she is reminiscent of the Greek mystery goddess Isis; cf. 9:15 note. **a crown of twelve stars:** the signs of the Zodiac, according to many commentators. cf. notes on 4:4, 5:6, 6:2–8, 8:8. **3. dragon with seven heads:** from Bab. mythology. **ten horns:** cf. Dan. 7:7. **4.** An astrological myth, the birth of Marduk the sun-god, may lie behind this idea, but cf. Dan. 8:10. **5.** Obviously our author intends this to refer to Jesus Christ, but it can include no more than his birth and ascension. In detail he has hardly adapted his source at all. We must not press all the details into Christian service, as is invariably attempted. cf. Isa. 66:7. **7-12.** This section, typical of pre-Christian Judaism (there is no need to go to Persian mythology) has merely a superficial connection with what goes before: no mention is made of the man-child. It looks as if sources have been laid alongside one another with a minimum of revision. **7. Michael:** one of the seven, if not the greatest of the seven, archangels of Judaism; he was guardian-angel and champion of Israel. In this role he predominantly figures in apocalyptic literature from Dan. onwards, Jewish and Christian, as well as in rabbinic literature. In Dan. 10:13–20, as national patron, he contends for Israel against the corresponding angels of Persia and Greece. It is probable that the reference is to Michael in Mal. 3:1 and Bar. 6:7. 'Mine angel' is the patron of Israel. But about the 2nd cent. B.C. there grew up another view about Michael, according to which he was the guardian of only the pious remnant in Israel (Ethiopic *Enoch* 20:5; Latin *Ascension of Isaiah* 9:23). The contest in which he takes part is now very different; it is that between good and evil represented by Michael and Satan respectively. This is the view of Rev. The struggle is not with the guardians of other nations but with the Deceiver who leads astray both Jew and Gentile alike. Michael's crusade is universal, and not national. The same idea occurs in Jude 9, in the *Testaments of the XII Patriarchs,* and in the *Testament of Abraham.* **fighting:** the best explanation of the unusual Gr. is to translate it: 'Michael and his b c d

921d angels *must* fight . . .' (Charles, ICC i, 322). **8. no longer any place for them :** cf. Dan. 2:35, but not LXX. **9. serpent . . . the deceiver :** cf. Gen. 3:13. **10f.** obviously contain Christian additions by the seer and changes (e.g. 'the righteous' to 'our brethren'). Probably all **11** was added to the source. The thought is very Johannine (Jn 16:33 ; 1 Jn 4:4, 5:4, 5). **then** in **12** resumes the thought of **10. 12a.** cf. Isa. 49:13. **13. woman :** in the present Christian context, the Church. **14-16 :** a notable example of an undigested piece of source-material ; it is at variance with the author's thesis that there will be universal Christian persecution. During the three and a half years of Antichrist's rule the Church is here said to be protected. cf. Dan. 12:7. **15** is peculiar in that there are no close Jewish parallels ; but a war of land and water is envisaged in the next verse, and this is a primitive mythological feature. **17. the rest of her offspring :** in the Jewish source these would be intended for the Jews who failed to escape before the sack of Jerusalem, perhaps : but, in this Christian context, the phrase seems to be a meaningless survival of revision.

e **XIII The Vision of the Two Beasts**—In this, two beasts rising, the one from the sea, the other from the land, now make us think of Dan. 7 ; in Rev. they must have some connection with the Roman Empire and Caesar-worship, possibly in the time of Nero. In that case, the dragon of ch. 12 may be assumed to have inspired Rome to make war on Christians, for the dragon gives the beast power and authority (13:2). Already, in the *Psalms of Solomon*, Pompey has been entitled the Dragon (2:29). From earliest Christian times Daniel's fourth beast, which rose from the sea, was interpreted of the Roman Empire (Charles, ICC i, 346). The observation that the three figures, the dragon and the two beasts, 'correspond to the Trinity' is not convincing (Torch Bible Commentary, 96), if Jewish sources lie behind.

f **1-10** concerns the first beast. **1. ten horns and seven heads :** like the dragon (12:3) and the beast (17:3). There seems to be a reference to the Roman emperors, but the idea of the seven-headed monster comes from Bab. mythology. It is difficult to decide whether the horns or the heads are supposed to represent the emperors. **a blasphemous name :** probably the title of the first emperor, Caesar Augustus, i.e. 'divine' Caesar. The following emperors made the same claim to divinity. **2.** Very reminiscent of Dan. 7, where in a vision the lion, the bear and the leopard rise from the sea. Commentators of a literal turn of mind complain that this composite beast is 'not plastically conceivable' (e.g. Charles, ICC i, 348). We need not attribute such oddities to later additions to the book ; they are due to the writer's extensive use of diverse sources. Here he has telescoped
g the vision of Daniel. **3. a mortal wound :** perhaps the beast is thought of as the counterpart to Christ (cf 5:6), the Antichrist. The healing of this mortal wound may refer to Caligula's serious illness, from which he recovered. It was Caligula who perpetrated the blasphemy of ordering his statue to be set up in the Temple, and that seems to be referred to in this chapter (v. 6). It reflects our author's use of earlier sources (e.g. a Caligula Apocalypse perhaps), since he himself is concerned with *Nero redivivus* rather than with Caligula (cf. below 17:8). RSV, after Goodspeed and Moffatt, may not be correct in translating **followed the beast**. The point seems rather that the world 'is amazed' to see Nero return from the abyss ; and so they *gazed* after him with wonder. **4. Who is like the beast . . . ?** This is reminiscent of the probable meaning of Michael's name : 'who is like God ?' **5a.** cf. Dan. 7:8 **6.** The blasphemous claims of the Caesars are meant : Domitian was 'dominus et deus noster'. **7a.** cf. Dan. 7:21 (Theod., not LXX). **8. written . . . in the book of life :** cf. 3:5 note, 17:8; Ps. 68:29 (RSV 69:28) ; Dan. 12:1. **of the Lamb that was slain :** probably a gloss of the author's, whereby the Jewish sources were made Christian with 921g
little inconvenience. Note how little there is in these chapters of a peculiarly Christian nature ; and this little can be detached without spoiling the sense. cf. Isa. 53:7. **10.** cf. Jer. 15:2. The meaning of this verse has nothing to do with the doctrine of pacifism, but it is an urge to accept unquestioningly whatever Providence sends, even martyrdom. RSV is based on the better-supported text, but Charles preferred that of Codex Alexandrinus (i, 355), which even more plainly advocates a spirit of resignation (viz. 'if any man is to be slain with the sword, he is to be slain with the sword').

11-18 concerns the second beast. **11. it spoke like** h
a dragon : difficult. There may be a corruption in the Gr. or the underlying Heb. (Charles, i, 358). **13.** It was expected in Jewish and early Christian thought that miracles would precede the coming of Antichrist. **15. those who will not worship the image :** cf. Dan. 3:6. The cult of the emperor is in mind. Speaking images were common, engineered by some form of trickery. **16. marked on the right hand or the forehead :** this method of identifying the emperor-worshippers is probably based on, and contrasted with, the practice of 1st-cent. Jews of weaving phylacteries on the left hand and on the brow. The suggestion that the mark was a Heb. letter written like a cross, because this passage is reminiscent of Ezek. 9:4, is plausible ; but to claim that our author has in mind the signing of the cross on the forehead in baptism or confirmation is to make him far too subtle (Torch Bible Comm., 99). His sources are clearly Jewish and often he is clumsy in
his use of them. **18. a human number :** Gr. says : i
'the number of a man'. Presumably the number is equivalent to the letters of a man's name, and therefore the beast is to be understood as being incarnate as an actual man. This man it would have been unwise for the author to name frankly. The Gr. word behind **reckon** means to calculate with numbers. The name *Neron Caesar* satisfies this numerical calculation, and it has the added advantage that it explains the variant reading '616', for that would be *Nero Caesar*. To reach this conclusion a reader would have to imagine the name to be written in Heb. characters, thus : נרון קסר.

XIV The Vision of the Lamb—This comprises a 922a
view of Jesus Christ the Lamb, on Mt Sion, with a hundred and forty-four thousand risen virgin martyrs. These saints are represented as having returned to earth to share in the glorious reign of a thousand years, the millennium. Are these to be identified (as Alford and Charles) with those who were sealed in 7:4–8 ? Their number is identical, and they are marked on the forehead. But others see here a reference to Christians in general, and in 7:4–8 a reference only to Jewish Christians. However, the allusions to the Lamb in this present section may well be the author's interpolations into the Jewish source, and thus in both places it is the elect in Judaism who were originally intended. Our author, or editor, fully understands the dramatic value of contrast. He passes directly from describing the beasts into a picture of the Lamb surrounded by his faithful virgins.

1-5 The Lamb on Sion—**1.** It should be realised b
that it is plain from the Gr. that these virgins who accompany the Lamb are men, not women ; in this verse, the feminine participle is simply due to the fact that **thousand** is fem. in Gr. RSV therefore does well to avoid the word 'virgin', but **chaste** (4) is not much better. They are male 'celibates'. It is beside the point to say that elsewhere in the NT celibacy is not particularly commended, and that therefore these saints are celibates only in the sense that they are not immoral. This author is not necessarily in line with the rest of the NT. To twist his words out of all resemblance to their real meaning, in the interest of making his ideas more palatable, is not in accord with the best traditions of Christian scholarship.

922b **4-5.** The idea of this author, that celibacy is a particularly high Christian calling (the **first fruits**), has induced Dr Charles to suspect that the reference is an interpolation of monkish scribes. He does not base this on solid evidence. Neither is there anything whatever to be said in favour of taking the Gr. word for 'celibate' as meaning here 'men who had kept the marriage-bond inviolate' (Andrews, in the original Peake's Commentary, p. 938*a*). **4b** reminds us of Lk. 9:57. **5.** cf. Zeph. 3:13.

c **6-13 The Fall of Rome**—Under the name of Babylon (cf. 1 Pet. 5:13) Rome's fall, and that of the emperor-worshippers, is foretold by three angels. **6. gospel** is here simply 'good news'. **7. Fear God:** cf. Ec. 12:13. **who made heaven and earth, the sea:** cf. 10:6*b*; Neh. 19:6; Ac. 4:24. **8. Fallen, fallen:** cf. Isa. 21:9. **Babylon the great:** cf. Dan. 4:27 (Gr.). It is quite inconsistent of RSV to translate the phrase as **the wine of her impure passion** in this verse, and then as 'the wine of whose fornication' in 17:2. There is nothing in the context to warrant such inconsistency. Fornication, as in the OT prophets, is to be understood metaphorically of idolatry. **10a.** cf. Ps. 75:8; Isa. 51:17; Jer. 25:15; *Psalms of Solomon* 8:15. **unmixed:** undiluted with water. **and in the presence of the Lamb:** not very natural, after the angels; but there is no need to explain it as a later gloss; the author probably glossed it on his sources in order to Christianise them. cf. *1 Enoch* 48:9. **11a.** cf. LXX of Isa. 34:10. **12. faith of Jesus:** rather, faith *in* Jesus; the translators have overlooked the Gr. objective genitive. cf. 2:13 note. **13. who die in the Lord** reminds us of 1 Th. 4:16.

d **14-20 Judgment on the World in general**—This will be described in greater detail in 19:11–16. Another dramatic change on the part of this author; the chapter which began serenely ends with a vindictive picture of wrath executed on the Church's enemies, and all this suffering imposed by God and actually taking place before the eyes of the Lamb (10–20). **14. seated upon the cloud:** cf. 1:7*a*. **a son of man:** cf. 1:13 note. **15-17.** Better sense is obtained if these verses are omitted. They may possibly have been inserted by a supposed editor of our author's work, or (far more probably) they reflect the author's method of conflating his sources, sometimes with little attempt to smooth out irrelevancies. **18.** In contemporary Jewish belief certain angels were considered to have power over the various elements (cf. *1 Enoch* 60:11–21). Gabriel was generally considered to be the angel over fire, but in the *Testament of Abraham* it is Purael (perhaps a Graecised form of Uriel). Some of the rabbis considered that the origin of all angels was in the fiery river mentioned in Dan. 7:10. Moreover we read in the Syriac *Apocalypse of Baruch* 6:4f.: 'I beheld and lo! four angels standing at the four corners of the city, each of them holding a torch of fire in his hands. And another angel descended from heaven and said to them: Hold your torches and do not light them till I tell you' (end of 1st cent. A.D.). Rev. makes much of this theme; we find again in 16:8f. that the fourth of the seven angels poured out his bowl and the contents scorched men with fire. No doubt the various Jewish and Christian apocalyptists were each borrowing from Jewish tradition. cf. also 7:1 note. Jl 3(4):13. **20. the winepress was trodden:** cf. Isa. 63:3; Lam. 1:15. **the city:** probably Jerusalem, not Rome; the number of stadia, 1,600, is possibly the length of Palestine. At this point many critics have felt that the author's chief apocalyptic source ended. It seems to be an end and nothing more needs to be said. If that is so, the Christian author did not agree with his source. He still has much to add about the judgment and especially about the joys of the blessed. Nevertheless it is very difficult to find much consistency in his scheme, which is full of anticipations and interpolations. This phenomenon will always be capable of several explanations, but it seems most reasonable to suppose that the author was not careful about neat 922d
arrangement and may not even have intended this to be the final edition of his book.

XV-XVI The Vision of the Seven Bowls—In a 923a
sense, all that has occurred since ch. 11 is a parenthesis. There the idea of judgment was conveyed through visions of trumpets, and now the idea is repeated by means of visions of bowls. There can hardly be any chronological conception lying behind this sequence.

XV The Bowls prepared—We now come to that part of the drama where judgment is described through the picture of bowls, just as previously it has been pictured by means of seals and trumpets. In this chapter, once again, either the author is very confused in his thoughts or he is conflating loosely more than one source. For instance, in v. 1 he is looking into heaven and sees the seven angels, whereas heaven is not opened and they do not emerge until v. 5. Probably he does not intend this new series of judgments to mark any advance in time.

2. who had conquered the beast is probably b
correct. The peculiar Gr. is literally (as RV) 'victorious from the beast', and may mean that they both conquered and escaped *from* him (i.e. by martyrdom)—a compressed phrase. Some grammarians suggest the meaning: 'who had *kept* themselves *from* the beast'. **3. and the song of the Lamb:** many commentators would ascribe this phrase to an interpolator. It is either an interpolation, or the author's attempt to make his sources Christian. The result sounds rather incongruous: the song of Moses and the song of the Lamb. Would Christian martyrs be likely to sing a song of Moses? Hence the source was probably referring to Jewish martyrs. There is no reference to the Lamb in the song itself, which incidentally displays the parallelism of Hebrew poetry. **Great and wonderful are thy deeds:** cf. Ps. 111:2, 139:14. **Just and true are thy ways:** cf. Ps. 145:17, combined with 119:151. **3*n*. the nations:** cf. Theodotion's version of Jer. 10:7. **4a. glorify thy name:** cf. Gr. of Ps. 85:9 (RSV 86:9), also 4*c*. **5. the temple of the tent of witness:** a difficult phrase. The first 'of' may merely be the equivalent of a comma in meaning (introducing a genitive of apposition). Another suggestion is, that in the Heb. source the phrase is a corruption of 'the temple of God'; the letters are very similar (Charles, ICC ii, 38). **6. robed in . . . c
linen:** RSV follows the same reading in the Gr. text as AV, but RV has: 'arrayed with *precious* stone'. RV follows the better MSS, but not the better sense. Probably all the MSS which give what appears to be the better reading have been corrupted at a very early date. cf. Dan. 10:5. **8. smoke:** like cloud, the symbol of God's majesty: Isa. 6:4. **no one could enter:** cf. Exod. 40:29. Dr Charles suggested a reason why no-one could enter the temple until the plagues were ended: the temple is to be understood figuratively as a place of *prayer*, and therefore no-one could *intercede* to prevent the judgment (ICC ii, 40).

XVI The Bowls poured—As Milligan pointed out, d
it is no use trying to determine the special meaning of the various objects which are said to be visited by the wrath of God, and we must concentrate on the general effect. The author's earliest readers may possibly have known what was meant in detail, but even that is doubtful. We certainly have little hope of finding the key. Probably the idea of universality is what the author meant to convey: no creature of God may expect to escape the judgment which will precede the return of Christ. **2. sores:** these and e
other plagues, reminiscent of those in Egypt in the time of Moses, are symbolical of some punishment destined to fall on Rome. cf. Exod. 9:10; Dt. 28:35. **3.** The second bowl. **every living thing:** cf. Gen. 1:21. **4.** The third bowl; cf. Exod. 7:20. **5. angel of water:** cf. notes on 7:1 and 14:18. **Just art thou . . . Holy:** same Gr. in Ps. 144(RSV 145):17. **6. blood to drink:** cf. Isa. 49:26. **7. just and**

923e **true are thy judgments:** cf. 19:2; Ps. 19:20. **8.** The fourth bowl. cf. notes on 7:1, 14:18. **10.** The fifth bowl. **throne of the beast:** probably the city of Rome itself. **darkness:** caused evidently by the smoke from the pit, 9:2; an echo of Exod. 10:21. **12.** The sixth bowl. **its water was dried up:** this would allow the Parthians from the East the better to march on Rome. There was widespread fear after Nero's death, that he would return *redivivus* at the head of a Parthian army and fight to regain his throne; but his victory would last but 'one hour' (17:12), for after this he and the Parthian leaders would make war on the Lamb and the Lamb would conquer (17:14), according to our author's belief. In this verse there is an echo of Exod. 14:21. **15.** The inappropriateness of this verse probably shows how carelessly the book has been compiled, although the author may have intended to revise it later. **like a thief** reflects our Lord's words (Mt. 24:43) and also
f 1 Th. 5:2, 4; 2 Pet. 3:10. cf. also Rev. 3:3. **16. Armageddon:** literally either 'mount of plagues' or 'mount of Megiddo'. We do not find the word anywhere else, and the meaning is very obscure. Megiddo was the battle-ground of kings in the OT (Jg. 5:19; 2 Kg. 23:29; Zech. 12:11), but nothing so subtle could have been in the author's mind. Again the solution lies in the Jewish source, of which we probably have only a part. **17.** The seventh bowl. **18. such as had never been since men were on the earth:** cf. Dan. 12:1. With Theodotion our author adds 'on the earth' to the Heb. text as we know it. **19.** Rome, though some take it as Jerusalem. **19b.** cf. 14:10*a* note. **20.** In apocalyptic the disappearance of mountains was one sign of the end of the world: *Assumption of Moses* 10:4; *1 Enoch* 1:6; *Sibylline Oracles* 8:234ff. **21. great hailstones:** like the seventh plague of Egypt; cf. Exod. 9:24. Here too the effect is the hardening of the heart against God. So ends this last series of plagues which are to descend upon mankind through the instrumentality of angels. We have now to turn in detail to the final struggle.

924a **XVII-XX 3 The Prophecy of the Fall of Babylon (Rome)**—The end draws near. The great enemy is probably Rome and the Caesar-worship associated with it, according to most interpreters. The final vision is a dramatic attempt to encourage Christians who are faced with martyrdom. Its message is that Rome ('the great harlot') will perish. Her tormentor ('the scarlet beast') will appear from out of the East, and then this tormentor of Rome will himself be destroyed by God. The beast 'was and is not and is to come'. Many take this of Nero, sprung to life again, leading the Parthian armies against Rome ('the great harlot' who was once carried by Nero, the beast: 17:7). Our author's original contribution to apocalyptic is this: the Lamb will eventually conquer Rome's conquerors (17:14, 16). The whole prophecy is full of OT allusions, especially to Tyre, Nineveh, and Babylon—ancient enemies and oppressors of God's people. Moreover, it is evident from a study of the language that we have traces of at least two distinct sources on which our author worked and which he attempted to revise. That is why the thought is not clear or easy to follow.

b **XVII 1-6 The Harlot on the Beast**—**1. the great harlot:** one would think this more appropriate of Jerusalem than of Rome. The Heb. prophets constantly accused the holy city of the spiritual sin of fornication, namely religious syncretism and imprudent associations with foreign kings; in v. 2 this city, whatever it is, is accused of just that kind of association with the kings of the earth. It is difficult to resist the conclusion that all this is very fittingly applied to Jerusalem. Such a conclusion is strengthened by the observation that the last words of ch. 18 ('in her was found the blood of prophets and of saints, and of all who have been slain on the earth') remind us vividly of words which Jesus used of Jerusalem in Mt. 23:35 ('that upon you may come all the righteous blood shed on earth, from the blood of innocent Abel to the blood of Zechariah. . . . O Jerusalem, Jerusalem, killing the prophets. . . .'). So once more the question arises whether Rev. is not really directed against militant and persecuting non-Christian Judaism, which arrested the spread of the Gospel in its earliest days, rather than secular Rome. On the other hand there are considerable difficulties in the acceptance of such a view and the rejection of the more usual identification with Rome. v. 12, for instance (the ten kings), would most naturally be a reference to Roman emperors, and the seven hills of v. 9 look like those on which Rome is built. **1. seated upon many** c
waters: cf. Jer. 51:13. This does not fit Rome, but it does fit Babylon which stands behind it, with its river and network of canals. **2.** cf. Isa. 23:17; Jer. 51:7; Nah. 3:4. **4. in her hand a golden cup:** cf. Jer. 51:7. A description of wealth and luxury. **5.** Wetstein quotes Seneca to illustrate that harlots in Rome wore their names placarded on their brows. **mystery:** in the NT the word is used of that which is only known or understood by the initiated; so here Babylon and all that is said of her must be interpreted in a sense known only to the readers. **6.** Some commentators have quoted Tacitus who describes the Neronian persecution of Christians: 'A great crowd was convicted both of arson and of hatred of the human race. Not only were they put to death, but put to death with insult, in that they were either dressed in the skins of beasts to perish by the worrying of dogs, or put on crosses or set on fire; and when daylight failed they were burnt as lights for the night.' **the blood of the saints and the blood of the martyrs:** it is hard to see what is the difference, since clearly these particular saints would be martyrs; we cannot very well translate the **and** by 'even' in this sentence; it is probably right to assume that the reference to 'martyrs' was added by the Christian author to his source, and to take 'saints' as referring to the Jewish martyrs in the Roman War of 66–70.

7-18 Interpretation of the Mystery—The beast, d
which hitherto has represented Rome, seems now to take personal form as one man, Nero. **8. to ascend from the bottomless pit:** i.e. to rise from the dead, but cf. 9:1 note, 11:7, 13:1. **perdition:** a case where RSV follows RV and AV in their imperfections; there is no reason for translating the same Gr. word as 'perdition' here and as 'destruction' when Jesus says, 'Broad is the way that leads to perdition'. The place is exactly the same and there seems to be no good reason why a modern English version should make the NT appear more complex than it is. cf. Mt. 7:13. According to contemporary Jewish thought life was lived along either of two ways, one broad and one narrow, and one departed from life by means of either of two gates, one broad and one narrow. The latter way and gate lead to life, the former to the place or condition which is referred to in this passage. The fulfilment of this prophecy comes at 19:20. **book of life:** cf. 3:5 note. **10. one is:** the author clearly is living in the time of the sixth king, or emperor; the five who are fallen will be Augustus, Tiberius, Caligula, Claudius and Nero. The present reign will thus be that of Vespasian, A.D. 69–79; the other who has not yet come and only remains a little while must then be Titus whose short reign was from A.D. 79 to 81.
11. the eighth: we are now well past the time of e
Vespasian in which it seemed, at first, our author was living. Perhaps it was the author of his source who lived in the reign of Vespasian; he himself seems to have lived in the reign of the eighth. To him this was Nero *redivivus*. Which emperor would this actually be? If we begin with Augustus and exclude the three doubtful emperors, Galba, Otho and Vitellius, we have Domitian as the eighth. This view is full of difficulties, for Domitian would hardly lead a Parthian invasion. It may be that Rev. was written just before the reign of Domitian (the author did not think the health of Titus would permit him to remain more

924e than 'a little while'), and that he expected that the next emperor would be Nero reincarnate. This view also has difficulties, for emperor-worship was not enforced until well into the reign of Domitian and certainly nothing occurred in the reign of Titus which could have provoked a book like Rev. The reign of Domitian, a second Nero in every way as far as the Church was concerned, is the most likely date for our author's activity. The difficulties in connection with the identification or juxtaposition of Domitian and Nero *redivivus* can only be solved on the supposition which we have had to put forward many times already: the author is working on several older pieces of material, each of them probably dating from a different reign. The details of these sources he did not take care to make consistent. It is the general effect that matters. Someone has aptly said that the art

f of this book is a kind of surrealism. **12. ten kings who have not yet received royal power:** it is difficult to know exactly who are meant. Some have vaguely suggested future powers; others the governors of Roman senatorial provinces. It is best to assume that they represent the satraps who ruled the Parthians. **14. called and chosen and faithful:** he may be consciously reproducing Mt. 20:16, 22:14. **15.** Linguistically this verse has every appearance of not being the work of our author (Charles, ICC ii, 72). **16.** The prophet Ezekiel had used these figures of Jerusalem, which are here apparently applied to Rome: Ezek. 23:25–9. **devour her flesh:** cf. Isa. 49:26.

g **XVIII The Judgment on Babylon**—An exultant cry of vengeance against the arch-foe of the Christian martyrs. 'Rejoice over her, O saints and apostles and prophets!' It is a recital of Rome's expected doom, and though saturated with OT allusions and figures of speech it falls very far short of poetry or true prophecy. The event proved it to be no more than wishful thinking as far as the immediate future was concerned, and in the long run as a matter of fact the very reverse happened; the Christian Church actually won over 'the great harlot' to the side of Christ! Either the author has not understood the Christian Gospel or else he is unthinkingly reproducing his Jewish sources; for the prayer, 'Repay her double for her deeds' (6), and, 'Give her a like measure of torment' (7), are the last word in vindictiveness and it is difficult to appreciate the tortuous reasoning of some Christian commentators in their attempt to prove that such prayers are Christlike. To the unbiased observer they are more like the Hasmonaean psalms. Perhaps the best that can be said in favour of this chapter has been said by E. F. Scott (*The Book of Revelation* (1939), 88f.). He thinks it is 'splendid poetry' and that it owes its fire and energy to the passion of hatred which runs through it. He makes the plea that Rome has not yet fallen, and that it is less culpable to exult beforehand than to trample 'on the enemy who lies prostrate under your feet'. He does not say that it would be better still to follow the example of Stephen and pray for one's persecutors. And might not the cruelty of Church powers in ages yet to come have drawn some inspiration and comfort from such words as these? However, E. F. Scott claims that the feeling of this chapter is not simply one of vengeance, but rather the joy of knowing that God is just, that he will defend the weak and punish the wicked. But that is best left in his hands, not made the subject of our prayers. Moreover, E. F. Scott discovers in the writer's words a tribute to the grandeur of Rome. That is the best that can be said of it. It is extravagant to claim that 'no one has ever written a more generous epitaph on a fallen foe'. If so, the cynic may well claim that Paul urged in vain: 'Bless those who persecute you; bless and do not curse them.'

h **1. the earth was made bright with his splendour:** cf. Ezek. 43:2. We are invited to go forward in imagination and see Rome's doom as already accomplished. 2. cf. 14:8; Isa. 13:21; *1 Baruch* 4:35.

haunt: the idea is rather that of a prison-house, 924h
e.g. 1 Pet. 3:19. In 19:3 'the smoke from her goes up for ever and ever', whereas here Rome is seen as a desolate ruin. **3.** cf. 17:2; Jer. 28(51):7. **have drunk:** cf. RSV*n*. The uncial MSS of great antiquity do not read this, but a rather impossible 'have fallen', which is almost certainly due to a mistake in copying. The later MSS, which read 'have drunk', are all following a brilliant guess as to the original meaning. **4.** cf. Jer. 51:45; Heb., not LXX; also 2 C. 6:17; Eph. 5:11. This verse provides a good example of the author's inconsistency. The saints are to leave Rome before her destruction, and yet they are all dead according to what has previously been said; the number of the martyrs is complete (ch. 15), and the bowls of judgment have already been poured out on a wholly heathen world. This illustrates the way in which he used his material; he was not a man with a tidy mind. **5.** cf. Jer. 28(51):9. **are heaped high as heaven:** the RSV rendering is very graphic; the Gr. is literally 'adhere' to heaven, however, which is not quite the same thing. Probably the older English versions and the Vulgate therefore are more correct in rendering it: 'reached' to heaven. The idea is not that they are stuck together in such a large mass that it reaches to heaven. The Jer. passage, in either Heb. or Gr., lends no support to that; and if our author had in mind 1 Esd. 8:72; Ezr. 9:6 or *4 Ezr.*
11:43, the same would be true. **6.** cf. Ps 137:8. i
It is not clear who exactly is addressed in this verse. Probably Nero *redivivus* and his Parthian hosts. C. Anderson Scott noted the 'striking contrast' between the sentiment expressed here and the comfortable words about being repaid double in Isa. 40:2, a 'gracious promise' (Cent.B, 268). **7c.** cf. the Heb. of Isa. 47:7–8. **8.** The thought of Isa. 47 still influences the dirge. **famine:** this would be due to the approaching Parthians who would cut off Rome's food supplies from the East. **pestilence** would follow, and then the burning of the city by fire (cf. 17:16). **9.** In the verses which follow, the dirge follows closely the doom pronounced by Ezekiel upon Tyre (26–8), in the same way that the last few verses have followed the prophet Isaiah closely. **9a.** cf. 17:1 note, 18:3. **11.** Rome's
commerce was vast at this time. **12.** This list of j
merchandise imported by Rome, though probably true enough to actual fact, is also closely based on the list given in Ezek. 27:12–24 of the imports of Tyre. **13. chariots:** this, however, has no parallel in Ezek.'s list. The Gr. word is very rare, and I suggest that in this context its presence is entirely due to misunderstanding of a probable Heb. original, which may have had *r^edhîdhî* (women's *finery*). In that case our author has simply transliterated it into Gr. as *rhedōn*, the nearest he could get in that language. In the Jerusalem Talmud the word *r^edhîdhā'* means a *veil* or *wrap*, and wraps like these were woven in Babylon, which gives point to their mention in this list. **slaves:** these may have been gladiators (Wetstein). **human souls:** this has a parallel in Ezek.'s list: 27:13. **14.** The dirge is now directly addressed to Rome itself. In this way the verse stands entirely alone, and many have thought that it has been misplaced, some restoring it after 21 and others after 23*d*. Once we admit the possibility that displacement has taken place in our text, there are a number of instances where the transposition of verses makes improved sense: the classic commentary of R. H. Charles should be consulted for these, but many are arbitrary and do not sound convincing. **18.** cf. Ezek. 27:32, of Tyre. **19a.** cf. Ezek. 27:30. Clearly the LXX is not being followed in this source, for it presupposes a different text. It would be a Heb. source. **20.** Charles transposes this verse to the very end of the chapter where, of course, it makes a very fitting climax. **apostles** may be an addition to the original Heb. source. **21.** Reminiscent of Jer. 51:63f. **22a.** cf. Ezek. 26:13. **22. minstrels:** Charles objected to this translation, though that is

924j really the meaning of the Gr., on the ground that a generic term is out of place in a list of specified performers. 'Singers' is what the context requires, and the word can just bear this meaning. **22f. millstone . . . lamp . . . bridegroom and bride** are all found in Jer. 25:10. 'The arts of civilized life would come to an end' (Charles). **23e.** cf. Isa. 23:8. **23f.** The reason for Rome's destruction : the shedding of the martyrs' blood and the seducing of other nations. The method of seduction is said to be by sorcery, and that was more fitting in its original context of Babylon than of Rome. Moreover, 24 reflects precisely what Jesus said concerning Jerusalem (Mt. 22:35). Rome was not responsible for many of the deaths of OT martyrs, and **all** is a very inclusive word.

925a **XIX 1-10.** From heaven now comes the response to the author's cry : 'Rejoice over her, O heaven !' The great multitude of heaven take up the cry from the seer and continue it with the same theme of exultant satisfaction that God's enemy, the harlot, is suffering her just punishment. At v. 4 the elders figure once again, with the four living creatures, adding their contribution of satisfaction and praise. A voice from the throne of God calls forth another song, which is sung by all the servants of God in heaven, presumably the great host of martyrs. The theme of the song is different : no longer satisfaction at the fall of Rome, but joy that the Kingdom of Christ is about to come. This is very much in accord with the practice of our author. He loves contrast, and often after a vision or song of judgment and horror he immediately presents a directly opposite state of affairs. No greater contrast can be imagined than that between the solemn vengeful dirge of ch. 18 and the lovely words of 19:6–10. His purpose is to encourage the faithful in a time of great trial. Over against the dark clouds of the present he always tries to set the sunshine of the future (e.g. after the dreadful hints of the wrath of the Lamb in ch. 6 comes the vision of the heavenly multitude which no man could number in ch. 7 ; after the hideous picture in the first half of ch. 11 comes the elders' song in the second half, culminating in a glimpse of the ark of God's covenant ; after the trials and destruction of all the faithful, who will not bear the mark of the beast, in ch. 13 there is immediately presented to the faithful a picture of the Lamb in heaven with his spotless loved ones). It is not so much in detailed arrangement as in this broad contrast that our author displays his artistry. Some have considered that in these verses at least he did not use any sources, but it should be observed that even here it is not until v. 7 that there is any reference to the Lamb or any other distinctively Christian phrase.

b **1.** Of what is this multitude composed ? Some have thought they are Christian martyrs, but their song comes later (5–8). Apparently they are choirs of angels. They are on the outer fringe of the throne, and the author appears to be working inwards towards the centre. **Hallelujah :** this important Christian word which has figured so extensively in liturgy and worship does not appear anywhere in the NT except in this present section. Incidentally a great number of Christian hymns are based entirely on Rev. This word is a transliteration into Gr., and thence into English, of the Heb. word which means 'Praise the Lord !' (end of Ps. 104, 105, 106). Pre-Christian Jews of the Dispersion had already made use of the transliteration in their synagogue worship ; it occurs in the LXX, both in the Ps. and elsewhere (cf. Tob. 13:18 ; 3 Mac. 7:13). **2a.** cf. 15:3, 16:7. **4. Amen :** cf. Ps. 106:48 (Heb.). **5.** The voice is probably not that of the Father or Christ, nor of an angel, but of a cherub or elder as they stood nearest the throne. **Praise our God :** not appropriate for the Father or Christ (the latter refers to '*my* God' in 3:12). cf Ps. 113:1, 134:1, 135:20. **servants :** probably the martyrs in our author's terminology, cf. 7:3, 19:2. **6.** cf. 1:15 note. **6f. the Lord . . . reigns. Let us rejoice and exult :** cf. Ps. 97:1. The second 925b part is strongly reminiscent of Mt. 5:12. **the marriage of the Lamb :** Hosea thought of Israel as the bride of Yahweh (2:19), and the same comparison occurs later in Isa. (54:1–8) and Ezek. (16:7), later still in *4 Ezra* 9 and in the parables of Jesus (Mt. 22 ; Lk. 14). In the NT epistles the figure is transferred to Christ and his Bride the Church. In Rev. the same conception will form the climax of the book, the New Jerusalem being the Bride of Christ (21:9f., 22:17, etc.), a symbol of her eternal union with him. The difficulty in this passage is, that while the new Israel is in mind as the bride, it seems that members of the Church are guests and not the bride ! Never does our author work out his magnificent conceptions in detail. **10. You must not do that :** it seems that angel-worship grew up very early in the Church, and this small incident may have been inserted for the benefit of any readers so inclined (cf. Col. 2:18 ; Heb. 2:5). This incident must have some great significance for the author, as it is repeated at 22:8. **testimony of Jesus :** it is not really possible to say whether the genitive in the Gr. is to be understood as subjective ('the testimony which Jesus bore') or as objective ('the testimony borne [by others] to Jesus'). cf. 1:2 note. **the testimony of Jesus is the spirit of prophecy :** difficult to understand. However, if the order of subject and predicate is reversed, it is clearer. True prophecy is (now) subject to Christian revelation. It is identical, in fact, with the testimony of Jesus (whether borne by or to him).

c

11-16 The Fifth Horseman—This idea takes us d back to ch. 6. Moreover, Christ is now a horseman, no longer a lamb, as in the previous paragraph. Nothing is said in detail about the defeat of Nero and the Parthians. What is now described is the next stage : the defeat of the kings and nations who had joined with Rome in days gone by, and who had recently beheld and wondered at Rome's total destruction. Now it is their turn. But nothing is said of the Parthians who had destroyed Rome. Their destruction is merely assumed. However, something is said of the beast (Nero) who leads them. Now he leads not apparently the Parthians, but the kings of the earth, to battle with the horseman. His fate is to be thrown into the lake of fire which burns with brimstone.

11a. cf. Ezek. 1:1. **Faithful and True :** this figure e on the horse must be Christ himself, for Christ was 'faithful' in 1:5 and 'true' in 3:7, and 'faithful and true' in 3:14. The idea of the Christ as a mighty warrior was no new one : cf. *Ps. of Solomon* 17:23–7. **in righteousness he judges :** cf. Isa. 11:4 (Heb., not LXX). **12a.** cf. 1:14, 2:18. **12c** Jews and early Christians ascribed a great deal of importance to the power of a name, e.g. in the healing of the cripple in Ac. 4:7. Among pagans too knowledge of a god's name bestowed magical powers. As the name is clearly secret it is not that divulged in the next verse : Word of God. We have no clue as to what our author intended. Some have thought the secret name was *Kyrios*, the Lord, in view of Phil. 2:11. It was a name full of significance, and at this time it would have to be secret as it was applied also to the Roman emperor. Others assume that the meaning is that no-one will know the name until the final consummation (in support cf. *Ascension of Isaiah* 9:5).

13. clad in a robe dipped in blood : the Christian f commentators of the type to which we have had reason to refer already, make the mistake of supposing that this is the horseman's own blood, in an attempt to soften the harshness of this portrait of Christ. Nothing could be farther from the truth, as the OT parallels show, cf. Isa. 63:1–3. Our author's Christ is certainly one who is red with the blood of his enemies. But who are these enemies ? They are not the nations with whom he is fighting at present, for their slaughter has not yet taken place. Dr Charles made the suggestion that it was the blood of the Parthian kings, whose slaughter has not been described, but merely

925f assumed (ICC, ii, 133). Other good MSS read: 'sprinkled with blood'. In either case, judgment and not redemption is the key-note here; the horseman is out to execute divine wrath, and we must beware of twisting the author's thoughts in order to make them reasonably Christian. **The Word of God:** the only parallel is John's Gospel (1:1ff.), if this refers, as it must, to Jesus Christ. But of course the phrase is used in an entirely different context in the two books. **14. armies of heaven:** a familiar idea in contemporary Jewish thought; cf. *Testament of Levi* 3:3; *2 Enoch* 17; *2 Esd.* 19:6; Mt. 26:53. **15.** An extraordinary verse but typical of this author. It conflates ideas from Ps. (2:9); Isa. (11:4, 63:3); and *Ps. of Solomon* (17:27, 39). **rule:** cf. 2:27 note. **16. on his thigh:** some have suggested that the girdle is meant, others that the name was inscribed upon a sword-hilt. **King of kings:** cf. 17:4; 1 Tim. 6:15; *1 Enoch* 9:4.

g **17-21 Final Doom of Rome**—Based on Ezek. 39, especially vv. 4, 20. **17. standing in the sun:** difficult, but probably a central position in heaven from which to issue the summons to the birds. **20. beast:** first mention since ch. 17. **the false prophet:** perhaps the second beast of ch. 13. In 16:13 we have three figures mentioned together: the dragon, the beast and the false prophet. The third mentioned here may be the third mentioned in chs. 12 and 13 ((i) the dragon: 12:13. (ii) the beast: 13:1. (iii) another beast: 13:11). The two figures of beast and false prophet have been compared with Ahriman and Azi-Dahâka; the Zend religion of the East influenced Judaism. Charles suggested that the false prophet was meant to represent the organised priesthood of Caesar-worship which was 'false' in the sense that all manner of impostures were used in order to beguile men into this worship. **lake of fire:** peculiar to Rev. In the NT the place of punishment is elsewhere the *valley* of fire (Gehenna) or the furnace. cf. 20:10, 14, 15, 21:8. **21. the rest:** these kings and their people, though slain, are not yet cast into the burning lake; however, their turn comes after the resurrection, in 20:15. Charles pointed out an interesting point of difference between this and what is found in another apocalypse (Jewish) of the 1st cent.: according to the *Ascension of Isaiah* (4:14) Beliar, who is the same as our beast, will be dragged into Gehenna along with his armies. Perhaps this isolation of the beast and false prophet in Rev., and their tasting of the fires before anyone else, is due to the artistry of our author.

h **XX 1-3 Satan bound**—Here we find that Satan is identified with the first of the three figures mentioned above (cf. 19:20 note), the dragon. There is a kind of trinity of evil in this book: the dragon, the beast and the false prophet. The description of Satan here has parallels in Jewish, Egyptian and Persian tradition. Two members of the trinity have been consigned to the lake of fire; the first member is destined instead to be bound with a chain in the pit for a thousand years, during the millennial reign of Christ, and after that to join them in the lake of fire. The pit is merely a temporary place of punishment. cf. 12:9 for Satan.

i **2. a thousand years:** the period of time during which Satan is bound may be symbolical of the period of the Church's life on earth. More probably the idea of the millennium is behind this, which is taken over in entirety from Jewish apocalyptic (cf. 20:4 note), and the author has not considered how pointless is this gap after the victory described in ch. 19. It is not clear why Satan should be bound for this long time, rather than that he should be immediately disposed of in the fiery lake, but Isa. 24:22, 23 may throw some light. There evil powers are consigned to be imprisoned and loosed again after many days; after that Yahweh shall reign on Zion. This prophecy may well have influenced our author, who says that Satan, chief of evil powers, **must be loosed** (i.e. God has decreed it in prophecy).

XX 4-XXII 5 The Final Judgment and the Holy City—When everything should be getting clearer as the drama mounts to a climax, unfortunately these chapters have seemed to some commentators confused and self-contradictory. Hitherto, although the details have not usually been clear, we have gained on the whole an impression of logical and coherent movement. Now we begin to meet with difficulties, especially in connection with the holy city. As Dr Charles pointed out, if a new heaven and earth appear in ch. 21, it is puzzling to find so many wicked people outside the gates of the new Jerusalem (22:15). A few of these inconsistencies and difficulties are listed by Dr Charles in his commentary (ii, 145–54). There is much to be said for his argument, but on the other hand it may be felt that he has slightly overestimated our author's concern for coherence and consistency. Sources are being adapted to the author's purpose, and it is not to be expected that they will always be blended with the same amount of skill. No doubt the whole of Rev. would be improved by revision and rearrangement, and in any case the theory that there are dislocations in 20:4 to 22:5 depends on the supposition that our author was really an editor. The subjective schemes for rearrangement on a large scale in these last chapters have little more than the ingenuity of Dr Charles to recommend them, and his own conviction that 1:1 to 20:3 is a unity and that the rest is not. He thought that the confusion was not due to scribal errors in the transmission of MSS, but because the author died when he had completed as far as this section. He left his materials behind for 'a faithful but unintelligent disciple' to use as he thought fit. 'The Seer's literary executor', as Charles called him, found two accounts of the heavenly Jerusalem and instead of keeping them distinct, or blending them, as his master would have done he rudely thrust them together: (*a*) the Jerusalem which would be the centre of the millennial kingdom: 21:9–22:2, 22:14, 15, 17; (*b*) another Jerusalem existing after the new heaven and earth has come: 21:1–4*c*, 22:3–5. For the purpose of this commentary we will follow the normal order, not that of Dr Charles, which nevertheless should be studied for its ingenuity and the good sense that it makes of the text. 926a

XX 4-15. In Charles' reconstruction this section comes after 22:17. It begins with a vision of the glorified martyrs, which follows quite naturally the description of the heavenly Jerusalem. It proceeds to describe the events at the end of the millennium, the loosing of Satan and the attack on the City by Gog and Magog; the latter are destroyed and Satan is cast into the fiery lake to be tormented for ever along with the other two members of the evil trinity. The great white throne then appears and a general judgment takes place. b

4-6 The First Resurrection—Elsewhere the NT does not envisage two resurrections, which are an invention of this author. It is not sound exegesis to spiritualise the first resurrection and yet to take the second literally. That is not what the author means. **4. those to whom judgment was committed:** these are either the saints of the Most High (Dan. 7:22, cf. also Dan. 7:9, 26) or the Apostles (Mt. 19:28). **for their testimony to Jesus and for the word of God:** cf. in the reverse order 1:2, 9, 6:9. In the first two RSV has rendered 'the testimony of Jesus', as if the genitive were subjective. It is unlikely that the author, for whom this is a significant phrase, would use it in two entirely different senses. **reigned with Christ a thousand years:** this, like the two resurrections, is a doctrine found nowhere else in the NT, but it has had a considerable influence on subsequent Christian thought and its presence is one reason why Rev. was so tardily accepted in some branches of the Church. The doctrine is that when he comes again, Christ will reign in bodily form on the earth for one thousand years. The closest approach to this expectation in the NT is perhaps 1 C. 15:23–8: 'He must c d

926d reign until he has put all his enemies under his feet. . . . When all things are subjected to him, then the Son himself will also be subjected to him who put all things under him.' This presupposes a temporary reign of Christ on earth, and that was no new idea in Jewish apocalyptic hope (cf. *1 Enoch* 91–104 ; *Psalms of Solomon* 11, 17, etc.). Sometimes the length was thought of as four hundred years, or even shorter, and sometimes as a thousand. Behind the latter number is the idea that in the life of the world, as at its creation, there are six days (millennia) of work to be followed by one day (millennium) of rest under Messiah, one day with God being as a thousand years (cf. 2 Pet. 3:8). These beliefs were probably not very old, no more than 200 years when our author wrote. Before that, and certainly in the teaching of the great prophets of the OT, the kingdom of Christ was an eternal kingdom on earth. Later, Jewish thought conceived that this world was too intrinsically evil to provide a permanent setting for the kingdom ; there would therefore be a temporary reign and after that the righteous would be translated to an eternal inheritance in heaven, beyond this earth entirely. Thus the apocalypse of John, together with other Christian apocalypses (e.g. *2 Baruch* 30 ; *4 Ezra* 7:28f.) reflect this comparatively recent development in Judaism of the teaching of Jeremiah, Deutero-Isaiah, Ezekiel, Jonah, Malachi, Haggai, Zechariah and Joel. Our author, however, appears to differ from previous and contemporary writers in his conception of the *length* of this earthly kingdom, a thousand years. Later books which refer to the thousand years include *2 Enoch* (known also as the Slavonic *Enoch* or the *Secrets of Enoch*, which in its present form can hardly be as early as the 1st cent.) 33:2, and the *Epistle of Barnabas* 15:2–8.

e **5.** This makes it plain that there is no *general* resurrection before the millennium ; the reign of Christ on earth will include only the martyrs and will be their reward. They partake of the first resurrection. Our author is original in one important respect : in keeping with the traditional Jewish teaching Paul stated his belief that any Christians who were still alive when Christ came again would share in the joys of resurrection with those who had died (1 C. 15:51f. ; 1 Th. 4:17) and presumably take part in the ensuing millennial reign. This author mentions no survivors among the saints at the coming of Christ, and we must conclude that he did not think there would be any. **6. share in :** verbally as Jn 13:8. **blessed and holy :** cf. *Jubilees* 2:23. **of God and of Christ :** a high Christology.

f **7-10 Satan loosed and conquered**—At the end of the reign of Christ Jerusalem will be attacked by heathen nations, led by Gog and Magog. This is in accord with contemporary Jewish expectation. **8. Gog and Magog :** they are taken from Ezek. 38 and 39 ; but in Jewish apocalyptic they also figure, and they symbolise Israel's enemies. They are also often mentioned in Rabbinic works in the same sense. **9. the beloved city :** the Jerusalem of the millennium. Presumably the author conceives that the old city, which he designated a spiritual Sodom and Egypt (11:8), has been destroyed by Rome already in A.D. 70. He may call it ' beloved ' because God loves it : Ps. 77:68, 87:2. But that is the old city. This millennial city may be called ' beloved ' because of Christ's residence therein for a thousand years. **the broad earth :** same Gr. phrase in Hab. 1:6. **9b.** cf. 2 Kg. 1:10.

927a **11-15 Final Resurrection and Last Judgment**—A great white throne of judgment appears. Heaven and earth disappear, including apparently the beloved city. **11a.** cf. Dan. 7:9, but here God alone judges for the throne is not plural. **11c.** cf. Dan. 2:35 (Theod.). **12. the dead :** that is the souls of all the dead, now risen with a body. **books were opened :** cf. Dan. 7:10 ; *4 Ezra* 6:20, *1 Enoch* 90:22. These contained deeds, not names. cf. note on 3:9. **another book . . . which is the book of life :** this was a register and contained names, not deeds ; cf. 3:9 note. 927a
13. This appears inconsistent, as there would not now be any sea. It is from the sea that the bodies of the dead come, and their souls come from Hades. The doctrine of a bodily resurrection was already accepted in Judaism and by Jesus. I am not convinced by the reasoning of those commentators who allege that this author did not teach the bodily resurrection of the wicked. Hades here appears to be the repository of the souls of the wicked, and the dead stand before the throne. cf. *1 Enoch* 51:1 (the soul and body raised separately and reunited at the Last Judgment). Dr Charles suggested the emending of sea to ' treasuries ' (i.e. the resting-places of righteous souls) ; it would then form a parallel with Hades (wicked souls) : ICC, ii, 196f. **Death and Hades :** cf. b
1:18 note. They also have appeared together in 6:8. Originally Hades was not exclusively for wicked souls, but the context suggests that for our author that was the case : it will be cast into the lake of fire. This is also true of contemporary Jewish thought. As far as Death is concerned, Paul shares this author's expectation : 1 C. 15:26, 54. **14. This is the second death, the lake of fire :** this does not make much sense, and it may well be, as has been suggested, originally a marginal gloss brought into the text from 21:8 where it is quite appropriate : for the individuals listed there the lake of fire was indeed the second death, but in this context it is a general statement and is very odd indeed. It was not the second death for Death and Hades. **15.** cf. *1 Enoch* 90:20, 24 ; also Theodotion's Dan. 12:1.

XXI 1-8 Descent of New Jerusalem—This is part c
of God's plan now that all evil is destroyed, the creation of a new heaven and earth. A very fitting climax to the book. **1.** cf. Isa. 65:17. **the sea was no more :** the sea was thought of both in the OT and in Bab. mythology as a devouring monster. The drying up of waters, the retiring of the sea into the abyss, and the failing of fountains, are part of contemporary apocalyptic. It is not merely the natural horror of the all-destructive sea. **2. holy city :** cf. Isa. 52:1. **new** distinguishes this city from the millennial Jerusalem ; it is the same city, but quite transformed, now the eternal dwelling-place of God and his people. We have a similar conception in other parts of the NT : Gal. 4:26 ; Phil. 3:20 ; Heb. 12:22. It is both rabbinical and Pauline. **3. the dwelling of God is with men :** RSV have been consistent here and 13:6 but not at 15:5. ' Dwelling ' of God is the correct idea, rather than tabernacle or tent. It is very reminiscent of Jn 1:14 ; the noun and the verb are used in the LXX of the Wilderness tabernacle. The Word and the Shekinah Glory were brought together in the Prologue of the Fourth Gospel, and so they are here : cf. 19:13. cf. Lev. 26:11, 12 ; Ezek. 37:27. **his people :** another link with the Fourth Gospel (10:16), especially if we read the plural. **4a.** cf. 7:17. **death shall be no more :** cf. Isa. 25:8 ; 1 C. 15:54 ; *2 Enoch* 65:10 ; *4 Ezra* 8:53 ; *2 Baruch* 21:23. **the former things have passed away . . . . Behold, I make all things new :** cf. Isa. 43:18–19. But also 2 C. 5:17 ; there are many reminiscences of Paul's words in the opening and closing chapters of Rev. **5. trustworthy and** d
true : it would be better to render ' faithful and true ', as the same epithets are rendered at 3:14 and 19:11. They qualify a different substantive, but that is no reason to disguise a characteristic expression of this author ; cf. also 22:6. **6. It is done :** RSV here follows the same text as AV, not RV. **6b.** cf. 22:17 ; Isa. 55:1 ; Jn 7:37. **7. he who conquers :** like the Letters to the churches, e.g. 3:5. Also like Paul again : Rom. 8:17 ; Gal. 4:7. **7b.** cf. 2 Sam. 7:14. **8. cowardly :** RSV gives the proper sense of the Gr. **faithless :** this also is better than RV, for it probably means the disloyal, not simply doubters. **polluted :** i.e. with the worship of the beast, emperor-worship.

927d **liars:** probably the frauds of heathen priests are included here ; cf. 22:15.

928a **XXI 9-XXII 5 Details of the City**—Charles would place all but the last three verses of this section before 20:4, 15. According to him, this city is not that of the previous sections (the eternal abode of God and the righteous) but the Jerusalem of the millennial period, where Christ will dwell temporarily, and which will be the centre for evangelistic activity among the nations during the thousand years. Thus, there are two future Jerusalems ; this is the first of them (cf. note at beginning of §926*a*). Some commentators take this Jerusalem to mean the Church which is now present in the midst of this world. **10.** cf. Mt. 4:8. But Ezek. 40:2ff. is very much in the author's mind. **11. the glory of God:** cf. Isa. 40:1 ; Ezek. 43:2, 4, 5. **jasper:** cf. 4:3. Probably either a diamond or opal. **12. twelve gates:** cf. Ezek. 48:31ff., each corresponding to one of the tribes. **twelve angels:** cf. Isa. 62:6. **twelve tribes:** their names are on the gates, and yet the names of the apostles are on the foundation ; Charles happily remarked that in this combination the author underlines the continuity of OT and Christian Church. cf. the same continuity in Mt. 19:28. **14. twelve apostles:** note that Paul is absent, significantly so according to those who see in Rev. an implicit attack on Paulinism. **16. four-square:** cf. Ezek. 48:16 ; *Sibylline Oracles* 5:251. Difficult to conceive. Babylon was a square, but not

b a cube ! **18-21:** the materials of the city. **18.** cf. Isa. 54:12. **19f.** Almost the same stones as in the high priest's breastplate (Exod. 28:17ff., 39:10ff.) and in Ezek.'s description of Tyre (28:13ff.) ; cf. also Isa. 54:11. Our author does not follow the LXX in his translation of the Heb. names of the stones. For the probable identification of these stones, cf. Charles, ICC, ii, 169f. **22.** Another link with the Gospel ; cf. Jn 4:21 (the Temple will cease to exist). **and the Lamb:** on the ground that this verse was originally a tristich like those before and after, Dr Charles suggested that some words have dropped out, viz. '[and the Lamb] is its Ark of the Covenant'. A fine idea, but of course highly subjective. **23.** cf. Isa. 60:19 ; Jn 8:12. The Shekinah and the Memra (Word) are joined together once more, as in Jn's Prologue ; cf. 21:3 note. There is also a parallel with the Light of the World conception in Jn. **24.** An example of the author's inconsistency or carelessness in the use of sources (or of his disciple, according to Dr Charles). The nations, from OT parallels, are heathen nations. What are they doing in the new heaven and the new earth? The scribal comment ('of the redeemed') has crept into some texts in order to hide the mistake. This is where the rearrangement of these last chapters by Charles, and his theory that there were two future Jerusalems, makes things much easier. cf. Isa. 60:3. The Jerusalem of the millennium would doubtless be a missionary centre for the evangelising of the peoples of the world who would be born during those thousand years. **25.** cf. Isa. 60:1, 2, 5, 11 ; Zech. 14:6, 7. **27. nothing unclean shall enter it:** cf. Isa. 52:1. **book of life:** cf. 3:5 note, 13:8, 17:8, 20:12.

c **XXII 1-5 The River and Tree of Life**—For parallels, cf. Gen. 2:9, 10 ; Jer. 2:13 ; Ezek. 47:1–12 (our author is closer to the Heb. than is the LXX); Jn 4:10 ; *1 Enoch* 24:4, 25:4f. ; *Jubilees* 10:10–13. Charles accepted only vv. 1 and 2 as belonging to the City of the millennial reign ; 3–5 describe the eternal joys of the blessed in the second heavenly City. **1. the river of the water of life:** cf. 'springs of living water' (7:17), 'the fountain of the water of life' (21:6). A pity once again that RSV is not more careful of consistency. In 7:17 and 21:6 the phrase is virtually the same ; but what is the connection between it and the river mentioned here? The river is that mentioned in Gen. 2:10 as being in Eden, and it does not seem to have much spiritual significance, unlike the water of life. Here, however, the river is said to consist of that life-giving water. **the throne of God and of the Lamb:** of God and the Son of Man in *1 Enoch* 62:3, 5. **2. the tree of life:** a generic singular, actually meaning 'trees'; not the single tree of life, as in Eden (Gen. 2:9, 3:22), but many trees as in Ezek. 47:7. The twelve kinds of fruit are also suggested by the Ezek. passage. **healing of the nations:** the best sense is undoubtedly made by understanding this, with Charles, as during the millennium. There would be no nations to be healed at the time when the eternal and final City is estab-lished. cf. Ezek. 47:12. **3.** According to the Charles d
reconstruction this follows straight after 21:4, where all old things were passing and God was making everything new. This is the eternal City. **anything accursed:** RSV gives a better interpretation than 'curse', and is also justified in introducing the second half of the verse by **but,** not 'and', because anything accursed is a barrier between God and man (Jos. 7:12); the second thought is a consequence of the first, not additional to it. cf. Zech. 14:11. **worship:** RSV avoids the unfortunate rendering of RV ('his servants shall do him service'), for the words which the latter renders 'servant' and 'service' are quite distinct in the author's mind and are not from the same root in Gr. The first word (servants) implies the correct idea, but their form of service is a very special one : that of the sanctuary, not bondage. **4a.** cf. Ps. 17:15. The beatific vision. This was denied to Moses, but the Jewish apocalyptists promised it to the faithful as the seventh and supreme bliss. **5a.** cf. 21:23 note. There is no direct OT parallel, but cf. *2 Baruch* 48:50. **shall:** how often this word occurs in connection with the eternal City ! Compare all the past tenses of ch. 20, which refer only to the millennium. **for ever and ever:** another contrast with the millennium. cf. the past tenses in 20:4.

At this point it should be added that some com- e
mentators have interpreted the City differently from the assumptions which lie behind the above notes. In particular, some take the new Jerusalem to be John's picture of the Church present in this world as well as the glorified Church which she is destined to be in the future. Her marriage with the Lamb is past already, according to this school of thought (e.g. W. Milligan, Ex.B, 364). This Church shines as a light in the world ; she reflects all the beauty of Christ to the nations and is ideally perfect. 'The thought of chronology must be banished from this book' (ibid., 367). The series of visions in Rev. is meant to display the present impact of the Church's appearance in history and its eternal significance. The City is not the future home of the people of God ; it *is* the people of God, now and always. Such a view accounts for a great many facts and removes the need to rearrange the text in the way that some com-mentators are compelled to do. In so far as it implies that our author is painting on a broad canvas and is concerned to make vivid impressions in a general way, not to give us a detailed key to the far-away future, I think it an excellent view. But the author did really make abundant use of current apocalyptic, and it would be hazardous to assume that he was merely using it to spiritualise the whole of it. Our opinion of his worth might go up considerably if we could think so. More likely he was a creature of his day and place, sharing the standard apocalyptic hopes, altering and adapting them here and there, Christianising them as far as possible. However, there is surely no reason why we ourselves should not read his book in a different way from that which he intended, in a contemporary and devotional way, finding in it broad principles illustrating the Church's present struggles, hope and glory.

6-21 Epilogue—The predominant impression is that 929a
of disconnection, and no doubt much improvement in sequence is effected by a rearrangement of sections. A suggestion of Charles is : 6–7, 18*a*, 16, 13, 12, 10, 8–9, 20–1. This is arranged on the principle that first we have the testimony of Jesus, and then that of

929a John. **6-7.** The testimony of Jesus. The visions are now complete; warnings and assurances follow. If we accept the suggestion of placing 21:6*b*–8 along with the Epilogue, as the opening words, we may describe them as the testimony of God. We therefore close the book with a threefold testimony, and the order of the personal agents of the revelation is that given in the opening words of Rev. ((1) God gave the revelation to Jesus Christ. (2) Jesus made it known by sending his angel to his servant John. (3) John bore witness). All three persons would thus appear at the end to make their final bow and confirm their
b testimony. **trustworthy and true:** cf. 21:5 note. **6f. prophets, prophecy:** the author is emphatic as to his close association with prophecy, either in the OT sense or perhaps as a member of the Christian order of prophets. In any case, he is sure that these things will happen soon; and, like the Christian prophet Agabus, he takes steps to make known to the Church that which the Holy Spirit has revealed to him. **spirits of the prophets:** probably the prophet's own spirit, inspired by the Spirit of God, as in 1 C. 14:32. **7. I am coming soon:** cf. 2:5, 16, 3:11, 16:15, 22:12. **Blessed is he:** this, the seventh beatitude of Rev., takes us back to the first in 1:3, a blessing on the reader, hearers and keepers of this prophetic book. The second beatitude was that on the Christian martyrs (14:13), the third on those who watch and keep their garments (16:15), the fourth on those who are invited to the marriage supper of the Lamb (19:9), the fifth on those who share the first resurrection (20:6), and the sixth (or seventh, if we reject the order of Charles) on those who wash their robes to have right to the tree of
c life (22:14). **8-9.** Probably a doublet of 19:9f. cf. note. **10.** A continuation of the testimony of Jesus. He urges John not to do the usual thing with an apocalypse by sealing it, but as the situation is urgent he must issue his book immediately. Contrast 10:4, however, where there is the usual command to seal. cf. Dan. 12:4, 9 (Theod.). In 10–15 it is not clear how much is spoken by the angel and how much by Christ. By closing the quotation marks after 11 and opening them again before 12, RSV assumes that the angel and not Christ is speaking in 10f. **11.** The wicked and righteous referred to are, of course, contemporaries of the author. It is strange that the possibility of repentance and restitution is not visualised. But the second coming of Christ was expected at any moment by the author. **still:** literally 'from now onwards'. **12a.** Either the reward which he brings, or the reward which is himself (genitive of quality); cf. Isa. 40:10. **12b.** cf. Ps. 62:12; Prov. 24:12; Mt. 16:27. **13.** What is said of the Father (1:8) is now claimed by Jesus, who has just claimed to be judge of all mankind (12). cf. the same phrase in 21:6.
d **14-15.** These verses certainly look rather out of place here. They break the solemnity of these final assurances, and introduce thoughts which are not only alien here but which would have been quite appropriate when the holy City was being discussed. Accepting the distinction mentioned above as to the two future Jerusalems, it seems clear that these verses belong to a description of the first rather than the second. The presence of sinners outside the gates is only appropriate of the millennial period, as after the new heaven and earth are created there would be no wicked ones left, and the righteous would not *enter* the second City, for that is their eternal and blissful home. Therefore, these verses might, on the above-mentioned hypothesis, have to be transposed as early as after 22:2. **wash their robes:** the better
reading, only slightly differing from the other in Gr. 929d
letters. It is a reference either to the general salvation of Christians or to salvation by martyrdom (cf. 2:7). **15.** Almost a repetition of 21:8. **dogs:** traditional description of the heathen Gentiles, but in view of the parallel between this verse and 21:8, they may be the 'polluted', i.e. Jews or Gentiles who have been contaminated with Caesar-worship. Paul applied the name to some of his fellow-countrymen (Phil. 3:2). **practises falsehood:** cf. Jn 3:21; 1 Jn 3:8.
16-20. The testimony of Christ continued. This is e
intended for a dramatic climax: the stepping forward of Jesus himself. **16. you:** it is not certain that the plural has any particular significance. **the root and the offspring of David:** cf. Isa. 11:1, 10; *Testament of Judah* 24:5. **the bright morning star:** cf. 2:28 note. But in the context here the meaning is likely to be Messianic; cf. Num. 24:17. **17.** This is as much out of place as 14–15, and like them would better be transposed to the same place in the millennial section. It contemplates the evangelisation of the heathen during that period. It is also another link with the Gospel of Jn (7:37), and it also goes closely with Rev. 21:6. **The Spirit:** i.e. probably the Spirit of Christ speaking through our author. This is in keeping with the usage of the word in this book, especially in chs. 2 and 3 ('what the Spirit says to the churches'). **the Bride:** the Church. Together with her Lord she is here represented as appealing to the heathen nations to repent and receive eternal life. In this interpretation, **'Come'** will not be taken as it most usually is: an appeal to Christ to hasten his second coming. Rather, it is the 'Come' of the Gospel appeal. Then **him who hears** is not the listener when Rev. is read aloud, but he who is converted by the Church's appeal and then joins her in
her missionary endeavour. **18b, 19.** cf. Dt. 4:2, f
12:32; *Epistle of Aristeas* 311. To some it has seemed that these two verses were not penned by our author. The petty literalness of these words has appeared as a contrast to the 'bold faith and confident hope' of the rest of the book (F. C. Porter, quoted in ICC, ii, 222). The style is a little different, too. Nevertheless it was a fairly common practice for writers to add this kind of warning to their books. **20. I am coming soon:** this is the *motif* of the whole book. To our author's mind, everything depends on this speedy return. He can see no other solution for the Church's ills. **Come, Lord:** the Gr. of the Aramaic 'Maranatha', an early Christian watchword.
21. The ending is like that of a NT epistle and takes g
us back to the Letters to the churches (chs. 1–3). Even there, however, he does not use the phrase **Lord Jesus.** cf. the Pauline epistles and Heb. It was not usual for apocalypses to end in this way, and it may indicate that Rev. was intended to be read aloud in the worship of the Church. **saints** is a Pauline word, but with a slightly different meaning. Throughout Rev. it describes the faithful and those who endure, not the great body of Christians.
A Note on the Rearrangement of Revelation.— 930a
Much attention has been given in the commentary to the possibility that better sense is achieved from the text if it is considerably rearranged in some parts. The most thorough exponent of this idea is still Dr R. H. Charles. For this reason there is appended a list of sections arranged in the order in which the seer either left his book or, in some cases, would have left it had he not died or been interrupted in some other way before the work was finished. One need not agree with the conclusions of this massive research on the part of Charles, but it would be convenient to see what it involves.

930b I 1–7, 9–17
II 1–26, 27*cab*, 28, 29
III 1–3*ab*
XVI 15

III 3*c*, 4–22 930b
IV 1–11
V 1–14
VI 1–17

930b VII 1–4, 5*ab*, 7, 8, 5*c*, 6, 9–17
VIII 1, 3, 4, 5, 2, 6, 13, 7–12
IX 1–21
X 1–11
XI 1–17, 18*abhcgdef*, 19
XII 1–17
XIII 1–5*a*, 6, 5*b*, 7–18
XIV 12, 13, 1, 2, 3*bc*, 4*cd*, 5–11, 14, 18–20
XV 2–8
XVI 1–4, 8–14, 16–21
XVII 1–13, 17, 16, 14, 18
XVIII 1–10, 11*a*, 23*e*, 11*b*, 12, 13, 15–19, 21, 14, 22*a–d*, 23*cd*, 22*e–h*, 23*ab*, 20, 23*f*, 24
XIX 1–4 930b
XVI 5*b*, 6, 7
XIX 5–9, 11–21
XX 1–3
XXI 9–27
XXII 1, 2, 14, 15, 17
XX 4*c–habi*, 5*b*, 6–15
XXI 5*a*, 4*d*, 5*b*, 1–4*c*
XXII 3–5
XXI 5*c*, 6*b*, 7, 8
XXII 6, 7, 18*a*, 16, 13, 12, 10, 8, 9, 20, 21

Verses omitted: I 8; XV 1; XVI 5*a*; XVII 15; XIX 10; XXII 11, 18*b*, 19.

Bibliography—Commentaries: W. Barclay, *Letters to the Seven Churches* (1957); R. H. Charles, *Revelation*, ICC (1920); Austin Farrer, *A Rebirth of Images* (1949); W. Hadorn, *Kommentar zur Apokalypse* (1928); Holtzmann-Bauer, *Die Offenbarung des Johannis*, HKNT (1908[3]); E. Lohmeyer, *Kommentar zur Apokalypse* (1926); W. Milligan, *Revelation*, Ex.B (1889); J. Moffatt, *Revelation*, EGT (1910), *A New Commentary on Holy Scripture*, ed. Gore (1928); J. B. Phillips, *The Book of Revelation* (1957); R. H. Preston and A. T. Hanson, *The Revelation of St John the Divine*, Torch Bible Commentaries (1949); C. A. Scott, *Revelation*, Cent.B (1902, 1912); T. Zahn, *Kommentar zur Apokalypse* (1924).

Other Literature: E. B. Allo, *L'Apocalypse de saint Jean* (1921[2]); I. T. Beckwith, *The Apocalypse of John* (1920); W. Bousset, *Der Antichrist* (1896), *Die Offenbarung Johannis* (1906); F. C. Burkitt, *Jewish and Christian Apocalypses* (1914); R. H. Charles, *Eschatology: Hebrew, Jewish and Christian* (1900), *Studies in the Apocalypse* (1915[2]), 'Schweich Lectures' (1919); M. Dibelius, *A Fresh Approach to the NT* (1936), 128f.; H. L. Goudge, *The Apocalypse and the Present Age*, in CQR (1916); H. A. Guy, *NT Prophecy* (1947); F. J Hort, *Apocalypse of St John, i–iii* (1908); R. J. Loenertz, o.p., *The Apocalypse of St John* (1947); A. Loisy, *L'Apocalypse de Jean* (1923); W. Milligan, *Lectures on the Apocalypse* (1892); H. Odeberg, *3 Enoch* (1928); J. Oman, *The Book of Revelation* (1919), *The Text of Revelation* 1928); F. C. Porter, *The Messages of the Apocalyptical Writers* (1911); W. M. Ramsay, *The Letters to the Seven Churches* (1904); I. Rohr, *Der Hebräerbrief und die Geheime Offenbarung des hl. Johannes* (1932[4]); A. Schlatter, *Das AT in der Johannes-Apokalypse* (1912); C. Schneider, *Die Erlebnisechtheit der Apokalypse des Johannes* (1930); R. Schütz, *Die Offenbarung des Johannes und Kaiser Domitian* (1933); E. F. Scott, *The Book of Revelation* (1939); E. Stauffer, *Christ and the Caesars* (1955); H. Wallace, 'Leviathan and the Beast in Revelation', in BA XI (1948), 61ff.

INDEX

All references are to the **Section Numbers** in the margins of the pages of the Commentary. Numbers in heavy type indicate the more important references.

LIST OF MAPS

Index of Place Names in Maps

INDEX OF PLACE NAMES IN MAPS

INDEX OF PLACE NAMES IN MAPS

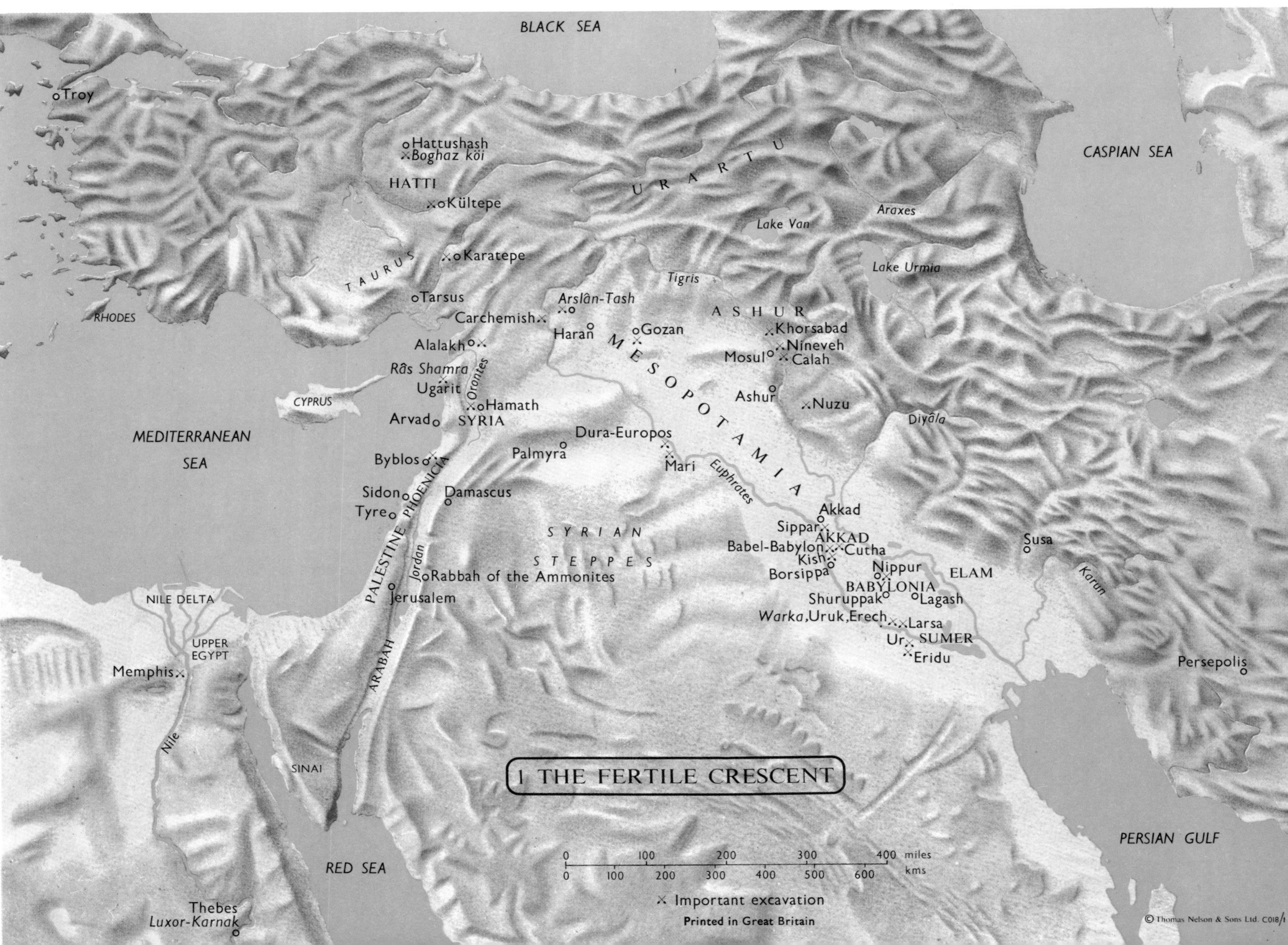

1 THE FERTILE CRESCENT
BLACK SEA
CASPIAN SEA
MEDITERRANEAN SEA
RED SEA
PERSIAN GULF
Troy
Hattushash
Boghaz köi
HATTI
Kültepe
Karatepe
TAURUS
Tarsus
RHODES
CYPRUS
URARTU
Lake Van
Araxes
Lake Urmia
Tigris
Arslân-Tash
Carchemish
Haran
Gozan
ASHUR
Khorsabad
Nineveh
Mosul
Calah
Ashur
Nuzu
Diyâla
MESOPOTAMIA
Alalakh
Râs Shamra
Ugarit
Orontes
Hamath
SYRIA
Arvad
Dura-Europos
Palmyra
Mari
Euphrates
Byblos
PHOENICIA
Sidon
Damascus
Tyre
SYRIAN STEPPES
PALESTINE
Jordan
Rabbah of the Ammonites
Jerusalem
ARABAH
Akkad
Sippar
AKKAD
Babel-Babylon
Cutha
Kish
Borsippa
Nippur
ELAM
BABYLONIA
Shuruppak
Lagash
Warka, Uruk, Erech
Larsa
Ur
SUMER
Eridu
Susa
Karun
Persepolis
NILE DELTA
UPPER EGYPT
Memphis
Nile
SINAI
Thebes
Luxor-Karnak
0 100 200 300 400 miles
0 100 200 300 400 500 600 kms
× Important excavation
Printed in Great Britain
© Thomas Nelson & Sons Ltd. C018/1

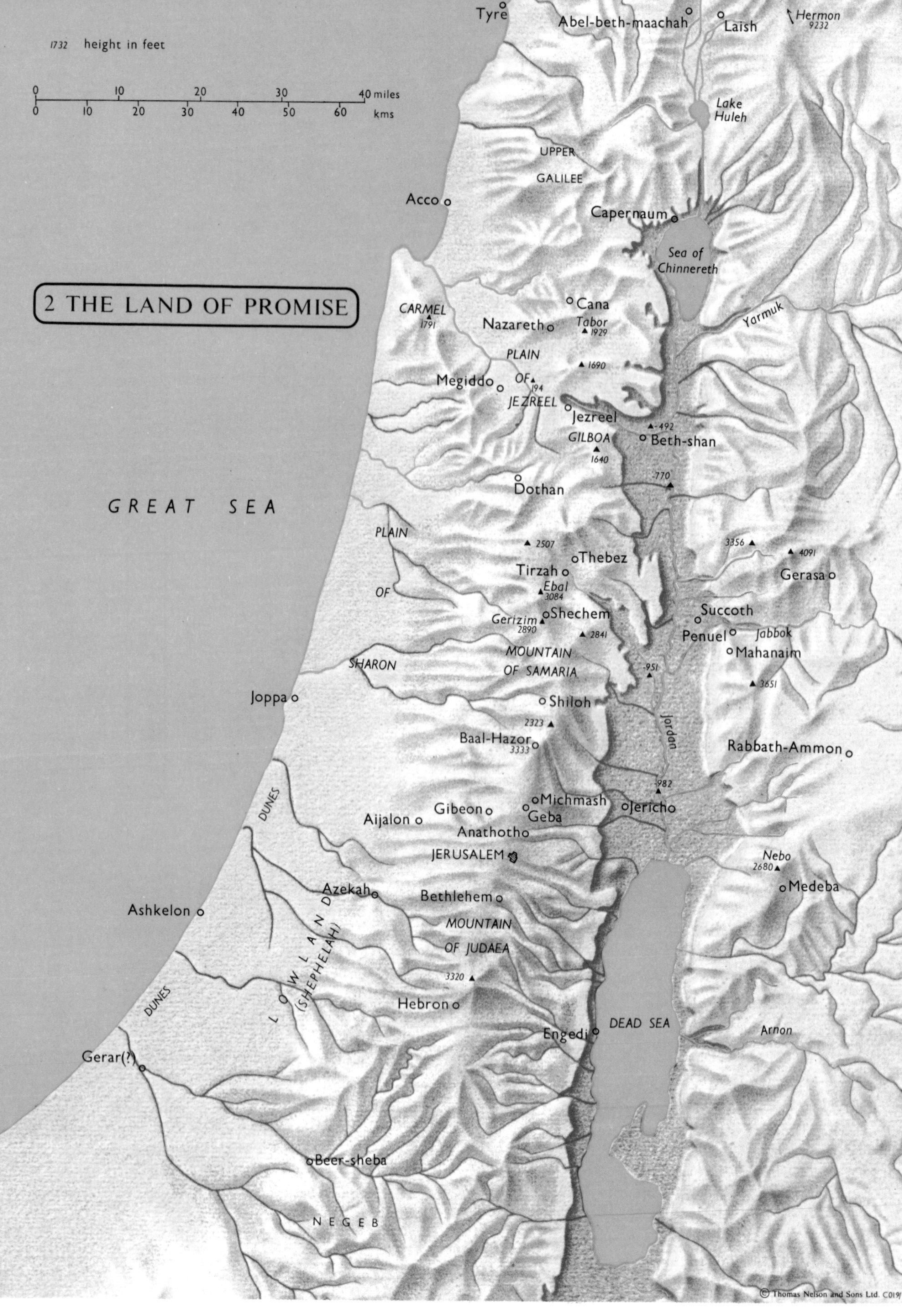

2 THE LAND OF PROMISE
1732 height in feet
0 10 20 30 40 miles
0 10 20 30 40 50 60 kms
Tyre
Abel-beth-maachah
Laish
Hermon 9232
Lake Huleh
UPPER GALILEE
Acco
Capernaum
Sea of Chinnereth
CARMEL 1791
Cana
Nazareth
Tabor 1929
Yarmuk
PLAIN OF JEZREEL
1690
Megiddo
194
Jezreel
-492
GILBOA
Beth-shan
1640
-770
Dothan
GREAT SEA
PLAIN OF SHARON
2507
Thebez
3356
4091
Tirzah
Gerasa
Ebal 3084
Succoth
Gerizim 2890
Shechem
Penuel
Jabbok
2841
Mahanaim
MOUNTAIN OF SAMARIA
-951
3651
Joppa
Shiloh
2323
Jordan
Baal-Hazor 3333
Rabbath-Ammon
-982
DUNES
Michmash
Jericho
Gibeon
Geba
Aijalon
Anathoth
JERUSALEM
Nebo 2680
Azekah
Medeba
Bethlehem
Ashkelon
LOWLAND (SHEPHELAH)
MOUNTAIN OF JUDAEA
3320
Hebron
DUNES
Engedi
DEAD SEA
Arnon
Gerar(?)
Beer-sheba
NEGEB

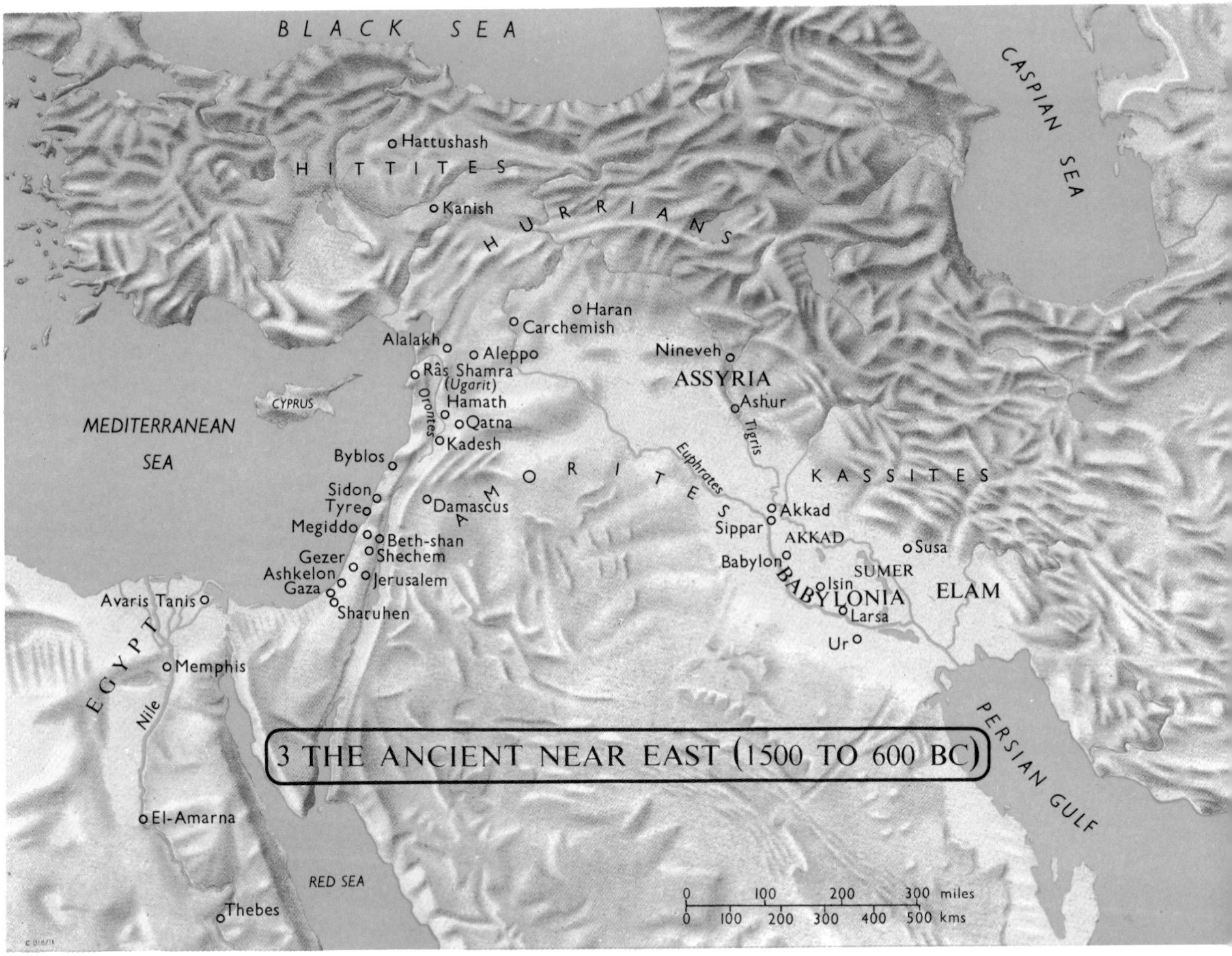

3 THE ANCIENT NEAR EAST (1500 TO 600 BC)

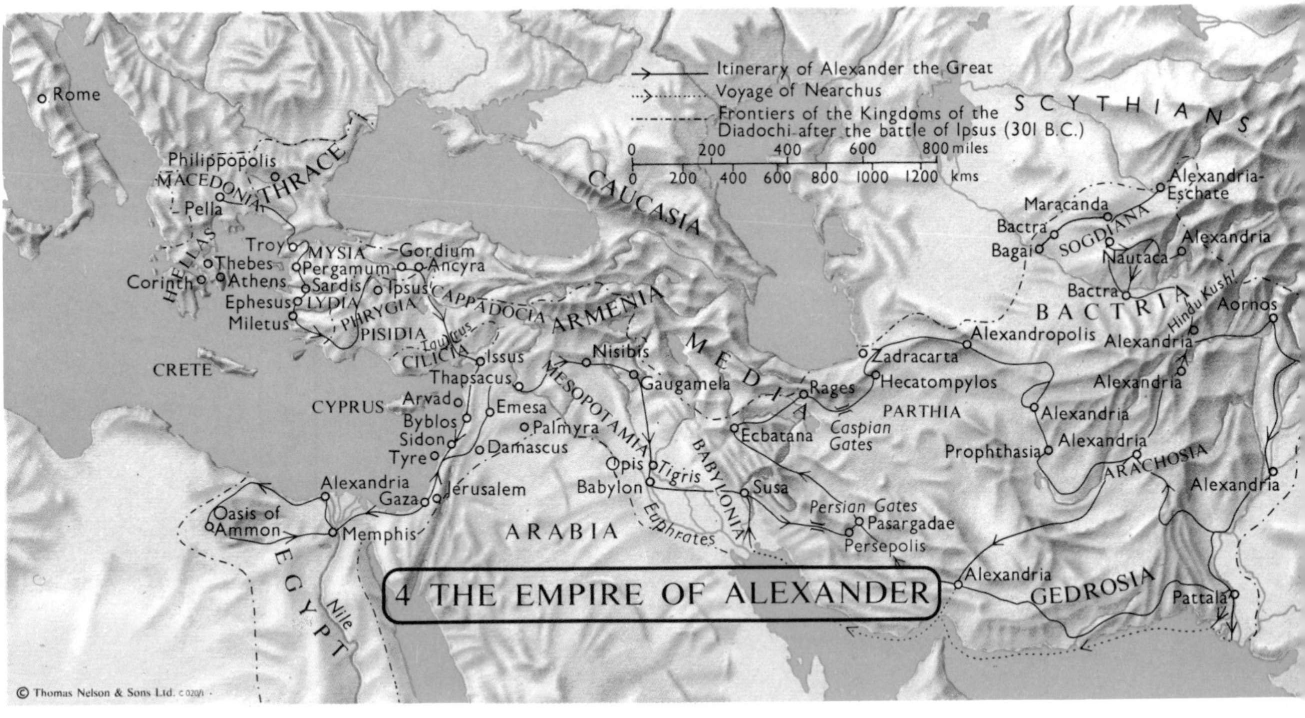

BLACK SEA
CASPIAN SEA
Hattushash
HITTITES
Kanish
HURRIANS
Haran
Carchemish
Alalakh
Aleppo
Nineveh
Râs Shamra
(Ugarit)
ASSYRIA
CYPRUS
Hamath
Ashur
Orontes
MEDITERRANEAN
SEA
Qatna
Kadesh
Tigris
Byblos
Euphrates
KASSITES
Sidon
AMORITES
Tyre
Damascus
Akkad
Megiddo
Sippar
Beth-shan
AKKAD
Susa
Gezer
Shechem
Babylon
SUMER
Ashkelon
Jerusalem
Isin
Gaza
BABYLONIA
ELAM
Avaris Tanis
Sharuhen
Larsa
Ur
Memphis
EGYPT
Nile
PERSIAN GULF
El-Amarna
RED SEA
Thebes

0 100 200 300 miles
0 100 200 300 400 500 kms

4 THE EMPIRE OF ALEXANDER

Itinerary of Alexander the Great
Voyage of Nearchus
Frontiers of the Kingdoms of the Diadochi after the battle of Ipsus (301 B.C.)

0 200 400 600 800 miles
0 200 400 600 800 1000 1200 kms

Rome
SCYTHIANS
Philippopolis
MACEDONIA
THRACE
CAUCASIA
Alexandria-Eschate
Pella
Maracanda
HELLAS
Troy
MYSIA
Gordium
Bactra
SOGDIANA
Alexandria
Thebes
Pergamum
Ancyra
Bagai
Nautaca
Corinth
Athens
Sardis
Ipsus
Ephesus
LYDIA
CAPPADOCIA
ARMENIA
Bactra
BACTRIA
Hindu Kush
Aornos
Miletus
PHRYGIA
MEDIA
Alexandropolis
Alexandria
PISIDIA
Taurus
Zadracarta
CRETE
CILICIA
Issus
Nisibis
Hecatompylos
Alexandria
Thapsacus
MESOPOTAMIA
Gaugamela
Rages
CYPRUS
Arvad
Emesa
PARTHIA
Alexandria
Byblos
Palmyra
Ecbatana
Caspian Gates
Sidon
Damascus
Prophthasia
Alexandria
Tyre
Opis
Tigris
ARACHOSIA
Alexandria
Jerusalem
Babylon
BABYLONIA
Susa
Alexandria
Gaza
Persian Gates
Oasis of Ammon
Memphis
ARABIA
Pasargadae
Persepolis
Euphrates
EGYPT
Nile
Alexandria
GEDROSIA
Pattala

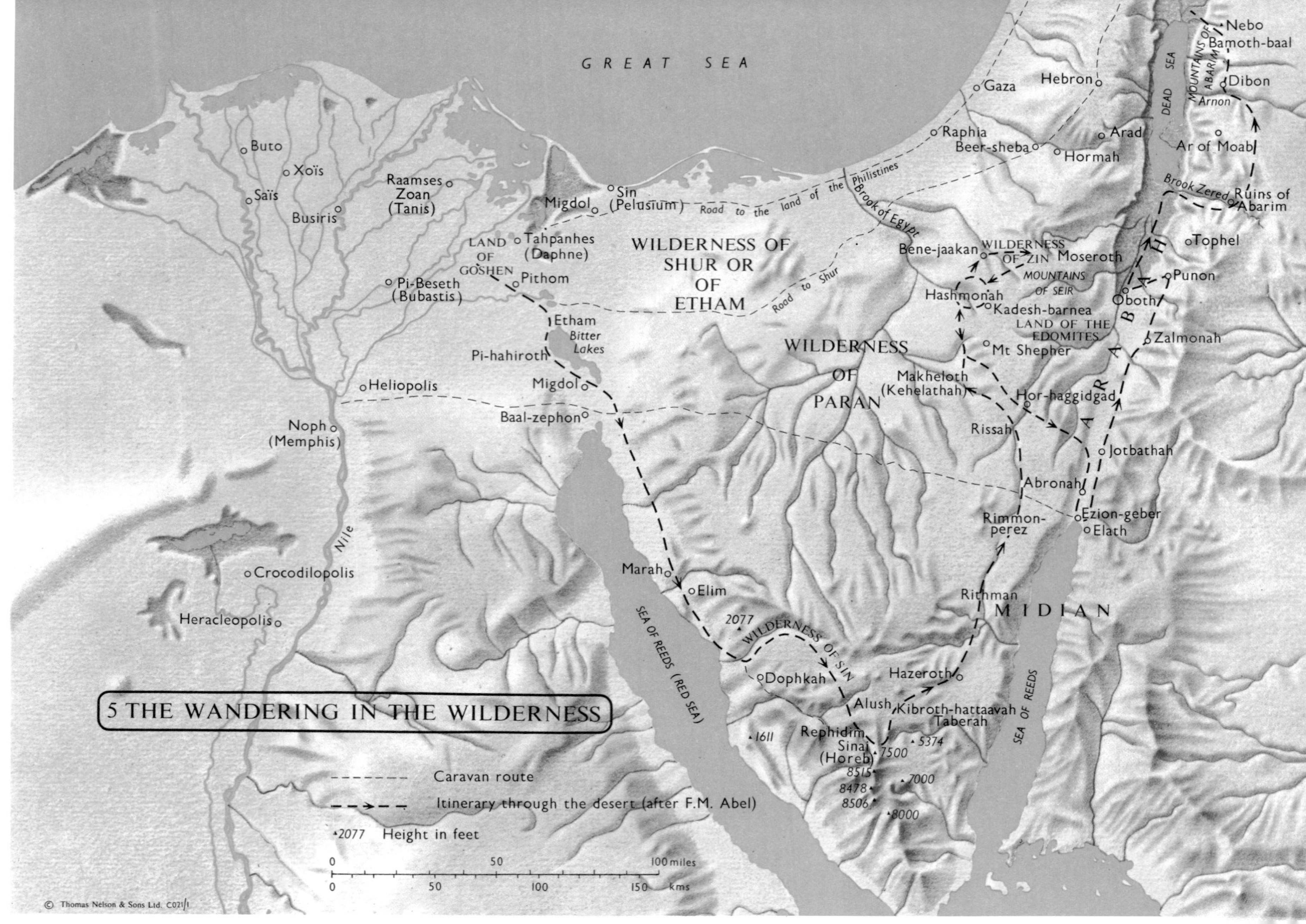
5 THE WANDERING IN THE WILDERNESS
GREAT SEA
DEAD SEA
Nebo
Bamoth-baal
MOUNTAINS OF ABARIM
Dibon
Arnon
Ar of Moab
Brook Zered
Ruins of Abarim
Tophel
Punon
Oboth
Zalmonah
ARABAH
Gaza
Hebron
Raphia
Arad
Beer-sheba
Hormah
Buto
Xoïs
Saïs
Busiris
Raamses
Zoan
(Tanis)
Migdol
Sin
(Pelusium)
Road to the land of the Philistines
Brook of Egypt
LAND OF GOSHEN
Tahpanhes
(Daphne)
Pithom
Pi-Beseth
(Bubastis)
WILDERNESS OF SHUR OR OF ETHAM
Road to Shur
Bene-jaakan
WILDERNESS OF ZIN
Moseroth
MOUNTAINS OF SEIR
Hashmonah
Kadesh-barnea
LAND OF THE EDOMITES
Mt Shepher
Etham
Bitter Lakes
Pi-hahiroth
Migdol
Heliopolis
Baal-zephon
Noph
(Memphis)
WILDERNESS OF PARAN
Makheloth
(Kehelathah)
Hor-haggidgad
Rissah
Jotbathah
Abronah
Ezion-geber
Elath
Rimmon-perez
Nile
Crocodilopolis
Heracleopolis
Marah
Elim
SEA OF REEDS (RED SEA)
2077
WILDERNESS OF SIN
Dophkah
Rithman
MIDIAN
Hazeroth
Alush
Kibroth-hattaavah
Taberah
SEA OF REEDS
Rephidim
Sinai
(Horeb)
1611
7500
5374
8515
8478
8506
7000
8000
Caravan route
Itinerary through the desert (after F.M. Abel)
2077 Height in feet
0 50 100 miles
0 50 100 150 kms

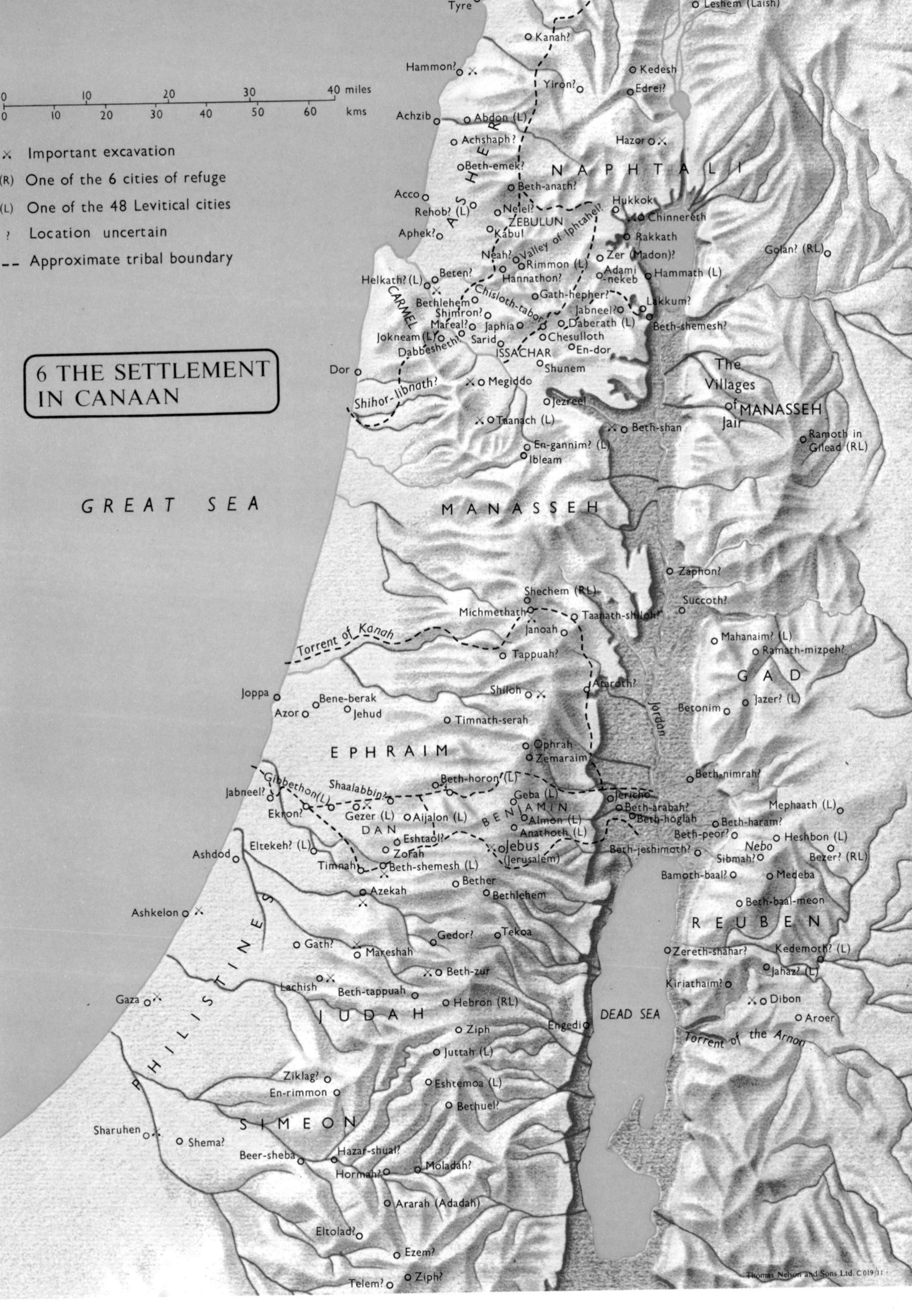
6 THE SETTLEMENT IN CANAAN
0 10 20 30 40 miles
0 10 20 30 40 50 60 kms
× Important excavation
(R) One of the 6 cities of refuge
(L) One of the 48 Levitical cities
? Location uncertain
Approximate tribal boundary
GREAT SEA
Tyre
Leshem (Laish)
Kanah?
Hammon?
Kedesh
Yiron?
Edrei?
Achzib
Abdon (L)
Achshaph?
Hazor
Beth-emek?
NAPHTALI
ASHER
Acco
Beth-anath?
Rehob? (L)
Neiel?
Hukkok
Chinnereth
ZEBULUN
Aphek?
Kabul
Valley of Iphtahel?
Rakkath
Golan? (RL)
Neah?
Rimmon (L)
Zer (Madon)?
Adami-nekeb
Hammath (L)
Helkath? (L)
Beten?
Hannathon?
CARMEL
Chisloth-tabor
Gath-hepher?
Bethlehem
Lakkum?
Shimron?
Jabneel?
Mareal?
Japhia
Daberath (L)
Beth-shemesh?
Jokneam (L)
Dabbesheth?
Sarid
Chesulloth
ISSACHAR
En-dor
Dor
Shunem
The Villages of Jair
Megiddo
Shihor-libnath?
Jezreel
MANASSEH
Taanach (L)
Beth-shan
Ramoth in Gilead (RL)
En-gannim? (L)
Ibleam
MANASSEH
Zaphon?
Shechem (RL)
Succoth?
Michmethath
Taanath-shiloh?
Janoah
Torrent of Kanah
Mahanaim? (L)
Tappuah?
Ramath-mizpeh?
GAD
Ataroth?
Joppa
Shiloh
Bene-berak
Jordan
Jazer? (L)
Azor
Jehud
Betonim
Timnath-serah
Ophrah
EPHRAIM
Zemaraim
Beth-nimrah?
Gibbethon (L)
Shaalabbin?
Beth-horon (L)
Jabneel?
Geba (L)
Jericho
Mephaath (L)
Ekron?
Gezer (L)
Aijalon (L)
BENJAMIN
Beth-arabah?
Almon (L)
Beth-hoglah
Beth-haram?
DAN
Anathoth (L)
Beth-peor?
Eltekeh? (L)
Eshtaol?
Nebo
Heshbon (L)
Ashdod
Zorah
Jebus (Jerusalem)
Beth-jeshimoth?
Sibmah?
Bezer? (RL)
Timnah
Beth-shemesh (L)
Bamoth-baal?
Medeba
Bether
Azekah
Bethlehem
Beth-baal-meon
Ashkelon
REUBEN
PHILISTINES
Gedor?
Tekoa
Gath?
Mareshah
Zereth-shahar?
Kedemoth? (L)
Beth-zur
Jahaz? (L)
Lachish
Kiriathaim?
Gaza
Beth-tappuah
Dibon
Hebron (RL)
JUDAH
DEAD SEA
Aroer
Engedi
Ziph
Torrent of the Arnon
Juttah (L)
Ziklag?
Eshtemoa (L)
En-rimmon
Bethuel?
SIMEON
Sharuhen
Shema?
Beer-sheba
Hazar-shual?
Moladah?
Hormah?
Ararah (Adadah)
Eltolad?
Ezem?
Telem?
Ziph?
Thomas Nelson and Sons Ltd. C019/11

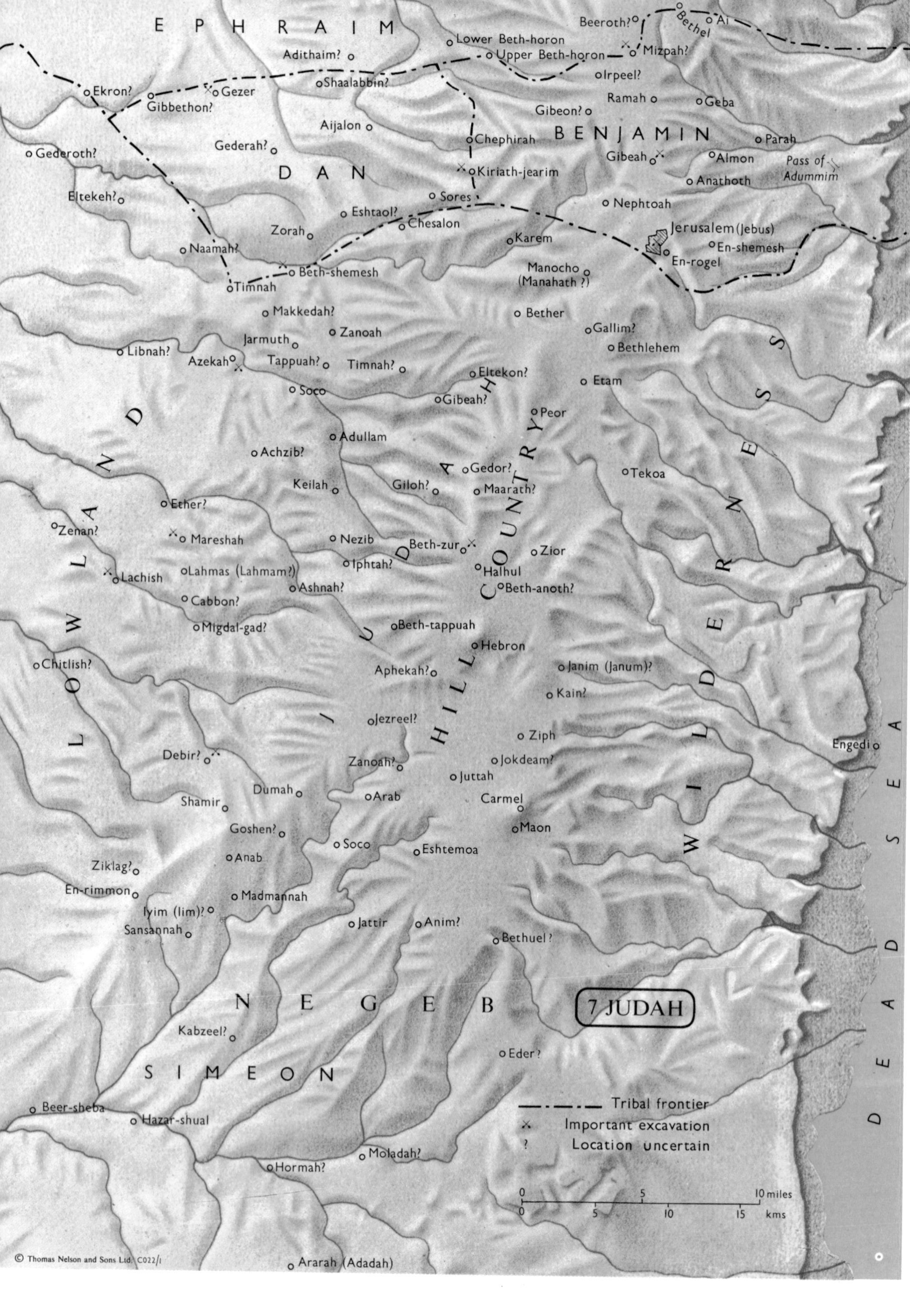

EPHRAIM
BENJAMIN
DAN
LOWLAND
JUDAH
HILL COUNTRY
WILDERNESS
NEGEB
SIMEON
DEAD SEA
Beeroth?
Bethel
Ai
Lower Beth-horon
Upper Beth-horon
Mizpah?
Adithaim?
Irpeel?
Ekron?
Gezer
Gibbethon?
Shaalabbin?
Ramah
Geba
Gibeon?
Aijalon
Chephirah
Parah
Gederoth?
Gederah?
Gibeah
Almon
Pass of Adummim
Kiriath-jearim
Anathoth
Eltekeh?
Sores
Nephtoah
Eshtaol?
Chesalon
Zorah
Jerusalem (Jebus)
Karem
En-shemesh
Naamah?
En-rogel
Beth-shemesh
Manocho (Manahath ?)
Timnah
Makkedah?
Bether
Zanoah
Gallim?
Jarmuth
Bethlehem
Libnah?
Azekah
Tappuah?
Timnah?
Eltekon?
Etam
Soco
Gibeah?
Peor
Adullam
Achzib?
Gedor?
Tekoa
Keilah
Giloh?
Maarath?
Ether?
Zenan?
Mareshah
Nezib
Beth-zur
Zior
Iphtah?
Lachish
Lahmas (Lahmam?)
Halhul
Ashnah?
Beth-anoth?
Cabbon?
Migdal-gad?
Beth-tappuah
Hebron
Chitlish?
Aphekah?
Janim (Janum)?
Kain?
Jezreel?
Ziph
Engedi
Debir?
Zanoah?
Jokdeam?
Juttah
Dumah
Arab
Carmel
Shamir
Goshen?
Maon
Soco
Eshtemoa
Anab
Ziklag?
En-rimmon
Madmannah
Iyim (Iim)?
Sansannah
Jattir
Anim?
Bethuel ?
7 JUDAH
Kabzeel?
Eder ?
Beer-sheba
Hazar-shual
Tribal frontier
Important excavation
Location uncertain
Moladah?
Hormah?
0
5
10 miles
0
5
10
15
kms
Ararah (Adadah)

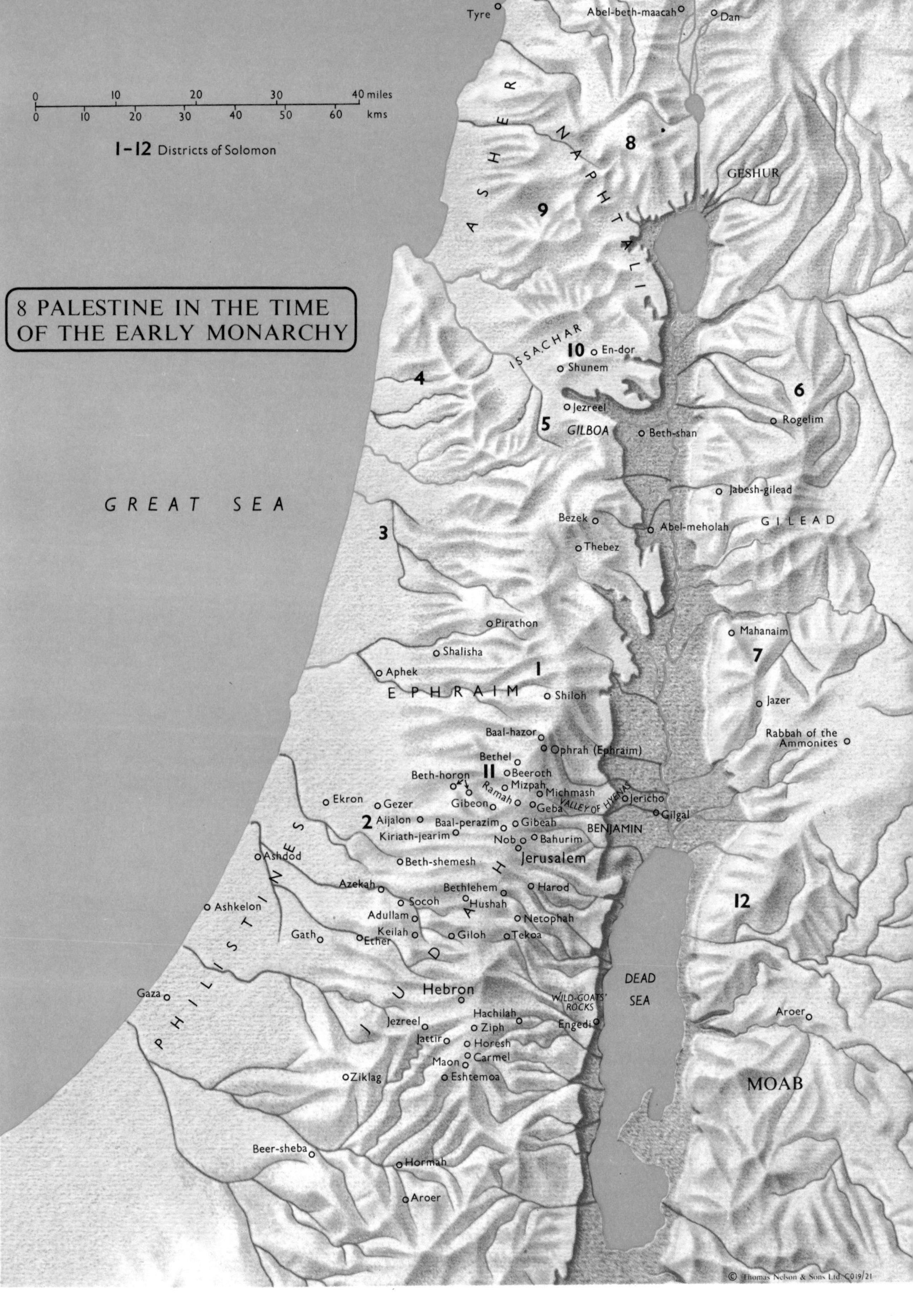
8 PALESTINE IN THE TIME
OF THE EARLY MONARCHY
0 10 20 30 40 miles
0 10 20 30 40 50 60 kms
1–12 Districts of Solomon
GREAT SEA
Tyre
Abel-beth-maacah
Dan
ASHER
NAPHTALI
8
9
GESHUR
ISSACHAR
10
En-dor
Shunem
4
6
Jezreel
5
GILBOA
Beth-shan
Rogelim
Jabesh-gilead
Bezek
Abel-meholah
GILEAD
3
Thebez
Pirathon
Mahanaim
Shalisha
7
Aphek
1
EPHRAIM
Shiloh
Jazer
Baal-hazor
Ophrah (Ephraim)
Rabbah of the
Ammonites
Bethel
II
Beeroth
Beth-horon
Mizpah
Ramah
Michmash
Ekron
Gezer
Gibeon
Geba
VALLEY OF HYENAS
Jericho
2
Aijalon
Baal-perazim
Gibeah
Gilgal
Kiriath-jearim
BENJAMIN
Nob
Bahurim
Ashdod
Jerusalem
Beth-shemesh
Azekah
Bethlehem
Harod
Socoh
Hushah
12
Ashkelon
Adullam
Netophah
Gath
Keilah
Ether
Giloh
Tekoa
PHILISTINES
JUDAH
DEAD
SEA
Gaza
Hebron
WILD-GOATS'
ROCKS
Hachilah
Jezreel
Ziph
Engedi
Aroer
Jattir
Horesh
Maon
Carmel
Ziklag
Eshtemoa
MOAB
Beer-sheba
Hormah
Aroer
© Thomas Nelson & Sons Ltd C019/21

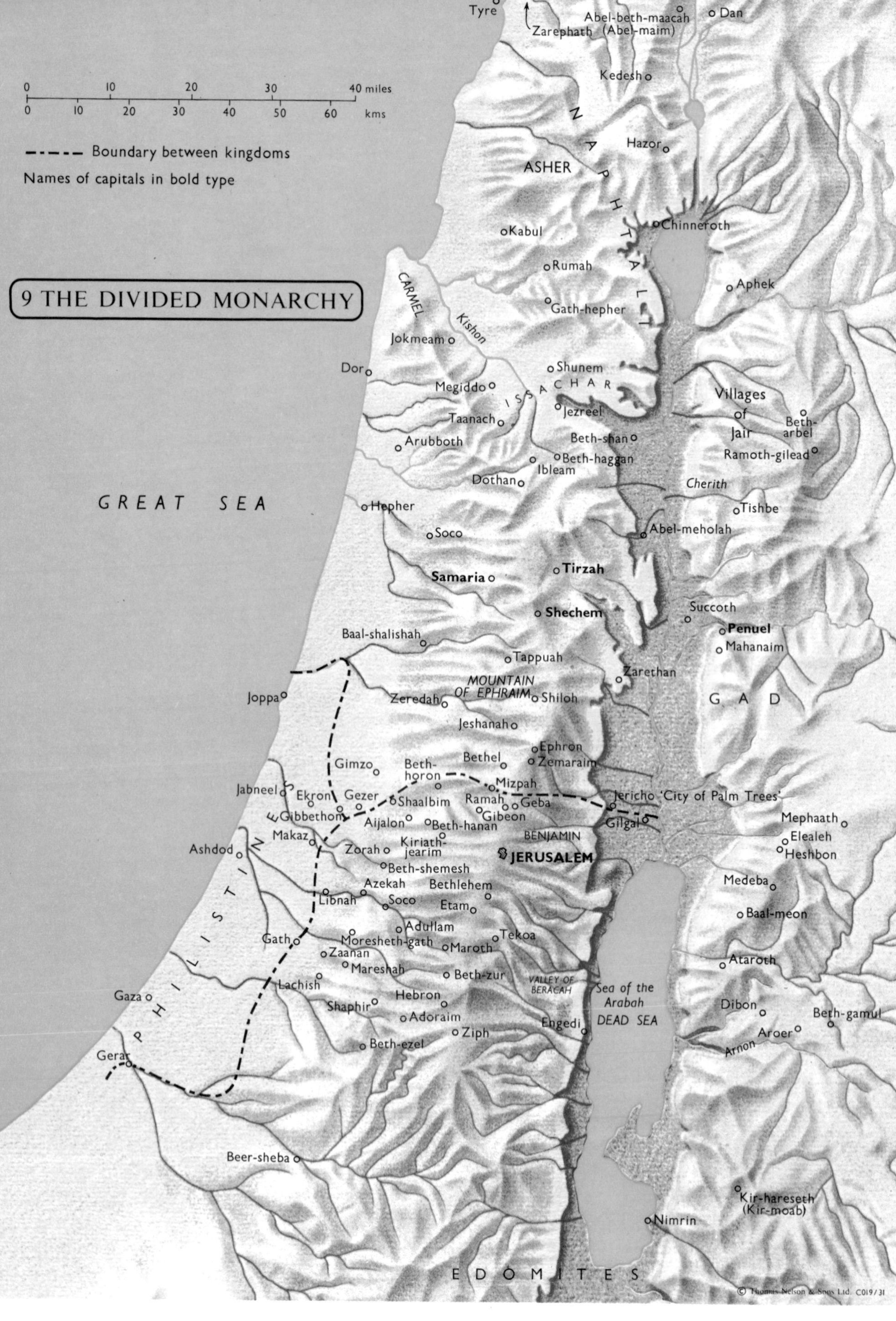
9 THE DIVIDED MONARCHY
0 10 20 30 40 miles
0 10 20 30 40 50 60 kms
Boundary between kingdoms
Names of capitals in bold type
GREAT SEA
Tyre
Zarephath
Abel-beth-maacah (Abel-maim)
Dan
Kedesh
NAPHTALI
Hazor
ASHER
Chinneroth
Kabul
Rumah
Aphek
CARMEL
Kishon
Gath-hepher
Jokmeam
Dor
Shunem
Megiddo
ISSACHAR
Villages of Jair
Taanach
Jezreel
Beth-arbel
Arubboth
Beth-shan
Ramoth-gilead
Ibleam
Beth-haggan
Dothan
Cherith
Hepher
Tishbe
Soco
Abel-meholah
Samaria
Tirzah
Shechem
Succoth
Penuel
Mahanaim
Baal-shalishah
Tappuah
Zarethan
MOUNTAIN OF EPHRAIM
Joppa
Zeredah
Shiloh
GAD
Jeshanah
Ephron
Bethel
Zemaraim
Gimzo
Beth-horon
Mizpah
Jabneel
Ekron
Gezer
Shaalbim
Ramah
Geba
Jericho 'City of Palm Trees'
Gibbethon
Gibeon
Aijalon
Beth-hanan
Gilgal
Mephaath
Makaz
BENJAMIN
Elealeh
Ashdod
Zorah
Kiriath-jearim
JERUSALEM
Heshbon
Beth-shemesh
Azekah
Bethlehem
Medeba
Libnah
Soco
Etam
Baal-meon
PHILISTINES
Adullam
Tekoa
Gath
Moresheth-gath
Maroth
Zaanan
Ataroth
Mareshah
Beth-zur
VALLEY OF BERACAH
Sea of the Arabah
DEAD SEA
Lachish
Gaza
Hebron
Dibon
Beth-gamul
Shaphir
Adoraim
Engedi
Aroer
Ziph
Arnon
Beth-ezel
Gerar
Beer-sheba
Kir-hareseth (Kir-moab)
Nimrin
EDOMITES
© Thomas Nelson & Sons Ltd. C019/31

10 PALESTINE IN THE TIME OF THE MACCABEES
0 10 20 30 40 miles
0 10 20 30 40 50 60 kms
GREAT SEA
Tyre
Kedesh
Plain of Hazor
Bascama
Ptolemais
Arbela
Lake of Gennesaret
GALILEE
The Great Plain
Dor
ARBATTA
Ephron
Scythopolis
SAMARIA
Samaria
Pharathon
Tephon
Joppa
Ramathaim
Timnath
Jazer
Adida
Birzaith
Lydda
Modin
Bethel
Ephraim
Beth-horon
Berea
Mizpah
Ekron
Dok
Jamnia
Capharsalama
Michmash
Jericho
Gezer
Adasa
Emmaus
Kedron
Jerusalem
Mount Zion
Azotus
Medeba
Bethbasi
Ashkelon
Nadabath
Beth-zechariah
Tekoa
Bezeth (Beth-zaitha)
Marisa
Beth-zur
PHILISTINES
Hebron
Gaza
DEAD SEA
Adora
IDUMAEA
AKRABATTINE

Printed in Great Britain

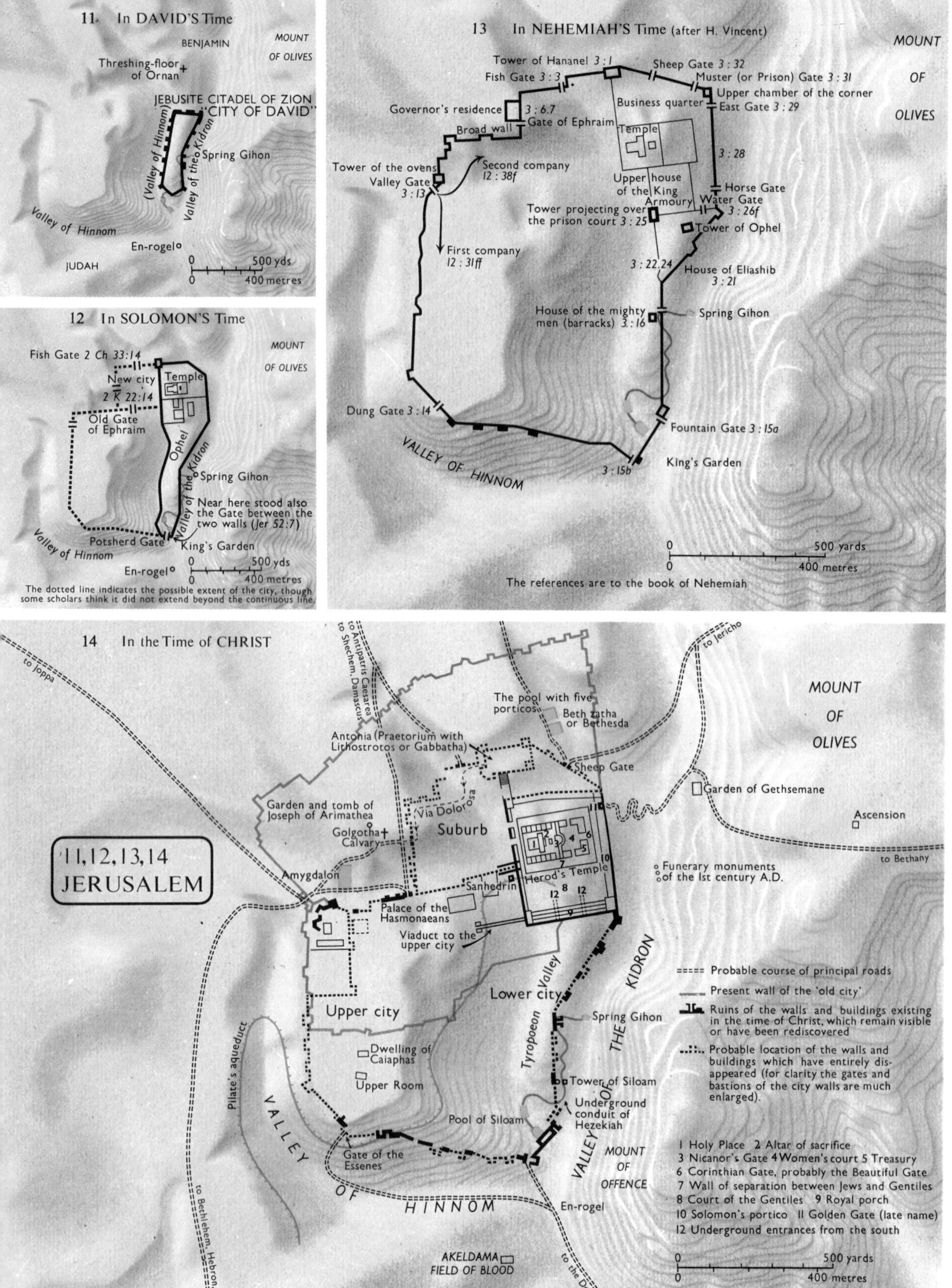

11 In DAVID'S Time
BENJAMIN
MOUNT OF OLIVES
Threshing-floor of Ornan
JEBUSITE CITADEL OF ZION
"CITY OF DAVID"
(Valley of Hinnom)
Valley of the Kidron
Spring Gihon
Valley of Hinnom
En-rogel
JUDAH
0 500 yds
0 400 metres
12 In SOLOMON'S Time
MOUNT OF OLIVES
Fish Gate 2 Ch 33:14
New city
2 K 22:14
Temple
Old Gate of Ephraim
Ophel
Valley of the Kidron
Spring Gihon
Near here stood also the Gate between the two walls (Jer 52:7)
Valley of Hinnom
Potsherd Gate
King's Garden
En-rogel
0 500 yds
0 400 metres
The dotted line indicates the possible extent of the city, though some scholars think it did not extend beyond the continuous line.
13 In NEHEMIAH'S Time (after H. Vincent)
MOUNT OF OLIVES
Tower of Hananel 3 : 1
Sheep Gate 3 : 32
Fish Gate 3 : 3
Muster (or Prison) Gate 3 : 31
Upper chamber of the corner
Business quarter
East Gate 3 : 29
Governor's residence
3 : 6.7
Gate of Ephraim
Broad wall
Temple
3 : 28
Tower of the ovens
Second company 12 : 38f
Valley Gate 3 : 13
Upper house of the King
Horse Gate
Armoury
Water Gate
3 : 26f
Tower projecting over the prison court 3 : 25
Tower of Ophel
First company 12 : 31ff
3 : 22.24
House of Eliashib 3 : 21
House of the mighty men (barracks) 3 : 16
Spring Gihon
Dung Gate 3 : 14
Fountain Gate 3 : 15a
VALLEY OF HINNOM
3 : 15b
King's Garden
0 500 yards
0 400 metres
The references are to the book of Nehemiah
14 In the Time of CHRIST
to Joppa
to Antipatris Caesarea
to Shechem, Damascus
to Jericho
MOUNT OF OLIVES
The pool with five porticos
Beth zatha or Bethesda
Antonia (Praetorium with Lithostrotos or Gabbatha)
Sheep Gate
Garden of Gethsemane
Garden and tomb of Joseph of Arimathea
Via Dolorosa
Ascension
Golgotha Calvary
Suburb
to Bethany
11,12,13,14
JERUSALEM
Funerary monuments of the Ist century A.D.
Amygdalon
Sanhedrin
Herod's Temple
Palace of the Hasmonaeans
Viaduct to the upper city
KIDRON
Tyropoeon Valley
Lower city
Upper city
Spring Gihon
THE
Pilate's aqueduct
Dwelling of Caiaphas
Upper Room
Tower of Siloam
Underground conduit of Hezekiah
Pool of Siloam
VALLEY OF HINNOM
Gate of the Essenes
VALLEY OF
MOUNT OF OFFENCE
En-rogel
AKELDAMA FIELD OF BLOOD
to Bethlehem, Hebron, Gaza
to the Dead Sea
Probable course of principal roads
Present wall of the 'old city'
Ruins of the walls and buildings existing in the time of Christ, which remain visible or have been rediscovered
Probable location of the walls and buildings which have entirely disappeared (for clarity the gates and bastions of the city walls are much enlarged).
1 Holy Place 2 Altar of sacrifice
3 Nicanor's Gate 4 Women's court 5 Treasury
6 Corinthian Gate, probably the Beautiful Gate
7 Wall of separation between Jews and Gentiles
8 Court of the Gentiles 9 Royal porch
10 Solomon's portico 11 Golden Gate (late name)
12 Underground entrances from the south
0 500 yards
0 400 metres

15 PALESTINE IN NEW TESTAMENT TIMES
GREAT SEA
SYRO-PHOENICIA
GALILEE
SAMARIA
JUDAEA
IDUMAEA
DECAPOLIS
PERAEA
NABATAEA
Damascus
Hermon 9232
Caesarea Philippi
Tyre
Ptolemais
Chorazin
Capernaum
Beth-saida
Magdala
Lake of Gennesaret
Tiberias
Hippos
Cana
Nazareth
Abila
Gadara
Nain
1690
194
Plain of Sharon
Caesarea
Scythopolis
1640
Pella
Aenon near Salim
3356
4091
Sebaste (Samaria)
2507
Gerasa
Shechem
Sychar
Gerizim
Jacob's Well
2841
Antipatris
3651
Alexandrium
Joppa
Arimathaea
2323
Lydda
Ephraim
Philadelphia
Emmaus
Jericho
Jamnia
Jerusalem
Bethany
Bethany (Bethabara)
Azotus
Kh. Qumrân
Bethlehem
Herodium
Ashkelon
3320
Machaerus
Hebron
DEAD SEA
Gaza
Engedi
Beer-sheba
Height in feet
Main road
Provincial boundary
0 10 20 30 40 50 miles
0 10 20 30 40 50 60 70 80 kms

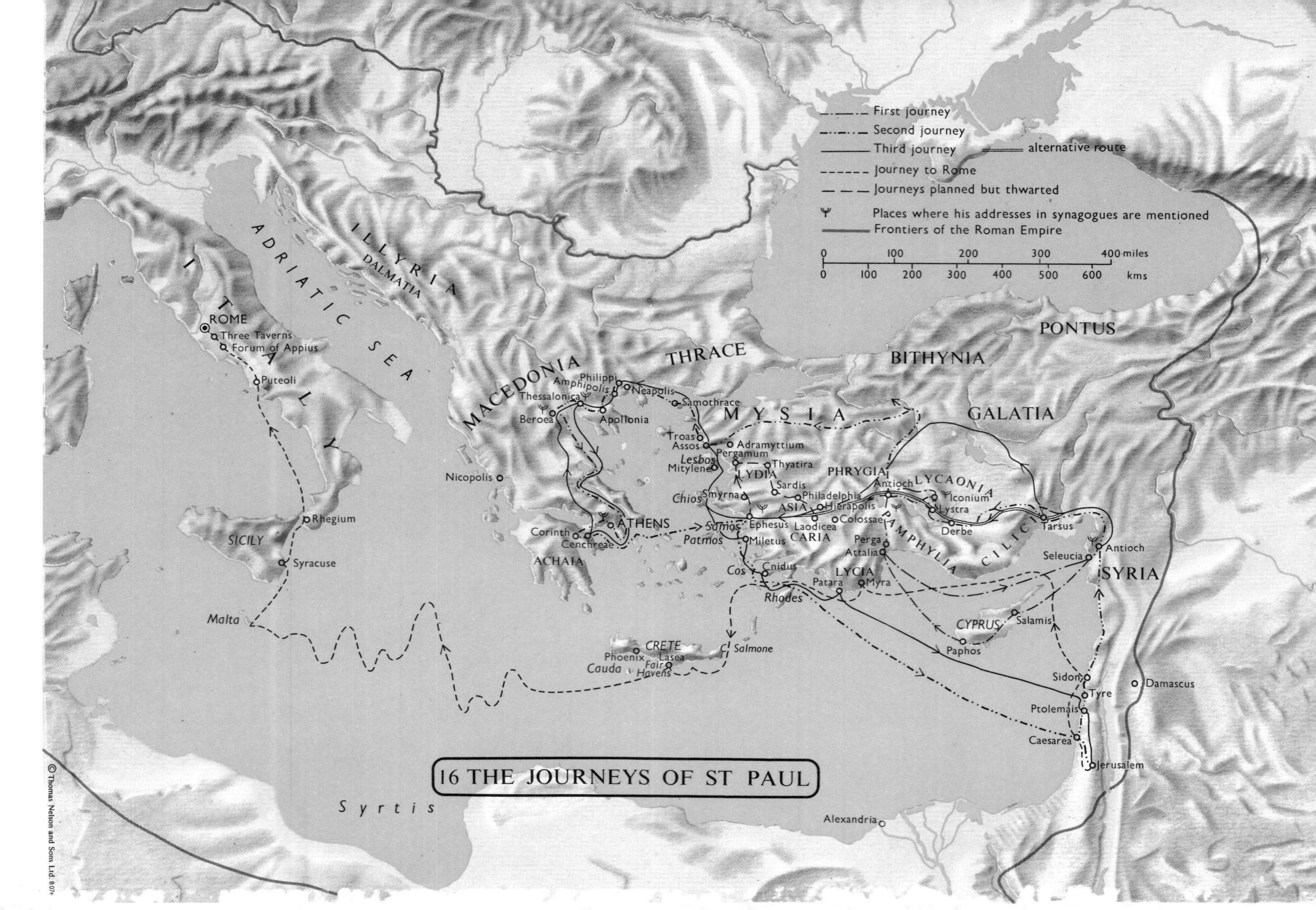

16 THE JOURNEYS OF ST PAUL

Introduction

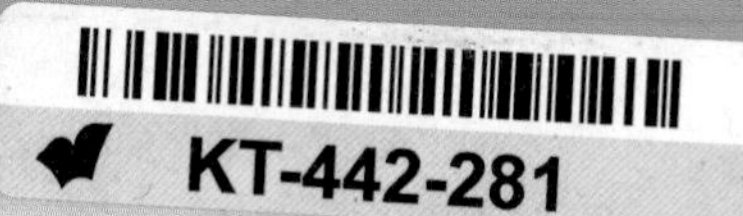

Advanced Chemistry has been written specially for the A-level specifications introduced in September 2000. Our central aim in writing this book has been to make chemistry accessible and stimulating without sacrificing rigour. With this in mind we have:

- organized content into double-page spreads so that you can find your way around the book easily and identify the information that you are looking for quickly (some spreads are clearly for use in the early terms of the course, while a few go beyond A level with the new Advanced Extension candidates in mind);
- given great emphasis to the visual presentation of concepts, by using hundreds of photographs and original diagrams, including images created with innovative molecular modelling software;
- researched original sources to ensure the accuracy of the data used in diagrams and tables;
- explained quantitative methods carefully and given extra maths help in boxes and in a dedicated 'Mathematics toolbox' appendix.

In addition, there are content summaries to help you to review topics effectively, hundreds of practice questions, and over fifty pages of examination questions to enable you to check your understanding and develop good exam technique.

You can use our website www.oup.com/uk/sciencegrids to tailor your use of the book to your particular specification.

We would like to acknowledge the many valuable contributions made to the early drafts of this book by Peter Atkins, one of today's great chemistry educators. We thank Peter for his helpful advice.

MJC would like to thank the Governors, Headmaster, colleagues, and students at Tonbridge School for their enthusiastic support during the writing of this book.

RF would like to thank her colleague David Dunevein at Abingdon College for his support and encouragement when she embarked on this project.

Both of us are very grateful to our respective families for their patience and support throughout.

We hope that you enjoy using our book and that it helps you to a greater understanding of chemistry, a subject that is central to our lives and our future.

Mike Clugston
Ros Flemming

Contents

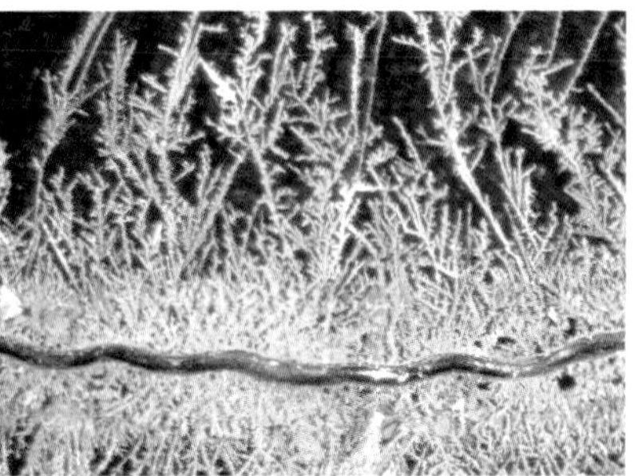

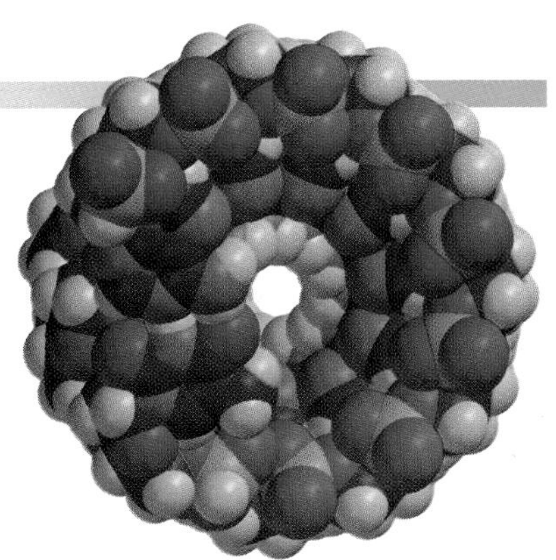

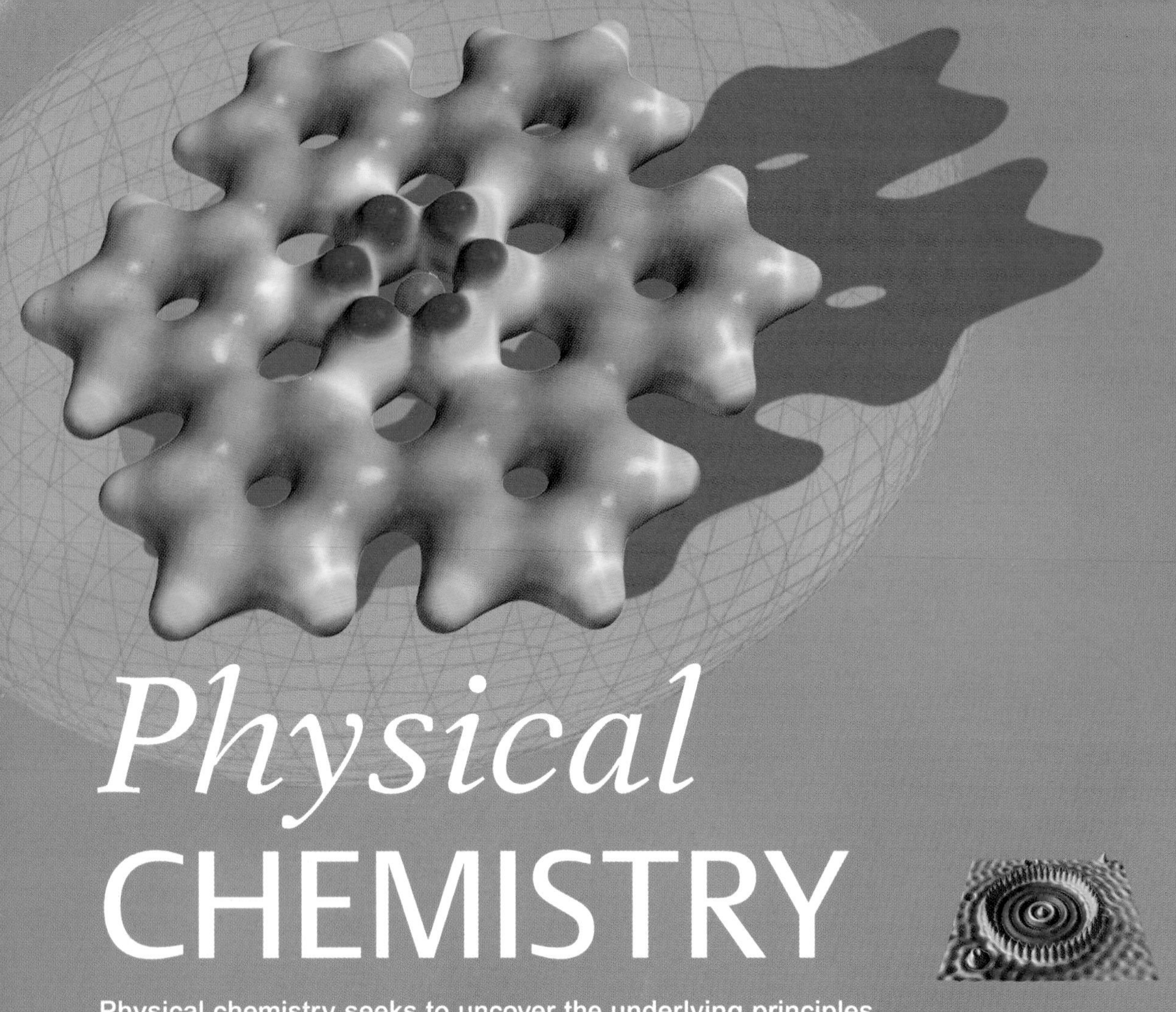

Physical CHEMISTRY

Physical chemistry seeks to uncover the underlying principles of chemistry. Our ideas were transformed by the discovery just over a hundred years ago of the electron (see chapter 2). Very recently, such spectacular images as those on the right have provided experimental confirmation of the wave nature of electrons when they are within atoms. This idea led to a thorough understanding of the structure of atoms and of the bonding between atoms (see chapters 3–5).

Bonding theory explains the structure of elements and compounds; structure and bonding together can explain the physical properties of substances, such as their melting and boiling points and their conductivities (see chapters 6 and 7). Gases (chapter 8) complete our survey of the behaviour of individual chemicals on their own.

We begin our study of chemical reactions in chapter 9 with an account of the masses and volumes of chemicals that react. This is followed by a discussion of the energy changes that accompany chemical reactions (chapter 10). The focus then shifts in a set of four chapters (11–14) to an investigation of competition between substances. This involves the general study of equilibrium followed by an examination of the two major classes of chemical reaction: acid–base and redox reactions. These four chapters conclude with an overview of the nature of spontaneous change towards equilibrium.

The final chapter in the physical chemistry section of the book (chapter 15) considers chemical kinetics. A reaction that is predicted by thermodynamics to be spontaneous may be too slow to be of any economic value. To investigate whether any particular substance is stable or not, we need to consider both thermodynamic stability and kinetic stability.

This image shows a ring of 48 iron atoms on a copper surface. The electrons in the surface scatter from the iron atoms. The ring of iron atoms forms a boundary, or 'corral', which traps electrons in its interior. The trapped electrons occupy the quantum states of the corral. Quantum corrals provide us with an opportunity to visualize the quantum behaviour of electrons in small confining structures.

1 Patterns in chemistry

Human beings are an inquisitive species. We have progressed from the Bronze Age to our current state of technological ability in just 5000 years. Throughout that time we have constantly observed the world around us and asked the questions: 'Why does that happen?' and 'How can I control what happens?' We try to answer these questions by carrying out experiments and searching for patterns in what we see and measure. Chemists are concerned with the study of matter – the structure of materials and how they interact. Chemistry aims to explain patterns in the behaviour of materials by formulating rules, theories, and laws to reveal the underlying nature of matter.

AN INTRODUCTION TO CHEMISTRY

OBJECTIVES

- The origins and scope of chemistry

Chemistry is the study of the elements and the compounds formed when they bond with each other. The subject is subdivided into three main branches: physical chemistry, inorganic chemistry, and organic chemistry. Physical chemistry is concerned with how the chemical structure of a substance affects its properties. It includes the study of chemical bonding and the structures of solids, liquids, and gases. Physical chemistry also investigates energy changes that accompany chemical reactions and how fast reactions happen. Inorganic chemistry is concerned with describing the properties and reactions of all elements and compounds other than those of carbon. Organic chemistry is concerned with the chemistry of carbon compounds. Its study centres particularly on the ability of carbon atoms to join with each other to form rings and long chains. There are also related branches of chemistry such as biochemistry, chemical engineering, and geochemistry.

Iron extraction uses chemical techniques discovered more than 3000 years ago. Converting iron into steel became much cheaper in the nineteenth century.

The origins of chemistry

The earliest uses of chemical processes were in the extraction of metals such as copper and iron, the firing of clays and sands to make ceramics and glasses, and the extraction and use of dyes. People were able to do all these things, but how could they explain what they saw happening? When thinking about the material world, people have always tried to find patterns and describe rules of behaviour. For example, when faced with sorting out a box of jumbled objects, the first thing anyone might try to do is sort them into groups of similar things. In the case of a collection of coloured marbles, a suitable procedure would be to sort them into different colours or sizes. The same was true of people at the dawn of civilization as they searched for a way of sorting out and explaining the non-living world around them.

At first, in the fifth century BC, their sorting was very broad. They concluded that there were four main categories of substance: fire, air, water, and earth. Each of these four categories was composed of pairs of the four fundamental qualities: hot, cold, wet, and dry. Everything in the whole of the non-living world had to fit one of these categories or a combination of them. At a simple level this classification works: mountains, deserts, rocks, and houses are all 'earthy'; all liquids are 'watery'; all gases are 'airy'; and all flames are 'fiery'. This scheme can also explain changes in materials. For example, when (cold–wet) water is boiled, the result is a form of (hot–wet) air, i.e. steam.

The early alchemists

The systematic study of chemistry as a subject started in Egypt about 1700 years ago. Writings by Zosimos (c. AD 300) describe chemical experiments and chemical apparatus. For the next thousand years, most chemical exploration sought ways of changing (or transmuting) cheap base metals such as lead into the precious metals, gold or silver. This work on transmutation was called alchemy (from the Arabic *al-kimia*: *al* = the, *kimia* = art of transmuting metals).

They did not succeed in their search but, almost accidentally, they developed many sound techniques of chemical manipulation. Modern chemistry was born during the seventeenth century when some of these early scientists started to investigate the mechanisms by which substances were changed. Alchemists continued their work during this period of transition, but their use of ghostly spirits and 'uncorporeal bodies' to explain their findings was gradually seen to make no sense.

Paracelsus

Theophrastus Bombast von Hohenheim (c. 1493–1541), a Swiss physician who called himself Paracelsus, attempted to move alchemy beyond simply striving to transmute metals. He declared that an equally valid aim for alchemists was to try to cure illness using chemicals as remedies. At that time four fluids of the human body called *humours* were thought to determine a person's physical and mental state. However, Paracelsus believed illness arose from specific external causes rather than from an imbalance of the *humours*.

The discovery of phosphorus in 1669 resulted from the alchemical investigations of Hennig Brandt of Hamburg. Brandt's starting material was urine. Phosphorus emits light (it is luminescent) by reaction with air; its name comes from the Greek for 'bringer of light'.

The foundation of modern chemistry

During the seventeenth century, the study of chemistry began to concentrate on the preparation, isolation, and use of new substances. In 1661, Robert Boyle wrote a landmark book called *The Sceptical Chymist*, in which he attacked the idea of the four categories (fire, air, water, and earth) and introduced the modern concept of chemical elements. During the following two centuries, Boyle's ideas took root and slowly developed. In 1789, in his *Elementary Treatise on Chemistry*, Antoine Lavoisier published a list of 33 chemical elements, many of which we recognize today. At that time, an element was thought of as a substance that cannot be broken down into two or more simpler substances. We know now that an **element** is a substance that contains only one sort of atom, and that an **atom** is the smallest particle of an element that can exist independently. Most of our modern chemical understanding rests on these two simple and fundamental points.

Antoine Lavoisier was the founder of modern chemistry. He showed that air contains oxygen and that water is a compound of oxygen and hydrogen. In 1789, using Boyle's definition of an element, he drew up the first table of chemical elements. This portrait is by Jacques-Louis David.

SUMMARY

- An element is a substance that cannot be broken down into two or more simpler substances.
- An element is a substance that contains only one sort of atom.
- An atom is the smallest particle of an element that can exist independently.

1.2

Elements: the search for patterns

OBJECTIVES

- Nineteenth-century attempts at classification

If you were a chemist working during the 1800s, you would have been living in exciting times. New elements were being discovered at an amazing rate. In 1807 Humphry Davy used electrolysis to isolate the new metals sodium and potassium. In 1808 he isolated the metals calcium, strontium, and barium. In 1810, Davy went on to show that chlorine is an element similar to iodine. During this period, chemists also began to investigate the *quantities* in which elements reacted with each other. From these investigations, each element was assigned an atomic mass.

Atomic mass

During the nineteenth century, the atomic masses of elements were calculated relative to hydrogen. One atom of this element was used as the arbitrary unit of mass. On this scale, oxygen had an atomic mass of 16, indicating that one atom of oxygen had a mass equal to the total mass of 16 atoms of hydrogen. The atomic mass for each element was calculated from carefully measuring the quantities of reactants and products involved in chemical reactions.

Atomic masses are now measured relative to one-twelfth of the mass of one atom of carbon-12, as we shall see later.

Döbereiner's triads

With about fifty elements clearly identified, chemists tried to group together elements that resembled each other. Following the process of classification started by the Ancient Greeks, they were looking for an underlying theory that would arrange elements into groups and explain their properties. The first real success came in 1817 when Johann Döbereiner noted that the metals calcium, strontium, and barium were very alike.

A decade later, once bromine had been discovered, he saw that the non-metals chlorine, bromine, and iodine were also very similar. Döbereiner also noted that the atomic mass of the middle element of each three was approximately the average of the atomic masses of the outer two elements. However, he was not able to suggest why this was so. Döbereiner believed that elements could be arranged in threes, or **triads** as he called them; but he could not find enough triads to construct a convincing theory to explain his classification.

Element	Atomic mass
Calcium	40.1
Strontium	87.6
Barium	137.3
Sulphur	32.1
Selenium	79.0
Tellurium	127.6
Chlorine	35.5
Bromine	79.9
Iodine	126.9

Three of Döbereiner's triads. In each triad, the atomic mass of the middle element falls approximately mid-way between the atomic masses of the outer two elements.

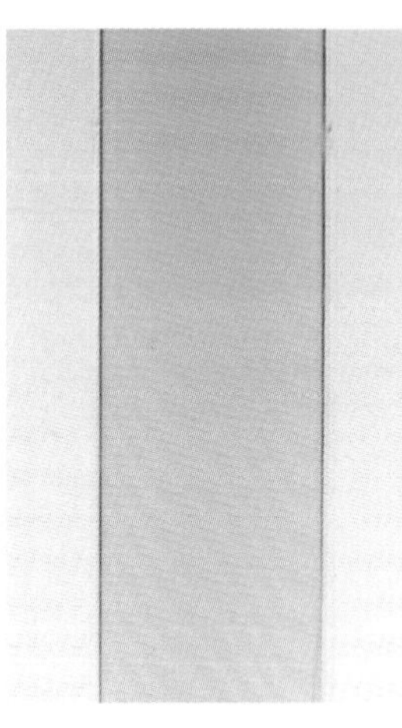

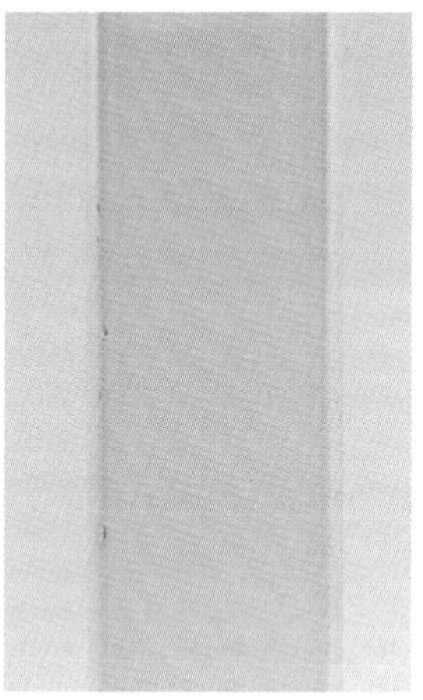

A Döbereiner triad. Chlorine, bromine, and iodine are all non–metals. Bromine (left) is a liquid with a brown vapour; chlorine (centre) is a gas; iodine (right) is a solid with a purple vapour. The atomic mass of bromine (79.9) is approximately equal to the average of the atomic masses of chlorine (35.5) and iodine (126.9) (the calculated average is 81.2).

Alexandre Béguyer de Chancourtois

In 1862, the French geologist Alexandre Béguyer de Chancourtois arranged the names of the elements in order of increasing atomic mass in a helical pattern around a cylinder. This procedure divided the elements into vertical columns. Each column contained some elements with similar properties. For example, lithium, sodium, and potassium appeared in one column; and oxygen, sulphur, selenium, and tellurium in another. (One problem was that he included some compounds and alloys thought to be elements at the time.) Béguyer de Chancourtois concluded that: 'The properties of substances are the properties of numbers.' His work was ignored by the majority of chemists, mainly because the diagram explaining his idea was omitted from the published paper.

William Odling

In 1864, William Odling published an article entitled 'On the Proportional Numbers of the Elements'. He grouped certain elements together and noticed that, for 'well-defined groups', their sequences of chemical properties and their sequences of atomic masses went in parallel with each other. Odling constructed a table of the elements to illustrate these relationships.

Newlands' octaves

John Newlands was the chief chemist in a London sugar refinery. In 1865 he noticed that, if the elements were written in order of their atomic masses, similar chemical properties appeared at every eighth element. Newlands likened this behaviour to a musical scale and suggested that the elements obeyed a *law of octaves*. Newlands had glimpsed the correct underlying pattern to the recurring properties of the elements, but he did not take the idea far enough. The real father of the modern periodic table was a Russian, Dmitri Mendeleyev.

SUMMARY

- Döbereiner identified groups containing three elements with similar properties. He called these groups *triads*.
- The triads included calcium–strontium–barium and chlorine–bromine–iodine.
- Newlands drew up a list of elements in order of increasing atomic mass and noted that every eighth element fell into a group with similar chemical properties.

John Newlands

Like Odling, he was born in a district of London called Southwark. Newlands' law of octaves represented an important step on the path to a systematic classification of the elements. However, his work was ridiculed.

When he presented his ideas to the Chemical Society in London, he was asked 'whether he had ever examined the elements according to the order of their initial letters?', and he was told that his work was 'not adapted for publication'. He did not receive the credit he deserved.

In later years it became clear that Newlands had anticipated Mendeleyev's 1869 periodic law. Belatedly, Newlands was awarded the Davy Medal of the Royal Society in 1887. A plaque was unveiled in 1998 at Elephant and Castle, London, to commemorate the centenary of his death.

PRACTICE

1 Look through this spread and list:
  - **a** the metals mentioned, and
  - **b** the non-metals mentioned.

2 Look up the following names and words in a large encyclopedia or on a computer. Arrange them into a sequence that shows the development of chemistry.

a	Bronze Age	**b**	Iron Age
c	Alchemy	**d**	Elements
e	Robert Boyle	**f**	Antoine Lavoisier
g	Joseph Priestley	**h**	Paracelsus
i	John Dalton.		

1.3

MENDELEYEV'S PERIODIC TABLE

OBJECTIVES

- How Mendeleyev constructed the first periodic table

Towards the end of the 1860s, chemists were on the verge of proposing a grand unifying model that would account for the properties of the elements. The 62 separate elements known in 1869 would soon be grouped and classified according to a set of clear rules. Newlands and others had glimpsed the underlying pattern in the properties of the elements. However, their understanding was incomplete and fragmented. It was the Russian Dmitri Mendeleyev who collected the elements together in a table that revealed the periodic (repeating) pattern in their properties.

The periodic law

We can arrange glass marbles systematically by referring to their colour or size. Mendeleyev arranged the 62 elements then known by referring to their atomic masses. Starting with hydrogen, he wrote out the elements in horizontal rows, in order of increasing atomic mass. This gathered elements with similar properties below one another in vertical groups. Mendeleyev's stroke of genius was to group elements according to their properties, even if he had to move some elements out of the strict sequence of increasing atomic mass. He looked at the arrangement of the elements in his table and was then able to state his periodic law, as follows:

- 'The elements, if arranged according to their atomic masses, show an evident periodicity of properties.'

A biographical note

Dmitri Ivanovich Mendeleyev was born in Tobolsk, Siberia, in 1834, the youngest of fourteen children. Mendeleyev became the most celebrated chemist of his generation, once the predictions he had made were verified.

Mendeleyev had divorced his first wife and then married a young art student. According to Russian Orthodox Law, he was a bigamist. No action was taken as Tsar Alexander II rejected criticism of his behaviour by saying: 'Yes, Mendeleyev has two wives, but I have only one Mendeleyev.'

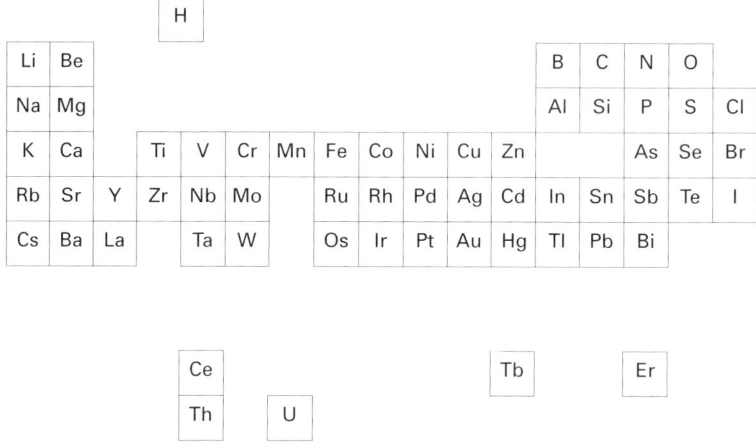

A modern outline of the periodic table incorporating the 62 elements known to Mendeleyev in 1869.

The shape of the periodic table

The illustration above shows the 62 elements known to Mendeleyev, positioned on an outline of a modern form of the periodic table. His original table successfully classified all the elements in Groups I to VII. The elements now referred to as 'transition metals' were scattered throughout the table in regions called 'subgroups'. These elements were later assigned to their own specific area created at the centre of the table.

Changing the order to fit the properties

The problem with arranging the elements in strict order of atomic mass is that the pattern does not match the properties of all the elements. For example, iodine ends up in the wrong place, away from bromine and chlorine. Mendeleyev had the courage to use his knowledge of the properties of the elements to bend his own rule; he simply exchanged some positions on the basis that the atomic masses known at the time might be inaccurate. Mendeleyev also had the foresight to realize that some elements had yet to be discovered.

The undiscovered elements

Having suggested that there must be undiscovered elements, Mendeleyev *left gaps* for them in his table in order to preserve the principle of periodicity. Most significantly, he went on to predict in detail the chemical properties that these unknown elements would have. There was a gap in his original table between silicon and tin, now occupied by germanium. Mendeleyev inserted an element he called 'eka-silicon' into this gap and he predicted its properties by inspection of the properties of the other elements in the group. The properties of germanium, isolated by Clemens Winkler in 1886, were in close agreement with Mendeleyev's predictions for eka-silicon. It is a further testimony to the brilliance of Mendeleyev's ideas that the later discovery of a completely new group of elements, the noble gases, did not disrupt his overall scheme.

Property	Eka-silicon, E (predicted)	Germanium, Ge (observed)
Atomic mass	72	72.6
Density	5.5 g cm^{-3}	5.35 g cm^{-3}
Oxide		
nature	white solid	white solid
formula	EO_2	GeO_2
density	4.7 g cm^{-3}	4.23 g cm^{-3}
Chloride		
boiling point	below 100 °C	84 °C
formula	ECl_4	$GeCl_4$
density	1.9 g cm^{-3}	1.84 g cm^{-3}

The properties of eka-silicon suggested by Mendeleyev compared with the actual properties of germanium.

This stamp commemorates the centenary of the introduction of the periodic table by Dmitri Mendeleyev. Gallium (Ga), unknown in 1869, is identified.

Lothar Meyer

As Mendeleyev was completing his periodic table, Lothar Meyer in Germany was also working with the concept of periodicity. He constructed a plot of the atomic volumes of the elements against their atomic masses. He calculated the atomic volume of each element by dividing its atomic mass by its density. The overall shape of the plot consisted of a series of periodically repeating peaks and troughs, illustrating the periodic nature of the atomic volumes of the elements.

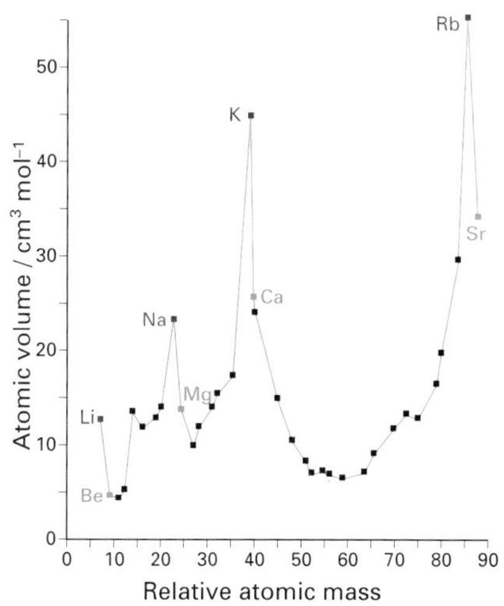

Lothar Meyer's curve of atomic volume against atomic mass would have looked similar to this one. Notice the elements at the peaks of the curve – lithium, sodium, potassium, and rubidium.

SUMMARY

- Mendeleyev was able to obtain groups containing similar elements by arranging the elements in order of increasing atomic mass.
- He left gaps or altered the order of the elements, to make better sense of their properties.
- Elements discovered later fitted in to the gaps in the table; their properties matched those predicted by Mendeleyev.

PRACTICE

1 Chemists greeted Mendeleyev's periodic law, which is only one sentence long, with a great deal of enthusiasm and approval. Why did it create so much excitement?

2 Why did the later discovery of the noble gases (helium, neon, argon, krypton, xenon, and radon) not affect the overall arrangement of Mendeleyev's periodic table?

3 Copy the outline of the periodic table given opposite. Add to it the symbols of the elements about whose chemistry you already know something. Is your chemical knowledge scattered randomly across the table or is there an underlying pattern?

4 You may have completed most of a whole period in question 3. Run your eye across it from left to right. Do you notice any trend in a property of the elements? Describe any trend that you see.

1.4

THE MODERN PERIODIC TABLE

OBJECTIVES

- The overall shape of the modern periodic table
- Groups of elements
- Periods of elements
- The metal/non-metal divide

Group numbering

The groups in the periodic table have traditionally been numbered with Roman numerals I to VIII, and that is the numbering system used in this book. (Note that some books use the Arabic numerals 1 to 8 for the groups, which can lead to confusion with the period numbers 1 to 7.)

By international agreement, modern forms of the periodic table number the groups 1 to 18.

Atomic mass and atomic number

Mendeleyev's original periodic table attempted to list elements in order of increasing atomic mass.

The modern periodic table lists elements by their atomic number, rather than by atomic mass. The atomic number of an element is the number of protons in its nucleus. Using atomic numbers avoids the problems encountered by Mendeleyev in trying to establish an order. Atomic number is explained fully in the next chapter.

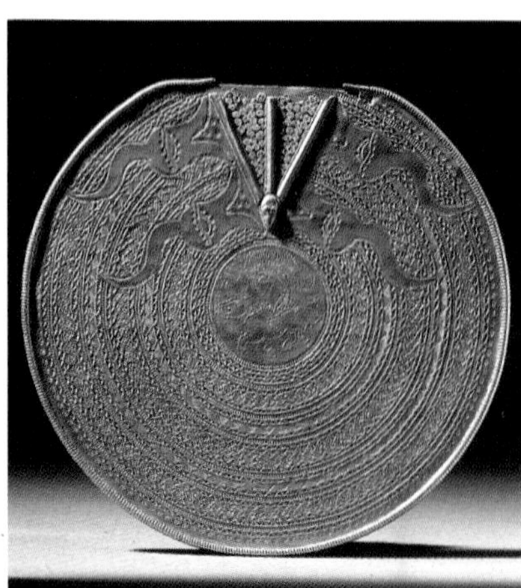

Gold is extremely malleable. This medallion was made by the Vikings.

A modern periodic table can appear very complicated. It is covered in unfamiliar chemical symbols; it also has a particular shape. If you can learn to read the table as a musician reads a musical score, then an enormous amount of information becomes available to you. In order to start to understand and make use of the periodic table, it is helpful first to define some regions within it. The vertical columns of the table are called **groups,** which are numbered I to VIII. Groups contain elements that have similar chemical properties to each other. The horizontal rows are called **periods**, which are numbered from 1 to 7.

Period \ Group	I	II											III	IV	V	VI	VII	VIII
①				H 1														He 2
②	Li 3	Be 4											B 5	C 6	N 7	O 8	F 9	Ne 10
③	Na 11	Mg 12											Al 13	Si 14	P 15	S 16	Cl 17	Ar 18
④	K 19	Ca 20	Sc 21	Ti 22	V 23	Cr 24	Mn 25	Fe 26	Co 27	Ni 28	Cu 29	Zn 30	Ga 31	Ge 32	As 33	Se 34	Br 35	Kr 36
⑤	Rb 37	Sr 38	Y 39	Zr 40	Nb 41	Mo 42	Tc 43	Ru 44	Rh 45	Pd 46	Ag 47	Cd 48	In 49	Sn 50	Sb 51	Te 52	I 53	Xe 54
⑥	Cs 55	Ba 56	La 57	Hf 72	Ta 73	W 74	Re 75	Os 76	Ir 77	Pt 78	Au 79	Hg 80	Tl 81	Pb 82	Bi 83	Po 84	At 85	Rn 86
⑦	Fr 87	Ra 88	Ac 89	Rf 104	Db 105	Sg 106	Bh 107	Hs 108	Mt 109									

Ce 58	Pr 59	Nd 60	Pm 61	Sm 62	Eu 63	Gd 64	Tb 65	Dy 66	Ho 67	Er 68	Tm 69	Yb 70	Lu 71
Th 90	Pa 91	U 92	Np 93	Pu 94	Am 95	Cm 96	Bk 97	Cf 98	Es 99	Fm 100	Md 101	No 102	Lr 103

The standard modern form of the periodic table. The deeper green colour identifies the metalloids, see opposite.

Metals and non-metals

The position of an element in the periodic table gives an indication of its overall properties. For example, run your eye across the elements in Period 3 (sodium to argon) of the periodic table above. Notice that there is a change from metals to non-metals. Overall, the majority of the elements in the table are metals. The relatively few non-metals are found on the right-hand side of the table.

Metallic elements

All the metallic elements, except mercury, are shiny solids. Metals are good electrical conductors, whereas most non-metals do not conduct electricity. Metals are *malleable*: they may be bent or pressed into different shapes. They are also *ductile*: they may be stretched to form, for example, thin wires. The most typically metallic elements are found in Groups I and II. Group I elements are called the alkali metals and include sodium and potassium. Group II elements include magnesium and calcium.

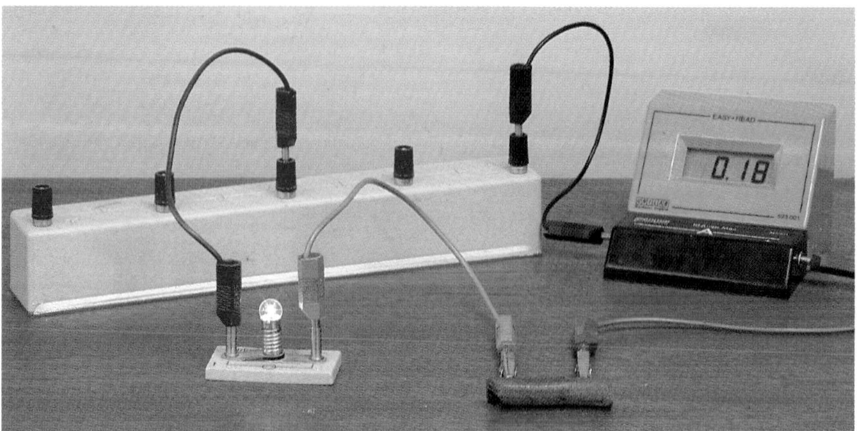

The alkali metal lithium, like all metals, is a good conductor of electricity.

[illegible]ic elements

[illegible]ost non-metals are electrical insulators, having an electrical conductivity at least one billion times smaller than that of a typical metal. They are also brittle when solid, and often have low melting and boiling points compared to typical metals. The most typically non-metallic elements are found in Group VII. These elements are called the **halogens** and include chlorine and bromine. Group VIII contains the **noble gases**, which include helium and neon.

Sulphur is a typical non-metal. It melts at 113 °C, is brittle, and is an electrical insulator. Compare these properties with those of a typical metal.

Metalloids

Look again at the right-hand side of the periodic table opposite. Notice the stepped line drawn rather like a staircase. This line roughly marks the division between metallic and non-metallic elements, with metals to its left and non-metals to its right. While Groups I and II contain metals and Groups VII and VIII contain non-metals, Groups III to VI contain both sorts of element. Group IV, for example, contains the non-metal carbon and the metals tin and lead. Metallic character increases as atomic number increases down the group. The elements silicon (Si) and germanium (Ge) are intermediate in nature between metals and non-metals. Together with arsenic (As), antimony (Sb), selenium (Se), and tellurium (Te), they are called **metalloids**. Because of their intermediate electrical conductivity, silicon and germanium are classed as *semiconductors*.

The 'transition' elements

The periodic table contains elements other than those in Groups I to VIII. The central regions of Periods 4, 5, and 6 contain transition elements such as titanium, iron, copper, silver, and gold. These elements are metallic. Note that two rows of metals are separated out at the bottom of the periodic table, the *lanthanides* Ce to Lu and the *actinides* Th to Lr.

Glenn Seaborg

Glenn Seaborg, the only person ever honoured in his lifetime with an element named after him (seaborgium, element 106), died in 1999.

SUMMARY

- The modern periodic table lists elements in order of their atomic number.
- Elements are arranged in vertical groups (I–VIII) and horizontal periods (1–7).
- Most elements are metals.
- Metals conduct electricity, and are malleable and ductile.
- Non-metals are found towards the top right-hand side of the periodic table.
- Most non-metals are insulators, are brittle when solid, and have lower melting and boiling points than metals.
- The diagonal band of metalloids in the periodic table acts like a fuzzy frontier between the metals and the non-metals.
- The six metalloids are silicon, germanium, arsenic, antimony, selenium, and tellurium.

PRACTICE

1 Give the names of the elements corresponding to the symbols: Li, Mg, Si, Br, K, Ag, Sn, F.

2 Give the symbol for each of the following elements: germanium, sulphur, calcium, gold, krypton, antimony, lead.

3 For the elements in questions 1 and 2, say whether each is a metal, a non-metal, or a metalloid.

4 Name a non-metal in Group III and a metal in Group VI.

5 Give the symbols and names of the elements corresponding to the atomic numbers: 23, 13, 56, 36, 38, 7.

The nuclear atom

In the previous chapter we discussed some of the early ideas about sorting and classifying elements. In this chapter we look in more detail at what we think an element actually is. We know that all matter is made up of very small particles called atoms. The idea of atoms originated with the Greek philosophers Leucippus and Democritus during the fifth century BC, but the concept remained ignored and undeveloped until it was reintroduced in the early nineteenth century by John Dalton. By measuring the masses of the elements taking part in chemical reactions, he was able to provide *indirect* evidence that matter is made up of atoms. It is only over the past few years that *direct* evidence for this has been obtained, using the scanning tunnelling microscope (STM).

IDEAS ABOUT ATOMS

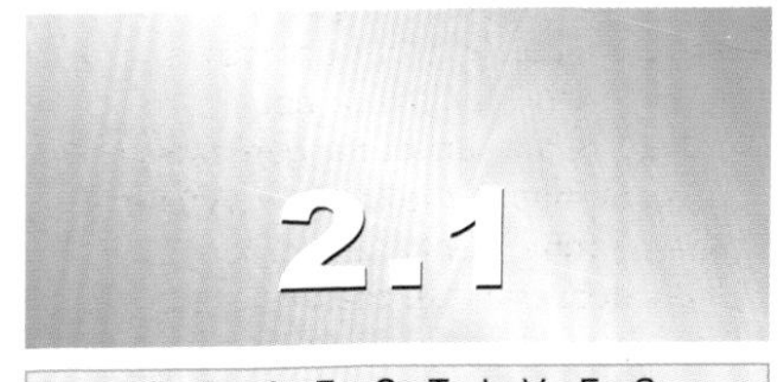

OBJECTIVES

- Matter is atomic rather than continuous
- Early ideas about atoms

For the past 2500 years people have asked the following question, in the form of a thought experiment: 'Can you go on cutting a piece of matter into ever smaller pieces, or is there a limit?' Zeno of Elea (born about 490 BC) thought that the answer was: 'Yes. Matter is continuous and fills space completely, rather like jelly.' In about 420 BC, Democritus took the opposite view. He held that matter is divided into small particles with empty space – a vacuum – between them. He also said that these particles, *atoms*, are hard and are in constant motion. He had no evidence to back up his assertions; they seemed to him to be simply the better idea.

A set of sixth-century multiplication tables gives the size of the 'smallest particle' as equivalent to 10^{-10} m, which is close to the modern value for the diameter of a typical atom. However, all these ideas about atoms were speculative, which means they were based solely on guessing and thinking.

Dalton was born in 1766 and left school at the age of twelve. He was fascinated by the weather, which he meticulously recorded for 57 years. As a life-long Quaker he shunned fame and would have been embarrassed to know that 40 000 people filed past his coffin as it lay in Manchester Town Hall. This is one of the earliest photographs of a scientist to exist (a Daguerrotype by Dancer).

John Dalton

John Dalton, a teacher from Manchester, is credited with developing the modern theory of the atom. He presented the idea in detail in his book *New System of Chemical Philosophy* in 1808. Following a long series of experiments Dalton suggested that:

- different elements have atoms which differ in mass;
- each element is characterized by the mass of its atoms.

The basis of Dalton's atomic theory is that all matter – elements, compounds, and mixtures – is composed of extremely small particles called atoms. Four *postulates* describe how these atoms behave:

1 The atoms in a given element are all of the same kind.

2 A compound contains atoms of two or more elements combined together in fixed proportions.

3 An atom retains its identity during a chemical reaction.

4 During a chemical reaction, the atoms in the reacting substances rearrange to form the products of the reaction.

Dalton also introduced the idea of chemical symbols. He was the first to find the correct formula for carbon dioxide, which he wrote down in symbols as ○●○. The open circles represent oxygen atoms and the filled circle represents a carbon atom. His system of circular symbols is no longer used. The current familiar system based on letters was devised by the Swede Jacob Berzelius in 1811.

Hydrogen ⊙ Sulphur ⊕
Nitrogen ⦶ Phosphorus
Carbon ● Copper Ⓒ
Oxygen ○ Lead Ⓛ
Carbon dioxide ○●○
Carbon monoxide ●○

Dalton's symbols for some atoms and two compounds. His formulae for carbon dioxide and carbon monoxide are correct, but he was not always so successful!

Direct evidence for atoms?

The scanning tunnelling microscope (STM) was invented in 1981. It creates images of surfaces, with a resolution that is sufficiently high to detect individual atoms. We perceive everyday objects around us by using our brains to analyse reflected light entering our eyes. The STM constructs an image by using a computer to analyse the electric current flowing between a surface and a very fine probe. More details of the STM are given in the box.

> **Principles of STM operation**
>
> Electricity does not usually escape from the surface of conducting wires, but if a second conductor is brought close enough to the wire, electrons cross the gap by a process called *tunnelling*. A tiny but measurable current flows.
>
> The STM uses a minute needle-like probe, tipped with tungsten, to scan the surface being examined. A very small potential difference is applied across the gap between the probe and the surface. When the probe encounters a bump on the surface, the gap becomes smaller and the current increases; when the probe encounters a dip, the gap becomes larger and the current decreases. When all the data have been collected, the computer generates a contour map of the surface. A very sharp probe is able to detect individual atoms in the surface being scanned.

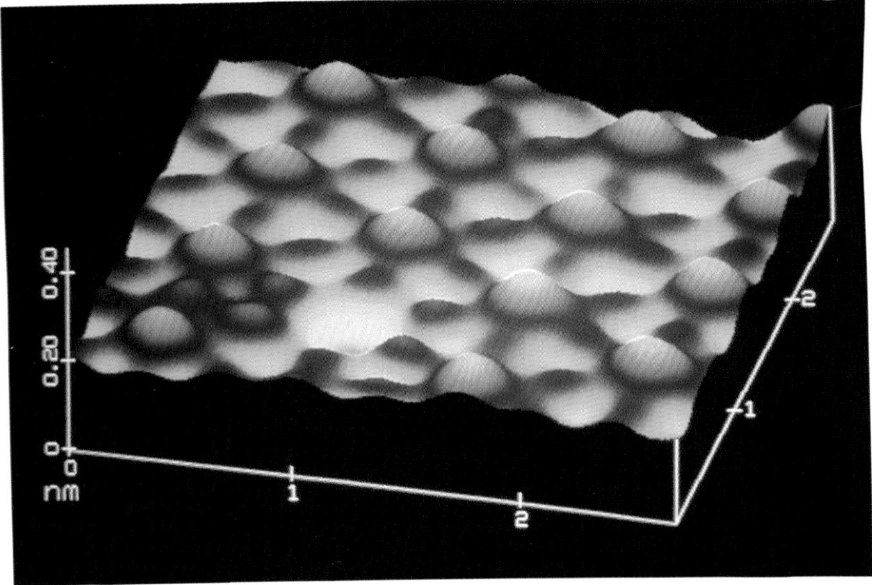

This STM image shows iodine atoms (on a platinum surface) as a series of peaks with pink tops. The colour was added to the image during computer analysis of the data from the probe. Note the 'vacancy' where an iodine atom is missing.

The STM image above of xenon atoms manipulated on a nickel surface must have pleased the sponsors of the research. The same company produced the image to the right using iron atoms on copper which contains the Kanji characters for 'atom' (the literal translation resembles 'original child').

SUMMARY

- Matter is made up of atoms.
- The atoms in a given element are all of the same kind.
- A compound contains atoms of two or more elements combined in fixed proportions.
- Atoms are very small – about 10^{-10} m in diameter.

> **Discussion point**
>
> Would you say that the STM enables us to *see* individual atoms?

PRACTICE

1 Dalton's atomic theory is based on four postulates. Give an example for each one of these, to explain what they mean.

2 The diameter of a typical atom is 10^{-10} m. How many atoms would cover the area of a printed full stop? You can assume that a full stop is 0.1 mm in diameter and that atoms are spherical.

2.2 THE DISCOVERY OF THE E[illegible]

OBJECTIVES

- Early evidence for atomic structure
- The negatively charged electron

Dalton's atomic theory of matter steadily gained acceptance during the second half of the nineteenth century, but there was still a long way to go before the modern theory became fully developed. Following Dalton's work it was at first thought that atoms could not be broken down into anything simpler. (In fact, the word 'atom' is derived from the Greek *atomos*, meaning 'indivisible'.) The first indication that atoms have an internal structure came with the discovery of the electron. The mass of the electron is far smaller than the mass of any atom so, the reasoning went, ordinary neutral atoms must also contain a massive positively charged part. We mainly owe our modern ideas on atoms to the experiments and thinking of three people: the Englishman J. J. Thomson, the New Zealander Ernest Rutherford, and the young Englishman Henry Moseley. The last two of these will take centre stage in the next spread.

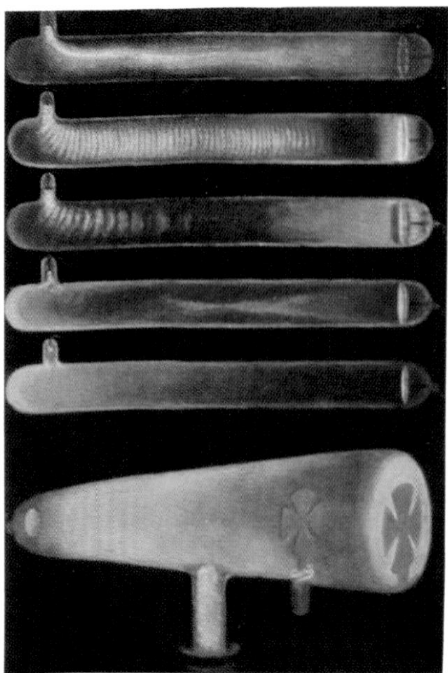

Cathode rays (electrons) stream from the cathode. As the pressure in the tube is reduced, a changing pattern of colourful lights occurs. At low pressure, the inner surface of the glass glows. A metal cross placed in the path of the electrons casts a sharp shadow, showing that they travel in straight lines.

J. J. Thomson and the electron

During the 1870s, physicists carried out experiments into the electrical conductivity of gases. They used a piece of apparatus called a 'discharge tube', which was a long glass tube fitted with a metal electrode at each end. When the gas inside was at very low pressure, a green glow appeared in the glass at the end of the tube furthest from the cathode (the negative electrode). Scientists proved that the glow was caused by invisible rays originating from the cathode and travelling away from it in straight lines. In 1895 the French physicist Jean Perrin placed a metal cylinder inside the tube to collect the 'cathode rays'. The charge on the cylinder showed that cathode rays are negatively charged.

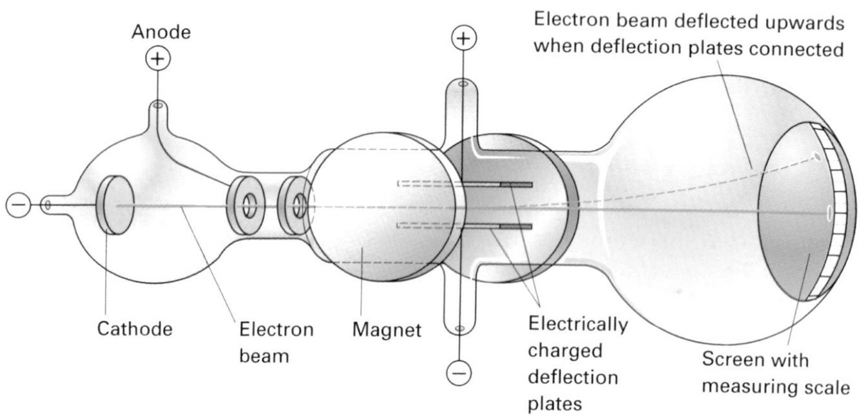

Thomson's apparatus for determining the charge/mass ratio (e/m) of electrons. The rays (electrons) from the cathode pass through a slit in the anode and exit from the slit as a narrow beam. The beam is deflected by a vertical electric field and a horizontal magnetic field, whose strengths are known. The beam strikes a fluorescent screen and appears as a dot on the measuring scale.

In 1897, J. J. Thomson deflected cathode rays with both electric and magnetic fields, and used his results to measure the ratio of their charge to their mass. He reasoned that, if cathode rays have mass, then they must be composed of a stream of particles. We now call these particles **electrons**. Thomson assumed the charge to be the same as the smallest charge observed during electrolysis, and so calculated the mass of an electron to be nearly 2000 times smaller than the mass of a hydrogen atom.

Joseph John (J. J.) Thomson (1856–1940) with the apparatus he used to determine the charge/mass ratio of the electron.

The 'plum pudding' model of the atom

Atoms have no overall charge; they are **neutral**. So, there must be a part of the atom that is positively charged, to balance the negative charge of the electrons. At the end of the nineteenth century, scientists understood that the atom had positively and negatively charged components, and that the negatively charged components had a very low mass.

J. J. Thomson proposed a model that described atoms as negatively charged electrons embedded in a sphere of positive charge. It became known as the 'plum pudding' model because the electrons were spread randomly throughout the positive charge like the dried fruit in a pudding. This model was soon shown to be inadequate.

The name 'electron'

The name 'electron' had been coined in 1891 by Johnstone Stoney, who suggested that this name would be appropriate for a fundamental electrically charged particle within atoms. Thomson called the very light particles found in this cathode-ray experiments 'corpuscles'. It was Hendrik Lorentz (see spread 14.4) who pointed out (in 1899) that Thomson had in fact found Stoney's electrons.

SUMMARY

- The electron has a negative charge; its mass is very small compared to that of an atom.
- Cathode rays are electrons.

PRACTICE

1 Look at the diagram of Thomson's *e/m* apparatus. Describe what would happen if you could reverse the + and – connections to the deflection plates.

2.3 THE NUCLEUS AND PROTONS

OBJECTIVES

- The nucleus contains protons
- Atomic number as a basis for the periodic table

Answers to questions often suggest further questions. In response to the question, 'What is inside atoms?', Thomson showed that they contain electrons. In this spread we explain how Rutherford subsequently demonstrated that a massive nucleus lies at their centre. A further conclusion was that the electrons surrounding the nucleus define the overall size of an atom. Of course, chemists were not content to let the matter rest at that point. They started thinking 'What is inside the nucleus?' Henry Moseley made the crucial breakthrough.

The Geiger–Marsden experiment

In 1909, Ernest Rutherford suggested to his colleague Hans Geiger that their young student Ernest Marsden might start a little research project. The project involved measuring the deflection of alpha particles as they struck a thin sheet of gold foil less than one micrometre (1 μm) thick. Alpha particles were known to be positively charged. Predictions based on Thomson's model of the atom suggested that the alpha particles would be deflected by a few degrees from the straight-ahead direction when they passed through the gold foil.

Geiger and Marsden made two unexpected observations. First, the vast majority of the alpha particles were deflected by less than one degree, showing that they must have passed through essentially empty space. Secondly, a few (about 1 in 8000) actually bounced *back* towards the source. Rutherford remarked that this was 'almost as incredible as if you had fired a 15-inch shell at a piece of tissue paper and it had bounced back and hit you'.

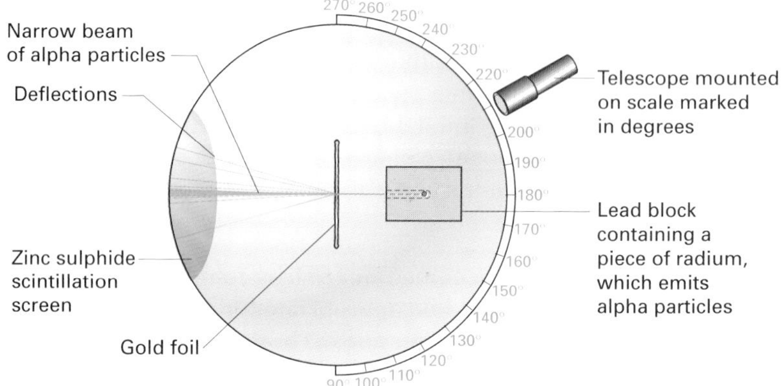

The Geiger–Marsden apparatus. A radioactive substance emits high-speed alpha particles. After passing through the foil, they produce visible scintillations (flashes of light) on a fluorescent screen. The angle of deviation of an alpha particle from the straight-ahead direction can be measured from the position of the flash on the screen.

The atom: mostly empty space

A new model of the atom was needed to account for the results of the Geiger–Marsden experiment. In 1911 Rutherford proposed that the atom has at its centre a very small positively charged **nucleus**, which contains almost all the mass of the atom. This nucleus is tiny and the rest of the atom is mostly empty space. (If you magnified an atom to the size of a football stadium, its nucleus would be about the size of a pea.) So, most of the alpha particles passed through empty space. Only very rarely would one travel close enough to the nucleus to be repelled strongly by the dense concentration of positive charge. Sufficient electrons surround the nucleus of an atom to balance the charge of the nucleus and to make the atom neutral overall.

Positive particles called protons

Between 1917 and 1921, Rutherford bombarded six different elements with alpha particles. He discovered that the nuclei of boron, nitrogen,

(a)

Alpha particles

Foil

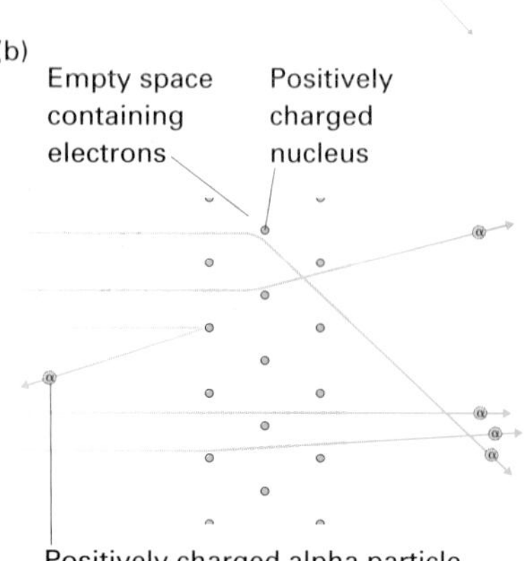

Diagram (a) summarizes the results of Geiger and Marsden and (b) shows Rutherford's interpretation of them. The size of the nucleus is greatly exaggerated for clarity.

fluorine, sodium, aluminium, and phosphorus all gave out the same positive particle, which was identical to the nucleus of the hydrogen atom. Because this was the first particle found in the nucleus, he called it the 'proton' (from the Greek *protos*, meaning 'first'). Rutherford concluded that protons made up the positive part of the nuclei of all elements. The proton carries a positive charge of exactly the same magnitude as the negative charge on the electron.

Radioactivity

α particles are helium nuclei;
β particles are electrons.
Exposure to radioctivity should be avoided where possible as radiation can damage human tissue. See spread 15.7 for an explanation of half-life.

The number of protons

The number of electrons in an atom equals the number of protons in its nucleus. The number of protons is called the **atomic number** (also called **proton number**) of the element concerned. In 1913 Henry Moseley found that when he bombarded elements with high-speed electrons, they emitted X-rays. He observed that the frequency of the emitted X-rays depended on the element used. Moseley plotted a graph of atomic number against the square root of the X-ray frequency. The result was a straight-line plot.

Henry Moseley 1887–1915

Moseley was killed in the Gallipoli Campaign during the First World War. The War Office only later understood the magnitude of the loss to science (and hence possibly to the war effort). From that point onwards, valuable scientists were never again allowed to serve in the Front Line.

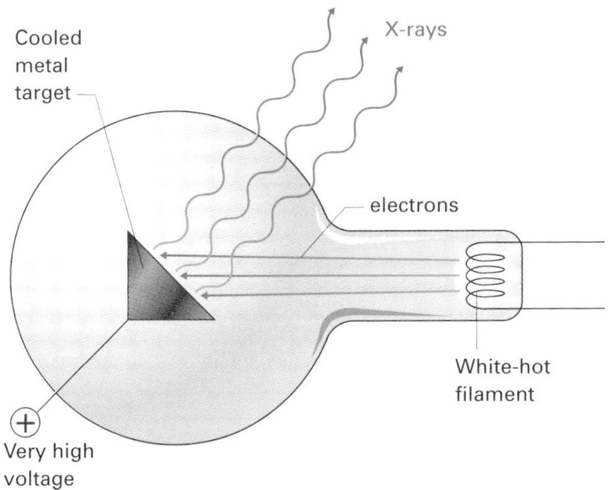

In a typical X-ray apparatus, a heated wire filament emits electrons. They accelerate towards a metal target, which has a very high positive voltage (typically 25 000 volts).

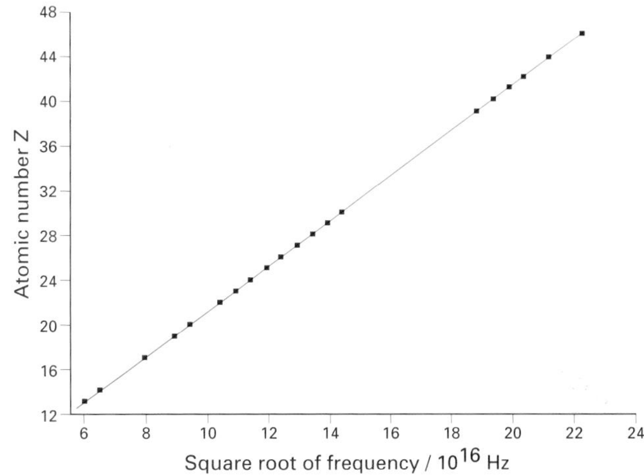

The plot of Moseley's results shows that there is a linear dependence between the atomic number of the element concerned and the square root of the frequency of the emitted X-rays.

It is easy to miss the importance of this result. Remember that Mendeleyev had arranged the elements in his periodic table in order of increasing relative atomic mass. He had then been forced to change the positions of some elements (notably iodine) to ensure that his vertical groups contained elements with similar properties. Moseley's graph listed the elements in their final order in the periodic table. Atomic number is therefore a more fundamental property of an element than its relative atomic mass. The atomic number of an element distinguishes it from all others because it specifies the number of protons in the nucleus.

The historical attraction Oxford Story recreates Moseley's study as it would have looked in 1913. His original apparatus is preserved in the Museum of Science which is also in Broad Street, Oxford.

SUMMARY

- The atom has at its centre a very small, positively charged nucleus.
- Amost all the mass of an atom is concentrated in the nucleus.
- The nucleus of an atom contains protons.
- The proton has a positive charge.
- The charge on a proton is equal in magnitude, and opposite in sign, to the charge on an electron.
- The total positive charge on the nucleus equals the total negative charge of the electrons.
- The atomic number of an element equals the number of protons in its nucleus.
- The atomic number of an element distinguishes that element from all others.

2.4

OBJECTIVES

- The discovery of the neutron
- Mass number
- Comparison of electrons, protons, and neutrons
- Isotopes

THE NUCLEUS AND NEUTRONS

Having discovered the proton, Rutherford was immediately faced with another problem. He could explain the *charge* on the nucleus of an atom in terms of the number of protons in it. However, there were always (except in the case of hydrogen) too few protons to explain the *mass* of the nucleus. He suggested that there must be another, uncharged, particle present in the nucleus. Rutherford introduced the term **neutron** for these particles in 1921, but they remained a theoretical speculation.

The neutron

Experimental evidence for the neutron was found in 1932, when James Chadwick bombarded the element beryllium with alpha particles. This bombardment produced a highly penetrating stream of particles, which could pass through many centimetres of solid lead and which was not deflected by electric or magnetic fields. Chadwick decided that the stream must consist of particles with almost the same mass as protons but with no charge. Chadwick had detected the neutrons postulated earlier by Rutherford. Protons and neutrons are collectively known as **nucleons** because they are both found in the nucleus.

The winning team – Ernest Rutherford and research colleagues at the Cavendish Laboratory, Cambridge, in 1920. James Chadwick (discoverer of the neutron) is at the extreme left of the middle row. J. J. Thomson (electron) and Ernest Rutherford (proton) are three and four places, respectively, to Chadwick's left. G. P. Thomson is sitting next to Chadwick.

The strong interaction

Why do nuclei not fly apart? They contain protons packed together in a very small space, but the protons do not seem to follow the rule that 'like charges repel, unlike charges attract'. The explanation is that neutrons and protons participate in an even stronger *attractive* force. This **strong interaction** is about 100 times stronger than charge repulsion or attraction, but only operates over very short distances in the nucleus (about 10^{-15} m).

Protons, neutrons, and mass number

An atom consists of a nucleus surrounded by electrons. The nucleus is positively charged because it contains positively charged protons. All atoms of the same element contain the same number of protons. The number of protons in an atom defines its atomic number and hence its identity as an element. Atoms of the same element all have the same atomic number.

Neutrons have almost the same mass as protons, so they contribute to the mass of an atom. The **mass number** (also called **nucleon number**) of an atom is defined as the sum of the numbers of protons and neutrons in the atom's nucleus. For example, the nucleus of a fluorine atom contains 9 protons and 10 neutrons. So, the atomic number of fluorine is 9 and its mass number is 19 (9 + 10).

Full symbols for atoms

An atom is defined by its atomic number. Chemists often incorporate the atomic number and the mass number into the symbol for an element. The full symbol for fluorine is $^{19}_{9}F$. The subscript 9 is the atomic number, and the superscript 19 is the mass number. From this full symbol you can work out that an atom of fluorine consists of 9 protons, 10 neutrons, and 9 electrons. As a further short-hand, the subscript (for the atomic number) can be omitted; thus you can write the symbol for fluorine as ^{19}F.

- The number of electrons in a neutral atom always equals the number of protons.
- The number of neutrons equals the mass number minus the atomic number.

Neutrons and isotopes

Atoms of the same element always have the same number of protons, but may have different numbers of neutrons. Atoms with the same number of protons but different numbers of neutrons are called **isotopes**. A **nuclide** is an isotope with a specified mass number. For example, naturally occurring chlorine consists of two isotopes, ^{35}Cl (17 protons and 18 neutrons) and ^{37}Cl (17 protons and 20 neutrons). The proportion of each isotope in a sample is called its **relative abundance**. The relative abundance of ^{35}Cl is 75.8% and of ^{37}Cl is 24.2%.

Isotopes and relative atomic mass

Most elements exist naturally as two or more different isotopes. The mass of an element therefore depends on the relative abundances of all the isotopes present in the sample. The **relative atomic mass** A_r of an element is defined as the mass of one atom of that element relative to 1/12th the mass of one atom of carbon-12 (i.e. ^{12}C = exactly 12). The relative atomic mass is the average of the masses of the stable isotopes of the element, weighted to take into account the relative abundance of each isotope. (Note that the term **relative isotopic mass** refers to the mass of a specific isotope.) For the example of chlorine given above, the relative atomic mass is calculated as follows:

$$A_r(\mathrm{Cl}) = \left(\frac{75.8}{100} \times 35\right) + \left(\frac{24.2}{100} \times 37\right) = 35.5$$

So the relative atomic mass of chlorine is 35.5.

SUMMARY

- The neutron has zero charge and almost the same mass as the proton.
- Protons and neutrons are called nucleons because they are found in the nucleus of an atom.
- The mass number is the sum of the numbers of protons and neutrons in the nucleus of an atom.
- Isotopes of an element have the same number of protons but different numbers of neutrons; they therefore have different masses.
- A nuclide is an isotope with a specified mass number.
- The relative atomic mass of an element is the average mass of one atom of the element relative to 1/12th the mass of one atom of carbon-12.

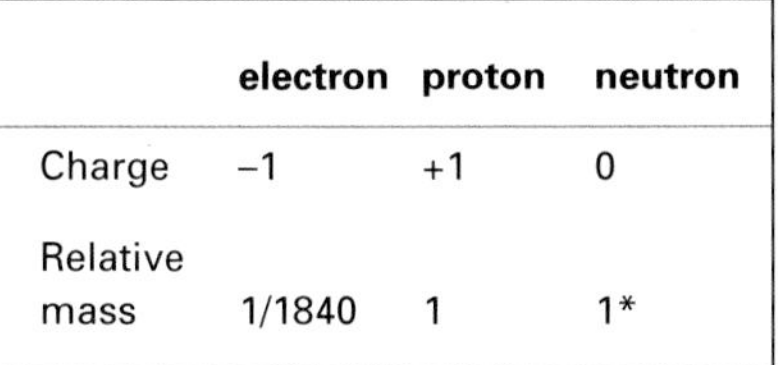

	electron	proton	neutron
Charge	−1	+1	0
Relative mass	1/1840	1	1*

*The charges and approximate relative masses of electrons, protons, and neutrons. *The mass of the neutron is 1.001 38 times the mass of the proton.*

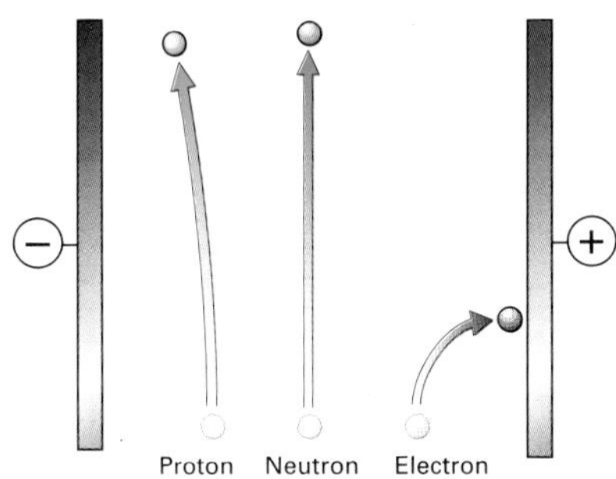

In an electric field, a neutron is not deflected, being neutral. A proton is deflected in the opposite direction to an electron; it is deflected less because it is heavier.

Symbols

The full symbols for protons, neutrons, and electrons are $^{1}_{1}p$, $^{1}_{0}n$, and $^{0}_{-1}e$.

Magnesium – three isotopes

The calculation of relative atomic mass is similar when the element has more than two isotopes. For example, naturally occurring magnesium has the following isotopic composition:

^{24}Mg = 79.0%, ^{25}Mg = 10.0%, ^{26}Mg = 11.0%

The relative atomic mass of magnesium is calculated as:

$$A_r(\mathrm{Mg}) = \left(\frac{79.0}{100} \times 24\right) + \left(\frac{10.0}{100} \times 25\right) + \left(\frac{11.0}{100} \times 26\right) = 24.3$$

Relative isotopic mass

The mass number of an isotope, the sum of the numbers of protons and neutrons, is an integer. Relative isotopic masses are, however, *not* integers, because protons and neutrons have very slightly different masses (see table above).

PRACTICE

1 Give the number of protons, neutrons, and electrons in:
a ^{35}Cl **b** ^{24}Mg **c** ^{235}U.

2 Give the atomic number and mass number for each of the isotopes in question 1.

3 Calculate the relative atomic mass of silicon with the following isotopic composition:
^{28}Si = 92.2%, ^{29}Si = 4.7%, ^{30}Si = 3.1%.

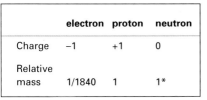

3 Masses of atoms and the mole

Chemists are interested in atoms and how they react together. They want to know about two main aspects of chemical reactions: the *qualitative* and the *quantitative*. Examples of qualitative questions are: 'What happens if I heat substance *x* with substance *y*?' and 'Why does that mixture explode when I drop it on the floor?' Quantitative questions are concerned with the 'how much' aspects of chemistry. A typical question would be: 'What mass of substance *x* will react with 10 g of substance *y*?' Quantitative questions are particularly important in the chemical industry: adding too much of a reagent will result in unnecessary cost and may also contaminate the product. The aim of this chapter is to show how you can calculate the quantities of reactants and products involved in chemical reactions. To do this you need to understand relative formula masses and the concept of the *mole*.

Finding the masses of atoms

3.1

OBJECTIVES

- Relative atomic mass
- Relative formula mass

During an earlier science course, you may have seen the following spectacular but *very* dangerous demonstration. Mix iron(III) oxide powder with aluminium powder in a clay crucible. Insert a strip of magnesium ribbon to act as a fuse, light the end of the ribbon, and move back to a safe distance. When the reaction has died down, a red-hot lump of iron will be found amongst the shattered remains of the crucible. The balanced chemical equation below shows the number of atoms involved and how they react together:

$$Fe_2O_3(s) + 2Al(s) \rightarrow 2Fe(l) + Al_2O_3(s)$$

The equation shows *how many atoms* react, but it does not indicate directly the *masses* that react. To find the answer to this question, we need to consider the masses of atoms themselves.

Iron(III) oxide and aluminium react to produce molten iron, which can weld railway lines together (the Thermit process). The correct masses must be used for a successful reaction.

Relative atomic mass

The masses of individual atoms are too small to be used in calculations on chemical reactions. So instead, the mass of an atom is expressed relative to a chosen standard atomic mass:

- The relative atomic mass of an element is the average mass of one atom of the element relative to 1/12th the mass of one atom of carbon-12.

The symbol for relative atomic mass is A_r.

On this scale, A_r for carbon-12 is *exactly* 12. The value of A_r for carbon given in a data book is 12.01 (to two decimal places). This figure illustrates the meaning of the phrase 'average mass of one atom of the element' in the definition above. Carbon occurs naturally as a mixture of carbon-12 (98.9%) and carbon-13 (1.1%). If the A_r value for a specific isotope is quoted, the name given is *relative isotopic mass* (see final spread in previous chapter).

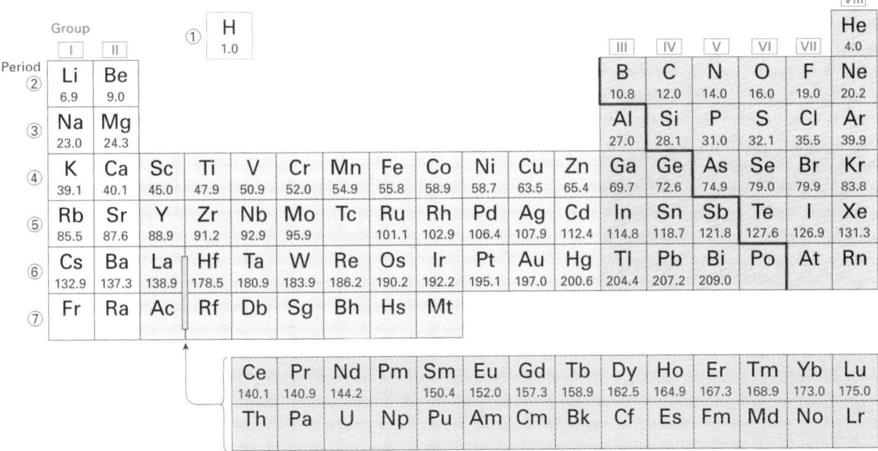

Periodic table of the elements showing relative atomic masses. Values are left out if an element has no stable isotope.

Relative atomic masses are known with great precision, usually to at least three decimal places. The values in the table above are consistently given to one decimal place. It is important to understand that, because A_r *compares* the masses of atoms, it does not itself have units. The scale is *relative*; one mass is divided by another mass and so the ratio has no units.

Relative formula mass

Atoms combine to form compounds. The formula of a compound shows the ratio in which the atoms combine. For example, the formula of water is H_2O; two atoms of hydrogen combine with one atom of oxygen. The formula of aluminium oxide is Al_2O_3; two atoms of aluminium combine with three atoms of oxygen. The idea of relative atomic masses can be extended to compounds:

- The **relative formula mass** of a compound is the sum of the relative atomic masses of all the atoms present in its formula.

The symbol for relative formula mass is M_r.

From the table above, A_r for hydrogen is 1.0, for oxygen is 16.0, and for aluminium is 27.0. The relative formula mass for water is:

$$(2 \times 1.0) + (1 \times 16.0) = 18.0$$

The relative formula mass for aluminium oxide is:

$$(2 \times 27.0) + (3 \times 16.0) = 102.0$$

These calculations allow us to compare the masses of atoms and compounds with each other. Calculating the actual masses that react depends on the idea of the *mole*, which is described later in this chapter. The concept of the 'mole' cannot be used successfully without a grasp of relative formula mass, so try the questions below to check your understanding.

Relative molecular mass

'Relative molecular mass' is the traditional name used for 'relative formula mass'. The modern name is better because the traditional term 'relative molecular mass' really refers only to compounds composed of molecules.

SUMMARY

- Relative atomic mass has no units.
- The relative formula mass (M_r) is the sum of the relative atomic masses of all the atoms present in the formula of a compound.

PRACTICE

1 Write down the relative atomic masses of: beryllium; boron; calcium; carbon; iron; manganese; phosphorus; sodium; xenon.

2 Calculate the relative formula masses of:

a N_2; CO_2; $CaCO_3$; H_2SO_4.

b ammonia; sulphur dioxide; methane; nitric acid.

3.2

OBJECTIVES

- The mass spectrometer
- Interpreting mass spectra

THE MASS SPECTROMETER

The relative atomic mass of an element is the average mass of one atom of the element relative to 1/12th the mass of one atom of carbon-12. In order to calculate the average mass, the masses of the isotopes of the element must be known, together with their relative abundances. These values are found using an instrument called the *mass spectrometer*.

Ions

A **positive ion** has more protons than electrons, whereas a **negative ion** has more electrons than protons.

The mass spectrometer

The diagram below illustrates the operating principles of a mass spectrometer. There are four main steps:

1 *Ionization*. A sample of the element is introduced as a vapour (the element may need to be heated if it is a solid). In the ionization chamber, an *electron gun* (a heated wire filament) produces a beam of high-energy electrons. When hit by the electron beam, an atom in the chamber can lose an electron and form a *positive ion*.

2 *Acceleration*. The acceleration chamber uses an *electric field* to accelerate the positive ions to high speed.

3 *Deflection*. The stream of fast-moving ions is deflected sideways as it passes through a *magnetic field*. The deflecting force depends only on the charge of the ions and not on their mass. So the same deflecting force acts on all singly positively charged ions. Lighter ions are therefore deflected more than heavier ions.

4 *Detection*. Ions of the same charge and mass will all follow one particular path. This stream of ions is detected by an instrument, such as an *electrometer*, that can detect charged particles.

A magnetic field can deflect a stream of charged particles. Here a fine beam of electrons is bent into a circle by a magnetic field at right angles to their direction of motion.

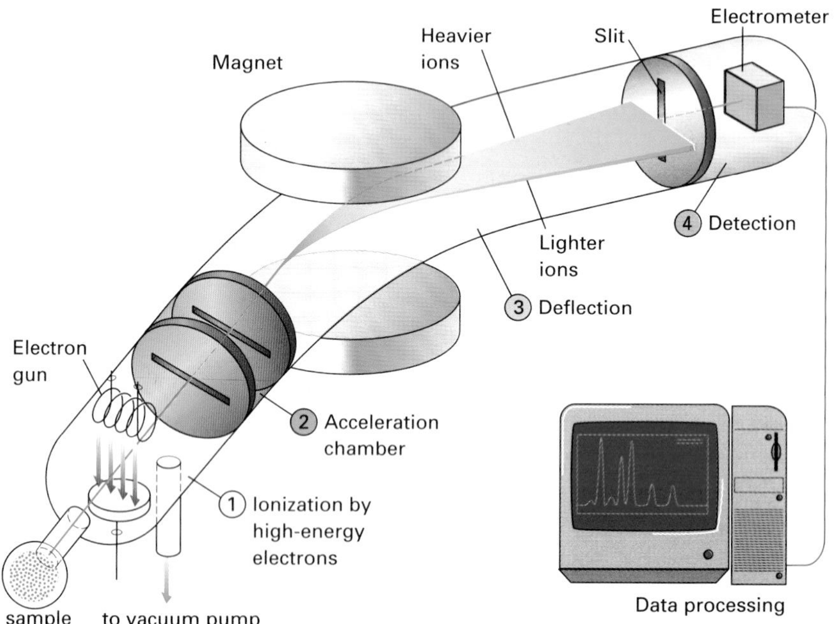

The principal parts of the mass spectrometer. Deflection only occurs within the magnetic field.

The need for a vacuum

The space inside a mass spectrometer is connected to a vacuum pump. The ions under investigation must be able to move freely. The machine would not work properly if the ions collided with the molecules of oxygen and nitrogen that are present in the atmosphere. So a vacuum is needed inside the apparatus.

The path of a given ion depends on its mass m and its charge e, and specifically on its m/e ratio. The energy of the electron gun is usually set to form only ions with a charge of 1+ (called **unipositive** ions). An ion will enter the detector only when the strength of the magnetic field has the appropriate value. In practice, the strength of the magnetic field is steadily increased. Ions of successively higher mass enter the detector, and all others strike the internal walls of the machine.

The stream of ions entering the detector makes an electric current. The magnitude of the current depends on the number of ions entering the detector per unit time. The relative abundances of different isotopes are calculated by comparing the magnitudes of their currents

Interpreting a mass spectrum

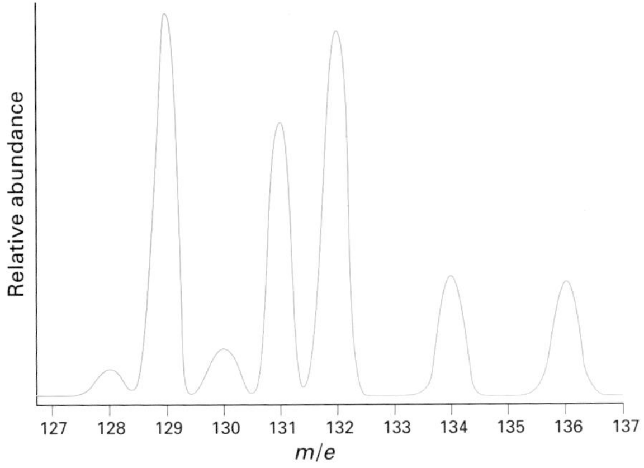

The mass spectrum for naturally occurring xenon. The horizontal axis is the mass-to-charge ratio m/e. As all ions are assumed to be unipositive, this measures the isotopic mass. The vertical axis shows the relative abundance.

A commercial mass spectrometer like this can be used to produce the spectrum shown to the left.

The mass spectrum (plural = spectra) for lead gives the following information:

Isotope	Detector current/arbitrary units
204	0.16
206	2.72
207	2.50
208	5.92

The total detector current is (0.16 + 2.72 + 2.50 + 5.92) = 11.30. The relative abundance of lead-206 is therefore $\frac{2.72}{11.30} \times 100\% = 24.1\%$. Similar calculations give the following results:

Isotope	Relative abundance/%
204	1.4
206	24.1
207	22.1
208	52.4

The relative atomic mass of lead can now be calculated:

$$A_r = \left(\frac{1.4}{100} \times 204\right) + \left(\frac{24.1}{100} \times 206\right) + \left(\frac{22.1}{100} \times 207\right) + \left(\frac{52.4}{100} \times 208\right)$$

$$= 207.2$$

SUMMARY

- The mass spectrometer produces positive ions by ionization, which are accelerated by an electric field; a magnetic field then deflects the paths of the ions, which are collected by a detector.
- The magnitudes of the detector currents of different isotopes are proportional to their relative abundances.
- The mass spectrometer can be used to determine relative atomic masses.

Data presentation

Most modern mass spectrometers are equipped with microprocessors, which provide a numerical display of the masses of the isotopes and their relative abundances. Simpler machines display results in the form of a trace called a *mass spectrum*. Both types of display give the information needed to calculate the relative atomic mass of an element.

Space probes

Mass spectrometers are frequent passengers on space probes. The Viking spacecraft found that the atmosphere of Mars was mostly carbon dioxide.

PRACTICE

1 A mass spectrometer provided the information on the right for a sample of naturally occurring germanium.
Calculate the relative atomic mass for germanium.

Isotope	Detector current/arbitrary units
70	6.83
72	9.13
73	2.60
74	12.17
76	2.60

THE MOLE

OBJECTIVES

- The mole
- Avogadro constant
- Molar mass
- Amount of substance

Chemical reactions change reactants into products. The atoms that make up the reactants rearrange to form the products. When carrying out a chemical reaction, the correct quantity of each reactant must be used for all the reactants to change into products. However, the balanced chemical equation for a reaction only gives precise information about the *numbers* of atoms involved. It is not possible to count out individual atoms: they are too small to be of any use in the measurement of reacting masses. Instead, chemists use the concept of the *mole*, which allows them to count atoms by weighing them.

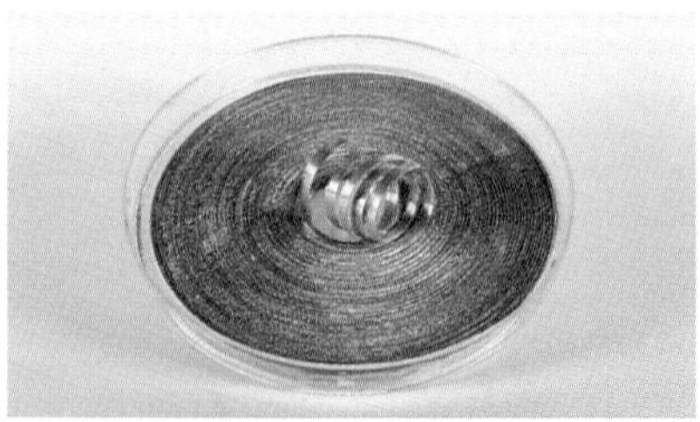

Each of these samples consists of one mole of an element. Each sample contains 6.02×10^{23} atoms. From top to bottom, the elements are magnesium, copper, mercury (which is very dense), carbon, and iodine.

The mole

A bank clerk (and the bank's customers!) would find it very tedious to count out individual coins to confirm that a customer had paid in the correct number of coins. Instead of counting them out individually, the clerks know the mass of a chosen number of each coin. For example, they count ten-pence pieces in collections of 50, and fifty-pence pieces in collections of 20. They can then weigh a bag of coins to confirm that the correct number of coins is present.

In a similar fashion, atoms are too small to be counted individually on a routine basis. So, chemists also count atoms by weighing a collection of them. The connection between the microscopic world of atoms and the everyday world of balances is that the mass of a particular fixed number of atoms is known.

The number of atoms in exactly 12 g of carbon-12 is chosen as the standard, because carbon-12 is the standard chosen for relative atomic mass:

- The number of atoms in exactly 12 g of carbon-12 is called one mole.
- The number of atoms per mole is called the **Avogadro constant**.

As a unit, we use the abbreviation 'mol' for mole. The symbol L is used for the Avogadro constant.

The mass of a single carbon-12 atom has been found (using a mass spectrometer) to be 1.993×10^{-23} g, and so the Avogadro constant L has the value

$$\begin{aligned} L &= \frac{\text{mass per mole of } ^{12}\text{C}}{\text{mass of one atom of } ^{12}\text{C}} \\ &= \frac{12\,\text{g mol}^{-1}}{1.993 \times 10^{-23}\,\text{g}} \\ &= 6.02 \times 10^{23}\,\text{mol}^{-1} \end{aligned}$$

The relative atomic mass of carbon-12 is exactly 12, by definition; that of magnesium-24 is 24. So one atom of magnesium-24 has twice the mass of one atom of carbon-12. However many atoms are chosen, a given number of magnesium-24 atoms always has twice the mass of the same number of atoms of carbon-12. So one mole of magnesium-24 atoms has twice the mass of one mole of carbon-12 atoms.

Molar mass

The mass per mole of an atom is called its **molar mass**, M. The molar mass has the same numerical value as the relative atomic mass, *but it also has units* of grams per mole (g mol^{-1}).

The concept of the mole can be extended to compounds. Once again, the mass per mole of the compound is called its **molar mass**. The molar mass of a compound has the same numerical value as the relative formula mass, but it also has units of grams per mole (g mol^{-1}). One mole of any object always contains 6.02×10^{23} copies of that object.

A very big number

One mole (1 mol) of particles contains 6.02×10^{23} of those particles. This number of grains of sand would cover the surface of the Earth to a depth of about 2 metres. The mole lives up to the meaning of its name: 'massive heap'.

There is nothing unusual in counting using a named collection of items: farmers count eggs in dozens (12); and shopkeepers sell sheets of paper in reams (500). Now we see that chemists count atoms using moles. The mole is simply the chemist's equivalent of the dozen or the ream. The numbers involved are much, much larger, but the principle is the same.

Amount of substance

The physical quantity **amount of substance** (symbol n) is measured in moles. **One mole** (1 mol) is the amount of any substance that contains the same number of particles as there are atoms in exactly 12 g of carbon-12. The particles (atoms, molecules, ions, etc.) need to be carefully specified.

For example, 1 mol C contains one mole of carbon atoms; 1 mol H_2O contains one mole of water molecules; 1 mol NaCl contains one mole of sodium chloride ion pairs, i.e. one mole of sodium ions and one mole of chloride ions. In each case, the *formula* indicates the species concerned.

> **Amount**
>
> Because the word 'amount' is used so imprecisely in everyday speech, we will emphasize the scientific use by using the term **amount in moles**.

Calculations: mass, molar mass, and amount in moles

The amount in moles (n) in a sample, the mass of the sample (m), and its molar mass (M) are related by the expression:

$$\text{amount in moles} = \frac{\text{mass}}{\text{molar mass}} \quad \text{or} \quad n = \frac{m}{M}$$

Suppose a sample of carbon has a mass of 3.0 g. The molar mass of carbon C is 12.0 g mol^{-1}. The amount in moles of carbon in the sample may be calculated by substitution into the above expression:

$$n = \frac{m}{M} = \frac{3.0\,\text{g}}{12.0\,\text{g mol}^{-1}} = 0.25\,\text{mol}$$

That is, 3.0 g of carbon contains 0.25 mol of carbon atoms.

The expression for amount in moles may be rearranged in two ways to make mass, or molar mass, the subject:

$$\text{mass} = \text{amount in moles} \times \text{molar mass} \quad \text{or} \quad m = nM$$

and

$$\text{molar mass} = \frac{\text{mass}}{\text{amount in moles}} \quad \text{or} \quad M = \frac{m}{n}$$

> **Mass calculation**
>
> What is the mass of 2.00 mol of neon [A_r(Ne) = 20.2]?
>
> We have
>
> amount in moles = 2.00 mol
>
> molar mass = 20.2 g mol^{-1}
>
> So
>
> mass = amount in moles × molar mass
>
> = (2.00 mol) × (20.2 g mol^{-1})
>
> = 40.4 g

> **Molar mass calculation**
>
> A pure sample of lithium has a mass of 1.39 g and contains 0.200 mol of lithium. What is the molar mass of lithium?
>
> We have
>
> mass = 1.39 g
>
> amount in moles = 0.200 mol
>
> So
>
> $$\text{molar mass} = \frac{\text{mass}}{\text{amount in moles}} = \frac{1.39\,\text{g}}{0.200\,\text{mol}} = 6.95\,\text{g mol}^{-1}$$

SUMMARY

- One mole is the amount of any substance that contains the same number of particles as there are atoms in exactly 12 g of carbon-12.
- The number of particles per mole (6.02×10^{23} mol^{-1}) is the Avogadro constant.
- The molar mass of a substance is its mass per mole. It has the same numerical value as the relative formula mass.

PRACTICE

1 Calculate the mass in grams of:

a 2 mol of carbon atoms [A_r(C) = 12.0]

b 0.5 mol of magnesium atoms [A_r(Mg) = 24.3]

c 0.01 mol of aluminium atoms [A_r(Al) = 27.0]

d 5 mol of sodium atoms [A_r(Na) = 23.0]

e 5 mol of sodium ions Na^+.

2 Calculate the mass in kilograms of:

a 1000 mol of iron atoms [A_r(Fe) = 55.9]

b 1×10^4 mol of tungsten atoms [A_r(W) = 183.9]

c 1×10^{-3} mol of hydrogen atoms [A_r(H) = 1.0].

3 Calculate the amount in moles (to 3 sig. figs) of atoms in:

a 23.0 g of sodium

b 62.0 g of phosphorus [A_r(P) = 31.0]

c 10.0 g of calcium [A_r(Ca) = 40.1].

3.4

Finding molar masses

OBJECTIVES

- Diatomic molecules
- Covalent compounds
- Ionic compounds

Some elements exist as separate atoms, e.g. He and Ne. Some elements exist as molecules consisting of two or more atoms joined together, e.g. O_2 and S_8. **Compounds** consist of two or more atoms of *different* elements bonded together, e.g. HCl, NH_3, NaBr, and H_2SO_4. The molar mass of any of these substances may be derived from its chemical formula. This spread shows you how.

Diatomic molecules

Elements such as neon consist of separate atoms. Therefore 1 mol Ne contains one mole of neon atoms. Elements such as oxygen (O_2), hydrogen (H_2), and chlorine (Cl_2) exist as diatomic molecules. A **diatomic molecule** contains two atoms. 1 mol O_2 contains 6.02×10^{23} oxygen *molecules*. It is also true to say that one mole of oxygen molecules contains two moles of oxygen atoms, because each oxygen molecule contains two atoms of oxygen.

Iodine consists of I_2 molecules. The relative atomic mass of iodine is 126.9. The molar mass of I_2 is therefore $2 \times 126.9 = 253.8$ g mol^{-1} Note that this sample is twice the size of that shown in the previous spread: this is one mole of I_2 ***molecules.***

A ball-and-stick model of an iodine molecule.

Worked examples on calculating the molar mass of a diatomic molecule

We shall look at two examples, oxygen O_2 and chlorine Cl_2.

The relative atomic mass of oxygen is 16.0.
1 mol of oxygen atoms O therefore has a mass of 16.0 g.
1 mol of oxygen *molecules* O_2 has a mass of
$2 \times (16.0\,g) = 32.0\,g$.

By similar reasoning,
1 mol of chlorine molecules Cl_2 [$A_r(Cl) = 35.5$] has a mass of
$2 \times (35.5\,g) = 71.0\,g$.
It follows that the molar mass of chlorine Cl_2 is 71.0 g mol^{-1}.

Covalent compounds

Covalent compounds consist of atoms bonded together to form molecules. Examples include carbon dioxide CO_2, water H_2O, and ammonia NH_3. The chemical formula of a covalent compound identifies the numbers of atoms of each element making up each molecule. The formula of carbon dioxide is CO_2, indicating that each molecule of carbon dioxide consists of one carbon atom bonded to two oxygen atoms.

Worked examples on calculating the molar mass of a covalent compound

We shall look at two examples, carbon dioxide CO_2 and ammonia NH_3.
One mole (1 mol) of carbon dioxide molecules contains 6.02×10^{23} carbon dioxide molecules. Each of these molecules contains one atom of carbon bonded to two atoms of oxygen.

The molar mass of carbon C is 12.0 g mol^{-1}.
The molar mass of oxygen O is 16.0 g mol^{-1}.
The molar mass of carbon dioxide CO_2 is therefore
$12.0\,g\,mol^{-1} + 2 \times (16.0\,g\,mol^{-1}) = 44.0\,g\,mol^{-1}$.
So, the mass of 1 mol CO_2 is 44.0 g.

By similar reasoning,
NH_3 has a molar mass of
$14.0\,g\,mol^{-1} + (3 \times 1.0\,g\,mol^{-1}) = 17.0\,g\,mol^{-1}$.

That very big number again!

Note that 44.0 g of carbon dioxide and 17.0 g of ammonia contain the same number of molecules (6.02×10^{23} molecules).

Ionic compounds

Ionic compounds consist of oppositely charged ions. Metal ions are positively charged and non-metal ions are negatively charged. For example, sodium chloride consists of sodium ions Na^+ and chloride ions

Cl^-. The formula NaCl tells you that sodium chloride consists of equal numbers of sodium and chloride ions. The formula for calcium chloride is $CaCl_2$, which tells you that a sample of calcium chloride contains twice as many chloride ions as calcium ions. Ionic compounds do not consist of molecules, so it is incorrect to speak about 'sodium chloride molecules'.

Worked examples on calculating the molar mass of an ionic compound

Again we consider two examples, sodium chloride NaCl and calcium bromide $CaBr_2$.

1 mol NaCl consists of one mole of sodium ions Na^+ and one mole of chloride ions Cl^-. Ions form when atoms gain or lose electrons. The mass of an electron is negligible compared to the masses of the protons and neutrons in an atom, so the mass of an ion is regarded as being the same as the mass of its parent atom.

The molar mass of the sodium ion Na^+ is $23.0\,g\,mol^{-1}$.
The molar mass of the chloride ion Cl^- is $35.5\,g\,mol^{-1}$.
The molar mass of sodium chloride NaCl is therefore
$23.0\,g\,mol^{-1} + 35.5\,g\,mol^{-1} = 58.5\,g\,mol^{-1}$.
So, the mass of 1 mol NaCl is 58.5 g.

By similar reasoning,
the molar mass of calcium bromide $CaBr_2$ is
$40.1\,g\,mol^{-1} + 2 \times (79.9\,g\,mol^{-1}) = 199.9\,g\,mol^{-1}$.

One mole of some ionic compounds. The green solid is hydrated nickel(II) chloride $NiCl_2 \cdot 6H_2O$, the pink solid is hydrated cobalt(II) chloride $CoCl_2 \cdot 6H_2O$, and the blue solid is hydrated copper(II) sulphate $CuSO_4 \cdot 5H_2O$. The orange solid is potassium dichromate(VI) $K_2Cr_2O_7$ and the white solid is sodium chloride NaCl.

SUMMARY

- The molar mass of a compound has the same numerical value as its relative formula mass.

PRACTICE

1 Calculate the molar masses of the following substances:
  - **a** ammonia NH_3
  - **b** ethanol CH_3CH_2OH
  - **c** sodium sulphate Na_2SO_4
  - **d** trioxygen (ozone) O_3.

2 Calculate the masses of:
  - **a** 2.0 mol of ammonia
  - **b** 0.20 mol of ethanol
  - **c** 2.5 mol of sodium bromide NaBr.

3 Calculate the amount in moles of each of the following:
  - **a** 2.57g of sulphur S_8
  - **b** 19.5 g of sodium chloride
  - **c** 4.9 g of sulphuric acid.

PRACTICE EXAM QUESTIONS

1

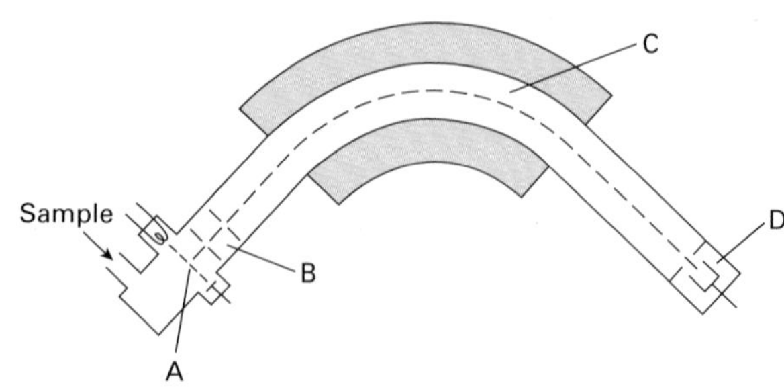

The simplified diagram shows the path of a $^{20}Ne^+$ ion through a mass spectrometer.

a Give the number of neutrons and the number of electrons in this ion. [2]

b Name the processes which occur in regions A, B, C, and D in the mass spectrometer. [4]

c i On a copy of the diagram of the mass spectrometer sketch the path which would be followed by a $^{21}Ne^+$ ion introduced into the spectrometer at the same time as the $^{20}Ne^+$ ion shown.

ii Explain why the paths travelled by the two ions differ. [2]

d The relative abundances of the two neon isotopes in a sample are 91.0% ^{20}Ne and 9.0% ^{21}Ne. Calculate a value for the relative atomic mass of neon. [2]
AQA (NEAB) 1995

2 a Give the meaning of the terms *mass number* of an isotope and *relative atomic mass* of an element. [2]

b Before atoms are deflected in a mass spectrometer they must be ionized and then accelerated.

i Explain briefly why the atoms need to be ionized.

ii What method is used to accelerate the ions? [2]

c The diagram below shows the mass spectrum of an element which has been ionized by removal of only one electron from each atom (forming mononuclear ions).

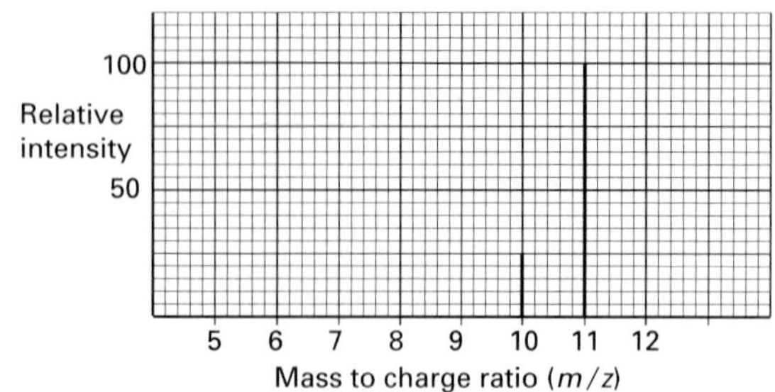

i Use the mass spectrum and your Periodic Table to identify this element. Give the symbol for one isotope of the element with its mass number and atomic number.

ii Use the information given on the mass spectrum to calculate a value for the relative atomic mass of the element. [5]

d Describe briefly how the spectrum in part **c** would differ if the ions were produced by removing two electrons from each atom and give a reason for your answer. [3]
AQA (NEAB) 1995

3 The table below shows some accurate relative atomic masses.

Atom	^1H	^{12}C	^6Li
Relative atomic mass	1.0078	12.0000	6.0149

a Why is ^{12}C the only atom with a relative atomic mass which is an exact whole number? [1]

b Calculate the mass of 1 mol of $^1H^+$ ions. The mass of a single electron is 9.1091×10^{-28} g. [Avogadro's number, L, is 6.0225×10^{23} mol^{-1}] [2]

c i Explain briefly the process by which a sample is ionized in a mass spectrometer.

ii Give **one** reason why it is important to use the minimum possible energy to ionize a sample in a a mass spectrometer.

iii After ionization and before deflection, what happens to the ions in a mass spectrometer; how is this achieved? [5]

d Why is it a good approximation to consider that the relative atomic mass of the $^6Li^+$ ion, determined in a mass spectrometer, is the same as that of ^6Li? [1]
AQA (NEAB) 1997

4 a A proton, a neutron, and an electron all travelling at the same velocity enter a magnetic field. State which particle is deflected the most and explain your answer. [2]

b Give two reasons why particles must be ionized before being analysed in a mass spectrometer. [2]

c A sample of boron with a relative atomic mass of 10.8 gives a mass spectrum with two peaks, one at m/z = 10 and one at m/z = 11. Calculate the ratio of the heights of the two peaks. [2]

d Compound **X** contains only boron and hydrogen. The percentage by mass of boron in **X** is 81.2%. In the mass spectrum of **X** the peak at the largest value of m/z occurs at 54.

i Use the percentage by mass data to calculate the empirical formula of **X**.

ii Deduce the molecular formula of **X**. [4]
AQA (NEAB) 1998 *(See also Chapter 9.)*

5 a State the meaning of the term *atomic number*. [1]

b What is the function of the electron gun and magnet in a mass spectrometer? [2]

c The mass spectrum of a pure sample of a noble gas has peaks at the following m/z values.

m/z	10	11	20	22
Relative intensity	2.0	0.2	17.8	1.7

i Give the complete symbol, including mass number, and atomic number for one isotope of this noble gas.

ii Give the species which is responsible for the peak at $m/z = 11$.

iii Use appropriate values from the data above to calculate the relative atomic mass of this sample of noble gas. [6]
AQA (NEAB) 1998

6 **a** Define the term *mole*. [2]

b A carbonate of metal **M** has the formula M_2CO_3. The equation for the reaction of M_2CO_3 with hydrochloric acid is given below

$M_2CO_3 + 2HCl \rightarrow 2MCl + CO_2 + H_2O$

0.245 g of M_2CO_3 was found to exactly neutralize 23.6 cm^3 of hydrochloric acid of concentration of 0.150 mol dm^{-3}. Carry out the following calculations and hence deduce the identity of **M**.

i Calculate the number of moles of hydrochloric acid. [1]

ii Calculate the number of moles of M_2CO_3. [2}

iii Calculate the relative molecular mass of M_2CO_3. [1]

iv Calculate the relative atomic mass of metal **M** and hence deduce its identity. [4]

c Here is a simplified diagram of a mass spectrometer which could also be used to determine the relative atomic mass of metal **M**.

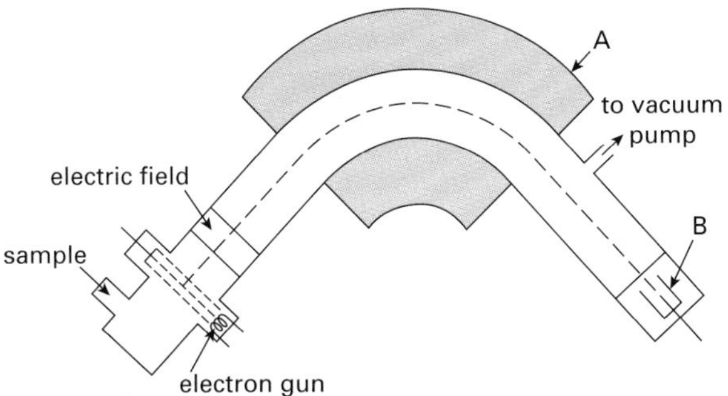

Give the names of the parts labelled **A** and **B**, and state the purpose of the parts labelled *electron gun* and *electric field*. [4]
AQA (AEB) 1997 *(See also Chapter 9.)*

7 **a** Complete the following table, giving the name, relative mass, and relative charge of each of the fundamental sub-atomic particles:

Particle	Relative mass	Relative charge
	1.0	
neutron		
		−1

[3]

b The element magnesium (atomic number 12) has three isotopes of mass numbers 24, 25, and 26, having abundances of 78.6%, 10.1%, and 11.3%, respectively.

Explain the meaning of the terms:

i atomic number, [1]

ii isotopes. [1]

c Before magnesium atoms can be deflected in a mass spectrometer, they must be ionized and then accelerated.

i Briefly explain why the atoms need to be ionized.

ii By what method are the ions accelerated? [1]

iii By what means are the ions deflected? [1]

d Define the term *relative atomic mass*. [2]

e Use the information given in **b** to:

i calculate the relative atomic mass of magnesium, giving your answer to two decimal places; [2]

ii draw the mass spectrum for magnesium on graph paper. [3]
AQA (AEB) 1996

4 Electrons in atoms

In the early years of the twentieth century, Rutherford's model of the atom consisted of a positively charged nucleus surrounded by a cluster of negatively charged electrons. It is well known that opposite charges attract each other, so how do the electrons remain apart from the nucleus? Rutherford's student, Niels Bohr, suggested that electrons orbit around the nucleus, rather like the planets around the Sun. The Bohr model allowed the structure of the hydrogen atom to be worked out. In the course of this chapter, you will come to understand that a whole new way of thinking about matter and energy is required, as the Bohr model failed for other atoms.

USING LIGHT TO FIND OUT ABOUT ATOMS

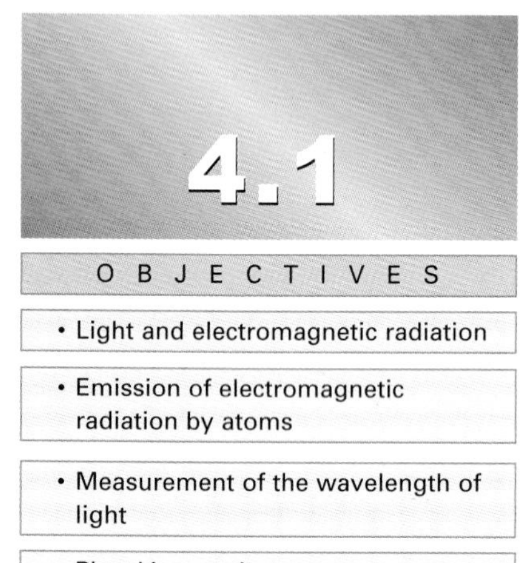

OBJECTIVES

- Light and electromagnetic radiation
- Emission of electromagnetic radiation by atoms
- Measurement of the wavelength of light
- Planck's equation

The modern theory of the atom rests on one main observed fact: atoms can emit light if they have absorbed energy (become excited). The wavelength of the light is characteristic of the element concerned. For example, sodium salts colour a Bunsen flame yellow; a discharge tube containing neon gas glows red. However, before attempting to link the colour of the radiated light to the internal structure of the atom, you must first understand something about the nature of light.

Light and electromagnetic radiation

Light is a form of electromagnetic radiation. **Electromagnetic radiation** is energy, associated with electric and magnetic fields, travelling as waves. A wave is described by its frequency (f) and its wavelength (λ). The frequency and wavelength of light are related by the equation:

$$c = f\lambda$$

where c is the speed at which the waves are travelling (the speed of light, $2.998 \times 10^8\,\mathrm{m\,s^{-1}}$). The unit of wavelength is the metre (m); the unit of frequency is the hertz (Hz). The whole range of frequencies of electromagnetic radiation is called the **electromagnetic spectrum**.

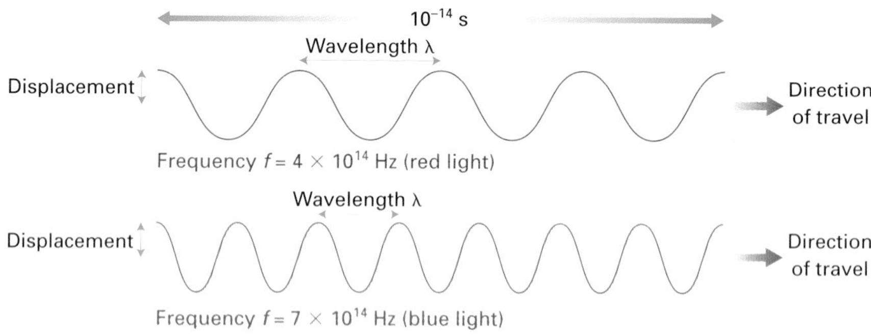

A transverse wave (such as a water wave or an electromagnetic wave) moves from one place to another at a characteristic speed. Its displacement is at right angles to its direction of travel. The wavelength λ is the distance between successive peaks (points of maximum displacement). The frequency f is the number of complete cycles of the wave that pass a stationary point in one second.

Using a spectrometer to measure wavelength

A light bulb emits light with a continuous range of wavelengths. The mixing together of this range of wavelengths produces the 'white' light that we see. Light from a coloured Bunsen flame or a discharge tube consists of a mixture of distinct, separate wavelengths. A **spectrometer** is an instrument that separates this light into its constituent wavelengths.

A diffraction grating in the spectrometer bends light of a particular wavelength λ through a specific angle. The lower the wavelength, the greater will be the angle of deviation. When the light is viewed through the telescope, each specific wavelength λ appears as a thin vertical line of coloured light. The telescope can be moved around the turntable to measure the angle of deviation for each line. We can then calculate the wavelength, and hence the frequency, of each line from its angle of deviation.

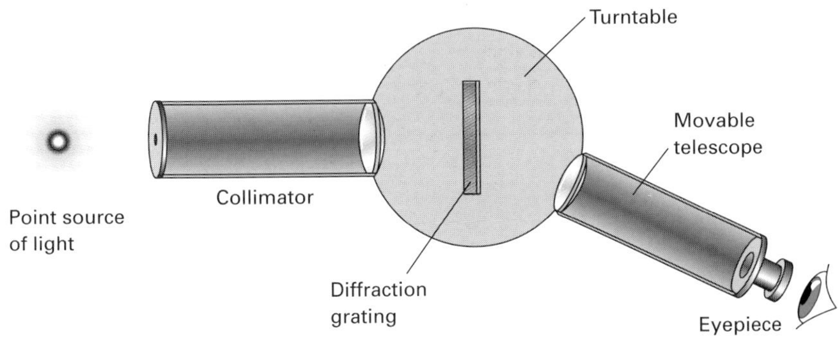

The main components of a spectrometer. The collimator produces a parallel beam of light from the point source. The diffraction grating consists of parallel slits scratched equal distances apart on a glass surface. The angle of deviation depends on the wavelength of the light and the distance between neighbouring slits.

Emission spectra

If you rotate the telescope of a spectrometer on its turntable, a number of separate coloured lines pass across your field of vision. The complete set of these lines laid out against a wavelength (or frequency) scale is a spectrum. When the spectrum is the result of light being *emitted* from *atoms*, it is called an **atomic emission spectrum**. An external energy source increases the energy of the atoms; and they lose energy as they emit electromagnetic radiation.

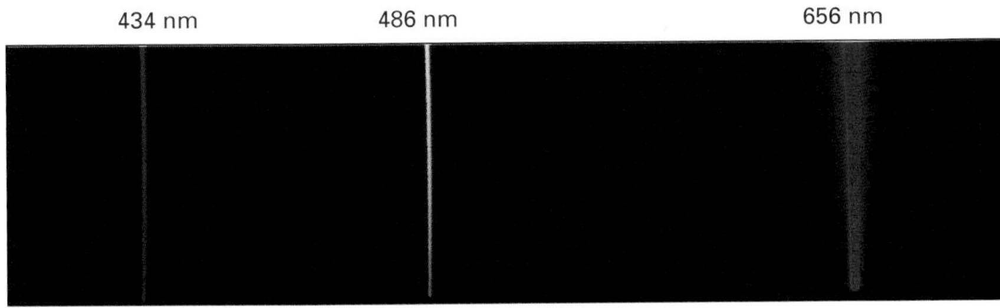

The emission spectrum of hydrogen. The wavelengths of the lines have values around 5×10^{-7} m (500×10^{-9} m, 500 nanometres, 500 nm). The corresponding frequencies are of the order of 6×10^{14} Hz.

Frequency and energy of light

Light is a form of energy. The lower the wavelength (and hence the higher the frequency), the greater is the energy of the light. Frequency f (hertz, Hz) and energy E (joules, J) are connected by an equation introduced by Max Planck in 1900:

$$E = hf$$

where h is the Planck constant (6.626×10^{-34} J s).

Measurements from a spectrometer show that the atoms in a Bunsen flame or discharge tube emit light at fixed wavelengths and hence fixed frequencies. Planck's equation indicates that energy is *directly proportional* to frequency; so these atoms emit *energy* in fixed quantities. Each fixed quantity of energy emitted is like a bundle or packet of energy. It is called a **quantum** (plural = quanta) of energy and corresponds to electromagnetic radiation of a specific frequency. Physicists needed to make a whole new range of models for the structure of the atom to fit in with this idea of quantized energy. We shall look at these in the following spreads.

SUMMARY

- Atoms can take in energy and then emit it as electromagnetic radiation at specific frequencies.
- Atoms emit fixed quantities of energy in packets called quanta.

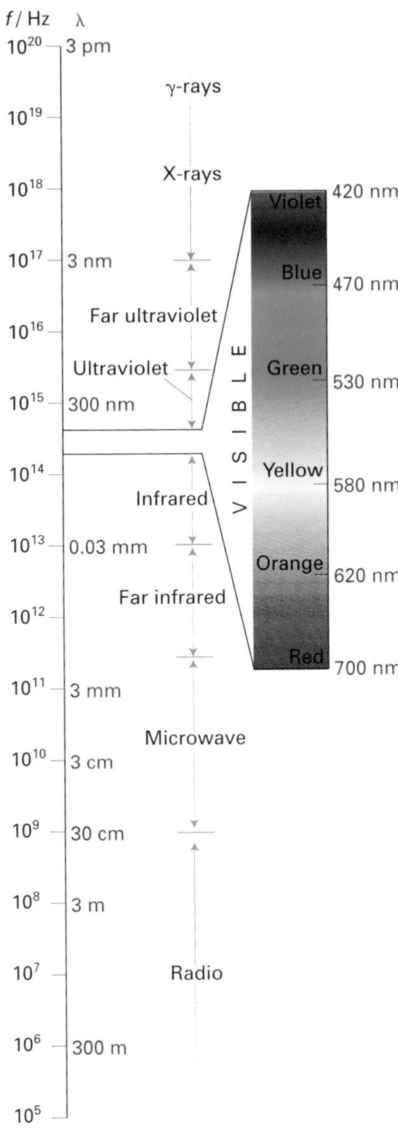

The electromagnetic spectrum.

Scientific methodology

Scientists observe something happening (a phenomenon), take measurements to gather data, and analyse the data in an attempt to explain the cause of the phenomenon. They often create a model, which behaves in a particular way to produce the observed effects. The modern model of the atom evolved over the past century.

The reflective thinker, writer, and TV personality Jacob Bronowski stated in his book *The Ascent of Man* that: 'The inside of the atom is invisible, but there is a window in it – a stained-glass window: the spectrum of the atom.' Deducing the structure of the atom from emission spectra is similar to deducing the existence of water and clouds from observing a rainbow.

4.2 THE HYDROGEN SPECTRUM AND SHELLS

OBJECTIVES

- Interpreting emission spectra
- The Bohr model of the atom
- Quantized energy levels (shells)
- Principal quantum numbers

Atoms are far too small for us to see their structure directly. We have to devise pictures and models that explain the results of experiments we carry out on them. This process is rather like poking at an elephant with sticks through the bars of a darkened cage. We then have to use the evidence gathered on the ends of our sticks to draw the elephant! Our unknown specimen is not an elephant, but the hydrogen atom. It is contained inside a discharge tube, and its outer skin is defined by its surrounding electrons. We poke at it with electrical energy and look at the electromagnetic radiation that results. We then try to conjure up a picture of the atom in our minds.

The hydrogen spectrum

An atom of hydrogen consists of just one proton with one surrounding electron. The emission spectrum of hydrogen is relatively simple compared to those of other elements. The complete spectrum of hydrogen consists of separate series of distinct wavelengths concentrated in the ultraviolet, visible, and infrared regions of the electromagnetic spectrum. The six series found are named after their discoverers. In order of increasing wavelength they are the Lyman series (ultraviolet), Balmer series (visible), Paschen, Brackett, Pfund, and Humphreys series (infrared). Each of these series is called a **line spectrum** because the film record from the spectrometer appears as a pattern of separate thin vertical lines.

The Balmer series

The Balmer series is the most straightforward part of the hydrogen emission spectrum to study because it occurs in the visible region of the electromagnetic spectrum. Each line in the series represents electromagnetic radiation of a specific single wavelength. (The purple line, for example, is at 434.05 nm.) The energy of the radiation may be calculated by using Planck's equation:

$E = hf$

Quantized energy levels

In 1913, Niels Bohr introduced his model of the hydrogen atom. He *assumed* that the electron within the hydrogen atom will *not* absorb or radiate energy so long as it stays in one of a number of circular **orbits**. His model of the atom was designed to explain the observation that the electromagnetic radiation emitted by an excited hydrogen atom has specific energies. These energies are fixed, or quantized. Bohr suggested that the energy of an electron in an atom must also be quantized, so the electron can only have certain discrete **energy levels** rather than a continuous range of possible energies. Each of these energy levels may be occupied by an electron of the appropriate energy.

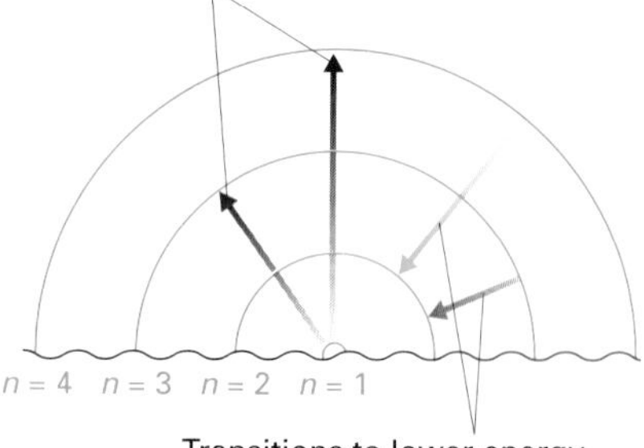
Excitation – transitions to higher energy levels
n = 4
n = 3
n = 2
n = 1
Transitions to lower energy levels emit energy in the form of electromagnetic radiation

If an atom collides with another atom, or absorbs radiation, this can increase the energy of an electron within the atom. The electron moves into a higher energy level. The atom emits electromagnetic radiation when the electron moves to a lower energy level.

When an atom is excited by absorbing energy, an electron jumps up to a higher energy level. In the Bohr model, the electron is then circling at a greater distance from the nucleus. The excited atom can emit energy in the form of electromagnetic radiation as the electron falls back down to a lower energy level. When an electron moves from one energy level to another, this is called an **electronic transition**. The emitted energy can be seen as a line in the spectrum (as viewed through a spectrometer, for example). If the electron energy levels were not quantized but could have any value, a *continuous* spectrum rather than a line spectrum would result.

The difference in energy ΔE between the two energy levels in this electronic transition, E(higher) and E(lower), is equal to the energy of the emitted radiation, E(radiation):

$$E(\text{radiation}) = E(\text{higher}) - E(\text{lower}) = \Delta E$$

If you combine this equation with Planck's equation, you can see that the frequency (f) of the radiation emitted depends on the energy level difference (ΔE) of the particular electronic transition:

$$\Delta E = hf$$

So, electronic transitions between energy levels result in emission of radiation of different frequencies and therefore produce different lines in the spectrum.

Differences

The Greek capital letter delta Δ is often used (as here) to describe a difference between two quantities. Here ΔE is a difference in energy.

Shells

Bohr labelled each of the energy levels in the hydrogen atom with a number called the **principal quantum number**, n. The energy level closest to the nucleus is labelled $n = 1$. The next energy levels are $n = 2$, $n = 3$, and so on. Each of these energy levels is called a **shell**. The principal quantum number defines the energy of the electron in a given shell. In an unexcited hydrogen atom, the electron is in the energy level $n = 1$. This state of lowest energy for the atom is called the **ground state**.

Bohr showed that the series in the high-energy ultraviolet region (the Lyman series) arises from electronic transitions from higher energy levels to the energy level $n = 1$. Each line in the Lyman series is due to electrons returning from a *particular* higher energy level to the energy level $n = 1$. The Balmer series arises from electronic transitions from higher energy levels to the energy level $n = 2$. Each line in the Balmer series is due to electrons returning from a *particular* higher energy level to the energy level $n = 2$.

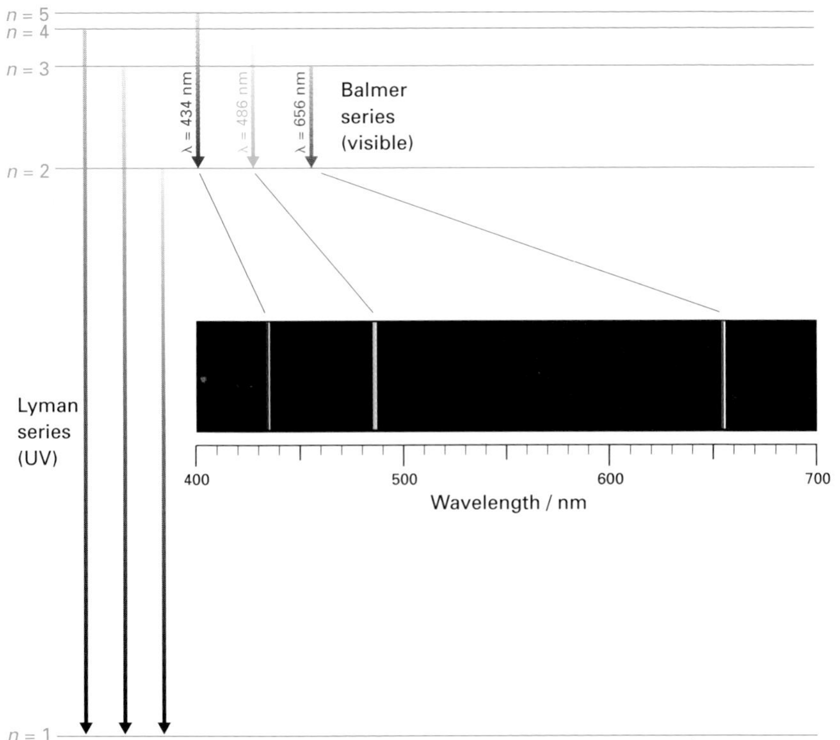

The Lyman series of lines results from electronic transitions from higher energy levels down to energy level n = 1. The Balmer series results from electronic transitions down to energy level n = 2.

Series in the infrared

The various series in the low-energy infrared region are caused by electrons returning to the energy levels $n = 3$ (Paschen series), $n = 4$ (Brackett series), $n = 5$ (Pfund series), and $n = 6$ (Humphreys series).

The convergence limit

The separate lines in a series become closer together as their wavelength decreases, i.e. as their frequency (and energy) increases. At the high-frequency end of the series, the lines are so close together that they form a continuous band of radiation, known as a **continuum**.

The start of this continuum, beyond which separate lines cannot be distinguished, is called the **convergence limit**. The convergence limit corresponds to the point at which the energy of an electron within the atom is no longer quantized. At that point, the nucleus has lost all influence over the electron; the atom has become **ionized**.

For the Lyman series, the convergence limit represents the ionization of the hydrogen atom:

$H(g) \rightarrow H^+(g) + e^-(g)$

SUMMARY

- Electrons within atoms occupy fixed energy levels.
- The energy of an electron in an atom is quantized; the electron may have only certain energies.
- Energy levels with the same principal quantum number are in the same shell.
- Atoms emit electromagnetic radiation when electrons move from a higher to a lower energy level.

PRACTICE

1 Draw an energy level diagram to show the electronic transitions responsible for the lowest-energy spectral lines in the Paschen series.

2 In no more than 60 words each, explain the meanings of the following terms:

a Quantized
b Principal quantum number
c Line spectrum
d Convergence limit.

4.3 THE SODIUM SPECTRUM AND SUBSHELLS

OBJECTIVES

- Shells
- s, p, and d subshells

Bohr's model of the atom used the idea of quantized electronic energy levels (shells) to explain the sequence of lines in the emission spectrum of hydrogen. He labelled the shells $n = 1$, $n = 2$, etc. in order of increasing energy. The Bohr model explains the emission spectrum of the hydrogen atom in terms of electronic transitions between shells. However, the emission spectrum of sodium is a good deal more complex. To explain this spectrum, there must be subdivisions of the Bohr shells, called *subshells*. The structure of the atom must be more complicated than Bohr thought.

The sodium spectrum

The hydrogen spectrum is simple throughout most of the visible region (corresponding to the Balmer series for electronic transitions to energy level $n = 2$). There is a single red line at 656 nm and then no further line until 486 nm. This red line originates from electronic transitions from energy level $n = 3$ to $n = 2$.

The sodium emission spectrum is more complex than the very simple hydrogen emission spectrum. If we look in particular at the region where wavelengths are greater than 550 nm, we find that, whereas there is a *single* line for hydrogen, there are *three* lines fairly close together for sodium, i.e.

- a green line at 569 nm;
- a yellow line at 589 nm;
- an orange line at 616 nm.

This observation suggests that there are more energy levels available in sodium than in hydrogen. In the sodium atom, the shells must be composed of **subshells**, each of which is at a different energy. It turns out that:

- For the shell $n = 1$, there is only one subshell, labelled 1s.
- For the shell $n = 2$, there are two subshells, labelled 2s and 2p. The 2p subshell is at a higher energy than the 2s subshell.
- For the shell $n = 3$, there are three subshells, labelled 3s, 3p, and 3d. These subshells increase in energy in the order 3s < 3p < 3d.

Wavelength

A wave of wavelength λ_1 has a *longer* wavelength than a wave of wavelength λ_2 if the numerical value of λ_1 is greater than the value of λ_2, i.e. the yellow sodium emission at 589 nm has a longer wavelength than the green emission at 569 nm.

f subshells

For the shells $n = 4$ and higher, there are *four* subshells: s, p, d, and f. The f subshell will be ignored for the moment.

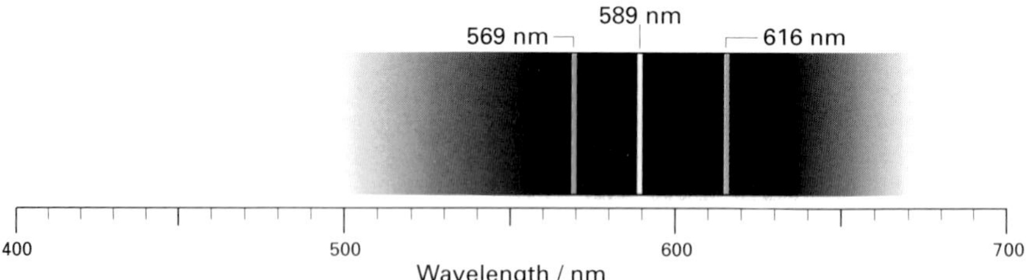

The visible region of the sodium emission spectrum. Note the green, yellow, and orange lines referred to in the text. There are numerous other lines at wavelengths below 550 nm. Lines at wavelengths greater than 616 nm are due to sodium ions Na^+ and not to sodium atoms themselves.

Absorption spectra

If continuous radiation (electromagnetic radiation of all wavelengths) passes through the vapour of an element, lines of certain wavelengths will be absorbed by the atoms and removed from the radiation. Looking through a spectrometer, you would see a series of black lines where wavelengths have been absorbed, against the background of continuous radiation. This is an **absorption spectrum**. The wavelengths of these lines correspond to the quantized energy taken in by the atoms to promote electrons from lower to higher energy levels. For example, excited hydrogen atoms in the photosphere of the Sun cause a dark line at 656 nm in the solar spectrum.

s, p, and d subshells – history

The letters used to label the subshells came from the descriptions of the series observed in the sodium spectrum. The series of lines had been given names that reflected their character in some way, e.g. 'sharp' because they *were* sharp. Each series arose from transitions in which the electron fell from a particular subshell. So it was natural to name the subshells after the associated series. The '**s**harp series' arose from transitions in which the electron fell from an s subshell. The '**p**rincipal series' (in which the electron fell from a p subshell) was so named because these lines also occurred in the absorption spectrum of sodium. The '**d**iffuse series' (in which the electron fell from a d subshell) was so named because of the characteristic visible difference from the sharp series.

Interpreting the sodium spectrum

We can explain the sodium atomic emission spectrum by assigning each line in the spectrum to an electronic transition on an energy level diagram. The diagram shows the energy levels corresponding to the subshells in the sodium atom. It is called a **Grotrian diagram**, after its originator, Walter Grotrian.

The most intense line, the yellow emission at 589 nm, is caused by an electronic transition from the 3p energy level down to the 3s energy level. Expressed more simply, the yellow line is the result of a 3p to 3s transition.

The orange line at 616 nm is the result of a 5s to 3p transition. This line is at a slightly longer wavelength than the yellow line. The frequency is therefore lower, corresponding to the smaller energy gap seen on the Grotrian diagram.

The green line at 569 nm is the result of a 4d to 3p transition. This line is at a slightly shorter wavelength than the yellow line. The frequency is therefore higher, corresponding to the larger energy gap seen on the Grotrian diagram.

At even shorter wavelength are emissions at 515 nm (6s to 3p), 498 nm (5d to 3p), and so on. At even longer wavelength, the 3d to 3p transition causes an intense line at 819 nm, which is in the infrared.

The Bohr model of the atom assumes that electrons are particles moving in orbits around the nucleus. This model became inadequate when it was understood in the 1920s that the electron can also behave as a *wave*. This startling discovery is explained in the next spread.

The ideas introduced in the next spread **will not be tested in exams** but are essential to explain why we now focus on the idea of *electron density*.

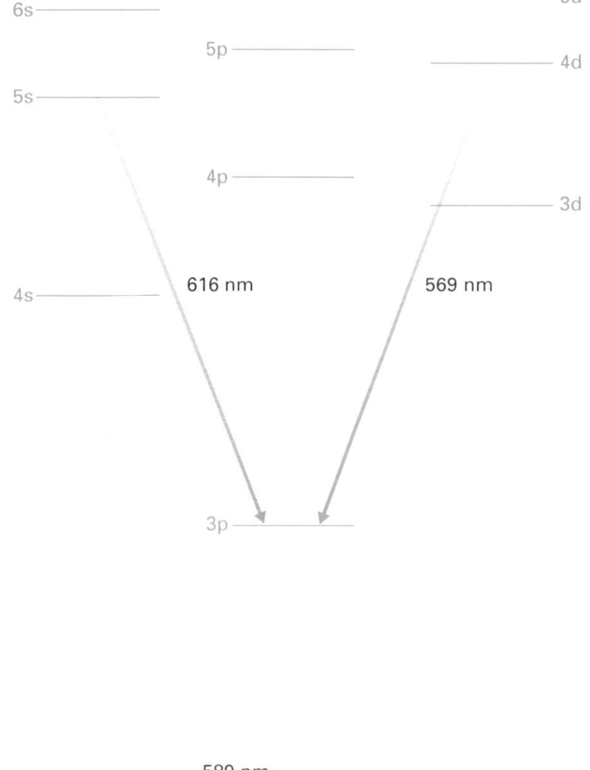

A Grotrian diagram (drawn accurately to scale) showing some of the electronic transitions responsible for the emission spectrum of sodium. Notice how the energies of the subshells get closer to each other as the principal quantum number increases.

SUMMARY

- Shells are labelled 1, 2, 3, etc. in order of increasing energy.
- Subshells are labelled s, p, d, and f.

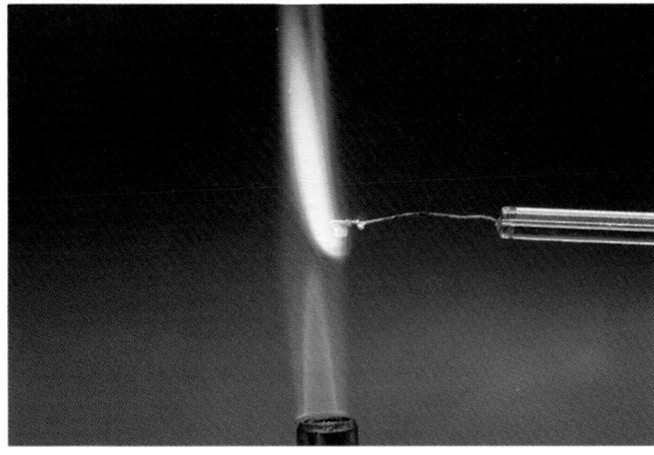

The test for sodium in the laboratory makes use of the bright yellow line in its spectrum: when heated in a flame, sodium colours the flame yellow.

PRACTICE

1 What subshells can occur in each of the following shells?

a $n = 1$
b $n = 2$
c $n = 3$
d $n = 4$.

2 Look at the Grotrian diagram for sodium, and arrange the following subshells of the sodium atom in order of *increasing* energy:
3s, 2p, 1s, 2s, 3d, 4s, 4p, 3p.

3 Look at the Grotrian diagram for sodium, and estimate the wavelength of the emission resulting from a 5d to 4p transition.

4.4

OBJECTIVES

- Wave–particle duality of the electron
- The uncertainty principle
- The Schrödinger equation
- Probability
- Atomic orbitals

Wave mechanics

Bohr attempted to construct a model of the atom which accounted for the data obtained from emission spectra. He assumed the electron to be a solid particle of matter and tried to describe its motion in terms of the mathematical equations of classical mechanics. Bohr's physical model of the atom was only partially convincing. In constructing it he ignored the inconvenient physical law which states that an orbiting charged particle such as an electron should lose energy and spiral in towards the nucleus. A completely new way of thinking was required to describe objects as small as atoms. The 1920s finally saw the emergence of our modern view of the atom and the branch of mathematics needed to describe it – wave mechanics (sometimes called quantum mechanics).

The electron: particle *and* wave

In 1924, Louis de Broglie presented a revolutionary idea in his doctoral thesis. He predicted that electrons, which were thought at the time to be particles, would also possess wave-like properties. One of the properties of waves is that they can be diffracted. This property means that when waves hit the edge of an object or pass through a narrow aperture, they bend around it and spread out, like the waves in a ripple tank. So, if electrons could behave like waves, it should be possible to diffract them, like light through a diffraction grating.

Three years after de Broglie's thesis appeared, G. P. Thomson provided experimental evidence which demonstrated that electrons can be diffracted in the same manner as X-rays. The conclusion was that electrons have both wave-like and particle-like properties. The realization that the electron shows **wave–particle duality** opened up a whole new theoretical method for describing the electronic structure of atoms based on the mathematics of waves.

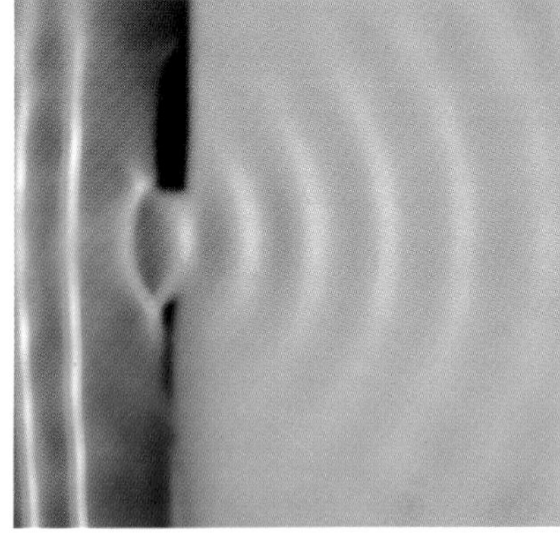

(a)

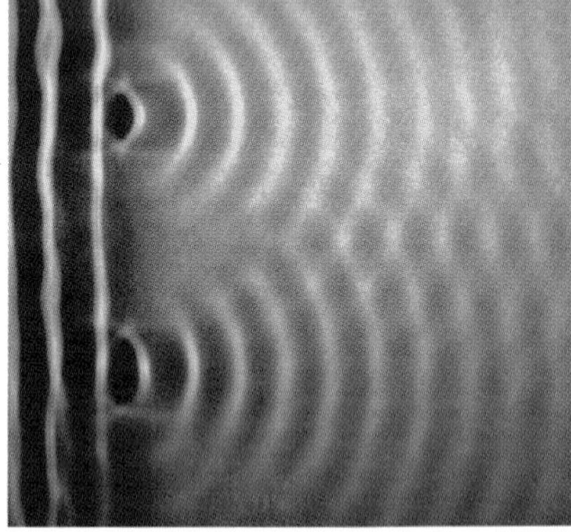

(b)

A wave spreads out when it passes through a small aperture. (The size of the aperture must be of the same order as the wavelength of the wave.) The waves from two or more apertures interfere with each other, forming a diffraction pattern of alternating maxima and minima.

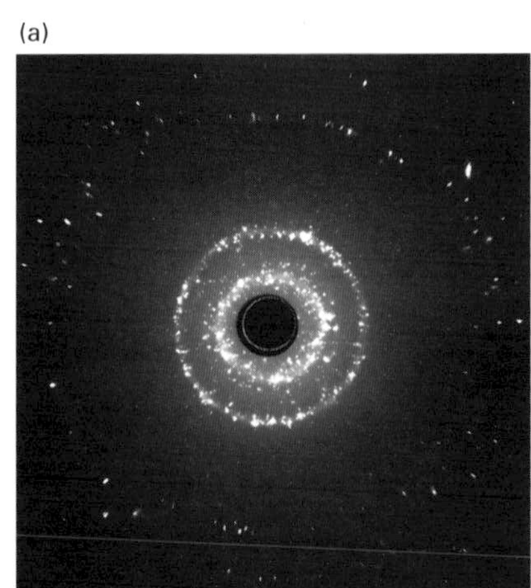

(a) The diffraction pattern produced by a beam of X-rays passing through aluminium foil. The rows of atoms in the metal act like the slits in a diffraction grating. (b) The diffraction pattern resulting from a beam of electrons.

The Thomsons

George Paget Thomson was the son of Joseph John (J. J.) Thomson, who discovered the electron. J. J. received the 1906 Nobel prize for physics for his work. G. P. shared the 1937 Nobel prize with Clinton Davisson for discovering electron diffraction.

The problem with the Bohr model

Any object moving in a circle must experience a force holding it in the circle; this force is called a **centripetal force**. This force produces an acceleration towards the centre of the circle. This applies equally to the Earth orbiting the Sun and to Bohr's electron orbiting the nucleus.

The difference between the astronomical model and Bohr's atomic model is that the electron is *charged*. The laws of electromagnetism explain that an *accelerating* charged particle should radiate electromagnetic radiation. The orbiting electron should gradually lose energy and spiral into the nucleus.

The Bohr model

Bohr's model of the atom can explain the observed emission spectrum of hydrogen. However, it fails to explain the spectra of atoms more complex than hydrogen. If a model cannot explain observations fully, then that model is limited or is built on false assumptions. The Bohr model is built on the false assumption that the electron exists as a solid particle of matter in an atom.

Heisenberg's uncertainty principle

In 1927, Werner Heisenberg published details of his uncertainty principle. The **uncertainty principle** states that it is impossible to measure accurately both the position and the velocity of an electron at the same time. The principle can be justified as follows. You view the world about you with the help of radiation (light rays) which reflects from objects and enters your eyes. To see an object as small as an electron would require radiation of extremely low wavelength and hence extremely high frequency. The energy of this radiation would alter the position and velocity of the electron you were trying to observe. Once scientists accepted the uncertainty principle, they stopped trying to construct Bohr-style models of the atom that attempted to define the positions of electrons exactly.

The Schrödinger equation

Erwin Schrödinger, working separately at almost the same time as Heisenberg, and following de Broglie's ideas, founded the mathematical technique called **wave mechanics**. This technique produced a *mathematical* model of the atom. The model is described by the **Schrödinger equation**, which allows for the uncertainty principle and the wave-like properties of the electron. Solutions of the Schrödinger equation account for the quantization of electronic energy levels.

The solution of the Schrödinger equation leads to the idea that there are regions of space around the nucleus where there is a high probability (but not an absolute certainty) of finding an electron of a given energy. These regions are called **atomic orbitals**. Because it does not try to define the *exact* position and path of an electron, the Schrödinger equation is consistent with the uncertainty principle.

The Schrödinger equation explains the existence of both shells and subshells, as described in spread 4.9.

SUMMARY

- The electron shows wave–particle duality.
- The Bohr model ignores one of the fundamental attributes of matter at the atomic level – uncertainty.
- The Schrödinger equation is a model of the atom based on the mathematics of waves.
- Solutions of the Schrödinger equation define regions of space where an electron is likely to be found: these regions are called atomic orbitals.

PRACTICE

1 Summarize each of the following in no more than 30 words:

a Bohr model of the atom
b Wave–particle duality
c The uncertainty principle
d Atomic orbital.

4.5

OBJECTIVES

- Atomic orbitals visualized as 90% boundary surfaces
- The shapes of the s, p, and d orbitals

Visualizing atomic orbitals

Atomic orbitals indicate the electron density for an electron of a given energy. When these electron densities are plotted in three dimensions they show the shapes that represent the various atomic orbitals. Atomic orbitals for the hydrogen atom have the same energies as the shells developed by Bohr. Atomic orbitals are labelled as s, p, or d, as they also naturally explain the subshells found from the atomic spectrum of sodium.

Electron density

Wave mechanics does not picture an electron as a point charge. Instead, the electron in an atomic orbital is imagined as being *smeared out*. The distribution of the electron is not uniform; rather, there is a high probability of finding the electron in some regions, and a low probability of finding it in others. This distribution of the probability of finding an electron at a certain position is the **electron density**. Regions of high probability have high electron density because the electron spends a greater proportion of its time in that region.

The 1s atomic orbital

An electron in the 1s atomic orbital has the lowest possible energy for an electron in that atom. The shape of the electron density in the 1s orbital is spherical. Look at the plot of the total electron density at r (distance from the nucleus) against r, shown below (c). It shows that the total electron density at the centre of the nucleus ($r = 0$) is zero, as might be expected. As the distance from the nucleus increases, so does the total electron density, until it reaches a maximum. The distance corresponding to the maximum total electron density is called the **Bohr radius** (a_0) and equals the radius of the orbit calculated by Bohr. Beyond the Bohr radius, the total electron density falls steadily, but does not reach zero. In theory, there is a finite (but *very* small) probability of the electron being found anywhere in the universe. Slicing the electron density in a plane through the nucleus produces circular contours. To get a picture of what is going on, we can find the 'shape' of the s orbital by defining a boundary surface that includes 90% of the electron density.

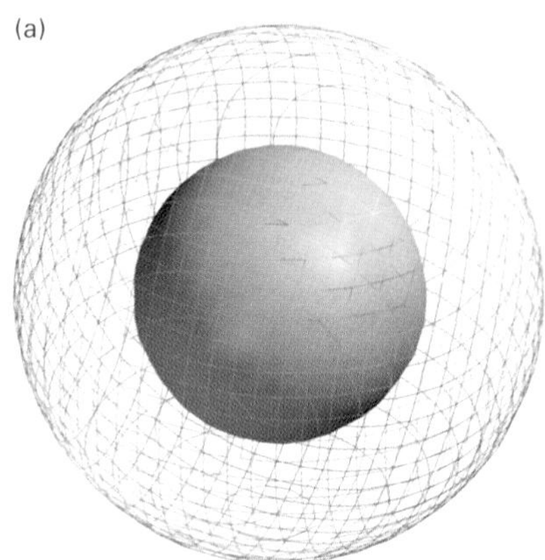

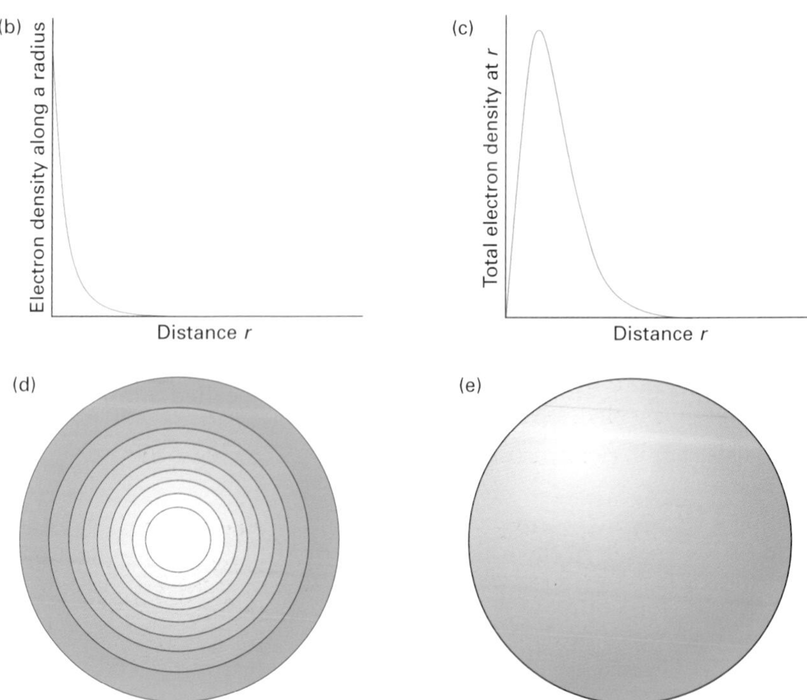

*The electron density in the 1s orbital is spherical. (a) The solid figure joins points of equal electron density; the wire-frame joins points where the electron density is ten times lower. (b) As you move out from the nucleus along any radius of the sphere that makes up the 1s orbital, the electron density falls steadily. (c) The total electron density at a particular distance from the centre of the sphere (rigorously called the **radial distribution function**) varies as shown here, because all points on the surface of the sphere (of area $4\pi r^2$) are at the same distance from the nucleus. (The maximum value corresponds to the Bohr radius. See appendix B.1.) (d) A cross-section through the electron density shows concentric circles, each successive circle including 10% more of the total electron density. The outer circle includes 90%. (e) To sketch an s orbital in the rest of the book, we will draw the 90% contour.*

The 2p atomic orbitals

There is just one 1s orbital and one 2s orbital, but there are three 2p orbitals of equal energy. The 2p orbitals are not spherically symmetrical about the nucleus. Electron density is more concentrated along one direction in space, so p orbitals must be drawn on three-dimensional axes to distinguish one orbital from another. Each orbital consists of two lobes with a region of zero electron density (a **node**) between them centred on the nucleus.

The three 2p orbitals are known as the $2p_x$, the $2p_y$, and the $2p_z$ orbitals. They are at right angles to each other.

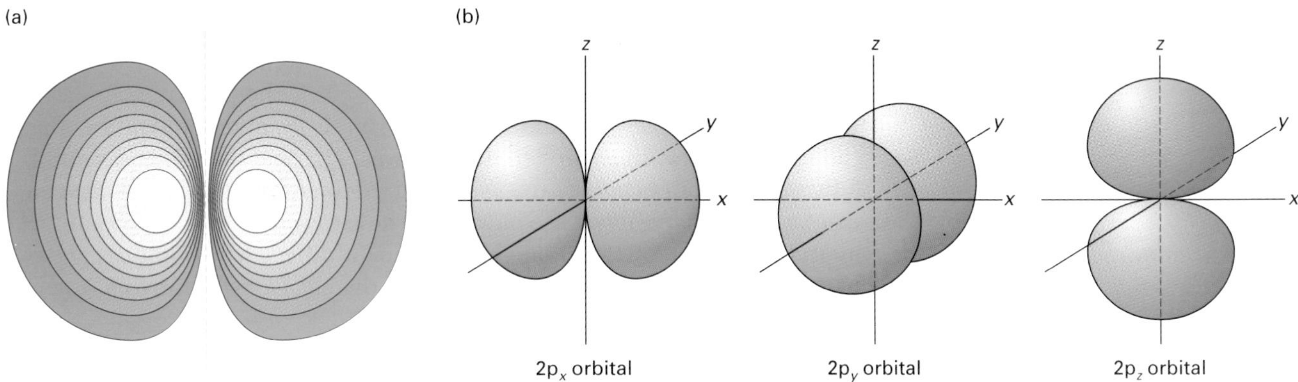

(a) Cross-section through the electron density of a 2p orbital: each successive contour includes 10% more of the total electron density. (b) The 90% boundary surfaces (i.e. 'the shapes') of the $2p_x$, the $2p_y$, and the $2p_z$ atomic orbitals.

The 3d atomic orbitals

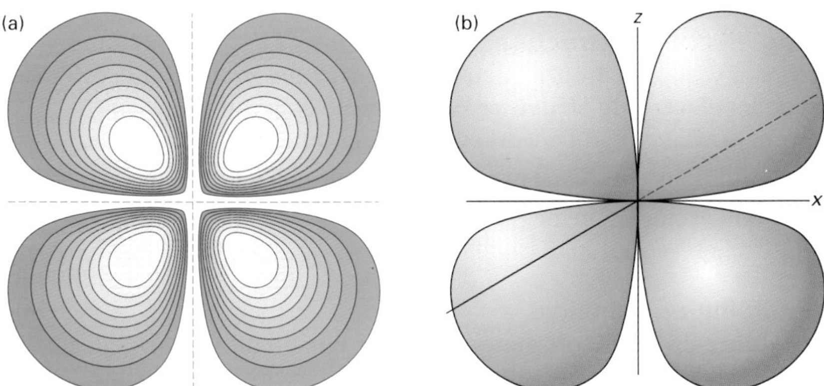

There are five 3d orbitals. This diagram shows (a) a cross-section through the electron density: each successive contour includes 10% more of the total electron density; (b) the shape of the $3d_{xz}$ orbital.

SUMMARY

- Solutions of the Schrödinger equation for atoms are called atomic orbitals.
- Atomic orbitals show the electron density for an electron of a given energy.
- The shape of an atomic orbital is visualized as a boundary surface within which the electron spends 90% of its existence.
- s orbitals are spherically symmetrical about the nucleus: they are sketched as circles.
- p orbitals have two opposing lobes, one on each side of the nucleus.

PRACTICE

1 Explain why it is not possible to draw 100% boundary surfaces for orbitals.

4.6

OBJECTIVES

- Electron spin
- Listing atomic orbitals in order of increasing energy
- Electrons-in-boxes notation
- Electronic structures

Atoms with more than one electron

Bohr's model of the atom explains the wavelengths of the lines in the hydrogen emission spectrum. It treats the electron as a particle and describes the various energy levels that it can occupy. Current theory relies on atomic orbitals, which define regions of space around the nucleus where there is a high electron density for an electron of a given energy. Atomic orbitals for the hydrogen atom have the same energies as the orbits of Bohr's model. But what about atoms other than hydrogen? Two questions now arise: what are the energies of the electrons in atoms with more than one electron, and what sort of quantized energy level does each occupy?

Hydrogen-like orbitals

It seems reasonable to assume that the orbitals in any atom will be much the same as those in hydrogen. In its lowest energy state, the electron in a hydrogen atom occupies the 1s orbital. Elements other than hydrogen can be built up by filling the atomic orbitals found for the hydrogen atom, that is 1s, 2s, 2p, 3s, 3p, etc. The main difference is that the *energy* of each atomic orbital will be affected by the electrons occupying other atomic orbitals.

Electron spin

Some of the electron's properties must be interpreted in terms of a property that scientists have chosen to call 'spin'. Picturing an electron spinning like the Earth on its axis is helpful, but simplistic. The human mind always prefers to visualize the unseen in pictorial terms.

Split lines and electron spin

High-resolution spectrometers show that the yellow line at 589 nm in the emission spectrum of sodium is actually split into two closely spaced lines. The explanation is that an electron can exist in one of two states, called 'spin up' and 'spin down'. Two electrons with the same spin state are said to have **parallel spins**.

Finding electronic structures

The way in which an atom's electrons are arranged in its atomic orbitals is called its **electronic structure** or electronic configuration. The electronic structure can be worked out using three basic rules:

- The building-up (*Aufbau*) principle
- The Pauli exclusion principle
- Hund's rule

Simplified electronic structures

In earlier science courses, you probably saw electronic structures written without identifying subshells. So sodium, for example, was Na 2,8,1 or Na 2.8.1.

The building-up principle

The **building-up principle** states that electrons fill atomic orbitals in order of increasing energy, subject to the Pauli exclusion principle.

The Pauli exclusion principle

This principle, introduced by Wolfgang Pauli, allows *no more than two electrons* to occupy any orbital. For example, the 1s orbital may contain one or two electrons only. The three orbitals ($2p_x$, $2p_y$, and $2p_z$) in the 2p subshell (which we saw in the previous spread) may contain a total of up to six electrons. Electron spin explains why the Pauli exclusion principle arises: two electrons occupying the same orbital must have **paired** (opposite) **spins**.

Hund's rule

Hund's rule is applied where orbitals of *equal* energy are available, for example $2p_x$, $2p_y$, and $2p_z$. The orbitals will first fill with one electron each with parallel spins before a second electron is added with the paired (opposite) spin.

Filling atomic orbitals with electrons

The Pauli exclusion principle says that an orbital can hold no more than two electrons. The first eight subshells are listed to the right in order of increasing energy. *It is important to learn this order.* For elements other than hydrogen, the electrons interact with each other and alter the relative energies of the orbitals. Energy levels become closer to each other than in the hydrogen atom, with the result that the energy of the 4s orbital can be below that of the 3d orbital. This is the case for sodium, for example, see spread 4.3. Similar changes occur with higher orbitals.

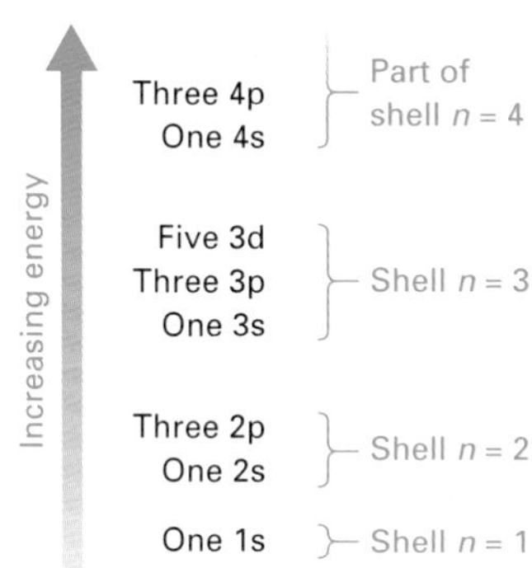

The relative energies of the 1s to 4p atomic orbitals for atoms with more than one electron. 4s orbitals are shown above 3d orbitals here, but they are actually of similar energy.

'Electrons-in-boxes' notation

A convenient way to represent electronic structures is a notation known as *'electrons-in-boxes'*. This notation shows each orbital as a box and the electrons as arrows in the boxes. The opposite spin of paired electrons is shown by arrows facing in opposite directions (usually up and down).

Although the 'electrons-in-boxes' notation is a useful visual aid, it is a tedious way to depict electronic structure routinely. We need an easier, shorter form. More usually, the occupied subshells are written in order of increasing energy with the number of electrons following as a superscript. For example, when there is only one electron in the 1s orbital, we write this as $1s^1$; similarly, $1s^2$ means two electrons are in the 1s orbital; and $2p^6$ means six electrons are in the 2p subshell (two each in the $2p_x$, $2p_y$, and $2p_z$ orbitals).

Element	Electrons-in-boxes					Shorter form of electronic structure
	1s	2s	2p			
			$2p_x$	$2p_y$	$2p_z$	
H	↑					$1s^1$
He	↑↓					$1s^2$
Li	↑↓	↑				$1s^22s^1$
Be	↑↓	↑↓				$1s^22s^2$
B	↑↓	↑↓	↑			$1s^22s^22p^1$
C	↑↓	↑↓	↑	↑		$1s^22s^22p^2$
N	↑↓	↑↓	↑	↑	↑	$1s^22s^22p^3$
O	↑↓	↑↓	↑↓	↑	↑	$1s^22s^22p^4$
F	↑↓	↑↓	↑↓	↑↓	↑	$1s^22s^22p^5$
Ne	↑↓	↑↓	↑↓	↑↓	↑↓	$1s^22s^22p^6$

'Electrons-in-boxes' notation and corresponding electronic structures in shorter form for the elements hydrogen to neon.

Ions

An ion with a charge of 1+ has one *less* electron than its parent atom. Such a *positive* ion is formed by the *loss* of an electron from the highest-energy occupied atomic orbital. The electronic structures of ions are presented in the same way as those of neutral atoms. For example, for sodium: Na $1s^22s^22p^63s^1$; Na^+ $1s^22s^22p^6$. Negative ions are represented in a similar manner, remembering that a *negative* ion has *more* electrons than its parent atom. For example, for chlorine: Cl $1s^22s^22p^63s^23p^5$; Cl^- $1s^22s^22p^63s^23p^6$.

Element	Atomic number	1s	2s	2p	3s	3p	3d	4s	4p
H	1	1							
He	2	2							
Li	3	2	1						
Be	4	2	2						
B	5	2	2	1					
C	6	2	2	2					
N	7	2	2	3					
O	8	2	2	4					
F	9	2	2	5					
Ne	10	2	2	6					
Na	11	2	2	6	1				
Mg	12	2	2	6	2				
Al	13	2	2	6	2	1			
Si	14	2	2	6	2	2			
P	15	2	2	6	2	3			
S	16	2	2	6	2	4			
Cl	17	2	2	6	2	5			
Ar	18	2	2	6	2	6			
K	19	2	2	6	2	6		1	
Ca	20	2	2	6	2	6		2	
Sc	21	2	2	6	2	6	1	2	
Ti	22	2	2	6	2	6	2	2	
V	23	2	2	6	2	6	3	2	
Cr	24	2	2	6	2	6	5	1	
Mn	25	2	2	6	2	6	5	2	
Fe	26	2	2	6	2	6	6	2	
Co	27	2	2	6	2	6	7	2	
Ni	28	2	2	6	2	6	8	2	
Cu	29	2	2	6	2	6	10	1	
Zn	30	2	2	6	2	6	10	2	
Ga	31	2	2	6	2	6	10	2	1
Ge	32	2	2	6	2	6	10	2	2
As	33	2	2	6	2	6	10	2	3
Se	34	2	2	6	2	6	10	2	4
Br	35	2	2	6	2	6	10	2	5
Kr	36	2	2	6	2	6	10	2	6

Electronic structures for the elements of atomic number Z = 1–36. The structures for chromium and copper are not as might be expected. This will be explained in Chapter 20.
Transition metal ions have electronic structures of the following form:
Fe^{2+} $1s^22s^22p^63s^23p^63d^6$
Cu^{2+} $1s^22s^22p^63s^23p^63d^9$
Note that the 4s electrons are always the first to be lost.

SUMMARY

- The building-up principle: electrons fill atomic orbitals in order of increasing energy.
- The Pauli exclusion principle: an atomic orbital can contain no more than two electrons. When two electrons occupy an atomic orbital, their spins must be paired.
- Hund's rule: when orbitals have the same energy, they first fill with one electron each (with parallel spins), before they start to pair up.

4.7

OBJECTIVES

- Patterns in electronic structures across periods and down groups

ELECTRONIC STRUCTURE AND THE PERIODIC TABLE

Mendeleyev constructed the first periodic table before anything was known about the structure of the atom. He organized it purely on the grounds of atomic mass and the properties of the elements. However, it is now known that chemical properties arise from the electronic structure of atoms and not from their relative masses. The shape of the periodic table may now be explained in terms of electronic structures.

Periods 1 and 2

The first shell, with principal quantum number n = 1, consists of just one s orbital. Period 1 therefore contains two elements: hydrogen H, with the electronic structure $1s^1$; and helium He, with the electronic structure $1s^2$. At the noble gas helium, the n = 1 shell is full.

The element lithium Li stands at the beginning of Period 2. The electronic structure of lithium is $1s^22s^1$. The second shell, with n = 2, has started to fill. This shell consists of one 2s orbital, which can contain two electrons, and three 2p orbitals, which can contain a total of six electrons. The n = 2 shell can therefore hold a maximum of eight electrons. Look at the outline periodic table below: the noble gas neon Ne marks the point at which the first shell (n = 1) and the second shell (n = 2) are both full.

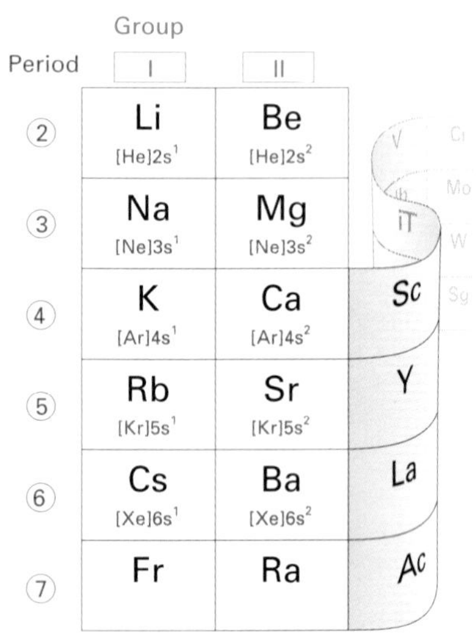

Period		III	IV	V	VI	VII	VIII
1	H $1s^1$						He $1s^2$
2		B $[He]2s^22p^1$	C $[He]2s^22p^2$	N $[He]2s^22p^3$	O $[He]2s^22p^4$	F $[He]2s^22p^5$	Ne $[He]2s^22p^6$
3		Al $[Ne]3s^23p^1$	Si $[Ne]3s^23p^2$	P $[Ne]3s^23p^3$	S $[Ne]3s^23p^4$	Cl $[Ne]3s^23p^5$	Ar $[Ne]3s^23p^6$
4	Zn	Ga $[Ar]3d^{10}4s^24p^1$	Ge $[Ar]3d^{10}4s^24p^2$	As $[Ar]3d^{10}4s^24p^3$	Se $[Ar]3d^{10}4s^24p^4$	Br $[Ar]3d^{10}4s^24p^5$	Kr $[Ar]3d^{10}4s^24p^6$
5	Cd	In $[Kr]4d^{10}5s^25p^1$	Sn $[Kr]4d^{10}5s^25p^2$	Sb $[Kr]4d^{10}5s^25p^3$	Te $[Kr]4d^{10}5s^25p^4$	I $[Kr]4d^{10}5s^25p^5$	Xe $[Kr]4d^{10}5s^25p^6$
6	Hg	Tl	Pb	Bi	Po	At	Rn

The periodic table with element symbols and short-form electronic structures up to barium Ba. Elements with electronic structures having full shells are the noble gases. As a short form, we use the symbols for the noble gases, enclosed in square brackets, to indicate electronic structures for full shells. For example, sodium Na $1s^22s^22p^63s^1$ can be written as Na $[Ne]3s^1$.

Groups

Notice how groups contain elements with similar electronic structures: Group I elements all end in ns^1; Group II elements all end in ns^2.

Period 3

Period 3 contains the sequence of elements from sodium Na to argon Ar, a total of eight elements. Period 3 fills the 3s and the 3p orbitals in the same way that Period 2 filled the 2s and the 2p orbitals. The third shell, with n = 3, consists of one 3s orbital, three 3p orbitals, and five 3d orbitals. You might expect the 3d to fill in the course of Period 3, but things are not that straightforward! The large number of electrons present causes the relative energies of the orbitals to change. The 4s orbital becomes lower in energy than 3d, and filling of the 3d orbitals is delayed until Period 4.

Period 4

Period 4 consists of a total of 18 elements, from potassium K to krypton Kr. The orbitals fill in the sequence 4s (potassium K, calcium Ca), 3d (scandium Sc to zinc Zn), and 4p (gallium Ga to krypton Kr).

Aluminium Al [Ne]$3s^2 3p^1$ is a metal. Silicon Si [Ne]$3s^2 3p^2$ is a metalloid. Phosphorus P [Ne]$3s^2 3p^3$ is a non-metal. These three elements, Al, Si, and P, have the sequential atomic numbers 13, 14, and 15, yet represent three different classes of element.

The s, p, d, and f blocks

The main body of the periodic table divides into three areas: the **s block**, the **p block**, and the **d block**.

- The s block, on the left, is where the s orbitals are filling.
- The p block, on the right, is where the p orbitals are filling.
- The d block, between the s and p blocks, is where the d orbitals of the previous shell are filling.

The two series of elements separated out at the bottom of the table make up the **f block**. There are 14 elements in each row (seven orbitals, two electrons each). The seven orbitals in each of the 4f and the 5f fill in the course of these series.

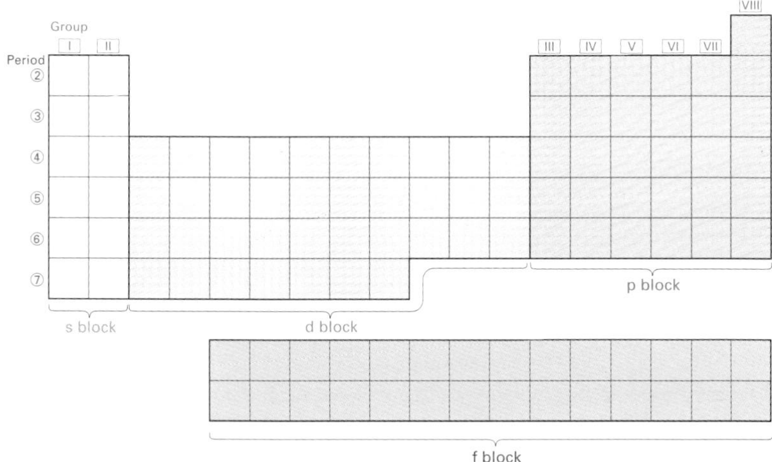

An outline of the periodic table showing the s, p, d, and f blocks.

SUMMARY

- The s block comprises Groups I and II (s orbitals filling – total two electrons).
- The p block comprises Groups III to VIII (p orbitals filling – total six electrons).
- The d block contains elements that have d orbitals filling (a total of 10 electrons for each of the 3d, 4d, and 5d subshells).

PRACTICE

1 In which block of the periodic table is each of the following elements?

a Strontium **b** Nickel
c Lithium **d** Arsenic
e Iron **f** Carbon.

2 Which orbitals are filling in the course of the following periods?

a Period 2 **b** Period 3
c Period 4.

4.8

OBJECTIVES

- First ionization energy
- Successive ionization energies

More evidence for shells and subshells: ionization energies

If you want to find out how something works, it is often a good idea to take it to pieces. Taking an atom to pieces involves removing the electrons one at a time, starting with the outermost. You already know that the process of removing electrons from an atom is called ionization. The energy needed to remove each successive electron from an atom is called the first, second, third, etc., ionization energy. The question is: can ionization energies confirm the arrangement of electrons in atoms?

Ionization energy

The **first ionization energy** is the minimum energy required to remove one electron from an isolated atom in the gas phase. In other words, it is the energy for the process:

$$E(g) \rightarrow E^{+}(g) + e^{-}(g)$$

where E represents an element. The value is usually quoted per mole of atoms. For example, the value for hydrogen is 1312 kJ mol^{-1}, and the value for sodium is 498 kJ mol^{-1}. All ionization energies are positive because it always *requires* energy to remove an electron. A plot of ionization energy against atomic number provides compelling evidence for the existence of shells and subshells.

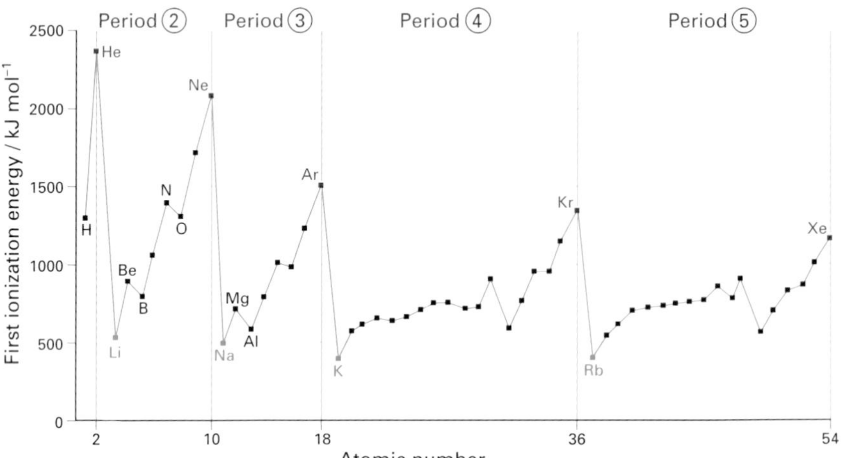

A plot of first ionization energy against atomic number for the elements hydrogen to xenon.

Evidence for shells

The noble gases helium to xenon stand at the peaks of the plot, where the values of first ionization energy are highest. These elements make up Group VIII: helium has one complete shell; neon has two complete shells; argon has completed the $n = 3$ shell (with the exception of the 3d subshell). Krypton and xenon follow a similar pattern.

Now turn your attention to the elements at the troughs in the plot, where the values of first ionization energy are lowest. These elements are all members of Group I. The outermost electrons of lithium, sodium, and potassium are all s electrons. From the graph we can see that the single s electron requires relatively little energy for removal compared with that needed to remove other electrons. This is because the s electrons are in 'new' shells further from the nucleus than the electrons in the preceding noble gases helium, neon, and argon. Note that the overall shape of the plot illustrates the periodic repetition of electronic structures that occurs in the periodic table.

Evidence for subshells

The plot of first ionization energies also provides evidence for subshells, although we need to look harder. See how the value *decreases* slightly between beryllium and boron, and between magnesium and aluminium. In both cases, the second element has its outermost electron in a new subshell (the p subshell) rather than an s subshell. As the p subshell is further from the nucleus, the attractive force is less and so the energy required to remove the electron is less.

There is also a decrease in ionization energy between nitrogen and oxygen. This decrease arises because nitrogen has three unpaired electrons in the 2p subshell, whereas oxygen has two unpaired electrons and two paired electrons. In the case of oxygen, the electron–electron repulsion between the two paired electrons in one p orbital makes one of the pair slightly easier to remove. The electronic structure of oxygen is therefore slightly less stable than the half-filled subshell in nitrogen, which contains no paired electrons. As a result, slightly less energy is required to remove an electron from oxygen than might otherwise be expected.

Some electronic structures

Beryllium	$_4Be$	[He]$2s^2$
Boron	$_5B$	[He]$2s^22p^1$
Nitrogen	$_7N$	[He]$2s^22p^3$
Oxygen	$_8O$	[He]$2s^22p^4$
Magnesium	$_{12}Mg$	[Ne]$3s^2$
Aluminium	$_{13}Al$	[Ne]$3s^23p^1$

Further evidence for shells

Further evidence for shells comes from the successive ionization energies needed to remove *all* the electrons from an atom. Look, for example, at removing all 11 electrons from a sodium atom. There is a significant increase in energy needed between removing the first and second electrons. There is another large increase between removing the ninth and tenth electrons. These observations suggest that the increases occur when the electron being removed has to come from a new shell, closer to the attractive charge of the nucleus. The pattern shows that the outermost $n = 3$ shell of sodium contains one electron, and the $n = 2$ shell has eight electrons, leaving two electrons in the innermost $n = 1$ shell.

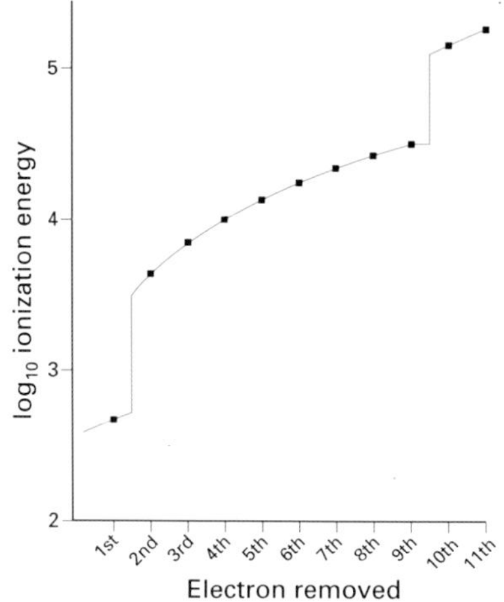

A plot of successive ionization energies for the sodium atom, $_{11}Na$ $1s^22s^22p^63s^1$. See spread 12.3 for the meaning of log_{10}.

Trends across a period

Each successive element in a period has one more proton than the previous one. As a result, the nuclear charge increases steadily. But the hold the nucleus has on the outer electrons does *not* change steadily. For successive elements across Period 3, electrons are added to the *same* outer shell. Since electrons in the same shell do not shield each other very well from the attraction of the nuclear charge, the *effective* nuclear charge experienced by the outermost electrons in each successive element increases. So the outermost electrons experience a greater attractive force towards the nucleus. The result is that the atomic radius *decreases* as the outermost electrons are pulled closer to the nucleus, as you go from sodium to argon, and the ionization energy *increases* significantly from sodium to argon.

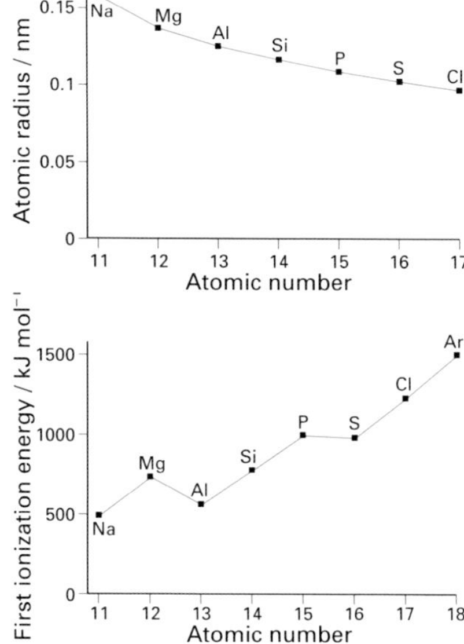

Plots of (a) atomic radius, and (b) first ionization energy against atomic number for Period 3.

SUMMARY

- Ionization energies provide evidence for shells and subshells.
- Atomic size decreases and first ionization energy generally increases across a period.

PRACTICE

1 Sketch a graph of the successive ionization energies of potassium. What does the shape of your graph tell you about the electronic structure of potassium?

2 The trend in ionization energies from lithium to neon is not smooth. Is the value for beryllium higher, or is the value for boron lower, than might be expected? Explain your answer.

3 Why do the ionization energies for the elements in the group helium to xenon show a downward trend?

4 The ionization energies of the d-block elements scandium to zinc are fairly similar. Refer to the electronic structures of these elements to explain this observation.

4.9

SOLVING THE SCHRÖDINGER EQUATION

OBJECTIVES

- The form of the Schrödinger equation
- Solutions of the Schrödinger equation
- Physical significance of the solutions

Principal quantum numbers

The Schrödinger equation for the hydrogen atom can only be solved analytically for certain values of *E*. The full set of solutions available can be labelled in terms of three quantum numbers. Remember that the Bohr model gave only one, the principal quantum number *n*. Solutions to the Schrödinger equation give values for *n* which concur with Bohr.

- *n* increases from 1 onwards in integer steps: 1, 2, 3, 4, etc.

Azimuthal quantum numbers

The second quantum number that arises from solutions of the Schrödinger equation is the **azimuthal quantum number** *l*. An s orbital has $l = 0$, a p orbital has $l = 1$, and a d orbital has $l = 2$.

- For any particular value of *n*, *l* can take all integer values from 0 to $n - 1$.

The first shell ($n = 1$) can therefore have only one subshell: 1s ($l = 0$). The second shell ($n = 2$) can have two subshells: 2s ($l = 0$) and 2p ($l = 1$). The third shell ($n = 3$) can have three subshells: 3s ($l = 0$), 3p ($l = 1$), and 3d ($l = 2$). *The Schrödinger equation provides a natural explanation for the existence of subshells.* (See spread 4.3.)

Magnetic quantum numbers

The third quantum number that arises from solutions of the Schrödinger equation is the **magnetic quantum number** m_l.

- For any particular value of *l*, m_l can take all integer values from $-l$ to l.

There is only **one s orbital** ($m_l = 0$) for any value of *n*. There are **three p orbitals** ($m_l = -1, 0, 1$) for $n \geq 2$, **five d orbitals** ($m_l = -2, -1, 0, 1, 2$) for $n \geq 3$, and **seven f orbitals** ($m_l = -3, -2, -1, 0, 1, 2, 3$) for $n \geq 4$. *The Schrödinger equation provides a natural explanation for the number of orbitals in each subshell.*

This spread looks at solutions of the Schrödinger equation, the mathematical model that gives us the shapes of atomic orbitals. **You are not expected to learn the contents of this spread**, but it gives more insight into the atomic orbital theory for students interested in mathematics. The Schrödinger equation gives a model of the atom based on the mathematics of waves, as we saw in spread 4.4 on wave mechanics. It is a *differential* equation. The two common techniques for solving such equations produce analytical solutions and numerical solutions. Early attempts to solve the equation focused on analytical solutions whereas numerical solutions are more common now, due to the advent of more powerful computers. In simple circumstances, the Schrödinger equation can even be solved on a graphical calculator, as shown below.

The Schrödinger equation

The form of the Schrödinger equation for the energy *E* of the 1s orbital in the hydrogen atom is as follows:

$$-\frac{h^2}{8\pi^2 m}\left[\frac{d^2\psi}{dr^2} + \left(\frac{2}{r}\right)\frac{d\psi}{dr}\right] - \frac{e^2}{4\pi\varepsilon_0 r}\,\psi = E\psi \qquad (1)$$

where *h* is the Planck constant, *m* is the mass of the electron, *e* is the charge on the electron, and ε_0 is a fundamental constant called the vacuum permittivity. The function ψ is called the **wave function**. The first (bracketed) term is the wave equation version of the kinetic energy of the electron. The second term is its potential energy due to electrostatic attraction to a single proton at a distance *r*.

Multiplying both sides of equation (1) by $(-8\pi^2 m/h^2)$ and collecting together fundamental constants using $a_0 = \varepsilon_0 h^2/\pi m e^2$, we find:

$$\frac{d^2\psi}{dr^2} + \left(\frac{2}{r}\right)\frac{d\psi}{dr} + \left(\frac{2}{a_0 r}\right)\psi = \left(\frac{-8\pi^2 mE}{h^2}\right)\psi \qquad (2)$$

The quantity a_0 has the units of length and is called the Bohr radius, the radius at which Bohr said the electron orbits the proton. The second and third terms cancel out if:

$$\frac{d\psi}{dr} = \frac{-\psi}{a_0}$$

This is the equation for exponential decay, whose solution is:

$$\psi = \psi_0 e^{-r/a_0}$$

The energy *E* for the 1s orbital is found by differentiating again, substituting into equation (2), and rearranging:

$$\frac{d^2\psi}{dr^2} = \frac{d}{dr}\left(\frac{d\psi}{dr}\right) = \frac{d}{dr}\left(\frac{-\psi}{a_0}\right) = \frac{\psi}{a_0^2}$$

$$\frac{1}{a_0^2} = \frac{-8\pi^2 mE}{h^2}$$

Thus,

$$E = \frac{-h^2}{8\pi^2 m a_0^2}$$

If you substitute the values $h = 6.626 \times 10^{-34}$ J s, $m = 9.109 \times 10^{-31}$ kg, $a_0 = 5.292 \times 10^{-11}$ m, and multiply by the Avogadro constant, 6.022×10^{23} mol^{-1}, to get the energy per mole, the numerical value is 1310 kJ mol^{-1} (to 3 sig. figs.), which is the ionization energy for the hydrogen atom, spread 4.8.

Using a graphical calculator

A graphical calculator can also be used to solve the Schrödinger equation numerically. With the substitutions:

$$x = \frac{r}{a_0}$$

and

$$E = -\frac{h^2}{8\pi^2 m a_0^{\,2}}$$

and using f in place of ψ for convenience, equation (2) (multiplied by $a_0^{\,2}$) simplifies to:

$$\frac{d^2f}{dx^2} + \left(\frac{2}{x}\right)\frac{df}{dx} + \left(\frac{2}{x}\right)f = f \qquad (3)$$

Equation (3), must be manipulated into a form suitable for use with a graphical calculator that can solve differential equations. Such a calculator usually needs a second-order differential equation (with a term $\frac{d^2f}{dx^2}$) to be re-written as a pair of first-order differential equations. This transformation is carried out as follows:

$$g = \frac{df}{dx}, \qquad (4)$$

$$\frac{dg}{dx} = \frac{d^2f}{dx^2}$$

$$= -\left(\frac{2}{x}\right)\frac{df}{dx} - \left(\frac{2}{x}\right)f + f$$

$$= -\left(\frac{2}{x}\right)g - \left(\frac{2}{x}\right)f + f \qquad (5)$$

This pair of equations (4 and 5) is now ready for solution once initial conditions are chosen. The following choice compares the value of ψ with its value at the origin (ψ_0):

$f = 1$ and $g = -1$ at $x = 0$

The solution is a *numerical* solution to the equation (which must avoid $x = 0$ itself, which leads to an infinite value). The result is shown to the right, a decaying exponential. See spread 4.5 for the related electron density (which is the square of the wave function).

If the pair of equations is solved again, with the term in front of the final f changed slightly (to simulate a value for the total energy *close to but different from* the true answer), the solution becomes unstable and does not correspond to physical reality. For example, for the equation:

$$\frac{dg}{dx} = -\left(\frac{2}{x}\right)g - \left(\frac{2}{x}\right)f + 1.01f$$

the numerical solution results in the lower figure shown to the right. The total energy is only *1% away from the true answer* and yet the solution is unacceptable as the value of the wave function rises to infinity (exceeding its initial value less than 12 Bohr radii from the nucleus).

The two plots shown provide graphic illustration of the quantization of energy. Quantization of energy arises naturally from the Schrödinger equation, whereas Bohr had to *assume* that energy is quantized.

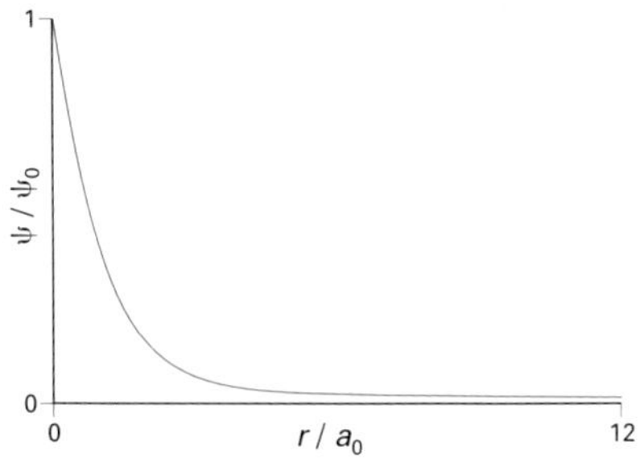

The numerical solution of the Schrödinger equation for the lowest-energy orbital (1s) is an exponential decay of the wave function ψ against distance from the nucleus.

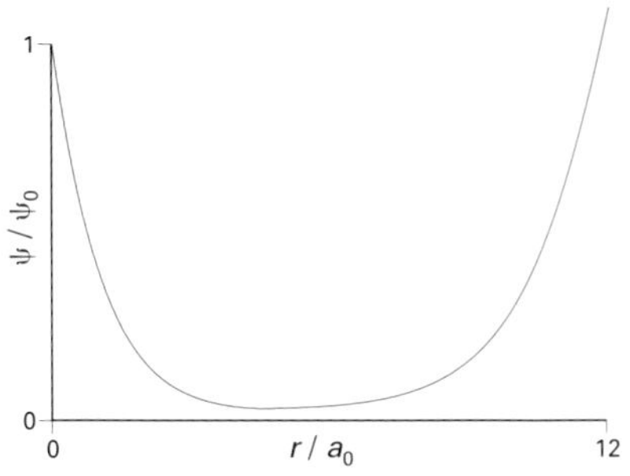

The plot of ψ against r, for a solution which does not correspond to physical reality.

Electron spin

The one failure of the Schrödinger equation is that it does not account for the existence of two electrons per orbital; it cannot explain electron spin or the Pauli exclusion principle.

PRACTICE EXAM QUESTIONS

1 The graph below shows the trend in first ionization energy from oxygen to magnesium.

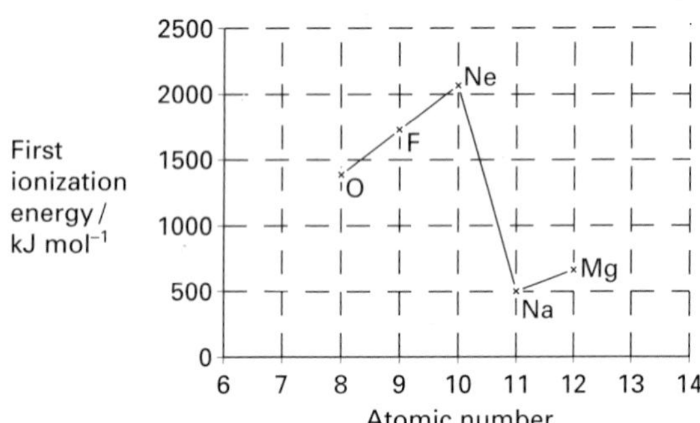

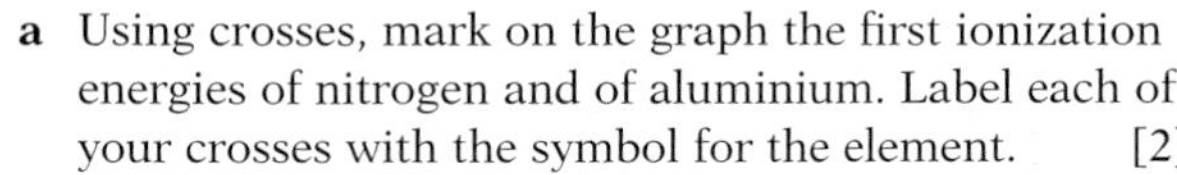

a Using crosses, mark on the graph the first ionization energies of nitrogen and of aluminium. Label each of your crosses with the symbol for the element. [2]

b Explain why the first ionization energy of neon is greater than that of sodium. [2]

c Of the elements neon, sodium, and magnesium, predict which one has the largest second ionization energy. Explain your answer. [3]

d Published values of electronegativity are available for oxygen, fluorine, sodium, and magnesium but not for neon.

i Explain why a value of electronegativity is not available for neon.

ii Of the elements oxygen, fluorine, sodium, and magnesium, predict which one has the smallest electronegativity value. [2]

e Explain, with reference to the bonding in sodium oxide, why this compound reacts with water to form a solution with a pH of 14. [3]

f What general type of oxide forms acidic solutions in water? Give the formula of one such oxide. [2]
AQA (NEAB) 1999 *(See also Chapters 16 and 17.)*

2 The diagram below shows the electronic structure of boron.

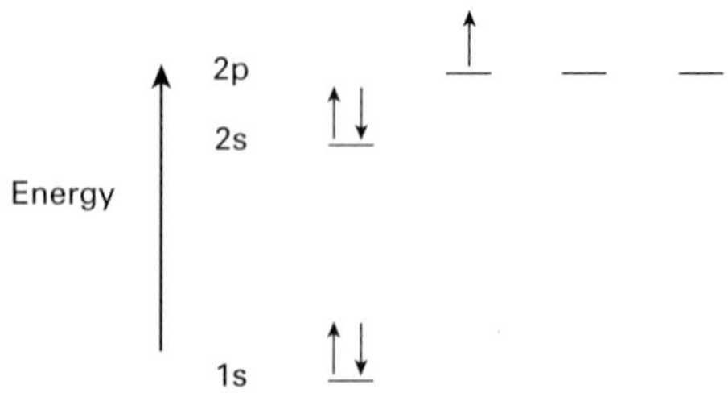

a The electrons are represented by arrows. What property of the electrons do these 'up' and 'down' arrows represent? [1]

b Suggest why electrons which occupy the 2p sub-levels have a higher energy than electrons in the 2s sub-level. [1]

c Complete the following energy level diagram to show the electronic structure of carbon. [2]

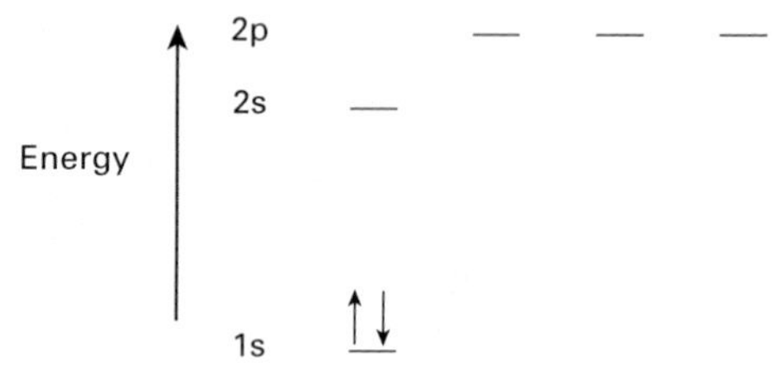

d Explain the meaning of the term *first ionization energy*. [2]

e Explain why oxygen has a lower first ionisation energy than nitrogen. [2]
AQA (NEAB) 1998

3 The following table contains ionization energy data.

Element	N	O	F	Ne	Na
First ionization energy / kJ mol⁻¹	1400	1310	1680	2080	494

a Explain the meaning of the term *first ionization energy* of an element. [2]

b Explain why neon has a higher first ionization energy than fluorine. [2]

c Explain why oxygen has a lower first ionization energy than nitrogen. [2]

d Explain why sodium has a lower first ionization energy than neon. [2]

e Predict an approximate value for the first ionization energy of carbon and explain your answer. [3]
AQA (NEAB) 1997

4 **a** Explain why the first ionization energy of aluminium is less than the first ionization energy of magnesium. [3]

b Explain why the first ionization energy of aluminium is less than the first ionization energy of silicon. [2]

c Explain why the second ionization energy of aluminium is greater than the first ionization energy of aluminium. [2]

d Write an equation to illustrate the third ionization energy of aluminium. [1]

e Explain why the third ionization energy of aluminium is much less than the third ionization energy of magnesium. [2]
AQA (NEAB) 1998

5 The Sun largely consists of a mixture of hydrogen and helium, the presence of each being detected by spectroscopy. The line emission spectrum of atomic hydrogen in the ultraviolet region of the electromagnetic spectrum is shown below.

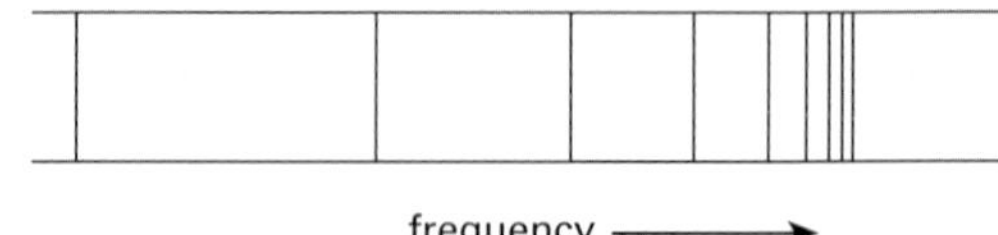

a Explain why this spectrum consists of lines which are converging.

(Up to 2 marks may be obtained for the quality of language in this part.) [7]

b Explain how the ionization energy of atomic hydrogen can be calculated from this spectrum. [2]
NICCEA 1998

6 a Define the second ionization energy of fluorine. [2]

b Using axis as below, sketch a graph to show the successive ionization energies of fluorine. Give reasons for the shape of the line you draw.

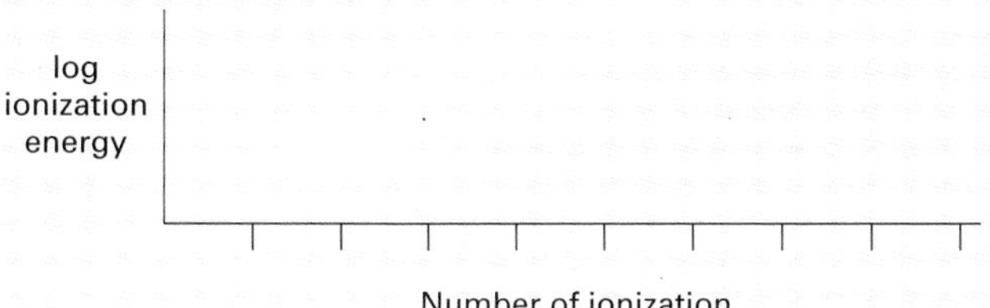

EDEXCEL 1997 [4]

7 a i Give the equation which represents the first ionization energy of oxygen atoms. [1]

ii Why is the first ionization energy of helium the largest of all the atoms? [2]

iii Why is the first ionization energy of oxygen atoms less than that of nitrogen atoms? [2]

iv Why do the first ionization energies of the atoms in Group 1 decrease as the atomic number increases? [2]

b i Write equations which represent the first and second electron affinities of oxygen atoms. [2]

ii The first electron affinity of oxygen atoms is -141 kJ mol^{-1} and the second is $+798$ kJ mol^{-1}. Suggest why the first is exothermic and the second endothermic. [2]

c Magnesium burns brightly in oxygen to give magnesium oxide, which contains the ions Mg^{2+} and O^{2-}. The formation of both these ions from their elements is strongly endothermic. Why, therefore, should magnesium combine with oxygen? [2]

d The table below gives the successive ionization energies of sodium.

No. of ionization	1	2	3	4	5	6
Energy / kJ mol^{-1}	496	4563	6913	9644	13352	16611

No. of ionization	7	8	9	10	11
Energy / kJ mol^{-1}	20115	25491	28934	141367	159079

What information about the electronic structure of sodium is provided by this data? [2]
EDEXCEL 1998 *(See also Chapter 10.)*

8 a Study the table of ionization energies below and answer the questions which follow.

Ionization energy / kJ mol^{-1}	1st	2nd	3rd	4th
Sodium	494	4560	6940	9540
Magnesium	736	1450	7740	10500
Aluminium	577	1820	2740	11600

Explain the relative magnitudes of the following:

i the 1st ionization energies of sodium and magnesium;

ii the 1st ionization energies of magnesium and aluminium;

iii the 2nd ionization energies of magnesium and aluminium;

iv the 3rd and 4th ionization energies of aluminium. [8]

b Consider the electron affinities for oxygen given below.

Electron affinity / kJ mol^{-1}	1st	2nd
	−142	+844

i Write equations representing the changes to which the 1st and 2nd electron affinities of oxygen relate.

ii Explain the relative magnitudes of the 1st and 2nd electron affinities of oxygen.

iii Given the endothermic nature of the 2nd electron affinity of oxygen, comment briefly on the thermodynamic stability of ionic metal oxides. [7]
EDEXCEL (ULEAC) 1993

9 The first ionization energies of the elements lithium to neon, in kJ mol^{-1}, are given below.

Li	Be	B	C	N	O	F	Ne
519	900	799	1090	1400	1310	1680	2080

a Write an equation representing the first ionization energy of oxygen. [1]

b i Explain why the ionization energies show an overall tendency to increase across the Period.

ii Explain the irregularities in this trend for B and O. [6]

c An element **X** has successive ionization energies as follows:

786; 1580; 3230; 4360; 16000; 20000; 23600; 29100 kJ mol^{-1}

i To which Group in the Periodic Table does **X** belong?

Explain your answer.

ii Write down the outer electronic configuration of an atom of **X**.

iii Suggest formulae for TWO chlorides of **X**. [5]
EDEXCEL (ULEAC) 1991

Chemical bonding

Excluding the 'exotic' elements produced in nuclear reactors, there are just 90 naturally occurring elements. These few elements combine to make over five million different compounds. A compound is any substance formed by the chemical combination of two or more elements in fixed proportions. The properties of a compound are usually completely different from the properties of its constituent elements. When atoms combine together to make compounds, there is a change in the arrangement of the electrons in the outermost shell of each atom. These electrons form links called **chemical bonds** between the atoms. The aim of this chapter is to investigate the nature of chemical bonds and to describe how they form.

BONDING REVISION

5.1

OBJECTIVES

- Ionic bonding
- Covalent bonding
- Bonding and properties

The sodium ion

A sodium *atom* Na has 11 protons in its nucleus. The nucleus is surrounded by 11 electrons. The atom is neutral overall, the total negative charge of the 11 electrons being exactly balanced by the total positive charge of the 11 protons, i.e. (+11) + (−11) = 0.

A sodium *ion* Na^+ forms when a sodium atom *loses* one electron. The ion has an overall charge of +1 because there are 11 protons in the nucleus with only 10 surrounding electrons, i.e. (+11) + (−10) = +1.

The chloride ion

A chlorine *atom* Cl has 17 protons in its nucleus. The nucleus is surrounded by 17 electrons.

A chloride *ion* Cl^- forms when a chlorine atom *gains* one electron. The ion has an overall charge of −1 because there are 17 protons in the nucleus with 18 surrounding electrons, i.e. (+17) + (−18) = −1.

In sodium chloride, Na^+ ions and Cl^- ions alternate in a three-dimensional lattice. The formula of sodium chloride is NaCl, which signifies that 1 mol of sodium ions is combined with 1 mol of chloride ions. It is incorrect to speak of 'a molecule of sodium chloride'.

In your earlier studies you have met two main types of bonding:

- ionic bonding,
- covalent bonding.

Before studying the subject of bonding in greater depth, this spread will revise the two basic principles underlying the formation of bonds: electron transfer and electron sharing. This spread uses simple concepts which will probably be familiar to you.

Ionic bonding

Ionic bonds form between metals and non-metals. The name 'ion' is used to describe any species that has unequal numbers of electrons and protons and so carries an electric charge. Metals lose one or more electrons and become positively charged ions. Non-metals gain one or more electrons and become negatively charged ions. Both types of ion usually have full outer shells of electrons, corresponding to the stable electronic structures of the noble gases. The oppositely charged ions attract each other to form a rigid three-dimensional lattice. Each ion in the lattice is surrounded by others of opposite charge.

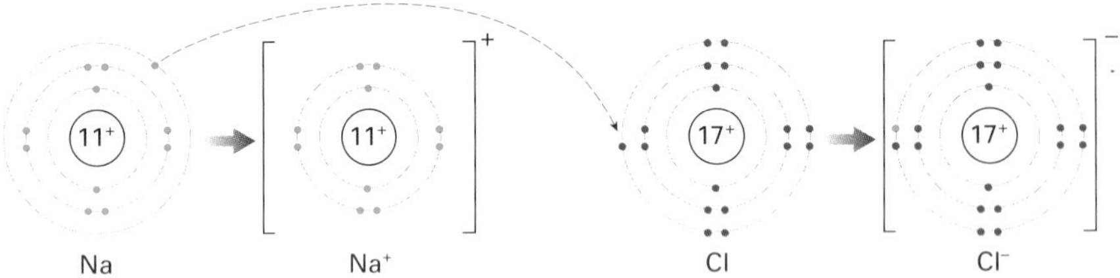

The formation of sodium and chloride ions from their atoms. The full inner shells of electrons are not usually shown.

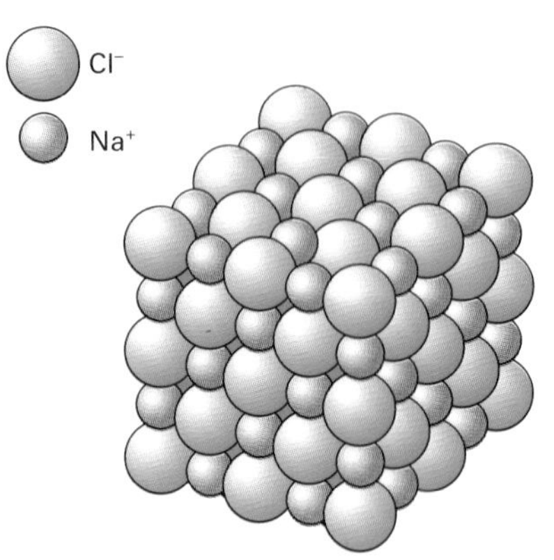

Cubic crystals of pure sodium chloride reflect the arrangement of the ions that make it up.

Covalent bonding

Covalent bonds form between non-metals, which share electrons in order to attain full outer shells. Each shared pair of electrons is regarded as one covalent bond. Covalent bonding between atoms results in the formation of **molecules**. The simplest examples are **diatomic molecules** (molecules that contain two atoms), such as the elements hydrogen H_2 and chlorine Cl_2.

$$:\ddot{\underset{..}{Cl}}\cdot + \cdot\ddot{\underset{..}{Cl}}: \longrightarrow :\ddot{\underset{..}{Cl}}:\ddot{\underset{..}{Cl}}:$$

Shared pair of electrons

The formation of a chlorine molecule. Two electrons, one from each chlorine atom, form a shared pair. Including this shared pair, each atom now has a full outer shell of electrons, corresponding to the electronic structure of the noble gas argon.

The shared pair of electrons is concentrated in the region of space between the two atomic nuclei. The nuclei are each attracted towards this region of negative charge concentrated between them. Covalent bonds are therefore the result of electrostatic attraction.

Covalent bonds form in the same manner between atoms of different elements. For example, one hydrogen atom and one chlorine atom combine to form a hydrogen chloride molecule HCl; hydrogen and oxygen atoms form water H_2O.

Looking forward

The model for ionic bonding described above was introduced by Walther Kossel in 1916. In the same year, Gilbert Lewis presented the theory of covalent bonding based on the sharing of electron pairs between atoms. The following two spreads will use Lewis's ideas to describe the bonding in a number of substances. Looking at the electron pairs present in molecules will then allow us to make predictions about their shapes.

SUMMARY

- Ionic bonds are the electrostatic forces of attraction between oppositely charged ions; the ions are the result of electron transfer between atoms.
- Covalent bonds result from atoms sharing electrons; there is an attraction between these electrons and the nuclei of the atoms.
- Ionic compounds generally have high melting points and high boiling points.
- Covalent compounds composed of small molecules have low melting points and low boiling points.

Properties of ionic compounds

The electrostatic forces of attraction between oppositely charged ions are strong. Ionic compounds have high melting points (T_m) and high boiling points (T_b) (e.g. sodium chloride: T_m = 801 °C, T_b = 1413 °C). Solid ionic compounds do not conduct electricity. When solid ionic compounds are melted, they *do* conduct electricity because the ions are then free to move.

Properties of covalent elements and compounds

The covalent bonds between atoms within a molecule are strong, but the forces of attraction *between molecules* are weak. Covalent compounds made up of small molecules have low melting points and low boiling points (e.g. hydrogen chloride HCl: T_m = −115 °C, T_b = −85 °C). Solid, liquid, and gas states all consist of covalently bonded molecules. Covalently bonded substances do not conduct electricity in any of these states because there are no free charged species (electrons or ions) present.

Chlorine gas consists of covalently bonded diatomic molecules (i.e. molecules in which two chlorine atoms are held together by a covalent bond).

PRACTICE

1 Give the symbols of the stable ions that may be formed by the following atoms:
- **a** Lithium
- **b** Aluminium
- **c** Oxygen
- **d** Potassium
- **e** Fluorine
- **f** Strontium
- **g** Nitrogen.

2 Draw diagrams to show what happens to the electrons when the ionic compound potassium sulphide is formed from the elements potassium and sulphur.

3 Draw diagrams to show how the following elements bond together to form covalent molecules. Give the formula of each molecule.
- **a** Hydrogen and fluorine
- **b** Oxygen and hydrogen
- **c** Nitrogen and hydrogen
- **d** Oxygen and fluorine.

OBJECTIVES

- Drawing Lewis structures
- Why electrons pair
- Bonding pairs and lone pairs

Lewis structures for covalent molecules – 1

You should already be familiar with drawing covalent molecules on paper, representing electrons as dots surrounding the symbols of each constituent element. These drawings are called Lewis structures. In the chlorine molecule Cl_2, one pair of electrons is shared between the two atoms. The sharing of a single electron pair constitutes a single covalent bond. This spread will look more closely at Lewis structures, and will show why electron pairs are central to the idea of covalent bonding.

(a)

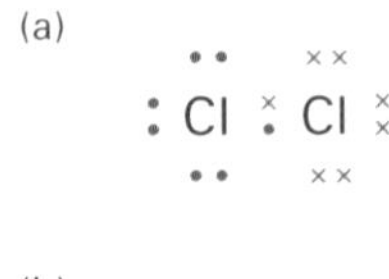

(b)

Cl Cl

(a) The dot-and-cross diagram and (b) the Lewis structure illustrating the bonding in the chlorine molecule. Note that the bond contains one electron from each of the contributing atoms. From now on we will use only Lewis structures in this book.

Lewis structures

Lewis structures use dots to represent electrons; **dot-and-cross diagrams** are similar to Lewis structures, but the electrons are shown as dots or crosses. Dot-and-cross diagrams help by showing the sources of the electrons involved in covalent bonds. However, dot-and-cross diagrams can be misleading, as they suggest that the electrons are somehow different from each other. Therefore, Lewis structures will be used throughout this text, with the dots of different intensity to show the sources of the electrons.

Electron pairs

A chlorine atom has 17 electrons; just *two* electrons are involved in the covalent bond between the atoms of a chlorine molecule. In this case it is clear that most of the electrons are not used for bonding. When two chlorine atoms form a covalent bond in Cl_2, each achieves the electronic structure of argon, a noble gas. The shared electrons involved in the formation of a covalent bond are called the **valence electrons**. The shell from which they originate is called the **valence shell** of the atom concerned. The valence shell is usually the *outermost* shell.

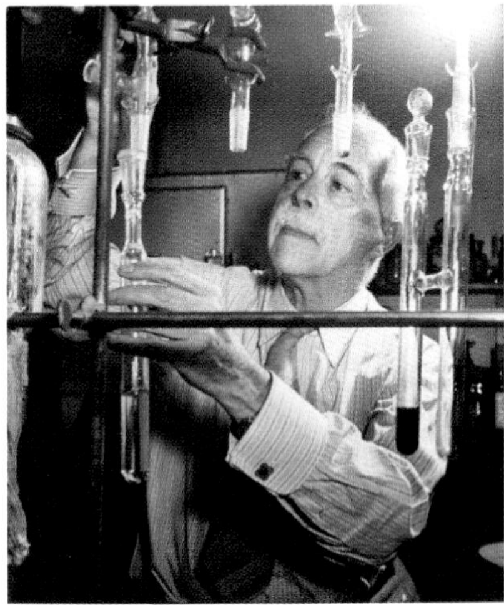

Gilbert Newton Lewis proposed the idea of covalent bonding and showed the importance of electron pairs in bonding. Lewis's treatment of covalent bonding was remarkable because the reasons for the formation of bonding pairs of electrons were not known at the time. Lewis first introduced his dot diagrams in 1916.

In the chlorine molecule Cl_2, the valence shell of each chlorine atom contains two electrons that are involved in bonding and six that are not. How are these electrons arranged? This question may be answered by considering the electronic structures of the atoms.

The atomic number of chlorine is 17. Its electronic structure in terms of occupied shells is therefore: Cl 2,8,7. This method of listing the electrons says little about the valence shell other than that it contains seven electrons. Stating the electronic structure in terms of atomic orbitals (as we did in the previous chapter) is more informative:

$$\text{Cl } 1s^2 2s^2 2p^6 3s^2 3p^5 \quad \text{or} \quad \text{Cl } [\text{Ne}]3s^2 3p^5$$

This structure shows that the valence shell ($n = 3$) is occupied by two s electrons and five p electrons (a total of seven electrons). The actual occupancy of the 3s and the 3p orbitals is shown by the electrons-in-boxes notation (shown left).

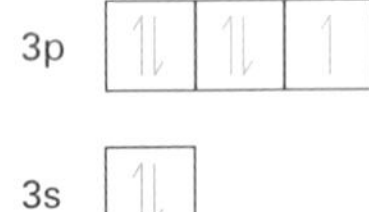

Electrons-in-boxes notation for 3s and 3p chlorine atomic orbitals. Note that there is no distinction between the three p orbitals. The unpaired electron could be in any one of them.

There is a pair of electrons in the 3s orbital. Two of the three equivalent 3p orbitals contain a pair of electrons each, while the remaining 3p orbital contains an unpaired electron. Look back to the Lewis structure for the chlorine atom and you will see that the electrons are grouped as three pairs with a single unpaired electron.

The bond in the chlorine molecule consists of a shared pair of electrons, which forms when two electrons (from atomic orbitals on two separate atoms) pair up and occupy a region of space between the two atoms. The electrons that form the bond are called a **bonding pair** of electrons. The bonding electrons must have opposite (paired) spins as a result of the Pauli exclusion principle. Each atom also has three pairs of electrons that are in the valence shell but do not take part in bonding. These electron pairs are called **lone pairs** (or non-bonding pairs).

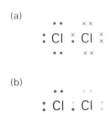

More Lewis structures

The Lewis structures for the covalently bonded molecules hydrogen chloride HCl, hydrogen H_2, and water H_2O are shown below. Each electron pair constitutes a single covalent bond. The bonding in the three molecules may be represented respectively as H—Cl, H—H, and H—O—H. A single line conventionally represents a single shared pair of electrons (a single covalent bond).

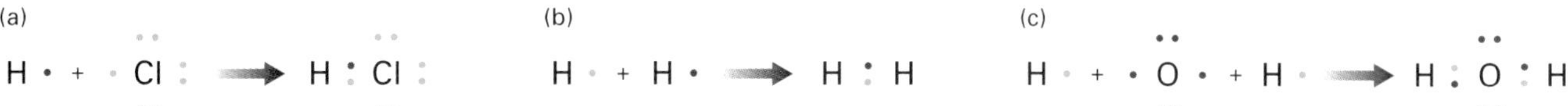

Lewis structures showing the formation of: (a) hydrogen chloride HCl; (b) hydrogen H_2; and (c) water H_2O.

The octet rule

When they combine to form molecules, many non-metal atoms share electrons in order to have eight electrons in their outermost (valence) shells. This electronic structure represents the particularly stable structure found in all the noble gases except helium. This pattern of electron sharing provides a useful rule of thumb, which helps to work out how atoms will bond together. Lewis called it the **octet rule** because atoms share electrons in order to achieve *eight* electrons in their valence shells. It is important to remember that hydrogen can only hold two electrons in its valence shell, so it can only share one pair of electrons (to gain the electronic structure of the noble gas helium).

For example, the ammonia molecule contains atoms of nitrogen and hydrogen. The electronic structures are N $1s^2 2s^2 2p^3$ and H $1s^1$. According to the octet rule, nitrogen must share *three* pairs of electrons with hydrogen atoms to bring the total population of its valence shell up from five electrons to eight.

Lewis structure showing the formation of ammonia NH_3. A single covalent bond forms between each hydrogen atom and the nitrogen atom.

Double bonds

A carbon atom has four electrons in the valence shell and so needs to share a total of four electron pairs. An oxygen atom has six electrons in the valence shell and so needs to share a total of two electron pairs. So two oxygen atoms combine with one carbon atom to form the molecule carbon dioxide. The bonding may therefore be represented as O=C=O, indicating the presence of two *double* covalent bonds. Each double covalent bond is conventionally represented by a double line.

The Lewis structure for carbon dioxide CO_2.

Triple bonds

A *triple* covalent bond forms between two atoms when each contributes *three* electrons. A total of six electrons are shared. This occurs, for example, in nitrogen N_2, represented as N≡N. Each triple covalent bond is conventionally represented by a triple line.

The Lewis structure for nitrogen N_2.

SUMMARY

- Lewis structures use dots to show the electrons involved in bonding pairs and lone pairs.
- The outer shells of atoms in molecules are usually full; i.e. the atoms have the electronic structures of the noble gases.
- A covalent bond forms when electrons from atomic orbitals on two separate atoms pair up and occupy the region of space *between* the two atoms.
- A single covalent bond is a shared electron pair.
- A double covalent bond consists of four electrons making up two shared pairs.
- A triple covalent bond consists of six electrons making up three shared pairs.

5.3

OBJECTIVES

- Failure of the octet rule
- Coordinate bonding

LEWIS STRUCTURES FOR COVALENT MOLECULES – 2

A single covalent bond consists of a shared pair of electrons. Double and triple covalent bonds result from the sharing of two and three pairs of electrons respectively. Atoms combine to form molecules – the atoms share electrons so that there are eight in their valence shells, following the octet rule. Lewis structures help us to explain this, and show the numbers of bonding pairs and lone pairs of electrons. However, there is a wide range of compounds whose formulae do not follow the octet rule. Their valence shells do not contain eight electrons. This spread takes a first look at this problem.

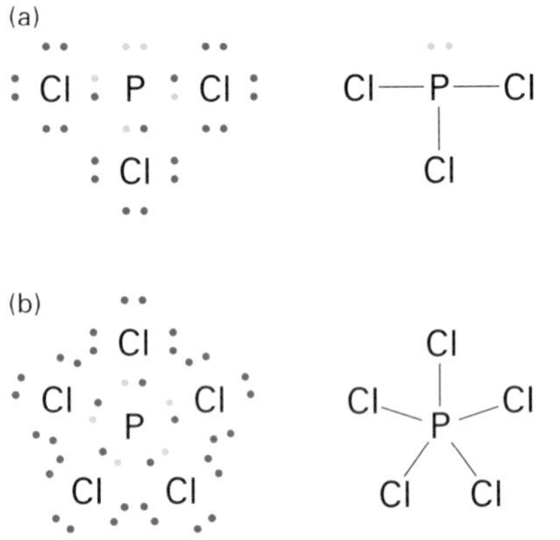

Lewis structures for (a) phosphorus trichloride (which follows the octet rule) and (b) phosphorus pentachloride (which does not follow the octet rule).

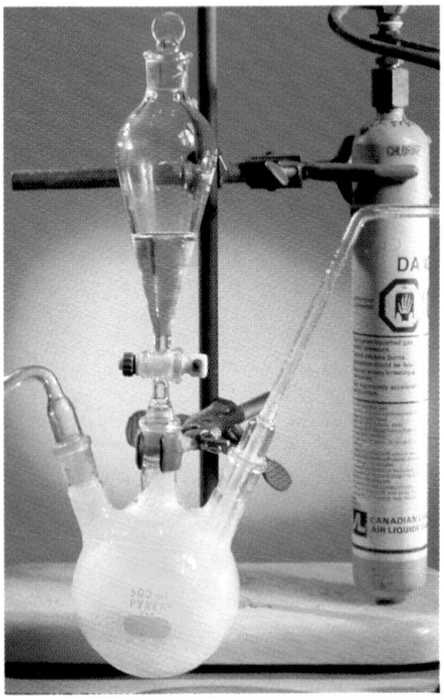

Phosphorus trichloride is a volatile liquid; it reacts with chlorine to form phosphorus pentachloride, which is a solid.

Expanding the octet

Phosphorus trichloride is a volatile liquid (T_b = 75 °C) which does not conduct electricity. This substance has the properties of a typical covalent compound, and the octet rule predicts correctly that phosphorus and chlorine atoms bond together to form molecules with the formula PCl_3.

Phosphorus trichloride reacts with chlorine to form phosphorus pentachloride. This substance contains phosphorus and chlorine in the mole ratio 1:5, and its properties suggest that it is covalently bonded. In the vapour state the molecules are completely separate from each other and have the formula PCl_5, although it has a more complicated structure in the solid state (but still with the same mole ratio).

The octet rule does not hold for the molecule PCl_5. Five P—Cl single covalent bonds involve five shared pairs of electrons, with the result that the valence shell of phosphorus contains a total of *ten* electrons. In this case, phosphorus is said to have 'expanded its octet', i.e. the valence shell contains more than eight electrons. You can still draw the Lewis structure of PCl_5, as shown to the left, but bear in mind that the electronic structure does not correspond to that of a noble gas and that it does not follow the octet rule.

Coordinate bonds

Aluminium is in Group III of the periodic table. The electronic structure of aluminium is Al [Ne]$3s^2 3p^1$ and so each atom can only contribute to three pairs of electrons in a molecule. Drawing the Lewis structure of aluminium chloride results in a molecule of formula $AlCl_3$ with three chlorine atoms each joined by a single covalent bond to an aluminium atom.

However, the actual formula of solid aluminium chloride (as determined by experiment) is Al_2Cl_6. This molecule consists of two $AlCl_3$ molecules joined together. The illustration below shows how this arrangement is achieved. Each of the aluminium atoms accepts a share in a lone pair of electrons donated by a chlorine atom attached to the *other* aluminium atom. Such a bond is referred to as a **coordinate bond** (or coordinate covalent bond or dative covalent bond) to emphasize the fact that *both* of the electrons in the shared pair originated from the *same* atom. The bond may be represented as an arrow, which shows the direction of the electron pair donation.

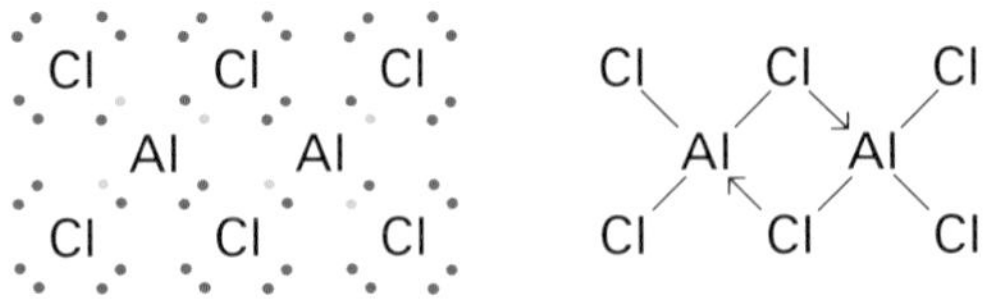

Lewis structure showing the electronic structure of Al_2Cl_6.

Compounds with an incomplete octet

Boron is also in Group III. Boron has the electronic structure B [He]$2s^2 2p^1$ and boron trichloride has the formula BCl_3. This substance has an incomplete octet because its valence shell contains fewer than eight electrons (BCl_3 does not follow the octet rule).

The octet of boron can only be completed if it accepts a share in a lone pair of electrons from another molecule, e.g. from an ammonia molecule. The bond that forms between boron and nitrogen is a coordinate bond because both the electrons have been donated by the nitrogen atom.

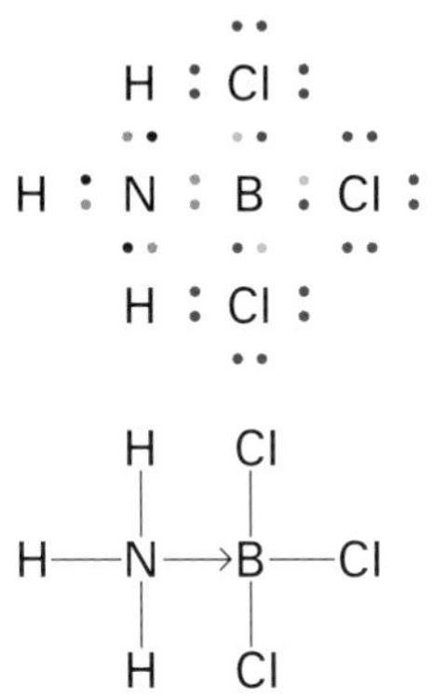

```
        ••
     H : Cl :
     ••   ••   ••
 H : N : B : Cl :
     ••   ••   ••
     H : Cl :
          ••

     H    Cl
     |    |
 H — N —→ B — Cl
     |    |
     H    Cl
```

Lewis structure showing the formation of a coordinate bond between ammonia and boron trichloride, in which boron obtains an octet of electrons in its valence shell.

An adduct

The illustration to the left shows the Lewis structure of boron trichloride and its acceptance of the lone pair of the nitrogen atom of an ammonia molecule to form an *adduct*. This adduct may be written in a shortened representation as $H_3N{:}\rightarrow BCl_3$.

Ions containing more than one atom

The only type of ion considered so far is formed when a single atom loses or gains electrons. Ions can also consist of covalently bonded atoms that have an unequal number of protons and electrons. A good example is the ammonium ion NH_4^+.

The ammonium ion contains four identical N—H bonds. Three bonding pairs of electrons are formed by the sharing of one electron from the nitrogen atom and one electron each from three hydrogen atoms. The fourth bonding pair results from a hydrogen ion H^+ accepting a share in the nitrogen lone pair. The species is a positive ion because the total number of protons is one greater than the total number of electrons.

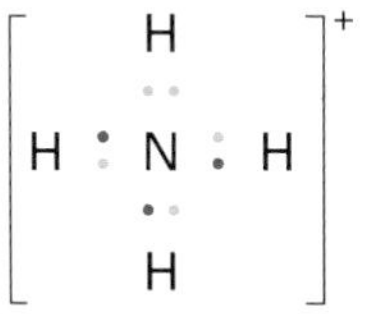

```
⎡     H     ⎤+
⎢     ••    ⎥
⎢ H : N : H ⎥
⎢     ••    ⎥
⎣     H     ⎦
```

Lewis structure showing the ammonium ion NH_4^+, which is formed from ammonia NH_3 and a hydrogen ion (proton) H^+.

SUMMARY

- A coordinate bond is a covalent bond in which one of the atoms donates both of the electrons in the shared pair.
- Expansion of the octet is possible in molecules such as phosphorus pentachloride PCl_5, in which the valence shell of the phosphorus atom contains ten electrons.
- Some compounds (such as boron trichloride BCl_3) have an atom with an incomplete octet.

PRACTICE

1 Draw Lewis structures for the following molecules, and write down the numbers of bonding pairs and lone pairs of electrons in the valence shells of the atoms concerned:

a Chlorine Cl_2
b Ammonia NH_3
c Hydrogen H_2
d Water H_2O
e Carbon dioxide CO_2
f Methane CH_4
g Oxygen O_2.

5.4

THE SHAPES OF MOLECULES – 1

OBJECTIVES

- Molecular shape from the VSEPR theory
- Five basic molecular shapes

Founders of the VSEPR theory

The VSEPR theory was introduced by Nevil Sidgwick and Herbert Powell, and was refined by Ronald Gillespie and Ronald Nyholm.

Understanding the shapes of molecules can help to explain many of their properties. This spread and the next describe how to predict the shapes of molecules by following a few simple rules.

The VSEPR theory

The best simple approach to determining the shape of a molecule is the **valence-shell electron-pair repulsion (VSEPR)** theory. This theory suggests that the electron pairs around an atom repel each other; bonding pairs and lone pairs arrange themselves to be as far apart as possible. The pairs take up this arrangement so that the potential energy due to their electrostatic repulsion is at a minimum.

In the case of molecules that have only bonding pairs and no lone pairs on the central atom, the total number of electron pairs equals the number of bonding pairs. It is quite straightforward to use the VSEPR theory to work out the shapes of these molecules, as follows:

1 Write a Lewis structure for the molecule.

2 Count the number of electron pairs around the central atom. (Treat multiple bonds in the same way as single bonds.)

3 Note the arrangement that this number of electron pairs will adopt:
two pairs = linear,
three pairs = trigonal planar,
four pairs = tetrahedral,
five pairs = trigonal bipyramidal,
six pairs = octahedral.

4 Write the symbol of the central atom and arrange the other atoms around it in the shape found in step 3.

The procedure is similar when there are one or more lone pairs on the central atom, as discussed in the next spread.

Balloons tied together will arrange themselves so that they are as far away from each other as possible. They form the same geometric arrangements as electron pairs in a molecule around a central atom. (a) Two balloons: linear; (b) three balloons: trigonal planar; (c) four balloons: tetrahedral; (d) five balloons: trigonal bipyramidal; (e) six balloons: octahedral.

Diatomic molecules

The simplest molecule of all is hydrogen H_2. It consists of two hydrogen atoms joined by a single covalent bond H—H. There are no electrons present in the molecule apart from the bonding pair. Hydrogen is a **linear** molecule because its two atoms are in a straight line (it is not possible to arrange them in any other way). All diatomic molecules are linear.

Linear molecules

Carbon dioxide CO_2 consists of two oxygen atoms each joined by a double covalent bond to one carbon atom, i.e. the arrangement of the atoms is O═C═O. There are two separate regions of high electron density, corresponding to the bonding electron pairs in the two C═O bonds. These two regions of high electron density repel each other and are therefore arranged so that they are as far apart as possible. The result is that CO_2 is a **linear** molecule. The arrangement of the electron pairs causes the three constituent atoms to be in a straight line. The bond angle O—C—O is 180°.

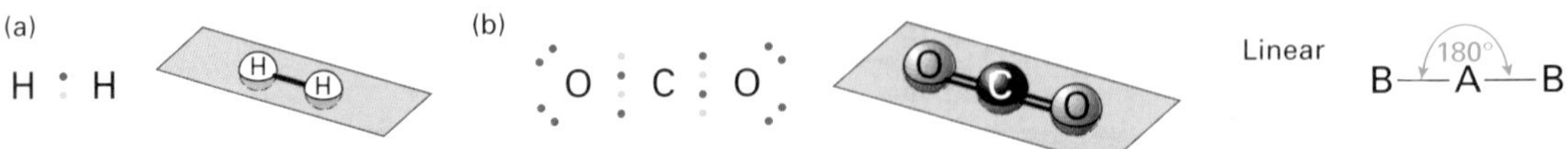

Two linear molecules: (a) hydrogen H_2 (diatomic molecules are all linear); and (b) carbon dioxide CO_2 (not all molecules with three atoms are linear). Beryllium chloride $BeCl_2$ (in the vapour) is another example of a linear molecule.

Trigonal planar molecules

Boron trichloride BCl_3 consists of three chlorine atoms each joined by a single covalent bond to one boron atom. There are three separate regions of high electron density, corresponding to the three B—Cl bonding pairs of electrons. These three bonding pairs repel each other equally, with the result that BCl_3 is a **planar** (flat) molecule. (Remember from your maths that a plane can always be drawn through any three points.) The arrangement of the electron pairs is **trigonal**: the three B—Cl bonds point towards the three corners of an equilateral triangle. The bond angles Cl—B—Cl are all equal at 120°. Boron trifluoride BF_3 has an identical structure.

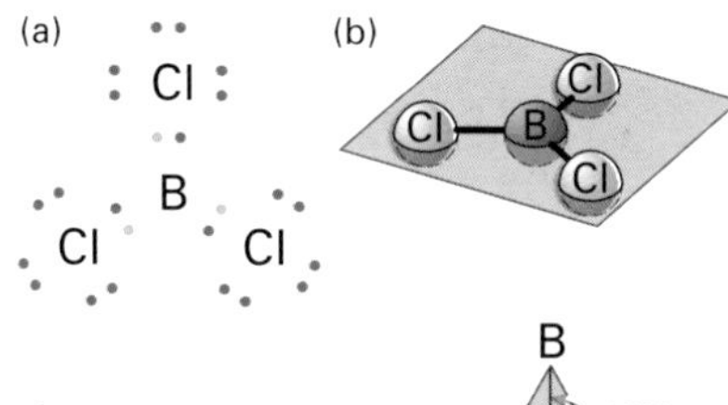

Boron trichloride BCl_3. (a) The Lewis structure shows that the central atom has three bonding pairs of electrons. (b) The arrangement of the electron pairs is trigonal planar.

Tetrahedral molecules

Methane CH_4 consists of four hydrogen atoms each joined by a single covalent bond to one carbon atom. There are four separate regions of high electron density, corresponding to the four C—H bonding electron pairs. These four bonding pairs repel each other equally. The arrangement of the electron pairs is **tetrahedral**: the four C—H bonds point towards the four corners of a regular tetrahedron. In other words, the four hydrogen atoms symmetrically surround the central carbon atom. The bond angles H—C—H are all equal at 109.5°. This angle is often referred to as the '**tetrahedral angle**', its precise value being 109°28′.

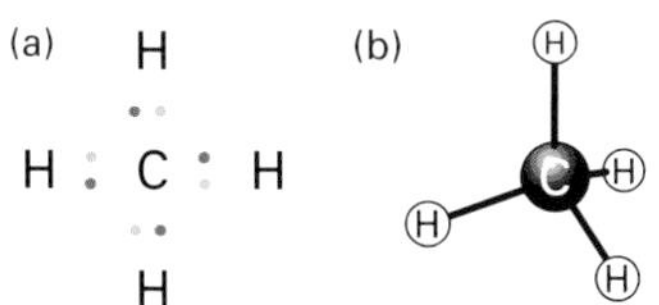

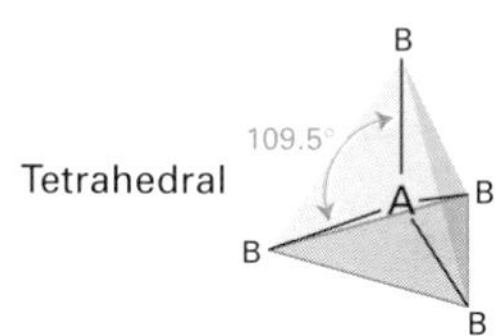

Methane CH_4. (a) The Lewis structure shows that the central atom has four bonding pairs of electrons. (b) The arrangement of the electron pairs is tetrahedral. (A tetrahedron is a three-dimensional shape with four triangular faces.)

Trigonal bipyramidal molecules

Phosphorus pentafluoride PF_5 consists of five fluorine atoms each joined by a single covalent bond to one phosphorus atom. There are five separate regions of high electron density, corresponding to the five P—F bonding electron pairs. The overall result is that the five P—F bonds point towards the five corners of a **trigonal bipyramid**. Phosphorus pentachloride PCl_5 has an identical structure.

The structure is not totally symmetrical: the bond angles F—P—F within the plane are 120°; the bonds above and below the plane are at 90°.

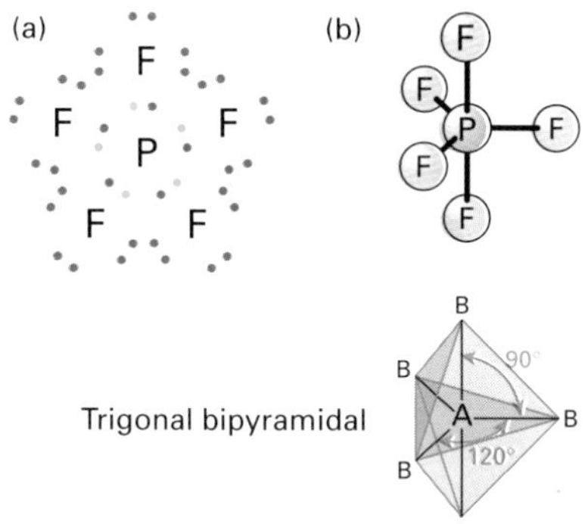

Phosphorus pentafluoride PF_5. (a) The Lewis structure shows that the central atom has five bonding pairs of electrons. (b) The arrangement of the electron pairs is trigonal bipyramidal. (A trigonal bipyramid consists of two pyramids with a common triangular base: bipyramid = two pyramids; trigonal = three-cornered.)

Octahedral molecules

Sulphur hexafluoride SF_6 consists of six fluorine atoms each joined by a single covalent bond to one sulphur atom. There are six separate regions of high electron density, corresponding to the six S—F bonding electron pairs. These six bonding pairs repel each other equally. The arrangement of the electron pairs is **octahedral**: the six S—F bonds point towards the six corners of a regular octahedron. In other words, the six fluorine atoms symmetrically surround the central sulphur atom. The bond angles F—S—F are all equal at 90°.

SUMMARY

- Molecular shapes can be predicted using the valence-shell electron-pair repulsion (VSEPR) theory.
- The number of electron pairs dictates the possible arrangements: linear (two electron pairs); trigonal planar (three electron pairs); tetrahedral (four electron pairs); trigonal bipyramidal (five electron pairs); and octahedral (six electron pairs).

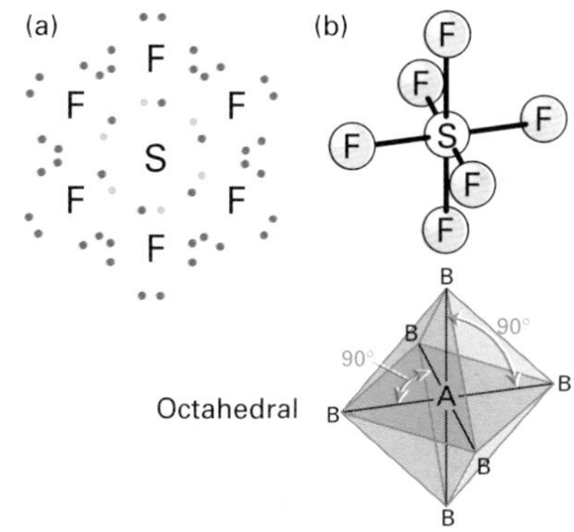

Sulphur hexafluoride SF_6. (a) The Lewis structure shows that the central atom has six bonding pairs of electrons. (b) The arrangement of the electron pairs is octahedral. (An octahedron is a three-dimensional shape with eight triangular faces.)

5.5

The shapes of molecules – 2

OBJECTIVES

- Effect of lone pairs on molecular shape
- Repulsion between bonding pairs and lone pairs contrasted
- Multiple bonds

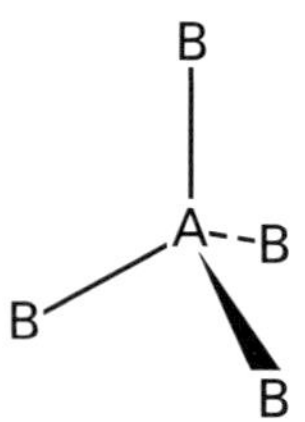

A representation of the tetrahedral arrangement. In this diagram, the solid lines each represent the axis of an electron pair (bonding pair or lone pair) in the plane of the paper; the wedge shape represents an axis coming out of the plane of the paper; and the dotted line represents an axis behind the plane of the paper.

(a)

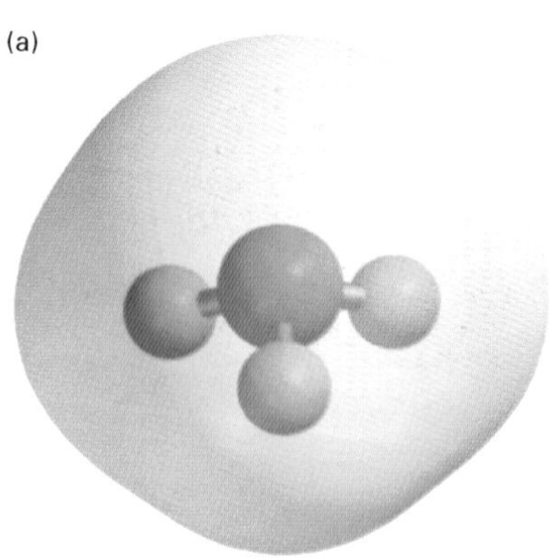

(b)

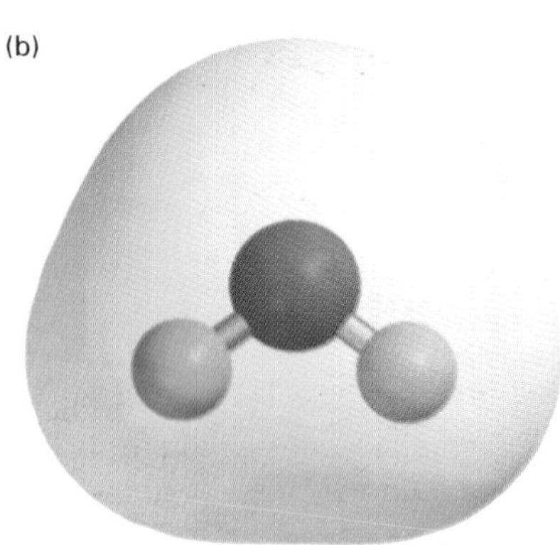

Electron density diagrams for (a) ammonia and (b) water. Each shows a contour of equal electron density and confirms the shapes suggested by the VSEPR theory. See following spread for details of the software used.

The previous spread introduced the idea of determining molecular shape by using the valence-shell electron-pair repulsion (VSEPR) theory. However, that introduction was limited to considering molecules that have only bonding pairs of electrons on the central atom. Lone pairs repel bonding pairs, and so they must also be taken into account when determining molecular shape.

The ammonia molecule

The Lewis structure for the ammonia molecule NH_3 shows that the central nitrogen atom has three bonding pairs and one lone pair. These four electron pairs are arranged tetrahedrally. However, the H—N—H bond angle is not 109.5° as expected for a regular tetrahedral arrangement. The angle is measured at 107°. This observation can be explained by assuming that:

- Lone pairs repel bonding pairs slightly more than bonding pairs repel each other.

So lone pair / lone pair repulsion is greater than lone pair / bonding pair repulsion, which in turn is greater than bonding pair / bonding pair repulsion.

Look at the illustration below. The *electron pairs* in ammonia are arranged tetrahedrally, as shown in part (b). Now focus just on the *atoms*, as shown in part (c). The atoms are arranged in the shape of a pyramid, so the shape of the *molecule* is **pyramidal**.

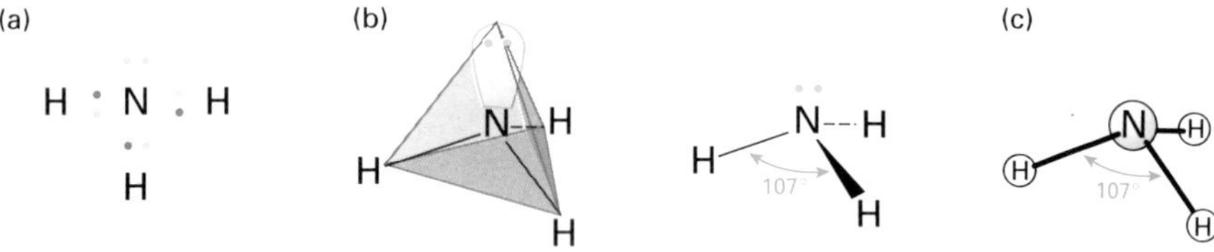

Ammonia NH_3. (a) The Lewis structure shows that the central atom has three bonding pairs and one lone pair. (b) The arrangement of the electron pairs is distorted tetrahedral. (c) The shape of the ammonia molecule (i.e. the arrangement of the atoms) is pyramidal.

The water molecule

The Lewis structure for the water molecule H_2O shows two bonding pairs and two lone pairs around the oxygen atom. This gives a total of four electron pairs. The VSEPR theory indicates that four electron pairs will adopt a tetrahedral arrangement in space. The lone pairs take up two of the tetrahedral positions, with the bonding pairs taking up the other two positions.

If we focus on the electron pairs in the water molecule, the observed structure confirms the expected arrangement. However, the H—O—H bond angle is 104.5° instead of the tetrahedral angle of 109.5°. As in the ammonia molecule, the angle is smaller than expected because a lone pair repels more strongly than a bonding pair, and so the lone pairs distort the shape by squeezing the angle between the O—H bonds. If we

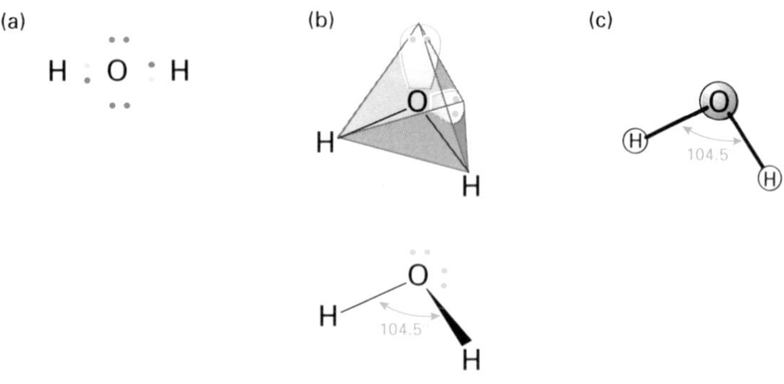

Water H_2O. (a) The Lewis structure shows that the central atom has two bonding pairs and two lone pairs. (b) The arrangement of the electron pairs is distorted tetrahedral. (c) The molecule is bent into a broad V-shape.

focus just on the atoms, we can consider the molecule to be bent into a broad **V-shape**.

The sulphur tetrafluoride molecule

The Lewis structure for the sulphur tetrafluoride molecule SF_4 shows four bonding pairs and one lone pair around the sulphur atom. These five electron pairs take up a trigonal bipyramidal arrangement, with the lone pair in an 'equatorial' position around the central sulphur atom, as shown in the diagram on the right.

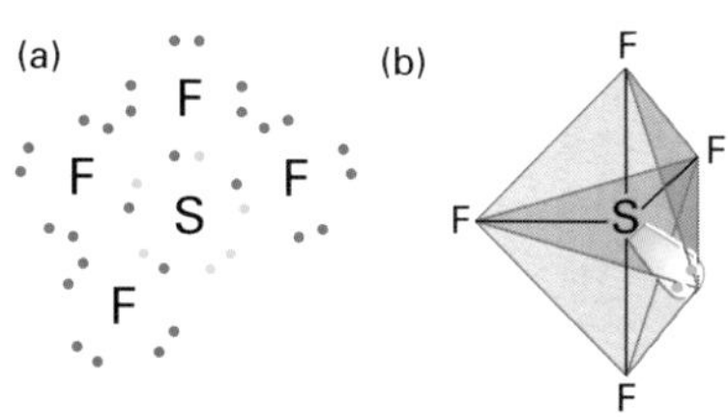

Sulphur tetrafluoride SF_4. (a) The Lewis structure. (b) The arrangement of the electron pairs. The three trigonal planar positions around the central atom are called the 'equatorial' positions. The two positions above and below the plane are called the 'axial' positions. The lone pair goes where the repulsions at the most acute angle (here 90°) are minimized.

Multiple bonds

Double bonds involve two bonding pairs of electrons and triple bonds involve three pairs.

A double bond is a single region of high electron density. Ethene $CH_2{=}CH_2$ therefore contains five regions of high electron density: the C=C double bond and the four C—H single bonds. The arrangement is therefore trigonal planar around each carbon atom, and the molecule as a whole is planar. The bond angles H—C—H are slightly *less* than 120° because the two electron pairs of the double bond repel the electrons in the C—H bonds to a *greater* extent than a single pair.

A triple bond is also a single region of high electron density.

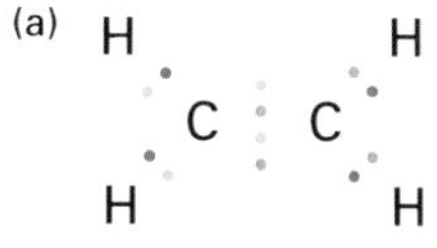

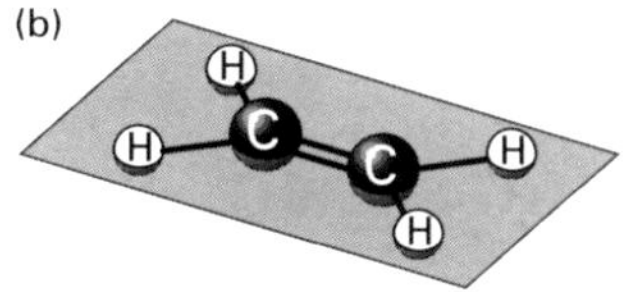

Ethene C_2H_4. (a) The Lewis structure. (b) The planar arrangement of the electron pairs.

VSEPR theory can be applied to ions

The VSEPR theory can be extended to the structure of ions as well as that of molecules. For example, the ammonium ion (NH_4^+) has exactly the same number of electrons as methane (CH_4): the two species are isoelectronic. The shape of the ammonium ion is exactly the same as that of the methane molecule, namely tetrahedral, because exactly the same number of bonding pairs and lone pairs are involved. As a second example, the oxonium ion H_3O^+, which will be centre stage in chapter 12 on acids and bases, is isoelectronic with ammonia, NH_3. Their shapes are the same, namely pyramidal. As a third example, the ion PCl_4^+ is isoelectronic with $SiCl_4$; both have four bonding pairs and no lone pairs, so both are tetrahedral.

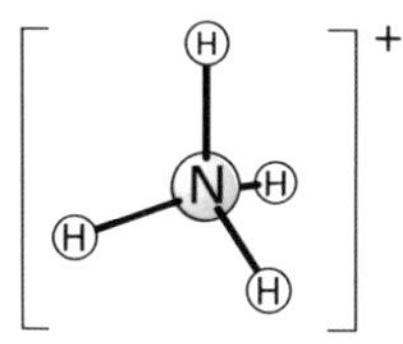

The ammonium ion is tetrahedral.

SUMMARY

- Lone pairs must be taken into account when determining molecular shape.
- Repulsion due to lone pairs is greater than repulsion due to bonding pairs.

PRACTICE

1 Draw Lewis structures for the following molecules. Using the VSEPR theory, sketch the arrangement of the electron pairs in space. Say what shape each molecule is.

- **a** Methane CH_4
- **b** Beryllium chloride $BeCl_2$
- **c** Tetrachloromethane CCl_4
- **d** Sulphur hexafluoride SF_6
- **e** Ammonium ion NH_4^+.

2 Draw Lewis structures for each of the following molecules. Draw the arrangement of the atoms and lone pairs. Say whether the bond angles are different from those expected for the regular geometrical shape.

- **a** Sulphur dioxide SO_2
- **b** Phosphine PH_3
- **c** Silicon tetrachloride $SiCl_4$
- **d** The ion PCl_4^+
- **e** Sulphur dichloride oxide SCl_2O.

5.6

Molecular orbital theory – ..

OBJECTIVES

- STM image shows interference
- Overlap of atomic orbitals
- Bonding and antibonding molecular orbitals

Wavefunction

John Pople shared the 1998 Nobel prize in Chemistry for his work on molecular orbital theory. He cofounded with Warren Hehre the company Wavefunction Inc., who have kindly supplied a number of electron density diagrams from their SPARTAN software.

Interference between two sources in a ripple tank.

In Chapter 4 you met the idea of atomic orbitals. Atomic orbitals define the regions of space around a nucleus where there is a high probability of finding an electron of a given energy (a high electron density). The electron density can be found from solutions of the Schrödinger equation for the atom concerned. Lewis structures represent covalent bonds as electron pairs shared between atomic centres. They do not explain *why* bonding electron pairs occupy these positions. A satisfactory explanation is provided by **molecular orbital theory** in which atomic orbitals overlap and combine to make molecular orbitals.

Visual 'proof'

Most of the electron density diagrams of atoms shown so far are pictures generated by a computer from solutions of the Schrödinger equation for that system of electrons and protons. They are visually convincing, with contours to show the magnitude of the electron density at each point. However, these pictures may seem a little contrived; they come from manipulating mathematical expressions. Can they really claim to answer the question 'What do atoms and molecules really look like?' The answer *yes they can!* is provided by some recent STM (scanning tunnelling microscope) images.

Look carefully at the STM image shown below. Until they understood what they were looking at, the workers who produced it thought their equipment had developed a fault. In fact, *the ripple effect on the surface layer of atoms in the crystal is the pattern resulting from the interference between electrons*. Interference is a phenomenon typical of waves.

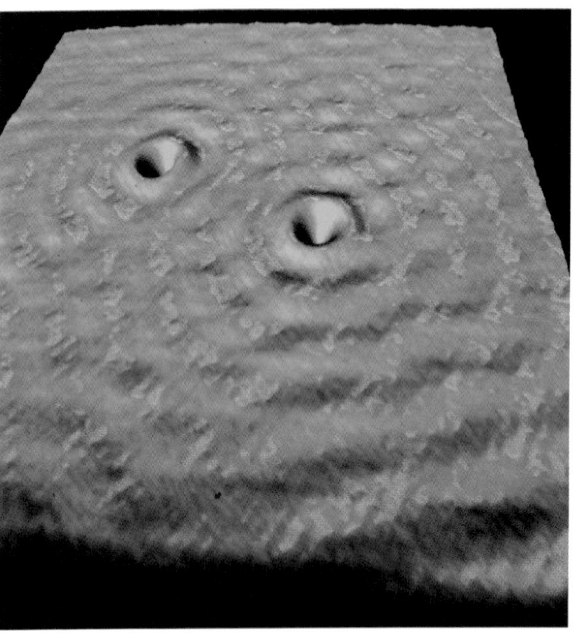

An STM image showing interference between electrons, confirming their wave nature. The two point defects (probably impurity atoms created in the preparation of the sample) scatter the surface state electrons, resulting in circular standing wave patterns

Forming molecular orbitals

Imagine two hydrogen atoms moving towards each other. Each atom has one electron contained in a 1s orbital. The electron density in each separate atomic orbital is described by the Schrödinger equation as spherically symmetrical about the atomic nucleus.

Where the two atomic orbitals **overlap**, electron density is redistributed and new molecular orbitals are created. These define the regions of space around a *set* of nuclei where there is a high probability of finding an electron. **Molecular orbitals** are the solutions of the Schrödinger equation for molecules, in the same way that atomic orbitals are the solutions for atoms.

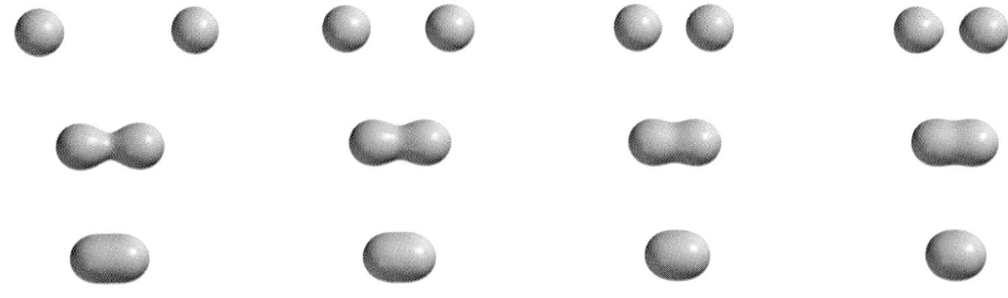

Electron density diagrams showing two hydrogen atoms approaching each other and forming a hydrogen molecule. Note the shift in the distribution of electron density as the nuclei get closer.

When the atoms are close together, the atomic orbitals interfere with each other. In a ripple tank, **constructive interference** results when waves of the same phase reinforce each other, and **destructive interference** results when waves of different phase cancel each other out. The same is true of the interference between atomic orbitals: the interference pattern is caused by orbitals of different phase interacting. In the diagrams, one phase is shown in red and the other phase in dark blue.

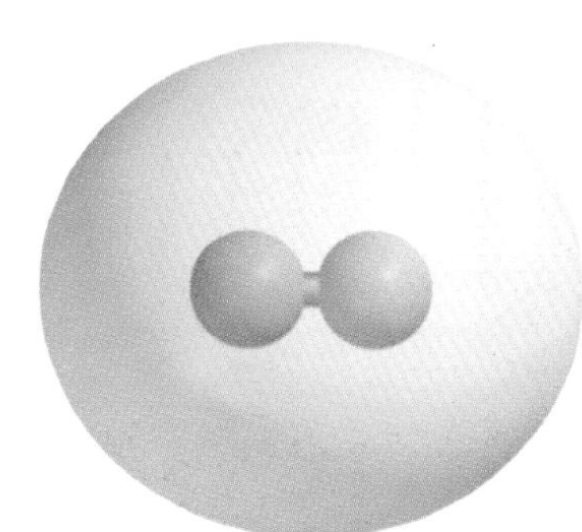

A contour of equal electron density for hydrogen H_2 at the equilibrium separation.

Bonding and antibonding molecular orbitals

Constructive interference between the two atomic orbitals (when they are in phase, shown by the same colour) *increases* the electron density between the two atoms and leads to a **bonding molecular orbital**. This orbital is of *lower* energy than that of either of the two individual atomic orbitals.

Destructive interference (when they are out of phase, shown by the different colours) *removes* electron density from between the nuclei and leads to an **antibonding molecular orbital**. This orbital is of *higher* energy than that of either of the two individual atomic orbitals.

The formation of these molecular orbitals may be represented on an energy level diagram.

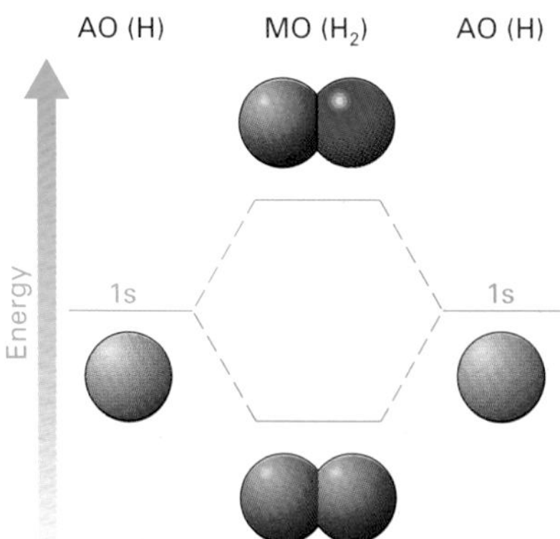

An energy level diagram showing two 1s atomic orbitals (AO) combining to form a lower-energy bonding molecular orbital (MO) and a higher-energy antibonding molecular orbital. The purple colour for the separate atoms signifies that the phase is unspecified.

The hydrogen molecule

In the case of the hydrogen molecule H_2, there is a total of two electrons (one electron per atom). Following the building-up principle, these electrons occupy the lowest energy orbital available, the bonding molecular orbital. The result is a single covalent bond containing two electrons; as required by the Pauli exclusion principle, the spins are paired. With two electrons in the bonding molecular orbital, the energy of the H_2 molecule is lower than that of the two separate atoms.

The non-existence of He_2

Molecular orbital theory explains very simply why helium atoms do not form a covalent bond with each other. A helium atom has two electrons contained in the 1s atomic orbital. The *hypothetical* helium molecule He_2 would therefore have a total of four electrons. These would need to be contained in molecular orbitals formed from the overlap of two 1s atomic orbitals. Referring to the energy level diagram, you can see that there would be two electrons in the bonding molecular orbital and two electrons in the antibonding molecular orbital. The energy of this arrangement is almost the same as the energy of two separate helium atoms. The energy of the system does not fall when two separate helium atoms approach each other closely. No covalent bond forms as it does in the case of hydrogen.

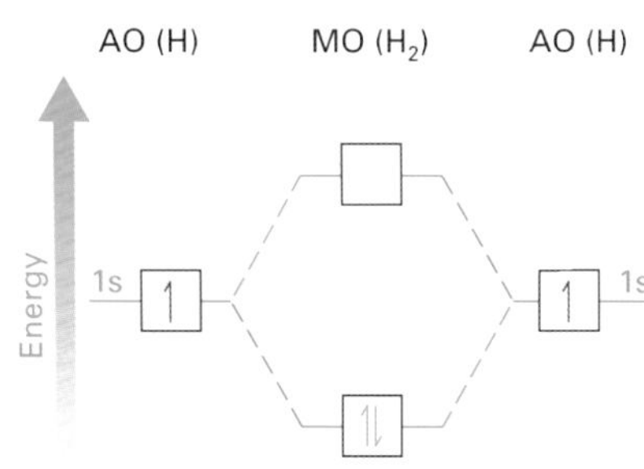

An energy level diagram for H_2 showing two electrons in the bonding molecular orbital of a hydrogen molecule. Note that the antibonding molecular orbital is empty. For the hypothetical molecule He_2, the bonding and the antibonding molecular orbitals would each contain two electrons; hence no bond forms between the two atoms.

SUMMARY

- Overlap of atomic orbitals leads to the formation of molecular orbitals.
- A bonding molecular orbital has a lower energy than either of the two atomic orbitals that overlap.
- An antibonding molecular orbital has a higher energy than either of the two atomic orbitals that overlap.

5.7 Molecular orbital theory – 2

OBJECTIVES

- σ and π molecular orbitals
- The O_2 molecule
- Electron density in covalent bonds

You should remember from the previous chapter that a p orbital has a very different shape from an s orbital. As a result, the overlap of two p orbitals to form molecular orbitals is significantly different from the overlap of two s orbitals. Overlap of two p orbitals forms two types of molecular orbital: sigma (σ) molecular orbitals and pi (π) molecular orbitals.

Sigma (σ) and pi (π) molecular orbitals

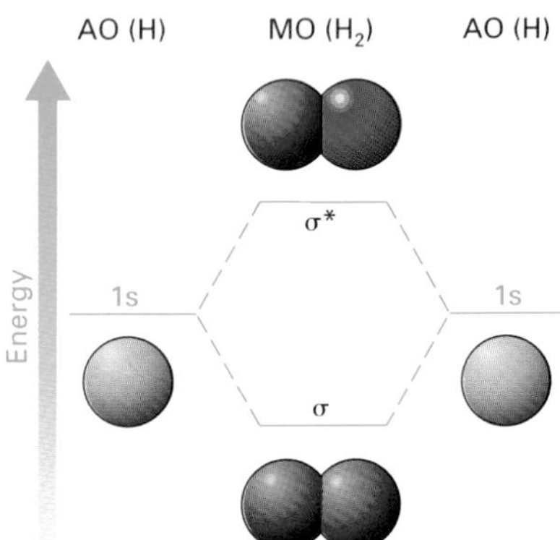

The overlap of two s orbitals produces σ and σ molecular orbitals. It is not possible to form π or π* molecular orbitals from s atomic orbitals.*

The overlap of two s orbitals produces a **sigma** (σ, the Greek letter corresponding to 's') bonding orbital when the two orbitals are in phase and a corresponding σ* antibonding orbital when they are out of phase.

Two electrons in a sigma bonding molecular orbital form a **sigma bond**.

There are *two* possible ways in which two p orbitals, the two lobes of which have opposite phase, can overlap. The first possibility is that they overlap end-on, giving rise to a sigma (σ) bonding molecular orbital when the overlapping lobes are in phase. (There will always be a corresponding antibonding orbital (σ*) when the overlapping lobes are out of phase.)

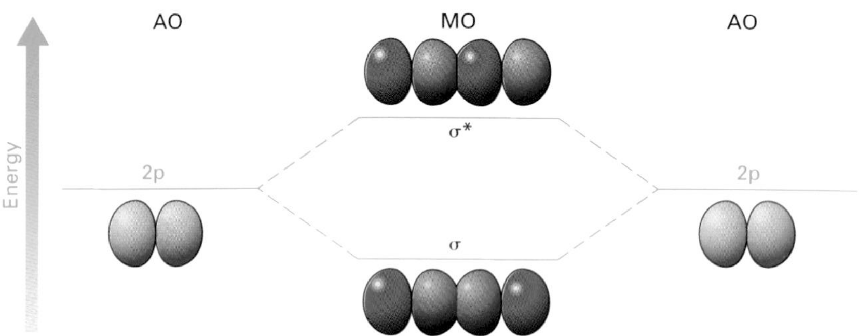

Overlap of two p orbitals end–on to form a sigma (σ) bonding molecular orbital and a sigma star (σ) antibonding molecular orbital.*

The second possibility is that the p orbitals at right angles to a sigma bond may overlap sideways. This arrangement gives rise to a **pi** (π) bonding molecular orbital when the orbitals are in phase. (Again, there is a corresponding antibonding orbital (π*) when the orbitals are out of phase.) Two electrons in a pi bonding molecular orbital form a **pi bond**. A pi bond is found in association with a sigma bond in molecules that contain a double covalent bond, such as ethene C_2H_4.

- A sigma molecular orbital is symmetrical about the internuclear axis (the imaginary line between the nuclei).
- A pi molecular orbital has a nodal plane (a plane in which the electron density is zero) along the internuclear axis.

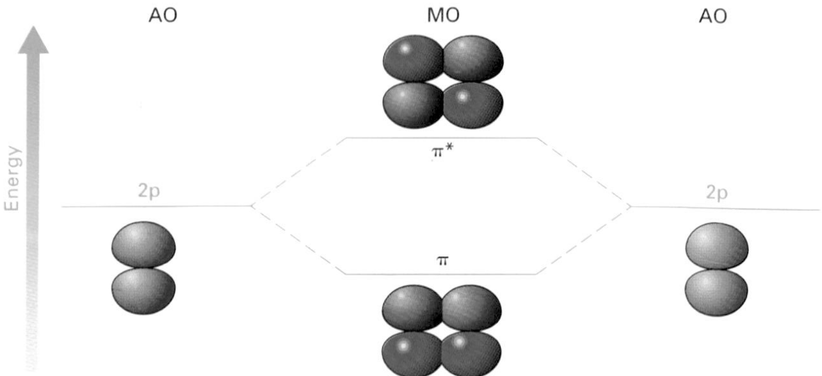

When two p orbitals overlap sideways, the resulting bonding is described as π bonding. When the orbitals overlap in phase (the lobes are the same colour), a π bonding molecular orbital is formed. When the orbitals overlap out of phase (the lobes of the orbitals are opposite colours), an antibonding (π) orbital is formed.*

The π bonding molecular orbital in ethene C_2H_4.

Solving the oxygen problem

Molecular orbital theory has been especially successful in explaining the detailed electronic structure of the oxygen molecule. The Lewis structure for this molecule shows two bonding electron pairs between the oxygen atoms and two lone pairs located on each atom. All the electron spins are paired. However, the demonstration illustrated in the photograph below shows that liquid oxygen is paramagnetic. A **paramagnetic** substance is attracted into a magnetic field. Substances that are paramagnetic contain one or more unpaired electrons. The Lewis structure for oxygen cannot explain this phenomenon.

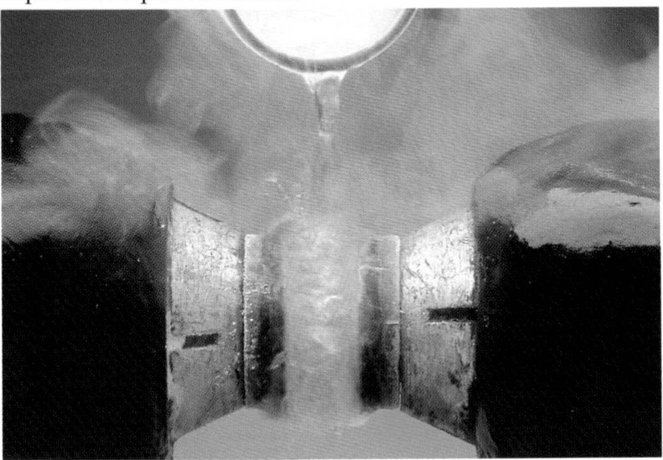

There is a powerful magnetic field between the jaws of this magnet. Liquid oxygen is attracted into this field. This phenomenon could not be explained before molecular orbital theory was introduced.

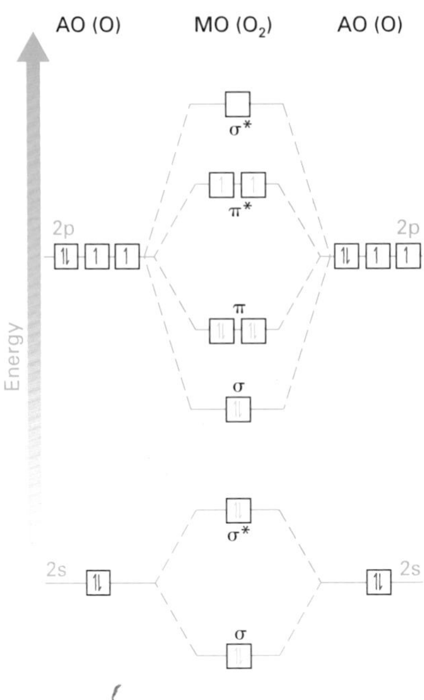

The energy level diagram for the formation of molecular orbitals from oxygen atomic orbitals. The molecular orbitals are filled according to the building-up principle and Hund's rule.

The energy level diagram for the atomic and molecular orbitals of oxygen is shown alongside. It can be seen that the electrons fill the orbitals following the building-up principle. The last two electrons have to fill the pair of antibonding π* molecular orbitals. The electrons go into the two orbitals of equal energy, with parallel spins (following Hund's rule, exactly as happens in atoms, spread 4.6). The two unpaired electrons in the antibonding orbitals cause the oxygen molecule to be paramagnetic.

The O_2^+ molecular ion

There is clear experimental evidence that antibonding molecular orbitals can physically exist.

The dioxygenyl ion O_2^+ (see spread 19.12) has a shorter and stronger bond than does the molecule O_2. This unusual situation occurs because the electron removed to form the ion comes from an antibonding molecular orbital. Removing the electron *strengthens* the overall bonding between the two atoms.

Electron density in covalent bonds

Molecular orbital theory can also describe the case where the original atomic orbitals that overlap have different energies. The resulting bonding molecular orbital more closely resembles the lower-energy atomic orbital and has a non-symmetrical distribution about the two atomic centres. This idea is central to the next spread.

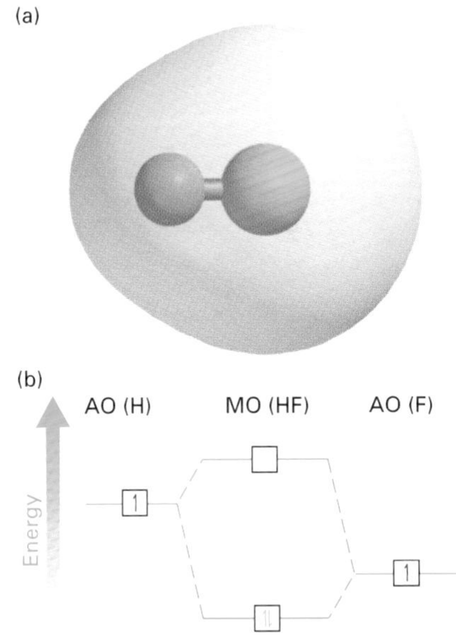

Hydrogen fluoride has a bonding molecular orbital formed from the overlap of the hydrogen 1s and one of the fluorine 2p atomic orbitals. (a) Electron density diagram. (b) Energy level diagram showing formation of the molecular orbital and electron occupancy.

SUMMARY

- Overlap of two s orbitals produces a σ bond.

PRACTICE

1 Draw the energy level diagrams for

a O_2^{2-} (peroxide ion)

b O_2^- (superoxide ion).

5.8 Bond polarity – 1

OBJECTIVES

- Electron density maps
- Polar covalent bonds
- Electronegativity

Lewis structures and the VSEPR theory can account for the shapes of a wide variety of molecules. The covalent bond is simply described as a pair of electrons shared between two atoms. In molecules where the atoms are of the same element, as in hydrogen H—H and chlorine Cl—Cl, equal sharing of the electron pair would be expected. However, where the atoms are of different elements, the sharing is *not* equal. A covalent bond in which the sharing is unequal is said to be a **polar covalent bond**. The unequal sharing of electron pairs is reflected in the properties of the compounds.

A reminder

Electron density describes how the charge of the electron is distributed. High electron density in a certain volume of space means that an electron has a high probability of being found there. Low electron density indicates that an electron has a low probability of being found there.

Electron density diagrams

Electrons in molecules inhabit particular regions of space. Bonding pairs are located in regions between the nuclei of the atoms that are bonded together. Lone pairs are located around a specific atom. Modern models of atomic and molecular structure concentrate on electron density. Electron density may be pictured in two main ways, as shown below.

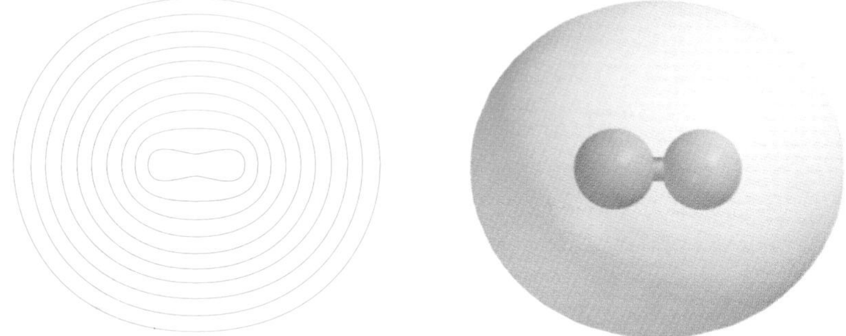

Two ways of picturing electron density in the hydrogen molecule H_2: (a) A contour map – showing lines of equal electron density. (b) An electron density diagram – a computer-generated plot using theoretically calculated values of electron density.

Evidence for unequal sharing

Compare the electron density diagrams shown below for the molecules hydrogen H_2, chlorine Cl_2, and hydrogen chloride HCl. The change is shown most clearly by calculating the electrostatic potential. An **electrostatic potential map** superimposes the colours representing the electrostatic potential onto a contour of equal electron density. A red colour indicates the most negative electrostatic potential and a blue colour indicates the most positive electrostatic potential. The potential increases in the order red < orange < yellow < green < blue.

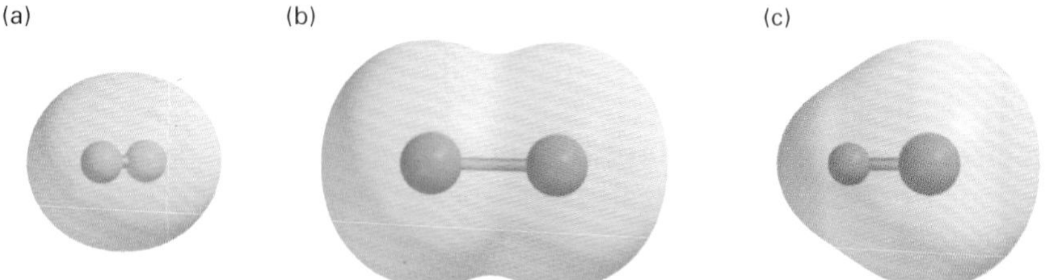

Electrostatic potential maps of (a) hydrogen, (b) chlorine, and (c) hydrogen chloride. The electron densities are symmetrical for hydrogen and chlorine but vary significantly from one end to the other in hydrogen chloride. The electrostatic potential shows that the hydrogen atom has a partial positive charge (blue).

You can see that, for hydrogen and chlorine, the electron density in both cases is symmetrically distributed between the two atoms. In the hydrogen chloride molecule, the electron density is *not* symmetrically distributed. The colour-coding shows there is greater electron density near the chlorine atom. The two bonding electrons that form the single covalent bond H—Cl are more likely to be found near the chlorine atom than near the hydrogen atom.

Hydrogen chloride exists as separate molecules of HCl. Gallium arsenide (a semiconductor used in the electronics industry) consists of a giant network of gallium and arsenic atoms covalently bonded to each other to form a solid lattice. The electron density diagram for the surface layer of a gallium arsenide crystal is shown below. It shows the high electron density between the two different atoms (gallium and arsenic) expected for a shared electron pair. However, careful inspection reveals that the electron density is slightly greater near the arsenic atom. This observation suggests that the electron pair is shared unequally. The arsenic atom has a greater share of the electron pair than the gallium atom.

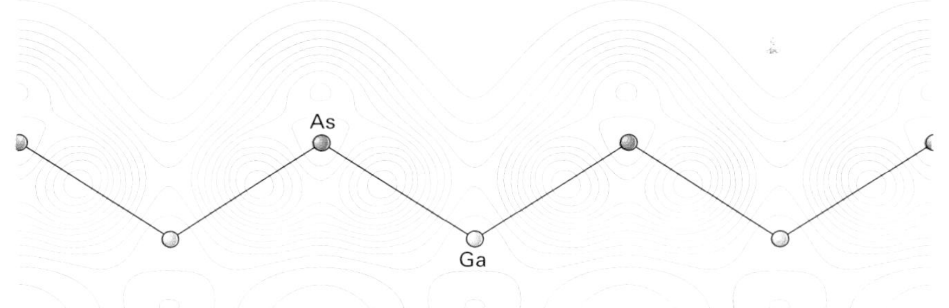

The experimental electron density for gallium arsenide. The peak of the electron density in the bond is closer to the arsenic atoms (coloured dark blue) than to the gallium atoms (coloured dark grey); arsenic is more electronegative than gallium.

Electronegativity

Where a covalent bond exists between two atoms that are not identical, one of the two will have a greater share of the electron pair. Unequal sharing happens because different atoms have different powers of attraction for electron pairs. The **electronegativity** of an atom gives a rough measure of its ability to attract a shared electron pair. Electronegativity is a relative quantity and is measured on the Pauling scale, ranging from 0.8 for caesium to 4.0 for fluorine. The atom with the greater electronegativity will have a larger share of the bonding pair of electrons. So the electron density will be skewed towards (i.e. higher near) the *more electronegative* atom. Thus in the example above, the maximum electron density occurs closer to arsenic (electronegativity 2.2) than to gallium (electronegativity 1.8).

Polar covalent bonds

When the electron pair forming a covalent bond is shared unequally between two atoms, the atom with the greater share acquires a partial negative charge because electron density is displaced towards it and electrons are negatively charged. This partial negative charge is written as δ–. The atom with the smaller share of the electron pair has a partial positive charge, written as δ+.

For example, consider the bond between hydrogen and chlorine in the hydrogen chloride molecule. Chlorine is more electronegative than hydrogen, and so electron density is higher near the chlorine atom. As a result, chlorine has a partial negative charge and hydrogen a partial positive charge. The bond is a polar covalent bond, as is indicated by the formula $H^{\delta+}$—$Cl^{\delta-}$.

SUMMARY

- A covalent bond between two different atoms is a polar covalent bond.
- The electronegativity of an atom is a measure of its ability to attract a shared electron pair.
- Electron density in a covalent bond is skewed towards the atom of higher electronegativity.
- The atom of higher electronegativity has a partial negative charge δ–.
- The atom of lower electronegativity has a partial positive charge δ+.

Some electronegativity values

A list of electronegativity values on the Pauling scale is shown below for a selection of elements. Two successive elements from each of Groups I to VII are shown. The elements across Period 3 are shown in **bold** type.

Group	Element	Electronegativity
I	**Sodium**	0.9
	Potassium	0.8
II	**Magnesium**	1.3
	Calcium	1.0
III	**Aluminium**	1.6
	Gallium	1.8
IV	Carbon	2.5
	Silicon	1.9
V	Nitrogen	3.0
	Phosphorus	2.2
VI	Oxygen	3.4
	Sulphur	2.6
VII	Fluorine	4.0
	Chlorine	3.2

(a)

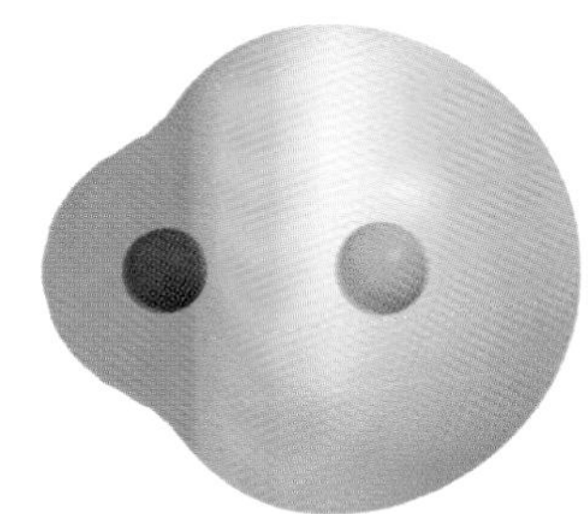

(b)

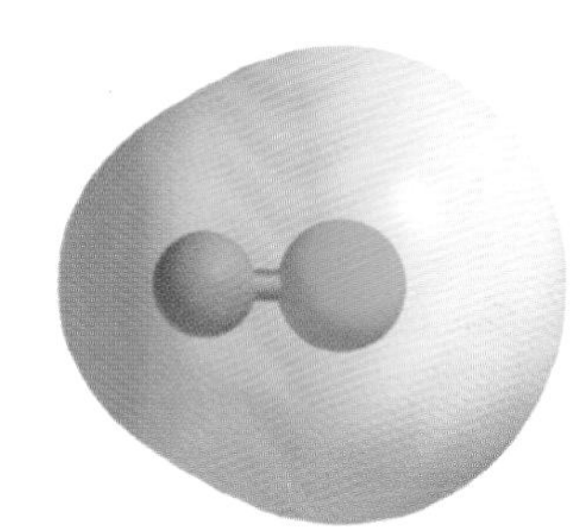

The electrostatic potential maps for the molecules LiH and HF. (a) Hydrogen is more electronegative than lithium and so the electrostatic potential shows that hydrogen has a partial negative charge (red). (b) Hydrogen is less electronegative than fluorine, and so the electrostatic potential shows that hydrogen has a partial positive charge (blue).

Bond polarity – 2

OBJECTIVES

- Polar covalent bonds
- Polar molecules

Polar covalent bonds result from the unequal sharing of bonding pairs of electrons in covalent molecules. Electrons are shared unequally when there are differences in the electronegativity values of the two atoms concerned. This spread looks at the presence of polar covalent bonds in molecules and their influence on the polarity of the molecule *as a whole*.

Electronegativity trends

There is a clear trend in electronegativity in the periodic table. Non-metals are elements that gain electrons to complete their outer shells. They have greater electronegativity values than metals, which lose electrons to achieve full outer shells. Electronegativity values generally decrease as atomic number increases down a group. They increase as atomic number increases across a period.

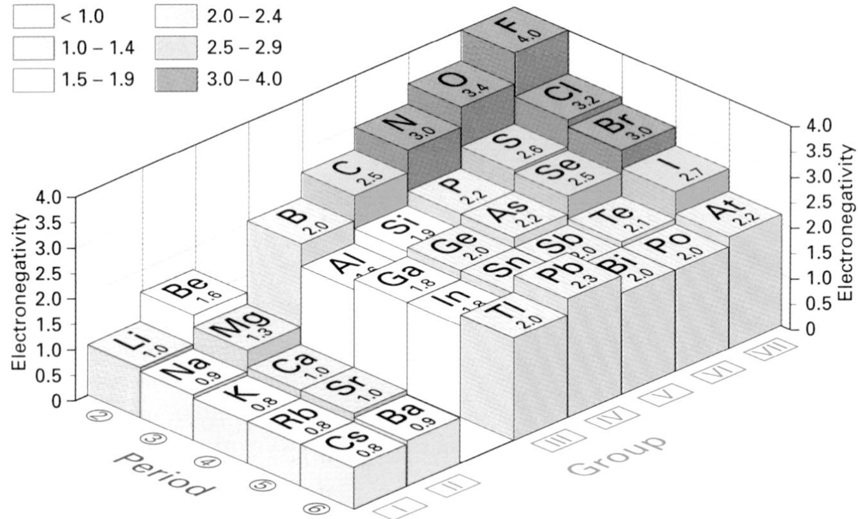

The elements and their electronegativity values arranged in a periodic table.

The hydrogen halides

The electronegativity of the halogens (Group VII) decreases in the order

F > Cl > Br > I

All these elements have greater electronegativity values than hydrogen, with the result that the hydrogen halides HX are polarized $H^{\delta+}$—$X^{\delta-}$. Fluorine is the most electronegative of the halogens. As a result the H—F bond is polarized to a greater extent than in the other hydrogen halides. The order of decreasing bond polarity is

H—F > H—Cl > H—Br > H—I

(a)

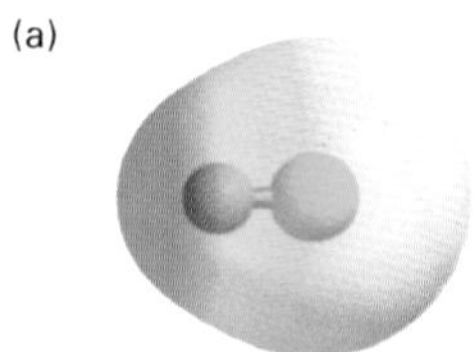

(b)

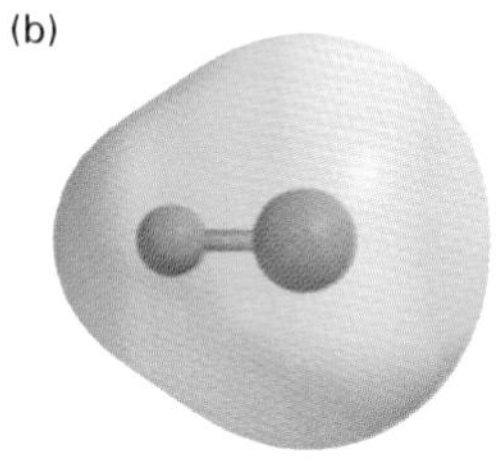

(c)

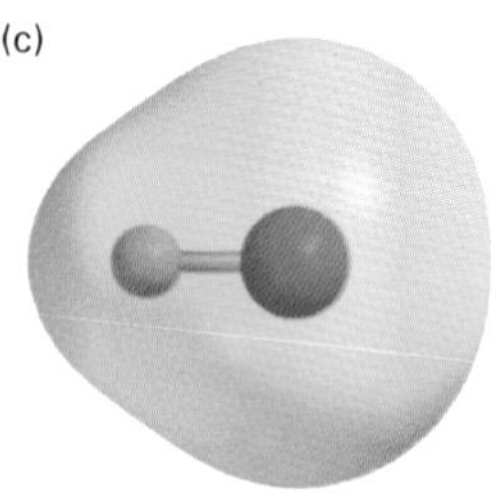

Electrostatic potential maps for (a) hydrogen fluoride HF; (b) hydrogen chloride HCl, and (c) hydrogen bromide HBr. Note that the colour-coding shows that the polarity decreases in the order HF > HCl > HBr.

Polar molecules

Hydrogen chloride, like all the hydrogen halides, has a polar covalent bond. It is said to be a **polar molecule**. The overall molecule has a **dipole**, that is, a pair of separated charges of opposite sign. Because the positive end of one molecule is attracted to the negative end of another, polar molecules interact with each other. These interactions affect the melting and boiling points of substances, and the types of reaction in which they take part. These effects will be discussed in depth in subsequent chapters.

(a) The hydrogen chloride molecule is a polar molecule. (b) A dipole can be represented as two opposite charges (+ and –) separated by a distance d.

Polar bonds but non-polar molecules

Carbon dioxide is a linear molecule. Both of the oxygen atoms are joined to the central carbon atom by a double covalent bond, so the molecule can be written as O=C=O. The electronegativity values for carbon and oxygen are 2.5 and 3.4 respectively. As a result, the C=O *bonds* are polarized, and can be written as $C^{\delta+}{=}O^{\delta-}$. However, in effect the carbon dioxide molecule O=C=O has *two* polarized bonds back-to-back, i.e. $O^{\delta-}{=}C^{\delta+}$ and $C^{\delta+}{=}O^{\delta-}$. These dipoles cancel out so that the *molecule* as a whole is **non-polar**.

Boron trifluoride has the formula BF_3. The arrangement of the electron pairs in the three B—F bonds is trigonal planar, spread 5.4. Although each B—F *bond* is polar ($B^{\delta+}$—$F^{\delta-}$), the *molecule* as a whole is non-polar: it has a zero dipole when considered *overall*.

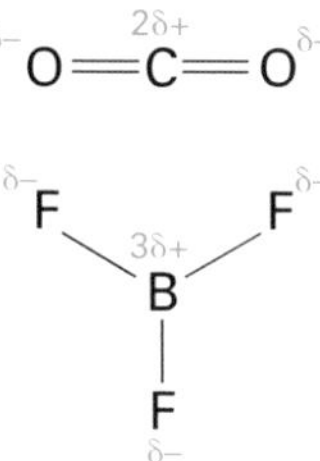

Although their molecules contain polar bonds, both carbon dioxide and boron trifluoride are non-polar molecules.

Water

Each of the hydrogen atoms in the water molecule H_2O is joined to the central oxygen atom by a single covalent bond. Writing the formula of water as H—O—H shows the two covalent bonds but does not take account of the two lone pairs of electrons on the oxygen atom. The arrangement of the four electron pairs (two bonding pairs and two lone pairs) is *distorted tetrahedral*. As a result, the bond angle H—O—H is 104.5°, as discussed in spread 5.5. If we focus just on the atoms, the water molecule is a broad V-shape. The O—H bonds are polar ($O^{\delta-}$—$H^{\delta+}$). The electrostatic potential map shows that the oxygen atom has a partial negative charge (indicated by the red colour). Because the two dipoles do not cancel out, the molecule as a whole is polar; that is, the molecule has a dipole.

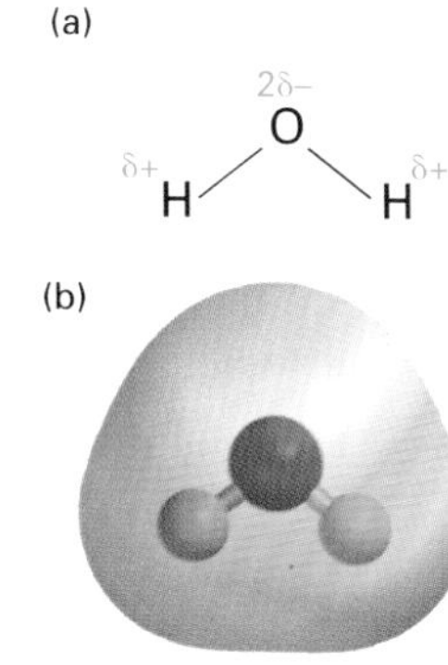

The water molecule: (a) Water has a dipole. (b) The electrostatic potential map, showing the polar nature of the overall molecule.

Ammonia

Each of the hydrogen atoms in the ammonia molecule NH_3 is joined to the central nitrogen atom by a single covalent bond. Writing the formula of ammonia as $:NH_3$ emphasizes the fact that the molecule has a lone pair on the nitrogen atom as well as three bonding pairs. The arrangement of the four electron pairs is *distorted tetrahedral* with H—N—H bond angles of 107°, spread 5.5. If we focus just on the atoms, the ammonia molecule is pyramidal. The N—H bonds are polar ($N^{\delta-}$—$H^{\delta+}$). The electrostatic potential map shows that the nitrogen atom has a partial negative charge (indicated by the red colour). Because the three dipoles do not cancel out, the overall molecule (like water) has a dipole. Notice how the hydrogens are less intensely blue than they are in water, because nitrogen is less electronegative than oxygen.

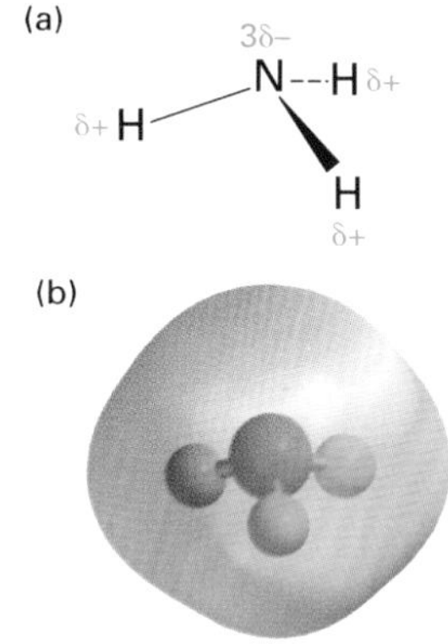

The ammonia molecule: (a) Ammonia has a dipole. (b) The electrostatic potential map, showing the polar nature of the overall molecule.

SUMMARY

- Polar covalent bonds result from the unequal sharing of bonding pairs of electrons in covalent molecules.
- Considered *overall*, a polar molecule has two oppositely charged regions: it acts as a dipole.
- The hydrogen halides, water, and ammonia are all polar molecules.
- CO_2 and BF_3 have polar bonds but are not polar molecules.

PRACTICE

1 For each of the following molecules, identify any polar bonds and label the constituent atoms appropriately δ+ or δ−. Say how you arrived at each decision.

a HBr **b** N_2 **c** ClF
d CCl_4 **e** CH_3Br **f** SO_2.

2 State whether each molecule in question 1 is polar or not, giving your reasons.

5.10

IONIC BONDING REVISI[illegible]

OBJECTIVES

- The relationship between polar covalent bonds and ionic bonds
- Ion formation and electronegativity differences

As the electronegativity difference between two covalently bonded atoms increases, the partial charges (δ+ and δ–) developed on the atoms become larger. As the partial charges increase, the bond becomes more and more polar. If the electronegativity difference is more than about 1.8 on the Pauling scale, the bond is so polar that we can describe the electrons as having transferred essentially completely to the more electronegative atom. The bonding is now ionic because the transfer of electrons from one atom to another creates oppositely charged **ions**.

Ions – another reminder

When electrons are transferred from one atom to another, the atoms end up with unequal numbers of electrons and protons, and become ions. A **positive ion** has more protons than electrons, whereas a **negative ion** has more electrons than protons.

Metals and non-metals

As you can see from the periodic table in the previous spread, generally the metals (on the left-hand side) have low values of electronegativity and the non-metals (on the right) have high values. When a metal combines with a non-metal there is a large difference in electronegativity, and so ionic bonding results. For example, all the metallic elements combine with oxygen to form oxides, and most metallic oxides are ionic. All metals also react with chlorine to give chlorides, and most metallic chlorides are ionic. The illustration shows the spectacular reaction between sodium and chlorine to produce sodium chloride. There are many other examples of ionic compounds, such as potassium fluoride, calcium chloride, and magnesium oxide.

State symbols

The bracket (s) indicates a solid; the bracket (g) indicates a gas.

The metallic element sodium combines with the non-metallic element chlorine to form the ionic compound sodium chloride:

$$2Na(s) + Cl_2(g) \rightarrow 2NaCl(s)$$

Note how different sodium chloride looks from sodium and chlorine. You need to think carefully about what is happening to the arrangement of electrons in these species. Remember that bonding tends to result in an outer octet of electrons for each atom.

Sodium and chlorine react together vigorously. Electrons transfer from the metal sodium to the non-metal chlorine.

Solid sodium metal, gaseous non-metallic chlorine, and the crystalline ionic compound sodium chloride.

Sodium (Na [Ne]$3s^1$) is in Group I of the periodic table. All the atoms of Group I have one electron in their valence shell. The ionization energy of sodium is quite low, so the metal readily loses this outermost electron. The nucleus is now surrounded by full shells only.

Chlorine is in Group VII of the periodic table. All the atoms of Group VII have seven electrons in their valence shell. Chlorine readily completes its octet of electrons by gaining an electron from another atom, such as sodium.

Sodium (Na 2,8,1) transfers the electron in its valence shell to the valence shell of chlorine (Cl 2,8,7), resulting in the sodium ion (Na^+ 2,8) and the chloride ion (Cl^- 2,8,8).

As a result of this transfer of one electron from sodium to chlorine, the sodium has lost one electron and become a sodium ion Na^+. The single positive charge indicates that the sodium ion has one more proton

...ons. The chlorine atom has gained one electron and ... a chloride ion Cl^-. The single negative charge indicates that the chloride ion has one more electron than it has protons. The electrostatic attraction between Na^+ and Cl^- ions bonds them together.

Electrons transfer readily from Group I atoms to Group VII atoms, for the reasons given in the previous three paragraphs. The compounds that result are most accurately described by the ionic model of bonding. Lewis structures help to picture the transfer of an electron from one atom to another.

Ionic compounds – lattices

Ionic compounds in the solid state consist of oppositely charged ions. The attraction between positive and negative ions constitutes an **ionic bond**. The ions arrange themselves so that each ion is surrounded by ions of opposite charge. The result is a regular three-dimensional array of alternating charges called an **ionic lattice**. This model for the solid ionic state is confirmed by electron density measurements.

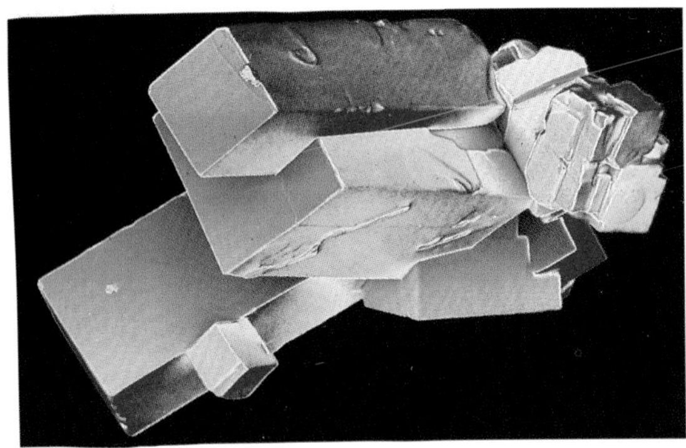

False-coloured scanning electron micrograph of sodium chloride.

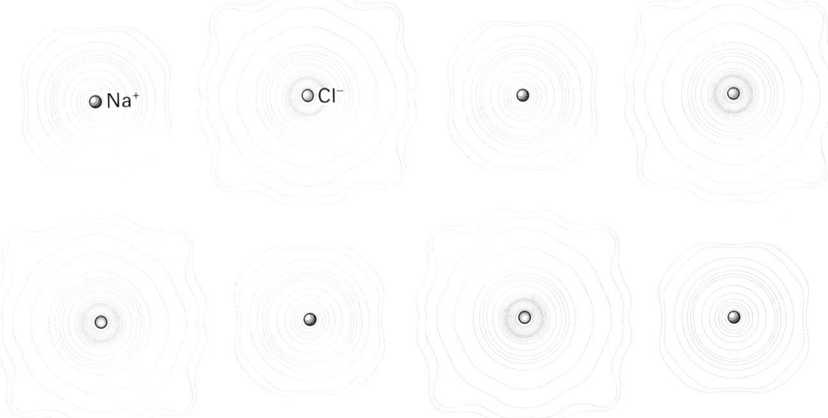

The experimental electron density for sodium chloride shows very little electron density between the sodium and the chloride ions. This picture supports the idea that electrons have been transferred from one atom to another to form ions. Diagrams like this are made by analysing the diffraction of X-ray beams by crystals of ionic compounds. Experimental measurement indicates 10.05 electrons per Na^+ ion.

Ionic bonding involves electron transfer. Covalent bonding involves electron sharing. The final spread of this chapter investigates compounds that exist between these two extremes.

SUMMARY

- Covalent bonds become more polar as the difference in the electronegativity values of the two bonded elements increases.
- An electronegativity difference greater than about 1.8 on the Pauling scale implies that the bond is sufficiently polar for the bonding to be ionic.
- Positive ions form when atoms lose electrons.
- Negative ions form when atoms gain electrons.
- Ions pack together in an array of alternating opposite charges to form a solid ionic lattice.

Magnesium and oxygen

The reaction between the Group II element magnesium and the Group VI element oxygen involves the transfer of two electrons from the magnesium atom to the oxygen atom. Magnesium has two valence electrons (Mg 2,8,2) and oxygen has six (O 2,6). The result is a magnesium ion with a double positive charge (Mg^{2+} 2,8) and an oxide ion with a double negative charge (O^{2-} 2,8).

Magnesium and chlorine

These two elements react together to form the ionic compound magnesium chloride $MgCl_2$. Each magnesium atom loses two electrons to form a magnesium ion:

$Mg \rightarrow Mg^{2+} + 2e^-$

These two electrons are separately accepted by two chlorine atoms to form two chloride ions:

$2e^- + 2Cl \rightarrow 2Cl^-$

PRACTICE

1 Use Lewis structures to explain how the following ionic compounds form:
  - a Potassium fluoride
  - b Calcium chloride
  - c Magnesium oxide.

2 Explain what you understand by each of the following terms:
  - a Polarity
  - b Ion
  - c Ionic lattice.

5.11 COVALENT OR IONIC

OBJECTIVES

- Ionic and covalent character
- Ionic and covalent bonding as extreme cases
- Polarizing power of ions
- Polarizability of ions

In the simplest model of ionic bonding, electrons transfer completely from one atom to another. Ions of opposite charge result, and the ions pack together to form a solid ionic lattice. Conversely, the simplest model of covalent bonding has electron pairs being shared between atoms. These two situations are extremes, and the actual arrangement in reality often lies somewhere between them. You already understand that a polar covalent bond has some ionic character. It is now time to consider the converse: how an ionic bond can acquire covalent character.

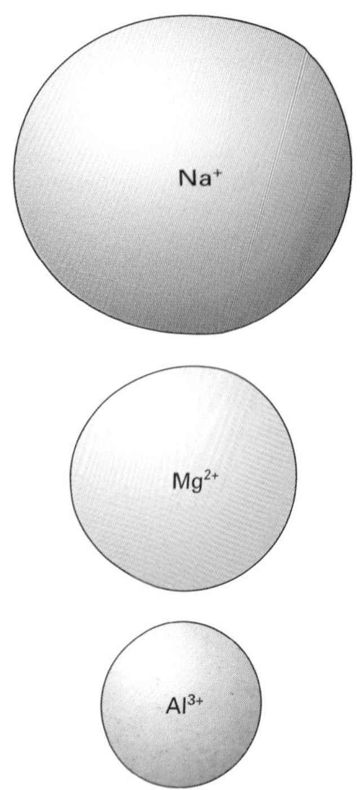

The relative sizes of the Na^+, Mg^{2+}, and Al^{3+} ions.

Covalent character – polarizing power of the positive ion

An ionic bond will acquire a degree of covalent character if the positive ion can attract electron density from the negative ion back into the region between the nuclei. The covalent character arises because the valence electrons will then be partially shared. The extent to which a positive ion can do this is called its **polarizing power**. The polarizing power of a positive ion depends on two factors, its charge and its size:

- The larger the positive charge on the ion, the greater is its attraction for the valence electrons. Doubling the charge doubles the force that a positive ion can exert.
- The smaller the size of the positive ion, the closer it is to the valence electrons, and the larger the force it exerts on them.

These two factors together combine to make up the **charge density** on the positive ion:

- The greater the charge density on the positive ion, the greater its polarizing power and the greater the covalent character of the bond it forms with a given negative ion.

The effect of polarizing power is illustrated by the chlorides of the metals of Period 3: NaCl, $MgCl_2$, and $AlCl_3$. The charge on the ions increases across the period: $Na^+ < Mg^{2+} < Al^{3+}$. The size of the ions decreases across the period: $Na^+ > Mg^{2+} > Al^{3+}$. The magnesium ion has a higher charge density than the sodium ion, because it has a greater charge *and* is smaller. The aluminium ion has the highest charge density because it is the smallest ion *and* has the greatest charge. The bonding in sodium chloride and in magnesium chloride is described adequately by the simple ionic model. However, the intensely polarizing Al^{3+} ion places the bonding in $AlCl_3$ on the borderline between ionic and covalent bond character.

The effect of polarizing power is also illustrated by silicon tetrachloride $SiCl_4$. The formation of purely ionic bonds in this compound would involve forming the Si^{4+} ion. This ion is so polarizing that it would attract back the electrons it had lost, so it is very unlikely to form. The bonding in $SiCl_4$ is essentially covalent.

Covalent character – polarizability of the negative ion

The extent to which a positive ion can pull electrons back into the space between the nuclei depends not only on its own polarizing power but also on how easy it is to polarize the negative ion. The **polarizability** of a negative ion measures the ease with which its electron density can be distorted towards the positive ion.

Polarizability increases with the charge on the negative ion and also increases with the number of electrons the ion has. Large, highly charged, negative ions can be polarized easily, and form bonds with greater covalent character. Small, singly charged ions are not easy to polarize. There is a clear trend in the polarizability of the ions of the Group VII elements. Fluoride ions have fewer electrons and are smaller than chloride ions. Fluoride ions are therefore less polarizable than chloride ions; all fluorides have greater ionic character than the

...chlorides. For example, aluminium fluoride is a ...stalline solid melting above 1000 °C. Anhydrous aluminium chloride (which is the dry form, with no water associated with it) shows much covalent character.

The iodide ion I^- is approximately 15% bigger than the chloride ion Cl^-. The iodide ion is therefore more polarizable than the chloride ion. The high charge density of the Na^+ ions distorts the electron density around the iodide ions in the NaI lattice and draws electron density into the region between the oppositely charged ions. NaI therefore has a degree of covalent character. The Cl^- ion is less distorted because it is smaller in size.

The combined effect of polarizing power and polarizability is illustrated by considering a series of compounds that all have the same total number of electrons: sodium fluoride NaF, magnesium oxide MgO, aluminium nitride AlN, and silicon carbide SiC. Passing along this series, the polarizing power of the positive ion increases as the ion becomes smaller and more highly charged, and the negative ion becomes more polarizable as its charge increases. Bonding character changes from ionic to covalent across this series.

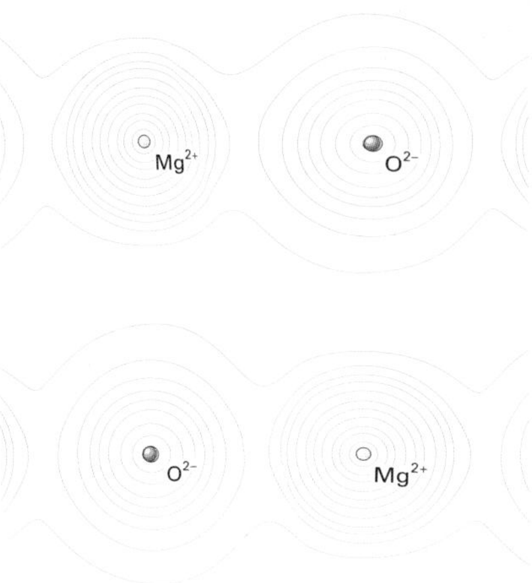

The experimental electron density for magnesium oxide. The minimum electron density between the ions is almost three times as large as that in sodium chloride, see previous spread.

Bond character and chemical properties

Sodium chloride and magnesium chloride both exist as crystalline solids at room temperature, and have the typical properties of ionic compounds (e.g. high melting point, aqueous solution conducts electricity). These compounds both dissolve in water without reaction. The solid crystalline lattice breaks down and the ions are surrounded by the polar water molecules:

$$NaCl(s) \rightarrow Na^+(aq) + Cl^-(aq)$$

Anhydrous aluminium chloride is not crystalline, has the relatively low melting point of 180 °C, and reacts violently with water:

$$AlCl_3(s) + 3H_2O(l) \rightarrow Al(OH)_3(s) + 3HCl(aq)$$

Many other covalent chlorides (e.g. silicon tetrachloride) react similarly with water:

$$SiCl_4(l) + 4H_2O(l) \rightarrow Si(OH)_4(s) + 4HCl(aq)$$

This behaviour suggests that the bonding in anhydrous aluminium chloride is also essentially covalent.

Hydrolysis

Reactions with water are referred to as **hydrolysis reactions**. The bracket (aq) indicates an aqueous solution; the bracket (l) indicates a liquid.

The reaction between silicon tetrachloride and water is vigorous. The glass rod is moistened with concentrated aqueous ammonia, which produces white fumes with the hydrogen chloride produced on hydrolysis.

SUMMARY

- The covalent character of an ionic bond depends on the polarizing power of the positive ion and the polarizability of the negative ion.
- The polarizing power of a positive ion depends on its charge density, which increases with increasing charge and decreasing size.
- The polarizability of a negative ion increases with increasing charge and increasing number of electrons.
- Bond character is reflected in the chemical properties of a compound.

PRACTICE

1 Using one of the following headings:
- non-polar covalent molecules,
- highly polar covalent molecules,
- an essentially ionic lattice,
- an ionic lattice with a marked degree of covalent character,

describe the bonding in each of the substances listed alongside.

a Methane CH_4
b Tetrachloromethane CCl_4
c Rubidium iodide RbI
d Sodium chloride NaCl
e Magnesium bromide $MgBr_2$
f Strontium oxide SrO
g Phosphine PH_3

Explain your reasoning in each case.

PRACTICE EXAM QUESTIONS

1 **a** Copy and complete the following table by giving, in each case, the formula of a molecule or ion which has the bond angle shown. Use a different molecule or ion for each angle. [4]

Bond angle	Formula of molecule or ion with this bond angle
90°	
109°28′	
120°	
180°	

b Draw a diagram of a water molecule and on your diagram indicate the value of the bond angle. [2]

c Explain why the value of the bond angle in part **b** is different from any of those values in part **a**. [2]

d Draw a diagram showing how two water molecules attract each other by hydrogen bonding.
AQA (NEAB) 1997

2 **a** The nitrogen and hydrogen atoms in an ammonia molecule are held together by covalent bonds. What is meant by the term *covalent bond*? [2]

b By referring to the formation of the ammonium ion from ammonia give the meaning of the term *coordinate bond*. [2]

c Suggest the difference in bond strength, if any, between the bond formed by co-ordination in the ammonium ion and the other N—H bonds. Explain your answer. [2]

d Give the bond angle in the ammonium ion and predict, with an explanation, an approximate value for the bond angle in the ammonia molecule. [3]

e Name the major force of attraction which exists between molecules in liquid ammonia and explain how this type of force arises. [12]
AQA (NEAB) 1995

3 **a** State the type of bonding in a crystal of potassium bromide. Write an equation to show what happens when potassium bromide is dissolved in water and predict the pH of the resulting solution. [3]

b When iodine reacts directly with fluorine, a compound containing 57.2% by mass of iodine is formed.

i Determine the empirical formula of this compound.

ii The empirical formula of this compound is the same as the molecular formula. Write a balanced equation for the formation of this compound. [4]

c **i** Sketch a diagram to show the shape of a BrF_3 molecule. Show on your sketch any lone pairs of electrons in the outermost shell of bromine and name the shape.

ii BrF_3 reacts with an equimolar am... fluoride to form an ionic compound which contains potassium ions. Give the formula of the negative ion produced, sketch its shape, show any lone pair(s) and indicated the value of the bond angle. [6]
AQA (NEAB) 1999 *(See also Chapter 9.)*

4 **a** Explain what is meant by the terms **ionic bond**, **covalent bond**, **dative covalent bond**. [3]

b Copy the table below and indicate whether each of the following molecules has an overall polarity. [3]

	Yes/No
Tetrachloromethane	
Carbon dioxide	
Methane	
Ethanol	
Trichloromethane	
Propanone	

c Below are given the atomic and ionic radii for a number of elements.

Atom	Radius / nm	Ion	Radius / nm
Na	0.157	Na^{+}	0.102
Mg	0.136	Mg^{2+}	0.072
Al	0.125	Al^{3+}	0.053
F	0.071	F^{-}	0.133
Cl	0.099	Cl^{-}	0.180
I	0.133	I^{-}	0.216

Give an explanation for each of the following:

i The magnesium atom is smaller than the sodium atom.

ii The sodium ion is smaller than the sodium atom.

iii Aluminium fluoride is ionic, aluminium iodide is covalent. [9]
EDEXCEL (ULEAC) 1996

5 **a** What is a polar covalent bond? [1]

b In what circumstances will a covalent bond be polar? [1]

c In what circumstances will an anion be polarized? [1]

d How does a polarized anion differ from an unpolarized anion? [1]

e **i** Draw diagrams to show the shapes of the following molecules and in each case show the value of the bond angle of the diagram.

I $BeCl_2$
II NCl_3
III SF_6

ii State which of the above molecules is most likely to form a coordinate bond with a hydrogen ion. Give a reason for your answer. [8]
AQA (NEAB) 1997

6 This question is about geometry and molecular shapes.

a Distinguish between the terms *covalent bond* and *dative bond (coordinate bond)*. [1]

b i When ammonia and boron trifluoride (BF_3) are mixed, a reaction occurs and a compound of molecular formula NBH_3F_3 is formed. Using the usual symbols for covalent and dative bonds, represent the molecular bonding in a diagram.

What geometry would you expect around the nitrogen atom in NBH_3F_3?

ii Boron trifluoride is a planar molecule but nitrogen trifluoride (NF_3) is pyramidal. Use the electron-pair repulsion theory to explain the difference in shape. [5]

c i What shape is molecular phosphorus pentachloride?

ii Five electron pairs arrange themselves as shown in the diagram. **X** is the central atom. Any lone pairs in such systems go into the equatorial plane.

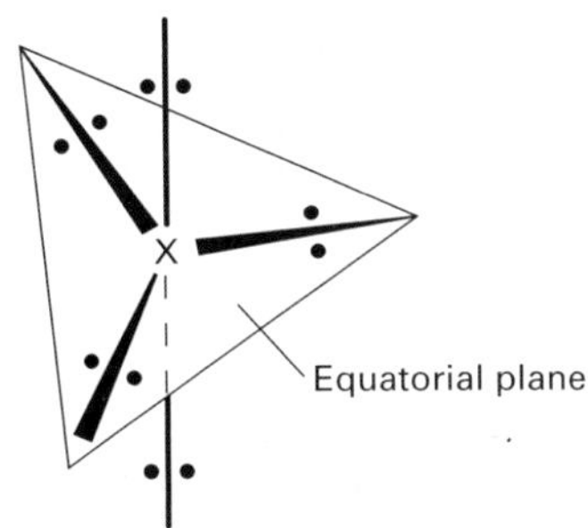

Use this fact to draw the shapes of the following molecules. You should indicate clearly the geometry about the central atom and show all lone pairs which are relevant to the shape.

Bromine trifluoride, BrF_3

Krypton difluoride, KrF_2 [5]

d A compound $Pt(NH_3)_2Cl_2$ is used in medicine as the modern drug cisplatin.

i Given that platinum(II) compounds are almost always square planar, draw the possible isomers of this compound and name the type of isomerism exhibited.

ii When $Pt(NH_3)_2Cl_2$ is synthesised in the laboratory the effectiveness of the resulting compound depends on the method of preparation. Suggest an explanation for this fact. [6]
EDEXCEL (ULEAC) 1991 *(See also Chapter 20.)*

7 Ammonia, NH_3, is a polar covalent molecule.

a State the general rules which determine the shape of a covalent molecule. [3]

b Draw the shape of the ammonia molecule. [1]

c Why is the bond angle in ammonia 107° rather than 109°28′? [1]

d Explain why the molecule of ammonia is polar. [1]
EDEXCEL 1997

8 a This part of the question concerns the hydrides CH_4, NH_3, and H_2O.

i Draw the shapes of each molecule, suggesting values for the bond angles.

ii State the type of intermolecular forces present for each hydride.

iii Account for the variation in bond angles in these molecules.

iv In which hydride are the intermolecular forces strongest? Explain how you decided upon your answer. [10]

b i Draw 'dot-and-cross' diagrams to show the structures of the ammonia molecule and of the ammonium ion.

ii Using the ammonium ion as an example, explain what is meant by the term dative covalent bond.

iii The ammonium ion has a tetrahedral shape. Explain what this suggests about the four N–H bonds. [5]
EDEXCEL (ULEAC) 1995 *(See also Chapter 7.)*

9 a Describe the motion of the ions in

i solid sodium chloride,

ii molten sodium chloride. [4]

b A lithium iodide crystal has some covalent character.

i Explain the meaning of the terms *covalent bond* and *some covalent character*.

ii Explain why lithium iodide has more covalent character than sodium iodide. [5]
AQA (NEAB) 1995

10 The table below shows electronegativity values for some atoms.

H	N	O	F	Cl	Cs
2.1	3.0	3.5	4.0	3.0	0.7

a What do you understand by the term **electronegativity**? [1]

b The nature of the bonding in substances depends partly on the electronegativities of the atoms concerned. *Use the data* in the table above to suggest the nature of the bonding in each of the following substances.

i caesium fluoride; [1]

ii water; [1]

iii chorine. [1]
EDEXCEL 1998

Solids

All around you are examples of the three main states of matter: solids, liquids, and gases. Solids are distinguished from liquids and gases by having definite shapes, whereas liquids and gases take on the shape of their containers. A definite external shape implies a regular internal structure where atoms, ions, or molecules are held in a fixed array. The previous chapter discussed the nature of ionic bonding between metallic and non-metallic elements as well as covalent bonding between non-metallic elements. The aims of this chapter are to investigate the forces that maintain the shapes of solids and to describe and explain their internal structures. It opens with an investigation of metallic solids.

Metallic solids: bonding and properties

6.1

OBJECTIVES

- Lattice structure of metals
- Delocalized valence electrons
- Electrical conductivity
- Physical properties

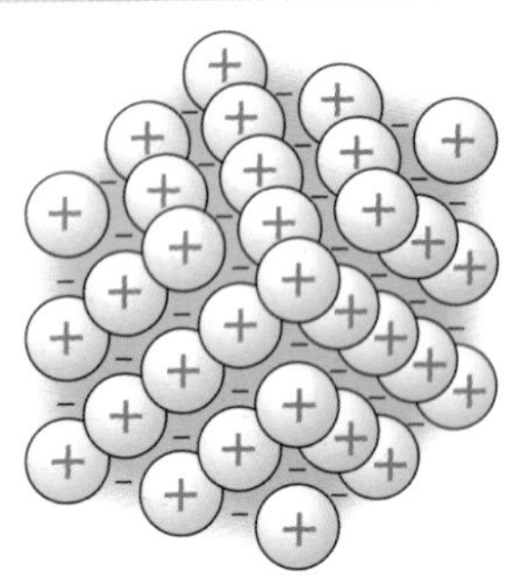

Metals consist of a regular array of metal ions surrounded by a 'sea' of delocalized valence electrons. Note that the overall structure remains electrically neutral.

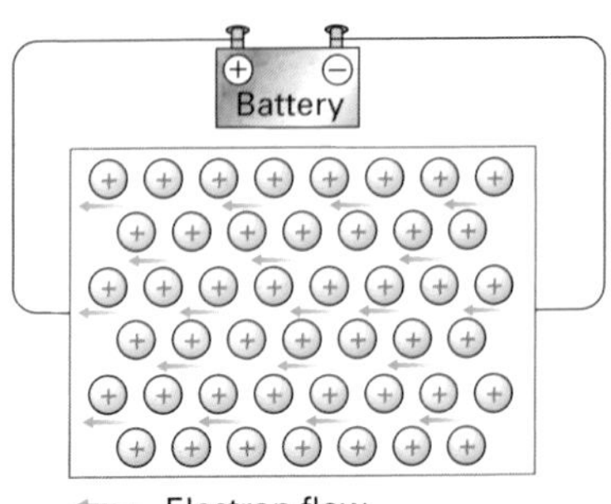

An electric current flowing through a metal is a flow of delocalized electrons. They flow from a region of negative electric potential to a region of positive potential.

Metallic elements all conduct electricity in the solid state. This observation cannot be explained by either an ionic or a covalent model of bonding. Ionic bonding requires the transfer of electrons to form oppositely charged ions; covalent bonding involves the sharing of electron pairs to form molecules. In neither model are there any species that are free to move around in the solid state. The bonding between metal atoms must be described by a different model.

Metallic bonding

When metal atoms are close to each other in the solid state, each atom loses control over one or more of its valence electrons. These electrons are no longer associated with a particular metal atom but are free to move throughout the solid piece of metal: the electrons are said to be **delocalized**. With valence electrons now delocalized, the metal atoms are effectively ionized. For example, the electronic structure of a sodium atom is Na $1s^22s^22p^63s^1$. The two inner shells are full. The 3s electron is delocalized, leaving each sodium atom as the sodium ion (electronic structure Na^+ $1s^22s^22p^6$). The bonding force is the attraction between the positive sodium ions and the delocalized electrons. The delocalized electrons are shared between all the sodium ions and act as a sort of 'glue' holding them together.

The whole system of ions and electrons has the lowest energy when the ions arrange themselves in a symmetrical pattern. In the solid state, **metallic bonding** therefore consists of regular arrangements of metal ions (called a **lattice**) surrounded by a 'sea' of delocalized electrons.

Electrical conductivity

An electric current is a flow of charged particles. In the case of metals, the charged particles are the delocalized valence electrons, which are free to move through the three-dimensional lattice of metal ions. Connecting a source of electric potential difference (e.g. a battery) across a piece of metal causes the electrons to move. The negative terminal of a battery has a negative potential, which means there is a surplus of electrons. The positive terminal has a positive potential, which means there is a deficit of electrons. Electrons flow through the metal from the negative to the positive terminal.

ermal conductivity

Thermal conductivity measures the rate of heat flow through a substance when one part of a sample is maintained at a higher temperature than the rest. The graph shows that the thermal conductivity of metals is linked closely to their electrical conductivities. This link indicates that electrons are the main conductors of heat through metals. In a metal, high temperature is represented by electrons with high kinetic energy and by metal ions with high vibrational energy. Energy is conducted through a piece of metal as the more energetic ('hotter') electrons collide with and speed up the slower, less energetic ('colder') electrons.

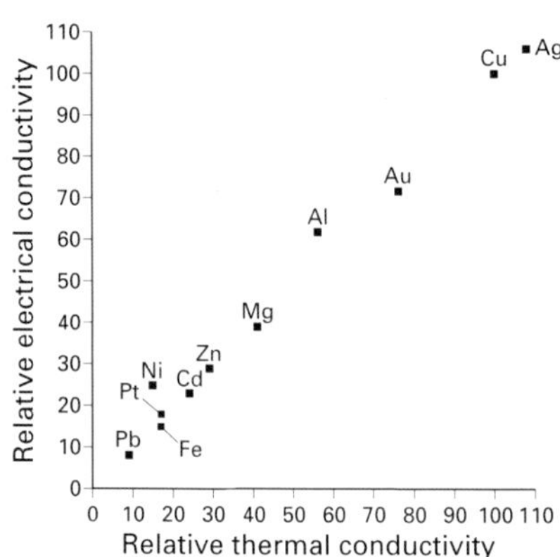

A scatter plot of relative thermal and electrical conductivities. The scales are relative to copper = 100.

Malleability and ductility

Metals are usually malleable: a **malleable** material may be beaten or pressed into new shapes. They are also usually ductile: a **ductile** material may be drawn out into a wire and made thinner by stretching. When metals are deformed, the metal ions in the solid structure slide past each other as the overall shape of the sample changes. The internal arrangement of ions and delocalized electrons allows this slippage to take place without significant disruption of the bonding forces.

When a metal is deformed, layers of metal ions can slip past one another without breaking up the whole structure.

Copper wire is made by drawing a thin cylinder of the metal through successively smaller holes. This process depends mainly on the property of ductility.

Car body panels are pressed from flat sheets of steel. This process takes advantage of both of the properties of malleability and ductility.

Metal crystals and alloys

A metal sample does not consist of a single regular lattice throughout its entire structure. The structure is broken up into tiny crystals, which may be seen through a microscope. The surface of a sample must first be carefully polished and then etched. When magnified, the surface appears to be divided into irregular areas. These areas are called grains; each **grain** represents a single crystal. The grains are separated by **grain boundaries**. We say that metals are polycrystalline.

Metals are mixed together to form **alloys**. The mechanical properties of alloys are controlled by the structures of the grains and by the composition of the grain boundaries.

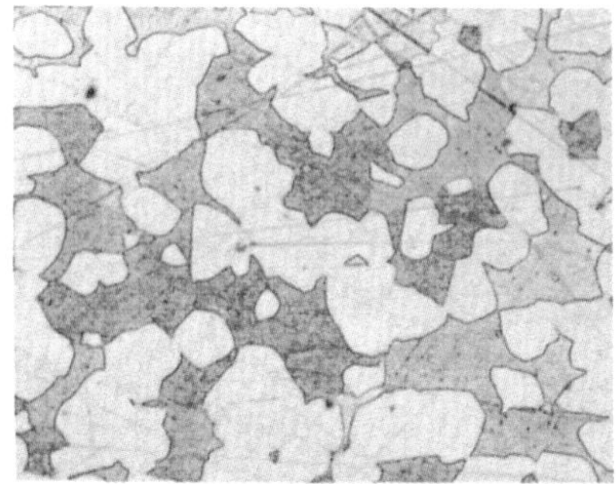

This magnified view of an etched and polished surface reveals the grains and grain boundaries in brass. ***Etching*** *is the removal of certain parts of a surface by means of a chemical reaction. It occurs selectively at the edges of the crystals, and so makes the edges much easier to see. The etching agent chosen depends on the type of metal: dilute nitric acid is used for iron or lead, and iron(III) chloride for copper.*

SUMMARY

- Metals consist of a regular array of metal ions surrounded by a 'sea' of delocalized valence electrons.
- The electrical and thermal conductivities of metals depend on the ability of the delocalized electrons to move freely.
- Metals are usually malleable and ductile because the metal ions can slip past each other without significantly disrupting the bonding forces.

PRACTICE

1 Explain why metals can conduct electricity in the solid state.

2 What do the terms *malleable* and *ductile* mean when applied to metals? Explain how pressing a sheet of steel to make a car body panel depends on both the malleability and the ductility of the steel.

3 Using a reference book or computer database, make a list of some alloys, along with their constituents, properties, and uses.

6.2

IONIC SOLIDS: BONDING AND PROPERTIES

OBJECTIVES

- Sodium chloride crystal structure
- Electrical conductivity
- Physical properties

Sodium chloride is a good example of an ionically bonded compound. A crystal of sodium chloride consists of equal numbers of sodium ions Na^+ and chloride ions Cl^-. Each ion is surrounded by six others of opposite charge. The crystal structure is a regular three-dimensional pattern of sodium ions alternating with chloride ions. Such a regular arrangement is called an **ionic lattice**. The internal structure gives solid ionic compounds a regular and sharply defined external shape. For sodium chloride, crystals grown by evaporating a solution have a cubic shape.

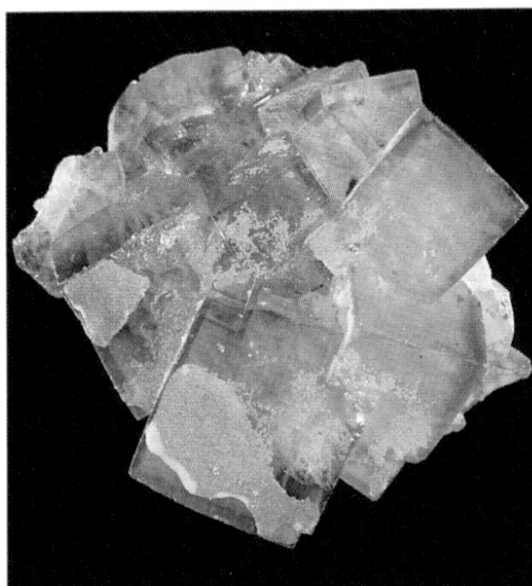

Fluorite CaF_2 and dolomite $CaCO_3 \cdot MgCO_3$ are both crystalline ionic compounds.

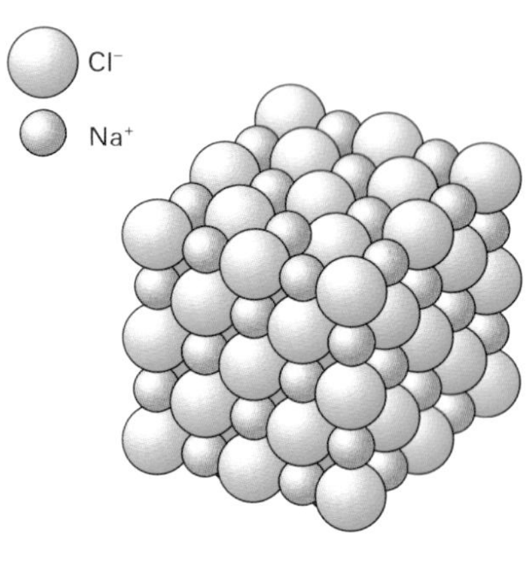

(a) A crystal of sodium chloride photographed in polarized light, (b) a space-filling model of the crystal lattice.

Melting ionic solids

Melting an ionic compound weakens the influence of the forces of attraction between the oppositely charged ions. The ions become free to move in the liquid state and are fairly independent of each other. The melting points of ionic compounds are generally high (e.g. T_m of sodium chloride = 801 °C), indicating that the forces of attraction between the ions are strong. Because ionic compounds have high melting points, they are always found as solids at room temperature. If a substance is a liquid or a gas at room temperature, we can safely assume that it does not have ionic bonding. On the other hand, a high melting point does not necessarily mean that a compound is ionic.

Solubility in water

Like many other ionic compounds, sodium chloride dissolves easily in water. The solid crystals gradually disappear as their constituent ions disperse throughout the solution. We can ask the question: if melting and dissolving both involve overcoming the forces of attraction between ions, why does melting take place at 801 °C while dissolving can take place at room temperature?

As we saw in spread 5.9, water is a V-shaped molecule with polar covalent bonds. The oxygen atom bears a partial negative charge and the hydrogen atoms each bear a partial positive charge. During solution, each positive sodium ion on the surface of the crystal attracts the partial negative charge on the oxygen atoms of water. Each negative chloride ion attracts the partial positive charges on the hydrogen atoms of the water molecules. The result is that the ions become surrounded by water molecules and are removed from their positions in the crystal lattice, as shown in spread 10.7.

Ion–dipole force

There is an attraction between a positive ion such as Na^+ and the negative end of the water dipole (the partial negative charge on the oxygen atom). This attractive force is called an **ion–dipole force**. The ion–dipole force between Na^+ and several water molecules almost exactly compensates for the attraction between the Na^+ and Cl^- ions.

If an ionic compound is soluble, the attractions between water molecules and the ions must be comparable with the energy required to separate the ions. This energy requirement is not always met and several ionic compounds, such as magnesium oxide and calcium carbonate, dissolve only to a very small extent in water.

Electrical conductivity

In general terms, an electric current will flow if charged particles are free to move when an electric potential difference is applied. Metals conduct electricity because they contain delocalized valence electrons. Ionic compounds conduct electricity when molten or when dissolved in water. In both cases, the electric current is carried by ions that are free to move. Solid ionic compounds do not conduct electricity because the ions cannot move freely.

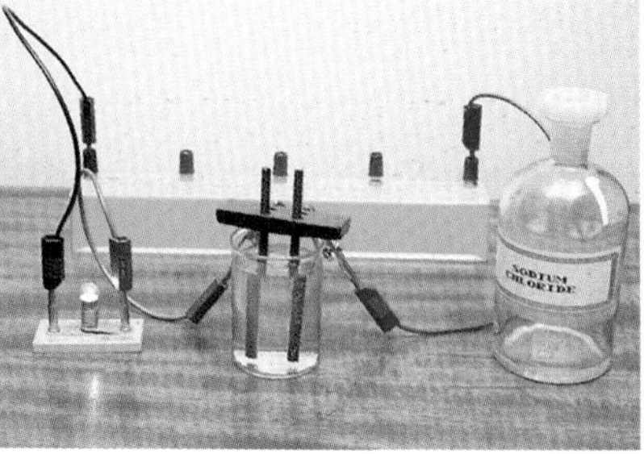

Sodium chloride conducts electricity when in aqueous solution.

Ionic crystals – hard and yet brittle

Ionic crystals are not malleable or ductile. They cannot be squeezed or beaten into new shapes or stretched to make them thinner. A crystal of sodium chloride shatters if an attempt is made to cut it with a knife. The ions in the crystal are moved so that each sodium ion is immediately next to another sodium ion, and each chloride ion is next to another chloride ion. Instead of being strongly attracted by their neighbours, the ions of like charge are strongly repelled and the crystal flies apart. Contrast this behaviour with that of metallic crystals, which do not shatter when cut or even when hit.

A sharp blow along specific planes of this potassium bromide crystal with a knife edge causes the crystal to split.

SUMMARY

- Solid ionic compounds consist of ions packed into a regular lattice.
- In the lattice, ions of one charge are surrounded by ions of the opposite charge.
- Ionic compounds have high melting points because of the strong forces of attraction between the ions.
- Aqueous solutions of ionic compounds contain separate ions each surrounded by water molecules.
- Ionic compounds conduct electricity when molten or when in aqueous solution because they contain ions that are free to move.
- Ionic compounds are brittle; they shatter when hit.

PRACTICE

1 For the ionic solid sodium chloride, draw a diagram to show the arrangement of a sodium ion and its nearest neighbours.

2 Draw the structures of the sodium ion and the chloride ion as they exist dissolved in water. Explain what happens as the solution evaporates and crystals of solid sodium chloride grow.

3 Write equations with state symbols to show:

a Solid sodium chloride melting

b Solid sodium chloride dissolving in water.

6.3

Giant covalent solids

OBJECTIVES

- Diamond
- Graphite
- Silica
- Glass
- Ceramics

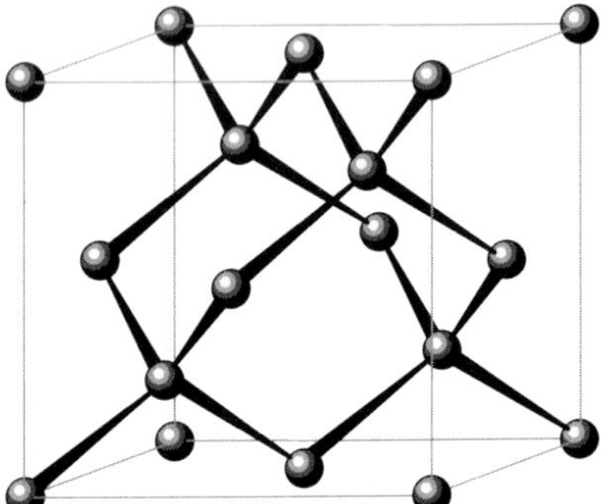

The three-dimensional structure of diamond.

*The diamond merchant Harry Winston sold three of the eight largest uncut diamonds ever found (*The Star of Sierra Leone, Presidente Vargas*, and* Jonker*). When this photograph appeared in* National Geographic *during his lifetime, his face was blacked out at the insistence of his life insurance company.*

Fullerite

See spread 19.4 for the structure of this third form of carbon.

Metallic and ionic solids are made up of ions held in place by electrostatic forces. In contrast, some covalent solids consist of networks of atoms, held in place by covalent bonds, that stretch throughout the whole structure. These substances are called **giant covalent solids**: they form the focus of this spread. Familiar examples include diamond, graphite, and silica. Giant covalent solids are sometimes also called **macromolecules** to reflect the immense size of the molecule involved.

Diamond

Diamond is a good example of a giant covalent solid. Each carbon atom in the structure is covalently bonded to four others. The bonding forces are uniform throughout the structure. As with ionic solids, giant covalent solids have very high melting points. The energy required to break the covalent bonds is very high. But, unlike most ionic solids, giant covalent solids do not dissolve in water because there are no ions to attract the water molecules.

The electronic structure of carbon is C $1s^22s^22p^2$. In diamond, the four valence electrons are all involved in bonding pairs located between the atoms of carbon. The other two electrons per atom are in a filled shell (n = 1). There are no free electrons and no ions present, so diamond does not conduct electricity. It is also the hardest substance known due to the strength of the carbon–carbon bonds and the geometrical rigidity of the structure. Many cutting tools are tipped with powdered diamond.

Graphite

Graphite is also a giant covalent solid, but its structure consists of two-dimensional layers of joined hexagonal rings rather than a three-dimensional network like diamond. Within a layer, each carbon atom is joined to three others by strong covalent bonds. The fourth valence electron from each carbon atom is delocalized within the layers. The delocalized electrons are free to move and so graphite can conduct electricity. The layers are not held tightly together and can slide over one another because of the weak forces of attraction between the layers (see the following chapter). This arrangement gives graphite a slippery feel and makes it a good high-temperature lubricant. Notice that the strong covalent bonds *within* the layers hold the carbon atoms close together; the weak forces *between* the layers result in a much wider separation. This wider separation explains why graphite's density (2.3 g cm^{-3}) is lower than diamond's (3.5 g cm^{-3}).

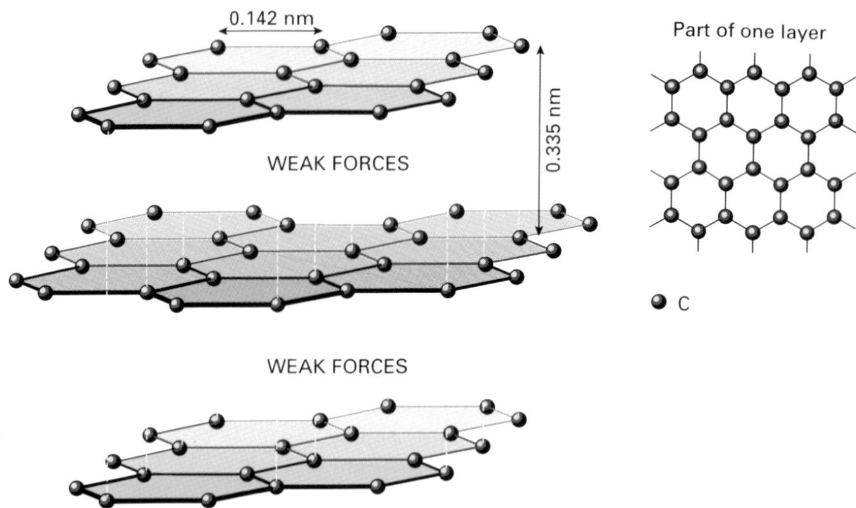

The structure of graphite. Compare the distance between the atoms within the layers with the distance between the layers.

Silica

Giant covalent solids can contain more than one sort of atom. Sand consists mostly of silicon dioxide, also called silica, whose formula is usually written as SiO_2. This formula gives the simplest ratio of the atoms concerned. Silica is a giant covalent solid with a structure similar to that of diamond. Because of its structure (i.e. strong covalent bonds, no ions, and no free electrons), silica is hard, has a high melting point, does not dissolve in water, and does not conduct electricity.

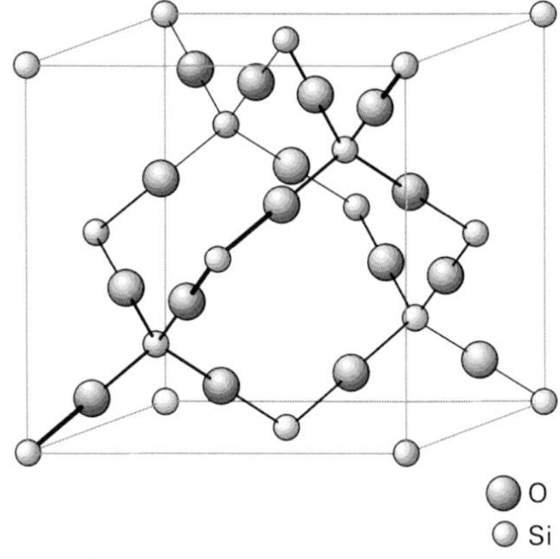

The silicon atoms in one form of silica adopt the diamond structure; there are oxygen atoms between each pair of silicon atoms.

Glass

All the giant covalent solids described above have regular structures. Glasses are made by melting silica with small amounts of other substances, but a glass does not have the regular structure of pure silica. The giant covalent structure is random, with ions from the other ingredients scattered throughout it. A glass does not have a distinct melting point.

Ceramics

Ceramics are manufactured solids that have a giant structure made up of two or more elements. The bonding can be either covalent, or ionic, or both. Familiar examples are bricks and porcelain, made by heating mixtures of sand and clays or feldspars to a high temperature (1500 °C) in a kiln. Clays and feldspars are aluminosilicates, spread 19.5, which contain aluminium, silicon, and oxygen, and often other metals such as magnesium. Because of their giant structure, ceramics typically show the following properties:

- They have high melting points.
- They are strong.
- They are good electrical and thermal insulators.

This glass building (Science Park at Futuroscope, Poitiers) echoes the shape of a quartz crystal, spread 17.4.

Superconductivity

Recent high-tech ceramics are of great interest because they exhibit **superconductivity**, which is the ability to conduct electricity without *any* resistance to current flow. Some metals develop this property, but only when cooled below 25 K by liquid helium (which is very expensive to make). Some ceramics become superconducting at much higher temperatures, above the boiling point of liquid nitrogen (77 K). Liquid nitrogen is cheaper than bottled water, which makes the technology affordable. These so-called 'high-temperature superconductors' offer the potential to store and transmit electricity without any loss of energy. A typical ceramic superconductor is an oxide of yttrium, barium, and copper, $YBa_2Cu_3O_7$.

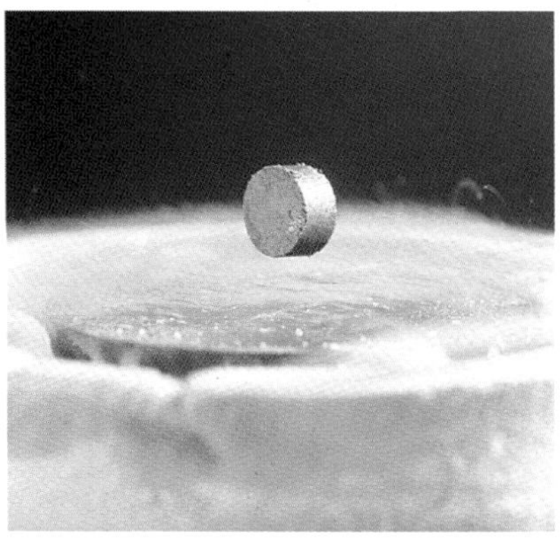

Placing a magnet over this superconductor induced an electric current in it. The current circulates without loss, creating a magnetic field, which opposes that of the magnet above. The magnet 'levitates'.

SUMMARY

- Giant covalent solids have high melting points.
- Most giant covalent solids are electrical insulators because all of the electrons either are in filled shells or are involved in covalent bonds.
- Diamond has a tetrahedral structure in which each carbon atom is bonded to four others.
- Graphite has a layered structure; within each hexagonal layer, each carbon atom is bonded to three others.
- Graphite is an electrical conductor because one valence electron per atom is delocalized within the layers.

PRACTICE

1 Explain why giant covalent substances are:
   a usually hard,
   b electrical insulators,
   c stable (i.e. do not decompose) at high temperatures.

2 Explain how graphite conducts electricity.

3 What type of bonds are present in silica? What type of bonds are present in sodium chloride? How do the strengths of these bonds compare? Give some evidence to support your argument.

6.4

DELOCALIZATION

OBJECTIVES

- Delocalization in metals and graphite
- Delocalization in benzene
- Delocalization in ions

As you read in the spread on bonding in metals at the beginning of this chapter, valence electrons in a metal are not associated with a particular metal atom but are free to move throughout the sample: the electrons are said to be **delocalized**. These delocalized electrons constitute a sort of 'glue' that holds the resulting metal ions in a regular lattice structure. Graphite is a form of carbon, which is a non-metallic element. The atoms are covalently bonded together in layers of hexagonal rings joined together. Although a non-metal, graphite conducts electricity because one valence electron per atom is delocalized within these layers. As you will see in later chapters, delocalization is present in many other substances and is an important idea in helping to explain their properties.

Graphite – a closer look

The concept of delocalization might seem to be a cunning invention to explain away the ability of graphite, a covalently bonded non-metallic element, to conduct electricity. However, the distances between the atoms (the **bond lengths**) in graphite show the bonding to be unusual.

The C—C single bond in diamond has a length of 0.154 nm. The C=C double bond in ethene $CH_2{=}CH_2$ is shorter at 0.134 nm. This is because the *two* pairs of electrons in the double bond draw the atoms closer together. The bond length between adjacent carbon atoms within the layers in graphite is 0.142 nm, a value *intermediate* between those for the C—C bond and the C=C bond. It is therefore reasonable to assume that the number of bonds between each pair of adjacent carbon atoms in graphite is between 1 and 2. Considering a simpler molecule, benzene, will explain why and how the bonds have this intermediate nature.

Benzene

Benzene is a compound of carbon and hydrogen with the formula C_6H_6. X-ray diffraction techniques confirm its structure as a hexagon of carbon atoms. Each carbon atom is joined to two carbon atoms, and to a hydrogen atom by a single covalent bond. All six carbon–carbon bonds have the same length, 0.139 nm. This value too is intermediate between the lengths for C—C and C=C.

The p orbitals on all six carbon atoms of the benzene ring overlap in phase to make this lowest-energy delocalized molecular orbital. See spread 23.1.

The electronic structure of carbon is C $1s^2 2s^2 2p^2$. So each carbon atom, in joining to two carbon atoms and one hydrogen atom, has so far not used one p orbital (out of three) and one valence electron (out of four). To understand what this means and to progress further, we need to apply molecular orbital theory.

Delocalization in benzene

The one p orbital per atom not so far used in bonding projects above and below the plane of the hexagonal ring. The p orbitals on adjacent carbon atoms overlap to form molecular orbitals which are spread over all six carbon atoms. The lowest-energy molecular orbital is shaped like two hexagonal doughnuts positioned above and below the plane of the ring. The pair of electrons in the lowest-energy molecular orbital bonds *all six atoms* together. (There are also two other bonding molecular orbitals of more complicated shape each containing a pair of electrons.) As shown to the left, this model is confirmed by a computer-generated electron density diagram.

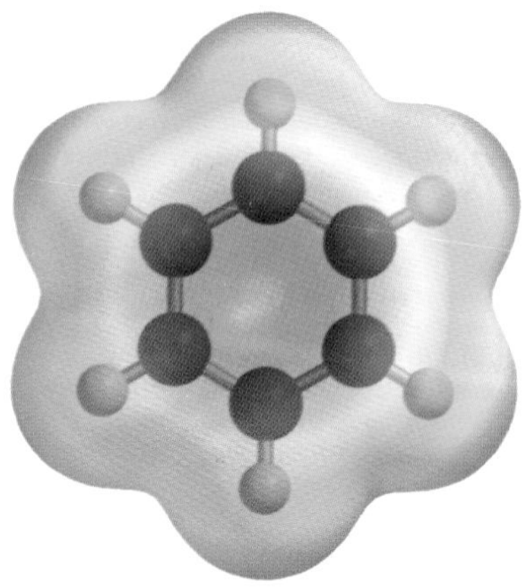

Electrostatic potential map for benzene: six bonding electrons enter the three delocalized orbitals to form a delocalized cloud of electrons. Note that the ball-and-stick model visible inside the electrostatic potential map shows atoms that are bonded; the number of bonds is intentionally not shown.

Graphite again

Benzene and graphite consist of hexagonal rings of carbon atoms. In benzene, each carbon atom is bonded to two other carbon atoms; a carbon–hydrogen bond extends out from each atom in the ring. In graphite, further carbon–carbon bonds extend out of each ring to link with other rings.

The p orbitals on each of the carbon atoms in graphite therefore overlap to form delocalized molecular orbitals, which cover the entire layer of joined hexagonal rings. Electrical conduction in graphite is therefore a flow of electrons within delocalized molecular orbitals.

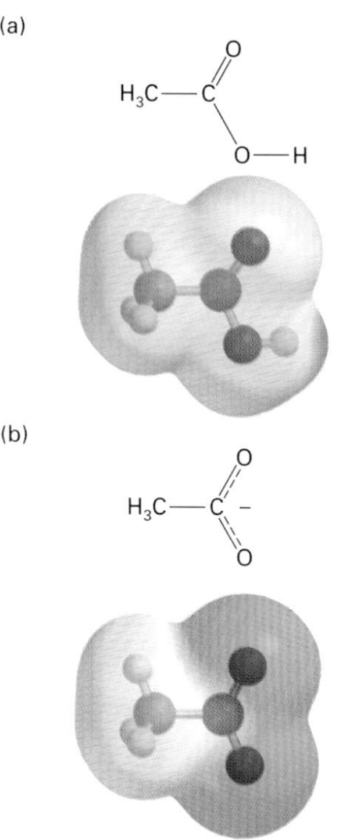

Electrostatic potential maps for (a) ethanoic acid and (b) the ethanoate ion. The two oxygen atoms are identical in the ion. Delocalization may be shown using dashed lines.

Delocalization in ions

The electrostatic potential map for ethanoic acid CH_3COOH shows that one of the oxygen atoms is bonded to a hydrogen atom and that the other oxygen atom is in a different environment. The heavy concentration of red shows that the carbon-oxygen double bond is strongly polar. The other red patch is around the other oxygen atom.

When a hydrogen ion H^+ is lost from ethanoic acid to form the ethanoate ion, the electron density shows a significant change has occurred. A simplistic analysis would suggest the formula CH_3COO^-. However, the electron density shows that the two oxygen atoms are no longer different. It is impossible to tell either to which oxygen atom the hydrogen was attached or which was the doubly bonded one. The ion is much better represented by the formula $CH_3CO_2^-$, the two oxygens now being equivalent. This will have important consequences for the acidity of organic acids, as explained in spread 27.1. The nitrate ion NO_3^- and the carbonate ion CO_3^{2-} are both delocalized; their shapes are trigonal planar. The sulphate ion SO_4^{2-} is also delocalized; its shape is tetrahedral.

The H_3^+ ion

This ion is the simplest example of delocalization. Three protons positioned at the corners of an equilateral triangle are held together by just two electrons shared between all three. This ion was first observed by mass spectrometry by J. J. Thomson in 1912, before a model existed which could explain its stability. The presence of H_3^+ has recently been discovered in the atmosphere of Jupiter.

Important features about delocalization

- Delocalization stabilizes a molecule or ion.

The reason for this lies in the wave nature of electrons. The more spread out a wave is, the less severe its curvature becomes; and hence its kinetic energy becomes lower.

- Most molecular orbitals are delocalized. The only exceptions to this occur in molecules that have exactly two atoms (diatomic molecules). See the discussion of the bonding in methane in spread 22.12.
- The lowest-energy orbital of each symmetry (σ or π) is easy to visualize: each atom has all the relevant orbitals in phase. See for example the shape of the lowest-energy π orbital in benzene shown on the opposite page.
- If n electron pairs in delocalized molecular orbitals bond $n+1$ atoms together (in CH_4 four electron pairs bond five atoms), n *localized* bonds can be made which give the correct electron density, albeit the wrong energy; see spread 22.12. When fewer than n electron pairs are involved, as is the case for the π electron pairs in benzene (three electron pairs bond six atoms), the localized picture fails to get *either* the electron density *or* the energy correct; see spread 23.1.

σ / π delocalization

The concept of delocalization is well accepted for π orbitals. That σ **orbitals are also delocalised** is not well recognized, because of point 4 alongside. Except in spread 22.12 this idea will not be raised again.

SUMMARY

- Delocalization is the extension of bonding electron density to cover more than two atomic centres.

PRACTICE

1 Look up spread 23.1 and then write an account of the delocalization in benzene.

6.5

METALLIC SOLIDS: STRUCTURES

OBJECTIVES

- Metallic crystal structures
- Simple cubic
- Body-centred cubic
- Hexagonal close packing
- Cubic close packing
- Coordination number

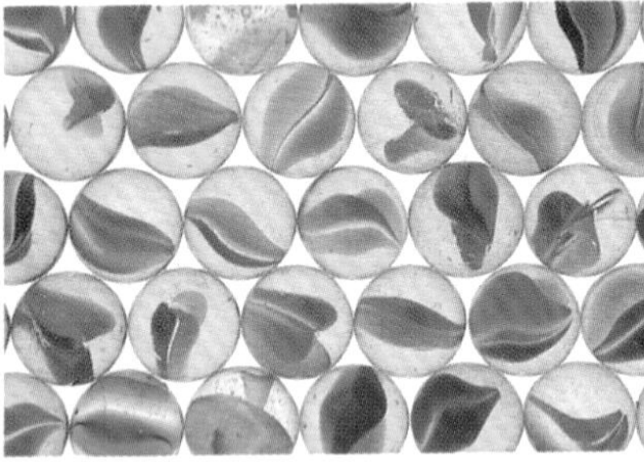

Packing of spheres in a layer: (a) square pattern where each sphere has four nearest neighbours; and (b) hexagonal pattern where each sphere has six nearest neighbours.

The unit cell

Crystals are made up from countless numbers of particles arranged in layers stacked together. The **unit cell** is the simplest pattern containing the appropriate particles that, when replicated, reproduces the overall arrangement of the lattice. Unit cells are usually represented by ball-and-stick models, which show the arrangement of the particles more clearly than space-filling models.

What are the actual structural arrangements in metals? What sorts of patterns do the ions adopt? Look at apples piled up on a market stall. A pile consists of flat layers in which the apples are as close as possible to each other. The apples in one layer fit into the hollows in the layer below. In this spread, we look at the four main structures that result when metal ions pack together.

Layers of metal ions

The simple model of a metallic crystal assumes that the ions are identical spheres which touch each other. It is helpful to think about the crystal lattice first in terms of the structure of each layer, and then in terms of how these layers fit together. There are two main ways in which spheres can be arranged in a single layer: a square pattern and a hexagonal pattern. The square pattern makes less efficient use of the space compared with the hexagonal pattern (i.e. there is a greater volume of empty space in the square pattern). Layers of spheres in either the square or the hexagonal pattern may then be stacked in different ways to make the four basic crystal structures: simple cubic, body-centred cubic, hexagonal close-packed, and cubic close-packed. To help us describe these structures, we shall give each layer a label, A, B, or C.

Simple cubic structure

This crystal structure results when square layers are placed exactly one on top of another. The layers repeat in the sequence AAA.... This means that the ions (spheres) in layers 2, 3, ... are in exactly the same positions as those in layer 1. This arrangement represents the least-efficient occupancy of space possible. The **coordination number** of an ion gives the number of its *nearest* neighbours. The coordination number for a simple cubic crystal structure is 6 because each ion has six nearest neighbours. The only metal with the simple cubic structure is polonium.

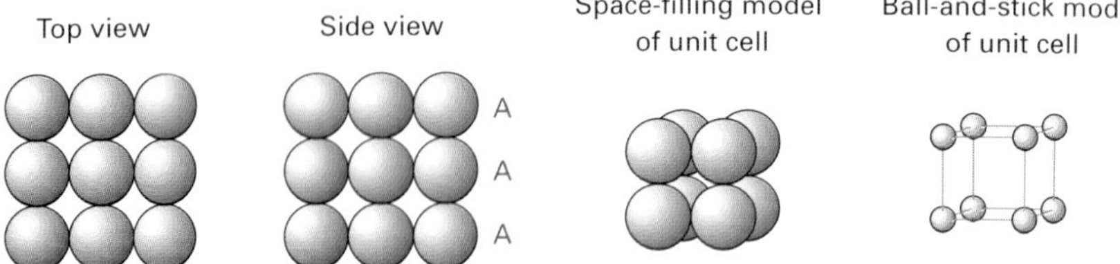

The simple cubic structure – showing the square layers stacked AAA....

Body-centred cubic structure

The ions in each square layer can be arranged to fit into the hollows between the ions in the layer immediately below. The square layers are then in the alternating sequence ABAB.... (This means that the ions in layers 1, 3, 5, ... are in exactly the same relative positions, but different from those in layers 2, 4, 6, ...) This is a more efficient use of space (68% of space is filled compared with only 52% for simple cubic). The coordination number is 8 and the unit cell is described as **body-centred cubic** (b.c.c.). Group I metals adopt the body-centred cubic structure, and their low densities reflect the relative openness of the b.c.c. structure, compared with the close packing described next.

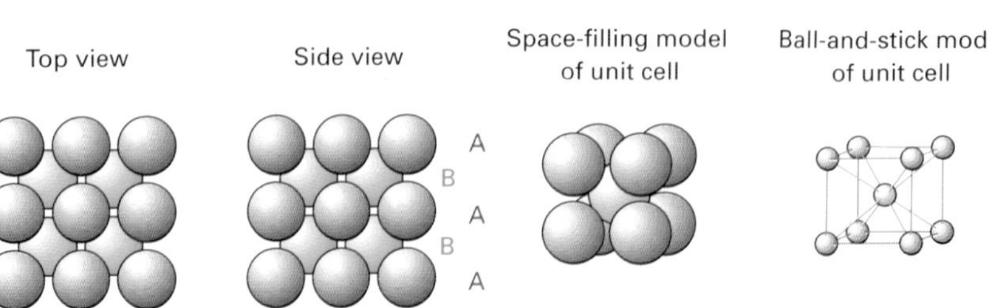

The body-centred cubic structure – showing the square layers stacked ABAB.... The layers have been coloured differently so that it is easier to see the arrangement, but all the spheres are identical.

Hexagonal close-packed structure

Hexagonal layers can stack one on another in the alternating sequence ABAB.... (Note that the labels A and B now refer to hexagonal layers.) The coordination number is 12, representing the most efficient use of space possible (74% of space is filled). The unit cell is called the **hexagonal close-packed** (h.c.p.) structure. Magnesium, zinc, and titanium are among the common metals to adopt the hexagonal close-packed structure in the solid state.

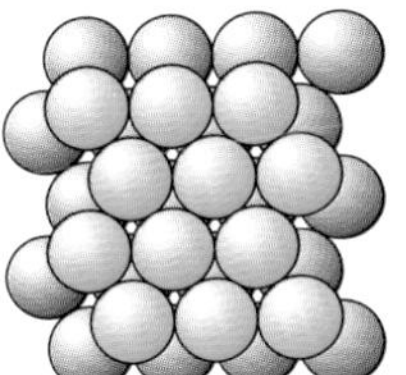

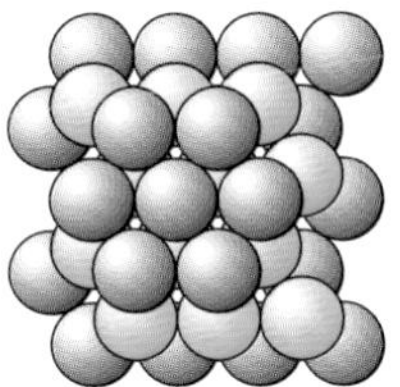

The ions in layer 3 lie directly above the ions in layer 1

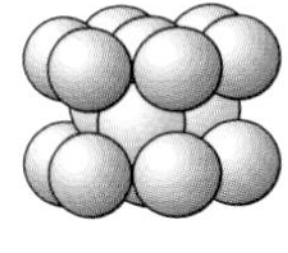

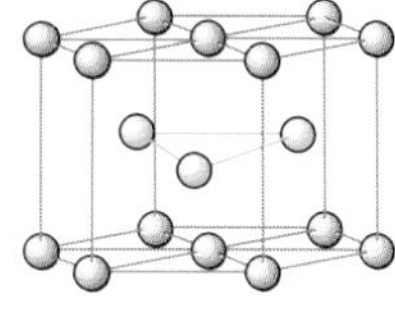

The hexagonal close-packed structure – showing the hexagonal layers stacked ABAB.... The layers have been coloured differently so that it is easier to see the arrangement, but all the spheres are identical.

Cubic close-packed structure

There is another way in which hexagonal layers can stack together. Instead of layer 3 being the same as layer 1, it can fit over the hollows in *both* the first two layers. This structure results in the sequence ABCABC.... The occupancy of space is the same as in the hexagonal close-packed structure (74%) and the coordination number is also 12. This unit cell is called the **cubic close-packed** structure, but may also be described as **face-centred cubic** (f.c.c.). The easiest way to understand the alternative name is to view *at an angle* from the close-packed planes. There is a sphere at each corner of the cube and also spheres at the centre of each of the faces. Aluminium, copper, silver, and gold are among the common metals to adopt the cubic close-packed structure in the solid state.

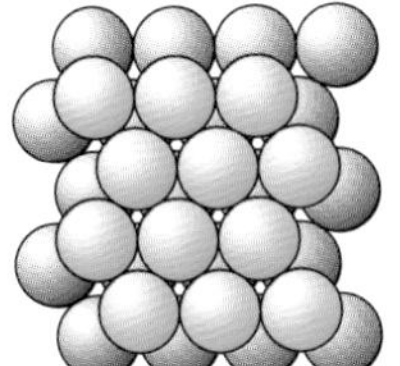

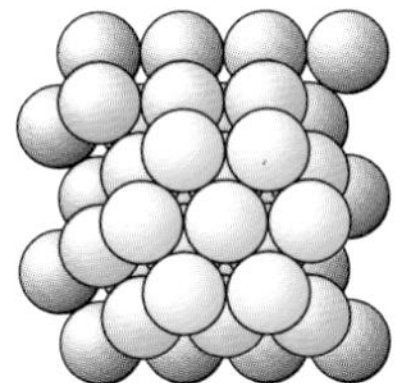

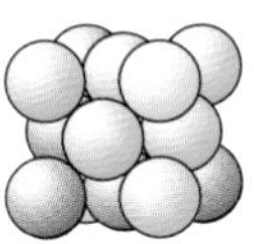

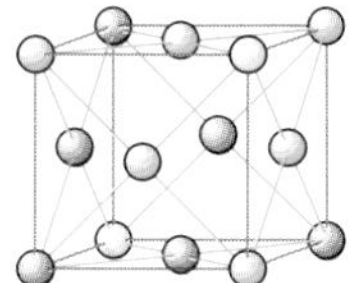

The cubic close-packed structure – showing the hexagonal layers stacked ABCABC.... Again, the layers have been coloured differently so that it is easier to see the arrangement, but all the spheres are identical.

SUMMARY

- Square layers stack AAA... to give the simple cubic structure or ABAB... to give the body-centred cubic structure.
- Hexagonal layers stack ABAB... to give the hexagonal close-packed structure or ABCABC... to give the cubic close-packed structure.
- Cubic close packing may also be called face-centred cubic.

PRACTICE

1 Give the coordination number for each of the following lattice structures:
  a Simple cubic
  b Body-centred cubic
  c Hexagonal close-packed
  d Face-centred cubic.

2 a Which of the four structures in question 1 are close-packed?
  b State what you understand by the term 'close packing'.
  c Give examples of structures that are not close-packed and say what distinguishes them from those which are.

3 Draw the ball-and-stick unit cells for each of the structures in question 1.

6.6

OBJECTIVES

- Caesium chloride structure
- Rock-salt (sodium chloride) structure

Ionic solids: structures

We have seen that metallic structures consist of *equal*-sized ions packed into crystalline lattices. There are four basic structures for arranging these metal ions: simple cubic, body-centred cubic, hexagonal close packing, and cubic close packing. So how do ionic substances, consisting of ions of generally *different* sizes, pack into regular lattices? As with metal ions in metallic structures, we can also think of the ions in ionic compounds as being spherical.

Ionic compounds

The crystals of ionic compounds are made up of ions that have opposite charges and generally different sizes. Packing these ions together presents a similar problem to packing oranges and grapefruit in the same box, with the additional complication that the positive and negative ions must be arranged to minimize repulsions and maximize attractions. The lattice adopted by ionic compounds depends largely on the relative numbers of ions and on their sizes. In this spread, we shall consider in detail two basic structures in which the ion ratio is 1:1.

The caesium chloride structure

The simplest structure found in ionic compounds is called the **caesium chloride structure**. In this structure, a simple cubic array of caesium ions interpenetrates a simple cubic array of chloride ions. It is not correct to refer to this structure as being body-centred cubic, because the ion at the centre of the unit cell has the *opposite* charge to the other ions. The arrangement of each constituent ion must be considered separately. There are eight caesium ions around each chloride ion, and eight chloride ions around each caesium ion. So the coordination number of each ion is 8.

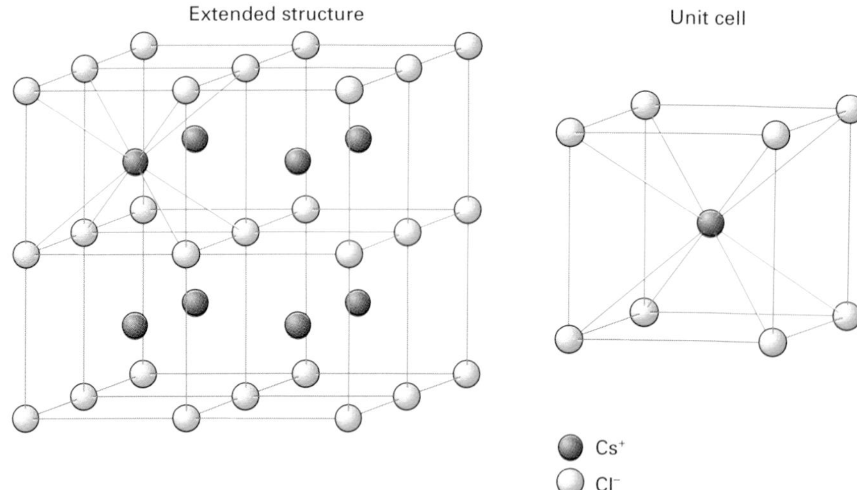

The caesium chloride structure.

Although the caesium chloride structure is the simplest way of packing ions of different sizes, it is not very common. It is found only in the chlorides, bromides, and iodides of caesium (Cs^+) and thallium(I) (Tl^+), where the positive and negative ions are of similar size. All the other alkali metal halides, including caesium fluoride, adopt the structure of sodium chloride, which we now consider.

The rock-salt (sodium chloride) structure

Sodium chloride is found naturally as rock salt. The crystal structure of sodium chloride is called the **rock-salt structure**. Each sodium ion is surrounded by six chloride ions. The coordination number of the sodium ion is 6. Similarly, each chloride ion is surrounded by six sodium ions. The coordination number of the chloride ion is also 6. Note that the sodium ion is significantly smaller than the chloride ion.

Look carefully at the diagram below. If we think just about the chloride ions in the rock-salt structure, we can see that they form a face-centred cubic array. The sodium ions similarly form a face-centred cubic array. The overall structure consists of two interpenetrating face-centred cubic arrays, one of sodium ions and one of chloride ions.

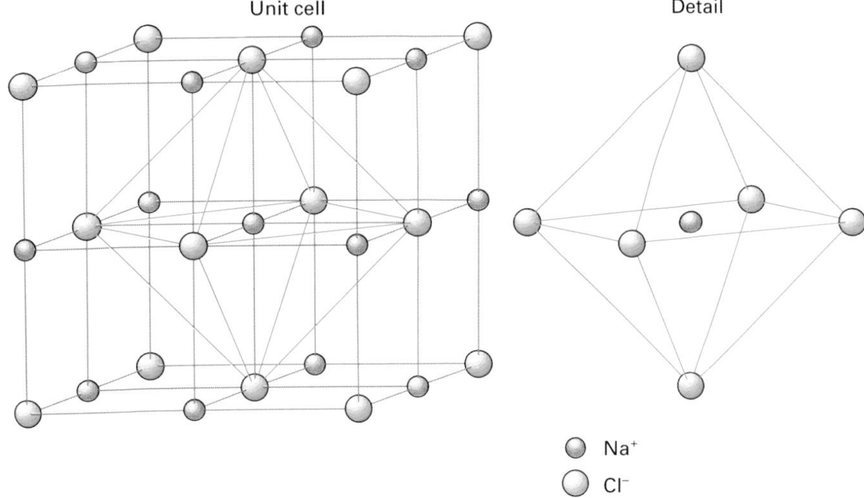

The rock-salt (sodium chloride) structure.

Compounds with the rock-salt (NaCl) structure

The rock-salt structure is by far the most common structure for compounds with a simple 1:1 ratio of ions. Examples include:

- seventeen Group I metal halides,
- silver chloride and silver bromide,
- magnesium oxide, calcium oxide, strontium oxide, and barium oxide,
- iron(II) oxide, cobalt(II) oxide, and nickel(II) oxide.

The structure is also adopted by compounds which show considerable covalent character, such as lead(II) sulphide PbS and titanium carbide TiC.

SUMMARY

- The lattice adopted by ionic compounds depends on the relative numbers of ions and on their sizes.
- Where the positive and negative ions are of approximately equal size, they may pack into the caesium chloride structure.
- The caesium chloride structure consists of two interpenetrating simple cubic arrays.
- The rock-salt (sodium chloride) structure consists of two interpenetrating face-centred cubic arrays.
- The rock-salt structure is by far the most important for compounds with a 1:1 ion ratio.

PRACTICE

1 Explain the meaning of both of the following sentences:

a The coordination number of the sodium ion in solid sodium chloride is 6.

b The coordination number of the chloride ion in the caesium chloride structure is 8.

2 Draw simple structures to represent the arrangement of the ions in the following:

a Thallium bromide (TlBr)

b Magnesium oxide (MgO).

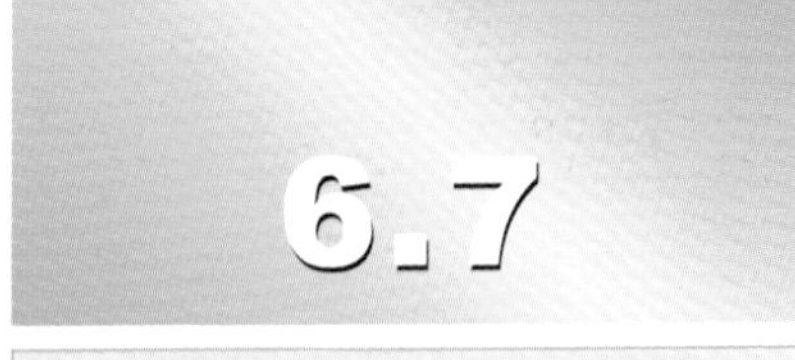

More about crystal structures

OBJECTIVES

- Fluorite structure
- Zinc-blende structure
- Crystal systems

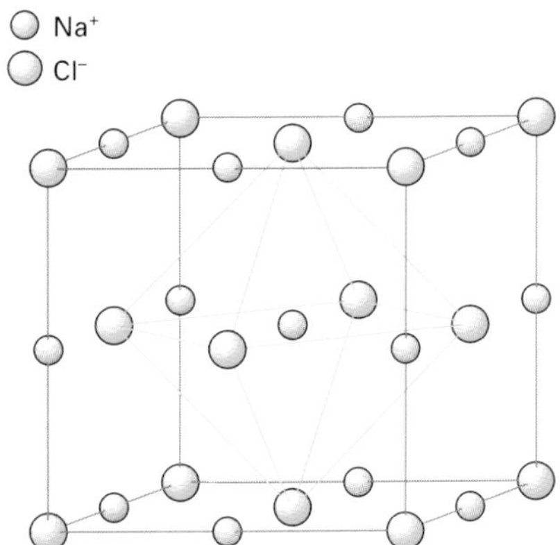

The rock-salt structure viewed as an f.c.c. array of chloride ions with all octahedral holes filled with sodium ions.

The caesium chloride and rock-salt structures described in the last spread are adopted by ionic compounds with a one-to-one ratio of ions. Compounds with a different ion ratio have different structures. Several examples related in simple ways to the rock-salt structure will be described in this spread.

The general structures met in any crystal will then be described. Every crystalline substance falls into one of the seven classes shown on the right-hand page.

The rock-salt structure revisited

The rock-salt structure described on the previous spread can be interpreted in another way. Imagine that the face-centred cubic (f.c.c.) array of chloride ions is expanded so that the chloride ions do not touch each other. The ions retain the geometrical arrangement of close packing, leaving holes in the structure. It can be seen that one type of hole has six spheres around it: this is called an **octahedral hole**. The rock-salt structure can therefore equally well be described as one in which *the chloride ions are in an f.c.c. array with all the octahedral holes filled with sodium ions*.

The fluorite structure

In addition to octahedral holes, there is one other type of hole: a **tetrahedral hole** has four spheres around it. There are twice as many tetrahedral holes as octahedral holes.

The most important structure adopted by compounds with a 2:1 ratio of ions is the **fluorite structure** (the mineral fluorite is calcium fluoride CaF_2, spread 6.2). In the fluorite structure, the positive (calcium) ions are in an f.c.c. array, with the negative (fluoride) ions in all the tetrahedral holes. The fluorite structure is adopted by, for example, the fluorides of calcium, strontium, and barium, and the oxide of uranium, UO_2. In the **anti-fluorite structure**, the *negative* ions are in the f.c.c. array, with the positive ions in all the tetrahedral holes. The antifluorite structure is adopted by, for example, the oxides of lithium, sodium, potassium, and rubidium.

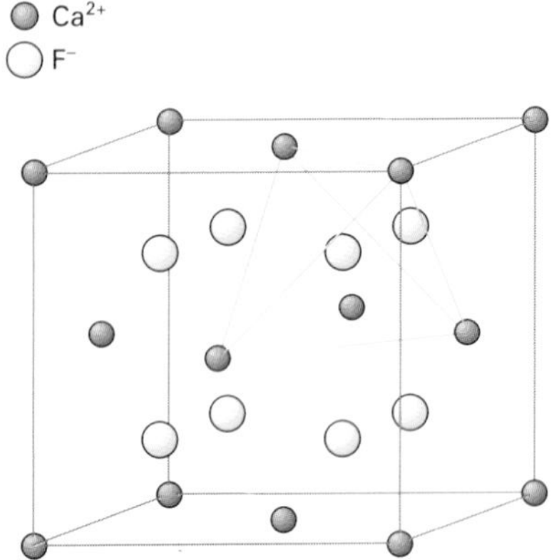

The fluorite structure.

The zinc-blende structure

Finally, another important structure can be created by filling only *half* of the tetrahedral holes. This gets us back to a 1:1 ion ratio. The mineral **zinc blende**, ZnS, gives its name to this structure. Note the close similarity with the diamond structure discussed in spread 6.3.

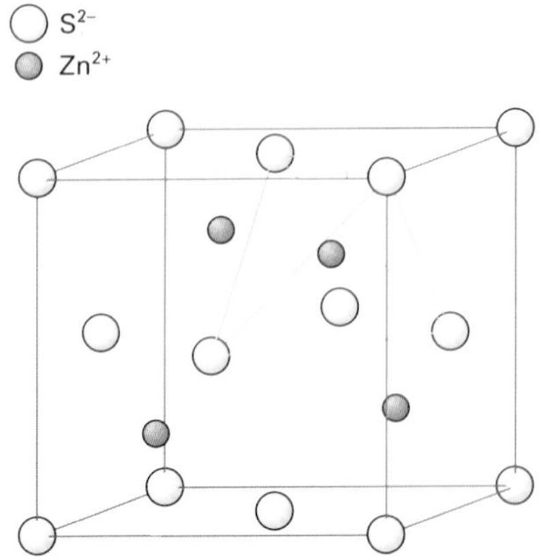

The zinc-blende structure.

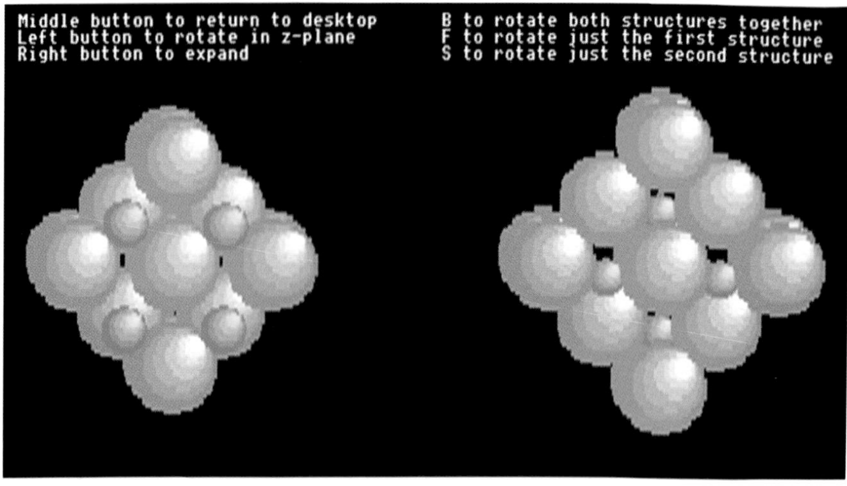

Computer programs such as ChemSoft are available which allow the user to display structures (sodium chloride (left) and zinc blende (right), for example), which can be expanded and rotated in three dimensions in real time. This is a great aid to understanding the structures better. See Appendix B.1 on the use of computers in chemistry.

The crystal systems

All substances crystallize in one of the following seven **crystal systems**. In the following three systems, the axes are at right angles:

- **cubic**, with three sides equal
- **tetragonal**, with two sides equal
- **orthorhombic**, with all sides unequal.

Tin is cubic at low temperatures ('grey tin'), transforming to a tetragonal structure ('white tin') at 13 °C; sulphur at room temperature is orthorhombic ('rhombic sulphur').

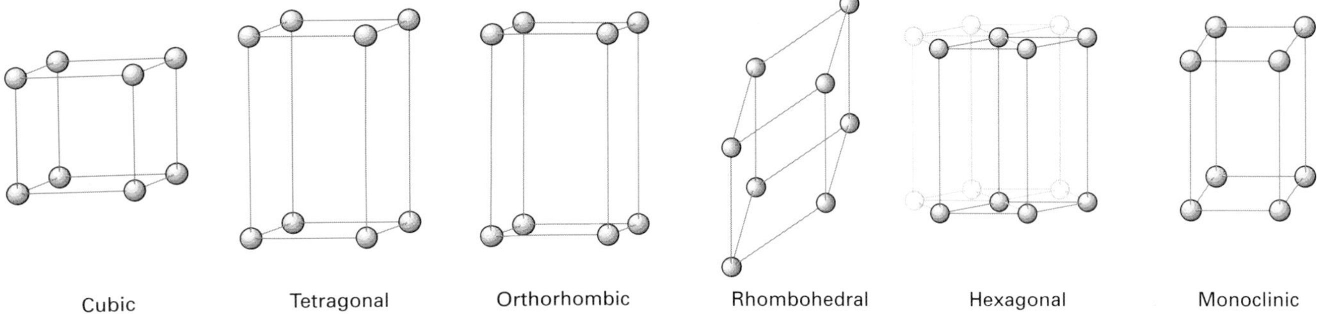

The cubic, tetragonal, and orthorhombic crystal systems have all axes at right angles.

The rhombohedral, hexagonal, and monoclinic crystal systems have at least one angle that is not a right angle.

The next set of three structures can be considered as distortions of each of the three structures above by *rotating* it.

- **Rhombohedral** is formed by rotating a cubic structure so that, although the angles remain the same, they are not right angles.
- **Hexagonal** is formed by rotating a tetragonal structure so that one angle becomes 120°.
- **Monoclinic** is formed by rotating an orthorhombic structure so that one angle is no longer a right angle.

Calcite, a form of calcium carbonate ($CaCO_3$), is rhombohedral, as is obvious from the photograph in spread 9.3; quartz, a form of silica (SiO_2), is hexagonal; just below 100 °C, rhombic sulphur changes into monoclinic sulphur.

The least symmetrical structure of all is **triclinic**, which has no equal angles and no sides equal. The most common example of a substance with this structure is hydrated copper(II) sulphate $CuSO_4{\cdot}5H_2O$.

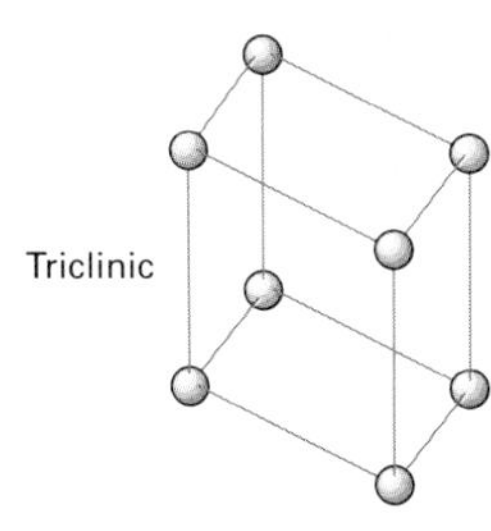

The triclinic crystal system is the least symmetrical.

Centred structures

Some of the above crystal systems can be found in a few variants. For example the cubic system has three variants: simple cubic, body-centred cubic, and face-centred cubic.

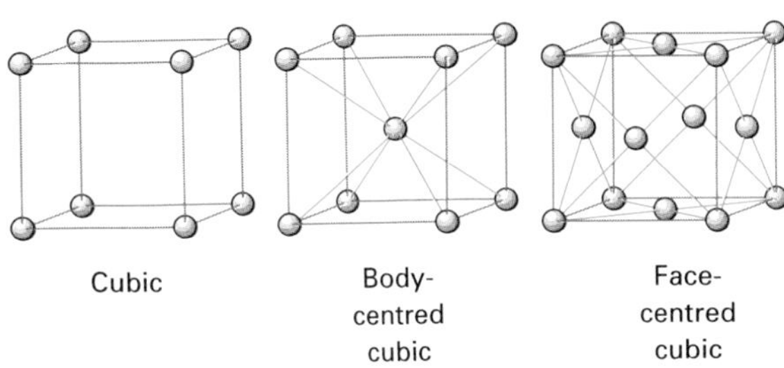

The cubic crystal system has three variants: simple cubic, body-centred cubic, and face-centred cubic.

Polonium is an example of an element which crystallizes as simple cubic, potassium as body-centred cubic, and platinum as face-centred cubic.

SUMMARY

- The most common structure for compounds with a 2:1 ion ratio is the fluorite (or antifluorite) structure.
- All crystals fall into one of the seven crystal systems.

PRACTICE

1 Explain how the tetragonal and orthorhombic systems differ from the cubic.

2 Give an example of an element which can form both orthorhombic and monoclinic crystals.

PRACTICE EXAM QUESTIONS

1 **a** The table below gives some data for an element in the Periodic Table. Copy and complete the table for the other elements shown. [6]

Element	Electronic configuration	Block
Sodium	$1s^2\ 2s^2 2p^6\ 3s^1$	s
Copper		
Gallium		
Phosphorus		

b Using the axes in the figure below, sketch the graph obtained when all the electrons are successively removed from an aluminium atom. [3]

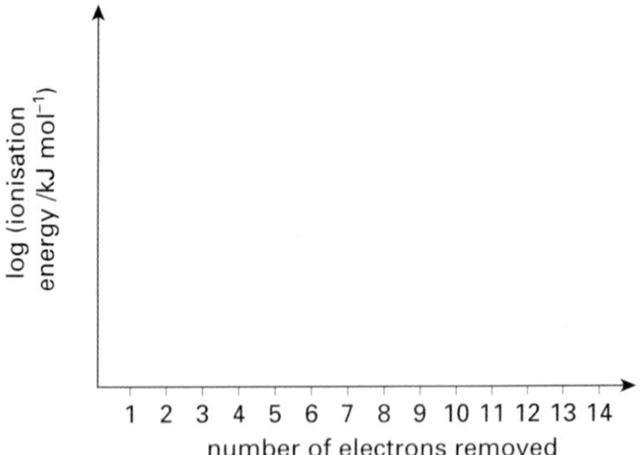

c The figure below shows the crystal structures of sodium and magnesium.

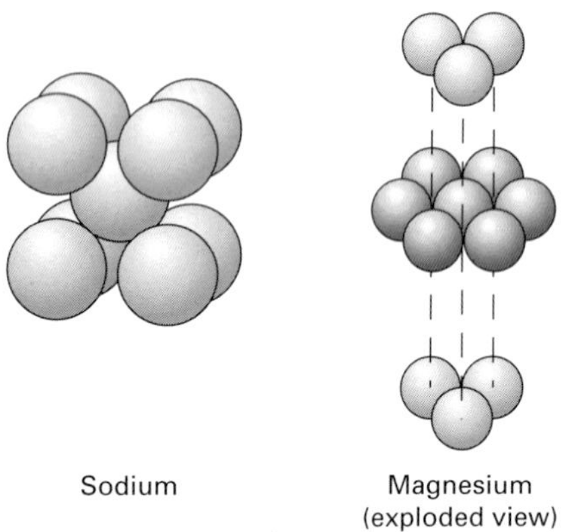

Give the name of the structure and state the coordination number of the atoms in each structure.
AQA (AEB) 1996 [4]

2 **a** The diagram below represents part of a sodium chloride crystal with the position of one sodium ion shown by a plus (+) sign in a circle.

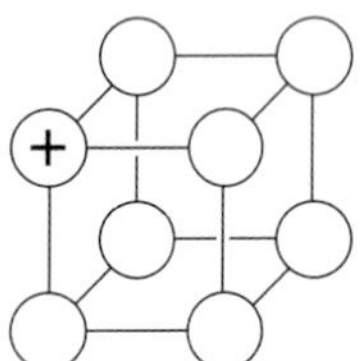

i Copy the diagram and mark with minus (–) signs all the circles in the above diagram which show the positions of chloride ions.

ii How many nearest sodium ions surround each chloride ion in a sodium chloride crystal? [2]

b Describe a simple test to show that sodium chloride is ionic. [2]

c A crystal of aluminium chloride vaporizes when heated to a relatively low temperature. In the gas phase, aluminium chloride exists as a mixture of $AlCl_3$ and Al_2Cl_6 molecules. The Al_2Cl_6 molecule is formed when $AlCl_3$ molecules are linked by two coordinate (dative covalent) bonds. The structure of Al_2Cl_6 is shown below with one of the coordinate bonds labelled.

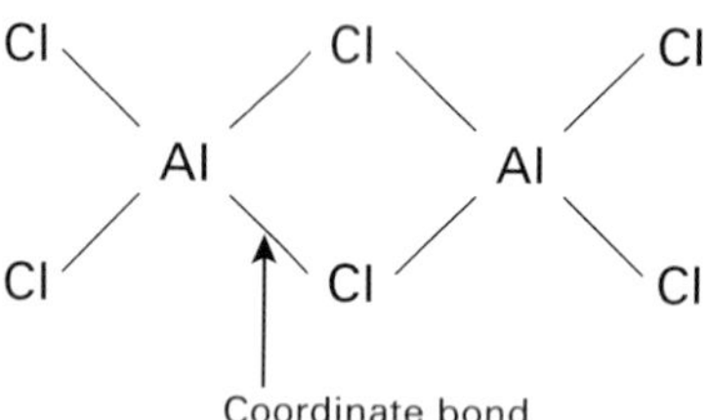

i Explain the meaning of the term *coordinate bond*.

ii Using an arrow, indicate on a copy of the diagram the other coordinate bond.

iii Explain briefly why solid aluminium chloride vaporizes at a relatively low temperature. [5]
AQA (NEAB) 1996

3 **a** Sodium chloride is a crystalline solid, melting point 801 °C. It is soluble in water.

i State the type of bonding present in sodium chloride. [1]

ii Describe, in terms of the motion and arrangement of the particles, what happens when solid sodium chloride is steadily heated from room temperature until it melts. [2]

iii Account for the relatively high melting point of sodium chloride and explain why it dissolves in water at room temperature. [3]

b In carbon dioxide the carbon atom is joined to each oxygen atom by a double covalent bond, O=C=O. Each of the double bonds is made up of one σ bond and one π bond.

Explain, either in words or in clear diagrams, what is meant by a

i σ bond;

ii π bond. [2]
EDEXCEL 1999

4 **a** Describe the bonding present in solid aluminium. Explain why aluminium is a conductor of electricity. [4]

b Aluminium combines readily with both dry fluorine and dry chlorine. Anhydrous aluminium chloride is a white solid which sublimes at about 200 °C; it reacts with water and dissolves in non-polar solvents. Aluminium fluoride is a crystalline solid up to a temperature in excess of 1290 °C; it is insoluble in non-polar solvents.

i Suggest, using the information above, the name of the bond type present in:

anhydrous aluminium chloride;

anhydrous aluminium fluoride. [2]

ii Give an explanation for the difference in bond type present in the two anhydrous aluminium halides. [3]

iii Explain why the bonding in anhydrous aluminium fluoride leads to a high melting temperature. [1]
EDEXCEL 1999

5 This question deals with bonding in molecules.

a Define the following terms, giving an example in each case:

i dative covalent bond.

ii Ionic bond. [4]

b Both aluminium chloride and molecular iodine sublime.

i Define the term sublimation.

ii Explain why aluminium chloride dissolves readily in water, whereas molecular iodine does not.

c Explain how metallic bonding accounts for the following characteristic properties of metals:

i high electrical conductivity,

ii high thermal conductivity. [2]
EDEXCEL (ULEAC) 1995

6 a Describe, with the aid of diagrams, the bonding and structure of:

i iodine; [3]

ii diamond [3]

b State and explain the effect, if any, of heat on separate samples of solid iodine and diamond. [4]

c Sodium chloride and caesium chloride have different crystal structures. Describe, with the aid of diagrams, the structure (stating the lattice type and coordination numbers) and bonding found in each solid. Explain why these salts have different crystal structures. [10]

d Copper metal has a high electrical conductivity. Using a diagram, show the bonding in copper metal and explain its high electrical conductivity. [5]
AQA (AEB) 1995

7 Electric cable is made of copper wire surrounded by poly(chloroethene) which is also called polyvinyl chloride, PVC. Another type of electric cable used in fire alarm systems has the copper wire surrounded by solid magnesium oxide, which acts as an insulator, the whole encased in a flexible copper tube, itself covered with PVC.

a Describe, with the aid of diagrams where appropriate,

i the bonding in copper, and hence explain how the metal conducts electricity;

ii the two types of bonding present in PVC, and hence explain why PVC acts as an insulator;

iii the bonding in magnesium oxide, giving the formulae of the particles, and hence explain why magnesium oxide does not conduct. [6]

b i Suggest **two** reasons why magnesium oxide is preferred to PVC as an insulator in fire alarm cabling.

ii Suggest why copper is used to encase the magnesium oxide. [2]
AQA (AEB) 1995

8 a Sodium chloride and caesium chloride have different ionic lattices.

i State what is meant by the term ionic lattice and briefly explain how such structures are held together. [3]

ii Draw diagrams to show the ionic arrangements found in caesium chloride and sodium chloride lattices; state the coordination number in each case. [5]

iii Use the information in the table below to explain why sodium chloride and caesium chloride have different crystal structures. [2]

Ion	Na^+	Cs^+	Cl^-
Ionic radius / nm	0.095	0.169	0.181

iv Give the name of a technique that can be used to determine crystal structure. [1]

b The reaction between phosphorus and fluorine produces a covalent compound of formula PF_5.

i Complete the electronic configuration of phosphorus. [1]

ii Draw a diagram to show the shape of the PF_5 molecule, state the bond angles present in the molecule, and give the name of this shape. [3]

iii Explain, in terms of the electron pairs present, why the molecule has this shape. [2]
AQA (AEB) 1995

7 Changes of state and intermolecular forces

The common states of matter are solid, liquid, and gas. The previous chapter discussed the structures of solids. This chapter will consider how structure affects the temperatures at which solids melt and liquids boil. **Melting** is the change of state from solid to liquid. **Boiling** is the change of state from liquid to gas. These changes happen for different substances over a wide range of temperatures. For example, ice cubes melt rapidly when taken from the freezer. Butter melts if left in the sun. On the other hand, have you ever seen table salt melt? Boiling water is familiar, but boiling salt is not. The reasons for these different behaviours lie in the forces between the particles that make up the solid.

States of matter

7.1

OBJECTIVES

- States of matter: solid, liquid, and gas
- Changes of state: melting, freezing, evaporation, boiling, condensation
- Arrangement of particles

Matter consists of particles, which are either atoms, molecules, or ions. For example, a sample of a noble gas (e.g. argon) consists of separate atoms; whereas carbon dioxide gas, liquid water, and solid sugar (sucrose) consist of molecules; and salt (sodium chloride) consists of ions. The forces between the particles that make up a substance determine whether it is a solid, a liquid, or a gas at a given temperature.

Solids

Solids are difficult to compress because the particles that make up a solid are very close to each other. Solids have fixed shapes because attractive forces bind the particles together in a fixed pattern. The particles vibrate about their fixed positions, and the magnitude of the vibrations becomes greater as the temperature increases.

(a) A solid has a fixed shape. (b) A liquid adopts the shape of the lowest part of its container. (c) A gas fills the whole of its container.

The temperature of this mixture of ice and water remains at 0 °C while both ice and water are still present.

Take ice out of the freezer and measure its temperature while it warms up. The temperature of the solid gradually increases as it takes in energy from its surroundings. Once the ice begins to melt, its temperature remains constant until melting is complete. This constant temperature is called the **melting point** (T_m). The energy the solid substance takes in during melting is needed to overcome the forces holding the particles together. It does not raise the temperature of the substance. During melting, the structure of the solid breaks down and the particles become free to move relative to each other. Once melting is complete, the energy supplied causes the temperature to rise again.

Liquids

Liquids can flow because the particles in a liquid can move past one another. However, the forces of attraction between the particles are strong enough to hold a liquid together in one place. A liquid takes up the shape of the vessel that holds it. It may also be poured from one container into another. The volume of a liquid is constant at a particular temperature, and its density usually decreases with increasing temperature. The particles are almost as close together as in the solid state, which makes liquids very difficult to compress.

Some US farmers spray crops with water during unseasonable frosts. While both liquid water and solid ice are present, the temperature of the mixture cannot fall below 0 °C, the freezing point of water. The crops do not suffer frost damage because the temperature of the ice- and water-coated plants does not fall below 0 °C.

As a liquid is heated, the total energy of the sample increases. This energy mostly takes the form of kinetic energy as the particles move from place to place. Random collisions cause the energy of each particle to change continually. As a result, some particles at the surface gain sufficient energy to overcome the forces holding them within the liquid. Some of the particles at the liquid surface enter the space above the liquid and become a gas. This change of state is called **evaporation**. Evaporation occurs at the surface of a liquid at any temperature, below the boiling point.

Gases

Gases can be compressed easily because the particles in a gas are widely separated. Gases have very low densities compared with liquids and solids. They expand to fill the space available uniformly. The total energy of the particles is sufficiently high to overcome completely the forces of attraction that hold them together in the liquid state.

The change of state from gas to liquid is called **condensation**. It occurs at temperatures below the boiling point when gas particles collide with insufficient energy to rebound from each other. Particles coalesce and droplets of liquid form.

SUMMARY

- Solids and liquids are extremely difficult to compress; gases can be compressed easily.
- The particles in solids and liquids are close to each other; those in gases are relatively far apart.
- Solids have fixed shapes; in crystalline solids, the particles are fixed in regular patterns.
- Liquids are mobile; they stay at the bottom of their container.
- Gases are mobile and uniformly fill their container.

Freezing

The opposite of melting is **freezing**, when a liquid changes into a solid. The temperature of a liquid stays constant as it freezes.

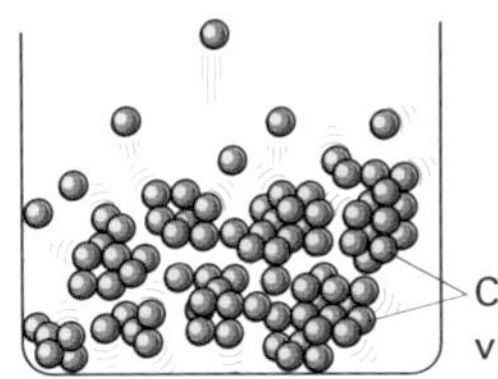

Evaporation occurs when particles in the liquid surface have energy greater than the forces of attraction between the particles.

Boiling

Boiling occurs when bubbles of vapour form *within the body of the liquid* (not just at the surface). A pure liquid boils at a fixed temperature called the **boiling point** (T_b). Energy supplied during boiling is needed to overcome the forces of attraction between the particles in the liquid state.

PRACTICE

1 Name each of the following state changes:
  - **a** Solid to liquid
  - **b** Liquid to solid
  - **c** Liquid to gas, at any temperature
  - **d** Liquid to gas, at a fixed, maximum temperature
  - **e** Gas to liquid.

7.2

Changes of state and the forces between particles

OBJECTIVES

- How structure affects melting and boiling points
- Atomic elements have very low melting and boiling points
- Metallic elements generally have high melting and boiling points
- Simple molecular substances have low melting and boiling points
- Giant covalent solids have very high melting and boiling points
- Ionic compounds have high melting and boiling points

Elements in the solid state have one of four main structures: atomic, metallic, simple molecular, or giant covalent. Compounds in the solid state have one of three main structures: simple molecular, giant covalent, or ionic. When solids melt, these structures break down. The temperature at which melting takes place depends on the forces between the particles that make up the solid.

Atomic elements

The noble gases helium to radon in Group VIII are the only elements that exist in the solid state as separate atoms arranged in an ordered lattice. The force of attraction between the atoms is very weak. As a consequence, the melting points of these elements are extremely low (e.g. solid argon, $T_m = -189\,°C$).

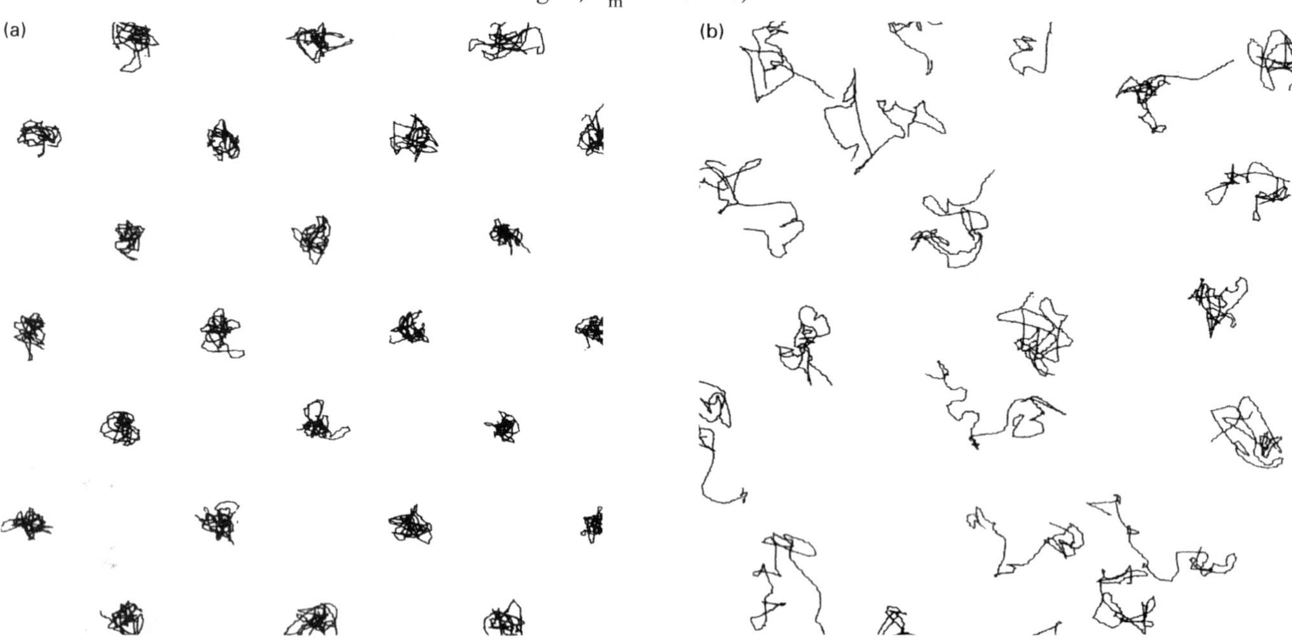

A computer simulation of the movement of the particles in argon (a) just below and (b) just above its melting point. Solid argon has the f.c.c. structure, spread 6.5.

The forces between atoms of the noble gases are also weak in the liquid state, with the result that their boiling points are less than 10 °C above the melting points (e.g. liquid argon, $T_b = -186\,°C$).

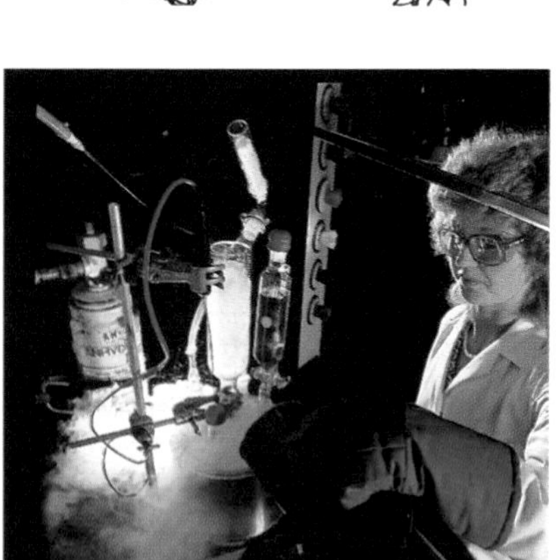

Liquid argon boils at −186 °C, less than 100 °C above absolute zero (−273 °C). It vaporizes rapidly at room temperature when outside its insulating flask.

Metallic elements

Metallic elements consist of a regular lattice of positively charged metal ions bonded together by a 'sea' of delocalized valence electrons. The bonding forces are strong and their effects are felt uniformly throughout the lattice. The melting points of the first three metals in Period 3 increase as follows: sodium, $T_m = 98\,°C$; magnesium, $T_m = 649\,°C$; and aluminium, $T_m = 660\,°C$. In general, Group I metals melt below 200 °C and Group II and the p-block metals usually melt below 1000 °C. These differences are due mainly to:

- the number of electrons delocalized from each atom;
- the size of the ions and their charge.

The small, highly charged Al^{3+} ions are held together strongly by three delocalized electrons per ion. The larger Na^{+} ions are only held together by one electron per ion, so sodium melts at a lower temperature.

Metals often boil at very high temperatures (e.g. iron, $T_b = 2750\,°C$). A metal atom must regain control over its required number of valence electrons before it is able to move into the gas phase as an isolated and independent atom.

Simple molecular elements and compounds

Simple molecular solids consist of covalently bonded molecules held together by weak **intermolecular forces** (the forces *between* molecules). Simple molecular solids melt when sufficient energy is provided to overcome these weak forces. The covalent bonds between the atoms in the molecules remain intact. Simple molecular substances therefore have relatively low melting points (e.g. oxygen O_2, $T_m = -219\,°C$; methane CH_4, $T_m = -183\,°C$; iodine I_2, $T_m = 114\,°C$; sulphur S_8, $T_m = 113\,°C$).

Simple molecular liquids contain molecules whose structure is similar to that in the solid state. The same weak intermolecular forces operate but the molecules have sufficient energy to move past each other. Simple molecular liquids boil at relatively low temperatures (e.g. O_2, $T_b = -183\,°C$; CH_4, $T_b = -161\,°C$).

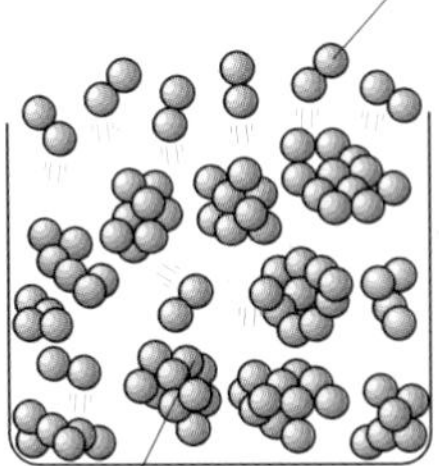
Many particles escaping from the surface
Large clumps of particles moving in opposite directions leave almost empty spaces (bubbles) containing only a few fast-moving particles

This diagram represents liquid oxygen O_2 boiling to form oxygen gas. Note that the covalent bonds between the oxygen atoms do not break.

Giant covalent elements and compounds

The structures of these substances consist of atoms covalently bonded to each other. The strong covalent bonds operate *throughout* the structure, making a sample of the substance effectively one enormous single molecule. Melting a giant covalent solid involves breaking these strong bonds. The liquid consists of separate free atoms. Melting points are therefore extremely high, e.g. diamond (elemental carbon) $T_m = 3550\,°C$. Boron nitride BN (a compound with the diamond structure) breaks down above 3000 °C to liberate atoms in the gas phase.

Ionic compounds

Ionic compounds consist of oppositely charged ions held together by strong electrostatic forces between the ions. These strong forces operate throughout the structure. The process of melting an ionic solid requires sufficient energy to break the strong bonds holding each ion to its neighbours. The melting points of ionic compounds are therefore generally high (e.g. sodium chloride NaCl, $T_m = 801\,°C$).

In the liquid state, ionic compounds consist of separate ions which are able to move past each other. Strong electrostatic forces operate between the ions, as in the solid state. The ions must achieve high energies before they can break free from each other and become a gas. Boiling points are therefore high (e.g. NaCl, $T_b = 1413\,°C$).

Sublimation

The change of state directly from solid to gas is called **sublimation**. The substance does not pass through the liquid state during sublimation. Carbon dioxide is a simple molecular substance that sublimes when heated, spread 7.7.

The sublimation of carbon dioxide CO_2. Solid carbon dioxide changes directly from solid to gas on warming up; 'dry ice' is used to produce smoke in this display at EuroDisney featuring the caterpillar from Alice in Wonderland.

SUMMARY

- Substances boil when their constituent particles have sufficient energy to break free from the forces holding the particles together.
- Melting and boiling points generally follow the sequence: atomic elements < simple molecular substances << metallic elements ≈ ionic compounds < giant covalent substances.

PRACTICE

1 The melting point of iron is 1536 °C and its boiling point is 2750 °C. Draw diagrams and write a description to explain the changes that take place at an atomic level when iron is heated from room temperature to 1600 °C.

2 Repeat the exercise outlined in question 1 for the following substances and temperature ranges:

a Argon ($T_m = -189\,°C$, $T_b = -186\,°C$) from −188 °C to −184 °C.

b Silicon (diamond structure: $T_m = 1410\,°C$, $T_b = 2355\,°C$) from room temperature to 1500 °C.

c Sodium chloride ($T_m = 801\,°C$, $T_b = 1413\,°C$) from 1200 °C to 1500 °C.

7.3 POLAR MOLECULES AND DIPOLE–DIPOLE FORCES

OBJECTIVES

- Bond polarity and polar molecules
- The effects of shape
- Dipole-dipole forces

	Dipole/D		Dipole/D
He	0	Ar	0
H_2	0	N_2	0
O_2	0	CH_4	0
CCl_4	0	CO_2	0
HF	1.91	HCl	1.08
HBr	0.80	HI	0.42
H_2O	1.85	NH_3	1.47
CH_3Cl	1.87	CH_3OH	1.71

The dipoles of some atoms and molecules in debyes (D). (One debye is 3.34×10^{-30} coulomb metre.)

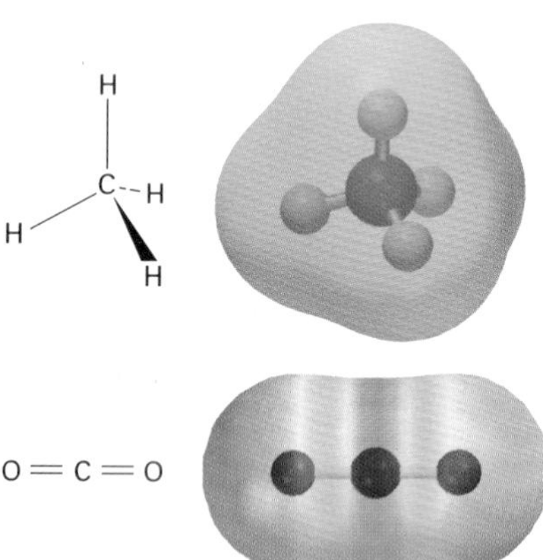

The individual bonds *in these molecules are polar. However, the molecules are symmetrical so the overall effects of the bonds cancel out and the* molecules *are non-polar. They have a dipole of zero.*

(a)

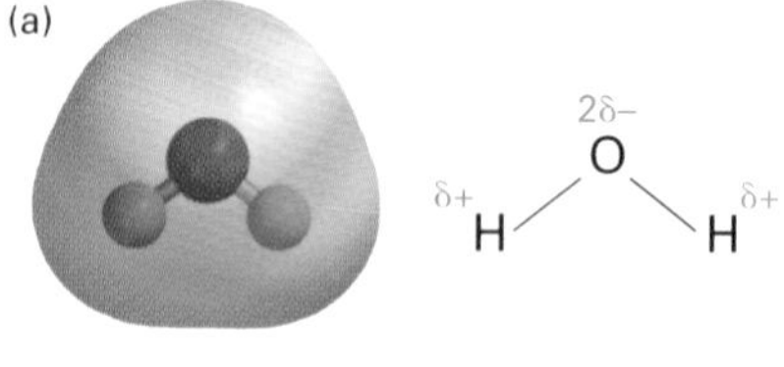

(b)

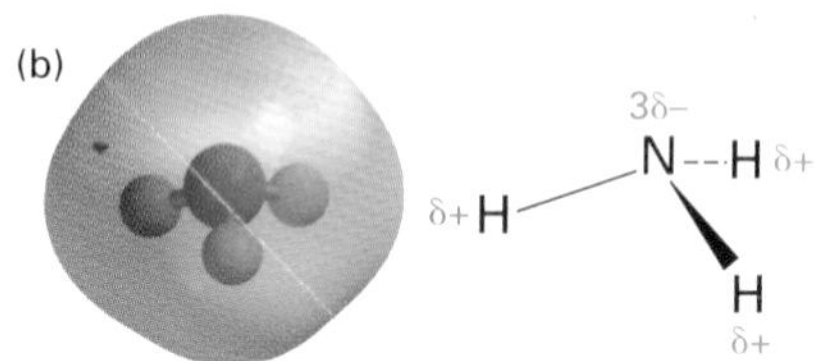

The individual bonds *in these molecules are polar. The molecules are non-symmetrical and so they are both polar* molecules.

Covalent bonds are the result of atoms sharing electron pairs. When an electron pair is shared in a bond between atoms of *different* elements, the sharing will be *unequal*. The bond will be polar and the atoms concerned will bear partial charges. For a diatomic molecule X—Y, the polarity of the bond $X^{\delta+}—Y^{\delta-}$ makes the molecule as a whole polar. Forces of attraction exist between polar molecules because of the electrostatic forces of attraction between the partial charges δ+ and δ– on separate molecules. This spread will continue the discussion started in the previous two chapters by investigating molecules containing polar bonds.

Dipoles

A polar molecule has a *dipole*. This term refers to the separation of charge in a molecule, causing it to behave as a pair of point charges of opposite sign separated from each other, spread 5.9. A non-symmetrical molecule that has polar bonds has a **permanent dipole**. The intermolecular forces between molecules that have permanent dipoles are called **dipole–dipole forces**.

Symmetrical polyatomic molecules

Most **polyatomic molecules** (molecules containing three or more atoms) contain polar bonds. However, the polarity of a molecule *as a whole* depends on its shape. A molecule is said to be **polar** if its overall charge distribution is equivalent to a pair of separated opposite charges.

Tetrachloromethane CCl_4 contains four polar $C^{\delta+}—Cl^{\delta-}$ bonds. However, the bonds are arranged tetrahedrally and the molecule is symmetrical. The four partial negative charges of the chlorine atoms are the same distance from the partial positive charge of the carbon atom. Tetrachloromethane is a non-polar molecule. There are no intermolecular dipole–dipole forces as the molecule has zero dipole.

Similarly a linear carbon dioxide molecule CO_2 has no dipole–dipole forces, despite the strong polarity of each C=O bond.

Non-symmetrical polyatomic molecules

Water H_2O and ammonia NH_3 are two familiar examples of non-symmetrical polyatomic molecules. The molecules are non-symmetrical because of the presence of lone pairs, two in the water molecule and one in ammonia.

Each oxygen–hydrogen bond in water is polarized $O^{\delta-}—H^{\delta+}$. The two lone pairs and the two bonding pairs take on the overall shape of a distorted tetrahedron. The two O—H bonds are thus arranged in a V-shape. As a result, the negative region of charge due to the oxygen atom is concentrated at one end of the molecule (at the point of the 'V'), spread 5.9. The positive region of charge due to the two hydrogen atoms is concentrated at the other end of the molecule. So the water molecule is a polar molecule.

In ammonia, each nitrogen–hydrogen bond is polarized $N^{\delta-}—H^{\delta+}$. The single lone pair and the three bonding pairs take on the overall shape of a distorted tetrahedron. The three N—H bonds are thus arranged in a pyramidal shape. The negative region of charge due to the nitrogen atom is concentrated at the apex of the pyramid and the positive region of charge due to the three hydrogen atoms is concentrated at the base, spread 5.9. So the ammonia molecule is a polar molecule.

Polar molecules and boiling points

Boiling involves the change from liquid (l) to gas (g). The molecules in the liquid state become widely separated in the gaseous state as intermolecular forces are overcome.

…ence of dipole–dipole forces can have a significant effect on the boiling point of a substance. For example, compare the boiling points of hydrogen chloride (–85 °C) and argon (–186 °C). The HCl molecule has exactly the same number of electrons as the Ar atom. But in the HCl molecule the electron density has been 'stretched out' along the direction of the bond, creating a molecule with a dipole. When HCl boils, the dipole–dipole forces *between* the HCl molecules must be overcome. There is no dipole in the Ar atom, so no such forces exist in argon. As a result of the dipole–dipole forces, HCl has the higher boiling point.

Dipole–dipole intermolecular forces between hydrogen chloride molecules.

Hydrogen halides revisited

Intermolecular forces are not simply restricted to dipole–dipole forces. The boiling points of the hydrogen halides reveal that there are *two other* factors at work.

First of all, the boiling point of hydrogen fluoride is anomalously high. To fit in with the overall trend in the group, the value should be in the region of –100 °C. Instead of having the lowest value, it actually has the highest value. The anomalously high boiling point of hydrogen fluoride is the result of a special variety of dipole–dipole force called *hydrogen bonding*. This effect will form the focus of the next-but-one spread.

The second consideration refers directly to the magnitude of the dipoles. The dipoles of the hydrogen halides decrease in the order HF > HCl > HBr > HI, as shown in the table opposite. The size of the dipole depends partly on the electronegativities of the halogens, which decrease in the sequence F (4.0) > Cl (3.2) > Br (3.0) > I (2.7). Putting the anomalous hydrogen fluoride to one side for the moment, the magnitudes of the dipoles indicate that dipole–dipole forces should decrease in the order HCl > HBr > HI, with the result that the boiling points should decrease in the same order. However, the boiling points *increase* in this order, i.e. HCl < HBr < HI. There must be another, more important, intermolecular force to consider: this is the *dispersion force*, which is discussed in the next spread.

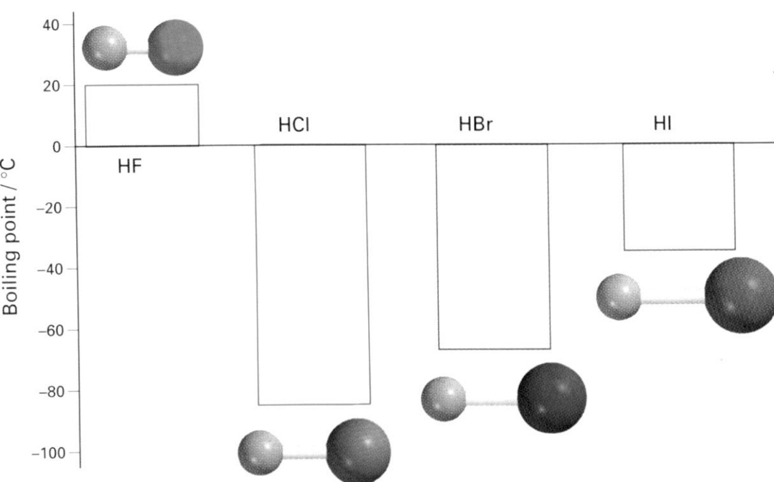

Hydrogen halide boiling points.

SUMMARY

- Polarity in molecules results from unequal sharing of electron pairs in covalent bonds.
- Unequal sharing of electron pairs results from differing electronegativity values.
- If dipole–dipole forces are the dominant intermolecular forces, boiling points increase with increasing polarity.

PRACTICE

1 Explain why tetrachloromethane CCl_4 is a non-polar molecule whereas trichloromethane $CHCl_3$ has a permanent dipole.

2 Explain why water H_2O is a more polar molecule than hydrogen sulphide H_2S (electronegativities: H, 2.2; O, 3.4; S, 2.6).

3 Explain the relationship between the terms 'polar bond' and 'polar molecule'.

7.4

DISPERSION FORC[...]

OBJECTIVES

- Origin of dispersion forces
- Polarizability
- Significance in noble gases and simple molecular substances

Strengths of forces

The strength of a force or bond is expressed as the energy per mole required to break the bond. Strengths have the following typical values:

Single covalent bonds
150–550 kJ mol^{-1}

Dipole–dipole forces
0–5 kJ mol^{-1}

Dispersion forces
1–15 kJ mol^{-1}

Two specific examples (values in kJmol^{-1}) are as follows:

	Dipole–dipole	Dispersion
HCl	0.2	2
NH_3	6	13

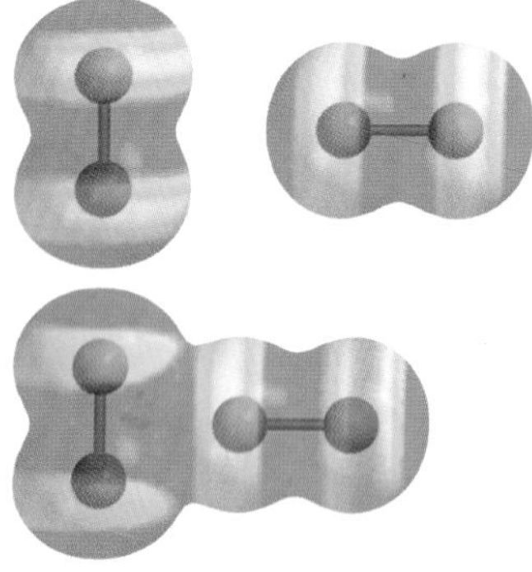

Electrostatic potential map of two chlorine molecules as they come closer to each other. The closer they approach the more polarized the molecule becomes.

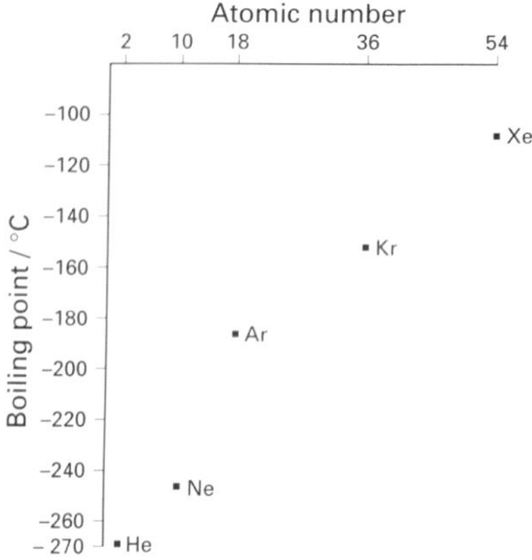

Plot of boiling point against atomic number for the noble gases. The forces between the atoms are dispersion forces, which increase as the number of electrons increases with increasing atomic number.

Dispersion forces are forces of attraction that operate between atoms and between molecules. They are weak, less than 5% of the strength of a covalent bond. Dispersion forces result from an instantaneous uneven distribution of electron density within atoms and molecules. The focus of this spread is to investigate the origin of dispersion forces, and to discuss their strengths relative to other bonding forces and their influence on the physical properties of various substances.

Origin of dispersion forces

On average, the electron density in a non-polar molecule (or an individual atom) is evenly distributed. At any one instant, however, the distribution may not be even and an **instantaneous dipole** will result. This *instantaneous* dipole will then cause the electrons in a neighbouring molecule to arrange themselves so that the force is attractive. An instantaneous dipole of this sort is also called an **induced dipole**. Dipoles flicker in and out of existence, inducing dipoles in other molecules in their vicinity. All these dipoles adjust to maintain an attractive force between the molecules by attracting or repelling electron density in the adjacent molecules.

The force between the instantaneous dipole of one molecule and that of another is a type of intermolecular force called the **dispersion force**. Dispersion forces exist between molecules with or without permanent dipoles, between ions, and between the single atoms of noble gases. Their influence is generally ignored in metals, in ionically bonded compounds, and in giant covalent solids, because other forces of attraction between the particles are much stronger. But dispersion forces are a significant feature to consider in molecules where permanent dipoles result in dipole–dipole forces.

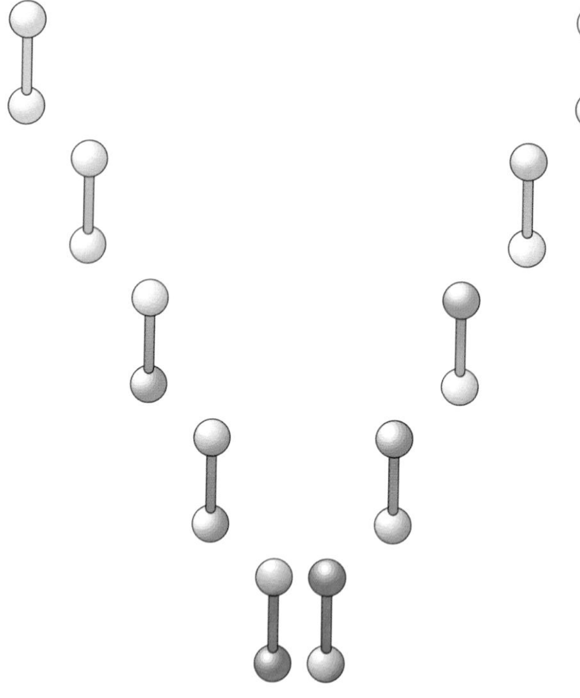

A schematic diagram explaining the origin of dispersion forces. When two non-polar molecules (such as two chlorine molecules) approach each other, instantaneous dipoles are produced that get into step. The opposite partial charges on the molecules then cause attraction. As the molecules approach closer, the instantaneous dipoles become larger in magnitude (shown by the greater intensity of colouring). The force is always an attraction but the direction of the dipole on an individual molecule is random; hence the diagram shows the direction switching twice.

Dispersion forces increase with (and are directly proportional to) increasing polarizability of the molecule concerned. **Polarizability** measures how easily the electron density is distorted when subjected to an external electric field. It depends on a number of factors; for example, polarizability generally increases with the surface area of the molecule and with the number of electrons present.

...n forces between atoms

The elements of Group VIII are called the noble gases. They have full shells and exist in all states (solid, liquid, or gas) as separate individual atoms. Dispersion forces are the only forces of attraction which operate between these atoms. As a result, melting and boiling points are extremely low, reflecting the weakness of these forces. However, the values of the melting and boiling points increase with increasing atomic number (see opposite). The atomic number indicates the number of electrons present and is hence a rough measure of the polarizability of the atom concerned.

Dispersion forces between molecules

The elements of Group VII (the halogens) exist as diatomic molecules, denoted generally as X_2. These molecules do not have permanent dipoles because each molecule consists of two atoms of the same element. There is a clear trend of increasing melting and boiling points with increasing atomic number (and hence increasing numbers of electrons). Melting and boiling points are higher overall than those of the noble gases. For example, compare chlorine Cl_2 with the noble gas krypton Kr. They have almost equal numbers of electrons (Cl_2, 34; Kr, 36), but the melting and boiling points for chlorine are a good deal higher than those for krypton. The reason for this difference is that the chlorine molecule consists of two atoms with a covalent bond between them. The electron density in chlorine is more spread out than that in the krypton atom and chlorine is therefore more polarizable.

Dispersion forces and molecular size

You should remember from your earlier studies that the alkanes have the general formula C_nH_{2n+2} and consist of chains of n carbon atoms with hydrogen atoms attached along the sides. The illustration alongside shows the structure of the alkane pentane C_5H_{12}. Data for the boiling points of the alkanes with one to eight carbon atoms are also given. Notice that, as the number of carbon atoms increases, so does the total number of electrons present in the molecule. The C—H bonds have low polarity because the electronegativities of carbon (2.5) and hydrogen (2.2) are very similar. As a result, dispersion forces are the only significant intermolecular forces in alkanes. The total number of electrons increases with increasing numbers of carbon and hydrogen atoms; boiling points therefore also increase.

SUMMARY

- Dispersion forces are significant when considering the melting and boiling points of the noble gases and of both polar and non-polar molecules.
- Dispersion forces are weak, less than 5% of the strength of a covalent bond.
- The magnitude of dispersion forces increases with the polarizability of the molecule, which generally increases with the number of electrons.

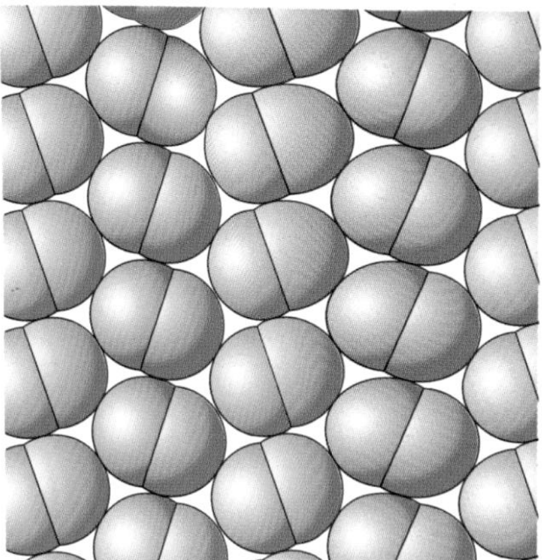

The structure of solid iodine. The molecules are held together by dispersion forces.

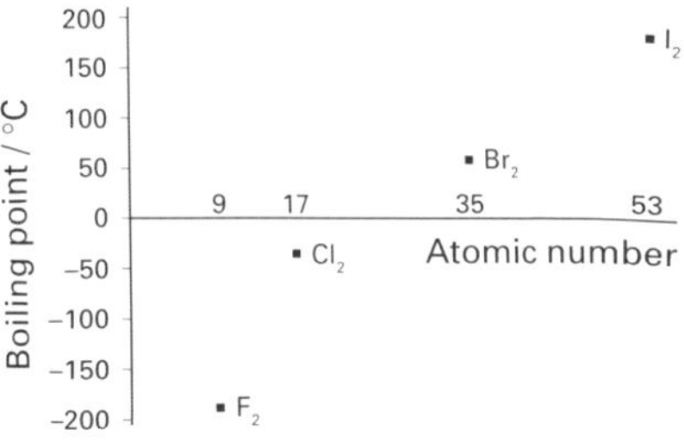

Plot of boiling point against atomic number for the halogens.

(a)

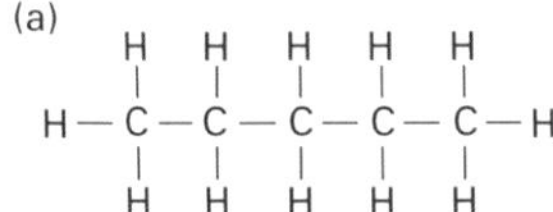

(b)

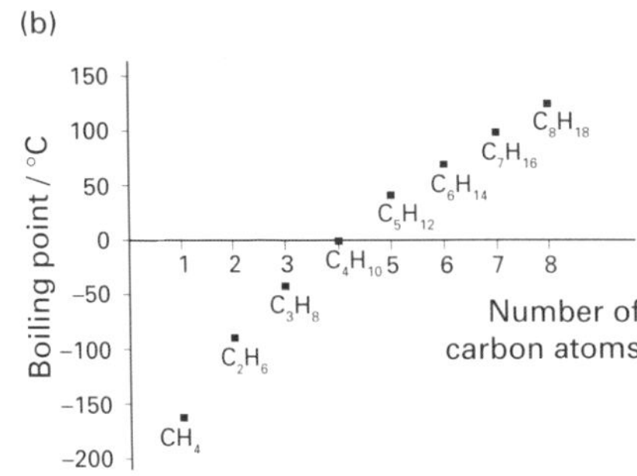

(a) The structure of pentane C_5H_{12}. (b) Boiling point data for the alkanes CH_4 to C_8H_{18}. These differences in boiling point allow mixtures of alkanes present in crude oil to be separated by fractional distillation, see spread 22.1.

PRACTICE

1 Describe the factors that influence the magnitude of dispersion forces.

2 Explain why dispersion forces are not taken into account when describing the bonding in a giant covalent solid such as diamond.

3 Explain why dispersion forces are a significant feature in maintaining the structure of graphite.

4 State the total number of electrons in each of bromine Br_2 and iodine monochloride ICl.
Which substance would you expect to have the higher boiling point? Explain your reasoning. [Electronegativities: chlorine Cl, 3.2; bromine Br, 3.0; iodine I, 2.7.]

7.5

HYDROGEN BOND

OBJECTIVES

- Relationship to other intermolecular forces
- Origin
- Effects on structure and boiling points
- Group trends in boiling point

Hydrogen bonding is the strongest of the intermolecular forces. It is a force of attraction that can have about 5% of the strength of a covalent bond. **Hydrogen bonds** form between molecules that contain a hydrogen atom bonded to one of the *small, highly electronegative* elements fluorine, oxygen, or nitrogen. Water H_2O is a good example of a molecule that has hydrogen bonds. When present, hydrogen bonding has a marked influence on melting and boiling points and on the structures of solids.

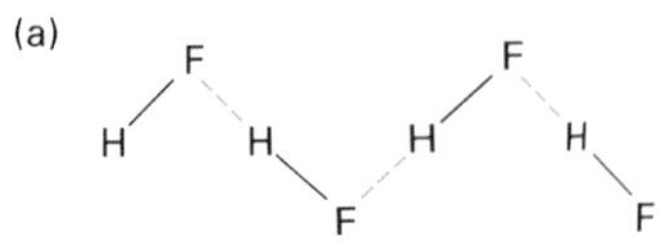

Hydrogen bonding in hydrogen fluoride $H^{\delta+}$—$F^{\delta-}$ causes the molecules to associate together in chains. Electronegativity values are: H, 2.2; F, 4.0. The hydrogen bonds are shown by orange dashed lines.

A special case: δ+ hydrogen

Any atom will have a partial positive charge (δ+) when it is bonded to another atom of greater electronegativity. Electron density is withdrawn from the atom with the lower electronegativity.

A covalently bonded hydrogen atom has a share of one bonding pair of electrons and no other shells. As a result, the hydrogen atom is significantly smaller than other atoms. The δ+ charge of the bonded hydrogen atom is therefore spread over a smaller volume and so its polarizing power is unusually high. The highly polarizing δ+ hydrogen atom then attracts electron density (commonly a lone pair) from a small, highly electronegative atom in another molecule. The δ+ hydrogen becomes 'sandwiched' between two small, highly electronegative atoms; it is covalently bonded to one atom and hydrogen-bonded to the other.

A computer-enhanced image of a snow crystal.

Water and the structure of ice

In liquid water, hydrogen bonds form as δ+ hydrogen atoms attract the lone pairs on oxygen atoms of nearby molecules. Water molecules group together in clumps, which are constantly losing and gaining molecules as a result of random collisions.

In ice, hydrogen bonding is maximized because the water molecules line up in an ordered way to form a regular lattice. In this ordered structure the water molecules are further apart than they are in the (more random) liquid state. As a result, at 0 °C ice is *less* dense than liquid water. This is unusual: in general, substances have *higher* densities in the solid state than in the liquid state.

Experiments show that the maximum density of water is at 4 °C. In cold weather ice forms on the top of a lake, while water at 4 °C sinks to the bottom and allows aquatic life to survive under the ice.

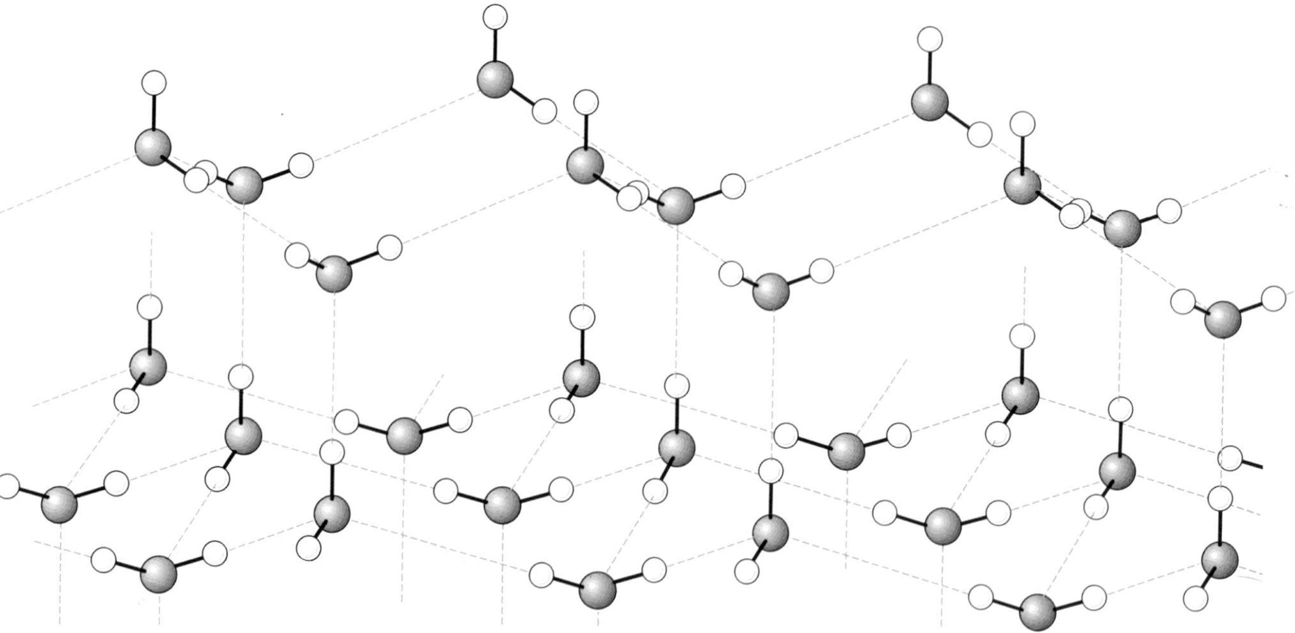

A three-dimensional network of hydrogen bonds holds water molecules in a regular and open lattice structure. Each oxygen atom forms two covalent bonds and two hydrogen bonds.

ogen bonding and boiling points

When a liquid boils, energy is required to overcome all the forces of attraction between the molecules in the liquid state. Look at the trends in boiling points for the hydrides of Groups V and VII. The values for ammonia NH_3 and hydrogen fluoride HF are anomalously high because there is hydrogen bonding between the molecules. On the other hand, there is a steady increase in the boiling points of the hydrides of Group IV consistent with a steady increase in the strength of the dispersion forces. Methane CH_4 does not have an anomalously high boiling point because there is no hydrogen bonding between molecules of methane.

Biochemistry

Hydrogen bonding also plays a crucial role in the structure and function of large organic molecules such as DNA, proteins, and enzymes, which contain covalently bonded H, O, and N atoms. The role of hydrogen bonding in biochemistry is discussed in chapter 30.

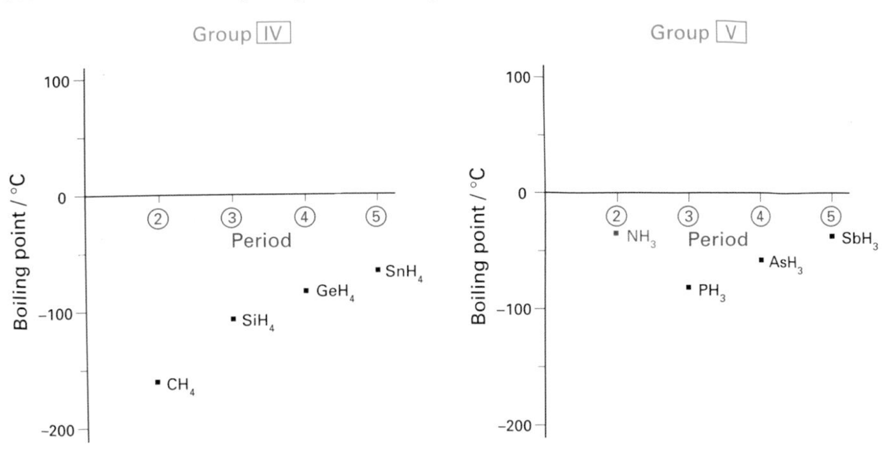

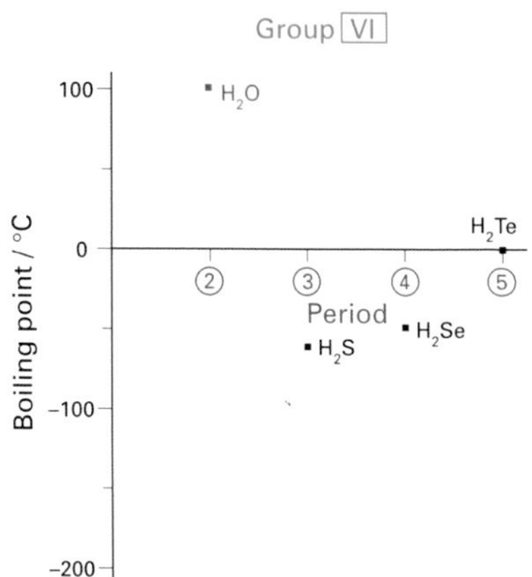

The boiling points for the hydrides of Groups IV, V, VI, and VII. Hydrogen bonding causes the hydrides NH_3, H_2O, and HF (highlighted in red) to have anomalously high boiling points.

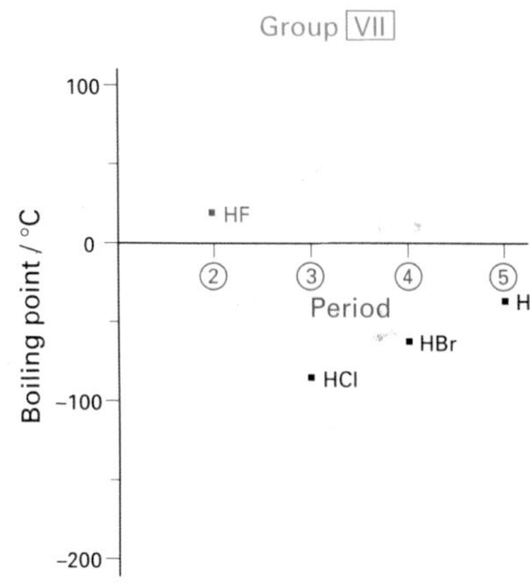

Water and the hydrides of Group VI

The most significant intermolecular force present in water is hydrogen bonding. The effect of the hydrogen bonds is for water H_2O to have a significantly higher boiling point than the other hydrides of Group VI (H_2S, H_2Se, and H_2Te). The steady upward trend in boiling points for the last three substances is due to increasing dispersion forces as the number of electrons present increases. Hydrogen bonds are not present in these compounds because the elements sulphur, selenium, and tellurium do not have sufficiently high electronegativity values.

SUMMARY

- Hydrogen bonds form between molecules that contain hydrogen bonded to fluorine, oxygen, or nitrogen atoms.
- Hydrogen bonds arise because a covalently bonded hydrogen atom has no electrons other than the bonding pair and is very small.
- Hydrogen bonding leads to unexpectedly high melting and boiling points, most importantly for water.
- Hydrogen bonding is especially important in biochemistry.

PRACTICE

1 Carbon, nitrogen, oxygen, and fluorine are the elements that stand at the heads of Groups IV, V, VI, and VII respectively. Explain why hydrogen bonds do not form between molecules of methane CH_4 whereas they do between the hydrides of the other named elements.

2 Water H_2O and ammonia NH_3 both show hydrogen bonding. Electronegativity values are: N, 3.0; O, 3.4; H, 2.2. Explain why the boiling point of ammonia is 133 °C *lower* than that of water: include reference to the structures of these molecules in your answer.

7.6

Further effects of intermolecular forces

OBJECTIVES

- Changes in intermolecular forces on mixing
- Criteria for miscibility
- Viscosity
- Surface tension

Mixing and entropy

The magnitude of the intermolecular forces is not the only criterion that determines the likelihood of mixing. Another important factor is entropy. **Entropy** is a measure of the *order* of a system: entropy increases when a system of particles becomes more disordered. Mixing two liquids together causes an increase in entropy. However, entropy must be considered *together with* the strengths of the intermolecular forces in order to make accurate predictions. The topic of entropy is discussed at length in chapter 14.

Hydrogen bonds are the predominant intermolecular force between water and ethanol molecules in a mixture of the two substances.

The intermolecular forces discussed so far in this chapter include those due to permanent dipoles (dipole–dipole forces), instantaneous dipoles (dispersion forces), and hydrogen bonds. These forces can help to explain the melting and boiling points of substances. This spread shows that knowledge of intermolecular forces can also help us to explain the miscibility of liquids, as well as viscosity and surface tension.

Mixing liquids

When two liquids mix, the molecules of one become surrounded by the molecules of the other. Changes in the intermolecular forces result from this process of mixing. For example, the separate liquids A and B have intermolecular forces between their molecules, which may be represented as A–A and B–B. Mixing the two liquids breaks down these two sets of intermolecular forces and establishes a new set A–B.

It is possible to predict whether liquids A and B will mix by comparing the intermolecular forces in the separate liquids (A–A and B–B) and in the mixture (A–B). The ability of liquids to mix, their **miscibility**, depends on the relative strengths of these three sets of intermolecular forces. If the intermolecular forces between molecules in the mixture are stronger than those between the molecules in the separate liquids, then mixing will occur.

Water and ethanol

Water H_2O and ethanol CH_3CH_2OH mix together in all proportions. A single, uniform, and homogeneous mixture results. The most significant intermolecular forces between water molecules are very strong hydrogen bonds. Ethanol possesses highly polar O—H bonds, which cause hydrogen bonds to form between its molecules. When the two liquids are mixed together, water forms hydrogen bonds with ethanol almost as readily as it does with itself.

Water and tetrachloromethane

Tetrachloromethane CCl_4 is a liquid organic solvent. It can dissolve a wide range of organic compounds such as greases and oils. Dispersion forces are the only intermolecular forces because the molecules have no dipole. Water and tetrachloromethane do not mix because the only forces of attraction between tetrachloromethane and water would be dispersion forces. These are very much weaker than the hydrogen bonds between the water molecules. The water molecules therefore remain firmly hydrogen-bonded to each other.

Miscibility

The hydrogen bonding between ethanol and water is strong enough to replace the hydrogen bonds in pure water and in pure ethanol. Water and ethanol are said to be totally **miscible** because they mix together to form a single liquid mixture.

Water and tetrachloromethane do not mix for the reasons just given. Water and tetrachloromethane are said to be **immiscible**: when shaken together, the two substances separate out into two distinct layers.

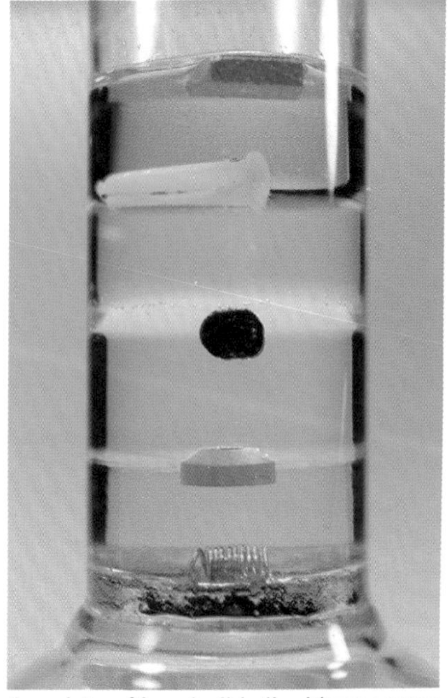

A variety of immiscible liquids; mercury is the densest and corn oil the least dense.

Viscosity

The viscosity of a fluid is a measure of its resistance to flowing when poured. For example, treacle and engine oil are more viscous than water, which in turn is more viscous than liquid nitrogen. Viscosity may be explained in terms of the intermolecular forces present in a liquid. Treacle is a highly concentrated solution of sucrose (sugar) in water. Each sucrose molecule $C_{12}H_{22}O_{11}$ has a total of eight polar O—H groups.

These groups form hydrogen bonds with water molecules, which themselves are hydrogen-bonded to each other and to other sucrose molecules. Hydrogen bonds must break and reform as treacle flows.

Molecules of engine oil consist of long alkane chains up to 30 carbon atoms long. The total number of electrons in each molecule is high, with the result that extensive dispersion forces hold oil molecules side by side in a tangled mass. These dispersion forces must break and reform as oil molecules move past each other in the flowing liquid.

Liquid nitrogen is far less viscous than water because the intermolecular forces in nitrogen are very weak dispersion forces. Note that liquid helium (T_b = –269 °C) has the lowest viscosity of all liquids.

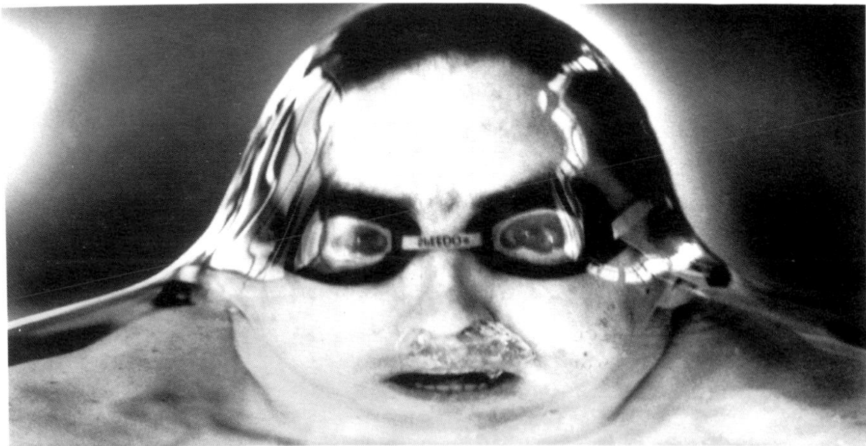

This remarkable prize-winning photo of the swimmer Matt Dunn taken by Tim Clayton was first published in the Sydney Morning Herald. *Dunn's head is surrounded by a thin film of water.*

Surface tension

Surface tension is a property of liquid surfaces that causes them to appear to be covered by a thin elastic 'skin' in a state of tension. Surface tension arises from the attractive forces between the molecules of the liquid. Surface tension causes falling drops of liquid and soap bubbles to have spherical shapes. Water has a high surface tension because there is strong hydrogen bonding between the molecules.

Producing bubbles of this size requires skill!

SUMMARY

- As an approximate rule, liquids mix when there are similar intermolecular forces between molecules in the mixture and between the molecules in the separate liquids.
- The magnitudes of viscosity and surface tension increase with increasing strength of intermolecular forces.

PRACTICE

1 Propane is a gas at room temperature; propan-2-ol and propanone are liquids.

```
     H   H   H
     |   |   |
 H — C — C — C — H        Propane
     |   |   |
     H   H   H

     H   OH  H
     |   |   |
 H — C — C — C — H        Propan–2–ol
     |   |   |
     H   H   H

         O
         ||
   H     C     H
    \   / \   /
     C       C            Propanone
   /  \     /  \
  H    H   H    H
```

a Referring to their structures, explain why propane is a gas and the other two substances are liquids.

b Which of the two liquids will have the higher boiling point? Explain your answer.

c Use diagrams to explain why propan-2-ol and propanone both dissolve in water.

2 Hexane is a liquid alkane with the formula C_6H_{14}. Explain with the aid of diagrams why it does not dissolve in water, but does dissolve in tetrachloromethane.

3 Explain why treacle is more viscous than engine oil.

7.7

OBJECTIVES

- Phase diagram for water
- Phase diagram for carbon dioxide
- Two-component phase diagrams
- Eutectic

PHASE DIAGRAMS

A '**phase**' is defined as a state of matter that is uniform throughout, not only in chemical composition but also in physical state. For a pure substance, the words 'phase' and 'state' have essentially the same meaning. Water's solid state could be described as the ice phase. When a *mixture* of two substances is considered, it is inappropriate to use the word 'state'. Two liquids that mix together, for example, form a single liquid phase, not a single liquid state.

The conditions of temperature and pressure under which different phases are stable can be shown on a phase diagram. A **phase diagram** describes which phase is most stable under particular conditions of temperature and pressure. We start first with the phase diagrams for two important pure substances and then consider the phase diagram for mixtures of two components.

Phase diagram for water

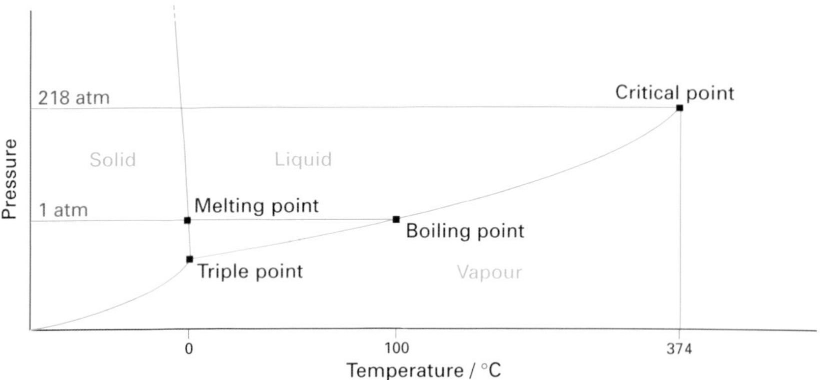

The phase diagram for water is shown above. At low temperatures under atmospheric pressure, the stable phase is the solid (ice). At 1 atm, the temperature at which ice and water are in equilibrium is called the **melting point** (0 °C, 273.15 K). This is shown by the line separating the solid and liquid phases. As this line is not vertical, the transition from solid to liquid takes place at different temperatures under different pressures. The line slopes backwards, which is unusual. The unusually open structure of ice is caused by hydrogen bonding, spread 7.5. Ice skating depends on this phenomenon. The pressure exerted by the skater on the narrow edge of the skates causes the melting point to lower and the ice melts locally (friction from the blade aids this process).

At temperatures between 0 °C and 100 °C under atmospheric pressure, the stable phase is liquid water. At 100 °C, the line representing the equilibrium between liquid and gas is reached and the temperature at which boiling takes place under atmospheric pressure is the **boiling point**. Again, the boiling point varies as the pressure varies. This phenomenon is well known to climbers because cooking takes much longer on the tops of mountains as water boils at a lower temperature. A 'three-minute' egg can require 30 minutes' cooking.

The unique point at which the three lines representing the solid/liquid, liquid/vapour, and solid/vapour equilibria meet is called the **triple point**, as it is the only condition of pressure and temperature at which all three phases are present. The triple point of water (at 611 Pa and 273.16 K) is chosen as the second fixed point on the Kelvin scale (the other being absolute zero).

At the other extreme of the liquid/vapour line is the **critical point**, above which it is not possible to liquefy a gas, however great the pressure. Indeed the term 'vapour' should only be used below the critical point, as it implies that it is possible to form a liquid. We will return to the idea of critical behaviour in the next chapter.

Phase diagram for carbon dioxide

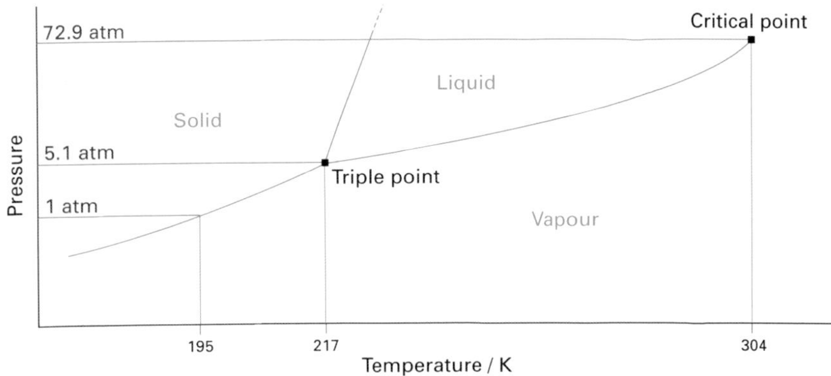

The phase diagram for carbon dioxide, shown above, is similar to that of water with two notable exceptions. First, the line joining solid and liquid slopes forwards, as is the common behaviour because the solid is more dense than the liquid. Second, the triple point lies *above* atmospheric pressure, and so carbon dioxide sublimes, spread 7.2. Ice too can sublime, but only if the pressure is below 611 Pa, the pressure of its triple point. When this happens on a cold winter's day, **hoarfrost** is formed. Frost, on the other hand, is just frozen dew.

Entropy again

The reason why the lowering of melting point takes place is that the entropy of the liquid is greater when there are two substances mixed together to form a solution.

Two-component phase diagrams

When two substances are present, such as two solids, the phase diagram usually consists of specifying the stable phase as temperature is changed at constant pressure. A typical example is shown to the right. Adding the other substance lowers the melting point of either component. So an alloy will typically melt at a lower temperature than the melting point of the lower-melting pure metal.

The lowest temperature that can be reached corresponds to the horizontal line. The point marked E corresponds to the composition that melts at the lowest temperature. This is called the **eutectic** (from the Greek for 'easily melted'). The eutectic can be distinguished from either pure A or pure B because adding a little of either component will increase its melting point. Microscopic examination shows that the solid with the eutectic composition consists of small individual crystals of the two components.

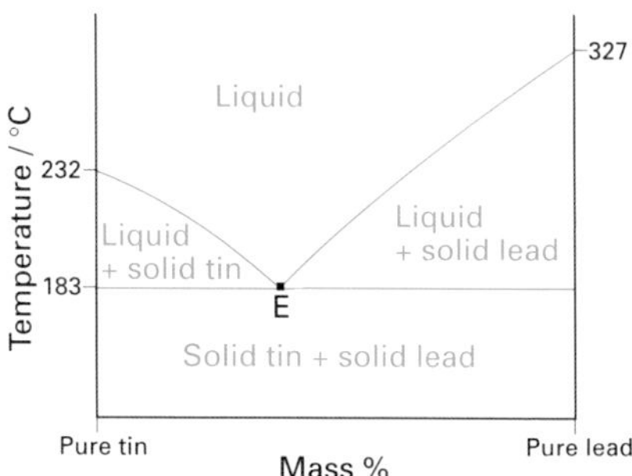

The phase diagram for mixtures of tin and lead; the point E marks the eutectic.

When a mixture of composition c_1 starts to cool, it remains solid until it reaches the line between the two phases (at c_2). At this temperature, pure lead will crystallize out. The composition of the remaining mixture gets more concentrated in tin and follows the line down to the point *e*, when all the rest of the mixture crystallizes out.

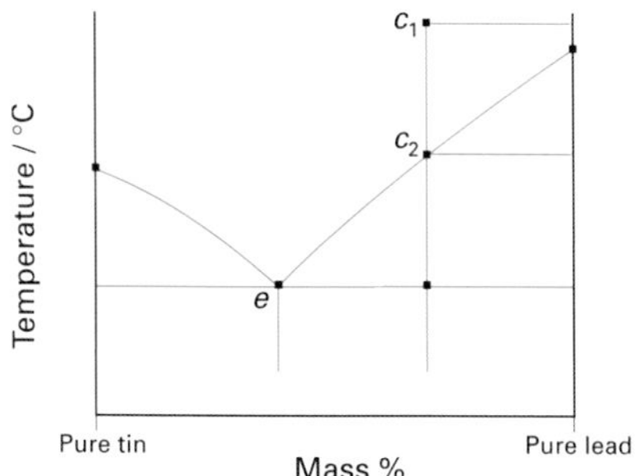

Cooling the mixture of composition c_1 first forms pure lead and then the eutectic.

Eutectics have a number of applications. For example, tin (T_m = 232 °C) and lead (T_m = 327 °C) form a eutectic (63% Sn, 37% Pb) that melts at the conveniently low temperature of 183 °C; this is used as electrical solder.

Common salt (sodium chloride) added to water lowers its melting point. The eutectic mixture melts at –21 °C. This is the reason that salt is spread on roads to prevent ice forming. However, reaching the eutectic composition could only occur by chance.

The phase diagram for potassium iodide and water is shown to the right. The line to the right of the eutectic represents the solubility curve for the salt in water.

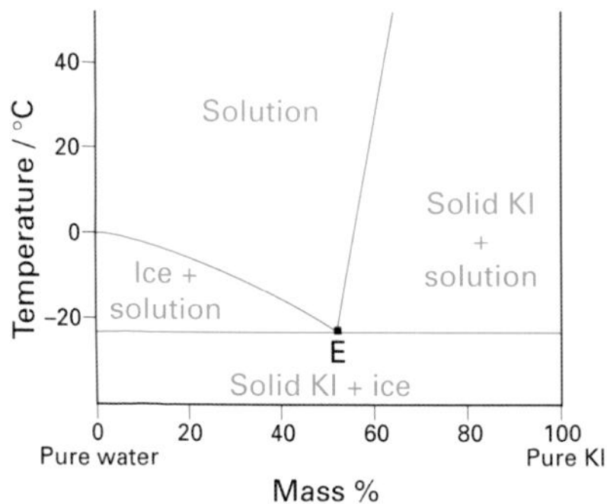

The phase diagram for potassium iodide and water.

SUMMARY

- A phase diagram describes which phase is most stable under particular conditions of temperature and pressure.
- The eutectic melts at the lowest temperature.

PRACTICE EXAM QUESTIONS

1 a i Copy the diagram below and by using the symbols δ+ and δ–, indicate the polarity of the covalent bonds shown. [3]

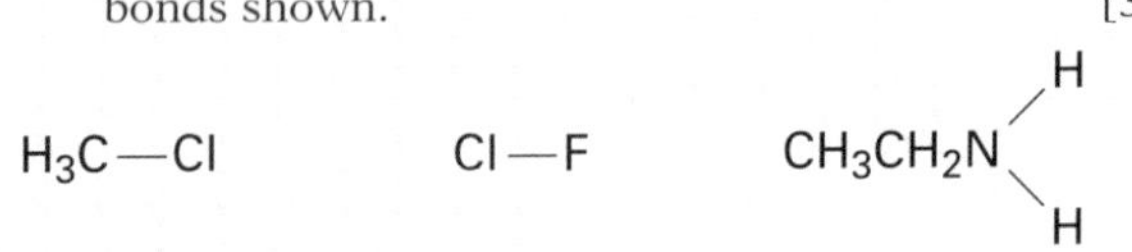

ii Explain the term *electronegativity*. [2]

b The diagram below shows the structure of ethanoic acid when dissolved in benzene.

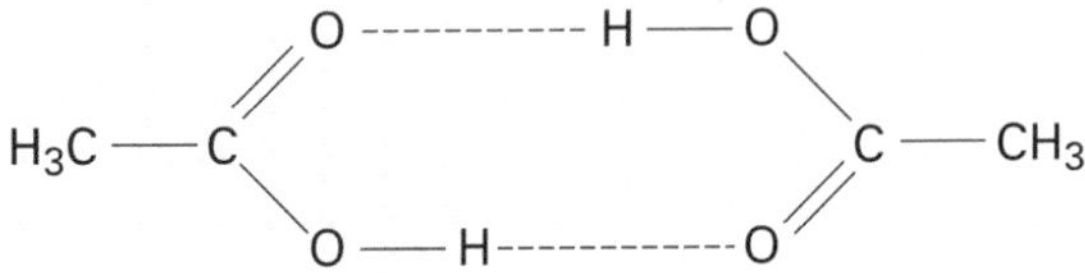

i Calculate the apparent relative molecular mass of ethanoic acid when dissolved in benzene. [2]

ii Give the name of the type of bonding shown by the dashed lines in the diagram above and explain how it arises. [4]

iii When ethanoic acid is dissolved in water the relative molecular mass is slightly less than half the value calculated in **b i**. Explain this observation by referring to the bonding shown in the diagram above. [3]
AQA (AEB) 1997

2 In order to counter the effects of accidental fires, many stores have fitted sprinkler devices. These are fitted with plugs, made of a mixture of two metals, which withstand the pressure of the water behind them. When the temperature rises above a particular value, water is released in a spray. The diagram below is a phase diagram for two such metals, A and B.

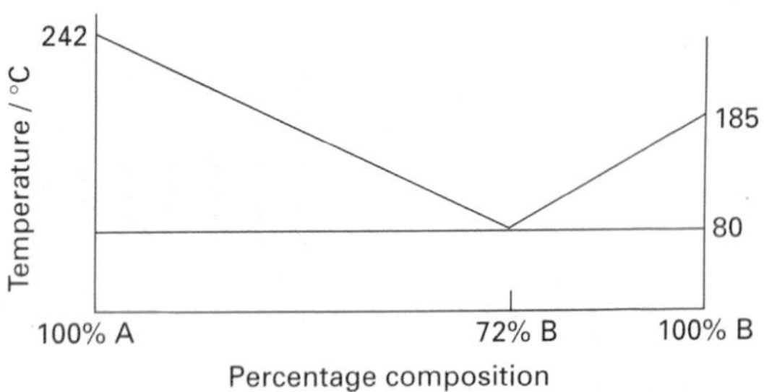

a i A fire starts in such a store and a plug with composition 60% B and 40% A is exposed to temperatures which rise from 20 °C to 300 °C over a short period of time. Explain, using a graph of temperature against time, what happens to the metallic mixture in the plug as the temperature rises. [4]

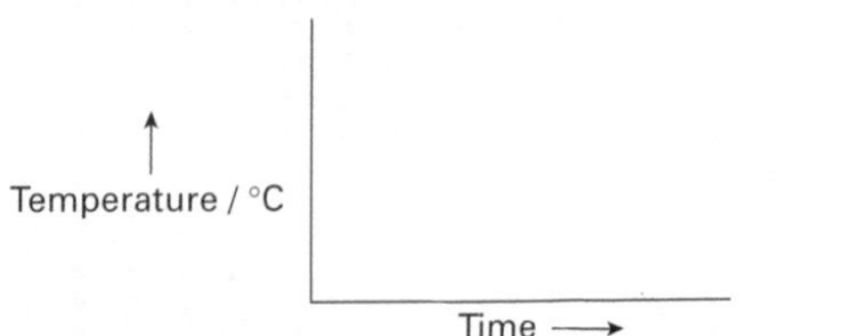

ii How would the graph differ if the plug had the composition of 72% B?

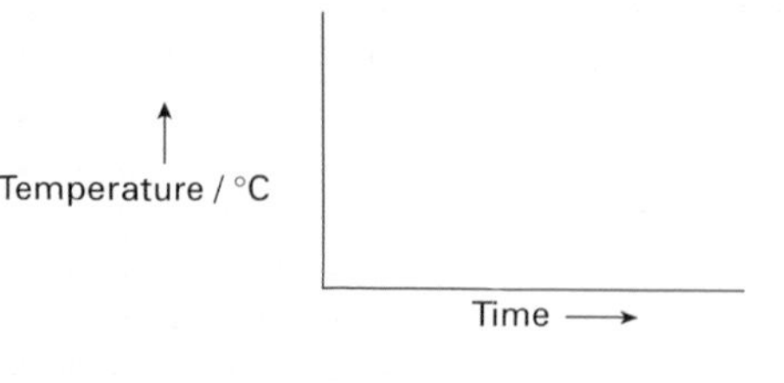

[3]

iii What is the name given to the mixture containing 72% B? [1]

b If the relative atomic masses of A and B are 127 and 181 respectively, calculate the mole fraction of A in this mixture. [2]
NICCEA 1998 *(See also Chapter 11.)*

3 a Define the term electronegativity. [2]

b The Diagram below shows the trend in the boiling points of the hydrides of the Group VI elements, oxygen to tellurium.

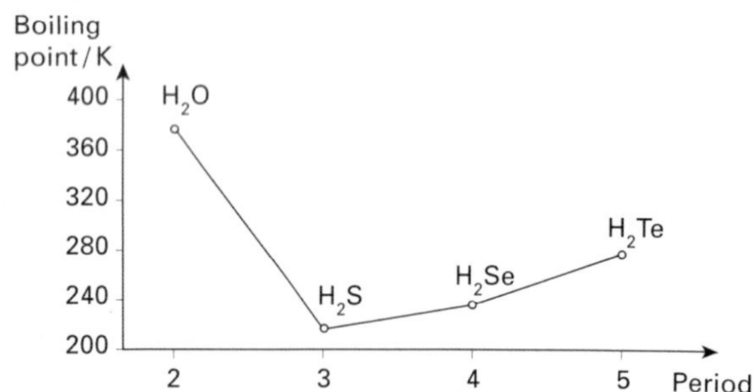

i Explain this rising trend in the boiling points of the compounds H_2S to H_2Te. [3]

ii Hydrogen bonding is said to account for the anomalously high boiling point of H_2O. With reference to the nature of the atoms involved, explain why intermolecular forces are so strong in H_2O. Draw a diagram, containing at least three molecules, to show hydrogen bonding in H_2O. [5]

c Protein molecules are composed of sequences of amino acid molecules joined together in long chains. The sequence of amino acids in a protein chain is illustrated below.

```
H        R    O     H    R    O     H    R    O
 \       |    ||    |    |    ||    |    |    ||
  N  —  C  —  C  —[ N  — C  — C ]— N  — C  — C — OH
 /       |                |      n        |
H        H                H               H
```

The protein chains are organized into complex three-dimensional structures. Briefly describe how the three-dimensional structure of a protein is held in place. [3]
AQA (AEB) 1998 *(See also Chapter 30.)*

4 Typical surface temperatures of the planets Mars, Jupiter, and Saturn are:
Mars, –60 °C; Jupiter, –140 °C; Saturn, –180 °C.

The surfaces of these planets contain methane, ammonia, and water. The phase diagrams of these three substances can be used to predict their physical states on these three planets. The values of the triple points are:

	Triple point / °C	Approx. pressure / kPa	$\log_{10}$ (pressure / kPa)
Methane	–170	10^1	1
Ammonia	–78	10^2	2
Water	0	1	0

a On the same sheet of graph paper and using the same axes, sketch the phase diagrams of methane, ammonia, and water. Plot the values of $\log_{10}$ (pressure) on the y-axis. Label the areas of the three phases on your phase diagram for water. [6]

b Use your sketch to predict whether each of these three substances exists as a solid, a liquid, or a gas on the surface of each of the three planets. [You may find it helpful to mark the planetary temperatures on your sketch.]

Mention any necessary assumptions for making your predictions. [4]
OCR (UCLES) 1994

5 **a** A sketch of the plot of the logarithms of the first seven successive molar ionization energies of silicon against the number of electrons removed is shown below.

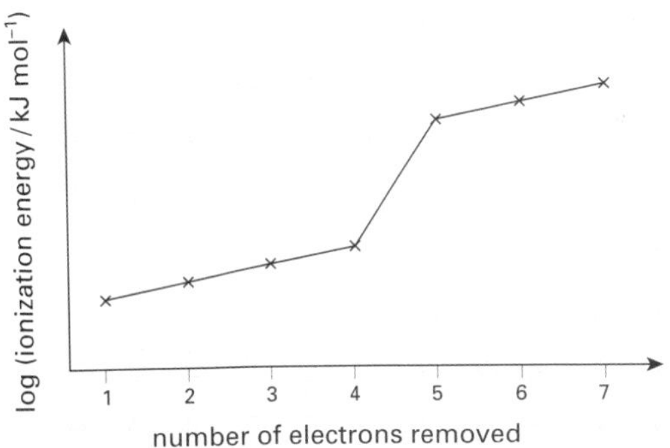

i Define the term *molar first ionization energy* of an element. [2]

ii Write an equation to represent the process whose energy change is equal to the molar second ionization energy of silicon. [2]

iii Explain the gradual increase in values as the second, third, and fourth electrons are removed. [2]

iv Explain why the molar fifth ionization energy is very much greater than the fourth. [2]

b The compounds silicon dioxide, SiO_2, and silicon tetrachloride, $SiCl_4$, both contain covalent bonding but their melting points are very different, being 1610 °C and –70 °C respectively.

i Give the name of the type of structure present in each of the compounds.

SiO_2 $SiCl_4$ [2]

ii Explain how the melting points of the two compounds are related to their structures. [4]
AQA (AEB) 1999

6 **a** Consider the information about halogens and hydrogen halides below, then answer the questions below.

	Fluorine	Chlorine	Bromine	Iodine
Electronegativity of halogen	4.0	3.0	2.8	2.5
Boiling point of hydrogen halide / K	293	188	206	238

i Define the term electronegativity. [2]

ii Briefly explain the steady increase in the boiling points of the hydrogen halides from HCl to HI. [2]

iii Explain why the boiling point of hydrogen fluoride is higher than that of any of the other hydrogen halides. [4]

b A carbonyl group (C=O) contains a double covalent bond between the carbon and oxygen atoms, which is made up of one σ bond and one π bond. Explain, in words or diagrams, what is meant by:

i a σ bond: [1]

ii a π bond. [1]

c **i** Draw a diagram to show the shape of the carbonate ion (CO_3^{2-}) and the bonding in it. [2]

ii State the similarity between the bonding in the carbonate ion and that present in the benzene molecule.
AQA (AEB) 1996 [1]

7 The table below shows some boiling temperatures (T_b) at a pressure of 100 kPa.

Substance	H_2	CH_4	HCl
T_b/K	21	112	188

a In liquid hydrogen, the atoms are held together by covalent bonds.

i What is a covalent bond?

ii How are the hydrogen molecules held together in liquid hydrogen? [2]

b Explain why methane has a higher boiling temperature than hydrogen. [2]

c **i** Give the meaning of the term *electronegativity*.

ii The electronegatives of hydrogen, carbon and chlorine are 2.1, 2.5, and 3.0, respectively. Use these values to explain why the boiling temperature of hydrogen chloride is greater than that of methane. [6]
AQA (NEAB) 1997

Gases

The properties of gases are very different from those of solids and liquids. Solids have fixed volumes and definite shapes. Liquids have a fixed volume but they flow and may be poured. As a result, liquids adopt the shape of the lower part of the container in which they are placed. In contrast, gases have neither definite shape nor fixed volume. They spread out to fill uniformly the whole of any space they enter. Solids and liquids expand when heated, but the extent of expansion depends on the substance present. When different gases are heated or compressed, they all behave in approximately the same manner, irrespective of the gas that is actually present. This chapter explores the distinctive properties of gases. The properties are explained in terms of the behaviour of the molecules that make up the gas.

GASES: THREE BASIC IDEAS

8.1

OBJECTIVES

- Boyle's law
- Charles's law
- Avogadro's principle

Gases may consist of separate atoms (e.g. argon Ar) or separate molecules (e.g. oxygen O_2, and carbon dioxide CO_2). At very high temperatures, gases may also consist of ions (e.g. $Na^+(g)$ and $Cl^-(g)$ from vaporized sodium chloride) or metal atoms (e.g. Na(g) from vaporized sodium). This chapter is mainly concerned with substances that are gases at room temperature and pressure. The vast majority of these gases are made up of simple molecules; so, for the sake of convenience, the term 'molecule' will be used to describe the particles in gases throughout this chapter. There are three important ideas describing the behaviour of gases: Boyle's law, Charles's law, and Avogadro's principle. They were discovered by these three scientists long ago in the history of modern science.

Applying Boyle's law

The **Heimlich manoeuvre** to relieve a person who is choking uses Boyle's law. Clasping the sufferer from behind and thrusting the fist forwards and upwards under the breastbone reduces the chest volume. The resulting pressure increase expels the blockage in the windpipe like a champagne cork.

Boyle's law

In 1662, Robert Boyle wrote down a law that summed up the experimental evidence he had gathered by measuring the volumes of air at different pressures. Expressed in modern language, **Boyle's law** is as follows:

- The volume of a fixed mass of gas (at constant temperature) is inversely proportional to its pressure.

In other words, if the pressure of a sample of gas is doubled, its volume is halved. Boyle's law may be expressed graphically, as shown below left, and can be written in symbols as $V \propto 1/p$.

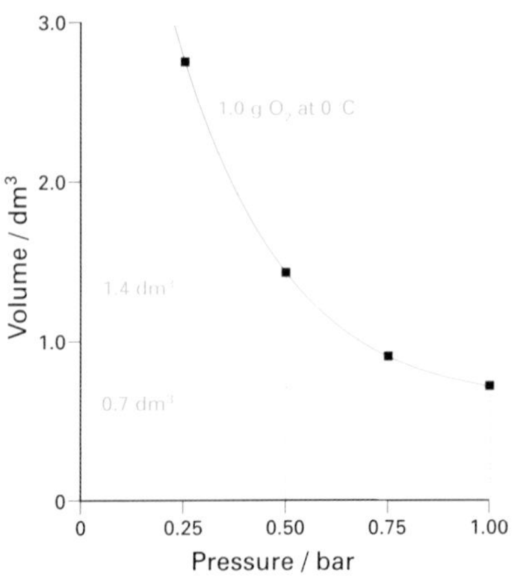

Boyle's law states that $V \propto 1/p$ or that pV = constant.

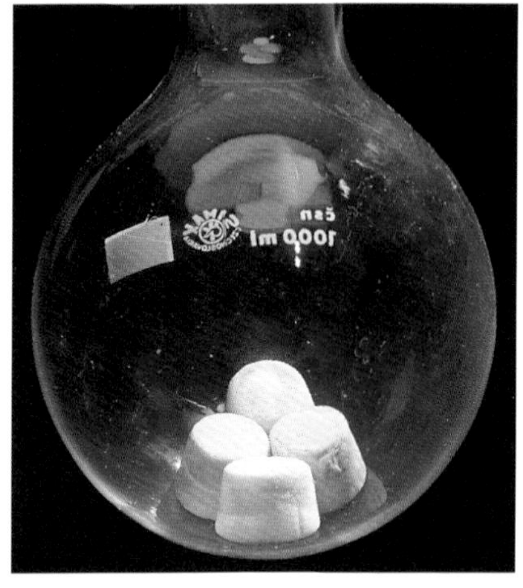

A vacuum pump reduces the pressure around marshmallows. Bubbles of air trapped inside them expand. The result is bigger marshmallows – until they are removed from the flask!

Charles's law

This law provides a quantitative version of the familiar 'rule of thumb' that heating a gas causes it to expand. **Charles's law** is as follows:

- The volume of a fixed mass of gas (at constant pressure) is directly proportional to the thermodynamic temperature.

Notice that the thermodynamic scale of temperature is used (see box to the right). Charles's law may be expressed graphically, as shown on the right, the plot of volume V against temperature T being a straight line, i.e. $V \propto T$. Extrapolating the graph to the point of zero volume suggests the idea of **absolute zero**, the lowest possible attainable temperature.

The air inside a balloon shrinks to a small volume when placed in liquid nitrogen at −196 °C. The air expands again when warmed to room temperature.

Jacques Charles

Jacques Charles stated his law in 1787, four years after he smashed the world altitude record. By using a hydrogen-filled balloon instead of a hot-air balloon, he reached 25 times the previous record height.

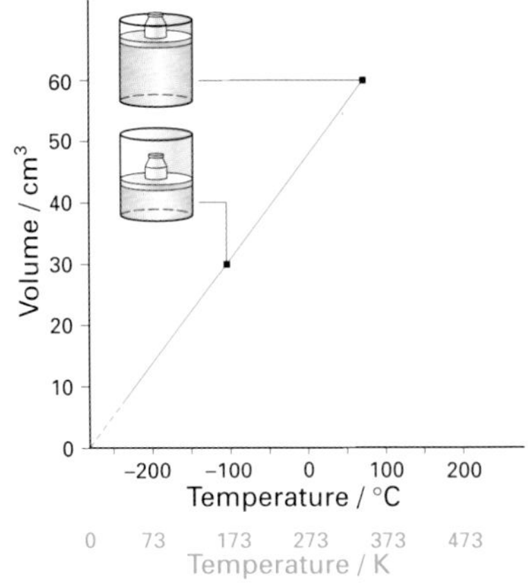

The relationship between volume and temperature is linear (the graph is a straight line), i.e. $V \propto T$.

Avogadro's principle

Amedeo Avogadro proposed a theoretical idea about gases in 1811. **Avogadro's principle** is as follows:

- Equal volumes of different gases at the same temperature and pressure contain the same number of molecules.

In other words, if there are x molecules of O_2 in 10 cm^3 of oxygen gas, then there are x molecules of N_2 in 10 cm^3 of nitrogen gas and there are x molecules of CO_2 in 10 cm^3 of carbon dioxide gas at the same temperature and pressure. Another way of putting this is that the volume of a gas depends on the amount in moles, $V \propto n$.

Working almost 200 years ago, Avogadro had no direct experimental evidence to support this statement. He simply talked about gases in terms of 'molecules'. Later experimental evidence showed the significance of Avogadro's principle, especially in recognizing that atoms can combine to form molecules.

Thermodynamic temperature

The work of Charles led to the idea of an absolute zero of temperature, now known to be −273 °C. This temperature is designated as the zero point (0 K) on the Kelvin temperature scale. The value of a temperature measured on the Kelvin scale (e.g. hydrogen boiling point = 20 K) is sometimes referred to as an 'absolute temperature' or, more correctly, as a 'thermodynamic temperature'; the latter will be used throughout this text. All temperatures measured on the Kelvin scale are thermodynamic temperatures.

An Italian stamp depicting Avogadro's principle.

SUMMARY

- Unlike solids and liquids, gases have neither definite shape nor fixed volume.
- Boyle's law: at constant temperature, $V \propto 1/p$ or pV = constant.
- Charles's law: at constant pressure, $V \propto T$ (T in kelvin).
- Avogadro's principle: equal volumes of different gases at the same temperature and pressure contain the same number of molecules.

PRACTICE

1 Jane puts her finger over the hole at the end of a bike pump. She pushes the plunger half way in. What is the pressure inside the pump?

2 A balloon contains 500 cm^3 of air at 300 K (27 °C). What is the volume of the balloon when it is placed in a freezer at 255 K (–18 °C)?

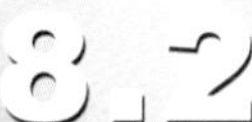

Ideal gases

OBJECTIVES

- The ideal gas equation
- The kinetic theory of gases

The greatest difference between gases and solids or liquids is that the molecules of a gas are very much further apart. Much of the chapter on solids was spent discussing the attractive forces that exist between the particles. When describing the behaviour of gases, it is assumed that there are no forces between the molecules. A gas in which there are no intermolecular forces is called an **ideal gas** (sometimes **perfect gas**). The behaviour of an ideal gas is described by the ideal gas equation. The molecular model of ideal gases is developed using the kinetic theory of gases. Real gases behave very much like ideal gases under normal conditions of temperature and pressure.

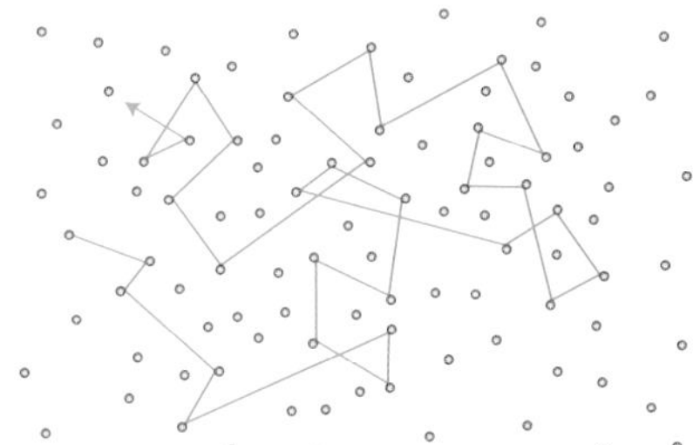

The path of a single molecule zig-zags randomly as the molecule repeatedly collides with other molecules.

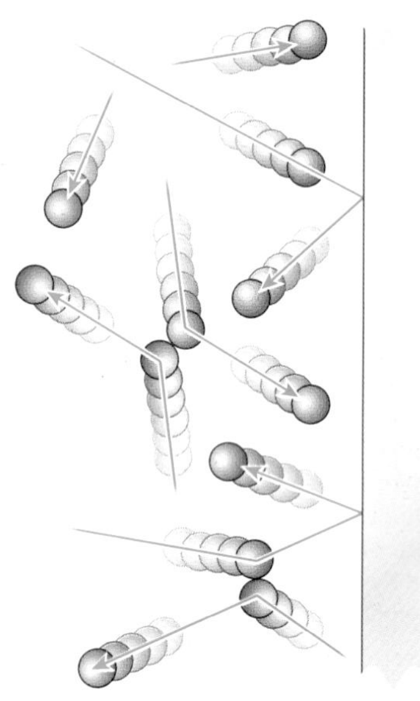

A gas exerts pressure as the molecules collide with and rebound from the walls of its container.

Pascals, bars, and atmospheres

Pressure is defined as force per unit area. The unit of pressure is the **pascal** (Pa): 1 Pa = 1 N m^{-2}. Atmospheric pressure at sea level is about 10^5 Pa (100 kPa); 1 **bar** is defined as 1×10^5 Pa. Weather forecasts give atmospheric pressures in millibars, mbar (1000 mbar = 1 bar). Finally, 1 **atmosphere** (atm) is equal to 101.325 kPa and is the pressure at which the boiling point of water is exactly 100 °C.

The ideal gas equation

Boyle's law and Charles's law are respectively expressed as:

$V \propto 1/p$ (at constant temperature) and

$V \propto T$ (at constant pressure)

Combining these expressions gives:

$V \propto T/p$ or $pV \propto T$

Adding a constant of proportionality results in the relationship:

$$pV = kT$$

where k is a constant for a fixed mass of a particular gas.

Avogadro's principle shows that the volume of a gas depends on the number of molecules. So the volume is proportional to the amount of gas (in moles), i.e. $V \propto n$. The behaviour of an ideal gas can therefore be described by the **ideal gas equation**:

$$pV = nRT$$

where R is a constant for all gases called the **gas constant**. Its value in SI units is $R = 8.31\,\mathrm{J\,K^{-1}\,mol^{-1}}$ or in other useful units $8.31\,\mathrm{Pa\,m^3\,K^{-1}mol^{-1}}$.

The kinetic theory of gases

An ideal gas follows the gas laws exactly. The **kinetic theory of gases** puts forward a model for gases that explains this behaviour. It makes the general assumption that an ideal gas is composed of independent molecules widely separated from each other, as described by the following four statements:

- The molecules in a gas are in continuous random motion.
- There are no intermolecular forces, so the only interactions between molecules are collisions.
- All collisions are perfectly 'elastic': the molecules bounce off each other without their total kinetic energy changing.
- The molecules themselves have no size, i.e. they occupy zero volume.

SI units and the ideal gas equation

SI units should be used consistently in calculations involving the ideal gas equation.

- The SI unit of pressure is the **pascal, Pa**, where 1 Pa = 1 N m^{-2}. Since the pascal is a very small unit, it is often more convenient to express pressures in bars or atmospheres (atm); 1 bar is 1×10^5 Pa and 1 atm is 1.01×10^5 Pa, so they are almost the same size. When using the ideal gas equation, however, the pressure should be converted to pascals.
- The SI unit of volume is the **cubic metre, m^3**, but the volume of a gas is most often expressed in cubic decimetres, dm^3; 1 m^3 = 1000 dm^3. Note that 1 dm^3 is the same volume as 1 litre. The diagram at the top of the opposite page shows how these units of volume are related. Again, when using the ideal gas equation, the volume should be converted to cubic metres.

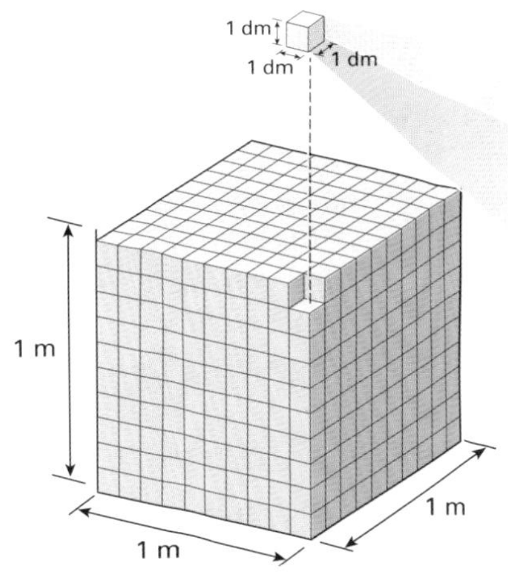

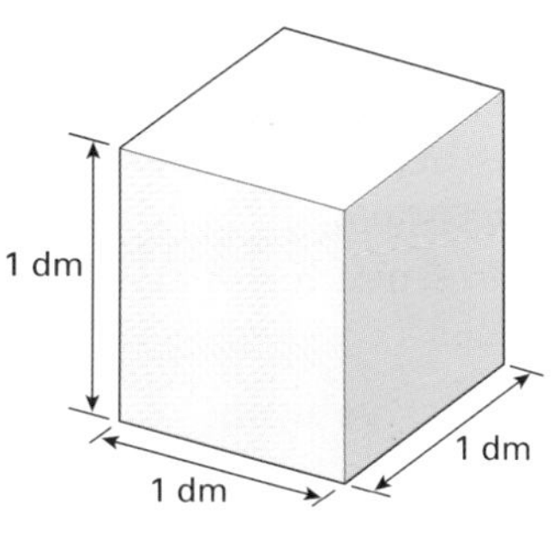

$1\ m^3 = 10 \times 10 \times 10\ dm^3$
$= 1000\ dm^3$

Relationship between the cubic metre and the cubic decimetre.

- The SI unit of temperature is the **kelvin, K**. Temperatures are most commonly measured in degrees celsius. Conversion to kelvins is very easy because 0 °C is equivalent to 273 K, so adding 273 to a temperature in degrees celsius converts it into a temperature (the *thermodynamic temperature*) in kelvins. When using the ideal gas equation, the temperature should be converted to kelvins.

Gas law summary

Boyle's law:
$V \propto 1/p$ (at constant n and T)
Charles's law:
$V \propto T$ (at constant n and p)
Avogadro's principle:
$V \propto n$ (at constant p and T)
The ideal gas equation:
$pV = nRT$

Kelvin scale

The thermodynamic temperature scale is often called the Kelvin scale (with a capital 'K'), after William Thomson, Lord Kelvin. The unit has a small letter when spelled out, kelvin, and is abbreviated to (capital) K. (Also note that it is **wrong** to say 'degrees Kelvin'.)

Worked example on calculating pressure

Question: Chloroethene is a chemical used to make the polymer PVC. A sample of the gas that contains 3.93 mol has a volume of 98.4 dm³ at 24 °C. What is the pressure of the gas?

Strategy: Use the ideal gas equation. Convert all quantities to SI units. Write the ideal gas equation in the form:

$$p = \frac{nRT}{V}$$

Answer:
$V = 98.4\,dm^3 = 98.4 \times 10^{-3}\,m^3$
$n = 3.93\,mol$
$T = (24 + 273)\,K = 297\,K$
So we get

$$p = \frac{nRT}{V}$$

$$= \frac{(3.93\,mol) \times (8.31\,Pa\,m^3\,K^{-1}\,mol^{-1}) \times (297\,K)}{(98.4 \times 10^{-3}\,m^3)}$$

$$= 9.86 \times 10^4\,Pa$$

A raincoat and umbrella made of the plastic PVC (short for polyvinyl chloride). Vinyl chloride is the traditional name for chloroethene. PVC results when molecules of chloroethene join to make long chains, spread 22.10. PVC has many other uses.

SUMMARY

- The molecules of an ideal gas:
  are in continuous random motion,
  experience no intermolecular forces,
  have perfectly elastic collisions,
  occupy zero volume.
- The ideal gas equation is: $pV = nRT$.
- SI units should be used in calculations involving the ideal gas equation.

PRACTICE

1. Calculate the volume of 0.5 mol of gas at 1×10^5 Pa and 20 °C.
2. What will be the volume of the gas in question 1 when the temperature is raised to 100 °C?
3. Calculate the pressure inside the cathode-ray tube in a television set, assuming that it contains 3.6×10^{-7} mol of gas in a volume of 5.0 dm³ at 20 °C.

8.3

O B J E C T I V E S

- The molar volume of an ideal gas
- Molar masses by experiment

Molar volume of an ideal gas

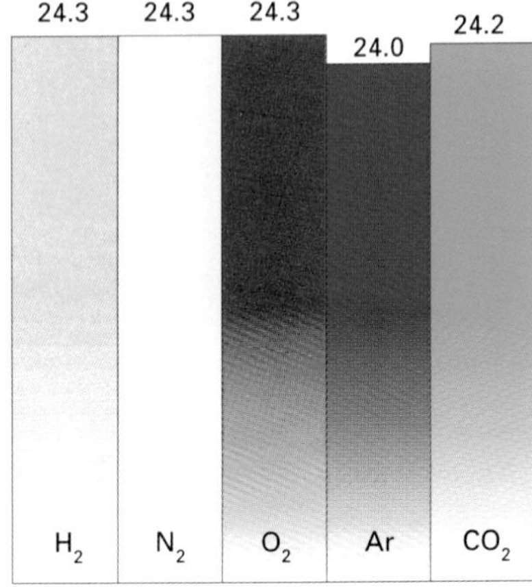

The volumes per mole of different gases are all very similar. Figures are given in $dm^3 \, mol^{-1}$ at 20 °C and 1 bar.

Conditions: *T* and *p*

The numerical value of the molar volume depends on the temperature and pressure of a gas. The usual conditions chosen are 20 °C and 1 bar. You should not refer to these conditions as 'room temperature and pressure' (because the conditions of the room in question are not specified!). For calculations, the conditions of a gas must be specified numerically.

The volume of one mole of an ideal gas at 20 °C and 1 bar is $24 \, dm^3$.

Avogadro's principle gives us some useful conclusions. As we saw in the previous two spreads, Avogadro's principle states that equal volumes of different gases contain the same number of molecules. Doubling the number of molecules present doubles the volume (at constant pressure). Also, according to the laws we met in the previous spread, doubling the number of molecules present will double the pressure (at constant volume).

The molar volume

Another way of stating Avogadro's principle is to say that:

- One mole of an ideal gas occupies the same volume under the same conditions of temperature and pressure.

This assertion leads to the idea of the **molar volume**, the volume per mole of any gas under stated conditions. You should find this idea easier to understand if you work through the following two examples.

Worked example on calculating the molar volume of a gas at room temperature and pressure

Question: What is the volume occupied by 1.00 mol of an ideal gas at 20 °C and 1.00 bar pressure?

Strategy: Use the ideal gas equation. Convert all quantities to SI units. Write the ideal gas equation in the form:

$$V = \frac{nRT}{p}$$

Answer:

$n = 1.00 \, \text{mol}$

$T = (20 + 273) \, \text{K} = 293 \, \text{K}$

$p = 1.00 \, \text{bar} = 1.00 \times 10^5 \, \text{Pa}$

So we get

$$V = \frac{nRT}{p} = \frac{(1.00 \, \text{mol}) \times (8.31 \, \text{Pa m}^3 \, \text{K}^{-1} \, \text{mol}^{-1}) \times (293 \, \text{K})}{(1.00 \times 10^5 \, \text{Pa})}$$

$$= 0.0243 \, \text{m}^3 = 24 \, \text{dm}^3 \quad \text{(2 sig. figs)}$$

Note: The units mol, Pa, and K cancel, leaving simply m^3, the SI unit of volume. In the more usual units of dm^3 ($1 \, m^3 = 1000 \, dm^3$) the equation predicts that the molar volume of an ideal gas at 20 °C and 1 bar (about room temperature and atmospheric pressure) is $\mathbf{24 \, dm^3 \, mol^{-1}}$. At standard temperature and pressure (273 K and 1.00 atm), abbreviated to STP, the molar volume of an ideal gas is $22.4 \, dm^3 \, mol^{-1}$. The volume is smaller because the temperature is lower.

Worked example on calculating the molar volume of a gas under alternative conditions

Question: On the surface of Venus the temperature is 470 °C and the pressure is 100 atm. What is the volume occupied by 1.00 mol of an ideal gas under these conditions?

Strategy: Use the ideal gas equation. Convert all quantities to SI units. Write the ideal gas equation in the form:

$$V = \frac{nRT}{p}$$

Answer:

$n = 1.00 \, \text{mol}$

$T = (470 + 273) \, \text{K} = 743 \, \text{K}$

$p = 100 \, \text{atm} = 1.01 \times 10^7 \, \text{Pa}$

So we get

$$V = \frac{nRT}{p} = \frac{(1.00 \, \text{mol}) \times (8.31 \, \text{Pa m}^3 \, \text{K}^{-1} \, \text{mol}^{-1}) \times (743 \, \text{K})}{(1.01 \times 10^7 \, \text{Pa})}$$

$$= 6.11 \times 10^{-4} \, \text{m}^3 = 0.61 \, \text{dm}^3 \quad \text{(2 sig. figs)}$$

Note: The molar volume is much less than on Earth because the atmospheric pressure is much greater.

Molar masses by experiment

We can use the idea of the molar volume of a gas to find out the molar mass of a volatile liquid, because a volatile liquid may be made into a gas easily. To do this we vaporize a known mass of the liquid and measure its volume. Then we assume that the vapour behaves as an ideal gas to work out its molar mass.

The experiment is carried out using the apparatus shown below. The steps are as follows:

1 Weigh the hypodermic syringe containing the volatile liquid (m_1).
2 Inject a small quantity of liquid into the gas syringe. Reweigh the hypodermic syringe (m_2) and hence find the mass of the vapour ($m = m_1 - m_2$).
3 Measure the volume of vapour that results in the gas syringe (V), the temperature (T), and the atmospheric pressure (p).

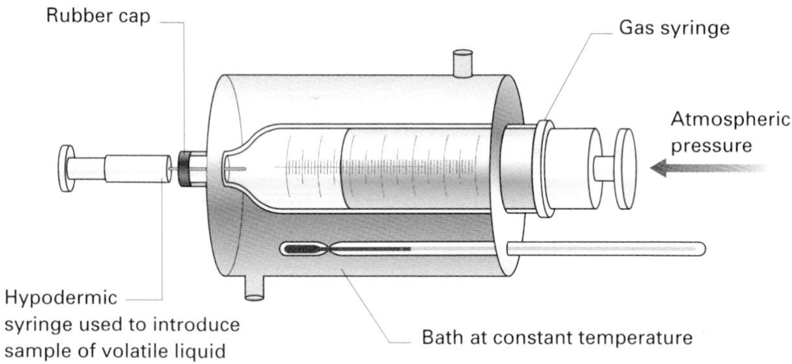

The apparatus for measuring the molar mass of a volatile liquid.

Reminder

Whenever starting a calculation involving gases, your first thought should be:

'The ideal gas equation is $pV = nRT$. How can I apply this equation to this problem?'

Calculating molar mass

Once we have carried out the experiment above, we are ready for the calculation. First we must ensure that all quantities are expressed in SI units. Then, from spread 3.3 on the mole, we know that the amount of gas in moles (n), the mass (m), and the molar mass (M) are related by the expression

$$n = \frac{m}{M} \qquad (1)$$

The ideal gas equation is

$$pV = nRT \qquad (2)$$

Substituting equation (1) into equation (2) gives us

$$pV = \frac{mRT}{M} \qquad (3)$$

Rearranging equation (3) to make M the subject of the equation gives

$$M = \frac{mRT}{pV} \qquad (4)$$

Now you can substitute your results from the experiment above into equation (4) and obtain a value for the molar mass M of the volatile liquid.

When fully pressurized at cruising altitude, a Jumbo Jet contains about one tonne of air. Knowledge of the pressure and temperature enables the calculation to be done.

SUMMARY

- The molar volume of an ideal gas at standard temperature and pressure (273 K, 1 atm) is $22.4\ dm^3\ mol^{-1}$.
- The molar volume of an ideal gas at 20 °C and 1 bar is $24\ dm^3\ mol^{-1}$.
- The molar mass of a volatile liquid may be measured using a gas syringe.

PRACTICE

1 On evaporation at 100 °C and 1.00 atm, 0.124 g of a volatile liquid hydrocarbon gave $45.3\ cm^3$ of vapour. Calculate the molar mass of the hydrocarbon.

2 The hydrocarbon in question 1 contained hydrogen and carbon in the mole ratio 2:1. What is the molecular formula of the hydrocarbon?

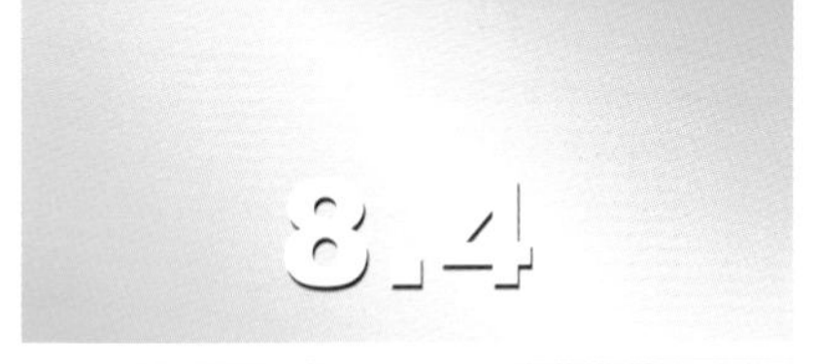

THE MOVEMENT OF GAS MOLECULES

OBJECTIVES

- Effusion
- Graham's law
- Diffusion
- The Maxwell–Boltzmann distribution

Bicycle tyres slowly deflate and balloons go limp and flabby. The walls of tyres and balloons are full of microscopic holes called pores. The molecules in a gas are in continuous random motion. If a molecule is by chance moving in the direction of a pore, it will enter it and eventually escape to the outside. This escaping tendency is called effusion. The rate of effusion of gases is linked to their molar masses. The model behind this leads to the idea of molecular kinetic energies and then to the Maxwell–Boltzmann distribution.

Rates of effusion and Graham's law

Effusion is the escape of gas molecules through a small hole. Experiments show that some gases effuse faster than others. This observation may be explained in terms of the kinetic energy of the molecules. Temperature is a measure of the average kinetic energy of the gas molecules. Average kinetic energy is proportional to the thermodynamic temperature.

The *average* kinetic energy of the molecules in the gas is constant at a given temperature.

You should remember the equation for kinetic energy from your earlier studies. So

$$\text{average KE} = \tfrac{1}{2}mv^2 = \text{constant}$$

$$mv^2 = \text{constant, which means} \quad v^2 = \frac{\text{constant}}{m} \quad \text{and} \quad v \propto \frac{1}{\sqrt{m}}$$

The speed of the molecules in the gas and therefore the rate of effusion is inversely proportional to the square root of the mass of the molecule. This means that lighter gases effuse faster at a given temperature because the molecules move faster.

This was discovered experimentally by Thomas Graham in 1832 before the kinetic theory of gases had been developed. He summarized his observations in a statement now known as **Graham's law**:

- The rate of effusion of a gas is inversely proportional to the square root of its relative formula mass, i.e. rate $\propto 1/\sqrt{M_r}$.

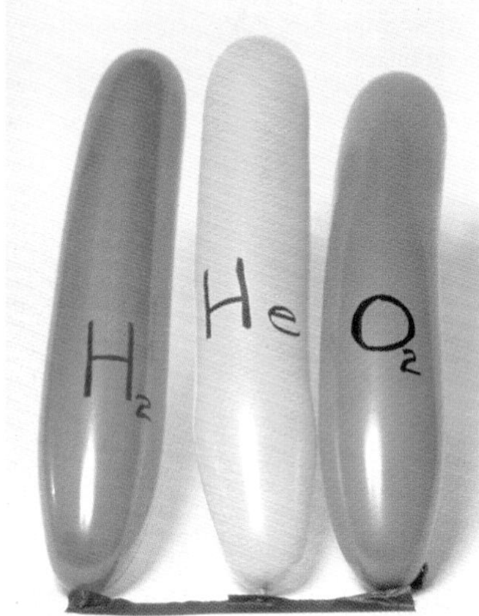

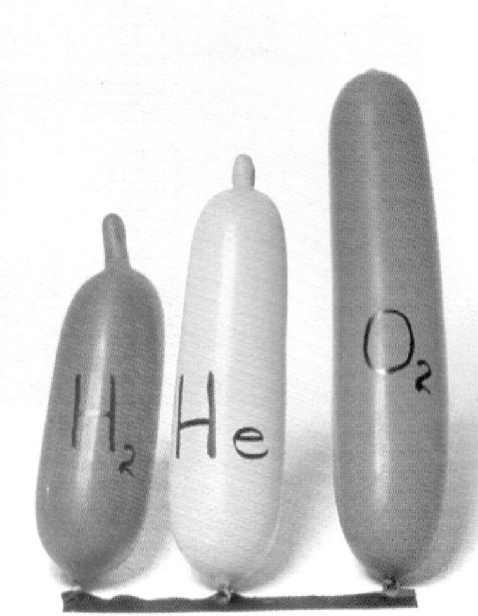

The rate of effusion is inversely proportional to the square root of the relative formula masses of the gases, which are: H_2, 2; He, 4; O_2, 32.

Diffusion

Diffusion is the mixing of one type of molecule throughout a space containing another type of molecule. For example, a bad smell diffuses until it uniformly fills a room. Experiments show that some gases diffuse faster than others. The process of gas diffusion obeys Graham's law, as shown by the illustration below: NH_3 diffuses faster as it is lighter than HCl.

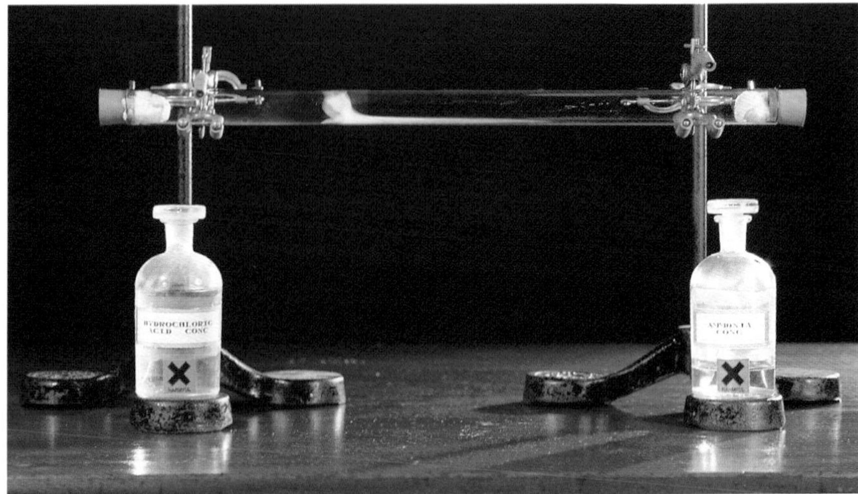

Ammonia NH_3 diffuses from the right-hand side of the tube and hydrogen chloride HCl from the left. The gases react to form solid ammonium chloride when they meet.

The Maxwell–Boltzmann distribution

Graham's law has been explained in terms of the *average* kinetic energy of the molecules. Since lighter gas molecules travel faster, they effuse faster. Many combinations of energy will, however, give the same average energy. For example, to produce an average of 4 kJ mol^{-1}, all the molecules could have that energy, or half of them could have 2 kJ mol^{-1} and the other half could have 6 kJ mol^{-1}. Alternatively, the molecules could have a wide spread of energies.

Clerk Maxwell looked at the problem of how many molecules in a gas had a particular energy, an area of study later reconsidered by Ludwig Boltzmann. Maxwell succeeded in calculating the probability of a gas molecule having a particular energy. For each energy, the **Maxwell–Boltzmann distribution** shows the fraction of molecules that have that energy. The energies of individual molecules in a gas are continually changing due to random collisions, but the calculations give the total fraction of molecules with that energy at a particular instant.

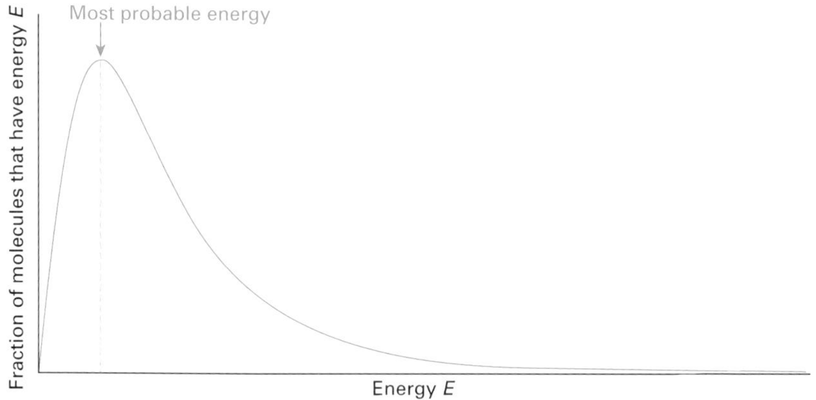

The Maxwell–Boltzmann distribution of molecular energies for a gas at a fixed temperature.

The highest point on the curve represents the most probable energy. The greatest fraction of molecules have this energy at a given instant. No molecules are stationary and a few molecules have exceptionally high energy. The area under the curve is *not symmetrical* about the most probable energy. There is a larger 'tail' at higher energy, and the graph drops off more sharply on the low-energy side.

At higher temperatures, the average energy of the molecules is greater. The range of the energies is also greater, with a higher chance of very high energy. The peak of the curve is broader and lower at higher temperature. The area under each of the curves represents the total number of molecules. This number is fixed, so the curve must have a lower peak at higher temperatures as more molecules have high energy.

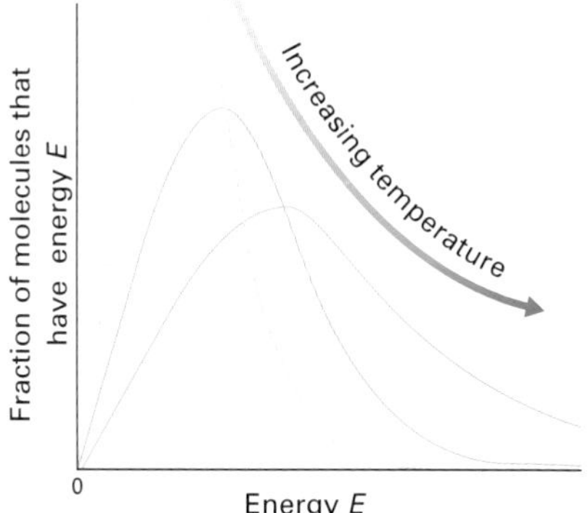

The Maxwell–Boltzmann distribution of molecular energies for a fixed mass of gas at three different temperatures. Spread 15.4 explains why the reaction rate varies with temperature.

SUMMARY

- Effusion is the escape of a gas through a small hole.
- The rate of effusion (and the rate of diffusion) of a gas is inversely proportional to the square root of its relative formula mass.
- Average molecular kinetic energy is proportional to the thermodynamic temperature of the gas.
- The fraction of molecules with a given energy is shown by the Maxwell–Boltzmann distribution. (Memorize the shape.)

PRACTICE

1 In an experiment, 100 cm^3 of a gas diffused out of a gas syringe in 14.1 s. The same volume of oxygen took 10 s. Calculate the relative formula mass of the unknown gas. Suggest an identity for the gas.

2 Arrange the following gases in order of increasing rate of effusion under the same conditions: ammonia NH_3; carbon dioxide CO_2; chlorine Cl_2; helium He; xenon Xe.

8.5 REAL GASES

OBJECTIVES

- Deviations of real gases from ideal gas behaviour

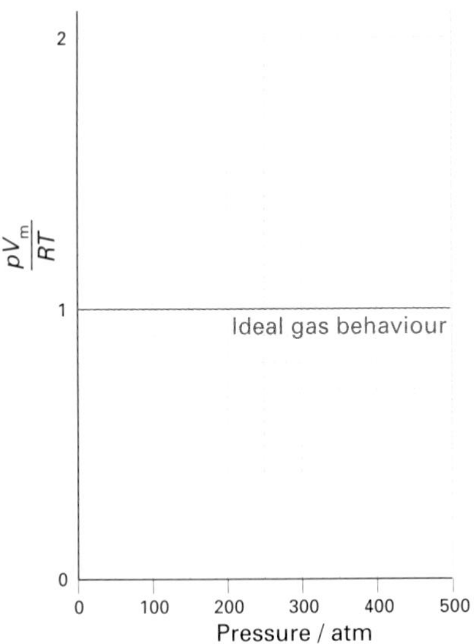

Isothermals

The plot of pV_m/RT against p shown above is called an **isothermal**. This term means that it is the result of measurements made at equal temperature.

Johannes Diderik van der Waals

The Dutch scientist Johannes van der Waals was the first person to take account of the forces between molecules in a gas. The general term 'van der Waals forces' is sometimes applied to intermolecular forces.

The ideal gas equation is an empirical law, which means that it is based on observations. The kinetic theory of gases is an attempt to explain the law by providing a model for the behaviour of gas molecules. Gases obey the ideal gas equation $pV = nRT$ under almost all common conditions of temperature and pressure. But are there any conditions under which the ideal gas equation is not valid? Two assumptions made by the kinetic theory about ideal gases are that (i) there are no intermolecular forces and (ii) the molecules themselves occupy zero volume. Real gases behave as ideal gases under conditions where these assumptions hold true. At high pressure and low temperature they do not, and real gases depart fairly significantly from ideal gas behaviour.

Real gases and ideal behaviour

It is important to note that deviations from ideal gas behaviour only occur under conditions of high pressure or low temperature, and that the deviations are usually quite small. The ideal gas equation remains an excellent approximation to the behaviour of real gases under normal laboratory conditions. A check for ideal behaviour depends on the following reasoning.

The ideal gas equation is:

$$pV = nRT$$

Remembering that the molar volume $V_m = V/n$, this rearranges to

$$\frac{pV_m}{RT} = 1$$

This relationship should apply for all values of pressure and temperature. The first diagram on spread 8.3 shows that the molar volume for many gases is within 2% of the ideal gas value at 20 °C and 1 bar, indicating that these real gases are behaving as an ideal gas. The assumptions made by the kinetic theory of gases apply to these gases *under these conditions*.

Deviations at moderately high pressure

Increasing the pressure on a gas forces its molecules closer to each other. When the pressure is high, the molecules are sufficiently close together for their intermolecular forces to become significant. So, the assumption underlying the kinetic theory of gases that there are no forces between molecules can no longer be made. The gas deviates from the ideal gas equation under these conditions. At high pressure (typically hundreds of atmospheres), the *attractive* forces between the molecules *decrease* the volume occupied by the gas: a real gas is more compact than an ideal gas would be under the same conditions.

Deviations at very high pressure

Remember that the kinetic theory of gases also assumes that the molecules themselves occupy zero volume. At *very* high pressure, the size of the molecules themselves becomes significant relative to their distance apart. Molecular size can no longer be ignored and the gas deviates from ideal behaviour. At very high pressures, the *repulsive* forces between the molecules *increase* the volume occupied by the gas: a real gas takes up more space than an ideal gas would under the same conditions.

Deviations at low temperature

Gases deviate from the ideal gas equation when the temperature is very low. As temperature decreases, the energies of the molecules decrease. The energy with which the molecules collide with each other is therefore less. At low temperatures, intermolecular forces become more significant. The molecules clump together as the collisions between them are not completely elastic and become more 'sticky'.

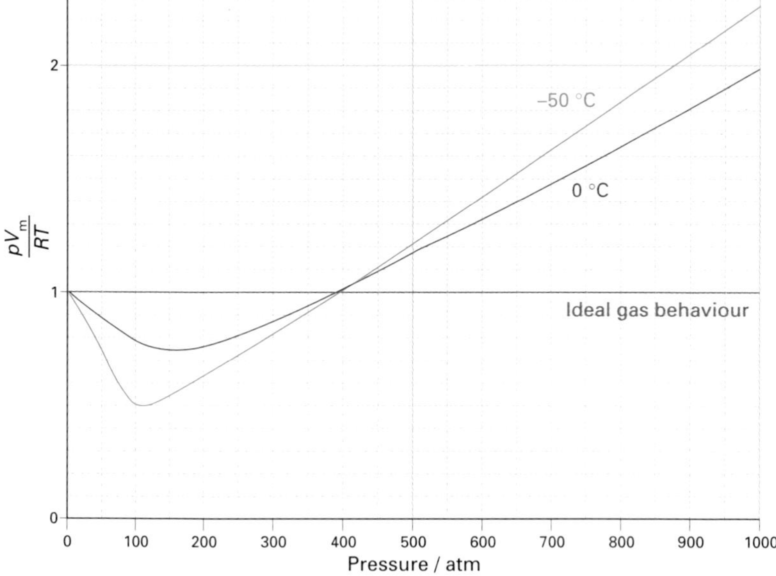

Plots of pV_m/RT against p for methane at 0 °C and at −50 °C at high pressures up to 1000 atm. The downward slopes of the plots at moderately high pressure result from the influence of attractive intermolecular forces. The subsequent upward slopes at very high pressures are due to repulsive forces operating between molecules where the size of the molecules themselves becomes significant.

Liquefaction of gases

A change of state occurs when a gas liquefies. At the point of liquefaction, at a sufficiently low temperature and high pressure, gas molecules collide and then stay close to each other. The collisions are no longer elastic and the gas condenses to form a liquid held together by attractive intermolecular forces. The temperature at which a gas liquefies depends on the pressure. There is a maximum temperature called the **critical temperature** above which a gas cannot be liquefied by the application of pressure alone. Values for ammonia, methane, and hydrogen are respectively 406 K, 191 K, and 33 K. As a result, liquid ammonia may be stored under pressure in steel containers at ambient temperature (20 °C). Liquid methane and hydrogen must be kept in refrigerated containers whose temperatures are below the relevant critical temperature.

Supercritical fluids

A modern method of making decaffeinated coffee depends on the properties of carbon dioxide above its critical temperature (31 °C). This supercritical fluid (SCF) can dissolve caffeine from raw coffee beans, without dissolving most of the substances responsible for coffee's taste and flavour. After pumping away the solution of caffeine in SCF carbon dioxide, the coffee beans are free of caffeine; any residual carbon dioxide disperses away. Older methods left a residue of organic solvent.

SUMMARY

- At high pressure, attractive forces between molecules become significant; the volume of a real gas is less than that of an ideal gas.
- At very high pressure, repulsive forces between molecules become significant; the volume of a real gas is greater than that of an ideal gas.
- At low temperatures, intermolecular forces become more significant.
- The critical temperature is the temperature above which a gas cannot be liquefied by the application of pressure alone.

PRACTICE

1 Which of the following pairs of gases would you expect to behave most like an ideal gas? Explain your answers.
 a Helium He and carbon dioxide CO_2
 b Helium He and xenon Xe
 c Carbon dioxide CO_2 and methane CH_4.

2 For both of the gases helium and carbon dioxide, sketch the plot of pV_m/RT against p you would expect for pressures ranging from 1 atm to 1000 atm. Compare and contrast the two plots and explain their shapes.

3 Explain the significance of critical temperature for the following observation:
'Camping gas' for small portable stoves is supplied as liquid butane C_4H_{10} in a disposable steel cartridge. The pressure of the gas above the liquid is about 3 atm.

Practice exam questions

1 **a** Discuss the bonding present in each of the following, indicating any bond polarity:

i hydrogen chloride molecule, HCl, [2]

ii ammonium chloride crystal, NH_4Cl, [2]

iii water molecule, H_2O. [2]

b Ice is a solid melting at 0 °C. Name the intermolecular bonding present in ice and explain the origin of this bonding. [2]

c Explain why solid iodine is much more volatile than solid sodium chloride. [2]

d Calculate the volume of 4.509 g of iodine vapour at 343 K and 1.01×10^5 Pa pressure, if the vapour contains only I_2 molecules. [3]

[The molar volume of a gas at 273 K and 1.01×10^5 Pa is 2.24×10^4 $cm^3\,mol^{-1}$.]
WJEC 1998

2 The equation $pV = nRT$ may be used in the determination of the relative molecular mass of a volatile liquid.

The diagram below shows the apparatus that could be used in this determination. A known mass of a volatile liquid is injected through the self-sealing rubber cap into the gas syringe, which is then heated in a boiling water bath for several minutes before the volume of the vapour in the syringe is noted. [15]

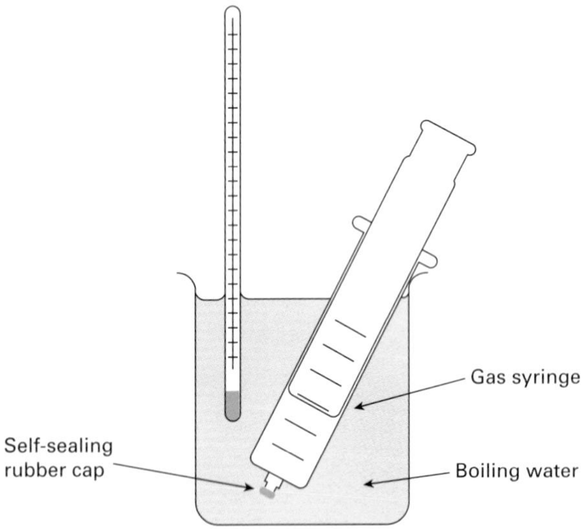

a **i** State what is meant by the term *volatile liquid*. Give the name of the equation $pV = nRT$, and state what the symbols n and R represent in this equation. [4]

ii Suggest why it is essential to leave the syringe in the boiling water bath for several minutes before reading the volume of the vapour. [2]

iii State **three** of the basic assumptions made in the kinetic theory of gases regarding the behaviour of gaseous molecules. [3]

b Using apparatus similar to that shown on the left, 0.167 g of ethanol, C_2H_5OH, was injected into a gas syringe and the syringe was then placed in a boiling water bath for several minutes. The atmospheric pressure was 101 300 Pa and the temperature of the bath was 100 °C. [5]

i Calculate the volume, in cm^3, of ethanol vapour that would have been produced under these conditions. [5]

$R = 8.314\,J\,K^{-1}\,mol^{-1}$

ii Explain why a gas syringe of 100 cm^3 capacity was found to be unsuitable. [1]
AQA (AEB) 1998

3 **a** With reference, where appropriate, to the kinetic theory of matter:

i Explain why a gas exerts a pressure; [2]

ii describe what happens as an ionic substance such as sodium chloride, melting point 801 °C, is steadily heated from room temperature until it melts; [2]

iii account for the relatively high melting points of ionic substances. [1]

b A volatile liquid, of mass 0.148 g, when vaporized occupies a volume of 63.0 cm^3 at a pressure of 1.01×10^5 Pa and a temperature of 100 °C. State the ideal gas equation and use it to calculate the relative molecular mass of the liquid. [5]
AQA (AEB) 1996

4 **a** **i** Copy the axis below and sketch a graph of V (the volume of an ideal gas) against $1/P$ (the reciprocal of its pressure) at a constant temperature. [1]

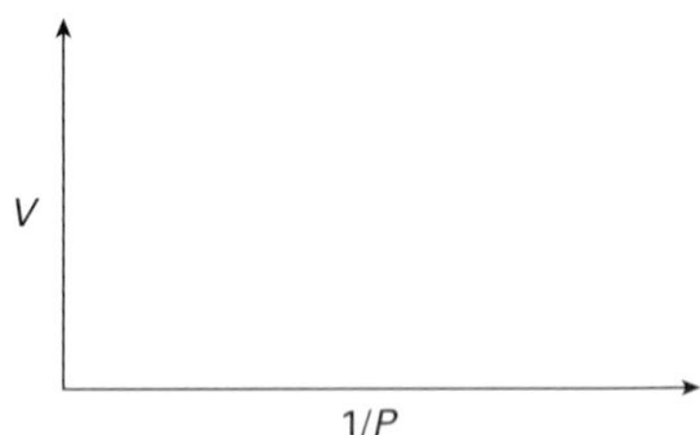

ii State **two** factors which cause real gases to deviate from ideal behaviour. [2]

b **i** Copy the axis below and sketch a graph to show the variation of the saturated vapour pressure of a liquid with temperature.

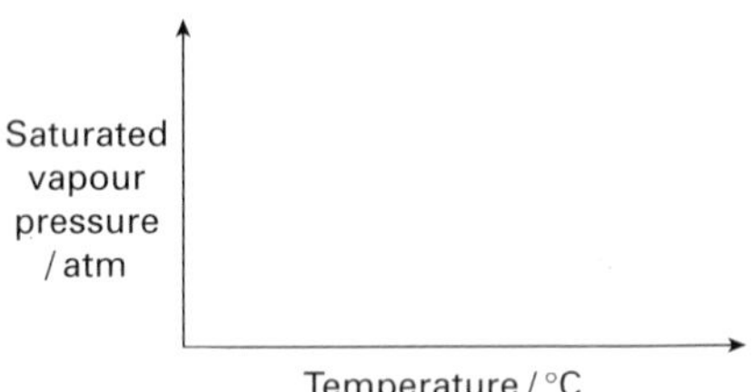

ii Explain why the boiling temperature of a liquid varies with the external pressure. [1]

iii Give **one** reason why some liquids are purefied by distillation under reduced pressure. [1]

c Calculate the molar mass of a volatile organic liquid, given that 0.597 g of the liquid when vaporized gives an ideal gas of volume 153 cm^3 at 100 °C and 1.01×10^5 Pa pressure (1 atmosphere).

[1 mole of an ideal gas occupies $2.24 \times 10^4 cm^3$ at 0 °C and 1.01×10^5 Pa pressure (1 atmosphere).] [3]
WJEC 1997 *(See also Chapter 22.)*

5 The kinetic theory of gases explains the physical properties of a gas in terms of the behaviour of its particles. A gas which obeys the assumptions made in this theory is said to be an ideal gas.

a Give the ideal gas equation. [1]

b 10.0 g of carbon dioxide were placed in a vessel of volume 5.00 dm^3 and the temperature maintained at 0 °C. Calculate the pressure exerted by the gas.

[The value of the gas constant R is 8.31 $J K^{-1} mol^{-1}$.] [3]

c Explain why the actual pressure exerted was found to be slightly less than the calculated value. [1]
OCR (UODLE) 1998

6 a i Draw a **labelled** diagram which shows the bonding in solid sodium. [2]

ii Use your diagram to explain two different physical properties which are **typical** of metals. [2]

b A mass spectrum of sodium vapour is shown in the following trace.

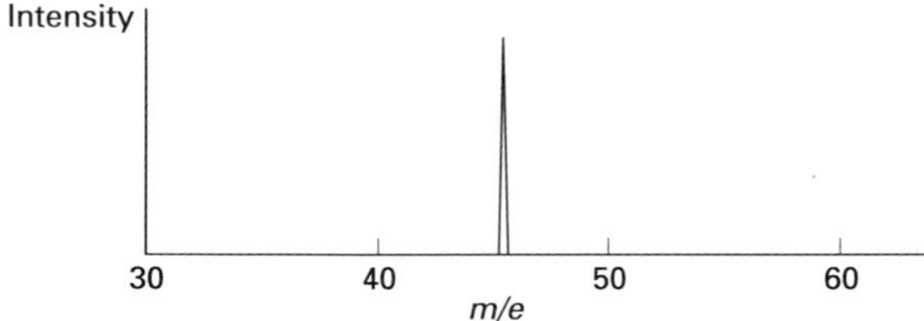

Explain the trace and draw a diagram showing the bonding in sodium under these conditions. [2]

c i A street lamp contains sodium vapour at a temperature of 20 °C and a pressure of 25 N m^{-2}. The volume of the tube containing the sodium is 50 cm^3. Calculate the mass of sodium in the lamp. [3]

ii What important assumption have you made in your calculation? [1]
[Gas constant R = 8.31 J $mol^{-1} K^{-1}$.]

d i Give the electron arrangement/configuration of the sodium **atom**, in terms of orbitals, in its ground state. [1]

ii Comment on the relative energies of the atomic orbitals given in **i**. [1]

iii Suggest the electron arrangement of a sodium atom in an **excited** state. [1]
OCR (UODLE) 1994

7 a State the ideal gas equation. [1]

b The density of ethanoic acid, CH_3COOH, in the vapour state, is 2.74 g dm^{-3} at 400 K and 101 kPa.

i Calculate the apparent relative molecular mass of the acid under these conditions. [Gas constant R = 8.31 $J K^{-1} mol^{-1}$.] [3]

ii Suggest why the measured relative molecular mass differs from 60. [1]

c The figure below shows the variation in pV plotted against p for one mole of argon, at a constant temperature.

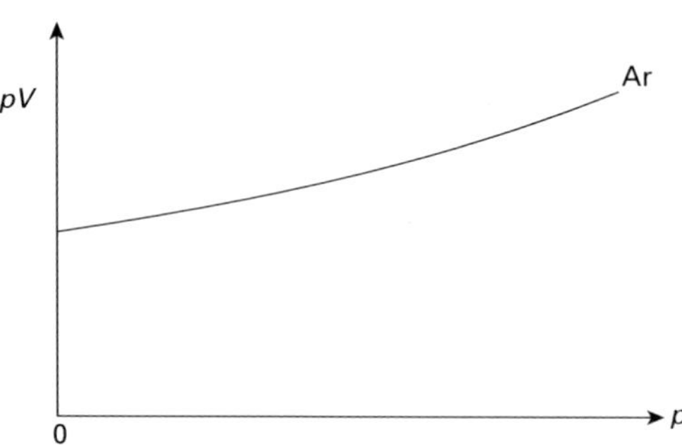

i Copy the figure and draw a line to show the behaviour of one mole of an ideal gas at the same temperature. [1]

ii Explain why argon does not behave as an ideal gas at pressures above zero. [2]
OCR (UODLE) 1996

Reacting masses and volumes

You were introduced to the idea of using the mole as a unit of quantity in chemistry in spread 3.3. You should now understand the term 'molar mass' and be able to work out the mass per mole of any element or compound. This chapter extends these ideas and shows you how to calculate the yields of reactions, the formulae of compounds from analysis data, the volumes of gases evolved in reactions, and the concentrations and volumes of reacting solutions. These are all essential skills for practical chemists carrying out reactions in the laboratory or in industry.

Calculating masses involved in reactions

OBJECTIVES

- Mass conservation
- The relationship between amount in moles, mass, and molar mass
- Calculating masses in reactions

In a chemical reaction, reactants change into products. A chemical reaction may be represented by a balanced chemical equation, showing the formulae of the reactants and products, and the changes that take place. For example:

$$CaCO_3(s) + 2HCl(aq) \rightarrow CaCl_2(aq) + H_2O(l) + CO_2(g)$$

There are two important facts about any chemical equation: first, all the atoms present in the reactants are also present in the products; and secondly, a balanced chemical equation shows the *numbers* of species – molecules, ions, atoms, etc. – taking part in the reaction. These two facts allow the *masses* of substances involved in reactions to be calculated. By the end of this spread, you should be able to calculate the mass of product to be expected from a given mass of reactant, and the mass of reactant required to produce a given mass of product.

Mass conservation

The **law of mass conservation** states that:

- The total mass of a system remains constant during a chemical reaction.

In other words, for the reaction

$$A + B \rightarrow C + D$$

the total mass of the products (C + D) is equal to the total mass of the reactants (A + B). A balanced chemical equation obeys the law of mass conservation.

The law may be easily demonstrated by carrying out a chemical reaction on the pan of a balance, as shown to the left.

Mass remains constant during a chemical reaction. Before reaction, a flask with aqueous silver nitrate and a measuring cylinder with potassium chromate(VI) are weighed. Mixing the solutions forms a solid precipitate of silver chromate(VI) and aqueous potassium nitrate. There is no change in mass, as indicated by the balance.

Moles and mole ratios

Calculations to find the masses of substances in chemical reactions always start from the balanced chemical equation for the reaction. The equation shows the amount in moles of each substance involved in the reaction. For example, the reaction between hydrogen and oxygen to produce water is:

$$2H_2(g) + O_2(g) \rightarrow 2H_2O(l)$$

This equation translates into plain language as: '2 moles of hydrogen molecules react with 1 mole of oxygen molecules to give 2 moles of water molecules'.

The ratios between the amounts in moles of reactants and the amounts in moles of products are called the **mole ratios** (previously called *stoichiometric ratios*). In this example, the mole ratios H_2:O_2:H_2O are 2:1:2. In other words, the amount in moles of hydrogen is twice the amount in moles of oxygen required to react with it; the amount in moles of hydrogen is the same as the amount in moles of water; and the amount in moles of water is twice the amount in moles of oxygen. The concept of mole ratio is the central idea on which the following calculations depend.

Mass-to-mass calculation

In this type of calculation, you might be asked to work out, for example, the mass of reactant needed to produce a certain mass of product or the mass of product that results from using a certain mass of reactant.
A calculation of this sort requires the balanced chemical equation and data about the mass of one reactant or product (A). The question will then ask you to work out the mass of another reactant or product (B). The route for the calculation follows a set path, with the following steps:

1 Use data about the mass of A to calculate the amount in moles of A.

2 Use the balanced chemical equation to state the mole ratio B:A.

3 Calculate the amount in moles of B.

4 Use the amount in moles of B to calculate the mass of B.

A mass-to-mass calculation therefore follows the sequence:

$$\text{Mass of A} \rightarrow \text{Moles of A} \xrightarrow{\text{Mole ratio B:A}} \text{Moles of B} \rightarrow \text{Mass of B}$$

Worked example of a mass-to-mass calculation

Sodium is produced in industry by the electrolysis of molten sodium chloride, spread 16.1.

Question: What mass of sodium chloride is needed to produce 1.00 kg of sodium?

Strategy: The calculation follows the four steps outlined above.

Answer:

Step 1 Use data about the mass of sodium to calculate its amount in moles.

We have

$$\text{amount in moles of Na} = \frac{\text{mass of Na}}{\text{molar mass of Na}}$$

so

$$n(\text{Na}) = \frac{1000\,\text{g}}{23.0\,\text{g mol}^{-1}} = 43.5\,\text{mol}$$

Step 2 Use the balanced chemical equation to state the mole ratio of NaCl:Na.

The balanced chemical equation for the reaction is

$2NaCl(l) \rightarrow 2Na(l) + Cl_2(g)$

The mole ratio of NaCl:Na is therefore 2:2, i.e. 1:1.

Step 3 Calculate the amount in moles of sodium chloride.

The amount of Na is 43.5 mol. The mole ratio NaCl:Na is 1:1. Therefore the amount of NaCl is 43.5 mol.

Step 4 Use the amount in moles of NaCl to calculate the mass of sodium chloride.

We have

mass of NaCl = amount in moles of NaCl × molar mass of NaCl

The molar mass of NaCl is $(23.0\,\text{g mol}^{-1} + 35.5\,\text{g mol}^{-1}) = 58.5\,\text{g mol}^{-1}$. Therefore:

$$m(\text{NaCl}) = (43.5\,\text{mol}) \times (58.5\,\text{g mol}^{-1}) = 2540\,\text{g (3 sig. figs)}$$
$$= 2.54\,\text{kg}$$

That is, 2.54 kg of sodium chloride is needed to produce 1.00 kg of sodium.

SUMMARY

- The total mass of the products in a chemical reaction is equal to the total mass of the reactants.
- Amount in moles = mass/molar mass; in symbols, $n = m/M$.
- A mass-to-mass calculation follows the path:
  $$\text{Mass of A} \rightarrow \text{Moles of A} \xrightarrow{\text{Mole ratio B:A}} \text{Moles of B} \rightarrow \text{Mass of B}$$

Reminder – amount in moles, mass, and molar mass

The molar mass (symbol M, unit g mol^{-1}) of a substance is defined as the mass (symbol m, unit g) present divided by the amount in moles (symbol n, unit mol), i.e.

$$\text{molar mass} = \frac{\text{mass}}{\text{amount in moles}}$$

or

$$M = \frac{m}{n}$$

The numerical value of the molar mass of a species is the same as its relative formula mass, but the molar mass has units, g mol^{-1}, whereas the relative formula mass does not.

Multiplying both sides of the equation above by n shows that the mass is equal to the amount in moles multiplied by the molar mass, i.e.

mass = amount in moles × molar mass

or

$m = nM$

Dividing both sides of the equation by M shows that the amount in moles is equal to the mass divided by the molar mass, i.e.

$$\text{amount in moles} = \frac{\text{mass}}{\text{molar mass}}$$

or

$$n = \frac{m}{M}$$

PRACTICE

1 Calculate the mass of sodium that results from the electrolysis of 50.0 g of molten sodium chloride.

2 Calculate the mass of chlorine that accompanies the production of 1.00 kg of sodium during the electrolysis of molten sodium chloride.

9.2

OBJECTIVES

- Aluminium production
- The 'top 10' chemicals
- A laboratory reaction
- Percentage yield

Further mass-to-mass calculations

The concept of molar mass is the key to carrying out mass-to-mass calculations. These calculations provide answers to questions of the sort: 'What mass of this reactant is required to produce *x* grams of that product?' or ' What mass of this product results from *y* grams of that reactant?' This spread provides further worked examples of mass-to-mass calculations, in both industrial and laboratory-based settings.

Bauxite and aluminium

The crash test result of the Jaguar XJ220, which has an aluminium frame. Unlike steel-framed cars there is no deformation of the area around the passengers and no bursting at the seams of the doors.

Aluminium is produced from the electrolysis of molten aluminium oxide, which is prepared from the ore *bauxite*. You should be familiar with the worked example given in the previous spread involving the extraction of sodium from sodium chloride. Answering the question 'What mass of aluminium oxide is needed to produce 1 kg of aluminium?' involves a similar calculation.

Worked example on aluminium production

Question: What mass of aluminium oxide is needed to produce 1.00 kg of aluminium?

Strategy: The calculation is carried out in the same four steps as in the previous spread.

Answer:

Step 1 We have

$$\text{amount in moles of Al} = \frac{\text{mass of Al}}{\text{molar mass of Al}}$$

so

$$n(\text{Al}) = \frac{1000\,\text{g}}{27.0\,\text{g mol}^{-1}} = 37.0\,\text{mol}$$

Step 2 The balanced chemical equation for the reaction is

$$2Al_2O_3(l) \rightarrow 4Al(l) + 3O_2(g)$$

The mole ratio Al_2O_3:Al is 2:4, i.e. 1:2.

Step 3 The amount of Al is 37.0 mol. The mole ratio Al_2O_3:Al is 1:2. Therefore the amount of Al_2O_3 is 37.0/2 = 18.5 mol.

Step 4 We have

$$\text{mass of } Al_2O_3 = \text{amount in moles of } Al_2O_3 \times \text{molar mass of } Al_2O_3$$

The molar mass of Al_2O_3 is $(27.0 \times 2) + (16.0 \times 3) = 102\,\text{g mol}^{-1}$.
Therefore

$$m(Al_2O_3) = (18.5\,\text{mol}) \times (102\,\text{g mol}^{-1}) = 1890\,\text{g (3 sig. figs)}$$
$$= 1.89\,\text{kg}$$

That is, 1.89 kg of aluminium oxide is needed to produce 1.00 kg of aluminium.

The Hall–Héroult cell for the extraction of aluminium. Graphite anodes dip into molten aluminium oxide dissolved in cryolite. The steel cell is also lined with graphite, which acts as the cathode. Oxygen gas is evolved at the anodes and liquid aluminium is produced at the cathode. The cell contents are kept molten at around 850 °C by the passage of the electric current.

The top 10 chemicals manufactured

The top 10 chemicals (ignoring water, steel, and sodium chloride) manufactured in the USA in 1995 are listed on the opposite page by mass in megatonnes. The top six are clear of the field; there is a tight bunch jostling for seventh place.

One megatonne is 10^6 tonnes, which is 10^9 kg or 10^{12} g. In terms of moles, the top three chemicals are nitrogen, ammonia, and ethene, in that order. The *amount in moles* of nitrogen manufactured is

$$\frac{30.9 \times 10^{12}\,\text{g}}{28.0\,\text{g mol}^{-1}} = 1.1 \times 10^{12}\,\text{mol}$$

which is more than one thousand billion moles.

Worked example on sulphuric acid production

Sulphuric acid, the chemical produced in highest mass, is produced in a series of reactions from elemental sulphur. The overall reaction may be represented as:

$2S + 2H_2O + 3O_2 \rightarrow 2H_2SO_4$

Question: What mass of sulphur was used to make the 43.3 megatonnes of sulphuric acid produced in the USA in 1995?

Strategy: The calculation follows the same steps as before, but now we do not list *all* the lines.

Answer:
43.3 megatonnes = 43.3×10^{12} g

The molar mass of H_2SO_4 is

$2 \times (1.0\ \text{g mol}^{-1}) + 32.1 + 4 \times (16.0\ \text{g mol}^{-1}) = 98.1\ \text{g mol}^{-1}$

We have

$$n(H_2SO_4) = \frac{43.3 \times 10^{12}\ \text{g}}{98.1\ \text{g mol}^{-1}} = 4.41 \times 10^{11}\ \text{mol}$$

The mole ratio of $S{:}H_2SO_4$ is 2:2, i.e. 1:1.

The amount in moles of sulphur required is the same as the amount in moles of sulphuric acid produced, i.e. 4.41×10^{11} mol. So

mass of sulphur = amount in moles of sulphur × molar mass of sulphur

$m(S) = (4.41 \times 10^{11}\ \text{mol}) \times (32.1\ \text{g mol}^{-1}) = 14.2 \times 10^{12}\ \text{g}$

That is, 43.3 megatonnes of sulphuric acid are produced from 14.2 megatonnes of sulphur.

We can express the success of a particular reaction as a **percentage yield**:

$$\text{percentage yield} = \frac{(\text{actual mass of product})}{(\text{theoretical mass of product})} \times 100$$

Worked example on calculating a percentage yield

Question: What mass of ethanol could form from fermentation of 90.0 g of glucose $C_6H_{12}O_6$? What is the percentage yield if 6.0 g of ethanol forms?

Strategy: The calculation follows the same steps. Then find the percentage yield.

Answer: As the molar mass of $C_6H_{12}O_6$ is
$6 \times (12.0\ \text{g mol}^{-1}) + 12 \times (1.0\ \text{g mol}^{-1}) + 6 \times (16.0\ \text{g mol}^{-1}) = 180\ \text{g mol}^{-1}$

$$n(C_6H_{12}O_6) = \frac{90.0\ \text{g}}{180\ \text{g mol}^{-1}} = 0.500\ \text{mol}$$

The chemical equation, spread 25.1, is:
$C_6H_{12}O_6(aq) \rightarrow 2CH_3CH_2OH(aq) + 2CO_2(g)$

The mole ratio of $CH_3CH_2OH{:}C_6H_{12}O_6$ is 2:1 so

$n(CH_3CH_2OH) = 2 \times (0.500\ \text{mol}) = 1.00\ \text{mol}$

The molar mass of CH_3CH_2OH is

$2 \times (12.0\ \text{g mol}^{-1}) + 6 \times (1.0\ \text{g mol}^{-1}) + 16.0\ \text{g mol}^{-1} = 46.0\ \text{g mol}^{-1}$

Hence the theoretical mass of ethanol = $(1.00\ \text{mol}) \times (46.0\ \text{g mol}^{-1}) = 46.0\ \text{g}$

$$\text{The percentage yield} = \frac{6.0\ \text{g}}{46.0\ \text{g}} \times 100 = 13\%$$

SUMMARY

Mass-to-mass calculations follow a set pathway:

- Use data about the mass to calculate the amount in moles of the substance whose mass is known.
- Use the balanced chemical equation to state the mole ratios of the substances in the question.
- Find the amount in moles of the substance whose mass is unknown.
- Use the amount in moles to find the unknown mass.

Chemical	Mass produced /megatonnes (10^{12} g)	Molar mass /g mol^{-1}
1 Sulphuric acid	43.3	98.1
2 Nitrogen	30.9	28.0
3 Oxygen	24.3	32.0
4 Ethene	21.3	28.1
5 Calcium oxide (lime)	18.7	56.1
6 Ammonia	16.1	17.0
7 Phosphoric acid	11.9	98.0
8 Sodium hydroxide	11.9	40.0
9 Propene	11.7	44.1
10 Chlorine	11.4	71.0

The top 10 chemicals produced in the USA in 1995.

How big is 14.2 megatonnes of sulphur? What size cube would it fill?

We know that

$$\text{density} = \frac{\text{mass}}{\text{volume}}$$

i.e.

$$\text{volume} = \frac{\text{mass}}{\text{density}}$$

The density of sulphur is 2.07 g cm^{-3}, which is equal to 2.07 tonnes m^{-3}. The mass of sulphur is 14.2×10^6 tonnes. The volume of this sulphur is

$$\text{volume} = \frac{14.2 \times 10^6\ \text{tonnes}}{2.07\ \text{tonnes m}^{-3}} = 6.86 \times 10^6\ \text{m}^3$$

This volume is equivalent to a cube of side 190 m. To put this value into perspective, the height of the Eiffel Tower in Paris is 300 m.

An industrial-scale pile of sulphur.

Finding empirical formulae

OBJECTIVES

- Empirical and molecular formulae
- Calculating empirical formulae from mass composition data

We can use calculations involving the masses of the elements that combine together to find the formulae of compounds. The specific version of the formula that can be found is the simplest whole-number ratio of the atoms present.

Empirical and molecular formulae

The **empirical formula** of a compound gives the simplest whole-number ratio of the atoms present. The **molecular formula** of a covalent compound that consists of small molecules gives the actual numbers of each of the atoms present in one molecule.

The molecular formula of a covalent compound that consists of small molecules is a whole-number multiple of the empirical formula. For example, the empirical formula of ethane is CH_3, as determined by various methods of analysis. Each molecule contains three times as many hydrogen atoms as there are carbon atoms. The relative formula mass corresponding to the empirical formula CH_3 is

$$12.0 + (3 \times 1.0) = 15.0$$

Experimental data show that the molar mass of ethane is $30.0\,g\,mol^{-1}$. The relative formula mass of ethane is therefore 30.0. This value, which corresponds to the molecular formula, is twice the value for the empirical formula. The molecular formula of ethane is therefore $(2 \times CH_3) = C_2H_6$. Each molecule of ethane contains two atoms of carbon and six atoms of hydrogen.

The formula of an ionic compound is an empirical formula. Ionic compounds do not exist as separate molecules but as giant lattices consisting of ions. The formula for common salt is NaCl. This empirical formula indicates that the ratio Na:Cl is 1:1. Empirical formulae may be calculated from data about the composition by mass.

Empirical formula calculations – the three steps

1 Find the amount in moles of each element present by dividing the mass of each element by its molar mass.

2 Find the ratio of the number of atoms of each element by dividing the amounts in moles by the smallest value found in step 1.

3 Convert these numbers into whole numbers, because atoms combine together in whole-number ratios.

The mineral calcite is a crystalline form of calcium carbonate $CaCO_3$. Calcite is birefringent, producing two refracted rays.

Worked example on the empirical formula of calcite

Data: The percentage by mass of the elements in calcite is 40.0% calcium, 12.0% carbon, and 48.0% oxygen.

Question: What is the empirical formula of calcite?

Strategy: Follow the three steps shown above.

Answer:

Step 1 Divide each mass by the molar mass of the element.

The data are given as percentages, and so this step will give the amount in moles of each element in 100 g of calcite. We get

$$\text{amount in moles of Ca} = \frac{40.0\,g}{40.1\,g\,mol^{-1}} = 0.998\,mol$$

$$\text{amount in moles of C} = \frac{12.0\,g}{12.0\,g\,mol^{-1}} = 1.00\,mol$$

$$\text{amount in moles of O} = \frac{48.0\,g}{16.0\,g\,mol^{-1}} = 3.00\,mol$$

Divide by the smallest value.

The smallest value in this case (0.998 mol) is very close to 1 mol, so we can move on to step 3.

Step 3   Convert to whole numbers.

We get

Ca:C:O = 1:1:3

The empirical formula of calcite is $CaCO_3$.

Worked example on the empirical formula of aspirin

Data: A sample of aspirin contains 6.00 g of carbon, 0.44 g of hydrogen, and 3.56 g of oxygen.

Question: What is the empirical formula of aspirin?

Strategy: We follow the same three steps as before.

Answer:

Step 1

We have

$$\text{amount in moles of C} = \frac{6.00\,\text{g}}{12.0\,\text{g mol}^{-1}} = 0.500\,\text{mol}$$

$$\text{amount in moles of H} = \frac{0.44\,\text{g}}{1.0\,\text{g mol}^{-1}} = 0.44\,\text{mol}$$

$$\text{amount in moles of O} = \frac{3.56\,\text{g}}{16.0\,\text{g mol}^{-1}} = 0.223\,\text{mol}$$

Step 2

The smallest value is the amount in moles of O (0.223 mol). So

$$\text{C} = \frac{0.500\,\text{mol}}{0.223\,\text{mol}} = 2.24$$

$$\text{H} = \frac{0.44\,\text{mol}}{0.223\,\text{mol}} = 2.0$$

$$\text{O} = \frac{0.223\,\text{mol}}{0.223\,\text{mol}} = 1.00$$

Step 3

The ratio C:H:O is 2.24:2.0:1.00. It is necessary to multiply by 4 to obtain numbers that are all near to whole numbers, i.e. 8.96:8.0:4.00. So C:H:O = 9:8:4.

The empirical formula of aspirin is $C_9H_8O_4$.

Crystals of aspirin $C_9H_8O_4$ viewed in polarized light. The aspirin molecule (below) consists of a six-membered ring of carbon atoms with two side-groups attached. The synthesis of this compound will be discussed later in the book.

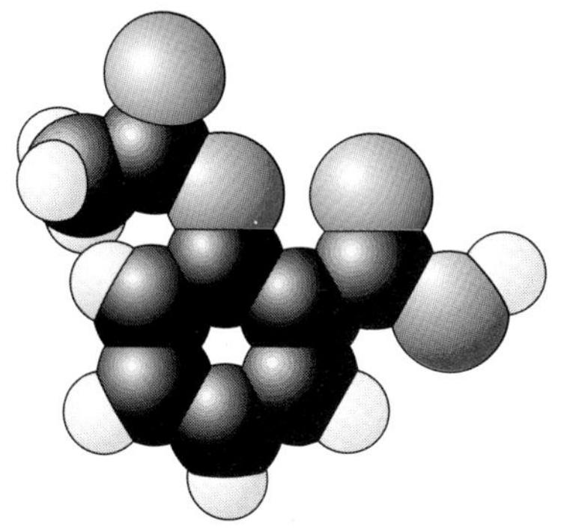

Aspirin

In the case of aspirin, the relative formula mass corresponding to the empirical formula $C_9H_8O_4$ is:

(9 × 12.0) + (8 × 1.0) + (4 × 16.0) = 180

Experimental data show that the relative formula mass of aspirin is 180. The molecular formula of aspirin is therefore the same as the empirical formula, i.e. $C_9H_8O_4$.

SUMMARY

- The empirical formula gives the simplest whole-number ratio of the atoms present in a compound.
- The molecular formula gives the actual numbers of each of the atoms present in one molecule of a covalent compound.
- Empirical formulae are found by calculating the mole ratio of the constituent elements from mass composition data.

PRACTICE

1 Calculate the empirical formula of the ore haematite. Its percentage composition is 70% iron and 30% oxygen.

2 Calculate the empirical formula of the ore iron pyrite (also known as 'fool's gold'). It was found that 1.00 g of the ore contains 0.47 g of iron and 0.53 g of sulphur.

Calculations invol...

OBJECTIVES

- Mass-to-volume calculations
- Volume-to-volume calculations

You should now be familiar with calculating the masses of substances involved in reactions, given a balanced chemical equation for the reaction and the mass of one of the reactants or products. Many reactions involve gases, as reactants and/or as products. For example, hydrogen gas is evolved when zinc granules react with dilute hydrochloric acid; and the gases hydrogen and oxygen react together to form water. The aim of this spread is to develop the concepts underlying mass-to-volume and volume-to-volume calculations, so enabling you to calculate the volumes of gases involved in chemical reactions.

Mass-to-volume calculations – overall strategy

In the reaction between zinc and excess hydrochloric acid, the volume of hydrogen evolved depends on the mass of zinc that has reacted. A typical question might ask you to calculate the volume of hydrogen evolved when, for example, 5.00 g of zinc reacts with excess hydrochloric acid. The strategy for this type of calculation follows a set path, with the following steps:

1 Use data about the mass of the solid to calculate the amount in moles of solid.

2 Use the balanced chemical equation to state the mole ratio of the gas to the solid.

3 Calculate the amount in moles of the gas.

4 Use the ideal gas equation $pV = nRT$ to calculate the volume of the gas at the stated conditions of temperature and pressure.

A mass-to-volume calculation therefore follows the path:

Mass of solid → Moles of solid $\xrightarrow{\text{Mole ratio gas:solid}}$ Moles of gas $\xrightarrow{\text{ideal gas equation}}$ Volume of gas

You will be asked to carry out a calculation for the reaction between zinc and hydrochloric acid in the practice questions at the end of the spread. The following worked example concentrates on a more practical use of a mass-to-volume reaction.

Excess reactant and limiting reactant

The phrase 'excess hydrochloric acid' implies that there is more than enough acid present to react with all the zinc added to it. When the reaction is complete, all the zinc has reacted, and some acid remains unused.

The substance that is completely used up is called the **limiting reactant**; it limits the yield of product. In the example to the right, the zinc metal is the limiting reactant and the acid is the reactant present in excess.

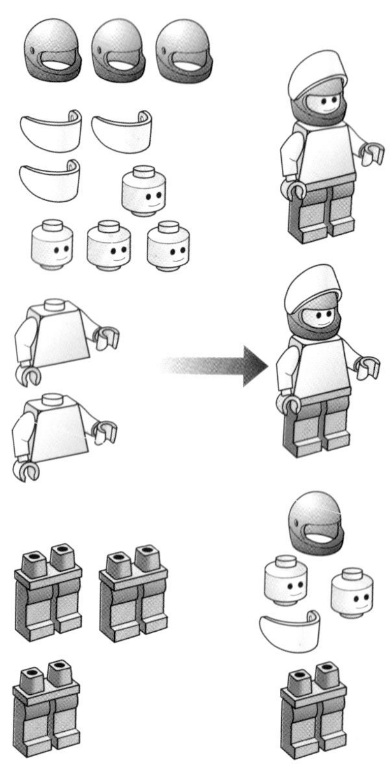

Only two figures can be made, because there are only two bodies. Bodies are limiting; the other components are present in excess.

The chemistry of an airbag

Airbags are fitted to many cars as safety equipment. An airbag has a sensor that can detect a severe front-end or rear-end collision. The airbag inflates about 20 milliseconds after the collision has been detected. Once fully inflated, it is designed to collapse gradually.

The most important chemical in most airbags is sodium azide NaN_3. When an impact has been detected, the NaN_3 is electrically ignited. It then decomposes very rapidly to produce sodium metal and nitrogen gas. It is the nitrogen gas that inflates the airbag. The equation for the decomposition is:

$$2NaN_3(s) \rightarrow 2Na(s) + 3N_2(g)$$

Worked example on an airbag

Data: An airbag contains 75 g of solid sodium azide. Assume that the temperature is 20 °C and the pressure is 1.00 bar.

Question: What is the volume of nitrogen gas produced?

Strategy: Follow the four steps shown above.

Answer:

Step 1 Calculate the amount in moles of solid.

The molar mass of NaN_3 is

$23.0\ \text{g mol}^{-1} + 3 \times (14.0\ \text{g mol}^{-1}) = 65.0\ \text{g mol}^{-1}$

$$\text{amount in moles of NaN}_3 = \frac{75.0\,\text{g}}{65.0\,\text{g mol}^{-1}} = 1.15\,\text{mol}$$

Step 2 State the mole ratio gas:solid.

The mole ratio N_2:NaN_3 = 3:2.

Step 3 Calculate the amount in moles of gas.

Therefore,

amount in moles of N_2 produced = $(\frac{3}{2}) \times 1.15\,\text{mol} = 1.73\,\text{mol}$

Step 4 Use the ideal gas equation to calculate the volume of gas.

The volume at 20 °C and 1.00 bar is obtained from the ideal gas equation $pV = nRT$. After dividing both sides by p, it can be written as

$$V = \frac{nRT}{p}$$

so for the airbag

$$V = \frac{(1.73\,\text{mol}) \times (8.31\,\text{Pa m}^3\,\text{K}^{-1}\,\text{mol}^{-1}) \times (293\,\text{K})}{(1.00 \times 10^5\,\text{Pa})}$$

$$= 0.042\,\text{m}^3 = 42\,\text{dm}^3 \text{ (2 sig. figs)}$$

The decomposition can therefore provide 42 litres of gas very quickly indeed. Manufacturers determine the optimum volume of gas required in the inflated airbag and then vary the mass of sodium azide accordingly.

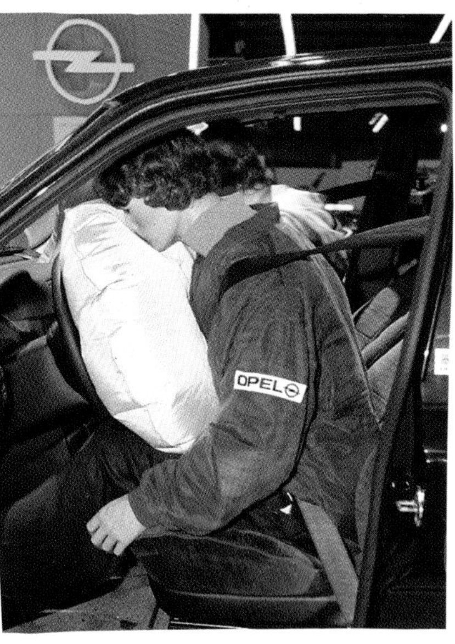

Sensors detect that a crash is happening and the airbag inflates within about 20 milliseconds. A canister of compressed gas would not operate with sufficient speed. The gas in the bag must be non-toxic and not flammable in case of leaks, so nitrogen is an ideal choice.

Volume-to-volume calculations

This type of calculation is extremely simple and straightforward, and may be carried out in a matter of seconds. For example, hydrogen and oxygen react to form water.

$$2H_2(g) + O_2(g) \rightarrow 2H_2O(l)$$

Avogadro's principle states that:

- Equal volumes of different gases contain the same number of molecules, under the same conditions of temperature and pressure.

A consequence of Avogadro's principle is that one mole of *any gas* has the same volume under stated conditions of temperature and pressure.

The balanced equation for the reaction between hydrogen and oxygen indicates that 2 mol of hydrogen reacts with 1 mol of oxygen. Thus, whatever the volume of hydrogen, half that volume of oxygen will be required for reaction, i.e. 50.0 cm^3 of hydrogen require 25.0 cm^3 of oxygen.

- The volumes of gases that react (and the volumes of the products if gaseous) are proportional to their mole ratio.

This is sometimes called **Gay-Lussac's law**, after Joseph Gay-Lussac.

Molar volume of a gas

In the calculations to the left, the ideal gas equation is used to convert the amount in moles of a gas to the volume of the gas. This equation includes the variables p and T and thus enables calculation of the volume under *any* conditions of temperature and pressure. However, a simpler expression may be used to convert the amount in moles of gas to gas volume:

$$\text{amount in moles} = \frac{\text{volume}}{\text{molar volume}}$$

This uses the molar volume of the gas. At 20 °C and 1 bar, you should remember, spread 8.3, that 1 mol of any gas occupies 24 dm^3, i.e.

molar volume of any gas is 24 $dm^3\,mol^{-1}$ (at 20 °C, 1 bar)

and this value can be used in the above expression under these conditions.

SUMMARY

- Mass-to-volume calculations follow the path: Mass of solid → Moles of solid $\xrightarrow{\text{Mole ratio gas:solid}}$ Moles of gas $\xrightarrow{\text{ideal gas equation}}$ Volume of gas.
- The limiting reactant is the substance that is completely consumed in the course of a reaction; its amount limits the amounts of products that may form.

PRACTICE

1 Zinc reacts with hydrochloric acid to produce hydrogen gas. Calculate:

a The volume of hydrogen produced at 293 K and 1.00 bar when 5.00 g of zinc reacts with excess dilute hydrochloric acid.

b The mass of zinc required to produce 1000 cm^3 of hydrogen at 293 K and 1.00 bar (excess acid present).

2 Calculate the volume of sulphur dioxide produced at 293 K and 1.00 bar when 5.00 g of sulphur burn in oxygen.

9.5 SOLUTION CONCE[NTRATION]

OBJECTIVES

- Solutes, solvents, and solutions
- Definition of molar concentration
- Calculating molar concentration
- Calculating amount in moles from molar concentration

Warning

Do *not* use the words 'strong' or 'weak' to refer to solutions of high or low concentration. These technical terms are used to describe acids and bases (see chapter 12).

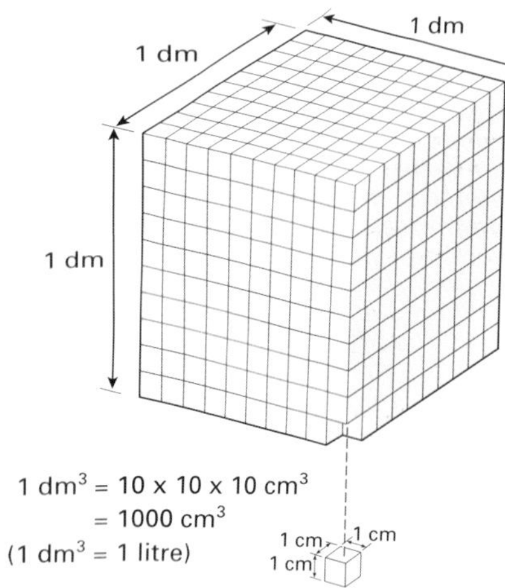

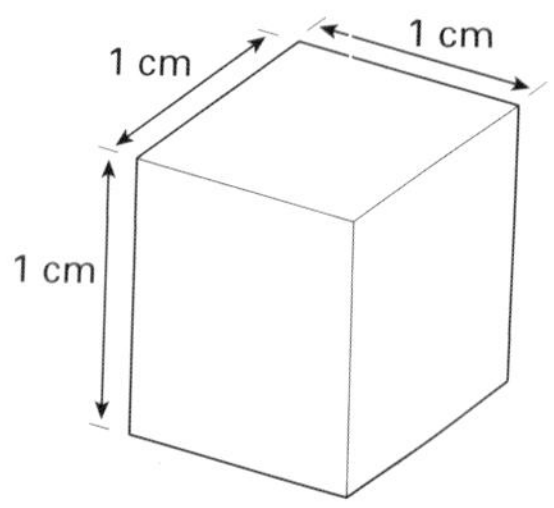

Volume interconversions. The SI unit of volume is the cubic metre (m^3), spread 8.2. Of more practical use for laboratory solutions are the cubic decimetre (dm^3) and the cubic centimetre (cm^3).

A **solution** consists of a substance dissolved in a solvent. The dissolved substance is called the **solute** and may be a solid, a liquid, or a gas. The **solvent** is almost always a liquid, although solid solutions can occur (e.g. some metal alloys). The **concentration** of a solution measures how much of a dissolved substance is present per unit volume of a solution. A solution is described as 'concentrated' if it consists of a large quantity of solute in a small quantity of solvent. A small quantity of solute in a large quantity of solvent results in a 'dilute' solution.

Solution concentration

The common unit of volume for solutions is the cubic decimetre (dm^3), also known as the litre (L or l): 1 cubic decimetre (1 dm^3) is equivalent to 1000 cubic centimetres (1000 cm^3); 1 cm^3 is also known as 1 ml (millilitre). The concentration of a solution is usually defined as the quantity of solute per unit volume of the solution.

The **mass concentration** of a solution may be written, for example, as mass per cubic decimetre; for example, the concentrations of the ions present in bottled spring water are usually stated in milligrams per cubic decimetre ($mg\,dm^{-3}$).

Molar concentration

Chemists usually express the concentration of a solution in terms of its molar concentration (a traditional name for this was molarity). By definition, the **molar concentration** (c) of a solution is equal to the amount in moles of a solute (n) divided by the volume (V) of the solution, i.e.

$$\text{molar concentration} = \frac{\text{amount in moles of solute}}{\text{volume of solution}}$$

or

$$c = \frac{n}{V}$$

Multiplying both sides of this equation by V makes the amount in moles of solute the subject of the expression, i.e.

amount in moles of solute = volume of solution × molar concentration

or

$$n = Vc$$

The units of molar concentration are moles per cubic decimetre ($mol\,dm^{-3}$).

Often a 0.1 $mol\,dm^{-3}$ solution is referred to as a 0.1 M solution.

Worked example 1

Question: The concentration of calcium ions in a sample of spring water is 100 $mg\,dm^{-3}$. Calculate the molar concentration of the calcium ions in $mol\,dm^{-3}$.

Answer: 1 dm^3 of water contains 100 mg of $Ca^{2+}(aq)$ ions. Dividing this mass by the molar mass of calcium (40.1 $g\,mol^{-1}$) gives the amount in moles of $Ca^{2+}(aq)$ ions, i.e.

$$\text{amount in moles of } Ca^{2+}(aq) = \frac{(100 \times 10^{-3}\,g)}{(40.1\,g\,mol^{-1})} = 2.5 \times 10^{-3}\,mol$$

This amount of calcium ions is present per dm^3 of solution. Therefore, the molar concentration of calcium ions is $2.5 \times 10^{-3}\,mol\,dm^{-3}$.

Worked example 2

Question: 250 cm^3 of a solution contains 5.85 g of sodium chloride. Calculate the molar concentration of sodium chloride in mol dm^{-3}.

Answer: We have

$$\text{amount in moles of NaCl} = \frac{\text{mass of NaCl}}{\text{molar mass of NaCl}} = \frac{5.85\ \text{g}}{58.5\ \text{g mol}^{-1}} = 0.100\ \text{mol}$$

Also

$$\text{molar concentration} = \frac{\text{amount in moles of solute}}{\text{volume of solution}} \qquad c = \frac{n}{V}$$

First convert the volume in cm^3 to a volume in dm^3 by dividing by 1000:

$$250\ \text{cm}^3 = \frac{250}{1000}\text{dm}^3 = 0.250\ \text{dm}^3$$

Therefore:

$$\text{molar concentration} = \frac{0.100\ \text{mol}}{0.250\ \text{dm}^3} = 0.400\ \text{mol dm}^{-3}$$

The molar concentration of the solution is 0.400 mol dm^{-3}.

*The **volume concentration** of a solution is usually stated as a percentage. This wine is labelled '13% vol.', which means that it contains 13 cm^3 of alcohol in 100 cm^3 of wine. Health workers call 10 cm^3 of alcohol '1 unit', so a 0.75 litre bottle of wine contains nearly 10 units of alcohol, sufficient in the UK to put you more than twice over the drink–drive limit.*

Worked example 3

Question: What volume of hydrogen gas (at 20 °C and 1 bar) can be produced from 250 cm^3 of 2.0 mol dm^{-3} hydrochloric acid and excess zinc?

Answer: We have

amount in moles of HCl = volume of HCl × molar concentration of HCl

First convert the volume in cm^3 to a volume in dm^3 by dividing by 1000:

$$250\ \text{cm}^3 = \frac{250}{1000}\ \text{dm}^3$$

So the amount in moles of HCl is

$$n(\text{HCl}) = V(\text{HCl}) \times c(\text{HCl}) = \left(\frac{250}{1000}\ \text{dm}^3\right) \times (2.0\ \text{mol dm}^{-3}) = 0.50\ \text{mol}$$

The chemical equation is:

$$\text{Zn(s)} + 2\text{HCl(aq)} \rightarrow \text{ZnCl}_2\text{(aq)} + \text{H}_2\text{(g)}$$

The mole ratio H_2:HCl is 1:2. So the amount in moles of H_2 produced is

$$n(\text{H}_2) = \tfrac{1}{2} \times n(\text{HCl}) = \tfrac{1}{2} \times 0.50\ \text{mol} = 0.25\ \text{mol}$$

The molar volume at 20 °C and 1 bar is 24 $dm^3\,mol^{-1}$. The volume of the 0.25 mol of hydrogen gas produced is therefore

$$(0.25\ \text{mol}) \times (24\ \text{dm}^3\text{mol}^{-1}) = 6.0\ \text{dm}^3\ \text{(2 sig. figs)}$$

Note: In the example in the previous spread, the volume of hydrogen produced was limited by the mass of zinc, because the *acid* was present in excess. Here, the *zinc* is in excess, and so the acid limits the volume of hydrogen.

Laboratory solutions

Laboratories are usually equipped with a selection of reagent bottles containing solutions of acids, alkalis, and other substances. Knowing the molar concentration of a reagent in solution allows you to calculate the amount of product to be expected from a reaction.

Zinc reacts with hydrochloric acid to produce hydrogen gas and aqueous zinc chloride. When excess zinc is present, the limiting reactant is the acid.

SUMMARY

- $\text{Molar concentration} = \dfrac{\text{amount in moles of solute}}{\text{volume of solution}}$

PRACTICE

1 Calculate the amount in moles of solute in 35.0 cm^3 of a solution that has a concentration of 0.100 mol dm^{-3}.

2 Calculate the volume of a solution that has a concentration of 0.25 mol dm^{-3} and contains 0.125 mol of solute.

9.6

OBJECTIVES

- Standard solutions
- Titration: burette, pipette, indicators

USING TITRATION TO MEASU[illegible] CONCENTRATION

Suppose you are in charge of the quality control department in a vinegar factory. How can you be sure that each batch of vinegar contains the right concentration of acid? The answer is to carry out a **titration**: add vinegar to a known volume of alkali, of known molar concentration, until the solution just becomes acidic. You know the molar concentration and volume of the alkali. You also know the volume of vinegar used. You can perform a calculation involving mole ratio, molar concentration, and volume to find the concentration of the acid in the vinegar. This spread gives details about the titration technique; the following spread discusses the necessary calculations.

Standard solutions

One of the solutions used in a titration must be a **standard solution**, a solution whose concentration is accurately known. A standard solution is made by adding a known mass of solute to the solvent and making up the solution to a known volume. The accuracy of a standard solution in the school laboratory depends partly on the accuracy with which the substances are weighed out or measured, and partly on the purity of the solute used. Chemical manufacturers supply many reagents of especially high purity for use in industry and in the laboratory.

Solid sodium hydroxide reacts with atmospheric carbon dioxide:

$$2NaOH(s) + CO_2(g) \rightarrow Na_2CO_3(s) + H_2O(l)$$

So, an accurate concentration cannot be given for aqueous sodium hydroxide made from an *ancient* sample of solid that may be only 95% pure. On the other hand, reagents such as solid sodium carbonate and ethanedioic acid $(COOH)_2$ are available to at least 99.9% purity. These reagents are used to make **primary standard solutions** whose concentrations may confidently be stated to high precision.

Making a standard solution

Suppose that you want to make a standard solution of sodium chloride. What mass of sodium chloride must you dissolve in 250 cm^3 of solution to obtain a concentration of 0.250 mol dm^{-3}?

We know that

amount in moles of solute = volume of solution × molar concentration

Therefore,

$$n(\text{NaCl}) = \left(\frac{250}{1000}\,\text{dm}^3\right) \times (0.250\,\text{mol dm}^{-3})$$
$$= 6.25 \times 10^{-2}\,\text{mol}$$

The molar mass of NaCl is $(23.0 + 35.5)\,\text{g mol}^{-1} = 58.5\,\text{g mol}^{-1}$. We also know that

mass = amount in moles × molar mass

Therefore,

$m(\text{NaCl}) = (6.25 \times 10^{-2}\,\text{mol}) \times (58.5\,\text{g mol}^{-1}) = 3.66\,\text{g}$

So you would need to dissolve 3.66 g of sodium chloride.

Performing a titration

A titration can determine the volume of one solution required to react exactly with a known volume of another solution. Titrations frequently involve the reaction of acids with bases. Titrations can also involve reactions other than acid–base reactions, such as redox reactions and reactions involving precipitations.

Whatever the type of reaction, all titrations follow the same overall method and involve the same major components, namely:

- A **burette** containing a solution of one of the reagents.
- A **flask** containing an accurately known volume of the other reagent solution, added using a **pipette**.
- An **indicator** (added to the contents of the flask) that gives a visual indication of when the reaction is complete.

One of the two solutions must be a standard solution and the other is of unknown concentration. The burette is used to add a measured volume of one reagent solution to the other reagent solution in the flask.

There are three main stages to any titration. For a titration in which reagent A runs from the burette into reagent B in the flask:

1 *Initial stage:* A and B react together. A is consumed and B remains in excess.

2 *Equivalence point:* Sufficient A has been added to B to consume all of B initially placed in the flask. The flask contains the products of the reaction only.

3 *Final stage:* Adding more A to the flask does not result in further reaction because B has already been completely consumed. A is now in excess in the flask.

(a)

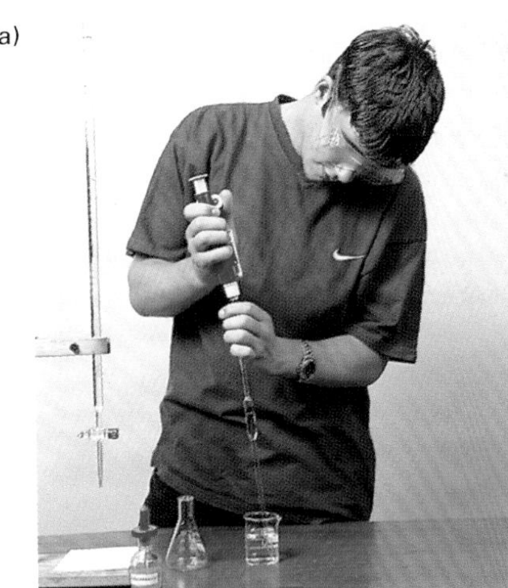

(b)

A titration involving dilute hydrochloric acid in the burette and aqueous sodium hydroxide in the flask. (a) Phenolphthalein indicator is then added to the aqueous sodium hydroxide, which turns pink (b). Hydrochloric acid is gradually added to the flask. Near the equivalence point, a small amount of base remains in the flask; the flask must be swirled after the addition of each drop of acid to ensure complete reaction. At the equivalence point, the addition of one more drop *of acid will neutralize all remaining base: acid is now in excess and the indicator becomes colourless.*

End point

The change in colour of the indicator marks the **end point** of the titration. The **equivalence point** marks the stage at which the reaction is complete: neither reagent is in excess. Within the volume of one drop of reagent added from the burette, the end point is usually the same as the equivalence point, if the indicator is chosen carefully.

For almost all titrations, an indicator is added that has one colour when one of the two reagents is in excess and another colour when the second reagent is in excess.

Indicators

The indicators chosen for acid–base titrations are usually different types of water-soluble dyes. The particular indicator chosen depends on the acid and base used in the titration. Examples of common acid–base indicators are given below, together with their colours in acidic and in basic solutions. The choice of indicators is discussed in spread 12.9.

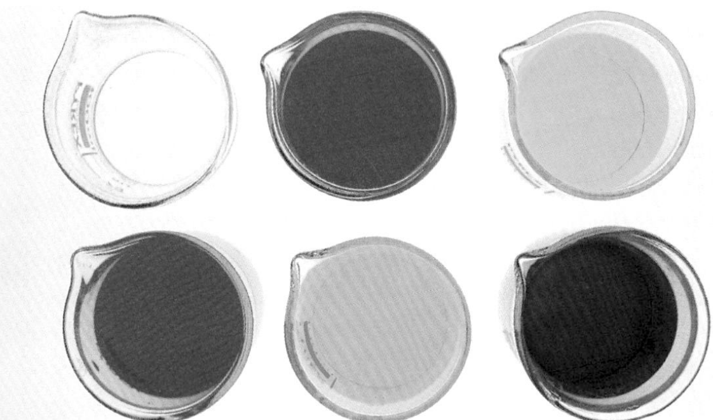

Common indicators and their colours in acidic (top) and in basic (bottom) solutions: (a) phenolphthalein, (b) methyl orange, and (c) bromothymol blue.

SUMMARY

- A titration can determine the volume of one solution required to react exactly with a known volume of another solution.
- The equivalence point occurs when neither reagent is in excess.
- An indicator is chosen that will change colour very close to the equivalence point of the reaction.

PRACTICE

1 Calculate the mass of sodium chloride that must be dissolved in 100 cm^3 of solution to give a molar concentration of 0.500 mol dm^{-3}.

2 Calculate the concentration of a standard solution that contains 1.70 g of silver nitrate dissolved in 250 cm^3 of solution.

9.7 ACID–BASE TITRATION CALCULATIONS

OBJECTIVES

- Calculating molar concentrations
- Industrial applications

Suppose you need to determine the concentration of a solution of a base, for example, aqueous sodium hydroxide. You have carried out a titration between this solution and a standard solution of an acid, for example hydrochloric acid. Taking the average of a number of separate titrations, you are able to make a statement that summarizes your results. A typical statement of results might be:

25.0 cm^3 of aqueous sodium hydroxide (molar concentration unknown) reacts exactly with 35.0 cm^3 of hydrochloric acid (molar concentration 0.250 mol dm^{-3}).

This spread starts by showing you how to calculate the molar concentration of the aqueous sodium hydroxide, and goes on to discuss other related types of calculation.

Burette reading

A burette can be read to the nearest 0.05 cm^3, which corresponds to half-way between the markings.

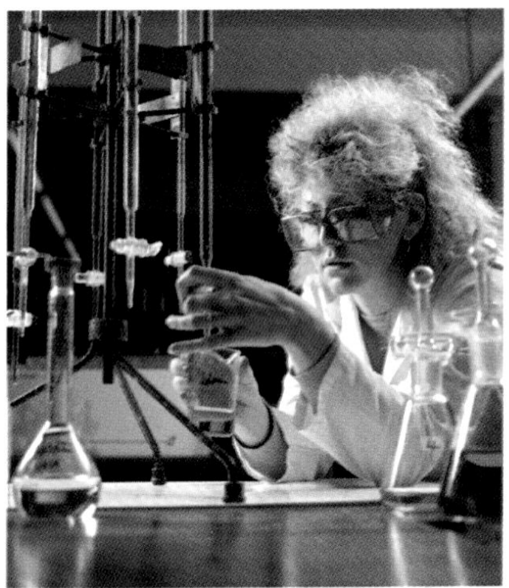

The quality control laboratory at British Steel.

Calculating the molar concentration

As in all mole calculations, this calculation starts by determining the amount in moles of the solution for which you know the molar concentration and have measured the volume used (in this case, the hydrochloric acid). The balanced chemical equation leads to the mole ratio between the acid and the base, which in turn leads to the amount in moles of the base (here, aqueous sodium hydroxide). Finally, the molar concentration of the base is calculated from the known volume and the amount in moles.

From the earlier spreads in this chapter we know that

$$\text{amount in moles} = \text{volume of solution} \times \text{molar concentration}$$

Therefore, for the acid

$$n(\text{HCl}) = \left(\frac{35.0}{1000}\,\text{dm}^3\right) \times (0.250\,\text{mol dm}^{-3}) \quad = 8.75 \times 10^{-3}\,\text{mol}$$

The balanced chemical equation is

$$\text{HCl(aq)} + \text{NaOH(aq)} \rightarrow \text{NaCl(aq)} + \text{H}_2\text{O(l)}$$

Therefore the mole ratio NaOH:HCl = 1:1. The amount in moles of NaOH present is 8.75×10^{-3} mol.

Now we use the equation

$$\text{molar concentration} = \frac{\text{amount in moles}}{\text{volume of solution}}$$

but this time for the base. First convert the volume of aqueous NaOH used to dm^3:

$$25.0\,\text{cm}^3 = \frac{25.0}{1000}\,\text{dm}^3 = 25.0 \times 10^{-3}\,\text{dm}^3$$

$$\text{Therefore, molar concentration of NaOH} = \frac{8.75 \times 10^{-3}\,\text{mol}}{25.0 \times 10^{-3}\,\text{dm}^3}$$

$$= 0.350\,\text{mol dm}^{-3}$$

Back titration

To find the molar concentration of ammonium ions, add a known excess of aqueous sodium hydroxide, then titrate the excess with standard hydrochloric acid, as shown alongside.

Worked example from industry

We now return to our vinegar factory, and consider the type of calculation that would be involved in the quality control laboratory.

Data: Vinegar must contain between 4% and 6% by mass of ethanoic acid (CH_3COOH) in water, i.e. the mass concentration of ethanoic acid is between 40 and 60 g dm^{-3}. Malt vinegar is made by extracting malt from barley and fermenting it with the aid of yeast. The result is a dilute solution of ethanol (an alcohol), which is then oxidized by atmospheric oxygen to give ethanoic acid. Batches of vinegar may be analysed by titration to ensure that the concentration of ethanoic acid falls within the prescribed limits. For example, suppose that 34.2 cm^3 of a sample of vinegar neutralized 25.0 cm^3 of aqueous sodium hydroxide (molar concentration = 0.500 mol dm^{-3}).

Questions: The relevant questions the quality controller asks are:

- What is the molar concentration of the vinegar in $mol\,dm^{-3}$?
- What is the mass concentration of the vinegar in $g\,dm^{-3}$?
- Is the batch from which the sample came fit for sale?

Answer: The calculation is similar to the one carried out above. We start with the equation

amount in moles = volume of solution × molar concentration

$$n(\text{NaOH}) = \left(\frac{25.0}{1000}\text{dm}^3\right) \times (0.500\,\text{mol dm}^{-3}) \quad = 1.25 \times 10^{-2}\,\text{mol}$$

The equation for the reaction is:

$CH_3COOH(aq) + NaOH(aq) \rightarrow Na^+CH_3CO_2^-(aq) + H_2O(l)$

Therefore, the mole ratio $CH_3COOH{:}NaOH = 1{:}1$. The amount in moles of CH_3COOH present is 1.25×10^{-2} mol.

The volume of aqueous CH_3COOH used is

$$34.2\,\text{cm}^3 = \left(\frac{34.2}{1000}\text{dm}^3\right) = 34.2 \times 10^{-3}\,\text{dm}^3$$

Now we can use

$$\text{molar concentration} = \frac{\text{amount in moles}}{\text{volume of solution}}$$

$$\text{molar concentration of CH}_3\text{COOH} = \frac{1.25 \times 10^{-2}\,\text{mol}}{34.2 \times 10^{-3}\,\text{dm}^3} = 0.365\,\text{mol dm}^{-3}$$

Finally we use

mass concentration = molar concentration × molar mass

The molar mass of CH_3COOH is

$2 \times (12.0\,g\,mol^{-1}) + 4 \times (1.0\,g\,mol^{-1}) + 2 \times (16.0\,g\,mol^{-1}) = 60.0\,g\,mol^{-1}$

mass concentration of $CH_3COOH = (0.365\,mol\,dm^{-3}) \times (60.0\,g\,mol^{-1})$

$= 22\,g\,dm^{-3}$ (2 sig. figs)

This concentration falls outside the limits of 40 to 60 $g\,dm^{-3}$, so the batch is *not* fit for sale, being too dilute.

Another industrial application

Large nickel–cadmium batteries are used for stand-by lighting systems in trains. The cells in these batteries contain an electrolyte consisting of aqueous potassium hydroxide. The problem is that the electrolyte slowly absorbs carbon dioxide from the atmosphere, decreasing the concentration of the potassium hydroxide and forming potassium carbonate in the solution:

$2KOH(aq) + CO_2(g) \rightarrow K_2CO_3(aq) + H_2O(l)$

The electrical resistance of the cell increases, with the result that performance is reduced. Cells can be returned to full efficiency by renewing the electrolyte. Manufacturers of these nickel–cadmium cells suggest that the electrolyte is replaced when the mass concentration of potassium carbonate reaches 75 $g\,dm^{-3}$. They suggest that chemical analysis of the electrolyte is carried out every two to three years, more frequently when batteries are operated close to vehicle exhausts or at high temperatures. The analysis involves titrating a sample of the electrolyte against boric acid (in the burette). Phenolphthalein indicator shows an end point when all the potassium hydroxide in the sample has been neutralized. Methyl orange indicator is then added, which shows an end point when all the potassium carbonate has been neutralized. The *difference* between the two burette readings for the two end points is then read off against a chart that shows potassium carbonate mass concentration.

SUMMARY

Calculation route for determining concentration:

- Calculate the amount in moles of the solution for which the volume and molar concentration data are available.
- Find the mole ratio from the balanced chemical equation.
- Use the mole ratio to determine the amount in moles of the second solution used in the titration.
- Calculate the molar concentration of the second solution from its volume and the amount in moles.

Delocalization

See spread 6.4 for the reason why the formula of sodium ethanoate is written as

$Na^+CH_3CO_2^-$.

PRACTICE

1 As a result of a series of titrations, it was found that 10.2 cm^3 of 0.100 $mol\,dm^{-3}$ sulphuric acid exactly neutralized 25.0 cm^3 of aqueous potassium hydroxide. Calculate the concentration of the aqueous potassium hydroxide in

a $mol\,dm^{-3}$ **b** $g\,dm^{-3}$.

2 Why do the nickel–cadmium cells mentioned in the box above deteriorate more rapidly when they are installed close to vehicle exhausts?

3 Imagine that you are the quality controller of our vinegar factory. To make as much profit as possible, you have to make the vinegar as weak as allowed. You carry out a titration using a vinegar sample with the minimum allowed concentration of ethanoic acid. What titration result would you expect for the volume of vinegar required to neutralize 25.0 cm^3 of the same aqueous sodium hydroxide?

PRACTICE EXAM QUESTIONS

1 50 kg of pure sulphuric acid were accidentally released into a lake when a storage vessel leaked. Two methods were proposed to neutralize it.

a The first proposal was to add a solution of 5 M (where M mol dm^{-3}) NaOH to the lake. Sodium hydroxide reacts with sulphuric acid as follows.

$2NaOH(aq) + H_2SO_4(aq) \rightarrow Na_2SO_4(aq) + 2H_2O(l)$

Calculate the volume of 5 M NaOH required to neutralise the sulphuric acid by answering the following questions.

i How many moles of sulphuric acid are there in 50 kg of the acid?

ii How many moles of sodium hydroxide are required to neutralize this acid?

iii Calculate the volume, in dm^3, of 5 M NaOH which contains this number of moles. [4]

b The second proposal was to add powdered calcium carbonate which reacts as follows.

$CaCO_3(s) + H_2SO_4(aq) \rightarrow CaSO_4(s) + H_2O(l) + CO_2(g)$

Calculate the mass of calcium carbonate required to neutralize 50 kg of sulphuric acid. [3]

c Suggest **two** reasons why the addition of calcium carbonate to neutralize the acid is the preferred method in practice. [2]
AQA (NEAB) 1995

2 **a** Sulphamic acid reacts with sodium hydroxide according to the following equation.

$NH_2SO_3H + NaOH \rightarrow NH_2SO_3Na + H_2O$

A standard solution of sulphamic acid was made by dissolving 5.210 g of the acid in water and making the volume up to exactly 250 cm^3 with more water.

i Calculate the number of moles of acid used and the molarity of the acid solution.

ii In a titration, 22.6 cm^3 of this acid solution were required to neutralize 25.0 cm^3 of sodium hydroxide solution. Calculate the molarity of the sodium hydroxide solution. [5]

b In a separate experiment sodium hydroxide was used to prepare a sample of Glauber's salt $Na_2SO_4.10H_2O$, by neutralisation with sulphuric acid followed by recrystallisation from aqueous solution.

$H_2SO_4 + 2NaOH \rightarrow Na_2SO_4 + 2H_2O$

Calculate the maximum mass of Glauber's salt which could be made from 5.0 g of sodium hydroxide. [4]
AQA (NEAB) 1995

3 A tank contained 4 m^3 of waste hydrochloric acid. It was decided to neutralize the acid by adding slaked lime, $Ca(OH)_2$.

a The concentration of the acid was first determined by titration of a 25.0 cm^3 sample against 0.121 M sodium hydroxide of which 32.4 cm^3 were required.

i Calculate the molarity of the hydrochloric acid in the sample.

ii Calculate the total number of moles of HCl in the tank. [4]

b Calculate the mass, in kg, of slaked lime required to neutralize the acid. Slaked lime reacts with hydrochloric acid according to the equation shown below.

$Ca(OH)_2 + 2HCl \rightarrow CaCl_2 + 2H_2O$ [3]

c The slaked lime was manufactured by roasting limestone and then adding water.

$CaCO_3 \rightarrow CaO + CO_2$

$CaO + H_2O \rightarrow Ca(OH)_2$

Calculate the mass of limestone which is required to produce 1 kg of slaked lime. [2]
AQA (NEAB) 1996

4 Elemental analysis of a salt **X** gave the following percentages by mass, the remainder being oxygen:

Silver: 71.05% Carbon: 7.89%

a Determine the empirical formula of the salt. [3]

b The relative molecular mass of **X** is 304. Use this to determine the molecular formula of **X**. [1]

c When heated, 5.00 g of **X** were decomposed completely to give a solid residue and 8.14×10^{-4} m^3 of carbon dioxide gas at 298 K and 100 kPa.

i Calculate the number of moles of **X** decomposed.

ii Use the volume of carbon dioxide gas to calculate the number of moles of carbon dioxide produced.

iii Using your answers to part **b** and parts **c i** and **ii**, identify the solid residue and write an equation for the thermal decomposition of **X**. [6]
AQA (NEAB) 1997

5 **a** An aqueous solution of hydrogen peroxide, H_2O_2, decomposes in the presence of a catalyst according to the equation:

$2H_2O_2(aq) \rightarrow 2H_2O(l) + O_2(g)$

i Calculate the number of moles of H_2O_2 required to produce 10 dm^3 of oxygen gas measured at room temperature and pressure.

[1 mole of any gas occupies a volume of 24 dm^3 at room temperature and pressure.] [2]

ii The number of moles calculated in **a i** is present in 1 dm^3 of H_2O_2 solution.

Calculate the volume of this solution required to make 250 cm^3 of a 0.100 mol dm^{-3} solution, by dilution with water. [2]

b Calculate the mass of potassium manganate(VII), $KMnO_4$, (M_r = 158) required to make 200 cm^3 of a solution having a concentration of 0.020 mol dm^{-3}. [2]

c When 20.0 cm^3 of the 0.100 mol dm^{-3} solution of H_2O_2 was acidified with dilute sulphuric acid and titrated against a 0.020 mol dm^{-3} solution of potassium manganate(VII), $KMnO_4$, 40.0 cm^3 of the latter were required for complete reaction.

[No experience of the reaction in the laboratory is needed to answer this question.]

i Calculate the number of moles of $KMnO_4$ in 40.0 cm^3 of 0.020 mol dm^{-3} solution. [1]

ii Calculate the number of moles of H_2O_2 in 20.0 cm^3 of 0.100 mol dm^{-3} solution. [1]

iii Hence deduce the number of moles of H_2O_2 which react with 1 mole of $KMnO_4$. [1]

iv Use the result from **c iii** to balance the following equation for the reaction taking place in the titration.

... $KMnO_4$ + ... H_2O_2 + ... H_2SO_4 →
... $MnSO_4$ + ... K_2SO_4 + ... H_2O + ... O_2 [2]

d The solution at the end of this reaction contains potassium sulphate and manganese(II) sulphate only.

i Write formulae for the cations present in this aqueous solution. [2]

ii Treatment of this solution with dilute sodium hydroxide gives a precipitate which does not dissolve in excess sodium hydroxide solution. Identify the precipitate by name or formula. [1]

e In addition to the normal oxide, sodium forms a peroxide, Na_2O_2. This reacts with carbon dioxide to form sodium carbonate and oxygen:

$$2Na_2O_2 + 2CO_2 \rightarrow 2Na_2CO_3 + O_2$$

i Calculate the volume of oxygen gas that would be formed by the reaction of 0.39 g of sodium peroxide with excess carbon dioxide.

[The molar volume of a gas at the temperature and pressure of the reaction should be taken as 24 dm^3 mol^{-1}.] [3]

ii How many molecules of oxygen would be present in this volume of oxygen?

[The Avogadro constant, *L*, is 6.02×10^{23} mol^{-1}.] [1]

iii Use oxidation numbers to identify the type of process that occurs in the formation of oxygen from the peroxide ion. [2]
EDEXCEL 1998 *(See also Chapter 13.)*

6 A solution of a weak acid H_2X was made by dissolving 2.25 g of solid H_2X in water to give 500 cm^3 of solution. On titration, 25.0 cm^3 of this solution was completely neutralized by 25.0 cm^3 of sodium hydroxide solution containing 0.100 mol dm^{-3}.

a Write an equation for the reaction. [1]

b i Calculate the number of moles of NaOH in 25.0 cm^3 of 0.100 mol dm^{-3} solution.

ii How many moles of H_2X would be required to react with this quantity of NaOH?

iii Calculate the relative molecular mass of H_2X.

iv A hydrated form of the acid also exists, $H_2X.yH_2O$. A solution containing 6.30 g dm^{-3} of the hydrated acid has the same (molar) concentration as the solution of the anhydrous acid, H_2X, originally used. Using this information and your answer from **b**, calculate the value of *y*. [8]

c The presence of sulphur dioxide in the atmosphere is the main cause of acid rain. Outline a method which could be used to estimate quantitatively the concentration of sulphur dioxide in a sample of air.
EDEXCEL 1996 [5]

7 a Define what is meant by the *molecular formula* of a compound. [1]

b A 0.130 g sample of a liquid compound **A** was vaporized at 100 °C (373 K) at a pressure of 1 atm (101 k Pa) and occupied a volume of 85.0 cm^3. Calulate the relative molecular mass of **A**. [2]

c Compound **A** has the following compsition by mass: C, 52.2%; H, 13.0%; O, 34.8%.

i Calculate the empirical formula of **A**.

ii Suggest an identity for **A** by giving a name or structural formula. [3]
OCR (UCLES) 1998

8 a The table below gives the accurate masses of two atoms

	^{1}H	^{12}C
Mass / g	1.6734×10^{-24}	1.9925×10^{-23}

i Calculate accurate values for the mass of one mole of each atom.

[The Avogadro constant (*L*) = 6.0225×10^{23}(–)mol^{-1}.]

ii Why is ^{12}C referred to when defining the relative atomic mass of an element? [3]

b i The carbon in a sample of pure graphite has a relative atomic mass of 12.011. Suggest why this value is different from the mass of one mole of ^{12}C which you have calculated in part **a i**.

ii This sample of graphite was burned completely in oxygen. The carbon dioxide produced occupied a volume of 1.85 dm^3 at 293 K and 98.0 kPa. Calculate the mass of carbon in the sample. [5]

c In a separate experiment, 1.54 g of carbon dioxide were produced and then absorbed in 50.0 cm^3 of a sodium hydroxide solution forming sodium carbonate (Na_2CO_3) in the solution. Calculate the molar concentration of the sodium carbonate in the solution. [3]
AQA (NAEB) 1996

10 Thermochemistry

Thermochemistry is the study of the energy changes that accompany chemical reactions. In the course of a chemical reaction, bonds between atoms are broken and new bonds are made as the atoms regroup to form new substances. As we saw in chapter 4, these processes of breaking and making bonds involve changes in energy. Energy is needed to break bonds and is given out when new bonds form. This means that the reaction is accompanied by a change in energy, mainly in the form of heat. So, during the reaction, heat flows into or out of the reaction mixture and it returns to its original temperature. Thermochemistry investigates this flow and uses it to help explain the structures of substances and the bonding within them. Thermochemistry is a part of the larger subject of **thermodynamics**, which studies the laws that govern the conversion of energy from one form to another. The subject of thermodynamics is developed further in chapter 14 on 'Spontaneous change towards equilibrium'.

Chemical reactions and energy

10.1

OBJECTIVES

- Understanding basic terminology

The solid fuel which propels the Space Shuttle is finely powdered aluminium mixed with ammonium perchlorate NH_4ClO_4. These substances are moulded with a small amount of iron catalyst into a solid plastic cylinder. When the fuel ignites, the ammonium perchlorate reacts with the aluminium to form white clouds of aluminium oxide. The temperature increases enormously and a mixture of high-pressure gases forms. These gases produce thrust as they expand rapidly and roar out of the rocket engine at high speed, carrying the other reaction products with them.

General definitions

Energy A measure of a system's capacity to do work. The unit of energy is the joule (J).

Work An energy transfer that is the result of a force moving a body through a distance. The unit of work is the joule (J).

Heat An energy transfer that is the result of a temperature difference between a system and its surroundings. The unit of heat is the joule (J).

Temperature The property of a system that determines the direction of heat flow between the system and its surroundings. Heat flows from the hotter region to the colder. The unit of temperature is the kelvin (K).

Thermochemical terminology

There are two groups of key terms specifically used in thermochemistry. The first group contains the two linked terms 'system' and 'surroundings'. The second group contains words which are used casually in everyday life but which you must use with great care in the context of this subject. These four related terms are 'energy', 'work', 'heat', and 'temperature'. The six terms can be illustrated in the context of the Space Shuttle rocket engine, as follows.

The **system** consists of the collection of substances involved in the chemical reaction. In its initial state, the system consists of all the reactants in the rocket fuel. In its final state, the system consists of all the products of the reaction. The **surroundings** consist of everything else in the **Universe** with the exception of the system:

- The Universe = the system + the surroundings.

As a result of the reaction, the *temperature* of the exhaust gases is greater than the temperature of the surroundings. *Heat* flows from the system to the surroundings. After some time, the temperatures of the system and the surroundings become equal again, as they were at the start before take-off.

The reaction inside the rocket engine evolves gases. These gases do *work* as they push outwards against the atmospheric pressure of the surroundings. The rocket transfers energy to its surroundings by doing work on the surroundings and by heating them up.

Chemical reactions and internal energy

As you watch a rocket taking off, it seems obvious that the chemical reactants in the fuel contain more energy than the chemical products in the exhaust plume. The energy contained within a system is called its **internal energy** (symbol U). Internal energy cannot easily be measured because it is the sum of the kinetic energies of all the particles in the system and their potential energies.

Hours after the rocket has launched the Shuttle into space, the exhaust products have cooled down to the same temperature as the surroundings. Some heat has transferred from the system to the surroundings. Also, the exhaust gases have expanded so that they are at atmospheric pressure; and the Shuttle is in orbit. The expanding gases have done some work. If the internal energy of the fuel is $U_{\text{reactants}}$ and the internal energy of the exhaust products is U_{products}, then:

$U_{\text{reactants}}$ is greater than U_{products}

The difference between these two values is given the symbol ΔU (Δ is the Greek capital letter 'delta' and is used to indicate change):

$$\Delta U = U_{\text{products}} - U_{\text{reactants}}$$

The reaction in this case results in a *decrease* in internal energy, and the expression above gives a *negative* value for ΔU for the Space Shuttle example (because $U_{\text{reactants}}$ is greater than U_{products}), signifying that the internal energy has *decreased*.

- The *decrease* in internal energy of the system results in an *increase* in the energy of the surroundings.

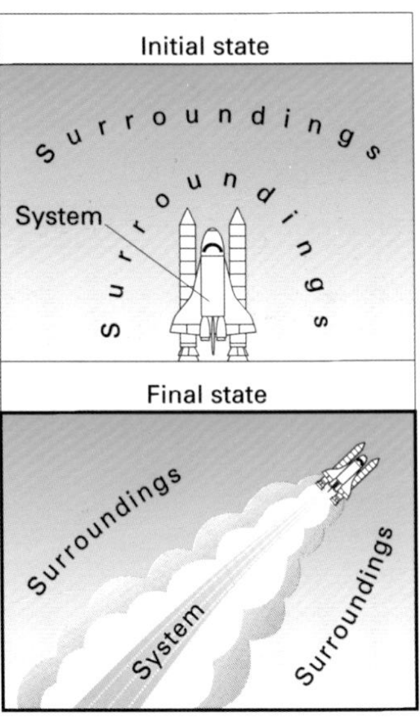

In the course of a chemical reaction, the system passes from its initial state into its final state. In the case of the rocket propellant, heat flows from the system to the surroundings; the system also does work on the surroundings.

A snowmaker uses the ideas of thermochemistry. It contains a mixture of compressed air and water vapour at about 20 atm pressure. Because of the large pressure difference to the outside atmosphere, when the mixture is sprayed into the atmosphere there is almost no heat exchanged with its surroundings. The large quantity of work done by the gas causes the mixture to cool, because of the law of energy conservation; snow forms because the mixture cools.

Practical considerations

The object of thermochemistry is to use measurements taken during practical experiments to explain the structure and bonding of substances. Changes in bonding during reactions involve changes in internal energy. It is necessary to make measurements that reflect the changes in internal energy. It is fairly straightforward to measure the heat evolved during a reaction by measuring the temperature change in a calorimeter, for example (see spread 10.4), and carrying out a relatively simple calculation. It is not so easy to measure the work done. It is helpful to define a quantity which is easy to measure; this quantity is 'enthalpy' and it is introduced in the following spread.

SUMMARY

- During a chemical reaction, energy is transferred between the system and the surroundings.
- Energy can be transferred as heat or as work.
- Heat flows as the result of a temperature difference between system and surroundings.

PRACTICE

1 Zinc and dilute hydrochloric acid react together according to the equation:

$Zn(s) + 2HCl(aq) \rightarrow ZnCl_2(aq) + H_2(g)$

The reaction takes place in an open test tube in a laboratory.

a What does the system consist of in its initial state?

b What does the system consist of in its final state?

c The reaction mixture becomes warmer. In which direction will heat flow?

d Does the system do work? Explain your answer.

e Does the internal energy of the system increase or decrease?

10.2

OBJECTIVES

- Enthalpy changes ΔH
- Exothermic reactions
- Endothermic reactions

ENTHALPY CHANGES

In a chemical reaction, existing bonds are broken and new bonds are made. Reactants are used up and products form. The internal energy of the system changes as it exchanges energy with the surroundings as heat or work. Changes in bonding are reflected in changes in internal energy. The problem is that internal energy cannot easily be measured. This problem is overcome by introducing and using a term called 'enthalpy', which is linked to internal energy but which can be measured more easily in practice.

Chemical changes and heat

A change in internal energy (ΔU) occurs when a system exchanges energy with its surroundings in the form of heat and/or work:

internal energy change = heat added to the system
+ work done on the system

Heat flows as the result of a temperature difference. If we know the mass of the system, its specific heat capacity (see spread 10.4), and use a thermometer to measure temperature difference, we can calculate the heat added to the system.

Work taking place during chemical reactions is more difficult to measure. In some chemical reactions work is obviously done, such as those that release a gas. The gas has to do work on the atmosphere to push the atmosphere out of the way and make room for itself. But it is inconvenient to collect the gas, and to measure its volume and the pressure of the surroundings, in order to calculate the work done. Some reactions take place at constant volume, such as precipitation reactions between solutions. In these cases, there is no change of volume and consequently no work is done. It is possible to study all chemical reactions in terms of changes in a quantity called 'enthalpy'.

Enthalpy

Enthalpy (symbol H) is a term that describes the heat content of a system. Just like internal energy, its actual value cannot be measured. However, an *enthalpy change* can easily be measured. An **enthalpy change** (ΔH, measured in joules, J) is defined as the heat added to the system under conditions of constant pressure:

enthalpy change = enthalpy of products − enthalpy of reactants

In symbols:

$$\Delta H = H_{\text{products}} - H_{\text{reactants}}$$

The typical practical procedure is to insulate the system from its surroundings, so that no heat can escape, and allow the temperature of the system to change during the reaction. You can then calculate the heat needed to bring the system back to its original temperature. This heat is the enthalpy change for the system:

ΔH = heat added to the system at constant pressure

For a reaction that evolves heat (i.e. heat flows *from* the system *to* the surroundings), the sign of ΔH is negative.

- A reaction with a negative value for ΔH is said to be **exothermic**.

For a reaction that absorbs heat (i.e. heat flows *from* the surroundings *to* the system), the sign of ΔH is positive.

- A reaction with a positive value for ΔH is said to be **endothermic**.

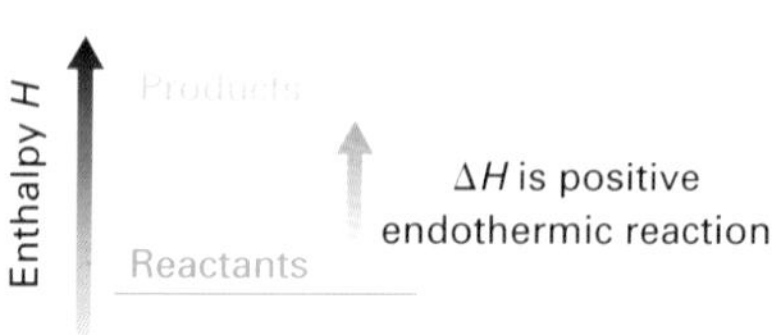

(a) For an exothermic reaction, the enthalpy change ΔH is negative. (b) For an endothermic reaction, the enthalpy change ΔH is positive.

Bond breaking and bond making

What actually happens when hydrogen burns in oxygen to form water vapour? The chemical equation is:

...$O_2(g) \rightarrow 2H_2O(g)$

...think about this reaction in terms of the bonds broken and made.

First of all, the molecules of hydrogen and oxygen must break apart to form separate atoms.

- Breaking the original bonds is an endothermic process.

Then the separate atoms combine in a new configuration to form molecules of water.

- Forming the new bonds is an exothermic process.

These changes may be represented on an **enthalpy profile diagram**, as shown to the right. Note that the reaction is exothermic overall.

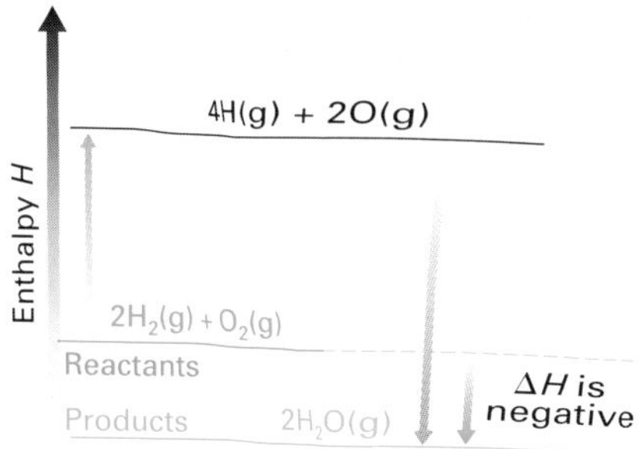

Breaking the bonds in the oxygen and hydrogen molecules is an endothermic process. Making the bonds in water is an exothermic process. The reaction is exothermic overall with $\Delta H = -242$ kJ per mole of water formed (at 298 K and 1 bar pressure), which we write as:

$2H_2(g) + O_2(g) \rightarrow 2H_2O(g)$;

Exothermic reactions

For an exothermic reaction, the enthalpy change ΔH is negative and heat flows from the system into the surroundings.

Endothermic reactions

For an endothermic reaction, the enthalpy change ΔH is positive and heat flows from the surroundings into the system.

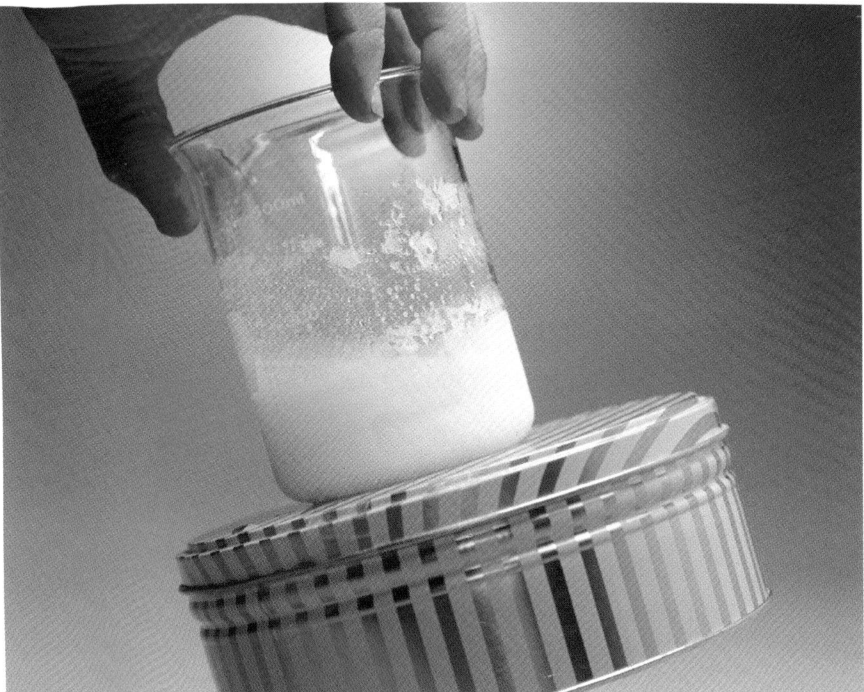

Solid hydrated barium hydroxide and excess solid ammonium nitrate react:
$Ba(OH)_2 \cdot 8H_2O(s) + 2NH_4NO_3(s) \rightarrow Ba(NO_3)_2(s) + 2NH_3(g) + 10H_2O(l)$
The water formed dissolves the excess ammonium nitrate and this process is highly endothermic. If the flask is placed on a wet biscuit tin, the water freezes and sticks the flask to the tin.

The reaction between glycerol (see spread 30.1) and potassium manganate(VII) is highly exothermic.

SUMMARY

- For an endothermic reaction, ΔH is positive.
- For an exothermic reaction, ΔH is negative.

PRACTICE

1 State, with reasons, whether each of the following processes is exothermic or endothermic:

a A match burning

b An ice cube melting

c Photosynthesis.

2 A chemical reaction usually involves the endothermic process of breaking the bonds of the reactants followed by the exothermic process of making the bonds of the products. Compare the magnitudes of these two processes:

a in a reaction that is exothermic overall,

b in a reaction that is endothermic overall.

10.3

OBJECTIVES

- A justification for using enthalpy
- Work done in expansion
- Comparing values of heat and work

ENTHALPY CHANGES EX... DETAIL

You will have noticed in the previous spreads of this chapter that few equations are expressed in symbols. The text speaks of 'internal energy', 'work', 'enthalpy', and 'heat', but does not often express these quantities in terms of their symbols. The reason for this approach is that much care must be taken with the signs used. Reference must be made to the direction of heat flow and to the distinction between the system and the surroundings. When reading this spread, you must always note whether a sign is positive or negative and explain the distinction in terms of what is actually happening in the experiment.

A justification for using enthalpies

The total energy of a system, its internal energy, may be increased either by heating the system or by doing work on it. The change in the thermodynamic quantity called 'enthalpy' is defined in such a way as to make it equal to the heat added at constant pressure. The reasoning below explains why thermochemistry concentrates on enthalpy changes rather than on internal energy changes.

If the heat added *to* a system is q and the work done *on* this system is w, then the change in the internal energy U is given by the expression:

$$\Delta U = q + w \qquad (1)$$

There are many ways in which work can be done. By far the most usual is when a gas evolved by a reaction expands against the pressure of the atmosphere. Consider the gas behind a piston expanding just a little against the constant pressure of the external atmosphere. Calculating the work done then depends on the definition of work:

$$\text{work} = \text{force} \times \text{distance moved in the direction of the force} \qquad (2)$$

Pressure is defined as force per unit area, i.e.

$$\text{pressure} = \text{force/area}$$

Rearranging this, we have

$$\text{force} = \text{pressure} \times \text{area} \qquad (3)$$

Substituting equation (3) into equation (2) gives

$$\text{work} = \text{pressure} \times \text{area} \times \text{distance moved}$$

i.e.

$$\text{work} = \text{pressure} \times \text{change in volume}$$

In the case of an expanding gas moving a piston, the system is doing work on the surroundings:

$$w = -p\Delta V$$

Remember that the sign is *negative* when the system *does* work.

When heat q is added to a system from the surroundings and the system does expansion work $p\Delta V$ on the surroundings, the internal energy change ΔU is expressed by the relationship:

$$\Delta U = q - p\Delta V \qquad (4)$$

If a chemical reaction involves a volume change, the work done must in principle be measured in order to calculate the internal energy change. It is difficult to measure the work done. To avoid measuring it, a new quantity called **enthalpy** is defined, as follows:

$$H = U + pV \qquad (5)$$

For small changes, the enthalpy change is:

$$\Delta H = \Delta U + p\Delta V + V\Delta p \qquad (6)$$

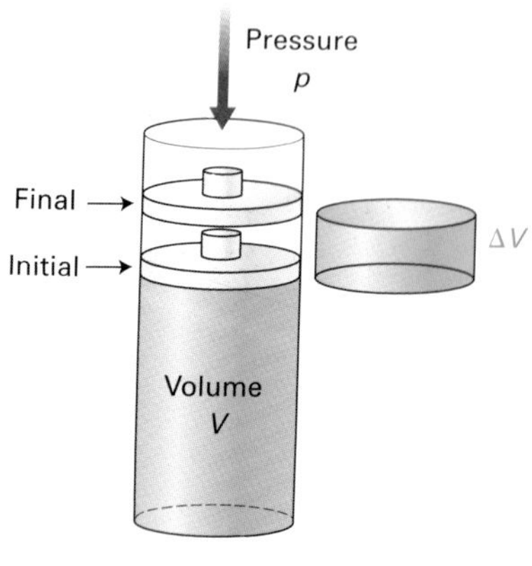

The pressure inside the cylinder is greater than the atmospheric pressure p outside. When the piston moves outwards, the volume inside the cylinder increases by ΔV. The gas inside the cylinder has done work.

...uation for the internal energy change (4) into (6), the end result of the derivation is that

$$\Delta H = q - p\Delta V + p\Delta V + V\Delta p$$

i.e.

$$\Delta H = q + V\Delta p \qquad (7)$$

If the change in pressure Δp is *zero*, then the enthalpy change is identical to the heat added to the system:

$$\Delta H = q \qquad \text{(at constant pressure)}$$

Chemical reactions almost always take place under conditions of constant pressure in an open laboratory because the atmospheric pressure is approximately constant.

In this way, the definition of enthalpy means that we can ignore the work term provided that the pressure is constant. The enthalpy change is the heat added to the system at constant pressure. Under conditions of constant pressure, a heat measurement *is* a measurement of an enthalpy change. The name 'enthalpy' appropriately comes from the Greek for 'inner warmth'.

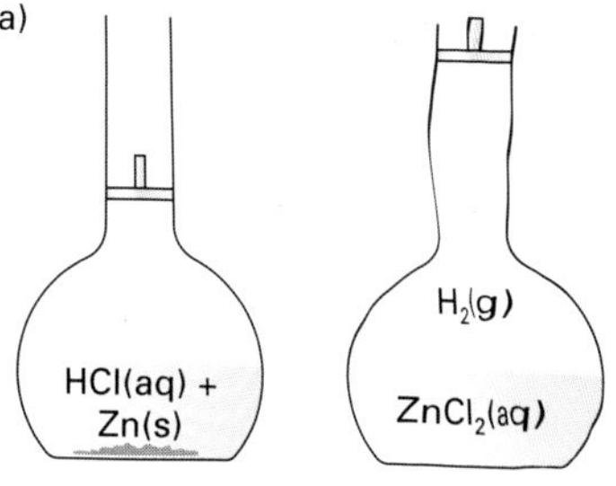

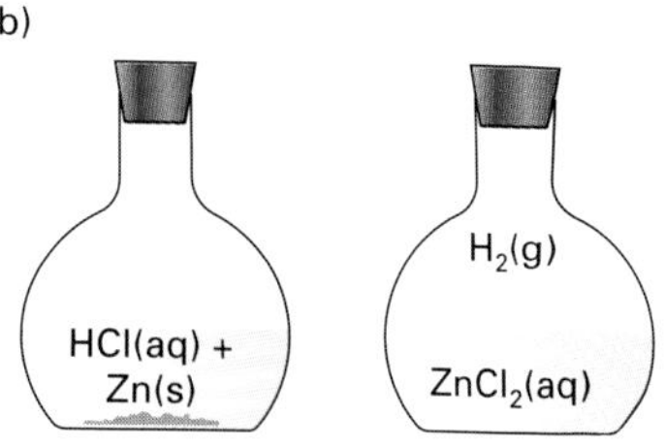

(a) At constant pressure, the reaction evolves gas, which expands and does work against the atmosphere. The enthalpy change = the heat added to the system. (b) If the same reaction takes place at constant volume, the reaction increases the pressure in the vessel and does more work on the bung. Now the heat added is not *equal to the enthalpy change.*

Worked example to measure work done in expansion

The enthalpy change per mole on vaporizing water at 100 °C and 1.0 bar is 40.7 kJ mol^{-1}. The molar volume of the liquid is 18 cm^{3}mol^{-1} and the molar volume of the vapour is 24 dm^{3}mol^{-1} (so the volume of the liquid is negligible). 1.0 bar is 1.0×10^5 Pa (N m^{-2}).

The work done on the surroundings is equal to $p\Delta V$. Therefore

$$\begin{aligned}\text{work done} &= (1.0 \times 10^5\,\text{N m}^{-2}) \times (24 \times 10^{-3}\,\text{m}^3\,\text{mol}^{-1}) \\ &= 2.4 \times 10^3\,\text{N m mol}^{-1} \\ &= 2.4\,\text{kJ mol}^{-1}\end{aligned}$$

This calculation shows that the work done is only about 6% of the enthalpy change.

SUMMARY

- The internal energy change $\Delta U = q + w$.
- When a system expands, the work done on the system equals $-p\Delta V$.
- The enthalpy change $\Delta H = q$ (at constant pressure).
- The enthalpy change is the heat added to the system at constant pressure.

PRACTICE

1 Zinc reacts with hydrochloric acid according to the chemical equation:

$Zn(s) + 2HCl(aq) \rightarrow ZnCl_2(aq) + H_2(g)$

1 mol of zinc liberates 24 dm^3 of gas at room temperature.

a Calculate the work done by the production of this volume of gas.

b Would the value of the enthalpy change be the same if this reaction were carried out at constant volume?

2 Explain why enthalpy H cannot easily be measured but an enthalpy change ΔH may be measured.

10.4 CALORIMETERS: MEASU[...] CHANGES

OBJECTIVES

- 'Coffee cup' calorimeter
- Flame calorimeter
- Bomb calorimeter

Specific heat capacity

In this spread we need to use the equation

$q = mc\Delta T$

that is

heat = mass of solution × its specific heat capacity × temperature change

The **specific heat capacity** is the heat required to raise the temperature of 1 g of a substance by 1 K. The specific heat capacity of pure water is 4.18 J $g^{-1}K^{-1}$.

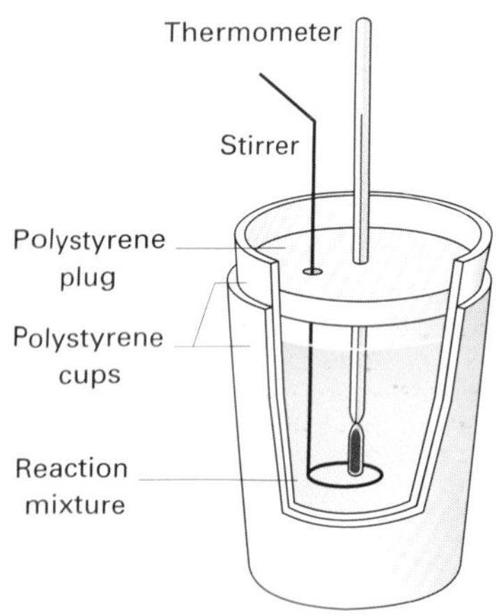

Two expanded polystyrene cups are placed one inside the other. An expanded polystyrene plug supports a thermometer and a wire stirrer. If the mass and specific heat capacity of the reaction mixture is large compared with that of the thermometer and stirrer, then the heat exchanged with the stirrer and thermometer is very much less than that exchanged with the reaction mixture, and we can make the assumptions mentioned to the right.

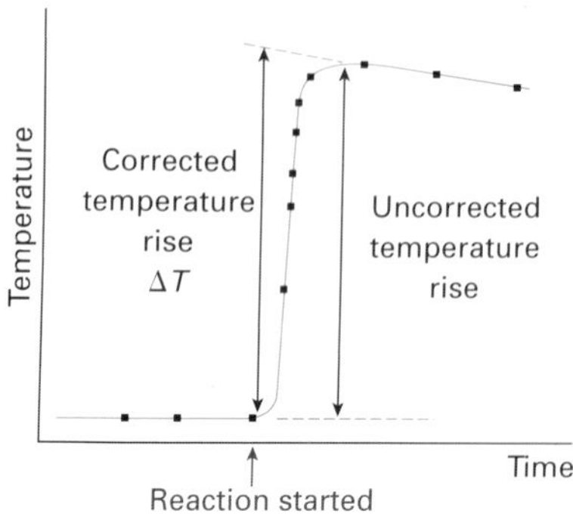

Cooling correction. Allowance may be made for heat lost from the calorimeter for an exothermic reaction by plotting a graph of temperature against time. Assuming that heat loss is constant during the experiment, a more accurate figure for the maximum temperature is obtained by extrapolating the graph back to the time of mixing.

A calorimeter is a piece of apparatus used to measure the enthalpy changes that accompany chemical reactions. Calorimeters are designed to insulate the reaction system thermally from its surroundings. The enthalpy change then causes a change in the temperature inside the calorimeter, which can be measured with a thermometer. The enthalpy change may then be calculated from a knowledge of the temperature change and the mass and specific heat capacity of the contents of the calorimeter. This spread describes three types of calorimeter.

The 'coffee cup' calorimeter

This simple type of calorimeter is suitable for changes that take place in aqueous solution. Examples include:

- neutralization reactions between an acid and a base;
- precipitation reactions where a solid forms on mixing two aqueous solutions;
- dissolving a solid to form an aqueous solution.

This calorimeter consists of an insulated cup containing an aqueous solution of the reacting substances. The chemical reaction that occurs is accompanied by an enthalpy change. This enthalpy change leads to a change in temperature of the calorimeter. The aqueous solution together with the cup, thermometer, and stirrer heat up or cool down. For the purposes of the calculation, we assume that all the heat is exchanged with the solution alone, and that the solution has the same specific heat capacity as pure water.

Worked example on measuring enthalpy of solution

The *enthalpy of solution* is the enthalpy change that accompanies the dissolution of 1.00 mol of a solid in a large excess of water. In this example, 8.00 g of ammonium nitrate (NH_4NO_3) was dissolved in 50.0 g of water in a simple expanded polystyrene calorimeter. The temperature fell by 10.1 °C.

Question: Calculate the enthalpy of solution for the process:

$NH_4NO_3(s) + \text{water} \rightarrow NH_4^+(aq) + NO_3^-(aq)$

Answer: The temperature fell as the solid dissolved: forming an aqueous solution of ammonium nitrate is an endothermic process, spread 10.2.

Step 1 Calculate the heat added from the change in temperature using $q = mc\Delta T$

where q = heat, m = mass, c = specific heat capacity, and ΔT = temperature change. Substituting values we get

$$q = (58.0\,g) \times (4.18\,J\,g^{-1}K^{-1}) \times (10.1\,K)$$
$$= 2.45 \times 10^3\,J = 2.45\,kJ$$

Step 2 Calculate the amount in moles of ammonium nitrate dissolved.

Molar mass of NH_4NO_3 = 2 × (14.0 g mol^{-1}) + 4 × (1.0g mol^{-1}) + 3 × (16.0g mol^{-1}) = 80.0 g mol^{-1}.

Amount in moles of NH_4NO_3 dissolved $= \frac{8.00\,g}{80.0\,g\,mol^{-1}} = 0.100\,mol$

Step 3 Calculate the enthalpy change per mole.

Solution of 0.100 mol of NH_4NO_3 required 2.45 kJ

Solution of 1.00 mol of NH_4NO_3 would require $\frac{2.45}{0.100}$ kJ = 24.5 kJ

The process is endothermic, so the accompanying enthalpy change is positive, i.e. $\Delta H = +24.5\,kJ\,mol^{-1}$

Note that the accepted value is +25.8 kJ mol^{-1}. The smaller value calculated in this example is the result of *heat losses* from the simple type of calorimeter used.

$$2H_2(g) + O_2(g) \rightarrow 2H_2O(g)$$

We will think about this reaction in terms of the bonds broken and made.

First of all, the molecules of hydrogen and oxygen must break apart to form separate atoms.

- Breaking the original bonds is an endothermic process.

Then the separate atoms combine in a new configuration to form molecules of water.

- Forming the new bonds is an exothermic process.

These changes may be represented on an **enthalpy profile diagram**, as shown to the right. Note that the reaction is exothermic overall.

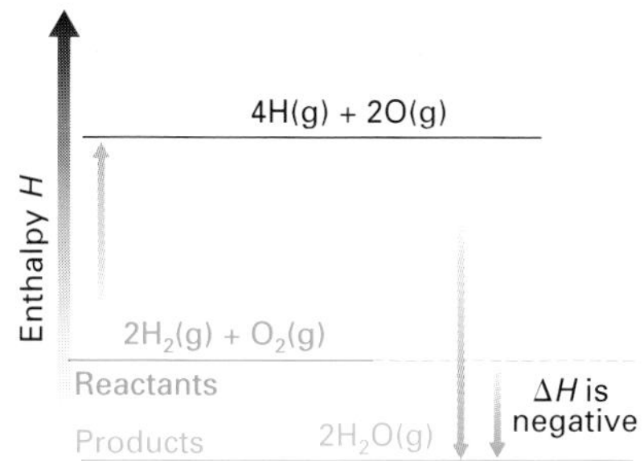

Breaking the bonds in the oxygen and hydrogen molecules is an endothermic process. Making the bonds in water is an exothermic process. The reaction is exothermic overall with $\Delta H = -242$ kJ per mole of water formed (at 298 K and 1 bar pressure), which we write as:

$2H_2(g) + O_2(g) \rightarrow 2H_2O(g);$

Exothermic reactions

For an exothermic reaction, the enthalpy change ΔH is negative and heat flows from the system into the surroundings.

Endothermic reactions

For an endothermic reaction, the enthalpy change ΔH is positive and heat flows from the surroundings into the system.

Solid hydrated barium hydroxide and excess solid ammonium nitrate react:
$Ba(OH)_2{\cdot}8H_2O(s) + 2NH_4NO_3(s) \rightarrow Ba(NO_3)_2(s) + 2NH_3(g) + 10H_2O(l)$
The water formed dissolves the excess ammonium nitrate and this process is highly endothermic. If the flask is placed on a wet biscuit tin, the water freezes and sticks the flask to the tin.

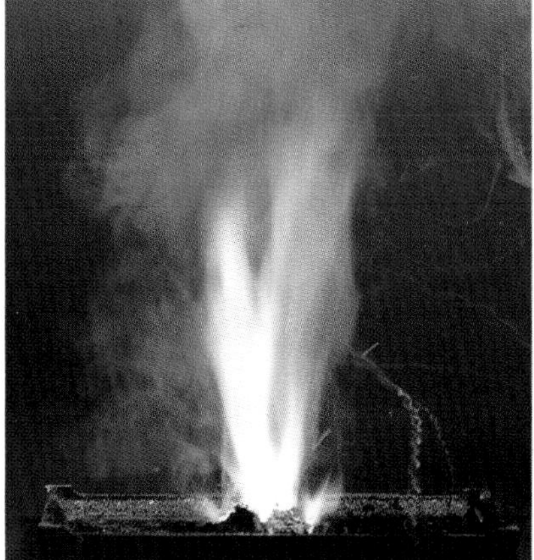

The reaction between glycerol (see spread 30.1) and potassium manganate(VII) is highly exothermic.

SUMMARY

- For an endothermic reaction, ΔH is positive.
- For an exothermic reaction, ΔH is negative.

PRACTICE

1 State, with reasons, whether each of the following processes is exothermic or endothermic:
  a A match burning
  b An ice cube melting
  c Photosynthesis.

2 A chemical reaction usually involves the endothermic process of breaking the bonds of the reactants followed by the exothermic process of making the bonds of the products. Compare the magnitudes of these two processes:
  a in a reaction that is exothermic overall,
  b in a reaction that is endothermic overall.

10.3

OBJECTIVES

- A justification for using enthalpy
- Work done in expansion
- Comparing values of heat and work

Enthalpy changes examined in detail

You will have noticed in the previous spreads of this chapter that few equations are expressed in symbols. The text speaks of 'internal energy', 'work', 'enthalpy', and 'heat', but does not often express these quantities in terms of their symbols. The reason for this approach is that much care must be taken with the signs used. Reference must be made to the direction of heat flow and to the distinction between the system and the surroundings. When reading this spread, you must always note whether a sign is positive or negative and explain the distinction in terms of what is actually happening in the experiment.

A justification for using enthalpies

The total energy of a system, its internal energy, may be increased either by heating the system or by doing work on it. The change in the thermodynamic quantity called 'enthalpy' is defined in such a way as to make it equal to the heat added at constant pressure. The reasoning below explains why thermochemistry concentrates on enthalpy changes rather than on internal energy changes.

If the heat added *to* a system is q and the work done *on* this system is w, then the change in the internal energy U is given by the expression:

$$\Delta U = q + w \qquad (1)$$

There are many ways in which work can be done. By far the most usual is when a gas evolved by a reaction expands against the pressure of the atmosphere. Consider the gas behind a piston expanding just a little against the constant pressure of the external atmosphere. Calculating the work done then depends on the definition of work:

$$\text{work} = \text{force} \times \text{distance moved in the direction of the force} \qquad (2)$$

Pressure is defined as force per unit area, i.e.

$$\text{pressure} = \text{force/area}$$

Rearranging this, we have

$$\text{force} = \text{pressure} \times \text{area} \qquad (3)$$

Substituting equation (3) into equation (2) gives

$$\text{work} = \text{pressure} \times \text{area} \times \text{distance moved}$$

i.e.

$$\text{work} = \text{pressure} \times \text{change in volume}$$

In the case of an expanding gas moving a piston, the system is doing work on the surroundings:

$$w = -p\Delta V$$

Remember that the sign is *negative* when the system *does* work.

When heat q is added to a system from the surroundings and the system does expansion work $p\Delta V$ on the surroundings, the internal energy change ΔU is expressed by the relationship:

$$\Delta U = q - p\Delta V \qquad (4)$$

If a chemical reaction involves a volume change, the work done must in principle be measured in order to calculate the internal energy change. It is difficult to measure the work done. To avoid measuring it, a new quantity called **enthalpy** is defined, as follows:

$$H = U + pV \qquad (5)$$

For small changes, the enthalpy change is:

$$\Delta H = \Delta U + p\Delta V + V\Delta p \qquad (6)$$

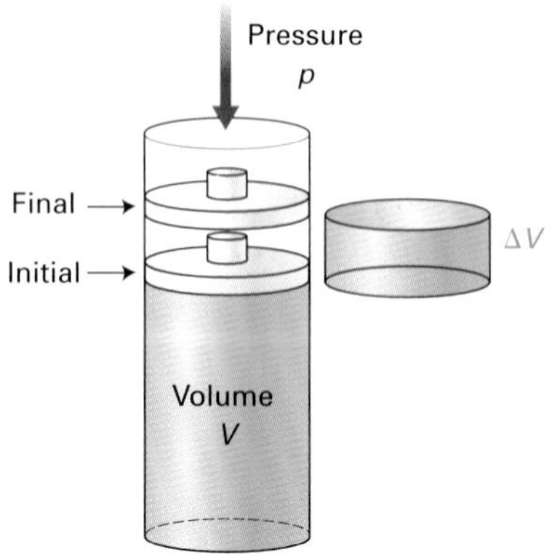

The pressure inside the cylinder is greater than the atmospheric pressure p outside. When the piston moves outwards, the volume inside the cylinder increases by ΔV. The gas inside the cylinder has done work.

Substituting the equation for the internal energy change (4) into equation (6), the end result of the derivation is that

$$\Delta H = q - p\Delta V + p\Delta V + V\Delta p$$

i.e.

$$\Delta H = q + V\Delta p \qquad (7)$$

If the change in pressure Δp is *zero*, then the enthalpy change is identical to the heat added to the system:

$$\Delta H = q \qquad \text{(at constant pressure)}$$

Chemical reactions almost always take place under conditions of constant pressure in an open laboratory because the atmospheric pressure is approximately constant.

In this way, the definition of enthalpy means that we can ignore the work term provided that the pressure is constant. The enthalpy change is the heat added to the system at constant pressure. Under conditions of constant pressure, a heat measurement *is* a measurement of an enthalpy change. The name 'enthalpy' appropriately comes from the Greek for 'inner warmth'.

(a)

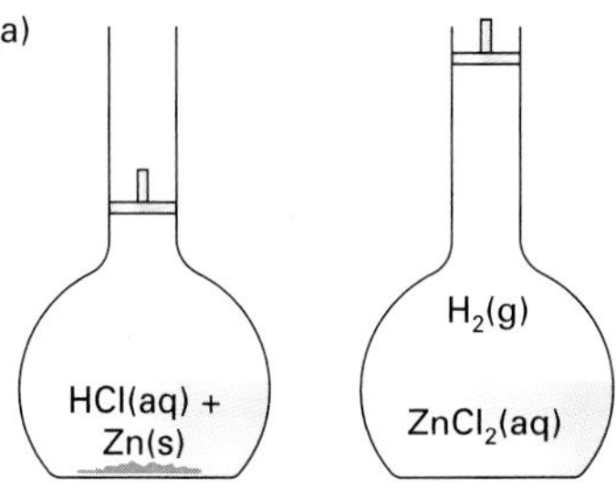

(b)

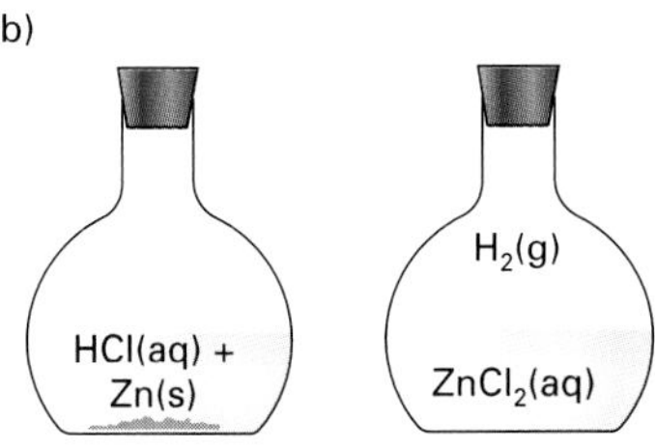

(a) At constant pressure, the reaction evolves gas, which expands and does work against the atmosphere. The enthalpy change = the heat added to the system. (b) If the same reaction takes place at constant volume, the reaction increases the pressure in the vessel and does more work on the bung. Now the heat added is not *equal to the enthalpy change.*

Worked example to measure work done in expansion

The enthalpy change per mole on vaporizing water at 100 °C and 1.0 bar is 40.7 kJ mol^{-1}. The molar volume of the liquid is 18 cm^3 mol^{-1} and the molar volume of the vapour is 24 dm^3 mol^{-1} (so the volume of the liquid is negligible). 1.0 bar is 1.0×10^5 Pa (N m^{-2}).

The work done on the surroundings is equal to $p\Delta V$. Therefore

$$\begin{aligned}\text{work done} &= (1.0 \times 10^5\,\text{N m}^{-2}) \times (24 \times 10^{-3}\,\text{m}^3\,\text{mol}^{-1})\\ &= 2.4 \times 10^3\,\text{N m mol}^{-1}\\ &= 2.4\,\text{kJ mol}^{-1}\end{aligned}$$

This calculation shows that the work done is only about 6% of the enthalpy change.

SUMMARY

- The internal energy change $\Delta U = q + w$.
- When a system expands, the work done on the system equals $-p\Delta V$.
- The enthalpy change $\Delta H = q$ (at constant pressure).
- The enthalpy change is the heat added to the system at constant pressure.

PRACTICE

1 Zinc reacts with hydrochloric acid according to the chemical equation:
Zn(s) + 2HCl(aq) → $ZnCl_2$(aq) + H_2(g)
1 mol of zinc liberates 24 dm^3 of gas at room temperature.
  a Calculate the work done by the production of this volume of gas.
  b Would the value of the enthalpy change be the same if this reaction were carried out at constant volume?

2 Explain why enthalpy H cannot easily be measured but an enthalpy change ΔH may be measured.

10.4

Calorimeters: measuring enthalpy changes

OBJECTIVES

- 'Coffee cup' calorimeter
- Flame calorimeter
- Bomb calorimeter

Specific heat capacity

In this spread we need to use the equation

$q = mc\Delta T$

that is

heat = mass of solution × its specific heat capacity × temperature change

The **specific heat capacity** is the heat required to raise the temperature of 1 g of a substance by 1 K. The specific heat capacity of pure water is $4.18\ \mathrm{J\ g^{-1}\ K^{-1}}$.

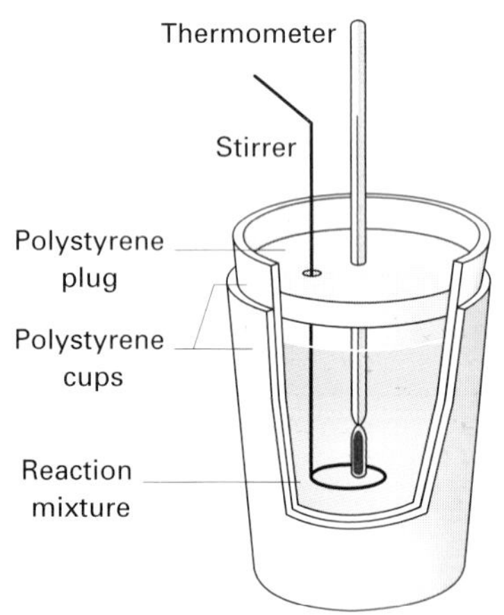

Two expanded polystyrene cups are placed one inside the other. An expanded polystyrene plug supports a thermometer and a wire stirrer. If the mass and specific heat capacity of the reaction mixture is large compared with that of the thermometer and stirrer, then the heat exchanged with the stirrer and thermometer is very much less than that exchanged with the reaction mixture, and we can make the assumptions mentioned to the right.

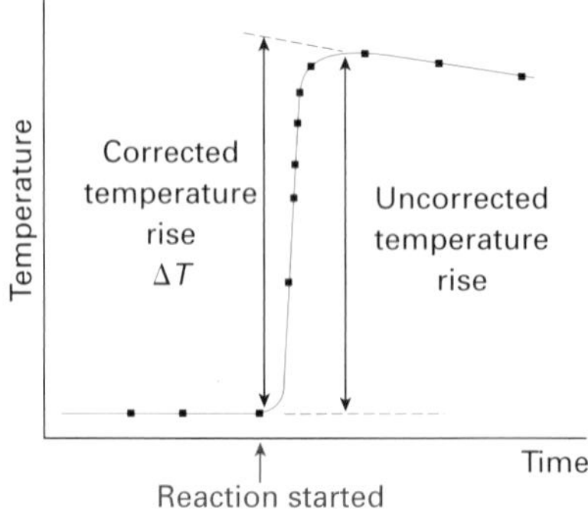

Cooling correction. Allowance may be made for heat lost from the calorimeter for an exothermic reaction by plotting a graph of temperature against time. Assuming that heat loss is constant during the experiment, a more accurate figure for the maximum temperature is obtained by extrapolating the graph back to the time of mixing.

A calorimeter is a piece of apparatus used to measure the enthalpy changes that accompany chemical reactions. Calorimeters are designed to insulate the reaction system thermally from its surroundings. The enthalpy change then causes a change in the temperature inside the calorimeter, which can be measured with a thermometer. The enthalpy change may then be calculated from a knowledge of the temperature change and the mass and specific heat capacity of the contents of the calorimeter. This spread describes three types of calorimeter.

The 'coffee cup' calorimeter

This simple type of calorimeter is suitable for changes that take place in aqueous solution. Examples include:

- neutralization reactions between an acid and a base;
- precipitation reactions where a solid forms on mixing two aqueous solutions;
- dissolving a solid to form an aqueous solution.

This calorimeter consists of an insulated cup containing an aqueous solution of the reacting substances. The chemical reaction that occurs is accompanied by an enthalpy change. This enthalpy change leads to a change in temperature of the calorimeter. The aqueous solution together with the cup, thermometer, and stirrer heat up or cool down. For the purposes of the calculation, we assume that all the heat is exchanged with the solution alone, and that the solution has the same specific heat capacity as pure water.

Worked example on measuring enthalpy of solution

The *enthalpy of solution* is the enthalpy change that accompanies the dissolution of 1.00 mol of a solid in a large excess of water. In this example, 8.00 g of ammonium nitrate (NH_4NO_3) was dissolved in 50.0 g of water in a simple expanded polystyrene calorimeter. The temperature fell by 10.1 °C.

Question: Calculate the enthalpy of solution for the process:

$NH_4NO_3(s) + \text{water} \rightarrow NH_4^+(aq) + NO_3^-(aq)$

Answer: The temperature fell as the solid dissolved: forming an aqueous solution of ammonium nitrate is an endothermic process, spread 10.2.

Step 1 Calculate the heat added from the change in temperature using $q = mc\Delta T$

where q = heat, m = mass, c = specific heat capacity, and ΔT = temperature change. Substituting values we get

$$q = (58.0\ \mathrm{g}) \times (4.18\ \mathrm{J\ g^{-1}\ K^{-1}}) \times (10.1\ \mathrm{K})$$
$$= 2.45 \times 10^3\ \mathrm{J} = 2.45\ \mathrm{kJ}$$

Step 2 Calculate the amount in moles of ammonium nitrate dissolved.

Molar mass of $NH_4NO_3 = 2 \times (14.0\ \mathrm{g\ mol^{-1}}) + 4 \times (1.0\ \mathrm{g\ mol^{-1}}) + 3 \times (16.0\ \mathrm{g\ mol^{-1}})$ $= 80.0\ \mathrm{g\ mol^{-1}}$.

Amount in moles of NH_4NO_3 dissolved $= \dfrac{8.00\ \mathrm{g}}{80.0\ \mathrm{g\ mol^{-1}}} = 0.100\ \mathrm{mol}$

Step 3 Calculate the enthalpy change per mole.

Solution of 0.100 mol of NH_4NO_3 required 2.45 kJ

Solution of 1.00 mol of NH_4NO_3 would require $\dfrac{2.45}{0.100}$ kJ = 24.5 kJ

The process is endothermic, so the accompanying enthalpy change is positive, i.e. $\Delta H = +24.5\ \mathrm{kJ\ mol^{-1}}$

Note that the accepted value is $+25.8\ \mathrm{kJ\ mol^{-1}}$. The smaller value calculated in this example is the result of *heat losses* from the simple type of calorimeter used.

The flame calorimeter

A more sophisticated instrument than a simple polystyrene cup is the flame calorimeter, which is used for measuring the enthalpy changes during combustion. A measured mass of the substance being investigated is combusted in a small burner. The heat released warms the surrounding vessel and the temperature rise is recorded. Unlike the polystyrene cup calorimeter, the flame calorimeter has a significant specific heat capacity. The heat capacity of a calorimeter containing a specified quantity of water is called the **calorimeter constant** (units $J\,K^{-1}$). If we know the calorimeter constant, we can calculate the enthalpy change directly from a measured temperature change.

There are two main sources of error when using a flame calorimeter:

1 Combustion products do not completely transfer their heat to the spiral copper heat exchanger. Therefore, the temperature rise of the apparatus is smaller than it should be.

2 Combustion of the sample may be incomplete. For example, a compound containing only carbon and hydrogen (a hydrocarbon) should burn to produce carbon dioxide and water only. Incomplete combustion results in carbon monoxide and carbon also being produced, with the result that the enthalpy change (and the resultant temperature rise) is less than the theoretical maximum value.

Calorimeter constant

The calorimeter constant (heat capacity) of a calorimeter may be calculated by measuring the temperature rise caused by a known quantity of electrical energy. This electrical energy is generated by an electric heater, the energy being given by

energy = voltage × current × time

Alternatively, the calorimeter may be calibrated by combusting a known mass of a substance whose enthalpy change on combustion is known.

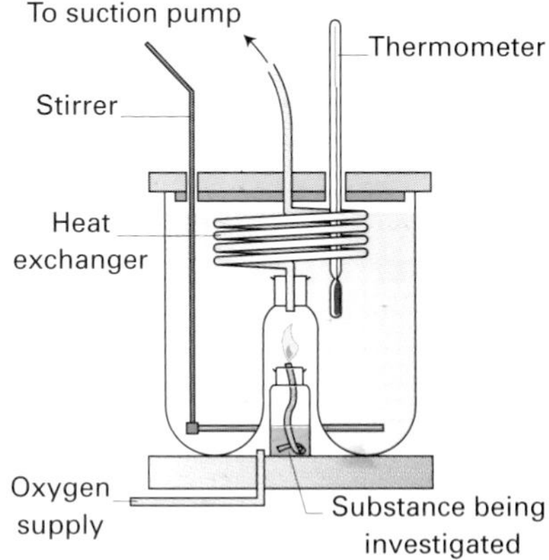

A flame calorimeter. A suction pump draws a steady stream of air through the apparatus so that hot combustion products flow through the copper heat exchanger coil.

The bomb calorimeter

A bomb calorimeter consists of a steel-walled pressure vessel in which a solid or liquid sample is burned in pure oxygen at 25 atm pressure. The main advantage of the bomb calorimeter is that the combustion is more likely to be complete due to the use of pure high-pressure oxygen.

Enthalpy changes are defined at constant *pressure*. The bomb calorimeter operates at constant *volume* and therefore measures the internal energy change for the reaction. Enthalpy changes calculated from bomb calorimeter data have to be corrected for work done as the result of a pressure change. The magnitude of the work done is typically a few per cent of the total energy change.

Insulation

The flame calorimeter is not thermally insulated. The maximum temperature of the calorimeter is obtained by plotting a cooling correction graph and extrapolating as described opposite.

SUMMARY

- Calorimeters are used to measure temperature changes resulting from enthalpy changes accompanying chemical reactions and physical changes.
- The heat is calculated from the temperature change by using the relationship $q = mc\Delta T$.
- The calorimeter constant is the heat required to raise the temperature of a given calorimeter and its contents by 1 K.

PRACTICE

1 Calculate the heat required to raise the temperature of 150 g of water by 25.0 °C. [For pure water $c = 4.18\,J\,g^{-1}\,K^{-1}$.]

2 The calorimeter constant of a flame calorimeter is $5.83 \times 10^3\,J\,K^{-1}$. The complete combustion of 3.20 g of methanol CH_3OH raises the temperature by 12.3 °C. Calculate the enthalpy change for the combustion of 1.00 mol of methanol.

10.5

STANDARD ENTHALPY CHANGES AND HESS'S LAW

OBJECTIVES

- Standard enthalpy changes
- Standard enthalpy change of formation
- Standard enthalpy change of combustion
- Hess's law

Standard state

The **standard state** of a substance is the substance in its pure form at 1 bar and the stated temperature. Although values are commonly quoted at 298 K (25 °C), measurements can be made at other temperatures. For example, the processes happening in a blast furnace occur at around 2000 K, see chapter 14.

Reference state

Some elements can exist in more than one form. The form used should be the one that is most stable at 1 bar and the stated temperature; this form is the element's **reference state**. For example, the standard enthalpy change of formation of gaseous carbon dioxide at 25 °C is the standard enthalpy change when carbon dioxide gas is formed from solid graphite (not diamond, which is the less stable form of carbon) and oxygen gas:

$C(s) + O_2(g) \rightarrow CO_2(g)$;

$\Delta H_f^\ominus$ (298 K) = –393.5 kJ mol^{-1}

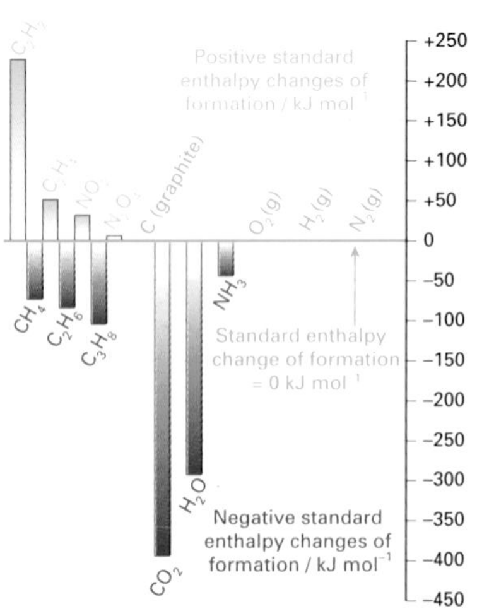

Standard enthalpy changes of formation are usually written in a table. Here they are compared diagrammatically.

All chemical reactions have an associated enthalpy change. For a given chemical reaction, the value of the enthalpy change depends on three factors: the amounts of the substances involved, the temperature, and the pressure at which the reaction is carried out. So if you quote an enthalpy change for a reaction, you need to state the conditions under which the reaction takes place. This leads to the idea of 'standard enthalpy changes', which are measured under certain fixed conditions. If we measure standard enthalpy changes, we can compare the values for different reactions. We can use measured standard enthalpy changes to calculate the standard enthalpy changes for related chemical reactions, giving us a value for a reaction that is difficult to measure practically.

Standard enthalpy changes

Data books list 'standard enthalpy changes' or, occasionally, 'standard molar enthalpy changes' or 'standard reaction enthalpies'. Standard enthalpy changes are given the symbol $\Delta H^\ominus$. The superscript $^\ominus$ signifies that

- all substances are in their *standard states* (see Box),
- the *pressure is 1 bar*, and
- the enthalpy change is measured *per mole* of the specified substance.

The physical state of a substance and the numerical value of the enthalpy change both depend on the temperature at which the reaction takes place. The temperature is indicated in brackets after the $\Delta H^\ominus$ symbol. For example, if the temperature at which the reaction takes place is 298 K, the full symbol for the standard enthalpy change is $\Delta H^\ominus$(298 K).

Standard enthalpy change of formation

This is defined as follows:

- The **standard enthalpy change of formation** $\Delta H_f^\ominus$ is the standard enthalpy change when a compound is formed from its *elements*.

Note that the *standard enthalpy change of formation* is also sometimes called the 'standard enthalpy of formation' or the 'standard formation enthalpy'.

For example, the standard enthalpy change of formation of aluminium oxide is represented as follows:

$$2Al(s) + \tfrac{3}{2}O_2(g) \rightarrow Al_2O_3(s); \qquad \Delta H_f^\ominus(298\text{ K}) = -1676\text{ kJ mol}^{-1}$$

Here:

- the temperature must be stated (in this case, 298 K),
- all substances are in their standard states at the stated temperature,
- pressure is 1 bar,
- the enthalpy change is measured per mole of the compound formed.

Values of standard enthalpy changes of formation are given in the diagram to the left. Note that the standard enthalpy change of formation of an element in its reference state (see Box) is zero, by definition.

Standard enthalpy change of combustion

The standard enthalpy change of combustion is defined in a very similar way to the standard enthalpy change of formation:

- The **standard enthalpy change of combustion** $\Delta H_c^\ominus$ is the standard enthalpy change when a substance is fully combusted in oxygen.

For example, the standard enthalpy change of combustion of methane is represented as follows:

$$CH_4(g) + 2O_2(g) \rightarrow CO_2(g) + 2H_2O(l);$$
$$\Delta H_c^{\ominus}(298\,K) = -890.7\ kJ\,mol^{-1}$$

Here:

- the temperature must be stated (in this case, 298 K),
- all substances are in their standard states at the stated temperature,
- pressure is 1 bar,
- the enthalpy change is measured per mole of the substance combusted.

Combustion can be used for many tasks, such as propulsion. The first round-the-world flight by a hot-air balloon took place in 1999. Many fuels are organic and include methane and the other constituents of natural gas.

Standard enthalpy change of reaction

The term 'standard enthalpy change of reaction' (or 'standard enthalpy of reaction') may be used for any reaction, not just combustion or formation.

Hess's law – calculating standard enthalpy changes

Germain Hess was a Russian chemist born in Switzerland. In 1840 he developed a thermochemical version of the law of energy conservation, now known as **Hess's law**:

- The standard enthalpy change for a reaction is independent of the route taken from the reactants to the products.

Hess's law may be used to calculate the standard enthalpy change for any reaction from known standard enthalpy changes. See the next spread.

For any reaction, we could consider it as taking place in two halves, making the products from their elements after having turned the reactants back into their elements. The latter step corresponds to the reverse of the standard enthalpy change of formation of the reactants.

Hence the overall standard enthalpy change is equal to the standard enthalpy change of formation of the products minus the standard enthalpy change of formation of the reactants:

$$\Delta H^{\ominus} = \Delta H_f^{\ominus}(\text{products}) - \Delta H_f^{\ominus}(\text{reactants})$$

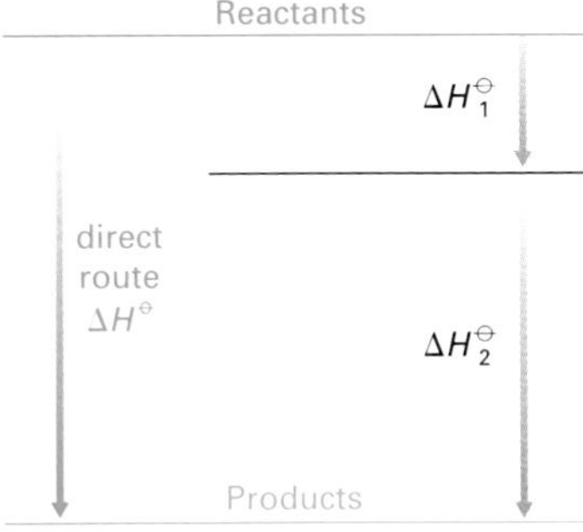

Hess's law summarized diagrammatically:
$\Delta H^{\ominus} = \Delta H_1^{\ominus} + \Delta H_2^{\ominus}$
where $\Delta H^{\ominus}$ refers to the direct route and $\Delta H_1^{\ominus}$ and $\Delta H_2^{\ominus}$ refer to the indirect route. Such a diagram is often called an enthalpy cycle.

SUMMARY

- The standard enthalpy change is the enthalpy change per mole for conversion of reactants in their standard states into products in their standard states, at a stated temperature.
- The standard state of a substance is the pure substance at 1 bar.
- The standard enthalpy change of formation is the standard enthalpy change when a compound is formed from its elements.
- The standard enthalpy change of combustion is the standard enthalpy change when a substance is fully combusted in oxygen.
- Hess's law states that the standard enthalpy change for a reaction is independent of the route taken from the reactants to the products.

10.6

OBJECTIVES

- Using Hess's law to do enthalpy calculations

HESS'S LAW EXAMPLES

Hess's law is very useful for performing calculations to find standard enthalpy changes for reactions, given appropriate data about other reactions. So long as the data given enable two routes to be taken from the same reactants to the same products, Hess's law guarantees that the standard enthalpy change calculated by either route must be the same. We will now do several examples to illustrate the law.

Data

The standard enthalpy changes of formation (in kJ mol^{-1}) are as follows:

$CH_4(g)$	–74.4
$CO_2(g)$	–393.5
$H_2O(l)$	–285.8

Worked example to calculate the standard enthalpy change of combustion of methane from standard enthalpy changes of formation

The chemical equation for the combustion of methane (the direct route) is:

$CH_4(g) + 2O_2(g) \rightarrow CO_2(g) + 2H_2O(l)$

Question: Calculate the standard enthalpy change of combustion of methane, using the values of the standard enthalpy change of formation for methane, carbon dioxide, and water shown in the margin.

Strategy: Use the equation
$\Delta H^\ominus = \Delta H_f^\ominus(\text{products}) - \Delta H_f^\ominus(\text{reactants})$

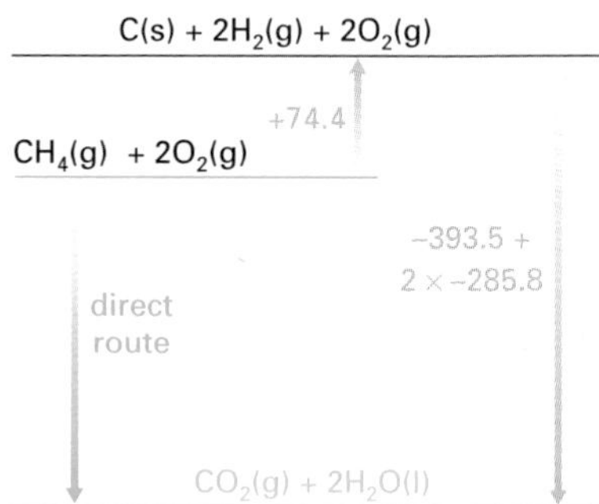

Answer:
Applying the principle explained above to this specific example, we get

$\Delta H^\ominus = \Delta H_f^\ominus(CO_2) + 2 \times \Delta H_f^\ominus(H_2O) - \Delta H_f^\ominus(CH_4) - 2 \times \Delta H_f^\ominus(O_2)$

where the numbers correspond to the mole ratios in the balanced equation.

Now substitute the values for the substances, remembering that the value for water is that for the liquid:

$\Delta H^\ominus = (-393.5\text{ kJ mol}^{-1}) + 2 \times (-285.8\text{ kJ mol}^{-1}) - (-74.4\text{ kJ mol}^{-1}) - 2 \times (0\text{ kJ mol}^{-1})$
i.e. we can write

$CH_4(g) + 2O_2(g) \rightarrow CO_2(g) + 2H_2O(l); \quad \Delta H_c^\ominus(298\text{ K}) = -890.7\text{ kJ mol}^{-1}$

Data

The standard enthalpy changes of combustion (in kJ mol^{-1}) are as follows:

C(s)	–393.5
$H_2(g)$	–285.8
$CH_4(g)$	–890.7

Worked example to calculate the standard enthalpy change of formation of methane from standard enthalpy changes of combustion

Question: Given the standard enthalpy changes of combustion shown in the margin, calculate the standard enthalpy change of formation of methane.

Strategy: Set up an enthalpy cycle that includes the data given and the unknown step.

Answer: The enthalpy cycle shows that the direct route (the combustion of the elements) gives the same standard enthalpy change as the indirect route in which the elements are combined into methane and then methane is combusted:

C(s) + 2H2(g) + 2O2(g)
$\Delta H_f^\ominus(CH_4)$
CH4(g) + 2O2(g)
–393.5 +
2 × –285.8
direct
route
–890.7
CO2(g) + 2H2O(l)

$(-393.5\text{ kJ mol}^{-1}) + 2 \times (-285.8\text{ kJ mol}^{-1}) = \Delta H_f^\ominus(CH_4) + (-890.7\text{ kJ mol}^{-1})$

Hence

$$\Delta H_f^\ominus(CH_4) = (-393.5\text{ kJ mol}^{-1}) + 2 \times (-285.8\text{ kJ mol}^{-1}) - (-890.7\text{ kJ mol}^{-1}) = -74.4\text{ kJ mol}^{-1}$$

Note: This calculation is essentially the reverse of the previous example.

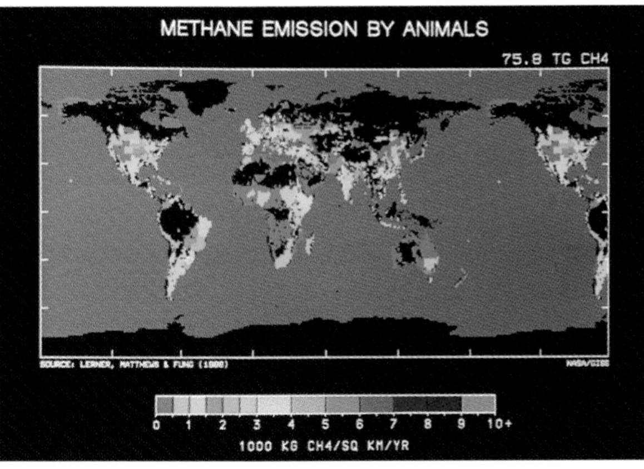

The intensity of methane emissions gives a clear view of the predominance of farming in different countries.

Worked example to calculate the standard enthalpy change of formation of nitromethane from standard enthalpy changes of combustion

Question: Given the standard enthalpy changes of combustion shown in the margin, calculate the standard enthalpy change of formation of nitromethane.

Strategy: Set up an enthalpy cycle that includes the data given and the unknown step.

Answer: The enthalpy cycle shows that the direct route (the combustion of the elements) gives the same standard enthalpy change as the indirect route in which the elements are combined into nitromethane and then nitromethane is combusted:

```
C(s) + 3/2 H2(g) + 1/2 N2(g) + 7/4 O2(g)

                ΔHf⦵ (CH3NO2)

-393.5 +        CH3NO2(l) + 3/4 O2(g)
(3/2) × -285.8
direct
route                       -709.2

CO2(g) + 3/2 H2O(l) + 1/2 N2(g)
```

$(-393.5\ \text{kJ mol}^{-1}) + (3/2) \times (-285.8\ \text{kJ mol}^{-1}) = \Delta H^{\ominus}_f(CH_3NO_2) + (-709.2\ \text{kJ mol}^{-1})$

Hence

$$\Delta H^{\ominus}_f(CH_3NO_2) = (-393.5\ \text{kJ mol}^{-1}) + (3/2) \times (-285.8\ \text{kJ mol}^{-1}) - (-709.2\ \text{kJ mol}^{-1})$$
$$= -113.0\ \text{kJ mol}^{-1}$$

Data

The standard enthalpy changes of combustion (in kJ mol^{-1}) are as follows:

C(s)	−393.5
H_2(g)	−285.8
CH_3NO_2(l)	−709.2

The combustion of nitromethane being evaluated in a test rig.

Worked example to calculate the standard enthalpy change of reaction from standard enthalpy changes of formation

Question: Calculate the standard enthalpy change for the following reaction:
$AlCl_3(s) + 6H_2O(l) = AlCl_3.6H_2O(s)$

Strategy: Use the equation $\Delta H^{\ominus} = \Delta H^{\ominus}_f(\text{products}) - \Delta H^{\ominus}_f(\text{reactants})$

Answer:

$$\Delta H^{\ominus} = \Delta H^{\ominus}_f(AlCl_3 \cdot 6H_2O(s)) - \Delta H^{\ominus}_f(AlCl_3(s) + 6H_2O(l))$$
$$= (-2680.0\ \text{kJ mol}^{-1}) - ((-704.2\ \text{kJ mol}^{-1}) + 6 \times (-285.8\ \text{kJ mol}^{-1}))$$
$$= -261\ \text{kJ mol}^{-1}$$

Note: Remember to multiply by the mole ratio in the equation.

Data

The standard enthalpy changes of formation (in kJ mol^{-1}) are as follows:

H_2O(l)	−285.8
$AlCl_3$(s)	−704.2
$AlCl_3 \cdot 6H_2O$(s)	−2680.0

SUMMARY

- Hess's law can be used to calculate the standard enthalpy change during reactions.

PRACTICE

1 Calculate the standard enthalpy change for the reaction
$CaO(s) + H_2O(l) \rightarrow Ca(OH)_2(s)$
given that the standard enthalpy changes of formation of calcium oxide, water, and calcium hydroxide are −635, −286, and −987 kJ mol^{-1} respectively.

2 Calculate the standard enthalpy change of formation of carbon monoxide given that the standard enthalpy changes of combustion of graphite and carbon monoxide are −393.5 and −283.0 kJ mol^{-1} respectively.

10.7 Some important enthalpy changes

OBJECTIVES

- Named standard enthalpy changes
- Breaking reactions into component steps

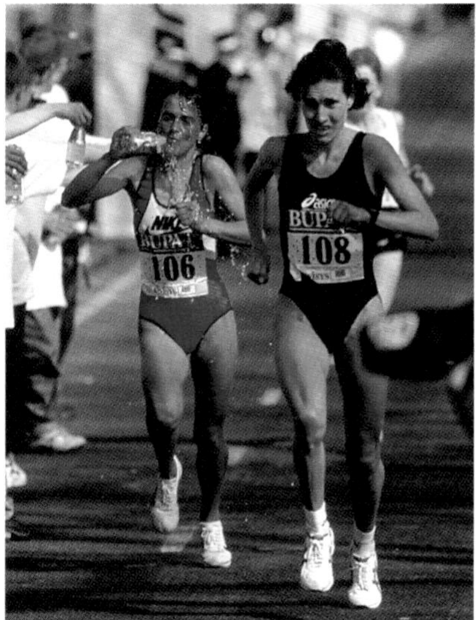

The heat needed to evaporate sweat is obtained from our hot bodies and so helps to keep us cool.

By now you should understand the meaning of the term 'standard enthalpy change'. You should also be able to carry out calculations involving Hess's law relating to standard enthalpy changes of combustion and standard enthalpy changes of formation. This spread introduces a further selection of important standard enthalpy changes. The spread concludes by showing you how to break reactions down and calculate the standard enthalpy changes for a series of steps.

Named standard enthalpy changes

It is conventional in all the following definitions to omit the word 'standard' preceding the name, despite the fact that they *are* standard enthalpy changes.

- The **enthalpy of fusion (melting)** is the standard enthalpy change accompanying the melting of a solid substance at its melting point. For example

  $Al(s) \rightarrow Al(l)$; $\Delta H^{\ominus}_{m}(933\,K) = +10.7\,kJ\,mol^{-1}$

- The **enthalpy of vaporization** is the standard enthalpy change accompanying the vaporization of a liquid substance at its boiling point. For example

  $H_2O(l) \rightarrow H_2O(g)$; $\Delta H^{\ominus}_{v}(373\,K) = +40.7\,kJ\,mol^{-1}$

- The **enthalpy of atomization** is the standard enthalpy change accompanying the production of separate gaseous atoms of an element. For example

  $\frac{1}{2}Cl_2(g) \rightarrow Cl(g)$; $\Delta H^{\ominus}_{at}(298\,K) = +121\,kJ\,mol^{-1}$
  $Na(s) \rightarrow Na(g)$; $\Delta H^{\ominus}_{at}(298\,K) = +108\,kJ\,mol^{-1}$

- The **first ionization enthalpy** is the standard enthalpy change accompanying the removal of one electron from an atom in the gas phase. For example

  $Na(g) \rightarrow Na^{+}(g) + e^{-}(g)$; $\Delta H^{\ominus}_{i.e.}(298\,K) = +498\,kJ\,mol^{-1}$

- The **second ionization enthalpy** is the standard enthalpy change accompanying the removal of a second electron from a singly positively charged ion in the gas phase. For example

  $Na^{+}(g) \rightarrow Na^{2+}(g) + e^{-}(g)$; $\Delta H^{\ominus}_{2nd\,i.e.}(298\,K) = +4560\,kJ\,mol^{-1}$

- The **electron-gain enthalpy** (previously called 'electron affinity') is the standard enthalpy change accompanying the addition of one electron to an atom in the gas phase. For example

  $Cl(g) + e^{-}(g) \rightarrow Cl^{-}(g)$; $\Delta H^{\ominus}_{e.g.}(298\,K) = -351\,kJ\,mol^{-1}$

  Note that the process of electron gain for chlorine is exothermic, so the enthalpy change has a negative sign.

- The **lattice enthalpy** is the standard enthalpy change accompanying breaking of a solid lattice into separate ions in the gas phase. For example

  $NaCl(s) \rightarrow Na^{+}(g) + Cl^{-}(g)$; $\Delta H^{\ominus}_{lat}(298\,K) = +787\,kJ\,mol^{-1}$

- The **enthalpy of hydration** is the standard enthalpy change accompanying the production of a hydrated ion from an ion in the gas phase. For example

  $Na^{+}(g) + water \rightarrow Na^{+}(aq)$; $\Delta H^{\ominus}_{hyd}(298\,K) = -406\,kJ\,mol^{-1}$

- The **enthalpy of solution** is the standard enthalpy change accompanying dissolving a solid in a large excess of water. For example

  $NaOH(s) + water \rightarrow NaOH(aq)$; $\Delta H^{\ominus}_{sol}(298\,K) = -42.7\,kJ\,mol^{-1}$

Lattice energy and ionization energy

Chapter 5 introduced the idea of removing electrons from atoms to form ions. The energy associated with that change was referred to as the 'ionization energy'. You will often find enthalpy changes being referred to colloquially as 'energies' rather than as 'enthalpies'. Similarly, 'lattice enthalpy' is often called 'lattice energy'.

Lattice formation enthalpy

Lattice enthalpy refers to the enthalpy change accompanying breaking of a solid lattice into separate ions in the gas phase. *Lattice formation enthalpy* refers to the opposite change, from gas-phase ions to form a solid. For example

$Na^{+}(g) + Cl^{-}(g) \rightarrow NaCl(s)$;
$\Delta H^{\ominus}_{lat\,for}(298\,K) = -787\,kJ\,mol^{-1}$

Compare this expression with the one for 'lattice enthalpy' alongside in the main text.

Lattice enthalpy

The magnitude of the lattice enthalpy depends on three main factors, which reflect how ions interact with each other. The three factors are:

1 *The charges on the ions*

The greater the charges on the ions, the greater the attraction between them, and the greater will be the lattice enthalpy. For example, sodium fluoride and magnesium oxide have similar structures. The halide is of the form M^+F^- and the oxide is $M^{2+}O^{2-}$. The attraction between the ions is proportional to the product of the charges. The lattice enthalpy of the oxide is expected to be *four times* that of the fluoride.

This prediction is quite close to the ratio of the observed values (1:4.2).

NaF $\Delta H^{\ominus}_{lat}(298\,K) = +926\,kJ\,mol^{-1}$
MgO $\Delta H^{\ominus}_{lat}(298\,K) = +3800\,kJ\,mol^{-1}$

2 *The distance between the ions*

The smaller the distance between the ions, the greater the attraction between them, and the greater will be the lattice enthalpy. For example, the sizes of the halide ions increase in the order $F^- < Cl^- < Br^- < I^-$. Lattice enthalpies for the sodium halides *decrease* in the same order (note that each substance has the same ionic charges).

The values for the sodium halides are:

NaF $\Delta H^{\ominus}_{lat}(298\,K) = +926\,kJ\,mol^{-1}$
NaCl $\Delta H^{\ominus}_{lat}(298\,K) = +787\,kJ\,mol^{-1}$
NaBr $\Delta H^{\ominus}_{lat}(298\,K) = +752\,kJ\,mol^{-1}$
NaI $\Delta H^{\ominus}_{lat}(298\,K) = +705\,kJ\,mol^{-1}$

The potassium ion is larger than the sodium ion, with the result that the values for the potassium halides are *smaller* than those for the corresponding sodium compounds.

The values for two potassium halides are:

KF $\Delta H^{\ominus}_{lat}(298\,K) = +821\,kJ\,mol^{-1}$
KCl $\Delta H^{\ominus}_{lat}(298\,K) = +717\,kJ\,mol^{-1}$

3 *The detailed crystal structure of the compound*

This last factor is usually the least important. The two factors discussed above have considered the interaction between only a single pair of ions. A real ionic crystal is far more complex, see spread 6.6.

Enthalpy of solution

Two processes take place when a solid dissolves in a solvent. First, the species in the solid become separated from each other. The standard enthalpy change for this endothermic process is the lattice enthalpy of the solid. Secondly, the separated species become surrounded by molecules of the solvent. This process is called **solvation**, or **hydration** when the solvent is water.

The illustration to the right shows water molecules clustering around the ions of dissolved sodium chloride. The attraction between the water molecules and the ions causes a total exothermic enthalpy of hydration of $\Delta H^{\ominus}_{hyd}(298\,K) = -783\,kJ\,mol^{-1}$ (for sodium chloride), i.e. the sum of

$$Na^+(g) + water \rightarrow Na^+(aq); \qquad \Delta H^{\ominus}_{hyd}(298\,K) = -406\,kJ\,mol^{-1}$$

(as given opposite) plus

$$Cl^-(g) + water \rightarrow Cl^-(aq); \qquad \Delta H^{\ominus}_{hyd}(298\,K) = -377\,kJ\,mol^{-1}$$

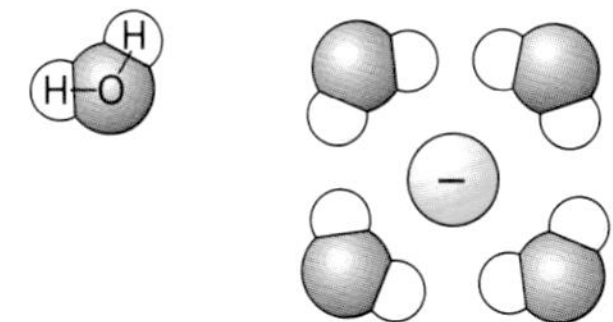

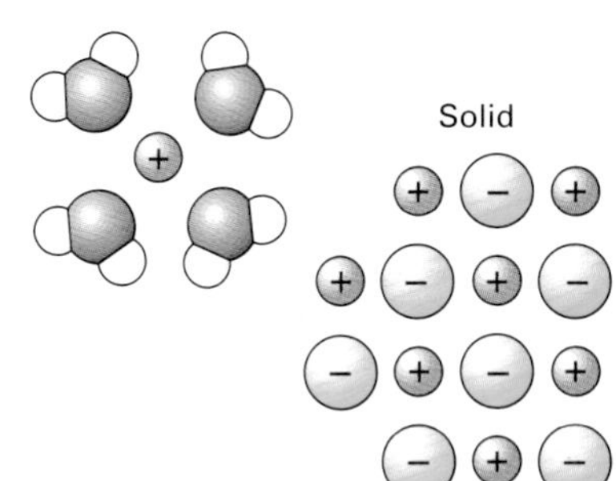

Solution takes place in two steps: the break-up of the lattice followed by hydration of the resulting ions.

The enthalpy of solution is the standard enthalpy change when a solid dissolves in a large excess of water. It is the sum of the lattice enthalpy and the total enthalpy of hydration of the ions. If a solid dissolves exothermically, the solution will become warm as it dissolves. If it dissolves endothermically, the solution will become cold. For example, when sodium chloride dissolves:

$$NaCl(s) + water \rightarrow Na^+(aq) + Cl^-(aq)$$

From above, the lattice enthalpy of sodium chloride is $\Delta H^{\ominus}_{lat}(298\,K) = +787\,kJ\,mol^{-1}$. So, for sodium chloride, the enthalpy of solution is

$$\begin{aligned}\Delta H^{\ominus}_{sol}(298\,K) &= \Delta H^{\ominus}_{lat}(298\,K) + \Delta H^{\ominus}_{hyd}(298\,K)\\ &= (+787\,kJ\,mol^{-1}) + (-783\,kJ\,mol^{-1})\\ &= +4\,kJ\,mol^{-1}\end{aligned}$$

The enthalpy of solution is *just* endothermic.

SUMMARY

- Lattice enthalpy depends on the charges on the ions, the distance between the ions, and the detailed crystal structure of the compound.
- The enthalpy of solution of an ionic compound is the sum of the lattice enthalpy and the total enthalpy of hydration of the ions.

10.8

OBJECTIVES

- Born-Haber cycle for sodium chloride
- Enthalpy of formation and stability

BORN–HABER CYCLES

Hess's law states that the value of the standard enthalpy change of a reaction is independent of the route taken. As a result, we can consider going from the reactants to the products by two different routes, in an enthalpy cycle. The values of the standard enthalpy changes for the direct and the indirect routes are equal, so we can calculate the value of a particular stage in the overall cycle. An enthalpy cycle used to calculate the standard enthalpy change of formation of ionic compounds is called a **Born–Haber cycle** after Max Born and Fritz Haber who developed it. A Born–Haber cycle pictures the formation of an ionic compound from its elements in a series of steps.

The Born–Haber cycle for sodium chloride

A diagram representing the formation of sodium chloride from its elements is shown below. The equation

$Na(s) + \frac{1}{2}Cl_2(g) \rightarrow NaCl(s)$

represents the *direct* route. The *indirect* route consists of five separate steps (temperature is 298 K throughout):

1 Atomize solid sodium

$Na(s) \rightarrow Na(g);\quad \Delta H^{\ominus}_{at} = +108\ kJ\ mol^{-1}$

2 Atomize chlorine gas

$\frac{1}{2}Cl_2(g) \rightarrow Cl(g);\quad \Delta H^{\ominus}_{at} = +121\ kJ\ mol^{-1}$

3 Form sodium ions from the sodium atoms

$Na(g) \rightarrow Na^+(g) + e^-(g);\quad \Delta H^{\ominus}_{i.e.} = +498\ kJ\ mol^{-1}$

4 Form chloride ions from the chlorine atoms

$Cl(g) + e^-(g) \rightarrow Cl^-(g);\quad \Delta H^{\ominus}_{e.g.} = -351\ kJ\ mol^{-1}$

5 Pack the sodium and chloride ions together to make solid sodium chloride

$Na^+(g) + Cl^-(g) \rightarrow NaCl(s);\quad \Delta H^{\ominus}_{lat\ for} = -787\ kJ\ mol^{-1}$

The sum of the standard enthalpy changes for this indirect route equals $-411\ kJ\ mol^{-1}$. This value is the same as the standard enthalpy change of formation of sodium chloride $\Delta H^{\ominus}_f = -411\ kJ\ mol^{-1}$. The standard enthalpy change corresponding to any one of the steps in a Born–Haber cycle may be calculated by applying Hess's law.

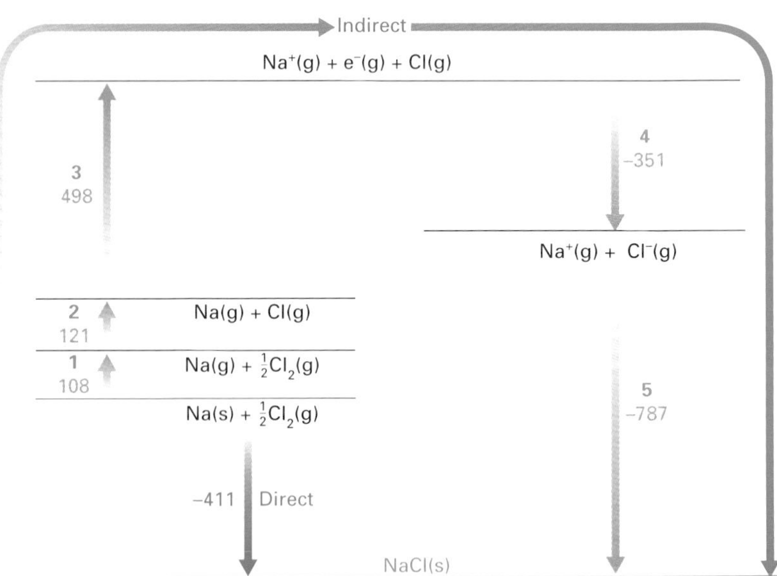

The direction of each arrow in this diagram signifies the sign of the enthalpy change: upwards represents an endothermic step; downwards an exothermic step. All figures are in kJ mol⁻¹.

Stability of ionic compounds

Overall the atomization and ionization processes (i.e. steps 1–4) in a Born–Haber cycle are endothermic (+376 kJ mol^{-1} for NaCl). When the ions in the gas phase pack together to form the solid compound (step 5), the process is exothermic (–787 kJ mol^{-1}). If a compound is to form, the exothermic lattice formation enthalpy must be large enough to compensate for the endothermic processes. As a general rule, the more negative the value of the standard enthalpy change of formation, the more stable the compound will be. (In this context, 'stability' refers to decomposition of the compound back to its elements on heating.) Conversely, an endothermic standard enthalpy change of formation indicates that the compound is likely to be thermally unstable or may not form at all.

Sodium reacts with oxygen to form sodium oxide Na_2O. The Born–Haber cycle for sodium oxide Na_2O shows that the exothermic lattice formation enthalpy is sufficiently large to compensate for the endothermic processes of atomization and ionization.

Note carefully that the *second* electron-gain enthalpy of oxygen is *endothermic*; once one electron has been gained, it repels further electrons.

Sodium does *not* react with oxygen to form the oxide NaO. The relevant Born–Haber cycle shows that the formation of the *hypothetical* ionic compound NaO would require the extremely endothermic step of forming Na^{2+} ions. The second electron would have to be removed from an inner shell closer to the nucleus, causing an enthalpy change of 4560 kJ mol^{-1}. Such a large endothermic process cannot be compensated for by the lattice formation enthalpy. The compound of formula NaO does not form because its standard enthalpy change of formation is too highly endothermic.

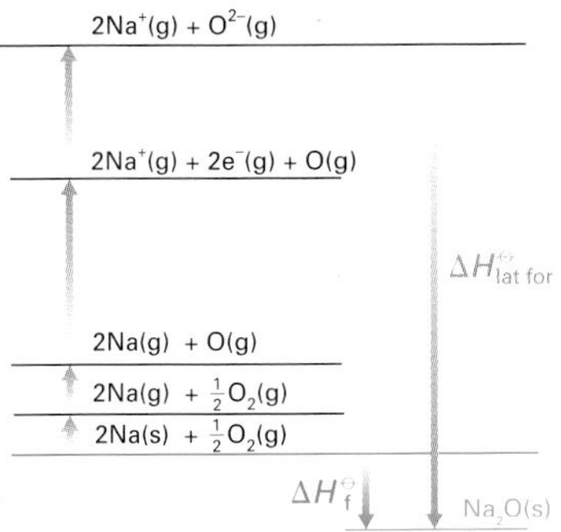

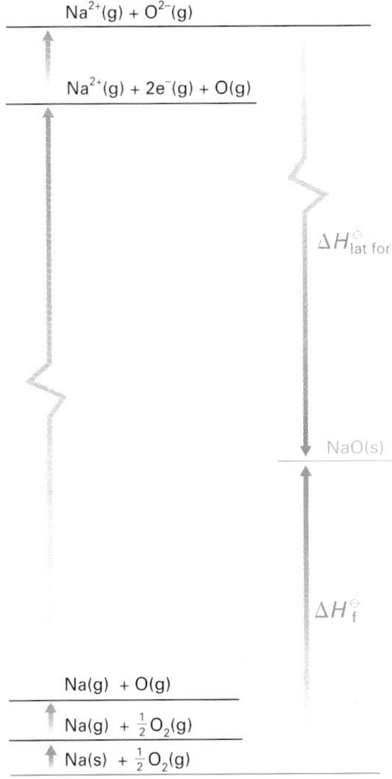

The Born–Haber cycles for (a) sodium oxide Na_2O and (b) the hypothetical compound NaO.

Born–Haber cycles and bond character

Lattice formation enthalpy terms refer to the change in which separated ions come together to form an ionic lattice. A model consisting of *separate uniformly charged spherical ions* represents a state of pure ionic bonding. Using this model, it is possible to calculate theoretical values for lattice formation enthalpies from a knowledge of the charges on the ions and the distance between the ions. Experimental values for lattice formation enthalpies are found from Born–Haber cycles in which the standard enthalpy changes of the various steps result from experimental data.

There is a discrepancy of just 2% between the theoretical and experimental values of lattice formation enthalpy for sodium chloride NaCl. The structure of sodium chloride closely resembles the model for pure ionic bonding. In the case of silver chloride AgCl, there is a discrepancy of 6%, indicating that the crystal lattice does not consist of separate spherical ions. Electron density concentrated *between* the two ions introduces a degree of covalent character to the bonding between the silver and chloride ions, so the lattice formation enthalpy differs from that predicted for a purely ionic compound.

Compound	**Theoretical value /kJ mol^{-1}**	**Experimental value /kJ mol^{-1}**
NaCl	–769	–787
NaBr	–732	–747
NaI	–682	–704
AgCl	–864	–915
AgBr	–830	–904
AgI	–808	–889

Theoretical and experimental values of lattice formation enthalpy. Notice that the discrepancy is more marked in AgBr and AgI than in AgCl. The bromide and iodide ions are larger than the chloride ion and are more polarizable, causing a greater deviation from pure ionic bonding.

SUMMARY

- Born–Haber cycles are an application of Hess's law to ionic compounds.
- Compounds with large negative standard enthalpy changes of formation are likely to be thermally stable with respect to their elements.
- Born–Haber cycles may be used to calculate the theoretical standard enthalpy changes of formation of ionic compounds to see how likely they are to exist.

10.9

Bond enthalpy

OBJECTIVES

- Bond enthalpy
- Average bond enthalpy
- Comparing calculation methods

Bonds

Bond breaking requires energy.

Bond making releases energy.

Bond enthalpies

Oxygen	O=O	+496 kJ mol^{-1}
Hydrogen	H—H	+436 kJ mol^{-1}
Water	O—H	+463 kJ mol^{-1}

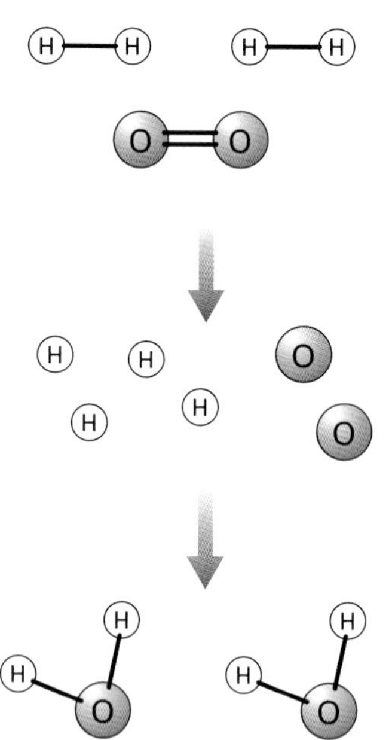

The reactants hydrogen H_2 (2 mol) and oxygen O_2 (1 mol) break into atoms, which combine to make 2 mol of the product, water H_2O.

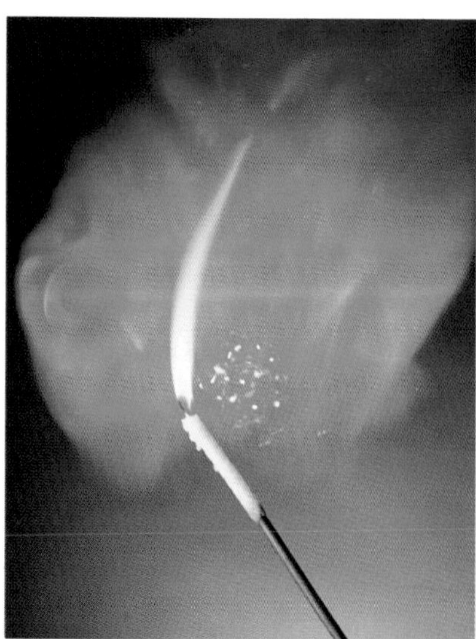

These bubbles are filled with hydrogen. They explode when ignited as the hydrogen meets the oxygen in the air.

You are already familiar with using standard enthalpy change of formation data in conjunction with Hess's law to calculate standard enthalpy changes of combustion. Another way of calculating the enthalpy changes of reactions involving covalent compounds is to consider the enthalpy associated with each covalent bond. Calculating the standard enthalpy change is then a matter of comparing the standard enthalpy change involved in *breaking* the bonds in the reactants with that involved in *making* new bonds to form the products. Adding the standard enthalpy changes for the two processes leads to the standard enthalpy change for the overall reaction.

Making and breaking bonds

The **bond enthalpy** (which is often colloquially but inaccurately called the 'bond energy') is the standard enthalpy change associated with breaking A—B bonds into A atoms and B atoms, all species being in the gas phase:

$$A\text{—}B(g) \rightarrow A(g) + B(g)$$

For example, the H—Cl bond enthalpy is the standard enthalpy change associated with breaking H—Cl molecules into H atoms and Cl atoms. The values of bond enthalpies are always positive because *breaking* a bond always requires energy. The enthalpy change for *making* a bond is equal in magnitude, but opposite in sign.

Calculations involving bond enthalpies

The calculation of the overall standard enthalpy change for any reaction can be thought of as follows:

1 The first step involves calculating the standard enthalpy change accompanying breaking the bonds in the reactant molecules.

2 The second step involves calculating the standard enthalpy change accompanying making the bonds in the product molecules.

3 Then we add together these standard enthalpy changes to obtain the overall standard enthalpy change.

We now show this method for a particular reaction. The equation for the formation of water in the gas phase is:

$$H_2(g) + \tfrac{1}{2}O_2(g) \rightarrow H_2O(g)$$

The steps are as follows:

Step 1 Break into atoms 1 mol of H_2 and ½ mol of O_2.

The total standard enthalpy change for breaking the molecules apart is:

$$1 \times (+436\ \text{kJ mol}^{-1}) + \tfrac{1}{2} \times (+496\ \text{kJ mol}^{-1}) = +684\ \text{kJ mol}^{-1}$$

i.e.

$$H_2(g) + \tfrac{1}{2}O_2(g) \rightarrow 2H(g) + O(g); \qquad \Delta H^\ominus(298\ \text{K}) = +684\ \text{kJ mol}^{-1}$$

Step 2 Form 2 mol of O—H bonds per mole of water produced.

Each water molecule has two O—H bonds, so we need to form 2 mol O—H per 1 mol H_2O. The value of the standard enthalpy change is negative because bonds are being made. The standard enthalpy change is therefore:

$$2 \times (-463\ \text{kJ mol}^{-1}) = -926\ \text{kJ mol}^{-1}$$

i.e.

$$2H(g) + O(g) \rightarrow H_2O(g); \qquad \Delta H^\ominus(298\ \text{K}) = -926\ \text{kJ mol}^{-1}$$

Step 3 Sum the standard enthalpy changes to calculate the overall standard enthalpy change:

$$(+684\ \text{kJ mol}^{-1}) + (-926\ \text{kJ mol}^{-1}) = -242\ \text{kJ mol}^{-1}$$

The standard enthalpy change of formation of water in the *gas* phase is –242 kJ mol^{-1}, spread 10.2.

Average bond enthalpies

The H—H bond enthalpy is quite straightforward because the H—H bond occurs only in the H_2 molecule. On the other hand, there are C—H bonds in many different compounds; for example, C—H bonds are present in every alkane. However, carbon atoms may be bonded together in various arrangements and to various other atoms. Because they may have these different environments, all C—H bonds do not have the same bond enthalpies. The bond enthalpies quoted in tables represent average (mean) bond enthalpies derived from the full range of molecules that contain a particular bond. The results of calculations using average bond enthalpies will therefore show discrepancies when compared with results from experiments with specific molecules.

Average bond enthalpies

Bond	Average bond enthalpy/kJ mol^{-1}
C—F	484
C—Cl	338
C—Br	276
C—I	238
C—H	413
C—C	348
C=C	612
C≡C	838
N—H	388
P—H	322
O—H	463
S—H	338
C=O	743

Worked example on methane

Question: Using average bond enthalpy values, calculate the standard enthalpy change of formation of methane. $\Delta H^{\ominus}_{at}$ for carbon is +717 kJ mol^{-1}. How does the answer obtained compare with the experimental value of –75 kJ mol^{-1}?

Answer: The equation for the reaction is:

$C(s) + 2H_2(g) \rightarrow CH_4(g)$

Step 1 Atomize the reactants.

Break into atoms 1 mol of carbon atoms and 2 mol of hydrogen molecules. The standard enthalpy change is:

$1 \times (+717\,kJ\,mol^{-1}) + 2 \times (+436\,kJ\,mol^{-1}) = +1589\,kJ\,mol^{-1}$

Step 2 Form 4 mol of C—H bonds.

The standard enthalpy change is:

$4 \times (-413\,kJ\,mol^{-1}) = -1652\,kJ\,mol^{-1}$

Step 3 Sum the standard enthalpy changes to calculate the overall standard enthalpy change.

The standard enthalpy change of formation is:

$(+1589\,kJ\,mol^{-1}) + (-1652\,kJ\,mol^{-1}) = -63\,kJ\,mol^{-1}$

i.e.

$C(s) + 2H_2(g) \rightarrow CH_4(g); \quad \Delta H^{\ominus}_{f}(298\,K) = -63\,kJ\,mol^{-1}$

Note: This *calculation* therefore gives the standard enthalpy change of formation of methane as –63 kJ mol^{-1}. The calculation uses the *average* bond enthalpy for C—H bonds in the full range of compounds, not just in methane.

The value determined *from experiment* is based on the standard enthalpy changes of combustion of carbon, hydrogen, and methane. Using experimental enthalpy of combustion data, the standard enthalpy change of formation for methane is found to be –75 kJ mol^{-1} using Hess's law. This latter figure is accepted as being the correct value.

There is a difference between results of calculations based on *average* bond enthalpies and results based on *specific* experimental data. However, bond enthalpies are easy to understand and to manipulate, and usually give an accurate enough indication of the standard enthalpy change of a reaction involving covalent substances.

SUMMARY

- Bond enthalpy is the standard enthalpy change associated with breaking A—B bonds into A atoms and B atoms, all species being in the gas phase.
- Average bond enthalpies represent the average value of the standard enthalpy changes required to break a particular covalent bond in the full range of molecules in which that bond may be found.
- Calculations based on average bond enthalpies lead to only approximate results when compared with values obtained from specific experimental data.

PRACTICE

1 Using the average bond enthalpy data given above:
- **a** Calculate the standard enthalpy change of formation of ethane C_2H_6 and of propane C_3H_8
- **b** Compare your two answers with one another and with the value of methane.

2 Calculate the standard enthalpy change of combustion for methane, given that the average bond enthalpy for the C=O bond is 743 kJ mol^{-1}.

10.10

OBJECTIVES

- Comparing calculation with experiment
- Insights into bonding

BOND ENTHALPIES AND BONDING

Bond enthalpy values may be used to calculate the standard enthalpy change for almost any reaction involving covalent substances. The average bond enthalpy value for a given bond is the average for that bond in all its different common environments. Using these *average* values for a *specific* chemical reaction may give unusual or anomalous results when compared to those obtained from experimental data. Such *anomalies* imply that a specific bond does not behave like the 'average bond' represented by the average bond enthalpy value. Studying these anomalies can lead to deeper understanding of the nature of the chemical bonds involved.

Strategy

Step 1 Write down the balanced chemical equation.

Step 2 Identify the bonds that are broken; assign average bond enthalpy values to each bond; breaking bonds is an endothermic process.

Step 3 Identify the bonds that are made; assign average bond enthalpy values to each bond; making bonds is an exothermic process.

Step 4 Sum the exothermic and the endothermic processes to give the overall reaction.

Step 5 Remember that bond enthalpy values refer to the gas phase; water formed from the gas phase must be converted to its standard state (liquid). The enthalpy of vaporization of liquid water is $+44\,kJ\,mol^{-1}$ at 298 K.

The standard enthalpy change of combustion of methane

In the following example, we will calculate the standard enthalpy change of combustion of methane from bond enthalpy values. We follow the steps shown on the left.

Step 1 The balanced chemical equation for this reaction is:

$$CH_4(g) + 2O_2(g) \rightarrow CO_2(g) + 2H_2O(l)$$

Step 2 We must break four C—H bonds (in the methane molecule) and two O═O bonds (in the two oxygen molecules). The standard enthalpy change is

$$4 \times (+413\,kJ\,mol^{-1}) + 2 \times (+496\,kJ\,mol^{-1}) = +2644\,kJ\,mol^{-1}$$

Step 3 We must make two C═O bonds (in the carbon dioxide molecule) and four O—H bonds (in the two water molecules). The standard enthalpy change is

$$2 \times (-743\,kJ\,mol^{-1}) + 4 \times (-463\,kJ\,mol^{-1}) = -3338\,kJ\,mol^{-1}$$

Step 4 We calculate the standard enthalpy change of combustion *in the gas phase* by summing the values calculated above. This gives

$$(+2644\,kJ\,mol^{-1}) + (-3338\,kJ\,mol^{-1}) = -694\,kJ\,mol^{-1}$$

Step 5 We now convert the water formed in the gas phase to a liquid. When water in the gas phase condenses to a liquid, it releases $44\,kJ\,mol^{-1}$ at 298 K. In this reaction, 2 mol of water form per mole of methane combusted, so the standard enthalpy change is

$$2 \times (-44\,kJ\,mol^{-1}) = -88\,kJ\,mol^{-1}$$

The prediction for the value of $\Delta H^\ominus_c$ for the reaction with liquid water as a product is:

$$(-694\,kJ\,mol^{-1}) + (-88\,kJ\,mol^{-1}) = -782\,kJ\,mol^{-1}$$

i.e.

$$CH_4(g) + 2O_2(g) \rightarrow CO_2(g) + 2H_2O(l);$$
$$\Delta H^\ominus_c(298\,K) = -782\,kJ\,mol^{-1}$$

Bonding implications

An average bond enthalpy term derives from a bond in a range of environments. A bond dissociation enthalpy refers to a specific bond in a specific molecule.

Bond broken	Bond dissociation enthalpy/ kJ mol^{-1}
CH_3CH_2—H	423
$(CH_3)_2CH$—H	413
$(CH_3)_3C$—H	403
The average bond enthalpy for the C—H bond is $413\,kJ\,mol^{-1}$	

The calculation in the example above gives the result $\Delta H^\ominus_c = -782\,kJ\,mol^{-1}$, which is far from the accepted standard enthalpy change of combustion ($-891\,kJ\,mol^{-1}$). The bond enthalpy value used for the C═O bonds in carbon dioxide assumes that each C═O bond is discrete (separate). In reality, electron density is not confined to the two C═O bonds separately. It is delocalized throughout the entire molecule, considerably strengthening each bond. As a result, the enthalpy required to break a C═O bond in carbon dioxide is significantly greater than that required to break the C═O bond in, for example, propanone CH_3COCH_3.

Spectroscopic measurements have determined the actual C═O bond enthalpy (called the **bond dissociation enthalpy**) in carbon dioxide to be $+804\,kJ\,mol^{-1}$. The value used in the calculation above ($+743\,kJ\,mol^{-1}$) is the *average* bond enthalpy for the C═O bond.

Repeating the calculation with $-804\,\text{kJ mol}^{-1}$ in place of $-743\,\text{kJ mol}^{-1}$ gives an answer of $-904\,\text{kJ mol}^{-1}$, very close to the experimentally based value of $-891\,\text{kJ mol}^{-1}$. The remaining error is due to the C—H and O—H values remaining as average values.

(a) O : C : O

O=C=O

(b) O—C—O

(c)

(a) The Lewis structure for carbon dioxide shows two electron pairs between each oxygen atom and the central carbon atom. (b) Overlap of the p orbitals in phase forms the molecular orbital (c). This is one of the two molecular orbitals, both of which are delocalized over both oxygen atoms and the central carbon atom (the other orbital is in the perpendicular plane).

Benzene

Average bond enthalpy values predict a standard enthalpy change of formation for the structure shown in (a) below of $+215\,\text{kJ mol}^{-1}$. The experimentally based value is $+49\,\text{kJ mol}^{-1}$. Benzene is thermodynamically more stable with respect to its elements than this structure suggests. Electron density diagrams show that there is equal electron density between each of the carbon atoms. There are six bonding electrons *delocalized* around the entire hexagonal ring of carbon atoms.

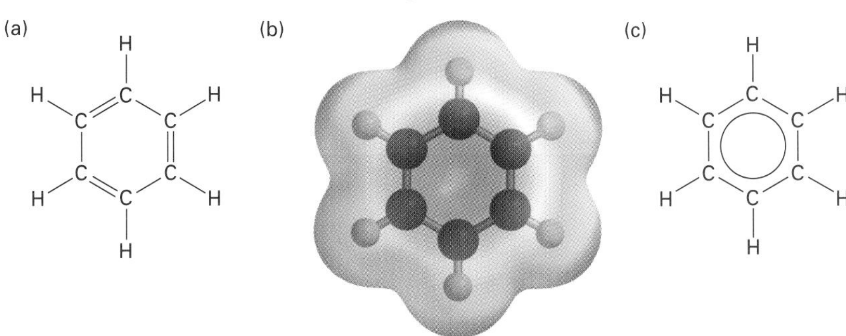

(a) The structure for benzene C_6H_6 suggested by Kekulé over 100 years ago. The structure shows carbon forming 4 covalent bonds and hydrogen forming 1. Six carbon atoms are held in a hexagonal ring structure by alternating C—C single and C=C double covalent bonds. (b) The electrostatic potential map for benzene showing that the carbon-carbon bonds are all the same length. (c) This modified structural formula indicates that the π electrons are delocalized.

Predictions using bond enthalpies

Despite discrepancies which are sometimes difficult to explain, average bond enthalpies are very useful for making general predictions. For example, the standard enthalpy changes of combustion of the alkanes are expected to increase in proportion to the number of carbon atoms present. On combustion, each additional CH_2 group will form one CO_2 molecule and one H_2O molecule. These predictions are borne out in practice and are a useful guide when choosing or designing fuels.

SUMMARY

- If results for $\Delta H^{\ominus}$ obtained from different calculations do not agree, this may be due to errors in assumptions about the nature of specific bonds.

PRACTICE

1. Butane and 2-methylpropane both have the molecular formula C_4H_{10}. Would you expect their standard enthalpy changes of combustion to be identical? Explain your answer.
2. Calculate the standard enthalpy change of combustion $\Delta H_c^{\ominus}(298\,\text{K})$ for ethane C_2H_6.
3. Estimate the standard enthalpy change of combustion of nonane C_9H_{20}.
4. The measured standard enthalpy change of formation of buta-1,3-diene $CH_2{=}CH{-}CH{=}CH_2$ is $+112\,\text{kJ mol}^{-1}$. Explain why the standard enthalpy change of formation calculated from average bond enthalpy terms is *more* endothermic than this value.

PRACTICE EXAM QUESTIONS

1 Below are some standard enthalpy changes including the standard enthalpy of combustion of nitroglycerine, $C_3H_5N_3O_9$:

$\frac{1}{2}N_2(g) + O_2(g) \rightarrow NO_2(g)$
$\Delta H^\ominus = +34\ kJ\ mol^{-1}$

$C(s) + O_2(g) \rightarrow CO_2(g)$
$\Delta H^\ominus = -394\ kJ\ mol^{-1}$

$H_2(g) + \frac{1}{2}O_2(g) \rightarrow H_2O(g)$
$\Delta H^\ominus = -242\ kJ\ mol^{-1}$

$C_3H_5N_3O_9(l) + \frac{11}{4}O_2(g) \rightarrow 3CO_2(g) + \frac{5}{2}H_2O(g) + 3NO_2(g)$
$\Delta H^\ominus = -1540\ kJ\ mol^{-1}$

a Standard enthalpy of formation is defined using the term *standard state*. What does the term *standard state* mean? [2]

b Use the standard enthalpy changes given above to calculate the standard enthalpy of formation of nitroglycerine. [4]

c Calculate the enthalpy change for the following decomposition of nitroglycerine. [3]

$C_3H_5N_3O_9(l) \rightarrow 3CO_2(g) + \frac{5}{2}H_2O(g) + \frac{3}{2}N_2(g) + \frac{1}{4}O_2(g)$

d Suggest one reason why the reaction in part **c** occurs rather than combustion when a bomb containing nitroglycerine explodes on impact. [1]

e An alternative reaction for the combustion of hydrogen, leading to liquid water, is given below.

$H_2(g) + \frac{1}{2}O_2(g) \rightarrow H_2O(l)$ $\Delta H^\ominus = -286\ kJ\ mol^{-1}$

Calculate the enthalpy change for the process $H_2O(l) \rightarrow H_2O(g)$ and explain the sign of $\Delta H^\ominus$ in your answer. [2]

AQA (NEAB) 1999

2 The tables below contain data which are needed to answer the questions.

Name	Hydrazine	Ethane
Formula of compound	N_2H_4	C_2H_6
Boiling temperature / K	387	184

Formula and state of compound	$C_2H_6(g)$	$CO_2(g)$	$H_2O(l)$
Standard enthalpy of formation (at 298 K) / kJ mol^{-1}	–85	–394	–286

a Suggest why hydrazine has a much higher boiling temperature than ethane. [2]

b When liquid hydrazine burns in oxygen it forms nitrogen and water. The standard enthalpy change for this reaction when one mole of hydrazine forms water in the liquid state is –624 kJ mol^{-1}.

i Write a balanced equation for the combustion of hydrazine in oxygen.

ii Calculate the standard enthalpy of formation of liquid hydrazine. [4]

c i Write an equation for the complete combustion of ethane.

ii Use the appropriate standard enthalpies of formation to calculate the standard enthalpy of combustion of ethane. [4]

d Suggest one reason why hydrazine is more suitable than ethane for use as a rocket fuel. [1]

AQA (NEAB) 1998

3 a Define the term *standard molar enthalpy change of formation*. [3]

b State *Hess's law*. [1]

c The equation below shows the reaction between ammonia and fluorine.

$NH_3(g) + 3F_2(g) \rightarrow 3HF(g) + NF_3(g)$

i Use the standard molar enthalpy change of formation ($\Delta H_f^\ominus$) data in the table below to calculate the molar enthalpy change for this reaction.

Compound	NH_3	HF	NF_3
$\Delta H_f^\ominus$/ kJ mol^{-1}	–46	–269	–114

[4]

ii Use the average bond enthalpy data in the table below to calculate a value for the molar enthalpy change for the same reaction between ammonia and fluorine.

$NH_3(g) + 3F_2(g) \rightarrow 3HF(g) + NF_3(g)$

Bond	N—H	F—F	H—F	N—F
Average bond enthalpy / kJ mol^{-1}	388	158	562	272

[3]

d The answer you have calculated in **c i** is regarded as being the more reliable value. Suggest why this is so. [3]

AQA (AEB) 1997

4 The relationship between enthalpy of solvation, enthalpy of solution, and lattice enthalpy for sodium chloride and water may be represented by the diagram below.

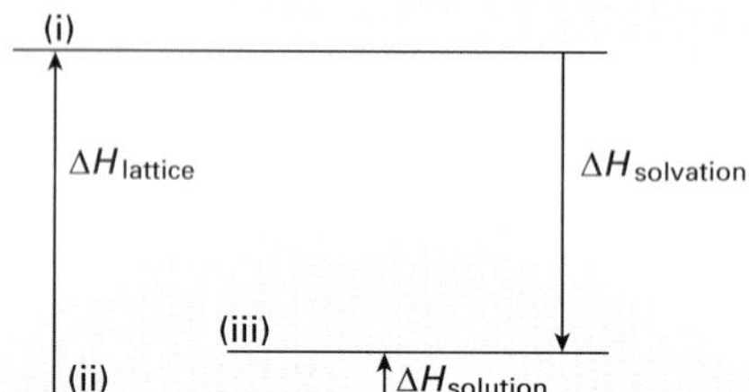

a Copy the diagram and on it, using symbols, indicate the species present at (i), (ii), and (iii). [6]

b Calculate the molar enthalpy of solution of sodium chloride if:

$\Delta H_{lattice} = +788\ kJ\ mol^{-1}$ and $\Delta H_{solvation} = -784\ kJ\ mol^{-1}$

$\Delta H_{solvation} =$ ________________ kJ mol^{-1} [2]

c State the tests you would carry out, giving experimental details, and observations you would make to correctly identify all three solutions labelled A, B, and C, suspected to be sodium chloride, potassium chloride, and lithium chloride. [4]

NICCEA 1998 *(See also chapter 16.)*

5 a A Born–Haber cycle for the formation of calcium oxide is shown below.

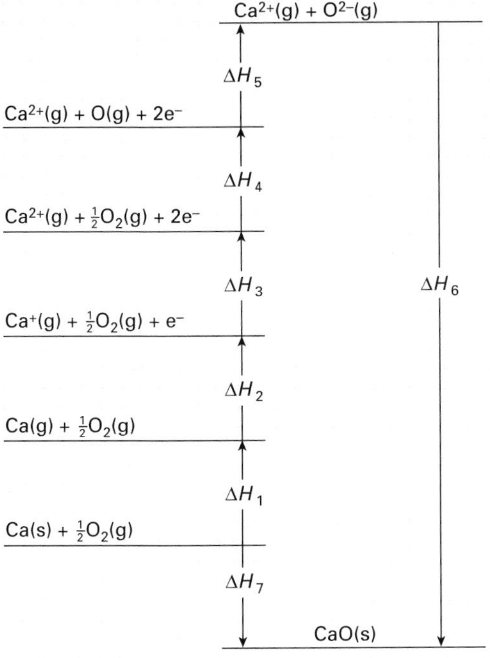

Data ΔH / kJ mol^{-1}:

$\Delta H_1 = +193$; $\Delta H_2 = +590$; $\Delta H_3 = +1150$; $\Delta H_4 = +248$; $\Delta H_6 = -3513$; $\Delta H_7 = -635$.

i Identify the change which represents the lattice enthalpy of CaO. [1]

ii Use the data above to calculate ΔH_5. [3]

iii Use this value of ΔH_5 to calculate the first electron affinity of oxygen, given that the second electron affinity of oxygen is +844 kJ mol^{-1}. [2]

b i What enthalpy change does the value of ΔH_2 represent? [1]

ii Would the value of ΔH_2 be larger or smaller for magnesium than it is for calcium? [1]

iii Explain your answer in **b ii.** [2]

c Given a sample of solid calcium chloride, contaminated with calcium carbonate, describe tests you would perform in order to confirm the presence of:

i calcium ions; [1]

ii chloride ions. [4]

EDEXCEL 1997 *(See also chapter 16 and 18.)*

6 Sodium bromide is formed from its elements at 298 K according to the equation

$Na(s) + \frac{1}{2}Br_2(l) \rightarrow NaBr(s)$

The lattice dissociation enthalpy of sodium bromide refers to the enthalpy change for the process

$NaBr(s) \rightarrow Na^+(g) + Br^-(g)$

The electron addition enthalpy refers to the process

$Br(g) + e^- \rightarrow Br^-(g)$

Use the information and the data in the table below to answer the questions which follow.

Standard enthalpies		$\Delta H^\ominus$ / kJ mol^{-1}
$\Delta H^\ominus_f$	formation of NaBr(s)	–361
$\Delta H^\ominus_{ea}$	electron addition to Br(g)	–325
$\Delta H^\ominus_{sub}$	sublimation of Na(s)	+107
$\Delta H^\ominus_{diss}$	bond dissociation of Br_2(g)	+194
$\Delta H^\ominus_{ion}$	first ionization of Na(g)	+498
$\Delta H^\ominus_L$	lattice dissociation of NaBr(s)	+753

a Construct a Born–Haber cycle for sodium bromide. Label the steps in the cycle with symbols like those used above rather than numerical values. [6]

b Use the data above and the Born–Haber cycle in part **(a)** to calculate the enthalpy of vaporization, $\Delta H^\ominus_{vap}$, of liquid bromine. [3]
NEAB 1998

7 Beer was brewed by the ancient Egyptians and is thought to have been among the rations of the builders of the Pyramids.

The ethanol and glucose composition of a beer is given in the table.

Constituent	Concentration / g dm^{-3}
Ethanol, C_2H_5OH	20
Glucose, $C_6H_{12}O_6$	20

Ethanol can be regarded as a food as well as a drug and is a more concentrated energy source than carbohydrate.

a Write a balanced equation for the complete combustion of ethanol. [1]

b i Define the term standard enthalpy change of combustion.

ii The standard enthalpy change of combustion of ethanol and of glucose may be taken as –1370 kJ mol^{-1} and –3000 kJ mol^{-1}, respectively.

Hence, calculate the enthalpy change per gram of ethanol and of glucose.

iii Calculate the total energy available in 1 dm^3 of the beer, as detailed in the table above. [5]
OCR (UCLES) 1998

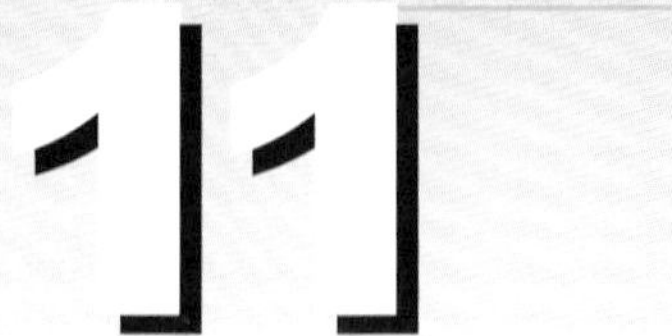

Chemical equilibrium

So far in this book, a chemical equation has implied that the reactants (the species on the left of the arrow) change completely to form the products (the species on the right of the arrow):

reactants → products

However, chemical reactions do not only move in the forward direction, from left to right in the chemical equation. This chapter explores the idea that chemical reactions also move in the backward direction, from right to left in the chemical equation. The relationship between the forward and the backward reactions and their effect on the overall yield of the reaction make up the study of *chemical equilibrium*.

THE NATURE OF DYNAMIC EQUILIBRIUM – 1

OBJECTIVES

- Static and dynamic equilibrium
- Forward and backward (reverse) reactions
- Reversible reactions

'Equilibrium' is a term used to denote balance. The two main types of equilibrium encountered in everyday life are static equilibrium and dynamic equilibrium. If you sit balanced against another person on a see-saw, you are in a state of *static* equilibrium. You do not have to move to maintain the state of balance. Dynamic equilibrium is very different. Imagine that you are on a downward-moving escalator and have set yourself the challenge: 'How can I remain at a fixed point between two floors?' You can achieve this objective only by climbing upwards at exactly the same speed as the escalator steps move downwards. In this way you establish a *dynamic* equilibrium, a balance between two objects actively moving in opposite directions.

Dynamic equilibrium for a physical process

Bromine is a dense poisonous fuming liquid. In a fume cupboard, pour some bromine into a large glass bottle and seal it with a stopper. Liquid bromine evaporates to form a vapour. To begin with, there is very little colour in the space above the liquid. But the red–brown colour of the vapour gradually darkens until the space is a uniformly dark shade. The colour change over time shows that the concentration of the bromine vapour increases until a maximum concentration is reached. After this initial change, the liquid and gaseous contents of the flask do not appear to alter their concentrations as time goes by (so long as the temperature remains constant). There will always be liquid bromine in the bottom of the flask with bromine vapour above. But, the equilibrium is not static.

Bromine vapour forms because the most energetic bromine molecules escape from the surface of the liquid: this process is called **vaporization** or **evaporation**. Also, the least energetic molecules in the vapour return to the liquid state: this process is called **condensation**. Vaporization and condensation are *both happening simultaneously* in the flask.

- When the concentration (colour) of the vapour remains steady, the rate of condensation equals the rate of vaporization.

Liquid bromine is in dynamic equilibrium with bromine vapour. This equilibrium process may be represented by a simple equation:

$$Br_2(l) \rightleftharpoons Br_2(g)$$

The symbol ⇌, two half-arrows, means that it is an equilibrium process. Written in this form, the equation means that, at equilibrium, bromine liquid is changing into bromine vapour at the same rate as bromine vapour is changing into bromine liquid:

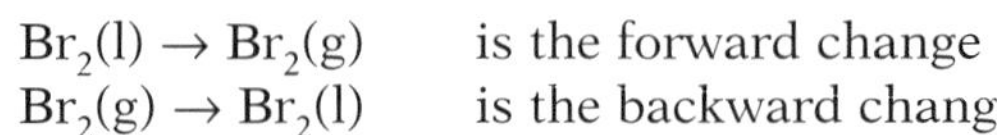

$Br_2(l) \rightarrow Br_2(g)$ is the forward change
$Br_2(g) \rightarrow Br_2(l)$ is the backward change

In a closed container, liquid bromine is in dynamic equilibrium with its vapour.

Chemical reactions and chemical equilibrium

Changes of state such as those detailed opposite are physical changes. A dynamic equilibrium will also develop during a chemical change. The balance of reactants and products at equilibrium is called the **equilibrium mixture** or equilibrium composition. All chemical reactions show a tendency to form an equilibrium mixture. The equilibrium mixture may consist mostly of reactants, which shows that very little reaction takes place overall. On the other hand, a reaction is commonly described as 'going to completion' if the equilibrium mixture consists mostly of products and hardly any reactants.

- **Chemical equilibrium** occurs when the concentrations (i.e. molar concentrations) of reactants and products remain constant.
- A **reversible reaction** describes the case where the equilibrium mixture contains significant amounts of the reactants.

Nitrogen, hydrogen, and ammonia

An example of a reversible reaction is the reaction between nitrogen and hydrogen at 450 °C to form ammonia:

$$N_2(g) + 3H_2(g) \rightleftharpoons 2NH_3(g)$$

Mixing nitrogen and hydrogen in a sealed reaction vessel under the right conditions will produce ammonia. The concentration of ammonia will reach a maximum value, but the concentrations of nitrogen and hydrogen do *not* fall to zero. Moreover, pure ammonia in a reaction vessel under the same conditions produces nitrogen and hydrogen. Whether starting from nitrogen and hydrogen or from ammonia, the system will always reach an equilibrium mixture of nitrogen, hydrogen, and ammonia. Once this state of chemical equilibrium is reached, the rates of the forward and backward reactions are the same and there is no further tendency for the composition to change.

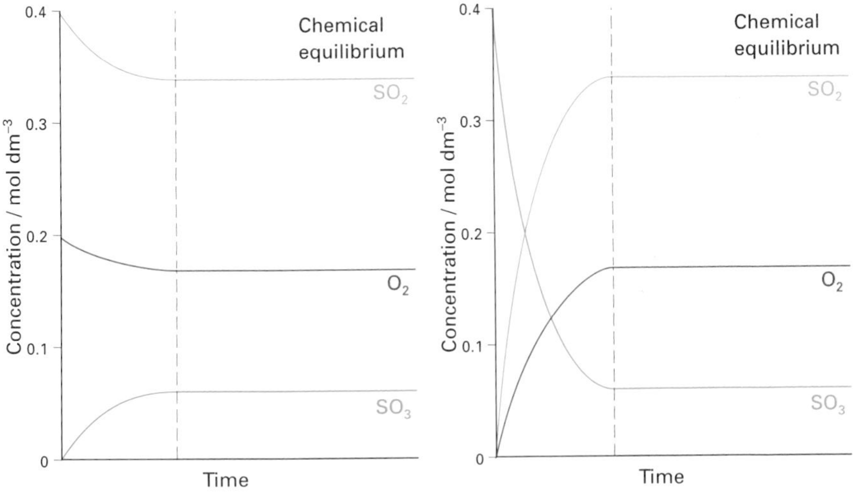

In the reaction $2SO_2(g) + O_2(g) \rightleftharpoons 2SO_3(g)$, the same concentrations are reached whether starting from pure reactants (SO_2 and O_2) or pure product (SO_3). After the time shown by the vertical dashed line, the composition does not change. This is the reversible reaction central to the manufacture of sulphuric acid (see alongside).

SUMMARY

- The forward reaction describes reactants changing into products.
- The backward reaction describes products changing back into reactants.
- Chemical equilibrium occurs when the concentrations of reactants and products remain constant.
- Chemical equilibrium is established when the rate of the forward reaction equals the rate of the backward reaction.

(a)

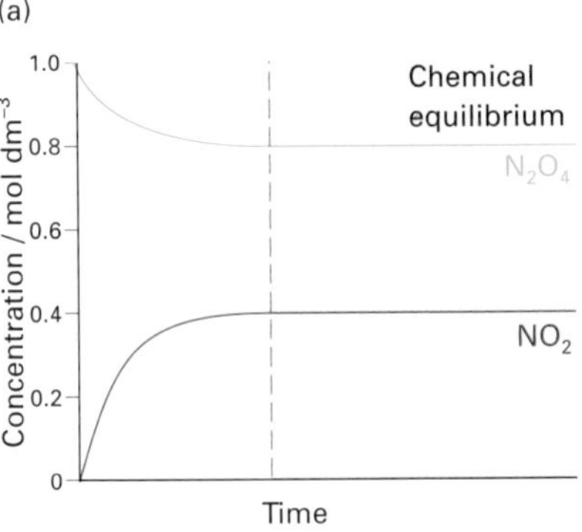

(b)

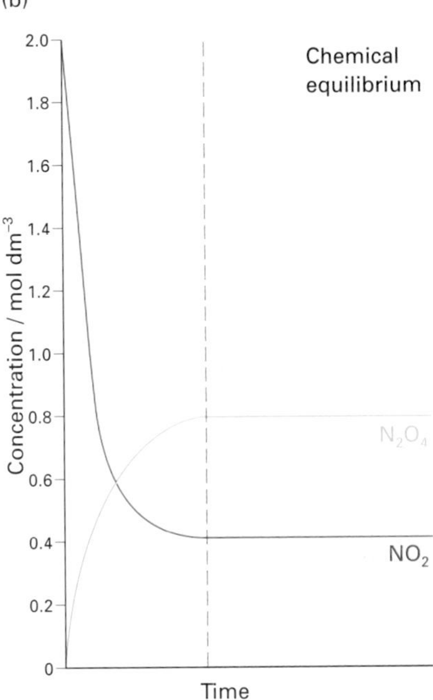

(a) Dinitrogen tetraoxide N_2O_4 decomposes into two molecules of nitrogen dioxide NO_2. (b) Two molecules of nitrogen dioxide combine to form dinitrogen tetraoxide. After the time shown by the vertical dashed line, the composition does not change. Whichever pure compound is chosen to start with, the same concentrations of the two compounds result once equilibrium is reached.

Large industrial plants, such as this one making sulphuric acid, often involve control of reversible reactions. Conditions of temperature and pressure are carefully controlled to produce the optimum yield.

11.2

OBJECTIVES

- Practical proof of the dynamic nature of chemical equilibrium
- Use of radioisotopes and 'heavy hydrogen'
- Ammonia, warfare, and food

THE NATURE OF DYNAMIC EQUILIBRIUM – 2

Nitrogen and hydrogen react to form ammonia; and ammonia decomposes to nitrogen and hydrogen. You are already aware that these two reactions make up a reversible reaction expressed as:

$$N_2(g) + 3H_2(g) \rightleftharpoons 2NH_3(g)$$

Once this system has reached chemical equilibrium, the equilibrium composition shows no further tendency to change. However, chemical reaction does *not* cease when equilibrium is reached. The reactants continue to react to form the products, and the products continue to react to form the reactants. Chemical equilibrium is *dynamic*; the forward and the backward reactions occur *at the same rate*.

Iodine-131

The full symbol for iodine-131 is $^{131}_{53}I$. During the decay of an iodine-131 nucleus, one neutron breaks down to form a proton and an electron (together with another sub-atomic particle called an antineutrino $\bar{\nu}_e$, which has zero charge and zero mass):

$$^1_0n \rightarrow {^1_1p} + {^0_{-1}e} + \bar{\nu}_e$$

The electron is ejected from the nucleus at high speed and may be detected as a beta particle (β) by a Geiger counter. This decay effectively adds a proton to the nucleus of the iodine-131, increasing its atomic number by one. The resulting nucleus contains 54 protons and 77 neutrons, which corresponds to the stable nuclide xenon-131. The overall change may therefore be represented by:

$$^{131}_{53}I \rightarrow {^0_{-1}\beta} + {^{131}_{54}Xe}$$

Practical proof that chemical equilibrium is dynamic

Substances called radioisotopes (radioactive isotopes) may be used to show that chemical equilibrium is dynamic. Look back at the chapter on 'The nuclear atom' to remind yourself about isotopes. **Radioisotopes** are isotopes that have unstable nuclei. An example is iodine-131, whose nuclei contain 53 protons and 78 neutrons. This isotope has four extra neutrons compared with the stable isotope iodine-127. As a result, iodine-131 is unstable. The nuclei in a sample of iodine-131 decay randomly, emitting radiation, which may be detected with a device called a Geiger counter. The radioisotope iodine-131 may be used to demonstrate the dynamic nature of a chemical equilibrium, as follows.

When a saturated solution of silver iodide (one that contains as much dissolved silver iodide as possible) is in contact with solid silver iodide, an equilibrium is set up between the solid silver iodide and the silver ions and iodide ions in solution:

$$AgI(s) \rightleftharpoons Ag^+(aq) + I^-(aq)$$

Even though no more solid silver iodide can dissolve, exchange continues between the solid silver iodide and the ions in solution. At equilibrium, the solid silver iodide is changing into aqueous silver ions and aqueous iodide ions at the same rate as the ions form solid silver iodide.

This exchange may be demonstrated by using a sample of radioactive solid silver iodide-131 and non-radioactive saturated aqueous silver iodide-127. Remember that overall the solution is saturated and no more solid can dissolve. The radioactive solid is added to the solution and the mixture is left to stand for several hours. After this time, the filtered solution is found to be radioactive. This effect can only happen if the equilibrium is dynamic, and there is exchange between the solid and the solution.

Heavy hydrogen

A similar experiment may be carried out using a *heavy* isotope instead of a *radioactive* one. A **heavy isotope** is an isotope having an extra neutron or neutrons. For example, deuterium (symbol D) is an isotope of hydrogen in which the nucleus of each atom consists of one proton and one neutron. It is often referred to by the name 'heavy hydrogen'.

We now return to the ammonia equilibrium mixture:

$$N_2(g) + 3H_2(g) \rightleftharpoons 2NH_3(g)$$

Some of the hydrogen in the $N_2/H_2/NH_3$ equilibrium mixture is replaced by an equal amount of heavy hydrogen D_2. The D_2 isotope behaves chemically in the same way as H_2 and will take part in the above reaction. So some NH_2D, NHD_2, ND_3, and HD will be detected later (by the use of a mass spectrometer). As in the previous example, this effect can only happen if there is an exchange of atoms between the ammonia and the nitrogen, hydrogen, and deuterium.

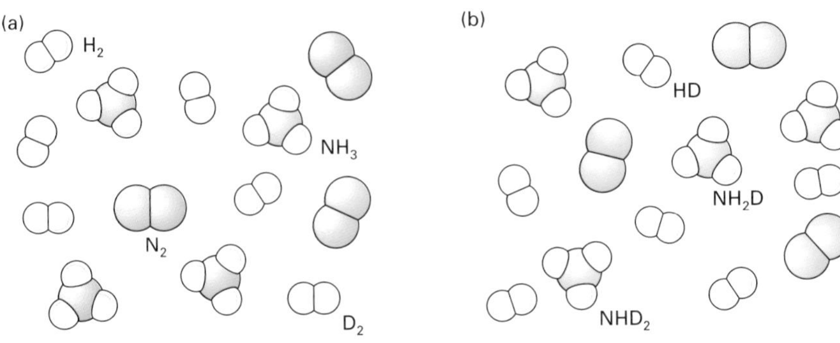

(a) Deuterium has just been substituted for some hydrogen in an equilibrium mixture of nitrogen/hydrogen/ammonia. (b) Some time later, the forward and the backward reactions have introduced deuterium atoms into ammonia and hydrogen molecules, producing HD, NH_2D, and NHD_2. ND_3 could also be found.

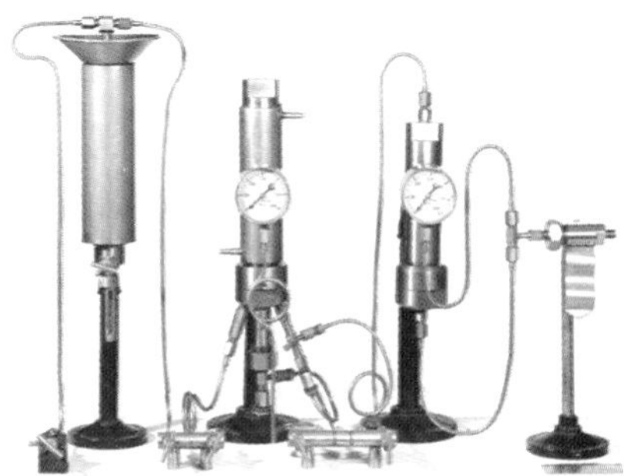

(a) Fritz Haber. (b) Haber's original laboratory apparatus for investigating the N_2/H_2 reaction at various temperatures and pressures.

Fritz Haber, Carl Bosch, and the ammonia synthesis

Fritz Haber was born in 1868 in Silesia (which is now Poland). In 1898 he became Professor of Physical Chemistry at the University of Dahlem, near Berlin. In 1908 he developed the synthesis of ammonia from nitrogen and hydrogen. Haber's chief discoveries were that high pressure was required and that iron catalyses the reaction.

Carl Bosch, who was born in Cologne in 1874, developed the process from the laboratory scale of Haber's experiments to the enormous industrial scale required. The first factory was built in 1913 at Ludwigshafen-Oppau by the Badische Anilin und Soda Fabrik (BASF).

At the start of the First World War, the British Navy blockaded all of Germany's ports. It was expected that the supply of nitrates for making explosives would dry up within a couple of years, as the only large-scale source of nitrates was in Chile. However, the Haber–Bosch process enabled the German chemical industry to make ammonia from nitrogen in the air and hydrogen synthesized from coke (carbon) and steam. Ammonia was then oxidized to make nitrates, which were then used to make explosives. Now independent of nitrate imports, Germany was able to fight on for four more years.

Ammonia is also used in the manufacture of ammonium and nitrate salts for use as plant fertilizers. The importance of ammonia for feeding the world's population was recognized by the award of the 1918 Nobel prize to Haber. In some ways Haber appeared an extraordinary choice for the first post-war prize. He had prolonged the fighting and also supervised the production of chlorine, the first gas to be used in warfare. Thirteen years later, Bosch won the 1931 Nobel prize for his contribution to solving the chemical engineering problems.

Human costs

Haber laboured to help his adopted country pay off the costs imposed on Germany by the armistice agreement signed at the end of the war. It should have been obvious to all that he was a patriot. However, in 1933 he faced an unexpected peril. Adolf Hitler had become Chancellor and Haber, of Jewish ancestry, was now in danger of imprisonment. He fled the country and died of a heart attack in Basle, Switzerland, just a few miles over the border from his beloved and ungrateful homeland. Haber's wife Clara, the first female Chemistry PhD from Dahlem, strongly disagreed with him about the use of chemical warfare. On the evening he was promoted for directing gas attacks, she committed suicide.

SUMMARY

- The concentrations of reactants and products do not change after they reach dynamic chemical equilibrium.
- Radioactive elements (radioisotopes) emit radiation, which can be detected by a Geiger counter.
- Radioisotopes and 'heavy' isotopes may be used to label substances and show how they react.
- The development of chemical processes can have profound social and political implications.

PRACTICE

1 In a closed container, liquid bromine is in dynamic equilibrium with its vapour.

a Explain the meaning of the term 'dynamic equilibrium'.

b Why would there no longer be an equilibrium if the stopper were removed from the bottle?

2 For the equilibrium

$N_2(g) + 3H_2(g) \rightleftharpoons 2NH_3(g)$

write down chemical equations for:

a the forward reaction,

b the backward reaction.

11.3

Le Chatelier's principle – 1

OBJECTIVES

- The response of an equilibrium to change
- The effect of concentration change
- The effect of pressure change

Equilibrium mixtures respond to external attempts to change the concentrations of their components. When a change in the concentration of one substance is made, the concentrations of all the other substances involved in the equilibrium will also change. The response of equilibrium systems to changes of concentration, pressure, and temperature was first summed up by Henri Le Chatelier in 1888. Le Chatelier's principle has important implications for many industrial processes, where conditions must be set to favour the production of a particular constituent in an equilibrium.

Statement of Le Chatelier's principle

The principle is a general rule-of-thumb for predicting the effect of changing conditions on the position of a dynamic equilibrium.
Le Chatelier's principle states that:

- If a system at equilibrium is subjected to a small change, the equilibrium tends to shift so as to *minimize* the effect of the change.

Le Chatelier's principle implies that changing the concentration of one substance causes a shift in the position of equilibrium which tends to minimize the change.

The effect of concentration change

The beaker on the left contains yellow CrO_4^{2-} ions. Adding sulphuric acid to a similar solution in the beaker on the right converts some CrO_4^{2-} to orange $Cr_2O_7^{2-}$ ions. The equilibrium has shifted to the right.

Sodium chromate(VI) is a yellow solid with the formula Na_2CrO_4. It dissolves in water to give a yellow solution containing the ions Na^+(aq) and CrO_4^{2-}(aq). Sodium dichromate(VI) is an orange solid with the formula $Na_2Cr_2O_7$. It dissolves in water to give an orange solution containing the ions Na^+(aq) and $Cr_2O_7^{2-}$(aq).

Adding acid H^+(aq) to a solution of chromate(VI) ions establishes the equilibrium:

$$\underset{\text{YELLOW}}{2CrO_4^{2-}(aq)} + 2H^+(aq) \rightleftharpoons \underset{\text{ORANGE}}{Cr_2O_7^{2-}(aq)} + H_2O(l)$$

The concentrations of the various substances present at equilibrium are constant.

Adding *more* acid will increase the concentration of H^+(aq) ions. This addition has the effect of disturbing the equilibrium. As a response, the balance between the various concentrations of the substances shifts to allow for the addition of H^+ ions. Some of the extra H^+ ions added react with the CrO_4^{2-} ions to form orange dichromate(VI) ions and so minimize the increase in concentration of H^+(aq).

- An equilibrium will shift to the right when the concentration of a reactant (a species on the left of the equation) is increased.

Adding alkali (containing OH^- ions) will reduce the hydrogen ion concentration by neutralization:

$$H^+(aq) + OH^-(aq) \rightarrow H_2O(l)$$

The position of the equilibrium will shift to the left to minimize the decrease in H^+(aq) ion concentration, forming yellow chromate(VI) ions.

The effect of pressure change – ammonia

The molecules in a gas are very far apart, and so gases can be compressed into a smaller volume by increasing the pressure. Under pressure in a smaller volume, the molecules of reacting gases are more likely to collide and to react together. In addition to such externally applied pressure, the reaction between gases might itself cause an overall change of volume (e.g. two gases reacting to form a solid or liquid) and thus pressure. Reactions involving gases are therefore sensitive to pressure change, and the position of equilibrium can be influenced by changes in pressure. Changing the equilibrium position changes the yield of the overall reaction.

Look again at the synthesis of ammonia from nitrogen and hydrogen:

$$N_2(g) + 3H_2(g) \rightleftharpoons 2NH_3(g)$$

There is 1 mol of N_2 and 3 mol of H_2 as reactants on the left of the equation (making 4 mol of gas altogether). On the right, there are only 2 mol of NH_3. Since 1 mol of any gas occupies the same volume, the forward reaction (from 4 mol to 2 mol) decreases the volume. If the pressure on the system is increased, Le Chatelier's principle says that the equilibrium will shift to minimize the pressure increase. The pressure will decrease if the equilibrium system contains fewer moles of gas. The equilibrium shifts to the right, increasing the concentration (and yield) of ammonia.

- In general, increasing the pressure shifts an equilibrium to whichever side of the equation has fewer gas-phase species.

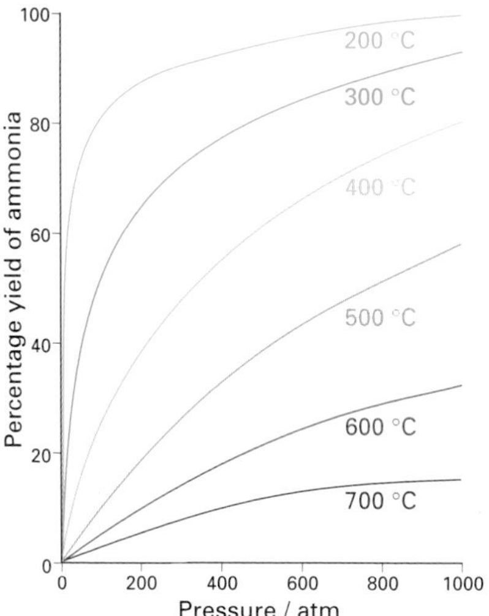

The quantitative effect of pressure on ammonia synthesis. At equilibrium, a larger percentage of ammonia is present at high pressure. In practice, there is a trade-off between initial costs and yield. UK plants operate at around 250 atm, but in France around 1000 atm is used. The higher pressure requires a greater initial investment (special chromium steel vessels are required), but the higher yield increases the profit in the long term.

The effect of pressure change – nitrogen dioxide

Another example of the effect of changing pressure is the dimerization of nitrogen dioxide NO_2. This red–brown gas is a major atmospheric pollutant from car exhausts. Two molecules of NO_2 tend to join together to form a colourless *dimer* called dinitrogen tetraoxide N_2O_4:

$$2NO_2(g) \rightleftharpoons N_2O_4(g)$$

In this equilibrium, there are more gas molecules on the left of the equation. Increasing pressure therefore shifts the equilibrium to the right, that is towards dimerization. This shift reduces the total number of molecules in the equilibrium system and so tends to minimize the pressure. Conversely, reducing the pressure shifts the equilibrium to the left, away from dimerization.

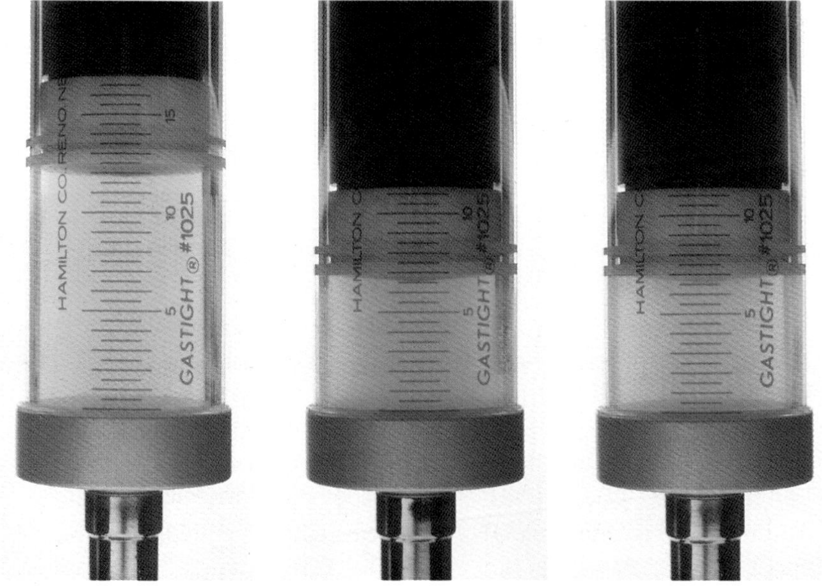

(a) Red–brown NO_2 and colourless N_2O_4 are at equilibrium in a gas syringe. (b) Pushing in the plunger increases the pressure. (c) After some time has passed, equilibrium has become re-established. The lighter colour indicates that the mixture contains a lower proportion of NO_2.

SUMMARY

- If a system at equilibrium is subjected to a small change, the equilibrium tends to shift so as to minimize the effect of the change.
- An equilibrium will shift to the right when the concentration of a reactant (a species on the left of the equation) is increased.
- An equilibrium will shift to the left when the concentration of a product (a species on the right of the equation) is increased.
- Increasing the pressure shifts an equilibrium to whichever side of the equation has fewer gas-phase species.

11.4

Le Chatelier's principle – 2

OBJECTIVES

- The effect of temperature change
- Industrial considerations
- Catalysts

The previous spread used Le Chatelier's principle to investigate the effects of changing concentration and pressure. This spread applies the principle to the effect of changing the temperature of an equilibrium system. It also considers the effect of catalysts on chemical equilibria.

The effect of temperature on an equilibrium between gases

You already know from the previous chapter that an endothermic reaction absorbs heat from the surroundings, whereas an exothermic reaction gives out heat to the surroundings. If an equilibrium is exothermic in the forward direction, then it is endothermic in the backward direction.

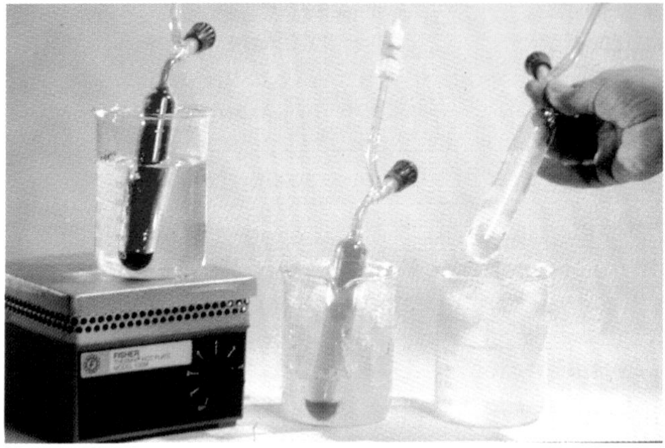

The dimerization of nitrogen dioxide at various temperatures. In hot water (left) red–brown NO_2 predominates; at 0 °C (middle) there is much less NO_2. In a freezing mixture (right) this equilibrium system appears almost colourless (nearly 100% N_2O_4).

For example, the dimerization of nitrogen dioxide

$$2NO_2(g) \rightleftharpoons N_2O_4(g)$$

is exothermic in the forward direction, because a bond is formed between the two nitrogen atoms and no other bonds are broken:

$$2NO_2(g) \rightarrow N_2O_4(g); \qquad \Delta H^{\ominus}(298\,K) = -24\,kJ\,mol^{-1}$$

The backward reaction, the decomposition of dinitrogen tetraoxide, is endothermic; the standard enthalpy change has the same magnitude as, but the opposite sign to, the forward reaction:

$$N_2O_4(g) \rightarrow 2NO_2(g); \qquad \Delta H^{\ominus}(298\,K) = +24\,kJ\,mol^{-1}$$

Le Chatelier's principle suggests that increasing the temperature shifts the equilibrium in the endothermic direction so that heat is absorbed and the temperature increase is minimized. That is, the concentration of NO_2 increases when the temperature is increased. Conversely, decreasing the temperature shifts the equilibrium in the direction that gives out heat. That is, the concentration of N_2O_4 increases when the temperature is decreased.

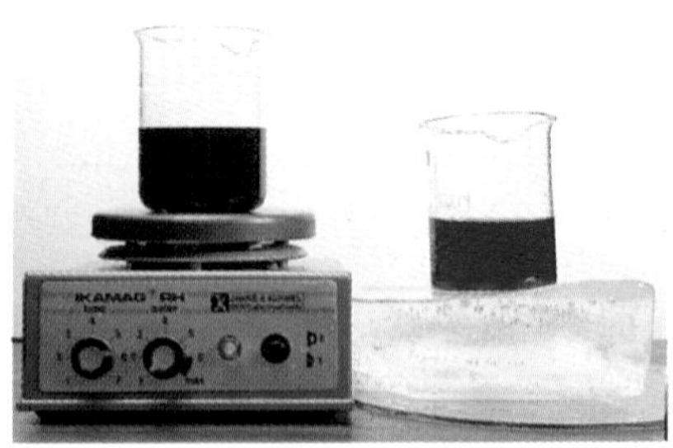

The pink $[Co(H_2O)_6]^{2+}$ ion predominates at low temperature and the blue $CoCl_4^{2-}$ ion at high temperature.

Test for water

You have probably already encountered anhydrous cobalt(II) chloride as a test for water. As the equilibrium equation shows, adding water to blue anhydrous cobalt(II) chloride produces a colour change to pink.

The effect of temperature on an equilibrium in solution

Dissolving cobalt(II) chloride in hydrochloric acid sets up the following equilibrium:

$$\underset{\text{BLUE}}{CoCl_4^{2-}(aq)} + 6H_2O(l) \rightleftharpoons \underset{\text{PINK}}{[Co(H_2O)_6]^{2+}(aq)} + 4Cl^-(aq)$$

The equilibrium as written is exothermic in the forward direction. If the temperature is increased, the mixture becomes blue. This colour change shows that the concentration of the chloro ion $CoCl_4^{2-}$ has increased. The equilibrium has shifted to the left (in the endothermic direction), thereby absorbing heat. If the temperature is decreased, more of the pink aqua ion $[Co(H_2O)_6]^{2+}$ forms as the equilibrium shifts to the right.

- In general, increasing the temperature shifts an equilibrium in the endothermic direction.

Temperature and the ammonia synthesis

The formation of ammonia from its elements is exothermic:

$$N_2(g) + 3H_2(g) \rightleftharpoons 2NH_3(g); \qquad \Delta H^{\ominus}(298\,K) = -92\,kJ\,mol^{-1}$$

As a result, Le Chatelier's principle predicts that the synthesis should be carried out at *low* temperature to obtain maximum yield. The yields at different temperatures are shown in the illustration on the right.

For industrial processes, the effect of temperature on the equilibrium yield is not the only consideration. The product must also be obtained as rapidly as possible, and so the rate of reaction is also important. As you might expect, reactions are slower at low temperatures and so a *compromise* has to be reached between yield and rate. The temperature used in the Haber–Bosch synthesis of ammonia is usually about 450 °C.

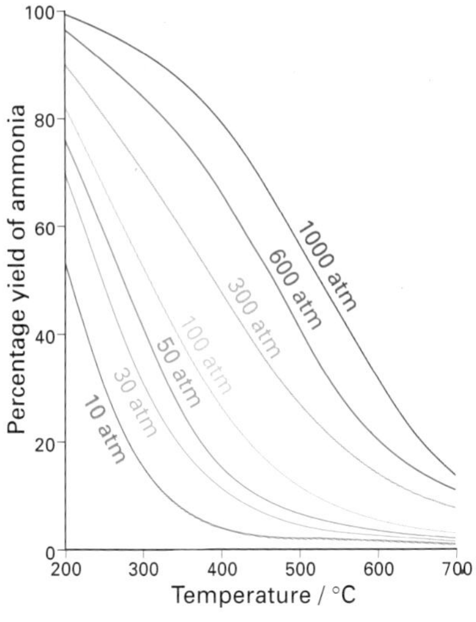

Graph of percentage yield against temperature at various pressures for the production of ammonia from nitrogen and hydrogen.

Catalysts

A **catalyst** is a substance that *speeds up* the rate of a chemical reaction. In the ammonia synthesis, a catalyst (iron) speeds up the rate at which equilibrium is reached. It does *not* affect the yield of ammonia. A catalyst increases the rates of the forward and the backward reactions *to the same extent*.

In some industrial processes, it may be uneconomical to keep the reaction going long enough for equilibrium to be reached. It may be necessary to compromise between the yield and the time taken to produce it.

SUMMARY

- If the forward reaction of an equilibrium is exothermic, then the backward reaction is endothermic; the standard enthalpy change has the same magnitude but opposite sign.
- An increase in temperature shifts an equilibrium in the endothermic direction; a decrease in temperature shifts an equilibrium in the exothermic direction.
- The temperature chosen for an industrial process is often a compromise between yield and rate.
- The equilibrium position is unaffected by the presence of a catalyst; equilibrium is reached faster in the presence of a catalyst.

PRACTICE

1 Consider the equilibrium:
$2CrO_4^{2-}(aq) + 2H^+(aq) \rightleftharpoons Cr_2O_7^{2-}(aq) + H_2O(l)$

a Give two ways of forcing the equilibrium to the right.

b Give two ways of forcing the equilibrium to the left.

c Describe the change in appearance of the solution when the equilibrium moves to the right.

2 What would be the effect of a decrease in pressure on each of the following equilibria?

a $N_2O_4(g) \rightleftharpoons 2NO_2(g)$

b $H_2(g) + I_2(g) \rightleftharpoons 2HI(g)$

c $CO(g) + 2H_2(g) \rightleftharpoons CH_3OH(g)$.

3 Ethanol CH_3CH_2OH is an important industrial compound made from the reaction between ethene C_2H_4 and steam. The three substances are involved in the equilibrium system:
$C_2H_4(g) + H_2O(g) \rightleftharpoons CH_3CH_2OH(g)$
How would you alter the pressure to increase the yield of ethanol?

4 An important step in the manufacture of sulphuric acid is the catalytic oxidation of sulphur dioxide SO_2 to sulphur trioxide SO_3:
$2SO_2(g) + O_2(g) \rightleftharpoons 2SO_3(g)$;
$\Delta H^{\ominus}(298\,K) = -197\,kJ\,mol^{-1}$
For each of the following changes, say how the equilibrium will react to the change and give your reasoning:

a Increase in temperature.

b Decrease in pressure.

c Reduction of catalyst efficiency by 50%.

11.5

THE EQUILIBRIUM CONSTANT K_c

OBJECTIVES

- Equilibrium position
- The equilibrium constant K_c
- Calculating K_c

A chemical equilibrium is a reversible chemical reaction in which the overall concentrations of reactants and products are not changing with time. An equilibrium may be described as 'lying to the left', indicating that the reactants predominate; or as 'lying to the right', if products predominate. The actual position of the equilibrium ('to the left' or 'to the right') is a basic property of any particular equilibrium, under fixed conditions. However, as we saw in the previous two spreads, the equilibrium position *does* change when the temperature, pressure, and concentrations change. The equilibrium position may be described in precise terms by combining the equilibrium concentrations to give a value for K_c, the equilibrium constant.

The general expression for K_c

An equilibrium expression may be written for any reaction. Consider the general equilibrium equation:

$aA + bB \rightleftharpoons cC + dD$

The expression for the **equilibrium constant** in terms of concentrations is:

$$K_c = \frac{[C]_{eq}^{c}[D]_{eq}^{d}}{[A]_{eq}^{a}[B]_{eq}^{b}}$$

where, for example, the term $[C]_{eq}^{c}$ means the concentration (mol dm^{-3}) of C at equilibrium raised to the power *c*.

The equilibrium constant K_c

Nitrogen and hydrogen react together to form ammonia:

$$N_2(g) + 3H_2(g) \rightleftharpoons 2NH_3(g)$$

The equation indicates that 1 mol of N_2 would react with 3 mol of H_2 to form 2 mol of NH_3, *if the reaction went to completion*. In fact, significantly less NH_3 results than the equation predicts because the reaction is reversible and the three species $N_2(g)$, $H_2(g)$, and $NH_3(g)$ are *all* present at chemical equilibrium.

The table below shows some experimental results for this equilibrium. Experiment 1 starts with nitrogen and hydrogen; experiment 2 starts with ammonia; experiment 3 starts with the concentrations indicated. The expression $[H_2]_{eq}$ means 'the concentration of hydrogen gas at equilibrium, in moles of hydrogen molecules H_2 per cubic decimetre'. $[H_2]_0$ refers to the concentration at the start of the reaction.

Results of three experiments for the ammonia synthesis reaction:
$N_2(g) + 3H_2(g) \rightleftharpoons 2NH_3(g)$ at 500 °C

Experiment	**Initial concentrations /mol dm^{-3}**	**Equilibrium concentrations /mol dm^{-3}**	**Equilibrium constant $K_c = \frac{[NH_3]_{eq}^2}{[N_2]_{eq}[H_2]_{eq}^3}$ /dm^6 mol^{-2}**
1	$[N_2]_0 = 1.00$ $[H_2]_0 = 1.00$ $[NH_3]_0 = 0$	$[N_2]_{eq} = 0.922$ $[H_2]_{eq} = 0.763$ $[NH_3]_{eq} = 0.157$	6.02×10^{-2}
2	$[N_2]_0 = 0$ $[H_2]_0 = 0$ $[NH_3]_0 = 1.00$	$[N_2]_{eq} = 0.399$ $[H_2]_{eq} = 1.197$ $[NH_3]_{eq} = 0.203$	6.02×10^{-2}
3	$[N_2]_0 = 2.00$ $[H_2]_0 = 1.00$ $[NH_3]_0 = 3.00$	$[N_2]_{eq} = 2.59$ $[H_2]_{eq} = 2.77$ $[NH_3]_{eq} = 1.82$	6.02×10^{-2}

Units

For the reaction:

$N_2(g) + 3H_2(g) \rightleftharpoons 2NH_3(g)$

the mathematical expression for K_c is:

$$K_c = \frac{[NH_3]_{eq}^{2}}{[N_2]_{eq}[H_2]_{eq}^{3}}$$

It contains concentrations expressed in units of mol dm^{-3}. The units for K_c *for this reaction* are therefore

$$\frac{(\text{mol dm}^{-3})^2}{(\text{mol dm}^{-3}) \times (\text{mol dm}^{-3})^3} = \text{dm}^6\,\text{mol}^{-2}$$

The units for K_c *for other reactions* may be different.

Look at the three main columns in the table. Each experiment starts with different initial concentrations. There is also a different set of concentrations for each of the equilibrium mixtures. However, substituting the equilibrium concentrations into the expression for K_c gives a constant numerical result, 6.02×10^{-2} dm^6 mol^{-2}.

Notice that the concentration of NH_3 is raised to the power of 2 and that of H_2 is raised to the power of 3. These powers are included because 2 mol of NH_3 and 3 mol of H_2 appear in the balanced equation.

- For K_c to have a constant value, the *concentrations* in an equilibrium expression must always be raised to powers corresponding to the mole ratios in the equation.
- No matter what concentrations of reactants or products are present at the start, a reaction always tends towards an equilibrium composition where the concentrations are related by K_c.
- The equilibrium constant is a constant for a particular reaction, at a constant temperature.

Esterification

The equilibrium discussed above takes place in the gas phase. An example of a *liquid-phase* equilibrium is the esterification reaction between an acid (ethanoic acid) and an alcohol (ethanol) to form an ester (ethyl ethanoate) and water, i.e.

$$\underset{\text{acid}}{CH_3COOH(l)} + \underset{\text{alcohol}}{CH_3CH_2OH(l)} \rightleftharpoons \underset{\text{ester}}{CH_3COOCH_2CH_3(l)} + \underset{\text{water}}{H_2O(l)}$$

The equilibrium concentrations of the four components may be determined by an acid–base titration, as shown in the next spread. The table below shows some experimental results that were obtained for this equilibrium.

Data for five experiments (at 373 K) showing initial concentrations of acid and alcohol, equilibrium concentrations of ester (and water), and associated K_c values.

Experiment	$[Acid]_0$ /mol dm^{-3}	$[Alcohol]_0$ /mol dm^{-3}	$[Ester]_{eq}$ /mol dm^{-3}	K_c
1	1.00	0.18	0.171	3.9
2	1.00	0.50	0.420	3.8
3	1.00	1.00	0.667	4.0
4	1.00	2.00	0.858	4.5
5	1.00	8.00	0.966	3.9

Taking experiment 3 as an example, the value for K_c is calculated as follows. The chemical equation indicates that 1 mol of ester requires the reaction of 1 mol of alcohol with 1 mol of acid. The equilibrium concentrations of acid and alcohol are

$(1.00 - 0.667)\ \text{mol dm}^{-3} = 0.333\ \text{mol dm}^{-3}$

Writing down the equation for K_c like that in the box opposite we get

$$K_c = \frac{[\text{ester}]_{eq}[\text{water}]_{eq}}{[\text{acid}]_{eq}[\text{alcohol}]_{eq}}$$

and substituting values

$$K_c = \frac{0.667 \times 0.667}{0.333 \times 0.333} = 4.0$$

Note that experiment 1 starts with an alcohol concentration more than five times smaller than experiment 3 and yet the values for K_c differ by just 2.5%. Experiment 5 starts with an alcohol concentration eight times larger than experiment 3 with the same resultant slight discrepancy.

- K_c remains essentially constant while the alcohol concentration changes by a factor of over 40.

SUMMARY

- K_c is the equilibrium constant for a chemical equilibrium expressed in terms of concentrations (mol dm^{-3}).
- A large numerical value of K_c indicates that the equilibrium lies to the right, i.e. products predominate in the equilibrium mixture.
- A small numerical value of K_c indicates that the equilibrium lies to the left, i.e. reactants predominate in the equilibrium mixture.
- The value of K_c is constant for a particular equilibrium reaction at a constant temperature.

Equilibrium constant and temperature

The value of the equilibrium constant is unaffected by changes in concentration or pressure. However, it *is* dependent on the temperature of the system. The response of an equilibrium to a change in temperature is to establish a new value for the equilibrium constant. Le Chatelier's principle cannot explain the *size* of this change. In a later chapter on 'Spontaneous change towards equilibrium', we show how thermodynamics provides quantitative predictions and also explain why K_c changes with temperature.

Units

Note that, unlike the situation for the $N_2/H_2/NH_3$ mixture, in the expression for the equilibrium constant for this esterification reaction, the units 'cancel out'. In this case, the units for K_c are

$$\frac{(\text{mol dm}^{-3}) \times (\text{mol dm}^{-3})}{(\text{mol dm}^{-3}) \times (\text{mol dm}^{-3})} = 1$$

and the equilibrium constant is just a number, i.e. it has no units.

PRACTICE

1 Write down the equilibrium constant for the following equilibria:

a $2NO_2(g) \rightleftharpoons N_2O_4(g)$

b $2SO_2(g) + O_2(g) \rightleftharpoons 2SO_3(g)$

11.6

OBJECTIVES

- Esterification equilibrium
- Thermostatic control of temperature
- 'Freezing' equilibrium reactions
- Analysis of results

AN EXPERIMENTAL DETERMINATION OF K_c

The equilibrium constant K_c is calculated from the concentrations of the substances in an equilibrium mixture. The value of K_c is a constant for a given equilibrium *at a constant temperature*. Changing the temperature alters the value of K_c; changing pressure or concentration does not. Equilibrium constants are derived from experimental data, and this spread gives details of the analysis of an equilibrium mixture and shows how to calculate K_c from the resulting data.

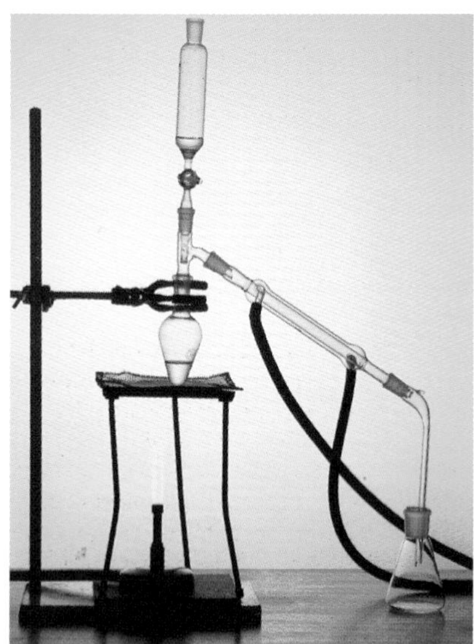

The apparatus for performing an esterification.

Esterification

The equilibrium reaction examined here takes place in the liquid state. It involves water, an alcohol (ethanol), an organic acid (ethanoic acid), and an ester (ethyl ethanoate). We looked at it briefly in the previous spread. The reaction is called 'esterification' because an ester forms as one of the products. The equation for the reaction is

$$\underset{\text{ETHANOIC ACID}}{CH_3COOH(l)} + \underset{\text{ETHANOL}}{CH_3CH_2OH(l)} \rightleftharpoons \underset{\text{ETHYL ETHANOATE}}{CH_3COOCH_2CH_3(l)} + \underset{\text{WATER}}{H_2O(l)} \quad (1)$$

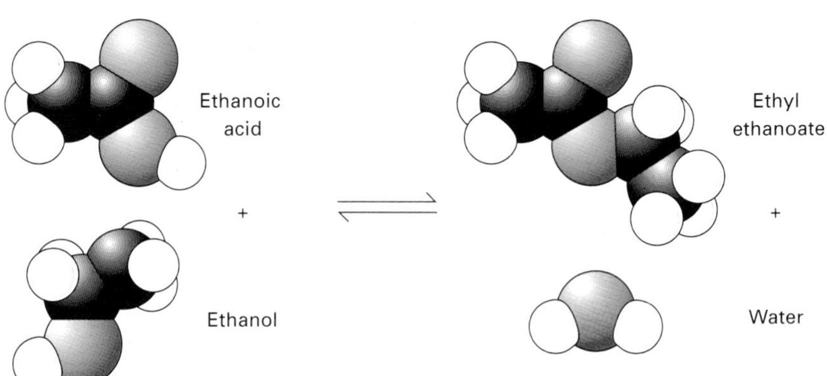

The esterification reaction.

Practical procedure

Mix 12.0 g (0.200 mol) of ethanoic acid in a conical flask with 9.20 g (0.200 mol) of ethanol and 18.0 g (1.00 mol) of water. Carefully add 4.90 g (0.050 mol) of concentrated sulphuric acid. This acid acts as a catalyst, which speeds up the attainment of equilibrium, but does not affect its position. Seal the flask with a bung and place it for a minimum of four days in a thermostatic water bath set at 25 °C. The total volume of the solution is 44.0 cm^3.

For the analysis of the mixture, set up a titration apparatus with aqueous sodium hydroxide (concentration 1.00 mol dm^{-3}) in the burette. Add base from the burette to the flask until the phenolphthalein indicator remains permanently pink. The base neutralizes the ethanoic acid remaining in the equilibrium mixture *plus* all the sulphuric acid added at the start as a catalyst.

For the purposes of the worked calculation below, assume that a total of 233 cm^3 of base was required.

Calculation

Step 1   Calculate the amount in moles of NaOH used in the titration.

We know from our previous work that

amount in moles = volume × concentration

so

$$\text{amount in moles of NaOH} = \left(\frac{233}{1000}\,\text{dm}^3\right) \times (1.00\,\text{mol dm}^{-3})$$

$$= 0.233\,\text{mol}$$

Step 2 Calculate the amount in moles of NaOH that reacts with the sulphuric acid.

Sulphuric acid reacts with sodium hydroxide:

$$H_2SO_4(aq) + 2NaOH(aq) \rightarrow Na_2SO_4(aq) + 2H_2O(l) \qquad (2)$$

We know that 0.050 mol H_2SO_4 was added at the start. Therefore the amount in moles of NaOH that reacts with the sulphuric acid according to equation (2) is

$$2 \times 0.050 = 0.100\ \text{mol}$$

Step 3 Calculate the amount in moles of ethanoic acid.

From Step 1, the total amount in moles of NaOH is 0.233 mol. Of this, in Step 2 we found that 0.100 mol reacts with the sulphuric acid. Therefore

$$0.233 - 0.100 = 0.133\ \text{mol}$$

reacts with the ethanoic acid present at equilibrium.

Ethanoic acid reacts with sodium hydroxide:

$$CH_3COOH(aq) + NaOH(aq) \rightarrow Na^+CH_3CO_2^-(aq) + H_2O(l) \qquad (3)$$

Therefore according to equation (3) there are 0.133 mol ethanoic acid present at equilibrium.

Step 4 Calculate the equilibrium constant K_c.

We are told that 0.200 mol of both ethanol and ethanoic acid were present at the start. We have worked out in Step 3 that 0.133 mol of ethanoic acid are present at equilibrium. Therefore according to equation (1) there is 0.133 mol of ethanol present at equilibrium. The increase in amount in moles of ester and water present at equilibrium is

$$0.200 - 0.133 = 0.067\ \text{mol}$$

A summary of the results is shown below:

	$CH_3COOH(l)$ +	$CH_3CH_2OH(l)$ $\rightleftharpoons$	$CH_3COOCH_2CH_3(l)$ +	$H_2O(l)$
Start/mol	0.200	0.200	0	1.00
Equilibrium/mol	0.133	0.133	0.067	1.067
Concentration /mol dm^{-3}	3.02	3.02	1.52	24.2

The values of the concentrations have been calculated from the expression:

$$\text{concentration} = \frac{\text{amount in moles}}{\text{volume}}$$

The equilibrium constant for reaction (1) is written in terms of concentrations as

$$K_c = \frac{[CH_3COOCH_2CH_3]_{eq}[H_2O]_{eq}}{[CH_3COOH]_{eq}[CH_3CH_2OH]_{eq}}$$

and substituting values from the last line of results above, we get

$$K_c = \frac{(1.52\ \text{mol dm}^{-3}) \times (24.2\ \text{mol dm}^{-3})}{(3.02\ \text{mol dm}^{-3}) \times (3.02\ \text{mol dm}^{-3})} = 4.0$$

Notice that the value of K_c for this equilibrium has no units – it is *dimensionless* – because the units in the numerator and denominator of the expression above cancel exactly.

SUMMARY

- A thermostatically controlled water bath is used to establish equilibria at temperatures above room temperature.
- An equilibrium involving an acid or a base may be analysed by acid–base titration.
- The equilibrium position is 'frozen' before titration by the addition of excess cold water.

'Freezing' a reaction

Before titrating, the equilibrium position is usually 'frozen' by the addition of a large volume of cold water (about 10 times the volume of the reaction mixture). This large dilution slows the rate at which the substances react together. Titration removes acid from the equilibrium and so alters the balance of the equilibrium, but the titration is completed before the reverse reaction replaces the ethanoic acid neutralized by the addition of base.

'Freezing' is particularly useful when the equilibrium is established at high temperature and the mixture is then titrated at room temperature.

Equilibrium concentrations

Remember that K_c is calculated from the equilibrium concentrations of the various substances (as indicated by the brackets [ ] in the equilibrium expression). Step 4 in the calculation converts amounts in moles into concentrations (mol dm^{-3}). The total volume of the mixture is 44.0 cm^3, equal to 0.044 dm^3.

Spreadsheets

The calculation of K_c follows a clearly defined route, irrespective of the actual amounts of the substances involved. A computer-based spreadsheet can be very useful in the calculation of K_c.

PRACTICE

1 Describe with full experimental detail how you would determine the equilibrium constant for the formation of ethyl ethanoate.

11.7

THE EQUILIBRIUM CONSTANT AND YIELD

OBJECTIVES

- Yield and equilibrium position
- Yield and the value of K_c
- Calculating yield

General strategy for calculating yield

Step 1 Write down the equation for the reaction, together with the expression for the equilibrium constant.

Step 2 Calculate the amounts in moles of acid and alcohol *at the start,* using the relationship:

$$\text{amount in moles} = \frac{\text{mass}}{\text{molar mass}}$$

Step 3 Find expressions for the amounts in moles *at equilibrium* on the basis that x mol of ester and x mol of water are formed.

Step 4 Substitute amounts in moles *at equilibrium* into the expression for the equilibrium constant. Arrange into quadratic form:

$ax^2 + bx + c = 0$

Step 5 Solve for x, using the quadratic formula:

$$x = \frac{-b \pm \sqrt{(b^2 - 4ac)}}{2a}$$

Step 6 Find the yield (in grams) from

mass = amount in moles (x) × molar mass

How can you calculate the yield of a chemical reaction? This task is straightforward in the case of reactions that 'go to completion'. In such reactions, essentially all the reactants change into products. Yield may be calculated from the balanced chemical equation and a knowledge of the amounts of the reactants. In the case of equilibrium reactions, calculating the yield is more complicated. Mixing the reactants leads to chemical equilibrium, where steady concentrations of reactants and products are present together. Product yield depends on the extent to which the equilibrium 'lies to the right', which in turn is reflected in the value of the equilibrium constant.

Calculating the yield of ethyl ethanoate

The reaction between ethanoic acid CH_3COOH and ethanol CH_3CH_2OH produces ethyl ethanoate $CH_3COOCH_2CH_3$ and water as products:

$$CH_3COOH(l) + CH_3CH_2OH(l) \rightleftharpoons CH_3COOCH_2CH_3(l) + H_2O(l)$$

The equilibrium constant has a value of 4.00 at 100 °C. The reaction may be used to make the ester, but the yield will be less than the amount indicated by the chemical equation.

Worked example on calculating yield

We consider the above reaction between ethanoic acid and ethanol.

Question: What mass of ethyl ethanoate is formed at equilibrium if 90.1 g of ethanoic acid is added to 92.1 g of ethanol at 100 °C? K_c for the reaction is 4.00 at 100 °C.

Strategy: We follow the steps outlined in the box on the left.

Answer:

Step 1 The equation for the reaction is given above. The expression for the equilibrium constant for the reaction is:

$$K_c = \frac{[CH_3COOCH_2CH_3]_{eq}[H_2O]_{eq}}{[CH_3COOH]_{eq}[CH_3CH_2OH]_{eq}}$$

Step 2 Calculate the amounts in moles of acid and alcohol *at the start* using the molar masses:

$$n(CH_3COOH) = \frac{90.1\,\text{g}}{\{(2 \times 12.0) + (4 \times 1.0) + (2 \times 16.0)\}\,\text{g mol}^{-1}}$$

$$= 1.50\,\text{mol}$$

$$n(CH_3CH_2OH) = \frac{92.1\,\text{g}}{\{(2 \times 12.0) + (6 \times 1.0) + (1 \times 16.0)\}\,\text{g mol}^{-1}}$$

$$= 2.00\,\text{mol}$$

Step 3 If x mol of $CH_3COOCH_2CH_3$ is formed, the chemical equation requires that x mol of H_2O is also formed and that the amounts of CH_3COOH and CH_3CH_2OH will each have *decreased* by x mol. *At equilibrium*, therefore, the amounts in moles can be expressed as:

$CH_3COOH = (1.50 - x)$ mol

$CH_3CH_2OH = (2.00 - x)$ mol

$CH_3COOCH_2CH_3 = x$ mol

$H_2O = x$ mol

Step 4 For each substance, its concentration is its amount in moles divided by the volume V of the mixture. For example, for CH_3COOH, at equilibrium its concentration is $(1.50 - x)$ mol/V. Substituting the expressions for the concentrations of all four substances into the expression for the equilibrium constant, and noting that we are given $K_c = 4.00$ in the question, we obtain:

$$K_c = \frac{(x\,\text{mol}/V) \times (x\,\text{mol}/V)}{\{(1.50 - x)\,\text{mol}/V\} \times \{(2.00 - x)\,\text{mol}/V\}} = 4.00$$

In this case (but *not* in all cases), the volume (V) and the units (mol) cancel, leaving:

$$4.00 = \frac{x^2}{(1.50 - x)(2.00 - x)}$$

Multiplying out the brackets gives:

$$(1.50 - x)(2.00 - x) = 3.00 - 1.50x - 2.00x + (-x)^2$$

$$= 3.00 - 3.50x + x^2$$

So

$$4.00 = \frac{x^2}{3.00 - 3.50x + x^2}$$

Multiply both sides by $(3.00 - 3.50x + x^2)$ to get rid of the denominator:

$$12.00 - 14.00x + 4.00x^2 = x^2$$

Subtract x^2 from each side,

$$12.00 - 14.00x + 4.00x^2 - x^2 = x^2 - x^2$$

$$12.00 - 14.00x + 3.00x^2 = 0$$

Arrange into the form $ax^2 + bx + c = 0$:

$$3.00x^2 - 14.00x + 12.00 = 0$$

i.e. $a = 3.00$, $b = -14.00$ (don't forget the minus sign), and $c = 12.00$.

Step 5 Solve using the quadratic formula given in the box above. Hence

$$x = \frac{14.00 \pm \sqrt{\{(-14.00)^2 - (4 \times 3.00 \times 12.00)\}}}{(2 \times 3.00)}$$

$$= 1.13 \text{ or } 3.54$$

The second *mathematical* solution is *chemically* impossible; you cannot form 3.54 mol of $CH_3COOCH_2CH_3$ from 1.50 mol of CH_3COOH. The amount in moles of $CH_3COOCH_2CH_3$ is therefore 1.13 mol.

Step 6 The yield (mass m) of $CH_3COOCH_2CH_3$ can therefore be found as

$$m = (1.13\,\text{mol}) \times \{(4 \times 12.0) + (8 \times 1.0) + (2 \times 16.0)\}\,\text{g mol}^{-1}$$

$$= 99\,\text{g}$$

K_c and equilibrium position

The magnitude of the equilibrium constant describes the equilibrium composition. Look again at the general expression for the equilibrium constant:

$$K_c = \frac{[C]_{eq}^{\,c}[D]_{eq}^{\,d}}{[A]_{eq}^{\,a}[B]_{eq}^{\,b}}$$

If the equilibrium mixture contains mostly products, $[C]_{eq}^{\,c}[D]_{eq}^{\,d}$ is much larger than $[A]_{eq}^{\,a}[B]_{eq}^{\,b}$ and K_c is large. As a general guide, if K_c has a value above about 1000, the reaction essentially goes to completion. If K_c is below about 0.001, there is too little reaction to be useful. If K_c is around 1, the reaction can sometimes be made useful by careful choice of reaction conditions, guided for example by Le Chatelier's principle.

SUMMARY

- $K_c > 1000$: reaction 'goes to completion'.
- $K_c < 0.001$: negligible reaction.
- K_c around 1: useful amounts of product may be obtained if reaction conditions are carefully chosen.

PRACTICE

1 The equation for the decomposition of phosphorus pentachloride PCl_5 is:
$PCl_5(g) \rightleftharpoons PCl_3(g) + Cl_2(g)$
The equilibrium constant $K_c = 0.19\,\text{mol dm}^{-3}$ at 250 °C. At equilibrium the mixture contains 0.200 mol dm^{-3} PCl_5 and 0.010 mol dm^{-3} PCl_3. Calculate the equilibrium concentration of Cl_2 and state the units.

2 Hydrogen iodide (1.00 mol) is introduced into a sealed vessel of volume 12 dm^3 at 425 °C. The equilibrium
$2HI(g) \rightleftharpoons H_2(g) + I_2(g)$
is quickly established. The value of the equilibrium constant K_c at this temperature is 0.018. Calculate the amounts in moles of hydrogen and iodine present in the equilibrium mixture.

GAS MIXTURES AND THE EQUILIBRIUM CONSTANT K_p

OBJECTIVES

- Partial pressure
- Mole fraction
- Calculating K_p

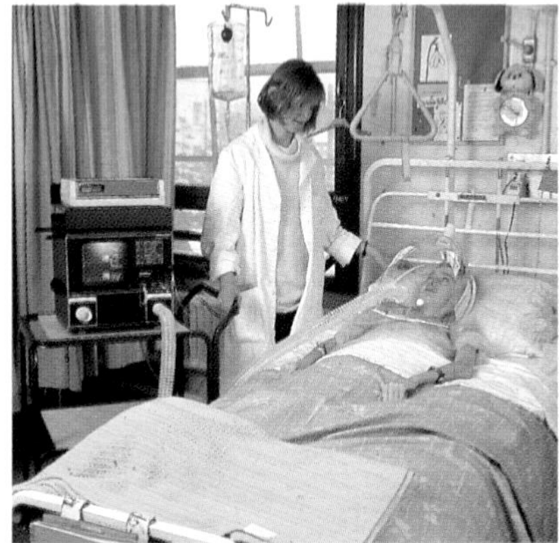

The measurement of the partial pressures of the gases carbon dioxide and oxygen enables a person's metabolic rate to be determined. The partial pressures of the exhaled and inhaled gases vary with the physical fitness, diet, and metabolism of each individual.

	Inhaled air	Exhaled air
$p(O_2)$/bar	0.21	0.16
$p(CO_2)$/bar	0.0003	0.04

$$x_A + x_B = \frac{n_A}{(n_A + n_B)} + \frac{n_B}{(n_A + n_B)} = \frac{(n_A + n_B)}{(n_A + n_B)} = 1$$

The composition of a solution is usually described in terms of the concentrations of its components. As a result, the equilibrium constant K_c for a reaction in solution is expressed in terms of concentrations. It is difficult to describe the composition of a gas mixture in terms of concentrations; the volume of a solution is fixed whereas the volume of a gas is not. A more natural measure is the *pressure*. The quantity of each gas in an equilibrium mixture is described in terms of the pressure that it exerts – its *partial pressure*. The equilibrium constant can be expressed in terms of these individual partial pressures: it is given the symbol K_p.

Partial pressure

The **partial pressure** of a gas in a mixture of gases is the pressure it would exert if it alone occupied the total volume occupied by the gas mixture. **Dalton's law** of partial pressures states that:

- The total pressure exerted by a mixture of gases is the sum of the partial pressures of the gases.

Dalton's law can be rephrased in terms of the mole fractions of each of the components of the mixture of gases. The **mole fraction** x_A of a component gas A is its fraction of the total amount in moles. In symbols, for a mixture of two component gases A and B:

$$x_A = \frac{n_A}{(n_A + n_B)}$$

where n_A = the amount in moles of gas A, and n_B = the amount in moles of gas B. A mole fraction, of course, has no units because it is a ratio. The sum of the mole fractions of all the components equals one (see box).

In terms of the mole fractions, the partial pressure p_A of a gas A equals the mole fraction x_A of the gas multiplied by the total pressure p_{tot}:

$$p_A = x_A p_{tot}$$

The partial pressure of a gas in a mixture is proportional to its mole fraction in the mixture. An equilibrium constant K_p can therefore be defined in terms of *partial pressures*, in the same way that the equilibrium constant K_c is defined in terms of *concentrations*.

The equilibrium constant K_p

When an equilibrium involves gases, the equilibrium constant can be expressed in terms of the partial pressures of the gases. Consider the general equilibrium

$$aA(g) + bB(g) \rightleftharpoons cC(g) + dD(g)$$

The equilibrium constant expression in terms of *partial pressures* is

$$K_p = \frac{p(C)_{eq}{}^c p(D)_{eq}{}^d}{p(A)_{eq}{}^a p(B)_{eq}{}^b}$$

where the subscript 'eq' indicates that the pressures are those once equilibrium has been reached, and, for example, the term $p(C)_{eq}{}^c$ means the partial pressure (usually expressed in bar or atm) of C at equilibrium, raised to the power c. Just as K_c is constant if concentration changes, K_p has the same value whatever the starting partial pressures.

For example, hydrogen, iodine, and hydrogen iodide react together:

$$H_2(g) + I_2(g) \rightleftharpoons 2HI(g)$$

Since the reaction occurs in the gas phase, it is more convenient to write the equilibrium in terms of partial pressures and so calculate K_p:

$$K_p = \frac{p(HI)_{eq}{}^2}{p(H_2)_{eq} p(I_2)_{eq}}$$

Data for the reverse reaction at 450 K show that, starting with 1.000 mol HI, 0.778 mol HI remains at equilibrium. The amounts in moles of hydrogen and iodine present at equilibrium may be found from this figure: i.e. if 0.778 mol HI remains, then the amount in moles of HI that must have decomposed is

$$1.000 - 0.778 = 0.222 \text{ mol}$$

The chemical equation shows that, in the backward reaction, 2 mol HI decomposes into 1 mol H_2 and 1 mol I_2. Therefore, 0.222 mol HI decomposes into 0.111 mol H_2 and 0.111 mol I_2. These amounts in moles must be converted to partial pressures for the calculation of K_p.

The mole fraction of each substance has the same numerical value as its amount in moles, i.e.

$$\text{mole fraction of HI } (x_{HI}) = \frac{0.778 \text{ mol}}{1.000 \text{ mol}} = 0.778$$

The total amount in moles present at equilibrium is (0.778 mol + 0.111 mol + 0.111 mol) = 1.000 mol

The partial pressures are proportional to the mole fractions. For example, at equilibrium the partial pressure of HI is given by

$$p(\text{HI})_{eq} = 0.778p_{tot}$$

where p_{tot} is the total pressure. The expression for the equilibrium constant becomes

$$K_p = \frac{(0.778p_{tot})^2}{(0.111p_{tot}) \times (0.111p_{tot})} = \frac{0.778^2}{0.111^2} = 49$$

Units

In *this* case, we do not need to know the actual value of the total pressure, because the p_{tot} terms cancel in the equation, and K_p has no units because

$$\frac{(\text{bar})^2}{(\text{bar} \times \text{bar})}$$

also cancels.

Le Chatelier revisited

An earlier spread in this chapter investigated the effect of pressure change on the ammonia synthesis equilibrium:

$$N_2(g) + 3H_2(g) \rightleftharpoons 2NH_3(g)$$

Le Chatelier's principle indicates that, if the pressure of this system is increased, the equilibrium will shift to minimize the pressure increase and the yield of ammonia will increase.

Writing the equilibrium expression for the reaction in terms of partial pressures shows *quantitatively* the effect of changing pressure:

$$K_p = \frac{p(NH_3)_{eq}^{\ 2}}{p(N_2)_{eq}p(H_2)_{eq}^{\ 3}}$$

According to Dalton's law, each partial pressure may be rewritten in terms of the mole fraction of the gas at equilibrium, x:

$$K_p = \frac{x(NH_3)^2p_{tot}^{\ 2}}{x(N_2)p_{tot}x(H_2)^3p_{tot}^{\ 3}}$$

Dividing top and bottom by $p_{tot}^{\ 2}$:

$$K_p = \frac{x(NH_3)^2}{x(N_2)x(H_2)^3p_{tot}^{\ 2}}$$

This expression shows that the equilibrium constant is proportional to a product of mole fractions divided by the square of the total pressure. As K_p is independent of pressure, K_p does not change if the pressure is changed. So if p_{tot} increases, the mole fraction term, $x(NH_3)^2/x(N_2)x(H_2)^3$, must also increase. But the sum of the mole fractions is always 1. So the mole fraction of ammonia, $x(NH_3)$, must increase while the mole fractions of nitrogen, $x(N_2)$, and hydrogen, $x(H_2)$, decrease.

Dinitrogen tetraoxide

For the dissociation of dinitrogen tetraoxide N_2O_4, the equilibrium constant K_p is

$$K_p = \frac{p(NO_2)_{eq}^{\ 2}}{p(N_2O_4)_{eq}}$$

Note that in this case K_p has units (e.g. bar).

Ethanol manufacture

The manufacture of ethanol by the direct hydration of ethene is a gas-phase reaction:

$$C_2H_4(g) + H_2O(g) \rightleftharpoons CH_3CH_2OH(g)$$

In a typical plant, 200 mol of ethene and 500 mol of steam are introduced into a reaction vessel at 300 °C and 65 atm pressure. Equilibrium is established rapidly in the presence of a phosphoric acid catalyst; the equilibrium mixture typically contains 180 mol of ethanol.

SUMMARY

- K_p is the equilibrium constant for gaseous equilibria; it is expressed in terms of the *partial pressures* of the gases involved in the equilibrium.
- The partial pressure of a gas in a mixture is equal to its mole fraction multiplied by the total pressure of the mixture.

11.9 HETEROGENEOUS EQUILIBRIA

OBJECTIVES

- Homogeneous and heterogeneous equilibria contrasted
- Heterogeneous equilibria and K_c, K_p
- Solubility products

All the chemical equilibria met so far have been **homogeneous equilibria**. The term 'homogeneous' means that all the component species are in the same physical state (phase). For example, the $N_2/H_2/NH_3$ system is a gas-phase equilibrium; and the $CrO_4^{2-}/H^+/Cr_2O_7^{2-}$ system is an aqueous equilibrium. **Heterogeneous equilibria** involve component species in more than one phase. For example, the ions $Ag^+(aq)$ and $Cl^-(aq)$ may be in equilibrium with solid AgCl(s):

$$AgCl(s) \rightleftharpoons Ag^+(aq) + Cl^-(aq)$$

This spread introduces some of the distinctive features of heterogeneous equilibria.

Heating limestone (calcium carbonate, $CaCO_3$) to a high temperature in a kiln causes decomposition to quicklime (calcium oxide, CaO).

K_c and the concentration of a solid

The concentration of a substance is defined as the amount in moles per unit volume. For a *solid*, this quantity is proportional to its density, which is its mass per unit volume. A large lump of material has the same density as a small lump. Unlike a solution or a gas, the concentration of a solid cannot change during a reaction. The solid may eventually all be used up; but, as long as any is present, *its concentration remains constant*.

When an equilibrium involves a solid, the concentration of the solid *is a constant*. Because the concentration of a solid cannot change during a reaction, it may be omitted from the expression for the equilibrium constant, K_c. For example, the decomposition of calcium carbonate is an important industrial process contributing to cement manufacture. It involves two solids and a gas:

$$CaCO_3(s) \rightleftharpoons CaO(s) + CO_2(g)$$

The concentration of each solid is a constant. So the expression for the equilibrium constant for this reaction, which is

$$K_c = \frac{[CaO]_{eq}[CO_2]_{eq}}{[CaCO_3]_{eq}} \quad (1)$$

can be reduced to

$$K_c' = [CO_2]_{eq} \quad (2)$$

The K_c in equation (1) is, however, a different number to K_c' in equation (2). The values of the concentrations of the solids have been included in the value of K_c'.

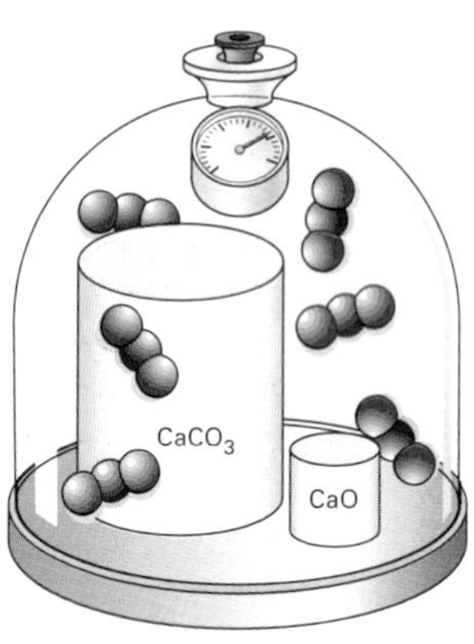

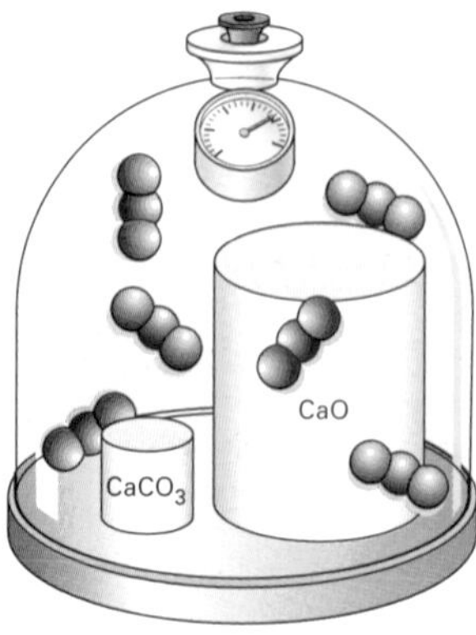

The concentration of a gas is proportional to its pressure. These two diagrams illustrate that the pressure of carbon dioxide is constant at a fixed temperature, regardless of the amounts of solid present.

K_p and the concentration of a solid

K_p is the equilibrium constant for a reaction expressed in terms of the partial pressures of the constituent gases. Because calcium oxide CaO and calcium carbonate $CaCO_3$ are solids, the amount of each substance present has no effect on the position of the equilibrium, for the same reasons as given above in the discussion about K_c. The expression for the equilibrium constant in terms of partial pressures is therefore:

$$K_p = p(CO_2)_{eq}$$

Precipitates and equilibria

Aqueous solutions are examples of homogeneous systems: they consist of a solute dissolved in water. A precipitation reaction happens when two solutions are mixed and a solid forms. For example, mixing aqueous silver nitrate with aqueous sodium chloride gives a precipitate of silver chloride. The formation of the precipitate is described by the equilibrium:

$$Ag^+(aq) + Cl^-(aq) \rightleftharpoons AgCl(s)$$

which lies far to the right. This equilibrium is heterogeneous.

A **saturated solution** is a solution that contains as much dissolved solid as the solvent can dissolve at a particular temperature. In a saturated solution of silver chloride, silver ions and chloride ions are in equilibrium with solid silver chloride:

$$AgCl(s) \rightleftharpoons Ag^+(aq) + Cl^-(aq)$$

and the equilibrium constant may be written as:

$$K_c = \frac{[Ag^+]_{eq}[Cl^-]_{eq}}{[AgCl]_{eq}}$$

The concentration of the solid is a constant and may be left out of the equilibrium expression. The resulting equilibrium constant is called the **solubility product**:

$$K_{sp} = [Ag^+]_{eq}[Cl^-]_{eq}$$

The following spread will describe the uses of solubility products.

It is sometimes possible to make a solution that contains a greater amount of solute than a saturated solution. Such a solution is called a ***supersaturated solution*** *and is unstable. Adding one crystal of solid to a supersaturated solution will cause the crystal to grow rapidly until the solution is only saturated.*

When clear aqueous solutions of lead(II) nitrate $Pb(NO_3)_2$ and potassium iodide KI are mixed, a precipitate of solid lead(II) iodide PbI_2 forms.

Solubility product

Consider the general reaction:

$A_aB_b(s) \rightleftharpoons aA^{n+}(aq) + bB^{m-}(aq)$

The solubility product is

$K_{sp} = [A^{n+}]_{eq}{}^a[B^{m-}]_{eq}{}^b$

The equilibrium may be established by placing the solid in contact with water, or by forming a precipitate by mixing together solutions of the ions.

Calcium hydroxide

Calcium hydroxide is a *sparingly soluble* solid, one that dissolves only to a very small extent in water:

$Ca(OH)_2(s) \rightleftharpoons Ca^{2+}(aq) + 2OH^-(aq)$

The solubility product for calcium hydroxide is:

$K_{sp} = [Ca^{2+}]_{eq}[OH^-]_{eq}{}^2$

The concentration of the hydroxide ion has been raised to the power 2 because two hydroxide ions are formed in the balanced equation.

SUMMARY

- The concentration of a solid is constant, regardless of the amount present.
- Equilibrium expressions for K_c and K_p do not include terms relating to solids involved in the heterogeneous equilibrium mixture.
- A saturated solution is a solution that contains as much dissolved solid as the solvent can dissolve at a particular temperature.
- A sparingly soluble solute is a substance that has a very low solubility in the solvent.
- The solubility product is the equilibrium constant expressed in terms of concentrations of the ions produced from a sparingly soluble solid in contact with its saturated solution.

PRACTICE

1 State what you understand by each of the following terms, giving examples to illustrate your meaning:

a Equilibrium
b Sparingly soluble
c Solution
d Homogeneous
e Heterogeneous
f Amount in moles
g Molar concentration.

2 Write equilibrium expressions for K_c, K_p, or K_{sp} as indicated for each of the following equilibrium systems:

a The thermal decomposition of limestone to quicklime:
$CaCO_3(s) \rightleftharpoons CaO(s) + CO_2(g)$ (K_p)

b Solid yellow lead(II) iodide in contact with water:
$PbI_2(s) \rightleftharpoons Pb^{2+}(aq) + 2I^-(aq)$ (K_{sp})

c The dissociation of water:
$H_2O(l) \rightleftharpoons H^+(aq) + OH^-(aq)$ (K_c).

11.10

OBJECTIVES

- Criteria for precipitation
- Qualitative analysis
- The common ion effect

SOLUBILITY PRODUCTS AND PRECIPITATES

If you mix two solutions containing ions, a solid precipitates if the ionic concentrations exceed those required for a saturated solution. For a sparingly soluble compound, the solubility product K_{sp} may be used to predict whether a precipitate will form. These predictions form the basis of much of qualitative analysis, which identifies substances by using specific reagents to form coloured precipitates.

Explaining precipitation

If you add dilute aqueous ammonia to a solution containing magnesium ions, magnesium hydroxide precipitates out from the solution. Repeat the experiment with a solution containing calcium ions, and no precipitate forms. These two practical results may be explained by considering the solubility products of calcium hydroxide $Ca(OH)_2$ and magnesium hydroxide $Mg(OH)_2$.

For both of the metal hydroxides, the expressions for the equilibrium reaction and the solubility product (using M to denote the metal) are:

$$M(OH)_2(s) \rightleftharpoons M^{2+}(aq) + 2OH^-(aq)$$

$$K_{sp} = [M^{2+}]_{eq}[OH^-]_{eq}^2$$

The equilibrium hydroxide ion concentration in dilute aqueous ammonia is typically $1.0 \times 10^{-3}\,mol\,dm^{-3}$, and hence $[OH^-]_{eq}^2 = 1.0 \times 10^{-6}\,mol^2\,dm^{-6}$. We now consider the solubility products of the two hydroxides.

The solubility product for *calcium hydroxide* is found from data tables to be $5.5 \times 10^{-6}\,mol^3\,dm^{-9}$, i.e.

$$K_{sp} = [Ca^{2+}]_{eq}[OH^-]_{eq}^2 = 5.5 \times 10^{-6}\,mol^3\,dm^{-9}$$

Substituting for $[OH^-]_{eq}^2$ from above, we get

$$[Ca^{2+}]_{eq} \times (1.0 \times 10^{-6}\,mol^2\,dm^{-6}) = 5.5 \times 10^{-6}\,mol^3\,dm^{-9}$$

Dividing both sides by $1.0 \times 10^{-6}\,mol^2\,dm^{-6}$

$$[Ca^{2+}]_{eq} = 5.5\,mol\,dm^{-3}$$

So a saturated solution of calcium hydroxide contains Ca^{2+} ions at a concentration of $5.5\,mol\,dm^{-3}$.

The solubility product for *magnesium hydroxide* is likewise found to be $1.1 \times 10^{-11}\,mol^3\,dm^{-9}$, i.e.

$$K_{sp} = [Mg^{2+}]_{eq}[OH^-]_{eq}^2 = 1.1 \times 10^{-11}\,mol^3\,dm^{-9}$$

Again, substituting for $[OH^-]_{eq}^2$ from above, we get

$$[Mg^{2+}]_{eq} \times (1.0 \times 10^{-6}\,mol^2\,dm^{-6}) = 1.1 \times 10^{-11}\,mol^3\,dm^{-9}$$

Dividing both sides by $1.0 \times 10^{-6}\,mol^2\,dm^{-6}$

$$[Mg^{2+}]_{eq} = 1.1 \times 10^{-5}\,mol\,dm^{-3}$$

So a saturated solution of magnesium hydroxide contains Mg^{2+} ions at a concentration of $1.1 \times 10^{-5}\,mol\,dm^{-3}$.

Most solutions of magnesium ions in the laboratory have concentrations greater than $1.1 \times 10^{-5}\,mol\,dm^{-3}$ and so $Mg(OH)_2(s)$ will precipitate if aqueous ammonia is added. It is unlikely that the calcium ion concentration in a solution will be as great as $5.5\,mol\,dm^{-3}$.

Qualitative analysis

Precipitation reactions may be used in **qualitative analysis** to identify ions in solution. For example, adding dilute aqueous sodium hydroxide to an aqueous solution containing metal ions often causes precipitation. This happens because many metal hydroxides are only very slightly soluble (**sparingly soluble**) in water, i.e. they have very low values of solubility product. So a precipitate forms according to rule 3 in the box on the right. Many of the metal hydroxides precipitated have characteristic colours, which helps to identify the original aqueous metal ion, spread 20.11.

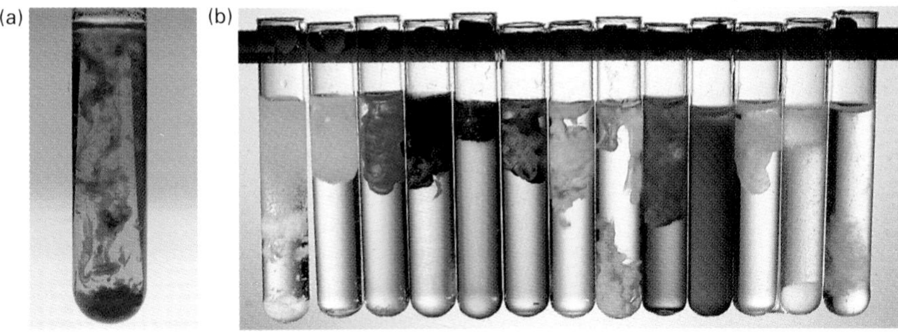

(a) When clear aqueous solutions of iron(III) nitrate $Fe(NO_3)_3$ and potassium hydroxide KOH are mixed, a precipitate of solid iron(III) hydroxide $Fe(OH)_3$ forms.
(b) Precipitates of sparingly soluble hydroxides.

Aqueous halide ions are identified by their precipitation reactions with aqueous silver nitrate. The general equation is:

silver nitrate +	metal halide ⇌	metal nitrate +	silver halide
SOLUBLE	SOLUBLE	SOLUBLE	INSOLUBLE PRECIPITATE

Silver *nitrate* is chosen because all nitrates have a high solubility in water. The nitrate ion in aqueous silver nitrate will not cause precipitation of metal nitrates from solutions to which it is added. The silver halides have characteristic colours, spread 18.6, so the halide ion can be identified.

The common ion effect

The solubility of a sparingly soluble compound is reduced further if another compound is added that contains an ion in common with it. For example, the expressions for the equilibrium reaction and solubility product for silver chloride are:

$$AgCl(s) \rightleftharpoons Ag^+(aq) + Cl^-(aq)$$

$$K_{sp} = [Ag^+]_{eq}[Cl^-]_{eq}$$

Adding sodium chloride (which is *very* soluble) to a saturated solution of silver chloride (which is only *sparingly* soluble) increases the chloride ion concentration. The value of K_{sp} for silver chloride must remain constant: but $[Cl^-]_{eq}$ has increased, so the equilibrium shifts to take up the extra Cl^- ions, and $[Ag^+]_{eq}$ must decrease. Thus the solubility of silver chloride is decreased; the production of a precipitate of silver chloride is correspondingly made more likely. The effect of the common Cl^- ion is to *reduce* the solubility of the silver chloride, so it precipitates.

The common ion effect is used in the Solvay process, the industrial preparation of sodium carbonate, spread 16.6. Carbon dioxide gas flows up a tower while brine (aqueous sodium chloride) saturated with ammonia flows down. The following equilibrium is established:

$$CO_2(g) + NH_3(aq) + NaCl(aq) + H_2O(l) \rightleftharpoons NH_4Cl(aq) + NaHCO_3(s)$$

The equilibrium shifts to the right because sodium hydrogencarbonate $NaHCO_3$ is almost insoluble in cold brine due to the common ion effect. The solid is filtered off and decomposed by heating to give the desired product (sodium carbonate).

SUMMARY

- A solid precipitates from solution when the product of the ionic concentrations in the solution exceeds the solubility product.
- Many metal ions form coloured hydroxide precipitates.
- The solubility of a sparingly soluble compound is reduced further on addition of another compound that contains a common ion.

Some basic rules

For an equilibrium such as

$AgCl(s) \rightleftharpoons Ag^+(aq) + Cl^-(aq)$

where a solid is in equilibrium with its ions in solution, the following rules hold:

1 If the product of the ionic concentrations on mixing two solutions is *exactly equal to* the solubility product, the mixed solution is saturated and no more solid will dissolve.

2 If the product of the ionic concentrations on mixing two solutions is *less than* the solubility product, the mixed solution is not saturated and a precipitate does not form.

3 If the product of the ionic concentrations on mixing two solutions is *greater than* the solubility product, the solubility of the solid is exceeded and a precipitate forms.

The brothers Solvay

Sodium carbonate is used in huge quantities to make glass. The Solvay process made this important raw material more cheaply than previous processes had done; as a result, the brothers Solvay made a large fortune. They funded the Solvay Congresses in the early twentieth century, which helped to solve the problem of the structure.of the atom.

PRACTICE EXAM QUESTIONS

1 Each of the equations **A**, **B**, **C**, and **D** represents a dynamic equilibrium.

A $N_2(g) + O_2(g) \rightleftharpoons 2NO(g)$ $\Delta H^\ominus = +180$ kJ mol^{-1}

B $N_2O_4(g) \rightleftharpoons 2NO_2(g)$ $\Delta H^\ominus = +58$ kJ mol^{-1}

C $3H_2(g) + N_2(g) \rightleftharpoons 2NH_3(g)$ $\Delta H^\ominus = -92$ kJ mol^{-1}

D $H_2(g) + I_2(g) \rightleftharpoons 2HI(g)$ $\Delta H^\ominus = -10$ kJ mol^{-1}

a Explain what is meant by the term dynamic equilibrium. [1]

b Explain why a catalyst does not alter the position of any equilibrium reaction. [2]

c The units of the equilibrium constant, K_c, for one of the above reactions are mol dm^{-3}. Identify the reaction **A**, **B**, **C**, or **D** which has these units for K_c and write the expression for K_c for this reaction. [2]

d The graphs below show how the yield of product varies with pressure for three of the reactions **A**, **B**, **C**, and **D** given above.

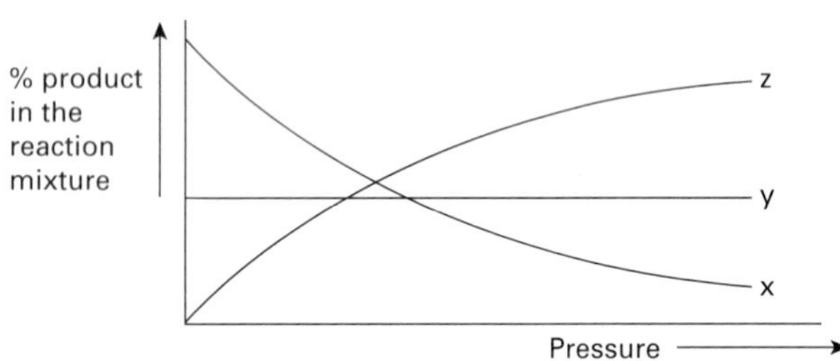

i Identify a reaction from **A**, **B**, **C**, and **D** which would have the relationship between yield and pressure shown in graphs x, y, and z.

ii Explain why an industrial chemist would not use a very low pressure for the reaction represented in graph x.

iii Explain why an industrial chemist may not use a very high pressure for the reaction represented in graph z.

iv Copy the above graphs and add a line to show how the product yield would vary with pressure if the reaction which follows curve z was carried out at a temperature higher than that of the original graph.
AQA (NEAB) 1999

2 At a temperature of 107 °C, the reaction

$CO(g) + 2H_2(g) \rightleftharpoons CH_3OH(g)$

reaches equilibrium under a pressure of 1.59 MPa with 0.122 mol of carbon monoxide and 0.298 mol of hydrogen present at equilibrium in a vessel of volume 1.04 dm^3.

Use these data to answer the questions that follow.

a Assuming ideal gas behaviour, determine the total number of moles of gas present. Hence calculate the number of moles of methanol in the equilibrium mixture. [3]

b Calculate the value of the equilibrium constant, K_c, for this reaction and state its units. [3]

c i Write an expression for the equilibrium constant K_p, for this equilibrium.

ii Calculate the mole fraction of each of the three gases present in the equilibrium mixture.

iii Calculate the partial pressure of hydrogen present in the equilibrium mixture.

iv Calculate the value of the equilibrium constant K_p, and state its units. [8]
AQA (NEAB) 1999

3 In the Contact Process for the production of sulphuric acid, highly purified sulphur dioxide and oxygen react together to form sulphur trioxide. The process is carried out in the presence of vanadium(V) oxide at about 700 K and at a pressure of 120 kPa

$2SO_2(g) + O_2(g) \rightleftharpoons 2SO_3(g)$
$\Delta H^\ominus = -190$ kJ mol^{-1}

Under these conditions, the partial pressures of sulphur dioxide and sulphur trioxide at equilibrium are 33 kPa and 39 kPa, respectively.

a What would be the effect on the yield of SO_3 of increasing the temperature? Explain your answer. [3]

b What would be the effect on the yield of SO_3 of increasing the total pressure? Explain your answer. [3]

c Determine the partial pressure and hence the mole fraction of oxygen in the equilibrium mixture. [3]

d i Write an expression for the equilibrium constant, K_p, for the reaction shown.

ii Calculate the value of the equilibrium constant, K_p, and state its units. [4]
AQA (NEAB) 1999

4 Phosphorus(V) chloride dissociates at high temperatures according to the equation

$PCl_5(g) \rightleftharpoons PCl_3(g) + Cl_2(g)$

83.4 g of phosphorus(V) chloride are placed in a vessel of volume 9.23 dm^3. At equilibrium at a certain temperature, 11.1 g of chlorine are produced at a total pressure of 250 kPa.

Use these data, where relevant, to answer the questions that follow.

a Calculate the number of moles of each of the gases in the vessel at equilibrium. [3]

b i Write an expression for the equilibrium constant K_c, for the above equilibrium.

ii Calculate the value of the equilibrium constant, K_c, and state its units. [4]

c i Write an expression for the equilibrium constant, K_p, for the above equilibrium.

ii Calculate the mole fraction of chlorine present in the equilibrium mixture.

iii Calculate the partial pressure of PCl_5 present in the equilibrium mixture.

iv Calculate the value of the equilibrium constant, K_p, and state its units. [7]
AQA (NEAB) 1998

5 Ammonia is manufactured by the Haber–Bosch process by mixing hydrogen and nitrogen at 700 K and 200 atmospheres pressure and using an iron catalyst with a potassium hydroxide promoter.

$N_2(g) + 3H_2(g) \rightleftharpoons 2NH_3(g)\ \Delta H^\ominus = -92\ \text{kJ mol}^{-1}$

a Explain the term **dynamic equilibrium**. [2]

b Explain why the use of high pressure favours ammonia formation. [2]

c Analysis of an equilibrium mixture, obtained by mixing nitrogen and hydrogen, showed 24.0 g of NH_3, 13.5 g of H_2, and 60.3 g of N_2 to be present. The total pressure of the system was 10 atmospheres.

i Copy this table and calculate the mole fraction of each of these substances present at equilibrium. [2]

N_2	H_2	NH_3
Mole fraction =	Mole fraction =	Mole fraction =

ii Calculate K_p and state its units. [4]

iii Explain the effect of increasing temperature on the value of K_p. [2]

d The reaction of ammonia with oxygen is exothermic:

$4NH_3 + 5O_2 \rightleftharpoons 4NO + 6H_2O$

However, mixtures of ammonia and oxygen do not catch fire spontaneously. Use this information to explain the difference between **kinetic** and **thermodynamic stability**. [4]
NICCEA 1998

6 Consider the equilibrium

$N_2O_4(g) \rightleftharpoons 2NO_2(g)$

a i Write an expression for K_c, indicating the units. [2]

ii 1 mol of dinitrogen tetraoxide, N_2O_4, was introduced into a vessel of volume 10.0 dm³ at a temperature of 70 °C. At equilibrium 50% had dissociated. Calculate K_c. [4]

	$\Delta H_f^\ominus$ / kJ mol⁻¹
N_2O_4	+9.70
NO_2	+33.9

iii Using the above data, calculate the enthalpy change for the forward reaction. [2]

iv If the same experiment is carried out at 100 °C, state qualitatively, giving your reasons, how the equilibrium composition will change. [2]

b Explain what you would do to increase the degree of dissociation of $N_2O_4(g)$ at constant temperature. [2]

c What is the effect of a catalyst on the following:

i the value of K_c; [1]

ii the equilibrium position; [1]

iii the rate of attainment of equilibrium? [1]

d Suggest why the reaction

$N_2 + 2O_2 \rightarrow 2NO_2$

is not a very useful method of making NO_2. [2]
EDEXCEL 1998

7 This question concerns the reaction

$H_2(g) + I_2(g) \rightleftharpoons 2HI(g)$

which, even at high temperatures, is slow.

	H—H	H—I	I—I	Cl—Cl	H—Cl
Bond energy / kJ mol⁻¹	436	299	151	242	431

a i Calculate ΔH for the reaction between hydrogen and iodine. [2]

ii Sketch an energy level diagram for this reaction. [2]

b Indicate on your sketch in **a ii**:

i ΔH for the reaction;

ii the activation energy for the forward reaction ($E_{a(F)}$);

iii the activation energy for the reverse reaction ($E_{a(R)}$). [3]

c For the analogous reaction for the formation of hydrogen chloride

$H_2(g) + Cl_2(g) \rightarrow 2HCl(g)$

suggest how you would expect the activation energy of the forward reaction to compare with that shown for the formation of HI. Give a reason for your answer. [2]

d The reaction for the formation of hydrogen iodide does not go to completion but reaches an equilibrium.

i Write an expression for the equilibrium constant, K_c, for this reaction. [1]

ii A mixture of 1.9 mol of H_2 and 1.9 mol of I_2 was prepared and allowed to reach equilibrium in a closed vessel of 250 cm³ capacity at 700 °C. The resulting equilibrium mixture was found to contain 3.0 mol of HI.

Calculate the value of K_c at this temperature. [3]
EDEXCEL 1998

12 Acid–base equilibrium

What sort of substances are acids? Your earliest experience of an acid may well have been as a small child when you bit into a lemon. After this first encounter, you soon came to associate sour, sharp tastes with citrus fruits (citric acid), vinegar (ethanoic acid), and unripe apples (malic acid or 2-hydroxybutanedioic acid). In the late seventeenth century, Robert Boyle characterized acids by their sourness and attempted to explain this property by suggesting that the atoms of acids are coated with spikes. However, not all sour-tasting substances are acids, and very few acids are safe to taste to see if they are sour! (*Remember: Never taste laboratory reagents!*) Human tongues have sense receptors that respond specifically to sourness, but we have no specific sensitivity to bases. As a crude approximation, bases may be regarded as the opposites of acids: they are substances that react with acids. This chapter presents more precise, chemical definitions of acids and bases.

ACIDS AND BASES AND THEIR PROPERTIES

12.1

OBJECTIVES

- Acidic solutions and the H^+ ion
- Basic solutions and the OH^- ion
- Neutralization
- Brønsted–Lowry theory

An early encounter with an acid – biting into a lemon.

Acids: a simple reminder

- Acids dissolve in water to give solutions of pH less than 7.
- Acids turn blue litmus red.
- Acids neutralize bases to give salts and water.
- Acids react with carbonates to give carbon dioxide gas.

The reaction between aqueous solutions of hydrochloric acid and sodium hydroxide is a typical acid–base reaction. Both solutions are good conductors of electricity; the electric current is carried by ions.

- Aqueous hydrochloric acid contains the ions $H^+(aq)$ and $Cl^-(aq)$.
- Aqueous sodium hydroxide contains the ions $Na^+(aq)$ and $OH^-(aq)$.

Acids and hydrogen ions

The ion common to all aqueous acids is the hydrogen ion or proton, H^+ (a proton results when a hydrogen atom loses its one electron). The simplest representation of the **aqueous hydrogen ion** is the symbol $H^+(aq)$. However, the hydrogen ion has a very large charge density, so each hydrogen ion attracts a lone pair of electrons on a neighbouring water molecule to form a single coordinate bond. The aqueous hydrogen ion is, therefore, more accurately described by the formula $H_3O^+(aq)$. The ion $H_3O^+(aq)$ is called the **oxonium ion** (or the **hydronium ion** or the **hydroxonium ion**).

The oxonium ion $H_3O^+(aq)$ forms when a hydrogen ion H^+ (a proton) from an acid bonds with a water molecule H_2O.

Bases and hydroxide ions

The ion common to all aqueous bases is the hydroxide ion, OH^-. This ion results when a soluble base dissolves in water. A base that is soluble in water is called an **alkali**. Dissolving an alkali in water gives an **alkaline** solution, which has a pH greater than 7. Some soluble bases (for example, sodium hydroxide) contain the hydroxide ion. The ion is released into solution as the substance dissolves:

$$NaOH(s) \rightarrow Na^+(aq) + OH^-(aq)$$

Some soluble bases generate hydroxide ions by reaction with water. For example, potassium oxide reacts as follows:

$$K_2O(s) + H_2O(l) \rightarrow 2K^+(aq) + 2OH^-(aq)$$

Neutralization reactions

Alkalis (soluble bases) and insoluble bases, such as copper(II) oxide CuO, *both* react with acids in **neutralization** reactions.

For example, aqueous hydrochloric acid and aqueous sodium hydroxide react according to the equation:

$$HCl(aq) + NaOH(aq) \rightarrow NaCl(aq) + H_2O(l)$$
$$\text{an acid} + \text{an alkali} \rightarrow \text{a salt} + \text{water}$$

The neutralization reaction can be written in terms of the ions involved as:

$$H^+(aq) + Cl^-(aq) + Na^+(aq) + OH^-(aq) \rightarrow H_2O(l) + Cl^-(aq) + Na^+(aq)$$

The ions $Cl^-(aq)$ and $Na^+(aq)$ do not take part in the reaction. Ions that do not take part in a reaction are called **spectator ions**. All neutralization reactions between solutions involve the reaction between aqueous hydrogen ions $H^+(aq)$ and aqueous hydroxide ions $OH^-(aq)$:

$$H^+(aq) + OH^-(aq) \rightarrow H_2O(l)$$

This reaction is more accurately represented in terms of the oxonium ion:

$$H_3O^+(aq) + OH^-(aq) \rightarrow 2H_2O(l)$$

An insoluble base such as copper(II) oxide can also neutralize an acid. For example:

$$H_2SO_4(aq) + CuO(s) \rightarrow CuSO_4(aq) + H_2O(l)$$
$$\text{an acid} + \text{a base} \rightarrow \text{a salt} + \text{water}$$

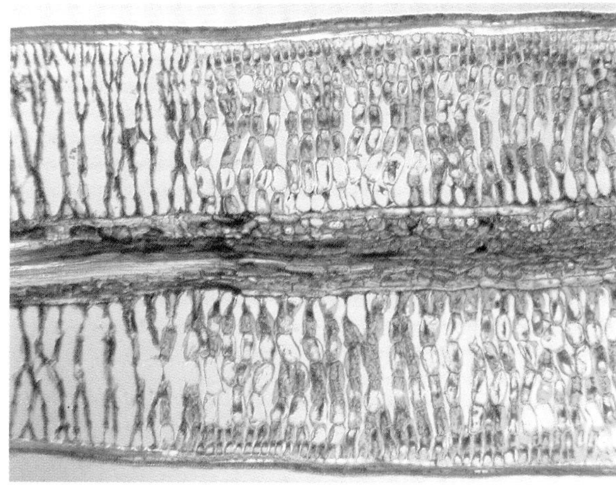

The spongy mesophyll of a leaf, with damage caused by acid rain visible on the left.

Brønsted–Lowry definitions

In aqueous solution, the underlying reaction in all acid–base neutralizations is

$$H_3O^+(aq) + OH^-(aq) \rightarrow 2H_2O(l)$$

Johannes Brønsted made a special study of acid–base reactions and in 1923 explained them in terms of **proton transfer**. Martin Lowry came to similar conclusions independently. According to the Brønsted–Lowry definition of acids and bases:

- A **Brønsted acid** is a proton donor.
- A **Brønsted base** is a proton acceptor.

During neutralization reactions, the oxonium ion acts as a Brønsted acid: it donates a proton to the hydroxide ion. The hydroxide ion acts as a Brønsted base: it accepts a proton from the oxonium ion.

SUMMARY

- Acidic solutions contain aqueous hydrogen ions $H_3O^+(aq)$.
- Basic solutions contain aqueous hydroxide ions $OH^-(aq)$.
- Acids neutralize bases.

Standard enthalpy changes of neutralization

The standard enthalpy changes of neutralization for the reactions between several different acids and bases are very similar. This observation supports the view that neutralization reactions involve the same ions in all cases, i.e.

$H^+(aq) + OH^-(aq) \rightarrow H_2O(l)$

Some typical values are given below:

Acid	Base	$\Delta H^\ominus$/kJ mol^{-1}
HCl	NaOH	–57.1
HCl	KOH	–57.2
HNO_3	NaOH	–57.3
HNO_3	KOH	–57.3

Acid rain

Rain water is naturally acidic because it contains dissolved carbon dioxide. The combustion of fossil fuels produces oxides of nitrogen and sulphur. These oxides dissolve in rain water and increase its acidity above natural levels. **Acid rain** is rain that is artificially more acidic than normal. The control of acidity is vital to living organisms, which have in-built systems for keeping the acidity of their tissues constant. The photograph alongside shows that trees are unable to cope with such dramatic increases in acidity.

Acid rain also leaches metals from soil and rocks into streams and lakes. These substances harm fish and other aquatic life-forms.

Monoprotic and diprotic acids

Many acids are called **monoprotic (monobasic) acids** because they can donate one mole of protons per mole of acid. Examples include hydrochloric and nitric acids, e.g.

$HCl(aq) + H_2O(l) \rightleftharpoons H_3O^+(aq) + Cl^-(aq)$

Some acids are called **diprotic (dibasic) acids** because they can donate two moles of protons per mole of acid. A common example is sulphuric acid H_2SO_4.

12.2

OBJECTIVES

- More on Brønsted acids and bases
- Acid–base reactions involve proton transfer
- Conjugate acid–base pairs

Acids and bases and proton transfer

You should now understand that solutions of acids contain oxonium ions $H_3O^+(aq)$, and that solutions of bases contain hydroxide ions $OH^-(aq)$. The previous spread treated acid–base neutralization in terms of the reaction between these two ions. You will recall that acids are substances that dissolve in water, donating protons to water molecules to produce oxonium ions; and bases are substances that neutralize these ions to form water. According to the Brønsted–Lowry theory of acids and bases, a Brønsted acid is a proton donor and a Brønsted base is a proton acceptor.

Brønsted acids

For an acid to behave as a proton donor, a base must be present to accept protons from it. Hydrochloric acid is a solution of hydrogen chloride gas in water. You can imagine this acidic solution forming in two steps, the first of which is simply the dissolution of the gas in water:

$$HCl(g) \rightarrow HCl(aq)$$

The second step happens when a hydrogen chloride molecule donates a proton to a water molecule. The hydrogen chloride acts as a Brønsted acid; the water acts as a Brønsted base:

$$HCl(aq) + H_2O(l) \rightleftharpoons H_3O^+(aq) + Cl^-(aq)$$

You should recognize the ion $H_3O^+(aq)$ as a Brønsted acid. It is the **conjugate acid** of H_2O, because it is formed when H_2O accepts a proton. The ion $Cl^-(aq)$ is the **conjugate base** of HCl, because it is formed when HCl donates a proton.

Non-aqueous solvents

Hydrogen chloride dissolves readily in benzene C_6H_6. Benzene is an example of a *non-aqueous* solvent. Hydrogen chloride does not behave as an acid when it is dissolved in benzene. There are no molecules present that can accept protons. For the same reason, dry hydrogen chloride gas is not acidic.

The covalent H—Cl bond breaks as both of the shared pair of electrons go over to the Cl atom. The proton H^+ released forms a new H—O bond with a lone pair of electrons on the H_2O molecule.

Brønsted bases

For a base to behave as a proton acceptor, an acid must be present to donate protons to it. Ammonia gas dissolves readily in water to produce a basic solution. You can imagine this basic solution forming in two steps, the first of which is simply the dissolution of the gas in water:

$$NH_3(g) \rightarrow NH_3(aq)$$

The second step happens when an ammonia molecule accepts a proton from a water molecule. The ammonia acts as a Brønsted base; the water acts as a Brønsted acid:

$$NH_3(aq) + H_2O(l) \rightleftharpoons NH_4^+(aq) + OH^-(aq)$$

You should recognize the ion $OH^-(aq)$ as a Brønsted base. It is the conjugate base of H_2O. The ion $NH_4^+(aq)$ is the conjugate acid of NH_3.

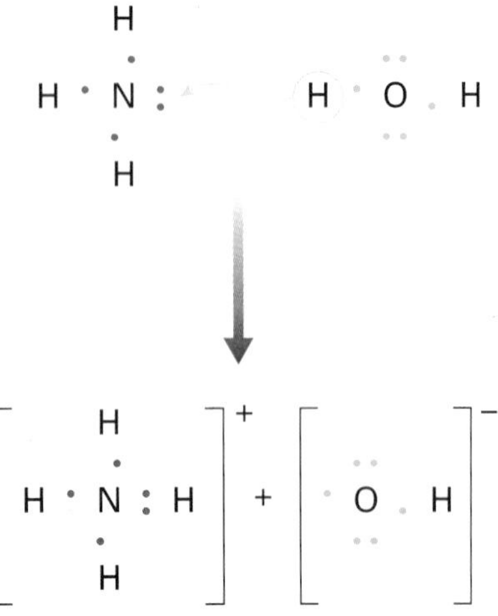

The Brønsted acid H_2O donating a proton to the Brønsted base NH_3. An H—O covalent bond breaks as both of the shared pair of electrons go over to the O atom. The proton H^+ released forms a new bond with the lone pair of electrons on the NH_3 molecule.

Neutralization reactions revisited

All neutralization reactions may be regarded as equilibria involving proton transfer. For example, the reaction between ammonia and hydrochloric acid in aqueous solution can be described by the following equilibrium:

$$NH_3(aq) + H_3O^+(aq) \rightleftharpoons NH_4^+(aq) + H_2O(l)$$

In the forward reaction, the base NH_3 accepts a proton from the acid H_3O^+. In the reverse reaction, the base H_2O accepts a proton from the acid NH_4^+. The acid NH_4^+ and the base NH_3 are a **conjugate acid–base pair** because they are related by the transfer of a proton. Similarly, the acid H_3O^+ and the base H_2O are a conjugate acid–base pair. In the reverse reaction, water is acting as a base:

$$\underset{\text{BASE}}{NH_3(aq)} + \underset{\text{ACID}}{H_3O^+(aq)} \rightleftharpoons \underset{\text{CONJUGATE ACID}}{NH_4^+(aq)} + \underset{\text{CONJUGATE BASE}}{H_2O(l)}$$

- The conjugate acid is the species that results when a base accepts a proton, e.g. the ammonium ion $NH_4^+(aq)$ is the conjugate acid of the base ammonia $NH_3(aq)$.
- The conjugate base is the species that results when an acid donates a proton, e.g. water $H_2O(l)$ is the conjugate base of the oxonium ion $H_3O^+(aq)$.

The hydroxide ion

The formula of the hydroxide ion is generally written as OH^-. However, it would be more correct to write the formula as HO^-. Remember that an oxygen atom has six electrons in its valence shell and a hydrogen atom has one electron. The Lewis structure for the hydroxide ion shows that the extra electron represented by the negative charge is used to complete *oxygen's* octet. It is therefore oxygen and not hydrogen that carries the negative charge.

(a) O (b) H• (c) [:O:H]⁻

The Lewis structures of (a) the oxygen atom, (b) the hydrogen atom, and (c) the hydroxide ion.

Sodium hydroxide should therefore have the formula NaHO, making the series H_2O, NaHO, Na_2O an obvious progression and similarly for H_3O^+, H_2O, HO^-. NaHO also lists the elements in the order of their electronegativities, following the general rule for formulae. Unfortunately, tradition dictates the illogical order NaOH.

SUMMARY

- Brønsted–Lowry theory explains acid–base reactions in terms of equilibria involving proton transfer.
- A Brønsted acid is a proton donor.
- A Brønsted base is a proton acceptor.
- Conjugate acid–base pairs are related by the transfer of a proton.

PRACTICE

1 State whether each of the following in aqueous solution can act as a Brønsted acid or a Brønsted base. Give reasons for your answers.

a HCl
b HI
c NaOH
d K_2O
e $Ca(OH)_2$
f NH_3.

2 For each of the following, give the formula of its conjugate base:

a HCl(aq)
b $H_3O^+(aq)$
c $H_2O(l)$.

3 For each of the following, give the formula of its conjugate acid:

a $NH_3(aq)$
b $HO^-(aq)$
c $H_2O(l)$.

4 Caves and potholes form in limestone, as carbon dioxide solution and rain water flow through and 'dissolve away' the rock:

$H_2O(l) + CO_2(aq) + CaCO_3(s) \rightleftharpoons Ca(HCO_3)_2(aq)$

Discuss this reaction in the light of the Brønsted-Lowry theory of acids and bases.

12.3

AQUEOUS HYDROGEN ION CONCENTRATION AND PH

OBJECTIVES

- pH as a measure of acidity
- Definition of pH
- pH measurement

Definition and meaning of $\log_{10}$

For any positive number *n*, the common **logarithm** (symbol $\log_{10}$) of *n* is the power to which the **base** (in this case, 10) must be raised to make *n*. For example, for the number 2,

$\log_{10} 2 = 0.3$ i.e. $2 = 10^{0.3}$

Logarithms to base 10 are often simply labelled 'LOG' or 'log' on a calculator.

Logarithms

The great advantage of logarithms is that they collapse very large numbers into more manageable ones. For example, the logarithm to base 10 of the Avogadro constant $6.0 \times 10^{23}\,mol^{-1}$ is 23.78. Similarly, very small numbers become more manageable. For example, the charge on the electron is 1.6×10^{-19} coulombs. The logarithm (to base 10) of this unwieldy number is −18.80. **Note that the units must be removed before a logarithm is taken.**

Antilogarithm

Finding the **antilogarithm** of a number is the reverse of the process of finding its logarithm. For example, the logarithm (to base 10) of the number 2 is 0.3. The antilogarithm (to base 10) of 0.3 is 2, i.e.

$\text{antilog}_{10} 0.3 = 10^{0.3} = 2$

Brønsted acids donate protons (hydrogen ions H^+) in aqueous solution. The **acidity** of a solution is a measure of the concentration of the aqueous hydrogen ion $H_3O^+(aq)$. The need to measure acidity quantitatively first arose at the end of the nineteenth century when brewers in Denmark were struggling to maintain the quality of their lager. They knew that the acidity of the lager was varying too much for the yeast to carry out optimum fermentation. But they could not control the acidity unless they could measure it. The Dane Søren Sørensen proposed the pH scale in 1909 for measuring acidity. The brewers were then able to provide the best conditions for their yeast. Chemists can now express the acidity of any solution as a simple number.

The pH scale

The name pH was chosen to conjure up the idea of the strength (*potenz* in German) of the hydrogen ions. It was known that aqueous hydrogen ion concentration, and therefore acidity, varies over a wide range. We shall see later in this chapter that solutions of concentration $1\,mol\,dm^{-3}$ (i.e. 1 mol of solute dissolved per dm^3 of solution) have aqueous hydrogen ion concentrations between 1 and $1 \times 10^{-14}\,mol\,dm^{-3}$. Because of this huge range of values, Sørensen adopted a *logarithmic* scale, where **pH** is defined as the negative logarithm, to base 10, of the aqueous hydrogen ion concentration $[H_3O^+]$ measured in $mol\,dm^{-3}$:

$$pH = -\log_{10}[H_3O^+]$$

For the sake of simplicity, this expression is sometimes written as:

$$pH = -\log_{10}[H^+]$$

The negative sign in the equation results in pH *increasing* as the aqueous hydrogen ion concentration *decreases*. For example, an aqueous hydrogen ion concentration of $1\,mol\,dm^{-3}$ gives a pH of:

$$pH = -\log_{10} 1 = 0.0$$

so this solution is highly acidic.

- The pH scale typically ranges from 0 to 14, but these limits are not absolute.
- **Acidic** solutions have pH values less than 7.
- **Basic** solutions have pH values greater than 7.
- **Neutral** water has a pH of 7.

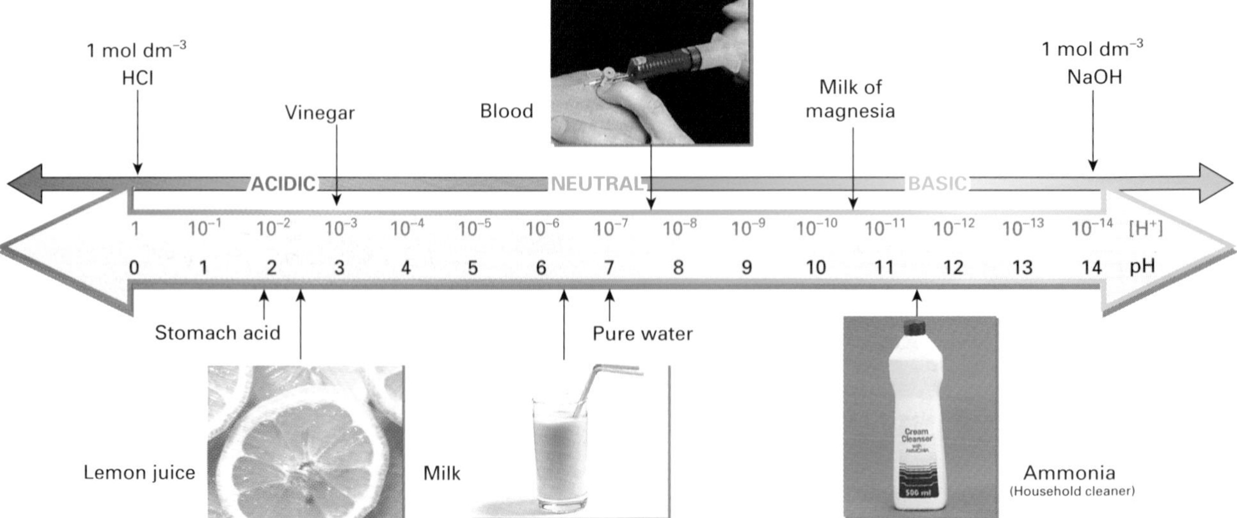

The pH scale and aqueous hydrogen ion concentration.

Measuring pH – indicators

Indicators are water-soluble dyes that have different colours in solutions of different pH. They may be used to indicate the approximate pH of a solution or reveal pH change.

Measuring pH – pH meters

A pH meter consists of three main parts: a pair of electrodes that dip into the solution being measured; an electronic circuit; and a readout device. The electrode pair develops a small voltage, whose magnitude depends on the solution's aqueous hydrogen ion concentration. The electronic circuit amplifies this voltage sufficiently to drive the readout device. On a digital pH meter, the pH is displayed directly. On an analogue pH meter, the pH is shown by a pointer moving across a scale. pH meters must be calibrated periodically: the calibration is checked by immersing the electrode in solutions of known pH, spread 12.11.

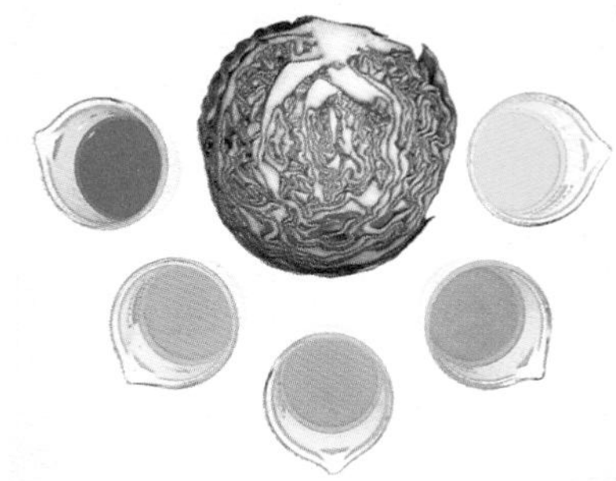

The juice of a red cabbage can act as an indicator. The solutions have (from left to right) pH values of 1, 4, 7, 10, and 13.

pH values and aqueous hydrogen ion concentrations

Worked example on calculating pH from $[H_3O^+]$

Question: The aqueous hydrogen ion concentration in human blood is $4 \times 10^{-8}\,mol\,dm^{-3}$. What is the pH of human blood?

Strategy: Substitute the concentration into the definition of pH given opposite.

Answer: We have

$pH = -\log_{10}[H_3O^+]$

Therefore, for human blood

$pH = -\log_{10}(4 \times 10^{-8}) = 7.4$ (1 decimal place)

Decimal places

The number of *decimal places* in a pH value is equal to the number of *significant figures* given in the concentration data.

It is often useful to determine aqueous hydrogen ion concentrations from pH values, obtained, for example, from pH meter measurements.

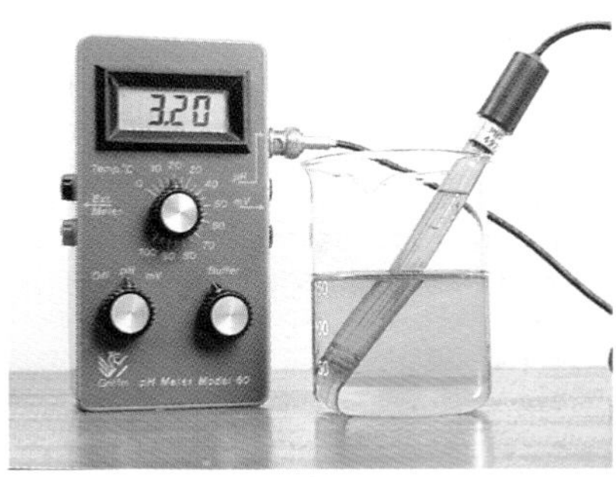

A digital pH meter measuring the pH of a solution containing aluminium ions. The solution is acidic because of the reaction between the metal ions and water molecules. The indicator, bromocresol green, turns yellow below pH 3.5; see the next but one spread.

Worked example on calculating $[H_3O^+]$ from pH

Question: A solution containing aqueous aluminium ions is quite acidic and has a pH of 3.2. What is the aqueous hydrogen ion concentration in the solution?

Answer: As before, pH is defined as:

$pH = -\log_{10}[H_3O^+]$

Multiply both sides of the equation by –1:

$\log_{10}[H_3O^+] = -pH$

Take the antilogarithm of both sides; add the units of $mol\,dm^{-3}$:

$[H_3O^+] = 10^{-pH}\,mol\,dm^{-3}$

Substitute the pH value given

$[H_3O^+] = 10^{-3.2}\,mol\,dm^{-3}$

i.e. the aqueous hydrogen ion concentration is $6 \times 10^{-4}\,mol\,dm^{-3}$

Note: We can check that the calculation has been performed correctly by evaluating $-\log_{10}(6 \times 10^{-4})$, whose value is 3.2.

PRACTICE

1 Calculate the pH of solutions with the following aqueous hydrogen ion concentration in $mol\,dm^{-3}$:
   a 0.1
   b 0.01
   c 0.05.

2 Calculate the aqueous hydrogen ion concentration corresponding to the following pH values:
   a 1.0
   b 2.5.

SUMMARY

- $pH = -\log_{10}[H_3O^+]$.
- The pH scale ranges typically from 0 to 14; neutral water has a pH of 7.
- Indicators and pH meters can be used to measure pH.

12.4 Strong acids

OBJECTIVES

- Strong and weak acids compared
- pH calculations for strong acids

The pH scale describes the aqueous hydrogen ion concentration of solutions. The lower the pH value, the greater the aqueous hydrogen ion concentration. Acidic solutions have pH values less than 7, and basic solutions have pH values greater than 7. As the pH decreases from 7, the acidity of the solution increases. The pH of an acidic solution depends on its concentration in mol dm^{-3}, and on the chemical properties of the acid itself – whether the acid is described as a *strong acid* or as a *weak acid*.

Strong and weak acids

The pH of 0.1 mol dm^{-3} aqueous hydrochloric acid is 1.0. The pH of 0.1 mol dm^{-3} aqueous ethanoic acid is 2.9 (see next spread). Both solutions have the same concentrations of acid yet different values of pH. The reason for this discrepancy is that hydrochloric acid is a strong acid and ethanoic acid is a weak acid.

Hydrochloric acid is described as a *strong* acid because the equilibrium

$$HCl(aq) + H_2O(l) \rightleftharpoons H_3O^+(aq) + Cl^-(aq)$$

lies essentially completely to the right. The acid is fully ionized in aqueous solution. Dissolving 1 mol of hydrogen chloride in water produces 1 mol of aqueous hydrogen ions. For example, a solution of hydrochloric acid of concentration 1 mol dm^{-3} has an aqueous hydrogen ion concentration $[H_3O^+] = 1$ mol dm^{-3}.

On the other hand, ethanoic acid is described as a *weak* acid because the equilibrium

$$CH_3COOH(aq) + H_2O(l) \rightleftharpoons H_3O^+(aq) + CH_3COO^-(aq)$$

lies to the left. Dissolving 1 mol of ethanoic acid in water does not result in 1 mol of aqueous hydrogen ions. For example, a solution of ethanoic acid of concentration 1 mol dm^{-3} has an aqueous hydrogen ion concentration $[H_3O^+] = 4 \times 10^{-3}$ mol dm^{-3}.

- A **strong acid** is *fully ionized* in aqueous solution. The aqueous hydrogen ion concentration is *equal* in magnitude to the concentration of the acid.
- A **weak acid** is *only partially ionized* in aqueous solution. The aqueous hydrogen ion concentration is *smaller* in magnitude than the concentration of the acid.

Ethanoate ion

The ion formed from ethanoic acid CH_3COOH, the ethanoate ion, is delocalized (see spread 6.4) and so should be written as $CH_3CO_2^-$.
To simplify, in this chapter we will use the formula CH_3COO^-.

Ionization of a weak acid HA. The equilibrium $HA(aq) + H_2O(l) \rightleftharpoons H_3O^+(aq) + A^-(aq)$ lies far to the left. Very few acid molecules HA are ionized; the aqueous hydrogen ion concentration is therefore lower than for a strong acid of the same concentration.

(a) A solution of ethanoic acid of concentration 0.1 mol dm^{-3}. This acid is a weak acid and is only partially ionized in aqueous solution. The low concentration of ions makes the solution a poor electrical conductor. (b) A solution of hydrochloric acid of concentration 0.1 mol dm^{-3}. This acid is a strong acid and is fully ionized in aqueous solution. The high concentration of ions makes the solution a good electrical conductor.

Identical samples of magnesium ribbon reacting with (a) 1.0 mol dm^{-3} hydrochloric acid, and (b) 1.0 mol dm^{-3} ethanoic acid. Hydrochloric acid is a strong acid (fully ionized in aqueous solution). The reaction is rapid because the solution contains aqueous hydrogen ions H_3O^+(aq) at a concentration of 1 mol dm^{-3}, pH = 0. Ethanoic acid is a weak acid (only partially ionized in aqueous solution). The reaction is much slower because the aqueous hydrogen ion concentration is 4×10^{-3} mol dm^{-3}, pH = 2.4.

Calculating the pH of strong acids

The pH of a strong acid depends only on its concentration because a strong acid is fully ionized.

For example, nitric acid is a strong acid:

$$HNO_3(aq) + H_2O(l) \rightarrow H_3O^+(aq) + NO_3^-(aq)$$

As a result, nitric acid at a concentration of 1×10^{-3} mol dm^{-3} contains aqueous hydrogen ions at a concentration of 1×10^{-3} mol dm^{-3}. So the pH of this solution is:

$$\begin{aligned} pH &= -\log_{10}[H_3O^+] \\ &= -\log_{10}(1 \times 10^{-3}) \\ &= 3.0 \end{aligned}$$

Worked example on calculating the pH of a strong acid

Question: Calculate the pH of the following concentrations of hydrochloric acid:
(a) 1 mol dm^{-3}
(b) 0.1 mol dm^{-3}
(c) 0.05 mol dm^{-3}

Strategy: Hydrochloric acid is a strong acid and so the aqueous hydrogen ion concentration is the same as the acid concentration.

Answer:

(a) pH = $-\log_{10} 1 = 0.0$
(b) pH = $-\log_{10} 0.1 = 1.0$
(c) pH = $-\log_{10} 0.05 = 1.3$

Negative pH values

A strong acid of concentration greater than 1 mol dm^{-3} will have a pH value *less than zero*. For example, 2 mol dm^{-3} aqueous hydrochloric acid has an aqueous hydrogen ion concentration of 2 mol dm^{-3}. The pH is therefore:

$$\begin{aligned} pH &= -\log_{10}[H_3O^+] \\ &= -\log_{10} 2 \\ &= -0.3 \end{aligned}$$

pH and concentration

For a strong acid, each dilution of the concentration by a factor of 10 increases the pH by one unit. For example, 0.1 mol dm^{-3} aqueous hydrochloric acid has a pH of 1.0. Adding 1 cm^3 of this solution to 9 cm^3 of water gives 0.01 mol dm^{-3} aqueous hydrochloric acid and results in a solution of pH 2.0. This result is a consequence of using the logarithm to base 10 in the definition of pH.

SUMMARY

- Strong acids are fully ionized in aqueous solution.
- Weak acids are only partially ionized in aqueous solution.
- The aqueous hydrogen ion concentration of a strong acid is equal in magnitude to the concentration of the acid.
- The pH of a strong acid depends only on its concentration.

PRACTICE

1 Explain the difference between the terms *acid concentration* and *acid strength*.

2 Calculate the pH value for both of the following solutions:
a Hydrochloric acid HCl(aq), 0.05 mol dm^{-3}
b Nitric acid, 2×10^{-3} mol dm^{-3}.

12.5

WEAK ACIDS

OBJECTIVES

- Acid ionization constant K_a
- Definition of pK_a
- pH calculations for weak acids
- Indicators and pK_{in}

The *strength* of an acid must not be confused with its *concentration*. Strength does not depend on the amount in moles present but on the extent to which the acid ionizes in solution. For example, ethanoic acid CH_3COOH is a weak acid because it is *not* fully ionized in aqueous solution. Hydrochloric acid is a strong acid because it *is* fully ionized. A solution of either acid containing 5 mol dm^{-3} is concentrated, whereas a solution containing 5×10^{-3} mol dm^{-3} is relatively dilute. This spread introduces the terms used to describe weak acids, then explains how to calculate pH values for weak acids.

The acid ionization constant K_a

The equilibrium set up when a weak acid HA dissolves in water is

$$HA(aq) + H_2O(l) \rightleftharpoons H_3O^+(aq) + A^-(aq)$$

The position of equilibrium depends on the nature of the acid HA. The acid HA and the base A^- form a conjugate acid–base pair. In the forward reaction, the acid HA donates its proton to the base H_2O. In the reverse reaction, the acid H_3O^+ donates a proton to the base A^-. The expression for the equilibrium constant is:

$$K_c = \frac{[H_3O^+]_{eq}[A^-]_{eq}}{[HA]_{eq}[H_2O]_{eq}}$$

The concentration of water is essentially constant because it is so large compared to the concentrations of the other species present. It may therefore be omitted from the equilibrium expression because shifting the equilibrium changes its value insignificantly. The resulting equilibrium constant is given a special symbol K_a, and is called the **acid ionization constant** or the **acid dissociation constant**:

$$K_a = \frac{[H_3O^+][A^-]}{[HA]}$$

Note that this equilibrium is reached so quickly that the subscript 'eq' may be omitted.

To calculate K_a from pK_a

From the main text we have

p$K_a = -\log_{10} K_a$

Multiply both sides of the equation by −1:

$\log_{10} K_a = -$pK_a

Take the antilogarithm of both sides of the expression, remembering to add the units of mol dm^{-3}:

$K_a = 10^{-pK_a}$ mol dm^{-3}

For example, the pK_a for ethanoic acid is 4.8. Substitute this value into the expression above and check you obtain the answer $K_a = 2 \times 10^{-5}$ mol dm^{-3}.

pK_a

The values of K_a span a wide range, for example from 0.65 for trichloroethanoic acid CCl_3COOH to 1×10^{-10} for phenol C_6H_5OH, and even smaller for other substances. Such a wide range of values is better accommodated by using a logarithmic scale defined in a similar manner to pH, i.e.

$$pK_a = -\log_{10} K_a$$

The lower the value of pK_a, the larger the value of K_a and the greater the ionization of the acid in water. For example, at the same concentrations, aqueous hydrofluoric acid (pK_a 3.2) is ionized to a greater extent than aqueous ethanoic acid (pK_a 4.8). Some typical K_a and pK_a values are given in the table below.

Acid ionization constants of some weak acids in water at 25 °C.

Compound	Ionization equilibrium	Ionization constant K_a /mol dm^{-3}	pK_a
Hydrofluoric acid	$HF + H_2O \rightleftharpoons H_3O^+ + F^-$	6.3×10^{-4}	3.2
Ethanoic acid	$CH_3COOH + H_2O \rightleftharpoons H_3O^+ + CH_3COO^-$	1.6×10^{-5}	4.8
Benzoic acid	$C_6H_5COOH + H_2O \rightleftharpoons H_3O^+ + C_6H_5COO^-$	6.3×10^{-5}	4.2
Phenol	$C_6H_5OH + H_2O \rightleftharpoons H_3O^+ + C_6H_5O^-$	1.3×10^{-10}	9.9

Calculating the pH of a weak acid

The extent of ionization, and hence the pH, of a weak acid depends both on its concentration and on its pK_a value. These two variables must *both* be taken into account when calculating the pH of a weak acid. For example, the pH of 0.1 mol dm^{-3} aqueous ethanoic acid (K_a 1.6×10^{-5} mol dm^{-3}) is calculated as follows.

The equilibrium equation for aqueous ethanoic acid is:

$$CH_3COOH(aq) + H_2O(l) \rightleftharpoons H_3O^+(aq) + CH_3COO^-(aq)$$

Applying the general equilibrium expression for K_a to ethanoic acid, this expression becomes:

$$K_a = \frac{[H_3O^+][CH_3COO^-]}{[CH_3COOH]}$$

The proportion of molecules ionized is very small. The value of $[CH_3COOH]$, the concentration of the un-ionized acid, is effectively equal to the original concentration of the solution, and may therefore be taken as 0.1 mol dm^{-3}. Also, the values of $[H_3O^+]$ and $[CH_3COO^-]$ must be equal because 1 mol of acid ionizes to give 1 mol of each ion, hence:

$$1.6 \times 10^{-5}\,\text{mol dm}^{-3} = \frac{[H_3O^+]^2}{0.1\,\text{mol dm}^{-3}}$$

$$[H_3O^+]^2 = (0.1\,\text{mol dm}^{-3}) \times (1.6 \times 10^{-5}\,\text{mol dm}^{-3})$$
$$= 1.6 \times 10^{-6}\,\text{mol}^2\,\text{dm}^{-6}$$
$$[H_3O^+] = \sqrt{(1.6 \times 10^{-6}\,\text{mol}^2\,\text{dm}^{-6})}$$
$$= 1.3 \times 10^{-3}\,\text{mol dm}^{-3}$$

Substitute this value into the expression for pH:

$$\text{pH} = -\log_{10}(1.3 \times 10^{-3})$$
$$= 2.9 \quad (1\text{ d.p.})$$

A short cut to this result is shown alongside.

A short cut

The pH, pK_a, and concentration A of a weak acid are related by the expression:

$\text{pH} = \frac{1}{2}pK_a - \frac{1}{2}\log_{10} A$

Its use is straightforward, as shown by the following example.

Suppose that we want to find the pH of a solution of ethanoic acid (pK_a 4.8) of concentration 0.1 mol dm^{-3}. We must substitute the data into the equation above, to obtain:

$$\text{pH} = \tfrac{1}{2}pK_a - \tfrac{1}{2}\log_{10} A$$
$$= (\tfrac{1}{2} \times 4.8) - (\tfrac{1}{2}\log_{10} 0.1)$$
$$= (\tfrac{1}{2} \times 4.8) - (\tfrac{1}{2} \times (-1.0))$$
$$= (2.4) - (-0.5)$$
$$= 2.9 \quad (1\text{ d.p.})$$

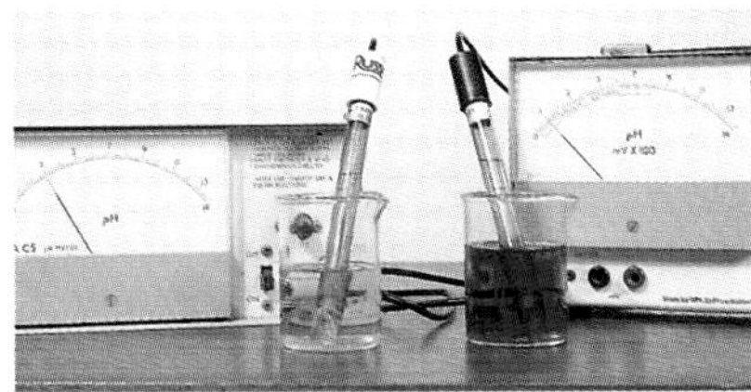

The pH meters show that 0.1 mol dm^{-3} aqueous ethanoic acid, a weak acid, has a pH of 2.9, whereas the same concentration of hydrochloric acid, a strong acid, has a pH of 1.0. The indicator thymol blue is orange at pH 1 and yellow at pH 2.9.

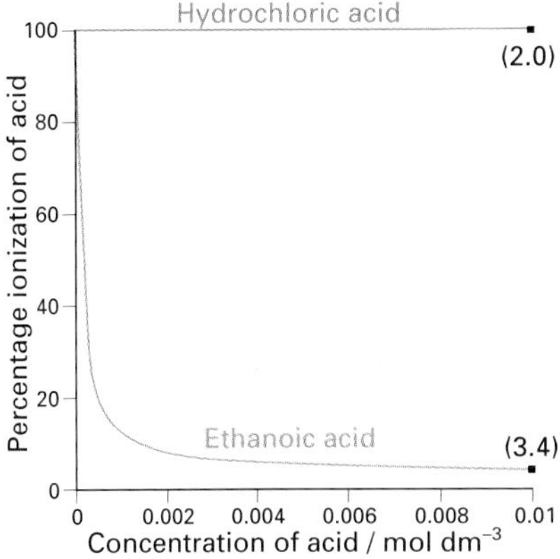

HCl is fully ionized at all concentrations. Ethanoic acid is just 4% ionized at 0.01 mol dm^{-3} concentration. Adding water to a solution of ethanoic acid forces the equilibrium $CH_3COOH(aq) + H_2O(l) \rightleftharpoons H_3O^+(aq) + CH_3COO^-(aq)$ to the right. The extent of ionization increases as the solution becomes more dilute. In extremely dilute solutions, the two acids have the same pH value. The figures in brackets are the pH values at 0.01 mol dm^{-3}.

Indicators as weak acids

As you already know, indicators are water-soluble dyes used to indicate the pH of solutions. They are weak acids of the general form HIn, which exist in aqueous solution in equilibrium with their conjugate base In^-:

$$HIn(aq) + H_2O(l) \rightleftharpoons H_3O^+(aq) + In^-(aq)$$

HIn(aq) and $In^-(aq)$ each have a different colour.

Changing the pH of a solution will bring about a change in the colour of an indicator added to it. The *range* of an indicator – the pH at which the colour change occurs – depends on the pK_a value of the indicator, designated pK_{in}. Typically the range of an indicator is one unit of pH either side of its pK_{in} value.

The indicator bromocresol green is green at pH 4.5; below pH 3.5 it is yellow, above pH 5.5 it is blue.

SUMMARY

- Weak acids are only partially ionized.
- K_a is the acid ionization constant for a weak acid: $K_a = \dfrac{[H_3O^+][A^-]}{[HA]}$
- $pK_a = -\log_{10} K_a$

12.6

Strong bases

OBJECTIVES

- The ionic product of water
- Aqueous hydrogen ion concentrations of basic solutions
- Strong and weak bases compared
- pH calculations for strong bases

Acidic solutions have pH values less than 7; basic solutions have pH values greater than 7. But how are we able to apply the pH scale, which measures *hydrogen ion* concentration, to basic solutions, which contain the *hydroxide ion* $OH^-(aq)$? The key lies in the fact that pure water spontaneously ionizes to a small extent to produce both hydrogen ions and hydroxide ions.

The ionization of water

Water can act as an *acid* when reacting with ammonia,

$$H_2O(l) + NH_3(aq) \rightleftharpoons NH_4^+(aq) + OH^-(aq)$$

and as a *base* when reacting with hydrochloric acid,

$$H_2O(l) + HCl(aq) \rightleftharpoons H_3O^+(aq) + Cl^-(aq)$$

Now imagine a situation in which water acts *simultaneously* as an acid and a base. One molecule donates a proton (and so acts as an acid) to a second molecule that accepts the proton (and so acts as a base):

$$2H_2O(l) \rightleftharpoons H_3O^+(aq) + OH^-(aq)$$

This process is called **self-ionization** because two identical neutral molecules create ions. The equilibrium constant is:

$$K_c = \frac{[H_3O^+]_{eq}[OH^-]_{eq}}{[H_2O]_{eq}^2}$$

The concentration of water is essentially constant because it is so large compared with the concentrations of the other species present. It can therefore be omitted from the equilibrium expression. The resulting equilibrium constant is called the **ionic product of water**, K_w:

$$K_w = [H_3O^+][OH^-]$$

This equilibrium is reached so quickly that the 'eq' subscript may be omitted. The value of K_w varies with temperature, as does the value of any equilibrium constant. It has an experimentally measured value at 25 °C of $1.0 \times 10^{-14}\,mol^2\,dm^{-6}$. You have seen that we do not need to know about K_w to calculate the pH of a strong acid. However, K_w is central to calculating the pH of basic solutions.

The pH of neutral water

In *neutral* water, the concentrations of hydrogen ions and hydroxide ions must be equal, i.e.

$[H_3O^+] = [OH^-]$

In neutral water at 25 °C the aqueous hydrogen ion concentration is $1 \times 10^{-7}\,mol\,dm^{-3}$ (because the square of 1×10^{-7} is 1×10^{-14}, the value of K_w). The pH of neutral water at 25 °C is therefore:

$$pH = -\log_{10}(1 \times 10^{-7}) = -(-7.0) = 7.0$$

Strong and weak bases

Sodium hydroxide is described as a strong base because it is essentially fully ionized in aqueous solution:

$$NaOH(aq) \rightarrow Na^+(aq) + OH^-(aq)$$

Dissolving 1 mol of solid sodium hydroxide in water results in 1 mol of aqueous hydroxide ions. For example, aqueous sodium hydroxide of concentration $1\,mol\,dm^{-3}$ has an aqueous hydroxide ion concentration $[OH^-] = 1\,mol\,dm^{-3}$.

Ammonia is described as a weak base because the equilibrium

$$NH_3(aq) + H_2O(l) \rightleftharpoons NH_4^+(aq) + OH^-(aq)$$

lies to the left. Dissolving 1 mol of ammonia gas in water does not result in 1 mol of aqueous hydroxide ions. For example, aqueous ammonia of concentration $1\,mol\,dm^{-3}$ has an aqueous hydroxide ion concentration $[OH^-] = 4 \times 10^{-3}\,mol\,dm^{-3}$.

- A **strong base** is *fully ionized* in aqueous solution. The aqueous hydroxide ion concentration is *equal* in magnitude to the concentration of the base.
- A **weak base** is *only partially ionized* in aqueous solution. The aqueous hydroxide ion concentration is *smaller* in magnitude than the concentration of the base.

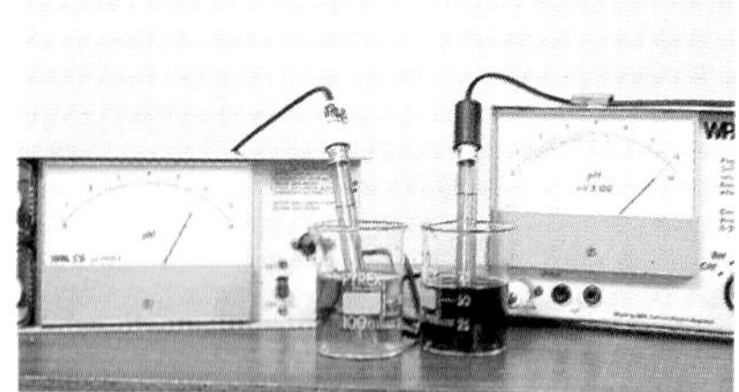

The pH meters show that 0.1 mol dm⁻³ aqueous ammonia, a weak base, has a pH of 11.1, whereas the same concentration of aqueous sodium hydroxide, a strong base, has a pH of 13.0. The indicator is alizarin yellow, see spread 12.9.

Neutralization enthalpies

The standard enthalpy change of neutralization for $NH_3(aq)$ and HCl(aq) is only $-52\,kJ\,mol^{-1}$, compared with $-57\,kJ\,mol^{-1}$ for NaOH (aq)/HCl(aq) and KOH(aq)/HCl(aq)

The value for $NH_3(aq)$ and the weak acid HCN(aq) is $-5\,kJ\,mol^{-1}$.

Calculating the pH of a strong base

The pH of a strong base depends only on its concentration because a strong base is fully ionized.

The calculation of pH for strong bases is of similar difficulty to that for strong acids. For example, aqueous sodium hydroxide at a concentration of 1 mol dm^{-3} has an aqueous hydroxide ion concentration of 1 mol dm^{-3}, i.e. $[OH^-] = 1$ mol dm^{-3}.

The aqueous hydrogen ion concentration multiplied by the aqueous hydroxide ion concentration must equal the ionic product of water:

$$K_w = [H_3O^+][OH^-] = 1 \times 10^{-14}\,\text{mol}^2\,\text{dm}^{-6}$$

Divide both sides of the equation by the aqueous hydroxide ion concentration:

$$[H_3O^+] = \frac{K_w}{[OH^-]}$$

$$= \frac{(1 \times 10^{-14}\,\text{mol}^2\,\text{dm}^{-6})}{(1\,\text{mol dm}^{-3})}$$

$$= 1 \times 10^{-14}\,\text{mol dm}^{-3}$$

Substituting this value into the expression for pH:

$$\text{pH} = -\log_{10}[H_3O^+] = -(-14.0) = 14.0$$

This calculation shows that aqueous NaOH at a concentration of 1 mol dm^{-3} has a pH of 14. This is the typical upper limit for pH.

Worked example on calculating aqueous hydroxide ion concentration from pH

Question: The measured pH of an aqueous base is 12.0. Calculate the corresponding hydroxide ion concentration.

Answer: First we use

$\text{pH} = -\log_{10}[H_3O^+]$

i.e.

$12.0 = -\log_{10}[H_3O^+]$

Multiply both sides by –1:

$\log_{10}[H_3O^+] = -12.0$

Taking the antilogarithm of both sides of the expression, remembering to add the units, gives:

$[H_3O^+] = 1 \times 10^{-12}$ mol dm^{-3}

Now we use

$K_w = [H_3O^+][OH^-] = 1 \times 10^{-14}$ mol^2 dm^{-6}

i.e.

1×10^{-14} mol^2 dm^{-6} $= 1 \times 10^{-12}$ mol dm^{-3} $\times [OH^-]$

Rearranging gives:

$$[OH^-] = \frac{1 \times 10^{-14}\,\text{mol}^2\,\text{dm}^{-6}}{1 \times 10^{-12}\,\text{mol dm}^{-3}}$$

$$= 1 \times 10^{-2}\,\text{mol dm}^{-3}$$

SUMMARY

- A strong base is fully ionized in aqueous solution; a weak base is only partially ionized.
- Water self-ionizes to a very small extent:
  $2H_2O(l) \rightleftharpoons H_3O^+(aq) + OH^-(aq)$
- The ionic product of water $K_w = [H_3O^+][OH^-]$.
- The value of K_w at 25 °C is 1.0×10^{-14} mol^2 dm^{-6}.

pOH and pK_w

Another way of doing pH calculations for bases involves introducing the quantity pOH, which is defined by analogy with pH as

pOH $= -\log_{10}[OH^-]$

From the equation shown alongside
$K_w = [H_3O^+][OH^-]$
taking the negative logarithm of both sides gives
$pK_w = \text{pH} + \text{pOH}$
where $\mathbf{p}K_w = -\log_{10}K_w$
$= -\log_{10}(1 \times 10^{-14})$
$= 14.0$ (at 25 °C)

For a strong base at a concentration of 1 mol dm^{-3}, pOH = 0.0
pH = 14.0 – pOH
= 14.0

pH and concentration

For a strong base, each dilution of the concentration by a factor of 10 decreases the pH by one unit. For example, 0.1 mol dm^{-3} aqueous sodium hydroxide has a pH of 13.0. This result is a consequence of using the logarithm to base 10 in the definition of pH.

PRACTICE

1 Calculate the pH of solutions with the following aqueous hydroxide ion concentrations in mol dm^{-3}:
  a 0.1
  b 0.01
  c 0.05.

2 Calculate the aqueous hydroxide ion concentration corresponding to the following pH values:
  a 13.0
  b 11.5.

12.7

WEAK BASES

OBJECTIVES

- Base ionization constant K_b
- Definition of pK_b
- pH calculations for weak bases

As you might expect, we can do calculations on weak bases in a similar way to those on weak acids. Weak bases are only partially ionized in solution and the extent of the ionization is reflected in their respective values of K_b, the base ionization constant. Calculating the pH values of aqueous *strong* bases involves the ionic product of water K_w, which relates the concentrations of aqueous hydrogen ions and aqueous hydroxide ions. This relationship is also important in pH calculations involving weak bases.

The base ionization constant K_b

Sodium hydroxide is a solid which dissolves readily in water. It is a strong base because it is fully ionized in solution:

$$NaOH(s) \rightarrow Na^+(aq) + OH^-(aq)$$

Ammonia is a gas which dissolves readily in water:

$$NH_3(g) \rightarrow NH_3(aq)$$

It is a weak base because the equilibrium

$$NH_3(aq) + H_2O(l) \rightleftharpoons NH_4^+(aq) + OH^-(aq)$$

lies to the left.

In general, any base B acts as a base when it accepts a proton, the equilibrium in aqueous solution being:

$$B(aq) + H_2O(l) \rightleftharpoons BH^+(aq) + OH^-(aq)$$

The equilibrium constant K_c is given by the expression:

$$K_c = \frac{[BH^+]_{eq}[OH^-]_{eq}}{[B]_{eq}[H_2O]_{eq}}$$

Water is present in large excess and its concentration is essentially constant. The **base ionization constant** is therefore expressed as:

$$K_b = \frac{[BH^+][OH^-]}{[B]}$$

Note that the equilibrium establishes itself very quickly and so the 'eq' subscript is not needed.

A comparison of K_a and K_b

For a weak acid HA:

$$\underset{\text{ACID}}{HA(aq)} + \underset{\text{BASE}}{H_2O(l)} \rightleftharpoons \underset{\text{CONJUGATE ACID}}{H_3O^+(aq)} + \underset{\text{CONJUGATE BASE}}{A^-(aq)}$$

$$K_a = \frac{[H_3O^+][A^-]}{[HA]}$$

For a weak base B:

$$\underset{\text{BASE}}{B(aq)} + \underset{\text{ACID}}{H_2O(l)} \rightleftharpoons \underset{\text{CONJUGATE ACID}}{BH^+(aq)} + \underset{\text{CONJUGATE BASE}}{OH^-(aq)}$$

$$K_b = \frac{[BH^+][OH^-]}{[B]}$$

pK_b

The pK_b value of a weak base is defined in a similar way to pH, i.e.

$$pK_b = -\log_{10} K_b$$

The lower the value of pK_b, the larger the value of K_b and the greater the ionization of the base in water. For example, at the same concentrations, aqueous ammonia $NH_3(aq)$ (pK_b 4.8) is ionized to a lesser extent than aqueous methylamine $CH_3NH_2(aq)$ (pK_b 3.4).

To calculate K_b from pK_b

From the main text we have

$pK_b = -\log_{10} K_b$

Multiply both sides of the equation by −1:

$\log_{10} K_b = -pK_b$

Take the antilogarithm of both sides of the expression, remembering to add the units of $mol\,dm^{-3}$:

$K_b = 10^{-pK_b}\,mol\,dm^{-3}$

For example, the pK_b for ammonia is 4.8. Substitute this value into the expression above and check you obtain the answer $K_b = 2 \times 10^{-5}\,mol\,dm^{-3}$.

Base ionization constants of some weak bases in water at 25 °C.

Compound	Ionization equilibrium	Ionization constant K_b /mol dm^{-3}	pK_b
Ammonia	$NH_3 + H_2O \rightleftharpoons NH_4^+ + OH^-$	1.6×10^{-5}	4.8
Methylamine	$CH_3NH_2 + H_2O \rightleftharpoons CH_3NH_3^+ + OH^-$	4.0×10^{-4}	3.4
Phenylamine	$C_6H_5NH_2 + H_2O \rightleftharpoons C_6H_5NH_3^+ + OH^-$	4.0×10^{-10}	9.4
Phenylmethylamine	$C_6H_5CH_2NH_2 + H_2O \rightleftharpoons C_6H_5CH_2NH_3^+ + OH^-$	2.5×10^{-5}	4.6

Calculating the pH of a weak base

The method of calculation follows a similar path to the one that uses K_a to find the pH of a weak acid.

As an example, we shall calculate the pH value of 0.1 mol dm^{-3} aqueous ammonia ($K_b = 1.6 \times 10^{-5}$ mol dm^{-3}).

The chemical equation for the equilibrium is:

$$NH_3(aq) + H_2O(l) \rightleftharpoons NH_4^+(aq) + OH^-(aq)$$

The expression for the base ionization constant is:

$$K_b = \frac{[NH_4^+][OH^-]}{[NH_3]}$$

Aqueous ammonia is only slightly ionized, so its concentration is effectively equal to the original concentration of the solution, i.e. $[NH_3] =$ 0.1 mol dm^{-3}. Substituting this value and the one for the base ionization constant $K_b = 1.6 \times 10^{-5}$ mol dm^{-3} gives:

$$1.6 \times 10^{-5}\,\text{mol dm}^{-3} = \frac{[NH_4^+][OH^-]}{0.1\,\text{mol dm}^{-3}}$$

The chemical equation indicates that the concentrations of ammonium ion and hydroxide ion are equal, i.e. $[NH_4^+] = [OH^-]$. So

$$1.6 \times 10^{-5}\,\text{mol dm}^{-3} = \frac{[OH^-]^2}{0.1\,\text{mol dm}^{-3}}$$

$$\begin{aligned}[OH^-]^2 &= (0.1\,\text{mol dm}^{-3}) \times (1.6 \times 10^{-5}\,\text{mol dm}^{-3}) \\ &= 1.6 \times 10^{-6}\,\text{mol}^2\,\text{dm}^{-6} \\ [OH^-] &= \surd(1.6 \times 10^{-6}\,\text{mol}^2\,\text{dm}^{-6}) \\ &= 1.3 \times 10^{-3}\,\text{mol dm}^{-3}\end{aligned}$$

The ionic product of water requires that:

$$[H_3O^+][OH^-] = 1 \times 10^{-14}\,\text{mol}^2\,\text{dm}^{-6}$$

Substituting the value for $[OH^-]$ from above:

$$[H_3O^+] \times (1.3 \times 10^{-3}\,\text{mol dm}^{-3}) = 1 \times 10^{-14}\,\text{mol}^2\,\text{dm}^{-6}$$

$$[H_3O^+] = 7.7 \times 10^{-12}\,\text{mol dm}^{-3}$$

Substituting this value into the expression for pH:

$$\begin{aligned}\text{pH} &= -\log_{10}[H_3O^+] \\ &= -\log_{10}(7.7 \times 10^{-12}) \\ &= 11.1\ (1\ \text{d.p.})\end{aligned}$$

Note: It is purely *coincidental* that pK_b for NH_3 and pK_a for CH_3COOH are both 4.8.

K_a values for weak bases

Aqueous ammonia is a weak base because it accepts protons from water:

$$NH_3(aq) + H_2O(l) \rightleftharpoons NH_4^+(aq) + OH^-(aq)$$

The base ionization constant K_b is given by the expression

$$K_b = \frac{[NH_4^+][OH^-]}{[NH_3]}$$

and has the value 1.6×10^{-5} mol dm^{-3}.

The conjugate acid of ammonia is the ammonium ion $NH_4^+(aq)$. It is a weak acid as shown by the equilibrium:

$$NH_4^+(aq) + H_2O(l) \rightleftharpoons H_3O^+(aq) + NH_3(aq)$$

The corresponding acid ionization constant K_a for the ammonium ion is

$$K_a = \frac{[H_3O^+][NH_3]}{[NH_4^+]}$$

and has the value 6.3×10^{-10} mol dm^{-3}.

Hence $pK_a(NH_4^+)$
= 9.2

In this manner, the K_a values of weak acids and the *conjugate acids* of weak bases may be given as a continuous list. Note that

$K_a \times K_b = [H_3O^+]\,[OH^-]$
$= 1 \times 10^{-14}$ mol^2 dm^{-6}
(K_w, the ionic product of water)

SUMMARY

- Weak bases are only partially ionized.
- K_b is the base ionization constant for a weak base:

$$K_b = \frac{[BH^+][OH^-]}{[B]}$$

- $pK_b = -\log_{10} K_b$

PRACTICE

1 Calculate the pH of a solution of ammonia, 0.2 mol dm^{-3}, $K_b = 1.6 \times 10^{-5}$ mol dm^{-3}.

2 Calculate the pH value of a solution of methylamine $CH_3NH_2(aq)$, 0.1 mol dm^{-3}, $pK_b = 3.4$.

3 Explain how the expression
$pK_a + pK_b = 14.0$
may be applied to any aqueous acid–base system.

12.8

OBJECTIVES

- Practical technique
- End point and equivalence point
- Titration curve for strong acid–strong base
- Calculation from results

Titration technique – a reminder

The usual method followed in a titration is to place a known volume of aqueous base in a conical titration flask. A few drops of indicator are then added to show the pH change during the titration. Acid is then run into the flask from a burette until the indicator changes colour. The colour change usually happens on addition of just one final drop of acid. The **end point** occurs when the indicator changes colour.

The **equivalence point** of a titration occurs when there are equal amounts of $H_3O^+(aq)$ and $OH^-(aq)$ ions in the titration flask. At this point, the neutralization is complete:

$H_3O^+(aq) + OH^-(aq) \rightarrow 2H_2O(l)$

ACID–BASE TITRATIONS – 1

Acids and bases neutralize each other when mixed together in aqueous solution. An acid–base titration is a technique used to measure the volumes of acid and base required for neutralization. If the concentration of one solution is known, then the concentration of the other may be calculated. There are four possible combinations of strong and weak acids and bases that may be considered for a titration. This spread investigates the simplest example of the four, focusing on the neutralization reaction between a strong acid and a strong base.

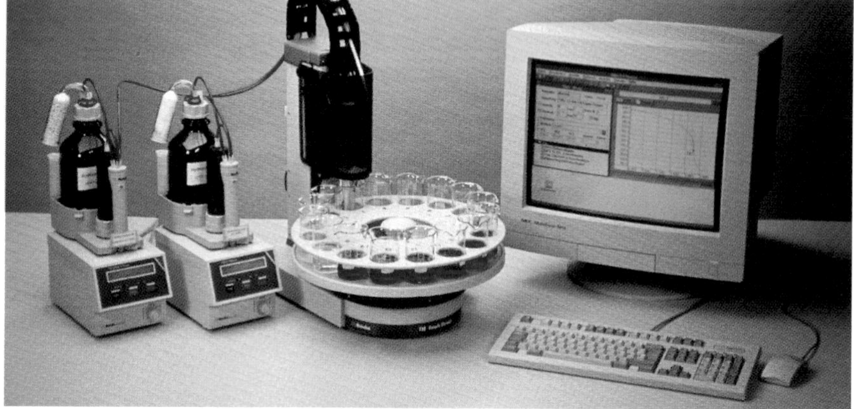

A commercially available automatic titrator.

Titration of a strong acid with a strong base

A **titration curve** shows the pH changes that occur when an aqueous acid reacts with an aqueous base. It is a graph of pH against volume (usually volume of added acid). The titration of a strong acid with a strong base causes a large pH change on neutralization, as shown in the graph below. Both the acid and the base are fully ionized. Very small volumes of acid or base cause large changes in pH when the reaction mixture is very close to the point of neutralization.

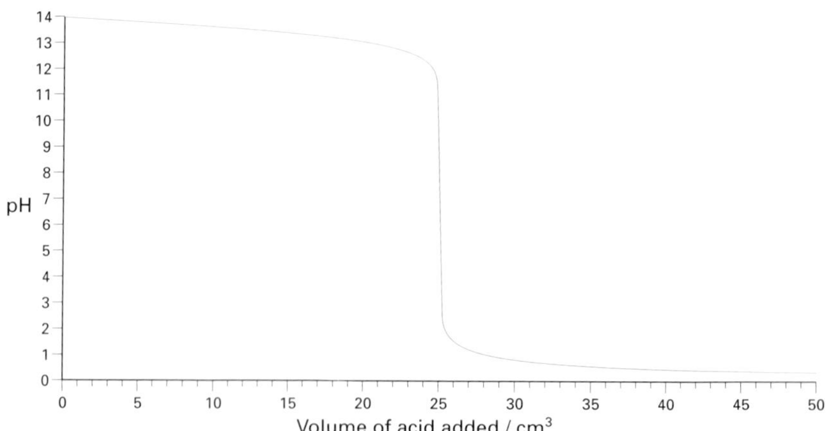

The equivalence point for a strong acid–strong base titration is at pH 7. The pH changes from 11 to 3 very rapidly so phenolphthalein (range pH 8–10), litmus (range pH 6–8), and methyl orange (range pH 3–5) would all be suitable indicators.

For example, imagine a titration of $25\,cm^3$ of $1\,mol\,dm^{-3}$ aqueous sodium hydroxide with hydrochloric acid of the same concentration. The total volume of solution at neutralization will be exactly twice the initial volume, because the equation shows that 1 mol of NaOH reacts with 1 mol of HCl:

$$NaOH(aq) + HCl(aq) \rightarrow NaCl(aq) + H_2O(l)$$

The equivalence point of this titration occurs when the amounts of acid and base are exactly equal. Now imagine overshooting the equivalence point by *just one drop*. A drop has a volume of approximately $0.05\,cm^3$.

The excess acid is equivalent to 0.05 cm^3 in 50 cm^3, a 1000-fold dilution. This dilutes the acid from a concentration of 1 mol dm^{-3} (in the burette) to 1×10^{-3} mol dm^{-3} (in the flask) and produces a pH of 3. Just one drop (0.05 cm^3) *before* neutralization, the sodium hydroxide concentration was 1×10^{-3} mol dm^{-3} and the solution had a pH of 11.

In such a titration, adding just two drops of acid at the equivalence point causes a very large change in pH from about 11 to about 3. This change is characteristic of a strong acid–strong base titration and is easy to detect by using any indicator with a range between pH 3 and pH 11. At the start, the base is in large excess; there is only a small change in pH because any acid added is neutralized by the base. If excess acid is added after reaching the equivalence point, the pH remains very low.

The indicator must be chosen with care to ensure that the end point coincides with the equivalence point. The actual pH changes that happen during an acid–base titration depend on the strengths of the acid and base concerned (described in the following spread). During a strong acid–strong base titration, the pH swings from 11 to 3 on the addition of two drops of acid. All common indicators change colour within this range, and so the end point (when the colour of the indicator changes) coincides with the equivalence point.

Reading a burette

The volume on a burette should be read to the nearest 0.05 cm^3.

Worked example on calculating concentration

Question: In a titration, 25.0 cm^3 of aqueous sodium hydroxide of concentration 1.00 mol dm^{-3} were exactly neutralized by 9.20 cm^3 of hydrochloric acid. Calculate the concentration of the acid.

Strategy: The calculation is carried out in four steps.

Answer: *Step 1* Write the balanced chemical equation for the reaction:
$HCl(aq) + NaOH(aq) \rightarrow NaCl(aq) + H_2O(l)$

Step 2 Calculate the amount in moles of sodium hydroxide:

$$n(\text{NaOH}) = \left(\frac{25.0}{1000}\,\text{dm}^3\right) \times (1.00\,\text{mol dm}^{-3}) = 0.0250\,\text{mol}$$

Step 3 Use the mole ratios indicated by the equation to calculate the amount in moles of HCl:

1 mol of HCl reacts with 1 mol of NaOH

Therefore the amount in moles of HCl is 0.0250 mol

Step 4 Calculate the concentration of the acid:

9.20 cm^3 (0.00920 dm^3) of the acid contains 0.0250 mol

$$\text{concentration} = \frac{\text{amount in moles}}{\text{volume}} = \frac{0.0250\,\text{mol}}{0.00920\,\text{dm}^3} = 2.72\,\text{mol dm}^{-3}$$

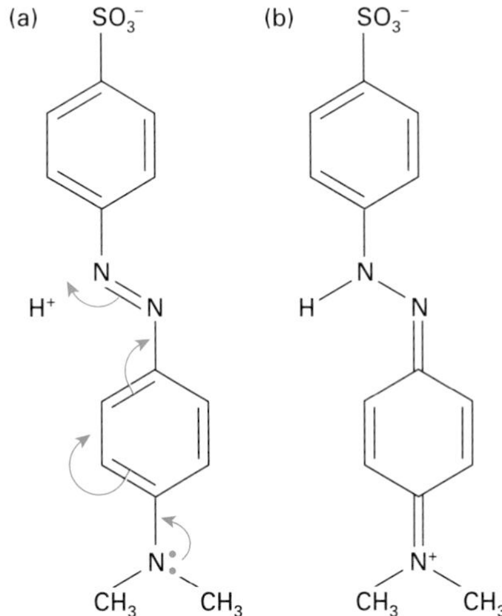

(a) Methyl orange in its base form. This structure predominates at pH 4.5 or greater and the solution colour is orange. (b) At pH 3 and below, the base form is protonated to give the conjugate acid, which is red.

Weak acids and bases

The titration curve for strong acid–strong base neutralization shows a large change in pH around the equivalence point. Choosing a suitable indicator is therefore a simple task. The following spread introduces neutralization reactions involving weak acids and bases. You will see that choosing an indicator is not so straightforward!

SUMMARY

- The end point of a titration occurs when the indicator changes colour.
- The equivalence point occurs when there are equal amounts of H_3O^+ and OH^- ions in the titration flask.
- Indicators with ranges between pH 3 and pH 11 are suitable for strong acid–strong base titrations.

12.9

ACID–BASE TITRATIONS – 2

OBJECTIVES

- Strong acid–weak base titrations
- Weak acid–strong base titrations
- Choice of indicator
- Weak acid–weak base conductometric titrations

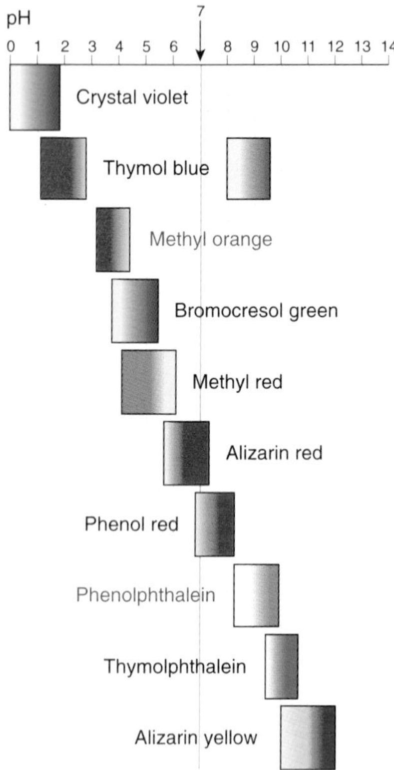

Common indicators and their ranges. The centre of the range is the value of pK_{in} *where* K_{in} *is the* indicator ionization constant.

The titration curve for a strong acid–strong base neutralization shows a large change in pH around the equivalence point. Any indicator with a range between pH 11 and pH 3 may be used. The titration curves for other combinations of strong/weak acid/base pairs offer a more limited change in pH. As a result, it is more difficult, if not impossible, to choose a suitable indicator.

Titration of a strong acid with a weak base

At the start of a strong acid–weak base titration, the weak base is in excess. Its pH is much lower (closer to 7) than that of a strong base because it is only partially ionized. When the weak base is just in excess (i.e. one drop before the equivalence point is reached), the pH will be only slightly greater than neutral (pH 7). (The exact pH value will depend on the K_b value of the weak base.) On adding excess strong acid (one drop after the equivalence point), a large change in pH value from 7 to about 3 occurs. A suitable indicator, such as methyl orange, will have a range between these two pH values: see spread 9.6.

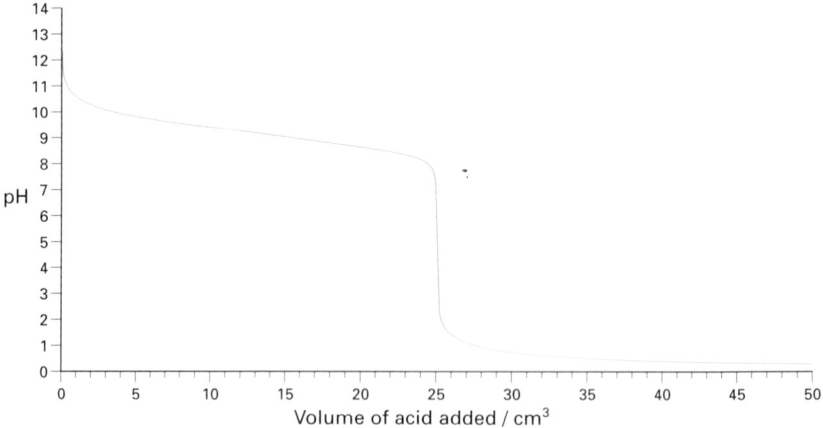

The titration curve of a strong acid (e.g. hydrochloric acid HCl) with a weak base (here ammonia NH_3*).*

Titration of a weak acid with a strong base

In this case, the strong base is in excess at the start of the titration and the weak acid is in excess at the end. You will see from the titration curve below that the large change in pH around the equivalence point occurs approximately between pH 11 and pH 7. A suitable indicator, such as phenolphthalein, will have a range between these two pH values.

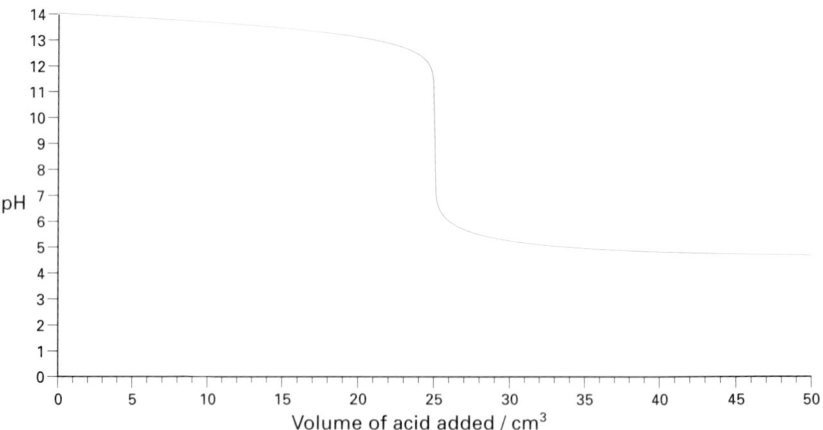

The titration curve of a weak acid (here ethanoic acid CH_3COOH*) with a strong base (e.g. sodium hydroxide NaOH).*

Choosing an indicator

The large changes of pH around the equivalence point can be summarized as follows:

- Strong acid–strong base: pH 11–3.
- Strong acid–weak base: pH 7–3.
- Weak acid–strong base: pH 11–7.

These regions of large pH change correspond to the near-vertical portions of the corresponding titration curves. In each case, a suitable indicator is one whose range falls within these pH limits. Note that the centre of the vertical region of a titration curve is called the **point of inflection**; it occurs at the point where the gradient of the curve changes direction.

It is possible to have two points of inflection in a titration, as shown in the figure on the right for the titration of sodium carbonate with hydrochloric acid. Two indicators are used in such a case, which is then called a **double indicator titration**. Two points of inflection also occur when a diprotic acid such as ethanedioic acid $(COOH)_2$ is titrated against sodium hydroxide.

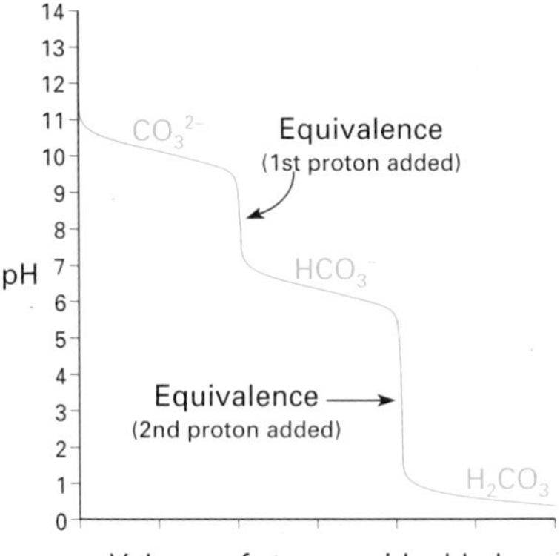

Two points of inflection. The titration curve for the weak base sodium carbonate Na_2CO_3 and the strong acid hydrochloric acid shows two points of inflection, i.e. two separate equivalence points. These two regions relate to the successive transfer of one and then two protons. The first corresponds to the conversion of carbonate to hydrogencarbonate:

$$CO_3^{2-}(aq) + H_3O^+(aq) \rightleftharpoons HCO_3^-(aq) + H_2O(l)$$

Phenolphthalein is a suitable indicator. The second equivalence point corresponds to the conversion of hydrogencarbonate to carbon dioxide:

$$HCO_3^-(aq) + H_3O^+(aq) \rightleftharpoons H_2CO_3(aq) + H_2O(l) \rightleftharpoons CO_2(aq) + 2H_2O(l)$$

Methyl orange is a suitable indicator.

Titration of a weak acid with a weak base

It is not possible to use an indicator to find the equivalence point of a titration involving a weak acid and a weak base. The variation of pH is too gradual for any indicator to show a distinct end point. Instead, a conductometric titration must be used.

At the start of the titration, the conductivity is not very great because the weak base in the titration flask is only partially ionized. Adding acid forms the salt, which is fully ionized. The conductivity rises steadily as more acid is added. Adding excess acid beyond the equivalence point barely changes the conductivity because the weak acid is also only partially ionized. The change in slope corresponding to the equivalence point is easy to detect.

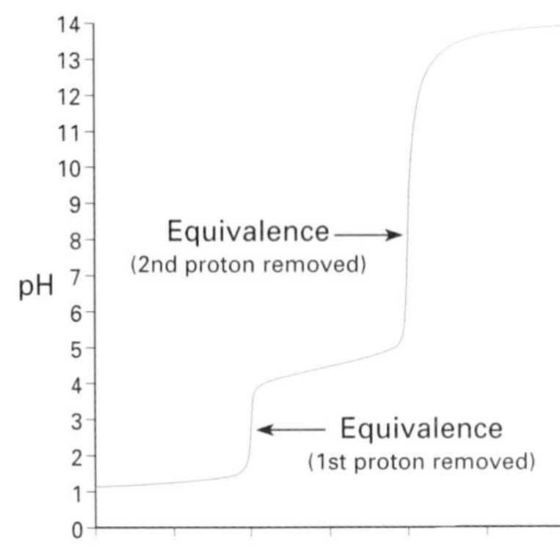

Ethanedioic acid / NaOH titration curve

SUMMARY

- The indicator range for a strong acid–weak base titration must fall between pH 7 and pH 3. Methyl orange is a useful choice.
- The indicator range for a weak acid–strong base titration must fall between pH 11 and pH 7. Phenolphthalein is a useful choice.
- Indicators cannot be used to find the equivalence point of a weak acid–weak base titration. A conductometric titration may be used.

PRACTICE

1 Explain the terms *end point* and *equivalence point* with reference to the titration of ethanoic acid $CH_3COOH(aq)$ (a weak acid) against sodium hydroxide $NaOH(aq)$ (a strong base).

2 For which class(es) of titration (strong acid–strong base, etc.) would each of the following indicators be suitable?
   a Alizarin yellow
   b Thymolphthalein
   c Bromocresol green.

3 In a titration, $36.2\,cm^3$ of $0.200\,mol\,dm^{-3}$ sulphuric acid $H_2SO_4(aq)$ neutralized $25.0\,cm^3$ of aqueous sodium hydroxide $NaOH(aq)$. Calculate the concentration of the aqueous sodium hydroxide.

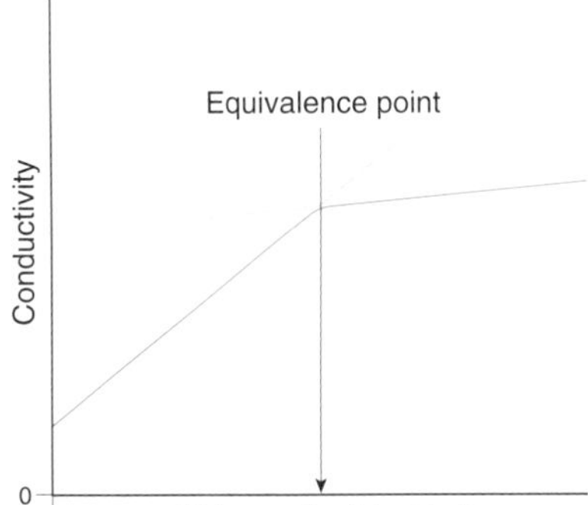

*The equivalence point in a weak acid–weak base neutralization may be determined by a **conductometric titration**, in which the electrical conductivity of the solution is measured.*

12.10

OBJECTIVES

- Acidic buffer solutions
- Basic buffer solutions

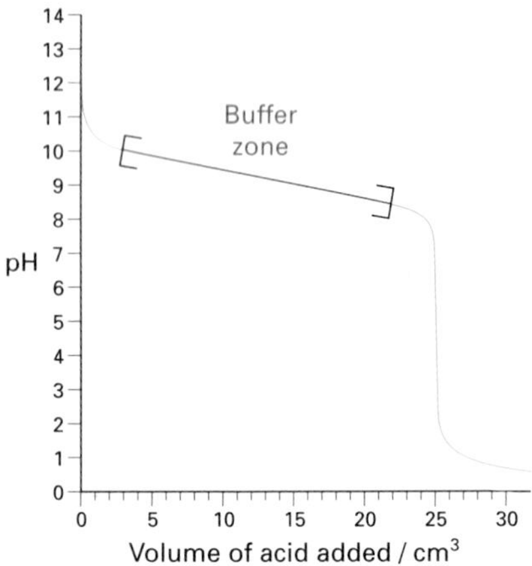

The titration curve resulting from the addition of the strong acid HCl(aq) to the weak base NH_3(aq). The buffer zone is highlighted in red.

Buffer solutions

Adding acid or base to a solution usually changes the value of its pH greatly. However, some mixtures, called **buffer solutions**, resist changes in pH despite small additions of acid or base. Buffer solutions may be made up to maintain specified acidic or basic pH values. This spread starts by identifying a region in a titration curve where buffer action is taking place, and then explains how to make buffer solutions.

Buffer action

Consider a titration in which the strong acid hydrochloric acid HCl(aq) is added to the weak base ammonia NH_3(aq). Initially the pH falls significantly; after this the titration curve shows only a moderate fall in pH, even though a strong acid is being added to the mixture. This portion of the titration curve, where buffer action is occurring, is called the **buffer zone**. The buffer present at this stage of the titration is a mixture of the weak base NH_3 and its salt NH_4^+, formed from the reaction between the acid and the base:

$$H_3O^+(aq) + NH_3(aq) \rightleftharpoons NH_4^+(aq) + H_2O(l)$$

This is an acid–base reaction, and the equilibrium lies far to the right.

Note that, in practice, buffer solutions are usually made by mixing suitable reactants in solution rather than by carrying out acid–base titrations.

Acidic and basic buffer solutions

Acidic buffer solutions maintain a nearly constant pH value less than 7. They consist of a solution of a weak acid and a salt that supplies the conjugate base of the weak acid. For example, an aqueous solution containing equal amounts in moles of ethanoic acid CH_3COOH and sodium ethanoate $Na^+CH_3COO^-$ constitutes an acidic buffer.

Basic buffer solutions maintain a nearly constant pH value greater than 7. They consist of a solution of a weak base and a salt that supplies the conjugate acid of the weak base. For example, an aqueous solution containing equal amounts in moles of ammonia NH_3 and ammonium chloride $NH_4^+Cl^-$ constitutes a basic buffer.

Acidic buffer action

First consider a solution of the weak acid CH_3COOH. The acid is partially ionized according to the equilibrium:

$$CH_3COOH(aq) + H_2O(l) \rightleftharpoons H_3O^+(aq) + CH_3COO^-(aq)$$

Le Chatelier's principle indicates that adding aqueous hydrogen ions H_3O^+ from a strong acid shifts the equilibrium (even further) to the left. Aqueous hydrogen ions are consumed, the concentration of CH_3COO^- ions decreases, and the concentration of CH_3COOH increases.

Conversely, adding aqueous hydroxide ions OH^- from a strong base will *remove* H_3O^+ ions and the equilibrium will shift to the right. The concentration of CH_3COO^- ions will increase and the concentration of CH_3COOH will decrease.

In the buffer, the salt $Na^+CH_3COO^-$ is also present. This salt is fully ionized in solution and supplies a large concentration of CH_3COO^- ions. So the buffer solution contains a large concentration of CH_3COO^- ions (from the salt) and a large concentration of CH_3COOH (the un-ionized acid).

The effect of adding acid to the buffer solution

When an acid is added, there is a large concentration of CH_3COO^- ions to react with the added H_3O^+ ions. The equilibrium

$$\underset{\text{FROM BUFFER}}{CH_3COO^-(aq)} + \underset{\text{ADDED}}{H_3O^+(aq)} \rightleftharpoons CH_3COOH(aq) + H_2O(l)$$

lies far to the right, and the pH remains almost unchanged.

The effect of adding base to the buffer solution

When OH^- ions from a base are added, they react with the high concentration of un-ionized CH_3COOH present. The equilibrium

$$\underset{\text{FROM BUFFER}}{CH_3COOH(aq)} + \underset{\text{ADDED}}{OH^-(aq)} \rightleftharpoons CH_3COO^-(aq) + H_2O(l)$$

lies far to the right, and the pH remains almost unchanged.

A natural (physiological) buffer system

Buffer solutions maintain optimum pH values for the biochemical processes taking place in living systems. The enzymes (biological catalysts) that enable biochemical reactions to take place can function only within a narrow range of pH. An important buffer system in human beings is the carbonate buffer consisting of carbonic acid H_2CO_3 and its conjugate base, the hydrogencarbonate ion HCO_3^-:

$$H_2CO_3(aq) + H_2O(l) \rightleftharpoons H_3O^+(aq) + HCO_3^-(aq)$$

Adding acid shifts the equilibrium to the left. Aqueous hydrogen ions are consumed (thus maintaining the pH value), reducing the concentration of HCO_3^- while increasing the concentration of H_2CO_3. Adding base shifts the equilibrium to the right. Aqueous hydrogen ions protonate the base and the concentration of HCO_3^- increases while the concentration of H_2CO_3 reduces.

Hyperventilation is needed to compensate for the low partial pressure of oxygen at high altitude. Climbers reaching the summit of K2 without additional oxygen have had their blood pH rise from 7.4 to 7.7.

SUMMARY

- Buffer solutions resist changes in pH despite small additions of acid or base.
- An acidic buffer consists of a weak acid and a salt that supplies its conjugate base.
- A basic buffer consists of a weak base and a salt that supplies its conjugate acid.
- Buffer solutions maintain optimum pH values for the biochemical processes taking place in living systems.

Basic buffer action

An example of a basic buffer pair is the salt ammonium chloride NH_4Cl dissolved in aqueous ammonia $NH_3(aq)$.

When aqueous hydrogen ions from an acid are added to this mixture, they react with the weak base NH_3. The equilibrium shifts to the right, taking up the added hydrogen ions:

$$NH_3(aq) + H_3O^+(aq) \rightleftharpoons NH_4^+(aq) + H_2O(l)$$

so the pH of the solution remains almost unchanged.

Adding base to this buffer solution introduces hydroxide $OH^-(aq)$ ions. The conjugate acid $NH_4^+(aq)$ donates protons to these hydroxide ions, shifting the following equilibrium to the right and resisting the change in pH:

$$NH_4^+(aq) + OH^-(aq) \rightleftharpoons NH_3(aq) + H_2O(l)$$

Buffers in industry

Many industrial processes take place successfully only within limited ranges of pH. Dyeing yarn and electroplating metals are two processes that are carried out in buffered solutions. Buffer solutions are also used to control the pH of shampoos.

PRACTICE

1 From the substances H_2CO_3, CH_3COOK, NH_3, CO_2, CH_3COOH and NH_4Cl, select:
  a an acidic buffer pair
  b a basic buffer pair.

2 Explain how a solution of a salt M^+A^- in a weak acid HA resists attempts to change its pH when aqueous hydrogen ions are added to it.

12.11

Buffer solutions: calculations

OBJECTIVES

- The Henderson–Hasselbalch equation
- Preparing buffer solutions

(a)

(b)

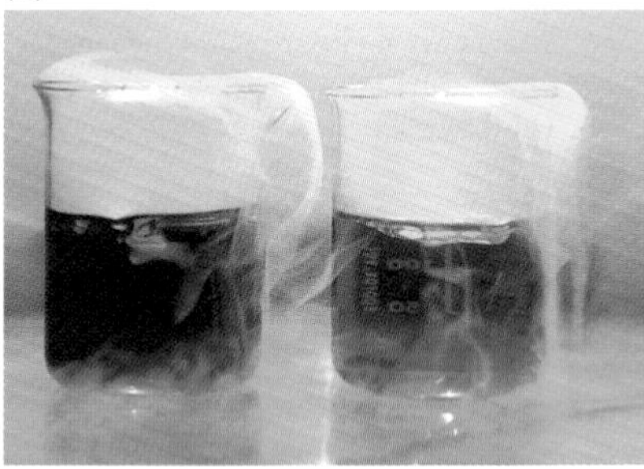

(a) Both beakers contain solutions at pH 7 initially (indicated by the green colour), but the one on the left is a buffer solution.

(b) Dry ice (solid carbon dioxide) added to both beakers has changed the pH significantly only for the pure water, which has become acidic (indicated by the yellow colour).

Buffer solutions resist attempts to change their pH by the addition of acid or base. They have applications in general chemistry and in physiological systems. This spread shows you how to calculate the pH of a buffer solution and how to predict the pH of the reaction mixture during the course of a titration. It also describes how to prepare buffer solutions of known pH. The key to these calculations lies in the Henderson–Hasselbalch equation, which describes the pH of a buffer solution in terms of the concentrations of the acid–base pairs present.

Deriving the Henderson–Hasselbalch equation

In general, the equilibrium established in a solution of a weak acid is:

$$HA(aq) + H_2O(l) \rightleftharpoons H_3O^+(aq) + A^-(aq)$$

The acid ionization constant for this reaction is:

$$K_a = \frac{[H_3O^+][A^-]}{[HA]}$$

Making $[H_3O^+]$ the subject of this equation:

$$[H_3O^+] = \frac{K_a[HA]}{[A^-]}$$

Taking the negative logarithm of both sides, remembering that $pH = -\log_{10}[H_3O^+]$:

$$\begin{aligned} pH &= -\log_{10}\left(\frac{K_a[HA]}{[A^-]}\right) \\ &= -\left\{\log_{10}K_a + \log_{10}\left(\frac{[HA]}{[A^-]}\right)\right\} \\ &= -\log_{10}K_a - \log_{10}\left(\frac{[HA]}{[A^-]}\right) \end{aligned}$$

But $pK_a = -\log_{10}K_a$, so:

$$pH = pK_a - \log_{10}\left(\frac{[HA]}{[A^-]}\right)$$

This equation may be rewritten as:

$$pH = pK_a + \log_{10}\left(\frac{[A^-]}{[HA]}\right)$$

or

$$pH = pK_a + \log_{10}\left(\frac{[\text{conjugate base}]}{[\text{acid}]}\right)$$

This equation is known as the **Henderson–Hasselbalch equation**.

Preparing buffer solutions

It is often necessary to prepare buffer solutions of known pH, for example when calibrating a pH meter. There are two main steps involved in selecting suitable substances and deciding their concentrations. Look carefully at the Henderson–Hasselbalch equation as applied to acidic buffers. There are two terms on the right-hand side, which determine the final pH of the solution. The first term is pK_a, whose value is responsible for the 'coarse selection' of pH. The second term involves the ratio [conjugate base]/[acid] and provides 'fine tuning' to the final pH.

So the strategy for preparing an acidic buffer solution of known pH is to select an acid whose pK_a is within about one pH unit of the desired pH. The ratio of salt and acid concentrations is then adjusted to achieve the desired pH. This 'fine tuning' allows the pH to be varied by about ±1 unit either side of the pK_a value.

Basic buffer solutions

The Henderson–Hasselbalch equation applies equally to basic buffer solutions. For example, the buffer solution containing aqueous ammonia NH_3 and ammonium chloride NH_4Cl establishes the equilibrium:

$$NH_4^+(aq) + H_2O(l) \rightleftharpoons H_3O^+(aq) + NH_3(aq)$$

The base is NH_3 and the conjugate acid is NH_4^+. In this example, the Henderson–Hasselbalch equation becomes:

$$pH = pK_a(NH_4^+) + \log_{10}\left(\frac{[NH_3]}{[NH_4^+]}\right)$$

or

$$pH = pK_a + \log_{10}\left(\frac{[\text{base}]}{[\text{conjugate acid}]}\right)$$

Worked example on calculating the pH of a buffer solution

Question: Consider an acidic buffer solution containing 0.1 mol dm^{-3} CH_3COONa and 0.1 mol dm^{-3} CH_3COOH, with pK_a 4.8. What is its pH?

Strategy: If the constituents of a buffer solution and their concentrations are known, then the pH can be calculated from the Henderson–Hasselbalch equation.

Answer: Ethanoic acid CH_3COOH is a weak acid and so is only partially ionized. Its concentration may be taken as 0.1 mol dm^{-3}. The conjugate base is the CH_3COO^- ion supplied by the salt CH_3COONa. This salt ionizes fully in solution, so the concentration of CH_3COO^- will equal the concentration of salt added, 0.1 mol dm^{-3}.

Substituting these values into the Henderson–Hasselbalch equation:

$$\text{pH} = \text{p}K_a + \log_{10}\left(\frac{[\text{conjugate base}]}{[\text{acid}]}\right)$$

$$= 4.8 + \log_{10}\left(\frac{0.1\ \text{mol dm}^{-3}}{0.1\ \text{mol dm}^{-3}}\right) \quad = 4.8 + \log_{10} 1.0 \quad = 4.8$$

For example, suppose you wish to prepare an acidic buffer with a pH of 4.0. A suitable weak acid would be ethanoic acid CH_3COOH because its pK_a is 4.8. The conjugate base is the ethanoate ion CH_3COO^-, which can be provided by the salt sodium ethanoate CH_3COONa. Ethanoic acid is available as a laboratory bench reagent with a concentration of 1.0 mol dm^{-3}.

The question now becomes: 'What mass of sodium ethanoate must I add to the ethanoic acid?' The Henderson–Hasselbalch equation is:

$$\text{pH} = \text{p}K_a + \log_{10}\left(\frac{[\text{conjugate base}]}{[\text{acid}]}\right)$$

Substituting the known quantities:

$$4.0 = 4.8 + \log_{10}\left(\frac{[\text{conjugate base}]}{1.0}\right)$$

$$4.0 = 4.8 + \log_{10}[\text{conjugate base}]$$

Rearranging:

$$\log_{10}[\text{conjugate base}] = -0.8$$

Taking the antilog of both sides, adding the units:

$$[\text{conjugate base}] = 0.16\ \text{mol dm}^{-3}$$

i.e. the concentration of the conjugate base is 0.16 mol dm^{-3}.

The molar mass of sodium ethanoate is 82.0 g mol^{-1}. So 0.16 mol of sodium ethanoate has a mass given by

$$\begin{aligned}\text{mass} &= \text{amount in moles} \times \text{molar mass}\\ &= (0.16\ \text{mol}) \times (82.0\ \text{g mol}^{-1})\\ &= 13\ \text{g}\end{aligned}$$

Therefore, an acidic buffer solution of pH 4.0 will result when 13 g of sodium ethanoate is added to 1.0 dm^3 of 1.0 mol dm^{-3} ethanoic acid.

SUMMARY

- The pH of an acid–base buffer pair is found from the general equation:

$$\text{pH} = \text{p}K_a + \log_{10}\left(\frac{[\text{base}]}{[\text{acid}]}\right)$$

- When half the acid in a solution is neutralized by a base, the concentrations of acid and conjugate base are equal and pH = pK_a.

Acidic buffer pH and pK_a

A weak acid HA is partially ionized with an acid ionization constant K_a. The equilibrium lies well to the left:

$$HA(aq) + H_2O(l) \rightleftharpoons H_3O^+(aq) + A^-(aq)$$

$$K_a = \frac{[H_3O^+][A^-]}{[HA]}$$

A salt M^+A^- of the weak acid HA ionizes fully in solution:

$$M^+A^-(aq) \rightarrow M^+(aq) + A^-(aq)$$

If equal amounts in moles of the salt and the weak acid are added together in solution, then their concentrations are equal, i.e.

$$[HA] = [A^-]$$

The expression for K_a becomes:

$$K_a = [H_3O^+]$$

The pH at this point may be calculated as follows. By taking the negative logarithm of both sides of the above equation we get:

$$-\log_{10}K_a = -\log_{10}[H_3O^+]$$

But, by definition,

$$-\log_{10}K_a = \text{p}K_a$$

$$-\log_{10}[H_3O^+] = \text{pH}$$

and so we can see that

$$\text{pH} = \text{p}K_a$$

The pH of a solution consisting of equal amounts in moles of weak acid and one of its salts is equal to the pK_a value of the weak acid concerned.

This statement applies also to the central point of the buffer zone of a titration curve. In the titration curve in spread 12.10, the centre of the buffer zone (at 12.5 cm^3 acid) is at pH = 9.2, the pK_a of ammonium ion, spread 12.7. Similarly, in spread 12.9, the two pK_a values for ethanedioic acid are 1.2 and 4.3.

pH may be measured accurately by using a pH meter, which incorporates a glass electrode similar to the one shown here. Buffer solutions of known pH are used to calibrate pH meters before use.

12.12

OBJECTIVES

- Lewis acids and bases
- Lewis and Brønsted–Lowry theories contrasted
- Coordinate bonds and complexes

LEWIS ACIDS AND BASES

The Brønsted–Lowry theory of acids and bases defines acids as proton donors and bases as proton acceptors. In the same year (1923), Gilbert Lewis, see spread 5.2, defined acids and bases in terms of the donation and acceptance of electron pairs. This definition broadens further the range of reactions described as 'acid–base' reactions. This spread applies the Brønsted–Lowry and Lewis theories to the reaction between hydrochloric acid and sodium hydroxide.

Brønsted–Lowry and Lewis theories

- A **Brønsted acid** is a proton donor.
- A **Brønsted base** is a proton acceptor.
- A **Lewis acid** is an electron-pair acceptor.
- A **Lewis base** is an electron-pair donor.

Hydrochloric acid and sodium hydroxide: a neutralization reaction

In aqueous solution, hydrochloric acid provides the aqueous hydrogen ion $H_3O^+(aq)$ and sodium hydroxide provides the aqueous hydroxide ion $OH^-(aq)$. These two ions react together, the $H_3O^+(aq)$ ion acting as an acid and the $OH^-(aq)$ ion as a base:

$$H_3O^+(aq) + OH^-(aq) \rightarrow 2H_2O(l)$$

As a Brønsted acid, H_3O^+ donates a proton, which is accepted by OH^- acting as a Brønsted base: see diagram (a) on the left.

Lewis theory provides an alternative, equally valid, view of the same reaction. As a *Lewis* base, OH^- donates a pair of electrons, which is accepted by a proton from H_3O^+ acting as a Lewis acid: see diagram (b) on the left.

In both cases, a pair of electrons forms a new bond between the proton and the hydroxide ion. Both of the theories describe the oxonium ion H_3O^+ as an acid and the hydroxide ion OH^- as a base.

The Lewis definition incorporates all Brønsted acids and bases. It is useful because it can also be used to describe reactions in which hydrogen ions are not involved, whilst applying the same terminology to more traditional acids. A good example is the reaction between ammonia and hydrogen chloride. In aqueous solution, these two substances neutralize each other on mixing:

$$NH_3(aq) + HCl(aq) \rightleftharpoons NH_4Cl(aq) + H_2O(l)$$

Ammonia and hydrogen chloride also react as covalent compounds in the gas phase to give white fumes of the ionic compound ammonium chloride:

$$NH_3(g) + HCl(g) \rightarrow NH_4Cl(s) \qquad [\text{i.e. } NH_4^+Cl^-(s)]$$

(a)

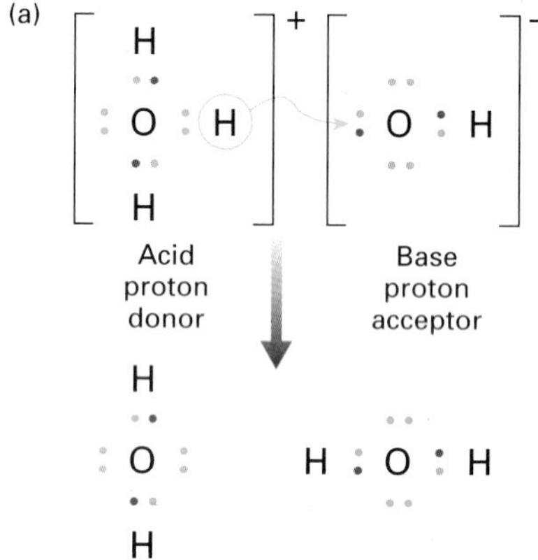

(b)

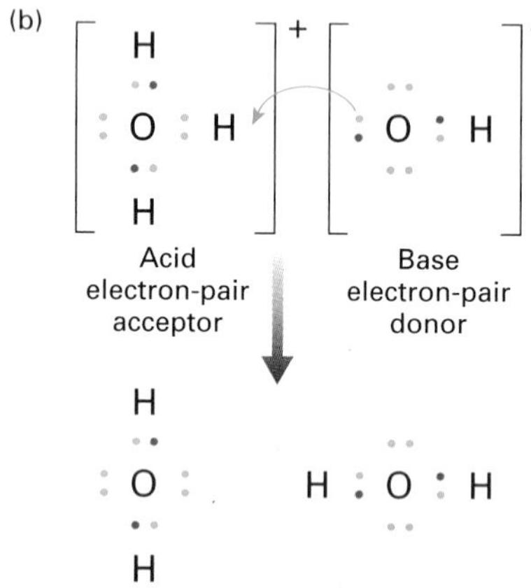

Lewis structures comparing (a) the Brønsted–Lowry and (b) the Lewis theories applied to the H_3O^+/OH^- acid–base neutralization reaction.

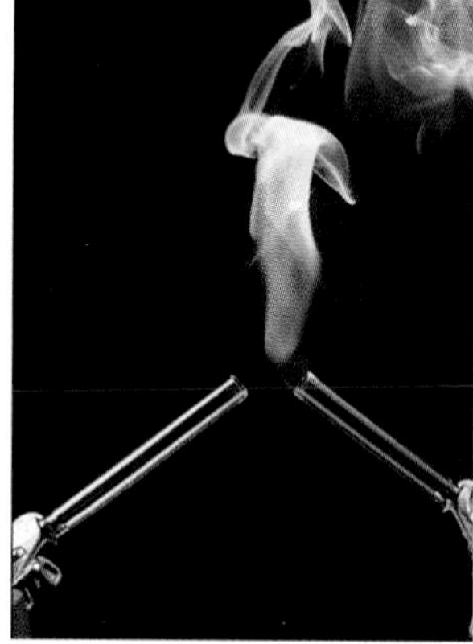

(a) Ammonia gas reacts with hydrogen chloride gas to produce clouds of solid ammonium chloride. The reaction is classified as an acid–base reaction by both Brønsted–Lowry theory and Lewis theory. (b) Ammonia reacts with boron trifluoride in a similar manner to hydrogen chloride. The reaction is classified as an acid–base reaction by Lewis theory only.

Brønsted–Lowry theory describes both of these reactions (aqueous and gas phase) as acid–base because they involve proton transfer. Ammonia may also be called a Lewis base because it donates a pair of electrons; hydrogen chloride is a Lewis acid because it accepts a pair of electrons.

The reaction between ammonia and the gas boron trifluoride also forms a solid product, as shown opposite:

$$NH_3(g) + BF_3(g) \rightarrow NH_3BF_3(s)$$

The product of the reaction is called an **adduct** because it is formed by the simple addition of one substance to another. Brønsted–Lowry theory does *not* recognize this reaction as an acid–base reaction because proton transfer does not take place. But from the standpoint of Lewis theory, the ammonia acts as a Lewis base because it donates an electron pair to form a bond. Boron trifluoride is a Lewis acid because it accepts a pair of electrons.

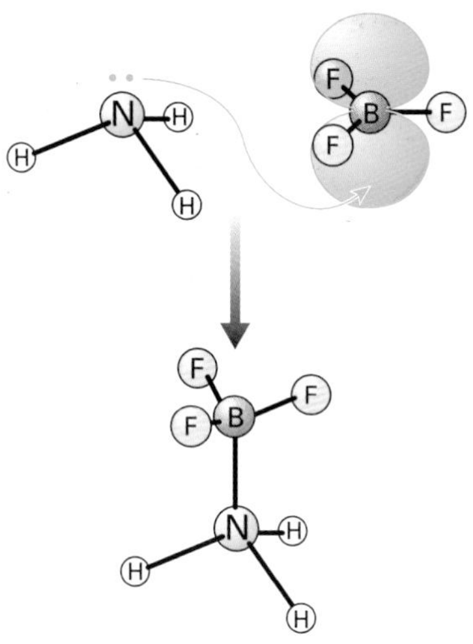

Boron trifluoride has an empty orbital in its valence shell. Ammonia donates a pair of electrons into this orbital to form a coordinate bond.

The formation of complex ions

Copper(II) sulphate dissolves in water to give a clear blue solution. A chemical equation representing this process is:

$$CuSO_4(s) + \text{water} \rightarrow Cu^{2+}(aq) + SO_4^{2-}(aq)$$

$Cu^{2+}(aq)$ is described as 'the aqueous copper(II) ion'. It behaves like all positively charged ions in aqueous solution, attracting the partial negative charge of the oxygen atoms of water molecules. However, the copper ion is small and bears a 2+ charge, with the result that it has a high charge density. The force of attraction is sufficient for oxygen atoms to donate a pair of electrons into vacant orbitals on the copper ion. In this way, the copper ion acts as a Lewis acid (an electron-pair acceptor) and the water molecules act as Lewis bases (electron-pair donors). Each copper ion forms a coordinate bond with each of six water molecules. The aqueous copper(II) ion $Cu^{2+}(aq)$ is therefore more accurately represented by the formula $[Cu(H_2O)_6]^{2+}$.

This structure is called a **complex ion** and is typical of the adducts formed between small, highly charged transition metal ions and substances that have lone pairs of electrons available to form coordinate bonds. Complex ions are Lewis acid–base adducts and are discussed in depth in chapter 20 on the transition metals.

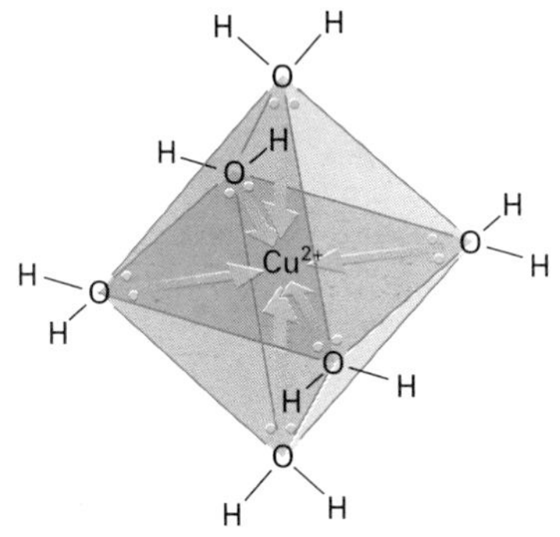

Blue aqueous copper(II) sulphate contains aqueous copper(II) ions $Cu^{2+}(aq)$. These ions are complex ions; their formula is better represented as $[Cu(H_2O)_6]^{2+}$ and their shape is octahedral.

SUMMARY

- A Lewis acid is an electron-pair acceptor.
- A Lewis base is an electron-pair donor.
- All Brønsted acids are Lewis acids; not all Lewis acids are Brønsted acids. (The same remarks apply to bases.)
- Many reactions cannot be described as acid–base reactions by Brønsted–Lowry theory, but may be described as acid–base reactions by Lewis theory. Such reactions include some that do not take place in aqueous solution.
- Complex ions result when Lewis bases form coordinate bonds with metal ions.

PRACTICE

1 Which of these reactions:

$NH_3(aq) + H_3O^+(aq) \rightarrow NH_4^+(aq) + H_2O(l)$

$2NH_3(aq) + Ag^+(aq) \rightleftharpoons [Ag(NH_3)_2]^+(aq)$

may be described as an acid–base reaction according to

a Brønsted–Lowry theory,

b Lewis theory?

Where appropriate, identify the substances acting as acids or bases, giving your reasoning in each case.

2 Liquid ammonia (T_b = –31°C) is slightly ionized in a similar manner to water:

$2NH_3$	$\rightleftharpoons$	NH_4^+	+	NH_2^-
AMMONIA		AMMONIUM ION		AMIDE ION

Identify the acid, the base, and the salt in the following reaction carried out in liquid ammonia ('am' means in solution in ammonia):

$NH_4Cl(am) + KNH_2(am) \rightarrow KCl(am) + 2NH_3(l)$

Explain your reasoning.

PRACTICE EXAM QUESTIONS

1 Propanoic acid occurs naturally in Swiss cheese in a concentration that can be as high as 1%. Its sodium and calcium salts are food additives used in processed cheeses to retard the formation of moulds.

a Propanoic acid is a weak acid with an acid dissociation constant of 1.22×10^{-5} mol dm^{-3}.

i Write an equation for the ionisation of propanoic acid. [2]

ii Calculate pK_a, for propanoic acid. [2]

b Sodium propanoate is made by the reaction of sodium hydroxide with propanoic acid.

i Write an equation for the reaction. [1]

ii If the reaction were carried out by titration using 0.1 M solutions of the hydroxide and the acid, state the name of a suitable indicator. [1]

c A mixture of sodium propanoate and propanoic acid acts as a buffer solution.

i What is meant by the term **buffer solution**? [2]

ii Explain how the mixture of sodium propanoate and propanoic acid acts as a buffer solution.

(Up to 2 marks may be obtained for the quality of language in this part.) [5]

iii Calculate the pH of the solution formed by adding 15.0 cm^3 of 0.1 M sodium hydroxide to 30.0 cm^3 of 0.1 M propanoic acid. [3]

iv Name a buffer solution found in a biological system and explain its importance. [2]
NICCEA 1998

2 **a** Explain the terms *acid* and *conjugate base* as used in the Brønsted–Lowry theory of acids and bases. [2]

b For each of the following reactions, give the name or formula of the acid and of its conjugate base.

i $NH_3 + HCl \rightarrow NH_4^+ + Cl^-$ [1]

ii $H_2SO_4 + HNO_3 \rightarrow HSO_4^- + H_2NO_3^+$ [1]

iii $NaNH_2 + NH_4Cl \rightarrow NaCl + 2NH_3$ [1]

c When ethanoic acid, CH_3COOH, dissolves in water, a solution of a weak acid is formed.

i Explain the difference between a *strong acid* and a *weak acid.* [2]

ii Write an equation to show the reaction of ethanoic acid with water. [1]

iii There are two conjugate acid–base pairs involved in the reaction in **c ii**. Copy the formulae, and use the symbols **A1** and **B1** to label one of the acid-base pairs, and the symbols **A2** and **B2** to label the other pair, by writing each symbol above the species to which it refers. [2]

d When dissolved in liquid ammonia, rather than in water, ethanoic acid becomes a strong Brønsted–Lowry acid.

i Write an equation to show the reaction between ethanoic acid and the ammonia solvent. [1]

ii Account for this increase in acid strength. [2]
AQA (AEB) 1996

3 The curves shown in **A**, **B**, and **C** below represent the variation of pH in three different acid–base titrations. In each case, 25.0 cm^3 of a solution **X** (0.1 M) is titrated with a solution **Y** (also 0.1 M).

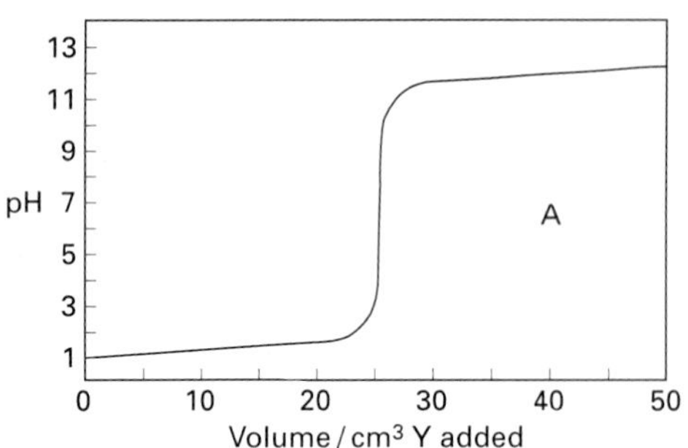

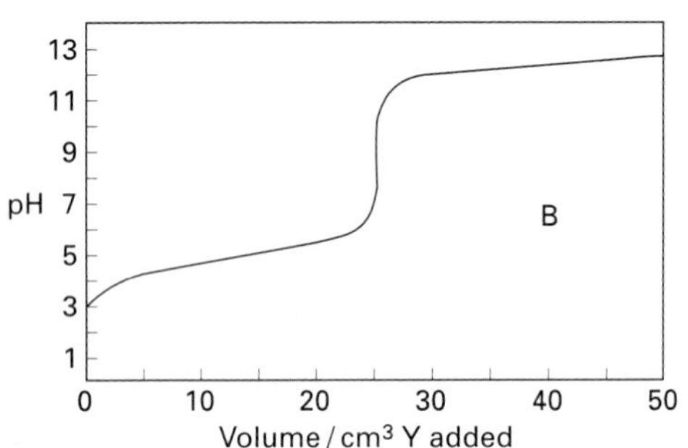

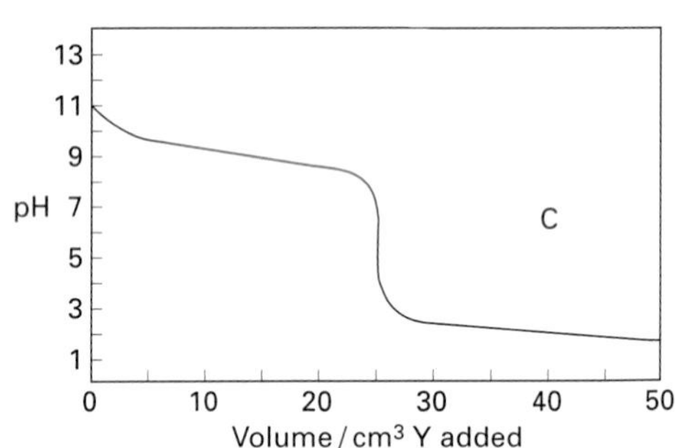

a State two possible components **X** and **Y** that would produce a titration curve similar to the one in **A** above. [2]

b Copy and complete the table below, by identifying the nature (i.e. strong acid/strong base/weak acid/weak base) of component **X** and component **Y** in curves **B** and **C** above. In **each** case give a reason to support your choice of the nature of both **X** and **Y**. [8]

Curve B	
Component X	**Component Y**
Nature of **X**	Nature of **Y**
Reason	Reason

Curve C	
Component X	**Component Y**
Nature of **X**	Nature of **Y**
Reason	Reason

c The pH of a 0.1 M solution of HA is 2.30. Calculate the value of K_a for this acid. [3]
AQA (NEAB) 1995

4 a i Aqueous ammonia is said to be a ***weak*** base. Explain what is meant by the term ***weak***. [1]

ii The expression for K_b for aqueous ammonia, $NH_3(aq)$, may be written as

$$K_b = \frac{[OH^-(aq)][NH_4^+(aq)]}{[NH_3(aq)]}$$

Write an expression for K_a for the aqueous ammonium ion, $NH_4^+(aq)$, given the equation

$NH_4^+(aq) \rightleftharpoons NH_3(aq) + H^+(aq)$. [1]

iii Hence write down an expression for the product $K_b \times K_a$. [1]

b i Write down an expression for the ionic product of water, K_w, and give its units. [2]

ii I. At 313 K, the numerical value of K_w is 2.91×10^{-14}. Calculate the pH of pure water at this temperature. [2]

II. The numerical value of K_w at 298 K is 1.01×10^{-14}.

Using Le Chatelier's principle, and the value of K_w at 313 K given in **b ii I.**, deduce the sign of $\Delta H^\ominus$ for the ionic dissociation of water. [2]

c In the reaction

$H_2O + H_2O \rightleftharpoons H_3O^+ + OH^-$

explain the role of the water molecules in terms of the Brønsted–Lowry theory of acids and bases. [2]
WJEC 1997

5 a Explain how an aqueous solution containing ethanoic acid and sodium ethanoate resists changes in pH when contaminated with small amounts of acid or alkali. [2]

b It can be shown that for solutions described in **a**

$$pH = pK_a + \log\frac{[\text{sodium ethanoate}]}{[\text{ethanoic acid}]}$$

where $pK_a = -\log K_a$.

i State the significance of the value of the pH when [sodium ethanoate] = [ethanoic acid]. [1]

ii Calculate the mass of sodium ethanoate which must be dissolved in 1 dm^3 of ethanoic acid of concentration 0.10 mol dm^{-3} to produce a solution with a pH value of 5.5 at 298 K. It can be assumed that there is no volume change on dissolving the salt.

[At 298 K the value of K_a for ethanoic acid is 1.8×10^{-5} mol dm^{-3}.] [3]

c i Name an indicator which would be suitable for the titration of aqueous ethanoic acid with aqueous sodium hydroxide, giving a reason for your choice. [1]

ii State whether the pH of an aqueous solution of pure ammonium chloride would be greater or less than 7 at 298 K, giving a reason for your answer. [1]

d The pH of human blood plasma is maintained at a value between 7.39 and 7.41 by the buffering action of dissolved carbon dioxide, hydrogencarbonate ions, and carbonic acid, H_2CO_3. Write equations to show what reactions may occur when the blood absorbs small amounts of acid or small amounts of alkali.

i Acid [1]

ii Alkali [1]
WJEC 1997

6 a The acid dissociation constant, K_a, of propanoic acid at room temperature is 1.35×10^{-5} mol dm^{-3}. Calculate the pH of each of the following aqueous solutions at room temperature:

i Propanoic acid of concentration 0.05 mol dm^{-3}. [2]

ii A solution containing 0.05 mol dm^{-3} propanoic acid and 0.05 mol dm^{-3} sodium propanoate. [2]

b The experimentally determined graphs below show the changes in pH when aqueous sodium hydroxide of concentration 0.1 mol dm^{-3} is added **separately** to 25 cm^3 of aqueous hydrochloric acid and 25 cm^3 of aqueous propanoic acid both of concentration 0.1 mol dm^{-3}. The ranges of two indicators are also shown.

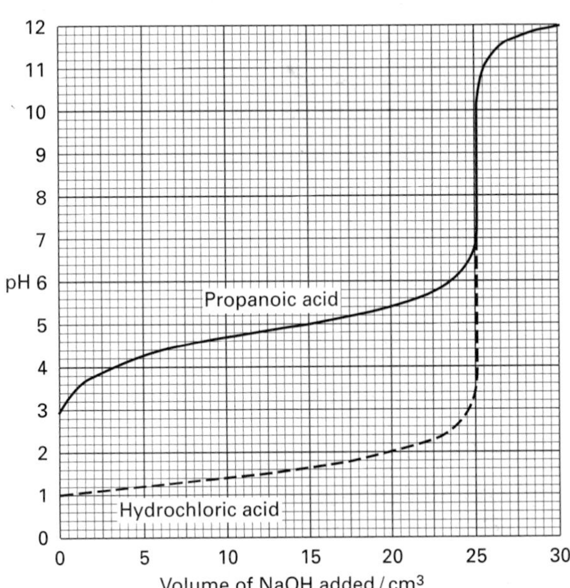

The pH ranges of two common indicators are

methyl orange	3.2 to 4.4
phenolphtalein	8.2 to 10

i State, giving a reason, which indicator or indicators would be suitable for the titration of each acid with aqueous sodium hydroxide. [2]

ii What is the value of the pH when the propanoic acid is half-neutralized? [1]

iii What is the significance of this value? [1]
WJEC 1997

13 Redox equilibrium

Redox reactions are reactions that involve the transfer of electrons between chemical species. Electron transfer from one place to another is a flow of electrons, and a flow of electrons is an electric current. The study of redox reactions is therefore the combined study of chemistry and electricity. In fact, an alternative title for this chapter could well be 'Electrochemistry'. We are all aware of a practical application of electrochemistry: the use of redox reactions inside batteries to generate an electric potential difference (voltage). A theoretical application uses knowledge about redox equilibria to predict whether chosen substances will take part in a redox reaction.

REDOX: OXIDATION AND REDUCTION

OBJECTIVES

- Oxygen and redox reactions
- Electron transfer and redox reactions
- Oxidants and reductants
- Half-equations

Magnesium Mg(s) burns in oxygen O_2(g) to form magnesium oxide MgO(s). Oxygen oxidizes magnesium; magnesium reduces oxygen. Magnesium loses electrons; oxygen gains electrons.

The term 'redox' is a contraction of the words *reduction* and *oxidation*. Oxidation and reduction take place together. One substance is reduced while the other is oxidized. In this introductory spread we look at an example of such a reaction and find the underlying process to be electron transfer.

The oxidation of magnesium

An example of a redox reaction is magnesium burning in oxygen to produce magnesium oxide:

$$2Mg(s) + O_2(g) \rightarrow 2MgO(s)$$

Magnesium is a metal, oxygen is a diatomic covalent gas, and magnesium oxide is an ionic compound containing Mg^{2+} and O^{2-} ions. A simple definition of redox reactions considers oxidation as the gain of oxygen atoms and reduction as the loss of oxygen atoms. Applying this definition to the burning of magnesium:

- magnesium is oxidized by oxygen;
- oxygen is reduced by magnesium.

The balanced chemical equation written above does not show electron transfer. Splitting the equation into two *half-equations* (below) reveals more clearly what is happening in the course of the reaction. One half-equation shows the loss of electrons and the other shows the gain of electrons.

- Magnesium loses electrons:

$$2Mg(s) \rightarrow 2Mg^{2+}(s) + 4e^-$$

- Oxygen gains electrons:

$$O_2(g) + 4e^- \rightarrow 2O^{2-}(s)$$

We can consider this reaction in terms of the underlying electron transfer:

- **Oxidation** is the loss of electrons (magnesium is oxidized).
- **Reduction** is the gain of electrons (oxygen is reduced).
- Oxidation is caused by the **oxidant** (or **oxidizing agent**): the oxidant (oxygen O_2) is itself reduced in the process (to O^{2-}).
- Reduction is caused by the **reductant** (or **reducing agent**): the reductant (magnesium Mg) is itself oxidized in the process (to Mg^{2+}).

The half-reaction described by the half-equation does *not necessarily* actually occur; the electrons may not become free in the way suggested. Half-equations are simply a useful way of thinking about the two component parts of a redox reaction. A half-equation must balance with respect to *charge* as well as with respect to the number of atoms. Notice how the sum of the charges on the left in the above equations equals the sum of the charges on the right.

Redox in the absence of oxygen

The example given above shows that the oxidation of magnesium may be interpreted in two ways: either as a gain of oxygen or as a loss of electrons. The idea of redox as electron transfer allows many reactions not involving oxygen to be classified as redox reactions. For example, the reaction between aqueous copper(II) sulphate and zinc metal is a redox reaction:

$$Zn(s) + CuSO_4(aq) \rightarrow ZnSO_4(aq) + Cu(s)$$

Remember that the formulae $CuSO_4(aq)$ and $ZnSO_4(aq)$ refer to ionic substances dissolved in water. $CuSO_4(aq)$ is therefore present as $Cu^{2+}(aq)$ and $SO_4^{2-}(aq)$ ions; $ZnSO_4(aq)$ is present as $Zn^{2+}(aq)$ and $SO_4^{2-}(aq)$ ions. The sulphate ion $SO_4^{2-}(aq)$ is a *spectator ion*; it does not take part in the chemical reaction and so we may disregard it.

The full balanced chemical equation is not very informative. However, the two half-equations reveal the redox nature of the reaction.

- The half-equation for zinc shows that the metal atoms are oxidized as the result of electron loss:

  $$Zn(s) \rightarrow Zn^{2+}(aq) + 2e^-$$

- The half-equation for copper shows that the aqueous copper(II) ions are reduced as the result of electron gain:

  $$Cu^{2+}(aq) + 2e^- \rightarrow Cu(s)$$

The balanced equation for the reduction of copper(II) ions by zinc results from adding together the two half-equations. In this example the combination is straightforward because both half-equations involve two electrons (note that we have not included the sulphate spectator ions):

$$Zn(s) + Cu^{2+}(aq) \rightarrow Zn^{2+}(aq) + Cu(s)$$

When a zinc strip is immersed in blue aqueous copper(II) sulphate, the result is copper metal and colourless aqueous zinc sulphate.

The outside of the Statue of Liberty is made from thin sheets of copper. Oxygen has oxidized the surface to copper(II) oxide. Further reaction with water and carbon dioxide has formed a blue-green coating of basic copper(II) carbonate of approximate formula $CuCO_3{\cdot}Cu(OH)_2$.

OIL RIG

A 'mnemonic' for remembering the rule about redox and electron transfer is OIL RIG:

Oxidation	**R**eduction
Is	**I**s
Loss (of electrons)	**G**ain (of electrons)

Oxidants and reductants

The terms 'oxidant' and 'oxidizing agent' have the same meaning. Similarly 'reductant' and 'reducing agent' mean the same. In this text we will use the more modern terms 'oxidant' and 'reductant'.

- An **oxidant** is a substance that oxidizes another species by removing electrons from it.
- A **reductant** is a substance that reduces another species by donating electrons to it.

SUMMARY

- An oxidation reaction is always accompanied by a corresponding reduction reaction.
- Oxidation is loss of electrons.
- Reduction is gain of electrons.
- A redox reaction may be expressed by two half-equations, one representing oxidation and the other reduction.

PRACTICE

1 For each of the following redox reactions:
  a $2Ca(s) + O_2(g) \rightarrow 2CaO(s)$
  b $CuO(s) + H_2(g) \rightarrow Cu(s) + H_2O(g)$
  c $2AgNO_3(aq) + Cu(s) \rightarrow 2Ag(s) + Cu(NO_3)_2(aq)$
  identify (i) the oxidant, (ii) the reductant, (iii) which species is oxidized, and (iv) which species is reduced.

2 For each of the reactions in question 1, write half-equations to show (i) electron loss during oxidation and (ii) electron gain during reduction.

13.2 OXIDATION NUMBERS – 1

OBJECTIVES

- Oxidation number and oxidation state
- Rules for assigning oxidation number
- Identifying redox reactions

Chlorine oxidizes iron (and iron reduces chlorine) when they combine to form iron(III) chloride $FeCl_3$:
$2Fe(s) + 3Cl_2(g) \rightarrow 2FeCl_3(s)$
$2Fe \rightarrow 2Fe^{3+} + 6e^-$
$3Cl_2 + 6e^- \rightarrow 6Cl^-$
The compound $FeCl_3$ has a high degree of covalent character; however, we can still treat it as ionic for the purposes of determining oxidation numbers.

Fluorine and oxygen

Oxygen usually has an oxidation number of −2. However, in the compound OF_2 (oxygen difluoride), oxygen has an oxidation number of +2. Fluorine is the only element that is more electronegative than oxygen. So fluorine, rather than oxygen, gains the electrons. Oxygen loses electrons, i.e. is oxidized. Its oxidation number changes from 0 (in O_2) to +2 (in OF_2).

Redox reactions are concerned with electron transfer. Loss and gain of electrons during these reactions reflect changes in the way the elements concerned bond with each other. Up to now you have probably described the bonding ability of elements in terms of their valencies. The valency of an element is determined by the number of electrons it controls. A more precise term for valency is *oxidation number*. Elements gain and lose electrons during redox reactions, with the result that their oxidation numbers change. Oxidation numbers indicate where the electrons are, and so help us with chemical book-keeping. Oxidation numbers are assigned to elements on the basis of how readily they react in redox reactions.

Electron transfer and oxidation number

Each element in any chemical species may be assigned an oxidation number. The **oxidation number** of an element is the number of electrons that need to be added to the element to make a neutral atom. For example, the iron ion Fe^{2+} requires the addition of two electrons to make a neutral atom. The oxidation number for iron in the Fe^{2+} ion is therefore +2. The **oxidation state** of this ion is written as iron(II) or as Fe(II); it is expressed in Roman numerals and describes the extent of oxidation of the species. The Fe^{3+} ion has an oxidation number of +3. The oxidation state of this ion is written as iron(III) or as Fe(III), indicating that it is a more highly oxidized species than Fe^{2+}.

When an iron(II) ion (Fe^{2+}) reacts to form an iron(III) ion (Fe^{3+}), iron loses one electron and is therefore oxidized:

$$Fe^{2+}(aq) \rightarrow Fe^{3+}(aq) + e^-$$

When it is oxidized, the oxidation number change for iron is from +2 to +3; the oxidation state change for iron is from Fe(II) to Fe(III).

- Oxidation involves an *increase* in oxidation number.

In the reverse process, *reduction*, an iron(III) ion gains one electron to become an iron(II) ion:

$$Fe^{3+}(aq) + e^- \rightarrow Fe^{2+}(aq)$$

When it is reduced, the oxidation number change for iron is from +3 to +2; the oxidation state change for iron is from Fe(III) to Fe(II).

- Reduction involves a *decrease* in oxidation number.

Rules for assigning oxidation numbers.

Rule No.	Rule	Examples for each rule
1	The sum of the oxidation numbers of all the atoms in any species must equal the charge on the species. For an atom or a molecule, the sum is zero. For an ion, the sum is the charge on the ion.	Nitrate ion NO_3^-: The overall charge on the ion is −1, so the sum of the oxidation numbers must be −1. The oxidation number total for the oxygen atoms (see rule 4) is $3 \times (-2) = -6$. So the oxidation number of nitrogen is +5.
2	The oxidation number of an element in its elemental state is zero. So the oxidation number of magnesium in Mg(s) is zero, as is the oxidation number of oxygen in $O_2(g)$.	Metallic iron: Oxidation number is 0. Nitrogen gas N_2: Oxidation number is 0.
3	The oxidation number of fluorine in its compounds is always −1. Fluorine is the most electronegative element and always gains electrons on bonding.	Sodium fluoride NaF: Oxidation number of sodium is +1 and that of fluorine is −1.
4	The oxidation number of oxygen in its compounds is usually −2, except if fluorine is present (or in certain unusual compounds such as peroxides or superoxides).	Carbon dioxide CO_2: Oxidation number of oxygen is −2 and that of carbon is +4. Water H_2O: Oxidation number of oxygen is −2 and that of hydrogen is +1.
5	Each shared electron pair is assigned to the more electronegative element.	Hydrogen chloride HCl: chlorine is more electronegative than hydrogen; oxidation number of hydrogen is +1 and that of chlorine is −1.

Identifying redox reactions

How can you tell whether a reaction is a redox reaction? The strategy is to work out the oxidation number for each element in the reaction. If none of the elements changes its oxidation number, the reaction *is not* a redox reaction.

- If there is any change in oxidation number, this indicates that the reaction *is* a redox reaction.

We will now apply this criterion to some reactions.

$$Fe(s) + S(s) \rightarrow FeS(s) \qquad (1)$$

The reactants are elements and therefore both have oxidation number 0. FeS is the compound iron(II) sulphide: the electron pairs are assigned to sulphur, which has the higher electronegativity value. The oxidation number of iron is +2 and that of sulphur is –2. Reaction (1) is a redox reaction.

$$NaOH(aq) + HCl(aq) \rightarrow NaCl(aq) + H_2O(l) \qquad (2)$$

There are no oxidation number changes, i.e. Na remains as +1, H as +1, Cl as –1, and O as –2. Reaction (2) is not a redox reaction; it is an acid–base reaction.

$$CuO(s) + H_2(g) \rightarrow Cu(s) + H_2O(g) \qquad (3)$$

The oxidation number of copper is +2 in copper(II) oxide CuO and 0 in copper Cu, indicating reduction. The oxidation number of hydrogen increases from 0 in the element to +1 in water. Reaction (3) is a redox reaction.

$$MnO_2(s) + 4HCl(aq) \rightarrow MnCl_2(aq) + Cl_2(g) + 2H_2O(l) \qquad (4)$$

Manganese is reduced from oxidation number +4 in MnO_2 to +2 in $MnCl_2$. Chlorine is oxidized from oxidation number –1 in HCl to 0 in the element Cl_2. The oxidation number of oxygen does not change. Reaction (4) is a redox reaction.

$$2H_2O_2(aq) \rightarrow 2H_2O(l) + O_2(g) \qquad (5)$$

The oxidation number of oxygen in peroxides is –1, in water it is –2, and in the element 0. The oxidation number of hydrogen does not change. Oxygen is both oxidized and reduced in this reaction. Reaction (5) is a redox reaction.

SUMMARY

- The oxidation number of an element is the number of electrons that need to be added to the element to make a neutral atom.
- A reaction is classed as a redox reaction if it involves a change in the oxidation number of any element taking part.
- Oxidation involves an increase in oxidation number.
- Reduction involves a decrease in oxidation number.

PRACTICE

1 In the reaction alongside, chlorine is produced by reaction of concentrated hydrochloric acid and potassium manganate(VII). Is the change chloride ion to chlorine gas an oxidation or a reduction?

Expressing oxidation numbers and oxidation states

The name of the compound of formula $CuSO_4$ is usually given as copper(II) sulphate (pronounced 'copper-two sulphate'). In this context, it is correct to say that:

- The *oxidation number* of copper is +2.
- The *oxidation state* of copper is written as copper(II) or Cu(II).
- $CuSO_4$ is the chemical formula of copper(II) sulphate.

Comment on redox reactions

Look at reaction (1) on the left. All reactions between two elements are *necessarily* redox reactions. The oxidation number of an uncombined element is always zero; the oxidation number of an element in a compound is never zero. So there is a change in oxidation number, and such reactions are redox reactions.

Look at reaction (5) on the left. Oxygen in the peroxide ion O_2^{2-} has an unusual oxidation number (–1), because two oxygen atoms bond to form the ion $^-O—O^-$. In the reaction, the oxidation number of oxygen both *increases* (to form O_2) and *decreases* (to form H_2O). This is a redox reaction in which the *same* element is both oxidized *and* reduced. Such a reaction is also called a **disproportionation** reaction.

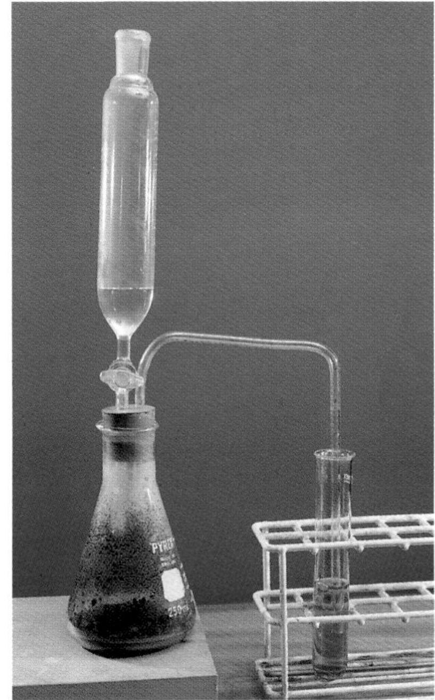

Gaseous chlorine oxidizes colourless aqueous bromide ions to red-brown bromine. This is an example of a redox reaction involving two non-metals: $Cl_2(g) + 2Br^-(aq) \rightarrow 2Cl^-(aq) + Br_2(l)$

13.3

OXIDATION NUMBERS – 2

OBJECTIVES

- Systematic naming of compounds
- Traditional and systematic names

The traditional names of many chemical substances date back to the nineteeth century. Many of these names are still in common use, especially those for acids (e.g. sulphuric acid H_2SO_4; sulphurous acid H_2SO_3) and their salts (e.g. sodium nitrate $NaNO_3$; potassium nitrite KNO_2). According to traditional nomenclature, an acid with the suffix '-ic' contains a larger amount of oxygen than one with the suffix '-ous'. (Look at the formulae of sulphuric and sulphurous acids.) In salts, the suffixes are '-ate' and '-ite', respectively representing greater and lesser amounts of oxygen. (Look at the formulae of sodium nitrate and potassium nitrite.) The modern systematic naming system uses the concept of oxidation number to help make the naming of chemical substances unambiguous.

A redox titration. (a) Potassium manganate(VII) acts as its own indicator during titration with aqueous iron(II) ions. Purple $MnO_4^-(aq)$ ions are reduced to pale pink $Mn^{2+}(aq)$ ions, while pale green $Fe^{2+}(aq)$ ions are oxidized to pale yellow $Fe^{3+}(aq)$ ions. The oxidation state changes for manganese and iron are:

Mn(VII) to Mn(II) (reduction)
Fe(II) to Fe(III) (oxidation)

(b) The purple colour of $MnO_4^-(aq)$ can be seen when all the $Fe^{2+}(aq)$ has reacted.

Systematic names

Oxidation numbers can be used to name compounds unambiguously. No confusion is possible when an element exhibits only one common oxidation state. For example, Group I elements always have an oxidation number of +1 in their compounds. Sodium is present in the ionic compound sodium oxide as Na(I). From rule 4 in the previous spread, the oxidation number of oxygen is –2. Because oxygen is present as O(–II), the formula must therefore be Na_2O. The oxygen is present in the compound as the ion O^{2-}. The name 'sodium oxide' is adequate to describe this substance.

On the other hand, 'iron oxide' presents a problem because there are two possible oxidation states of iron, iron(II) and iron(III). Oxygen is present as O(–II). The compound FeO is therefore 'iron(II) oxide' and Fe_2O_3 is 'iron(III) oxide'. Similarly, MnO_2 is 'manganese(IV) oxide'.

When two non-metals are combined, the rules for naming are very different. The common name of the compound simply describes the number of atoms present. Thus CO_2 is 'carbon dioxide', CO is 'carbon monoxide', SO_2 is 'sulphur dioxide', SO_3 is 'sulphur trioxide', and N_2O_4 is 'dinitrogen tetraoxide'. This form of nomenclature is only used for simple covalent compounds containing non-metals.

Oxoanions and $KMnO_4$

Oxoanions are negatively charged ions that contain elements combined with oxygen. A common example is the ion MnO_4^- present in the substance $KMnO_4$, traditionally called 'potassium permanganate'. A solution contains the ions $K^+(aq)$ and $MnO_4^-(aq)$. The naming of MnO_4^- needs careful thought. You must first assign an oxidation number of –2 to oxygen. Now recognize that there are four oxygen atoms in the anion, and that the anion has an overall charge of –1. As a result, manganese is assigned an oxidation number of +7. The oxoanion MnO_4^- is therefore described as the manganate(VII) ion; $KMnO_4$ is called 'potassium manganate(VII)'. Note that an oxidation number of +7 does *not* imply that MnO_4^- contains the ion Mn^{7+}.

Traditional and systematic names

The following table will help you to move freely between the two naming systems. Only the *systematic name* should be used for acids and oxoanions containing metals. The *traditional names* are suitable where there is no chance of ambiguity. For example, the traditional name 'sulphuric acid' is less cumbersome for the substance H_2SO_4. Using this traditional name for the acid matches the use of the name 'sulphur trioxide' for SO_3 rather than the systematic name 'sulphur(VI) oxide'.

Acids and oxoanions: traditional and systematic names (the names in **bold** *are the ones that we shall use).*

Traditional name	Formula	Systematic name	
sulphuric acid	H_2SO_4	sulphuric(VI) acid	↑
sulphate ion	SO_4^{2-}	sulphate(VI) ion	
sulphurous acid	H_2SO_3	sulphuric(IV) acid	
sulphite ion	SO_3^{2-}	sulphate(IV) ion	
nitric acid	HNO_3	nitric(V) acid	
nitrate ion	NO_3^-	nitrate(V) ion	
nitrous acid	HNO_2	nitric(III) acid	
nitrite ion	NO_2^-	nitrate(III) ion	non-metals
permanganate ion	MnO_4^-	**manganate(VII) ion**	metals
chromate ion	CrO_4^{2-}	**chromate(VI) ion**	
dichromate ion	$Cr_2O_7^{2-}$	**dichromate(VI) ion**	↓

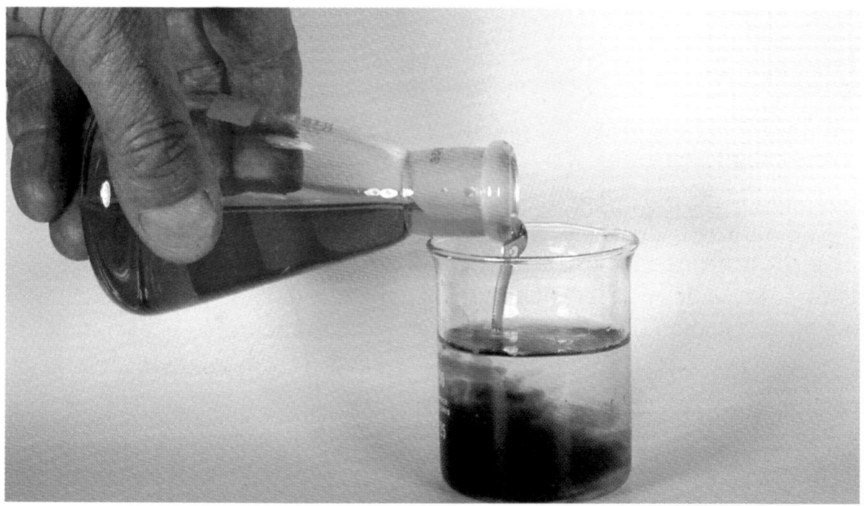

Orange dichromate(VI) ions poured into aqueous iron(II) ions results in a green solution. The ionic equation for the reaction (see next spread)

$$Cr_2O_7^{2-}(aq) + 6Fe^{2+}(aq) + 14H^+(aq) \rightarrow 2Cr^{3+}(aq) + 6Fe^{3+}(aq) + 7H_2O(l)$$

shows that dichromate(VI) ions are reduced to chromium(III) ions by iron(II) ions in acidified aqueous solution; the iron(II) ions are oxidized to iron(III).

SUMMARY

- Systematic names of substances include information about oxidation states.

Naming chlorine oxoanions

Chlorine forms four oxoanions. The systematic names for the ions ClO_4^-, ClO_3^-, ClO_2^-, and ClO^- are respectively chlorate(VII), chlorate(V), chlorate(III), and chlorate(I). The traditional names are perchlorate, chlorate, chlorite, and hypochlorite. See spread 10.1.

No ambiguity

The names actually only become unambiguous when the number of oxygen atoms is also specified. So the fully systematic name for MnO_4^- is tetraoxomanganate(VII) ion.

Reminder about oxidation number changes

- If the oxidation number of an element **increases** during a reaction, the element has been **oxidized**.
- If the oxidation number of an element **decreases** during a reaction, the element has been **reduced**.

PRACTICE

1 Give the oxidation numbers of each of the elements in the following species:
 a H_2O
 b K_2O
 c $AlCl_3$
 d NO_3^-
 e OF_2.

2 State whether each of the following may be classed as a redox reaction or not. Explain your reasoning by writing and discussing the full balanced chemical equations and half-equations:
 a Carbon dioxide gas being evolved from a mixture of calcium carbonate and dilute hydrochloric acid.
 b Chlorine gas being evolved from a heated mixture of manganese(IV) oxide and concentrated hydrochloric acid.

3 Name the following species:
 a H_2SO_4
 b H_2SO_3
 c NaClO
 d ClO_3^-
 e MnO_2
 f CuO.

13.4

REDOX REACTIONS AND TITRATIONS

OBJECTIVES

- Manganate(VII) ion as oxidant
- Dichromate(VI) ion as oxidant
- Thiosulphate ion as reductant
- Calculations for a redox titration

In this dichromate(VI)/iron(II) titration, the intense orange colour of $Cr_2O_7^{2-}(aq)$ ions changes to green as they are reduced to $Cr^{3+}(aq)$.

Starch as an indicator

None of the ions present in the iodine/thiosulphate reaction is highly coloured. Starch, which forms a deep blue complex with iodine, can be used as an indicator to show a clear end point for the reaction. A small quantity of starch solution is added just before the end point when the iodine solution is a pale straw colour, i.e. when most of the iodine has reacted. The end point is when the intense blue colour of the starch–iodine complex finally disappears.

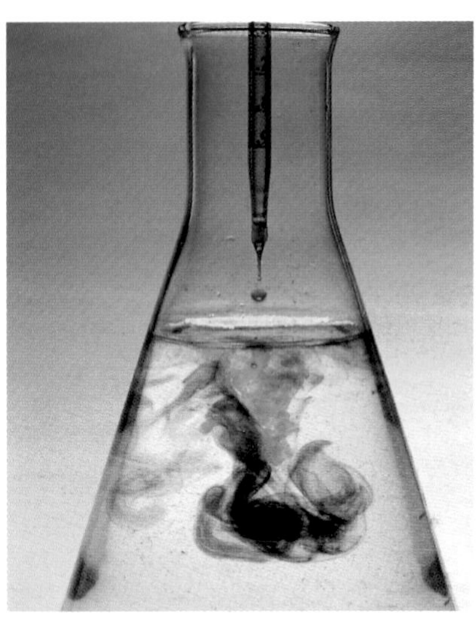

The intense blue starch–iodine complex consists of iodine molecules lying inside long spirals of starch molecules. Thiosulphate ions reduce this complex to colourless iodide ions.

The previous chapter introduced you to the idea of using the method of titration to measure the concentrations of acids and bases in acid–base reactions. A **redox titration** uses the same technique but is applied to the reactants in a redox reaction. There are three reagents most commonly used in redox titrations: manganate(VII) ion, dichromate(VI) ion, and thiosulphate ion.

The manganate(VII) ion as an oxidant

Potassium manganate(VII) $KMnO_4$ can act as an oxidant in acidic solution. The half-equation for the reduction of manganate(VII) ion under these conditions is:

$$MnO_4^-(aq) + 8H^+(aq) + 5e^- \rightarrow Mn^{2+}(aq) + 4H_2O(l) \qquad (1)$$

Manganate(VII) ion is commonly used to determine the concentration of aqueous iron(II) ions $Fe^{2+}(aq)$, which it oxidizes to $Fe^{3+}(aq)$: see previous spread. The half-equation for the oxidation of iron(II) ions is:

$$Fe^{2+}(aq) \rightarrow Fe^{3+}(aq) + e^- \qquad (2)$$

This reaction supplies only one electron so the half-equation (2) must be multiplied by *five* before adding to the manganate(VII) half-equation (1). Doing this, we obtain the ionic equation for the redox reaction:

$$MnO_4^-(aq) + 5Fe^{2+}(aq) + 8H^+(aq) \rightarrow Mn^{2+}(aq) + 5Fe^{3+}(aq) + 4H_2O(l)$$

i.e. Mn(VII) is reduced to Mn(II); Fe(II) is oxidized to Fe(III).

- For titration calculations, the mole ratio is 5 mol Fe^{2+} to 1 mol MnO_4^-.

The dichromate(VI) ion as an oxidant

Potassium dichromate(VI) $K_2Cr_2O_7$ can act as an oxidant in acidic solution. The half-equation for the reduction of dichromate(VI) ion is:

$$Cr_2O_7^{2-}(aq) + 14H^+(aq) + 6e^- \rightarrow 2Cr^{3+}(aq) + 7H_2O(l) \qquad (3)$$

This reaction provides its own indicator because the colour changes as excess orange $Cr_2O_7^{2-}(aq)$ mixes with green $Cr^{3+}(aq)$ at the equivalence point. As in the example for manganate(VII) given above, iron(II) is a suitable source of electrons. But now we need to multiply the half-equation (2) by *six* before adding it to equation (3). Doing this, we get the ionic equation for the redox reaction:

$$Cr_2O_7^{2-}(aq) + 6Fe^{2+}(aq) + 14H^+(aq) \rightarrow 2Cr^{3+}(aq) + 6Fe^{3+}(aq) + 7H_2O(l)$$

i.e. Cr(VI) is reduced to Cr(III); Fe(II) is oxidized to Fe(III).

- For titration calculations, the mole ratio is 6 mol Fe^{2+} to 1 mol $Cr_2O_7^{2-}$.

The thiosulphate ion as a reductant

Sodium thiosulphate $Na_2S_2O_3$ can act as a reductant in acidic solution. The half-equation for the oxidation of thiosulphate ion $S_2O_3^{2-}$ to tetrathionate ion $S_4O_6^{2-}$ is:

$$2S_2O_3^{2-}(aq) \rightarrow S_4O_6^{2-}(aq) + 2e^- \qquad (4)$$

Iodine is a suitable oxidant to accept the electrons, itself being reduced to iodide ions:

$$I_2(aq) + 2e^- \rightarrow 2I^-(aq) \qquad (5)$$

We obtain the overall ionic equation for the redox reaction between iodine and thiosulphate ions by adding together half-equations (4) and (5):

$$I_2(aq) + 2S_2O_3^{2-}(aq) \rightarrow 2I^-(aq) + S_4O_6^{2-}(aq)$$

i.e. I(0) is reduced to I(–I); S(+2) is oxidized to S(+2.5). [You should note that the oxidation number of sulphur in tetrathionate is +2.5. This number cannot be written in Roman numerals, so the change is expressed here in terms of oxidation numbers, not oxidation states.]

- For titration calculations, the mole ratio is 1 mol I_2 to 2 mol $S_2O_3^{2-}$.

Worked example on a redox titration calculation

Data: Potassium iodate KIO_3 oxidizes potassium iodide KI to form iodine I_2 in acidic solution. In a laboratory reaction, 20.0 cm^3 of aqueous potassium iodate containing 3.00 g KIO_3 per dm^3 reacted with excess potassium iodide. The liberated iodine required 16.8 cm^3 of 0.100 mol dm^{-3} aqueous sodium thiosulphate for complete reaction.

Question: Calculate the mole ratio between iodine and iodate ion and hence suggest an ionic equation for the reaction.

Answer:

Step 1 Calculate the amount in moles of thiosulphate ion used in the titration.

From earlier chapters we know that

amount in moles = volume of solution × molar concentration

So substituting the quantities given above for the thiosulphate ion $S_2O_3^{2-}$:

$$\text{amount in moles of } S_2O_3^{2-} = \left(\frac{16.8}{1000}\,dm^3\right) \times (0.100\,mol\,dm^{-3})$$
$$= 1.68 \times 10^{-3}\,mol$$

Step 2 Calculate the amount in moles of iodine liberated, using the ionic equation:

$I_2(aq) + 2S_2O_3^{2-}(aq) \rightarrow 2I^-(aq) + S_4O_6^{2-}(aq)$

The equation shows that 1 mol I_2 reacts with 2 mol $S_2O_3^{2-}$. So

$$\text{amount in moles of } I_2 = \frac{1.68 \times 10^{-3}\,mol}{2}$$
$$= 8.40 \times 10^{-4}\,mol$$

Step 3 Calculate the amount in moles of potassium iodate in the original solution.

The aqueous KIO_3 contained 3.00 g dm^{-3}. The molar mass of KIO_3 is

$39.1\,g\,mol^{-1} + 126.9\,g\,mol^{-1} + 3 \times (16.0\,g\,mol^{-1}) = 214\,g\,mol^{-1}$

Therefore

$$\text{molar concentration of aqueous } KIO_3 = \frac{3.00\,g\,dm^{-3}}{214\,g\,mol^{-1}}$$
$$= 0.0140\,mol\,dm^{-3}$$

We now use

amount in moles = volume of solution × molar concentration

So substituting the quantities for the potassium iodate:

$$\text{amount in moles of } KIO_3 = \left(\frac{20.0}{1000}\,dm^3\right) \times (0.0140\,mol\,dm^{-3})$$
$$= 2.80 \times 10^{-4}\,mol$$

Step 4 Calculate the ratio of these two amounts, I_2/IO_3^-, and then convert it to a whole-number ratio.

The amounts in moles of I_2 and IO_3^- found in steps 2 and 3 are 8.40×10^{-4} mol and 2.80×10^{-4} mol respectively. The simplest ratio is

$$\frac{I_2}{IO_3^-} = \frac{8.40 \times 10^{-4}\,mol}{2.80 \times 10^{-4}\,mol} = \frac{8.40}{2.80} = \frac{3}{1}$$

Step 5 Suggest an ionic equation for the reaction.

According to this calculation, 3 mol of iodine I_2 results from the reaction of 1 mol of iodate IO_3^- with excess iodide. The equation for the reaction is:

$IO_3^-(aq) + 5I^-(aq) + 6H^+(aq) \rightarrow 3I_2(aq) + 3H_2O(l)$

I(V) is reduced to I(0); I(–I) is oxidized to I(0).

Titrations and equations

Calculations such as this example were originally used to work out chemical equations. All required careful experimental evaluation of the amounts of one chemical needed to react with another. Although chemical reactions are rarely found in this manner from first principles, it is useful to see how one was actually determined.

SUMMARY

- $MnO_4^-(aq) + 8H^+(aq) + 5e^- \rightarrow Mn^{2+}(aq) + 4H_2O(l)$
- $Cr_2O_7^{2-}(aq) + 14H^+(aq) + 6e^- \rightarrow 2Cr^{3+}(aq) + 7H_2O(l)$
- $I_2(aq) + 2S_2O_3^{2-}(aq) \rightarrow 2I^-(aq) + S_4O_6^{2-}(aq)$

PRACTICE

1 Give two examples of solutions which can be used as oxidants in redox titrations. Describe the colour changes that occur.

2 Write down the equation for the reaction between iodine and sodium thiosulphate. How may the end point be detected?

13.5

OBJECTIVES

- Non-metal oxidants
- Metal reductants
- Displacement reactions and relative strengths

Oxidants and reductants

Several species may be conveniently classified as oxidants or reductants. If they are present in a reaction mixture, there is a strong likelihood that a redox reaction is taking place. You have already met many different examples of redox reactions in this chapter. This spread includes some further examples and introduces the idea of comparing the strengths of oxidants and of reductants.

Oxygen gas as an oxidant

Elemental (molecular) oxygen O_2 usually acts as an oxidant in reactions. It was oxygen that historically gave its name to the process of oxidation. The most obvious examples of redox reactions are those in which oxygen reacts with an element to form its oxide.

Oxygen acts as an oxidant because it has a very high electronegativity value: the rules for assigning oxidation numbers (which we met earlier in this chapter) assign to oxygen any electron pairs shared with *any* other element (except fluorine).

(a) 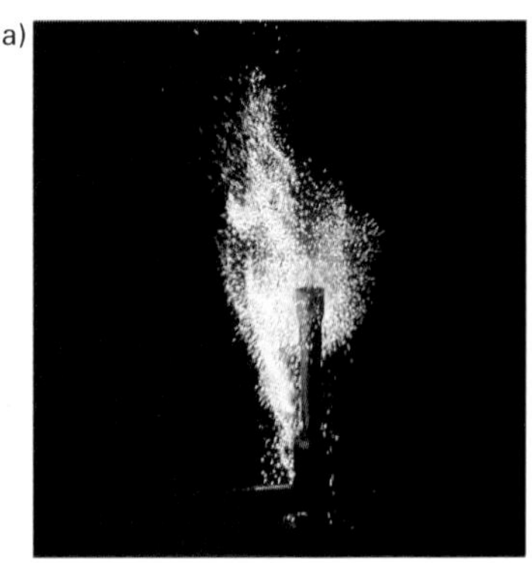

(b) 

(a) Oxidation of a metallic element: iron filings oxidize to a mixture of iron(II) oxide and iron(III) oxide when sprinkled into a non-luminous Bunsen flame:
$3Fe(s) + 2O_2(g) \rightarrow Fe_2O_3{\cdot}FeO(s)$
(b) Oxidation of a non-metallic element: heated molten sulphur burns in oxygen with a blue flame to produce sulphur dioxide gas:
$S(l) + O_2(g) \rightarrow SO_2(g)$

The halogen bromine reacts violently with phosphorus to form phosphorus tribromide PBr_3. Bromine is more electronegative than phosphorus so in forming PBr_3 the phosphorus has been oxidized. A later view of the same reaction is shown in spread 18.1.

Halogens as oxidants

Oxygen acts as an oxidant because it has a high electronegativity value (3.4) and so removes electrons from (oxidizes) most other species. The halogens fluorine and chlorine also have high electronegativity values (fluorine 4.0, chlorine 3.2). Fluorine is an extremely powerful oxidant and chlorine is comparable with oxygen.

Non-metal displacement reactions

Redox reactions may be considered as a competition between two species for control of electrons. For example, chlorine removes electrons from aqueous bromide ions, oxidizing them to bromine (spread 13.2):

$$Cl_2(g) + 2Br^-(aq) \rightarrow 2Cl^-(aq) + Br_2(l)$$

Chlorine is a more powerful oxidant than bromine, under these conditions, so the reverse reaction does not occur to any significant extent.

Gases as reductants

Hydrogen, carbon monoxide, and methane can all act as reductants. For example, each will reduce heated copper(II) oxide to copper:

$$H_2(g) + CuO(s) \rightarrow Cu(s) + H_2O(g)$$
$$CO(g) + CuO(s) \rightarrow Cu(s) + CO_2(g)$$
$$CH_4(g) + 4CuO(s) \rightarrow 4Cu(s) + CO_2(g) + 2H_2O(g)$$

These gases have important roles to play as reductants in industry. Amongst many other uses, hydrogen reduces vegetable oils in the manufacture of margarine. Carbon monoxide reduces iron ore in the blast furnace to make iron:

$$3CO(g) + Fe_2O_3(s) \rightarrow 2Fe(l) + 3CO_2(g)$$

Methane reduces steam in the presence of a nickel catalyst to produce hydrogen, used in the Haber–Bosch synthesis of ammonia:

$$CH_4(g) + H_2O(g) \rightarrow CO(g) + 3H_2(g)$$

It is important to remember, however, that it not possible to classify substances uniquely as *either* oxidants *or* reductants. The same substance may be an oxidant in one reaction and a reductant in another. Redox behaviour depends on *both* the reacting substances.

Metal reductants

Potassium	K	Decreasing power as a reductant in aqueous solution ↓
Calcium	Ca	
Aluminium	Al	
Zinc	Zn	
Iron	Fe	
Lead	Pb	
Copper	Cu	
Silver	Ag	

Metals as reductants

Most metallic elements act as reductants, donating electrons to other species. For example, aluminium will reduce iron(III) oxide to metallic iron in the very vigorous 'Thermit' reaction, see spread 3.1:

$$Fe_2O_3(s) + 2Al(s) \rightarrow Al_2O_3(s) + 2Fe(l)$$

i.e. Fe(III) is reduced to Fe(0); Al(0) is oxidized to Al(III).

From your earlier work you may remember a list of metals called 'the reactivity series'. This list orders the metals according to their overall chemical reactivity. In general terms:

- A more reactive metal will reduce the oxide of a less reactive metal.

So you would expect zinc to reduce lead oxide, but you would not expect lead to reduce aluminium oxide.

- A more reactive metal will displace a less reactive metal from a solution containing ions of the less reactive metal.

So you would expect zinc to displace copper ions, spread 13.1, but you would not expect lead to displace zinc ions.

As another example, the reaction between copper metal and aqueous silver ions is

$$Cu(s) + 2Ag^+(aq) \rightarrow 2Ag(s) + Cu^{2+}(aq)$$

Copper is acting as the reductant, donating electrons to the silver ions. Copper metal is a more powerful reductant than silver, so the reverse reaction does not take place to any significant extent.

Copper metal reacts with aqueous silver ions to produce silver. Its nickname, the 'Christmas tree' reaction, is easy to understand.

The relative power of a metal as a reductant is therefore linked to its overall chemical reactivity, from potassium as the most powerful to silver as the weakest. This correlation is an approximate guideline only, and in the next few spreads we will introduce more precise ideas.

SUMMARY

- The non-metals fluorine, oxygen, chlorine, and bromine often act as oxidants.
- Metallic elements often act as reductants.
- The reactivity series of metals lists the elements in order of their strengths as reductants in aqueous solution.

PRACTICE

1 State the changes in oxidation number that happen to each of the elements involved in the following reactions:
  - **a** Methane burning in oxygen.
  - **b** Bromine displacing iodide ions from aqueous solution.
  - **c** Nickel displacing copper(II) ions from aqueous solution to form nickel(II) ions.
  - **d** The catalytic oxidation of methane to produce methanol $2CH_4(g) + O_2(g) \rightarrow 2CH_3OH(g)$

2 For each of the reactions in question 1, identify (i) the oxidant and (ii) the reductant. Give reasons for your answers.

13.6

Redox and electrochemical cells

OBJECTIVES

- Half-equations and half-cells
- Electrochemical cells
- Potential difference and e.m.f.

Some substances generally react as oxidants and others generally react as reductants. To predict whether a redox reaction will take place between two species, it is necessary to make measurements. The key to this problem is to separate the two species physically and to monitor the *direction* of electron flow between them. We need to remember that electrons flow *from* the reductant *to* the oxidant during a redox reaction.

Metal displacement reactions

The previous spread introduced the idea of displacement reactions between a metal and the aqueous ions of another metal. We saw in spread 13.1 the example of immersing a strip of zinc metal in aqueous copper(II) ions, resulting in the following redox reaction:

$$Zn(s) + Cu^{2+}(aq) \rightarrow Zn^{2+}(aq) + Cu(s)$$

This chemical equation can be separated into two half-equations:

$$Zn(s) \rightarrow Zn^{2+}(aq) + 2e^-$$

i.e. zinc is the reductant; it loses electrons and is oxidized.

$$Cu^{2+}(aq) + 2e^- \rightarrow Cu(s)$$

i.e. copper(II) ion is the oxidant; it gains electrons and is reduced.

A displacement reaction also takes place between nickel metal and aqueous copper(II) ions:

$$Ni(s) + Cu^{2+}(aq) \rightarrow Ni^{2+}(aq) + Cu(s)$$

There are again two half-equations. One describes the oxidation of nickel:

$$Ni(s) \rightarrow Ni^{2+}(aq) + 2e^-$$

and the other describes the reduction of aqueous copper(II) ions:

$$Cu^{2+}(aq) + 2e^- \rightarrow Cu(s)$$

We might now ask an important question: 'Is it possible to measure the reducing powers of zinc and nickel and other metals to compare them?' The answer is 'yes', using measurements from half-cells.

Silvery-coloured nickel metal reacts with blue aqueous Cu^{2+} ions to form a red-brown deposit of copper and green aqueous Ni^{2+} ions. This is the result $1\frac{1}{2}$ hours after mixing.

Half-cells

Look again at the $Zn(s)/Cu^{2+}(aq)$ displacement reaction. It is possible to separate the reactions represented by the two half-equations given above. We can do so by carrying out each reaction in an electrochemical half-cell. A typical **electrochemical half-cell** consists of a metal in contact with an aqueous solution of its ions.

Imagine that a strip of zinc is placed in a beaker containing aqueous zinc ions (from zinc sulphate, for example). A dynamic equilibrium is quickly established between the surface of the metal and the aqueous ions:

$$Zn^{2+}(aq) + 2e^- \rightleftharpoons Zn(s)$$

The electrons liberated by the backward reaction are delocalized throughout the whole of the metal strip. In this context, the metal strip is called an **electrode** because electrons may enter or leave through it.

A similar equilibrium can be set up in a second beaker containing a copper electrode immersed in aqueous copper(II) ions (from copper(II) sulphate, for example):

$$Cu^{2+}(aq) + 2e^- \rightleftharpoons Cu(s)$$

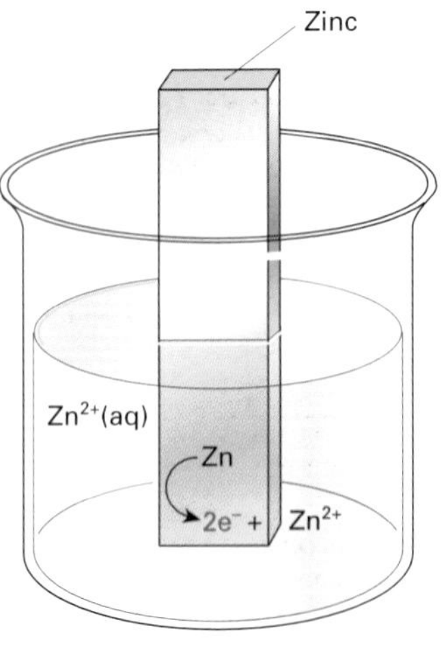

The zinc half-cell consists of a strip of zinc metal immersed in aqueous Zn^{2+} ions.

Half-cells and electric potential

Any half-cell may be described by the corresponding redox half-equation, which we can write in general terms for a metal/metal ion half-cell using M for the metal and *n* for the number of charges:

$$M^{n+}(aq) + ne^- \rightleftharpoons M(s)$$

In terms of general chemical reactivity, zinc is more reactive than copper. You may therefore assume that the equilibrium in the zinc half-cell lies further to the left than does the equilibrium in the copper half-cell. As a result, there are more electrons on the zinc electrode than on the copper electrode.

As there are more electrons on the zinc electrode, its electric potential is more negative than that on the copper electrode. The zinc electrode is said to have a **negative potential** with respect to the copper electrode. (It is equally correct to say that the copper electrode has a **positive potential** with respect to the zinc electrode.)

Electrons and ions

Note that there are no free electrons in the solution: they remain delocalized throughout the electrode. The reaction takes place on the surface of the electrode where the metal is in contact with the aqueous ions.

Electrochemical cells

As shown in the diagram below, two half-cells may be connected together to make an **electrochemical cell**. The two electrodes are connected by wires to a voltmeter, which measures the **potential difference** (p.d.) between them. In this example, the voltmeter reading is 1.1 volts (symbol: V) when the solutions have concentrations of 1 mol dm^{-3} and the temperature is 298 K. This value is not affected by the size or shape of the electrodes.

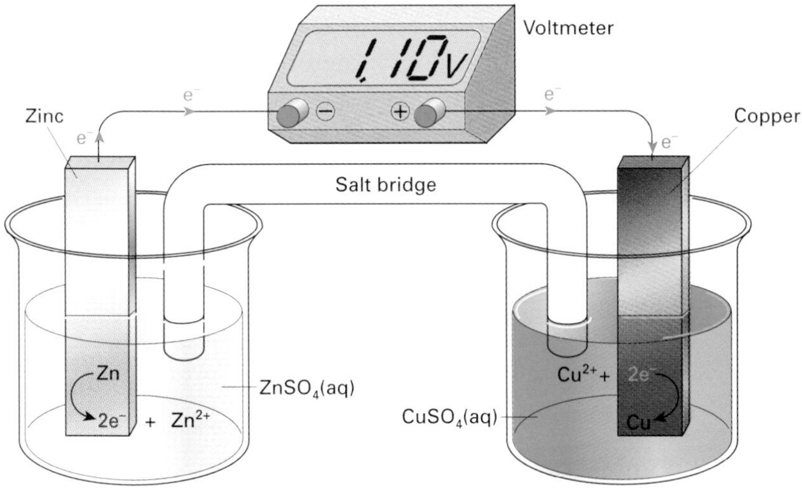

This apparatus separates into two beakers the reactions represented by the two half-equations for the zinc/copper(II) displacement reaction. See next spread.

The voltmeter indicates that the copper electrode is positive with respect to the zinc electrode. If the two electrodes are connected directly together by a wire, then electrons flow towards the positive (copper) electrode. The zinc electrode loses electrons and so the equilibrium

$$Zn^{2+}(aq) + 2e^- \rightleftharpoons Zn(s)$$

shifts to the left. Zinc metal reacts and the concentration of zinc ions increases. The copper electrode gains electrons and so the equilibrium

$$Cu^{2+}(aq) + 2e^- \rightleftharpoons Cu(s)$$

shifts to the right. Copper(II) ions accept electrons and a deposit of copper metal forms on the surface of the copper electrode.

The copper/zinc electrochemical cell has a measured e.m.f. of 1.1 V. The copper/nickel cell has a measured e.m.f. of 0.59 V. The zinc half-cell generates a more negative potential than does the nickel half-cell.

- Reductants are electron donors: therefore in aqueous solutions zinc must be a more powerful reductant than nickel.

The following spreads show how the direction of electron flow and the measured values of e.m.f. may be used to predict the outcome of redox reactions.

Measuring potential difference

A high-resistance digital voltmeter measures the potential difference (p.d.) between two half-cells. It allows little current to flow, but does indicate the direction in which a current *would* flow if the electrodes were directly connected together. The p.d. measured when negligible current flows is called the 'electromotive force' (**e.m.f.**) and is the maximum voltage that a cell can develop. If the voltmeter does allow an appreciable current to flow, then the p.d. measured is lower, because of the internal resistance of the cell.

Metals that react with water

For the most reactive reductants such as sodium, it is not possible to use a piece of the metal as an electrode immersed in an aqueous solution, because the metal would react with water. Instead we use an amalgam of the metal dissolved in liquid mercury as the electrode. Connection is then made to the external circuit and voltmeter via a platinum wire dipping into the amalgam.

The salt bridge

The **salt bridge** completes the electric circuit by allowing charged species to flow between the solutions. This flow of ions ensures that the contents of each half-cell remain electrically neutral while electrons flow from one electrode to the other. A simple salt bridge consists of a piece of filter paper soaked in saturated aqueous potassium chloride. A salt bridge which does not dry out so easily can be made using a glass tube filled with saturated aqueous potassium chloride in jelly form.

SUMMARY

- A half-cell contains the species that take part in a half-equation.
- The difference in electric potential between two half-cells is measured by a voltmeter. The unit of potential difference is the volt (symbol: V).

13.7

OBJECTIVES

- The standard hydrogen electrode
- Standard electrode potentials
- Cell diagrams

Sea level

Altitude in the U.K. is measured against an arbitrary zero, which is defined as the mean sea level at Newlyn, Cornwall.

STANDARD ELECTRODE POTENTIALS – 1

From previous work in this chapter, you should now understand that half-cells contain oxidized and reduced species, which are in equilibrium with each other. Two half-cells may be joined together to make an electrochemical cell, in which electrons flow from the electrode with the more negative potential to the electrode with the more positive potential. Whichever has the more negative potential is the stronger reductant. This spread shows that measuring each half-cell against a standard reference allows each to be assigned a 'standard electrode potential'.

The standard hydrogen electrode

It is only possible to measure a potential *difference*. It is not possible to measure the potential of an isolated electrode and assign an absolute value of potential to it. Chemists have found a way around this problem by agreeing the specification of a *standard half-cell*, which has a value of zero potential assigned to it. The potentials of other half-cells may then be measured against this arbitrary standard of zero potential. This standard half-cell is the **standard hydrogen electrode** shown below left.

The standard hydrogen electrode consists of a platinum electrode immersed in acid of pH 0 (i.e. where $[H^+(aq)] = 1\,mol\,dm^{-3}$) with hydrogen gas at standard pressure (1 bar) passing over it.

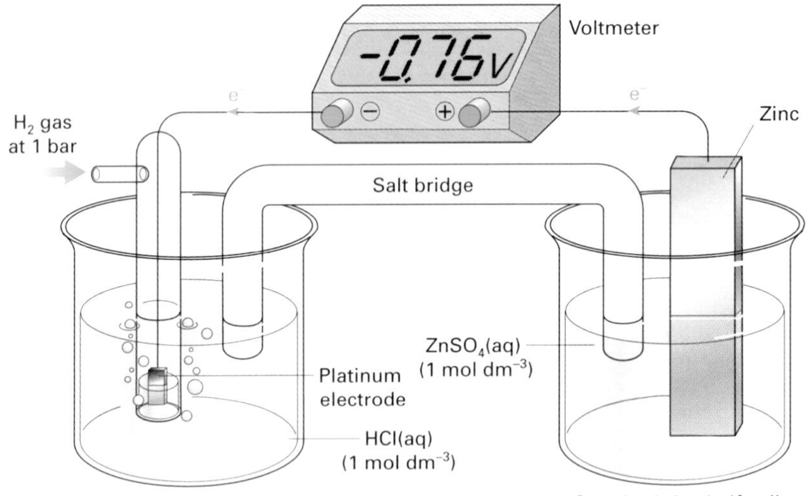

An electrochemical cell consisting of a standard hydrogen electrode and a standard zinc half-cell. The measured standard electrode potential for the redox equilibrium $Zn^{2+}(aq) + 2e^- \rightleftharpoons Zn(s)$ is –0.76 V.

The redox half-equation for the standard hydrogen electrode is:

$$2H^+(aq) + 2e^- \rightleftharpoons H_2(g) \qquad E^\ominus = 0\,V$$

The symbol $E^\ominus$ represents the **standard electrode potential** of a half-cell, which is the e.m.f. measured between a standard hydrogen electrode and a *standard* metal half-cell (set up using an aqueous solution of the metal ion at a concentration of $1\,mol\,dm^{-3}$) at 298 K.

By convention, standard electrode potentials are always recorded as standard *reduction* potentials. The reaction is written with the reduced species on the right, i.e.

$$\text{oxidized species} + ne^- \rightleftharpoons \text{reduced species}$$

Some examples are given in the table to the left.

Standard electrode potentials for metal/metal ion half-cells.

Oxidized species	⇌	Reduced species	$E^\ominus$/V
$K^+(aq) + e^-$	⇌	K(s)	–2.92
$Ca^{2+}(aq) + 2e^-$	⇌	Ca(s)	–2.87
$Mg^{2+}(aq) + 2e^-$	⇌	Mg(s)	–2.37
$Al^{3+}(aq) + 3e^-$	⇌	Al(s)	–1.66
$Zn^{2+}(aq) + 2e^-$	⇌	Zn(s)	–0.76
$Fe^{2+}(aq) + 2e^-$	⇌	Fe(s)	–0.44
$2H^+(aq) + 2e^-$	⇌	$H_2(g)$	0
$Cu^{2+}(aq) + 2e^-$	⇌	Cu(s)	+0.34
$Ag^+(aq) + e^-$	⇌	Ag(s)	+0.80

The sign of the $E^\ominus$ value

The $E^\ominus$ value for the zinc half-cell is –0.76 V. The minus (–) sign signifies that the electric potential on the zinc electrode is more negative than the potential on the standard hydrogen electrode. The $E^\ominus$ value for the copper half-cell is +0.34 V. The plus (+) sign signifies that the standard hydrogen electrode has the more negative potential.

Cell diagrams

An electrochemical cell results when two half-cells are connected together. A **cell diagram** is an agreed way of depicting cells on paper. For example, combining hydrogen and zinc half-cells gives the overall cell diagram:

$$Pt(s)\,|\,H_2(g)\,|\,H^+(aq)\,||\,Zn^{2+}(aq)\,|\,Zn(s)$$

By convention:

- The two parallel lines represent the salt bridge.
- Each single line represents the change of phase between aqueous ions and solid metal.
- The electrodes through which electrons flow are placed at the start and the finish of the cell diagram.
- The standard hydrogen electrode is placed on the left-hand side.

In the case of the zinc/copper electrochemical cell, the cell diagram is:

$$Zn(s)\,|\,Zn^{2+}(aq)\,||\,Cu^{2+}(aq)\,|\,Cu(s)$$

By convention, the cell diagram is written with:

- the half-cell undergoing oxidation on the left of the diagram
- the half-cell undergoing reduction on the right of the diagram.

So, when the electrodes are directly connected, electrons flow from the zinc half-cell to the copper half-cell. Reduction therefore takes place in the $Cu^{2+}(aq)|Cu(s)$ half-cell and oxidation in the $Zn(s)|Zn^{2+}(aq)$ half-cell.

The zinc half-cell is identified as the half-cell undergoing oxidation because its standard electrode potential is more negative than that of the copper half-cell. Look at the table of $E^\ominus$ values and you should understand that:

- Oxidation will take place in the half-cell with the more negative standard electrode potential.
- Reduction will take place in the half-cell with the less negative (more positive) standard electrode potential.

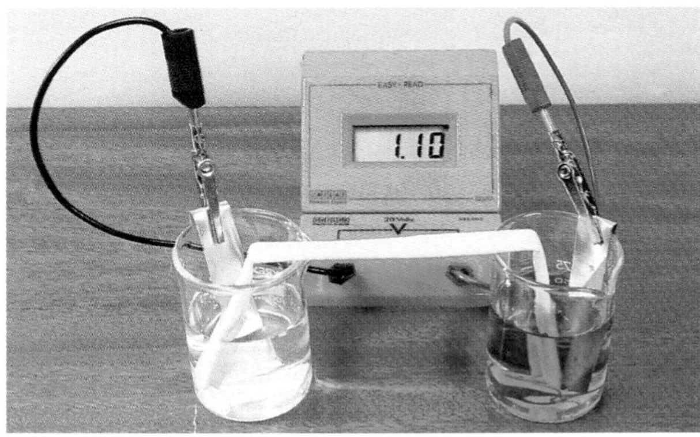

An electrochemical cell consisting of $Zn^{2+}(aq)/Zn(s)$ and $Cu^{2+}(aq)/Cu(s)$ half-cells. The standard cell e.m.f. is +1.10V. If the electrodes are connected directly together, copper(II) ions are reduced and zinc metal is oxidized.

SUMMARY

- $E^\ominus$ is the standard electrode potential of a half-cell, measured against a standard hydrogen electrode at 298 K; solutions are at 1 mol dm^{-3}.
- The standard hydrogen electrode has a platinum electrode, H_2 gas at 1 bar, and acid at pH 0; it is assigned an arbitrary $E^\ominus$ of 0 V.
- Cell diagrams are written with the half-cell undergoing oxidation on the left and the half-cell undergoing reduction on the right, starting with one electrode and finishing with the other.
- The e.m.f. of a cell is the potential difference measured when negligible current flows.
- The standard cell e.m.f. is equal to the difference between the $E^\ominus$ values for the two half-cells concerned.

Oxidant/reductant power

The standard electrode potentials for the zinc and the copper half-cells are −0.76 V and +0.34 V respectively. So zinc metal (with the more negative $E^\ominus$ value) is a more powerful reductant than copper.

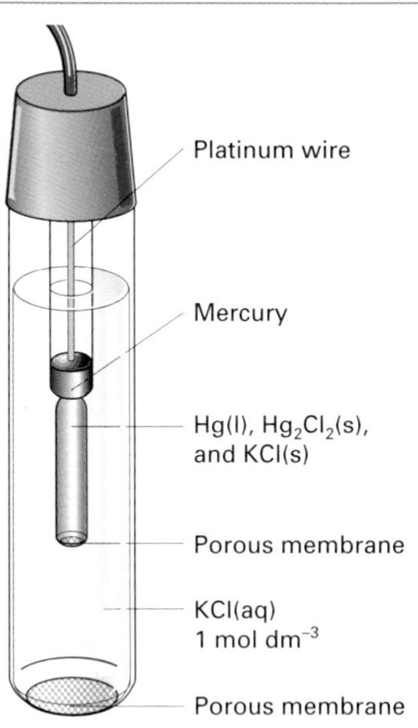

The 'standard calomel electrode' is easier to set up than a standard hydrogen electrode. ('Calomel' is the traditional name for mercury(I) chloride Hg_2Cl_2.) Its $E^\ominus$ value is +0.27 V and it is used as a secondary standard electrode against which to measure other electrode potentials. The redox reaction in the calomel half-cell is $Hg_2Cl_2(s) + 2e^- \rightleftharpoons 2Hg(l) + 2Cl^-(aq)$

Standard cell e.m.f.

The **standard cell e.m.f.** is the difference in the standard electrode potentials of the two half-cells as calculated from the expression:

$E^\ominus$(cell) = $E^\ominus$(right-hand electrode) − $E^\ominus$(left-hand electrode)

'Right' and 'left' signify the reactions as written in the cell diagram. For example, for the cell:

$Zn(s)\,|\,Zn^{2+}(aq)\,||\,Cu^{2+}(aq)\,|\,Cu(s)$

we have

$$E^\ominus(\text{cell}) = E^\ominus(Cu^{2+},Cu) - E^\ominus(Zn^{2+},Zn) = (+0.34\,V) - (-0.76\,V) = +1.10\,V$$

A high-resistance voltmeter connected to this electrochemical cell would indicate this value of e.m.f., as shown in the photo on the left.

Redox and $E^\ominus$ values: a reminder

The half-cell with the more negative ('lower') $E^\ominus$ will reduce the half-cell with the less negative $E^\ominus$.

13.8

OBJECTIVES

- Metal reactivity series and $E^\ominus$ values
- Other half-cells
- $E^\ominus$ values and predictions

STANDARD ELECTRODE POTENTIALS – 2

The *metal reactivity series* can be used to compare the relative reactivities of different metals. This spread starts by comparing the reactivity series with the relative reducing powers of metals according to their $E^\ominus$ values. There is an important distinction that we must draw between the *feasibility* of a chemical reaction and the *rate* at which it happens. The spread concludes with examples that use $E^\ominus$ values to explain which redox reactions happen.

Metal reactivity series and corresponding $E^\ominus$ values.

Metal reactivity series	Increasing reactivity ↑	Increasing reductant strength ↑	Standard electrode potential/V	
K			K	−2.92
Na			Ca	−2.87
Ca			Na	−2.71
Mg			Mg	−2.37
Al			Al	−1.66
Zn			Zn	−0.76
Fe			Fe	−0.44
Pb			Pb	−0.13
			H_2	0
Cu			Cu	+0.34
Ag			Ag	+0.80

Metal reactivity and $E^\ominus$ values

The metal reactivity series lists metals in order of general chemical reactivity. Metals generally react by losing electrons to form positive ions. The more readily a metal loses electrons, the more reactive it is – and the greater its strength as a reductant. Metals higher up the series can reduce the ions of those lower down.

The standard electrode potential of a metal also indicates its strength as a reductant. The more negative the value of the standard electrode potential of a metal, the greater is its strength as a reductant. Hence, you might expect the metal reactivity series and standard electrode potentials to list metals in the *same* order. However, you must remember that the metal reactivity series is based on observing a *range* of reactions, such as displacement reactions between solid metals and solid metal oxides. Standard electrode potentials refer *specifically* to reactions taking place in aqueous solution.

The table (left) compares the metal reactivity series with the **electrochemical series**, which ranks metals according to their standard electrode potentials. The obvious discrepancy is the relative positions of sodium and calcium. Calcium is a stronger reductant than sodium according to $E^\ominus$ values, but the metal reactivity series suggests that calcium is *less* reactive than sodium. This discrepancy arises because calcium reacts at a much slower *rate*, in displacement reactions for example, which in turn happens because *two* electrons must be removed, not one as for sodium.

Note also that aluminium reacts readily with oxygen in the air, forming a layer of stable aluminium oxide on its surface. This impervious oxide coat often causes aluminium to exhibit lower reactivity than its position in the metal reactivity series indicates.

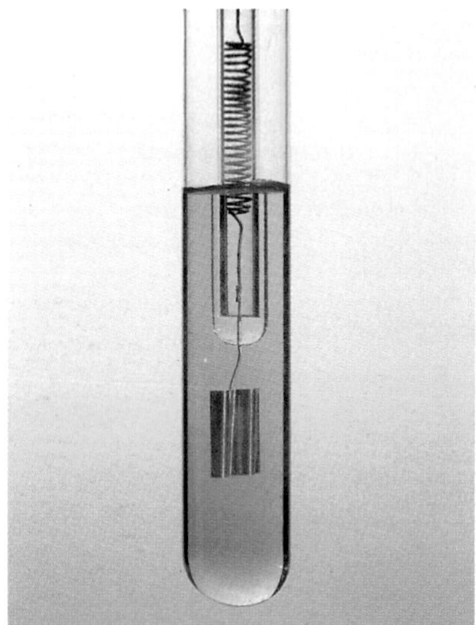

This half-cell consists of a platinum electrode dipping into an aqueous mixture of iron(II) and iron(III) ions.

Displacement reactions involving non-metals

With the exception of the standard hydrogen electrode, all the redox half-cells considered so far have consisted of a metal in contact with an aqueous solution of its ions. The photograph alongside shows a different type of half-cell involving iron ions. The platinum electrode is the point at which electrons enter or leave the system; the electrode does not take part in the redox reaction. Earlier in this chapter we introduced the concept of non-metal displacement reactions, including the reactions between halogens and aqueous solutions of halide ions. A typical example is the reaction between chlorine and bromide ions, spread 13.2:

$$Cl_2(g) + 2Br^-(aq) \rightarrow 2Cl^-(aq) + Br_2(l)$$

The relevant half-equations

$$Cl_2(g) + 2e^- \rightarrow 2Cl^-(aq)$$
$$2Br^-(aq) \rightarrow Br_2(l) + 2e^-$$

indicate that chlorine is reduced and bromide ions are oxidized, i.e. chlorine acts as an oxidant and bromide ion as a reductant. As with metal/metal ion half-cells, each of these reactions can be set up as a redox half-cell.

Halogen/halide standard electrode potentials.

Oxidized species	⇌	Reduced species	$E^\ominus$/V
$F_2(g) + 2e^-$	⇌	$2F^-(aq)$	+2.87
$Cl_2(g) + 2e^-$	⇌	$2Cl^-(aq)$	+1.36
$Br_2(l) + 2e^-$	⇌	$2Br^-(aq)$	+1.07
$I_2(s) + 2e^-$	⇌	$2I^-(aq)$	+0.54

Combining a standard halogen/halide half-cell with a hydrogen electrode allows the standard electrode potential to be measured. Values are shown in the table opposite. As mentioned in the previous spread, the equilibrium for a standard electrode potential is always written with the reduced species on the right:

$$\text{oxidized species} + ne^- \rightleftharpoons \text{reduced species}$$

The oxidizing power of the halogens in aqueous solution decreases in the order $F_2 > Cl_2 > Br_2 > I_2$. The reducing power of the aqueous halide ions decreases in the order $I^- > Br^- > Cl^- > F^-$. See spread 18.3.

Using standard electrode potentials to predict the outcome of redox reactions

Worked example 1

Question: Explain why zinc reacts with dilute hydrochloric acid to form hydrogen gas but copper cannot.

Answer: The balanced chemical equation for the reaction between zinc and hydrochloric acid is

$Zn(s) + 2HCl(aq) \rightarrow H_2(g) + ZnCl_2(aq)$

Because the chloride ions are spectator ions, the ionic equation is

$Zn(s) + 2H^+(aq) \rightarrow H_2(g) + Zn^{2+}(aq)$

The ionic half-equations are

$Zn(s) \rightarrow Zn^{2+}(aq) + 2e^-$

$2H^+(aq) + 2e^- \rightarrow H_2(g)$

The relevant standard electrode potentials are

$Zn^{2+}(aq) + 2e^- \rightleftharpoons Zn(s);\quad E^\ominus = -0.76\,V$

$2H^+(aq) + 2e^- \rightleftharpoons H_2(g);\quad E^\ominus = 0\,V$

Electrons flow from the half-cell of more negative potential to the half-cell of more positive potential, i.e. from Zn^{2+}/Zn to H^+/H_2. Zinc metal is oxidized and hydrogen ions are reduced.

In the case of *copper*, the relevant standard electrode potential is

$Cu^{2+}(aq) + 2e^- \rightleftharpoons Cu(s);\quad E^\ominus = +0.34\,V$

In a copper/hydrogen electrochemical cell, electrons flow in the direction *opposite* to that required for copper metal to reduce aqueous hydrogen ions to hydrogen gas.

Worked example 2

Question: Copper *does* react with concentrated nitric acid, forming nitrogen dioxide (not hydrogen) according to the equation:

$Cu(s) + 4HNO_3(aq) \rightarrow Cu(NO_3)_2(aq) + 2NO_2(g) + 2H_2O(l)$

Explain why.

Answer: The relevant standard electrode potentials are

$Cu^{2+}(aq) + 2e^- \rightleftharpoons Cu(s);\quad E^\ominus = +0.34\,V$

$NO_3^-(aq) + 2H^+(aq) + e^- \rightleftharpoons NO_2(g) + H_2O(l);\quad E^\ominus = +0.80\,V$

Electrons flow from the more negative copper half-cell to the more positive nitrate half-cell. Copper is the reductant and *nitrate ion* is the oxidant.

SUMMARY

- Predictions using standard electrode potentials only apply to redox reactions taking place in aqueous solution.
- Standard electrode potentials may indicate that a reaction is feasible: however, the reaction rate may be so slow as to make the reaction appear not to happen.
- The concentrations of the ions concerned must be close to the standard concentration of $1\,mol\,dm^{-3}$ in order to apply $E^\ominus$ values.

Powerful oxidants and reductants

Powerful oxidants generally have standard electrode potentials more positive than about +1 V. For example, oxygen:

$O_2(g) + 4H^+(aq) + 4e^- \rightleftharpoons 2H_2O(l)$
$E^\ominus = +1.23\,V$

Fluorine is the strongest common oxidant:

$F_2(g) + 2e^- \rightleftharpoons 2F^-(aq);\quad E^\ominus = +2.87\,V$

Powerful reductants generally have standard electrode potentials more negative than about −1 V.

Potassium is the strongest common reductant:

$K^+(aq) + e^- \rightleftharpoons K(s);\quad E^\ominus = -2.92\,V$

The problem of reaction rate

Standard electrode potentials may be used to predict the outcome of redox reactions. However, it is important to note that these predictions do not take account of the *rate* of a reaction. A reaction that is predicted to occur may do so at a rate too slow to observe.

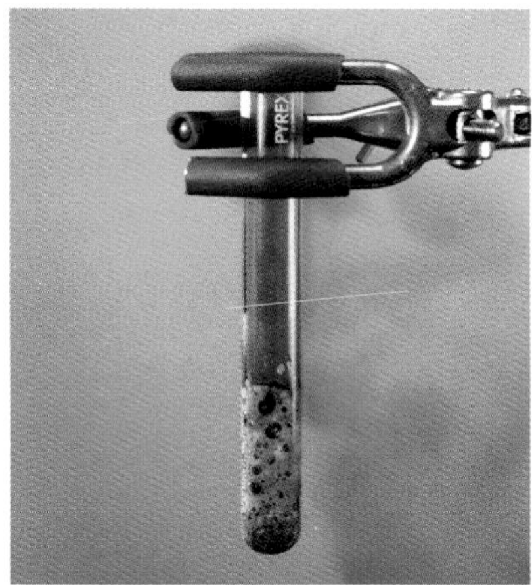

Copper metal reacts with concentrated nitric acid to give brown fumes of nitrogen dioxide.

Non-standard conditions

OBJECTIVES

- Changing concentration
- Nernst equation

Zinc and copper strips immersed in an electrolyte (lemon juice) can generate a potential difference despite *the ionic concentrations being far away from 1 mol dm*$^{-3}$.

All the redox reactions discussed so far have concerned aqueous solutions at 1 mol dm^{-3} concentration. Chemists are always looking for ways of controlling reactions and making use of them. This spread investigates the effect of non-standard conditions on redox equilibria, which may lead to a successful reaction.

Non-standard conditions

Standard electrode potentials may be used to predict whether a redox reaction will occur or not. If a reaction is feasible, then the greater the value of the standard cell e.m.f., the further to the right will be the chemical equilibrium for the overall reaction. When ion concentration is different from 1 mol dm^{-3}, the electrode potential for a cell may be greater or smaller than the standard electrode potential. Equilibrium position may be controlled by a suitable choice of concentrations.

Altering conditions to change the value of the cell e.m.f. will change the value of the equilibrium constant. For example, the power of an oxidant such as manganate(VII) ion is affected by the pH of its solution. The standard electrode potentials for manganate(VII) ion as oxidant are:

$$MnO_4^-(aq) + 8H^+(aq) + 5e^- \rightleftharpoons Mn^{2+}(aq) + 4H_2O(l) \qquad (1)$$

Mn(VII) to Mn(II) $\quad E^\ominus = +1.51$ V

$$MnO_4^-(aq) + 4H^+(aq) + 3e^- \rightleftharpoons MnO_2(s) + 2H_2O(l) \qquad (2)$$

Mn(VII) to Mn(IV) $\quad E^\ominus = +1.69$ V

Many reductants will reduce purple Mn(VII) to almost colourless Mn(II) via equilibrium (1) or to a brown suspension of manganese(IV) oxide via equilibrium (2).

Le Chatelier's principle indicates that, when $[H^+(aq)] < 1$ mol dm^{-3}, both equilibria will shift to the left. The values of their electrode potentials will become less positive and they will become less powerful as oxidants.

The Nernst equation

The potential E of a half-cell (measured against a standard hydrogen electrode) deviates from the standard electrode potential $E^\ominus$ according to the relationship:

$$E = E^\ominus + \frac{(0.059\,\text{V})}{z}\log_{10}\frac{[\text{oxidized species}]}{[\text{reduced species}]}$$

(z is the number of electrons transferred when the oxidized species changes into the reduced species). This relationship is called the **Nernst equation**, after Walther Nernst who developed the relationship. The Nernst equation provides a 'fine tuning' around $E^\ominus$ in a similar way to the Henderson-Hasselbalch equation for buffer solutions, spread 12.11.

The alkene cyclohexene will reduce alkaline manganate(VII) ions to green aqueous manganate(VI) ions. The worked example opposite explains why this happens.

Worked example on using the Nernst equation

Question: What is the electrode potential *at pH 14* for these two reductions of manganate(VII) ion, MnO_4^-:

(a) $MnO_4^-(aq) + e^- = MnO_4^{2-}(aq)$

(b) $MnO_4^-(aq) + 8H^+(aq) + 5e^- = Mn^{2+}(aq) + 4H_2O(l)$

Strategy: Route (a) can be done by inspection: it has the same value as the standard electrode potential, +0.56 V, as no aqueous hydrogen ions are involved in the reduction. For route (b), the Nernst equation must be used as aqueous hydrogen ions are involved in the reduction and the pH is not 0.

Answer: The Nernst equation applied to route (b) gives:

$$E = E^{\ominus} + \frac{(0.059\,\text{V})}{5}\log_{10}[H^+]^8$$

where $E^{\ominus}$ is the standard electrode potential and five electrons are involved. This equation may be manipulated as follows, using the rules for logarithms (toolbox):

$$E = E^{\ominus} + (8/5)(0.059\,\text{V})\log_{10}[H^+]$$

Recognizing $\text{pH} = -\log_{10}[H^+]$ leads to the equation

$$E = E^{\ominus} - (8/5)(0.059\,\text{V})\,\text{pH}$$

At pH 14, the electrode potential is (+1.51 V) – (8/5)(0.059 V) × 14 = +0.19 V.

Note: In *alkaline* solution, manganate(VII) ions can form the manganate(VI) ion, MnO_4^{2-}, which is a green solution. Alkaline manganate(VII) ions are used as a colour test for alkenes. The normal reduction to colourless manganese(II) ions, does *not* occur as it is now much more weakly oxidizing (has a lower electrode potential).

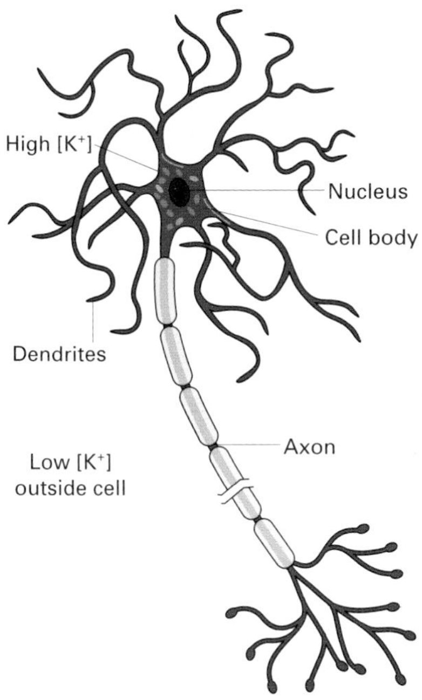

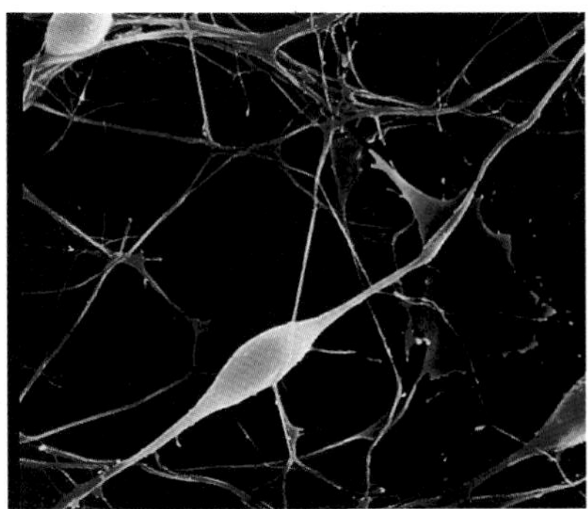

*A **concentration cell** generates a potential from two half-cells containing the same element, but with ions at different concentrations. A biochemical example occurs in nerve cells which have potassium ions at a concentration 25 times greater inside than outside the cell. The potential difference across a nerve cell membrane is about –70 mV. Electrical nerve impulses result from a change in this potential as sodium and potassium ions move across the membrane.*

The Nernst equation and nerve cells

One particularly important application of the Nernst equation arises when the two half-cells contain the same element, but with ions at different concentrations. Such a concentration cell can generate a potential. A biochemical example occurs in nerve cells. There are different concentrations of potassium ions inside and outside the cell. The potential across the nerve cell membrane can be approximated as:

$$E = -(0.059\,\text{V})\log_{10}\left\{\frac{[K^+,\text{ inside}]}{[K^+,\text{ outside}]}\right\}$$

As the potassium concentration is about 25 times larger inside the cell, the membrane *resting potential* can be predicted to be

$$E = -(0.059\text{V})\log_{10} 25 = -82\,\text{mV}$$

This is reasonably close to the actual value of –70 mV.

The Nernst equation and the effect of strong base

Although the concentration of *any* ion will affect the electrode potential, because $E^{\ominus}$ specifically refers to a concentration of 1 mol dm^{-3}, the only ion whose concentration can be altered easily over a wide range is the aqueous hydrogen ion. Its concentration can be changed by 14 orders of magnitude, simply by adding 1 mol dm^{-3} acid and then 1 mol dm^{-3} base.

In general, the presence of strong base causes the *higher* of two oxidation states to be preferentially stabilized, which is particularly important for the transition metals (see chapter 20). This is also relevant to the discussion of rusting in spread 13.12.

SUMMARY

- Standard electrode potentials are measured at pH 0.
- In strongly basic solutions, electrode potentials may be very different from those at pH 0.
- Strong base preferentially stabilizes the higher of two oxidation states.

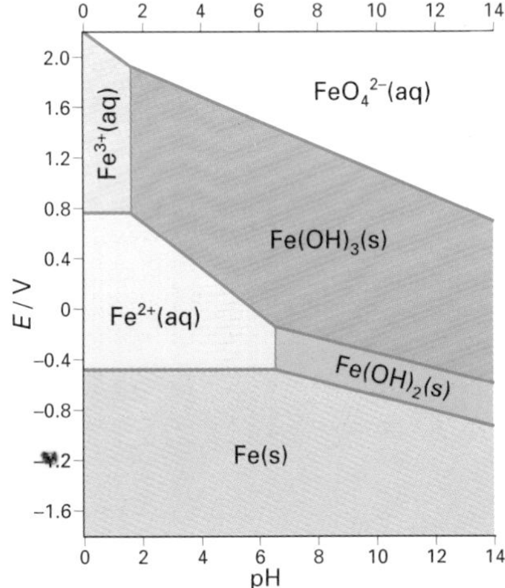

The variation of electrode potential E with changing pH. Note that iron(III) is preferentially stabilized at high pH.

USING REDOX REACTIONS: GALVANIC CELLS

OBJECTIVES

- Primary and secondary cells
- Electrodes and electrolytes
- Anode and cathode reactions

Switch on an electric torch or start a car engine and you are using electrical energy provided by redox reactions inside electrochemical cells. You already know that redox reactions involve a transfer of electrons and that moving electrons constitute an electric current. The everyday devices we usually call 'batteries' depend on these effects. They work by producing energy from chemical reactions inside a convenient portable package.

Galvanic cells

A **galvanic cell** (or **voltaic cell**) is an electrochemical cell used as a source of electric potential difference. Redox reactions inside the cell cause an electric current to flow in an external circuit, where useful work can be done. The first reliable galvanic cell, using the reaction between zinc and copper(II) sulphate, was invented in the early nineteenth century by John Daniell, though his cell was hardly portable. He developed the cell in response to the urgent need for an electricity supply to power the new technology of telegraphy.

Galvanic cells are classified as either primary or secondary cells. Both types of cell consist of two electrodes in contact with a liquid ('wet' cells) or moist paste ('dry' cells), called the electrolyte. Electrons flow in the electrodes and ions flow through the electrolyte. By definition:

- The **anode** is the site of oxidation, i.e. electrons are lost at the anode.
- The **cathode** is the site of reduction, i.e. electrons are gained at the cathode.

A **primary cell** may be used only once; it is thrown away when exhausted. In a chemical context, the term 'exhausted' means that current flow has ceased; the cell is discharged because the chemical contents have reached equilibrium. A common example of a primary cell is an alkaline dry cell used in torches and portable radios.

When a **secondary cell** is exhausted, it may be recharged by passing an electric current through it in the opposite direction to the current flow during discharge. In this manner, the discharge reactions are reversed and the original chemical state of the cell is restored.

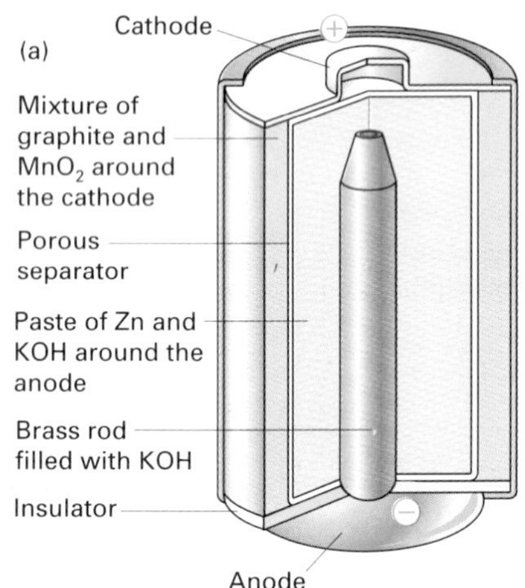

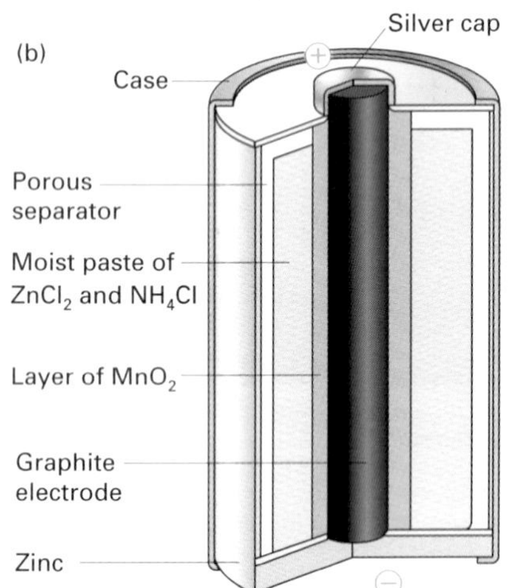

Alkaline dry cells (a) maintain operating voltage better at high current drain than the older type of carbon–zinc dry cells (b) (sometimes called Leclanché cells). Alkaline dry cells are marketed as 'high-power batteries' or as 'longer-lasting'.

The alkaline dry cell

The anode is a paste of powdered zinc with an electrolyte of potassium hydroxide, and the cathode is manganese(IV) oxide in the same electrolyte. The electrode reactions are

Anode: $Zn(s) + 2OH^-(aq) \rightarrow Zn(OH)_2(s) + 2e^-$
Cathode: $MnO_2(s) + 2H_2O(l) + e^- \rightarrow Mn(OH)_3(s) + OH^-(aq)$

This 'alkaline dry cell' produces a voltage of 1.5 V and is commonly known as a 'torch battery'.

The secondary nickel–cadmium cell

The **nickel–cadmium** (**nicad**) **cell** has an anode of cadmium and a cathode of nickel(III) hydroxide, of approximate formula $Ni(OH)_3$. The electrolyte is potassium hydroxide. The electrode reactions are

Anode: $Cd(s) + 2OH^-(aq) \rightarrow Cd(OH)_2(s) + 2e^-$
Cathode: $Ni(OH)_3(s) + e^- \rightarrow Ni(OH)_2(s) + OH^-(aq)$

This type of cell produces a voltage of 1.25 V and is widely used in portable equipment such as lap-top computers and mobile telephones. They may be recharged several hundred times during their life.

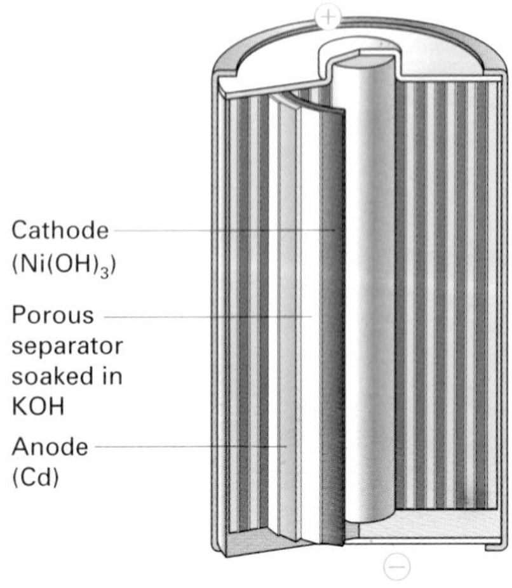

A rechargeable nickel–cadmium cell.

The secondary lead–acid cell

The **lead–acid cell** has an anode of spongy lead covering a lead–antimony alloy grid. The cathode is lead(IV) oxide in pockets on a lead–antimony alloy grid. The electrolyte is aqueous sulphuric acid. The electrode reactions are

Anode: $Pb(s) + SO_4^{2-}(aq) \rightarrow PbSO_4(s) + 2e^-$
Cathode: $PbO_2(s) + 4H^+(aq) + SO_4^{2-}(aq) + 2e^- \rightarrow PbSO_4(s) + 2H_2O(l)$

Typically, six cells are connected in series to produce a **battery** with a total voltage of 12 V. The most common use of these batteries is in cars.

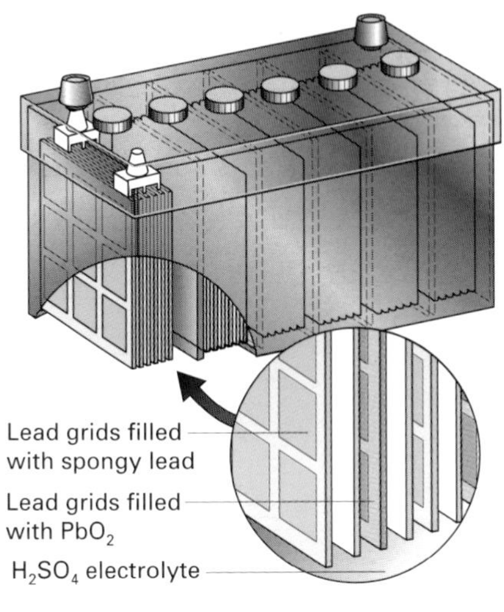

A lead–acid cell. These cells give off oxygen and hydrogen gas during recharging and must be periodically 'topped up' with pure water. 'Maintenance-free' batteries for cars use a calcium–lead alloy, which decomposes the water less rapidly.

Fuel cells

Fuel cells are galvanic cells that oxidize a gaseous fuel to produce an electric current. Fuel cells on-board manned space vehicles consume hydrogen and oxygen, producing electricity and drinking water. Fuel cells operate continuously as long as the reactants are supplied.

The electrode reactions are
Anode: $H_2(g) + 2OH^-(aq) \rightarrow 2H_2O(l) + 2e^-$
Cathode: $O_2(g) + 2H_2O(l) + 4e^- \rightarrow 4OH^-(aq)$

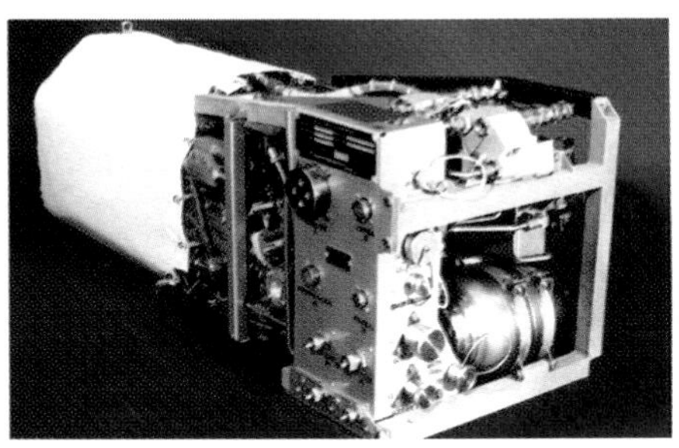

A hydrogen–oxygen fuel cell used in the space program. It is about 70% efficient and is pollution-free.

New developments

A disadvantage of the lead–acid battery is that it is heavy and so delivers little energy per kilogram. When used to power a low-pollution electric town car, lead–acid batteries provide only a limited range. A more suitable alternative for this application is the **sodium–sulphur** battery, which will supply at least four times the energy of other batteries of the same mass. The main problem is that it has to operate at 300 °C.

Another recent innovation is a novel version of the **zinc–air** secondary cell, which was first introduced in the late nineteenth century. The innovation involves replenishing the cell by physically removing the used-up zinc electrodes and fitting new ones by machine. The used electrodes are then recycled. A 650 kg zinc–air battery pack has already managed to produce a range of 185 miles per charge. A conventional lead–acid battery pack weighing 900 kg would be lucky to last about 35 miles.

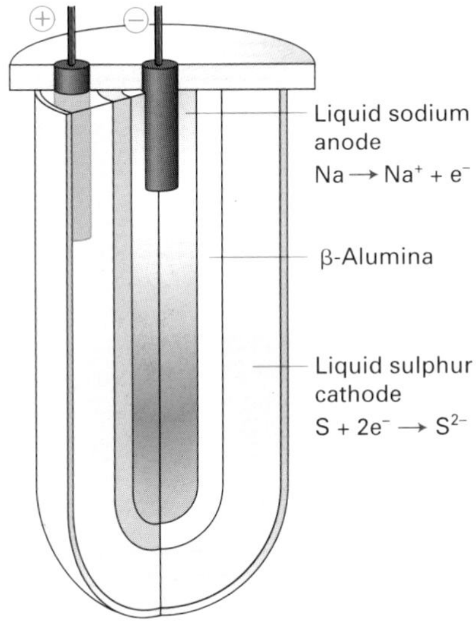

A sodium–sulphur cell. $Na^+(l)$ ions migrate through the β-alumina (a form of Al_2O_3) in the opposite direction to $S^{2-}(l)$ ions.

SUMMARY

- The anode is the site of oxidation.
- The cathode is the site of reduction.

PRACTICE

1. Write chemical equations to represent the anode and cathode reactions taking place in a Daniell cell when it provides an electric current.
2. Explain why it may not be practicable to power electric cars by:
   a rechargeable nickel–cadmium cells,
   b fuel cells.
3. Write chemical equations to represent the anode and cathode reactions during the recharging of a lead–acid cell.
4. Giving appropriate examples, explain and contrast the meanings of the terms: half-cell; cell; battery.

13.11

OBJECTIVES

- Electrolysis of molten substances
- Electrolysis of aqueous solutions
- Electroplating
- The Faraday constant

USING REDOX REACTIONS: ELECTROLYTIC CELLS

A galvanic cell uses chemical reactions to generate electricity, but an electrolytic cell does the opposite. An electrolytic cell uses electricity to cause chemical change. **Electrolysis** uses electrical energy to drive a chemical reaction in a direction opposite to that in which it naturally proceeds. As you will see, the uses of electrolytic cells include decomposing solutions and molten substances and the purification and plating of metals.

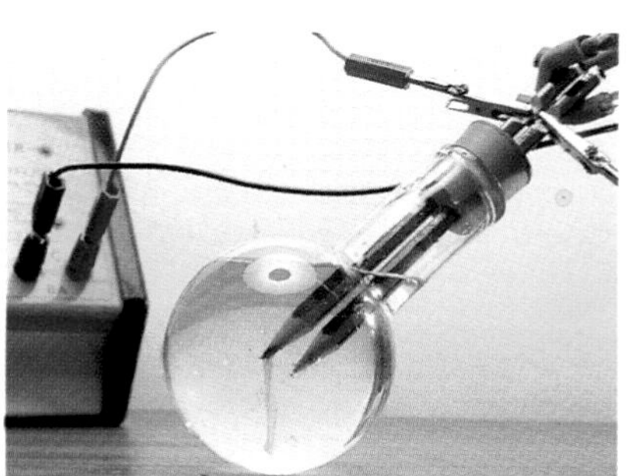

Electrolysis of aqueous potassium iodide produces iodine and hydrogen gas.

The principles of electrolytic cells

An **electrolytic cell** consists of two electrodes immersed in an electrolyte. The **electrolyte** may be either a molten ionic substance or a solution of an ionic substance in water. In either case, the electrolyte will contain positive and negative ions that are free to move. The electrodes are connected to a source of e.m.f., which removes electrons from one electrode and transfers them to the other electrode, via the external circuit. One electrode (the **anode**) bears a *positive* electric charge. The other electrode (the **cathode**) bears a *negative* electric charge.

Positively charged ions from the electrolyte are attracted towards the negatively charged cathode. Positive ions are therefore called **cations** because they are attracted to the cathode. Negatively charged ions (called **anions**) from the electrolyte are attracted towards the positively charged anode. Electron transfer reactions (that is, reduction at the cathode and oxidation at the anode) take place when these ions reach the electrode surfaces. In summary:

- Reduction occurs at the cathode where cations gain electrons from the cathode.
- Oxidation occurs at the anode where anions lose electrons to the anode.

The reactions that take place during electrolysis depend on a number of factors including:

- the state of the electrolyte;
- the concentration of the solution;
- the positions of the elements involved in the electrochemical series.

Cathodes

Note that the *sign* of the cathode is *opposite* in an electrolytic cell to that in a galvanic cell. It is the site of reduction in both cases.

Practical points – 1

The voltage applied to the cell must be sufficiently large to drive a current through it *against* the natural cell e.m.f. generated by the substances concerned. The reactions

$Na^+(l) + e^- \rightarrow Na(l)$

$2Cl^-(l) \rightarrow Cl_2(g) + 2e^-$

form the basis of the industrial extraction of sodium metal and chlorine gas from molten sodium chloride, spread 16.1.

The electrolysis of a molten substance

When an ionic solid is melted, its ions are free to move in the liquid. We shall consider sodium chloride as a typical example. Molten sodium chloride produces *two* ionic species, $Na^+(l)$ and $Cl^-(l)$. In an electrolytic cell, the $Na^+(l)$ cations are reduced at the cathode to produce molten sodium metal:

$$Na^+(l) + e^- \rightarrow Na(l)$$

The $Cl^-(l)$ anions are oxidized at the anode to produce chlorine gas:

$$2Cl^-(l) \rightarrow Cl_2(g) + 2e^-$$

The electrolysis of an aqueous solution

When an ionic solid dissolves in water, its aqueous ions are free to move. At the same time, water ionizes partially to provide a small concentration of aqueous hydrogen and hydroxide ions:

$$H_2O(l) \rightleftharpoons H^+(aq) + OH^-(aq)$$

We shall continue with sodium chloride as our example. When sodium chloride dissolves in water, it produces $Na^+(aq)$ and $Cl^-(aq)$ ions. Water provides $H^+(aq)$ and $OH^-(aq)$ ions. Aqueous sodium chloride therefore contains a total of *four* ionic species. Which two of these will react (be **discharged**) to form products at the electrodes?

Standard electrode potentials.

Oxidized species	⇌	Reduced species	$E^\ominus/V$
$2H^+(aq) + 2e^-$	⇌	$H_2(g)$	0
$Na^+(aq) + e^-$	⇌	$Na(s)$	−2.71
$O_2(g) + 4H^+(aq) + 4e^-$	⇌	$2H_2O(l)$	+1.23
$Cl_2(g) + 2e^-$	⇌	$2Cl^-(aq)$	+1.36

Considering the anions, chloride ion is discharged rather then hydroxide ion: chlorine gas, *not* oxygen, is usually evolved at the anode. The main reason for this result is that the concentration of chloride ions is far greater than usual. The industrial electrolysis of brine uses *saturated* aqueous sodium chloride. The high concentration of chloride ion causes the actual electrode potentials of Cl^- and OH^- to become very similar.

Now consider the cations. A list of standard electrode potentials shows that $H^+(aq)$ is a more powerful oxidant than $Na^+(aq)$, and so will be discharged (reduced) at the cathode as $H_2(g)$. In other words, hydrogen ions are more easily reduced than sodium ions, which remain in solution.

Practical points – 2

As electrolysis proceeds, aqueous hydrogen ions are discharged and hydroxide ions remain in solution. Water dissociates to maintain the value of K_w, the ionic product of water. The products of the electrolysis of aqueous sodium chloride are therefore hydrogen gas, chlorine gas, and aqueous sodium hydroxide, spread 18.2.

Electroplating and electrolytic purification

A metal that has a *positive* standard electrode potential is more readily reduced than hydrogen, and so will be discharged at the cathode in preference to hydrogen. One such metal is copper. In an electrolysis cell with an electrolyte of copper(II) ions, the cathode becomes plated with a layer of copper metal:

$$\text{Cathode:} \quad Cu^{2+}(aq) + 2e^- \rightarrow Cu(s)$$

If a copper anode is used, it undergoes the following oxidation:

$$\text{Anode:} \quad Cu(s) \rightarrow Cu^{2+}(aq) + 2e^-$$

(The anode is termed a *soluble anode*.) As a result, the concentration of copper(II) ions in the solution remains constant. This reaction is the basis of copper-plating and the industrial purification of copper. Using aqueous copper(II) sulphate as the electrolyte, an impure copper anode dissolves while pure copper plates onto the cathode. Impurities in the anode do not dissolve, but drop down to form a layer of 'anode sludge' at the bottom of the cell.

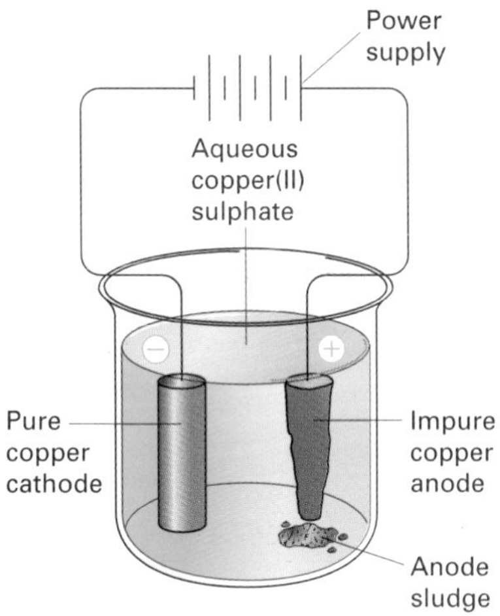

Extremely pure copper is required for electricity cables and water pipes. Precious metals such as gold and platinum are recovered from the 'anode sludge'.

The Faraday constant

The Faraday constant F is the magnitude of the charge per mole of electrons. It is expressed in coulombs per mole ($C\,mol^{-1}$), where one coulomb (1 C) is the total charge carried by one ampere (1 A) of electric current flowing for one second (1 s). It forms the link between the quantity of electricity and the amount in moles of substance discharged. The Faraday constant can be readily calculated by multiplying the charge e on a single electron by the number of electrons per mole L (the Avogadro constant):

$$F = eL = (1.602 \times 10^{-19}\,C) \times (6.022 \times 10^{23}\,mol^{-1})$$
$$= 96\,500\,C\,mol^{-1} \text{ (3 sig. figs)}$$

The Faraday constant may be used to calculate the charge required to deposit a particular mass of substance during electrolysis, as shown in the box (right).

How much metal?

We can calculate the mass of metal deposited during electrolysis by using the Faraday constant.

For example, 1 mol of silver Ag has a mass of 108 g. Silver ions $Ag^+(aq)$ discharge at the cathode during electrolysis:

$Ag^+(aq) + e^- \rightarrow Ag(s)$

So 96 500 C deposit 108 g of silver.

As a second example, 1 mol of copper Cu has a mass of 63.5 g. Copper(II) ions $Cu^{2+}(aq)$ discharge at the cathode during electrolysis:

$Cu^{2+}(aq) + 2e^- \rightarrow Cu(s)$

But now we need two moles of electrons per mole of Cu^{2+} ions. Therefore, we need $2 \times 96\,500$ C to deposit 63.5 g of copper.

SUMMARY

The products obtained during electrolysis depend on a number of factors, including:

- the state of the electrolyte – molten or aqueous;
- the relative concentrations of the ions in an aqueous electrolyte;
- the relative values of the electrode potentials that apply to the conditions of the electrolysis cell.

PRACTICE

1 The anode and cathode in an electrolytic cell are made from copper; the electrolyte is aqueous copper(II) sulphate. What mass of copper will be transferred if a current of 0.5 A flows for 15 min?

13.12

OBJECTIVES

- Cause of rusting
- Mechanism of rusting
- Prevention of rusting

The hull of the Titanic has rusted since it sank in 1912.

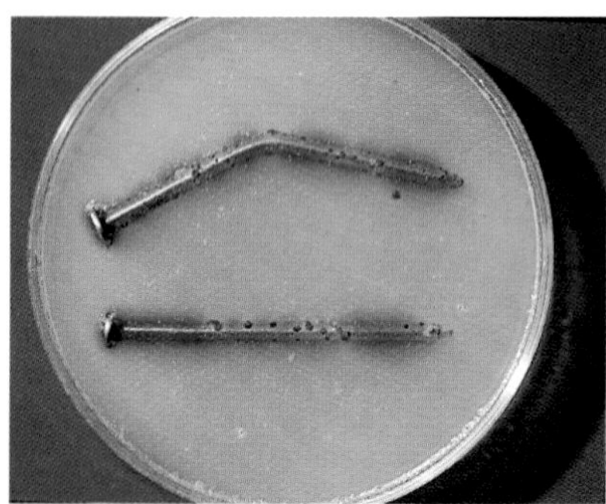
Nails placed in 'ferroxyl' indicator. 'Ferroxyl' indicator is a mixture of aqueous potassium hexacyanoferrate(III), which gives a blue colour with iron(II) ions, spread 20.11, and phenolphthalein, which indicates the presence of hydroxyl ions by turning pink in basic solution, spread 12.9.

RUSTING

One of the most important redox reactions is the corrosion or rusting of iron. It is estimated that this costs the UK in excess of £5 billion each year. Iron and steel objects have a natural tendency to rust. We first need to understand why rusting occurs before we can suggest strategies for reducing the rate of rusting.

The cause of rusting

Rusting can be predicted on the basis of standard electrode potentials. Oxygen has a standard electrode potential for the reaction

$$O_2(g) + 4H^+(aq) + 4e^- \rightarrow 2H_2O(l)$$

of $E^\ominus = +1.23$ V, spread 13.8; oxygen is a strong oxidant. Iron has a standard electrode potential for

$$Fe^{2+}(aq) + 2e^- \rightarrow Fe(s)$$

of $E^\ominus = -0.44$ V; iron is a moderately strong reductant. So oxygen should oxidize iron in aqueous solution.

It is well known that two of the requirements for rusting are the presence of water and of oxygen. An approximate equation describing rusting is:

$$4Fe(s) + 3O_2(g) + 2xH_2O(l) \rightarrow 2Fe_2O_3.xH_2O(s)$$

Notice how the exact number of water molecules present in rust is uncertain.

The mechanism of rusting

We can examine the mechanism of rusting in more detail. A steel nail which has a drop of 'ferroxyl' indicator added shows two important aspects of the reaction.

A blue mass forms, indicating that iron(II) ions are present. This *anodic process* is the oxidation of iron:

$$Fe(s) \rightarrow Fe^{2+}(aq) + 2e^-$$

The pink colour indicates that hydroxyl ions are present. This *cathodic process* is the reduction of oxygen:

$$O_2(g) + 2H_2O(l) + 4e^- \rightarrow 4OH^-(aq)$$

Combining these two half-equations, multiplying the first by two, we find

$$2Fe(s) + O_2(g) + 2H_2O(l) \rightarrow 2Fe^{2+}(aq) + 4OH^-(aq)$$

The iron(II) hydroxide so formed is then rapidly oxidized under basic conditions, see spreads 13.9 and 20.5, to red-brown hydrated iron(III) oxide, best represented by the approximate formula $Fe_2O_3.xH_2O$. The rust flakes off the surface (partly because rust has a lower density than iron). This exposes more surface and rusting continues.

Prevention of rusting

Iron and steel objects can be protected against rusting in a variety of ways. Painting would be perfectly adequate, as long as the surface is not damaged. In the case of a car, this is extremely unlikely to be the case once stone chips occur. Rusting can occur *anywhere* under the paint once the surface is damaged as the metal surface is a conductor and the electrons released by iron can travel through the rest of the car to the hole, where oxygen is then reduced.

A more intelligent solution results from consulting the table on spread 13.7. A metal with a *more negative* standard electrode potential will give up its electrons more readily than iron does. So if a more strongly reducing metal is attached to the iron, that protective metal will be oxidized in place of the iron. The protective metal is termed a **sacrificial anode**. To protect an object as large as a ship, pieces of magnesium ($E^\ominus = -2.37$ V) are attached to the hull. Replacement blocks are then substituted when the protective metal becomes depleted.

The same principle is applied to protecting cars using zinc ($E^{\ominus}$ = –0.76 V) in a process called **galvanizing**. Car manufacturers that use 100 per cent galvanized bodywork can offer longer warranties against body corrosion. Note that this slows the rate of corrosion, but does not prevent the iron from corroding once the zinc has been exhausted and so it does not protect indefinitely. Actually the situation is rather less simple than it appears at first sight. Zinc ions *do* go into solution in place of iron ions; aqueous zinc ions are colourless, as explained in spread 20.11, and escape visual detection: the car actually still disintegrates, only its decay is less easily seen!

Scanning electron micrograph of resprayed paint (blue) poorly bonded to the original paint of a rusty car.

Making rusting more severe

Standard electrode potentials can also help us understand how rusting can be made more severe. The rate of rusting is accelerated if iron is in contact with a metal with a less negative standard electrode potential, such as tin ($E^{\ominus}$ = –0.14 V) or copper ($E^{\ominus}$ = +0.34 V). Tin-plated cans rust very quickly when opened, which explains why food should be removed rapidly (aluminium cans do not suffer in the same way). Gustav Eiffel, the designer of the Statue of Liberty in New York harbour, was aware that his support structure, built of iron, would rust if it contacted the copper cladding. He attempted to prevent this by placing asbestos pads between the metals. Unfortunately, contact anywhere along the structure can cause corrosion and Eiffel's original iron framework has had to be completely replaced.

A similar reaction can be demonstrated in the laboratory by wrapping a copper wire around a piece of zinc. When placed in acid, bubbles of hydrogen can be seen on the copper as well as on the zinc. It is well known that copper metal itself does not reduce hydrogen ions, spread 13.8. The electrons required for the reduction have come from the zinc; they are available at the copper as it is in electrical contact. The solution remains colourless when all the zinc has reacted, as aqueous zinc ions are colourless.

Rusting occurs faster when salt is present, which happens in winter as salt is spread on roads to try to keep them free from ice. The salt increases the conductivity of the water, which is the limiting factor in the rate of rusting as water's conductivity is much lower than that of the metal with which it is in contact.

SUMMARY

- Iron rusts in the presence of water and oxygen.
- The anodic process is the oxidation of iron: $Fe(s) \rightarrow Fe^{2+}(aq) + 2e^-$
- Iron can be protected using a sacrificial anode; zinc is used in galvanizing.
- Rusting is more severe with salt present.

PRACTICE

1 Describe the anodic and cathodic process that occur during rusting.

2 How can you slow down the rate of rusting? Can you stop it permanently.

13.13

Principles of metal extraction

OBJECTIVES

- Carbon reduction
- Electrolysis
- Batch processes

The ideas introduced in this chapter can be used to understand the different extraction techniques used to win metals from their ores. The most widely applicable method is electrolysis; this is also the most expensive. Hence, this is the preferred option in industry only if it is not possible to extract the metal more cheaply by other methods. In this section we will examine the reasons why the various techniques can be used.

The least reactive metals

Some metals have been used since prehistory. They are the ones that are the least reactive (have the most positive standard electrode potentials). A famous example is gold. Because it is so unreactive, it exists in the environment 'native', which means uncombined with another element. In the previous two hundred years there have been a number of 'gold rushes', as for example in 1849 in California. If fortunate, a prospector could literally pick up a piece of gold. Hence no chemical techniques need to be employed to extract gold.

Gold has been prized for millennia and many of the most beautiful artefacts handed down from previous generations have been made of gold. One example is the saltcellar designed by Benvenuto Cellini.

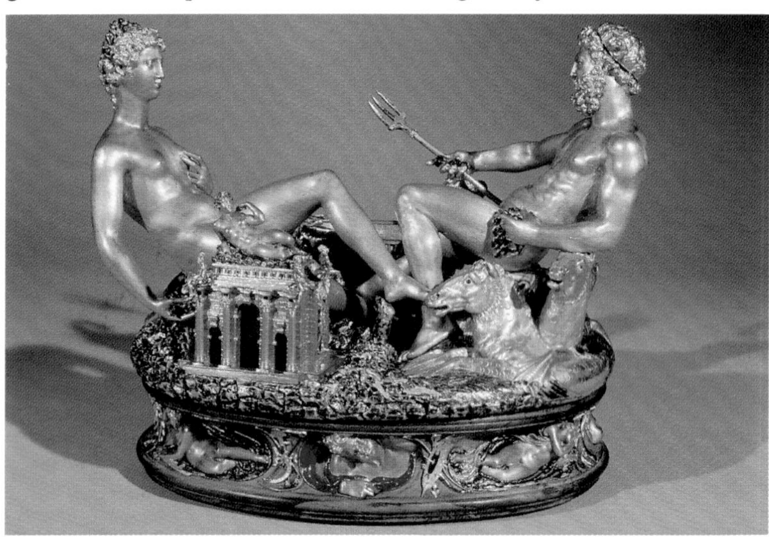

This magnificent saltcellar was made by Benvenuto Cellini in the sixteenth century for King Francis I of France.

The fairly reactive metals

When the metal is rather more reactive than gold, it will be found in the environment combined with other elements, most commonly with oxygen. The oxide will then need to be converted to the element. As has been explained in this chapter, conversion of an oxide to the element involves reduction. The choice of reductant needs to be carefully considered. Cost is a very significant factor and crucial for industrial success. The cheapest widely available reductant is the element carbon.

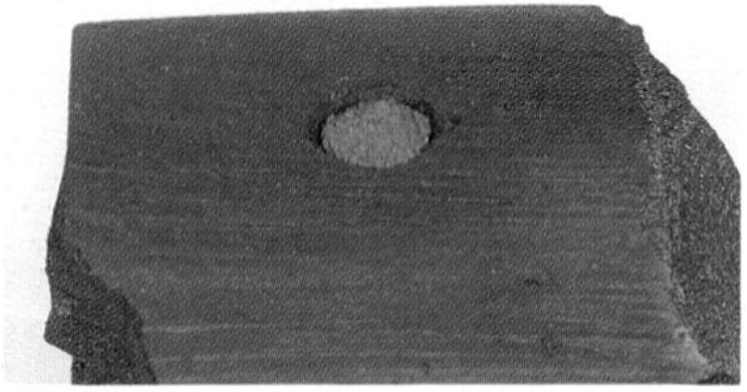

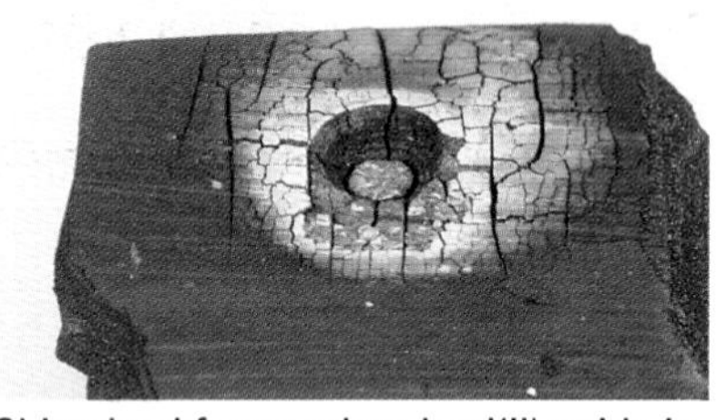

Shiny lead forms when lead(II) oxide is heated with carbon.

In the photograph alongside, lead(II) oxide is shown having been heated with carbon; shiny lead may be seen in places throughout the hole in the block. The equation for the reaction is

$$PbO(s) + C(s) = Pb(s) + CO(g)$$

Iron has been extracted from its oxide ore haematite for over two thousand years by heating with carbon in a blast furnace. The temperature is crucial to the extraction process; the next chapter explains why the extraction requires high temperatures and also introduces the idea that both carbon and carbon monoxide (formed from carbon in the furnace) can be effective reductants. Iron is frequently converted into steel (spread 20.2).

Andrew Carnegie became one of the richest people in the world at the turn of the twentieth century by gaining effective control of steel manufacture in the US. He built Carnegie Hall, New York, famous for its concerts and recitals.

The most reactive metals

Iron is the most familiar metal in everyday life for two reasons. The extraction technique is relatively inexpensive and the metal is very abundant in nature. However, there is one metal which is even more abundant, aluminium. Despite its abundance, elemental aluminium was not made until the nineteenth century because the temperature needed for extraction by carbon is uneconomically high, as explained in spread 14.6.

The extraction of aluminium, and that of other very reactive metals such as sodium and potassium, had to wait for a new technological advance. This was the discovery of electrolysis, which itself relied on the batteries first made around 1800.

Sodium and potassium proved easier to extract than aluminium. The principles of electrolysis require that the electrolyte is either molten or in solution (as discussed in a previous spread). The problem with aluminium is that its ore bauxite (hydrated aluminium oxide) has an enormously high melting point (over 2000 °C), thus preventing electrolysis at an economical temperature. Sodium chloride on the other hand melts at 801 °C, so its extraction is easier than that of aluminium.

The technological problems involved in the electrolysis of aluminium were overcome by Charles Hall, as described in spread 19.2. Like Carnegie, chemical manufacture made Hall extremely rich. As with iron manufacture the process is continuous, a typical Hall cell producing a little over a tonne of aluminium per day.

Year	1852	1855	1858	1888	1895	1900	1950
Price of aluminium metal / $ per kg	1200	250	25	11.5	1.15	0.73	0.40
		→| Introduction of $Na/AlCl_3$ process		→| Introduction of Hall electrolysis			

The price of aluminium per kilogram fell significantly when the Hall process was introduced in the 1880s. The other major drop occurred in 1855 when it was first extracted in a batch process using sodium metal reducing aluminium chloride. Aluminium is now the second most widely used metal, after iron.

Batch processes

Metals required on a less extravagant scale than iron and aluminium do not need to be manufactured continuously. They can be made when needed in a **batch process**, the name being derived from the bread produced in a single baking in a baker's oven.

For example, aluminium can be used to extract chromium (spread 20.3); the driving force for the process is the extremely high lattice energy of aluminium oxide. The technique is very similar to that of the Thermit process shown in spread 3.1.

Similarly, magnesium can be used to extract titanium (spread 20.3). Titanium is the ninth most abundant element in the environment. Yet the fact that it is extracted in a batch process using a metal that itself must be extracted using the expensive option of electrolysis makes titanium a rare and prized metal. The monument commemorating the exploration of space erected in Moscow is made from titanium.

To celebrate their achievement of the first successful space flight by Yuri Gagarin and their subsequent exploration of space, the Russians built this monument out of titanium.

SUMMARY

- The least reactive metals, such as gold, are found 'native'.
- The fairly reactive metals, such as iron, are extracted by carbon reduction at high temperatures.
- The most reactive metals are extracted by electrolysis (as for aluminium) or by using an even more reactive metal, in a batch process (as for titanium).

PRACTICE

1 Explain the principles behind the extraction of metals.

PRACTICE EXAM QUESTIONS

1 a In terms of transfer of electrons, what is meant by the term *reduction*? [1]

b Name the electrode relative to which standard electrode potentials are measured, and give one reason why this electrode is not often used in experimental determinations of standard electrode potentials. [2]

c In both of the overall redox reactions given below, the reaction can be separated into two redox half-equations. In each case, identify the two redox half-equations, and state which species is being reduced.

i $2Ag^+(aq) + Cu(s) \rightarrow 2Ag(s) + Cu^{2+}(aq)$

ii $5S_2O_8^{2-}(aq) + 2Mn^{2+}(aq) + 8H_2O(l) \rightarrow$
$10SO_4^{2-}(aq) + 2MnO_4^-(aq) + 16H^+(aq)$ [6]
AQA (NEAB) 1997

2 a Standard electrode potentials, $E^\ominus$, are measured relative to a standard reference electrode. What is the standard reference electrode and what is its potential? [2]

b State three conditions which must apply when values of $E^\ominus$ are being determined. [3]

c What is the function of a *salt bridge*, and what might it contain? [2]

d What is meant by the *Electrochemical Series*? [2]

e Consider the following standard electrode potentials.

$Fe^{2+}(aq) + 2e^- \rightarrow Fe(s)$ $E^\ominus/V = -0.44$

$Zn^{2+}(aq) + 2e^- \rightarrow Zn(s)$ $E^\ominus/V = -0.76$

State which species is reduced if these two half-cells are joined together in an electrochemical cell. Explain your answer. [3]
AQA (NEAB) 1996

3 Use the standard potentials in the list below, as appropriate, to answer the questions that follow.

	$E^\ominus$/V
$MnO_4^-(aq) + 8H^+(aq) + 5e^- \rightarrow Mn^{2+}(aq) + 4H_2O(l)$	+1.51
$Cl_2(g) + 2e^- \rightarrow 2Cl^-(aq)$	+1.36
$Cr_2O_7^{2-}(aq) + 14H^+(aq) + 6e^- \rightarrow 2Cr^{3+}(aq) + 7H_2O(l)$	+1.33
$Fe^{3+}(aq) + e^- \rightarrow Fe^{2+}(aq)$	+0.78
$Fe^{3+}(aq) + 3e^- \rightarrow Fe(s)$	−0.04
$Fe^{2+}(aq) + 2e^- \rightarrow Fe(s)$	−0.44

a The two half-cells above which involve metallic iron are joined to produce an electrochemical cell. Using standard notation, give the conventional representation for this cell, calculate its standard potential, and write an equation for the spontaneous reaction that occurs. [6]

b Potassium manganate(VII) and potassium dichromate(VI) are both strong oxidizing agents. Which of the two is **not** used for the quantitative estimation of iron(II) ions in a solution of iron(II) chloride? Use data from the table to justify your choice. [3]

c Equimolar solutions of acidified potassium manganate(VII), manganese(II) sulphate, potassium dichromate(VI) and chromium(III) sulphate are mixed and allowed to come to equilibrium.

i State which ion is oxidised and which is reduced.

ii Use half-equations to construct the equation for the overall reaction that occurs. [5]
AQA (NEAB) 1998

4 a Select **three** different general methods for the extraction of metals. For **each** method you select, state the starting materials, the conditions used and give one example of a metal extracted by this method. [9]

b i Indicate the essential chemistry involved in the removal of carbon from impure iron in the manufacture of steel.

ii Give **two** reasons why steel is less expensive to produce than titanium.

iii Give **one** reason why titanium is used for certain applications despite the extra cost of this metal as compared to steel.
AQA (NEAB) [5]

5 The apparatus below was used to measure the **standard** electrode potential of the Fe/Fe^{3+} electrode, copper being the positive electrode.

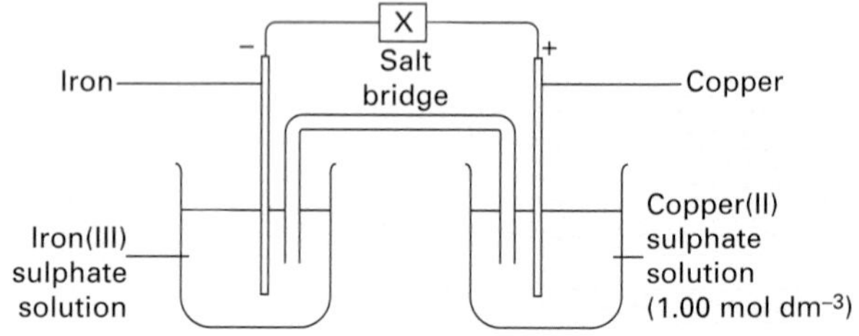

a i Name the instrument which could be used at **X** to measure the e.m.f. of the cell. Indicate its main characteristic.

ii What is the concentration of the Fe^{3+} ions in the iron(III) sulphate solution? [3]

b i What is the function of the salt bridge?

ii What might it contain?

iii Why is the salt bridge used and not a piece of wire? [3]

c i The e.m.f. of the cell is +0.38 V. Given that the standard electrode potential of the Cu^{2+}/Cu electrode is +0.34 V, calculate the standard electrode potential of the Fe^{3+}/Fe electrode and explain your reasoning.

ii Give the conventional representation of the cell.

iii Write an equation, with state symbols, to represent the cell reaction. [7]

d Use the data below to explain concisely why zinc is used in preference to tin for coating steel which is used to manufacture cars. [3]

	$E^\ominus$/V
$Sn^{2+}(aq) + 2e^- \rightleftharpoons Sn(s)$	−0.14
$Fe^{2+}(aq) + 2e^- \rightleftharpoons Fe(s)$	0.44
$Zn^{2+}(aq) + 2e^- \rightleftharpoons Zn(s)$	−0.76

EDEXCEL 1996

6 A student set up 4 standard half-cells each containing one of the metals A, B, C and D. These half-cells were then used to make different electrochemical cells. The table below shows the standard cell potential, $E^\ominus_{cell}$, and the positive terminal of each electrochemical cell.

Cell	Metals used	$E^\ominus_{cell}$ / V	Positive terminal
1	**A** and **B**	+1.10	**B**
2	**B** and **C**	+0.46	**C**
3	**B** and **D**	+0.47	**B**

a Draw a labelled diagram of cell 1. [3]

b Deduce the order of reactivity of the metals **A, B, C** and **D**. [3]

c Outline a method the student may have used to identify the positive terminal. [1]

d Calculate the standard cell potential of a cell made from the half-cells containing **A** and **D**. [1]
OCR (UCLES) 1998

7 This question concerns the lead-acid battery.

The following data will be required.

	$E^\ominus$/V
$PbO_2(s) + 4H^+(aq) + SO_4^{2-}(aq) + 2e^- \rightleftharpoons PbSO_4(s) + 2H_2O(l)$	+1.69
$PbSO_4(s) + 2e^- \rightleftharpoons SO_4^{2-}(aq) + Pb(s)$	−0.36

a The lead-acid battery is one form of storage cell. What substance is used for:

i the negative pole; [1]

ii the positive pole; [1]

iii the electrolyte. [1]

b Give the equation for the overall cell reaction during discharge. [2]

c Calculate the e.m.f. of the cell. [2]

d A storage cell, as used in the lead-acid battery, is a simple cell in which the reactions are reversible i.e. once the chemicals have been used up they can be re-formed.

Write an equation for the chemical reaction which occurs on charging. [1]

e Give one disadvantage of such batteries for use in cars. [1]

f **i** State the essential requirement for the rusting of iron in water. [1]

ii Explain why corrosion of iron results in deep pitting of the metal surface. [1]

iii Explain why sheet iron which has been fabricated to a particular shape, sometimes under high pressure, is more likely to corrode than a single strip of pure iron. [2]

iv An underground iron pipe is less likely to corrode if bonded at intervals to magnesium stakes. Give a reason for this. Explain why aluminium would be a poor substitute for the magnesium. [2]
EDEXCEL 1998

8 Aluminium/air electrochemical cells can be used to power golf trolleys and invalid carriages. One electrode is made of aluminium while the other is made by bubbling air through an inert porous material. The electrolyte is usually sodium hydroxide solution. The equations for the reactions taking place at the electrodes are:

I $Al(s) + 3OH^-(aq) \rightarrow Al(OH)_3(s) + 3e^-$

II $O_2(g) + 2H_2O(l) + 4e^- \rightarrow 4OH^-(aq)$

a Which electrode acts as the cathode of the cell? [1]

b Write an equation for the overall cell reaction. [1]

c Suggest one reason why the efficiency of the cell may be reduced over a period of time. [1]
EDEXCEL 1999

9 **a** Explain why each of the following reactions can be classified as redox processes. Give a balanced equation for each reaction.

i chlorine reacting with aqueous potassium iodide;

ii chlorine reacting with hydrogen;

iii iron(II) ions reacting with acidified aqueous manganate(VII) ions. [5]

b **i** Explain why electrolysis is a redox process.

ii Describe, including the electrode reactions, the industrial extraction of aluminium from purified aluminium oxide. [7]
OCR (UCLES) 1999 *(See also Chapters 18 and 19)*

14 Spontaneous change towards equilibrium

Stir a spoonful of sugar into a cup of coffee and the solid sugar *spontaneously* dissolves in the solution. Mix together aqueous silver ions and aqueous iodide ions and a yellow precipitate of silver iodide *spontaneously* forms. The Universe is full of spontaneous changes of this sort. Bicycles roll down hills, hot coffee cools down, our bodies age, and the steel bodies of motor cars rust slowly back to the ore from which the iron was originally extracted. **Spontaneous changes** are changes that have a natural tendency to occur. The question should now arise in your mind: 'Yes: but what makes spontaneous changes happen?' Developing an answer to this question is the aim of this chapter. At its end you should be able to complete the sentence: 'Spontaneous changes happen because ....'

Spontaneity and spreading

14.1

OBJECTIVES

- System and surroundings
- Criterion for spontaneous change

The concept of *stability* is a useful point from which to start this topic. A stable substance, or mixture of substances, is one that does not change its structure or composition. Think about stirring sugar into your coffee. Kept in isolation, sugar and water are both *stable* substances. Each compound will remain unchanged for an indefinite period of time. Pouring sugar into water makes an *unstable* system. The state of the system spontaneously changes to make a solution. When the solution has formed, the system is more stable. **Spontaneous change**, change that has a natural tendency to occur, causes a system to move from a less stable state to a more stable state. So what *causes* spontaneous change?

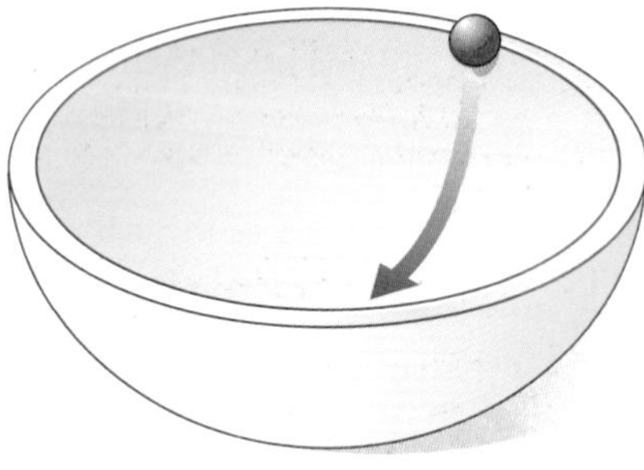

When it is at the rim, the ball has minimum kinetic energy and maximum potential energy. When it is at the bottom of the bowl, the ball has maximum kinetic energy and minimum potential energy. In the absence of friction and air resistance, this system does not *tend towards the position of minimum potential energy.*

Spontaneous change and energy

The concept of energy change is often used to explain things that happen in the world. For example, think of a frictionless ball sliding down the inside edge of a large frictionless bowl. The ball travels down to the bottom of the bowl and up the opposite side. It is tempting to say that the ball is in an unstable state at the rim, and that it is more stable when it has fallen to the point of lowest potential energy, at the bottom of the bowl. However, there is no overall energy change happening in this theoretical system because *the total energy of the ball remains constant*. In the absence of friction, the ball will continue to oscillate and its total energy remains constant.

A real ball oscillating in a real bowl *does* spontaneously reach a final

The direction of spontaneous change. A block of hot metal cools to the temperature of its surroundings. A block that is at the same temperature as its surroundings does not spontaneously become hotter.

System and surroundings: a reminder

Chemical changes and physical changes of state are accompanied by changes in energy. The substances undergoing the change are called 'the system'; everything else outside the system is called 'the surroundings'. An energy change in the system causes the temperature of the system to change. If the system and the surroundings are in contact, heat then flows between the system and the surroundings.

state of minimum potential energy at the bottom of the bowl. However, the reason the ball settles at the bottom is not because that is the system's state of minimum potential energy. It is more accurate to say that friction causes *energy to spread out* from the ball. Kinetic and potential energy that were concentrated in the ball have *spread out* as heat into the ball, into the bowl, and into the surrounding air.

Pendulums

A frictionless pendulum swinging in a vacuum is another example of a theoretical system in which the energy remains constant and does not spread out into the surroundings.

Spontaneous change and the state of matter

This change in our way of thinking about a situation helps to explain the physical change of sugar dissolving in a cup of coffee. Using ideas from thermochemistry, you might suggest that sugar dissolves in water because the change is *exothermic*. That is, the system gives out heat as the solution forms, because the energy of the separate hydrated sugar molecules is less than the energy of sugar molecules in a solid sugar crystal.

However, many substances have an *endothermic* enthalpy of solution. According to an argument based solely on enthalpy changes, these substances would not be expected to dissolve spontaneously in water. But, for example, ammonium nitrate *does* dissolve:

$$NH_4NO_3(s) \rightarrow NH_4^+(aq) + NO_3^-(aq); \quad \Delta H^{\ominus}_{sol}(298\,K) = +25.8\,kJ\,mol^{-1}$$

The positive value of the enthalpy change shows that heat has flowed from the surrounding water to increase the energies of the $NH_4^+(aq)$ and $NO_3^-(aq)$ ions (compared with their energies when in the solid state). While energy has not spread out during this spontaneous change, matter *has* spread out. As in all cases of dissolution, a solid ordered lattice has broken down and spread out into a more disordered state. The spreading out of matter – not the enthalpy change – is the common factor in the formation of solutions.

- Spontaneous changes are those that cause energy and/or matter to spread out.

You should now understand that the spreading out of energy and/or matter gives direction to spontaneous changes. Simply considering just decreases in energy does not lead to an adequate model that explains observations.

The next spread develops the idea of 'spreading out' by quantifying and measuring it. To proceed further, you must get to grips with a concept called 'entropy', and apply it to chemical as well as physical changes.

The direction of spontaneous change. A gas spontaneously diffuses to fill its container uniformly. For an ideal gas, there is no exchange of energy with the surroundings.

Spontaneity and rate

As in previous chapters, we must also consider the *rate* at which a reaction occurs. For example, hydrogen and oxygen are unstable with respect to water:

$H_2(g) + \frac{1}{2}O_2(g) \rightarrow H_2O(l);$
$\Delta H^{\ominus}(298\,K) = -286\,kJ\,mol^{-1}$

The reaction is highly exothermic. However, at room temperature (298 K), the rate of reaction is so slow as to be effectively zero. So, even though the reaction is spontaneous at room temperature, it occurs at a rate too slow to observe. Spontaneous does *not* mean fast.

SUMMARY

- The structure and composition of a stable system do not change over time.
- Spontaneous change moves a system from a less stable state to a more stable state.
- Spontaneous change cannot be accounted for solely in terms of the system tending to a state of lower energy.
- Spontaneous changes are those that cause energy and/or matter to spread out.

PRACTICE

1 Describe each of the following changes in terms of the spreading out of matter or of energy. Where appropriate, describe changes in the structure of the system and changes in the energy distribution.
   a Melting ice.
   b The exothermic neutralization of aqueous hydrochloric acid by aqueous sodium hydroxide.
   c Gas diffusion.
   d The combustion of a liquid fuel.

2 Suggest why a spontaneous endothermic precipitation reaction is unlikely to occur.

14.2

Entropy – 1

OBJECTIVES

- Entropy and disorder
- Entropy and phase change
- Entropy changes in system and surroundings
- Second law of thermodynamics and spontaneous change

The previous spread revealed that spontaneous change involves an increase in disorder: either energy or matter or both must spread out. A large negative (exothermic) standard enthalpy change is *not* a sufficient criterion for spontaneous change. There are many endothermic changes which are spontaneous (such as the dissolution of ammonium nitrate). This spread introduces the concept of *entropy change* as a means of describing and quantifying disorder. The following spread uses calculations involving entropy to identify and predict spontaneous changes.

Disorder and entropy

Entropy is a measure of the disorder of a system. The entropy of a system increases when the matter or energy in the system spreads out or becomes more random in its arrangement. For example, entropy increases when a solid melts to produce a liquid, when a liquid vaporizes to produce a gas, and when substances dissolve or mix together. Entropy also increases when a substance is heated with no change of state. For example, heating a liquid increases the speed of the particles and the number of collisions per second; the entropy of the liquid increases as its particles become more disordered. At the same time, entropy increases as energy from the source of heat spreads out into the liquid.

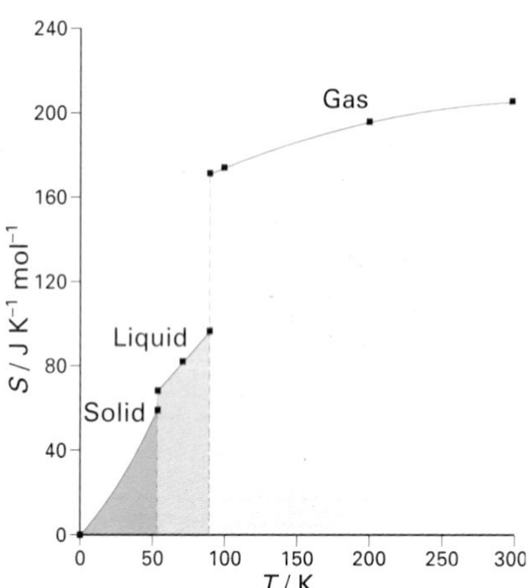

The entropy ***S*** *of a substance (in this case oxygen) increases as its temperature* ***T*** *increases. There is a sharp increase in entropy at the melting point as the structure changes from solid to the more random arrangement of particles in a liquid. There is an even greater increase in entropy at the boiling point because the particles are much more widely spread out.*

Numerical values for entropy

Entropy is given the symbol S. Just as the enthalpy change ΔH was important, so it is the entropy *change* ΔS that is important. In general terms, the **entropy change** ΔS in a system is defined as:

$$\Delta S = q/T$$

where q is the heat added to the system from the surroundings and T is the thermodynamic temperature (in kelvin) at which the heat is transferred. To understand the significance of this expression, think about heating a system that is undergoing a change of state (e.g. ice melting). Heating the system does not increase the temperature of the system: it just makes the matter in the system more disordered.

Worked example on calculating entropy changes

Data: The enthalpy change during melting of ice ΔH_{fus} is +6.01 kJ mol^{-1} at 273 K; the enthalpy change during vaporization of water ΔH_{vap} is +40.7 kJ mol^{-1} at 373 K.

Question: Calculate the entropy change per mole when (a) ice melts at 0 °C and (b) water vaporizes at 100 °C. Remember that the enthalpy change equals the heat added to the system at constant pressure.

Answer:

(a) The equation is

$H_2O(s) \rightarrow H_2O(l)$; $\quad \Delta H_{fus}(273\,K) = +6.01\,kJ\,mol^{-1}$

So

$$\Delta S = \frac{q}{T} = \frac{\Delta H_{fus}}{T} = \frac{+6010\,J\,mol^{-1}}{273\,K} = +22.0\,J\,K^{-1}\,mol^{-1}$$

(b) The equation is

$H_2O(l) \rightarrow H_2O(g)$; $\quad \Delta H_{vap}(373\,K) = +40.7\,kJ\,mol^{-1}$

So

$$\Delta S = \frac{q}{T} = \frac{\Delta H_{vap}}{T} = \frac{+40\,700\,J\,mol^{-1}}{373\,K} = +109\,J\,K^{-1}\,mol^{-1}$$

Comment

In both cases (a) and (b) in the worked example, heat has been added to the system (the water). This energy input has increased the internal energy of the water molecules.

At the molecular level, the increase in disorder is much greater in the case of vaporization than in the case of melting. This difference is reflected in the values of the entropy changes:

$\Delta S = +109\,J\,K^{-1}\,mol^{-1}$ for vaporization,

$\Delta S = +22\,J\,K^{-1}\,mol^{-1}$ for melting.

System *and* surroundings

The total entropy change for any process can be broken down into the entropy change in the system, ΔS_{sys}, plus the entropy change in the surroundings, ΔS_{surr}. In an exothermic reaction, heat disperses from the system into the surroundings. Remember that, for an exothermic reaction, the enthalpy change for the system, ΔH, is negative; so the enthalpy change for the surroundings, $-\Delta H$, has a positive value.

In terms of entropy change, the significance of the heat released by an exothermic reaction into the surroundings depends on how hot the surroundings already are. The hotter they are, the less effect a given heat transfer will have. Quantitatively, the size of the entropy change in the surroundings is *inversely* proportional to the temperature:

$$\Delta S_{surr} = \frac{q}{T} \quad \text{or} \quad \Delta S_{surr} = \frac{-\Delta H}{T}$$

(The surroundings are always assumed to be so large that no change in temperature results.)

Combining the entropy changes in the system and the surroundings:

$$\Delta S_{tot} = \Delta S_{sys} + \Delta S_{surr}$$

which becomes

$$\Delta S_{tot} = \Delta S_{sys} - \frac{\Delta H}{T}$$

By convention, ΔS refers to the system, so the expression becomes:

$$\Delta S_{tot} = \Delta S - \frac{\Delta H}{T}$$

You should notice that the term $-\Delta H/T$, which is used to represent the entropy change in the *surroundings*, is expressed in terms that describe the *system* only.

The second law of thermodynamics

The system plus the surroundings taken together constitute the Universe. An observed fact is that, when any change takes place, the total entropy of the Universe ΔS_{tot} tends to increase. This observation is expressed as the **second law of thermodynamics**, simply stated as:

- The total entropy of the Universe always tends to increase; it never goes down.

As a result, ΔS_{tot} for any change is always greater than (or equal to) zero (the special case where it is zero is dealt with in spread 14.5). A negative total entropy change is not possible. For a spontaneous change to occur:

$$\Delta S_{tot} > 0$$

So substituting the equation above gives

$$\Delta S - \frac{\Delta H}{T} > 0 \quad \text{for a spontaneous change}$$

Now if we multiply through by T, the criterion for spontaneous change becomes:

$$T\Delta S - \Delta H > 0$$

Note that, as in any equation, the units are the same on both sides of this inequality, so the units of ΔH and of $T\Delta S$ are J mol^{-1}.

SUMMARY

- Entropy change $\Delta S = q/T$ (units $\text{J K}^{-1}\text{mol}^{-1}$).
- Entropy increases with the temperature of the system.
- For a spontaneous change, the total entropy tends to increase.
- For spontaneous change, $\Delta S_{tot} > 0$, or alternatively $T\Delta S - \Delta H > 0$

The first law of thermodynamics

The **first law of thermodynamics** states that:

- Energy cannot be created or destroyed.

The significance of this law to a system and its surroundings is that the enthalpy change in the surroundings is *exactly equal* in magnitude, and *opposite* in sign, to the enthalpy change in the system.

Spontaneous change

For a spontaneous change,

$\Delta S_{tot} > 0$ so $T\Delta S - \Delta H > 0$

Imagine a system consisting of solid ice and liquid water in equilibrium at 0 °C. Now imagine two situations:

1. If the surroundings have a temperature slightly greater than 0 °C (e.g. 10 °C, 283 K), heat flows *into* the system. Then from our data and calculations in the worked example opposite:

$H_2O(s) \rightarrow H_2O(l)$;
$\Delta H = +6.01\ \text{kJ mol}^{-1}$
$\Delta S = +22.0\ \text{J K}^{-1}\text{mol}^{-1}$

The value of $T\Delta S - \Delta H$ in this case is

$[283\ \text{K} \times (+22.0\ \text{J K}^{-1}\text{mol}^{-1})] - (+6010\ \text{J mol}^{-1})$
$= +200\ \text{J mol}^{-1}$ (1 sig. fig.)

This is greater than zero, so the ice melting is spontaneous.

2. If the surroundings have a temperature slightly below 0 °C (e.g. −10 °C, 263 K), heat flows *out of* the system. The value of $T\Delta S - \Delta H$ in this case is

$[263\ \text{K} \times (+22.0\ \text{J K}^{-1}\text{mol}^{-1})] - (+6010\ \text{J mol}^{-1})$
$= -200\ \text{J mol}^{-1}$ (1 sig. fig.)

This is less than zero, indicating that the total entropy would go down if the ice melted under these conditions – so melting is not spontaneous, but *freezing* is spontaneous.

PRACTICE

1 Explain whether entropy increases or decreases in the following changes:
  a melting of ice
  b boiling of water
  c decomposition of calcium carbonate.

14.3 Entropy – 2

OBJECTIVES

- Spontaneous change and $T\Delta S - \Delta H > 0$
- Standard entropy values
- Standard entropy change

A lime kiln in Iraq. The decomposition of calcium carbonate to produce quicklime (calcium oxide) is a highly endothermic process:
$CaCO_3(s) \rightarrow CO_2(g) + CaO(s)$;
$\Delta H^\ominus = +178\,kJ\,mol^{-1}$
There is no spontaneous decomposition at low temperature. At high temperature, the release of carbon dioxide gas increases the entropy of the system sufficiently to make the change spontaneous, i.e. to satisfy the requirement that $T\Delta S^\ominus > \Delta H^\ominus$. Limestone hills do not decompose to CO_2 and CaO until heated in a lime kiln!

You should by now understand that the criterion for spontaneous chemical or physical change is that the total entropy change must be greater than zero, i.e. $\Delta S_{tot} > 0$. In other words, the total entropy of the Universe always tends to increase; it never goes down. The previous spread established the role of entropy and concentrated on physical changes. This spread introduces methods of calculation that can be applied to chemical reactions. However, our first task is to develop the point made in the previous spread about considering *both* enthalpy changes and entropy changes.

Two special cases

The general expression for spontaneous change described in the previous spread is

$$T\Delta S - \Delta H > 0$$

There are two special cases relating to this general expression.

First, if the enthalpy change ΔH is negligible, the processes that occur spontaneously are those that increase the entropy of the system so that $T\Delta S > 0$. Examples include the diffusion and mixing of gases. A similar example is dissolving a salt that has a small enthalpy of solution, such as sodium chloride ($+4\,kJ\,mol^{-1}$). The salt dissolves because the particles can spread out into the solution rather than staying 'locked up' in the ordered crystal structure of the solid.

A second special case arises when the entropy change ΔS (and thus $T\Delta S$) is negligible. In this case the term $-\Delta H$ must be greater than zero, and this can only occur if the enthalpy change is negative. This conclusion explains why most reactions that occur spontaneously are exothermic. The fundamental reason for these *exothermic* reactions being spontaneous is that the entropy of the surroundings increases, as heat is released into them.

Both entropy change *and* enthalpy change must be considered in order to explain spontaneous endothermic processes. Endothermic processes have positive values for ΔH and can therefore only occur if the entropy change is positive and sufficiently large that:

$$T\Delta S > \Delta H$$

Spontaneous *endothermic* changes, such as the evolution of carbon dioxide when a dilute acid is added to a hydrogencarbonate, must be accompanied by a large increase in entropy in order that the total entropy of the Universe increases, i.e. to obey the second law of thermodynamics.

Standard entropies

The standard entropy of a substance at a specified temperature is the entropy change per mole that results from heating the substance from 0 K to the specified standard temperature. Here we look at how standard entropies are calculated.

At 0 K (–273 °C) the entropy of a perfect crystalline solid is zero. Heating a substance increases its temperature and increases its entropy. Remember that the heat q added to a system is related to the temperature change via the heat capacity C, which is equal to the mass multiplied by the specific heat capacity, spread 10.4:

$$q = C\Delta T \qquad (1)$$

The value of C itself depends on the temperature, so equation (1) applies only if the temperature change, ΔT, is small. Measuring the heat capacity of a substance down to very low temperatures allows the entropy at any temperature to be calculated, as follows.

Entropy change is defined as

$$\Delta S = \frac{q}{T} \qquad (2)$$

Combining equations (1) and (2) gives the entropy change for a small change in temperature,

$$\Delta S = \frac{C\Delta T}{T}$$

The **standard entropy** (symbol $S^\ominus$) of a substance is the sum of all the entropy changes resulting from heating the substance from 0 K to the specified temperature, i.e. written mathematically

$$S^\ominus = \sum_{T=0}^{T=\text{specified}} \frac{C\Delta T}{T} \quad \text{or} \quad \int_0^{\text{specified}} \frac{C}{T}\,dT$$

Data books usually list standard entropies of elements and compounds at 298 K, i.e. under the heading $S^\ominus$(298 K). (The standard pressure is 1 bar, as was the case for standard enthalpies.)

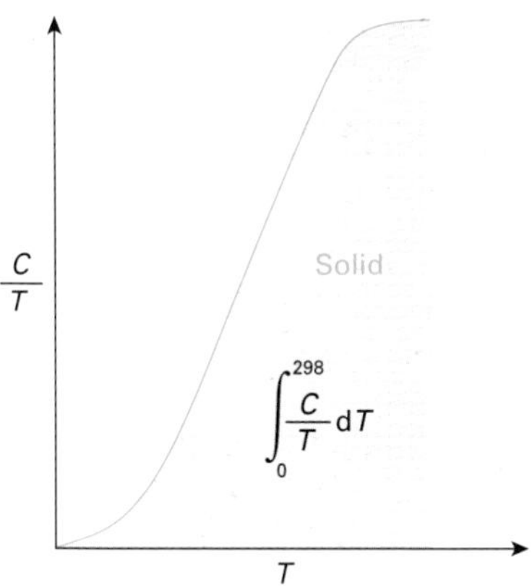

*The standard entropy of a solid at 298 K may be determined graphically by plotting **C/T** against **T** for values of **T** between 0 K and 298 K. The area under the curve is the standard entropy of the substance. Note that, if a phase change occurs below 298 K, then the corresponding* ***ΔS = ΔH/T*** *must be included.*

Substance	Formula	$S^\ominus$(298 K) /J K^{-1} mol^{-1}
Hydrogen	H_2	131
Nitrogen	N_2	192
Oxygen	O_2	205
Carbon dioxide	CO_2	214
Carbon monoxide	CO	198
Ammonia	NH_3	192
Water	H_2O	70
Ethanol	CH_3CH_2OH	161
Benzene	C_6H_6	173
Diamond	C	2.4
Graphite	C	5.7
Aluminium	Al	28
Lead	Pb	65
Calcium oxide	CaO	38
Calcium carbonate	$CaCO_3$	92

Standard entropies of substances at 298 K (25 °C).

Standard entropy change

You should remember, spread 10.5, that *standard enthalpy change* is defined as the enthalpy change per mole for conversion of reactants in their standard states into products in their standard states, at a stated temperature. The *standard entropy change* $\Delta S^\ominus$ is defined in the same manner.

- The **standard entropy change** is the entropy change per mole for conversion of reactants in their standard states into products in their standard states, at a stated temperature.

In symbols, we can write this as

$$\Delta S^\ominus = S^\ominus(\text{products}) - S^\ominus(\text{reactants})$$

The following example shows how the standard entropy change may be calculated for the decomposition of ammonia:

$$2NH_3(g) \rightarrow N_2(g) + 3H_2(g)$$

The standard entropies of ammonia, nitrogen, and hydrogen are 192, 192, and 131 J K^{-1} mol^{-1} respectively. So

$$\begin{aligned}\Delta S^\ominus &= S^\ominus(N_2) + 3S^\ominus(H_2) - 2S^\ominus(NH_3)\\ &= (192\,\text{J K}^{-1}\text{mol}^{-1}) + 3 \times (131\,\text{J K}^{-1}\text{mol}^{-1}) - 2 \times (192\,\text{J K}^{-1}\text{mol}^{-1})\\ &= +201\,\text{J K}^{-1}\text{mol}^{-1}\end{aligned}$$

The standard entropy change (per mole of reaction as written) is +201 J K^{-1} mol^{-1}. So we can write

$$2NH_3(g) \rightarrow N_2(g) + 3H_2(g); \qquad \Delta S^\ominus(298\,\text{K}) = +201\,\text{J K}^{-1}\text{mol}^{-1}$$

The standard entropy change is positive, which signifies that there has been an increase in disorder. An inspection of the chemical equation confirms this: 2 mol of gas changes into 4 mol of gas. The following spreads show how to use the actual value of $\Delta S^\ominus$ to make predictions about spontaneity.

Comparing standard entropies

Gases generally have larger standard entropies than liquids, which in turn have larger values than solids. Also, different substances in the same state can have different entropies. For example, diamond has a lower entropy than lead, partly because the carbon atoms in diamond are connected together by rigid bonds. Substances made up from heavy atoms generally have higher entropies than those made up from light atoms, e.g. N_2(g) has a higher entropy than H_2(g). Water H_2O has a lower entropy than ethanol CH_3CH_2OH.

SUMMARY

- Exothermic reactions occur because the heat released increases the entropy of the surroundings.
- Endothermic reactions can only occur if the entropy change in the reaction is positive and large enough that $T\Delta S > \Delta H$.
- A value of standard entropy may be measured for any substance.
- The standard entropy change $\Delta S^\ominus$ is the entropy change per mole for conversion of reactants in their standard states into products in their standard states, at a stated temperature.

14.4

OBJECTIVES

- Standard Gibbs energy change $\Delta G^{\ominus}$
- Spontaneous change: $\Delta G^{\ominus} < 0$
- Calculating temperature for reaction

STANDARD GIBBS ENERGY CHANGE

We have now clearly established the criterion for spontaneous change: the total entropy change (system plus surroundings) must be greater than zero ($\Delta S_{tot} > 0$). Simply expressed, spontaneous changes cause the entropy of the Universe to increase. However, as we saw in the previous spreads, deciding whether a reaction will be spontaneous requires knowledge of the entropy change ΔS, the enthalpy change ΔH, and the temperature T. It would be far more convenient to consider just one factor instead of several; that single factor is the standard Gibbs energy change.

Conditions

The entropy change in the surroundings is equal to $-\Delta H^{\ominus}/T$ when the change is carried out at:
(a) constant temperature T and
(b) 1 bar pressure (so that the heat added is equal to $\Delta H^{\ominus}$). The negative sign means that an exothermic reaction causes an *increase* in the entropy of the surroundings.

Defining standard Gibbs energy change

The criterion for spontaneous reaction is given in the previous two spreads. Now, at 1 bar, if we use the *standard* enthalpy change and the *standard* entropy change in this criterion to obtain a simple expression for spontaneity at the temperature T:

$$T\Delta S^{\ominus} - \Delta H^{\ominus} > 0$$

If the sign of both sides is changed, we arrive at an alternative expression for the criterion for spontaneous change:

$$\Delta H^{\ominus} - T\Delta S^{\ominus} < 0$$

The search throughout this chapter has been for a single quantity that will define spontaneity. The **standard Gibbs energy change** ('Gibbs energy' is sometimes called 'free energy') combines the three quantities above in one term and is defined at constant temperature as:

$$\Delta G^{\ominus} = \Delta H^{\ominus} - T\Delta S^{\ominus}$$

So, the Gibbs energy *decreases* in any spontaneous change.

- **The criterion for spontaneous change is that $\Delta G^{\ominus} < 0$.**

Both $\Delta H^{\ominus}$ and $T\Delta S^{\ominus}$ are measured in kJ mol^{-1}: $\Delta G^{\ominus}$ therefore also has units kJ mol^{-1}. A reaction with a negative value for $\Delta G^{\ominus}$ is said to be **exergonic**; this echoes the name 'exothermic' (spread 10.2).

- Exergonic reactions are spontaneous.

Josiah Willard Gibbs (1839–1903). When asked to name the most important scientist of his generation (after himself!), Albert Einstein immediately stated: Hendrik Lorentz (who discovered relativity at the same time as Einstein) but added 'I never met Willard Gibbs; perhaps, had I done so, I might have placed him alongside Lorentz.'

Standard Gibbs energy change

Standard Gibbs energy change is defined in the same way as the standard enthalpy change and the standard entropy change:

- The **standard Gibbs energy change** $\Delta G^{\ominus}$ is the Gibbs energy change per mole for conversion of reactants in their standard states into products in their standard states, at a stated temperature.

In simple terms, the criterion for spontaneous change is that $\Delta G^{\ominus} < 0$. When applied to a formation reaction, the standard Gibbs energy change of formation is related to the standard enthalpy and entropy changes of formation by

$$\Delta G_f^{\ominus} = \Delta H_f^{\ominus} - T\Delta S_f^{\ominus}$$

Data books provide values of standard Gibbs energy change of formation for a wide range of substances. For elements, $\Delta G_f^{\ominus}$ is by definition zero (as is the standard enthalpy change of formation).

Using $\Delta G_f^{\ominus}$ terms

Standard enthalpy changes may be calculated indirectly by using cycles based on Hess's law. Standard Gibbs energy changes may be manipulated in the same way. The standard Gibbs energy changes of formation of the reactants and of the products are obtained from data books. The standard Gibbs energy change $\Delta G^{\ominus}$ is given by

$\Delta G^{\ominus} = \Delta G_f^{\ominus}(\text{products}) - \Delta G_f^{\ominus}(\text{reactants})$

Worked example on methane

Question: Calculate the standard Gibbs energy change of combustion of methane from the standard Gibbs energy changes of formation of the substances involved in the reaction.

Answer: The first step is to write down the chemical equation, which is

$CH_4(g) + 2O_2(g) \rightarrow CO_2(g) + 2H_2O(l)$

With reference to the combustion of methane, the standard Gibbs energy change is given by

$\Delta G^{\ominus}_{c} = [\Delta G^{\ominus}_{f}(CO_2) + 2\Delta G^{\ominus}_{f}(H_2O)] - [\Delta G^{\ominus}_{f}(CH_4) + 2\Delta G^{\ominus}_{f}(O_2)]$

Substituting the relevant values:

$\Delta G^{\ominus}_{c} = [-394\,\text{kJ mol}^{-1} + 2 \times (-237\,\text{kJ mol}^{-1})] - [-50\,\text{kJ mol}^{-1} + 2 \times (0\,\text{kJ mol}^{-1})]$

$= -818\,\text{kJ mol}^{-1}$

So, the standard Gibbs energy change of combustion of methane is $-818\,\text{kJ mol}^{-1}$.

Comment – 1

The significance of the result for methane (negative sign, value in the order of hundreds of kJ mol^{-1}) will become clear in due course. For the present, you need simply to be familiar with this method of calculation.

Worked example on calcium carbonate

This example uses the expression for the standard Gibbs energy change to find the temperature at which $\Delta G^{\ominus}$ becomes negative. Remember, when $\Delta G^{\ominus}$ becomes negative, the reaction becomes spontaneous.

Question: The decomposition of calcium carbonate is an important process in the extraction of iron in a blast furnace (see the final spread in this chapter). Calculate the standard enthalpy change for the decomposition of calcium carbonate at 298 K. Also calculate the standard entropy change at 298 K. From these values, determine an approximate value for the decomposition temperature of the carbonate.

Answer:

Step 1 We first calculate the standard enthalpy change by combining the relevant standard enthalpy changes of formation in a Hess's law cycle. The equation for the decomposition is

$CaCO_3(s) \rightarrow CaO(s) + CO_2(g)$

So

$\Delta H^{\ominus} = \Delta H^{\ominus}_{f}(CaO) + \Delta H^{\ominus}_{f}(CO_2) - \Delta H^{\ominus}_{f}(CaCO_3)$

$= (-635\,\text{kJ mol}^{-1}) + (-394\,\text{kJ mol}^{-1}) - (-1208\,\text{kJ mol}^{-1})$

$= +179\,\text{kJ mol}^{-1}$

Step 2 We next calculate the standard entropy change in a similar manner. So

$\Delta S^{\ominus} = S^{\ominus}(CaO) + S^{\ominus}(CO_2) - S^{\ominus}(CaCO_3)$

$= (38\,\text{J K}^{-1}\text{mol}^{-1}) + (214\,\text{J K}^{-1}\text{mol}^{-1}) - (92\,\text{J K}^{-1}\text{mol}^{-1})$

$= +160\,\text{J K}^{-1}\text{mol}^{-1}$

Step 3 The reaction is spontaneous when $\Delta G^{\ominus}$ is negative, i.e. when

$\Delta H^{\ominus} - T\Delta S^{\ominus} < 0$

So, decomposition occurs when $T\Delta S^{\ominus} > \Delta H^{\ominus}$

i.e. when

$$T > \frac{\Delta H^{\ominus}}{\Delta S^{\ominus}}$$

Substituting the values calculated above:

$$T > \frac{+179\,000\,\text{J mol}^{-1}}{+160\,\text{J K}^{-1}\text{mol}^{-1}} \quad \text{i.e. } T > 1120\,\text{K} \quad \text{(3 sig. figs)}$$

The minimum temperature for the decomposition of calcium carbonate is 1120 K.

Comment – 2

In the earlier chapter on 'thermochemistry' we found that the standard *enthalpy* change of combustion of methane is $\Delta H^{\ominus}_{c} = -891\,\text{kJ mol}^{-1}$. The standard *Gibbs energy* change of combustion of methane worked out above is less negative ($\Delta G^{\ominus}_{c} = -818\,\text{kJ mol}^{-1}$) because in the combustion three moles of gas are consumed and only one mole of gas is formed: remember that the values are at 298 K so water is a liquid. This unfavourable entropy change causes the difference ($T\Delta S^{\ominus}$) between the two values.

Data – at 298 K or 1120 K?

The decomposition of calcium carbonate is strongly endothermic at room temperature (298 K); limestone hills do not spontaneously decompose. The predicted decomposition temperature is 1120 K, which is close to the actual value of 1170 K (900 °C). Using values for the standard enthalpy change and standard entropy change *at 1120 K* rather than 298 K would give even closer agreement with the observed decomposition temperature.

The concept of Gibbs energy helps to determine the feasibility of all reactions – from the functioning of an oil refinery to the biochemistry of the living cell.

SUMMARY

- Standard Gibbs energy change is defined *at constant temperature* as $\Delta G^{\ominus} = \Delta H^{\ominus} - T\Delta S^{\ominus}$
- A spontaneous change is accompanied by a decrease in standard Gibbs energy, i.e. $\Delta G^{\ominus} < 0$.
- The standard Gibbs energy change may be calculated from standard Gibbs energy changes of formation $\Delta G^{\ominus}_{f}$.
- Standard Gibbs energy changes may be used to calculate the temperature at which a reaction becomes spontaneous.

$\Delta G^{\ominus}$ and $E^{\ominus}$

There is a direct proportionality between the standard Gibbs energy and the standard cell e.m.f.:

$\Delta G^{\ominus} = -zFE^{\ominus}$

where z is the number of electrons transferred and F is the Faraday constant, spread 13.11.

14.5

Gibbs energy and chemical equilibrium

OBJECTIVES

- $\Delta G^\ominus = 0$ as a special case
- Gibbs energy vs composition diagrams
- Standard Gibbs energy and equilibrium constant

$\Delta G^\ominus$

The standard Gibbs energy change $\Delta G^\ominus$ is the difference between the standard Gibbs energy changes of formation of the pure products and the pure reactants. Under the conditions of the reaction, each substance is *not pure*; it is mixed with the other substances. The actual Gibbs energy change, established at a fixed composition of the reaction mixture, also contains a component due to mixing. The Gibbs energy of mixing is negative.

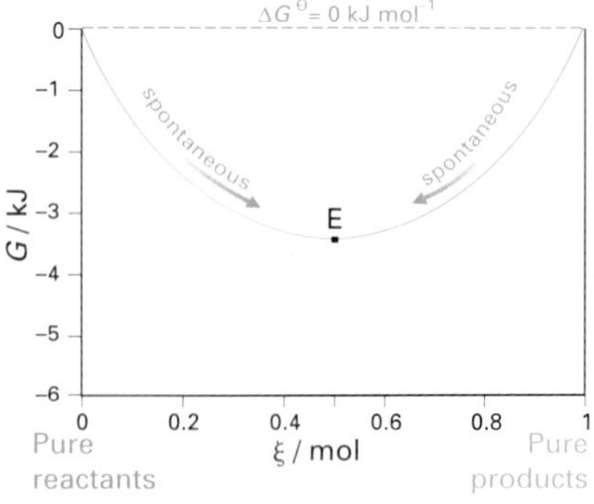

*The plot of Gibbs energy **G** vs extent of reaction for an imaginary reaction where $\Delta G^\ominus = 0$. In this example, the Gibbs energies of the reactants and the products are equal. Reaction spontaneously proceeds in either direction towards equilibrium E because the Gibbs energy of mixing of reactants and products is negative. Note that the Gibbs energy of mixing depends only on the number of species in the balanced chemical equation, and not on any energy terms.*

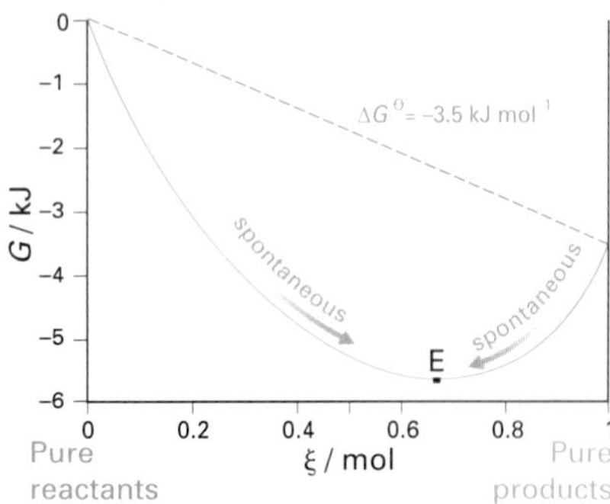

*The plot of Gibbs energy **G** vs extent of reaction for the formation of ethyl ethanoate. An extent of reaction of 0.67 mol corresponds to an equilibrium constant of*

$$\frac{(0.67\ \text{mol}) \times (0.67\ \text{mol})}{(0.33\ \text{mol}) \times (0.33\ \text{mol})} = 4$$

See spread 11.5.

All the chemical equations written so far in this chapter have been represented as if they go to completion. The format has been: 'reactants' → 'products'. However, you should remember that all reactions form an *equilibrium mixture* of reactants and products, chapter 11. The position of the equilibrium is described by the equilibrium constant K. If the standard Gibbs energy change is the indicator for spontaneity of reaction, there should be a connection between $\Delta G^\ominus$ and K.

Gibbs energy of mixing

An important point to note is that standard Gibbs energy changes concern the change from *pure* reactants to *pure* products. Consider the imaginary reaction A + B → C + D for which $\Delta G^\ominus = 0\ \text{kJ mol}^{-1}$.

Does any reaction actually happen?

Entropy measures the disorder of a system. When two substances are mixed, there is an increase in disorder and so an increase in entropy. The **entropy of mixing** ΔS_{mix} is the entropy change due to the mixing of substances. The entropy of mixing is greatest when the two substances are present in equal proportions. There is an increase in entropy resulting from the mixing of reactants and products, which in turn means that the Gibbs energy *decreases* as the **Gibbs energy of mixing** is

$$\Delta G_{mix} = -T\Delta S_{mix}$$

In simple terms, the criterion for a spontaneous reaction is that $\Delta G^\ominus$ *is less than zero*. However, what would happen if $\Delta G^\ominus$ *equals* zero? Some reactants form products because the Gibbs energy of mixing favours a 50:50 equilibrium mixture over either pure reactants or pure products. The composition of the equilibrium mixture will be half-way between pure reactants and pure products. The **extent of reaction** ξ (the Greek letter xi) is defined such that pure reactants correspond to a value of 0 mol; pure products correspond to a value of 1 mol. For $\Delta G^\ominus = 0\ \text{kJ mol}^{-1}$, equilibrium occurs when $\xi = 0.5$ mol.

Equilibria favouring products

The example given on the left relates to an equilibrium reaction where $\Delta G^\ominus = 0$, i.e. the Gibbs energies of the reactants and products are equal. The diagram below left shows the plot of Gibbs energy vs extent of reaction when the Gibbs energy of the products is less than that of the reactants (i.e. $\Delta G^\ominus < 0$). The standard Gibbs energy change for the forward reaction is represented by the line joining pure reactants and pure products. If there were no mixing term, a *tiny* negative $\Delta G^\ominus$ would cause the composition to slide all the way down to products. A minimum in the Gibbs energy occurs because of the Gibbs energy of mixing.

Equilibrium occurs where Gibbs energy reaches a minimum

We can now state the exact criterion for any spontaneous reaction:

- Any composition of a reaction mixture will change spontaneously in the direction of decreasing Gibbs energy; no further change occurs when the Gibbs energy reaches its minimum value.
- In mathematical terms, the gradient is zero at equilibrium: $dG/d\xi = 0$.

The more negative the value for the standard Gibbs energy change $\Delta G^\ominus$, the steeper is the slope of the line from pure reactants to pure products, and the further towards the products the equilibrium lies.

Conversely, an equilibrium favours the reactants when the Gibbs energy of the products is greater than that of the reactants. Note that Gibbs energy of mixing is especially significant only where $\Delta G^\ominus$ lies between about $+35\ \text{kJ mol}^{-1}$ and $-35\ \text{kJ mol}^{-1}$, as explained opposite.

Standard Gibbs energy change and the equilibrium constant

Standard Gibbs energy change and the equilibrium constant are linked together by the simple expression:

$$\Delta G^{\ominus} = -RT \ln K$$

where R is the gas constant ($8.31\,\mathrm{J\,K^{-1}\,mol^{-1}}$), T is the thermodynamic temperature, and $\ln K$ is the natural logarithm (see box) of the equilibrium constant. The significance of this relationship is shown below:

How the values of K and $\Delta G^{\ominus} = -RT\ln K$ are related to the equilibrium position.

Standard Gibbs energy change, $\Delta G^{\ominus}$/kJ mol^{-1}	Equilibrium constant K	Equilibrium position
More negative than −35	Greater than 10^6	'Reaction effectively complete'
Between −35 and 0	Between 10^6 and 1	Products predominate
Between 0 and +35	Between 1 and 10^{-6}	Reactants predominate
More positive than +35	Smaller than 10^{-6}	'Effectively no reaction'

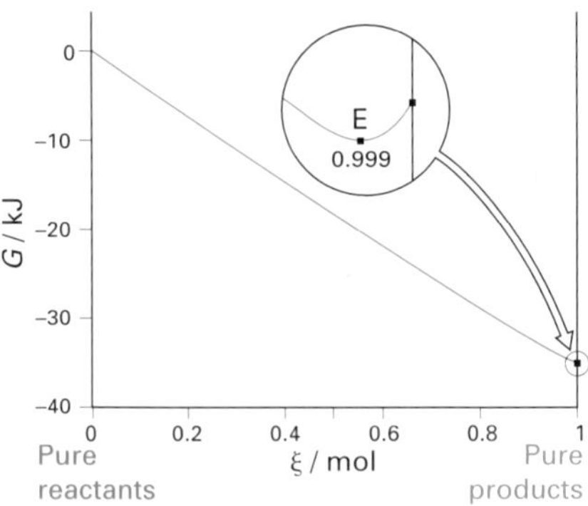

If $\Delta G^{\ominus}$ has a large negative value, Gibbs energy is at a minimum when the concentration of products in the equilibrium mixture E is much greater than the concentration of reactants. Then $K \gg 1$, and the reaction goes almost to completion (i.e. the equilibrium lies very far to the right).

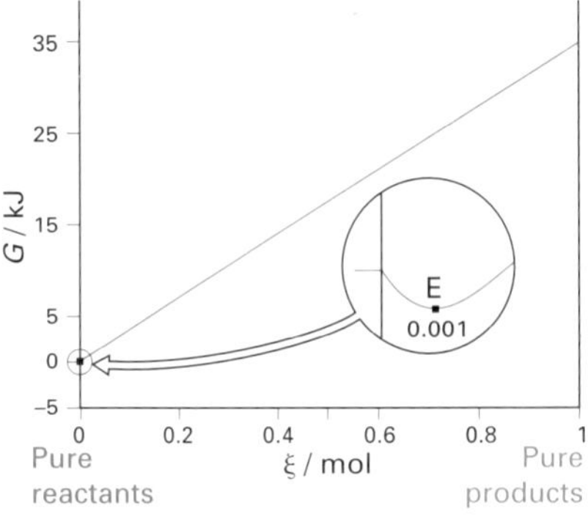

If $\Delta G^{\ominus}$ has a large positive value, Gibbs energy is at a minimum when the concentration of products in the equilibrium mixture E is much smaller than the concentration of reactants. Then $K \ll 1$, and the reaction 'does not go' (i.e. the equilibrium lies very far to the left).

Worked example on calculating an equilibrium constant

Question: Calculate the value of the equilibrium constant at 25 °C for the esterification reaction:

$$CH_3COOH(l) + CH_3CH_2OH(l) \rightleftharpoons CH_3COOCH_2CH_3(l) + H_2O(l)$$

Answer:

Step 1 We first use a data book to find the standard Gibbs energy changes of formation of the reactants and products. We find the values:

$-389.9\,\mathrm{kJ\,mol^{-1}}$ (CH_3COOH)

$-174.8\,\mathrm{kJ\,mol^{-1}}$ (CH_3CH_2OH)

$-331.1\,\mathrm{kJ\,mol^{-1}}$ ($CH_3COOCH_2CH_3$)

$-237.1\,\mathrm{kJ\,mol^{-1}}$ (H_2O)

Step 2 Now we calculate $\Delta G^{\ominus}$ for the forward reaction:

$$\Delta G^{\ominus} = [(-331.1) + (-237.1)]\,\mathrm{kJ\,mol^{-1}} - [(-389.9) + (-174.8)]\,\mathrm{kJ\,mol^{-1}}$$
$$= -3.5\,\mathrm{kJ\,mol^{-1}}$$

The small negative value of the standard Gibbs energy change shows that an equilibrium slightly favouring the products will be established.

Step 3 Finally we insert values into the equation $\Delta G^{\ominus} = -RT\ln K$ and solve for K:

$$-3500\,\mathrm{J\,mol^{-1}} = -(8.31\,\mathrm{J\,K^{-1}mol^{-1}}) \times (298\,\mathrm{K}) \times \ln K$$

$$\ln K = \frac{-3500\,\mathrm{J\,mol^{-1}}}{-(8.31\,\mathrm{J\,K^{-1}\,mol^{-1}}) \times (298\,\mathrm{K})}$$
$$= 1.4$$

Now by reference to the box we find that

$K = e^{1.4} = 4$ (1 sig. fig.)

Note: The value for K may be used to calculate the composition of the equilibrium mixture (see the earlier chapter on 'chemical equilibrium'). The value calculated here from Gibbs energy changes matches the experimental value.

Natural logarithms

These are like common logarithms, but to a different base, the number we call 'e'. For any positive number n, the **natural logarithm** (symbol ln or $\log_e$) of n is the power to which the base (in this case, e) must be raised to make n. For example, for the number 2,

$\ln 2 = 0.693$ i.e. $2 = e^{0.693}$

Natural logarithms are probably labelled 'ln' on a calculator.

For our purposes here, we need to do the reverse of finding the natural logarithm. If we have

$\ln K = n$ then $K = e^n$

so we need to use the button labelled 'e^x' on the calculator.

SUMMARY

- Equilibrium occurs where the Gibbs energy reaches its minimum value.
- Equilibrium constant and standard Gibbs energy change are connected by the expression $\Delta G^{\ominus} = -RT\ln K$
- When $\Delta G^{\ominus}$ is large and positive, the reaction 'does not go'.
- When $\Delta G^{\ominus}$ is large and negative, the reaction 'goes to completion'.

14.6

OBJECTIVES

- Criterion for spontaneous decomposition of a metal oxide
- Carbon as a reductant
- Ellingham diagrams and predicting conditions

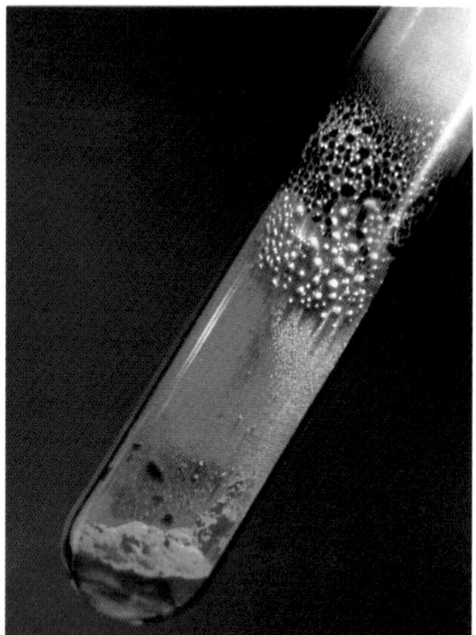

The decomposition of mercury(II) oxide to produce metallic mercury and oxygen gas.

K and ΔG⊖

Remember that, for a reaction to favour products, the equilibrium constant K must be greater than 1. When $\Delta G^\ominus = 0$, $K = 1$, and reactants and products are present in equal concentrations.

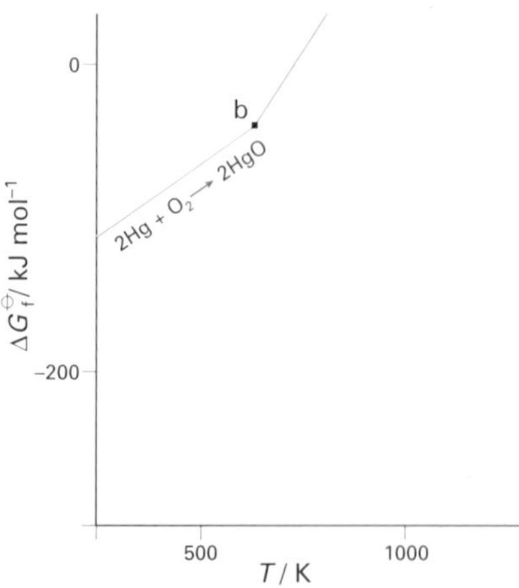

Gaseous oxygen reacts with mercury to form solid mercury(II) oxide. The standard entropy change of formation is therefore negative and the gradient of the line is positive. The gradient becomes steeper at b, the boiling point of the metal, because the solid oxide is now being formed from two *gaseous species, oxygen and the metal.*

GIBBS ENERGY AND METAL EXTRACTION

You are now well used to searching data books to enable you to calculate standard entropy, enthalpy, and Gibbs energy changes. However, you should bear in mind that the $^\ominus$ symbol in, for example, $\Delta G^\ominus$ refers to a pressure of 1 bar and a stated temperature that is *not necessarily 298 K.* The value of $\Delta G^\ominus$ for a reaction depends on the temperature. In this spread we look at how the temperature dependence of $\Delta G^\ominus$ determines the conditions under which metals may be extracted from their ores.

Changing metal oxides into metals

If you heat mercury(II) oxide alone at about 450 °C, it spontaneously decomposes into mercury and oxygen. But to extract zinc from its oxide ore, the ore must be reduced with carbon at about 1000 °C. The extraction of aluminium by carbon reduction would require a temperature greater than 2000 °C, too high for commercial use. The differences in behaviour between these metals may be explained by looking closely at the standard Gibbs energy changes for the reactions at different temperatures.

The dependence of $\Delta G^\ominus$ on temperature

When we are considering the extraction of metals from their oxide ores, the standard Gibbs energy change of particular interest is $\Delta G^\ominus_f$, the standard Gibbs energy change of formation of the oxide. The standard Gibbs energy change of formation is given by the equation:

$$\Delta G^\ominus_f = \Delta H^\ominus_f - T\Delta S^\ominus_f$$

The standard enthalpy change of formation $\Delta H^\ominus_f$ and the standard entropy change of formation $\Delta S^\ominus_f$ may be assumed to be roughly independent of temperature. Rewriting the relationship as

$$\Delta G^\ominus_f = -\Delta S^\ominus_f T + \Delta H^\ominus_f$$

gives the formula of a straight-line graph of the type

$$y = mx + c$$

That is, a plot of $\Delta G^\ominus_f$ against T gives a straight line with a gradient of $-\Delta S^\ominus_f$. The diagram to the left shows this plot for mercury(II) oxide. In the formation of the oxide, one mole of oxygen gas is destroyed, so $\Delta S^\ominus$ is strongly *negative* and the line generally slopes upwards.

The decomposition of mercury(II) oxide

As the temperature increases, the value of $\Delta G^\ominus_f$ for the reaction

$$2Hg + O_2(g) \rightarrow 2HgO(s)$$

becomes less negative, especially after mercury becomes a gas (at point b on the diagram). At approximately 750 K the value becomes zero; at this temperature, mercury, oxygen, and mercury(II) oxide exist together in an equilibrium with a K value of around 1. At higher temperatures, $\Delta G^\ominus_f$ becomes positive for this reaction, and therefore the standard Gibbs energy change for the *decomposition* of mercury(II) oxide

$$2HgO(s) \rightarrow 2Hg(g) + O_2(g)$$

becomes negative. Above 750 K, mercury(II) oxide spontaneously decomposes to its elements.

The majority of metal oxides remain stable up to extremely high temperatures. However, many metals can be extracted from their oxides with the assistance of a reductant, which is commonly carbon or carbon monoxide.

Ellingham diagrams

An **Ellingham diagram** consists of graphs of the standard Gibbs energy changes of formation for the metal oxides as a function of temperature. In an Ellingham diagram, the $\Delta G_f^\ominus$ values are quoted per mole of oxygen gas. As with the example of Hg/HgO given opposite, the gradients of the metal/metal oxide plots are generally positive. Many metals such as iron, lead, and zinc are produced by heating an oxide ore with carbon. Conditions in the metal smelting furnace may vary, so that the reductant is either carbon itself or carbon monoxide. Ellingham diagrams also contain the plots for the formation of the oxides of carbon:

$$2C(s) + O_2(g) \rightarrow 2CO(g) \quad (a)$$
$$2CO(g) + O_2(g) \rightarrow 2CO_2(g) \quad (b)$$

Notice that the line (a) for the conversion of carbon to carbon monoxide slopes *downwards*. The line slopes in this direction because 2 mol of carbon monoxide gas are produced for every 1 mol of oxygen gas used, and so the entropy change is positive. This downward-sloping line will eventually cross the upward-sloping line for the conversion of a metal to its oxide. Above the temperature at which the lines cross, carbon can reduce the metal oxide to the metal. Above 1000 K carbon can reduce iron(II) oxide. Zinc is also manufactured by carbon reduction at temperatures greater than 1200 K. However, the temperatures required for titanium, aluminium, and calcium are uneconomically high.

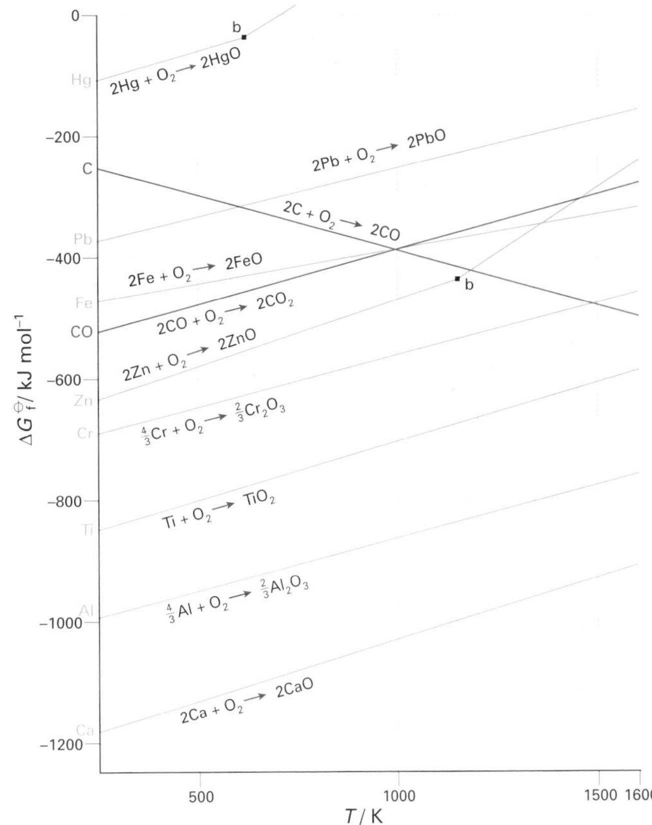

An Ellingham diagram showing the relationship between standard Gibbs energy change and temperature, for the oxides of carbon and various metal oxides. For zinc, the slope becomes significantly greater at the boiling point (b).

Generally, the reduction of the metal oxide may proceed by one of two possible pathways:

1. metal oxide + carbon → metal + carbon monoxide
2. metal oxide + carbon monoxide → metal + carbon dioxide

- A carbon–oxygen system will reduce a metal–oxygen system when the $\Delta G_f^\ominus$ value of the former is more negative than the $\Delta G_f^\ominus$ value of the latter.

Iron and the blast furnace

The extraction of iron in a blast furnace is a complex process that occurs in a number of steps. However, the final stage can be treated as the reduction of iron(II) oxide. Look at the Ellingham diagram plots for the formation of iron(II) oxide from its elements, and for the formation of carbon dioxide from carbon monoxide. Carbon monoxide will reduce iron(II) oxide at temperatures *up to* 1000 K – the point where the plot for $\Delta G_f^\ominus$(CO_2 from CO) cuts the line for $\Delta G_f^\ominus$(FeO from Fe):

$$FeO(s) + CO(g) \rightarrow Fe(s) + CO_2(g)$$

At temperatures *above* 1000 K, carbon acts as the reductant:

$$FeO(s) + C(s) \rightarrow Fe(s) + CO(g)$$

A blast furnace, showing the molten iron being run off.

SUMMARY

- The standard Gibbs energy is a function of temperature.
- Plots of $\Delta G_f^\ominus$ against T for metal oxides generally have positive gradients.
- Metal oxides spontaneously decompose into their elements at sufficiently high temperatures, when the value of $\Delta G_f^\ominus$ for the oxide becomes *positive*.
- Ellingham diagrams may be used to predict the temperature at which the reduction of a metal oxide by carbon or carbon monoxide becomes feasible.

PRACTICE EXAM QUESTIONS

1 The effect of temperature on chemical equilibrium is given by the equation

$\Delta G^\ominus = -RT \ln K_c$

Use this information, where relevant, in answering the questions that follow.

a To what does the symbol c refer in the equilibrium constant which is written K_c? [1]

b Derive an expression which shows the dependence of the logarithm of the equilibrium constant, ln K_c, on temperature, T, standard enthalpy change, $\Delta H^\ominus$, and standard entropy change $\Delta S^\ominus$. [2]

c Assuming that $\Delta H^\ominus$ and $\Delta S^\ominus$ do not vary with temperature, use the expression you derived in **b** above to explain how the magnitude of ln K_c varies with *increase* in temperature for

i an exothermic reaction,

ii an endothermic reaction. [4]

AQA (NEAB) 1995

2 The diagram below shows apparatus used to measure the standard e.m.f. of an electrochemical cell.

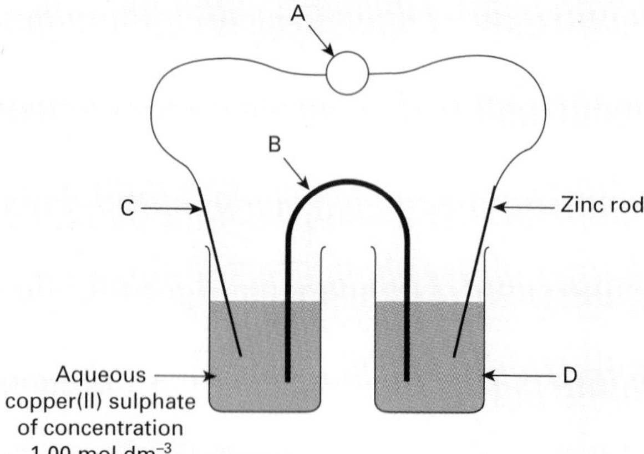

a i Give the name of each piece of apparatus **A** to **C**. [3]

ii Give the formula and concentration of the cation in solution **D**. [1]

iii State the condition required for this measurement. [1]

b The table below shows the standard electrode potentials for copper and zinc.

Electrode system	$E^\ominus$/V
$Zn^{2+}(aq) + 2e^- \rightleftharpoons Zn(s)$	–0.76
$Cu^{2+}(aq) + 2e^- \rightleftharpoons Cu(s)$	+0.34

i Write an equation to show the overall reaction in the cell. [1]

ii Calculate the e.m.f. of this cell. [1]

iii Calculate the free energy change, $\Delta G^\ominus$, for the reaction in **b i**.

[Faraday constant = 96 500 C mol^{-1}.] [3]

iv In which direction will the electrons move through **A** in the digram? [1]

AQA (AEB) 1996

3 The feasibility of a chemical reaction depends on the standard free energy change, $\Delta G^\ominus$, which is related to the standard enthalpy and entropy changes by the equation

$\Delta G^\ominus = \Delta H^\ominus - T\Delta S^\ominus$

Use this information, where relevant, in answering the questions that follow.

a Ice melts at atmospheric pressure only if the surrounding temperature rises about 0 °C.

i State the signs of the enthalpy and entropy changes during melting.

ii Explain why ice does not melt at temperatures below 0 °C. [4]

b When sodium hydrogencarbonate is added to dilute hydrochloric acid, the temperature of the reaction mixture drops. Despite this, the reaction is spontaneous. Explain how this can be. [3]

c Give the signs of enthalpy change, of the entropy change and of the free energy change for the combustion of propane. In **each** case give a reason for your answer. [6]

AQA (NEAB) 1995

4 a The graph below shows the variation of ΔG with temperature for three reactions relevant to the extraction of iron from iron oxide.

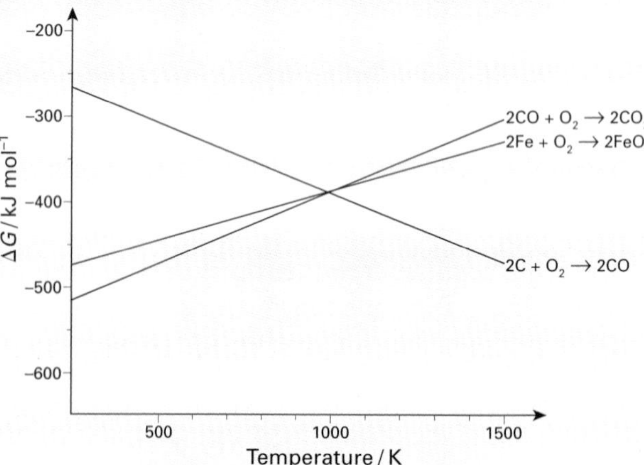

i Use this diagram to estimate values of ΔG at 800 K for the following reactions:

$2C + O_2 \rightarrow 2CO$

$2CO + O_2 \rightarrow 2CO_2$

$2Fe + O_2 \rightarrow 2FeO$ [3]

ii Calculate the values of ΔG for the following reactions at 800 K:

$FeO + C \rightarrow CO + Fe$

$FeO + CO \rightarrow CO_2 + Fe$ [3]

iii Use the values obtained in **a ii** to explain why carbon monoxide, rather than carbon, acts as the reducing agent at 800 K. [2]

iv Use **Figure 3** to estimate the minimum temperature at which carbon becomes capable of reducing iron oxide to iron. [1]

v Use the relevant equation given in **a ii** to explain why the reduction of iron oxide to iron using carbon as the reducing agent results in an increase in the entropy of the system. [2]

b The table below shows some values for standard electrode potentials.

Electrode system	$E^{\ominus}$/V
$Fe^{2+}(aq) + 2e^- \rightleftharpoons Fe(s)$	–0.44
$H^+(aq) + e^- \rightleftharpoons \frac{1}{2}H_2(s)$	0.00

i Give the emf of the cell. [1]

ii State which would be the positive electrode. [1]

iii Write an equation to show the overall reaction in the cell [1]

iv Write down the cell diagram that represents the overall reaction in the cell. [2]

v Give the name of an instrument that could be used to measure the emf of the cell. [1]
AQA (NEAB) 1998

5 When zinc foil is placed in aqueous lead(II) nitrate solution, an exothermic reaction takes place. The enthalpy change can be measured using an electrical compensation calorimeter, and the following data were obtained in such an experiment in which an excess of zinc powder was added.

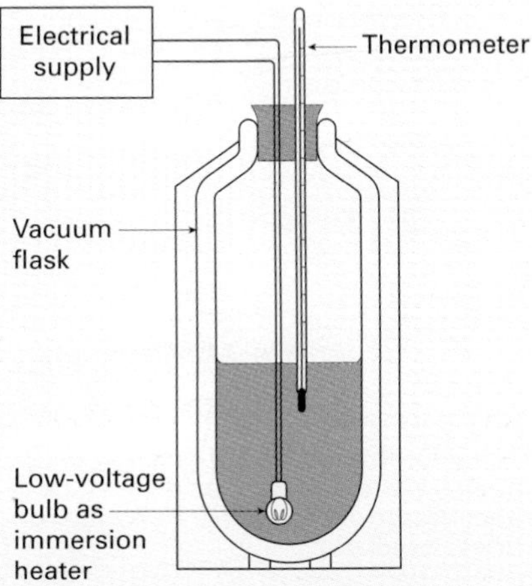

Output of immersion heater = 25.0 W (1 W = 1 J s^{-1})
Volume of 0.5 M lead(II) nitrate solution = 100 cm^3
Temperature rise in solution after reaction = 12.5 °C
Time taken for immersion heater to raise temperature by 12.5 °C = 305 s.

a Write two half-equations to represent the changes which take place when zinc reacts with lead(II) nitrate solution. [2]

b What are the two main advantages of the electrical compensation calorimeter over other simple methods for measuring enthalpy changes? [2]

c Calculate a value for the standard molar enthalpy change for this reaction from the data. [2]

d The same reaction can be used in an electrochemical cell. Under standard conditions this gives an e.m.f. of 0.63 V.

i Write down a conventional cell diagram for this cell.

ii Which is the positive electrode in this cell? Explain your reasoning.

iii State the names and concentrations of suitable solutions that could be used to set up the cell under standard conditions.

iv Draw a diagram to show how this cell could be set up in a laboratory, and its e.m.f. measured. You should clearly label the electrode materials and the solutions: the position of the salt bridge should be shown but details of its composition are not required. [6]

e i Calculate the entropy change at 298 K in the system during this reaction, using the relationships:

$\Delta G^{\ominus} = -zFE^{\ominus} = \Delta H^{\ominus} - T\Delta S^{\ominus}_{system}$
$[F = 9.65 \times 10^4 \text{ C mol}^{-1}]$

ii Calculate the entropy change at 298 K for the surroundings in this reaction ($\Delta S^{\ominus}_{surroundings}$).

iii Calculate the value of $\Delta S^{\ominus}_{system} + \Delta S^{\ominus}_{surroundings}$ for this reaction at 298 K, and explain clearly the significance of the result of this calculation. [5]
EDEXCEL (ULEAC) 1986

6 a Entropy is often linked with the idea of order and disorder. Write an equation for a chemical reaction in which the amount of *disorder* increases and state the sign of the entropy change which accompanies this reaction. [2]

b The combustion of graphite involves an increase in entropy from reactants to products of +3 J K^{-1} mol^{-1}. The standard entropy of oxygen is 205 J K^{-1} mol^{-1} and that of carbon dioxide is 214 J K^{-1} mol^{-1}. Calculate the standard entropy of graphite and suggest why it has a relatively low value. [4]

c i Write an equation that relates ΔG to ΔH and ΔS in a reaction.

ii Derive an equation which relates ΔS to ΔH when $\Delta G = 0$. [2]

d For certain reversible processes such as boiling and freezing, the Gibbs free energy change is zero. When water freezes, 6.0 kJ mol^{-1} of heat energy are evolved. Use the equation you derived in part **c ii** to calculate the entropy change in 54 g of water when it freezes at 0 °C. [4]
AQA (NEAB) 1996

Chemical kinetics

Two questions are frequently asked about a chemical reaction. They are: 'Will it happen?' and 'How fast does it happen?' As we saw in earlier chapters, thermodynamics answers the first question by considering the implications of changes in enthalpy and especially Gibbs energy associated with chemical reactions. However, there are many reactions that, whilst thermodynamically feasible, proceed extremely slowly. Once we know that a reaction is feasible, knowledge about its rate (How fast?) is clearly of equal importance. This chapter is concerned with chemical kinetics – measuring the rates of reactions and trying to understand in detail how reactants change into products.

REACTION RATE

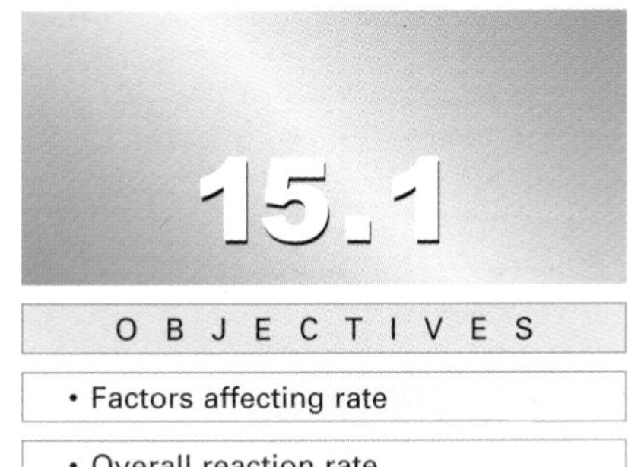

OBJECTIVES

- Factors affecting rate
- Overall reaction rate

Imagine a car travelling at a speed of 80 kilometres per hour ($km\,h^{-1}$) down the motorway. Each second, about 50 separate combustion cycles happen in the engine. Each cycle involves drawing a fuel/air mixture into the combustion chamber, compressing the mixture, burning it, and expelling the exhaust gases. The rate of this oxidation reaction is extremely rapid, taking less than five milliseconds. At the same time, a patch of rust hidden inside one of the doors is slowly growing. Rusting is the corrosion of iron (a reaction with oxygen and water). The rate of this oxidation reaction is extremely slow. It may take years before the first tell-tale brown spots appear under the gleaming paintwork.

A number of different factors affect the rates of reactions. We will summarize them now. Most of these factors are dealt with in this chapter, whereas others are studied elsewhere in this book.

Rate and collisions

In any reaction, the reactant species must collide with sufficient energy for reaction to happen. The reactant species could be molecules, atoms, or ions; for simplicity we will use the term 'molecules' from now on. Collisions break chemical bonds in the reactants; new bonds form between the fragments to create the products.

The effect of temperature on the reaction between magnesium and water (both beakers contain an indicator that changes from colourless to purple in the presence of the basic solution formed by the reaction): hot water at 80 °C (left) and cold water at 20 °C.

The effect of concentration on the reaction between magnesium and dilute sulphuric acid: (a) H_2SO_4(aq) of concentration 1.0 $mol\,dm^{-3}$; and (b) H_2SO_4(aq) of concentration 0.2 $mol\,dm^{-3}$.

Rate and temperature

Increasing the temperature of the reactants increases the rate of a reaction. At higher temperatures, the molecules are moving with greater average speed and so collide more frequently and with greater energy.

Rate and concentration

Increasing the concentration of the reactants increases the rate of a reaction. At greater concentration, there are more molecules in a given volume. Distances between these molecules are therefore reduced and there is an increased number of collisions per second.

Other factors

- *Pressure*: For reactions involving gases, increasing the pressure of a gas increases its concentration. A given volume contains a greater amount in moles of the gas.
- *Surface area*: In a reaction involving a solid, breaking the solid into smaller pieces increases its total surface area. There is more contact with the other reactant(s) and so the rate of reaction increases.

(a) 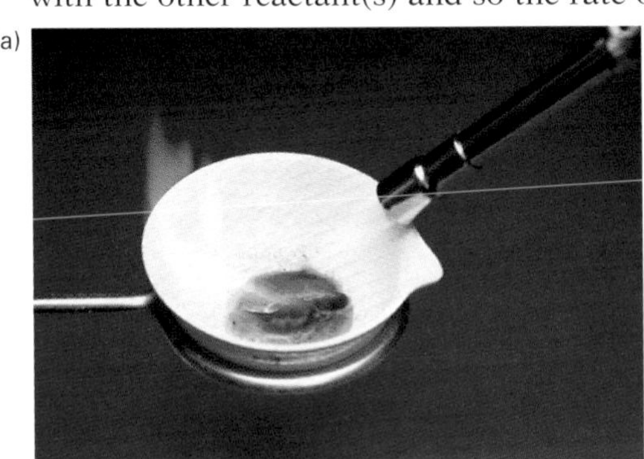 (b) 

Lycopodium powder consists of the dusty spores of a common moss. (a) The spores burn with difficulty when piled together in a dish. (b) When sprayed into a flame, combustion is rapid because the spores are very well mixed with oxygen.

- *Light*: Some reactions are much more vigorous when carried out in bright light. Light is a form of electromagnetic radiation. If the frequency of the light is great enough, then the energy carried by each quantum of light may be sufficient to break a bond in one of the reactants and create a short-lived, reactive species (called a **reactive intermediate**) from which the products form.
- *Catalysts*: A catalyst is a substance that increases the rate of a chemical reaction without itself undergoing a permanent change.

Overall rate and instantaneous rate

You can measure the overall rate of a reaction by starting a clock as you mix the reactants and then stopping the clock when the reaction is complete. If you know the increase in concentration of a product, then the overall rate *with respect to that product* is given by

$$\text{rate of reaction} = \frac{\text{increase in concentration of product}}{\text{time}}$$

As in the box above, concentration is measured in moles per cubic decimetre ($mol\,dm^{-3}$) and time in seconds (s).

However, it may be obvious from watching a reaction that the *instantaneous* rate changes as the reaction proceeds. Rate usually decreases as time goes by because the reactant concentration is decreasing. (Returning to the car analogy, the *overall* speed for a journey may be $80\,km\,h^{-1}$. The *instantaneous* speed may vary between zero and $120\,km\,h^{-1}$.)

SUMMARY

- The rate of a chemical reaction is the change in concentration per unit time.
- The rate of a reaction depends chiefly on temperature and on reactant concentration.
- Other factors that may affect reaction rate include pressure, light, the presence of a suitable catalyst, and the surface area of a solid reactant.

Car speed and reaction rate

From your science lessons in past years, you should remember that

$$\text{speed} = \frac{\text{change in distance}}{\text{time}}$$

So a car that travels 80 kilometres in one hour has an overall speed of

$$\frac{80\,km}{1\,h} = 80\,km\,h^{-1}$$

When we need to talk about how fast a reaction is, we use a similar expression, but using 'rate of reaction' and 'change in concentration':

$$\text{rate of reaction} = \frac{\text{change in concentration}}{\text{time}}$$

So a chemical reaction in which the concentration changes by $0.10\,mol\,dm^{-3}$ in 120 seconds has an overall rate of

$$\frac{0.10\,mol\,dm^{-3}}{120\,s} = 8.3 \times 10^{-4}\,mol\,dm^{-3}\,s^{-1}$$

(The units here are moles per cubic decimetre per second.)

Light

A mixture of the gases methane CH_4 and chlorine Cl_2 shows little sign of reaction. Fire a photographic flash gun close to the mixture and there will be an explosive reaction. Electromagnetic radiation forms highly reactive chlorine atoms, which trigger the reaction.

A sample of aqueous hydrogen peroxide $H_2O_2(aq)$ decomposes over a period of months into oxygen and water. If a platinum catalyst is immersed in the sample, the reaction is complete in a matter of minutes.

15.2

SOME PRACTICAL TECHNIQUES

OBJECTIVES

- Titration
- Colorimetry
- Conductivity
- Flash photolysis
- Measuring gas volume

Chemical kinetics investigates the rates at which chemical reactions take place. The rate of a reaction is the rate of change in concentration of one of the products or reactants. The units of rate are usually moles per cubic decimetre per second ($mol\,dm^{-3}\,s^{-1}$). Some practical investigations directly monitor the concentration of one of the reactants or products as the reaction proceeds. Other investigations measure other variables such as mass or volume. All these measurements must be converted into changes in concentration over specified periods of time in order to calculate rate. This spread introduces the main methods of monitoring changes in the composition of reaction mixtures. Some are dealt with in more detail elsewhere in this book.

Titration

The reaction between aqueous hydrogen peroxide and acidified potassium iodide

$$H_2O_2(aq) + 2H^+(aq) + 2I^-(aq) \rightarrow I_2(aq) + 2H_2O(l)$$

may be investigated by monitoring the concentration of iodine. At measured (but *not* necessarily equal) time intervals, samples of the reaction mixture are extracted. The reaction in each sample taken is **quenched** (slowed down very significantly) by diluting in ice-cold water. Each sample is then titrated against standard aqueous sodium thiosulphate, and the concentration of the iodine is calculated. (We will look at this example in more detail in the next spread.)

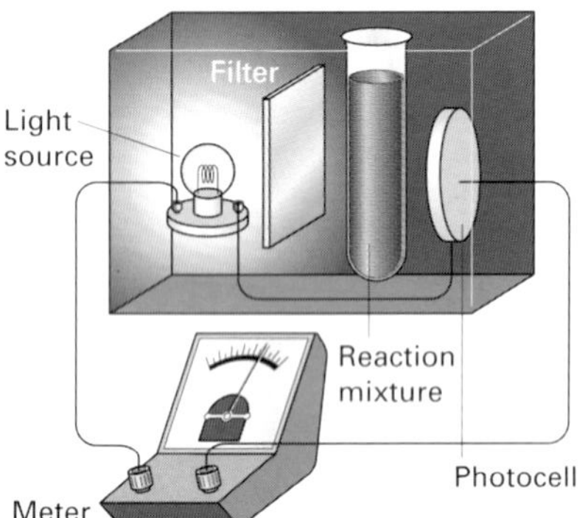

*A **colorimeter** indicates concentration by measuring the intensity of light shining through a coloured reaction mixture. The colorimeter produces an electrical signal, which can be analysed by computer.*

Colorimetry

Some reaction mixtures show a steady change of colour as the reaction proceeds. For example, colourless ethanedioate ions ($C_2O_4^{2-}$) reduce purple manganate(VII) ions (MnO_4^-) to colourless manganese(II) ions (Mn^{2+}) in acidic solution:

$$2MnO_4^-(aq) + 16H^+(aq) + 5C_2O_4^{2-}(aq) \rightarrow 2Mn^{2+}(aq) + 10CO_2(g) + 8H_2O(l)$$

The concentration of manganate(VII) ion may be monitored over time by using a colorimeter. Light of a fixed wavelength shines through the reaction mixture and onto a photocell. The photocell develops an e.m.f. proportional to the intensity of the light. If the photocell has been calibrated with solutions of known concentration, the e.m.f. can be converted to manganate(VII) ion concentration values.

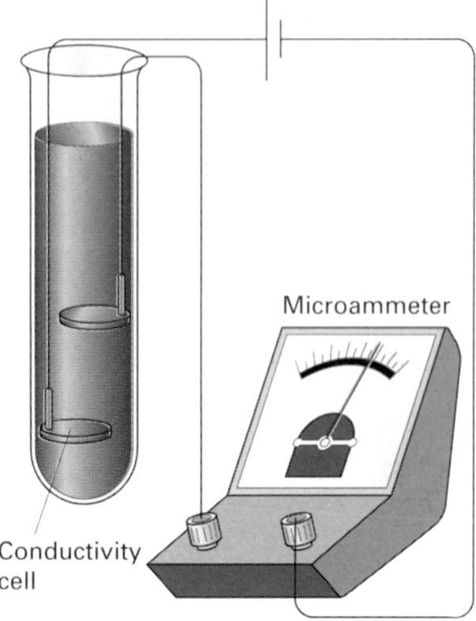

A conductivity cell. The smallest possible current is passed through the cell to limit electrolytic effects.

Conductivity

Look again at the above ionic equation for the reaction between manganate(VII) and ethanedioate ions. You should notice that the reactants include a total of 23 ions, whilst amongst the products there are just two ions. The electrical conductivity of a solution is proportional to the concentration of its ions and the charges they bear. The conductivity of the reaction mixture may be monitored over time by carrying out the reaction in a conductivity cell. As with the colorimeter, conductivity apparatus may be calibrated with solutions of known concentration. Readings of conductivity as the reaction proceeds may then be converted to concentrations of the ions present.

Laser flash photolysis and femtosecond spectroscopy

Some reactions are extremely rapid. The technique of **laser flash photolysis** uses a very short burst of light from a laser to start a reaction that is sensitive to light. Spectroscopic techniques, chapter 32, then monitor the concentration of the reactive intermediate formed. A particularly neat version of the technique uses the same laser to start the reaction and to measure the response of the system, as shown in the illustrations at the top of the opposite page.

A very short pulse of light of femtosecond duration (1 femtosecond = 1 fs = 10^{-15} s) starts out from a laser and is split into two beams. The direct beam causes the reaction to start; the indirect beam is delayed by being sent over a longer path to the reaction chamber. This *probe pulse arrives a few femtoseconds later and causes the reaction mixture to absorb light, which is analysed to reveal the concentrations of the species present.*

Free Na atoms
Na in NaI molecule
Absorption intensity
Time delay / ps

When excited by a laser pulse, the ion pair Na^+I^- becomes a covalently bonded pair NaI, which rapidly decomposes into separate atoms Na and I. The lower graph shows the intensity of the absorption by the molecule NaI. The upper graph shows the absorbance of free Na atoms (and hence their concentration).

Measuring the volume of gas produced

The decomposition of aqueous hydrogen peroxide occurs rapidly in the presence of a catalyst:

$$2H_2O_2(aq) \rightarrow 2H_2O(l) + O_2(g)$$

This reaction may be monitored by measuring the volume of oxygen gas evolved as a function of time elapsed after adding the catalyst.

The measured volume of gas may then be used to calculate the corresponding concentration of the reactant, hydrogen peroxide. The rate of the reaction is then expressed as

$$\text{rate of reaction} = \frac{\text{decrease in concentration of reactant}}{\text{time}}$$

Which product or reactant?

Look again at the reaction between aqueous hydrogen peroxide and acidified potassium iodide:

$$H_2O_2(aq) + 2H^+(aq) + 2I^-(aq) \rightarrow I_2(aq) + 2H_2O(l)$$

The reaction produces 2 mol of water for every 1 mol of iodine produced. Rate of reaction is defined as

$$\text{rate of reaction} = \frac{\text{change in concentration}}{\text{time}}$$

The rate of change in concentration with respect to water is therefore *twice* the rate of change in concentration with respect to iodine.

How this is dealt with in a formal way to give a unique rate for any reaction is explained in spread 15.7.

Temperature control

Reaction rates are obtained by monitoring the change in concentration of one substance with time. Rate is dependent on temperature, so reactions should be carried out in a thermostatically controlled water bath.

SUMMARY

- Concentration can be monitored using techniques such as titration, colorimetry, and conductivity.
- Ultra-fast reactions can be studied using laser flash photolysis.

PRACTICE

1 Suppose you mix acidified potassium iodide with aqueous hydrogen peroxide. You titrate the iodine in the sample against 0.20 mol dm^{-3} aqueous sodium thiosulphate and obtain the results shown (1 mol of iodine I_2 reacts with 2 mol of thiosulphate $S_2O_3^{2-}$). Calculate the rate of the reaction (include units) during:

a the first 15 minutes,

b the final 15 minutes.

Results:

t/min	Volume of $S_2O_3^{2-}$(aq)/cm^3
0	0
15	15.0
30	24.5
45	28.5
60	30.0
75	30.0

15.3

OBJECTIVES

- Rate changes during a reaction
- Plotting concentration–time graphs
- Finding rates from concentration–time graphs

INSTANTANEOUS REACTION RATE

The previous spread concluded by asking you a question about the reaction between acidified potassium iodide and aqueous hydrogen peroxide. Simply by looking at the experimental data (reproduced again below), it should be obvious that the reaction rate changes in the course of the reaction. The rate is greatest at the start of the reaction because the reactant concentration has its maximum value. The rate is zero at the end of the reaction because the concentration of one or more reactants is zero. How can you measure this changing rate and how can the results be expressed on paper? These are the problems tackled by this spread.

The practical procedure

The balanced chemical equation for the peroxide/iodide reaction is

$$H_2O_2(aq) + 2H^+(aq) + 2I^-(aq) \rightarrow I_2(aq) + 2H_2O(l)$$

The method of analysis is as follows:

1 Mix acidified potassium iodide with aqueous hydrogen peroxide; start the clock.

2 Every 15 minutes remove a 10.0 cm^3 sample from the reaction mixture and pour it into 100 cm^3 of water at 5 °C.

3 Titrate the iodine in the sample against 0.200 mol dm^{-3} aqueous sodium thiosulphate (1 mol of iodine I_2 reacts with 2 mol of thiosulphate $S_2O_3^{2-}$).

Typical results are shown in the table to the left. Note that the reaction is complete by 60 minutes: there is no increase in the volume of thiosulphate used and therefore no increase in the concentration of iodine in the reaction mixture.

Results for the titration of 0.200 mol dm^{-3} aqueous sodium thiosulphate against the iodine liberated from the reaction between acidified potassium iodide and aqueous hydrogen peroxide.

t/min	Volume of $S_2O_3^{2-}$/cm^3
0	0
15	15.0
30	24.5
45	28.5
60	30.0
75	30.0

Calculating concentrations

The rate of this reaction will be stated in terms of the concentration of the product, iodine. Iodine concentration is calculated from each of the titration results. The calculation for t = 15 min is as follows:

The volume of 0.200 mol dm^{-3} $S_2O_3^{2-}$ used is 15.0 cm^3.

Now we need to use

amount in moles = volume × concentration

So

$$\text{amount in moles of } S_2O_3^{2-} = \left(\frac{15.0}{1000}\,\text{dm}^3\right) \times (0.200\,\text{mol dm}^{-3})$$
$$= 3.00 \times 10^{-3}\,\text{mol}$$

The equation for the titration reaction is:

$$I_2(aq) + 2S_2O_3^{2-}(aq) \rightarrow 2I^-(aq) + S_4O_6^{2-}(aq)$$

From this, the mole ratio I_2:$S_2O_3^{2-}$ = 1:2. So

$$\text{amount in moles of } I_2 = \tfrac{1}{2} \times 3.00 \times 10^{-3}\,\text{mol}$$
$$= 1.50 \times 10^{-3}\,\text{mol}$$

This amount in moles was in a 10.0 cm^3 sample removed from the reaction mixture. Now we need to use

$$\text{concentration} = \frac{\text{amount in moles}}{\text{volume}}$$

So

$$\text{iodine concentration} = \frac{1.50 \times 10^{-3}\,\text{mol}}{10.0 \times 10^{-3}\,\text{dm}^3}$$
$$= 0.150\,\text{mol dm}^{-3}$$

Successive calculations along exactly the same lines as the above give the results shown in the table to the left.

Results showing the concentration of iodine at 15-minute intervals.

t/min	Concentration of I_2(aq) /mol dm^{-3}
0	0
15	0.150
30	0.245
45	0.285
60	0.300
75	0.300

Time and average rate

The results obtained in the course of the reaction may be plotted to give the graph shown on the right. The results in the graph show that the reaction produces a concentration of 0.300 mol dm^{-3} of iodine in 56 minutes, after which the reaction is complete. Rate is defined as:

$$\text{rate} = \frac{\text{change in concentration}}{\text{time}}$$

Therefore, the *overall* rate of the reaction is

$$\frac{0.300\,\text{mol dm}^{-3}}{56 \times 60\,\text{s}} = 8.9 \times 10^{-5}\,\text{mol dm}^{-3}\,\text{s}^{-1}$$

The rate *during the first 15 minutes* is

$$\frac{0.150\,\text{mol dm}^{-3}}{15 \times 60\,\text{s}} = 1.7 \times 10^{-4}\,\text{mol dm}^{-3}\,\text{s}^{-1}$$

These rates are average values, taken over a period of time. However, the requirement is usually for information about the magnitude of the rate *at a particular time*.

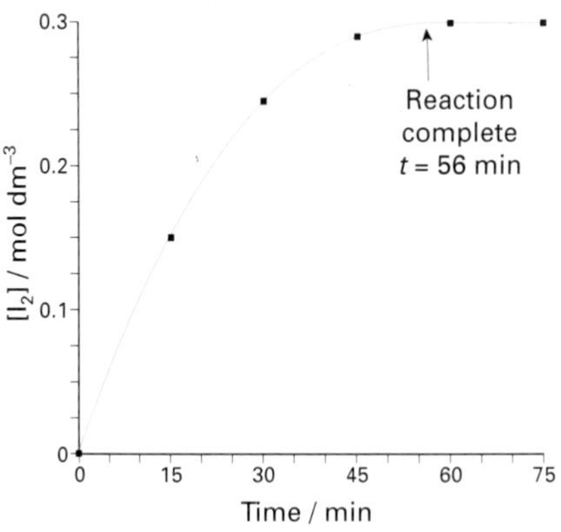

The graph of iodine concentration vs time.

Instantaneous rates

There are several important points to note about this graph:

- The rate of reaction is greatest at the start of the reaction (at t = 0 min).
- The graph becomes horizontal when the reaction is finished, i.e. when the gradient is zero.
- A time of just less than 60 minutes (about 56 minutes) elapsed from the start of the reaction to its completion. (Note that, from our results in the table, all we can say is that *the reaction was finished by the time we took our sample at 60 minutes*. On drawing the graph, we can say that *the reaction was finished just before we took our sample at 60 minutes*.)

To find the rate of reaction at a certain time, it is necessary to find the slope (gradient) of the tangent to the graph at that time.

- The instantaneous rate of reaction is equal to the slope (gradient) of the tangent to the concentration–time graph.

The technique is shown in the drawings alongside, using the graph obtained earlier from the experimental data and shown at the top of this page.

We calculate the instantaneous rate at t = 30 min as follows:

The line AB is the tangent to the graph at t = 30 min.

The rate of reaction at t = 30 min is equal to the slope of this line. So

$$\text{gradient AB} = \frac{\text{change in concentration}}{\text{time}}$$

$$= \frac{MR}{RT} = \frac{(y_2 - y_1)}{(x_2 - x_1)}$$

$$= \frac{(0.310 - 0.175)\,\text{mol dm}^{-3}}{60 \times (45.0 - 15.0)\,\text{s}}$$

$$= \frac{0.135\,\text{mol dm}^{-3}}{60 \times 30\,\text{s}}$$

$$= 7.5 \times 10^{-5}\,\text{mol dm}^{-3}\,\text{s}^{-1}$$

Remember that this value is for the rate of reaction at a given time – in the same way that the speedometer of a car will indicate 20 km h^{-1} as it is slowing down to a halt from an initial speed of 80 km h^{-1}.

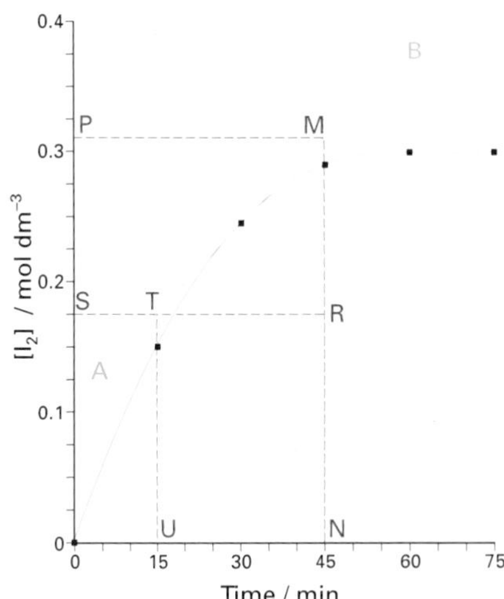

The construction lines that are necessary to find the rate at time t = 30 min:
1 Draw the tangent (AB) to the graph at t = 30 min.
2 At any convenient point M (x_2, y_2) on AB, draw the vertical line MRN (cuts the x-axis at x_2) and the horizontal line MP (cuts the y-axis at y_2).
3 At any other convenient point T (x_1, y_1) on AB, draw the vertical line TU (cuts the x-axis at x_1) and the horizontal line RTS (cuts the y-axis at y_1).

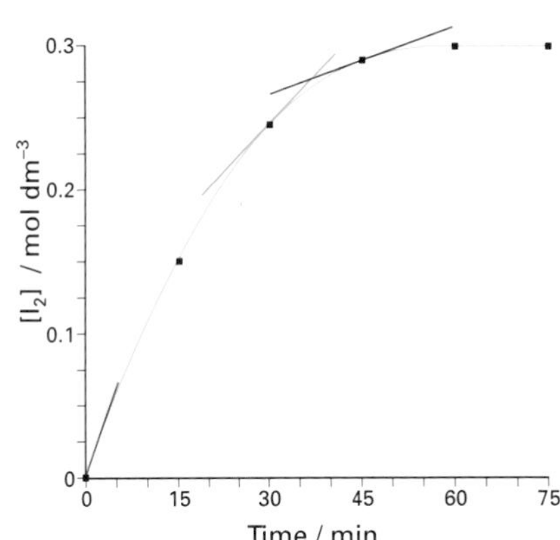

The slope is steepest at t = 0 min; it is less steep at t = 45 min than at t = 30 min. The reaction gets slower.

SUMMARY

- Reaction rate is at a maximum at the start of the reaction; it is zero at the end of the reaction.
- Experimental results are used to plot concentration–time graphs.
- The rate at a given time is equal to the slope of the tangent to the concentration graph at that time.

15.4

REACTION RATE AND COLLISION THEORY

OBJECTIVES

- Temperature and kinetic energy
- Distribution of molecular energies
- Activation energy
- Reaction profiles

Reactant species: a reminder

The reactant species that collide in the course of chemical reactions may include molecules, atoms, or ions. For the sake of simplicity, we refer to reactant species simply as 'molecules'.

Temperature, energy, and speed

If we set T = thermodynamic temperature (in kelvin), E_k = kinetic energy, v = molecular speed, and m = molecular mass, then

$E_k \propto T$

and, by definition,

$E_k = \frac{1}{2}mv^2$

so,

$E_k \propto v^2$

and

$v^2 \propto T$

i.e.

$v \propto \sqrt{T}$

There are two assumptions about chemical reactions that it seems reasonable to make: molecules must physically meet before they can react; and molecules must collide with sufficient energy for reaction to take place. This spread examines these two assumptions and explores their influence on reaction rates. You will also see how they form the basis of 'collision theory' and the idea of 'activation energy'.

Temperature and average kinetic energy

Reactions occur faster at higher temperatures. For example, the reactions that cause milk and other food products to 'go off' occur more slowly at lower temperatures, which is why food is stored in a fridge. The even lower temperatures in a freezer keep food fresh for longer still.

The average kinetic energy of the molecules in a substance is proportional to its thermodynamic temperature. The kinetic energy of each of these molecules is proportional to the square of its speed. At higher temperature, the average speed of the molecules is greater. The greater average speed of molecules at higher temperatures has two consequences: the molecules collide more often, and each collision is more energetic.

Increasing the temperature from 25 °C to 35 °C causes the rate of the decomposition of dinitrogen pentaoxide N_2O_5:

$$2N_2O_5(g) \rightarrow 4NO_2(g) + O_2(g)$$

to increase by a factor of *four* (i.e. a 400% increase). You might conclude that the increase in reaction rate is due to the increase in molecular speed resulting in an increase in the collision frequency. However, increasing the temperature between these limits increases the average speed by just 2%. It seems the effect of temperature is far greater than can be explained simply by the molecules colliding more often.

The distribution of molecular energies

The molecules in a gas are continuously colliding with each other. The directions of the molecules are forever changing as they collide. An instantaneous 'snapshot' of a group of molecules would show a range of energies, from almost zero to very high values. This range may be represented by the Maxwell–Boltzmann distribution (see below and spread 8.4), which illustrates the distribution of molecular energies in a gas.

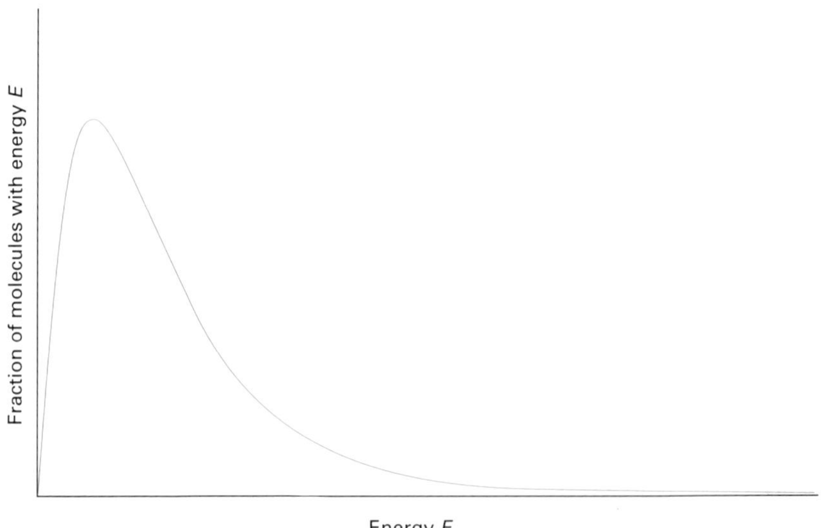

The Maxwell–Boltzmann distribution of molecular energies in a gas. You should note the following:
- *Only very small fractions of the molecules have either extremely high or extremely low energies.*
- *The curve is not symmetrical; the average energy is to the right of the peak of the curve.*

Activation energy

At the start of this spread, we made two assumptions: that molecules must come together to react; and also that they must collide with at least a certain minimum energy for reaction to occur. This minimum energy is called the **activation energy**, and it varies from one reaction to another. If the reactants collide with an energy at least equal to the activation energy, the collision is 'successful' and products will form. If the energy of the collision is less than the activation energy, the collision will be 'unsuccessful' and the molecules will simply rebound from each other unchanged.

The distribution of molecular energies shows how activation energy is the key to the dependence of reaction rate on temperature. The diagram below shows two superimposed molecular energy distributions at two temperatures, where T_2 is greater than T_1. At higher temperatures, there are many more energetic molecules, so the likelihood of a 'successful' collision increases rapidly with increase in temperature.

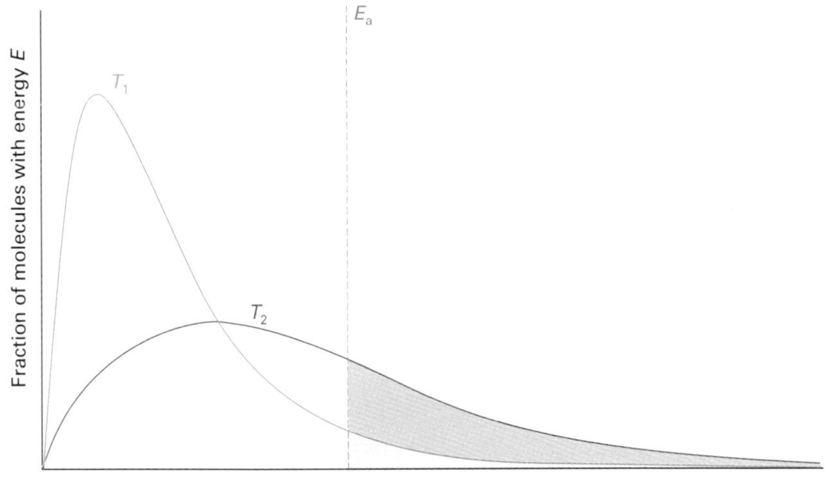

The distribution of molecular energies at two temperatures (T_2 is significantly higher than T_1). You should note the following:
- *The area under each distribution curve is proportional to the total number of molecules.*
- *There is a wider range of molecular energies at the higher temperature (T_2). The peak of the curve lies at higher energies at higher temperatures; the average energy also increases at higher temperatures.*
- *The activation energy is represented by the vertical line labelled E_a. The fraction of molecules that have at least this energy is much greater at the higher temperature than at the lower temperature (shown by the shading).*

(a)

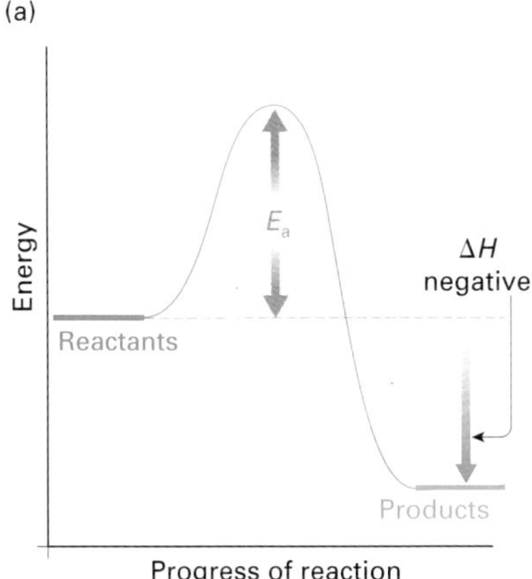

(b)

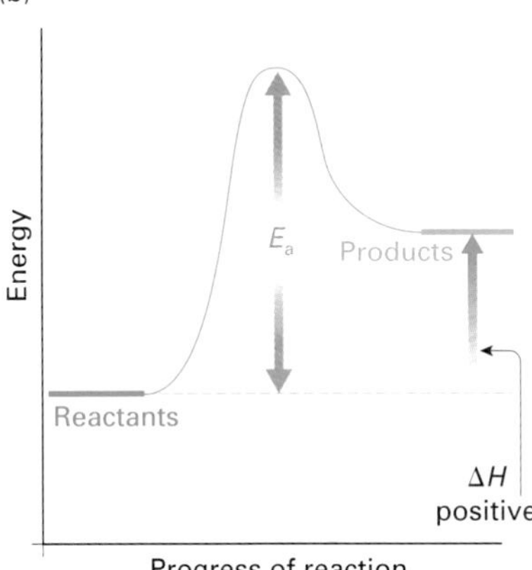

Reaction profiles for (a) exothermic and (b) endothermic reactions. E_a is the activation energy barrier that reactants must overcome before they can change into products. ΔH indicates the overall enthalpy change for the reaction.

Reaction profiles

The activation energy may be shown on diagrams called 'reaction profiles'. These diagrams illustrate the role of activation energy as an energy barrier that must be overcome by reactants before they may form products. A question now needs to be answered: 'What state have the reactants reached at the point represented by the top of the reaction profile (the **transition state**)?' The answer will be discussed later in this chapter, as it is fundamental to understanding the action of catalysts.

SUMMARY

- The average energy of molecules is proportional to the thermodynamic temperature.
- The distribution of molecular energies is shown by the Maxwell–Boltzmann distribution.
- The energy of reactant molecules must be at least equal to the activation energy before reaction can take place.

PRACTICE

1 Explain each of the following terms or phrases, as used in the text above:
a Average energy **b** Distribution of energy **c** Energy barrier **d** 'Successful' collision **e** 'Unsuccessful' collision **f** Activation energy.

RATE EQUATIONS AND ORDER OF REACTION

OBJECTIVES

- Rate and concentration
- Rate equations
- Order of reaction

Is there a relationship between the rate of a reaction and the concentration of the reactants? For a reaction to occur, the reactants have to collide. Higher concentration leads to a greater chance of the reactants colliding. So, at first sight, it seems reasonable to expect that the rate of a reaction *does* depend on the concentration of the reactants. Starting from this apparently common-sense point of view, two questions then arise: 'Can we express the rate of reaction *mathematically* in terms of reactant concentrations' and 'Can we then go on to *predict* the rate of a reaction?' The answer to both questions is 'Yes' – but we need to proceed with care!

The iodine clock reaction.
(a) The flask contains the reactants, peroxodisulphate $S_2O_8^{2-}$(aq) ions and iodide ions, together with thiosulphate $S_2O_3^{2-}$(aq) ions and starch indicator. (b) As the thiosulphate is exhausted, the blue starch–iodine complex forms.

The iodine clock reaction

The peroxodisulphate ion $S_2O_8^{2-}$ oxidizes iodide ions according to the reaction:

$$2I^-(aq) + S_2O_8^{2-}(aq) \rightarrow I_2(aq) + 2SO_4^{2-}(aq)$$

You can monitor the rate of this reaction in a convenient way by adding a fixed volume of aqueous thiosulphate ions to the reaction mixture together with a few drops of starch solution. The thiosulphate very rapidly reduces the iodine formed in the above reaction:

$$I_2(aq) + 2S_2O_3^{2-}(aq) \rightarrow 2I^-(aq) + S_4O_6^{2-}(aq)$$

When all the thiosulphate has reacted, free iodine rapidly forms a blue complex with the starch.

Experimental data for the peroxodisulphate/iodide reaction.

Experiment no.	Initial concentrations/mol dm^{-3} $[S_2O_8^{2-}]$	$[I^-]$	Initial rate of reaction /mol dm^{-3} s^{-1}
1	0.038	0.030	7.0×10^{-6}
2	0.076	0.030	14.0×10^{-6}
3	0.076	0.060	28.0×10^{-6}

Analysing the results

The table of results shows that doubling the concentration of peroxodisulphate (using the same concentration of I^-) *doubles* the rate of the reaction. For this reaction, reaction rate is proportional to peroxodisulphate concentration. In symbols:

$$\text{rate} \propto [S_2O_8^{2-}]$$

You will see from the table of results that the same relationship exists between rate and iodide concentration. In symbols:

$$\text{rate} \propto [I^-]$$

These two expressions may be combined with a constant of proportionality k to express the rate of the reaction in terms of the concentrations of both reactants:

$$\text{rate} = k[S_2O_8^{2-}][I^-]$$

The constant k is called the **rate constant**. (It may also be called the **rate coefficient**, because the value of k depends on temperature and so is not truly constant.)

The order of a reaction

In general, for a reaction between A and B, experimental results can be analysed to show that:

$$\text{rate} = k[A]^m[B]^n$$

Such an equation is called a **rate equation**. The power to which the concentration of A is raised in the experimental rate equation is called the **order** of reaction with respect to A. The order with respect to A is m and the order with respect to B is n. The overall order is the sum of the individual orders: $m + n$ in this case.

- Once the rate constant and order with respect to reactants A and B are known, the rate may be predicted at any concentrations of A and B.

The rate of the peroxodisulphate/iodide reaction above is directly proportional to the concentration of the peroxodisulphate ions; the rate is also directly proportional to the concentration of the iodide ions. This may be expressed as:

$$\text{rate} = k[S_2O_8^{2-}][I^-]$$

This rate equation indicates that the reaction is:

- first order with respect to peroxodisulphate ion;
- first order with respect to iodide ion;
- second order overall.

Note that orders must be determined *experimentally* and may not, as here, be equal to the mole ratios in the balanced chemical equation.

Determining order

One method of finding the order is to carry out a number of separate experiments with different initial concentrations and measure the *initial* rates of reaction, i.e. measure the time taken to produce a small fixed concentration of product.

- If *doubling* the concentration of A has *no effect* on the rate, the reaction is **zero order** with respect to A:

  $$\text{rate} = k[A]^0 \qquad \text{i.e. rate} = k$$

- If *doubling* the concentration of A *doubles* the rate, the rate and the concentration are directly proportional, and the reaction is **first order** with respect to A:

  $$\text{rate} = k[A]^1 \qquad \text{i.e. rate} = k[A]$$

- If *doubling* the concentration of A *increases* the rate by a *factor of four*, the reaction is **second order** with respect to A:

  $$\text{rate} = k[A]^2$$

SUMMARY

- The rate equation expresses the rate of a reaction in terms of the concentration of each reactant raised to a specific power.
- The power to which the concentration of a reactant is raised in the rate equation is the order of the reaction with respect to that reactant.
- The overall order of a reaction is the sum of the orders in the rate equation.

Units

In the rate equation

rate = $k[S_2O_8^{2-}][I^-]$

rate has units of $\text{mol dm}^{-3}\,\text{s}^{-1}$ and the concentration of each reactant is expressed as mol dm^{-3}. So, for *this* reaction, k has units $\text{mol}^{-1}\,\text{dm}^3\,\text{s}^{-1}$. The units of k vary, depending on the overall order.

Predicting the rate

Dinitrogen pentaoxide gas N_2O_5 decomposes according to the chemical equation:

$2N_2O_5(g) \rightarrow 4NO_2(g) + O_2(g)$

This reaction is first order with respect to N_2O_5 as shown by the rate equation:

rate = $k[N_2O_5]$

At 298 K the value of k is $3.4 \times 10^{-5}\,\text{s}^{-1}$. The instantaneous rate of this reaction may be calculated simply by substituting into the rate expression. For example, if the concentration of N_2O_5 is $1.0\,\text{mol dm}^{-3}$:

rate = $(3.4 \times 10^{-5}\,\text{s}^{-1}) \times (1.0\,\text{mol dm}^{-3})$

$= 3.4 \times 10^{-5}\,\text{mol dm}^{-3}\,\text{s}^{-1}$

Too many experiments

A disadvantage of this approach is that sufficient quantities of the reactants must be available to perform several experiments. These quantities are not always available, especially if the material is expensive or difficult to obtain. Later in this chapter we will look at a more elegant approach to determining order.

PRACTICE

1 The results shown refer to the oxidation of bromide ion by bromate ion in acidic solution. The equation for the reaction is:

$5Br^-(aq) + BrO_3^-(aq) + 6H^+(aq)$
$\rightarrow 3Br_2(aq) + 3H_2O(l)$

a Find the orders with respect to each of the three reactants.

b State the overall order of the reaction.

c Write the rate equation.

d Calculate the value of the rate constant and state its units.

e Calculate the rate when the concentrations of all three reactants are $0.2\,\text{mol dm}^{-3}$.

Results

$[Br^-]$ /mol dm^{-3}	$[BrO_3^-]$ /mol dm^{-3}	$[H^+]$ /mol dm^{-3}	Initial rate /mol dm^{-3} s^{-1}
0.10	0.10	0.10	8.0×10^{-4}
0.10	0.20	0.10	1.6×10^{-3}
0.20	0.20	0.10	3.2×10^{-3}
0.10	0.10	0.20	3.2×10^{-3}

15.6

Using order to find reaction mechanisms

OBJECTIVES

- Determining order from rate–concentration graphs
- Reaction mechanisms
- Order as evidence for mechanisms
- Rate-limiting step

The previous spread showed how the order of a reaction may be found by carrying out a series of separate reactions. If we know the order, we can calculate the rate constant, which in turn allows us to calculate the rate at given reactant concentrations. This spread shows how we may determine the order with respect to a reactant from a single reaction that is continuously monitored throughout its progress. Once we know the order for each reactant, we can suggest possible reaction mechanisms for the overall reaction.

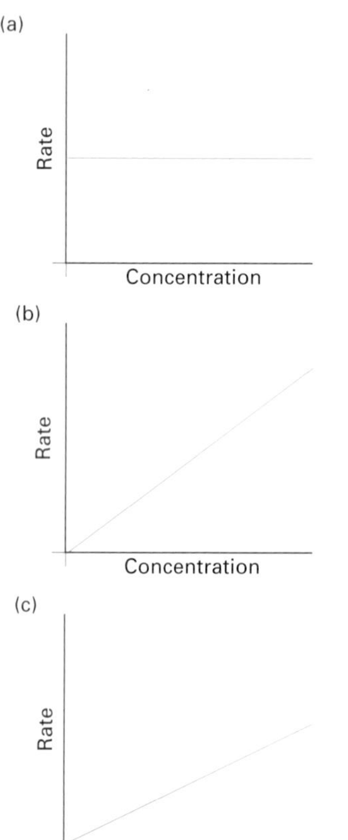

The three types of rate–concentration graphs used to indicate order with respect to a given reactant A.
(a) A zero-order reaction: rate = $k[A]^0 = k$
(b) A first-order reaction: rate = $k[A]^1 = k[A]$
(c) A second-order reaction: rate = $k[A]^2$

Order from rate–concentration graphs

The concentration of a reactant falls as time elapses. If we monitor the concentration of a reactant during the course of a reaction, we will be able to plot a concentration–time graph. We can then draw a tangent at a point on this graph. The slope of the tangent gives the instantaneous rate of the reaction at that particular concentration. (The technique is detailed earlier in this chapter.)

We need to do this at several points on the concentration–time graph. Then we plot another graph. This time, the value of the instantaneous rate that we have found is plotted against concentration. The shape of our rate–concentration graph may then be used to determine order with respect to that reactant. There are three possible cases:

- For a zero-order reaction, the graph of rate as a function of concentration will be a horizontal straight line that cuts the vertical axis at k.
- For a first-order reaction, the graph of rate as a function of concentration will be a straight line of slope k passing through the origin.
- For a second-order reaction, the graph of rate as a function of the *square* of the concentration will be a straight line of slope k passing through the origin.

The iodination of propanone

The reaction between iodine and propanone CH_3COCH_3 is extremely slow, even at high temperatures:

$$I_2(aq) + CH_3COCH_3(aq) \rightarrow CH_3COCH_2I(aq) + HI(aq)$$

However, the addition of dilute acid provides $H^+(aq)$ ions, which catalyse the reaction and cause it to happen in a matter of minutes at 25 °C. The iodine concentration may be determined by titration. Details of a typical reaction mixture are given below together with expected results and their manipulation to find the order with respect to iodine.

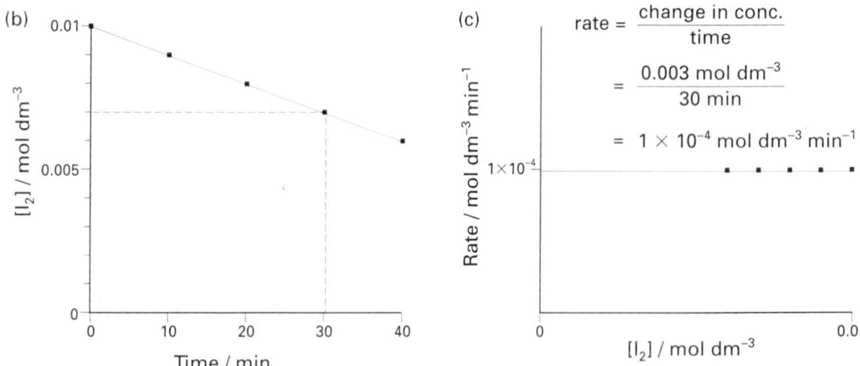

The experiment to determine the order of reaction with respect to iodine for the reaction between iodine and propanone. (a) Initial concentrations of the reaction mixture. (b) The results plotted as a graph (iodine concentration vs time). (c) The graph of rate vs iodine concentration.

The graph of rate against iodine concentration is a straight line parallel to the horizontal axis. This result shows that the reaction is zero order with respect to iodine, i.e. the rate is *independent* of the concentration of iodine. This is a strange result when you bear in mind that iodine is one of the reactants. Other kinetic studies show that the reaction is first order with respect to propanone and, perhaps more surprisingly, first order with respect to the catalyst (hydrogen ions from the dilute acid).

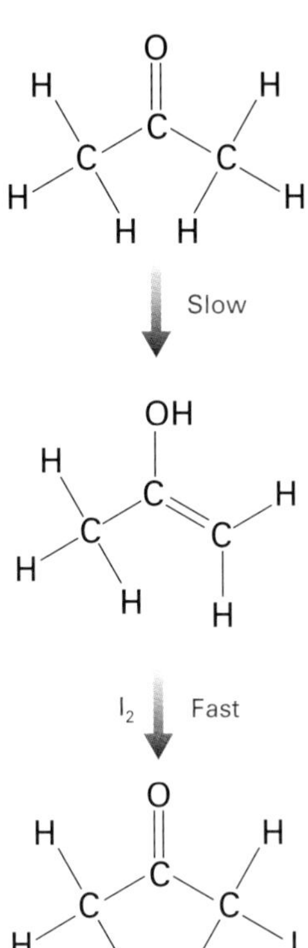

The suggested two-step reaction mechanism for the iodination of propanone.

Suggesting a reaction mechanism

A reaction **mechanism** is a detailed step-by-step account of how an overall reaction happens. It specifically states all intermediate stages and mentions all intermediate species formed, even though some do not appear as products. The kinetic observations suggest that the mechanism for the iodination of propanone occurs in at least two steps.

Rate is directly proportional to both propanone and aqueous hydrogen ion concentrations (both are first order), indicating that these two substances react together in a first step. In this first step, propanone is changed into a more reactive form (called the enol form). This is a *slow step* in comparison to the next one.

Rate is independent of iodine concentration (zero order). Because it does not affect the overall rate of the reaction, the second step must be a *fast step* in comparison to the first one. In this second step, the double bond between the two carbon atoms reacts rapidly with iodine to form the products of the reaction. The complete reaction mechanism is shown on the right.

Comment

This investigation shows that it is possible to find out important details about a reaction by interpreting information about orders of reaction derived from *experimental* data.

Overall rate

The reaction above takes place in two steps. The first step is the slower of the two and is therefore called the **rate-limiting step** (sometimes called the *rate-determining step*). Increasing the rate of the second (faster) step will not increase the overall rate.

The enol form of propanone is referred to as the **reactive intermediate**. It reacts rapidly with the iodine and, in the process, regenerates the catalyst $H^+(aq)$.

(a)

(b)

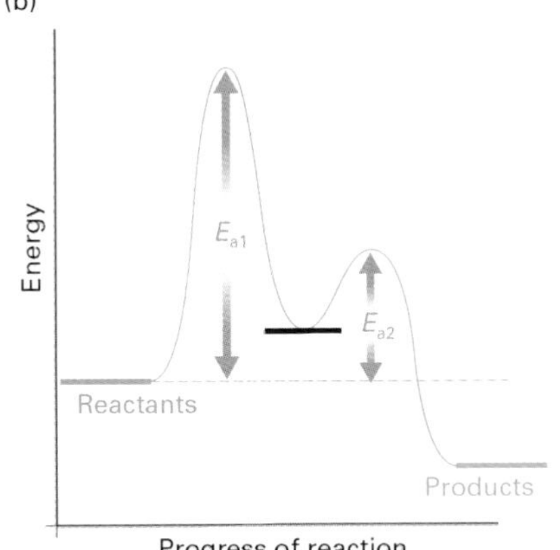

(a) This two-step reaction is like an assembly-line system. The overall rate of production is limited by the slowest step in the process. (b) The corresponding reaction profile includes two separate energy barriers E_{a1} and E_{a2}. Notice that E_{a2} is much smaller than E_{a1}, which explains the relative rates of the two steps.

SUMMARY

- A reaction mechanism describes in detail how reactants turn into products.
- The rate-limiting step is the slowest step in a multi-step reaction.

PRACTICE

1 Explain the meaning of the term *first-order* reaction.

15.7 Using calculus to find order

OBJECTIVES

- Using mathematics to find how rate depends on concentration
- Solving rate equations for zero- and first-order reactions
- First order and exponential decay
- Half-life

Formal definition

The formal definition of the rate of a reaction is best presented in mathematical form. For a reaction $aA + bB = cC + dD$ the rate can be defined uniquely by dividing the rate of change of any species by its mole ratio. That is rate = $\left(\frac{1}{c}\right)\frac{d[C]}{dt} = \left(\frac{1}{d}\right)\frac{d[D]}{dt} = -\left(\frac{1}{a}\right)\frac{d[A]}{dt} = -\left(\frac{1}{b}\right)\frac{d[B]}{dt}$

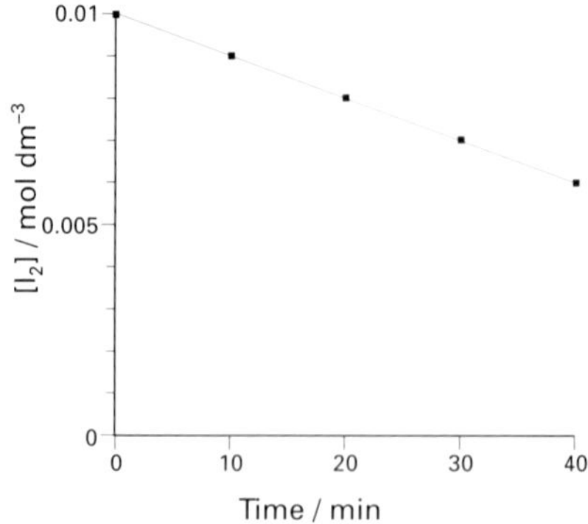

The graph of iodine concentration against time in the reaction between iodine and propanone is a straight line, so the reaction is zero order with respect to iodine.

The substance being investigated in a rate experiment may not be available in unlimited quantities. In this case, the technique of doing multiple experiments with different initial concentrations and measuring the initial rates is too wasteful in material. It would be better to monitor the concentration as a function of time during a single experiment. This is the technique commonly used in research laboratories.

The disadvantage of this approach is that the analysis of the data becomes more complicated. The rate equations need to be solved mathematically and then appropriate graphs drawn. This spread introduces the mathematical solutions and explains how to analyse the experimental data.

Writing a rate equation mathematically

We can write a rate equation mathematically by recognizing that it corresponds to the time differential of a concentration c. If we are considering one of the *reactants*, the concentration of the reactant will decrease as the reaction proceeds. The rate of reaction can be written as

$$\text{rate} = -\frac{dc}{dt}$$

Zero order

For a zero-order reaction, the rate is proportional to the concentration raised to the power zero. As any number raised to the power zero is equal to one, the rate is a *constant*, k, and the rate equation for a zero-order reaction is

$$\text{rate} = kc^0 = k$$

$$-\frac{dc}{dt} = k$$

Multiplying by –1 gives the equation

$$\frac{dc}{dt} = -k \qquad (1)$$

The solution of this equation is

$$c = c_0 - kt$$

where c_0 is the concentration at time zero. The solution can be differentiated to give equation 1; c_0 and k are constants.

The concentration in a zero-order reaction falls linearly with time, from the value c_0 at time zero. The slope of the line is $-k$. See, for example, the graph of the iodine concentration in the iodination of propanone shown alongside.

First order

For a first-order reaction, the rate is proportional to the concentration raised to the power one. The rate equation for a first-order reaction is

$$\text{rate} = kc$$

$$-\frac{dc}{dt} = kc$$

Multiplying by –1 gives the equation

$$\frac{dc}{dt} = -kc \qquad (2)$$

The solution to this equation involves an exponential, as this is the function whose differential is itself (see maths toolbox). Therefore the solution for the concentration as a function of time is as follows:

$$c = c_0 e^{-kt} \qquad (3)$$

Differentiating this equation produces equation 2:

$$\frac{dc}{dt} = c_0 \times (-k)e^{-kt} = -kc$$

Equation 3 is called an exponential decay: the concentration decays exponentially from the value c_0 at time zero. Taking natural logarithms (see maths toolbox) of this equation gives the following equation for the natural log of the concentration:

$$\ln c = \ln c_0 - kt$$

which is the equation of a straight line with a slope of $-k$.

So to prove that a reaction is first order it is necessary to plot the *natural log* of the concentration as a function of time. If the reaction is first order, this graph will be a straight line (see figure alongside).

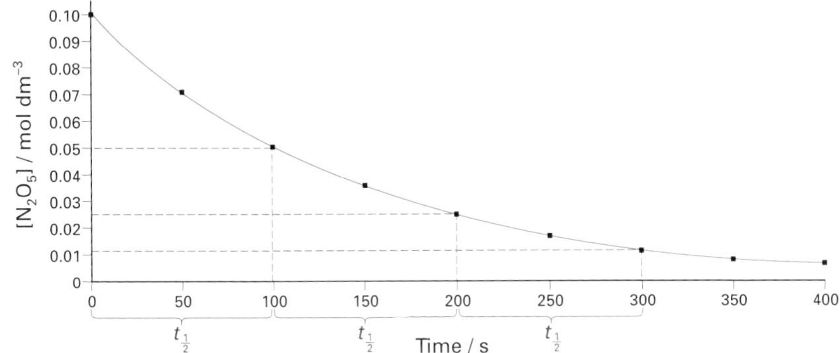

Plot of concentration of N_2O_5 against time for the reaction $2N_2O_5(g) \rightarrow 4NO_2(g) + O_2(g)$ at 70 °C. The graph shows that the concentration falls exponentially. The half-life $t_{½}$, discussed below, is constant for a first-order reaction.

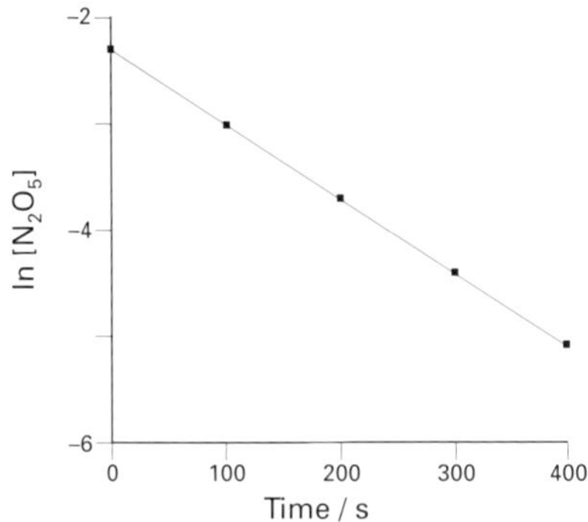

The reaction $2N_2O_5(g) \rightarrow 4NO_2(g) + O_2(g)$ is first order with respect to the reactant, as the natural log *graph is a straight line.*

In this experiment, the concentration is being displayed on the screen on the left. The exponential decay can be clearly seen.

Radioactive decay and half-life

An important example of a first-order reaction is radioactive decay. The emission of alpha or beta particles obeys a first-order rate equation (equation 2) because the probability of radioactive decay depends only on the number of radioactive atoms remaining.

The **half-life** of a first-order reaction is the time taken for the concentration to fall to half its original value. It is clearly related to the rate constant, the exact relationship being derived as follows.

$$c = c_0 e^{-kt}$$

Divide both sides by c_0 and take natural logs to find

$$\ln(c/c_0) = -kt$$

At the half-life $t_{½}$, the concentration c has become $½c_0$ and so

$$\ln(½) = -kt_{½}$$

Multiplying through by −1, using the rules of logarithms, gives the final answer that

$$\ln 2 = kt_{½}$$

Note that the half-life is independent of concentration.

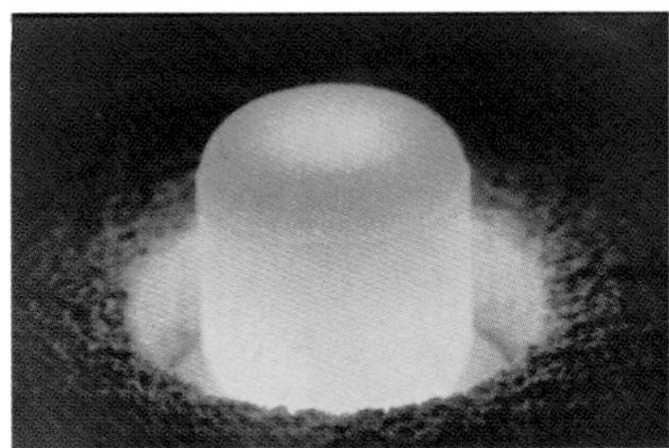

The radioactive element curium (named after Marie Curie), photographed in the dark, illuminated only by the radiation it emits itself.

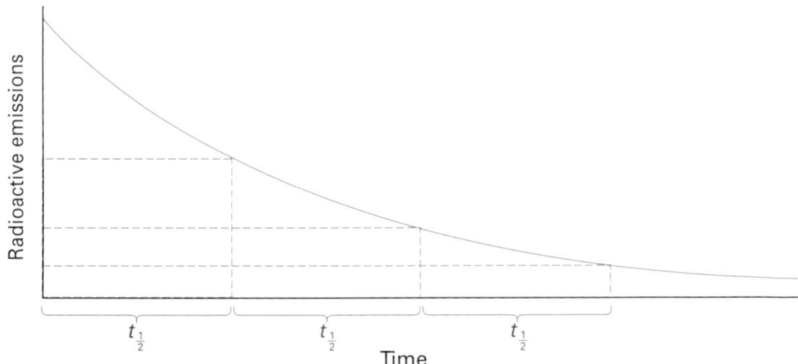

The half-life is the time taken for the concentration (the radioactive emissions in this instance) to fall to half its original value.

SUMMARY

- For a first-order reaction, the concentration decays exponentially.
- Radioactive decay is an example of a first-order reaction.

PRACTICE

1 Explain the meaning of the term *half-life*. For a first-order reaction, how many half-lives does it take for the concentration to reach one eighth of its original value?

15.8

OBJECTIVES

- Finding the activation energy for a reaction
- The Arrhenius equation
- Applications of the Arrhenius equation

ACTIVATION ENERGY AND THE ARRHENIUS EQUATION

It may seem that the activation energy for a reaction is a concept that has been pulled like a rabbit from a hat. This is not the case; it is a measurable quantity. Detailed mathematical analysis allows the value of the activation energy to be extracted from experimental data. The Swede Svante Arrhenius suggested an empirical (based on observation and experiment) equation which could be used to measure the activation energy. It turned out to be consistent with the equations of thermodynamics.

The Arrhenius equation

Svante Arrhenius suggested how to calculate the activation energy from the rates of reaction at different temperatures. The Arrhenius equation predicts that the rate constant, k, defined in previous spreads, is related to the temperature by:

$$\ln k = \ln A - E_a/RT$$

The second term involves the activation energy E_a, the gas constant R (spread 8.2), and the thermodynamic temperature T (in kelvin). Each reaction has a particular value of A and E_a.

A Cyalume™ light stick glows more brightly in warm water than in iced water.

Although the Arrhenius equation seems complicated, it is actually the equation of a straight line ($y = mx + c$). To see this, think of $\ln k$ (the rate variable) as equivalent to y and $1/T$ (the temperature variable) as equivalent to x. The gradient, m, of the line is then the constant $-E_a/R$. The intercept, c, is the constant $\ln A$. A graph of $\ln k$ against $1/T$ is called an **Arrhenius plot**.

The figure below shows an Arrhenius plot of the data in the table on the effect of temperature on the decomposition of dinitrogen pentaoxide N_2O_5. It is clear that the graph is a straight line. The activation energy can be found from the gradient which equals $-E_a/R$ (where R is 8.31 J $K^{-1}mol^{-1}$). For this reaction, the activation energy is 105 kJ mol^{-1}.

T/°C	k/s^{-1}	$\ln k$	$1/(T/K)$
25	3.4×10^{-5}	−10.29	3.36×10^{-3}
35	1.4×10^{-4}	−8.87	3.25×10^{-3}
45	5.0×10^{-4}	−7.60	3.14×10^{-3}
55	1.5×10^{-3}	−6.50	3.05×10^{-3}
65	4.9×10^{-3}	−5.32	2.96×10^{-3}

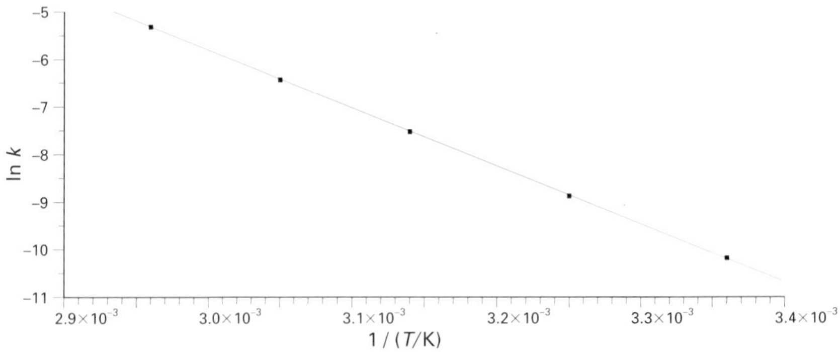

An Arrhenius plot for the decomposition of dinitrogen pentaoxide at different temperatures (shown in the table).

This sort of analysis can also be carried out for reactions in solution. Aqueous hydrochloric acid added to aqueous sodium thiosulphate causes a precipitate of sulphur to form: the time taken for the precipitate to obscure a card placed underneath the flask is measured. The third column in the table opposite on the sulphur precipitation ('sulphur clock') reaction, headed k, has been calculated as follows. The rate of reaction is the change in concentration divided by the time, t, taken for the change. Because the same concentration of sulphur is needed to hide the card, the relative rate is simply found by calculating $1/t$.

The table opposite shows how the relative rate varies as the temperature is increased from 25 °C to 65 °C. It is clear that this is not a linear change. The figure opposite shows an Arrhenius plot of the data in the table. This graph *is* a good straight line.

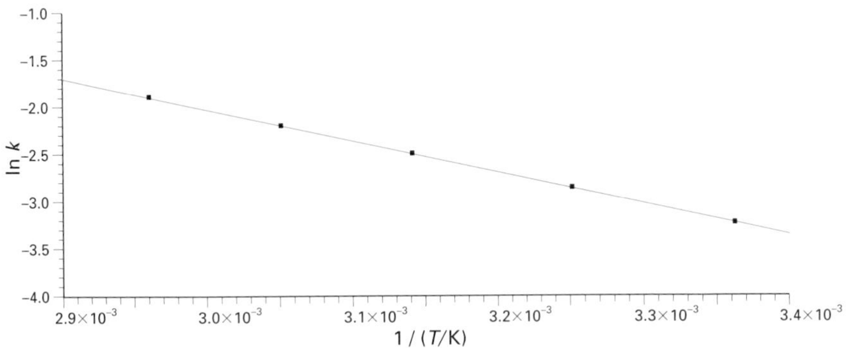

An Arrhenius plot for the sulphur precipitation reaction at different temperatures. See the previous table for 1/(T/K) values.

T/°C	t/s	k/s^{-1}	ln$k$
25	25.3	0.040	−3.23
35	17.9	0.056	−2.88
45	12.5	0.080	−2.53
55	9.0	0.111	−2.20
65	6.6	0.152	−1.88

The activation energy can be found from the gradient of the graph, which equals $-E_a/R$. For this reaction, the activation energy is 39 kJ mol^{-1}.

The Arrhenius plot is widely used to analyse the effect of temperature on reaction rate. The figure alongside shows data obtained by General Motors to monitor the effectiveness of their catalytic converters.

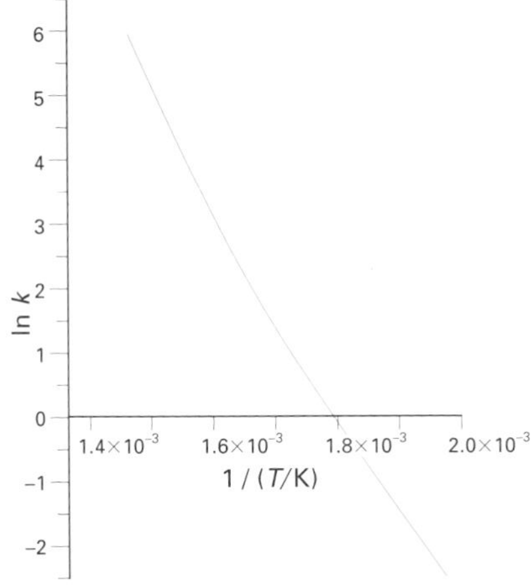

The effectiveness of a catalytic converter analysed using an Arrhenius plot. The reaction involved is discussed in the following spread.

The Arrhenius equation can be rearranged by taking exponentials of both sides, since natural logarithms ln and exponentials e^x are inverse operations. The resulting equation is

$$k = A\, e^{-E_a/RT}$$

The first factor on the right hand side of the equation, A, is called the **pre-exponential factor**. For gaseous reactants, it roughly takes account of the rate of collision. As only a certain small fraction of the collisions are successful, this needs to be multiplied by a second factor which depends on the activation energy to find the rate constant.

Worked example on using the Arrhenius equation

Question: The activation energy for a certain reaction is 50 kJ mol^{-1}. What is the effect on the rate constant of increasing the temperature by 10 K around room temperature (assumed to be 15 °C which is 288 K)?

Strategy: Substitute into the Arrhenius equation. Calculate the ratio of the rate constants at the two temperatures. The first factor in the Arrhenius equation is the pre-exponential factor and this is a constant for the reaction so it will cancel, leaving only the exponential term. So the effect of temperature will be explained by the second factor involving the activation energy.

Answer: The ratio of rate constants is

$$k(25\,°\text{C})/k(15\,°\text{C}) = \frac{\exp((-50\,000 \text{ J mol}^{-1})/(8.31 \text{ J K}^{-1}\text{mol}^{-1})*(298 \text{ K}))}{\exp((-50\,000 \text{ J mol}^{-1})/(8.31 \text{ J K}^{-1}\text{mol}^{-1})*(288 \text{ K}))}$$

$$= 2.0$$

Note: The rate doubles for a 10 °C rise in temperature if the activation energy is 50 kJ mol^{-1}.

Tropical fireflies flash faster on warm nights. The change in their flash rate produces an Arrhenius plot with an activation energy of about 50 kJ mol^{-1}.

SUMMARY

- The activation energy may be found using an Arrhenius plot.
- An Arrhenius plot is a graph of ln k against $1/T$ with T measured in kelvin: its gradient is $-E_a/R$.

15.9

OBJECTIVES

- General catalytic behaviour
- Alternative reaction routes
- Common features

CATALYSIS

Catalysts are substances that increase the rates of a wide variety of chemical reactions. They can be recovered at the end of the reaction, unchanged in mass or chemical composition. Industrial catalysts are used in the manufacture of an enormous variety of products, from margarine to plastics to fertilizers to cracking of crude oil; see spread 22.3. **Enzymes** are biological catalysts, which allow living systems to function. This spread looks at the general principles underlying catalyst function. The following two spreads deal with the two main categories of catalytic activity in greater depth.

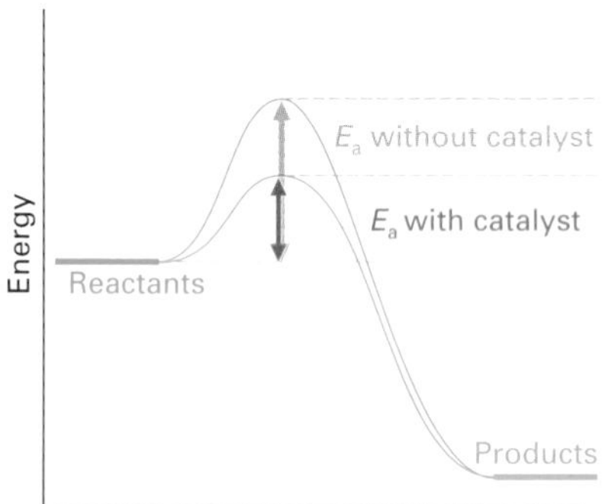

The reaction profiles for (a) an uncatalysed reaction and (b) the same reaction with a suitable catalyst present.

Catalytic activity

Reaction profiles show that the activation energy acts as an energy barrier, which the reactants must overcome before they can change into products. Most chemical reactions proceed by a distinct route, which includes one or more intermediate steps. The reaction mechanism describes the steps by which a reaction takes place. When a reaction mixture includes a suitable catalyst, the reaction can occur by an *alternative route of lower activation energy* than the uncatalysed reaction. At the same temperature, a greater proportion of the reactant molecules will therefore have sufficient energy to overcome the (lower) energy barrier for the catalysed reaction, and so the rate is increased.

There are two important classes of catalysts: heterogeneous catalysts and homogeneous catalysts.

Autocatalysis

Autocatalysis occurs when a product of a reaction increases the rate of the reaction. For example, in the reduction of manganate(VII) ions:

$2MnO_4^-(aq) + 5C_2O_4^{2-}(aq) + 16H^+(aq) \rightarrow 2Mn^{2+}(aq) + 10CO_2(g) + 8H_2O(l)$

the Mn^{2+} ions produced catalyse the reaction.

Heterogeneous catalysis

- A **heterogeneous catalyst** is in a different phase from the reactants.

An example of heterogeneous catalysis is the use of iron in the Haber–Bosch synthesis in which nitrogen and hydrogen react to form ammonia. The rate of this reaction is imperceptible at room temperature, and increasing the temperature and the pressure has relatively little effect because of the extremely high bond energy of the N≡N triple covalent bond. However, the equilibrium

$$N_2(g) + 3H_2(g) \rightleftharpoons 2NH_3(g)$$

is rapidly established in the presence of finely divided iron, which acts as a heterogeneous catalyst.

The catalysed reaction mechanism depends on the reactant molecules attaching themselves to the metal surface: the N≡N bond is broken as the molecules attach (this is called **dissociative adsorption**). Reaction occurs on the surface, and the ammonia molecules then detach (desorb) from the metal surface.

Margarine

Another important industrial application of heterogeneous catalysis is in the 'hardening' of vegetable oils in the production of margarine. Oil molecules contain large numbers of C=C double covalent bonds. Hydrogen reacts with these bonds in the presence of a nickel catalyst to produce molecules with C—C single bonds. The greater the proportion of these single bonds, the higher the melting point of the product. Liquid oils become solid fats.

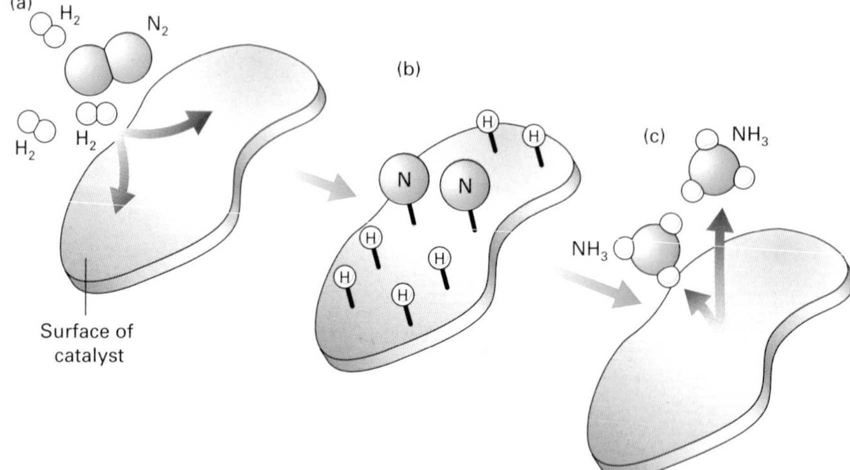

The reaction mechanism for the catalytic reduction of nitrogen by hydrogen on an iron surface. This diagram shows the three stages: (a) inward diffusion of reactants and (b) attachment to the catalyst surface; followed by reaction to form products; and (c) outward diffusion of products.

Homogeneous catalysis

- A **homogeneous catalyst** is in the same phase as the reactants.

An example of homogeneous catalysis is the use of aqueous cobalt(II) chloride in the reaction between hydrogen peroxide and an aqueous solution of Rochelle salt (sodium potassium 2,3-dihydroxybutanedioate). When the catalyst is added, the reaction happens very much more quickly. During the reaction, the aqueous cobalt(II) chloride changes colour from pink to green before reverting to pink at the end, spread 20.6. This observation shows that the catalyst takes an *active* part in a reaction rather than being an inactive spectator.

The bombardier beetle stores hydrogen peroxide, water, and noxious substances in an abdominal sac. When threatened, it injects a catalyst into this mixture. The almost instantaneous exothermic decomposition of hydrogen peroxide generates steam, which ejects the contents of the sac as a hot and highly offensive spray.

Common features of catalysts

- *Catalysts may be very specific.*

A catalyst is generally specific to a single reaction or to a class of very similar reactions. For example, the enzyme urease catalyses the hydrolysis of urea, NH_2CONH_2, but not the hydrolysis of the molecule CH_3CONH_2. Platinum catalyses a number of hydrogenation reactions (addition of H_2) but not *all* addition reactions.

- *Catalysts do not affect the equilibrium position.*

Catalysts do not affect the equilibrium position, nor do they affect the value of the equilibrium constant. The position of equilibrium does not depend on the route taken by a reaction. The forward and backward reactions are speeded up *to the same extent*.

- *Small quantities of catalyst can usually achieve a huge increase in rate.*

Just 2 g of platinum can catalyse the decomposition of one million litres of hydrogen peroxide. One molecule of the enzyme triose-phosphate isomerase can catalyse the reaction of 400 000 molecules per second (the limiting factor is the rate of diffusion of reactant molecules to the enzyme).

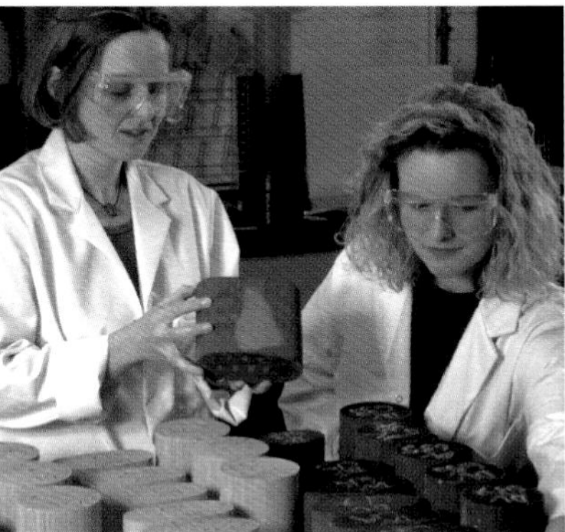

Catalytic converters in the exhaust systems of modern cars show all the main features of a heterogeneous catalyst. The catalyst consists of about 2 g of finely divided platinum/rhodium, on a rigid ceramic support. The primary effect is to catalyse the conversion of the pollutants carbon monoxide and nitrogen monoxide to carbon dioxide and nitrogen:
$2CO(g) + 2NO(g) \rightarrow 2CO_2(g) + N_2(g)$
Note that leaded petrol will rapidly poison a catalytic converter.

- *The state of subdivision of the catalyst is significant.*

Solid catalysts are more effective when finely divided (very finely powdered), because they present a larger surface area to the reactants.

- *Catalysts may be poisoned by some other substances.*

Catalysts may be poisoned, and hence be rendered ineffective, by substances such as lead, arsenic, and the cyanide ion CN^-. Such substances bind strongly to the catalyst surface and block the adsorption of reactant molecules. These substances also often act as poisons to living organisms, binding to the active sites in enzymes and blocking their biological activity.

Catalysts may be physically altered over time. The platinum/rhodium gauze used as a catalyst in the Ostwald process (the catalytic oxidation of ammonia; see spread 19.9) becomes crystallized over time. This roughens the surface and decreases the mechanical strength.

SUMMARY

- A catalyst speeds up a reaction by providing an alternative route of lower activation energy.
- A catalyst is specific to a single reaction or to a class of similar reactions.
- A heterogeneous catalyst is in a different phase from the reactants.
- A homogeneous catalyst is in the same phase as the reactants.
- A catalyst does not alter the equilibrium position.

PRACTICE

1 Cover the text of this spread and define each of the following terms in one sentence each: reaction profile; reaction mechanism; homogeneous catalyst; heterogeneous catalyst; autocatalyst; poison; enzyme.

2 Explain what is meant by *catalytic activity*, including in your answer the terms 'activation energy', 'energy distribution', and 'reaction route'.

15.10

Heterogeneous catalysis

OBJECTIVES

- Surface adsorption
- Mechanism of heterogeneous catalysis
- Industrial considerations

By definition, a heterogeneous catalyst is in a different phase from the reactants. The most common situation involves a solid catalyst in contact with liquid or gaseous reactants. For example, you should already be familiar with the laboratory preparation of oxygen by the catalytic decomposition of aqueous hydrogen peroxide by solid manganese(IV) oxide. This spread examines the mechanism of heterogeneous catalysis in detail and discusses the role of catalyst promoters and supports in industrial applications.

Adsorption

Adsorption describes the attachment of a species to the *surface* of a solid. A given catalyst surface has a finite number of **active sites** at which reactants may adsorb. When adsorption occurs by dispersion forces, it is described as **physisorption**; when it occurs by formation of a covalent bond, it is described as **chemisorption**. Chemisorption to transition metal catalysts often involves vacant d orbitals accepting electron density from the adsorbed molecules. Catalytic activity depends critically on the strength of the adsorption. The bond must be *strong* enough to bind the reactants, but *weak* enough to break again to release the product. So, for hydrogenation reactions, tungsten (W) forms too strong a bond, whereas silver (Ag) forms too weak a bond. Nickel (Ni) and platinum (Pt) are about right.

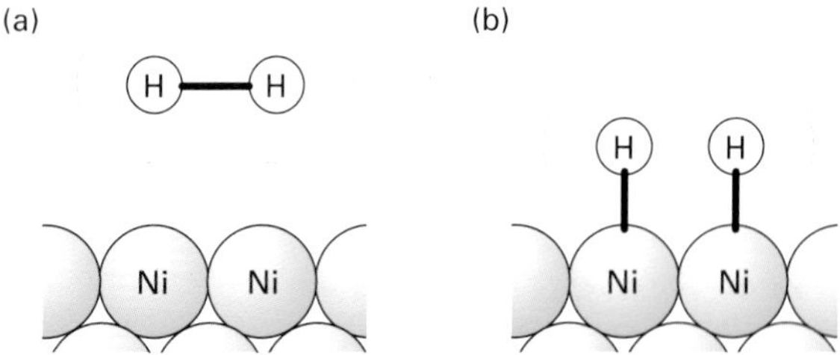

(a) Physisorption and (b) chemisorption of hydrogen on a nickel surface.

Various types of catalyst bead used in different stages of the Haber–Bosch synthesis of ammonia. Each bead is designed to present an optimum surface area to the reactants.

Adsorption and the Haber–Bosch synthesis

The reaction between nitrogen and hydrogen to form ammonia proceeds in a series of steps.

The first step is the adsorption of nitrogen and hydrogen onto the surface of the iron catalyst. The process of adsorption of nitrogen breaks the N≡N triple covalent bond and results in separate nitrogen atoms bound to the metal surface. Similarly, hydrogen molecules break up on attaching to the surface. The attachment to the surface is by chemisorption in both cases, involving the donation of electron density from nitrogen and hydrogen atoms into vacant d orbitals on the iron atoms.

The next step is the formation of three N—H bonds between atoms on the surface. The final step involves the desorption of the ammonia molecule from the surface. See previous spread.

The hydrogenation of ethene

Adsorption to metal surfaces is not limited to diatomic molecules. The hydrogenation of ethene to ethane is catalysed by nickel:

$$\underset{\text{ETHENE}}{CH_2{=}CH_2(g)} + H_2(g) \rightarrow \underset{\text{ETHANE}}{CH_3{-}CH_3(g)}$$

The first step involves the dissociative adsorption of hydrogen. An adsorbed hydrogen atom then approaches an ethene molecule and bonds to it ($H^\bullet$ represents a hydrogen atom and its associated electron):

$$CH_2{=}CH_2 + H^\bullet \rightarrow {}^\bullet CH_2{-}CH_3$$

This reaction forms a radical ${}^\bullet CH_2{-}CH_3$, which has an unpaired electron on a carbon atom. (A **radical** is an atom or molecule that contains one or more unpaired electrons.) The radical uses this unpaired electron to bond to the metal surface. Reaction with another adsorbed hydrogen atom follows:

$$^{\bullet}CH_2—CH_3 + H^{\bullet} \rightarrow CH_3—CH_3$$

The final step is the desorption of the product ethane.

Catalyst poisons

The function of a heterogeneous catalyst depends critically on the strength of adsorption of reactant and product molecules. Catalyst poisons are substances that bind strongly to the surface and do not readily desorb.

Hydrogen in the Haber–Bosch synthesis is derived from natural gas. Any sulphur impurities mixed with methane from a gas well must be removed. If they are not, the sulphur atoms will rapidly poison the iron catalyst by binding strongly to the active sites and blocking the adsorption of hydrogen and nitrogen.

In a similar manner, a vehicle's catalytic converter will be poisoned if leaded fuel is burned in the engine, because lead bonds strongly to the platinum/rhodium surface.

Promoters

The effectiveness of a heterogeneous catalyst may be improved by the use of a promoter. A **promoter** is a substance that does not catalyse the reaction itself, but *does* further increase the rate when used with the catalyst. Promoters improve the surface area and also the electronic structure of the surface. The iron catalyst in the Haber–Bosch process for manufacturing ammonia is promoted by the oxides of potassium, calcium, and aluminium.

Catalyst supports

Heterogeneous catalysis of a reaction takes place where the reactant molecules meet the catalyst surface. Catalytic activity is affected by the surface area of the catalyst and not by its thickness. Many heterogeneous catalysts are expensive, e.g. platinum and rhodium. Efficient and cost-effective use can be made of these substances by depositing very thin layers of them on an inexpensive carrier material or **support**. Catalytic converters used in vehicle exhaust systems consist of a platinum/rhodium mixture on a ceramic support.

SUMMARY

- Heterogeneous catalysts are frequently transition metals or their compounds.
- Reaction takes place between reactant molecules adsorbed onto the catalyst surface.
- Catalyst poisons are substances that bind strongly to the surface and are not readily desorbed.
- Catalyst promoters improve the effectiveness of catalysts.
- Thin layers of expensive or mechanically weak catalyst materials can be deposited on the surfaces of strong, cheap supports.

(a)

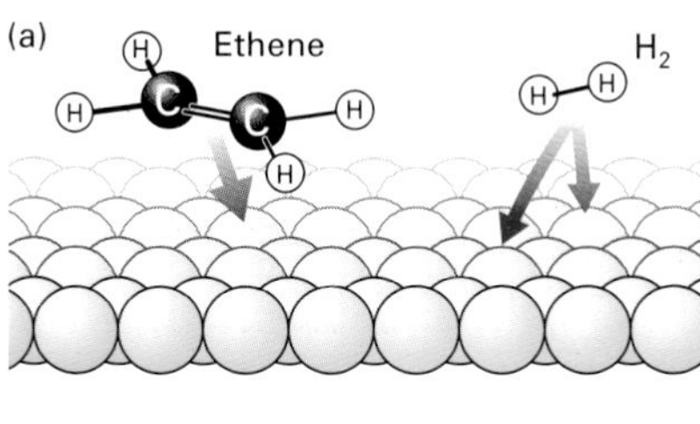

(b)

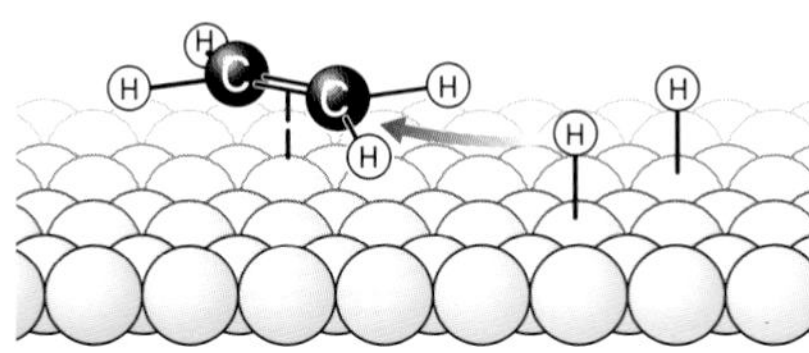

(c)

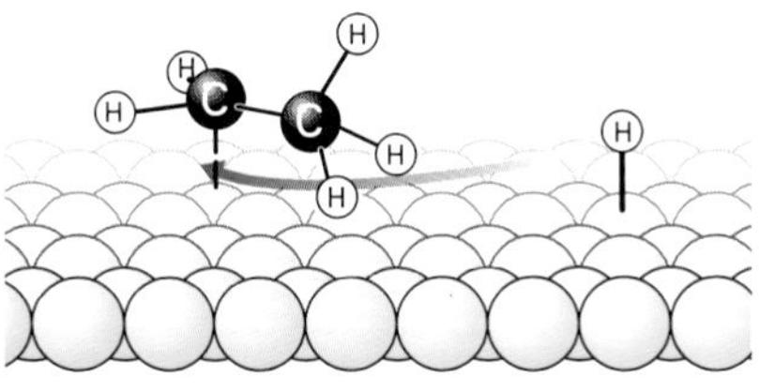

(d)

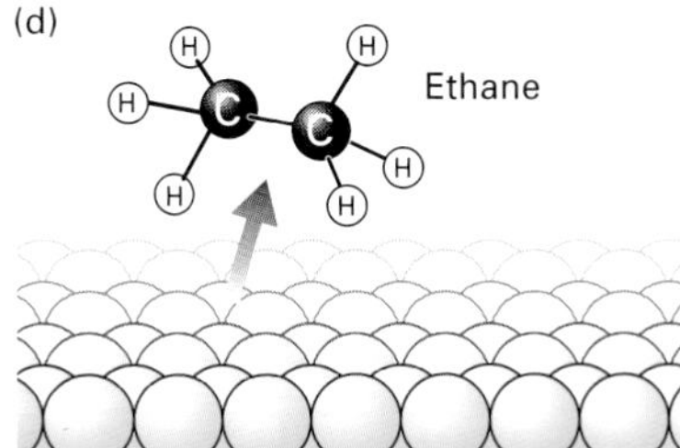

The four main steps in the catalytic hydrogenation of ethene: (a) Hydrogen atoms adsorb onto the surface; as does an ethene molecule. (b) Ethene reacts with a hydrogen atom; the radical $^{\bullet}CH_2—CH_3$ *forms and attaches to the surface by means of the unpaired electron. (c) The radical reacts with another hydrogen atom to form* $CH_3—CH_3$*, which desorbs from the surface (d).*

Supports – another use

Some catalyst materials lack sufficient physical strength to be used on their own. A support stops the catalyst surface from collapsing. An example is the silica support for the phosphoric acid catalyst used in the direct hydration of ethene.

PRACTICE

1 Draw Lewis structures of the hydrocarbon species to illustrate each of the stages in the catalytic hydrogenation of ethene to ethane.

2 Suggest a mechanism for the reaction $H_2(g) + I_2(g) \rightarrow 2HI(g)$ using a platinum catalyst. Explain why the activation energy of the catalysed reaction is approximately one-fifth that of the uncatalysed reaction.

15.11

Homogeneous catalysis

OBJECTIVES

- Mechanisms
- Transition metal ion catalysis
- Enzymes
- Acid catalysis

Inhibitors

The decomposition of hydrogen peroxide may be slowed down by the addition of ethanol. A substance that slows down a reaction is called an **inhibitor** (or, infrequently, a **negative catalyst**).

By definition, a homogeneous catalyst is in the same phase as the reactants. Whilst heterogeneous catalysis typically involves gases reacting on a solid catalytic surface, homogeneous catalysis typically involves liquid mixtures or substances in solution. All catalysts operate by making available reaction routes of lower activation energy; however, you will see that the mode of operation of homogeneous catalysts is distinctly different to that of heterogeneous catalysts.

Hydrogen peroxide (again)

Aqueous hydrogen peroxide $H_2O_2(aq)$ slowly decomposes to water and oxygen gas over a number of weeks. Adding a small quantity of bromine causes a similar sample to decompose in just a few minutes. The mechanism for the reaction involves two steps, as follows:

$$\mathbf{H_2O_2(aq)} + Br_2(aq) \rightarrow 2Br^-(aq) + 2H^+(aq) + \mathbf{O_2(g)} \qquad (1)$$

$$\mathbf{H_2O_2(aq)} + 2Br^-(aq) + 2H^+(aq) \rightarrow \mathbf{2H_2O(l)} + Br_2(aq) \qquad (2)$$

$$\text{overall } \mathbf{2H_2O_2(aq)} \rightarrow \mathbf{2H_2O(l)} + \mathbf{O_2(g)}$$

You can see that bromine acts as a catalyst because it is involved in the reaction mechanism but emerges unchanged at the end of the two steps concerned.

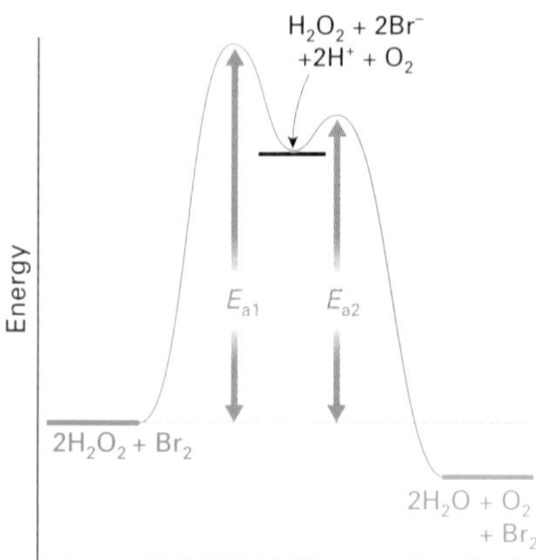

The reaction profile for the decomposition of hydrogen peroxide catalysed by bromine. The profile includes two separate energy barriers E_{a1} and E_{a2}. The peak of each 'hump' on the curve represents the transition state formed between (1) H_2O_2 and Br_2 and (2) H_2O_2 and H^+/Br^-.

Two-step reaction profiles

Reaction profiles imply that a transition state, spread 15.4, exists between the arrangement of atoms called 'the reactants' and the arrangement called 'the products'. The catalysed decomposition of hydrogen peroxide discussed above occurs in two steps. The reaction profile has two peaks with a trough between them. Each peak represents a transition state. Reactants achieve this transition state when they come together with energy at least equal to the activation energy for that step. At the transition state, an activated complex exists which is in equilibrium with the reactants and which may decompose to form the products. The groups of atoms (activated complex) corresponding to these transition states cannot be isolated. The trough on the reaction profile represents the **intermediate species**, in this case, $Br^-(aq)$ and $H^+(aq)$.

Transition metal ions

Many redox reactions may be catalysed by transition metal ions. These ions alternate between two oxidation states, transferring electrons between the oxidant and the reductant. For example, peroxodisulphate ions $S_2O_8^{2-}(aq)$ oxidize iodide ions to iodine (peroxodisulphate is reduced to sulphate):

$$S_2O_8^{2-}(aq) + 2I^-(aq) \rightarrow 2SO_4^{2-}(aq) + I_2(aq)$$

The uncatalysed reaction is slow, due largely to both the reactants bearing negative charges (which repel them from each other).

The two half-equations are:

Reduction: $S_2O_8^{2-}(aq) + 2e^- \rightarrow 2SO_4^{2-}(aq)$

Oxidation: $2I^-(aq) \rightarrow I_2(aq) + 2e^-$

Iron(II) ions catalyse the reaction by acting as an intermediate in the transfer of electrons from iodide to peroxodisulphate.

Step 1 Peroxodisulphate oxidizes Fe(II) to Fe(III):

$$S_2O_8^{2-}(aq) + 2Fe^{2+}(aq) \rightarrow 2SO_4^{2-}(aq) + 2Fe^{3+}(aq)$$

Step 2 Iron(III) ion oxidizes iodide ion to iodine:

$$2Fe^{3+}(aq) + 2I^-(aq) \rightarrow 2Fe^{2+}(aq) + I_2(aq)$$

Note that step 2 reduces iron(III) back to iron(II).

Enzymes

Enzymes act as homogeneous catalysts in living systems. They consist of complex protein chains coiled into specific shapes. Part of an enzyme, often containing a transition metal ion, is the active site where reaction takes place. Reactant molecules must fit the shape of the active site, rather like two jigsaw puzzle pieces fitting together, or a key fitting into a lock. Enzyme names often indicate the substances on which they act and end in *–ase*. For example, *peroxidase* is an enzyme found in mammalian livers and is responsible for decomposing harmful peroxides. It is interesting to note that the activation energy for the uncatalysed decomposition of hydrogen peroxide is 75 kJ mol^{-1}, whereas the corresponding values for the reaction catalysed by platinum and peroxidase are 49 kJ mol^{-1} and 23 kJ mol^{-1} respectively.

NB. Enzymes are discussed at greater length in spreads 30.6 and 30.7.

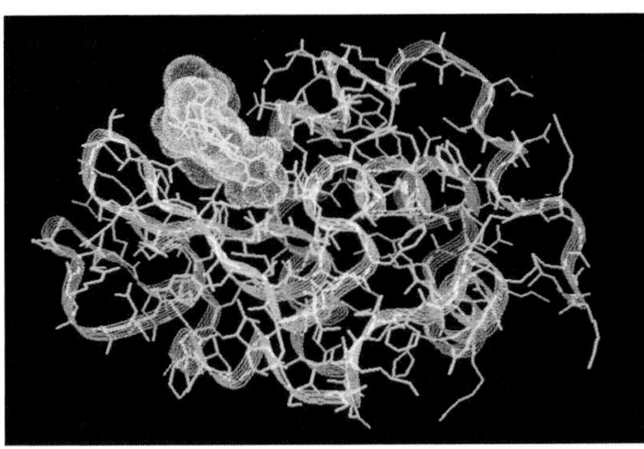

The lysozyme molecule (M_r 14 100). This enzyme occurs in tears and nasal mucus and is responsible for destroying bacteria. The active site binds to specific chemical groupings on the bacterial cell wall and breaks them apart.

Depletion of the ozone layer

15–50 km above the Earth's surface, intense sunlight forms ozone (trioxygen O_3) from atmospheric oxygen (dioxygen O_2). The 'ozone layer' protects surface life by absorbing ultraviolet radiation from solar radiation. Chlorofluorocarbons (CFCs) found use as refrigerants and in plastics manufacture. A typical CFC is dichlorodifluoromethane CF_2Cl_2. Escaping into the ozone layer, it is broken down by UV radiation to give highly reactive radicals e.g.

$CF_2Cl_2 \rightarrow {}^{\cdot}CF_2Cl + Cl^{\cdot}$

The chlorine atom catalyses the decomposition of ozone to oxygen:

$O_3 + Cl^{\cdot} \rightarrow O_2 + ClO^{\cdot}$

$ClO^{\cdot} + O_3 \rightarrow 2O_2 + Cl^{\cdot}$

Acid catalysed esterification

Esterification is the reaction between a carboxylic acid and an alcohol to produce an ester, e.g. ethanoic acid CH_3COOH reacts with ethanol CH_3CH_2OH to form an equilibrium mixture, spread 11.5, also containing ethyl ethanoate $CH_3COOCH_2CH_3$ and water:

$$CH_3COOH(l) + CH_3CH_2OH(l) \rightleftharpoons CH_3COOCH_2CH_3(l) + H_2O(l)$$

The equilibrium constant K_c for the reaction is 4.0 at 80 °C. The uncatalysed reaction takes many weeks to reach equilibrium. However, the addition of concentrated sulphuric acid causes equilibrium to be established in a few hours. Note that the value of the equilibrium constant is identical for both catalysed and uncatalysed reactions (at the same temperature). The mechanism for this reaction, highlighting the role of the catalyst, is discussed in detail in spread 27.3.

SUMMARY

- A homogeneous catalyst is in the same phase as the reactants.
- Transition metal ions catalyse redox reactions by acting as intermediates in the electron-transfer process.
- Enzymes are highly-specific biological homogeneous catalysts.

PRACTICE

1 Explain the relationships between the three terms *intermediate species, transition state,* and *activated complex.*

2 The redox reaction between dichromate(VI) and iodide ions

$14H^+(aq) + Cr_2O_7^{2-}(aq) + 6I^-(aq) \rightarrow 2Cr^{3+}(aq) + 3I_2(aq) + 7H_2O(l)$

is catalysed by minute amounts of copper(II) ions.

a Write half-equations for the oxidation and the reduction reactions contained in the equation above.

b Outline an experimental procedure to show that the reaction is catalysed by copper(II) ions.

c Suggest a mechanism to explain the function of copper(II) as a catalyst in this reaction.

PRACTICE EXAM QUESTIONS

1 a A fixed mass of marble is reacted with dilute hydrochloric acid at a constant temperature. Explain why the rate of the reaction is increased if the lumps of marble are reduced in size. [2]

b The initial rate of the reaction between substances **A** and **B** was measured in a series of experiments and the following rate equation was deduced:

rate = $k[\mathbf{A}][\mathbf{B}]^2$

i Copy and complete the table of data below for the reaction between **A** and **B**.

Expt	Initial [A] / mol dm^{-3}	Initial [B] / mol dm^{-3}	Initial rate / mol dm^{-3} s^{-1}
1	0.020	0.020	1.2×10^{-4}
2	0.040	0.040	
3		0.040	2.4×10^{-4}
4	0.060	0.030	
5	0.040		7.2×10^{-4}

ii Using the data for Experiment 1, calculate a value for the rate constant, *k*, and state its units.
AQA (NEAB) 1999 [7]

2 a The diagram below shows the Maxwell–Boltzmann energy distribution curves for molecules of a gas under two sets of conditions **A** and **B**. The total area under curve **B** is the same as the total area under curve **A**.

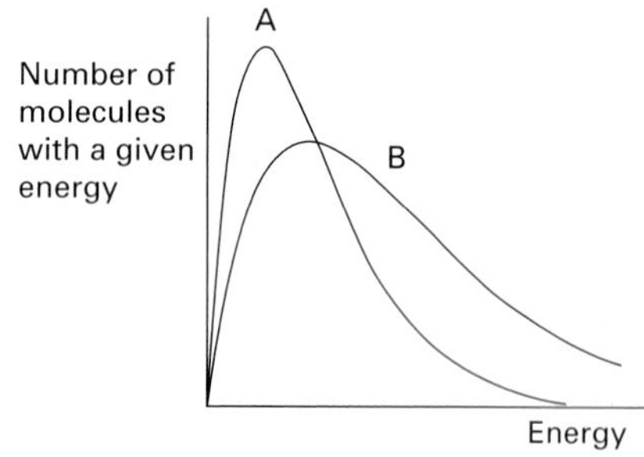

i What change of condition is needed to produce curve **B** from curve **A**?

ii What is represented by the total area under curve **A**?

iii Why is the total area under curve **B** the same as that under curve **A**? [3]

b i Explain the meaning of the term activation energy.

ii In a reaction involving gas molecules, if all other conditions are kept constant, state the effect, if any, on the value of the activation energy when a catalyst is added and the volume of the vessel is decreased. [3]

c Explain why reactions between solids usually occur very slowly, if at all. [2]
AQA (NEAB) 1998

3 a State the difference between homogeneous and heterogeneous catalysis. [2]

b Explain the term activation energy. [2]

c A rate equation for a reaction between reagents A and B is

rate = $k[\mathrm{A}]^n$

i State the meaning of all the terms other than *rate* which appear in this equation.

ii What can be deduced from the absence of reagent B from the rate equation? [4]

d In the examples below, decide whether the catalyst is homogeneous or heterogeneous, and explain how it provides an alternative route of lower activation energy in each case.

i The Contact Process

ii Enzyme catalysed reactions [6]

e Suggest **two** different measures that can be taken to maximize the efficiency and minimize the costs associated with a very expensive heterogeneous catalyst. [2]
AQA (NEAB) 1999 *(See also Chapters 19 and 30)*

4 The following information refers to a procedure to determine the *order of reaction* with respect to iodide ions for the reaction represented by the equation

$$2I^-(aq) + H_2O_2(aq) + 2H^+(aq) \rightarrow 2H_2O(l) + I_2(aq)$$

Rate is measured by the time taken for the iodine produced to react with a small *fixed amount* of sodium thiosulphate added to the constant volume system.

The faster the iodine is produced, the shorter the time taken for the sodium thiosulphate to be used up.

The reciprocal of this time can be used as a measure of the initial rate of reaction. The results are given below.

Experiment	[KI(aq)]/ mol dm^{-3}	Time (*t*) / s	Reciprocal of time (1/*t*)/s^{-1}
I	0.004	74	0.0135
II	0.006	49.4	0.0202
III	0.008	37	0.0270
IV	0.010	30	0.0333
V	0.012	25	0.0400

a i In the experiments the concentrations of acid and hydrogen peroxide were far more concentrated than that of potassium iodide. Explain why this was necessary. [1]

ii In each of the experiments the aqueous hydrogen peroxide was always added last. State why this was necessary. [1]

iii Explain why the volume of the system was kept constant for all the experiments. [1]

b i Copy showing the axes and plot, a graph of the initial rate ($\frac{1}{t}$) on the vertical axis against the concentration of potassium iodide used on the horizontal axis.

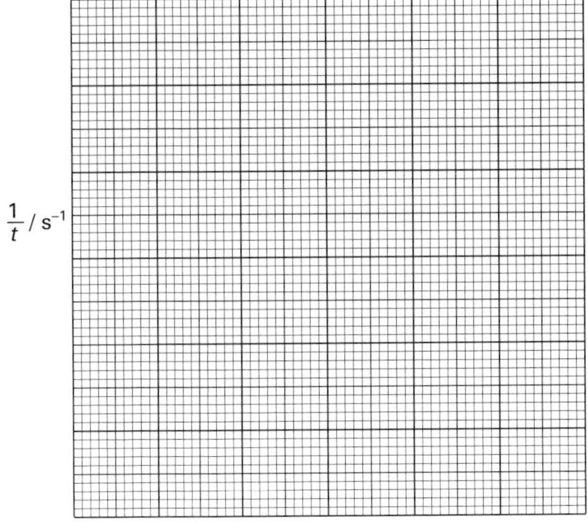

ii Use your graph to determine the order, n, of the reaction with respect to iodide ions. Carefully state your reasoning. [3]

c Further studies show that the rate equation for the reaction is

Rate (mol $dm^{-3}s^{-1}$) = $k[I^-(aq)^n][H_2O_2(aq)]$

i From this overall rate equation, state what can be deduced about the role of aqueous hydrogen ions. [1]

ii State the units of k in the above rate equation. [1]
WJEC 1998

5 a The Arrhenius equation, $k = Ae^{-E/RT}$, may be expressed in the following form:

$\ln k = \ln A - E/RT$

The decomposition of a gas, **Q**, was studied at a number of different temperatures (T), and the value of k was obtained at each temperature. Values were calculated for $1/T$ and for $\ln k$. A plot of $\ln k$ against $1/T$ is shown below.

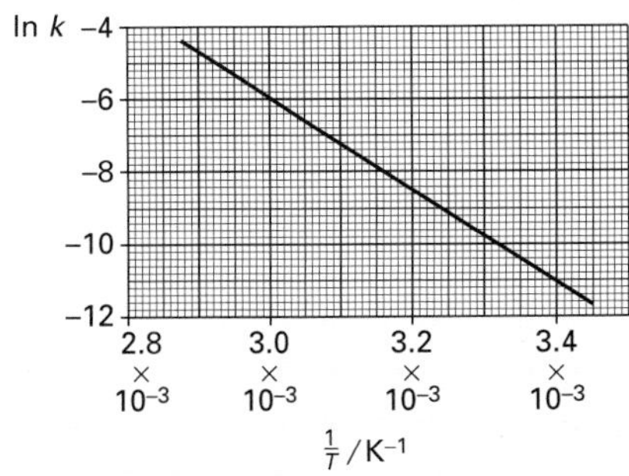

i What do the symbols k and A in the Arrhenius equation represent? [2]

ii Determine the gradient for the graph, $-E/R$. [2]

iii Using the gradient obtained in **a ii**, deduce the value of the activation energy, E, for the decomposition of **Q**. Include the units for E in your answer.

$R = 8.314\ J\ K^{-1}\ mol^{-1}$ [4]

b In separate reactions between sulphur dioxide and oxygen, an increase in the concentration of SO_2 from 0.180 mol dm^{-3} to 0.540 mol dm^{-3} was found to increase the initial rate of reaction by a factor of 9.

i State what is meant by the term *order of reaction*. [2]

ii Explain why the rate of the above reaction is increased by an increase in the concentration of SO_2. [2]

iii Deduce, using the information given above and showing your working, the order of the reaction with respect to SO_2. [2]
AQA (AEB) 1998

6 This question is about the reaction between bromomethane and aqueous hydroxide ions

$CH_3Br + OH^- \rightarrow CH_3OH + Br^-$

a An increase in temperature increases the rate of this reaction.

Explain this increase by referring to the collision frequency and the collision energy of the molecules. [3]

b By sketching the energy distribution of the molecules at a given temperature, T, show how the presence of a catalyst will increase the rate of the reaction. [3]

c Define the following terms used in reaction kinetics.

i Overall order of reaction [1]

ii Rate constant [1]

Time / min	0	10	20	30	40	50	60	70
$[CH_3Br]$/mol dm^{-3}	0.100	0.074	0.057	0.043	0.033	0.025	0.019	0

d In the reaction between bromomethane and aqueous hydroxide ions at constant temperature the concentration of bromomethane at various times is given in the table.

i Plot a graph to show that the reaction is first order with respect to bromomethane. [4]

ii If the concentration of the hydroxide ion doubles, all other factors remaining constant, the rate of the reaction doubles. What is the order of reaction with respect to the hydroxide ion? [1]

iii Hence write a rate equation for this reaction. [1]

iv Based on the kinetic information obtained above write the mechanism for the reaction between CH_3Br and aqueous OH^- ions. [3]
EDEXCEL 1997 (See also Chapter 24)

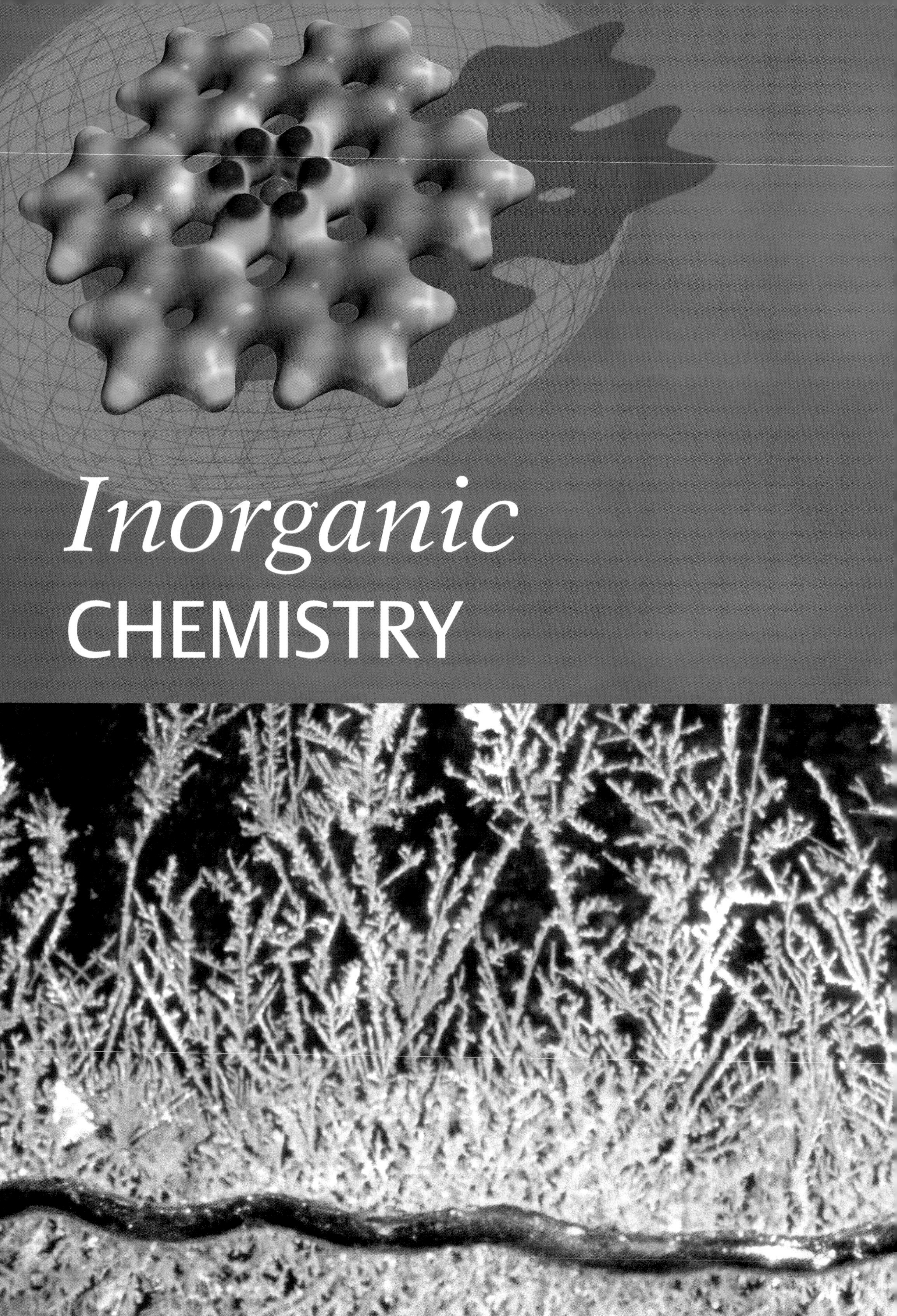
Inorganic
CHEMISTRY

Inorganic chemistry studies the behaviour of the elements and their compounds, with the single exception of the element carbon (whose study is called organic chemistry). The most important unifying principle is the periodic table. (A simple introduction to the periodic table was given in chapter 1; further insight was provided in chapter 4, where the idea of the s, p, and d blocks was introduced.)

We study the periodic table in a particular order. The s block, which occurs on the far left of the periodic table, is looked at first (chapter 16). The general variation across the periodic table is considered (chapter 17), and then we turn to the halogens (chapter 18), the most important group of elements towards the right of the periodic table.

The halogens form a part of the p block. We have attempted to give a balanced approach to the most important elements in the p block in chapter 19.

The final area studied is the transition metals, which form the major part of the d block (chapter 20). They offer a visually interesting conclusion to the study of inorganic chemistry: much of the colour seen around us in nature is caused by transition metal compounds. Transition metals are also very important in biochemistry, being involved in the transport of electrons between species, as well as being central to the function of important molecules such as haemoglobin. Before studying the vital area of biochemistry, we first need to know about organic chemistry, the study of which begins in chapter 21.

A light micrograph of crystalline silver deposited on a copper wire. Copper wire is suspended in aqueous silver nitrate. The copper reacts with the silver ions, and silver is deposited as crystals on the wire. In time, all of the silver is displaced, leaving aqueous copper(II) nitrate. Magnification x65.

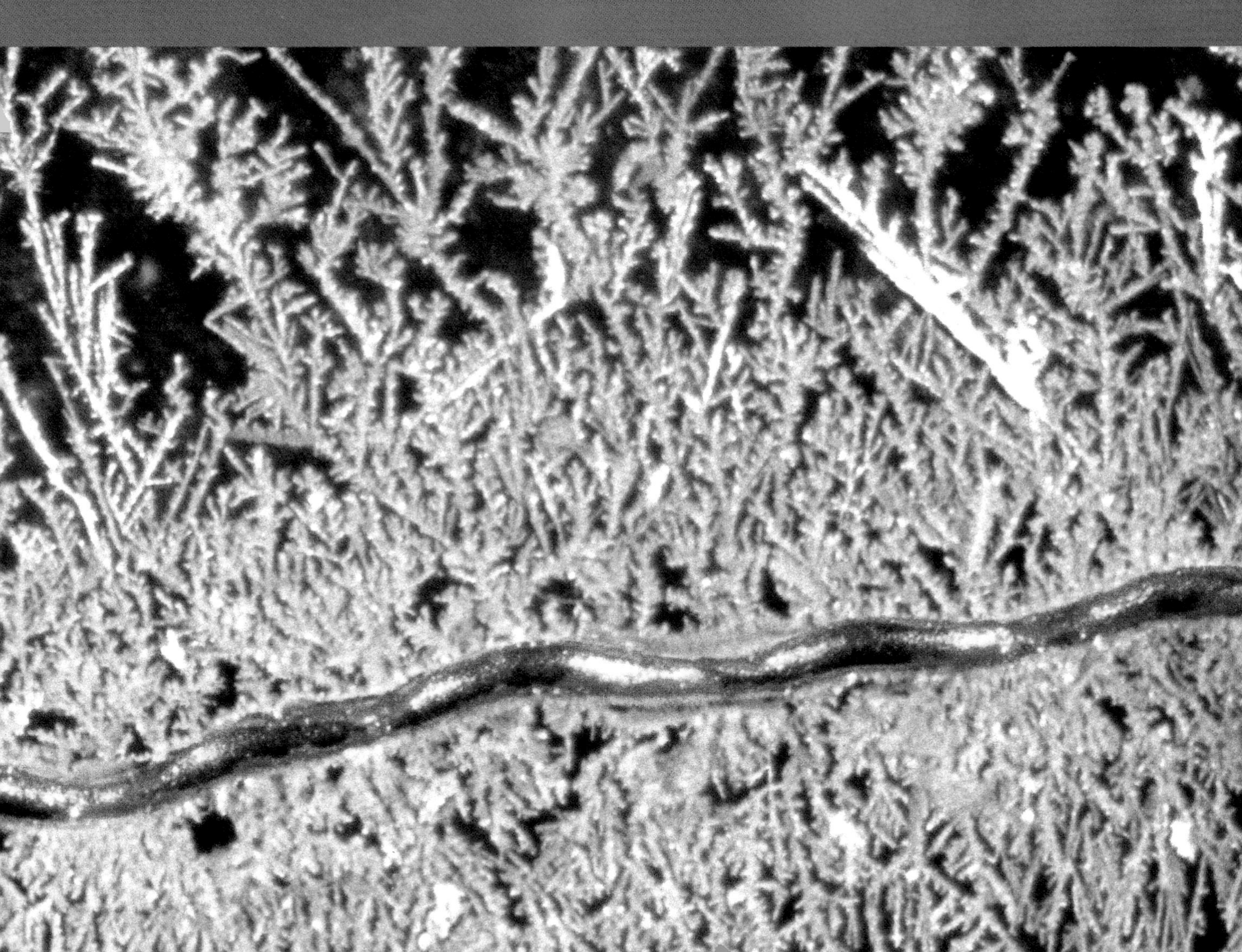

The s-block elements

The s-block elements consist of the metals contained in Groups I and II of the periodic table. These two groups are referred to as the s block because the elements in them have a valence-shell electronic structure of either ns^1 (Group I) or ns^2 (Group II). Group I contains the elements lithium to francium, and Group II contains the elements beryllium to radium. Compared to most other metals, the s-block metals have generally greater chemical reactivity. In this chapter, we shall look at the properties of these two groups of metals (with the exception of the radioactive elements francium and radium), and at the underlying reasons for their distinct identity.

Group I and Group II metals: an overview

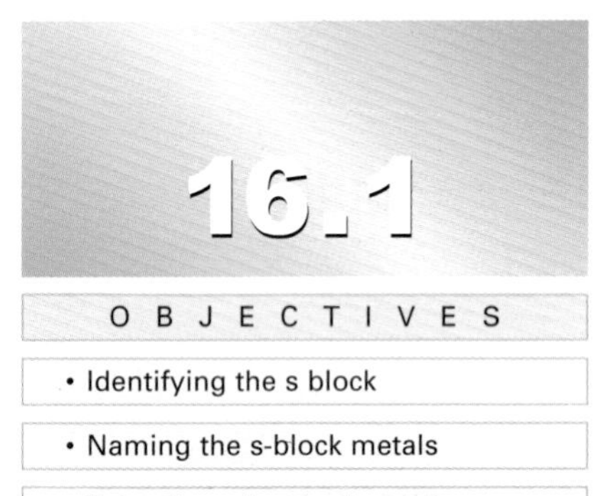

OBJECTIVES

- Identifying the s block
- Naming the s-block metals
- Extraction of s-block metals

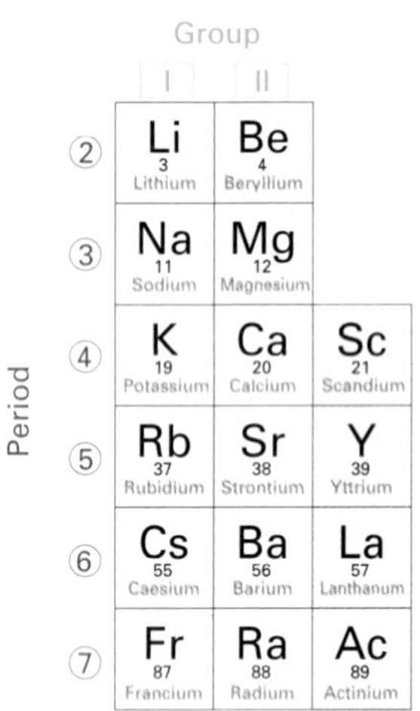

The s block comprises Groups I and II and occupies the extreme left-hand side of the periodic table.

Downs cell

Electrolysis of aqueous sodium chloride reduces hydrogen ions in preference to the sodium ions; see spread 18.2. *Molten* sodium chloride contains sodium ion as the only positive ion. Some calcium chloride is added to the electrolyte because the mixture of chlorides melts at a lower temperature (about 600 °C) than the melting point of pure sodium chloride (801 °C), spread 7.7. Each Downs cell consumes about 200 kW at a current of about 25 000 A.

The Group I elements show the typical properties of metals: a freshly cut surface is shiny, electrical and thermal conductivities are high, and the elements are ductile and malleable. The presence of just one electron in the valence shell leads to these elements forming compounds containing the M^+ ion.

The Group II elements likewise show typical properties of metals, although beryllium shows some anomalies (see later spread in this chapter). There are two electrons in the valence shell, so the elements magnesium to barium form compounds containing the M^{2+} ion.

For historical reasons, the Group I and Group II elements are sometimes known respectively as the **alkali metals** and the **alkaline earth metals**.

Extraction of s-block metals

The s-block metals cannot be manufactured by the reduction of an oxide by carbon because the temperature required is too high to be economic. They are generally extracted by electrolysis of a molten salt, usually the chloride. For example, metallic sodium is manufactured in a Downs cell from molten sodium chloride at a temperature of about 600 °C.

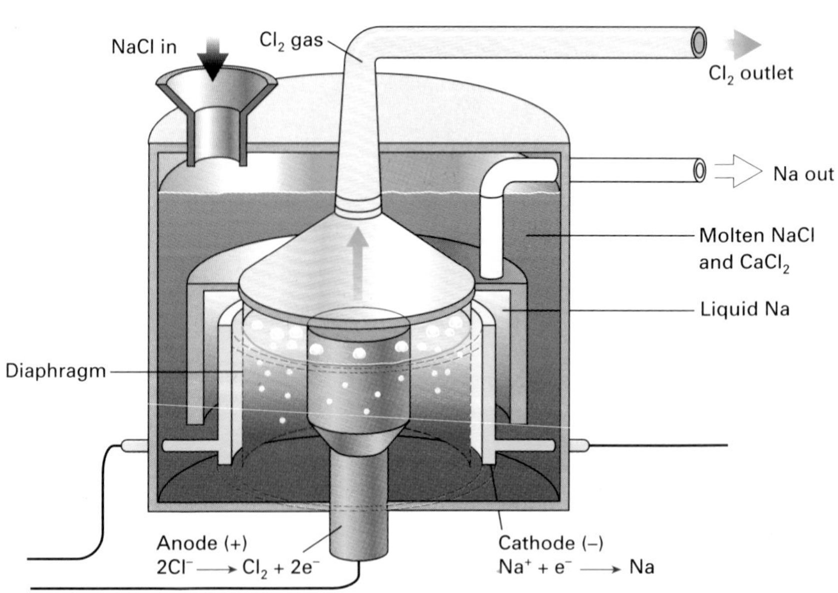

A Downs cell consists of a cylindrical graphite anode (which resists the attack of chlorine) and a steel cathode constructed in the shape of a ring. At the cathode, sodium ions are reduced to form sodium metal (which is molten at this temperature). At the anode, chloride ions are oxidized to form chlorine gas. The diaphragm keeps the molten sodium and gaseous chlorine apart. If the products were to come into contact, they would react, re-forming sodium chloride.

The s-block elements: table of data

For the purposes of this chapter, Group I includes the elements lithium to caesium, and Group II includes the elements beryllium to barium. The anomalous behaviour of lithium and beryllium will be covered separately in a later spread in this chapter. The radioactive elements francium and radium will not be covered here.

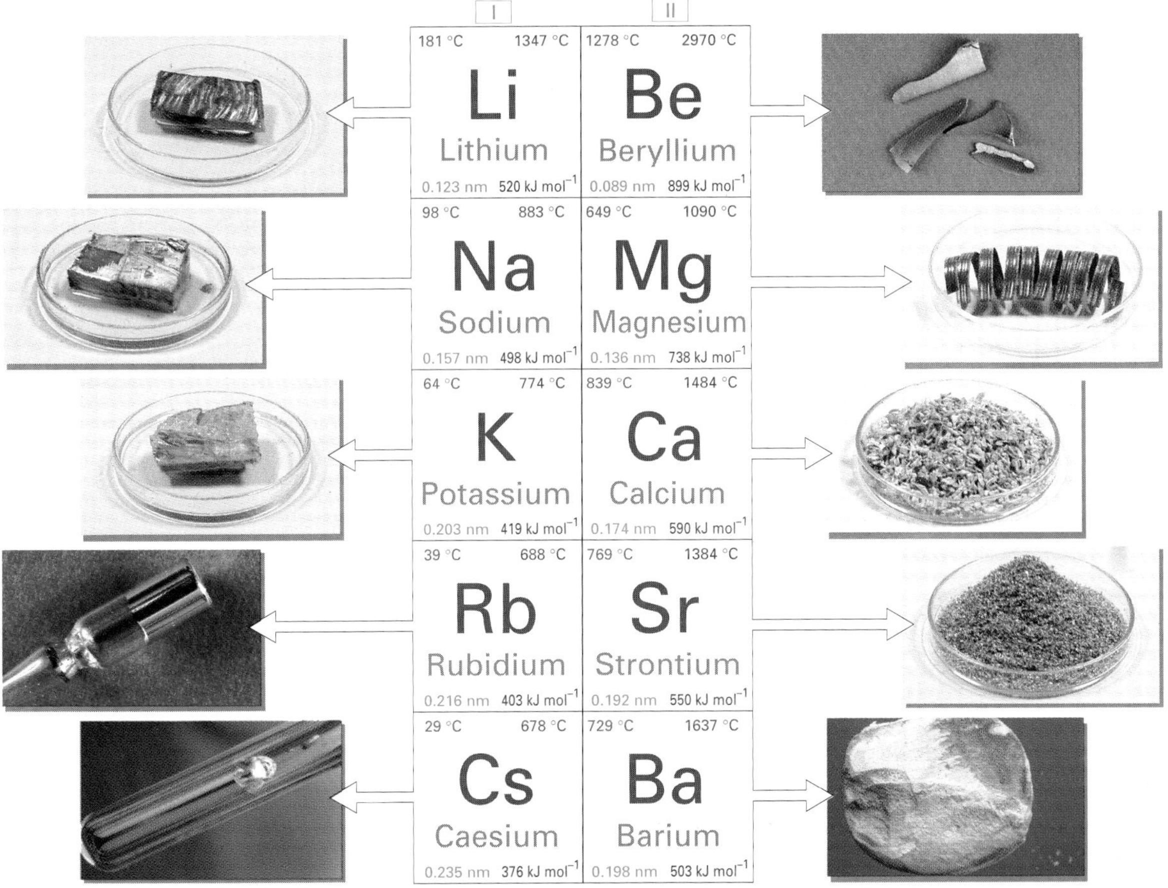

The major physical properties of the s-block elements: clockwise from top left = melting point, boiling point, first ionization energy, atomic radius. The Group I metals are very reactive: lithium, sodium, and potassium are coated with compounds that form on their surface. Rubidium and caesium are so reactive that they must be stored in sealed vessels.

SUMMARY

- The Group I metals studied are lithium, sodium, potassium, rubidium, and caesium.
- The Group II metals studied are beryllium, magnesium, calcium, strontium, and barium.
- The valence-shell electronic structures of the s-block metals are ns^1 (Group I) and ns^2 (Group II).
- The s-block metals are extracted by electrolysis of a molten salt.

Ionization energy: a reminder

In the chapter on 'Thermochemistry', where we were considering enthalpy changes, we associated the term 'ionization *enthalpy*' with the removal of electrons from atoms to form ions. In the earlier chapter on 'Electrons in atoms', we associated the term 'ionization *energy*' with the same change. You will often find enthalpy changes being referred to colloquially as 'energies' and we will do so here.

PRACTICE

1 Plot separate graphs for Group I and Group II elements to illustrate the trends in each of the following properties:

- **a** Melting point
- **b** Boiling point
- **c** Atomic radius
- **d** First ionization energy.

When plotting your graphs, space each element equally along the x-axis in order of increasing atomic number.

2 For each of the plots that you produced in question 1, make a general comment about the trend in the property as the atomic number increases.

16.2 Some group trends

OBJECTIVES

- Trends in:
  atomic radius and ionic radius
  ionization energy
  melting point
  electronegativity
- Oxidation number

The s-block elements have distinctive characteristics that distinguish them from the metals in other regions of the periodic table. Within the s block, Group I and Group II are clearly distinguishable from each other, in particular because they have different oxidation numbers in their compounds. Within each group, properties such as atomic radius, ionization energy, and melting point show clear trends. This spread gives an overview of these properties of the s-block elements, and describes the trends within Group I and Group II.

Atomic radii

In the earlier chapter on 'Electrons in atoms', we looked at the shapes and sizes of atomic orbitals. In terms of probability, we saw that the orbitals of an atom extend to infinity. So, describing the size of an atom (its radius) necessarily requires an arbitrary decision about where the boundary of an atom is.

The s-block elements have one or two valence electrons in orbitals outside filled shells of electrons. These filled shells are reasonably effective at shielding the valence electrons from the attraction of the nucleus. As a result, the atomic radii of the s-block metals are generally about 50% greater than those of other metals.

Comparisons

The average value for the atomic radii of the Group I metals is 0.187 nm; for the Group II metals it is 0.158 nm. For comparison, the average value for the d-block elements scandium to zinc is 0.122 nm. The atomic radius of the p-block metal aluminium is 0.125 nm.

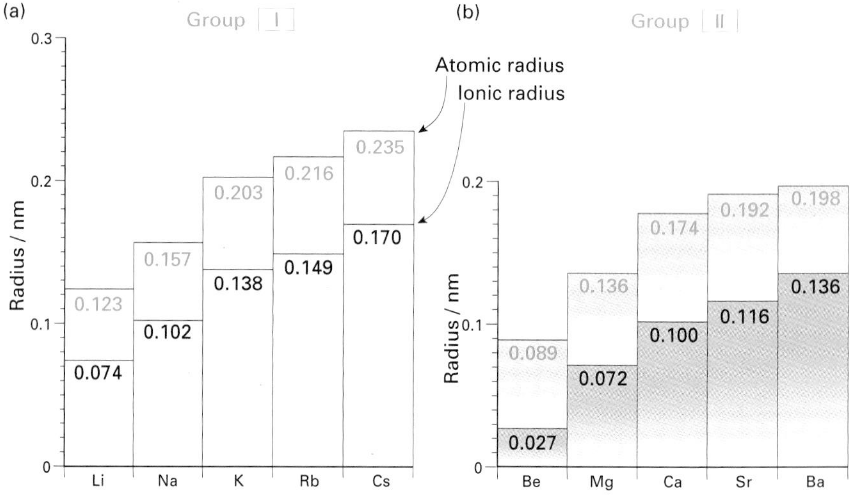

Atomic radius increases as atomic number increases from lithium to caesium (Group I) and from beryllium to barium (Group II). Each successive element in a group has an extra filled shell of electrons. Ionic radii increase similarly. All ions are smaller than their parent atoms as electrons have been lost.

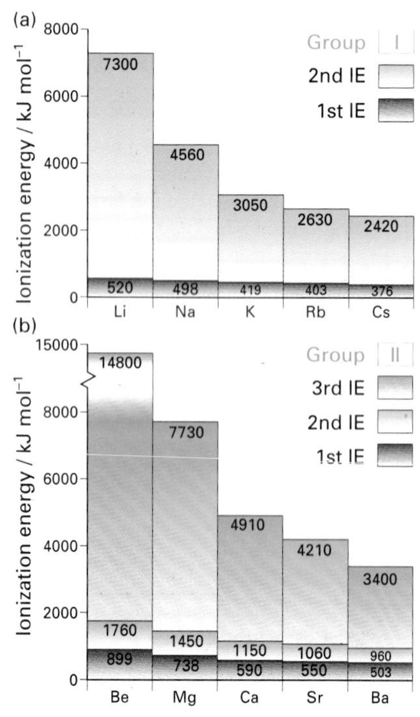

(a) The first and second ionization energies of the Group I elements.
(b) The first, second, and third ionization energies of the Group II elements.

Ionization energies

The first ionization energy of an element involves removing an electron from its outermost orbital. The s-block elements have relatively large atomic radii and therefore have low values of ionization energy. For example

Group I: $Na(g) \rightarrow Na^+(g) + e^-(g)$; $\Delta H^\ominus = +498\,kJ\,mol^{-1}$

Group II: $Mg(g) \rightarrow Mg^+(g) + e^-(g)$; $\Delta H^\ominus = +736\,kJ\,mol^{-1}$

In each group, the atomic radius increases with increasing atomic number, and there is a corresponding decrease in the value of the ionization energy, as the electron being ionized is further from the nucleus. Within a given period, the Group II ion M^{2+} is smaller than the corresponding Group I ion M^+. This effect is due to the fact that the same number of electrons are under the control of more protons.

Group I elements have one electron in their valence shell. The energy required to remove that electron is relatively low (+498 kJ mol^{-1} for sodium), and so the elements readily form ions with a single positive charge. The second ionization energy is much greater because an electron needs to be removed from an inner shell much closer to the nucleus. For example, the second ionization energy of sodium is +4560 kJ mol^{-1}, about nine times greater than the first ionization energy. As a result, Group I elements do not form ions with a double positive charge.

Group II elements have two electrons in their valence shell. The first and second ionization energies are relatively low in value. The *third* ionization energies are large by comparison, corresponding to the removal of an electron from an inner shell much closer to the nucleus. So, Group II elements do form ions with a double positive charge.

Compared to other metals, the Group I elements are unusually soft. Sodium may be cut with a knife. Forces of attraction between the Na^+ ions and the delocalized electrons in the metallic lattice are relatively low. Because sodium is so reactive, it is stored under oil; some of that protective oil is visible here.

Melting points

Larger atoms tend to have smaller first ionization energies because the valence electron concerned is further from the nucleus. Larger positive ions have lower charge density, so they have a smaller attraction for the delocalized electrons within the metallic structure. As a result, melting points within a group generally decrease with increasing atomic number. Within a given period, the Group II metal has a higher melting point than its Group I counterpart because each atom delocalizes *two* electrons into the metallic lattice, increasing the forces of attraction between the metal ions and the delocalized electrons.

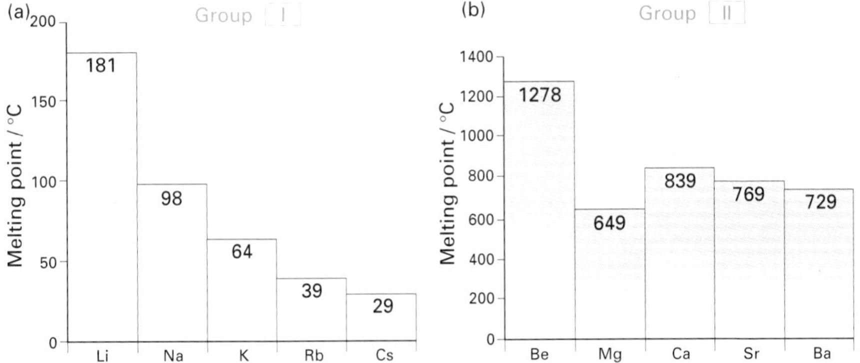

Melting points (T_m) of (a) Group I elements and (b) Group II elements.

Electronegativity: a reminder

If you need to revise electronegativity, you should look back at the chapter on 'Chemical bonding'. Electronegativity is measured on the Pauling scale. Metals are elements which lose electrons when they form compounds. They have smaller electronegativities than non-metals. The smaller the electronegativity, the more metallic is the element.

Electronegativity

We can see from the values given on the right that, in a given group, metallic character increases with increasing atomic number. Within a given period, the Group I metal has greater metallic character than the corresponding Group II metal.

Pauling electronegativity values for s-block elements.

Group I element	Pauling electronegativity
Li	1.0
Na	0.9
K	0.8
Rb	0.8
Cs	0.8
Group II element	**Pauling electronegativity**
Be	1.6
Mg	1.3
Ca	1.0
Sr	1.0
Ba	0.9

Oxidation numbers

Group I elements have an oxidation number of +1 in all their compounds, corresponding to the loss of the single ns^1 electron from the valence shell. Examples include the sodium ion Na^+ in sodium chloride NaCl, the potassium ion K^+ in potassium oxide K_2O, and the lithium ion Li^+ in lithium carbonate Li_2CO_3. The highly endothermic formation of the doubly charged ion prevents the element from reaching higher oxidation states.

Group II elements have an oxidation number of +2 in all their compounds, corresponding to the loss of both ns^2 electrons from the valence shell. Examples include the ions Mg^{2+} in magnesium oxide MgO, and Ca^{2+} in calcium carbonate $CaCO_3$. Both the ns^2 electrons can be removed during the formation of such compounds: the endothermic formation of the doubly charged ion M^{2+} is compensated for by the highly exothermic formation of the solid ionic lattice from its separate ions (see the earlier chapter on 'Thermochemistry').

SUMMARY

- Within a group, the variations in atomic radius, first ionization energy, and melting point are due to the different number of electron shells in the atoms or ions.
- Group I compounds contain the M^+ ion. Group II compounds contain the M^{2+} ion.

PRACTICE

1 Describe and explain the trend in the ionization energies of the elements in Group II.

16.3

OBJECTIVES

- Trends in reactivity with water and oxygen
- Comparison between Groups I and II
- Trends in reactivity

Reactions with water and oxygen

The valence shells of Group I and Group II elements contain one and two electrons respectively. When the elements react to form compounds, these electrons are lost and positively charged ions form. The elements have relatively low ionization energies, which decrease with increasing atomic number. This spread gives details of the reactions of the elements with water and oxygen, and explains trends in reactivity in terms of trends in the values of ionization energies.

Reaction with water

The Group I metals are powerful reductants in aqueous solution. Their common name 'alkali metals' comes from their ability to reduce water to form alkalis (soluble bases) and hydrogen gas. For example, the reaction of sodium with water is:

$$2Na(s) + 2H_2O(l) \rightarrow 2NaOH(aq) + H_2(g)$$

The reaction of Group I elements with water increases in vigour with increasing atomic number. All the Group I metals are so reactive that they must be stored under oil to prevent reaction with water or air.

(a)

(b)

(c)

(d)

(a) Lithium reacts steadily with water in an unspectacular manner. (b) Sodium floats on water. The exothermic reaction melts the metal and the hydrogen released propels it across the surface. (c) The hydrogen that forms during the very exothermic reaction of potassium with water ignites. (d) Caesium reacts explosively, shattering its glass container.

Group II metals react less vigorously than their Group I counterparts. Beryllium does not react with water, and magnesium reacts only very slowly. Reactivity increases down the group Ca–Sr–Ba, with calcium approaching the reactivity of sodium. As with the Group I elements, the hydroxide is formed and hydrogen is evolved:

$$Ca(s) + 2H_2O(l) \rightarrow Ca(OH)_2(aq) + H_2(g)$$

An advanced explanation

The elements of Group II have two electrons that must be removed when they act as reductants. On average they react with water less quickly than the Group I elements. For example, calcium reacts about as vigorously with water as does sodium. You might expect calcium to be *more* reactive than sodium, because it has the more negative standard electrode potential. However, the *rate* of reaction of calcium is lower because *two* electrons must be removed when it reacts, so the activation energy for the reaction is greater than for sodium.

(a)

(b)

(a) The rate of reaction of magnesium with cold water is imperceptibly slow. It does react more rapidly with steam. (b) Calcium reacts steadily with water. Calcium hydroxide has only limited solubility and gradually appears as a white cloudiness.

Reaction with oxygen

All Group I elements react with oxygen to form the oxide M_2O (where we use M to denote any Group I metal). For example, potassium reacts as follows:

$$4K(s) + O_2(g) \rightarrow 2K_2O(s)$$

All Group II elements react with oxygen to form the oxide MO (where now M denotes any Group II metal). For example, calcium reacts as follows:

$$2Ca(s) + O_2(g) \rightarrow 2CaO(s)$$

All Group II oxides are white ionic solids with extremely high melting points. Magnesium reacts very vigorously with oxygen, spread 13.1, to form magnesium oxide. Magnesium oxide is a particularly stable compound, which explains why magnesium reacts with carbon dioxide, as illustrated alongside.

Magnesium is a sufficiently powerful reductant to continue burning when placed between two pieces of dry ice (solid carbon dioxide). The reaction products are magnesium oxide and carbon:
$2Mg(s) + CO_2(g) \rightarrow 2MgO(s) + C(s)$

Peroxides and superoxides

In their reaction with oxygen, all the Group I metals from sodium to caesium and the Group II metals strontium and barium also form *peroxides*. A **peroxide** contains the ion O_2^{2-}, for example Na_2O_2 (Group I) and BaO_2 (Group II). The Group I metals from potassium to caesium also form *superoxides*. A **superoxide** contains the ion O_2^-, for example KO_2.

Trends in reactivity

Group I elements react more vigorously with water than their Group II counterparts. In each group, reactivity increases with increasing atomic number. The reason for these differences is that the elements form positive ions in the course of their reaction. Group I metals lose one electron and Group II metals lose two. The energy required for this change is the ionization energy.

In both groups, ionization energy decreases with increasing atomic number. The lower the ionization energy, the lower the activation energy for reaction, and so the faster the reaction. (Note that the word 'reactivity' here actually refers to the *rate* of a reaction.) So, the trends in reactivity *within* the two groups and the differences in reactivity *between* the two groups may be explained with reference to the ionization energies of the elements.

Underwater chemistry

Potassium superoxide is used to purify the air in submarines and in emergency breathing apparatus. It both removes the waste products of respiration and supplies fresh oxygen:

$4KO_2(s) + 4CO_2(g) + 2H_2O(g) \rightarrow 4KHCO_3(s) + 3O_2(g)$

Building with magnesium

The relatively slow rate of reaction between magnesium and water allows magnesium alloys to be used for construction. Magnesium has a low density (1.7 g cm^{-3}, compared with 2.7 g cm^{-3} for aluminium and 7.9 g cm^{-3} for iron), making it the least dense constructional metal. However, its strength as a reductant becomes important at high temperatures. In battle, disastrous fires have occurred in naval ships that used magnesium in their superstructures: the magnesium reacts violently once ignited.

SUMMARY

- The reactivity of the Group I elements with water is greater than that of the Group II elements.
- Reactivity increases with increasing atomic number.
- The rate of reaction with water depends on the activation energy, which in turn depends on the ionization energy.

PRACTICE

1 Write chemical equations for the reactions of rubidium and barium with water and with oxygen. For each of the four reactions, discuss the changes in oxidation state that take place.

2 Look at the illustrations on the left-hand page and make statements about the densities of the elements concerned. Are you able to comment on the densities of the s-block elements that are not illustrated?

3 Potassium is more dense than mineral oil and less dense than water. Describe how, with the aid of standard laboratory glassware, you would use these three substances to produce hydrogen *safely*. Give details of the *function* of your design – how it would work.

4 The text above states: 'The lower the ionization energy, the lower the activation energy for reaction, and so the faster the reaction.' Explain this statement with respect to the trend in the reactivity of the Group II metals.

16.4

OBJECTIVES

- Oxides and water
- Sodium hydroxide
- Trends in solubility of hydroxides
- The limewater test
- Base character

The s-block oxides and hydroxides

As noted in the previous spread, all the s-block metals form stable oxides. In this spread we shall investigate the properties of these oxides, particularly their solubility and their reaction with water to form hydroxides. You will see that both the oxides and hydroxides are ionic, and that they act principally as bases in their reactions with other substances. (Note that beryllium oxide has anomalous properties, which are specifically addressed in a later spread in this chapter.)

The solubility of the Group I and Group II hydroxides. Solubility data are given in grams of solid per 100 cm³ of water.

Group I hydroxide	Solubility
LiOH	13
NaOH	42
KOH	107
RbOH	180
CsOH	395
Group II hydroxide	**Solubility**
$Be(OH)_2$	ss*
$Mg(OH)_2$	0.0009
$Ca(OH)_2$	0.18
$Sr(OH)_2$	0.41
$Ba(OH)_2$	5.6

* ss = sparingly soluble.

Group I oxides

The Group I metal oxides do not simply dissolve in water, they *react* with it. For example, sodium oxide reacts with water to form aqueous sodium hydroxide:

$$Na_2O(s) + H_2O(l) \rightarrow 2NaOH(aq)$$

Group I metal oxides are ionic, and it is the oxide ion that reacts to form the hydroxide ion:

$$O^{2-}(s) + H_2O(l) \rightarrow 2OH^-(aq)$$

The resulting solutions are strongly basic because they contain a high concentration of the aqueous hydroxide ion.

Sodium hydroxide

Sodium hydroxide is typical of Group I hydroxides. Because it is cheap, it is the reagent of choice when a strongly basic solution is required. It is a white waxy solid usually supplied in the form of pellets. It is stable to heat, melting to a clear, colourless liquid at 318 °C. It dissolves in water exothermically to give a solution that is a strong base.

The three main classes of reaction involving sodium hydroxide are:

- Neutralization of acids (see spread 12.1)

$$H_3O^+(aq) + OH^-(aq) \rightarrow 2H_2O(l)$$

- Precipitation of hydroxides (see spread 11.10)

$$Zn^{2+}(aq) + 2OH^-(aq) \rightarrow Zn(OH)_2(s)$$

- Hydrolysis in organic chemistry

$$CH_3CH_2Br(l) + OH^-(aq) \rightarrow CH_3CH_2OH(aq) + Br^-(aq)$$

Note that these reactions of aqueous sodium hydroxide (and of all Group I hydroxides) involve the aqueous hydroxide ion $OH^-(aq)$ acting as a Lewis base (see chapter on 'Acid–base equilibrium'). (The Group I metal ion M^+ takes no part in the reactions and is a 'spectator' ion.)

Pellets of sodium hydroxide. This substance is ***deliquescent****, which means that it absorbs water from the air to such an extent that it forms a concentrated solution. It must therefore be kept in an airtight container. This sample has been left for a short time and is already glistening.*

Group II oxides and hydroxides

There is a significant difference between the two groups of s-block elements in the solubility of their oxides. The oxides of the Group I metals react with water to form soluble hydroxides. Most of the oxides of the Group II metals are much less soluble in water. We can explain this effect by considering the energy changes that take place during dissolution.

The only Group II oxide to form a strong base in water is barium oxide:

$$BaO(s) + H_2O(l) \rightarrow Ba(OH)_2(aq)$$

Barium hydroxide is fully ionized in water. The other Group II hydroxides are far less soluble than those of Group I. Look at the table above and you will see that calcium hydroxide is only very slightly soluble and that magnesium hydroxide is even less so. Saturated solutions of these Group II hydroxides are only weakly basic, because the concentration of aqueous hydroxide ion is very low. In general, hydroxide solubility *increases* as the atomic number of the Group II metal increases. The main reason for this trend is that the lattice enthalpy decreases significantly as the ionic radius increases.

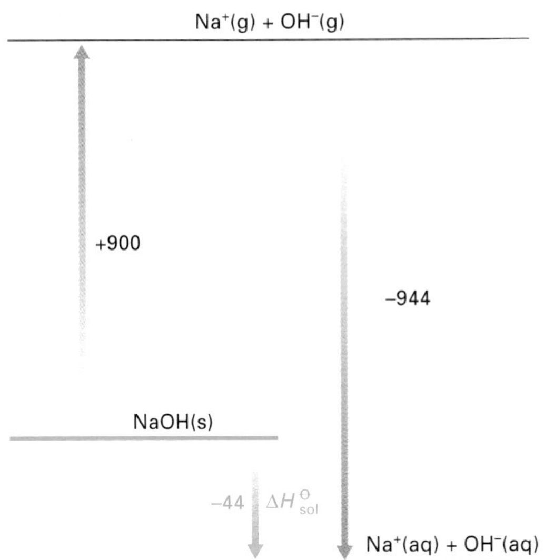

Enthalpy cycle for the dissolution of sodium hydroxide. The two most significant factors to consider about dissolving a metal hydroxide are the lattice enthalpy and the enthalpy of hydration; see spread 10.7.
(a) Breaking the ionic lattice into separate ions involves the highly endothermic lattice enthalpy $\Delta H^\ominus_{lat}$:
Group I: $NaOH(s) \rightarrow Na^+(g) + OH^-(g)$
Group II: $Mg(OH)_2(s) \rightarrow Mg^{2+}(g) + 2OH^-(g)$
(b) Hydrating the ions involves the highly exothermic *enthalpy of hydration $\Delta H^\ominus_{hyd}$:*
$OH^-(g) \rightarrow OH^-(aq)$
Group I: $Na^+(g) \rightarrow Na^+(aq)$
Group II: $Mg^{2+}(g) \rightarrow Mg^{2+}(aq)$
The lattice enthalpy for magnesium hydroxide is extremely large (3000 kJ mol^{-1}) because of the double charge on the Mg^{2+} ion. The magnitude of the enthalpies of hydration of the Mg^{2+} ion plus two OH^- ions is smaller than the magnitude of the lattice enthalpy. The reaction is therefore endothermic overall (+4 kJ mol^{-1}): $Mg(OH)_2$ is sparingly soluble. Sodium hydroxide has a much lower lattice enthalpy and the solution process is exothermic overall (−44 kJ mol^{-1}).

Magnesium, calcium, and strontium hydroxides are usually made by mixing aqueous sodium hydroxide with an aqueous salt of the metal. For example, for magnesium chloride:

$$MgCl_2(aq) + 2NaOH(aq) \rightarrow Mg(OH)_2(s) + 2NaCl(aq)$$

Magnesium hydroxide is only weakly basic, which is useful for its application as an antacid in indigestion tablets. The milky-white suspension is called 'milk of magnesia'.

Whilst they have limited reaction with water, all Group II oxides *do* react with an acid to form a salt and water. They may therefore be classified as *basic oxides*. For example, magnesium oxide reacts with hydrochloric acid to form magnesium chloride and water:

$$MgO(s) + 2HCl(aq) \rightarrow MgCl_2(aq) + H_2O(l)$$

SUMMARY

- All s-block oxides and hydroxides are basic; they can act as Brønsted bases.
- All Group I oxides react with water to form a solution of the hydroxide.
- All Group I hydroxides are stable to heat, but they dissolve readily in water.
- All Group II metal oxides and hydroxides (except those of barium) are weak bases with limited solubility in water. The solubility increases with increasing atomic number of the metal.

The limewater test for carbon dioxide

The test to identify carbon dioxide involves bubbling the gas through a solution of **limewater** (saturated aqueous calcium hydroxide), which has pH = 12. A milky precipitate of calcium carbonate forms:

$Ca(OH)_2(aq) + CO_2(g) \rightarrow CaCO_3(s) + H_2O(l)$

The precipitate reacts with excess carbon dioxide to form (a colourless solution of) aqueous calcium hydrogencarbonate:

$CaCO_3(s) + CO_2(g) + H_2O(l) \rightarrow Ca(HCO_3)_2(aq)$

Quicklime and slaked lime

Calcium oxide is called **quicklime**. It is produced in industry by roasting **limestone** (calcium carbonate). Quicklime may be used to neutralize acids and is especially useful for spreading on soils that are too acidic. Quicklime absorbs water to form calcium hydroxide, which is called **slaked lime**. Mixed with water and sand to make mortar (for bonding brick walls), it slowly sets by reaction with atmospheric carbon dioxide to form interlaced crystals of calcium carbonate.

PRACTICE

1 Write chemical equations for the following reactions (include state symbols):
  a Potassium oxide and water
  b Strontium oxide and water
  c Magnesium oxide and nitric acid
  d Magnesium nitrate and aqueous sodium hydroxide.

2 Which of the two solutions resulting in (a) and (b) in question 1 will be more strongly basic? Give your reasoning.

3 Write equations for the chemical changes discussed in the box above headed 'Quicklime and slaked lime':
  a Production of quicklime
  b Neutralizing soil acidity
  c Formation of slaked lime.

16.5

THE S-BLOCK HALIDES

OBJECTIVES

- Bonding in the halides
- Trends in halide solubility
- Enthalpy changes and solubility

The s-block metals are highly reactive compared with other metals. The halogens are highly reactive non-metals. As you might expect, all the Group I and Group II metals react with all the halogens to form halides. In this spread we look at the methods of producing these halides, and we explore their bonding character and the reasons for their differing solubilities in water. The emphasis throughout is not so much on the properties themselves as on trends and the reasons for them.

Perhaps the most remarkable use of sodium chloride (and sugar) is in the rehydration tablets that help keep dehydrated patients alive. They are very effective *and* cheap.

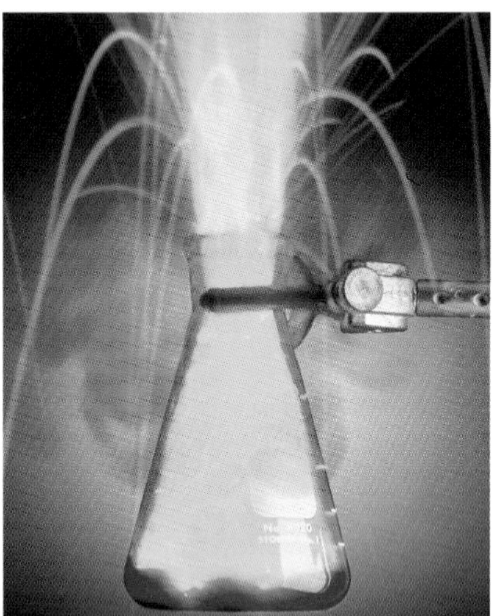

Sodium reacts very vigorously with bromine to form sodium bromide.

Sodium chloride (like all other Group I halides) consists of oppositely charged ions arranged in a regular crystalline lattice.

Group I halides

The halides of the Group I metals are all white crystalline solids. They are made either by directly combining the elements in a redox reaction, e.g.

$$2Na(s) + Br_2(l) \rightarrow 2NaBr(s)$$

or by a neutralization reaction, e.g.

$$HBr(aq) + NaOH(aq) \rightarrow NaBr(aq) + H_2O(l)$$

All Group I halides have the rock-salt structure (see earlier chapter on 'Solids'), with the exception of CsCl, CsBr, and CsI, which have the caesium chloride structure. All are ionic; they are soluble in water and their aqueous solutions conduct electricity.

Group II halides

The halides of the Group II metals are off-white crystalline solids. CaF_2, SrF_2, BaF_2, $SrCl_2$, and $BaCl_2$ all have the fluorite structure (see chapter on 'Solids'). Group II halides are predominantly ionic, with the exception of the compounds of beryllium. They may all be produced by direct combination of the elements. For example, magnesium and chlorine react:

$$Mg(s) + Cl_2(g) \rightarrow MgCl_2(s)$$

Reactivity decreases in the order $F_2 > Cl_2 > Br_2 > I_2$ and in the order $Ba > Sr > Ca > Mg > Be$.

Bonding character

The bonding in the chlorides is predominantly *ionic*. Ionic character and melting point increase with increasing atomic number of the metal. However, beryllium chloride has a relatively low melting point, which suggests that it has significant *covalent* character; see spread 16.8. Remember that covalent character increases where the cation has small size and high charge, that is, high charge density. For example, the small lithium ion has a greater charge density than the (larger) sodium ion, so its compounds have a relatively greater covalent character. Beryllium compounds have greater covalent character than the corresponding lithium compounds because the beryllium ion is *doubly* charged and so will have greater charge density.

The melting points of the Group II metal chlorides.

Group II chloride	Melting point/°C
$BeCl_2$	415
$MgCl_2$	714
$CaCl_2$	772
$SrCl_2$	874
$BaCl_2$	962

Melting point and the nature of the anion

Bonding character also depends on the nature of the anion. For example, the melting points of the halides of magnesium show a decrease as halide ionic radius increases with atomic number: see table opposite. Covalent character also increases when the anion has high polarizability. Covalent character increases in the order fluoride < chloride < bromide < iodide.

The solubility of the s-block halides. Solubility data are given in grams of solid per 100 cm³ of water.

Cation	F^-	Cl^-	Br^-	I^-
Li^+	0.27	64	145	165
Na^+	4.2	36	116	184
K^+	92	34	53	128
Rb^+	131	77	98	152
Cs^+	367	162	124	44
Be^{2+}	reacts	reacts	s*	dec†
Mg^{2+}	0.008	54	102	148
Ca^{2+}	0.0016	75	142	209
Sr^{2+}	0.011	54	100	178
Ba^{2+}	0.12	38	104	205

* s = soluble (no figure available). † dec = decomposes.

Solubility

The solubilities of the s-block halides in water are summarized above.

Note the following points from the table:

- The covalent character of the beryllium halides results in their reacting with water (BeF_2, $BeCl_2$) or even decomposing (BeI_2).
- Solubility of the Group II halides generally increases in the order fluoride < chloride < bromide < iodide.

Remember that solubility is mainly affected by two opposing factors: the endothermic lattice enthalpy required to break the solid lattice into separate ions, and the exothermic enthalpy of hydration of the ions by water molecules. Both the lattice enthalpy and the enthalpy of hydration of the positive ions become smaller as the ions become larger. As an approximate guide, solubility increases with increasing enthalpy of solution; low solubility results where the lattice enthalpy exceeds the enthalpy of hydration, i.e. where the enthalpy of solution is endothermic overall.

SUMMARY

- The s-block halides may be made by direct combination of the elements.
- The bonding in the s-block halides is predominantly ionic.
- The bonding of beryllium halides and, to a lesser extent, lithium halides show significant covalent character.

The melting points of the magnesium halides.

Magnesium halide	Melting point/°C
MgF_2	1263
$MgCl_2$	714
$MgBr_2$	711
MgI_2	634

The enthalpies of solution ($\Delta H^\ominus_{sol}$) given by
$\Delta H^\ominus_{sol} = \Delta H^\ominus_{lat} + \Delta H^\ominus_{hyd}(\text{metal}) + \Delta H^\ominus_{hyd}(F^-)$
and the solubilities of the Group I fluorides. Solubility data are given in grams of fluoride per 100 cm³ of water.

Group I fluoride	$\Delta H^\ominus_{sol}$ /kJ mol⁻¹	Solubility
LiF	+5	0.27
NaF	+1	4.2
KF	−18	92
RbF	−26	131
CsF	−37	367

Solubility and the entropy factor

Lattice enthalpies and the corresponding enthalpies of hydration are only an approximate guide to the solubility of a substance in water. Another factor is the entropy change (see the chapter on 'Spontaneous change ...') that takes place on dissolution. The ordered crystal lattice breaks down and the ions become randomized throughout the solution. This loss of order (increase in entropy) can be more significant than the enthalpy changes.

PRACTICE

1 Give the chemical equation for the preparation of the following:

  a Rubidium bromide by a neutralization method

  b Magnesium bromide by direct combination.

2 Arrange the following halides in order of increasing covalent character: magnesium iodide; potassium fluoride; potassium bromide. Give details of your reasoning.

3 Suggest reasons why the Group I fluorides show a much greater range of solubilities than the other Group I halides.

4 Look at the solubilities for the Group II fluorides. Suggest why the solubilities of the fluorides MgF_2 to BaF_2 are far smaller than those of all other s-block halides.

16.6

Carbonates and hydrogencarbonates

OBJECTIVES

- Reaction with acid
- Thermal decomposition of carbonates
- Carbonates in industry

Solution pH

Solutions of Group I carbonates are basic as the result of hydrolysis. For example, sodium carbonate dissolves to give aqueous ions:

$Na_2CO_3(s) \rightarrow 2Na^+(aq) + CO_3^{2-}(aq)$

Water acts as a Brønsted acid and protonates the carbonate ion. The pH becomes greater than 7 because the aqueous hydroxide ion $OH^-(aq)$ forms:

$CO_3^{2-}(aq) + H_2O(l) \rightleftharpoons OH^-(aq) + HCO_3^-(aq)$

The resulting hydrogencarbonate ion may itself then be protonated by water, further increasing the concentration of hydroxide ion:

$HCO_3^-(aq) + H_2O(l) \rightleftharpoons OH^-(aq) + H_2CO_3(aq)$

This equation indicates that solutions of hydrogencarbonates are also basic. However, these two equilibria lie to the left, so aqueous s-block carbonates have pH values about 11. Values for aqueous s-block hydrogencarbonates are lower (pH 8–9).

The stalactites that hang from the roofs of some caves form as follows. Rain water dissolves atmospheric carbon dioxide, producing (dilute) carbonic acid:
$H_2O(l) + CO_2(g) \rightarrow H_2CO_3(aq)$
This then percolates through carbonate rocks to form hydrogencarbonates:
$H_2CO_3(aq) + CaCO_3(s) \rightarrow Ca(HCO_3)_2(aq)$
The carbonate rock is slowly 'dissolved away' over millions of years to form caves. Water containing the dissolved calcium (or magnesium) hydrogencarbonates drips from the roof, and the water evaporates. The aqueous hydrogencarbonates decompose to form insoluble carbonates:
$Ca(HCO_3)_2(aq) \rightarrow CaCO_3(s) + H_2O(l) + CO_2(g)$
These carbonates are deposited to form stalactites (and build up the accompanying stalagmites on the floor below).

Both carbonates and hydrogencarbonates are salts of carbonic acid $H_2CO_3(aq)$, formed when carbon dioxide gas dissolves in water. Carbonates are compounds that contain the CO_3^{2-} ion, and hydrogencarbonates are compounds that contain the HCO_3^- ion. With the exception of beryllium, there is a complete series of s-block carbonates and hydrogencarbonates. A wide variety of s-block carbonate minerals exist, two of great commercial importance.

Solubility in water

The s-block carbonates are white solids. The Group I carbonates have the general formula M_2CO_3 and (with the exception of lithium carbonate) are soluble in water. The Group II carbonates have the general formula MCO_3 and are insoluble in water.

The Group I hydrogencarbonates have the general formulae $MHCO_3$; they exist as white solids which are soluble in water. Aqueous Group II hydrogencarbonates (except that of beryllium) may be obtained by bubbling carbon dioxide gas through an aqueous suspension of the carbonate, see spread 16.4:

$$CaCO_3(s) + CO_2(g) + H_2O(l) \rightarrow Ca(HCO_3)_2(aq)$$

If the solution is evaporated in an attempt to isolate the solid, the hydrogencarbonate decomposes by reversal of the above reaction.

Calcium and magnesium hydrogencarbonates are responsible for the temporary hardness of water.

Reactions with acid

Carbonates evolve carbon dioxide gas when added to acid:

$$MgCO_3(s) + 2HCl(aq) \rightarrow CO_2(g) + H_2O(l) + MgCl_2(aq)$$
$$CO_3^{2-}(s) + 2H^+(aq) \rightarrow CO_2(g) + H_2O(l)$$

Similarly, hydrogencarbonates evolve carbon dioxide gas when added to acid:

$$NaHCO_3(s) + HCl(aq) \rightarrow CO_2(g) + H_2O(l) + NaCl(aq)$$
$$HCO_3^-(s) + H^+(aq) \rightarrow CO_2(g) + H_2O(l)$$

Thermal decomposition

Of the Group I carbonates, only lithium carbonate decomposes on heating, giving carbon dioxide and lithium oxide:

$$Li_2CO_3(s) \rightarrow CO_2(g) + Li_2O(s)$$

All the others melt, with no significant decomposition. The hydrated crystalline forms of the Group I carbonates lose water on moderate heating. For example, sodium carbonate decahydrate:

$$Na_2CO_3{\cdot}10H_2O(s) \rightarrow Na_2CO_3(s) + 10H_2O(g)$$

Solid Group I hydrogencarbonates decompose when heated. For example:

$$2NaHCO_3(s) \rightarrow Na_2CO_3(s) + CO_2(g) + H_2O(g)$$

Group II carbonates decompose on heating:

$$CaCO_3(s) \rightarrow CaO(s) + CO_2(g)$$

Thermal stability

The carbonates of the Group II elements have different thermal stabilities, so they decompose at different temperatures when heated. The order of stability of the carbonates is Mg < Ca < Sr < Ba. To suggest reasons for this trend, consider calcium carbonate and barium carbonate. Calcium carbonate is stable up to about 900 °C; the corresponding figure for barium carbonate is about 1350 °C.

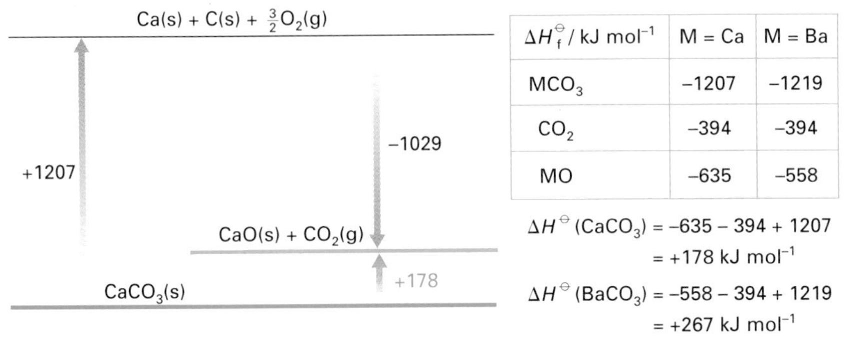

$\Delta H^\ominus_f$ / kJ mol^{-1}	M = Ca	M = Ba
MCO_3	−1207	−1219
CO_2	−394	−394
MO	−635	−558

$\Delta H^\ominus(CaCO_3) = -635 - 394 + 1207 = +178\ \text{kJ mol}^{-1}$

$\Delta H^\ominus(BaCO_3) = -558 - 394 + 1219 = +267\ \text{kJ mol}^{-1}$

Enthalpy cycle showing the decomposition of two Group II carbonates in terms of the standard enthalpy changes of formation of the constituents.

The difference in the standard enthalpy change for these two decompositions results from the difference in the values of the standard enthalpy change of formation of barium oxide compared with that of calcium oxide. Calcium oxide is more stable (has a more negative standard enthalpy change of formation) than barium oxide because its lattice enthalpy is larger, due to the calcium ion being smaller. So, calcium carbonate decomposes at a *lower* temperature than barium carbonate because calcium oxide is *more stable* than barium oxide.

By the same reasoning, magnesium carbonate decomposes more readily than calcium carbonate because magnesium oxide is more stable than calcium oxide, due to the magnesium ion being smaller than the calcium ion. Magnesium oxide has extremely high thermal stability and so is used as refractory (heat-resistant) bricks in furnaces.

Carbonates in industry

Calcium carbonate occurs as chalk, marble, and limestone. Finely ground chalk is incorporated in some toothpastes and cosmetics. Slabs of marble give a high-quality finish to buildings; and blocks may be carved to form sculptures. Millions of tonnes of crushed limestone are used each year to build roads. The most important chemical use of limestone is in the smelting of iron ore (see the later chapter on 'The transition metals').

Sodium carbonate is by far the most commercially important Group I carbonate. It is manufactured by the Solvay process, as outlined below.

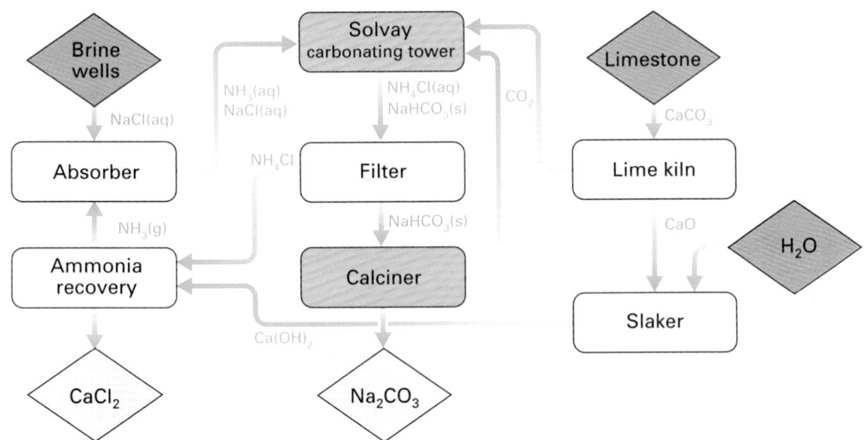

Flow scheme for the Solvay process. Carbon dioxide is passed up a carbonating tower (25 metres tall), down which flows an aqueous mixture of ammonia and concentrated sodium chloride:

$CO_2(g) + NH_3(aq) + NaCl(aq) + H_2O(l) \rightarrow NaHCO_3(s) + NH_4Cl(aq)$

The high concentration of sodium ion causes the solubility of sodium hydrogencarbonate $NaHCO_3$ to be exceeded through the common ion effect (see chapter on 'Acid–base equilibrium'). Solid $NaHCO_3$ forms; it is filtered off and then decomposed by heating in rotating calciners (30 metres long) to obtain the carbonate:

$2NaHCO_3(s) \rightarrow Na_2CO_3(s) + H_2O(g) + CO_2(g)$

The carbon dioxide is recycled.

SUMMARY

- All s-block carbonates and hydrogencarbonates exist, with the exception of the beryllium compounds. They react with strong acids to give carbon dioxide gas.
- Group I carbonates are stable to heat, with the exception of lithium carbonate. All are soluble in water and form basic solutions.
- Group II carbonates are insoluble in water, and decompose when strongly heated.
- The thermal stabilities of the Group II carbonates increase with increasing atomic number.

Decomposition and entropy

Calcium carbonate does not decompose at 298 K because the reaction is strongly endothermic: limestone hills do *not* spontaneously decompose! However, reaction occurs above 900 °C because the entropy increase due to the release of carbon dioxide gas exceeds the entropy decrease in the surroundings due to the endothermic nature of the reaction (see the chapter on 'Spontaneous change...' and especially spread 14.4).

In the blast furnace

Limestone decomposes at about 900 °C:

$CaCO_3(s) \rightarrow CaO(s) + CO_2(g)$

The calcium oxide acts as a **flux** (a substance that reacts with unwanted impurities in the furnace to produce a waste product called a **slag**).

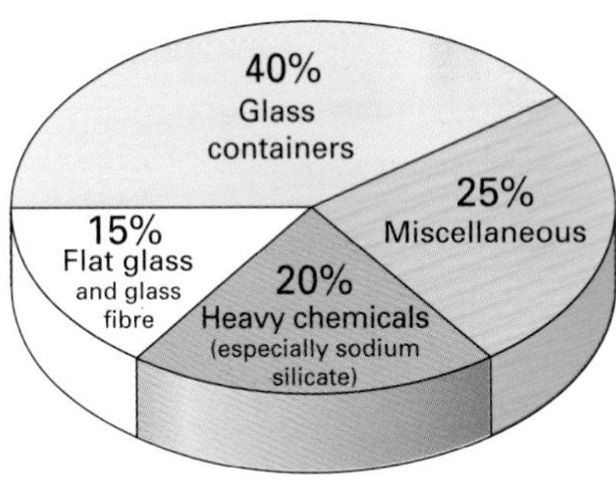

The major uses of sodium carbonate.

Trona

Although the Solvay process is still important world-wide, an alternative process has been gaining importance, especially in the USA. This involves mining the mineral *trona*, which is especially abundant in Wyoming. Trona has the approximate formula $Na_2CO_3{\cdot}NaHCO_3{\cdot}2H_2O$. Heating the ore decomposes it and produces sodium carbonate.

16.7

THE S-BLOCK NITRATES AND SULPHATES

OBJECTIVES

- Action of heat on nitrates
- Solubilities
- Barium sulphate

Nitrates and sulphates are salts containing respectively the ions NO_3^- and SO_4^{2-}. There is a full range of compounds consisting of s-block metal ions with either nitrate or sulphate ions. All these compounds exist as white crystalline solids or, when dehydrated, as white amorphous powders. As you might expect from reading the previous spreads in this chapter, the Group I and the Group II compounds show a distinct difference in behaviour, with lithium compounds being between the two.

Nitrates

Moderate heating decomposes Group I nitrates (except $LiNO_3$) to nitrites, which contain the ion NO_2^-:

$$2NaNO_3(s) \rightarrow 2NaNO_2(s) + O_2(g)$$

(More extreme temperatures form the oxide, nitrogen dioxide, and oxygen.)

Heating decomposes any Group II nitrate, and lithium nitrate, directly to the oxide. The difference in behaviour between Group I and Group II arises because the Group II oxides have more negative standard enthalpy changes of formation than the Group I oxides (see the previous spread for an explanation). Nitrogen dioxide (seen as brown fumes) and oxygen are evolved. For example:

$$2Ca(NO_3)_2(s) \rightarrow 2CaO(s) + 4NO_2(g) + O_2(g)$$

Sodium nitrate is the only nitrate to occur naturally in substantial amounts. Deposits of the sodium nitrate mineral *Chile saltpetre*, now largely mined out, are found in rainless areas of Chile. These deposits were the only source of nitrate before the introduction of the Haber–Bosch and Ostwald processes (see the chapter on 'The p-block elements'), which use atmospheric nitrogen to produce ammonia and then nitric acid. Much of the nitric acid now produced is used to make potassium and ammonium nitrate fertilizers. A minor use of potassium nitrate is in the gunpowder incorporated in fireworks.

Nitrate solubility

In common with all other nitrates, the s-block metal nitrates are soluble in water:

$Mg(NO_3)_2(s) \rightarrow Mg^{2+}(aq) + 2NO_3^-(aq)$

Potassium nitrate

Potassium nitrate is the only other nitrate ore. Major deposits are found in India.

Sulphates

The s-block sulphates are relatively stable to heat, decomposing only at high temperature. They have no significant chemical properties other than precipitating insoluble sulphates from solution. For example, for lead sulphate:

$$SO_4^{2-}(aq) + Pb^{2+}(aq) \rightarrow PbSO_4(s)$$

Of the Group I sulphates, sodium sulphate is a key chemical for making brown wrapping paper and corrugated cardboard. Potassium sulphate is used in glass-making and as a fertilizer ('sulphate of potash'). Group II sulphates occur naturally as the minerals *celestine* $SrSO_4$ and *barytes* $BaSO_4$. The main ores containing calcium are *gypsum* $CaSO_4{\cdot}2H_2O$ and *anhydrite* $CaSO_4$. The magnesium ore $MgSO_4{\cdot}7H_2O$ is called *Epsom salts*. In purified form it is used as a laxative and to make artificial snow on film sets.

Plaster of Paris is an insoluble form of calcium sulphate $2CaSO_4{\cdot}H_2O$. When mixed with water it forms $CaSO_4{\cdot}2H_2O$, expanding when it hydrates and hardening to a rigid, ceramic-like material. It is used for plaster-casts to immobilize broken bones, in dental work, and for gypsum wallboard ('plasterboard') in the construction industry.

This 2500 year old panel found in Pharaoh Rawer's tomb at Giza is made out of alabaster, a fine-grained form of gypsum $CaSO_4{\cdot}2H_2O$.

Sulphate solubility

In common with all other Group I salts, the sulphates are soluble in water. Group II sulphates show varying solubility: magnesium sulphate is soluble, calcium sulphate is sparingly soluble, and barium sulphate is very insoluble. Trends of this sort exist because solubility is a balance between the endothermic lattice enthalpy $\Delta H^{\ominus}_{lat}$ required to break the lattice into ions, and the exothermic enthalpy of hydration $\Delta H^{\ominus}_{hyd}$ accompanying the subsequent hydration of the ions. For example:

$$BaSO_4(s) \rightarrow Ba^{2+}(g) + SO_4^{2-}(g); \quad \Delta H^{\ominus}_{lat} = +2374\,kJ\,mol^{-1}$$
$$Ba^{2+}(g) + SO_4^{2-}(g) \rightarrow Ba^{2+}(aq) + SO_4^{2-}(aq); \quad \Delta H^{\ominus}_{hyd} = -2355\,kJ\,mol^{-1}$$

The lattice enthalpies of the three sulphates are quite similar because the sulphate ion is a very large ion; the changing size of the metal ion has little effect. On the other hand, the enthalpies of hydration become significantly smaller as metal ion size increases. The sum of the enthalpy of hydration and the lattice enthalpy therefore becomes correspondingly more endothermic (less favourable to solution) with increasing atomic number.

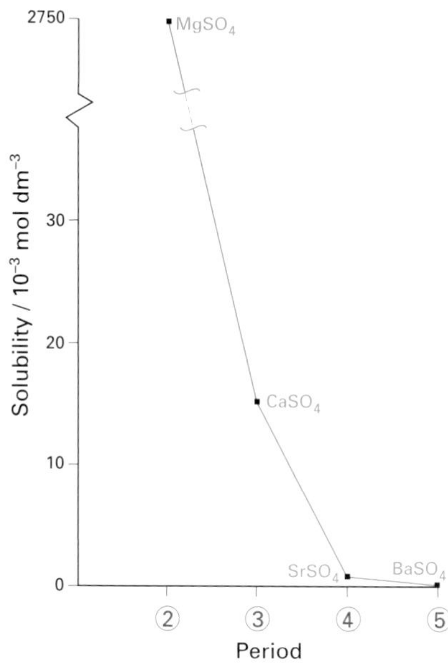

The solubility of Group II salts. The same decreasing trend as for sulphates is observed for other Group II salts with large, doubly charged negative ions such as carbonate CO_3^{2-}, ethanedioate $C_2O_4^{2-}$, and chromate(VI) CrO_4^{2-}.

Barium sulphate

Barium sulphate is extremely insoluble in water, and this feature is used both in the laboratory and in diagnostic medicine. In the laboratory, barium ions are used to identify aqueous sulphate ions. Addition of acidified barium nitrate (or barium chloride) to a solution containing sulphate ions causes a white precipitate of barium sulphate to form:

$$Ba^{2+}(aq) + SO_4^{2-}(aq) \rightarrow BaSO_4(s)$$

The acid is necessary to prevent the false detection of sulphite ion SO_3^{2-}. Barium sulphite $BaSO_3$ is also insoluble, and would form as a white precipitate. However, the acid reacts with sulphite ion: sulphur dioxide gas forms and the Ba^{2+} ions remain in solution. (Similarly, any carbonate ion present reacts to form carbon dioxide gas.)

Barium sulphate is used in medicine, as described in the caption to the photograph alongside.

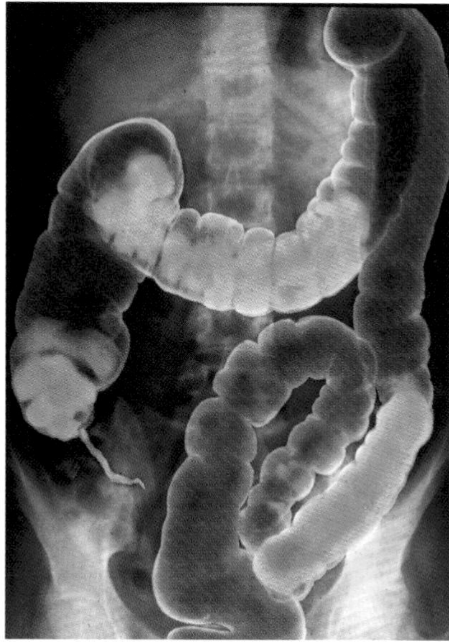

Barium sulphate is highly insoluble and is opaque to X-rays. This radiograph shows the human upper intestinal tract. The patient swallowed a suspension of barium sulphate about an hour before the X-ray was taken.

SUMMARY

- All s-block nitrates are soluble in water.
- All Group I sulphates are soluble in water. The solubility of the Group II sulphates decreases as atomic number increases.
- Group I nitrates (except $LiNO_3$) decompose to the nitrite and oxygen when heated.
- Lithium nitrate and Group II nitrates decompose to the oxide, nitrogen dioxide, and oxygen when heated.
- Acidified barium nitrate added to aqueous sulphate ions produces a white precipitate of barium sulphate.

PRACTICE

1 Barium ions $Ba^{2+}(aq)$ are highly poisonous. Explain why barium sulphate is used in preference to barium nitrate when taking X-ray pictures of the sort illustrated above.

2 a Why are minerals containing Group II sulphates so much more common than minerals containing Group I sulphates?

b Why are deposits of sodium nitrate found only in rainless regions of the world?

3 Suggest how 'plaster of Paris' is manufactured from gypsum.

16.8

ANOMALOUS BEHAVIOUR OF LITHIUM AND BERYLLIUM

OBJECTIVES

- Increased covalent character
- Amphoteric beryllium hydroxide
- Diagonal relationships
- Thermal decomposition of lithium carbonate

The ionic radii of the s-block elements. Notice that each Group II ion is smaller than the corresponding Group I ion, because the same number of electrons is under the control of one more proton. The lithium ion in Group I is about the same size as the magnesium ion in Group II. The sodium ion is about 50% larger than the lithium ion.

Group I ion	Radius/nm
Li^+	0.074
Na^+	0.102
K^+	0.138
Rb^+	0.149
Cs^+	0.170
Group II ion	**Radius/nm**
Be^{2+}	0.027
Mg^{2+}	0.072
Ca^{2+}	0.100
Sr^{2+}	0.116
Ba^{2+}	0.136

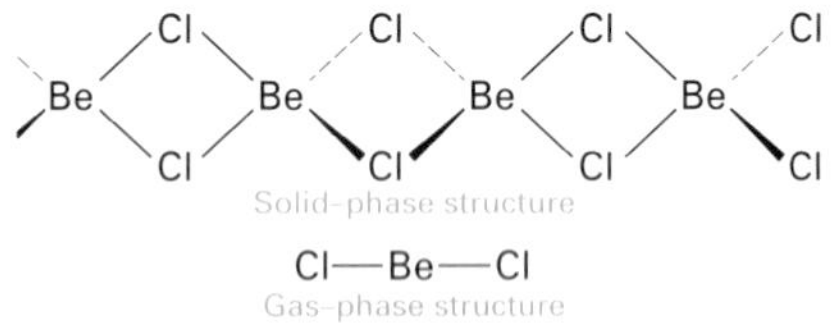

Solid-phase structure

Cl—Be—Cl

Gas-phase structure

Solid anhydrous beryllium chloride consists of chains of beryllium and chlorine atoms bonded by covalent and coordinate bonds. In the gas phase, at temperatures around 900 °C, the compound consists of linear $BeCl_2$ molecules.

Lithium and beryllium stand at the head of Group I and Group II respectively. Many of the properties of these elements and their compounds are unlike those of the other members of their group. For example, lithium is the only Group I metal able to reduce nitrogen gas, this reaction being typical of Group II metals. Molten beryllium compounds are poor conductors of electricity, indicating that the liquid does not contain a substantial concentration of free ions. The main reason for these anomalous properties is the small size of each ion and hence the tendency towards covalent bonding.

Lithium: charge density

The very small lithium ion has a larger charge density than the sodium ion, so its compounds have a greater tendency towards covalency. The increased covalency is demonstrated by the lower solubility of lithium fluoride in water (spread 16.5), and by the fact that some lithium compounds are soluble in organic solvents. Organic solvents are generally non-polar when compared with the polar solvent water. Ionic solutes dissolve in polar solvents; covalent solutes dissolve in non-polar solvents. Lithium chloride has sufficient covalent character to be soluble in ethoxyethane; lithium iodide dissolves in both methanol and propanone.

The lithium ion is the smallest of the Group I metal ions, and so its ionic compounds have the largest lattice enthalpies. For example, the lattice enthalpy of lithium nitride is sufficient to compensate for the very strongly endothermic step of creating N^{3-} ions from a nitrogen N_2 molecule (containing a strong N≡N triple covalent bond). The reaction is therefore exothermic overall.

Beryllium: charge density

The compounds of beryllium tend to have significant covalent character because the beryllium ion is very small and doubly charged. It has the highest charge-to-radius ratio of all ions, with the exception of the hydrogen ion H^+, and its high charge density makes it highly polarizing. The Be^{2+} ion distorts the electron cloud around an adjacent negatively charged ion. Electron density becomes concentrated between the two ion centres, giving the bond substantial covalent character.

Beryllium: amphoteric character of hydroxide

Beryllium acts as a metal when it reacts with sulphuric acid:

$$Be(s) + H_2SO_4(aq) \rightarrow BeSO_4(aq) + H_2(g)$$

Adding aqueous sodium hydroxide to aqueous beryllium sulphate precipitates beryllium hydroxide:

$$BeSO_4(aq) + 2NaOH(aq) \rightarrow Na_2SO_4(aq) + Be(OH)_2(s)$$

Beryllium hydroxide acts as a base when it reacts with an acid:

$$Be(OH)_2(s) + 2HCl(aq) \rightarrow BeCl_2(aq) + 2H_2O(l)$$

All the behaviour mentioned so far is typical of a Group II metal such as calcium. However, beryllium hydroxide acts as an *acid* when it reacts with aqueous sodium hydroxide:

$$Be(OH)_2(s) + 2NaOH(aq) \rightarrow Na_2Be(OH)_4(aq)$$

Beryllium hydroxide shows both acidic and basic properties; it is therefore said to be **amphoteric**. In this respect it is similar to aluminium hydroxide, which also reacts with both acids and bases. Amphoteric behaviour is typical of the metallic elements closest in position in the periodic table to the non-metals.

Notice the similarities between the properties of lithium and those of magnesium, and between the properties of beryllium and those of aluminium. These *diagonal relationships* are due to the pairs of atoms concerned having similar electronegativities. Remember that electronegativity is a measure of the ability of an atom to attract electron density. Electronegativity increases as atomic number increases across a period in the periodic table; it decreases as atomic number increases down a group.

Because they have significant covalent character, beryllium salts (like lithium salts) are soluble in organic solvents. They also tend to hydrolyse when added to water. For example, beryllium chloride dissolves in water very exothermically. Strong coordinate bonds form between the beryllium ion and four water molecules, so that the beryllium ion exists in solution as a *complex ion* with the formula $[Be(H_2O)_4]^{2+}(aq)$.

Coordination number of beryllium

Solid beryllium chloride and beryllium sulphate have the chemical formulae $BeCl_2{\cdot}4H_2O$ and $BeSO_4{\cdot}4H_2O$ respectively. The beryllium ion exists as the complex ion $[Be(H_2O)_4]^{2+}$, in which the beryllium ion has a coordination number of 4. Note that all elements of Period 2 have this maximum coordination number (4). Higher coordination numbers involve d orbitals. For the elements of Period 2, the energies of the vacant 3d orbitals are too high compared with the occupied orbitals in the $n = 2$ shell, so no higher coordination numbers are possible.

Thermal decomposition of lithium carbonate

Unlike the other Group I carbonates, lithium carbonate decomposes when heated. This behaviour is typical of Group II carbonates. The metal ions in the Group I oxides have a charge of 1+; those in the Group II oxides have a charge of 2+. As a result, the Group I oxides have lower lattice enthalpies than the Group II oxides. Group I carbonates are therefore more stable than Group II carbonates because the formation of the Group I oxides is less exothermic.

The lithium ion Li^+ is very small, so lithium oxide is more stable than other Group I oxides. Lithium carbonate is therefore relatively less stable when heated. For the same reasons, other lithium oxosalts (such as $LiNO_3$) decompose more readily than the oxosalts of other Group I metals.

SUMMARY

- The properties of lithium and its compounds are often similar to those of magnesium (rather than to those of other Group I elements) – this is a 'diagonal relationship'.
- The beryllium ion has the second highest charge density of all ions, so it has great polarizing power. Its compounds with non-metals therefore have a high degree of covalent character.
- The properties of beryllium and its compounds are often similar to those of aluminium (rather than to those of other Group II elements) – this is another 'diagonal relationship'.

Comparisons

- The solubilities of lithium salts often resemble those of magnesium salts rather than those of other Group I elements.
- Anhydrous beryllium chloride is similar to aluminium chloride. Both are deliquescent white solids, i.e. they absorb sufficient water from the atmosphere to form a concentrated solution.

Oxoanions, oxoacids, and oxosalts

Oxoanions are anions that contain oxygen; common examples are NO_3^- and SO_4^{2-}. **Oxoacids** are acids that form oxoanions; e.g. HNO_3, H_2SO_4 (so HCl and HF are *not* oxoacids). In an oxoacid, the hydrogen atoms are bonded directly to oxygen. **Oxosalts** are salts of oxoacids, so they contain oxoanions; e.g. Li_2CO_3, $CaSO_4$.

Lithium and nerve impulses

The transmission of impulses along nerves depends on the movement of sodium and potassium ions across the nerve membrane (see spread 13.9). Lithium ions mimic these ions and modify the impulse transmission. Lithium carbonate may be administered to patients with psychiatric disorders (such as manic depression) to help prevent swings of mood.

PRACTICE

1 Suggest reasons why the beryllium ion Be^{2+} is *so* small compared with the other Group II metal ions. (It is less than *half* the size of the Mg^{2+} ion.)

2 Lithium reacts with atmospheric nitrogen to form an ionic nitride Li_3N. Explain why you would also expect magnesium but not sodium to form a nitride.

3 The sum of the first and second ionization energies of beryllium is $+2660\,kJ\,mol^{-1}$ and of strontium is $+1610\,kJ\,mol^{-1}$. What implications do these figures have for the ch§aracter of the bonding in the chlorides of these elements?

4 What do you understand by the term 'hydrolyse'? Explain why beryllium salts hydrolyse when added to water, but strontium salts do not.

16.9

OBJECTIVES

- The s-block elements and flame colours
- Biochemical roles of s-block elements

The s-block elements: flame tests and living systems

All the common compounds of the alkali metals (the elements of Group I) are soluble. As a result, the metal ions cannot be identified by precipitation. The first part of this spread shows how flame tests may be used to identify these ions, as well as those of calcium, strontium, and barium. The spread concludes by introducing a completely different aspect of the s-block elements: their role in the biochemical reactions that support life. This discussion is continued at greater depth in the later chapter on 'Biochemistry'.

Flame test colours

The characteristic colours for the Group I metals are:

- lithium: crimson-red
- sodium: yellow
- potassium: lilac
- rubidium: deep red
- caesium: sky blue

Some of the Group II metals also give flame colours:

- calcium: brick-red
- strontium: crimson
- barium: yellow–green (apple green)

Interference by sodium

The intensity of the colour is much greater for sodium than it is for potassium, so a small amount of sodium impurity can disguise the potassium colour. The presence of the potassium colour can be confirmed by looking at the flame through 'cobalt blue' glass. The blue glass absorbs the yellow sodium light, while allowing the lilac still to be seen.

Flame tests

An s-block element (with the exceptions of beryllium and magnesium) may be identified by a **flame test**. The unknown compound is vaporized in a flame. The electrons in its atoms are promoted into higher orbitals by the energy from the burning gas. The excited atoms then lose energy and undergo an electronic transition to a lower energy level, giving off the extra energy in the form of electromagnetic radiation. In the case of most s-block elements, the frequency of this radiation falls in the visible region. The electronic transitions are different for each element, so an s-block element in the unknown compound may be identified by the colour of the flame.

Neither beryllium nor magnesium colours a flame because their emissions lie outside the visible region of the electromagnetic spectrum.

The procedure for carrying out a flame test involves the following steps:

1. Clean a nichrome or platinum wire by dipping it in concentrated hydrochloric acid and placing it in a non-luminous Bunsen flame.
2. Continue this cleaning process until no colour at all is produced when the wire is in the flame.
3. Moisten the wire with concentrated hydrochloric acid, dip it in the unknown compound, and hold it in the flame again.
4. Check the colour observed against the list on the left or the photos below.

(a)

(b)

(c)

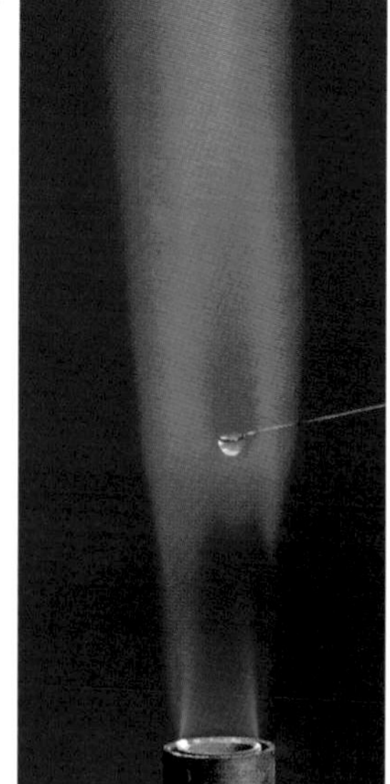

(d)

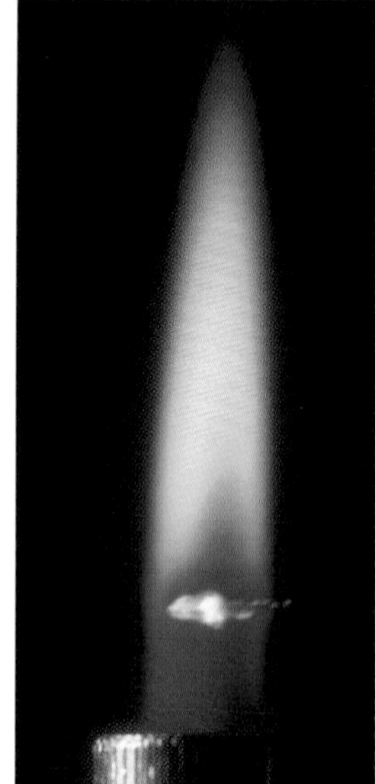

The flame colours for: (a) lithium, (b) potassium, (c) strontium, and (d) barium. Sodium is shown in spread 4.3.

The s-block elements in living systems

The s-block elements are important in biochemistry. In organisms, sodium is the principal cation in the fluid *outside* cells, and potassium is the principal cation in the fluid *inside* cells. The ions of sodium and potassium (together with chloride ion) are fundamental to many biochemical processes, e.g. in maintaining the balance between fluid pressures inside and outside the cells within an organism, in stabilizing certain species such as DNA, and in nerve action; see spread 13.9.

Magnesium is necessary for the stability of many biochemical anions. For example, adenosine triphosphate is the predominant supplier of energy in living cells. Its name is usually abbreviated to ATP, as if it were uncharged. In fact, it should be written as $ATP^{4-}{\cdot}Mg^{2+}$. The magnesium ion decreases the overall charge of the species, and so increases its stability.

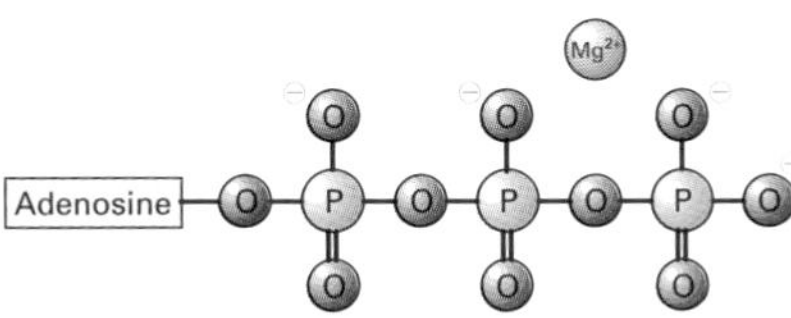

The complex $ATP^{4-}{\cdot}Mg^{2+}$.

Chlorophyll is an exceptionally important (and complex) compound of magnesium. This green pigment takes in energy from sunlight during photosynthesis. This fuels the growth of the plants. The green plants are at the bottom of many food chains, and so are very important sources of energy for the processes of life.

Calcium is also vital for a range of biochemical functions, which include: as a constituent of bones, shells, and teeth; in the transmission of impulses across the synapses where nerves meet; in the control of fertilization, permitting one sperm only to enter the egg; and in muscle contraction.

The concentration of calcium ion varies from 10^{-6} to $10^{-2}\,mol\,dm^{-3}$ in the environment, except in biological systems where it is rigorously controlled by hormones to be very close to $10^{-3}\,mol\,dm^{-3}$. This concentration allows precipitation of carbonates (mollusc shells), phosphates (bones), and ethanedioates (plant structures). There is little room for error in the control of calcium ion concentration. In people, ageing is accompanied by loss of calcium ions from bone, which progressively loses its structural strength. The arteries may become calcified when the control systems no longer work properly. They become clogged with calcium salts and other debris, diminishing the blood flow.

SUMMARY

- A flame test can identify all s-block elements, with the exception of beryllium and magnesium.
- Electrons move to vacant outer orbitals when metal atoms are excited in the flame; visible light is emitted as the electrons move back to lower orbitals.
- The flow of an impulse along a nerve fibre depends on a change of sodium ion and potassium ion concentration inside the nerve fibre.
- Magnesium is fundamental to the action of chlorophyll and ATP.
- The control of calcium ion concentration is important for human health.

Anions and cations: a reminder

By definition, **anions** are ions that bear a negative charge; **cations** are ions that bear a positive charge.

Fireworks incorporate metal salts with gunpowder to make coloured effects. Which metals could be responsible for each of the colours in these bursting fireworks?

Toxic beryllium

The beryllium ion can replace the magnesium ion in biochemically active molecules. The beryllium ion mimics the magnesium ion, but it is smaller and so has a higher charge density. The ion is very toxic because it binds tightly to a site usually occupied by magnesium and so disrupts biochemical processes.

PRACTICE

1 Explain why the presence of magnesium in a compound cannot be established by a flame test.

2 Calcium ions are present in the cell sap of plants. Suggest why calcium ions do not bind to chlorophyll molecules.

3 Suggest why cadmium and mercury are toxic.

PRACTICE EXAM QUESTIONS

1 **a** The following table shows some physical properties of two s-block metals.

Metal	Hardness	Melting temperature / °C	Density / g cm^{-3}
Caesium	Very soft	28.7	1.9
Barium	Quite hard	714	3.51

i Suggest reasons for the differences in the physical properties of caesium and barium as shown in the table. The metals have the same crystal structure. [3]

ii Caesium gets its name from the blue colour it or its salts impart to a Bunsen flame. What process within the atom is responsible for the emission of this colour? [1]

iii If the light emitted from excited caesium atoms is passed through a spectrometer, what would you expect to see? [1]

b Sodium burns in excess oxygen to give a yellow solid, Y.

i Y contains 58.97% sodium. Find its empirical formula. [2]

ii The relative molecular mass of Y is 78. What is its molecular formula? [1]

iii If Y is reacted with ice-cold dilute sulphuric acid, a solution of Z is obtained which will react with potassium manganate(VII) solution. Describe the experimental procedure you would use to determine the mole ratio in which Z and potassium manganate(VII) react together. [3]
EDEXCEL 1997

2 Sodium and sodium hydroxide are both manufactured by electrolytic processes.

a Name the electrolyte used in the manufacture of:

i sodium;

ii sodium hydroxide. [2]

b **i** What is produced at the anode during the manufacture of sodium hydroxide? Write an equation for its formation.

ii What other gaseous product might be given off at the anode under other conditions? Write an equation for its formation. [5]

c Suggest a reason why the product in **b i** is formed in the industrial process rather than that in **b ii**. [3]

d Describe what you would observe when dilute sodium hydroxide solution is added dropwise to a solution of aluminium sulphate until in excess. Give the formulae of the aluminium-containing species present in the original solution, and responsible for the observations you have described. [6]
EDEXCEL 1996 *(See also Chapter 19)*

3 **a** **i** Complete the electronic configuration of a calcium atom: $1s^2$.... [1]

ii Describe the bonding present in solid calcium. [4]

b **i** Write an equation for the reaction of calcium with water. Identify the oxidation numbers of all the atoms involved by writing the numbers underneath each symbol in the equation. [2]

ii State which substance in **b i** has been oxidized and write a half-equation to show the oxidation process. [2]

iii What is the common name of the solution formed by the reaction of calcium with water? Suggest the likely pH of the solution. [2]

c What would be **observed** if aqueous sodium hydroxide were added dropwise, until in excess, to aqueous solutions of:

i magnesium chloride;

ii barium chloride? [2]

d Account for the observations in **c**, giving any relevant ionic equations. [3]
AQA (AEB) 1998

4 Magnesium oxide, MgO, is a white solid with a high melting temperature which is used as a furnace lining.

i State **two** ways in which magnesium oxide can be obtained giving a balanced equation in each case. [4]

ii Using **outer** electrons only, draw a dot-and-cross diagram showing the bonding in magnesium oxide. [2]

iii State why magnesium oxide is described as a basic oxide. [1]

iv One industrial method for obtaining magnesium from magnesium oxide involves heating magnesium oxide with silicon at a high temperature in the absence of air.

$$2MgO + Si \rightarrow 2Mg + SiO_2$$

I. State why the process must be carried out in the absence of air. [1]

II. Calculate the mass of silicon required to convert completely 500 kg of magnesium oxide into magnesium. [3]
WJEC 1998

5 **a** Magnesium occurs naturally as the mineral *carnallite*, $KCl{\cdot}MgCl_2{\cdot}6H_2O{\cdot}$

i State what is **observed** and give a balanced equation for the reaction which occurs when a solution of carnallite is treated with sodium hydroxide solution. [2]

ii State how to test for the presence of chloride ions in the carnallite solution, giving details of the reagents added, **observation**, and an **ionic** equation for any precipitation reaction which may occur. [3]

b Both magnesium sulphate and barium sulphate occur naturally as minerals but only magnesium sulphate is soluble in water.

i Explain, in terms of hydration and lattice enthalpies, the reason why only one of the compounds is soluble in water. [2]

ii Name **two** features of magnesium sulphate which identify it as a **typical ionic compound**. [1]

c State why magnesium is an essential element for plant growth. [1]
WJEC 1998 *(See also Chapter 18)*

6 a i Write an equation for the reaction of barium with water. [1]

ii Would the reaction in **a i** occur more vigorously or less vigorously than the reaction of calcium with water? Identify one contributory factor and use it to justify your answer. [2]

iii Write an equation for the action of heat on solid barium carbonate. [1]

iv At a given high temperature which of the two carbonates, barium carbonate or calcium carbonate, would decompose more easily? [1]

v How would you distinguish between solutions of barium chloride and calcium chloride? State in each case what you would see as a result of the test on each solution. [2]

b 1.71 g of barium reacts with oxygen to form 2.11 g of an oxide **X**.

i Calculate the formula of **X**. [2]

ii Give the formula of the anion present in **X**. [1]

iii What is the oxidation number of oxygen in this anion? [1]

iv Sodium forms an oxide, **Y**, which contains this same anion. Give the formula of **Y**. [1]

c Treatment of either **X** or **Y** with dilute sulphuric acid leads to the formation of the sulphate of the metal, together with an aqueous solution of hydrogen peroxide, H_2O_2.

i Write an equation for the reaction of **Y** with dilute sulphuric acid. [1]

ii The hydrogen peroxide solution produced may be separated from the other reaction product. Explain briefly why this is easier to achieve if **X** is used as the initial reagent rather than **Y**. [2]
EDEXCEL 1998

7 a i Using the data provided, construct a Born-Haber cycle for magnesium chloride, $MgCl_2$, and from it determine the electron affinity of chlorine. [5]

	ΔH / kJ mol^{-1}
Enthalpy of atomisation of chlorine	+122
Enthalpy of atomisation of magnesium	+148
First ionization energy of magnesium	+738
Second ionization energy of magnesium	+1451
Lattice enthalpy of magnesium chloride	−2526
Enthalpy of formation of magnesium chloride	−641

ii The theoretically calculated value for the lattice enthalpy of magnesium chloride is –2326 kJ mol–1. Explain the difference between the theoretically calculated value and the experimental value given in data in a i, in terms of the bonding of magnesium chloride. [3]

a The table below gives some information about the sulphates of elements in Group 2.

Sulphate	Solubility / mol dm^{-3}	Lattice enthalpy / kJ mol^{-1}	Hydration enthalpy of M^{2+} / kJ mol^{-1}
$CaSO_4$	4.6×10^{-2}	−2480	−1650
$SrSO_4$	7.1×10^{-2}	−2484	−1480
$BaSO_4$	9.4×10^{-2}	−2374	−1360

i Suggest an explanation for the trend shown in the hydration enthalpies of the cations. [2]

ii Comment on the trend in the solubilities of these sulphates in relation to the lattice and hydration enthalpies given in the table. [4]

iii Barium sulphate, which is opaque to X-rays, is used for the 'barium meal' to enable X-ray pictures to be taken of the gut. Barium ions are very toxic; why is this not a problem here? [1]

iv Give the equation for the reaction of barium with cold water. [2]

v Suggest the practical procedure by which you might convert the solution of the product in the reaction in **iv** into a reasonably pure sample of barium sulphate. [3]
EDEXCEL 1998 *(see also Chapter 18)*

8 a i Describe what would be seen if dilute sodium hydroxide solution was added, until in excess, to aqueous solutions of magnesium nitrate and barium nitrate. [2]

ii Account for the observations given in **i** and write any relevant ionic equations. [3]

b i State, and explain, the trend in the thermal stability of Group 2 carbonates. [3]

ii Suggest, with a reason, how the thermal stability of sodium carbonate differs from that of magnesium carbonate. [2]

c One of the industrial processes for the manufacture of magnesium is similar in principle to that used for the manufacture of sodium.

i What type of process is used for the manufacture of sodium? [1]

ii Suggest which compound of magnesium could be used in its manufacture by a similar process and give its probable source. [2]

iii State the essential condition for this process, and write an ionic equation to represent the formation of magnesium. [2]

iv State the name of the other product of the process and give one of its uses. [2]

d i When LiCl is heated in a bunsen flame a characteristic red flame is seen. Explain why lithium compounds produce a coloured flame in these circumstances. [2]

ii Lithium chloride can be made by burning lithium in chlorine. Give a reason why rubidium chloride is not normally prepared in the laboratory in a similar way. [1]
EDEXCEL 1999

17 Trends across a period

The periodic table is made up from elements arranged in vertical groups and horizontal periods. Look at successive elements as atomic number increases down a group. You will see that the number of valence electrons remains constant, while the number of filled inner shells increases. Now look at successive elements across a period. The filled inner shells of electrons remain constant, while the number of valence electrons steadily increases. The previous chapter considered the elements lithium to caesium and beryllium to barium arranged vertically in Groups I and II. In this chapter we consider the elements sodium to argon arranged horizontally in Period 3. We discuss their properties and the trends in those properties, explaining them in terms of the electronic structures of the elements concerned.

PERIOD 3: SODIUM TO ARGON

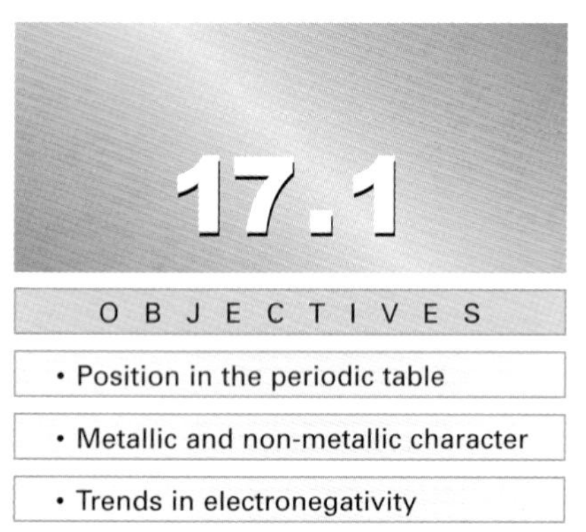

17.1

OBJECTIVES

- Position in the periodic table
- Metallic and non-metallic character
- Trends in electronegativity

The elements sodium to argon are in Period 3 of the periodic table. They represent the most straightforward unbroken trend in properties across the periodic table. By comparison, Period 2 – the elements lithium to neon – includes elements that stand at the heads of their respective groups. As you will know from the previous chapter, these elements often have anomalous properties when compared with the other members of their group. Period 4 – the elements potassium to krypton – is interrupted by the d-block elements scandium to zinc. So in this spread we look at Period 3 in the context of the periodic table as a whole, and at the trend in the metallic/non-metallic nature of the elements.

Period 3 in the periodic table

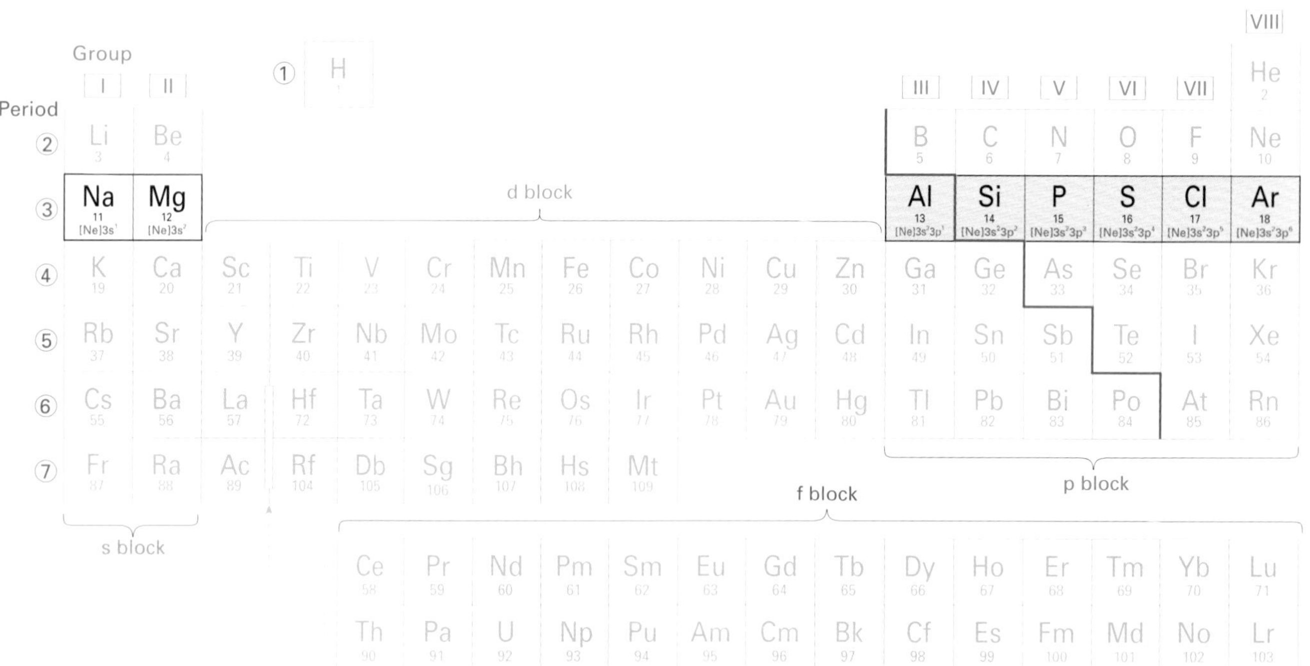

The elements of Period 3 in the periodic table. Note the successive filling of the 3s and 3p orbitals.

There are eight elements in Period 3, from sodium (atomic number $Z = 11$) to argon ($Z = 18$). All the elements have filled inner electron shells corresponding to the noble gas neon ([Ne] = $1s^2 2s^2 2p^6$). The two elements sodium and magnesium are members of the s block, with the electronic structures Na [Ne]$3s^1$ and Mg [Ne]$3s^2$ respectively. The six elements from aluminium to argon are members of the p block, where the three 3p orbitals fill, as shown above.

Metallic and non-metallic character

Metals are good electrical conductors and they are malleable and ductile. This behaviour is due to the presence of delocalized electrons in their solid structure. Metals tend to lose electrons during chemical reactions. Electronegativity is a measure of an element's ability to attract a shared electron pair to itself. Typical metals have electronegativities smaller than 1.7; typical non-metals have electronegativities greater than 2.4.

The elements sodium (Na), magnesium (Mg), and aluminium (Al) are metals. They have conductivities at least one-third that of copper, are malleable, and have electronegativities between 0.9 and 1.6. The elements phosphorus (P), sulphur (S), chlorine (Cl), and argon (Ar) are non-metals. They have extremely low or negligible conductivities, the solid elements are brittle, and their electronegativities range from 2.2 to 3.2. The element silicon (Si) is a metalloid. It is a semiconductor with intermediate conductivity, its electronegativity is 1.9 (less than the values for the unreactive metals tin and lead), yet it is brittle, indicating a non-metallic structure.

Electrical conductivity, electronegativity, and malleability data for the elements of Period 3.

Element	Electrical conductivity*	Electronegativity (Pauling scale)	Malleability
Sodium	37	0.9	good
Magnesium	38	1.3	good
Aluminium	64	1.6	good
Silicon	16	1.9	brittle
Phosphorus	10^{-16}	2.2	brittle
Sulphur	10^{-22}	2.6	brittle
Chlorine	negligible	3.2	–
Argon	negligible	–	–

* Relative scale based on Cu = 100.

The general trend is from metallic to non-metallic across the period. The following two spreads will look at trends in other physical properties of these elements.

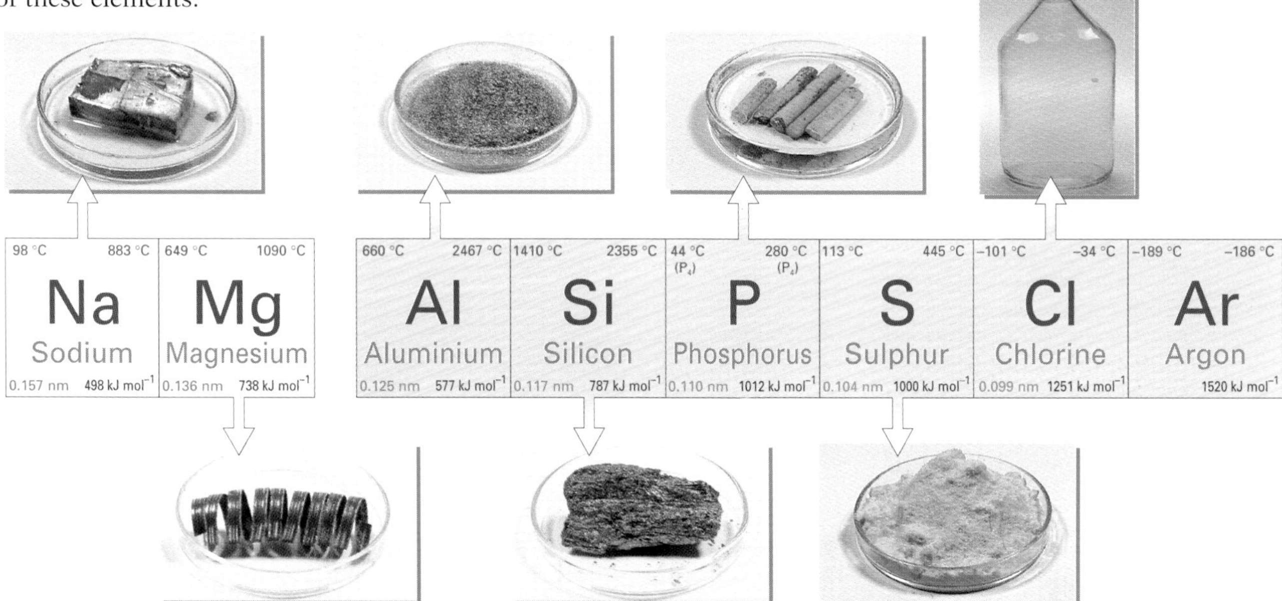

A summary of the major properties of the elements of Period 3 (the elements sodium to argon). The noble gas argon is a colourless gas.

SUMMARY

- As the atomic number of the elements increases across a period, the trend is from metallic to non-metallic character.
- Metals have electronegativities smaller than 1.7; non-metals have electronegativities greater than 2.4.

PRACTICE

1 Sketch an outline periodic table. Add a horizontal arrow above the table, pointing to the right. Add a vertical arrow to the left of the table, pointing downwards. Label each arrow twice to show overall trends in:
  a electronegativity,
  b metallic or non-metallic character.

2 Using information from this spread only [*Don't* cheat!], suggest electronegativities for the elements caesium, barium, fluorine, and carbon. Comment on the metallic/non-metallic character of each.

17.2

OBJECTIVES

- The trend in melting point
- Bonding in the elements
- Some uses of the elements

Melting points, bonding, and structure

The melting point of an element gives a direct indication of the forces between the particles that make up the solid element. A high melting point indicates metallic bonding or the presence of a giant covalent structure. A lower melting point is associated with covalently bonded molecules held in a solid lattice by weak dispersion forces. An extremely low melting point suggests a structure consisting of separate *atoms* held together by dispersion forces only. All these structural types are encountered in the elements of Period 3.

Melting points: sodium to argon

The graph of melting point (T_m) against increasing atomic number shows a distinct overall shape. There is a steady upward trend (sodium to silicon), followed by a sharp fall (silicon to phosphorus), and then an overall more gradual decline (phosphorus to argon). You should be able to identify the elements sodium, magnesium, and aluminium as metals; silicon is a metalloid; phosphorus, sulphur, chlorine, and argon are non-metals. Note also that the four non-metals fall into two groups: phosphorus and sulphur have melting points significantly greater than those of chlorine and argon (both of which are gases at 20 °C and 1 bar). These eight elements between them represent distinctly different types of structure.

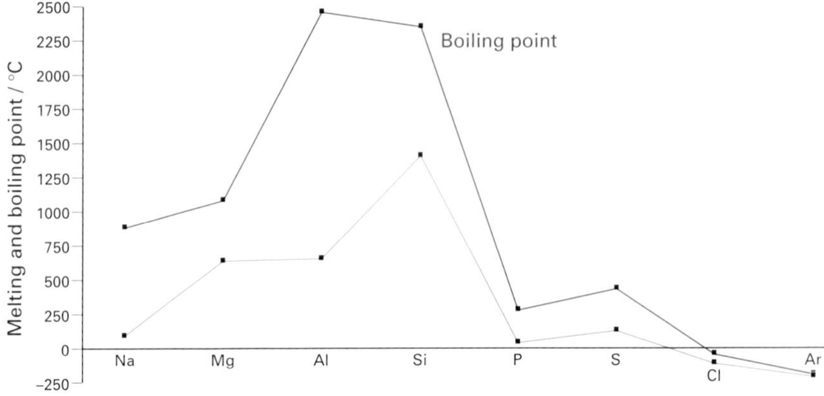

Trends in the melting and boiling points of the Period 3 elements.

The metals sodium, magnesium, and aluminium

The three elements sodium, magnesium, and aluminium have metallic structures consisting of a regular lattice of metal ions (Na^+, Mg^{2+}, and Al^{3+} respectively). These ions are surrounded by delocalized valence electrons, which come from the one, two, and three valence electrons per atom respectively.

The metalloid silicon

The atoms in solid silicon are bonded together covalently, with the atoms arranged in the diamond structure (a giant covalent structure – see chapter on 'Solids'). Each silicon atom is bonded to four other silicon atoms; to melt silicon requires breaking all these covalent bonds. This needs a large amount of energy, so silicon has the highest melting point in Period 3. Silicon has a melting point of 1410 °C.

Phosphorus

Phosphorus exists in several crystalline forms (**allotropes**), the two most important of which are named according to their colour. Red phosphorus (T_m = 590 °C) consists of chains of phosphorus atoms. White phosphorus (T_m = 44 °C) consists of individual P_4 molecules. The bonds within these small tetrahedral molecules are very strained, which makes white

Na, Mg, Al – facts and uses

Sodium

Liquid sodium is an ideal heat-exchange medium, because it has a high thermal conductivity and a high boiling point (883 °C). It is also little affected by radiation (it has a low neutron capture cross-section). For these reasons, liquid sodium is used to cool the small compact cores of 'fast breeder' nuclear reactors.

Magnesium

Low density alloys for the aircraft industry include mixtures of magnesium with zirconium and thorium. Magnesium is also used in the nuclear industry. Mixed with 0.8% aluminium and 0.5% beryllium to make the alloy 'Magnox', it is used to contain the uranium fuel in gas-cooled nuclear reactors.

Aluminium

The low density of aluminium makes it one of the metals most used for construction. Its malleability means that items with complex cross-sections may be made by extrusion: heated to about 200 °C, the metal is forced through a shaped die, just like toothpaste squeezed from a tube. Its low density and high strength mean that it can be used to construct aircraft and the overhead electricity cables slung from pylons.

Semiconductors

At temperatures above absolute zero, thermal energy causes some of the four valence electrons of silicon to become delocalized and move freely through the lattice. These electrons impart some conductivity to the silicon. So silicon (Group IV, Period 3) is a semiconductor: its electrical conductivity is intermediate between those of metals and those of non-metals. The conductivity can be altered and controlled by adding impurity atoms that contain three or five valence electrons. The 'silicon chips' so important in the electronic circuitry of computers, radios, and TVs rely on semiconduction for their function. Note that germanium (Group IV, Period 4) is also a semiconductor, as is gallium arsenide, which is composed of the two elements either side of germanium in Period 4.

phosphorus very reactive. White phosphorus must be stored under water because it ignites spontaneously in air above 35 °C.

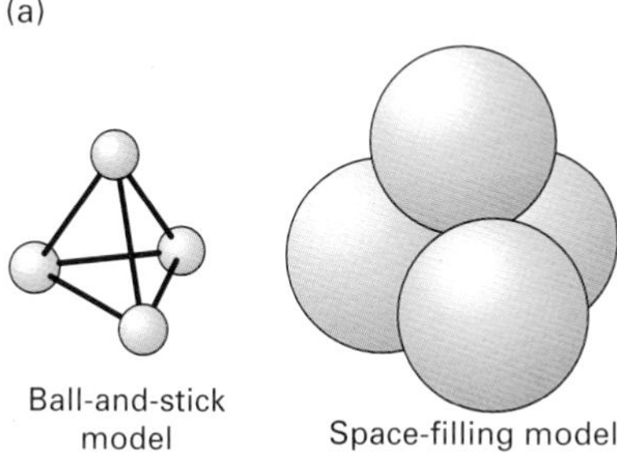

(a) The structure of white phosphorus. (b) White and red phosphorus.

Sulphur

There are two allotropes of sulphur: rhombic sulphur (T_m = 113 °C) and monoclinic sulphur (T_m = 119 °C). Both are composed of S_8 crown-shaped molecules and differ only in the arrangement in which the molecules are packed; see spread 6.7. At temperatures slightly above the melting point, liquid sulphur consists of separate S_8 crown-shaped ring molecules. The dispersion forces holding S_8 molecules together are stronger than those holding P_4 molecules together because there is virtually double the number of electrons. As a result, sulphur melts at a higher temperature than phosphorus. Sulphur occurs as the element in volcanic areas, including those found on Io, one of the moons of the planet Jupiter.

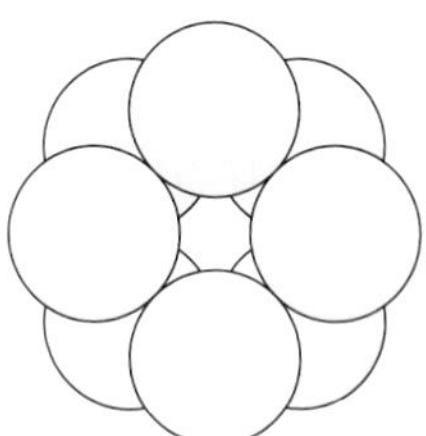

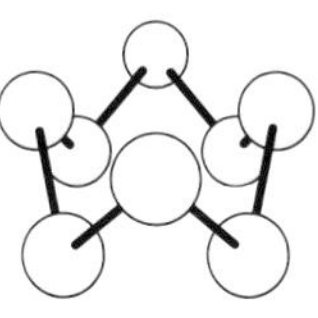

(a) The S_8 molecule. (b) Sulphur pool in Yellowstone National Park.

Chlorine

Solid chlorine consists of covalently bonded Cl_2 molecules held in a regular lattice by dispersion forces. The melting point is low because these dispersion forces are weak. Liquid and gaseous chlorine consist of separate Cl_2 molecules.

Argon

Solid argon consists of separate atoms held in a regular lattice by dispersion forces. These forces are extremely weak, so argon has a very low melting point.

SUMMARY

- The melting points across Period 3 rise with increasing atomic number until silicon, after which they fall dramatically.
- Sodium, magnesium, and aluminium have metallic structures bonded by delocalized valence electrons.
- Silicon has a giant covalent structure.
- P_4, S_8, and Cl_2 are simple covalent molecules.
- The individual atoms in solid Ar are held together by dispersion forces only.

PRACTICE

1 Many of the ideas in this spread were covered in the chapter on 'Solids'. Refer to that chapter and make sketches that illustrate the structures of the following:
  - **a** Magnesium
  - **b** Silicon
  - **c** Solid chlorine (include dispersion forces in your sketch)
  - **d** Solid argon.

2 Explain why the bonds between the phosphorus atoms in the P_4 molecule are said to be 'strained'.

3 Explain the difference between the melting points of red and white phosphorus in terms of structure and bonding.

4 Suggest why the melting point of sodium is so much lower than those of magnesium and aluminium.

17.3

EFFECTS OF ATOMIC SIZE

OBJECTIVES

- Trends in atomic radius
- Trends in ionization energy
- Trends in oxidation number

The value of the atomic radius of an element gives a measure of its size. The size of an atom has an influence on its ionization energy, which is the minimum energy required to remove one or more of the outermost electrons. In turn, the ionization energy influences the valency of an element expressed as the oxidation number. The values of these three interlinked attributes – atomic radius, ionization energy, and oxidation number – all show clear trends as the atomic numbers of the elements increase across a period.

Trends in atomic radius

In each period of the periodic table, the Group I metal is the element with the largest atomic radius. Each Group I metal has one valence electron outside filled inner shells which partially shield that electron from the nuclear charge. In Periods 2 and 3, the atomic radius decreases steadily as atomic number increases from Group I to Group VII. The steady increase in nuclear charge pulls all electrons closer to the nucleus. In Period 4, the trend seen in the previous two periods is less smooth because of the d-block elements, in which the *inner* 3d subshell is filling.

Shielding

Each successive element across a period contains one more proton and electron. The extra electron might be expected to **shield** (cancel out the attraction of) the extra proton. This shielding is only *partially* successful; electron density is smeared out (as explained in the chapter on 'Electrons in atoms'), whereas the protons are definitely located in the nucleus.

This lack of perfect shielding means that the **effective nuclear charge** experienced by an electron increases across a period; the increasing nuclear charge outweighs the effect of an extra electron *in the same shell.*

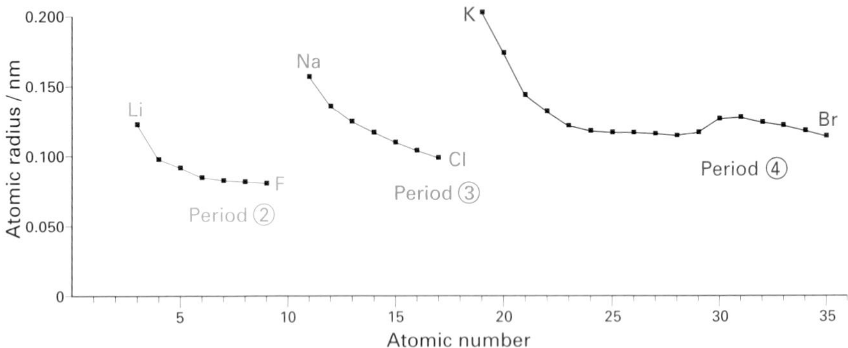

Plots of atomic radius against atomic number for Periods 2, 3, and 4.

First ionization energy

Atomic size decreases across a period as atomic number increases. It is therefore reasonable to expect the first ionization energy to increase as the valence electron becomes closer to the nucleus. While this is generally true, there are two other points of interest to note: 'dips' at Groups III and VI.

First ionization energy

The first ionization energy is the minimum energy required to remove one electron from an isolated atom in the gas phase, represented for a general element E as:

$E(g) \rightarrow E^{+}(g) + e^{-}(g)$

(Values are usually quoted per mole.)

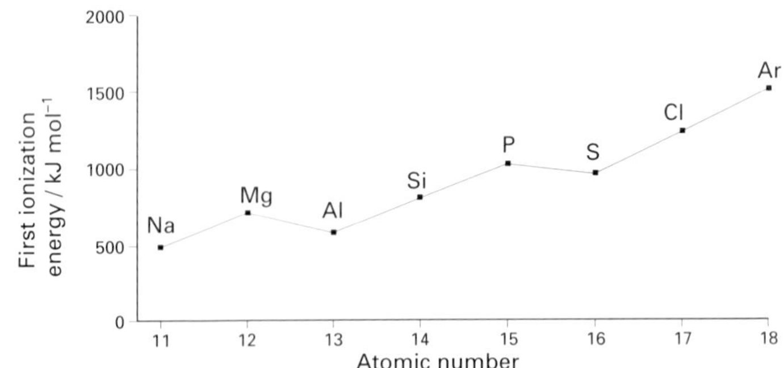

Plot of first ionization energy against atomic number for Z = 11 (Na) to Z = 18 (Ar). The plot shows that there is a periodic variation in ionization energy across Period 3.

The Group III/Group VI 'dips'

In Periods 2 and 3, there is a small dip in the plot at the Group III elements and at the Group VI elements. The dip at beryllium/boron (in Period 2) provides evidence for electron subshells (see the chapter on 'Electrons in atoms'). In Period 3, the first ionization energies of aluminium and sulphur are lower than expected. In the case of the pair of elements Mg/Al, the electron that is removed in Al is from the 3p subshell, which is further from the nucleus than the 3s electron that is removed from Mg. It therefore requires less energy to remove this electron during ionization. In the case of the pair of elements P/S, the 3d electrons in phosphorus all occupy separate orbitals. The fourth p electron in sulphur must enter one of these orbitals, resulting in increased electron repulsion and a *lower* ionization energy than otherwise expected.

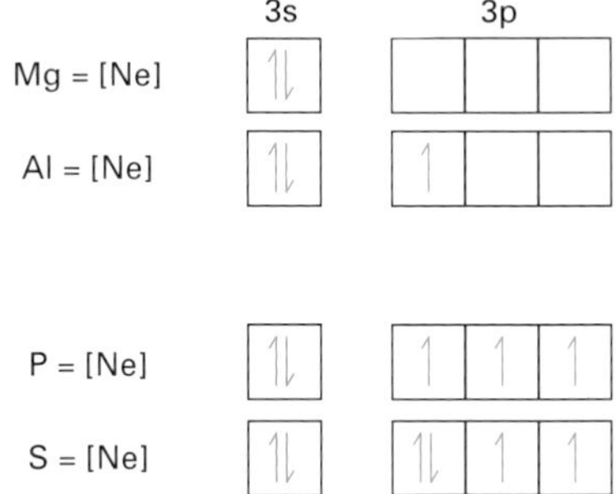

The electronic structures of Mg, Al, P, and S.

The d-block elements

There is a smaller overall change in ionization energy across the d-block elements than through the s-block and p-block elements. This is because d-block elements lose an outer s electron during ionization, rather than an electron from the inner incomplete d subshell. For example, the electronic structure of scandium is $[Ar]3d^1 4s^2$ and that of nickel is $[Ar]3d^8 4s^2$. Both elements lose a 4s electron of similar energy during ionization, so the ionization energies are similar.

Filling d orbitals

Period 4 includes the elements scandium to zinc (10 elements) and Period 5 includes the elements yttrium to cadmium (10 elements). The five 3d orbitals fill in the course of Period 4 and the five 4d orbitals fill in Period 5.

Oxidation numbers

There is a general increase in first ionization energy as atomic number increases across Period 3. The relatively low values for the metals sodium, magnesium, and aluminium indicate that a positive oxidation number can be expected. In the s block, sodium (Group I) loses its single outer s electron and exhibits an oxidation number of +1 in all its compounds. Magnesium (Group II) has an oxidation number of +2 only, corresponding to the loss of both valence electrons. The p-block elements have a greater range of oxidation numbers.

The highest oxidation numbers are most likely to be found in fluorides, oxides, or oxoanions, because fluorine and oxygen are the most powerful oxidants. In Period 3, the highest oxidation number increases smoothly from +1 for sodium to +7 for chlorine, corresponding to the element concerned losing or sharing *all* of the electrons in its valence shell when forming a compound. However, ionization energy increases across the period, so the non-metals are much less likely to attain positive oxidation numbers than the s-block metals. In fact, the elements from silicon to chlorine exhibit *negative* oxidation numbers, which means that they *gain* rather than lose electrons to make up their octet. The trends in oxidation number exert a strong influence over the trends in chemical properties discussed later.

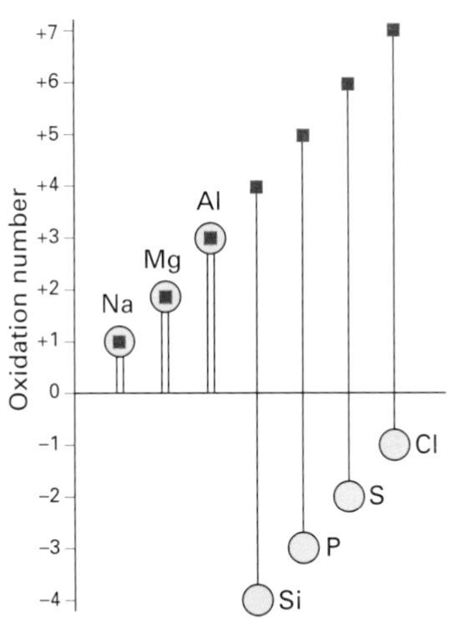

The oxidation numbers of the elements Na to Cl.

SUMMARY

- Within any period, atomic radii, ionization energies, and oxidation numbers all show a periodic change in their values.
- With increasing atomic number across Periods 2 and 3, atomic radii decrease, ionization energies increase (with small dips at Groups III and VI), and maximum oxidation number increases.
- The trends noted in Periods 2 and 3 (s- and p-block elements only) are repeated in later periods with the inclusion of a break corresponding to the d-block elements.
- The highest possible oxidation number of an element in its compounds is equal to the number of its valence electrons.

PRACTICE

1 Sketch the plots for atomic radius against atomic number for Periods 2, 3, and 4. Add an outline of the plot you would expect for Period 5. Label the regions occupied by s-, p-, and d-block elements.

2 The plot of first ionization energy against atomic number shows a series of peaks and troughs.

   a Explain why Group I elements are found at the troughs and Group VIII elements at the peaks.

   b Explain the trend in the ionization energies of the noble gases.

3 Write down the electronic structures of magnesium, aluminium, sulphur, and phosphorus. In each case, identify the electron lost during the process of ionization, represented in general as:

$E(g) \rightarrow E^+(g) + e^-(g)$

4 Construct an oxidation number diagram for the elements of Period 2, like the one given above for Period 3.

17.4

REACTIONS WITH OXYGEN

OBJECTIVES

- The oxides of Period 3
- Melting point and structure of oxides

White phosphorus spontaneously ignites in air at temperatures above 35 °C. Such substances are said to be ***pyrophoric****. A piece of white phosphorus also spontaneously ignites when placed in oxygen.*

All the Period 3 elements except silicon and chlorine react directly with oxygen to form oxides. There is a full range of oxides representing all the common oxidation states of the elements concerned. As you might expect, the properties of the oxides change steadily across the period as atomic number increases. This spread interprets the melting points of the oxides in terms of their bonding and structure; the next looks at their acid–base character.

The oxides of Period 3

The oxides of the elements of Period 3 have the following names and chemical formulae. Note that phosphorus, sulphur, and chlorine form more than one oxide, so more than one oxidation number is possible.

Oxide name	Formula	Oxidation number of the Period 3 element
Sodium oxide	Na_2O	+1
Magnesium oxide	MgO	+2
Aluminium oxide	Al_2O_3	+3
Silicon dioxide	SiO_2	+4
Phosphorus(III) oxide	P_4O_6	+3
Phosphorus(V) oxide	P_4O_{10}	+5
Sulphur dioxide	SO_2	+4
Sulphur trioxide	SO_3	+6
Dichlorine oxide	Cl_2O	+1
Chlorine dioxide	ClO_2	+4
Dichlorine heptaoxide	Cl_2O_7	+7

Direct combination of the elements

Sodium (Na), magnesium (Mg), aluminium (Al), phosphorus (P), and sulphur (S) all burn in oxygen to form an oxide. The balanced chemical equations are as follows:

$$4Na(s) + O_2(g) \rightarrow 2Na_2O(s)$$
$$2Mg(s) + O_2(g) \rightarrow 2MgO(s)$$
$$4Al(s) + 3O_2(g) \rightarrow 2Al_2O_3(s)$$
$$P_4(s) + 5O_2(g) \rightarrow P_4O_{10}(s)$$
$$S_8(s) + 8O_2(g) \rightarrow 8SO_2(g)$$

Melting points of the oxides

The plot of the melting point of the oxides of the elements Na to Cl shows a sharp initial rise followed by a steady decline; the values for P_4O_{10}, SO_3, and Cl_2O_7 are significantly lower. The overall shape of this plot indicates that there is a trend in the bonding and structure of the oxides. Remember that high melting points are associated with ionic or giant covalent structures, and low melting points with solids consisting of simple covalent molecules.

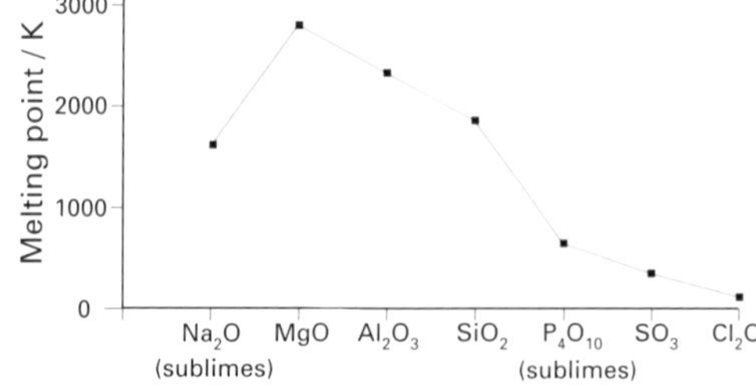

Plot of melting point for the oxides of the elements of Period 3. Note that, where an element has more than one oxide, the oxide corresponding to the highest oxidation number (as shown in the box on the left) is given.

Oxidation numbers

The formulae of the oxides show a smooth increase in *highest* oxidation number as atomic number increases across the period.

Na_2O	+1
MgO	+2
Al_2O_3	+3
SiO_2	+4
P_4O_{10}	+5
SO_3	+6
Cl_2O_7	+7

The *highest* oxidation number is equal to the number of valence electrons in the element, i.e. the maximum oxidation number is the same as the group number.

It was this clear trend that convinced Mendeleyev that his periodic table would prove useful.

Sodium, magnesium, and aluminium oxides

The oxides of metals are predominantly ionic, with the extent of covalent character increasing from sodium to aluminium, in line with the increasing charge density of the ions Na^+, Mg^{2+}, and Al^{3+}. The melting points are all relatively high. The very high value for MgO explains its use as a refractory lining.

Quartz is a mineral form of silica that crystallizes as molten rocks solidify underground. Quartz is ***piezoelectric****, generating a potential difference when a stress is applied; this property explains its use in oscillators.*

Silicon dioxide (silica)

The oxide of the metalloid silicon is essentially covalent. Silicon dioxide SiO_2 is called *silica*, and it has a giant covalent structure, as illustrated in the chapter on 'Solids'. The formula SiO_2 gives the empirical formula of the substance, i.e. the simplest whole-number ratio of the atoms. Yellow sand is silica with impurities such as iron(III) oxide.

The oxides of phosphorus

The oxides of phosphorus may be treated as molecules of formulae P_4O_6 and P_4O_{10}. Because the molecules are quite large, the dispersion forces are sufficiently strong for both oxides to exist as solids at room temperature. (Remember that dispersion forces are approximately proportional to the number of electrons in the molecule.)

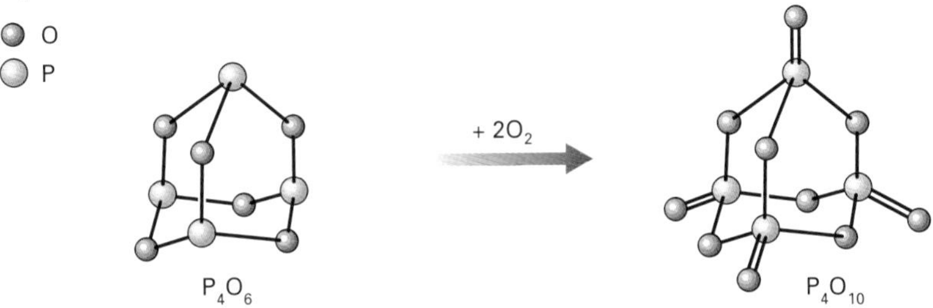

The structures of the molecules P_4O_6 and P_4O_{10}.

The oxides of sulphur

Sulphur dioxide SO_2 exists as individual molecules. The dipole–dipole and dispersion forces between SO_2 molecules are weak, so sulphur dioxide is a gas at room temperature. Sulphur trioxide SO_3 is composed mainly of rings of three molecules and chains whose length is not fixed. Below 17 °C, sulphur trioxide exists as a solid held together by the dispersion forces between the rings.

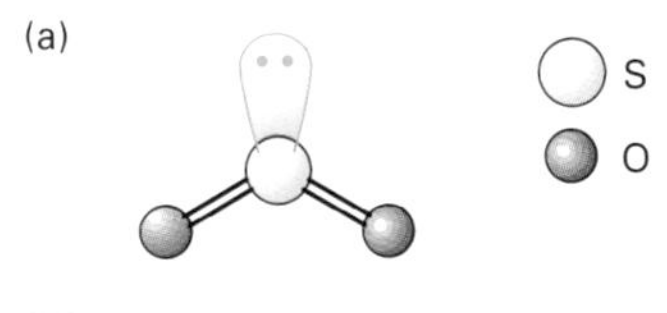

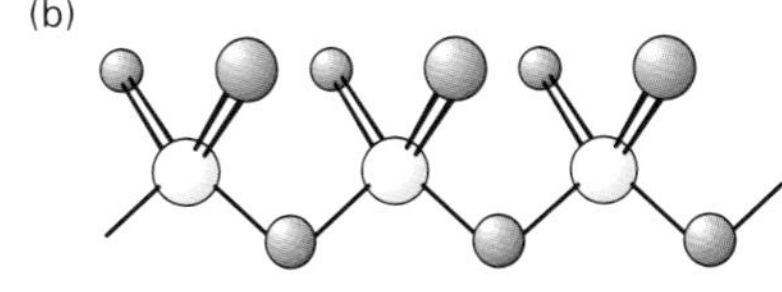

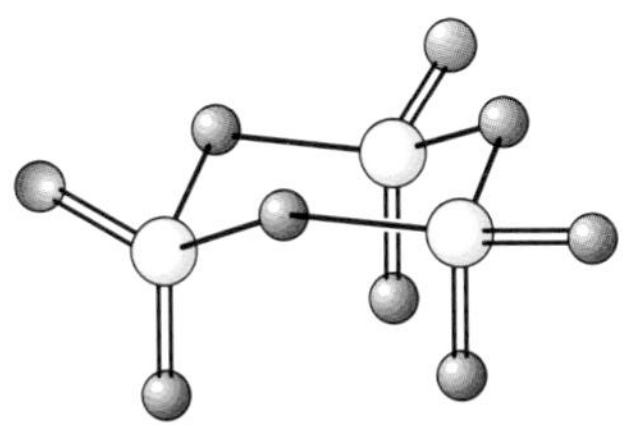

(a) The structure of an SO_2 molecule. (b) SO_3 molecules join together to make chains and rings. Sulphur uses its d orbitals to expand its valence shell.

The oxides of chlorine

The oxides of chlorine are highly reactive and unstable. Cl_2O and ClO_2 exist as separate molecules. These oxides therefore have low melting points and exist as gases at room temperature and pressure. The highest oxide of chlorine (Cl_2O_7) has greater dispersion forces and exists as an oily liquid under the same conditions.

SUMMARY

- As atomic number increases across Period 3, the oxide structure changes from ionic (Na_2O, MgO, Al_2O_3), to giant covalent (SiO_2), to simple molecular (P_4O_{10}, SO_2, Cl_2O_7).
- The melting points of the oxides follow the trend: Na_2O, MgO, Al_2O_3, SiO_2 – high; P_4O_{10}, SO_3, Cl_2O_7 – low.
- The melting point of SO_3 is greater than expected because it forms chains and three-membered rings.

PRACTICE

1 Write balanced chemical equations for the following reactions:

  a The combustion of phosphorus in a limited supply of oxygen to produce phosphorus(III) oxide.

  b The catalytic oxidation of sulphur dioxide by oxygen to produce sulphur trioxide.

2 Suggest why silicon reacts only very slowly with oxygen, even when at red-heat (temperature approximately 850 °C).

3 Outline the trends in melting points, structure, and bonding that you would expect for the oxides of Period 2.

17.5

OBJECTIVES

- Sodium and magnesium oxides are basic
- Aluminium oxide is amphoteric
- Non-metal oxides are acidic
- Trends in pH of aqueous solutions

ACID–BASE CHARACTER OF THE OXIDES

As the atomic number of the elements increases across Period 3 from sodium to chlorine, we shall see that there is a clear trend in the acid–base character of the oxides. The oxides of the metals on the left-hand side of the period are basic; the oxides of the non-metals on the right-hand side of the period are acidic. In this spread we discuss the nature of each oxide in turn. We conclude by summarizing these properties to show the overall trend across the period.

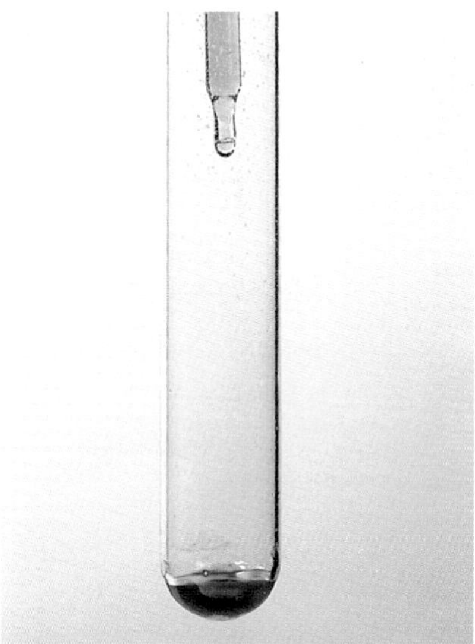

Solid sodium oxide $Na_2O(s)$ reacts with water exothermically. The product is aqueous sodium hydroxide $NaOH(aq)$, which turns the indicator blue.

Sodium and magnesium hydroxides

Sodium hydroxide NaOH is a strong base. It dissolves readily in water and ionizes fully to give a solution with pH ≈ 14:

$NaOH(s) \rightarrow Na^+(aq) + OH^-(aq)$

Magnesium hydroxide is only partially ionized in aqueous solution. The low hydroxide ion concentration results in a solution of pH ≈ 10:

$Mg(OH)_2(s) \rightleftharpoons Mg^{2+}(aq) + 2OH^-(aq)$

Hydrated aluminium oxide

It is much easier to demonstrate the chemical properties of aluminium oxide if the hydrated form is used. It forms when aqueous aluminium ions react with aqueous sodium hydroxide:

$Al^{3+}(aq) + 3OH^-(aq) \rightarrow Al(OH)_3(s)$

Although the formula of the precipitate has been shown as if it were a simple hydroxide, it is better represented as $Al_2O_3{\cdot}3H_2O$ (or, more realistically, as $Al_2O_3{\cdot}xH_2O$, where x can vary from 1 to 3).

Sodium oxide

Sodium oxide is a white solid. It reacts with water to give strongly basic aqueous sodium hydroxide with a pH of about 14:

$$Na_2O(s) + H_2O(l) \rightarrow 2NaOH(aq)$$

The oxide reacts vigorously with acids to produce an aqueous solution of a salt. For example

$$Na_2O(s) + H_2SO_4(aq) \rightarrow Na_2SO_4(aq) + H_2O(l)$$

These reactions show sodium oxide to be a *basic* oxide.

Magnesium oxide

Magnesium oxide is a white powder which is only slightly soluble in water. The aqueous solution is weakly basic with a pH of approximately 10:

$$MgO(s) + H_2O(l) \rightarrow Mg(OH)_2(aq)$$

The oxide reacts readily with acids to produce an aqueous solution of a salt. For example

$$MgO(s) + 2HCl(aq) \rightarrow MgCl_2(aq) + H_2O(l)$$

These reactions show magnesium oxide to be a *basic* oxide.

Aluminium oxide

Aluminium oxide Al_2O_3 is a white solid which is very insoluble in water. The hydrated oxide behaves as if it had the approximate formula $Al(OH)_3$. It acts as a base when it reacts with excess acid:

$$Al(OH)_3(s) + 3H^+(aq) \rightarrow Al^{3+}(aq) + 3H_2O(l)$$

The hydrated oxide acts as an acid when it reacts with excess aqueous sodium hydroxide to form a complex ion called the *tetrahydroxoaluminate* ion (sometimes abbreviated to aluminate ion):

$$Al(OH)_3(s) + OH^-(aq) \rightarrow [Al(OH)_4]^-(aq)$$

Aluminium oxide therefore has the properties of both a basic and an acidic oxide: it is an *amphoteric* oxide; see spread 16.8.

Silica

Silica SiO_2 has a giant covalent structure, and so is highly insoluble in water. It reacts only with highly concentrated alkalis or at high temperature. For example, it reacts with molten sodium hydroxide at 350 °C to form sodium silicate:

$$SiO_2(s) + 2NaOH(l) \rightarrow Na_2SiO_3(l) + H_2O(g)$$

The oxides of phosphorus

Phosphorus(V) oxide P_4O_{10} reacts with water to form aqueous phosphoric acid, which has a pH of about 1:

$$P_4O_{10}(s) + 6H_2O(l) \rightarrow 4H_3PO_4(aq)$$

Anhydrous phosphoric acid exists as deliquescent colourless crystals which melt at T_m = 42 °C. (Phosphorus(III) oxide P_4O_6 reacts with water to form aqueous phosphonic acid H_3PO_3.)

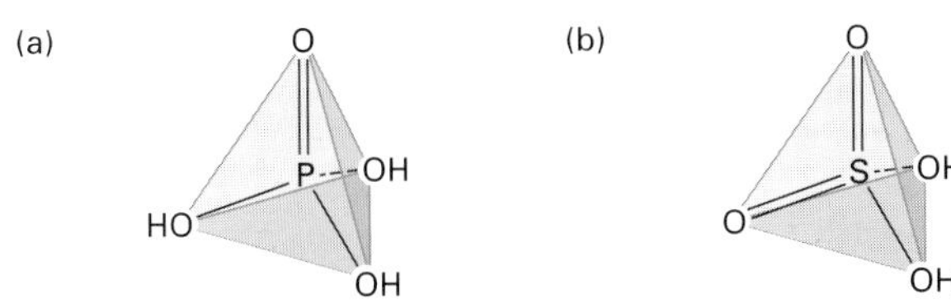

Oxoacid structures: (a) phosphoric acid; and (b) sulphuric acid.

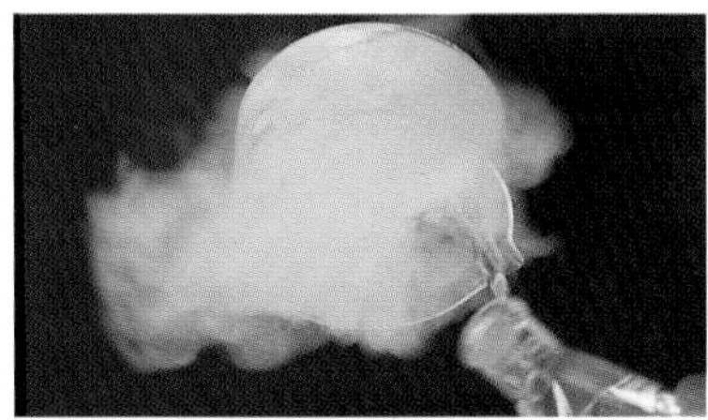

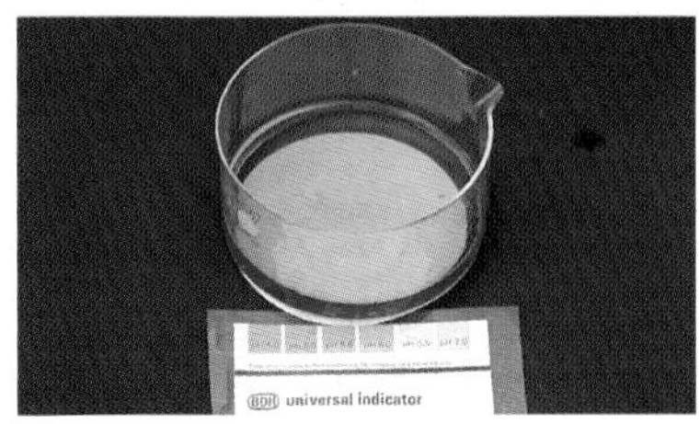

(a) Solid phosphorus(V) oxide P_4O_{10}(s) reacts with water very exothermically. (b) The product is aqueous phosphoric acid H_3PO_4(aq), which turns the indicator red.

The oxides of sulphur

Sulphur dioxide SO_2 is a gas with moderate solubility in water, forming an aqueous solution (pH ≈ 1) of sulphurous acid:

$$SO_2(g) + H_2O(l) \rightleftharpoons H_2SO_3(aq)$$

The acid cannot be isolated in the anhydrous state, as it decomposes back to the gas.

Sulphur trioxide SO_3 is a solid (T_m = 17 °C and T_b = 45 °C), which reacts with water to form aqueous sulphuric acid:

$$SO_3(s) + H_2O(l) \rightarrow H_2SO_4(aq)$$

Sulphuric acid is a strong acid and the aqueous solution has a pH close to 0. The anhydrous acid may be isolated as an oily liquid which boils at T_b = 338 °C.

Oxoacids and oxoanions: a reminder

Oxoacids are acids that contain oxygen. Oxoanions are anions that contain oxygen. Oxosalts are salts containing oxoanions.

The oxides of chlorine

The chemical properties of the chlorine oxides are dominated by their tendency to explode. However, about 100 000 tonnes of chlorine dioxide ClO_2 are manufactured each year. This explosive yellow gas is used to bleach wood pulp in the paper-making industry. It produces good whiteness without destroying the fibrous texture.

Dichlorine oxide Cl_2O reacts with water to give aqueous hypochlorous acid HClO(aq). Dichlorine heptaoxide Cl_2O_7 reacts with water to give aqueous perchloric acid $HClO_4$(aq). The redox properties of perchloric acid and the other oxoacids of Period 3 will be dealt with in the following spread.

The properties of some oxides of the elements of Period 3. Note particularly the increasing acidity of the oxides and the corresponding decrease in the pH of their aqueous solutions.

Formula of oxide	Na_2O	MgO	Al_2O_3	SiO_2	P_4O_{10}	SO_2	SO_3
State of oxide at 25 °C	solid	solid	solid	solid	solid	gas	liquid
Bonding and structure in oxide	ionic lattice	ionic lattice	ionic lattice	giant covalent	covalent molecular	covalent molecular	covalent molecular
Effect of adding oxide to water	reacts to form strongly basic aqueous NaOH	reacts to form weakly basic aqueous $Mg(OH)_2$	does not react with water	does not react with water	reacts to form weakly acidic aqueous H_3PO_4	reacts to form weakly acidic aqueous H_2SO_3	reacts to form strongly acidic aqueous H_2SO_4
Aqueous solution pH	14	10	7	7	1	1	0
Nature of oxide	basic	basic	amphoteric	acidic	acidic	acidic	acidic

SUMMARY

- Sodium oxide and magnesium oxide are basic.
- Aluminium oxide is amphoteric.
- The non-metal oxides in Period 3 are acidic.
- The pH of an aqueous solution of the oxides decreases across the period: recall the actual values above.

PRACTICE

1 Describe the trend in the bonding and structure of the oxides of Period 3. Also describe the trend in the pH of their aqueous solutions.

17.6 The oxoacids

OBJECTIVES

- Non-metal oxoacids
- Trends in oxidizing power of oxoacids

Many of the oxides of the elements of Period 3 react with water to form aqueous solutions. The oxides of the non-metals phosphorus, sulphur, and chlorine form a range of covalent oxoacids such as phosphoric acid and sulphuric acid. Some of these oxoacids exhibit oxidizing properties during redox reactions with suitable reductants. A clear trend in oxidizing power emerges.

Some oxoacids of phosphorus, sulphur, and chlorine.

Name of acid	Simple formula	More exact formula
Phosphoric	H_3PO_4	$(HO)_3PO$
Sulphurous	H_2SO_3	$(HO)_2SO$
Sulphuric	H_2SO_4	$(HO)_2SO_2$
Hypochlorous	HClO	HOCl
Chlorous	$HClO_2$	HOClO
Chloric	$HClO_3$	$HOClO_2$
Perchloric	$HClO_4$	$HOClO_3$

The oxoacids of phosphorus, sulphur, and chlorine

There is a large number of oxoacids containing these three elements. Details of the acids covered by this text are listed on the left. The second, more cumbersome, formula makes clear their status as oxoacids, by showing that the hydrogen atoms are bonded directly to oxygen.

Phosphoric acid

Phosphoric acid H_3PO_4 is non-volatile and does not act as an oxidant. It is therefore the acid of choice when preparing hydrogen bromide or hydrogen iodide. For example, HBr can be prepared by heating solid sodium bromide with concentrated aqueous phosphoric acid:

$$H_3PO_4(aq) + NaBr(s) \rightarrow NaH_2PO_4(aq) + HBr(g)$$

(Concentrated sulphuric acid cannot be used as it would oxidize the bromide ion to bromine – see below.) H_3PO_4 ionizes in three stages to form $H_2PO_4^-$, HPO_4^{2-}, and PO_4^{3-} ions. The pK_a values for the successive loss of the three protons are pK_{a1} = 2.2, pK_{a2} = 7.2, and pK_{a3} = 12.3. The pK_{a2} value is very close to neutral; one of the two important buffer solutions in nature is the 'phosphate buffer' $H_2PO_4^-/HPO_4^{2-}$; see spread 12.10.

Notation: pK_{a1} and pK_{a2}

pK_{a1} refers to the loss of the first proton from a diprotic acid, and pK_{a2} refers to the loss of a second proton. For example:

$H_2SO_3(aq) + H_2O(l) \rightleftharpoons H_3O^+(aq) + HSO_3^-(aq)$; p$K_{a1}$ = 1.9

$HSO_3^-(aq) + H_2O(l) \rightleftharpoons H_3O^+(aq) + SO_3^{2-}(aq)$; p$K_{a2}$ = 7.2

Sulphurous acid

Sulphurous acid H_2SO_3 contains the element sulphur with oxidation number +4. It is a weak acid (pK_{a1} = 1.9, pK_{a2} = 7.2), forming salts containing the hydrogensulphite HSO_3^- and sulphite SO_3^{2-} ions. Sulphurous acid is an infamous constituent of acid rain. Sulphurous acid also acts as a reductant, and is oxidized to sulphate ion:

$$H_2SO_3(aq) + H_2O(l) \rightleftharpoons SO_4^{2-}(aq) + 4H^+(aq) + 2e^-$$

For example, sulphurous acid will reduce iron(III) ions to iron(II):

$$2Fe^{3+}(aq) + H_2SO_3(aq) + H_2O(l) \rightleftharpoons 2Fe^{2+}(aq) + SO_4^{2-}(aq) + 4H^+(aq)$$

Sulphuric acid

Sulphuric acid H_2SO_4 is a *strong* acid in aqueous solution. It forms *normal salts* such as sodium sulphate Na_2SO_4 and *acid salts* such as sodium hydrogensulphate $NaHSO_4$. Concentrated sulphuric acid (96% H_2SO_4, 4% H_2O) has three distinctive properties:

1 It is the *most involatile* acid.

That is, it is the acid with the highest boiling point, 338 °C. It can therefore be used to produce more volatile acids, displacing hydrogen chloride and nitric acid when heated with their salts:

$$H_2SO_4(aq,conc) + NaCl(s) \rightarrow NaHSO_4(aq) + HCl(g)$$
$$H_2SO_4(aq,conc) + NaNO_3(s) \rightarrow NaHSO_4(aq) + HNO_3(l)$$

2 It is a *powerful oxidant*.

For example, it oxidizes bromide ion to bromine. Concentrated sulphuric acid is reduced to sulphur dioxide (the oxidation number of sulphur goes from +6 to +4):

$$H_2SO_4(aq,conc) + NaBr(s) \rightarrow NaHSO_4(aq) + HBr(aq)$$
$$H_2SO_4(aq,conc) + 2HBr(aq) \rightarrow Br_2(aq) + 2H_2O(l) + SO_2(g)$$

Sulphuric acid

Sulphuric acid is crucial to a large number of industrial processes. More than 10 000 tonnes are manufactured in the UK each day, more than for any other oxoacid. To show explicitly that it is an oxoacid (that is, that the hydrogen atoms are bonded directly to oxygen), the formula may be written as $(HO)_2SO_2$ (see the previous spread for the detailed structure of the molecule).

Concentrated sulphuric acid similarly oxidizes iodide ion to iodine, and is itself reduced to SO_2. However, the iodide ion is a sufficiently powerful reductant to reduce the sulphuric acid to elemental sulphur (oxidation number 0) and further to H_2S (oxidation number −2); see the following chapter for further details. Concentrated sulphuric acid is not a sufficiently powerful oxidant to oxidize chloride ion to chlorine (as in 1 above).

3 It is a powerful *dehydrating agent*.

This means that it chemically removes the elements of water from a compound. It can for example dehydrate sugar (sucrose $C_{12}H_{22}O_{11}$), as shown alongside.

Concentrated sulphuric acid dehydrates sucrose by removing 11 molecules of water from each $C_{12}H_{22}O_{11}$ molecule. The result is carbon and steam:
$C_{12}H_{22}O_{11}(s) \rightarrow 12C(s) + 11H_2O(g)$

Ionization of $H_2SO_4(aq)$

$H_2SO_4(aq)$ is a strong acid and so is fully ionized in water:

$H_2SO_4(aq) + H_2O(l) \rightarrow H_3O^+(aq) + HSO_4^-(aq)$

The hydrogensulphate ion is, however, only partially ionized ($pK_a = 1.9$):

$HSO_4^-(aq) + H_2O(l) \rightleftharpoons H_3O^+(aq) + SO_4^{2-}(aq)$

Oxoacids of chlorine

These acids are prepared in solution by adding a strong acid to a salt of the chlorine oxoacid. For example, aqueous hypochlorous acid HClO results when sulphuric acid is added to solid sodium hypochlorite:

$$NaClO(s) + H^+(aq) \rightarrow HClO(aq) + Na^+(aq)$$

The acid is only partially ionized ($pK_a = 7.4$) and is therefore a weak acid:

$$HClO(aq) + H_2O(l) \rightleftharpoons H_3O^+(aq) + ClO^-(aq)$$

Note that the oxygen atom bears the negative charge. Chlorine has oxidation number +1 in HClO. Its salts, such as sodium hypochlorite NaClO, are important bleaches in the home and in industry, acting by oxidation.

Oxidizing power increases in the order

$$HClO < HClO_2 < HClO_3 < HClO_4.$$

Perchloric acid $HClO_4$ is an extremely powerful oxidant and can react explosively with organic matter. Perchloric acid is also a strong acid.

Trends in oxidizing power

Sulphuric acid H_2SO_4 is a stronger oxidant than phosphoric acid H_3PO_4; perchloric acid $HClO_4$ is stronger still. The oxoacids of chlorine with lower oxidation numbers are also oxidants, although less powerful than $HClO_4$.

SUMMARY

- Non-metal oxides react with water to form oxoacids, which contain hydrogen atoms bonded directly to oxygen.
- Oxidizing power of the oxoacids of phosphorus, sulphur, and chlorine increases with increasing oxidation state in the overall order P(V) < S(VI) < Cl(VII).
- Sulphuric acid is the most involatile acid and a powerful oxidant and dehydrating agent.
- Sulphuric acid and perchloric acid are strong acids.

PRACTICE

1 Arrange the oxoacids of chlorine in order of increasing acid strength.

2 a Draw three-dimensional representations of all the oxoacids described in this spread.

b For each of your sketches in (a), draw the Lewis structure and indicate the mechanism by which each acid dissociates.

3 Compare and discuss the pK_a data given in this spread.

17.7

The chlorides of Period 3

OBJECTIVES

- Formulae
- Formation
- Trends in melting point
- Bonding trends
- Reactions with water

All the elements of Period 3 from sodium to phosphorus react directly with chlorine to form chlorides. The metallic elements form ionic chlorides, and the non-metallic elements form covalent chlorides. As with the elements themselves and their oxides, there is a trend in properties of these chlorides as the atomic number of the element increases across the period. This spread deals with the formation of the chlorides and their reactions with water.

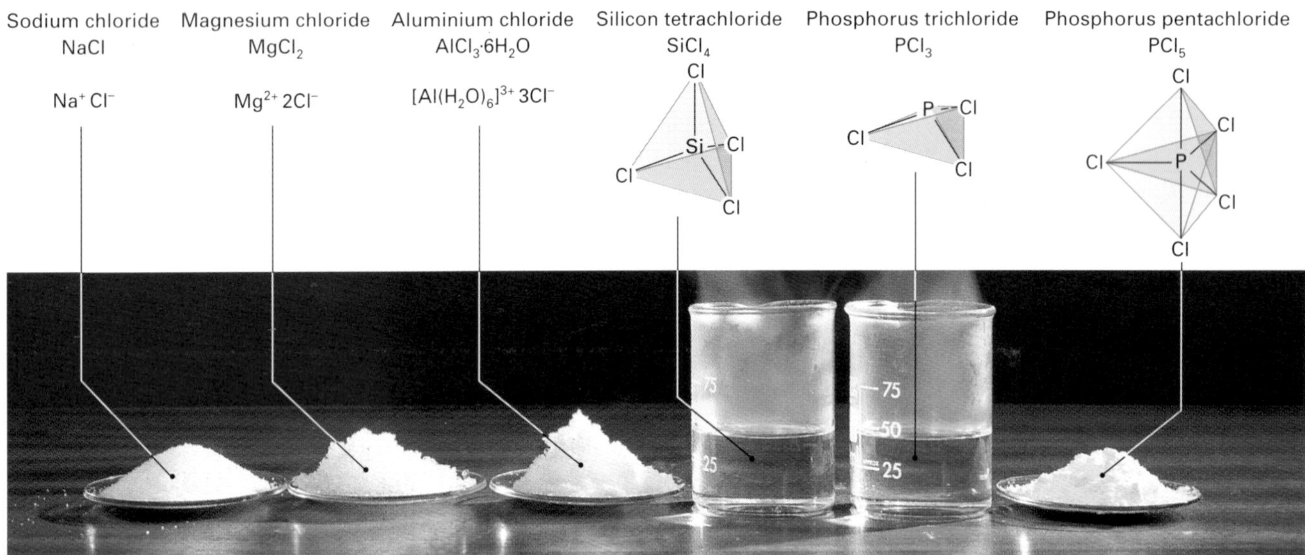

Physical state, formula, and bonding of the chlorides of the elements of Period 3.

Oxidation numbers

Oxidation number increases from +1 to +5 in the sequence of chlorides from sodium chloride to phosphorus pentachloride: Na(I) in NaCl; Mg(II) in $MgCl_2$; Al(III) in $AlCl_3$; Si(IV) in $SiCl_4$; and P(V) in PCl_5. Note that phosphorus also forms a chloride of formula PCl_3. Sulphur forms a number of chlorides, such as S_2Cl_2, which are not important enough to describe in detail.

The reaction of magnesium metal with chlorine gas is highly exothermic.

Sodium and magnesium chlorides

The chlorides of sodium and magnesium are formed by heating the metal in air until it burns, and then lowering it into a vessel containing chlorine. Sodium and magnesium both continue to burn in chlorine, with the white product coating the walls of the reaction vessel:

$$2Na(s) + Cl_2(g) \rightarrow 2NaCl(s)$$
$$Mg(s) + Cl_2(g) \rightarrow MgCl_2(s)$$

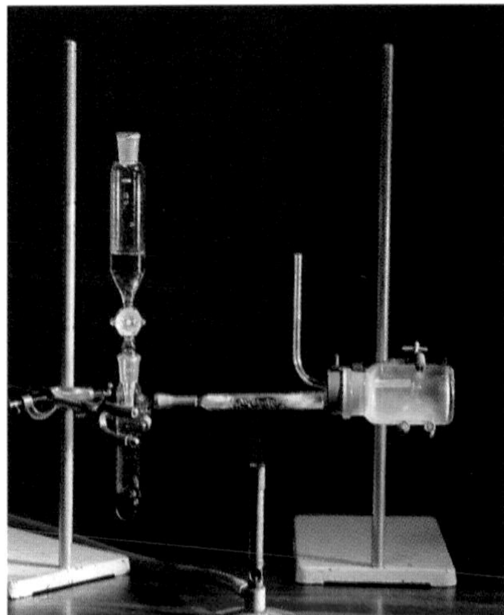

The reaction in the tube on the left supplies chlorine. Aluminium chloride condenses inside the flask seen on the right.

Aluminium chloride

Aluminium chloride reacts very readily with water, so it must be synthesized under anhydrous conditions. In the apparatus shown to the left, a stream of dry chlorine is passed over heated aluminium. The aluminium chloride product vaporizes and is carried through the apparatus by the flow of chlorine gas. It condenses as a white powder:

$$2Al(s) + 3Cl_2(g) \rightarrow Al_2Cl_6(s)$$

Similar apparatus may be used to synthesize the chlorides of the non-metals of Period 3.

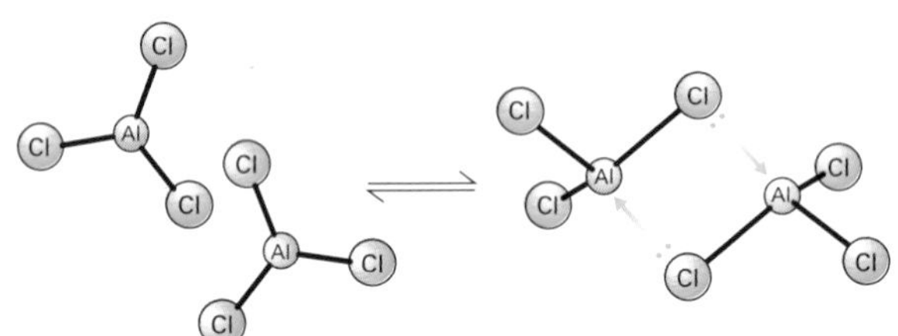

The structure of Al_2Cl_6. This anhydrous form results from $AlCl_3$ molecules forming dimers: chlorine atoms donate lone pairs of electrons into vacant orbitals in the valence shell of the aluminium atoms.

Silicon tetrachloride

The apparatus is similar to that used for the synthesis of aluminium chloride. However, $SiCl_4$ is a liquid at room temperature; the product is condensed in a water-cooled side-arm tube (which replaces the flask):

$$Si(s) + 2Cl_2(g) \rightarrow SiCl_4(l)$$

The chlorides of phosphorus

Heating phosphorus in excess chlorine forms the pentachloride PCl_5; excess phosphorus forms the trichloride PCl_3:

$$P_4(s) + 10Cl_2(g) \rightarrow 4PCl_5(s) \qquad \text{(excess } Cl_2\text{)}$$
$$P_4(s) + 6Cl_2(g) \rightarrow 4PCl_3(l) \qquad \text{(excess } P_4\text{)}$$

The pentachloride is a solid and the trichloride is a liquid at 25 °C and 1 bar. The hot product vapours must be condensed.

Phosphorus pentachloride

The structure of *solid* phosphorus pentachloride is unusual. It exists as the ion pair $PCl_4^+ \, PCl_6^-$. The PCl_4^+ ion has a tetrahedral shape; the PCl_6^- ion has an octahedral shape.

Bonding in the chlorides and reaction with water

The chlorides of sodium and magnesium are predominantly ionic. They are white solids with high melting points, which dissolve in water to form a neutral solution (pH 7):

$$NaCl(s) \rightarrow Na^+(aq) + Cl^-(aq)$$

All the other chlorides of Period 3 have significant covalent character and *react* with water. These reactions are called **hydrolysis** reactions.

Aluminium forms two solid chlorides, one of which is anhydrous (Al_2Cl_6) and the other hydrated ($AlCl_3{\cdot}6H_2O$). The anhydrous chloride (see opposite) *reacts* with water, evolving hydrogen chloride gas:

$$Al_2Cl_6(s) + 6H_2O(l) \rightarrow 2Al(OH)_3(s) + 6HCl(g)$$

Some HCl dissolves in the water to give hydrochloric acid, a strong acid with pH ≈ 0. This behaviour is characteristic of covalent chlorides.

The hydrated chloride consists of a complex cation $[Al(H_2O)_6]^{3+}$ bonded ionically to three chloride ions. The formula of the solid is therefore more accurately expressed as $[Al(H_2O)_6]Cl_3$. It dissolves in water, as is typical of an ionic solid, to form the ions $[Al(H_2O)_6]^{3+}(aq)$ and $Cl^-(aq)$. The solution is slightly acidic (pH ≈ 3), for reasons discussed in the chapter on 'The p-block elements'.

The chlorides of silicon and phosphorus are predominantly covalent. They all react with water (are hydrolysed) rather than simply dissolving in water; $SiCl_4$ and PCl_3 fume in air (see opposite):

$$SiCl_4(l) + 2H_2O(l) \rightarrow 4HCl(g) + SiO_2(s)$$
$$PCl_5(s) + 4H_2O(l) \rightarrow 5HCl(g) + H_3PO_4(aq)$$

The hydrochloric acid formed turns the solution strongly acidic, with pH ≈ 0.

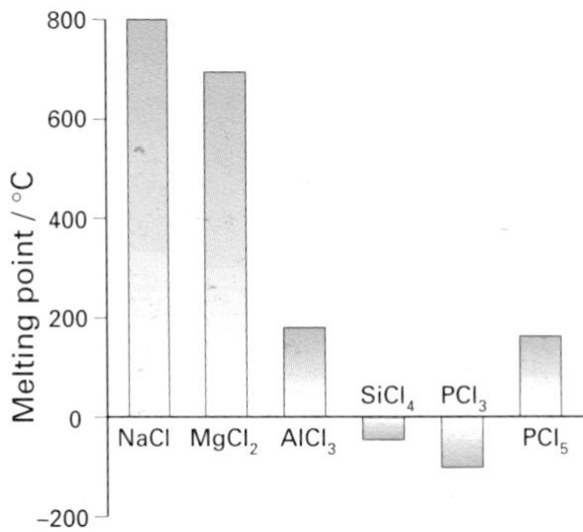

A bar chart of the melting points of the chlorides in period 3.

Phosphorus trichloride is hydrolysed by water to aqueous phosphonic acid $H_3PO_3(aq)$ and hydrogen chloride: $PCl_3(l) + 3H_2O(l) \rightarrow H_3PO_3(aq) + 3HCl(aq)$ Some of the hydrogen chloride dissolves in the water to give an aqueous solution with a pH close to zero, which turns universal indicator red.

SUMMARY

- All the elements of Period 3 react directly with chlorine to form chlorides.
- The bonding in aluminium chloride is on the borderline between ionic and covalent.

Formula of chloride	NaCl	$MgCl_2$	$AlCl_3$	$SiCl_4$	PCl_5
State of chloride at 25 °C	solid	solid	solid	liquid	solid
Bonding and structure in chloride	ionic lattice	ionic lattice	see text	covalent molecular	covalent molecular
Effect of adding chloride to water	dissolves	dissolves	see text	reacts	reacts
Aqueous solution pH	7	7	3	0	0

PRACTICE

1 Describe the bonding and structure of the chlorides of sodium to phosphorus.

17.8

OBJECTIVES

- Bonding character of the hydrides
- Reactions with water
- Trends in the hydrides

THE HYDRIDES: FROM IONIC TO COVALENT

Hydrides are compounds that contain hydrogen and one other element. There is a complete range of hydrides for the Period 3 elements, but the non-metal hydrides are much more important than the metal hydrides. The metal hydrides contain the hydride ion H^-, whereas the non-metal hydrides contain covalently bonded hydrogen atoms. The behaviour of the hydrides varies greatly, depending on the nature of the bonding within them. As you would expect by now, there is a trend in properties across the period from sodium hydride to hydrogen chloride.

The hydrides of Period 3

Hydride name	Formula
Sodium hydride	NaH
Magnesium hydride	MgH_2
Aluminium hydride	AlH_3
Silane	SiH_4
Phosphine	PH_3
Hydrogen sulphide	H_2S
Hydrogen chloride	HCl

Sodium hydride

Sodium hydride is a solid ionic hydride which reacts with water to form hydrogen gas and aqueous sodium hydroxide:

$$NaH(s) + H_2O(l) \rightarrow NaOH(aq) + H_2(g)$$

The hydride ion H^- is unstable in water as shown in the photograph below left for the case of calcium hydride. Hydride ion reduces a hydrogen atom in the water molecule, forming hydroxide ion and hydrogen gas:

$$H^-(s) + H_2O(l) \rightarrow OH^-(aq) + H_2(g)$$

The hydride ion is a powerful reductant, and so ionic hydrides exist only where the metal has a low electronegativity.

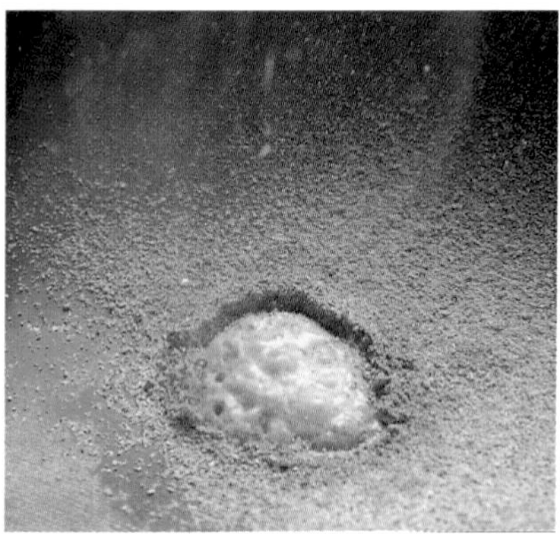

Calcium (Period 4) forms a solid hydride CaH_2. It reacts with water to form hydrogen, which is burning here with a yellow flame.

Aluminium hydride and the tetrahydridoaluminate ion

The hydride AlH_3 has little importance, but the closely related AlH_4^- ion is very important in organic chemistry. In the AlH_4^- ion, four hydrogen atoms are covalently bonded to a central aluminium atom. This ion is a powerful reductant and is stable only in the presence of metal ions with low electronegativity such as Li^+. Lithium tetrahydridoaluminate $LiAlH_4$ (also called lithium aluminium hydride) is a white solid which is used as a powerful reductant throughout organic chemistry, e.g. spread 26.2.

Silane

Silicon is in Group IV of the periodic table along with carbon. There is a series of silicon hydrides similar to the series of carbon hydrides (called *alkanes*, i.e. methane CH_4, ethane C_2H_6, propane C_3H_8, etc.). The first and most important of these is silane SiH_4, a gas which boils at $T_b = -112\,°C$. Four hydrogen atoms are covalently bonded to a central silicon atom. Unlike methane, which is only mildly reducing, silane is a powerful reductant and spontaneously ignites in air:

$$SiH_4(g) + 2O_2(g) \rightarrow SiO_2(s) + 2H_2O(l)$$

Silane is hydrolysed by water (containing a trace of alkali) to hydrated silica and hydrogen gas:

$$SiH_4(g) + 2H_2O(l) \rightarrow SiO_2(s) + 4H_2(g)$$

Phosphine

Phosphine PH_3 is a poisonous gas ($T_b = -87\,°C$) which is almost insoluble in water. Its structure is similar to that of ammonia, the hydride of the Group V element nitrogen. Phosphine is a strong reductant, and is able to precipitate copper and silver from aqueous solutions of their salts. For example:

$$4Cu^{2+}(aq) + PH_3(g) + 4H_2O(l) \rightarrow 4Cu(s) + H_3PO_4(aq) + 8H^+(aq)$$

Hydrogen sulphide

Hydrogen sulphide H_2S is a gas ($T_b = -61\,°C$) which smells of 'bad eggs'. In solution, hydrogen sulphide is weakly acidic and is the parent acid of a series of salts called *sulphides*, e.g. sodium sulphide Na_2S.

Hydrogen sulphide is formed by adding a strong acid to a sulphide such as iron(II) sulphide:

$$FeS(s) + 2HCl(aq) \rightarrow FeCl_2(aq) + H_2S(g)$$

Hydrogen sulphide is a strong reductant, able to reduce sulphur dioxide:

$$2H_2S(g) + SO_2(g) \rightarrow 3S(s) + 2H_2O(l)$$

The reaction is catalysed by a trace of water.

Hydrogen chloride

Hydrogen chloride HCl is a gas (T_b = −85 °C) which dissolves very easily in water to form hydrochloric acid. Hydrochloric acid is a strong acid, being essentially fully ionized in solution:

$$HCl(g) + H_2O(l) \rightarrow H_3O^+(aq) + Cl^-(aq)$$

Trends in the hydrides

The trend in the bonding in the hydrides is similar to that in the chlorides. The elements on the extreme left of the period tend to form ionic hydrides, and the elements on the extreme right tend to form covalent hydrides.

The oxidation states of the Period 3 element in hydrides vary in the sequence: Na(I) in NaH; Mg(II) in MgH_2; Al(III) in AlH_4^-; Si(IV) in SiH_4; P(III) in PH_3; S(−II) in H_2S; and Cl(−I) in HCl. Note the change of oxidation number from positive on the left to negative on the right. Hydrogen has an electronegativity only *just* larger than that of phosphorus.

Where the hydrides dissolve in water or react with it, pH falls steadily in the sequence NaH (pH 14) to PH_3 (pH 7) to HCl (pH 0).

With the exception of hydrogen chloride, the hydrides are strong reductants.

Size

The covalent radius of the hydrogen atom H is 0.037 nm. The ionic radius of the hydride ion H^- is 0.208 nm. Compare these figures with those for the chlorine atom Cl (0.099 nm) and the chloride ion Cl^- (0.181 nm).

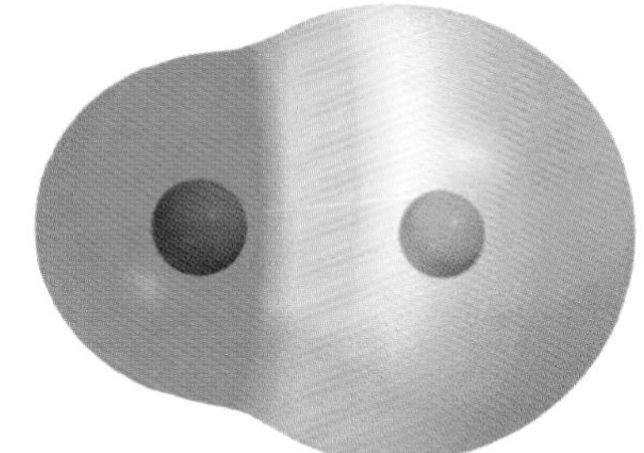

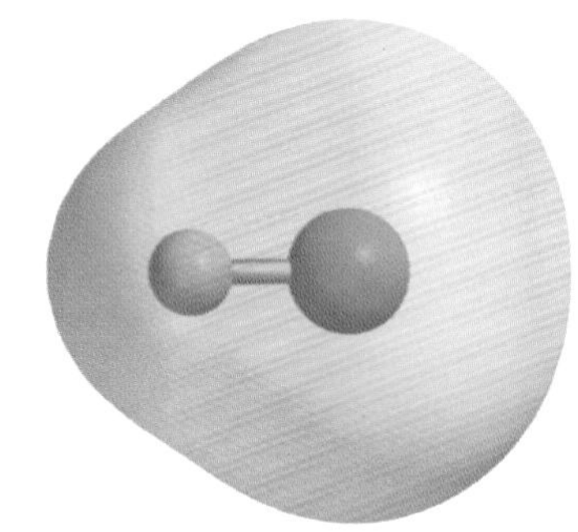

Electrostatic potential maps show that sodium hydride NaH has a large charge separation (is essentially ionic), with hydrogen partially negatively charged. Hydrogen chloride HCl is polar covalent with hydrogen partially positively charged. The other hydrides of the Period 3 elements show a steady change in bonding character between these two extremes.

SUMMARY

- The hydrides show trends across the period, from ionic to covalent compounds.
- Sodium hydride is an ionic solid which reacts with water to form an aqueous solution of pH ≈ 14.
- Hydrogen chloride is a covalent gas which reacts with water to form an aqueous solution of pH ≈ 0.

PRACTICE

1 Draw Lewis structures for the following species:
  - **a** The hydride ion H^-
  - **b** Silane SiH_4
  - **c** Phosphine PH_3
  - **d** Hydrogen sulphide H_2S
  - **e** Hydrogen chloride HCl
  - **f** The tetrahydridoaluminate ion AlH_4^-.

2 For each of the species in question 1(b) to (f), draw its shape showing the arrangement of its bonds, remembering to include lone pairs of electrons.

3 The text above states that: 'In solution, hydrogen sulphide is weakly acidic …'. Write a chemical equation to illustrate this observation.

4 Explain why the hydride ion H^- is larger than most other monatomic (single-atom) ions.

5 Plot a graph of the boiling points of the hydrides SiH_4 to HCl. Comment on the shape of the plot. Explain any trend you can point out in terms of the intermolecular forces present.

PRACTICE EXAM QUESTIONS

1 **a** The graph below shows the melting points of the elements sodium to argon.

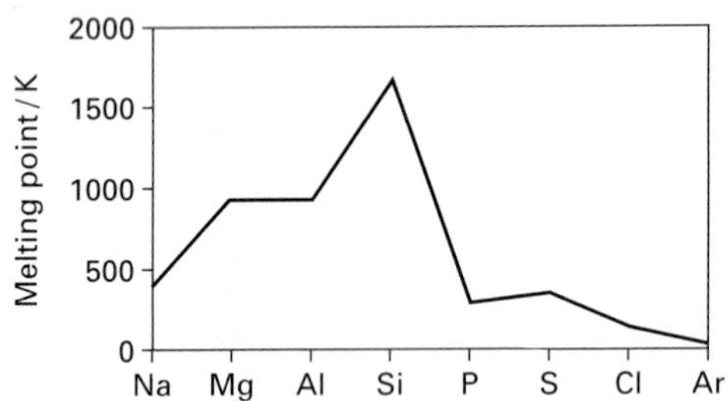

By reference to their structure and bonding, explain the melting points of the elements from sodium to argon. [5]

b The graphs below show the trends in atomic radius and molar first ionization energy for Group 1 elements.

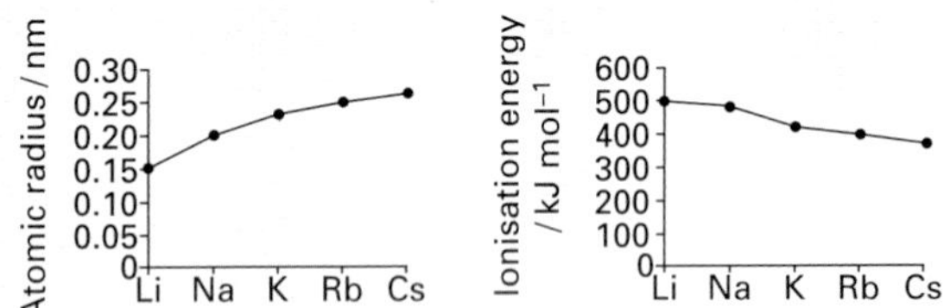

Explain why the atomic radius increases and the ionization energy decreases as the group is descended. [4]

c Write balanced equations to show the reaction of water with:

i sodium: [1]

ii sodium oxide; [1]

iii sodium hydride. [1]

d Suggest a pH value for the solution formed when sodium hydride reacts with water. [1]
AQA (AEB) 1999

2 The elements of the third period are as follows:

Na Mg Al Si P S Cl Ar

All of your answers below should relate to these elements.

a Which elements can exist:

i as diatomic molecules at room temperature;

ii as macromolecular structures? [2]

b Which pairs of elements combine to produce compounds with formulae of the type *XY*? [2]

c Two elements form chlorides with formula, of the type XCl_3. Draw displayed formulae for these two chlorides, and suggest values for the bond angles. [4]

d **i** One element combines with oxygen to form an oxide which reacts with water to give a strongly alkaline solution. Name the element, and write a balanced equation for the oxide reacting with water.

ii One element combines with oxygen to form an oxide of the type XO_2, which reacts with water to given an acidic solution. Name the element and write a balanced equation for the oxide reacting with water. [4]
OCR (UCLES) 1998

3 **a** Explain the meaning of the term periodic trend when applied to trends in the Periodic Table. [2]

b Explain why atomic radius decreases across Period 2 from lithium to fluorine. [2]

c The table below shows the melting temperatures, T_m, of the Period 3 elements.

Element	Na	Mg	Al	Si	P	S	Cl	Ar
T_m / K	371	923	933	1680	317	392	172	84

Explain the following in terms of structure and bonding.

i Magnesium has a higher melting temperature than sodium.

ii Silicon has a very high melting temperature.

iii Sulphur has a higher melting temperature than phosphorus.

iv Argon has the lowest melting temperature in Period 3. [8]
AQA (NEAB) 1998

4 **a** In the table below, give the formulae of the chlorides of the elements of Period 3, other than silicon.

Element	Na	Mg	Al	Si	P	S
Formula of chloride				$SiCl_4$		

[2]

b Calculate the percentage by mass of silicon in silicon tetrachloride. [2]

c **i** Draw a dot-and-cross diagram to show the bonding in silicon tetrachloride.

ii Draw the shape of this molecule.

Explain your answer in terms of the electron-pair repulsion theory.

iii State the shape of a molecule of $AlCl_3$ and explain why it is different from that of $SiCl_4$. [6]

d **i** Give an equation for the reaction of $SiCl_4$ with cold water.

ii How does the behaviour of carbon tetrachloride with cold water compare with this? Explain any differences. (4)
EDEXCEL 1996

5 **a** Define the term **electronegativity**. [2]

b State and explain the trend in electronegativity across Period 3 from sodium to chlorine. [4]

c **i** What is the trend in bond type in the oxides of the Period 3 elements from sodium to sulphur?

ii Explain how this trend is related to the differences in electronegativity between the Period 3 element and oxygen. [3]

d Write an equation for the reaction of phosphorus(V) oxide, P_4O_{10}, with water. [2]
AQA (NEAB) 1998

6 **a** Describe the nature of the attractive forces which hold the particles together in magnesium metal and in magnesium chloride. [4]

b Name the type of bond between aluminium and chlorine in aluminium chloride and explain why the bonding in aluminium chloride differs from that in magnesium chloride. [3]

c Write an equation, including state symbols, to show what happens when magnesium chloride dissolves in water. Explain, in terms of bonding, the nature of the interaction between water and magnesium in this solution. [3]
AQA (NEAB) 1998

7 **a** Write equations to show what happens when the following oxides are added to water and predict approximate values for the pH of the resulting solutions.

i sodium oxide;

ii sulphur dioxide. [4]

b What is the general relationship between bond type in the oxides of the Period 3 elements and the pH of the solutions which result from addition of the oxides to water? [2]

c Write equations to show what happens when the following chlorides are added to water and predict approximate values for the pH of the resulting solutions:

i magnesium chloride;

ii silicon tetrachloride. [4]
AQA (NEAB) 1997

8 The table below shows electronegativity values for some atoms.

Atom	H	N	O	F	Cl	Cs
	2.1	3.0	3.5	4.0	3.0	0.7

a What do you understand by the term electronegativity? [1]

b The nature of the bonding in substances depends partly on the electronegativities of the atoms concerned. Use the data in the table above to suggest the nature of the bonding in each of the following substances.

i caesium fluoride; [1]

ii water; [1]

iii chlorine. [1]

c Ammonia, NH3, is a polar covalent molecule.

i State the general rules which determine the shape of a covalent molecule. [3]

ii Draw the shape of the ammonia molecule [1]

iii Why is the bond angle in ammonia 107° rather than 109° 28′? [1]

iv Explain why the molecule is polar [1]

d Each of the elements sodium to chlorine in Period 3 will react with oxygen given suitable conditions.

i Choose an element from this period which gives a basic oxide, and write equations both for its reaction with oxygen and to illustrate the basic nature of the oxide. [2]

ii Choose an element which forms an amphoteric oxide and write equations which illustrate this amphoteric nature. [2]

iii Carbon dioxide reacts readily with dilute aqueous sodium hydroxide whereas silicon dioxide does not. Explain this difference and suggest conditions under which silicon dioxide would react. [2]
EDEXCEL 1997

The halogens

The halogens are the non-metallic elements fluorine (F), chlorine (Cl), bromine (Br), iodine (I), and astatine (At) that make up Group VII of the periodic table. They are p-block elements; the p orbitals are incompletely filled and the valence shell has the structure ns^2np^5. The halogens have generally greater chemical reactivity than other non-metals. They also have wide application in industrial processes and are often present in finished products. The properties of the halogens and their compounds (with the exception of the radioactive element astatine) form the subject of this chapter.

Group VII elements: an overview

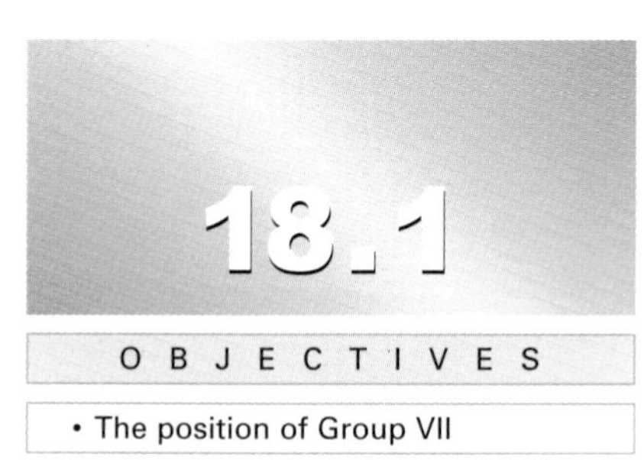

OBJECTIVES

- The position of Group VII
- Naming the halogens
- Trends in boiling point
- Bonding in compounds

The halogens show the typical properties of non-metals: they have low melting and boiling points, when solid they are brittle, and when liquid they are extremely poor conductors of electricity. All halogens have seven electrons in the valence shell, so they all show similar chemical properties. The p orbitals are incompletely filled, being one electron short of the eight required for a full shell ns^2np^6. They form two main classes of compounds: ionic compounds containing the halide ion X^-, and covalent compounds where electrons are shared with other atoms.

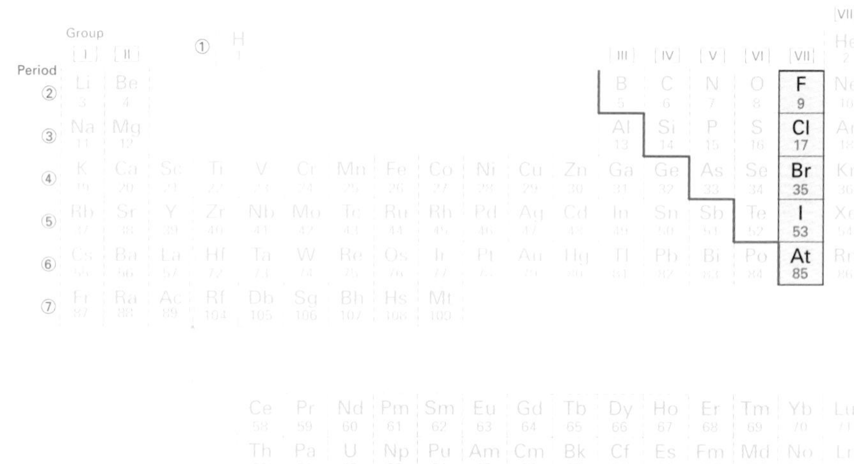

The halogens form Group VII of the periodic table. (Astatine is a radioactive element; its chemistry will not be dealt with in this text.)

Bromine reacts vigorously with red phosphorus. An earlier view of the same reaction is shown in spread 13.5.

The elements

The elements exist as diatomic molecules containing a single covalent bond X—X (where we use X to mean any halogen). The number of electrons increases with atomic number, resulting in an increase in the dispersion forces between the molecules (see spread 7.4). As a result, the melting and boiling points of the halogens increase as atomic number increases in the order $F_2 < Cl_2 < Br_2 < I_2$. Fluorine and chlorine are gases, bromine is a liquid, and iodine is a solid at 25 °C (298 K) and 1 bar.

: Cl : Cl :

Cl—Cl

Two halogen atoms share a pair of electrons to form a single covalent bond.

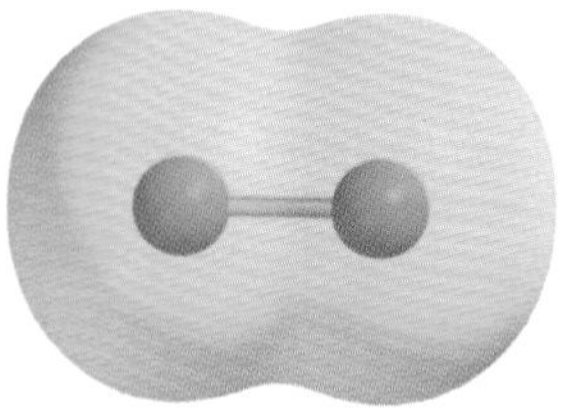

The electrostatic potential map of the chlorine molecule Cl_2. Note the concentration of electron density (forming the bond) between the two atomic centres. The symmetrical electron density shows that the molecule is non-polar.

Halogen compounds

The *binary compounds* (compounds in which just *two* elements are combined) containing halogens are called **halides**. Each of the four halogens shows similar formulae in their compounds. For example, the ionic sodium halides are sodium fluoride NaF, sodium chloride NaCl, sodium bromide NaBr, and sodium iodide NaI. All are white crystalline solids which are soluble in water. Halogens have an oxidation number of −1 in ionic compounds. Electronegativity decreases in the order F > Cl > Br > I, and so the covalent character of ionic compounds increases in the order fluoride < chloride < bromide < iodide. Aluminium fluoride melts above 1000 °C; aluminium chloride is more covalent and melts at 180 °C.

A similar pattern is noted in the covalent compounds. For example, the hydrogen halides are hydrogen fluoride HF, hydrogen chloride HCl, hydrogen bromide HBr, and hydrogen iodide HI. All are gases (at 25 °C and 1 bar) and are readily soluble in water, forming acidic solutions. The halogens have an oxidation number of −1 in the hydrogen halides. With the exception of fluorine, the halogens can also exhibit other oxidation numbers in some of their covalent compounds.

Group VII

	F	Cl	Br	I
Electronegativity	4.0	3.2	3.0	2.7

The variation in electronegativity for the halogens.

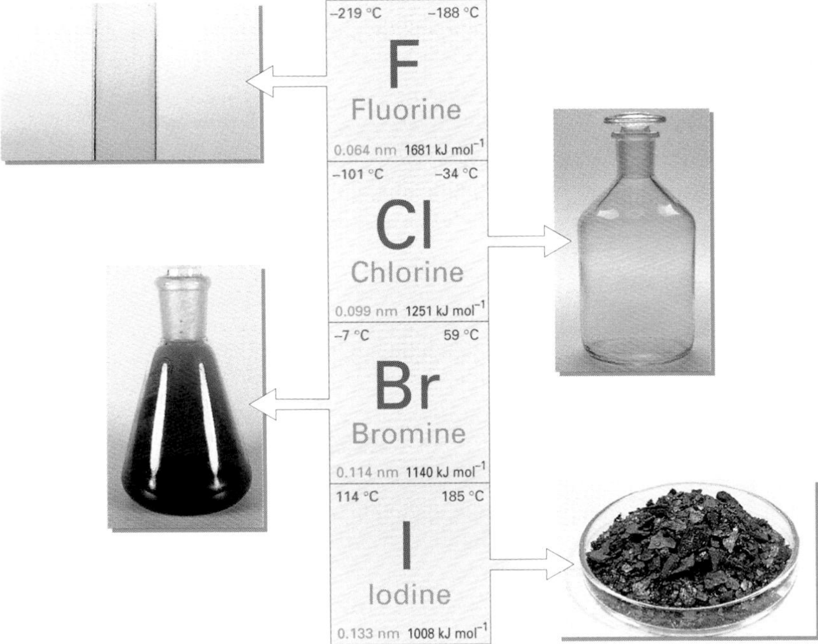

This chart summarizes the major properties of the Group VII elements fluorine to iodine.

SUMMARY

- The halogens are the elements in Group VII.
- They are non-metals with outer-shell electronic structures ns^2np^5.
- They form ionic compounds with metals, and covalent compounds with non-metals.
- As atomic number *increases* from fluorine to iodine: melting point, boiling point, and atomic radius *increase*; ionization energy and electronegativity *decrease*.

PRACTICE

1 Explain why the melting points of the halogens vary.

2 Draw Lewis structures to show the bonding in hydrogen bromide.

3 Draw diagrams to show how sodium and bromine bond together in sodium bromide.

4 Explain why sodium iodide melts at a lower temperature (661 °C) than sodium chloride (801 °C). Base your answer on a discussion of the character of the bonding, supported by data from the chart above.

5 Explain why a solution of hydrogen iodide in water is acidic.

6 Explain what influence, if any, the atomic radius of a halogen has on its:

a electron-gain enthalpy,

b ionization energy,

c melting point.

18.2

OBJECTIVES

- Chlorine and fluorine: by electrolysis
- Bromine and iodine: by displacement
- Industrial roles

Manufacture and uses

The halogens play an important role in an enormous number of modern manufacturing processes, and occur widely in many finished products. Chlorine is by far the most important halogen commercially. Millions of tonnes are manufactured each year from common salt, sodium chloride. In turn, chlorine plays a key role in the production of the halogens bromine and iodine. Together with fluorine, these elements are involved in the production of plastics, dyestuffs, pharmaceuticals and drugs, refrigerants, and photographic film.

Uses of chlorine and its compounds

- Cl_2 – sterilizing water
- Cl_2 – recovery of tinplate from cans
- Cl_2 – making hydrochloric acid
- NaClO – bleaches for textiles and paper
- PVC – plastic
- Anaesthetics (e.g. halothane), disinfectants (e.g. TCP)
- Chlorinated hydrocarbon solvents.

The greatest percentage use is PVC (27%), followed by water purification, bleaches, and then solvents.

Chlorine

The electrolysis of sodium chloride in the **chlor–alkali industry** produces chlorine, hydrogen, and sodium hydroxide. The two technologies currently used, the 'membrane cell' and the 'diaphragm cell', have several features in common. The electrolyte in both cells is saturated **brine** (aqueous sodium chloride) containing about 25% by mass of NaCl. The electrode reactions are the same in both cells.

At the anode, chloride ions lose electrons and are oxidized to chlorine gas, i.e.

at the anode: $2Cl^-(aq) \rightarrow Cl_2(g) + 2e^-$

The anode resists attack by chlorine because it is made from titanium with an inert coating of ruthenium(IV) oxide RuO_2. The high concentration of chloride ions in the solution results in chlorine being formed at the anode by oxidation of chloride ions. (If the chloride ion concentration were too low, oxygen would form from the oxidation of water.)

At the cathode (made from steel or nickel), water is reduced to hydrogen gas and hydroxide ions are formed, i.e.

at the cathode: $2H_2O(l) + 2e^- \rightarrow H_2(g) + 2OH^-(aq)$

At the anode

If the chloride ion concentration is low, oxygen is liberated at the anode from the oxidation of water, i.e.

self-ionization:
$H_2O(l) \rightleftharpoons H^+(aq) + OH^-(aq)$

at the anode:
$4OH^-(aq) \rightarrow O_2(g) + 2H_2O(l) + 4e^-$

The key problem in the manufacture is that the products of the electrolysis, i.e. Cl_2 and OH^-, react with each other. The **diaphragm cell** uses a porous asbestos diaphragm to keep the products separate. The **membrane cell** uses a polymer ion-exchange membrane that allows only cations to pass through it. The electrolyte is removed from the electrolysis cell and evaporated. The less-soluble sodium chloride crystallizes, leaving sodium hydroxide dissolved in the solution for later recovery.

'Mercury cells'

An earlier type of cell used a flowing mercury cathode. These 'mercury cells' have now been withdrawn from use because the inevitable loss of mercury caused environmental damage. The most notorious case occurred in the coastal town of Minamata in Japan during the 1950s. Contaminated waste from a new factory entered the food chain through plankton and fish, eventually causing babies to be born with severe abnormalities.

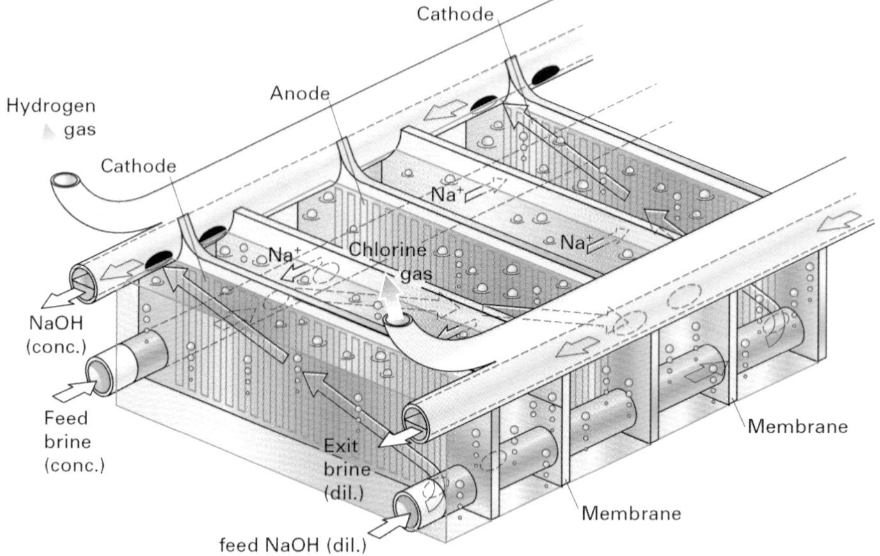

The membrane cell. The electrode processes are the same for the diaphragm cell; only the means of separating the products differs.

Fluorine

Fluorine is extracted by the electrolysis of a molten mixture of HF and KHF_2 at about 100 °C. Fluorine is released at the anode and hydrogen at the cathode. The extraction is extremely hazardous because fluorine will react violently with any moisture, oil, or grease present. The products combine explosively if allowed to mix, and so are kept apart by a diaphragm dipping below the electrolyte surface.

Bromine and iodine

The manufacture of these two halogens depends on the relative ease of oxidation of the halide ions:

$$2X^-(aq) \rightarrow X_2(aq) + 2e^-$$

The order is $I^- > Br^- > Cl^-$, which indicates that chlorine will displace both iodide and bromide ions, forming iodine and bromine respectively, as shown in the following spread.

Bromine may be produced from seawater, which contains about 0.006% by mass of bromide ion. Seawater is treated with chlorine and the free bromine is helped to vaporize by blowing air through the mixture:

$$2Br^-(aq) + Cl_2(aq) \rightarrow 2Cl^-(aq) + Br_2(aq)$$

The reaction is a redox reaction: each chlorine atom removes an electron from a bromide ion.

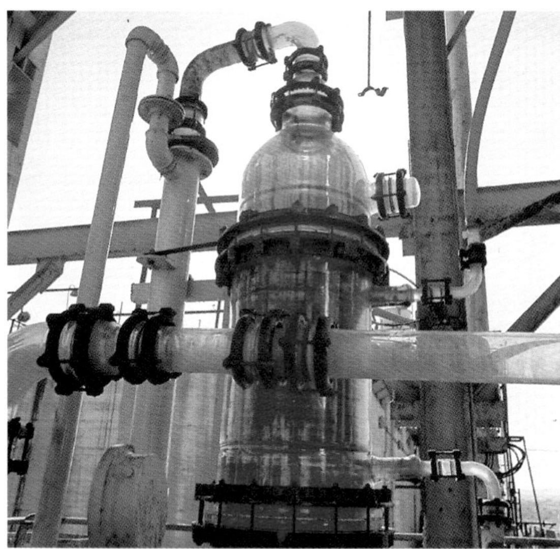

The red-brown element bromine is manufactured by the oxidation of bromide ions by chlorine.

Iodine is also present in seawater, at a concentration of less than one part per million. Some types of seaweed extract iodine during growth to the extent that their ash after combustion contains about 0.5% by mass of iodine. The ash is dissolved in dilute sulphuric acid to give aqueous iodide ion, and iodine is displaced from this solution by chlorine:

$$2I^-(aq) + Cl_2(aq) \rightarrow 2Cl^-(aq) + I_2(aq)$$

SUMMARY

- Chlorine (and sodium hydroxide) is manufactured by the electrolysis of saturated aqueous sodium chloride.
- Bromine and iodine are manufactured by using chlorine to displace the halogen from an aqueous solution of the halide.

PRACTICE

1 Explain why fluorine cannot be manufactured by the electrolysis of an aqueous fluoride compound.

Uses of fluorine and its compounds

- PTFE – 'non-stick' plastics and coatings
- UF_6 – uranium isotope separation
- BF_3 – petroleum industry catalysts
- Na_3AlF_6 – cryolite in aluminium smelting
- NaF – fluoridation of water.

Note that the previously very widely used chlorofluorocarbon (CFC) refrigerants and propellants (such as 'Freon' CCl_2F_2) are now banned in most countries, because of their adverse effect on the atmospheric ozone layer.

Uses of bromine and its compounds

- $C_2H_4Br_2$ – petrol additive (dominant use in 1980s, now obsolescent)
- AgBr – photographic film emulsion
- Medicines and drugs (2% of total use)
- Halons – fire extinguishers, e.g. $CBrClF_2$
- Synthesis of organic chemicals.

Note that the mass of bromine manufactured is one-hundredth that of chlorine.

Uses of iodine and its compounds

- Iodine ointment for skin ulcers
- Antiseptics (e.g. triiodomethane CHI_3)
- Antibacterial agents
- Polarizing light filters.

Iodine

The main source of the element is sodium iodate $NaIO_3$, which is present as an impurity in the mineral form of sodium nitrate, Chile saltpetre.

18.3

HALOGENS AND HALIDES: REDOX BEHAVIOUR

OBJECTIVES

- Halogens: relative oxidizing strength
- Halogen/halide displacement
- Halides: relative reducing strength
- Laboratory preparation of chlorine

Standard electrode potentials

The oxidizing ability of the halogens in aqueous solution is reflected in their standard electrode potentials. The more positive the value, the greater the oxidizing power of the halogen.

$F_2(g) + 2e^- \rightleftharpoons 2F^-(aq)$ $E^\ominus = +2.87\,V$

$Cl_2(g) + 2e^- \rightleftharpoons 2Cl^-(aq)$ $E^\ominus = +1.36\,V$

$Br_2(l) + 2e^- \rightleftharpoons 2Br^-(aq)$ $E^\ominus = +1.07\,V$

$I_2(s) + 2e^- \rightleftharpoons 2I^-(aq)$ $E^\ominus = +0.54\,V$

Recognition of halogens in organic solvents

The halogens exist as covalent diatomic molecules. Their solubility in the polar solvent water is limited, but they have greater solubility in organic solvents such as tetrachloromethane. Where water and this solvent are in contact, a halogen dissolves preferentially in the organic solvent. The solutions have distinctive colours: chlorine – pale yellow/green; bromine – red/brown; iodine – purple.

Iodine solutions

Iodine is brown in oxygen-containing solvents, such as water and ethanol. It is purple in solvents that do not contain oxygen, such as 1,1,1-trichloroethane and tetrachloromethane.

Fluorine as an oxidant

There are further examples of the great strength of fluorine as an oxidant. For example, it is the only element that is able to combine with the noble gas krypton. Sulphur forms a hexafluoride SF_6 (containing S(VI)) but there is no equivalent compound for the other halogens. Fluorine is so powerful an oxidant that it can oxidize water to molecular oxygen:

$2F_2(g) + 2H_2O(l) \rightarrow 4HF(aq) + O_2(g)$

In the manufacture of bromine and iodine, chlorine displaces the elements from their respective ions, bromide Br^- and iodide I^-. These displacement reactions follow the rule that a halogen in a *higher* position (of lower atomic number) in Group VII will oxidize a halide ion from *lower* in the group to the corresponding halogen. For example, chlorine added to aqueous iodide ion gives iodine and aqueous chloride ion; there is no reaction when bromine is added to aqueous chloride ion. These displacement reactions depend on the relative ability of the halogens to act as oxidants. Displacement reactions are redox reactions.

Halogen displacement: a reminder

The order of reactivity of the halogens can be demonstrated by reacting chlorine with aqueous bromide and iodide ions. In both cases, chlorine oxidizes the halide ion to the corresponding halogen and is itself reduced to chloride ion:

$$Cl_2(g) + 2Br^-(aq) \rightarrow Br_2(aq) + 2Cl^-(aq)$$
$$Cl_2(g) + 2I^-(aq) \rightarrow I_2(aq) + 2Cl^-(aq)$$

Chlorine is said to have 'displaced' bromine or iodine from solution.

Halogen/halide displacement reactions: upper layer aqueous; lower layer tetrachloromethane. (a) Chlorine water added to fluoride: no reaction. (b) Chlorine oxidizes bromide: red bromine in the lower layer. (c) Chlorine oxidizes iodide: purple iodine in the lower layer.

Oxidizing power

Fluorine is the strongest oxidant of all the elements. Chlorine is also a very strong oxidant. Bromine is a little weaker as an oxidant, and iodine weaker still. This trend is demonstrated very clearly by the compounds formed by iron when it combines directly with the halogens. Fluorine and chlorine form iron(III) fluoride and iron(III) chloride respectively; these compounds have iron in its higher oxidation state. Bromine forms both iron(III) bromide and iron(II) bromide.

Iodine is too weak an oxidant to form the higher oxidation state and so only forms iron(II) iodide. Indeed, iron(III) ions can oxidize iodide ions to form iodine and iron(II) ions:

$$2Fe^{3+}(aq) + 2I^-(aq) \rightarrow 2Fe^{2+}(aq) + I_2(s)$$

Reduction of iodine by thiosulphate

Fluorine, chlorine, and bromine can all oxidize thiosulphate ion $S_2O_3^{2-}$ to sulphate ion. Iodine is too weak an oxidant to achieve this. Instead it oxidizes thiosulphate ion to tetrathionate ion:

$$I_2(aq) + 2S_2O_3^{2-}(aq) \rightarrow 2I^-(aq) + S_4O_6^{2-}(aq)$$

The oxidation number of sulphur in thiosulphate is +2. Note that the oxidation number of sulphur in tetrathionate is +2.5, that is, not a whole number. As we saw in the chapter on 'Redox equilibrium', this very specific reaction for iodine is extremely useful in the quantitative analysis of oxidants, as follows.

The oxidant is first added to excess iodide ion to produce iodine, and then the liberated iodine is titrated against standard sodium thiosulphate. Sodium thiosulphate has the advantage that it is one of the few reductants that is not oxidized by air. The end point of the titration is easily seen using starch as an indicator added just as the end point is near and the iodine solution has become straw-coloured. Starch forms a deep blue complex in the presence of small quantities of iodine. The end point is when the last trace of blue is removed to leave a colourless solution.

Halide ions as reductants

A trend that follows directly from the fact that the *halogens* become weaker oxidants from fluorine to iodine is that the *halide ions* become stronger reductants from fluoride to iodide. That is, the strength of the halide ions as reductants is in the order $I^- > Br^- > Cl^- > F^-$.

Iodide ion is a common reductant in acidic solution. A useful illustration is the reaction of iodide ions with copper(II) ions, the result being a dull-looking precipitate of copper(I) iodide:

$$2Cu^{2+}(aq) + 4I^-(aq) \rightarrow 2CuI(s) + I_2(aq)$$

The dull colour is caused by the presence of iodine. This contaminant may be removed by adding aqueous sodium thiosulphate to the mixture. The iodine is reduced to iodide ion, revealing the white precipitate of copper(I) iodide.

$Cu^{2+}(aq)$ and $Cl^-(aq)$

Unlike iodide ion, chloride ion does not reduce copper(II) ions; instead it forms a green complex $CuCl_4^{2-}$. No redox reaction has occurred: copper remains in oxidation state Cu(II).

Laboratory preparation of chlorine

Chlorine may be prepared by oxidizing concentrated hydrochloric acid using a suitably strong oxidant. A common oxidant which works at room temperature is potassium manganate(VII) $KMnO_4$:

$$2KMnO_4(s) + 16HCl(aq) \rightarrow 2KCl(aq) + 2MnCl_2(aq) + 5Cl_2(g) + 8H_2O(l)$$

Manganese(IV) oxide is also successful, although only when the reaction mixture is heated:

$$MnO_2(s) + 4HCl(aq) \rightarrow MnCl_2(aq) + Cl_2(g) + 2H_2O(l)$$

Note that fluorine cannot be obtained from the fluoride ion by chemical oxidation. This reaction requires a more powerful oxidant than fluorine – difficult if not impossible to obtain under normal laboratory circumstances. (Fluorine is manufactured by *electrolysis*, as discussed in the previous spread.)

Preparing chlorine. Concentrated hydrochloric acid is added from the funnel to solid manganese(IV) oxide in the flask. Warming the mixture releases chlorine. Chlorine is denser than air, so the gas is collected by downward delivery.

SUMMARY

- The oxidizing power of the halogens decreases in the order $F_2 > Cl_2 > Br_2 > I_2$.
- The general chemical reactivity of the halogens follows the order of their oxidizing power.
- Iodine reacts quantitatively with thiosulphate ion: $I_2(aq) + 2S_2O_3^{2-}(aq) \rightarrow 2I^-(aq) + S_4O_6^{2-}(aq)$
- A halogen will displace a halide that has a greater atomic number than itself.
- Halide ions may act as reductants; the order of reactivity is $I^- > Br^- > Cl^- > F^-$.
- Iodide ion is the most commonly used halide reductant.

Oxidation numbers

The reactions described above show that the halogens have oxidation number 0 as elements and oxidation number −1 as halide ions. You will encounter higher oxidation numbers in the following spreads.

PRACTICE

1 Decide whether a reaction takes place in each of the following mixtures, and write a balanced chemical equation where appropriate:

a Chlorine and aqueous bromide ions

b Bromine and aqueous iodide ions

c Bromine and aqueous chloride ions.

2 Chlorine gas is dissolved in 1,1,1-trichloroethane. The solution is shaken with an aqueous solution of sodium bromide and then allowed to stand. Describe what you would expect to see after the mixture had been standing for five minutes.

18.4

Halogens in solution

OBJECTIVES

- Halogen solubility in water
- Halogen reactivity with base
- Disproportionation reactions

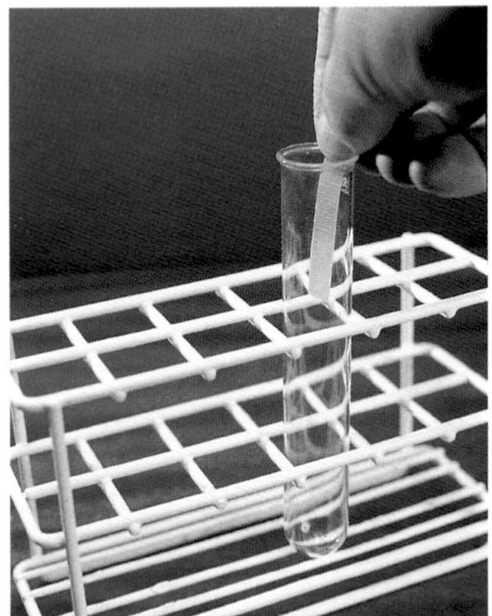

Testing for chlorine. Chlorine gas bleaches a piece of moist litmus paper held in it. The paper must be moist so that the chlorine may dissolve and react to form hypochlorous acid, which bleaches the paper. A red colour (indicating acidity) may be seen very briefly first.

Other names

See spread 13.3 for alternative names used for the halogen oxoanions.

Pool water pH

The optimal pH range for bather comfort and efficiency of disinfection is 7.3 to 7.4. The pH can be controlled by adding sodium hydrogensulphate to reduce pH or sodium carbonate to increase it.

The halogens dissolve in or react with water to varying extents and show a variety of behaviours. The nature of the behaviour depends largely on the strength of the halogen as an oxidant. For example, fluorine oxidizes water vigorously. The other halogens undergo a series of reactions in which higher halogen oxidation states are reached.

Fluorine plus water

Unlike the other halogens, fluorine *oxidizes* water to oxygen, i.e.

$$2F_2(g) + 2H_2O(l) \rightarrow 4HF(aq) + O_2(g)$$

oxidation state changes: F(0) to F(–I); O(–II) to O(0)

Small amounts of hydrogen peroxide H_2O_2 and oxygen difluoride OF_2 are also formed. The solution contains essentially no dissolved fluorine gas, as it all reacts.

Chlorine plus water

Chlorine dissolves in water to give **chlorine water** $Cl_2(aq)$, and some chlorine then reacts with the water. Some oxidation of water occurs, especially in bright light, but the main reaction is **disproportionation**, which is a reaction in which a species is both oxidized and reduced:

$$Cl_2(aq) + H_2O(l) \rightleftharpoons HCl(aq) + HClO(aq)$$

oxidation state changes: Cl(0) to Cl(–I) and Cl(I)

The product HClO(aq) is called **hypochlorous acid**.

Hypochlorous acid and hypochlorite ion

Aqueous hypochlorous acid is a weak acid that ionizes to give the **hypochlorite ion** ClO^-:

$$HClO(aq) + H_2O(l) \rightleftharpoons H_3O^+(aq) + ClO^-(aq)$$

The hypochlorite ion ClO^- contains chlorine with an oxidation number of +1. It is an oxidant, especially in acidic solution. It will, for example, oxidize iodide ion to iodine:

$$2I^-(aq) + ClO^-(aq) + 2H^+(aq) \rightarrow I_2(aq) + Cl^-(aq) + H_2O(l)$$

The hypochlorite ion acts as a powerful disinfectant and bleach. Disinfectant action depends on its ability to oxidize organic material and thereby to disrupt the life processes of bacteria. Sodium hypochlorite is the active constituent in domestic bleaches and sterilizing fluids (e.g. *Milton*). 'Bleaching powder' contains calcium hypochlorite, and is used commercially for water treatment and for bleaching paper and textiles. Bleaching action depends on the ability of hypochlorite ions to break up the structures of organic colouring matter.

Hypochlorous acid is a good bactericide. 'Chlorine' is therefore used to kill bacteria in swimming pools and drinking water. As you might expect, it is important to use the optimum quantities in each case, with increased concentrations being required in swimming pools. The source of chlorine is often granular calcium hypochlorite $Ca(ClO)_2$ or tablets of 'Trichlor'.

Chlorine plus cold dilute aqueous sodium hydroxide

The equilibrium mixture of chlorine in water is acidic. If aqueous base is added, the equilibrium is shifted much further to the right. For example, sodium hypochlorite is produced when chlorine reacts with *cold* aqueous sodium hydroxide:

$$Cl_2(g) + 2NaOH(aq) \rightarrow NaCl(aq) + NaClO(aq) + H_2O(l)$$

Similarly, the reaction between chlorine and aqueous calcium hydroxide forms calcium hypochlorite:

$$2Cl_2(g) + 2Ca(OH)_2(aq) \rightarrow CaCl_2(aq) + Ca(ClO)_2(aq) + 2H_2O(l)$$

A solution of hypochlorite ion disproportionates at temperatures above about 75 °C to form chloride ion Cl^- and **chlorate ion** ClO_3^-. Note again the changes in oxidation state:

$$3ClO^-(aq) \rightarrow 2Cl^-(aq) + ClO_3^-(aq)$$

oxidation state changes: Cl(I) to Cl(–I) and Cl(V)

Bromine plus water or aqueous sodium hydroxide

Bromine undergoes a similar reaction with water to that of chlorine. The result is hydrobromic acid HBr(aq) and hypobromous acid HBrO(aq):

$$Br_2(aq) + H_2O(l) \rightleftharpoons HBr(aq) + HBrO(aq)$$

However, the equilibrium lies far to the left. Unless the solution is kept at around 0 °C, the **hypobromite ion** BrO^- disproportionates further to give bromide ion Br^- and **bromate ion** BrO_3^-:

$$3BrO^-(aq) \rightarrow 2Br^-(aq) + BrO_3^-(aq)$$

oxidation state changes: Br(I) to Br(–I) and Br(V)

Reacting aqueous bromine with aqueous sodium hydroxide encourages the disproportionation and increases the concentration of bromate ion.

Iodine plus water or aqueous sodium hydroxide

Iodine has very low solubility in water. However, it dissolves in water containing a high concentration of iodide ions, e.g. KI(aq). An equilibrium is established in which iodide ion reacts with iodine to form the **triiodide ion**:

$$I^-(aq) + I_2(s) \rightleftharpoons I_3^-(aq)$$

The solution behaves as if it is a solution of $I_2(aq)$.

The concentration of HIO(aq) in this solution is negligible. Reacting iodine with aqueous sodium hydroxide does not increase the concentration of **hypoiodite ion** $IO^-(aq)$. This species disproportionates to give the **iodate ion** IO_3^-:

$$3IO^-(aq) \rightarrow 2I^-(aq) + IO_3^-(aq)$$

oxidation state changes: I(I) to I(–I) and I(V)

SUMMARY

- Fluorine oxidizes water to give oxygen and hydrofluoric acid.
- Chlorine and bromine dissolve in water and disproportionate to give hypochlorous and hypobromous acids HXO.
- The concentrations of the hypohalite ions ClO^- and BrO^- may be increased by reacting the halogen with a base, e.g. $Cl_2(g) + 2NaOH(aq) \rightarrow NaCl(aq) + NaClO(aq) + H_2O(l)$
- The hypohalous acids are weak acids with stabilities in the order HClO > HBrO > HIO.
- Hypochlorite ion disproportionates to form chloride ion $3ClO^-(aq) \rightarrow 2Cl^-(aq) + ClO_3^-(aq)$

Decomposition

The hypochlorite ion slowly decomposes on standing as a result of two separate reactions. The first involves disproportionation to chloride and chlorate ClO_3^-:

$3ClO^-(aq) \rightarrow 2Cl^-(aq) + ClO_3^-(aq)$

oxidation state changes: Cl(I) to Cl(–I) and Cl(V)

The second reaction evolves oxygen gas, and is observed especially in sunlight:

$2ClO^-(aq) \rightarrow 2Cl^-(aq) + O_2(g)$

oxidation state changes: Cl(I) to Cl(–I); O(–II) to O(0)

Sodium hypochlorite

This substance can be made commercially by the electrolysis of cooled brine. The electrolysis cell is arranged so that the chlorine produced at the anode mixes with the sodium and hydroxide ions in the solution.

Do not mix with acid!

Some toilet cleaners used to contain solid calcium hypochlorite $Ca(ClO)_2$, the approximate formula for 'bleaching powder'. The label usually warned against 'mixing with other proprietary cleaners which may contain acid'. Some limescale removers contained 30% hydrochloric acid. If these two cleaning chemicals were used together, an unpleasant mixture resulted that reacts according to the following chemical equation:

$Cl^-(aq) + ClO^-(aq) + 2H^+(aq) \rightarrow Cl_2(aq) + H_2O(l)$

Choking fumes of poisonous chlorine gas were given off! The acid reverses the equilibrium for the reaction of chlorine with water.

PRACTICE

1 Give the formulae of each of the following:

a Hypochlorous acid
b Hypochlorite ion
c Chlorate ion.

2 For each of the species in question 1, give the oxidation number of the halogen concerned.

18.5 THE HYDROGEN HALIDES

OBJECTIVES

- Physical properties
- Preparation
- Oxidation of hydrogen halides
- Acidic properties

Hydrogen halide boiling points

Hydrogen halide	Boiling point/°C
HF	19
HCl	−85
HBr	−66
HI	−36

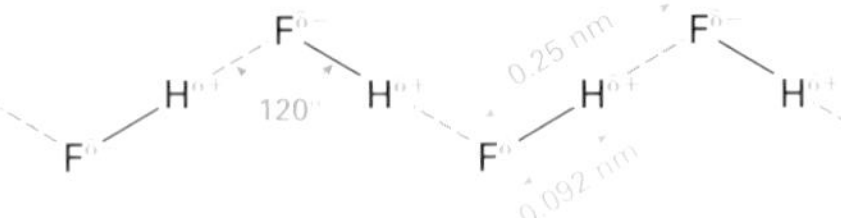

Hydrogen bonding occurs in hydrogen fluoride, due to the high electronegativity of fluorine and hence the extreme polarity of the $H^{\delta+}$—$F^{\delta-}$ bond.

Laboratory apparatus for the preparation of the hydrogen halides. A concentrated acid is run onto a halide salt. Heating the mixture drives off the volatile hydrogen halide, which is dried by concentrated sulphuric acid and collected by downward delivery. (HCl, HBr, and HI are all more dense than air.)

The hydrogen halides are compounds containing a halogen and hydrogen only. They have the formula HX, where the halogen is bonded to hydrogen by a single covalent bond. They are all gases at 25 °C and 1 bar, and may be prepared by the action of a suitable concentrated acid on a halide salt. However, the redox properties of the hydrogen halides differ widely, so the acid used for preparation must be chosen with care.

Physical properties

The boiling points of the hydrogen halides increase from HCl to HI, because the dispersion forces increase as the number of electrons increases. The anomalously high boiling point of HF arises because there is hydrogen bonding between the highly polar molecules. This polarity results from the fact that fluorine is a small, highly electronegative element. See the chapter on 'Changes of state and ...'.

Laboratory preparation

Hydrogen chloride can be made by heating a chloride salt with concentrated (96%) sulphuric acid:

$$NaCl(s) + H_2SO_4(aq, conc.) \rightarrow HCl(g) + NaHSO_4(aq)$$

The action of concentrated sulphuric acid with (a) NaCl, (b) NaBr, and (c) NaI. The products seen are: (b) some bromine, and (c) copious iodine vapour.

Concentrated sulphuric acid is a powerful oxidant. It may not be used to prepare HBr and HI because these substances are reductants and so are oxidized by concentrated sulphuric acid to bromine and iodine respectively. For example

$$2HBr(aq) + H_2SO_4(aq, conc.) \rightarrow 2H_2O(l) + SO_2(g) + Br_2(g)$$

Hydrogen iodide reduces concentrated sulphuric acid further, to sulphur and hydrogen sulphide. A summary of these reactions is given below.

Hydrogen bromide and hydrogen iodide are prepared by using phosphoric acid, an involatile acid that is *not* an oxidant. For example

$$NaI(s) + H_3PO_4(aq, conc.) \rightarrow HI(g) + NaH_2PO_4(aq)$$

Summary table showing the products of reaction between sodium halides and concentrated sulphuric acid.

Halide	Observations	Products	Oxidation states
NaCl	Steamy fumes	HCl	Cl(−I)
NaBr	Steamy fumes	HBr	Br(−I)
	Brown fumes	Br_2	Br(0)
	Colourless gas	SO_2	S(+IV)
NaI	Steamy fumes	HI	I(−I)
	Purple fumes	I_2	I(0)
	Colourless gas	SO_2	S(+IV)
	Yellow solid	S	S(0)
	Smell of bad eggs	H_2S	S(−II)

Manufacture

Hydrogen chloride and hydrogen bromide are manufactured by direct combination of the elements. Hydrogen fluoride cannot be manufactured in this way because hydrogen reacts explosively with fluorine at temperatures down to –200 °C. Mixtures of hydrogen and chlorine also react explosively when exposed to a spark or to bright light, but a jet of hydrogen burns steadily in an atmosphere of chlorine. Hydrogen and bromine react more slowly, and commercial production requires a temperature of 300 °C and a platinum catalyst. This trend of decreasing ease of production of the hydrogen halides fits the pattern of the general chemical reactivity of the halogens and parallels the very large variation in standard enthalpy change of formation.

Thermal stability

Dipping a red-hot wire into hydrogen iodide gas produces copious violet clouds of iodine:

$$2HI(g) \rightarrow H_2(g) + I_2(g)$$

The order of ease of such decomposition of the hydrogen halides is the opposite of the order of reactivity between hydrogen and the halogens. The trend in ease of decomposition depends mainly on the strength of the hydrogen–halogen bond as measured by the bond enthalpy. The size of the atoms increases from fluorine to iodine; therefore the bond length increases and the bond enthalpy *decreases* in this order.

Hydrogen halides as acids

Dry, gaseous, hydrogen halides are not acidic; they do not affect dry indicator paper. However, their aqueous solutions *are* acidic. For example, hydrogen chloride dissolves readily in water to form hydrochloric acid:

$$HCl(g) + H_2O(l) \rightarrow H_3O^+(aq) + Cl^-(aq)$$

One surprise is that hydrofluoric acid is a *weak* acid (pK_a 3.45) whereas the other hydrogen halides all form strong acids (see the chapter on 'Acid–base equilibrium'). This is because the H—F bond is particularly strong and hydrogen bonding between hydrogen fluoride molecules and water molecules inhibits the ionization of HF. The other hydrogen halides do not show hydrogen bonding.

Hydrogen fluoride

This substance attacks glass. It is prepared by heating calcium fluoride with concentrated sulphuric acid:

$CaF_2(s) + H_2SO_4(aq, conc.) \rightarrow$
$CaSO_4(aq) + 2HF(g)$

$\Delta H_f^\ominus$ (298 K) for HX(g)

Hydrogen halide	$\Delta H_f^\ominus$ (298 K) /kJ mol^{-1}
HF	–273
HCl	–92
HBr	–36
HI	+27

Bond lengths and enthalpies

Bond	Bond length /nm	Bond enthalpy /kJ mol^{-1}
H—F	0.092	562
H—Cl	0.127	431
H—Br	0.141	366
H—I	0.161	299

SUMMARY

- Hydrogen halides are produced by the action of concentrated sulphuric acid or concentrated phosphoric acid on a metal halide salt.
- An aqueous solution of HF is weakly acidic; HCl, HBr, and HI are all strong acids in aqueous solution.
- Reducing power is in the order (powerfully reducing) HI > HBr > HCl > HF (non-reducing).
- Bond enthalpy (and hence thermal stability) follows the order HF > HCl > HBr > HI.

PRACTICE

1 Write balanced chemical equations for the laboratory preparation of HF, HCl, HBr, and HI.

2 Sketch the apparatus you would use to prepare a sample of dry hydrogen bromide. [Note that a suitable drying agent is solid anhydrous calcium bromide.]

3 Write balanced chemical equations for the following:

a The manufacture of HCl by burning hydrogen in an atmosphere of chlorine.

b The dissolution of HI gas in water to make an acidic solution.

c Liquid anhydrous HF protonating itself (thus accounting for the moderate electrical conductivity of the liquid).

4 Explain why hydrogen bonding occurs in hydrogen fluoride but not in the other hydrogen halides.

5 Explain why HI is a more powerful reductant than HCl.

Some ionic halides

OBJECTIVES

- Chemical tests for halide ions
- Solubility of silver halides

Halogens

The name 'halogen' comes from the Greek for 'salt former'.

The physical properties of the halogens vary considerably, from gaseous fluorine and chlorine to liquid bromine and solid iodine. However, the ionic compounds that they form have similar formulae and are indistinguishable by appearance alone. For example, the compounds NaF, NaCl, NaBr, and NaI are all white crystalline solids which are soluble in water. While the physical properties are similar, the chemical properties are distinctive to each compound. These chemical properties form the basis of this spread. It ends with more details about the anomalous behaviour of fluorides.

Oxidation number

Ionic halides contain the halide ions F^-, Cl^-, Br^-, and I^-. These ions form when a halogen accepts one electron to complete its valence shell of electrons. The oxidation number of −1 is found in all the ionic halides of metals. The formula of the Group I halides is MX; the formula of the Group II halides is MX_2.

Adding nitric acid

The solution to be tested for halide ions is acidified with nitric acid before adding the aqueous silver nitrate. The presence of this acid prevents the formation of other insoluble silver compounds, such as silver carbonate. The carbonate would react with the acid to form carbon dioxide gas.

A chemical test for halide ions

The silver halides are used to identify the chloride, bromide, and iodide ions. These halides may be identified in a solution by adding acidified silver nitrate and observing the colour of the precipitate formed. Silver fluoride is soluble and its solution is colourless, so the fluoride ion cannot be identified by the test. Silver chloride, silver bromide, and silver iodide, however, are insoluble in water and are precipitated. The colours of the precipitates are as follows:

- Silver chloride is white.
- Silver bromide is cream.
- Silver iodide is yellow.

The ionic equation for the precipitation of the chloride, for example, is

$$Ag^+(aq) + Cl^-(aq) \rightarrow AgCl(s)$$

Confirmation is obtained by observing the behaviour when aqueous ammonia is added to these precipitates:

- Silver chloride dissolves in dilute aqueous ammonia.
- Silver bromide dissolves in concentrated aqueous ammonia.
- Silver iodide remains as a precipitate in both dilute and concentrated aqueous ammonia.

Actually, the precipitate does not simply *dissolve* to give the aqueous ions $Ag^+(aq)$ and $X^-(aq)$. What happens is that a *complex ion* (see chapter on 'The transition metals') is formed between the silver ion and ammonia:

$$AgCl(s) + 2NH_3(aq) \rightarrow [Ag(NH_3)_2]^+(aq) + Cl^-(aq)$$

Remember that bromide and iodide ions may also be identified from their reaction with concentrated sulphuric acid (see the previous spread).

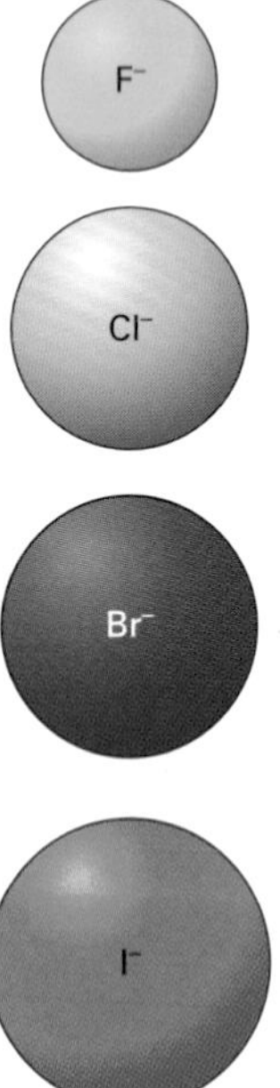

Halide ionic radii (to scale).

Tubes 1, 3, 5: Precipitates of silver chloride (white), silver bromide (cream), and silver iodide (yellow). The solids are light-sensitive and darken over time. Tubes 2, 4, 6: The effect on the precipitates of adding concentrated aqueous ammonia.

Trends in solubility

Why is silver chloride more soluble than silver iodide in aqueous ammonia? Solubility involves a balance between lattice enthalpy and enthalpy of hydration. Lattice enthalpy and enthalpy of hydration both become smaller when the anion is larger. The value of both of these enthalpy changes will therefore be smaller for silver iodide than for silver chloride because the iodide ion is larger than the chloride ion. The lower enthalpy of hydration for the iodide ion is mainly responsible for the lower solubility of silver iodide.

Quantitatively, the enthalpy of solution can be calculated by adding the (endothermic) lattice enthalpy and the (exothermic) enthalpies of hydration of both the silver and halide ions (see box). The enthalpy of solution of AgCl is +66 kJ mol^{-1}. For AgI the enthalpy of solution is +112 kJ mol^{-1}, i.e. AgI is less likely to dissolve than AgCl. These endothermic values should be compared with the enthalpy of solution of AgF, which is exothermic (–20 kJ mol^{-1}).

The enthalpy change on forming a complex ion with ammonia is exothermic. The value is *just* sufficient to take AgCl into solution, but is not large enough to give the same result with AgI.

Adding the enthalpies

Silver chloride	/kJ mol^{-1}
$\Delta H^{\ominus}_{lat}$	+915
$\Delta H^{\ominus}_{hyd}(Ag^+)$	–472
$\Delta H^{\ominus}_{hyd}(Cl^-)$	–377
$\Delta H^{\ominus}_{sol}(AgCl)$	+66

Silver iodide	/kJ mol^{-1}
$\Delta H^{\ominus}_{lat}$	+889
$\Delta H^{\ominus}_{hyd}(Ag^+)$	–472
$\Delta H^{\ominus}_{hyd}(I^-)$	–305
$\Delta H^{\ominus}_{sol}(AgI)$	+112

Silver fluoride	/kJ mol^{-1}
$\Delta H^{\ominus}_{lat}$	+967
$\Delta H^{\ominus}_{hyd}(Ag^+)$	–472
$\Delta H^{\ominus}_{hyd}(F^-)$	–515
$\Delta H^{\ominus}_{sol}(AgF)$	–20

More about solubility

Ionic chlorides, bromides, and iodides of a given metal tend to have fairly similar solubilities in water, but the solubilities of the fluorides are often anomalous. You have already seen above that the silver halides are all insoluble with the exception of silver fluoride. On the other hand, calcium fluoride is *insoluble*, whereas the other halides of calcium are soluble.

Water of crystallization

The small size and large enthalpy of hydration of the fluoride ion mean that some fluorides retain water molecules as they crystallize. These water molecules are called **water of crystallization**. For example, crystalline potassium fluoride may have the formula $KF.2H_2O$. The other potassium halides crystallize with the formulae KCl, KBr, and KI, i.e. with no associated water of crystallization.

SUMMARY

- The halide ions all have an oxidation number of –1.
- A solution of silver nitrate acidified with dilute nitric acid is used to test for chloride, bromide, and iodide ions. The precipitates that form are white, cream, and yellow respectively. Aqueous ammonia is used to confirm the results.
- The enthalpy of solution for an ionic halide is the sum of the endothermic lattice enthalpy and the exothermic enthalpy of hydration.

PRACTICE

1 Why is nitric acid, and not sulphuric or hydrochloric acid, used to acidify solutions in the silver nitrate test?

2 Why would sodium carbonate not give a precipitate if you used it in the silver nitrate test?

3 Write the chemical formulae of the following substances:

a Strontium bromide
b Silver iodide
c Caesium fluoride
d Copper(II) bromide
e Chromium(III) chloride.

4 Use the following data to predict the relative enthalpies of solution of calcium fluoride and calcium chloride:

Calcium fluoride	/kJ mol^{-1}
$\Delta H^{\ominus}_{lat}$	+2630
$\Delta H^{\ominus}_{hyd}(Ca^{2+})$	–1587
$\Delta H^{\ominus}_{hyd}(F^-)$	–515
Calcium chloride	**/kJ mol^{-1}**
$\Delta H^{\ominus}_{lat}$	+2258
$\Delta H^{\ominus}_{hyd}(Ca^{2+})$	–1587
$\Delta H^{\ominus}_{hyd}(Cl^-)$	–377

PRACTICE EXAM QUESTIONS

1 **a** State and explain the trend in the electronegativity of the halogens down Group VII. [3]

b State and explain the trend in boiling temperatures of the halogens down Group VII. [3]

c The relative molecular masses of bromine, Br_2, and iodine monochloride, ICl, are almost the same, yet their boiling temperatures are quite different. Account for this difference in boiling temperature. [4]
AQA (NEAB) 1999

2 Hydrogen iodide can be prepared by adding water to a mixture of red phosphorus and iodine, and then warming gently.

a Construct the following equations:

i phosphorus and iodine forming phosphorus tri-iodide;

ii phosphorus tri-iodide and water reacting to form hydrogen iodide and phosphoric(III) acid, H_3PO_3. [2]

b What would you expect to see when hydrogen iodide reacts with:

i aqueous silver nitrate, followed by aqueous ammonia;

ii warm concentrated sulphuric acid? [3]
OCR (UCLES) 1998

3 **a** **i** How does concentrated sulphuric acid react with sodium chloride? Write an equation for the reaction. Suggest an appropriate temperature at which it might be carried out.

ii Sodium iodide does not react in this way. Give an equation for the reaction which occurs and explain the difference. [4]

b By reference to the structure and bonding in hydrogen fluoride explain why it is a much weaker acid than the other halogen hydrides. [3]

c Given samples of chloride and iodide salts, how would you distinguish them other than by using concentrated sulphuric acid? [3]

d **i** On the basis of the redox potentials

	$E^{\ominus}$/V
$Cl_2 + 2e^- \rightleftharpoons 2Cl^-$	+1.36
$Br_2 + 2e^- \rightleftharpoons 2Br^-$	+1.09

explain what occurs when chlorine is bubbled into a solution containing bromide ions.

ii What is the industrial significance of this reaction? [5]
EDEXCEL 1996

4 **a** Phosphorus forms trihalides of formula PX_3 for X = F, Cl, Br and I, and pentahalides, PX_5, for X = F, Cl and Br.

i Give the name of the type of bonding present in PCl_3 and draw a dot-and-cross diagram to show it. (Only the outer electrons need be shown.) [2]

ii Draw a diagram to show the shape of the molecule of PCl_3 and briefly explain why the molecule has the shape given. [4]

iii Outline a suitable method for the preparation of PCl_5 in the laboratory. [4]

iv Give the formulae of the species present in solid phosphorus pentachloride. [2]

v Phosphorus pentafluoride is a gas at room temperature and pressure while phosphorus pentachloride is a solid. Suggest an explanation for this difference in physical states. [3]

vi Suggest why phosphorus pentaiodide is unknown. [1]

b PCl_5 can be used as a reagent in preparative organic chemistry as indicated in the scheme below:

$$\underset{\mathbf{R}}{C_3H_7OH} \longrightarrow \underset{\mathbf{S}}{C_2H_5COOH} \xrightarrow[\text{room temperature}]{PCl_5} \mathbf{T}$$

i Give the name and the graphical formula of compound **T**. [2]

ii Give **one** reason why care must be taken when phosphorus pentachloride is added to **S**, and one relevant observation. Write a balanced equation for the reaction. [3]

iii Draw the **two** graphical formulae for the isomeric alcohols of formula C_3H_7OH and state, with a reason, which isomer must be compound **R**. [4]

iv Give the names of the reagents required to convert **R** into **S** in the laboratory and identify the practical steps involved in obtaining a sample of **S**. [3]
AQA (AEB) 1997 *(See also Chapter 25)*

5 **a** Outline the process by which chlorine is manufactured from brine. [2]

b Describe how chlorine reacts with:

i hot, aqueous sodium hydroxide;

ii aqueous potassium bromide;

iii ethene.

In each case, describe what is seen, write an equation and identify the type of reaction occurring. [8]
OCR (UCLES) 1994

6 **a** What oxidation numbers do the elements sodium to phosphorus show in their chlorides? Outline the reactions, if any, of these chlorides with water and relate these reactions to the bonding present. [5]

b Sulphur and chlorine can react together to form S_2Cl_2. When 1.00 g of this sulphur chloride reacted with water, 0.36 g of a yellow precipitate was formed, together with a solution containing a mixture of sulphurous acid, H_2SO_3, and hydrochloric acid.

i Use the above data to deduce the equation for the reaction between S_2Cl_2 and water. [3]

ii What volume of 1.00 mol dm^{-3} sodium hydroxide would be required to neutralize the final solution?
OCR (UCLES) 1994 [2]

7 The major natural source of fluorine is the mineral fluorspar, which is mainly calcium fluoride, CaF_2.

a i Construct a Born–Haber cycle for the formation of CaF_2 from its elements.

ii Use the cycle to calculate the lattice energy of $CaF_2(s)$. Incorporate the following data as well as relevant data given in the *Data Booklet*.

$\Delta H^{\ominus}_{at}(Ca) = +178$ kJ mol^{-1}

$F(g) \rightarrow F^-(g)$; $\Delta H^{\ominus} = -328$ kJ mol^{-1}
(this is the electron affinity of fluorine)

$\Delta H^{\ominus}_f(CaF_2) = -1220$ kJ mol^{-1} [5]

b The first stage in liberating the fluorine from CaF_2 is to grind this compound up and react it with concentrated sulphuric acid. The products are hydrogen fluoride and calcium sulphate, $CaSO_4$.

i Write a balanced equation for this reaction.

ii Calculate the enthalpy change for this reaction, by using the following data in addition to those given above:

$\Delta H^{\ominus}_f(H_2SO_4) = -814$ kJ mol^{-1}

$\Delta H^{\ominus}_f(HF) = -271$ kJ mol^{-1}

$\Delta H^{\ominus}_f(CaSO_4) = -1434$ kJ mol^{-1}

iii Should the reaction be heated or cooled? Give a reason for your answer. [5]
OCR (UCLES) 1994

8 a This question concerns the essential features of the electrolytic process by which sodium hydroxide is manufactured in a diaphragm cell.

i Identify the electrolyte used. [1]

ii Give the equation for the reaction at the anode. [1]

iii Give the equation for the reaction at the cathode. [1]

iv Give the equation for the overall reaction occurring in the cell. [1]

b i How would the electrolytic process be modified in order to manufacture sodium chlorate(I)? [1]

ii Write an equation to show how sodium chlorate(I) is formed. [1]

iii Give one large scale use of sodium chlorate(I). [1]

c Chlorate(I) ions are capable of undergoing **disproportionation**.

i What is meant by the term disproportionation? [1]

ii Write an ionic equation for the disproportionation of sodium chlorate(I). Indicate the oxidation numbers of chlorine in each species in which it occurs. [2]

iii Write two ionic half-equations for this process which illustrate your definition of disproportionation. [4]
EDEXCEL 1998

9 This question concerns the chemistry of halides.

a Describe and explain the trend in thermal stability of the hydrogen halides. [2]

b Halide ions react with concentrated sulphuric acid in different ways.

i Chloride ions react to give hydrogen chloride as the only gaseous product. Iodide ions react to give hydrogen iodide, HI, and other gaseous products. Identify two of these gaseous products.

ii Explain why these halide ions do not react in the same way with concentrated sulphuric acid. [3]

c An aqueous solution containing an unknown halide ion was acidified with nitric acid; aqueous silver nitrate was then added. A cream precipitate was obtained which dissolved in concentrated aqueous ammonia.

Identify the halide ion. [1]

d Aqueous KI was used to obtain I_2 by electrolysis. A current of 1.56 A was passed through the aqueous KI until 3.81 g of I_2 were collected at one electrode.

Calculate how many moles of I_2 were collected. [1]
OCR (UCLES) 1998

10 Commercial bleaches contain sodium hypochlorite (sodium chlorate(I)), which acts as an oxidizing agent. The concentration of sodium hypochlorite in solution can be determined by reaction with acidified potassium iodide solution.

$NaOCl + 2KI + H_2SO_4 \rightarrow I_2 + H_2O + NaCl + K_2SO_4$

The liberated iodine is titrated with standard sodium thiosulphate solution:

a Which species is oxidised in this equation? [1]

b Explain the term **standard** sodium thiosulphate solution. [1]

c Name a suitable indicator for this titration, stating the expected colour change at the end point. [3]

d Write the equation for the reaction between iodine and sodium thiosulphate. [2]

e 15.0 cm^3 of a bleach sample was diluted to 250 cm^3 with de-ionized water. 25.0 cm^3 portions of the solution were treated with excess acidified potassium iodide solution and then titrated with 0.1 M sodium thiosulphate solution. The average titre was found to be 25.2 cm^3. Calculate the concentration of sodium hypochlorite in the original bleach sample. [4]
NICCEA 1998

19 The p-block elements

The p block includes all the elements in Groups III to VIII inclusive in the periodic table. You have already encountered details of some p-block elements earlier in this book: the chapter on 'Trends across a period' included the elements aluminium, silicon, phosphorus, sulphur, and chlorine; and the chapter on 'The halogens' included the elements fluorine, chlorine, bromine, and iodine. The s-block elements are mostly highly reactive metals, while most d-block elements are relatively unreactive metals with high melting points. By comparison, the p-block elements show an enormously wide range of properties, from highly reactive non-metals, to mildly reactive metals, to chemically inert gases. However, there are patterns to be discovered amongst all this variety. As always, electronic structure and bonding dictate both the physical natures of the elements and the chemical properties they exhibit.

OBJECTIVES

- Position of the p block
- The p-block elements studied elsewhere
- The p-block elements in this chapter
- Introductory data

THE P-BLOCK ELEMENTS TO BE STUDIED

The position of the p block in the periodic table is shown below, with the elements studied in this chapter highlighted. You will notice that there are some elements, in addition to the halogens, that will *not* be discussed here in detail. Gallium, indium, and thallium of Group III, arsenic, antimony, and bismuth of Group V, and selenium, tellurium, and polonium of Group VI will be mentioned, but for comparison only. These elements fall outside the scope of this book because they are rare and have unusual properties and uses. Study of their detailed chemical properties is generally only carried out in universities and industrial research departments.

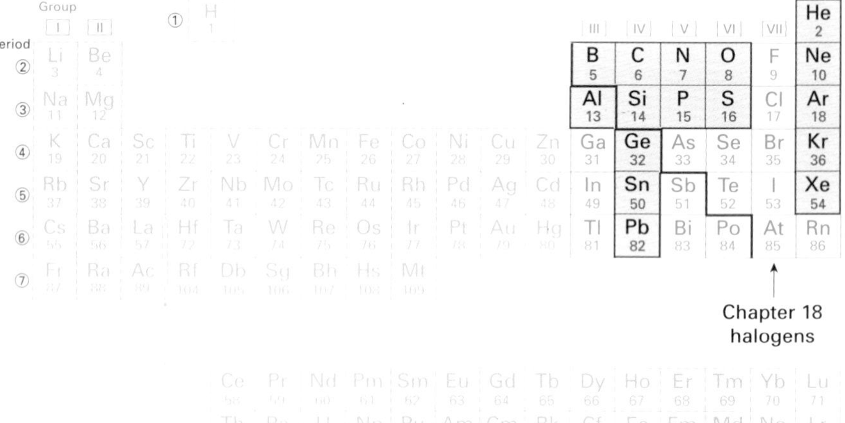

The position of the p block in the periodic table. Elements to be studied in this chapter are highlighted.

Electronic structures

The electronic structure of all p-block elements in Groups III to VII corresponds to the electronic structure of a noble gas together with a full outer s subshell and an incomplete p subshell. For example, the electronic structure of silicon Si (Period 3, Group IV) is $[Ne]3s^2 3p^2$. In addition, the p-block elements of Periods 4 and 5 have a complete inner d subshell, e.g. germanium Ge is $[Ar]3d^{10}4s^2 4p^2$. The p-block elements of Period 6 also have a complete f subshell, e.g. lead Pb is $[Xe]4f^{14}5d^{10}6s^2 6p^2$.

Two points that you should note are that the outermost orbitals are p orbitals, and that the total number of s and p electrons is equal to the group number. For example, the electronic structures of the three elements given above all end with ns^2np^2. Each of these elements is therefore a member of Group IV (i.e. 2 + 2 = 4). The element sulphur S has the electronic structure $[Ne]3s^23p^4$ and is therefore a member of Group VI.

The p-block elements for study in this chapter

- *Group III*: the non-metal boron and the metal aluminium.
- *Group IV*: the non-metal carbon, the metalloids silicon and germanium, and the metals tin and lead.
- *Group V*: the non-metals nitrogen (a gas) and phosphorus (a solid).
- *Group VI*: the non-metals oxygen (a gas) and sulphur (a solid).
- *Group VIII*: the noble gases helium, neon, argon, krypton, and xenon.

> **Metal or non-metal?**
>
> Remember that, within a *group*, metallic character *increases* with increasing atomic number *Z* of the element. In Group IV, carbon (*Z* = 6) is a non-metal, germanium (*Z* = 32) is a metalloid, and lead (*Z* = 82) is a metal.
>
> Within a *period*, metallic character *decreases* with increasing atomic number. In Period 3, aluminium (*Z* = 13) is a metal, silicon (*Z* = 14) is a metalloid, and phosphorus (*Z* = 15) is a non-metal.

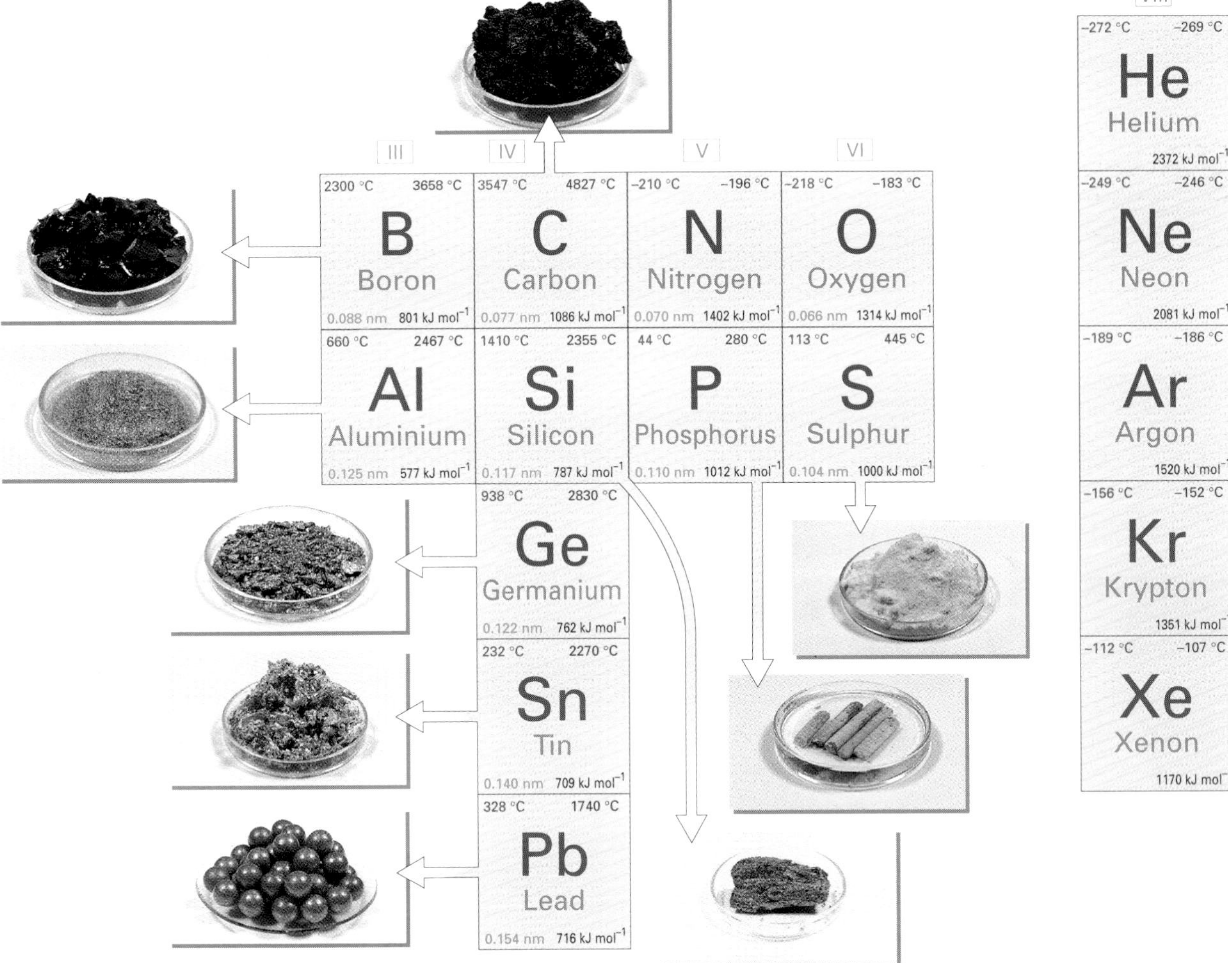

This chart summarizes the major properties of the p-block elements, with particular emphasis on those elements discussed in this chapter. The noble gases, nitrogen, and oxygen are all colourless gases.

SUMMARY

- The p-block elements in Groups III to VII inclusive have incompletely filled p orbitals.
- The elements of Group IV show the greatest change in character, from non-metallic (carbon) to metallic (lead).

PRACTICE

1 By inspecting the electronic structures only, identify the group number for each of the following p-block elements:

a $[He]2s^22p^2$ **b** $[Ne]3s^23p^6$

c $[Ar]3d^{10}4s^24p^4$

2 Sort the p-block elements to be studied under the three headings: 'Metal', 'Metalloid', and 'Non-metal'.

19.2

Group III: boron and aluminium

OBJECTIVES

- Boron and aluminium compared
- Manufacture of aluminium
- Uses of aluminium
- Boron and aluminium oxides compared

Hypothetical ionic boron compounds

The boron B^{3+} ion is extremely small and highly charged. The resulting high charge density would make the B^{3+} ion highly polarizing. In an ionic lattice, B^{3+} ions would withdraw electron density from neighbouring anions, concentrating it between the boron ions and the anions; the bonding becomes covalent.

Solid structures

Boron (melting point T_m = 2300 °C) has a unique covalent structure based on B_{12} molecules shaped as an icosahedron, a 20-sided polyhedron. Aluminium (T_m = 660 °C), on the other hand, has a close-packed metallic structure.

Charles Hall. His chemistry professor convinced him there was a fortune to be made if aluminium could be manufactured cheaply. The price of aluminium fell by a factor of 50 between 1855 and 1890. Earlier, no king nor emperor could afford to build a statue of himself out of aluminium: the first was that of Charles Hall, which stands in Oberlin College, Ohio.

The Group III elements are, in order of increasing atomic number, boron (B), aluminium (Al), gallium (Ga), indium (In), and thallium (Tl). All have a valence-shell electronic structure of ns^2np^1; all, except for boron, are metals. This spread and the following one concentrate mainly on the chemistry of aluminium.

Metallic and non-metallic character

Boron is a hard, brittle solid with poor electrical conductivity. Aluminium is a typical metal, being shiny, malleable, ductile, and with good electrical and thermal conductivities. Both boron and aluminium show an oxidation number of +3. The compounds of boron are all covalent; those of aluminium have considerable covalent character.

The reason that boron does not form ionic compounds is the extremely large value of the standard enthalpy change of formation of the B^{3+} ion ($\Delta H^{\ominus}$ = +6888 kJ mol^{-1}). To form an ionic solid, this endothermic step must be balanced by the exothermic lattice formation enthalpy. Compounds of boron are therefore essentially exclusively covalent.

The manufacture of aluminium

Aluminium is manufactured by the Hall process (or **Hall–Héroult process**). In 1886, Charles Hall in the USA and Paul Héroult in France independently developed the modern process for the extraction of aluminium by electrolysis. (Both were also 23 years old.) Electrolysis is very expensive but is necessary as carbon reduction is not possible, spread 13.13. The process uses an electrolyte of aluminium oxide, produced by purifying the ore *bauxite*, dissolved in molten cryolite (sodium hexafluoroaluminate Na_3AlF_6) at 950 °C. The melting point of aluminium oxide is 2070 °C, far too high for it to be used alone as an electrolyte. An electric current of about 100 000 A is passed through the liquid, heating it. Aluminium is formed by reduction at the cathode, spread 9.2, according to the electrode reaction:

$$Al^{3+}(l) + 3e^- \rightarrow Al(l)$$

Oxide ions are oxidized to oxygen at the anode: $2O^{2-}(l) \rightarrow O_2(g) + 4e^-$. The carbon anode is eroded as its surface is attacked by the oxygen.

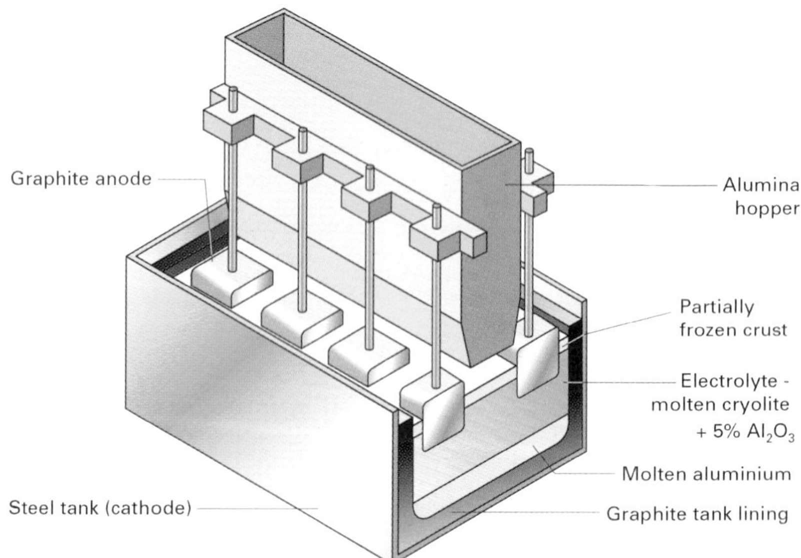

The Hall cell for the industrial extraction of aluminium.

Reactions of the elements

Boron is relatively inert, because of the short and strong B—B bonds. It ignites above 700 °C in air, forming the oxide B_2O_3 and the nitride BN. It does not react with dilute acids or aqueous bases, but combines at high temperatures with chlorine to form boron trichloride BCl_3.

The chemistry of aluminium is much more interesting.

- Aluminium burns when heated in oxygen

$$4Al(s) + 3O_2(g) \rightarrow 2Al_2O_3(s)$$

Aluminium is a strong reductant (standard electrode potential $E^\ominus = -1.66\,V$; compare with iron $E^\ominus = -0.44\,V$). However, its apparent reactivity is lower than that expected from these data. Aluminium does indeed react with air and water when exposed, but the reaction stops at the metal surface. The transparent aluminium oxide coat formed by this reaction is very thin indeed, about 10 nm (equivalent to a few atoms), but this layer protects the metal from further reaction. Note that an oxide layer does not always give protection. The rust that forms on iron is also an oxide, but rusting is a *corrosive* process, not a protective one.

- Aluminium reacts with acids and aqueous bases

Cleaned aluminium reacts with *acids* to give hydrogen and a solution of a salt:

$$2Al(s) + 6HCl(aq) \rightarrow 2AlCl_3(aq) + 3H_2(g)$$

It also reacts with concentrated aqueous *bases* to give an aqueous aluminate salt:

$$2Al(s) + 2NaOH(aq) + 6H_2O(l) \rightarrow 2NaAl(OH)_4(aq) + 3H_2(g)$$

- Aluminium combines directly with chlorine when heated (spread 17.7)

$$2Al(s) + 3Cl_2(g) \rightarrow 2AlCl_3(s)$$

Aluminium chloride has predominantly covalent character, and will be discussed further in the next spread.

Oxide character

Boron oxide B_2O_3 is *acidic*, as you would expect for an oxide of a non-metal. It reacts readily with water to form boric acid (a weak acid, $pK_{a1} = 9.2$):

$$B_2O_3(s) + 3H_2O(l) \rightarrow 2H_3BO_3(aq)$$

Aluminium oxide is *amphoteric*; see spread 17.5. It is insoluble in water but reacts with acids and bases:

in acids $\quad Al_2O_3(s) + 6H^+(aq) \rightarrow 2Al^{3+}(aq) + 3H_2O(l)$

in bases $\quad Al_2O_3(s) + 3H_2O(l) + 2OH^-(aq) \rightarrow 2[Al(OH)_4]^-(aq)$

The $[Al(OH)_4]^-$ ion is called the tetrahydroxoaluminate ion (usually abbreviated to 'aluminate ion').

SUMMARY

- All Group III elements have the valence-shell electronic structure ns^2np^1.
- All Group III elements, with the exception of boron, are metals.
- The compounds of boron are covalent; the compounds of aluminium are on the borderline between ionic and covalent, but AlF_3 and Al_2O_3 are predominantly ionic.
- Boron oxide is acidic; aluminium oxide is amphoteric.

Aluminium in the nineteenth century

In the nineteenth century, aluminium was rare and highly prized. At the Paris Exposition of 1855, it was exhibited next to the crown jewels. At state banquets, Emperor Napoleon III gave his favoured guests aluminium, rather than gold, cutlery. The Washington Monument was topped with aluminium in 1885.

Aluminium powder reacts vigorously with oxygen.

Aluminium alloys (e.g. with copper, zinc, magnesium, and silicon) are strong and corrosion-resistant. Unlike iron, it is maintenance-free. Aluminium's density is about one-third that of iron, which explains its extensive use in the Apollo Lunar Excursion Module (LEM). Other uses include aircraft, window frames, overhead electricity cables, and soft drink cans.

PRACTICE

1 Write a balanced chemical equation for each of the following reactions:
   - **a** The reduction of boron oxide by magnesium to form boron.
   - **b** The reduction of boron tribromide by hydrogen to form boron.
   - **c** Reacting aluminium metal with sulphuric acid.
   - **d** Precipitating aluminium hydroxide from a solution of aluminium sulphate.
   - **e** Heating aluminium hydroxide to form aluminium oxide.
   - **f** Reacting aluminium oxide with sulphuric acid.

2 Explain why boron
   - **a** is extremely hard, and
   - **b** has a high melting point (above 2000 °C).

3 Explain why sodium chloride is ionic whereas aluminium chloride is on the borderline between ionic and covalent.

19.3

Group III: the acidity of aluminium compounds

OBJECTIVES

- Acidic nature of $Al^{3+}(aq)$
- Reactions with anions
- Aluminium and boron halides as Lewis acids

The aluminium ion Al^{3+} has a particularly high charge density due to its triple positive charge and small size. As a result, this ion has properties in solution which are different from those of 'well-behaved' ions such as Na^+ and Mg^{2+}. The symbol $Al^{3+}(aq)$ has a different meaning to the symbols $Na^+(aq)$ and $Mg^{2+}(aq)$. A further unusual property of aluminium (and boron) is electron deficiency in simple covalent compounds such as $AlCl_3$: the presence of just six electrons in the valence shell (rather than the usual eight) allows them to accept lone pairs from other atoms. Boron and aluminium halides are thus able to act as Lewis acids.

Aluminium chloride

The halides of aluminium may be prepared by direct combination of the elements on heating. They are borderline ionic/covalent with the exception of aluminium fluoride, which contains the Al^{3+} ion. Aluminium chloride is a solid that **sublimes** (changes directly from solid to gas) at 180 °C, to produce an equilibrium mixture of $AlCl_3$ and Al_2Cl_6 (for comparison, NaCl *melts* at T_m = 801 °C and $MgCl_2$ at T_m = 714 °C). The formation of the dimer Al_2Cl_6 is dealt with in spread 17.7.

With the exception of AlF_3, the anhydrous halides are hydrolysed by water:

$$Al_2Cl_6(s) + 6H_2O(l) \rightarrow 2Al(OH)_3(s) + 6HCl(g)$$

The solution equilibria of aluminium

The sodium ion Na^+, the magnesium ion Mg^{2+}, and the aluminium ion Al^{3+} all have 10 electrons. Each has the electronic structure $1s^22s^22p^6$. The aqueous sodium and magnesium ions, $Na^+(aq)$ and $Mg^{2+}(aq)$, consist of the metal ion surrounded by a number of water molecules making up a layer called the 'hydration sphere'. Water molecules are polar and the δ– oxygen atoms are attracted towards the positively charged metal ions.

An aluminium ion Al^{3+} has a much greater charge density than either Mg^{2+} or Na^+ because it is smaller and more highly charged. The high charge density makes the aluminium ion more strongly polarizing than sodium or magnesium ions. The aluminium ion attracts electron density from the lone pairs on the oxygen atoms of water molecules into its empty 3s, 3p, and 3d orbitals. Each aluminium ion becomes symmetrically surrounded by six water molecules, forming a complex ion (see the next chapter) with the formula $[Al(H_2O)_6]^{3+}$. Note that, although the water molecules are written as H_2O in this formula, bond formation is between the *oxygen* atom and the central aluminium ion.

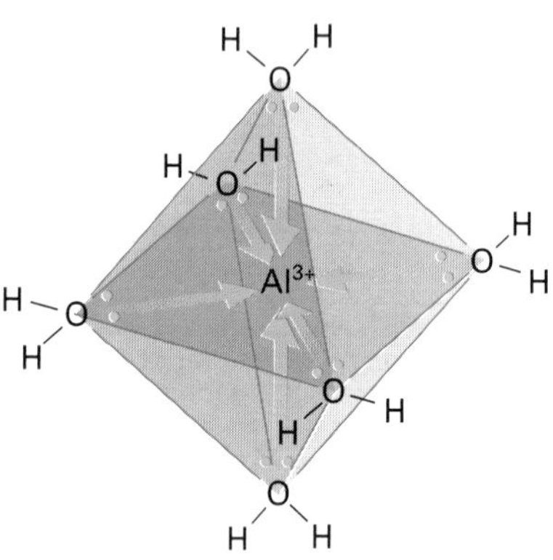

The structure of the $[Al(H_2O)_6]^{3+}$ complex ion. The six water molecules are referred to as ligands. They are evenly distributed about the central aluminium ion, giving the complex octahedral symmetry.

The acidic character of $Al^{3+}(aq)$

The high charge density of the central aluminium ion withdraws electron density from the O—H bonds in the water molecules, so weakening them. The hydrated complex ion is therefore likely to lose a proton and behave as an acid. The aluminium ion can act as a Brønsted acid (by donating a proton to a water molecule); for details see the chapter on 'Acid–base equilibrium'. As a result aqueous solutions of aluminium ions are about as acidic as aqueous solutions of ethanoic acid.

The first equilibrium established is:

$$[Al(H_2O)_6]^{3+}(aq) + H_2O(l) \rightleftharpoons H_3O^+(aq) + [Al(H_2O)_5OH]^{2+}(aq)$$

The complex ion on the right-hand side has a hydroxo ligand in addition to five water ligands. It can lose a further proton and form a complex ion with *two* hydroxo ligands:

$$[Al(H_2O)_5OH]^{2+}(aq) + H_2O(l) \rightleftharpoons H_3O^+(aq) + [Al(H_2O)_4(OH)_2]^+(aq)$$

This process occurs a third time; the difference is that the complex with three hydroxo ligands is uncharged and precipitates out of the solution:

$$[Al(H_2O)_4(OH)_2]^+(aq) + H_2O(l) \rightleftharpoons H_3O^+(aq) + Al(H_2O)_3(OH)_3(s)$$

All these equilibria can be shifted towards the products by adding a base to remove the aqueous hydrogen ions H_3O^+. Adding a small quantity of a base (e.g. aqueous sodium hydroxide) to aqueous aluminium ions therefore causes the precipitation of hydrated aluminium hydroxide $Al(OH)_3$. Further reaction can be achieved by adding more base. The solid hydroxide 'redissolves' (showing amphoteric behaviour):

$$Al(OH)_3(s) + OH^-(aq) \rightarrow [Al(OH)_4]^-(aq)$$

Note that this ion is *tetrahedral* in shape because four OH^- ligands surround the central Al^{3+} ion.

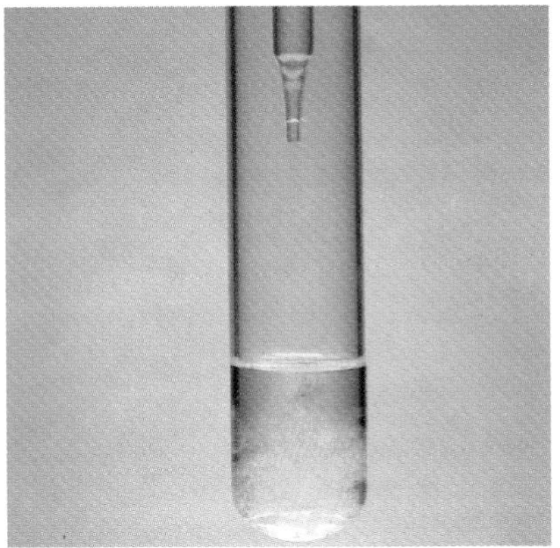

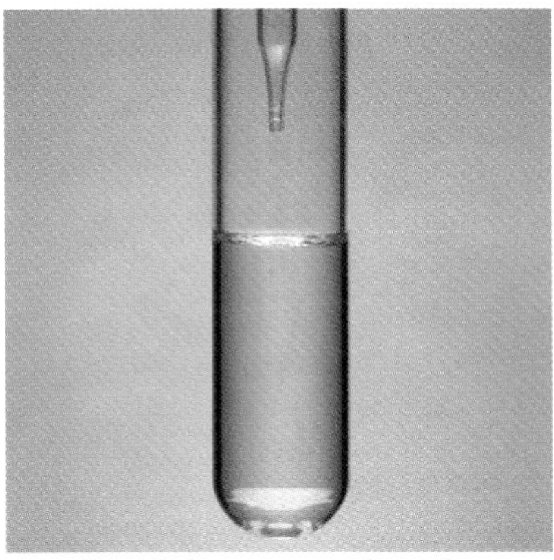

(a) Adding a small quantity of aqueous sodium hydroxide to aqueous aluminium ions causes a white precipitate of aluminium hydroxide $Al(OH)_3$. (b) Adding excess aqueous sodium hydroxide causes the precipitate to 'redissolve'.

Adding solid sodium carbonate to aqueous aluminium chloride causes the rapid release of carbon dioxide gas and precipitation of aluminium hydroxide. See spread 20.8 for more detail on the similar reaction of iron(III) ions and sodium carbonate. The process also occurs with anions from other weak acids, such as sulphide ion S^{2-} or sulphite ion SO_3^{2-}.

Further Lewis acid behaviour

The halides of boron and aluminium act as Lewis acids (spread 12.12) by accepting lone pairs. This behaviour is to be expected because the valence shells of the central atoms in $AlCl_3$ and BF_3, for example, contain just six electrons. During the reaction as a Lewis acid, the central atom gains a share in a further two electrons to complete the octet, as, for example, in the reaction between boron trifluoride BF_3 (Lewis acid) and ammonia NH_3 (Lewis base) to form the adduct $H_3N{:}\!\rightarrow BF_3$; see spread 12.12.

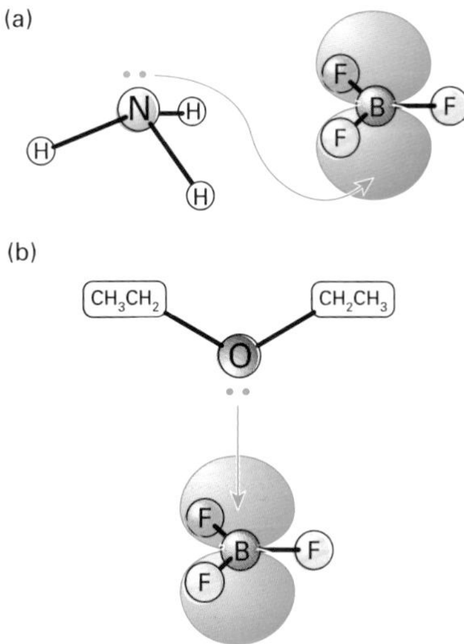

Boron trifluoride BF_3 is electron-deficient. It acts as a Lewis acid by accepting lone pairs from (a) ammonia NH_3 or (b) ethoxyethane $CH_3CH_2—O—CH_2CH_3$.

SUMMARY

- The Al^{3+} ion has a very high charge density; it is highly polarizing.
- The aqueous Al^{3+} ion, usually written as $Al^{3+}(aq)$, exists as a complex ion with the formula $[Al(H_2O)_6]^{3+}$.
- Aqueous aluminium salts are acidic; the ion $[Al(H_2O)_6]^{3+}$ protonates water molecules.
- Boron and aluminium halides have an incomplete octet. They can act as Lewis acids by accepting lone pairs from Lewis bases, thus forming adducts.

PRACTICE

1 Draw the structures of each of the following species:
  a $Al(OH)_3{\cdot}3H_2O$
  b $[Al(OH)_4]^-$
  c The adduct formed between BCl_3 and NH_3.

2 Describe what you would see when aqueous sodium hydroxide is slowly added with shaking to a solution of aluminium sulphate. In your answer, include balanced chemical equations and details of complex ion structure.

3 Draw Lewis structures to show the arrangement of valence electrons in boric acid and in the borate anion. Suggest shapes for these species.

4 Explain how the hydration sphere of water molecules around the aqueous sodium ion $Na^+(aq)$ differs from that in the aqueous aluminium ion $Al^{3+}(aq)$.

19.4 Group IV: carbon to lead

OBJECTIVES

- The elements
- Melting point and conductivity trends
- 'Buckyballs'

The Group IV elements are, in order of increasing atomic number, carbon (C), silicon (Si), germanium (Ge), tin (Sn), and lead (Pb). Carbon is a non-metal, silicon and germanium are metalloids, and tin and lead are metals. All have a valence-shell electronic structure of ns^2np^2. Of all the groups in the periodic table, Group IV shows the clearest trend from non-metallic to metallic character with increasing atomic number.

Crystalline tin results when molten tin cools slowly. Tin is a typical metal, consisting of ions arranged in a metallic lattice bonded by delocalized valence electrons.

Structures of the elements

The physical structures of the elements of Group IV are suggested by their melting points and electrical conductivities. The structures of the carbon allotropes, diamond and graphite, are described in the chapter on 'Solids'. Diamond has a giant covalent structure in which each atom is linked to four other atoms by single covalent bonds. Graphite has a layered giant covalent structure. Such structures are associated with very high melting points. The electrical conductivity of diamond is very low, confirming the lack of delocalized electrons. Graphite has an electrical conductivity 10^{15} times greater, owing to the presence of delocalized valence electrons; see spread 6.4.

Silicon and germanium have similar structures to diamond. However, their electrical conductivities are 10^{14} (Si) and 10^{11} (Ge) times greater than that of diamond. These elements are *semiconductors*: they have conductivities intermediate between those of metals and those of non-metals, in keeping with their classification as metalloids. A small proportion of the localized bonding electrons break free from the covalent bonds and delocalize throughout the solid structure.

Tin and lead are metals, as confirmed by their high electrical conductivities.

Melting point and electrical conductivity data for the Group IV elements.

Element	Melting point /K	Electrical conductivity /S m^{-1}
C*	3800	7×10^4
C†	3820	1×10^{-11}
Si	1683	1×10^3
Ge	1211	2.2
Sn	505	9×10^6
Pb	601	5×10^6

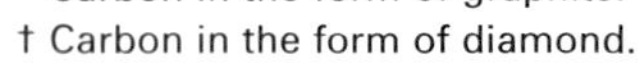

* Carbon in the form of graphite.
† Carbon in the form of diamond.

The story of fullerite – the third carbon allotrope

Since the early 1970s, Harry Kroto of Sussex University had been fascinated by the unsolved problem of the 'diffuse interstellar bands'. This is a set of black absorption bands seen in the visible spectrum of the interstellar medium (the stuff between the stars!) obtained using an optical telescope. These absorption features had puzzled astronomers for more than six decades. Kroto's research interests in long-chain carbon molecules with multiple bonds made him hope that they would provide the long-awaited answer. In attempting to solve this problem, in the 1980s he made by chance an even greater discovery.

In their laboratories at Rice University in Texas, Bob Curl and Rick Smalley had the equipment needed to bombard targets with very high-energy lasers. Kroto tried to persuade them to experiment with carbon, rather than silicon, which was their preferred target at the time. Eighteen months after the three first collaborated, Curl and Smalley invited Kroto to visit Texas to observe their experiments with carbon.

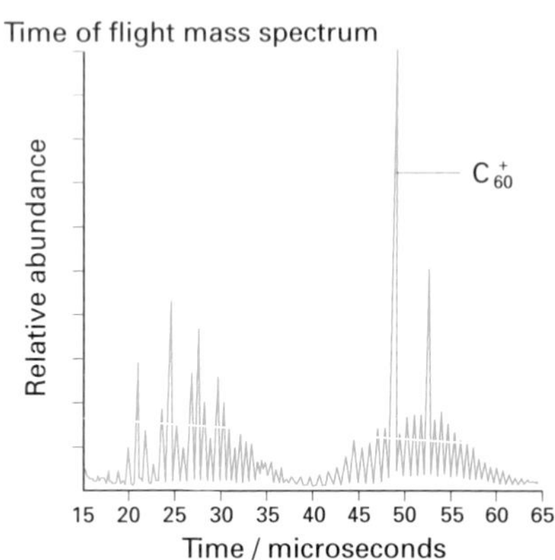

Mass spectrum showing the peak corresponding to C_{60}.

Their apparatus enabled any species created by the impact of the laser beam on the target to be analysed by mass spectrometry (see the chapters on 'Masses of atoms…' and 'Techniques of … identification'). The illustration to the left shows the mass spectrum recorded on 4 September 1985. The signal of mass 720 units was exceptionally strong, suggesting a stable molecule of formula C_{60}. The problem was to determine the structure of such a molecule.

Just five days later the team members were celebrating the end of their collaboration and the return of Kroto to England. Over dinner, they had bounced around ideas about C_{60}, suggesting that it was some sort of closed structure. Kroto kept thinking of the geodesic dome designed by the architect Buckminster Fuller for the *EXPO '67* exhibition in Montreal. Buckminster Fuller's dome was a closed structure made almost exclusively of hexagons, with just a few pentagons to enable it to close into a spherical dome. Exactly how many carbon atoms arranged in hexagons and pentagons would be able to curve into a sphere? After consulting the models, they realized that the number of pentagons needed was 12 and the number of carbon atoms was exactly 60.

(a) The architectural form known as a geodesic dome, composed of interlocking hexagons and pentagons. (b) The structure of C_{60}: note the structural similarity to the geodesic dome. The model is held by Harry Kroto.

Physical data

Modern data books now include data on the C_{60} carbon allotrope:

electrical conductivity	1.7×10^{-6} S m^{-1}
density	1.72 g cm^{-3}

The structure onto which the team had stumbled during their meal was much more familiar than they had suspected at first. It has exactly the same shape as a football with its white (hexagonal) and black (pentagonal) patches! Kroto, Curl, and Smalley were sure that they had found the answer to the structure: C_{60} is a geodesic sphere shaped like a football. However, they had no proof for their structure, and had to wait five long years for the confirmation. Kroto named C_{60} **buckminsterfullerene** in honour of Buckminster Fuller's architectural designs.

In the end, the team was almost beaten to the final proof of the structure by Wolfgang Krätschmer and Donald Huffman and their co-workers. This group had been studying soot produced by applying an electric arc to sticks of graphite. They managed to isolate in 1990 a red solution of C_{60} in benzene. They evaporated the solution to produce crystals of a solid they called **fullerite**. They examined fullerite using X-ray diffraction and confirmed the spherical structure. Later in the same year, Kroto's team provided the final proof by observing a single-line ^{13}C NMR spectrum (see the chapter on 'Spectroscopy and structure'), which showed that all the carbon atoms are in identical environments in C_{60}.

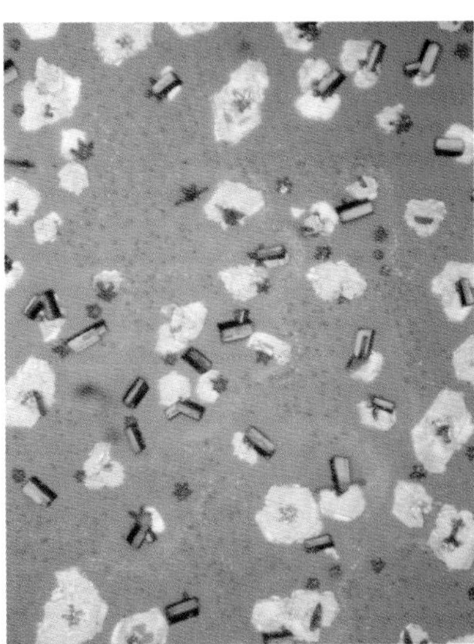

Crystals of fullerite.

Carbon cycle

The **carbon cycle** is a sequence of events in the environment by which carbon, in the form of carbon dioxide, is removed from the atmosphere and incorporated into carbon compounds during photosynthesis (see the chapter on 'Biochemistry'). Subsequently this carbon is returned to the atmosphere as a by-product of respiration. Note also that the oceans can dissolve carbon dioxide, as discussed in the next spread.

'Buckyballs'

There is a whole family of spherical carbon molecules, of which C_{60} is the most stable. The similarity of these molecules to a football earned them the familiar name of 'buckyballs'. They may be isolated from the soot resulting from burning paraffin wax in a Bunsen flame. It is hoped that buckyballs will have commercial applications as lubricants and as superconductors.

SUMMARY

- Carbon is a non-metal; silicon and germanium are metalloids; tin and lead are metals.
- Graphite and diamond are two allotropes of carbon; they have giant covalent structures.
- Carbon in the form of graphite is the only non-metallic element classed as an electrical conductor.
- Fullerite C_{60}, the solid form of buckminsterfullerene, is a third allotropic form of carbon.

The ultimate recognition

For their discovery of buckminsterfullerene, Kroto, Curl, and Smalley were awarded the 1996 Nobel prize for chemistry.

19.5

GROUP IV: THE CHEMISTRY OF THE ELEMENTS – 1

OBJECTIVES

- Oxidation numbers
- Oxide character
- Silicates and carbonates

The oxidation numbers exhibited by Group IV elements in their compounds. The more stable oxidation number is in bold.

Element	Oxidation number
C	+2, **+4**
Si	**+4**
Ge	**+4**
Sn	+2, **+4**
Pb	**+2**, +4

The 'inert pair effect'

The increase in stability of the lower oxidation number with increasing atomic number is sometimes called the 'inert pair effect'.

Carbon monoxide

This gas is prepared in the laboratory by using warm concentrated sulphuric acid to dehydrate methanoic acid HCOOH:

$HCOOH(l) \rightarrow H_2O(l) + CO(g)$

Carbon monoxide burns with a pale blue flame to form carbon dioxide:

$2CO(g) + O_2(g) \rightarrow 2CO_2(g)$

Carbon monoxide's most notorious characteristic is its ability to bind tightly to haemoglobin in the blood. In this way it prevents haemoglobin from carrying oxygen around the body. Carbon monoxide gas forms as the result of incomplete combustion in petrol engines, and also in poorly ventilated gas fires, causing preventable deaths.

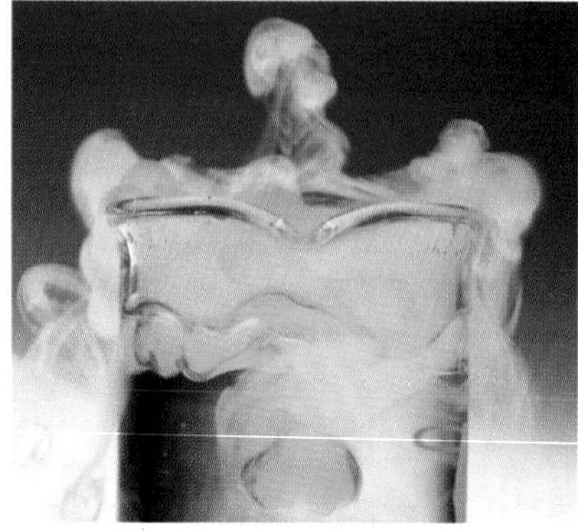

Solid carbon dioxide dissolves to produce some weak carbonic acid, $CO_2(g) + H_2O(l) \rightleftharpoons H_2CO_3(aq)$ Hence rainwater is naturally acidic.

The chemistry of the elements carbon to lead shows a clear trend from non-metallic to metallic properties. Consequently, the character of the bonding in the corresponding compounds shows a trend from covalent to ionic. Predominantly covalent bonds form when the element shares its four valence electrons ns^2np^2 to form four covalent bonds, as in silicon dioxide SiO_2. Ionic bonds form when the element loses the two outer p electrons to become a doubly charged ion M^{2+}, as, for example, in lead(II) nitrate $Pb(NO_3)_2$. As you might expect, the high values of ionization energy involved mean that ionic M^{4+} compounds are uncommon.

Oxidation numbers

The most common oxidation number in Group IV is +4, as in the compounds carbon dioxide CO_2, silicon tetrachloride $SiCl_4$, and lead(IV) oxide PbO_2. The state with an oxidation number of +2 becomes increasingly stable with increasing atomic number. For example, when the elements are heated with oxygen, they form the oxides CO_2, SiO_2, GeO_2, SnO_2, and PbO. Note that the elements have an oxidation number of +4 in all these oxides except lead(II) oxide PbO.

In carbon monoxide CO, carbon exhibits an oxidation number of +2 and thus stands outside the overall trend. This covalent compound is important as a reductant in industry, for example in the blast furnace where it reduces iron(III) oxide to iron (see next chapter). Tin and lead also form halides in which their oxidation number is +2. These compounds are predominantly ionic, containing the Sn^{2+} and Pb^{2+} ions.

Oxide character

As a general rule, the oxides of non-metals are acidic, the oxides of metalloids are usually amphoteric, and the oxides of most metals are basic, although some are amphoteric. As a result of the Group IV trend from non-metal to metal down the group, you might expect the oxides to become less acidic (i.e. more basic) as the atomic number of the element increases. Such a steady trend is *not* encountered in practice, because of the presence of more than one oxidation state for tin and lead.

Carbon dioxide CO_2 is an acidic gas. It dissolves in water to give an acidic solution (pH ≈ 5, as shown below left by the colour of universal indicator):

$$CO_2(g) + H_2O(l) \rightleftharpoons H_2CO_3(aq)$$
$$H_2CO_3(aq) + H_2O(l) \rightleftharpoons H_3O^+(aq) + HCO_3^-(aq)$$

It neutralizes bases to give carbonate salts:

$$CO_2(g) + 2NaOH(aq) \rightarrow Na_2CO_3(aq) + H_2O(l)$$

Silicon dioxide SiO_2 is also acidic, but it is a solid with a high melting point (1610 °C). Silicon dioxide reacts with molten bases to give silicates (in the same manner that carbon dioxide gives carbonates):

$$SiO_2(s) + 2NaOH(l) \rightarrow Na_2SiO_3(l) + H_2O(g)$$

Lead(II) oxide PbO is amphoteric; it reacts both with bases and with acids. Lead(II) oxide reacts with nitric acid as follows:

$$PbO(s) + 2HNO_3(aq) \rightarrow Pb(NO_3)_2(aq) + H_2O(l)$$

The oxides of lead

There are three oxides of lead: lead(II) oxide PbO,which is a yellow solid used to make lead glass which sparkles brilliantly, lead(IV) oxide PbO_2, which is a brown solid used in the lead–acid battery, and 'red lead' Pb_3O_4, which is named after its characteristic colour. Red lead is a mixed oxide, an array of oxide ions with two Pb^{2+} ions and one Pb^{4+} ion for each set of four O^{2-} ions. When red lead reacts with nitric acid, it turns to a brown suspension because PbO is more basic than PbO_2, hence leaving the brown solid behind.

The structures of CO_2 and SiO_2

The dramatically different physical properties of carbon dioxide and silicon dioxide are due to the different bonding in the two compounds. Carbon dioxide is a gas composed of individual small CO_2 molecules with carbon–oxygen double bonds. Silicon dioxide is a solid with a giant covalent structure similar to that of diamond; see spread 6.3.

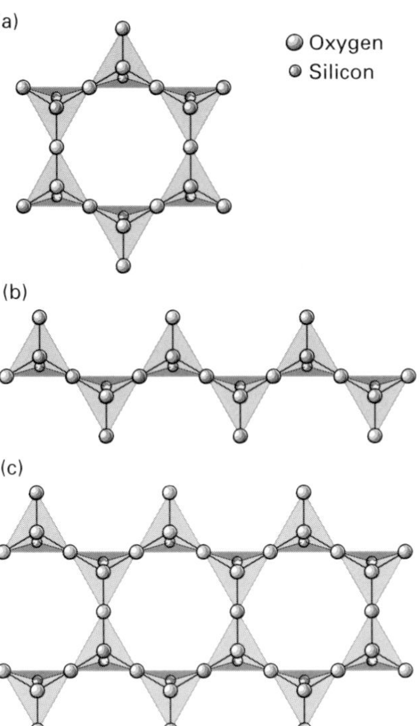

Silicate structures: (a) ring (b) single chain (c) double chain.

Silicates and carbonates

Silicates account for over 90% of the rocks in the Earth's crust. The difference between the structures of silicates and carbonates mirrors the difference described above between the structure of silicon dioxide and carbon dioxide. Carbonates contain the carbonate ion, CO_3^{2-}, which has a double bond, delocalized between the three oxygen atoms and the carbon atom. The very important compound calcium carbonate was discussed in the chapter on 'The s-block elements'. Silicates are based instead on SiO_4 tetrahedra, with silicon–oxygen *single* bonds, linked together by sharing oxygen atoms at their vertices.

This sharing can result in rings, chains, double chains, sheets, and 3D networks. **Beryl** ($Be_3Al_2Si_6O_{18}$) is an example of a silicate containing a six-membered ring. Sodium silicate Na_2SiO_3 forms single-stranded chains; the notorious fibrous silicate **asbestos** has double chains. Sheet silicates are widely abundant and include kaolinite, micas, and talc. The most abundant of all minerals are **feldspars**, which are complex mixtures of 3D network **aluminosilicates** (silicates also containing aluminium); the alkali feldspars have the formula $Na_xK_{1-x}AlSi_3O_8$.

Clay minerals

Clays are layered aluminosilicates. Clays are the raw materials for some of our most ancient artefacts, such as pottery and bricks. An approximate equation describing the weathering of a potassium feldspar into a clay by the action of water and atmospheric carbon dioxide is:

$$2KAlSi_3O_8 + CO_2 + 2H_2O = K_2CO_3 + 4SiO_2 + Al_2Si_2O_5(OH)_4$$

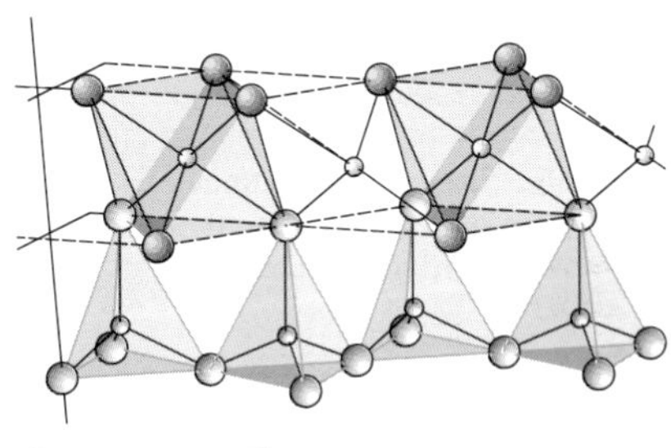

The structure of kaolinite.

The structure of clay minerals is built up from two units: SiO_4 tetrahedra and AlO_6 octahedra. One layer of SiO_4 tetrahedra sharing corners with one layer of AlO_6 octahedra forms the 1:1 mineral **kaolinite** (china clay). The idealized composition of kaolinite is $Al_2Si_2O_5(OH)_4$.

Two layers of SiO_4 tetrahedra sharing corners with one layer of AlO_6 octahedra forms the 2:1 mineral **pyrophyllite**. The idealized composition of pyrophyllite is $Al_2Si_4O_{10}(OH)_2$. A closely related mineral in which two aluminiums are replaced by three magnesiums is talc $Mg_3Si_4O_{10}(OH)_2$. The layers are electrically neutral, and there are therefore only weak forces between the layers. Talc has the lowest value of 1 on the Mohs scale of hardness (diamond having the other extreme value of 10).

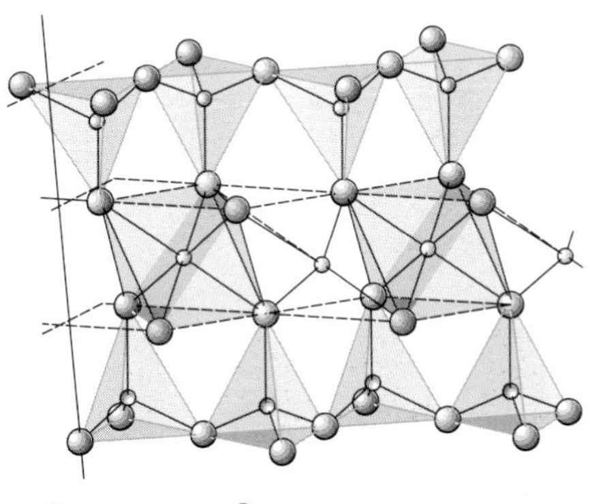

The structure of pyrophyllite.

Replacement of one quarter of the silicons in pyrophyllite with aluminium creates negatively-charged layers, which can be balanced with positive ions (cations) such as potassium, to form muscovite (white mica) $KAl_3Si_3O_{10}(OH)_2$. This replacement, which depends ultimately on charge balance, is not specific for potassium ion, so such minerals allow cation exchange, where one cation takes the place of another. Plants get their cationic nutrients, such as iron(III), in a similar way from the soil.

SUMMARY

- The trend down the group is from non-metallic to metallic character.
- The most common oxidation number (except for lead) is +4.
- Tin and lead form ionic compounds containing Sn^{2+} and Pb^{2+} ions (i.e. oxidation number +2). Pb(II) is the stable oxidation state for lead.

PRACTICE

1 Explain why ionic compounds of Group IV containing M^{4+} ions are uncommon.

OBJECTIVES

- Structure and bonding in the tetrahalides
- Hydrolysis of the tetrachlorides
- Environmental issues

GROUP IV: THE CHEMISTRY OF THE ELEMENTS – 2

The chemistry of the Group IV elements carbon to lead shows a clear trend from non-metallic to metallic properties down the group. Where oxidation numbers of +2 and +4 are available, compounds in which the element has oxidation number +2 tend to be predominantly ionic, and those in which the element has oxidation number +4 tend to be predominantly covalent in character. This spread concentrates particularly on the chemistry of the chlorides of the Group IV elements.

The Group IV tetrachlorides.

Tetra-chloride	State at 25 °C and 1 bar	Boiling point/°C
CCl_4	liquid	77
$SiCl_4$	liquid	58
$GeCl_4$	liquid	87
$SnCl_4$	liquid	114
$PbCl_4$	liquid	decomp

The tetrahalides in general

All the tetrahalides of the Group IV elements are known, with the exception of the bromide and iodide of lead. Lead(IV) is an oxidant, and bromides and iodides are readily oxidized. Lead(IV) fluoride has appreciable ionic character, but lead(IV) chloride is predominantly covalent.

Structure and bonding in the tetrahalides

The predominant oxidation number for the elements carbon to tin is +4. However, remember that the stability of the state with oxidation number +2 increases down the group. Thermodynamically stable tin(II) compounds are available (but they are strong reductants), and the more stable state for lead is Pb(II). The tetrahalides all contain the Group IV element with oxidation number +4. Formulae, physical state, and boiling point data are summarized on the left.

The relatively low boiling points suggest that the bonding character of these compounds is predominantly covalent. This view is confirmed by their poor electrical conductivity in the liquid state and their ability to dissolve in non-polar (organic) solvents. Each of these tetrachlorides exists as discrete molecules of general formula ECl_4. The central Group IV element is attached to four chlorine atoms by four single covalent bonds. The shape of the molecule is tetrahedral.

Hydrolysis of the tetrachlorides

Tetrachloromethane CCl_4 (previously called carbon tetrachloride) is immiscible with water and does not react with it. The C—Cl bond is strong (average bond enthalpy = 338 kJ mol^{-1}). However, the hydrolysis reaction

$$CCl_4(l) + 2H_2O(l) \rightarrow CO_2(g) + 4HCl(aq)$$

is favoured thermodynamically and will occur, given sufficient time (many years). This reaction proceeds at an extraordinarily slow rate.

The Si—Cl bond in silicon tetrachloride $SiCl_4$ is far more polar than the C—Cl bond in CCl_4; it is also longer and weaker. As a result, silicon tetrachloride gives off fumes in moist air and is hydrolysed rapidly by water:

$$SiCl_4(l) + 2H_2O(l) \rightarrow SiO_2(s) + 4HCl(aq)$$

The products of the reaction are hydrogen chloride fumes and a white precipitate of hydrated silicon dioxide.

The ease of hydrolysis decreases in the order Si > Ge > Sn >Pb as metallic character increases down the group.

Because silicon has 3d orbitals close enough in energy to the occupied 3p orbitals, (a) the incoming water molecule can form a bond with the silicon before *the existing bonds are broken (b). Such a reaction mechanism is not possible for carbon because the 3d orbitals are too far away in energy from its 2p orbitals. Cyan highlights changes in an individual step.*

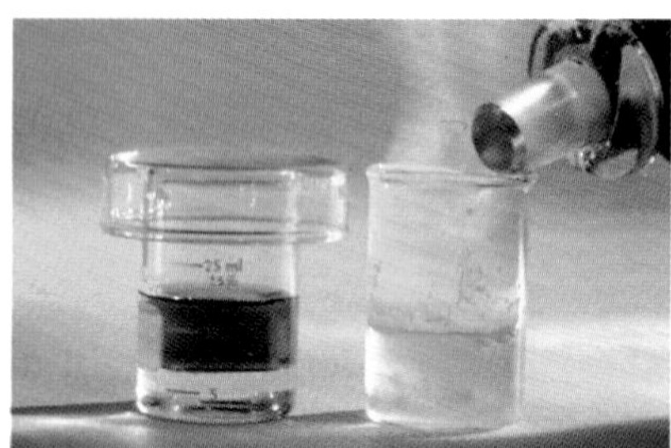

(a) Tetrachloromethane reacts extraordinarily slowly with water. (b) Silicon tetrachloride is rapidly hydrolysed by water. The hydrogen chloride gas released forms white fumes with the top of a bottle of concentrated aqueous ammonia. Some HCl dissolves in water, turning the indicator yellow.

Comparing tin and lead

The most stable oxidation number for tin is +4 and that for lead is +2. The increased stability of the lower oxidation state for lead is illustrated by lead(IV) chloride. It has a tendency to decompose near room temperature to form the more stable lower oxidation state:

$$PbCl_4(l) \rightarrow PbCl_2(s) + Cl_2(g)$$

This tendency is also illustrated when the 2+ ions of tin and lead react with acidified potassium dichromate(VI). Tin(II) ions are oxidized by the dichromate(VI) ions, and the colour changes from orange ($Cr_2O_7^{2-}$ ions) to green (Cr^{3+} ions). Lead(II) ions are not oxidized by dichromate(VI). Instead, a yellow precipitate of lead(II) chromate(VI) $PbCrO_4$ forms.

Heavy metals and the environment

Lead is called a 'heavy metal' because it has a high relative atomic mass. Other common heavy metals are cadmium and mercury. Lead in particular causes problems in the environment because it is a cumulative poison that is poorly excreted by humans. Small ingested quantities accumulate in the body over a period of years, ultimately causing damage to the central nervous system.

Because lead is malleable and ductile, it has been used for water pipes for centuries. In hard water areas, an impervious coating forms on the inside of the pipe. But soft water does not cause such a coating, and the water in the pipe becomes contaminated with lead. It has been suggested that the fall of the Roman Empire was due to richer administrators being able to afford piped water in their villas. The only suitable metal available at that time was lead. Neurological decay resulted in societal decay! Today, lead water pipes have mainly been replaced, with copper or plastic.

Until recently, vehicles used petrol that contained tetraethyllead as an 'anti-knocking' agent. Exhaust systems emitted tiny particles of lead compounds which contaminated the air and roadsides. Surveys revealed that children living near busy roads had elevated levels of lead in their blood and performed less well in cognitive and psychomotor tests. Modern cars now run on 'unleaded' petrol (that does not contain lead additives).

Franklin's naval expedition in 1847 to find the Northwest Passage (from the North Atlantic to the North Pacific, around the 'top' of Canada) ended with the deaths of all 147 men. The expedition was the first to use cooked canned food rather than salted and pickled preserves. The cans were made from sheet steel assembled with tin–lead solder. The lead leached into the food and slowly poisoned the men. Hair from bodies preserved in the ice was recently analysed and showed high lead content: the concentration increased the closer to the scalp the sample was taken.

SUMMARY

- Group IV compounds are predominantly covalent, with the oxidation number +4 being preferred.
- The stability of compounds of Group IV elements with oxidation number +2 increases with increasing atomic number.
- Lead(II) ionic compounds are more stable than lead(IV) covalent compounds.
- The tetrachlorides of Si, Sn, and Pb all hydrolyse to give HCl and hydrated oxides.
- Lead is a cumulative poison, particularly affecting the central nervous system.

PRACTICE

1 Draw Lewis structures of CCl_4 and $GeCl_4$. Sketch the shape of $SnCl_4$.

Electrode potentials

Tin(II) ions will reduce orange dichromate(VI) to green chromium(III). Lead(II) ions do not bring about this change. The different outcomes may be understood by looking at the standard electrode potentials:

$E^{\ominus}(Sn^{4+}/Sn^{2+}) = +0.15\,V$

$E^{\ominus}(Cr_2O_7^{2-}/Cr^{3+}) = +1.33\,V$

$E^{\ominus}(Pb^{4+}/Pb^{2+}) = +1.69\,V$

Tin(II) ion reduces dichromate(VI), but lead(II) ion cannot reduce dichromate(VI).

Sheet lead is durable and easily beaten into shape to fit traditional roofs. People who work regularly with lead in the building industry have the level of lead in their blood measured twice yearly.

Lead: physiological and biological data

Lead is moderately toxic by ingestion and affects the gut and central nervous system. Lead compounds can be carcinogenic and teratogenic.

Biological role: none

Toxic intake: 50 mg

Levels in humans:

Blood/mg dm^{-3}: 0.2

Bone/p.p.m.: about 15

Liver/p.p.m.: about 10

Muscle/p.p.m.: about 1

19.7

Group V: nitrogen and phosphorus – 1

OBJECTIVES

- Reactivity of the elements
- Oxidation numbers
- Oxides
- Biochemistry

Bismuth is the only member of Group V with all the attributes of a typical metal (although antimony has some metallic character). Bismuth is usually encountered in the laboratory as its oxoanion, the bismuthate(V) ion BiO_3^-. Bismuthate(V) is so strong an oxidant that it can oxidize manganese(II) ions (pale pink) to manganate(VII) ions (deep purple), hence providing a test for manganese.

Arsenic the poison

Arsenic, usually in the form of its oxide As_2O_3, is famous as a poison. It binds to the active sites in a variety of enzymes, inhibiting their biochemical function and ultimately causing death. Note that arsenic also poisons industrial catalysts such as nickel and platinum.

Nitrogen monoxide reacts with oxygen

When nitrogen monoxide NO forms in the presence of oxygen, it immediately reacts to produce nitrogen dioxide NO_2:

$2NO(g) + O_2(g) \rightarrow 2NO_2(g)$

colourless brown

Pain relief and anaesthesia

Dinitrogen oxide N_2O acts as an anaesthetic. It is a constituent of *Entonox*, the gas mixture that is sometimes given to ease pain in childbirth, and is also used as a short-lasting general anaesthetic in dental surgery.

The Group V elements are, in order of increasing atomic number, nitrogen (N), phosphorus (P), arsenic (As), antimony (Sb), and bismuth (Bi). Metallic character increases with increasing atomic number. Nitrogen and phosphorus are non-metals, arsenic and antimony are metalloids, and bismuth is a metal. All have a valence-shell electronic structure of ns^2np^3. This spread and the following one will concentrate on the chemistry of nitrogen and phosphorus, with some reference to the remaining elements where they illustrate group trends.

Nitrogen and phosphorus: reactivity

The elements nitrogen and phosphorus have very different structures and therefore very different reactivities. Nitrogen is a gas at room temperature (melts at $T_m = -210\,°C$, boils at $T_b = -196\,°C$). A nitrogen molecule N_2 consists of two atoms bonded by a triple covalent bond (N≡N). This very strong bond (bond enthalpy $+944\,kJ\,mol^{-1}$) makes nitrogen extremely stable and unreactive.

Phosphorus, on the other hand, is very reactive. It has several allotropes, none of which has the sort of strong bonding found in nitrogen. Of these allotropes, white phosphorus ($T_m = 44\,°C$) is particularly reactive, since the P_4 molecule has a highly strained tetrahedral structure (see the chapter on 'Trends across a period').

Oxidation numbers

The valence-shell electronic structure of the Group V elements is ns^2np^3. All elements can show an oxidation number of +3 by forming covalent bonds, for example with chlorine. All elements except nitrogen readily show an oxidation number of +5 by using a vacant d orbital. Phosphorus forms two chlorides, PCl_3 and PCl_5. Nitrogen and phosphorus can also exhibit an oxidation number of −3.

For example, nitrides can be formed when nitrogen reacts with certain s-block elements. When heated with air, magnesium forms the nitride Mg_3N_2 as well as the oxide MgO. Similarly lithium reacts with nitrogen to form the compound Li_3N. Both Mg_3N_2 and Li_3N contain the nitride ion N^{3-}.

The oxidation number −3 is also shown in the important compounds ammonia and phosphine, which are discussed in the following spread.

The oxides of nitrogen

The oxides of nitrogen and phosphorus are generally acidic, as is usual for oxides of non-metals. The three main oxides of nitrogen are the colourless gases nitrogen monoxide NO and dinitrogen oxide N_2O and the brown gas nitrogen dioxide NO_2. Remember that NO_2 exists in equilibrium with its dimer N_2O_4, the position of the equilibrium depending on the temperature and pressure (see the chapter on 'Chemical equilibrium'). The similar electronegativities of nitrogen and oxygen (3.0 and 3.4 respectively) imply that the N—O bonds will have only slight polarity. The boiling points are NO −152 °C, N_2O −89 °C, and N_2O_4 +21 °C. These values fit the trend of increasing strength of dispersion forces as the number of electrons increases.

'Smog' was first used to describe a poisonous mixture of smoke, fog, and other chemicals that caused London air pollution; as late as 1952 4,000 people died of respiratory diseases in a particularly severe week's smog. The Clean Air Act introduced in 1956 in the UK drastically improved the urban atmosphere. **Photochemical smog** (containing nitrogen oxides, ozone, together with organic compounds) has proved harder to avoid, especially in cities such as Los Angeles. Both NO and NO_2 have an unpaired electron (count the total number of electrons in the molecules).

A series of complex reactions involving radicals such as these, and involving absorption of radiation, create a number of dangerous chemicals. Humans, animals, plants, and even polymers all suffer damage.

Laboratory preparations

Nitrogen monoxide NO is prepared by pouring 50% nitric acid onto copper:

$$3Cu(s) + 8HNO_3(aq) \rightarrow 3Cu(NO_3)_2(aq) + 4H_2O(l) + 2NO(g)$$

Dinitrogen oxide N_2O is obtained by heating ammonium nitrate (produced in the reaction vessel from a mixture of ammonium chloride and sodium nitrate) very carefully:

$$NH_4NO_3(s) \rightarrow N_2O(g) + 2H_2O(g)$$

Nitrogen dioxide NO_2 is obtained when powdered lead(II) nitrate is heated:

$$2Pb(NO_3)_2(s) \rightarrow 2PbO(s) + 4NO_2(g) + O_2(g)$$

The lead(II) nitrate crackles as it produces brown fumes of nitrogen dioxide.

NO_x

High-temperature combustion of fuels, e.g. near the spark plug in a petrol engine, produces both NO and NO_2, as well as carbon dioxide and carbon monoxide. The term NO_x is often used to mean NO or NO_2 or a mixture of both. NO_x reacts with water and so contributes to the problem of acid rain. Most NO_x can be removed from car exhausts by catalytic converters (see the chapter on 'Chemical kinetics'). As the exhaust gases pass through the catalytic converter, NO_x reacts with carbon monoxide to form nitrogen and carbon dioxide; see spread 15.9.

The oxides of phosphorus

As we saw in the chapter on 'Trends across a period', the two oxides of phosphorus, phosphorus(III) oxide P_4O_6 and phosphorus(V) oxide P_4O_{10}, are molecular solids. Both structures bear a striking similarity to that of white phosphorus, as each is based on a tetrahedron of four phosphorus atoms. The oxide P_4O_6 forms when phosphorus burns in a limited supply of oxygen, and P_4O_{10} forms when it burns in a plentiful supply of oxygen. Both oxides dissolve in water to form acidic solutions.

Nitrogen and phosphorus in biochemistry

Both nitrogen and phosphorus play vital roles in biochemistry. The total mass of nitrogen in an average 70 kg person is 1.8 kg; the corresponding value for phosphorus is 780 g.

Nitrogen is found in amino acids and the proteins that are built from them; see the chapter on 'Biochemistry'.

Phosphorus is an essential element in nucleic acids (DNA and RNA) and in adenosine triphosphate ATP, the carrier of chemical energy in all organisms. The availability of phosphorus in seawater is a limiting factor on the growth of plankton, and hence affects the biomass that occurs higher in marine food chains.

Hydroxyapatite $Ca_5(OH)(PO_4)_3$ is a phosphate mineral found in skeletons and teeth. Hydroxyapatite is piezoelectric, capable of changing shape in response to mechanical stress. This property allows bone to be the internal skeleton of multicellular organisms.

Nitrogen fixation

One of the most important processes in nature is nitrogen fixation, which enables leguminous plants (such as peas, beans, and clover) to make use of atmospheric nitrogen. Nitrogen fixation is carried out by bacteria such as *Rhizobium* in root nodules of the plants. Atmospheric nitrogen is converted into nitrate ion, which is then available for biochemical syntheses.

SUMMARY

- Oxidation numbers of nitrogen and phosphorus vary from –3 to +5.
- Nitrogen and phosphorus have important biochemical roles.

PRACTICE

1 Give the oxidation number of the Group V element in each of the following compounds:

a	NH_3	**f**	HNO_3
b	NO	**g**	NO_2^-
c	N_2O	**h**	BiO_3^-
d	NO_2	**i**	P_4O_{10}
e	HNO_2	**j**	BiOCl.

2 Elemental nitrogen exists as simple covalent molecules consisting of two triply bonded nitrogen atoms. Suggest reasons why phosphorus does not similarly form triply bonded P_2 molecules.

3 Correlate material from the chapter on 'Trends across a period' relating to phosphorus with the information in this spread.

19.8

OBJECTIVES

- Oxoacids
- Hydrides

GROUP V: NITROGEN AND PHOSPHORUS – 2

This spread focuses on the oxoacids and hydrides of nitrogen and phosphorus. The most important oxoacid of nitrogen is nitric acid HNO_3. The most important oxoacid of phosphorus is phosphoric acid H_3PO_4. As discussed in the chapter on 'Trends across a period', all these substances are formed by reacting oxides with water. Of the hydrides, ammonia NH_3 should be very familiar to you by now. It is often used as an example in connection with its synthesis, solubility, basic character (Brønsted–Lowry and Lewis), and range of salts. However, *all* the Group V elements form hydrides. There are some interesting differences to be noted between the properties of ammonia and those of phosphine PH_3, the hydride of phosphorus.

Oxoacids

When nitrogen dioxide reacts with water, it disproportionates to form **nitrous acid** HNO_2 (containing N(III)) and **nitric acid** HNO_3 (containing N(V)):

$$2NO_2(g) + H_2O(l) \rightarrow HNO_2(aq) + HNO_3(aq)$$

The salts of nitrous acid are called nitrites and contain the **nitrite ion** NO_2^-. The salts of nitric acid are called nitrates, and contain the **nitrate ion** NO_3^-. Nitric acid is an important reagent because it can act both as an acid and as an oxidant.

Nitric acid as a strong acid

Nitric acid is a strong acid. When added to water it becomes essentially fully ionized:

$$HNO_3(aq) + H_2O(l) \rightarrow H_3O^+(aq) + NO_3^-(aq)$$

To show that nitric acid is an oxoacid, its formula may be written as $HONO_2$.

Nitric acid as an oxidant

Nitric acid is a strong oxidant. For example, metallic copper does not react with hydrochloric acid, but *does* react with concentrated nitric acid. Copper metal is oxidized to blue aqueous copper(II) ions and a red–brown gas (nitrogen dioxide) is produced:

$$Cu(s) + 4HNO_3(aq, conc.) \rightarrow Cu(NO_3)_2(aq) + 2H_2O(l) + 2NO_2(g)$$

Copper and nitric acid

Note that, in the reaction between metallic copper and concentrated nitric acid, *nitrate ions* are reduced, not hydrogen ions. This result is unusual because acids usually react with metals to form hydrogen by reduction of hydrogen ions. See the chapter on 'Redox equilibrium'.

Ammonia and phosphine

All the Group V elements form hydrides of the general formula MH_3. They are named ammonia (NH_3), phosphine (PH_3), arsine (AsH_3), stibine (SbH_3), and bismuthine (BiH_3). Thermal stability decreases in the order $NH_3 > PH_3 > AsH_3 > SbH_3 > BiH_3$. Bismuthine is so unstable that it can only be obtained in very small amounts under controlled conditions. All the Group V hydrides are predominantly covalent compounds.

Ammonia is produced in the laboratory by heating an ammonium salt with a base. The usual mixture chosen is solid ammonium chloride and soda-lime (a mixture of solid sodium hydroxide and solid calcium hydroxide):

$$NH_4Cl(s) + NaOH(s) \rightarrow NH_3(g) + H_2O(g) + NaCl(s)$$

The gas is dried by passing it through calcium oxide; it is then collected by upward delivery (density of ammonia relative to air = 0.59).

Phosphine may be produced in the laboratory by heating calcium phosphide with water:

$$Ca_3P_2(s) + 6H_2O(l) \rightarrow 3Ca(OH)_2(aq) + 2PH_3(g)$$

The gas is collected over water.

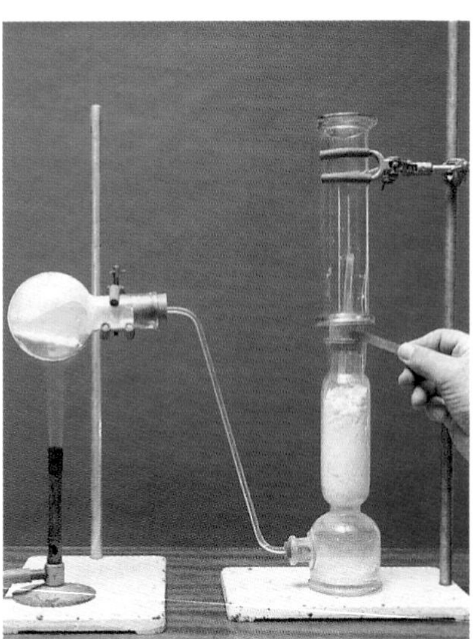

Apparatus for the laboratory preparation of ammonia. The damp litmus paper will turn blue showing that aqueous ammonia is basic.

Molecular shape

The molecules of both ammonia and phosphine are pyramidal. The H—N—H bond angle is 107° whereas the H—P—H bond angle is 93°. The P—H bonds are longer (0.142 nm) than the N—H bonds (0.101 nm), and so they have smaller electron density and therefore less mutual repulsion.

(a)

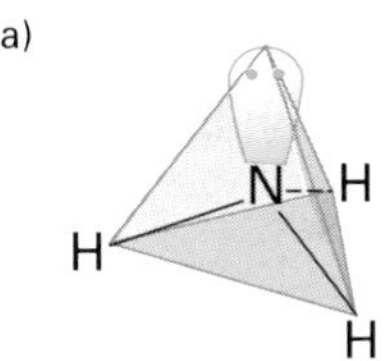

(b)

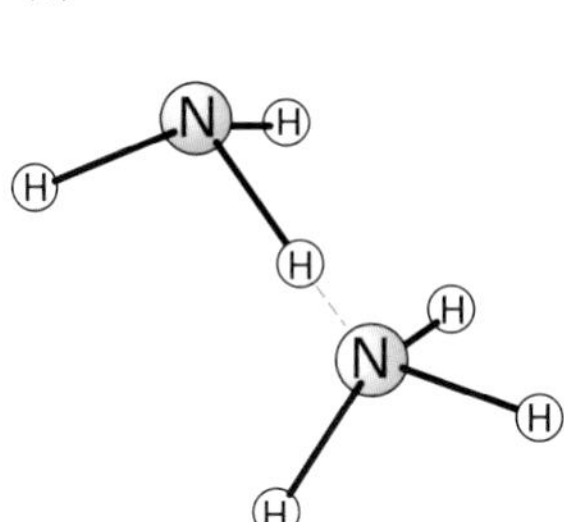

(a) The ammonia molecule. The tetrahedral angle is 109.5°. The 107° bond angles result because greater lone pair to bonding pair repulsions decrease the angle. (b) Hydrogen bonding in ammonia.

Boiling points

The boiling point of ammonia is −33 °C. If you consider dispersion forces alone, you would expect the boiling point of phosphine to be higher. However, phosphine boils at the *lower* temperature of −87 °C. The presence of hydrogen bonds (see the chapter on 'Changes of state and intermolecular forces') between ammonia molecules causes its boiling point to be higher than that expected on the basis of dispersion forces alone.

Water solubility

Because of the hydrogen bonds that form between ammonia and water molecules, ammonia is extremely soluble in water. The electronegativity of phosphorus (2.2) is equal to that of hydrogen (2.2), so the phosphine molecule is essentially non-polar and its solubility in water is very low.

Basic properties and salt formation

In solution, ammonia acts as a weak Brønsted base, accepting a proton from a water molecule:

$$NH_3(g) \rightarrow NH_3(aq)$$
$$NH_3(aq) + H_2O(l) \rightleftharpoons NH_4^+(aq) + OH^-(aq)$$

The resulting solution is basic: saturated aqueous ammonia has a pH of 11. Ammonia also acts as a Lewis base by donating a pair of electrons to a hydrogen atom on a water molecule. There are many examples of complex ions containing ammonia in the next chapter on 'The transition metals'.

Ammonia readily forms solutions of salts with acids; and evaporation of the solution yields stable crystalline solids. For example:

$$NH_3(aq) + HNO_3(aq) \rightarrow NH_4NO_3(aq)$$
$$NH_3(aq) + H^+(aq) \rightarrow NH_4^+(aq)$$

Ammonium nitrate is a valuable fertilizer, see next spread. Phosphine is a much weaker base than ammonia. Phosphonium salts form only with difficulty and are unstable. For example, phosphonium iodide decomposes above 50 °C:

$$PH_4I(aq) \rightarrow PH_3(g) + HI(aq)$$

Redox properties. Ammonia acts as a reductant when passed over heated copper(II) oxide (a black solid):
$3CuO(s) + 2NH_3(g) \rightarrow$
$3Cu(s) + 3H_2O(g) + N_2(g)$
Oxidation state changes:
Cu(II) to Cu(0); N(−III) to N(0)
Phosphine is a more powerful reductant than ammonia. It can precipitate copper and silver from their aqueous ions. Ammonia only forms a complex ion.

SUMMARY

- Nitric acid is an oxidizing acid; hydrochloric acid is not. (Reminder: sulphuric acid is oxidizing only when concentrated.)
- The boiling point of ammonia is greater than that of phosphine because there are hydrogen bonds between ammonia molecules.
- The solubility of ammonia in water is greater than that of phosphine because ammonia forms hydrogen bonds with water.
- Phosphine is a much weaker base than ammonia.

PRACTICE

1 Draw and label a diagram of the apparatus you would use to prepare and collect phosphine.

2 Draw labelled sketches to show how hydrogen bonding occurs between molecules of ammonia in the liquid phase.

3 Draw Lewis structures to show the electron arrangements in
 a PH_3
 b NH_4^+

4 Compare the reactions between:
 a Iron metal and nitric acid
 b Iron metal and hydrochloric acid.

5 Use the concept of electronegativity to explain why ammonia has a higher boiling point than phosphine. Sketch a graph of the boiling points of the Group V hydrides and explain its shape.

19.9

THREE IMPORTANT INDUSTRIAL PROCESSES

OBJECTIVES

- Ammonia: the Haber–Bosch process
- Nitric acid: the Ostwald process
- Sulphuric acid: the Contact process

The German chemist Baron Justus von Liebig commented in 1843 that the level of commercial prosperity of a country could be judged by the amount of sulphuric acid it consumed each year. This acid is one of a number of 'heavy chemicals' which are central to the manufacture of an enormous range of substances, from fertilizers and dyestuffs, to detergents, explosives, and artificial fibres. The production of the 'heavy chemicals' sodium hydroxide and chlorine from the electrolysis of brine was described in the previous chapter. This spread draws together the manufacture of ammonia, nitric acid, and sulphuric acid.

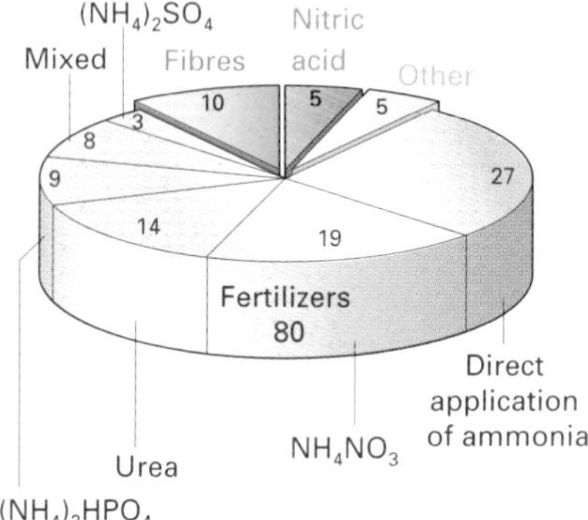

Ammonia uses: over 100 million tonnes of ammonia are manufactured each year world-wide.

Ammonia: the Haber–Bosch synthesis

Ammonia (NH_3) is manufactured from nitrogen and hydrogen by the Haber–Bosch synthesis. Hydrogen is produced in the 'primary reformer' from the reaction between methane and steam, using a nickel catalyst at about 750 °C and 30 atm:

$$CH_4(g) + H_2O(g) \rightleftharpoons CO(g) + 3H_2(g)$$

The methane must be desulphurized to avoid poisoning the catalyst.

Air is added to this gas mixture in the 'secondary reformer'. The oxygen is removed by reaction with some of the hydrogen. Carbon monoxide is removed in the 'shift reactor' by reaction with more steam in the presence of a freshly produced, finely divided Fe_3O_4 catalyst at 400 °C. The final mixture contains nitrogen and hydrogen in a ratio of 1:3.

In the synthesis reaction vessel, nitrogen, hydrogen, and ammonia exist together in the following equilibrium:

$$N_2(g) + 3H_2(g) \rightleftharpoons 2NH_3(g); \qquad \Delta H^\ominus = -92\ \text{kJ mol}^{-1}$$

Le Chatelier's principle (see the chapter on 'Chemical equilibrium') indicates that low temperature and high pressure increase the yield. In practice, a pressure of 250 atm and a temperature of 450 °C are used, giving a conversion of about 15%. The temperature is a compromise between yield and rate. A catalyst of iron is used, which is made more active by using the oxides of potassium, calcium, and aluminium as promoters.

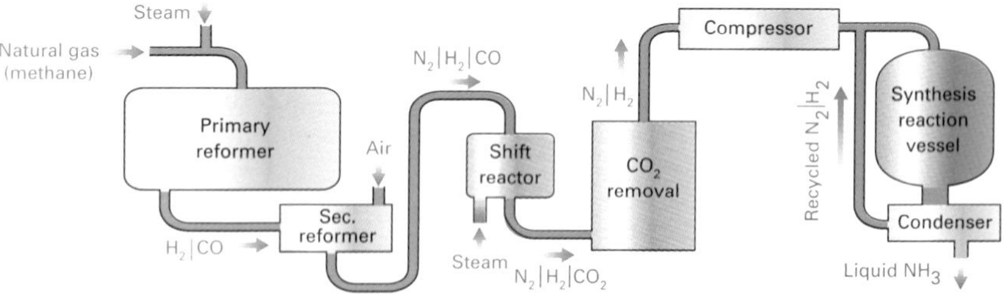

Flow diagram of the Haber–Bosch process for the synthesis of ammonia from its elements.

Nitric acid: the Ostwald process

The fertilizers (see box) that contain nitrogen are made from nitric acid, which is made from ammonia. The conversion of ammonia to nitric acid (HNO_3) is ingenious in its careful control of oxidation state change. Nitrogen has its lowest oxidation number of −3 in ammonia; it has its highest oxidation number of +5 in nitric acid.

The first stage of the process involves the catalytic oxidation of ammonia to nitrogen monoxide. A mixture of purified air and ammonia passes through a woven platinum–rhodium gauze at 850 °C:

$$4NH_3(g) + 5O_2(g) \rightarrow 4NO(g) + 6H_2O(g)$$

oxidation state changes: O(0) to O(−II); N(−III) to N(+II)

The conversion efficiency is about 96%.

Fertilizers and eutrophication

The demand for increased food production to keep the increasing world population alive resulted in much more efficient growth of crops during the twentieth century. Artificial fertilizers replace the nutrients taken out of the soil by plants, especially the three essential elements for plant growth, nitrogen N, phosphorus P, and potassium K. The main fertilizers are nitrates and phosphates. These inorganic fertilizers include potassium nitrate KNO_3, ammonium nitrate NH_4NO_3, and 'superphosphate' $Ca(H_2PO_4)_2$. Most commercial fertilizers are labelled with the amounts of nitrogen, phosphorus, and potassium that they contain. They are termed **NPK fertilizers** when they contain all three nutrients.

If more fertilizers are applied than is necessary, the excess may dissolve in rain water and run off into rivers and other watercourses. There, the fertilizers stimulate the growth of green and blue-green algae. This growth may become excessive and deprive the water of oxygen and light, and so cause other aquatic plants and animals to die. The watercourses become choked with decaying plant and animal matter. The excessive over-feeding and subsequent collapse of the water's ecosystem in this way is called **eutrophication**. Lake Balaton, the largest lake in Europe, turned visibly green in places in 1982 before the pollution problem was addressed.

The second stage of the manufacture involves cooling the nitrogen monoxide and mixing it with air; oxidation to nitrogen dioxide occurs:

$$2NO(g) + O_2(g) \rightarrow 2NO_2(g)$$

oxidation state changes: O(0) to O(–II); N(+II) to N(+IV)

The mixture of NO_2 and air then passes through an absorption tower containing water, in which the overall reaction is:

$$4NO_2(g) + O_2(g) + 2H_2O(l) \rightarrow 4HNO_3(aq)$$

oxidation state changes: O(0) to O(–II); N(+IV) to N(+V)

The acid that results is fairly concentrated (60%). This concentration is sufficient for most applications.

Sulphuric acid: the Contact process

Sulphuric acid (H_2SO_4) is manufactured by the Contact process. The first step involves burning molten sulphur in air to produce sulphur dioxide:

$$S(l) + O_2(g) \rightarrow SO_2(g)$$

Sulphur dioxide contains sulphur with oxidation number +4; sulphuric acid contains sulphur with oxidation number +6. Further oxidation is therefore required to obtain sulphuric acid from sulphur dioxide.

This oxidation involves an equilibrium reaction, so the conditions must be carefully controlled to maximize the yield. The catalyst, spread 19.11, is vanadium(V) oxide V_2O_5, with potassium sulphate K_2SO_4 as a promoter, on a silica support. The equilibrium is:

$$2SO_2(g) + O_2(g) \rightleftharpoons 2SO_3(g); \qquad \Delta H^{\ominus} = -197\,\text{kJ mol}^{-1}$$

This reaction is exothermic: too high a temperature will cause the yield to be unacceptably low (equilibrium shifts to the left); too low a temperature results in an unacceptably low reaction rate. The best compromise temperature for this reaction is found to be 450 °C. Pressure is typically 2 atm. Under these conditions, conversion exceeds 99.5%.

The product from the reaction is sulphur trioxide, which is absorbed in concentrated sulphuric acid:

$$SO_3(g) + H_2SO_4(l) \rightarrow H_2S_2O_7(l)$$

The resulting liquid is called *oleum*. It is then diluted with water to form the oily concentrated acid, which is 96–98% pure H_2SO_4:

$$H_2S_2O_7(l) + H_2O(l) \rightarrow 2H_2SO_4(l)$$

This round-about method is used because if sulphur trioxide is added directly to water, it produces a stable mist, rather than dissolving in it.

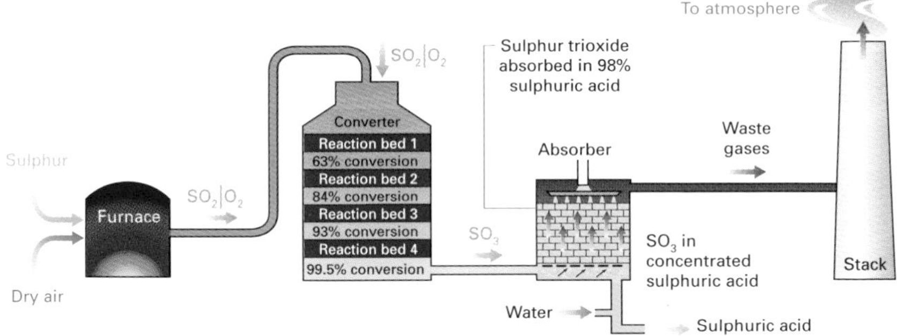

Flow diagram of the Contact process for the synthesis of sulphuric acid from water and the elements sulphur and oxygen. The absorber tower is packed with ceramic rings to ensure good contact between the acid and the gas. Most plants use two *absorbers, the other after the reaction bed 3 which has been omitted for clarity.*

SUMMARY

- Ammonia is manufactured from nitrogen (source: air) and hydrogen (source: methane). The catalyst is iron at 450 °C and 250 atm.
- Nitric acid is manufactured from ammonia, oxygen (source: air), and water. The catalyst is platinum–rhodium at 850 °C.
- Sulphuric acid is manufactured from sulphur (source: mining), oxygen (source: air), and water. The catalyst is vanadium(V) oxide at 450 °C.

Nitric acid uses

Nitric acid is used in the manufacture of fertilizers (70% is used for NH_4NO_3 production), medicines, dyestuffs, and explosives. Its manufacture from ammonia is therefore of considerable commercial and social significance.

The platinum–rhodium gauze used in the Ostwald process.

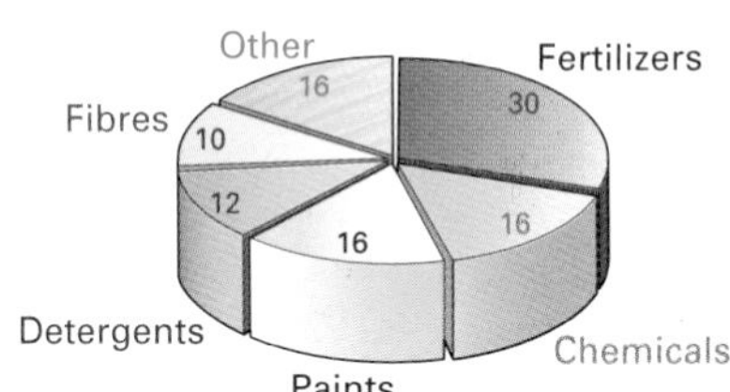

Sulphuric acid uses: over 150 million tonnes of sulphuric acid are manufactured every year throughout the world, a greater mass than for any other chemical.

19.10

Group VI: oxygen and sulphur – 1

OBJECTIVES

- Allotropes of oxygen
- Allotropes of sulphur
- Oxides and sulphides

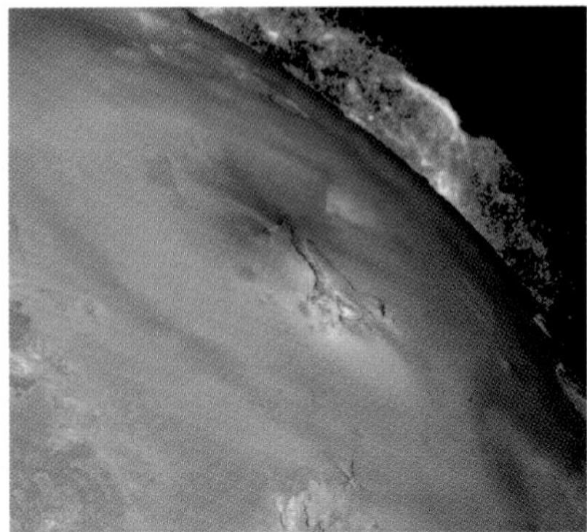

The active volcanoes on Io, one of the moons of the planet Jupiter, emit streams of sulphur.

Uses of oxygen

The chief industrial use of oxygen is steel-making, where it is blown into molten iron to oxidize and remove impurities. The gas is also used in some breathing apparatuses (e.g. for mountaineers and hospital patients). Mixed with oxygen, the gas ethyne (acetylene) burns at over 3000 °C, hot enough to cut and weld steel.

Uses of sulphur

The chief industrial use of sulphur is in the manufacture of sulphuric acid (described in the previous spread). Sulphur is used in its powdered elemental form to dust grape vines to prevent fungal growth. The sulphonamides (spread 23.6) are a group of antibiotics containing the $—SO_2NH_2$ group; they are used to treat infections of the gut and urinary system.

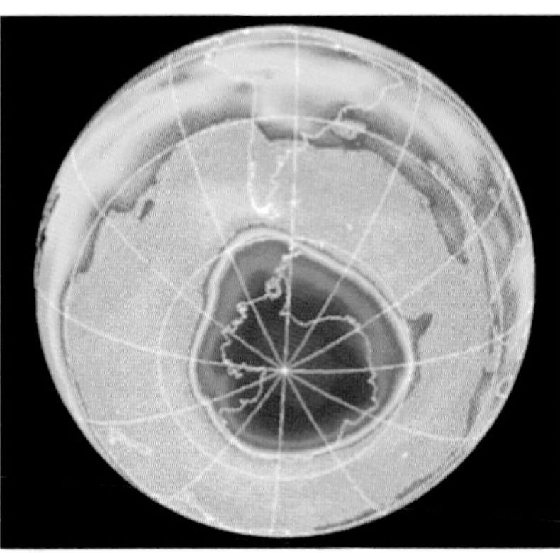

Ozone is crucial for the survival of life on Earth. The ozone layer in the upper atmosphere partially blocks harmful ultraviolet rays from the Sun. Depletion of ozone in the upper atmosphere, first discovered in the 1970s, has caused world-wide concern. See spread 24.4.

The Group VI elements are, in order of increasing atomic number, oxygen (O), sulphur (S), selenium (Se), tellurium (Te), and polonium (Po). All have a valence-shell electronic structure of ns^2np^4. Oxygen and sulphur are non-metals, selenium and tellurium are metalloids, and polonium is a metal. Radioactive polonium has a simple cubic structure, which is unique among elements. You are already familiar with a good deal of the chemistry of oxygen and sulphur. This spread provides some more general background information about the elements and points to other chapters where more detailed information may be obtained.

Occurrence

Oxygen is the most common element in the Earth's crust, accounting for 46% of its solid constituents, 89% of water, and 21% of the atmosphere. It is obtained industrially from the fractional distillation of liquid air, itself produced by compressing and cooling air from the atmosphere. Oxygen is produced in the laboratory either (1) by adding hydrogen peroxide to manganese(IV) oxide or (2) by heating potassium chlorate with manganese(IV) oxide. In both cases the manganese(IV) oxide is acting as a catalyst, and the reactions are:

$$2H_2O_2(aq) \rightarrow 2H_2O(l) + O_2(g) \qquad (1)$$

$$2KClO_3(s) \rightarrow 2KCl(s) + 3O_2(g) \qquad (2)$$

Sulphur is found in the elemental state in volcanic areas. It is also present as hydrogen sulphide H_2S at concentrations of up to 6% in natural gas (methane) wells. The methane and hydrogen sulphide that make up the natural gas are both products of microbial action on organic matter. Sulphur is also extracted from crude oil (petroleum) during refining.

Allotropes of oxygen

The two allotropes of oxygen (O_2 and O_3) are both gases at 25 °C and 1 bar. The systematic names are dioxygen and trioxygen respectively. However, O_2 is usually referred to as 'oxygen' and O_3 as 'ozone'.

Ozone at ground level is hazardous as it is an extremely vigorous oxidant. It forms in the high-voltage discharge in sparking electrical equipment, where oxygen molecules split into oxygen atoms, which then combine with O_2 to form O_3. (Similar reactions initiated by solar radiation produce ozone in the atmosphere.) At low concentrations, ozone's strength as an oxidant is put to good use in the sterilization of water, for example in some swimming pools. Ozone has two advantages over chlorination: it kills micro-organisms more rapidly and there is no risk of forming potentially carcinogenic (cancer-inducing) chlorinated organic compounds.

Allotropes of sulphur

The two important solid allotropes of sulphur are rhombic sulphur and monoclinic sulphur, spread 6.7. Below 96 °C, rhombic sulphur is the stable allotrope; monoclinic sulphur is the stable allotrope above this temperature. Both are composed of ring-shaped S_8 molecules and differ only in the pattern in which these molecules pack (see the chapter on 'Trends across a period').

Oxides and sulphides

Oxides form when oxygen is heated with most elements; the oxygen acts as an oxidant by gaining electrons and forming the oxide ion O^{2-}. In the case of the s-block metals, the peroxide ion O_2^{2-} and the superoxide ion O_2^- may form (see the chapter on 'The s-block elements').

Sulphides form similarly when sulphur is heated with most elements. These compounds contain the sulphide ion S^{2-} in which sulphur has undergone reduction by gaining electrons.

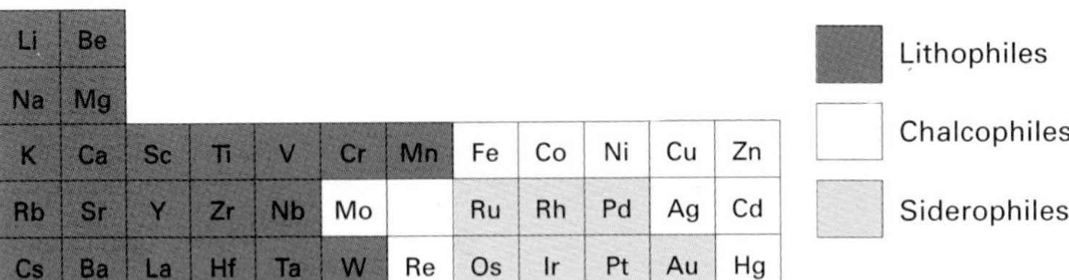

*The **lithophiles** tend to occur as oxides, silicates, sulphates, or carbonates. The **siderophiles** tend to occur native (in the elemental form). The **chalcophiles** tend to occur as suphides. The element Tc (between Mo and Ru) is essentially unknown in nature.*

At first glance, the formation of the O^{2-} ion appears energetically highly unfavourable:

First electron-gain enthalpy of oxygen $-148\ kJ\ mol^{-1}$
Second electron-gain enthalpy of oxygen $+850\ kJ\ mol^{-1}$

However, the expenditure in producing the doubly charged ion is more than compensated by the lattice formation enthalpy of most oxides:

Lattice formation enthalpy of MgO $-3800\ kJ\ mol^{-1}$
Lattice formation enthalpy of BaO $-3050\ kJ\ mol^{-1}$

The ionization enthalpies of oxygen show that the formation of positive ions is highly unlikely, thus confirming its non-metallic nature:

First ionization enthalpy of oxygen $+1314\ kJ\ mol^{-1}$
Second ionization enthalpy of oxygen $+3390\ kJ\ mol^{-1}$

The non-metallic character is also confirmed by its electronegativity of 3.4.

Sulphur is a less powerful oxidant than oxygen. Sulphides also have greater covalent character than the corresponding oxides. This is because the electronegativity of sulphur (2.6) is lower than that of oxygen (3.4).

The majority of sulphides are extremely insoluble in water, with the exception of ammonium and Group I sulphides. The precipitates shown formed when hydrogen sulphide gas was bubbled into solutions of: (a) Fe^{2+}(aq); (b) Cd^{2+}(aq); and (c) Sb^{3+}(aq).

SUMMARY

- Oxygen and sulphur are both found as the elements: O_2(g) and S_8(s) respectively.
- Ozone O_3 is another allotrope of oxygen O_2.
- The two main allotropes of sulphur, monoclinic and rhombic, differ in the packing of the S_8 ring-shaped molecules.
- Sulphides are more covalent than the corresponding oxides because the electronegativity of sulphur is lower (O, 3.4; S, 2.6).
- The majority of metal sulphides are insoluble in water; the coloured precipitates may be used to identify metal cations.

Biochemistry

Oxygen is essential to most organisms for respiration – the oxidation of carbohydrates to carbon dioxide and water with the release of chemical energy. Death usually results after four minutes of oxygen starvation.

Sulphur is also an essential biochemical element. Links form between sulphur atoms at different points in a protein chain. These links are called **disulphide bridges** and they help to hold the protein chain in the correct shape for it to function correctly. Insulin is a hormone that controls the concentration of glucose in the blood: insulin deficiency causes diabetes. The shape of the insulin molecule (and hence its function) is partly controlled by disulphide bridges.

Selenium

Selenium is important as a trace element in biological systems. In the late twentieth century, in northern central China, the local population suffered from a deficiency disease called Kashin–Beck syndrome, which caused muscular problems. The soil (and therefore the food crops grown in it) were found to have a very low selenium content. The soil is now treated with salts containing the selenate ion SeO_4^{2-} and the syndrome has effectively disappeared.

PRACTICE

1 Explain why the ozone layer is crucial for survival of life on Earth.

19.11

GROUP VI: OXYGEN AND SULPHUR – 2

OBJECTIVES

- Oxidation numbers
- Sulphur dioxide – sulphurous acid
- Sulphur trioxide – sulphuric acid

Oxygen and sulphur combine to make two oxides of sulphur, sulphur dioxide SO_2 and sulphur trioxide SO_3. These acidic oxides dissolve in water to form sulphurous acid H_2SO_3 and sulphuric acid H_2SO_4 respectively. These acids in turn give rise to a total of four series of stable, crystalline salts. Before looking more closely at these substances, this spread opens with an assessment of the oxidation numbers of oxygen and sulphur.

Oxidation state summary

Oxidation state	Found in
O(–II)	H_2O, CuO
O(II)	only OF_2
S(–II)	H_2S, CuS
S(II)	SCl_2
S(IV)	SO_2, SO_3^{2-}
S(VI)	SO_3, SO_4^{2-}

Oxidation numbers

By far the most common oxidation number for oxygen is –2; sulphur shows a wider range of oxidation numbers, including –2, +2, +4, and +6, because sulphur has d orbitals of suitable energy to involve in bonding, whereas oxygen does not. Particular use of d orbitals is made in compounds containing S(VI), e.g. SF_6.

In the definition of oxidation number, any shared electron pairs are assigned to the more electronegative atom. As oxygen is second only to fluorine in electronegativity, oxygen is always in a negative oxidation state except when combined with fluorine, e.g. OF_2 contains O(II) while H_2O contains O(–II).

Metal sulphides resemble the oxides in their chemical formulae and contain sulphur with oxidation number –2. While oxide ores are the most important sources for most elements, sulphide ores are especially important sources for the chalcophiles (see previous spread). Examples include zinc blende ZnS, copper pyrites $CuFeS_2$, and stibnite Sb_2S_3, used as eye-shadow since Biblical times.

The halides of sulphur also show a range of oxidation numbers; of the halogens, only fluorine can oxidize sulphur to oxidation number +6 in sulphur hexafluoride SF_6. Chlorine forms S_2Cl_2 and SCl_2, but not SCl_6. Sulphur is found with oxidation numbers +4 and +6 in its oxides and oxoacids. The oxides, SO_2 and SO_3, have been discussed in the chapter on 'Trends across a period'.

Sulphur dioxide and sulphurous acid

Sulphur dioxide is produced when sulphur burns in air:

$$S_8(s) + 8O_2(g) \rightarrow 8SO_2(g)$$

when a metal sulphide is heated in air, e.g.:

$$2CuS(s) + 3O_2(g) \rightarrow 2CuO(s) + 2SO_2(g)$$

and when an acidified solution of a sulphite is boiled, e.g.:

$$Na_2SO_3(aq) + H_2SO_4(aq) \rightarrow Na_2SO_4(aq) + SO_2(g) + H_2O(l)$$

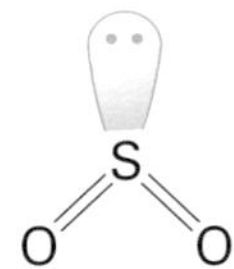

The Lewis structure for sulphur dioxide. Note that there are two S═O bonds and one lone pair. VSEPR theory (see the chapter on 'Chemical bonding') indicates that the molecule will be V-shaped; the O═S═O angle is 119°.

The sulphur atom at the centre of the sulphur dioxide molecule has a lone pair because the two oxygen atoms form covalent bonds with only four of the six electrons on the sulphur atom. The shape of the molecule is therefore V-shaped.

Sulphur dioxide is an acidic gas. It dissolves in water to give **sulphurous acid**:

$$SO_2(g) \rightarrow SO_2(aq)$$
$$SO_2(aq) + H_2O(l) \rightleftharpoons H_2SO_3(aq)$$

Sulphurous acid is a weak dibasic acid:

$$H_2SO_3(aq) + H_2O(l) \rightleftharpoons H_3O^+(aq) + HSO_3^-(aq)$$
$$HSO_3^-(aq) + H_2O(l) \rightleftharpoons H_3O^+(aq) + SO_3^{2-}(aq)$$

Neutralization of sulphurous acid by base forms two series of salts, the **hydrogensulphites** (e.g. sodium hydrogensulphite $NaHSO_3$) and the **sulphites** (e.g. sodium sulphite Na_2SO_3):

$$H_2SO_3(aq) + 2NaOH(aq) \rightarrow Na_2SO_3(aq) + 2H_2O(l)$$

Aqueous sulphites produce sulphur dioxide when acidified:

$$SO_3^{2-}(aq) + 2H^+(aq) \rightarrow SO_2(g) + H_2O(l)$$

Sulphur dioxide gas and sulphite ions are also reductants; they oxidize to sulphate ion in aqueous solution. The test for sulphur dioxide gas in the laboratory uses a piece of filter paper soaked in acidified potassium dichromate(VI). A change in colour from orange to green is a positive test for a reductant.

Sulphur trioxide and sulphuric acid

Sulphur trioxide (T_m = 17 °C, T_b = 45 °C) is produced in the laboratory (and in industry) by passing dry sulphur dioxide and air over a heated vanadium(V) oxide catalyst (as shown on the right):

$$2SO_2(g) + O_2(g) \rightleftharpoons 2SO_3(g)$$

Sulphur trioxide is acidic. It reacts violently with water to give **sulphuric acid** (often in the form of a stable acidic mist):

$$SO_3(g) + H_2O(l) \rightarrow H_2SO_4(aq)$$

Sulphuric acid is a dibasic acid; it forms two series of salts, the **hydrogensulphates** (e.g. sodium hydrogensulphate $NaHSO_4$) and the **sulphates** (e.g. sodium sulphate Na_2SO_4). Unlike aqueous sulphites, the aqueous sulphate ion is not affected by the presence of acid or base.

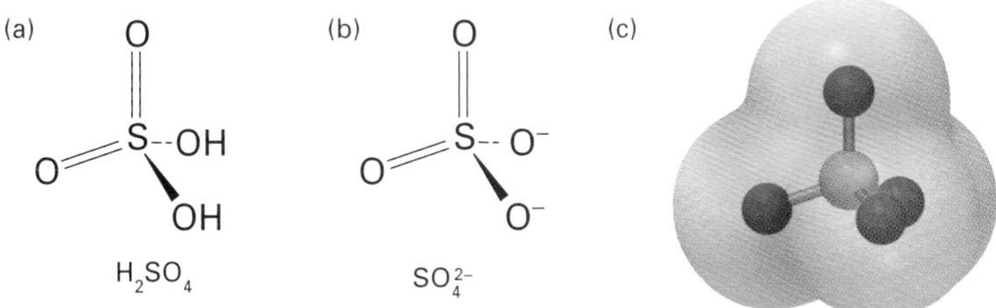

(a) The sulphuric acid molecule has a distorted tetrahedral shape. (b) The sulphate ion has a regular tetrahedral shape. (c) The electrostatic potential map shows that electron density is delocalized equally throughout the four S—O bonds, proving that the simple structure shown is not adequate for the electronic structure in the ion.

SUMMARY

- Oxidation numbers: oxygen −2 (+2 with fluorine); sulphur −2, +2, +4, + 6.
- SO_2 dissolves in water to give sulphurous acid H_2SO_3.
- H_2SO_3 is the parent acid of the hydrogensulphite and sulphite salts.
- SO_2 and SO_3^{2-} are reductants.
- SO_3 reacts violently with water to give sulphuric acid H_2SO_4.
- H_2SO_4 is the parent acid of the hydrogensulphate and sulphate salts.

Food preservation

The reducing properties of sulphur dioxide make it useful as an antioxidant in food. Sulphite ions can also be used as antioxidants and are often more convenient than gaseous sulphur dioxide. In the presence of acids, they release free sulphur dioxide. A disadvantage is that SO_2 can cause an asthma attack in people who are sensitive to it.

Acid rain

Sulphur dioxide from the combustion of sulphur-contaminated fuels is a major contributor to acid rain. The main source of atmospheric SO_2 is coal-fired power stations. Sulphur dioxide dissolves in rain water to form sulphurous acid. Ultraviolet radiation in the upper atmosphere can initiate oxidation to SO_3, and sulphuric acid then forms.

Acid ionization

See the chapter on 'Trends across a period' for the ionization of sulphurous and sulphuric acids.

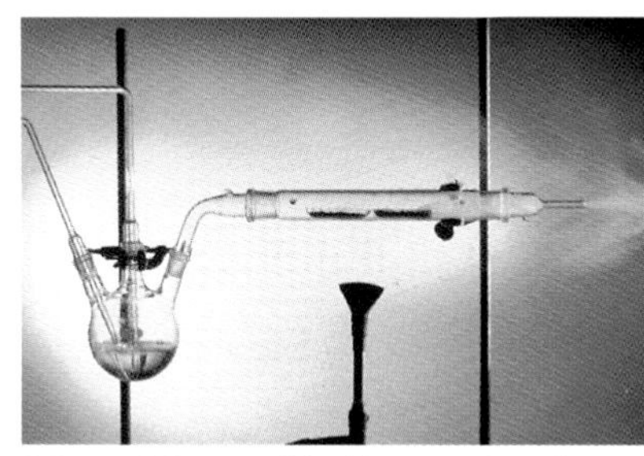

SO_2 and O_2 are dried by passing them through concentrated sulphuric acid. They combine on the surface of the V_2O_5 catalyst. SO_3 fumes in moist air. It can be condensed as a solid inside a cool dry flask.

PRACTICE

1 Give the oxidation state of the Group VI element(s) in each of the following substances:
- **a** H_2SO_3
- **b** H_2SO_4
- **c** OF_2
- **d** Cl_2O
- **e** H_2Se
- **f** K_2SO_3
- **g** $Te(OH)_6$.

2 Write a balanced ionic equation for the reaction between aqueous sodium sulphite and dilute hydrochloric acid.

3 Write a balanced chemical equation for each of the following reactions:
- **a** Roasting solid iron(II) sulphide FeS
- **b** Heating solid potassium chlorate $KClO_3$
- **c** Bubbling hydrogen sulphide gas H_2S into a solution of copper(II) sulphate $CuSO_4$.

4 Explain why the following observations hold for the first and second electron-gain enthalpies ($\Delta H^{\ominus}_{e.g.}$) for oxygen and sulphur:
- **a** The first for oxygen is exothermic, but the second is highly endothermic.
- **b** The first for sulphur is *greater* than that for oxygen, whereas the second for sulphur is *smaller* than that for oxygen.

19.12

Group VIII: the noble gases

OBJECTIVES

- Full valence shells
- Compounds of xenon and krypton
- 'Inert gases' or 'noble gases'?

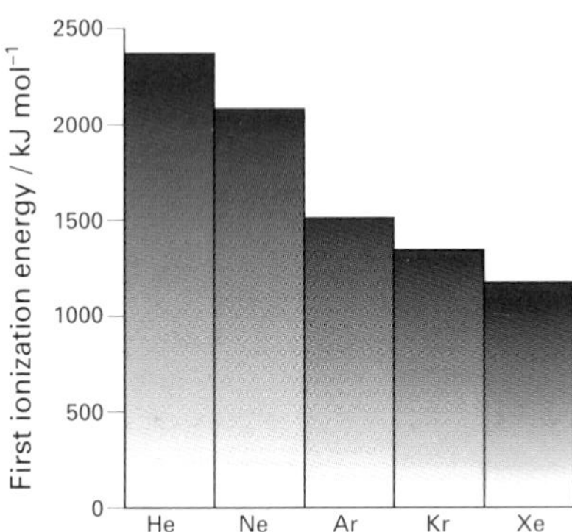

The first ionization energies of the noble gases decrease with increasing atomic number.

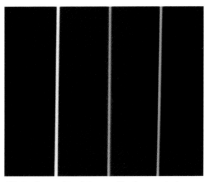

Light is emitted from discharge tubes as electrically excited electrons fall back to lower energy levels. The tubes contain helium (left), neon (centre), and argon (right).

He, Ne, and Ar *are* inert

The lack of any reactivity among the first three members of Group VIII can be understood in terms of their ionization energies. The values decrease with increasing atomic number because the electron being ionized is further from the attraction of the nucleus. Xenon forms compounds most readily because the ionization energy required is the lowest in the group.

The Group VIII elements are, in order of increasing atomic number, helium (He), neon (Ne), argon (Ar), krypton (Kr), and xenon (Xe). The sixth member of the group is radon (Ra). This element is radioactive and its study falls outside the scope of this book. All are colourless gases at room temperature. All the elements have full valence shells with an electronic structure ns^2np^6 (a complete octet), except He ($1s^2$). The members of this group were once regarded as being totally inert. However, compounds of xenon and krypton have been prepared.

Physical state

The noble gases have similar properties because the atoms all have a full valence shell. As a result, they show a great reluctance to combine with any other elements. The atoms do not interact to form molecules, as in the case of O_2, N_2, H_2, etc. They are therefore the only gases that exist as separate atoms.

The boiling points of the noble gases are extremely low. Helium boils within 5 K of absolute zero. The boiling points of the noble gases increase as their atomic number increases down Group VIII. The only forces between the atoms are dispersion forces (spread 7.4), which become larger as the size of the atoms increases. Larger atoms are more polarizable, because they have more electrons. Dispersion forces increase with increasing atomic number, as each atom has one more full shell of electrons compared with the previous noble gas.

Differences

Demonstrating the difference between the noble gases is fairly difficult, short of determining the values of a physical property such as relative atomic mass. They do, however, emit different colours of light when excited at low pressure in a discharge tube. The discharge excites the atoms, which causes them to produce their characteristic atomic emission spectrum. The spectrum varies from one element to another because the electronic energy levels vary. Atomic emission is used to distinguish between the noble gases as well as for the illuminated displays called 'neon lights'. Despite the name, these lights contain not just neon, but various noble gases to create the different colours.

Inert or noble?

The elements of Group VIII were called the 'inert gases' for 60 years after they were discovered just before the turn of the twentieth century. They were given this name because they appeared to react with no other element. They seemed to have no chemical properties (other than having no chemical properties!). While this observation remains true for the first three elements (helium, neon, and argon), the chemical research community was startled in 1962 by the discovery of the first compounds of xenon.

Xenon is now known to form a range of compounds with fluorine and oxygen, the two most electronegative elements. Examples include XeF_2, XeF_4, and XeF_6 together with XeO_3 and $XeOF_2$. There are fewer compounds of krypton because its ionization energy is higher. Again, the compounds consist mainly of fluorides such as the colourless solid KrF_2.

Once chemists knew that xenon reacted, the name for the group had to be changed. One suggestion was 'rare gases', but this was a poor choice, because argon is the third most abundant gas in the atmosphere (at about 1%). The name 'noble gases' has been chosen to replace 'inert gases'. It is reminiscent of the name 'noble metals' (for metals such as gold and platinum that do not react readily).

The preparation of xenon compounds

Louis Pasteur, who made important discoveries in chemistry, medicine, and microbiology, once said: 'In the field of observation, chance favours only the prepared mind.' The following discovery provides a good example of this general principle.

Neil Bartlett, a British-born Canadian chemistry professor, was working with the compound platinum(VI) fluoride PtF_6. One morning, instead of a red gas, his apparatus contained an orange solid. Rather than simply washing out the apparatus and starting again, Bartlett asked himself how the change had occurred. When he found a tiny hole in the apparatus, he suspected that air could have entered the apparatus overnight.

Analysis of the solid confirmed his guess. The solid had the formula O_2PtF_6. This unusual compound contained the ions O_2^+ (called dioxygenyl ion, spread 5.7) and PtF_6^-. This was an extraordinary discovery, as it meant that molecular oxygen, O_2, had been *oxidized* by loss of an electron. Platinum(VI) fluoride is such a powerful oxidant that it can oxidize molecular oxygen.

Following up the discovery, Bartlett wondered how much energy was needed to remove one electron from *molecular* oxygen. Data books showed the ionization energy to be 1175 kJ mol^{-1}. Bartlett then remembered that this value was very close indeed to the ionization energy of xenon, 1170 kJ mol^{-1}. He reasoned that, if this powerful oxidant could remove an electron from molecular oxygen, then maybe it could also remove one from xenon.

His colleagues were politely amused when Bartlett asked for some xenon 'so that I can try some reactions'. Their amusement turned to great excitement when he was able to prepare $XePtF_6$, the noble gas analogue of O_2PtF_6. Within a short space of time, xenon compounds exhibiting a wide range of oxidation states were prepared. The elements of Group VIII were no longer 'inert'; they were merely 'noble'.

(a)

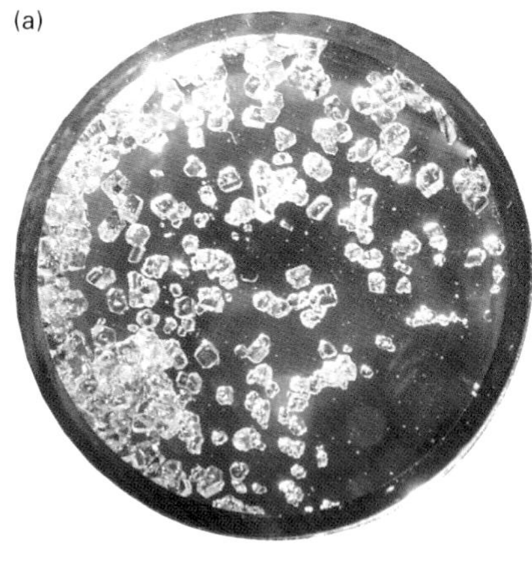

(b)

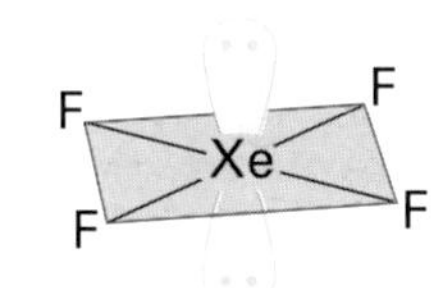

(a) Crystals of xenon tetrafluoride XeF_4. (b) The structure of the molecule XeF_4.

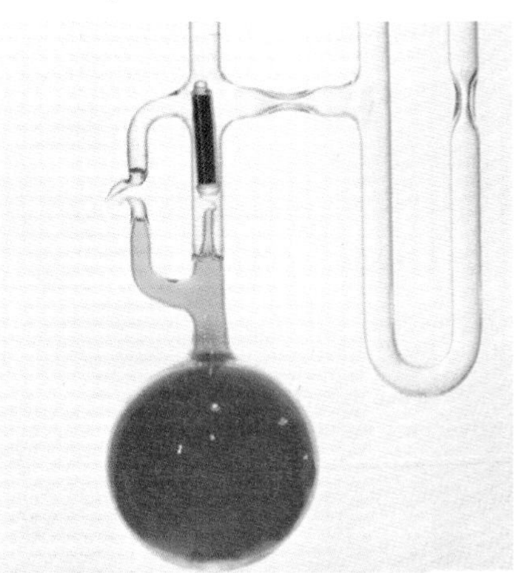

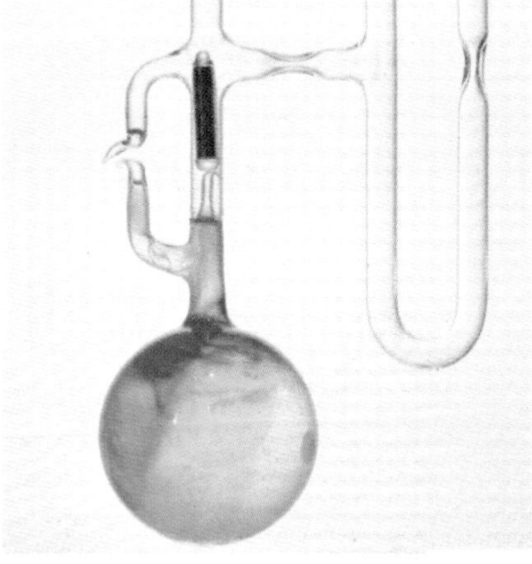

The preparation of the first xenon compound. (a) The apparatus contains the red gas PtF_6, and a seal to xenon gas. (b) After the seal is broken, it contains $XePtF_6$.

SUMMARY

- The Group VIII elements exist as separate atoms.
- The Group VIII elements have extremely low melting and boiling points; they are all gases at 25 °C and 1 bar.
- Helium, neon, and argon *are* inert; they do not form compounds.
- Xenon and, to a much lesser extent, krypton form compounds with the highly electronegative elements fluorine and oxygen.

PRACTICE

1 Describe the structure of and explain the bonding in solid argon.

2 Comment on the relative values of the boiling points of the noble gases.

PRACTICE EXAM QUESTIONS

1 Aluminium is produced commercially by the electrolysis of a 5% solution of aluminium oxide in molten cryolite. The cathode and anode can be made of carbon and the temperature of the electrolyte is maintained at around 1200 K.

a i Explain, with reference to economic considerations, why pure molten aluminium oxide is not used as the electrolyte. [2]

ii Write an equation for the reaction at the cathode and indicate the physical state of the aluminium as it is formed. [2]

iii Write an equation for the reaction at the anode and explain why the regular replacement of anodes is necessary. [3]

b The electrolysis uses large quantities of electricity. Identify the **two** main processes that have high electrical energy requirements. [2]

c Aluminium is readily recycled.

i Give **two** benefits of recycling rather than extracting aluminium from its ore. [2]

ii Identify **one** cost, other than electrical energy, in the process of recycling aluminium. [1]
AQA (NEAB) 1999

2 a i Describe what you would observe when anhydrous aluminium chloride is added to an excess of water. Write an equation for the reaction.

ii Write an equation to show why an aqueous solution containing aluminium ions is acidic.

iii Describe what you would observe when solid sodium carbonate is added to a solution containing aluminium ions. Write an equation (or equations) for the reaction which occurs. [8]

b i Describe what is observed when dilute ammonia solution is added, dropwise until in excess, to a solution containing aluminium ions. Give the formula of the final aluminium-containing species.

ii How would your observations differ if dilute sodium hydroxide solution was used instead of dilute ammonia solution?
Give the formula of any different aluminium-containing species formed. [4]
AQA (NEAB) 1997

3 a From the compounds of the Group IV elements C, Si, Ge, Sn and Pb choose an appropriate example for **each** of the following.

	Type of compound	Name or formula of example
(i)	A strongly reducing oxide	
(ii)	A giant covalent oxide	
(iii)	A strongly reducing chloride	
(iv)	A covalent chloride which is **not** hydrolysed by water	

[4]

b i When metallic tin is placed in a solution of iodine in an organic solvent, a covalent compound of empirical formula, SnI_x, is formed which dissolves in the solvent.
When 0.4814 g of tin (an excess) was placed in a solution of iodine in the organic solvent, all the iodine reacted and formed SnI_x which dissolved in the solvent. Recovery of the covalent iodide yielded 1.987 g of product and 0.1048 g of unreacted tin. Determine the value of x. [2]

ii If the empirical formula and molecular formula of the covalent iodide are the same, state the shape of the molecule of SnI_x. [1]

c The element carbon exists as diamond and graphite which are covalent solids.

i State **two** ways in which the **structures** of these two forms of carbon differ. [2]

ii A third form of carbon C_{60}, called fullerene, is known, in which the carbon atoms form the shape of a football made up of five and six membered rings. State a physical method by which the existence of C_{60} particles could be verified. [1]
WJEC 1998

4 This question is concerned with elements in Group IV.

a Complete the following table:

Element	Formula of chloride of element in its highest oxidation state	Formula of oxide of element in its lowest oxidation state
Carbon		
Silicon		
Lead		

[2]

b A bottle of the chloride of silicon produces 'steamy' fumes when left open on the bench. A bottle of the chloride of carbon produces no such fumes. Explain these observations, giving equations where appropriate. [5]

c Lead(IV) oxide oxidizes hydrochloric acid according to the following equation:

$$PbO_2 + 4HCl \rightarrow PbCl_2 + Cl_2 + 2H_2O$$

Write two ionic half-equations for this process. [2]

d Explain why carbon dioxide is a gas at room temperature whereas silicon dioxide is a solid with a melting point of 1710 °C. [3]
EDEXCEL 1996

5 Ammonia, NH_3, and phosphine, PH_3, are the hydrides of the first two elements in Group V.

a i Draw a dot-and-cross diagram for the ammonia molecule. [1]

ii Sketch and explain the shape of the ammonia molecule. [3]

iii Ammonia molecules have σ-bonds. What do you understand by a **σ-bond**? [1]

iv Draw a charge-cloud (orbital) representation of the ammonia molecule. [1]

b Some physical properties of ammonia and phosphine are given in the following table:

	Boiling temperature / °C	Solubility in water / mol dm^{-3}
Ammonia	−33	31.1
Phosphine	−88	8.88×10^{-4}

i By reference to the nature of the intermolecular forces in both molecules, suggest reasons for the difference in boiling temperatures. [3]

ii Suggest why ammonia is much more soluble in water than phosphine. [2]

c Ammonium salts are widely used as fertilisers. One standard method for the analysis of ammonium salts (except the chloride) is to react them in a solution with methanal, HCHO. This forms a neutral organic compound together with an acid which can be titrated with standard alkali. For ammonium nitrate the equation for this reaction is:

$$4NH_4NO_3 + 6HCHO \rightarrow (CH_2)_6N_4 + 4HNO_3 + 6H_2O$$

15.0 g of a fertiliser containing ammonium nitrate as the only ammonium salt was dissolved in water and the solution made up to 1.00 dm^3 with pure water.

25.0 cm^3 portions of this solution were treated with saturated aqueous methanal solution and allowed to stand for a few minutes.

The liberated nitric acid was then titrated with 0.100 mol dm^{-3} NaOH solution. The volume of NaOH solution used was 22.3 cm^3. What percentage by mass of the fertiliser was ammonium nitrate? [4]
EDEXCEL 1997

6 a Compare and contrast the properties of the Group IV chlorides by completing the table below.

	Tetrachloromethane	Silicon tetrachloride	Lead(II) chloride
physical state at room temperature			
electrical conductivity when liquid			
effect of adding water at room temperature			
type of bonding			

[5]

b i Write an equation for one of the Group IV oxides reacting with a base.

ii Write an equation for one of the Group IV oxides reacting with an acid. [2]

c i Which Group IV metal forms divalent ions that readily decolorize acidified, aqueous potassium manganate(VII)?

ii Use the redox half-equations in the *Data Booklet* to write a balanced equation for the reaction in **c i**. [2]
OCR (UCLES) 1994

7 a Sulphuric acid is produced in the UK by the Contact Process. The sulphur dioxide needed for this process is obtained by burning elemental sulphur, which is imported in the liquid state.

i State *one* advantage and *one* disadvantage of transporting sulphur in the liquid state. [2]

ii Write equations to show the conversion of sulphur to sulphur trioxide. [2]

b The figure below shows diagrammatically a sulphuric acid converter.

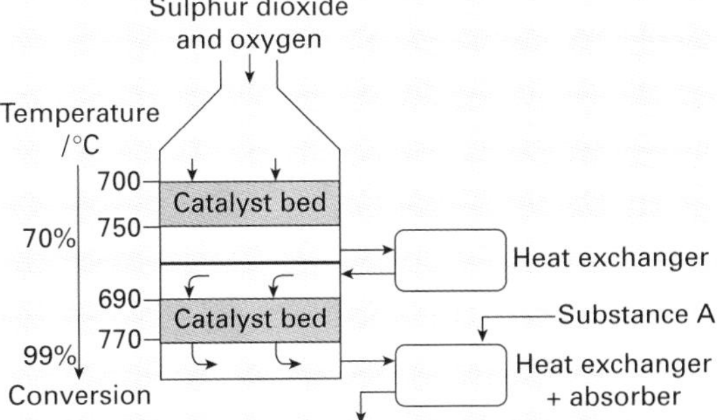

i Is the reaction between sulphur dioxide and oxygen endothermic or exothermic? [1]

ii Give the name of a catalyst used in this process. [1]

iii Give *two* reasons why heat exchangers are used in the Contact Process. [2]

iv Why is more than one catalyst bed used? [2]

v Give the name of substance A, shown in the diagram above which enters the absorber, and then write an equation for the process occurring in the absorber. [3]

c Give *two* reasons why a sulphuric acid plant should *not* be sited near a residential area. [2]
AQA (AEB) 1996

8 Copper and silicon(IV) oxide have properties that make them widely used materials.

a Copper is a good conductor of electricity whereas silicon(IV) oxide is not. Explain why this is so. [2]

b Suggest why silicon(IV) oxide has a higher melting point than copper. [2]

c Silicon(IV) oxide is known as a ceramic material. It is used to make hot plates for electric cookers. Suggest three reasons why it is used for this purpose. [3]

d Suggest one advantage and one disadvantage of using pure copper as the material of an axe-head.
OCR (UCLES) 1996

20 The transition metals

The transition metals have been of great importance throughout history. For example, gold jewellery and decorative artefacts were first made around 5000 BC. Two of the main stages of human development, namely the Bronze Age (3500–1100 BC) and the Iron Age (1100 BC – AD 100), are marked by the discovery and use of the two transition metals copper (bronze is an alloy of copper and tin) and iron. During the twentieth century, the catalytic activity of transition metals was exploited to make many key industrial processes possible. The transition metals are important in our modern industrialized society as catalysts and structural metals. When present in compounds, they show a range of distinctive properties.

20.1 The elements titanium to copper

OBJECTIVES

- Variable oxidation states and catalytic activity
- Coloured ions and complex formation
- Partially filled d subshell explains properties

Origin of the name

The name *transition* metals refers to the transition from the element calcium, in which the 3d orbitals are too high in energy to be used, to the element zinc, in which the 3d electrons are too strongly held to take part in chemical reactions.

The transition metals occupy the central region of the periodic table in Periods 4, 5, and 6. A set of five d orbitals fills with a total of 10 electrons in the course of each period. This chapter will concentrate on the chemistry of elements selected from the first row of the d block, the Period 4 elements scandium Sc to zinc Zn.

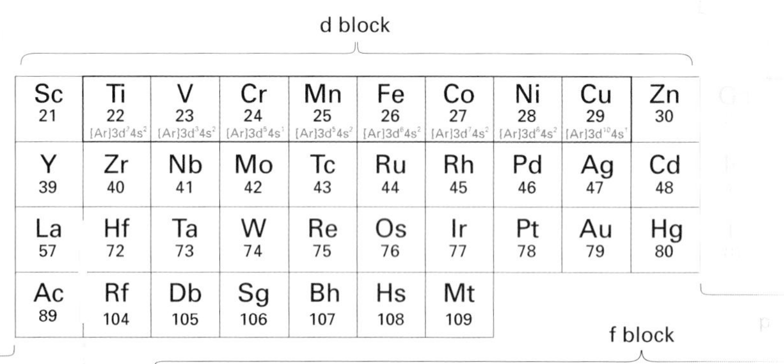

The position of the d block in the periodic table.

The first row of the d block: scandium to zinc

Calcium is the metal immediately before scandium in Period 4. All the elements of the first row of the d block have greater first ionization energies than calcium. Notice that both the atomic radius and the ionization energy have similar values from titanium Ti to copper Cu. Atomic size decreases overall across Periods 2 and 3 (see the chapter on 'Trends across a period') because the increasing nuclear charge attracts the electrons in the outer orbitals more strongly. Throughout this first row of the d block, however, size changes very little. The electrons are being added to *inner* d orbitals, where they are much more effective at shielding the outer s electrons from the increasing nuclear charge. As a result, the ionization energy also increases very little across the period, because the outer 4s electrons are well shielded from the nuclear charge.

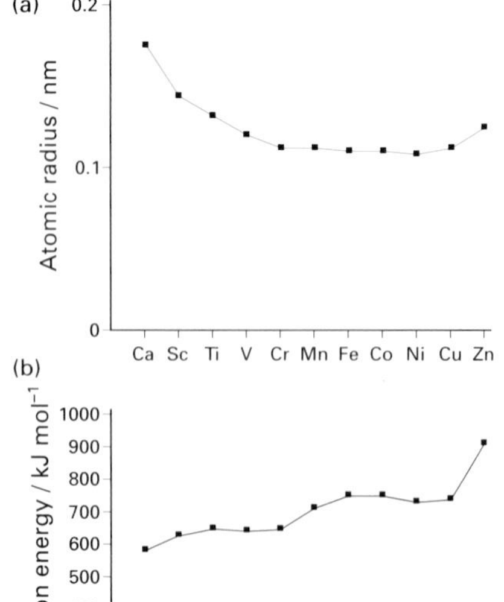

(a) The atomic radius decreases quite sharply from calcium to chromium, after which there is little change in the value. (b) The first ionization energy shows a rather gentle general increase across the d block, with a sharp increase from copper to zinc.

'Transition metals' or 'd-block elements'?

All the d-block elements of Period 4, with the exception of zinc, have much higher melting points and higher densities than calcium. Notice also that, with the exception of scandium and zinc, they show variable oxidation states in their compounds. Many d-block elements, again with the exception of scandium and zinc, have aqueous ions that are coloured. So, a transition metal is defined as follows:

- A **transition metal** (a transition element) is a d-block element forming at least one stable ion that has a *partially filled* d subshell.

Scandium and zinc are d-block elements but they are *not* transition metals. Each metal forms just one ion: there are *no* d electrons present in Sc^{3+}, and the d subshell is *full* in Zn^{2+}. This explains why scandium and zinc do not form coloured aqueous ions. Colour is due to electronic transitions between d orbitals (see the final spread in this chapter), so needs at least one d electron – and a vacant orbital in which to put it!

1660 °C 3287 °C Ti Titanium 0.132 nm 658 kJ mol⁻¹
1887 °C 3377 °C V Vanadium 0.122 nm 650 kJ mol⁻¹
1857 °C 2672 °C Cr Chromium 0.117 nm 653 kJ mol⁻¹
1244 °C 1962 °C Mn Manganese 0.117 nm 717 kJ mol⁻¹
1535 °C 2750 °C Fe Iron 0.116 nm 759 kJ mol⁻¹
1495 °C 2870 °C Co Cobalt 0.116 nm 760 kJ mol⁻¹
1453 °C 2732 °C Ni Nickel 0.115 nm 737 kJ mol⁻¹
1084 °C 2567 °C Cu Copper 0.117 nm 745 kJ mol⁻¹

The major properties of the transition metals titanium to copper.

Electronic structures

The 3d orbitals are filling as atomic number increases from Ti to Cu. Look at the sequence of electronic structures opposite. You would expect the 3d subshell to fill with electrons smoothly from one to ten. However, there are two places where the filling does not follow this expected sequence. Chromium has the electronic structure $3d^5 4s^1$ and not $3d^4 4s^2$; and copper has the electronic structure $3d^{10} 4s^1$ and not $3d^9 4s^2$. This is because the 3d and 4s orbitals are very close in energy; as electrons are added across the period, their *relative* energies change. At chromium, it is energetically favourable for all the orbitals to be half-full; in agreement with Hund's rule, the five electrons have unpaired spins (see the chapter on 'Electrons in atoms'). At copper, it is energetically favourable to fill the d orbitals completely, leaving the 4s orbital with an unpaired electron, as the 3d orbitals are now lower in energy than the 4s orbitals.

Ion formation

When the transition metals of Period 4 form ions, they lose the (outermost) 4s electrons *before* they lose the (inner) 3d electrons. For example, the Ti^{2+} ion is formed by losing the two 4s electrons rather than the two 3d electrons. The Ti^{2+} ion has the structure $[Ar]3d^2$ instead of $[Ar]4s^2$. Both Mn^{2+} and Fe^{3+} have the structure $[Ar]3d^5$.

$$[H_3N\!:\rightarrow Ag^+ \leftarrow :NH_3]^+$$

Complex ions. Lone pairs are found on ions or molecules such as Cl^-, H_2O, NH_3, and CN^-. Transition metals can act as Lewis acids by accepting these lone pairs (they go into vacant d orbitals). This illustration shows the linear structure of the complex ion $[Ag(NH_3)_2]^+$ (see information about the 'silver nitrate test' in the chapter on 'The halogens').

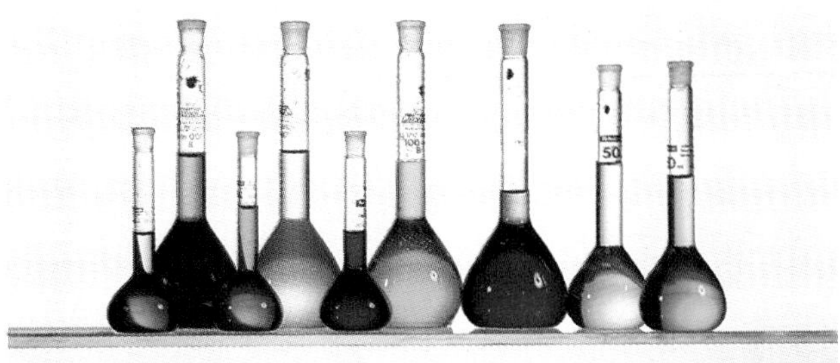

Common transition metal ions in aqueous solution (from left to right) Cr^{2+}, Cr^{3+}, $Cr_2O_7^{2-}$, Mn^{2+}, MnO_4^-, Fe^{3+}, Co^{2+}, Ni^{2+}, Cu^{2+}.

SUMMARY

- Transition metal characteristics are:
  - variable oxidation states
  - catalytic activity
  - complex ion formation
  - formation of coloured ions.
- Transition metal characteristics result when a d-block element forms at least one stable ion that has a partially filled d subshell.
- The first row of transition metals comprises the eight elements titanium to copper.

PRACTICE

1 State the four common characteristics of transition metals.

20.2

IRON AND STEEL

OBJECTIVES

- The blast furnace
- Steel-making
- Specialist steels

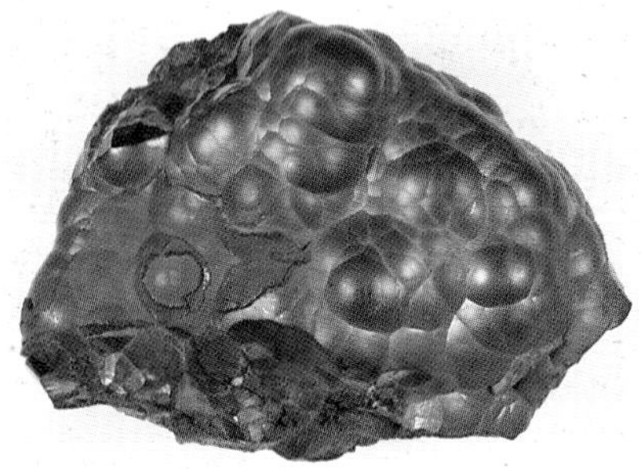

Kidney iron ore is a form of haematite Fe_2O_3 found as red-brown rounded nodules.

Iron is the most widely used of all metals because it is abundant and relatively cheap to extract from its ores. Millions of tonnes are produced each year. As well as iron ore, the extraction uses coal and limestone mined from the ground together with oxygen from the air. Iron is used commercially in the form of steels, which consist of iron mixed with controlled amounts of other elements. Over 90% of all metallic objects are made out of steel. The chief drawback is that the cheaper types of steel corrode to produce a hydrated oxide (called rust; see spread 13.12), which is structurally weak.

Iron ores and their treatment

The most important ore of iron is haematite, containing iron(III) oxide Fe_2O_3. High-grade haematite ores have iron concentrations over 60%, while low-grade ores may have an iron content of 20%. Other iron ores include magnetite Fe_3O_4 and siderite $FeCO_3$. The carbonate ore siderite is first roasted in air to convert it to iron(III) oxide:

$$4FeCO_3(s) + O_2(g) \rightarrow 2Fe_2O_3(s) + 4CO_2(g)$$

Sulphide ores on roasting produce some sulphur dioxide, which is a potential pollutant.

Iron smelting: the blast furnace

Oxides of iron can be reduced to the metal using carbon, as we saw in the chapters on 'Redox equilibrium' and 'Spontaneous change…'. The industrial process takes place in a **blast furnace**, shown below. The raw materials and the chemical reactions are described in the box on the left.

The chemistry of the blast furnace

Three solid raw materials are loaded into the top of the blast furnace:

- *Coke* (C) This is a form of carbon made by heating coal in the absence of air. It is the fuel and the source of the reductant.
- *Iron ore* (Fe_2O_3) This is the source of the iron. It is usually crushed haematite or roasted carbonate ore.
- *Limestone* ($CaCO_3$) This combines with high-melting-point impurities in the ore to form a liquid slag. Limestone is also a secondary source of the reductant.

A high-pressure blast of heated air enters the furnace. A series of chemical reactions take place:

1. Coke burns in the air:
   $C(s) + O_2(g) \rightarrow CO_2(g)$
2. Limestone decomposes:
   $CaCO_3(s) \rightarrow CaO(s) + CO_2(g)$
3. Coke reduces the carbon dioxide:
   $C(s) + CO_2(g) \rightarrow 2CO(g)$
4. Carbon monoxide reduces the iron oxide ore:
   $Fe_2O_3(s) + 3CO(g) \rightarrow 2Fe(l) + 3CO_2(g)$
5. Impurities in the ore (mostly silica) react with calcium oxide to form a liquid slag:
   $CaO(s) + SiO_2(s) \rightarrow CaSiO_3(l)$

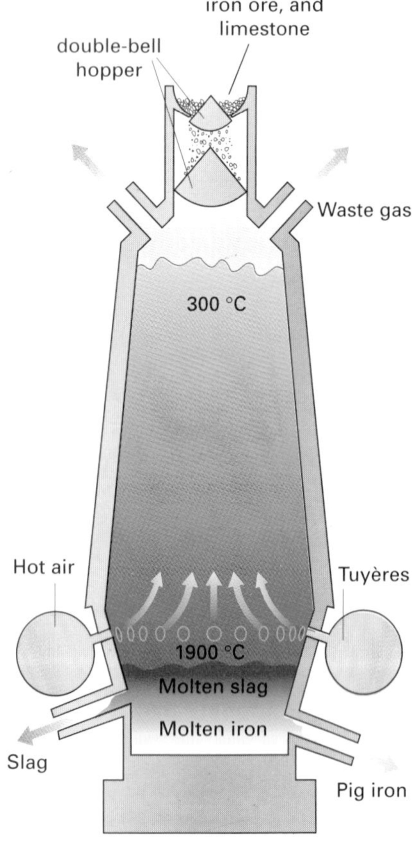

A modern blast furnace is a steel structure lined with refractory firebrick and is up to 30 metres high. The air blast is preheated to about 900 °C by heat exchangers (visible on the far left), which extract heat from burning the waste gases leaving the top of the furnace. This also greatly reduces levels of the pollutant carbon monoxide. A modern furnace produces around 10 000 tonnes of iron per day.

The liquid iron falls to the bottom of the furnace as it is formed, and the liquid slag floats on top of it. This protects the iron from oxidation by the air blast. Slag and iron are run off separately at intervals of about four hours. Slag is used to make building blocks and road foundations.

The manufacture of mild steel

Impure **pig iron**, the iron that comes out of a blast furnace, is very brittle. It contains about 4% carbon from the coke, together with nitrogen from the air blast, and silicon from impurities in the ore. The physical properties of iron improve dramatically when the carbon content is below 0.2%. Lowering the carbon content of iron and carefully controlling the amounts of other substances present is called steel-making. **Mild steel** is a tough steel that contains approximately 0.15% carbon. Pig iron is usually converted to mild steel by the **basic oxygen process**. Oxygen is blasted into molten iron through a water-cooled lance to oxidize the excess carbon to carbon dioxide. The 'basic' part of the name refers to the basic lining of the furnace and to the basic substances called fluxes that are added. These combine with the acidic impurities (oxides of other non-metals) to form a slag which can be removed from the iron.

A basic oxygen converter contains up to 300 tonnes of molten pig iron mixed with up to 30% scrap steel. The oxygen lance oxidizes the chief non-metallic impurities, carbon, phosphorus, and nitrogen.

Removal of S

Sulphur is removed by blowing powdered magnesium into the melt; this reacts with sulphur to form magnesium sulphide, which is removed with the slag.

Recycling

Recycling scrap steel makes a helpful contribution to our care of the environment, as is the case with recycling aluminium cans.

Alloy steels

Alloy steels have specific properties that suit their end-use. These properties are achieved by controlling the percentages of non-metals in the steel and by adding controlled quantities of other transition metals. For example, vanadium is used as an alloying agent in **ferrovanadium steel**, forming a carbide V_4C_3 that gives a fine grain to the steel and increases its resistance to wear. Ferrovanadium steel is used in springs.

High-tensile structural steels have a maximum of 0.3% carbon with 0.9% of both chromium and manganese, and 0.4% of copper. **Stainless steels** resist corrosion much better than iron itself. They typically contain 18% chromium and 8% nickel. Stainless steels for use above 450 °C also contain titanium. **Hadfield steel**, containing 13% manganese, is particularly frustrating for safe-crackers, as the metal becomes harder the more it is hit. **Armour plate** and some bicycle frames are made from steel containing 3% chromium and 0.5% molybdenum. **High-speed steels** include vanadium and cobalt as important constituents in a wide variety of wear-resistant alloy steels used to make cutting tools. **Alnico steel** contains iron, aluminium, nickel, and cobalt and is used to make permanent magnets.

Galvanizing involves immersing a steel or iron object in a tank of molten zinc; see spread 13.12. **Galvanized steel** or iron has a thin protective coating of zinc on its surface. The coating acts in two ways. It *physically* prevents water and oxygen reaching the iron below. But it continues to protect the iron or steel underneath in a more important *chemical* way, even if it is scratched or partly worn off. Zinc is more reactive than iron (it has a more negative standard electrode potential), so it will lose electrons more easily than iron. In contact with water and oxygen (from damp air, for example), it is therefore the zinc that is oxidized and preferentially corrodes away, rather than the iron rusting.

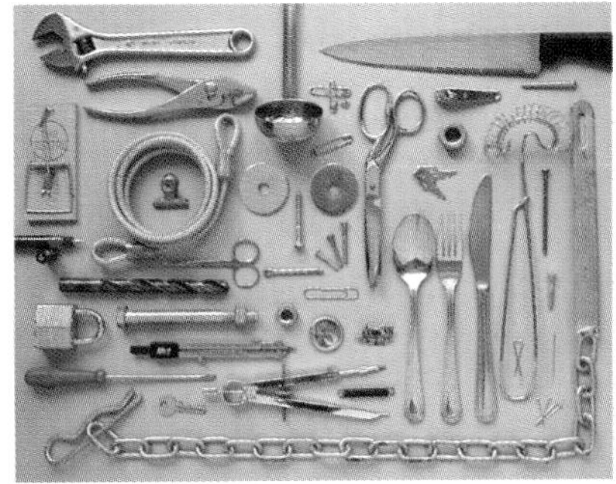

A selection of objects made from steel.

SUMMARY

- Pig iron is obtained by reduction of iron ore by carbon.
- Steel is made from pig iron by oxidizing most, but not all, of the carbon in the pig iron using a water-cooled oxygen lance.
- The properties of steels may be controlled by the addition of other transition metals.
- Stainless steels contain chromium and nickel alloyed with iron.
- Vanadium, manganese, and cobalt add toughness and hardness to steels.

20.3

OBJECTIVES

- Manufacture and uses of chromium
- Manufacture and uses of titanium
- Manufacture and uses of copper

Manufacture and uses of three transition metals

Chromium, titanium, and copper are three transition metals with widely differing end-uses. The extraction method of each of these metals reflects its general reactivity and how readily it can be oxidized. Unlike iron, none of these three metals is extracted by carbon reduction in a blast furnace. Chromium would require a temperature 500 °C hotter than for iron for this process to be thermodynamically feasible. Titanium also is too strongly bonded to oxygen: furthermore, it forms a carbide with carbon. In the case of copper, the metal is so unreactive (i.e. the metal ions are so easily reduced) that a separate reductant is not required. Simply heating the ore causes decomposition to the metal. A further distinction is that iron, which is needed in huge quantities, is produced by a *continuous* process (the blast furnace), in which reactants are added and products are removed continuously over a long time. These three metals, which are required in smaller quantities, are each produced by a *batch* process; see spread 13.13. Batch processes are necessarily more costly than continuous processes.

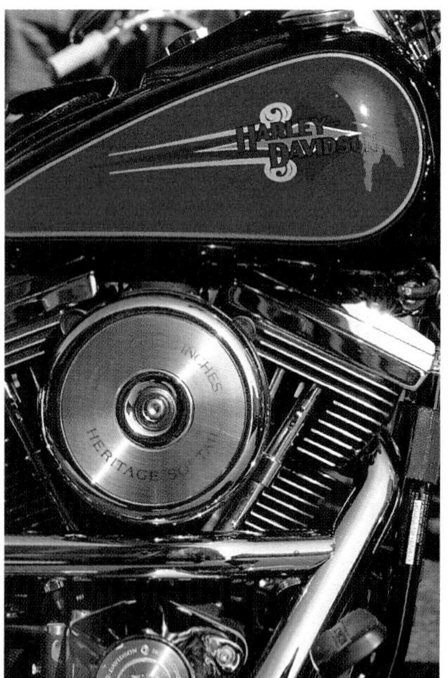
Uses of chromium-plated steel. The layer of chromium plate is only a few hundredths of a millimetre thick. It protects the underlying steel and improves its appearance.

The manufacture of chromium

Chromium is a bright, shiny metal which forms a transparent and protective oxide layer on its surface. This makes chromium very useful for coating readily corroded metals such as iron.

The only commercially important chromium ore is chromite $FeCr_2O_4$ (i.e. $FeO{\cdot}Cr_2O_3$), 95% of the world's supplies of which are in South Africa. The element is extracted and mixed with nickel to make heat-resisting alloys, or with iron and nickel to make stainless steels. The presence of chromium also hardens steel. 'Chromium plate' is a thin protective and decorative layer of chromium electroplated onto steel.

If pure chromium is required (e.g. for electroplating), the ore is first concentrated and converted to chromium(III) oxide. The oxide is then reduced by the Thermit process, in which a powdered mixture of chromium(III) oxide and aluminium is ignited; see spread 3.1:

$$Cr_2O_3(s) + 2Al(s) \rightarrow 2Cr(l) + Al_2O_3(s)$$

The result of this highly exothermic reaction is a pool of molten chromium at the bottom of the refractory container.

If a ferrochrome alloy for use in steel-making, rather than pure chromium, is required, then concentrated chromite ore is reduced by carbon in an electric arc furnace:

$$FeCr_2O_4(s) + 4C(s) \rightarrow Fe(l) + 2Cr(l) + 4CO(g)$$

The manufacture of titanium: the Kroll process

Titanium is the ninth-commonest element in the Earth's crust. It has just over half the density of steel but comparable tensile strength (strength under tension, i.e. when pulled). Titanium is a reactive metal but it forms a protective oxide coating on its surface in the same way as aluminium does.

The main titanium ores are rutile TiO_2 and ilmenite $FeTiO_3$ (i.e. $FeO{\cdot}TiO_2$). Extraction is difficult because molten titanium reacts strongly with non-metals such as nitrogen, oxygen, and especially carbon: these impurities would render the metal brittle. The first stage is to produce titanium(IV) chloride (T_b = 136 °C) by heating the oxide with chlorine and carbon at about 900 °C:

$$TiO_2(s) + 2C(s) + 2Cl_2(g) \rightarrow TiCl_4(g) + 2CO(g)$$

The chloride is then reduced by magnesium at 1000 °C in an inert atmosphere of argon:

$$TiCl_4(g) + 2Mg(l) \rightarrow Ti(s) + 2MgCl_2(l)$$

In a Kroll reactor, the reduction of titanium(IV) chloride produces up to 3 tonnes of titanium, which must be bored or machined out of the cooled reactor. (This is a good example of a batch process.) Further processing is needed to remove magnesium and magnesium chloride impurities.

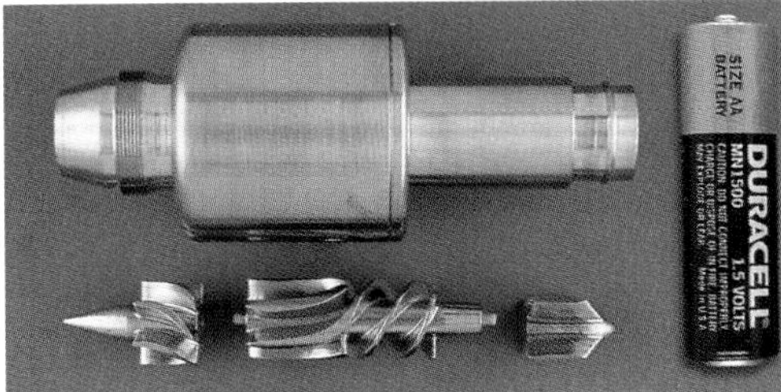

Titanium alloy is used to make the tiny turbine in this heart bypass pump. The shape of the blades required careful design to achieve a sufficient flow rate while avoiding cell damage. (The battery is shown for scale.)

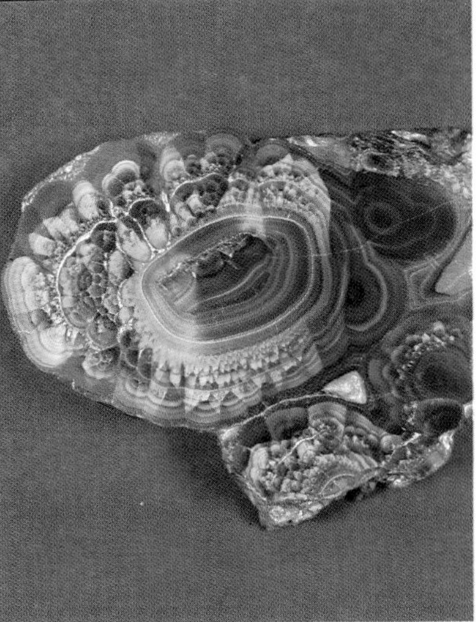

The ore malachite.

The manufacture of copper

Copper is used as the pure metal, which resists corrosion and is an excellent conductor of heat and electricity. It polishes to a bright shine and so is decorative. **Bronze** is an alloy of about 90% copper with tin. **Brass** is an alloy of copper and zinc. **Coinage metals** contain about 75% copper together with nickel.

The chief copper ore is copper pyrite (chalcopyrite) $CuFeS_2$ (i.e. $CuS{\cdot}FeS$). Other commercial ores include copper glance Cu_2S, cuprite Cu_2O, azurite $2CuCO_3{\cdot}Cu(OH)_2$, and malachite $CuCO_3{\cdot}Cu(OH)_2$. Lumps of copper metal called 'native copper' are occasionally found, illustrating the low reactivity of copper compared to most other metals.

Most copper ores contain only a few per cent of the metal. The ore is concentrated by 'froth flotation', in which air is bubbled through a tank containing water, very finely powdered ore, and detergent. Copper-containing particles rise with the bubbles; waste (called 'gangue') sinks. The copper-containing froth can be skimmed off.

The next steps are most easily understood if we start from the ore Cu_2S. When roasted in air, copper(I) sulphide forms copper(I) oxide and sulphur dioxide:

$$2Cu_2S(l) + 3O_2(g) \rightarrow 2Cu_2O(l) + 2SO_2(g)$$

The oxide then reacts with unchanged ore to give the molten metal:

$$2Cu_2O(l) + Cu_2S(l) \rightarrow 6Cu(l) + SO_2(g)$$

The product contains 2–3% of impurities, mainly iron and sulphur. These impurities harden the metal and make it quite unsuitable for its major use in the manufacture of bendable wires and malleable copper piping. Electrolytic refining (see the chapter on 'Redox equilibrium') gives copper of almost 100% purity.

The electrical conductivity of pure copper is second only to that of silver. Its high ductility enables it to be drawn into wires. Good malleability means that wires and pipes may be bent when they are fitted into buildings.

SUMMARY

- Chromium is produced by the Thermit process: the reduction of chromium(III) oxide by aluminium.
- Uses of chromium include in stainless steels and as chromium plate.
- Titanium is produced by the reduction of gaseous titanium(IV) chloride by magnesium in an inert argon atmosphere.
- Titanium metal is strong and has a low density; titanium alloys perform well in high-temperature or corrosive environments.
- Copper is produced by roasting the ore in air.
- The use of copper in pipes and electrical wires depends on its chemical inertness, high ductility, malleability, and electrical conductivity.

PRACTICE

1 Write out the metal reactivity series, showing the relative reactivities of the metals calcium, iron, lead, tin, silver, sodium, and zinc. Insert copper, chromium, and titanium into this list. Justify your choice of position for each of the last three metals.

20.4

VARIABLE OXIDATION STATES – 1

OBJECTIVES

- Range of oxidation states
- Bonding with 3d and 4s electrons
- Reduction of vanadium(V)
- Assigning oxidation states

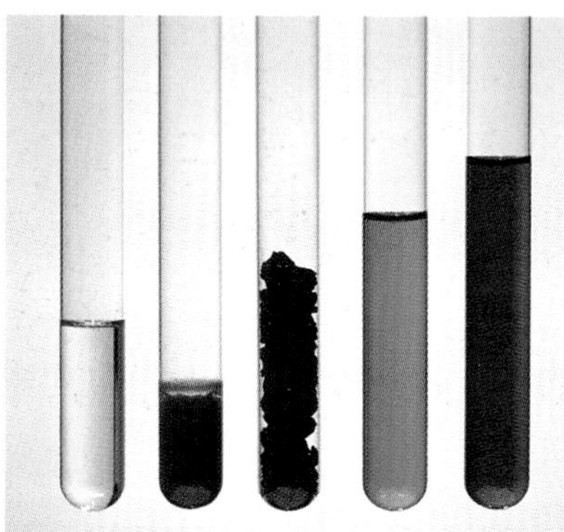

Compounds showing the common oxidation states of manganese. All are shown here as aqueous solutions, with the exception of manganese(III) hydroxide $Mn(OH)_3$ and manganese(IV) oxide MnO_2. (a) Mn^{2+}(aq), (b) $Mn(OH)_3$(s), (c) MnO_2(s), (d) MnO_4^{2-}(aq), and (e) MnO_4^-(aq).

One of the characteristic properties of the transition metals is that they have variable oxidation states. This is because the five inner d orbitals are at a similar energy level as the single outer s orbital. In the transition metals, d electrons as well as s electrons are involved in bonding. Ionic bonds form when 4s and then 3d electrons are lost to produce positively charged ions. Covalent bonds form as unpaired electrons pair up with those on other atoms.

Electronic structures and oxidation states

You can see the wide range of oxidation states shown by the elements of the first row of transition metals below. Manganese, for example, shows most oxidation numbers from +2 to +7 inclusive. Notice that the *maximum* oxidation number is equal to the total number of 3d and 4s electrons for the elements titanium to manganese inclusive. As you might expect, compounds containing transition metals in higher oxidation states tend to be covalent, e.g. the manganate(VII) ion MnO_4^- is a covalently bonded oxoanion containing manganese with oxidation number +7. In this ion the two 4s electrons and all five 3d electrons are used for bonding. Lower oxidation states tend to involve ionic bonding, e.g. manganese(II) chloride contains the Mn^{2+} ion.

The figure alongside compares the first four ionization energies for aluminium and chromium, both of which are normally found in oxidation state III. The sum of the first three ionization energies differs by less than two per cent. However, the fourth ionization energy, from M^{3+} to M^{4+}, varies greatly. In aluminium, the fourth electron has to be taken from an *inner* (2p) orbital, much closer to the nucleus. Hence the huge rise in ionization energy and the fact that aluminium is never seen in oxidation state IV. Chromium's significantly lower fourth ionization energy can be compensated by the increased lattice energy caused by the higher charged ion. So chromium compounds in oxidation state IV exist, the most famous being chromium(IV) oxide, CrO_2, colloquially dubbed 'chrome dioxide' by the audio and video tape industry.

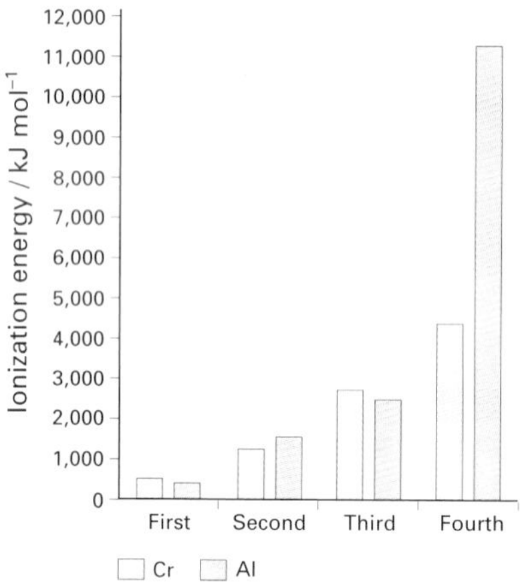

Comparison of the first four ionization energies of chromium and aluminium.

The main oxidation states (bold indicating the most important) and the electronic structures of the elements titanium to copper. Compounds containing a transition metal in its higher oxidation state tend to be oxidants. See spread 13.4 for redox titrations involving $Cr_2O_7^{2-}$ and MnO_4^-.

oxidation number								
+7				**+7**				
+6			**+6**	+6	+6			
+5		**+5**						
+4	**+4**	**+4**		**+4**				
+3	**+3**	+3	**+3**	+3	**+3**	**+3**	+3	
+2	+2	+2	+2	**+2**	**+2**	**+2**	**+2**	**+2**
+1								+1
Element	**Ti**	**V**	**Cr**	**Mn**	**Fe**	**Co**	**Ni**	**Cu**
Electronic structure	[Ar]$3d^24s^2$	[Ar]$3d^34s^2$	[Ar]$3d^54s^1$	[Ar]$3d^54s^2$	[Ar]$3d^64s^2$	[Ar]$3d^74s^2$	[Ar]$3d^84s^2$	[Ar]$3d^{10}4s^1$

Titanium(IV) chloride reacts vigorously with water to form copious clouds of titanium(IV) oxide. This reaction is used to produce smoke trails during aerobatic displays.

Bond character: $TiCl_3$ and $TiCl_4$

The illustration to the left shows two chlorides of titanium. Titanium(IV) chloride is a liquid at room temperature, confirming that it is covalent. In common with other covalent chlorides, it fumes in moist air as the result of hydrolysis. By contrast, titanium(III) chloride is a solid. It dissolves in water to form a solution containing the Ti^{3+}(aq) ion, i.e. $[Ti(H_2O)_6]^{3+}$. This behaviour is typical of ionic chlorides. The reason for the difference in bonding is the higher charge density of Ti^{4+} compared with Ti^{3+}, making the bonds in titanium(IV) compounds more covalent.

Vanadium: V(V), V(IV), V(III), and V(II)

A striking illustration of variable oxidation states is shown by the chemistry of vanadium. The highest oxidation states occur when the element combines with the highly electronegative element oxygen. Vanadium shows its oxidation number +5 in the vanadate(V) ion. When zinc reduces ammonium vanadate(V) in concentrated hydrochloric acid, the solution changes from yellow to blue-green, and eventually violet as the oxidation number changes from +5 through to +2:

$VO_2^+(aq)$ →	$VO^{2+}(aq)$ →	$V^{3+}(aq)$ →	$V^{2+}(aq)$
V(V)	V(IV)	V(III)	V(II)
yellow	blue	blue-green	violet

In a similar way, zinc can reduce dichromate(VI) ions $Cr_2O_7^{2-}$ in acidic solution via chromium(III) ions Cr^{3+} to chromium(II) ions Cr^{2+}. To prepare a transition metal in a low oxidation state, the general process is

1 add an acid

2 add a reductant

Zinc is the reductant in this case. See spread 20.10 for preparing a complex in a high oxidation state.

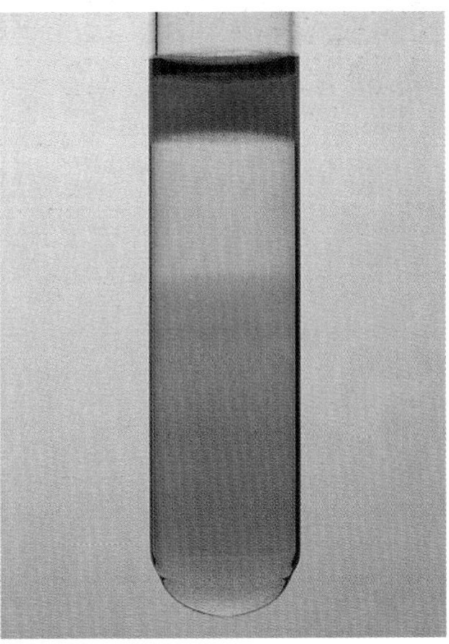

The oxidation states of vanadium may be demonstrated by carefully pouring a layer of aqueous potassium manganate(VII) over aqueous V^{2+} ions. After a few hours, coloured layers develop in the vanadium solution. The ion species are (from the lowest upwards): $V^{2+}(aq)$ – violet; $V^{3+}(aq)$ – blue-green; $VO^{2+}(aq)$ – blue; $VO_2^+(aq)$ – pale yellow. The green band in the middle is a mixture of the colours of VO_2^+ and VO^{2+}. The brown and pink layers at the top contain $MnO_2(s)$ and $MnO_4^-(aq)$ respectively.

Worked example on assigning oxidation states

Question: Find the oxidation states of the transition metal(s) in each of the following reactions. Comment on whether the reaction is a redox reaction or not.

(a) $2Fe(s) + 3Cl_2(g) \rightarrow 2FeCl_3(s)$

(b) $Fe(s) + 2HCl(g) \rightarrow FeCl_2(s) + H_2(g)$

(c) $2CrO_4^{2-}(aq) + 2H^+(aq) \rightarrow Cr_2O_7^{2-}(aq) + H_2O(l)$

(d) $MnO_4^-(aq) + 5Fe^{2+}(aq) + 8H^+(aq) \rightarrow Mn^{2+}(aq) + 5Fe^{3+}(aq) + 4H_2O(l)$

Strategy: You may need to look back at the rules in the chapter on 'Redox equilibrium': see the box on the right.

Answer:

(a) The oxidation state of elemental iron is Fe(0). In $FeCl_3$, chlorine is the more electronegative element and has the oxidation state Cl(–I). Therefore the oxidation state of iron in $FeCl_3$ is Fe(III). Iron has been oxidized.

(b) The oxidation state of elemental iron is Fe(0). In $FeCl_2$, chlorine is the more electronegative element and has the oxidation state Cl(–I). Therefore the oxidation state of iron in $FeCl_2$ is Fe(II). Iron has been oxidized.

(c) Chromium in the chromate(VI) ion CrO_4^{2-} has the oxidation state Cr(VI). Chromium in the dichromate(VI) ion $Cr_2O_7^{2-}$ also has the oxidation state Cr(VI). The reaction is not a redox reaction.

(d) The oxidation number of the iron ion is equal to its charge. The change in oxidation state is therefore from Fe(II) to Fe(III). A redox reaction has occurred: iron has been oxidized. Manganese has the oxidation state Mn(VII) in the manganate(VII) ion MnO_4^-. In the ion Mn^{2+}, the oxidation number is equal to the charge on the ion, so the oxidation state is Mn(II). Manganese has been reduced from Mn(VII) to Mn(II).

Strategy for finding oxidation states

You find the oxidation states of each element by applying the rules listed in the earlier chapter on 'Redox equilibrium'. Assign an oxidation number –2 to oxygen and remember that the sum of the oxidation numbers of the elements in an ion is equal to the charge on the ion. If the oxidation states for each element are the same on both sides of the chemical equation, then the reaction is not a redox reaction. If they are different, the reaction is a redox reaction.

Comment on reactions (a) and (b)

Notice how it takes the strong oxidant chlorine to force iron into the higher oxidation state Fe(III), whereas the weaker oxidant hydrogen chloride results only in oxidation state Fe(II).

Comment on reaction (d)

You should look back at the chapter on 'Redox equilibrium' for a discussion of redox titrations involving the iron(II) ion and the manganate(VII) ion.

Copper(I)

The only transition metal for which the oxidation number +1 is important is copper. Copper(I) oxide, for example, is formed by reduction of Fehling's solution using an aldehyde (see the chapter on 'Aldehydes and ketones'). Similarly, iodide ions can reduce aqueous copper(II) ions to a precipitate of copper(I) iodide; see spread 18.3. As the iodine produced reacts quantitatively with thiosulphate ion, this can be used to estimate the copper content in alloys such as brass. Aqueous copper(I) solutions are not stable: see the next spread.

SUMMARY

- Variable oxidation states result from the outermost s and d orbitals having similar energies.

20.5

VARIABLE OXIDATION STATES – 2

OBJECTIVES

- Using standard electrode potentials
- Common oxidants and reductants
- Ions with oxidation numbers +2 and +3

All the transition metals titanium to copper can exist in two or more positive oxidation states. A species changing from a higher to a lower oxidation state is reduced and acts as an oxidant. A species changing from a lower to a higher oxidation state is oxidized and acts as a reductant. The likelihood of a given species being an oxidant or reductant is shown by its standard electrode potential; see the chapter on 'Redox equilibrium'.

What standard electrode potentials mean

- Oxidants tend to have large positive standard electrode potentials

For example, cobalt(III) ion tends to be oxidizing, removing electrons from other species and itself being reduced to cobalt(II) ion:

$$Co^{3+}(aq) + e^- \rightleftharpoons Co^{2+}(aq); \quad E^\ominus = +1.82\,V$$

- Reductants tend to have large negative standard electrode potentials

For example, chromium(II) ion tends to be reducing, donating electrons to other species and itself being oxidized to chromium(III) ion:

$$Cr^{3+}(aq) + e^- \rightleftharpoons Cr^{2+}(aq); \quad E^\ominus = -0.41\,V$$

- The half-cell with the more negative $E^\ominus$ will cause reduction; see spread 13.7.

For example, chromium(II) ion will reduce cobalt(III) ion in the redox reaction:

$$Cr^{2+}(aq) + Co^{3+}(aq) \rightarrow Cr^{3+}(aq) + Co^{2+}(aq)$$

Colours of some aqueous ions

Ion	Colour
$Ti^{3+}(aq)$	purple
$V^{2+}(aq)$	violet
$V^{3+}(aq)$	blue-green
$Cr^{2+}(aq)$	blue
$Cr^{3+}(aq)$	green
$Mn^{2+}(aq)$	pale pink
$Fe^{2+}(aq)$	green
$Fe^{3+}(aq)$	brown
$Co^{2+}(aq)$	pink
$Ni^{2+}(aq)$	green
$Cu^{2+}(aq)$	blue

See spreads 20.1, 20.4, 20.6, and 20.8 for photographs of these ions; spreads 20.8 and 20.11 explain the origin of the colours.

Reductants

Transition metals change from reducing to oxidizing as their oxidation state increases. In their *lower* oxidation states, the ions tend to be reductants. Metallic chromium and the Cr^{2+} ion are reductants.

- Chromium displaces hydrogen from acids to produce the blue $Cr^{2+}(aq)$ ion.

The relevant standard electrode potentials are:

$$Cr^{2+}(aq) + 2e^- \rightleftharpoons Cr(s); \quad E^\ominus = -0.91\,V$$
$$2H^+(aq) + 2e^- \rightleftharpoons H_2(g); \quad E^\ominus = 0\,V$$

Electrons flow from chromium to hydrogen, thus bringing about the overall change:

$$Cr(s) + 2H^+(aq) \rightarrow Cr^{2+}(aq) + H_2(g)$$

- Chromium(II) ion rapidly reduces oxygen in air to form the green chromium(III) ion.

The overall change is:

$$4Cr^{2+}(aq) + O_2(g) + 4H^+(aq) \rightarrow 4Cr^{3+}(aq) + 2H_2O(l)$$

Again, this change may be predicted from standard electrode potentials:

$$Cr^{3+}(aq) + e^- \rightleftharpoons Cr^{2+}(aq); \quad E^\ominus = -0.41\,V$$
$$O_2(g) + 4H^+(aq) + 4e^- \rightleftharpoons 2H_2O(l); \quad E^\ominus = +1.23\,V$$

- Iron(II) ion is a weak reductant that reduces strong oxidants like chlorine.

The overall change:

$$2Fe^{2+}(aq) + Cl_2(aq) \rightarrow 2Fe^{3+}(aq) + 2Cl^-(aq)$$

is confirmed by standard electrode potential data:

$$Fe^{3+}(aq) + e^- \rightleftharpoons Fe^{2+}(aq); \quad E^\ominus = +0.77\,V$$
$$Cl_2(aq) + 2e^- \rightleftharpoons 2Cl^-(aq); \quad E^\ominus = +1.36\,V$$

Green iron(II) hydroxide forms when aqueous base is added to aqueous iron(II) ions. The precipitate oxidizes on contact with air to red-brown iron(III) hydroxide. See spread 13.9.

Oxidants

Transition metal ions in *higher* oxidation states tend to be oxidants.

- Iron(III) is a moderately strong oxidant, reacting with copper to produce $Cu^{2+}(aq)$ ions.

The overall change:

$$2Fe^{3+}(aq) + Cu(s) \rightarrow 2Fe^{2+}(aq) + Cu^{2+}(aq)$$

may be predicted from standard electrode potentials:

$$Fe^{3+}(aq) + e^- \rightleftharpoons Fe^{2+}(aq); \quad E^\ominus = +0.77\,V$$
$$Cu^{2+}(aq) + 2e^- \rightleftharpoons Cu(s); \quad E^\ominus = +0.34\,V$$

(This reaction is used to etch copper in the manufacture of printed circuit boards in the electronics industry.)

- The purple manganate(VII) ion $MnO_4^-(aq)$ is a commonly used oxidant in acidic solution.

$$MnO_4^-(aq) + 8H^+(aq) + 5e^- \rightarrow Mn^{2+}(aq) + 4H_2O(l); \quad E^\ominus = +1.51\,V$$

In *basic* solution its final reduction product is manganese(IV) oxide:

$$MnO_4^-(aq) + 2H_2O(l) + 3e^- \rightarrow MnO_2(s) + 4OH^-(aq); \quad E = +0.59\,V$$

Note that here we have E not $E^\ominus$, because the reaction refers to non-standard conditions – there is an excess of base (see spread 13.9 in the chapter on 'Redox equilibrium').

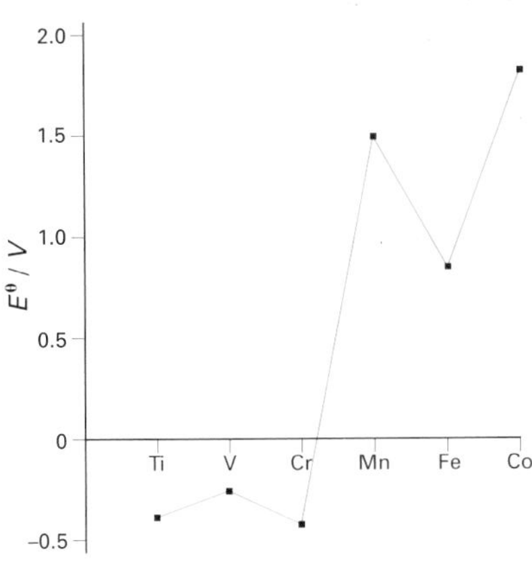

Graph of standard electrode potentials for M(III)/M(II) for transition metals Ti to Co. (In aqueous solution, the M(III) oxidation state is too unstable for either Ni or Cu to have a value.)

The M(II) and M(III) oxidation states

Both oxidation numbers +2 and +3 are possible for each of the elements from titanium to copper, and it is not obvious which is the more stable ion in aqueous solution. The standard electrode potential for the M^{3+}/M^{2+} half-cell (see the graph to the right) tells us which is the more stable ion for each transition metal M. The negative values for titanium, vanadium, and chromium indicate that the higher oxidation state is preferred and that a strong reductant such as metallic zinc ($E^\ominus = -0.76\,V$) must be used to reduce them to oxidation state II.

- A useful reductant to reduce Cr^{3+} to Cr^{2+} or V^{3+} to V^{2+} is zinc (see the previous spread)

Zinc amalgam has reduced acidified vanadate(V) ions to vanadium(II) ions, V^{2+}, which are violet coloured. The reaction takes about a week.

The high positive standard electrode potential for Mn(III)/Mn(II) indicates that the most stable state for manganese is Mn^{2+}. For iron, *both* oxidation states can exist under normal conditions, as its standard electrode potential is much less positive. The drop from manganese to iron is due to the electronic structures of the ions concerned. Mn^{3+} has a $3d^4$ electronic structure, while the electronic structure of Mn^{2+} is $3d^5$. Fe^{3+} and Fe^{2+} are $3d^5$ and $3d^6$ respectively. The extra stability associated with a half-filled d subshell (see the chapter on 'Electrons in atoms') makes the change from Mn^{3+} to Mn^{2+} very favourable; the change from Fe^{3+} to Fe^{2+} is less favourable (i.e. the electrode potential is less positive) than expected. For cobalt, as for manganese, the more stable state is normally Co^{2+}; however

- Aqueous base makes the higher oxidation state relatively more stable, as explained in spread 20.10.

Disproportionation reactions can occur in compounds in which a transition metal has an intermediate oxidation state.

$Cu^+(aq)$

Copper(I) ion disproportionates in aqueous solution. The relevant standard electrode potentials are:

$Cu^{2+}(aq) + e^- \rightleftharpoons Cu^+(aq) \quad E^\ominus = +0.15\,V$

$Cu^+(aq) + e^- \rightleftharpoons Cu\,(s) \quad E^\ominus = +0.52\,V$

The disproportionation reaction is

$2Cu^+(aq) \rightarrow Cu(s) + Cu^{2+}(aq)$

for which $E^\ominus = (+\,0.52\,V) - (+0.15\,V)$

$= +\,0.37\,V$

SUMMARY

- For a given transition metal, higher oxidation states are often oxidants, lower ones are often reductants.
- Higher oxidation states usually exist as covalently bonded (charged or neutral) molecules containing the transition metal with electronegative elements such as oxygen.
- The feasibility of a redox reaction is indicated by the standard electrode potentials (under *standard* conditions).

PRACTICE

1 Give examples of species in their common oxidation states for
- **a** chromium
- **b** manganese
- **c** iron.

20.6

Catalytic activity

OBJECTIVES

- Homogeneous catalysis – role of variable oxidation states
- Transition metals in enzymes
- Heterogeneous transition metal catalysts

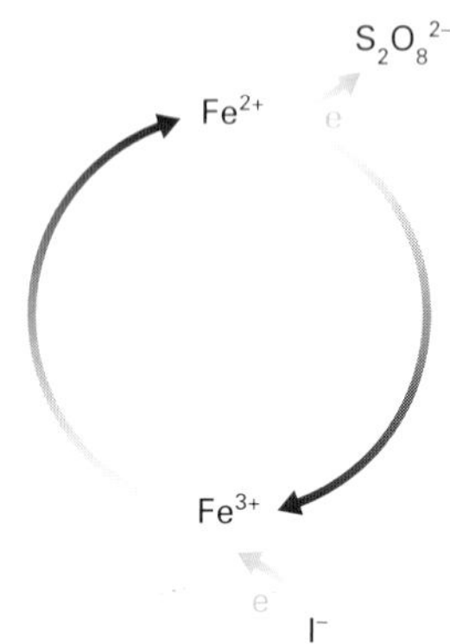

Summary diagram showing iron alternating between the states with oxidation numbers +2 and +3 as $S_2O_8^{2-}$ removes electrons and I^- donates them.

Catalysts speed up chemical reactions by providing an alternative route of lower activation energy (see the chapter on 'Chemical kinetics'). Transition metals show catalytic activity. Homogeneous catalysis involves a catalyst that is in the *same* phase as the reactants. Heterogeneous catalysis involves a catalyst that is *not* in the same phase as the reactants. Heterogeneous catalysts are generally used as the metals or as solid compounds; liquid- or gas-phase reactions take place at their surfaces.

Homogeneous transition metal catalysis

Many transition metal compounds can act as homogeneous catalysts because they readily interconvert between oxidation states. In this way, they act as intermediaries for the exchange of electrons between the reactants. A good example is the reaction (outlined in spread 15.11) between peroxodisulphate ions $S_2O_8^{2-}$ and iodide ions I^-:

$$2I^-(aq) + S_2O_8^{2-}(aq) \rightarrow I_2(aq) + 2SO_4^{2-}(aq)$$

This redox reaction is much faster when Fe^{2+} ions are present

The standard electrode potential of the Fe^{3+}/Fe^{2+} system is:

$$Fe^{3+}(aq) + e^- \rightleftharpoons Fe^{2+}(aq); \qquad E^\ominus = +0.77\,V$$

This value lies *between* the values of the relevant half-equations:

$$S_2O_8^{2-}(aq) + 2e^- \rightleftharpoons 2SO_4^{2-}(aq); \qquad E^\ominus = +2.01\,V$$
$$I_2(aq) + 2e^- \rightleftharpoons 2I^-(aq); \qquad E^\ominus = +0.54\,V$$

When Fe^{2+} ions are also present in the solution, peroxodisulphate ions oxidize Fe^{2+} ions *faster* than they oxidize I^- ions:

$$2Fe^{2+}(aq) + S_2O_8^{2-}(aq) \rightarrow 2SO_4^{2-}(aq) + 2Fe^{3+}(aq)$$

The Fe^{3+} ions can oxidize I^- ions *faster* than $S_2O_8^{2-}$ ions can:

$$2I^-(aq) + 2Fe^{3+}(aq) \rightarrow I_2(aq) + 2Fe^{2+}(aq)$$

The result of the reaction is the same, whether catalysed or uncatalysed. In the catalysed reaction, the route has a lower activation energy and so the reaction is faster. The Fe^{2+} ions are regenerated.

Seeing is believing! In the redox reaction between Rochelle salt (sodium potassium 2,3-dihydroxybutanedioate) and hydrogen peroxide, the change in oxidation state of the catalyst can actually be seen. The catalyst, which consists of cobalt(II) ions, changes from pink to green – the colour of cobalt(III) – at the start of the effervescent reaction, and reverts back to pink again at the end of the reaction.

Transition metals in enzymes

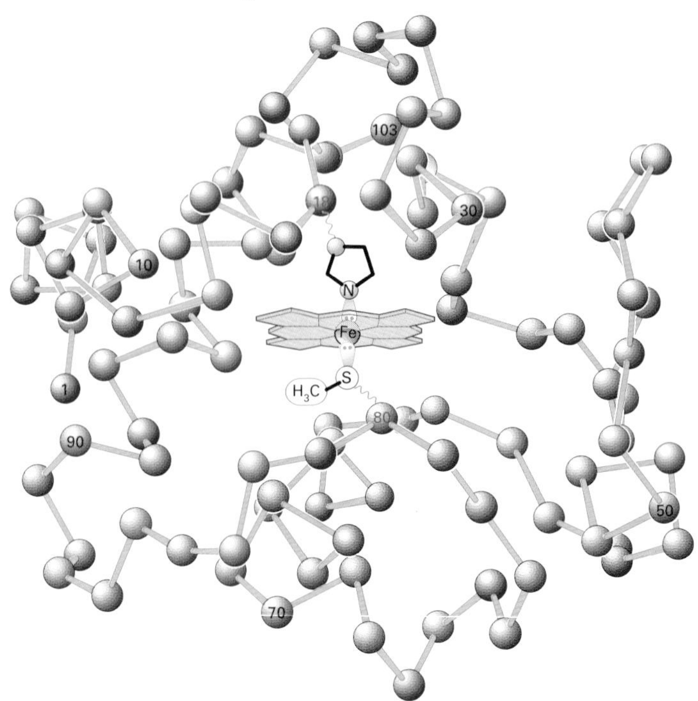

An outline structure of the enzyme cytochrome c. Cytochromes are involved in the biochemical electron-transport chain, i.e. respiration in mitochondria and photosynthesis in chloroplasts. The iron alternates between the Fe(II) and the Fe(III) oxidation states.

Heterogeneous transition metal catalysis

The mechanism of heterogeneous catalysis is discussed at the end of the chapter on 'Chemical kinetics'. With few exceptions, the catalyst is a solid and the reactants are usually gases. The activation energy is lowered because the catalyst adsorbs the reactants onto its surface and holds them close together in an orientation that favours reaction. Transition metals are very good at this because partially filled d orbitals can accept electron density from the adsorbed molecules. There are many important examples of heterogeneous catalysis using transition metals, some of which are mentioned below:

- Titanium(IV) chloride is used in the Zeigler–Natta polymerization (see the chapter on 'Alkanes and alkenes') of ethene to produce poly(ethene).
- Vanadium(V) oxide is used in the Contact process for making sulphuric acid (see the previous chapter). In this reaction, sulphur dioxide is oxidized by vanadium(V) oxide, which is reduced to vanadium(IV) oxide. The latter is then reoxidized by oxygen to vanadium(V) oxide.

$$SO_2(g) + V_2O_5(s) \rightarrow SO_3(g) + 2VO_2(s)$$

$$4VO_2(s) + O_2(g) \rightarrow 2V_2O_5(s)$$

- Manganese(IV) oxide catalyses the decomposition of hydrogen peroxide (see the chapter on 'Chemical kinetics').
- Metallic iron is the catalyst in the Haber–Bosch synthesis of ammonia (see the previous chapter).
- Nickel, palladium, and platinum are used as catalysts in making margarine from vegetable oils by hydrogenation (see the chapter on 'Alkanes and alkenes').
- Platinum and rhodium are used in the Ostwald process for making nitric acid (see the previous chapter).
- Platinum–rhodium alloy is used in vehicle exhaust system catalytic converters (see the chapter on 'Chemical kinetics').

Enzymes

Enzymes catalyse the biochemical reactions that support life. Many enzymes contain transition metals bonded within the structure of a protein. The transition metal alternates between oxidation states, and so allows other electron-transfer (redox) reactions to take place at a suitable rate. The role of enzymes is discussed in greater detail in the chapter on 'Biochemistry'.

Crystals of palladium (a transition metal of Period 5), a very good catalyst for hydrogenation.

SUMMARY

- A transition metal catalyst transfers electrons from the reductant to the oxidant. In doing so, it alternates between two oxidation states.
- A homogeneous transition metal catalyst system has a standard electrode potential *intermediate* between those of the redox systems being oxidized and reduced.
- Many enzymes consist of a transition metal bonded within the structure of a protein; such enzymes catalyse the biochemical electron-transport chain.
- On the surfaces of heterogeneous transition metal catalysts, incoming species donate electron density into vacant d orbitals.

PRACTICE

1 Explain why Fe(II)/Fe(III) would *not* catalyse the peroxodisulphate/iodide reaction if its standard electrode potential were *minus* 0.77 V.

2 Draw a labelled reaction profile diagram (see chapter on 'Chemical kinetics') to illustrate the uncatalysed and the catalysed reactions between peroxodisulphate ion and iodide ion in solution.

3 The redox reaction between 2,3-dihydroxybutanedioate ions (found in Rochelle salt) and hydrogen peroxide is represented by the following chemical equations:

$(CHOHCO_2^-)_2(aq) + 2H_2O(l) \rightarrow$
$4CO_2(g) + 8H^+(aq) + 10e^-$
$2H^+(aq) + H_2O_2(aq) + 2e^- \rightarrow 2H_2O(l)$

a What substance is being reduced and what substance is being oxidized?

b Write an *overall* equation for this reaction.

c Suggest the mechanism by which $Co^{2+}(aq)$ ions catalyse this reaction.

d Suggest why the solution is pink at the start and finish of the reaction, yet green during it.

20.7

OBJECTIVES

- Ligands and bonding
- Coordination number
- Shapes

Lewis acids and bases

In a complex, the metal ion acts as a Lewis acid (see chapter on 'Acid–base equilibrium') because it accepts electron pairs. Each donating species (ligand) acts as a Lewis base.

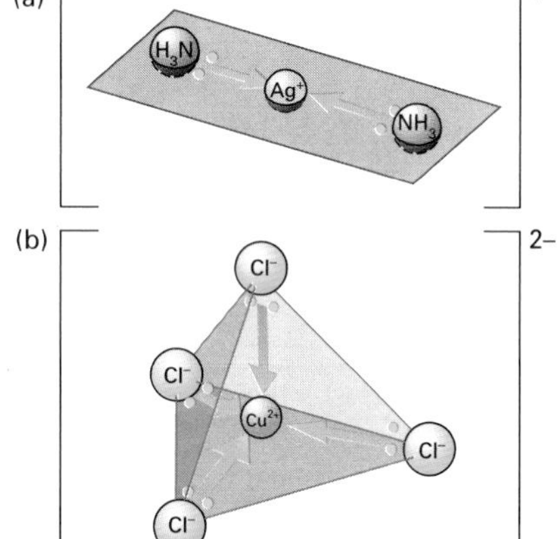

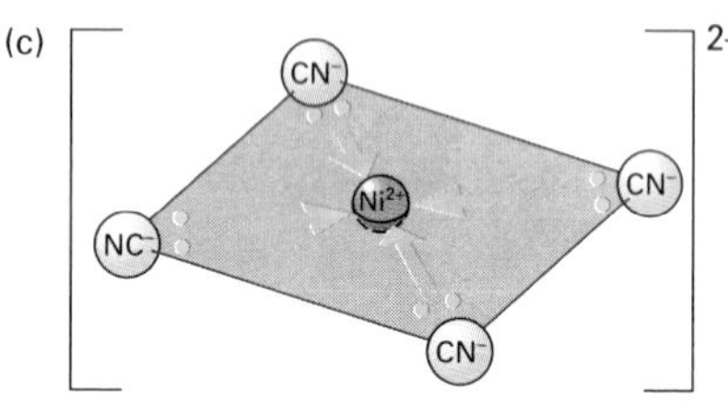

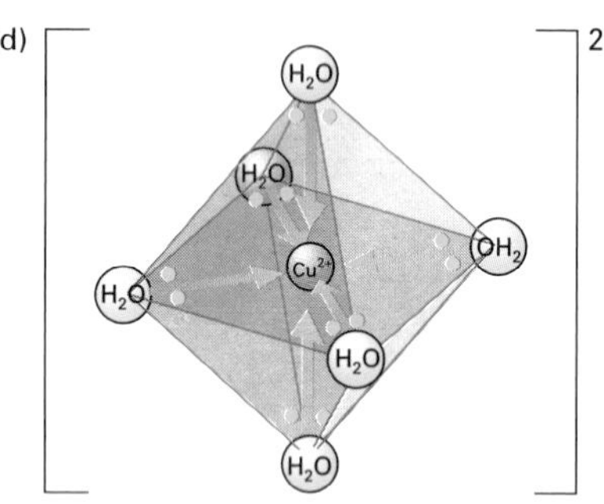

The four main shapes of complexes: (a) Linear – coordination number 2, e.g. $[Ag(NH_3)_2]^+$. (b) Tetrahedral – coordination number 4, e.g. $CuCl_4^{2-}$. $FeCl_4^{2-}$ and $CoCl_4^{2-}$ are also tetrahedral. (c) Square planar – coordination number 4 (rare, tends to occur in complexes where the metal ion has d^8 electronic structure), e.g. Ni^{2+} in $[Ni(CN)_4]^{2-}$. (d) Octahedral – coordination number 6, e.g. $[Cu(H_2O)_6]^{2+}$. $[V(H_2O)_6]^{3+}$, $[Cr(H_2O)_6]^{3+}$, $[Mn(H_2O)_6]^{2+}$, and $[Fe(H_2O)_5SCN]^{2+}$ are also octahedral.

TRANSITION METAL COMPLEXES: KEY FACTS

Complexes consist of a central metal ion surrounded by molecules or ions that form coordinate bonds (see the chapter on 'Chemical bonding') with it. Transition metals form a larger range of complexes than elements from other regions of the periodic table. This is partly because transition metals have d orbitals available for the formation of coordinate bonds. The metal ions also often have high positive charges (e.g. Cr^{3+}, Fe^{3+}), and the resulting high charge density strongly attracts the lone pairs on other species. This spread looks at these topics, and also introduces the terminology relating to complexes and describes their various shapes.

Some definitions

The species that donate electron pairs to the central metal ion are called **ligands**. The **coordination number** is the number of atoms donating electron pairs to the central metal ion and is most commonly 2, 4, or 6. The **shape** of a complex is its geometrical arrangement in space.

Ligands

Ligands donate at least one pair of electrons. Each electron pair forms a single coordinate bond with the central metal ion. Some ligands are negative ions, including cyanide CN^-, halide such as Cl^-, and hydroxide OH^- ions. Some ligands are uncharged molecules that have lone pairs to donate, such as water $:OH_2$ and ammonia $:NH_3$. These ligands are referred to as **monodentate** (or **unidentate**) because each ligand donates just one electron pair. Some other ligands are *bidentate*, because each ligand donates two electron pairs. Bidentate and polydentate ligands will be discussed in later spreads in this chapter.

Shape and coordination number

The shapes of complex ions can be predicted by using rules similar to those of VSEPR theory (see the chapter on 'Chemical bonding') for predicting the shapes of molecules. As a general rule (for monodentate ligands):

- Two ligands give a *linear* shape.
- Four ligands usually give a *tetrahedral* shape, although occasionally the shape may be *square planar*. Tetrahedral complexes are common with larger, negatively-charged ligands such as Cl^-.
- Six ligands give an *octahedral* shape. Octahedral complexes are common with small uncharged ligands such as H_2O and NH_3.

Naming complexes

There are four parts to the name of a complex. The first two parts identify the number and nature of the ligands present. The final two parts give the metal ion present and its oxidation state. With electrically neutral ligands, the charge on the complex simply equals the oxidation state of the metal ion. If the complex is negatively charged, the ending is changed to *-ate* and sometimes the Latin name for the metal is chosen. The four examples alongside are called respectively:

(a) diamminesilver(I) (b) tetrachlorocuprate(II)
(c) tetracyanonickelate(II) (d) hexaaquacopper(II)

The charge on the central ion

The *overall* charge on the complex depends on the charge on the central ion, and the *total* charge due to the ligands. Remember that ligands are usually either neutral (H_2O, NH_3) or negatively charged (F^-, CN^-), as shown by the following two examples.

Worked example on finding the charge on the central ion

Question: Find the charge on the central cobalt ion in (a) $[Co(NH_3)_6]Cl_3$ and (b) $CoCl_4^{2-}$.

Answer: (a) This formula corresponds to solid hexaamminecobalt(III) chloride. When dissolved in water, it ionizes to give $Cl^-(aq)$ ions and the aqueous complex ion $[Co(NH_3)_6]^{3+}(aq)$. The ammonia ligands are neutral; therefore the charge on the central cobalt ion is 3+.

(b) Each chloride ligand bears a charge of 1–. The total charge due to the ligands is therefore 4–. The overall charge on the complex is 2–; therefore the charge on the central cobalt ion is 2+.

Note: A **cationic complex** has a positive charge; an **anionic complex** has a negative charge.

Copper(II) complexes change colour depending on the ligand. The tubes on the left have concentrated and dilute hydrochloric acid added. The tubes on the right have dilute and concentrated aqueous ammonia added.

Complexes and colour

Complex formation is often accompanied by a change in colour. Perhaps the most familiar is the formation of a deep blue solution when aqueous ammonia is added to aqueous copper(II) sulphate. The aqueous $Cu^{2+}(aq)$ ion exists in solution as the hexaaquacopper(II) complex, $[Cu(H_2O)_6]^{2+}$. Addition of aqueous ammonia displaces four of the water ligands, forming the tetraamminediaquacopper(II) complex, $[Cu(NH_3)_4(H_2O)_2]^{2+}$. Notice that ammonia does not displace all six of the water ligands, in the case of *copper*; two waters remain. Aqua ions can also exist in the solid state, as in $CoCl_2{\cdot}6H_2O$.

SUMMARY

- Complex ions consist of a central metal ion surrounded by ligands.
- Ligands donate electron pairs into vacant orbitals on the central metal ion. The bonding type is thus coordinate bonding.
- The number of atoms donating electron pairs to the central metal ion is its coordination number.
- Coordination number 2: linear shape.
- Coordination number 4: usually tetrahedral shape.
- Coordination number 6: octahedral shape.

Use of square brackets

When a complex ion contains a ligand that has *more than one atom*, such as water, the formula for the complex needs to have two types of brackets, round ones surrounding the ligand and square ones surrounding the whole complex. An example is $[Cu(H_2O)_6]^{2+}$. If the ligand is a simple ion, no brackets are needed: although square brackets are sometimes included for chloride complexes such as $CuCl_4^{2-}$; they are very rarely used for the logically equivalent oxide complexes such as CrO_4^{2-}.

Silver complexes

Three important linear complexes of silver are

$[Ag(NH_3)_2]^+$, used in Tollens' reagent (spread 26.4)

$[Ag(S_2O_3)_2]^{3-}$, used in photographic fixing

$[Ag(CN)_2]^-$, used in electroplating

Some more names

- Hexaaquairon(III)

Here *hexa* = six, and the ligands are *aqua* = water, i.e. six H_2O ligands. The central ion is Fe^{3+}, i.e. iron has oxidation number +3. The formula is $[Fe(H_2O)_6]^{3+}$.

- Hexaamminenickel(II)

Here *ammine* = ammonia. The formula is $[Ni(NH_3)_6]^{2+}$.

- Hexacyanoferrate(III)

Here *cyano* = cyanide ion CN^-, and *ferr* = iron (Latin *ferrum*, the central ion being Fe^{3+}). The formula is $[Fe(CN)_6]^{3-}$.

Changes of shape

Hydrated cobalt(II) chloride $CoCl_2{\cdot}6H_2O$ contains the hexaaqua complex ion $[Co(H_2O)_6]^{2+}$. When heated, the pink solid turns blue as the water is driven off and the tetrachloro complex $CoCl_4^{2-}$ is formed. The shape of the complex changes from octahedral for the hexaaqua complex to tetrahedral for the tetrachloro complex. The negatively charged chloride ions repel each other more than the uncharged water molecules repel one another.

PRACTICE

1 For each of the following complexes, give (i) the charge on the central transition metal ion and (ii) its coordination number:

a $[Co(NH_3)_6]^{3+}$
b $[Cu(NH_3)_4(H_2O)_2]^{2+}$
c $[Fe(CN)_6]^{4-}$
d $[Co(NH_3)_6]Cl_3$
e $CuCl_4^{2-}$
f $K_4[Fe(CN)_6]$
g Na_2CoCl_4
h $[Cu(CN)_2]^-$.

2 Sketch the shape of each of the complex ions in question 1.

3 Define each of the following terms, using the complex $[Ni(CN)_4]^{2-}$ to illustrate your answer:

a Ligand
b Coordination number
c Shape.

20.8

OBJECTIVES

- Ligand substitution reactions
- Types of ligand
- Applications

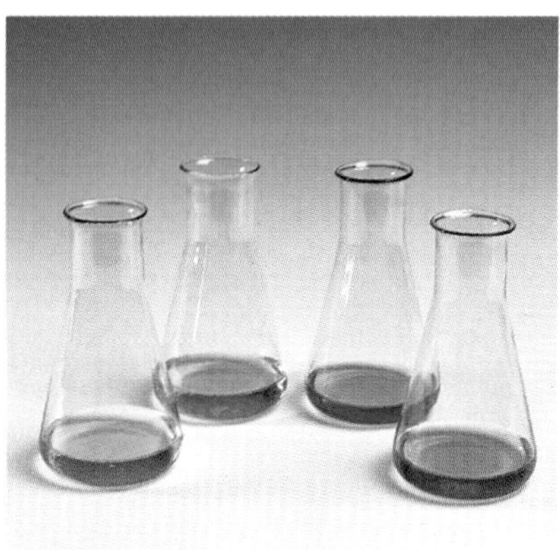

A ligand substitution reaction in which one, two, and three en ligands (see opposite) substitute for two water molecules each around a nickel(II) ion: $[Ni(H_2O)_6]^{2+}$ is green, $[Ni(en)_3]^{2+}$ is pink.

Stability constants for Cu^{2+} complexes

Ligand	$\log_{10} K_{stab}$
Cl^-	5.6
NH_3	13.3
EDTA	18.8
CN^-	27.3

EDTA will displace NH_3 and Cl^-.

CN^- will displace all other ligands.

Toxic cyanide

Cyanide ion has a high value of stability constant with respect to all transition metals. Many enzymes – particularly those responsible for respiration – contain a transition metal complexed with amino acids or other biological groups. Cyanide ion displaces these ligands and thus renders enzymes inoperative. Death rapidly follows as the energy-producing pathways in the organism cease functioning.

Changes of shape

Replacing small uncharged ligands with charged ligands may cause an octahedral complex to change its shape to tetrahedral. For example, adding concentrated hydrochloric acid to octahedral (6-coordinate) $[Cu(H_2O)_6]^{2+}$(aq) forms tetrahedral (4-coordinate) $CuCl_4^{2-}$(aq). The colour change is from blue to green to yellow when the acid is in excess.

TRANSITION METAL COMPLEXES: SOME REACTIONS

Complexes may undergo reactions in which incoming ligands substitute for existing ligands. These **ligand substitution reactions** (or ligand exchange reactions) are equilibrium reactions, and have associated equilibrium constants. The extent to which one species of ligand will substitute for another therefore depends on the relative concentrations of the ligands and the enthalpy/entropy changes associated with the reaction. Some ligands are able to donate more than one electron pair per ligand. These ligands usually donate 2, 4, or 6 electron pairs. They have wide applications to analytical chemistry as well as to the medical and industrial fields.

Nickel(II) – a substitution reaction

Solid nickel(II) chloride exists as yellow crystals. It dissolves in water to give a green solution containing the complex $[Ni(H_2O)_6]^{2+}$(aq). Pouring an excess of aqueous ammonia into this solution results in a colour change from green to violet. Ammonia ligands NH_3 replace all six water ligands:

$$[Ni(H_2O)_6]^{2+}(aq) + 6NH_3(aq) \rightleftharpoons [Ni(NH_3)_6]^{2+}(aq) + 6H_2O(l)$$

The acidic character of M^{3+}(aq)

The acidity of the aqueous aluminium ion Al^{3+}(aq) was covered in the previous chapter. In a similar way, transition metal aqua ions with a charge of 3+ are notably acidic; their acidity is much greater than that of aqua ions with a charge of 2+ because of their higher charge density. For example, a piece of litmus placed in an aqueous solution containing iron(III) ions turns red. The following equilibrium is set up:

$$[Fe(H_2O)_6]^{3+}(aq) + H_2O(l) \rightleftharpoons H_3O^+(aq) + [Fe(H_2O)_5OH]^{2+}(aq)$$

The acidity of the solution means that when aqueous sodium carbonate is added to aqueous iron(III) ions, carbon dioxide gas is given off and a red-brown precipitate of iron(III) hydroxide $Fe(OH)_3$ forms. Similarly, when aqueous sodium carbonate is added to aqueous chromium(III) ions, carbon dioxide gas is given off and a green precipitate of chromium(III) hydroxide $Cr(OH)_3$ forms. Note that *no* metal(III) carbonate is formed.

The hydroxo complex, although a minor component of the mixture, absorbs light much more strongly than the hexaaqua ion does and so dominates the perceived colour. The colour of the unionized hexaaqua ion is seen in the solid state, where hydrated ammonium iron(III) sulphate (colloquially called 'ferric alum') is coloured pale purple. The aqueous iron(III) ions, Fe^{3+}(aq), appear yellow-brown. A similar effect occurs for other ions such as chromium(III), for which the hexaaqua ion is violet but the hydroxo complex, formed when it is dissolved in water, is green.

The stability constant

A solution of an iron(II) salt such as iron(II) sulphate $FeSO_4$ contains the hexaaquairon(II) complex $[Fe(H_2O)_6]^{2+}$(aq). Addition of cyanide ions displaces water ligands to produce the hexacyanoferrate(II) complex $[Fe(CN)_6]^{4-}$(aq). Each step in the displacement of water by cyanide ion constitutes an equilibrium reaction and has an associated equilibrium constant.

$$[Fe(H_2O)_6]^{2+}(aq) + 6CN^-(aq) \rightleftharpoons [Fe(CN)_6]^{4-}(aq) + 6H_2O(l)$$

The equilibrium constant for the overall reaction is called the **stability constant** K_{stab} (note that the *outer* square brackets indicate the concentration, whereas the inner ones are part of the formula of the complex):

$$K_{stab} = \frac{[[Fe(CN)_6]^{4-}]}{[[Fe(H_2O)_6]^{2+}][CN^-]^6}$$

The stability constant of a complex is a measure of its stability with respect to its constituent species. The larger the value, the more stable the complex. Stability constants have a wide range of values. They are usually expressed as their logarithm $\log_{10} K_{stab}$ in order to make the numbers more easily manageable.

- Comparing stability constants indicates the likelihood of one ligand species substituting for another.

For example, the K_{stab} values at 298 K for $[Cu(NH_3)_4(H_2O)_2]^{2+}$ and $[Cu(CN)_4]^{2-}$ are 2×10^{13} and 2×10^{27} respectively. Cyanide ligands CN^- will therefore displace ammonia ligands NH_3 from the complex $[Cu(NH_3)_4(H_2O)_2]^{2+}$. Ammonia ligands will not displace cyanide ligands from the complex $[Cu(CN)_4]^{2-}$ to any significant extent. (Note the common tetrahedral shape of a complex with four *anionic* ligands.)

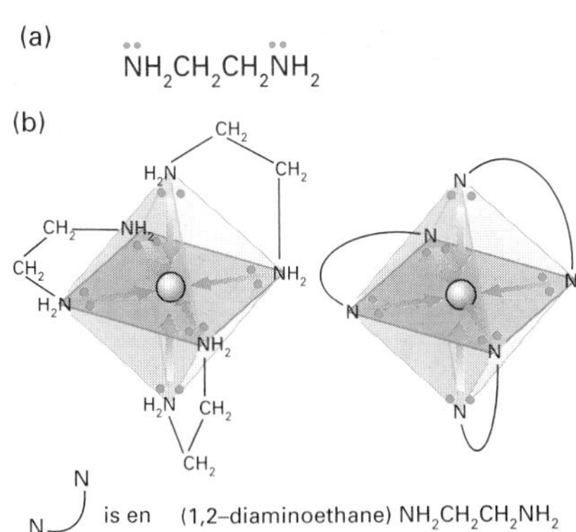

(a) The 1,2-diaminoethane ligand (en) with two available lone pairs. This bidentate ligand is neutral. (b) Structure of a metal-en complex.

Polydentate ligands

Ligands such as CN^- and NH_3 are referred to as monodentate ligands because they possess only one lone pair of electrons that may be used to form a ligand-metal bond. A ligand that donates two electron pairs is called a **bidentate ligand**. For example, the molecule 1,2-diaminoethane $NH_2CH_2CH_2NH_2$ (often known by its older name ethylenediamine and abbreviated to en) has two nitrogen atoms that can both donate their lone pair. Another example of a bidentate ligand is ethanedioate (oxalate) ion $C_2O_4^{2-}$, as in the complex $[Fe(C_2O_4)_3]^{3-}$. **Polydentate** (or **multidentate**) **ligands** donate more than two electron pairs. An example of a polydentate ligand is EDTA.

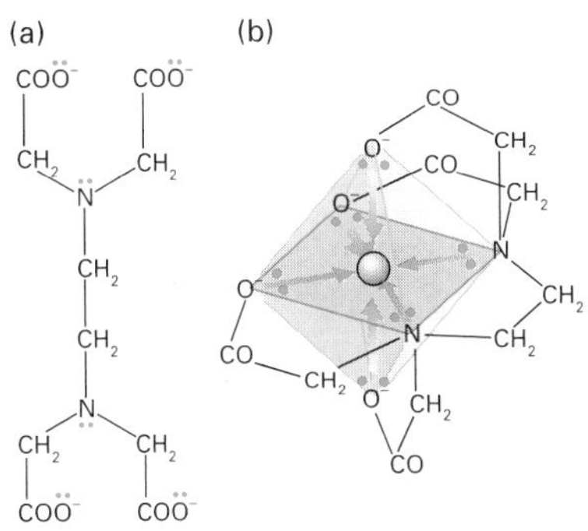

(a) Ethylenediaminetetraacetate EDTA: a hexadentate ligand. Each EDTA bears a total charge of 4–. (b) The structure of a metal-EDTA complex. The complex consists of a metal ion and a single EDTA and has an octahedral shape.

The porphyrin ligand in the haem group in haemoglobin is also polydentate.

The fact that polydentate ligands generally form very stable complexes is called the **chelate effect**: EDTA forms a much more stable complex than ammonia does, despite the fact that four of the atoms complexing in EDTA are also nitrogen atoms. The explanation for the chelate effect is that a single EDTA ligand liberates *six* water molecules, a process that is very favourable entropically (see the chapter on 'Spontaneous change...').

Applications

Unlike cyanide ion, EDTA is non-toxic. It has medical uses in extracting aqueous ions from the body fluids of patients suffering from poisoning by the aqueous ions of toxic metals such as lead and cadmium. EDTA acts as a *sequestering agent*, forming a complex with the toxic ion and preventing its physiological chemical effect. Other sequestering agents are present in soap powders and detergents and soften water by removing the $Ca^{2+}(aq)$ and $Mg^{2+}(aq)$ ions.

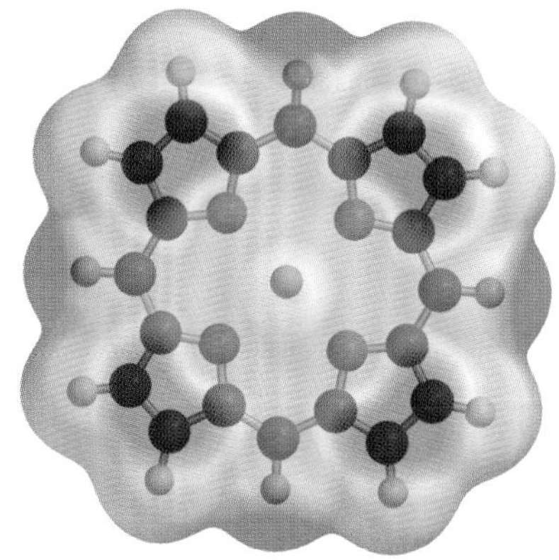
Haem, part of the haemoglobin molecule, has an Fe^{2+} complexed by a tetradentate porphyrin ligand. The electrostatic potential map shown here corresponds to the simplest porphyrin. Note that the porphyrin ring is delocalized; this cannot be shown accurately in the next but one spread where the actual haem group is drawn.

Standard solutions of EDTA may be used in complexometric titrations to estimate the concentrations of aqueous metal ions, especially magnesium and calcium. One mole of EDTA effectively removes one mole of aqueous metal ions, the end point of the reaction being indicated by a dyestuff that itself complexes with the metal ion. The dyestuff has one colour when complexed with the metal and another colour when displaced free into the solution by EDTA.

SUMMARY

- Complexes may undergo ligand substitution reactions in which incoming ligands displace existing ligands.
- Metal(III) aqua ions are acidic.
- Ligands of greater value of stability constant substitute for those of lower value.
- Bidentate ligands donate two electron pairs.
- Polydentate ligands donate more than two electron pairs.

PRACTICE

1 Draw the structure of the complex $[Cu(en)_2(H_2O)_2]^{2+}$. Suggest its geometry.

20.9

OBJECTIVES

- Geometric (*cis–trans*) isomerism
- Optical isomerism

Square planar complexes

In general, if M is a metal ion and X and Y are monodentate ligands, square planar complexes with the formula MX_2Y_2 show geometric isomerism.

ISOMERISM IN TRANSITION METAL COMPLEXES

Isomers are compounds that have the same molecular formula but different structures. Some transition metal complexes show isomerism. The form of isomerism most common in transition metal complexes is stereoisomerism, in which ligands are arranged differently in space around the central metal ion. Stereoisomerism can take two forms, geometric isomerism and optical isomerism. Each form has its own distinctive properties.

Geometric isomerism

Geometric isomers of complexes have a different arrangement of ligands around the central ion. For example, there are two geometric isomers of the square planar complex $[Pt(NH_3)_2Cl_2]$, which are called *cis-* and *trans*-diamminedichloroplatinum(II). The prefix *cis-* indicates that the two ammine ligands are next to each other in the complex ion structure. The prefix *trans-* indicates that the two ammine groups are on opposite sides of the structure. The isomer *cis*-$[Pt(NH_3)_2Cl_2]$ is called 'cisplatin' and is a highly effective anti-cancer agent. The *trans* isomer does not have anti-cancer properties. Geometric isomerism is sometimes known as ***cis–trans* isomerism.**

(a)

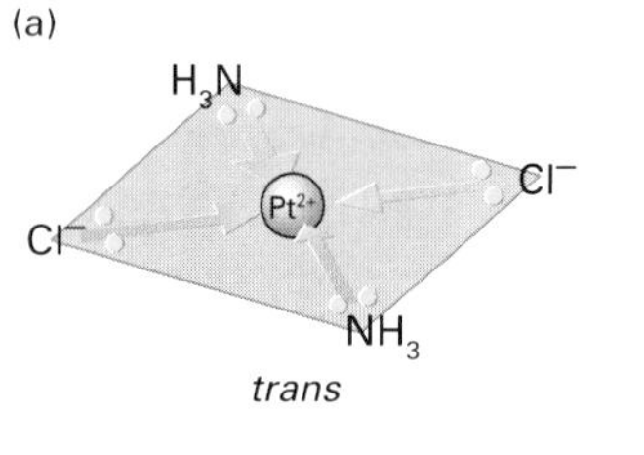

(b)

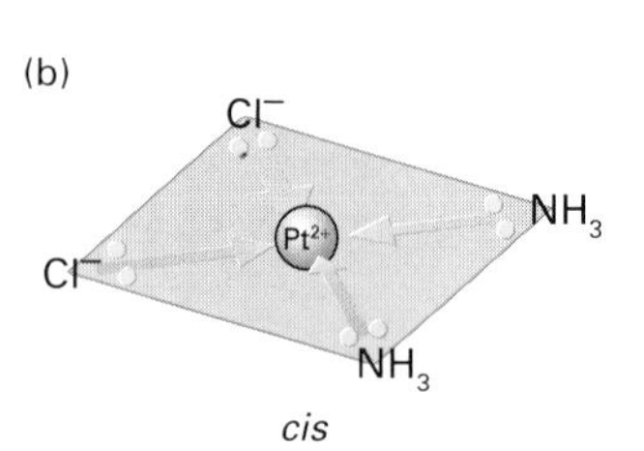

(c)

(a) The trans *isomer of* $[Pt(NH_3)_2Cl_2]$. *(b) The* cis *isomer of* $[Pt(NH_3)_2Cl_2]$.
(c) Crystalline cisplatin.

Octahedral complexes

In general, if M is a metal ion and X and Y are monodentate ligands, octahedral complexes with the formula MX_2Y_4 show geometric isomerism.

The octahedral tetraamminediaquacopper(II) complex ion $[Cu(NH_3)_4(H_2O)_2]^{2+}$ exists only as the *trans* isomer, in which the two water ligands are on opposite sides of the structure. The *cis* isomer does not exist, because of bonding and orbital energy constraints. However, there are *two* isomers of the tetraamminedichlorocobalt(III) ion $[Co(NH_3)_4Cl_2]^+$, as illustrated below.

(a)

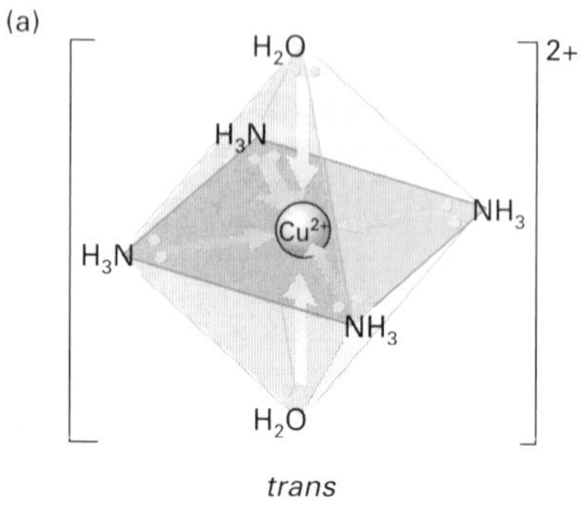

(b)

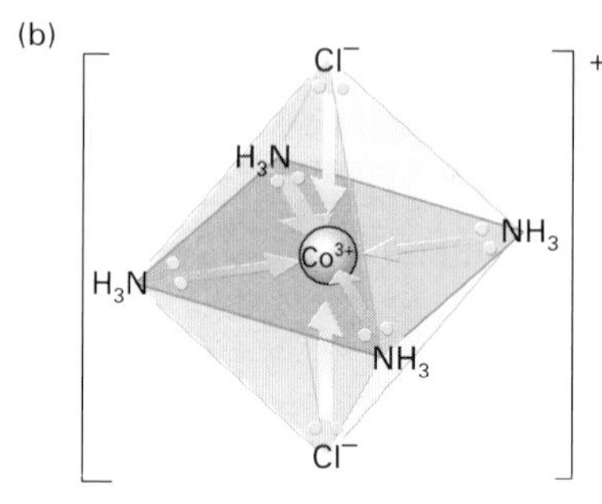

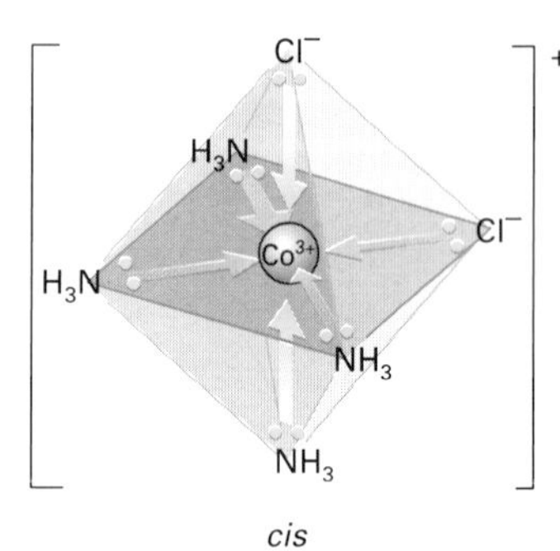

(a) The single trans *isomer of* $[Cu(NH_3)_4(H_2O)_2]^{2+}$. *(b) The* trans *and* cis *isomers of* $[Co(NH_3)_4Cl_2]^+$.

Optical isomerism

Look again at the structure of the *cis*-tetraamminedichlorocobalt(III) ion $[Co(NH_3)_4Cl_2]^+$. Imagine a ligand substitution reaction in which two pairs of ammonia molecules are replaced by two molecules of the bidentate ligand 1,2-diaminoethane ('en'). There are two possible structures for the *cis* isomer of the bis(en)dichlorocobalt(III) ion, *cis*-$[Co(en)_2Cl_2]^+$. (Note that here we use the prefix 'bis'. This denotes 'two' and is used instead of 'di' with bidentate ligands.)

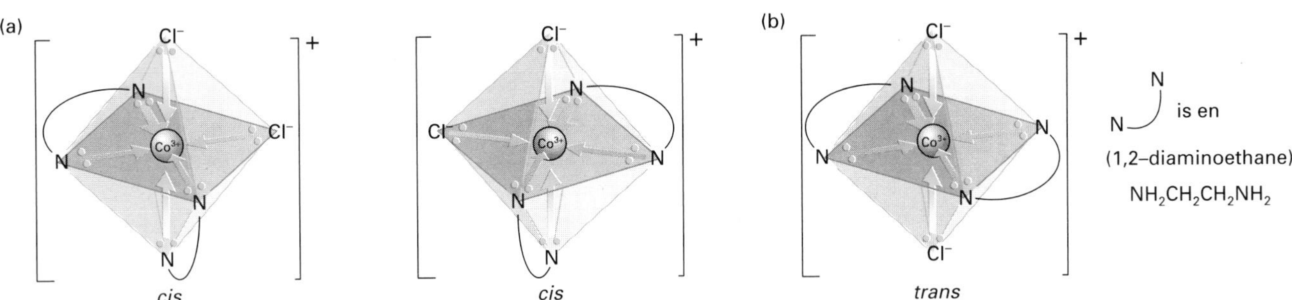

(a) The cis *isomer of $[Co(en)_2Cl_2]^+$ and its mirror image are not superimposable. They form a pair of optical isomers. (b) The* trans *isomer has a plane of symmetry. It is superimposable on its mirror image.*

The two *cis* isomers are called **chiral** because they exist as mirror images of, and are not superimposable on, each other, in the same way that your left hand is a mirror image of your right hand. These chiral isomers are also called **optical isomers** because their solutions have the ability to rotate the plane of plane-polarized light. Optical isomers are said to be optically active; one isomer will rotate the plane of plane-polarized light in one direction, the second isomer in the opposite direction. (Optical isomerism is described in more detail in the chapter on 'Organic nitrogen compounds'.)

There is only one isomer of *trans*-bis(en)dichlorocobalt(III) ion. The *trans* isomer and its mirror image are superimposable because the *trans* isomer has a plane of symmetry.

Optical isomers also occur when there are three bidentate ligands. Examples include $[Fe(C_2O_4)_3]^{3-}$ and $[Ni(en)_3]^{2+}$.

Symmetry

The number 8 has two planes of symmetry (imagine slicing it in half with either a vertical cut, or a horizontal cut). The number 3 has one plane of symmetry (slice it horizontally), but the number 9 has no plane of symmetry.

SUMMARY

- Stereoisomers have the same ligands, but they are arranged differently in space.
- There are two kinds of stereoisomerism – geometric (*cis–trans*) isomerism and optical isomerism.
- Optical isomers are mirror images of each other.
- Chiral species are not superimposable on their mirror images.

PRACTICE

1 Explain why the tetraaquadichlorocobalt(III) complexes show geometric isomerism.

2 For the isomers of the complex $[Cr(en)_2Cl_2]^+$, sketch the pairs of structures that are:
  a geometric isomers,
  b optical isomers.

3 Explain why the *trans* isomer of $[Co(en)_2Cl_2]^+$ is not optically active.

4 Sketch the possible isomers of the complex $[Co(en)_3]^{3+}$. Select a pair that show optical isomerism.

20.10 OTHER REACTIONS OF COMPLEX IONS

OBJECTIVES

- Formation of an ammine complex of cobalt
- Redox reactions of transition metals in biochemistry

The presence of base stabilizes the higher oxidation states in transition metal complexes (see spread 13.9). A particularly famous application of this principle was the preparation by ligand substitution reaction of the ammine complexes of cobalt. Studying the chemistry of these substances helped Alfred Werner in 1893 to formulate his 'theory of coordination compounds', in which the concepts of oxidation state and coordination number were introduced for the first time. Ligand substitution reactions are also of great importance in the field of biochemistry. This spread looks at these topics and concludes by outlining how haemoglobin transports molecular oxygen in mammals.

Higher oxidation states

To prepare a metal complex that contains the metal in a high oxidation state, the general process is

1 add a base

2 add an oxidant.

In the example alongside, the base is ammonia, and the oxidant is air. An alternative oxidant is aqueous hydrogen peroxide. So for example addition of hydrogen peroxide to aqueous chromium(III) ions Cr^{3+} in sodium hydroxide results in yellow aqueous chromate(VI) ions CrO_4^{2-}.

Stages in the preparation of a hexaamminecobalt(III) solution.

Preparing an ammine complex of cobalt

• The outline procedure

Werner found that the addition of aqueous ammonia to aqueous cobalt(II) chloride gave a blue-green precipitate of cobalt(II) hydroxide. Treating the precipitate with concentrated aqueous ammonia in the absence of air formed a pale brown (straw-coloured) solution of the hexaamminecobalt(II) complex. This solution rapidly oxidized in the presence of air to give a dark brown mixture containing the hexaamminecobalt(III) ion, $[Co(NH_3)_6]^{3+}$.

• The detailed steps

In acidic solution, the Co(II) oxidation state is more stable than the Co(III) state, as indicated by the standard electrode potential:

$$Co^{3+}(aq) + e^- \rightleftharpoons Co^{2+}(aq); \qquad E^{\ominus} = +1.82\,V$$

The value of this electrode potential becomes much less positive in basic solution (provided by excess aqueous ammonia), showing that the Co(III) oxidation state is now much *more* stable than it is under acidic conditions:

$$[Co(NH_3)_6]^{3+}(aq) + e^- \rightleftharpoons [Co(NH_3)_6]^{2+}(aq); \qquad E = +0.11\,V$$

The steps followed in Werner's preparation involve the following changes:

1 Dissolving cobalt(II) chloride in water gives pink aqueous $Co^{2+}(aq)$ ions present as the hexaaqua complex $[Co(H_2O)_6]^{2+}$.

$$CoCl_2(s) \rightarrow Co^{2+}(aq) + 2Cl^-(aq)$$

2 Adding concentrated aqueous ammonia forms a blue-green precipitate of cobalt(II) hydroxide $Co(OH)_2(s)$.

Aqueous ammonia forms the following equilibrium in water:

$$NH_3(aq) + H_2O(l) \rightleftharpoons NH_4^+(aq) + OH^-(aq)$$

The aqueous hydroxide ion causes the precipitation of cobalt(II) hydroxide (see spread 11.10):

$$Co^{2+}(aq) + 2OH^-(aq) \rightarrow Co(OH)_2(s)$$

3 Adding excess concentrated aqueous ammonia forms a straw-coloured solution containing the hexaamminecobalt(II) ion, $[Co(NH_3)_6]^{2+}(aq)$.

$$Co(OH)_2(s) + 6NH_3(aq) \rightarrow [Co(NH_3)_6]^{2+}(aq) + 2OH^-(aq)$$

4 Warming the solution and bubbling air through it oxidizes Co(II) to Co(III). A dark brown solution containing the hexaamminecobalt(III) complex $[Co(NH_3)_6]^{3+}(aq)$ together with others such as the pentaamminechlorocobalt(III) ion $[Co(NH_3)_5Cl]^{2+}(aq)$ results.

A biological substitution reaction

An earlier spread in this chapter discussed the role of transition metal ions in homogeneous catalysis. Simple *aqueous* species catalyse reactions by alternating between two oxidation states. The ion in an upper oxidation state accepts an electron from a reductant and is reduced to a lower state. Passing the electron to the oxidant, the catalyst then reverts to the upper oxidation state. In this manner, transition metal ions mediate in redox reactions by passing electrons from reductant to oxidant.

Many biological systems use *complexed* transition metal ions to mediate in biochemical reactions. For example, energy is generated in higher animals by the enzyme-mediated oxidation of sugars, particularly glucose. The oxidant is oxygen from the air. In the lungs, oxygen from the air is taken up into haemoglobin in the blood. Mammalian haemoglobin is an iron-containing protein complex with a relative formula mass of 64 450. It is haemoglobin that is the red pigment in red blood cells. The iron is present as the Fe^{2+} ion complexed by a tetradentate haem ligand; see spread 20.8.

The square planar shape is particularly prone to further coordination. A fifth position is coordinated by the amino acid histidine, which itself is part of the surrounding protein chain. The sixth position can be coordinated by the π-electron density in multiply bonded substances such as O_2, CO, and CN^-. Haemoglobin therefore takes up molecular oxygen in the lungs, forming oxyhaemoglobin. This is transported around the body in the bloodstream, and the oxygen is released in regions of low oxygen concentration. Note that the oxidation number of the complexed iron is +2 in *both* haemoglobin and oxyhaemoglobin.

Much of the detailed mechanism of the action of haemoglobin is now understood, through the pioneering work of Max Perutz. Deoxyhaemoglobin, lacking oxygen, contains a *'high-spin'* iron(II) ion which is converted into a *'low-spin'* iron(II) ion in the oxygenated state. The terms 'high-spin' and 'low-spin' depend on recognizing that the energy levels of the d orbitals are split, which will be explained in the next spread. The low-spin ion is smaller and as a result the iron ion can now slip into the plane of the haem ring.

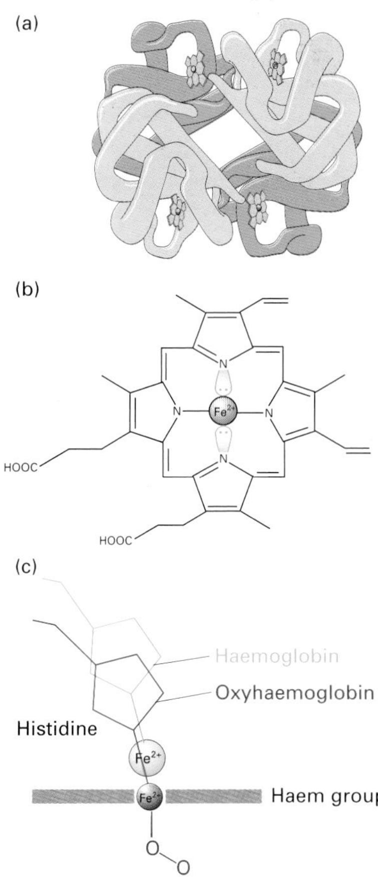

(a) Haemoglobin: the Fe^{2+} ion is located within a protein structure consisting of folded chains of amino acids. (b) The Fe^{2+} ion forms bonds with each of four nitrogen atoms on the haem ligand. Histidine, present in another section of the protein, forms a fifth coordinate bond to the Fe^{2+} ion. (c) Oxygen binds reversibly to the Fe^{2+} ion in haemoglobin to form oxyhaemoglobin. Note that CO and CN^- bind more strongly than O_2 and are strong poisons.

SUMMARY

- Higher oxidation states are stabilized by the addition of base.
- The presence of the base aqueous ammonia allows a cobalt(II) complex to be oxidized to cobalt(III) by the action of atmospheric oxygen alone.
- Transition metal complexes in living systems mediate in biochemical reactions. The metal ion is usually surrounded by and complexed by a protein of very high relative formula mass.

PRACTICE

1 Explain the action of cyanide ions as a poison.

2 Use the equilibrium expression
$Hb + O_2 \rightleftharpoons HbO_2$
where Hb refers to the haemoglobin molecule, to explain why haemoglobin complexes with oxygen in the lungs and releases oxygen elsewhere in the body tissues.

3 Lack of iron in the diet or poor uptake of iron from the diet can lead to a complaint called *anaemia*, in which the haemoglobin content of the blood is lowered. Suggest the major symptoms experienced by a person suffering from anaemia. Explain their origins.

4 There are three hydrates of the salt chromium(III) chloride $CrCl_3{\cdot}6H_2O(s)$: they are violet $[Cr(H_2O)_6]Cl_3$, green $[Cr(H_2O)_5Cl]Cl_2{\cdot}H_2O$, and green $[Cr(H_2O)_4Cl_2]Cl{\cdot}2H_2O$. Explain what you would expect to see when solutions of equal concentration of these compounds are each treated with an equal excess of aqueous silver nitrate.

20.11 Coloured ions

OBJECTIVES

- Complementary colours
- d orbitals are split by a ligand field
- d–to–d transitions
- Charge transfer transitions
- Qualitative analysis

Look at aqueous $Ti^{3+}(aq)$ ions, shown on the left, and you see a purple colour. The solution absorbs green light from the continuous spectrum of white light. When white light passes through the solution, the colour you perceive is white minus green, which leaves purple. The absorption of light takes place by electronic transitions between different energy levels (see the chapter on 'Electrons in atoms'). In many transition metal ions, the differences between the energy levels correspond to energies within the visible spectrum. There are two ways in which this can come about.

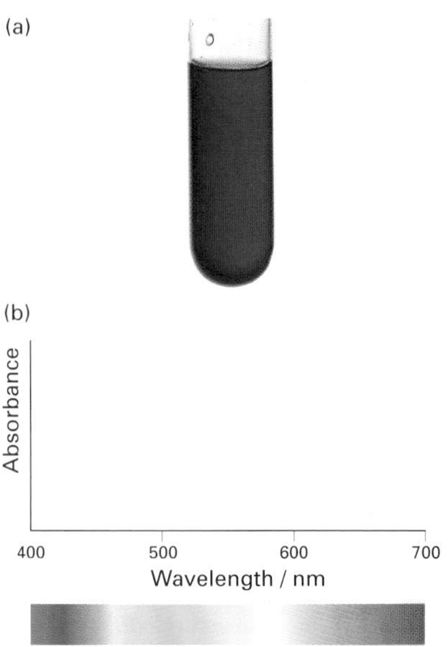

(a) A solution containing the complex ion $[Ti(H_2O)_6]^{3+}(aq)$. (b) The absorption spectrum of $[Ti(H_2O)_6]^{3+}(aq)$.

d-to-d transitions

In an isolated atom or ion, the five d orbitals have the same energy. When ligands are present, some d orbitals are closer than others to the ligands, because of their distribution in space. The ligands may be roughly regarded as clouds of negative charge, which push the orbitals closest to them to slightly higher energy levels. In an octahedral complex, two of the d orbitals point along the axes *directly at* the ligands; these orbitals are at a higher energy level than the other three d orbitals. This is called **ligand field splitting**. The energy difference between the split d orbitals corresponds to frequencies within the visible spectrum.

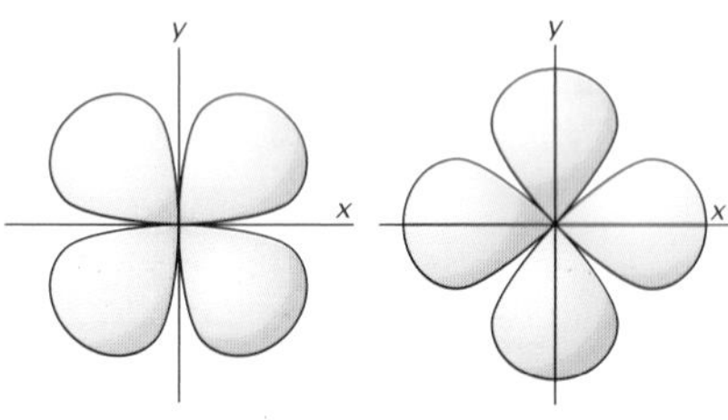

Three of the five d orbitals point between the axes; two point along the axes.

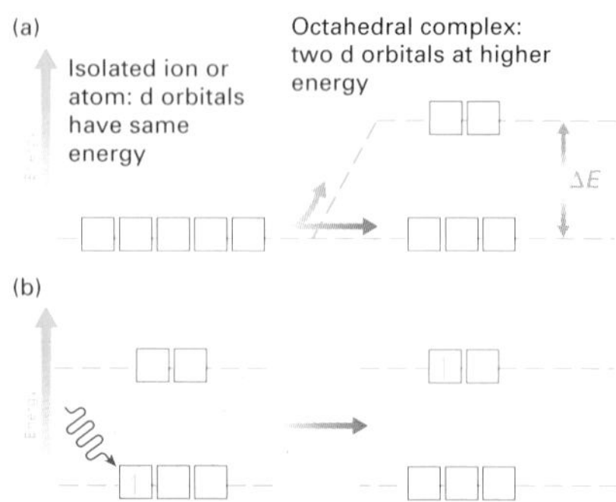

(a) The splitting of d orbitals by an octahedral ligand field. (b) An electron absorbs radiation (of frequency f such that $\Delta E = hf$) and is promoted to a higher-energy orbital. Note that the electron usually returns to its original energy level by an alternative route that does not emit visible radiation.

The opportunity now exists for an electron to be excited from a lower-energy to a higher-energy d orbital, *provided* that there is at least one electron present to be excited *and* that there is space for it in one of the orbitals of higher energy. The condition for this **d-to-d transition** to occur and hence for an ion to be coloured is:

- the ion must have a partially filled d subshell.

(This confirms why neither $Zn^{2+}(aq)$ nor $Sc^{3+}(aq)$ are coloured.)

The frequency of the light absorbed, and so the colour seen, depends on the energy difference between the two levels. The energy difference between the split d orbitals (and hence the colour) depends on:

- the nature and oxidation state of the metal ion;
- the nature and number of the ligands.

Changing the ligands around a given metal ion changes the colour perceived. For example, the hexaaquacopper(II) ion $[Cu(H_2O)_6]^{2+}$ is pale blue; the tetrachlorocuprate(II) complex $CuCl_4^{2-}(aq)$ is yellow –green (spread 20.8); the complex $[Cu(NH_3)_4(H_2O)_2]^{2+}$ is deep blue. All three complexes are coloured as a result of d-to-d transitions.

A further consequence of ligand field splitting is that ions with between four and seven electrons can have them arranged in two ways. For example Fe^{2+} has six electrons. One possible electronic structure has all six in the lower energy level, in which case their spins must be paired and the ion is described as **low-spin**. Alternatively, four can be in the lower level and two in the higher; following Hund's rule, there are four unpaired electrons and the ion is described as **high-spin**.

Charge transfer transitions

An electron may be transferred from the *ligand* to the central metal ion in a **charge transfer transition**. When such a transfer occurs, it causes a much more intense absorption, as in the deep purple of manganate(VII) ions or the bright orange of dichromate(VI) ions.

The ease with which an electron transfers depends on the oxidizing power of the central ion. As the oxidizing power increases, the ion accepts the electron more readily and so the transition energy falls. For the vanadate(V) ion VO_4^{3-} the energy is high and the absorption lies in the ultraviolet; for the strongly oxidizing chromate(VI) ion CrO_4^{2-} the absorption extends into the blue end of the visible and the solution appears yellow. The very strongly oxidizing manganate(VII) ion MnO_4^- absorbs in the green and thus appears purple.

Colour and qualitative analysis

Addition of limited quantities of aqueous hydroxide ions to an aqua complex causes the metal hydroxide to precipitate. The hydroxides of transition metals are characteristically coloured, and this may be used to identify the metal ion. Those hydroxides that are amphoteric (e.g. chromium(III) hydroxide) 'dissolve' in excess aqueous sodium hydroxide. The addition of aqueous ammonia may have the same effect as adding aqueous sodium hydroxide because it also is a base. However, adding an excess of aqueous ammonia can dissolve the hydroxide precipitate by forming an *ammine* complex. These reactions are summarized in the following chart:

Tests for identifying some transition metal ions.The nature of the precipitates in oxidation state +3 are complex and they have been approximated as $M(OH)_3$.

Ion	Effect of adding dilute NaOH(aq)	Effect of adding dilute NH_3(aq)
Cr^{3+}(aq)	Green precipitate of $Cr(OH)_3$ 'redisssolves' in excess as it is amphoteric, forming $[Cr(OH)_6]^{3-}$	Green precipitate of $Cr(OH)_3$ 'redissolves' in excess, forming $[Cr(NH_3)_6]^{3+}$
Mn^{2+}(aq)	White precipitate of $Mn(OH)_2$	As for NaOH(aq)
Fe^{3+}(aq)	Red-brown precipitate of $Fe(OH)_3$	As for NaOH(aq)
Fe^{2+}(aq)	Green precipitate of $Fe(OH)_2$ turning brown on standing because of oxidation by air	As for NaOH(aq)
Co^{2+}(aq)	Blue-green precipitate of $Co(OH)_2$	Blue-green precipitate of $Co(OH)_2$; in excess gives a dark brown solution, on standing, as cobalt(III) ammine complex forms
Ni^{2+}(aq)	Green precipitate of $Ni(OH)_2$	Green precipitate of $Ni(OH)_2$; in excess gives a violet-purple solution as nickel(II) ammine complex forms
Cu^{2+}(aq)	Blue precipitate of $Cu(OH)_2$	Blue precipitate of $Cu(OH)_2$; in excess gives a dark blue solution as copper(II) ammine complex forms

Many transition metal compounds are used as pigments, including those of titanium, iron, and copper: Monastral blue is a porphyrin complex of copper. Note that titanium(IV) oxide TiO_2, which is much used in paints, is white because Ti^{4+} contains no *d electrons.*

Zinc

Zinc forms a *white* precipitate of $Zn(OH)_2$ on addition of small quantities of either dilute aqueous sodium hydroxide or dilute aqueous ammonia. The zinc ion Zn^{2+} has a full d subshell, so no d-to-d transition can occur. The precipitate 'redissolves' in excess of either reagent, forming $[Zn(OH)_4]^{2-}$ or $[Zn(NH_3)_4]^{2+}$ respectively.

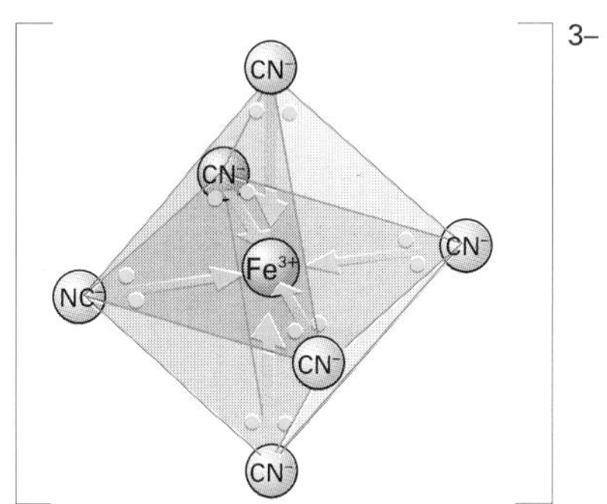

Aqueous potassium hexacyanoferrate(III) $K_3[Fe(CN)_6]$ contains the complex ion $[Fe(CN)_6]^{3-}$(aq).

Testing for Fe^{2+}(aq) and Fe^{3+}(aq)

Adding aqueous thiocyanate ions SCN^-(aq) to iron(III) ions Fe^{3+}(aq) forms the deep blood-red complex ion $[Fe(H_2O)_5SCN]^{2+}$. Iron(II) ions Fe^{2+}(aq) do not form this complex. But the colour formed with iron(III) is so intense that care is needed with this test. If iron(II) has been partially oxidized by air and there is even a small amount of iron(III) present in it, the red colour will still appear in this test. The result needs to be compared with a similar test on a known solution containing iron(III), and the intensity of the colours compared to be sure of a positive result.

A second test for Fe^{2+}(aq) and Fe^{3+}(aq) relies on adding hexacyanoferrate(II) ions $[Fe(CN)_6]^{4-}$ to iron(III) ions or hexacyanoferrate(III) ions $[Fe(CN)_6]^{3-}$ to iron(II) ions. The result is an extremely deep blue colour known as **Prussian blue** (and used traditionally for architects' 'blueprints'). This insoluble compound has the formula $Fe(III)_4[Fe(II)(CN)_6]_3$. Notice that *both* oxidation states have to be present to give the deep colour, which is due to a charge transfer transition.

The formation of Prussian blue. Here, aqueous hexacyanoferrate(III) ions $[Fe(CN)_6]^{3-}$ are being added to aqueous iron(II) sulphate.

SUMMARY

- Some transition metal compounds are coloured because they absorb certain colours from incident white light.
- An octahedral ligand field causes the d orbitals to split into two separate groups of differing energy.
- Coloured ions have fewer than 10 electrons and at least one partially filled d orbital.
- Transition metal ions may be identified by the formation of specific coloured species.

PRACTICE EXAM QUESTIONS

1 a Iron can be obtained from its oxide, Fe_2O_3, by reaction with carbon, aluminium, or hydrogen. Write an equation for the reaction in each case. [3]

b State, with an explanation, which of the reducing agents used above is likely to lead to:

i the cheapest iron;

ii the purest iron. [4]

c State two compounds formed during the extraction of iron in the blast furnace which lead to environmental pollution. In each case identify the type of pollution caused. [4]

d Outline the essential chemistry of the process for converting crude iron into a carbon steel. [2]
AQA (NEAB) 1999

2 a Give *two* physical properties of iron metal which show it to be a typical d-block element. [2]

b i Complete the following ground-state electronic configurations, where [Ar] represents the ground-state configuration of the argon atom:

Fe [Ar] Fe^{2+} [Ar] [2]

ii Explain why the Fe^{2+} ion might be expected to be less stable than the Fe^{3+} ion. [2]

c i State the colour of aqueous solutions of iron(II) salts. Give the formula and shape of the complex ion responsible for the colour. [3]

ii What colour change slowly occurs if a solution containing this ion is allowed to stand? Explain your answer. [3]

d i What would be observed if aqueous potassium iodide were added to an aqueous solution containing Fe^{3+} ions? Explain any observations in terms of the reaction taking place. [3]

ii Write an ionic equation for the reaction. [1]

e Explain why compounds of d-block elements are often coloured. [3]
AQA (AEB) 1998

3 a i Explain the meaning of the term ligand.

ii Explain the meaning of the term bidentate as applied to a ligand. [2]

b i Anhydrous cobalt(II) chloride is a Lewis acid. Explain the meaning of the term Lewis acid.

ii Give the formula and shape of each of the complex ions formed when anhydrous cobalt(II) chloride is added separately to water and to concentrated hydrochloric acid.

iii Give a reason for the difference in shape of the complex ions formed in part **b ii** above.

iv Give a reason for the difference in colour of the complex ions formed in part **b ii** above. [7]

c 1,2–Diaminoethane, $NH_2CH_2CH_2NH_2$, acts as a bidentate ligand. Deduce the formula of the complex ion formed when cobalt(II) chloride is treated with an excess of 1,2–diaminoethane in the absence of air. (You may write 'en' as the formula of the ligand.) [2]
AQA (NEAB) 1998

4 a Copy the boxes below and give the electronic structure of the vanadium atom and the V^{2+} ion:

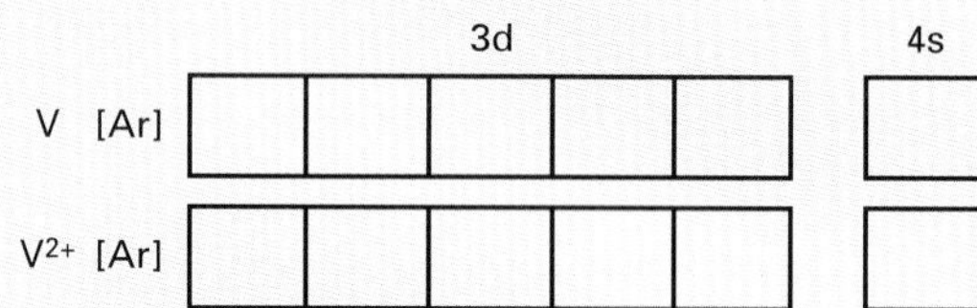

b i Suggest why the hydrated ion $[V(H_2O)_6]^{2+}$ is coloured.

ii Name the types of bonding within ions of this type. [3]

c Ammonium vanadate, NH_4VO_3, dissolves in aqueous sodium hydroxide with the evolution of a colourless gas. The solution becomes yellow after acidification. The gas has a pungent odour and produces a pale blue precipitate with copper(II) sulphate solution. The precipitate dissolves as more gas is passed in, to give a deep blue solution.

i Write an ionic equation for the reaction of the cation in NH_4VO_3 with alkali.

ii Name the pale blue precipitate.

iii Give the formula of the ion responsible for the colour of the deep blue solution.

iv Ammonium vanadate, on treatment with sulphuric acid, gives a yellow colour due to the $[VO_2]^+$ ion. Addition of zinc to the solution causes the solution colour to change to blue, then green, then violet. Give the oxidation number of vanadium in the vanadium-containing ions in each coloured solution. [5]

d The industrial production of sulphur trioxide from sulphur dioxide and oxygen is catalysed by vanadium(V) oxide. It has been proposed that the first stage of the reaction is

$$SO_2 + V_2O_5 \rightarrow SO_3 + 2VO_2$$

Write an equation for the second stage, thus showing the behaviour of vanadium(V) oxide as a catalyst. [1]

e Give the systematic name for each of these ions:

i $[VO_2]^+$

ii $[Cr(NH_3)_4Cl_2]^+$. [2]

f Draw and describe the shape of the ion in **e ii**. [2]
EDEXCEL 1996

5 a Transition metals and their compounds can act as heterogeneous catalysts. Explain what is meant by both *heterogeneous* and *catalyst*. [2]

b State one feature of transition metals which makes them able to act as catalysts. [1]

c Write an equation for a reaction which is heterogeneously catalysed by a transition metal or one of its compounds. State the catalyst used. [2]

d When an acidified solution of ethanedioate ions is titrated with a solution of potassium manganate(VII), the colour of the manganate(VII) ions disappears slowly at first, but then more rapidly as the end point is reached. Explain this observation. [3]
AQA (NEAB) 1997

6 **a** Give **three** changes which can result in a change of colour during the reaction of a transition metal ion. [3]

b For **each** of the observations described below, state which change or changes you have given in part **a** is responsible for the change in colour.

i A pale blue aqueous solution of copper(II) sulphate turns deep blue when added to an excess of aqueous ammonia.

ii A pink aqueous solution of cobalt(II) chloride turns blue when added to an excess of concentrated hydrochloric acid. [3]

c **i** Explain what is meant by the term *homogeneous catalyst*.

ii Which property of the transition metals makes their compounds particularly useful as catalysts?

iii The conversion of sulphur dioxide into sulphur trioxide by reaction with oxygen is catalysed industrially by vanadium(V) oxide. Write equations to show the catalytic role of vanadium(V) oxide in this reaction. [5]
AQA (NEAB) 1995

7 **a** List **three chemical** characteristics of the transition elements. [3]

b Give **one** example, of your own choice, of the ***chemical*** use of a named transition metal of the 3d series or one of its compounds in a major industrial process. State the chemical property on which the use depends. [1]

c Copy and complete the boxes below by inserting arrows to show the ground state electronic configuration of:

i a chromium atom;

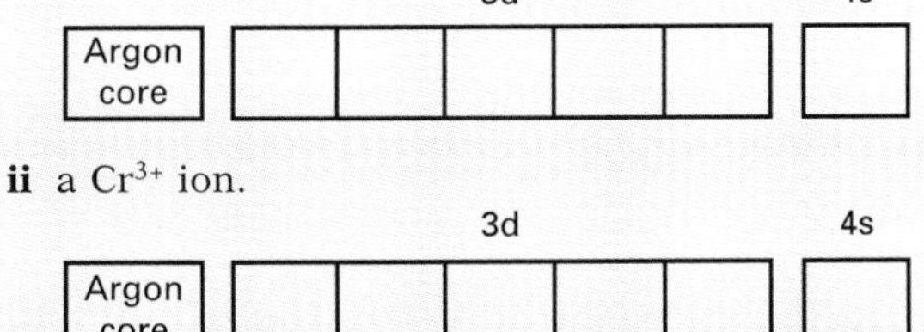

ii a Cr^{3+} ion.

[2]

d In acidic aqueous solution the dichromate(VI) ion, $Cr_2O_7^{2-}$, is a powerful oxidizing agent. The oxidation of iron(II) ions by dichromate(VI) ions may be represented by

$$Cr_2O_7^{2-}(aq) + 14H^+(aq) + 6Fe^{2+}(aq) \rightarrow 2Cr^{3+}(aq) + 6Fe^{3+}(aq) + 7H_2O(l)$$

i Deduce the change in the oxidation state of chromium in this reaction. [1]

ii Calculate the number of moles of $Fe^{2+}(aq)$ in 25.00 cm^3 of acidic aqueous iron(II) sulphate containing 12.15 g dm^{-3} of iron(II) sulphate, $FeSO_4$, (M_r = 151.91). [2]

iii Calculate the volume of aqueous potassium dichromate(VI) of concentration 0.0200 mol dm^{-3} that will completely oxidize the number of moles of $Fe^{2+}(aq)$ in **d ii**. [2]

e State what you would expect to see if aqueous sodium hydroxide was added slowly to a solution of aqueous chromium(III) sulphate until the alkali was in excess. [2]
WJEC 1997

8 **a** When concentrated hydrochloric acid is added to aqueous copper(II) sulphate until in excess, a yellow solution containing the complex ion **P** is formed.

Give the formula of the complex ion **P**. [1]

b The addition of a slight excess of iron filings to aqueous copper(II) sulphate produces a solution of an ion **Q** and a solid which is then removed by filtration.

i Write the ionic equation for this reaction. [1]

ii Give two observations that could be made. [1]

iii In aqueous solution, **Q** exists as a complex ion. Give the formula of this complex ion. [1]

c Describe the charge and shape of each of the ions **P** and **Q**, using the appropriate words from the following list: anionic, cationic, neutral, octahedral, planar, and tetrahedral. [2]

d The addition of aqueous sodium hydroxide to the solution containing **Q** produces a precipitate of iron(II) hydroxide which, when filtered, slowly turns into a brown solid, **R**, on the filter paper.

i State the colour of the iron(II) hydroxide. [1]

ii Give the formula of **R**. [1]

iii With what does the iron(II) hydroxide react to produce R? [1]

iv What type of reaction occurs in the formation of both **Q** and **R**? [1]
AQA (AEB) 1996

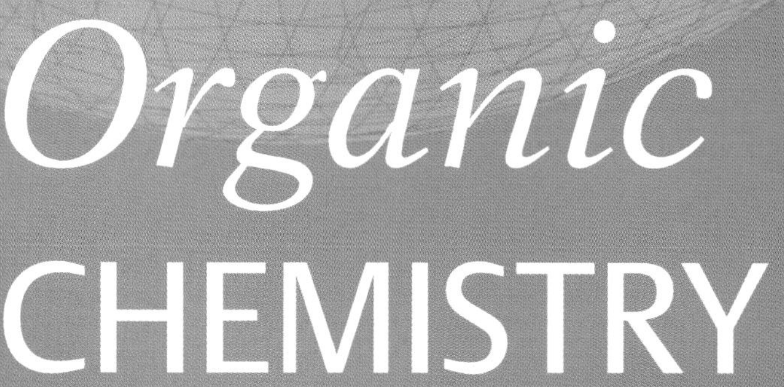

Organic CHEMISTRY

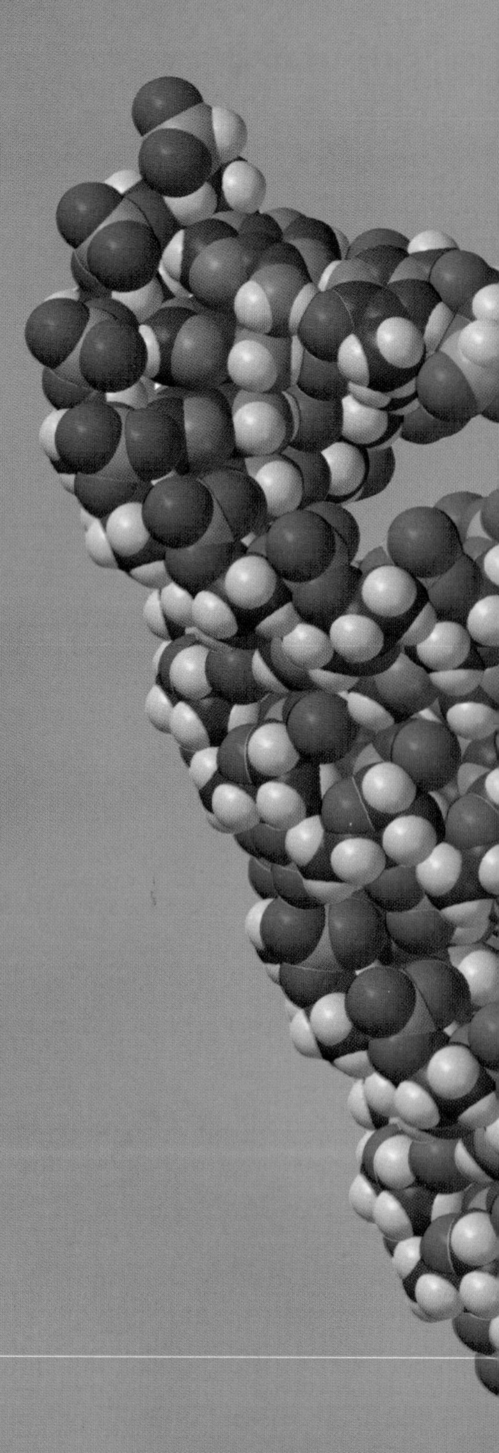

Organic chemistry involves the study of the compounds formed by carbon. There are over five million known, so their investigation is greatly simplified by considering the behaviour of a few significant classes of molecules (chapter 21). The most important classes are covered in turn, starting with the simplest compounds: those that contain only carbon and hydrogen atoms (chapters 22 and 23).

The next pair of chapters introduce atoms that create significant polarity in the bonding within the organic compounds, which has very significant effects on the types of reaction the molecules undergo. Halogen atoms are present in the halogenoalkanes (chapter 24); oxygen atoms forming single bonds are present in the alcohols (chapter 25).

Oxygen atoms are also capable of forming double bonds, and so the consequences of such a bond are discussed in the next two chapters, on aldehydes and ketones (chapter 26) and carboxylic acids (chapter 27). The final important element in organic chemistry is nitrogen, and chapter 28 surveys some of the molecules that contain nitrogen atoms. Chapter 29 seeks to draw together some of the ideas presented earlier and includes a discussion of the efforts organic chemists make to synthesize chemicals of significant value, especially to medicine, such as ibuprofen.

Chapter 30 tries to provide an insight into the exceptionally important area of biochemistry, arguably the most significant application of chemistry. In particular, the illustrations provided should prove helpful.

The final two chapters in the book, while not falling specifically under the heading 'organic chemistry', revolve around the separation and identification of chemicals. Powerful and widely used techniques such as chromatography (chapter 31) and spectroscopy (chapter 32) were introduced in the 20th century and transformed our ability to identify the structure of molecules.

Since 1950, advances have come most quickly in the area of biochemistry. In the second half of the 20th century, the detailed mechanism by which genetic information is passed from one generation to another via the replication, transcription, and translation of DNA was revealed. With little doubt, this is the most profound idea science has discovered during that period of time. At the heart of molecular biology is the double helix structure of the DNA molecule, shown here. You can read an account of this fascinating discovery in spreads 30.8–10.

There are still big questions to be answered. For example, it is unclear how (in full molecular detail) a single cell in the body differentiates to produce the appropriate limbs and organs. Maybe you will be the person who provides one of the vital links in this continuing quest.

Two computer-generated images of a space-filling model of DNA. The beauty of this molecule is even more apparent on the computer display, since the image can be rotated to show the three-dimensional structure to better effect. Here we have selected two views: one showing the grooves in the molecule and one looking down the inside of the double helix.

21 Introduction to organic chemistry

Organic chemistry is the study of the compounds of carbon. Carbon compounds are far more numerous than those of other elements because carbon atoms are able to bond together to form a wide range of chains and rings. The subject is called *organic chemistry* because living organisms are composed mainly of carbon compounds. Organic chemistry is the chemistry of life. It also includes the chemistry of an enormous range of substances, including food, fuels, textiles, plastics, drugs, dyes, explosives, pesticides, and paint. Most of the world's energy comes from burning carbon-based fuels, and the organic chemical industry is essential to most national economies. Major international crises have occurred over the supply and trade of carbon-containing substances such as crude oil, natural gas, coal, and their products. This chapter explores the basic principles of organic chemistry while giving you some feel for its scope. With *over four million* separate compounds, it would seem to be a vast subject. However, you will learn to group this huge array of organic compounds into separate families (called homologous series), each with its own distinct set of properties. This grouping together of compounds that react in a similar way makes studying them much simpler.

Organic chemistry and the carbon atom

21.1

OBJECTIVES

- Fuels and materials
- Basis of life
- Chains and rings of carbon atoms

Catenation

Elements other than carbon, especially other members of Group IV, are able to catenate. Silicon atoms bond to each other, but molecules containing more than eight silicon atoms are unstable. Sulphur atoms can form *very* long chains, especially in the liquid at a temperature of 170 °C, but sulphur cannot form complex molecules because each atom can only form two bonds, so chains cannot be branched. Carbon is unique in its ability to form molecules of almost any size and shape.

The basic structure of any organic compound – be it plastic, protein, medicine, fuel, or fibre – consists of a skeleton of carbon atoms joined together in chains and rings. The ability of an element to form chains of atoms bonded together is called **catenation.** This spread gives examples of the types of carbon skeleton possible. Later spreads will discuss the actual shapes of organic molecules and the conventions used to name them.

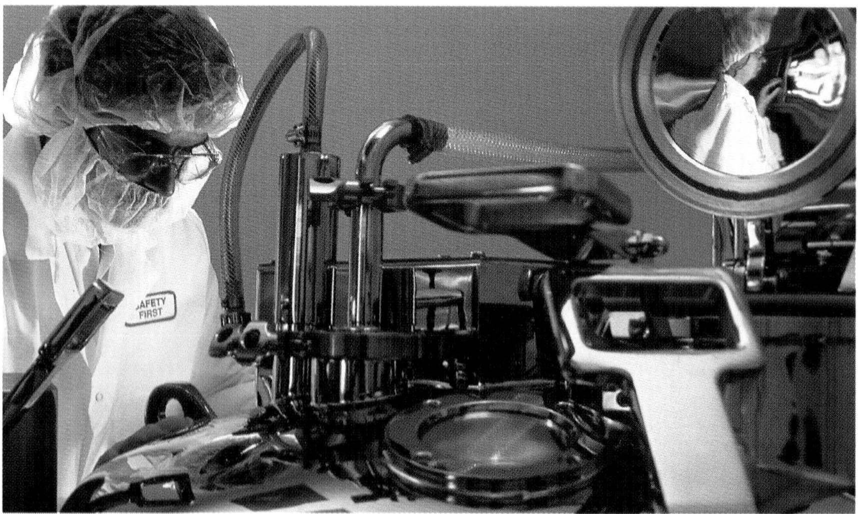

The economies of industrialized societies are underpinned by their chemical industries. Chemical companies generate some of the highest turnovers and the largest profits in British industry. Industrialized societies spend typically 10–25% of their income on fuel for transport, cooking, and heating. These fuels are provided by the organic chemical industry, whose function is to make useful compounds from readily available raw materials. The organic sector uses fossil-fuels (coal, crude oil, and natural gas) and resources from living organisms as its raw materials.

The carbon atom

The carbon atom has four electrons in its valence shell. It can share each of these electrons with another atom to form *four* covalent bonds. The simplest organic compound is methane CH_4, which consists of a central carbon atom bonded to four separate atoms of hydrogen. A molecule of methane may be described in a number of different ways, as shown at the top of the opposite page.

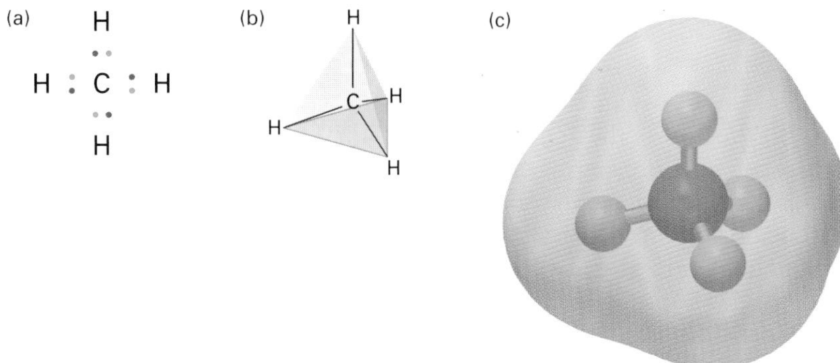

Various representations of the methane molecule CH_4. (a) The Lewis structure shows the arrangement of the bonding electron pairs. (b) VSEPR theory indicates that the molecule has a tetrahedral shape. (c) An electrostatic potential map confirms both the shape and the electron distribution suggested in (a) and (b). Note that there is very little polarity in the molecule.

Chains and rings of carbon atoms

Carbon is unique in that its atoms can bond together to make chains and rings of almost unlimited size and complexity. At the same time, bonds remain free to join with other atoms. Most of the diagrams below show only the carbon skeleton of some chains and rings; each line represents a bonding electron pair. Most of the diagrams do *not* show three-dimensional structure: they are *projections* onto the flat two-dimensional page. Carbon skeletons may also consist of branched chains or of two or more rings fused together:

(a) A single carbon atom and the four bonds it can form. (b) Two carbon atoms joined by a single covalent bond; six further bonds can be formed. (c) Five carbon atoms joined together to make a single chain. (d) and (e) Five and six carbon atoms joined to make ring-shaped structures.

A branched-chain carbon skeleton.

Kinetic and thermodynamic stability

Another reason why carbon forms so many compounds is that its compounds are *kinetically* very stable. The activation energy required to break a carbon–carbon bond is high. At normal temperatures compounds with carbon–carbon bonds are very stable. Once the activation energy is overcome at high temperatures, carbon compounds combust readily in the presence of oxygen. The reactions are highly exothermic because carbon compounds are thermodynamically unstable relative to their combustion products. It is this combination of a high activation energy and exothermic combustion that makes many organic compounds very useful as fuels.

SUMMARY

- Carbon compounds form the basis of living organisms. They form an enormous range of materials and fuels central to the function of any modern industrialized society.
- Catenation is the ability of an element to form chains with itself.
- Carbon catenates to form molecules of almost any size or shape.

Inorganic carbon chemistry

Organic chemistry studies carbon compounds, but a few carbon compounds such as carbon monoxide, carbon dioxide, metal carbonates, and carbon disulphide traditionally come under the umbrella of *inorganic* chemistry.

Hydrocarbons

Hydrocarbons are compounds that contain carbon and hydrogen only. Examples include the commercially important substances methane CH_4, benzene C_6H_6, and ethene C_2H_4.

Bond strengths

Bond	Bond enthalpy /kJ mol^{-1}
C—C	348
C=C	612
C≡C	838
C—H	413
C—O	360

Standard enthalpy changes of combustion

Compound	$\Delta H_c^\ominus$ /kJ mol^{-1}
Hydrogen H_2	−286
Methane CH_4	−891
Octane C_8H_{18} (in petrol)	−5512
Sucrose $C_{12}H_{22}O_{11}$ (sugar)	−5644

21.2 ORGANIC MOLECULES

OBJECTIVES

- Five types of formulae
- Saturated and unsaturated molecules
- Homologous series

Empirical formula

The empirical formula, spread 9.3, shows the simplest whole-number *ratio* of the numbers of each type of atom present. The molecular formula shows the *actual* numbers of each type of atom present. The empirical formula of lactic acid (2-hydroxypropanoic acid) is CH_2O; its molecular formula is $C_3H_6O_3$.

The properties of organic molecules frequently depend on their shape as well as on the atoms they contain. As a result, chemists have developed various ways of representing the three-dimensional shapes of molecules, especially organic molecules, on two-dimensional sheets of paper. This spread begins with a discussion of empirical and molecular formulae, with which you are already familiar. The shortcomings of these formulae lead to the development of two types of formulae that represent molecular shape. The spread ends by listing the 10 basic carbon skeletons on which many common organic compounds are based.

Writing molecular formulae

It is possible to represent organic molecules in a number of different ways. The **molecular formula** (see chapter on 'Reacting masses and volumes') of a compound shows the actual numbers of each type of atom present. For example, the molecular formula of ethanol is C_2H_6O. A problem immediately arises because the molecular formula of the compound methoxymethane is also C_2H_6O. The molecular formula does *not* distinguish between these two compounds.

(a) CH_3CH_2OH

(b) CH_3OCH_3

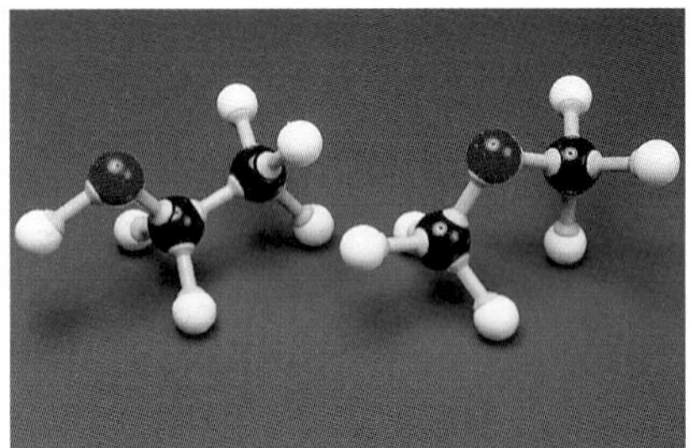

Displayed and shortened structural formulae: (a) ethanol; and (b) methoxymethane.

Shortened and displayed structural formulae

The **structural formula** provides more information because it specifies exactly which atoms are bonded together. The **shortened structural formulae** of ethanol and methoxymethane are CH_3CH_2OH and CH_3OCH_3 respectively. (The CH_3CH_2 group is sometimes written as C_2H_5, ethanol being represented as C_2H_5OH; this description is less clear and should be avoided.)

Structural formulae can also be *drawn* to show the bonds between atoms or groups of atoms. Such a **displayed formula** (or **graphic formula**) projects the three-dimensional structure of a molecule onto a flat two-dimensional page. As a result, bond angles are distorted and appear generally to be 90° or 180°.

Drawing stereochemical formulae

The **stereochemical formula** represents bond angles more accurately. It shows each atom separately and all the bonds present; it also attempts to represent the shape of the molecule. It is agreed among chemists that:

- A bond in the plane of the paper is shown as a solid line.
- A bond going behind the paper is shown as a dashed line (or as a diminishing wedge or as a 'striped' wedge).
- A bond coming in front of the paper is shown as an enlarging wedge.

Applying these rules, the tetrahedral shape of methane appears as shown below, together with the stereochemical formulae of ethanol and methoxymethane. Stereochemical formulae are only rarely used (but see spreads 22.8 and 28.6).

Stereochemical formulae: (a) methane; (b) ethanol; and (c) methoxymethane.

Shorthand methods

The structural formulae of larger molecules containing rings and long chains of carbon atoms are tedious to draw out in full. A shorthand form of representation is often used, which makes the following assumptions:

- Each single line represents a single covalent bond between two carbon atoms; the symbols for the carbon atoms are not included.
- All other elements except for hydrogen are represented by their chemical symbols.

- The ends of all bonds are assumed to be occupied by hydrogen, unless otherwise indicated by a different chemical symbol.

The examples on the right show the **skeletal formulae** for cyclohexane C_6H_{12} and hexane C_6H_{14}.

(a)

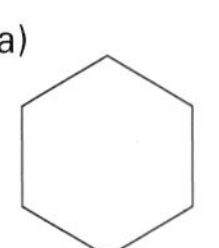

(b)

Skeletal formulae: (a) cyclohexane; and (b) hexane.

Saturated and unsaturated molecules

A molecule in which *all* the carbon atoms have four single covalent bonds is called a **saturated** molecule. A molecule containing one or more multiple bonds (i.e. double or triple covalent bonds) is said to be **unsaturated**.

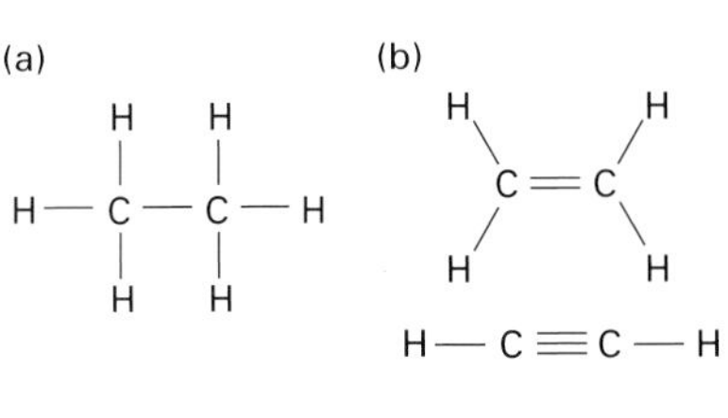

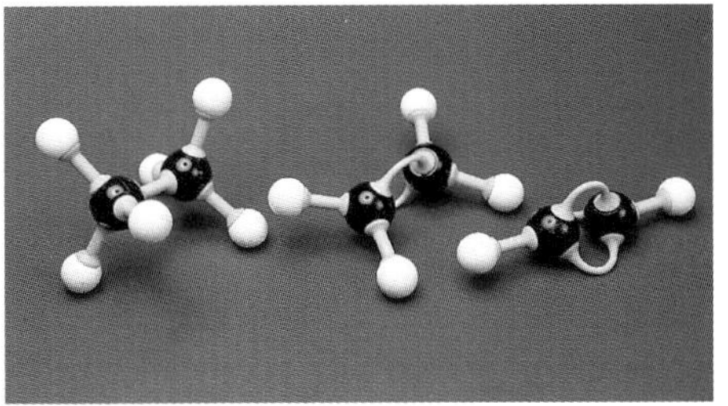

(a) A saturated molecule. (b) Unsaturated molecules.

Homologous series

The arrangement of carbon atoms may be thought of as the **skeleton** of an organic molecule. All the atoms of other elements are attached to that skeleton. The simplest skeleton is a single carbon atom; the next simplest consists of two carbon atoms bonded together. Then there can be chains of three, four, five, or more carbon atoms. A series of carbon compounds differing from each other only by the addition of more —CH_2— groups to increase the length of the carbon chain is called a **homologous series**. Compounds are named according to internationally agreed rules published by the International Union of Pure and Applied Chemistry (**IUPAC**) as explained in the next spread.

Meth-
Eth-
Prop-
But-
Pent-
Carbon skeleton
Hex-
Hept-
Oct-
Non-
Dec-
Prefix

Carbon skeletons. Specific series of compounds (homologous series) are formed by attaching particular types or groups of atoms to each of these carbon chains. The name of each compound begins with the prefix that refers to the length of the carbon chain. For example, attaching hydrogen atoms only to these carbon chains results in a homologous series called the alkanes. The simplest member CH_4 is called methane; $C_{10}H_{22}$ is called decane. Notice that many of the names are similar to those used to describe polygons (e.g. pentagon, octagon, etc.).

SUMMARY

- The empirical formula shows the simplest whole-number ratio of the numbers of each type of atom present in a molecule.
- The molecular formula shows the actual numbers of each type of atom present in a molecule.
- The structural formula shows exactly which atoms are bonded together. It may be shortened or displayed.
- The stereochemical formula represents the individual atoms in a molecule, the bonds between the atoms, and the angles between the bonds.
- A saturated molecule contains single covalent bonds only.
- An unsaturated molecule contains one or more multiple (double or triple) covalent bonds.
- The members of a homologous series differ from each other only in the length of the carbon chain.

PRACTICE

1 Copy the 10 carbon skeletons shown above. To each, add the bonds and hydrogen atoms necessary to produce the alkane homologous series from methane to decane.

2 Why are the compounds in question 1 referred to as being *saturated*?

3 Give the following for the compound propane C_3H_8:

a Molecular formula
b Shortened structural formula
c Displayed formula.

4 Draw the structural formulae corresponding to each of the following skeletal formulae:

a   **b**

21.3

OBJECTIVES

- Naming alkanes
- Structural isomers
- Chain isomers

Structural isomerism

The first organic compounds which we shall study are the hydrocarbons, which consist of a carbon skeleton to which only hydrogen atoms are attached. The simplest skeletons take the form of a single chain or a branched chain. The name of an organic compound gives information about its structure, and understanding how to name hydrocarbons prepares you for the study of more complex organic molecules containing elements other than carbon and hydrogen.

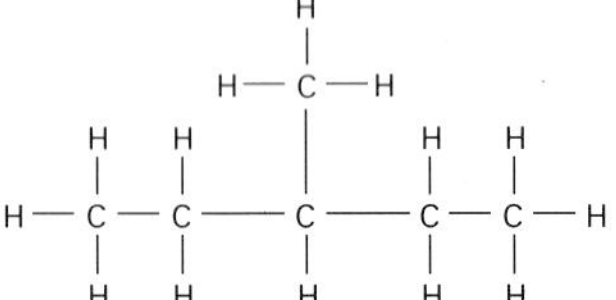

3-Methylpentane.

2-Methylpentane.

Name this hydrocarbon.

Straight-chain and branched-chain hydrocarbons

An organic compound with a straight-chain or branched-chain carbon skeleton that does *not* contain a benzene ring, spread 23.1, is called an **aliphatic** compound. The simplest aliphatic compounds are the **alkanes**, which contain carbon–carbon single bonds only. To find the IUPAC name for an alkane, you must carry out the following steps:

1 Identify the *longest* unbroken carbon chain (called the **main chain**), count the number of carbon atoms in it, and name appropriately as meth-, eth-, prop-, but-, pent-, etc. (see the previous spread).

2 Identify any shorter branches (called **side chains**) attached to this main chain as methyl (CH_3—), ethyl (CH_3CH_2—), propyl ($CH_3CH_2CH_2$—) groups, etc.

3 Number the carbon atoms at which the branches are attached by counting the carbon atoms of the main chain from the end that will give the lower number at the first point of difference.

For example, the first compound to the left is 3-methylpentane. The name consists of:

- *-ane* because the compound only contains carbon–carbon single bonds and so is an alkane;
- *pent-* because there are five carbons in the main chain;
- *methyl-* because the branch contains one carbon atom;
- *3-* because the branch is attached at the third carbon atom, no matter from which end of the main chain you count.

The second compound to the left would be called 2-methylpentane counting from one end of the main chain or 4-methylpentane counting from the other end. The correct name is 2-methylpentane because it contains the *lower* number.

The flame front of fuel burning in the cylinder of a petrol engine. A major component of petrol is octane C_8H_{18}. The straight-chain isomer (which occurs naturally in crude oil) gives explosive combustion that can result in engine 'knocking'. Combustion is smoother when the branched-chain isomers (such as the one in the worked example) are also used.

Worked example on naming an alkane

Question: Name the compound shown to the left.

Strategy: Follow the steps mentioned in the text above.

Answer:

Step 1 Count the carbon atoms in the longest unbroken chain and name it.

The longest unbroken chain is five carbon atoms long and so the substance is a *substituted* pentane. The term *substituted* generally means that one or more hydrocarbon groups (e.g. methyl CH_3—) or atoms other than hydrogen (e.g. Cl—) are attached to the main chain.

Step 2 Count the carbon atoms in each side chain and name them.

The side chains all contain a single carbon atom and so they are all methyl groups. There are three methyl groups, so the substance is a trimethylpentane.

Step 3 Number the carbon atoms to which the side chains are attached, keeping the numbers as low as possible.

Numbering from the left gives two methyl groups on carbon 2 and one on carbon 4, i.e. 2,2,4-.... Numbering from the right gives one methyl group on carbon 2 and two on carbon 4, i.e. 2,4,4-.... Numbering from the left gives the lower number at the first point of difference. So the IUPAC name is 2,2,4-trimethylpentane.

Structural isomerism

Alkanes with four or more carbon atoms can show different arrangements of the carbon atoms. For example, there are two structures (and two different substances) that have the molecular formula C_4H_{10}, namely butane and 2-methylpropane.

Molecules that share the same molecular formula but have different structural formulae are called **structural isomers**. There are three structures for the hydrocarbon C_5H_{12}, corresponding to the molecules pentane, 2-methylbutane, and 2,2-dimethylpropane.

(a) (b) (c)

The three isomers with molecular formula C_5H_{12}: (a) pentane; (b) 2-methylbutane; and (c) 2,2-dimethylpropane.

Structural isomers with different arrangements of the carbon skeleton are often called **chain isomers**. Chain isomers may have different *physical* properties because the different shapes will alter the strength of the dispersion forces. For example, pentane boils at 36 °C, 2-methylbutane at 28 °C, and 2,2-dimethylpropane at 10 °C. Their *chemical* properties, however, are virtually the same because they are all alkanes.

(a) (b)

Twisting the end of a molecule (by rotating a single carbon–carbon bond) does not *create an isomer. For example, a bent chain is not an isomer of a straight chain, as shown in this example of pentane C_5H_{12}. Molecules are only isomeric if changing from one isomer to another involves breaking bonds and reassembling the molecule in a different way. Bond angles are represented as 90° in these structural formulae, which can be misleading. In reality, bond angles in alkanes are very close to the tetrahedral angle (109° 28′).*

(a)

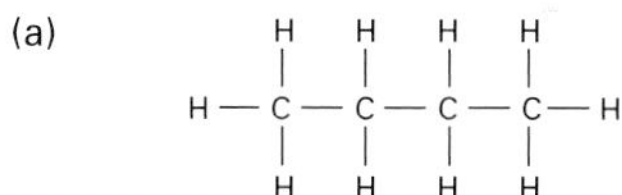

(b)

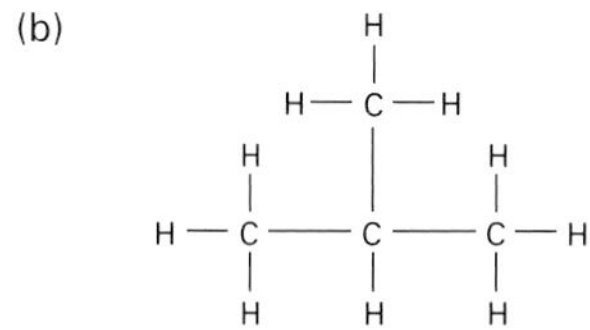

Space-filling models for the two isomers with molecular formula C_4H_{10}: (a) butane; and (b) 2-methylpropane.

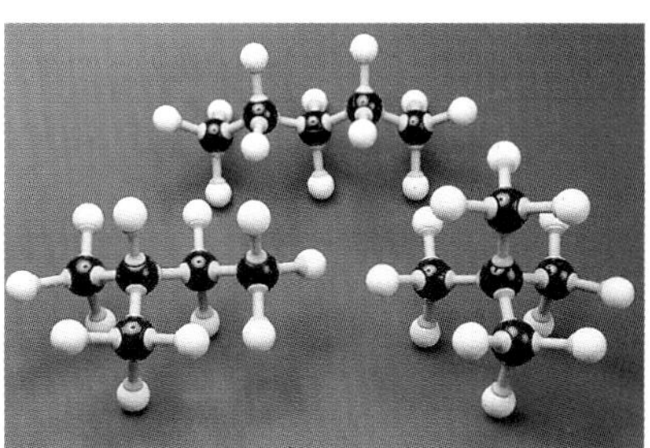

The three isomers with molecular formula C_5H_{12}.

SUMMARY

- The name of an organic compound is based on the number of atoms in the longest unbroken carbon chain.
- The carbon atoms in the main chain are numbered so that the positions of side chains are given the lower number at the first point of difference.
- Structural isomers have the same molecular formula but different molecular structures, i.e. the atoms are bonded together in different sequences.
- Chain isomers have different arrangements of their carbon skeletons.
- Structural isomers have similar chemical properties but different physical properties.

PRACTICE

1 Draw all the possible isomers of hexane C_6H_{14} and give the name of each.

2 Draw structural formulae for each of the following alkanes:
  a 2,2-Dimethylbutane
  b 2-Methyl-4-ethylhexane
  c Cyclohexane C_6H_{12}.

3 A student gave the name of a hydrocarbon as 2-methyl-2-ethylbutane. Give the *correct* name.

4 a Draw the structural formula of the most highly branched isomer of octane.
  b Suggest why this isomer combusts more smoothly than the straight-chain isomer.
  c Which of these two isomers has the higher boiling point? Give reasons why this isomer gives rise to the higher value.

21.4

FUNCTIONAL GROUPS

OBJECTIVES

- Functional groups
- Positional isomers
- Functional group isomers

The simplest organic molecules are the hydrocarbons, which consist of hydrogen atoms attached to a skeleton of carbon atoms. More complex substances result when hydrogen atoms are replaced by atoms of other elements. These atoms make up functional groups, which have significant effects on the properties of the substances. We will not look at the properties of the various functional groups in this introductory chapter. At this stage you simply need to recognize the groups, name them, and name molecules that contain them.

(a)

```
    H   H
    |   |
H — C — C — O — H
    |   |
    H   H
```

(b)

CH_3OH

CH_3CH_2OH

$CH_3CH_2CH_2OH$

$CH_3CH_2CH_2CH_2OH$

(a) Ethanol. (b) The simplest members of the alcohol homologous series.

Functional groups

Atoms other than carbon or hydrogen or groups of such atoms attached to the main carbon chain are called **functional groups**. As with hydrocarbons, the systematic IUPAC name of a substance that has a functional group allows you to determine its structural formula. For example, look at the structural formula of ethanol shown to the left. The first part of the name *ethan-* shows the length of the carbon chain (two carbon atoms in a saturated molecule CH_3CH_2—). The second part of the name (*-ol*) indicates the presence of the alcohol functional group —OH. There is a complete homologous series of alcohols (i.e. methanol, ethanol, propanol, butanol, etc.) that are based on the alkane homologous series. In each case, a hydrogen atom in an alkane molecule is replaced by a **hydroxyl group** —OH.

There are various different series of organic compounds, each with its own functional group. Examples include the ketones, aldehydes, carboxylic acids, ethers, and halogenoalkanes. The formulae and structures of these compounds are shown below. Note that, when writing a general formula for a homologous series containing a functional group, the symbol **R** ('residue') may be used to denote an alkyl group such as CH_3— or CH_3CH_2—.

Alcohols	Ketones	Aldehydes	Carboxylic acids	Ethers	Halogeno-alkanes
R — OH	R — C(=O) — R′	R — C(=O) — H	R — C(=O) — O — H	R — O — R′	R — X (X = F, Cl, Br, I)

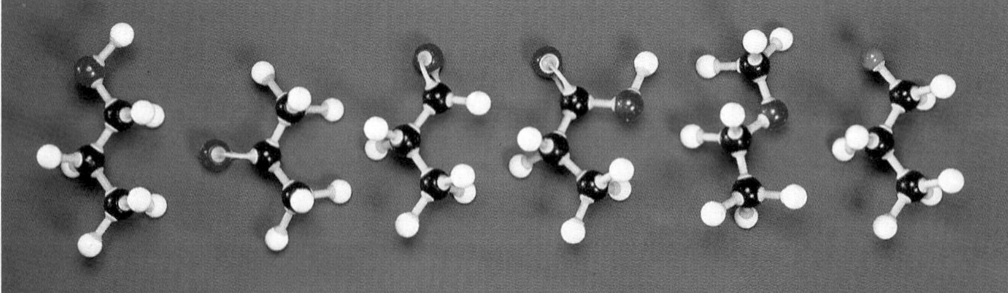

The structural formulae of some important homologous series containing functional groups: (a) alcohols, (b) ketones, (c) aldehydes, (d) carboxylic acids, (e) ethers, and (f) halogenoalkanes.

Chemical and physical properties

Functional groups determine the chemical reactions that a molecule can undergo, so *all members of a homologous series have very similar chemical properties*. The length of the carbon chain does not affect chemical properties because the C—C and C—H bonds have large bond enthalpies and so do not react easily. The chain length mainly affects physical properties such as melting point and boiling point. As additional —CH_2— units are added, the molecules have larger dispersion forces, and so the melting and boiling points increase.

Naming molecules with different functional groups

The four compounds shown below have names including 'but-', because the longest carbon chain consists of four carbon atoms (corresponding to the alkane butane). The other part of each name denotes the functional group present. The position of the functional group must be given in the name if there is any chance of ambiguity. For example, in (b), the hydroxyl group is attached to carbon atom 1 (butan-1-ol). It could also be attached to carbon atom 2 (butan-2-ol). These two substances both have the molecular formula $C_4H_{10}O$ but different structures. Functional groups give rise to *isomerism*.

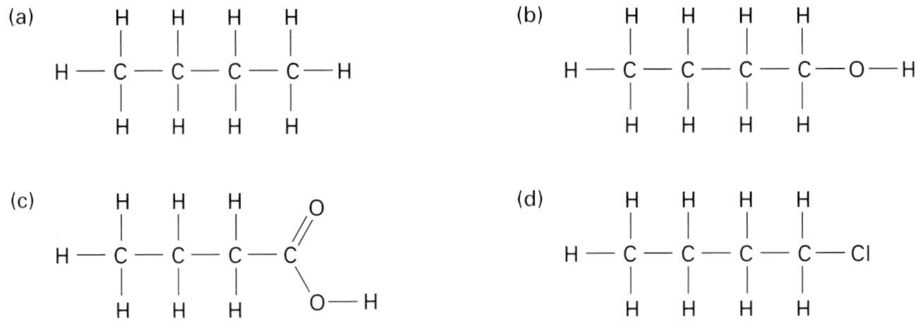

Naming molecules with functional groups: (a) butane; (b) butan-1-ol; (c) butanoic acid; and (d) 1-chlorobutane.

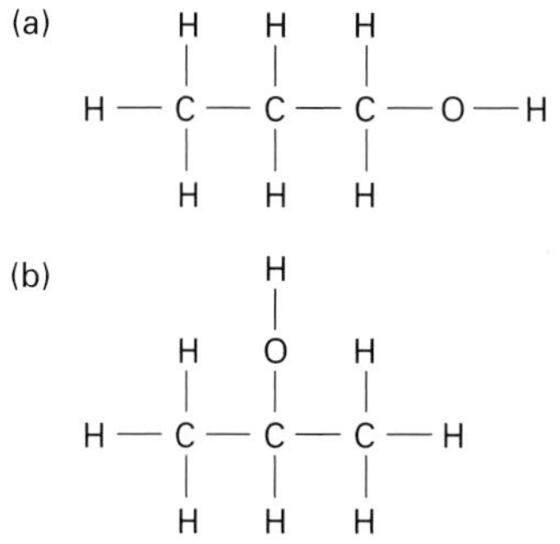

Isomers

Structural isomers can arise from placing a *functional group in a different position* on the chain. For example, C_3H_8O is the molecular formula for both propan-1-ol and propan-2-ol, but the functional group —OH occurs at position 1 or 2, giving different structural formulae.

These structural isomers are sometimes called **positional isomers**. The *physical* properties of positional isomers may vary slightly; for example, propan-1-ol boils at 97 °C whereas propan-2-ol boils at 82 °C. Their *chemical* properties may also vary because of the different position of the functional group on the carbon skeleton.

Structural isomers may also have *different functional groups*. The molecular formula C_3H_6O may correspond to propanal CH_3CH_2CHO (an aldehyde) or to propanone CH_3COCH_3 (a ketone) – see illustrations to the right. These structural isomers are sometimes called **functional group isomers**. Functional group isomers not only have different physical properties but they also have *different chemical properties* because the functional group is different.

Methoxymethane CH_3OCH_3 (see spread 21.2) is an ether; it is a functional group isomer of ethanol CH_3CH_2OH. Hydrogen bonding between ethanol molecules results in a much higher boiling point for ethanol (78 °C) than for methoxymethane (–25 °C). Ethanol reduces aqueous dichromate(VI) ions, turning the solution from orange to green. Methoxymethane does not react with aqueous dichromate(VI) ions.

Hydrocarbons revisited

The simplest hydrocarbons are saturated and are the homologous series called the **alkanes**. If a double bond is present, then the result is the homologous series of **alkenes**. The first few members of this series are shown to the right. The double bond in alkenes is called a functional group because it gives the series its distinctive chemical properties.

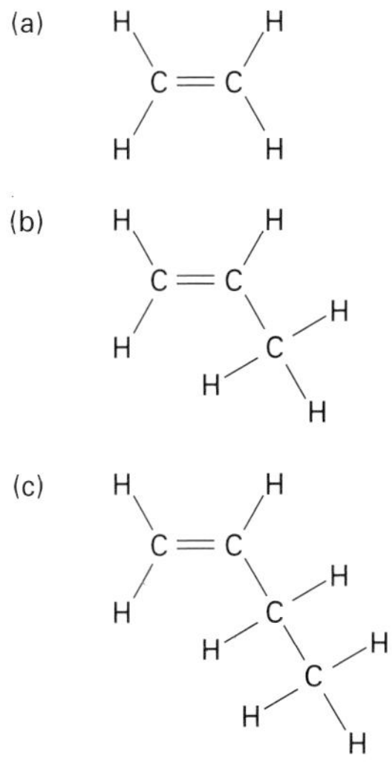

SUMMARY

- A functional group is an atom other than carbon or hydrogen (e.g. —Cl), a group of atoms (e.g. —OH), or a carbon–carbon double bond.
- The length of the carbon chain has little effect on the properties of a homologous series containing a functional group.
- Structural isomers of compounds that have functional groups may be positional isomers or functional group isomers.

Positional isomers of C_3H_7OH: (a) propan-1-ol $CH_3CH_2CH_2OH$; and (b) propan-2-ol $CH_3CH(OH)CH_3$.

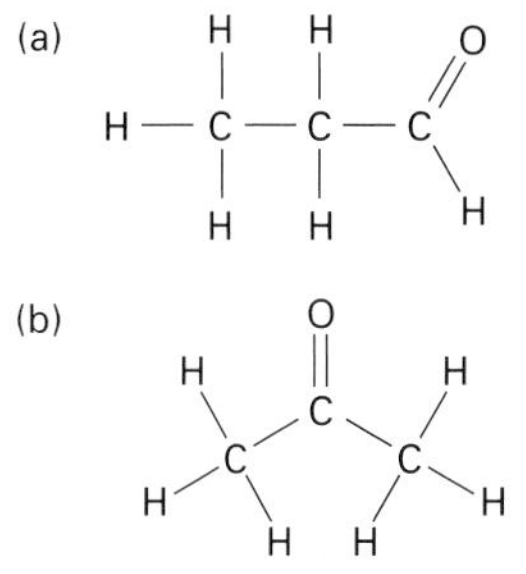

Functional group isomers with molecular formula C_3H_6O: (a) propanal CH_3CH_2CHO; and (b) propanone CH_3COCH_3.

Straight-chain alkenes: (a) ethene; (b) propene; (c) but-1-ene. Note that (c) has an isomer but-2-ene in which the double bond is between carbon atoms 2 and 3. The lower number is used to describe the position of the double bond.

PRACTICE

1 Draw the structural formulae of all possible isomers corresponding to each of the following molecular formulae:

a C_4H_{10} **c** C_4H_9Cl
b C_5H_{12} **d** $C_4H_{10}O$.

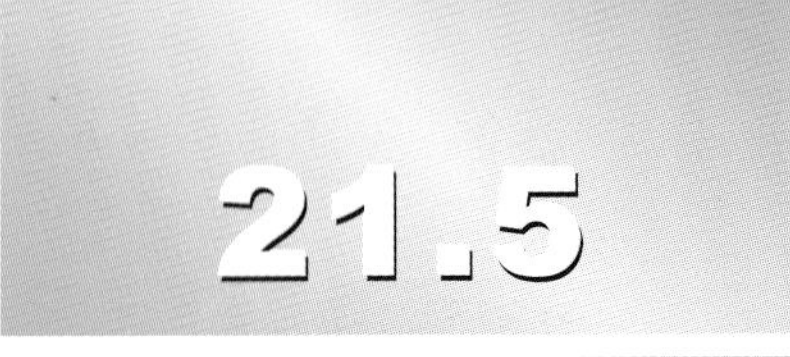

The reactions of organic compounds – 1

OBJECTIVES

- Molecular sites vulnerable to attack
- Nucleophiles and electrophiles
- Substitution and addition

The reactions of organic compounds fall into a small range of distinct types. Apart from combustion, in which the molecular structure is completely destroyed, reactions tend to involve only part of the molecule, usually the functional groups. These act as reactive sites, reacting with other chemicals. You will meet the specific reactions of functional groups in the following chapters. The aim of the last two spreads in this chapter is to introduce the *types of reaction* undergone by organic molecules.

The site of attack

Alkanes are very unreactive. The carbon–carbon and carbon–hydrogen bonds do not break easily because they have high average bond enthalpies (C—C, 348 kJ mol^{-1}; C—H, 413 kJ mol^{-1}). The elements have similar electronegativities (C, 2.5; H, 2.2) and so the bonds have little polarity.

Molecules with functional groups are generally more reactive. For example, the halogenoalkane bromoethane reacts to form ethanol when heated with aqueous base:

$$CH_3CH_2Br(aq) + OH^-(aq) \rightarrow CH_3CH_2OH(aq) + Br^-(aq)$$

Comparing bromoalkanes with alkanes, we can see that:

1 The C—Br bond is weaker than the C—C and C—H bonds (average C—Br bond enthalpy 276 kJ mol^{-1}).

2 The electronegativity of bromine is 3.0, so the C—Br bond is polarized $C^{\delta+}$—$Br^{\delta-}$.

H–C(H)(H)–C(H)(H)–Br + :O–H

↓

H–C(H)(H)–C(H)(H)–O–H + :Br⁻

Because the C—Br bond is polarized, the 'attacking' aqueous hydroxide ion $OH^-(aq)$ is attracted towards the δ+ charge on the carbon atom. A C—OH bond forms (average bond enthalpy 360 kJ mol^{-1}) as the weaker C—Br bond breaks. Cyan highlights the parts of the species that are changing.

Reactive sites

Functional groups in molecules contain reactive sites that are attacked by incoming species. A **reactive site** is a region of higher or lower electron density.

Electron-deficient sites include:

- atoms with a partial δ+ charge because they are bonded to a more electronegative atom;
- positive ions.

Electron-rich sites include:

- atoms with a partial δ– charge because they are bonded to a less electronegative atom;
- negative ions
- double bonds between carbon atoms;
- lone pairs.

Successful reactions

Bond enthalpies and electronegativities are not the only factors that determine whether a reaction is successful. The nature of the products of the reaction, the conditions of temperature and pressure, and entropy changes (see chapter on 'Spontaneous change ...') all play a part in deciding the likelihood of a reaction taking place.

(a) (b)

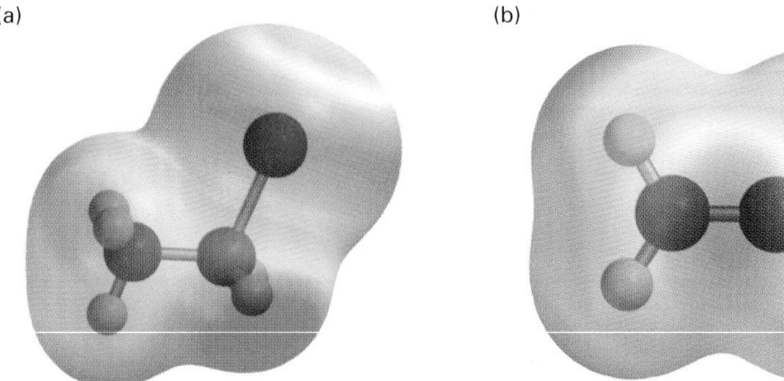

Reactive sites: electrostatic potential maps (see spread 5.8) of functional groups. (a) An electron-deficient site ($C^{\delta+}$) and an electron-rich site ($Br^{\delta-}$) in bromoethane. (b) An electron-rich site resulting from the increased electron density at the carbon–carbon double bond in ethene, indicated by the red colour.

The attacking species

Two important classes of reagent are used in organic reactions: these classes are called nucleophiles and electrophiles.

- **Nucleophiles** are species that are electron-pair donors.

Nucleophiles include negatively charged ions such as CN^-, OH^-, or Cl^-, as well as molecules bearing lone pairs of electrons like H_2O or NH_3. Nucleophiles attack the partially positively charged (δ+) atoms of polar covalent bonds such as the $C^{\delta+}$ in halogenoalkanes, aldehydes, or ketones. Nucleophiles donate electron pairs to form new bonds.

- **Electrophiles** are species that are electron-pair acceptors.

Electrophiles are typically positive ions like H^+ or NO_2^+. Electrophiles attack the partially negatively charged (δ–) atoms of polar covalent bonds. They also often attack the regions of high electron density in the double bond in alkenes and other double-bonded structures. Electrophiles accept electron pairs to form new bonds.

(a)

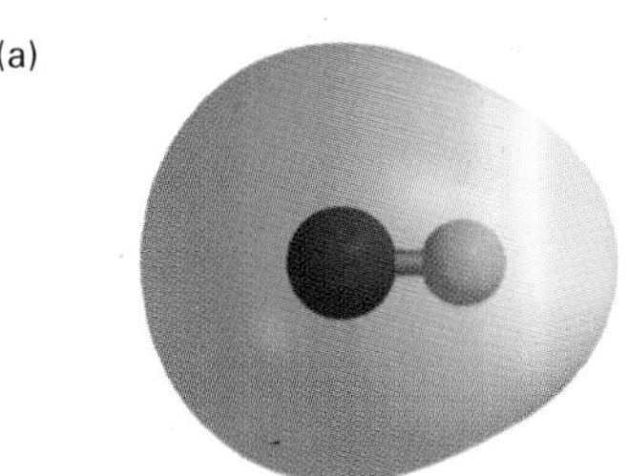

(b)

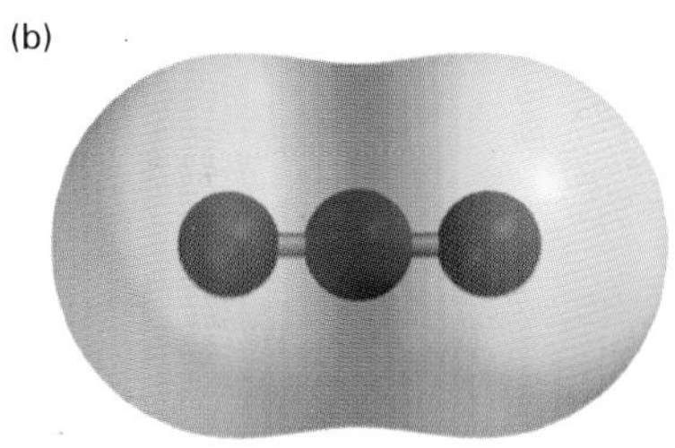

Electrostatic potential maps of a nucleophile and an electrophile. (a) The hydroxide ion OH^- is a nucleophile: note the high electron density due to the negative charge. (b) The nitronium ion NO_2^+ is an electrophile: note the low electron density due to the positive charge.

Types of reactions

When an electrophile or a nucleophile attacks an organic molecule, several different reactions can follow. Two common types of reaction are substitution reactions and addition reactions.

- In a **substitution** reaction, an atom or group (X) in a molecule is *replaced* by another (Y). Substitution reactions are typical of saturated compounds.

Look again at the reaction between bromoethane and aqueous hydroxide ions described at the start of this spread. This reaction is classed as a substitution reaction because the hydroxyl group —OH substitutes for the bromine atom —Br.

- In an **addition** reaction, two molecules *add* together to form one larger one, as in the addition of a molecule X—Y across a double bond. Addition reactions are typical of unsaturated compounds.

Not all compounds undergo all types of reaction; for example, alkanes take part only in substitution reactions. To become a good synthetic organic chemist, you need to understand the properties of particular chemical bonds, and how and why they react. You need to know how to introduce different atoms into a given molecule. Planning a chemical synthesis involves considering the nature of the partial charges (if any) present in the molecule. Having located these 'points of weakness', you must then choose a reactant that will introduce the group you want into the molecule. You must consider whether there are other groups of atoms close by that will obstruct attack by your chosen reagent. This apparently complex task is made much easier if you have a sure grasp of the terms introduced in this spread and in the one that follows.

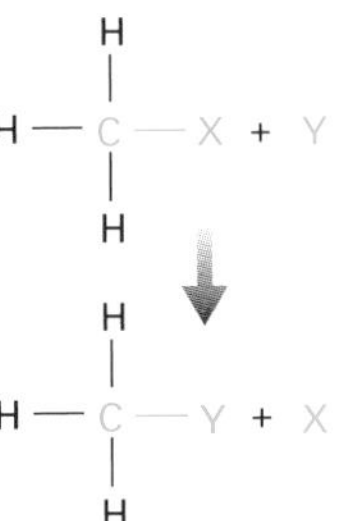

Substitution of X by Y.

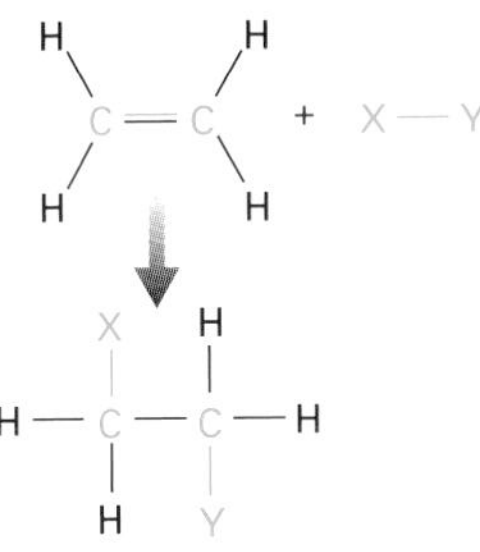

Addition of an incoming molecule X—Y across a carbon–carbon double bond.

SUMMARY

- Reagents attack regions of low or high electron density in organic molecules.
- Regions of low electron density (electron deficiency) result when highly electronegative atoms bonded to carbon atoms withdraw electron density from the bonds that join them.
- Regions of high electron density result around highly electronegative atoms or around double bonds.
- Nucleophiles are species that are electron-pair donors and attack regions of low electron density.
- Electrophiles are species that are electron-pair acceptors and attack regions of high electron density.

Saturated and unsaturated compounds

You should remember that:

- *Saturated compounds* have only single covalent bonds between their atoms; for example, the alkanes are saturated hydrocarbons.
- *Unsaturated compounds* have one or more double bonds between their atoms; for example, carbon–carbon C=C double bonds in alkenes; and carbon–oxygen C=O double bonds in aldehydes and ketones.

21.6

The reactions of organic compounds – 2

OBJECTIVES

- Heterolytic fission
- Curly arrows
- Homolytic fission
- Radicals
- Oxidation

Organic compounds may contain regions of low electron density, which may be attacked by reagents that are nucleophiles, and regions of high electron density, which may be attacked by reagents that are electrophiles. Chemical reactions are concerned with the breaking and making of bonds. This spread starts by looking at the *ways* in which bonds can break, and ends with an introduction to the oxidation of organic compounds.

Heterolytic fission. The electron density in the C—Cl bond is displaced towards the chlorine atom. The bond breaks when the electron pair transfers entirely to the chlorine atom. Heterolytic bond fission should be shown by one double-headed curly arrow.

Breaking bonds: heterolytic fission

The breaking of bonds is often described as **bond fission**. When a covalent bond breaks, there are two ways in which the electron pair can be redistributed. During the process known as **heterolytic fission** (or **heterolysis**), *both* the electrons in the bond transfer to *one* of the two atoms:

$$A—B \rightarrow A^+ + B^-$$

An ion pair results. Heterolytic fission produces *ions* because one atom gains an extra electron and the other loses one. The illustration to the left shows the heterolytic fission of a C—Cl bond. The species that result are highly reactive. They may form a new bond with an attacking reagent, or if not they may simply recombine. Polar covalent bonds often break heterolytically because the electron pair is already displaced towards one of the atoms.

The movement of an electron pair is shown by using a double-headed **curly arrow**. The arrow *starts* at the origin of the electron pair (in the case shown above left, the covalent bond between C and Cl). The arrow *ends* at the new position of the electron pair (in the case shown, on chlorine).

Homolytic fission. Each chlorine atom receives one of the pair of electrons making up the single covalent bond. Homolytic bond fission may be shown by two single-headed curly arrows.

Breaking bonds: homolytic fission

Alternatively, during the process known as **homolytic fission** (or **homolysis**), the *two* atoms keep *one* electron each:

$$A—B \rightarrow A^\bullet + B^\bullet$$

The electron pair that formed the single covalent bond is shared equally between the two atoms. Homolytic fission produces atoms or groups of atoms containing an *unpaired electron*. A species with an unpaired electron is called a **radical** (or sometimes a **free radical**). The unpaired electron is represented as a raised dot in diagrams.

A radical is a high-energy species. It is *very reactive* because forming a covalent bond by pairing with another electron is a highly exothermic process, releasing about 150–400 kJ mol^{-1}. Homolytic fission is typical of non-polar bonds such as the Cl—Cl bond in the Cl_2 molecule.

Fish hooks

In bond fission, electrons move from bonding orbitals positioned between atoms to orbitals located on individual atoms. A double-headed curly arrow shows the movement of an electron pair, as in heterolytic fission.

A single-headed curly arrow (sometimes called a 'fish hook') shows the movement of a single electron, as in homolytic fission.
Some chemists do not use 'fish hooks' to avoid confusion with double-headed curly arrows, whose use is both universal and exceptionally important. We colour 'fish hooks' differently to avoid confusion.

Causes of bond fission

Molecules are constantly colliding with each other. Bond fission occurs when they collide with sufficient energy and at the correct angle to each other. Non-polar bonds are more likely to undergo homolytic fission, particularly in the presence of ultraviolet light (see the following chapter). If a bond is already polarized (e.g. C—Cl), then the fission is likely to be heterolytic; the atom with the higher electronegativity gains a full negative charge.

Heterolytic bond fission can also be caused by the approach of an attacking species. For example, a nucleophile has a region of high electron density that will repel electron density in a functional group. As the nucleophile approaches closer and closer, electron density transfers more and more to the most electronegative atom within the group. Eventually the electron density is completely displaced onto the most electronegative atom, and this atom is no longer bonded to the group.

Oxidation of organic molecules

The term 'oxidation' originally referred to the gain of oxygen (see chapter on 'Redox equilibrium') or to the loss of hydrogen. This definition can quite often enable you to identify oxidation in equations representing organic reactions. Oxidation in organic chemistry is frequently carried out using potassium dichromate(VI) $K_2Cr_2O_7$ in acidic solution as the oxidant. For example, ethanol can be oxidized in two stages. During the first stage, hydrogen is removed from the molecule; during the second stage oxygen is added to the molecule (as shown below).

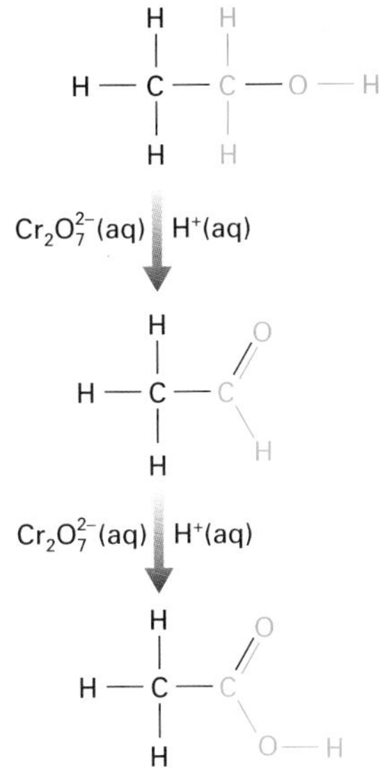

H—C(H)(H)—C(H)(H)—O—H

$Cr_2O_7^{2-}$(aq) H^+(aq)

H—C(H)(H)—C(=O)—H

$Cr_2O_7^{2-}$(aq) H^+(aq)

H—C(H)(H)—C(=O)—O—H

The oxidation of ethanol (CH_3CH_2OH) to ethanoic acid (CH_3COOH).

You are now familiar with the basic principles that underpin the reactions of organic molecules. We can now apply these principles to the reactions of specific functional groups and their homologous series.

Reduction

The process of reduction is the opposite of oxidation. An organic molecule is reduced when it loses oxygen or gains hydrogen. Ethanoic acid may be converted into ethanol by reduction, spread 27.8. Specific reduction reactions are discussed in later chapters.

SUMMARY

- In heterolytic fission, both electrons in a bond move to one of the two bonded atoms.
- Heterolytic fission tends to occur in polar bonds; the result is a pair of oppositely charged ions.
- In homolytic fission, the electron pair in a bond is split equally between the two bonded atoms.
- Homolytic fission tends to occur in non-polar bonds; the result is two radicals.
- A molecule is oxidized when it gains oxygen or loses hydrogen.
- A molecule is reduced when it loses oxygen or gains hydrogen.

PRACTICE

1 a Name two electrophiles and two nucleophiles.
b In a molecule of ethanol CH_3CH_2OH, which atom would an electrophile attack? Which atom would a nucleophile attack?

2 State whether each of the following reactions represents substitution or addition. Give reasons for your answer.
a $CH_3CHBrCH_3 + OH^- \rightarrow CH_3CH(OH)CH_3 + Br^-$
b $CH_3CH{=}CH_2 + H_2 \rightarrow CH_3CH_2CH_3$
[Hint: start by drawing structural formulae for each of the compounds in these reactions.]

3 For each of the reactions in question 2:
a Which part of the organic molecule is attacked by the incoming reagent?
b Which part of the reagent species attacks the organic molecule?
c Which bonds are broken and which bonds are made?

4 Using the molecule $(CH_3)_3CBr$ as an example, describe how the C—Br bond may undergo:
a homolytic fission;
b heterolytic fission.

5 Draw structural formulae for the ketone CH_3COCH_3 and the alcohol $CH_3CH(OH)CH_3$. Explain why conversion of the alcohol to the ketone is described as an oxidation reaction.

22 Alkanes and alkenes

The organic chemical industry produces millions of tonnes of products each year. These products may be fuels or materials such as plastics and fibres. They may also be the chemicals required for manufacturing processes, such as isoprene (2-methylbuta-1,3-diene) used to make the synthetic rubber for car tyres. Whatever the end product, the major raw materials are alkanes together with the alkenes derived from them. Alkanes are saturated hydrocarbons. They have few chemical properties because they have no functional groups. Alkenes are unsaturated hydrocarbons – they contain carbon–carbon double bonds. Substituting other elements for hydrogen atoms in alkanes and adding atoms to alkenes are the first steps to introducing the functional groups that allow the synthesis of almost any conceivable end product.

THE OIL INDUSTRY: FRACTIONATION

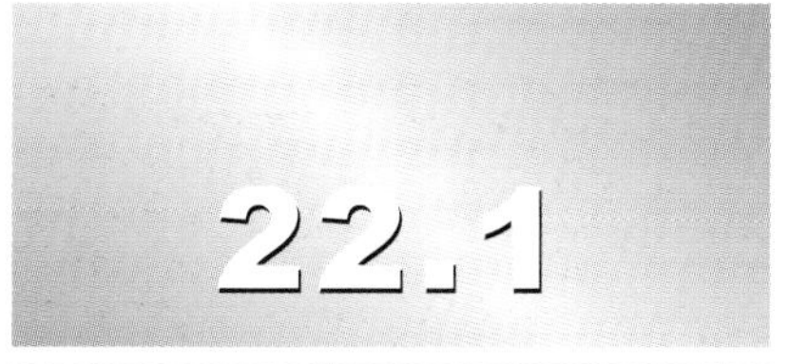

OBJECTIVES

- Raw materials for the chemical industry
- Fractional distillation
- How fractionating columns work
- Fractions

The alkanes and the alkenes are two homologous series of hydrocarbons, their molecules consisting of hydrogen and carbon only. One of the major sources of alkanes is crude oil (also known as petroleum). Another major source is natural gas, which is found either dissolved in crude oil or else in underground reservoirs containing gases alone. Crude oil is a mixture of hundreds of different hydrocarbons, most of which are alkanes. This introductory spread shows how crude oil is separated by industrial-scale fractional distillation. It also discusses how fractional distillation is carried out in the laboratory and introduces you to ideas about vapour pressure that explain this process.

Fractional distillation of crude oil

The different components of a mixture have *different boiling points*, and fractional distillation separates the components as a result of this property. Fractional distillation of crude oil results in a series of **fractions**, each consisting of a mixture of hydrocarbons boiling within a given temperature range. The substances within a fraction may be separated by further distillation. The boiling point of a fraction increases with the number of carbon atoms, because of stronger dispersion forces, spread 7.4.

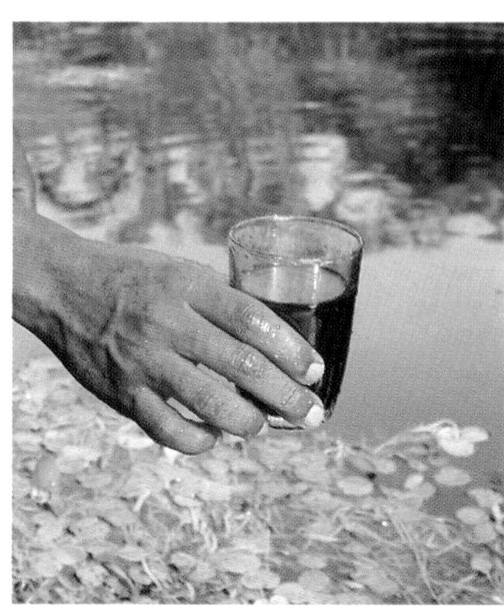

The actual composition of crude oil depends on where it was found. This sample comes from Ogoniland, Nigeria.

An oil refinery converts crude oil into a wide range of products. Some of the products are ready for use, e.g. gasoline (C_5–C_8) and kerosene/paraffin (C_{10}–C_{14}). Some of the products are used as chemical feedstocks for the manufacture of organic chemicals, e.g. gases (C_1–C_4) and naphtha (C_8–C_{10}).

Natural gas

Crude oil is the major source of alkanes. The second most important source of alkanes is natural gas, which is a mixture consisting mostly of methane CH_4 (at least 85%), ethane (up to 10%), propane (about 3%), and butane. Trace amounts of carbon dioxide, nitrogen, oxygen, and sometimes helium may also be present.

Theory and practice of fractional distillation

At a fixed temperature, the total vapour pressure above a liquid mixture depends on the vapour pressure of each pure component liquid and on the proportion of each liquid in the mixture. The total vapour pressure of a mixture of two liquids varies linearly with the composition of the mixture. The liquid boils when the total vapour pressure equals the external atmospheric pressure. See following spread for details.

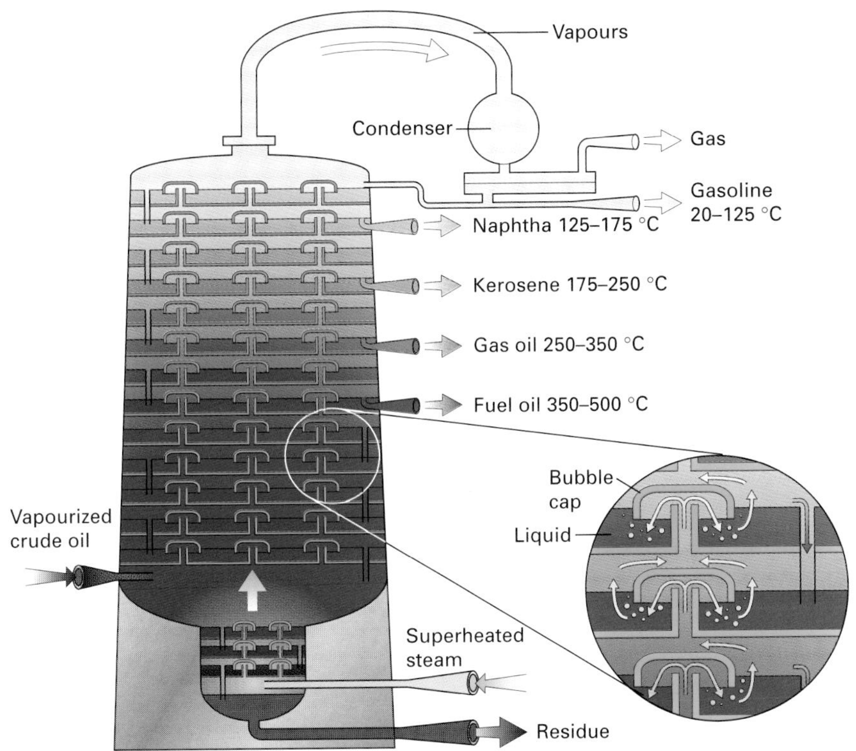

An industrial-scale fractionating column. Crude oil is pre-heated to about 450 °C in a furnace. It vaporizes on entering the fractionating column. Superheated steam maintains the temperature in the lower regions and ensures that the vapours rise through the column. Bubble caps cause rising vapour to mix intimately with the falling liquid that has condensed at each level. Liquid is either drawn off or is re-routed to a lower level. The boiling point in a fraction increases with the number of carbon atoms.

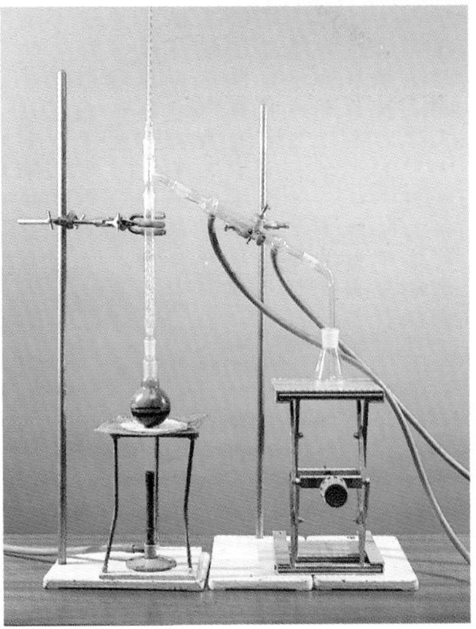

Laboratory-scale fractional distillation apparatus. When separating two liquids, the more volatile component distils over at a constant temperature as read by the thermometer. During this time, the less volatile component condenses and falls as a liquid down the column.

Imagine a liquid mixture consisting of 1 mol of each of two substances. As the temperature increases, the vapour pressures of each of the two liquids increase. However, the vapour pressure of the more volatile component increases to a greater extent. The vapour above the boiling liquid mixture becomes richer in the more volatile component. Condensing this vapour produces a *liquid* richer in the more volatile component. Repeated evaporation and condensation stages can completely separate the liquid mixture into its two components. This is what happens in a fractionating column.

In the laboratory-scale fractional distillation apparatus shown at top right, rising vapour and falling liquid meet and mix on the surface of the glass beads that fill the fractionating column. In an industrial-scale fractionating column, **bubble caps** allow the falling liquid to equilibrate fully with the rising vapour. Note that both columns have a temperature gradient; they are cooler at the top and hotter at the bottom.

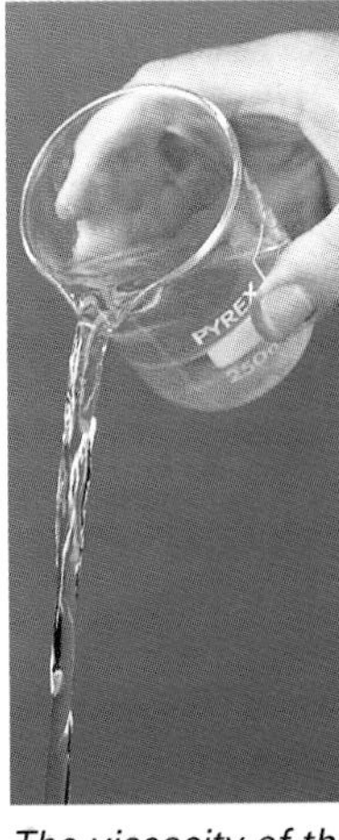

The viscosity of the different fractions increases with increasing dispersion forces, which in turn increase with the number of carbon atoms in a hydrocarbon molecule. (a) The liquid fraction C_5 to C_8. (b) The liquid fraction C_{20} to C_{30}.

SUMMARY

- Crude oil and natural gas are the major raw materials of the organic chemical industry. They contain a high proportion of alkanes.
- Fractional distillation separates crude oil into fractions – mixtures of hydrocarbons boiling within a given temperature range.
- The boiling point of a hydrocarbon depends largely on the number of carbon atoms in its skeleton.
- A fractionating column allows intimate mixing between ascending vapour and descending liquid.

22.2

OBJECTIVES

- Raoult's law
- Fractional distillation explained
- Deviations from Raoult's law
- Azeotropes

Fractional distillation and Raoult's law

It is possible to separate the fractions of crude oil using fractional distillation. This spread concentrates on explaining in detail how it is possible to separate a mixture of volatile liquids, such as crude oil. The principle depends on a law called Raoult's law. Fractional distillation will successfully separate a mixture of liquids that follows Raoult's law. At the end of the spread, we consider what happens when a liquid mixture deviates from Raoult's law.

Raoult's law: vapour pressure/composition varies linearly

Raoult's law states that, at a constant temperature, the total vapour pressure above a mixture of two liquids varies linearly with the composition of the mixture expressed as mole fractions, see spread 11.8. The vapour pressure of each component of the mixture varies as follows:

$$p_A = x_A p^*_A$$

where p_A is the vapour pressure of component A, p^*_A is its vapour pressure when pure, and x_A is the mole fraction of A in the liquid mixture. This law was first introduced by François Raoult, who made painstaking measurements of the vapour pressures of various mixtures. Raoult's law applies very well when the liquids in the mixture have similar intermolecular forces, which is the case for hydrocarbons with similar numbers of carbon atoms.

- A mixture that follows Raoult's law is called an **ideal solution**.

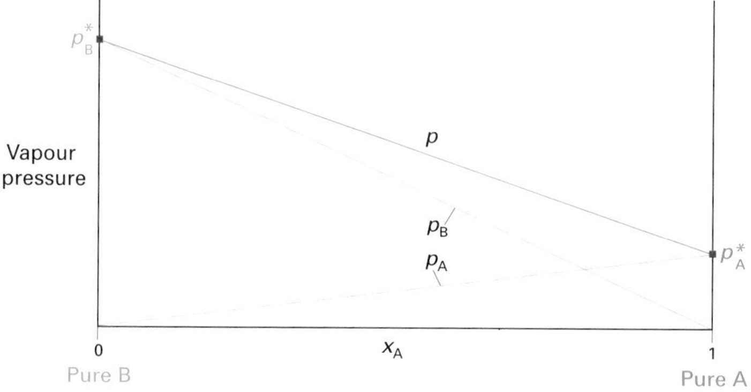

The vapour pressure at constant temperature of a mixture of two liquids varies linearly with the composition of the mixture expressed as mole fractions. This is Raoult's law.

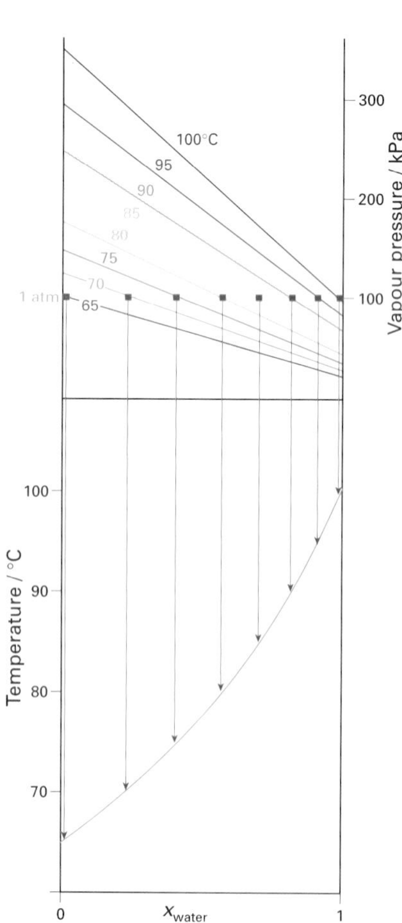

As the vapour pressure of the more volatile component (methanol) rises faster as the temperature is raised, the straight-line vapour pressure graph becomes a curved boiling-point graph.

Boiling-point curves

As the temperature increases, the vapour pressures of both the liquids in the mixture increase. However, the vapour pressure of the *more volatile* liquid increases more significantly, so a graph of the temperature at which the mixture boils when plotted against composition is a curve. Look at the diagrams alongside to see how this happens. This shows the conversion of a vapour pressure diagram into a boiling point curve, for a mixture of methanol and water.

The vapour above the boiling liquid mixture is richer in the more volatile component, so the composition of the vapour lies on the *other* side of the straight line joining the boiling points. This creates a cigar-shaped boiling-point/composition graph: see opposite.

To understand how to read this graph, consider heating a liquid of composition c_1 (which is richer in water, which has a higher boiling point). The vapour in equilibrium with the boiling liquid (at the same temperature) has the composition c_2. When this condenses, the liquid becomes richer in the more volatile component. If this process of boiling and condensing continues, the diagram shows that the mixture can be separated into its two components: pure methanol boils off first. When all the methanol has boiled off, water then starts to boil off.

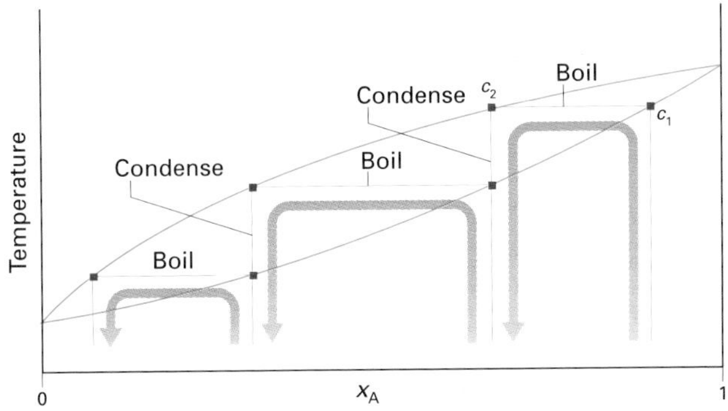

The vapour above the boiling liquid mixture is richer in the more volatile component. When the mixture of composition c_1 boils and then condenses, a liquid of composition c_2 forms.

The bubble caps in the industrial-scale apparatus, see previous spread, are the main means of establishing equilibrium at different temperatures between the falling liquid and the rising vapour. As long as the column is long enough and the number of bubble caps sufficient, it is possible to separate a ideal solution into its pure components.

- It is possible to separate an ideal solution into its pure components by fractional distillation.

Deviations from Raoult's law: azeotropes

Some liquid mixtures have boiling-point/composition graphs that do not look like the one shown above. Such mixtures are said to deviate from Raoult's law. For example, ethanol and water shows a graph which differs in a very important fashion from the methanol/water example discussed immediately above, despite the fact that ethanol is the next compound in the homologous series after methanol. There is a point on the graph, close to pure ethanol, where the vapour and liquid compositions become identical. Boiling this particular composition causes no further separation to occur: this particular mixture boils without change in composition and is called an **azeotrope**. Formation of an azeotrope occurs because the intermolecular forces between the components in the mixture vary too greatly.

Boiling an equal mixture (in terms of mole fraction) of ethanol and water causes a similar enrichment in the more volatile ethanol in a similar manner to that of an ideal mixture, until the azeotropic composition is reached, when no further separation occurs. Boiling a mixture of ethanol and water will produce the azeotropic mixture of 96% ethanol (by mass) and water.

- It is impossible to separate fully a mixture that forms an azeotrope by fractional distillation.

Further separation of the azeotropic mixture of ethanol and water requires a different strategy, such as using chemical drying by standing over calcium oxide.

Other mixtures form a maximum boiling azeotrope rather than a minimum boiling one, as was the case for ethanol/water. An example of a mixture forming a maximum boiling azeotrope is nitric acid/water. In this case, the deviation is more severe than for ethanol and the azeotrope occurs at 68 per cent nitric acid (by mass). So separation of an equal mixture of nitric acid and water by fractional distillation cannot concentrate the acid more than the azeotropic composition. This azeotropic mixture is typically labelled as concentrated nitric acid.

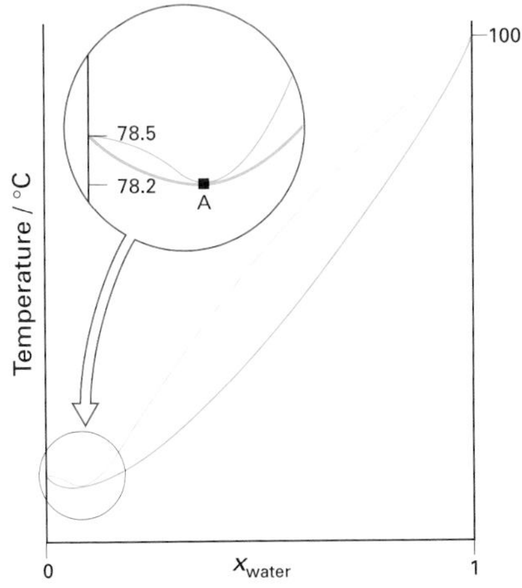

The boiling point / composition graph for ethanol and water. A marks the azeotrope.

SUMMARY

- Raoult's law: the vapour pressure of a liquid mixture varies linearly with its composition (as mole fractions).
- A mixture that follows Raoult's law is called an ideal solution.
- An azeotropic mixture boils without change in composition.

22.3

THE OIL INDUSTRY: CRACKING

OBJECTIVES

- Alkanes are very unreactive
- Radical reactions
- Fractions and their uses
- Cracking

The alkanes in crude oil and natural gas are currently the most abundant and relatively cheap source of organic compounds. The alkanes, however, are very unreactive molecules. They contain C—C and C—H bonds only, and do not have any regions of high electron density because there are no double bonds. The bonds have low polarity, because carbon and hydrogen have similar electronegativities (C 2.5; H 2.2), so there are no centres of partial charge to attract electrophiles or nucleophiles. So, radicals are the only species reactive enough to overcome the high activation energy required to break the strong C—C and C—H bonds. The three most important radical reactions that alkanes undergo are:

- Thermal cracking
- Substitution with the halogens chlorine and bromine
- Combustion

This spread covers the topic of cracking; the next two spreads will deal with substitution and combustion.

General formulae

The general formula for an alkane is C_nH_{2n+2}, where n is the number of carbon atoms. The general formula for an alkene is C_nH_{2n}.

Cracking

Carbon–carbon bonds are strong, so the skeleton of an organic molecule usually remains intact when reactions happen at functional groups. However, carbon–carbon bonds *can* be broken by cracking.

The table below shows that the percentage composition of crude oil does not match the market demand. One of the most important industrial processes at a refinery is **cracking** because it breaks down large molecules into smaller ones. When the original molecule is an alkane, the product molecules are a smaller alkane and an alkene. For example, octane could break into hexane and ethene:

$$C_8H_{18} \rightarrow C_6H_{14} + C_2H_4$$

or into pentane and propene:

$$C_8H_{18} \rightarrow C_5H_{12} + C_3H_6$$

Structural formulae show how a molecule of octane splits to form hexane (an alkane) and ethene (an alkene).

Ethene and propene are particularly useful for making the polymers poly(ethene) and poly(propene), traditionally known as polythene and polypropylene respectively, spread 22.9.

There are two main cracking processes, which occur under different reaction conditions and proceed by different reaction mechanisms.

The composition of North Sea crude oil. The market demands a greater proportion of alkanes with smaller numbers of carbon atoms.

Fraction	Number of carbon atoms in molecules	Percentage of fraction from distillation	Approximate demand for fraction (%)	Typical use for fraction
Gas	1–4	2	4	refinery fuel
Gasoline	5–8	12	22	petrol
Naphtha	8–10	12	5	cracking
Kerosene	10–14	12	8	jet fuel
Gas oil	14–19	19	23	diesel
Fuel oil	19–35	43	38	power stations

Changing molecules

There are three main processes used to match the raw material, the fractions from crude oil, to the requirements of consumers.

- **Cracking** breaks large molecules into smaller molecules.
- **Reforming** rearranges the atoms in a molecule to make a new structure.
- **Polymerization** joins small molecules to make very large ones.

Thermal cracking

In **thermal cracking** the alkane is heated to between 800 and 900 °C, for about half a second, sometimes in the presence of superheated steam. These high temperatures are sufficient to cause the strong carbon–carbon bonds to break. The reaction depends on the favourable entropy increase (see chapter on 'Spontaneous change...') caused by forming two species in place of one. At high temperatures, this increase in entropy compensates for the unfavourable endothermic enthalpy change.

The species initially formed are radicals. A carbon–carbon bond undergoes homolytic fission, leaving each carbon with a single unpaired electron. For example, octane could break down into a hexyl radical and an ethyl radical:

$$C_8H_{18} \rightarrow C_6H_{13}^{\bullet} + C_2H_5^{\bullet}$$

The raised dot indicates an unpaired electron. These radicals can then undergo a number of reactions. For example, they can *lose a hydrogen atom* to form a stable molecule. The ethyl radical becomes ethene in such a reaction:

$$C_2H_5^{\bullet} \rightarrow C_2H_4 + H^{\bullet}$$

The hydrogen atoms, which are also radicals because they have an unpaired electron, may combine together to form hydrogen gas:

$$H^{\bullet} + H^{\bullet} \rightarrow H_2$$

Hydrogen gas is a useful by-product of thermal cracking.

The radicals formed may also *remove a hydrogen atom* from another molecule. For example, the ethyl radical can remove a hydrogen atom from octane to give ethane and an octyl radical:

$$C_2H_5^{\bullet} + C_8H_{18} \rightarrow C_2H_6 + C_8H_{17}^{\bullet}$$

There is always a mixture of products from cracking, including a high percentage of alkanes. However, the choice of reaction conditions does to some extent control the product mixture. The mixture is cooled and then separated by fractional distillation.

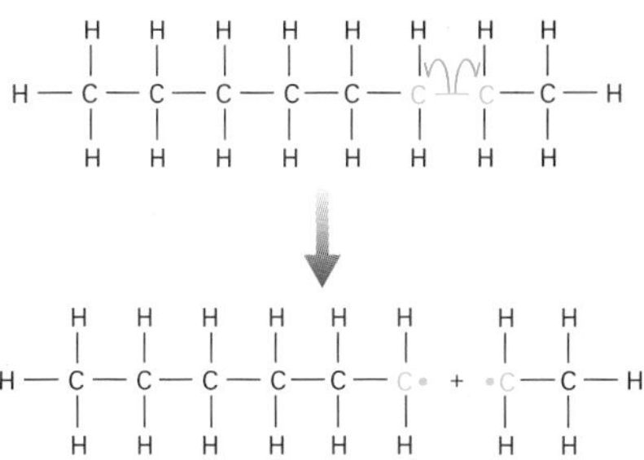

Structural formulae show how a molecule of octane splits to form two radicals – the hexyl and the ethyl radicals.

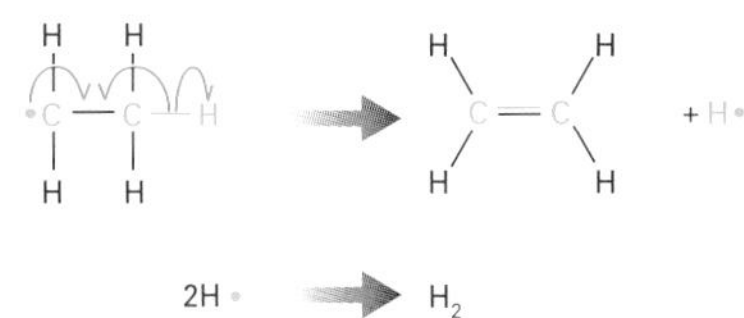

The ethyl radical loses a hydrogen atom to become ethene. Two hydrogen atoms then combine to form a molecule of hydrogen gas.

Catalytic cracking

Catalytic cracking (often abbreviated to 'cat-cracking') does not require such high temperatures as thermal cracking but does require a catalyst. A temperature of 500 °C is common, and the catalyst is often a finely divided mixture of silica SiO_2 and aluminium oxide Al_2O_3. The mechanism involves ions (carbocations, see spread 22.8) rather than radicals. Cracking dodecane $C_{12}H_{26}$ with a zeolite (a sodium aluminosilicate) catalyst gives a mixture in which just over half of the hydrocarbons contain four or five carbon atoms.

An industrial catalytic cracker operates at a temperature of 500 °C. The catalyst is often a mixture of SiO_2 and Al_2O_3.

Comparing thermal and catalytic cracking

The greatest difference between the products from the two types of cracking is that the carbon skeleton undergoes rearrangement to a greater extent in catalytic cracking. In a **rearrangement** reaction, carbon–carbon bonds are broken and reformed at different positions in the carbon skeleton, usually making it more branched. This result is put to good use in a related industrial process called reforming. The main purpose of **reforming** is to cause molecules to rearrange themselves to give branched-chain alkanes. These alkanes burn more steadily than their straight-chain isomers in internal combustion engines. Reforming also produces a significant quantity of aromatic hydrocarbons, such as benzene (see next chapter).

SUMMARY

- Alkane molecules are chemically unreactive because they do not have functional groups and the C—C and C—H bonds have high bond enthalpies.
- Cracking, reforming, and polymerization are used to match crude oil composition to market demand.
- Crude oil generally contains a higher proportion of relatively large molecules than the market requires.
- Cracking breaks large alkane molecules into a mixture of alkenes and smaller alkanes.
- Thermal cracking uses high temperatures alone; catalytic cracking uses more moderate temperatures and a catalyst.

PRACTICE

1 Use structural formulae to show how a molecule of octane forms pentane and propene.

22.4

THE ALKANES

OBJECTIVES

- Substitution by chlorine and bromine
- Combustion

Boiling points

The boiling points of the alkanes were explained in terms of dispersion forces in spread 7.4.

Nomenclature

The overall reaction between an alkane and chlorine involves substitution of one or more chlorine atoms for hydrogen atoms. The reactive intermediates are radicals; the process is therefore called **radical substitution**. The reaction is termed 'dirty' as there is a mixture of products in which no one substance dominates.

Bromination

Bromination follows exactly the same mechanism as chlorination. In the case of iodination, substitution to form CH_3I is *endothermic* by 59 kJ mol^{-1} (for chlorination it is exothermic by 99 kJ mol^{-1}). The reaction is therefore energetically unfavourable; iodination does not occur under these conditions.

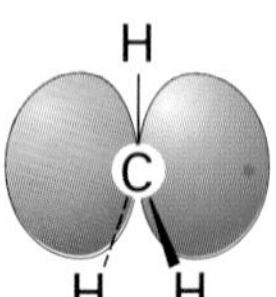

The methyl radical. Note that, whereas methane CH_4 is tetrahedral, the methyl radical $CH_3^{\bullet}$ is planar.

The alkanes have the general formula C_nH_{2n+2}. They lack functional groups, and so their chemistry is restricted to combustion and substitution reactions. Radicals are the only species reactive enough to overcome the high activation energy required to break the strong C—C and C—H bonds. The combustion of alkanes provides many of our energy requirements, from petrol burning in car engines to methane burning in domestic cookers. While the *overall* equations are fairly straightforward, combustion involves the formation and reaction of *intermediate* radicals in a series of extremely rapid reactions, which are complex and difficult to investigate experimentally. In this spread we will concentrate on the mechanism of the radical substitution of chlorine for hydrogen in an alkane, and only deal briefly with combustion, which will be considered in detail in the next spread.

Substitution by the halogens chlorine and bromine

Halogen radicals such as $Cl^{\bullet}$ or $Br^{\bullet}$ may be produced from halogen molecules by shining ultraviolet light on the halogen (or by heating to high temperatures). Radicals form when ultraviolet light provides the energy needed to cause homolytic fission of the halogen–halogen covalent bond. Replacing hydrogen atoms in an alkane molecule with chlorine or bromine atoms is called **chlorination** or **bromination** respectively. For example, exposing a mixture of methane and chlorine to ultraviolet light results in the formation of chloromethane CH_3Cl:

$$CH_4(g) + Cl_2(g) \xrightarrow{\text{UV light}} CH_3Cl(g) + HCl(g)$$

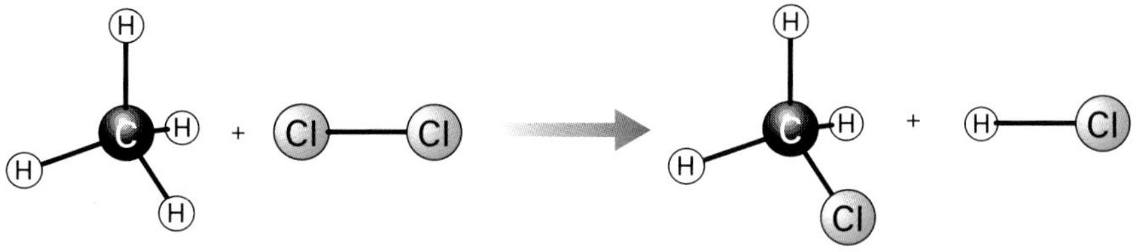

The radical substitution of chlorine in methane.

The mechanism of the chlorination of alkanes (chain reaction)

The reaction between an alkane and chlorine is a chain reaction: a **chain reaction** is a series of reactions in which a product of one reaction starts the next reaction in the chain.

The chain reaction is started when a reactive species is formed. The first step, called **chain initiation**, is the homolytic fission of a chlorine–chlorine bond to form two chlorine radicals, caused by absorption of ultraviolet light:

$$Cl_2 \rightarrow 2Cl^{\bullet} \qquad (1)$$

The chlorine radical is highly reactive and is likely to react with any radical or molecule that it meets.

The chlorine radical removes one of the hydrogen atoms from methane to form the stable molecule hydrogen chloride. The remaining species is the **methyl radical**, which has an unpaired electron resulting from homolytic fission of the bond:

$$Cl^{\bullet} + CH_4 \rightarrow HCl + CH_3^{\bullet} \qquad (2)$$

The methyl radical is also highly reactive. It reacts with chlorine as follows:

$$CH_3^{\bullet} + Cl_2 \rightarrow CH_3Cl + Cl^{\bullet} \qquad (3)$$

Chain propagation and termination

The *pair* of reactions (2) and (3) is called **chain propagation** because the chlorine radical destroyed in reaction (2) is regenerated in reaction (3). The regenerated chlorine radical may then react with more methane. The reactions 'keep the chain going'; they *propagate* the chain. One CH_4 molecule and one Cl_2 molecule are consumed, generating one CH_3Cl molecule and one HCl molecule, as given by the overall equation above this box.

The alternating destruction and creation of chlorine radicals continues until one of several reactions ends, or terminates, the chain reaction. The **chain termination** reactions always involve *two* radicals reacting together to make a relatively unreactive molecule, e.g.

$CH_3^\bullet + Cl^\bullet \rightarrow CH_3Cl$
$Cl^\bullet + Cl^\bullet \rightarrow Cl_2$
$CH_3^\bullet + CH_3^\bullet \rightarrow CH_3CH_3$

The presence of ethane in the product mixture provides strong evidence in support of this proposed mechanism.

Further substitution

Substitution reactions do not stop when just one hydrogen has been replaced. They continue until all the hydrogen atoms have been replaced. After some time, CH_3Cl molecules will be present in significant amounts. A chlorine radical colliding with CH_3Cl can produce HCl and a $CH_2Cl^\bullet$ radical, which can go on to form CH_2Cl_2. Further substitutions will result in a mixture of substitution products: CH_3Cl, CH_2Cl_2, $CHCl_3$, and CCl_4.

Combustion

As with the reaction of alkanes with chlorine, combustion is a radical chain reaction. The complication for combustion is that, as well as chain initiation, propagation, and termination, a further chain process called chain branching is possible.

Chain branching occurs when one reactant radical produces two product radicals. A common example is the reaction between a hydrogen molecule and an oxygen atom (which is a *biradical* $O^{\bullet\bullet}$ containing two unpaired electrons, spread 4.6) to produce a hydrogen atom (which is a radical $H^\bullet$) and the hydroxyl radical ($HO^\bullet$).

$$H_2 + O^{\bullet\bullet} \rightarrow H^\bullet + HO^\bullet$$

Chain branching can lead to an enormous increase in the rate of the reaction, because the number of radicals *doubles* after each reaction step. If the conditions during combustion favour chain branching, then an explosion occurs.

Cutting using a torch fuelled by propane.

SUMMARY

- Alkanes contain only C—C and C—H single bonds, which have high bond enthalpies.
- Only radicals (possessing unpaired electrons) are sufficiently reactive to break these bonds and force alkanes to undergo reaction.
- Chlorination and bromination substitute halogen atoms for hydrogen atoms in alkanes.
- Chlorination and bromination are radical chain reactions, involving the radicals $Cl^\bullet$ and $Br^\bullet$.
- Chain reactions proceed by means of chain initiation, chain propagation, and chain termination. (The exact steps for chlorination should be noted carefully.)
- Combustion is a complex radical chain reaction involving the oxygen biradical $O^{\bullet\bullet}$.

PRACTICE

1 Describe the mechanism of methane bromination.

22.5

PLUSES AND MINUSES OF COMBUSTION

OBJECTIVES

- Liquid and gaseous fuels
- The 'greenhouse effect'
- Energy density of a fuel
- Biofuels
- Waste disposal

We saw in the last spread that the combustion reactions of alkanes provides many of our energy needs. However, we need to be aware of the problems that combustion can bring as well. This spread considers the advantages and disadvantages of combustion and the continuing search for the best alternatives.

Fuels

A good fuel must obviously have a high exothermic standard enthalpy change of combustion so that it is an efficient provider of heat. But that is not the only consideration; a fuel must also be safe, cheap, and practical to transport. Ideally then, the combustion reaction of a fuel must have a high activation energy, so that it does not easily catch fire when it is being transported, but it also needs to have a high energy yield for the mass or volume carried. Ideally too, a fuel should not contribute to pollution by producing toxic combustion products or those which will contribute to the 'greenhouse effect'.

Liquid fuels are relatively easy to transport and store compared to gases. The alkane octane C_8H_{18} and the alcohol ethanol CH_3CH_2OH are both liquids which can be used as fuels. However, their combustion reactions both produce CO_2 which is a greenhouse gas. Hydrogen gas H_2 is also a good fuel, but it is awkward to transport and store and forms an explosive mixture with air. Hydrogen has the added advantage that it burns to form water which neither pollutes nor contributes to global warming. The alkanes methane CH_4 and butane C_4H_{10} are gases used as fuels. Methane is the chief constituent of the natural gas which is piped to our houses. Methane is cheap to produce because it occurs in large amounts naturally. Butane is bottled under pressure so that it liquefies, and is familiar to many as camping gas. However, methane and butane both produce CO_2 when you burn them and are greenhouse gases in their own right.

Calculating the energy density of a fuel

The **energy density** of a fuel can be calculated as the energy generated per unit mass or per unit volume of the fuel. For example, if 0.200 g of fuel yields 15.7 kJ of heat, the energy density is given by:

$$\text{energy density} = 15.7 \times 1000/0.200$$
$$= 78\,500 \text{ kJ kg}^{-1}$$

Equally, if 0.200 cm^3 of fuel yields 15.7 kJ of heat, the heat from 1 dm^3 of fuel will be given by the same calculation except the units will be kJ dm^{-3}.

Waste disposal

There are two basic methods available for the disposal of waste, landfill and incineration.

In **landfill**, the waste is compacted into natural or man-made cavities in the landscape. The most obvious objection is the eye-sore that this represents and the encouragement it gives to rats and other vermin. Microbiological action in organic landfill waste leads to the production of methane which is an explosion and fire hazard. Methane is also a greenhouse gas and, to avoid it being released to the atmosphere, action is being taken to collect it from landfill sites and either flame it off or use it as fuel. Microbiological action can also lead to toxic products such as hydrogen sulphide gas. Liquid leaching from landfill sites and polluting the ground water is yet another problem. This danger can be lessened by lining the site with impermeable material.

A reminder about the greenhouse effect

Just as the glass of a greenhouse prevents the energy entering the greenhouse from the Sun being re-radiated out, so that the greenhouse warms up, certain gases in the atmosphere keep the Earth warm by the same effect – called the 'greenhouse effect'. However, there is concern that build up of certain gases, particularly CO_2, is causing an *enhanced* greenhouse effect which may lead to 'global warming'.

Incinerators use combustion reactions to dispose of waste.

Landfill is an increasingly expensive way of disposing of wastes, due to the shortage of suitable sites and the cost of meeting higher environmental standards. So increasing amounts of waste are being burnt in incinerators. Incineration sterilizes the material for final disposal and reduces it in volume by about 90 per cent. Also, most new incinerators are designed to use the heat from burning rubbish to generate electricity.

However, it is the products of combustion that go up the incinerator flue into the atmosphere which must concern us. A large proportion of domestic waste is organic in origin and produces CO_2 (and H_2O) on combustion and so contributes to the greenhouse effect. Toxic gases such as carbon monoxide together with soot are produced by incomplete combustion. Sulphur-containing compounds produce sulphur dioxide and nitrogen-containing compounds produce NO_2; both can cause acid rain, spread 19.7. But by far the greatest concern is that an insufficiently high temperature can lead to chlorinated compounds producing dioxins.

Dioxins is the name given to a whole range of highly toxic compounds that consist of two benzene rings connected via two oxygen atoms.

O O Cl Cl O O Cl Cl

dibenzodioxin

TCDD, tetrachlorodibenzodioxin

TCDD, tetrachlorodibenzodioxin, is a particularly dangerous product of incomplete combustion of the chlorinated polymer PVC.

In 1977 it was discovered that burning wood produced some dioxins. Burning anything that has a combination of carbon, oxygen, hydrogen, and chlorine, such as the polymer PVC, has the potential of producing dioxins. The largest source of dioxins in cities has been incinerators for burning domestic waste. However, incinerators have been greatly improved in recent years by passing the flue gases through carbon filters. This reduces the amount of dioxin released to trillionths of a gram of dioxin per cubic metre of gas emitted.

This negative effect must be balanced against the positive effects that a modern incinerator burns about 750 000 tonnes of waste a year, and generates electricity at the same time. The energy it provides saves the burning of 300 000 tonnes of fossil fuel. Added to this, an incinerator may in fact destroy more dioxins in the waste than it emits to the atmosphere.

SUMMARY

- A good fuel must have a highly exothermic standard enthalpy change of combustion.
- A good fuel must be cheap and easy to transport safely.
- Biofuels have net zero effect on atmospheric CO_2.
- Incineration has advantages over landfill in waste disposal.

Biofuels

These are fuels derived from biological sources. For example, a fuel known as 'biodiesel' is made from the oil extracted from rape seeds. Another biofuel is wood taken from sustainable forests. These fuels release CO_2 when they burn, but because the plants they come from also fix CO_2 from the atmosphere while they grow and photosynthesize, their use has a net zero impact on atmospheric CO_2 levels and so does not contribute to the greenhouse effect.

A reminder about pollution from car engines

Because petrol and diesel consist mostly of alkanes, burning them releases CO_2, as we have seen. The poisonous gas carbon monoxide, CO, is produced when alkanes are burned in a limited supply of oxygen (incomplete combustion) as can happen in an internal combustion engine. Internal combustion engines also pollute the atmosphere with oxides of nitrogen (collectively known as NO_x) and unburned hydrocarbons. Most of these pollutants can be removed by fitting a catalytic converter to the exhaust system of the engine, spread 15.9.

PRACTICE

1 Discuss the advantages and disadvantages of liquid and gaseous fuels.

2 Discuss the merits of incineration over landfill as a method for disposing of domestic waste.

22.6

OBJECTIVES

- Structure from VSEPR theory
- σ and π bonds
- Geometrical isomers

BONDING IN ALKENES

Lewis structures give a reasonable model for the structures of methane and ethane; and the VSEPR theory predicts that methane has tetrahedral geometry. However, the final spread in the chapter shows that a fuller account of the bonding is given by considering the overlap of atomic orbitals to give molecular orbitals. Bonds form between atoms when these molecular orbitals are occupied by pairs of electrons. In ethane, a C—C single bond forms between the two carbon atoms. However, ethene has a C=C double bond. This spread investigates the bonding in ethene, first by the Lewis/VSEPR theory and then by using the idea of molecular orbitals.

Lewis structures and electron-pair repulsions

Ethene has the molecular formula C_2H_4. A Lewis structure suggests that each carbon atom can complete its octet of electrons by forming one C=C double bond and two C—H single bonds. The H—C—H angle at each end of the molecule is about 118° rather than the 120° expected from a regular trigonal planar shape. This is because the C=C double bond repels the C—H single bonds to a slightly greater extent than would a C—C single bond (as a result of the increased electron density in the C=C double bond).

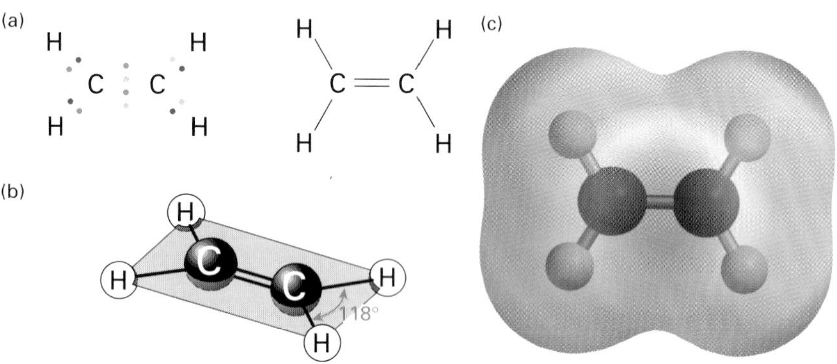

(a) The Lewis structure of ethene shows that each carbon atom donates two electrons to form one C=C bond and two more electrons to form two C—H bonds. (b) The ethene molecule has trigonal planar geometry. (c) The electrostatic potential map for ethene. Note the red colour indicating the high electron density in the double bond.

Ethene: overlapping atomic orbitals

As in spread 5.7, imagine two carbon atoms approaching each other. The first atomic orbitals to overlap are the 2p orbitals that point along the line of approach. A **sigma (σ) molecular orbital** results, which is symmetrical about the internuclear axis. This molecular orbital contains two electrons that bond the carbon atoms to each other, forming a single **sigma (σ) bond**.

As the carbon atoms approach even closer, the two 2p orbitals at right angles to those forming the sigma bond overlap *sideways* above and below the sigma bond. This overlap gives rise to another sort of molecular orbital called a **pi (π) molecular orbital**. It contains a pair of electrons that constitute a **pi (π) bond**. The π orbital is at a higher energy level than the σ orbital. The two carbon atoms now have a double covalent bond between them, consisting of one sigma bond and one pi bond; they are sharing two pairs of electrons. The carbon–hydrogen bonds form in a way similar to those in methane, see the final spread in the chapter.

Bonding electrons

Ethene consists of two carbon atoms and four hydrogen atoms. Four electrons ($2s^22p^2$) are available for bonding from each carbon atom; each hydrogen atom has the $1s^1$ electron available. The total number of bonding electrons to be contained in the molecular orbitals is therefore 2 × 4 = 8 from the carbon atoms and 4 × 1 = 4 from the hydrogen atoms, making a total of 12 electrons. They form six bonds: a C=C double bond and 4 C—H single bonds.

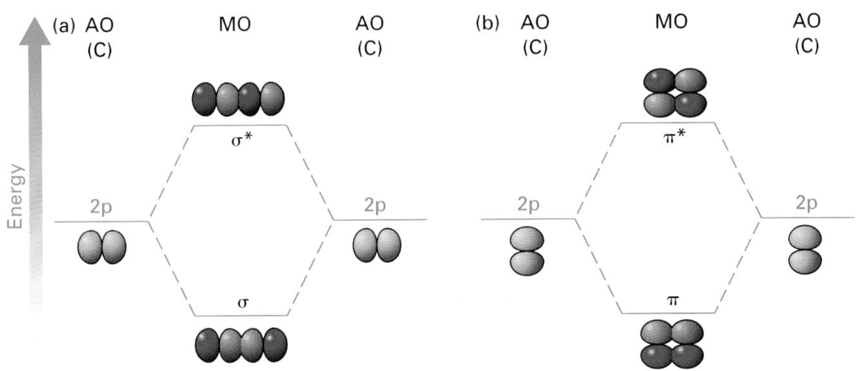

The formation of bonding (and antibonding) molecular orbitals in ethene: (a) the C—C sigma (σ) bond; (b) the C—C pi (π) bond. The C—H bonds form as described for methane in the spread 'Bonding in methane' at the end of the chapter.

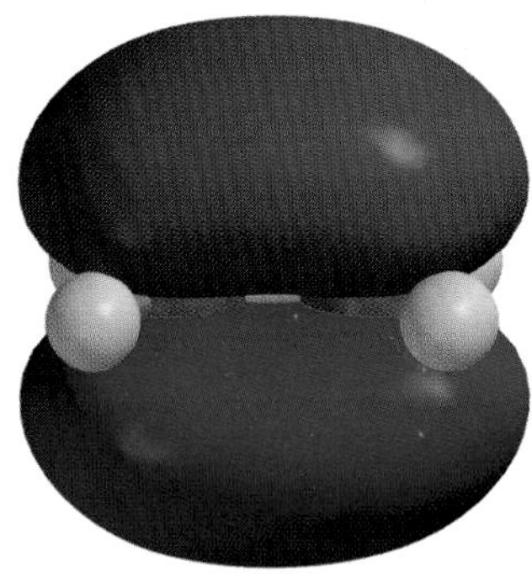

The π molecular orbital of ethene.

The C═C bond and isomerism

Rotation about a C—C single bond is possible. For example, the two —CH_3 groups in ethane may alter their relationship to each other as they 'spin' like propellers at each end of the molecule. But twisting a π bond would weaken it, as the sideways overlap would be reduced. So, the π bond is rigid, and rotation about a C═C double bond is not possible. This *restricted rotation* about a double bond means that the two ═CH_2 groups in ethene are fixed with respect to each other. As a result, there is a type of isomerism particular to alkenes.

Compounds that contain double bonds can show geometric isomerism (also known as *cis–trans* isomerism). The groups around a double bond are fixed in space relative to each other because the double bond is a rigid structure and the carbon atoms at each end cannot move relative to each other. For example, the but-2-ene molecule has two alternative arrangements in space: *cis*-but-2-ene has the two methyl groups on the *same* side of the double bond, whereas *trans*-but-2-ene has the two methyl groups on *opposite* sides of the double bond.

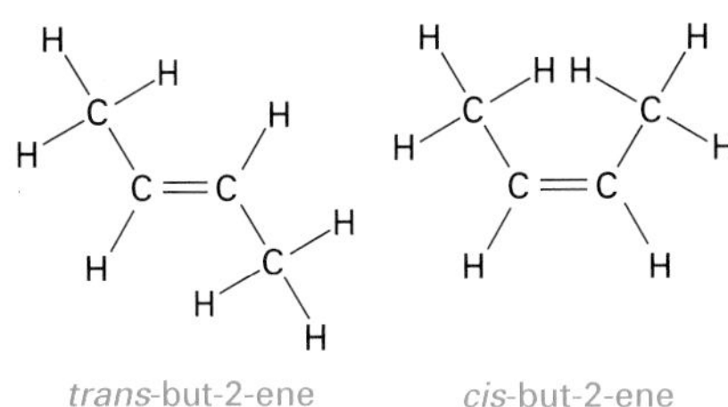

Geometrical isomers of but-2-ene C_4H_8. The chemical reactions of the double bond in these two isomers are the same. But their physical properties are slightly different: cis*-but-2-ene boils at 4 °C whereas* trans*-but-2-ene boils at 1 °C because the molecules pack together differently, with resulting different values of dispersion force.*

Retinol

The chemical name for vitamin A is retinol. Green plants contain compounds, particularly the red/orange carotenes found in carrots and tomatoes, that the body can change into the vitamin. Retinol is converted into the aldehyde retinal in the liver. Retinal is a constituent of rhodopsin, the light-sensitive pigment that occurs in the rod cells in the retina of the eye. Part of the structure of retinal consists of four alternating single and double carbon–carbon bonds. A key reaction in the process that enables us to see is the conversion of a *cis*- arrangement of one of these double bonds to the *trans*- arrangement.

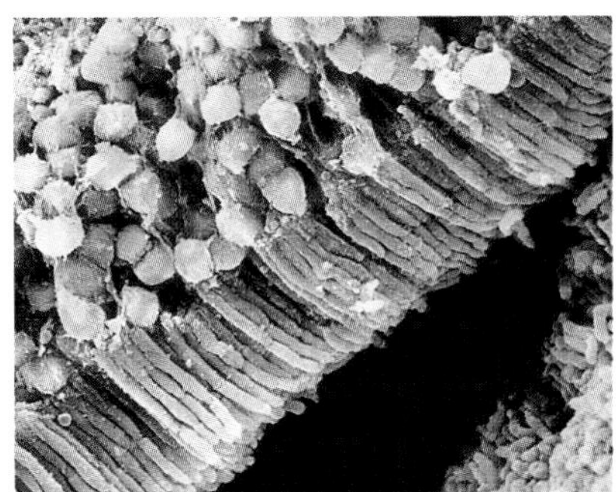

*Rod cells in the human retina. This type of light-sensitive cell contains rhodopsin and is responsible for vision in dim light. When light reaches rhodopsin, it converts 11-*cis*-retinal to all-*trans*-retinal and the rhodopsin molecule breaks up. This causes electrical changes in the rod cell, which can set up a nerve impulse. This is the first part of the complex process of sight in* all *animal eyes. Maximum sensitivity of these cells occurs when the light input to the retina is 10 000 quanta per second, equivalent to one quantum per rod cell every three minutes!*

SUMMARY

- A sigma (σ) molecular orbital results from s–s, s–p, or p–p atomic orbital overlap. It is symmetrical about the axis between the two atomic nuclei.
- A pi (π) molecular orbital results from sideways p–p atomic orbital overlap. It is not symmetrical about the axis between the two atomic nuclei.
- Rotation about a C—C single bond is possible, but rotation about a C═C double bond is restricted.
- Many alkenes show geometrical isomerism (*cis-trans* isomersim) as a result of the restricted rotation about the C═C double bond.

PRACTICE

1. Draw a Lewis structure showing the valence-shell electronic structure for propene.
2. Sketch the shape of the propene molecule indicated by VSEPR theory, showing the bond angles.
3. Explain why there are no geometrical isomers of but-1-ene.

22.7

OBJECTIVES

- Radical addition
- Electrophilic addition
- Bromine water test

Cycloalkenes

Cyclohexene, a six-membered ring containing a double bond, can be hydrogenated to cyclohexane, see spread 23.1.

Polyunsaturated

Polyunsaturated oils contain two or more double bonds. The prefix 'poly' usually means 'many'!

ALKENES AND ADDITION – 1

Alkenes have the general formula C_nH_{2n} compared with C_nH_{2n+2} for the alkanes. Alkenes have greater overall reactivity than alkanes. The carbon–carbon double bond in alkenes is a centre of high electron density, which makes this homologous series more reactive. Like alkanes, alkenes can react by slow radical substitution (as discussed earlier in this chapter). However, alkenes undergo more rapid reactions involving the double bond between the carbon atoms. This functional group allows alkenes to react by *addition*, in which an incoming group splits and joins with the carbon atoms at each end of the double bond.

Addition of hydrogen to alkenes

Mixtures of hydrogen and an alkene are stable at room temperature. However, in the presence of a catalyst of finely divided nickel at about 150 °C, hydrogen adds across the double bond to form an alkane. For example, ethene is *hydrogenated* to ethane:

$$CH_2{=}CH_2(g) + H_2(g) \xrightarrow{Ni} CH_3CH_3(g)$$

Alternative catalysts for this **hydrogenation reaction** are palladium and platinum, which can be used at room temperature.

The mechanism of hydrogenation involves radicals, and the reaction between ethene and hydrogen is classed as **radical addition**. Ethene adsorbs on to the surface of the catalyst. Hydrogen molecules also adsorb, breaking into hydrogen atoms, which are radicals. One hydrogen atom combines with ethene to form an ethyl radical, which remains adsorbed on the catalyst. When a second hydrogen atom combines, the resulting ethane desorbs from the catalyst.

The addition of hydrogen to unsaturated vegetable oils is used industrially to make margarine. Hydrogenation lowers the number of double bonds in the polyunsaturated vegetable oils, 'hardening' the substance to make it a solid at room temperature.

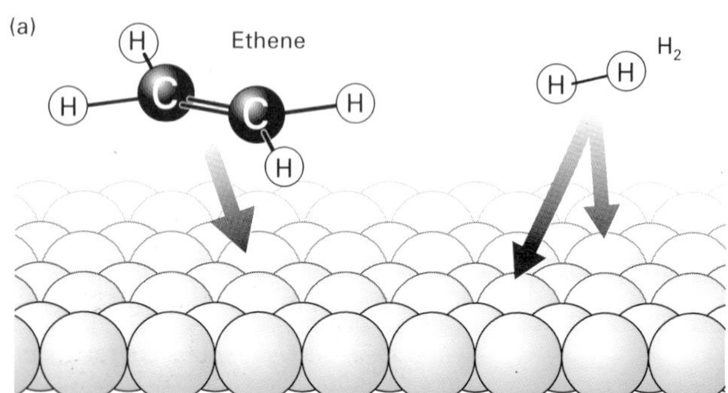

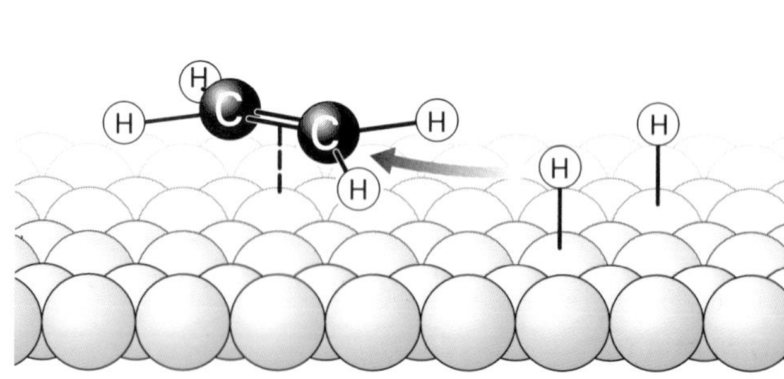

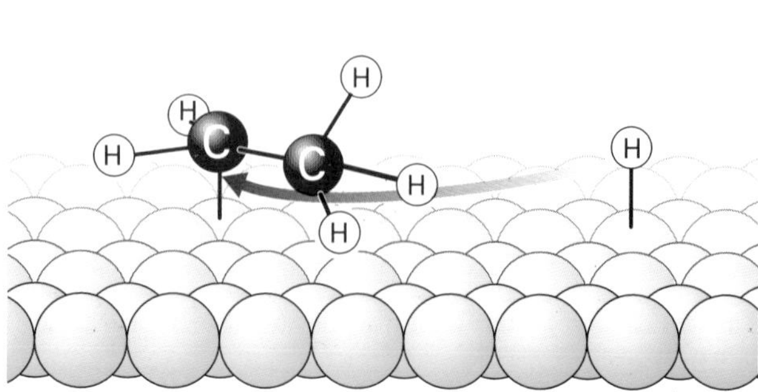

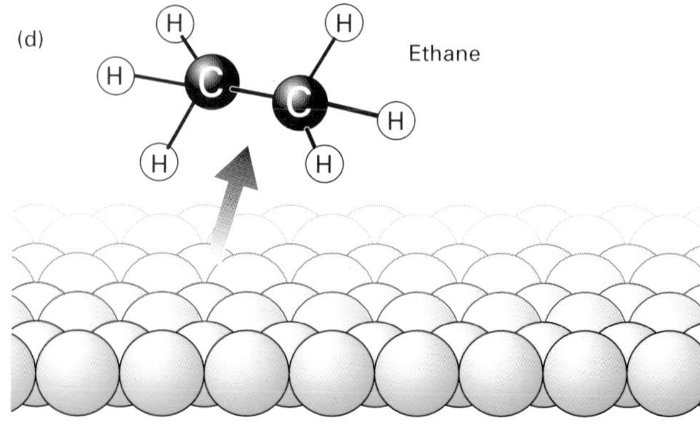

(a) Hydrogen and ethene adsorb on to the metal surface by donating electron density into vacant d orbitals on the catalyst metal atoms. (b) and (c) Hydrogen atoms (radicals) interact with the electron density in the ethene double bond, and bond with the carbon atoms. (d) The product ethane desorbs from the surface of the catalyst.

Addition of hydrogen halides or halogens to alkenes

Slow substitution between an alkane and a halogen results in a halogenoalkane. The results are unpredictable because substitution can replace more than one hydrogen atom on the alkane molecule, producing a mixture of products. Reacting an alkene with a hydrogen halide is a much more rapid reaction with a more predictable outcome. For example, ethene and hydrogen bromide react in aqueous solution:

$$CH_2{=}CH_2 + HBr \rightarrow CH_3CH_2Br$$

Hydrogen bromide ionizes in aqueous solution

$$HBr(aq) \rightarrow H^+(aq) + Br^-(aq)$$

and the reaction between ethene and hydrogen bromide is classed as **electrophilic addition** because the attacking species is the H^+ ion, which is attracted to the high electron density in the alkene C=C double bond. The full mechanism of the reaction is given in the following spread.

A good yield of product is obtained by bubbling ethene gas through concentrated hydrobromic acid and then distilling the mixture to isolate bromoethane. This reaction is straightforward to perform in industry because ethene is readily available from the cracking of the naphtha fraction of crude oil. The reaction takes place at room temperature and pressure.

Reacting a halogen (rather than a hydrogen halide) with an alkene also results in addition. For example, bromine and ethene react to form 1,2-dibromoethane:

$$CH_2{=}CH_2 + Br_2 \rightarrow BrCH_2CH_2Br$$

This reaction is also classed as an electrophilic addition, as will be explained in the next spread.

Molecules of sunflower oil (right) contain greater numbers of C=C double bonds than are found in peanut oil: sunflower oil is more polyunsaturated. As a result, sunflower oil decolourizes a dilute solution of iodine in ethanol more rapidly than peanut oil does.

The bromine water test

Bromine dissolves in water to form a red/brown solution, which is referred to in the laboratory as 'bromine water'. This solution is used in the **'bromine water test'** to distinguish between saturated and unsaturated hydrocarbons, which is carried out as follows:

1 Place the test substance in a test tube: if a gas, fill and stopper the tube; if a liquid, use a few drops.

2 Add a 1 cm depth of bromine water: shake, and allow the contents of the tube to settle.

3 If the test substance contains carbon–carbon double bonds, the liquid in the tube will be colourless. *An alkene decolourizes bromine water*. If the test substance is saturated, the colour of the bromine water will be unaffected.

A similar test with an alcoholic solution of iodine is used to detect double bonds in unsaturated oils (see top right).

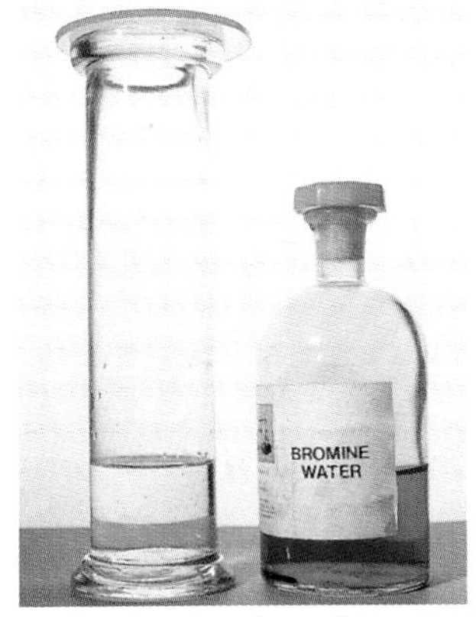

Ethene decolourizes bromine water.

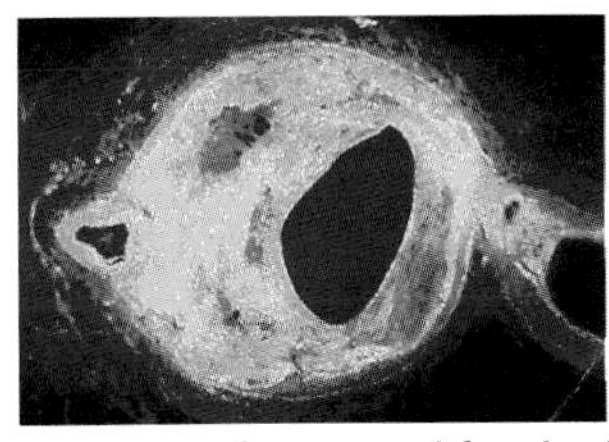

The presence of saturated fats in the diet can cause excess cholesterol in the body. Raised levels of blood cholesterol are associated with atherosclerosis, a condition in which fatty substances are deposited on the insides of artery walls, slowing and eventually stopping the flow of blood through the artery.

SUMMARY

- When mixed with a halogen such as bromine, alkanes undergo slow substitution reactions whereas alkenes undergo rapid addition reactions.
- Hydrogen halides add to alkenes to make the halogenoalkane; halogens can also add to alkenes.
- An alkene will rapidly decolourize bromine water.

PRACTICE

1 Explain why the catalytic addition of hydrogen to ethene is described as 'radical addition', whereas the addition of hydrogen bromide is described as 'electrophilic addition'.

2 Describe what you would expect to *see* when propene gas is bubbled into an aqueous solution of bromine.

22.8 ALKENES AND ADDITION – 2

OBJECTIVES

- Mechanism: HBr + alkene
- Mechanism: Br_2 + alkene
- Markovnikov's rule

Remember that a double-headed curly arrow indicates the movement of an electron pair.

Alkanes undergo substitution by means of radical chain reactions involving species with unpaired electrons. Alkenes undergo addition reactions. The previous spread gave details of several alkene reactions, including the addition of hydrogen bromide and bromine to ethene. You were also introduced to the bromine water test for unsaturation. This spread explains the mechanisms underlying these reactions. Addition reactions also proceed by a series of steps. However, the species involved are not radicals but *ions*.

Addition of hydrogen bromide to ethene

Step (1): Electron density in the ethene π bond attracts the H^+ ion (an electrophile). The electrostatic potential map, spread 22.6, shows that the high electron density lies above and below the plane, so the following stereochemical formulae would be preferable:

Step (2): The final product forms when the carbocation reacts with the bromide ion (a nucleophile).

Hydrobromic acid is a strong acid, spread 12.4, and its solution therefore contains a high concentration of the ions $H^+(aq)$ and $Br^-(aq)$. The hydrogen ion is an electrophile, spread 21.5, because it has a positive charge. When ethene is bubbled through aqueous hydrobromic acid, the first step is the attack of the electrophile H^+ on the ethene molecule:

$$CH_2{=}CH_2 + H^+ \rightarrow CH_3CH_2^+ \qquad (1)$$

The resulting species contains a carbon atom bearing a positive charge. Because the charge is positive, the species is called a **carbocation** (sometimes less accurately termed a carbonium ion). The carbon–carbon linkage in $CH_3CH_2^+$ has a single σ bond in place of the double bond present in $CH_2{=}CH_2$. The electron pair that formed the π bond between the two carbon atoms now forms a carbon–hydrogen bond.

The carbocation can be attacked by a nucleophile, which provides an electron pair to form the new bond. The bromide ion in the solution is a nucleophile, and in the second step of the reaction it attacks the carbocation to form bromoethane:

$$CH_3CH_2^+ + Br^- \rightarrow CH_3CH_2Br \qquad (2)$$

The overall result of these two steps is the addition of hydrogen and bromine across the double bond. The reaction is classed as an **electrophilic addition**, because the *first* step involves attack by an electrophile (H^+).

Addition of bromine to ethene

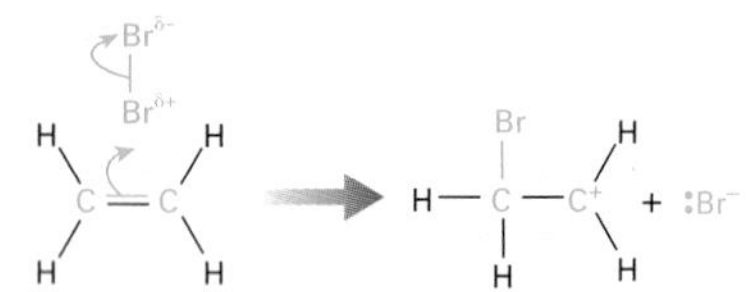

Step (1): The bromine molecule becomes polar as it approaches the region of high electron density in the ethene π bond. Ultimately, the π electrons form a bond with the δ+ bromine atom; the electron pair in the Br—Br bond migrates to the δ– bromine atom, giving it a full negative charge and breaking the bond.

Step (2): The final product forms when the carbocation reacts with the bromide ion (a nucleophile). This step is virtually identical to that shown in step (2) in the previous mechanism box.

The addition of bromine to ethene is another example of electrophilic addition. The bromine–bromine bond is not polar, so bromine is not apparently an electrophile. However, as the bromine molecule approaches the high electron density of the double bond, the electrons of the bromine–bromine bond are repelled: the approaching end of the molecule becomes partially positively charged. This end of the molecule acts as an electrophile and is attracted closer to the electron density in the double bond. The closer the bromine molecule approaches to the alkene π bond, the more polar it becomes. The bromine–bromine bond ultimately undergoes heterolytic fission; at the same time, a bond forms between one of the carbon atoms and the nearest ($Br^{\delta+}$) bromine atom, using the electrons of the double bond. The result is a carbocation and a bromide ion:

$$CH_2{=}CH_2 + Br_2 \rightarrow BrCH_2CH_2^+ + Br^- \qquad (1)$$

The bromide ion now attacks the carbocation. The final result is the addition of two bromine atoms across the double bond:

$$BrCH_2CH_2^+ + Br^- \rightarrow BrCH_2CH_2Br \qquad (2)$$

In the bromine *water* test, water (a nucleophile) is present in such huge excess that it attacks the carbocation instead of the bromide ion in an alternative second step. After loss of a proton (H^+), 2-bromoethanol forms:

$$BrCH_2CH_2^+ + H_2O \rightarrow BrCH_2CH_2OH_2^+ \rightarrow BrCH_2CH_2OH + H^+ \qquad (2')$$

Markovnikov's rule

There is only one possible product in the electrophilic addition of HBr to ethene because the ethene molecule is a 'symmetrical' alkene – you cannot distinguish the two ends of the molecule either side of the double bond. If, however, the alkene molecule is *not* symmetrical about its double bond, two different products could result.

Where there is a choice of product in an electrophilic addition, the product that will be dominant can be predicted by **Markovnikov's rule**:

- The dominant product of electrophilic addition of HX to an unsymmetrical alkene has the hydrogen atom attached to the carbon atom that had more hydrogen atoms at the start.

Markovnikov's rule

Vladimir Markovnikov introduced his rule in the same year (1869) as Dmitri Mendeleyev introduced the periodic table.

Explanation for Markovnikov's rule

We shall consider the case of adding hydrogen bromide HBr to propene $CH_3CH{=}CH_2$. Does the Br atom add to the $CH{=}$ carbon atom or to the $={CH_2}$ carbon atom? In practice, the addition of HBr to propene results in a much greater quantity of 2-bromopropane than 1-bromopropane:

$CH_3CH{=}CH_2 + HBr \rightarrow CH_3CHBrCH_3$ (almost exclusively)
$CH_3CH{=}CH_2 + HBr \rightarrow CH_3CH_2CH_2Br$ (very little)

The explanation for this lies in the effect of an alkyl group (such as a methyl group) on the electron density in a molecule, compared with the effect of a hydrogen atom. A hydrogen atom has no electrons other than those in its bond. A methyl group has electron pairs in the three carbon–hydrogen bonds. In a carbocation, these electrons can be attracted towards the positive charge. Electron density feeds towards the charge, lowering the overall value of the positive charge and stabilizing the ion. A methyl group is described as **electron-donating**.

In the first step of the addition of HBr to propene, two possible carbocations may be formed:

$CH_3CH{=}CH_2 + H^+ \rightarrow CH_3CH^+CH_3$ (1)
$CH_3CH{=}CH_2 + H^+ \rightarrow CH_3CH_2CH_2^+$ (2)

The dominant carbocation (1) identified by Markovnikov's rule has *two* methyl groups attached to the charged carbon, which can stabilize the charge. The second carbocation (2) has only one alkyl group (an ethyl group) and two hydrogen atoms attached to the charged carbon. The carbocation is less stable because the charge is stabilized less. The more stable carbocation goes on to be attacked by a bromide ion to give the dominant product:

$CH_3CH^+CH_3 + Br^- \rightarrow CH_3CHBrCH_3$ (3)

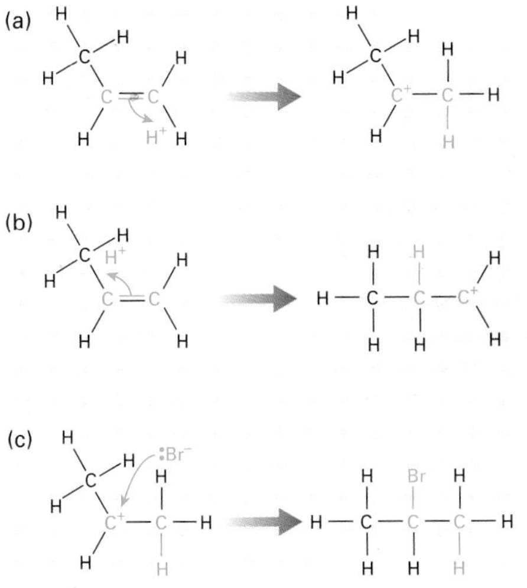

(a) A hydrogen ion could attack a terminal carbon atom to form this carbocation. (The charged atom is attached to two alkyl groups.)

(b) A hydrogen ion could attack the central carbon atom to form this carbocation. (The charged atom is attached to one alkyl group.)

(c) A bromide ion is attracted to the more stable carbocation and forms the product.

SUMMARY

- The first stage of an alkene electrophilic addition reaction involves attack on the C=C π bond by an electrophile; the result is a positively charged carbocation.
- The second stage of an alkene electrophilic addition reaction involves attack on the charged carbocation by a nucleophile.
- Markovnikov's rule: The dominant product of electrophilic addition of HX to an unsymmetrical alkene has the hydrogen atom attached to the carbon atom that had more hydrogen atoms at the start.

PRACTICE

1 Explain why carbocations are attacked by nucleophiles and not by electrophiles.

2 Suggest reasons why alkene addition reactions are generally faster than alkane substitution reactions.

3 Write chemical equations involving structural formulae to explain the mechanisms in the reactions between the following:

a Propene and bromine
b Propene and hydrogen bromide
c But-1-ene and hydrogen bromide.

22.9

Converting alkenes to alcohols

OBJECTIVES

- Ethanol from ethene
- Diols

The addition of water to an alkene produces an alcohol: the reaction is called **hydration**. There is an abundant supply of alkenes in industry, and alcohols are important solvents. This reaction is therefore used in industry to produce millions of tonnes of various alcohols every year. The reaction may also be carried out in the laboratory under somewhat different conditions, the products of the reaction depending on the actual conditions chosen. (The mechanisms for some reactions are enclosed in boxes, which you may ignore if you do not require this level of detail.)

Ethanol: the industrial process

Ethanol is important in industry because it is widely used as a solvent. The main method of making ethanol is the **direct hydration of ethene**.

Hydration of ethene

An H^+ ion from the catalyst (phosphoric acid) attacks the π bond of ethene. The ethene is protonated as it forms a bond with the hydrogen ion. As the proton H^+ does not have any electrons to bring to a bond, both of the bonding electrons come from the carbon–carbon π bond. As a result, the carbon atom that does not bond to the incoming hydrogen ion effectively loses an electron and becomes positively charged:

$$CH_2{=}CH_2 + H^+ \rightarrow CH_3CH_2^+$$

Water is a nucleophile and so is attracted to the carbocation:

$$CH_3CH_2^+ + H_2O \rightarrow CH_3CH_2OH_2^+$$

Finally, a proton is lost, regenerating the H^+ ion and forming ethanol:

$$CH_3CH_2OH_2^+ \rightarrow CH_3CH_2OH + H^+$$

This is very similar to the final step in the mechanism for the bromine water test (in the previous spread).

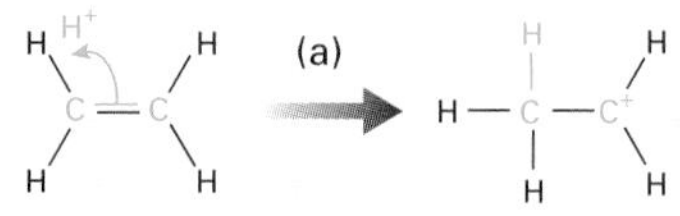

(a) An H^+ ion protonates ethene to form a carbocation.

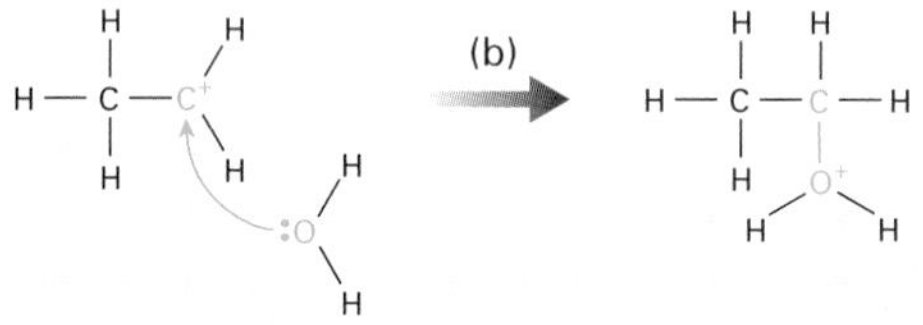

(b) Water acts as a nucleophile: oxygen donates a lone pair to the carbocation.

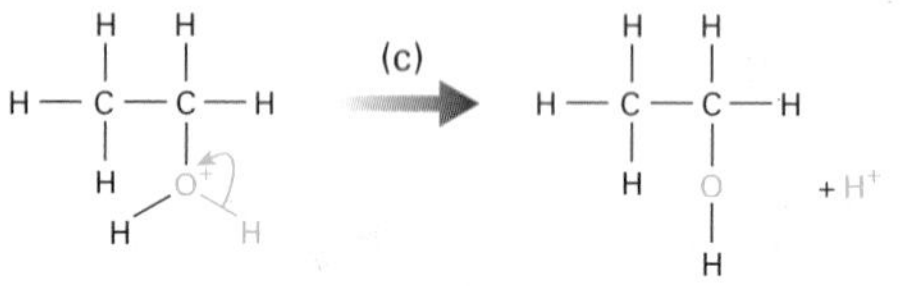

(c) Ethanol forms as the ion loses a proton (deprotonates).

Ethene and steam react together at a temperature of 300 °C and a pressure of about 70 atm in the presence of a phosphoric acid catalyst held on a Celite (silica) support:

$$CH_2{=}CH_2 + H_2O \rightarrow CH_3CH_2OH$$

The phosphoric acid supplies H^+ ions that act as a catalyst: they take part in the reaction but are regenerated at the end. The overall reaction is reversible. The forward reaction is exothermic and so is favoured by low temperature. A compromise has to be reached when choosing the temperature because low temperatures lower the rate of reaction. Since one mole of gaseous product is produced from two moles of gaseous reactants, the forward reaction is favoured by high pressure.

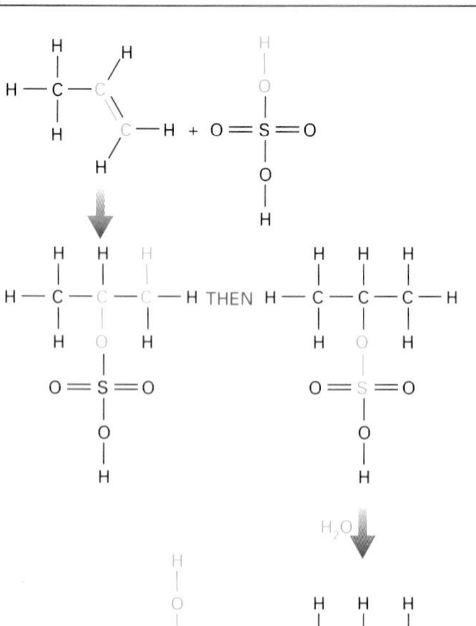

Propene reacts with water to form propan-2-ol, following Markovnikov's rule (see previous spread).

Ethanol: the laboratory reaction

Concentrated sulphuric acid is used as the catalyst in the laboratory reaction to add water to ethene. Concentrated sulphuric acid H_2SO_4 may be looked upon as H—OSO_2OH (i.e. H—X), see spread 19.11, which adds across the C=C double bond in the usual manner:

$$CH_2{=}CH_2 + H{-}OSO_2OH \rightarrow CH_3CH_2OSO_2OH$$

The addition compound ethyl hydrogensulphate $CH_3CH_2OSO_2OH$ reacts with water to produce ethanol and reform the catalyst H_2SO_4:

$$CH_3CH_2OSO_2OH + H_2O \rightarrow CH_3CH_2OH + H_2SO_4$$

Adding *two* —OH groups across a double bond

Alcohols with two hydroxyl groups per molecule are called **diols**. Ethane-1,2-diol (common name *ethylene glycol*) is an important industrial chemical. It is mixed into the water in vehicle cooling systems during the winter as an 'antifreeze'. Ethane-1,2-diol is also the raw material for making polyester fibres (e.g. Terylene), spread 27.6.

Ethane-1, 2-diol in industry

The industrial production of ethane-1,2-diol is carried out in two stages, the first of which involves the oxidation of ethene by air using a silver catalyst at 300 °C and 15 atm. The product is a cyclic compound (a cyclic ether; considered in more detail in spread 25.6) epoxyethane:

$$CH_2{=}CH_2(g) + \tfrac{1}{2}O_2(g) \xrightarrow{Ag} CH_2(O)CH_2(g)$$

Epoxyethane is then hydrolysed by dilute acid:

$$CH_2(O)CH_2(g) \xrightarrow{H^+(aq),\ H_2O(l)} HOCH_2CH_2OH$$

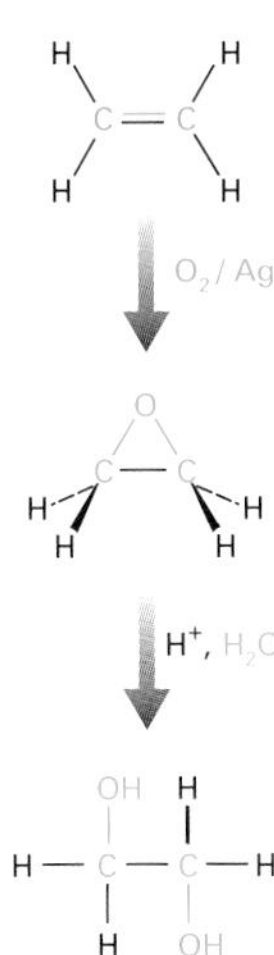

The manufacture of ethane-1,2-diol from ethene. Note the structure of the intermediate epoxyethane.

The laboratory reaction to add two —OH groups requires the use of a mild oxidant. Cold alkaline potassium manganate(VII) adds an —OH group to each side of an alkene double bond to give a diol. For example, ethene reacts to form ethane-1,2-diol:

$$CH_2{=}CH_2 \xrightarrow{MnO_4^-(aq)/\ OH^-(aq)} HOCH_2CH_2OH$$

This reaction may be used as a test for alkenes because the purple colour of the manganate(VII) ion changes to green aqueous manganate(VI) ion, spread 13.9. However, ethane-1,2-diol can be further oxidized under more strongly oxidizing conditions (see chapter on 'Organic synthesis reactions').

Ethane-1,2-diol (ethylene glycol) is used as antifreeze to prevent the water that cools an engine from freezing and damaging the engine as it expands. This is the engine from the Vauxhall Lotus Carlton, the fastest production saloon car ever made.

SUMMARY

- Adding water across an alkene C=C double bond involves protonation by an acid catalyst followed by attack by water acting as a nucleophile.
- The industrial manufacture of ethanol adds steam to ethene with the aid of a phosphoric acid catalyst at 300 °C and 70 atm.
- Oxidation by alkaline manganate(VII) ion adds an —OH group to each of the carbon atoms in an alkene C=C double bond; the result is a diol.
- The change in colour by purple alkaline manganate(VII) ions acts as a test for the C=C double bond.

PRACTICE

1 Draw a flow diagram representing the industrial manufacture of ethanol from ethene. The conversion process operates at 70% efficiency, so you will need to separate unused reactants from products and recycle them. [Boiling points: water, 100 °C; ethanol, 78 °C; ethene, −104 °C]

2 Draw structural formulae to represent the following reactions:

a The industrial manufacture of ethanol from ethene.

b The action of cold dilute aqueous potassium manganate(VII) on propene.

c The protonation of propene to form a carbocation.

22.10 THE POLYMERIZATION OF ETHENE

OBJECTIVES

- Discovery of polythene
- Addition polymerization
- Other addition polymers

The ethene molecule contains a C═C double bond, which can undergo addition reactions. In the polymerization of ethene, the molecule *adds to itself* to produce a saturated hydrocarbon chain that consists of repeating —CH_2CH_2— units. The resulting solid substance is called **polythene** (also poly(ethene) or polyethylene) and has many uses. Polythene is an example of a **polymer**, a large molecule made up of many identical repeating sub-units called **monomers**. Physical properties such as hardness depend on the number of carbon atoms (typically 40 000 to 800 000) in the polythene chain. Polythene was the first synthetic hydrocarbon polymer to be produced. We then discuss four other important polymers based on alkenes.

'Poly bags' and polythene food wrapping films have molecular chains with around 40 000 carbon atoms each. As the number increases, the polymer material becomes harder and more rigid. Milk containers have around 60 000 carbon atoms per molecule and bleach bottles around 80 000. When the number reaches 800 000, the material can be used in artificial ice rinks.

The accidental discovery of polythene

Starting in 1932, research was carried out at the ICI chemical works in Cheshire into the effects of high pressure on chemical reactions. Over 50 reactions were investigated but none appeared interesting. One of the 'failures' (in March 1933) was the reaction between ethene and benzaldehyde (C_6H_5CHO) at 1400 atm and 170 °C. A white waxy solid resulted, which was thought to be a polymer of ethene. Repeating the experiment with ethene alone caused a massive explosion.

In December 1935, the ethene experiment was repeated, with stronger equipment. As became clear later, the ethene was contaminated with traces of oxygen. Pumping ethene into the reaction vessel caused the pressure to increase: it then suddenly dropped as oxygen initiated the polymerization. The resulting polymer proved to be chemically inert and an excellent insulator. It was initially tested in the manufacture of cables. Commercial production started in 1939, one of the first wartime uses being the insulation of airborne radar aerials. Polythene later became the first polymer whose production exceeded 1 million tonnes per year.

Serendipity

The discovery of polythene is an example of serendipity – a useful and unexpected discovery made by accident.

Low-density poly(ethene), LDPE

Originally made by the high-pressure polymerization of ethene, LDPE has a density of around 0.92 g cm^{-3} and a melting point of around 110 °C. The polymer has considerable chain branching, leading to an open structure. LDPE is used as an electrical insulator and in packaging.

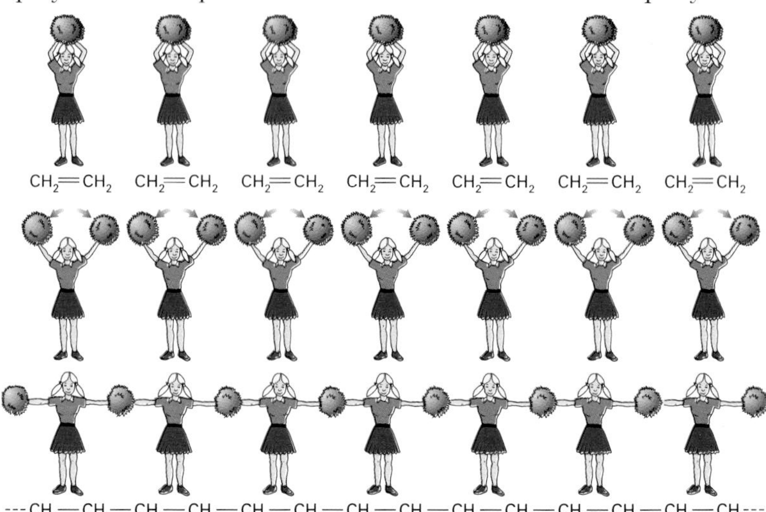

Polythene is formed by the addition polymerization *of ethene – the ethene monomers take part in an addition reaction across the double bond. The process can be pictured as the molecules using an internal linkage (the π bond) to create external linkages between each other.*

The variety of addition polymers

Ethene polymerizes to give a polymer of general formula $-[CH_2CH_2]_n-$. The general case is that the substituted alkene $CH_2{=}CHG$, where G is a side group, will polymerize to give the polymer $-[CH_2CHG]_n-$. Some common examples are shown below. PTFE, poly(tetrafluoroethene) is unusual in that four hydrogen atoms are substituted: the polymer is $-[CF_2CF_2]_n-$.

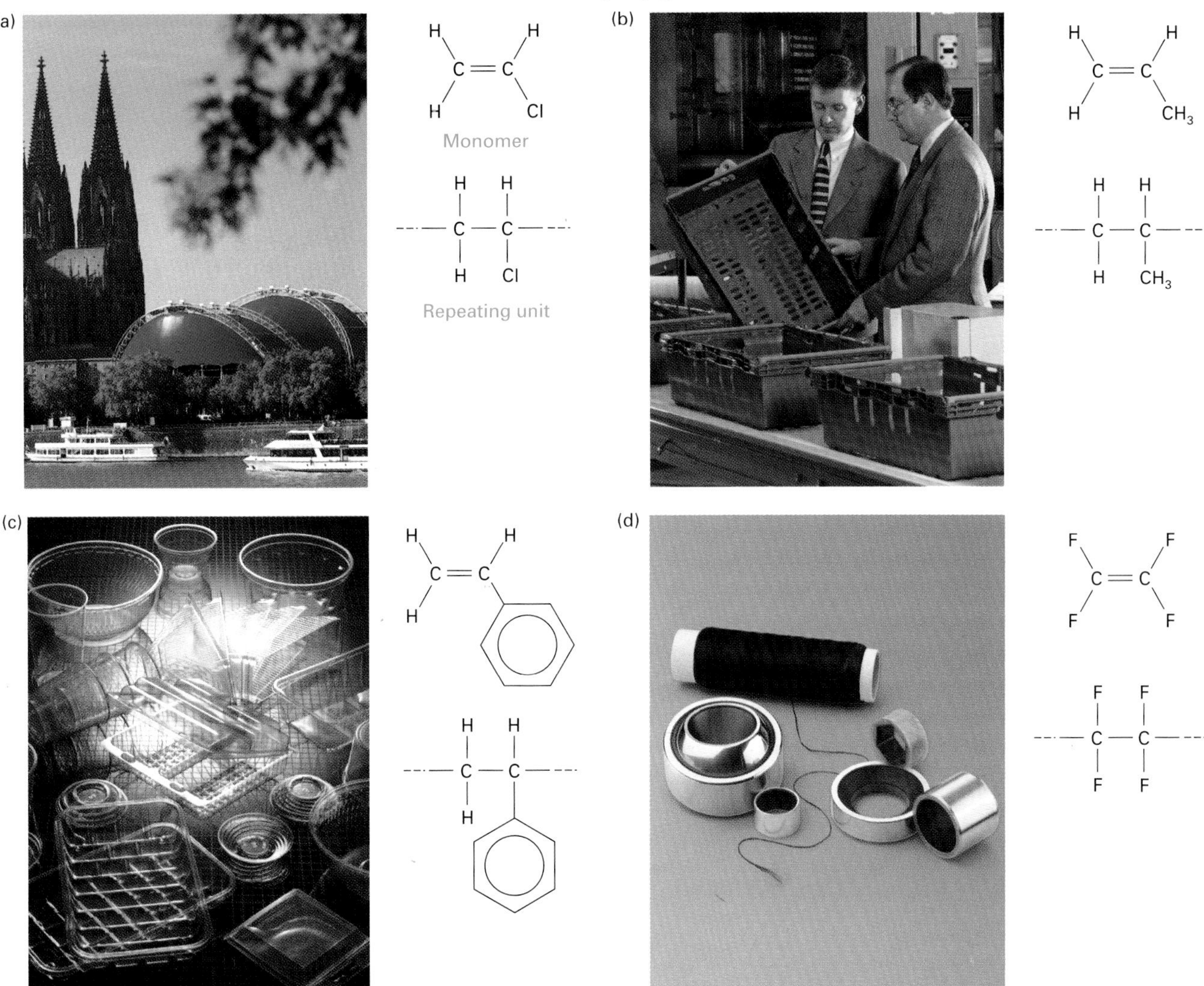

Some common addition polymers based on ethene derivatives together with their monomer and repeating unit. (a) PVC, (b) polypropylene, (c) polystyrene, and (d) PTFE.

SUMMARY

- Ethene undergoes addition to itself to form poly(ethene).
- Poly(ethene) is a polymer made up of ethene monomers. Its molecules are long chains consisting of repeating $-CH_2CH_2-$ units. Chains are between 10^4 and 10^6 carbon atoms long.
- Increasing chain length leads to increased density, hardness, and melting point.
- For a given number of $-CH_2CH_2-$ units, increasing the degree of chain branching decreases the density, hardness, and melting point.
- Low-density poly(ethene) (LDPE) results from high-pressure polymerization (1400 atm and 170 °C).

PRACTICE

1 List two uses each for LDPE, PP, PS, PVC, and PTFE.

22.11 THE MECHANISM OF POLYMERIZATION

OBJECTIVES

- Ziegler-Natta catalysis
- Polymer chains and properties
- Polymer geometry

Ethene $CH_2{=}CH_2$ undergoes addition polymerization by using the C=C π bond to form bonds between its molecules. The resulting polymer chain consists of thousands of $-CH_2CH_2-$ units joined together like beads on a necklace. The hydrogen atoms of ethene do not play a part in the polymerization reaction. Replacing one or more of the ethene hydrogen atoms by other atoms, or groups of atoms, results in polymer chains with repeating side groups. Side groups may be chosen to give polymers with specific desired properties. You will also see that the *arrangement* of the side groups along the polymer chain has an influence on the properties of the resulting polymer. This arrangement is affected by the mechanism of polymerization.

Mechanism of high-pressure polymerization

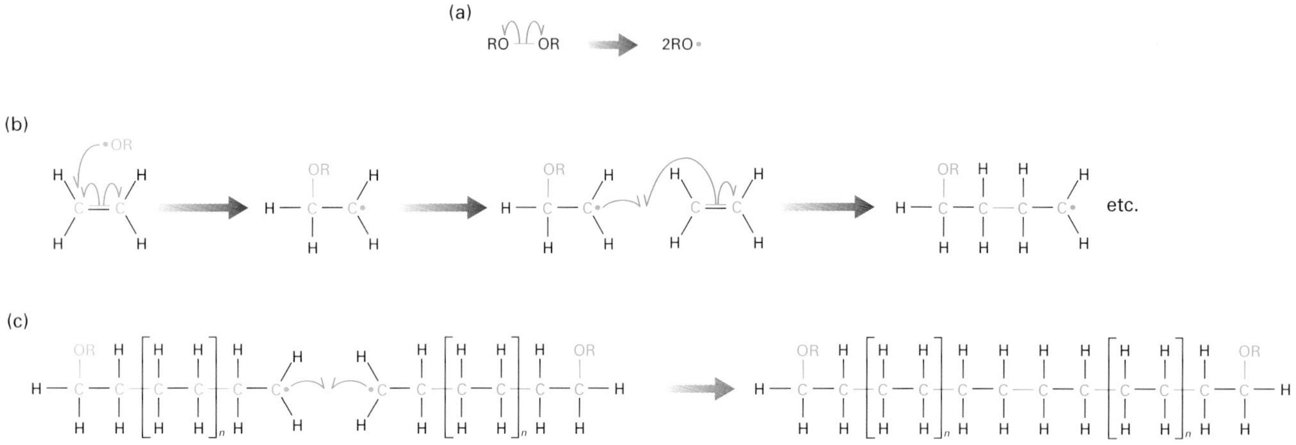

(a) RO—OR → 2RO•

(b)

(c)

The mechanism of commercial high-pressure addition polymerization (1400 atm and 170 °C) to form LDPE. (a) Initiation: radicals are generated from the decomposition of an organic peroxide. (b) Propagation: ethene adds to the radical; the unpaired electron is situated on the end carbon atom. (c) Termination: two radicals combine.

High-density poly(ethene), HDPE

This material is produced by Ziegler–Natta catalysis and has a very small degree of chain branching. As a result, the polymer chains are able to pack more closely than in LDPE, which has branched chains. HDPE is therefore harder and more rigid than LDPE, has a density of around 0.96 g cm^{-3}, and a melting point of around 135 °C. It is used to make containers.

Mechanism of polymerization with Ziegler–Natta catalysts

During the 1950s, Karl Ziegler and Giulio Natta discovered how to polymerize ethene at just 2 atm pressure and 70 °C. The key was a catalyst mixture consisting of titanium(IV) chloride $TiCl_4$ with triethylaluminium $Al(CH_2CH_3)_3$. Polymerization proceeds steadily as ethene passes into the catalyst mixture, allowing for a continuous manufacturing process. The equipment for the high-pressure production process is far more costly and this can only be carried out as a batch process. The mechanism of the Ziegler–Natta polymerization is complex and still only partially understood. The main points are summarized below.

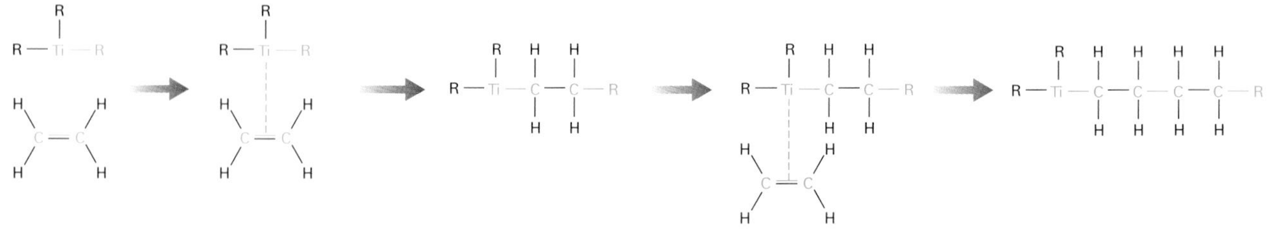

A summary of the Ziegler–Natta polymerization of ethene to form HDPE. The process is called coordination polymerization *because coordination compounds (complexes) form as electron density from the ethene π bond is donated into d orbitals on an atom of titanium (the catalyst). One end of the growing hydrocarbon chain is attached to a titanium atom, while incoming ethene molecules form a coordination complex with the same titanium atom.*

Chain structure and polymer properties

The previous spread showed that chain length and chain branching in polythene affect the physical properties of the polymer material. Properties such as stiffness are particularly influenced by the manner in which the polymer chains interact with each other. The inclusion of side groups (e.g. —Cl in PVC, —CH_3 in polypropylene, —C_6H_5 in polystyrene) introduces extra factors that influence the interaction between chains.

First, the side groups may cause the polymer chains to align, which makes the material more **crystalline** (i.e. having a regular and repeated arrangement of atoms). For example, polythene is a substance that is fairly **amorphous** (i.e. lacking regular, crystalline structure), with the polymer chains in a random arrangement; whereas in polystyrene, interactions between the side groups lead to a more ordered and crystalline structure with increased hardness.

Secondly, different arrangements of the side groups along the polymer chain are possible. Polymerization of phenylethene (styrene) $CH_2{=}CHC_6H_5$ by means of a Ziegler–Natta catalyst results in an **isotactic polymer** with all the phenyl —C_6H_5 groups situated on the *same* side of the chain. Catalysts may also be tailored to produce the **syndiotactic polymer**, in which the phenyl side groups regularly *alternate* from one side of the chain to the other. Isotactic and syndiotactic polymers are called **stereoregular polymers**. Polymerization by radicals is a much more random process and results in the formation of the **atactic polymer**, in which the phenyl groups have a *random* arrangement along opposite sides of the polymer chain.

The three classes usually have significantly different properties. Physical properties depend on the interaction between the chains, which in turn depends on the type and extent of interaction between side groups. The positioning of the side groups with respect to each other has a marked effect on the opportunities for interaction between one chain and another. For example, atactic polystyrene softens and can be moulded at a much lower temperature than the isotactic form. Isotactic polypropylene can be used to make jug kettles.

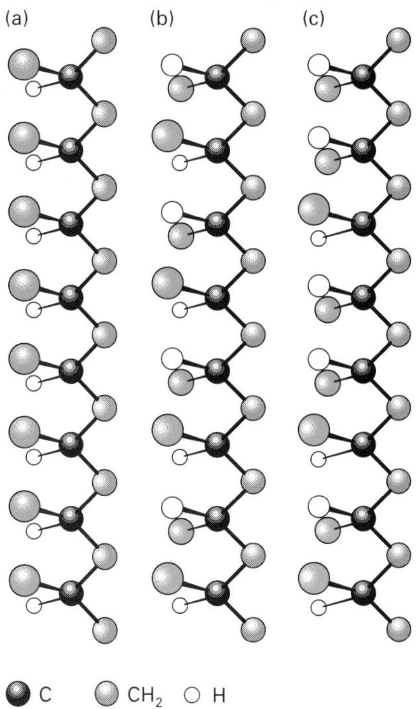

Polymer geometry: (a) isotactic (all groups on the same side of the hydrocarbon chain); (b) syndiotactic (alternating sides); and (c) atactic (random).

Isotactic pvc. The regular arrangement of the chloro side groups in the isotactic form allows the chains to approach each other more closely.

SUMMARY

- Ethene $CH_2{=}CH_2$ undergoes addition polymerization to give a polymer (polythene) of general formula $-\!\!\!\!+CH_2CH_2+\!\!\!\!-_n$.
- A substituted alkene $CH_2{=}CHG$ undergoes addition polymerization to give a polymer of general formula $-\!\!\!\!+CH_2CHG+\!\!\!\!-_n$.
- The side groups of isotactic polymers are all situated on the same side of the chain; in syndiotactic polymers, they regularly alternate; the arrangement in atactic polymers is random.
- Polymers produced by Ziegler–Natta catalysts are isotactic or syndiotactic; polymers produced by radical polymerization are atactic.
- Ziegler–Natta catalysis (based on titanium(IV) chloride and triethylaluminium) produces high-density poly(ethene) (HDPE) at low pressure (2 atm and 70 °C).

22.12

OBJECTIVES

- Structures from VSEPR theory
- Bonding in methane
- Electron density models
- Delocalization

BONDING IN METHANE

Alkanes contain carbon–carbon single bonds only. You should already be familiar with drawing Lewis structures to show the electronic structure in these types of molecules. However, it is now necessary to consider the bonding in these molecules more carefully. This spread starts by looking at two very different representations of the methane molecule. One is the Lewis structure, first put forward about 90 years ago. The other is the structure derived from overlapping atomic orbitals to form molecular orbitals; the quantitative calculations on which this model relies have only been possible since the early 1990s.

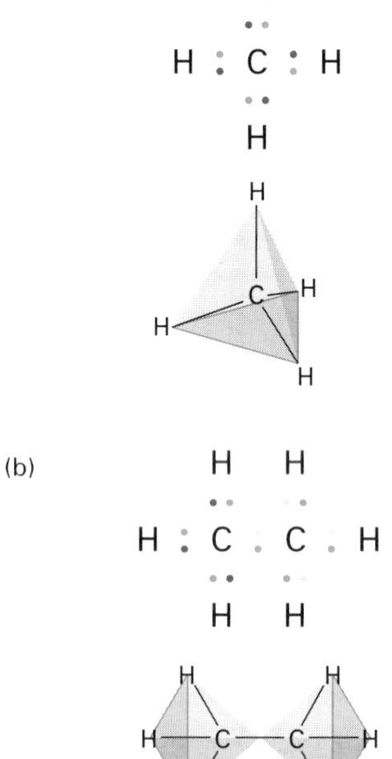

(a) Methane CH_4 has the shape of a regular tetrahedron. Four equivalent C—H bonds repel each other equally, giving a bond angle of 109.5°. (b) The shape of the ethane molecule is equivalent to two methane molecules joined together.

Lewis structures and VSEPR

Lewis structures show the electronic structures of the valence shells in a covalently bonded molecule. VSEPR (valence-shell electron-pair repulsion) theory suggests three-dimensional shapes for molecules by considering the repulsion between electron pairs in bonds and lone pairs (when present). The shapes obtained for methane and ethane are shown alongside.

Methane: overlapping atomic orbitals

The electronic structures of carbon and hydrogen are $1s^22s^22p^2$ and $1s^1$ respectively. The valence shell in the carbon atom consists of the single 2s atomic orbital together with the three 2p atomic orbitals. The valence shell in the hydrogen atom consists of the single 1s atomic orbital. Now consider what happens as four hydrogen atoms approach a carbon atom and then bond together to form methane.

As the atoms approach, the atomic orbitals on the carbon atom overlap with those on the hydrogen atoms. Two sorts of overlap occur in methane. In the first, the 1s orbital on each of the four hydrogen atoms overlaps with the 2s orbital on the carbon atom. The combined volume of space that they now share is called a **molecular orbital**. This single molecular orbital is occupied by a pair of electrons *that bonds all five atoms together*.

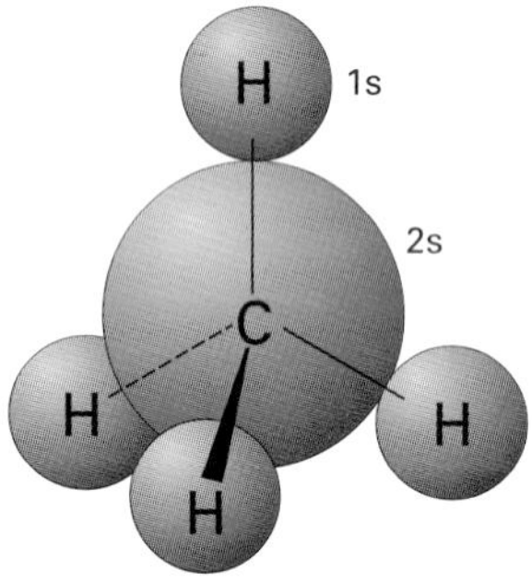

The formation of a bonding molecular orbital by the overlap of the carbon 2s orbital with the 1s orbitals of the four hydrogen atoms. The resulting molecular orbital is delocalized over all five atoms.

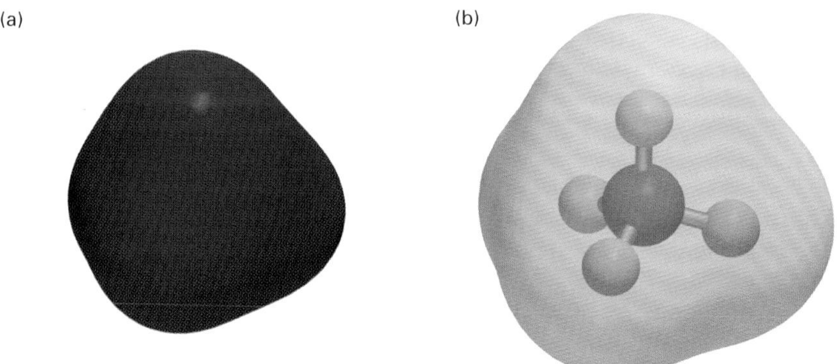

(a) The lowest-energy bonding molecular orbital formed by the overlap shown above is delocalized over all five atoms. The shape of this one orbital resembles the shape of the whole molecule, shown in the electrostatic potential map (b).

The second sort of overlap occurs between the four hydrogen 1s orbitals and the three carbon 2p orbitals. The result is three molecular orbitals containing six electrons that bond all five atoms together. These three orbitals have identical energies, but they are significantly higher in energy than the orbital arising from the overlap of the hydrogen 1s and carbon 2s orbitals. As a result, there are two sets of molecular orbitals in methane representing different energy levels.

There is a general result (see spread 6.4) that when 4 molecular orbitals are delocalized over 5 atoms, a set of 4 *localized* orbitals may be generated mathematically, each lying between a bonded pair of atoms; this reconstitutes the simple picture for methane of four equal bonds arranged tetrahedrally. Such a localization scheme provides a useful link with the Lewis structure: the electron density is accurately represented.

On the other hand, the *energies* of the molecular orbitals are actually very significantly different: the most stable delocalized molecular orbital involving overlap with the carbon 2s is *more than twice* as stable as the three molecular orbitals formed from the overlap with 2p. This feature does not appear in the localization scheme. The delocalized approach is confirmed both by computer calculation and by experimental measurement: there are two *different* ionization energies for the methane molecule. (This measurement was made by a spectroscopic technique called photoelectron spectroscopy.)

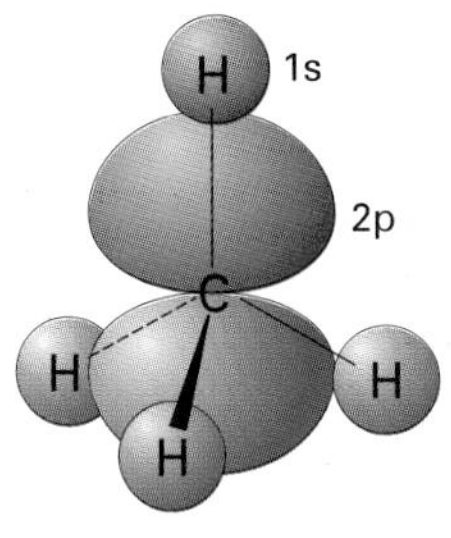

The formation of a bonding molecular orbital by the overlap of a carbon 2p orbital with the 1s orbitals of the four hydrogen atoms. The other two carbon 2p orbitals form similar molecular orbitals.

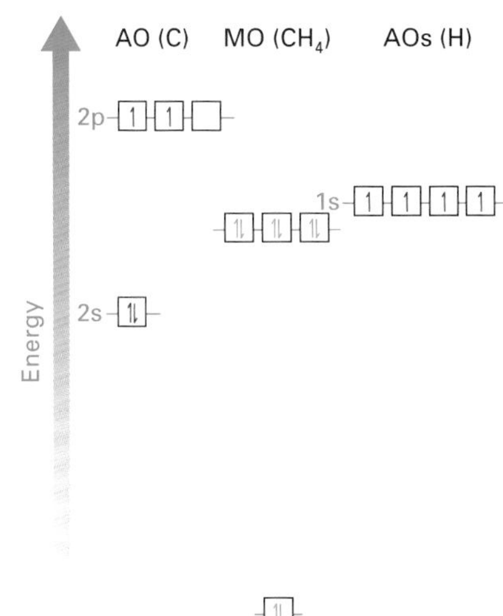

The bonding orbital formed by overlap of the carbon 2s is much *more stable than the three equivalent bonding orbitals formed by overlap of the carbon 2p. (The figure is drawn to scale.)*

SUMMARY

- Molecular orbitals result from the overlap of atomic orbitals on separate atoms.
- Each molecular orbital can hold a maximum of two electrons.
- Computer-generated electron density models show the distribution in space of the electrons in a molecule and illustrate its overall shape.
- The lowest-energy bonding molecular orbital in methane results from overlap of the carbon 2s and the four hydrogen 1s orbitals.
- The lowest-energy bonding molecular orbital in methane is delocalized over all five atoms.

PRACTICE

1 Draw a Lewis structure showing the valence-shell electronic structure for propane.

2 Sketch the shape of the propane molecule indicated by VSEPR theory, showing the bond angles.

3 Sketch the overlap of orbitals that forms the lowest-energy bonding molecular orbital in ethane.

Chapter 22 Reactions summary

- Cracking:

  alkane → smaller alkane + alkene

  $C_8H_{18} \rightarrow C_6H_{14} + C_2H_4$

- Alkane substitution:

  $CH_4 + Cl_2 \xrightarrow{UV} CH_3Cl + HCl$

  Mechanism: radical chain reaction

- Hydrocarbon combustion:

  $CH_4 + 2O_2 \rightarrow CO_2 + 2H_2O$

- Addition of hydrogen to an alkene:

  $CH_2{=}CH_2 + H_2 \xrightarrow{Ni} CH_3CH_3$

- Addition of hydrogen halide to an alkene:

  $CH_2{=}CH_2 + HBr \rightarrow CH_3CH_2Br$

  Mechanism: electrophilic addition

- Markovnikov addition to an unsymmetrical C=C bond:

  $CH_3CH{=}CH_2 + HBr \rightarrow CH_3CHBrCH_3$ (predominantly)

- Addition of bromine to an alkene:

  $CH_2{=}CH_2 + Br_2 \rightarrow BrCH_2CH_2Br$

- Action of bromine water on an alkene:

  $CH_2{=}CH_2 + Br_2(aq) \rightarrow BrCH_2CH_2OH$

  Bromine water is decolourized

- Addition of water to an alkene (acid catalyst):

  $CH_2{=}CH_2 + H_2O \rightarrow CH_3CH_2OH$

- Alkenes may be polymerized: examples include polythene, polypropylene, polystyrene, PVC, and PTFE.

Practice exam questions

1 The diagram below represents the industrial fractional distillation of crude oil.

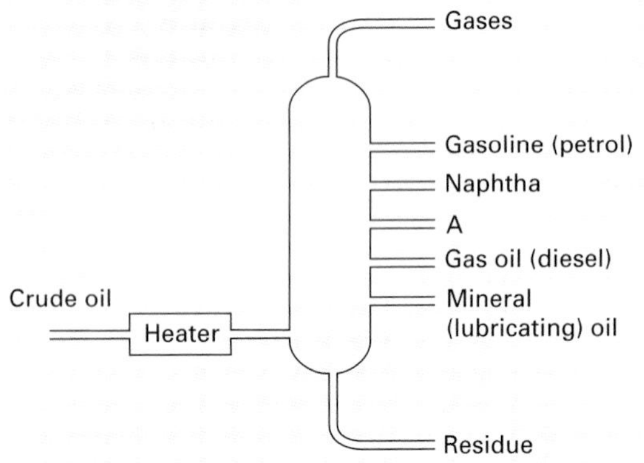

a Identify fraction **A**. [1]

b What property of the fractions allows them to be separated in the column? [1]

c Give **one** use each for the naphtha fraction and the gas oil fraction other than in diesel engines. [2]

d The gases include butane which is used as bottled fuel by campers.

i Write an equation for the complete combustion of butane.

ii Suggest a reason why gas oil would be unsuitable fuel for campers. [3]

e Why cannot the residue be further separated into paraffin waxes and tar by strong heating? [1]

AQA (NEAB) 1995

2 **a i** State Raoult's law for an ideal mixture of two liquids. [2]

ii Benzene and methylbenzene may be separated by fractional distillation. Sketch the general form of the boiling-point/composition diagram for such a mixture and use it to explain the basis on which fractional distillation rests.

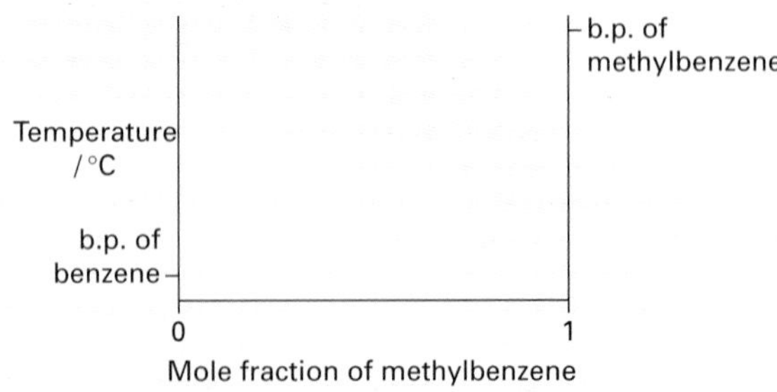

iii The first stage in the refining of crude oil (petroleum) is fractional distillation. State two ways in which the commercial fractional distillation of crude oil differs from the fractional distillation of a simple ideal mixture of two liquids. [6]

b i All lighter (more volatile) fractions from petroleum distillation are useful as fuels. Suggest two reasons why the liquid fractions with 8 to 12 carbon atoms per molecule are used as motor fuels, rather than the gaseous ones containing from one to four carbon atoms. [2]

ii Benzene is added to unleaded petrol to compensate for the absence of tetraethyllead. Both compounds are hazardous; which hazard is associated with benzene, other than its flammability? [1]

iii Tetraethyllead or benzene is added to petrol to prevent **pre-ignition**. What is pre-ignition, and why is it a problem? [2]

iv Suggest two reasons why unleaded fuel has been promoted by government and the petroleum industry. [2]

EDEXCEL 1997

3 When irradiated with ultraviolet light, methane reacts with chlorine to form a mixture containing several organic products.

a Name the type of mechanism involved. [1]

b Explain why ultraviolet light is needed. [2]

c Write an equation to show the formation of chloromethane from chlorine and methane. [1]

d Another product has a relative molecular mass of 85. Identify this product and write that part of the mechanism which shows its formation from chloromethane. [3]

e Explain how a small amount of ethane is formed in the process and name the mechanistic step which leads to its formation. [2]

f Give the major product formed when methane reacts with a large excess of chlorine. [1]

AQA (NEAB) 1995

4 Alkenes such as but-2-ene are used by the petrochemical industry to produce many useful materials. Some reactions of but-2-ene are shown below.

a Draw structures to represent possible compounds **A**–**D** in the reactions of but-2-ene below.

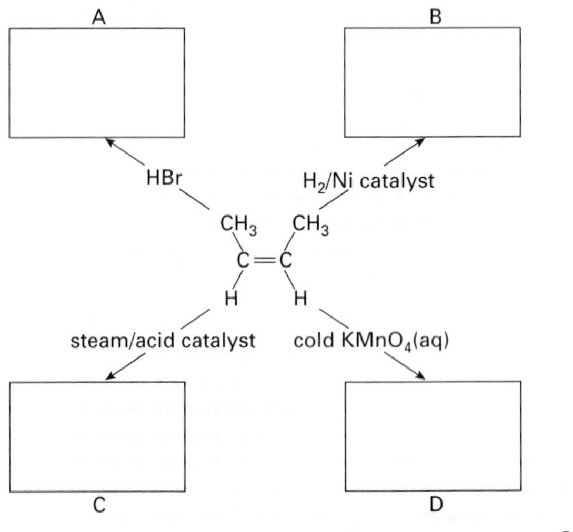

[4]

b Bromine reacts with but-2-ene in an addition reaction.

i What type of reagent is bromine in this reaction?

ii Complete the mechanism below for this reaction.

$$\begin{array}{c}CH_3 \quad CH_3\\ \diagdown \;\; \diagup \\ C=C \\ \diagup \;\; \diagdown \\ H \quad\quad H\end{array} \longrightarrow \qquad \longrightarrow H-\underset{Br}{\underset{|}{\overset{CH_3}{\overset{|}{C}}}}-\underset{Br}{\underset{|}{\overset{CH_3}{\overset{|}{C}}}}-H$$

$$\begin{array}{c}Br\\ |\\ Br\end{array}$$

c But-2-ene can be converted into buta-1,3-diene by a process called dehydrogenation. Buta-1,3-diene is used to make synthetic rubber.

i Suggest the structure of buta-1,3-diene.

ii Construct an equation for the dehydrogenation of but-2-ene.
OCR (UCLES) 1998 [2]

5 Low density poly(ethene) is used for packaging and plastic bags. The exothermic reaction by which poly(ethene) is made is shown by the following equation:

$nC_2H_4 \rightarrow (C_2H_4)_n$

a Write the structural formulae, showing all the bonds, of

i ethene;

ii poly(ethene), showing three repeating units. [2]

b Explain why typical conditions used in the process are a high pressure of 2000 atmospheres and a relatively low temperature of 200 °C. [4]

c The reaction proceeds via a free radical mechanism. The production of poly(ethene) may be initiated by the reaction.

$$R\cdot + CH_2{=}CH_2 \longrightarrow R-CH_2-CH_2\cdot$$

Suggest an equation to show how

i a subsequent stage occurs;

ii the polymerisation might terminate. [4]

d High density poly(ethene), used for articles such as buckets and crates, is made under other conditions, using a catalyst.

i Suggest why this form of poly(ethene) has a higher density.

ii Other than density, suggest ONE physical property which would be different for high density poly(ethene). [2]

e Draw a representative length of the molecule of poly(2-methylpropene), showing three repeating units. [1]

f i Write the structural formula, showing all covalent bonds, for the product obtained by reacting 2-methylpropene with bromine.

ii Write the structural formula of the compound formed by the reaction of aqueous sodium hydroxide with the product of the reaction in **f i**.
EDEXCEL 1996 [2]

6 Poly(chloroethene), PVC, is manufactured on a large scale from ethene. The process is essentially in three stages.

Stage 1 The formation of 1,2-dichloroethane from ethene.

Stage 2 The formation of chloroethene from 1,2-dichloroethene.

Stage 3 The polymerization of chloroethene.

a **Stage 1**, in some processes, may be carried out by the reaction below

$CH_2{=}CH_2 + \frac{1}{2}O_2 + 2HCl \rightarrow$
$CH_2Cl{-}CH_2Cl + H_2O;$
$\Delta H^\ominus = -242\ \text{kJ mol}^{-1}$

at a pressure of 5 atmospheres and a temperature of 570 K. A copper(II) chloride catalyst is used and the reaction vessel cooled.

i State one reason why the reaction vessel is cooled. [1]

ii The gases are washed to remove any unreacted hydrogen chloride. Give the name of a common aqueous solution which could be used. [1]

iii State what influence the presence of a catalyst has on the operating temperature and the economics of **Stage 1**. [2]

b **Stage 2** is brought about by thermal cracking. The reaction mechanism involves three steps.

$CH_2Cl{-}CH_2Cl \rightarrow CH_2Cl{-}CH_2\cdot + Cl\cdot$

$CH_2Cl{-}CH_2Cl + Cl\cdot \rightarrow HCl + CH_2Cl{-}CHCl\cdot$

$CH_2Cl{-}CHCl\cdot \rightarrow CH_2{=}CHCl + Cl\cdot$

i Write down the initiation step for **Stage 2.** [1]

ii Write down an equation for the overall reaction in **Stage 2**. [1]

iii The product, chloroethene (boiling temperature −13 °C), has to be separated from unchanged liquid 1,2-dichloroethane (boiling temperature 84 °C). State how this may be achieved. [1]

iv State what happens to the 1,2-dichloroethane recovered in **b iii**. [1]

c In **Stage 3** chloroethene undergoes polymerization.

i Draw the repeating unit in the polymer.

ii Give **one** everyday domestic use of the poly(chloroethene). [1]

iii Apart from the necessity to deal carefully with chloroethene, which is highly toxic, state **two** other safety considerations which would be necessary at a plant manufacturing PVC.
WJEC 1997 [2]

23 Arenes

The **arenes** are an enormous group of compounds based on the benzene ring C_6H_6. This ring gives distinctive properties to any molecule that contains it. By comparison, aliphatic organic compounds are based on chains of carbon atoms. **Alicyclic** organic compounds contain a ring structure other than benzene; their properties are similar to those of aliphatic compounds. The chemistry of the arenes is so distinctive that it is usually studied separately in its own right. This chapter concentrates on the reactions of benzene and of arenes containing functional groups attached to a single benzene ring. Later chapters will deal with the properties of these functional groups in aliphatic compounds.

THE UNIQUE CHARACTER OF BENZENE

23.1

OBJECTIVES

- Alicyclics and arenes compared
- Delocalized electrons
- Delocalized π cloud

The benzene molecule consists of six carbon atoms joined to form a ring. Benzene is a hydrocarbon in which each carbon atom is joined to two other carbon atoms and to a single hydrogen atom. Molecules of cyclohexane and cyclohexene also consist of six carbon atoms joined in a ring. However, the properties of these compounds are very different from those of benzene. The reasons for these differences lie in the character of the bonds between the carbon atoms in each of the different types of ring. Cyclohexane, cyclohexene, and benzene all have six-membered rings of carbon atoms: so how do they differ?

Alicyclic compounds: cycloalkanes

The carbon atoms in cycloalkanes are joined to form a ring structure. These compounds are named by prefixing the appropriate alkane name with 'cyclo'. For example, cyclohexane has the formula C_6H_{12}. It is saturated and reacts by substitution only, in the same manner as aliphatic (straight-chain and branched-chain) alkanes.

In general, cycloalkanes are as unreactive as aliphatic alkanes, undergoing just the same types of radical processes. The two exceptions are cyclopropane and cyclobutane. Their bond angles are 60° and 90° respectively, compared with the normal tetrahedral angle of 109°. The ring structure is **strained** and causes these two compounds to be more reactive than their straight-chain analogues propane and butane.

Alicyclic compounds may consist of hydrocarbon rings with functional groups attached. For example, attaching an —OH group to cyclohexane C_6H_{12} results in the compound cyclohexanol $C_6H_{11}OH$ (in the same manner that attaching this group to ethane CH_3CH_3 results in the aliphatic compound ethanol CH_3CH_2OH). Cyclohexanol has almost identical chemical properties to ethanol.

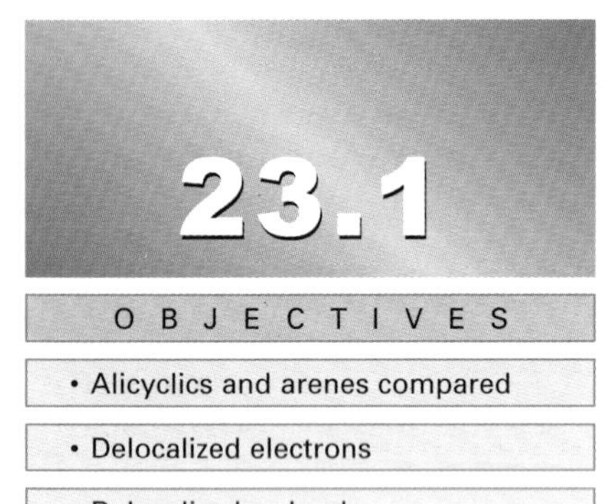

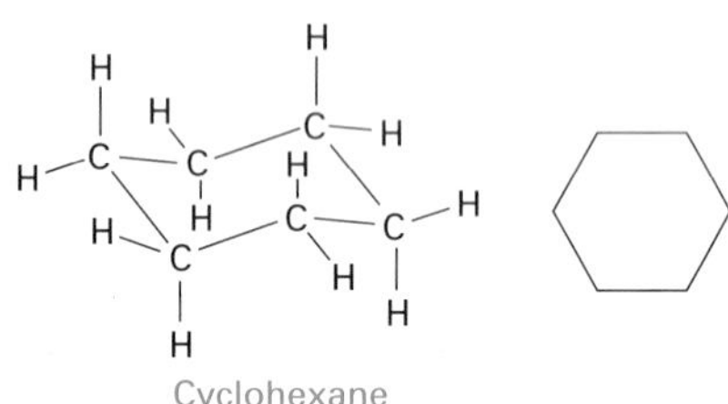

Displayed and skeletal formulae for two alicyclic compounds. Note that neither of these molecules is flat – the carbon atoms are not all in the same plane.

Aromatic arenes

Benzene C_6H_6 is the parent molecule of all arene compounds. Arenes were earlier called 'aromatic' compounds because they have characteristic (strongly 'aromatic') smells.

Alicyclic compounds: cycloalkenes

These compounds are similar to cycloalkanes in their overall structure, but contain one or more C═C double bonds. For example, cyclohexene has the formula C_6H_{10} and contains one C═C double bond and five C—C single bonds. It is unsaturated and reacts mainly by addition, in the same manner as aliphatic alkenes. The structures of cyclopropene and cyclobutene are strained for the same reasons as are the corresponding cycloalkanes. These two cycloalkenes therefore have greater reactivity than propene and butene.

Arenes: benzene

Benzene is a liquid (T_b = 80 °C) available from the fractional distillation of crude oil and also made from gasoline by catalytic reforming, spread 22.3. The molecular formula of benzene is C_6H_6. Using the standard form of single and double covalent bonds, Friedrich August Kekulé proposed the structure shown to the right in 1865. However, the following points show the Kekulé structure to be incorrect:

- The Kekulé structure contains three double bonds. Molecules with several double bonds are usually quite reactive and take part in addition reactions, spread 22.7. Benzene is relatively *unreactive*, slow *substitution* reactions being most common.
- The Kekulé structure suggests alternating double and single bonds. Double bonds are shorter than single bonds, but X-ray analysis of solid benzene shows a regular hexagon with all the bonds *the same length*, intermediate between a typical single and double bond.
- The Kekulé structure would be correctly described as cyclohexa-1,3,5-triene (triene because it has three double bonds). On this basis, the standard enthalpy change (see chapter on 'Thermochemistry') associated with hydrogenating the three unsaturated C═C bonds would be expected to be three times that for hydrogenating the one double bond of cyclohexene ($-120\,kJ\,mol^{-1}$). However, the experimental value of $-208\,kJ\,mol^{-1}$ is much smaller than the predicted value of $-360\,kJ\,mol^{-1}$.

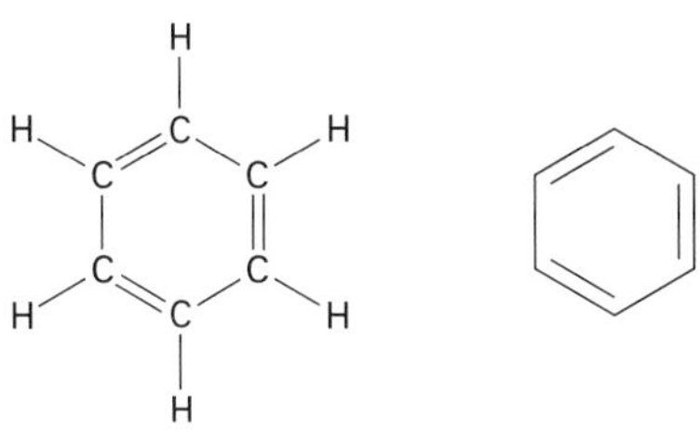

The Kekulé structure (displayed formula) for benzene with its skeletal version. Note that the carbon atoms are in one plane, i.e. benzene is 'flat'. The hydrogen atoms are also coplanar with the carbon atoms.

The enthalpies of hydrogenation show that benzene actually has a *more stable* structure than the Kekulé structure (by about $150\,kJ\,mol^{-1}$). The explanation is that the p orbitals at right angles to the plane of the carbon ring do not just overlap in pairs to form bonds, but all six overlap together.

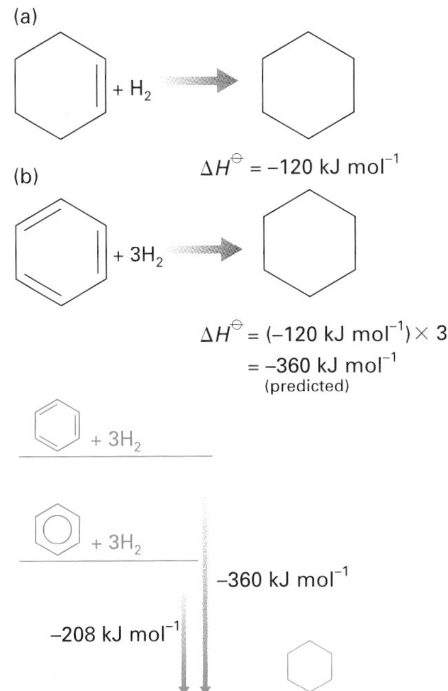

The standard enthalpy changes of hydrogenation for cyclohexa-1,3,5-triene and benzene.

Delocalization of electrons in the benzene ring

A molecule of benzene contains a total of 30 valence electrons (four for each of the six carbon atoms, and one for each of the six hydrogen atoms). Of these electrons, 12 are involved in six C—H σ bonds, and another 12 form six C—C σ bonds. These bonds establish the basic planar hexagonal **sigma framework** of the molecule. The remaining six electrons are not associated with any particular pair of carbon atoms. They are **delocalized** in ring-shaped molecular orbitals above and below the main hydrocarbon skeleton.

Each carbon atom uses its 2s and two of its 2p atomic orbitals to form the σ framework of the benzene molecule. The remaining 2p atomic orbitals all combine together to form a set of delocalized π molecular orbitals. The six remaining valence electrons fill three bonding molecular orbitals, each of which is delocalized (together constituting a delocalized π cloud). The lowest-energy orbital arises from overlap of all six orbitals in phase, spread 6.4. Thus the total number of π bonds is correctly described by the Kekulé structure, but the detailed electron density is not.

Delocalization, spread 6.4, lowers the energy of the structure by an amount often described as the **delocalization enthalpy** (or delocalization energy) (about $150\,kJ\,mol^{-1}$). This delocalized electronic structure has a dominant influence on the properties of molecules that contain benzene rings. The delocalization is now emphasized using the following symbol for benzene:

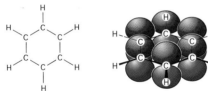

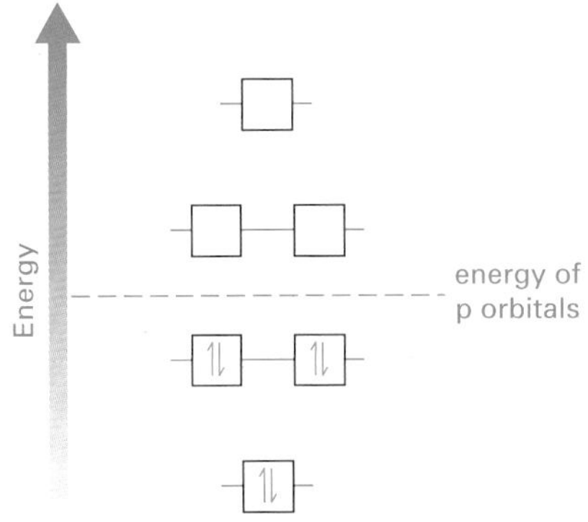

The three bonding orbitals are each occupied by two electrons: the shape of the lowest energy orbital is shown above left. The other two bonding orbitals (lying below the energy of the p orbitals) have more complicated shapes; the average electron density resembles that of the lowest-energy orbital. (The three antibonding orbitals, of even more convoluted shape, are not occupied.)

SUMMARY

- Arenes contain the benzene ring C_6H_6, which is unsaturated but does not contain localized C═C carbon–carbon double bonds.
- Three bonding electron pairs in benzene are delocalized in molecular orbitals above and below the plane of the ring.

23.2

HALOGENATION OF ARENES

OBJECTIVES

- Naming arenes
- Electrophilic substitution
- Attack by radicals

Naming arenes

Naming arenes is generally simple: most are named as substituted benzenes. Examples include methylbenzene, chlorobenzene, and nitrobenzene. Most exceptions switch to using the name 'phenyl' for the group C_6H_5— Hence the molecule $C_6H_5CH{=}CH_2$ is phenylethene; the molecule C_6H_5OH is phenol.

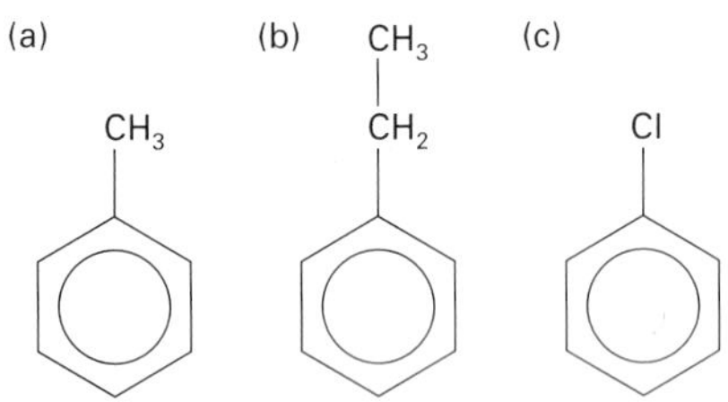

Structural formulae of substituted arenes: (a) methylbenzene (toluene); (b) ethylbenzene; (c) chlorobenzene.

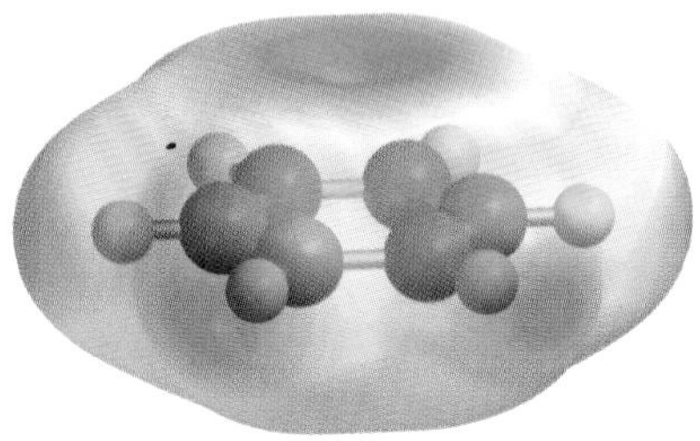

The electrostatic potential map for benzene: note the high electron density above (and below) the ring.

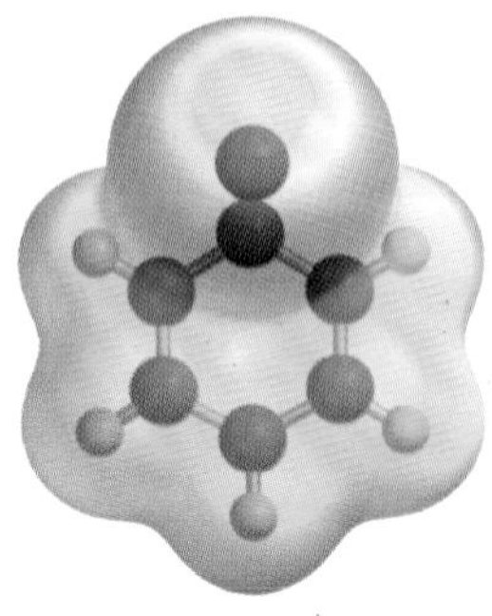

The electrophilic Cl^+ ion attacks benzene on top, where the electron density is high, to form this Wheland intermediate.

Simple arenes generally consist of a functional group or a carbon chain attached to a benzene ring. Despite the unsaturated nature of benzene, it does not readily undergo addition reactions. Most functional groups and carbon chains are introduced into the benzene molecule by means of *substitution* reactions. As you will see, this type of reaction allows the delocalized π cloud of electrons to remain intact.

Addition of halogens to benzene is difficult

The unsaturated benzene molecule does not readily undergo electrophilic addition reactions (which are common for alkenes), because saturating the carbon–carbon bonds destroys the delocalized π cloud. Remember that this delocalized structure is particularly stable. Although benzene is unsaturated, it does not decolorize bromine water (the usual test for unsaturation).

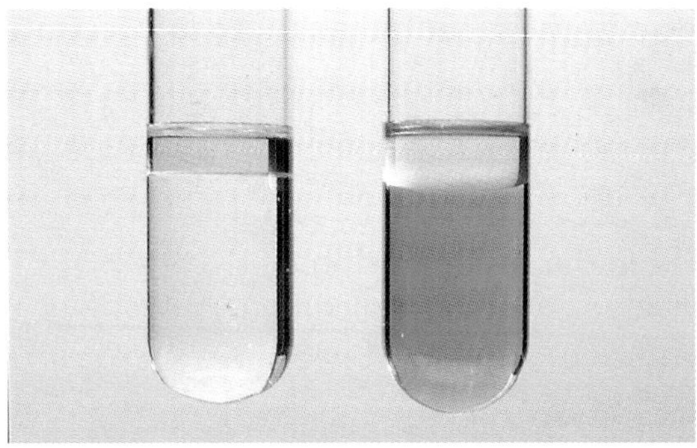

(a) Bromine water is decolourized by cyclohexene, which contains a bonding pair of electrons localized between *two adjacent carbon atoms in a C═C double bond.*
(b) Benzene does not decolourize bromine water: benzene contains three pairs of bonding π electrons that are delocalized *over six carbon atoms.*

Electrophilic substitution

Benzene usually undergoes electrophilic *substitution* reactions in which the delocalized π cloud is preserved. The product of such a substitution reaction with a halogen is a **halogenoarene** such as chlorobenzene. To *substitute* a halogen for hydrogen in benzene, a catalyst called a '**halogen carrier**' is needed as well as the halogen itself, as the π cloud is more stable than the simple π bond in an alkene.

The six-membered carbon skeleton in the benzene molecule is sandwiched between the two halves of the delocalized π electron cloud. The π cloud is a region of high electron density, coloured red in the image alongside. Benzene is therefore attacked by electrophiles; nucleophiles would be repelled. Halogen carriers make the halogen strongly electrophilic. They cause heterolytic fission of the Cl—Cl bond in the chlorine molecule (or polarize it to form $Cl^{\delta+}$—$Cl^{\delta-}$). The electrophilic Cl^+ ion then attacks the ring. Typical halogen carrier catalysts are Lewis acids such as aluminium chloride $AlCl_3$ or iron(III) chloride $FeCl_3$. Metallic iron is also often used because it reacts with chlorine to form iron(III) chloride within the reaction mixture. Equivalent bromine-carrying catalysts, $FeBr_3$ and $AlBr_3$, are used with bromine to make bromoarenes.

- Electrophilic substitution is the characteristic reaction of all arenes.

The mechanism of electrophilic substitution starts with attack by the electrophilic Cl^+ ion on benzene. As the electrostatic potential map alongside shows, the high electron density is above (and below) the plane, hence this is the direction of attack. An intermediate called a **Wheland intermediate** forms, in which the positive charge is shared by the five other carbon atoms in the ring (see next spread but one). This intermediate loses a proton to form chlorobenzene. Overall:

$$C_6H_6 + Cl^+ \rightarrow C_6H_5Cl + H^+$$

(a)

$Cl_2 + AlCl_3 \rightarrow Cl^+ + AlCl_4^-$

(b) (c) (d)

The mechanism of halogen substitution. (Note that, although chlorine is shown here, the same mechanism applies to bromination.) (a) Chlorine donates electron density into a vacant orbital on the aluminium atom in aluminium chloride. (b) The benzene π cloud attracts the Cl^+ ion. The Cl^+ ion bonds to carbon; four π electrons are shared by five carbon atoms (c). (d) The molecule loses a proton (deprotonates) to form the product. This regains the delocalization energy of the benzene ring.

Attack by radicals on side chains

Radicals normally attack alkanes indiscriminately. For example, the radical reaction between chlorine and an alkane in the presence of ultraviolet light gives a wide range of products (see previous chapter). In the case of an alkylbenzene, radical attack occurs preferentially at the carbon atom nearest the ring. For example, the radical chlorination (Cl_2, UV) of ethylbenzene $C_6H_5CH_2CH_3$ results in one dominant product, $C_6H_5CHClCH_3$.

Chlorine substitutes at this position because the radical formed during the attack is much more stable than alternative radicals. The unpaired electron is delocalized with the π cloud.

(a) Less stable radical. (b) More stable radical with its electron delocalized with the ring. Being more stable, it will stand a better chance of reacting to form the product.

Chlorine radical or chlorine ion

Remember that, if the chlorine species attacking the arene is the electrophilic Cl^+ ion, attack will not occur at the alkyl side chain. Instead the electrophile will attack the benzene ring, and substitute a chlorine for a hydrogen in the ring. The products of chlorination are therefore strongly dependent on the exact nature of the species that attacks and hence on the reaction conditions.

To *add* chlorine to benzene itself, it is necessary to use the same vigorous conditions as those required to *substitute* chlorine for hydrogen in an alkane. In the presence of ultraviolet light, chlorine *adds* to benzene in a radical chain reaction to form the saturated halogeno compound 1,2,3,4,5,6-hexachlorocyclohexane, which has eight structural isomers, one of which is the 'organochlorine' insecticide *Lindane*:

$$C_6H_6(l) + 3Cl_2(g) \rightarrow C_6H_6Cl_6(l)$$

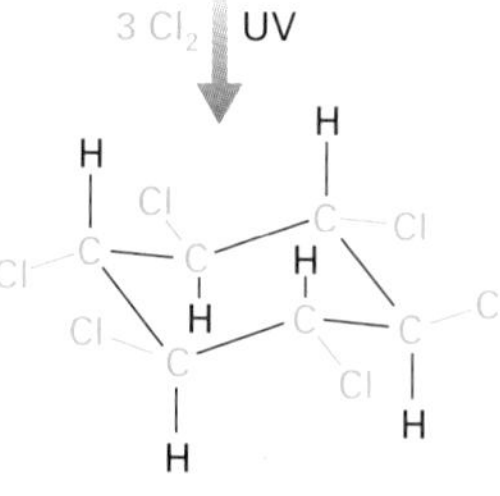

Adding chlorine to benzene destroys the delocalized π cloud of electrons. The product molecule is saturated.

SUMMARY

- Arenes most commonly react by electrophilic substitution.
- Halogen carriers polarize halogens so they become electrophiles capable of attracting electron density from the benzene ring π cloud.
- Halogen carriers include $FeCl_3$ and $AlCl_3$ for chlorination and $FeBr_3$ and $AlBr_3$ for bromination.

PRACTICE

1 In the chlorination of benzene by electrophilic substitution, chlorine and the halogen carrier $AlCl_3$ form Cl^+ and $AlCl_4^-$.
  - **a** Why is $AlCl_3$ described as being 'electron-deficient'?
  - **b** Why are Lewis acids used as halogen carriers?
  - **c** How many electrons are delocalized around the benzene ring (i) in the reaction intermediate $[C_6H_6Cl]^+$ and (ii) in the product C_6H_5Cl?

2 Draw structural formulae to show the reactant, reaction intermediate, and product in the radical reaction between propylbenzene and chlorine in the presence of ultraviolet light.

23.3 Nitration and nitrobenzene

OBJECTIVES

- Nitrating mixture
- Nitrating benzene
- Nitrating nitrobenzene
- TNT

The nitro group $—NO_2$ is a very important functional group when attached to a benzene ring. Nitrobenzene is a yellow oily liquid ($T_m = 6\,°C$; $T_b = 211\,°C$) which smells of bitter almonds. It is far more important commercially than is chlorobenzene (discussed in the previous spread). Nitrobenzene is the starting material for the production of a wide variety of substances, including dyes and explosives, see spreads 28.3 and 28.4 for details. The colours of the clothes you are wearing are probably courtesy of a few teaspoonsful of nitrobenzene – as are the continuing tragic effects of the land mines hidden in abandoned battlefields around the world.

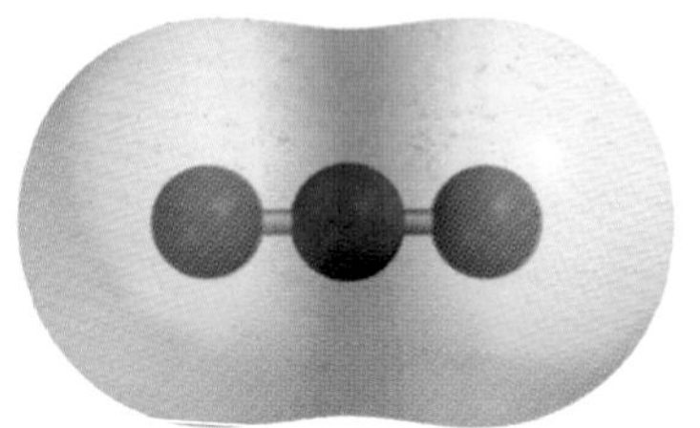

The nitrogen atom of the nitronium ion NO_2^+ carries most of the positive charge (indicated by the blue colour).

The nitrating mixture

Substituting a nitro group into a benzene ring is called **nitration**. The reagent that brings about the reaction is called a **nitrating mixture**. When nitrating benzene itself, the nitrating mixture consists of concentrated nitric acid and concentrated sulphuric acid, at a temperature of about 50 °C. These two acids react together to produce a powerful electrophile called the **nitronium ion** NO_2^+.

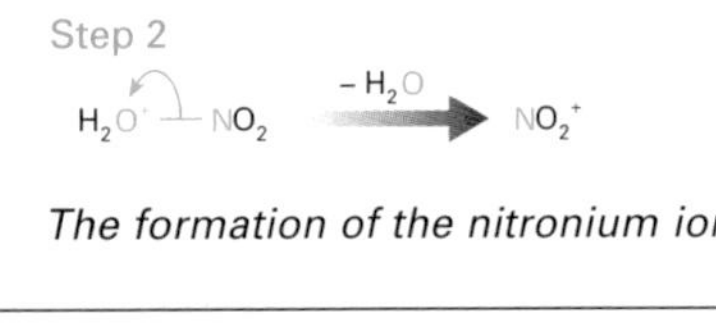

The formation of the nitronium ion.

The overall reaction is:

$HNO_3 + 2H_2SO_4 \rightarrow NO_2^+ + H_3O^+ + 2HSO_4^-$

The nitronium ion can be thought of as forming in two steps.

Step 1 Sulphuric acid protonates nitric acid HNO_3 (more correctly written as $HONO_2$, spread 19.8):

$HONO_2 + H_2SO_4 \rightarrow H_2O^+—NO_2 + HSO_4^-$

Step 2 The protonated nitric acid then loses water:

$H_2O^+—NO_2 \rightarrow NO_2^+ + H_2O$

The ion NO_2^+ is a powerful electrophile because it has a full positive charge.

Nitrating benzene

The overall reaction for the preparation of nitrobenzene may be represented by the chemical equation:

$$C_6H_6 + NO_2^+ \rightarrow C_6H_5NO_2 + H^+$$

The actual substitution reaction happens in the following three distinct steps.

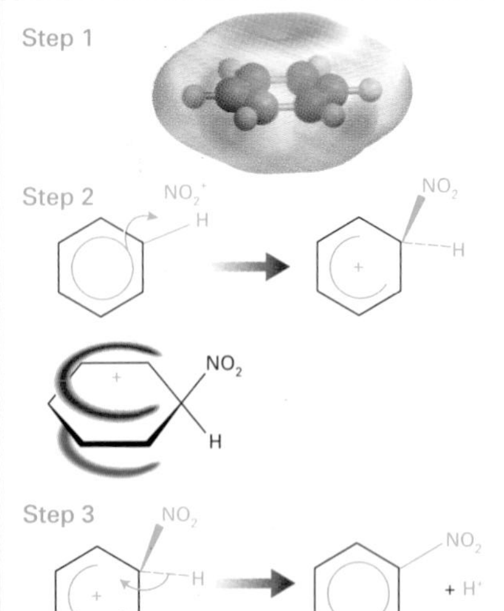

The mechanism for the nitration of benzene.

Step 1 The NO_2^+ ion is attracted to the high electron density in the π cloud of delocalized electrons above and below the plane of the benzene ring.

Step 2 An electron pair from the ring forms a bond between one of the carbon atoms and the attacking electrophile. This carbon atom has now formed four single bonds and so *no longer contributes to the delocalized system*. The intermediate species is positively charged because the positively charged electrophile did not bring any bonding electrons with it; *both* the electrons of the new C—N bond came from the ring.

Step 3 The pair of electrons in the C—H bond returns to the delocalized orbitals on the benzene ring. The hydrogen atom no longer possesses its valence electron and so is ejected as the ion H^+.

Note that, in step 2, the benzene ring exists as a positively charged ion. This situation is equivalent to the carbocation formed when an electrophile attacks an alkene (see previous chapter). In that case a nucleophile attacks the carbocation, resulting in an *addition* reaction. In the case of the benzene ring, such a reaction would mean a significant loss of delocalization, which is energetically unfavourable. Instead, the intermediate deprotonates, which restores the delocalized system over all six carbon atoms and results in overall *substitution*.

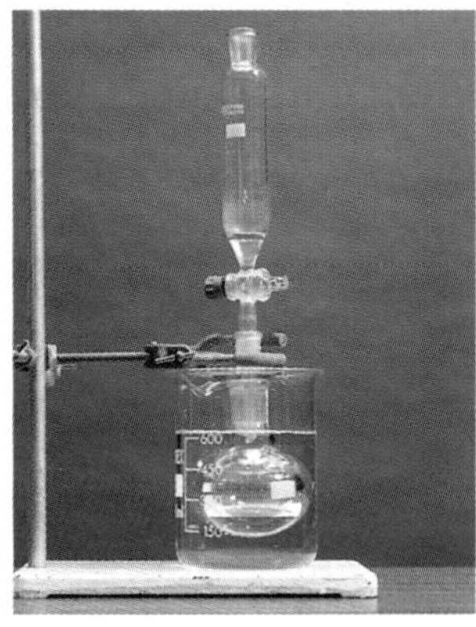

Apparatus for the nitration of benzene. The nitrating mixture is prepared in the flask. Benzene is slowly run in from the funnel while the flask is cooled in water. Then the flask is heated to 50 °C by a water bath to convert the benzene to nitrobenzene.

Dinitrobenzene

The nitration of benzene takes place at 50 °C. If the temperature is increased to 100 °C, a second nitro group will substitute. When two or more groups are attached to a ring, their relative positions are indicated by numbering the six carbon atoms that make up the ring. In this *disubstitution* of benzene by nitro groups, 1,3-dinitrobenzene (T_m = 90 °C) will result. The reason for the production of this particular isomer will be explained in the following spread.

Nitration of substituted benzene rings

The nitrating mixture will also nitrate other substituted benzene rings. For example, phenol (C_6H_5OH) forms 2,4,6-trinitrophenol (formerly known as picric acid). Methylbenzene forms 2,4,6-trinitromethylbenzene (formerly known as trinitrotoluene, **TNT**). Notice that both these reactions happen readily in comparison to the nitration of nitrobenzene, which requires higher temperatures. The influence of functional groups on the rates of further substitution reactions will be dealt with in the following spread.

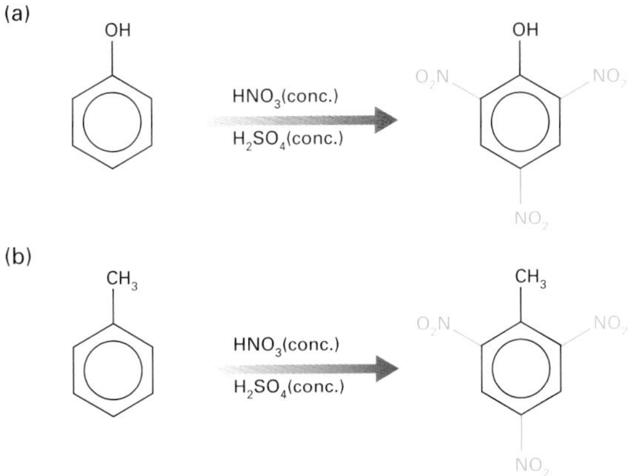

(a) Phenol consists of a hydroxyl (—OH) group attached to a benzene ring. The nitrating mixture readily converts it to bright yellow 2,4,6-trinitrophenol. This substance was used as a high explosive, particularly during the First World War. (b) Methylbenzene converts eventually and with difficulty to 2,4,6-trinitromethylbenzene.

The reaction of nitrobenzene to form 1,3-dinitrobenzene.

A space-filling model of 2,4,6-trinitromethylbenzene (top). This is the high explosive trinitrotoluene (TNT).

SUMMARY

- The formula of the nitro group is $—NO_2$.
- The nitro group is substituted into the benzene ring by the nitrating mixture, which consists of concentrated nitric acid and concentrated sulphuric acid.
- The nitrating mixture produces the powerfully electrophilic nitronium ion NO_2^+.
- Further nitro groups may be substituted into nitrobenzene, at higher temperatures.

PRACTICE

1 Draw Lewis structures to show the electronic structures of nitric acid and sulphuric acid. Show how these molecules interact to produce the nitronium ion NO_2^+.

2 With reference to the nitration of benzene to form nitrobenzene:

a Why is the NO_2^+ ion described as an electrophile?

b Why does the nitro group substitute into the benzene ring and not add to it?

c Each product molecule contains one nitro group only and does not go on to further substitution. Explain why.

3 Methylbenzene nitrates to form 2,4,6-trinitromethylbenzene. Look at the photograph of the space-filling model above and suggest why the formation of 2,3,4,5,6-pentanitromethylbenzene is highly unlikely.

23.4

OBJECTIVES

- The 2-/4-directing and 3-directing groups
- Activating and deactivating groups
- Wheland intermediate

THE EFFECT OF AN EXISTING FUNCTIONAL GROUP

Arenes most commonly react by undergoing electrophilic substitution of hydrogen atoms attached to the benzene ring. When the arene already has a functional group attached to the ring, this group may have two distinct effects on subsequent substitution reactions. First, the existing group may activate (or deactivate) the ring, making the ring respectively more (or less) likely than benzene to substitute further hydrogen atoms. Secondly, an existing group may direct incoming groups to specific positions on the ring relative to itself. As you will see, the key to this behaviour is the charged reaction intermediate – the so-called 'Wheland intermediate'.

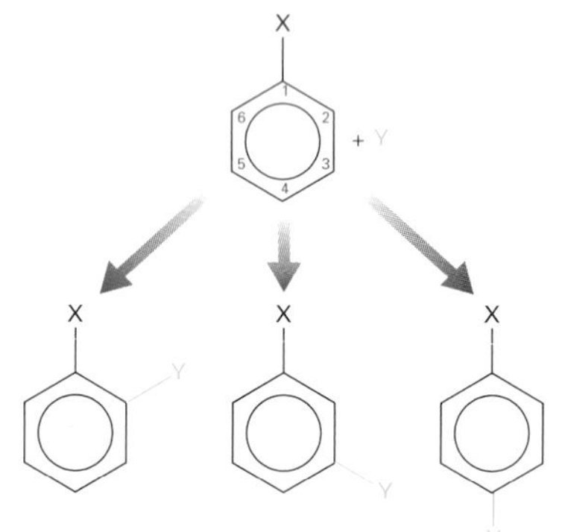

The three possible isomers of a disubstituted benzene compound.

Directing incoming groups

When one group is already attached to a benzene ring, a second incoming group may attach itself at three possible positions. The nature of the first group 'directs' (controls) the position where the second substitutes. For example, nitration is a reaction that substitutes a —NO_2 functional group for a hydrogen atom on the benzene ring. Nitration of nitrobenzene forms 1,3-dinitrobenzene. On the other hand, nitration of methylbenzene forms a mixture of 2- and 4-nitromethylbenzene. (Positions 2 and 6 are identical owing to the symmetry of the ring, as are positions 3 and 5.) Extreme conditions cause three nitro groups to be attached to form 2,4,6-trinitromethylbenzene (TNT). Note that two of the hydrogen atoms remain; they are *not* substituted by nitro groups.

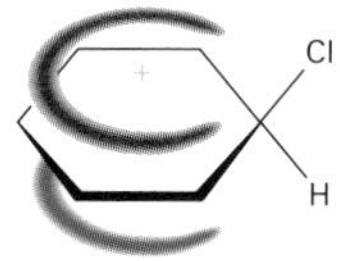

Electrophilic substitution of benzene – a reminder. The electrophilic substitution of benzene proceeds via a Wheland *intermediate. This has a positive charge; the incoming group and the departing hydrogen atom are both bonded to one of the carbon atoms of the benzene ring.*

The 2-/4-directing methyl group

In the Wheland intermediate, electrons are delocalized around five carbon atoms. However, it is most important to note that the positive charge is *not* spread *evenly* around these five carbon atoms, as shown by the colour coding in its electrostatic potential map alongside. Consider the nitration of methylbenzene. There are three possible Wheland intermediates corresponding to the final products 2-, 3-, and 4-nitromethylbenzene (see the diagrams below). In the intermediate, the positive charge is concentrated on the carbon atoms in positions 2, 4, and 6 *relative to the incoming electrophile*. If an electron-donating group (see the previous chapter) is already present in any of these positions, it will donate electron density, lessening the positive charge on the ring, and so stabilize the Wheland intermediate. The Wheland intermediate leading to the 1,2- and 1,4- isomers will have lower energy than the Wheland intermediate leading to the 1,3- isomer.

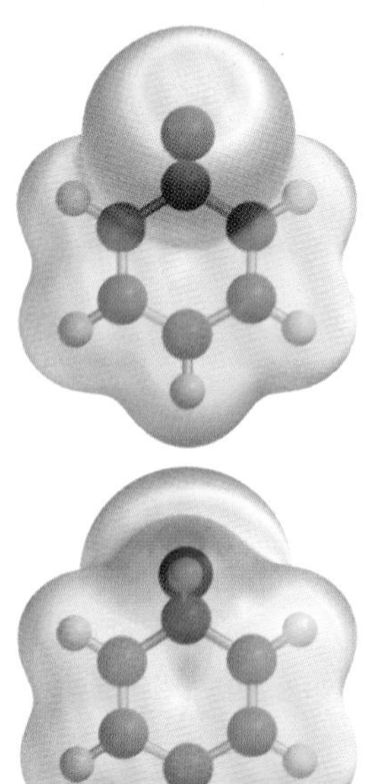

The electron density in the Wheland intermediate is not evenly distributed as is made clear by this electrostatic potential map, which is a view from underneath (compared with the image on the spread before last).

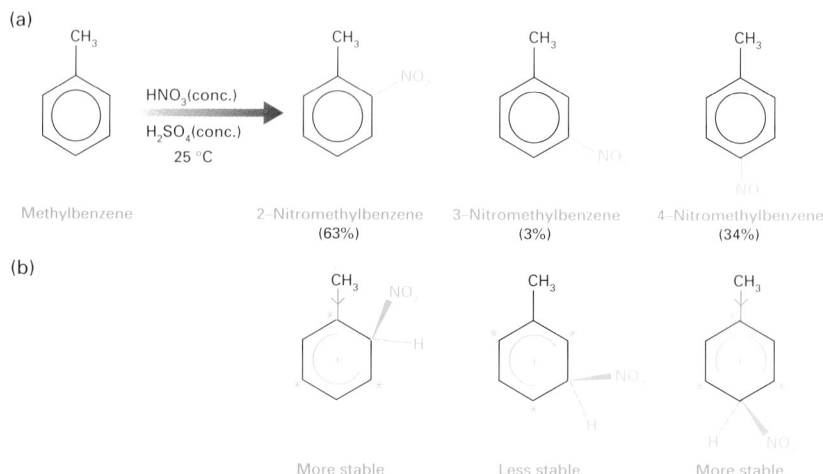

(a) The nitration of methylbenzene produces more of the 2- and 4- isomers than of the 3- isomer. (b) The Wheland intermediates leading to 2-nitromethylbenzene, 3-nitromethylbenzene, and 4-nitromethylbenzene. The positions at which the positive charge is concentrated are labelled with a star (positions 2, 4, and 6 relative to the incoming —NO_2 group). The —CH_3 group donates electron density to the ring and therefore stabilizes the two intermediates with an adjacent positive charge.

The ring-activating methyl group

The nitration of methylbenzene requires a temperature some 25°C lower than that required for the nitration of benzene. The methyl group therefore has the effect of activating the ring to further substitution. By stabilizing the 1,2- and 1,4- Wheland intermediates, the methyl group lowers the activation energy and increases the rate of the reaction. In general:

- An *electron-donating group* attached to a benzene ring will *increase* the rate of further substitution relative to benzene; it will also direct the incoming group to the 2 or 4 position.

2-/4- directing
— OH strongly activating
— CH_3 } activating
— R (other alkyl groups) }

3- directing
— NO_2 strongly deactivating
— $C(=O)CH_3$ deactivating

The influence of existing groups.

The 3-directing deactivating groups

Electron-withdrawing groups, such as the nitro —NO_2 group, deactivate the ring relative to benzene. As before, the positive charge on the Wheland intermediate is concentrated on the carbon atoms in positions 2, 4, and 6 *relative to the incoming electrophile*. The presence of an electron-withdrawing group in any of these positions *destabilizes* the Wheland intermediate by increasing the positive charge on the ring. This effect is reduced if the second group attaches to the 3 (or the equivalent 5) position relative to the existing nitro group. More severe conditions are needed for the nitration of nitrobenzene than for the nitration of benzene; the nitro group deactivates the ring to further substitution.

- An *electron-withdrawing group* attached to a benzene ring will *decrease* the rate of further substitution relative to benzene; it will also direct the incoming group to the 3 position.

Phenol

The hydroxyl group stabilizes the Wheland intermediate by another rmechanism, namely extending the delocalization out onto the oxygen atom. This is possible only in the 2- and 4- positions and so phenol is also 2-/4-directing.

(a)

NO_2 — HNO_3(conc.), H_2SO_4(conc.), $T \sim 100$ °C → NO_2, NO_2

(b)

Less stable — More stable — Less stable

(a) The nitration of nitrobenzene produces 1,3-dinitrobenzene and very little of the 1,2- and 1,4- isomers. (b) The Wheland intermediates leading to 1,2-dinitrobenzene, 1,3-dinitrobenzene, and 1,4-dinitrobenzene. The positions at which the positive charge is concentrated are labelled with a star (positions 2, 4, and 6 relative to the incoming —NO_2 group). The existing —NO_2 group withdraws electron density from the ring and therefore destabilizes the two intermediates with an adjacent positive charge.

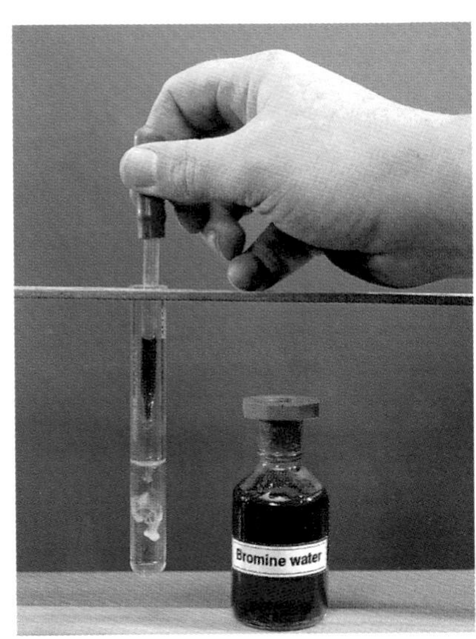

The —OH group in phenol C_6H_5OH activates the ring to substitution. Phenol decolourizes bromine water (remember that benzene does not); the product is an immediate white precipitate of 2,4,6-tribromophenol.

2,4,6-tribromophenol

The equivalent chlorine molecule, 2,4,6-trichlorophenol, is known as TCP: TCP is a well-known antiseptic.

SUMMARY

- Disubstituted arenes have three isomers; the 1,2-, the 1,3-, and the 1,4- isomers.
- Electrophilic substitution reactions involve a positively charged Wheland intermediate. The charge is delocalized around five of the carbon atoms of the benzene ring.
- The positive charge of the Wheland intermediate is concentrated at positions 2, 4, and 6 relative to the position of the incoming electrophile.
- Electron-donating groups activate the ring and direct incoming groups to positions 2 and 4 relative to the existing group.
- Electron-withdrawing groups deactivate the ring and direct incoming groups to position 3 relative to the existing group.

PRACTICE

1 Give the formula(e) of the major disubstituted product(s) of each of the following reactions. State also whether the ring will be activated or deactivated by the existing functional group.

a Nitration of ethylbenzene
b Nitration of nitrobenzene.

23.5

THE FRIEDEL–CRAFTS REACTION

OBJECTIVES

- The Friedel–Crafts reaction
- Alkylation
- Acylation
- Oxidation of alkyl groups

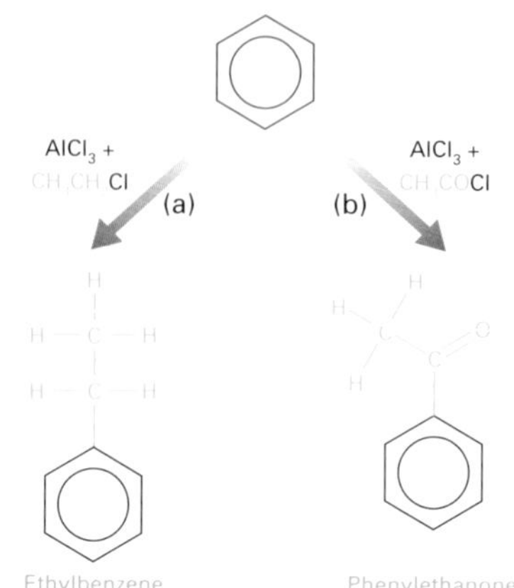

(a) Alkylation and (b) acylation reactions.

Friedel and Crafts

The Friedel–Crafts reaction arose from an unexpected laboratory accident in 1877. James Crafts, a native Bostonian, was collaborating in Paris with Charles Friedel, whom he had met sixteen years earlier on a previous trip to Europe. Crafts had actually returned to Paris mainly because of ill health. Because of the change of climate (along with their discovery!), his health improved dramatically. Crafts did eventually return to the USA and in 1897 was elected President of the Massachusetts Institute of Technology (MIT).

Aeroplanes of the Second World War era were propelled by high-performance piston engines that required high-octane fuel. The yield of this fuel from refining techniques at that time was very low. Friedel–Crafts alkylation of benzene and its hydrocarbon derivatives produced suitable fuel, which made great contributions to the war effort of the Allies.

Synthesis in organic chemistry involves making complex molecules from simpler starting materials. You are familiar with substituting chlorine, bromine, and nitro groups into benzene and its derivatives. These groups are described as *functional groups*; they can undergo further changes in subsequent reactions. Many arenes contain relatively inert alkyl groups attached to the benzene ring. Attaching alkyl groups involves a number of problems.

The Friedel–Crafts reaction

The **Friedel–Crafts reaction** attaches extra carbon atoms to a benzene ring. In this reaction, the arene reacts with a halogen-containing organic molecule. The whole of the molecule attached to the chlorine atom substitutes into the benzene ring. There are two variants of the Friedel–Crafts reaction: **alkylation** attaches an alkyl group (—R); and **acylation** attaches an acyl group (—COR).

In both cases the C—Cl bond in the attacking molecule is polarized, $C^{\delta+}$—$Cl^{\delta-}$ (because carbon has a lower electronegativity than chlorine). However, the halogeno compound alone is not a sufficiently powerful electrophile to attack the benzene ring. Adding a Lewis acid such as aluminium chloride breaks the C—Cl bond producing an electrophile, which can successfully attack the benzene ring.

Friedel–Crafts alkylation

If the halogen reagent in a Friedel–Crafts reaction is a halogenoalkane, the attached group is an alkyl group and the reaction is called a Friedel–Crafts alkylation. For example, chloroethane CH_3CH_2Cl (in industry C_2H_4 and HCl are used in place of CH_3CH_2Cl) reacts with benzene in the presence of an aluminium chloride $AlCl_3$ catalyst (under *anhydrous* conditions, as $AlCl_3$ hydrolyses) to give ethylbenzene $C_6H_5CH_2CH_3$, which is an intermediate in the manufacture of polystyrene:

$$CH_3CH_2Cl + C_6H_6 \xrightarrow{AlCl_3} C_6H_5CH_2CH_3 + HCl$$

The reaction takes place in a series of steps, as follows:

Step 1 The chloroethane donates electron density into a vacant valence orbital on electron-deficient aluminium chloride (the $AlCl_3$ is thus acting as a Lewis acid):

$CH_3CH_2Cl + AlCl_3 \rightarrow CH_3CH_2^+ + AlCl_4^-$

giving rise to the ethyl carbocation, which is a powerful electrophile.

Step 2 The electrophile attacks the benzene ring, forming the Wheland intermediate (see opposite page):

$C_6H_6 + CH_3CH_2^+ \rightarrow [C_6H_6CH_2CH_3]^+$

Step 3 The Wheland intermediate deprotonates, forming the product (ethylbenzene in this example) by substitution, and thus reforming the delocalized π cloud of the benzene ring, and the catalyst is regenerated:

$[C_6H_6CH_2CH_3]^+ \rightarrow C_6H_5CH_2CH_3 + H^+$

$AlCl_4^- + H^+ \rightarrow AlCl_3 + HCl$

The main problem with Friedel–Crafts *alkylation* is that the alkyl group is electron-donating and *activates* the ring (see previous spread), making it more susceptible to further attack. The initial product is *more* reactive than the original benzene, and there is a good chance that further alkyl groups will substitute as well, giving a mixture of products. The required product then has to be separated out from the mixture.

Friedel–Crafts acylation

This reaction is similar to the alkylation reaction above, except that the acyl group —COR becomes attached to the benzene ring.

> For example, ethanoyl chloride CH_3COCl reacts with the halogen carrier $AlCl_3$ as follows:
>
> $CH_3COCl + AlCl_3 \rightarrow [CH_3CO]^+ + AlCl_4^-$
>
> The ethanoyl ion $[CH_3CO]^+$ is a powerful electrophile. It attacks the benzene ring, which undergoes an electrophilic substitution reaction. The chemical equation for the overall reaction is:
>
> $CH_3COCl + C_6H_6 \xrightarrow{AlCl_3} C_6H_5COCH_3 + HCl$
>
> The compound formed in a Friedel–Crafts acylation is a *ketone*, phenylethanone $C_6H_5COCH_3$ in this example.

Friedel–Crafts *acylation* produces a product that is *less* reactive than the original benzene. The acyl group withdraws electron density and so deactivates the ring (see previous spread), making it less susceptible to further electrophilic attack. As a result, the initial product is unlikely to react with a second acyl group. Unlike the case of Friedel–Crafts alkylation, acylation gives one predominant product.

Step 1

Step 2

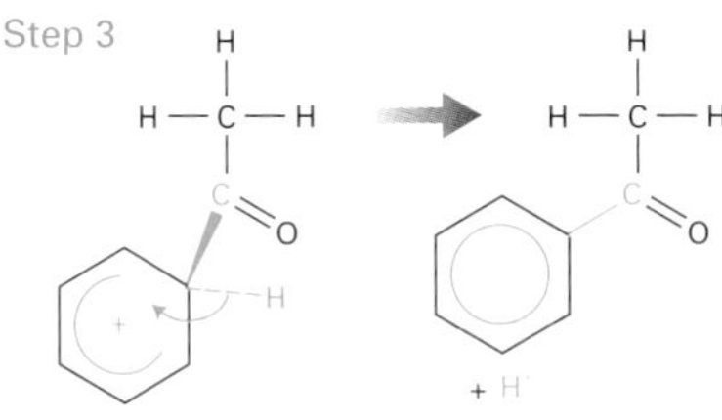

Friedel–Crafts acylation.
Step 1: Formation of the electrophile.
Step 2: Formation of Wheland intermediate.
Step 3: Deprotonation.

Oxidizing an alkyl group

Alkanes are almost completely unaffected by oxidants. Alkenes split their carbon chains when treated with powerful oxidants such as hot concentrated acidified manganate(VII) ions (see chapter on 'Organic synthesis reactions'). In complete contrast, alkyl groups attached to a benzene ring undergo oxidation relatively readily. The whole alkyl group is oxidized to a carboxyl group —COOH.

> For example, alkaline potassium manganate(VII) oxidizes methylbenzene to benzoic acid (after neutralization):
>
> $C_6H_5CH_3 \xrightarrow{[O]} C_6H_5COOH + H_2O$
>
> (here the symbol [O] indicates oxidation). The product always has a carboxyl group attached directly to the benzene ring. Methylbenzene, ethylbenzene, or any other benzene derivative with an alkyl side chain (however long) will produce the *same* product, *benzoic acid*. The rest of the side chain is destroyed, forming carbon dioxide and water. For example,
>
> $C_6H_5CH_2CH_3 \xrightarrow{[O]} C_6H_5COOH + CO_2 + 2H_2O$
>
> The resulting benzoic acid is stabilized by delocalization of the carboxyl group with the benzene ring.

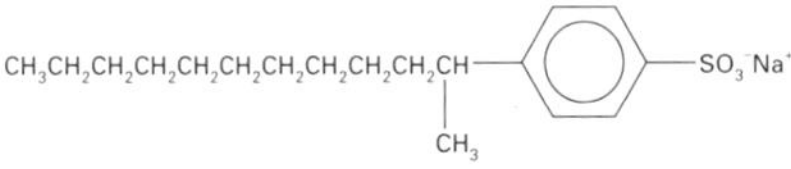

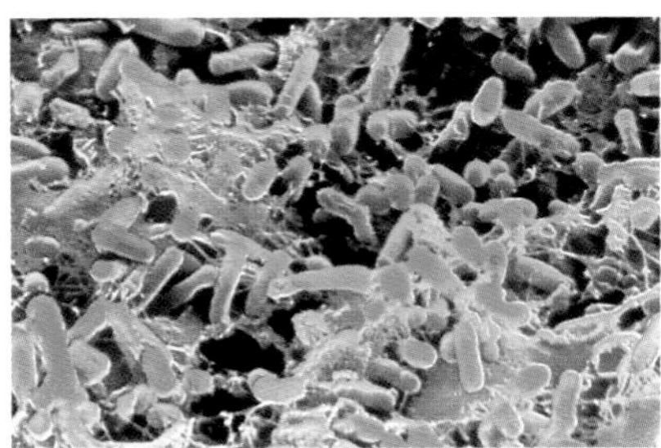

The Friedel–Crafts reaction is extremely useful in industry. Synthetic rubber, plastics, detergents, and high-octane unleaded petrol all depend on this one reaction. For example, the common biodegradable synthetic detergent sodium dodecylbenzenesulphonate has the 12-carbon side chain attached by a Friedel–Crafts reaction. (The next spread describes how the sulphonate group can be attached.) Bacteria, such as Escherichia coli *(shown magnified 42 000 times) can degrade this detergent.*

SUMMARY

- Friedel–Crafts alkylation attaches an alkyl group (e.g. the ethyl group $—CH_2CH_3$) to a benzene ring.
- Friedel–Crafts acylation attaches an acyl group (e.g. the ethanoyl group $—COCH_3$) to a benzene ring.
- Friedel–Crafts reactions use a Lewis acid catalyst such as aluminium chloride.
- For alkylation, use a halogenoalkane, e.g. chloroethane CH_3CH_2Cl.
- For acylation, use an acyl chloride, e.g. ethanoyl chloride CH_3COCl.
- Alkylbenzene compounds all oxidize to benzoic acid C_6H_5COOH, regardless of the length of the alkyl group attached to the benzene ring.

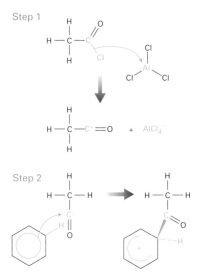

PRACTICE

1 Starting with benzene, outline the reaction(s) you would use to produce:

a Propylbenzene

b Diphenylmethanone ($C_6H_5COC_6H_5$)

c Benzoic acid.

2 Draw structural formulae to describe the mechanism of the Friedel–Crafts reaction being used to attach an ethyl group to a benzene ring.

23.6

SULPHONATION OF BENZENE

OBJECTIVES

- Benzenesulphonic acid
- Preparation
- Uses

Benzene undergoes reactions and forms compounds which are unlike those of aliphatic compounds. For example, phenol C_6H_5OH is acidic, whereas hexan-1-ol $C_6H_{13}OH$ is neutral; ethylbenzene $C_6H_5CH_2CH_3$ forms an acid on oxidation, whereas octane C_8H_{18} does not react. The final spread of this chapter introduces the sulphonate group —SO_2OH. Joining this group to the benzene ring by a carbon–sulphur bond forms benzenesulphonic acid. This compound is of great industrial importance in the manufacture of detergents, dyestuffs, and drugs. The alkyl analogue is unstable in the presence of water and is of no commercial interest. As before, the delocalized electrons around the benzene ring are the key to the stability of the arene compound.

Sulphonation of benzene

Benzene is sulphonated by refluxing it with concentrated sulphuric acid. The formula of this acid is usually written as H_2SO_4. However, the form $(HO)_2SO_2$ (see chapter on 'Trends across a period') reminds you that it is an oxoacid, with two —OH groups and two oxygen atoms attached to a central sulphur atom.

The actual electrophile is sulphur trioxide SO_3 and the overall reaction may be represented as:

$$C_6H_6 + SO_3 \rightarrow C_6H_5SO_2OH$$

The resulting product is benzenesulphonic acid, which is a colourless oily liquid. The reaction proceeds in a series of steps.

Step 1

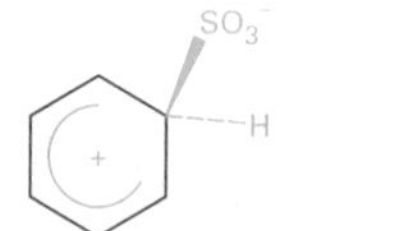

Step 2

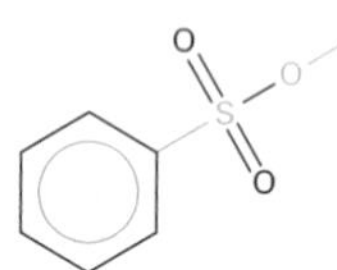

Step 3

The mechanism of the sulphonation of benzene.

Step 1 Concentrated sulphuric acid contains a proportion of free sulphur trioxide as a result of the equilibrium:

$H_2SO_4 \rightleftharpoons SO_3 + H_2O$

Although it is a neutral molecule, sulphur trioxide is a powerful electrophile because oxygen has a greater electronegativity than sulphur, and so the sulphur atom has a significant partial positive charge.

Step 2 The sulphur trioxide electrophile is attracted to the delocalized π cloud of the benzene ring and forms a Wheland intermediate by bonding with a carbon atom on the ring:

$SO_3 + C_6H_6 \rightarrow [C_6H_6]^+SO_3^-$

Note that the intermediate bears a negative charge on the —SO_3^- group and a positive charge delocalized around the benzene ring.

Step 3 The benzene ring deprotonates from the carbon atom attached to the —SO_3^- group. Another proton then adds on to the sulphonate group:

$[C_6H_6]^+SO_3^- \rightarrow C_6H_5SO_2OH$

Acid character

Benzenesulphonic acid is a weak acid:

$$C_6H_5SO_2OH + H_2O \rightleftharpoons H_3O^+ + C_6H_5SO_3^-$$

It forms salts on reaction with base. For example,

$$C_6H_5SO_2OH + NaOH \rightarrow Na^+C_6H_5SO_3^- + H_2O$$

The salt $Na^+C_6H_5SO_3^-$ is called sodium benzenesulphonate.

The sulphonic acid group in benzenesulphonic acid is stabilized by delocalization of its electron density around the benzene ring. The three oxygen atoms in the ion $C_6H_5SO_3^-$ are all equivalent, as shown in the electrostatic potential map alongside.

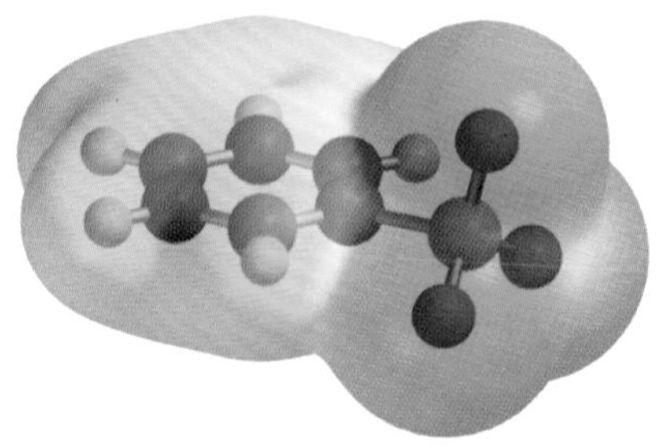

Delocalization of electron density within the benzenesulphonate ion.

Applications

Benzenesulphonates are widely used as a feedstock from which detergents are made, see previous spread. The sulphonate group introduces a polar region into an otherwise non-polar molecule, improving its overall solubility in water. Sulphonic acid groups are also present in some dyes. Their acidic groups attach the dye molecules to basic amino groups in wool or silk. In the case of cotton, sulphonic acid groups form ester linkages with the hydroxyl groups on the cellulose fibres of the cotton. A family of antibiotics called the *sulphonamides* have very similar molecular structures to sulphonates (see spread 28.7).

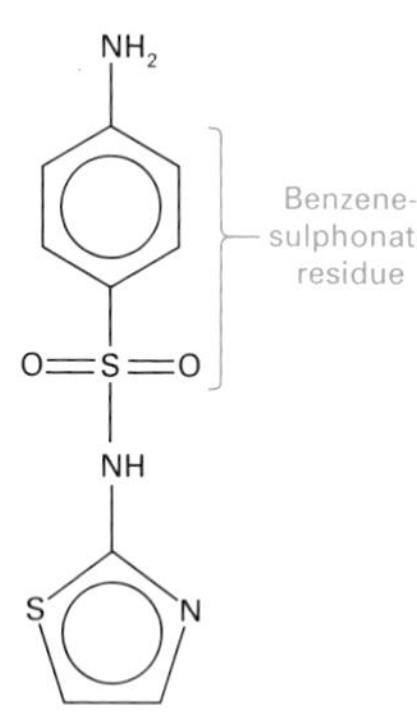

The structure of the sulphonamide antibiotic sulphathiazole, effective against Staphylococci.

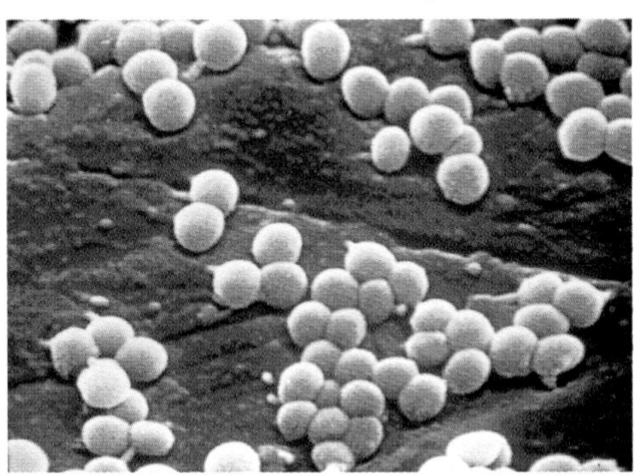

The bacteria Staphylococci *form clusters resembling grapes.*

SUMMARY

- The sulphonic acid group has the formula —SO_2OH.
- Benzenesulphonic acid is a weak acid in solution, forming salts such as $Na^+C_6H_5SO_3^-$.
- The sulphonating agent is concentrated sulphuric acid; it provides the electrophile sulphur trioxide SO_3.
- The sulphonic acid and sulphonate groups are highly polar, increasing the water solubility of molecules to which they are attached.
- Derivatives of benzenesulphonic acid include detergents, dyestuffs, and drugs.

PRACTICE

1 Draw structural formulae and Lewis structures for sulphuric acid and sulphur trioxide.

2 Use 'curly arrows' to show how electron pairs move to break and make bonds when:

a sulphuric acid protonates water;

b benzenesulphonic acid protonates water.

3 Explain why it is difficult to substitute a second sulphonic acid group into the benzenesulphonic acid molecule.

4 What would you expect to see when benzenesulphonic acid is added to aqueous potassium carbonate? Write a *balanced* chemical equation for the reaction.

Chapter 23 Reactions summary

- Chlorine substitution using a Lewis acid as a halogen carrier:
  $C_6H_6 \xrightarrow{Cl_2/AlCl_3} C_6H_5Cl$
- Bromine substitution using a Lewis acid as a halogen carrier:
  $C_6H_6 \xrightarrow{Br_2/AlBr_3} C_6H_5Br$
- The nitrating mixture producing the nitronium ion:
  $HNO_3 + 2H_2SO_4 \rightarrow NO_2^+ + H_3O^+ + 2HSO_4^-$
- Preparation of nitrobenzene:
  $C_6H_6 + NO_2^+ \xrightarrow{50\,°C} C_6H_5NO_2 + H^+$
  Further nitration forms 1,3-dinitrobenzene.
- Friedel–Crafts alkylation:
  $C_6H_6 + CH_3CH_2Cl \xrightarrow{AlCl_3} C_6H_5CH_2CH_3 + HCl$
- Friedel–Crafts acylation:
  $C_6H_6 + CH_3COCl \xrightarrow{AlCl_3} C_6H_5COCH_3 + HCl$
- Oxidation of alkyl side chain (however long) on benzene:
  $C_6H_5CH_2CH_3 \xrightarrow{[O]} C_6H_5COOH + CO_2 + 2H_2O$
- Sulphonation of benzene by concentrated sulphuric acid:
  $C_6H_6 + SO_3 \rightarrow C_6H_5SO_2OH$

PRACTICE EXAM QUESTIONS

1 Alkylation of an aromatic compound can be carried out using the Friedel–Crafts reaction. For example, benzene reacts with chloromethane in the presence of aluminium chloride to give methylbenzene.

$$C_6H_6 + CH_3Cl \xrightarrow{AlCl_3} C_6H_5CH_3 + HCl$$

a Hydrogen chloride is produced as the reaction proceeds. Describe how you could show when the reaction had finished. [2]

b The chloromethane reacts with aluminium chloride to give $CH_3^+[AlCl_4]^-$.

$CH_3Cl + AlCl_3 \rightarrow CH_3^+[AlCl_4]^-$

i The carbonium ion, CH_3^+, is an **electrophile**. Explain this term.

ii The mechanism for the reaction of CH_3^+ with a benzene ring is similar to that of the nitronium ion with benzene. Using a flow scheme suggest a mechanism for the reaction of CH_3^+ with benzene.[5]

c A problem with alkylation is that the reaction does not stop at methylbenzene; further alkylation of the benzene ring takes place to form dimethylbenzenes.

i Draw the structures of the three dimethylbenzenes and give the systematic name of **one** of them.

ii State a technique by which you could separate a mixture of the dimethylbenzenes. [5]

d One molecule of benzene reacts with one molecule of a chloroalkane to form an alkylbenzene:

$$RCl + C_6H_6 \xrightarrow{AlCl_3} C_6H_5R + HCl$$

The percentage composition by mass of the alkylbenzene is 90.0% carbon and 10.0% hydrogen.

i Calculate the empirical formula of the alkylbenzene.

ii Determine the molecular formula of the alkylbenzene. Explain your method. [4]

e Acylation of the benzene ring can occur with an acyl chloride.

$$C_6H_6 + CH_3COCl \xrightarrow{AlCl_3} X + HCl$$

Draw the structure of the product X. [2]
NICCEA 1997

2 The following is a modified account of a method for the preparation of phenylethanone, $C_6H_5COCH_3$.

- Place 3 g of finely powdered anhydrous aluminium chloride and 7.5 cm^3 (6.6 g) of dry benzene in a 50 cm^3 round-bottomed flask.
- Fit the flask with a reflux condenser and place in a cold water bath in a fume cupboard.
- Slowly add, down the condenser, 2 cm^3 (2.2 g) of ethanoyl chloride.
- Heat the flask in a water bath at 50 °C for 30 minutes, or until no further hydrogen chloride is evolved.
- Pour the reaction mixture into a 100 cm^3 flask containing 20 cm^3 of water, and shake vigorously.
- Transfer to a separating funnel and discard the lower aqueous layer.
- Add a dilute solution of sodium hydroxide to the separating funnel. Shake the mixture, and again discard the aqueous layer.
- Dry the organic layer with anhydrous calcium chloride and fractionally distil, collecting the fraction boiling between 195 °C and 205 °C.
- The yield of phenylethanone is 2 g.

a i Give the equation for the reaction between ethanoyl chloride and benzene, using structural formulae. [2]

ii Suggest a mechanism for this reaction. [3]

b Suggest reasons for each of the following steps in the preparation:

i finely powdering the aluminium chloride; [1]

ii drying the benzene; [1]

iii adding the ethanoyl chloride slowly; [1]

iv using a fume cupboard; [1]

v shaking the product with sodium hydroxide solution. [1]

c The benzene is in excess in this preparation, being used as the solvent also.

i Calculate the mass of phenylethanone which could theoretically be obtained from this preparation based on the mass of ethanoyl chloride used. [The molar mass of ethanoyl chloride is 78.5 g mol^{-1} and that of phenylethanone is 120 g mol^{-1}.] [3]

ii What is the percentage yield in this preparation? [1]

iii Suggest reasons why the actual yield for organic reactions generally is significantly less than the theoretical yield. [2]
EDEXCEL 1999

3 The following passage gives a method for the preparation of nitrobenzene. Place 35 cm^3 of concentrated nitric acid in a 500 cm^3 flask, and add slowly 40 cm^3 of concentrated sulphuric acid, keeping the mixture cool during the addition by immersing the flask in cold water. Place a thermometer in the nitrating mixture, and add very slowly 29 cm^3 of benzene. The benzene should be added about 3 cm^3 at a time, and the contents of the flask thoroughly mixed after each addition; the temperature of the mixture must not be allowed to rise above 40 °C, and the flask must be cooled in cold water if necessary.
When all the benzene has been added, fit a reflux condenser to the flask, and heat the latter in a water

bath at 60 °C for 45 minutes. During this period the flask should be removed from the water bath from time to time and vigorously shaken.
After this heating period, pour the contents of the flask into a large excess of cold water (about 300 cm^3), and stir the mixture vigorously. Decant off as much of the upper aqueous layer as possible, and transfer the residue to a separating funnel. Run off the lower nitrobenzene layer into a beaker, and reject the aqueous layer. Then wash the nitrobenzene successively first with an equal volume of cold water and then with dilute sodium carbonate solution.
Transfer the nitrobenzene to a small flask, add some granular calcium chloride, and leave until the liquid is quite clear. Filter the nitrobenzene into a small, dry flask, and distil, collecting the fraction which boils between 207 °C and 211 °C.

(Adapted from Mann F.G. & Saunders, B.C., *practical Organic Chemistry*, 4th edn: Longman, 1960.)

a Suggest reasons for each of the following:

i the use of a mixture of concentrated nitric and sulphuric acids; [2]

ii the slow addition of the benzene to the nitrating mixture; [1]

iii the need to keep the temperature below 40 °C during the addition; [1]

iv the need to keep the reaction temperature at 60 °C; [1]

v the necessity to shake the mixture from time to time; [2]

vi the addition of the reaction mixture to an excess of cold water. [1]

vii the need to wash with water and then with sodium carbonate solution. [1]

viii the distillation between 207 °C and 211 °C. [1]

b Nitrobenzene can be nitrated further to give 1,3-dinitrobenzene:

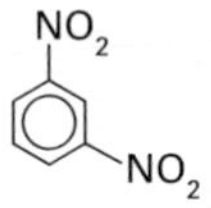

NO_2 / NO_2

By analogy with the reduction of nitrobenzene to phenylamine, suggest reagents and conditions by which 1,3-dinitrobenzene can be converted to 1,3-diaminobenzene. [3]

c Nomex is a du Pont fibre, used for flame-retardant clothing, which can resist temperatures of 1000 °C for 12 seconds, enough to have enabled the Benetton Formula 1 team to have survived a serious fire during the 1994 Grand Prix season. Nomex is a polymer which could in principle be made from 1,3-diaminobenzene and benzene-1,3-dicarboxylic acid:

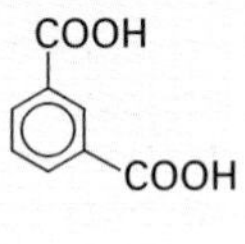

NH_2 / NH_2 COOH / COOH

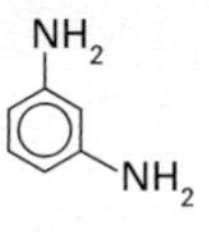

i Draw a representative length of the Nomex polymer chain. [2]

ii What type of polymer is Nomex? [1]

iii Dicarboxylic acids are not usually used in making this type of polymer. They are generally made from acid chlorides. Suggest why this is so. [2]

iv Suggest how benzene-1,3-dicarboxylic acid could be converted to its diacid chloride, and draw its structure. [2]

EDEXCEL 1998

4 a Under different reaction conditions, methylbenzene reacts with chlorine by different reaction mechanisms. One product of each reaction is shown in the figure below.

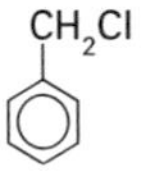

CH_2Cl CH_3 / Cl

(chloromethyl)benzene 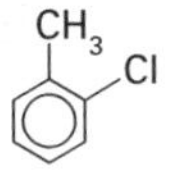   2–chloromethylbenzene

In each reaction other organic products are also formed.

i For the reaction leading to the formation of (chloromethyl)benzene give:

the reaction conditions;

the formula of another organic product of the reaction. [2]

ii For the reaction leading to the formation of 2-chloromethylbenzene give:

the reaction conditions;

the formula of another organic product which is isomeric with 2-chloromethylbenzene. [2]

b The reaction giving (chloromethyl)benzene as a product is a free radical substitution. Write equations to show the following steps in the reaction mechanism:

i the initiation step; [1]

ii two propagation steps; [2]

iii two termination steps. [2]

c Give the name of the type of mechanism involved in the reaction which gives 2-chloromethylbenzene as a product. [1]

d When the compound with the formula shown in the figure below reacts with aqueous sodium hydroxide, one of the chlorine atoms is replaced.

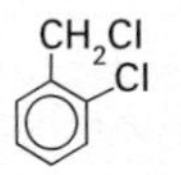

CH_2Cl / Cl

i Draw the structure of the product of the reaction. [1]

ii Explain the difference in the reactivities of the two chlorine atoms. [4]

AQA (AEB) 1997

24 Organic halogeno compounds

There are two main reasons for making an organic compound: it may be useful in its own right, or it may be a route to some other molecule. Halogeno compounds consist of a halogen atom attached to a carbon skeleton. Their immediate uses are restricted because some are toxic and have damaging effects on the environment. However, they are extremely useful as intermediates for making other types of molecule. The carbon–halogen bond is polar and polarizable, and so reagents may attack it in order to substitute other functional groups. Inserting a halogen into a carbon skeleton often represents the first stage in a multi-step synthetic pathway.

POLAR CARBON–HALOGEN BONDS

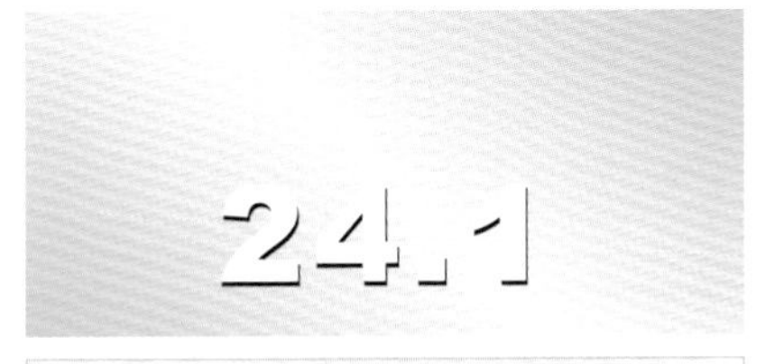

OBJECTIVES

- Chloro-, bromo-, and iodoalkanes
- Preparation outlines
- Halogenoalkanes react by nucleophilic substitution
- Halogenoalkanes and halogenoarenes

(a)

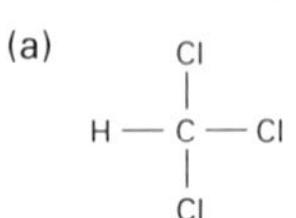

(b) (c)

(d) (e)

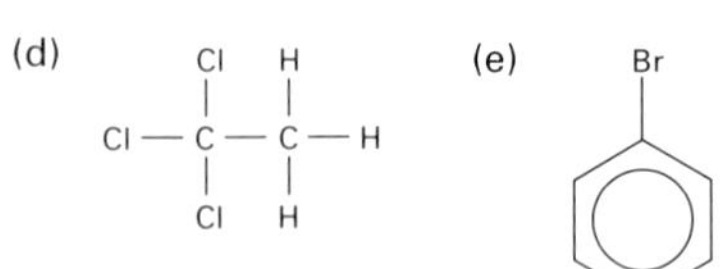

Structural formulae of some halogeno compounds: (a) trichloromethane; (b) 1-bromobutane; (c) 2-chloropropane; (d) 1,1,1-trichloroethane; and (e) bromobenzene.

Electronegativities: a reminder

Atom	Electronegativity
C	2.5
H	2.2
Cl	3.2
Br	3.0
I	2.7

The halogeno compounds of most interest are the chlorides, bromides, and iodides. Halogen atoms may be attached to alkyl, alicyclic, or aryl carbon skeletons. As you might expect, the alkyl halides and alicyclic halides have similar properties, which are distinctly different from those of the aryl halides (see previous chapter). This introductory spread is concerned with naming the various types of organic halides, revising the reactions by which they are prepared, and outlining the main type of reaction that halogenoalkanes undergo.

Naming halogeno compounds

The names of **halogenoalkanes** (also called **haloalkanes**) result from prefixing the name of the parent alkane with chloro-, bromo-, or iodo-, and indicating, where necessary, the number of the carbon atom to which the halogen is attached. The number of halogens in each molecule is indicated by the prefix di-, tri-, etc. The products of the reaction between chlorine and methane (see chapter on 'Alkanes and alkenes') contain only one carbon atom, so their names are chloromethane (CH_3Cl), dichloromethane (CH_2Cl_2), trichloromethane ($CHCl_3$), and tetrachloromethane (CCl_4). In a similar manner, the names of halogenoarenes result from adding the appropriate halogeno prefix to the name of the arene, e.g. bromobenzene.

Bond polarity and polarizability

Halogens are electronegative atoms. Attaching a halogen atom to a carbon atom creates a polar covalent bond. Therefore, the carbon–halogen bond provides a δ+ carbon atom for attack by nucleophiles. Furthermore, carbon–halogen bonds, especially C—I bonds, are polarizable by approaching nucleophiles. For this reason, introducing halogen atoms is a useful way of starting the synthesis of complex substances from the hydrocarbons obtained from refining and cracking crude oil.

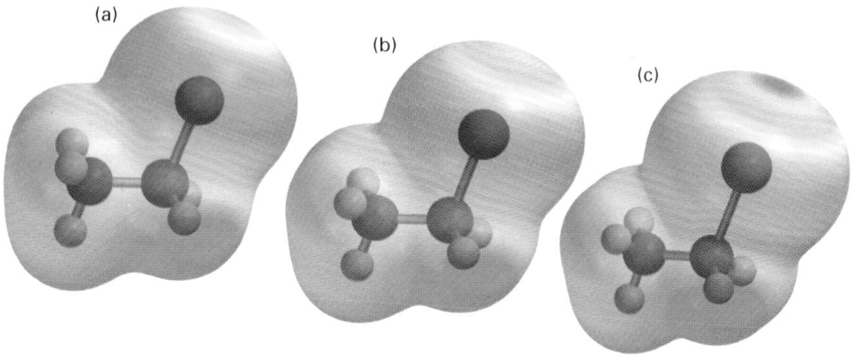

Electrostatic potential maps of the halogenoethanes. Note that the atomic radii are: Cl, 0.099 nm; Br, 0.114 nm; I, 0.133 nm. (a) The C—Cl bond (length 0.177 nm). (b) The C—Br bond (length 0.193 nm). (c) The C—I bond (length 0.214 nm).

Making halogenoalkanes

There are three main methods of attaching halogen atoms (X) to a carbon skeleton, as described in earlier chapters:

- Radical substitution of an alkane

  $CH_3CH_3 + Cl_2 \xrightarrow{UV} CH_3CH_2Cl + HCl$
  (and all other possible products up to CCl_3CCl_3)

- Electrophilic addition of HX or X_2 to an alkene

  $CH_2{=}CH_2 + HBr \rightarrow CH_3CH_2Br$
  $CH_2{=}CH_2 + Br_2 \rightarrow BrCH_2CH_2Br$

Reaction by nucleophilic substitution

The carbon–halogen bond in halogenoalkanes usually reacts by *nucleophilic substitution*. Nucleophiles are electron-pair donors and are attracted to the δ+ carbon atom of the carbon–halogen bond. Furthermore, the approaching nucleophile repels electron density towards the polarizable halogen atom, thus *inducing* a larger dipole in the bond. The carbon–halogen bond eventually breaks and the incoming nucleophile takes its place.

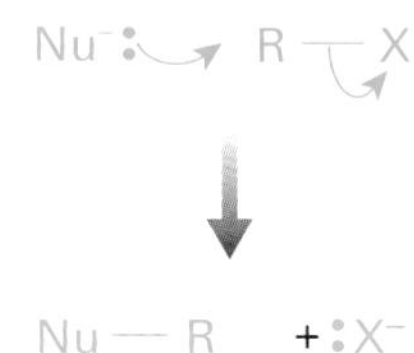

The approach and attack of a nucleophile on a halogenoalkane, causing a substitution reaction.

Reaction rates: halogenoarenes and halogenoalkanes

In halogenoarenes, a lone pair of the halogen atom is delocalized with the aromatic ring. This strengthens the carbon–halogen bond and makes it much harder to break: the C—X bond enthalpy is larger for a halogenoarene than for the corresponding halogenoalkane. (Note that the aryl C—Cl bond length is 0.169 nm compared with the alkyl C—Cl bond length of 0.177 nm.) For this reason, the chlorine atom in chlorobenzene C_6H_5Cl is *not* substituted by aqueous sodium hydroxide to give phenol C_6H_5OH, whereas chloroethane CH_3CH_2Cl forms ethanol CH_3CH_2OH. We shall therefore now concentrate on halogenoalkanes.

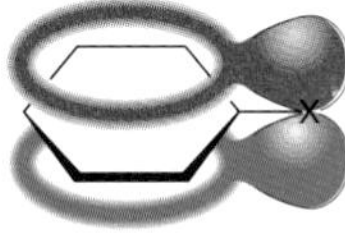

Lone pair from the halogen atom feeds into the delocalized π cloud. The electronegative halogen atom withdraws electron density from the delocalized π cloud strengthening the C—X bond.

SUMMARY

- Attaching a halogen to an alkane provides a means of substituting other functional groups.
- The carbon–halogen bond reacts because it is polarized and polarizable.
- The carbon–halogen bonds decrease in strength (and so increase in reactivity) in the order Cl > Br > I and increase in length in the order Cl < Br < I.
- Halogenoarenes are generally very much less reactive than halogenoalkanes.
- Halogenoalkanes react by nucleophilic attack on the carbon atom of the carbon–halogen bond.

PRACTICE

1 Draw structural formulae for the following substances:
   - a Chloroethane
   - b Bromobutane
   - c 2-Bromopropane
   - d 2-Iodobutane
   - e 2,2-Dichloropropane
   - f 1,4-Dibromobenzene.

2 a Describe the relationship between the length of a bond and its strength.
   b Compare the C—Cl bond lengths in chlorobenzene and chloroethane.
   c Use your answers to (a) and (b) and any other information to explain why chlorobenzene is much less reactive than chloroethane.

3 With reference to carbon–halogen bond strengths (see next spread), suggest an order of reactivity for the halogenoalkanes: chloroethane, bromoethane, and iodoethane.

4 Write a balanced equation for the reaction between chloroethane and aqueous sodium hydroxide. Identify the attacking nucleophile and the atom on the chloroethane molecule that it attacks.

24.2

Reactions with hydroxide, cyanide, and ammonia

OBJECTIVES

- Hydroxide ion as a nucleophile
- Cyanide ion as a nucleophile
- Ammonia as a nucleophile
- Relative reaction rates Cl/Br/I
- Primary, secondary, and tertiary halogenoalkanes

Heating a reaction mixture in a flask with a vertical condenser is called 'heating under reflux' or 'refluxing'. Organic reactions are often slow and reactants may need heating together for several hours. The reflux condenser ensures that volatile substances are not lost during prolonged boiling; rising vapours condense and fall back into the flask.

Water

Water H_2O is a weaker nucleophile than hydroxide ion OH^-, but water can hydrolyse halogenoalkanes to the same products as aqueous hydroxide ion:

$CH_3CH_2Br(aq) + H_2O(l) \rightarrow CH_3CH_2OH(aq) + Br^-(aq) + H^+(aq)$

However, the rate of reaction is very much slower.

Bond strengths

Bond	Average bond enthalpy/kJ mol^{-1}
C—C	348
C—H	413
C—F	484
C—Cl	338
C—Br	276
C—I	238

The strength of the C—F bond results in the fluoroalkanes being unreactive. They are of little use in organic synthesis compared with other halogenoalkanes.

The major reason for introducing a halogen, and therefore bond polarity, into an organic molecule is to make nucleophilic substitution reactions possible. The carbon–fluorine bond is very strong and therefore difficult to break. However, nucleophilic substitution readily converts chloro-, bromo-, and iodoalkanes into other useful molecules. A nucleophile is attracted to the δ+ carbon atom bonded to the halogen. Typical attacking nucleophiles are hydroxide ion OH^-, cyanide ion CN^-, and ammonia NH_3. The result in all cases is the removal of a halide ion and its substitution by the incoming nucleophile. These reactions are easy to carry out and give a good yield of a relatively pure product.

Hydroxide ion as a nucleophile

- Reaction of a halogenoalkane RX with hydroxide ion OH^- produces an *alcohol* ROH, thus replacing a halogen atom with an *oxygen* atom:

$$CH_3CH_2Br(aq) + OH^-(aq) \rightarrow CH_3CH_2OH(aq) + Br^-(aq)$$

This reaction is described as **hydrolysis**. It is carried out by refluxing the halogenoalkane with dilute aqueous potassium (or sodium) hydroxide. After the hydrolysis is complete, the alcohol may be isolated by fractional distillation of the reaction mixture.

Cyanide ion as a nucleophile

- Reaction of a halogenoalkane RX with cyanide ion CN^- produces a *nitrile* RCN, thus adding a *carbon* atom to the carbon skeleton:

$$CH_3CH_2Br + CN^- \rightarrow CH_3CH_2CN + Br^-$$

The halogenoalkane is heated under reflux with potassium cyanide dissolved in ethanol. This reaction is very useful in synthesis. The cyanide (nitrile) group converts readily to other useful functional groups, especially the —COOH group (see later chapter on 'Organic synthesis reactions').

Ammonia as a nucleophile

- Reaction of a halogenoalkane RX with ammonia NH_3 produces an *amine* RNH_2, thus replacing a halogen atom with a *nitrogen* atom:

$$CH_3CH_2Br + NH_3 \rightarrow CH_3CH_2NH_3^+ + Br^-$$

The halogenoalkane is usually heated with an excess of ammonia dissolved in ethanol. Adding base then liberates the amine:

$$CH_3CH_2NH_3^+ + OH^- \rightarrow CH_3CH_2NH_2 + H_2O$$

But the amine produced is also a nucleophile, and so will attack and further substitute the halogenoalkane:

$$CH_3CH_2Br + CH_3CH_2NH_2 \xrightarrow{OH^-} (CH_3CH_2)_2NH + H_2O + Br^-$$

The reaction of ammonia with a halogenoalkane has a low yield, and the mixture of products obtained because of the further substitution results in this reaction being little used.

Halogen and rate of reaction

The rate of nucleophilic substitution depends on which halogen is present. Carbon–halogen bonds have different strengths, as seen in the box alongside. The C—Cl bond is stronger than the C—Br bond, which is stronger than the C—I bond. It is the carbon–halogen bond that breaks during a nucleophilic substitution reaction. As a result, iodoalkanes substitute faster than bromoalkanes, and bromoalkanes substitute faster than chloroalkanes.

Hydrolysing halogenoalkanes and then adding acidified silver nitrate shows how the rate of reaction varies with the halogen. Covalently bonded halogenoalkanes do not react with Ag^+. However, hydrolysis of the halogenoalkane releases halide ions into solution, as described above. The halide ions immediately precipitate out as insoluble silver halide:

$$RX(aq) + OH^-(aq) \rightarrow ROH(aq) + X^-(aq)$$
$$Ag^+(aq) + X^-(aq) \rightarrow AgX(s)$$

When the three halogenoethanes CH_3CH_2Cl, CH_3CH_2Br, and CH_3CH_2I react with silver nitrate in ethanol solution, the yellow colour of silver iodide forms faster than the cream colour of silver bromide, which itself forms faster than the white colour of silver chloride.

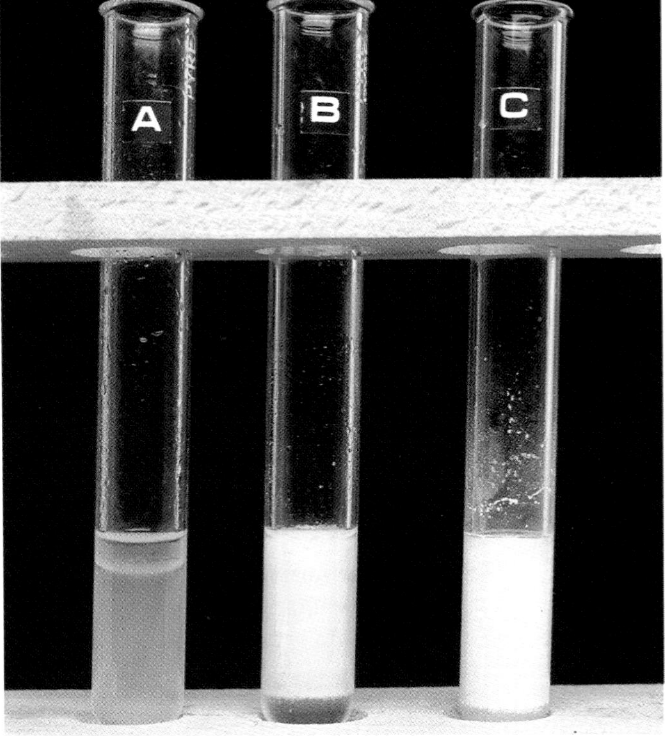

(a) CH_3CH_2Cl: faintest of white precipitates.
(b) CH_3CH_2Br: significant cream precipitate.
(c) CH_3CH_2I: distinct yellow precipitate.

Grignard reaction

Halogenoalkanes also undergo one other very important reaction, the Grignard reaction (see spread 29.2).

(a) CH_3-CH_2-Br (H, C, H)

Bromoethane,
a primary halogenoalkane

(b) $CH_3-CH(CH_3)-Br$

2-bromopropane,
a secondary halogenoalkane

(c) $CH_3-C(CH_3)_2-Br$

2-bromo-2-methylpropane,
a tertiary halogenoalkane

The relative reaction rates also depend on the structure of the halogenoalkane, as explained in the next spread.

SUMMARY

- The halogen of a halogenoalkane may be substituted by an attacking nucleophile.
- Hydroxide ion hydrolyses halogenoalkanes to alcohols.
- Halogenoalkanes show varying rates of hydrolysis in the order RI > RBr > RCl.
- Cyanide ion adds a carbon atom to form a nitrile RCN.
- Ammonia forms amines RNH_2; but further substitution occurs and the reaction is of little use.

PRACTICE

1 Write structural formulae to show the reaction between each of the following:

a Bromoethane and hydroxide ion
b Chloroethane and cyanide ion
c Iodoethane and water.

2 Heating iodoethane with aqueous ammonia in a sealed tube forms ethylamine $CH_3CH_2NH_2$. The reaction effectively substitutes an ethyl group for a hydrogen atom on the ammonia molecule. Further products form as ethylamine reacts with iodoethane. Give the structural formulae of two further products.

3 Halogenoalkanes are almost insoluble in water, but they dissolve readily in ethanol. Explain why ethanol is added to the mixture of aqueous silver ion and halogenoalkane described in the illustration above.

24.3

Rates and reaction mechanisms

OBJECTIVES

- The S_N2 mechanism
- The S_N1 mechanism

Hydroxide ions hydrolyse halogenoalkanes to alcohols. The previous spread showed that the reaction rates for halogenoalkanes increase in the sequence chloride < bromide < iodide. The reaction rate also depends on the detailed structure of the halogenoalkane. This spread considers the *order* of each reaction (see chapter on 'Chemical kinetics'), and then goes on to explain these orders in terms of the different reaction mechanisms involved.

Primary and tertiary halogenoalkane hydrolysis

Halogenoalkanes are classified depending on the number of alkyl groups attached to the carbon atom bonded to the halogen (see previous spread):

- **primary** if there is *one* alkyl group
- **secondary** if there are *two* alkyl groups
- **tertiary** if there are *three* alkyl groups

Bromobutane is a primary halogenoalkane, and 2-bromo-2-methylpropane is a tertiary halogenoalkane. Both have the molecular formula C_4H_9Br; each is hydrolysed by hydroxide ion to the corresponding alcohol. Investigating the chemical kinetics of these hydrolysis reactions reveals the following information:

- Bromobutane hydrolysis is *first* order with respect to bromobutane and *first* order with respect to hydroxide ion.
- 2-Bromo-2-methylpropane hydrolysis is *first* order with respect to 2-bromo-2-methylpropane and *zero* order with respect to hydroxide ion.

These data indicate that the two reactions proceed by different reaction mechanisms.

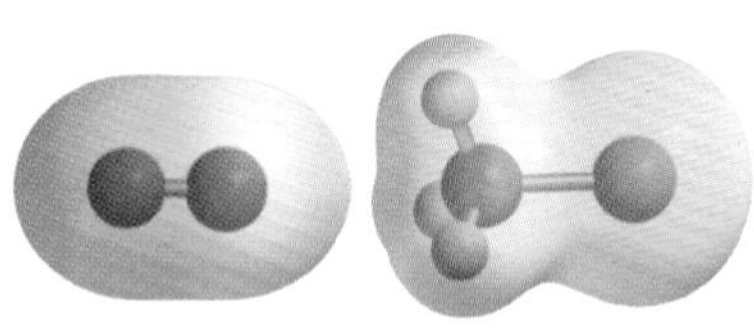
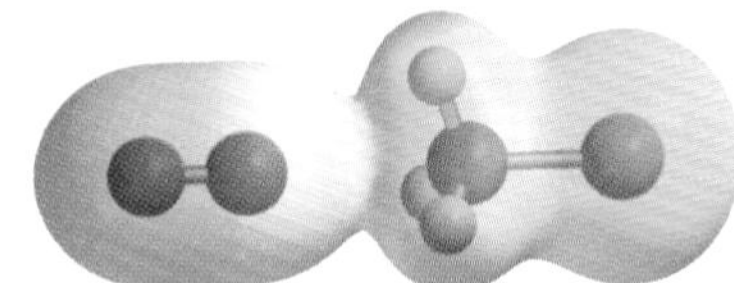
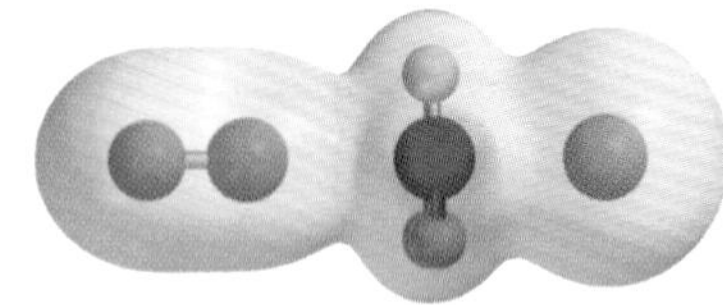
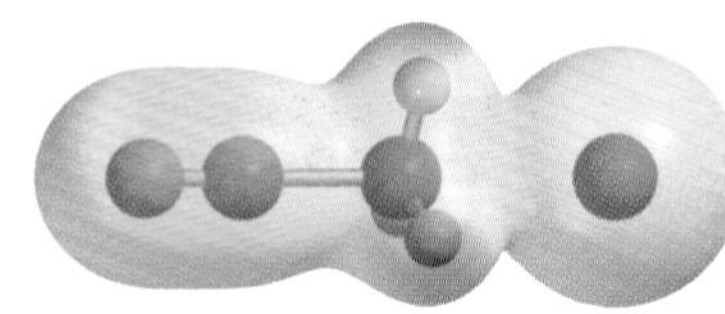
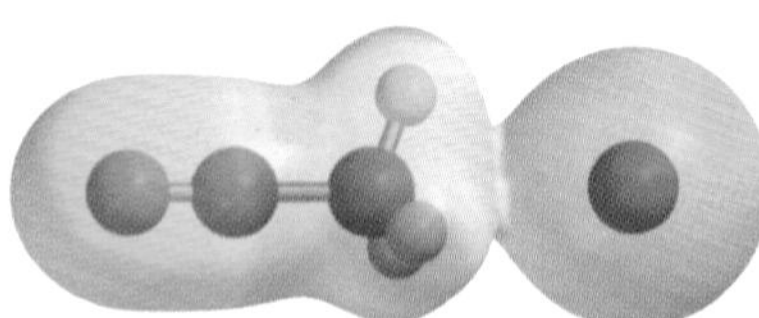

Five stages in the S_N2 reaction between cyanide ion and a halogenoalkane.

S_N2 inversion

The tetrahedral arrangement of the molecule around the δ+ carbon atom has flipped, like an umbrella turning inside out. This is called **Walden inversion**. Its experimental observation confirms that the molecule is attacked from the opposite side to the halogen.

Bromoethane and the S_N2 reaction mechanism

For a *primary* halogenoalkane reacting with dilute aqueous sodium hydroxide, the kinetics shows that the reaction is second order overall. The rate depends on the concentrations of *both* the halogenoalkane *and* the hydroxide ion (the nucleophile):

$$\text{rate} = k[\text{RX}][\text{OH}^-]$$

This shows that both the halogenoalkane and the OH^- ion must be involved in the rate-limiting step (see chapter on 'Chemical kinetics'). The following mechanism fits the observed kinetics.

The OH^- ion is attracted to the δ+ carbon atom of the C—X bond. It approaches the molecule from the opposite side to the halogen, where its attack is not impeded by the bulky halogen with its δ– charge.

A transition state forms in which the halogen atom and the oxygen atom are both *partially* bonded to the carbon atom. Note that the transition state involves a p orbital on the carbon atom attached to the halogen, and so forces a 'reverse-side' attack by the incoming nucleophile.

The halide ion leaves the transition state and the product is formed.

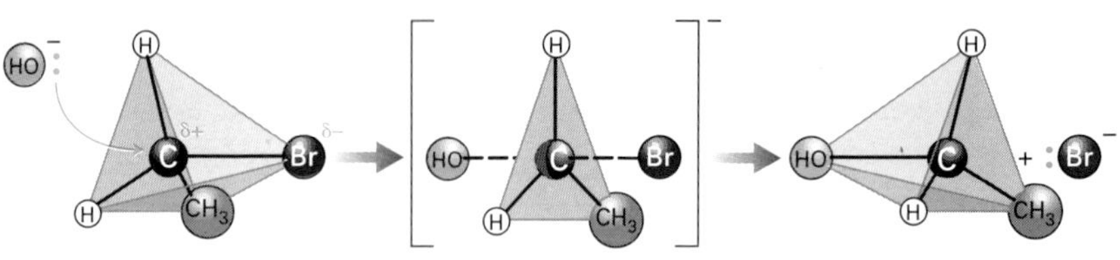

The mechanism of the S_N2 reaction of hydroxide ion with bromoethane.

Primary halogenoalkanes are said to react by an $\mathbf{S_N2}$ mechanism – S for substitution, N for nucleophilic, 2 for bimolecular. (The term 'bimolecular' means that there are two species involved in the rate-limiting step.) According to this mechanism, bond breaking and bond making happen *simultaneously*.

2-Bromo-2-methylpropane and the S_N1 reaction mechanism

For a *tertiary* halogenoalkane reacting with dilute aqueous sodium hydroxide, the kinetics are different: the reaction is *first order* overall. The rate depends *only* on the concentration of the halogenoalkane:

$$\text{rate} = k[\text{RX}]$$

The concentration of the hydroxide ion does not have any effect on the rate of reaction, indicating that the OH^- ion is not involved in the rate-limiting step. The mechanism is discussed below.

Comparing the structure of a primary and a tertiary halogenoalkane shows that the reaction mechanisms are likely to be different. The δ+ carbon atom in a tertiary halogenoalkane is surrounded by large alkyl groups, which obstruct the attack of the nucleophile. This effect is called **steric hindrance**. The hydrolysis of a tertiary halogenoalkane proceeds by the following steps.

Step 1 In the course of random collisions, the halide ion ionizes by heterolytic fission. The result of this rate-limiting step is a carbocation and a halide ion:

$$(CH_3)_3C\text{—}Br \rightarrow (CH_3)_3C^+ + Br^-$$

Step 2 The carbocation attracts a hydroxide ion OH^- and bonds to it, forming the product. This step happens much faster than step 1, so the overall rate does not depend on the hydroxide ion concentration. Notice also that the S_N1 mechanism does not necessarily involve an inversion because an OH^- ion can attack from either side of the *planar* carbocation.

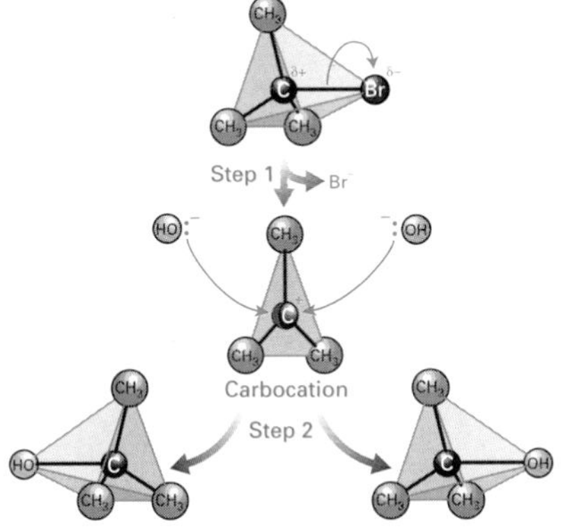

The mechanism of the S_N1 reaction.

The electrostatic potential map for the carbocation $(CH_3)_3C^+$.

Tertiary halogenoalkanes are said to react by an $\mathbf{S_N1}$ mechanism – S for substitution, N for nucleophilic, 1 for unimolecular. According to this mechanism, bond making happens *after* bond breaking.

SUMMARY

- Primary, secondary, and tertiary halogenoalkanes have respectively one, two, and three alkyl groups on the carbon atom bonded to the halogen.
- Primary halogenoalkanes substitute by the S_N2 reaction mechanism. The C—X bond breaks as the bond with the incoming nucleophile forms.
- Tertiary halogenoalkanes substitute by the S_N1 reaction mechanism. The C—X bond breaks before any reaction with the incoming nucleophile occurs. The reaction proceeds via a carbocation.

Intermediate carbocations

The intermediate tertiary carbocation is particularly stable due to the electron-donating effect of the *three* alkyl groups attached to the positive carbon atom (see chapter on 'Alkanes and alkenes'). The hydrolysis of a primary halogenoalkane does not follow this mechanism because the primary carbocation is far less stable, having just one alkyl group attached to the positive carbon atom.

Leaving groups

The reaction rate in nucleophilic substitution reactions depends to a certain extent on the nature of the leaving group. The **leaving group** is the species that becomes displaced from the carbon atom and leaves the molecule. In the example alongside, bromide ion is the leaving group.

Secondary halogenoalkanes

Kinetic data are more complicated in the case of secondary halogenoalkanes because the S_N1 and S_N2 mechanisms are approximately equally likely.

24.4

Elimination reactions and uses of halogeno compounds

OBJECTIVES

- Elimination vs. substitution
- Direct uses and drawbacks
- The ozone layer
- Alternatives

Halogeno compounds are extremely useful as *intermediates* in the synthesis of more complex molecules. The carbon–halogen bond can be substituted; halogenoalkanes can also eliminate, as discussed below. Halogeno compounds also have many direct uses. They are relatively straightforward to produce industrially, and may be used as anaesthetics, aerosol propellants, foaming agents, refrigerants, insecticides, herbicides and fire extinguishers. However, we now know that some of them cause thinning of the ozone layer, thus endangering all life on Earth.

Elimination reactions

We shall now compare substitution and elimination reactions. As we have seen, dilute aqueous potassium (or sodium) hydroxide will *substitute* hydroxide ion for the halide ion:

$$CH_3CH_2Br + OH^- \xrightarrow[\text{dilute}]{\text{(aq)}} CH_3CH_2OH + Br^-$$

However, hot concentrated sodium hydroxide in ethanol ('alcoholic sodium hydroxide') will *eliminate* hydrogen bromide, leaving an alkene:

$$(CH_3)_3CBr + OH^- \xrightarrow[\text{hot concentrated}]{\text{(ethanol)}} (CH_3)_2C{=}CH_2 + H_2O + Br^-$$

In the substitution reaction, the hydroxide ion acts as a nucleophile and attacks the δ+ carbon atom. In the elimination reaction, the hydroxide ion acts as a *base* and removes a hydrogen ion. To some extent, substitution and elimination are always in competition because the attacking reagent OH^- is both a nucleophile and a base. In general:

- Substitution is fastest with primary halogenoalkanes.
- Elimination is fastest with tertiary halogenoalkanes.

Anaesthetics

In 1956 a team at ICI developed 'Halothane', $CF_3CHBrCl$. It was the first effective and non-explosive general anaesthetic. Currently, the two most common general anaesthetics are Isoflurane $CF_3CHClOCHF_2$ and Sevoflurane $(CF_3)_2CHOCH_2F$, which, like Halothane, contain the trifluoromethyl group.

BCF

Bromochlorodifluoromethane ('BCF') $CBrClF_2$ makes a good fire extinguisher, blanketing a fire in a dense, non-flammable, oxygen-excluding vapour. Combustion is a radical reaction. At high temperatures BCF molecules produce bromine radicals, which combine with the radicals present in the flame and inhibit the combustion process.

Solvents

Simple chloroalkanes are very good solvents. Some, such as 1,1,1-trichloroethane CCl_3CH_3 and tetrachloromethane CCl_4, were once familiar 'organic' solvents used to dissolve non-polar solutes. (They are now mostly considered too toxic for common use.) They dissolve grease well and were used for 'dry' cleaning.

CFCs and ozone layer depletion

Compounds in which some or all of the hydrogen atoms of an alkane have been replaced by chlorine or fluorine are called **chlorofluorocarbons**, abbreviated to **CFCs**. CFCs are even less reactive than alkanes because the C—F bond is extremely strong, spread 24.2. They are also non-toxic, volatile liquids which do not easily catch fire. These properties made them very useful as aerosol propellants, refrigerants, and as 'blowing agents' for making expanded ('foamed') plastics such as those used in heat-insulating packaging. CFCs (and BCF) have one very unfortunate property. When released during use, they diffuse unchanged into the upper atmosphere. Under the influence of intense ultraviolet radiation in the **stratosphere** (altitude of 11–50 km; the layer below 11 km is called the **troposphere**), they decompose to form radicals. These radicals react

Substitute or eliminate?

2-Bromopropane $CH_3CHBrCH_3$ can react with potassium hydroxide by *substitution* to give $CH_3CH(OH)CH_3$ or by *elimination* of HBr to give $CH_3CH{=}CH_2$. The actual outcome depends on the reaction conditions chosen.

The carbocation $(CH_3)_3C^+$ formed during the S_N1 mechanism (see previous spread) may lose a proton instead of reacting with a nucleophile. The result is an elimination reaction: Br^- is lost in the first step and H^+ in the second.

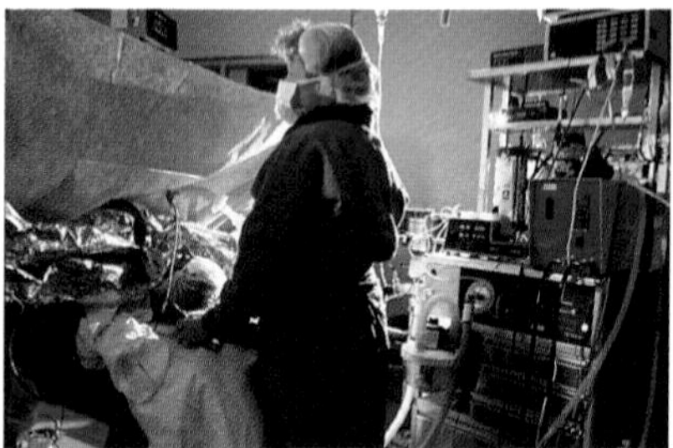

Sevoflurane is a very effective general anaesthetic.

Health and safety

Some halogenoalkanes such as tetrachloromethane CCl_4 are toxic. They are no longer permitted for use as solvents at all. Legislation to control substances hazardous to health (in the UK these are called the 'COSHH Regulations') requires companies to seek safer alternative solvents.

The international agreement for environmental protection called the 'Montreal Protocol' (1996) effectively banned the use of chlorinated solvents in industrialized countries. The new generation of replacement solvents are based on cyclic siloxanes.

with the ozone formed at this altitude and break it down, producing the 'hole in the ozone layer' (see spread 19.10). As ozone shields the surface of the Earth from harmful ultraviolet radiation, its depletion is causing ultraviolet levels at the Earth's surface to increase. The average depletion at the latitude of London is about 0.35% per year.

The main culprit is the chlorine radical $Cl^{\bullet}$. The carbon–chlorine bond is the weakest in the molecule, so it is the easiest to break. The depletion of the ozone occurs by reaction of the chlorine radical with ozone:

$$Cl^{\bullet} + O_3 \rightarrow ClO^{\bullet} + O_2$$

Furthermore, by initiating a *chain* reaction, one chlorine radical can destroy thousands of ozone molecules. Searches for replacements have focused on molecules that do not contain chlorine. Useful, but more expensive, alternatives are **hydrofluorocarbons** (HFCs) such as CH_2FCF_3. Manufacture started in 1990 and increased 10-fold over the next two years. HFCs produce almost zero ozone depletion, and are non-toxic and non-flammable.

F. Sherwood Rowland (left) predicted that the ozone layer would be depleted by the use of CFCs before the problem was first detected. Here he is receiving the Nobel prize from the King of Sweden.

The rise and fall of DDT

The insecticide DDT is a complex halogenoarene and an extremely effective insecticide. Developed in 1939, it acts as a nerve poison, which causes convulsions, paralysis, and death of insects. Furthermore, no documented human death has been attributed to DDT. Malaria, typhus, and sleeping sickness are diseases that have long been established in Africa and in Southern Europe. These diseases are caused by parasites spread by biting insects. The death toll in Italy from malaria was 400 000 in 1945. By using DDT to kill the mosquitoes that carry the parasites, this figure was brought down to 40 in 1968. The World Health Organization suggests that five million human lives were saved in the first eight years of the use of DDT; one billion people (a sixth of the Earth's population) have had their lives improved. However, DDT is so unreactive that it passes unchanged along food chains. As a consequence, there is now a world-wide ban on the use of DDT.

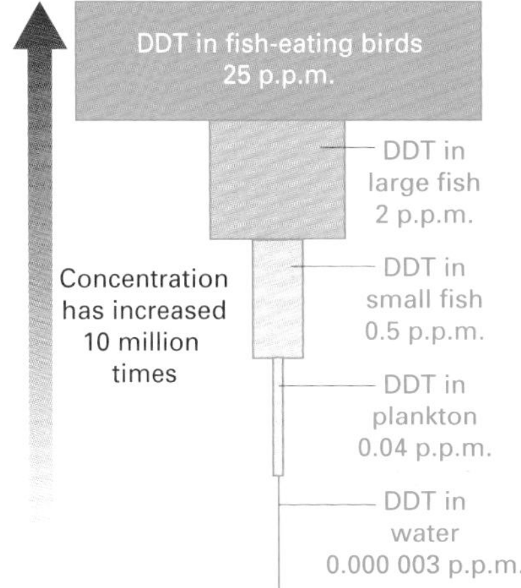

Because DDT is very unreactive, it remains unchanged in the bodies of organisms. Organisms high up in the food chain accumulate high concentrations of DDT and suffer toxic effects.

SUMMARY

- Halogenoalkanes undergo elimination to form alkenes when heated with a concentrated solution of hydroxide ions in alcohol.
- Halogenoalkanes are used as solvents, anaesthetics, and fire extinguishers.

PRACTICE

1 Explain why the chemical properties of hydrofluorocarbons such as CH_2FCF_3 lead to them being described as 'ozone-friendly'.

2 Ultraviolet radiation increases the incidence of skin cancers (especially in pale-skinned people) and causes cataracts to form in unprotected eyes. Suggest why developing countries wish the industrialized countries to phase out CFCs before they do so themselves.

Chapter 24 Reactions summary

- Radical substitution of an alkane:
  $CH_3CH_3 + Cl_2 \xrightarrow{UV} CH_3CH_2Cl + HCl$
  and all other possible products up to CCl_3CCl_3.
- Electrophilic addition of HX or X_2 to an alkene:
  $CH_2{=}CH_2 + HBr \rightarrow CH_3CH_2Br$
  $CH_2{=}CH_2 + Br_2 \rightarrow BrCH_2CH_2Br$
- Reaction with hydroxide ion to give an alcohol:
  $CH_3CH_2Br + OH^- \rightarrow CH_3CH_2OH + Br^-$
- Reaction with cyanide ion to give a nitrile:
  $CH_3CH_2Br + CN^- \rightarrow CH_3CH_2CN + Br^-$
- Reaction with ammonia to give an amine (after neutralization):
  $CH_3CH_2Br + NH_3 \rightarrow CH_3CH_2NH_3^+ + Br^-$
  $CH_3CH_2NH_3^+ + OH^- \rightarrow CH_3CH_2NH_2 + H_2O$
- Elimination to yield an alkene:
  $(CH_3)_3CBr \xrightarrow[\text{hot concentrated}]{OH^-\text{ (ethanol)}} (CH_3)_2C{=}CH_2 + H_2O + Br^-$
- The S_N2 mechanism (spread 24.3) should be noted.

PRACTICE EXAM QUESTIONS

1 **a** Explain what is meant by the term nucleophilic substitution. [2]

b Explain why 1-bromopropane reacts with nucleophiles but propane itself does not. [2]

c Write an equation and a mechanism for the reaction of 1-bromopropane with an excess of ammonia. [4]

d Give the starting materials and state the conditions for the preparation of CH_3CH_2CN by nucleophilic substitution. [3]
AQA (NEAB) 1995

2 **a** Give the structural formula of 2-bromo-3-methylbutane. [1]

b Write an equation for the reaction between 2-bromo-3-methylbutane and dilute aqueous sodium hydroxide. Name the type of reaction taking place and outline a mechanism. [4]

c Two isomeric alkenes are formed when 2-bromo-3-methylbutane reacts with ethanolic potassium hydroxide. Name the type of reaction occurring and state the role of the reagent. Give the structural formulae of the two alkenes. [4]
AQA (NEAB) 1995

3 Under appropriate reaction conditions, 2-bromo-3-methylbutane, $(CH_3)_2CHCHBrCH_3$, can be converted into an alcohol or into two isomeric alkenes.

a Name the type of reaction taking place and give the role of the reagent when 2-bromo-3-methylbutane reacts with **aqueous** potassium hydroxide. Give the structure of the alcohol and outline a mechanism for this reaction. [5]

b **i** Name the type of reaction taking place and give the role of the reagent when 2-bromo-3-methylbutane reacts with **ethanolic** potassium hydroxide.

ii One of the reaction products is 2-methylbut-2-ene. Outline a mechanism for the formation of this compound and give the structure of the second alkene which is also formed. [7]
AQA (NEAB) 1997

4 **a** There are four **structural** isomers of molecular formula C_4H_9Br. The formulae of two of these isomers are given.

```
    H   H   H   H                 H  CH3 H
    |   |   |   |                 |   |   |
H — C — C — C — C — H         H — C — C — C — H
    |   |   |   |                 |   |   |
    H   H   Br  H                 H   Br  H
```

Isomer 1 **Isomer 2**

i Draw the remaining two structural isomers. [2]

ii Give the name of **Isomer 2**. [1]

b All four structural isomers of C_4H_9Br undergo similar reactions with ammonia.

i Give the name of the mechanism involved in these reactions. [1]

ii Draw the structural formula of the product formed by the reaction of **Isomer 1** with ammonia. [1]

iii Select the isomer of molecular formula C_4H_9Br that would be the most reactive with ammonia. State the structural feature of your chosen isomer that makes it the most reactive of the four isomers. [2]

c The elimination of HBr from **Isomer 1** produces two structural isomers, compounds **A** and **B**.

i Give the reagent and conditions required for this elimination reaction. [3]

ii Give the structural formulae of the two isomers, **A** and **B**, formed by elimination of HBr from **Isomer 1**. [2]

d Ethene, C_2H_4, reacts with bromine to give 1,2-dibromoethane.

i Give the name of the mechanism involved. [1]

ii Show the mechanism for this reaction. [3]
AQA (NEAB) 1998

5 **a** Outline a mechanism for the reaction of 1-bromopropane with an excess of ammonia. [4]

b Explain how you could distinguish between samples of 1-bromopropane and 2-bromopropane using

i infrared spectroscopy

ii low-resolution proton NMR spectroscopy. [4]
AQA (NEAB) 1998 *(See also Chapter 31 and 32.)*

6 **a** **i** One product of the reaction of ethene with aqueous bromine in the presence of sodium chloride is 1,2-dibromoethane. Give the mechanism for the formation of 1,2-dibromoethane.

ii Give the structural formula of ONE other compound formed.

iii Explain mechanistically why the following compound is not formed.

```
     H   H
     |   |
Cl — C — C — Cl
     |   |
     H   H
```

[6]

b **i** Give a reagent, and the conditions under which it might be used, to convert 1,2-dibromoethane to ethane-1,2-diol.

ii How would the rate of this reaction differ if 1,2-diiodoethane was used instead of 1,2-dibromoethane at the same temperature?

Explain your answer. [4]
EDEXCEL 1996

7 **a** Myrcene has the molecular formula $C_{10}H_{16}$ (M_r = 136) and its structure is shown as **A** below. This compound is produced by pine trees in North America. Unfortunately, it attracts females of the beetle *Dendroctonus brevicomins*, which lays eggs in the tree. The drilling of the tree injects pathogenic fungus, causing the tree's death.

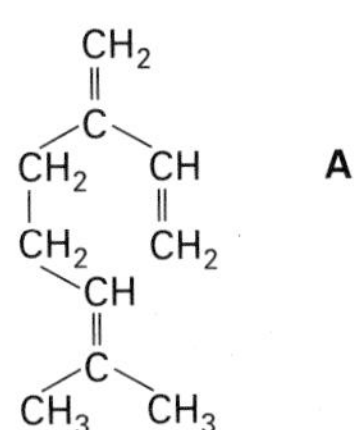

A

i State what you would see when bromine dissolved in an inert organic solvent is added to myrcene. [1]

ii A sample of Myrcene weighing 2.72 g is reacted with a 1.00 mol dm^{-3} solution of bromine; 60.0 cm^3 was required. Show that this is consistent with the structure of myrcene. [3]

b Myrcene reacts with hydrogen bromide to give **B**:

CH_3 Br
C
CH_2 HC—Br
CH_2 CH_3
CH_2
CH_3—C—Br
CH_3

B

The double bonds can be regenerated by an elimination reaction; one elimination product among many is **C**:

CH_3
C
CH CH
CH_2 CH_2
CH
C
CH_3 CH_3

C

i State the reagents and conditions required to form **C** from **B**. [2]

ii Explain why products other than Myrcene itself are produced in this elimination reaction. [2]

iii What type of isomerism is shown by the bromo compound **B** which is not shown by Myrcene itself? Give a reason. [2]
EDEXCEL 1998

8 **a** When 3-bromo-2-methylpentane, $(CH_3)_2CHCHBrCH_2CH_3$, reacts with aqueous potassium hydroxide, an alcohol is formed.

i Name the type of reaction taking place and give the role of the reagent.

ii Give the structure of the alcohol formed and outline a mechanism for its formation. [5]

b **i** Give the structural formula of the product obtained when the alcohol formed in part **a** is treated with acidified potassium dichromate(VI).

ii This product shows dominant peaks at *m/z* values of 57 and 71 in its mass spectrum. Give the structures of the species responsible for these two peaks.

Peak at *m/z* = 57.
Peak at *m/z* = 71. [3]

c When 3-bromo-2-methylpentane reacts with ethanoic potassium hydroxide, two isomeric alkenes are formed.

i Name the type of reaction taking place and give the role of the reagent.

ii One of the reaction products is 2-methylpent-2-ene. Give the structure of this alkene and outline a mechanism for its formation.

iii Give the structure of the second alkene which is also formed in this reaction. What type of stereoisomerism is shown by this compound? [8]
AQA (NEAB) 1999

9 **a** **i** Give the structure of 3-bromopentane.

ii Name and outline the mechanism for the reaction taking place when 3-bromopentane is converted into pent-2-ene in the presence of a strong base.

iii What type of stereoisomerism is shown by pent-2-ene? [7]

b **i** Give the structures of the two carbocation intermediates formed when pent-2-ene reacts with hydrogen bromide.

ii Name the two isomeric organic products which result from this reaction.

iii Indicate why these two products are obtained in approximately equal amounts. [5]
AQA (NEAB 1998)

25 Alcohols

There are two main categories of oxygen-containing organic compounds. In the first category, an oxygen atom has a *single* bond to two other atoms. The most familiar compounds of this kind are the **alcohols**, which contain the —OH group attached to an alkyl group. If the —OH group is directly attached to a benzene ring, the compounds are called **phenols**. If the oxygen atom is sandwiched between two alkyl groups to give an R—O—R′ type structure, the result is an **ether**. This chapter discusses the properties of all three of these classes of molecule, with the main emphasis on alcohols. In the second category of oxygen-containing compounds, an oxygen has a **double** bond to a carbon atom. In the following two chapters you will meet the **carbonyl group** ⊃C═O, present in **aldehydes** and **ketones**, and, at the highest level of oxidation, the **carboxylic acids** (that contain the —COOH group), and their derivatives.

An introduction to alcohols

OBJECTIVES

- Structure of alcohols
- Manufacture of ethanol
- Uses of alcohols

Carbonyl group symbol

Typographically we have used the symbol ⊃C═O, to represent the carbonyl group

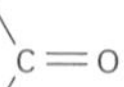

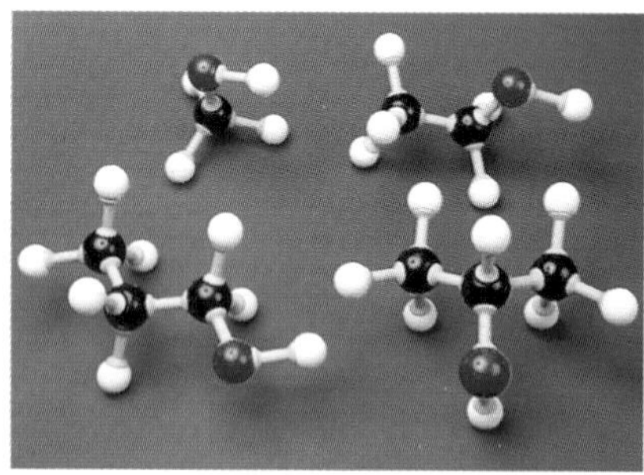

The structures of some alcohols: methanol, ethanol, and the two propanol isomers, propan-1-ol and propan-2-ol; see spread 21.4.

IR spectra

The presence of an —OH group in an alcohol can be detected by infrared spectroscopy, chapter 32.

Alcohols consist of a covalently bonded hydroxyl group —OH attached to a carbon skeleton. In the case of common aliphatic alcohols, the carbon skeleton is an alkyl group. While there are many different alcohols, the most widely used is ethanol CH_3CH_2OH. This substance is so well known that its everyday name is simply 'alcohol'.

The manufacture of ethanol

Two main processes are currently used to make ethanol. The process chosen depends on economic factors and on the end use of the product.

The first process is **fermentation**, which has been used for thousands of years to make ethanol. The illustration below shows an industrial-scale fermentation reaction in a modern brewery. The process uses a sugar such as sucrose (from sugar cane or sugar beet) or glucose (from the digestion of starch). In fermentation, the sugars are slowly decomposed by enzymes produced by organisms called yeasts. The process is **anaerobic** – it takes place in the absence of oxygen. For example, glucose is fermented by a series of enzymes to form ethanol and carbon dioxide:

$$C_6H_{12}O_6 \rightarrow 2CH_3CH_2OH + 2CO_2$$

When the concentration of ethanol reaches about 13%, the yeasts and their enzymes no longer function and fermentation stops. Distillation is used to achieve higher concentrations of ethanol in the end product.

Modern brewing takes place on an industrial scale. Most beers contain about 3–6% ethanol; distilled spirits contain about 40% ethanol. This fermentation vat is in Jamaica.

The second process used to produce ethanol is the **direct hydration of ethene**, which uses ethene as a chemical feedstock. Ethene is currently available in huge quantities from the cracking of crude oil (see chapter on 'Alkanes and alkenes'). Ethene and steam react together in the presence of a phosphoric acid catalyst. This catalyst is chosen because ethene is susceptible to attack by electrophiles; the hydrogen ion H^+, which is characteristic of all acids, is an electrophile. Phosphoric acid, H_3PO_4, is the second least volatile acid after sulphuric acid, and so it may be used at moderately high temperatures. The actual conditions are 300 °C and 70 atm pressure. The phosphoric acid catalyst is supported on a silica-based material called Celite. The overall reaction is represented by the following chemical equation:

$$CH_2{=}CH_2(g) + H_2O(g) \rightarrow CH_3CH_2OH(g)$$

Some uses of alcohols

- The lower alcohols – methanol, ethanol, and propanol – are mainly used as solvents. Ethanol is the major component in methylated spirits.
- Large quantities of methanol produced by the catalytic oxidation of methane are oxidized to methanal HCHO, which is used as a chemical feedstock to make so-called 'formaldehyde' resins such as melamine.
- Methanol is used as a petrol additive to improve combustion. It is also the current fuel in the motor racing series Champ Cars in the US.
- Ethanol has a wide range of applications, including the extraction of essences from fruits and spices, as a dispersant for dyes in lacquers, and as a solvent for fragrances in perfumes and after-shave lotions.
- Ethanol is the active constituent of alcoholic drinks. In humans, it suppresses inhibitions and thereby brings more enjoyment, and misery, to the world than all other drugs put together.
- Propan-2-ol is the solvent in ink-jet printer ink, many cosmetics, and certain food flavourings. It is also present in a wide range of cleaning fluids for items such as compact discs and the record/playback heads in tape machines.

SUMMARY

- Alcohols contain the hydroxyl group —OH bonded to an alkyl group.
- Ethanol is produced by (i) the fermentation of sugars by yeasts or (ii) the direct hydration of ethene.
- The lower alcohols are widely used as solvents.
- Methanol and propan-2-ol are raw materials for the plastics industry.

Fermentation and direct hydration of ethene compared

Direct hydration links the price of ethanol to the price of ethene which is linked to the price of crude oil. On the other hand, fermentation of sugars is seen as a means of using agricultural surplus; ethanol production by this means is subsidized by the EU, bringing the price down. Although the actual production cost of ethanol by direct hydration is less, the price is dependent on price stability in the oil markets. Environmentally, there is no waste from the catalytic hydration of ethene, but fermentation produces carbon dioxide, which contributes to the enhanced greenhouse effect.

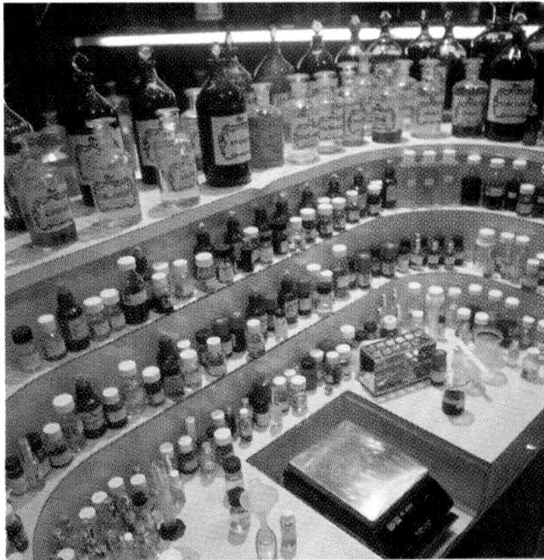

Perfumes frequently contain ethanol as solvent.

Biochemistry

The —OH group is present in many important molecules, including retinol, menthol, cholesterol, vitamin C, adrenaline, and the anabolic steroid stanozolol abused by Ben Johnson, the disqualified 'winner' of the 1988 Olympic 100 m Gold medal).

PRACTICE

1 Explain each of the following terms/phrases in the context of this spread:
   - a Alkyl group
   - b Crude oil fractions
   - c Anaerobic decomposition
   - d Ethene is susceptible to attack by electrophiles.

2 Explain why ethanol from the direct hydration of ethene is rarely used in the manufacture of alcoholic drinks.

3 Phosphoric acid is the catalyst used in the direct hydration of ethene. Suggest reasons for each of the following:
   - a Concentrated sulphuric acid is not used as the catalyst.
   - b Concentrated hydrochloric acid is not used as the catalyst.
   - c High pressure (70 atm) is used.

25.2 POLARITY IN ALCOHOLS

OBJECTIVES

- Effects of hydrogen bonding
- Nucleophilic substitution: halogenoalkanes
- Chlorinating agents
- Reaction with sodium

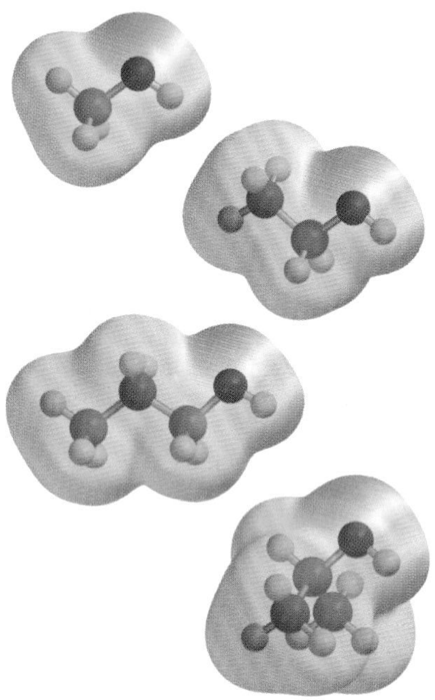

The electrostatic potential maps for methanol, ethanol, propan-1-ol, and propan-2-ol show the polarity of the C—O—H bonds.

Alcohols contain the functional group —OH attached to an alkyl group. Oxygen is more electronegative than either carbon or hydrogen. As a result, the oxygen atom is charged δ– and the adjacent hydrogen and carbon atoms are charged δ+. Because of the polarity of the —OH group, alcohol molecules hydrogen-bond with each other and with water when in aqueous solution (see chapter on 'Changes of state and intermolecular forces'). Also, as in the case of the halogenoalkanes (see previous chapter), nucleophiles are attracted to the δ+ carbon atom in the molecule. Nucleophilic substitution follows, in which the hydroxyl group —OH is replaced by the incoming nucleophile.

Hydrogen bonding

Considering dispersion forces alone would suggest that the boiling point of an alcohol should be about the same as that of the alkane with the same number of electrons (see chapter on 'Changes of state and intermolecular forces'). But alcohols have much *higher* boiling points than these corresponding alkanes: e.g. ethanol CH_3CH_2OH (26 electrons), T_b = 78 °C; propane $CH_3CH_2CH_3$ (26 electrons), T_b = –42 °C. This is because hydrogen bonding between the molecules of ethanol raises the boiling point of ethanol relative to propane.

When an alcohol is mixed with water, hydrogen bonds form between the alcohol molecules and the water molecules. As a result, the lower alcohols are miscible with water. As the length of the hydrocarbon chain increases, solubility in water decreases.

Nucleophilic substitution by HBr

Hydrogen bromide is a polar molecule in which the hydrogen and bromine atoms bear partial charges $H^{\delta+}$—$Br^{\delta-}$. In aqueous solution, HBr exists as the ions H^+ and Br^-. The Br^- ion is a nucleophile because of its negative charge. Aqueous hydrogen bromide (hydrobromic acid) is often produced *in situ* by adding potassium bromide (or sodium bromide) to concentrated sulphuric acid.

Heating an alcohol together with potassium bromide in concentrated sulphuric acid produces a halogenoalkane:

$$ROH + HBr \xrightarrow[\text{KBr}]{\text{conc. } H_2SO_4} RBr + H_2O$$

Concentrated sulphuric acid is run in to a flask containing the alcohol from a dropping funnel, while the mixture is cooled. Solid potassium bromide is then added, and the bromoalkane product is distilled into a cooled receiver.

Iodoalkanes may also be produced by this method. However, concentrated *phosphoric acid* must be used, to avoid the problem of concentrated sulphuric acid oxidizing iodide ions to iodine (see the chapter on 'The halogens').

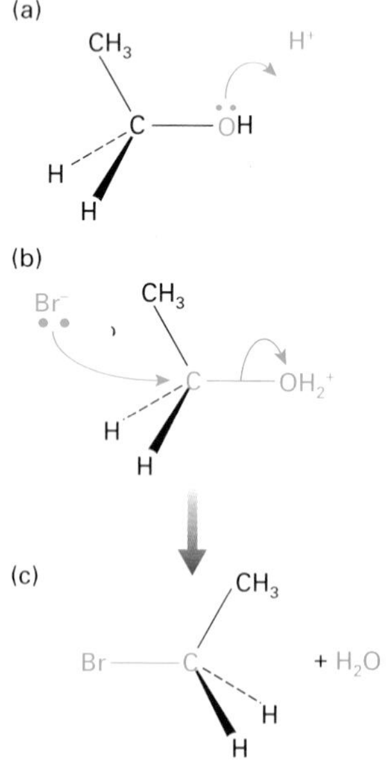

Mechanism for the nucleophilic substitution reaction between ethanol and potassium bromide in concentrated sulphuric acid. (a) Protonation of the alcohol's oxygen atom (which donates a lone pair to form a single covalent bond). (b) Reverse-side attack by the Br⁻ nucleophile. (c) The C—Br bond forms and the C—O bond breaks: water is liberated.

In a reaction of this sort, substitution occurs and OH^- 'leaves' the molecule. The OH^- group is said to be a 'poor leaving group' because the carbon–oxygen bond is short and consequently very strong. Because of this, the hydroxide ion leaves only with great difficulty. To make the reaction proceed more readily, a reactive intermediate is created that has a better leaving group.

The first step is the protonation of the alcohol by the concentrated acid:

$$CH_3CH_2OH + H^+ \rightarrow CH_3CH_2OH_2^+$$

The leaving group is now water H_2O, which is a good leaving group.
The nucleophilic bromide ion attacks the protonated alcohol to form the bromoalkane:

$$CH_3CH_2OH_2^+ + Br^- \rightarrow CH_3CH_2Br + H_2O$$

Chlorinating agents

A **chlorinating agent** is a substance that replaces a hydroxyl group —OH with a chlorine atom —Cl.

The most important chlorinating agents are:

- Phosphorus trichloride PCl_3
- Phosphorus pentachloride PCl_5
- Sulphur dichloride oxide (thionyl chloride) SCl_2O

PCl_3 and SCl_2O are liquids, and the reaction is carried out by heating the alcohol and the chlorinating agent under reflux. The equation for the reaction of sulphur dichloride oxide with ethanol is:

$$CH_3CH_2OH + SCl_2O \rightarrow CH_3CH_2Cl + SO_2 + HCl$$

Reaction of an alcohol with solid PCl_5 occurs at room temperature:

$$CH_3CH_2OH + PCl_5 \rightarrow CH_3CH_2Cl + PCl_3O + HCl$$

The production of HCl gas on adding phosphorus pentachloride is a useful test for an alcohol.

Phosphorus pentachloride

Solid PCl_5 contains the ions PCl_4^+ and PCl_6^-. The PCl_4^+ ion performs a similar role to the H^+ ion in the HBr example given opposite, weakening the carbon–oxygen bond and assisting the nucleophilic substitution reaction. The PCl_4^+ ion and the H^+ ion both act as *Lewis* acids (see chapter on 'Acid–base equilibrium'), accepting a lone pair from the oxygen atom in the hydroxyl group on the alcohol molecule.

Iodination

The hydroxyl group can be replaced by an iodine atom by using phosphorus and iodine.

The reaction between alcohols and sodium

Nucleophilic substitution reactions break the polar C—OH bond. The polar O—H bond is broken when an alcohol is reduced by sodium. Hydrogen gas is slowly released, forming a solution of the product **alkoxide ion** RO^- in ethanol (et):

$$2ROH(l) + 2Na(s) \rightarrow 2Na^+RO^-(et) + H_2(g)$$

The reaction is very similar to the reaction of sodium with water:

$$2HOH(l) + 2Na(s) \rightarrow 2Na^+HO^-(aq) + H_2(g)$$

If the mixture resulting from the reaction between sodium and ethanol is carefully evaporated, the solid product is sodium ethoxide:

$$2CH_3CH_2OH(l) + 2Na(s) \rightarrow 2Na^+CH_3CH_2O^-(s) + H_2(g)$$

The alkoxides are useful nucleophiles, as you will see in a later spread.

Sodium reacts less vigorously with ethanol than it does with water. Hydrogen is steadily evolved and a solution containing the ethoxide ion forms.

SUMMARY

- There is extensive hydrogen bonding between alcohol molecules, and between alcohol molecules and water molecules.
- Hydrogen bonding results in the alcohols having relatively high boiling points and good miscibility with water.
- The C—OH bond is polarized $C^{\delta+}$—$O^{\delta-}$; it reacts when nucleophiles attack the $\delta+$ carbon atom.
- Hydrogen bromide (produced *in situ* from potassium bromide and concentrated sulphuric acid) causes nucleophilic substitution of the —OH group in alcohols.
- Chlorinating agents (PCl_3, PCl_5, and SCl_2O) replace the —OH group with a chlorine atom.
- The production of HCl gas on adding phosphorus pentachloride is a useful test for an alcohol.
- Alcohols react with sodium to produce an alkoxide and hydrogen gas.

PRACTICE

1. Explain why decan-1-ol $CH_3(CH_2)_8CH_2OH$ has only limited solubility in water, whereas ethanol CH_3CH_2OH is miscible with water in all proportions.
2. Give details of the reagents and the practical procedures required to prepare each of the following substances from a named alcohol:
   - **a** 1-Chloropropane
   - **b** 2-Bromopropane.
3. Explain why sodium metal reacts more slowly with ethanol CH_3CH_2OH than with water HOH.
4. Draw Lewis structures to show the formation of the ethoxide ion by the action of sodium on ethanol.

25.3

OBJECTIVES

- Elimination vs. substitution
- Dehydration

(a)

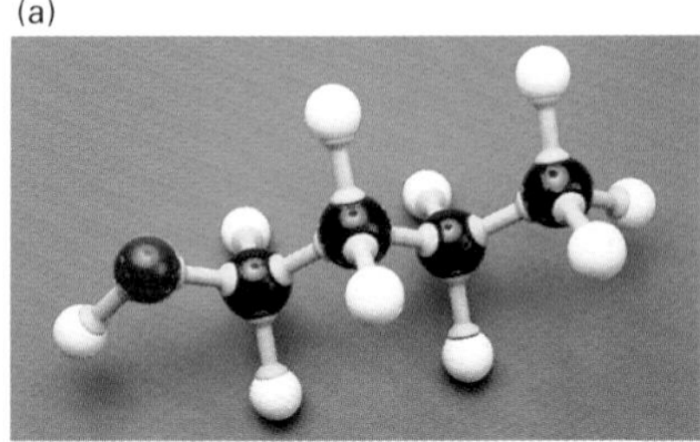

(b)

(c)

Three alcohols of molecular formula C_4H_9OH: (a) butan-1-ol is a primary alcohol; (b) butan-2-ol is a secondary alcohol; and (c) 2-methylpropan-2-ol is a tertiary alcohol.

(a)

CH_3 H H C O H H O C CH_3 H H

(b)

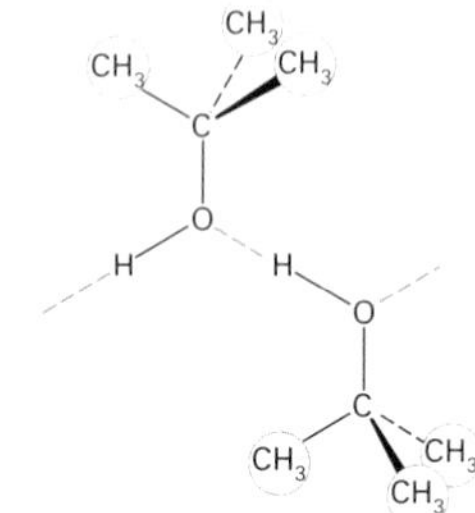

Hydrogen bonding between adjacent molecules of (a) a primary alcohol and (b) a tertiary alcohol. Note that steric hindrance by three alkyl groups inhibits close approach between tertiary alcohol molecules.

PRIMARY, SECONDARY, AND TERTIARY ALCOHOLS AND DEHYDRATION

You know that alcohols contain the functional group —OH attached to an alkyl group. The most typical reactions of alcohols involve nucleophilic substitution reactions in which the —OH group is replaced by an incoming group such as a halogen. However, substitution reactions generally take place in competition with elimination reactions (see previous chapter). In the case of alcohols, elimination reactions involve the formation of a carbon–carbon double bond as the —OH group and a hydrogen atom are removed from across a carbon–carbon single bond. Substitution and elimination reactions both involve the —OH functional group. Which of the two reactions predominates depends on the nature of the hydrocarbon chain attached to the functional group.

The three classes of alcohols

There are three main classes of alcohols: primary, secondary, and tertiary alcohols. As for the halogenoalkanes, spread 24.3, this classification is based on the number of alkyl groups (R) attached to the carbon atom bearing the —OH group:

- in a **primary alcohol**, it has one R group and two hydrogen atoms;
- in a **secondary alcohol**, it has two R groups and one hydrogen atom;
- in a **tertiary alcohol**, it has three R groups.

Comparing physical properties

The electronegativity of oxygen is 3.4 and that of hydrogen is 2.2. As a result, the O—H bond is polarized $O^{\delta-}$—$H^{\delta+}$. This bond polarity has an effect on the intermolecular forces in alcohols. The structures of three alcohols of molecular formula C_4H_9OH are given on the left. Now look at their boiling points:

- butan-1-ol (a primary alcohol) 117 °C
- butan-2-ol (a secondary alcohol) 99 °C
- 2-methylpropan-2-ol (a tertiary alcohol) 82 °C

These alcohols have the same molecular formula. Weak dispersion forces are proportional to the number of electrons, so are comparable in these molecules. The most significant intermolecular force is hydrogen bonding, which depends both on the polarity of the O—H bond and on the structure of the molecule. The strength of the hydrogen bonding in an alcohol increases in the order tertiary < secondary < primary.

The illustration to the left shows that the —OH group in the tertiary alcohol is surrounded by methyl groups. These groups prevent the close approach of other molecules and inhibit the formation of hydrogen bonds. Such hindering of a chemical reaction (or, in this case, hydrogen bonding) by the arrangement of the atoms in space is called **steric hindrance**. The primary alcohol allows closer approach by adjacent —OH groups and increases the extent of hydrogen bonding.

Elimination of water

Alcohols are manufactured by adding water to an alkene, using phosphoric acid as a catalyst (see earlier in this chapter). This reaction may be reversed to eliminate water from an alcohol and produce an alkene. The elimination process involves **dehydration**, i.e. the removal of a molecule of water. Alcohols are dehydrated by warming with concentrated sulphuric acid at about 180 °C:

$$CH_3CH_2OH \longrightarrow CH_2{=}CH_2 + H_2O$$

As with the hydration reaction, a strong acid acts as a catalyst. Remember that a catalyst will always catalyse the reverse reaction as well as the forward reaction. The acid first protonates the oxygen atom of the alcohol, to form $[CH_3CH_2OH_2]^+$, then water is lost, forming a carbocation; finally the catalytic hydrogen ion is regenerated.

Dehydration is most likely for tertiary alcohols because the intermediate carbocation is stabilized by the three alkyl groups attached to it. Remember that the stability of carbocations decreases in the order tertiary > secondary > primary, spread 22.8. Of the isomers of C_4H_9OH, the one that dehydrates most easily is the *tertiary* alcohol 2-methylpropan-2-ol:

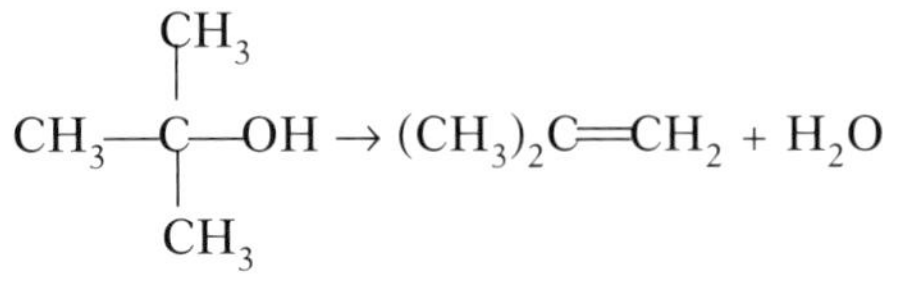

$$CH_3-\overset{\displaystyle CH_3}{\underset{\displaystyle CH_3}{\overset{|}{\underset{|}{C}}}}-OH \rightarrow (CH_3)_2C{=}CH_2 + H_2O$$

Another method of dehydration

An alcohol is dehydrated when its vapour passes over heated powdered aluminium oxide. The powder offers a large surface area on which the decomposition takes place. The chemical equation for the dehydration of ethanol under these conditions is also:

$CH_3CH_2OH \rightarrow CH_2{=}CH_2 + H_2O$

(a) The oxygen atom of the tertiary alcohol, with its two lone pairs, provides a site for protonation by the catalyst, concentrated sulphuric acid.

(b) The protonated alcohol loses water; water, as mentioned in the previous spread, is a good leaving group. This loss creates a tertiary carbocation, which is stabilized by three electron-donating methyl groups.

(c) The tertiary carbocation loses a proton, regenerating the catalyst (H^+).

The product of dehydration is an alkene.

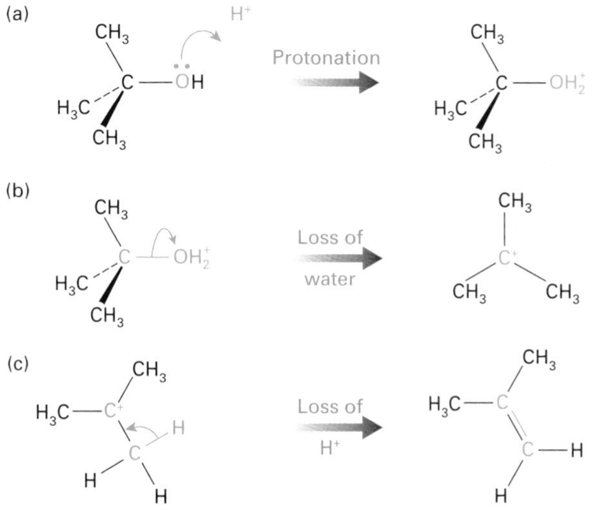

Mechanism for the production of 2-methylpropene by elimination of water from 2-methylpropan-2-ol.

The full mechanism is given below.

SUMMARY

- Elimination reactions in alcohols bring about dehydration and the formation of an alkene.
- Ease of dehydration increases in the order primary < secondary < tertiary alcohols.
- Ethanol is dehydrated to ethene using concentrated sulphuric acid at 180 °C.

Dehydration conditions

Reaction conditions must be controlled to favour dehydration rather than the reverse reaction. Dehydration is favoured by high temperature (about 180 °C) because the reaction is endothermic. The entropy change is in favour of dehydration because one molecule decomposes to make two molecules.

PRACTICE

1 Draw structural formulae for each of the following substances and state whether each is a primary, a secondary, or a tertiary alcohol:
- **a** Butan-2-ol
- **b** 2-Methylbutan-2-ol
- **c** Cyclohexanol.

2 Arrange the alcohols in question 1 in order of increasing boiling point. Give reasons for your answer.

3 Give details of reagents and the practical procedures required to prepare each of the following substances from a named alcohol:
- **a** Propene
- **b** But-2-ene.

4 Suggest a reaction mechanism (complete with structural formulae) to explain the dehydration of ethanol using concentrated sulphuric acid as a catalyst to produce ethene. Include the following steps: (i) protonation of the alcohol; and (ii) loss of water.

25.4 OXIDATION OF ALCOHOLS

OBJECTIVES

- Combustion
- Oxidation of primary, secondary, and tertiary alcohols

Oxidation may take place by the process of combustion in oxygen or by chemical reaction with oxidants such as acidified potassium dichromate(VI). Like most organic compounds, alcohols combust readily. Complete combustion of primary, secondary, and tertiary alcohols always produces water and carbon dioxide. The products of chemical oxidation by potassium dichromate(VI) are more specific to the class of alcohol: primary alcohols yield aldehydes and carboxylic acids; secondary alcohols yield ketones; tertiary alcohols do not react.

Brandy contains up to 40% ethanol. It ignites readily and burns with a clear non-sooty flame.

Oxidation: combustion

Alcohols burn in air to form carbon dioxide and water. The molecular structure is completely destroyed and the constituent atoms oxidize to carbon dioxide and water. An example is the combustion of ethanol:

$$CH_3CH_2OH(l) + 3O_2(g) \rightarrow 2CO_2(g) + 3H_2O(l)$$

This reaction is strongly exothermic, and ethanol is used as a fuel in areas where it can be produced cheaply, e.g. in Brazil where conditions are suitable for growing sugar cane. In the UK, ethanol is sold as a fuel in the form of 'methylated spirits', which contains added methanol (about 5%) and a blue dye to make it unsuitable for drinking.

Oxidation and oxidants

It is also possible to oxidize an alcohol in ways that keep the carbon skeleton intact. Two oxidants are commonly used for this: potassium dichromate(VI), which contains the $Cr_2O_7^{2-}$ ion; and potassium manganate(VII), which contains the MnO_4^- ion. Used in acidified solution, both these oxidants change colour when reduced. This change is a useful sign that the organic compound has been oxidized.

Oxidation of the hydroxyl group —OH of an alcohol involves the removal of a hydrogen atom from the carbon atom bearing the hydroxyl group. The reaction product depends on the position of the —OH group in the alcohol, and on the reaction conditions used. Whereas all three classes of alcohol react in the same way during nucleophilic substitution, they differ greatly in their behaviour on oxidation.

Oxidation: primary alcohols

The structure of a *primary* alcohol is RCH_2OH. The —OH group is attached to a carbon atom bearing *two* hydrogen atoms. Oxidation (indicated in outline by the symbol [O]) removes one of these hydrogen atoms together with the hydrogen atom in the —OH group. The result is an aldehyde RCHO:

$$RCH_2OH \xrightarrow{[O]} RCHO$$

For example, ethanol is converted to ethanal CH_3CHO:

$$CH_3CH_2OH \xrightarrow{[O]} CH_3CHO$$

The oxygen atom is doubly bonded to the carbon atom, forming a carbonyl group ⊃C═O. The illustration to the left gives structural formulae for these molecules.

$Cr_2O_7^{2-}/H^+$

The oxidation of ethanol to ethanal.

Aldehydes and ketones

See the following chapter for more details on aldehydes and ketones, such as their reduction to alcohols (26.2) and how to distinguish between them (26.4).

Further oxidation: carboxylic acids

The aldehyde functional group —CHO consists of a hydrogen atom attached to the carbonyl ⊃C═O carbon atom. This structure may be oxidized further. The result is a carboxylic acid RCOOH:

$$RCHO \xrightarrow{[O]} RCOOH$$

Overall, the primary alcohol ethanol oxidizes in two stages: first to the aldehyde (ethanal) and then to the carboxylic acid (ethanoic acid):

$$CH_3CH_2OH \xrightarrow{[O]} CH_3CHO \xrightarrow{[O]} CH_3COOH$$

$Cr_2O_7^{2-}/H^+$

The oxidation of ethanal to ethanoic acid.

Oxidants are generally very unspecific in their reaction. Oxidizing a primary alcohol produces an aldehyde. Leaving the aldehyde product in contact with the oxidant will allow further oxidation to the carboxylic acid. This may be avoided by distilling the aldehyde away from the reaction mixture as it forms. The aldehyde lacks hydrogen bonding (hydrogen is bonded to *carbon*, not oxygen) and so has a lower boiling point than the corresponding alcohol.

Colour changes on heating alcohols with acidified potassium dichromate(VI): primary and secondary alcohols reduce orange $Cr_2O_7^{2-}$(aq) to blue-green Cr^{3+}(aq). Tertiary alcohols (right) have no effect.

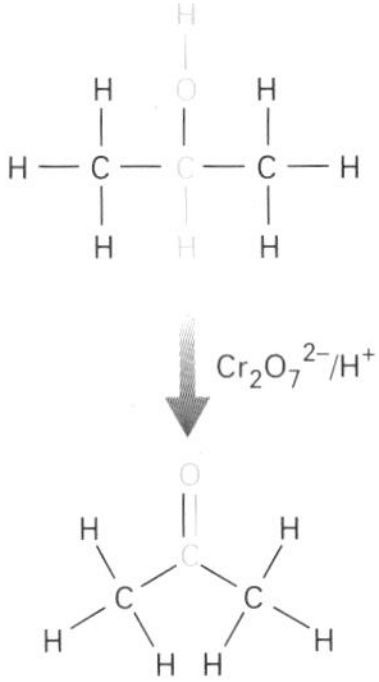

The oxidation of propan-2-ol to propanone.

Oxidation: secondary alcohols

The structure of a *secondary* alcohol is RR′CHOH. The —OH group is attached to a carbon atom bearing *one* hydrogen atom. As in the case of primary alcohols, oxidation removes this hydrogen atom together with the hydrogen atom in the —OH group. The result is a ketone RR′C═O. Note that ketones and aldehydes both contain the carbonyl group ⊃C═O. There is no hydrogen atom attached to the carbon atom of the carbonyl group in ketones, just two alkyl groups. In general terms:

$$\text{RR'CHOH} \xrightarrow{[O]} \text{RR'CO}$$

Ketones resist further oxidation.

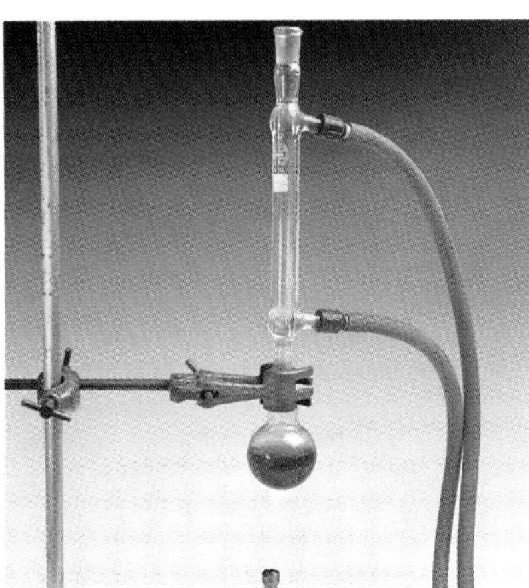

Refluxing a secondary alcohol with acidified potassium dichromate(VI) produces a ketone.

Tertiary alcohols are not easily oxidized

The structure of a *tertiary* alcohol is RR′R″COH. In this case, there are no hydrogen atoms attached to the carbon atom bearing the hydroxyl group. As a result, tertiary alcohols *cannot* be oxidized (except under extreme conditions, when carbon–carbon bonds break).

SUMMARY

- Primary alcohols are oxidized to aldehydes and then to carboxylic acids.
- Secondary alcohols are oxidized to ketones.
- Primary and secondary alcohols are oxidized by acidified potassium dichromate(VI) or acidified potassium manganate(VII).
- Tertiary alcohols are not readily oxidized.

PRACTICE

1 Methoxymethane and ethanol both have the molecular formula C_2H_6O. Explain in terms of molecular structure why ethanol (T_b = 78 °C) has a much higher boiling point than methoxymethane (T_b = −28 °C).

2 Acidified potassium dichromate(VI) was added to each of the following substances:

a Propanone
b 2-Methylpropan-2-ol
c Propan-2-ol

Write the structural formula for the product (if any).

25.5 PHENOLS AND ETHERS

OBJECTIVES

- Phenols and alcohols contrasted
- Ether synthesis
- Ethers are inert

The *alcohols* are a class of compounds in which a hydroxyl group —OH is attached directly to an alkyl group. By comparison, the *phenols* are a class of compounds in which the —OH group is attached directly to a benzene ring. The properties of alcohols and phenols are distinctly different. Different properties are also shown by the *ethers*, which consist of an oxygen atom joined to two separate alkyl groups. The lack of a hydroxyl group means that ethers are chemically inert.

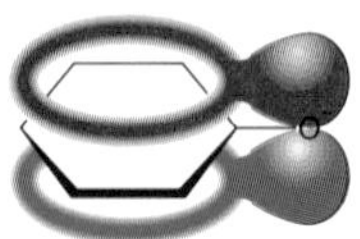

Aqueous ethanol has a pH of 7. The alkoxide ion is formed only in the presence of a powerful reductant. Sodium is capable of reducing alcohols to hydrogen gas. In contrast, aqueous phenol has a pH of about 4 (phenol is partially miscible with water). The —OH group attached to a benzene ring shows acidic properties. The negative ion is stabilized by delocalization of the negative charge, as shown in the electrostatic potential map below.

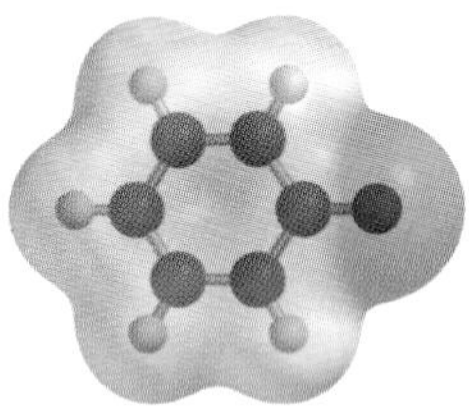

The polar O—H bond in alcohols and phenols

The O—H bond is polarized $O^{\delta-}$—$H^{\delta+}$. Complete charge separation would cause the bond to break, resulting in the loss of a proton H^+ and a negative charge on the oxygen atom. However, aqueous solutions of alcohols are neutral. The terminal hydrogen atom on the —OH group is not acidic and does not protonate water to form the aqueous hydrogen ion (oxonium ion) $H_3O^+(aq)$. Moreover, alcohols do not act as acids in the presence of aqueous hydroxide ion $OH^-(aq)$ from bases such as aqueous sodium hydroxide.

In contrast, a solution of phenol is acidic (≈ pH 4):

$$C_6H_5OH + H_2O \rightleftharpoons H_3O^+ + C_6H_5O^-$$

Loss of a proton is possible in phenol because the negative charge in the **phenoxide ion** is delocalized around the benzene ring. Phenol reacts with strong bases to form salts:

$$C_6H_5OH + NaOH \rightarrow Na^+C_6H_5O^- + H_2O$$

Alcohols do not show this behaviour in solution or with aqueous bases because the negative charge remains localized on the oxygen atom.

Phenylmethanol

This compound has the formula $C_6H_5CH_2OH$. The —OH group is not attached directly to the benzene ring, and so its properties are the same as those of an *alcohol*.

Phenol acidity

Phenol is not a strong enough acid to liberate carbon dioxide from aqueous sodium carbonate. Sodium phenoxide $Na^+C_6H_5O^-$ is the salt of a *weak* acid. The acid is regenerated on addition of *strong* acid:

$Na^+C_6H_5O^- + HCl \rightarrow C_6H_5OH + NaCl$

Test for phenol

A characteristic test for a phenol is the formation of a purple colour with aqueous iron(III) chloride.

A comparison of the properties of phenol and ethanol.

Property or reaction	Phenol C_6H_5OH	Ethanol CH_3CH_2OH
Solubility in water at 20 °C	Partially miscible	Miscible in all proportions
pH of solution	approx. pH 4	pH 7
Action of CH_3COOH	No reaction	Forms ester* $CH_3CH_2OCOCH_3$
Action of CH_3COCl	Rapid reaction, good yield of $C_6H_5OCOCH_3$	Rapid reaction, good yield of $CH_3CH_2OCOCH_3$
Action of bromine water	Immediate reaction to give 2,4,6-tribromophenol	No reaction
Action of $Cr_2O_7^{2-}/H^+$	Gives a complex mixture of products	Forms ethanal, then ethanoic acid
Action of sodium	Evolves $H_2(g)$	Evolves $H_2(g)$

* See the chapter on 'Carboxylic acids and their derivatives'.

Ethers

The alkoxide ion RO^- is negatively charged and is therefore a nucleophile. Alkoxides dissolved in ethanol react with halogenoalkanes. The alkoxide ion substitutes for the halide ion to form an ether. An **ether** consists of an oxygen atom with two single covalent bonds each joined to a separate alkyl group.

The most important ether is ethoxyethane $CH_3CH_2OCH_2CH_3$ (diethylether, or in everyday use just 'ether').

The reaction in which an alkoxide ion substitutes for the halide ion is called the **Williamson synthesis** of an ether. The diagram shows the mechanism for this reaction.

For example, sodium ethoxide when refluxed with bromoethane forms ethoxyethane:

$CH_3CH_2O^- + CH_3CH_2Br \rightarrow CH_3CH_2OCH_2CH_3 + Br^-$

The alkoxide ion RO^- is a nucleophile, in a similar way to the hydroxide ion HO^-. Halogenoalkanes react with nucleophiles; the reaction follows the typical nucleophilic substitution mechanism of halogenoalkanes (see previous chapter). One advantage of the Williamson synthesis is that the alkoxide can have a different number of carbon atoms from the halogenoalkane and unsymmetrical ethers can be made this way: sodium methoxide, $Na^+CH_3O^-$, will react with bromoethane to give methoxyethane $CH_3OCH_2CH_3$.

Alexander William Williamson had to overcome considerable adversity in his desire to be a chemist. He had lost an arm and the use of an eye in childhood. His inquiring mind remained thankfully intact. Despite being essentially an organic chemist, he made major contributions to physical chemistry too, as he was for example the first person to formulate the idea of chemical equilibrium.

The reaction between ethoxide ion and bromoethane.

Ethers are generally unreactive and are mostly used as solvents. Note that ethers have lower boiling points than the corresponding alcohols. For example, the ether methoxybutane $CH_3—O—CH_2CH_2CH_2CH_3$ and the alcohol pentan-1-ol both have the molecular formula $C_5H_{12}O$. As a result, the dispersion forces between the molecules of each compound should be similar. However, methoxybutane boils at 70 °C and pentan-1-ol at 138 °C, confirming the absence of hydrogen bonds in the ether.

Ethers and petrol

In response to the need to remove lead from petrol, alternative petrol additives have been developed to prevent engine damage through 'knocking'. One such additive is an ether derived from methanol, methyl tertiary butyl ether (MTBE, $CH_3OC(CH_3)_3$). Petrol may contain 15% MTBE. Production of this chemical has increased from virtually zero in the 1970s to several million tonnes per year.

Ethoxyethane is being used here to extract chromium peroxide $CrO(O_2)_2$ from the reaction between hydrogen peroxide and acidified potassium dichromate(VI). A deep blue solution results.

SUMMARY

- The —OH group is acidic when *directly* attached to a benzene ring in a phenol.
- Alcohols and phenols have distinctly different properties.
- Alcohols react at the O—H or the C—O bond; phenols react at the O—H bond or undergo substitution reactions involving hydrogen atoms on the benzene ring.

PRACTICE

1 Explain why phenol is acidic in solution, whereas phenylmethanol is neutral.

2 Draw structural formulae to illustrate the reactions listed in the phenol/ethanol comparison table opposite.

3 Give details of a possible laboratory synthesis of MTBE.

25.6

OBJECTIVES

- Epoxyethane
- Ethane-1,2-diol
- Propane-1,2,3-triol

ALCOHOLS WITH MORE THAN ONE —OH GROUP

All of the alcohols met so far have been **monohydric** alcohols: each alcohol molecule (whether primary, secondary, or tertiary) has contained just *one* hydroxyl group —OH. Alcohols with *two* hydroxyl groups are called **dihydric** alcohols; those with *three* hydroxyl groups are called **trihydric** alcohols. The term **polyhydric** describes a molecule that contains a large number of hydroxyl groups. Common polyhydric alcohols include the sugars, which will be described in the chapter on 'Biochemistry'. This spread concentrates on di- and trihydric alcohols, two of which have great commercial importance.

Epoxyethane and ethane-1,2-diol

Epoxyethane is one of the most useful compounds made industrially from ethene. The molecule has one oxygen atom that is attached to two carbon atoms to form a triangular ring. The compound is therefore a *cyclic ether*. This arrangement is an example of a **heterocyclic** compound, where the ring contains another atom in place of carbon. (In contrast, in alicyclic compounds all the atoms in the ring are carbon.)

Epoxyethane is manufactured from ethene obtained from the cracking of crude oil fractions. The reaction is carried out by passing a mixture of ethene and oxygen over a silver catalyst at 300 °C and 15 atm. Below its boiling point of 11 °C, the epoxyethane produced is a colourless volatile liquid.

Considerable care must be taken in the formation and handling of epoxyethane, as it is both flammable and explosive. Furthermore, epoxyethane may irritate the respiratory system and may cause neurological disorders.

The bond angles in the epoxyethane ring are about 60°, so the structure is extremely strained. The molecule is very responsive to reactions that involve opening the ring, thereby relieving the strain. Ethers such as ethoxyethane $CH_3CH_2OCH_2CH_3$ do not have this strained ring structure and are generally unreactive. As discussed earlier in this chapter, the reactions of alcohols often involve the protonation of oxygen before the main reaction can occur. In the case of epoxyethane, dilute sulphuric acid acts as a catalyst and causes the molecule to react with water, forming ethane-1,2-diol $HOCH_2CH_2OH$ (a dihydric alcohol, traditionally called **ethylene glycol**):

$$CH_2(O)CH_2 + H_2O \rightarrow HOCH_2CH_2OH$$

Ethane-1,2-diol is used as antifreeze in car cooling systems (see spread 22.9) and in the manufacture of polyester fabrics, including the synthetic fibre Terylene (see chapter on 'Carboxylic acids and their derivatives').

Trihydric alcohols

A common trihydric alcohol is propane-1,2,3-triol (traditionally called *glycerol* or *glycerine*: the latter name should be avoided). This trihydric alcohol is an extremely viscous liquid due to the high degree of hydrogen bonding between its molecules. It occurs widely in Nature as a component of fats and oils (see spread 30.1 on 'Lipids' in the chapter on 'Biochemistry'). Heating propane-1,2,3-triol with a nitrating mixture of concentrated sulphuric and nitric acids results in **nitroglycerine**. This substance is the 'active ingredient' in dynamite, used for blasting rock out of quarries and when building structures such as roads.

Epoxides

Epoxides contain oxygen atoms in their molecules as part of a three-membered ring. Epoxides are cyclic ethers. They react with compounds such as phenols to form polymeric epoxy resins.

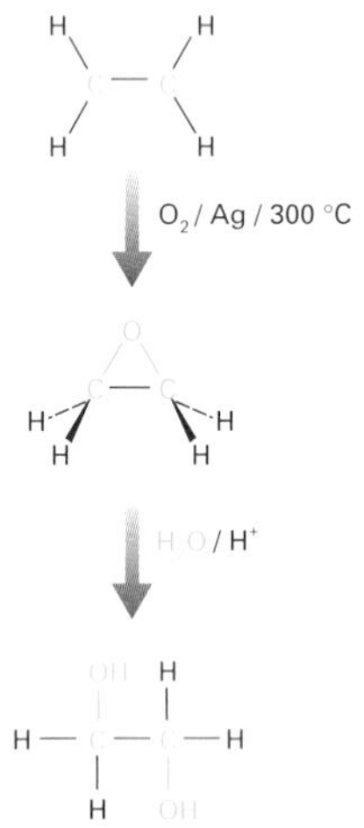

O_2 / Ag / 300 °C

H_2O / H^+

The industrial conversion of ethene to epoxyethane and then to ethane-1,2-diol. Note that epoxyethane is hazardous, being both flammable and explosive.

Alkoxy alcohols

Epoxyethane reacts with an alcohol in the presence of an acid catalyst to yield a compound that is both an ether and an alcohol.

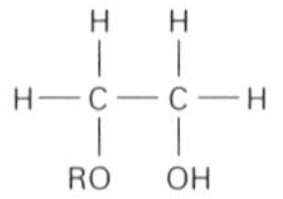

H—C(H)(RO)—C(H)(OH)—H

These alkoxy alcohols are useful as solvents, and in the production of plasticisers and non-ionic detergents. For example, an alkoxy alcohol is used as a solvent for cellulose ethanoate in the manufacture of films, lacquers, and varnishes.

$$\mathrm{H{-}\underset{ONO_2}{\overset{H}{C}}{-}\underset{ONO_2}{\overset{H}{C}}{-}\underset{ONO_2}{\overset{H}{C}}{-}H}$$

Pure nitroglycerine is a shock-sensitive liquid: it will explode if dropped. Working at the end of the nineteenth century, Alfred Nobel absorbed nitroglycerine into kieselguhr (a type of clay). The result was dynamite, *which explodes only when detonated. He hoped his invention would alleviate the dangers experienced by miners and other labourers. However, Nobel was greatly disappointed by the use of dynamite in warfare. He sold the explosives factories that had made him a rich man, and set up a fund to award annual prizes for outstanding work in the fields of science, writing, and the advancement of world peace. The first Nobel prizes were awarded in 1901: they have their origins in a trihydric alcohol.*

SUMMARY

- Oxidation of ethene over a silver catalyst at 300 °C and 15 atm forms epoxyethane, a cyclic ether.
- Acidic hydrolysis of epoxyethane produces ethane-1,2-diol.
- Dihydric alcohols contain two hydroxyl groups, e.g. ethane-1,2-diol ('ethylene glycol'), used as an antifreeze additive.
- Trihydric alcohols contain three hydroxyl groups, e.g. propane-1,2,3-triol ('glycerol'), used to make nitroglycerine.

PRACTICE

1 Explain why, compared to ethanol, ethane-1,2-diol:
  - **a** is more viscous;
  - **b** has much higher melting and boiling points.

2 Explain why the structure of epoxyethane is described as 'strained'. What effect do you think this factor will have on the general reactivity of the molecule?

3 To what extent do you think propane-1,2,3-triol is soluble in water? Give reasons for your answer.

Chapter 25 Reactions summary

- Fermentation of glucose by yeast:
  $C_6H_{12}O_6 \rightarrow 2CH_3CH_2OH + 2CO_2$
- Direct hydration of ethene (phosphoric acid catalyst, 300 °C, and 70 atm):
  $CH_2{=}CH_2(g) + H_2O(g) \rightarrow CH_3CH_2OH(g)$
- Nucleophilic substitution of the —OH group by a halide:
  $CH_3CH_2OH + HBr \xrightarrow[\text{KBr}]{\text{conc. } H_2SO_4} CH_3CH_2Br + H_2O$
- Chlorination of ethanol by SCl_2O (or PCl_3, PCl_5):
  $CH_3CH_2OH + SCl_2O \rightarrow CH_3CH_2Cl + SO_2 + HCl$
- Elimination of water (dehydration) from ethanol (conc. sulphuric acid catalyst, 180 °C):
  $CH_3CH_2OH \rightarrow CH_2{=}CH_2 + H_2O$
- Combustion of ethanol:
  $CH_3CH_2OH(l) + 3O_2(g) \rightarrow 2CO_2(g) + 3H_2O(l)$
- Oxidation of a primary alcohol to an aldehyde and then to a carboxylic acid:
  $CH_3CH_2OH \xrightarrow{[O]} CH_3CHO \xrightarrow{[O]} CH_3COOH$
- Oxidation of a secondary alcohol to a ketone:
  $RR'CHOH \xrightarrow{[O]} RR'C{=}O$
- Tertiary alcohols do not oxidize.
- Synthesis of epoxyethane and subsequent hydrolysis:
  $CH_2{=}CH_2 \xrightarrow[300\,°C]{Ag} H_2C{-}CH_2 \text{ (bridged by O)} \xrightarrow[H^+]{+H_2O} HOCH_2CH_2OH$

PRACTICE EXAM QUESTIONS

1 Butan-1-ol can be oxidized by acidified potassium dichromate(VI) using two different methods.

a In the first method, butan-1-ol is added dropwise to acidified potassium dichromate(VI) and the product is distilled off immediately.

i Using the symbol [O] for the oxidizing agent, write an equation for this oxidation of butan-1-ol, showing clearly the structure of the product. State what colour change you would observe.

ii Butan-1-ol and butan-2-ol give different products on oxidation by this first method. By stating a reagent and the observation with each compound, give a simple test to distinguish between these two oxidation products. [6]

b In a second method, the mixture of butan-1-ol and acidified potassium dichromate(VI) is heated under reflux. Identify the product which is obtained by this reaction. [1]

c Give the structures and names of two branched chain alcohols which are both isomers of butan-1-ol. Only isomer 1 is oxidised when warmed with acidified potassium dichromate(VI). [4]
AQA (NEAB) 1997

2 The infrared spectrum of ethanol is shown below.

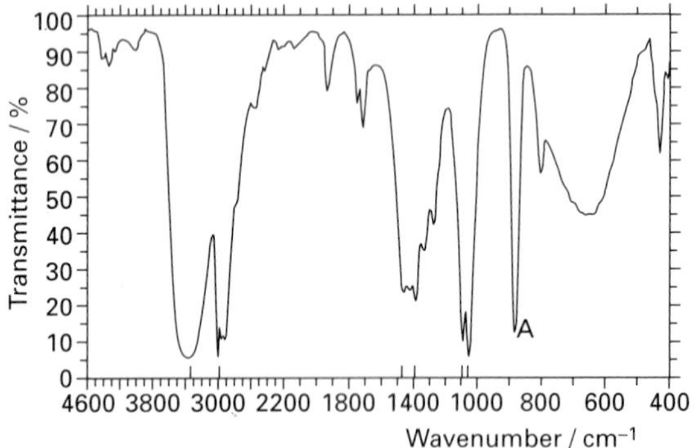

Table of infrared absorption data

Bond	Wavenumber / cm^{-1}
C—H	2840–3300
C—C	750–1100
C=C	1610–1680
C=O	1680–1750
C—O	1000–1300
O—H	3230–3550

a Using this table of data, identify a bond that could be responsible for the absorption labelled A on the spectrum. [1]

b i With the aid of the spectrum, suggest an approximate range for the fingerprint region.

ii How does the fingerprint region enable a compound to be identified? [3]

c Modern roadside breathalysers measure the absorption due to ethanol at 2950 cm^{-1}. Propanone, which is often found in the breath of diabetics, also absorbs at 2950 cm^{-1} but the breathalyser is able to distinguish between ethanol and propanone and to eliminate any signal from the latter.

i Suggest why the absorption at 3340 cm^{-1} is not used to analyse the amount of alcohol in a person's breath.

ii At what wavenumber approximately would a breathalyser indicate strong absorption of propanone but almost none for ethanol?

iii Describe a simple chemical test which would enable you to distinguish between ethanol and propanone. Give the reagent(s) used and the observation with each compound. [6]
AQA (NEAB) 1995 *(See also Chapter 32.)*

3 a Why is it necessary, in the direct synthesis of epoxyethane from ethene and air, to have efficient removal of the heat generated? [1]

b i Explain briefly why epoxyethane is highly reactive and write an equation for the reaction between one mole of epoxyethane and one mole of ethanol.

ii Give the repeating unit of the polymer formed when one mole of ethanol reacts with an excess of epoxyethane. (5)

c Predict, by means of an equation, how one mole of epoxyethane reacts with one mole of ammonia. (1)
AQA (NEAB) 1997

4 Three different reactions of propan-2-ol are shown below.

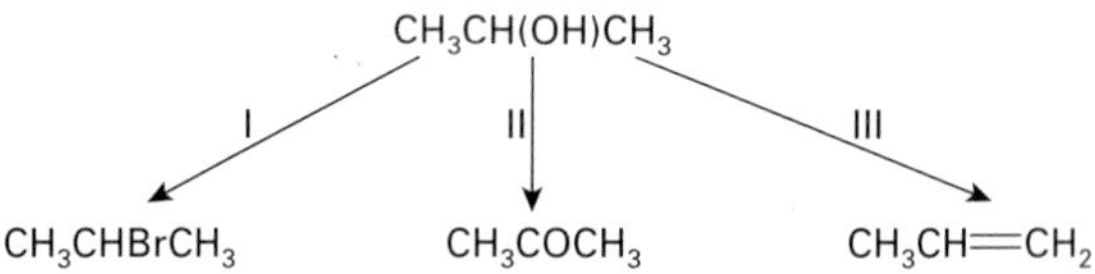

a For each of the reactions I, II, and III, give suitable reagents and conditions. [6]

b If 2-methylpropan-2-ol, $(CH_3)_3COH$, was used as the starting material in **a** instead of propan-2-ol, identify the organic products, if any, of reactions I, II and III. You should indicate if no reaction occurs. [3]
EDEXCEL 1998

5 There are four alcohols of molecular formula $C_4H_{10}O$ which are structural isomers.

Three of these alcohols are given below.

$CH_3CH_2CH_2CH_2OH$
butan-1-ol

$CH_3CH(OH)CH_2CH_3$
butan-2-ol

$(CH_3)_3COH$
2-methylpropan-2-ol

a Give the structural formula of the fourth alcohol that is isomeric with those above. [1]

b On heating with concentrated sulphuric acid, butan-2-ol is converted into a mixture of alkenes.

i Give the name of the type of reaction taking place. [1]

ii Give the structural formula of one of the alkenes formed. [1]

c i Give the name or structural formula of the organic compound produced when butan-1-ol is heated with acidified potassium dichromate(VI) and the product is removed by distillation as it forms. [1]

ii Give the name or structural formula of the organic compound produced when butan-1-ol is heated under reflux for 20 minutes with acidified potassium dichromate(VI). [1]

iii Give the structural formula of the organic product formed when butan-2-ol is heated under reflux for 20 minutes with acidified potassium dichromate(VI). [1]

iv State the type of reaction occurring in **c iii**. [1]

d When 2-methylpropan-2-ol is heated with a carboxylic acid in the presence of a catalyst, an ester, $C_6H_{12}O_2$, is formed.

i Give the structural formula of this ester of molecular formula $C_6H_{12}O_2$. [1]

ii Give the name of the carboxylic acid needed to form the ester in **d i**. [1]

iii Suggest a suitable catalyst for the reaction [1]

e Lucas' test may be used to distinguish between the three alcohols butan-1-ol, butan-2-ol and 2-methylpropan-2-ol. A mixture of anhydrous zinc chloride and hydrochloric acid is warmed with each of the three alcohols under identical conditions.

i Describe how the results of Lucas' test lead to the identification of the three alcohols. [2]

ii Give the name and the structural formula of the organic compound formed by butan-2-ol in Lucas' test. [2]

AQA (AEB) 1998 *(See also Chapter 27.)*

6 Alcohols and ethers have the same general formula, $C_nH_{2n+2}O$. Ethers contain a C—O—C linkage as, for example, in methoxypropane, $H_3C—O—CH_2CH_2CH_3$.

a i Give the number of peaks in the low-resolution proton NMR spectrum of methoxypropane and the ratio of the areas under the peaks in the spectrum.

ii Draw the structure of an ether which is an isomer of methoxypropane and which produces only 2 peaks in its low-resolution proton NMR spectrum. [3]

b i Alcohols can be prepared from haloalkanes by reaction with hydroxide ions. Name and outline the mechanism for the preparation of propan-1-ol from bromopropane.

ii Ethers can be prepared from haloalkanes by a similar reaction. Complete the following equation which shows the formation of methoxypropane.

$$\_\_\_\_\_ + BrCH_2CH_2CH_3 \rightarrow CH_3OCH_2CH_2CH_3 + Br^-$$ [5]

c Ethers are not oxidized by acidified potassium dichromate(VI). Name the type of alcohol which is also not oxidized by acidified potassium dichromate(VI) and draw the structure of an alcohol of this type which is an isomer of methoxypropane. [2]

d Write an equation for the complete combustion of methoxypropane in an excess of oxygen. [1]

e Ethers and alcohols can be distinguished by studying their infrared spectra. Using the table of data given below, state where, other than in the fingerprint region, their infrared spectra will be different and explain what causes this difference. [2]

Table of infrared absorption data

Bond	Wavenumber/cm^{-1}
C—H	2850–3300
C—C	750–1100
C=C	1620–1680
C=O	1680–1750
C—O	1000–1300
O—H in alcohols	3230–3550
O—H in acids	2500–3000

AQA (NEAB) 1997 *(See also Chapter 32.)*

26 Aldehydes and ketones

Aldehydes and ketones are two classes of compound that both contain the carbonyl group. The **carbonyl group** consists of an oxygen atom attached to a carbon atom by a double covalent bond, usually represented by the formula ⊃C═O. The carbon atom is referred to as the **carbonyl carbon atom**. **Aldehydes** have the structure RCHO where R is an alkyl or aryl group (methanal has the formula HCHO). **Ketones** have the structure RR′CO where R and R′ are alkyl or aryl groups. Both these types of **carbonyl compound** show the reactions of the ⊃C═O carbonyl group. In aldehydes, the hydrogen atom attached to the carbonyl group leads to different behaviour on oxidation compared to that seen with ketones.

INTRODUCTION TO THE CARBONYL GROUP

26.1

OBJECTIVES

- Aldehydes
- Ketones
- Nucleophilic addition reactions
- Addition of HCN

Carbonyl group symbol

Typographically we have used the symbol ⊃C═O, to represent the carbonyl group

$>C=O$

Rate of reaction

The rate of nucleophilic addition to the carbonyl group increases with the size of the positive charge on the carbon atom. Groups that release electron density towards the carbonyl group will decrease the value of the charge. The order of reactivity is therefore:

$(H)(H)C=O$ methanal > $(R)(H)C=O$ aldehyde > $(R)(R')C=O$ ketone

Remember that the geometry of the R groups ('steric hinderance', see previous chapter) will also influence reaction rates.

Aldehydes and ketones are of immense industrial importance. Propanone CH_3COCH_3 (traditionally called *acetone*) is a ketone widely used as a solvent. Its derivative methyl isobutyl ketone (MIBK) is an important solvent used in the manufacture of plastics. Propanone is also used to form methacrylates, which are the chemical feedstocks for making plastics such as Perspex and acrylic resins. Propanone reacts with phenol to form bisphenol A, which is used to make epoxy resins. Methanal is an industrially important aldehyde used to make plastics such as 'Melamine', spread 29.4. All these substances and their various uses stem from the unique properties of the carbonyl group ⊃C═O and the opportunities it offers for chemical synthesis.

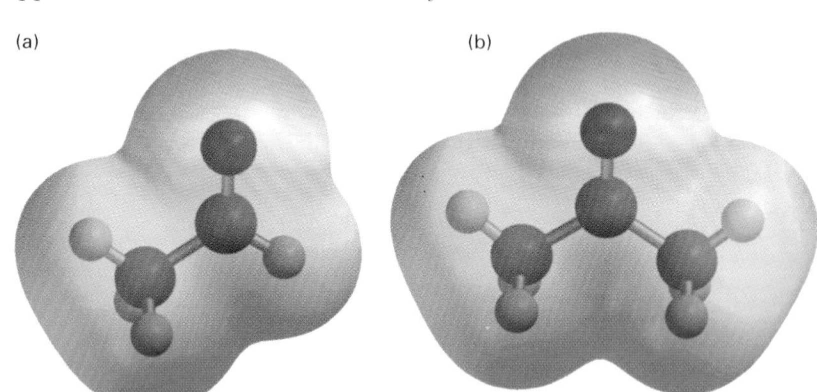

Electrostatic potential maps of (a) ethanal and (b) propanone show the polar nature of the carbonyl group ⊃C═O. The oxygen atom is δ– (shown by red colour); the carbon atom is δ+. Remember that Spartan intentionally does not show the number of bonds; see spread 6.4.

The carbon–oxygen double bond

The structure of the C═O bond makes it a useful starting point for the synthesis of other molecules. At first sight, the C═O bond looks similar to the C═C bond, and indeed both react to saturate the double bond by addition. However, the oxygen atom is much more electronegative than carbon and will attract electron density in the double bond towards itself. The bond is polarized $C^{\delta+}=O^{\delta-}$, thus offering *two* main centres of reactivity, the $C^{\delta+}$ atom and the $O^{\delta-}$ atom. Remember that the C═C bond is non-polar.

- The C═C bond is attacked by electrophiles. The characteristic reaction of alkenes is *electrophilic addition*.
- The $C^{\delta+}$ atom in the ⊃C═O bond is attacked by nucleophiles. There are two possible outcomes: *nucleophilic addition* reactions and *condensation* reactions, which involve nucleophilic addition followed by elimination.

Nucleophilic addition of HCN

Nucleophilic addition of hydrogen cyanide HCN to a carbonyl compound makes the carbon chain longer. Cyanide ions CN^- are nucleophiles and so will attack the $C^{\delta+}$ carbonyl carbon atom. This reaction produces a nitrile that has a hydroxyl group attached to the carbon bearing the nitrile group. These molecules are called **hydroxynitriles**. For example, the reaction of hydrogen cyanide with ethanal (a two-carbon molecule) produces a molecule with a three-carbon chain, as shown below.

The addition of HCN to the carbonyl group in the aldehyde ethanal.

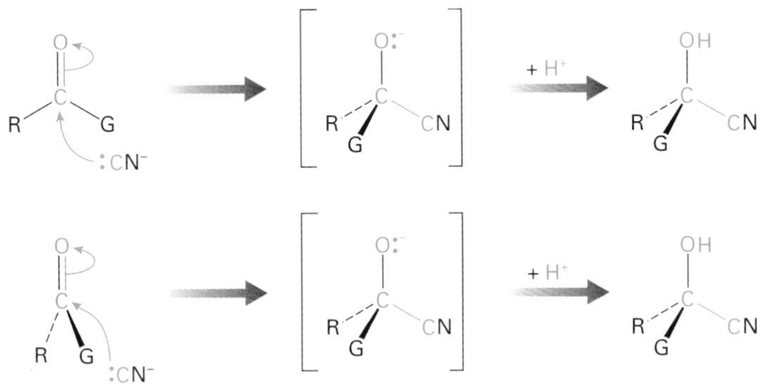

Nucleophilic addition to a carbonyl group leads to an alcohol with a carbon–nucleophile single bond. Note that there is no other product.
The view of the addition of cyanide immediately above gives a more accurate picture of the attack of the ion. Group G is either another R group or a hydrogen.

In general, nucleophilic addition of HCN to an aldehyde or a ketone forms a hydroxynitrile. In the next spread we will study another nucleophilic addition reaction, before turning to condensation reactions in spread 26.3.

SUMMARY

- The formula of the carbonyl group is ⊃C═O.
- Aldehydes have the formula RCHO.
- Ketones have the formula RR′CO.
- The carbonyl group is polarized $C^{\delta+}{=}O^{\delta-}$.
- The most characteristic reaction of the carbonyl group is attack by a nucleophile on the carbonyl carbon atom, leading either to a nucleophilic addition reaction or, after elimination, to a condensation reaction.
- HCN adds to aldehydes and ketones to form hydroxynitriles.

C═O and C═C comparison

In the nucleophilic addition to a carbonyl group, an important feature is that *oxygen* carries the negative charge in the species produced when the nucleophile has attacked. A similar reaction at the C═C bond of alkenes would be very unfavourable as a carbon atom is much less stable than oxygen when carrying a negative charge.

Cyanide

Use of cyanides requires carefully controlled conditions because of the cyanide ion's severe toxicity.

Aldehydes and ketones in Nature

The aldehyde retinal (see chapter on 'Alkanes and alkenes') is important to the function of the human eye. The aldehyde CH_2CHCHO (propenal) is a major component of bonfire and barbecue smoke and is partly responsible for making your eyes water. The ketone $CH_3COCOCH_3$ (butanedione) gives butter and stale sweat their characteristic smells. Carvone is the main constituent of oil of spearmint; zingerone is the active ingredient in ginger. The sex hormones progesterone and testosterone are ketones.

PRACTICE

1 Draw structural formulae for each of the following substances:
- **a** Ethanal
- **b** Propanone
- **c** Propanal
- **d** 2-Methylpropanal
- **e** Butanone
- **f** Pentan-2-one
- **g** Pentan-3-one.

2 Give the name and draw the structural formula of the compound that results from each of the following nucleophilic addition reactions:
- **a** Ethanal + hydrogen cyanide
- **b** Propanal + hydrogen cyanide
- **c** Propanone + hydrogen cyanide.

26.2

OBJECTIVES

- $NaBH_4$
- $LiAlH_4$
- Reduction of aldehydes and ketones

Reduction of aldehydes and ketones

The previous chapter discussed the oxidation of alcohols. To summarize the reactions: oxidation of primary alcohols produces aldehydes; oxidation of secondary alcohols produces ketones. Both these oxidation reactions may be carried out using moderately powerful oxidants such as acidified potassium dichromate(VI). This spread shows that the oxidation of alcohols to produce these carbonyl compounds can be reversed by the action of suitable reductants. Sodium tetrahydridoborate $NaBH_4$ is commonly used for reducing carbonyl compounds. An alternative reagent is the more powerful reductant lithium tetrahydridoaluminate $LiAlH_4$.

$NaBH_4$ and $LiAlH_4$

Sodium tetrahydridoborate $NaBH_4$ and lithium tetrahydridoaluminate $LiAlH_4$ are two common reductants that produce the hydride ion H^-. The hydride ion acts as a nucleophile, attacking the δ+ carbonyl carbon atom in aldehydes and ketones. The hydride ion H^- is also present in sodium hydride Na^+H^-, but sodium hydride is too unstable for use with most organic compounds. The two complexes BH_4^- and AlH_4^- supply hydride ions in a steady and controlled manner during reaction; they are sometimes referred to as 'hydride ion carriers'.

$$Na^+\left[\begin{array}{ccc} & H & \\ H & : B : & H \\ & H & \end{array}\right]^- \qquad Li^+\left[\begin{array}{ccc} & H & \\ H & : Al : & H \\ & H & \end{array}\right]^-$$

Boron and aluminium are both Group III elements. Their hydrides BH_3 and AlH_3 are Lewis acids (see chapter on 'Acid–base equilibrium'), and so can accept the electron pair from a hydride ion to form the complexes BH_4^- and AlH_4^-.

Sodium tetrahydridoborate.

Sodium tetrahydridoborate $NaBH_4$

Sodium tetrahydridoborate is a white crystalline solid which reduces aldehydes and ketones. This reductant can be used either in aqueous solution or in alcoholic solution.

- $NaBH_4$ reduces aldehydes to primary alcohols:

  $$RCHO \xrightarrow{NaBH_4} RCH_2OH$$

For example, ethanal is reduced to ethanol, using [H] to indicate reduction:

$$CH_3CHO \xrightarrow{[H]} CH_3CH_2OH$$

- $NaBH_4$ reduces ketones to secondary alcohols:

  $$RR'CO \xrightarrow{NaBH_4} RR'CHOH$$

For example, propanone is reduced to propan-2-ol:

$$(CH_3)_2CO \xrightarrow{[H]} (CH_3)_2CHOH$$

In both cases, the oxygen atom has not been removed from the molecule, but the carbon–oxygen double bond has been made into a single bond and the molecule has gained two hydrogen atoms. The mechanism is shown at the top of the opposite page.

Reduction of aldehydes and ketones

The reduction of a carbonyl group by $NaBH_4$ is carried out in two stages: (a) the addition of sodium tetrahydridoborate to the carbonyl compound, followed by (b) protonation to produce the final product.

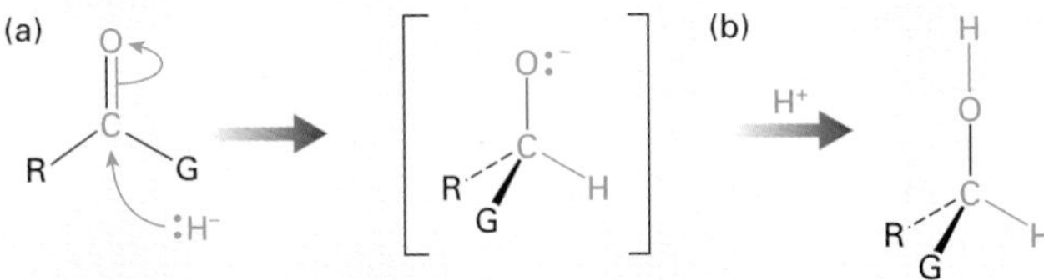

Reduction of a carbonyl group by $NaBH_4$. (a) A hydride ion H^- carries out nucleophilic attack on the δ^+ carbonyl carbon atom. (b) Protonation by the solvent forms the product.

Lithium tetrahydridoaluminate $LiAlH_4$

Lithium tetrahydridoaluminate is a more powerful reductant than sodium tetrahydridoborate. $LiAlH_4$ reduces water too vigorously for it to be used in aqueous solution. As a result, anhydrous conditions are needed when reducing aldehydes and ketones using this reagent. Dry ether (ethoxyethane, spread 25.5) is the solvent commonly used; water is added later to complete the reaction. $LiAlH_4$ acts by a similar mechanism to $NaBH_4$, reducing aldehydes to primary alcohols, and reducing ketones to secondary alcohols.

Familiar name

The names 'sodium tetrahydridoborate' and 'lithium tetrahydridoaluminate' are not convenient to use when asking a colleague to hand you a bottle of reagent. The latter is frequently contracted to 'lithal'.

Comparing with other reductants

Compounds with carbon–carbon double bonds are reduced by catalytic hydrogenation using hydrogen passed over the surface of a heated catalyst. For example, ethene is hydrogenated to ethane:

$$CH_2{=}CH_2 + H_2 \xrightarrow[150\,°C]{Ni} CH_3CH_3$$

The most usual catalysts are the transition metals nickel, palladium, and platinum, spread 22.7. The reaction mechanism is a radical process rather than a nucleophilic one because it involves hydrogen *atoms* adsorbed on the surface of the catalyst (see the chapter on 'Alkanes and alkenes').

Other, more specific, reduction processes are also common in organic chemistry. Two examples are sodium metal reacting with alcohols (see the previous chapter), and tin and hydrochloric acid used to reduce nitrobenzene to phenylamine (see the chapter on 'Organic nitrogen compounds').

SUMMARY

- $NaBH_4$ reduces aldehydes and ketones in aqueous or alcoholic solution.
- $LiAlH_4$ reduces aldehydes and ketones in anhydrous solution in ether: water is added to complete the reaction.
- Aldehydes are reduced to primary alcohols.
- Ketones are reduced to secondary alcohols.
- Reduction occurs by hydride ion attack on the carbonyl carbon atom, followed by protonation.

PRACTICE

1 Give the name and structural formula for the product that results from reducing each of the following substances with $NaBH_4$:
   a Propanone
   b Butanal
   c 2-Methylpropanal.

2 Lithium tetrahydridoaluminate $LiAlH_4$ and sodium tetrahydridoborate $NaBH_4$ have similar structures. Explain why $LiAlH_4$ is the more powerful reductant.

3 Suggest a mechanism for the reaction between lithium tetrahydridoaluminate and the carbonyl group.

4 Indicate briefly how you would obtain a sample of ethane from ethanol.

26.3

CONDENSATION REACTIONS

OBJECTIVES

- Addition–elimination
- DNP

The carbonyl carbon atom bears a partial positive charge $C^{\delta+}$ and so is attacked by nucleophiles. As a result, the characteristic reaction of aldehydes and ketones is *nucleophilic addition*. As discussed in an earlier spread, straightforward addition of a nucleophile H—Nu to a carbonyl group ⊃C═O results in the formation of an alcohol with a single carbon–nucleophile bond ⊃C(OH)Nu. However, there is another type of product that can result from the initial nucleophilic attack on a carbonyl group. The addition product can eliminate water, resulting in the formation of a carbon–nucleophile *double* bond.

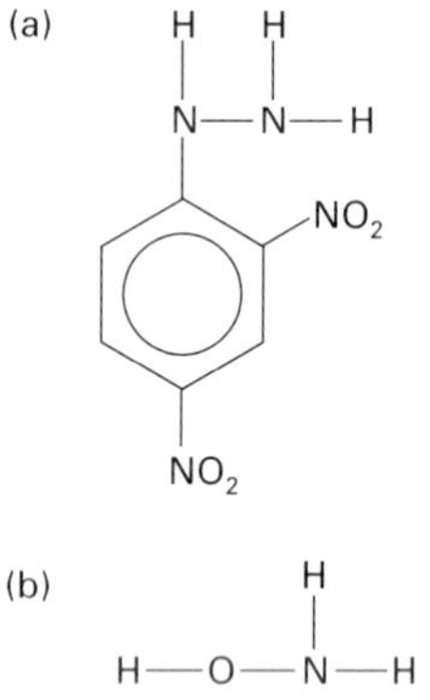

Addition–elimination is condensation

Nucleophilic addition to a carbonyl group may be followed by the elimination of a molecule of water. The oxygen atom in the water molecule originates as the carbonyl oxygen atom and the two hydrogen atoms come from the nucleophile. This class of reaction is called an **addition–elimination** or **condensation** reaction.

This reaction pathway often happens when the electron pair on the attacking nucleophile is the lone pair on a nitrogen atom. The elimination of water results because H—O bonds are stronger than H—N bonds.

There is a series of important nitrogen-containing nucleophiles with the general formula XNH_2. Aldehydes and ketones undergo condensation reactions with these nucleophiles. In general terms:

Aldehyde: $RHC{=}O + XNH_2 \rightarrow RHC{=}NX + H_2O$

Ketone: $RR'C{=}O + XNH_2 \rightarrow RR'C{=}NX + H_2O$

The mechanism for this reaction is outlined below.

(a) H H N—N—H NO₂ ... NO₂ (b) H—O—N—H

Nitrogen-containing nucleophiles with the general formula XNH_2:
(a) 2,4-dinitrophenylhydrazine;
(b) hydroxylamine.

Two possible outcomes of nucleophilic addition to the carbonyl group.

(a) The formation of an alcohol with a carbon–nucleophile *single* bond.

(b) The formation of a carbon–nucleophile double bond by addition and *then* elimination.

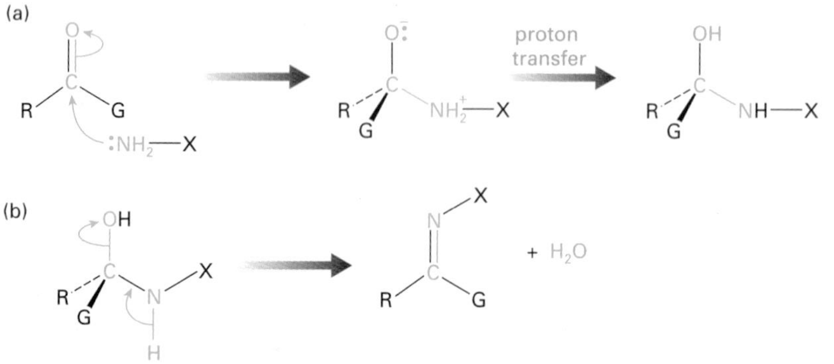

(a) Nucleophilic addition and (b) condensation. G may be R′ or H.

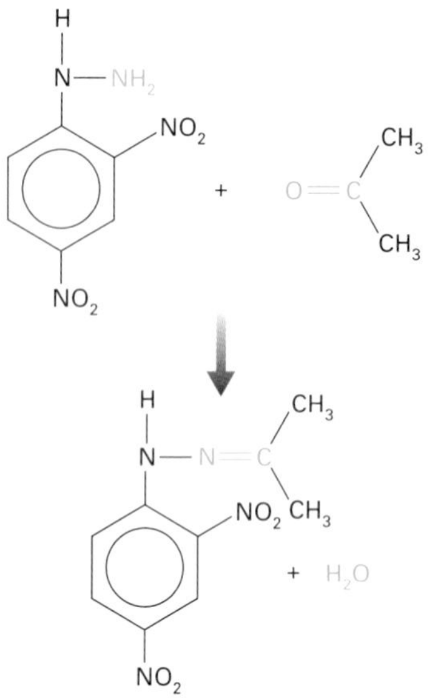

DNP derivatives

DNP is an abbreviation for 2,4-dinitrophenylhydrazine. Aldehydes and ketones undergo rapid condensation reactions in aqueous solution with this substance to form insoluble derivatives called 2,4-dinitrophenylhydrazones. These DNP derivatives are yellow–orange solids. The production of a yellow–orange precipitate on adding an unknown compound to DNP is a positive test for a carbonyl compound (an aldehyde or a ketone). The derivatives also have sharp and characteristic melting points. An aldehyde or ketone may therefore be positively identified by measuring the melting point of its DNP derivative.

The condensation reaction between DNP and propanone. The yellow–orange solid melts sharply at 128 °C. Note that the DNP derivative of propanal (isomeric with propanone) melts at 155 °C.

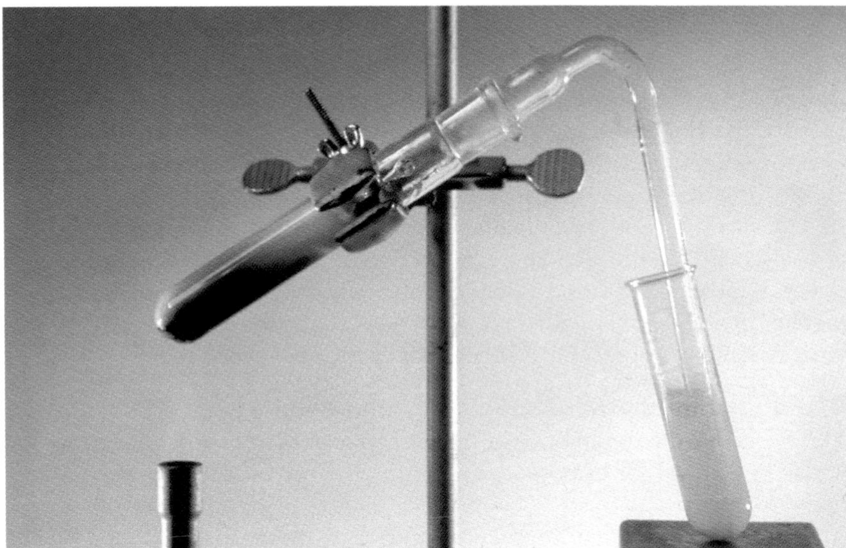

Ethanol is oxidized by potassium dichromate(VI), which turns green, to ethanal and the ethanal is distilled into DNP solution, which forms a yellow-orange precipitate of ethanal 2,4-dinitrophenylhydrazone.

Hydroxylamine derivatives (oximes)

Condensing hydroxylamine $HONH_2$ with an aldehyde or ketone yields the **oxime**. These derivatives usually melt at significantly lower temperatures than the DNP equivalent (e.g. 46 °C for the oxime of ethanal, $CH_3HC{=}NOH$, compared with 168 °C for the DNP derivative). Again, measuring the melting point of an oxime can lead to the identification of the aldehyde or ketone.

SUMMARY

- Carbonyl compounds undergo condensation reactions by nucleophilic addition of compounds of the form XNH_2 to the carbonyl carbon atom followed by elimination of a water molecule to form the structure $\supset C{=}NX$.
- DNP is 2,4-dinitrophenylhydrazine.
- Formation of a yellow-orange precipitate of a DNP derivative indicates the presence of an aldehyde or ketone.
- The melting points of crystalline DNP derivatives enable specific aldehydes and ketones to be identified.

PRACTICE

1 Using structural formulae, write chemical equations to show the reaction between each of the following pairs of reagents:

a Hydroxylamine and cyclohexanone

b 2,4-Dinitrophenylhydrazine and ethanal.

2 Look at the illustration on the opposite page that shows the mechanism of a general addition–elimination (condensation) reaction. Draw Lewis structures to show how bonds are broken and made during the stages of:

a nucleophilic addition;

b the elimination of water.

3 There are two possible outcomes of nucleophilic addition to the carbonyl group: (i) the formation of an alcohol with a carbon–nucleophile single bond and (ii) the formation of a carbon–nucleophile double bond. Discuss the two sorts of reagent that lead to the two possible outcomes, giving examples of each.

26.4

Oxidation of aldehydes

OBJECTIVES

- Aldehydes: reducing properties
- Tollens' reagent
- Fehling's solution
- Ketones resist oxidation

Reminder: aldehyde and ketone preparation

Aldehydes are prepared by the oxidation of a primary alcohol. For example,

$$CH_3CH_2OH \xrightarrow{Cr_2O_7^{2-}(aq)/H^+(aq)} CH_3CHO$$

Ketones are prepared by the oxidation of a secondary alcohol. For example,

$$(CH_3)_2CHOH \xrightarrow{Cr_2O_7^{2-}(aq)/H^+(aq)} (CH_3)_2CO$$

Practical details are given in the previous chapter.

Tollens' reagent

The test was introduced by Bernhard Tollens (1841-1918), hence the position of the apostrophe. Tollens discovered the molecular formula of glucose (see spread 30.2) in 1888.

Both aldehydes and ketones contain the carbonyl group $\supset C{=}O$. The carbonyl carbon atom in ketones joins with two separate alkyl groups to give the general structure RR′CO. In aldehydes, the carbonyl carbon atom is bonded to a hydrogen atom to give the general structure RCHO. The most important difference between these two structures is the presence of the hydrogen atom in aldehydes. The —CHO grouping gives reducing properties to the aldehyde molecule, and so enables aldehydes and ketones to be distinguished by simple chemical tests. Ketones do not have reducing properties: they resist attempts to oxidize them.

Distinguishing between aldehydes and ketones

Aldehydes have reducing properties: it is possible to oxidize them to carboxylic acids, for example by warming them with acidified potassium manganate(VII):

$$RCHO \xrightarrow{MnO_4^-(aq)/H^+(aq)} RCOOH$$

Ketones do not have reducing properties and so are not oxidized under similar conditions. This distinction forms the basis of two very simple tests that distinguish between the two types of carbonyl compound.

Tollens' reagent: the 'silver mirror' test

Tollens' reagent is sometimes called 'ammoniacal silver nitrate'. It is made as follows. A small quantity of aqueous sodium hydroxide is added to aqueous silver nitrate, forming a precipitate of hydrated silver oxide Ag_2O. Addition of aqueous ammonia causes the precipitate to form a solution containing the silver ammine complex $[Ag(NH_3)_2]^+(aq)$. On warming, aldehydes reduce Tollens' reagent, which is colourless, to a grey precipitate of metallic silver. In a thoroughly cleaned glass container, the precipitate forms as a *silver mirror*. Ketones do not react with Tollens' reagent.

Left: The 'silver mirror' test with Tollens' reagent. Aldehydes reduce the ammine complex of silver $[Ag(NH_3)_2]^+(aq)$ to metallic silver. Ketones do not react with Tollens' reagent. Right: The test with Fehling's solution. Aldehydes reduce a $Cu^{2+}(aq)$ complex to a brick-red precipitate of Cu_2O. Ketones do not react with Fehling's solution.

Fehling's solution

Fehling's solution contains a complex of Cu^{2+}. It is made by mixing 'Fehling's A' (aqueous copper(II) sulphate) with 'Fehling's B' (an alkaline solution of sodium potassium 2,3-dihydroxybutanedioate (sodium potassium tartrate)). On warming, aldehydes reduce Fehling's solution, which is blue, to a brick-red precipitate of copper(I) oxide Cu_2O. (Methanal reduces the solution further to metallic copper.) Ketones do not react with Fehling's solution.

Worked example on identifying aldehydes and ketones

Question: A substance **A** has the molecular formula $C_4H_{10}O$. It oxidizes to the carbonyl compound **B** (C_4H_8O). **B** gives a brick-red precipitate with Fehling's solution. Passing the vapour of **A** over heated aluminium oxide forms **C** (C_4H_8). **C** reacts with hydroiodic acid HI(aq) forming **D** (C_4H_9I). **D** may be hydrolysed and then oxidized to **E** (C_4H_8O). **E** contains a carbonyl group but does not react with Fehling's solution. Identify **A** to **E** and explain the reactions.

Strategy: Find one substance that you can positively identify with no ambiguity and then work from that substance. It is often better to start with the last substance in the sequence, rather than initially concentrating on the first step.

Answer: Compound **E** is a carbonyl compound that contains four carbon atoms. It must be a ketone because it does not react with Fehling's solution. The only four-carbon ketone is butanone. Therefore **E** must be butanone $CH_3CH_2COCH_3$.

E is butanone, so **D** must be the iodoalkane $CH_3CH_2CHICH_3$, which hydrolyses to the corresponding secondary alcohol, $CH_3CH_2CH(OH)CH_3$, which oxidizes to butanone.

C is an alkene to which HI will add to form the iodoalkane **D**. However, the position of the double bond is uncertain at this stage.

B must be an aldehyde because it is a carbonyl compound that reacts with Fehling's solution. The straight-chain four-carbon aldehyde is butanal $CH_3CH_2CH_2CHO$. **B** is formed by oxidation of **A**; therefore, **A** must be the primary alcohol $CH_3CH_2CH_2CH_2OH$ (butan-1-ol).

C is formed by dehydration of **A** and hence the double bond occupies the 1,2-position $CH_3CH_2CH{=}CH_2$ (but-1-ene). When HI adds to **C**, Markovnikov's rule (see chapter on 'Alkanes and alkenes') states that the product will be $CH_3CH_2CHICH_3$, **D**.

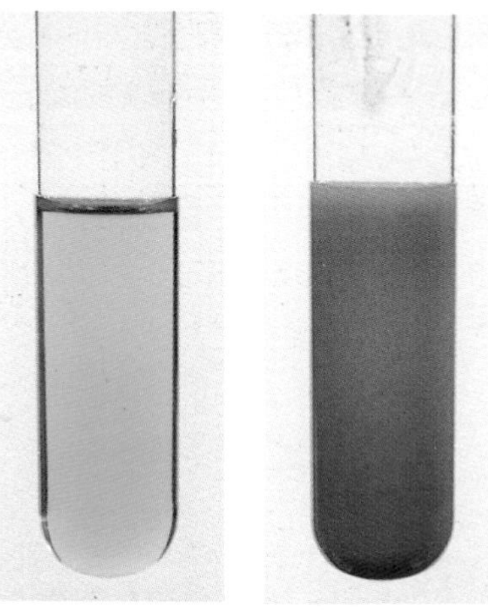

***Benedict's solution** (favoured more by biologists than chemists) is very similar to Fehling's solution, but uses citrate ions instead of tartrate ions. On warming, aldehydes reduce the Cu^{2+} complex to brick-red copper(I) oxide. Ketones do not react with Benedict's solution.*

Comment

The ketone **E** (butanone) is an isomer of the aldehyde **B** (butanal). 2-Methylpropanal $(CH_3)_2CHCHO$ is a branched-chain isomer of the aldehyde **B**. This isomer would behave almost identically to butanal. It is therefore a better strategy to identify the carbon chain as unbranched (by identifying **E**) rather than starting at **A** and working forwards, in which case it would be necessary to consider both the straight-chain and branched-chain alternatives.

SUMMARY

- Aldehydes are reductants; ketones are not.
- Aldehydes are readily oxidized to carboxylic acids.
- Aldehydes reduce Tollens' reagent, which is colourless, to a silver mirror.
- Aldehydes reduce Fehling's solution, which is blue, to a brick-red precipitate of copper(I) oxide.
- Ketones do not react with Tollens' reagent or with Fehling's solution.

PRACTICE

1 To what substance is ethanal converted when it reacts with Fehling's solution?

2 Substances **P** and **Q** are carbonyl compounds and both have the molecular formula C_3H_6O. **P** gives a positive result with Fehling's solution; **Q** gives a negative result with Tollens' reagent. Give the names and structural formulae of substances **P** and **Q**.

3 Substance **A** has the molecular formula C_4H_9Br. Hydrolysis with boiling aqueous sodium hydroxide gives **B** ($C_4H_{10}O$). Treating **B** with acidified potassium dichromate(VI) gives a carbonyl compound **C** (C_4H_8O).
- **a** Give the structural formulae and names of the substances **A**, **B**, and **C**.
- **b** Give the name and structural formula of an isomer of **C** that would give a positive result with Tollens' reagent.

4 Three compounds are an aldehyde, a ketone, and an alcohol. Identify them from the following information.
- **a** **A** forms a yellow-orange precipitate on reaction with DNP; **A** does not change the colour of Fehling's solution.
- **b** **B** does not form a precipitate on reacting with DNP; **B** does not change the colour of Fehling's solution.
- **c** **C** forms a yellow-orange precipitate on reaction with DNP; **C** deposits a silver mirror on the inside of the test tube when treated with Tollens' reagent.

26.5

OBJECTIVES

- C=C position
- Oxidative cleavage

Some worked examples from analysis

One of the problems often facing an organic chemist is to identify an unknown substance. The task of analysis involves discovering the molecular formula, the structure of the carbon skeleton, the functional groups present, and the positions of those groups on the skeleton. Data come from a wide range of sources, from simple test tube experiments to sophisticated techniques such as mass spectrometry and nuclear magnetic resonance (see the last two chapters in this book). The task is then to arrive at a structural formula that fits the data. While much of the process involves logical analysis of data, chemists also need to trust their intuition and test out hunches.

Manganate(VII) summary

Hot acidified potassium manganate(VII) splits an alkene molecule at the C=C double bond. For example,

$CH_2{=}CH_2 \rightarrow 2CH_2O$

Dilute alkaline potassium manganate(VII) changes from purple to green as it oxidizes the C=C bond. For example,

$CH_2{=}CH_2 \rightarrow HOCH_2CH_2OH$

The position of a double bond

Vigorous oxidation breaks a carbon–carbon double bond, splitting an alkene molecule into two parts. The process is called **oxidative cleavage**. Oxidation of the C=C bond produces two carbonyl groups where the double bond was, i.e.

$$\supset C{=}C\subset \xrightarrow{[O]} \supset C{=}O + O{=}C\subset$$

Oxidation is carried out either by hot acidified potassium manganate(VII) or by ozone O_3. Each of the two carbonyl compounds may then be identified, for example by forming the DNP derivatives and measuring their melting points.

Worked example 1

Question: Identify the alkene that forms propanone and ethanal on heating with hot acidified potassium manganate(VII).

Strategy: The carbon–oxygen double bonds occupy the same positions in the carbonyl compounds as the carbon–carbon double bond occupied in the alkene.

Answer: The diagram below shows the two halves of the molecule being reassembled to form the alkene $(CH_3)_2C{=}CHCH_3$.

Note: Selective cleavage of a double bond can also be achieved by reaction with ozone in a process called **ozonolysis**. The initial product from the addition of ozone is hydrolysed to form the separate carbonyl compounds.

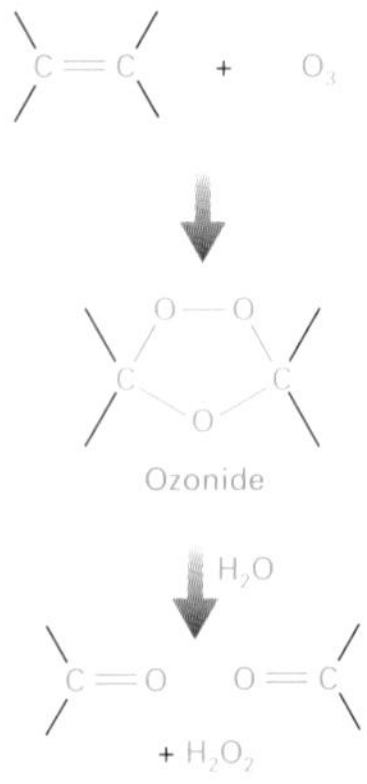

Ozonolysis occurs in two steps: (a) The formation of an ozonide. (b) Hydrolysis of the ozonide by water to form two carbonyl compounds.

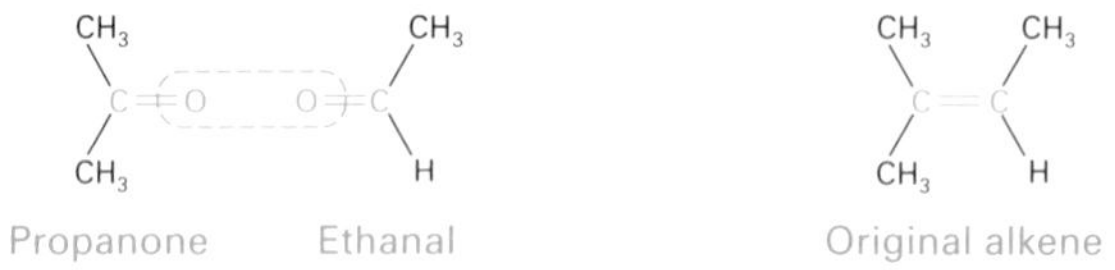

Determining the alkene structure by combining the two carbonyl compounds that result from oxidative cleavage.

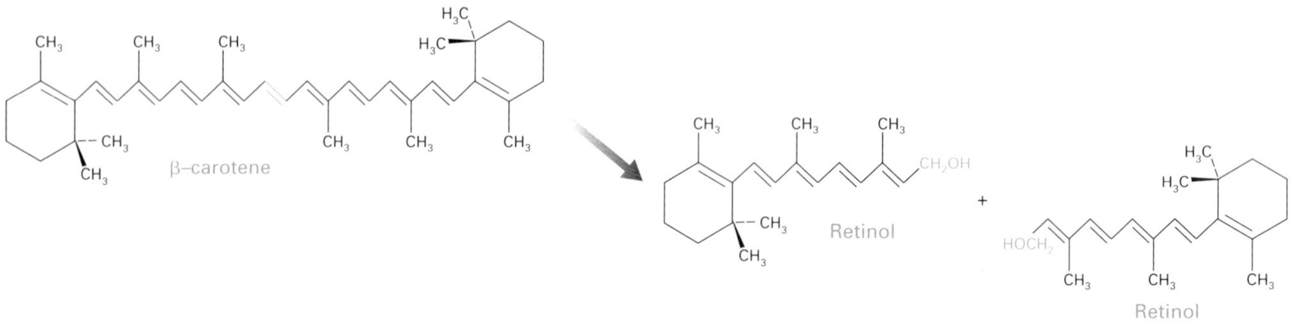

Fission at a double bond occurs in our own human biochemistry. Carrots contain β-carotene, which undergoes enzymatic oxidative cleavage (which produces two alcohols rather than two carbonyl compounds) to produce two molecules of retinol (vitamin A). The oxidized form, retinal, is a constituent of the visual pigment rhodopsin present in the retina, spread 22.6. So – it is actually true that carrots can help you to see better.

Worked example 2

Question: A substance **S** has the molecular formula C_4H_9Br. After boiling with aqueous sodium hydroxide, a product **T**, of formula $C_4H_{10}O$, was formed. On oxidation, **T** formed **U** (C_4H_8O), which reacted to form a DNP derivative but gave no reaction with Fehling's solution. Identify **S**, **T**, and **U**. Name a reagent that can convert **U** into **T**.

Strategy: Find one substance that you can positively identify with no ambiguity and then work from that substance. It is often better to start with the last substance in the sequence, rather than initially concentrating on the first step.

Answer: Because it reacted to form a DNP derivative, **U** is a carbonyl compound. A carbonyl compound that does not react with Fehling's solution must be a ketone. There is only one ketone of formula C_4H_8O: therefore **U** is butanone $CH_3COCH_2CH_3$. A ketone is formed by oxidation of a secondary alcohol. Therefore **T** is butan-2-ol $CH_3CH(OH)CH_2CH_3$. **S** must be the *secondary* halogenoalkane, $CH_3CHBrCH_2CH_3$. A suitable reagent to convert butanone (**U**) to butan-2-ol (**T**) is $NaBH_4$.

*A flow scheme of the reactions of substances **S**, **T**, and **U**. It is good practice always to summarize your answers to analysis questions in this form.*

SUMMARY

- Oxidation by hot acidified potassium manganate(VII) splits an alkene double bond (by oxidative cleavage) to form two separate carbonyl compounds.
- Ozone adds across a double bond to form an ozonide; hydrolysis results in two separate carbonyl compounds.
- The structure of an alkene is determined by fitting together the structures of the carbonyl compounds formed on oxidative cleavage of the original C═C bond.

PRACTICE

1 An alkene **N** (of formula C_6H_{12}) gave two compounds **M** (of formula C_3H_6O) and **P** (of formula C_3H_6O) on oxidative cleavage. On warming with Fehling's solution, **M** produced a brick-red precipitate but there was no reaction with **P**. Name the compounds **N**, **M**, and **P** (giving your reasoning), and draw the structural formula of each.

2 An alkene **P** (of formula C_6H_{10}) gave a single compound **Q** (of formula $C_6H_{10}O_2$) on oxidative cleavage. **Q** formed an orange precipitate on warming with DNP. It also gave a positive result with Fehling's solution and Tollens' reagent. Suggest possible names for the compounds **P** and **Q** (giving your reasoning), and draw the structural formula of each.

3 Compound **A** is an iodoalkane. Warming **A** with dilute aqueous sodium hydroxide forms **B**, which is oxidized to **C** by acidified potassium dichromate(VI). **C** does not react with Fehling's solution but does form a DNP derivative. Boiling **A** with alcoholic potassium hydroxide solution forms **D** by elimination. Oxidative cleavage of **D** results in **E** (HCHO) and **F** (C_3H_6O), both of which give a silver mirror with Tollens' reagent. Name the compounds **A** to **F** (giving your reasoning), and draw the structural formula of each.

26.6

OBJECTIVES

- Reaction at the α-carbon atom
- The triiodomethane (iodoform) test

THE TRIIODOMETHANE (IODOFORM) REACTION

The reactions of the carbonyl group described so far include nucleophilic addition and condensation (nucleophilic addition–elimination). These reactions are confined to the carbon atom and the oxygen atom that make up the carbonyl group ⊃C═O. However, the influence of the carbonyl group reaches further along the molecule than you might suppose. The carbon atom, and its associated hydrogen atoms, *next to* the carbonyl group have greater reactivity than expected for a hydrocarbon CH_2 group. The hydrogen atoms may be substituted with halogen atoms. This behaviour is the basis of the triiodomethane reaction, a useful test that establishes the presence of two particular molecular structures.

The α-carbon atom

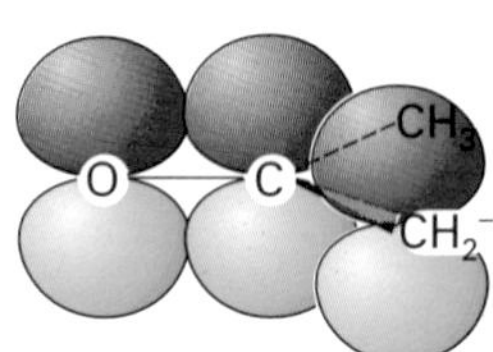

Delocalization of the lone pair on carbon with the π bond of the carbonyl group.

The **α-carbon atom** in a carbonyl compound is the carbon atom *next to* the one bearing the functional group. The carbonyl group ⊃C═O has a potentially useful effect on the C—H bonds of the α-carbon atom. When a hydrogen atom is removed from the α-carbon atom, the C═O double bond helps to delocalize the negative charge left on the α-carbon atom. Delocalization lowers the energy of the negative ion and so makes subsequent reaction much more likely to happen. As a result, the C—H bonds of the α-carbon atom are relatively easy to break. The mechanism is shown below for a typical reaction.

(a) CH_3COCH_2–H + :OH^- $\xrightarrow{-H_2O}$ (b) $:CH_2^-COCH_3$ $\xrightarrow{I_2}$ (c) $ICH_2COCH_3 + I^-$

Mechanism of iodination of the α-carbon atom.

The iodination of propanone, spread 15.6, is a good example of a reaction that occurs at the α-carbon atom C—H bond. We shall use this particular example to illustrate the general mechanism:

(a) Base causes the C—H bond to break heterolytically.

(b) The negative ion is stabilized by delocalization of the charge by overlap of the p orbitals on the atomic centres C—C═O.

(c) The ion can then react with a halogen, such as iodine. Note that all three hydrogen atoms on the α-carbon may be substituted by iodine as shown below.

$CH_3COCH_3 \longrightarrow CH_3COCH_2I \longrightarrow CH_3COCHI_2 \longrightarrow CH_3COCI_3$

All three of the α-carbon hydrogen atoms may be replaced by halogen.

The triiodomethane (iodoform) test

The substitution by iodine is the basis of a test for carbonyl compounds that contain the structure —$COCH_3$. Iodine in basic solution reacts with these compounds to form triiodomethane CHI_3. This substance forms a yellow precipitate and has a characteristic antiseptic smell. The reaction is known as the **triiodomethane test** or **iodoform test**. The reaction occurs in two stages. First, the iodine substitutes for all three of the hydrogen atoms in the methyl group as outlined above:

$$CH_3CH_2COCH_3 \xrightarrow{I_2/OH^-} CH_3CH_2COCI_3$$

Then excess base hydrolyses the molecule causing the C—C bond to break, releasing triiodomethane:

$$CH_3CH_2COCI_3 \xrightarrow{OH^-} CH_3CH_2CO_2^- + CHI_3$$

The mechanism is shown at the top of the opposite page.

Alcohols

Secondary alcohols that contain the structure —$CH(OH)CH_3$ are oxidized by iodine to the —$COCH_3$ structure and so they also give a positive triiodomethane test. The triiodomethane reaction is also a method of breaking a C—C bond and removing a methyl —CH_3 group. It is therefore a method of shortening a chain by a *single* carbon atom.

The mechanism for the formation of triiodomethane from propanone in the triiodomethane test is as follows. (Note that triiodopropanone forms as shown in the mechanism box on the opposite page.)

(a) Base carries out nucleophilic attack on the carbonyl carbon atom.

(b) The C—CI_3 bond breaks to form ethanoic acid and the CI_3^- ion, the three electronegative iodine atoms helping to stabilize the negative charge.

(c) Ethanoic acid transfers a proton to the CI_3^- ion to form triiodomethane and the ethanoate ion.

(a) $CH_3COCI_3 + {:}OH^- \rightarrow CH_3C(O^-)(OH)CI_3$

(b) $CH_3C(O^-)(OH)CI_3 \rightarrow {:}CI_3^- + CH_3COOH$

(c) ${:}CI_3^- + CH_3COOH \rightarrow CH_3CO_2^- + CHI_3$

Mechanism of the triiodomethane test.

SUMMARY

- The α-carbon atom in a carbonyl compound is the carbon atom *next to* the one bearing the carbonyl group.
- The hydrogen atoms on the α-carbon atom in an aldehyde or ketone are substituted in basic solution by halogens.
- Compounds containing the structure —$COCH_3$ or —$CH(OH)CH_3$ form a precipitate of triiodomethane CHI_3 when treated with a basic solution of iodine.
- The triiodomethane reaction is a useful method in chemical synthesis for shortening a carbon chain by a single carbon atom.

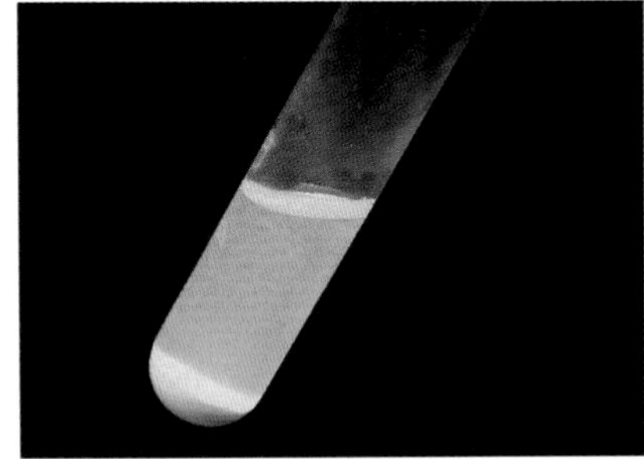

The yellow precipitate of triiodomethane (iodoform).

PRACTICE

1 Draw structural formulae for the two molecular structures, either of which will give a positive triiodomethane reaction.

2 Give examples of three-, four-, and five-carbon compounds that will give a positive reaction to the triiodomethane test.

3 Outline the practical method you would use to produce propanoic acid from butanone.

4 The hydrogen atoms attached to the α-carbon atom of an aldehyde or ketone are sometimes described as being 'acidic'. What evidence can you find in this spread to support this statement?

Chapter 26 Reactions summary

- Oxidation of a primary alcohol to form an aldehyde:
  $CH_3CH_2OH \xrightarrow{Cr_2O_7^{2-}/H^+} CH_3CHO$
- Oxidation of a secondary alcohol to form a ketone:
  $(CH_3)_2CHOH \xrightarrow{Cr_2O_7^{2-}/H^+} (CH_3)_2CO$
- Nucleophilic addition of HCN to ethanal:
  $CH_3CHO + HCN \rightarrow CH_3CH(OH)CN$
- Nucleophilic addition of HCN to propanone:
  $(CH_3)_2CO + HCN \rightarrow (CH_3)_2C(OH)CN$
- Reduction of an aldehyde to a primary alcohol:
  $CH_3CHO \xrightarrow{NaBH_4} CH_3CH_2OH$
- Reduction of a ketone to a secondary alcohol:
  $(CH_3)_2CO \xrightarrow{NaBH_4} (CH_3)_2CHOH$
- Condensation between propanone and DNP:

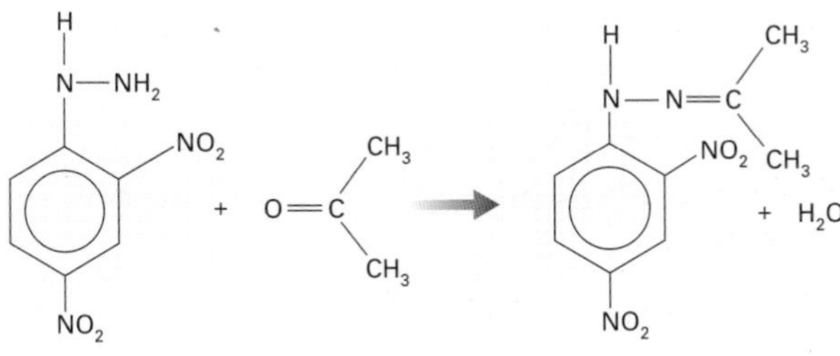

A yellow–orange precipitate on reaction with DNP confirms the presence of a carbonyl compound.

- Oxidation of an aldehyde to a carboxylic acid:
  $CH_3CHO \xrightarrow{MnO_4^-/H^+} CH_3COOH$
  This reaction distinguishes an aldehyde from a ketone.
- Aldehydes reduce Tollens' reagent, which is colourless, to a silver mirror. Ketones do not react.
- Aldehydes reduce Fehling's solution, which is blue, to a brick-red precipitate of copper(I) oxide. Ketones do not react.
- Oxidative cleavage at an alkene double bond:
  $\supset C{=}C\subset \xrightarrow{[O]} \supset C{=}O + O{=}C\subset$
  The oxidant is either hot acidified potassium manganate(VII) or ozone.
- The triiodomethane test is a test for the presence of —$COCH_3$ or —$CH(OH)CH_3$

A positive result is a yellow precipitate of CHI_3.

PRACTICE EXAM QUESTIONS

1 **a** Outline the reaction of propanone with the following reagents. Give the equation for the reaction, the conditions, and the name of the organic product.

i Hydrogen cyanide. [3]

ii Sodium tetrahydridoborate (sodium borohydride). [3]

b **i** Give the mechanism for the reaction in **a i**. [3]

ii What type of mechanism is this? [1]

iii What feature of the carbonyl group makes this type of mechanism possible? Explain how this feature arises. [2]

iv Explain briefly, by reference to its structure, why ethene would not react with HCN in a similar way. [1]

EDEXCEL 1998

2 **a** Give a chemical test by which you could distinguish between ethanal and propanone. State the reagent(s) and conditions for the test, describe what you would observe, and give the name or formula of the organic product. [4]

b Consider the following series of reactions involving ethanal, then answer the questions which follow.

S ←HCN(l)— CH_3CHO —2,4-Dinitrophenylhydrazine→ T

CH_3CHO —$NaBH_4$→ U

i Draw graphical formulae to show the structures of compounds **S**, **T** and **U**. [3]

ii Give the name of compound **T** and describe its appearance. [2]

c Give the name and an outline of the mechanism for the reaction of ethanal with HCN(l) to produce compound **S**. [4]

AQA (AEB) 1996

3 **a** Give the structural formula to show clearly the organic product formed from each of the following mixtures. If you consider no reaction occurs, you should state 'no reaction'.

i 1-bromobutane with KOH in water;

ii 1-bromobutane with KOH in alcohol;

iii propanal with hydrogen cyanide;

iv 1-bromopropane with potassium cyanide;

v propan-1-ol with ammoniacal silver nitrate;

vi propanone with ammoniacal silver nitrate;

vii propan-1-o1 with acidified potassium dichromate(VI), heated under reflux;

viii propan-2-ol with acidified potassium dichromate(VI), heated under reflux. [8]

b For each of the four reactions **a i–iv**, state what type of reaction is occurring. [4]

c **i** Give the mechanism for the reaction of hydrogen cyanide with propanal. [3]

ii If the pH of this reaction mixture is too low or too high, the reaction is very slow. Explain why in both cases. [2]

EDEXCEL 1997

4 Propenal, $CH_2{=}CHCHO$, is one of the materials that gives crispy bacon its sharp odour. In the following question assume that the carbon–carbon double bond and the aldehyde group in propenal behave independently.

a Give the structural formulae of the compounds formed when propenal reacts with:

i hydrogen bromide; [2]

ii hydrogen cyanide; [1]

iii 2,4-dinitrophenylhydrazine. [2]

b **i** Give the mechanism for the reaction between hydrogen cyanide and the aldehyde group. You may represent the aldehyde group as

[3]

ii The reaction in **i** occurs best in slightly acidic conditions. It is slower if the pH is high or low. Suggest reasons why this is so. [3]

c Explain why lithium tetrahydridoaluminate (lithium aluminium hydride), $LiAlH_4$, reacts only with the ⊃C=O bond and not with the ⊃C=C⊂ bond, even though these bonds have the same electronic structure. [2]

d Suggest reactions, giving equations and conditions, which would convert propenal into a compound which would react with iodine in the presence of sodium hydroxide solution. [4]

EDEXCEL 1998

5 **a** Compound **W** can be converted into three different organic compounds as shown by the reaction sequence below. Give the structures of the new compounds **X**, **Y**, and **Z**.

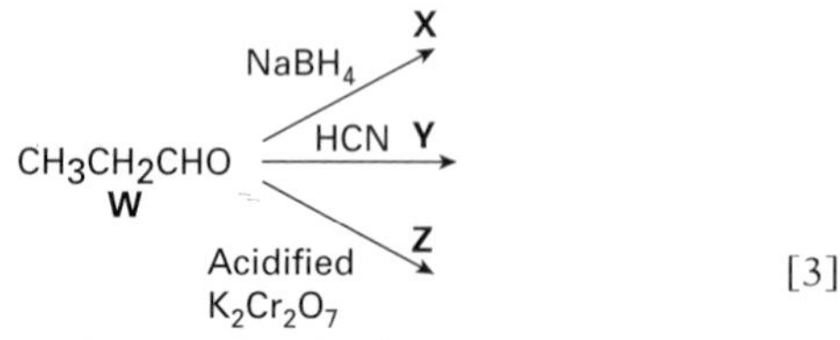

[3]

b Outline a mechanism for the formation of **Y**.

c The infrared spectra shown opposite are those of the four compounds **W**, **X**, **Y** and **Z**. [4]

i Using the table of infrared absorption data given opposite, identify which compound would give rise to each spectrum by labelling each spectrum with the letter **W**, **X**, **Y**, or **Z**.

ii Suggest the wavenumber of the absorption caused by the C≡N bond. (The wavenumber of this absorption is outside the fingerprint region.) [5]

Table of infrared absorption data

Bond	Wavenumber/cm^{-1}
C—H	2850–3300
C—C	750–1100
C=C	1620–1680
C=O	1680–1750
C—O	1000–1300
O—H in alcohols	3230–3550
O—H in acids	2500–3000

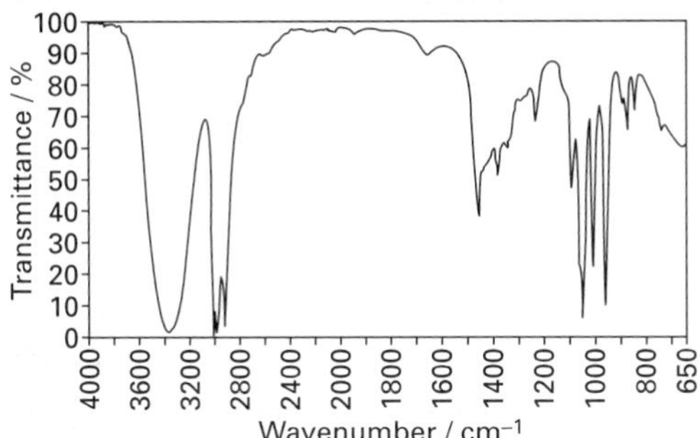

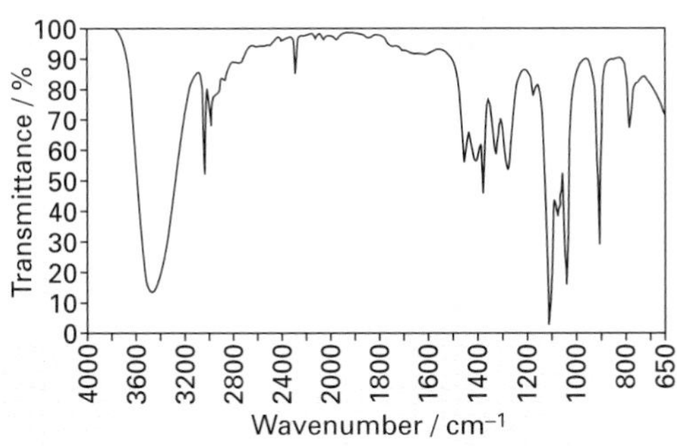

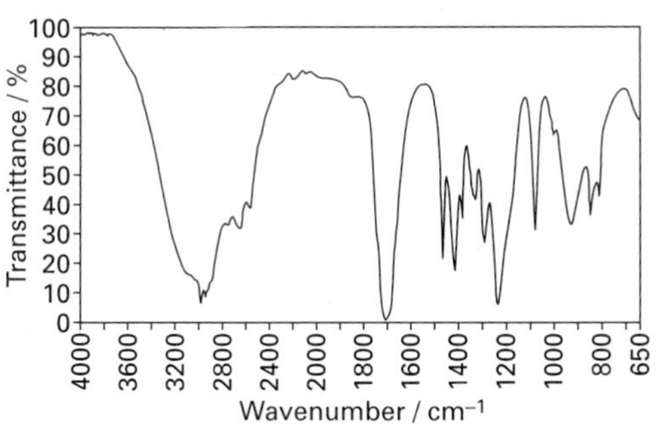

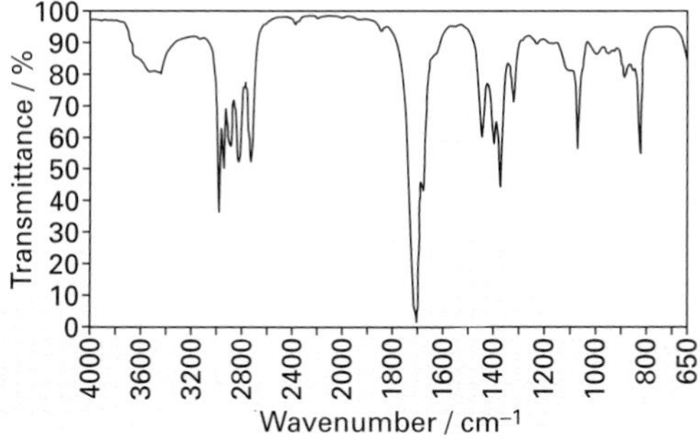

AQA (NEAB) 1998 *(See also Chapter 32.)*

6 a i Copy and complete the table below which shows some of the reactions of propanal. [6]

Reactant	Reagent(s)	Organic product	
		Name	**Graphic formula**
CH_3CH_2CHO	Fehling's solution		
CH_3CH_2CHO	$NaBH_4$		
CH_3CH_2CHO		2-hydroxybutanenitrile	

ii Describe and explain what you would see in the reaction of propanal with Fehling's solution. [3]

iii Give another example of this type of reaction with propanal. [2]

b For each of the following reactions, give the name of the type of mechanism involved and the formula of the attacking inorganic species.

i $CH_3CH_2CH_2Br + NaOH \rightarrow CH_3CH_2CH_2OH + NaBr$ [2]

ii $CH_2CH_2 + HBr \rightarrow CH_3CH_2Br$ [2]

AQA (AEB) 1997

7 The polymer poly(methyl 2-methylpropenoate) (Perspex) can be made by a process which involves the following reactions.

$(H_3C)_2C{=}O \xrightarrow[\text{Step 1}]{\text{Reagent A}} CH_3{-}C(CH_3)(CN){-}OH \xrightarrow{\text{Step 2}} H_2C{=}C(CH_3)COOH$

$H_2C{=}C(CH_3)COOH \xrightarrow[\text{Reagent B}]{\text{Step 3}} H_2C{=}C(CH_3)COOCH_3 \rightarrow \text{Perspex}$

a i Identify Reagent **A**.

ii Name and outline the mechanism for the reaction in Step 1. [6]

b i Name Reagent **B**.

ii Name the type of reaction occurring and give a substance which would act as a catalyst for the reaction in Step 3. [3]

c Draw the repeating unit of Perspex.

d Write an equation for the reaction between the product of Step 2 with sodium hydroxide, showing clearly the structure of the new product. [2]

AQA (NEAB) 1997

27 Carboxylic acids and their derivatives

Carboxylic acids RCOOH contain the functional group —COOH. Aldehydes and ketones contain the carbonyl group ⊃C═O, and alcohols contain the hydroxyl group —OH. You might assume that carboxylic acids have a blend of the properties of aldehydes, ketones, and alcohols, but this is not the case. The carboxylic acid group has its own distinctive and unique properties. **Carboxylic acid derivatives** include acyl chlorides RCOCl, esters RCOOR′, and amides $RCONH_2$. In acyl chlorides, a chlorine replaces the —OH group of the parent acid. In esters, the H atom is replaced by an alkyl or aryl group. The first spread of this chapter is devoted to the properties of carboxylic acids; the remaining spreads consider their derivatives.

An introduction to carboxylic acids

27.1

OBJECTIVES

- Preparation of carboxylic acids
- Carboxylic acids as weak acids
- Charge is delocalized in the carboxylate ion
- Comparison with ethanol and phenol

Carboxylic acids are the most important class of organic acids. They neutralize bases to form salts, and their aqueous solutions have pH values below 7. Acid behaviour is described in the chapter on 'Acid–base equilibrium': Brønsted–Lowry theory defines acids as proton donors. You will see that Brønsted–Lowry theory describes the behaviour of organic acids in exactly the same way as it describes the behaviour of inorganic acids.

The preparation of carboxylic acids

Aliphatic carboxylic acids are prepared by the oxidation of primary alcohols (see chapter on 'Alcohols'). For example, refluxing ethanol with acidified potassium dichromate(VI) produces the aldehyde ethanal, which is then oxidized to ethanoic acid:

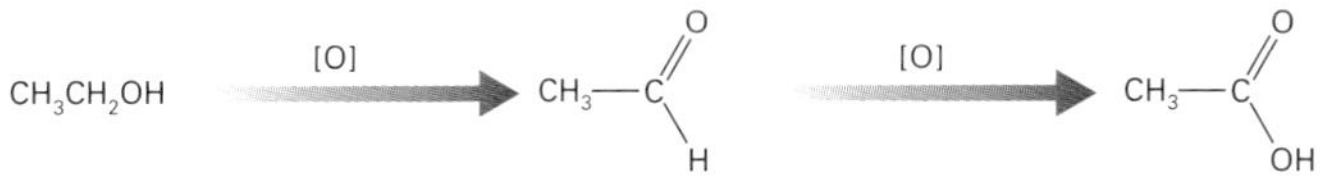

$$CH_3CH_2OH \xrightarrow{[O]} CH_3CHO \xrightarrow{[O]} CH_3COOH$$

Aromatic carboxylic acids consist of a carboxylic acid group attached *directly* to a benzene ring. They are prepared by the oxidation of an alkyl group attached to a benzene ring. For example, refluxing methylbenzene with alkaline potassium manganate(VII) produces benzoic acid (after neutralization):

$$C_6H_5CH_3 \xrightarrow{[O]} C_6H_5COOH$$

Preparing benzoic acid

Note that methylbenzene, ethylbenzene, or any other benzene compound with an alkyl side chain (however long) will produce the *same* product, benzoic acid (see chapter on 'Arenes'). The rest of the side chain is destroyed, forming carbon dioxide and water. For example

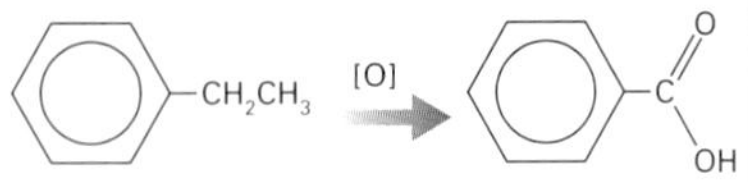

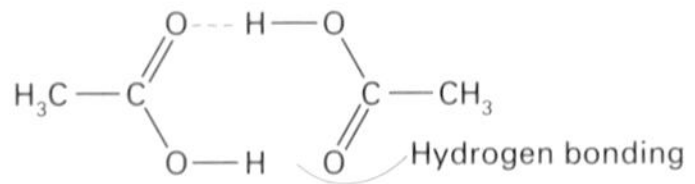

$$C_6H_5CH_2CH_3 \xrightarrow{[O]} C_6H_5COOH$$

Physical properties

The lower aliphatic carboxylic acids are colourless liquids, usually with sharp or distinctive smells. Boiling points are higher than would be expected by considering their relative formula masses only; the molecules form dimers by means of hydrogen bonding. Pure ethanoic acid CH_3COOH boils at 118 °C and melts at 17 °C. On cold days, it freezes to form needle-shaped crystals, hence the name 'glacial ethanoic acid'.

Benzoic acid (systematically called benzenecarboxylic acid) C_6H_5COOH is the simplest aromatic carboxylic acid. It is a white crystalline solid (T_m = 122 °C; T_b = 249 °C). Compared with ethanoic acid, a larger proportion of this molecule consists of a non-polar hydrocarbon skeleton. It has only limited solubility in water at 25 °C but dissolves fairly readily in hot water.

Hydrogen bonding

Two hydrogen bonds form between molecules of ethanoic acid, holding the molecules together in a dimer.

Acid behaviour

Carboxylic acids are weak acids. For example:

$$CH_3COOH(aq) + H_2O(l) \rightleftharpoons H_3O^+(aq) + CH_3CO_2^-(aq)$$

Aqueous ethanoic acid of concentration 1 mol dm^{-3} has a pH of 2.4 (corresponding to an acid ionization constant K_a of 2×10^{-5} mol dm^{-3}). The negative charge on the resulting **ethanoate ion** ($CH_3CO_2^-$) is stabilized by delocalization, the two oxygen atoms now being identical (see the diagram top right and spread 6.4).

Benzoic acid acts as a proton donor in the same way as ethanoic acid:

$$C_6H_5COOH(aq) + H_2O(l) \rightleftharpoons H_3O^+(aq) + C_6H_5CO_2^-(aq)$$

It has an acid ionization constant of 6×10^{-5} mol dm^{-3}.

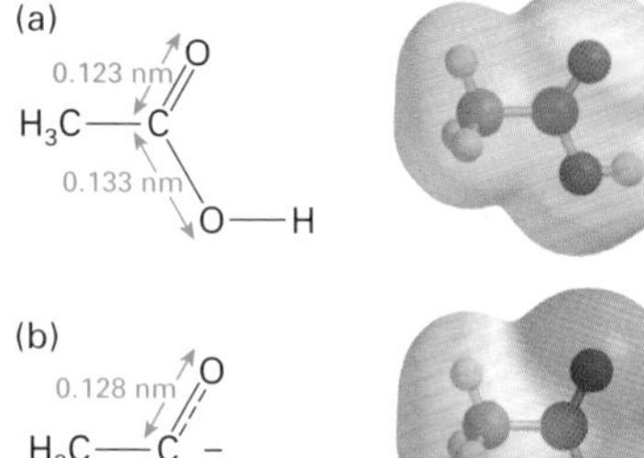

Electrostatic potential maps. (a) The un-ionized ethanoic acid molecule: the C—O bond is longer than the C=O bond. (b) The ethanoate ion: the negative charge in the ethanoate ion is delocalized. Both C—O bonds are equivalent, having the same bond lengths and electron densities (intermediate between C—O and C=O).

Carboxylic acids, alcohols, and phenols

Brønsted acidity is associated with proton transfer from a molecule, usually to water. Wherever there is a C—O—H group in an organic molecule, the potential exists for proton transfer. However, the detailed structure of the organic molecule affects how readily the proton transfers. Remember that water self-ionizes slightly in the liquid state:

$$2H_2O(l) \rightleftharpoons H_3O^+(aq) + OH^-(aq); \qquad pK_w = 14.0 \text{ at } 25\,°C$$

Water provides a useful comparison for the acidity of organic compounds. The order of acid ionization is alcohols < water < phenols < carboxylic acids. The reasons for this order can be seen in the stabilities of the ions formed, as shown below.

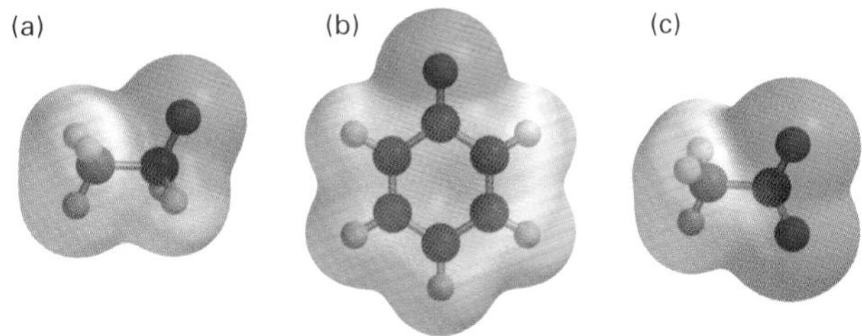

(a) The ethanol molecule has a hydroxyl group attached to an alkyl group. Alkyl groups do not delocalize the negative charge on the alkoxide ion, RO^-. So, alcohols are not acidic because the alkoxide ion does not form readily (see spread 25.2). (b) The phenol molecule has a hydroxyl group attached to a benzene ring, which involves delocalized electrons. The negative charge on the phenoxide ion $C_6H_5O^-$ becomes partially delocalized with the benzene ring. As a result, phenols are much more acidic than alcohols because the phenoxide ion forms readily. (c) The ethanoic acid molecule has a hydroxyl group attached to a carbonyl group. As explained above, the negative charge on the carboxylate ion RCO_2^- is delocalized with the C=O double bond. Carboxylic acids are therefore more acidic than phenols.

The major consequence of this order of acidities is that ethanoic acid is acidic enough to produce carbon dioxide when reacted with sodium carbonate or sodium hydrogencarbonate: phenol is not acidic enough to react.

SUMMARY

- The carboxylic acid functional group has the formula —COOH.
- Carboxylic acids are weak acids: $RCOOH + H_2O \rightleftharpoons H_3O^+ + RCO_2^-$
- The charge on the carboxylate ion is delocalized, the two oxygen atoms being equivalent.

Salts

Salts form when carboxylic acids neutralize bases. For example, sodium ethanoate is a white crystalline solid, which may be isolated by evaporation following the reaction:

$CH_3COOH(aq) + NaOH(aq) \rightarrow$
$Na^+CH_3CO_2^-(aq) + H_2O(l)$

—COOH and —CO_2^-

The formula for an un-ionized carboxylic acid group is written as —COOH (and not as —CO_2H) to show that the two oxygen atoms are *not* equivalent. The formula for the carboxylate ion is written as —CO_2^- (and not as —COO^-) to show that the two oxygen atoms *are* equivalent.

pK_a values

$CH_3CH_2OH(aq) + H_2O(l) \rightleftharpoons H_3O^+(aq) + CH_3CH_2O^-(aq)$

pK_a for ethanol = 16.0

$C_6H_5OH(aq) + H_2O(l) \rightleftharpoons H_3O^+(aq) + C_6H_5O^-(aq)$

pK_a for phenol = 9.9

$CH_3COOH(aq) + H_2O(l) \rightleftharpoons H_3O^+(aq) + CH_3CO_2^-(aq)$

pK_a for ethanoic acid = 4.8

PRACTICE

1 Explain, with the aid of equations, why ethanoic acid is described as a 'weak acid'.

2 Carbon dioxide gas is evolved when sodium hydrogencarbonate reacts with aqueous ethanoic acid. With respect to this reaction:

a Write a balanced chemical equation.

b Show how ethanoic acid acts as a Brønsted acid.

c Name and give the formula of the species acting as a base.

27.2

ACYL CHLORIDES AND ACYLATION

OBJECTIVES

- Acyl chlorides
- Acid anhydrides
- Acylating agents

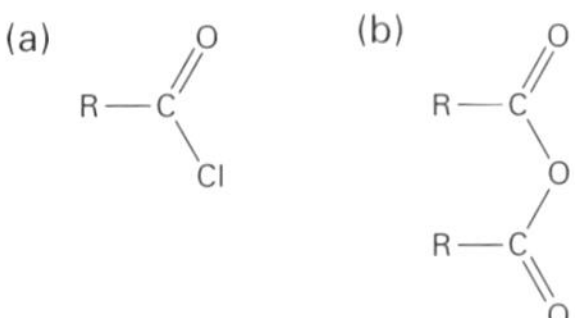

Carboxylic acid derivatives: (a) acyl chlorides; (b) acid anhydrides.

Carboxylic acid derivatives include **acyl chlorides** RCOCl. The **acid anhydrides** $(RCO)_2O$ are another group of carboxylic acid derivatives, consisting of two acid molecules condensed together. The uses of acyl chlorides and acid anhydrides as acylating agents are discussed in this spread.

Acyl chlorides: preparation

The chlorinating agents (see spread 25.2 in the chapter on 'Alcohols') PCl_3, PCl_5, and SCl_2O convert carboxylic acids into acyl chlorides:

$$RCOOH + PCl_5 \rightarrow RCOCl + PCl_3O + HCl$$
$$RCOOH + SCl_2O \rightarrow RCOCl + SO_2 + HCl$$

For example, ethanoic acid CH_3COOH reacts with PCl_5 or SCl_2O to give **ethanoyl chloride** CH_3COCl. Note that the chlorinating agents for carboxylic acids are the same as those for alcohols.

Acid anhydrides: preparation

Acid anhydrides are prepared by refluxing an acyl chloride with the sodium salt of the corresponding carboxylic acid. For example, ethanoyl chloride and sodium ethanoate react to form ethanoic anhydride:

$$CH_3COCl + NaCH_3CO_2 \rightarrow (CH_3CO)_2O + NaCl$$

Acid anhydrides are liquids with high boiling points and limited solubility in water. Their reactions are similar to those of acyl chlorides, but are less violent, and so acid anhydrides are often chosen in industry to avoid excessively vigorous reaction.

A drop of water on a glass rod causes the vapour of ethanoyl chloride to 'fume' as it is hydrolysed by the water. The fumes are hydrogen chloride gas.

Acylating agents

Substitution of RCO— for a hydrogen atom in a molecule is called **acylation**. For example, substitution of CH_3CO— for a hydrogen atom is called **ethanoylation** (traditionally called 'acetylation'). There are two main types of acylating agents: acyl chlorides (e.g. ethanoyl chloride CH_3COCl) and acid anhydrides (e.g. ethanoic anhydride $(CH_3CO)_2O$).

The C—Cl bond in acyl chlorides is more reactive than that in chloroalkanes. Both the chlorine atom *and* the oxygen atom withdraw electron density from the carbon atom, increasing its partial positive charge δ+. Also, the double bond allows the new bond to form before the old one is broken. The chlorine atom is removed from the acyl chloride during acylation. The chloride ion is referred to as a 'good leaving group'. The result is that acyl chlorides engage in *nucleophilic substitution* reactions, which replace the chlorine atom with a nucleophile.

The mechanism of acylation involves the following stages:

(a) Nucleophilic attack at the carbonyl carbon atom to form a **tetrahedral intermediate**.

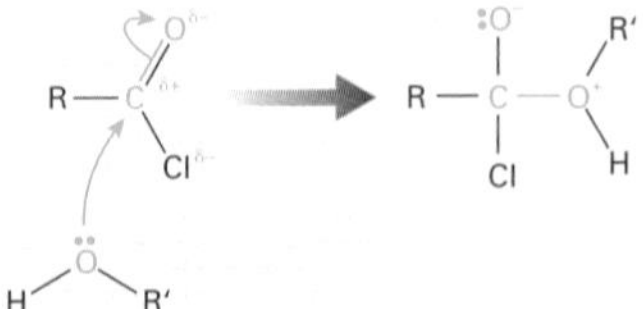

(b) Loss of a chloride ion as the double bond reforms.

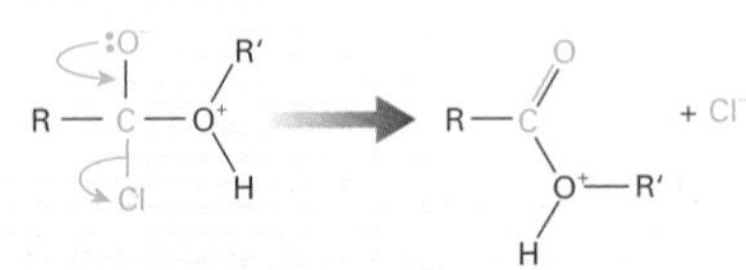

(c) Loss of a proton.

General mechanism of acylation. The reaction occurs by nucleophilic addition of the alcohol, followed by elimination of HCl (in two stages).

Acylation reactions

Acyl chlorides (such as ethanoyl chloride) perform the following reactions:

- Acyl chlorides react with water to form carboxylic acids

  $CH_3COCl(l) + H_2O(l) \rightarrow CH_3COOH(aq) + HCl(g)$

This reaction is described as **hydrolysis** of the acyl chloride, see opposite, because the C—Cl bond has been split by water. Viewed from the point of view of the *water*, a hydrogen atom has been substituted by CH_3CO—.

- Acyl chlorides react with alcohols to form esters

  $CH_3COCl(l) + CH_3CH_2OH(l) \rightarrow CH_3COOCH_2CH_3(l) + HCl(g)$

Viewed from the point of view of the *alcohol*, a hydrogen atom has been substituted by CH_3CO—.

- Acyl chlorides react with phenols to form esters

  $CH_3COCl(l) + C_6H_5OH(aq) \rightarrow CH_3COOC_6H_5(s) + HCl(g)$

- Acyl chlorides react with ammonia to form amides

  $CH_3COCl(l) + NH_3(aq) \rightarrow CH_3CONH_2(aq) + HCl(g)$

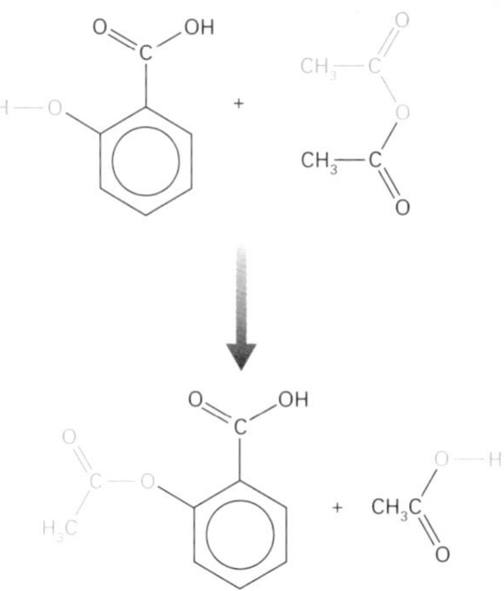

The acylation of 2-hydroxybenzoic acid by ethanoic anhydride (which reacts in a more controlled fashion than ethanoyl chloride). Note that only half of the ethanoic anhydride molecule takes part in the acylation; the other half forms the leaving group.

Aspirin

The manufacture of aspirin involves an example of acylation. The starting material is 2-hydroxybenzoic acid (salicylic acid), which contains a carboxylic acid group and a hydroxyl (phenol) group. Ethanoic anhydride reacts to substitute an ethanoyl group for the hydrogen atom on the hydroxyl group. The resulting compound is 2-ethanoyloxybenzoic acid (acetylsalicylic acid) or 'aspirin'.

The Salix alba *tree (here, in Tealham Moor, Somerset) and the history of aspirin. In 1763, the Reverend Edmund Stone noticed that an extract from the bark of the English willow* Salix alba *was able to reduce fever. Fifty years later, the active ingredient was isolated, and after a further fifty years it was successfully synthesized. The active ingredient was called salicylic acid. Unfortunately, treatment often caused severe stomach pains for the patients. (Salicylic acid is now used in creams for removing warts.) Felix Hoffman's father suffered these stomach pains, and his son decided to search for a less acidic derivative. Hoffman found in 1898 that the ester formed by ethanoylating salicylic acid was even more effective at reducing inflammation and yet was better tolerated. He named this derivative 'aspirin': a- for the acetyl (ethanoyl) group, and -spir- for spirsäure, the German word for salicylic acid.*

SUMMARY

- Carboxylic acid derivatives include RCOCl (acyl chlorides), RCOOR′ (esters), $RCONH_2$ (amides), and $(RCO)_2O$ (acid anhydrides).
- Acyl chlorides are more vigorous acylating agents than acid anhydrides.
- Acylation substitutes the acyl group RCO— for a hydrogen atom on alcohols, phenols, and ammonia.
- Acylation of an alcohol gives an ester; acylation of phenol gives an ester; and acylation of ammonia gives an amide.

PRACTICE

1 Draw a structural formula for each of the following acylating agents:
  - **a** Ethanoyl chloride
  - **b** Benzoyl chloride
  - **c** Propanoic anhydride.

2 Each of the acylating agents in question 1 reacts with ethanol to form an ester.
  - **a** Use molecular formulae to write a chemical equation for each of the three reactions.
  - **b** Repeat part (a) using structural formulae.
  - **c** Which of the three acylating agents reacts most slowly?

3 Suggest a mechanism for the hydrolysis reaction between ethanoyl chloride and water.

27.3

OBJECTIVES

- Structure
- Occurrence in Nature
- Laboratory preparations

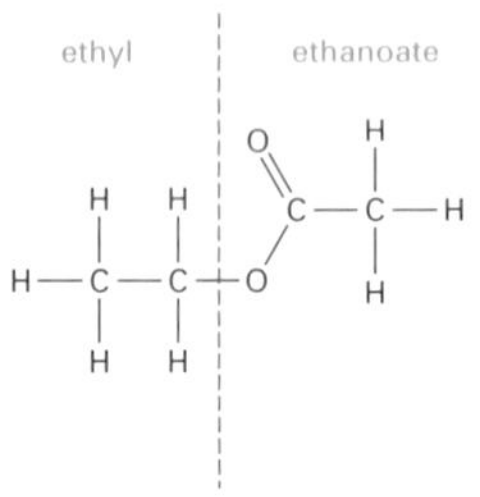

ethyl | ethanoate

The name of the ester ethyl ethanoate derived from ethanol and ethanoic acid.

Structural formulae of esters

Note that the structure $CH_3CH_2OCOCH_3$ (ethyl ethanoate) presents the alcohol group first, followed by the acid group. This is often reversed, so that the structure of ethyl ethanoate may be written as $CH_3COOCH_2CH_3$. In general, you may find esters written as ROCOR′ or as R′COOR, where R is the alcohol alkyl group and R′ is the alkyl group of the carboxylic acid. In this book we shall generally use the second of these alternatives.

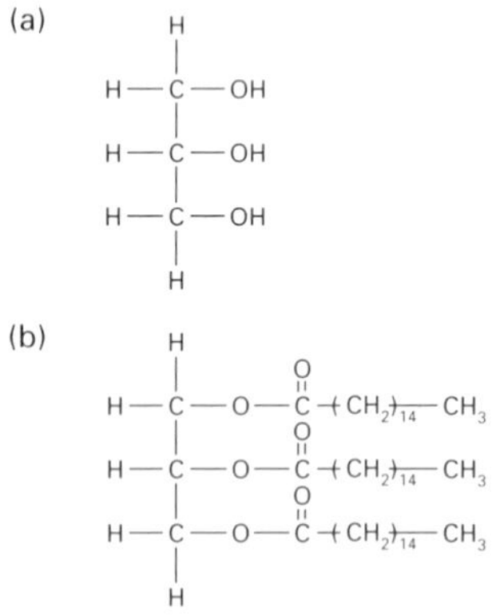

(a)

(b)

Fats and oils in both plants and animals are esters of the trihydric alcohol propane-1,2,3-triol (glycerol) (see chapter on 'Alcohols'). (a) The structure of propane-1,2,3-triol. (b) One of the constituents of palm tree oil.

Esters – 1

Esters are carboxylic acid derivatives. They are found widely in Nature in fats and oils (see chapter on 'Biochemistry'), and are responsible for the aroma of many fruits. Esters are formed in the laboratory by the reaction of alcohols with carboxylic acids, acyl chlorides, or acid anhydrides. This spread covers the production and uses of esters; the following spread looks at hydrolysis reactions, which split esters into their component alcohol and carboxylic acid fragments.

Ester structure

Esters may be regarded as consisting of two parts, one deriving from an alcohol and the other from a carboxylic acid. For example, the structure of ethyl ethanoate is $CH_3CH_2OCOCH_3$ (or $CH_3COOCH_2CH_3$, see box). This ester results from reacting the alcohol ethanol CH_3CH_2OH with the carboxylic acid ethanoic acid CH_3COOH. The names of esters consist of the name of the alcohol's alkyl group (methyl, ethyl, etc.) followed by the name of the ion corresponding to the carboxylic acid (methanoate, ethanoate, etc.).

The occurrence and uses of esters

Esters occur widely in Nature. Look down the list of compounds in a mango, and you will see that it is easy to pick out the esters. Simply look for the names that have the form ...yl ...oate. Volatile esters of low relative formula mass usually have distinctive and pleasant fruity aromas, which add to the taste and flavour of fruits. Many of the 'artificial flavours' listed as the ingredients of processed foods, snacks, and confectionery are synthesized esters. For example, the aroma of a chocolate 'rum truffle' is courtesy of a few milligrams of ethyl methanoate $HCOOCH_2CH_3$. Esters are also used as solvents in perfumes and in plasticizers.

Some of the compounds present in an average mango. Spot the esters.

Esterification: alcohol and carboxylic acid

Esterification is the formation of an ester and water from an alcohol and a carboxylic acid, spread 11.7. For example, ethanol and ethanoic acid react in the presence of a concentrated sulphuric acid catalyst to form the ester ethyl ethanoate:

$$CH_3CH_2OH(l) + CH_3COOH(l) \rightleftharpoons CH_3COOCH_2CH_3(l) + H_2O(l)$$

In this reaction, it is the C(O)—OH bond in the acid that breaks and *not* the C—OH bond in the alcohol. This reaction mechanism is confirmed by using an alcohol that is labelled with the isotope ^{18}O. On separation of the reaction products, it is found that it is the ester that contains the labelled oxygen and not the water:

$$CH_3CH_2{}^{18}OH(l) + CH_3COOH(l) \rightleftharpoons CH_3CO^{18}OCH_2CH_3(l) + H_2O(l)$$

The detailed mechanism is shown below.

The reaction mechanism involves a lone pair on the oxygen atom of the alcohol. The alcohol acts as a nucleophile and attacks the carbonyl carbon atom of the carboxylic acid. The rate at which the reaction reaches equilibrium is increased by using concentrated sulphuric acid as a catalyst. The equilibrium mixture still contains considerable amounts of the reactants. Notice that the bonds *made* are the same as the bonds *broken*, so a *very* small enthalpy change can be expected for the reaction.

The steps shown are as follows:

(a) Protonation of the carboxylic acid.

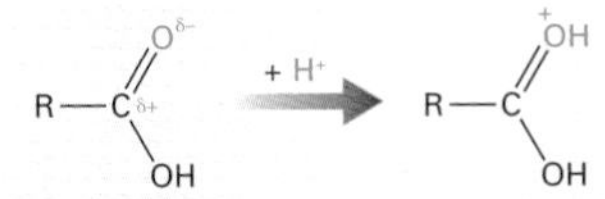

(b) Nucleophilic attack by the alcohol oxygen lone pair.

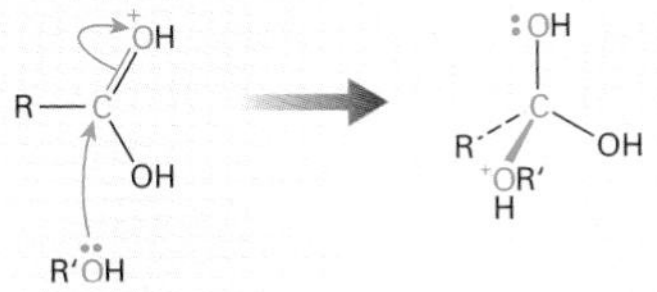

(c) Proton transfer.

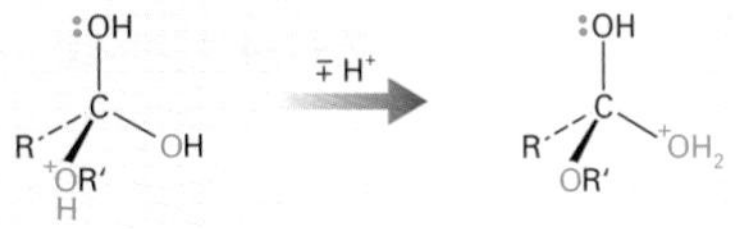

(d) Elimination of water.

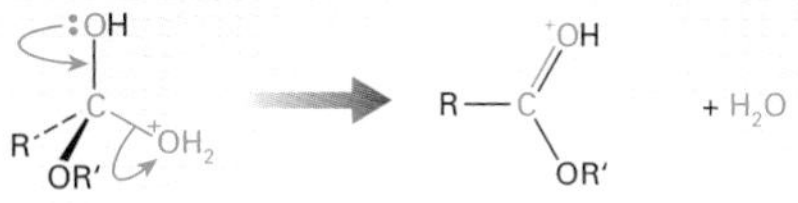

(e) Elimination of a proton.

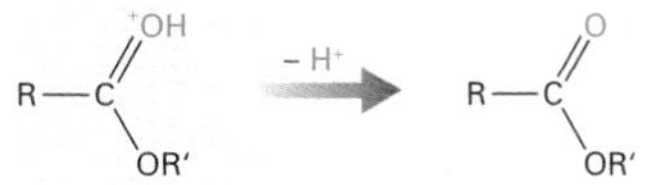

Detailed mechanism of esterification.

Esterification: alcohol and acyl chloride

The synthesis of an ester starting from a carboxylic acid such as ethanoic acid is bound to give a small yield because the equilibrium constant is very close to 1 ($K_c \approx 4$ for ethyl ethanoate at 25 °C). It is much better practice to use an acyl chloride, as the reaction is then much faster and more complete. This behaviour is to be expected because the carbon–halogen bond is being replaced by a stronger carbon–oxygen bond:

$$ROH(l) + R'COCl(l) \rightarrow R'COOR(l) + HCl(g)$$

Ethanoyl chloride acylates ethanol to form ethyl ethanoate:

$$CH_3CH_2OH(l) + CH_3COCl(l) \rightarrow CH_3COOCH_2CH_3(l) + HCl(g)$$

Benzoyl chloride C_6H_5COCl benzoylates ethanol to form ethyl benzoate:

$$CH_3CH_2OH(l) + C_6H_5COCl(l) \rightarrow C_6H_5COOCH_2CH_3(l) + HCl(g)$$

SUMMARY

- An ester molecule consists of an alcohol and a carboxylic acid condensed together.
- Many fats and oils are esters of the trihydric alcohol propane-1,2,3-triol (glycerol).
- Esterification between a carboxylic acid and an alcohol is an equilibrium reaction.
- Esterification of an alcohol with an acyl chloride results in a much higher yield than with a carboxylic acid.
- Esters are used in flavourings, as solvents in perfumes, and in plasticisers.

Acid anhydrides

Esters also form when acid anhydrides $(RCO)_2O$ react with alcohols. The reaction is slower than when acyl chlorides are used.

Esterification: phenol and benzoyl chloride

Phenols are much weaker nucleophiles than alcohols and do not form esters so readily with carboxylic acids. The preferred reactants to produce phenyl benzoate $C_6H_5OCOC_6H_5$ are phenol in aqueous sodium hydroxide with benzoyl chloride C_6H_5COCl. Phenol reacts with the aqueous base to form the phenoxide ion:

$C_6H_5OH(s) + OH^-(aq) \rightarrow C_6H_5O^-(aq) + H_2O(l)$

The phenoxide ion is a stronger nucleophile than phenol, and reacts readily with the benzoyl chloride:

$C_6H_5O^-(aq) + C_6H_5COCl(l) \rightarrow C_6H_5COOC_6H_5(s) + Cl^-(aq)$

27.4

Esters – 2

OBJECTIVES

- Ester hydrolysis
- Soap-making
- Mechanism and isotopic labelling

One of the methods of preparing esters is to react together an alcohol with a carboxylic acid. This process can be reversed by a reaction called **ester hydrolysis**. Esters are hydrolysed to alcohols and carboxylic acids or their salts. The sodium salts of long-chain carboxylic acids are used to make toilet soap and soap flakes. The main purpose of this spread is to describe the mechanism of the hydrolysis reaction and to compare it with the mechanism for esterification.

Ester hydrolysis

Ester, water, alcohol, and acid exist together in the following equilibrium:

$$CH_3COOCH_2CH_3(l) + H_2O(l) \rightleftharpoons CH_3CH_2OH(l) + CH_3COOH(l)$$

The equilibrium mixture (see chapter on 'Chemical equilibrium') is established by mixing either alcohol and acid, or ester and water. Concentrated sulphuric acid catalyses ester formation (the reverse reaction) and therefore must also catalyse ester hydrolysis (the forward reaction). However, ester hydrolysis gives a much higher yield when a *base* is used as a catalyst. Hydroxide ions are better nucleophiles than water, and will attack the carbonyl carbon more readily. More importantly, with base the equilibrium will shift to the right because the OH^- ion will deprotonate the acid to form the salt:

$$CH_3COOH(l) + NaOH(aq) \rightarrow Na^+CH_3CO_2^-(aq) + H_2O(l)$$

The products of ester hydrolysis using sodium hydroxide are the alcohol and the sodium salt of the acid:

$$CH_3COOCH_2CH_3(l) + NaOH(aq) \rightarrow CH_3CH_2OH(l) + Na^+CH_3CO_2^-(aq)$$

Liberating the acid

The carboxylic acid itself can be formed from its salt by adding a strong acid such as hydrochloric acid after the hydrolysis is complete:

$Na^+CH_3CO_2^-(aq) + HCl(aq) \rightarrow$
$CH_3COOH(aq) + NaCl(aq)$

Soap-making

Soaps are the sodium salts of long-chain carboxylic acids. Soft 'toilet' soap is generally made by hydrolysing the esters present in vegetable oils. The basic hydrolysis of esters is sometimes called **saponification** (derived from sapo, the Latin word for 'soap'). During soap-making, a mixture of vegetable oils and aqueous sodium hydroxide or potassium hydroxide is heated with steam. Hydrolysis yields propane-1,2,3-triol (glycerol) and salts of long-chain carboxylic acids.

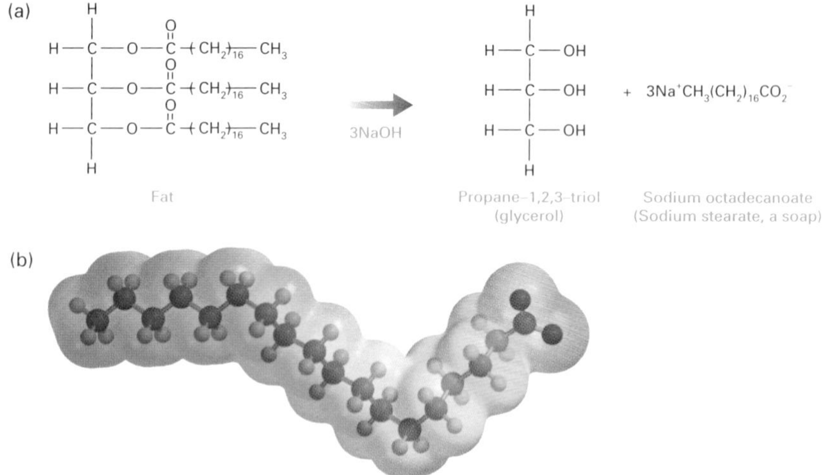

(a) A soap produced by base-catalysed hydrolysis of a fat. (b) The electrostatic potential map of sodium octadecanoate shows the polar 'head' of the octadecanoate ion.

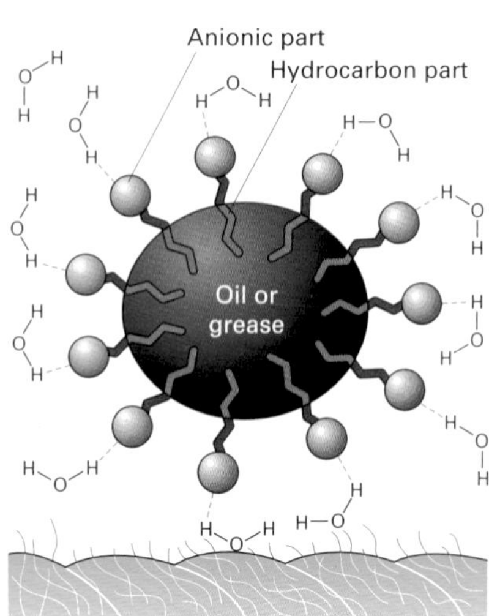

Soap functions because the polar anionic part of the species is solvated by water; the non-polar hydrocarbon part of the species dissolves in oil or grease.

Base-catalysed ester hydrolysis

Hydrolysis is the opposite reaction to esterification. However, esterification between an alcohol and a carboxylic acid is an *acid-catalysed* process. The mechanism of *base-catalysed* hydrolysis is not simply the reverse of the esterification mechanism (see previous spread). As an introduction to the mechanism of hydrolysis, look at the structure of the ester shown earlier. There are two carbon–oxygen bonds that could be broken, RCOO—R′ *or* RCO—OR′.

The mechanism of base-catalysed ester hydrolysis starts with the attack of the (nucleophilic) hydroxide ion on the carbonyl carbon atom. The carbonyl group is polar due to the presence of the electronegative oxygen atom. Note that this first step is the rate-limiting step. The result is an intermediate that has a tetrahedral shape (a **tetrahedral intermediate**) and a negatively charged oxygen atom. This rate-limiting step is consistent with the order of reaction (see chapter on 'Chemical kinetics'), which is second order overall, thus showing that *two* species take part in the rate-limiting step. In the next step, the tetrahedral intermediate breaks down by fission of the RO—COR′ bond to form an alkoxide ion and a carboxylic acid. Finally, a proton transfers from the acid to the alkoxide ion to form the alcohol.

(a) Nucleophilic attack by hydroxide ion on the δ+ carbon atom forming a tetrahedral intermediate.

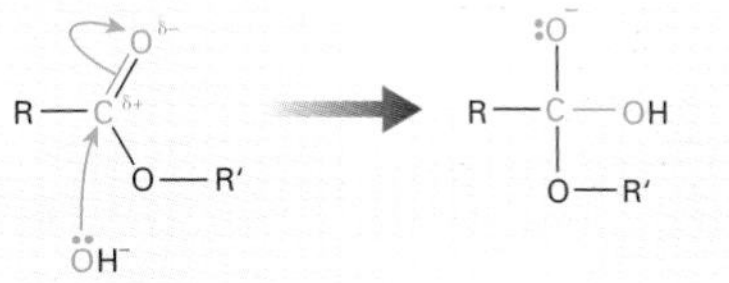

(b) Breakdown of tetrahedral intermediate.

(c) Proton transfer from carboxylic acid to alkoxide ion.

$$RCOOH + R'O^- \longrightarrow RCO_2^- + R'OH$$

Mechanism of base-catalysed ester hydrolysis.

More evidence from isotopic labelling

In 1951 the American chemist Myron Bender investigated the hydrolysis of ethyl benzoate in which the carbonyl oxygen was the isotope ^{18}O, $CH_3CH_2OC^{18}OC_6H_5$. The tetrahedral intermediate (see above) had a labelled carbonyl oxygen but the incoming OH^- was not labelled. If the tetrahedral intermediate forms as suggested, the hydrogen of the OH^- group could swap to the negatively charged, labelled, oxygen very easily. The swap would result in an identical intermediate except that the hydroxyl oxygen would now be labelled rather than the carbonyl oxygen. This swap could not happen if this intermediate did not form.

Bender's flash of genius was to recognize that if this swap happened and the intermediate then broke down to reform the starting materials rather than the products (the reaction is reversible), the reaction mixture would contain some *unlabelled* ester. The hydroxide ion would contain the labelled oxygen instead. Bender therefore looked for *unlabelled* ester at various stages during the reaction, and he found it, thus confirming the suggested mechanism.

Labelling

A molecule containing a radioactive (e.g. ^{14}C) or a stable (e.g. ^{18}O) isotope of an element is called a **labelled compound**. A radioactive isotope in a reaction product may be detected by a Geiger counter; a stable isotope is usually detected by a mass spectrometer. Bender measured the density of the ester.

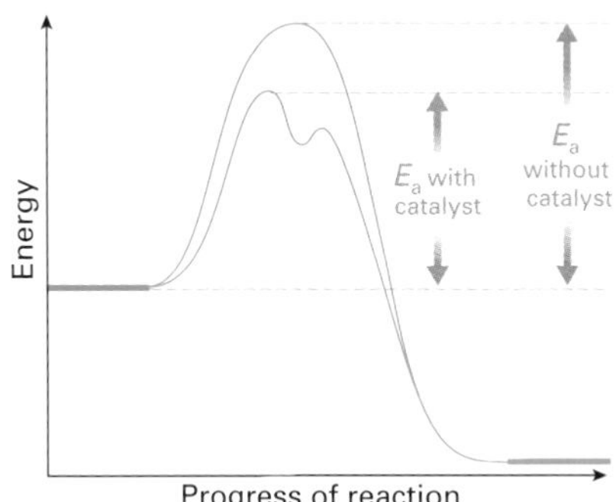

Acid-catalysed ester hydrolysis has a reaction profile in which the catalysed route involves an intermediate, the protonated ester, which then reacts with water. The reaction profile for base-catalysed ester hydrolysis resembles the figure in spread 15.9.

SUMMARY

- Esterification of an alcohol and a carboxylic acid is an acid-catalysed reaction; ester hydrolysis is base-catalysed.
- During base-catalysed hydrolysis, fission occurs at the RO—COR′ bond.
- A reaction mechanism may be explored by labelling a reactant molecule with an isotope such as ^{18}O. Products are separated and analysed for the presence of the isotope.

PRACTICE

1 Draw a structural formula for each of the following esters:
  - a Methyl propanoate
  - b Phenyl ethanoate
  - c Ethyl benzoate
  - d Phenyl benzoate.

2 Give the names and structural formulae of the products that result from the base-catalysed hydrolysis of the four esters listed in question 1.

3 Give the name and structural formula of an acyl chloride and the substance that reacts with it to form each of the esters listed in question 1.

4 Explain with the help of structural formulae and chemical equations the meanings of the three points listed in the 'Summary' section above.

5 Does the work of Myron Bender confirm that hydrolysis involves fission of the RO—COR′ bond? Explain your answer with the help of structural formulae.

27.5

OBJECTIVES

- Preparation
- Acid–base properties
- Typical reactions

Odours, aromas, stenches, and smells

People differ in their descriptions of smells. However, the penetrating aroma of ammonia reminds parents of babies' nappies long overdue for changing (bacteria metabolize urea in urine to ammonia). Amines smell distinctly fishy, the amine from rotting fish being called 'putrescine'. People who keep pet mice will recognize the smell associated with amides – a sure sign that the cage is due for cleaning out.

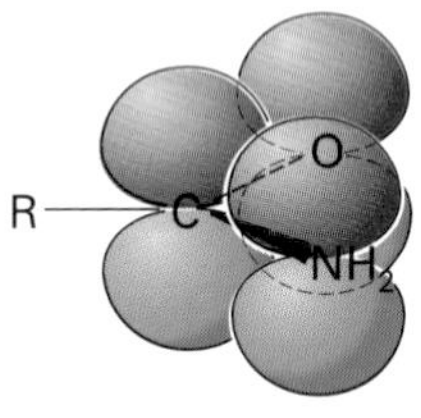

Delocalization in the amide group. Amides are not basic because the nitrogen lone pair is no longer available for protonation. Instead, it is delocalized with the carbonyl group. An amide such as ethanamide CH_3CONH_2 has a delocalization enthalpy (see chapter on 'Arenes') of about 45 kJmol^{-1}, i.e. the measured standard enthalpy change of formation is 45 kJmol^{-1} more exothermic than that calculated from bond enthalpy terms.

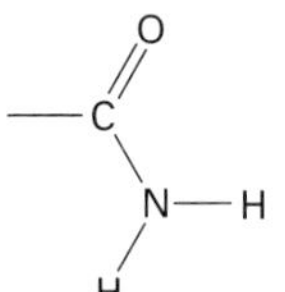

The planar shape and bond angles of the amide group.

AMIDES

Amides contain the functional group —$CONH_2$. Amides may also be regarded as carboxylic acid derivatives: they are named after the corresponding carboxylic acid with the ending '...oic acid' replaced by '...amide'. Hence CH_3CONH_2 is called *ethanamide*. Whilst the amide group would appear to consist of a carbonyl group ⊃C═O attached to an amine group —NH_2, it is more useful to look on —$CONH_2$ as a separate functional group. The amide group has its own unique chemistry, which is not simply a blend of carbonyl and amine group reactions.

Physical properties

Methanamide $HCONH_2$ is a liquid with a high boiling point, whereas all other amides are white solids. The low volatility is due to hydrogen-bonded dimers forming, as in carboxylic acids. The lower members of the amide homologous series are water-soluble.

Preparation of amides

- Ammonia reacts with an acyl chloride (e.g. ethanoyl chloride) to form an amide:

$$CH_3COCl + NH_3 \rightarrow CH_3CONH_2 + HCl$$

- Primary amines react similarly with ethanoyl chloride to form a substituted amide. For example:

$$CH_3COCl + CH_3NH_2 \rightarrow CH_3CONHCH_3 + HCl$$

The C—N bond in the —CONH— group of a substituted amide is the peptide bond, discussed more fully in the next chapter. Amides are used to protect amine groups during synthesis reactions, as mentioned in the following chapter.

- Amides also result from heating the ammonium salts of carboxylic acids:

$$NH_4^+C_6H_5CO_2^- \rightarrow C_6H_5CONH_2 + H_2O$$

The yield is poor unless the ammonium salt is heated with excess of the parent acid to reduce the degree of ionization:

$$NH_4^+C_6H_5CO_2^- \rightleftharpoons C_6H_5COOH + NH_3$$

Acid–base character

Amides are extremely weak acids, but show greater acidic character than ammonia:

$$RCONH_2(aq) + H_2O(l) \rightleftharpoons H_3O^+(aq) + RCONH^-(aq); \quad pK_a \approx 16$$

$$NH_3(aq) + H_2O(l) \rightleftharpoons H_3O^+(aq) + NH_2^-(aq); \quad pK_a \approx 33$$

Amides are at least 10^{10} times weaker bases than ammonia:

$$RCONH_2(aq) + H_2O(l) \rightleftharpoons RCONH_3^+(aq) + OH^-(aq); \quad pK_b \approx 15$$

$$NH_3(aq) + H_2O(l) \rightleftharpoons NH_4^+(aq) + OH^-(aq); \quad pK_b = 4.8$$

Amides are therefore regarded as being essentially neutral in water. For example, aqueous ethanamide has a pH of 7.

Chemical properties

Amides are much weaker bases than amines. Amides are also much weaker nucleophiles than amines. For example, primary amines react with halogenoalkanes to produce secondary and tertiary amines and quaternary ammonium salts; there is no reaction between amides and halogenoalkanes.

- *Hydrolysis*

Amides hydrolyse when refluxed in acidic or in basic solution. Acidic hydrolysis results in the carboxylic acid and the ammonium ion.

For example

$$CH_3CONH_2 + H_3O^+ \rightarrow CH_3COOH + NH_4^+$$

Hydrolysis by base results in the carboxylate ion and ammonia. For example

$$CH_3CONH_2 + OH^- \rightarrow CH_3CO_2^- + NH_3$$

(a) Attack by hydroxide ion on the amide, forming a tetrahedral intermediate.

(b) Breakdown of the tetrahedral intermediate, by loss of the amide ion leaving group (NH_2^-).

(c) Proton transfer from ethanoic acid to amide ion.

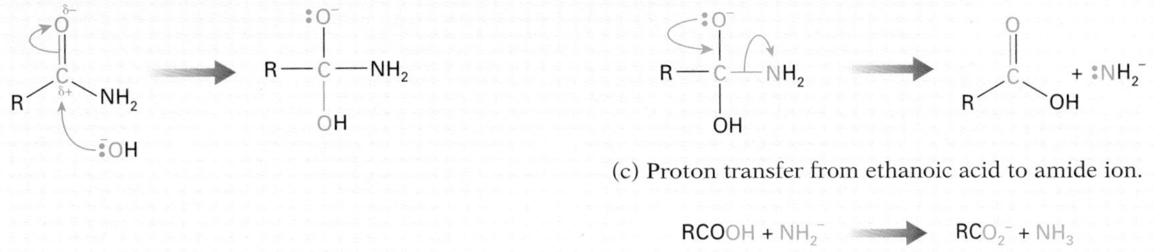

$$RCOOH + NH_2^- \rightarrow RCO_2^- + NH_3$$

Hydrolysis of an amide by base.

- *Dehydration*

Heating an amide with a dehydrating agent such as phosphorus(V) oxide produces a nitrile. For example

$$C_6H_5CONH_2 \xrightarrow{P_4O_{10}} C_6H_5CN + H_2O$$

- *Reduction*

Powerful reductants such as lithium tetrahydridoaluminate reduce amides to primary amines (see spread 27.8). For example

$$CH_3CONH_2 \xrightarrow{[H]} CH_3CH_2NH_2$$

- *Amine production*

Amides react with a mixture of bromine in aqueous potassium hydroxide to produce amines containing *one less carbon atom*. For example

$$\underset{\text{ethanamide}}{CH_3CONH_2(aq)} + Br_2(aq) + 4KOH(aq) \rightarrow \underset{\text{methylamine}}{CH_3NH_2(aq)} + K_2CO_3(aq) + 2KBr(aq) + 2H_2O$$

The significance of this reaction (sometimes called the *Hofmann degradation reaction*) to multi-step organic synthesis is discussed in the chapter on 'Organic synthesis…'.

SUMMARY

- Amides are formed by reacting acyl chlorides with ammonia, or by heating the ammonium salts of carboxylic acids.
- Amides are essentially neutral in aqueous solution: the nitrogen lone pair is delocalized and is not available for protonation.
- Amides are hydrolysed to carboxylic acids by refluxing with either acid or base.
- Amides are dehydrated to nitriles and reduced to primary amines.
- Reaction with bromine in aqueous potassium hydroxide produces an amine with one less carbon atom (Hofmann degradation).

PRACTICE

1 Give the name and structural formula of all of the substances that result when propanamide reacts with each of the following reagents:

a NaOH(aq)

b $H_2SO_4(aq)$

c P_4O_{10}

d $LiAlH_4$

e Br_2/KOH.

27.6

OBJECTIVES

- Polyesters
- Copolymers
- PET, Terylene, and Mylar
- Polycarbonates

CONDENSATION POLYMERIZATION: POLYESTERS

Polymer molecules consist of long chains of repeating units. The simplest example of a polymer is polythene (also called poly(ethene)). It is made by a process of *addition polymerization* (see chapter on 'Alkanes and alkenes') in which thousands of ethene molecules $CH_2{=}CH_2$ add together to form a long-chain polymer. Addition polymerization involves *one functional group* only, the carbon–carbon double bond. **Condensation polymerization** forms polymers by condensation reactions (see previous chapter) between *different functional groups*. One of the simplest examples of condensation polymerization is the reaction used to form polyesters.

Polycotton

Look at the wash labels attached to shirts, trousers, skirts, sheets, and duvet covers. You will see that one of the commonest modern textiles is polycotton, a mixture of cotton and polyester fibres. The strength and crease-resistance of the polyester adds to the 'feel' and durability of cotton.

Polyesters

A condensation reaction involves the combination of two molecules to make a larger molecule, accompanied by the elimination of a small molecule, spread 26.3. Esterification may be classed as a condensation reaction, in which an alcohol and a carboxylic acid react to form an ester, with the elimination of water. A single molecule bearing both an alcohol group and a carboxylic acid group can act as a monomer and undergo a condensation polymerization reaction.

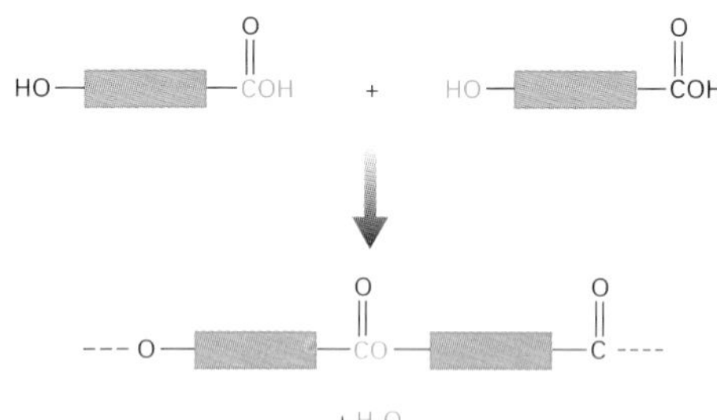

The monomer molecule is a difunctional molecule. A difunctional molecule *bears two functional groups. The alcohol group on one molecule condenses to form an ester linkage with the carboxylic acid group on another molecule. Polymer chains many thousands of monomer units long can result.*

Copolymers

A **copolymer** results from the reaction between two different monomer molecules. A polyester may be formed by condensation between two different difunctional molecules, one of which bears *two* alcohol groups and the other *two* carboxylic acid groups. The majority of commercial polyesters are copolymers.

A polyester forms from the reaction between two different monomer molecules.

The polyester Mylar is used to make the sails on sailboards. It does not 'wet' and is light and 'rip-proof'.

PET, Terylene, Dacron, and Mylar

Polyesters are made industrially from diacids (or, more usually, the corresponding but more reactive diacyl chlorides) together with dialcohols. PET was first produced in 1941 as a result of the work of the British chemist John Winfield. PET can be made by heating ethane-1,2-diol ('ethylene glycol', spread 25.6) with benzene-1,4-dicarboxylic acid ('terephthalic acid'). PET (or PETE) is an abbreviation of the traditional name polyethylene terephthalate. It is now the most widely used polyester: for example, the plastic containers for fizzy drinks are made of PET; drawn into filaments or blown into films, PET is also used in the form of yarn and textiles (Terylene in the UK, Dacron in the USA) and as the backing film for audio tapes (Mylar).

$$HO-CH_2-CH_2-OH \quad + \quad CH_3OC(=O)-C_6H_4-C(=O)OCH_3$$

$$\downarrow$$

$$\cdots-C_6H_4-CO-O-CH_2-CH_2-O-OC-C_6H_4-\cdots$$

$$+\ CH_3OH \qquad +\ CH_3OH$$

PET

The industrial production of PET often uses the dimethyl ester instead of the free acid.

The human-powered Gossamer Albatross *first flew across the English Channel in 1979. Its wings were covered with a thin layer of Mylar polyester film.*

Intermolecular bonding

Polyesters have polar bonds included in their structures. Interaction between these permanent dipoles results in attractive forces between separate polymer chains. Chemists modify the properties of polyesters by choosing carefully the positions and types of polar bond in the polyester chain.

Polycarbonates

A special class of polyester, the polycarbonates, results from the reaction between dialcohols and derivatives of carbonic acid, such as carbonyl chloride (phosgene) $COCl_2$. Polycarbonates are exceptionally hard materials, which are used to make bullet-proof windows, riot shields, bicycle safety helmets, and car bumpers. Some polycarbonates are sufficiently optically clear to be used for spectacle lenses, in which application they are at least ten times more resistant to breakage than conventional glass.

The polycarbonate Lexan was used to make this helmet visor. The Space Shuttle is reflected in the visor. The 'safety specs' you wear during chemistry practical work are most likely made from a polycarbonate material, as are American football helmets.

SUMMARY

- Condensation polymers result from the polymerization of *difunctional* molecules – molecules bearing two functional groups.
- A copolymer is the result of a polymerization reaction between two different molecules.
- Dialcohols react with diacids to form polyesters.
- PET is a common commercial polyester formed from the reaction between ethane-1,2-diol and benzene-1,4-dicarboxylic acid.
- Polycarbonates are formed from the reaction between dialcohols and derivatives of carbonic acid, such as carbonyl chloride $COCl_2$.

27.7

OBJECTIVES

- Polyamides
- Nylon
- Aramid fibres

Condensation polymerization: polyamides

Condensation polymers form between molecules bearing functional groups that undergo condensation reactions. As discussed in the previous spread, polyesters form between diacyl chlorides and dialcohols. Polyamides are another common class of condensation copolymer. They result from the condensation of diacyl chlorides and diamines to form the substituted amide group —CONH—. Nylons are the most common polyamides. Proteins, spread 30.5, are natural polyamides.

The substituted amide group

As discussed in spread 27.5, amides have the general formula $RCONH_2$. A substituted amide has the general formula RCONHR′; an alkyl group R′ is attached to the nitrogen atom in place of one of the hydrogen atoms. A polyamide can be formed from the reaction between a diacyl chloride and a diamine, as shown below.

$$CH_3{-}CH_2{-}NH_2 + Cl{-}C(=O){-}CH_3 \rightarrow CH_3{-}CH_2{-}NH{-}C(=O){-}CH_3 + HCl$$

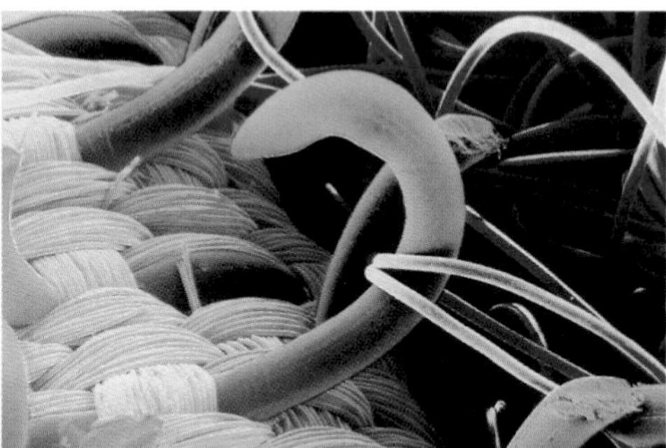

Condensation reaction between ethylamine and ethanoyl chloride to give the substituted amide N-ethylethanamide. A false-colour scanning electron micrograph of a Velcro fastener. One half has a surface with nylon loops; the other has a surface with hooks.

Nylon uses

One of the first uses of nylon was women's sheer 'silk stockings', introduced to critical acclaim at the 1939 New York World's Fair. The all-nylon 'drip-dry' shirt of the 1950s did not require ironing, unlike its conventional cotton counterpart. However, it felt like wearing a plastic bag! Modern all-nylon products include rope and twine, as well as the Velcro fastener. Nylon is frequently blended with other fibres to increase their wear-resistance. Mixed with wool staple, it makes hard-wearing carpets.

Nylon-6,6

A copolymer results when a diacyl chloride reacts with a diamine to form repeating substituted amide groups. The monomers each have two functional groups – they are difunctional molecules. For example, the reaction between hexane-1,6-dioyl chloride and 1,6-diaminohexane forms the polymer known as nylon-6,6 (pronounced 'six-six'). This name signifies that both monomers contain six carbon atoms; hence there are six carbon atoms between each of the repeating substituted amide groups in the polymer. A range of different nylon polymers results from using diamines and diacyl chlorides containing different numbers of carbon atoms.

$$H{-}NH{-}(CH_2)_6{-}NH{-}H + Cl{-}C(=O){-}(CH_2)_4{-}C(=O){-}Cl \rightarrow {-}{-}{-}NH{-}(CH_2)_6{-}NH{-}C(=O){-}(CH_2)_4{-}C(=O){-}{-}{-} + HCl$$

The condensation reaction between 1,6-diaminohexane and hexane-1,6-dioyl chloride forms nylon-6,6.

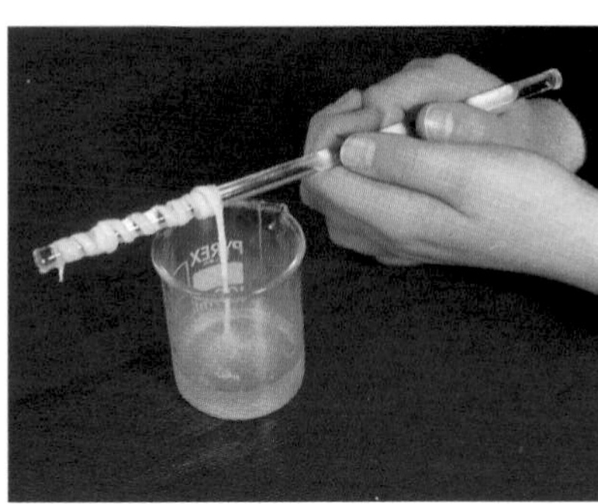

The laboratory demonstration of the formation of nylon-6,6. The reaction occurs at the interface between two immiscible liquids. The lower liquid is tetrachloromethane containing dissolved hexane-1,6-dioyl chloride; the upper liquid is an aqueous solution of 1,6-diaminohexane.

Wallace Carothers and the naming of nylon

Wallace Hume Carothers was born in 1896 in Iowa. After obtaining degrees from the Universities of Illinois and Harvard, in 1928 he took up the post of 'Head of Organic Research' at the Du Pont company in Delaware. By 1931 his team had developed the first synthetic condensation polymers.

The raw product of the polymerization reaction was of little commercial use. However, younger members of the research team chanced upon an accidental discovery that led to the material becoming a huge commercial success. While Carothers was away from the laboratory, they engaged in some high-spirited horseplay, which centred on the question: 'Just how far will this stuff stretch?' Pulling on the ends of a sample – technically called 'cold drawing' – they found that it became very silky in appearance and increased in strength. Pulling the fibre aligned the polymer chains; hydrogen bonding between the chains gave a degree of crystallinity similar to that in silk.

The original name of Du Pont's first polyamide was '66 polyamide', but this did not sound appealing enough to catch the popular imagination. One reason for the huge commercial success was that stockings made from the material did not 'run' (form 'ladders' when snagged). The name 'Norun' was therefore suggested, but this did not satisfy the Du Pont management. Spelling the name backwards as 'Nuron' eventually led to 'Nylon' – the greatest commercial success the company ever had.

Hydrogen bonding between the polyamide chains in nylon-6,6.

Aramid fibres

Aramids are particularly useful variants of polyamides in which the —CONH— group is directly attached to benzene rings. The aramid fibre with the amide groups attached to the 1 and 3 positions of the benzene molecule (Nomex) has exceptional heat- and flame-resistant qualities. Woven Nomex undergarments are worn by fire-fighters, racing drivers, and fighter aircraft pilots. Attaching the amide groups to the 1 and 4 positions gives an exceptionally strong material (Kevlar, made by reaction of benzene-1, 4-dicarboxylic acid and benzene-1, 4-diamine) used to make bullet-proof vests and the chassis of some racing cars.

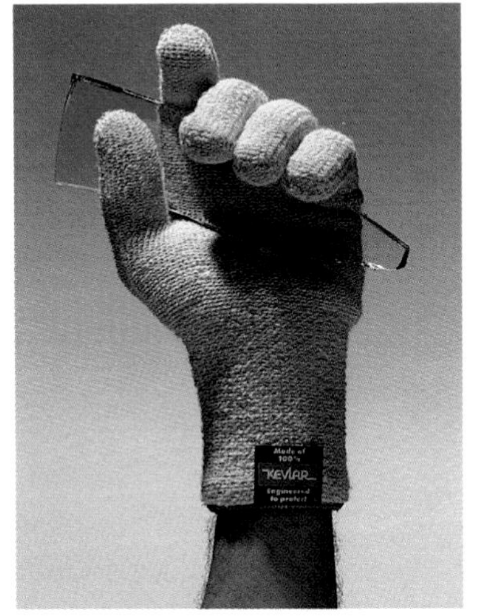

Aramids have extremely high tensile strengths, coupled with toughness, wear- and temperature-resistance, and low density. The 1,4-disubstituted aramids are particularly strong materials.

SUMMARY

- Polyamides contain the substituted amide (or peptide) linkage —CONH—.
- Polyamides form from condensation reactions between diacyl chlorides and diamines.
- Nylon-6,6 is the polyamide resulting from the reaction between 1,6-diaminohexane and hexane-1,6-dioyl chloride.
- The name 'nylon-6,6' signifies that both monomer molecules contain six carbon atoms.

Biodegradable polymers

Both polyesters and polymides can be hydrolysed; see spreads 27.4 and 27.5. This allows them to be broken down in the environment more readily than any poly(alkene).

PRACTICE

1 Explain the following terms, giving examples:
  - **a** Polyester
  - **b** Polyamide
  - **c** Copolymer
  - **d** Difunctional molecule
  - **e** Condensation polymerization.

2 Give the structural formulae of two monomers suitable for the production of nylon-4,4.

3 Draw the structural formula of a section of the polymer molecule that results from the reaction between propane-1,3-diol and benzene-1,3-dioyl chloride.

27.8 REDUCTION OF ACID DERIVATIVES

OBJECTIVES

- Reduction of acyl chlorides
- Reduction of esters
- Reduction of amides

The three major classes of carboxylic acid derivatives are the acyl chlorides, the esters, and the amides. All of these can be reduced by strong reductants.

Reduction reactions

Carboxylic acid derivatives have the general structure

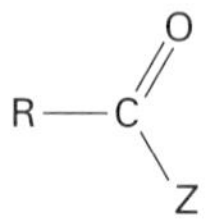

R—C(=O)—Z

where Z is Cl (acyl chlorides), OR′ (esters), or NH_2 (amides). All these derivatives are reduced by lithium tetrahydridoaluminate. A more powerful reductant than $NaBH_4$ (see the previous chapter) is required due to the delocalization of the lone pair on the Z group with the carbonyl group.

- An acyl chloride is reduced to an alcohol:

$$\underset{\text{ethanoyl chloride}}{CH_3COCl} \xrightarrow{LiAlH_4} \underset{\text{ethanol}}{CH_3CH_2OH}$$

Note that the parent acid is also reduced:

$$CH_3COOH \xrightarrow{LiAlH_4} CH_3CH_2OH$$

- An ester is reduced to *two* alcohols:

$$\underset{\text{propyl ethanoate}}{CH_3CH_2CH_2OCOCH_3} \xrightarrow{LiAlH_4} \underset{\text{propan-1-ol}}{CH_3CH_2CH_2OH} + \underset{\text{ethanol}}{CH_3CH_2OH}$$

- An amide is reduced to an amine:

$$\underset{\text{ethanamide}}{CH_3CONH_2} \xrightarrow{LiAlH_4} \underset{\text{ethylamine}}{CH_3CH_2NH_2}$$

Lithium tetrahydridoaluminate is a useful reagent, but it is expensive and requires absolutely anhydrous conditions. Sodium in ethanol is frequently a suitable alternative:

$$ROCOR' \xrightarrow{Na/CH_3CH_2OH} ROH + R'CH_2OH$$

The reaction products are the same as with lithium tetrahydridoaluminate, but with the added complication that the liberated alcohols will react with the sodium to form their respective alkoxide ions; see spread 25.2. At the end of the reaction, the excess sodium is removed and water is then added to reform the alcohols. Fractional distillation can then be used to separate the three alcohols from the reaction mixture.

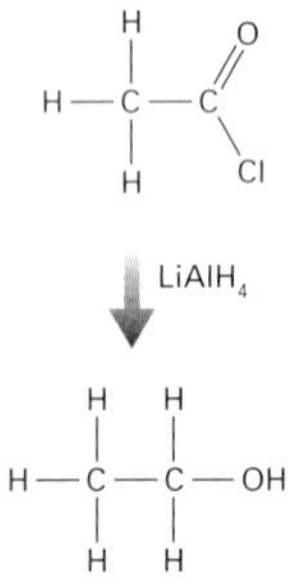

H—C(H)(H)—C(=O)—Cl —LiAlH₄→ H—C(H)(H)—C(H)(H)—OH

Reduction of ethanoyl chloride to ethanol.

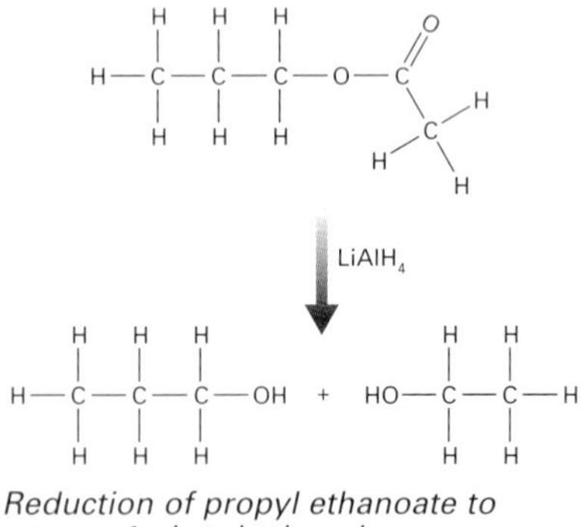

H—C(H)(H)—C(H)(H)—C(H)(H)—O—C(=O)—C(H)(H)H —LiAlH₄→ H—C(H)(H)—C(H)(H)—C(H)(H)—OH + HO—C(H)(H)—C(H)(H)—H

Reduction of propyl ethanoate to propan-1-ol and ethanol.

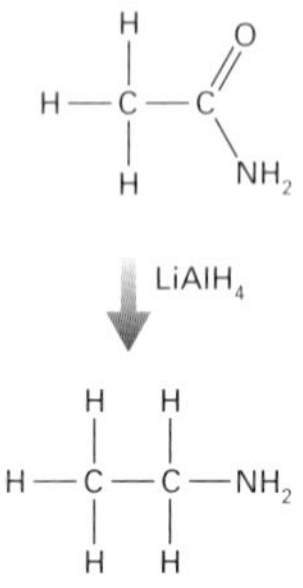

H—C(H)(H)—C(=O)—NH₂ —LiAlH₄→ H—C(H)(H)—C(H)(H)—NH₂

Reduction of ethanamide to ethylamine.

Worked example on reduction

Question: **A**, $C_4H_8O_2$, is reduced by lithium tetrahydridoaluminate to **B**, $C_4H_{10}O$. **B** is dehydrated to form **C**, C_4H_8. **C** reacts with HBr(aq) to form $(CH_3)_3CBr$. Draw structural formulae for **A**, **B**, and **C**.

Strategy: The loss of one oxygen on reduction suggests the reduction of an acid (an ester would produce *two* products).

Answer: **C** must be an alkene to add HBr; it must be $(CH_3)_2C{=}CH_2$. The alcohol **B** therefore must be $(CH_3)_2C(OH)CH_3$ or $(CH_3)_2CH—CH_2OH$. **B** has to be formed by reduction of an acid; only the second suggestion fits that piece of data.

Hence **B** is $(CH_3)_2CH—CH_2OH$ and
A is $(CH_3)_2CH—COOH$.

SUMMARY

- Esters, acids, and acyl chlorides are reduced by $LiAlH_4$ to alcohols.
- Amides are reduced by $LiAlH_4$ to amines.

PRACTICE

1 Write chemical equations for the reduction of each of the following substances. Name the products formed and give their structural formulae:
   a Ethyl ethanoate
   b Methyl propanoate
   c Ethyl benzoate
   d Phenyl benzoate
   e Ethanoyl chloride
   f Benzoyl chloride.

2 Give the structural formula of ethanamide, together with the name and formula of the product of its reduction.

Chapter 27 Reactions summary

- Aliphatic carboxylic acids – from oxidation of primary alcohols via aldehydes by acidified potassium dichromate(VI):
  $CH_3CH_2OH \xrightarrow{[O]} CH_3CHO \xrightarrow{[O]} CH_3COOH$
- Aromatic carboxylic acids – from oxidation of any alkylbenzene by alkaline potassium manganate(VII):
  $C_6H_5CH_3 \xrightarrow{[O]} C_6H_5COOH$
- Carboxylic acids – protonation of water:
  $CH_3COOH(aq) + H_2O(l) \rightleftharpoons H_3O^+(aq) + CH_3CO_2^-(aq)$
- Carboxylic acids – salt formation:
  $CH_3COOH(aq) + NaOH(aq) \rightarrow Na^+CH_3CO_2^-(aq) + H_2O(l)$
- Preparation of acyl chlorides:
  $RCOOH + SCl_2O \rightarrow RCOCl + SO_2 + HCl$
- Acyl chloride with water (hydrolysis):
  $CH_3COCl + H_2O \rightarrow CH_3COOH + HCl$
- Acyl chloride with alcohol to form ester:
  $CH_3COCl + CH_3CH_2OH \rightarrow CH_3COOCH_2CH_3 + HCl$
- Acyl chloride with ammonia to form amide:
  $CH_3COCl + NH_3 \rightarrow CH_3CONH_2 + HCl$
- Esterification – alcohol with carboxylic acid to form ester (conc. sulphuric acid catalyst):
  $CH_3CH_2OH(l) + CH_3COOH(l) \rightleftharpoons CH_3COOCH_2CH_3(l) + H_2O(l)$
- Base-catalysed hydrolysis of ester:
  $CH_3COOCH_2CH_3(l) + NaOH(aq) \rightarrow CH_3CH_2OH(l) + Na^+CH_3CO_2^-(aq)$
- Substituted amide from acyl chloride and amine:
  $RCOCl + R'NH_2 \rightarrow RCONHR' + HCl$
- Amide from heating the ammonium salt of a carboxylic acid:
  $NH_4^+C_6H_5CO_2^- \rightarrow C_6H_5CONH_2 + H_2O$
- Acidic hydrolysis of an amide:
  $CH_3CONH_2 + H_3O^+ \rightarrow CH_3COOH + NH_4^+$
- Basic hydrolysis of an amide:
  $CH_3CONH_2 + OH^- \rightarrow CH_3CO_2^- + NH_3$
- Dehydration of an amide:
  $C_6H_5CONH_2 \xrightarrow{P_4O_{10}} C_6H_5CN + H_2O$
- Reduction of an amide by $LiAlH_4$:
  $CH_3CONH_2 \xrightarrow{[H]} CH_3CH_2NH_2$
- Amine production by Hofmann degradation reaction:
  $CH_3CONH_2(aq) + Br_2(aq) + 4KOH(aq) \rightarrow CH_3NH_2(aq) + K_2CO_3(aq) + 2KBr(aq) + 2H_2O(l)$
- Reduction of acyl chloride:
  $CH_3COCl \xrightarrow{LiAlH_4} CH_3CH_2OH$
- Reduction of ester:
  $CH_3CH_2CH_2OCOCH_3 \xrightarrow{LiAlH_4} CH_3CH_2CH_2OH + CH_3CH_2OH$

PRACTICE EXAM QUESTIONS

1 The molecular formulae of some compounds that can be prepared from ethanoic acid are given in the scheme below.

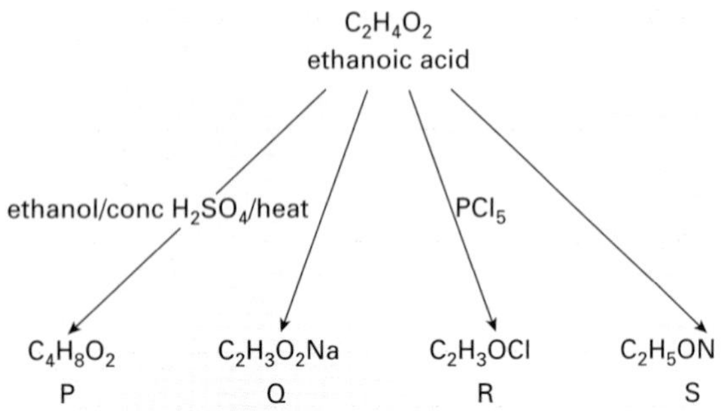

a i Give the name and graphical formula of **P**. [2]

ii Give the name of the type of reaction which occurs when **P** is formed from ethanoic acid. [1]

b Ethanoic acid can be obtained from P.

i Give the name of the reagent(s) and state the conditions required. [2]

ii Write a balanced equation for the reaction. [1]

c i State the reagent and reaction conditions that could be used for converting ethanoic acid into **Q**. [2]

ii Give the name and graphical formula of the organic product of the reaction between anhydrous samples of **Q** and **R**. [2]

iii State how the product formed in **c ii** could be converted into ethanoic acid and write an equation for the reaction. [2]

d i Give the name and graphical formula of the amide, **S**. [2]

ii State the reagent(s) and reaction conditions that could be used for converting ethanoic acid into **S**. [2]

iii Write a balanced equation for the reaction between **S** and aqueous hydrochloric acid. [1]
AQA (AEB) 1999

2 a Write balanced equations for the following hydrolysis reactions:

i ethanamide and aqueous sodium hydroxide; [2]

ii propanenitrile and aqueous hydrochloric acid; [2]

iii ethanoyl chloride and water; [2]

iv ethanoic anhydride and water. [2]

b What difference is there in the conditions needed for the hydrolyses shown in **a iii** and **a iv**? [1]

c Give the formulae of **two** organic compounds that would react together to give each of the following products:

i CH_3COOCH_3 [2]

ii $CH_3CH_2NHCOCH_3$ [2]
AQA (AEB) 1996

3 Citric acid is used in foodstuffs as an antioxidant and, together with its sodium salt, as an acidity regulator. It occurs naturally in fruit juices.

The formula of citric acid is

$$HO-\underset{CH_2COOH}{\overset{CH_2COOH}{\underset{|}{\overset{|}{C}}}}-COOH$$

a i Assuming citric acid behaves in aqueous solution as a monoprotic acid:

$$RCOOH + H_2O \rightleftharpoons RCO_2^- + H_3O^+$$

write an expression for K_a for this acid. [1]

ii Calculate the pH of lemon juice which contains citric acid at a concentration of 0.200 mol dm^{-3}. [K_a for citric acid = 7.4×10^{-4} mol dm^{-3}.]

b The use of citric acid together with its salt, sodium citrate, as an acidity regulator depends on the ability of this mixture to act as a buffer.

i What is the function of a buffer solution? [2]

ii Describe how the mixture of citric acid and sodium citrate achieves this buffering action. Give equations for the TWO reactions you describe. [3]

ii Calculate the pH of a buffer solution containing 0.200 mol dm^{-3} of citric acid and 0.400 mol dm^{-3} of sodium citrate. [2]

c Citric acid forms a liquid ester which has the structural formula

$$HO-\underset{CH_2COOC_2H_5}{\overset{CH_2COOC_2H_5}{\underset{|}{\overset{|}{C}}}}-COOC_2H_5$$

i Describe a test you could use to show that the ester contains an —OH group. [2]

ii What reagent would you use to hydrolyse the ester? [1]

iii Treatment of the products of the reaction in **c ii** leads to the production of a pure sample of citric acid. How would you show the presence of the —COOH group in the citric acid other than by the use of an indicator? [2]
EDEXCEL 1998

4 *Terylene* has the following repeat unit.

$$-CO-\langle\bigcirc\rangle-CH_2CH_2CH_2-O-$$

a Draw the displayed formulae of the two monomers used to make *Terylene*.

b State the type of polymerization which occurs when *Terylene* is made.

c Explain why holes form when aqueous sodium hydroxide is spilled on a *Terylene* shirt. [4]
OCR (UCLES) 1998

5 a An organic compound A has a molar mass of 46 g mol^{-1} and the following elemental composition by mass:

C 52.13% H 13.15%; O 34.72%

Determine the molecular formula of **A**. [2]

b The organic compound **A** has an infrared spectrum which shows the following features:

Absorption at 2900 cm^{-1}
C—H stretching frequency

Absorption at 3300 cm^{-1}
O—H stretching frequency

Absorption at 1050 cm^{-1}
C—O stretching frequency

Absorption at 1400 cm^{-1}
C—H bending frequency

The shape and position of the —OH peak indicates substantial hydrogen bonding.

i Explain, briefly, what is meant by the term *hydrogen bonding*. [1]

ii By reference to the infrared spectrum and your answer to **a** deduce the structure of **A**.

Give three reasons in support of your answer. [4]

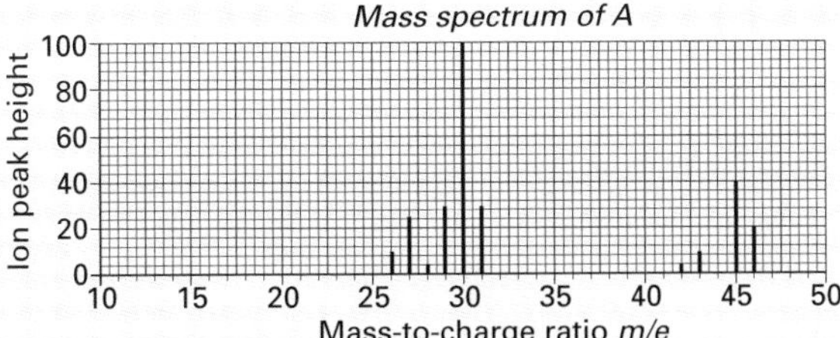

c The mass spectrum of A is given above.

Using the structural formula of **A** deduced above, suggest formulae for the positive ions responsible for *m/e* peaks at 45, 31, and 29. [3]

d i When **A** is treated with ethanoyl chloride, a compound **B** is formed containing 4 carbon atoms.

Give the name and structure of **B** and state to which class of organic compounds it belongs. [3]

ii State how you would carry out the addition of ethanoyl chloride to the compound, **A**, paying particular attention to safety. [2]
OCR (UCLES) 1997

6 a The figure below shows the infrared absorption spectrum for 'Nylon-6,6'.

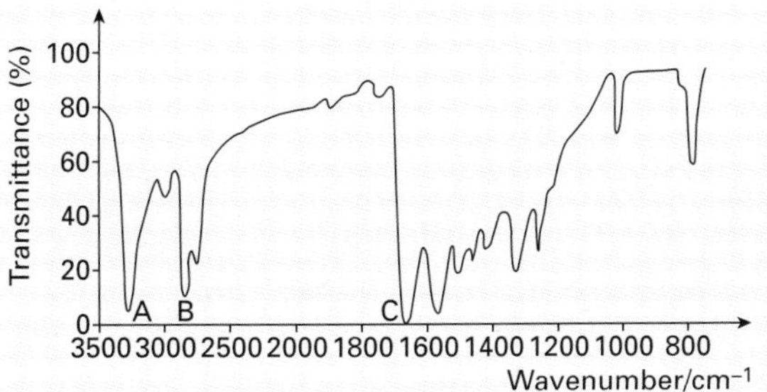

The table below shows some characteristic infrared absorptions.

Molecule or group	Bond absorbing	Wavenumber/cm^{-1}
Alkyl	C—H	2960–2850
	C—H	1460–1370
Aldehyde	C—H	3250–3200
	C═O	1740–1650
Alkene	C—H	3095–3075
	C—H	990–3300
Amide	N—H	3500–3300
Alcohol	C—O	1200–1050
	O—H	3650–3590

i Using the data in the table, identify the cause of the absorption peaks **A**, **B** and **C** in the figure. [3]

ii Draw graphical formulae of two monomers that can be used to produce 'Nylon-6,6'. [4]

b In an experiment involving enzymes, a student used urease, which is found in plants. Urease converts urea to ammonia. The student took some urea solution and added 3 drops of litmus solution, followed by drops of dilute hydrochloric acid until the solution just changed to a red colour. A small quantity of 1% urease solution was then added and the solution quickly changed colour to blue.

i Explain why the colour of the solution becomes blue. [2]

ii Complete and balance the following equation for the reaction in which urea is hydrolysed. [2]

$$(H_2N)_2C{=}O + H_2O \rightarrow$$

iii The student repeated the experiment, using ethanamide (CH_3CONH_2) in place of urea. There was no change in the colour of the solution when the urease was added. Explain this observation in terms of the activity of the enzyme. [3]

iv Suggest how the enzyme urease could be denatured in this reaction. [1]
AQA (AEB) 1997 *(See also Chapters 30 and 32.)*

7 Nylon 6,6 has the formula

$$—(CH_2)_4—CONH—(CH_2)_6—NHCO—(CH_2)_4—CONH—(CH_2)_6—NHCO—$$

a Give the formulae of the two monomers which combine to make nylon 6,6. [2]

b What is the name of the other product in this polymerization? [1]

c Suggest, including an equation, what will happen if nylon 6,6 is boiled with dilute acid. [4]
NICCEA 1998

28 Amines and amino acids

Amines and amino acids are organic compounds that contain one or more nitrogen atoms. These different classes of compounds have some underlying properties that derive from the presence of nitrogen. However, the similarities are no more marked than those seen in the alcohols, ketones, and carboxylic acids, which all contain oxygen. This chapter concentrates on amines and amino acids. The study of aromatic amines includes a treatment of diazo compounds; the study of amino acids leads into the topic of optical activity.

ORGANIC NITROGEN COMPOUNDS

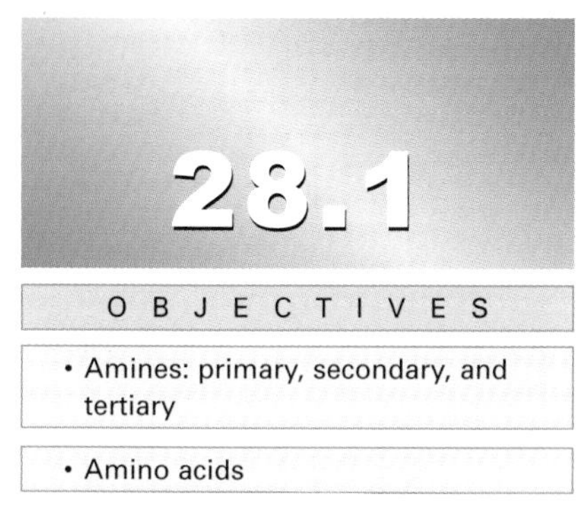

OBJECTIVES

- Amines: primary, secondary, and tertiary
- Amino acids

You have already met amides, which are carboxylic acid derivatives that contain the functional group —$CONH_2$. Central to this chapter are two other classes of nitrogen-containing organic compounds – amines and amino acids. **Amines** have an amine group —NH_2 (sometimes one or more of the hydrogen atoms is substituted). **Amino acids** have an amine group —NH_2 *and also* a carboxylic acid group —COOH attached to the molecule. We shall also look at nitriles, which have a carbon–nitrogen triple bond —C≡N, and diazo compounds, which contain a nitrogen–nitrogen double bond —N=N—.

Some molecules that contain nitrogen. From left to right, the molecules are methylamine CH_3NH_2, dimethylamine $(CH_3)_2NH$, trimethylamine $(CH_3)_3N$, ethanamide CH_3CONH_2, and ethanenitrile CH_3CN.

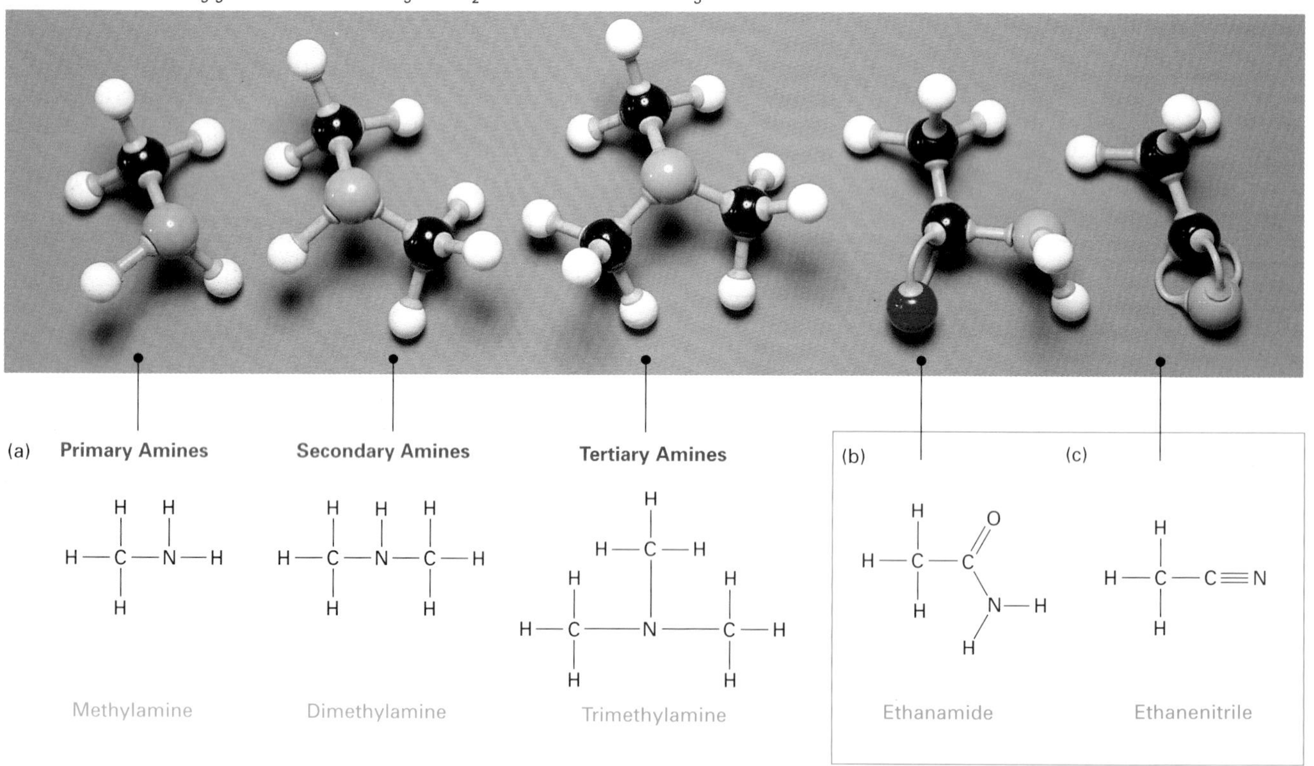

There are other nitrogen-containing molecules apart from amines. On the right are two examples: ethanamide CH_3CONH_2, and ethanenitrile CH_3CN.

Amines

The name of an amine depends on the alkyl or aryl groups present.

Formula	Name
CH_3NH_2	methylamine
$C_6H_5NH_2$	phenylamine
$(CH_3CH_2)_2NH$	diethylamine
$(CH_3CH_2)_3N$	triethylamine

Amines

Amines are organic compounds derived from ammonia in which alkyl (or aryl) groups substitute for some of the hydrogen atoms of the NH_3 molecule. **Primary**, **secondary**, and **tertiary amines** correspond to the substitution of one, two, and three hydrogen atoms respectively. Methylamine, ethylamine, and dimethylamine are gases; other common amines are liquids.

The organic equivalents of the ammonium ion are the **quaternary ammonium salts** $R_4N^+A^-$ in which four groups are attached to a central positively charged nitrogen atom. A^- is an anion such as OH^-, Cl^-, SO_4^{2-}, etc. Quaternary ammonium salts with two long-chain alkyl groups can act as cationic surfactants. Fabric softeners contain cationic surfactants to give a soft feel to cleaned garments; they must be cationic because detergents are usually anionic; see spread 23.5.

Remember that the structures of primary, secondary, and tertiary *alcohols* depend on the number of alkyl groups *attached to the carbon atom* bearing the —OH functional group. Hence, $CH_3CH_2CH_2CH_2OH$ (butan-1-ol) is a primary alcohol, $CH_3CH(OH)CH_2CH_3$ (butan-2-ol) is a secondary alcohol, and $(CH_3)_3COH$ (2-methylpropan-2-ol) is a tertiary alcohol. The structures of primary, secondary, and tertiary amines depend on the number of alkyl groups *attached directly to the nitrogen atom* of the functional group. So, CH_3NH_2 (methylamine) is a primary amine, $(CH_3)_2NH$ (dimethylamine) is a secondary amine, and $(CH_3)_3N$ (trimethylamine) is a tertiary amine.

Quaternary Ammonium Salt

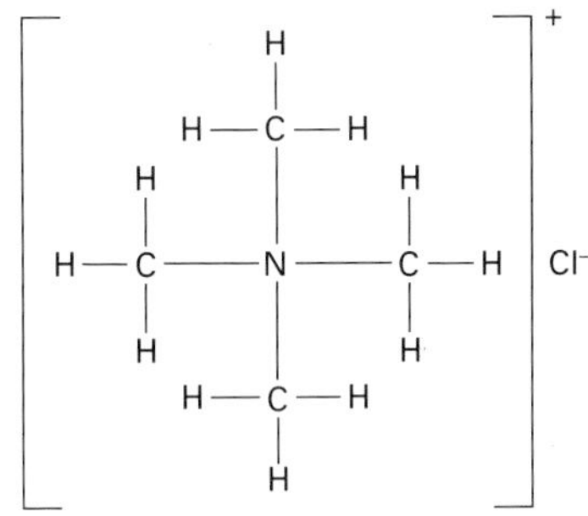

Tetramethylammonium chloride

The biochemically important species acetylcholine is $CH_3COOCH_2CH_2N^+(CH_3)_3$.

Amino acids

The amine group is also present in amino acids. Amino acids contain both the amine group —NH_2 and the carboxylic acid group —COOH. Naturally occurring amino acids are the chief constituents of proteins. These α-amino acids have the general structure

$$H_2N\text{—}CH(R)\text{—}C(=O)\text{—}O\text{—}H$$

The prefix 'α' signifies that the amine group is attached to the carbon atom that itself is attached *directly* to the carboxylic acid group.

The amino acid γ-aminobutanoic acid (also known as GABA) is a neurotransmitter found in nerve synapses in the brain. This is a γ-amino acid and has the structure

$$HO\text{—}C(=O)\text{—}\overset{\alpha}{CH_2}\text{—}\overset{\beta}{CH_2}\text{—}\overset{\gamma}{CH_2}\text{—}NH_2$$

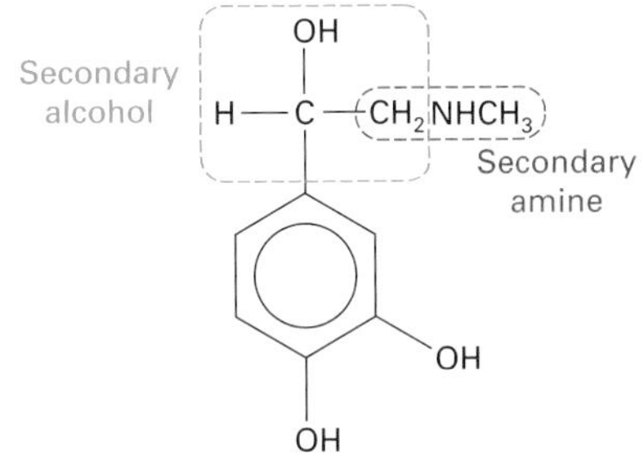

Adrenaline (also known as epinephrine) is a secondary amine. (It is also a secondary alcohol.) Adrenaline is a hormone produced by the adrenal glands, which are situated above the kidneys. Adrenaline increases heart rate as part of the 'fight or flight' response to danger or stress. It is used to treat anaphylactic shock.

SUMMARY

- Nitrogen-containing organic compounds include:
  primary amines RNH_2
  secondary amines R_2NH
  tertiary amines R_3N
  quaternary ammonium salts $R_4N^+A^-$
  amides $RCONH_2$
  nitriles RCN
  α-amino acids $H_2NCHRCOOH$
  diazo compounds RNNR
- Some quaternary ammonium salts can be used as cationic surfactants.

PRACTICE

1 Draw structural formulae for each of the following nitrogen-containing compounds:

a Ethylamine
b Methylethylamine
c Dimethylethylamine
d Trimethylethylammonium chloride
e Tetramethylammonium sulphate
f Propanamide
g Ethanenitrile
h 2-Aminopropanoic acid (alanine).

28.2

OBJECTIVES

- Amines as bases
- Amines as nucleophiles

Aliphatic amines

Aliphatic amines are organic compounds that contain at least one alkyl group bonded directly to a nitrogen atom. The lone pair on the nitrogen atom results in amines and ammonia having similar chemical behaviour. Amines are described as Brønsted bases when they accept a proton. They are described as Lewis bases or nucleophiles when they engage in reactions that involve the donation of this lone pair.

Pharmaceuticals

Many pharmaceuticals, for example the local anaesthetic procaine

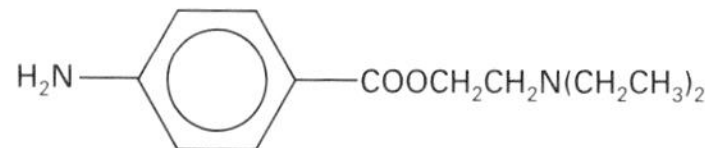

are manufactured as their 'hydrochlorides': this is usually because an amine group within the molecule is protonated.

Amines as bases

Ammonia acts as a Brønsted base when it accepts a proton from a Brønsted acid. For example, the neutralization of aqueous ammonia by dilute acid:

$$NH_3(aq) + H_3O^+(aq) \rightarrow NH_4^+(aq) + H_2O(l)$$

Amines can act in a similar manner. For example, a primary amine such as ethylamine $CH_3CH_2NH_2$ acts as a Brønsted base when it accepts a proton from a Brønsted acid. For example, ethylamine reacts with hydrochloric acid to form a substituted ammonium salt. The amine group is protonated:

$$CH_3CH_2NH_2(aq) + H_3O^+(aq) \rightarrow CH_3CH_2NH_3^+(aq) + H_2O(l)$$

Substituted ammonium salts may be isolated in the solid state, e.g. ethylammonium chloride $CH_3CH_2NH_3^+Cl^-(s)$. Strong bases displace weak bases from their salts. For example, the free amine is regenerated by adding aqueous sodium hydroxide to a solution of ethylammonium chloride:

$$CH_3CH_2NH_3^+Cl^-(aq) + NaOH(aq) \rightarrow CH_3CH_2NH_2(aq) + NaCl(aq)$$

Ammonia acts as a Lewis base when it donates a pair of electrons to a Lewis acid. For example, the formation of the nickel(II) complex:

$$6NH_3(aq) + Ni^{2+}(aq) \rightarrow [Ni(NH_3)_6]^{2+}(aq)$$

Primary amines also react with nickel(II) ions to form a solution that contains the nickel(II) ion complexed by the amine:

$$6CH_3CH_2NH_2(aq) + Ni^{2+}(aq) \rightarrow [Ni(NH_2CH_2CH_3)_6]^{2+}(aq)$$

The complex formed between (left) Cu^{2+} ions and an amine (here, ethylamine) is very similar in appearance and properties to that formed between (right) Cu^{2+} ions and ammonia.

pK_b values

There are small differences in the basicity of primary, secondary, and tertiary amines, but they all have pK_b values within one or two units of that of ammonia:

ammonia	NH_3	pK_b = 4.8
methylamine	CH_3NH_2	pK_b = 3.4
ethylamine	$CH_3CH_2NH_2$	pK_b = 3.2

For aliphatic amines, base strength increases with the size and number of alkyl groups attached to the nitrogen atom. Alkyl groups donate electron density towards the nitrogen atom, increasing the ability of the nitrogen atom to donate its lone pair of electrons.

Test for ammonia

The familiar test for ammonia, turning moist litmus paper blue, is not definitive; amines are volatile and their vapours also turn litmus blue.

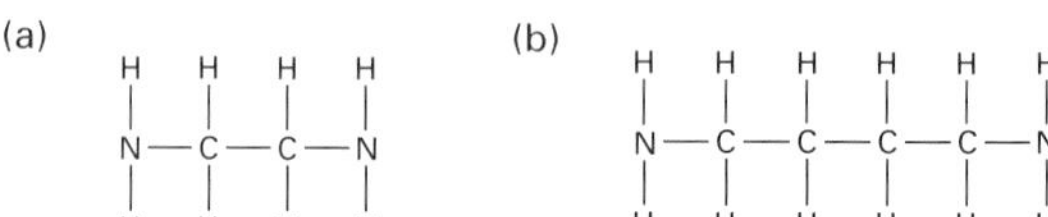

The difference a couple of —CH_2— groups can make! (a) 1,2-Diaminoethane, traditionally called 'ethylenediamine' and abbreviated to en, is a common bidentate ligand (see chapter on 'The transition metals'). It has a very slight odour, but is otherwise inoffensive as a laboratory reagent. (b) Putrescine has the systematic name 1,4-diaminobutane. It has the clinging smell of putrescent rotting fish.

Amines as nucleophiles

The presence of the lone pair on the nitrogen atom results in amines being nucleophiles. For example, primary and secondary amines are acylated by acyl chlorides. The following reaction mechanism makes clear the nucleophilic attack by the lone pair on the acyl chloride δ+ carbon atom; see spread 27.7.

(a) The carbonyl carbon atom in ethanoyl chloride has a δ+ charge due to the electronegative oxygen and chlorine atoms. This carbon atom undergoes nucleophilic attack by the lone pair of electrons on the amine nitrogen atom.

(b) The C—Cl bonding pair of electrons reverts to the chlorine atom, which leaves as the chloride ion Cl^-.

(c) The N—H bonding pair of electrons reverts to the nitrogen atom. Hydrogen leaves as the hydrogen ion H^+.

Acylation of ethylamine by ethanoyl chloride.

Amines can be produced by heating excess ammonia in ethanol with a chloroalkane. The primary amine forms as follows:

$$RCl + NH_3 \rightarrow RNH_2 + HCl$$

Unfortunately, the product is itself a nucleophile and can react with more chloroalkane to form successively secondary and tertiary amines and ultimately a quaternary ammonium salt:

$$RCl + RNH_2 \rightarrow R_2NH + HCl$$
$$RCl + R_2NH \rightarrow R_3N + HCl$$
$$RCl + R_3N \rightarrow R_4N^+Cl^-$$

At each step the lone pair on the nitrogen atom carries out nucleophilic attack on the δ+ carbon atom of the chloroalkane. Separation of the mixture is difficult; this reaction is therefore rarely used for the preparation of amines.

A more controlled method of producing *primary* aliphatic amines is to reduce a nitrile with lithium tetrahydridoaluminate; see spread 27.8:

$$CH_3C{\equiv}N \xrightarrow[\text{[H]}]{} CH_3CH_2NH_2$$

See also the Gabriel synthesis in the last spread in this chapter.

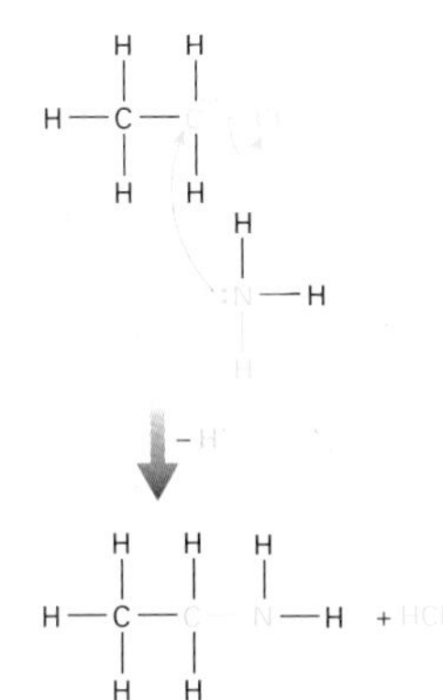

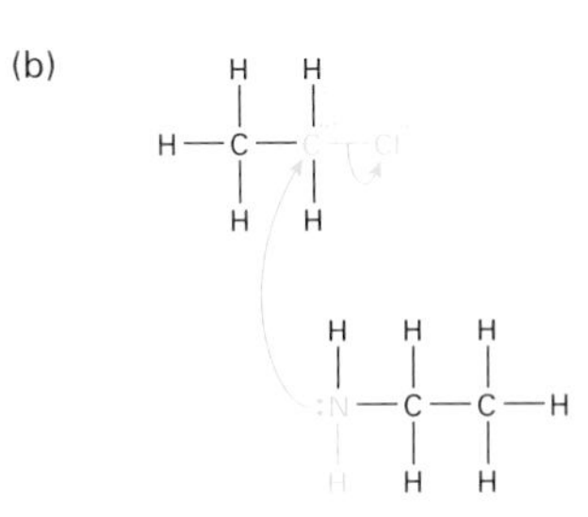

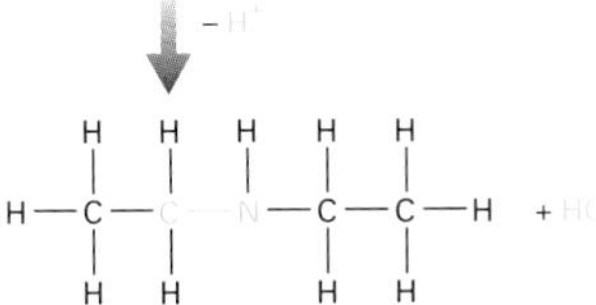

(a) Ethylamine results from the nucleophilic attack of ammonia on chloroethane. (b) Diethylamine results from the nucleophilic attack of ethylamine on chloroethane.

SUMMARY

- Amines react as substituted ammonia molecules.
- Amines act as Brønsted bases when they neutralize strong acids to form substituted ammonium salts.
- The free amine is regenerated when a substituted ammonium salt reacts with a strong base.
- Amines are weak bases; primary amines have slightly lower pK_b values than ammonia.
- Amines act as nucleophiles: the nitrogen lone pair attacks the δ+ carbon atom on halogenoalkanes and acyl chlorides.
- Amines react as Lewis bases when their nitrogen atom donates its lone pair of electrons, e.g. in transition metal complex formation.

PRACTICE

1. Interpret the reaction $CH_3CH_2NH_2 + H_3O^+ \rightarrow CH_3CH_2NH_3^+ + H_2O$ in terms of a Lewis acid–Lewis base reaction.
2. Explain why the reaction $6CH_3CH_2NH_2(aq) + Ni^{2+}(aq) \rightarrow [Ni(NH_2CH_2CH_3)_6]^{2+}(aq)$ can be interpreted by Lewis acid–base theory but not by Brønsted-Lowry acid–base theory.

28.3

Aromatic amines

OBJECTIVES

- Phenylamine preparation
- Aliphatic and aromatic amines compared
- Phenylamine as a nucleophile

A reminder

Aliphatic amines can be produced by the reaction of ammonia with a halogenoalkane (see previous spread), e.g. chloroethane:

$CH_3CH_2Cl + NH_3 \rightarrow CH_3CH_2NH_2 + HCl$

Note that secondary and tertiary amines and ultimately a quaternary ammonium salt also form.

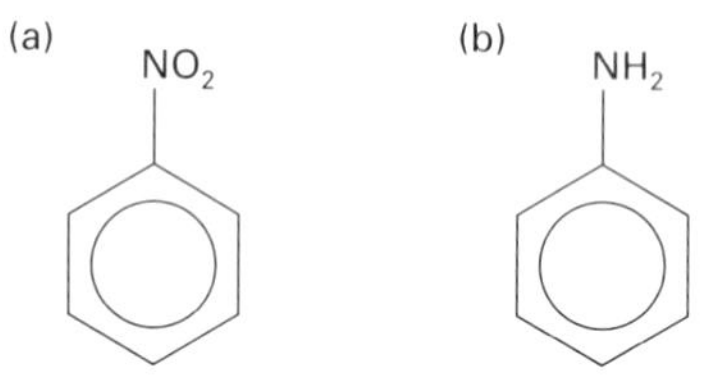

(a) Nitrobenzene has a nitrogen atom attached directly to the benzene ring. (b) The structure of phenylamine suggests that it will result from reduction of nitrobenzene.

You should recognize aliphatic amines as organic bases. These substances act as Lewis bases when they donate the lone pair of electrons on their nitrogen atom. The presence of the nitrogen lone pair also makes aliphatic amines act as nucleophiles, which attack centres of positive charge. Aromatic amines consist of an amine —NH_2 group attached to a benzene ring. The ring incorporates a system of delocalized π electrons. This delocalized system is capable of delocalizing the lone pair on the nitrogen atom. For this reason, aromatic amines do not have similar properties to aliphatic amines.

Aromatic amine synthesis

It is not possible to make aromatic amines in a similar manner to aliphatic amines. The reason is that ammonia reacts much more slowly with chloroarenes than with chloroalkanes. Ammonia is a nucleophile: its lone pair of electrons is attracted to centres of positive charge. The delocalized π electron cloud of a chloroarene *repels* the lone pair of an approaching ammonia molecule. The C—Cl bond is also stronger in the chloroarene due to delocalization of electron density from the ring with the bond, spread 24.1. The route to aromatic amines such as phenylamine $C_6H_5NH_2$ is therefore less direct.

Phenylamine: laboratory preparation

Instead of using chlorobenzene, nitrobenzene $C_6H_5NO_2$ (see the chapter on 'Arenes') is chosen as the starting material for the synthesis of phenylamine $C_6H_5NH_2$ (traditionally called aniline). Studying the structures of these molecules shows that nitrobenzene must lose oxygen and gain hydrogen. This change is a reduction and the most effective laboratory reductant is a mixture of granulated tin and concentrated hydrochloric acid. Phenylamine is very weakly basic and the reduction medium is acidic. The product is the salt phenylammonium chloride $C_6H_5NH_3^+Cl^-$:

$$C_6H_5NO_2(l) \xrightarrow{Sn/HCl} C_6H_5NH_3^+Cl^-(aq)$$

(a)

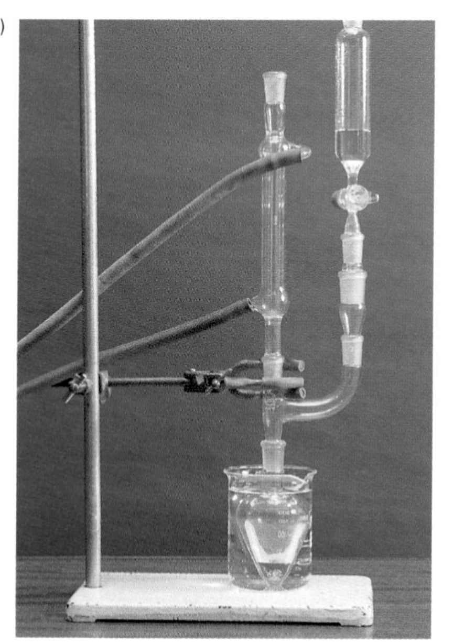

(b)

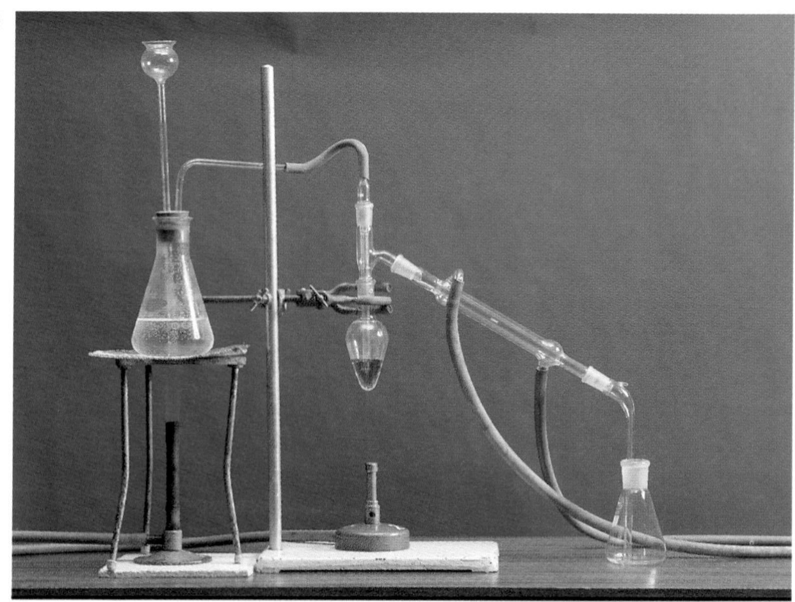

Stages in the preparation of phenylamine. (a) Place granulated tin and nitrobenzene in a flask. Fit a reflux condenser and slowly add concentrated hydrochloric acid, cooling the flask if necessary. Remove the condenser and heat the open flask in a boiling water bath for about one hour. Cool the mixture and add concentrated aqueous sodium hydroxide to produce the free amine by removing a proton from the nitrogen atom:

$C_6H_5NH_3^+Cl^-(aq) + NaOH(aq) \rightarrow C_6H_5NH_2(l) + H_2O(l) + NaCl(aq)$

(b) Steam distil the mixture until the milky emulsion of phenylamine no longer appears in the distillate. The mixture of phenylamine and steam (bubbled through the reaction mixture) boils just below 100 °C, at which temperature phenylamine decomposes much less than it does at its boiling point.

Phenylamine: properties

Aromatic amines are far less soluble in water than are aliphatic amines. Solubility depends partly on the polarity of a molecule. Aromatic amines are less polar because charge is delocalized around the benzene ring.

Phenylamine $C_6H_5NH_2$ (pK_b 9.4) is a much weaker base than ammonia (pK_b 4.8), by a factor of about 10^5. The reason for this difference is that the nitrogen lone pair is delocalized with the benzene ring and so is substantially more difficult to protonate. Phenylamine is, however, sufficiently basic to be protonated by strong acids to form salts containing the **phenylammonium ion** $C_6H_5NH_3^+$.

As for aliphatic amines, phenylamine reacts with acyl chlorides.

- Phenylamine reacts with ethanoyl chloride:

$$C_6H_5NH_2 + CH_3COCl \rightarrow C_6H_5NHCOCH_3 + HCl$$

The reaction is carried out by mixing the reagents. The product is called *N*-phenylethanamide (acetanilide) and hydrogen chloride forms as a by-product.

- Phenylamine reacts with benzoyl chloride:

$$C_6H_5NH_2 + C_6H_5COCl \rightarrow C_6H_5NHCOC_6H_5 + HCl$$

The reaction is carried out by shaking the reagents with aqueous sodium hydroxide. The product is called *N*-phenylbenzamide (benzanilide); water and sodium chloride form as by-products.

The presence of the amine group in phenylamine activates the benzene ring to electrophilic substitution (see the chapter on 'Arenes'). For example, shaking phenylamine with bromine water rapidly produces 2,4,6-tribromophenylamine:

$$C_6H_5NH_2 + 3Br_2(aq) \longrightarrow Br_3C_6H_2NH_2 + 3HBr$$

Industry

The production of phenylamine is particularly important in industry. It is the precursor of a range of important dyes, some of which were crucial to the development of antibiotics. The following spread discusses the *diazotization reaction*, which is fundamental to the production of these substances.

SUMMARY

- In aromatic amines, electron density from the nitrogen lone pair is delocalized with the benzene ring.
- Aliphatic amines have lower pK_b values and are more powerful nucleophiles than aromatic amines.
- Aromatic amines react more slowly with acyl chlorides than do aliphatic amines.
- The amine group activates the benzene ring to electrophilic substitution into the 2, 4, and 6 positions.

Phenylamine and medicines

The acylation of a derivative of phenylamine leads to the pain-relieving medicine paracetamol (acetaminophen). Its formula is:

p-$HOC_6H_4NHCOCH_3$

The 'para-' signifies the 4-isomer.

(a)

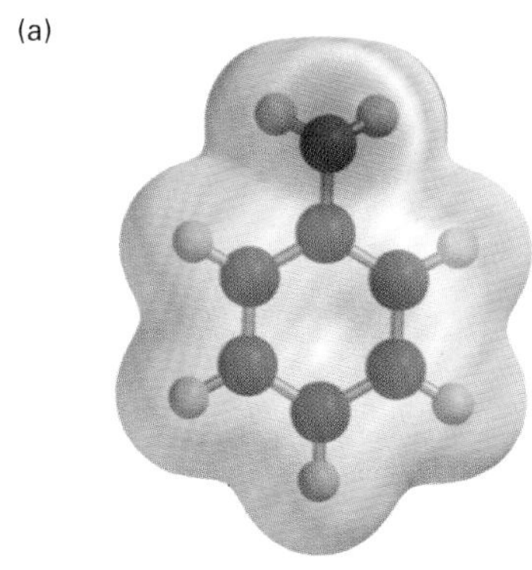

(b)

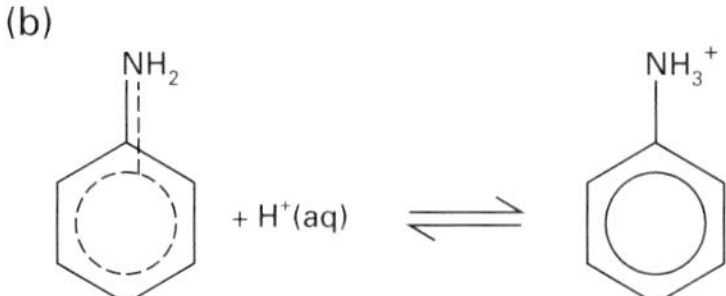

(c)

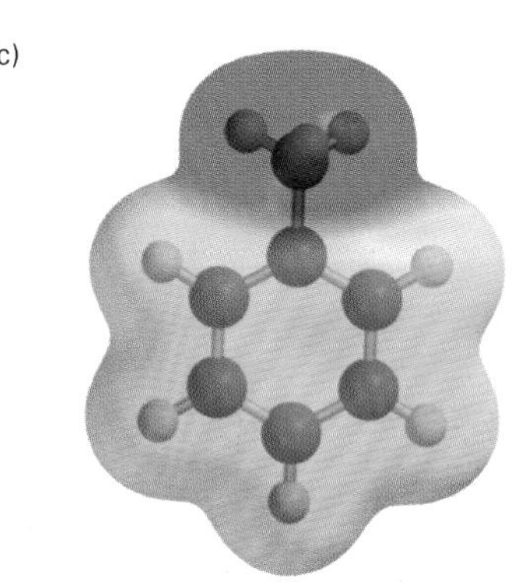

Phenylamine as a base.
(a) Phenylamine (an aromatic amine) is a weaker base than ethylamine (an aliphatic amine) due to delocalization of the nitrogen lone pair with the benzene ring. (b) The phenylammonium ion forms when phenylamine acts as a base (donating its nitrogen lone pair). (c) Delocalization stabilization is absent in the phenylammonium ion because there is no lone pair.

PRACTICE

1 Look at the photographs and captions on the stages in the preparation of phenylamine (opposite page).

  a Why is a reflux condenser fitted during the addition of the concentrated hydrochloric acid?

  b Why is no condenser required during heating on the water bath?

  c Why is concentrated aqueous sodium hydroxide added at the end of the reduction?

2 Suggest a mechanism for the reaction between phenylamine and ethanoyl chloride to produce *N*-phenylethanamide:
$C_6H_5NH_2 + CH_3COCl \rightarrow C_6H_5NHCOCH_3 + HCl$

3 Phenylamine reacts with benzoyl chloride to produce *N*-phenylbenzamide:
$C_6H_5NH_2 + C_6H_5COCl \rightarrow C_6H_5NHCOC_6H_5 + HCl$
Explain why this reaction is slower than the acylation reaction in question 2, and why aqueous sodium hydroxide is included in the reaction mixture.

28.4 PHENYLAMINE AND DIAZOTIZATION

OBJECTIVES

- Benzenediazonium salts
- Substitution reactions
- Coupling reactions
- Diazo dyes and drugs

(a)

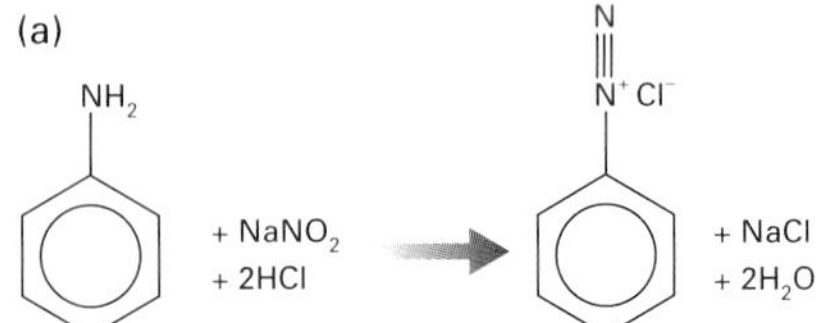

(b)

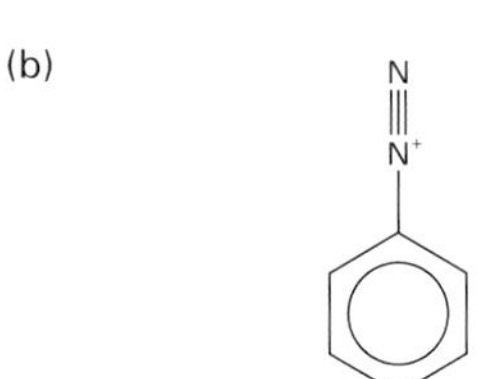

(c)

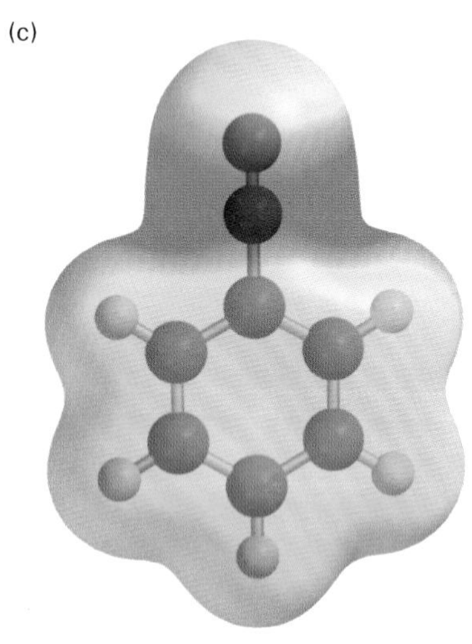

(a) The overall diazotization reaction may be represented by this chemical equation. (b) Classical bonding considerations indicate this structure for the diazonium ion. (c) The electrostatic potential map confirms that the nitrogen atom nearer the ring carries most of the positive charge (blue colour).

Diazonium salts

Aromatic diazonium salts are reasonably stable in solution if they are kept cold. This is because the benzene ring delocalizes the charge on the ion. It is not possible to make aliphatic diazonium salts, because the lack of delocalization makes them extremely unstable. They decompose immediately, releasing nitrogen gas.

Phenylamine (aniline) was originally manufactured from benzene obtained from the distillation of coal tar. This tar has a similar constitution to crude oil and was one of the by-products from heating coal to produce coke and coal gas. The synthetic dyestuff industry began in 1856 when William Perkin discovered a mauve dye while attempting to synthesize quinine, a cure for malaria. Many of the dyes subsequently developed became known as 'aniline' or 'coal tar' dyes. These dyes contain the diazo —N=N— group and are called 'diazo' dyes (or azo dyes). The dyestuffs industry that produces them has a total annual turnover of billions of pounds world-wide, a substantial proportion of which depends on just one chemical reaction – *diazotization*.

Diazotization

The **diazotization reaction** uses nitrous acid HNO_2 (HONO) to convert phenylamine $C_6H_5NH_2$ into the diazonium salt **benzenediazonium chloride** $C_6H_5N_2^+Cl^-$. Nitrous acid decomposes very readily and so cannot be stored. It is prepared *in situ* (within the reaction mixture) from a mixture of sodium nitrite $NaNO_2$ and an acid, i.e.

$$NaNO_2(aq) + HCl(aq) \rightarrow HNO_2(aq) + NaCl(aq)$$

The temperature must be kept below 5 °C in an ice-bath during diazotization otherwise the main product decomposes, losing its nitrogen atoms as nitrogen gas N_2. Temperature control is critical because below 0 °C the rate of diazotization becomes very slow.

Replacing the nitrogen atoms

- *Phenol*

When the temperature rises to around 50 °C, the diazonium ion reacts with water to produce phenol:

$$C_6H_5N_2^+Cl^-(aq) + H_2O(l) \rightarrow C_6H_5OH(aq) + N_2(g) + HCl(aq)$$

Note that, in this reaction, water is acting as a nucleophile.

- *Chlorobenzene*

Other nucleophiles may be used to attack diazonium salts. For example, chloride ions from hydrochloric acid (with copper(I) chloride CuCl as a catalyst) react to form chlorobenzene in the **Sandmeyer reaction** (named after the Swiss Traugott Sandmeyer):

$$C_6H_5N_2^+Cl^- \xrightarrow{HCl/CuCl} C_6H_5Cl + N_2$$

Similar reactions occur with bromide ion and iodide ion (iodide ion does not need a catalyst because it is a more powerful nucleophile). This reaction is the best way of attaching a halogen atom to a benzene ring.

Coupling to the diazo group

Diazonium salts also undergo a type of reaction known as **coupling**. A simple example is the reaction of a diazonium salt (kept below 5 °C) with an aromatic compound such as phenol C_6H_5OH in alkaline solution. The reaction produces an intense orange–yellow precipitate of (4-hydroxyphenyl)azobenzene:

$$C_6H_5N_2^+Cl^- + C_6H_5OH \rightarrow HOC_6H_4N{=}NC_6H_5 + HCl$$

In a similar manner, an aromatic amine couples via its carbon atom at position 4 to form a diazo compound, as shown below. Similar diazo compounds are much used in the dyestuffs industry.

H2N—C6H4—H + Cl N≡N—C6H5 → H2N—C6H4—N=N—C6H5 + HCl

Coupling phenylamine with the benzenediazonium ion to produce (4-aminophenyl) azobenzene. In all reactions of this type, the attacking molecule couples to the diazo group by the carbon atom in position 4 with respect to its functional group.

Diazo dyes and antibiotics

Before 1900, the vast majority of diseases simply had to be left to run their course because no chemotherapy treatment was available. The first breakthrough came in 1907 when Paul Ehrlich used the diazo dye 'Tyrian red' to treat sleeping sickness and other diseases caused by parasitic trypanosomes. He was awarded the Nobel prize in the following year for this life-saving discovery. In 1909 he introduced Salvarsan, an arsenic-containing molecule designed to treat syphilis.

Ehrlich did not rest on his laurels. He wished to find a compound that would be effective against a wider range of diseases. As a medical student, he had noticed that several synthetic dyes selectively stained biological tissue. He wondered if he could alter such a dye to deliver a 'magic bullet' to kill certain disease-causing pathological microorganisms.

Other scientists joined in the search, and nowhere was activity more intense than at the huge German dye manufacturers I. G. Farben. One particular dye, Prontosil, had achieved impressive results on mice that had been infected with *Streptococcus* bacteria. As the research was at the early stage, it was not felt acceptable to test the compound on humans. However, in 1935 the youngest daughter of Gerhard Domagk, a doctor at I. G. Farben, contracted a severe case of streptococcal infection from a pin prick. With his daughter close to death, Domagk gambled that Prontosil might possibly cure her. It did – she became the first of many to owe their lives to the effects of Prontosil.

Active metabolites

Prontosil is a diazo dye. It was initially suspected that this structure was responsible for its antibacterial activity. Ernest Fourneau of the Pasteur Institute later showed that human metabolism breaks down Prontosil to 4-aminobenzene-sulphonamide (sulphanilamide). This breakdown product (metabolite) is the chemical substance responsible for the destruction of the *Streptococcus* bacterium. (We shall discuss sulpha drugs more fully in the last spread in this chapter.)

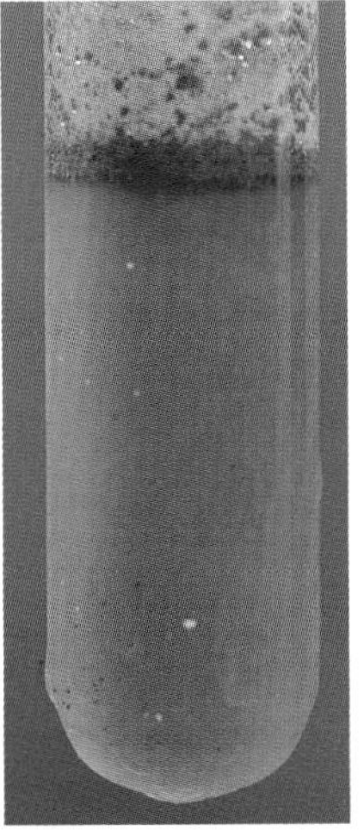

Diazo dyestuffs are used to dye natural and synthetic fibres. Compared to earlier natural dyestuffs, they have greater wash- and light-fastness, and more intense colours. They can also be used in plastics and paints. Their use in food is diminishing.

SUMMARY

- Diazotization forms the benzenediazonium ion $C_6H_5N_2^+$ by the action of nitrous acid HNO_2 on phenylamine $C_6H_5NH_2$.
- The diazo group has the formula —N═N—.
- Nucleophiles such as halide ion and water replace the $—N_2^+$ group on the benzenediazonium ion.
- Phenol and phenylamine couple to the benzenediazonium ion $C_6H_5N_2^+$ to form diazo compounds $C_6H_5N{=}NC_6H_4X$. The X group is in the 4 position relative to the diazo linkage.

PRACTICE

1 Most of the chemical equations given in this spread are written as shortened structural formulae. Rewrite them using *displayed* formulae.

2 A solution of benzenediazonium chloride reacts with the secondary amine *N*-methylphenylamine $C_6H_5NHCH_3$. Draw the structural formula of the product of this coupling reaction.

3 Suggest why iodide ion is a more powerful nucleophile than chloride ion in the reaction with the benzenediazonium ion.

Amino acids

OBJECTIVES

- The α-amino acids
- Zwitterions
- Condensation reactions
- Polypeptides and proteins

A molecular model of the simplest amino acid, glycine.

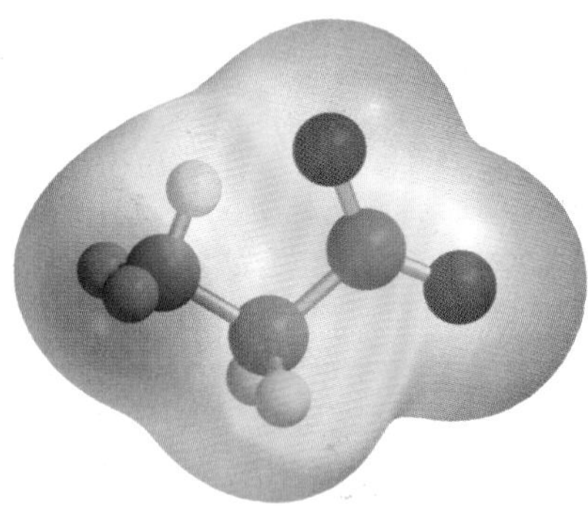

Amino acids typically exist as zwitterions: the protonated amine group is blue and the carboxylate group is red.

Zwitterions

The charges on the zwitterions mean that amino acids move in an electric field. This property is the basis of their separation by electrophoresis (see the chapter on 'Techniques of preparation...').

Amino acids are substances whose molecules contain both a basic —NH_2 group and an acidic —COOH group. They are very important in biochemistry as the monomers that make up the natural polyamide polymers called proteins (see chapter on 'Biochemistry'). Almost all naturally occurring amino acids are α-amino acids in which the amine group is attached to the α-carbon atom of a carboxylic acid. As a result, they have the general formula

$$\mathrm{H_2N{-}CH(R){-}C({=}O){-}O{-}H}$$

Whilst amino acids contain both a basic amine group and a carboxylic acid group, the overall acid–base nature depends on the balance of acidic and basic groups in the R group.

General physical properties

Amino acids have high melting points and low solubility in non-polar solvents. For example, glycine (aminoethanoic acid) NH_2CH_2COOH is a crystalline solid. Propanoic acid CH_3CH_2COOH and butylamine $CH_3CH_2CH_2CH_2NH_2$ have similar relative formula masses to aminoethanoic acid but are liquids. These properties point to amino acid molecules having a significantly polar nature. In both the solid state and in solution, they exist as 'inner salts' or '**zwitterions**'. The hydrogen atom from the carboxylic acid group protonates the basic amine group, i.e.

$$NH_2CH_2COOH \rightarrow {}^{+}NH_3CH_2CO_2^{-}$$

Natural amino acids

There are about 20 naturally occurring amino acids. As stated above, almost all are α-amino acids with the general formula $RCH(NH_2)COOH$. The only part of the molecule that varies is the R group. If the R group does not contain any acidic or basic groups, the amino acid is neutral overall. If there are more acidic groups, the amino acid is acidic (aspartic acid, glutamic acid); if there are more basic groups, the amino acid is basic (asparagine, arginine, lysine).

Glycine: $H_2N{-}CH(H){-}COOH$

Alanine: $H_2N{-}CH(CH_3){-}COOH$

Serine: $H_2N{-}CH(CH_2OH){-}COOH$

Threonine: $H_2N{-}CH(CH(OH)CH_3){-}COOH$

Phenylalanine: $H_2N{-}CH(CH_2C_6H_5){-}COOH$

Glutamic acid: $H_2N{-}CH(CH_2CH_2COOH){-}COOH$

Histidine: $H_2N{-}CH(CH_2{-}\text{imidazolyl (N, NH)}){-}COOH$

Cysteine: $H_2N{-}CH(CH_2SH){-}COOH$

Some of the amino acids occurring in proteins.

Amino acids, polypeptides, and proteins

Amino acids undergo condensation reactions (see the chapter on 'Aldehydes and ketones') to form a substituted amide R—CONH—R′. For example, for glycine and alanine

$$NH_2CH_2COOH + NH_2CH(CH_3)COOH \rightarrow$$
$$NH_2CH_2CONHCH(CH_3)COOH + H_2O$$

The C—N bond in the —CONH— **peptide link** is called the **peptide bond**. The result of the reaction is a **dipeptide** molecule, which retains an amine group at one end and a carboxylic acid group at the other. Further amino acid molecules may condense with this product to extend the chain length. Chains consisting of up to 20 amino acids are called **oligopeptides**; longer chains are called **polypeptides**. Proteins consist of one or more polypeptide chains coiled into a complex and distinctive structure (see the chapter on 'Biochemistry').

The amino acids glycine and alanine condense to form a dipeptide, with the elimination of water. Note that there are two possible products (Gly–Ala and Ala–Gly). In natural systems, the choice of product is controlled by the structure of DNA.

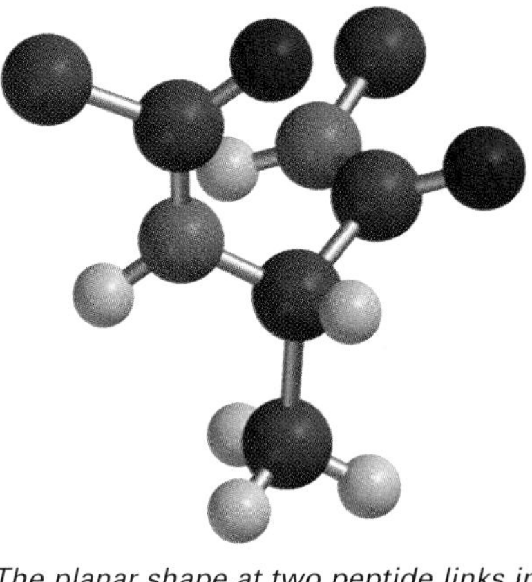

The planar shape at two peptide links in a portion of a protein. Remember that Spartan intentionally does not show the number of bonds; see spread 6.4.

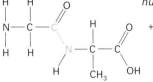

General chemical properties

Amino acids undergo the typical reactions of primary amines and carboxylic acids:

- Salt formation with acids

  $NH_2CH_2COOH(aq) + HCl(aq) \rightarrow [^+NH_3CH_2COOH]Cl^-(aq) + H_2O(l)$
- Salt formation with base

  $NH_2CH_2COOH(aq) + NaOH(aq) \rightarrow Na^+ \, NH_2CH_2CO_2^-(aq) + H_2O(l)$

One distinctive feature of α-amino acids is that the carbon atom highlighted in the formula $RCH(NH_2)COOH$ is attached to four different groups. As a result, these substances can show optical activity. This topic forms the focus of the following spread.

Crystals of phenylalanine. Amino acids may be isolated as crystalline solids. They have good solubility in water.

Catabolism and anabolism

Digesting the proteins in food involves an overall process called *catabolism*. Protein structure is broken down to liberate the component amino acids. The synthesis, in living systems, of proteins from amino acids is an example of *anabolism*. See the chapter on 'Biochemistry'.

SUMMARY

- Amino acids contain both a primary amine group and a carboxylic acid group.
- Naturally occurring amino acids are usually α-amino acids of general formula $RCH(NH_2)COOH$.
- The carboxylic acid group protonates the amine group to form a zwitterion $^+NH_3CHRCO_2^-$.
- Two amino acid molecules condense with the elimination of water to form a dipeptide containing a peptide link —CONH—, i.e. a dipeptide is a substituted amide.
- Polypeptides contain more than 20 amino acids condensed together. Proteins are natural polypeptides.

PRACTICE

1 Explain the relationship between amino acids, polypeptides, and proteins.

2 Suggest a mechanism for the condensation reaction between two molecules of glycine (aminoethanoic acid) to form a dipeptide containing the peptide link —CONH—.

3 Give the structural formulae of the species you would expect to be present on dissolving solid glycine (aminoethanoic acid) in the following:

a Dilute hydrochloric acid
b Pure water
c Dilute aqueous sodium hydroxide.

4 Suggest approximate pH values for solutions of the following amino acids in pure water:

a Glycine (aminoethanoic acid)
b Aspartic acid (2-aminobutanedioic acid)
c Serine (2-amino-3-hydroxypropanoic acid)
d Lysine (2,6-diaminohexanoic acid).

AMINO ACIDS AND OPTICAL ACTIVITY

OBJECTIVES

- Plane-polarized light
- Chiral molecules
- Enantiomers

The general formula of the naturally occurring α-amino acids is $RCH(NH_2)COOH$. With the exception of glycine (where R = H), all these substances contain a carbon atom that is attached to four different groups. These four groups are situated at the corners of a tetrahedron, and are bonded to a carbon atom placed at its centre. As you saw with the inorganic examples in the chapter on 'The transition metals', it is possible for such a compound to exist in two forms that are non-superimposable mirror images of each other. These two optically active isomers will rotate the plane of plane-polarized light in opposite directions to each other.

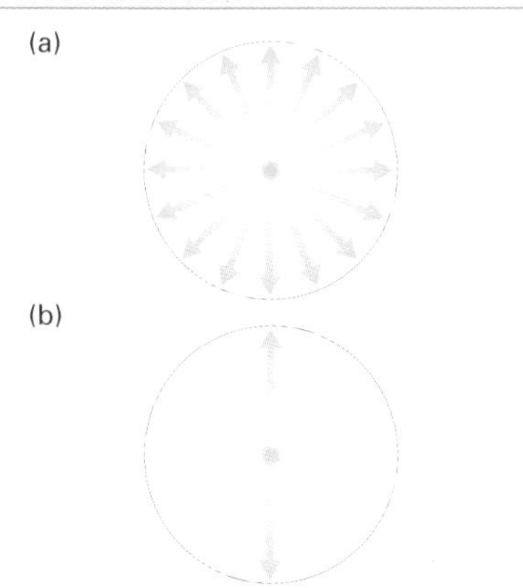

(a) A cross-sectional diagram of a ray of ordinary light travelling directly towards you. The electric field vibrates in all planes. (b) A ray of plane-polarized light. The electric field vibrates in one plane only.

Polarized light

Light (a form of electromagnetic radiation) is a transverse wave motion, which means that its electric field vibrates at right angles to the direction of motion. In ordinary light, there is an infinite number of planes of vibration for the electric field. Passing this light through a Polaroid filter or certain types of prism results in **plane-polarized light**. The vibration is in one direction (plane) only, depending on how the filter is aligned. Note that laser light is plane-polarized.

The asymmetric carbon atom

A carbon atom is said to be an **asymmetric carbon atom** if it is joined to four different atoms or groups. In the terminology introduced in spread 20.9, such a carbon atom is referred to as a '**chiral centre**'. A compound containing one chiral centre can exist in two forms that are non-superimposable mirror images of each other. These two isomeric forms are called **optical isomers** or **enantiomers**.

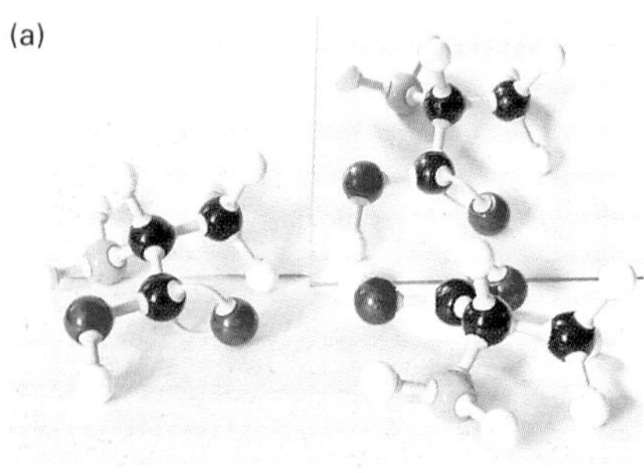

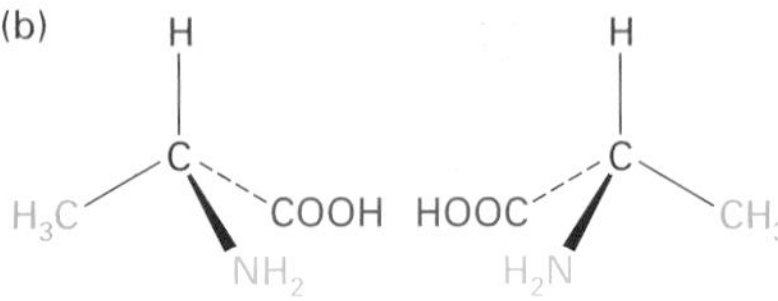

(a) Two non-superimposable mirror images (enantiomers). (b) The two enantiomers of the amino acid alanine (2-aminopropanoic acid) $H_2NCH(CH_3)COOH$. Under identical conditions, samples of the two enantiomers rotate the plane of plane-polarized light through the same angle, but in opposite directions.

Demonstrating optical activity

Optical activity is measured by an instrument called a **polarimeter**. Rays of light of a single frequency (monochromatic light) are polarized as they pass through a polarizing filter. A similar filter is fitted to the eyepiece. This filter is rotated until the light is extinguished. The polarizers are then said to be 'crossed'; their polarizing effects are at right angles to each other. A solution of the substance under investigation is then placed between the two polarizers. If the solution is optically active, then the plane of polarization will be rotated, and light will be seen through the eyepiece. Rotating the eyepiece polarizer can again extinguish the light.

If the eyepiece polarizer must be rotated clockwise – to the right – when viewed looking towards the light source, then the substance is said to be '**dextrorotatory**'; a '**laevorotatory**' substance requires rotation anticlockwise – to the left. The two isomers are known as the + (plus) form and the – (minus) form. The extent of rotation depends on the concentration of the solution, its temperature, the frequency of the light, and the distance the beam travels through the sample. Standard conditions are usually $1\,g\,cm^{-3}$, 25 °C, sodium light (589 nm), and 10 cm respectively.

Properties of enantiomers

Enantiomers have the same physical properties, with the exception that they rotate the plane of plane-polarized light in opposite directions. Their chemical properties are also identical, unless they are reacting with other chiral molecules.

The tube is filled with a saturated solution of cane sugar in water. When plane-polarized light is shone through the tube, bands of light of different colours can be seen along the length of the tube: blue, yellow-green, and red-brown can be seen.

The significance of optical activity

Reaction mechanisms

A reaction such as

$$CH_3-C(=O)-H + HCN \longrightarrow CH_3-C(OH)(CN)-H$$

results in a product that has an asymmetric carbon atom. However, the reaction always gives a mixture that contains equal amounts of the two enantiomers (a racemic mixture). The cyanide group can attack the planar carbonyl carbon atom from either above or below the molecule. Hydrolysis in acid produces racemic 2-hydroxypropanoic acid (lactic acid); see spread 29.1. An optically active product would indicate attack from one side only. Lactic acid in Nature is almost exclusively one enantiomer.

Living systems

With the exception of glycine, all amino acids obtained from proteins are optically active because the α-carbon atom is a chiral centre. Naturally occurring amino acids all have the amine group, the carboxylic acid group, the hydrogen atom, and the R group arranged in space in the same way (see the chapter on 'Biochemistry'). Organisms cannot metabolize the isomeric substances that are arranged differently at the chiral centre.

When chiral molecules of different substances react together, the situation can be likened to a hand trying to fit into a pair of gloves. The right hand fits snugly into a right glove, but not so comfortably into a left glove. The chiral nature of amino acids (and of many other natural compounds) can give rise to some surprising physiological effects.

- The odours of spearmint and caraway seed are caused by the two enantiomers of carvone. Although infrared and ultraviolet spectrometers (see the chapter on 'Techniques of preparation, ...') cannot distinguish the difference, our noses can!
- One enantiomer of the amino acid asparagine tastes bitter whereas the other tastes sweet.
- Only one of the enantiomers of LSD causes hallucinations.
- One enantiomer of morphine relieves pain strongly and is not greatly addictive, whereas the other is strongly addictive and not nearly so effective at relieving pain.
- Bacteria incorporate non-human enantiomers into their cell walls to protect themselves against attack by our immune systems.
- One enantiomer of dopamine (3,4-dihydroxyphenylalanine) is used to treat the debilitating illness Parkinson's disease. The other enantiomer is not found in Nature.

SUMMARY

- The electric field in light vibrates at right angles to its direction of motion. Plane-polarized light vibrates in one plane only.
- An asymmetric carbon atom is bonded to four different atoms or groups, forming a chiral centre.
- Compounds with an asymmetric carbon atom exist as isomeric pairs called enantiomers; they are non-superimposable mirror images of each other.
- A (+) enantiomer rotates the plane of plane-polarized light clockwise; a (–) enantiomer rotates the light anticlockwise.
- All naturally occurring amino acids (except glycine) are optically active.

Racemic mixtures

A solution that contains equal amounts (in moles) of the two enantiomers does not show optical activity. It is called a **racemic mixture**. The rotating effect of one form exactly cancels out the effect of the other.

Stereoisomerism

Stereoisomers differ in their spatial arrangement. There are two types of stereoisomers: optical isomers and geometric isomers, spread 22.6.

Frances Kelsey. The drug 'Thalidomide' was introduced in Europe in the late 1950s to relieve morning sickness during pregnancy. Evidence slowly emerged that it was teratogenic, causing malformations of the foetus. Children were born with greatly shortened and distorted limbs. The thalidomide molecule is chiral. One enantiomer is teratogenic; the other alleviates morning sickness and is not teratogenic. The drug sold in Europe was a racemic mixture. Frances Kelsey was a pharmacologist working for the US Federal Drug Administration. Every drug used in the USA has to pass the scrutiny of the FDA. Kelsey was concerned about initial reports of nervous disorders in animals, and hesitated to grant a licence for Thalidomide, instead requesting further evidence. Before the manufacturers could respond, the human disaster in Europe had unfolded. US mothers who gave birth in the early 1960s have reason to give thanks for Kelsey's diligence. President Kennedy presented her with the Distinguished Federal Civilian Award in 1962.

28.7 SOME ADVANCED IDEAS

OBJECTIVES

- Gabriel synthesis of amines
- Sulpha drugs
- Protection of an amine group
- Phase transfer catalysis

Nitrogen-containing compounds are useful in synthesis because the nitrogen atoms act as centres of reactivity. The ability of nitrogen to donate its lone pair of electrons is a major factor in their reactions. The advanced reactions in this spread are not simply laboratory curiosities. The Gabriel synthesis of amines is the first of several stages in the manufacture of penicillin. The sulphanilamides are another important group of antibiotic drugs synthesized from standard organic reagents. The whole subject of multi-step synthetic pathways is covered in greater detail in the following chapter.

Gabriel synthesis for primary amines

The yield of primary amine is very poor when using the conventional reaction of a halogenoalkane with ammonia (see earlier in this chapter). The Gabriel synthesis shown below is a great improvement. The nitrogen atom in the Gabriel reagent carries a full negative charge and is therefore a more powerful nucleophile than the nitrogen atom in ammonia.

The mechanism of Gabriel synthesis. The reaction is carried out in a polar solvent that does not donate protons, e.g. dimethylsulphoxide $(CH_3)_2SO$.

(a) The Gabriel reagent attacks the halogenoalkane: the carbon skeleton of the halogenoalkane becomes joined to the nitrogen atom of the Gabriel reagent. Only one halogenoalkane can react.

(b) Hydrolysis of the resulting compound gives a *primary* amine in high yield.

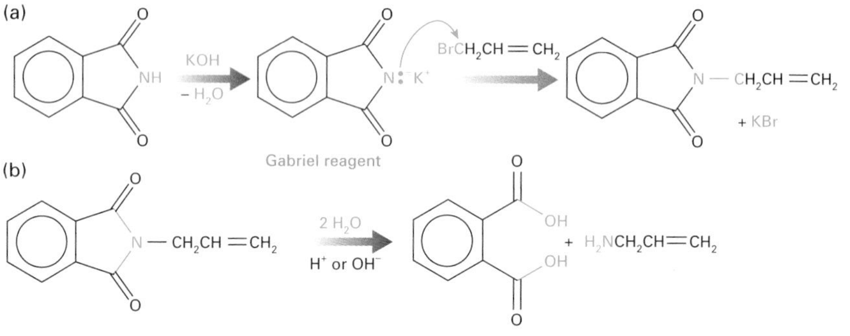

(a) KOH, $-H_2O$; Gabriel reagent (N: K^+); $BrCH_2CH{=}CH_2$ → N—$CH_2CH{=}CH_2$ + KBr

(b) N—$CH_2CH{=}CH_2$ —($2H_2O$, H^+ or OH^-)→ OH, OH + $H_2NCH_2CH{=}CH_2$

The Gabriel synthesis of an amine.

The synthesis of a sulpha drug

The industrial manufacture of a sulpha drug requires a four-stage synthesis, shown in the box below. The first (and last) steps are required because the amine group is generally too reactive.

The molecule sulphalinamide (4-aminobenzenesulphonamide) itself is too toxic for widespread use. The modern group of sulpha drugs are derivatives of this substance, and have a common structure that involves the replacement of one hydrogen in the sulphonamide group —SO_2NH_2 to give —SO_2NHR, as in sulphapyridine where R is [pyridyl ring, N]

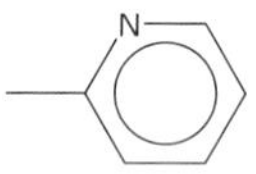

The mechanism of the synthesis of sulphanilamide.

(a) The amine group is protected in the first step by reaction with ethanoyl chloride (or ethanoic anhydride) to form a substituted amide, which is much less reactive, e.g.
$RNH_2 + CH_3COCl \rightarrow RNHCOCH_3 + HCl$

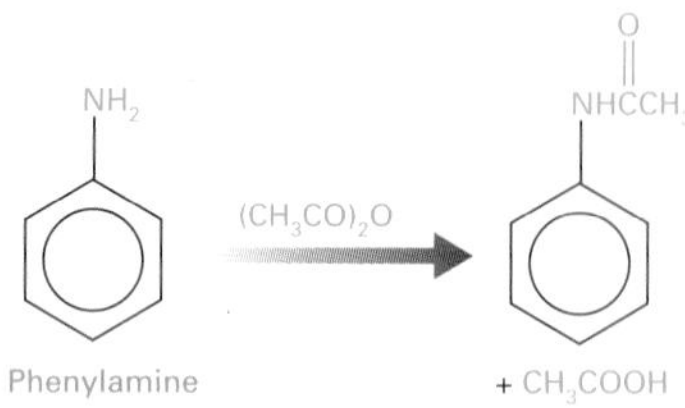

Phenylamine (NH_2) —$(CH_3CO)_2O$→ $NHCCH_3$ (O) + CH_3COOH

(b) The second step is similar to sulphonation of the benzene ring (see chapter on 'Arenes').

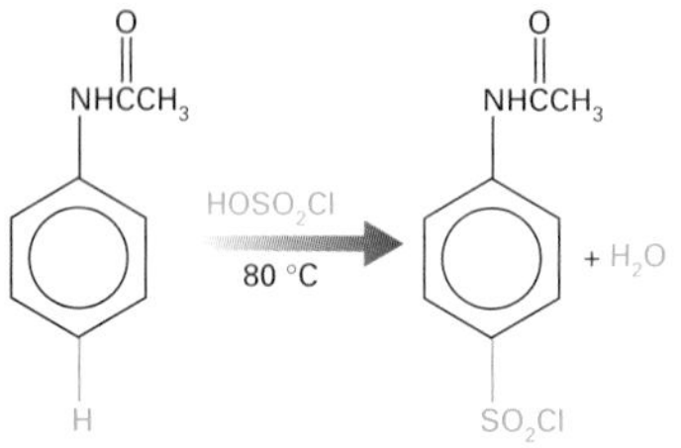

$NHCCH_3$ (H) —$HOSO_2Cl$, 80 °C→ $NHCCH_3$ (SO_2Cl) + H_2O

(c) In the third step, nucleophilic substitution replaces a halogen atom by the nitrogen atom of an amine group.

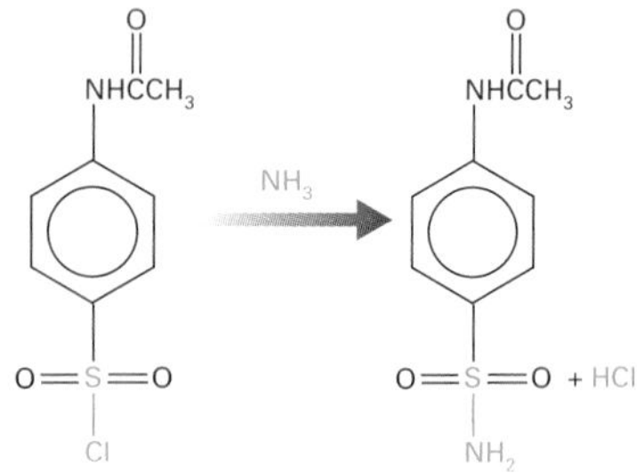

$NHCCH_3$ (O=S=O, Cl) —NH_3→ $NHCCH_3$ (O=S=O, NH_2) + HCl

(d) The protecting CH_3CO— group is finally removed by acidic hydrolysis, to give sulphanilamide, with the structure:

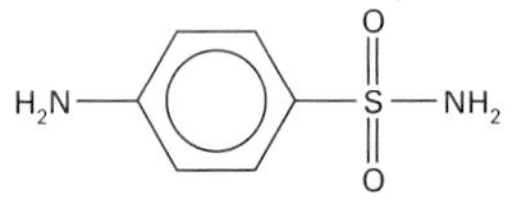

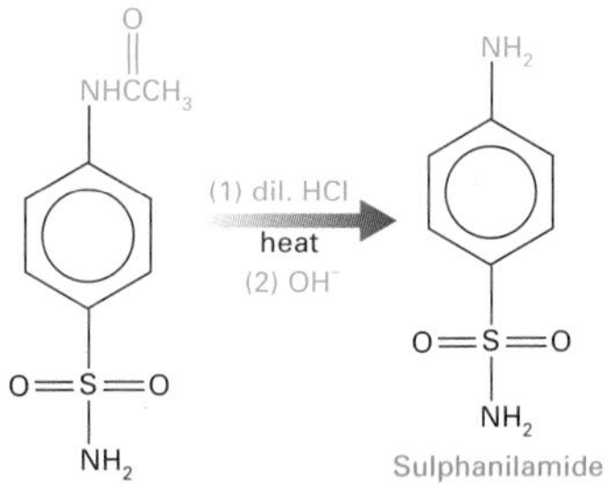

H_2N—C₆H₄—$S(=O)_2$—NH_2

$NHCCH_3$ (O=S=O, NH_2) —(1) dil. HCl, heat, (2) OH^-→ NH_2 (O=S=O, NH_2) Sulphanilamide

The synthesis of sulphanilamide.

Phase transfer catalysis

An increasingly common strategy for encouraging reactions to occur between organic compounds and ionic compounds involves a process called phase transfer catalysis. Immiscible liquids are mixed, carrying the inorganic nucleophile from the aqueous phase into the organic phase. For example, stirring a mixture of 1-chlorooctane with aqueous sodium cyanide for several days gives a negligible yield of the nitrile. Adding a small quantity of a quaternary ammonium salt (which contains the R_4N^+ ion) causes the mixture to produce a yield of more than 90% of the nitrile within 2 hours, according to the equation:

$$R{-}Cl + Na^+CN^- \rightarrow R{-}CN + Na^+Cl^-$$

Without the quaternary ammonium salt, the sodium ion of the sodium cyanide is hydrated and the cyanide ion is forced to remain in the aqueous layer to preserve electrical neutrality. In the presence of quaternary ammonium ions, the rigorous demarcation between the two liquid phases is removed. The quaternary ammonium ions can migrate from the inorganic layer (the aqueous phase) into the organic layer, partly because they are more weakly hydrated than sodium ions, and partly because the organic groups are attracted by the dispersion forces of the organic solvent. To maintain electrical neutrality within each phase, each quaternary ammonium ion takes a cyanide ion with it and so allows the reactants (cyanide and halogenoalkane) to meet in the organic phase.

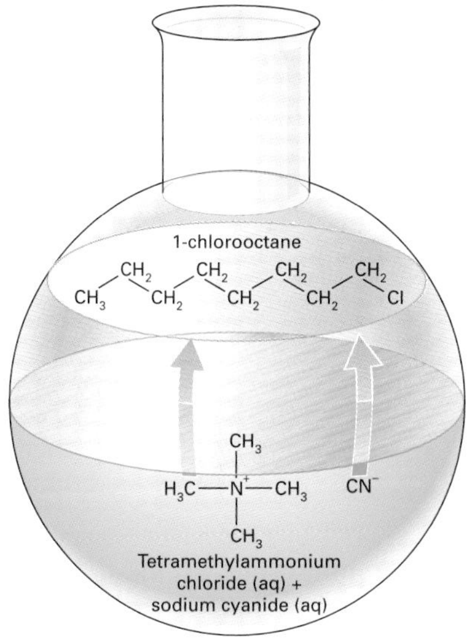

1-Chlorooctane and aqueous tetramethylammonium chloride with sodium cyanide form two immiscible layers. The ion pair tetramethylammonium cyanide can migrate into the organic layer; this is the basis of phase transfer catalysis in this reaction.

SUMMARY

- The Gabriel reagent produces primary amines in much greater yield than the reaction between ammonia and halogenoalkanes.
- Amine groups may be protected during multi-stage syntheses by reaction with an acyl halide to form a substituted amide (and hydrolysed back to the amine at the completion of the synthesis).
- Phase transfer catalysis uses a quaternary ammonium salt to carry a nucleophile from the aqueous phase into the organic phase, where reaction takes place.

Chapter 28 Reactions summary

- Amine as a base:
  $CH_3CH_2NH_2 + H_3O^+ \rightarrow CH_3CH_2NH_3^+ + H_2O$
- Regeneration of free amine:
  $CH_3CH_2NH_3^+Cl^-(aq) + NaOH(aq) \rightarrow$
  $CH_3CH_2NH_2(aq) + NaCl(aq)$
- Amine as ligand in complex formation:
  $6CH_3CH_2NH_2(aq) + Ni^{2+}(aq) \rightarrow [Ni(NH_2CH_2CH_3)_6]^{2+}(aq)$
- Successive formation of primary, secondary, and tertiary amine, and quaternary ammonium salt:
  $RCl + NH_3 \rightarrow RNH_2 + HCl$
  $RCl + RNH_2 \rightarrow R_2NH + HCl$
  $RCl + R_2NH \rightarrow R_3N + HCl$
  $RCl + R_3N \rightarrow R_4N^+Cl^-$
- Amine from the reduction of a nitrile by $LiAlH_4$:
  $CH_3C{\equiv}N \xrightarrow{[H]} CH_3CH_2NH_2$
- Aromatic amine from the reduction of a nitro compound:
  $C_6H_5NO_2(l) \xrightarrow{Sn/HCl} C_6H_5NH_3^+Cl^-(aq)$
  $C_6H_5NH_3^+Cl^- + NaOH \rightarrow C_6H_5NH_2 + H_2O + NaCl$
- Phenylamine reacts with ethanoyl chloride:
  $C_6H_5NH_2 + CH_3COCl \rightarrow C_6H_5NHCOCH_3 + HCl$
- Formation of 2,4,6-tribromophenylamine from phenylamine:
  $C_6H_5NH_2 + 3Br_2 \longrightarrow Br_3C_6H_2NH_2 + 3HBr$
- Diazotization of phenylamine:
  $C_6H_5NH_2 + NaNO_2 + 2HCl \rightarrow C_6H_5N_2^+Cl^- + NaCl + 2H_2O$
- Substitution reactions with the benzenediazonium ion:
  $C_6H_5N_2^+Cl^-(aq) + H_2O(l) \rightarrow C_6H_5OH(aq) + N_2(g) + HCl(aq)$
  $C_6H_5N_2^+Cl^- \xrightarrow{HCl/CuCl} C_6H_5Cl + N_2$
- Coupling reactions with the benzenediazonium ion:
  $C_6H_5N_2^+Cl^- + C_6H_5OH \rightarrow HOC_6H_4N{=}NC_6H_5 + HCl$
- Amino acid zwitterion formation:
  $NH_2CH_2COOH \rightarrow {}^+NH_3CH_2CO_2^-$
- Formation of peptide link between amino acids:
  $2NH_2CHRCOOH \rightarrow NH_2CHR{-}CONH{-}CHRCOOH + H_2O$

PRACTICE EXAM QUESTIONS

1 **a** Explain why ethylamine is a Brønsted–Lowry base. [2]

b Why is phenylamine a weaker base than ethylamine? [2]

c Ethylamine can be prepared from the reaction between bromoethane and ammonia.

i Name the type of reaction taking place and outline a mechanism.

ii Give the structures of **three** other organic substitution products which can be obtained from the reaction between bromoethane and ammonia. [2]

d Write an equation for the conversion of ethanenitrile into ethylamine and give one reason why this method of synthesis is superior to that in part **c**.
AQA (NEAB) 1997 [2]

2 (Phenylmethyl)amine, $C_6H_5CH_2NH_2$, can be prepared from (bromomethyl)benzene, $C_6H_5CH_2Br$, and also from benzenecarbonitrile, C_6H_5CN.

a **i** Write an equation for the conversion of (bromomethyl)benzene into (phenylmethyl)amine. Name the type of reaction taking place and explain why a low yield of product is obtained.

ii Name the type of reaction involved in the conversion of benzenecarbonitrile into (phenylmethyl)amine. Write an equation for this reaction and suggest a suitable reagent or a combination of reagent and catalyst. Explain why this method of preparation gives a high yield of product. [4]

b State which of the two amines, (phenylmethyl)amine and phenylamine, $C_6H_5NH_2$, is the weaker base, and explain your choice. [3]
AQA (NEAB) 1997

3 Consider the compound A

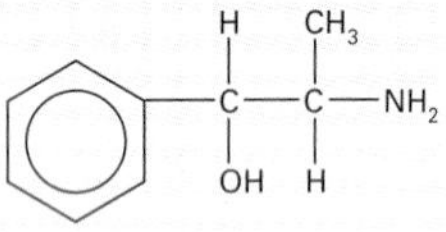

(benzene ring)–C(H)(OH)–C(H)(CH_3)–NH_2

which is related to the hormone adrenaline.

a Draw the structures of the organic product(s) which you would expect from the reaction of A with

i phosphorus pentachloride; [1]

ii dilute hydrochloric acid; [1]

iii ethanoyl chloride; [2]

iv hot alkaline potassium manganate(VII); [1]

v hot concentrated sulphuric acid. [1]

b Suppose that you have to purify a sample of A by recrystallization from trichloromethane. This solvent is toxic by inhalation and skin absorption but is not flammable.

i What safety precautions would you take in using this solvent? [2]

ii Describe in detail how you would recrystallize a sample of about 5 g of A. [5]

iii What simple test would you use to determine the purity of your recrystallized material? [2]
EDEXCEL 1997

4 **a** Explain the term *polymerization*. [1]

b Polymers found in natural materials can be formed by the reaction between amino acids.

i Draw the graphical formula of the product formed when two molecules of alanine, $CH_3CH(NH_2)COOH$, react together. [1]

ii Give the name of the important linkage formed and draw a ring round it on the formula drawn in **b i**. [2]

iii Give the name of the type of naturally occurring polymer containing this linkage. [1]

c Poly(ethene) is an example of a synthetic polymer. It is manufactured in two main forms, low density poly(ethene) and high density poly(ethene). [1]

i Write an equation to represent the polymerization of ethene. [1]

ii What is the main structural difference between the polymer chains in the two main forms of poly(ethene)? Explain how this difference affects the densities of the polymers. [3]

iii Give **one** further physical property that is affected by the structural difference given in **c ii**. [1]

iv Low density poly(ethene) is manufactured via a free radical mechanism. Draw a graphical formula to represent the free radical formed between a free radical, **R•**, and a molecule of ethene in the reaction. [1]

v What type of catalyst is used in the manufacture of high density poly(ethene)? [1]

d Poly(ethene) is non-biodegradable. [1]

i Explain the term *non-biodegradable*.

ii Give **one** environmental benefit of using biodegradable plastics. [1]

iii Developing biodegradable plastics involves compromise. Suggest **one** factor that requires careful consideration and explain your choice.
AQA (AEB) 1998 [2]

5 Consider the following reaction scheme:

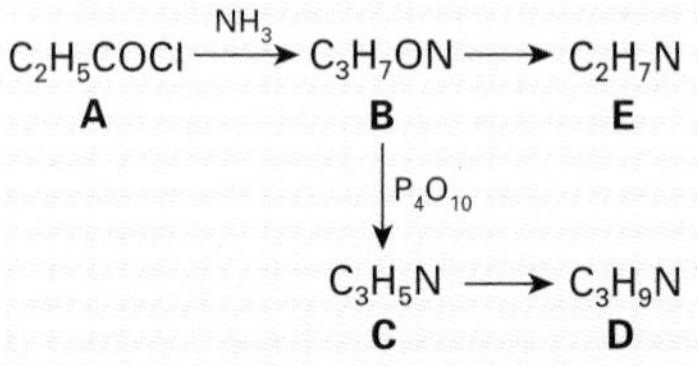

$$\underset{\mathbf{A}}{C_2H_5COCl} \xrightarrow{NH_3} \underset{\mathbf{B}}{C_3H_7ON} \longrightarrow \underset{\mathbf{E}}{C_3H_7N}$$

$$\mathbf{B} \xrightarrow{P_4O_{10}} \underset{\mathbf{C}}{C_3H_5N} \longrightarrow \underset{\mathbf{D}}{C_3H_9N}$$

Compounds **D** and **E** have the same functional group.

a Identify, using structural formulae, the compounds **B** and **C** and the functional group in both **D** and **E**.[3]

b i Give the reagents and conditions necessary for the conversion of compound **C** into compound **D**. [2]

ii Give the reagents and conditions necessary for the conversion of compound **B** into compound **E**. [2]

c i Give an equation to represent the reaction that takes place when compound **C** is boiled with dilute hydrochloric acid. [2]

ii State the type of reaction taking place in **i**. [1]

d i What structural feature of the functional group present in both **D** and **E** enables them each to react with dilute hydrochloric acid. [1]

ii Using the structural formulae, give an equation to represent the reaction of compound **D** with dilute hydrochloric acid. [2]

e A compound C_6H_7N having the same functional group as **D** and **E** reacts with nitrous acid in the presence of hydrochloric acid. The resulting solution reacts with alkaline 2-naphthol to give a red precipitate.

i Give the equation representing the reaction of C_6H_7N with nitrous acid, using structural formulae. [2]

ii Show the structure of the product which is formed with 2-naphthol. [1]

iii What is the significance of compounds of this type? [1]
EDEXCEL 1997

6 a Give the structural formulae, showing all covalent bonds, for all the isomers of C_4H_9Br, and name them. [3]

b The compounds in **a** all react on heating with aqueous sodium hydroxide by a nucleophilic substitution reaction. For one of these isomers, the reaction at a given temperature was found to be first order with respect to the organic molecule and first order overall.

i Explain what is meant by the term *nucleophile*.

ii Identify the nucleophile in this reaction.

iii Write the rate expression for this reaction.

iv Give the mechanism for this reaction using the isomer most likely to react in this way. Explain briefly your choice of isomer. [9]

c i Identify the isomer in **a** that is chiral and explain briefly why it is chiral.

ii Assuming that one of the optical isomers of the compound given in **c i** reacts with sodium hydroxide by the same mechanism as in **b iv**, explain how the nature of the intermediate results in a product which is not optically active. [4]
EDEXCEL 1996

7 N-Phenylethanamide can be prepared from benzene in three steps:

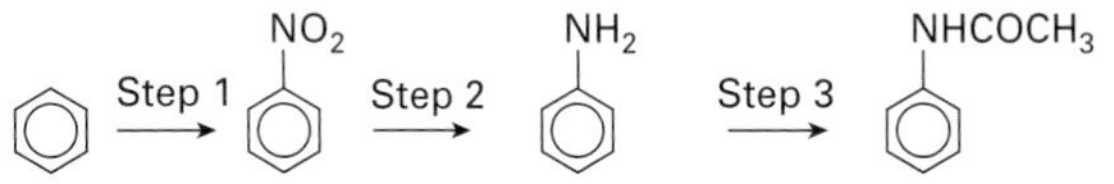

benzene —Step 1→ $C_6H_5NO_2$ —Step 2→ $C_6H_5NH_2$ —Step 3→ $C_6H_5NHCOCH_3$

a Give the reagents required to carry out Step 1 and write an equation for the formation of the reactive inorganic species present. Name and outline the mechanism for the reaction between this species and benzene.

b Name the type of reaction taking place in Step 2 and suggest a suitable reagent or combination of reagents.

c Write an equation for the reaction occurring in Step 3. Name and outline the mechanism for this reaction. [7]
AQA (NEAB) 1999

8 a Define the following terms, and illustrate them by drawing graphical formulae for the stated examples.

i Structural isomerism, showing the appropriate isomers of C_4H_{10}. [4]

ii Geometrical isomerism, showing the appropriate isomers of C_4H_8. [4]

iii Optical isomerism, showing the appropriate isomers of $CH_3CH(OH)COOH$. [4]

b The figure below shows the chain structure of a dipeptide made from alanine and cysteine.

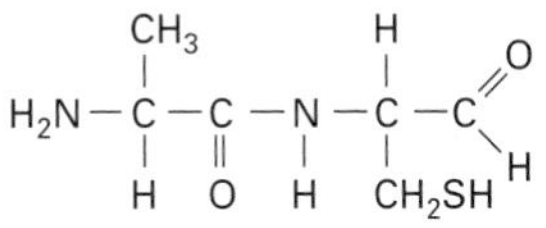

$H_2N-CH(CH_3)-C(=O)-NH-CH(CH_2SH)-CHO$

i Copy the figure and mark any chiral centres of with an asterisk (*). [2]

ii Draw the graphical formulae of the two amino acids alanine and cysteine. [2]

iii Describe how you would show the optical activity of an aqueous solution of one of the optical isomers of alanine. [3]
AQA (AEB) 1997

29 Organic synthesis: changing the carbon skeleton

The aim of organic synthesis is to make a required product from readily available precursors. Most simply described, organic synthesis starts with a chosen substance, and adds or removes carbon atoms and associated functional groups. A complete synthesis may involve many steps, and so the final yield may be very small. For example, a four-step synthesis with a reasonable 30% conversion efficiency per step will produce less than 1 g of product from 100 g of starting material. Such a synthetic route may look feasible on paper, but the economic considerations of the pharmaceutical or dyestuffs industry would make it a complete 'non-starter'. However, the task at this stage of your chemical understanding is simply to suggest synthesis methods based on the most straightforward route possible.

THE SYNTHESIS OF IBUPROFEN

Ibuprofen is a hugely profitable and useful medicine. It is classified in pharmacology as a non-steroidal anti-inflammatory drug (or NSAID in short). Ibuprofen is mostly used to treat pain resulting from inflammation, e.g. rheumatism, pulled muscles, and back-ache. The side-effects of ibuprofen are far less significant than those of many other NSAID compounds. For this reason, ibuprofen along with aspirin are the only NSAIDs licensed in the UK for non-prescription 'over-the-counter' sale. The synthesis of ibuprofen is straightforward, and you are already familiar with most of the reactions involved.

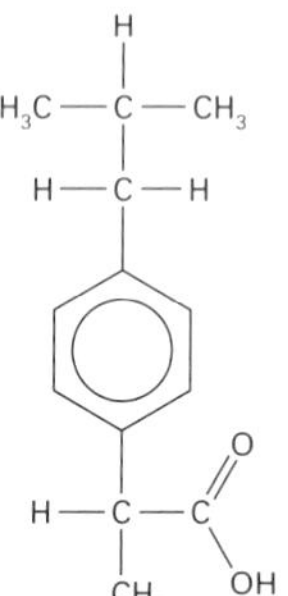

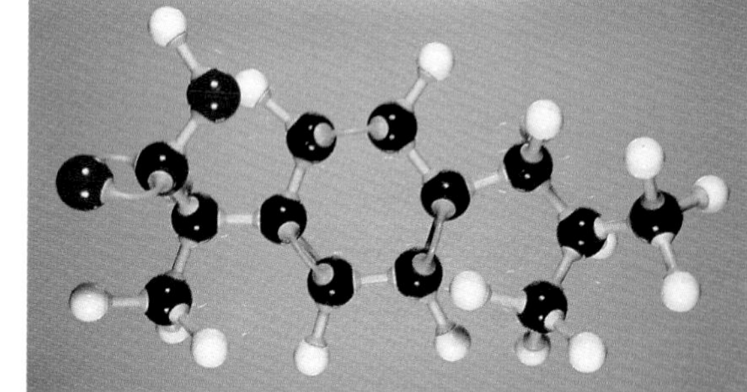

More than 30 types of preparation containing ibuprofen are currently available from pharmacists. They range from gels and sprays for muscle sprains to tablets for the relief of period pains and head-ache. Ibuprofen is a carboxylic acid with a relatively simple molecular structure.

Step 1 Friedel–Crafts acylation

The starting material for the synthesis of ibuprofen is (2-methylpropyl)benzene $(CH_3)_2CHCH_2C_6H_5$. The $(CH_3)_2CHCH_2$— group remains unchanged throughout the synthesis and will therefore be represented by the symbol R– throughout the five steps.

The first step involves Friedel–Crafts acylation (see the chapter on 'Arenes') to introduce an ethanoyl CH_3CO— group in the 4 position on the benzene ring:

$$RC_6H_5 + CH_3COCl \xrightarrow{AlCl_3} RC_6H_4COCH_3 + HCl$$

The acyl group deactivates the benzene ring to further substitution after one group has joined.

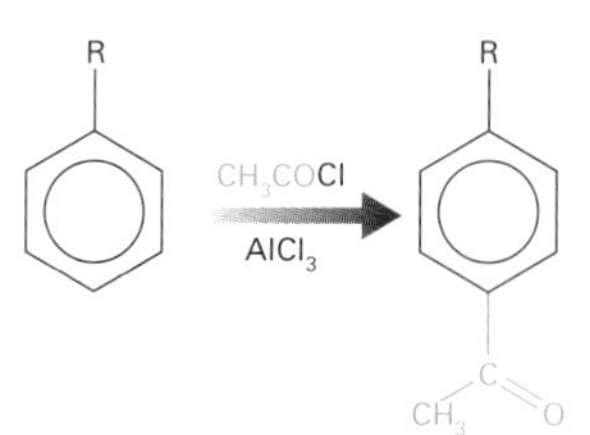

Step 1: Introducing an ethanoyl group in the 4 position to the R group on the benzene ring.

Step 2 Reduction

Reduction of the carbonyl group ⊃C═O by sodium tetrahydridoborate produces a secondary alcohol group ⊃CHOH (see the chapter on 'Aldehydes and ketones'):

$$RC_6H_4COCH_3 \xrightarrow{NaBH_4} RC_6H_4CH(CH_3)OH$$

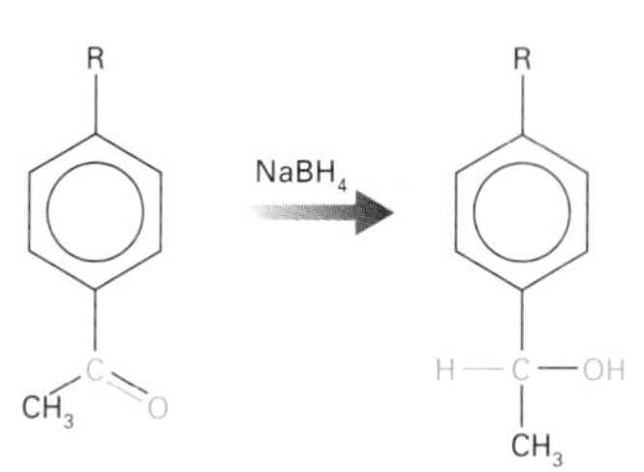

Step 2: Reducing the ketone group to a secondary alcohol.

Step 3 Bromination

The hydroxyl group can be brominated by reaction with phosphorus tribromide PBr_3 in a similar way that PCl_3 reacts (see chapter on 'Alcohols'). PBr_3 is produced *in situ* by the addition of red phosphorus and bromine to the reaction mixture:

$$RC_6H_4CH(CH_3)OH \xrightarrow{P(red)/Br_2} RC_6H_4CH(CH_3)Br$$

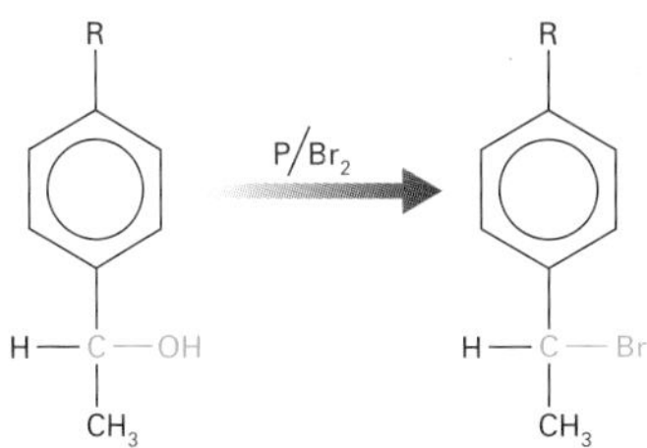

Step 3: Bromination of the alcohol group.

Step 4 Chain lengthening with the cyanide ion

The aim of the *overall* synthesis is to join a carboxylic acid group —COOH to the carbon atom that was attached in the first step to the 4 position on the benzene ring. This fourth step introduces an extra carbon atom at that point in the molecule. Cyanide ion CN^- substitutes for Br^- in a nucleophilic substitution reaction (see the chapter on 'Organic halogeno compounds'). The reaction is carried out using potassium cyanide in ethanol. Ethanol is a polar organic solvent and so will dissolve both the organic halogenoalkane and the ionic cyanide. The mixture is then heated under reflux; the product is a nitrile:

$$RC_6H_4CH(CH_3)Br \xrightarrow{KCN/ethanol} RC_6H_4CH(CH_3)CN$$

Note that this reaction is suitable for use with phase transfer catalysis techniques (see the previous chapter).

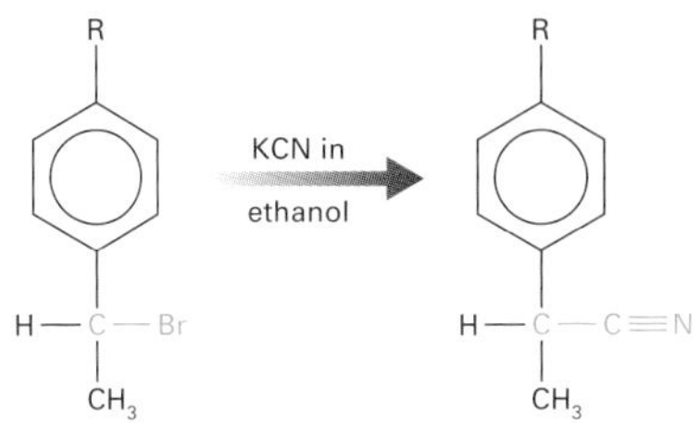

Step 4: Nucleophilic substitution of bromine by cyanide ion.

Step 5 Producing the carboxylic acid group

The most important reaction of nitriles is hydrolysis to form a carboxylic acid. The reaction is carried out by refluxing the nitrile with aqueous acid. Hydrolysis causes the nitrile group to lose nitrogen in the form of ammonia. In acidic solution, the ammonia is protonated to form the ammonium ion. For example:

$$CH_3CH_2CN + H_3O^+ + H_2O \rightarrow CH_3CH_2COOH + NH_4^+$$

(Note that, when hydrolysis by *base* is carried out, the carboxylic acid reacts to form a salt and ammonia *gas* is released.)

This reaction forms the final step of this synthesis, in which the ibuprofen molecule is produced:

$$RC_6H_4CH(CH_3)CN \xrightarrow{H^+(aq)} RC_6H_4CH(CH_3)COOH$$

Each batch of ibuprofen then goes through many stages of purification, recrystallization, and testing before being incorporated into the final packaged product ready for use. Note that the carbon atom next to the benzene ring is a chiral centre; see spread 28.6.

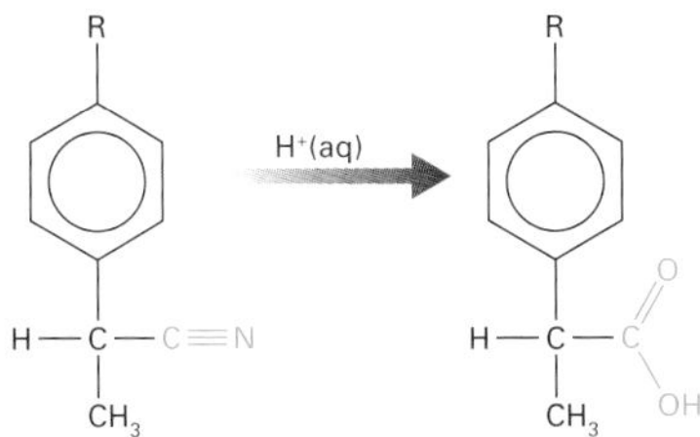

Step 5: Acid hydrolysis of the cyanide group to produce a carboxylic acid.

Millipedes have a defence mechanism that relies on the production of hydrogen cyanide HCN from the hydrolysis of the hydroxynitrile $C_6H_5CH(OH)CN$. A millipede can produce enough hydrogen cyanide to kill a small mouse. Note that the laboratory preparation of this hydroxynitrile would involve the addition of HCN to the aldehyde C_6H_5CHO. Millipedes reverse this reaction using a completely different enzyme-mediated biochemical pathway.

Lactic acid

Addition of hydrogen cyanide HCN to ethanal CH_3CHO followed by hydrolysis in acid produces 2-hydroxypropanoic acid (lactic acid) $CH_3CH(OH)COOH$.

Chiral drugs

The (+) enantiomer of ibuprofen is a much more effective painkiller, so pharmaceutical companies actively search for ways of making this enantiomer preferentially.

Nucleophilic carbon

The cyanide ion is a nucleophile that contains a carbon atom bearing a full negative charge. Cyanide is therefore a useful reagent for adding one carbon atom to a carbon chain. How can more than one carbon atom be added? The answer is to produce a nucleophile consisting of a carbon chain in which one of the carbon atoms bears a negative charge. Grignard reagents provide such nucleophiles; see the following spread.

SUMMARY

- Acidic hydrolysis of a nitrile produces a carboxylic acid:

  $RCN \xrightarrow{H^+(aq)} RCOOH$

29.2

Grignard reagents and other organometallics

OBJECTIVES

- Carbon as a nucleophilic centre
- The Grignard reaction
- Organometallics

The use of the cyanide ion to form nitriles adds just *one* extra carbon atom to a carbon skeleton. **Grignard reagents** are compounds that have the general formula RMgX, where X is a halogen. They are classed as **organometallic compounds** because they contain a metal (magnesium) bonded to a carbon atom in an alkyl group. During the Grignard reaction, the organometallic reagent adds across the carbonyl group of aldehydes or ketones. The R group of the Grignard reagent attaches to the carbonyl carbon, thus joining together the two carbon skeletons. There are some limitations to the types of carbon skeletons that may be joined using Grignard reagents. However, Grignard reagents are a very powerful tool for the synthesis of more complex organic molecules. They can add more than one carbon atom to the skeleton.

(a)

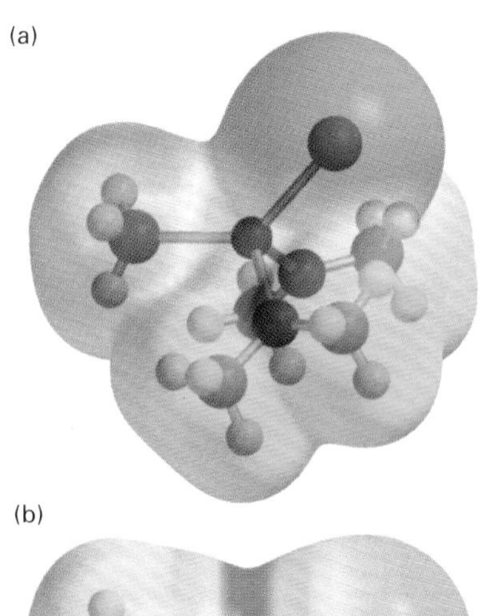

(b)

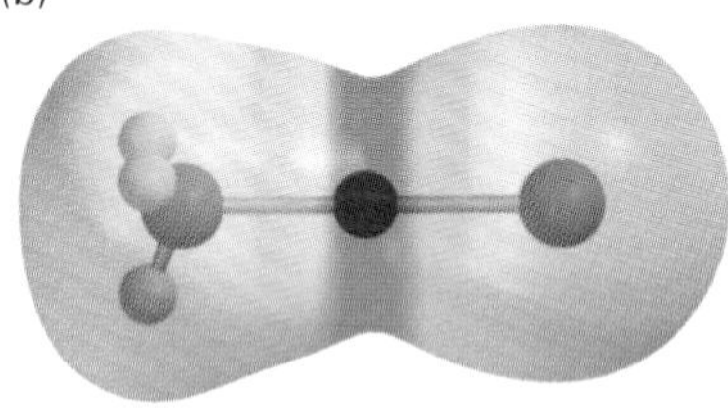

There is evidence to suggest that (a) Grignard reagents are chemically associated by coordinate bonding with the ether solvent in which they are prepared. However, the structure shown in (b) is adequate to explain the reagent's behaviour. Note the high partial positive charge on the magnesium atom shown by the blue colour.

Preparation of Grignard reagents

Grignard reagents are not very stable, and so they must be freshly prepared and used immediately. A Grignard reagent is made by dissolving a halogenoalkane in dry ethoxyethane (ether) and allowing it to stand over turnings of magnesium metal. A vigorous exothermic reaction takes place in which the magnesium disappears as the mixture turns cloudy and boils. The following equation illustrates the reaction for iodoethane:

$$CH_3CH_2I + Mg \xrightarrow{\text{ether}} \underset{\text{ethylmagnesium iodide}}{CH_3CH_2MgI}$$

Although the formula is written in the form RMgX, there is evidence that the actual structure is more complex. The bonds to the magnesium atom are highly polar covalent bonds. Grignard reagents may be thought of as forming a free **carbanion** R^-, an ion in which a carbon atom carries a full negative charge. However, in reality Grignard reagents do not dissociate fully to form $R^-[^+Mg\ I]$, and the situation is more complex than this.

The Grignard reaction

Grignard reagents include a carbon atom bonded to a significantly *less* electronegative atom. The C—Mg bond is very polar, the electron density being pulled towards the carbon, giving the carbon atom a partial *negative* charge δ–. Grignard reagents therefore contain a powerfully *nucleophilic* carbon atom which attacks δ+ carbon atoms on other molecules. The **Grignard reaction** specifically adds a Grignard reagent to the carbonyl group of an aldehyde or ketone. In the carbonyl group ⊃C═O, a carbon atom is joined to a *more* electronegative oxygen atom. This carbon atom has a partial positive charge δ+ and is liable to attack by incoming nucleophiles. The reaction happens in two steps: addition of the Grignard reagent, followed by hydrolysis in acid. Yields of these reactions can be up to 90% or even greater.

- With methanal, the product is a primary alcohol:

$$RMgI + HCHO \xrightarrow{H_2O} RCH_2OH + Mg(OH)I$$

- With other aldehydes, the product is a secondary alcohol:

$$RMgI + R'CHO \xrightarrow{H_2O} RR'CH(OH) + Mg(OH)I$$

- With ketones, the product is a tertiary alcohol:

$$RMgI + R'R''CO \xrightarrow{H_2O} RR'R''COH + Mg(OH)I$$

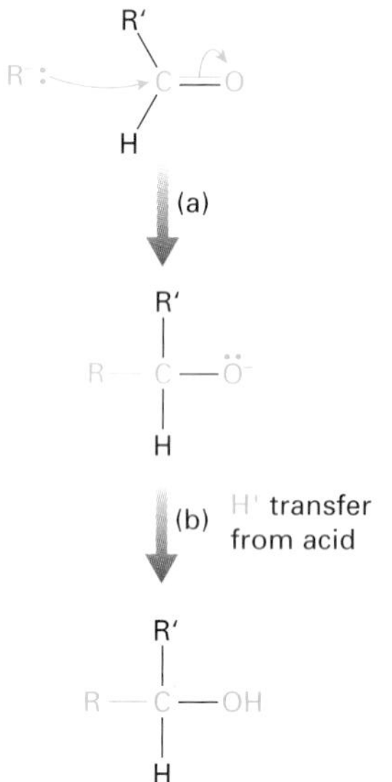

(a) An addition reaction of a Grignard reagent (b) Hydrolysis of the addition product.

- With carbon dioxide, the product is a carboxylic acid:

$$RMgI + CO_2 \rightarrow RCOOMgI \xrightarrow{H_2O} RCOOH + Mg(OH)I$$

Note that reaction between the Grignard reagent and CO_2 effectively converts a halogenoalkane into a carboxylic acid with one extra carbon atom in the chain. This conversion may also be achieved by reacting the halogenoalkane with potassium cyanide to form the nitrile, followed by acid hydrolysis to form the carboxylic acid (see the previous spread).

(a) $HCHO$ —(i) CH_3CH_2MgI (ii) H^+ from acid→ $CH_3CH_2CH_2OH$ Propan-1-ol

(b) CH_3CHO —(i) CH_3MgI (ii) H^+ from acid→ $CH_3CH(OH)CH_3$ Propan-2-ol

(c) $(CH_3)_2C{=}O$ —(i) CH_3MgI (ii) H^+ from acid→ $(CH_3)_3COH$ 2-Methylpropan-2-ol

(d) $O{=}C{=}O$ —(i) CH_3CH_2MgI (ii) H^+ from acid→ CH_3CH_2COOH Propanoic acid

Examples of the addition reactions of Grignard reagents.

Other organometallic compounds

Two common organometallic compounds are tetraethyllead $(CH_3CH_2)_4Pb$ and triethylaluminium $(CH_3CH_2)_3Al$. Tetraethyllead was added to some grades of petrol (UK 'four star') to improve its octane rating. Its use has now been stopped, because of fears about the adverse effects of high levels of lead in the environment.

Triethylaluminium forms part of the Ziegler–Natta catalyst used in the industrial polymerization of substituted alkenes (see the chapter on 'Alkanes and alkenes'). It is made by reacting chloroethane with aluminium:

$$3CH_3CH_2Cl + 2Al \rightarrow (CH_3CH_2)_3Al + AlCl_3$$

SUMMARY

- Grignard reagents are a class of organometallic compounds with the general formula RMgX.
- Grignard reagents add across carbonyl groups: an organic product results from subsequent hydrolysis.
- RMgX + methanal → a primary alcohol.
- RMgX + other aldehydes → a secondary alcohol.
- RMgX + ketones → a tertiary alcohol.
- RMgX + CO_2 → a carboxylic acid.

Degree of chain extension

In all these reactions, the product has more carbon atoms than the original carbonyl compound. The number of carbon atoms added depends on the Grignard reagent used.

Victor Grignard

Victor Grignard was born in Cherbourg, the son of a sailmaker. He was 'a simple man with much common sense and a practical mind'. He described his reagent in his doctoral thesis of 1901.
His technique caught on quickly. In 1908, 500 papers using Grignard reagents were published. The Nobel prize was awarded to him in 1912.

PRACTICE

1 Give the name and structural formula of the compound that results from reacting ethylmagnesium bromide with water.

2 Give the names and structural formulae of the compounds that result from hydrolysis following the addition of ethylmagnesium bromide to the following substances:

a Propanal
b Cyclohexanone
c Carbon dioxide
d Butanone.

3 Outline the synthesis of butan-2-ol from bromoethane, involving the use of standard inorganic reagents only.

29.3 The Diels–Alder reaction

OBJECTIVES

- Conjugated dienes
- Dienophile
- 1,4-Cycloaddition

Two of the three most useful reactions for making carbon–carbon bonds have already been described: the Friedel–Crafts reaction (see the chapter on 'Arenes') and the Grignard reaction (see previous spread in this chapter). The third is called the Diels–Alder reaction. It has the added advantage of making *two* carbon–carbon bonds. The **Diels–Alder reaction** involves addition of a compound that has two double bonds, called a **diene**, to a reagent called a **dienophile**. A cyclic product is formed. For example, the reaction joins together the diene butadiene with the dienophile ethene to form the cyclic adduct cyclohexene. The diene must be a *conjugated* diene, which means that the two C═C double bonds are separated by exactly *one* C—C single bond.

Otto Diels and Kurt Alder

The Diels–Alder reaction was developed by Otto Diels and Kurt Alder in 1928. It proved to be of such value in the synthesis of cyclic compounds that they were awarded the 1950 Nobel prize for chemistry.

1,4-Cycloaddition

The simplest example of a Diels–Alder addition is that between butadiene and ethene. (Butadiene is more correctly called buta-1,3-diene.) However, the yield is low (20%) and a high temperature is required. The reaction is referred to as a '1,4-cycloaddition', because carbon atoms 1 and 4 of the diene add across the double bond of the alkene to produce a cyclic product.

The 1,4-cycloaddition of butadiene to ethene to form cyclohexene.

The yield of this addition reaction is higher when the dienophile has electron-withdrawing groups attached, such as —COOH, —COR, —CN, etc. Notice that the double bond of the dienophile reverts to a single bond.

The mechanism of the Diels–Alder 1,4-cycloaddition reaction is as follows:

(a) The mechanism may be regarded as a migration of the π electrons from the three C═C double bonds. Note that the reaction does not depend on the creation of a charge centre on a carbon atom; it involves a concerted interaction of the orbitals in the reacting molecules.

(b) The electron-withdrawing group X on the dienophile increases the yield.

(c) Ball-and-stick models show the stereochemistry of the reaction.

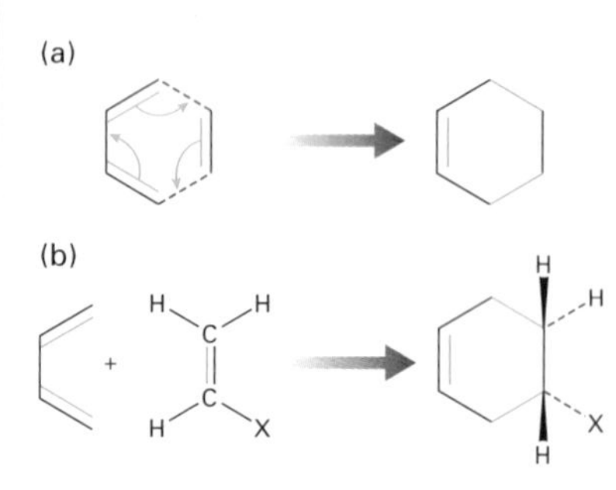

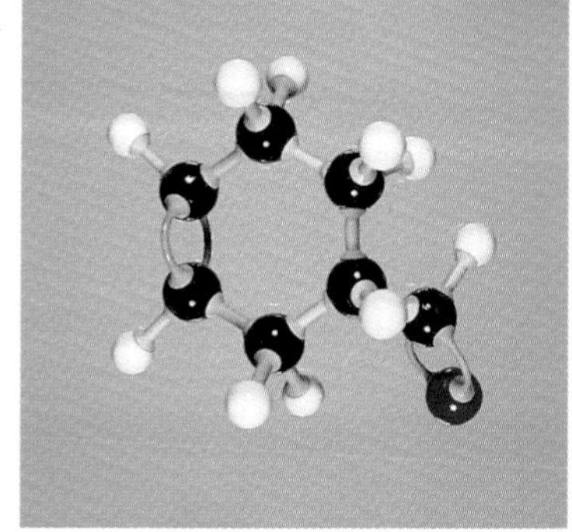

The Diels–Alder 1,4-cycloaddition reaction.

Diels–Alder reactions and natural products

Many naturally occurring or physiologically active substances contain ring structures. The Diels–Alder reaction is extremely useful during the synthesis of such molecules. For example, animals excrete substances called pheromones into the atmosphere in order to affect the behaviour of other animals that detect them. Female fruit flies produce a pheromone that is a sexual attractant. It is effective at concentrations as low as a few tens of molecules per cubic centimetre of air. Artificially produced pheromones synthesized using the Diels–Alder reaction are used to bait traps for insect pests.

A pheromone-baited trap for a bark beetle in Zurich, Switzerland.

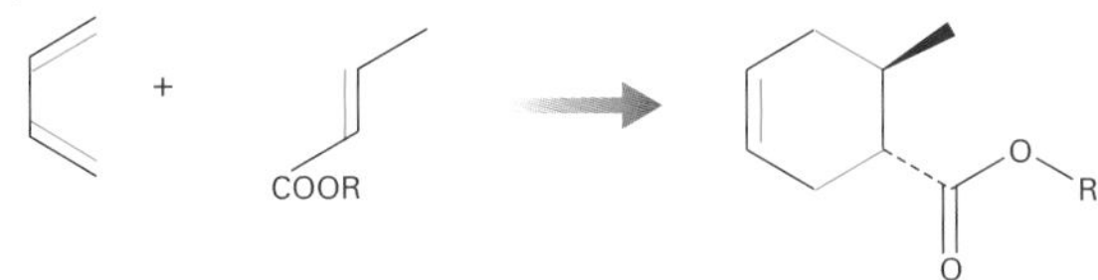

The synthesis of siglure, which mimics the pheromone secreted by the Mediterranean fruit fly. $R = -CH(CH_3)CH_2CH_3$

Robert Burns Woodward

R. B. Woodward is generally regarded as the greatest synthetic chemist of the twentieth century. Together with Roald Hoffmann, he established the mechanism of the Diels–Alder reaction, and was then able to use it for crucial steps of the syntheses of enormous biologically active molecules. In 1951, he produced an intermediate from which he finally prepared cortisone. Woodward synthesized the alkaloid reserpine (then used in the treatment of high blood pressure) in 1956. He achieved a total synthesis of chlorophyll in 1960, and of vitamin B_{12} in 1971.

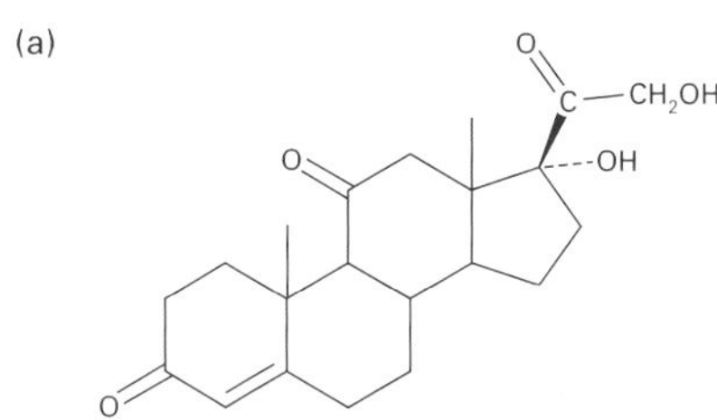

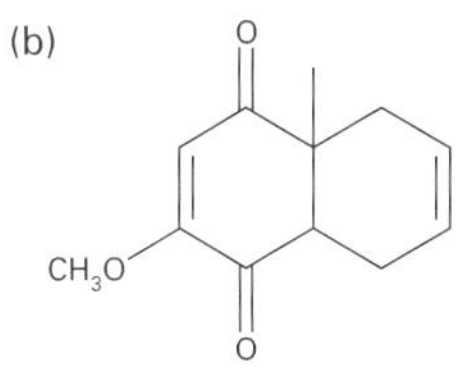

(a) The complex fused ring structure of the steroid hormone cortisone may be synthesized with the help of Diels–Alder cycloaddition reactions. (b) The intermediate synthesized by Woodward that enabled cortisone to be produced synthetically. Cortisone treatment reduces inflammation in severe allergic and rheumatic diseases such as asthma and rheumatoid arthritis.

SUMMARY

- A conjugated diene has two C═C double bonds separated by one C—C single bond.
- Diels–Alder 1,4-cycloaddition adds a conjugated diene to a dienophile to form a ring structure consisting of six carbon atoms.
- An example of the Diels–Alder reaction is the addition of butadiene to ethene to form cyclohexene.
- Yields are increased if the dienophile has electron-withdrawing groups.
- The Diels–Alder reaction is of great use in producing ring structures for synthetic hormones.

PRACTICE

1 Give the structural formulae of the following dienes and dienophiles. In each case give the structural formulae of the Diels–Alder adduct formed by the reaction.

- **a** Buta-1,3-diene; ethene
- **b** Penta-1,3-diene; ethene
- **c** Buta-1,3-diene; propenenitrile $CH_2{=}CH{-}CN$
- **d** Penta-1,3-diene; propenenitrile
- **e** Cyclohexa-1,3-diene; propenenitrile.

2 The structures shown below were formed by Diels–Alder cycloaddition. Give the structural formulae and names of the diene and dienophile from which each was formed.

(a) (b) 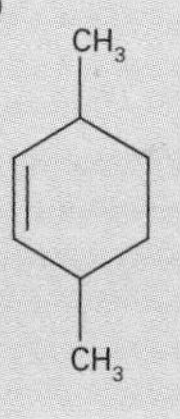 (c)

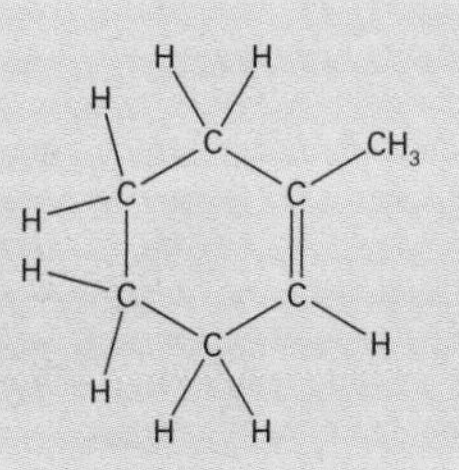

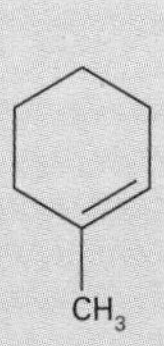

29.4

Revisiting polymerization – 1

OBJECTIVES

- Polymerization reactions
- Polymer properties
- Thermosoftening polymers
- Thermosetting polymers

Polymers consist of long-chain molecules containing bonds formed by polymerization reactions. The two main classes of polymers are natural polymers and synthetic polymers. Natural polymers include the structural proteins and enzymes which are fundamental to the function of living systems. These polymers will be discussed in the following chapter. Synthetic polymers include addition polymers such as polythene and PVC, together with condensation polymers such as polyesters (e.g. Terylene) and polyamides (e.g. nylon). The chemical reactions responsible for the formation of addition polymers were introduced in the chapter on 'Alkanes and alkenes'; condensation polymerization was discussed in the chapter on 'Carboxylic acids and their derivatives'. This spread and the next one develop these ideas within the context of organic synthesis reactions and the design of molecules that show desired properties.

The general principle of addition polymerization: the monomer phenylethene (styrene) $CH_2{=}CHC_6H_5$ polymerizes to give the polymer polystyrene.

Revision: addition polymers

Typical addition polymers result when the π electrons in substituted alkene monomers form C—C σ bonds between the molecules. Thus a monomer $CH_2{=}CHG$ gives rise to a polymer of general formula $\left[CH_2CHG \right]_n$: the structure within the brackets is called the **repeating unit** (or **repeat unit**). Examples include polythene (G = H), polypropylene (G = CH_3), polystyrene (G = C_6H_5), and PVC (G = Cl).

Revision: condensation polymers

Condensation copolymers result from monomer molecules that possess two functional groups. During the polymerization process, condensation reactions take place between groups on adjacent molecules. The principle is illustrated by the formation of a polyamide, in which a diacid molecule condenses with a diamine molecule to form a peptide link —CONH— between the molecules.

An amine group $—NH_2$ on a diamine molecule condenses with a carboxylic acid group —COOH on a diacid. A molecule of water is eliminated and the molecules become connected by a substituted amide group —CONH—.

Controlling polymer properties

Two very important properties of polymers are tensile strength and softening temperature. Tensile strength determines the structural uses to which a material can be put; softening temperature affects the way in which it can be moulded or extruded. These properties are largely controlled by the forces of attraction between the polymer chains, which in turn are affected by the atoms or groups attached to the carbon skeleton and the way they are arranged along the chain.

For example, there are two distinct forms of polystyrene. Using a Ziegler–Natta catalyst (spread 22.11) for the polymerization of phenylethene (styrene) $CH_2{=}CHC_6H_5$ gives an *isotactic* polymer with all the phenyl groups on *one* side of the chain. Radical polymerization gives *atactic* polystyrene in which the arrangement of the phenyl groups is *random*.

'Tactic'

Giulio Natta's wife coined the term *tactic* to describe the arrangement of side groups along a polymer carbon chain:

- **Atactic** = a random arrangement
- **Isotactic** = side groups all along the same side
- **Syndiotactic** = side groups alternate

When the pattern is regular (iso- and syndiotactic), the polymer is described as being 'stereoregular'.

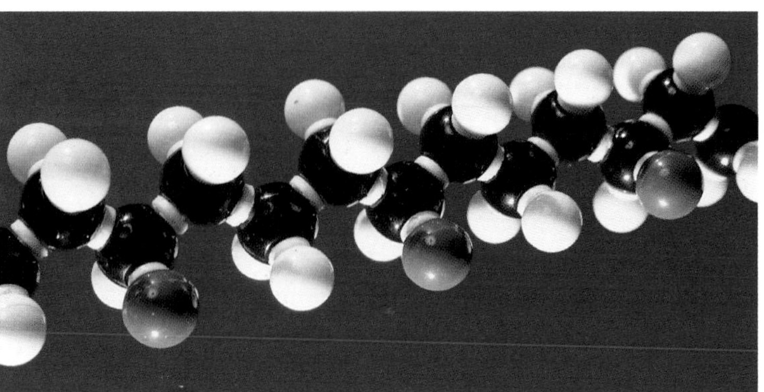

Isotactic PVC. The regular arrangement of the chloro side groups in the isotactic form allows the chains to approach each other more closely.

The regular structure of the isotactic polymer allows dispersion forces to attract the molecules closer to each other. Intermolecular forces are therefore weaker in the atactic form, which can be softened and moulded at a lower temperature than the isotactic form, and which is more soluble in most solvents.

Intermolecular forces

The intermolecular forces between hydrocarbon polymer chains such as polythene and polystyrene are limited to weak dispersion forces. The presence of polar groups allows for stronger dipole–dipole interactions, an example being the commercial fibre Orlon, which is an addition polymer made from propenenitrile $CH_2{=}CHCN$. Much stronger intermolecular forces are produced by hydrogen bonding. This type of force is more common in condensation polymers such as nylon.

Thermoplastics and thermosets

All the polymers described so far are called '**thermosoftening polymers**', or 'thermoplastics'. Increasing the temperature overcomes the intermolecular forces; the chains are able to slide past each other and the material softens. Thermoplastics can be repeatedly heated and cooled without changing their properties.

Another class of synthetic polymeric materials are the '**thermosetting polymers**', or 'thermosets'. Thermosetting polymers are usually made from liquids that are mixed and heated in a mould. The monomer molecules link with each other by forming bonds between the different chains; such bonds are called **cross-links**. A hard product results that has a three-dimensional network of covalent bonds interconnecting the polymer chains. Thermosets can be shaped only once.

Melamine

Methanal

Monomers

The monomers join by cross-links
$—NHCH_2NH—$
formed in condensation reactions between NH_2 groups on neighbouring rings with the methanal

Melamine (2,4,6-triamino-1,3,5-triazine) reacts with methanal to form the thermoset material commonly called 'Melamine'. It can be moulded to produce durable and shatterproof cups, saucers, and plates.

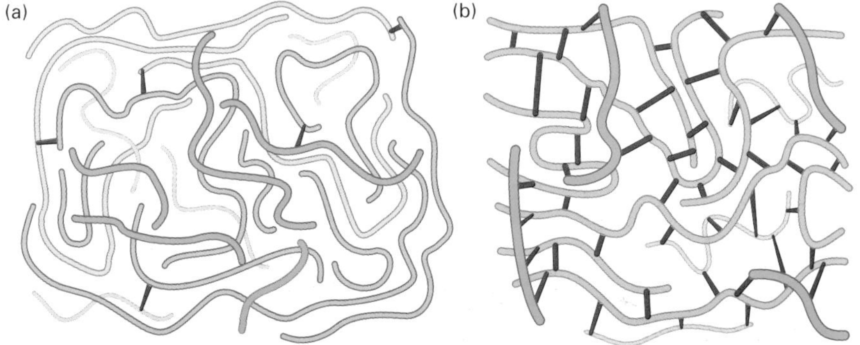

(a) Thermoplastics have polymer chains with weak intermolecular forces between them. There are few covalent cross-links between chains. (b) Thermosets have a covalently bonded three-dimensional network. There is extensive cross-linking.

SUMMARY

- Polymers may be natural or synthetic.
- Synthetic polymers may be formed by addition or condensation polymerization.
- Polymers may be thermosoftening or thermosetting.

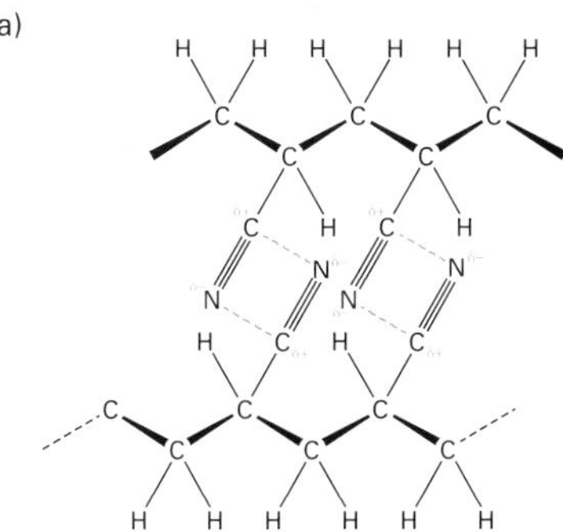

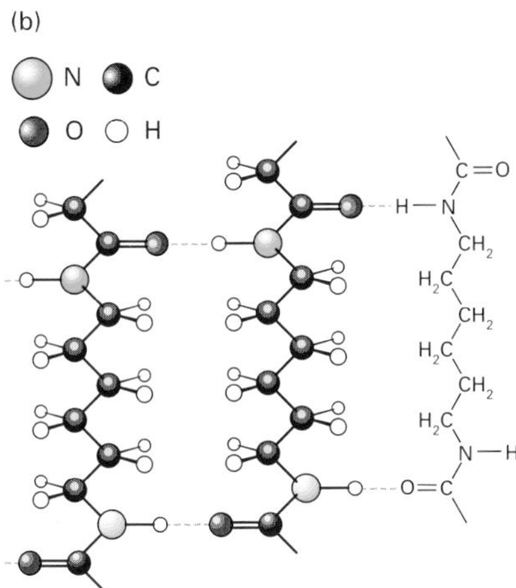

Interactions between polymer chains.
(a) Dipole–dipole forces in Orlon.
(b) Hydrogen bonding in nylon .

Chief distinctions

- **Thermoplastics** soften when heated, are permanently deformed when a force is applied, and harden when cooled.
- **Thermosets** are hard polymeric materials that do not soften when heated, and can be shaped only once.

Recycling plastics

Thermosets are very difficult to recycle. The task of recycling thermoplastics has been simplified by coding individual plastics, thus making their identification easy. For example:

29.5

REVISITING POLYMERIZATION – 2

OBJECTIVES

- Staudinger's vision
- Chain and step polymerization
- Copolymers
- Rubber

Hermann Staudinger's foresight

The idea that polymers consist of long-chain molecules was first put forward in the 1920s by Hermann Staudinger, to the disbelief of his contemporaries. Subsequent studies have shown Staudinger to be correct, but he was two years into his retirement before his insight led to him being awarded the Nobel prize for chemistry. Turning his attention to the natural polymers in living systems, Staudinger made the prediction in 1936 that: 'Every gene macromolecule possesses a definite structure which determines its function in life.' Modern molecular biology describes in precisely these terms the role of DNA in the synthesis of proteins and the inheritance of characteristics. The next chapter will focus on biochemistry.

A synthetic polymer can be classified as an addition polymer or as a condensation polymer, according to the type of reaction that formed it. A synthetic polymer may also be classified as thermosoftening or thermosetting, according to the extent of cross-linking and the consequent behaviour on heating. This spread introduces the idea of classifying a polymer according to the mechanism of its formation; it leads to the categories of *step polymers* and *chain polymers*. The vision of Hermann Staudinger links the ideas underlying this chapter to those of the next one.

Chain polymerization

An example of chain polymerization is the reaction between ethene molecules to produce polythene. During the reaction, the monomer concentration decreases steadily with time. Polymer chains of high molar mass form extremely rapidly. The reaction mixture contains monomer, polymer chains of high molar mass, and a small number of growing polymer chains. The polymer yield increases with reaction time, but the polymer molar mass does not.

The process of chain polymerization most often occurs when monomers add together. 'Addition polymerization' is often used as an alternative name, but the two terms are not synonymous. Chain polymerization can only produce thermoplastics (and not thermosets).

The chain reaction mechanism

The chapter on 'Alkanes and alkenes' discussed the chain reaction involved in the chlorination of methane. The reaction involves radicals (species with unpaired electrons) and proceeds by steps: chain initiation; chain propagation; chain termination. Chain polymerization follows the same overall reaction mechanism. The most common types of monomer to polymerize in this manner are derivatives of ethene such as chloroethene and phenylethene.

Chain polymerization is readily started by heating an initiator such as dibenzoyl peroxide $(C_6H_5CO)_2O_2$. The molecule breaks down to yield two radicals of formula $C_6H_5CO_2^{\bullet}$, which loses carbon dioxide to form the phenyl $C_6H_5^{\bullet}$ radical. Polymerization then proceeds as shown below. The resulting chains are atactic and mostly linear, with a certain amount of chain branching. The process of chain termination finally halts the growth of the chain.

(a) $C_6H_5^{\bullet}$ + $CH_2{=}CH(C_6H_5)$ → $C_6H_5{-}CH_2{-}\dot{C}H(C_6H_5)$

(b) $C_6H_5{-}CH_2{-}\dot{C}H(C_6H_5)$ + $CH_2{=}CH(C_6H_5)$ → $C_6H_5{-}CH_2{-}CH(C_6H_5){-}CH_2{-}\dot{C}H(C_6H_5)$

(c) $C_6H_5{+}CH_2CH(C_6H_5){+}_n{-}CH_2\dot{C}H(C_6H_5)$ $\xrightarrow{+\,C_6H_5^{\bullet}}$ $C_6H_5{+}CH_2CH(C_6H_5){+}_n{-}CH_2CH(C_6H_5){-}C_6H_5$

The radical polymerization of phenylethene. (a) Initiation: the initiator joins with the monomer to form a radical. (b) Propagation: as the chain grows, the unpaired electron continues to be located at the end of the chain. (c) Termination: one possible termination step occurs when a growing chain combines with an initiator radical.

Step polymerization

Step polymerization builds up a polymer in a number of stages. The monomer concentration decreases rapidly with reaction time; the average molar mass also increases steadily with time. Long reaction times are need to produce large polymer chains. The reaction mixture contains polymer molecules with a wide range of chain length, from dimers up to those of very high molar mass.

The process of step polymerization most often happens when monomers condense together. 'Condensation polymerization' is often used as an alternative name, but the two terms are not synonymous. For example, polyurethanes (much used for furniture foam) are made by step polymerization but the reaction does not involve condensation. Step polymerization can produce thermoplastics *and* thermosets.

Three monomers – acrylonitrile, (propenenitrile), butadiene, and styrene – polymerize to make the copolymer acrylonitrile–butadiene–styrene, known as ABS. It is a very tough material, used to make suitcases and children's toy bricks.

Copolymers

Copolymers are made from two or more monomers. The polyester Terylene and the polyamide nylon-6,6 described earlier are examples of copolymers, as are many other condensation polymers. If the monomers are A and B, then the polymer chain has the structure ...ABABAB.... Copolymers can be designed to have particular physical properties by using monomers that can polymerize with themselves or with each other. Polymer structure then takes the random form ...AABBBBAABBBA.... An example is Saran, a copolymer of PVC and poly(1,1-dichloroethene) used as a film for wrapping food.

(a)

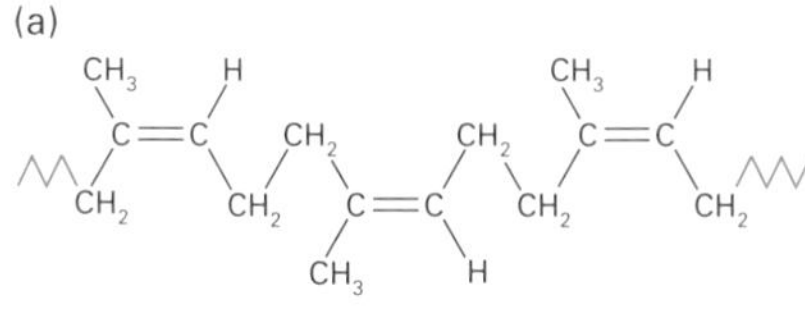

(b)

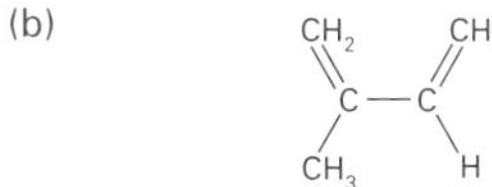

(c)

(a) Natural rubber is poly(cis-2-methylbuta-1,3-diene); the monomer was formerly known as isoprene.
(b) The monomer unit of natural rubber.
(c) Vulcanized rubber is used to make tyres. The extent of cross-linking is controlled carefully to give the product the required hardness, wear resistance, and elasticity.

Elastomers

An elastomer is a material that can rapidly recover its original shape after being deformed. The most important example is vulcanized rubber. The structure of natural rubber illustrates the requirements for elastomeric properties: long flexible chains, weak intermolecular forces, and some cross-linking. The all-*cis* configuration limits the approach of adjacent chains and results in low dispersion forces. The all-*trans* isomer occurs naturally as gutta percha, which is hard and non-elastic.

Vulcanization, heating rubber with sulphur, forms disulphide cross-links. Vulcanized rubber is used to manufacture car tyres.

SUMMARY

- Chain polymerization: proceeds by chain initiation, propagation, and termination; the reaction mixture contains monomer, polymer chains of high molar mass, and a small number of growing chains.
- Step polymerization: chain length increases steadily with time; the reaction mixture contains polymer molecules with a wide range of chain length.
- Copolymers are made from two or more monomers.
- Vulcanization of rubber introduces disulphide cross-links between polymer chains.

Chapter 29 Reactions summary

- Preparation of Grignard reagent:
  $CH_3CH_2I + Mg \xrightarrow{\text{ether}} CH_3CH_2MgI$
- Grignard reagent with carbon dioxide:
  $RMgI + CO_2 \xrightarrow{H_2O} RCOOH + Mg(OH)I$
- Grignard reagent with methanal:
  $RMgI + HCHO \xrightarrow{H_2O} RCH_2OH + Mg(OH)I$
- Grignard reagent with other aldehydes:
  $RMgI + R'CHO \xrightarrow{H_2O} RR'CH(OH) + Mg(OH)I$
- Grignard reagent with ketones:
  $RMgI + R'R''CO \xrightarrow{H_2O} RR'R''COH + Mg(OH)I$
- Diels–Alder 1,4-cycloaddition:

PRACTICE EXAM QUESTIONS

1 a Normal electric wiring consists of copper wire surrounded by polyvinyl chloride (PVC). In one type of electric wiring used in fire alarm systems, a copper wire is surrounded by solid magnesium oxide to act as insulator, the whole being encased in a copper tube covered with PVC.

i Describe the bonding in copper metal and hence explain how it conducts electricity.

ii What type of bonding is present in PVC? Hence explain why it can be used as an insulator.

iii What type of bonding is present in magnesium oxide? Hence explain how it can act as an insulator.

iv Suggest why magnesium oxide is preferred to PVC alone as an insulator in fire alarm systems. [12]

b Magnesium reacts with bromoethane to form a Grignard reagent. Write the equation for this reaction and give the necessary conditions. [3]

c Name and give the structures of the products when the Grignard reagent from **b** is reacted with:

i propanone;

ii butanal. [4]

d i Describe a chemical test which would distinguish between the products of **c i** and **c ii**.

ii Explain briefly why in each case neither of the final liquid products of the reactions in **c i** and **c ii** has any effect on the plane of plane-polarized light which is passed through it. [6]

EDEXCEL 1996

2 Propranolol is a chiral compound used in some 40 pharmaceutical preparations for the treatment of high blood pressure and cardiac pain. It is a base and is usually used as its hydrochloride salt, which is a white powder soluble to the extent of 50 g dm^{-3} in cold water and much more so in hot.

Propranolol is manufactured from glycidyl butanoate

$CH_3CH_2CH_2-C(=O)-O-CH_2CH-CH_2$ (with O bridging CH and CH_2)

which is a chiral ester. This is made from glycidol, which has a boiling point of 56 °C, and butanoyl chloride, the latter being made from butan-1-ol via butanoic acid.

The esterification gives a racemic mixture of the ester but propranolol requires only one of the optical isomers in this mixture.

Butan-1-ol is made commercially from natural gas; it can also be made from an aldehyde and a Grignard reagent, but this is not economic. The alcohol is oxidized to butanoic acid, which is then converted to the acid chloride and then the ester.

a i What is meant by the term **chiral**?

ii Draw the two stereoisomers of glycidol,

CH_2-CHCH_2-OH (with O bridging CH_2 and CH)

iii How is chirality detected experimentally? [5]

b Write the equations, stating briefly the necessary conditions, to show how you would bring about the following:

i conversion of butan-1-ol to butanoic acid;

ii conversion of butanoic acid to butanoyl chloride;

iii reaction of butanoyl chloride with glycidol. [6]

c i Suggest how butan-1-ol could be prepared using a Grignard reagent and an aldehyde.

ii State how the Grignard reagent you have suggested can be prepared from a halogenoalkane. [5]

d Suggest why only one of the optical isomers of propranolol is effective as a drug. [1]

e Give experimental details of how you could purify propranolol hydrochloride by recrystallization. How would you assess its purity? [7]

f How would you liberate the base propranolol from its hydrochloride salt? [1]

EDEXCEL 1996

3 Poly(phenylethene) is obtained by a chain polymerization reaction.

a Explain what is meant by chain polymerization. [2]

b The degree of polymerization is governed by physical changes taking place during the polymerization process.

i Describe the physical changes that take place during the polymerization.

ii Explain the principles underlying suspension polymerization in terms of the changes outlined in **i**.

Briefly describe the use of suspension polymerization in the manufacture of poly(phenylethene). [8]

OCR (UCLES) 1994

4 a Polymers are extensively used in the manufacture of synthetic fibres during which the relative molecular mass must be carefully controlled.

Explain the importance of the relative molecular mass of such polymers in the production and end-use of fibres. [4]

b Several polyamides are in current production in the synthetic fibre industry, including nylon 6, nylon 66, nylon 610, and nylon 11.

i Suggest the structural formula of the monomer that could be used in the manufacture of nylon 11.

ii Predict, with reasons, how you would expect the crystalline melting point of nylon 11 to compare with that of nylon 66. [4]

c After cleaning out some dilute acid bottles, a laboratory technician noticed that small holes had appeared in her nylon stockings.

Suggest a reason for this. [2]
OCR (UCLES) 1995

5 **a** Describe briefly the types of bonding present in polymers. [5]

b How do the bonds and molecular interactions within a polymer contribute to;

i the properties of the polymer,

ii the relative ease of processing thermoplastics? [5]
OCR (UCLES) 1995

6 This question concerns the addition polymer poly(propene), and the condensation polymer nylon.

a **i** Draw a structural formula for part of the poly(propene) chain showing clearly the repeating unit. [2]

ii Suggest why, when poly(propene) is heated, it softens over a range of temperature rather than melting sharply at a particular temperature. [2]

b Nylon-6,6 is made from a diamine, $H_2N(CH_2)_6NH_2$, and a diacid chloride, $ClOC(CH_2)_4COCl$.

i Draw the structural formula of a representative length of the polymer chain. [2]

ii Using nylon-6,6 and poly(propene) as examples, explain the essential difference between condensation and addition polymerization reactions. [3]

iii Suggest why a diacid chloride is employed to make nylon rather than the corresponding dicarboxylic acid. [1]

iv Nylon fibre is about twice as strong as poly(propene) fibre. Suggest in terms of the intermolecular forces in the polymers why this is so. [2]

c Nylon is an extremely good electrical insulator. Conducting polymers can however be made by polymerising ethyne, HC≡CH. Poly(ethyne) shows stereoisomerism. A section of the cis- form is shown below:

```
  H   H           H   H
  |   |           |   |
  C===C           C===C
 /     \         /     \
        C===C           C===C
        |   |           |   |
        H   H           H   H
```

i Draw a diagram of a section of the trans- form of poly(ethyne). [2]

ii Suggest why poly(ethyne) conducts electricity. [2]
AQA (NEAB) 1999 *(See also Chapter 32.)*

7 **a** **i** Describe the type of bonding which holds together the monomer units in a large polymer molecule.

ii Separate molecules or segments of a polymer chain are held together by secondary bonding.

Give **two** examples of secondary bonding found in polymer systems.

iii Give **two** physical properties of polymers which involve the making or breaking of secondary bonding. [5]

b **i** What is meant by the terms *thermosetting* and *thermoplastic* when applied to polymer systems?

ii Give **one** advantage and **one** disadvantage connected with the use of thermoplastics.

iii What is commonly the limiting factor in the use of thermosetting polymers? [5]
OCR (UCLES) 1994

30 Biochemistry

Biochemistry studies the chemistry of life. Biochemists seek to describe the chemical structures of organisms and to explain the reactions that underlie the processes of life. Organisms are as much a part of the chemical world as any other class of object. Everything in the world, living or non-living, is composed of an assortment of atoms selected from the known elements. Organisms therefore consist of a collection of chemical substances that work together to produce the familiar set of properties and functions we recognize as 'life'. We can move towards understanding biochemistry by studying the structure and function of the types of molecules found in organisms. These substances fall into four broad categories: **lipids**, **carbohydrates**, **proteins**, and **nucleic acids**. The major part of this chapter treats each of these categories in turn. The final spread shows how these substances work together to support the metabolism of the living cell.

LIPIDS

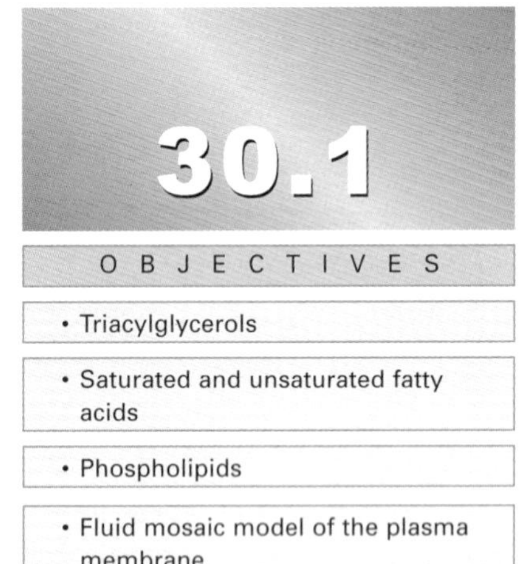

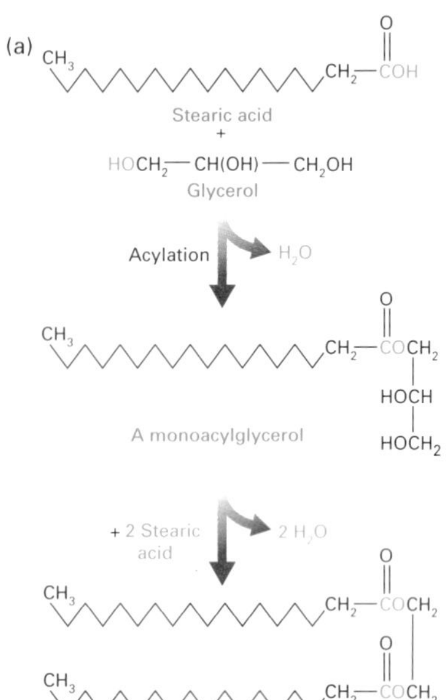

The formation of a triacylglycerol from long-chain fatty acids and the triol glycerol. Note that the three acyl groups could in principle be different; for simplicity, they are shown here to be identical.

Lipid is the general name given to a wide range of substances, found in organisms, that are largely insoluble in water but soluble in non-polar organic solvents. This spread looks at two types of lipid: **acylglycerols** and **phospholipids**. Examples of acylglycerols include the fats and oils used as food stores and the waxes used for waterproofing. Chemically, they are *esters* formed from long-chain carboxylic acids and the alcohol **glycerol**. The long-chain carboxylic acids are often referred to as 'fatty acids'. Note that glycerol has the systematic IUPAC name *propane-1,2,3-triol*, spread 25.6. The shorter familiar name 'glycerol' will be used here. The phospholipids are a major component of the **plasma membranes** of cells and play a pivotal role in their structure and function.

Acylglycerols

Acylglycerols are fatty acid esters of the triol glycerol $HOCH_2CH(OH)CH_2OH$. Esterification can occur at one, two, or all three of the hydroxyl groups of the triol, producing mono-, di-, and triacylglycerols respectively. The most common fatty acid esters found in living systems are **triacylglycerols** (or **triglycerides**), in which long-chain fatty acids attach by acylation reactions (see chapter on 'Carboxylic acids and their derivatives') to all three hydroxyl groups on the triol.

Saturated and unsaturated fatty acids

Different lipids contain various different fatty acids. The carbon chain of the fatty acid may be *saturated*, as is common in animal lipids, or *unsaturated*, as is more common in plant lipids. The phrase 'high in polyunsaturates, low in saturates' is often used in advertisements to describe butter substitutes (margarine, etc.) made from vegetable oils. A polyunsaturated fatty acid contains more than one carbon–carbon double bond. An excess of saturated fats in the diet can cause a high concentration of the substance cholesterol.

Cholesterol

Cholesterol has a structure based on four alicyclic hydrocarbon rings fused together. It is present in food and is also manufactured in the liver. It is an essential component of plasma membranes and of blood plasma. In the body it is converted to bile acids and many hormones such as the male and female sex hormones testosterone, oestrogen, and progesterone. There is medical evidence to show that increased levels of blood cholesterol are associated with a condition called *atherosclerosis*, in which lipids accumulate on the inner walls of arteries, ultimately restricting or even obstructing blood flow (see spread 22.7).

Phospholipids

Phospholipids are a major constituent of plasma membranes. In a **phospholipid**, two of the hydroxyl groups of glycerol are esterified by fatty acids, but the third is esterified by phosphoric acid. The phosphate group is frequently bound to a nitrogen-containing group. The illustration to the right shows the molecular structure of a lecithin (phosphatidylcholine, the most abundant animal phospholipid).

A phospholipid has two distinct regions. The phosphate group constitutes a polar and hence **hydrophilic** ('water-loving') region, and the fatty acid chains form a **hydrophobic** ('water-hating') region. One important result of this is that, in aqueous environments, phospholipid molecules arrange themselves as a double layer called a **bilayer**, in which all the hydrophobic ends point inwards *away from* the water phase.

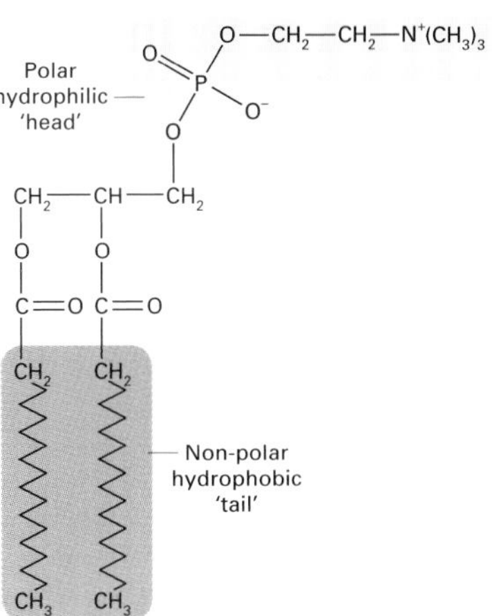

The two regions of a phospholipid molecule: the polar hydrophilic 'head' and the non-polar hydrophobic 'tail'.

Phospholipids and plasma membranes

The fundamental structure of the plasma membranes of cells consists of a phospholipid bilayer in which proteins and other molecules float, thus forming what is described as a **fluid mosaic**. This extremely flexible structure includes all the molecules responsible for the complex functions of the membrane. These functions include controlling the transport of substances across the membrane, enabling the cell to be 'recognized' as part of the organism, and various membrane-bound reactions such as the electron transport chain.

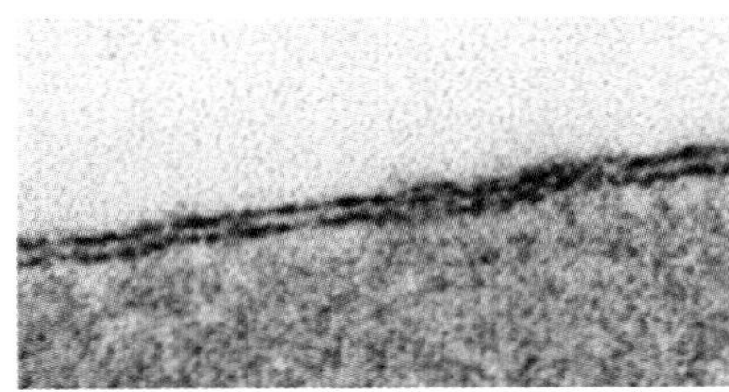

The plasma membrane of a red blood cell.

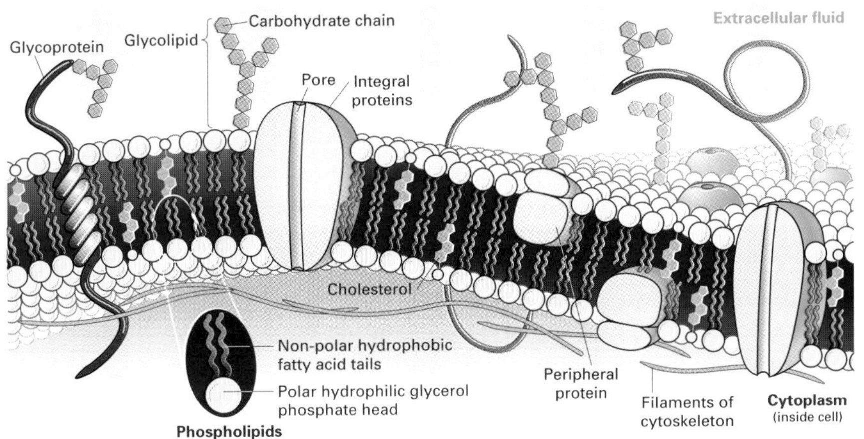

The fluid mosaic model of the plasma membrane. The sheet-like surface of the membrane consists of a phospholipid bilayer (shown alongside in greater detail). Globular proteins are embedded in the bilayer with tree-shaped carbohydrate structures joined to the external surface.

SUMMARY

- Two main classes of lipids are the acylglycerols and the phospholipids.
- Acylglycerols are fats, oils, and waxes consisting of glycerol esterified with fatty acids.
- The fatty acids in acylglycerols may be saturated, unsaturated, or polyunsaturated.
- Phospholipids are diacylglycerols with a phosphate group attached to the third hydroxyl group of the glycerol molecule.
- Plasma membranes have a fluid mosaic structure.

PRACTICE

1 Draw a displayed structural formula for each of the following fatty acids:

a $CH_3(CH_2)_{10}COOH$ (lauric acid)

b $CH_3(CH_2)_4CH{=}CHCH_2CH{=}CH(CH_2)_7COOH$ (*cis,cis*-linoleic acid).

2 Draw the structural formula of the triacylglycerol that results from the esterification of lauric acid at two of the hydroxyl groups of glycerol and *cis,cis*-linoleic acid at the third.

3 A common group found in phospholipids is the ethanolamine group:

$$-\overset{\overset{\displaystyle O}{\|}}{\underset{\underset{\displaystyle O^-}{|}}{P}}-OCH_2CH_2NH_3^+$$

Sketch the interaction expected between this hydrophilic group and water molecules.

30.2

CARBOHYDRATES: MONOSACCHARIDES

OBJECTIVES

- Monosaccharides
- D and L nomenclature
- Ring structures
- α and β anomers

Instant energy

Because carbohydrates are partially oxidized compared with lipids, lipids release more energy per gram than carbohydrates do in complete oxidation. Carbohydrates provide more 'instant access' energy.

The simplest carbohydrates are the monosaccharides such as glucose and fructose, which are important intermediates in the respiration of food to release energy. These two substances are classed as **monosaccharides** because they are not hydrolysed by hydrochloric acid. Monosaccharides however can join together (by a condensation reaction) to form longer chains. Sucrose is a **disaccharide** because dilute acid splits it by hydrolysis into glucose and fructose (both monosaccharides). Disaccharides and polysaccharides are described in the next two spreads. Whatever their complexity, all carbohydrates contain the elements carbon, hydrogen, and oxygen, and have the general formula $C_x(H_2O)_y$.

Monosaccharides

Chemically, the monosaccharides are aldehydes or ketones that also have several hydroxyl groups attached to their carbon skeletons. For example, glucose is known as an **aldose** and has an aldehyde structure at carbon atom number 1 (C1 for short). On the other hand, fructose is known as a **ketose** and has a ketone structure at carbon atom C2.

Glucose and fructose molecules both have the molecular formula $C_6H_{12}O_6$. They both have six carbon atoms and so are called **hexoses**. Monosaccharides that have three carbon atoms are called **trioses**, those with four are **tetroses**, those with five are **pentoses**, and so on. Ribose is the most important pentose. Monosaccharides dissolve easily in water due to the presence of a large number of polar hydroxyl groups, which hydrogen-bond with water molecules.

(a)	Carbon number	(b)
CHO	①	CH_2OH
H—C—OH	②	C=O
HO—C—H	③	HO—C—H
H—C—OH	④	H—C—OH
H—C—OH	⑤	H—C—OH
CH_2OH	⑥	CH_2OH

(a) Glucose: an aldohexose. Note that the molecule is drawn with the carbonyl group at the top. The carbon atoms are numbered from the top to the bottom of each molecule.
(b) Fructose: a ketohexose.

Chiral centres and optical activity

Look at the structural formula of glucose. You should be able to point out chiral centres (see spread on 'Amino acids and optical activity' in the chapter on 'Amines and amino acids') where carbon atoms are attached to four different groups. These molecules can therefore exist in different enantiomeric forms, some of which may be optically active. The actual shape (stereochemistry) of a monosaccharide molecule may be described by comparing it to a reference standard, glyceraldehyde (2,3-dihydroxy-propanal). This substance has only one chiral centre, which means that it can exist as two enantiomers (see below). The enantiomer with the —OH group on the left is given the label L and the enantiomer with the —OH group on the right is given the label D.

L-Glucose	Carbon number	D-Glucose
CHO	①	CHO
HO—C—H	②	H—C—OH
H—C—OH	③	HO—C—H
HO—C—H	④	H—C—OH
HO—C—H	⑤	H—C—OH
CH_2OH	⑥	CH_2OH

L- and D-glucose.

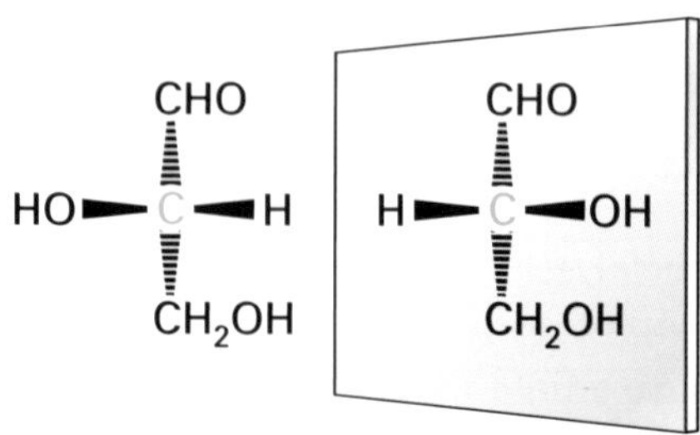

L-Glyceraldehyde D-Glyceraldehyde

L- and D-glyceraldehyde.

L-Ribose	Carbon number	D-Ribose
CHO	①	CHO
HO—C—H	②	H—C—OH
HO—C—H	③	H—C—OH
HO—C—H	④	H—C—OH
CH_2OH	⑤	CH_2OH

L- and D-ribose.

This definition leads to two 'families' of compounds. The L carbohydrates are structurally related to L-glyceraldehyde (at the chiral centre closest to the bottom of the carbohydrate molecule, shown by a coloured carbon atom), and the D carbohydrates are structurally related to D-glyceraldehyde. The two forms of glucose are shown to the left. It is important to note that the labels L and D do *not* relate to the direction of rotation of plane-polarized light (which is described as (+) for dextrorotatory, and (–) for laevorotatory). *Most naturally occurring carbohydrates are D-carbohydrates*: so the label 'D' will be dropped from now on.

Open-chain and ring structures

The glucose and fructose molecules in the illustrations opposite are shown as open-chain structures. However, there is evidence that these molecules exist as *ring* structures when in solution. This happens because the shape and flexibility of the molecule bring the aldehyde or ketone carbonyl group close to one of the hydroxyl groups, and they react to form a cyclic structure. Glucose ($C_6H_{12}O_6$) forms a six-membered **pyranose** ring structure; fructose ($C_6H_{12}O_6$) and ribose ($C_5H_{10}O_5$) both form five-membered **furanose** ring structures.

> **Sugars**
>
> Sugars have a definite, fixed molar mass: they may be monosaccharides, disaccharides etc. The molar mass of a polysaccaride may vary.

(a) α–glucose (Axial) ⇌ ($\pm H^+$) glucose: open-chain aldehyde form ⇌ ($\pm H^+$) (b) β–glucose (Equatorial)

A molecule of glucose undergoes an internal reaction that results in a ring structure. A new chiral centre is formed after reaction at carbon atom number 1 (C1) (called the anomeric centre*). Two possible isomers (called* anomers*) result: (a) α-glucose: attack from above means that the hydroxyl group attached to C1 is in the axial position (pointing out from the plane of the ring). (b) β-glucose: attack from below means that the hydroxyl group attached to C1 is in the equatorial position (pointing into the plane of the ring). The β isomer is more stable for glucose (64% exists in this form). The α isomer has the hydroxyl group on the carbon atom on the 'opposite' side of the ring from the end CH_2OH group, numbered 6. The β isomer has them on the 'same' side.*

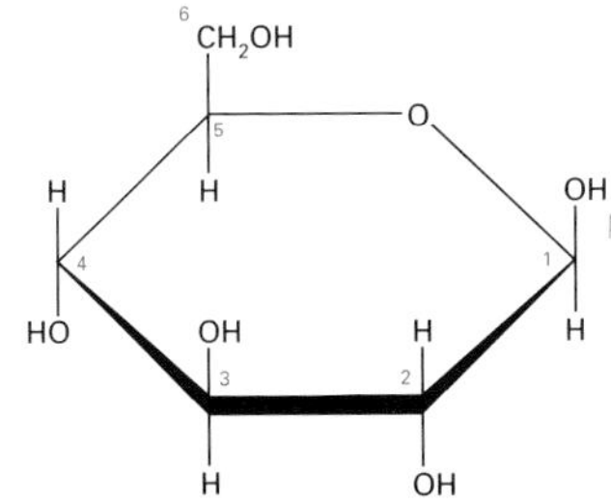

Haworth projection for β-glucose.

Haworth projections

Haworth projections show the structures of carbohydrates in a way that makes comparisons easier. The conventions for D and L and α and β isomers are as follows:

- The —CH_2OH group attached to C5 is written *up* for D sugars and *down* for L sugars.
- The —OH group attached to C1 is written *down* for the α isomer and *up* for the β isomer.

Note that Haworth projections give the false impression that the six-membered pyranose ring is flat; in reality it resembles a chair.

SUMMARY

- Carbohydrates have the general formula $C_x(H_2O)_y$.
- The simplest carbohydrates are the monosaccharides.
- Carbohydrates contain chiral centres. The structures of D and L isomers are related to the defined structures of D- and L-glyceraldehyde.
- Most naturally occuring carbohydrates are D-carbohydrates.
- Monosaccharides form ring structures in solution. α and β isomers result that differ in the position of the hydroxyl group at carbon atom number 1.

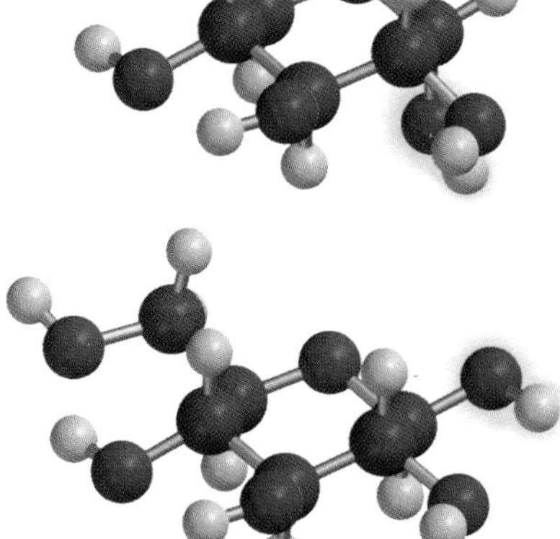

α- and β-glucose. The blue background highlights the position of the hydroxyl group on C1.

PRACTICE

1 Draw structural formulae to illustrate the differences between the chain structures of D- and L-glucose.

2 Draw structural formulae and Haworth projections to show the differences between the four ring structures: α-D-glucose, β-D-glucose, α-L-glucose, and β-L-glucose. Give your reasoning.

30.3

CARBOHYDRATES: DISACCHARIDES

OBJECTIVES

- The glycosidic link
- Reducing and non-reducing sugars
- Sucrose

The simplest carbohydrates are the monosaccharides such as glucose and fructose. Two monosaccharide molecules can link together by a condensation reaction to form a disaccharide. Examples include sucrose, which is cane sugar, and lactose, which is a constituent of milk. This spread investigates disaccharides and discusses the nature of the linkage that joins the monosaccharide units together.

Disaccharides

Disaccharides consist of two monosaccharide units joined together by a **glycosidic link**. A glycosidic link is made by the reaction between the carbonyl group of one molecule and a hydroxyl group of another molecule. In the case of the disaccharide maltose, two molecules of glucose condense together, forming a glycosidic link between carbon atom 1 on the first glucose molecule and carbon atom 4 on the second.

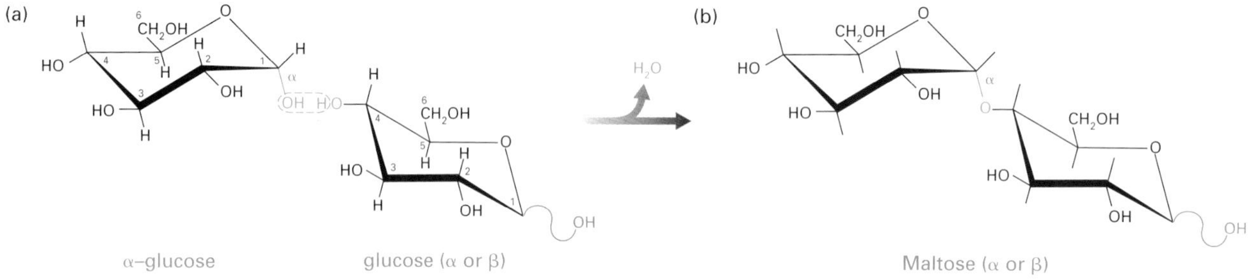

(a) α–glucose   glucose (α or β)   (b) Maltose (α or β)

As we saw in the previous spread, the isomers of glucose can interconvert by the ring opening and reclosing, so the wiggly green line on the second glucose molecule shows that either isomer can form maltose. Exactly as for glucose, the right-hand ring in maltose can open and α and β isomers can interconvert. However, the left-hand ring cannot open: it is locked into the α position. Maltose is an α-glycoside.

Enzyme hydrolysis

Enzymes can bring about hydrolysis of disaccharides. Enzyme-catalysed hydrolysis is far more specific than the acid-catalysed reaction. For example, the enzyme maltase catalyses the hydrolysis of α-glycosides much more rapidly than that of β-glycosides.

Acid hydrolysis

Disaccharides hydrolyse when warmed with dilute hydrochloric acid. For example, 1 mole of the disaccharide maltose yields 2 moles of the monosaccharide glucose.

α- and β-glycosides

A glycosidic link can be arranged in different ways, giving rise to a difference in biochemical properties. Look again at the displayed structure of maltose. The oxygen atom of the glycosidic link lies *outside the plane* of the left-hand glucose ring. Maltose is therefore said to have an α-glycosidic link; maltose is an α-glycoside.

Now look at the structure of cellobiose below. Like maltose, it is also a disaccharide built from two glucose molecules. However, the glycosidic link lies *in the plane* of the left-hand glucose ring. Cellobiose is therefore said to have a β-glycosidic link; cellobiose is a β-glycoside.

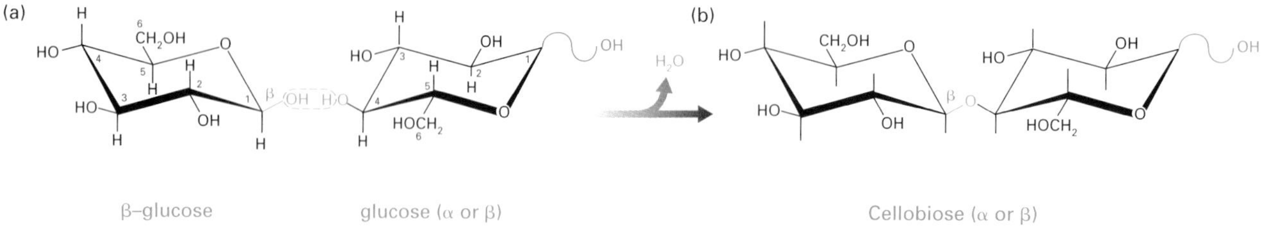

(a) β–glucose   glucose (α or β)   (b) Cellobiose (α or β)

The isomers of glucose can interconvert by the ring opening and reclosing, so the wiggly green line on the second glucose molecule shows that either isomer can form cellobiose. Exactly as for glucose, the right-hand ring in cellobiose can open and α and β isomers can interconvert. However, the left-hand ring cannot open: it is locked into the β position. Cellobiose is a β-glycoside.

(a) α–glucose β–fructose $\xrightarrow{-H_2O}$ (b) Sucrose

Unlike the situation with maltose or cellobiose, the sucrose molecule has the glycosidic link between the anomeric centres of both rings. The molecule results from a condensation reaction between α-glucose and β-fructose. The carbon atom that is the centre for interconversion between the α and β isomers in fructose (carbon atom 2) is no longer able to do so once permanently locked into a β-glycosidic link. The sucrose molecule is unique (there are no α and β isomers).

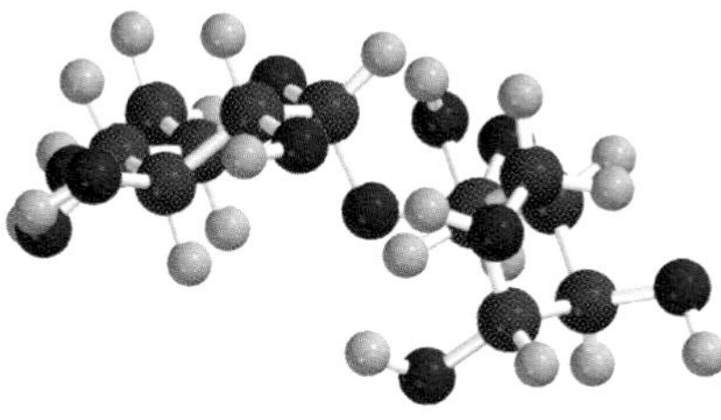

The sucrose molecule as produced by Spartan. Representing as complicated a molecule as this in two dimensions using either artwork or a screen shot is exceptionally difficult.

Reducing and non-reducing sugars

In solution, the ring forms of monosaccharides are in equilibrium with the open-chain forms, which bear aldehyde or ketone groups. Carbonyl groups in aldehydes act as reductants (being oxidized to carboxylic acids), so aldoses would be expected to react positively with Fehling's or Tollens' reagents (see chapter on 'Aldehydes and ketones'). Ketones do not normally give a positive reaction to these tests because they do not readily oxidize. However, *ketoses* do give a positive result due to the presence of a hydroxyl group attached to the carbon atom next to the carbonyl carbon. Thus, *all* monosaccharides are **reducing sugars**.

Disaccharides may be reducing or non-reducing. To form the open-chain structure from the ring structure, a carbonyl group must be present. If this carbonyl group was involved in forming the glycosidic link of a disaccharide, then that disaccharide will be a **non-reducing sugar**. Look at the structural formulae above and you will see that maltose is a reducing disaccharide but sucrose is non-reducing. You should note that:

- **Reducing sugars** have formed the glycosidic link using a hydroxyl group present in the open-chain structure, and so a carbonyl group remains on one monosaccharide. This can therefore form an anomeric centre, and *two forms* exist: there is an α-maltose and a β-maltose.
- **Non-reducing sugars** have formed the glycosidic link using a hydroxyl group formed on making the ring structure of the molecule, and so no carbonyl group remains. This cannot therefore form anomers, and only *one form* exists: sucrose is a unique molecule.

Benedict's solution

Benedict's solution, spread 26.4, is a more sensitive test for reducing sugars than Fehling's solution. The reagent is a mixture of aqueous copper(II) sulphate with a basic solution of sodium citrate. When boiled with a reducing sugar, the pale blue solution forms a red precipitate. Detection of glucose in urine is a common test for diabetes.

SUMMARY

- A glycosidic link forms by the reaction of a carbonyl group on one monosaccharide with a hydroxyl group on another monosaccharide.
- The α-glycosidic link forms when the bridging oxygen atom is outside the plane of the two monosaccharide rings.
- The β-glycosidic link forms when the bridging oxygen atom is in the plane of the two monosaccharide rings.
- All monosaccharides are reducing sugars.
- Disaccharides are reducing if a carbonyl group remains on one monosaccharide.

PRACTICE

1 Prepare a 10-minute talk (with overhead projector transparencies and other visual aids) to explain:

a the similarities and differences between the α- and β-glycosides;

b the structure that a disaccharide needs to have for it to reduce Benedict's solution.

30.4 Carbohydrates: polysaccharides

OBJECTIVES

- Starch
- Amylose and amylopectin
- Cellulose
- Glycogen
- Amylase

Polysaccharides are natural condensation polymers made up of monosaccharides joined by glycosidic links to form long chains. They are important as carbohydrate energy stores and are fundamental to the structure of plants and fungi. They are also present in the plasma membranes of animal and bacterial cells. This spread concentrates on three glucose-based polysaccharides: starch, cellulose, and glycogen. You will see that, in common with disaccharides, the properties of these polysaccharides depend to a great extent on the type of glycosidic link (α or β) between the monosaccharide units from which they are constructed.

Some polysaccharide sources. (a) Bananas are a source of starch. Digestion in animals breaks down starch into glucose, which circulates in the bloodstream. The human brain requires the energy from two teaspoonfuls of glucose each hour. This glucose comes mainly from sugars (mono- and disaccharides) and starch-based foodstuffs. (b) Chitin (pronounced ki-tin) is a polysaccharide found in the body shells (exoskeletons) of many invertebrate animals, especially arthropods. Chitin is probably the second most abundant organic compound on Earth. The copepods (aquatic crustaceans about 1 mm long) alone produce 10^9 tonnes of chitin per year.

The α and β angles

The α-glycosidic link lies outside the plane of one of the monosaccharide rings that it joins; the β-glycosidic link lies in the plane of the rings. As a result, the α link holds the rings at a more acute angle to each other than does the β link.

Starch: amylose and amylopectin

Starch from plant sources is a major direct or indirect energy source in the diets of animals. Plants make glucose by photosynthesis, and this may be converted to starch for storage. A typical starch polymer chain consists of around 2500 glucose molecules. Starch is used as a carbohydrate store in roots, tubers, seeds, and fruits. Plant cells store starch in the form of *starch grains*, which usually contain variable proportions of the two polysaccharides *amylose* and *amylopectin*.

Amylose and **amylopectin** are both polymers of glucose. Amylose has a structure consisting of glucose units joined by α-(1–4)-glycosidic links. Amylopectin has a branched structure: the chains have the same arrangement as in amylose, branches forming by means of α-(1–6)-glycosidic links. The α-glycosidic link in amylose and amylopectin results in a coiled molecule most suited for storage in starch grains. This contrasts with the β-glycosidic link present in cellulose.

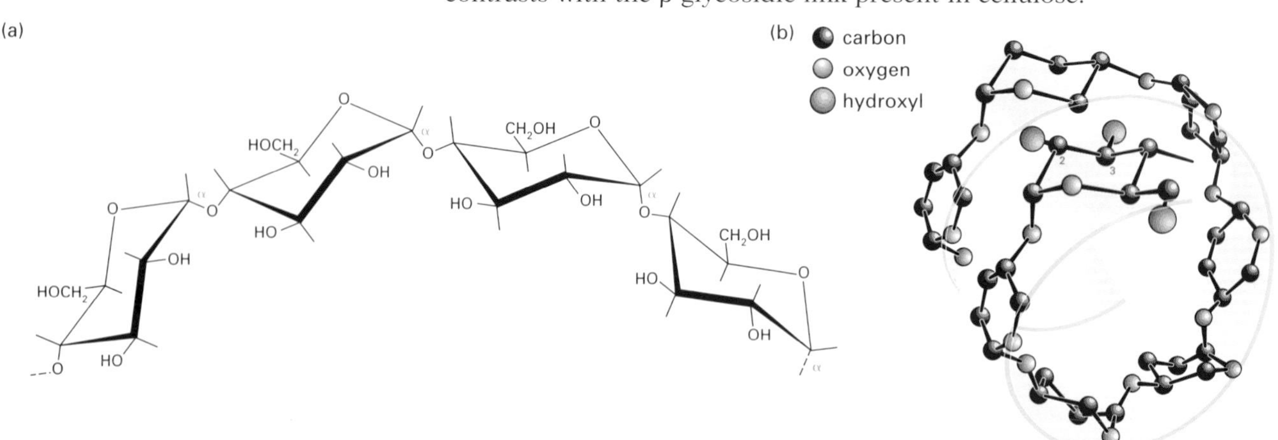

(a) Part of the structure of amylose. (b) The coiled structure of starch results from the angle of the α-glycosidic link. This enables intramolecular hydrogen bonding between the hydroxyl group on C2 with the glycosidic link and the hydroxyl group on C3 with the oxygen atom in the ring.

Cellulose

Cellulose, the main structural component of plant cell walls, is the most abundant organic compound on Earth. It accounts for more than half the carbon in the biosphere. In common with starch, cellulose is a polymer of glucose. However, the (1–4)-glycosidic links between the glucose molecules are at the β angle, resulting in a linear chain structure. Compared with the spiral structure of starch, this shape is more suited to the formation of the rigid walls of plant cells.

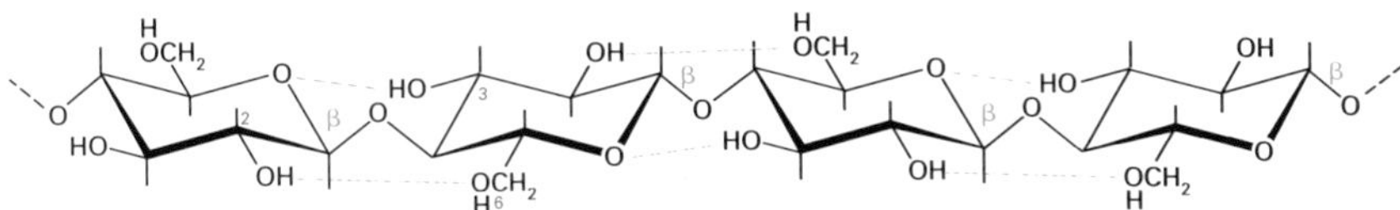

Part of the structure of cellulose. The linear structure of cellulose results from the angle of the β-glycosidic link. Alternate rings are rotated by 180°, which allows hydrogen bonding between the hydroxyl group on C2 with that on C6 and between the hydroxyl group on C3 with the oxygen atom in the ring. Compare this structure with that of amylose.

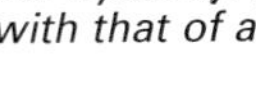

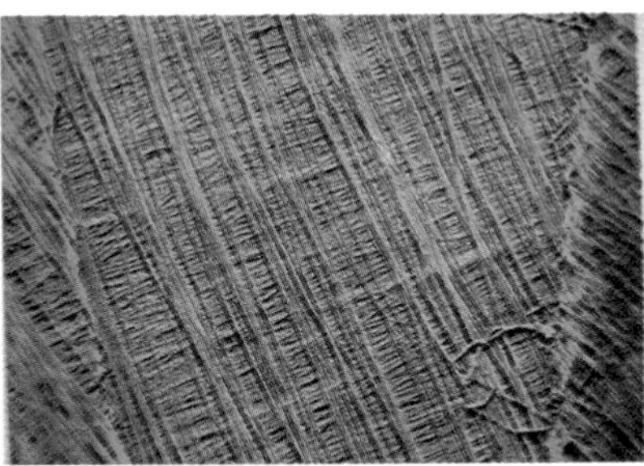

Cellulose fibres in the cell wall of the alga Chaetomorpha, *which grows in freshwater pools.*

Glycogen

Starch and cellulose are produced by plants: cellulose is a structural material and starch acts as a food store. Glycogen is the storage carbohydrate of animals. It is very similar to amylopectin, but has a more extensively branched structure. In mammals, starch is digested to glucose. Excess glucose is polymerized and stored in the liver as glycogen. The balance between stored glycogen and free glucose in the blood is controlled largely by the two hormones insulin (promotes conversion of glucose to glycogen) and glucagon (promotes conversion of glycogen to glucose).

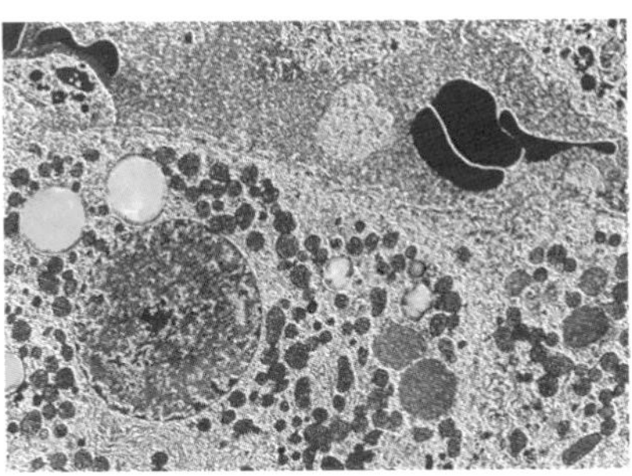

Glycogen granules (pink/red) in the cytoplasm of a liver cell. The glucose units making up these granules probably originated in the starch grains of a plant cell.

Enzyme hydrolysis

Mammals such as humans digest starch by means of a group of catalytic enzymes called *amylases*. These enzymes split the α-glycosidic link to produce a mixture of glucose and the disaccharide maltose. However, human amylases cannot hydrolyse β-glycosidic links. Because of this, we cannot digest cellulose. Herbivores such as cattle and sheep have bacteria in their stomachs that produce an enzyme that digests the cellulose in plant material, breaking it down to the mono- and disaccharides that the body can use.

All enzymes are proteins – this is the subject of the following spread.

SUMMARY

- Polysaccharides are natural polymers consisting of monosaccharides joined by glycosidic links.
- Starch, cellulose, and glycogen are all polysaccharides made up from glucose.
- Starch consists of glucose units linked by α-(1–4)-glycosidic links to form amylose (straight chain) and amylopectin (branched chain).
- The α angle in amylose and amylopectin results in a coiled molecule whose structure is maintained by intramolecular hydrogen bonding.
- Cellulose is a linear polymer consisting of glucose units linked by β-(1–4)-glycosidic links.

PRACTICE

1 Compare and contrast the structures and uses of starch, cellulose, and glycogen.

2 Suggest reasons for the presence of 4 mol dm^{-3} hydrochloric acid in the digestive fluids in the stomachs of mammals.

30.5 PROTEINS

OBJECTIVES

- Primary structure
- Secondary structure
- Tertiary structure
- Quaternary structure
- Fibrous and globular proteins

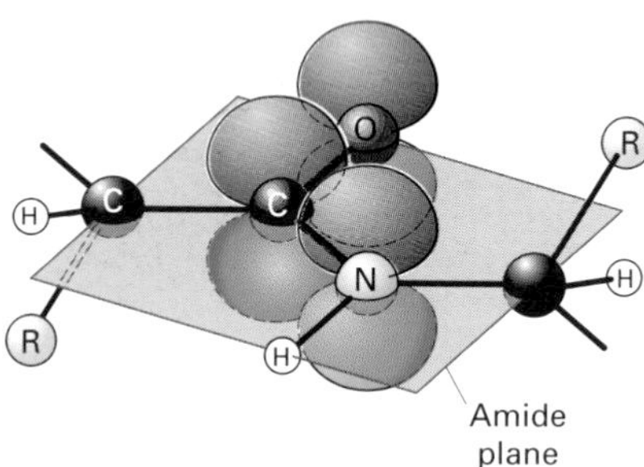

The p orbitals on carbon and oxygen that form the π bond can also overlap with the p orbital on nitrogen, when this is arranged as in the illustration to cause a structure delocalized over all the atoms. This delocalization is the reason why the peptide link must be planar.

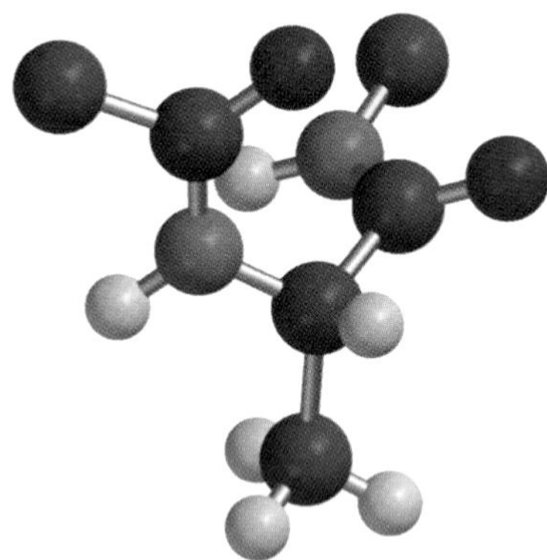

Each peptide link is planar (remember that Spartan uses ball-and-stick models to show atoms that are bonded; the number of bonds is not *shown)*

Proteins are naturally occurring condensation polymers (see chapter on 'Carboxylic acids and their derivatives'), consisting of chains of amino acid groups. As noted in the chapter on 'Amines and amino acids', there are about 20 naturally occurring amino acids. The human body can synthesize some of these, while others, called the **essential amino acids**, must be present in our food. There are four levels of structure used to describe proteins: primary, secondary, tertiary, and quaternary. The illustrations included in this spread show how these structures relate to the proteins myoglobin and haemoglobin, the oxygen-carrying components of cells.

Primary structure

The **primary structure** of a protein describes the sequence of amino acids present. Each amino acid is joined to the next via a **peptide link**, which forms between the carboxyl group of one amino acid and the amine group of the next. Chemists would describe a protein as a polyamide, see spread 27.7. Writing out the full amino acid structure for each amino acid in a protein would be very tedious, and so primary structure is usually depicted by a three-letter short-hand notation, e.g. **ala** for alanine, **leu** for leucine, and so on, arranged in the appropriate sequence.

The sequence of amino acids in a protein is determined experimentally by reacting the amino acid at one end of the molecule with a substance that creates a coloured or fluorescing derivative. The protein is then hydrolysed by a highly specific enzyme that removes only the terminal amino acid. The marked amino acid is identified by chromatography (see next chapter). Repeating the process many times determines the full primary structure.

H_2N—Val(1)—Leu—Ser—Glu—Gly(5)—Glu—Trp—Gln—Leu—Val(10)—Leu

—Ala—Lys(145)—Tyr—Lys—Glu—Leu—Gly(150)—Tyr—Gln—Gly—COOH

This sequence of amino acids gives the primary structure of sperm whale myoglobin.

Secondary structure

The chain of amino acids that makes up the primary structure of a protein can fold itself in two ways, depending on the sequences of amino acids that are next to each other. Hydrogen bonds hold the folded structures in place. This folding of the primary structure is called the **secondary structure**.

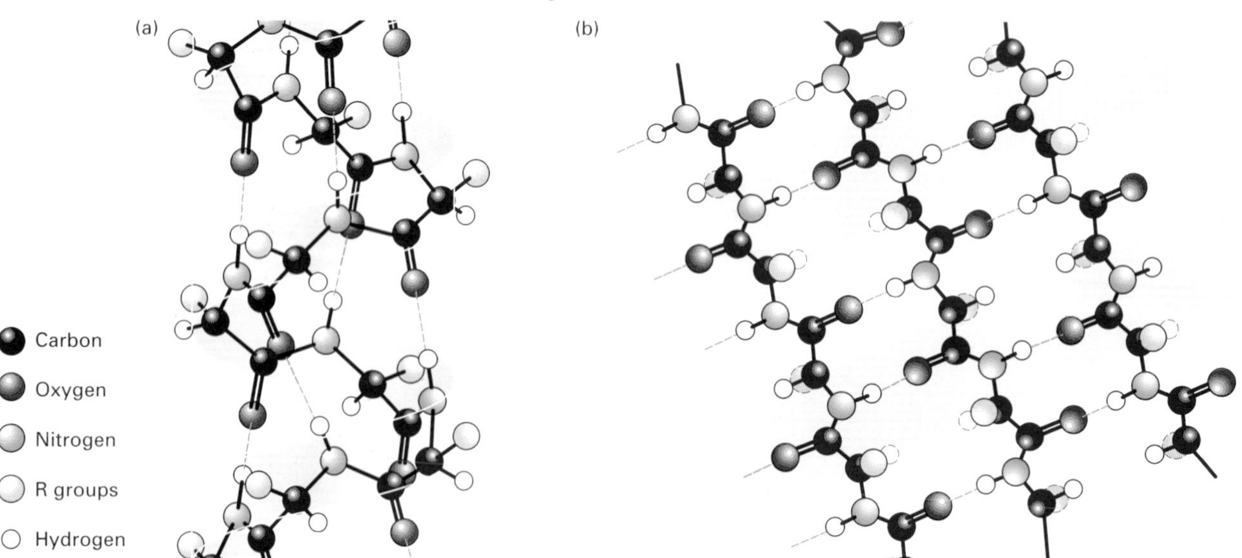

Hydrogen bonding gives rise to the two forms of secondary structure: (a) the ***alpha helix****; and (b) the* ***beta pleated sheet*** *(here, three-stranded).*

Tertiary structure

There is overall folding of the chain held by interactions between more distant amino acids. This is called the **tertiary structure**. These interactions include hydrogen bonds and **disulphide bridges** (covalent bonds that form between sulphur atoms on the oxidation of two cysteine amino acids, spread 28.5) as well as ionic interactions and intermolecular forces.

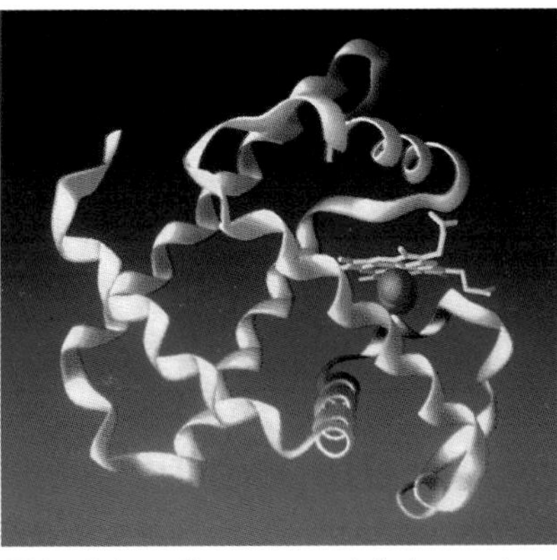

This ribbon diagram model shows the tertiary structure of myoglobin. The position of the oxygen molecule when it binds to the haem group is shown in red (and at exaggerated scale).

Quaternary structure

Finally, some structure results from interaction between separate protein chains. This is called **quaternary structure**. Not all proteins have a quaternary structure; myoglobin, for example, has only one chain. Haemoglobin has a quaternary structure that includes four protein chains – it has two alpha chains and two beta chains. (Note that the terms 'alpha and beta chains' should not be confused with the terms 'alpha helix' and 'beta pleated sheet' used to describe secondary structure.)

Fibrous and globular proteins

The proteins present in organisms may conveniently be divided into two classes. **Fibrous proteins** have long molecules, which are strengthened by many cross-links between the chains. Fibrous proteins form structures such as muscle fibres. **Globular proteins** are smaller and are much more round and compact. Globular proteins have many roles, particularly as **enzymes** and certain **hormones** (carriers of biochemical messages). The structure of proteins, and hence their function, can be disrupted by a number of factors, such as high temperature. The proteins are then said to be **denatured**; this will be considered in detail in the next spread on enzymes.

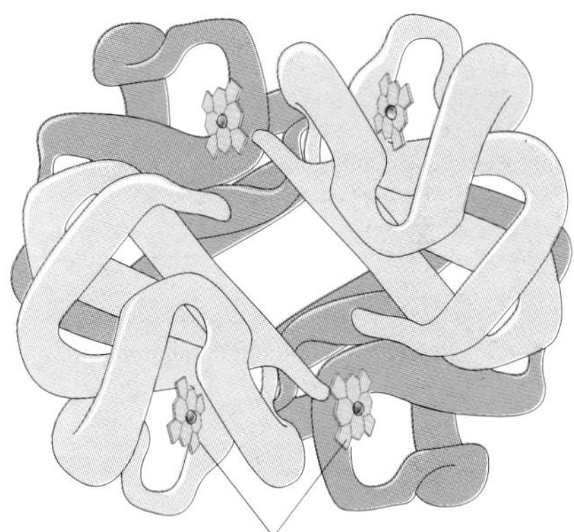

The quaternary structure of haemoglobin consists of two alpha chains and two beta chains arranged at the corners of a tetrahedron.

SUMMARY

- Proteins are condensation polymers of amino acids.
- The structure of proteins is considered at four levels: primary, secondary, tertiary, and quaternary.
- Primary structure: the amino acid sequence in the polypeptide chain.
- Secondary structure: the alpha helix and beta pleated sheet held by hydrogen bonding between adjacent sections of polypeptide chain.
- Tertiary structure: folding of a protein molecule held by interactions between distant amino acids.
- Quaternary structure: fitting together two or more separate protein chains to give the final physiologically active protein.
- Proteins may be fibrous or globular.
- Proteins may be denatured.

Hydrolysis

Acidic hydrolysis (see spread 27.5) of proteins, for example by hot hydrochloric acid, forms amino acids, see spread 28.5.

PRACTICE

1 Refer to the amino acid structures in the chapter on 'Amines and amino acids'.
  a Show how threonine and alanine condense together to make a dipeptide.
  b Explain why lysine, a basic amino acid, and glutamic acid may together be responsible for the tertiary structure of a protein.

2 The atoms in the peptide link are in the same plane. There is limited rotation about the C—N bond. Explain why the carbonyl (⊃C═O) oxygen atom and the imino (⊃N—H) hydrogen atom do not align *cis* to each other. [Hint: refer to the R groups on each α-amino acid.]

3 Which of the three structural considerations – secondary, tertiary, or quaternary – determines whether a protein is globular or fibrous? Give the reason for your answer.

30.6

Enzymes – 1

OBJECTIVES

- Lowering of activation energy
- Active site
- Lock-and-key and induced-fit models
- Denaturation

Enzymes are globular proteins that act as biological catalysts. They increase the rate of biochemical reactions, which would otherwise be so slow that life would not be possible. For example, respiration releases energy from the oxidation of glucose. The overall reaction may be represented as:

$$C_6H_{12}O_6 + 6O_2 \rightarrow 6CO_2 + 6H_2O$$

At the temperature of 37 °C found in the human body, the reaction as written proceeds at a negligible rate. However, glucose is oxidized in organisms by means of a complex metabolic pathway called **glycolysis**, which involves a large number of different enzymes, see final spread in this chapter. Each enzyme is specific to one reaction in the pathway. The overall process of glycolysis produces as much energy per molecule of glucose as does the combustion of glucose in air (following Hess's law; see the chapter on 'Thermochemistry').

The active site

In common with all catalysts, enzymes speed up a reaction by providing an alternative route of *lower activation energy* (see chapter on 'Chemical kinetics'). They do this by binding the reactant molecule, called the **substrate**, and holding it in a favourable orientation for reaction. The mechanism may be summarized as:

enzyme + substrate → enzyme/substrate complex → enzyme + product

Note that the enzyme, like any other catalyst, is released *unchanged* at the end of the reaction.

Equilibrium constants

In common with other catalysts, enzymes do not alter the position of an equilibrium, i.e. they do not change the value of the equilibrium constant. Enzyme action causes equilibrium to be achieved more rapidly.

The part of the enzyme molecule that binds the substrate is known as the **active site**. There are two models used to describe how the active site works. In one, the *lock-and-key model*, the active site accurately fits its particular substrate molecule (as shown in the illustration below). Alternatively, the *induced-fit model* visualizes the active site changing shape slightly in response to its particular substrate. In both cases the active site is *very specific* to the substrate.

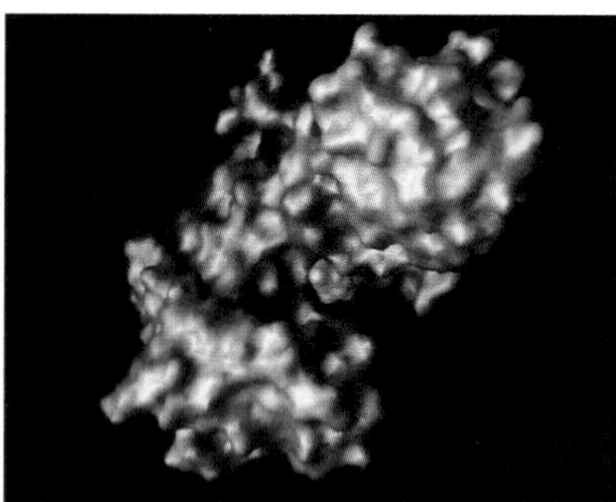

Computer graphics model of hexokinase. When glucose (orange) enters the active site, it causes the protein to change shape, illustrating the induced-fit model.

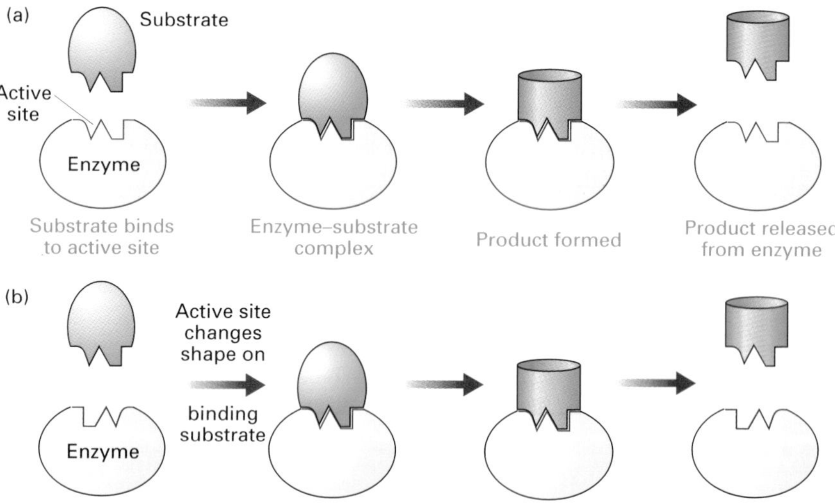

Two models for binding a substrate (reactant) to an enzyme: (a) lock-and-key model; and (b) induced-fit model. Note that the reaction occurs after the substrate has bound to the enzyme; release of the product leaves the enzyme in its initial state and shape.

TIM

The enzyme triose-phosphate isomerase (abbreviated name TIM) interconverts two triose monosaccharides. TIM is spectacularly efficient: one molecule (M_r = 43 000) can catalyse the reaction of 400 000 substrate molecules per second, the limiting factor being the rate of diffusion of substrate to the enzyme. TIM is a component of a variety of biochemical pathways. In muscle, it is involved in the respiration of carbohydrate to produce energy; in green plants, it is involved in the photosynthetic reactions that produce carbohydrates. Its role in the photosynthetic pathway is the reverse of its role in respiration. TIM illustrates many of the general properties of enzymes:

- Enzymes greatly increase the rate of reactions that otherwise would be too slow.
- Enzymes are globular proteins consisting of coiled polypeptide chains.
- Enzymes are highly specific: a given enzyme catalyses a single reaction or a limited class of reactions.
- Substrate and product bind reversibly to the active site.
- The names of most enzymes end in *-ase*, this suffix often being added to the name of the substrate.

TIM catalyses just one reaction out of many hundreds in the biochemical pathway that connects carbohydrate with carbon dioxide, water, and energy. In animals, this pathway is catabolic; in plants, anabolic (see spread 30.11). TIM interconverts glyceraldehyde 3-phosphate (an aldotriose, spread 30.2) with dihydroxypropanone phosphate (a ketotriose).

Denaturation

Most enzymes are destroyed by high temperature because the increased kinetic energy causes the protein structure to break down. Loss of tertiary structure means that the enzyme no longer has the specific shape required for its correct function. The loss of biochemical activity through structural change is called **denaturation**.

The graph to the right plots reaction rate against temperature for an enzyme-catalysed reaction. Note that the optimum temperature for this enzyme is about 45 °C. Above this temperature, the reaction rate falls as the enzyme starts to denature and lose its function. Different enzymes have their own optimum temperature; for human enzymes, the optimum is around 37 °C (body temperature).

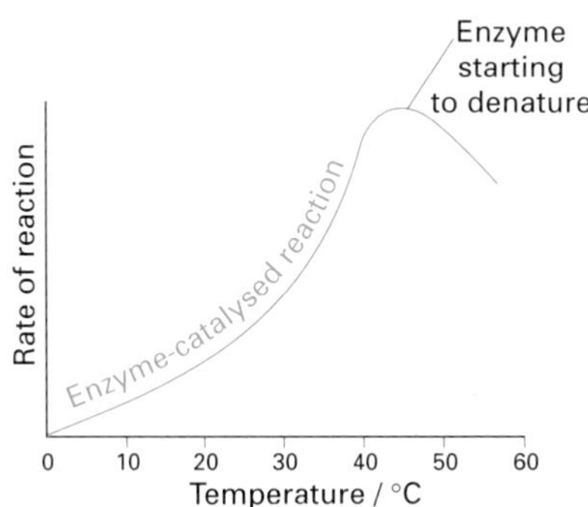

Temperature dependence of enzyme-catalysed reactions. Lactase is an enzyme that breaks the disaccharide lactose ('milk sugar') into the monosaccharides galactose and glucose. The enzyme is denatured at temperatures above about 45 °C, causing the reaction rate to decrease.

Extremes of pH also cause denaturation, and each enzyme also has an optimum pH at which it works best. The illustration below shows a graph of reaction rate against pH for the enzyme fumarase.

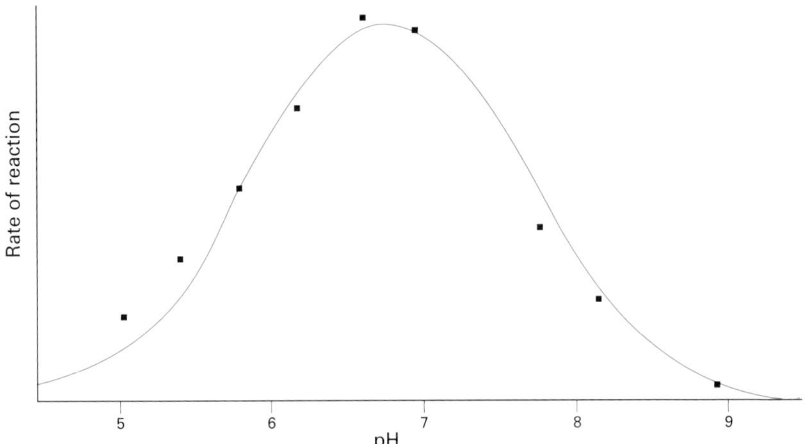

Fumarase has an optimum pH of about 6.5.

The process of cooking (heating) a protein food denatures the protein. For example, boiling an egg causes the protein albumin in the white portion to coagulate and harden. Decreasing the pH also brings about denaturation, as when pickling in vinegar. Note that denaturation destroys an enzyme *irreversibly*.

SUMMARY

- Enzymes are biological catalysts.
- Enzymes have an active site that binds to the substrate.
- Enzyme action is described by the lock-and-key and induced-fit models.
- Enzymes are denatured by high temperature and extremes of pH.

30.7 Enzymes – 2

OBJECTIVES

- Enzyme inhibition
- Immobilized enzymes
- Cofactors

Enzymes are specific to the reactions they catalyse. They are sensitive to temperature and pH, high or low values of these causing denaturation and hence loss of activity. Enzymes can also be *poisoned* in the same manner as non-biological catalysts (see chapter on 'Chemical kinetics'), and they can be *inhibited*, which decreases activity. Some enzymes are active only in the presence of a substance called a **cofactor**, which acts to 'switch on' the enzyme. Despite the sensitivity of enzymes to their environment, they are used increasingly in industrial processes. Most enzymes act only on a specific substrate, and this specificity as well as excellent conversion efficiencies makes enzymes ideal for carrying out the conversion of a given organic substance in industry.

Enzyme inhibition

Enzyme action can be **inhibited** by the presence of another molecule, with the result that activity decreases. Inhibition may be irreversible, in which case the enzyme is permanently 'poisoned'. This happens when the inhibitor forms a covalent bond with the enzyme which is difficult to break. Conversely, reversible inhibition is an important mechanism for controlling enzyme reactions. A **competitive inhibitor** is a molecule that competes with the substrate for position at the active site. The enzyme molecule 'recognizes' the inhibitor molecule as substrate and so binds to it, but cannot convert it into product. Competitive inhibitors are often chemically very similar to the substrate molecule. A **non-competitive inhibitor** does not bind to the active site, but changes the shape of the active site when it binds to another part of the enzyme. A non-competitive inhibitor is often a heavy metal ion. The enzyme is thus prevented from binding to its substrate. The illustration below shows the distinguishing features of competitive and non-competitive inhibition.

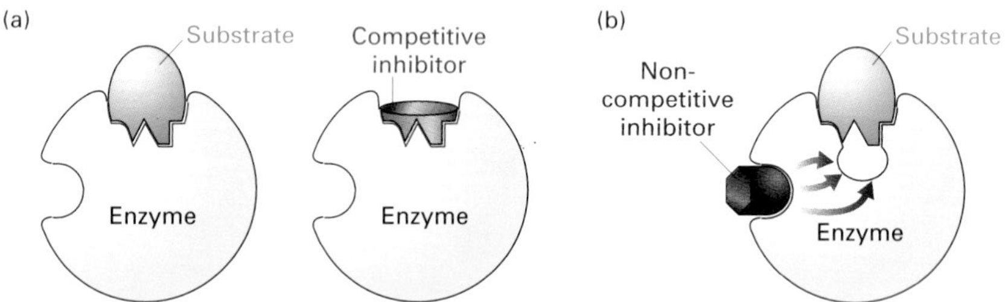

The mechanism of inhibition. (a) Competitive inhibition: both substrate and inhibitor can bind to the active site on the enzyme and hence compete for it. (b) Non-competitive inhibition: the inhibitor binds to a site elsewhere on the enzyme.

Immobilized enzymes

Many enzyme-catalysed reactions have become industrially important. For example, corn syrup is a cheap source of the sugar glucose. Glucose can be converted into the much sweeter (and therefore more valuable) sugar fructose by the enzyme glucose isomerase. A major problem lies in separating the contaminating and expensive enzyme from the product after the reaction.

Immobilization is an industrial process whereby an enzyme is attached to a solid support that does not interfere with its catalytic activity. There are several methods of attaching the enzyme to its support. For example, the enzyme may be trapped within the framework of a polymer, or it may be adsorbed onto the surface of an inert substance such as stainless steel, glass, or cellulose. The support is usually in the form of small beads, which can easily be separated from the product after reaction. The enzyme may be re-used many times. Immobilizing enzymes in this way mirrors the situation in living cells. The majority of enzymes in organisms are anchored within organelles – minute structures inside cells that have a specific specialized function.

Commercial uses

Enzymes are used in a number of commercial enterprises. Prominent among these are the industries based on fermentation (spread 25.1) and the use of enzymes in biological washing powders.

Cofactors

Some enzymes cannot function without the presence of a cofactor. **Vitamins** are substances that must be present in small amounts in food to maintain health, and many vitamins are cofactors. Two important cofactors are **NAD^+** (nicotinamide adenine dinucleotide) and **$NADP^+$** (nicotinamide adenine dinucleotide phosphate), which are synthesized from the B vitamin **niacin**. NAD^+ and $NADP^+$ are examples of a type of cofactor known as a **coenzyme**, because they must be present for the enzyme to work, but they are not bound to it, or are bound reversibly. NAD^+ and $NADP^+$ are essential to the functioning of certain dehydrogenase enzymes that catalyse redox reactions. They are involved in the transport of electrons and hydrogen ions during the oxidation of food to release energy (respiration).

FAD (flavin adenine dinucleotide) is synthesized from the B vitamin **riboflavin**. FAD is a type of cofactor known as a **prosthetic group**, because it binds tightly to the enzyme with which it works. FAD is associated with the enzyme succinate dehydrogenase, for example. **Coenzyme A** is a cofactor synthesized from the B vitamin **pantothenic acid**, which is present in cereal grains, egg yolk, liver, and peas. Coenzyme A is involved in reactions that transfer acyl groups, and it occupies a central position in metabolism (see last spread in this chapter). Some cofactors are metal ions, for example Ca^{2+}, Mg^{2+}, and Fe^{2+}. They form complexes with the lone pair on some amino acids, thus sustaining the tertiary structure of the protein.

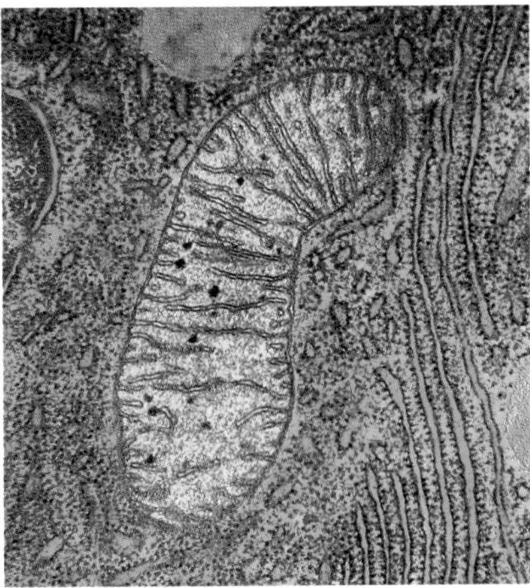

Mitochondrion: the 'powerhouse' of the cell. Mitochondria are constructed mostly from lipids and proteins. They contain the enzymes and coenzymes that control the energy-releasing reactions of respiration. The reactions take place in the numerous microgranules that coat the highly-folded inner membrane.

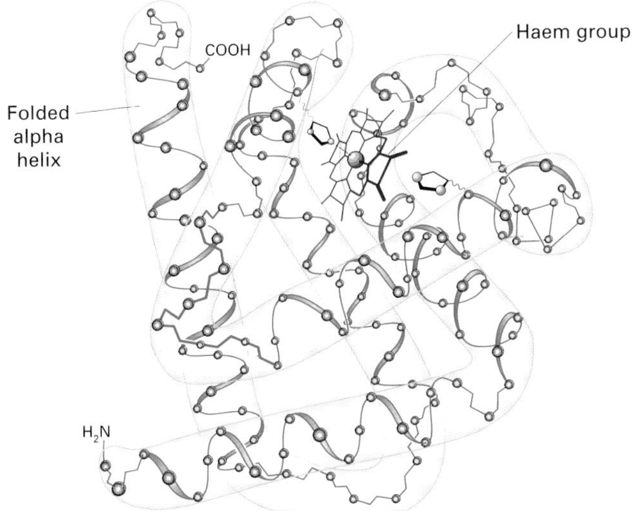

Myoglobin acts as a store for oxygen. An oxygen molecule attaches directly to the Fe^{2+} ion at the centre of a haem group. This group holds the myoglobin polypeptide chain in its tertiary structure.

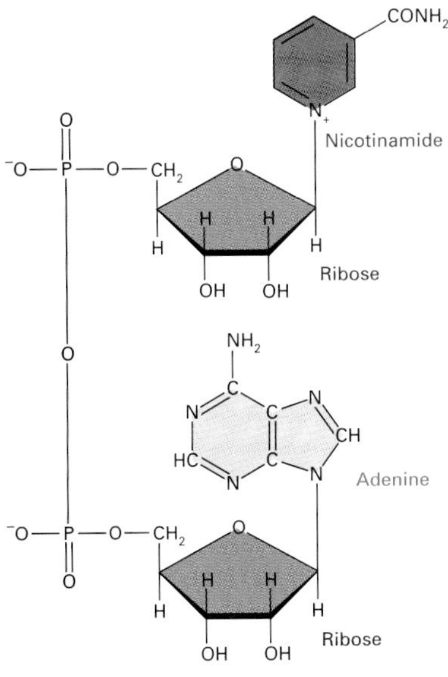

The structure of NAD^+. The molecule consists of the two nitrogen-containing bases nicotinamide and adenine, each bonded to the monosaccharide ribose. Nucleotides are discussed in detail in the next spread. (The lengths of two P—O bonds on the left are exaggerated.)

SUMMARY

- Enzyme inhibitors may be competitive or non-competitive.
- Enzymes used in industrial reactions are often immobilized.
- Some enzymes cannot work without the presence of a cofactor.
- Important cofactors are NAD^+, $NADP^+$, and FAD.

PRACTICE

1 Pectin is a polysaccharide that forms a gel with sucrose. It is widely used as an additive in commercial jam-making. Pectin is present in the germinated grains used for brewing beer. Explain why brewers add the digestive enzyme pectinase to beer during fermentation. Suggest the action of this enzyme.

2 Explain the relationship between the terms 'cofactor' and 'prosthetic group'.

3 An inhibitor lowers the rate at which an enzyme converts substrate to product. Why might a biological system need an inhibitor?

4 Explain the differences between:
- **a** Reversible and non-reversible inhibition
- **b** Competitive and non-competitive inhibition.

30.8

NUCLEIC ACIDS – 1

OBJECTIVES

- Nucleosides and nucleotides
- Nucleic acids as polynucleotides
- RNA and DNA
- Ribose and deoxyribose
- Nitrogenous bases

Nucleotides

Nucleotides are widespread throughout biological systems. For example, you have already met NAD^+ (nicotinamide adenine dinucleotide) and FAD (flavin adenine dinucleotide). These two substances each consist of just *two* nucleotides bonded together. Nucleic acids are polymers consisting of chains of *thousands* of nucleotides.

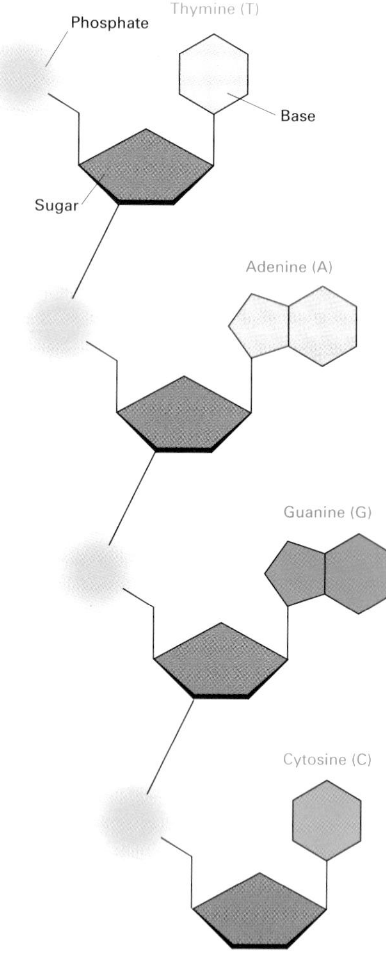

Nucleic acids are polymer chains consisting of phosphate groups alternating with sugar residues. Nitrogenous bases project from the sugar residues of the sugar–phosphate backbone.

Nucleic acids are the molecules responsible for storing information in a cell and for determining inherited characteristics in an organism. The structure of nucleic acids encodes the information necessary to synthesize all the proteins in an organism. The nucleic acid DNA controls inheritance as its structure is copied and passed on through successive generations. This spread introduces the fundamental structure of nucleic acids; the following two spreads discuss their function.

Outline structure

Nucleic acids are **polynucleotides** – they are polymer chains made up from repeating nucleotide units. A **nucleotide** consists of a phosphate group attached to a nucleoside; a **nucleoside** consists of a nitrogenous (nitrogen-containing) organic base attached to a sugar residue.

The sugar residues in DNA and RNA

There are two types of nucleic acid: **deoxyribonucleic acid (DNA)** and **ribonucleic acid (RNA)**. Both nucleic acids have the same general structure but contain different sugar residues. As the names imply, DNA contains deoxyribose and RNA contains ribose.

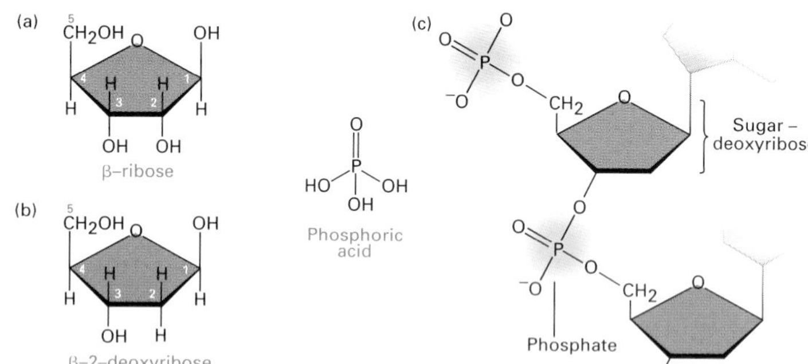

Ribose and deoxyribose. (a) Ribose normally exists as a five-membered ring; the base forms a β-glycosidic link with ribose and so the ring drawn has the systematic name β-ribose. (b) Deoxyribose has the same structure as ribose, with the exception that the hydroxyl group on carbon atom 2 is replaced by a hydrogen atom. Systematic name is β-2-deoxyribose. (c) Deoxyribose bonds to two phosphate groups by means of ester links involving the hydroxyl groups on carbon atoms 3 and 5 to form the sugar–phosphate backbone of DNA.

The nitrogenous bases

Each type of nucleic acid has *four* different nitrogenous bases. DNA contains **adenine** (A), **guanine** (G), **cytosine** (C), and **thymine** (T). RNA has adenine, guanine, cytosine, and **uracil** (U). Cytosine, thymine, and uracil belong to a class of compounds called the **pyrimidines**, whose structures are based on a single nitrogen-containing ring. Adenine and guanine are **purines**, based on two fused nitrogen-containing rings.

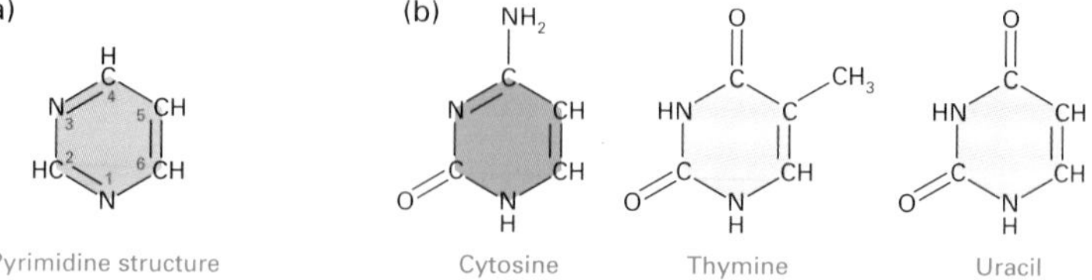

(a) Pyrimidine structure: in a nucleic acid, pyrimidines bond via the nitrogen atom at position 1 to carbon atom 1 on the sugar. (b) The chemical structures of the pyrimidines cytosine, thymine, and uracil.

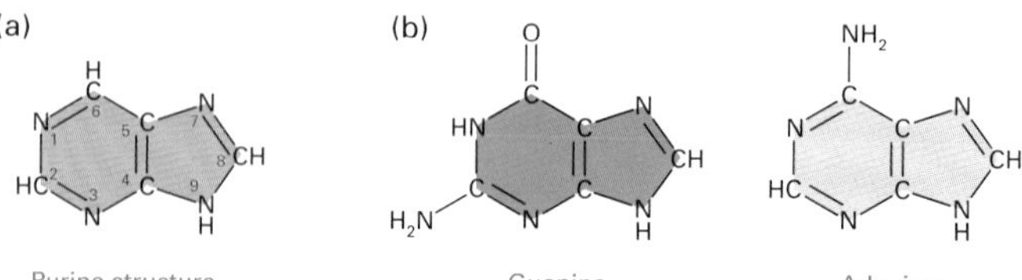

(a) Purine structure: in a nucleic acid, purines bond via the nitrogen atom at position 9 to carbon atom 1 on the sugar. (b) The chemical structures of the purines guanine and adenine.

Detailed chemical structure

As you will see in the following spread, the full structure of DNA involves *two* polynucleotide chains twisted together. The diagrams below show the structures of the single polynucleotide chains of RNA and DNA. The actual bases present in a portion of DNA depend on the function of that portion.

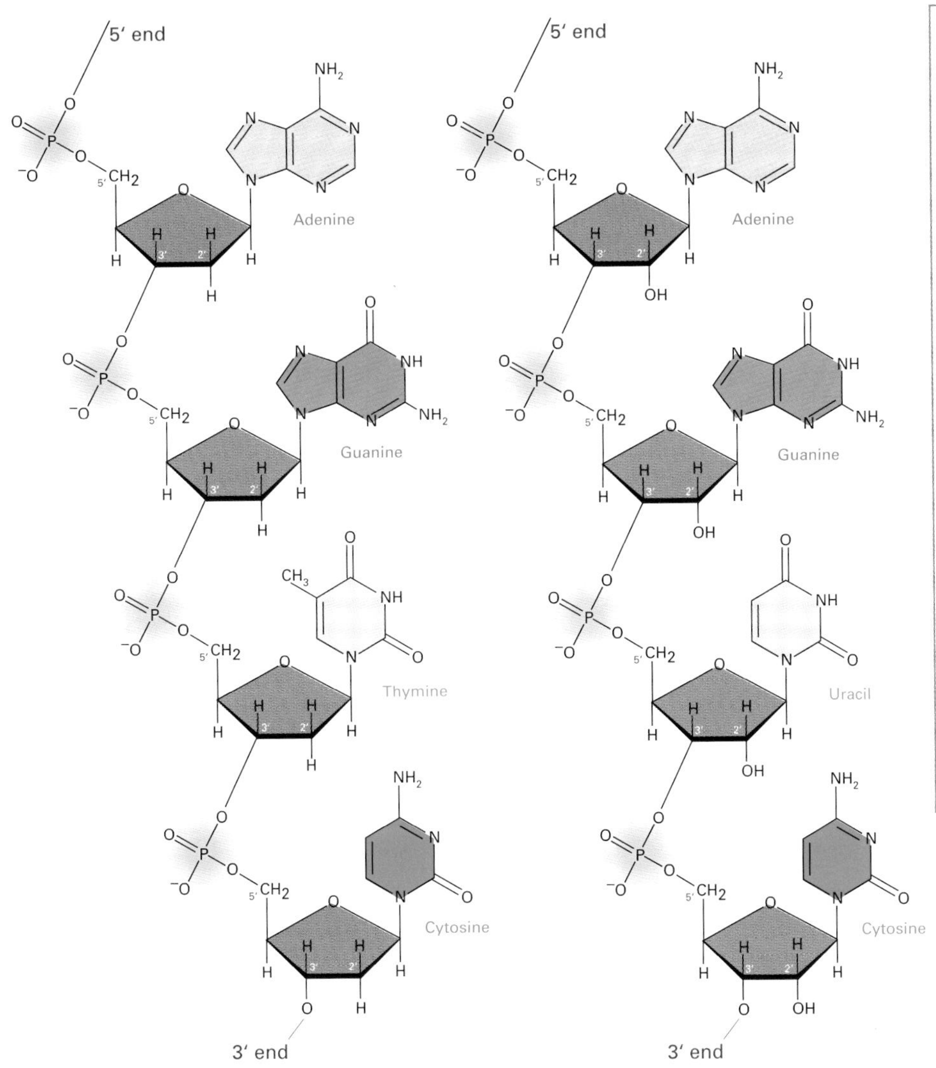

The chemical structures of the polynucleotides making up DNA (left) and RNA (right). The primes refer to positions in the sugar rings (numbers without primes refer to the position in the bases).

The unravelling of DNA

In 1950, the underlying control mechanism for life's processes was not understood. It *was* clear that lipids and carbohydrates were not sufficiently complex to be responsible. Most research workers, including Max Perutz at Cambridge (see spread 20.10), suspected that proteins held the key to life, as they obviously *did* have sufficient complexity.

In 1951, a young post-doctoral student, Jim Watson, asked to work in Perutz's group. Watson was a 'believer' that the molecules that control life are the nucleic acids. The next couple of years saw Watson successfully prove his hunch. He and Francis Crick were crucially aided by the diffraction photograph (shown on the next spread) taken by Rosalind Franklin. Watson and Crick came up with a structure for DNA which accounted in detail for the X-ray pattern. Immediately they had found the structure, they were able to suggest a mechanism for self-replication and hence explain genetic inheritance.

SUMMARY

- Nucleic acids have a backbone of alternating phosphate and sugar groups from which nitrogenous bases project.
- Nucleoside = nitrogenous base + sugar; nucleotide = nucleoside + phosphate.
- DNA (deoxyribonucleic acid) and RNA (ribonucleic acid) differ in the sugar residue that each contains.
- DNA contains the nitrogenous bases adenine, guanine, cytosine, and thymine. RNA contains uracil instead of thymine.

PRACTICE

1 Explain the difference between a nucleoside and a nucleotide.

2 Draw the structures of β-ribose and β-2-deoxyribose.

30.9

NUCLEIC ACIDS – 2

OBJECTIVES

- Complementary base pairing
- Double helix
- Replication

The nucleic acid DNA contains polynucleotide chains that consist of phosphate groups alternating with deoxyribose sugar residues bearing nitrogenous bases. The structures of these nitrogenous bases are absolutely fundamental to the functioning of the DNA molecule because they form hydrogen bonds with each other in a very specific manner. These hydrogen bonds hold *two* polynucleotide chains together to give DNA molecules their distinctive shape of a *double helix*.

Interactions between the bases

In DNA, the shapes of and partial charges on the molecules dictate that adenine can *only* hydrogen-bond effectively with thymine, and guanine can *only* hydrogen-bond with cytosine. This restriction is called **complementary base pairing**.

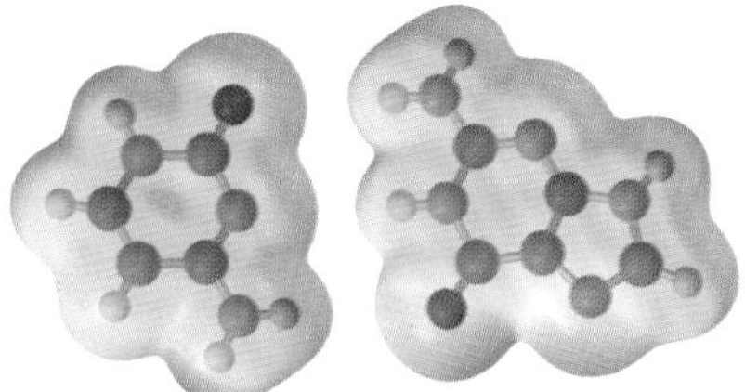

The electrostatic potential map of a cytosine–guanine pair showing how the complementary base pair hydrogen-bonds. The base pair thymine–adenine (T–A) forms only two hydrogen bonds, unlike the three hydrogen bonds formed by the C–G pair.

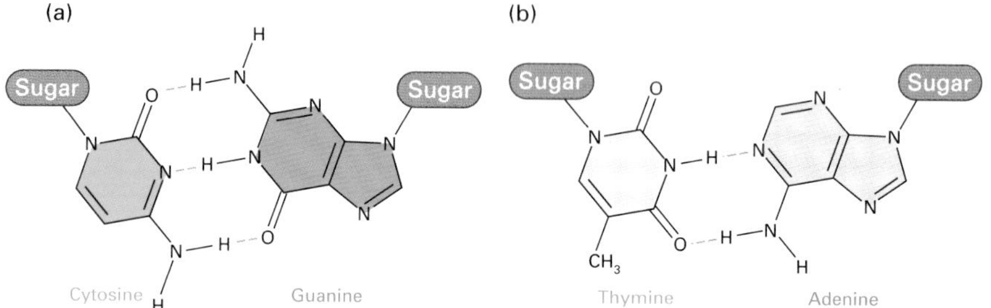

Specific hydrogen bonding between nitrogenous bases: (a) cytosine–guanine (three hydrogen bonds); and (b) thymine–adenine (two hydrogen bonds).

The chemical structure of DNA

DNA consists of two strands of polynucleotide chain held together by hydrogen bonds between complementary bases. The resulting structure of DNA is a double helix in which each strand spirals about the other. DNA can make exact copies of itself. This is how it passes on hereditary information to successive generations. Copies of DNA are made during cell division.

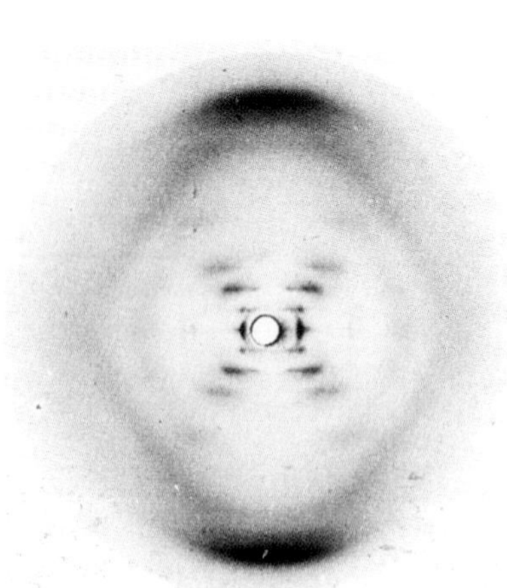

An X-ray diffraction photograph of crystalline DNA prepared by Rosalind Franklin in 1953. This is the photograph that provided Francis Crick and James Watson with the necessary information to deduce their Nobel prize-winning structure of DNA. The X-shaped pattern at the centre indicates the presence of a helix. The arcs at the top and bottom of the picture show that the structure repeats every 3.4 nm along the axis of the helix.

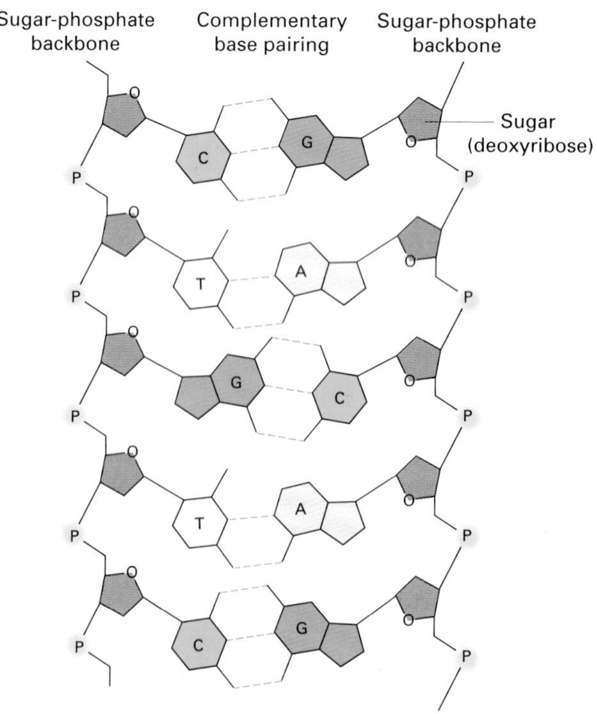

A DNA molecule consists of two polynucleotide chains held together by complementary base pairing. There are 10 base pairs per turn of the sugar–phosphate helix. On the opposite page, we show how the shape of the phosphate group and the carbon atom C5 outside the ring causes the bonds to successive bases (shown in red) to be twisted relative to each other by 36°, forming one of the two helical strands.

Replication

The complete **genetic code** of an organism is called its **genome**. Genetic information is stored in DNA in the sequence of base pairs along the polynucleotide chains. The DNA is packaged in structures called **chromosomes** in the nucleus of each cell. Each cell contains an identical copy of the genome, which carries all the information needed to determine the structure of the entire organism and to control the function of its cells. Sections of the code are switched 'on' or 'off' depending on the type and function of each specific cell. The key property that enables a nucleic acid molecule to perform its function is the ability to make exact copies of itself. This process is called **replication**.

Complementary base pairing allows replication to take place by a mechanism first proposed by Meselson and Stahl. In this mechanism, the double helix of DNA 'unzips', revealing unpaired bases. Free nucleotides present in the cell then pair with these bases and form a chain exactly like the original complementary chain. The mechanism is termed '**semi-conservative**'. This term indicates that the two daughter double-stranded DNA molecules each contain *one* of the parent strands.

In the following spread, you will see how the information stored in the structure of DNA is used to control protein synthesis within cells.

The Meselson and Stahl experiment

Matthew Meselson and Franklin Stahl grew the bacterium *E. coli* in a medium in which the only source of nitrogen was the heavy isotope ^{15}N. After several generations, the bacterial DNA was shown to contain only ^{15}N in its bases. These bacteria were then transferred to a medium containing ordinary ^{14}N. The bacteria were allowed to reproduce, and their DNA was analysed from generation to generation. It was noted that, after a single generation, the DNA was a hybrid of light and heavy forms. In subsequent generations, the light form gradually became dominant. These results were consistent with the semi-conservative mechanism.

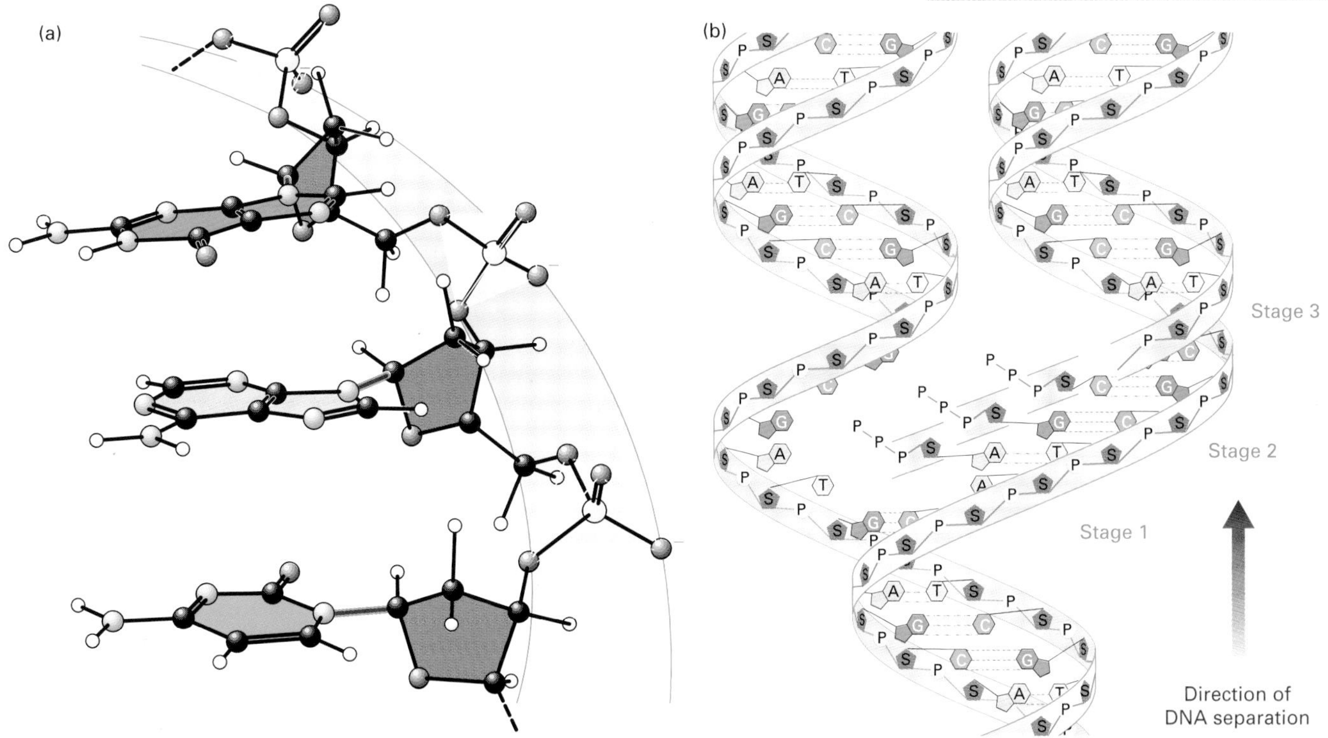

(a) An accurate represention of the three-dimensional structure, showing how the bases twist relative to each other. (b) An outline of DNA replication shown in three stages. Stage 1: The double helix of DNA uncoils and separates. Stage 2: Exposed bases act as a template, which selects complementary bases (as nucleoside triphosphates) from the surroundings. Stage 3: The nucleotides join in sequence to make a new strand of nucleic acid.

SUMMARY

- DNA consists of two polynucleotide chains that are held together by complementary base pairing.
- In complementary base pairing, adenine forms hydrogen bonds with thymine, and guanine with cytosine.
- The two polynucleotide chains in DNA are held in the shape of a double helix.
- DNA replicates by (a) breaking the hydrogen bonding between the complementary bases and then (b) using the two polynucleotide strands as templates: complementary bases (as nucleotides) join in sequence along each strand to form two identical strands of DNA.

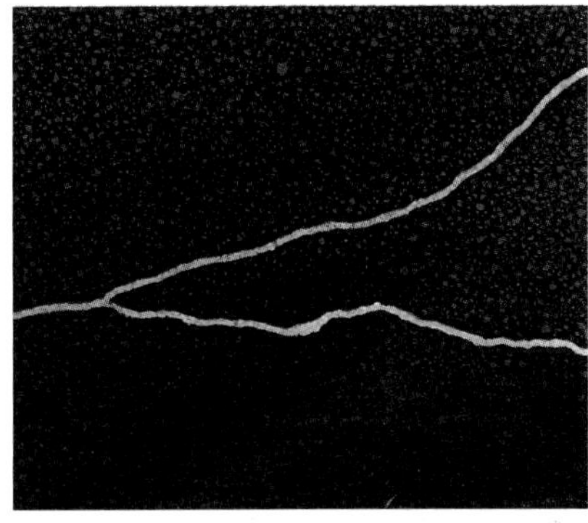

The double helix of DNA uncoils to produce two strands in this false-colour image.

30.10

NUCLEIC ACIDS – 3

OBJECTIVES

- Transcription into RNA
- Translation of RNA into protein
- Triplet code
- Protein synthesis
- Anti-viral drugs

A genetic disorder

Sickle-cell anaemia is a disease in which red blood cells are distorted and have a reduced ability to transport oxygen. In normal haemoglobin, the amino acid at position 6 in the β-polypeptide chain is glutamic acid. In sickle-cell anaemia, this amino acid is valine. This change in one amino acid has come about because of a faulty sequence of nucleotides in the section of DNA that codes for haemoglobin synthesis. This disease is hereditary: it can be passed from parents to their children. An *advantage* of this faulty sequence of nucleotides is that it protects carriers of sickle-cell anaemia from the worst effects of malaria, which is constantly present in the areas of Africa where sickle-cell anaemia is most common.

The previous two spreads discussed the structure of DNA. They also described the ability of DNA to make exact copies of itself and so pass on hereditary information. This spread looks at how the information is stored in a genetic code, and how that code is deciphered into instructions that control the synthesis of proteins. Remember that the architecture of an organism depends mainly on the presence of structural proteins; the metabolism of an organism is controlled by enzymes, which are also proteins. The form and function of all organisms depend on their proteins, which in turn depend on the message encoded in their DNA.

DNA and RNA

DNA is the molecule that carries the genetic code. It is located in the chromosomes contained in the nuclei of cells. RNA is the form into which the code is copied. RNA is transported out of the nucleus into the cytoplasm, where it controls the amino acid sequence during protein synthesis.

Messenger RNA

RNA is a single-stranded molecule that is formed by **transcription** from DNA. The DNA molecule 'unzips' to reveal its bases, as in replication. However, in transcription, it is free *ribo*nucleotides (and not *deoxyribo*nucleotides) that base-pair to it and form an RNA molecule. The RNA molecule thus formed, called **messenger RNA (mRNA)**, then moves out of the nucleus of the cell and attaches to another cell organelle called a ribosome. **Ribosomes** are the sites at which proteins are assembled, during a process called **translation**. RNA is responsible for deciphering the genetic code into protein.

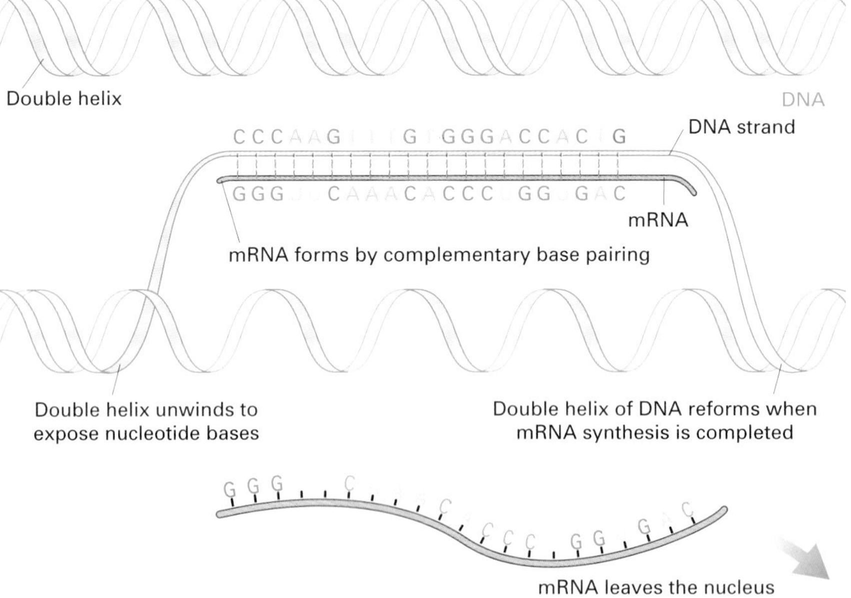

Double helix
DNA
DNA strand
mRNA
mRNA forms by complementary base pairing
Double helix unwinds to expose nucleotide bases
Double helix of DNA reforms when mRNA synthesis is completed
mRNA leaves the nucleus

Transcription. All body cells contain identical DNA (with the exception of sperm and ova, the cells that join together to form a new individual in reproduction). However, complex organisms such as humans contain cells that are specialized, arranged in tissues with differing functions. During transcription, the portion of DNA relevant to the function of that cell uncoils and acts as a template for the formation of a complementary chain of messenger RNA.

The triplet code

The primary structure of a protein consists of a chain of amino acids connected by peptide links. There are about 20 naturally occurring amino acids. The structure of DNA includes the four nitrogenous bases adenine, guanine, cytosine, and thymine. The code for each amino acid (called a **codon**) is a *sequence of three bases*.

There are 64 different *triplets* (sequences of three bases) that can be made up by the four bases. As a result, some amino acids are encoded by more than one codon. The codons for some amino acids are given on the right. Of the 64 codons, 61 code for amino acids and 3 act as 'stop' signals that switch off the protein synthesis when the end of the polypeptide chain has been reached.

Amino acid	Codons
Alanine	GCU, GCC, GCA, GCG
Arginine	AGA, AGG, CGU, CGC, CGA, CGG
Glutamine	GAA, GAG
Glycine	GGU, GGC, GGA, GGG
Histidine	CAU, CAC
Lysine	AAA, AAG
Phenylalanine	UUU, UUC
Proline	CCU, CCC, CCA, CCG

The codons in mRNA that code for a few amino acids.

Transfer RNA, messenger RNA, and protein synthesis

Protein synthesis takes place at ribosomes located in the cytoplasm. One end of a messenger RNA molecule attaches to a ribosome, which moves along it three bases at a time. Molecules of another type of RNA, called **transfer RNA (tRNA)**, bind to free amino acids in the cytoplasm. Transfer RNA molecules each carry a specific amino acid. They also each have their own base triplet, and this binds to the complementary triplet on the messenger RNA. In this way the messenger RNA determines the order of amino acids. Peptide links form between adjacent amino acids, and the protein chain steadily grows. The illustration below summarizes the process of protein synthesis.

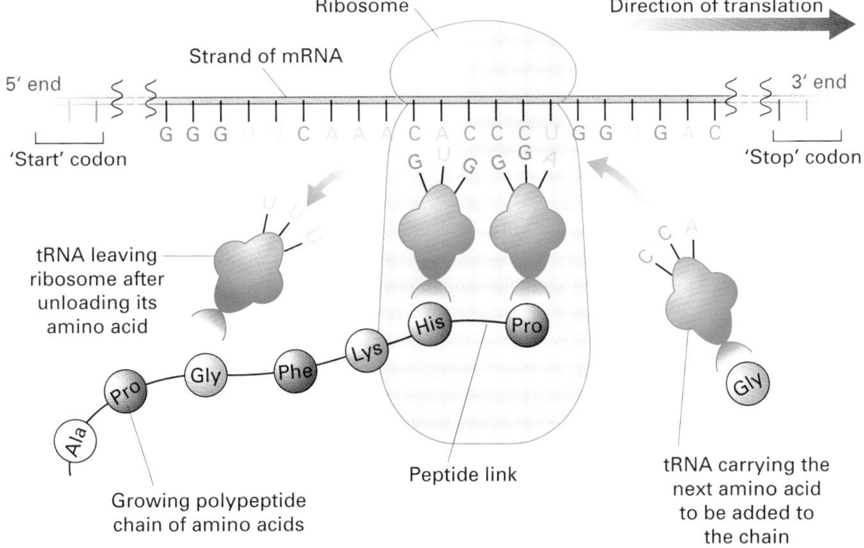

Protein synthesis taking place at a ribosome.

SUMMARY

- The genetic code for each amino acid carried on DNA and messenger RNA is a sequence of three bases – a codon.
- Transcription of DNA forms messenger RNA.
- Translation of the code on messenger RNA results in protein synthesis, which takes place at the ribosomes.

Viruses and anti-viral drugs

Bacteria are microscopic organisms. Some bacteria reproduce in the body and cause disease, for example by producing toxins (e.g. typhoid fever, Salmonella 'food poisoning'). Antibiotics are drugs that act against bacteria by disrupting their life processes. Viruses are thousands of times smaller than bacteria, and consist mainly of nucleic acid inside a protein coat. Viruses cause diseases such as the common cold and chickenpox. They inject DNA or RNA into a human (or other host) cell. This viral nucleic acid then overrides the normal function of the cell and instructs it to make more virus particles. The cell ultimately bursts and releases thousands of new viruses, which invade more host cells. Outside host cells, viruses are completely inert; unlike bacteria, viruses do not have life processes or an internal metabolism, and are therefore not affected by antibiotics. A recently developed range of anti-viral drugs are based on the acyclovir molecule. Acyclovir closely resembles the structure of guanine plus ribose, lacking part of the ring and most importantly one of the two hydroxyl groups used to make the polynucleotide chain. A virus incorporating acyclovir cannot continue to build a chain and dies.

PRACTICE

1 Explain the meaning of each of the following terms:
   a Genome
   b Replication
   c Complementary base pairing
   d Nucleic acid.

2 Explain the differences between:
   a A nucleoside and a nucleotide
   b RNA and DNA
   c The functions of transfer RNA and messenger RNA
   d The processes of transcription and replication.

3 Explain why adenine pairs with thymine across the two nucleic acid strands in DNA, whereas adenine and guanine do not pair.

4 Write down the amino acid sequence for the peptide corresponding to the following set of DNA codons:
TTC/CGA/CCC/AAG

30.11

OBJECTIVES

- Anabolism and catabolism
- Photosynthesis
- Glycolysis
- Krebs cycle

Metabolism

Metabolism is the term that refers to the sum total of all the chemical reactions taking place within an organism. There are two broad categories of chemical reactions: **catabolism** refers to any process in which substances are broken down; **anabolism** refers to processes that build up molecules. The catabolic and anabolic processes together make up an organism's metabolism. Reactions usually take place in a series of steps called a **metabolic pathway.** A major concern of any organism is the supply and handling of energy resources. The concluding spread of this chapter considers some of the metabolic pathways associated with this highly important function.

Photosynthesis

It was shown in Chapter 14 that, for a reaction to be spontaneous, the standard Gibbs energy change $\Delta G^{\ominus}$ must be negative. Biochemists call such a reaction **exergonic**. Anabolism involves reactions which are endergonic, for which $\Delta G^{\ominus}$ is positive. These reactions can only occur if Gibbs energy is supplied by coupling them so that an endergonic reaction is 'driven' by an exergonic one.

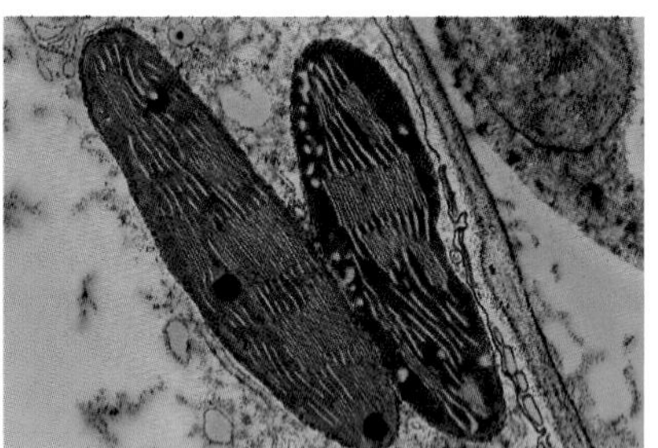

Coloured transmission electron micrograph of two chloroplasts seen in the leaf of a pea plant Pisum sativum.

The process of photosynthesis is fundamental to life on Earth because it harnesses the energy of the Sun to drive an endergonic process. This metabolic pathway starts in small green organelles called **chloroplasts** in the cells of plants. Overall:

$$6CO_2 + 6H_2O \rightarrow C_6H_{12}O_6 + 6O_2$$

This simple equation represents two very complex processes: splitting water to produce oxygen and fixing carbon dioxide to produce sugars.

The splitting of water is called the *light reaction* because it requires the energy of sunlight. The first reaction of photosynthesis is the absorption of light by the green pigment **chlorophyll** which is a complex of magnesium. Activation of chlorophyll by light provides the energy required to synthesize the reductant NADPH.

$$NADP^+ + H_2O \xrightarrow{\text{light/chlorophyll}} NADPH + H^+ + \tfrac{1}{2}O_2$$

The *dark reaction* fixes carbon dioxide to form a series of more-complex organic molecules such as sugars.

Respiration

A major catabolic process is respiration. **Respiration** takes place inside the cells, the net effect being the oxidation of glucose to carbon dioxide and water:

$$C_6H_{12}O_6 + 6O_2 \rightarrow 6CO_2 + 6H_2O$$

This equation is the same as the one written for the burning of glucose in oxygen when the energy released by the reaction appears as heat.

Glycolysis

The first stage of respiration is called **glycolysis** which means 'glucose-splitting'. Glycolysis occurs in the cytoplasm of the cell. The six-carbon molecule of glucose is converted into two three-carbon molecules of **pyruvate** $CH_3COCO_2^-$. The pyruvate is then combined with a very important coenzyme (spread 30.7) called coenzyme A to form **acetyl coenzyme A** (acetyl CoA).

Acetyl coenzyme A holds a key position in metabolism. It is the product not only of the oxidation of carbohydrate by glycolysis, but also of the oxidation of fatty acids and glycerol obtained from the digestion of fats. The metabolic uses of carbohydrate, lipid, and protein from the diet therefore all converge on acetyl CoA as a common intermediate. Acetyl CoA, from whatever source, then enters the Krebs cycle where it is catabolized to carbon dioxide and water in a cyclic series of reactions.

Krebs cycle

The Krebs cycle, discovered by Hans Krebs, is simplified by counting the number of carbon atoms involved at each stage. Two carbon atoms come into the cycle at stage ① ; one carbon atom leaves the cycle at stage ③ and another leaves at stage ④.

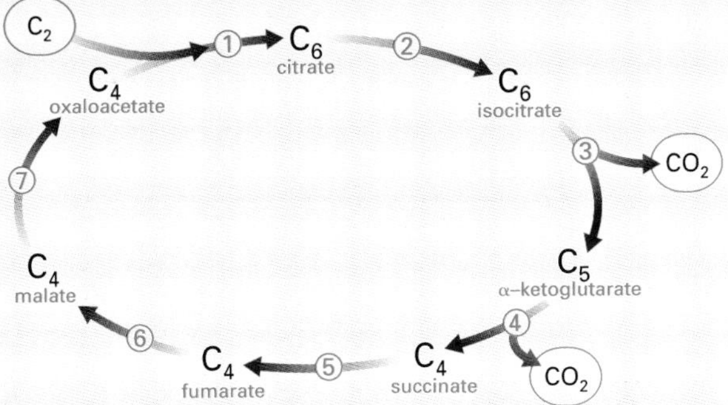

The Krebs cycle

① Incorporation of the two carbon atoms

This stage is the most unfamiliar, involving the addition of acetyl coenzyme A ($CH_3COSCoA$) across the carbonyl bond, followed by hydrolysis

Oxaloacetate $\xrightarrow{CH_3COSCoA}$ $HO-C(CO_2^-)(CH_2COSCoA)(CH_2CO_2^-)$ $\xrightarrow{+H_2O,\ -HSCoA,\ -H^+}$ Citrate

② Isomerization

This stage occurs by dehydration followed by hydration, with the oxygen attaching to the carbon on the opposite side of the double bond.

Citrate $\xrightarrow{-H_2O}$ $(CO_2^-CH_2)(CO_2^-)C=C(H)(CO_2^-)$ $\xrightarrow{+H_2O}$ Isocitrate

③ Oxidative decarboxylation

This stage occurs by oxidation (loss of hydrogen atoms) followed by loss of carbon dioxide.

Isocitrate $\xrightarrow{NAD^+ \rightarrow NADH + H^+}$ $CO_2^-CH_2-CH(CO_2^-)-C(=O)CO_2^-$ $\xrightarrow{-CO_2,\ +H^+}$ α–ketoglutarate

④ Oxidative decarboxylation

This stage is the most complex, despite the simple change to the molecule and involves a complex of enzymes. It is specifically the carboxyl group attached to the carbonyl that is lost. The resulting succinate molecule is symmetrical. Up to this point the acetyl group is intact: in succinate the distinguishing green colour is absent.

α–ketoglutarate $\xrightarrow{NAD^+ + H_2O \rightarrow NADH + H^+ + CO_2}$ Succinate

⑤ Oxidation

This stage involves oxidation (loss of hydrogen atoms).

Succinate $\xrightarrow{FAD \rightarrow FADH_2}$ Fumarate

⑥ Hydration

This stage involves hydration of a double bond: as the molecule is symmetrical, it does not matter which carbon is attacked.

Fumarate $\xrightarrow{+H_2O}$ Malate

⑦ Oxidation

This stage involves oxidation (loss of hydrogen atoms).

Malate $\xrightarrow{NAD^+ \rightarrow NADH + H^+}$ Oxaloacetate

SUMMARY

- The processes that break down molecules are called catabolic.
- The processes that build up molecules are called anabolic.

PRACTICE EXAM QUESTIONS

1 a The graphical formulae of alanine and glycine, two important amino acids, are given in the figure below.

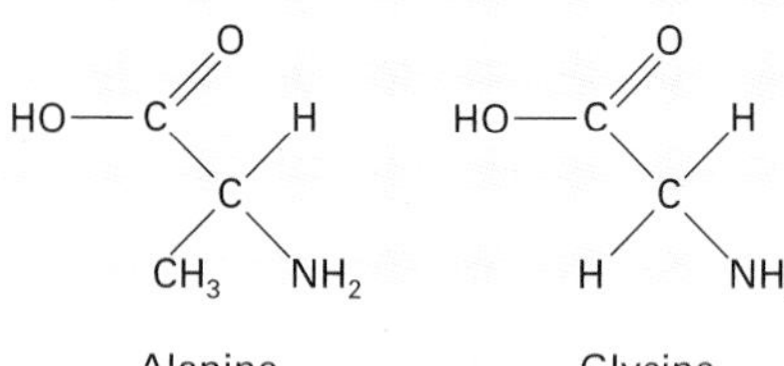

i State, with a reason, which of these two amino acids can exist as optical isomers. [2]

ii Show the formation of a peptide link between these two amino acids. [2]

b Outline the procedure for determining the primary structure of a peptide. [4]

c Suggest two reasons why fluothane, $CF_3CHBrCl$, replaced ether, $C_2H_5OC_2H_5$, as an anaesthetic in the 1950s. [2]

d Chlorofluorocarbons have found widespread use as refrigerants, aerosol propellants, and foam producers. Recently they have been replaced by other compounds, and their manufacture has been restricted.

i Why did chlorofluorocarbons find widespread use as aerosol propellants? [2]

ii Explain the dangers to the environment of chlorofluorocarbons. [3]
AQA (AEB) 1997

2 Diagrams **A**, **B**, **C** and **D** represent carbohydrates.

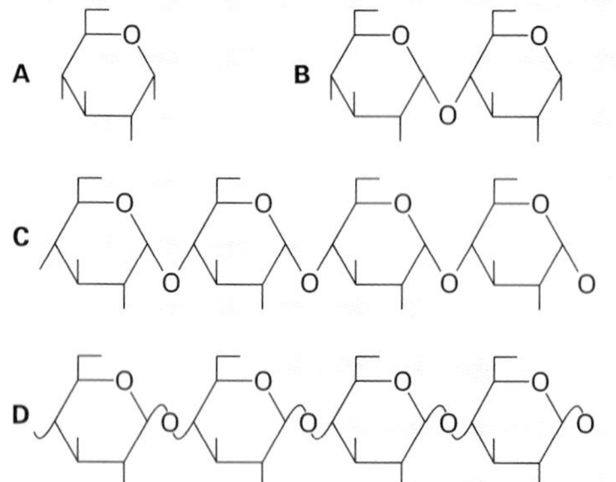

a Name and draw a displayed formula for the molecule drawn as **A**. [1]

b **B** can be converted into **A**.

i Write a molecular equation for the conversion of **B** into **A** and state what type of reaction it is.

ii Two different methods can be used for this conversion. For each, state the reagents used and the conditions necessary. [5]

c Explain the structural differences between **C** and **D** and the consequent roles that each has in nature. [4]
OCR (UCLES) 1998

3 The base pairing in DNA is A ... T and G ... C.

The base pairing in RNA is A ... U and G ... C.

a Draw a block diagram of the double helix of DNA, showing three repeat units. [2]

b Explain how DNA both replicates itself and also leads to the formation of RNA. [4]

c A sequence of bases in one strand of DNA is

– T – G – G – A – C – T – A – A – C –

State the corresponding base sequence in

i the complementary strand of DNA,

ii the RNA derived from this complementary strand of DNA. [2]

d There are about 3×10^9 base pairs in one strand of human DNA. About 10^5 sections of the DNA strand are involved in protein synthesis and, on average, 10^3 base pairs are required for each protein.

What percentage of the DNA strand is involved in protein synthesis? [2]
OCR (UCLES) 1998

4 Integral proteins and bilayers are important components in cell membranes.

a What is the function of integral proteins in membranes? Explain why the bilayers cannot perform this function.

A research team in California has synthesized 'molecular channels' which have uniform diameters of only a few nanometres. These molecular channels are called nanotubes and could be used to inject drug molecules or metal ions into malignant cells or into bacteria. Nanotubes are made from rings of cyclic peptides stacked on top of each other. Alternate rings consist of natural amino acids and synthetic amino acids which have the opposite optical activity. The nanotubes form when rings of cyclic peptides stack up from a solution. [1 nanometre = 10^{-9} metres]

b Draw a displayed formula for a cyclic tripeptide, using R to represent the side chain of each amino acid. Label the chiral atoms of the ring with an asterisk(*). [4]

c i Suggest how nanotubes of differing diameters can be made.

ii Suggest how the surface characteristics of the nanotubes might be varied for use in different cell walls. [2]
OCR (UCLES) 1998

5 Recent techniques have allowed DNA from various sources to be broken down by enzymes (called restriction endonucleases). These enzymes cut DNA molecules at specific places in the sequence of base pairs.

The various fragments that result from the enzyme action are separated by gel electrophoresis carried out in a buffer of pH 7 and constant potential difference.

a Describe, using a block diagram, the structure of the nucleotides which make up nucleic acids. State briefly how these are arranged in DNA. [4]

b Describe how the enzyme functions in this example and state what sort of reaction occurs. [2]

c Explain, in terms of the structure of the nucleotide, why the DNA fragments move towards the positive electrode in the electrophoresis separation. [2]
OCR (UCLES) 1994

6 **a** Explain what enzymes are and how they function in biochemical processes. [5]

b Several deaths occur each year by poisoning due to the accidental swallowing of ethane-1,2-diol (glycol) which is widely used as a solvent or as anti-freeze for car radiators. The glycol is oxidized in the body to ethanedioic acid (oxalic acid) which is poisonous.

If the patient can be treated quickly enough, large doses of brandy (which contains a high percentage of ethanol) are given.

Explain how the ethanol from the brandy acts as a competitive inhibitor and how its action suppresses the oxalic acid poisoning. Include in your answer the formulae of the organic substances involved. [5]
OCR (UCLES) 1995

7 **a** Plant material is composed largely of carbohydrates, an important constituent of the human diet.

Explain why some plants, e.g. potatoes, may be utilized as a source of energy whereas others, e.g. cabbage, provide mainly roughage. [4]

b During jam-making, fruit is boiled with sugar solution.

Some jam was added to water and warmed: the resulting mixture was filtered. A sample of the resulting solution gave a red-brown precipitate on treatment with alkaline Cu^{2+} ions and warming. A sample of the original fruit/sugar mixture gave no reaction before boiling but, after acidification, the resulting solution also produced a red-brown precipitate on warming with alkaline Cu^{2+} ions.

Suggest the possible identities of the two sugars present in the jam. Explain your reasoning. [4]

c Suggest why frozen vegetables may have a higher nutritional value then so-called 'fresh vegetables'. [2]
OCR (UCLES) 1995

8 **a** Describe the β-pleated sheet structure of the protein which constitutes the main material of meat. Your answer should include a suitable diagram, which also shows the bonding between the strands. [5]

b **i** What is the function of haemoglobin and of myoglobin in the living animal?

ii Explain why unwrapped minced beef for sale at a meat counter is bright red, whereas a slice of raw beef cut from the centre of a joint may be purplish-red.

iii Uncooked minced beef, prepacked in supermarket displays, is wrapped in a plastic film which is permeable to air. Explain why air is allowed to reach the meat. [5]
OCR (UCLES) 1998

9 The major components of membranes are phospholipids and proteins. The phospholipids form a bilayer which is interspersed with protein molecules. Transport proteins extend across the membranes and catalyse the transport of specific molecules and ions into and out of the cell. Transport can be passive or active.

a Give the full structural formula of a typical phospholipid. Describe the nature of the different parts of a phospholipid. (If you are unable to draw a structural formula, marks can be scored by a simple labelled diagram of a phospholipid.) [3]

b Explain, using your answer to **a**, how bilayers are constructed. State the nature of the chemical attractions at each end of a phospholipid. [3]

c Explain what is meant by active transport. Describe briefly one common example of active transport. [4]
OCR (UCLES) 1994

10 What is meant by each of the terms *primary, secondary, tertiary* and *quaternary* as applied to the structure of proteins? Where possible, illustrate your answer with examples of the chemical bonding involved in each structure. [10]
OCR (UCLES) 1994

11 **a** 'Terylene' is a polymer derived from benzene-1,4-dicarboxylic acid and ethane-1,2-diol.

i Draw graphical formulae to represent benzene-1,4-dicarboxylic acid and ethane-1,2-diol. [2]

ii What type of polymer is 'Terylene' ? [1]

iii Draw the structure of the repeat unit of this polymer. [2]

b **i** Explain the term *biodegradable*. [1]

ii State **one** environmental benefit of using biodegradable plastics. [1]

c Starch is an important constituent in foodstuffs. It can be hydrolysed by boiling with mineral acid in a test tube.

i Give the name of a source of starch. [1]

ii What is the product of the hydrolysis of starch? [2]

d **i** Amylase is an enzyme that brings about the same hydrolysis in the body. Suggest why amylase cannot be substituted for the mineral acid in the procedure described in **c**. [2]

ii Suggest the pH environment within which amylase can function best as a catalyst. [1]
AQA (AEB) 1996

Techniques of preparation, separation, and identification

It is often easy to overlook the fact that chemistry is a practical subject. Much current information about the properties of elements and their compounds is the result of careful experimentation and observation. The early chemists used primitive apparatus and had few measuring instruments. Modern apparatus is much more convenient to use, and instruments are available today that can probe to the heart of a molecular structure. This chapter looks at some of the practical techniques used to investigate molecules. The first spread discusses some of the techniques you can use to prepare and separate a pure sample of a substance of interest. The rest of this chapter describes three important techniques for identifying substances – electrophoresis, chromatography, and mass spectrometry.

USING SIMPLE APPARATUS

31.1

OBJECTIVES

- 'Quickfit' and distillation
- Separatory funnels
- Solvent extraction
- Buchner funnel
- Recrystallization

Distillation and condensers

- Heating 'under reflux' – see chapter on 'Alcohols' (spread 25.4 on 'Oxidation of alcohols').
- Fractional distillation – see chapter on 'Alkanes and alkenes' (spread 22.1 on 'The oil industry: fractionation').
- Steam distillation – see chapter on 'Amines and amino acids' (spread 28.3 on 'Aromatic amines').

Purifying a liquid product

A liquid product is first dried by leaving it in contact with a small quantity of a substance that absorbs water, such as anhydrous sodium sulphate, for about 30 minutes. The final purification of a liquid product involves redistilling it and collecting the fraction that emerges from the condenser very close to the boiling point of the product (typically ±2 °C).

You should be familiar with carrying out chemical reactions in test tubes where your concern is to observe accurately the reaction taking place and make a record of the results. In preparative chemistry, the object is to make something safely, to obtain a good yield, and to make the sample pure enough for its intended use. 'Test tube' chemistry in the laboratory will rarely achieve these aims, and is certainly not suitable for industrial preparations. The most convenient apparatus for small-scale laboratory and industrial preparations is glass apparatus known as Quickfit™, which is made from borosilicate glass and has standard-size ground glass joints, so that different pieces of equipment can be fitted together easily.

Condensers

The function of a condenser is to provide a cool surface on which vapours produced in a reaction may condense. An air condenser relies on the surrounding air to cool the vapour inside. You will more commonly use a Leibig condenser, in which tap water passes through an outer jacket to make the inner surface colder.

Separatory funnels

Once a reaction has been completed, the product must be separated from the reaction mixture. If an organic product is a liquid, a separatory funnel (traditionally called a 'separating funnel') can be used, for example, to wash out excess acid. This technique relies on the organic product and the aqueous phase used for washing being immiscible.

Using a separatory funnel.
(a) With the stopper out to allow the escape of any evolved gases, initially mix the liquids by gentle swirling. This step is particularly important when washing with a carbonate to remove excess acid.
(b) Now give the funnel about 20 vigorous shakes, pausing half way to allow any gases to escape.
(c) Support the funnel while the contents settle and two layers form. One layer is the organic product and the other is the aqueous washing solution. Pour off the lower layer, but always keep both liquids until the organic product has been isolated. Even experienced chemists sometimes discard the wrong layer!

Solvent extraction

If the organic product is more soluble in an organic solvent than it is in water, a technique called solvent extraction can be used to separate the product from its aqueous solution. Under these conditions, the dissolved substance (the solute) becomes unequally distributed between the two solvents. It is **partitioned** between the two solvents.

The two liquids are shaken together in a separatory funnel, and the solute dissolves preferentially in the organic layer. The layers are separated and the solute is recovered by evaporation of the organic solvent.

During the manufacture of penicillin, the product is extracted from its aqueous solution using solvent extraction by trichloromethane. Evaporation of the highly volatile trichloromethane gives pure crystalline penicillin. The large-scale manufacture of penicillin was developed by Norman Heatley, who was awarded the first ever honorary Doctorate in Medicine from Oxford University.

The apparatus for vacuum filtration: a Buchner flask fitted with a Buchner funnel.

Filtration under reduced pressure

Evaporating the solvent from a solution will make the solution more concentrated. A small quantity of solid crystallizes when the solubility of the solid is exceeded. More solid appears as the volume of the solution decreases further. The solvent will also be able to dissolve many of the impurities produced in the reaction along with the desired product. It is therefore not wise to evaporate *all* of the solvent. Evaporation is usually carried out until there is a suspension of the solid product in a small volume of its saturated solution.

Filtration under reduced pressure is the quickest method of separating the solid from its suspension. The apparatus includes a Buchner funnel: the Buchner flask has thick walls to withstand the partial vacuum and a side-arm for attaching a pump to suck the air out. The mixture of crude product is poured gently onto the centre of the filter paper. The partial vacuum in the flask results in rapid filtration.

The ideal solvent

The ideal solvent for recrystallization should:

- not react with the compound;
- have a boiling point lower than the melting point of the compound to be recrystallized;
- be non-toxic and non-flammable.

Above all, the solid product should be very soluble in the hot solvent and *much* less soluble in it when cold.

Recrystallization

A solid product can be purified by recrystallization. The impure solid is dissolved in the minimum volume of a hot solvent and filtered to remove insoluble impurities. The resulting hot, saturated solution of the product, together with any soluble impurities, is then allowed to cool *slowly*, whereupon crystals of pure compound will separate from the solution. These can be filtered out of the solution. The impurities have a much lower concentration and so remain in solution. The crystals of product are tested for purity by melting-point determination (see box).

Lead(II) iodide, recrystallized from hot acidic solution, forms yellow crystals which give an appearance of spangles to the suspension.

SUMMARY

- A condenser provides a cold surface on which vapours may condense.
- Condensers are used for reflux and for distillation.
- A separatory funnel is used for separating immiscible liquids, generally during a purification process involving washing with an aqueous solution.
- Solvent extraction separates an organic product from an aqueous solution.
- Solid products are separated from suspensions in liquids by filtration under reduced pressure.
- Solid products are purified by recrystallization.
- The purity of a solid is checked by melting-point determination.

Melting-point determination

A pure substance will have a *sharp* melting point: it does not melt slowly over a range of temperature (as does an impure substance).

31.2

ELECTROPHORESIS

OBJECTIVES

- Electrophoresis
- PAGE
- Isoelectric point
- DNA 'fingerprints'

Electrophoresis is a method of separation and identification that separates molecules based on how easily they form ions. The ions migrate in a buffered solution under the influence of an applied electric field. The electric field causes positive ions to move towards the cathode and negative ions to move towards the anode. The different ions in a mixture migrate at different rates, and so can be separated. Electrophoresis is particularly useful for separating molecules of high molar mass such as proteins and nucleic acids.

(a) $R-C(H)(NH_3^+)-COOH$

(b) $R-C(H)(NH_2)-CO_2^-$

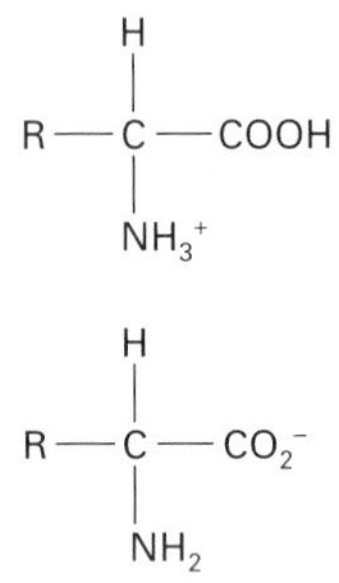

Amino acid structure at (a) low pH and (b) high pH.

Amino acids and pH

Protein structure is discussed in the previous chapter. Proteins consist of chains of amino acids bonded together by peptide links. As shown to the left, an amino acid contains a carbon atom bonded to an amine group, a carboxylic acid group, and an R group. The R groups are different for different amino acids, and may themselves contain groups that can ionize. The overall charge on a protein depends on the balance of these ionizable groups at a particular pH.

At low pH, amine groups $—NH_2$ are protonated to form $—NH_3^+$, but carboxyl groups are not ionized. The result is a net positive charge. Conversely, at high pH, amine groups are not protonated, but carboxyl groups —COOH are ionized to form $—CO_2^-$. The result is a net negative charge. At pH values between these extremes, the balance of protonation and ionization depends on the particular pK_a values of the R groups.

Polyacrylamide gel electrophoresis

The medium on which electrophoresis is carried out is commonly a **polyacrylamide gel**. This form of the technique is known as **PAGE**, which stands for **p**oly**a**crylamide **g**el **e**lectrophoresis. A gel is a network of polymer molecules with a random structure. The aqueous solution moves through the spaces, or pores, within the network of the gel. Gels of different pore sizes are available for separating molecules of different sizes. The gel acts as a sort of sieve; molecules larger than the average pore size are held back, whereas molecules smaller than the average pore size move through more quickly.

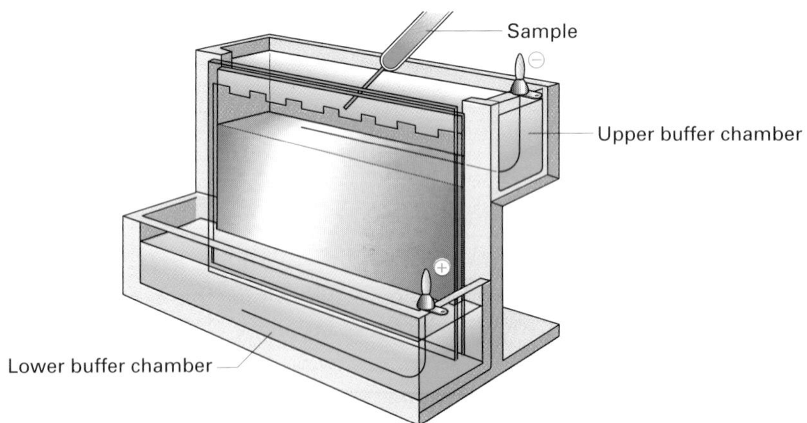

A PAGE cell. Samples are applied in slots in the top of the gel.

The mixture under examination is placed on the centreline of the gel plate. Ions travel towards the anode or the cathode depending on their charge and at speeds depending on their size. Once separation has been achieved, the gel is stained to reveal the individual constituents. A commonly used staining reagent is ninhydrin, which is available in aerosol canisters. On spraying and heating, amino acids and proteins show up as a blue-purple stain. Alternatively, sometimes the components fluoresce under ultraviolet light: in this case a permanent copy is obtained by blotting with radiographic paper. A typical example is shown opposite.

The isoelectric point

At one particular pH, a protein will have no net charge because it contains an equal number of positively and negatively charged groups. This pH is called the **isoelectric point** of the protein, and its characteristic value, found by electrophoresis, may be used to identify the protein. Electrophoresis can also be used to *separate* proteins, because at any given pH the speed with which a protein migrates depends on its particular net charge. Different proteins will travel at different rates through the gel.

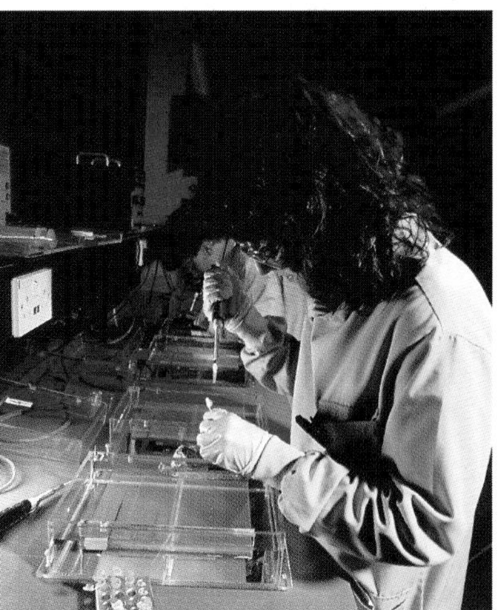

DNA fingerprinting. Preparation of the agarose electrophoresis gel used to separate fragments of DNA into bands.

Genetic fingerprinting

One of the major modern uses of electrophoresis is in separating the components of DNA in the technique of **DNA fingerprinting**.

The DNA of one person is different from the DNA of any other person. The pattern produced by the electrophoresis of DNA taken from a tissue sample can be used to identify the individual from whom the tissue came, just as a fingerprint can be used to identify a particular person. The sample can be extremely small: a smear of blood, the root of a hair, or a flake of skin is enough.

The technique depends on a group of enzymes known as restriction endonucleases. These enzymes act as a sort of 'molecular scissors' that break up a chain of DNA in a predictable way. DNA is extracted from a sample of tissue and is then treated with restriction endonucleases. Electrophoresis of the resulting fragments of DNA gives a pattern unlike that from any other individual except an identical twin. This pattern can therefore be used to identify an individual from tissue inadvertently left at the scene of a crime. Also, common features between the DNA fingerprints of two people can be used to establish hereditary relationships including, for example, the paternity of a child.

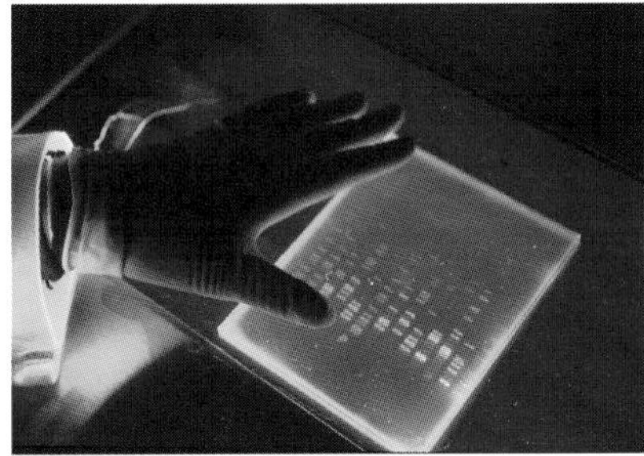

An electrophoresis gel fluorescing to reveal the components of the original mixture. The positions of the constituents are noted. The constituents may be isolated by cutting up the gel and washing each section.

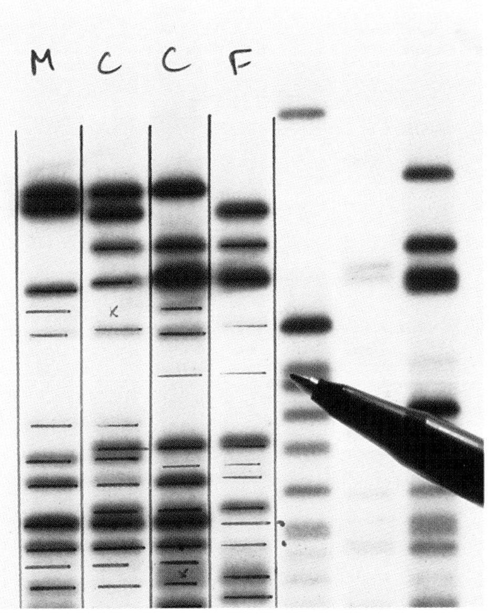

DNA fingerprints of two children (C). Red matches bands common with their mother (M); blue matches bands common with their father (F).

SUMMARY

- Electrophoresis depends on the migration of ions in a buffered solution under the influence of an electric field.
- Electrophoresis is used for separating large molecules such as proteins, nucleic acids, and their breakdown products.
- The isoelectric point is the pH at which a protein has no net charge.
- Electrophoresis may be used for both identification and separation.

PRACTICE

1 Explain why the amino acid glycine NH_2CH_2COOH migrates towards the anode at high pH and towards the cathode at low pH.

2 Would you expect the isoelectric point for the amino acid aspartic acid $HOOCCH_2CH(NH_2)COOH$ to be greater or less than 7? Explain your answer.

31.3

OBJECTIVES

- General principles
- Paper chromatography
- TLC
- Column chromatography

CHROMATOGRAPHY – 1

Filtration, distillation, and solvent extraction are all useful techniques to separate a significant quantity of product. Chromatography can be used to separate complex mixtures containing very *small* quantities of different substances. There are many different types of chromatography, but in each case there are two phases: a **mobile phase** that moves and a **stationary phase** that stays still. The different components of the mixture become *partitioned* (see first spread in this chapter) or *adsorbed* to different extents between the two phases.

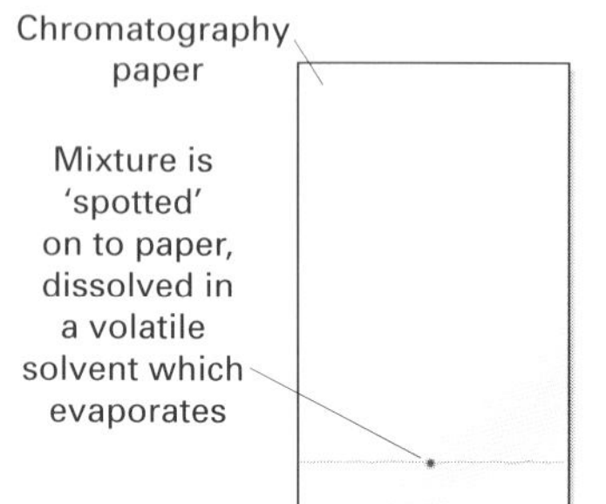

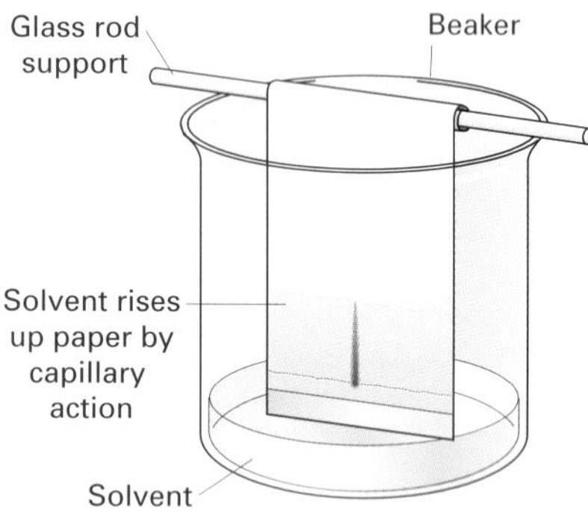

Chromatography paper is a thick absorbent paper rather like filter paper. (a) The mixture to be separated is applied as a spot a short distance from one end of the paper. (b) The end below the spot is dipped into the solvent. Each component of the mixture is carried a different distance by the moving solvent. When the solvent nears the top, the level the solvent has reached is marked on the paper, which is removed from the solvent and dried. The separate components may be directly visible, or are made visible either by staining or by fluorescing under a UV lamp.

Paper chromatography

A sheet of paper consists largely of cellulose fibres. Cellulose is a polysaccharide (see previous chapter) composed of glucose molecules, which have a large number of hydroxyl groups. Water molecules hydrogen-bond to these groups, so that a sheet of 'dry' paper contains around 10% by mass of water. This water acts as the stationary phase in the technique of paper chromatography. The mobile phase is a solvent consisting of an aqueous solution or an organic solvent such as ethanol or ethanoic acid. The mixture to be separated is dissolved in this mobile phase, which moves along the paper. The movement comes about by capillary action, which results from the forces between the solvent and the solid fibres of the paper.

Thin-layer chromatography

Thin-layer chromatography (**TLC**) is a technique similar to paper chromatography. The stationary phase is a solid; the mobile phase is a liquid. TLC uses a thin layer of a material such as silica (silicon dioxide SiO_2) or alumina (aluminium oxide Al_2O_3) coated onto a glass, plastic, or aluminium plate. The separated substances may be recovered for further analysis or reaction by selectively scraping patches from the plate and dissolving the substance in a suitable solvent. The detection by TLC of the molecule pregnanediol in urine is a positive test for pregnancy.

The R_f value

The R_f value compares the distance moved by each component of the solute with the distance moved by the solvent during the experiment. The $\boldsymbol{R_f}$ **value** (or **retention factor**) of a component of the solute is given by

$$R_f = \frac{\text{distance moved by component of solute}}{\text{distance moved by solvent}}$$

The R_f value may be used to identify a component by comparing it with the R_f values of known substances. The R_f value is dependent on the solute and on the nature of the stationary and mobile phases (such as the solvents used); it is not dependent on the distance travelled by the solvent.

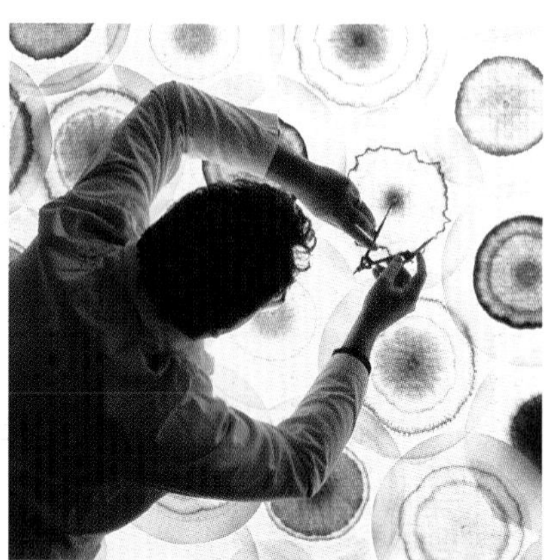

Paper chromatography uses paper of varying shapes and sizes!

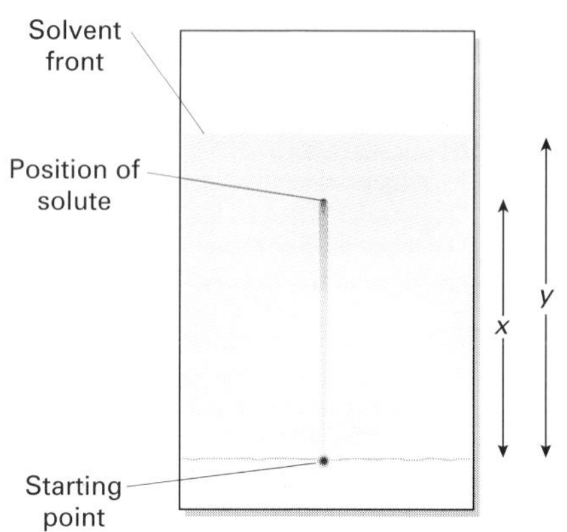

The chromatrography paper after removal when the solvent has reached the top.

The R_f value is here given by

$$R_f = \frac{\text{distance moved by solute}}{\text{distance moved by solvent}} = \frac{x}{y}$$

Column chromatography

Column chromatography is a convenient technique for physically separating the components of a mixture for further use, rather than for identification. The stationary phase is a powder packed into a vertical column of quite large diameter (about 1–2 cm) and wetted with solvent. The mixture is applied to the top of the column, followed by solvent, which runs through under gravity. The components of the mixture adsorb onto the surface of the solid to different extents. The different components emerge from the bottom of the column at different times.

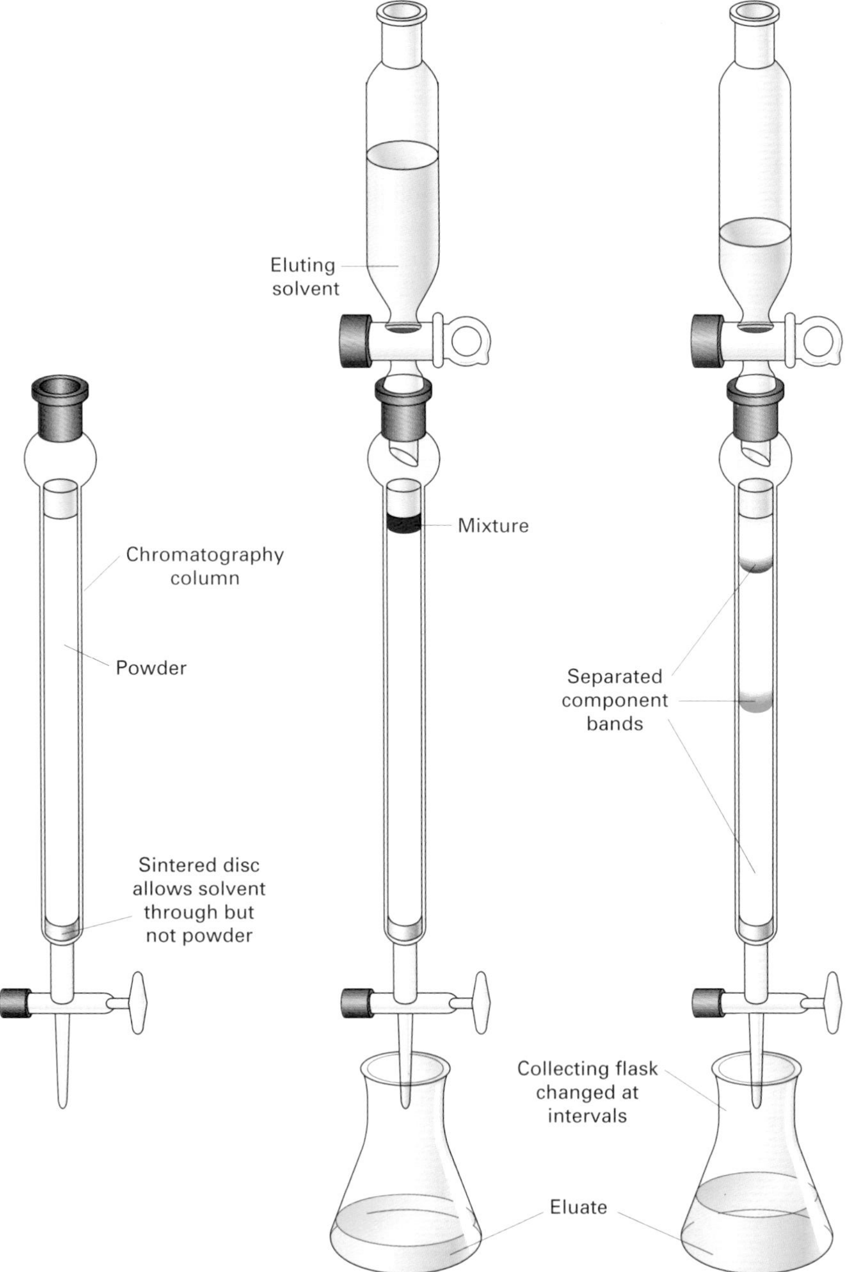

Column chromatography. The mixture in this illustration contains coloured components that appear as coloured bands at different places down the column.

SUMMARY

- All types of chromatography involve a mobile phase and a stationary phase.
- The different compounds separate because they are partitioned or are adsorbed to different extents.
- The ratio of the distance moved by a component of the solute to the distance moved by the solvent is called the component's R_f value.

TLC of the pigments in Poa annua *annual meadow grass: the second and third green bands are chlorophylls.*

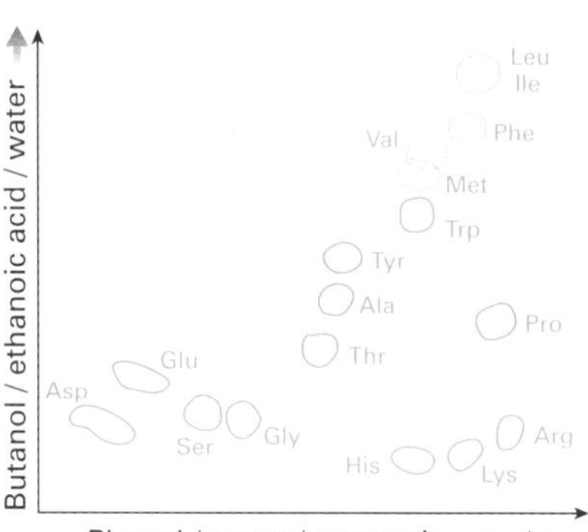

A sophisticated version of thin-layer chromatography is two-dimensional TLC. In this technique, separation is carried out in two stages. The plate is first dipped into one solvent mixture, left for a time, removed, and dried. It is then turned through 90° and dipped into the second solvent mixture, left for a time, removed, and dried. Separation is particularly effective using this method: the amino acids are almost completely separated.

Column chromatography in action.

CHROMATOGRAPHY – 2

OBJECTIVES

- HPLC
- GLC

This spread introduces two important chromatographic techniques: high-performance liquid chromatography (HPLC) and gas–liquid chromatography (GLC). You will see that HPLC is a development of column chromatography described in the previous spread. GLC works by a similar principle, but uses an inert gas to carry the components of a gaseous mixture through the apparatus.

High-performance liquid chromatography (HPLC)

Although it is useful for demonstrating liquid chromatography, column chromatography operating by the force of gravity is no longer used much in laboratories. Instead, chemists use **high-performance liquid chromatography**; in this technique, the stationary phase is held in a column and the mobile phase is forced through under pressure. Separation is much faster. A common stationary phase consists of silica particles with long-chain alkanes adsorbed onto their surfaces. A common mobile phase is methanol.

The separated components of the mixture are usually detected by UV spectroscopy (see next chapter) as they pass through a flow cell between a UV source and detector. The output of the detector is recorded as a **chromatogram**.

HPLC can be used for identification as well as for separation. The components of a mixture are identified by the time they take to pass through the system. The time between injection and the appearance of a peak on the chromatogram is called the **retention time**. Identical substances will have the same retention times under the same conditions.

HPLC may be used commercially for the identification of the stimulants theobromine and caffeine. Calibration with standard solutions (i.e. of known concentration) allows the concentrations of theobromine and caffeine in drinking chocolate and tea to be worked out from the chromatograms. (a) Calibrating the machine with standard solutions of theobromine and caffeine. (b) Drinking chocolate extract. (c) Tea extract.

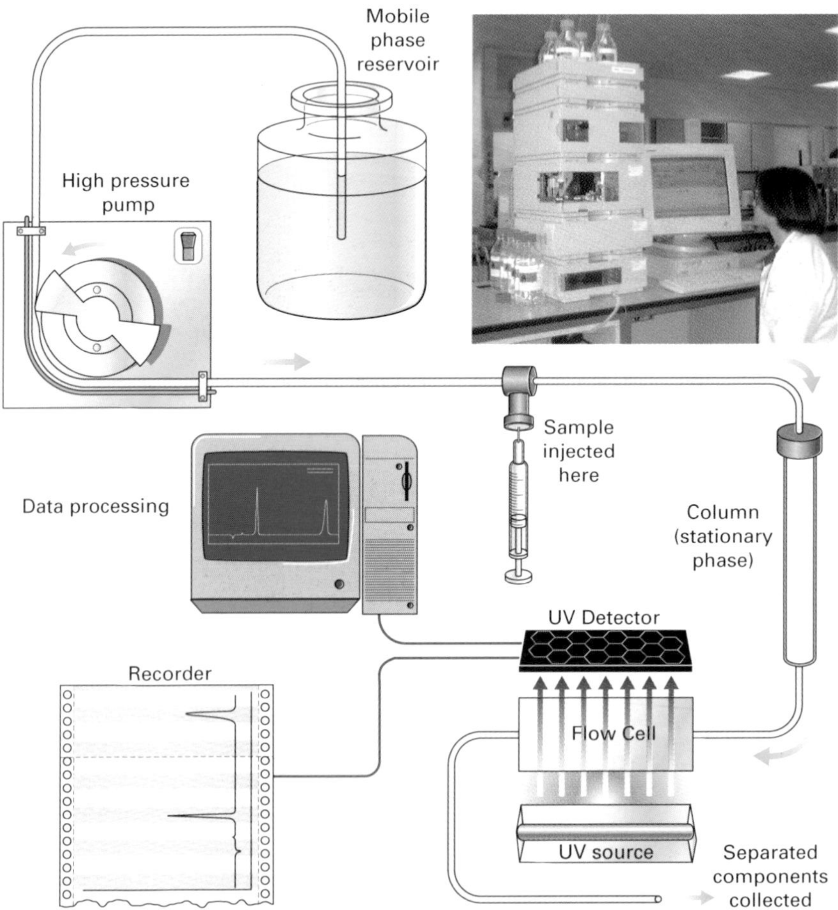

An HPLC system. The photo shows an HPLC system in use. One particular use of this technique is chiral separation, which is able to separate the (+) and (–) forms of optical isomers. Although these isomers have the same functional groups and molecular formula, their differing structures around a chiral centre (their stereochemistry) affects the strength of their adsorption onto a chiral stationary phase.

Gas–liquid chromatography

In common with all the chromatographic techniques described so far, gas–liquid chromatography (**GLC**) uses a stationary phase and a mobile phase. This method is used to separate and identify volatile liquids that do not decompose at temperatures around their boiling points. GLC is generally used for identifying the components of a mixture, and measuring their concentrations. For example, evidence given in Court during prosecutions of drunk drivers usually comes from a gas chromatogram of the defendant's breath.

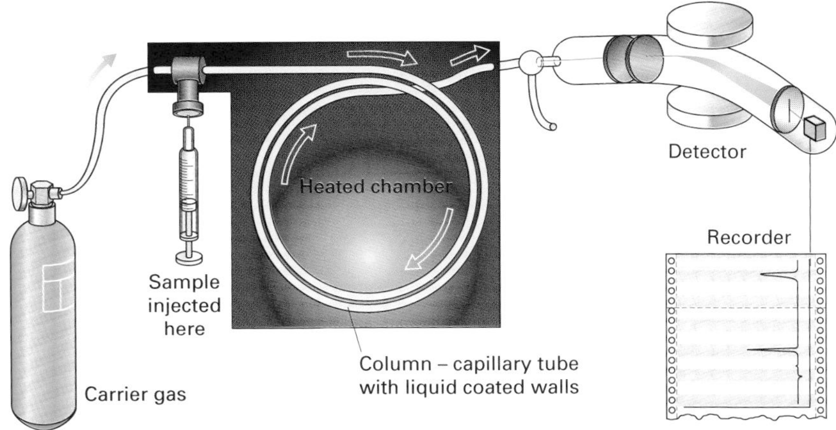

The stationary phase in a GLC apparatus consists of a liquid coated onto the walls of a long, thin capillary tube. The mobile phase is an unreactive gas such as helium or nitrogen. The sample is injected into a heated entrance port, where it immediately vaporizes. The vapour is carried into the column by the mobile phase, which is usually referred to as the *carrier gas*. The carrier gas does not play any part in the separation except to carry the sample along. At the end of the column, the separated components of the mixture pass through a detector, typically a mass spectrometer, see following spread. As in HPLC, the components are identified by their retention times. The relative quantity of each constituent is proportional to the area under its peak in the chromatogram.

Gas-liquid chromatography/mass spectrometry used in forensic analysis. Mass spectrometry is discussed further in the following spread.

SUMMARY

- In HPLC the solvent is pumped through a column under pressure.
- The time between sample injection and the appearance of a peak in HPLC is called the retention time.
- In GLC the stationary phase is a liquid coated onto the walls of a long, thin capillary tube.
- In GLC the mobile phase is an unreactive carrier gas such as helium or nitrogen.

Nomenclature

Chromatography is the technique.

Chromatograph is the apparatus.

Chromatogram is the result that can be seen – e.g. coloured bands or spots; a graph drawn by a plotter driven by a detector.

A gas–liquid chromatograph. The detector here is a mass spectrometer. GLC columns used for analysis are usually narrow, and can analyse very small samples down to $10^{-7}\,dm^3$ (0.1 μl). GLC can also be used for separation, in which case the columns tend to be wider and are packed with a powdered inert solid.

LC–MS

Current HPLC systems are also frequently interfaced with mass spectrometers: LC–MS provides a powerful and robust addition to the analyst's arsenal, with a number of commercial instruments reducing the price of this once specialized equipment. Interfacing HPLC with NMR spectrometers is under development.

PRACTICE

1. Describe three different techniques involving chromatography, including one example of its use.
2. Use the chromatogram opposite to comment on the remark that there is more caffine in tea than in coffee.

31.5

Mass spectrometry

OBJECTIVES

- Fragmentation
- The molecular ion peak
- Interpreting mass spectra
- Fragmentation patterns

In spread 3.2 we looked at mass spectrometry as a means to determine the relative *atomic* masses and relative abundances of isotopes. Mass spectrometry is also used to analyse *molecules*, particularly organic molecules. The mass spectrometer breaks molecules into ionized fragments. These may be detected and displayed as a spectrum, analysis of which gives information about *molecular* mass and structure.

FAB

Molecules with high relative formula mass may be dislodged from a solid sample by a stream of rapidly moving atoms (called **fast atom bombardment**).

Fragmentation

When a *molecule* is bombarded with high-energy electrons, it loses an electron to form a positive ion and absorbs energy, causing it to break into fragments. These positively charged fragments appear in the mass spectrum. The *tallest* peak in the spectrum is due to the fragment produced in greatest quantity. This peak is called the **base peak**. The relative abundances of all other peaks in the spectrum are measured as a percentage of the abundance of the base peak. The base peak may not be the molecular ion peak (see below).

High-resolution mass spectrometers

Modern mass spectrometers can measure masses to four or five decimal places, so molecules with almost exactly the same mass can be distinguished. For example, a compound whose relative formula mass M_r is 123 (to the nearest whole number) could be $C_6H_5NO_2$ or $C_8H_{13}N$. Precise values of the relevant relative atomic masses are:

^{12}C = 12.00000 (by definition)

^{1}H = 1.00782

^{14}N = 14.00307

^{16}O = 15.99492

Using these figures,
$M_r(C_6H_5NO_2)$ = 123.0320
and
$M_r(C_8H_{13}N)$ = 123.1047
the two substances can therefore be easily distinguished.

The molecular ion peak

The **molecular ion peak** is produced by the loss of just one electron from the *complete* molecule. So the mass at which the molecular ion peak is found represents the relative formula mass of the molecule. The molecular ion peak will usually be found within the cluster of peaks of greatest mass in the spectrum, but sometimes it may be very weak or even absent. To determine which one of the cluster of highest-mass peaks represents the molecular ion, the various isotopes that may be present in the molecule must be considered.

The *m/e* ratio for the singly charged molecular ion is labelled M. Peaks of mass 1 or 2 units heavier than the molecular ion are called M+1 and M+2 peaks respectively. They are due to the presence of isotopes that are 1 or 2 mass units heavier than the most abundant isotope.

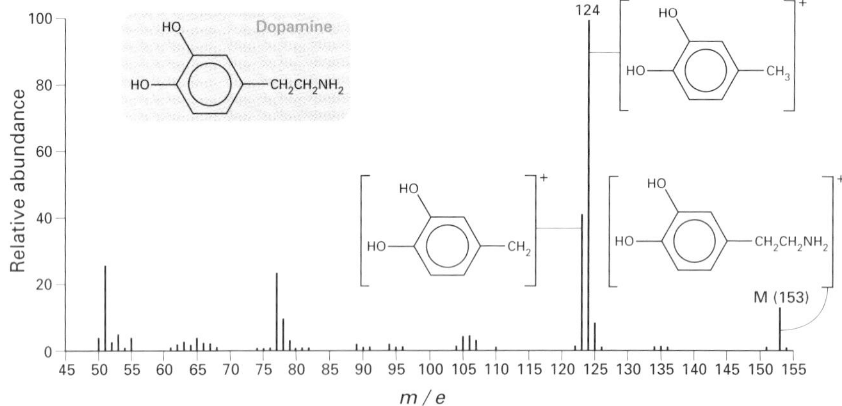

A (simplified) mass spectrum of dopamine, which is a neurotransmitter in the brain. Knowledge of its structure has led to the synthesis of L-dopamine, used to treat some of the symptoms of Parkinson's disease. The molecular ion peak at m/e = 153 corresponds to an ion of formula $C_8H_{11}O_2N^+$. The peak at m/e = 124 (the base peak) corresponds to the ion $C_7H_8O_2^+$. This ion results from fission of the $C_6H_3(OH)_2CH_2—CH_2NH_2$ bond (producing $C_6H_3(OH)_2CH_2^+$) followed by capture of a hydrogen atom from other molecular fragments. This structure allows the delocalization of the positive charge with the benzene ring π cloud.

Molecular and structural formulae

Note that identifying the molecular ion leads only to the *molecular* formula. Modern instruments, using specialized ionization techniques (such as ionspray), can be tuned to emphasize the molecular ion peak. Obtaining the structural formula requires further analysis; see the following chapter.

The M+1 peak

An M+1 peak in a molecule containing carbon is probably due to one of the ^{12}C atoms being replaced by a ^{13}C atom. The relative abundance of ^{13}C in Nature is 1% of that of ^{12}C, so a ^{12}C atom will be replaced by a ^{13}C atom 1% of the time. For a molecule with two carbon atoms, a molecule 1 mass unit heavier will therefore occur 2 × 1 or 2% of the time. So, you may expect to see an M+1 peak with an abundance of 2% of the molecular ion peak abundance. The relative abundance of the M+1 peak increases linearly with the number of carbon atoms.

The M+2 peak

The heavier isotopes of chlorine and bromine are each 2 mass units heavier than the lighter isotopes. The natural abundance of ^{81}Br is 98% that of ^{79}Br. The mass spectrum of a compound containing a bromine atom therefore has M and M+2 peaks of *almost equal intensity*.

The natural abundance of ^{37}Cl is 33% that of ^{35}Cl. The mass spectrum of a compound containing a chlorine atom therefore has an M+2 peak that is one-third the intensity of the molecular ion peak.

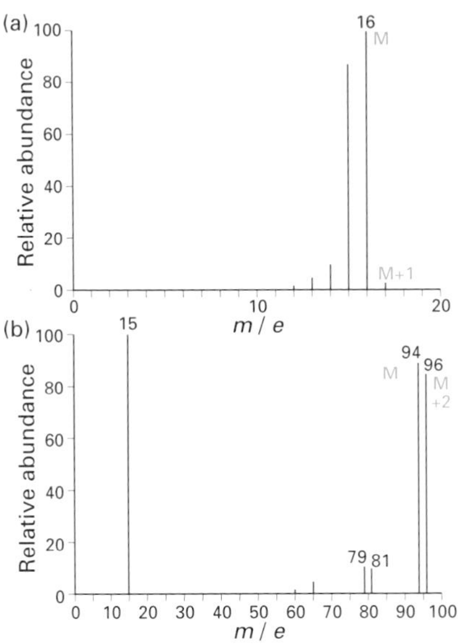

(a) The mass spectrum of methane CH_4 showing the molecular ion peak at m/e = 16 and the (much smaller) M+1 peak at m/e = 17. (b) The (simplified) mass spectrum of bromomethane showing the M+2 peak.

Fragmentation patterns

The molecular ion has an unpaired electron, and so is both a carbocation and a radical; a radical contains an unpaired electron and is unstable. When a molecular ion fragments, the most common result is another carbocation fragment (which will appear in the mass spectrum) together with a neutral fragment with an unpaired electron (which will not be detected), e.g. a methyl radical $CH_3^{\bullet}$.

Fragmentation of the molecular ion occurs most easily at positions that give the most stable carbocation fragments. The stability of carbocations increases with the number of alkyl groups attached to the positive carbon atom, spread 22.8. This can be to used to predict how, for example, an alkane is likely to fragment. The **fragmentation pattern** produced is characteristic and acts as a fingerprint for the parent molecule. With the *m/e* values for various fragments determined in this way, the various peaks in a mass spectrum may be allocated to specific fragments. A substance can be identified by comparing its mass spectrum against a library held on a computer database.

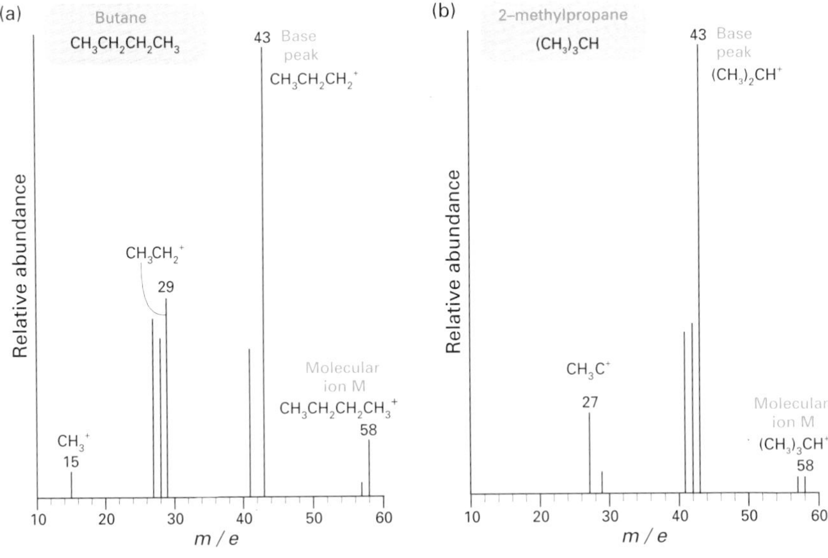

The (simplified) mass spectra of two isomers. (a) Butane. The main fragments are identified. (b) 2-Methylpropane. Note the following 2 major changes. The peak at 29 is very much smaller, as the fragment $CH_3CH_2^+$ cannot be formed. The relative heights of 57 and 58 are the same because breaking the $(CH_3)_3C$—H bond creates a tertiary carbocation, which is relatively very stable. As for butane, the base peak is formed by the loss of one methyl group.

Carbocation stability

A tertiary carbocation R_3C^+ is more stable than the secondary carbocation R_2HC^+, which is more stable than the primary carbocation RH_2C^+, which is more stable than H_3C^+. The fragment RCO^+ is also generally more stable.

Nitrogen

Most organic compounds have masses that are even numbers. A clue to the presence of nitrogen in a molecule arises because, although nitrogen has an even mass (14), it forms an *odd* number of bonds (3). Therefore, the presence of a single nitrogen atom will result in an *odd*-numbered relative formula mass. See box opposite.

Practical techniques

It is possible to predict the fragments likely to form from a given structure. Conversely, deducing the likely identity of the fragments observed gives information about the original molecular structure from which they derive. In practice, a single analytical technique can rarely be used alone to obtain detailed structural information. Mass spectrometry and infrared spectroscopy (see next chapter) are so commonly used together that they are now frequently combined in one single instrument. Sensor outputs are linked to a computer, which displays a three-dimensional pictorial representation of the molecule.

SUMMARY

- The molecular ion peak is produced by loss of one electron from the complete molecule.
- The M+1 peak shows the number of carbon atoms present in a molecule.
- The M+2 peak identifies compounds containing chlorine and bromine.
- A molecular ion of odd mass suggests the presence of nitrogen.
- The fragmentation pattern produced is characteristic of the molecular structure.
- Fragmentation occurs at positions that give stable carbocations.

PRACTICE EXAM QUESTIONS

1 **a** The organic compound **M** is introduced into a mass spectrometer.

i What information can be obtained from the precise value of the mass of the molecular ion $\mathbf{M^{+\cdot}}$?

ii Suggest why it is usually possible to detect a small peak at one mass unit higher than that of the molecular ion.

iii Write a general equation for the fragmentation of a molecular ion $\mathbf{M^{+\cdot}}$ into two new species. Explain briefly why only one of these species can be detected. [4]

b **i** The relative intensities of the peaks at $m/z = 50$ and $m/z = 52$ present in the mass spectrum of chloromethane are in the ratio of approximately 3 to 1, respectively. Suggest why two molecular ion peaks are found.

ii Write an equation for the fragmentation of $CH_3Cl^{+\cdot}$, giving rise to a peak at $m/z = 15$. [4]

AQA (NEAB) 1997

2 Mass spectrometry is an important analytical technique used in a variety of applications.

a The table below shows the relative abundances of isotopes of strontium obtained from the mass spectrum of a sample of the element.

Nucleon (mass) number	Relative abundance
84	0.60
86	9.90
87	7.00
88	82.50

i Calculate a value for the relative atomic mass of strontium from the data, showing your working.

ii Suggest why a sample of strontium from a different source may have a slightly different relative atomic mass. [3]

b The high resolution mass spectrum of the products of combustion of a plastic shows peaks at *m/e* values of 27.0109, 29.9980, and 30.0105.

Using the table below identify the components of the mixture responsible for these peaks. Show how you arrive at your conclusions.

Element	Relative atomic mass
Hydrogen, ^{1}H	1.0078
Carbon, ^{12}C	12.0000
Nitrogen, ^{14}N	14.0031
Oxygen, ^{16}O	15.9949

i *m/e* 27.0109

ii *m/e* 29.9980

iii *m/e* 30.0105 [3]

c The mass spectrum shown below was obtained from compound **E**, which contains carbon, hydrogen, and oxygen only.

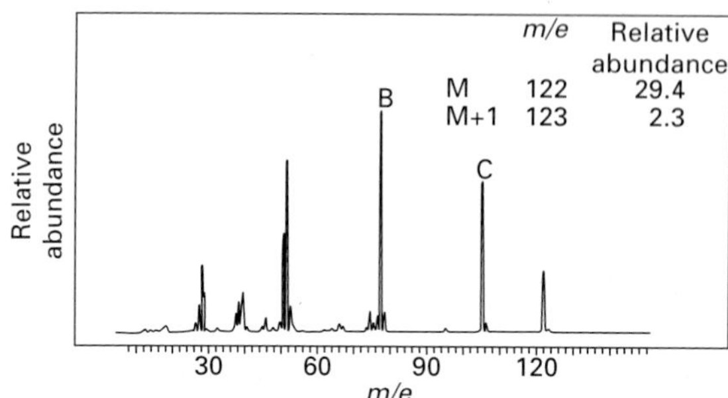

i Using the data provided, show how you can confirm that compound **E** contains seven carbon atoms.

ii Suggest the formulae of the molecular ions responsible for the peaks labelled B and C. [4]

d Suggest a structure for **E**, and identify the functional group present. [2]

OCR (UCLES) 1998

3 This question concerns the compounds in the following reaction scheme:

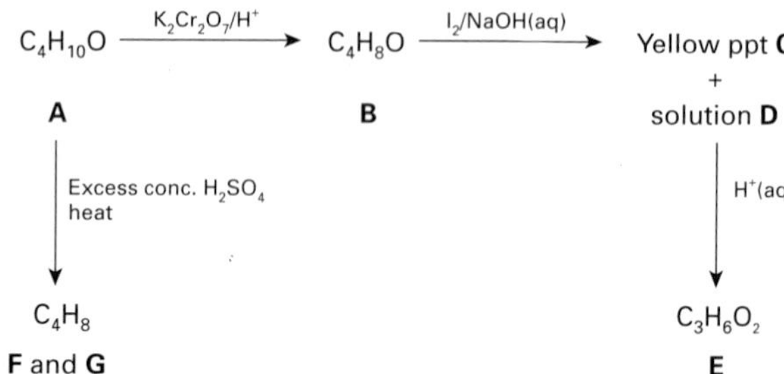

a **F** and **G** are compounds which both decolourize bromine water. **F** has two stereoisomers.

i What functional group is present in both **F** and **G**? [1]

ii Give the structural formulae of both stereoisomers of **F**. [2]

iii Explain how these two isomers arise. [2]

iv Write the structural formula of **G**. [1]

b **B** cannot be oxidized by acidified potassium dichromate(VI) solution.

i Write the structural formula of **B**. [1]

ii Draw the general structural features of molecules which can be detected by the reaction with iodine and alkali. [2]

iii Give the structure of the substance in solution **D**, and of the product **E**. [2]

c The mass spectrum of **A** gives peaks at *m/e* 29 and 45, amongst others. That at 45 is the largest.

This spectrum shows no molecular ion peak, which would be expected at *m/e* 74. **A** is chiral.

i Give the structural formula for **A**. [1]

ii Identify the ions responsible for the peaks at *m/e* 45 and 29, and hence suggest why the molecule shows no molecular ion peak. [3]

d **A** is miscible with benzene and the mixture formed shows a positive deviation from Raoult's law and forms an azeotrope.

i **A** boils at 99 °C, benzene at 80 °C. Sketch a possible boiling point/composition diagram for a mixture of A with benzene. [3]

ii Explain why a mixture of **A** with benzene shows a large positive deviation from Raoult's law. [3]

iii The infrared spectrum of **A** is shown below. The very broad peak at 3500 cm^{-1} is due to the presence of an —OH group. This peak becomes much narrower when diluted with benzene and moves to 3600 cm^{-1}.

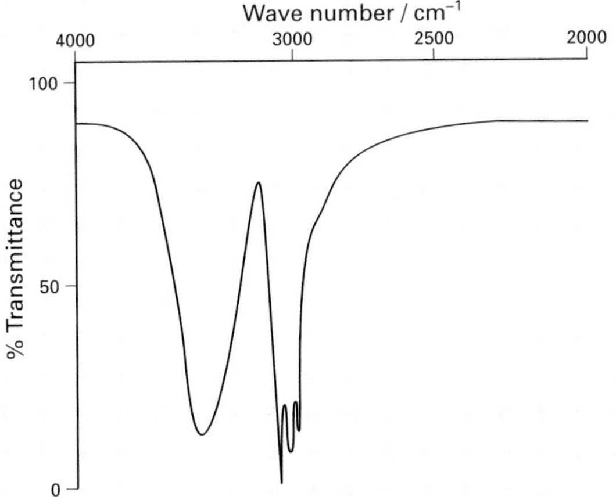

Suggest why the —OH absorption peak changes as **A** is diluted with benzene. [2]
EDEXCEL 1998

4 **a** The figure below shows part of the mass spectrum of an organic compound with the molecular formula $C_2H_8N_2$.

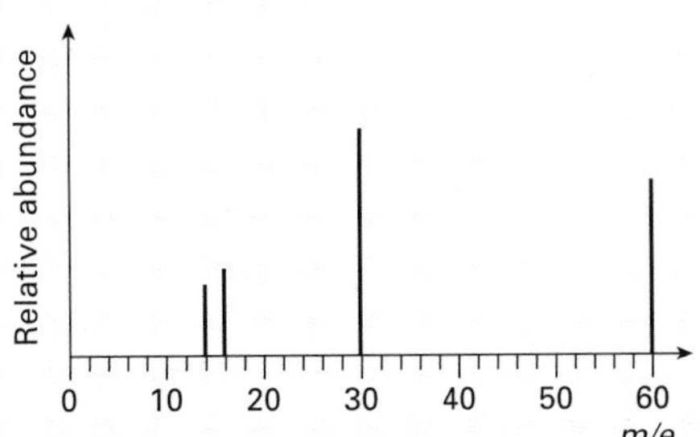

i What is the relative molecular mass of the compound? [1]

ii Suggest the formula of the fragment that corresponds to each of the following masses:

30 mass units; [1]

16 mass units; [1]

14 mass units. [1]

iii Give the name of a functional group in the original molecule. [1]

b Compounds can exhibit structural, geometrical, and optical isomerism. Explain what is meant by *geometrical isomerism*. [2]

c The following formulae represent compounds which exist as geometrical isomers. Draw formulae to show **both** isomers for each compound

i C_4H_8 [2]

ii $[Cr(H_2O)_4Cl_2]^+$ [2]
AQA (AEB) 1996

5 **a** **i** Define the terms:

Relative molecular mass

Isotope.

ii Calculate the relative atomic mass of carbon which contains two main isotopes ^{12}C(98.9%) and ^{13}C (1.10%). Give your answer to an appropriate number of significant figures. [6]

b The diagram below shows a simplified mass spectrum for an organic compound X which contains carbon, hydrogen, and oxygen only. The infrared spectrum of X indicates the presence of a C=O group.

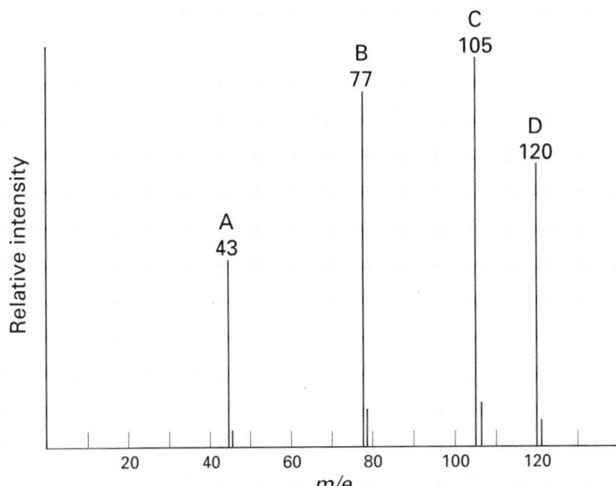

i Deduce from the mass spectrum the relative molecular mass of X.

ii Account for the very small peaks that occur next to each of the peaks A, B, C, and D at masses of 44, 78, 106 and 121 respectively. [3]

c **i** Estimate the number of carbon atoms present in ion D and hence explain why compound X is likely to be aromatic and to have the formula $C_6H_5COCH_3$.

ii Deduce the formulae of the ions responsible for peaks B and C.

iii Suggest a reason for the absence of a recorded peak at *m/e* = 15. [7]

d Give the reagents and the result of a simple chemical test to show the presence of the carbonyl group in X.
EDEXCEL 1997 [2]

32 Spectroscopy and structure

Once a substance has been separated from a reaction mixture and purified, we then need to identify its structure. The previous chapter introduced mass spectrometry for finding molecular formulae. This chapter describes the use of (i) atomic emission and absorption, (ii) ultraviolet and visible, (iii) infrared, and (iv) nuclear magnetic resonance spectroscopy. Spectroscopy involves the interaction of electromagnetic radiation with matter. These techniques allow the structural formulae of molecules to be determined.

Atomic spectroscopy

32.1

OBJECTIVES

- Spectroscopy: general principles
- Emission and absorption spectra
- Atomic spectra: AES and AAS

Flame photometry

A flame photometer is a simple instrument for detecting emission spectra. It is used in hospital laboratories to detect Na^+ and K^+ in blood serum and urine. The flame burns natural gas, and the sample to be analysed is sprayed into it as an aerosol. Optical filters are placed between the flame and the detector to isolate the strong emission lines, spread 16.9, from Na, K, Li, Ca, or Ba.

Earlier we explained how the emission spectrum of hydrogen provides valuable information about the arrangement of electrons in atoms. Obtaining an *emission* spectrum, however, requires special conditions such as high temperature or low pressure. The instruments for obtaining and analysing emission spectra are often expensive. Information about energy levels can be obtained more cheaply and for a much wider range of substances using absorption spectroscopy. This technique detects the *absorption* of electromagnetic energy that accompanies a transition to a higher energy level. The overall result is an absorption spectrum.

Atomic emission spectroscopy (ICP-AES)

Although the instruments remain very expensive, atomic emission spectroscopy (AES) has been revolutionized by a device called the **inductively coupled plasma (ICP) torch**. A plasma, see below, is a gas containing a high proportion of cations and electrons. In the ICP torch, argon gas is made into a plasma by exciting it with a powerful radio-frequency source. The energy heats the argon by induction to temperatures around 10 000 K. The sample to be analysed is made into an aerosol and is carried into the plasma by the argon flowing through the central tube of the torch.

As the sample enters the torch, it atomizes and is excited into various higher energy levels. The radiation emitted as these excited energy levels return to the lowest energy level is analysed as in any other form of spectrometer. The very significant difference between ICP-AES and atomic absorption spectroscopy (see opposite page) is that no radiation source is required, and so the spectra of many different elements may be analysed together.

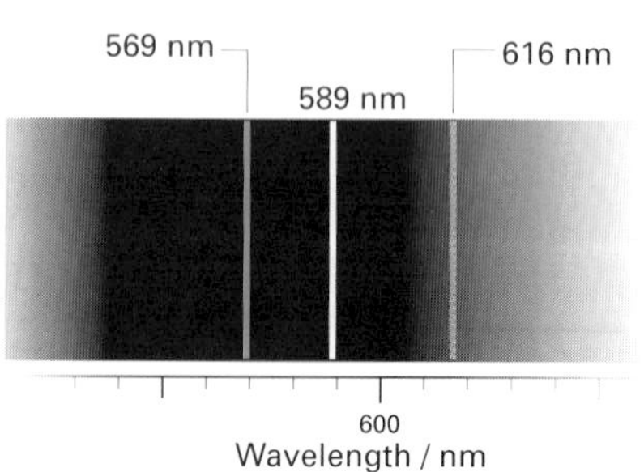

The atomic emission spectrum of sodium showing the intense yellow line at 589 nm. This emission is due to electronic transitions from the 3p energy level down to the 3s energy level. The green line at 569 nm is the result of 4d to 3p transitions; the orange line at 616 nm results from 5s to 3p transitions. See spread 4.3.

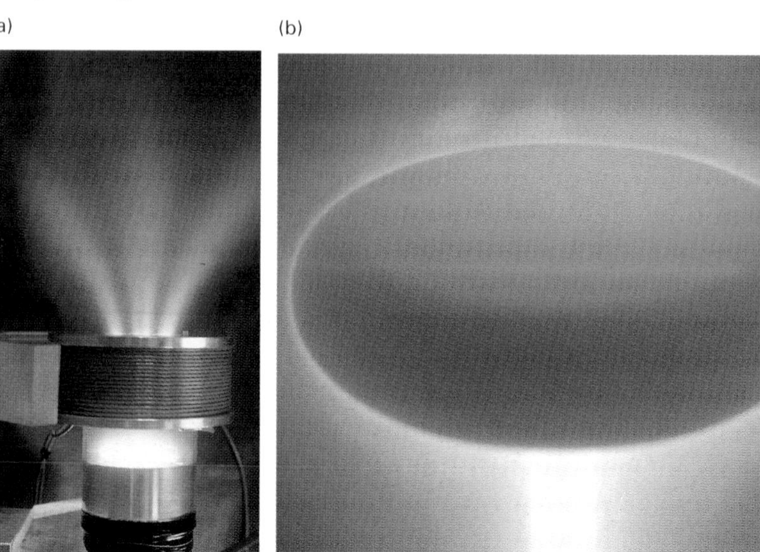

(a) A hollow-anode nitrogen plasma source used to manufacture light-emitting-diodes (LEDs). (b) Nitrogen plasma around a titanium electrode.

Atomic absorption spectroscopy (AAS)

If you heat a compound to a sufficiently high temperature, it will usually break apart to form atoms in the gas phase. Atomic absorption spectroscopy atomizes a sample at high temperatures (around 3000 K) in an oxygen–ethyne flame. When electromagnetic radiation is shone through the sample, the electrons in the atoms absorb energy and are promoted to higher energy levels. The energy absorbed in each transition corresponds to a particular wavelength of radiation.

Atomic absorption spectroscopy is able to detect just one element at a time. The instrument shines radiation from a hollow cathode discharge tube at the flame containing the vaporized sample. The cathode is made from the element being investigated, so it emits radiation of wavelengths characteristic of that element. Any atoms of that element present in the flame absorb energy at these wavelengths, and the radiation emerging from the flame is measured by the instrument. A typical atomic absorption spectrum shows a series of sharp lines. The extent of the absorption depends on the relative quantity of the element in the sample, allowing the concentration of the element in the sample to be determined.

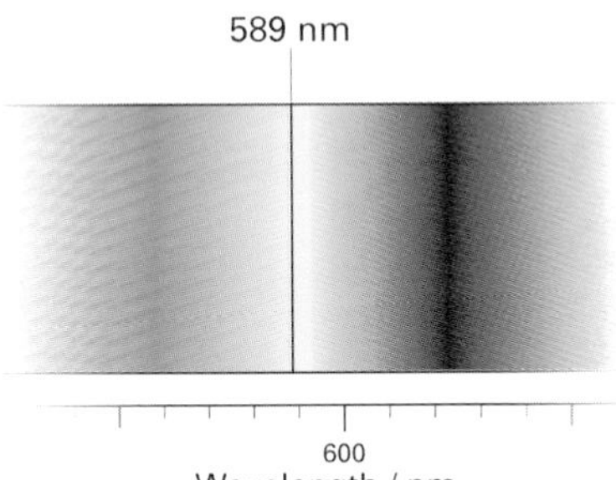

The atomic absorption spectrum of sodium, extending over the same region of wavelengths as the emission spectrum shown opposite. Compare the two spectra and note that both emission and absorption occur at 589 nm.

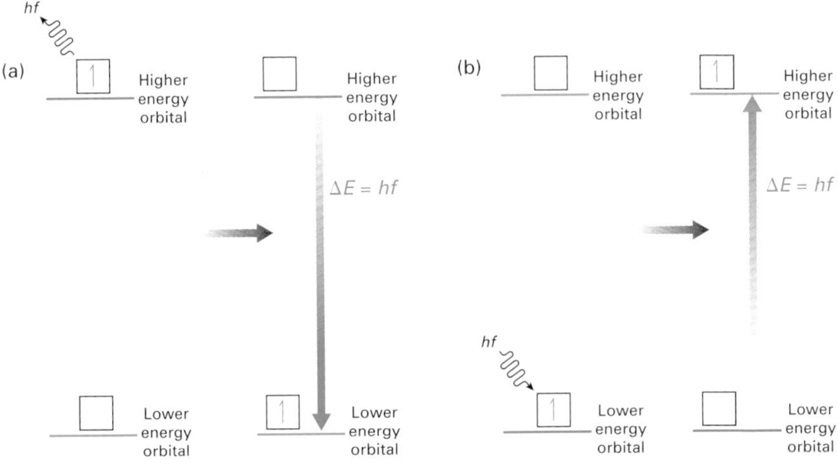

Comparing the mechanisms of emission and of absorption. (a) Emission. An atom emits a quantum of electromagnetic radiation when an electron in a higher energy level makes a transition to a lower energy level. The frequency f of the radiation is given by $\Delta E = hf$, where ΔE is the difference between the two energy levels and h is the Planck constant. (b) Absorption. An atom absorbs a quantum of electromagnetic radiation of the correct energy, causing an electron to make a transition to a higher energy level. The frequency f of the radiation is also given by $\Delta E = hf$.

Photon

A quantum of electromagnetic radiation is called a photon.

SUMMARY

- Atomic emission spectroscopy depends on an atom emitting a quantum of electromagnetic radiation when an electron in a higher energy level makes a transition to a lower energy level.
- Atomic absorption spectroscopy depends on an atom absorbing a quantum of electromagnetic radiation when an electron in a lower energy level makes a transition to a higher energy level.
- The frequency of emitted or absorbed radiation is given by $\Delta E = hf$.
- In atomic absorption spectroscopy only one element is detected at a time.

PRACTICE

1 Explain why the absorption spectrum for atomic sodium contains fewer lines than its emission spectrum.

32.2

OBJECTIVES

- Transitions between molecular energy levels
- Chromophores
- Conjugation

UV/Vis and metal ions

Ultraviolet and visible spectroscopy can also be used to determine the concentration of metal ions in solution after addition of an appropriate ligand to intensify the colour, spread 20.11.

Ultraviolet and visible spectroscopy

Atomic emission and absorption spectra involve transitions of electrons between energy levels (orbitals) in atoms. **Ultraviolet and visible (UV/Vis) spectroscopy** probes the same region of the electromagnetic spectrum, but the spectra result from electronic transitions between *molecular* energy levels. The chapter on 'Chemical bonding' introduced the idea of molecular orbitals forming from the redistribution of electron density when atomic orbitals overlap. The various possible molecular orbitals represent different quantized energy levels for molecules in the same way as atomic orbitals do for atoms. An electron in a molecule can absorb a quantum of radiation and make a transition between these molecular energy levels, just as an electron in an atom can between atomic energy levels. Analysis of the resulting spectra can lead to identifying the bonds present in a molecule.

Energy level transitions in molecules

A single covalent bond results from the formation of a sigma (σ) molecular orbital, and a double bond also involves the formation of a pi (π) molecular orbital. An unfavourable energy level called an **antibonding orbital** is always formed along with a **bonding orbital,** spread 5.6. Antibonding orbitals are given the symbols σ^* and π^*. Orbitals containing lone pairs of electrons are called **non-bonding orbitals** and are given the symbol n. Stable, unexcited molecules generally have electrons in bonding and non-bonding orbitals. Absorption of energy can promote these electrons to antibonding orbitals.

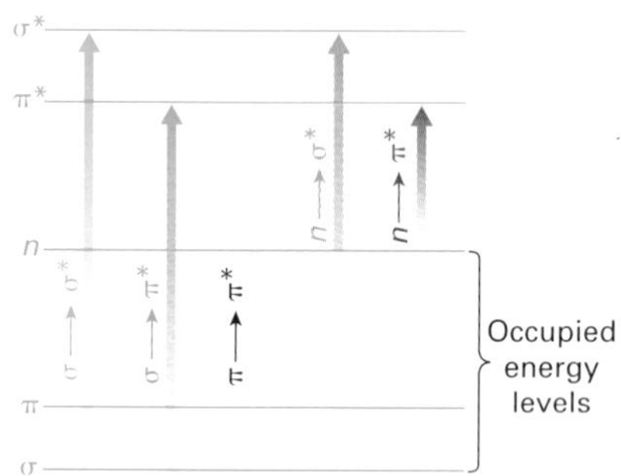

The typical relative energy levels of molecular orbitals and the electronic transitions that can occur between them.

Chromophores

The energy required to make an electronic transition in a molecule depends on how strongly the electrons are attracted by the nuclei of the bonded atoms. So the characteristic energy of a transition is a property of a *group of atoms*. A group of atoms producing such a characteristic absorption is called a **chromophore**.

Different transitions are possible in different chromophores. In molecules such as alkanes that only contain sigma bonds and do not contain any lone pairs, only one electronic transition is possible, i.e. $\sigma \rightarrow \sigma^*$. The energy required for this transition is relatively large. It represents the absorption of ultraviolet radiation of wavelengths too short for detection by most instruments.

Where lone pairs are present as well as sigma bonds, $n \rightarrow \sigma^*$ transitions become possible. The energy of these transitions comes within the range of ultraviolet wavelengths that *can* be measured experimentally: —NH_2 and —OH groups absorb in this way in the wavelength range 175–200 nm. (Remember that the frequency f of the radiation is given by $f = \Delta E/h$; and the wavelength λ is given by $\lambda = c/f$, where c is the speed of light.)

If a double bond is present, a $\pi \rightarrow \pi^*$ transition becomes possible. In alkenes this transition occurs at an energy corresponding to a wavelength around 175 nm; and in carbonyl compounds at around 188 nm.

In an unsaturated molecule that also contains a lone pair, an $n \rightarrow \pi^*$ transition is also possible. C=O typically absorbs in this way at wavelengths around 275–290 nm, —N=N— at around 340 nm, and R—NO_2 at around 270 nm.

(a)

(b)

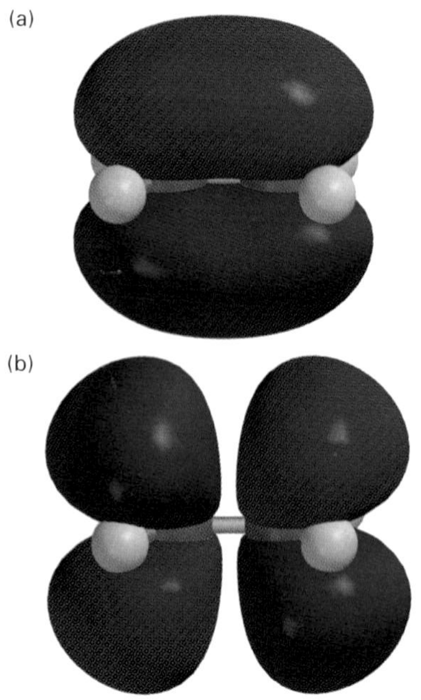

Electron density diagrams for ethene's molecular orbitals: (a) π, and (b) π^*.

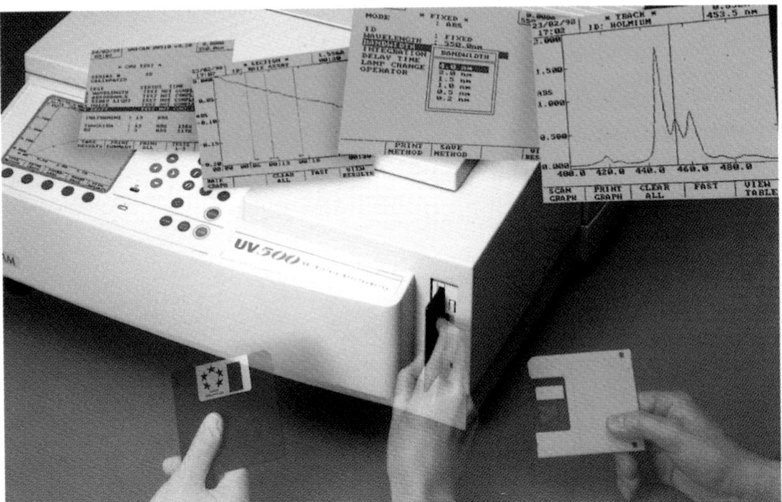

An ultraviolet spectrometer. When it is necessary to measure absorption across a range of wavelengths, a scanning ultraviolet/visible spectrometer *is used. This generates a beam of radiation that scans through each wavelength in turn over the range from about 200 nm to about 800 nm. The output of the instrument, the spectrum, is usually a plot of absorption against wavelength. Modern instruments include data processing electronics that can be used to store the measured spectrum and carry out qualitative comparisons against a library of examples.*

Class	Transition	λ_{max} / nm
ROH	$n \to \sigma^*$	180
RCHO	$\pi \to \pi^*$	190
	$n \to \pi^*$	290
R_2CO	$\pi \to \pi^*$	180
	$n \to \pi^*$	280
RCOOH	$n \to \pi^*$	205
RCOOR′	$n \to \pi^*$	205
$RCONH_2$	$n \to \pi^*$	210

Typical absorptions of single isolated chromophores.

Conjugation

Conjugation occurs where there are alternating double and single bonds in a molecule (see chapter on 'Organic synthesis: ...'). In a conjugated molecule, electron density is delocalized over molecular orbitals stretching across all the atomic centres involved. Conjugation decreases the energy required for a $\pi \to \pi^*$ transition, and so causes a shift to longer wavelength; it also increases the intensity of absorption. The effect of conjugation is important because it shifts the absorption wavelength to a region of the spectrum much more readily detected using simple instruments. In fact, in extreme cases it shifts it into the *visible* region and the substance is coloured.

Conjugation effects

The C=C double bond in ethene absorbs at 175 nm; whereas the C=C—C=C conjugated bonds in butadiene absorb at 217 nm and in 2-methylbutadiene at 220 nm. Conjugation changes the wavelength by 42 nm; adding the methyl group causes a change of only 3 nm.

(a)

(b)

Organic compounds that are coloured by virtue of conjugated double bonds. (a) β-Carotene. (b) Methyl orange.

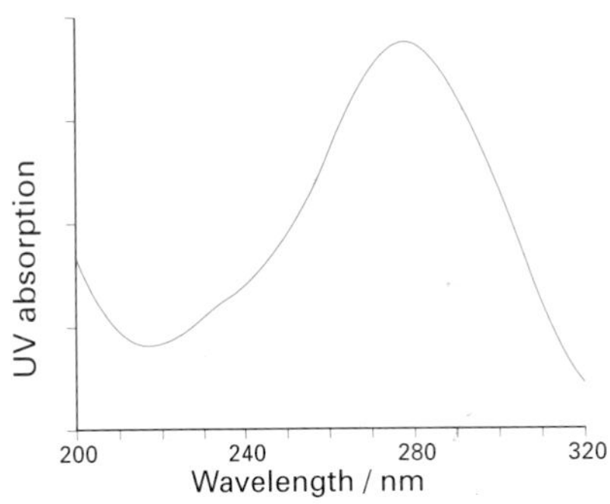

The ultraviolet spectrum of propanone in cyclohexane.

SUMMARY

- UV/Vis spectroscopy is used to detect electronic transitions between molecular energy levels.
- A group of atoms producing a characteristic absorption is called a chromophore.
- Conjugation progressively decreases the energy required for a $\pi \to \pi^*$ transition.

PRACTICE

1 Explain how absorption spectra could be used to determine atmospheric composition, as for example in the planet revolving around 51 Pegasus.

32.3

INFRARED SPECTROSCOPY – 1

OBJECTIVES

- Vibrational and rotational energy levels
- Stretching and bending vibrations
- Active and inactive bonds
- The infrared spectrometer

Rotational transitions

- **Electronic transitions** involve energies in the region of 100–400 kJ mol^{-1} and correspond to UV/Vis spectra.
- **Vibrational transitions** involve energies in the region of 20 kJ mol^{-1} and correspond to IR spectra.
- **Rotational transitions** involve energies in the region of 0.01 kJ mol^{-1} and correspond to the microwave region. These spectra are difficult to observe and are not discussed further in this text.

Electronic transitions between molecular orbitals giving rise to UV/Vis absorption are not the only types of quantized transition that can occur in molecules. Molecules can interact with electromagnetic radiation in more ways than atoms can. The absorption of energy can cause bonds to stretch, bend, or twist in characteristic ways that distort the electron density. These transitions take place at lower energies than electronic transitions, with the result that vibrational and rotational energy changes are detected by infrared (IR) spectroscopy.

Vibrational transitions

Some molecules absorb radiation of infrared wavelengths, which causes changes in the **modes of vibration** (the various ways in which the molecule vibrates). The wavelengths absorbed correspond to transitions between quantized energy levels. The simplest modes of vibration are **stretching** and **bending**. These modes and some more complicated vibrations are shown in the illustration below. The wavelength of absorption is characteristic of the type of bond present, so infrared absorption spectra give two sorts of structural information:

- Certain groups of atoms give rise to characteristic absorptions, which can be used to identify specific functional groups. It is thus a *'bond-spotting'* technique.
- Molecules with different structures have different vibrational energy levels, and so the infrared spectrum of a compound is like a *'fingerprint'* which is not shared by any other compound. Compounds with identical infrared spectra are identical.

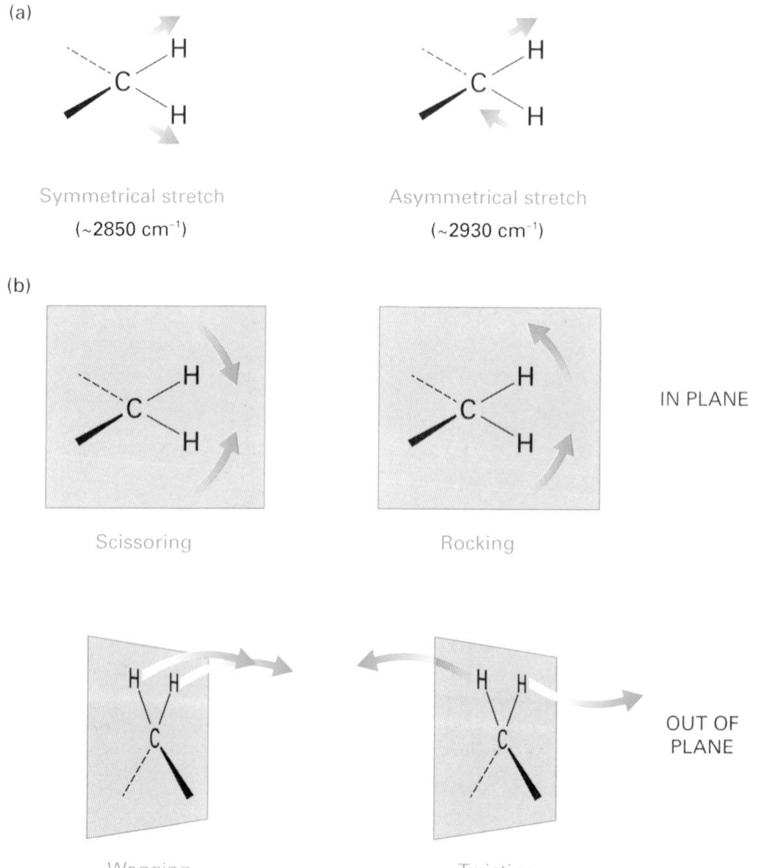

The modes of vibration. (a) Stretching vibrations. (b) Bending vibrations. Note that the traditional unit used in infrared spectroscopy is cm^{-1}*. This measures the* ***wavenumber*** *and is the reciprocal of the wavelength in centimetres (1/cm).*

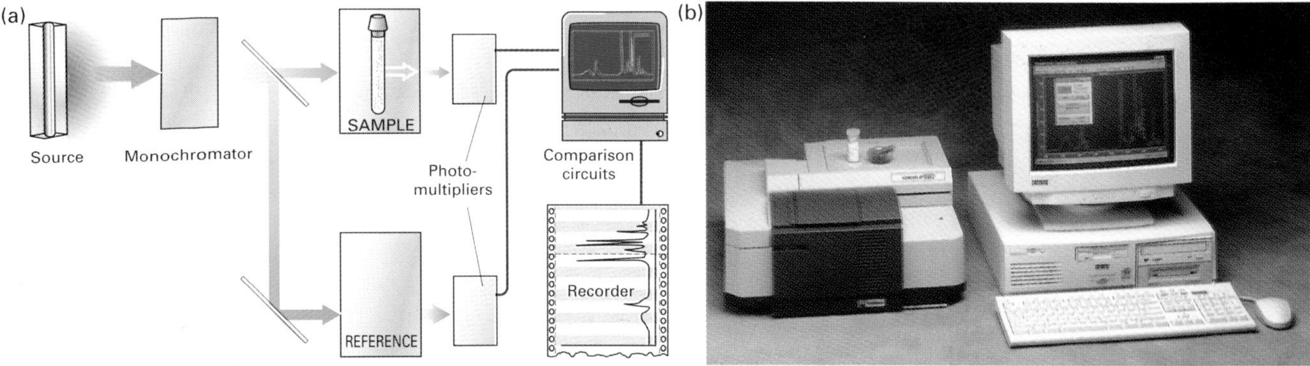

(a) A double-beam infrared spectrometer. (b) An FT-IR spectrometer

Active and inactive bonds

Not all bonds absorb energy at infrared wavelengths. For energy to be transferred from the infrared radiation, a bond must have an electric dipole, spread 5.9, that changes as it vibrates. Symmetrical bonds, such as those in H_2 or Cl_2, will not absorb, nor will symmetrical bonds that are also symmetrically substituted either side of the bond, e.g. the C=C bond in ethene. These bonds are '**IR-inactive**'. As shown below right, carbon monoxide is a linear diatomic molecule with one **IR-active** mode of vibration. In comparison, carbon dioxide is a linear triatomic molecule: two IR-active modes of vibration are shown with one IR-inactive one.

Sample preparation

For IR spectroscopy (and also for UV/Vis spectroscopy), special materials must be used to contain the sample in order to avoid distortion of the absorption spectrum by the material of the 'container'. **Potassium bromide** is the most commonly used material, because it is transparent at infrared wavelengths. Windows made from a single crystal of potassium bromide are available, which can be used to make 'cells' to contain gases or liquids. Alternatively, a thin film of liquid can be sandwiched between two windows.

FT-IR spectroscopy

Older infrared spectrometers work on the same basic principle as UV/Vis machines, scanning wavelengths from about 2500 nm (4000 cm^{-1}) to 25 000 nm (400 cm^{-1}) and comparing sample and reference beams. Because of the time taken to scan the large range of wavelengths, these instruments have now been largely superseded by **Fourier transform (FT-IR) spectrometers**, which pass several wavelengths through the sample at the same time and analyse the results using the mathematical technique of Fourier analysis. This takes a complex waveform and works out the amplitudes of each single-frequency component in it. The analysis is carried out by a computer (inside the instrument), which then plots the spectrum.

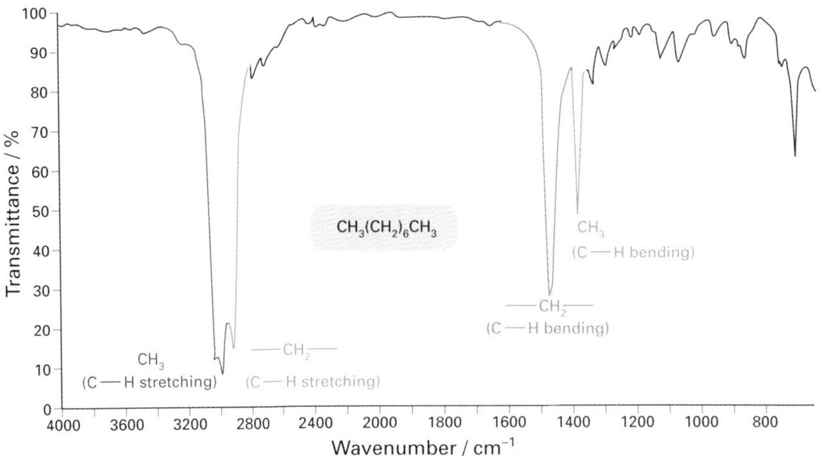

*The infrared absorption spectrum for octane. The standard method of display shows percentage transmission, rather than absorption. This produces downward 'peaks' of the curve at the wavenumbers where a molecule absorbs radiation. The pattern within the '**fingerprint region**' (1500–400 cm^{-1}) is specific to each molecule, and can be used for identification purposes.*

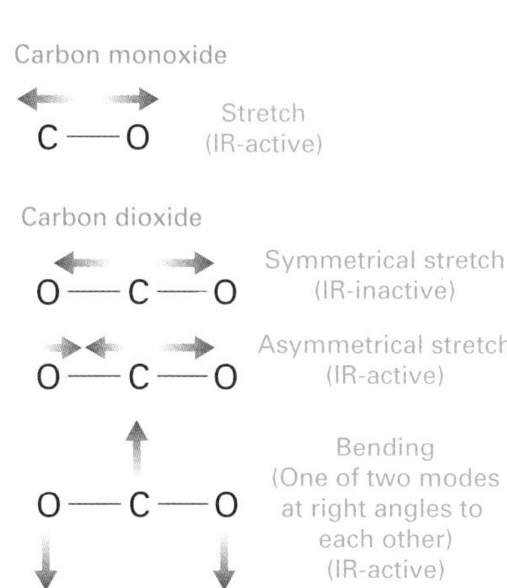

Symmetrical stretching of the CO_2 molecule does not alter the overall dipole moment of the molecule. This vibrational mode is therefore IR-inactive. The nature of the bonding in these molecules is not *represented (see spread 10.10).*

SUMMARY

- Infrared spectroscopy is used to detect vibrational transitions.
- For a bond to be infrared-active, it must have an electric dipole that changes as it vibrates.
- Infrared spectra can be used to identify specific bond vibrations and to identify complete molecules by using their infrared 'fingerprint'.
- A material transparent to infrared, such as potassium bromide, must be used to contain the sample.

32.4

Infrared spectroscopy – 2

OBJECTIVES

- Correlation charts
- Interpretation of IR spectra

Bond-spotting

Alcohols are identified from the O—H absorption and carbonyl compounds from the C═O absorption.

Golden Gate

An infrared spectrum may be obtained very quickly using a variant called the Golden Gate, in which an infrared beam is directed upwards through a diamond wafer onto a thin film of the sample. The beam passes through a very thin layer of the sample before being reflected back downwards towards the detector. The sample is placed on the diamond wafer either as a liquid or as a solid (which is then crushed against the diamond wafer by a metal plate). A spectrum may be collected in about 40 seconds. The instrument is then cleaned by wiping the diamond wafer with a suitable solvent, leaving it ready for the next sample.

To interpret the infrared spectra of substances and deduce their molecular structures, spectroscopists apply their analytical skills together with an almost intuitive 'feel' for complex spectra gained from experience. Automatic data processing techniques are available that compare measured spectra with libraries of known spectra. Remember that the pattern within the '**fingerprint region**' (1500–400 cm^{-1}) is specific to each molecule, and may be used to identify an unknown substance by comparison of its spectrum with those of previously identified substances. To aid the novice, **correlation charts** list the characteristic absorptions of different isolated functional groups. A simplified correlation chart is shown below. The aim of this spread is to show the interpretation of a number of different IR spectra, and then to help you to make your own interpretations of the spectra of unnamed substances.

A simplified correlation chart.

Bond	Type of compound	Range / cm^{-1}	Bond	Type of compound	Range / cm^{-1}
C—H	Alkanes	2850 – 2960	C═C	Arenes	1500 – 1600
	Alkenes	3010 – 3095	C—O	Alcohols, ethers, carboxylic acids, esters	1000 – 1300
	Arenes	3030 – 3080	C═O	Aldehydes, ketones, carboxylic acids, esters	1680 – 1750
	Aldehydes	2710 – 2730			
O—H	Alcohols (H-bonded)	3230 – 3550	C—N	Amines	1180 – 1360
	Carboxylic acids (H-bonded)	2500 – 3000	C≡N	Nitriles	2210 – 2260
N—H	Amines	3320 – 3560	N—O	Aryl nitro derivatives	1330 – 1550

Interpreting IR spectra

Look at each of the following four IR spectra and compare the absorptions with the values given in the correlation chart. Note that the characteristic frequencies of some of the functional groups are not always clearly defined.

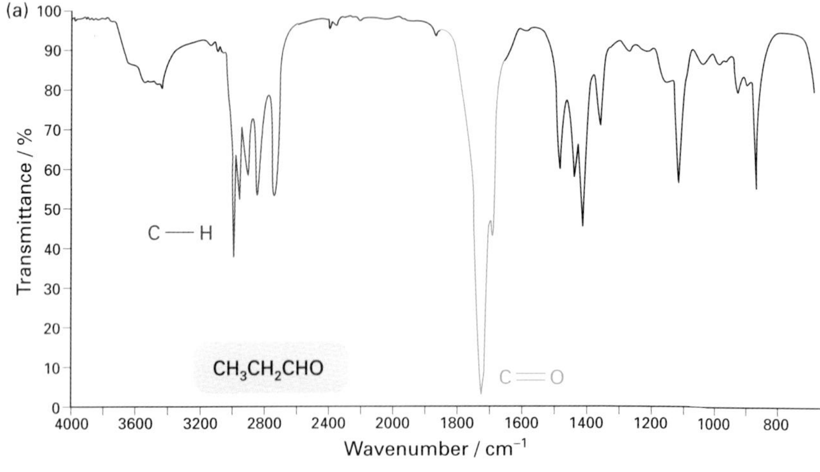

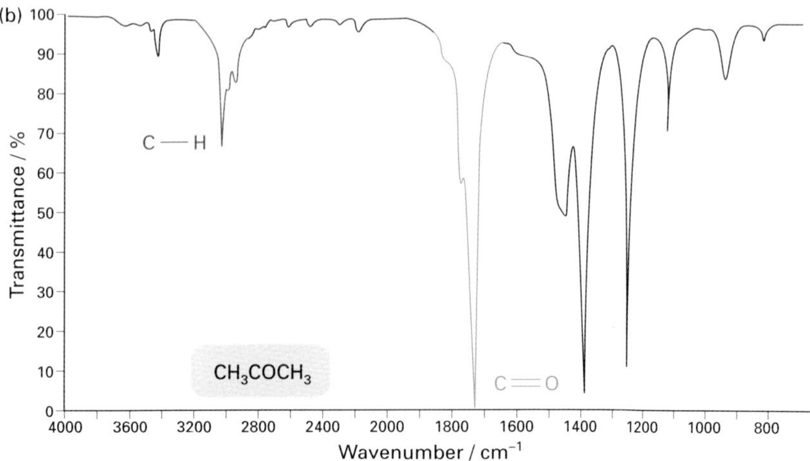

IR spectra of (a) propanal and (b) propanone.

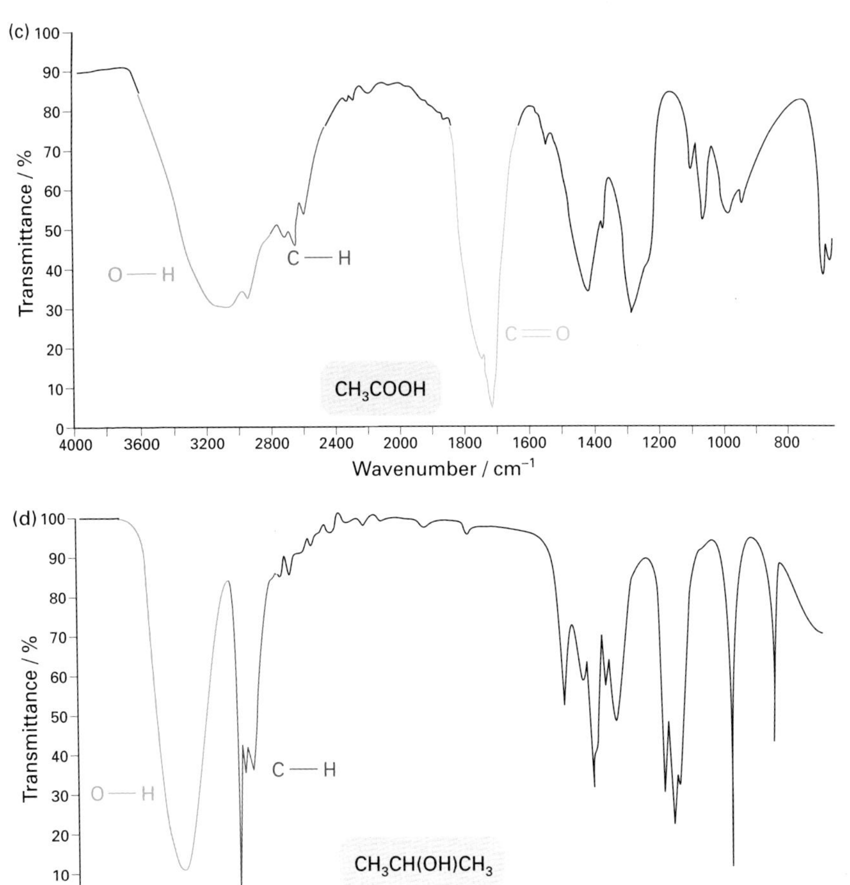

IR spectra of (c) ethanoic acid and (d) propan-2-ol.

Broad O—H

Notice the broad O—H absorption in a carboxylic acid.

SUMMARY

- Inspect the region 3600–1500 cm^{-1} for the characteristic absorptions of O—H, N—H, C=O, C=C, etc.
- The region 1500–400 cm^{-1} is the fingerprint region.
- The region 2500–1800 cm^{-1} frequently contains no peaks.

PRACTICE

1 Describe the modes of vibration in the following:

a Carbon monoxide

b Carbon dioxide

c Water

d Sulphur dioxide.

State which modes are IR-inactive, giving reasons for your choices.

2 Describe as fully as you can the structures of the molecules giving rise to the IR spectra shown below.

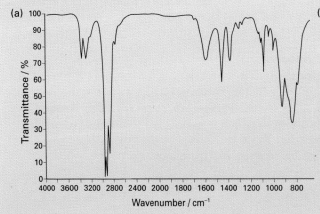

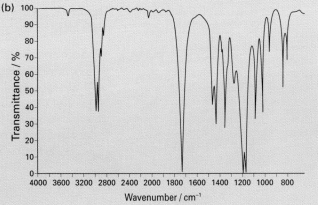

The infrared spectra of: (a) a compound of molecular formula C_3H_9N; and (b) a compound of molecular formula $C_4H_8O_2$.

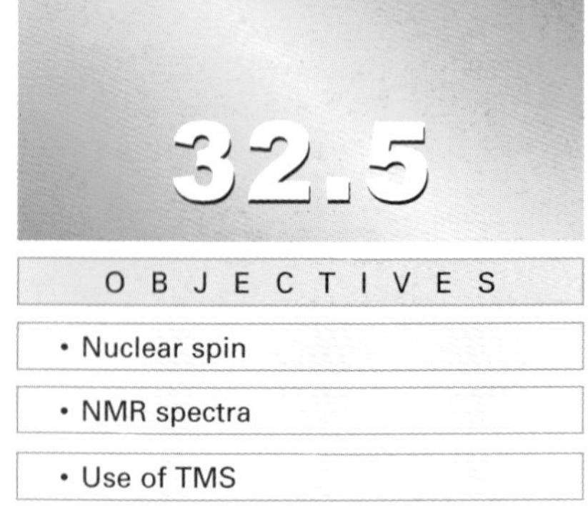

NUCLEAR MAGNETIC RESONANCE (NMR) – 1

OBJECTIVES

- Nuclear spin
- NMR spectra
- Use of TMS

Whereas IR spectroscopy provides information about the types of bonds in a molecule, nuclear magnetic resonance (**NMR**) spectroscopy gives different information about the arrangement of specific atoms in a molecule. The sample is placed in a very strong magnetic field and its absorption of electromagnetic radiation is measured. The nuclei of certain atoms, most importantly hydrogen, absorb strongly under these circumstances. The actual magnetic field experienced by each hydrogen nucleus in a molecule depends on the extent to which electrons shield the nucleus from the applied field. This shielding in turn depends on the arrangement of the electrons around each nucleus. Thus, the magnetic field experienced by an individual hydrogen nucleus depends on its position within the molecule. As with IR spectra, the full interpretation of NMR spectra can be as much an art as an exact science, but NMR spectroscopy is of great value in the fields of research and analytical chemistry.

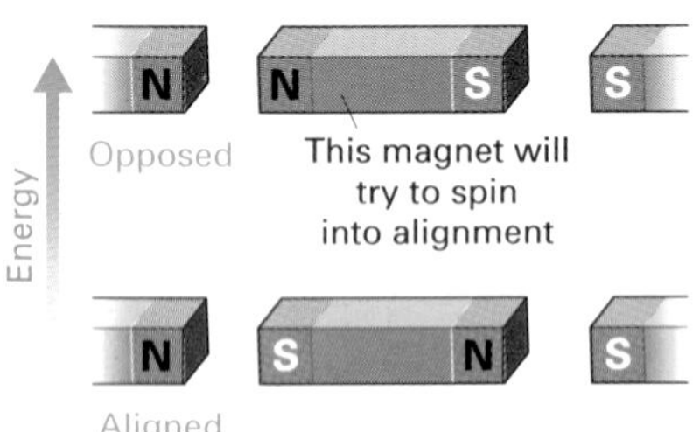

Aligned (lower-energy) and opposed (higher-energy) arrangements of bar magnets.

Nuclear spin

The phenomenon of *electron* spin (either 'up' or 'down') was introduced in the chapter on 'Electrons in atoms'. The nuclei of atoms that have an odd mass number also possess spin. The two nuclei that are most often studied in NMR spectroscopy are hydrogen (^{1}H), as mentioned above, and carbon-13 (^{13}C), because they both possess spin. NMR applied to the hydrogen nucleus is often called 'proton magnetic resonance' (**PMR**): we will concentrate exclusively on proton NMR. Carbon-13 NMR was useful in identifying buckminsterfullerene, spread 19.4.

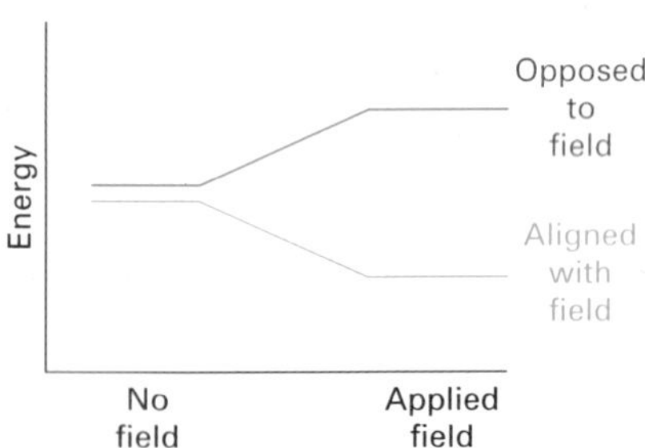

The spin states of a proton both in the absence and the presence of an applied magnetic field.

Proton NMR spectroscopy

Like the electron, the proton (the hydrogen nucleus ^{1}H) has two possible spin states available to it. These spin states have the *same energy* until a magnetic field is applied. The spin of the nucleus may then align itself either with the field or opposed to it, as shown on the left. The spin state that is aligned with the field is now at a lower energy than the spin state that is opposed to the field. The precise energy difference between the spin states depends on the strength of the magnetic field experienced by the nucleus.

The nuclei aligned with the applied field can change their spin to the opposite state if they absorb energy that matches the energy required for the transition (in the same way that energy of the correct magnitude is required for an electronic transition from a lower energy level to a higher one). As with other types of spectroscopy, the energy absorbed can be measured. Because the energy difference is very small, the wavelength of the electromagnetic radiation absorbed is *much* longer than for UV/Vis or for IR spectroscopy, and lies in the radio-frequency range, around 100 MHz.

Proton-free solvents

Proton NMR are obtained using samples dissolved in solvents that do not contain protons, such as CCl_4 or deuterated solvents, in which all H atoms are the deuterium isotope ^{2}H.

Producing NMR spectra

The sample substance, either a pure liquid or in solution, is placed in a cylindrical sample tube, which is spun on its axis between the poles of a powerful electromagnet (typically between 2 and 10 tesla). Around the sample tube is a probe coil, which is connected to a radio-frequency generator and a receiver. To produce a spectrum, the applied magnetic field is varied by means of extra electromagnet coils.

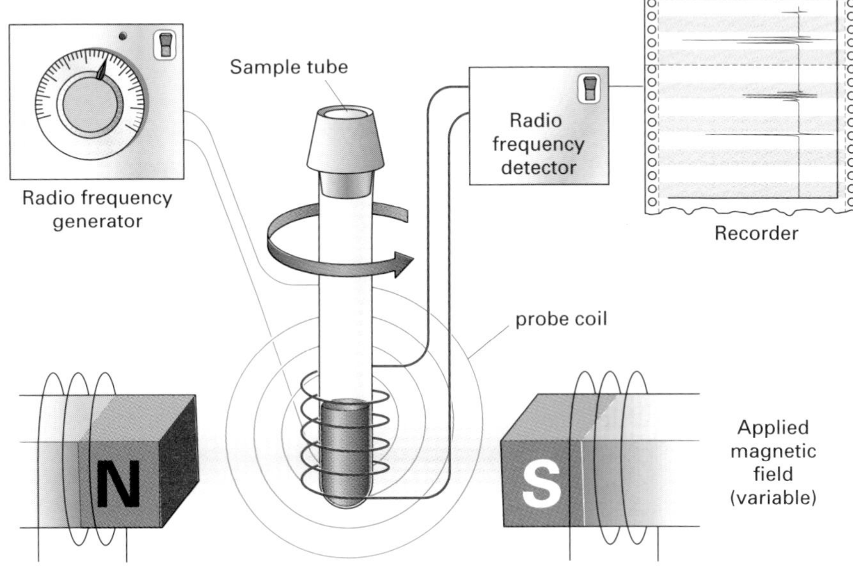

The main parts of an NMR spectrometer.

Chemical shift and TMS

A particular proton within a molecule will absorb electromagnetic radiation at a particular frequency called its **resonance frequency**. The resonance frequencies of protons in different environments are different but very close together. It is very difficult to measure frequencies with enough precision to make out these very small differences. So, instead of trying to measure the *exact* resonance frequency of any proton, a **reference compound** is added to the sample, and the resonance frequency of each proton in the sample is measured *relative to the resonance frequency of the protons in the reference compound*. This technique enables a frequency *difference* to be measured (which is much easier) rather than an exact frequency. Tetramethylsilane (**TMS**), $(CH_3)_4Si$, is universally used as the reference compound for proton NMR because its methyl groups are particularly well shielded. The resonances of the protons in the sample are described in terms of how far they are 'shifted' from those of TMS.

The size of this shift varies with the magnitude of the applied magnetic field, which itself depends on the design of the spectrometer and, in particular, on the frequency corresponding to the applied magnetic field. To enable data from different workers and different instruments to be compared, the chemical shift has been *defined* to be independent of applied magnetic field strength (and thus spectrometer radio-frequency used). The **chemical shift** δ is the shift in Hz of the proton in question divided by the operating frequency in MHz of the spectrometer used, i.e.

$$\delta = \frac{\text{shift in Hz}}{\text{spectrometer frequency in MHz}}$$

The units of chemical shift are parts per million (p.p.m.).

SUMMARY

- Nuclei of atoms that have an odd mass number, such as hydrogen, possess a spin, which can align with or against an applied magnetic field.
- NMR measures the energy needed to change the spin state, and this energy depends on the environment of the atom.
- Tetramethylsilane (TMS) is used as a reference compound for proton NMR spectra.
- The chemical shift is the shift in Hz of the proton in question (relative to TMS) divided by the frequency in MHz of the spectrometer used.

Body scanners

NMR using other nuclei, such as ^{13}C and ^{31}P, has found widespread use in medicine. ^{31}P NMR can be used, for example, to determine the extent of damage following a heart attack.
A recent development is the whole-body scanner. The whole-body scanner allows visualization of the entire body by placing the patient inside the magnet of a very large NMR machine. (There is no need to spin the sample!) Molecules in different tissues of the body are in different environments, and so it is possible to distinguish them using NMR. With the aid of a computer, the results can be displayed as a colour map of the organs in the body. In medicine, the technique is known as **magnetic resonance imaging** (MRI) because people are apprehensive of the word 'nuclear'.

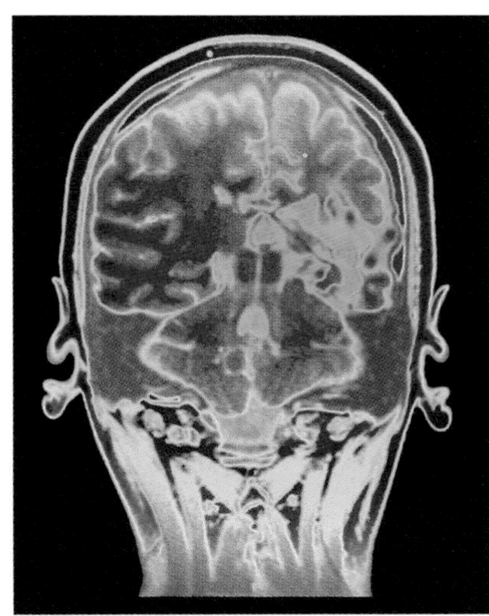

An MRI image of a human head. False-colour imaging (produced by software in the machine) allows the different tissues to be distinguished.

NMR spectra

You are now familiar with the principles underlying the production of NMR spectra. The following two spreads introduce examples of actual spectra and explain how to interpret them.

OBJECTIVES

- Chemical equivalence
- Peak area and proton numbers

NUCLEAR MAGNETIC RESONANCE (NMR) – 2

The previous spread covered the basic principles of nuclear magnetic resonance spectroscopy. This spread looks in detail at how the environment of protons in a molecule can vary, and how to derive structural information from a proton NMR spectrum.

Chemical equivalence

Protons that are in the same environment in a molecule will have identical chemical shifts. They are said to be **chemically equivalent** and give rise to a single peak in the NMR spectrum of the compound. For example, a benzene molecule contains six hydrogen atoms attached to the six carbon atoms in a regular planar hexagonal ring, spread 23.1. The nucleus of each of these atoms is in an identical environment, as shown by the single peak in the NMR spectrum given below. The protons of the six hydrogen atoms in benzene are chemically equivalent.

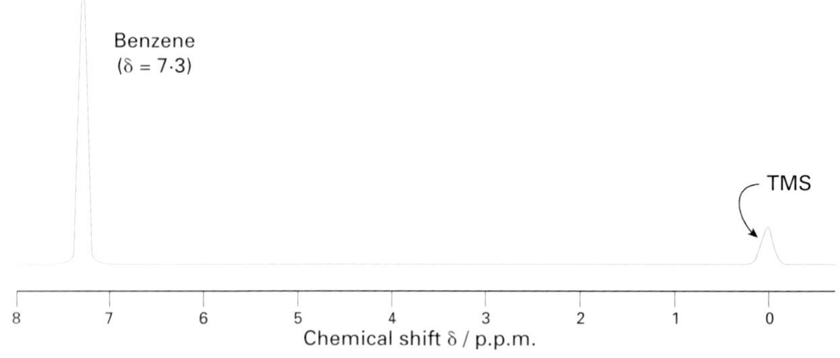

The NMR spectrum of benzene C_6H_6.

Table of approximate chemical shifts and corresponding proton environments. Here R is an alkyl group.

Type of proton	Chemical shift δ/p.p.m.
RCH_3	0.9
R_2CH_2	1.3
R_3CH	1.5
$R_2C{=}CH_2$	5
C_6H_5–H	7.3
C_6H_5–CH_3	2.3
R–C(=O)–CH_3	2.3
R–C(=O)–H	9.7

Values for chemical shifts

The value of the chemical shift of a peak in an NMR spectrum tells us about the particular type of proton environment. A table of values for chemical shifts gives us information about the types of molecular structure next to the proton that has that particular chemical shift. Note that chemical shifts alone do not often let us find the precise structure of a molecule.

Interpreting NMR spectra

Protons in different environments will have different chemical shifts, and so each peak in the NMR spectrum represents a different 'type' of proton. Ethyl ethanoate $CH_3COOCH_2CH_3$ has *three* different types of proton corresponding to the two methyl groups —CH_3 and the —CH_2— part of molecule. The two methyl groups are not equivalent, so the NMR spectrum of ethyl ethanoate will have three separate peaks, as shown below.

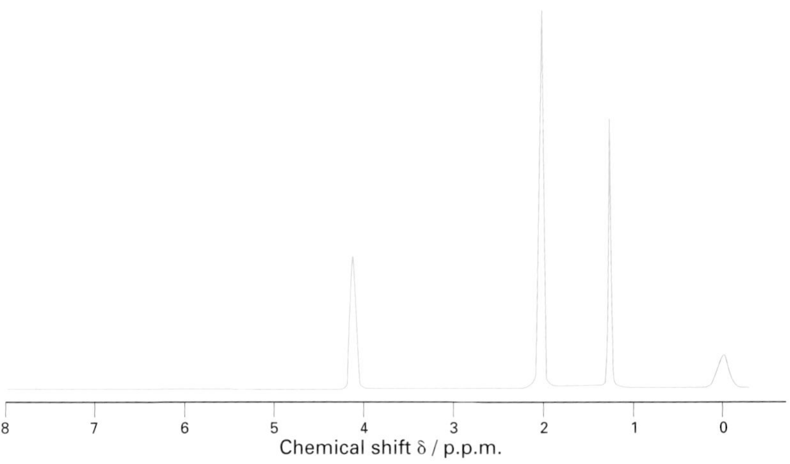

The NMR spectrum of ethyl ethanoate $CH_3COOCH_2CH_3$. There are three different groups of protons, each in its own magnetic environment and each chemically equivalent. See following spread for more details.

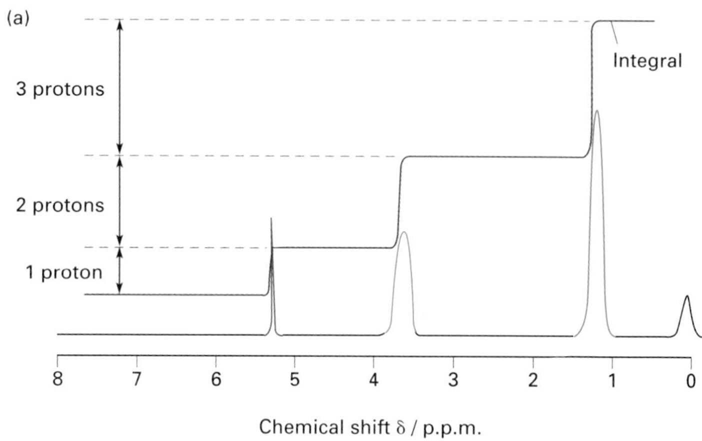

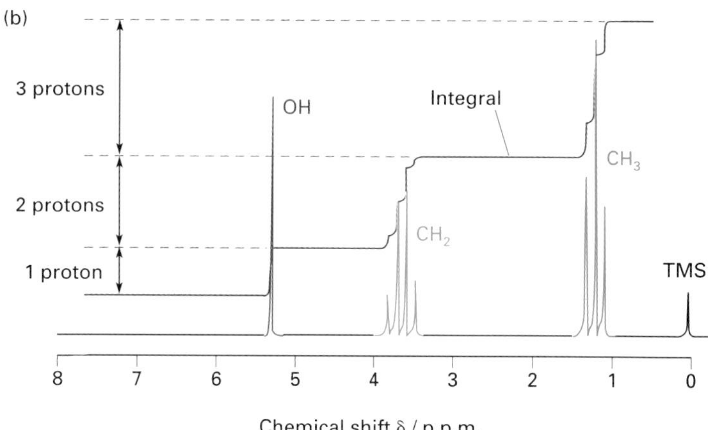

The NMR spectrum of ethanol (a) at low resolution and (b) at high resolution. The additional trace with vertically rising sections 'integrates' the area under each peak. The height of each vertical section is proportional to the area under the peak.

High resolution

Even more details can be extracted from the spectra at high resolution, as explained in the following spread.

Peak areas

The area under each peak in an NMR spectrum is proportional to the number of protons generating that peak. The area is calculated automatically by the instrument by numerical integration, and can be displayed as a line above each peak, the height of which is proportional to the area. Note that the height of the line does not give the exact number of hydrogen atoms, just the *relative number* within that molecule. It is therefore necessary to look at the areas under all the peaks and work out the simplest ratio between them.

For example, the three peaks in the NMR spectrum for ethanol (above) have relative areas of 1, 2, and 3 respectively. The *true* number of protons must be deduced from other information about the molecule, some of which may be deduced from high-resolution NMR spectra, which will be introduced in the next spread.

The three peaks in ethanol correspond to the proton of the hydroxyl (—OH) group, the two protons of the —CH_2— group, and the three protons of the end methyl (—CH_3) group from left to right of the spectrum above. Confirmation of this interpretation requires the high-resolution spectrum discussed in detail in the following spread.

SUMMARY

- Chemically equivalent protons give rise to a single peak in the NMR spectrum.
- Values of chemical shift can be used to indicate the chemical environment of the protons in a molecule.
- The area under each peak in the NMR spectrum is proportional to the number of protons generating that peak.

PRACTICE

1 Identify the type of proton giving rise to each of the *three* peaks in the NMR spectrum of ethanol. Give reasons for your choices.

2 Explain why propanone gives a *single* NMR peak.

3 Explain why 1,4-dimethylbenzene gives *two* separate NMR peaks.

4 Sketch the NMR spectra for the following:

a 1,1,2-Trichloroethane

b 1,1,1-Trichloroethane.

32.7

OBJECTIVES

- High-resolution spectra
- Spin–spin splitting
- $n + 1$ rule

NUCLEAR MAGNETIC RESONANCE (NMR) – 3

All the NMR spectra described so far (except the last) have been of low resolution; they do not show the fine detail of the high-resolution spectra produced by modern instruments. You already know that the area under each peak in an NMR spectrum is proportional to the number of protons generating that peak. Comparing the areas gives the ratios of the different types of proton in a molecule. This section shows how analysis of the fine structure leads to detail about the relative positions of the protons within the molecule.

Spin–spin splitting

The chemical shift of protons in a molecule is slightly altered by other adjacent non-equivalent protons because their respective magnetic fields are close enough to interact. A neighbouring proton with a field aligned with the applied field will have a slightly deshielding effect because its field will add to the applied field. If the field of a neighbouring proton is opposed to the applied field, it will effectively reduce the applied field and so have a shielding effect. The protons are said to be **coupled**.

The effect of coupling on the NMR spectrum is that each type of proton does not necessarily give a single resonance peak. This phenomenon is known as **spin–spin splitting** and becomes evident at high resolution.

- The number of peaks arising from splitting indicates how many protons are *adjacent* to a particular given proton.
- If the number of adjacent protons is n, the peak will split into (n + 1) peaks:
  - **one** adjacent proton produces two closely spaced peaks (a **doublet**),
  - **two** adjacent protons produce three closely spaced peaks (a **triplet**),
  - **three** adjacent protons produce four closely spaced peaks (a **quartet**).

Ethanol at high resolution

See previous spread for spectrum. The —CH_2— peak is split into a quartet by the adjacent —CH_3 group. The —CH_3 peak is split into a triplet by the adjacent —CH_2— group.

Each line within a peak has a relative intensity that can be worked out by a simple mathematical technique called Pascal's triangle.

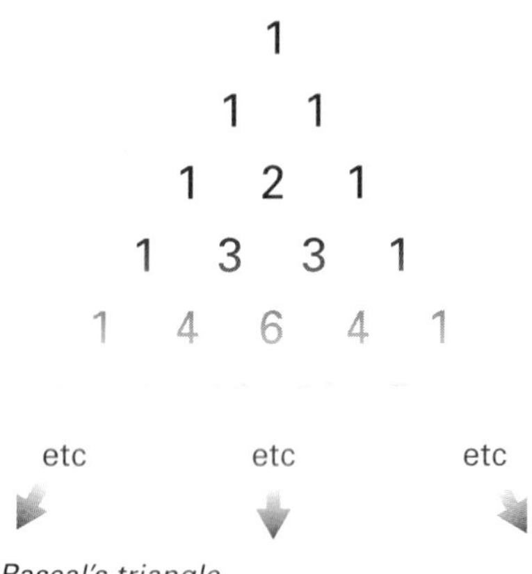

Pascal's triangle.

Each number in the triangle is the sum of the two integers above it to the left and to the right. A doublet therefore has two equal peaks (relative intensities 1:1); a triplet has three peaks (relative intensities 1:2:1) and a quartet has four peaks (relative intensities 1:3:3:1).

Interpreting a high-resolution NMR spectrum

Look at the NMR spectrum of 1,1,2-trichloroethane shown below. The low-resolution spectrum consists of two peaks, indicating that there are two types of proton in the molecule. Integrating each peak to obtain the area under it indicates that the two types of proton are present in the ratio 1:2.

The high-resolution spectrum (opposite) shows that the signal arising from the single proton C**H**Cl_2CH_2Cl is split into three (1:2:1) peaks by the pair of equivalent protons $CHCl_2$C**H**$_2$Cl. The signal arising from the pair of equivalent protons $CHCl_2$C**H**$_2$Cl is split into two (1:1) peaks by the single proton C**H**Cl_2CH_2Cl.

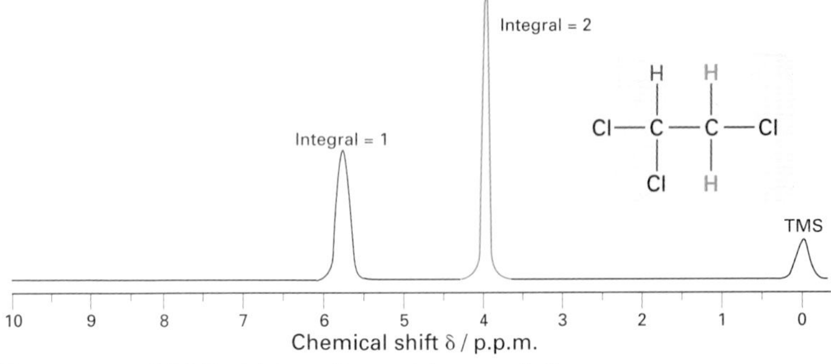

NMR spectrum of 1,1,2-trichloroethane at low resolution.

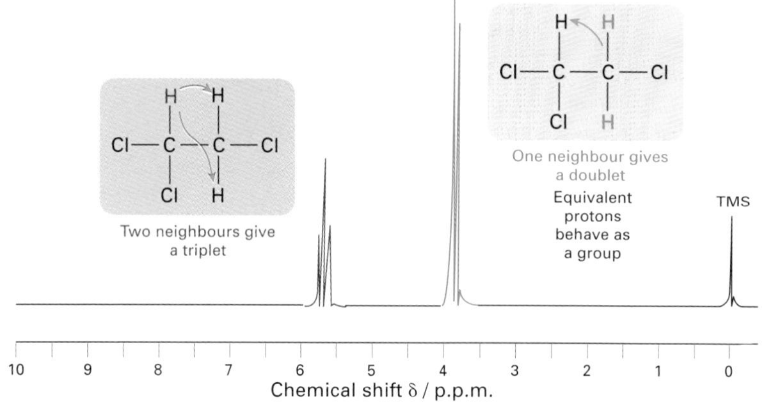

NMR spectrum of 1,1,2-trichloroethane at high resolution.

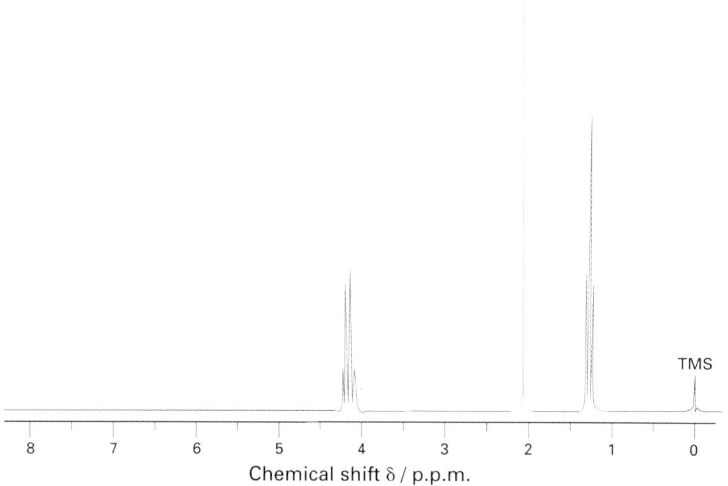

The high-resolution NMR spectrum of ethyl ethanoate.

SUMMARY

- Spin–spin splitting yields information about neighbouring protons.
- If the number of adjacent equivalent protons is n, the peak will split into $(n + 1)$ peaks.
- Pascal's triangle can be used to predict the relative intensifies of split peaks.

Ethyl ethanoate

The single peak near 2.1 p.p.m. must be due to the CH_3 connected to the carbonyl group, as it is a singlet (which means there are no adjacent protons).
The peak near 4.1 p.p.m. is a quartet, owing to the $—CH_2—$ group being attached to a $—CH_3$.
The peak near 1.3 p.p.m. is a triplet, confirming that the $—CH_2—$ group is the neighbour of this $—CH_3$ group.

NMR

NMR is one of the most powerful techniques currently used for structure determination in organic chemistry. Modern NMR spectrometers are fully computer controlled and, when coupled with automatic sample changers, provide continuous data acquisition and processing. This high level of automation, together with easy to use software packages, allows wider access to the instruments and frees the chemist to focus on data *interpretation* rather than mere data acquisition and processing.

PRACTICE

1 The NMR spectrum shown to the right was obtained from iodoethane. Explain the splitting pattern observed.

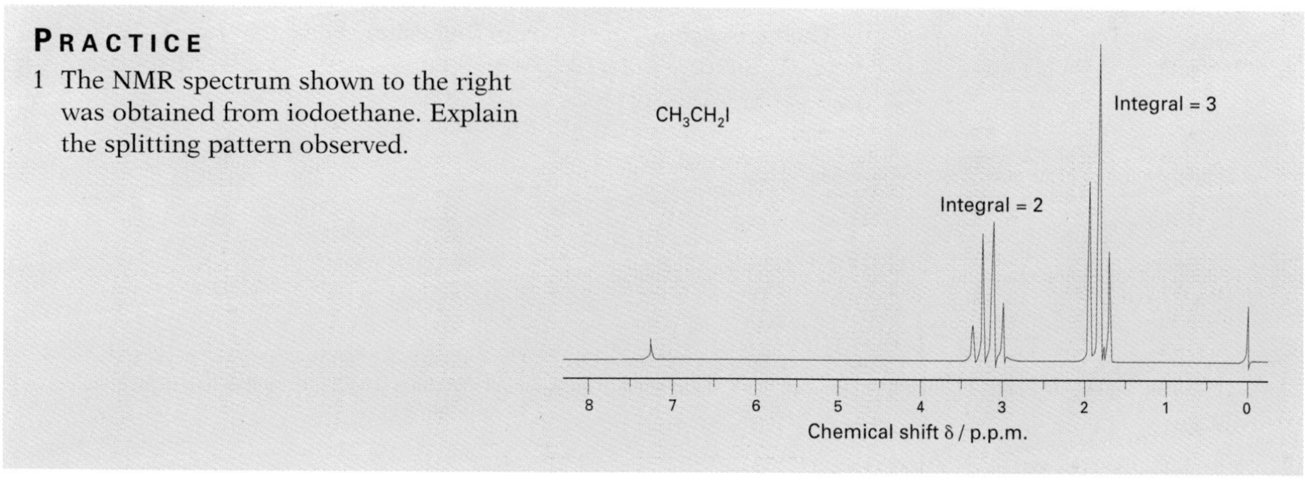

PRACTICE EXAM QUESTIONS

1 **a** Outline the principles on which atomic absorption spectroscopy is based. [3]

b Briefly describe the main differences in the principles on which atomic absorption spectroscopy and flame emission spectroscopy are based. [2]

c The urine of a patient admitted to hospital with suspected 'heavy-metal' poisoning was analysed by using atomic absorption spectroscopy. The spectrum shown below was obtained.

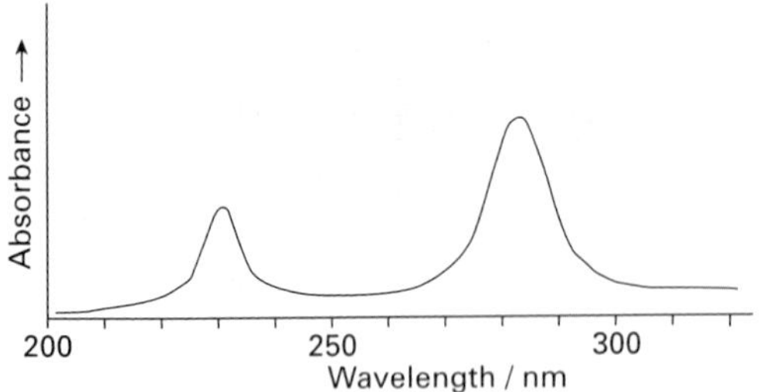

Wavelength of absorption / nm	Element	Possible source
229	Cadmium	Coloured pigments for pottery
254	Mercury	Seafood from contaminated water
283	Lead	Old water pipes, pottery glazes, old paint

Use the data in the table above to identify the likely source of the poisoning, indicating the evidence you have used. [3]

OCR (UCLES) 1998

2 **a** The infrared spectrum shown below is that of compound **X** which has the molecular formula $C_4H_8O_2$.

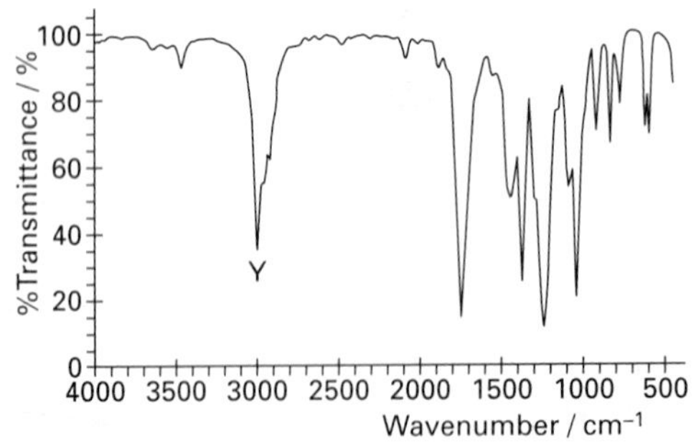

Table of infrared absorption data

Bond	Wavenumber/cm^{-1}
C—H	2850–3300
C—C	750–1100
C═C	1620–1680
C═O	1680–1750
C—O	1000–1300
O—H (alcohols)	3230–3550
O—H (acids)	2500–3000

i Use the table of infrared data to help you identify the bond responsible for the absorption marked **Y**.

ii Draw the structures of the two carboxylic acids having the molecular formula $C_4H_8O_2$ and explain why **X** cannot be either of these. [5]

b The fingerprint regions of the infrared spectra of **X** and of three other compounds are shown below labelled **I**, **II**, **III**, and **IV**.

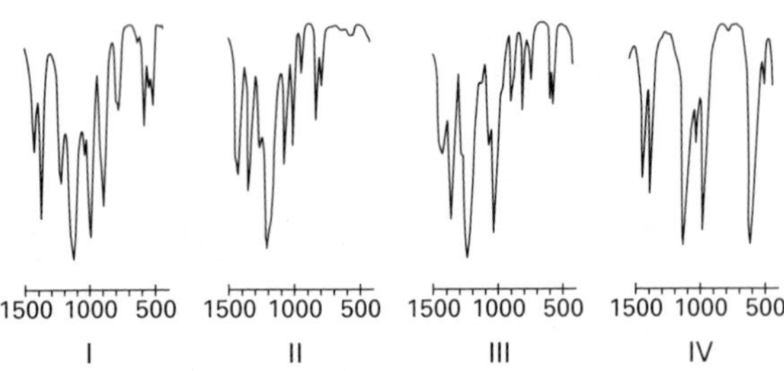

Which one of the fingerprint regions above is that of **X**? [1]

Compound **X** has three peaks with ratio of areas 3:2:3 in its low-resolution proton NMR spectrum. Draw two possible structures for compound **X**. [2]

AQA (NEAB) 1999

3 **a** For each of the following molecules, state how many absorptions you would expect to see in its infrared spectrum:

i H_2O

ii CO_2

iii CO. [3]

b **i** State two analytical uses of infrared spectroscopy.

ii Give a reason why infrared spectroscopy is suitable for each use. [4]

c The infrared spectrum shown below was obtained from compound **A**, known to contain carbon, hydrogen, and oxygen only. The M_r of compound **A** is 88. Identify the functional groups found in the compound and suggest a structure for **A**, indicating how you arrive at your conclusion. [3]

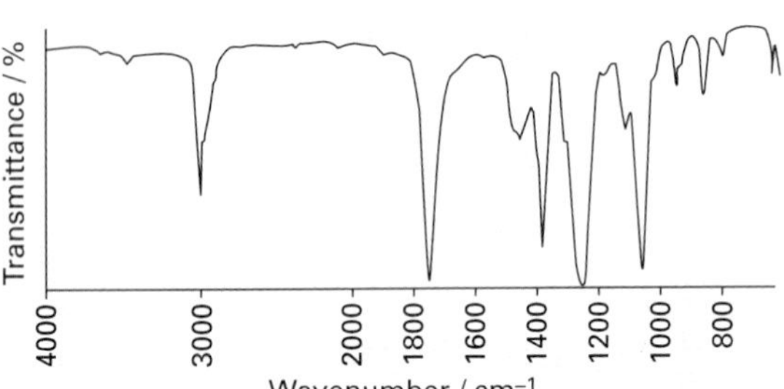

OCR (UCLES) 1998

4 **a** **i** Outline why a proton can occupy two different energy states when subjected to an external magnetic field.

ii The NMR spectrum of ethanal, CH_3CHO, contains two absorptions, a 1:1 doublet and a 1:3:3:1 quartet. Outline why these splitting patterns occur. [4]

b The two NMR spectra shown below were obtained from compounds F and G, which have the same empirical formula, $C_3H_6O_2$.

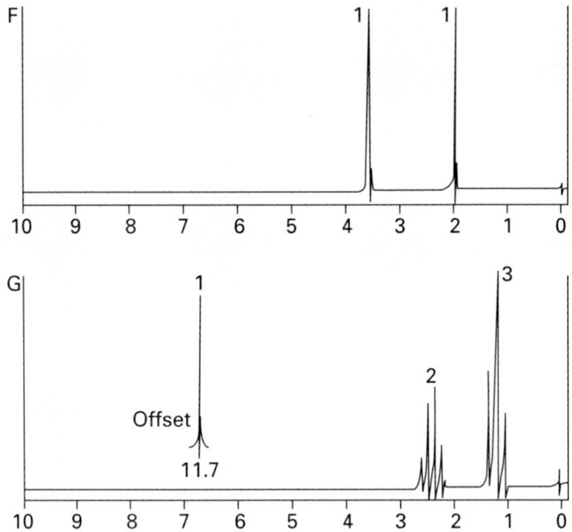

Identify the groups responsible for the absorptions in each spectrum, and hence deduce the structures of the two compounds. [6]
OCR (UCLES) 1998

5 The proton NMR spectrum of an alcohol, **A**, $C_5H_{12}O$, is shown below.

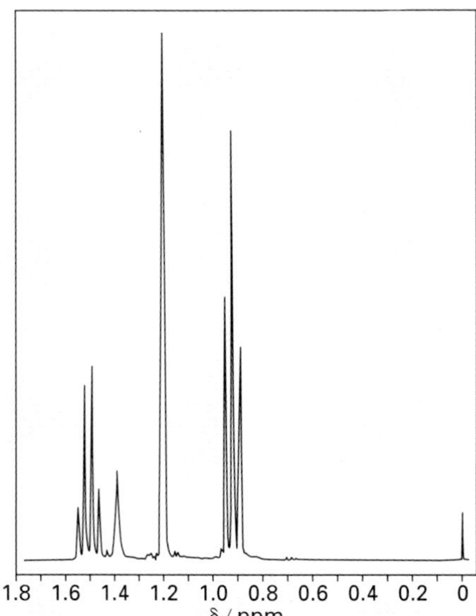

The measured integration trace gives the ratio 0.90 to 0.45 to 2.70 to 1.35 for the peaks at δ 1.52, 1.39, 1.21, and 0.93, respectively.

a What compound is responsible for the signal at δ = 0? [1]

b How many different types of proton are present in compound **A**? [1]

c What is the ratio of the numbers of each type of proton? [1]

d The peaks at δ 1.52 and δ 0.93 arise from the presence of a single alkyl group. Identify this group and explain the splitting pattern. [3]

e What can be deduced from the single peak at δ 1.21 and its integration value? [1]

f Give the structure of compound *A*. [1]
AQA (NEAB) 1999

6 **a** **i** Explain what is meant by the term *null* in infrared spectroscopy.

ii Ethanol is a good solvent for many organic compounds. Explain why ethanol is not a suitable solvent for use in producing infrared spectra of such compounds. [3]

b The infrared spectrum shown was obtained from a compound **J** of formula $C_5H_7O_2N$.

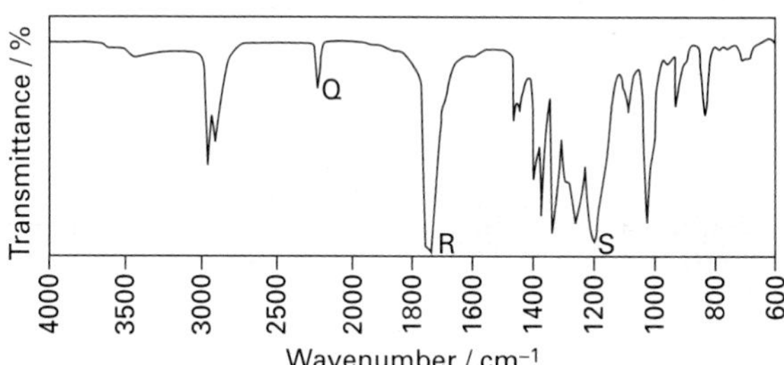

Identify the bonds responsible for the absorptions labelled **Q**, **R**, and **S**, and hence suggest a structure for **J**.

c The mass spectrum shown was obtained from a compound **K**.

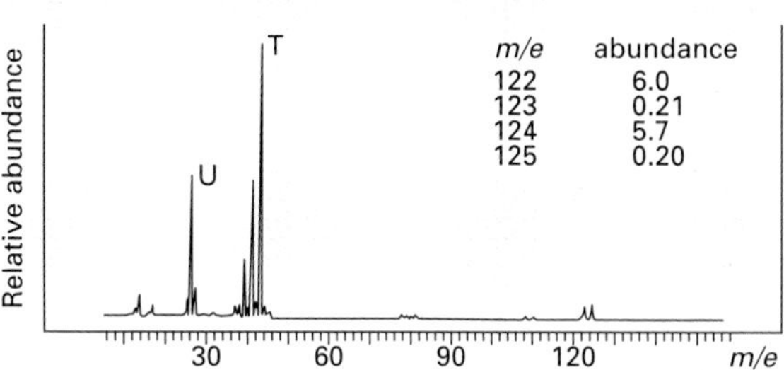

i Deduce what fragment has been lost in forming the peak labelled **T**.

ii Deduce what fragment has been lost from **T** in forming peak **U**.

iii Suggest a formula for **K**. [3]
OCR (UCLES) 1998

Mathematics toolbox: Standard form, uncertainty, and significant figures

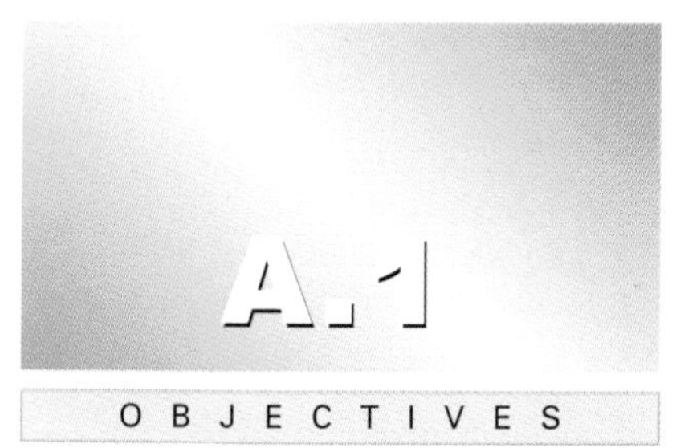

OBJECTIVES

- Standard form
- Uncertainty
- Significant figures

Examples of standard form

101 is 1.01×10^2

0.000 001 03 is 1.03×10^{-6}

126.5 is 1.265×10^2

Communicating data numerically is an important skill. You need to know the conventions for writing down the information. You also need to understand just what it is you are communicating, the certainty of the information, and the significance of figures.

Standard form

In chemistry, we often meet very large or very small numbers. A method of writing numbers that allows this very wide range to be covered is known as **standard form** or **scientific notation**. In standard form a number is written in two parts that are multiplied together. The first part is a number that is always greater than or equal to 1 and less than 10, and this is multiplied by 10 raised to any power that is an integer.

$$\text{standard form} = \pm a \times 10^{p}$$

The power of 10 (p) represents the number of moves of the decimal point in a that we need to make if the number we want is less than 1 or greater than 10. If the number is less than 1, the value of p is negative and the decimal point is moved to the left. For a number greater than 10, we move the decimal point to the right in the same way:

$$0.000\,012\,34 = 1.234 \times 10^{-5}$$

$$918 = 9.18 \times 10^{2}$$

Uncertainty

When scientists say that there is an **uncertainty** in a measurement, they do not mean that they are unsure of its value. Uncertainties, which are sometimes less helpfully called errors, are not mistakes. An uncertainty is a natural variation in a measurement that comes about for a variety of reasons:

- No instrument is exactly accurate.
- Different people may be using different types of instrument.
- No two people read an instrument in exactly the same way.
- The instrument's adjustment may have changed.

No matter how carefully we set up experiments, problems like these always arise. Scientists try to estimate how big an effect such problems may have on an experiment, and they may quote an uncertainty in the measurement.

If you read a scientific paper you will find that the numerical results include a second number and a '±' symbol. For example, a time may be quoted as $4.6 \pm 0.6 \times 10^{-8}$ s. This means that the author believes that the measurement result is 4.6×10^{-8} s but suspects that it may be as large as 5.2×10^{-8} s ($5.2 = 4.6 + 0.6$) or that it could be as small as 4.0×10^{-8} s ($4.0 = 4.6 - 0.6$). This defines the range of uncertainty that is unavoidably part of the experiment.

Worked example on uncertainty

Question: A burette may be read to the nearest 0.05 cm^3 (see spread 9.7). Given that the titre in an experiment is 25 cm^3, estimate the percentage uncertainty in the answer caused by the uncertainty in this titre.

Answer: The percentage uncertainty is

$$(0.05\,cm^3)/(25\,cm^3) \times 100 = 0.2$$

This particular reading causes a 0.2% uncertainty in the final answer.

Significant figures

The digits reported in a measurement are called the **significant figures** (sig. figs or s.f.). For example, 2.5 cm^3 has 2 sig. figs; 25.2 cm^3 has 3 sig. figs. Calculators quote answers to as many figures as the display will allow. For example, if you divide 10 by 6 on your calculator, it may report the answer 1.6666667. If you are dealing with experimental data, however, it is important to think about how many significant figures it is reasonable to quote.

Generally, it is a good rule to quote calculated values to the same number of significant figures as the data used in the calculation. So, for example, it would be wrong to go from data quoted to two significant figures to a result (calculated from those data) given to three or more significant figures. Equally, though, sometimes whole numbers are given to just one figure because it is obviously exact. Say, for example, you were dealing with four discrete objects. It would be unnecessary to limit the results of calculations using that 4 to just one significant figure. Counting is exact; measurements are always uncertain. You must always consider the certainty of any measurement.

Some confusion can arise over the significance of zeros in a measurement. It is important to distinguish between legitimately measured zeros and ones that are just used to mark the position of the decimal point. The last zeros after the decimal point, as in 25.0 cm^3, are significant because they were measured. If the measurement could be made to ±0.05 cm^3, 25.0 means that the volume is somewhere between 24.95 and 25.05 cm^3. However, some zeros are 'captive'. These may or may not be significant. If you measure 30.7 g, then the zero is significant because it was measured. The zeros in the value 0.035 g are not significant; they are just used to indicate powers of 10. So 0.035 g has two significant figures, but 0.0350 g has three significant figures because the last zero was measured (if it was).

Using significant figures in calculations

You must not quote more significant figures in your answer than the minimum number you had in your data. This means that you often have to round off your result. Round *up* if the last digit is above 5 and round *down* if it is below 5. For numbers ending in 5, always round to the nearest even number to avoid compounding rounding-off errors in your answer.

Do not round off as you work through a calculation, only at the end. In practice, carry all digits in the memory of your calculator until you get the final answer and then round this off in a single step. For example, the result 30.348 rounds to 30.3 to 3 sig. figs but 30.35 to 4 sig. figs.

Significant figures and standard form

A number like 782 000 000 might have been rounded to three significant figures or might be accurate to nine significant figures. It is impossible to tell which just by looking at it. If, however, the number is given in standard form, then all the figures are significant. So

1.60×10^{-19} is 3 sig. figs

1.602×10^{-19} is 4 sig. figs

$1.602\,18 \times 10^{-19}$ is 6 sig. figs

Decimal places

The decimal places are the digits that follow the decimal point. Again, we must be consistent in the number of decimal places we quote. In addition or subtraction, the number of decimal places quoted in the result should be the same as the *smallest number of decimal places* in the data.

When multiplying or dividing, revert to the rule that the number of *significant figures* should be the same as the *smallest number of significant figures* in the data.

A.2

OBJECTIVES

- Substituting into equations
- Manipulating equations
- What is a graph?
- Drawing graphs
- Information from graphs
- The equation of a straight line

Mathematics toolbox: Equations and graphs

An equation is characterized by the equals sign. For example,

$$5y = x - 3$$

Equations are algebraic, with both numbers and letters. Usually you are in the position of knowing all the terms except one in an equation. You will then substitute the correct value for each letter before you can carry out the calculation. For example, if $x = 18$ in the above equation, then:

$$5y = 18 - 3$$
$$5y = 15$$
$$y = 3$$

Manipulating equations

An equation demands that the relationship denoted by the equals sign is maintained. However, you often need to move quantities about to obtain the answer you need, for example to change the subject of an equation. The important thing to remember is that *you must do the same thing to both sides of the equation* so that the equals sign is not violated. The following steps are commonly used in manipulating equations.

- Add the same quantity to both sides
  For
  $$x - 3 = 5y$$
  adding 3 to both sides gives
  $$x = 5y + 3$$

- Subtract the same quantity from both sides
  For
  $$x + 5 = 7y$$
  subtracting 5 from both sides gives
  $$x = 7y - 5$$

- Multiply the whole equation by the same quantity
  For
  $$\frac{x + 9}{5} = 8y$$
  multiplying both sides by 5 gives
  $$x + 9 = 40y$$

- Divide the whole equation by the same quantity
  For
  $$x + 3 = 2y$$
  dividing both sides by 2 gives
  $$\frac{x + 3}{2} = y$$

- Raise both sides to the same power
  For
  $$x + 3 = 2y$$
  squaring both sides gives
  $$(x + 3)^2 = (2y)^2$$
  $$(x + 3)^2 = 4y^2$$

- Take roots of both sides
  For
  $$x^2 = 4y^2 + 9$$
  taking the square root of both sides gives
  $$x = \pm\sqrt{(4y^2 + 9)}$$

If you are unsure whether you have performed an operation correctly, a good check is to substitute simple numbers into the equation. *If one side is not equal to the other, you have done something wrong.*

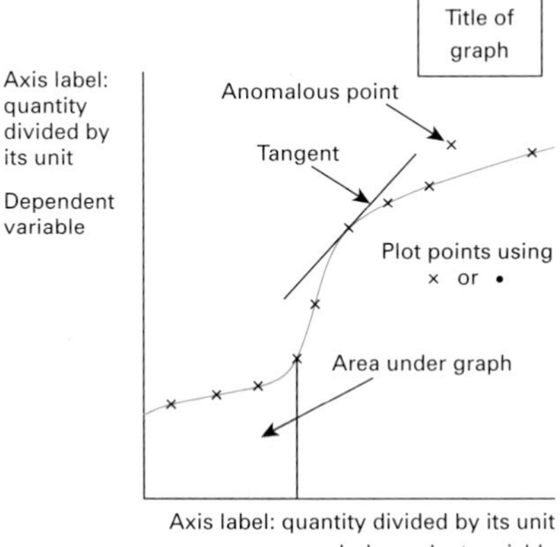

The parts of a graph.

Why use graphs?

A graph is a visual aid. When the results of an experiment are presented as a graph, it is immediately clear if they show a pattern. A graph will immediately reveal the scatter there is of the points about a smooth curve. The scatter is an indication of the size of the random errors involved in the experiment. Any gaps in your evidence will be plain as well. A graph also makes it easy to make estimations between measured points.

Drawing graphs

- Plot the **independent variable** on the horizontal axis or x-axis. You select values for the independent variable in an experiment.
- Plot the **dependent variable** on the vertical axis or y-axis. The dependent variable is the result of your alterations to the independent variable.
- Look at the range of values for both variables and choose a scale for both axes so that the plot fills most of the available space. (The scale need not be the same for both axes.) In some cases, this may mean leaving out the zero or origin from one or both axes.
- Choose a simple scale that will be straightforward to use. Make 10 small divisions represent 1, 2, or 5 (or these numbers multiplied by factors of 10 like 10, 0.2, and 500).
- Do not expect numbers from experimental measurements to give you a perfectly smooth curve or straight line. Draw the line of best fit for the plotted points, ignoring any obviously anomalous point. It is often a good idea to sketch your graph as you take your readings. This means you can take extra readings to fill in any missing detail or repeat the reading of an obviously anomalous point. In case you need to make an alteration, plot the points and draw the best-fit line with a soft lead pencil.

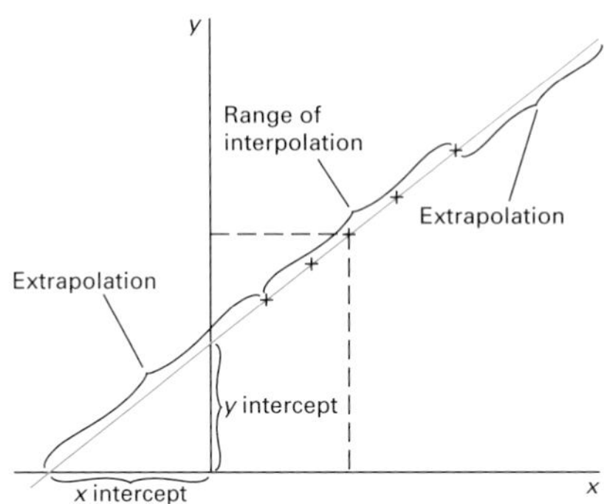

Graph showing interpolated and extrapolated points and intercepts.

The equation of a straight line

If the dimensions of x and y are related by the expression

$$y = mx + c$$

and you plot y (vertical axis) against x (horizontal axis), you will obtain a straight line. The gradient of the straight line is m, and the intercept on the y axis is c.

Information from graphs

Once the line of best fit is drawn, you can read any value of x in terms of y and vice versa by reading from the value on one axis, crossing to the line of best fit, and reading off the value of the other axis at that point. Points between the experimental readings may be found by **interpolation**. Extending the curve outside the experimental range is called **extrapolation**.

The **gradient** is the slope of a line at a point. To calculate the gradient of a straight-line graph, draw the largest convenient triangle using the line. The gradient is found from the equation

gradient = change in y coordinate/change in x coordinate

If the best-fit line is curved, you can only obtain the gradient for one point at a time. You will need to construct a **tangent** to the curve at that point, and then use the triangle method.

A tangent has the slope of the line at the point where it touches the curve. There are several methods of constructing tangents. To draw a tangent by eye, hold your ruler against the curve at the point where you want to construct the tangent so that it does not obscure the curve. Adjust the slope of the ruler so that the curve falls away equally on both sides of the point of contact.

The gradient of anything plotted against time will give you a rate of change.

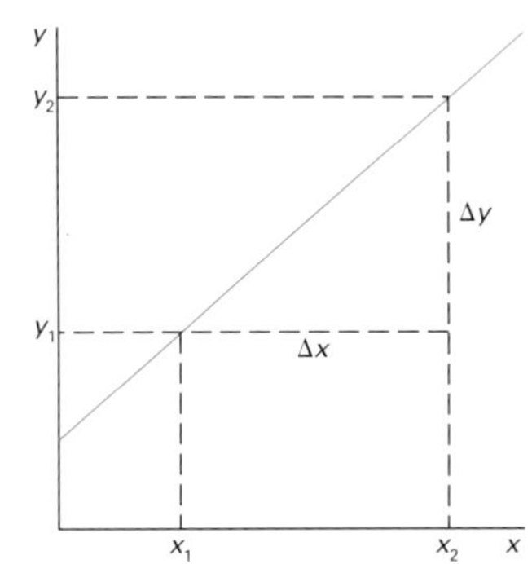

Determining the gradient:
gradient = $(y_2 - y_1)/(x_2 - x_1)$,
gradient = $\Delta y/\Delta x$

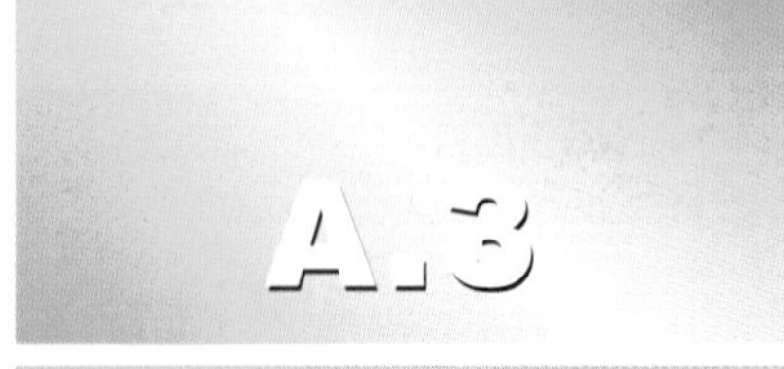

MATHEMATICS TOOLBOX: LOGARITHMS AND EXPONENTIALS

OBJECTIVES

- Common logarithms
- Natural logarithms
- Calculations using logarithms
- The exponential function
- Graphs of exponential functions

Theory of logarithms

If a number y can be written in the form a^x, then the power x is called the **logarithm** of y to the base a. For example, $1000 = 10^3$, so $3 = \log_{10} 1000$. You can check this using the 'log' function on your calculator.

Common logarithms

The logarithm of a number to base 10 is the power that the number 10 has to be raised to in order to equal that number. Logarithms having a base of 10 are called **common logarithms**, and $\log_{10}$ is often abbreviated to 'log' or 'lg'.

Natural logarithms

Logarithms having a base of e, where e is a mathematical constant approximately equal to 2.718, are called **natural logarithms** or sometimes Napierian or hyperbolic logarithms. Log_e is often abbreviated to 'ln'.

Rules of logarithms

- To multiply two numbers, we add their logs:

  $\log(a \times b) = \log a + \log b$

- To divide two numbers, we subtract their logs:

  $\log(a/b) = \log a - \log b$

- To raise a number to a power, we multiply its log by the power:

  $\log a^n = n \log a$

To do the opposite operation, to find the number from its log, we use the antilogarithm or 10^x (log) key, which is usually found as the second (shifted) function on the log key.

The examples below and alongside show how one particular current calculator works. NB Older calculators may require step 3 to be done first (possibly with the minus sign put in after the number), in which case step 4 is probably not needed. For instance to find the antilog of –3.2

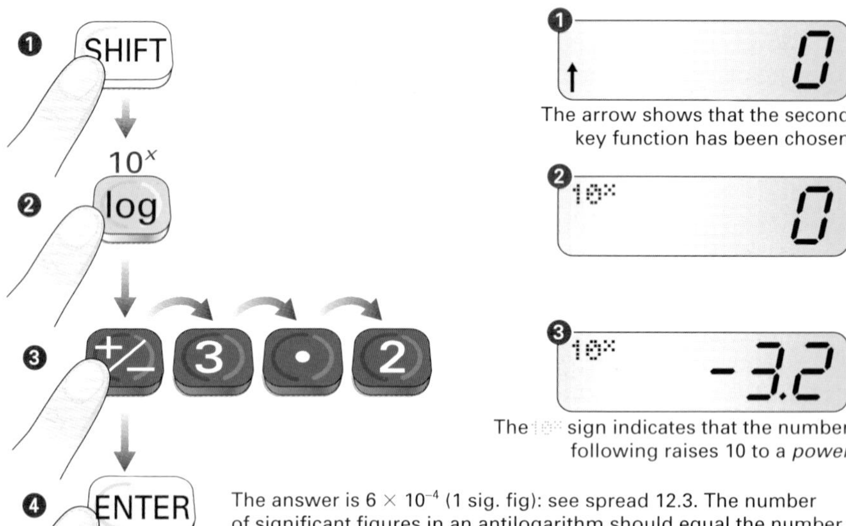

SHIFT
10^x
log
+/–
3
•
2
ENTER
The arrow shows that the second key function has been chosen
The sign indicates that the number following raises 10 to a *power*

The answer is 6×10^{-4} (1 sig. fig): see spread 12.3. The number of significant figures in an antilogarithm should equal the number of decimal places in a logarithm. Try entering –3.3 and the answer becomes 5×10^{-4} (1 sig. fig); a change in the first decimal place changes the first significant figure of the antilogarithm.

The exponential function

The mathematical constant e, which has a value of approximately 2.718, is called the exponent. A function that contains e^x is called an exponential function. e^x is a function that increases at a rate proportional to its own magnitude.

Know your calculator

There are many different calculators on the market and they often execute functions such as logarithms in slightly different ways. It is well worth checking how your *particular* calculator executes logarithms and exponentials. The examples below and alongside show how one particular current calculator works. NB Older calculators may require steps 1 and 2 below to be done *in reverse*, in which case step 3 is probably not needed.

Say you want to find the common logarithm of 6.0×10^{23}, as is needed in spread 12.3:

1. Press the key labelled 'log' or 'LOG':

log

2. Enter your given number, remembering to press the 'enter exponent' key (usually labelled EE or EXP):

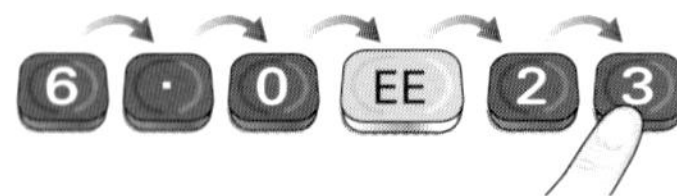

6
0
EE
2
3

3. Press the key which causes the calculation to be performed (usually labelled ENTER or EXE or =):

ENTER

The answer you will find is 23.78 (2 d.p.). In spread 12.3 we stated that the number of *decimal places* in a pH value (which uses logs) should equal the number of *significant figures* in your given number: repeat the exercise above using 5.9 in place of 6.0 and the final answer changes to 23.77 (2 d.p.); a change in the second significant figure changes the second decimal place of the logarithm.

The exponent is important because all the natural laws of growth and decay are of the form $y = ae^x$

Logarithms to the base e, natural logarithms, were developed to simplify calculations involving the exponential function.

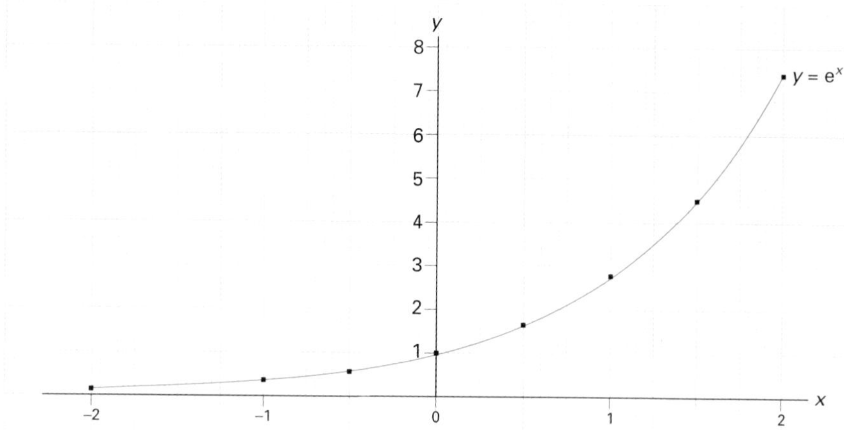

A graph of the curve $y = e^x$. This is called a growth curve.

You can find the value of e^x using the e^x function key on a scientific calculator. The degree of precision given by the calculator is often far greater than is appropriate. The selection of the appropriate number of significant figures is harder than in the case of a common antilogarithm; a rough rule of thumb is to use one more significant figure than there are decimal places in the given number. For example, $e^{-3.2}$ is 0.042 (2 sig. figs), whereas $e^{-3.3}$ is 0.037 (2 sig. figs).

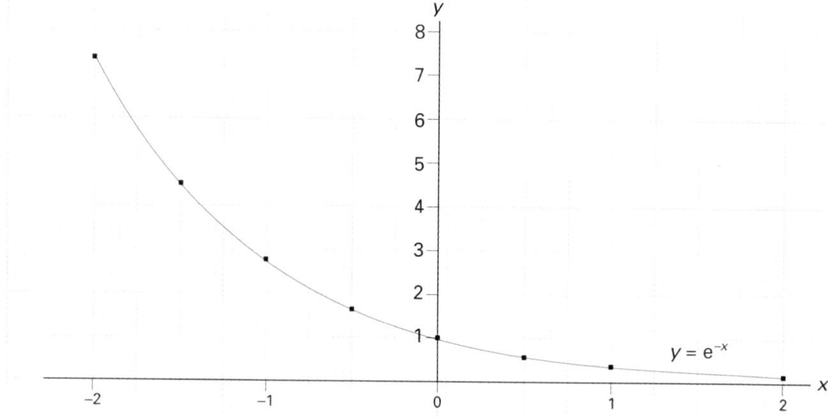

A graph of the curve $y = e^{-x}$. This is called a decay curve.

Graphs of exponential functions

For graphs of the form $y = e^{kx}$, where k is a constant and can be positive or negative, 'k' has the effect of altering the scale of x. For graphs of the form $y = Ae^{kx}$, where A is a constant, 'A' has the effect of altering the scale of y. Hence, every curve of the form $y = Ae^{kx}$ has the same general shape, and A and k are called scale factors of the graph.

Practical uses of growth and decay curves

Experimental data start from a given time, so time has only positive values. Hence, only the terms to the right of the y axis are used.

ln graphs

If $y = Ae^{kx}$ then, by taking natural logarithms, we find that

$$\begin{aligned} \ln y &= \ln (Ae^{kx}) \\ &= \ln A + \ln (e^{kx}) \\ &= \ln A + kx \end{aligned}$$

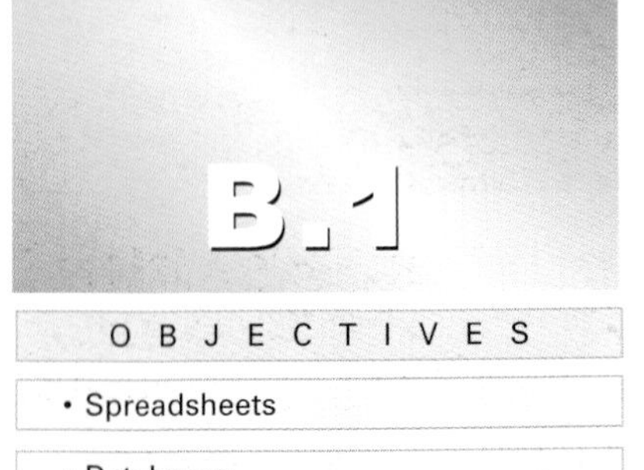

OBJECTIVES

- Spreadsheets
- Databases
- Computer-generated graphs
- Visualization software
- Modelling

THE USES OF COMPUTERS IN CHEMISTRY

The uses of computers in chemistry are particularly widespread. We introduce several of the areas where they are helpful in this spread.

Details on the availability of the various different pieces of software mentioned here may be obtained from one of the authors (MJC), care of the publishers. (MJC gratefully acknowledges the help of former students – most notably Paul Collins and James Whyte – with programming some of the software demonstrated here.)

Spreadsheets

One simple use of a computer involves a spreadsheet to take the tedium out of routine calculations. The example shown below relates to the esterification equilibrium discussed in spread 11.6.

Expt	Titre	OrigVol *acid*	OrigVol *water*	OrigVol *alc*	OrigVol *ester*
1	18.6	6.0	12.0	6.0	6.0
2	17.1	9.0	3.0	9.0	9.0
3	34.4	9.0	12.0	0.0	9.0
4	15.1	6.0	9.0	9.0	6.0

n(acid) *start*	n(water) *start*	n(alc) *start*	n(ester) *start*	n(acid) *eq*	n(water) *eq*	n(alc) *eq*	n(ester) *eq*	K_c
0.105	0.664	0.103	0.061	0.102	0.666	0.100	0.064	4.12
0.157	0.166	0.154	0.092	0.094	0.229	0.091	0.155	4.19
0.157	0.664	0.000	0.092	0.197	0.624	0.040	0.052	4.14
0.105	0.498	0.154	0.061	0.082	0.521	0.131	0.085	4.13

Spreadsheet for the esterification equilibrium.

Significant figures

The volumes are given to the nearest 0.1 cm^3; this means that the volumes are correct to either 3 sig. figs (for the titres) or 2 sig. figs (for the original volumes). The third significant figure is retained throughout to avoid rounding errors. The final figure for K_c is shown to 3 sig. figs; the third figure cannot be regarded as correct.

The various different starting compositions are entered into the spreadsheet and the necessary formulae are specified in the various cells. Entering the titres found in a particular experiment can update the sheet instantaneously. The values above represent such an application. Note how the final column, the value for K_c, is almost constant. Providing a shortcut compared with the long-winded and tedious calculation steps (helpfully avoiding the chances of errors cropping up!) frees the student to focus on the important conclusion about the chemistry involved.

Databases

Computers have large memory capacities, allowing storage of huge quantities of data, with fast access available. It is, for example, possible to access a database with essentially all known crystal structures or spectral data. This research tool can be used to find out whether a newly made compound has been fully characterised before. Suitable software is routinely provided with newer spectroscopic equipment.

On a smaller scale, but more useful in educational situations, the periodic table program in ChemSoft is able to provide all the usual data on the elements (melting point, boiling point, ionization energy, and so on). Graphs can be drawn of the variation across periods and down groups. An example is shown below.

Lanthanides and actinides

The correct positioning of the lanthanides and actinides is controversial. In this text, we follow the exam Boards' traditional placing. The program follows current international opinion at research level.

(a)

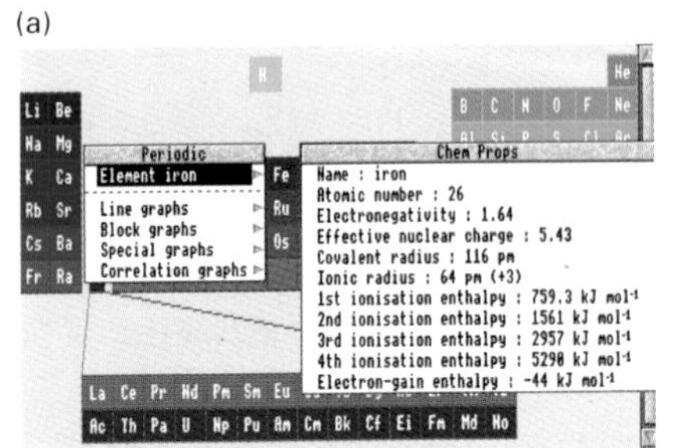

(b)

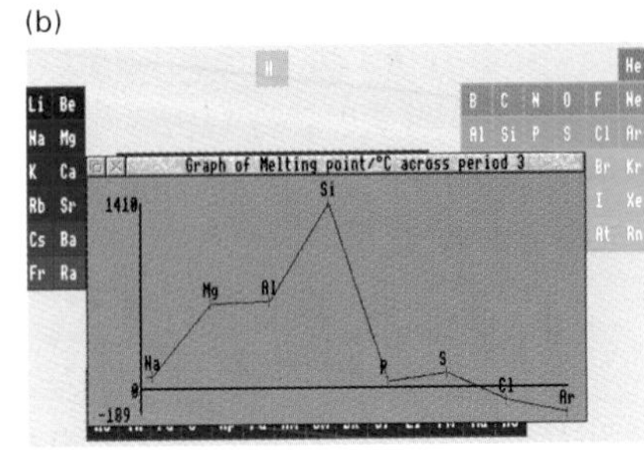

(a) One selection of the data available for an element. (b) Graph of the melting points across Period 3.

In addition, the correlation between data sets may be investigated. Some of the possible permutations will produce little additional understanding (discovery date and density would be a pair unlikely to warrant study). On the other hand, relative atomic mass and atomic number show close correlation.

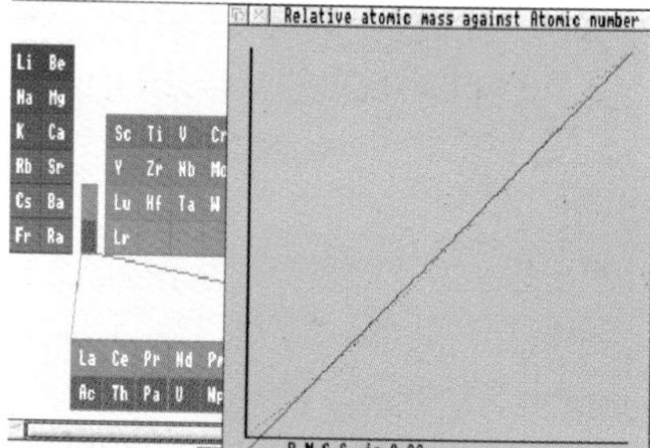

The correlation between relative atomic mass and atomic number.

'Calculate and display' software

Computer-generated graphs are more accurately drawn than are easily possible by hand, assuming the program has been coded correctly! The graphs of pH against volume shown on spreads 12.8 and 12.9 were originally calculated by a computer program written by one of the authors (MJC). The program allows the user to choose any particular weak acid for example; on specification of the pK_a value, the program will then accurately calculate and display the pH curve in a matter of seconds. It is encouraging that specifications suggest using computers to generate such graphs.

Similar programs for the Maxwell–Boltzmann distribution, Boyle's law curves, shapes of atomic orbitals, and the extent of ionization of a weak acid (among others) are also available.

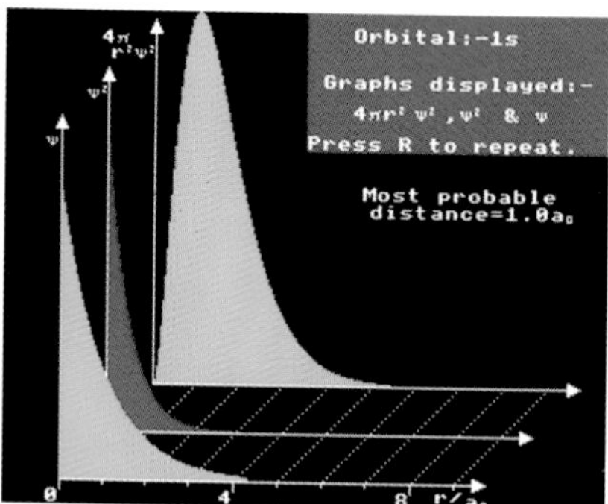

Plots of the wave function ψ, its square ψ^2, together with the electron density, which is equal to $4\pi r^2\psi^2$.

Visualization software

One of the most important application of computers relies on their unrivalled ability to display objects in three dimensions, enabling objects such as crystal structures or molecules to be rotated in real time.

We mentioned in spread 6.7 that the very impressive structure program in ChemSoft enables the most important crystal structures (including f.c.c., h.c.p., rock-salt, fluorite, zinc blende, and several others) to be displayed, resized, and rotated. The octahedral and tetrahedral holes may be highlighted to allow the structure around a specific atom or ion to be investigated. This makes the structures come alive in a visually appealing way.

Modelling

Modelling also aims to take advantage of the display facility of computers, applied mainly to organic molecules. Organic molecules may be rotated to view the detailed electron densities and to inspect the various reactive sites (as explained in spread 21.5).

Such software may be used (most especially by biotechnology companies) to investigate the match of a potential drug to the receptor site on its chosen target.

We have been very fortunate to benefit from the kindness of Wavefunction Inc, and its co-founder and CEO Warren Hehre, who provided many images from their Spartan software package. A number of other companies provide similar packages, mostly for the university sector. We are also grateful to Oxford Molecular, and its founder and CEO Graham Richards, for providing other useful images from software such as CAChe.

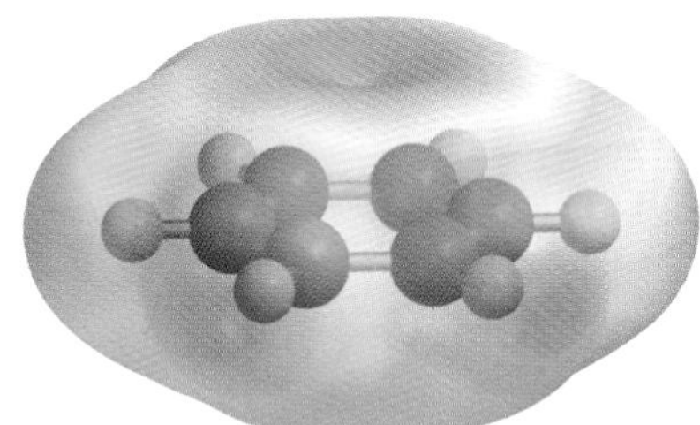
The electrostatic potential map for benzene confirms the high electron density, shown by the red colour, above (and below) the plane of the ring.

A wide range of different molecules may be displayed and manipulated on screen. These may be tailored to show a number of properties. For example, the electron density may be displayed as an electrostatic potential map, spread 5.8. This image may be examined to identify centres of partial charge which will attract nucleophiles or electrophiles for example.

Alternatively, the shape of different molecular orbitals for a selection of the most important molecules can be shown. This can be used to decide which atoms have substantial involvement in for example the so-called frontier orbitals, which are the ones most important in molecular collisions. The frontier orbitals are the highest occupied molecular orbital (HOMO) and lowest unoccupied molecular orbital (LUMO). See for example the p and p* orbitals for ethene shown in spread 32.2. The shape of the lowest-energy bonding molecular orbital has particular significance for the concept of delocalization, spread 6.4.

The lowest energy bonding molecular orbital for methane is delocalized over all five atoms, see spread 22.12.

A particularly effective use of the technology is to allow visualization of the steps in a mechanism, such as that for nucleophilic substitution shown in spread 24.3.

C.1

THE PERIODIC TABLE

OBJECTIVES

- Origin of some names
- Name and symbol
- Atomic number and relative atomic mass

Chemistry is all about the elements and the compounds formed between them. Some elements (such as carbon and gold) have been known since prehistoric times, whereas others (such as fermium and lawrencium) were discovered in the second half of the twentieth century. This spread gives a little historical background to the discovery and naming of the elements.

Element	Atomic no.	Symbol	Isolation	Origin of name and symbol (if different)
aluminium	13	Al	1825, Oersted	Latin *alumen*, alum
argon	18	Ar	1894, Rayleigh/Ramsay	Greek *argos*, inert
barium	56	Ba	1808, Davy	Greek *barys*, heavy
boron	5	B	1808, Davy	Arabic *buraq*, borax, + -on, as in carbon
bromine	35	Br	1826, Balard	Greek *bromos*, stench
caesium	55	Cs	1860, Bunsen/Kirchhoff	Latin *caesius*, sky blue
calcium	20	Ca	1808, Davy	Latin *calx*, lime
carbon	6	C	prehistoric	Latin *carbo*, charcoal
chlorine	17	Cl	1774, Scheele	Greek *chloros*, yellow-green
cobalt	27	Co	1735, Brandt	German *Kobold*, goblin
copper	29	Cu	prehistoric	Latin *cuprum*, *cyprium*, Cyprus
curium	96	Cm	1944, Seaborg/Ghiorso	Pierre and Marie Curie
europium	63	Eu	1901, Demarçay	Europe
fermium	100	Fm	1952, Ghiorso	Enrico Fermi
fluorine	9	F	1886, Moissan	Latin *fluere*, flow
germanium	32	Ge	1886, Winkler	Latin *Germania*, Germany
gold	79	Au	prehistoric	Anglo-Saxon *gold*; Au: Latin *aurum*
hafnium	72	Hf	1923, von Hevesy	Latin *Hafnia*, Copenhagen
helium	2	He	1895, Ramsay	Greek *helios*, Sun
hydrogen	1	H	1766, Cavendish	Greek *hydr* + *gen*, water-forming
iodine	53	I	1811, Courtois	Greek *iodes*, violet
iron	26	Fe	prehistoric	Anglo-Saxon *iron*; Fe: Latin *ferrum*
krypton	36	Kr	1898, Ramsay/Travers	Greek *kryptos*, hidden
lawrencium	103	Lr	1961, Ghiorso	Ernest Lawrence
lead	82	Pb	prehistoric	Anglo-Saxon *lead*; Pb: Latin *plumbum*
magnesium	12	Mg	1808, Davy	Greek *Magnesia*, district in Greece
mendelevium	101	Md	1955, Ghiorso/Seaborg	Dmitri Mendeleyev
mercury	80	Hg	prehistoric	the planet Mercury; Hg: Latin *hydragyrum*
neon	10	Ne	1898, Ramsay/Travers	Greek *neos*, new
oxygen	8	O	1774, Priestley/Scheele	Greek *oxys* + *gen*, acid-forming
phosphorus	15	P	1669, Brandt	Greek *phosphoros*, light bringer
platinum	78	Pt	prehistoric	Spanish *platina*, silver
plutonium	94	Pu	1940, Seaborg	the planet Pluto
polonium	84	Po	1898, Marie Curie	Poland
potassium	19	K	1807, Davy	English *potash*; K: Latin *kalium*
radium	88	Ra	1898, Curie	Latin *radius*, ray
rubidium	37	Rb	1861, Bunsen/Kirchhoff	Latin *rubidus*, red
selenium	34	Se	1817, Berzelius	Greek *selene*, Moon
silver	47	Ag	prehistoric	Anglo-Saxon *silver*; Ag: Latin *argentum*
sodium	11	Na	1807, Davy	English *soda*; Na: Latin *natrium*
strontium	38	Sr	1808, Davy	Strontian, place in Scotland
sulphur	16	S	prehistoric	Sanskrit *sulvere*
tellurium	52	Te	1783, von Reichenstein	Latin *tellus*, Earth
tungsten	74	W	1783, d'Elhuyar	Swedish *tung sten*, heavy stone; W: *wolfram*
uranium	92	U	1841, Peligot	the planet Uranus
vanadium	23	V	1801, del Rio	*Vanadis*, Scandinavian goddess of beauty
xenon	54	Xe	1898, Ramsay/Travers	Greek *xenon*, stranger
ytterbium	70	Yb	1878, de Marignac	Ytterby, place in Sweden
zinc	30	Zn	prehistoric	German *Zink*

Period	I	II											III	IV	V	VI	VII	VIII
1	$_{1}$H Hydrogen 1.0																	$_{2}$He Helium 4.0
2	$_{3}$Li Lithium 6.9	$_{4}$Be Beryllium 9.0											$_{5}$B Boron 10.8	$_{6}$C Carbon 12.0	$_{7}$N Nitrogen 14.0	$_{8}$O Oxygen 16.0	$_{9}$F Fluorine 19.0	$_{10}$Ne Neon 20.2
3	$_{11}$Na Sodium 23.0	$_{12}$Mg Magnesium 24.3											$_{13}$Al Aluminium 27.0	$_{14}$Si Silicon 28.1	$_{15}$P Phosphorus 31.0	$_{16}$S Sulphur 32.1	$_{17}$Cl Chlorine 35.5	$_{18}$Ar Argon 39.9
4	$_{19}$K Potassium 39.1	$_{20}$Ca Calcium 40.1	$_{21}$Sc Scandium 45.0	$_{22}$Ti Titanium 47.9	$_{23}$V Vanadium 50.9	$_{24}$Cr Chromium 52.0	$_{25}$Mn Manganese 54.9	$_{26}$Fe Iron 55.8	$_{27}$Co Cobalt 58.9	$_{28}$Ni Nickel 58.7	$_{29}$Cu Copper 63.5	$_{30}$Zn Zinc 65.4	$_{31}$Ga Gallium 69.7	$_{32}$Ge Germanium 72.6	$_{33}$As Arsenic 74.9	$_{34}$Se Selenium 79.0	$_{35}$Br Bromine 79.9	$_{36}$Kr Krypton 83.8
5	$_{37}$Rb Rubidium 85.5	$_{38}$Sr Strontium 87.6	$_{39}$Y Yttrium 88.9	$_{40}$Zr Zirconium 91.2	$_{41}$Nb Niobium 92.9	$_{42}$Mo Molybdenum 95.9	$_{43}$Tc Technetium (98)	$_{44}$Ru Ruthenium 101.1	$_{45}$Rh Rhodium 102.9	$_{46}$Pd Palladium 106.4	$_{47}$Ag Silver 107.9	$_{48}$Cd Cadmium 112.4	$_{49}$In Indium 114.8	$_{50}$Sn Tin 118.7	$_{51}$Sb Antimony 121.8	$_{52}$Te Tellurium 127.6	$_{53}$I Iodine 126.9	$_{54}$Xe Xenon 131.3
6	$_{55}$Cs Caesium 132.9	$_{56}$Ba Barium 137.3	$_{57}$La Lanthanum 138.9	$_{72}$Hf Hafnium 178.5	$_{73}$Ta Tantalum 180.9	$_{74}$W Tungsten 183.9	$_{75}$Re Rhenium 186.2	$_{76}$Os Osmium 190.2	$_{77}$Ir Iridium 192.2	$_{78}$Pt Platinum 195.1	$_{79}$Au Gold 197.0	$_{80}$Hg Mercury 200.6	$_{81}$Tl Thallium 204.4	$_{82}$Pb Lead 207.2	$_{83}$Bi Bismuth 209.0	$_{84}$Po Polonium (209)	$_{85}$At Astatine (210)	$_{86}$Rn Radon (222)
7	$_{87}$Fr Francium (223)	$_{88}$Ra Radium (226)	$_{89}$Ac Actinium (227)	$_{104}$Rf Rutherfordium (261)	$_{105}$Db Dubnium (262)	$_{106}$Sg Seaborgium (263)	$_{107}$Bh Bohrium (262)	$_{108}$Hs Hassium (265)	$_{109}$Mt Meitnerium (266)									

$_{58}$Ce Cerium 140.1	$_{59}$Pr Praseodymium 140.9	$_{60}$Nd Neodymium 144.2	$_{61}$Pm Promethium (145)	$_{62}$Sm Samarium 150.4	$_{63}$Eu Europium 152.0	$_{64}$Gd Gadolinium 157.3	$_{65}$Tb Terbium 158.9	$_{66}$Dy Dysprosium 162.5	$_{67}$Ho Holmium 164.9	$_{68}$Er Erbium 167.3	$_{69}$Tm Thulium 168.9	$_{70}$Yb Ytterbium 173.0	$_{71}$Lu Lutetium 175.0
$_{90}$Th Thorium (232)	$_{91}$Pa Protactinium (231)	$_{92}$U Uranium (238)	$_{93}$Np Neptunium (237)	$_{94}$Pu Plutonium (244)	$_{95}$Am Americium (243)	$_{96}$Cm Curium (247)	$_{97}$Bk Berkelium (247)	$_{98}$Cf Californium (251)	$_{99}$Es Einsteinium (252)	$_{100}$Fm Fermium (257)	$_{101}$Md Mendelevium (258)	$_{102}$No Nobelium (259)	$_{103}$Lr Lawrencium (262)

C.2 THERMODYNAMIC PROPERTIES

OBJECTIVES

- Standard enthalpy change of formation
- Standard entropy
- Standard Gibbs energy change of formation

Aluminium Al(s)

Barium Ba(s)

Copper Cu(s)

Iron Fe(s)

Substance	$\Delta H^{\ominus}$(298 K)/kJ mol^{-1}	$S^{\ominus}$(298 K)/J K^{-1} mol^{-1}	$\Delta G^{\ominus}$(298 K)/kJ mol^{-1}
Ag(s)	0	+43	0
AgCl(s)	−127	+96	−110
Al(s)	0	+28	0
$AlCl_3$(s)	−704	+111	−629
Al_2O_3(s)	−1676	+51	−1582
Ar(g)	0	+155	0
BF_3(g)	−1136	+254	−1119
Ba(s)	0	+63	0
$BaCl_2$(s)	−859	+124	−810
BaO(s)	−554	+70	−525
Br_2(l)	0	+152	0
C(s, graphite)	0	+6	0
CH_4(g)	−74	+186	−50
C_2H_6(g)	−84	+230	−32
C_2H_4(g)	+53	+220	+68
C_2H_2(g)	+228	+201	+211
CH_3CHO(l)	−192	+160	−128
CH_3CH_2OH(l)	−278	+161	−175
CH_3COOH(l)	−485	+160	−390
CH_3NO_2(l)	−113	+172	−14
CO(g)	−111	+198	−137
CO_2(g)	−394	+214	−394
Ca(s)	0	+42	0
$CaCO_3$(s)	−1208	+92	−1129
$CaCl_2$(s)	−795	+105	−749
CaH_2(s)	−182	+41	−143
CaO(s)	−635	+38	−603
Cl_2(g)	0	+223	0
CsCl(s)	−443	+101	−415
Cu(s)	0	+33	0
$CuCl_2$(s)	−220	+108	−176
CuO(s)	−157	+43	−130
$CuSO_4$(s)	−771	+109	−662
F_2(g)	0	+203	0
Fe(s)	0	+27	0
$FeCl_2$(s)	−342	+118	−302
$FeCl_3$(s)	−400	+142	−334
Fe_2O_3(s)	−824	+87	−742
Fe_3O_4(s)	−1118	+146	−1015

Substance	$\Delta H^{\ominus}$(298 K)/kJ mol^{-1}	$S^{\ominus}$(298 K)/J K^{-1} mol^{-1}	$\Delta G^{\ominus}$(298 K)/kJ mol^{-1}
H_2(g)	0	+131	0
HBr(g)	−36	+199	−53
HCl(g)	−92	+187	−95
HF(g)	−273	+174	−275
HI(g)	+27	+207	+2
HNO_3(l)	−174	+156	−81
H_2O(l)	−286	+70	−237
H_2O(g)	−242	+189	−229
H_2SO_4(l)	−814	+157	−690
I_2(s)	0	+116	0
K(s)	0	+65	0
KCl(s)	−437	+83	−409
KOH(s)	−425	+79	−379
Mg(s)	0	+33	0
$MgCl_2$(s)	−641	+90	−592
MgO(s)	−602	+27	−569
N_2(g)	0	+192	0
NO_2(g)	+33	+240	+51
N_2O_4(g)	+9	+304	+98
NH_3(g)	−46	+193	−16
Na(s)	0	+51	0
NaCl(s)	−411	+72	−384
Na_2O(s)	−414	+75	−376
NaOH(s)	−426	+64	−380
O_2(g)	0	+205	0
O_3(g)	+143	+239	+163
P_4(s, white)	0	+41	0
PCl_3(l)	−320	+217	−272
Pb(s)	0	+65	0
$PbCl_2$(s)	−359	+136	−314
PbO(s)	−217	+69	−188
S_8(s, rhombic)	0	+32	0
SF_6(g)	−1221	+291	−1117
SO_2(g)	−297	+248	−300
SO_3(s)	−455	+71	−374
$SiCl_4$(l)	−687	+240	−620
SiO_2(s)	−911	+41	−856
TiO_2(s)	−944	+51	−889
V_2O_5(s)	−1551	+131	−1420
Zn(s)	0	+42	0
$ZnCl_2$(s)	−415	+111	−369
ZnO(s)	−351	+44	−321

Potassium K(s)

Magnesium Mg(s)

Lead Pb(s)

Sulphur S_8(s)

Suggested answers to selected practice and exam questions

Please note: the following suggested answers and solutions are intended as a guide for the reader. The respective exam boards have not supplied the answers and solutions to past exam questions nor are they in any way responsible for their accuracy or correctness.
In some answers, one extra unjustified significant figure is retained to avoid rounding error at the end.

Chapter 1

Practice questions

Spread 1.4

1 Lithium, magnesium, silicon, bromine, potassium, silver, tin, fluorine.

2 Ge, S, Ca, Au, Kr, Sb, Pb

5 Vanadium, V; aluminium, Al; barium, Ba; krypton, Kr; strontium, Sr; nitrogen, N

Chapter 2

Practice questions

Spread 2.1

2 Simplistically, the ratio of the areas is equal to the square of the ratio of the radii; hence 10^{12} (NB A more sophisticated answer would recognize that close-packed spheres occupy only 74% of space; see spread 6.5)

Spread 2.4

1 **a** 17 protons, 18 neutrons, 17 electrons
b 12 protons, 12 neutrons, 12 electrons
c 92 protons, 143 neutrons, 92 electrons

2 **a** Atomic number: 17, mass number: 35
b Atomic number: 12, mass number: 24
c Atomic number: 92, mass number: 235

3 28.1

Chapter 3

Practice questions

Spread 3.1

1 9.0, 10.8, 40.1, 12.0, 55.8, 54.9, 31.0, 23.0, 131.3

2 **a** 28.0, 44.0, 100.1, 98.1; **b** 17.0, 64.1, 16.0, 63.0

Spread 3.2

1 72.7

Spread 3.3

1 **a** 24.0 g; **b** 12.15 g; **c** 0.27 g; **d** 115 g; **e** 115 g

2 **a** 55.9 kg; **b** 1839 kg; **c** 1.0×10^{-6} kg

3 **a** 1.00 mol; **b** 2.00 mol; **c** 0.249 mol

Spread 3.4

1 **a** 17.0 g mol^{-1}; **b** 46.0 g mol^{-1}; **c** 142 g mol^{-1}; **d** 48.0 g mol^{-1}

2 **a** 34.0 g; **b** 9.2 g; **c** 257.3 g

3 **a** 0.010 mol; **b** 0.33 mol; **c** 0.050 mol

Exam questions

1 **a** Neutrons: 10; electrons: 9
b A: ionization; B: acceleration; C: deflection; D: detection
c i For $^{21}Ne^+$ the path would curve above the line shown (and hit the top wall of the magnet)
ii The extent of deflection depends on the mass of the ion – lighter ions are deflected more
d $(91.0 \times 20 + 9.0 \times 22)/100 = 20.2$ to 3 sig. figs (NB The question should read 9.0% ^{22}Ne)

2 **a** See spread 2.4
b i The path of neutral atoms is not affected by an electric or a magnetic field
ii An electrostatic field (charged plates)
c i Boron (atomic number 5); ^{10}B and ^{11}B
ii $(25 \times 10 + 100 \times 11)/125 = 10.8$
d Peaks would be at 5 and 5.5 with the same ratio of heights; the *x*-axis is mass/charge, and the charge would double

3 **a** ^{12}C is the standard against which other atoms are compared – it is exactly 12 by definition
b Mass of 1 mol H atoms = 1.0078 g; mass of 1 mol electrons $= 9.1091 \times 10^{-28} \times 6.0225 \times 10^{23} = 5.4860 \times 10^{-4}$ g; mass of 1 mol H^+ ions $= (1.0078\text{ g}) - (5.4860 \times 10^{-4}\text{ g}) = 1.0073$ g
c i An electron is removed by electron bombardment
ii To avoid multiply charged ions being formed
iii They are accelerated by an electrostatic field (charged plates)
d The mass of the electron lost is very small compared to the mass of the atom

4 **a** The electron; it has the lowest mass/charge ratio
b See **2 b i**
c $(a \times 10 + b \times 11)/100 = 10.8$; $a + b = 100$; $a = 20$, $b = 80$; $a{:}b = 1{:}4$
d i In 100 g of sample, B = 81.2 g and H = 18.8 g; in moles, B = 81.2/10.8 = 7.52 and H = 18.8/1 = 18.8; simplest ratio = 1:18.8/7.52 = 1:2.5 or 2:5; empirical formula = B_2H_5
ii Mass of empirical formula is 26.6; 54 is approx. 2×26.6, so molecular formula is B_4H_{10}

5 **a** See spread 2.3
b Electron gun: ionizes atoms; magnet: deflects and separates ions of different masses
c i $^{20}_{10}Ne$ and $^{22}_{10}Ne$
ii $^{22}Ne^{2+}$
iii $M_r = (17.8 \times 20 + 1.7 \times 22)/(17.8 + 1.7) = 20.2$

6 **a** See spread 3.3
b i $Vc = (0.0236\text{ dm}^3) \times (0.150\text{ mol dm}^{-3}) = 0.003\,54$ mol
ii $(0.003\,54\text{ mol})/2 = 0.001\,77$ mol
iii $M = (0.245\text{ g})/(0.001\,77\text{ mol}) = 138\text{ g mol}^{-1}$, so $M_r = 138$
iv $2M + 12 + 3 \times 16 = 138$, so M = 39; M is potassium
c A: magnetic field; B: detector; electron gun: ionizes sample; electric field: accelerates ions

7 **a**

Particle	Relative mass	Relative charge
proton	1.0	1
neutron	1.0	0
electron	1/1840	−1

b See spreads 2.3 and 2.4
c i So that they will be affected by the electric and magnetic fields
ii Charged plates (electric field)
iii Magnetic field
d See spread 2.4
e i $(78.6 \times 24 + 10.1 \times 25 + 11.3 \times 26)/100 = 24.3$ (NB An answer to 2 d.p. is unjustified, given integer values for the isotopes: compare the answer to spread 3.2, question 1 with the periodic table)
ii Peaks at 24, 25, 26 in the ratio 78.6:10.1:11.3

Chapter 4

Practice questions

Spread 4.7

1 **a** s; **b** d; **c** s; **d** p; **e** d; **f** p

2 **a** 2s, 2p; **b** 3s, 3p; **c** 4s, 3d, 4p

Exam questions

1 **a** N: atomic number 7, ionization energy slightly higher than that of O; Al: atomic number 13, ionization energy slightly lower than that of Mg
b Na has an electron in a higher shell than the electrons in Ne, which is further from the nucleus and less tightly bound to the atom
c Na: an electron removed from the same shell as for Ne but an extra proton in the nucleus means there is a stronger attractive force on the electrons
d i Ne does not form any bonds with any atoms; hence the value for the electronegativity is not measurable

ii Na; the lowest first ionization energy and the least affinity for electrons

e On dissolving the sodium oxide, ions are separately hydrated; the small oxide ion bonds strongly with the H atoms in the water causing the O—H bonds to break, forming OH^- ions; the excess of these ions increases the pH

f A non-metal oxide, or the oxide of an element in a high positive oxidation state, e.g. SO_3

2 a Spin

b 2p is slightly further from the nucleus

c Spin pair in 2s and two up arrows in two 2p orbitals

d See spread 4.8

e O has additional repulsion from a second electron in one of the 2p orbitals (Note also that a *half-filled* subshell (as for the 2p in N) is particularly stable; the origin of this stability is complex)

3 a See **2 d**

b Ne has an extra proton, so the attraction for the electrons in the 2p is greater than for F

c See **2 e**

d Na has an electron in the 3s that is further away from the nucleus than the 2p of Ne; hence less energy is required to remove it

e The average difference between O, F, and Ne is 385, so C should be approx. 1400 − 385 = 1015

4 a 3p (Al) is at slightly higher energy than 3s (Mg) and so requires less energy to remove it

b Si has an extra proton in the nucleus, so there is extra force on the outer electrons, so more energy is required for their removal

c The same nuclear charge attracts fewer electrons more strongly

d $Al^{2+}(g) \rightarrow Al^{3+}(g) + e^-(g)$

e The 3rd ionization energy of Mg removes an electron from an inner shell (2p), which requires much more energy; the 3rd electron from Al comes from 3s

5 a Lines occur because the atoms have fixed energy levels and transitions between an upper energy level and a lower one cause emission of light; lines in the ultraviolet end on the energy level with $n = 1$; the energy levels get closer together as the energy increases, so the lines converge

b The convergence limit, where the lines merge, corresponds to an electron at the edge of the atom; the ionization energy is the energy corresponding to that frequency: $E = hf$

6 a The minimum energy required per mole to remove one electron from singly positively charged fluorine ions in the gaseous state

b Generally upward with a steeper upward kink after the 7th electron

7 a i $O(g) \rightarrow O^+(g) + e^-(g)$

ii There is only a pair of electrons in the lowest shell and one more proton in the nucleus compared to H, so He has the greatest attraction for (outer) electrons

iii See **2 e**

iv The outer electron is in progressively higher shells down the group, which are further from the nucleus; hence progressively less energy is required to remove it

b i $O(g) + e^-(g) \rightarrow O^-(g)$; $O^-(g) + e^-(g) \rightarrow O^{2-}(g)$

ii The second electron is repelled by the negatively charged O^- ion, so energy has to be supplied to push it into the ion

c The energy given out when the oppositely charged ions are attracted together to form an ionic crystalline lattice more than compensates for the energy required to form the ions

d The arrangement is 2, 8, 1 (the 2nd ionization energy is much greater than the 1st, so there is one electron in the outer shell; the 2nd to 9th show a steady increase and are in the 2nd shell; the 10th and 11th are much higher and so are in the 1st shell)

8 a i Mg has an extra proton (as before)

ii Al: 1st electron in higher subshell (as before)

iii Electrons from the same subshell but Al has an extra proton

iv The 4th electron is removed from an inner shell, so much more energy is required

b i See **7 b i**

ii See **7 b ii** (NB Values given in this question are different from those in **7**)

iii They are stable because of the ionic bond – strong electrostatic attraction means a lot of energy is given out when the lattice forms (see **7 c**)

9 a See **7 a i**

b i There is increasing charge on the nucleus, which implies increasing attraction for electrons in the same shell

ii B: the electron in 2p has higher energy than the 2s of Be; see **2 e**

c Group IV: the first four ionization energies show a steady increase; then there is a large jump

---

Chapter 5

Exam questions

1 a Possible answers include SF_6, CH_4, $AlCl_3$, $BeCl_2$

b See spread 5.5

c The lone pairs are more repulsive than bond pairs are

d See spread 7.5

2 a A covalent bond is the attraction between the nuclei of the bonded atoms and a shared pair of electrons

b A coordinate bond is a normal covalent bond where the shared pair of electrons is donated by one of the atoms

c There is no difference: attraction is between N and identical H nuclei; electrons are indistinguishable

d Ammonium ion: 109°; ammonia molecule: 107°; the lone pair occupies more space closer to the nucleus so there is a greater repulsive force, which pushes the bonds closer together

e H bonding. N—H bonds are polar; δ^+ on H is attracted to the lone pair on the adjacent δ^- N atom

3 a Ionic; $KBr(s) + aq \rightarrow K^+(aq) + Br^-(aq)$; pH 7

b i 57.2% I, 42.8% F; moles: 57.2/126.9 = 0.451, 42.8/19.0 = 2.25; simplest ratio: 0.451:2.25 = 1:5; empirical formula: IF_5

ii $I_2 + 5F_2 \rightarrow 2IF_5$

c i T-shaped (2 lone pairs)

ii BrF_4^-; square planar, 90°

4 a Ionic bond: electrostatic attraction between oppositely charged ions; covalent bond: see **1 a**; dative covalent bond: see **1 b**

b No, no, no, yes, yes, yes

c i Mg has an extra proton

ii Ion has lost the outer shell electron and is left with an inner core of electrons; hence it is smaller (also, the remaining electrons feel a stronger attraction to the nucleus, as there is one fewer electron overall)

iii I^- is large and has high polarizability; Al^{3+} has high charge density, so Al shares the I electrons forming a covalent molecule; F^- is small with low polarizability

5 a Two nuclei attract a shared pair of electrons; one nucleus (more electronegative) has a greater attraction, so the electrons are shared unequally

b When the two atoms have different electronegativities

c When it is close to a cation with a high charge density

d In an unpolarized anion the distribution of electrons is symmetrical, which is not the case in a polarized anion

e i **I** linear; **II** pyramidal; **III** octahedral

ii NCl_3, the only one with a lone pair

6 a A dative or coordinate bond is a normal covalent bond in which both the shared electrons are donated by one of the atoms

b i $H_3N \rightarrow BF_3$; tetrahedral

ii There are four pairs of electrons around the N; mutual repulsion moves them to the tetrahedral positions; there are only three pairs of electrons around the boron atom in BF_3; mutual repulsion pushes them as far apart as possible i.e. to bond angles of 120°, trigonal planar

c i Trigonal bipyramidal

ii BrF_3 is T-shaped; KrF_2 is linear

d i Geometrical or *cis–trans* isomerism; Cl atoms are either adjacent (*cis*) or opposite (*trans*)

ii Only one of the isomers is an active drug; some methods of preparation produce a mixture of the isomers while some selectively produce one isomer or the other

7 a VSEPR theory: the shape is determined by the number of electron pairs in the valence shell of the central atom; repulsion between electron pairs decides the final shape since lone pair/lone pair repulsion > lone pair/bond pair repulsion > bond pair/bond pair repulsion

b Pyramidal

c The greater repulsion of the lone pair pushes the bond pairs closer together

d Nitrogen has a higher electronegativity than the hydrogen atoms, so the electron density in the bonds is uneven, the N having the bigger share *and* the shape is pyramidal

8 a i CH_4: tetrahedral, 109°; NH_3: pyramidal, 107°; H_2O: V-shaped, 104°

ii Methane: dispersion forces; ammonia and water: hydrogen bonds plus dispersion plus dipole–dipole

iii Repulsion from the lone pair(s) pushes the bond pairs together in ammonia and water – more so in water where there are two lone pairs

iv Water: O is the most electronegative, so O—H bonds are the most polar, hence the strongest are hydrogen bonds; also since the Os have two lone pairs, each water molecule can hydrogen bond to four other molecules

b i See spreads 5.2 and 5.3

ii See **6 a** (the ammonium ion is a poor example)

iii All the N—H bonds are identical and indistinguishable

9 a i Vibrations around fixed lattice positions

ii Ions are able to move away from lattice positions, but they remain fairly close together; movement is random

b i Covalent bond – see **6 a**; in LiI the small lithium ion attracts and shares some of the valence electrons in the polarizable iodide ion; there is thus a partial covalent character to the bond between the ions

ii Li^+ is smaller than Na^+ and thus it has a higher charge density

10 a A measure of an atom's ability to attract shared electron pairs

b i Ionic; **ii** Covalent (polar); **iii** Covalent

Chapter 6

Practice questions

Spread 6.5

1 a 6; **b** 8; **c** 12; **d** 12

Exam questions

1 a Copper: $1s^22s^22p^63s^23p^63d^{10}4s^1$, d block
Gallium: $1s^22s^22p^63s^23p^63d^{10}4s^24p^1$, p block
Phosphorus: $1s^22s^22p^63s^23p^3$, p block

b Graph shows steady increase with steep rises between 3 and 4, and 11 and 12

c Sodium: body-centred cubic, 8; magnesium: hexagonal close-packed, 12

2 a i On ions next to the + shown and diagonally opposite through the cube

ii 6

b It conducts electricity when molten

c i Electron pair donated by one of the atoms sharing the bond

ii Opposite on the central 'square' of bonds

iii If it is largely covalent, then there are only weak forces *between* molecules

3 a i Ionic

ii Vibration of ions increases as temperature rises; at melting point ions move out of lattice sites and move randomly

iii There are strong electrostatic forces between ions, hence a lot of energy is required to overcome them; there is strong attraction for polar water molecules; the formation of hydrated ions compensates for the lattice energy

b i A shared pair of electrons with high electron density between nuclei

ii A shared pair of electrons with electron density in two lobes above and below the axis between the two nuclei; see figures on spread 5.7

4 a Metallic bonding; ions packed close together, ions held together by mutual attraction for the valence shell electrons; the valence shell electrons are relatively free to move from one atom to another and hence conduct electricity

b i Covalent: $AlCl_3$; ionic: AlF_3

ii Al and F: there is a large difference in electronegativity; Al and Cl: there is a smaller difference in electronegativity, so that a partial covalent bond forms with Al^{3+} and polarizable Cl^-

iii Strong electrostatic attraction between ions requires a large input of energy to overcome forces

5 a i See **2 c i**; $H_3N \rightarrow BF_3$

ii Electrostatic attraction between oppositely charged ions: NaCl

b i Solid turns to gas state on heating with no intervening liquid state

ii $AlCl_3$ attracts the polar water molecule strongly; iodine is non-polar so there is no strong attraction for water molecules

c i Valence electrons are delocalized and relatively free to move between ions

ii Moving electrons carry energy from one ion to the next; also ions are close packed, so, when ions vibrate more and hit adjacent ions, they pass on energy

6 a i I–I is a simple molecule loosely packed in the crystal lattice; see spread 7.4

ii Tetrahedral structure: each atom bonded to four others; giant covalent: see spread 6.3

b Iodine sublimes at low temperature because there are weak dispersion forces between the molecules; diamond has a very high melting point because there are strong covalent bonds between all the atoms

c NaCl: interlocking face-centred cubic, coordination 6,6; CsCl: interlocking simple cubic, coordination 8,8; both ionic; coordination numbers are determined by radius ratios: Na^+ is smaller than Cs^+ so has a smaller ratio (see **8 a iii**)

d See **4 a**

7 a i See **4 a**

ii Covalent bonds between atoms in the PVC molecule; weak intermolecular forces between molecules; all electrons are localized; hence it is a non-conductor

iii Ionic, Mg^{2+} and O^{2-}, electrons are localized; hence it is a non-conductor

b i High melting point; non-flammable

ii MgO is brittle and needs to be protected from fracture by bending or impacts

8 a i The arrangement of ions in the crystal; electrostatic attraction between oppositely charged ions

ii See the figures in spread 6.6; NaCl: 6,6; CsCl: 8,8

iii Radius ratios: $Na^+/Cl^- = 0.52$; $Cs^+/Cl^- = 0.93$; for NaCl it is much smaller, hence NaCl has a lower coordination number

iv X-ray crystallography

b i P $[Ne]3s^23p^3$

ii Trigonal bipyramidal, angles 90° and 120°

iii 5 bond pairs, 0 lone pairs, total 5; the repulsion between pairs is equal

Chapter 7

Practice questions

Spread 7.4

4 70

Exam questions

1 a i $C^{\delta+}$—$Cl^{\delta-}$; $Cl^{\delta+}$—$F^{\delta-}$; $N^{\delta+}$—$H^{\delta-}$
ii See spread 5.8
b i $(CH_3COOH) \times 2 = (24 + 32 + 4) \times 2 = 120$
ii Hydrogen bond
iii Molecules not dimerized and are hydrated by forming H-bonds with water molecules, and there is some dissociation into ethanoate and oxonium ions

2 a i Graph shows steady rise to 80 °C; mixture starts to melt at 80 °C, forming liquid A, but a solid remains until the temperature reaches 120–140 °C, when the solid mixture completes melting
ii Graph shows steady rise to 80 °C then remains horizontal for some time before then rising steadily; the mixture melts at 80 °C, temperature remains constant until all solid has melted
iii A eutectic mixture
b In 100 g of mixture, $n(A) = (28\,g)/(127\,g\,mol^{-1}) = 0.220\,mol$; $n(B) = (72\,g)/(181\,g\,mol^{-1}) = 0.398\,mol$; mole fraction of A $= 0.220/(0.220 + 0.398) = 0.36$

3 a See **1 a ii**
b i Number of electrons in the molecule increases from S to Te; thus the size of the dispersion forces increases; this results in increasing attraction between the molecules
ii O is the smallest and most electronegative of the Group VI elements and its bonds with H are highly polar, thus the δ^+ on the H atom is strongly attracted to the δ^- O on adjacent molecules; dotted lines between O of one atom and H of adjacent molecule (chain of three)
c Hydrogen bonds between N—H and C=O; see figures in spread 30.5

4 a Graph
b (What does 'surface' mean for Jupiter and Saturn?) Assuming temperature given is the same at all depths of atmosphere (a false assumption), Mars – low pressure; methane: gas; ammonia: gas; water: solid; Jupiter – pressure increases with depth; methane – all three states possible; gas at high altitudes, then liquid, possibly solid very deep where pressure greatest; ammonia: gas at high altitudes; solid lower; water largely solid; some vapour at top of atmosphere and possibly liquid at very high pressures deep in the atmosphere; Saturn – methane: gas at high altitudes, then solid (no liquid); ammonia: as Jupiter; water: as Jupiter, except liquid less likely

5 a i See spread 4.8
ii $Si^+(g) \rightarrow Si^{2+}(g) + e^-(g)$
iii Same nuclear charge as more electrons removed means that there is more attraction for the remaining electrons in the shell
iv The 5th electron is taken from a lower energy level than the 4th, so considerably more energy must be supplied
b i Giant covalent; simple molecular
ii In silicon dioxide there are strong covalent bonds linking all the atoms together which require a lot of energy to break them; hence it has a high melting point; silicon tetrachloride has only weak forces between molecules; little energy is required to overcome these forces, hence a low melting point

6 a i See **1 a ii**
ii Increasing the number of electrons in valence shells means that dispersion forces increase down the group; hence the force between molecules increases and so the energy required increases
iii Strong H bonding in HF means that there is a more powerful force between molecules, and a higher temperature is required
b i Shared pair of electrons with high electron density between nuclei
ii Shared pair of electrons with electron density in two lobes above and below the axis between the two nuclei; see figures in spread 5.7
c i Trigonal planar: all angles 120°; delocalized π bond
ii Both have a skeleton of sigma bonds with delocalized π bonding

7 a i See **1 a ii**
ii Dispersion forces
b Methane has more electrons; hence dispersion forces are stronger
c i See **1 a ii**
ii HCl has a bigger difference in electronegativity, hence bond is more polar and molecule has larger dipole, hence there is greater force between molecules; methane has no overall dipole because of tetrahedral arrangement of H atoms

Chapter 8

Practice questions

Spread 8.1

1 a 2 atm
2 425 cm^3

Spread 8.2

1 0.011 m^3
2 0.015 m^3
3 0.18 Pa

Spread 8.3

1 84.0 g mol^{-1}
2 C_6H_{12}

Spread 8.4

1 16; CH_4

Exam questions

1 a i Polar covalent bonds; Cl is more electronegative than H, so Cl δ^- and H δ^+
ii Polar covalent bonds in the ammonium ion between the N and H atoms (N δ^-, H δ^+); ionic bonds between ammonium ions and chloride ions
iii Polar covalent bonds between O and H (O δ^-, H δ^+)
b Hydrogen bonding (see spread 7.5)
c Sodium chloride: there is strong electrostatic attraction between oppositely charged ions; hence a lot of energy is required to separate ions; in iodine, there are only relatively weak dispersion forces between molecules, so much less energy is required to separate the molecules
d $n(I_2) = (4.509\,g)/(253.8\,g\,mol^{-1}) = 0.01777\,mol$; volume $= (0.01777\,mol) \times (2.24 \times 10^4\,cm^3\,mol^{-1}) \times (343\,K)/(273\,K) = 500\ cm^3$ (3 sig. figs)

2 a i Volatile means that it readily evaporates and forms a vapour; ideal gas equation: n = amount of gas in moles, R = the gas constant
ii So that the syringe and contents uniformly reach the temperature of the boiling water bath
iii Particles in constant motion; volume of particles is negligible; there are no interactions between particles other than collisions; collisions are perfectly elastic
b i $n(CH_3CH_2OH) = (0.167\,g)/(46.0\,g\,mol^{-1}) = 3.63 \times 10^{-3}\,mol$; $V = nRT/p = (3.63 \times 10^{-3}\,mol) \times (8.314\,Pa\,m^3\,K^{-1}\,mol^{-1}) \times (373\,K)/(101\,300\,Pa) = 1.11 \times 10^{-4}\,m^3 = 111\,cm^3$
ii Volume of the gas exceeds volume of the syringe

3 a i Gas particles impact the walls of the containing vessel and rebound; change in velocity means there is change in momentum; with many particles hitting a specific area every second, the combined force of the particles exerts a pressure
ii As temperature increases, ions vibrate more violently about the lattice sites; at 801 °C the ions start to move away from their lattice sites
iii A lot of energy is required to overcome the strong electrostatic forces holding ions in their lattice site
b $pV = nRT$; $n = pV/RT = (1.01 \times 10^5\,Pa) \times (63.0 \times 10^{-6}\,m^3)/((8.31\,Pa\,m^3\,K^{-1}\,mol^{-1}) \times (373\,K))$; $n = 0.00205\,mol$; molar mass $= (0.148\,g)/n = 72.2\ g\,mol^{-1}$

4 a i A straight line through the origin
ii Particles do not have a negligible volume: there are forces acting between particles; collisions are not perfectly elastic
b i Slightly concave rising curve (almost parabolic) not starting from the origin
ii A liquid boils at the temperature for which its saturated vapour pressure is equal to the external pressure
iii Some liquids decompose at temperatures below their boiling point at normal atmospheric pressure
c $p_1V_1/T_1 = p_2V_2/T_2$ for the same amount in moles, so $V_1 = (T_1/T_2)V_2 = (273/373) \times 153\,cm^3 = 112.0\,cm^3$;
$n = (112.0\,cm^3)/(2.24 \times 10^4\,cm^3\,mol^{-1}) = 5.00 \times 10^{-3}\,mol$;
$M = (0.597\,g)/(5.00 \times 10^{-3}\,mol) = 119\,g\,mol^{-1}$ (3 sig. figs)

5 a $pV = nRT$
b $n(CO_2) = (10.0\,g)/(44.0\,g\,mol^{-1}) = 0.2273\,mol$;
$p = (nRT/V) = (0.2273\,mol) \times (8.31\,Pa\,m^3\,K^{-1}\,mol^{-1}) \times (273\,K)/(5.00 \times 10^{-3}\,m^3) = 1.03 \times 10^5\,Pa$
c In real gases there are attractive forces between molecules that reduce the pressure

6 a i Separate ions and delocalized sea of electrons
ii Delocalized electrons allow conduction of electricity; since all ions are the same, layers of ions can roll over each other to new stable positions; thus metal is malleable/ductile
b In the vapour, sodium exists as diatomic molecules, Na—Na, with one pair of shared electrons
c i $n(Na) = pV/RT = (25\,Pa) \times (50 \times 10^{-6}\,m^3)/((8.31\,Pa\,m^3\,K^{-1}\,mol^{-1}) \times (293\,K)) = 5.13 \times 10^{-7}\,mol$;
$m(Na) = (5.13 \times 10^{-7}\,mol) \times (23.0\,g\,mol^{-1})$
$= 1.2 \times 10^{-5}\,g$ (2 sig. figs)
ii The assumption that sodium vapour behaves as an ideal gas
d i $1s^2 2s^2 2p^6 3s^1$
ii The energy levels increase from the 1s to the 3s
iii $1s^2 2s^2 2p^6 3p^1$

7 a $pV = nRT$
b i n(acid) in $1\,dm^3$ of vapour $= (101 \times 10^3\,Pa) \times (1 \times 10^{-3}\,m^3)/((8.31\,Pa\,m^3\,K^{-1}\,mol^{-1}) \times (400\,K))$
$= 3.04 \times 10^{-2}\,mol$;
molar mass $= (2.74\,g)/(3.04 \times 10^{-2}\,mol)$
$= 90\,g\,mol^{-1}$ (2 sig. figs)
ii Some of the molecules are dimers, with a mass of 120; the calculated value is an average for the molecules in the gas
c i A horizontal line
ii Atoms do not have a negligible volume (especially at high pressures) (NB There are also attractions, so the shape in the question is incorrect at low pressures)

Chapter 9

Practice questions

Spread 9.1
1 19.7 g — 2 1.54 kg

Spread 9.3
1 Fe_2O_3 — 2 FeS_2

Spread 9.4
1 a $1.8\,dm^3$; **b** 2.7 g — 2 $3.7\,dm^3$

Spread 9.5
1 $3.5 \times 10^{-3}\,mol$ — 2 $0.50\,dm^3 = 500\,cm^3$

Spread 9.6
1 2.93 g — 2 $0.04\,mol\,dm^{-3}$

Spread 9.7
1 a $0.0816\,mol\,dm^{-3}$; **b** $4.58\,g\,dm^{-3}$
3 $30.0\,cm^3$

Exam questions

1 a i $n(H_2SO_4) = (50\,000\,g)/(98.1\,g\,mol^{-1}) = 510\,mol$
ii $n(NaOH) = 2 \times (510\,mol) = 1020\,mol$
iii $V(NaOH) = (1020\,mol)/(5\,mol\,dm^{-3}) = 204\,dm^3$
b i $n(CaCO_3) = 510\,mol$; M_r $CaCO_3 = 40 + 12 + 16 \times 3 = 100$; mass $= (510\,mol) \times (100\,g\,mol^{-1})$
$= 51\,kg$ (2 sig. figs)
c NaOH is strongly alkaline: local concentrations could do more damage than the acid; NaOH produces a soluble product that could damage water, plants, and animals; solid calcium carbonate is less dangerous to transport and spread

2 a i M_r(acid) $= 14 + 2 + 32 + 3 \times 16 + 1 = 97$;
n(acid) used $= (5.210\,g)/(97\,g\,mol^{-1}) = 0.0537\,mol$;
concentration $= (0.0537\,mol)/(0.25\,dm^3)$
$= 0.215\,mol\,dm^{-3}$
ii $n(NaOH) = n$(acid), so $c(NaOH) = (0.215\,mol\,dm^{-3}) \times (22.6/25) = 0.194\,mol\,dm^{-3}$
b $M_r(NaOH) = 23 + 16 + 1 = 40$;
$n(NaOH) = (5.0\,g)/(40\,g\,mol^{-1}) = 0.125\,mol$;
n(salt) formed $= (0.125\,mol)/2 = 0.0625\,mol$;
M_r(salt) $= 2 \times 23 + 32 + 4 \times 16 + 10 \times 18 = 322$;
mass of salt $= (0.0625\,mol) \times (322\,g\,mol^{-1}) = 20.1\,g$

3 a i c(acid) $= (0.121\,mol\,dm^{-3}) \times (32.4/25.0)$
$= 0.1568\,mol\,dm^{-3}$
ii $n(HCl) = (0.1568\,mol\,dm^{-3}) \times (4 \times 10^3\,dm^3)$
$= 627.2\,mol$
b n(lime) $= (627.2\,mol)/2 = 313.6\,mol$;
M_r(lime) $= 40.1 + 2 \times 16.0 + 2 \times 1.0 = 74.1$;
mass required $= (313.6\,mol) \times (74.1\,g\,mol^{-1})$
$= 23.2 \times 10^3\,g = 23.2\,kg$
c n(lime) $= (1000\,g)/(74.1\,g\,mol^{-1}) = 13.50\,mol$;
n(limestone) needed $= 13.50\,mol$;
M_r(limestone) $= 40.1 + 12.0 + 3 \times 16.0 = 100.1$;
mass of limestone $= (13.50\,mol) \times (100.1\,g\,mol^{-1})$
$= 1.35 \times 10^3\,g = 1.35\,kg$

4 a Ag: 71.05; C: 7.89; O: 21.06; moles: 71.05/107.9 $= 0.658$; $7.89/12.0 = 0.658$; $21.06/16.0 = 1.32$; ratio: $1:1:(1.32/0.658) = 2$; empirical formula $= AgCO_2$
b Empirical formula; mass $= 108 + 12 + 32 = 152$;
$M_r = 304 = 2 \times 152$; molecular formula $= Ag_2C_2O_4$
c i $n(X) = (5.00\,g)/(304\,g\,mol^{-1}) = 0.016\,45\,mol$
ii n(gas) $= pV/RT = (100 \times 10^3\,Pa) \times (8.14 \times 10^{-4}\,m^3)/((8.31\,Pa\,m^3\,K^{-1}\,mol^{-1}) \times (298\,K)) = 0.032\,87\,mol$
iii Ratio of $X:CO_2 = 0.016\,45:0.032\,87 = 1:2.00 = 1:2$;
$Ag_2C_2O_4 \rightarrow 2Ag + 2CO_2$; residue is silver; proof: mass of $CO_2 = (0.032\,87\,mol) \times (44.0\,g\,mol^{-1}) = 1.45\,g$;
mass of residue $= 5.00\,g - 1.45\,g = 3.55\,g$; mass of Ag in $X = 2 \times (0.016\,45\,mol) \times (107.9\,g\,mol^{-1}) = 3.55\,g$

5 a i $n(O_2) = (10\,dm^3)/(24\,dm^3\,mol^{-1}) = 0.417\,mol$
$n(H_2O_2) = 2n(O_2) = 0.83\,mol$ (2 sig. figs)
ii $n(H_2O_2) = (0.100\,mol\,dm^{-3}) \times (0.250\,dm^3)$
$= 0.0250\,mol$;
volume $= (0.0250\,mol)/(0.833\,mol\,dm^{-3})$
$= 0.0300\,dm^3 = 30\,cm^3$ (2 sig. figs)
b $n(KMnO_4) = (0.200\,dm^3) \times (0.020\,mol\,dm^{-3})$
$= 0.0040\,mol$;
$m(KMnO_4) = (0.0040\,mol) \times (158\,g\,mol^{-1})$
$= 0.63\,g$ (2 sig. figs)
c i $n(KMnO_4) = (0.0400\,dm^3) \times (0.020\,mol\,dm^{-3})$
$= 8.0 \times 10^{-4}\,mol$
ii $n(H_2O_2) = (0.0200\,dm^3) \times (0.100\,mol\,dm^{-3})$
$= 2.0 \times 10^{-3}\,mol$
iii $n(H_2O_2)/n(KMnO_4) = 2.0 \times 10^{-3}/8.0 \times 10^{-4} = 2.5$
iv $2KMnO_4 + 5H_2O_2 + 3H_2SO_4 \rightarrow 2MnSO_4 + K_2SO_4 + 8H_2O + 5O_2$
(NB This question has inconsistent precision)
d i K^+ and Mn^{2+}
ii Manganese(II) hydroxide
e i $M_r(Na_2O_2) = 2 \times 23.0 + 2 \times 16.0 = 78.0$;
$n(Na_2O_2) = (0.39\,g)/(78.0\,g\,mol^{-1}) = 0.0050\,mol$;
$n(O_2) = \frac{1}{2}n(Na_2O_2) = 0.0025\,mol$;
$V(O_2) = (0.0025\,mol) \times (24\,dm^3\,mol^{-1}) = 0.060\,dm^3$
$= 60\,cm^3$
ii Number $= (0.0025\,mol) \times (6.02 \times 10^{23}\,mol^{-1})$
$= 1.5 \times 10^{21}$

iii Ox(O) in peroxide = −1; Ox(O) in oxygen = 0; Ox(O) in carbonate = −2; hence oxygen has been oxidized and reduced, i.e. disproportionation

6 a $H_2X + 2NaOH \rightarrow Na_2X + 2H_2O$
b i $n(NaOH) = (0.025\,dm^3) \times (0.100\,mol\,dm^{-3}) = 0.0025\,mol$
ii $n(H_2X) = \frac{1}{2}n(NaOH) = 0.00125\,mol$
iii This amount is in 25 cm^3; hence the amount in 500 cm^3 = (500/25) × (0.00125 mol) = 0.025 mol; 2.25 g is equivalent to 0.025 mol; M_r = 2.25/0.025 = 90
iv Mass of H_2X in 1 dm^3 = 2 × 2.25 = 4.5 g; hence, mass of water = 6.3 g − 4.5 g = 1.8 g; $n(H_2O) = (1.8\,g)/(18\,g\,mol^{-1}) = 0.10\,mol$; $n(H_2X) = 2 \times (0.025\,mol) = 0.05\,mol$; $n(H_2O)/n(H_2X) = 0.10/0.05 = 2$
c Shake a measured sealed volume of air with a measured mass of water; titrate the solution formed with standard aqueous sodium hydroxide

7 a See spread 9.3
b From spread 8.3, $M = mRT/pV$ = (0.130 g) × (8.31 Pa m^3 K^{-1} mol^{-1}) × (373 K)/((101 × 10^3 Pa) × (85.0 × 10^{-6} m^3)) = 46.9 g mol^{-1} (The data in the question is slightly out: 46.0 was meant)
c i Divide by mass of atom: 52.2/12.0 = 4.35; 13.0/1.0 = 13.0; 34.8/16.0 = 2.175; 4.35:13.0:2.175 = 2:6:1; empirical formula = C_2H_6O
ii Ethanol, CH_3CH_2OH, or methoxymethane, CH_3OCH_3

8 a i $^1H = 1.6734 \times 10^{-24} \times 6.0225 \times 10^{23} = 1.0078\,g$
$^{12}C = 1.9925 \times 10^{-23} \times 6.0225 \times 10^{23}$ = 12.000 g (5 sig. figs)
ii ^{12}C given the value 12 is the standard against which other atoms are compared; it is useful as it is a component of a large number of compounds
b i Naturally occurring carbon has a small percentage of other isotopes of carbon such as ^{13}C
ii $C + O_2 \rightarrow CO_2$; use $pV = nRT$: $n(CO_2) = pV/RT$ = (98.0 × 10^3 Pa) × (1.85 × 10^{-3} m^3)/((8.31 Pa m^3 K^{-1}mol^{-1}) × (293K)) = 0.07446 mol; $n(C) = n(CO_2)$; $m(C)$ = (0.07446 mol) × (12.0 g mol^{-1}) = 0.894 g
c $CO_2 + 2NaOH \rightarrow Na_2CO_3 + H_2O$; $n(CO_2)$ = (1.54 g)/(44.0 g mol^{-1}) = 0.0350 mol; $n(NaOH)$ = 2 × (0.0350 mol) = 0.0700 mol; $c(NaOH)$ = (0.0700 mol)/(0.0500 dm^3) = 1.4 mol dm^{-3}

Chapter 10

Practice questions

Spread 10.4

1 15.7 kJ

Spread 10.6

1 −66 kJ mol^{-1}

Spread 10.9

1 a −84 kJ mol^{-1}; −105 kJ mol^{-1}

2 −760 kJ mol^{-1}

Exam questions

1 a See spread 10.5
b $\Delta H_f^\ominus$(nitro) − 1540 = 3 × (−394) + 5/2 × (−242) + 3 × 34 = − 1685, so $\Delta H_f^\ominus$(nitro) = −1685 + 1540 = −145 (all in kJ mol^{-1})
c $\Delta H_f^\ominus$(reaction) − 145 = 3 × (−394) + (5/2) × (−242) = −1642 (all in kJ mol^{-1})
d A decomposition reaction is more exothermic than combustion
e $\Delta H_f^\ominus(l \rightarrow g)$ = −242 − (−286) = +44 kJ mol^{-1}; the process is endothermic, so heat needs to be added

2 a Hydrazine has polar bonds and hydrogen bonding between molecules; hence more energy is needed to separate the molecules than in ethane, which only has weak dispersion forces
b i $N_2H_4 + O_2 \rightarrow N_2 + 2H_2O$
ii $\Delta H_f^\ominus$(hydrazine) −624 = 2 × (−286), so $\Delta H_f^\ominus$ = +52 kJ mol^{-1}
c i $C_2H_6 + 7/2O_2 \rightarrow 2CO_2 + 3H_2O$
d Hydrazine uses less oxygen; the energy given out per mole of oxygen used is greater for hydrazine than for ethane; liquids are easier to handle

3 a See spread 10.5
b See spread 10.5
c i $\Delta H_f^\ominus$ − 46 = 3 × (−269) − 114, so $\Delta H_f^\ominus$ = −875 (all in kJ mol^{-1})
ii Bonds broken: 3(N—H): 3 × 388; 3(F—F): 3 × 158; total = 1638; bonds made: 3(H—F): 3 × (−562); 3(N—F): 3 × (−272); total = −2502; $\Delta H_f^\ominus$ = bonds broken + bonds made = 1638 − 2502 = −864 (all in kJ mol^{-1})
d Bond enthalpies are averages for the bonds of a particular type in a compound and are only approximate, e.g. breaking the three N—H bonds in ammonia in turn requires three different quantities of energy; enthalpies of formation can be obtained either directly by experiment or from enthalpy of combustion measurements and are thus more accurate

4 a i Gaseous ions Na^+ and Cl^- and liquid water
ii NaCl crystal lattice and liquid water
iii Hydrated ions $Na^+(aq)$ and $Cl^-(aq)$ in liquid water
b $\Delta H_f^\ominus$(solution) =788 − 784 = +4 (all in kJ mol^{-1})
c Flame tests; clean flame wire by heating and dipping in conc. HCl; dip hot wire in solution and hold in flame; flame colour yellow: sodium, lilac: potassium, red: lithium; silver nitrate test for chloride: white precipitate when nitric acid and aqueous silver nitrate added

5 a i ΔH_6 (lattice formation enthalpy)
ii $\Delta H_1 + \Delta H_2 + \Delta H_3 + \Delta H_4 + \Delta H_5 + \Delta H_6 = \Delta H_7$ = −635 − (193 + 590 + 1150 + 248 − 3513) = +697 (all in kJ mol^{-1})
iii ΔH_5 = 1st E.A. + 2nd E.A. + 697 = 1st E.A. + 844; 1st E.A. = 697 − 844 = −147 kJ mol^{-1}
b i 1st ionization enthalpy
ii Larger for magnesium
iii Magnesium is a smaller atom with the valence shell closer to the nucleus and hence bound more tightly
c i Flame test: calcium gives an brick-red flame
ii Dissolve the solid in dilute nitric acid (the carbonate reacts and effervesces), then add a few drops of aqueous silver nitrate; a white precipitate suggests chloride; add excess aqueous ammonia: the precipitate dissolves, confirming the presence of chloride ions

6 a

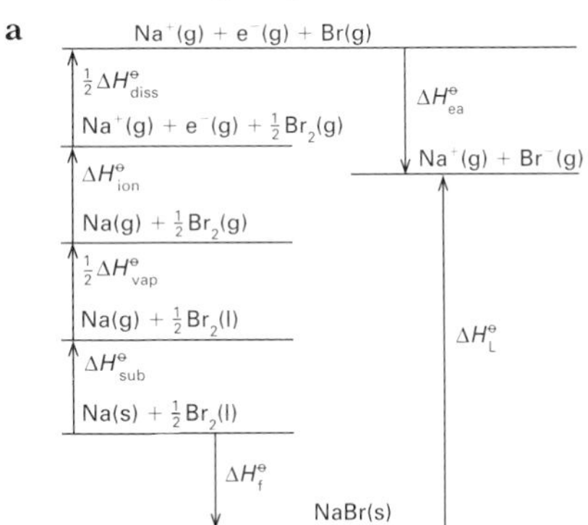

b $\frac{1}{2}\Delta H_{vap}^\ominus$ = −361 − (107 + 498 + 194/2 − 325 − 753) = +15 so $\Delta H_{vap}^\ominus$ = +30 (all in kJ mol^{-1})

7 a $CH_3CH_2OH + 3O_2 \rightarrow 2CO_2 + 3H_2O$
b i See spread 10.5
ii Ethanol: M_r = 46.0; hence the energy released by 1 g = 1370/46 =29.8 kJ; glucose: M_r = 180; hence the energy released by 1 g = 3000/180 = 16.7 kJ

iii Total energy from ethanol = 20 × 29.8 = 596 kJ; total energy from glucose = 20 × 16.7 = 334 kJ; total energy from 1 dm^3 of beer = 930 kJ (2 sig. figs)

Chapter 11

Practice questions

Spread 11.7

1 3.8 mol dm^{-3}

2 0.13 mol H_2 and 0.13 mol I_2

Exam questions

1 a See spread 11.1
  b The position of equilibrium is independent of the rate at which equilibrium is reached
  c B; $K_c = [NO_2]^2/[N_2O_4]$
  d i x: B; y: A or D; z: C
    ii Reaction will not be fast enough
    iii It may become too expensive to make the containment vessels
    iv z is the ammonia synthesis, which is exothermic, so the yield is lower at higher temperature

2 a Using $pV = nRT$, $n = pV/RT$; n(total) = ((1.59 × 10^6 Pa) × (1.04 × 10^{-3} m^3))/((8.31 Pa m^3 K^{-1} mol^{-1}) × (380 K)) = 0.524 mol; $n(CH_3OH)$ = 0.524 mol − 0.122 mol − 0.298 mol = 0.104 mol
  b $[CH_3OH]$ = (0.104 mol)/(1.04 dm^3) = 0.100 mol dm^{-3}; $[H_2]$ = (0.298 mol)/(1.04 dm^3) = 0.2865 mol dm^{-3}; $[CO]$ = (0.122 mol)/(1.04 dm^3) = 0.1173 mol dm^{-3}; $K_c = [CH_3OH]/[H_2]^2[CO]$ = (0.100 mol dm^{-3})/((0.2865 mol dm^{-3})^2 × (0.1173 mol dm^{-3})) = 10.4 dm^6 mol^{-2} (3 sig. figs)
  c i $K_p = p(CH_3OH)/p(CO)p(H_2)^2$
    ii $x(CO)$ = 0.122/(0.524) = 0.2328; $x(H_2)$ = 0.298/0.524 = 0.5687; $x(CH_3OH)$ = 0.105/0.524 = 0.1985
    iii $p(H_2)$ = 0.5687 × (1.59 MPa) = 0.904 MPa
    iv $p(CO)$ = 0.2328 × (1.59 MPa) = 0.370 MPa; $p(CH_3OH)$ = 0.1985 × (1.59 MPa) = 0.316 MPa; K_p = (0.316 MPa)/((0.370 MPa) × (0.904 MPa)^2) = 1.0 MPa^{-2} (2 sig. figs)

3 a Increasing temperature → lower yield of sulphur trioxide; the reaction is exothermic, so an increase in temperature favours the backward reaction and reduces the equilibrium constant
  b Increasing p → higher yield of sulphur trioxide; the number of gas moles decreases in the reaction, so the reaction shifts in the direction that minimizes the increase in pressure
  c $p(O_2)$ = 120 kPa − 33 kPa − 39 kPa = 48 kPa; $x(O_2)$ = 48/120 = 0.4
  d i $K_p = p^2_{SO_3}/p^2_{SO_2}p_{O_2}$
    ii K_p = (39 kPa)^2/((33 kPa)^2 × (48 kPa)) = 0.029 kPa^{-1}

4 a $n(Cl_2)$ = (11.1 g)/(71.0 g mol^{-1}) = 0.156 mol; $n(PCl_3)$ = 0.156 mol; PCl_5 used up = 0.156 mol; $n(PCl_5)$ at start = (83.4 g)/(208.5 g mol^{-1}) = 0.400 mol; $n(PCl_5)$ at equilibrium = 0.400 mol − 0.156 mol = 0.244 mol
  b i $K_c = [PCl_3] \times [Cl_2]/[PCl_5]$
    ii $[PCl_3] = [Cl_2]$ = (0.156 mol)/(9.23 dm^3) = 0.01690 mol dm^{-3}; $[PCl_5]$ = (0.244 mol)/(9.23 dm^3) = 0.02644 mol dm^{-3}; K_c = (0.01690 mol dm^{-3})/(0.02644 mol dm^{-3}) = 0.011 mol dm^{-3} (2 sig. figs)
  c i $K_p = p(PCl_3) \times p(Cl_2)/p(PCl_5)$
    ii $x(Cl_2)$ = 0.156/(2 × 0.156 + 0.244) = 0.281
    iii $p(PCl_5)$ = (0.244/(2 × 0.156 + 0.244)) × (250 kPa) = 110 kPa
    iv K_p = (0.281 × 250 kPa)^2/110 kPa = 45 kPa

5 a Forward and backward reactions still occurring, but the concentrations of the reactants and products do not change
  b The number of gas moles decreases in the forward reaction so there is a decrease in pressure; equilibrium favours the direction that minimizes change in external pressure, so high pressure favours the forward reaction
  c i $n(NH_3)$ = (24.0 g)/(17.0 g mol^{-1}) = 1.41 mol; $n(H_2)$ = (13.5 g)/(2.0 g mol^{-1}) = 6.75 mol; $n(N_2)$ = (60.3 g)/(28.0 g mol^{-1}) = 2.15 mol; n(total) = 10.31 mol; $x(NH_3)$ = (1.41 mol)/(10.31 mol) = 0.137; $x(H_2)$ = (6.75 mol)/(10.31 mol) = 0.655; $x(N_2)$ = (2.15 mol)/(10.31 mol) = 0.209;
    ii Pressures are 1.37 atm NH_3, 6.55 atm H_2, 2.09 atm N_2; $K_p = p^2_{NH_3}/p_{N_2}p^3_{H_2}$ = (1.37 atm)^2/((0.209 atm) × (6.55 atm)^2) = 3.2 × 10^{-3} atm^{-2} (2 sig. figs)
    iii Reaction is exothermic, so increasing the temperature favours the backward reaction, decreasing the yield and reducing K_p
  d Thermodynamic stability refers to the enthalpy change (strictly Gibbs energy change) for the reaction, which in this case is negative, i.e. the products are at a lower energy level (more stable) than the reactants; kinetic stability refers to the rate at which the change occurs; if the reaction is slow (i.e. there is a high activation energy barrier for the reactants to surmount) then the reactants are said to be kinetically stable

6 a i See **1 c**
    ii 0.5 mol N_2O_4 forms 1 mol NO_2; volume is 10.0 dm^3, so $[N_2O_4]$ = 0.05 mol dm^{-3}; $[NO_2]$ = 0.1 mol dm^{-3}; so K_c = (0.1 mol dm^{-3})^2/(0.05mol dm^{-3}) = 0.2 mol dm^{-3}
    iii ΔH°_f = 2 × (+33.9 kJ mol^{-1}) − (+9.70 kJ mol^{-1}) = +58.1 kJ mol^{-1}
    iv The dissociation will increase because the reaction is endothermic
  b Decrease the pressure
  c i Faster
    ii None
    iii Faster
  d The bonds in the reactants are stronger than those in the products

7 a i Bonds broken: H—H and I—I = (+436 kJ mol^{-1}) + (+151 kJ mol^{-1}) = +587 kJ mol^{-1}; bonds made: 2 × H—I = 2 × (−299 kJ mol^{-1}) = −598 kJ mol^{-1}; so ΔH = (+587 kJ mol^{-1}) + (−598 kJ mol^{-1}) = −11 kJ mol^{-1}
    ii Energy goes up, reaches a transition state, and then falls to just below the original energy level
  b i Energy down from reactants to products;
    ii Energy up from reactants to transition state
  c Higher activation energy because the Cl—Cl bond is stronger than the I—I bond
  d i $K_c = [HI]^2/[H_2][I_2]$
    ii 1.5 mol H_2 and 1.5 mol I_2 react to form 3.0 mol HI, so the amount in moles left of H_2 and I_2 = 1.9 mol − 1.5 mol = 0.4 mol; $[H_2] = [I_2]$ = (0.4 mol)/(0.25 dm^3) = 1.6 mol dm^{-3}; [HI] = 3.0 mol/(0.25 dm^3) = 12 mol dm^{-3}; $K_c = [HI]^2/[H_2][I_2]$ = (12 mol dm^{-3})^2/(1.6 mol dm^{-3})^2 = 56

Chapter 12

Practice questions

Spread 12.7

1 11.3 2 11.1

Spread 12.9

1 0.579 mol dm^{-1}

Exam questions

1 a i $C_2H_5COOH(aq) \rightleftharpoons H^+(aq) + C_2H_5COO^-(aq)$
    ii pK_a = 4.91
  b i $C_2H_5COOH(aq) + NaOH(aq) \rightarrow C_2H_5COONa(aq) + H_2O(l)$
    ii Phenolphthalein
  c i A solution that resists change in pH despite small additions of acid or base

ii Addition of acid or base shifts the equilibrium, so counteracting the addition; e.g. if acid is added, the excess hydrogen ions cause the equilibrium to shift to the left, the propanoate ions combine to form more propanoic acid molecules, and the hydrogen ion concentration remains almost constant
iii Volume of NaOH added neutralizes the same volume of acid = 15 cm^3; volume of acid remaining = 15 cm^3, since amounts of acid and salt are equal; pK_a = pH
iv Carbon dioxide/hydrogencarbonate ions; maintains a constant pH – structure of proteins (e.g. enzymes) sensitive to changes in pH

2 a See spread 12.2
b HCl, Cl^-, H_2SO_4, HSO_4^-; NH_4^+, NH_3
c i and ii See spread 12.4
iii CH_3COOH **A1**, $CH_3CO_2^-$ **B1**, H_3O^+ **A2**, H_2O **B2**
d i $CH_3COOH + NH_3 \rightarrow NH_4^+ + CH_3CO_2^-$
ii Ammonia is a base, encouraging the deprotonation to occur

3 a X: strong base (e.g. sodium hydroxide)
Y: strong acid (e.g. hydrochloric)
b Curve B – X: weak acid, pH higher at start than for strong acid in A, equivalence point above pH 7; Y: strong base, final pH similar to A; curve C – X: weak base, pH lower at start than it would be for a strong base of same concentration, Y: strong acid, final pH same as start in A, equivalence point below pH 7
c $[H^+] = 5.0 \times 10^{-3}$ mol dm^{-3};
$K_a = (5.0 \times 10^{-3}\,\text{mol dm}^{-3})^2/(0.1\,\text{mol dm}^{-3})$
$= 2.5 \times 10^{-4}$ mol dm^{-3}

CHAPTER 13

Exam questions

1 a Reduction is the gain of electrons by a species
b The standard hydrogen electrode; difficult to maintain standard conditions (e.g. pressure of hydrogen gas) and hence reliable cell emf; risk of ignition of hydrogen gas
c i $Ag^+(aq) + e^- \rightarrow Ag(s)$; $Cu(s) \rightarrow Cu^{2+}(aq) + 2e^-$; the silver ions are reduced
ii $S_2O_8^{2-}(aq) + 2e^- \rightarrow 2SO_4^{2-}(aq)$;
$Mn^{2+}(aq) + 4H_2O(l) \rightarrow$
$MnO_4^-(aq) + 8H^+(aq) + 5e^-$; the $S_2O_8^{2-}$ is reduced

2 a Hydrogen electrode; 0 V
b No current drawn from cell; solutions of 1 mol dm^{-3}; temperature: 298 K; pressure: 1 bar
c To provide electrical contact betwen the two half-cells; potassium chloride
d Table of redox half-equations (usually written as reduction reactions) in order of their standard electrode potentials (most negative at the top)
e Iron(II) ions reduced to Fe: Zn has the greater potential to lose electrons and donates electrons to the iron(II) ions

3 a $Fe(s) | Fe^{2+}(aq) || Fe^{3+}(aq) | Fe(s)$
emf = (−0.04 V) − (−0.44 V) = + 0.4 V
$3Fe(s) + 2Fe^{3+}(aq) \rightarrow 3Fe^{2+}(aq) + 2Fe(s)$
b Manganate(VII); the manganate(VII) standard half-cell has a more positive potential than the chlorine half-cell and will oxidize chloride ions to chlorine, thus interfering with the estimation of the iron
c i The manganate(VII) will oxidize the chromium(III)
ii $6MnO_4^-(aq) + 10Cr^{3+}(aq) + 11H_2O(l) \rightarrow$
$6Mn^{2+}(aq) + 5Cr_2O_7^{2-}(aq) + 22H^+(aq)$

4 a Method 1: reduction by carbon (blast furnace); the metal ore; the reducing agent; high temperature, e.g. iron; method 2: electrolysis of molten metal compound; metal compound; high temperature, e.g. aluminium; method 3: reduction by stronger reduction agent, e.g. Thermit process
b i Carbon oxidized by oxygen
ii Raw materials cheaper, less energy required (lower temperatures)
iii Titanium able to withstand higher temperatures

5 a i Digital voltmeter; high resistance
ii 1 mol dm^{-3}
b i Provides electrical contact between the solutions in the two half-cells
ii Aqueous potassium chloride
iii It is the ions in the solution which are the charge carriers, not free electrons as in the metal wire
c i emf = $E^\ominus$(r.h. electrode) − $E^\ominus$(l.h. electrode) = + 0.38 V
= +0.34 V − $E^\ominus(Fe^{3+}/Fe)$, so $E^\ominus(Fe^{3+}/Fe)$
= +0.34 V − 0.38 V = −0.04 V
ii $Fe(s) | Fe^{3+}(aq) | Cu^{2+}(aq) | Cu(s)$
iii $2Fe(s) + 3Cu^{2+}(aq) \rightarrow 2Fe^{3+}(aq) + 3Cu(s)$
d Zinc has a more negative standard electrode potential than iron, i.e. it will reduce any iron(II) formed and will be oxidized itself, so even if the surface is scratched to expose the iron, the zinc will prevent rusting occurring; tin has a more positive standard electrode potential than iron; if tinplate is scratched, the iron will oxidize and prevent the tin from being oxidized, so rusting is accelerated

6 a $A|A^{n+}||B^{n+}|B$
b C most reactive, then B, D, A
c Used a digital voltmeter
d $E^\ominus$ = (+1.10 V) − (+0.47 V) = +0.63 V

7 a i Pb
ii PbO_2
iii H_2SO_4
b $Pb(s) + PbO_2(s) + 2H_2SO_4(aq) \rightarrow 2PbSO_4 + 2H_2O(l)$
c $E^\ominus$ = (+1.69 V) − (−0.36 V) = +2.05 V
d Opposite of the equation above
e They are heavy
f i Oxygen also needed
ii Rusting more severe where there is already an indentation
iii Corrosion more likely where this is stress
iv Magnesium corrodes preferentially as Mg is more reactive than Fe

8 a II
b $4Al(s) + 3O_2(g) + 6H_2O(l) \rightarrow 4Al(OH)_3(s)$
c The electrodes get coated in the non-conducting aluminium

9 a i $Cl_2 + 2KI \rightarrow I_2 + 2KCl$
ii $Cl_2 + H_2 \rightarrow 2HCl$
iii See spread 13.4
b i The reactions at the electrodes involve the gain and loss of electrons
ii See spread 19.2

CHAPTER 14

Exam questions

1 a Conservation
b $\Delta H^\ominus - T\Delta S^\ominus = -RT\ln K_c$; so $\ln K_c = \Delta S^\ominus - \Delta H^\ominus/T$
c i As T increases, if $\Delta H^\ominus$ is negative, the second term gets less positive and so the value of K_c falls
ii If $\Delta H^\ominus$ is positive, the second term above gets less negative and so the value of K_c rises

2 a i A: digital voltmeter; B: salt bridge; C: copper wire
ii Zn^{2+}; 1 mol dm^{-3}
iii Zero current
b i $Zn(s) + Cu^{2+}(aq) \rightarrow Zn^{2+}(aq) + Cu(s)$
ii $E^\ominus$ = (+0.34 V) − (−0.76 V) = +1.10 V
iii $\Delta G^\ominus = -zFE^\ominus = -2 \times (96\,500\,\text{C mol}^{-1}) \times (+1.10\,\text{V})$
= −212 kJ mol^{-1}
iv From Zn to Cu

3 a i $\Delta H_f^\ominus$ is positive, $\Delta S_f^\ominus$ is positive
ii Below 0, $|T\Delta S_f^\ominus| < |\Delta H_f^\ominus|$ so $\Delta G_f^\ominus$ is positive and the reaction is not spontaneous
b $\Delta H_f^\ominus$ for reaction is positive, and overall $\Delta S_f^\ominus$ is also positive as gas is released; $|T\Delta S_f^\ominus| > |\Delta H_f^\ominus|$, so $\Delta G_f^\ominus$ is negative, and the reaction goes

c $\Delta H_f^{\ominus}$ is negative, so more energy is released by new bonds made than is required to break bonds in reactants; $\Delta S_f^{\ominus}$ is positive, so there is an increase in the number of molecules during the reaction, and hence $\Delta G_f^{\ominus}$ is negative

4 a i $-350\,kJ\,mol^{-1}$ (CO); $-420\,kJ\,mol^{-1}$ (CO_2); $-410\,kJ\,mol^{-1}$ (Fe)

ii FeO + C: $\Delta G_f^{\ominus} = (+410 - 350)/2 = +30\,kJ\,mol^{-1}$; FeO + CO: $\Delta G_f^{\ominus} = (+410 - 420)/2 = -5\,kJ\,mol^{-1}$

iii Only the reaction with CO is feasible at 800K because $\Delta G_f^{\ominus}$ is negative for this reaction but positive for the reaction with C

iv Approx. 1000 K (where the C line crosses and falls below the Fe line)

v Both reactants are solid: low S; one of the products is a gas: high S, so change is positive

5 a $Zn(s) \rightarrow Zn^{2+}(aq) + 2e^-$; $Pb^{2+}(aq) + 2e^- \rightarrow Pb(s)$

b It takes account of heat lost from the calorimeter; you do not have to assume the specific heat capacity of the solution is the same as for pure water

c Energy given out = $(25.0\,J\,s^{-1}) \times (305\,s) = 7625\,J$; n(lead) used = $(0.5\,mol\,dm^{-3}) \times (0.1\,dm^3) = 0.05\,mol$; energy released per mole lead = $(7625\,J)/0.05 = 152.5\,kJ$; $\Delta H_f^{\ominus} = -152.5\,kJ\,mol^{-1}$

d i $Zn(s)|Zn^{2+}(aq)|Pb^{2+}(aq)|Pb(s)$

ii Lead; it is the one being reduced (taking up electrons)

iii 1 M aqueous lead nitrate and zinc nitrate

iv See question 8, chapter 13

e i $\Delta G^{\ominus} = -zFE^{\ominus} = -2 \times (9.65 \times 10^4\,C\,mol^{-1}) \times (0.63\,V) = -121.6\,kJ\,mol^{-1} = \Delta H^{\ominus} - T\Delta S^{\ominus}$, so $T\Delta S^{\ominus} = \Delta H^{\ominus} - \Delta G^{\ominus} = (152.5\,kJ\,mol^{-1}) - (-121.6\,kJ\,mol^{-1}) = -30.9\,kJ\,mol^{-1}$; thus $\Delta S_f^{\ominus}$(system) $= (-30.9 \times 10^3\,J\,mol^{-1})/(298\,K) = -103.7\,J\,K^{-1}\,mol^{-1}$ (answer correct as given)

ii $\Delta S_f^{\ominus}(surr) = -\Delta H_f^{\ominus}/T = (+152.5 \times 10^3\,J\,mol^{-1})/(298\,K) = +511.7\,J\,K^{-1}\,mol^{-1}$

iii $\Delta S^{\ominus}(sys) + \Delta S^{\ominus}(surr) = -103.7\,J\,K^{-1}\,mol^{-1} + 511.7\,J\,K^{-1}\,mol^{-1} = 408\,J\,K^{-1}\,mol^{-1}$; this is equal to $-\Delta G_f^{\ominus}/T$, so if $\Delta S_f^{\ominus}$(total) is positive, the reaction is spontaneous, which it is

6 a Any reaction where a solid becomes a liquid or gas, or liquid becomes gas, or where the number of particles increases, e.g.
$2Na(s) + 2H_2O(l) \rightarrow 2Na^+(aq) + 2OH^-(aq) + H_2(g)$

b $214 - 205 - S^{\ominus}$(graphite) = 3, so $S^{\ominus}$(graphite) = $6\,J\,K^{-1}\,mol^{-1}$; graphite is solid, and has a highly ordered lattice with strong bonds between atoms; hence low $S^{\ominus}$

c i Given in **1**

ii When $\Delta G_f^{\ominus} = 0$, $T\Delta S_f^{\ominus} = \Delta H_f^{\ominus}$, or $\Delta S_f^{\ominus} = \Delta H_f^{\ominus}/T$

d $\Delta S_f^{\ominus} = 6000/273 = 22\,J\,K^{-1}\,mol^{-1}$; M_r(water) = 18, hence $54\,g = (54\,g)/(18\,g\,mol^{-1}) = 3\,mol$; total entropy change $= (3\,mol) \times (22\,J\,K^{-1}\,mol^{-1}) = 66\,J\,K^{-1}$

Chapter 15

Exam questions

1 a Reducing the size of the lumps increases the surface area of the marble in contact with the acid, hence providing a greater probability that the acid will collide with and react with the marble and increasing the rate of reaction

b i Expt 2: compared to expt 1, concentration of A and B doubles, hence the rate is multiplied by $2 \times 2^2 = 8$: $8 \times 1.2 \times 10^{-4} = 9.6 \times 10^{-4}$; expt 3: concentration of B is the same as in 2 but the rate is 1/4 of the rate in expt 2, so [A] = 1/4 of 0.04 = 0.01; expt 4: compared to expt 1, we have [A] × 3, [B] × 1.5, so rate = $1.2 \times 10^{-4} \times 3 \times 1.5^2 = 8.1 \times 10^{-4}$; expt 5: compared to 1, we have [A] doubled, rate × 6, so $6 = 2 \times b^2$, where $b = 1.732$, so [B] = $1.732 \times 0.02 = 0.035$

ii In expt 1, $1.2 \times 10^{-4} = kx$, $0.02 \times 0.022k = 15\,mol^{-2}\,dm^6\,s^{-1}$

2 a i Increased temperature

ii The total number of molecules

iii There is no change to the number of molecules

b i The minimum energy particles must have for collisions to bring about a reaction

ii Catalyst: causes activation energy to decrease (rate to increase); if volume is reduced, pressure increases, but there is no effect on the activiation energy (but rate increased)

c Few particles move from their lattice positions and so there are few collisions between the reactants and few have sufficient kinetic energy to produce a reaction

3 a Homogeneous: same phase as reactants; heterogeneous: different phase

b See **2 b i**

c i k: rate constant, the constant of proportionality in rate expression (gradient of line of rate against [A]); [A]: concentration of reactant A; n: the order of the reaction with respect to reactant A

ii The order of reaction with respect to B is zero

d i Heterogeneous; reactants adsorbed onto surface of the catalyst; weak bonds formed between reactants and catalyst which weaken bonds in reactants, allowing molecules close together on catalyst surface to form new bonds

ii Homogeneous; reactant molecules fit into and bond with active sites on enzyme molecules; this weakens bonds in the reactant molecules allowing reactions to take place

e Increase the surface area of the catalyst, e.g. by making it into porous pellets (vanadium(V) oxide) or coating it onto an inert substrate (e.g. platinium on ceramic in catalytic converters); recover and re-use the catalyst after use

5 a i k: the rate constant; A: the pre-exponential factor

ii Gradient = $-12\,500\,K$

iii $E = (-12\,500\,K) \times (-8.31\,J\,K^{-1}\,mol^{-1}) = 104\,kJ\,mol^{-1}$

b i Order: the powers of the concentration in the rate expression, e.g. rate = $k[A]^x$, where x is the order with respect to A

ii Increased concentration means that there are more collisions between reactant molecules and hence a greater probability that the reaction will occur

iii Proportional increase in concentration = 0.54/0.18 = 3; rate increases by factor of $9 = 3^2$; reaction is second order; rate is proportional to concentration squared

Chapter 16

Exam questions

1 a i Barium has stronger metallic bonding; because 2 electrons in outer shell are involved in bonding, not 1; barium atoms are smaller than caesium atoms

ii Electrons dropping from higher to lower energy levels

iii Discrete lines

b i NaO; **ii** Na_2O_2

iii Weighed mass of Y reacted with known volume of H_2SO_4(aq); titrate aliquots with $KMnO_4$(aq) of known concentration

2 a i Molten NaCl; **ii** Aqueous NaCl

b i Cl_2; $2Cl^- \rightarrow Cl_2 + 2e^-$

ii O_2; $4OH^- \rightarrow 2H_2O + O_2 + 4e^-$

c Although OH^- is easier to oxidize ($E^{\ominus}$ is less positive under standard conditions), concentration of Cl^- is much higher

d White precipitate ($[Al(OH)_3(H_2O)_3]$) formed from colourless solution ($[Al(H_2O)_6]^{3+}$), which redissolves in excess to give colourless solution ($[Al(OH)_4]^-$)

3 a i $1s^2 2s^2 2p^6 3s^2 3p^6 4s^2$

ii Ca atoms lose outer electrons to form cations in a sea of delocalized electrons; held together by strong electrostatic forces of attraction

b i $Ca + 2H_2O \rightarrow Ca(OH)_2 + H_2$
0   +1 −2   +2 −2 +1   0

ii Ca is oxidized; $Ca \rightarrow Ca^{2+} + 2e^-$

iii Calcium hydroxide (limewater); 11

c i White precipitate after a few drops
ii No obvious change
d $Mg^{2+}(aq) + 2OH^-(aq) \rightarrow Mg(OH)_2(s)$
$Mg(OH)_2$ is much less soluble than $Ba(OH)_2$, which is a strong base; fewer drops of NaOH(aq) are required

4 i Method 1: heat magnesium in oxygen
$2Mg(s) + O_2(g) \rightarrow 2MgO(s)$
Method 2: heat carbonate, nitrate, or hydroxide
$MgCO_3(s) \rightarrow MgO(s) + CO_2(g)$
ii $[Mg]^{2+}\ [O]^{2-}$
iii It contains O^{2-} ions, which can act as proton acceptors
iv I Magnesium oxidizes when heated in air
II 175 kg

5 a i White precipitate; $Mg^{2+}(aq) + 2OH^-(aq) \rightarrow Mg(OH)_2(s)$
ii Reagents: add $AgNO_3(aq)$ acidified with $HNO_3(aq)$; observation: white precipitate which does not dissolve in $HNO_3(aq)$; equation: $Ag^+(aq) + Cl^-(aq) \rightarrow AgCl(s)$
b i Lattice enthalpies for both compounds are similar; hydration enthalpy of Mg^{2+} is much greater than that of Ba^{2+}
ii High melting point/hard/cleaves/conducts only when liquid or aqueous
c Required for chlorophyll production

6 a i $Ba + 2H_2O \rightarrow Ba(OH)_2 + H_2$
ii More vigorously; the lower ionization energy of Ba means that electrons are lost more easily
iii $BaCO_3(s) \rightarrow BaO(s) + CO_2(g)$
iv Calcium carbonate
v Flame test; calcium: brick-red; barium: yellow-green
b i BaO_2; **ii** O_2^{2-}; **iii** -1; **iv** Na_2O_2
c i $Na_2O_2 + H_2SO_4 \rightarrow Na_2SO_4 + H_2O_2$
ii $BaSO_4$ is insoluble and could be removed by filtering

7 a i $-348\ kJ\ mol^{-1}$; the Born–Haber cycle
ii The theoretical lattice enthalpy is based on a purely ionic model, so the experimental lattice enthalpy would be different because magnesium chloride has some covalent character
b i As the cation radius increases (from Ca to Ba), the ions have less attraction to water
ii The sulphates become less soluble (from $CaSO_4$ to $BaSO_4$), because the cationic radius increases, so the hydration enthalpy increases; the decrease in lattice enthalpy is only slight in comparison
iii Barium sulphate is very insoluble, so there are few barium ions free to poison the patient
iv $Ba(s) + 2H_2O(l) \rightarrow Ba(OH)_2(aq) + H_2(g)$
v Add dilute sulphuric acid, filter the barium sulphate precipitate formed, and dry

8 a i The aqueous magnesium nitrate would immediately form a white precipitate with sodium hydroxide; the aqueous barium nitrate would not form a precipitate with a few drops of NaOH, but when excess is added, a white precipitate would form
ii Magnesium hydroxide is insoluble and hence precipitates immediately; $Mg^{2+}(aq) + 2OH^-(aq) \rightarrow Mg(OH)_2(s)$; barium hydroxide is much more soluble and so would only form a precipitate if NaOH was added in large amounts; $Ba^{2+}(aq) + 2OH^-(aq) \rightarrow Ba(OH)_2(s)$
b i As the atomic number increases, the Group II carbonates become more stable, because the cation radius increases, so the cations polarize the carbonate anion less, so the carbonates require higher temperatures to decompose; more importantly, the lattice energy of the oxide formed would be less
ii Sodium carbonate is much more stable to heat because the sodium ion only has a 1^+ charge, so the sodium ion does not polarize the carbonate so much
c i Electrolysis of molten sodium chloride
ii Magnesium chloride, from dried-up salt lakes
iii High temperature to melt the salt, and electricity; $Mg^{2+} + 2e^- \rightarrow Mg$

iv Chlorine; examples of uses: manufacture of bleach, PVC, insecticides
d i The electronic energy levels around a lithium ion are fixed; the flame heat promotes electrons to a high energy level; when the electrons fall down energy levels, light is emitted; as the energy levels around the ions are fixed, the energy released is fixed, so a particular colour is produced
ii Rubidium is much more reactive, so burning it in chlorine would be too dangerous

---

CHAPTER 17

Exam questions

1 a The first three elements have a relatively high melting point owing to their metallic bonding; silicon in the middle has a very high melting point owing to a giant covalent lattice; the last elements have low melting points owing to the weak intermolecular forces between the simple molecules
b As atomic number increases in Group I, the atomic radius increases, because there is an increased number of electron shells; the ionization energies decrease as the electron shells increase, producing an increased distance from the nucleus to the outer
c i $2Na(s) + 2H_2O(l) \rightarrow 2NaOH(aq) + H_2(g)$
ii $Na_2O(s) + H_2O(l) \rightarrow 2NaOH(aq)$
iii $NaH(s) + H_2O(l) \rightarrow NaOH(aq) + H_2(g)$
d 14

2 a i Cl_2
ii Si, P (red)
b NaCl; MgS
c $AlCl_3$: trigonal planar, 120°; PCl_3: pyramidal, less than 109°
d i Sodium: $Na_2O + H_2O \rightarrow 2NaOH$
ii Sulphur: $SO_2 + H_2O \rightarrow H_2SO_3$

3 a The way that the properties of the elements (and their compounds) show a repeating pattern when ordered by atomic number
b The number of protons in the nucleus increases and electrons in the same shell shield poorly, so the nucleus increasingly attracts electrons
c i Mg has stronger metallic bonding because 1 more electron per atom is involved in the delocalized sea
ii Si has a giant covalent structure; therefore very strong covalent bonds must be broken
iii S_8 has stronger dispersion forces between molecules than P_4
iv In Ar there are only very weak dispersion forces between individual atoms

4 a NaCl; $MgCl_2$; $AlCl_3$; Al_2Cl_6; PCl_3/PCl_5; S_2Cl_2
b 16.5%
c i Cl, Cl Si Cl, Cl **ii**
4 bond pairs (and 0 lone pairs) repel each other equally to the corners of a tetrahedron
iii $AlCl_3$ has 3 bond pairs (and 0 lone pairs) which repel each other equally to the corners of a triangle
d i $SiCl_4 + 2H_2O \rightarrow SiO_2 + 4HCl$
ii CCl_4 does not react because the outer shell of the C atom does not have a vacant orbital to accept a lone pair from a water molecule (see artwork in spread 19.6)

5 a A measure of the attraction of an atom for a shared pair of electrons (in a covalent bond)
b Electronegativity increases, because the number of protons increases and the added electron shields poorly, so the effective nuclear charge increases, so the strength of attraction for electrons increases
c i Ionic $\rightarrow$ covalent
ii As atoms become more electronegative, the difference in electronegativity decreases, so electrons are shared rather than transferred
d $P_4O_{10} + 6H_2O \rightarrow 4H_3PO_4$

6 a Metallic bonding in Mg: strong force of attraction between cations and delocalized electrons; ionic bonding in $MgCl_2$: strong force of attraction between oppositely charged ions
b Covalent/ionic borderline, because Al is more electronegative than Mg; the difference in electronegativity is less, *or* Al^{3+} has a higher charge density than Mg^{2+}, so it polarizes Cl^- more
c $MgCl_2(s) + aq \rightarrow Mg^{2+}(aq) + 2Cl^-(aq)$; the force of attraction between positive Mg^{2+} and polar water molecules (or coordinate covalent bonds $\rightarrow [Mg(H_2O)_6]^{2+}$)

7 a i $Na_2O + H_2O \rightarrow 2NaOH$; pH = 14
ii $SO_2 + H_2O \rightarrow H_2SO_3$; pH = 1
b Ionic oxides give basic solutions, covalent give acidic
c i $MgCl_2(s) + aq \rightarrow Mg^{2+}(aq) + 2Cl^-(aq)$; pH = 7
ii $SiCl_4(l) + 2H_2O(l) \rightarrow SiO_2(s) + 4HCl(g)$; pH = 0

8 a Electronegativity is a measure of the attraction of an atom to a shared electron pair in a covalent bond
b i Ionic; ii Covalent (polar); iii Covalent
c i The electron pairs around a central atom move as far apart as possible, to decrease the repulsion between them; lone pair – lone pair repulsion is greater than lone pair – bonding pair repulsion, which is greater than bonding pair – bonding pair repulsion
ii Ammonia has a pyramidal shape; draw the lone pair straight up, with one bond in the plane of the paper at 107° from the lone pair, and then the other two bonds off the other way, one into the paper and one out
iii The lone pair repels more effectively than the N—H bonding pairs, so the lone pair pushes the bonding pairs together
iv The N—H bond is polar owing to the difference in electronegativity of the N and H atoms; the whole molecule is polar because the polar bonds do not cancel each other since they are off to one side of the molecule
d i $2Mg + O_2 \rightarrow 2MgO$; $MgO + 2HCl \rightarrow MgCl_2 + H_2O$
ii $Al_2O_3 + 6H^+ \rightarrow 2Al^{3+} + 3H_2O$; $Al_2O_3 + 3H_2O + 2OH^- \rightarrow 2[Al(OH)_4]^-$;
iii CO_2 is more acidic; SiO_2 requires molten NaOH at high temperatures

Chapter 18

Exam questions

1 a It decreases; as the number of shells increases, the distance from the nucleus increases
b It increases; more electrons increase the strength of the dispersion forces
c Br_2 is non-polar, while ICl is polar, because Cl is more electronegative than I; therefore dipole–dipole forces exist as well as dispersion forces

2 a i $2P + 3I_2 \rightarrow 2PI_3$
ii $PI_3 + 3H_2O \rightarrow H_3PO_3 + 3HI$
b i Yellow precipitate then no change
ii Black solid/purple vapour (rotten egg smell)

3 a i $NaCl(s) + H_2SO_4(l) \rightarrow NaHSO_4(s) + HCl(g)$; at room temperature
ii I^-/HI is a stronger reductant than Cl^-/HCl, therefore $H_2SO_4 + 8HI \rightarrow 4I_2 + H_2S + 4H_2O$
b Ionization: $HF + H_2O \rightarrow H_3O^+ + F^-$; it is less with HF, because the H—F bond is strongest
c Add $AgNO_3(aq)$; white precipitate with Cl^-, yellow precipitate with I^-
d i $2Br^-(aq) + Cl_2(g) \rightarrow Br_2(l) + 2Cl^-(aq)$
$E^\ominus$ for the reaction is positive ((1.36 – 1.09) V) and therefore it is energetically feasible
ii It allows the production of Br_2 from seawater

4 a i Covalent bonding; the diagram should show the three covalent bonds in the PCl_3 as three pairs of dots and crosses; the P also has a lone pair of electrons
ii The diagram should show a pyramidal shape like that of ammonia; the electron pairs repel until they are as far apart as possible
iii Drip PCl_3 through dry chlorine gas using ice-cold apparatus
iv PCl_4^+ and PCl_6^-
v PCl_5 has an unexpected ionic structure, which causes an increased melting point
vi PI_5 is unknown because it is not possible to fit five large iodine atoms around the relatively small phosphorus atom
b i Propanoyl chloride, CH_3CH_2COCl; the graphical formula would show all the bonds
ii There is a vigorous production of HCl (seen as white fumes) which can be violent; the HCl fumes would form concentrated hydrochloric acid, which could harm the experimenter
iii Graphical formulae would show all the bonds; the diagrams would show propan-1-ol, $CH_3CH_2CH_2OH$ and propan-2-ol, $CH_3CH(OH)CH_3$; R is propan-1-ol
iv Add R to potassium manganate(VII) (or potassium dichromate) with dilute sulphuric acid and heat under reflux; the product would be purified by fractional distillation

5 a Chlorine is produced by electrolysis of brine using a steel cathode and titanium anode
b i $3Cl_2(g) + 6NaOH(aq) \rightarrow NaClO_3(aq) + 5NaCl(aq) + 3H_2O(l)$; the green chlorine gas produces a colourless solution, by disproportionation
ii $Cl_2(g) + 2Br^-(aq) \rightarrow Br_2(l) + 2Cl^-(aq)$; the chlorine oxidizes the bromide ions to bromine; the green chlorine produces a brown solution; a redox reaction
iii $Cl_2(g) + C_2H_4(g) \rightarrow ClCH_2CH_2Cl(l)$; the green chlorine gas reacts with ethene to make a colourless oily liquid; the chlorine adds to the ethene by electrophilic addition

6 a Main oxidation states: Na: +1; Mg: +2; Al: +3; Si: +4; P: +3 and +5; ionic chlorides dissolve in water;
$NaCl(s) \rightarrow Na^+(aq) + Cl^-(aq)$;
$MgCl_2(s) \rightarrow Mg^{2+}(aq) + 2Cl^-(aq)$;
covalent chlorides hydrolyse and produce white hydrogen chloride fumes;
$Al_2Cl_6(s) + 3H_2O(l) \rightarrow 2Al(OH)_3(s) + 6HCl(g)$;
$SiCl_4(l) + 2H_2O(l) \rightarrow SiO_2(s) + 4HCl(g)$;
$PCl_3(l) + 3H_2O(l) \rightarrow H_3PO_3(aq) + 3HCl(g)$;
$PCl_5(l) + 4H_2O(l) \rightarrow H_3PO_4(aq) + 5HCl(g)$;
b i $2S_2Cl_2(l) + 3H_2O(l) \rightarrow 3S(s) + H_2SO_3(aq) + 4HCl(g)$
ii $22.2\,cm^3$

7 a i The Born–Haber cycle should include $2 \times \Delta H^\ominus_{at}(F)$, and 2 × E.A. of fluorine
ii $-2640\,kJ\,mol^{-1}$
b i $CaF_2 + H_2SO_4(l) \rightarrow CaSO_4(s) + 2HF(g)$
ii $+58\,kJ\,mol^{-1}$
iii The reaction should be heated; the equilibrium will shift right with increasing temperature, so the forward reaction will be favoured, because the reaction is endothermic

8 a i Aqueous NaCl (brine)
ii $2Cl^- \rightarrow Cl_2 + 2e^-$
iii $2H^+ + 2e^- \rightarrow H_2$, or $2H_2O + 2e^- \rightarrow H_2 + 2OH_2$
iv $2NaCl + 2H_2O \rightarrow 2NaOH + Cl_2 + H_2$
b i Remove the diaphragm so that Cl_2 and NaOH can react
ii $2NaOH + Cl_2 \rightarrow NaCl + NaOCl + H_2O$
iii Bleach
c i Simultaneous oxidation and reduction of the same species in a reaction
ii $3ClO^- \rightarrow 2Cl^- + ClO_3^-$
+1 −1 +5
iii $ClO^- + 4OH^- \rightarrow ClO_3^- + 2H_2O + 4e^-$
$ClO^- + H_2O + 2e^- \rightarrow Cl^- + 2OH^-$

9 a As the atomic number increases, the halogen atomic radius increases, so the hydrogen halide bonds become weaker, so the hydrogen halides become less stable to heat
b i Hydrogen sulphide, H_2S, and some sulphur dioxide, SO_2
ii The iodide ions have more electron shells, so there is a

greater distance from the nucleus to the outer electrons, so the outer electrons are more weakly held, so the iodide ions are easily oxidized by sulphuric acid (Using $E^\ominus$ values would be better)

c Bromide ion

d 0.015 mol I_2

10 **a** Iodide ions

b Standard means that the solution is made accurately to a particular concentration; this is only possible because the thiosulphate salt can be made pure

c Starch, blue-black to colourless.

d $S_2O_3^{2-}(aq) + I_2(aq) \rightarrow S_4O_6^{2-}(aq) + 2I^-(aq)$

e 3.36 mol dm^{-3}

Chapter 19

Exam questions

1 **a i** Al_2O_3 has a very high melting point, so energy costs would be high

ii $Al^{3+} + 3e^- \rightarrow Al(l)$

iii $2O^{2-} \rightarrow O_2 + 4e^-$; hot oxygen reacts with graphite anodes to form gaseous CO_2 and CO

b Electrode reactions, heating the melt

c i Conservation of resources, less environmental damage

ii Labour

2 **a i** Reaction is vigorous, exothermic, with steamy fumes $Al_2Cl_6 + 6H_2O \rightarrow 2Al(OH)_3 + 6HCl$ (simplified)

ii $[Al(H_2O)_6]^{3+}(aq) + H_2O \rightleftharpoons [Al(H_2O)_5(OH)]^{2+}(aq) + H_3O^+(aq)$

iii Effervescence, gas turns limewater cloudy, white precipitate of $Al(OH)_3$
$2H^+(aq) + CO_3^{2-}(aq) \rightarrow H_2O(l) + CO_2(g)$

b i White precipitate forms, which does not react with excess; $Al(OH)_3(H_2O)_3$, *or* $Al(OH)_3$

ii White precipitate would react with excess; forms $[Al(OH)_4]^-$

3 **a i** CO; **ii** SiO_2; **iii** $SnCl_2$; **iv** CCl_4

b i $x = 4$; **ii** Tetrahedral

c i Diamond: 3D lattice, tetrahedral arrangement of atoms; graphite: 2D lattice/layers of atoms, trigonal planar arrangement of atoms

ii Mass spectrometry

4 **a** CCl_4, CO; $SiCl_4$, SiO_2; $PbCl_4$, PbO

b $SiCl_4$ hydrolyses to produce HCl fumes;
$SiCl_4 + 2H_2O \rightarrow SiO_2 + 4HCl$
there is no hydrolysis with CCl_4 because there are no vacant orbitals in the outer shell of the C atom (see artwork in spread 19.6)

c $PbO_2 + 4H^+ + 2e^- \rightarrow Pb^{2+} + 2H_2O$; $2Cl^- \rightarrow Cl_2 + 2e^-$

d CO_2 has a simple molecular structure – only dispersion forces have to be broken; SiO_2 has a giant covalent structure, and therefore covalent bonds must be broken

5 **a i** See spread 5.5

ii See spread 5.5; 3 bond pairs and 1 lone pair repel each other to the corners of the tetrahedron

iii A bond formed by collinear overlap of atomic orbitals

b i In both cases there are dispersion and dipole–dipole forces between molecules; NH_3 forms H bonds as well

ii H bonds can form between H_2O and NH_3 molecules

c 47.6%

6 **a** CCl_4: liquid/poor/immiscible, no reaction/covalent;
$SiCl_4$: liquid/poor/hydrolyses, produces white fumes and white precipitate/covalent;
$PbCl_2$: solid/good/insoluble solid/ionic

b i $CaO(s) + SiO_2(s) \rightarrow CaSiO_3(s)$ in blast furnace (several answers possible)

ii $PbO(s) + 2HNO_3(aq) \rightarrow Pb(NO_3)_2(aq) + H_2O(l)$ (other reactions of tin and lead oxides are possible)

c i Tin

ii $2MnO_4^-(aq) + 5Sn^{2+}(aq) + 16H^+(aq) \rightarrow 2Mn^{2+}(aq) + 5Sn^{4+}(aq) + 8H_2O(l)$

7 **a i** It can be moved in pipes; it has to be kept hot

ii $S(l) + O_2(g) \rightarrow SO_2(g)$; $2SO_2(g) + O_2(g) \rightleftharpoons 2SO_3(g)$

b i Exothermic

ii Vanadium(V) oxide

iii To cool the gases (increases yield) and to raise steam ('recycle' energy)

iv The cooler the bed, the greater the yield of SO_3 (Le Chatelier's principle)

v Conc. H_2SO_4; $H_2SO_4 + SO_3 \rightarrow H_2S_2O_7$

c Possibility of loss of harmful gases, e.g. SO_2/ugly/leak of acid could occur

8 **a** Copper is a good conductor because it has metallic bonding where the electrons are free to move; SiO_2 is a poor conductor because the electrons are held in strong covalent bonds

b SiO_2 has a giant covalent structure, so all the strong Si—O bonds need to break to make the oxide liquid; copper is easier to turn into a liquid because the metallic bonds are not so strong

c SiO_2 is an electrical insulator, has a high melting point, and is hard (scratch resistant)

d Advantage: copper is easy to melt and pour into axe-head moulds; disadvantage: copper is not hard so the axe edge will blunt easily

Chapter 20

Exam questions

1 **a** $Fe_2O_3 + 3C \rightarrow 2Fe + 3CO$
$Fe_2O_3 + 2Al \rightarrow 2Fe + Al_2O_3$
$Fe_2O_3 + 3H_2 \rightarrow 2Fe + 3H_2O$

b i Carbon; it is cheapest/most plentiful

ii Hydrogen; byproduct is a gas and there is no contamination by a solid reductant

c SO_2, acid rain; CO_2, global warming

d O_2 blown through molten iron; impurities oxidized to gases or acidic solids that can be removed by calcium oxide

2 **a** High melting point/dense/hard

b i $[Ar]3d^64s^2$; $[Ar]3d^6$

ii Fe^{3+} has a stable half-filled subshell ($3d^5$)

c i Pale green; $[Fe(H_2O)_6]^{2+}$; octahedral

ii It turns brown (depending on pH); Fe^{2+} oxidized to Fe^{3+} by aerial O_2

d i Orange-brown solution is produced; I^- is oxidized to I_2 by Fe^{3+}

ii $2Fe^{3+} + 2I^- \rightarrow 2Fe^{2+} + I_2$

e Associated ligands split the 3d subshell into 2 energy levels; promotion of electrons between levels absorbs visible light of a particular wavelength

3 **a i** A molecule or ion with a lone pair that can make a coordinate covalent bond with a metal ion

ii 1 molecule or ion that can make 2 coordinate bonds with the same metal ion

b i Electron pair acceptor

ii $[Co(H_2O)_6]^{2+}$, octahedral; $[CoCl_4]^{2-}$, tetrahedral

iii Cl^- ions repel each other

iv Different ligands/different coordination number

c $[Co(en)_3]^{2+}$

4 **a** V: $[Ar]3d^34s^2$; V^{2+}: $[Ar]3d^3$

b i Because of the partially filled d subshell (see **2 e**)

ii Coordinate covalent

c i $NH_4^+ + OH^- \rightarrow NH_3 + H_2O$

ii Copper(II) hydroxide

iii $[Cu(NH_3)_4(H_2O)_2]^{2+}$

iv +4; +3; +2

d $2VO_2 + \frac{1}{2}O_2 \rightarrow V_2O_5$

e i Dioxovanadium(V)

ii Tetraamminedichlorochromium(III)

f Octahedral

5 **a** Heterogeneous: in different phase to reactants; catalyst: speeds up a reaction, recoverable at end

b Variable oxidation states
c See answer to chapter 19, exam question 7
d MnO_4^- is reduced to pale pink Mn^{2+}; Mn^{2+} catalyses the reaction so it gets progressively faster as $[Mn^{2+}]$ increases (= autocatalysis)

6 **a** Change in oxidation state; ligand exchange; coordination number change
b i Ligand exchange
ii Ligand exchange and coordination number change
c i A catalyst in the same phase as the reactants
ii Variable oxidation state
iii See **4 d**

7 **a** Coloured ions; variable oxidation state; complex formation; catalytic properties
b Example: V_2O_5, Contact process; variable oxidation state
c i $[Ar]3d^54s^1$; **ii** $[Ar]3d^3$
d i $+6 \rightarrow +3$; **ii** 2.00×10^{-3}; **iii** 16.7 cm^3
e Green precipitate forms which reacts with excess to give a green solution

8 **a** $CuCl_4^{2-}$
b i $Fe(s) + Cu^{2+}(aq) \rightarrow Fe^{2+}(aq) + Cu(s)$
ii The solid is bronze coloured; the solution becomes green rather than blue
iii $[Fe(H_2O)^6]^{2+}$
c P: anionic, tetrahedral; **Q**: cationic, octahedral
d i Green; **ii** $Fe(OH)_3$;
iii Oxygen in the air; **iv** Oxidation

CHAPTER 21

Practice questions

Spread 21.3

3 3,3-dimethylpentane

CHAPTER 22

Exam questions

1 **a** Kerosine
b Different boiling points
c Naphtha: cracking; diesel: industrial furnaces/central heating
d i $2C_4H_{10} + 13O_2 \rightarrow 8CO_2 + 10H_2O$
ii Not volatile, viscous liquid
e Decomposes/combusts

2 **a i** Partial vapour pressure = mole fraction × vapour pressure of pure component
ii Ideal behaviour; draw liquid and vapour lines and use tie lines (horizontal lines joining the liquid and vapour lines) to explain purification
iii Oil has many more than two components; fractions are themselves mixtures; fractions are taken from many levels, not just the top and bottom
b i It is easier/safer to transport liquids/more can be contained in the same space
ii Carcinogenicity
iii The mixture explodes too soon/before the spark/it causes engine damage/fewer mpg
iv Lead compounds cause damage to the central nervous system

3 **a** Homolytic/(free) radical substitution
b It breaks the Cl—Cl bond to form radicals
c $CH_4 + Cl_2 \rightarrow CH_3Cl + HCl$
d CH_2Cl_2
$CH_3Cl + Cl\cdot \rightarrow \cdot CH_2Cl + HCl$
$\cdot CH_2Cl + Cl_2 \rightarrow CH_2Cl_2 + Cl\cdot$
e $\cdot CH_3$ radicals collide in a termination step
$2\cdot CH_3 \rightarrow CH_3CH_3$
f CCl_4

4 **a** A: 2-bromobutane $CH_3CH_2CHBrCH_3$
B: butane $CH_3CH_2CH_2CH_3$
C: butan-2-ol $CH_3CH_2CH(OH)CH_3$
D: butane-2,3-diol $CH_3CH(OH)CH(OH)CH_3$
b i Electrophile
ii See spread 22.8
c i $CH_2{=}CH{-}CH{=}CH_2$
ii $C_4H_8 \rightarrow C_4H_6 + H_2$

5 **a i** $CH_2{=}CH_2$
ii $-CH_2-CH_2-CH_2-CH_2-CH_2-CH_2-$
(C—H bonds not shown)
b High pressure shifts the position of equilibrium to the right, increasing yield/increases rate; low temperature shifts the position of equilibrium to the right, increasing yield, as the reaction is exothermic;
compromise so that the rate is not too low
c i $R-CH_2CH_2\cdot + CH_2{=}CH_2$
$\rightarrow R-CH_2-CH_2-CH_2-CH_2\cdot$
ii Any two radicals forming a bond, e.g.
$2R-CH_2-CH_2\cdot \rightarrow R-CH_2-CH_2-CH_2-CH_2-R$
d i The chains are unbranched
ii Higher melting point/stronger
e

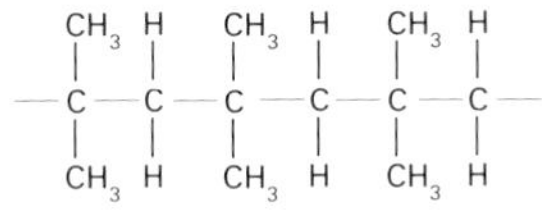

```
  CH3 H   CH3 H   CH3 H
   |  |    |  |    |  |
 --C--C----C--C----C--C--
   |  |    |  |    |  |
  CH3 H   CH3 H   CH3 H
```

f i 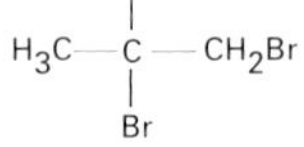 (Not all bonds are shown)

```
      CH3
       |
H3C----C----CH2Br
       |
       Br
```

ii

```
      CH3
       |
H3C----C----CH2OH
       |
       OH
```

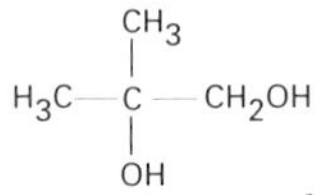

6 **a i** The reaction is exothermic
ii Sodium hydroxide/sodium carbonate/limewater
iii The same rate can be achieved at a lower temperature; lower temperatures increase the yield by shifting the position of equilibrium to the right
b i $CH_2ClCH_2Cl \rightarrow CH_2ClCH_2\cdot + Cl\cdot$
ii $CH_2ClCH_2Cl \rightarrow CH_2{=}CHCl + HCl$
iii Fractional distillation
iv Recycled
c i CH_2CHCl
ii Poly(chloroethene) = PVC, raincoats, pipes, etc.
iii HCl is a strongly acidic gas; hydrocarbon–oxygen mixtures are explosive

---

CHAPTER 23

Exam questions

1 **a** Test with ammonia gas; when no more white smoke is produced, the reaction is over
b i Can accept a pair of electrons
ii Electrophilic substitution (see spread 23.5)
c i 1,2-dimethylbenzene 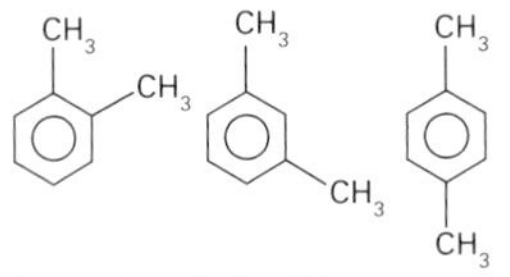
(structures of 1,2-, 1,3- and 1,4-dimethylbenzene: benzene rings with two CH_3 groups)
ii Fractional distillation
d i C_3H_4
ii C_9H_{12}; C_6H_5R with R = C_3H_7
e $C_6H_5COCH_3$

2 **a i** $C_6H_6 + CH_3COCl \rightarrow C_6H_5COCH_3 + HCl$ (SF needed)
ii Electrophilic substitution (see spread 23.5)
b i A large surface area to give a fast reaction
ii H_2O hydrolyses $AlCl_3$ and CH_3COCl
iii The reaction is exothermic/could get out of control
iv Harmful: HCl; carcinogenic: benzene fumes
v It removes acids
c i (2.2 g) × (120/78.5) = 3.4 g
ii 59%
iii Side reactions/incomplete reactions/losses during purification

3 **a i** It produces a higher concentration of NO_2^+ than in just conc. HNO_3

ii The reaction is exothermic and the temperature must be kept low

iii To prevent further nitration

iv For a good rate

v Because acids and benzene are immiscible

vi It dilutes/removes excess acid

vii It removes any acid dissolved in nitrobenzene

viii It separates nitrobenzene from other volatile components

b Sn/conc. HCl/heat under reflux

c i

—HN NHCO CO—

ii Condensation or polyamide

iii The acid chlorides are more reactive and so react faster and give a better yield

iv PCl_5 or SCl_2O at room temperature

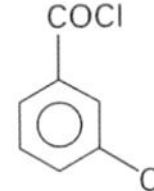

4 a i Cl_2/UV; $C_6H_5CHCl_2$ and $C_6H_5CCl_3$

ii Cl_2/$AlCl_3$/dry +

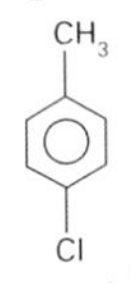

b See spread 22.4 for radical substitution

c Electrophilic substitution

d i CH_2OH / Cl

ii Cl in ring is attached and cannot be substituted owing to overlap of the Cl p orbital with the delocalized π cloud

---

CHAPTER 24

Exam questions

1 a Replacement of an atom or group by another in a reaction initiated by an electron-rich species donating a pair of electrons

b The electronegative Br atom makes the C atom electron deficient

c $CH_3CH_2CH_2Br + NH_3 \rightarrow CH_3CH_2CH_2NH_2 + HBr$ nucleophilic substitution (S_N2)

d CH_3CH_2Br/KCN dissolved in ethanol heat under reflux

2 a $CH_3CHBrCH(CH_3)_2$

b $CH_3CHBrCH(CH_3)_2 + NaOH$
$\rightarrow CH_3CH(OH)CH(CH_3)_2 + NaBr$
substitution
S_N1 or S_N2 (see spread 24.3)

c Elimination; base;
$CH_2{=}CHCH(CH_3)_2$ and $CH_3CH{=}C(CH_3)_2$

3 a Nucleophilic substitution, $(CH_3)_2CHCH(OH)CH_3$; the mechanism is based on nucleophilic substitution; S_N1 or S_N2 would be acceptable

b i Elimination; the KOH is acting as a base (proton acceptor)

ii See spread 24.4

4 a i

$CH_3CH_2CH_2CH_2Br$; $CH_3CH(CH_3)CH_2Br$

ii 2-bromomethylpropane

b i Nucleophilic substitution

ii $CH_3CH_2CH(NH_2)CH_3$

iii Isomer 2; it is a tertiary bromide

c i NaOH dissolved in ethanol/heat

ii $CH_3CH_2CH{=}CH_2$ and $CH_3CH{=}CHCH_3$

d i Electrophilic addition

ii See spread 22.8

5 a See spread 24.3 for nucleophilic substitution with the ammonia as the nucleophile (S_N2). Repeated nucleophilic substitution occurs, resulting in a succession of products: $CH_3CH_2CH_2NH_2$, $(CH_3CH_2CH_2)_2NH$, $(CH_3CH_2CH_2)_3N$, and $(CH_3CH_2CH_2)_4N^+$

b i IR would only differ in the fingerprint region

ii $CH_3CH_2CH_2Br$ would show 3 peaks; $(CH_3)_2CHBr$ would show 2 peaks

6 a i Electrophilic addition (see spread 22.8)

ii CH_2BrCH_2OH or CH_2BrCH_2Cl

iii The first step involves an electrophile; Cl^- is a nucleophile and can react only after electrophilic addition has occurred

b i Heat under reflux with NaOH(aq)

ii Faster because the C—I bond is weaker

7 a i Decolourized

ii Mole ratio of A:Br_2 = 1:3; this is consistent with 3 C=C bonds

b i NaOH dissolved in ethanol/heat under reflux

ii H atom on any adjacent carbon could be eliminated, producing different products

iii Optical – there are two chiral C atoms in B

8 a i Substitution; nucleophile

ii $(CH_3)_2CHCH(OH)CH_2CH_3$
(see spread 24.3 for mechanism)

b i $(CH_3)_2CHCOCH_2CH_3$

ii 57: $CH_3CH_2CO^+$
71: $(CH_3)_2CHCO^+$

c i Elimination; base

ii $(CH_3)_2C{=}CHCH_2CH_3$
see spread 24.3 for mechanism

iii $(CH_3)_2CHCH{=}CHCH_3$
geometric

9 a i $CH_3CH_2CHBrCH_2CH_3$

ii Elimination (see spread 24.4)

iii Geometric

b i $CH_3CH_2{}^+CHCH_2CH_3$; $CH_3{}^+CHCH_2CH_2CH_3$

ii 3-bromopentane; 2-bromopentane

iii They are both formed from similarly stable secondary carbocations

---

CHAPTER 25

Exam questions

1 a i $CH_3CH_2CH_2CH_2OH + [O] \rightarrow CH_3CH_2CH_2CHO$
orange → green

ii Butan-1-ol produces butanal; if Fehling's solution, blue solution → brick-red precipitate
butan-2-ol produces butanone – no change with Fehling's solution

b $CH_3CH_2CH_2COOH$

c Isomer 1 = methylpropan-1-ol $CH_3CH(CH_3)CH_2OH$

Isomer 2 = methylpropan-2-ol $CH_3C(CH_3)(OH)CH_3$

2 a C—C

b i 700–1500

ii Complex pattern is unique to that compound

c i Too broad/not specific for ethanol

ii 1700

iii Several possibilities: PCl_5, $KMnO_4/H_2SO_4$(aq), $K_2Cr_2O_7/H_2SO_4$(aq); DNP, (see text for details)

3 a Higher temperatures would increase loss of $CH_2 = CH_2$ as CO_2 and H_2O or reaction is exothermic; therefore lower temperatures favour better yields

b i See **1**

$CH_3CH_2OH + CH_2$—CH_2 (epoxide, O) → $CH_3CH_2OCH_2CH_2OH$

ii $CH_3CH_2(OCH_2CH_2)_nOH$

c

H_2C—CH_2 (epoxide, O) $+ NH_3 \rightarrow H_2NCH_2CH_2OH$

4 a Reaction I: KBr + conc. H_2SO_4 + heat *or* PBr_3 (P + Br_2) room temperature; reaction II: named oxidant e.g. $Cr_2O_7^{2-}$(aq) + H_2SO_4(aq) + heat; reaction III: conc. H_2SO_4, 180 °C *or* pass vapour over hot Al_2O_3

b Reaction I: $(CH_3)_3CBr$; reaction II: no reaction; reaction III: $(CH_3)_2C{=}CH_2$

5 a $(CH_3)_2CHCH_2OH$

b i Elimination

ii $CH_3CH_2CH{=}CH_2$; $CH_3CH{=}CHCH_3$ but-1-ene; (*cis*- and *trans*-) but-2-ene

c i Butanal

ii Butanoic acid

iii $CH_3CH_2COCH_3$

iv Oxidation

d i $CH_3COOCH(CH_3)_3$

ii Ethanoic acid

iii Conc. H_2SO_4

e i The rate of formation of a white precipitate increases in the order:
butan-1-ol → butan-2-ol → 2-methylpropan-2-ol

ii 2-chlorobutane/$CH_3CHClCH_2CH_3$

6 a i 4 peaks: 3:2:2:3

ii CH_3CH_2—O—CH_2CH_3

b i Nucleophilic substitution (S_N2); see spread 25.5

ii CH_3O^-

c Tertiary
$(CH_3)_3COH$

d $C_4H_{10}O + 6O_2 \rightarrow 4CO_2 + 5H_2O$

e Broadened peak between 3230 and 3550 only in alcohols

CHAPTER 26

Practice questions

Spread 26.3

2 P: propanal, CH_3CH_2CHO; Q: propanone, CH_3COCH_3

3 a A: $CH_3CH_2CHBrCH_3$; B: $CH_3CH_2CH(OH)CH_3$
C: $CH_3CH_2COCH_3$

b $CH_3CH_2CH_2CHO$

4 a ketone; **b** alcohol; **c** aldehyde

Spread 26.4

1 N: $CH_3CH_2CHC(CH_3)_2$; M: CH_3CH_2CHO; P: CH_3COCH_3

3 A: 2-iodobutane, $CH_3CH_2CHICH_3$;
B: butan-2-ol, $CH_3CH_2CH(OH)CH_3$;
C: butanone, $CH_3CH_2COCH_3$;
D: but-1-ene, $CH_3CH_2CHCH_2$;(assuming no but-2-ene forms);
E: methanal, HCHO;
F: propanal, CH_3CH_2CHO

Exam questions

1 a i $CH_3COCH_3 + HCN \rightarrow CH_3COH(CN)CH_3$
aqueous/pH 5
2-hydroxy(-2-)methylpropanenitrile

ii $CH_3COCH_3 + 2[H] \rightarrow CH_3CH(OH)CH_3$
aqueous
propan-2-ol

b i See spread 26.1

ii Nucleophilic addition

iii Electron-deficient C atom
C is bonded to an electronegative O atom

iv Ethene is susceptible to electrophilic not nucleophilic attack due to 'electron-rich' ⊃C=C⊂

2 a Any named *oxidant* + conditions + observations, e.g. Fehling's or Tollens'; only ethanol reacts

b i S = $CH_3CH(OH)CN$
T = CH_3(H)C=NNH–$C_6H_3(NO_2)_2$ (2,4-dinitrophenyl)
U = CH_3CH_2OH

ii Ethanol-2,4-dinitrophenylhydrazone yellow–orange precipitate

c Nucleophilic addition; (see spread 26.1)

3 a i $CH_3CH_2CH_2CH_2OH$

ii $CH_3CH_2CH{=}CH_2$ **iii**

iv $CH_3CH_2CH_2CN$

v No reaction

vi No reaction

vii CH_3CH_2COOH

viii CH_3COCH_3

b i Nucleophilic substitution

ii Elimination

iii Nucleophilic addition

iv Nucleophilic substitution

c i Nucleophilic addition (see spread 26.1)

ii See **4 b ii**

4 a i $CH_3CHBrCHO$; **ii** $CH_2CHCH(OH)CN$

iii CH_2CH(H)C=NNH–$C_6H_3(NO_2)_2$ (2,4-dinitrophenyl)

b i Nucleophilic addition (see spread 26.1)

ii High pH $[H^+]$ is low, therefore 2nd step becomes very slow; low pH CN^- is protonated, therefore $[CN^-]$ is low and 1st step becomes very slow

c $LiAlH_4$ (contains H^-) is a nucleophilic reagent; only >C=O is susceptible to nucleophilic attack as carbon–carbon bond has no polarity

d I_2/NaOH = iodoform reagent, therefore convert it to $CH_3CH(OH)CHO$ by, e.g., using H_2O/H^+(aq)

5 a X = $CH_3CH_2CH_2OH$
Y = $CH_3CH_2CH(OH)CN$
Z = CH_3CH_2COOH

b See spread 26.1

c i Y, X, Z, W; **ii** 2900–3000

6 a i Propanoic acid CH_3CH_2COOH
propan-l-ol $CH_3CH_2CH_2OH$
HCN $CH_3CH_2CH(OH)CN$

ii Blue solution → brick-red precipitate
propanal reduces Cu^{2+} to Cu_2O

iii Any named oxidant e.g. Tollens'

b i Nucleophilic substitution (S_N2); OH^-

ii Electrophilic addition; H^+

7 a i HCN

ii Nucleophilic addition (see spread 26.1)

b i Methanol

ii Esterification; conc. H_2SO_4

c [–C(H)(H)–C(CH_3)($COOCH_3$)–]$_n$

d $CH_2{=}C(CH_3)COOH + NaOH \rightarrow$
$CH_2{=}C(CH_3)CO_2^-Na^+ + H_2O$

CHAPTER 27

Exam questions

1 a i Ethyl ethanoate $CH_3COOCH_2CH_3$ (linear abbreviation)

ii Esterification

b i H_2SO_4(aq) / heat

ii $CH_3COOCH_2CH_3 + H_2O \rightleftharpoons CH_3COOH + CH_3CH_2OH$

c i NaOH(aq)/room temperature

ii Ethanoic anhydride $(CH_3CO)_2O$ (linear abbreviation)

iii Add water and warm
$(CH_3CO)_2O + H_2O \rightarrow 2CH_3COOH$

d i Ethanamide CH_3CONH_2 (linear abbreviation)

ii Add NH_3(aq), heat to evaporate water and heat solid (dehydrates)

iii $CH_3CONH_2 + H_2O + HCl \rightarrow CH_3COOH + NH_4^+ + Cl^-$

2 a i $CH_3CONH_2 + NaOH \rightarrow CH_3CO_2^-Na^+ + NH_3$
ii $CH_3CH_2CN + 2H_2O + HCl \rightarrow CH_3CH_2COOH + NH_4^+ + Cl^-$
iii $CH_3COCl + H_2O \rightarrow CH_3COOH + HCl$
iv $(CH_3CO)_2O + H_2O \rightarrow 2CH_3COOH$
b iii Vigorous at room temperature, whereas **iv** slow at room temperature
c i (CH_3COOH or) $CH_3COCl + CH_3OH$
ii $CH_3COCl + CH_3CH_2NH_2$

3 a i $K_a = [RCO_2^-][H_3O^+]/[RCOOH]$
ii pH = 1.9
b i A buffer solution resists a change in pH on the addition of small amounts of acid or alkali
ii The citric acid reacts with alkali; $RCOOH(aq) + OH^-(aq) \rightarrow RCOO^-(aq) + H_2O(l)$; the citrate ion reacts with acid; $RCOO^-(aq) + H^+(aq) \rightarrow RCOOH(aq)$
iii pH = 3.4
c i Add PCl_5 and there will be vigorous production of smoky fumes (of HCl)
ii Aqueous sodium hydroxide
iii Sodium hydrogencarbonate would effervesce

4 a $HOOCC_6H_4COOH$ and $HOCH_2CH_2OH$ (linear abb.)
b Condensation
c NaOH hydrolyses ester

5 a C_2H_6O
b i See spread 7.5; **ii** CH_3CH_2OH
c 45: $CH_3CH_2O^+$; 31: CH_2OH^+; 29: $CH_3CH_2^+$
d i Ethyl ethanoate; $CH_3COOCH_2CH_3$; ester
ii Add slowly to dry ethanol at room temperature

6 a i A: N—H; B: C—H (alkyl); C: C=O
ii $H_2N(CH_2)_6NH_2$ and $ClOC(CH_2)_4COCl$ (linear abbreviation)
b i NH_3 is produced, which is basic
ii $(NH_2)_2CO + H_2O \rightarrow 2NH_3 + CO_2$
iii Enzymes are specific and cannot hydrolyse ethanamide at an appreciable rate
iv H bonds are disrupted by ethanamide

7 a $H_2N(CH_2)_6NH_2$
$ClOC(CH_2)_4COCl$
b Hydrogen chloride
c Hydrolyses $—OC(CH_2)_4CONH(CH_2)_6NH— + 2H_2O \rightarrow H_2N(CH_2)_6NH_2 + HOOC(CH_2)_4COOH$

Chapter 28

Exam questions

1 a Can act as a proton acceptor owing to lone pair on N atom
b Lone pair is delocalized by overlap with benzene π system
c i Nucleophilic substitution (see spreads 24.3 and 28.2)
ii $(CH_3CH_2)_2NH$; $(CH_3CH_2)_3N$; $(CH_3CH_2)_4N^+$
d $CH_3CN + 4[H] \rightarrow CH_3CH_2NH_2$
only the primary amine is formed

2 a i $C_6H_5CH_2Br + NH_3 \rightarrow C_6H_5CH_2NH_2 + HBr$
nucleophilic substitution
(possibly $NH_3 + HBr \rightarrow NH_4Br$)
secondary, tertiary amines and quaternary salt are also produced
ii Reduction
$C_6H_5CN + 4[H] \rightarrow C_6H_5CH_2NH_2$
$LiAlH_4$ (or H_2/Ni)
other amines cannot be formed
b Phenylamine
lone pair on N atom is delocalized with the benzene π system

3 a i $C_6H_5CHClCH(CH_3)NH_2$
ii $C_6H_5CH(OH)CH(CH_3)NH_3^+Cl^-$
iii $C_6H_5(OCOCH_3)CH(CH_3)NHCOCH_3$
iv C_6H_5COOH
v $C_6H_5CH{=}C(CH_3)NH_2$

b i Perform in fume cupboard/wear gloves
ii See spread 31.1
iii Determine melting point

4 a Joining many small molecules (monomers) to form a long chain polymer
b i $H_2NCH(CH_3)CONHCH(CH_3)COOH$ (linear abbreviation)
ii Peptide (amide)
iii (Polypeptides) proteins
c i $n\ CH_2{=}CH_2 \rightarrow [CH_2—CH_2]_n$
ii Low density has more branched chains which cannot pack so closely
iii Melting point
iv $R - CH_2CH_2\cdot$
v Ziegler–Natta
d i Not broken down in the environment (by organisms) / does not rot
ii Will not 'clutter' the environment
iii More prone to hydrolysis

5 a B = $CH_3CH_2CONH_2$
C = $CH_3CH_2C{\equiv}N$
functional group = $–NH_2$
b i Reduce with e.g. $LiAlH_4$
ii NaOH(aq), $Br_2(l)$
c i $CH_3CH_2CN + 2H_2O + HCl \rightarrow CH_3CH_2COOH + NH_4^+ + Cl^-$
ii Hydrolysis
d i Lone pair on N atom
ii $CH_3CH_2CH_2NH_2 + HCl \rightarrow CH_3CH_2CH_2NH_3^+ + Cl^-$
e i $C_6H_5NH_3^+ + HNO_2 \rightarrow C_6H_5N_2^+ + 2H_2O$
ii See spread 28.4
iii Used as dyes

6 a $CH_3CH_2CH_2CH_2Br$, $CH_3CH_2CHBrCH_3$, $(CH_3)_3CBr$, $(CH_3)_2CHCH_2Br$
b i A nucleophile is an electron pair donor
ii Hydroxide ion
iii Rate = $k[C_4H_9Br]$
iv The mechanism is S_N1, so the halogenoalkane loses the Br^- in the first step, the rate-determining step, and then the hydroxide ion reacts with the carbocation produced in the second, fast step; tertiary halogenoalkanes tend to undergo S_N1, so $(CH_3)_3CBr$ should appear in the mechanism
c i $CH_3CH_2C^*HBrCH_3$ is chiral, as indicated by the '*'; this C has four different groups attached and so is optically active
ii The intermediate forms a carbocation that is trigonal planar; the hydroxide ion may attack from either side of the carbocation and so produces two optically active isomers in equal amounts; the isomers twist the plane of polarized light equally in opposite directions, so the mixture is not optically active

7 a Conc. H_2SO_4 + conc. HNO_3
$2H_2SO_4 + HNO_3 \rightarrow NO_2^+ + H_3O^+ + 2HSO_4^-$
electrophilic substitution (see spread 23.3)
b Reduction; Sn/conc. HCl
c $C_6H_5NH_2 + CH_3COCl \rightarrow C_6H_5NHCOCH_3 + HCl$
condensation (nucleophilic addition then elimination); see spread 28.2

8 a i Arrangement of C atoms in backbone differs
$CH_3CH_2CH_2CH_3$ and $(CH_3)_3CH$ (linear abbreviation)
ii When a pair of groups is on the same or opposite sides of a double bond

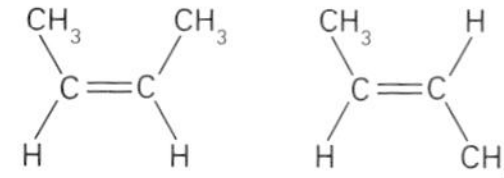

iii When a pair of molecules are non-superimposable mirror images

COOH COOH
C H H C
CH3 OH HO CH3

b **i** N—C*—C—N—C*—C
ii See spread 28.5
iii Use a polarimeter; (see spread 28.6)

Chapter 29

Exam questions

1 **a** **i** Metallic, delocalized electron sea conducts
ii Covalent, no delocalized electrons
iii Ionic, therefore cannot conduct as a solid
iv MgO has a much higher melting point than PVC (giant ionic lattice structure versus molecular)
b $CH_3CH_2Br + Mg \rightarrow CH_3CH_2MgBr$ (dry ether solvent, I_2 catalyst, heat under reflux)
c **i** $CH_3CH_2C(CH_3)_2OH$ 2-methylbutan-2-ol
ii $CH_3CH_2CH(OH)CH_2CH_2CH_3$ hexan-3-ol
d **i** test with any common oxidant e.g. $KMnO_4$ (see spread 25.4 for details)
ii For **c i** the product is not chiral for **c ii**, although products are chiral, a racemic mixture is produced (carbonyls are planar and can be attacked by the Grignard from either side)

2 **a** **i** Mirror image is not superimposable
iii By using a polarimeter to detect/measure optical activity
b **i** $CH_3CH_2CH_2CH_2OH + 2[O] \rightarrow CH_3CH_2CH_2COOH + H_2O$; heat under reflux with $KMnO_4(aq)/H_2SO_4(aq)$ or similar
ii $CH_3CH_2CH_2COOH + PCl_5 \rightarrow CH_3CH_2CH_2COCl + HCl + POCl_3$; room temperature
iii

$H_2C—CH_2$ (epoxide ring with O) $+ NH_3 \rightarrow H_2NCH_2CH_2OH$

room temperature
c **i** React $CH_3CH_2CH_2MgBr$ with HCHO then HCl(aq)
ii See **1 b**
d Enzymes (the target) are stereospecific.
e See spread 31.1 for details of recrystallization assess purity by determining melting point
f Add NaOH(aq)

3 **a** See spread 29.5
b **i** The liquid mixture of monomers thickens as the monomer molecules react in the presence of an initiator to produce long-chain molecules; the reaction is exothermic, so the mixture becomes hotter
ii The monomer, poly(phenylethene), is immiscible with water, so when the two liquids are mixed, a suspension is formed; the heat generated is absorbed by the water, so the temperature does not get too high

4 **a** If the molecule chains are too short, the softening point of the product would be too low, and the product would be too soft and weak; if the chains are too long, then the softening point may be too high, making it difficult to melt the polymer and mould it; it also may become too brittle
b **i** A ring structure of 11 carbon atoms and one nitrogen atom, including an amide link
ii Nylon 11 would have many more amide links than nylon 66, so there would be more hydrogen bonding between the nylon 11 chains than the nylon 66 chains, so the crystalline melting point of nylon 11 would be much higher than that for nylon 66
c The nylon amide links are hydrolysed by acid

5 **a** Covalent bonds; dispersion forces between chains; polyamides (nylon) hydrogen bond
b **i** The covalent bonds make the polymers insulators and quite resistant to chemical change; the hydrogen bonds make the polymers have high melting points
ii The intermolecular forces between the polymer molecules influence the processing of thermoplastics because if the intermolecular forces are weak, then the plastic would soften easily when heated; if the polymer molecules hydrogen bond, then the melting point may be so high that the polymer would not soften easily

6 **a** **i** See spread 22.10
ii Chain length varies/behaves as a mixture
b **i** See spread 27.7
ii Condensation: small molecule like H_2O or HCl is formed as a byproduct (= addition followed by elimination) Addition: no byproduct
iii Acid chloride is more reactive
iv H bonds between —CONH— links on neighbouring chains
c **i** Copy the diagram but with each bond having the *trans* geometry (groups across the bond) rather than *cis*
ii The conjugated double bonds allow delocalization and hence conduction

7 **a** **i** Covalent bonding, in which atoms share electrons
ii Polyamide chains are held together by hydrogen bonding; polyesters and polyhalogenoalkenes (i.e. PVC) are held by dipole–dipole attraction
iii Melting and mechanical strain, which pulls the polymer chains apart
b **i** Thermosetting plastics are polymers that solidify as they are formed and will not melt when heated; thermoplastics are polymers that will soften after being made
ii Advantage: thermoplastics may be extruded and moulded; disadvantage: they have low softening points and so cannot be used at high temperatures and are often weak
iii Whether the thermosetting plastic can be made in the mould

Chapter 30

Exam questions

1 **a** **i** Alanine is chiral
ii $CH_3CH(NH_2)CONHCH_2COOH$ or other way around
b Edman degradation (1) modify N terminus; (2) mild acid hydrolysis releases modified N terminus; (3) released amino acid identified by chromatography; (4) repeat process
c Less toxic, not flammable
d **i** Volatile, low toxicity, inertness
ii Broken by UV in stratosphere to chlorine radicals which lead to destruction of ozone etc.

2 **a** A is glucose (see spread 30.2 for graphical formula)
b **i** $B + H_2O \rightarrow 2A$; this is hydrolysis
ii Either an enzyme (a yeast, at 35 °C) or aqueous hydrochloric acid could be used and heated under reflux
c C is starch, used as a food store; D is cellulose; see spread 30.4 for the consequences of the α and β glycosidic links

3 **a** and **b** See spreads 30.8–10
c **i** – A – C – C – T – G – A – T – T – G –
ii – U – G – G – A – C – U – A – A – C –
d 3.3%

4 **a** Active transport of substances across the cell membrane; the bilayers repel most substances
b **i**
ii The side chains of the peptides could be made non-polar or polar, depending on the membrane
c **i** Increase the number of C atoms between amino and carboxyl groups
ii Change the side chains, i.e. vary the proportion with hydrophilic and hydrophobic groups

5 **a** See spreads 30.8–10
b The enzyme fits certain combinations of base pairs; when it contacts the correct sequence it holds on to the chain and breaks it
c Phosphate groups are negatively charged

6 **a** See spreads 30.6 and 30.7

b Ethanol competes for active sites of oxidative enzymes which oxidize glycol, giving the body time to eliminate the glycol before it is oxidized

7 **a** Potatoes contain starch for which humans have the digestive enzyme; cabbage has cellulose for which humans do not have the enzyme
b The first jam had a sugar with an aldehyde group which it is likely to be glucose; the second jam contained a disaccharide which contained no aldehyde group, but when boiled in acid, the disaccharide split to make glucose
c Vitamins break down naturally in fresh vegetables; the low temperature of the frozen vegetables slows the breakdown of the vitamins

8 **a** See spread 30.5
b i Haemoglobin: transfer of O_2 from lungs to tissues; myoglobin: storage of O_2 in tissues
ii Residual respiration in tissues uses O_2 bound to myoglobin; myoglobin near surface is recharged with O_2 from air
iii To keep it red/attractive

9 **a** and **b** See spread 30.1
c Active transport is the movement of a solute across a biological membrane from a region of low to high solute concentration, requiring the input of energy and the involvement of enzymes and specific transport proteins; sodium pump involves Na^+ ion

10 The primary protein structure is the sequence of covalently bonded amino acids; the secondary structure is the chain of amino acids forming a helix held by hydrogen bonds; the tertiary structure is the helix bent to form globular or planar structures held by hydrogen bonds or —S—S— bridges; the quaternary structure is the folds in the tertiary structure, held by hydrogen bonds

11 **a i** The graphical formula should show all bonds; $HOCO—C_6H_4—COOH$ and $HOCH_2CH_2OH$
ii polyester
iii $[—CO—C_6H_4—CO—OCH_2CH_2O—]_n$
b i Biodegradable means it will break down naturally in a short time
ii The plastics would break down so would not fill landfill sites, or they could even be used as a source of energy
c i Potatoes, wheat, rice, maize
ii Glucose
d i Mineral acid in a food stuff would harm the person.
ii Around pH 7

Chapter 31

Exam questions

1 **a i** M_r; **ii** due to ^{13}C; **iii** $M^{+\cdot} \rightarrow P\cdot + Q^+$
only one carries a positive charge and is accelerated towards detector: the other is a radical
b i There are two isotopes ^{35}Cl and ^{37}Cl whose abundance ratio is 3:1
ii $CH_3Cl^{+\cdot} \rightarrow CH_3^+ + Cl\cdot$

2 **a i** 87.7; **ii** Different relative abundances of isotopes
b i HCN; **ii** NO; **iii** HCHO
c i M+1 peak is approx 7% of M peak
ii $B = C_6H_5^+$ $C = C_6H_5CO^+$
d C_6H_5COOH; $-COOH$

3 **a i** C═C; **ii** *Cis-* and *trans-*
iii Restricted rotation around C═C; **iv** $CH_3CH_2CH═CH_2$
b i $CH_3CH_2COCH_3$; **ii** $—COCH_3$ or $—CH(OH)CH_3$
iii D: $CH_3CH_2CO_2^-Na^+$ E: CH_3CH_2COOH
c i $CH_3CH_2CH(OH)CH_3$; **ii** 29: $CH_3CH_2^+$ 45: $CH_3CH(OH)^+$
most parent molecules fragment
d i See spread 22.2, which assumes Raoult's law
ii Positive deviation means that there is more vapour than expected from Raoult's law, because the forces between the two molecules are poorly matched; they have stronger forces with their own kind (such as hydrogen bonding for the alcohol)

iii Broadening caused by hydrogen bonding, which gets less prevalent on dilution

4 **a i** 60; **ii** 30: CH_2NH_2; 16: NH_2; 14: CH_2
iii Amine
b See spread 22.6
c i See spread 22.6
ii This is very similar to $[Co(NH_3)_4Cl_2]^+$, as in spread 20.9

5 **a i** Relative molecular mass; the weighted mean of the mass numbers of a sample of an element, using 1/12 of a carbon-12 atom as one unit; isotopes have the same atomic number (proton number) but different mass number (number of neutrons)
ii 12.0
b i 120
ii The small peaks are due to the molecular ions containing one ^{13}C atom
c i A molecule with mass 120 (which must contain 1 oxygen atom) must contain at least 8 carbon atoms; with one less C-atom it would be difficult to think of a possible molecule; with one more carbon atom there would not be spare mass for enough hydrogen atoms
ii B: 77; $C_6H_5^+$; C: 105; $C_6H_5CO^+$
iii The CH_3^+ ions would be removed/would not be detected as the analysis concentrated on the larger fragments
d Add 2,4-dinitrophenylhydrazine, and a brightly coloured solid would be made if the compound contained a C═O group

Chapter 32

Exam questions

1 **a** See spread 32.1
b See spread 32.1
c Cadmium and lead from pottery glazes

2 **a i** C—H
ii $CH_3CH_2CH_2COOH$
$(CH_3)_2CHCOOH$
no broadened O—H peak evident
b III
c $CH_3COOCH_2CH_3$ and $CH_3CH_2COOCH_3$

3 **a** H_2O: 3
CO_2: 2
CO: 1
b See spreads 32.3 and 32.4
c Any isomers of C_3H_7COOH
absorbances corresponding to carboxylic
C═O ; C—O— ; —O—H

4 **a i** See spread 32.5
ii See spread 32.7
b F: CH_3COOCH_3
G: CH_3CH_2COOH

5 **a** $Si(CH_3)_4$
b 4
c 2:1:6:3
d $CH_3CH_2–$
splitting of δ 1.52 due to neighbouring $—CH_3$; splitting of δ 0.93 due to neighbouring $—CH_2$
e Single peak, therefore no spin–spin coupling, no H atom on adjacent group; 6 of these H atoms
f $CH_3CH_2C(CH_3)_2—OH$

6 **a i** Paste made from solid sample
ii Interactions (e.g. H bonding) between ethanol and test substance complicate interpretation
b Q: C≡C or C≡N
R: C═O
S: C—O, C—N
c i T has a mass of 43, which suggests $C_3H_7^+$
ii U has a mass of 28, which suggests $C_2H_4^+$
iii The M+2 peak of similar height to the M peak suggests that bromine is present: this confirms that T is mass 43, because 43 + 79 = 122; K may be $(CH_3)_2CHBr$

Index

D

Acknowledgements

Photographs and computer-generated images

(FPNY = Fundamental Photographs New York; GSF = GeoScience Features; LGPL = Leslie Garland Picture Library; SPL = Science Photo Library; (t) = top; (b) = bottom; (l) = left; (r) = right; (c) = centre.)

10–11 IBM Corporation, Research Division, Almaden Research Centre; 12 Crown Copyright/Health and Safety Laboratory/SPL; 13(l) Derby Museum and Art Gallery, Derbyshire UK/Bridgeman Art Library; 13(r) The Metropolitan Museum of Art, Purchase, Mr and Mrs Charles Wrightsman Gift, in honour of Everett Fahy, 1977 (1977.10), photo: © 1989 Metropolitan Museum of Art (detail); 14(bl) Andrew Lambert/LGPL; 14(tl, tc, tr, br) GSF; 18(l) Statens Historiska Museum Stockholm/Werner Forman Archive; 18(r) Andrew Lambert/LGPL; 19 Lawrence Migdale/SPL; 20 Science Museum/Science and Society Picture Library; 21(bl, br) IBM Corporation, Research Division, Almaden Research Center; 21(t) scan courtesy of Purdue University, image courtesy of Digital Instruments, Veeco Metrolology Group, Santa Barbara, CA, USA; 22 Jean-Loup Charmet/SPL; 23 Cavendish Laboratory, University of Cambridge; 25 The Oxford Story exhibition; 26 Cavendish Laboratory, University of Cambridge; 28 Thermit Welding (GB) Ltd; 30 Peter Gould; 31 Tek Image/SPL; 32 GSF; 34 GSF; 35 Charles D. Winters/Timeframe Photography Inc.; 39 Dept of Physics, Imperial College/SPL; 43 Jerry Mason/SPL; 44(bl) Mr Fred Wondre, Dept of Physics, University of Oxford; 44(br) Dr Tongguang Zhai, Department of Materials Science, University of Oxford; 44(t) Peter Gould; 51 GSF; 58 GSF; 59 Charles D. Winters/SPL; 60 Bancroft Library, University of California Archives no. 13.596; 62 Bochsler Photographics+Imaging, Burlington, Canada; 64 Martin Sookias; 68 IBM Corporation, Research Division, Almaden Research Center; 71 © Richard Megna/FPNY; 76(l) © Andy Washnik ñ CORPRICOM; 76(r) © Richard Megna/FPNY; 77 Dr Jeremy Burgess/SPL; 79 Andrew Lambert/LGPL; 83(l) Nubar Alexanian/Corbis; 83(tr) Rover, Oxford; 83(br) Andrew Syred/Microscopix; 84(t) J C Revy/SPL; 84(r) Michael W Davidson/SPL; 84(b) GSF; 85(b) Charles D. Winters/Timeframe Photography; 85(t) Andrew Lambert/LGPL; 86 Fred Ward, Black Star /Colorific!; 87(t) Tony Craddock/SPL; 87(b) Robert Harding Picture Library; 90 Charles D. Winters/Timeframe Photography; 94 ChemSoft, with thanks to James Whyte; 98(tc) Yoav Levy/Phototake Inc/Robert Harding Picture Library; 98(tr) © Richard Megna/FPNY; 98(r) Charles D. Winters/SPL; 98(b) Adam Hart-Davis/SPL; 99 Dan Guravitch/SPL; 100(t) from Mark Ladd: Introduction to Physical Chemistry 3rd edn, Cambridge University Press 1998; 100(b) Geoff Tompkinson/SPL; 101 Mike Clugston; 106 Mehan Kulyk/SPL; 108 Runk/Schoenberger from Grant Heilman; 109(t) Tim Clayton/Sidney Morning Herald; 109(b) D. Wells/The Image Works; 114 Andrew Lambert/LGPL; 115(t) Charles D. Winters/Timeframe Photography; 117 L. S. Stepanowicz/The Picture Cube; 118 Martin Sookias; 119 Ken McVeigh/Tony Stone Worldwide; 120(l) Bochsler Photographics+Imaging, Burlington, Canada; 120(r) Andrew Lambert/LGPL; 126 Andrew Lambert/LGPL; 128(t) MIRA; 129 David Nunuk/SPL; 128(b) Chris Fairclough/Image Select; 130 Lester V. Bergman/Corbis; 131 Alfred Pasieka/SPL; 133 Auto Express/Quadrant Picture Librart; 135(t) Martin Sookias; 135(b) © Richard Megna/FPNY; 137(tl, b) Andrew Lambert/LGPL; 137(tr) Ken Karp; 138 British Steel plc; 142 NASA/SPL; 143 Chris Barry/Action-Plus Photography; 145(l) Charles D. Winters/Timeframe Photography; 145(r) Lawrence Migdale/SPL; 151 Robert Smith/Rex Features; 153(t) NASA Goddard Institute for Space Studies/SPL; 153(b) Crown Copyright/Health and Safety Laboratory/SPL; 154 Neil Tingle/Action-Plus Photography; 158 © Richard Megna/FPNY; 164 GSF; 165 Simon Fraser/SPL; 167(t) Hulton Getty; 167(b) BASF; 168 James Scherer/Houghton Mifflin Company; 169 © Richard Megna/FPNY; 170(t) Bochsler Photographics+Imaging, Burlington, Canada; 170(b) Andrew Lambert/LGPL; 174 Andrew Lambert/LGPL; 178 St Bartholomewís Hospital/SPL; 180 Bryan Pickering/Corbis; 181 David Taylor/SPL; 182 © Richard Megna/FPNY; 183(l) Dr E. R. Degginger; 183(r) Andrew Lambert/LGPL; 186 Leslie Garland/LGPL; 187 Alfred Pasieka/SPL; 190(t) Adam Hart-Davis/SPL; 190(bl) Corel Professional Photos; 190(bc) Oxford University Press; 190(bc) Martin Sookias; 191 Andrew Lambert/LGPL; 192 Andrew Lambert/LGPL; 193 Andrew Lambert/LGPL; 195(b) Dr E. R. Degginger; 195(t) Andrew Lambert/LGPL; 196 Andrew Lambert/LGPL; 200 Metrohm; 205 Jason Burke/Eye Ubiquitous; 206 Mike Clugston; 207 Andrew Lambert/LGPL; 208 Ken Karp; 209 Andrew Lambert/LGPL; 212 Bochsler Photographics+Imaging, Burlington, Canada; 213(b) Andrew Lambert/LGPL; 213(t) Robert Harding Picture Library; 214 Andrew Lambert/LGPL; 215 Andrew Lambert/LGPL; 216 Andrew Lambert/LGPL; 217 GSF; 218(t) Andrew Lambert/LGPL; 218(b) Paul Silverman/FPNY; 220(tl) Charles D. Winters/Timeframe Photography; 220(tr) Charles D. Winters/SPL; 220(b) Ken Karp; 221 Jerry Mason/SPL; 222 Andrew Lambert/LGPL; 224 © Andy Washnik – CORPRICOM; 225 Andrew Lambert/LGPL; 226 Andrew Lambert/LGPL; 227 Andrew Lambert/LGPL; 228(t) Peter Gould; 228(b) Andrew Lambert/LGPL; 229 Dr Dennis Kunkel/Phototake NYC/Robert Harding Picture Library; 231 NASA/Glenn Research Center; 232 Andrew Lambert/LGPL; 234(t) Kevin Wisniewski/Rex Features; 234(b) Andrew Lambert/LGPL; 235 Dr Jeremy Burgess/SPL; 236(t) Kunsthistorisches Museum Vienna/photo: Erich Lessing/AKG London; 236(b)

GSF; 237 Philip Craven/Robert Harding Picture Library; 240 Manley Prim Photography; 241 Andrew Lambert/LGPL; 244 Dean Conger/Corbis; 246 SPL; 250 Bochsler Photographics+Imaging, Burlington, Canada; 251 Paolo Koch/Robert Harding Picture Library; 254 Andrew Lambert/LGP; 255(tl, tr) Charles D. Winters/Timeframe Photography; 255(b) © Richard Megna/FPNY; 257 Physics Dept, Imperial College/SPL; 262 © Richard Megna/FPNY; 267(t) Geoff Tompkinson/SPL; 267(b) US Dept of Energy/SPL; 268 © Richard Megna/FPNY; 269 Dr Ivan Polunin/NHPA; 271(t) Thomas Eisner, Daniel Aneshansley, Cornell University; 271(bc) Johnson Matthey; 272 Oxford University Press; 275 Clive Freeman/The Royal Institution/SPL; 278–279 SPL; 281 (lithium, sodium, potassium, calcium, magnesium , strontium) GSF; 281 (beryllium, rubidium) Russ Lappa/SPL; 281 (cesium, barium) Lester V. Bergman/Corbis; 283 GSF; 284(t) (all except cesium) Andrew Lambert/LGPL; 284(t) (cesium) still from BBC Open University video The elements organised in the periodic table; 284(b) Bochsler Photographics+Imaging, Burlington, Canada; 285 © Andy Washnik – CORPRICOM; 286 GSF; 288(t) Phototake/Robert Harding Picture Library; 288(b) © Richard Megna/FPNY; 290 James Davis Worldwide Photographic Travel Library; 292 The Egyptian Museum, Cairo/Werner Forman Archive; 293 CNRI/SPL; 296(a) David Taylor/SPL; 296(b) Jerry Mason/SPL; 296(c) E. R. Degginger/SPL; 296(d) Lester V. Bergman/Corbis; 297 A. R. Lampshire/Robert Harding Picture Library; 301 (all except chlorine) GSF; 301 (chlorine) Charles D. Winters/SPL; 303(l) T. Waltham/Robert Harding Picture Library; 303(r) © Richard Megna/FPNY; 306 Andrew Lambert/LGPL; 307 Hartmann/Sachs/Phototake NYC/Robert Harding Picture Library; 308 Andrew Lambert/LGPL; 309 GSF; 311 David Taylor/SPL; 312 Andrew Lambert/LGPL; 313 Andrew Lambert/LGPL; 314 Charles D. Winters/Timeframe Photography; 318 Ken Karp; 319 (fluorine, iodine) GSF; 319 (bromine) Andrew Lambert/LGPL; 319 chlorine Charles D. Winters/SPL; 321 Srulik Haramaty/Phototake NYC/Robert Harding Picture Library; 322 GSF; 323 Bochsler Photographics+Imaging, Burlington, Canada; 324(t) Andrew Lambert/LGPL; 324(b) Frank Herholdt/Tony Stone Images; 326(t) James Scherer/Houghton Mifflin Company; 326(b) Andrew Lambert/LGPL; 328 Andrew Lambert/LGPL; 333 GSF; 334 Oberlin College Archives, Ohio; 335(t) Andrew Lambert/LGPL; 335(b) Digital imagery copyright 1999 PhotoDisc, Inc.; 337(l) © Richard Megna/FPNY; 337(r) Andrew Lambert/LGPL; 338 AT&T Archives; 339(tl) John Mead/SPL; 339(tr) Geoff Tompkinson/SPL; 339(b) Donald Huffman, University of Arizona; 340 © Richard Megna/FPNY; 342 Bochsler Photographics+Imaging, Burlington, Canada; 343 Niall MacLeod/Corbis; 344 GSF; 346 Andrew Lambert/LGPL; 347 Andrew Lambert/LGPL; 349 James L. Amos/Corbis; 350 NASA; 351 GSF; 353 Bochsler Photographics+Imaging, Burlington, Canada; 354 Runk/Schoenberger from Grant Heilman; 355(t) Keenan & Wood: General College Chemistry, 5th edn, Harper & Row, New York 1976; 355(br) Argonne National Laboratory; 359(t) (all except cobalt, nickel and chromium) GSF; 359(t) (nickel) Lester V. Bergman/Corbis; 359(t) (chromium) Klaus Guldbrandsen/SPL; 359 (cobalt) Russ Lappa/SPL; 359(b) Andrew Lambert/LGPL; 360(t) GSF; 360(b) J Allan Cash; 361(t) British Steel plc; 361(r) David Cumming/Eye Ubiquitous; 361(b) Leslie Garland/LGPL; 363(tl) Courtesy of Micromed Technology, Inc.; 363(tr) GSF; 363(b) Leslie Garland/LGPL; 364 Houghton Mifflin Company; 364 Richard Megna/FPNY; 365 James Scherer/Houghton Mifflin Company; 366 GSF; 367 Mike Clugston; 368 Andrew Lambert/LGPL; 369 Eye of Science/SPL; 371 GSF; 372 Jerry Mason/SPL; 374 NIH/Phototake; 376 Andrew Lambert/LGPL; 378 © Richard Megna/FPNY; 379(t) Martin Sookias; 379(b) Andrew Lambert/LGPL; 384 Geoff Tompkinson/SPL; 386 Andrew Lambert/LGPL; 387 Andrew Lambert/LGPL; 388 Volker Steger/SPL; 389 Andrew Lambert/LGPL; 390 Andrew Lambert/LGPL; 396(l) Sarah Leigh Lewis/Panos Pictures; 396(r) Mike Taylor/LGPL; 397 Andrew Lambert/LGPL; 400 Ian McKinnell/Ace; 403 James Holmes/SPL; 404 Warren Gretz/NREL/US Dept of Energy/SPL; 407 Prof. P. Motta/Dept of Anatomy/University La Sapienza Rome/SPL; 409(t, c) Andrew Lambert/LGPL; 409(b) Custom Medical Stock Photo/SPL; 413 Vauxhall Motors Ltd; 414(l) Martin Sookias; 414(r) Courtesy of Ice-Nook/MNS Holdings, Ontario, Canada, web site: http://www.pathcom.com/~mns; 415(tl) Courtesy of European Council of Vinyl Manufacturers; 415(tr, bl) BASF; 415(br) DuPont; 424 Andrew Lambert/LGPL; 427(t,c) Andrew Lambert/LGPL; 427(b) Craig Hammell/The Stock Market; 429 Andrew Lambert/LGPL; 430 Colin Smedley/Skyscan; 431 CNRI/SPL; 433 BSIP/SPL; 438 Andrew Lambert/LGPL; 439 Peter Gould; 442 BSIP Leca/SPL; 443 Camera Press; 446 Jonathan Blair/Corbis; 447 Gail Mooney/Corbis; 449 Andrew Lambert/LGPL; 450 Andrew Lambert/LGPL; 451 Anthony Blake Photo Library; 453(l) Peter Gould; 453(r) Jerry Mason/SPL; 455 Mike Clugston; 457 Craig Aurness/Corbis; 462 Andrew Lambert/LGPL; 465 Bochsler Photographics+Imaging, Burlington, Canada; 466(l) James Scherer/ Houghton Mifflin Company; 466(r) Andrew Lambert/LGPL; 467 Andrew Lambert/LGPL; 471 Peter Gould; 476 Andrew Lambert/LGPL; 477 David Woodfall/NHPA; 478 Corel Professional Photos; 484 Corel Professional Photos; 485(t) Jim Sugar/Corbis; 485(b) Digital imagery ñ copyright 1999 PhotoDisc, Inc.; 486(t) Dr Jeremy Burgess/SPL; 486(b) Andrew Lambert/LGPL; 487 DuPont; 492 Andrew Lambert/LGPL; 493 David Parker/SPL; 494 Andrew Lambert/LGPL; 496 Andrew Lambert/LGPL; 496 Andrew Lambert/LGPL; 499(l) Andrew Lambert/LGPL; 499(r) Jeremy Hofner/Panos Pictures; 500 Andrew

Lambert/LGPL; 501 Alfred Pasieka/SPL; 502(t) GSF; 502(t) Mike Clugston, Andrew Worrall, David Braybrook, Jill Jordan; 503 Topham Picturepoint; 508 GSF; 509 K. G. Preston-Mafham/Premaphotos Wildlife; 512 GSF; 513 Eric Soder/NHPA; 514 Andrew Lambert/LGPL; 517(t) Mike Clugston; 517(b) Barnabas Bosshart/Corbis; 521 NIBSC/SPL; 526(l) Ecoscene; 526(r) J. C. Revy/SPL; 527(t) Biophoto Associates; 527(b) CNRI/SPL; 529 Ken Eward/SPL; 530 Ken Eward/SPL; 533 Bill Longcore/SPL; 536 Kings College London; 537 Dr Gopal Murti/SPL; 540 Dr Kari Lounatmaa/SPL; 544 Andrew Lambert/LGPL; 545(l) Mike Clugston; 545(r) Andrew Lambert/LGPL; 546 James Holmes/Cellmark Diagnostics/SPL; 547(t) Phillippe Plailley/SPL; 547(b) David Parker/SPL; 548 Geoff Tompkinson/SPL; 549(t) Sinclair Stammers/SPL; 549(b) Digital imagery – copyright 1999 PhotoDisc, Inc.; 550 Hichrom; 551(t) Unicam Chromatography; 551(b) SmithKline Beecham; 556(t) Lawrence Berkeley National Laboratory/SPL; 556(b) Jean Collomber/SPL; 559 Spectronic Unicam; 561 Spectronic Unicam; 565 Simon Fraser/Royal Victoria Infirmary, Newcastle on Tyne/SPL.

In a few cases we have been unable to trace the copyright holder prior to publication. If notified, the publishers will be pleased to amend the acknowledgements in any future edition.

Picture research by Anne Lyons

We gratefully acknowledge the generosity of Dr Warren Hehre of Wavefunction, Inc. in creating and providing images throughout the book generated with Spartan software.

Exam questions

We are grateful to the following examination boards for their kind permission to reproduce past examination paper questions:
The Associated Qualifications Authority (AQA), including the Associated Examination Board (AEB) and the Northern Examinations and Assessment Board (NEAB); Edexcel, including London Examinations; the Northern Ireland Council for the Curriculum, Examinations and Assessment (NICCEA); Oxford, Cambridge and RSA Examinations (OCR), including the University of Oxford Delegacy of Local Examinations (UODLE) and the University of Cambridge Local Examinations Syndicate (UCLES); and the Welsh Joint Examinations Committee (WJEC).